WE BUY FOR CASH
HIGHEST PRICES PAID

We are one of the largest Stamp Auction Houses in Europe and are constantly looking to buy better stamps, sets and souvenir sheets as well as entire collections and rare classical stamps of

GERMANY
States
Empire
French Occupation
Russian Occupation
Federal Republic
Berlin
Saar
Local Issues
Colonies
Zeppelin
Inselpost

EUROPE
Austria
Belgium
France
Great Britain
Liechtenstein
Luxembourg
Netherlands
Norway
Spain
Sweden
Switzerland

In dealing directly with us you can profit from the higher prices for these stamps in Europe.

RUDOLF STELTZER
STAMP AUCTIONS

Rudolfstraße 13-17, Frankfurt/Main, GERMANY

U.S. AGENT
HARALD STELTZER

121 West Acton Rd., Stow, Mass. 01775; (617) 897-6994

QUESTIONNAIRE:

Scott's last reader questionnaire was contained in Vol. 3 of the 1978 Catalogue. Approximately 30 percent of the readers responded. From this information we were able to plan several ways for Scott to improve its publications: (1) the use of a higher quality paper stock was recommended and adopted (2) statistical information regarding stamp price movements was widely requested and the results of our efforts to satisfy this need are presented herein as a special supplement (see between pages US44 & US45) (3) rapidly changing prices and price premiums for never hinged material indicated the need for Scott's *StampMarket Update,* our new quarterly and (4) the *For the Record* section has been continued, but many newly popular countries have been brought into the main Catalogue.

We hope your response to this questionnaire will assist us to further improve our products. For your convenience we have included a postage free envelope; however, if the envelope is missing we would appreciate your mailing the questionnaire to Scott, 3 East 57th Street, New York, N.Y. 10022 Attn: Reader Survey.

Please ✔ The Appropriate Response

1. How did you acquire this Catalogue?
   (a) ___ Gift ___ Philatelic dealer ___ Mail order ___ Bookstore
   Other (specify) ___________
   (b) ___ Purchased individual vol. Purchased, or will purchase set
   (c) Price paid for Vol. $ ___________
   (d) Most recent previous purchase of
   Vol. 1 ___ 1979 ___ 1978 ___ 1977 ___ Prior ___ First time (Skip to Q.3)

2. Comparison with previous Catalogues:

	Much better	Better	Same	Worse	Much worse
Paper Stock:					
Cover Material:					
Prices:					
Completeness of listings:					

3. Advertising. A portion of the increased production costs, especially the paper stock, has been offset by increased advertising revenues. Please help our advertisers by answering the following:
   (a) The quantity of advertising in this Catalogue is:
   ___ Too much ___ Acceptable ___ Don't care
   (b) I ___ did look ___ did not look at the Yellow Pages
   (c) I ___ used ___ plan to use ___ will not use the Reader Service Cards found behind the Yellow Pages.

4. Please study the U.S. Statistical Supplement presented between pages U.S.44 and U.S.45 .
   (a) I find this information ___ Very informative ___ Mildly interesting
   ___ Of no interest
   (b) This information___ should ___ should not be included as a regular part of the Catalogue.
   (c) I would like to see similar information for the following countries:
   ____
   ____

5. Stamp Collecting Interests:
   ☐ World-Wide ☐ Topical ☐ By Country
   (a) If World-Wide, do you use ☐ Scott's International
   ☐ Other ___________
   (b) If topical, what are the subjects?
   1.___________ 2.___________ 3.___________ 4.___________
   (c) If by country, which countries do you collect?
   1.___________ 2.___________ 3.___________ 4.___________

6. Name ________________________________

Address ________________________________

City ________________ State ____________ Zip ____________

A. Are You: ☐ Male ☐ Female ☐ Married ☐ Single

B. Age: ☐ 15-25 ☐ 26-35 ☐ 36-50 ☐ 51-65 ☐ Over 65

C. Age of children ☐ None ____ Years ____ Years ____ Years

D. Occupation ________________________________

E. Annual Income (in thousands) ☐ $8-15 ☐ $16-25 ☐ $26-30 ☐ Over $30

F. In the past year, how much did you spend adding to your stamp collection?
☐ Under $100 ☐ $100-$250 ☐ $250-$500 ☐ $500-$1000 ☐ Over $1000

G. Do you purchase the majority of your stamps from:
☐ Auction House ☐ Out of town dealers ☐ New Issue Service
☐ Approval Service

The next question is most important. Please give us your most thoughtful answer. How can we improve future Scott Catalogues?

____

____

____

____

____

____

____

____

____

7. **Scott Publications to Supplement the Catalogue**

Scott publishes two products to supplement our annual Catalogues. *Scott's Monthly Stamp Journal,* which publishes the New Issues that are constantly being added to the Catalogue but will not appear in the Catalogue until the next edition, and the *Scott StampMarket Update,* which is published quarterly and keeps collectors up-to-date on the current prices of collectible stamps.

A. SCOTT'S MONTHLY STAMP JOURNAL

(a) ____ I currently subscribe to this magazine
____ I do not know of this magazine
____ I no longer subscribe to this magazine

(b) I ____ do ____ do not collect new issues. If so, I collect new issues from the following countries:

____

____

(c) I purchase new issues from (check all applicable):
____ U.S.P.S. ____ Retail dealers
____ Mail order service ____ Stamp shows

B. SCOTT STAMPMARKET UPDATE

____ I currently subscribe to this quarterly
____ I do not know of this quarterly
____ I no longer subscribe to this quarterly

STANDARD POSTAGE STAMP CATALOGUE

1980

One Hundred and Thirty-sixth Edition
in Four Volumes

VOLUME III

EUROPEAN COUNTRIES and COLONIES
INDEPENDENT NATIONS of
AFRICA, ASIA, LATIN AMERICA
G—O

SCOTT PUBLISHING CO.
3 East 57th St., New York, N.Y. 10022

BERT TAUB, *Publisher*
FRANK TRUMBOWER, *President*

Chief Catalogue Editor—JAMES B. HATCHER

New Issues Editor—LILLY B. FREED

Staff Editors—WILLIAM W. CUMMINGS, RICHARD GORDON, IRVING KOSLOW, STEVEN Y. MARDIGUIAN, IRWIN SIEGEL, BERT TAUB

Associate Editors—GEORGE A. McNAMARA, WILLIAM N. SALOMON

ACKNOWLEDGMENT

The Editor cordially thanks all those many good friends of Scott who have helped this year or in previous years in the task of revising the Standard Catalogue. They have generously shared their stamp knowledge with others through this medium.

No list of aides can be complete, and several helpers prefer anonymity. The following men are chiefly those who have undertaken to assist on one or more specific countries:

Bruce W. Ball
John K. Bash
Ivan Bedic
Herbert J. Bloch
William G. Bogg
John R. Boker, Jr.
Paul Brenner
George W. Brett
Victor Bukinik

Alex A. Cohen
Herbert E. Conway

Ellery Denison
Pandelis J. Drossos

Daniel S. Franklin
Roger K. Frigstad

Frank P. Geiger
Frederick H. Gloeckner
Brian M. Green
Irving I. Green
David Gronbeck-Jones

Mihran B. Hagopian
Calvet M. Hahn
J. Hannaney
Leo John Harris
Harrison D. S. Haverbeck
Clifford O. Herrick
Juan J. Holler
Robert L. Huggins
J. R. Hughes

Abdullah Izadi

Lewis S. Kaufman

Ernest A. Kehr
Allen D. Kerr

Irving Lapiner
Jim Lemmon
Arthur L. Levine
Andrew Levitt

Robert L. Markovits
Joseph C. Martin

Robert P. Odenweller

Souren Panirian
Frank E. Patterson III
Gilbert N. Plass
Henrik Pollak
Charles Prant

Alex Rendon
Stanley J. Richmond
Col. Milo D. Rowell

Otto G. Schaffling
Alfredo M. Seiferheld
F. Burton Sellers
James N. Sissons
Lt. Col. James W. Smith
Sherwood Springer
Willard F. Stanley
John Stark

M. N. Thacker

John M. Wilson
Paul B. Woodward
William W. Wylie

Among the organizations that have helped are:

AMERICAN AIR MAIL SOCIETY
Gerhard Wolff, c/o Elmer Fox, Westheimer & Co., 540 Investment Bldg., Washington, D.C. 20005

AMERICAN PHILATELIC SOCIETY
P.O. Box 800, State College, Pa. 16801

AMERICAN REVENUE ASSOCIATION
Sherwood Springer, 3761 West 117th St., Hawthorne, Calif. 90250

AMERICAN STAMP DEALERS' ASSOCIATION
840 Willis Ave., Albertson, N.Y. 11507

ARABIAN PHILATELIC ASSOCIATION
Aramco Box 1929, Dhahran, Saudi Arabia

BRAZIL PHILATELIC ASSOCIATION
T.E. Gaughan, Thompson Drive, Washingtonville, N.Y. 10992.

BUREAU ISSUES ASSOCIATION
16 Sammis Lane, White Plains, N.Y. 10605

CANADIAN STAMP DEALERS' ASSOCIATION
L. A. Davenport, Apt. 308, 7 Jackes Ave., Toronto, Ont., Canada M4T 1E3

CANAL ZONE STUDY GROUP
Alfred R. Bew, Sec'y., 29 S. South Carolina Ave., Atlantic City, N.J. 08401

CHINA STAMP SOCIETY
Ellery Denison, Pres., 7207 Thirteenth Pl., Takoma Park, Md. 20012

CONFEDERATE STAMP ALLIANCE
Jack Solomon, 612 East Park Avenue, Long Beach, New York 11561

COSTA RICA COLLECTORS, Society of
Rt. 3, Box 72, Marble Falls, TX 78654

CROATIAN PHILATELIC SOCIETY
260 Vancouver St., London, Ontario, Canada N5W 4R8

CZECHOSLOVAK PHILATELY, Society for
87 Carmita Ave., Rutherford, N.J. 07070

EIRE PHILATELIC ASSOCIATION
John J. Blessington, Sec'y., 4302 St. Clair Ave., Studio City, Calif. 91604

ESTONIAN PHILATELIC SOCIETY
Rudolf Hamar, Pres., 243 E. 34th St., New York, N.Y. 10016

FRANCE & COLONIES PHILATELIC SOCIETY
Walter Parshall, Sec'y., 103 Spruce St., Bloomfield, N.J. 07003

FRIEDL EXPERT COMMITTEE
10 East 40th St., New York, N.Y. 10016

GERMANY PHILATELIC SOCIETY
c/o Fred Behrendt, Sec'y, P.O. Box 563, Westminster, Maryland 21157

GUATEMALA COLLECTORS, International Society of
Richard Canman, Pres., 175 W. Jackson Blvd., Chicago, Ill. 60604

HELLENIC PHILATELIC Society of America
Maurice R. Friend, M.D., Sec'y., 262 Central Park West, New York, N.Y. 10024

JAPANESE PHILATELY, International Society for
Lois M. Evans, Sec'y., P.O. Box 961, State College, Pa. 16801

KOREA STAMP SOCIETY
Forrest W. Calkins, Sec'y., P.O. Box 1057, Grand Junction, Colo. 81501

MEXICO-ELMHURST PHILATELIC SOCIETY INTERNATIONAL
Mrs. Judith Saks, 2310 Veteran, West Los Angeles, CA 90064

NETHERLANDS PHILATELIC SOCIETY
Julius Mansbach, Sec'y., 6323 N. Francisco, Chicago, Ill. 60645

OCEANIA PHILATELIC SOCIETY
William Hagan, Pres., 1523 East Meadowbrook Drive, Loveland, OH 45140

PHILATELIC FOUNDATION
270 Madison Ave., New York, N.Y. 10016

POLONUS PHILATELIC SOCIETY
864 N. Ashland Ave., Chicago, Ill. 60622

PORTUGUESE PHILATELY, International Society for
Robert L. Huggins, 69 Woodland Ave., Glen Ridge, N.J. 07028

ROSSICA, Society of Russian Philately
Norman Epstein, Treas., 33 Crooke Ave., Brooklyn, N.Y. 11226

EL SALVADOR, Associated Collectors of
Joseph D. Hahn, P.O. Box 522, State College, Pa. 16801

SCANDINAVIAN COLLECTORS CLUB
Box 175, Ben Franklin Sta., Washington, D.C. 20044

SOCIETY OF PHILATELIC AMERICANS
Robert B. Brandeberry, P.O. Box 9041, Wilmington, Del. 19809

UNITED POSTAL STATIONERY SOCIETY
Central Office, P.O. Box 1407, Bloomington, Ill. 61701

Soft-Cover Edition: ISBN 0-89487-025-4

Library of Congress Card No. 2-3301

CONTENTS OF VOLUME III

See Index at back of book for page numbers

Nations of Europe, Africa, Asia and their colonies, and Latin America appear alphabetically in Vols. II, III and IV.

Vol. II runs from A to F (Territory of the Afars and Issas through Funchal).

Vol. III covers G to O (Gabon through Oltre Giuba).

Vol. IV covers P to Z (Panama through Zambezia).

See Vol. I for United States and Affiliated Territories, United Nations, and British Commonwealth of Nations.

SPECIAL NOTICES

This Catalogue lists adhesive postage stamps of the various countries. For the United States additional listings cover revenue stamps and postal stationery.

To facilitate identification, the following style of listing is used:

Korea

94 A50 14wn deep blue 50 25
a. 14wn light blue 20.00 12.50

The number (94) in the first column is the index or identification number; the letter and number combination (A50) indicates the design and refers to the illustration having this (A50) designation; next comes the denomination (14wn) followed by the color (deep blue); the prices are in two columns at the right, the first (50) being that of an unused stamp and the last (25) of a canceled one. This is known as a major listing or variety.

Variations from so-called "normal" stamps are listed in small type and designated by lowercase letters of the alphabet. These are called minor varieties. When they immediately follow the major listing in the catalogue the original index and design numbers are understood to be the same. In the preceding example, the minor variety, No. 94a, differs from the major variety, No. 94, only in shade; its design, perforation, etc., remain unchanged.

When year, perforation, watermark or printing method is mentioned, the description applies to all succeeding listings until a change is noted. The heading note "Without Gum" applies only to the set it precedes.

When a stamp is printed in black on colored paper, the color of the paper alone is given in italics.

With stamps printed in two or more colors, the color given first is that of the frame or outer parts of the design starting at upper left corner. The colors that follow are those of the vignette or inner parts of the design.

For some sets which include both vertical and horizontal format stamps, a single illustration is used, with the various designs and formats described beneath the illustration.

ABBREVIATIONS

The most frequently used abbreviations are:

Imperf. = Imperforate. Perf. = Perforated. Wmk. = Watermark. Unwmkd. = Unwatermarked. Litho. = Lithographed. Photo. = Photogravure. Engr. = Engraved. Typo. = Typographed.

When no color is given for an overprint or surcharge, it is understood to be in black. Abbreviations are sometimes used, as (B) or (Bk) Black, (Bl) Blue, (R) Red, (G) Green, etc.

NEW ISSUE LISTINGS

Scott's Chronicle of New Issues appears regularly in the Scott's Monthly Stamp Journal and reports new listings.

CONDITION

Condition is the all-important factor of price. Prices quoted are for stamps in fine condition. Extra fine copies often bring higher prices, while unused stamps without gum or with partial gum usually sell for less than copies with full original gum. Prices given in this Catalogue for unused stamps are for specimens which have the major part of the original gum on the back, except, of course, those varieties which were issued without gum. In certain countries, such as Brunswick, a note indicates that prices are for specimens without gum. **Slightly defective stamps which are off-center, heavily canceled, faded or stained are usually sold at large discounts. Damaged stamps which are torn or mutilated or have serious defects seldom bring more than a small fraction of the price of a fine specimen.**

Standards of condition vary greatly in the stamps of different countries. Early United States, Great Britain, Victoria and Japan stamps, for example, were poorly perforated and as a rule heavily canceled. They cannot be obtained in as fine condition as stamps from countries where more care was taken in perforating and lighter cancellations applied.

PRICES

The prices appearing in this Catalogue were estimated after careful study of available wholesale and retail offerings together with recommendations and information submitted by many of the leading philatelic societies. These and other factors were considered in determining the figures which the editors consider represent the proper or present price basis for a fine specimen when offered by an informed dealer to an informed buyer. Sales are frequently made at lower figures occasioned by individual bargaining, changes in popularity, temporary over-supply, local custom, the "vest pocket dealer," or the many other reasons which cause deviations from any accepted standard. Sales at higher prices are usually because of exceptionally fine condition, unusual postal markings, unexpected political changes or newly discovered information. While the minimum price of a stamp is fixed at 3c to cover the dealer's labor and service cost of sorting, cataloguing and filling orders individually, the sum of these list prices does not properly represent the "value" of a packet of unsorted or unmounted stamps sold in bulk which generally consists of only the cheaper stamps.

Prices in italics indicate infrequent sales, lack of pricing information, or that the market value is fluctuating excessively. The condition of early issues of many countries varies greatly. In some instances very fine to superb copies are rarely obtainable. Many of these older issues are priced in italics because the actual value is determined by the condition of each individual stamp.

The absence of price does not necessarily indicate that the stamp is scarce or rare. In the United States listings, a dash in the price column means that the stamp is known in a stated form or variety, but that information is lacking or insufficient for pricing.

Unused prices are for stamps that have been hinged. Where used prices are considerably higher than unused, the price applies to a stamp showing a distinct postmark of origin including a contemporary date.

Beginning around 1900, sometimes earlier, prices for sets are given for most issues of five or more stamps. Unless otherwise noted, the set price excludes minor varieties. The parenthetical number in the set-price line tells the number of stamps in the priced total. Set prices are the sum of the individual prices.

Many countries sell canceled-to-order stamps at a marked reduction of face value. (Exceptions include Australia, Netherlands, France and Switzerland, which sell or have sold CTO stamps at full face value.) It is almost impossible to identify such stamps, if the gum has been removed, as the official government canceling devices are used. Examples on cover and used in the proper period are worth more.

Price Changes affecting this Catalogue are published regularly in Scott's Monthly Stamp Journal. (Subscribe and follow Scott's Chronicle of New Issues as well as the Price Changes.)

HOW TO ORDER FROM YOUR DEALER

It is not necessary to write the full description of a stamp as listed in this Catalogue. All that is needed is the name of the country, the index number and whether unused or used. For example, "Japan No. 422 unused" is sufficient to identify the stamp of Japan listed as: "422 A206 5y brown."

ADDENDA and NUMBER CHANGES

Stamps received too late to be included in the body of the Catalogue are listed in the Addenda at the back of this volume.

A list of stamps whose catalogue numbers have been changed from those of the preceding edition appears at the back of this volume.

Certain currently unlisted stamps are mentioned in "For the Record" at the back of this volume.

EXAMINATION

Scott Publishing Co. cannot undertake to pass upon genuineness or condition of stamps, due to the time and responsibility involved, but refers collectors to the several expert committees which undertake this work. Neither can Scott Publishing Co. undertake to appraise or identify. The Company cannot take responsibility for unsolicited stamps or covers.

INFORMATION FOR COLLECTORS

The anatomy of a stamp can be divided into the following parts: paper, watermark, separation, impression, design and gum.

PAPER

Paper is a material composed of a compacted web of cellulose fibers formed into sheets. The fibers most often used for the paper on which stamps are printed are mulberry bark, wood, straw and certain grasses, with linen or cotton rags added for greater strength. These fibers are ground, bleached and boiled until they are reduced to a slushy pulp known as "stuff." Sizing, or weak glue, and coloring matter may be added to the pulp. Thin coatings of pulp are poured on sieve-like frames which allow the water to run off while retaining the matted pulp. When it is almost dry, the appearance of the pulp is converted by mechanical processes. It may be passed through smooth or engraved rollers (dandy rolls) or placed between cloth in a press that flattens and dries the product under pressure, thus forming a sheet of paper.

Stamp paper falls broadly into two divisions–"wove" and "laid." The differences in appearance are caused by the surface of the frame onto which the pulp is first fed. If the surface is smooth and even, the paper will be of uniform texture throughout, showing no light and dark areas when held up to a light. This is called **Wove Paper.** Early paper making machines poured the pulp on to continuously circulating webs of felt, but modern machines feed the pulp on to a cloth-like screen made of closely interwoven fine wires. This paper, when held up to a light, will show little dots or points, very close together. Technically, it is called "wire wove," but because it is the most common form, it is generally known as "wove paper." Any United States or British stamp printed after 1880 will furnish an example of wire wove paper.

The frames utilized for **Laid Paper** are made of closely spaced parallel wires, with cross wires at wider intervals. Obviously a greater thickness of the pulp will settle between the wires, and the paper, when held up to a light, will show alternate light and dark lines. The spacing and the thickness of the lines may vary, but on any one sheet of paper, they are all alike. (Russia Nos. 31-38.)

If the lines are spaced quite far apart, like the ruling on a writing tablet, the paper is called **Batonné** from the French word meaning a staff. Batonné paper may be either wove or laid. If it is laid, fine laid lines can be seen between the batons. The laid lines, which are actually a form of watermark, may be geometrical figures such as squares, diamonds, rectangles, or wavy lines.

When the lines form little squares, the paper is called **Quadrille.** When they form rectangles instead of squares, the paper is called **Oblong Quadrille.** (Mexico–Guadalajara Nos. 38-41.)

Paper is also classified as thick or thin, hard or soft, and by color if dye was added during production, such as yellowish, greenish, bluish and reddish.

Pelure Paper is an extremely thin, hard and often brittle paper. It is sometimes bluish or grayish. (Serbia No. 170.)

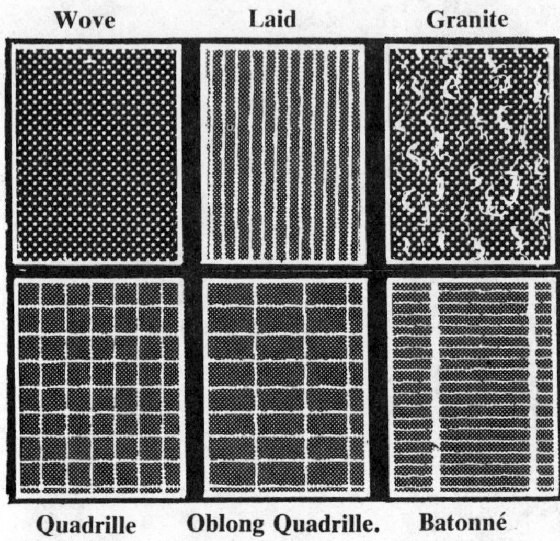

Native Paper is a term applied to the handmade papers on which some of the early stamps of the Indian States were printed. Japanese paper, originally made of mulberry fibers and rice flour, is part of this group. (Japan Nos. 1-18.)

Manila Paper, often used to make stamped envelopes and wrappers, is a coarse textured stock, usually smooth on one side and rough on the other. It is made in a variety of colors.

Silk Paper, introduced by the British in 1847 as a safeguard against counterfeiting, has scattered bits of colored silk thread in it. Silk-thread paper has continuous threads of colored silk arranged so that one or more threads run through the stamp or postal stationery. (Great Britain Nos. 5-8.)

Granite Paper, not to be confused with either of the silk papers, is filled with minute fibers of various colors and lengths in the paper substance. (Austria Nos. 172-175.)

Chalky Paper is coated with a chalk-like substance to discourage the cleaning and reuse of canceled stamps. As the design is imprinted on the water-soluble coating of the stamp, any attempts to remove a cancellation will destroy the stamp. **Collectors are warned not to soak these stamps in any fluid.** If one is to be removed from envelope paper, a good way is to wet the paper from underneath until the gum dissolves enough to slip the stamp off it. (St. Kitts-Nevis Nos. 89-90.)

India Paper, originally introduced from China about 1750, is sometimes referred to as China Paper. It is a thin, opaque paper often used for plate and die proofs by many countries.

Double Paper in philately has two distinct meanings. The first, used experimentally as a means to discourage re-use,is two-ply paper, usually of a thick and thin sheet, joined together during the process of manufacture. Any attempt to remove a cancellation would destroy the design which is printed on the thin paper. The second occurs on the rotary press when the printer glues the end of one paper roll onto the next roll to save time in feeding the paper through the press. Stamp designs are printed over the joined paper and if overlooked by inspectors, may get into post-office stocks.

Goldbeater's Skin, used for the 1886 issue of Prussia, was made of a tough translucent paper. The design was printed in reverse on the back of the stamp, and the gum applied on top of the printing. It is impossible to remove them from the paper to which they are affixed without destroying the design.

Ribbed Paper has an uneven, corrugated surface made by passing it through ridged rollers. (Exists on some copies of U.S. No. 163.)

Various other substances that have been used for stamp manufacture include aluminum, copper, silver and gold foil, plastic, silk and cotton fabrics. Most of these are considered novelties designed for sale to novice collectors.

WATERMARKS

Watermarks are an integral part of the paper as they are formed in the process of manufacture. They consist of small designs such as crowns, stars, anchors, letters, etc. formed of wire or cut from metal that are soldered to the surface of the dandy roll or mold. These pieces of metal (referred to as "bits") impress a design into the paper which may be seen by holding the stamp up to the light. They are more easily seen in a watermark detector, a small black tray. The stamp is placed face down in the tray and dampened with carbon tetrachloride or lighter fluid, which brings up the watermark in dark lines against a lighter background.

WARNING. Some inks used in the photogravure process dissolve in watermark fluids. (See SOLUBLE PRINTING INKS.) There are also electric watermark detectors that come with plastic discs of various colors. When the light is turned on the watermark can be seen through the disc that neutralizes the color of the stamp.

Watermarks may be found reversed, inverted, sideways or diagonal, as seen from the back of the stamp, depending on the position of the printing plates or the manner in which paper was fed through the press. On machine-made paper they normally read from right to left. In a "multiple watermark" the design is repeated closely throughout the sheet. In a "sheet watermark" the design appears only once on the sheet, but extends over many stamps. Individual stamps may carry only a small fraction or none of the watermark.

"Marginal watermarks" occur in the margins of sheets or panes of stamps. Outside the border of some papers a large

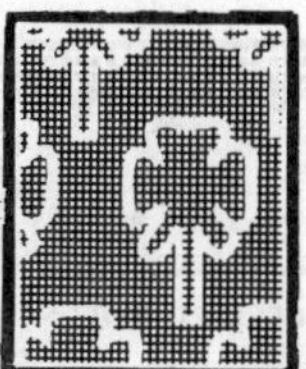

Multiple Watermarks of Crown Agents and Burma

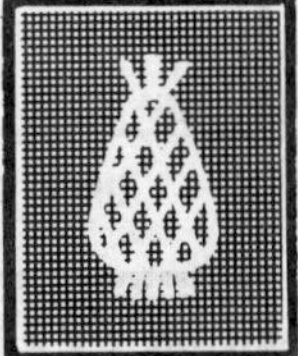

Watermarks of Uruguay, Vatican and Jamaica

row of letters may spell the name of the country or of the manufacturer of the paper. Careless press feeding may cause parts of these letters to show on stamps of the outer rows. **For easier reference watermarks are numbered in the Scott Catalogue. See numerical index of Watermarks at back of this volume.**

SEPARATION

Separation is the general term used to describe methods of separating stamps. The earliest issues, such as the 1840 Penny Blacks, did not have any means provided for separating and were intended to be cut apart with scissors. These are called imperforate stamps. As many stamps that were first issued imperforate were later issued perforated, care must be observed in buying imperforate stamps to be sure they are really imperforate and not perforated copies that have been trimmed. Although sometimes priced as singles, it is recommended that imperforate varieties of normally perforated stamps be collected in pairs or larger pieces as indisputable evidence of their imperforate character.

Separation is effected by two general methods, rouletting and perforating. In rouletting the paper is cut partly or wholly through, but no paper is removed. In perforating a part of the paper is removed. Rouletting derives its name from the French roulette, a spur-like wheel. As the wheel is rolled over the paper, each point makes a small cut. The number of cuts made in two centimeters determines the gauge of the roulette. This is fully explained under "Perforation."

ROULETTING: The shape and arrangement of the teeth on the wheels varies. French names are usually used to describe the various roulettes:

Percé en lignes: rouletted in lines. The paper receives short, straight cuts in lines. (Mexico No. 500.)

Percé en points: pin-perforated. Round, equidistant holes are pricked through the paper, but no paper is removed, which distinguishes it from a small perforation. (Mexico Nos. 242-256.)

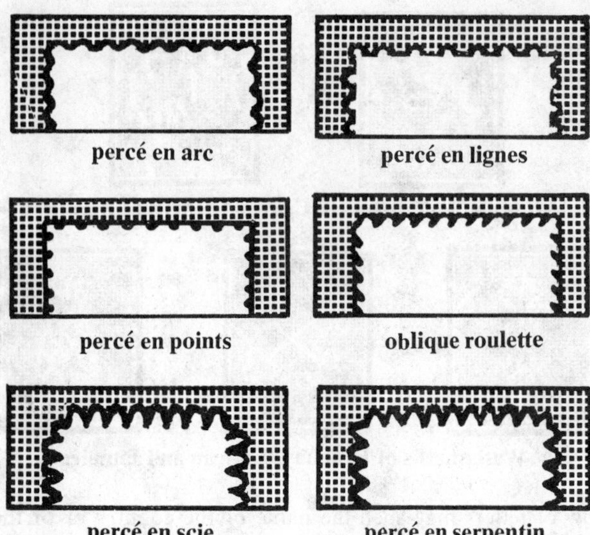

Percé en arc and percé en scie: pierced in an arc or saw-toothed rouletted, forming half circles or small triangles. (Hanover Nos. 25-29.)

Percé en serpentin: serpentine roulette. The cuts form a serpentine or wavy line. (Brunswick Nos. 13-22.)

PERFORATION: The second chief style of separation of stamps, and the one which is in universal use today, is called perforating. By this process the paper between the stamps is cut away in a line of holes, usually round, leaving little bridges of paper between the stamps to hold them together. These little bridges, which project from the stamp when it is torn from the sheet are called the teeth of the perforation. As the size of the perforation is sometimes the only way to differentiate between two otherwise identical stamps, it is necessary to be able to measure and describe them. This is done with a perforation gauge, a ruler-like device that has dots to show how many perforations can be counted in the space of 2 centimeters, the space universally adopted as the length in which perforations are measured. Run your stamp along the gauge until the dots on it fit exactly into the perforations. If the number alongside the dots into which it fits is 11, this means that 11 perforations fit between two centimeters and the stamp is described as "perf. 11." If the gauge of the perforations on the top and bottom of a stamp differs from that on the sides, it is called a "compound perforation." In measuring compound perforations the gauge at the top and bottom is always given first, then the sides. Thus a stamp that measures 10½ at top and bottom and 11 at the sides is described as "10½ x 11." (U.S. No. 1526.)

A perforation with small holes and teeth close together is called a "fine perforation." One with large holes and teeth far apart is a "coarse perforation." If the holes are jagged rather than clean cut, it is called "rough perforation." Blind perforations are the slight impressions left by the perforating pins if they fail to puncture the paper. Multiples showing blind perfs may command a slight premium over normally perforated stamps.

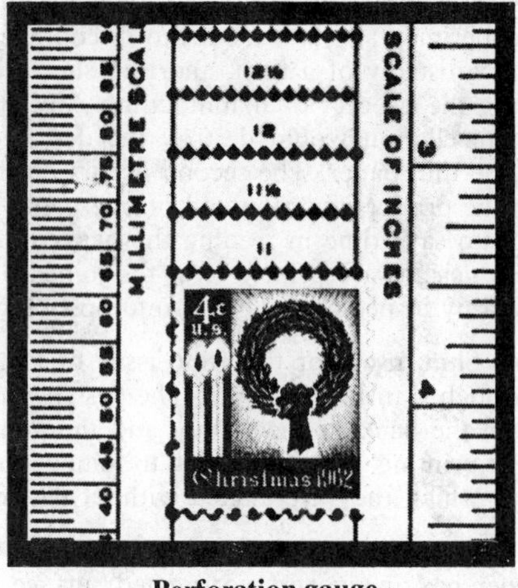

Perforation gauge

PRINTING PROCESSES

ENGRAVING (Intaglio): Master Die—The initial operation in the engraving process is the making of the master die. The die is a small flat block of soft steel on which the stamp design is recess engraved in reverse.

The original art is reduced photographically to the appropriate size, and serves as a tracing guide for the initial outline of the design. After the engraving is completed, the die is hardened to withstand the stress and pressures of subsequent transfer operations.

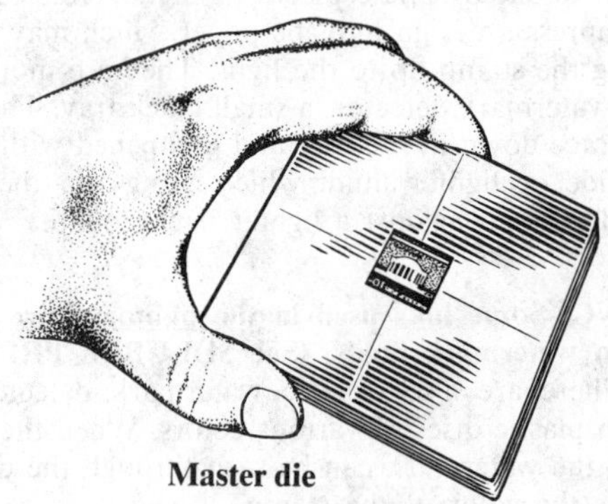

Master die

Transfer Roll—The next operation is the making of the transfer roll which, as the name implies, is the medium used to transfer the subject from the die to the plate. A blank roll of soft steel, mounted on a mandrel, is placed under the bearers of a transfer press, so as to allow it to roll freely on its axis. The hardened die is placed on the bed of the press and the face of the transfer roll is brought to bear on the die under pressure. The bed is then rocked back and forth under increasing pressure until the soft steel of the roll is forced into every engraved line of the die. The resulting impression on the roll is known as a "relief" or a "relief transfer." When the required number of reliefs are "rocked in," the soft steel transfer roll is also hardened.

A "relief" is the normal reproduction of the design on the die in reverse. A "defective relief" may occur during the "rocking in" process due to a minute piece of foreign material lodging on the die, or other causes. Imperfections in the steel of the transfer roll may result in a breaking away of parts of the design. If the damaged relief is continued in use, it will transfer a repeating defect to the plate. Sometimes reliefs are deliberately altered. "Broken relief" and "altered relief" are terms used to designate these changed conditions.

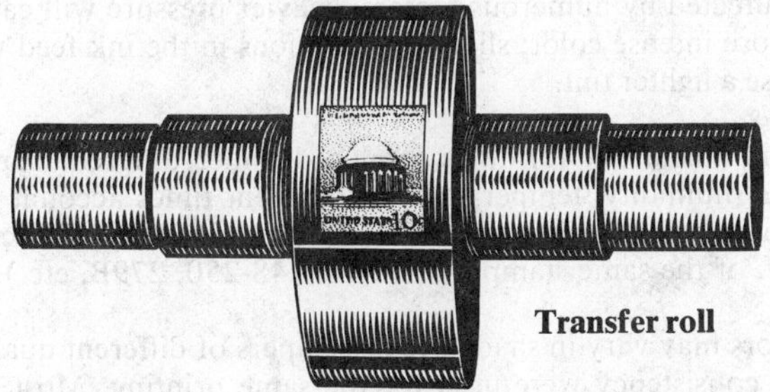

Transfer roll

Plate—The final step in the procedure is the making of the printing plate. A flat piece of soft steel replaces the die on the bed of the transfer press and one of the reliefs on the transfer roll is brought to bear on it. The position on the plate is determined by position dots, which have been lightly marked on the plate in advance. After the position of the relief is determined, pressure is brought to bear and, by following the same method used in making the transfer roll, a transfer is entered, This transfer reproduces in reverse and in detail the design of the relief. As many transfers are entered on the plate as there are to be subjects.

After the required transfers have been entered, the position dots, layout dots and lines, scratches, etc. are generally burnished out. Any required *guide lines, plate numbers* or other *marginal markings* are added. A proof impression is then taken and if "certified" (approved), the plate is machined for fitting to the press, hardened and sent to the plate vault ready for use.

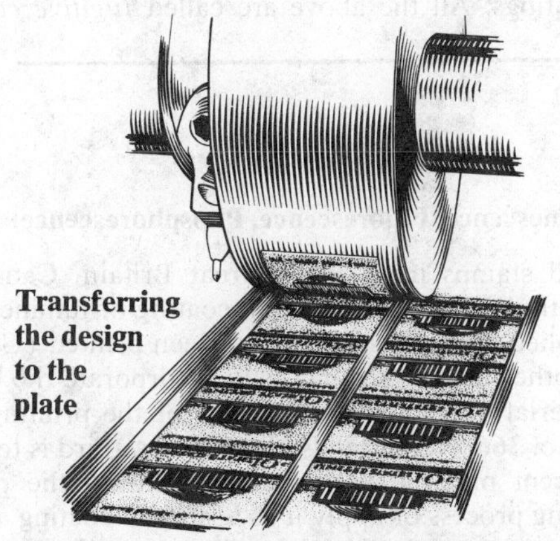

Transferring the design to the plate

On press, the plate is inked and the surface automatically wiped clean, leaving the ink only in the depressed lines. Damp paper under pressure is forced down into the engraved depressed lines, thereby receiving the ink. Consequently, the lines on engraved stamps are slightly raised; and, conversely, slight depressions occur on the back of the stamp.

The expressions *taille douce,* engraved, line engraved and steel plate all designate substantially the same processes for producing engraved stamps.

Rotary Press—Engraved stamps were printed only with flat plates until 1915, when rotary press printing was introduced. *Rotary press plates,* after being certified, require additional machining. They are curved to fit the press cylinder and "gripper slots" are cut into the back of each plate to receive the "grippers," which hold the plate securely on the press, after which the plate is hardened. Stamps printed from rotary press plates are usually longer or wider than the same stamps printed from flat press plates. The stretching of the plate during the curving process causes this enlargement.

Re-entry—In order to execute a re-entry the transfer roll is reapplied to the plate, usually at some time after it has been put to press. Thus worn-out designs can be resharpened by carefully re-entering the transfer roll. If the transfer roll is not precisely in line with the impression on the plate, the registration will not be true and a double transfer will result. After a plate has been curved for the rotary press, it is impossible to make a re-entry.

Double Transfer—A description of the condition of a transfer on a plate that shows evidence of a duplication of all, or a portion of the design. It is usually the result of the changing of the registration between the transfer roll and the plate during the rocking-in of the original entry.

It is sometimes necessary to remove the original transfer from a plate and repeat the process a second time. If the finished re-transfer shows indications of the original impression due to incomplete erasure, the result is also a double transfer.

Re-engraved—Either the die that has been used to make a plate or the plate itself may have its "temper" drawn (softened) and be re-cut. The resulting impressions from such a re-engraved die or plate may differ slightly from the original issue, and are known as "re-engraved."

Short Transfer—It sometimes happens that the transfer roll is not rocked its entire length in entering a transfer on a plate, with the result that the finished transfer fails to show the complete design. This is known as a "short transfer." (U.S. No. 8, type III of 1851-56 1c.)

TYPOGRAPHY (Letterpress, Surface Printing)—As related to the printing of postage stamps, typography is the reverse of engraving. It includes all printing wherein the design is raised above the surface area, whether it is wood, metal, or in some instances hard rubber.

The master die is made in much the same manner as the engraved die. However, in this instance the area not being utilized as a printing surface is cut away, leaving the surface area raised. The original die is then reproduced by stereotyping or electrotyping. The resulting electrotypes are assembled in the required number and format of the desired sheet of stamps. The plate used in printing the stamps is an electroplate of these assembled electrotypes.

Ink is applied to the raised surface and the pressure of the press transfers the ink impression to the paper. Again, as opposed to engraving, the fine lines of typography are impressed on the surface of the stamp. When viewed from the back (as on a typewritten page) the corresponding linework will be raised slightly above the surface.

PHOTOGRAVURE (Rotogravure, Heliogravure)–In this process the basic principles of photography are applied to a sensitized metal plate, as opposed to photographic paper. The design is photographically transferred to the plate through a halftone screen, breaking the reproduction into tiny dots. The plate is treated chemically and the dots form depressions of varying depths, depending on the degrees of shade in the design. The depressions in the plate hold the ink, which is lifted out when the paper is pressed against the plate, in a manner similar to that of engraved printing.

LITHOGRAPHY–This process is based on the principle that oil and water will not mix. The design is drawn by hand or transferred from an engraving to the surface of a lithographic stone or metal plate in a greasy (oily) ink. The stone (or plate) is wet with an acid fluid, causing it to repel the printing ink in all areas not covered by the greasy ink.

Transfers are made from the original stone or plate by means of transfer paper. A series of duplicate transfers are grouped and these in turn are transferred to the final printing plate.

Photolithography–The application of photographic processes to lithography. This process allows greater flexibility of design, relating to use of halftone screens combined with linework.

Offset–A development of the lithographic process. A rubber-covered blanket cylinder takes up the impression from the inked lithographic plate. From the "blanket" the impression is *offset* or transferred to the paper. Because of its greater flexibility and speed, offset printing has largely displaced lithography. Since the processes and results are almost identical, stamps printed by either method are designated as lithographed.

Sometimes two or even three printing methods are combined in producing stamps.

EMBOSSED (RELIEF) PRINTING–A method in which the design is sunk in the metal of the die and the printing is done against a yielding platen, such as leather or linoleum, which is forced up into the depression of the die, thus forming the design on the paper in relief.

Embossing may be done without color (Sardinia Nos. 4-6); with color printed around the embossed area (Great Britain No. 5 and most U.S. envelopes); and with color in exact registration with the embossed subject (Canada Nos. 656-657).

INK COLORS: Pigments or dyes, usually of mineral origin, are used in the manufacture of inks or colored papers on which stamps are printed. The tone of any given color may be affected by numerous factors: heavier pressure will cause a more intense color; slight interruptions in the ink feed will cause a lighter tint.

Hand-mixed ink formulas produced under different conditions (humidity, temperature) at different times account for notable color variations in early printings, mostly 19th century, of the same stamp (U.S. Nos. 248-250, 279B, etc.).

Colors may vary in shade because papers of different quality and consistency were used for the same printing. Most pelure papers, for example, show a richer color when compared to wove or laid papers. (Russia No. 181a.)

The very nature of the printing processes can cause a variety of differences in shades or hues of the same stamp. Some of these shades are scarcer than others, and are of particular interest to the advanced collector.

SOLUBLE PRINTING INKS. WARNING. Most stamp colors are permanent. That is, they are not seriously affected by light or water. Some colors may fade from excessive exposure to light. Other stamps are printed in inks which dissolve easily in water or in benzine, carbon tetrachloride or other fluids used to detect watermarks. These inks were often used intentionally to prevent the removal of cancellations.

Benzine affects most photogravure printings. Water affects all aniline prints, those on safety paper, and some photogravure printings. All the above are called *fugitive colors.*

TAGGED STAMPS

(Luminescence, Fluorescence, Phosphorescence)

Some tagged stamps have bars (Great Britain, Canada), frames (South Africa), or an overall coating of luminescent material applied after the stamps have been printed (United States). Another tagging method is to incorporate the luminescent material into some or all colors of the printing ink (Australia No. 366, Netherlands No. 478). A third is to mix the luminescent material with the pulp during the paper manufacturing process or apply it as a surface coating afterwards. These are called "fluorescent" papers. (Switzerland Nos. 510-514, Germany No. 848.)

The treated stamps show up in specific colors when exposed to ultraviolet light. The wave length of the luminescent material determines the colors and activates the triggering mechanism of the electronic machinery for sorting, facing or canceling letters.

Various fluorescent substances have been used as paper whiteners, but the resulting "hi-brite papers" show up differently under ultraviolet light and do not trigger the machines. They are not noted in the Catalogue.

Introduced in Great Britain in 1959 on an experimental basis, tagging in its various forms is now used by many countries to expedite the handling of mail. Following Great Britain were Germany ('61); Canada and Denmark ('62); United States, Australia, Netherlands and Switzerland ('63); Belgium and Japan ('66); Sweden and Norway ('67); Italy ('68); Russia ('69), and so forth.

Certain stamps were issued both with and without the luminescent factor. In these instances, the "tagged" variety is listed in the United States, Canada, Great Britain and Switzerland, and is noted in some of the other countries.

GUM

The gum on a stamp's back may be smooth, crinkly, dark, white, colored or tinted, and either obvious or virtually invisible as on Canada No. 453 or Rwanda Nos. 287-294. Most stamp gumming has been carried out with adhesives using gum arabic or dextrine as a base, but certain polymers such as polyvinyl alcohol (PVA) have been used extensively since World War II. The PVA gum which Harrison & Sons of Great Britain introduced in 1968 is dull, slightly yellowish and almost invisible.

Stamps having full **original gum** sell for more than those from which the gum has been removed. Reprints may have gum differing from the originals.

REPRINTS AND REISSUES

Reprints are impressions of stamps (usually obsolete) made from the original plates or stones. If valid for postage and from obsolete issues, they are called reissues. If they are from current issues, they are *second, third,* etc. *printings.* If designated for a particular purpose, they are called *special printings.*

When reprints are not valid for postage, but made from original dies and plates by authorized persons they are *official reprints*–to distinguish them from *private reprints* made from original plates and dies by private hands. *Official reproductions* or imitations are made from new dies and plates by government authorization.

For the 1876 Centennial, the U.S. government made official imitations of its first postage stamps, which are listed as Nos. 3-4; official reprints of the demonetized pre-1861 issues; reissued the 1869 stamps and made special printings of the current 1875 denominations. An example of the private reprint is that of the New Haven postmaster's provisional.

Most reprints differ slightly from the original stamp in some characteristic such as gum, paper, perforation, color, watermark (or lack thereof). Sometimes the details have been followed so meticulously that only a student of that stamp can tell the reprint from the original.

REMAINDERS AND CANCELED TO ORDER

Some countries sell their stock of old stamps when a new issue replaces them. The **remainders** are usually canceled with a punch hole, a heavy line or bar, or a more or less regular cancellation to avoid postal use. The most famous merchant of remainders was Nicholas F. Seebeck, who arranged printing contracts between the Hamilton Bank Note Co., of which he was a director, and several Central and Latin American countries in the 1880's and 1890's. The contracts provided that the plates and all remainders of the yearly issues became the property of Hamilton, and Seebeck saw to it that ample stock remained. The "Seebecks," both remainders and reprints, were standard packet fillers for decades.

Some countries also issue stamps **canceled to order** (CTO), either in sheets with original gum or stuck onto pieces of paper or envelopes and canceled. Such CTO items generally are worth less than postally used stamps. Most can be detected by the presence of gum. However, as the CTO practice goes back at least to 1885, the gum inevitably has been washed off some stamps so they could pass for postally used. The normally applied postmarks usually differ slightly and specialists can tell the difference. When applied individually to envelopes by philatelically minded persons, CTO material is known as *favor canceled* and generally sells at large discounts.

CINDERELLAS AND FACSIMILES

Cinderella is a catchall term used by collectors of phantoms, fantasies, bogus items, municipal issues, exhibition seals, local revenues, transportation stamps, labels, poster stamps, etc. Cinderellas are not issued by any national government for postal purposes. Some cinderella collectors include local postage issues, telegraph stamps, essays and proofs, forgeries and counterfeits.

A fantasy is an adhesive created for a nonexisting stamp issuing authority. Fantasy items range from imaginary countries (Kingdom of Sedang or Principality of Trinidad) to nonexisting locals (Winans City Post), or nonexisting transportation lines (McRobish & Co.'s Acapulco-San Francisco Line). On the other hand, if the entity exists and might have issued stamps or did issue other stamps, the items are *bogus* stamps. These would include the Mormon postage stamps of Utah, S. Allan Taylor's Guatemala and Paraguay inventions, the propaganda issues for the South Moluccas and the adhesives of the Page & Keyes local post of Boston.

Both fantasies and bogus issues are sometimes called *phantoms.*

Facsimiles are copies or imitations made to represent original stamps, but which do not pretend to be originals. A catalogue illustration is such a facsimile. Illustrations from the Moëns catalogue of the last century were occasionally colored and passed as stamps. Since the beginning of stamp collecting, facsimiles have been made for collectors as space fillers or for reference. They often carry the words "facsimile," "falsch" (German), "sanko" or "mozo" (Japanese), or "faux" (French) overprinted on the face or stamped on the back. Naturally, they have only curio value.

COUNTERFEITS OR FORGERIES

Postal counterfeits or **postal forgeries** are unauthorized imitations of stamps intended to deprive the post of revenue. They often command higher prices than the genuine stamps they imitate. Sales are illegal and governments can, and do, prosecute.

The first postal forgery was of Spain's 4-cuartos carmine of 1854, No. 25. The forgers lithographed it, though the original was typographed. Apparently they were not satisfied and soon made an engraved forgery which is fairly common, unlike the scarce lithographed counterfeit. Postal forgeries quickly followed in Spain, Austria, Naples, Sardinia and the Roman States.

An infamous counterfeit to defraud the government is the 1-shilling Great Britain "Stock Exchange" forgery of 1872 used on telegrams at the exchange that year. It escaped detection until a stamp dealer noticed it in 1898. Recent postal counterfeits include the U.S. 4c Lincoln and the 8c Eisenhower as well as Canada's 6c orange of 1968 (which was later faked in turn).

Because the governments concerned did not issue them, the *wartime propaganda* stamps of both World Wars may be classed as postal counterfeits. They were put out by other governments or resistance groups.

Philatelic forgeries or *counterfeits* are unauthorized imitations of stamps designed to deceive and defraud collectors. Such spurious items first appeared on the market around 1860 and most old-time collections contain one or more. Many are crude and easily spotted even by the non-specialist, but some can deceive the better-than-average collector.

An important supplier of these early philatelic forgeries was the Hamburg printer, Gebrüder Spiro. Many others indulged in this craft including S. Allan Taylor, George Hussey, James Chute, Georges Foure, Benjamin & Sarpy, Julius Goldner, E. Oneglia and L. H. Mercier. Among the noted 20th century forgers are Francois Fournier, Jean Sperati and the prolific Raoul DeThuin.

Most classic rarities, many medium priced stamps and, in this century, cheap stamps on a wholesale basis destined for beginners' packets, have been fraudulently produced. However, few new philatelic forgeries have appeared in recent decades and virtually no new frauds of valuable classics. Successful imitation of engraved work is virtually impossible. It has proven far easier to produce a fake by altering a genuine stamp than to duplicate a stamp completely.

REPAIRS AND FAKES

Most collectors will not object to restoration of a stamp or cover, although they will not accept repairs on the same basis. *Restoration* in this sense includes cleaning with a soft eraser or soap and water. It may include the ironing out of a crease or removal of a cellophane tape stain. Removal of old hinges is acceptable. Some collectors believe that freshening of a stamp is valid restoration, whether done by the removal of oxides, "toning," or the effect of wax paper left on stamps shipped to the tropics between such sheets. Regumming may have been acceptable restoration half a century ago, but today it is considered faking. Restored stamps or covers do not normally sell at a discount, and may even change hands at a premium.

Repairs include filling in thin spots, mending tears by reweaving, adding a missing corner or perforation "tooth." Repaired stamps sell at substantial discounts.

Fakes are genuine stamps altered in some way to make them more desirable and sold without revealing the alterations. According to one major student, 30,000 varieties of fakes were known in the 1950's. The number has grown. The widespread existence of fakes makes it important for collectors to study their philatelic holdings and relevant literature. For the same reason they should buy from reputable dealers who will guarantee their stamps and make full prompt refund should a purchase be declared not genuine by some mutually agreed-upon authority. Because fakes always have some genuine characteristics, it is not always possible to obtain unanimity among expert students regarding specific items. These students may change their opinions as philatelic knowledge increases. More than 80 per cent of all fakes on the market today are regummed, reperforated or altered in regard to overprints, surcharges or cancellations.

Stamps can be chemically treated to alter or eliminate colors. For example a pale rose can be recolored into a blue of a higher value, or a "missing color" variety created. Designs may be changed by "painting," or a stroke or dot added or bleached out to turn an ordinary variety into a scarce stamp. Part of a stamp can be bleached and reprinted in a different version, achieving an inverted center or frame. Margins can be added or repairs done so deceptively that the stamp moves from the repaired to the fake category.

The fakers have not left the backs of stamps untouched. They may create false watermarks or add fake grills (or press out genuine ones). A thin India paper proof may be glued onto a thicker backing to "create" an issued stamp, or a cardboard proof may be shaved down. Silk threads have been impressed in and stamps have been split so that a rare paper variety, from a cheap stamp, can be applied as a back to falsely identify the stamp. However, the most common back treatment is regumming.

Some operators openly advertise "foolproof" application of "original gum" to stamps that lack it. This is faking, not counterfeiting. As few early stamps have survived without being hinged, the large number of never-hinged examples now offered for sale suggests the extent of regumming that has been and is being done. Regumming may be used to hide repairs and thin spots, but dipping in watermark fluid will often reveal these flaws.

The fakers also tamper with separations. Ingenious ways to add margins are known, and perforated wide-margin stamps may be falsely represented as imperforate when trimmed. Reperforating is commonly done to create scarce coil or perforation varieties and to eliminate the straight-edge stamps found in sheet margin positions of many earlier issues. Custom has made straight edges less desirable and the fakers have obliged by reperforating them so extensively that many are now uncommon if not rare.

Another main field of the faker is that of the overprint, surcharge and cancellation. The forging of rare surcharges or overprints began in the 1880's or 1890's. These forgeries are sometimes difficult to detect, but the better experts have probably identified almost all of them. Only occasionally are the overprints or cancellations removed to create unoverprinted stamps or unused items. The SPECIMEN overprints are sometimes removed–scraping and repainting is one way –to create unoverprinted varieties. Cheap revenues or pen-canceled stamps are used to generate "unused" stamps for further faking by adding other markings. The quartz lamp and a high-powered magnifying glass help in detecting cancellation removals.

The big problem, however, is the addition of overprints, surcharges or cancellations–many quite dangerous. Plating of the stamps or the overprint can be an important detecting method.

Fake postmarks can range from numerous spurious fancy cancellations, to the host of markings applied to transatlantic covers to create rare uses. With the advance of cover collecting and the wide interest in postal history, a fertile new field for fakers arose. Some have tried to create entire covers. Others specialize in adding stamps, tied by fake cancellations, to genuine stampless covers, or replacing cheaper or damaged stamps with more valuable ones. Detailed study of rates and postmarks (including the analysis of "breaks" in each handstamp over a period), ink analysis, etc. will usually unmask the fraud.

TERMINOLOGY

BOOKLETS: Many countries have issued stamps in small booklets for the convenience of users. They are usually sold by the post office at a small premium. Booklets have been issued in all sizes and forms, often with advertising on the covers, on the panes of stamps or on the interleaving. The panes may be printed from special plates or made from regular sheets. All panes from booklets issued by the United States and many from those of other countries are straight edged on the bottom and both sides, but perforated between the stamps. Any unit in the pane, either printed or blank, which is not a postage stamp, is called a *label* in the catalogue listings.

CANCELLATIONS: The marks or obliterations put on a stamp by the postal authorities to show that it has done service and is no longer valid for postage. If it is made with a pen, it is called a pen cancellation. When the location of the post office appears in the cancellation, it is called a town cancellation. When it calls attention to a cause or celebration, it is a slogan cancellation. Many other types and styles of cancellations exist, such as duplex, numerals, targets, etc.

COIL STAMPS–Stamps issued in rolls for use in affixing and vending machines. Those of the United States, Canada, etc., are perforated horizontally or vertically only, with the outer edges imperforate. Coil stamps of some countries (Great Britain) are perforated on all four sides.

COVERS: Envelopes, with or without adhesive postage stamps, which have passed through the mail and bear postal or other markings of philatelic interest. Before the introduction of envelopes (1840), people folded letters and wrote the address on the outside. Many people covered their letters with an extra sheet of paper on the outside for the address. Hence the word "cover." Used air letter sheets, stamped envelopes, and other items of postal stationery are also referred to as "covers."

ERRORS: Stamps having some unintentional deviation from the normal. Errors include, but are not limited to, mistakes in color, paper or watermark; inverted centers (or frames), surcharges or overprints, and double impressions. A factually wrong or misspelled inscription, if it appears on all examples of a stamp, is not classified as a philatelic error. (Panama No. J1).

OVERPRINTED AND SURCHARGED STAMPS: Overprinting is wording placed on stamps to alter the place of use ("Canal Zone" on U.S. issues); to adapt them for a special purpose ("Porto" on Denmark's 1913-20 regular issues for use as postage dues, Nos. J1-J7); or for a special occasion (Guatemala Nos. 374-378).

The term **surcharge** is used when the overprint changes or restates the value (1923 "Inflation Issues" of Germany; Australia No. 580).

Surcharges and overprints may be handstamped, typeset or, occasionally, lithographed or engraved.

PRECANCELS: Stamps canceled by the issuing government before they are sold at the post office. Precanceling is done to expedite the handling of large mailings.

In the United States precancellations generally identify the point of origin. That is, the city and state names (or initials) appear, usually centered by an arrangement of parallel lines.

In France the abbreviation **Affranchts** in a semicircle together with the word **Postes** is the general form. Belgian precancellations are usually a square box in which the name of the city appears. Netherlands' precancellations have the name of the city enclosed between a large and small circle, sometimes called a "life-saver."

Precancellations of other countries usually follow these patterns, but may be any arrangement of bars, boxes and city names.

PROOFS AND ESSAYS: Proofs are impressions taken from an approved die, plate or stone in which the design and color are the same as the stamp issued to the public. Trial color proofs are impressions taken from approved dies, plates or stones in varying colors. An essay is the impression of a design that differs in some way from the stamp as issued.

PROVISIONALS: Stamps issued on short notice and intended for temporary use pending the arrival of regular (definitive) issues. They are usually issued to meet contingencies: changes in government or currency; shortage of necessary postage values, or military occupation.

In the 1840's, postmasters in certain American cities issued stamps that were valid only at specific post offices. Postmasters of the Confederate States also issued stamps with limited validity. These are known as Postmasters' Provisionals.

SE-TENANT: Joined together, referring to an unsevered pair, strip or block of stamps differing in design, denomination or overprint (U.S. Nos. 1530-1537).

TETE BECHE: A pair of stamps in which one is upside down in relation to the other. Some of these are the result of intentional sheet arrangement (Morocco Nos. B10-B11). Others occurred when one or more electrotypes were accidentally placed upside down on the plate (Colombia No. 57a). Separation of course destroys the tête bêche variety.

SPECIMENS: One of the regulations of the Universal Postal Union requires member nations to send samples of all stamps they put into service to the International Bureau in Switzerland. These are then sent to all other member nations as samples of what stamps are valid for postage. Many are overprinted, handstamped or initial-perforated "Specimen," "Canceled" or "Muestra." Some are marked with bars across the denominations (China), punched holes (Czechoslovakia) or back inscriptions (Mongolia).

Stamps distributed to government officials or for publicity purposes, and stamps submitted by private security printers for official approval may also receive such defacements.

These markings prevent postal use, and all such items are generally known as "specimens."

CLASSIFICATION OF STAMPS

Thė various functions of stamps are classified by their names. Postage stamps; air post stamps; postage due stamps for unpaid postage, collected at time of delivery; late fee stamps, a special fee for forwarding a letter after regular mail delivery; registration stamps, fee for keeping special record of letter and ensuring its delivery; special delivery and express stamps, for delivery of letter in advance of regular delivery. With the exception of regular postage, all numbers in the catalogue include a prefix letter denoting the class to which the stamp belongs. (B=Semi-Postal; C=Air Post; E=Special Delivery; J=Postage Due; O=Official; CO=Air Post Official; etc.).

CATALOGUE TERMS TRANSLATED

English	French	German	Spanish	Italian
Air mail	Poste aérienne	Flugpost	Correo aéreo	Posta aerea
Back	Verso	Rückseitig	Dorso	Dorso
Background	Fond	Hintergrund	Fondo	Sfondo
Bar	Barre	Balken	Barra	Barra
Bisected stamp	Timbre coupé	Halbiert	Partido en dos	Frazionato
Block of four	Bloc de quatre	Viererblock.	Bloque de cuatro	Blocco di quattro
Booklet	Carnet	Heftchen	Cuadernillo	Libretto
Bottom	Bas	Unten	Abajo	Basso
Bright	Vif	Lebhaft	Vivo	Vivo
Broken	Interrompu	Unterbrochen	Interrumpido	Interrotto
Cancellation	Oblitération	Entwertung	Matasello	Annullamento
Cancellation to order	Oblitération de complaisance	Gefälligkeitsabstempelung	Matasello de complacencia	Annullamento di compiacenza
Canceled	Annulé	Gestempelt	Cancelado	Annullato
Center	Centre du timbre	Mittelstück	Centro	Centro
Centering	Centrage	Zentrierung	Centrado	Centratura
Chalky paper	Papier couché	Kreidepapier	Papel estucado	Carta gessata
Circle	Cercle	Kreis	Circulo	Circolo
Coat of arms	Armoiries	Wappen	Escudo de armas	Arme
Coil	Rouleau de timbres	Markenrolle	Rollo de sellos	Rollo di francobolli
Color	Couleur	Farbe	Color	Colore
Comb perforation	Dentelure en peigne	Kammzähnung	Dentado de peine	Dentalletura e pettine
Commemorative	Commémoratif	Gedenkausgabe	Conmemorativo	Commemorativo
Corner	Angle	Ecke	Esquina	Angolo
Counterfeit	Faux	Fälschung	Falsificación	Falsificazione
Cover	Lettre	Brief	Carta	Lettera
Crescent	Croissant	Halbmond	Media luna	Luna crescente
Crown	Couronne	Krone	Corona	Corona
Cut square	Coupure	Ausschnitt	Recorte	Ritaglio
Dark	Foncé	Dunkel	Oscuro	Oscuro
Date	Date	Datum	Fecha	Data
Definitive	Définitif	Freimarken	Definitivo	Definitivo
Design	Dessin	Zeichnung	Diseño	Disegno
Die	Matrice	Urstempel	Cuño	Conio
District	District	Bezirk	Distrito	Distretto
Double	Double	Doppelt	Doble	Doppio
Dull	Terne	Trüb	Turbio	Smorto
Embossing	Impression en relief	Prägedruck	Impresión en relieve	Rilievo
Engraved	Gravé	Graviert	Grabado	Inciso
Error	Erreur	Fehler	Error	Errore
Essay	Essai	Probedruck	Ensayo	Saggio
Figure	Chiffre	Ziffer	Cifra	Cifra
Forerunner	Précurseur	Vorläufer	Precursor	Precursore
Forgery	Faux	Fälschung	Falsificación	Falsificazione
Frame	Cadre	Rahmen	Marco	Cornice
Genuine	Authentique	Echt	Auténtico	Autentico
Glossy paper	Papier glacé	Glanzpapier	Papel lustre	Carta patinata
Granite paper	Papier mélangé de fils de soie	Faserpapier	Papel con filamentos	Carta con fili di seta
Gum	Gomme	Gummi	Goma	Gomma
Gutter	Interpanneau	Zwischensteg	Espacio blanco entre dos grupos	Interspazio
Half	Moitié	Hälfte	Mitad	Metà
Handstamp	Cachet à la main	Handstempel	Matasello manual	Annullamento manuale

English	French	German	Spanish	Italian
Imperforate	Non-dentelé	Geschnitten	Sin dentar	Non dentellato
Inscription	Inscription	Inschrift	Inscripción	Dicitura
Inverted	Renversé	Kopfstehend	Invertido	Capovolto
Issue	Emission	Ausgabe	Emisión	Emissione
King	Roi	König	Rey	Re
Kingdom	Royaume	Königreich	Reino	Regno
Laid	Vergé	Gestrichen	Listado	Vergato
Large	Grand	Gross	Grande	Grosso
Late fee stamp	Timbre pour lettres en retard	Verspätungsmarke	Sello para cartas retardadas	Francobollo per le lettere in ritardo
Left	Gauche	Links	Izquierda	Sinistro
Light	Clair	Hell	Claro	Chiaro
Line perforation	Dentelure en lignes	Linienzähnung	Dentado en linea	Dentellatura lineare
Lithography	Lithographie	Steindruck	Litografia	Litografia
Lozenges	Losanges	Rauten	Rombos	Losanghe
Margin	Marge	Rand	Borde	Margine
Multiple	Multiple	Mehrfach	Multiple	Multiplo
Narrow	Étroit	Eng	Estrecho	Stretto
Network	Burelage	Netz	Burelage	Rete
Newspaper stamp	Timbre pour journaux	Zeitungsmarke	Sello para periódicos	Francobollo per giornali
Not issued	Non émis	Nicht verausgabt	No emitido	Non emesso
Numeral	Chiffre	Ziffer	Cifra	Numerale
Occupation	Occupation	Besetzung	Occupación	Occupazione
Official stamp	Timbre de service	Dienstmarke	Sello de servicio	Francobollo servizio
Oval	Ovale	Eiförmig	Óvalo	Ovale
Overprint	Surcharge	Aufdruck	Sobrecarga	Soprastampa
Pair	Paire	Paar	Pareja	Coppia
Pale	Pâle	Blass	Pâlido	Pallido
Pane	Panneau	Gruppe	Grupo	Gruppo
Paper	Papier	Papier	Papel	Carta
Parcel post stamp	Timbre pour colis postaux	Paketmarke	Sello para paquete postal	Francobollo per pacchi postali
Pen canceled	Oblitéré à plume	Federzugentwertung	Cancelado a pluma	Annullato a penna
Perforated	Dentelé	Gezähnt	Dentado	Dentellato
Perforation	Dentelure	Zähnung	Dentar	Dentellatura
Photogravure	Héliogravure	Rastertiefdruck	Fotograbado	Rotocalco
Piece	Fragment	Briefstück	Fragmento	Frammento
Pin perforation	Percé en points	In Punkten durchstochen	Horadado con alfileres	Perforato a punti
Plate	Planche	Platte	Plancha	Lastra
Postage due stamp	Timbre-taxe	Portomarke	Sello de tasa	Segnatasse
Postage stamp	Timbre-poste	Briefmarke	Sello de correos	Francobollo postale
Postal forgery	Faux pour servir	Postfälschung	Falso por correo	Falso per posta
Postal tax stamp	Timbre surtaxe obligatoire	Zwangszuschlagsmarke	Sello de sobretasa obligatorio	Francobollo per sopratassa obligatorio
Postmark	Oblitération postale	Poststempel	Matasello	Bollo
Price	Prix	Preis	Precio	Prezzo
Printing	Impression	Druck	Impresión	Stampa
Private	Privé	Privat	Privado	Privato
Proof	Epreuve	Druckprobe	Prueba de impresión	Prova
Quadrille	Quadrillé	Gegittert	Cuadriculado	Quadriglia
Quarter	Un quart	Viertel	Un cuarto	Quarto
Recess printing	Impression en taille douce	Tiefdruck	Grabado	Incisione
Reengraving	Regravure	Neugravierung	Regrabado	Rincisione

English	French	German	Spanish	Italian
Reentry	Double frappe	Nachgravierung	Regrabado	Doppia incisione
Registration stamp	Timbre pour lettre recommandée	Einschreibemarke	Sello de certificado	Francobollo per lettere raccomandate
Reprint	Réimpression	Nachdruck	Reimpresión	Ristampa
Revenue stamp	Timbre fiscal	Stempelmarke	Sello fiscal	Francobollo fiscale
Reversed	Retourné	Umgekehrt	Invertido	Rovesciato
Ribbed	Cannelé	Geriffelt	Acanalado	Scanalatura
Right	Droite	Rechts	A la derecha	Destro
Rotary printing	Impression par cylindre	Walzendruck	Impresión cilindrica	Stampa rotativa
Roulette	Perçage	Durchstich	Picadura	Foratura
Rouletted	Percé	Durchstochen	Picado	Forato
Semipostal stamp	Timbre de bienfaisance	Wohltätigkeitsmarke	Sello de beneficencia	Francobollo di beneficenza
Serpentine roulette	Percé en serpentin	Schlangenartiger Durchstich	Picado a serpentina	Perforazione a serpentina
Set	Série	Satz	Serie	Serie
Set price	Prix de la série	Satzpreis	Precio por serie	Prezzo per serie
Se-tenant	Se-tenant	Zusammendruck	Combinación	Combinazione
Shade	Nuance	Tönung	Tono	Gradazione di colore
Sheet	Feuille	Bogen	Hoja	Foglio
Side	Côté	Seite	Lado	Lato
Small	Petit	Klein	Pequeño	Piccolo
Souvenir sheet	Bloc commémoratif	Block, gedenkblock	Hojita-bloque conmemorativa	Foglietto commemorativo
Special delivery stamp	Timbre pour exprès	Eilmarke	Sello de urgencia	Francobollo per espressi
Specimen	Spécimen	Muster	Muestra	Saggio
Strip	Bande	Streifen	Tira	Striscia
Surcharge	Surcharge	Zuschlag	Sobrecarga	Soprastampa
Surtax	Surtaxe	Zuschlag	Sobretasa	Sopratassa
Tête bêche	Tête-bêche	Kehrdruck	Tête-bêche	Tête-bêche
Thick	Épais	Dick	Grueso	Spesso
Thin	Mince	Dünn	Delgado	Smilzo
Tinted paper	Papier teinté	Getöntes papier	Papel coloreado	Carta colorata
Top	Haut	Oben	Arriba	Alto
Typography	Typographie	Buchdruck	Tipografía	Tipografia
Unused	Neuf	Ungebraucht	Nuevo	Nuovo
Used	Oblitéré	Gebraucht	Usado	Usato
War tax stamp	Timbre d'impôt de guerre	Kriegssteuermarke	Sello de impuesto de guerra	Francobollo per tassa di guerra
Watermark	Filigrane	Wasserzeichen	Filigrana	Filigrana
Wide	Espacé	Weit	Ancho	Largo
With	Avec	Mit	Con	Con
Without	Sans	Ohne	Sin	Senza
Worn	Usé	Abgenutzt	Gastado	Usato
Wove paper	Papier ordinaire	Einfaches Papier	Papel avitelado	Carta unita

CATALOGUE COLORS TRANSLATED

English	French	German	Spanish	Italian
Apple green	Verte-pomme	Apfelgrün	Verde manzana	Verde mela
Bister	Bistre	Bister	Bistre	Bistro
Black	Noir	Schwarz	Negro	Nero
Blue	Bleu	Blau	Azul	Azzurro
Brick red	Rouge-brique	Ziegelrot	Rojo ladrillo	Rosso di mattone
Bronze	Bronze	Bronze	Bronce	Bronzo
Brown	Brun	Braun	Castaño, pardo	Bruno
Buff	Chamois	Sämisch	Anteado	Camoscio
Carmine	Carmin	Karmin	Carmin	Carminio
Cerise	Cerise	Kirschrot	Color de ceresa	Color ciliegia
Chalky blue	Bleu terne	Kreideblau	Azul turbio	Azzurro smorto
Chamois	Chamois	Sämisch	Anteado	Camoscio
Chestnut	Marron	Kastanienbraun	Castaño rojo	Marrone
Chocolate	Chocolat	Schokoladebraun	Chocolate	Cioccolato
Chrome yellow	Jaune-chrome	Chromgelb	Amarillo cromo	Giallo croma
Citron	Citron	Zitronengelb	Cidra	Cedro
Claret	Lie de vin	Weinrot	Rojo vinoso	Vinaccia
Cobalt	Cobalt	Kobaltblau	Cobalto	Cobalto
Copper red	Rouge-cuivre	Kupferrot	Rojo cobre	Rosso di rame
Cream	Crème	Rahmfarbe	Crema	Crema
Crimson	Cramoisi	Karmesin	Carmesi	Cremisi
Emerald	Vert-émeraude	Smaragdgrün	Esmeralda	Smeraldo
Flesh	Chair	Fleischfarben	Carne	Carnicino
Gray	Gris	Grau	Gris	Grigio
Green	Vert	Grün	Verde	Verde
Indigo	Indigo	Indigo	Azul indigo	Indaco
Lake	Lie de vin	Lackfarbe	Laca	Lacca
Lemon	Jaune-citron	Zitronengelb	Limón	Limone
Lilac	Lilas	Lila	Lila	Lilla
Magenta	Magenta	Magentarot	Magenta	Magenta
Mauve	Mauve	Malvenfarbe	Malva	Malva
Milky blue	Bleu laiteux	Milchblau	Azul lechoso	Azzurro di latte
Moss green	Vert mousse	Moosgrün	Verde musgo	Verde muscosa
Multicolored	Polychrome	Mehrfarbig	Multicolores	Policromo
Ocher	Ocre	Ocker	Ocre	Ocra
Olive	Olive	Oliv	Oliva	Oliva
Orange	Orange	Orange	Naranja	Arancio
Pink	Rose	Rosa	Rosa	Rosa
Plum	Prune	Pflaumenfarbe	Color de ciruela	Prugna
Prussian blue	Bleu de Prusse	Preussischblau	Azul de Prusia	Azzurro di Prussia
Purple	Pourpre	Purpur	Púrpura	Porpora
Red	Rouge	Rot	Rojo	Rosso
Rose	Rose	Rosa	Rosa	Rosa
Rosine	Rose vif	Lebhaftrosa	Rosa vivo	Rosa vivo
Royal blue	Bleu-roi	Königsblau	Azul real	Azzurro reale
Rust	Brun-rouille	Rostbraun	Castaño oxidado	Castagna
Sage green	Vert-sauge	Salbeigrün	Verde salvia	Verde salvia
Salmon	Saumon	Lachs	Salmón	Salmone
Scarlet	Écarlate	Scharlach	Escarlata	Scarlatto
Sea green	Vert de mer	Seegrün	Verde mar	Verde mare
Sepia	Sépia	Sepia	Sepia	Seppia
Sienna	Terre de Sienne	Siena	Siena	Siena
Sky blue	Bleu ciel	Himmelblau	Azul celeste	Azzurro cielo
Slate	Ardoise	Schiefer	Pizarra	Ardesia
Steel blue	Bleu acier	Stahlblau	Azul acero	Azzurro acciaio
Straw	Jaune-paille	Strohgelb	Amarillo pajizo	Giallo pallido
Turquoise blue	Bleu-turquoise	Türkisblau	Azul turquesa	Azzurro turchese
Ultramarine	Outremer	Ultramarin	Ultramar	Oltremare
Vermilion	Vermillon	Zinnober	Cinabrio	Vermiglione
Violet	Violet	Violett	Violeta	Violetto
Yellow	Jaune	Gelb	Amarillo	Giallo

List of Colonies, Former Colonies, Offices and Territories Controlled by Parent States

BELGIUM

Belgian Congo
Ruanda-Urundi

DENMARK

Danish West Indies
Faroe Islands
Greenland
Iceland

FRANCE

Colonies, Past and Present, and Controlled Territories

Afars and Issas, Terr. of
Alaouites
Alexandretta
Algeria
Alsace and Lorraine
Ajouan
Annam & Tonkin
Benin
Cambodia (Khmer)
Cameroun
Castellorizo
Chad
Cilicia
Cochin China
Comoro Islands
Dahomey
Diego Suarez
Djibouti (Somali Coast)
Fezzan
French Congo
French Equatorial Africa
French Guiana
French Guinea
French India
French Morocco
French Polynesia (Oceania)
French Southern & Antarctic Territories
French Sudan
French West Africa
Gabon
Germany
Ghadames
Grand Comoro
Guadeloupe
Indo-China
Inini
Ivory Coast
Laos
Latakia
Lebanon
Madagascar
Martinique
Mauritania
Mayotte
Memel
Middle Congo
Mohéli
New Caledonia
New Hebrides
Niger Territory
Nossi-Bé
Obock
Reunion
Rouad, Ile
Ste.-Marie de Madagascar
St. Pierre & Miquelon
Senegal
Senegambia & Niger
Somali Coast
Syria
Tahiti
Togo
Tunisia
Ubangi-Shari
Upper Senegal & Niger
Upper Volta
Viet Nam
Wallis & Futuna Islands

Post Offices in Foreign Countries

China
Crete
Egypt
Turkish Empire
Zanzibar

GERMANY

Early States

Baden
Bavaria
Bergedorf
Bremen
Brunswick
Hamburg
Hanover
Lubeck
Mecklenburg-Schwerin
Mecklenburg-Strelitz
Oldenburg
Prussia
Saxony
Schleswig-Holstein
Wurttemberg

Former Colonies

Cameroun (Kamerun)
Caroline Islands
German East Africa
German New Guinea
German South-West Africa
Kiauchau
Mariana Islands
Marshall Islands
Samoa
Togo

ITALY

Early States

Modena
Parma
Romagna
Roman States
Sardinia
Tuscany
Two Sicilies
  Naples
  Neapolitan Provinces
  Sicily

Former Colonies, Controlled Territories, Occupation Areas

Aegean Islands
  Calimno (Calino)
  Caso
  Cos (Coo)
  Karki (Carchi)
  Leros (Lero)
  Lipso
  Nisiros (Nisiro)
  Patmos (Patmo)
  Piscopi
  Rodi (Rhodes)
  Scarpanto
  Simi
  Stampalia
Castellorizo
Corfu
Cyrenaica
Eritrea
Ethiopia (Abyssinia)
Fiume
Ionian Islands
  Cephalonia
  Ithaca
  Paxos
Italian East Africa
Libya
Oltre Giuba
Saseno
Somalia (Italian Somaliland)
Tripolitania

Post Offices in Foreign Countries

"Estero"*

Austria
China
  Peking
  Tientsin
Crete
Tripoli
Turkish Empire
  Constantinople
Turkish Empire (cont.)
  Durazzo
  Janina
Jerusalem
Salonika
Scutari
Smyrna
Valona

* Stamps overprinted "ESTERO" were used in various parts of the world.

NETHERLANDS

Netherlands Antilles (Curacao)
Netherlands Indies
Netherlands New Guinea
Surinam (Dutch Guiana)

PORTUGAL

Colonies, Past and Present, and Controlled Territories

Angola
Angra
Azores
Cape Verde
Funchal
Horta
Inhambane
Kionga
Lourenço Marques
Macao
Madeira
Mozambique
Mozambique Co.
Nyassa
Ponta Delgada
Portuguese Africa
Portuguese Congo
Portuguese Guinea
Portuguese India
Quelimane
St. Thomas & Prince Isls.
Tete
Timor
Zambezia

RUSSIA

Allied Territories and Republics, Occupation Areas

Armenia
Aunus (Olonets)
Azerbaijan
Batum
Estonia
Far Eastern Republic
Georgia
Karelia
Latvia
Lithuania
North Ingermanland
Ostland
Russian Turkestan
Siberia
South Russia
Tannu Tuva
Transcaucasian
  Federated Republics
Ukraine
Wenden (Livonia)
Western Ukraine

SPAIN

Colonies, Past and Present, and Controlled Territories

Agüera, La
Cape Juby
Cuba
Elobey, Annobon & Corisco
Fernando Po
Ifni
Mariana Islands
Philippines
Puerto Rico
Rio de Oro
Rio Muni
Spanish Guinea
Spanish Morocco
Spanish Sahara
Spanish West Africa

Post Offices in Foreign Countries

Morocco
Tangier
Tetuan

COMMON DESIGN TYPES

Pictured in this section are issues where one illustration has been used for a number of countries in the Catalogue. Not included in this section are overprinted stamps or those issues which are illustrated in each country.

EUROPA

Europa Issue, 1956

The design symbolizing the cooperation among the six countries comprising the Coal and Steel Community is illustrated in each country.

Belgium	444–445
France	805–806
Germany	748–749
Italy	715–716
Luxembourg	318–320
Netherlands	368–369

Europa Issue, 1958

"E" and Dove

CD1

European Postal Union at the service of European integration.

1958, Sept. 13

Belgium	478–479
France	889–890
Germany	790–791
Italy	750–751
Luxembourg	341–343
Netherlands	375–376
Saar	317–318

Europa Issue, 1959

6-Link Endless Chain

CD2

1959, Sept. 19

Belgium	479–498
France	929–930
Germany	805–806
Italy	791–792
Luxembourg	354–355
Netherlands	379–380

Europa Issue, 1960

19-Spoke Wheel

CD3

First anniversary of the establishment of C.E.P.T. (Conférence Européenne des Administrations des Postes et des Télécommunications.)

The spokes symbolize the 19 founding members of the Conference.

1960, Sept.

Belgium	518–519
Denmark	379
Finland	376–377
France	970–971
Germany	818–820
Great Britain	377–378
Greece	688
Iceland	327–328
Ireland	175–176
Italy	809–810
Luxembourg	374–375
Netherlands	385–386
Norway	387
Portugal	866–867
Spain	941–942
Sweden	562–563
Switzerland	400–401
Turkey	1493–1494

Europa Issue, 1961

19 Doves Flying as One

CD4

The 19 doves represent the 19 members of the Conference of European Postal and Telecommunications Administrations, C.E.P.T.

1961–62

Belgium	536–537
Cyprus	201–203
France	1005–1006
Germany	844–845
Great Britain	383–384
Greece	718–719
Iceland	340–341
Italy	845–846
Luxembourg	382–383
Netherlands	387–388
Spain	1010–1011
Switzerland	410–411
Turkey	1518–1520

Europa Issue 1962

Young Tree with 19 Leaves

CD5

The 19 leaves represent the 19 original members of C.E.P.T.

1962–63

Belgium	546–547
Cyprus	219–221
France	1045–1046
Germany	852–853
Greece	739–740
Iceland	348–349
Ireland	184–185
Italy	860–861
Luxembourg	386–387
Netherlands	394–395
Norway	414–415
Switzerland	416–417
Turkey	1553–1555

Europa Issue, 1963

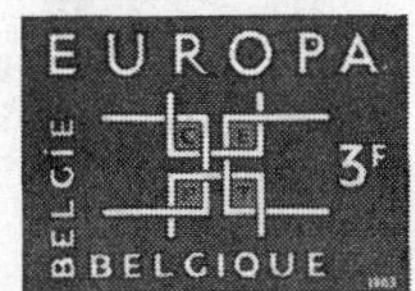

Stylized Links, Symbolizing Unity

CD6

1963, Sept.

Belgium	562–563
Cyprus	229–231
Finland	419
France	1074–1075
Germany	867–868
Greece	768–769
Iceland	357–358
Ireland	188–189
Italy	880–881
Luxembourg	403–404
Netherlands	416–417
Norway	441–442
Switzerland	429
Turkey	1602–1603

Europa Issue, 1964

Symbolic Daisy

CD7

5th anniversary of the establishment of C.E.P.T. The 22 petals of the flower symbolize the 22 members of the Conference.

1964, Sept.

Austria	738
Belgium	578–579
Cyprus	244–246
France	1109–1110
Germany	897–898
Greece	801–802
Iceland	367–368
Ireland	196–197
Italy	894–895
Luxembourg	411–412
Monaco	590–591
Netherlands	428–429
Norway	458
Portugal	931–933
Spain	1262–1263
Switzerland	438–439
Turkey	1628–1629

Europa Issue, 1965

Leaves and "Fruit"

CD8

1965

Belgium	600–601
Cyprus	262–264
Finland	437
France	1131–1132
Germany	934–935
Greece	833–834
Iceland	375–376
Ireland	204–205
Italy	915–916
Luxembourg	432–433
Monaco	616–617
Netherlands	438–439
Norway	475–476
Portugal	958–960
Switzerland	469
Turkey	1665–1666

Europa Issue, 1966

Symbolic Sailboat

CD9

1966, Sept.

Andorra, French	172
Belgium	622–628
Cyprus	275–277
France	1163–1164
Germany	963–964
Greece	862–863
Iceland	384–385
Ireland	216–217
Italy	942–943
Liechtenstein	415
Luxembourg	440–441
Monaco	639–640
Netherlands	441–442
Norway	496–497
Portugal	980–982
Switzerland	477–478
Turkey	1718–1719

Europa Issue, 1967

Cogwheels

CD10

1967

Andorra, French	174–175
Belgium	641–642
Cyprus	297–299
France	1178–1179
Greece	891–892
Germany	969–970
Iceland	389–390
Ireland	232–233
Italy	951–952
Liechtenstein	420
Luxembourg	449–450
Monaco	669–670
Netherlands	444–447
Norway	504–505
Portugal	994–996
Spain	1465–1466
Switzerland	482
Turkey	B120–B121

Europa Issue, 1968

Golden Key with C.E.P.T. Emblem
CD11

1968

Andorra, French	182–183
Belgium	664–665
Cyprus	314–316
France	1209–1210
Germany	983–984
Greece	916–917
Iceland	395–396
Ireland	242–243
Italy	979–980
Liechtenstein	442
Luxembourg	466–467
Monaco	689–691
Netherlands	452–453
Portugal	1019–1021
San Marino	687
Spain	1526
Turkey	1775–1776

Europa Issue, 1969

"EUROPA" and "CEPT"
CD12

Tenth anniversary of C.E.P.T.

1969

Andorra, French	188–189
Austria	837
Belgium	683–684
Cyprus	326–328
Denmark	458
Finland	483
France	1245–1246
Germany	996–997
Great Britain	585
Greece	947–948
Iceland	406–407
Ireland	270–271
Italy	1000–1001
Jugoslavia	1003–1004
Liechtenstein	453
Luxembourg	474–475
Monaco	722–724
Netherlands	475–476
Norway	533–534
Portugal	1038–1040
San Marino	701–702
Spain	1567
Sweden	814–816
Switzerland	500–501
Turkey	1799–1800
Vatican	470–472

Europa Issue, 1970

Interwoven Threads
CD13

1970

Andorra, French	196–197
Belgium	708–709
Cyprus	340–342
France	1271–1272
Germany	1018–1019
Greece	985, 987
Iceland	420–421
Ireland	279–281
Italy	1013–1014
Jugoslavia	1024–1025
Liechtenstein	470
Luxembourg	489–490
Monaco	768–770
Netherlands	483–484
Portugal	1060–1062
San Marino	729–730
Spain	1607
Switzerland	515–516
Turkey	1848–1849

Europa Issue, 1971

"Fraternity, Cooperation, Common Effort"—CD14

1971

Andorra, French	205–206
Belgium	742–743
Cyprus	365–367
Finland	504
France	1304
Germany	1064–1065
Greece	1029–1030
Iceland	429–430
Ireland	305–306
Italy	1038–1039
Jugoslavia	1052–1053
Liechtenstein	485
Luxembourg	500–501
Malta	425–427
Monaco	797–799
Netherlands	488–489
Portugal	1094–1096
San Marino	749–750
Spain	1675–1676
Switzerland	531–532
Turkey	1876–1877

Europa Issue, 1972

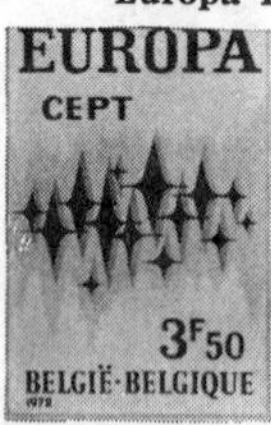

Sparkles, Symbolic of Communications
CD15

1972

Andorra, French	210–211
Andorra, Spanish	62
Belgium	768–769
Cyprus	380–382
Finland	512–513
France	1341
Germany	1089–1090
Greece	1049–1050
Iceland	439–440
Ireland	316–317
Italy	1065–1066
Jugoslavia	1100–1101
Liechtenstein	504
Luxembourg	512–513
Malta	450–453
Monaco	831–832
Netherlands	494–495
Portugal	1141–1143
San Marino	771–772
Spain	1718
Switzerland	544–545
Turkey	1907–1908

Europa Issue, 1973

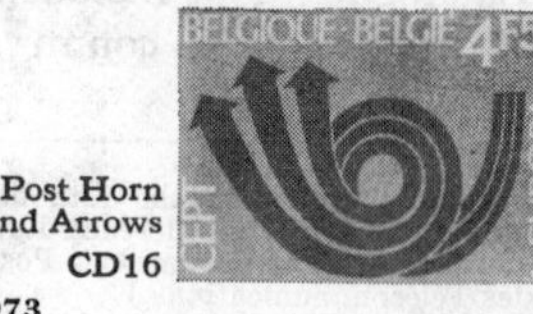

Post Horn and Arrows
CD16

1973

Andorra, French	319–320
Andorra, Spanish	76
Belgium	782–783
Cyprus	396–398
Finland	526
France	1367
Germany	1114–1115
Greece	1090–1092
Iceland	447–448
Ireland	329–330
Italy	1108–1109
Jugoslavia	1138–1139
Liechtenstein	528–529
Luxembourg	523–524
Malta	469–471
Monaco	866–867
Netherlands	504–505
Norway	604–605
Portugal	1170–1172
San Marino	802–803
Spain	1753
Switzerland	580–581
Turkey	1935–1936

PORTUGAL & COLONIES

Vasco da Gama Issue

Fleet Departing—CD20

Fleet Arriving at Calicut
CD21

Embarking at Rastello—CD22

Muse of History
CD23

Flagship San Gabriel, da Gama and Camoens
CD24

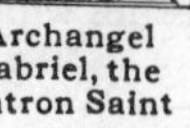

Archangel Gabriel, the Patron Saint
CD25

Flagship San Gabriel
CD26

Vasco da Gama
CD27

Fourth centenary of Vasco da Gama's discovery of the route to India.

1898

Azores	93–100
Macao	67–74
Madeira	37–44
Portugal	147–154
Port. Africa	1–8
Port. India	189–196
Timor	45–52

Pombal Issue

POSTAL TAX

Marquis de Pombal
CD28

Planning Reconstruction of Lisbon, 1755
CD29

Pombal Monument, Lisbon
CD30

Sebastiao José de Carvalho e Mello, Marquis de Pombal (1699–1782), statesman, rebuilt Lisbon after earthquake of 1755. Tax was for the erection of Pombal monument. Obligatory on all mail on certain days throughout the year.

1925

Angola	RA1–RA3
Azores	RA9–RA11
Cape Verde	RA1–RA3
Macao	RA1–RA3
Madeira	RA1–RA3
Mozambique	RA1–RA3
Portugal	RA11–RA13
Port. Guinea	RA1–RA3
Port. India	RA1–RA3
St. Thomas & Prince Islands	RA1–RA3
Timor	RA1–RA3

Pombal Issue

POSTAL TAX DUES

Marquis de Pombal
CD31

Planning Reconstruction of Lisbon, 1755
CD32

Pombal Monument, Lisbon
CD33

1925

Angola	RAJ1–RAJ3
Azores	RAJ2–RAJ4
Cape Verde	RAJ1–RAJ3
Macao	RAJ1–RAJ3
Madeira	RAJ1–RAJ3
Mozambique	RAJ1–RAJ3
Portugal	RAJ2–RAJ4
Port. Guinea	RAJ1–RAJ3
Port. India	RAJ1–RAJ3
St. Thomas & Prince Islands	RAJ1–RAJ3
Timor	RAJ1–RAJ3

Vasco da Gama
CD34

Mousinho de Albuquerque
CD35

Dam
CD36

Prince Henry the Navigator
CD37

Affonso de Albuquerque
CD38

1938–39

Angola	274–291
Cape Verde	234–251
Macao	289–305
Mozambique	270–287
Port. Guinea	233–250
Port. India	439–453
St. Thomas & Prince Islands	302–319, 323–340
Timor	223–239

Plane over Globe
CD39

1938–39

Angola	C1–C9
Cape Verde	C1–C9
Macao	C7–C15
Mozambique	C1–C9
Port. Guinea	C1–C9
Port. India	C1–C8
St. Thomas & Prince Islands	C1–C18
Timor	C1–C9

Lady of Fatima Issue

Our Lady of the Rosary, Fatima, Portugal
CD40

1948–49

Angola	315–318
Cape Verde	266
Macao	336
Mozambique	325–328
Port. Guinea	271
Port. India	480
St. Thomas & Prince Islands	351
Timor	254

A souvenir sheet of 9 stamps was issued in 1951 to mark the extension of the 1950 Holy Year. The sheet contains: Angola No. 316, Cape Verde No. 266, Macao No. 336, Mozambique No. 325, Portuguese Guinea No. 271, Portuguese India Nos. 480, 485, St. Thomas & Prince Islands No. 351, Timor No. 254.

The sheet also contains a portrait of Pope Pius XII and is inscribed "Encerramento do Ano Santo, Fatima 1951." It was sold for 11 escudos.

Holy Year Issue

Church Bells and Dove
CD41

Angel Holding Candelabra
CD42

Holy Year, 1950.

1950–51

Angola	331–332
Cape Verde	268–269
Macao	339–340
Mozambique	330–331
Port. Guinea	273–274
Port. India	490–491, 496–503
St. Thomas & Prince Islands	353–354
Timor	258–259

A souvenir sheet of 8 stamps was issued in 1951 to mark the extension of the Holy Year. The sheet contains: Angola No. 331, Cape Verde No. 269, Macao No. 340, Mozambique No. 331, Portuguese Guinea No. 275, Portuguese India No. 490, St. Thomas & Prince Islands No. 354, Timor No. 258, some with colors changed. The sheet contains doves and is inscribed "Encerramento do Ano Santo, Fatima 1951." It was sold for 17 escudos.

Holy Year Conclusion Issue

Our Lady of Fatima
CD43

Conclusion of Holy Year. Sheets contain alternate vertical rows of stamps and labels bearing quotation from Pope Pius XII, different for each colony.

1951

Angola	357
Cape Verde	270
Macao	352
Mozambique	356
Port. Guinea	275
Port. India	506
St. Thomas & Prince Islands	355
Timor	270

Medical Congress Issue

Medical Examination
CD44

First National Congress of Tropical Medicine, Lisbon, 1952.
Each stamp has a different design.

1952

Angola	358
Cape Verde	287
Macao	364
Mozambique	359
Port. Guinea	276
Port. India	516
St. Thomas & Prince Islands	356
Timor	271

POSTAGE DUE STAMPS

CD45

1952

Angola	J37–J42
Cape Verde	J31–J36
Macao	J53–J58
Mozambique	J51–J56
Port. Guinea	J40–J45
Port. India	J47–J52
St. Thomas & Prince Islands	J52–J57
Timor	J31–J36

Sao Paulo Issue

Father Manuel da Nobrega and View of Sao Paulo
CD46

400th anniversary of the founding of Sao Paulo, Brazil.

1954

Angola	385
Cape Verde	297
Macao	382
Mozambique	395
Port. Guinea	291
Port. India	530
St. Thomas & Prince Islands	369
Timor	279

Tropical Medicine Congress Issue

Securidaca Longipedunculata
CD47

Sixth International Congress for Tropical Medicine and Malaria, Lisbon, Sept. 1958.
Each stamp shows a different plant.

1958

Angola	409
Cape Verde	303
Macao	392
Mozambique	404
Port. Guinea	295
Port. India	569
St. Thomas & Prince Islands	371
Timor	289

Sports Issue

Flying
CD48

Each stamp shows a different sport.

1962

Angola	433–438
Cape Verde	320–325
Macao	394–399
Mozambique	424–429
Port. Guinea	299–304
St. Thomas & Prince Islands	374–379
Timor	313–318

Anti-Malaria Issue

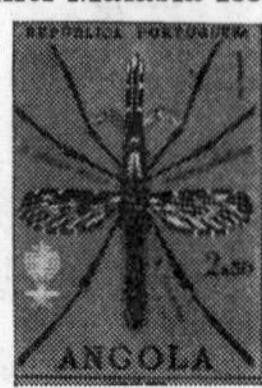

Anopheles Funestus and Malaria Eradication Symbol

CD49

World Health Organization drive to eradicate malaria.

1962

Angola	439
Cape Verde	326
Macao	400
Mozambique	430
Port. Guinea	305
St. Thomas & Prince Islands	380
Timor	319

Airline Anniversary Issue

Map of Africa, Super Constellation and Jet Liner

CD50

Tenth anniversary of Transportes Aéreos Portugueses (TAP).

1963

Angola	490
Cape Verde	327
Mozambique	434
Port. Guinea	318
St. Thomas & Prince Islands	381

National Overseas Bank Issue

Antonio Teixeira de Sousa

CD51

Centenary of the National Overseas Bank of Portugal.

1964, May 16

Angola	509
Cape Verde	328
Port. Guinea	319
St. Thomas & Prince Islands	382
Timor	320

ITU Issue

ITU Emblem and St. Gabriel

CD52

Centenary of the International Communications Union.

1965, May 17

Angola	511
Cape Verde	329
Macao	402
Mozambique	464
Port. Guinea	320
St. Thomas & Prince Islands	383
Timor	321

National Revolution Issue

St. Paul's Hospital, and Commercial and Industrial School

CD53

40th anniversary of the National Revolution.

Different buildings on each stamp.

1966, May 28

Angola	525
Cape Verde	338
Macao	403
Mozambique	465
Port. Guinea	329
St. Thomas & Prince Islands	392
Timor	322

Navy Club Issue

Mendes Barata and Cruiser Dom Carlos I

CD54

Centenary of Portugal's Navy Club.

Each stamp has a different design.

1967, Jan. 31

Angola	527–528
Cape Verde	339–340
Macao	412–413
Mozambique	478–479
Port. Guinea	330–331
St. Thomas & Prince Islands	393–394
Timor	323–324

Admiral Coutinho Issue

Admiral Gago Coutinho and his First Ship

CD55

Centenary of the birth of Admiral Carlos Viegas Gago Coutinho (1869–1959), explorer and aviation pioneer.

Each stamp has a different design.

1969, Feb. 17

Angola	547
Cape Verde	355
Macao	417
Mozambique	484
Port. Guinea	335
St. Thomas & Prince Islands	397
Timor	335

Administration Reform Issue

Luiz Augusto Rebello da Silva

CD56

Centenary of the administration reforms of the overseas territories.

1969, Sept. 25

Angola	549
Cape Verde	357
Macao	419
Mozambique	491
Port. Guinea	337
St. Thomas & Prince Islands	399
Timor	338

Marshal Carmona Issue

Marshal A. O. Carmona

CD57

Birth centenary of Marshal Antonio Oscar Carmona de Fragoso (1869–1951), President of Portugal.

Each stamp has a different design.

1970, Nov. 15

Angola	563
Cape Verde	359
Macao	422
Mozambique	493
Port. Guinea	340
St. Thomas & Prince Islands	403
Timor	341

Olympic Games Issue

Racing Yachts and Olympic Emblem

CD59

20th Olympic Games, Munich, Aug. 26–Sept. 11.

Each stamp shows a different sport.

1972, June 20

Angola	569
Cape Verde	361
Macao	426
Mozambique	504
Port. Guinea	342
St. Thomas & Prince Islands	408
Timor	343

Lisbon-Rio de Janeiro Flight Issue

"Santa Cruz" over Fernando de Noronha

CD60

50th anniversary of the Lisbon to Rio de Janeiro flight by Arturo de Sacadura and Coutinho, March 30-June 5, 1922.

Each stamp shows a different stage of the flight.

1972, Sept. 20

Angola	570
Cape Verde	362
Macao	427
Mozambique	505
Port. Guinea	343
St. Thomas & Prince Islands	409
Timor	344

WMO Centenary Issue

WMO Emblem

CD61

Centenary of international meteorological cooperation.

1973, Dec. 15

Angola	571
Cape Verde	363
Macao	429
Mozambique	509
Port. Guinea	344
St. Thomas & Prince Islands	410
Timor	345

FRENCH COMMUNITY

Colonial Exposition Issue

People of French Empire

CD70

Women's Heads

CD71

France Showing Way to Civilization

CD72

"Colonial Commerce"

CD73

International Colonial Exposition, Paris 1931.

1931

Cameroun	213–216
Chad	60–63
Dahomey	97–100
Fr. Guiana	152–155
Fr. Guinea	116–119
Fr. India	100–103
Fr. Polynesia	76–79
Fr. Sudan	102–105
Gabon	120–123
Guadeloupe	138–141
Indo-China	140–142
Ivory Coast	92–95
Madagascar	169–172
Martinique	129–132
Mauritania	65–68
Middle Congo	61–64
New Caledonia	176–179
Niger	73–76
Reunion	122–125
St. Pierre & Miquelon	132–135
Senegal	138–141
Somali Coast	135–138
Togo	254–257
Ubangi-Shari	82–85
Upper Volta	66–69
Wallis & Futuna Isls.	85–88

Paris International Exposition Issue

Colonial Arts Exposition Issue

"Colonial Resources"

CD74 CD77

Overseas Commerce

CD75

Exposition Buildings and Women

CD76

"France and the Empire"

CD78

Cultural Treasures of the Colonies

CD79

Souvenir sheets contain one imperf. stamp.

1937

Cameroun	217–222A
Dahomey	101–107
Fr. Equatorial Africa	27–32, 73
Fr. Guiana	162–168
Fr. Guinea	120–126
Fr. India	104–110
Fr. Polynesia	117–123
Fr. Sudan	106–112
Guadeloupe	148–154
Indo-China	193–199
Inini	41
Ivory Coast	152–158
Kwangchowan	120
Madagascar	191–197
Martinique	179–185
Mauritania	69–75
New Caledonia	208–214
Niger	72–83
Reunion	167–173
St. Pierre & Miquelon	165–171
Senegal	172–178
Somali Coast	139–145
Togo	258–264
Wallis & Futuna Isls.	89

Curie Issue

Pierre and Marie Curie

CD80

40th anniversary of the discovery of radium. The surtax was for the benefit of the International Union for the Control of Cancer.

1938

Cameroun	B1
Dahomey	B2
France	B76
Fr. Equatorial Africa	B1
Fr. Guiana	B3
Fr. Guinea	B2
Fr. India	B6
Fr. Polynesia	B5
Fr. Sudan	B1
Guadeloupe	B3
Indo-China	B14
Ivory Coast	B2
Madagascar	B2
Martinique	B2
Mauritania	B3
New Caledonia	B4
Niger	B1
Reunion	B4
St. Pierre & Miquelon	B3
Senegal	B3
Somali Coast	B2
Togo	B1

Caillié Issue

René Caillié and Map of Northwestern Africa

CD81

Death centenary of René Caillié (1799–1838), French explorer.

All three denominations exist with colony name omitted.

1939

Dahomey	108–110
Fr. Guinea	161–163
Fr. Sudan	113–115
Ivory Coast	160–162
Mauritania	109–111
Niger	84–86
Senegal	188–190
Togo	265–267

New York World's Fair Issue

Natives and New York Skyline

CD82

1939

Cameroun	223–224
Dahomey	111–112
Fr. Equatorial Africa	78–79
Fr. Guiana	169–170
Fr. Guinea	164–165
Fr. India	111–112
Fr. Polynesia	124–125
Fr. Sudan	116–117
Guadeloupe	155–156
Indo-China	203–204
Inini	42–43
Ivory Coast	163–164
Kwangchowan	121–122
Madagascar	209–210
Martinique	186–187
Mauritania	112–113
New Caledonia	215–216
Niger	87–88
Reunion	174–175
St. Pierre & Miquelon	205–206
Senegal	191–192
Somali Coast	179–180
Togo	268–269
Wallis & Futuna Isls.	90–91

French Revolution Issue

Storming of the Bastille

CD83

150th anniversary of the French Revolution. The surtax was for the defense of the colonies.

1939

Cameroun	B2–B6
Dahomey	B3–B7
Fr. Equatorial Africa	B4–B8, CB1
Fr. Guiana	B4–B8, CB1
Fr. Guinea	B3–B7
Fr. India	B7–B11
Fr. Polynesia	B6–B10, CB1
Fr. Sudan	B2–B6
Guadeloupe	B4–B8
Indo-China	B15–B19, CB1
Inini	B1–B5
Ivory Coast	B3–B7
Kwangchowan	B1–B5
Madagascar	B3–B7, CB1
Martinique	B3–B7
Mauritania	B4–B8
New Caledonia	B5–B9, CB1
Niger	B2–B6
Reunion	B5–B9, CB1
St. Pierre & Miquelon	B4–B8
Senegal	B4–B8, CB1
Somali Coast	B3–B7
Togo	B2–B6
Wallis & Futuna Isls.	B1–B5

Plane over Coastal Area

CD85

All five denominations exist with colony name omitted.

1940

Dahomey	C1–C5
Fr. Guinea	C1–C5
Fr. Sudan	C1–C5
Ivory Coast	C1–C5
Mauritania	C1–C5
Niger	C1–C5
Senegal	C12–C16
Togo	C1–C5

Colonial Infantryman

CD86

1941

Cameroun	B13B
Dahomey	B13
Fr. Equatorial Africa	B8B
Fr. Guiana	B10
Fr. Guinea	B13
Fr. India	B13
Fr. Polynesia	B12
Fr. Sudan	B12
Guadeloupe	B10
Indo-China	B19B
Inini	B7
Ivory Coast	B13
Kwangchowan	B7
Madagascar	B9
Martinique	B9
Mauritania	B14
New Caledonia	B11
Niger	B12
Reunion	B11
St. Pierre & Miquelon	B8B
Senegal	B14
Somali Coast	B9
Togo	B10B
Wallis & Futuna Isls.	B7

Cross of Lorraine and Four-motor Plane

CD87

1941–5

Cameroun	C1–C7
Fr. Equatorial Africa	C17–C23
Fr. Guiana	C9–C10
Fr. India	C1–C6
Fr. Polynesia	C3–C9
Fr. West Africa	C1–C3
Guadeloupe	C1–C2
Madagascar	C37–C43
Martinique	C1–C2
New Caledonia	C7–C13
Reunion	C18–C24
St. Pierre & Miquelon	C1–C7
Somali Coast	C1–C7

Transport Plane

CD88

Caravan and Plane—CD89

1942

Dahomey C6–C13
Fr. Guinea C6–C13
Fr. Sudan C6–C13
Ivory Coast C6–C13
Mauritania C6–C13
Niger C6–C13
Senegal C17–C25
Togo C6–C13

Red Cross Issue

Marianne
CD90

The surtax was for the French Red Cross and national relief.

1944

Cameroun B28
Fr. Equatorial Africa B38
Fr. Guiana B12
Fr. India B14
Fr. Polynesia B13
Fr. West Africa B1
Guadeloupe B12
Madagascar B15
Martinique B11
New Caledonia B13
Reunion B15
St. Pierre & Miquelon B13
Somali Coast B13
Wallis & Futuna Isls. B9

Eboué Issue

Félix Eboué
CD91

Félix Eboué, first French colonial administrator to proclaim resistance to Germany after French surrender in World War II.

1945

Cameroun 296–297
Fr. Equatorial Africa 156–157
Fr. Guiana 171–172
Fr. India 210–211
Fr. Polynesia 150–151
Fr. West Africa 15–16
Guadeloupe 187–188
Madagascar 259–260
Martinique 196–197
New Caledonia 274–275
Reunion 238–239
St. Pierre & Miquelon 322–323
Somali Coast 238–239

Victory Issue

Victory
CD92

European victory of the Allied Nations in World War II.

1946, May 8

Cameroun C8
Fr. Equatorial Africa C24
Fr. Guiana C11
Fr. India C7
Fr. Polynesia C10
Fr. West Africa C4
Guadeloupe C3
Indo-China C19
Madagascar C44
Martinique C3
New Caledonia C14
Reunion C25
St. Pierre & Miquelon C8
Somali Coast C8
Wallis & Futuna Isls. C1

Chad to Rhine Issue

Leclerc's Departure from Chad
CD93

Battle at Cufra Oasis
CD94

Tanks in Action, Mareth
CD95

Normandy Invasion
CD96

Entering Paris
CD97

Liberation of Strasbourg
CD98

"Chad to the Rhine" march, 1942–44, by Gen. Jacques Leclerc's column, later French 2nd Armored Division.

1946, June 6

Cameroun C9–C14
Fr. Equatorial Africa C25–C30
Fr. Guiana C12–C17
Fr. India C8–C13
Fr. Polynesia C11–C16
Fr. West Africa C5–C10
Guadeloupe C4–C9
Indo-China C20–C25
Madagascar C45–C50
Martinique C4–C9
New Caledonia C15–C20
Reunion C26–C31
St. Pierre & Miquelon C9–C14
Somali Coast C9–C14
Wallis & Futuna Isls. C2–C7

UPU Issue

French Colonials, Globe and Plane
CD99

75th anniversary of the Universal Postal Union.

1949, July 4

Cameroun C29
Fr. Equatorial Africa C34
Fr. India C17
Fr. Polynesia C20
Fr. West Africa C15
Indo-China C26
Madagascar C55
New Caledonia C24
St. Pierre & Miquelon C18
Somali Coast C18
Togo C18
Wallis & Futuna Isls. C10

Tropical Medicine Issue

Doctor Treating Infant
CD100

The surtax was for charitable work.

1950

Cameroun B29
Fr. Equatorial Africa B39
Fr. India B15
Fr. Polynesia B14
Fr. West Africa B3
Madagascar B17
New Caledonia B14
St. Pierre & Miquelon B14
Somali Coast B14
Togo B11

Military Medal Issue

Medal, Early Marine and Colonial Soldier
CD101

Centenary of the creation of the French Military Medal.

1952

Cameroun 332
Comoro Isls. 39
Fr. Equatorial Africa 186
Fr. India 233
Fr. Polynesia 179
Fr. West Africa 57
Madagascar 286
New Caledonia 295
St. Pierre & Miquelon 345
Somali Coast 267
Togo 327
Wallis & Futuna Isls. 149

Liberation Issue

Allied Landing, Victory Sign and Cross of Lorraine
CD102

10th anniversary of the liberation of France.

1954, June 6

Cameroun C32
Comoro Isls. C4
Fr. Equatorial Africa C38
Fr. India C18
Fr. Polynesia C23
Fr. West Africa C17
Madagascar C57
New Caledonia C25
St. Pierre & Miquelon C19
Somali Coast C19
Togo C19
Wallis & Futuna Isls. C11

FIDES Issue

Plowmen
CD103

Efforts of FIDES, the Economic and Social Development Fund for Overseas Possessions (Fonds d' Investissement pour le Developpement Economique et Social.)

Each stamp has a different design.

1956

Cameroun 326–329
Comoro Isls. 43
Fr. Polynesia 181
Madagascar 292–295
New Caledonia 303
Somali Coast 268
Togo 331

Flower Issue

Euadania
CD104

Each stamp shows a different flower.

1958–9

Cameroun 333
Comoro Isls. 45
Fr. Equatorial Africa 200–201
Fr. Polynesia 192
Fr. So. & Antarctic Terr. 11
Fr. West Africa 79–83
Madagascar 301–302
New Caledonia 304–305
St. Pierre & Miquelon 357

Somali Coast 270
Togo 348–349
Wallis & Futuna Isls. 152

Human Rights Issue

Sun, Dove and U. N. Emblem

CD105

10th anniversary of the signing of the Universal Declaration of Human Rights.

1958

Comoro Isls. 44
Fr. Equatorial Africa 202
Fr. Polynesia 191
Fr. West Africa 85
Madagascar 300
New Caledonia 306
St. Pierre & Miquelon 356
Somali Coast 274
Wallis & Futuna Isls. 153

C.C.T.A. Issue

Map of Africa and Cogwheels

CD106

10th anniversary of the Commission for Technical Cooperation in Africa south of the Sahara.

1960

Cameroun 335
Cent. African Rep. 3
Chad 66
Congo, P.R. 90
Dahomey 138
Gabon 150
Ivory Coast 180
Madagascar 9
Mali 117
Mauritania 104
Niger 89
Upper Volta 89

Air Afrique Issue, 1961

Modern and Ancient Africa, Map and Planes

CD107

Founding of Air Afrique (African Airlines).

1961–62

Cameroun C37
Cent. African Rep. C5
Chad C7
Congo, P.R. C5
Dahomey C17
Gabon C5
Ivory Coast C18
Mauritania C17
Niger C22
Senegal C31
Upper Volta C4

Anti-Malaria Issue

Malaria Eradication Emblem

CD108

World Health Organization drive to eradicate malaria.

1962, Apr. 7

Cameroun B36
Cent. African Rep. B1
Chad B1
Comoro Isls. B1
Congo, P.R. B3
Dahomey B15
Gabon B4
Ivory Coast B15
Madagascar B19
Mali B1
Mauritania B16
Niger B14
Senegal B16
Somali Coast B15
Upper Volta B1

Abidjan Games Issue

Relay Race

CD109

Abidjan Games, Ivory Coast, Dec. 24–31, 1961.

Each stamp shows a different sport.

1962

Chad 83–84
Cent. African Rep. 19–20
Congo, P.R. 103–104
Gabon 163–164
Niger 109–111
Upper Volta 103–105

African and Malagasy Union Issue

Flag of African and Malagasy Union

CD110

First anniversary of the Union.

1962, Sept. 8

Cameroun 373
Cent. African Rep. 21
Chad 85
Congo, P.R. 105
Dahomey 155
Gabon 165
Ivory Coast 198
Madagascar 332
Mauritania 170
Niger 112
Senegal 211
Upper Volta 106

Telstar Issue

Telstar and Globe Showing Andover and Pleumeur-Bodou

CD111

First television connection of the United States and Europe through the Telstar satellite, July 11–12, 1962.

1962–63

Andorra, French 154
Comoro Isls. C7
Fr. Polynesia C29
Fr. So. & Antarctic Terr. C5
New Caledonia C33
Somali Coast C31
St. Pierre & Miquelon C26
Wallis & Futuna Isls. C17

Freedom From Hunger Issue

World Map and Wheat Emblem

CD112

United Nations Food and Agriculture Organization's "Freedom from Hunger" campaign.

1963, Mar. 21

Cameroun B37–B38
Cent. African Rep. B2
Chad B2
Congo, P.R. B4
Dahomey B16
Gabon B5
Ivory Coast B16
Madagascar B21
Mauritania B17
Niger B15
Senegal B17
Upper Volta B2

Red Cross Centenary Issue

Centenary Emblem

CD113

Centenary of the International Red Cross.

1963, Sept. 2

Comoro Isls. 55
Fr. Polynesia 205
New Caledonia 328
St. Pierre & Miquelon 367
Somali Coast 297
Wallis & Futuna Isls. 165

African Postal Union Issue

UAMPT Emblem, Radio Masts, Plane and Mail

CD114

Establishment of the African and Malagasy Posts and Telecommunications Union, UAMPT.

1963, Sept. 8

Cameroun C47
Cent. African Rep. C10
Chad C9
Congo, P.R. C13
Dahomey C19
Gabon C13
Ivory Coast C25
Madagascar C75
Mauritania C22
Niger C27
Rwanda 36
Senegal C32
Upper Volta C9

Air Afrique Issue, 1963

Symbols of Flight

CD115

First anniversary of Air Afrique and inauguration of DC-8 service.

1963, Nov. 19

Cameroun C48
Chad C10
Congo, P.R. C14
Gabon C18
Ivory Coast C26
Mauritania C26
Niger C35
Senegal C33

Europafrica Issue

Europe and Africa Linked Together

CD116

Signing of an economic agreement between the European Economic Community and the African and Malagasy Union, Yaoundé, Cameroun, July 20, 1963.

1963–64

Cameroun 402
Chad C11
Cent. African Rep. C12
Congo, P.R. C16

Gabon	C19
Ivory Coast	217
Niger	C43
Upper Volta	C11

Human Rights Issue

Scales of Justice and Globe

CD117

15th anniversary of the Universal Declaration of Human Rights.

1963, Dec. 10

Comoro Isls.	58
Fr. Polynesia	206
New Caledonia	329
St. Pierre & Miquelon	368
Somali Coast	300
Wallis & Futuna Isls.	166

PHILATEC Issue

Stamp Album, Champs Elysées Palace and Horses of Marly

CD118

"PHILATEC," International Philatelic and Postal Techniques Exhibition, Paris, June 5-21, 1964.

1963–64

Comoro Isls.	60
France	1078
Fr. Polynesia	207
New Caledonia	341
St. Pierre & Miquelon	369
Somali Coast	301
Wallis & Futuna Isls.	167

Cooperation Issue

Maps of France and Africa and Clasped Hands

CD119

Cooperation between France and the French-speaking countries of Africa and Madagascar.

1964

Cameroun	409–410
Cent. African Rep.	39
Chad	103
Congo, P.R.	121
Dahomey	193
France	1111
Gabon	175
Ivory Coast	221
Madagascar	360
Mauritania	181
Niger	143
Senegal	236
Togo	495

ITU Issue

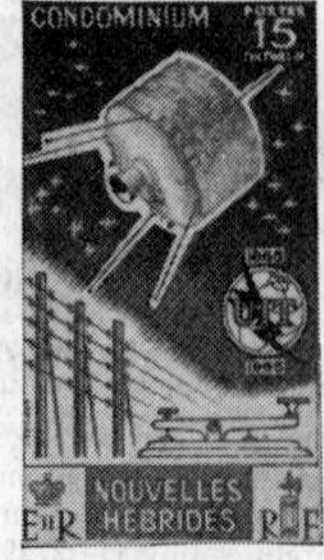

Telegraph, Syncom Satellite and ITU Emblem

CD120

Centenary of the International Telecommunication Union.

1965, May 17

Comoro Isls.	C14
Fr. Polynesia	C33
Fr. So. & Antarctic Terr.	C8
New Caledonia	C40
New Hebrides	124–125
St. Pierre & Miquelon	C29
Somali Coast	C36
Wallis & Futuna Isls.	C20

French Satellite A-1 Issue

Diamant Rocket and Launching Installations

CD121

Launching of France's first satellite, Nov. 26, 1965.

1965–66

Comoro Isls.	C15–C16
France	1137–1138
Fr. Polynesia	C40–C41
Fr. So. & Antarctic Terr.	C9–C10
New Caledonia	C44–C45
St. Pierre & Miquelon	C30–C31
Somali Coast	C39–C40
Wallis & Futuna Isls.	C22–C23

French Satellite D-1 Issue

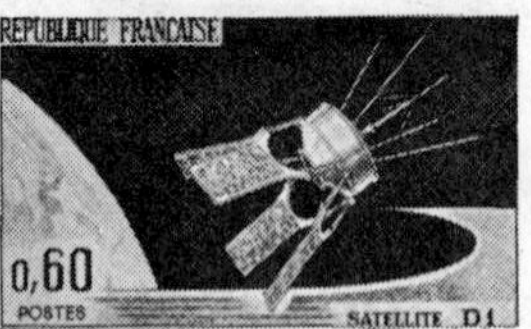

D-1 Satellite in Orbit

CD122

Launching of the D-1 satellite at Hammaguir, Algeria, Feb. 17, 1966.

1966

Comoro Isls.	C17
France	1148
Fr. Polynesia	C42
Fr. So. & Antarctic Terr.	C11
New Caledonia	C46
St. Pierre & Miquelon	C32
Somali Coast	C49
Wallis & Futuna Isls.	C24

Air Afrique Issue, 1966

Planes and Air Afrique Emblem

CD123

Introduction of DC-8F planes by Air Afrique.

1966

Cameroun	C79
Cent. African Rep.	C35
Chad	C26
Congo, P.R.	C42
Dahomey	C42
Gabon	C47
Ivory Coast	C32
Mauritania	C57
Niger	C63
Senegal	C47
Togo	C54
Upper Volta	C31

African Postal Union Issue, 1967

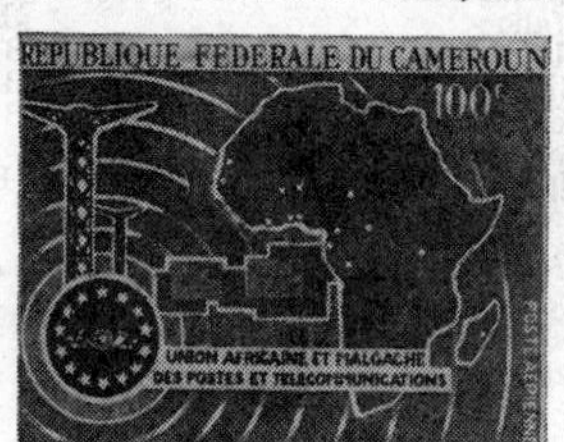

Telecommunications Symbols and Map of Africa

CD124

Fifth anniversary of the establishment of the African and Malagasy Union of Posts and Telecommunications, UAMPT.

1967

Cameroun	C90
Cent. African Rep.	C46
Chad	C37
Congo, P.R.	C57
Dahomey	C61
Gabon	C58
Ivory Coast	C34
Madagascar	C85
Mauritania	C65
Niger	C75
Rwanda	C1–C3
Senegal	C60
Togo	C81
Upper Volta	C50

Monetary Union Issue

Gold Token of the Ashantis, 17–18th Centuries

CD125

Fifth anniversary of the West African Monetary Union.

1967, Nov. 4

Dahomey	244
Ivory Coast	259
Mauritania	238
Niger	204
Senegal	294

Togo	623
Upper Volta	181

WHO Anniversary Issue

Sun, Flowers and WHO Emblem

CD126

20th anniversary of the World Health Organization.

1968, May 4

Afars & Issas	317
Comoro Isls.	73
Fr. Polynesia	241–242
Fr. So. & Antarctic Terr.	31
New Caledonia	367
St. Pierre & Miquelon	377
Wallis & Futuna Isls.	169

Human Rights Year Issue

Human Rights Flame

CD127

International Human Rights Year.

1968, Aug. 10

Afars & Issas	322–323
Comoro Isls.	76
Fr. Polynesia	243–244
Fr. So. & Antarctic Terr.	32
New Caledonia	369
St. Pierre & Miquelon	382
Wallis & Futuna Isls.	170

2nd PHILEXAFRIQUE Issue

Gabon No. 131 and Industrial Plant

CD128

Opening of PHILEXAFRIQUE, Abidjan, Feb. 14.

Each stamp shows a local scene and stamp.

1969, Feb. 14

Cameroun	C118
Cent. African Rep.	C65
Chad	C48
Congo, P.R.	C77
Dahomey	C94
Gabon	C82
Ivory Coast	C38–C40
Madagascar	C92
Mali	C65
Mauritania	C80
Niger	C104
Senegal	C68
Togo	C104
Upper Volta	C62

Concorde Issue

Concorde in Flight
CD129

First flight of the prototype Concorde super-sonic plane at Toulouse, Mar. 1, 1969.

1969

Afars & Issas	C56
Comoro Isls.	C29
France	C42
Fr. Polynesia	C50
Fr. So. & Antarctic Terr.	C18
New Caledonia	C63
St. Pierre & Miquelon	C40
Wallis & Futuna Isls.	C30

Development Bank Issue

Bank Emblem—CD130

Fifth anniversary of the African Development Bank.

1969

Cameroun	499
Chad	217
Congo, P.R.	181-182
Ivory Coast	281
Mali	127-128
Mauritania	267
Niger	220
Senegal	317-318
Upper Volta	201

ILO Issue

ILO Headquarters, Geneva, and Emblem
CD131

50th anniversary of the International Labor Organization.

1969–70

Afars & Issas	337
Comoro Isls.	83
Fr. Polynesia	251-252
Fr. So. & Antarctic Terr.	35
New Caledonia	379
St. Pierre & Miquelon	396
Wallis & Futuna Isls.	172

ASECNA Issue

Map of Africa, Plane and Airport
CD132

10th anniversary of the Agency for the Security of Aerial Navigation in Africa and Madagascar (ASECNA, Agence pour la Sécurité de la Navigation Aérienne en Afrique et à Madagascar).

1969–70

Cameroun	500
Cent. African Rep.	119
Chad	222
Congo, P.R.	197
Dahomey	269
Gabon	260
Ivory Coast	287
Mali	130
Niger	221
Senegal	321
Upper Volta	204

U.P.U. Headquarters Issue

U.P.U. Headquarters and Emblem
CD133

New Universal Postal Union headquarters, Bern, Switzerland.

1970

Afars & Issas	342
Algeria	443
Cameroun	503-504
Cent. African Rep.	125
Chad	225
Comoro Isls.	84
Congo, P.R.	216
Fr. Polynesia	261-262
Fr. So. & Antarctic Terr.	36
Gabon	258
Ivory Coast	295
Madagascar	444
Mali	134-135
Mauritania	283
New Caledonia	382
Niger	231-232
St. Pierre & Miquelon	397-398
Senegal	328-329
Tunisia	535
Wallis & Futuna Isls.	173

De Gaulle Issue

General de Gaulle, 1940
CD134

First anniversary of the death of Charles de Gaulle, (1890-1970), President of France.

1971–72

Afars & Issas	356-357
Comoro Isls.	104-105
France	1322-1325
Fr. Polynesia	270-271
Fr. So. & Antarctic Terr.	52-53
New Caledonia	393-394
Reunion	377, 380
St. Pierre & Miquelon	417-418
Wallis & Futuna Isls.	177-178

African Postal Union Issue, 1971

Carved Stool, UAMPT Building, Brazzaville, Congo
CD135

10th anniversary of the establishment of the African and Malagasy Posts and Telecommunications Union, UAMPT.

Each stamp has a different native design.

1971, Nov. 13

Cameroun	C177
Cent. African Rep.	C89
Chad	C94
Congo, P.R.	C136
Dahomey	C146
Gabon	C120
Ivory Coast	C47
Mauritania	C113
Niger	C164
Rwanda	C8
Senegal	C105
Togo	C166
Upper Volta	C97

West African Monetary Union Issue

African Couple, City, Village and Commemorative Coin
CD136

10th anniversary of the West African Monetary Union.

1972, Nov. 2

Dahomey	300
Ivory Coast	331
Mauritania	299
Niger	258
Senegal	374
Togo	825
Upper Volta	280

African Postal Union Issue, 1973

Telecommunications Symbols and Map of Africa
CD137

11th anniversary of the African and Malagasy Posts and Telecommunications Union (UAMPT).

1973, Sept. 12

Cameroun	574
Cent. African Rep.	194
Chad	272
Congo, P.R.	289
Dahomey	311
Gabon	320
Ivory Coast	361
Madagascar	500
Mauritania	304
Niger	287
Rwanda	540
Senegal	393
Togo	849
Upper Volta	285

Philexafrique II—Essen Issue

II-349

Buffalo and Dahomey No. C33
CD138

II-350

Wild Ducks and Baden No. 1
CD139

Designs: Indigenous fauna, local and German stamps.

Types CD138–CD139 printed horizontally and vertically se-tenant in sheets of 10 (2x5). Label between horizontal pairs alternately commemorates Philexafrique II, Libreville, Gabon, June 1978, and 2nd International Stamp Fair, Essen, Germany, Nov. 1–5.

THE ONLY MOUNT
WORTHY OF THE NAME SCOTT
NEW
ScottMounts
Superb new generation hingeless mounts with 5 features no other mount offers
Hingeless Mounts do very special things for stamps. 100% inert, they prevent chemical deterioration, eliminate tearing and abrasion, make hinges and hinge marks passé, and dress a collection beautifully. We've sworn we'd never put the prestigious Scott name on any mount until we found a better one. Now we have. We call it ScottMount.
Check these exclusive ScottMount features:
1 Opaque, black or clear backing The onyx backing of a ScottMount is completely opaque, offering stamp framing far more brilliant, far sharper than any other mount.
2 Crystal-clear face The total clarity of the ScottMount face vividly enhances the color and detail of a stamp. We have diffused the face of the mount just enough to prevent reflections.
3 Better adhesion Two layers of gum assure 100% contact. One adheres to the mount, the other to the page. Little chance of mounts popping off, yet they can be peeled off easily.
4 Resealable packaging Unlike throw-away packaging used for other mounts, most ScottMount packets are re-useable as storage trays. Open our package, take out the mounts you need, then reseal it.
5 Compatible with other mounts ScottMounts are entirely compatible in sizes and shapes with similar type mounts.
SCOTT®
Serving collectors since 1863.
. . . THE AUTHORITY

SCOTT'S STANDARD POSTAGE STAMP CATALOGUE

GABON

(gȧ'bôn')

LOCATION—On the west coast of Africa, at the equator.

GOVT.—Republic (former French colony).

AREA—102,089 sq. mi.

POP.—530,000 (est. 1977).

CAPITAL—Libreville.

Gabon was originally under the control of French West Africa. In 1886 it was made a separate colony. In 1888 it was united with French Congo. In 1904 Gabon was granted a certain degree of colonial autonomy which prevailed until 1934 when it merged with French Equatorial Africa. Gabon Republic was proclaimed Nov. 28, 1958.

100 Centimes = 1 Franc

Stamps of French Colonies of 1881–86 Handstamp Surcharged in Black:

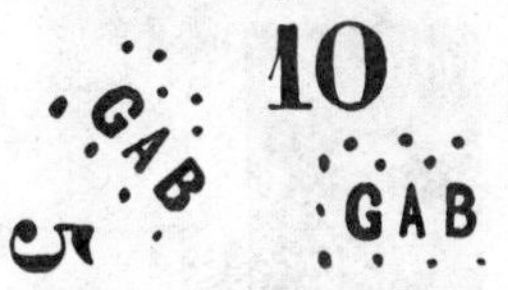

a b

1886 *Perf. 14x13½* **Unwmkd.**

1 A9 (*a*) 5c on 20c red, *green* 200.00 200.00
2 " (*b*) 10c on 20c red, *green* 185.00 185.00
3 " (") 25c on 20c red, *green* 17.50 15.00
   e. 56 dots around "GAB" 1000.00 200.00
4 " (") 50c on 15c blue 700.00 650.00
5 " (") 75c on 15c blue 750.00 700.00

Nos. 1–3 exist with double surcharge of numeral; No. 3 with "GAB" double or inverted, or with "25" double.

On Nos. 3 and 5 the surcharge slants down; on No. 4 it slants up. The number of dots varies.

Counterfeits of Nos. 1–15 exist.

Handstamp Surcharged in Black **15**

1888-89

6 A9 15c on 10c *lavender* 2000.00 475.00
7 " 15c on 1fr bronze green, *straw* 800.00 400.00
8 " 25c on 5c green, *greenish* 500.00 72.50
9 " 25c on 10c *lavender* 1500.00 600.00
10 " 25c on 75c car., *rose* 1200.00 500.00

A well informed dealer can help the collector build his collection. He is the one to turn to when philatelic property must be sold.

Postage Due Stamps of French Colonies Handstamp Surcharged in Black

GABON
TIMBRE
15

1889 ***Imperf.***

11 D1 15c on 5c black 65.00 55.00
12 " 15c on 30c black 1750.00 1500.00
13 " 25c on 20c black 35.00 25.00

Nos. 11 and 13 exist with "GABON," "TIMBRE" or "25" double; "TIMBRE" or "15" omitted, etc.

A8

1889 **Typeset**

14 A8 15c *rose* 550.00 325.00
15 " 25c *green* 325.00 225.00

Ten varieties of each. Nos. 14–15 exist with "GAB" inverted or omitted, and with small "f" in "Francaise."

Navigation and Commerce

A9

1904–07 **Typo.** ***Perf. 14x13½***

Name of Colony in Blue or Carmine.

16 A9 1c *lilac blue* 20 20
   a. "GABON" double 75.00
17 " 2c brown, *buff* 20 20
18 " 4c claret, *lavender* 40 40
19 " 5c yellow green 75 75
20 " 10c rose 2.00 2.00
21 " 15c gray 2.00 2.00
22 " 20c red, *green* 3.50 3.50
23 " 25c blue 2.00 2.00
24 " 30c yellow brown 4.00 4.00
25 " 35c *yellow* ('06) 7.00 7.00
26 " 40c red, *straw* 5.00 5.00
27 " 45c *gray grn.* ('07) 10.00 10.00
28 " 50c brown, *azure* 4.00 4.00
29 " 75c dp. vio., *orange* 6.00 6.00
30 " 1fr bronze green, *straw* 12.00 12.00
31 " 2fr violet, *rose* 27.50 27.50
32 " 5fr lilac, *lavender* 50.00 50.00
Nos. 16–32 (17) 136.55 136.55

Fang Warrior

A10

Libreville

A11

Fang Woman

A12

Inscribed: "Congo Français".

1910 ***Perf. 13½x14***

33 A10 1c choc. & orange 40 40
34 " 2c black & chocolate 40 40
35 " 4c violet & deep blue 60 60
36 " 5c olive gray & green 75 75
37 " 10c red & carmine 1.00 1.00
38 " 20c choc. & dk. vio. 1.00 1.00
39 A11 25c dp. blue & choc. 75 75
40 " 30c gray black & red 8.00 8.00
41 " 35c dk. vio. & green 4.00 4.00
42 " 40c choc. & ultra. 6.00 6.00
43 " 45c carmine & vio. 10.00 10.00
44 " 50c blue green & gray 17.50 17.50
45 " 75c org. & chocolate 30.00 30.00
46 A12 1fr dk. brn. & bis. 32.50 32.50
47 " 2fr car. & brown 100.00 100.00
48 " 5fr blue & choc. 85.00 85.00
Nos. 33–48 (16) 297.90 297.90

A13

A15

A14

Inscribed: "Afrique Equatoriale."

1910–22

49 A13 1c chocolate & orange 6 6
50 " 2c black & chocolate 8 8
   a. 2c gray black & deep olive 10 10
51 " 4c violet & deep blue 6 6
52 " 5c olive gray & green 15 8
53 " 5c gray black & ochre ('22) 8 8
54 " 10c red & carmine 18 13
55 " 10c yellow green & blue green ('22) 8 8
56 " 15c brown violet & rose ('18) 15 15
57 " 20c olive brown & dark violet 1.65 1.65
58 A14 25c dp. blue & choc. 17 15
59 A14 25c Prussian blue & black ('22) 25 25
60 " 30c gray black & red 9 8
61 " 30c rose & red ('22) 15 15
62 " 35c dk. vio. & green 30 15
63 " 40c choc. & ultra. 15 15
64 " 45c carmine & violet 10 10
65 " 45c black & red ('22) 30 30
66 " 50c blue green & gray 8 8
67 " 50c dark blue & blue ('22) 10 10
68 " 75c org. & chocolate 1.40 1.35
69 A15 1fr dk. brn. & bistre 65 65
70 " 2fr carmine & brown 1.10 1.00
71 " 5fr blue & chocolate 1.85 1.85
Nos. 49–71 (23) 9.18 8.73

Stamps of 1904–07 Surcharged in Black or Carmine

05 10

e f

1912

Surcharged Type "e"

72 A9 5c on 2c brown, *buff* 20 20
73 " 5c on 4c claret, *lavender* (C) 20 20
74 " 5c on 15c gray (C) 15 15
75 " 5c on 20c red, *green* 15 15
76 " 5c on 25c blue (C) 15 15
77 " 5c on 30c pale brown (C) 15 15

Surcharged Type "f"

78 A9 10c on 40c red, *straw* 10 10
79 " 10c on 45c *gray green* (C) 20 20
80 " 10c on 50c brown, *azure* (C) 20 20
81 " 10c on 75c deep violet, *orange* 20 20
82 " 10c on 1fr bronze green, *straw* 25 25
83 " 10c on 2fr violet, *rose* 20 20
   a. Inverted surch 75.00 75.00
84 " 10c on 5fr lilac, *lavender* 85 85
Nos. 72–84 (13) 3.00 3.00

Two spacings between the surcharged numerals are found on Nos. 72 to 84.

Stamps of 1910–22 Overprinted in Black, Blue or Carmine

AFRIQUE EQUATORIALE FRANÇAISE

1924–31

85 A13 1c brown & orange 6 6
86 " 2c black & choc. (Bl) 6 6
87 " 4c violet & indigo 6 6
88 " 5c gray black & ochre 8 8
89 " 10c yellow green & blue green 8 8
   a. Double ovpt. (Bk+Bl) 35.00 35.00
90 " 10c dark blue & brown ('26) (C) 10 10
91 " 15c brown violet & rose (Bl) 12 12
92 " 15c rose & brown violet ('31) (Bl) 20 20
93 " 20c olive brown & dark violet (C) 18 18
   a. Inverted ovpt. 35.00 35.00

Overprinted AFRIQUE EQUATORIALE FRANÇAISE

94 A14 25c Prussian blue & black (C) 17 17
95 " 30c rose & red (Bl) 8 8
96 " 30c blk. & org. ('26) 10 10
97 " 30c dark green & blue green ('28) 25 25
98 " 35c dark violet & green (Bl) 8 8

99 A14 40c chocolate & ultra. (C) 12 12
100 " 45c black & red (Bl) 15 15
101 " 50c dark blue & blue (C) 10 10
102 " 50c car. & green ('26) 8 8
103 " 65c deep blue & red org. ('28) 1.25 1.25
104 " 75c org. & brn. (Bl) 25 25
105 " 90c brown red & rose ('30) 85 85

Overprinted like Nos. 85 to 93.

106 A15 1fr dark brown & bistre 35 35
107 " 1.10fr dull green & rose red ('28) 1.65 1.35
108 " 1.50fr pale blue & dark blue ('30) 30 30
109 " 2fr rose & brown 35 35
110 " 3fr red violet ('30) 1.85 1.65
111 " 5fr deep blue & chocolate 1.25 1.25
Nos. 85–111 (27) 10.17 9.67

Types of 1924–31 Issues Surcharged with New Values in Black or Carmine.

1925-28

112 A15 65c on 1fr olive green & brown 20 20
113 " 85c on 1fr olive green & brown 20 20
114 A14 90c on 75c brown red & cerise ('27) 60 60
115 A15 1.25fr on 1fr dark blue & ultra. (C) 10 10
116 " 1.50fr on 1fr light blue & dark blue ('27) 25 25
117 " 3fr on 5fr magenta & olive brown 1.10 1.10
118 " 10fr on 5fr orange brown & green ('27) 4.00 4.00
119 " 20fr on 5fr red violet & orange red ('27) 4.00 4.00
Nos. 112–119 (8) 10.45 10.45

Bars cover the old denominations on Nos. 114–119.

Colonial Exposition Issue.

Common Design Types

1931 ***Perf. 12½***

Name of Country in Black.

120 CD70 40c deep green 75 70
121 CD71 50c violet 30 25
122 CD72 90c red orange 75 70
123 CD73 1.50fr dull blue 1.00 70

Timber Raft on Ogowe River
A16

Count Savorgnan de Brazza
A17

Village of Setta Kemma
A18

1932-33 Photo. ***Perf. 13x13½***

124 A16 1c brown violet 6 6
125 " 2c black, *rose* 6 6
126 " 4c green 8 8
127 " 5c greenish blue 10 10
128 " 10c red, *yellow* 10 10
129 " 15c red, *green* 25 15
130 " 20c deep red 20 20
131 " 25c brown red 8 8
132 A17 30c yellow green 45 40
133 " 40c brown violet 30 20
134 " 45c black, *dull green* 50 40
135 " 50c red brown 25 20
136 " 65c Prussian blue 1.50 1.25
137 " 75c black, *red orange* 75 65
138 " 90c rose red 1.00 65
139 " 1fr yellow green, *blue* 6.00 5.00
140 A18 1.25fr deep violet ('33) 55 40
141 " 1.50fr dull blue 1.00 60
142 " 1.75fr deep green ('33) 65 40
143 " 2fr brown red 6.25 5.50
144 " 3fr yellow green, *blue* 1.50 1.25
145 " 5fr red brown 1.65 1.65
146 " 10fr black, *red orange* 8.00 7.00
147 " 20fr dark violet 13.50 10.00
Nos. 124–147 (24) 44.78 36.38

Republic

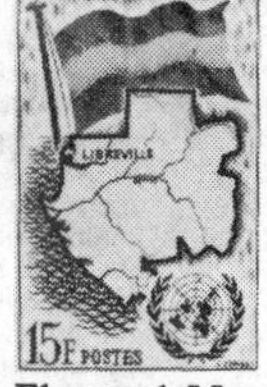

Prime Minister Leon Mba
A19

Flag and Map of Gabon and U.N. Emblem
A20

Design: 25fr, Leon Mba, profile.

Engraved.

1959, Nov. 28 ***Perf. 13*** **Unwmkd.**

148 A19 15fr chocolate 25 12
149 " 25fr dark brown & greenish black 40 13

Issued to commemorate the first anniversary of the proclamation of the Republic.

Imperforates

Most Gabon stamps from 1959 onward exist imperforate in issued and trial colors, and also in small presentation sheets in issued colors.

C.C.T.A. Issue

Common Design Type

1960, May 21 Engr. ***Perf. 13***

150 CD106 50fr violet brown & Pruss. blue 1.00 90

1961, Feb. 9

151 A20 15fr multicolored 35 20
152 " 25fr " 45 30
153 " 85fr " 1.65 1.00

Gabon's admission to United Nations.

Combretum—A21

Designs: 1fr, 5fr, Tulip tree (vert.). 2fr, 3fr, Yellow cassia.

1961, July 4 ***Perf. 13*** **Unwmkd.**

154 A21 50c rose red & grn. 5 5
155 " 1fr slate green, red & bistre 5 5
156 A21 2fr dk. grn. & yellow 8 8
157 " 3fr olive grn. & yel. 20 20
158 " 5fr multicolored 25 25
159 " 10fr green & rose red 35 25
Nos. 154–159 (6) 98 88

President Leon Mba
A22

1962 **Engraved**

160 A22 15fr indigo, carmine & green 25 10
161 " 20fr brown black, carmine & grn. 30 15
162 " 25fr brn., car. & grn. 35 20

Abidjan Games Issue

Common Design Type

Designs. 20fr, Foot race, start. 50fr, Soccer.

1962, July 21 Photo. ***Perf. 12½x12***

163 CD109 20fr dark & lt. blue, brn. & black 30 25
164 " 50fr dark & lt. blue, brn. & black 80 55

Abidjan Games. See No. C6.

African-Malgache Union Issue

Common Design Type

1962, Sept. 8 ***Perf. 12½x12***

165 CD110 30fr emerald, bluish grn., red & gold 1.00 75

Issued to commemorate the first anniversary of the African and Malgache Union.

Captain Ntchorere and Flags of France and Gabon—A23

1962, Nov. 23 ***Perf. 12***

166 A23 80fr multicolored 1.20 90

Issued to honor Capt. Ntchorere, who died for France, June 7, 1940.

Space Communications Issue

Waves Around Globe
A23a

Design: 100fr, Orbit patterns around globe.

1963, Sept. 19 Photo. ***Perf. 12½***

167 A23a 25fr ultra., grn. & org. 40 35
168 " 100fr green, ultra. & red brown 1.60 1.60

Issued to publicize space communications.

Common Design Types pictured in section at front of book.

Human Rights Issue

UNESCO Emblem, Scales and Tree—A23b

1963, Dec. 10 Engraved ***Perf. 13***

169 A23b 25fr green, dark gray & red brown 35 30

Issued to commemorate the 15th anniversary of the Universal Declaration of Human Rights.

World Meteorological Day Issue

Barograph and WMO Emblem
A23c

1964, March 23 ***Perf. 13*** **Unwmkd.**

170 A23c 25fr olive bister, slate green & ultra. 45 40

Issued to commemorate the United Nations Fourth World Meteorological Day, March 23.

Arms of Gabon
A24

Photogravure

1964, June 15 ***Perf. 13x12½***

171 A24 25fr ocher & multi. 35 25

Tarpon—A25

Designs: 60fr, Gorilla (vert.). 80fr, Buffalo.

1964, July 15 Engraved ***Perf. 13***

172 A25 30fr brown red, blue & black 50 30
173 " 60fr brown, green & brown red 1.00 50
174 " 80fr dark blue, green & red brown 1.20 90

Cooperation Issue

Common Design Type

175 CD119 25fr gray, dk. brn. & light blue 45 35

Dissotis Rotundifolia
A26

Flowers: 5fr, Gloriosa superba. 15fr, Eulophia horsfallii.

1964, Nov. 16 Photo. *Perf. 12x12½*

Flowers in Natural Colors

176 A26 3fr deep green 10 7
177 " 5fr green 12 8
178 " 15fr dark brown 28 20

Sun and IQSY Emblem
A27

1965, Feb. 25 ***Perf. 12½x12***

179 A27 85fr multicolored 1.65 1.25

International Quiet Sun Year, 1964–65.

Morse Telegraph—A28

1965, May 17 Engraved ***Perf. 13***

180 A28 30fr multicolored 50 40

Issued to commemorate the centenary of the International Telecommunication Union.

Manganese Crusher, Moanda
A29

Design: 60fr, Uranium mining, Mounana.

1965, June 15 ***Perf. 13*** **Unwmkd.**

181 A29 15fr bright blue, purple & red 20 18
182 " 60fr brown, bright blue & red 90 60

Issued to publicize Gabon's mineral wealth.

Field Ball A30 **Okoukoue Dance** A31

1965, July 15 Engraved ***Perf. 13***

183 A30 25fr bright green, black & red 45 30

Issued to commemorate the First African Games, Brazzaville, July 18–25. See No. C35.

1965, Sept. 15 ***Perf. 13***

Design: 60fr, Mukudji dance.

184 A31 25fr brn., grn. & yel. 40 25
185 " 60fr blk., dark red & brown 90 65

Abraham Lincoln
A32

1965, Sept. 28 Photo. ***Perf. 12½x13***

186 A32 50fr violet blue, blk., gold & buff 75 50

Centenary of death of Abraham Lincoln.

Old and New Post Offices and Mail Transport—A33

1965, Dec. 18 Engraved ***Perf. 13***

187 A33 30fr blue, bright grn. & chocolate 45 30

Issued for Stamp Day, 1965.

Balumbu Mask
A34

Designs: 10fr, Fang ancestral figure, Byeri. 25fr, Fang mask. 30fr, Okuyi mask, Myene. 85fr, Bakota leather mask.

1966, Apr. 18 Photo. ***Perf. 12x12½***

188 A34 5fr red, brn., black & buff 10 10
189 " 10fr brt. greenish bl., dk. brn. & yel. 20 15
190 " 25fr multicolored 45 25
191 " 30fr maroon, yellow & black 55 35
192 " 85fr multicolored 1.50 1.00
Nos. 188–192 (5) 2.80 1.85

Issued to commemorate the International Negro Arts Festival, Dakar, Senegal, Apr. 1–24.

WHO Headquarters, Geneva
A35

1966, May 3 Photo. ***Perf. 12½x13***

193 A35 50fr org. yel., ultra. & black 75 45

Issued to commemorate the inauguration of the World Health Organization Headquarters, Geneva.

Mother Learning to Write A36 **Soccer Player** A37

1966, June 22 Photo. ***Perf. 12x12½***

194 A36 30fr multicolored 50 30

UNESCO literacy campaign.

1966, July 15 Engraved ***Perf. 13***

Design: 90fr, Player facing left.

195 A37 25fr brown, green & ultra. 40 25
196 " 90fr ultra. & dk. pur. 1.50 90

Issued to commemorate the 8th World Cup Soccer Championship, Wembley, England, July 11–30. See No. C45.

Timber Industry
A38

Design: 85fr, Offshore oil rigs.

1966, Aug. 17 ***Perf. 13***

197 A38 20fr red brn., lilac & dark green 35 20
198 " 85fr dk. brn., brt. bl. & brt. green 1.25 65

Economic development.

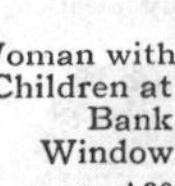

Woman with Children at Bank Window
A39

1966, Sept. 23 Engraved ***Perf. 13***

199 A39 25fr brt. bl., vio. brn. & slate green 35 20

Issued to publicize Savings Banks.

Scouts Around Campfire
A40

Design: 50fr, Boy Scout pledging ceremony (vert.).

1966, Oct. 17 Engraved ***Perf. 13***

200 A40 30fr slate blue, car. & dk. brown 45 20
201 " 50fr Prus. blue, brn. red & dk. brn. 80 45

Issued to honor Gabon's Boy Scouts.

Sikorsky S-43 Hydroplane and Map of West Africa
A41

1966, Dec. 17 Photo. ***Perf. 12½x12***

202 A41 30fr multicolored 50 25

Issued for Stamp Day and to commemorate the 30th anniversary of the first airmail service from Libreville to Port Gentil.

Hippopotami
A42

Animals: 2fr, African crocodiles. 3fr, Water chevrotain. 5fr, Chimpanzees. 10fr, Elephants. 20fr, Leopards.

1967, Jan. 5 Photo. ***Perf. 13x14***

203 A42 1fr multicolored 5 5
204 " 2fr " 8 7
205 " 3fr " 10 8
206 " 5fr " 12 10
207 " 10fr " 25 10
208 " 20fr " 40 20
Nos. 203-208 (6) 1.00 60

Lions International Emblem
A43

Design: 50fr, Lions emblem, map of Gabon and globe.

1967, Jan. 14 ***Perf. 12½x13***

209 A43 30fr multicolored 45 20
210 " 50fr blue & multi. 75 40
a. Strip of 2+ label 1.25 1.25

Issued to commemorate the 50th anniversary of Lions International. No. 210a contains one each of Nos. 209–210 and label with commemorative inscription.

Carnival Masks
A44

1967, Feb. 4 Photo. ***Perf. 12x12½***

211 A44 30fr brn., yel. bister & blue 50 30

Libreville Carnival, Feb. 4–7.

"Transportation" and Tourist Year Emblem
A45

1967, Feb. 15 ***Perf. 12½x13***

212 A45 30fr multicolored 50 30

International Tourist Year, 1967.

Olympic Diving Tower, Mexico City A46 **Symbolic of Atomic Energy Agency** A47

Designs: 30fr, Sun, snow crystals and Olympic rings. 50fr, Ice skating rink and view of Grenoble.

1967, March 18 Engraved ***Perf. 13***

213 A46 25fr dk. vio., greenish blue & ultra. 40 20
214 " 30fr green, red lilac & maroon 45 25
215 " 50fr ultra., green & brown 80 50

1968 Olympic Games.

1967, Apr. 15 Engraved ***Perf. 13***

216 A47 30fr red brn., dk. grn. & ultramarine 50 25

International Atomic Energy Agency.

Pope Paul VI, Papal Arms and Libreville Cathedral
A48

1967, June 1 Engraved *Perf. 13*

217 A48 30fr ultra., green & black 50 25

Issued to commemorate the "Populorum progressio" encyclical by Pope Paul VI concerning underdeveloped countries.

Flags, Tree, Logger, Map of Gabon and Mask

A49

1967, June 24 Engraved *Perf. 13*

218 A49 30fr multicolored 50 25

Issued to commemorate EXPO '67, International Exhibition, Montreal, Apr. 28–Oct. 27, 1967.

Europafrica Issue, 1967

Map of Europe and Africa and Products

A50

1967, July 18 Photo. *Perf. 12½x12*

219 A50 50fr multicolored 75 30

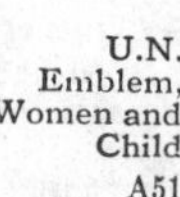

U.N. Emblem, Women and Child

A51

1967, Aug. 10 Engr. *Perf. 13*

220 A51 75fr brt. bl., dk. brn. & emerald 1.10 60

United Nations Commission for Women.

19th Century Mail Ships—A52

Design: No. 222, Modern mail ships.

1967, Nov. 17 Photo. *Perf. 12½*

221 A52 30fr multicolored 50 40
222 " 30fr " 50 40

Stamp Day. Nos. 221–222 printed se-tenant.

Draconea Fragrans

A53

Trees: 10fr, Pycnanthus angolensis. 20fr, Disthemonanthus benthamianus.

1967, Dec. 5 Engraved *Perf. 13*

Size: 22x36mm.

223 A53 5fr blue, emerald & brown 15 10
224 " 10fr green, dk. green & blue 20 12
225 " 20fr rose red, green & olive 35 18
Nos. 223–225, C61–C62 (5) 3.10 1.65

For booklet pane see No. C62a.

WHO Regional Office

A54

1968, Apr. 8 Engraved *Perf. 13*

226 A54 20fr multicolored 35 20

Issued to commemorate the 20th anniversary of the World Health Organization.

Dam, Power Station and UNESCO Emblem

A55

1968, June 18 Engraved *Perf. 13*

227 A55 15fr lake, orange & Prussian blue 20 10

Issued to publicize the Hydrological Decade (UNESCO), 1965–1974.

Pres. Albert Bernard Bongo

A56

Design: 30fr, Pres. Bongo and arms of Gabon in background.

1968, June 24 Photo. *Perf. 12x12½*

228 A56 25fr grn., buff & blk. 30 15
229 " 30fr rose lilac, light blue & black 40 20

Port Gentil Refinery Issue

Tanker, Refinery, and Map of Area Served—A56a

1968, July 30 Photo. *Perf. 12½*

230 A56a 30fr multicolored 45 25

Issued to commemorate the opening of the Port Gentil (Gabon) Refinery, June 12, 1968.

Open Book, Child and UNESCO Emblem—A57

1968, Sept. 10 Engraved *Perf. 13*

231 A57 25fr violet blue, dull red & brown 35 20

Issued for International Literacy Day.

Coffee

A58

Design: 40fr, Cacao.

1968, Oct. 15 Engraved *Perf. 13*

232 A58 20fr blue green, red & dark green 30 15
233 " 40fr slate green, ocher & brown 55 25

"La Junon"

A59

1968, Nov. 23 Engraved *Perf. 13*

234 A59 30fr ocher, dk. green & purple 50 30

Issued for Stamp Day.

Lawyer, Globe and Human Rights Flame

A60

1968, Dec. 10

235 A60 20fr black, bl. green & carmine 30 15

International Human Rights Year.

Okanda Gap

A61

Designs: 15fr, Barracuda. 25fr, Kinguele Waterfall (vert.). 30fr, Sitatunga trophies (vert.).

1969, Mar. 28 Engraved *Perf. 13*

236 A61 10fr brown, blue & slate green 15 12
237 " 15fr brn. red, emerald & indigo 25 12
238 " 25fr bl., pur. & olive 35 15
239 " 30fr multicolored 40 20

Year of African Tourism, 1969.

Mvet (Musical Instrument)

A62

Musical Instruments: 30fr, Ngombi harp. 50fr, Ebele and Mbe drums. 100fr, Medzang xylophone.

1969, June 6 Engraved *Perf. 13*

240 A62 25fr plum, olive & deep carmine 35 20
241 A62 30fr red brown, olive & dark brown 40 25
242 " 50fr plum, olive & deep carmine 65 40
243 " 100fr red brown, olive & dark brown 1.40 70
a. Min. sheet of 4 4.00 4.00

No. 243a contains one each of Nos. 240–243. Size: 130x100mm.

Aframomum Polyanthum (Zingiberaceae)

A63

Tree of Life

A64

African Plants: 2fr, Chlamydocola chlamydantha (Sterculiaceae). 5fr, Costus dinklagei (Zingiberaceae). 10fr, Cola rostrata (Sterculiaceae). 20fr, Dischistocalyx grandifolius (Acanthaceae).

1969, July 15 Photo. *Perf. 12x12½*

244 A63 1fr multicolored 5 5
245 " 2fr lt. olive & multi. 9 5
246 " 5fr multicolored 10 8
247 " 10fr slate & multi. 25 15
248 " 20fr yellow & multi. 35 25
Nos. 244–248 (5) 84 58

1969, Aug. 17 Photogravure

249 A64 25fr multicolored 35 20

National renovation.

Drilling for Oil on Land

A65

Workers and ILO Emblem

A66

Design: 50fr, Offshore drilling station.

1969, Sept. 13 *Perf. 12x12½*

250 A65 25fr multicolored 30 20
251 " 50fr " 60 45
a. Strip of 2+label 1.10 1.10

Issued to commemorate the 20th anniversary of the ELF-SPAFE oil operations in Gabon. No. 251a contains one each of Nos. 250–251 and label with commemorative inscription.

1969, Oct. 29 Engraved *Perf. 13*

252 A66 30fr blue, slate green & dp. carmine 40 25

Issued to commemorate the 50th anniversary of the International Labor Organization.

Arms of Port Gentil

A67

Canoe Mail Transport

A68

Coats of Arms: 20fr, Lambarene. 30fr, Libreville.

1969, Nov. 19 Photo. *Perf. 12*

253 A67 20fr red, gold, silver & black 25 10

254 A67 25fr bl., blk. & gold 30 13
255 " 30fr blue & multi. 35 15

See also Nos. 267–269, 291–293, 321–326, 340–345, 409–415.

1969, Dec. 18 Engraved *Perf. 13*

256 A68 30fr brt. grn., greenish bl. & red brn. 45 30

Issued for Stamp Day 1969.

Satellite, Globe, TV Screen and ITU Emblem
A69

1970, May 17 Engraved *Perf. 13*

257 A69 25fr dk. blue, dk. red brown & black 40 25

International Telecommunications Day.

U.P.U. Headquarters Issue
Common Design Type

1970, May 20 Engraved *Perf. 13*

258 CD133 30fr brt. grn., brt. rose lilac & brown 50 30

Geisha and African Drummer
A70

1970, May 27 Photo. *Perf. 12½x12*

259 A70 30fr ultra. & multi. 40 25

Issued to publicize EXPO '70 International Exhibition, Osaka, Japan, Mar. 15–Sept. 13.

ASECNA Issue
Common Design Type

1970, Aug. 26 Engraved *Perf. 13*

260 CD132 100fr bright green & blue green 1.40 85

U.N. Emblem, Globe, Dove and Charts
A71

1970, Oct. 24 Photo. *Perf. 12½x12*

261 A71 30fr Prus. bl. & multi. 45 30

25th anniversary of the United Nations.

Bushbucks
A72

Designs: 15fr, Pels scaly-tailed flying squirrel. 25fr, Gray-cheeked monkey (vert.). 40fr, African golden cat. 60fr, Sevaline genet.

1970, Dec. 14 Photo. *Perf. 12½x13*

262 A72 5fr yel. grn. & multi. 15 10
263 " 15fr red org. & black 30 20
264 " 25fr violet & multi. 45 25
265 " 40fr red & multi. 60 35
266 " 60fr blue & multi. 90 40
Nos. 262–266 (5) 2.40 1.30

Certain unlisted issues of Gabon, starting in 1970, are mentioned and briefly described in "For the Record" at the back of this volume.

Arms Type of 1969

Coats of Arms: 20fr, Mouila. 25fr, Bitam. 30fr, Oyem.

1971, Feb. 16 Photo. *Perf. 12*

267 A67 20fr vermilion, black, silver & gold 25 8
268 " 25fr emerald, gold & black 30 12
269 " 30fr emerald, gold, black & red 35 15

Men of Four Races and Emblem
A73

1971, March 21 Engraved *Perf. 13*

270 A73 40fr multicolored 50 30

International year against racial discrimination.

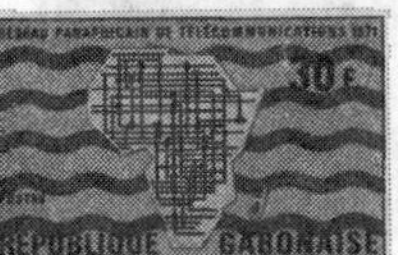

Map of Africa and Telecommunications System
A74

1971, Apr. 30 Photo. *Perf. 13*

271 A74 30fr orange & multi. 35 25

Pan-African telecommunications system.

Charaxes Smaragdalis
A75

Butterflies: 10fr, Euxanthe crossleyi. 15fr, Epiphora rectifascia. 25fr, Imbrasia bouvieri.

1971, May 26 Photo. *Perf. 13*

272 A75 5fr yellow & multi. 12 8
273 " 10fr blue & multi. 25 8
274 " 15fr green & multi. 33 15
275 " 25fr olive & multi. 50 25

Hertzian Center, Nkol Ogoum
A76

1971, June 17 Engraved *Perf. 13*

276 A76 40fr green, black & dark carmine 55 35

3rd World Telecommunications Day.

Mother Nursing Child
A77

1971, Aug. 17 Engraved *Perf. 13*

277 A77 30fr lilac rose, sepia & ocher 40 30

15th anniversary of the Gabonese social security system.

U.N. Headquarters and Emblem
A78

1971, Sept. 30 Photo. *Perf. 13*

278 A78 30fr red & multi. 35 20

10th anniversary of Gabon's admission to the United Nations.

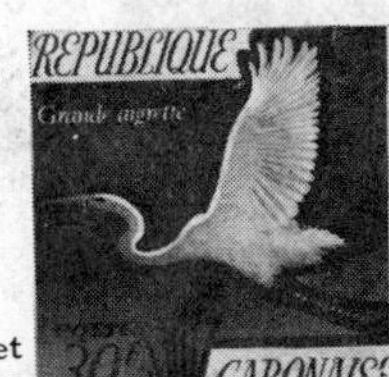

Large Egret
A79

Birds: 40fr, African gray parrot. 50fr, Woodland Kingfisher. 75fr, Cameroon bareheaded rock-fowl. 100fr, Gold Coast touraco.

1971, Oct. 12 Litho. *Perf. 13*

279 A79 30fr multicolored 40 25
280 " 40fr " 60 35
281 " 50fr " 75 40
282 " 75fr " 1.00 45
283 " 100fr " 1.25 55
Nos. 279–283 (5) 4.00 2.00

Asystasia Volgeliana
A80

Designs: Flowers of Acanthus Family after paintings by Noel Hallé.

1972, Apr. 4 Photo. *Perf. 13*

284 A80 5fr pale citron & multi. 12 8
285 " 10fr multicolored 18 10
286 " 20fr " 35 25
287 " 30fr lilac rose & multi. 50 30
288 " 40fr dk. grn. & multi. 65 50
289 " 65fr red & multi. 90 65
Nos. 284–289 (6) 2.70 1.88

Louis Pasteur
A81

1972, May 15 Engraved *Perf. 13*

290 A81 80fr dp. org., purple & green 85 30

Sesquicentennial of the birth of Louis Pasteur (1822–1895), scientist and bacteriologist.

Arms Type of 1969

Coats of Arms: 30fr, Franceville. 40fr, Makokou. 60fr, Tchibanga.

1972, June 2 Photo. *Perf. 12*

291 A67 30fr silver & multi. 35 20
292 " 40fr grn. & multi. 45 18
293 " 60fr blk., grn. & silver 75 25

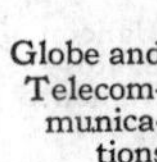

Globe and Telecommunications Symbols
A81a

1972, July 25 *Perf. 13x12½*

294 A81a 40fr blk., yel. & org. 45 25

4th World Telecommunications Day.

Nat King Cole
A82

Black American Jazz Musicians: 60fr, Sidney Bechet. 100fr, Louis Armstrong.

1972, Sept. 1 Photo. *Perf. 13x13½*

295 A82 40fr blue & multi. 50 30
296 " 60fr orange & multi. 80 45
297 " 100fr multicolored 1.25 75

Blanding's Rear-fanged Snake
A83

Designs: 2fr, Beauty snake. 3fr, Egg-eating snake. 15fr, Striped ground snake. 25fr, Jameson's mamba. 50fr, Gabon viper.

1972, Oct. 2 Litho. *Perf. 13*

298 A83 1fr lemon & multi. 5 5
299 " 2fr red brn. & multi. 6 5
300 " 3fr brn. org. & multi. 10 6
301 " 15fr multicolored 30 18
302 " 25fr green & multi. 40 20
303 " 50fr multicolored 75 35
Nos. 298–303 (6) 1.66 89

Dr. Armauer G. Hansen, Lambarene Leprosarium
A84

1973, Jan. 28 Engraved *Perf. 13*

304 A84 30fr Prus. grn., slate green & brown 40 30

Centenary of the discovery of the Hansen bacillus, the cause of leprosy.

Charaxes Candiope
A85

Designs: Various butterflies.

1973, Feb. 23 Lithographed *Perf. 13*
Multicolored

305 A85 10fr *shown* 15 7
306 " 15fr *Eunica pechueli* 20 8
307 " 20fr *Cyrestis camillus* 30 15
308 " 30fr *Charaxes castor* 45 25
309 " 40fr *Charaxes ameliae* 50 32
310 " 50fr *Pseudacrea boisduvali* 75 35
Nos. 305–310 (6) 2.35 1.22

Balloon of Santos-Dumont, 1901
A86

History of Aviation: 1fr, Montgolfier's balloon, 1783 (vert.). 3fr, Octave Chanute's biplane, 1896. 4fr, Clement Ader's Plane III, 1897. 5fr, Louis Bleriot crossing the Channel, 1909. 10fr, Fabre's hydroplane, 1910.

1973, May 3 Engraved *Perf. 13*

311 A86 1fr grn., slate green & dark red 5 5
312 " 2fr slate green & bright blue 8 5
313 " 3fr bl., slate & org. 8 5
314 " 4fr lilac & dk. pur. 10 6
315 " 5fr slate grn. & org. 15 8
316 " 10fr rose lilac & Prus. blue 18 10
Nos. 311–316 (6) 64 39

1977 Coil Stamp

316A A86 10fr aquamarine 10 6

No. 316A has red control numbers on back of every 10th stamp.

INTERPOL Emblem
A87

1973, June 26 Engraved *Perf. 13*

317 A87 40fr magenta & ultra. 40 20

50th anniversary of the International Criminal Police Organization (INTERPOL).

Earth Station "2 Decembre"
A88

1973, July 2 Engraved *Perf. 13*

318 A88 40fr slate green, blue & brown 40 20

Party Headquarters, Libreville—A89

1973, Aug. 17 Photogravure

319 A89 30fr multicolored 30 15

African Postal Union Issue
Common Design Type

1973, Sept. 12 Engraved *Perf. 13*

320 CD137 100fr red lilac, pur. & blue 90 60

11th anniversary of Afro-Malagasy Union of Posts and Telecommunications, UAMPT.

Arms Type of 1969

Coats of Arms: 5fr, Gamba. 10fr, Ogowe-Lolo. 15fr, Fougamou. 30fr, Kango. 40fr, Booue. 60fr, Koula-Moutou.

1973–74 Photogravure *Perf. 12*

321 A67 5fr bl. & multi. ('74) 8 3
322 " 10fr black, red & gold ('74) 12 5
323 A67 15fr green & multi. ('74) 15 8
324 " 30fr red & multi. 35 12
325 " 40fr " " 40 13
326 " 60fr emerald & multi. 60 15
Nos. 321–326 (6) 1.70 56

Issue dates: Nos. 321–323, Feb. 13, 1974; Nos. 324–326, Oct. 4, 1973.

St. Teresa of Lisieux
A90

REPUBLIQUE GABONAISE
20F
POSTES 1973
XXV
25e ANNIVERSAIRE DE LA DECLARATION UNIVERSELLE DES DROITS DE L'HOMME

Human Rights Flame
A91

Design: 40fr, St. Teresa and Jesus carrying cross.

1973, Dec. 4 Photo. *Perf. 13*

327 A90 30fr black & multi. 35 25
328 " 40fr " " 45 35

Birth centenary of St. Teresa of the Infant Jesus (Thérèse Martin, 1873–1897), Carmelite nun.

1973, Dec. 10 Engraved

329 A91 20fr grn., red & ultra. 20 12

25th anniversary of the Universal Declaration of Human Rights.

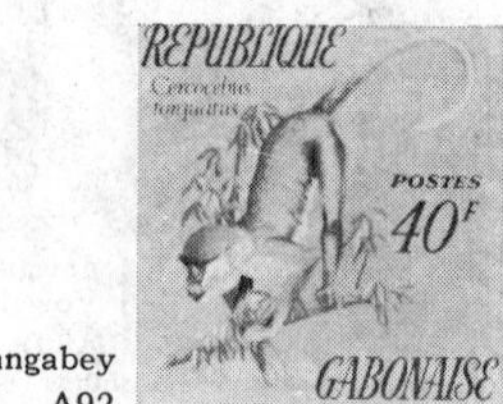

Mangabey
A92

Monkeys: 60fr, Cercopithecus cephus. 80fr, Mona monkey.

1974, Mar. 20 Lithographed *Perf. 14*

330 A92 40fr gray grn. & multi. 35 20
331 " 60fr lt. blue & multi. 50 30
332 " 80fr lilac rose & multi. 65 40

Ogowe River at Lambarene
A93

Designs: 50fr, Cape Estérias. 75fr, Poubara rope bridge.

1974, July 30 Photo. *Perf. 13x13½*

333 A93 30fr multicolored 25 15
334 " 50fr " 40 25
335 " 75fr " 60 40

Manioc
A94

Design: 50fr, Palms and dates.

1974, Nov. 13 Photo. *Perf. 13x12½*

336 A94 40fr org. red & multi. 35 20
337 " 50fr bister & multi. 40 20

UDEAC Issue

Presidents and Flags of Cameroun, CAR, Congo, Gabon and Meeting Center—A95

1974, Dec. 8 Photogravure *Perf. 13*

338 A95 40fr multicolored 35 20

See No. C156.

Hôtel du Dialogue—A96

1975, Jan. 20 Photo. *Perf. 13*

339 A96 50fr multicolored 40 25

Opening of Hôtel du Dialogue.

Arms Type of 1969

Coats of Arms: 5fr, Ogowe-Ivindo. 10fr, Moabi. No. 342, Moanda. No. 343, Nyanga. 25fr, Mandji. No. 345, Mekambo. No. 346, Omboué. 60fr, Minvoul. 90fr, Mayumba.

1975–77 Photo. *Perf. 12*

340 A67 5fr red & multi. 5 3
341 " 10fr gold & multi. 8 5
342 " 15fr red, silver & blk. 12 5
343 " 15fr blue & multi. 10 5
344 " 25fr green & multi. 20 10
345 " 50fr blk., gold & red 40 20
346 " 50fr multicolored 40 20
347 " 60fr " 50 15
348 " 90fr " 70 40
Nos. 340–348 (9) 2.55 1.23

Issue dates: Nos. 340–342, Jan. 21, 1975. Nos. 343–345, Aug. 17, 1976. Nos. 346–348, July 12, 1977.

Map of Africa with Lion's Head, and Lions Emblem—A97

1975, May 2 Typo. *Perf. 13*

349 A97 50fr green & multi. 40 30

Lions Club 17th congress, District 403, Libreville.

Hertzian Wave Transmitter Network, Map of Gabon—A98

1975, July 8 Engraved *Perf. 13*

350 A98 40fr multicolored 40 25

City and Rural Women, Car, Train and Building—A99

1975, July 22 Engr. *Perf. 13*

351 A99 50fr car., bl. & brn. 50 30

International Women's Year 1975.

Scoutmaster Ange Mba, Emblems and Rope
A100

Design: 50fr, Hand holding rope, Scout, camp, Boy Scout and Nordjamb 75 emblems.

1975, July 29

352 A100 40fr multicolored 40 25
353 " 50fr green, red & dark brown 50 30

Nordjamb 75, 14th Boy Scout Jamboree, Lillehammer, Norway, July 29–Aug. 7.

Lutjanus Goreensis
A101

Fish: 40fr, Galeoides decadactylus. 50fr, Sardinella aurita. 120fr, Scarus hoefleri.

1975, Sept. 22 Litho. *Perf. 14*

354 A101 30fr multicolored 25 15
355 " 40fr " 35 25
356 " 50fr " 40 30
357 " 120fr " 1.00 70

Agro-Industrial Complex—A102

1975, Dec. 15 Litho. *Perf. 12½*

358 A102 60fr multicolored 50 35

Inauguration of Agro-Industrial Complex, Franceville.

Tchibanga Bridge—A103

Bridges of Gabon: 10fr, Mouila. 40fr, Kango. 50fr, Lambaréné (vert.).

1976, Jan. 30 Engr. *Perf. 13*

359 A103 5fr multicolored 5 4
360 " 10fr " 8 6
361 " 40fr " 32 25
362 " 50fr " 40 30

Telephones 1876 and 1976, Satellite, A. G. Bell—A104

1976, Mar. 10 Engr. *Perf. 13*

363	A104	60fr dk. bl., grn. & slate green	50	35

Centenary of first telephone call by Alexander Graham Bell, Mar. 10, 1876.

Msgr. Jean Remy Bessieux—A105

1976, Apr. 30 Engr. *Perf. 13*

364	A105	50fr grn., bl. & sepia	40	30

Death centenary of Msgr. Bessieux.

Athletes, Torch, Map of Africa, Games Emblem—A106

1976, June 25 Photo. *Perf. 13x12½*

365	A106	50fr multicolored	40	30
366	"	60fr orange & multi.	50	35

First Central African Games (Zone 5), Libreville, June–July.

Moto-bécane, France A107

Motorcycles: 5fr, Bultaco, Spain. 10fr, Suzuki, Japan. 20fr, Kawasaki, Japan. 100fr, Harley-Davidson, U.S.

1976, July 20 Litho. *Perf. 12½*

367	A107	3fr multicolored	6	3
368	"	5fr org. & multi.	8	4
369	"	10fr blue & multi.	10	8
370	"	20fr multicolored	15	10
371	"	100fr car. & multi.	80	60
		Nos. 367-371 (5)	1.19	85

Rice A108

Design: 60fr, Pepper plants.

1976, Oct. 15 Litho. *Perf. 13x13½*

372	A108	50fr multicolored	40	20
373	"	60fr "	50	35

1977, Apr. 22 Litho. *Perf. 13x13½*

Designs: 50fr, Banana plantation. 60fr, Peanut market.

374	A108	50fr multicolored	40	30
375	"	60fr "	50	35

Telecommunications Emblem and Telephone A109

1977, May 17 *Perf. 13*

376	A109	60fr multicolored	50	35

World Telecommunications Day.

View of Oyem A110

Designs: 50fr, Cape Lopez. 70fr, Lebamba Cave.

1977, June 9 Litho. *Perf. 12½*

377	A110	50fr multicolored	40	30
378	"	60fr "	50	35
379	"	70fr "	55	40

Conference Hall—A111

1977, June 23 Photo. *Perf. 13x12½*

380	A111	100fr multicolored	80	55

Meeting of the Organization for African Unity, Libreville.

Arms of Gabon A112

1977 Engraved *Perf. 13*

Size: 22x36mm.

381	A112	50fr blue	40	30

Size: 17x23mm.

382	A112	60fr orange	50	15
	a.	Booklet pane of 5	2.75	
383	A112	80fr red	65	50

No. 381 issued in coils, No. 382 in booklets only.

Issue dates: Nos. 381–382, June 23. No. 383, Sept.

Modern Buildings, Libreville—A113

1977, Aug. 17 Litho. *Perf. 12*

387	A113	50fr multicolored	40	30

National Festival 1977.

Paris to Vienna, 1902—A114

Renault Automobiles: 10fr, Coupé 12 CV, 1921. 30fr, Torpédo Scaphandrier, 1925. 40fr, Reinastella 40 CV, 1929. 100fr, Nerva Grand Sport, 1937. 150fr, Voiturette 1 CV, 1899. 200fr, Alpine Renault V6, 1977.

1977, Aug. 30 Engr. *Perf. 13*

388	A114	5fr multicolored	5	4
389	"	10fr "	10	8
390	"	30fr "	25	20
391	"	40fr "	30	22
392	"	100fr "	80	50
		Nos. 388-392 (5)	1.50	1.04

Miniature Sheet

393	A114	sheet of 2+label	3.75	3.75
	a.	150fr multicolored	1.50	1.50
	b.	200fr "	2.00	2.00

Louis Renault, French automobile pioneer, birth centenary. Nos. 383a–393b are perf. on 3 sides, without perforation between stamps and center label showing dark brown portrait of Renault. Size: 170x90mm.

See Nos. 395–400.

Globe A115

1978, Feb. 21 Engr. *Perf. 13x12½*

394	A115	80fr multicolored	65	50

World Leprosy Day.

Automobile Type of 1977

Citroen Cars: 10fr, Cabriolet, 1922. 50fr, Taxi, 1927. 60fr, Berline, 1932. 80fr, Berline, 1934. 150fr, Torpedo, 1919. 200fr, Berline, 1948. 250fr, Pallas, 1975.

1978, May 9 Engr. *Perf. 13*

395	A114	10fr multicolored	10	8
396	"	50fr "	50	35
397	"	60fr "	60	40
398	"	80fr "	80	50
399	"	200fr "	2.00	1.00
		Nos. 395-399 (5)	4.00	2.33

Miniature Sheet

400	A114	Sheet of 2	4.25	4.25
	a.	150fr multicolored	1.50	
	b.	250fr "	2.50	

Andre Citroen (1878–1935), automobile designer and manufacturer. No. 400 shows Eiffel Tower in green and brown between stamps. Size: 170x100mm.

Ndjole on Ogowe River—A116

Views: 40fr, Lambarene lake district. 50fr, Owendo Harbor.

1978, May 17 Litho. *Perf. 12½*

401	A116	30fr multicolored	30	20
402	"	40fr "	40	25
403	"	50fr "	50	30

The only foreign revenue stamps listed in this Catalogue are those authorized for prepayment of postage.

Sternotomis Mirabilis A117

Anti-Apartheid Emblem A118

Coleoptera: 60fr, Analeptes trifasciata. 75fr, Homoderus mellyi. 80fr, Stephanorrhina guttata.

1978, June 21 Photo. *Perf. 12½x13*

404	A117	20fr multicolored	20	12
405	"	60fr "	60	40
406	"	75fr "	75	45
407	"	80fr "	80	50

1978, July 25 Engr. *Perf. 13*

408	A118	80fr multicolored	80	50

Anti-Apartheid Year.

Arms Type of 1975

Coats of Arms: 5fr, Oyem. 40fr, Okondja. 60fr, Mimongo.

1978, Aug. 17 Photo. *Perf. 12*

409	A67	5fr multicolored	5	4
413	"	40fr "	40	25
415	"	60fr bl., gold & blk.	60	40

Acropolis and UNESCO Emblems—A119

1978, Oct. 24 Engr. *Perf. 13*

419	A119	80fr multicolored	80	50

UNESCO campaign to save the Acropolis, Athens.

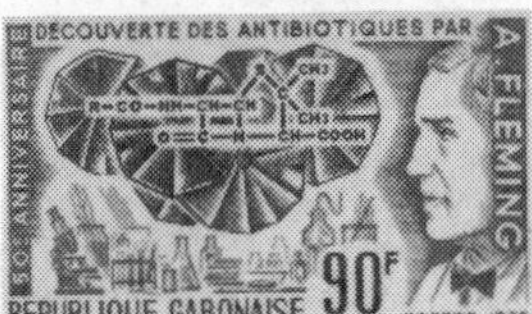

Penicillin Formula, Equipment and Dr. Fleming—A120

1978, Nov. 21 Engr. *Perf. 13*

420	A120	90fr multicolored	90	55

Alexander Fleming's discovery of antibiotics, 50th anniversary.

The Visitation A121

Design: 80fr, Massacre of the Innocents. Woodcarvings from St. Michael's Church, Libreville.

1978, Dec. 15 Photogravure

421	A121	60fr gold & multi.	60	40
422	"	80fr " "	80	50

Christmas 1978.

Train and Map
A122

1978, Dec. 27 Litho. ***Perf. 12½***

423	A122	60fr multicolored	60	40

Inauguration of Trans-Gabon Railroad, Libreville to Njolé.

Arms Type of 1969

Coats of Arms: 5fr, Ogowe-Maritime. 10fr, Lastoursville. 15fr, M'Bigou.

1979, Mar. 21 Photo. ***Perf. 12***

424	A67	5fr multicolored	5	3
425	"	10fr "	10	7
426	"	15fr "	15	8

SEMI-POSTAL STAMPS.

No. 37 Surcharged in Red

1916 *Perf. 13½x14* **Unwmkd.**

B1 A10 10c+5c red & carmine 6.00 6.00
a. Double surch. 45.00 45.00

Same Surcharge on No. 54 in Red.

B2 A13 10c+5c red & carmine 8.00 7.00
a. Double surch. 45.00 45.00

No. 54 Surcharged in Red

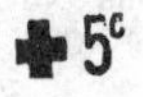

1917

B3 A13 10c+5c carmine & red 25 25

Republic

Anti-Malaria Issue

Common Design Type

1962, Apr. 7 Engr. *Perf. 12½x12*

B4 CD108 25fr+5fr yel. green 60 60

Issued for the World Health Organization drive to eradicate malaria.

Freedom from Hunger Issue

Common Design Type

1963, Mar. 21 *Perf. 13* **Unwmkd.**

B5 CD112 25fr+5fr dark red, green & brown 60 60

AIR POST STAMPS

Dr. Albert Schweitzer—AP1

Engraved

1960, July 23 *Perf. 13* **Unwmkd.**

C1 AP1 200fr green, dull red brn. & ultra. 4.50 2.50

Issued to honor Dr. Albert Schweitzer, medical missionary.

Workmen Felling Tree—AP2

1960, Oct. 8

C2 AP2 100fr red brown, grn. & blk. 2.00 1.10

Issued to commemorate the Fifth World Forestry Congress, Seattle, Washington, Aug. 29–Sept. 10.

Olympic Games Issue

French Equatorial Africa No. C37 Surcharged in Red Like Chad No. C1.

1960, Dec. 15

C3 AP8 250fr on 500fr greenish black, black & slate 6.00 6.00

Issued to commemorate the 17th Olympic Games, Rome, Aug. 25–Sept. 11.

Lyre-tailed Honey Guide—AP3

1961, May 30 *Perf. 13*

C4 AP3 50fr slate green, red brown & ultra. 90 60

See also Nos. C14–C17.

Air Afrique Issue

Common Design Type

1962, Feb. 17 Engraved *Perf. 13*

C5 CD107 500fr slate green, blk. & bis. 7.50 4.50

Issued to commemorate the founding of Air Afrique (African Airlines).

Abidjan Games Issue

Long Jump

AP3a

1962, July 21 Photo. *Perf. 12x12½*

C6 AP3a 100fr dk. & lt. blue, brown & blk. 2.00 1.10

Issued to publicize the Abidjan Games.

Breguet 14, 1928—AP4

Development of air transport: 20fr, Dragon biplane transport. 60fr, Caravelle jet. 85fr, Rocket-propelled aircraft.

1962, Sept. 4 Engraved *Perf. 13*

C7 AP4 10fr dull red brown & slate 45 20
C8 " 20fr dark blue, slate & ochre 50 35
C9 " 60fr dark slate grn., blk. & brown 1.25 1.00
C10 " 85fr dk. blue, black & orange 2.25 2.00
a. Souv. sheet of 4 5.00 5.00

Gabon's first philatelic exhibition, Libreville, Sept. 2–9.

No. C10a contains one each of Nos. C7–C10 with black marginal inscription. Size: 129x99½mm.

No. C1 Surcharged in Red: "100F/JUBILE GABONAIS/1913-1963"

1963, Apr. 18

C11 AP1 100fr on 200fr 1.75 1.35

Issued to commemorate the 50th anniversary of Dr. Albert Schweitzer's arrival in Gabon.

Post Office, Libreville—AP5

1963, Apr. 28 Photo. *Perf. 13x12*

C12 AP5 100fr multicolored 1.35 1.00

African Postal Union Issue

Common Design Type

1963, Sept. 8 *Perf. 12½* **Unwmkd.**

C13 CD114 85fr brt. carmine, ocher & red 1.25 90

Bird Type of 1961

Birds: 100fr, Johanna's sunbird. 200fr, Blue-headed bee-eater (vert.). 250fr, Crowned hawk-eagle (vert.). 500fr, Narina trogon (vert.).

1963–64 Engraved *Perf. 13*

C14 AP3 100fr dk. grn., vio. bl. & car. 1.75 80
C15 " 200fr olive, violet blue & red 3.50 1.75
C16 " 250fr green, black & dk. brn. ('64) 4.50 2.25
C17 " 500fr multicolored 8.50 4.00

1963 Air Afrique Issue

Common Design Type

1963, Nov. 19 Photo. *Perf. 13x12*

C18 CD115 50fr light vio., gray, black & green 75 60

Europafrica Issue

Common Design Type

1963, Nov. 30 *Perf. 12x13*

C19 CD116 50fr violet, yellow & dk. brown 1.25 75

Chiefs of State Issue

Map and Presidents of Chad, Congo, Gabon and CAR

AP5a

1964, June 23 *Perf. 12½*

C20 AP5a 100fr multicolored 1.60 1.10

See note after Central African Republic No. C19.

Europafrica Issue, 1964

Globe and Emblems of Industry and Agriculture

AP6

1964, July 20 *Perf. 12x13*

C21 AP6 50fr red, olive & bl. 85 60

See note after Cameroun No. 402.

Start of Race—AP7

Athletes (Greek): 50fr, Massage at gymnasium (vert.). 100fr, Anointing with oil before game (vert.). 200fr, Four athletes.

1964, July 30 Engraved *Perf. 13*

C22 AP7 25fr slate green, dk. brown & orge. 40 30
C23 " 50fr dark brown, slate green & orange brn. 80 55
C24 " 100fr violet bl., olive green & dark brown 1.60 1.10
C25 " 200fr dark brown, magenta & orange red 3.25 2.35
a. Min. sheet of 4 6.25 6.25

Issued for the 18th Olympic Games, Tokyo, Oct. 10–25, 1964. No. C25a contains one each of Nos. C22–C25. Size: 191x99mm.

Communications Symbols

AP7a

1964, Nov. 2 Litho. *Perf. 12½x13*

C26 AP7a 25fr lt. grn., dark brn. & light red brown 35 30

See note after Chad No. C19.

John F. Kennedy

AP8

1964, Nov. 23 Photo. *Perf. 12½*

C27 AP8 100fr green, orange & black 1.75 1.40
a. Souv. sheet of 4 7.00 7.00

Issued in memory of Pres. John F. Kennedy (1917–1963). No. C27a contains four stamps with black marginal inscription. Size: 90x129mm.

Telephone Operator, Nurse and Police Woman—AP9

1964, Dec. 5 Engraved *Perf. 13*

C28 AP9 50fr car., blue & chocolate 80 50

Social evolution of Gabonese women.

World Map and ICY Emblem AP10

1965, Mar. 25 *Perf. 13* **Unwmkd.**

C29 AP10 50fr org., Pruss. blue & greenish bl. 80 55

International Cooperation Year.

Merchant Ship, 17th Century—AP11

Designs: 25fr, Galleon, 16th century (vert.). 85fr, Frigate, 18th century (vert.). 100fr, Brig, 19th century.

1965, Apr. 22 Photo. *Perf. 13*

C30 AP11 25fr lilac & multi. 50 35
C31 " 50fr yel. & multi. 1.00 55
C32 " 85fr multicolored 1.50 1.00
C33 " 100fr " 2.00 1.25

Red Cross Nurse Carrying Sick Child—AP12

1965, June 25 Engraved *Perf. 13*

C34 AP12 100fr brown, slate green & red 1.50 1.00

Issued for the Gabonese Red Cross.

Women's Basketball AP13

1965, July 15 **Unwmkd.**

C35 AP13 100fr sepia, red orange & brt. lilac 1.50 1.00

African Games, Brazzaville, July 18–25.

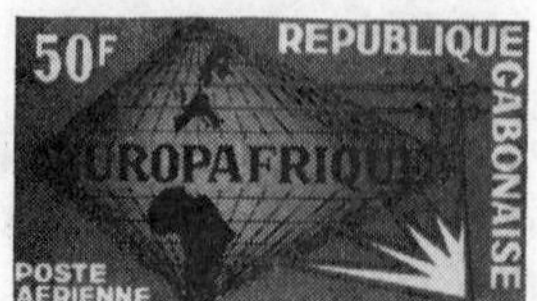

Maps of Europe and Africa AP14

1965, July 26 Photo. *Perf. 13x12*

C36 AP14 50fr multicolored 1.50 45

See note after Cameroun No. 421.

Pres. Leon Mba AP15

1965, Aug. 17 *Perf. 12½*

C37 AP15 25fr multicolored 40 30

Fifth anniversary of independence.

Sir Winston Churchill and Microphones—AP16

1965, Sept. 28 Photo. *Perf. 12½*

C38 AP16 100fr gold, black & blue 1.60 1.10

Issued in memory of Sir Winston Spencer Churchill (1874–1965), statesman and World War II leader.

Dr. Albert Schweitzer—AP17

Embossed on Gold Foil

Die-cut Perf. 14½, Approx.

1965, Dec. 4

C39 AP17 1000fr gold 32.50 32.50

Issued in memory of Dr. Albert Schweitzer (1875–1965), medical missionary, theologian and musician.

Pope John XXIII and St. Peter's AP18

1965, Dec. 10 Photo. *Perf. 13x12½*

C40 AP18 85fr multicolored 1.25 85

Issued in memory of Pope John XXIII.

Anti-Malaria Treatment AP19

Design: 100fr, First aid.

1966, Apr. 8 Photo. *Perf. 12½*

C41 AP19 50fr dk. grn., brn., black & red 75 50
 a. Min. sheet of four 3.50 3.50
C42 " 100fr dk. grn., brn., black & red 1.60 90
 a. Min. sheet of four 7.00 7.00

Issued for the Red Cross. No. C41a contains four No. C41, No. C42a four No. C42. Size: 115x155mm.

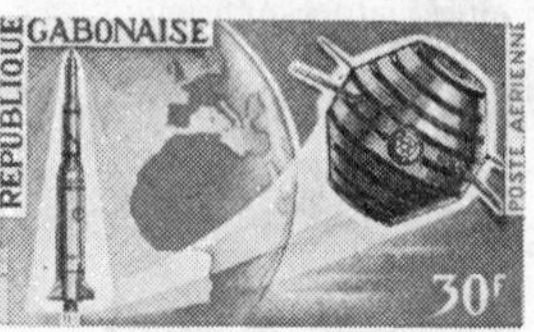

Diamant Rocket, A-1 Satellite and Map of Africa—AP20

Design: 90fr, FR-1 satellite, Diamant rocket and earth.

1966, May 18 Engraved *Perf. 13*

C43 AP20 30fr dk. pur., brt. bl. & red brn. 50 35
C44 " 90fr bright lilac, red & pur. 1.35 75

French achievements in space.

Soccer and World Map—AP21

1966, July 15 Engraved *Perf. 13*

C45 AP21 100fr slate & brown red 1.75 1.00

Issued to commemorate the 8th World Soccer Cup Championship, Wembley, England, July 11–30.

Symbols of Industry and Transportation AP22

Student and UNESCO Emblem AP23

1966, July 26 Photo. *Perf. 12x13*

C46 AP22 50fr multicolored 85 40

Issued for the 3rd anniversary of the economic agreement between the European Economic Community and the African and Malgache Union.

Air Afrique Issue, 1966

Common Design Type

1966, Aug. 31 Photo. *Perf. 13*

C47 CD123 30fr org., black & gray 40 20

Issued to commemorate the introduction of DC-8F planes by Air Afrique.

1966, Nov. 4 Engraved *Perf. 13*

C48 AP23 100fr dull bl., ocher & black 1.50 85

Issued to commemorate the 20th anniversary of UNESCO (United Nations Educational, Scientific and Cultural Organization).

Libreville Airport—AP24

1966, Nov. 21 Engraved *Perf. 13*

C49 AP24 200fr dp. blue & red brown 3.00 1.20

Inauguration of Libreville Airport.

Farman 190—AP25

Planes: 300fr, De Havilland Heron. 500fr, Potez 56.

1967, Apr. 1 Engraved *Perf. 13*

C50 AP25 200fr ultra., lilac & bl. green 3.50 1.10
C51 " 300fr brn., lilac & brt. blue 5.00 1.50
C52 " 500fr brn. carmine, dark green & indigo 8.00 4.75

Planes, Runways and ICAO Emblem—AP26

1967, May 19 Engraved *Perf. 13*

C53 AP26 100fr plum, brt. blue & yel. grn. 1.50 85

International Civil Aviation Organization.

Blood Donor and Bottles AP27

Jamboree Emblem and Symbols of Orientation AP28

Design: 100fr, Human heart and transfusion apparatus.

1967, June 26 Photo. *Perf. 12½*

C54 AP27 50fr ocher, red & slate 75 40
 a. Souv. sheet of 4 3.00 3.00
C55 " 100fr yellow green, red & gray 1.60 90
 a. Souv. sheet of 4 7.00 7.00

Issued for the Red Cross. No. C54a contains 4 No. C54 in 2 vertical tête bêche pairs; slate marginal inscription and Red Cross. No. C55a contains 4 No. C55 in 2 vertical tête bêche pairs; gray marginal inscription and red cross. Size: 115x154 mm.

1967, Aug. 1 Engraved *Perf. 13*

Design: 100fr, Jamboree emblem, maps and Scouts of Africa and America.

C56 AP28 50fr multicolored 75 45
C57 " 100fr brt. grn., dp. car. & blue 1.50 85

Issued to commemorate the 12th Boy Scout World Jamboree, Farragut State Park, Idaho, Aug. 1–9.

African Postal Union Issue, 1967

Common Design Type

1967, Sept. 9 Engraved *Perf. 13*

C58 CD124 100fr dull blue, olive & red brown 1.40 75

Mission Church—AP29

1967, Oct. 18 Engr. *Perf. 13*

C59 AP29 100fr brt. bl., dk. grn. & blk. 1.40 50

Issued to commemorate the 125th anniversary of the arrival of American Protestant missionaries in Baraka-Libreville.

U.N. Emblem, Sword, Book and People
AP30

Konrad Adenauer
AP31

1967, Nov. 7 Photo. *Perf. 13*

C60 AP30 60fr dk. red, violet blue & bis. 1.00 30

U.N. Commission on Human Rights.

Tree Type of Regular Issue

Designs: 50fr, Baillonella toxisperma. 100fr, Aucoumea klaineana.

1967, Dec. 5 Engraved *Perf. 13*

Size: 26½x47½mm.

C61 A53 50fr green, brt. blue & brown 80 40
C62 " 100fr multicolored 1.60 85
a. Bklt. pane (1 each #223–225 & C61–C62 with gutter btwn.) 3.25 3.25

1968, Feb. 20 Photo. *Perf. 12½*

C63 AP31 100fr black, dull org. & red 1.50 75
a. Souv. sheet of 4 6.00 6.00

Issued in memory of Konrad Adenauer (1876–1967), chancellor of West Germany (1949–63). No. C63a contains four No. C63. Margin with black inscription and 1967 CEPT (Europa) emblem. Size: 120½x170mm.

Madonna of the Rosary by Murillo
AP32

Paintings: 90fr, Christ in Bonds, by Luis de Morales. 100fr, St. John on Patmos, by Juan Mates (horiz.).

1968, July 9 Photo. *Perf. 12½x12*

C64 AP32 60fr multicolored 1.00 50
C65 " 90fr " 1.35 75
C66 " 100fr " 1.65 1.00

See Nos. C77, C102–C104, C132–C133, C146–C148.

Europafrica Issue

Stylized Knot
AP32a

1968, July 23 Photo. *Perf. 13*

C67 AP32a 50fr yellow brown, emerald & light ultra. 80 40

See note after Congo Republic No. C69.

Support for Red Cross—AP33

Design: 50fr, Distribution of Red Cross gifts.

1968, Aug. 13

C68 AP33 50fr multicolored 70 35
C69 " 100fr " 1.50 75
a. Bklt. pane (1 #C68, 1 #C69 with gutter btwn.) 2.50 2.50

Issued for the Red Cross.

High Jump—AP34

Designs: 30fr, Bicycling (vert.). 100fr, Judo (vert.). 200fr, Boxing.

1968, Sept. 3 Engraved

C70 AP34 25fr dark brown, magenta & gray 30 18
C71 " 30fr brick red, Prus. blue & dark brown 40 22
C72 " 100fr brt. blue, dark brown & dull yellow 1.40 70
C73 AP34 200fr emerald, gray & dk. brn. 2.75 1.40
a. Bklt. pane (1 each #C70–C71 & C72–C73 with gutter btwn.) 6.00 6.00

Issued to publicize the 19th Summer Olympic Games, Mexico City, Oct. 12–27.

Pres. Mba, Flag and Arms of Gabon
AP35
Embossed on Gold Foil

1968, Nov. 28 *Perf. 14½*

C74 AP35 1000fr gold, green, yellow & dk. blue 14.00 14.00

Issued to commemorate the first anniversary of the death of President Léon Mba (1902–1967).

Pres. Bongo, Maps of Gabon and Owendo Harbor
AP36

Design: 30fr, Owendo Harbor.

1968, Dec. 16 Photo. *Perf. 12½*

C75 AP36 25fr multicolored 40 20
C76 " 30fr " 50 25
a. Strip of 2 + label 1.10 1.00

Issued to commemorate the laying of the foundation stone for Owendo Harbor, June 24, 1968. No. C76a contains one each of Nos. C75–C76 and label with arms of Gabon and commemorative inscription.

PHILEXAFRIQUE Issue

Painting Type of 1968

Design: 100fr, The Convent of St. Mary of the Angels, by Francois Marius Granet.

1969, Jan. 8 Photo. *Perf. 12½x12*

C77 AP32 100fr multi. 1.60 1.60

Issued to publicize PHILEXAFRIQUE Philatelic Exhibition in Abidjan, Feb. 14–23. Printed with alternating brown label.

Mahatma Gandhi
AP37

Portraits: 30fr, John F. Kennedy. 50fr, Robert F. Kennedy. 100fr, Rev. Dr. Martin Luther King, Jr.

1969, Jan. 15 *Perf. 12½*

C78 AP37 25fr pink & black 40 18
C79 " 30fr lt. yel. green & black 45 20
C80 " 50fr lt. blue & blk. 75 35
C81 " 100fr bright rose lilac & black 1.50 65
a. Souv. sheet of 4 3.50 3.50

Issued to honor exponents of non-violence. No. C81a contains one each of Nos. C78–C81. Black marginal inscription. Size: 120x160mm.

2nd PHILEXAFRIQUE Issue

Common Design Type

1969, Feb. 14 Engraved *Perf. 13*

C82 CD128 50fr green, indigo & red brown 90 50

Issued to commemorate the opening of PHILEXAFRIQUE, Abidjan, Feb. 14.

Battle of Rivoli, by Henri Philippoteaux—AP39

Paintings: 100fr, The Oath of the Army, by Jacques Louis David. 250fr, Napoleon with the Children on the Terrace in St. Cloud, by Louis Ducis.

1969, Apr. 23 Photo. *Perf. 12½x12*

C83 AP39 50fr brn. & multi. 1.25 75
C84 " 100fr grn. & multi. 2.25 1.50
C85 " 250fr lilac & multi. 6.00 4.00

Birth bicentenary of Napoleon I.

Red Cross Plane, Nurse and Biafran Children—AP40

Design: 20fr, Dispensary, ambulance and supplies. 25fr, Physician and nurse in children's ward. 30fr, Dispensary and playing children.

1969, June 20 Photo. *Perf. 14x13½*

C86 AP40 15fr lt. ultra., dk. brn. & red 25 15
C87 " 20fr emerald, blk., brn. & red 35 20
C88 " 25fr greenish blue, dark brown & red 40 25
C89 " 30fr org. yel., dk. brn. & red 45 25

Red Cross help for Biafra.

A souvenir sheet contains four stamps similar to Nos. C86–C89, but lithographed and rouletted 13x13½. Gray margin with red inscription and Red Cross. Size: 118x75mm. Sold in cardboard folder. Price $1.20.

Astronauts and Lunar Landing Module, Apollo 11—AP41

Embossed on Gold Foil

Die-cut Perf. 10½x10

1969, July 25

C90 AP41 1000fr gold 14.00 14.00

See note after Algeria No. 427.

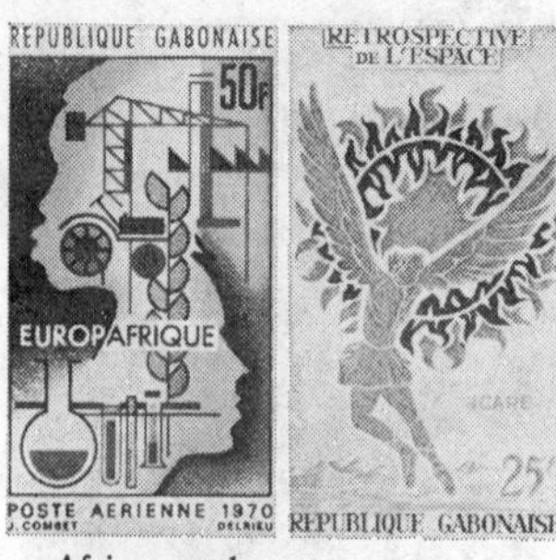

African and European Heads and Symbols AP42 — Icarus and Sun AP43

Europafrica Issue, 1970

1970, June 5 Photo. ***Perf. 12x13***

C91 AP42 50fr multicolored 75 35

1970, June 10 Engraved ***Perf. 13***

Designs: 100fr, Leonardo da Vinci's flying man, 1519. 200fr, Jules Verne's space shell approaching moon, 1865.

C92 AP43 25fr ultra., red & orange 40 25
C93 " 100fr ocher, plum & slate green 1.40 90
C94 " 200fr gray, ultra. & dk. carmine 3.25 1.75
a. Miniature sheet of 3 5.25 5.25

No. C94a contains one each of Nos. C92–C94. Size: 128x99mm.

UAMPT Emblem
AP44

Embossed on Gold Foil

1970, June 18 ***Die-cut Perf. 12½***

C95 AP44 200fr gold, yellow grn. & blue 2.75 1.65

Issued to commemorate the meeting of the Afro-Malagasy Union of Posts and Telecommuncations (UAMPT), Libreville, June 17–23.

Throwing Knives
AP45

Gabonese Weapons: 30fr, Assegai and crossbow (vert.). 50fr, War knives (vert.). 90fr, Dagger and sheath.

1970, July 10 Engraved ***Perf. 13***

C96 AP45 25fr brt. green, red brn. & indigo 35 12
C97 " 30fr brt. green, red brn. & slate 45 25
C98 " 50fr brt. green, red brn. & slate 65 40
C99 " 90fr brt. green, red brn. & slate 1.35 70
a. Miniature sheet of 4 3.00 3.00

No. C99a contains one each of Nos. C96–C99. Size: 169x99½mm.

Japanese Masks, Mt. Fuji and Torii at Miyajima
AP46

Embossed on Gold Foil

1970, July 31 ***Die-cut Perf. 10***

C100 AP46 1000fr multi. 15.00 15.00

Issued to publicize EXPO '70 International Exhibition, Osaka, Japan, Mar. 15–Sept. 13.

Pres. Albert Bernard Bongo
AP47

Lithographed; Gold Embossed

1970, Aug. 17 ***Perf. 12½***

C101 AP47 200fr multi. 3.00 1.60

10th anniversary of independence.

Painting Type of 1968

Paintings: 50fr, Portrait of a Young Man, School of Raphael. 100fr, Portrait of Jeanne d'Aragon, by Raphael. 200fr, Madonna with Blue Diadem, by Raphael.

1970, Oct. 16 Photo. ***Perf. 12½x12***

C102 AP32 50fr multicolored 80 40
C103 " 100fr blue & multi. 1.60 75
C104 " 200fr brn. & multi. 3.25 1.75

Issued to commemorate the 450th anniversary of the death of Raphael (1483–1520).

Presidents Bongo and Pompidou
AP48

1971, Feb. 11 Photo. ***Perf. 13***

C105 AP48 50fr multicolored 75 30

Visit of Georges Pompidou, President of France.

Flowers and Plane
AP49

Flowers and Planes: 25fr, Carnations. 40fr, Roses. 55fr, Daffodils. 75fr, Orchids. 120fr, Tulips.

1971, May 7 Litho. ***Perf. 13½x14***

C106 AP49 15fr yel. & multi. 25 15
C107 " 25fr multicolored 40 20
C108 " 40fr pink & multi. 60 30
C109 " 55fr blue & multi. 75 40
C110 " 75fr multicolored 1.20 65
C111 " 120fr grn. & multi. 1.75 1.00
a. Souvenir sheet of 2 3.25 3.25
Nos. C106–C111 (6) 4.95 2.70

"Flowers by air." No. C111a contains one each of Nos. C110–C111. Red margin with portraits of Orville and Wilbur Wright. Size: 134x80mm.

Napoleon's Death Mask
AP50

Designs: 200fr, Longwood, St. Helena, by Jacques Marchand (horiz.). 500fr, Sarcophagus in Les Invalides, Paris.

1971, May 12 Photo. ***Perf. 13***

C112 AP50 100fr gold & multi. 1.75 85
C113 " 200fr " " 3.25 1.50
C114 " 500fr " " 7.00 3.50

Sesquicentennial of the death of Napoleon Bonaparte (1769–1821).

Charles de Gaulle—AP51

Designs: 40fr, President de Gaulle. 80fr, General de Gaulle. 100fr, Quotation.

1971, June 18 Photo. ***Perf. 12½***

C115 AP51 Souv. sheet of 5 5.00 5.00
a. 40fr dark red & multicolored 50 50
b. 80fr dark green & multicolored 50 50
c. 100fr green, brown & yellow 1.25 1.25

In memory of Gen. Charles de Gaulle (1890–1970), President of France. No. C115 has green marginal inscriptions. Size: 150x139mm.

Red Crosses
AP52

1971, June 29

C116 AP52 50fr multicolored 75 40

For the Red Cross of Gabon.

Uranium—AP53

Design: 90fr, Manganese.

1971, July 20 Photo. ***Perf. 13x12½***

C117 AP53 85fr blue & multi. 1.10 60
C118 " 90fr yel. & multi. 1.25 75

Landing Module over Moon
AP54

Embossed on Gold Foil

1971, July 30 ***Die-cut Perf. 10***

C119 AP54 1500fr multi. 20.00 20.00

Apollo 11 and 15 U.S. moon missions.

African Postal Union Issue, 1971

Common Design Type

Design: 100fr, Bakota copper mask and UAMPT building, Brazzaville, Congo.

1971, Nov. 13 Photo. ***Perf. 13x13½***

C120 CD135 100fr bl. & multi. 1.40 70

Ski Jump and Miyajima Torii
AP55

Design: 130fr, Speed skating and Japanese temple.

1972, Jan. 31 Engr. ***Perf. 13***

C121 AP55 40fr henna brown, slate grn. & violet blue 60 25
C122 " 130fr henna brown, slate grn. & violet blue 1.85 65
a. Strip of 2 + label 3.00 2.50

11th Winter Olympic Games, Sapporo, Japan, Feb. 3–13. No. C122a contains one each of Nos. C121–C122 and center label with Sapporo '72 emblem. Size: 159x100mm.

The Basin and Grand Canal, by Vanvitelli—AP56

Paintings: 70fr, Rialto Bridge, by Canaletto (erroneously inscribed Caffi; vert.) 140fr, Santa Maria della Salute, by Vanvitelli (vert.).

1972, Feb. 7 Photo. ***Perf. 13***

C123 AP56 60fr gold & multi. 75 20
C124 " 70fr " " 1.20 30
C125 " 140fr " " 2.40 70

UNESCO campaign to save Venice.

Souvenir Sheet

No. C115 Surcharged in Brown and Gold

1972, Feb. 11 *Perf. 12½*

C126 AP51 Souv. sheet of 5 7.00 7.00
- *a.* 60fr on 40fr multi. 75 75
- *b.* 120fr on 80fr multi. 1.50 1.50
- *c.* 180fr on 100fr multi. 2.25 2.25

Publicity for the erection of a memorial for Charles de Gaulle. Nos. C126a–C126b have surcharge and Cross of Lorraine in gold, 2 bars obliterating old denomination in brown; No. C126c has surcharge, cross and bars in brown. Two Lorraine Crosses and inscription (MEMORIAL DU GENERAL DE GAULLE) in brown added in margin.

Hotel Inter-Continental, Libreville—AP57

1972, Feb. 26 Engraved *Perf. 13*

C127 AP57 40fr bl., slate grn. & org. brn. 50 20

No. C51 Surcharged

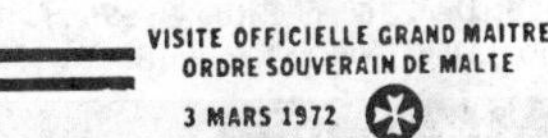

1972, Mar. 3

C128 AP25 50fr on 300fr multicolored 75 50

Official visit of the Grand Master of the Knights of Malta, March 3.

Discobolus, by Alcamenes AP58

Designs: 100fr, Doryphoros, by Polycletus. 140fr, Borghese gladiator, by Agasias.

1972, May 10 Engraved *Perf. 13*

C129 AP58 30fr rose claret & gray 40 15
C130 " 100fr rose claret & gray 1.35 35
C131 " 140fr rose claret & gray 1.85 50
- *a.* Miniature sheet of 3 4.00 4.00

20th Olympic Games, Munich, Aug. 26–Sept. 10. No. C131a contains one each of Nos. C129–C131. Size: 129x99mm.

Painting Type of 1968

Paintings: 30fr, Adoration of the Magi, by Peter Brueghel, the Elder (horiz.). 40fr, Madonna and Child, by Marco Basaiti.

1972, Oct. 30 Photo. *Perf. 13*

C132 AP32 30fr gold & multi. 40 25
C133 " 40fr " " 50 25

Christmas 1972.

Nos. C129–C131 Surcharged with New Value, Two Bars and Names of Athletes.

1972, Dec. 5 Engraved *Perf. 13*

Rose Claret & Gray

C134 AP58 40fr on 30fr (*Morelon*) 50 30
C135 " 120fr on 100fr (*Keino*) 1.50 75
C136 " 170fr on 140fr (*Spitz*) 2.25 1.20

Gold medal winners in 20th Olympic Games: Daniel Morelon, France, Bicycling (C134); Kipchoge Keino, Kenya, steeplechase (C135); Mark Spitz, USA, swimming (C136).

Globe with Space Orbits, Simulated Stamps—AP59

1973, Feb. 20 Photo. *Perf. 13*

C137 AP59 100fr multi. 1.25 65
- *a.* Souvenir sheet of 4 5.50 5.50

PHILEXGABON 1973, Philatelic Exhibition, Libreville, Feb. 19–26. No. C137a contains 4 No. C137, perf. 12x12½. Multicolored margin. Size: 169x139mm. No. C137a exists imperf.

DC10-30 "Libreville" over Libreville Airport—AP60

1973, Mar. 19 Typo. *Perf. 13*

C138 AP60 40fr blue & multi. 50 28

Kinguélé Hydroelectric Station—AP61

Design: 40c, Kinguélé Dam.

1973, June 19 Engraved *Perf. 13*

C139 AP61 30fr slate grn. & dark olive 30 25
C140 " 40fr slate grn., dk. olive & blue 40 30
- *a.* Strip of 2+label 75 75

Hydroelectric installations at Kinguélé. Nos. C139–C140 printed se-tenant with label in between carrying slate green inscription.

M'Bigou Stone Sculpture, Woman's Head AP62

Design: 200fr, Sculpture, man's head.

1973, July 5

C141 AP62 100fr black, blue & brown 1.20 80
C142 " 200fr grn., sepia & slate grn. 2.50 1.50

No. C116 Surcharged with New Value, 2 Bars, and Overprinted in Ultramarine: "SECHERESSE SOLIDARITE AFRICAINE"

1973, Aug. 16 Photo. *Perf. 12½*

C143 AP52 100fr on 50fr multi. 1.20 75

African solidarity in drought emergency.

Astronauts and Lunar Rover on Moon—AP63

1973, Sept. 6 Engraved *Perf. 13*

C144 AP63 500fr multi. 5.50 3.50

Apollo 17 U.S. moon mission, Dec. 7–19, 1973.

Presidents Houphouet Boigny (Ivory Coast) and De Gaulle—AP64

1974, Apr. 30 Engr. *Perf. 13*

C145 AP64 40fr rose lilac & indigo 35 20

30th anniversary of the Conference of Brazzaville.

Painting Type of 1968

Impressionist Paintings: 40fr, Pleasure Boats, by Claude Monet (horiz.). 50fr, Ballet Dancer, by Edgar Degas. 130fr, Young Girl with Flowers, by Auguste Renoir.

1974, June 11 Photo. *Perf. 13*

C146 AP32 40fr gold & multi. 35 20
C147 " 50fr " " 40 25
C148 " 130fr " " 1.10 60

Astronaut on Moon, Eagle and Emblems AP65

1974, July 20 Engraved *Perf. 13*

C149 AP65 200fr multi. 1.60 1.10

First men on the moon, 5th anniversary.

UPU Emblem, Letters, Pigeon AP66

Design: 300fr, UPU emblem, letters, pigeons (diff.).

1974, Oct. 9 Engraved *Perf. 13*

C150 AP66 150fr lt. blue & Prus. bl. 1.50 90
C151 " 300fr orange & claret 3.00 1.60

Centenary of Universal Postal Union.

Space Docking, US and USSR Crafts AP67

1974, Oct. 23 Engraved *Perf. 13*

C152 AP67 1000fr green, red & slate 8.00 5.25

Russo-American space cooperation.

Soccer and Games Emblem—AP68

Designs: Soccer actions.

1974, Oct. 25

C153 AP68 40fr green, red & brown 40 25
C154 " 65fr red, brown & green 60 35
C155 " 100fr green, red & brown 1.00 60
- *a.* Souvenir sheet of 3 2.25 2.25

World Cup Soccer Championship, Munich, June 13–July 7. No. C155a contains one each of Nos. C153–C155 and 3 labels showing Games emblem and soccer field. Red marginal inscription. Size: 170x100mm.

UDEAC Issue

Presidents and Flags of Cameroun, CAR, Gabon and Congo AP68a

1974, Dec. 8 Photogravure *Perf. 13*

C156 AP68a 100fr gold & multi. 90 55

Annunciation, Tapestry, 15th Century—AP69

Design: 40fr, Visitation from 15th century tapestry, Notre Dame de Beaune (vert.).

1974, Dec. 11

C157	AP69	40fr gold & multi.	40	25
C158	"	50fr " "	50	30

Christmas 1974.

Dr. Schweitzer and Lambarene Hospital—AP70

1975, Jan. 14 Engraved *Perf. 13*

C159	AP70	500fr multi.	4.00	2.75

Dr. Albert Schweitzer (1875–1965), medical missionary, birth centenary.

Crucifixion, by Bellini AP71

Painting: 150fr, Resurrection, Burgundian School, c. 1500.

1975, Apr. 8 Photo. *Perf. 13½*

Size: 26x45mm.

C160	AP71	140fr gold & multi.	1.40	75

Size: 36x48mm.

Perf. 13

C161	AP71	150fr gold & multi.	1.50	75

Easter 1975.

Marc Seguin Locomotive, 1829 AP72

Locomotives: 25fr, The Iron Duke, 1847. 40fr, Thomas Rogers, 1895. 50fr, The Soviet 272, 1934.

1975, Apr. 8 Engraved *Perf. 13*

C162	AP72	20fr multicolored	15	10
C163	"	25fr "	20	15
C164	"	40fr "	35	20
C165	"	50fr lilac & multi.	40	25

Swimming Pool, Montreal Olympic Games' Emblem—AP73

Designs: 150fr, Boxing ring and emblem. 300fr, Stadium, aerial view, and emblem.

1975, Sept. 30 Litho. *Perf. 13x12½*

C166	AP73	100fr multi.	80	50
C167	"	150fr "	1.20	80
C168	"	300fr "	2.40	1.65
		a. Miniature sheet of 3	4.50	4.50

Pre-Olympic Year 1975. No. C168a contains one each of Nos. C166–C168. Size: 170x100mm.

No. C152 Surcharged in Violet Blue: "JONCTION / 17 Juillet 1975"

1975, Oct. 20 Engr. *Perf. 13*

C169	AP67	1000fr multi.	8.00	5.50

Apollo-Soyuz link-up in space, July 17, 1975.

Annunciation, by Maurice Denis—AP74

Painting: 50fr, Virgin and Child with Two Saints, by Fra Filippo Lippi.

1975, Dec. 9 Photo. *Perf. 13*

C170	AP74	40fr gold & multi.	40	25
C171	"	50fr " "	50	30

Christmas 1975.

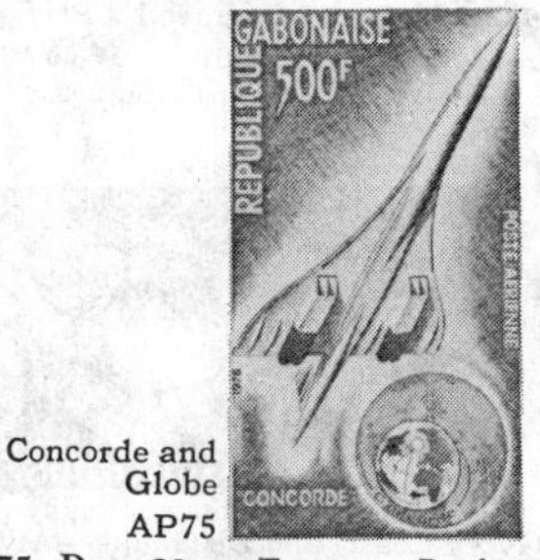

Concorde and Globe AP75

1975, Dec. 29 Engr. *Perf. 13*

C172	AP75	500fr bl., vio. bl. & red	4.00	2.75

First commercial flight of supersonic jet Concorde, Paris to Rio de Janeiro, Jan. 21, 1976.

No. C172 Surcharged

= 1000F
21 Janv. 1976
1er Vol
Commercial de
CONCORDE

1976, Jan. 21

C173	AP75	1000fr on 500fr	8.00	5.50

First commercial flight of supersonic jet Concorde from Paris to Rio de Janeiro, Jan. 21.

Slalom and Olympic Games Emblem—AP76

Design: 250fr, Speed skating and Winter Olympic Games emblem.

1976, Apr. 22 Engr. *Perf. 13*

C174	AP76	100fr black, blue & red	80	60
C175	"	250fr black, blue & red	2.00	1.40
		a. Souvenir sheet	3.00	3.00

12th Winter Olympic Games, Innsbruck, Austria, Feb. 4–15. No. C175a contains 100fr and 250fr stamps in continuous design with additional inscription and skier between, but without perforations between the design elements.

Size of perforated area: 125x27mm.; size of sheet: 169x90mm.

Jesus Between the Thieves AP77

Design: 130fr, St. Thomas putting finger into wounds of Jesus. Both designs after wood carvings in Church of St. Michael, Libreville.

1976, Apr. 28 Litho. *Perf. 12½x13*

C176	AP77	120fr multi.	1.00	65
C177	"	130fr "	1.10	75

Easter 1976. See Nos. C188–C189.

Boston Tea Party—AP78

Designs: 150fr, Battle of New York. 200fr, Demolition of statue of George III.

1976, May 3 Engr. *Perf. 13*

C178	AP78	100fr multi.	80	60
C179	"	150fr "	1.20	80
C180	"	200fr "	1.60	1.00
		a. Triptych (#C178–C180) + 2 labels	4.00	3.50

American Bicentennial. No. C180a contains one each of Nos. C178–C180 and Prussian blue labels showing Washington and Jefferson.

Issued in sheets of 5 triptychs.

Nos. C178–C180a Overprinted: "4 JUILLET 1976"

1976, July 4 Engr. *Perf. 13*

C181	AP78	100fr multi.	80	60
C182	"	150fr "	1.20	80
C183	"	200fr "	1.60	1.00
		a. Triptych (#C181–C183) + 2 labels	4.00	3.50

Independence Day. Overprint applied to each stamp of triptych.

Running AP79

Designs (Olympic Rings and): 200fr, Soccer. 260fr, High jump.

1976, July 27 Litho. *Perf. 12½*

C184	AP79	100fr multi.	80	60
C185	"	200fr "	1.60	1.00
C186	"	260fr "	2.00	1.40
		a. Souvenir sheet of 3	4.50	4.50

21st Olympic Games, Montreal, Canada, July 17–Aug. 1. No. C186a contains one each of Nos. C184–C186, perf. 13, marginal inscription, Olympic rings and maple leaf. Size: 150x120mm.

Unused prices are for stamps that have been hinged.

Presidents Giscard d'Estaing and Bongo—AP80

1976, Aug. 5 Photo. *Perf. 13*

C187	AP80	60fr blue & multi.	50	35

Visit of Pres. Valèrie Giscard d'Estaing of France.

Sculpture Type of 1976

Designs: 50fr, Presentation at the Temple. 60fr, Nativity. Designs after wood carvings in Church of St. Michael, Libreville.

1976, Dec. 6 Litho. *Perf. 12½x13*

C188	AP77	50fr multicolored	40	25
C189	"	60fr "	50	35

Christmas 1976.

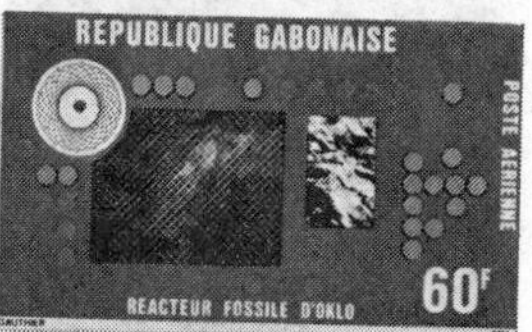

Oklo Fossil Reactor Station—AP81

1976, Dec. 15 Litho. *Perf. 13*

C190	AP81	60fr red & multi.	50	35

The Last Supper, by Juste de Gand AP82

Painting: 100fr, The Deposition, by Nicolas Poussin.

1977, Mar. 25 Litho. *Perf. 12½*

C191	AP82	50fr gold & multi.	40	30
C192	"	100fr " "	80	60

Easter 1977.

Air Gabon Plane and Insigne—AP83

1977, June 3 Litho. *Perf. 12½*

C193	AP83	60fr multicolored	50	35

Air Gabon's first intercontinental route.

Beethoven, Piano and Score—AP84

1977, June 15 Engr. *Perf. 13*

C194	AP84	260fr slate	2.00	1.40

Ludwig van Beethoven (1770–1827), composer.

Lindbergh and Spirit of St. Louis—AP85

1977, Sept. 13 Engr. *Perf. 13*

C195 AP85 500fr multi. 4.00 2.50

Charles A. Lindbergh's solo transatlantic flight from New York to Paris, 50th anniversary.

Soccer—AP86

1977, Oct. 18 Photo. *Perf. 13x12½*

C196 AP86 250fr multi. 2.00 1.35

Elimination games, World Soccer Cup, Buenos Aires, 1978.

Viking on Mars AP87

1977, Nov. 17 Engr. *Perf. 13*

C197 AP87 1000fr multi. 8.00 4.00

Viking, U.S. space probe.

No. C172 Overprinted:
"PARIS NEW-YORK / PREMIER VOL / 22.11.77"

1977, Nov. 22 Engr. *Perf. 13*

C198 AP75 500fr multi. 4.00 3.00

Concorde, first commercial flight, Paris to New York.

Lion Hunt, by Rubens—AP88

Rubens Paintings: 80fr, Hippopotamus Hunt. 200fr, Head of Black Man (vert.).

1977, Nov. 24 Litho. *Perf. 13*

C199 AP88 60fr gold & multi. .50 35
C200 " 80fr " " 65 50
C201 " 200fr " " 1.60 1.20
a. Souvenir sheet of 3 2.75 2.75

Peter Paul Rubens (1577–1640), 400th birth anniversary.

No. C201a contains one each of Nos. C199–C201; multicolored margin with black control number. Size: 176x136mm.

Adoration of the Kings, by Rubens—AP89

Design: 80fr, Flight into Egypt, by Rubens.

1977, Dec. 15 Litho. *Perf. 12½*

C202 AP89 60fr gold & multi. 50 35
C203 " 80fr " " 65 50

Christmas 1977; 400th birth anniversary of Peter Paul Rubens (1577–1640).

Paul Gauguin, Self-Portrait AP90

Design: 150fr, Flowers in vase and Maori statuette.

1978, Feb. 8 Litho. *Perf. 12½x12*

C204 AP90 150fr multi. 1.20 60
C205 " 300fr " 2.40 1.25

Paul Gauguin (1848–1903), French painter, 75th death anniversary.

Pres. Bongo, Map of Gabon, Plane and Train AP91

Litho.; Gold Embossed

1978, Mar. 12 *Perf. 12½*

C206 AP91 500fr multi. 4.00 2.00

10th anniversary of national renewal.

Soccer and Argentina '78 Emblem AP92

Designs (Argentina '78 Emblem and): 120fr, Three soccer players. 200fr, Jules Rimet Cup (vert.).

1978, July 18 Engr. *Perf. 13*

C207 AP92 100fr red, green & brown 80 40
C208 AP92 120fr green, red & brown 1.00 60
C209 " 200fr brn. & red 1.60 80
a. Miniature sheet of 3 3.50 3.50

11th World Cup Soccer Championship, Argentina, June 1–25. No. C209a contains Nos. C207–C209. Size: 180x100mm.

Nos. C207–C209a Overprinted in Ultramarine:

a. ARGENTINE / HOLLANDE / 3–1
b. BRESIL / ITALIE / 2–1
c. CHAMPION / DU MONDE 1978 / ARGENTINE

1978, July 21 Engr. *Perf. 13*

C210 AP92 (*a*) 100fr multi. 80 40
C211 " (*b*) 120fr " 1.00 50
C212 " (*c*) 200fr " 1.60 80
a. Souvenir sheet of 3 3.75 3.75

Argentina's victory in World Cup Soccer Championship. Overprints on No. C212a are black. Size: 180x100mm.

Dürer (age 13), Self-portrait AP93

Design: 250fr, Lucas de Leyde, by Dürer.

1978, Sept. 15 Engr. *Perf. 13*

C213 AP93 100fr red brown & slate 80 40
C214 " 250fr black & red brown 2.00 1.00

Albrecht Dürer (1474–1528), German painter.

Philexafrique II—Essen Issue

Common Design Types

Designs: No. C215, Gorilla and Gabon No. 280. No. C216, Stork and Saxony No. 1.

1978, Nov. 1 Litho. *Perf. 13x12½*

C215 CD138 100fr multi. 80 40
C216 CD139 100fr " 80 40

Nos. C215–C216 printed se-tenant.

Wright Brothers and Flyer AP94

1978, Dec. 19 Engr. *Perf. 13*

C217 AP94 380fr multi. 3.00 1.50

75th anniversary of 1st powered flight.

Pope John Paul II AP95

Design: 200fr, Popes Paul VI and John Paul I, St. Peter's Basilica and Square (horiz.).

1979, Jan. 24 Litho. *Perf. 12½*

C218 AP95 100fr multi. 80 40
C219 " 200fr " 1.60 80

Sculpture Type of 1976

Designs: 100fr, Disciples recognizing Jesus in the breaking of the bread. 150fr, Jesus appearing to Mary Magdalene. Designs after wood carvings in Church of St. Michael, Libreville.

1979, Apr. 10 Litho. *Perf. 12½x13*

C220 AP77 100fr multi. 1.00 50
C221 " 150fr " 1.50 75

Easter 1979.

AIR POST SEMI-POSTAL STAMPS

Ramses II Paying Homage to Four Gods, Wadi-es-Sabua
SPAP1

Engraved

1964, March 9 *Perf. 13* **Unwmkd.**

CB1	SPAP1	10fr+5fr dk. bl. & bister brn.	55	55
CB2	"	25fr+5fr dk. car. rose & vio. bl.	75	75
CB3	"	50fr+5fr slate grn. & claret	1.00	1.00

Issued to publicize the UNESCO world campaign to save historic monuments in Nubia.

POSTAGE DUE STAMPS.

Postage Due Stamps of France Overprinted **GABON** **A. E. F.**

1928 *Perf. 14x13½* **Unwmkd.**

J1	D2	5c light blue	8	8
J2	"	10c gray brown	8	8
J3	"	20c olive green	10	10
J4	"	25c bright rose	25	25
J5	"	30c light red	35	35
J6	"	45c blue green	45	45
J7	"	50c brown violet	40	40
J8	"	60c yellow brown	50	50
J9	"	1fr red brown	55	55
J10	"	2fr orange red	85	85
J11	"	3fr bright violet	90	90
		Nos. J1-J11 (11)	4.51	4.51

Chief Makoko, de Brazza's Aide
D3

Count Savorgnan de Brazza
D4

Typographed.

1930 *Perf. 13½x14*

J12	D3	5c dark blue & olive	15	15
J13	"	10c dark red & brown	25	25
J14	"	20c green & brown	30	30
J15	"	25c light blue & brown	50	50
J16	"	30c bistre brown & Prussian blue	50	50
J17	"	45c Prussian blue & olive	50	50
J18	"	50c red violet & brown	90	90
J19	"	60c gray lilac & blue black	1.50	1.50
J20	D4	1fr bistre brown & blue black	2.35	2.35
J21	"	2fr violet & brown	3.00	3.00
J22	"	3fr deep red & brown	3.00	3.00
		Nos. J12-J22 (11)	12.95	12.95

Scott's editorial staff cannot undertake to identify, authenticate or appraise stamps and postal markings.

Fang Woman
D5

1932 Photogravure *Perf. 13x13½*

J23	D5	5c dark blue, *blue*	20	20
J24	"	10c red brown	40	40
J25	"	20c chocolate	60	60
J26	"	25c yellow green, *blue*	40	40
J27	"	30c carmine rose	60	60
J28	"	45c red orange, *yellow*	1.75	1.75
J29	"	50c dark violet	60	60
J30	"	60c dull blue	80	80
J31	"	1fr black, *red orange*	1.60	1.60
J32	"	2fr dark green	3.00	3.00
J33	"	3fr rose lake	2.00	2.00
		Nos. J23-J33 (11)	11.95	11.95

Republic

Pineapple—D6

Fruit: No. J35, Mangos. No. J36, Avocados. No. J37, Tangerines. No. J38, Coconuts. No. J39, Grapefruit. No. J40, Oranges. No. J41, Papaya. No. J42, Breadfruit. No. J43, Guavas. No. J44, Lemons. No. J45, Bananas.

Engraved

1962, Dec. 10 *Perf. 11* **Unwmkd.**

J34	D6	50c red brn., yel. & grn.	5	5
J35	"	50c red brn., yel. & grn.	5	5
J36	"	1fr grn., yellow & red	5	5
J37	"	1fr green, yellow & red	5	5
J38	"	2fr ocher & green	10	10
J39	"	2fr ocher & green	10	10
J40	"	5fr grn., yel. & brn.	15	15
J41	"	5fr grn., yel. & brn.	15	15
J42	"	10fr green, yel. & red	30	30
J43	"	10fr green, yel. & red	30	30
J44	"	25fr brn., yel. & green	60	60
J45	"	25fr brn., yel. & green	60	60
		Nos. J34-J45 (12)	2.50	2.50

The two stamps of the same denomination are printed together in the sheet, se-tenant at the base.

Charaxes Candiope
D7

Butterflies: 10fr, Charaxes ameliae. 25fr, Cyrestis camillus. 50fr, Charaxes castor. 100fr, Pseudacrea boisduvali.

1978, July 4 **Litho.** *Perf. 13*

J46	D7	5fr multicolored	5	5
J47	"	10fr "	10	10
J48	"	25fr "	25	20
J49	"	50fr "	50	35
J50	"	100fr "	1.00	75
		Nos. J46-J50 (5)	1.90	1.45

OFFICIAL STAMPS

Map of Gabon
O1

Flag of Gabon
O2

Designs: 25fr, 30fr, Flag of Gabon. 50fr, 85fr, 100fr, 200fr, Coat of Arms.

Photogravure

1968 *Perf. 14* **Unwmkd.**

O1	O1	1fr olive & multi.	6	6
O2	"	2fr multicolored	6	6
O3	"	5fr lilac & multi.	8	6
O4	"	10fr emerald & multi.	15	8
O5	"	25fr brown & multi.	30	15
O6	"	30fr orange & multi.	45	25
O7	"	50fr multicolored	75	30
O8	"	85fr "	1.10	50
O9	"	100fr yellow & multi.	1.25	65
O10	"	200fr gray & multi.	2 50	1.40
		Nos. O1-O10 (10)	6.70	3.51

1971-78 Typo. *Perf. 13x14*

O11	O2	10fr gray & multi.	15	15
O12	"	30fr multi. ('78)	25	20
O13	"	40fr " ('72)	55	25
O14	"	50fr red & multi. ('76)	40	20
O15	"	60fr multi. ('77)	50	35
O16	"	80fr " ('77)	60	55
O17	"	100fr " ('78)	80	60
O18	"	500fr " ('78)	4.00	3.00
		Nos. O11-O18 (8)	7.25	5.30

GEORGIA

(jôr'jyȧ; jôr'jĭ·ȧ)

LOCATION—In the southern part of Russia, bordering on the Black Sea and occupying the entire western part of Trans-Caucasia.

GOVT.—A Soviet Socialist Republic.

AREA—25,760 sq. mi. (1920).

POP.—2,372,403 (1920).

CAPITAL—Tiflis.

Georgia was formerly a province of the Russian Empire and later a part of the Transcaucasian Federation of Soviet Republics. Stamps of Georgia were replaced in 1923 by those of Transcaucasian Federated Republics.

100 Kopecks = 1 Ruble

Tiflis

A 6k local stamp, imperforate and embossed without color on white paper, was issued in November, 1857, at Tiflis by authority of the viceroy. The square design shows a coat of arms.

National Republic.

St. George

A1 A2

Perf. 11½, Imperf.

1919		Lithographed	Unwmkd.	
12	A1	10k blue	10	15
13	"	40k red orange	10	15
		a. Tête bêche pair	6.00	6.00
14	"	50k emerald	10	15
15	"	60k red	10	20
16	"	70k claret	10	25
17	A2	1r orange brown	10	25
		Nos. 12-17 (6)	60	1.15

Queen Thamar

A3

1920		*Perf. 11½, Imperf.*		
18	A3	2r red brown	15	25
19	"	3r gray blue	15	25
20	"	5r orange	25	50

Nos. 12–20 with parts of design inverted, sideways or omitted are fraudulent varieties.

Overprints meaning "Day of the National Guard, 12, 12, 1920" (5 lines) and "Recognition of Independence, 27, 1, 1921" (4 lines) were applied, probably in Italy, to remainders taken by government officials who fled when Russian forces occupied Georgia.

"Constantinople" and new values were unofficially surcharged on stamps of 1919–20 by a consul in Turkey.

Soviet Socialist Republic.

Soldier with Flag — A5

Peasant Sowing Grain — A6

Industry and Agriculture

A7

1922		*Perf. 11½*	Unwmkd.	
26	A5	500r rose	1.50	1.25
27	A6	1000r bistre brown	1.50	1.25
28	A7	2000r slate	3.00	2.00
29	"	3000r brown	3.00	2.00
30	"	5000r green	2.50	2.00
		Nos. 26-30 (5)	11.50	8.50

Nos. 26 to 30 exist imperforate but were not so issued. Price for set, $25.

Nos. 26–30 Handstamped with New Values in Violet

1923				
36	A6	10,000r on 1000r bistre brown	1.50	1.50
		a. Black surcharge	3.50	3.50
		b. 20,000r on 1000r bis. brown	250.00	
37	A7	15,000r on 2000r slate, blk. surch.	2.50	2.50
		a. Violet surcharge	10.00	10.00
38	A5	20,000r on 500r rose	1.50	1.50
		a. Black surcharge	2.00	2.00
39	A7	40,000r on 5000r grn.	1.50	1.50
		a. Black surcharge	5.00	5.00
40	A7	80,000r on 3000r brn.	2.00	1.50
		a. Black surcharge	5.00	5.00
		Nos. 36-40 (5)	9.00	8.50

There were two types of the handstamped surcharges, with the numerals 5⅓ mm. and 6⅓ mm. high. The impressions are often too indistinct to measure or even to distinguish the numerals.

Double and inverted surcharges exist, as is usual with handstamps.

Printed Surcharge in Black.

43	A6	10,000r on 1000r bistre brown	5.00	5.00
44	A7	15,000r on 2000r slate	3.00	3.00
45	A5	20,000r on 500r rose	1.25	1.25
46	A7	40,000r on 5000r grn.	2.00	2.00
47	"	80,000r on 3000r brn.	2.50	2.50
		Nos. 43-47 (5)	13.75	13.75

Nos. 43, 45, 46 and 47 exist imperforate but were not so issued. Price $4 each.

Russian Stamps of 1909–18 Handstamp Surcharged

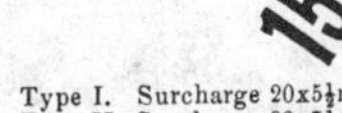

Type I. Surcharge 20x5½mm.
Type II. Surcharge 22x7½mm.

1923		*Perf. 14½x15*		
48	A14	10,000r on 7k light blue	40.00	30.00
49	A11	15,000r on 15k red brown & blue (I)	3.00	2.75
		a. Type II	2.75	2.50

Same Surcharge Handstamped on Armenia No. 141.

50	A11	15,000r on 5r on 15k red brn. & bl. (I)	40.00	50.00
		a. Type II		

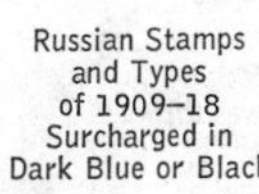

Russian Stamps and Types of 1909–18 Surcharged in Dark Blue or Black

1923		*Perf. 11½, 14½x15*		
51	A14	75,000r on 1k orange	1.75	2.00
		a. Imperf.	100.00	100.00
52	A14	200,000r on 5k claret	2.50	3.00
53	A8	300,000r on 20k blue & carmine (Bk)	3.00	3.50
		a. Dark blue surcharge	150.00	150.00
54	A14	350,000r on 3k red	5.00	6.00
		a. Imperf.	6.00	7.00

Imperf.

55	A14	700,000r on 2k green	6.00	7.50
		a. Perf. 14½x15	35.00	35.00
		Nos. 51-55 (5)	18.25	22.00

SEMI-POSTAL STAMPS.

SP1 SP2

SP3 SP4

Surcharge in Red or Black

1922		*Perf. 11½.*	Unwmkd.	
B1	SP1	1000r on 50r violet (R)	35	35
B2	SP2	3000r on 100r brown red (Bk)	35	35
B3	SP3	5000r on 250r gray green (Bk)	35	35
B4	SP4	10,000r on 25r blue (R)	35	35

Nos. B1–B4 exist imperf. but were not so issued. Price about twice that of perf.

GERMAN EAST AFRICA

(jûr'mȧn ēst ăf'rĭ·kȧ)

LOCATION—In East Africa, bordering on the Indian Ocean.

GOVT.—Former German Colony

AREA—384,180 sq. mi.

POP.—7,680,132 (1913).

CAPITAL—Dar-es Salaam.

Following World War I, the greater part of this German Colonial possession was mandated to Great Britain. The British ceded to the Belgians the provinces of Ruanda and Urundi. The Kionga triangle was awarded to the Portuguese and became part of the Mozambique Colony. The remaining area became the British Mandated Territory of Tanganyika.

64 Pesa = 1 Rupee

100 Heller = 1 Rupee (1905)

100 Centimes = 1 Franc (1916)

Numeral of Value — A1

German Imperial Eagle — A2

Stamps of Germany Surcharged in Black.

1893		*Perf. 13½x14½.*	Unwmkd.	
1	A1	2pes on 3pf brown	47.50	50.00
2	"	3pes on 5pf green	55.00	50.00
3	A2	5pes on 10pf car.	38.50	25.00
4	"	10pes on 20pf ultra.	27.50	19.00
5	"	25pes on 50pf red brown	50.00	32.50

The surcharge is in three lengths (14¼, 15¼ and 16¼mm.) on Nos. 2 and 3; two lengths (15¼ and 16¾mm.) on No. 4, and two lengths (16¾ and 17½mm.) on No. 5.

A3 A4

1896		Black Surcharge.		
6	A3	2pes on 3pf dk. brn.	2.75	*8.00*
		a. 2pes on 3pf light brown	38.50	40.00
		b. 2pes on 3pf grayish brown	5.50	5.50
7	A3	3pes on 5pf green	3.25	4.50
8	A4	5pes on 10pf carmine	3.25	4.50
9	"	10pes on 20pf ultra.	8.50	5.50
10	"	25pes on 50pf red brown	32.50	38.50

Kaiser's Yacht "Hohenzollern"

A5 A6

1900		Typographed	*Perf. 14*	
11	A5	2p brown	2.25	2.25
		a. Imperf. (pair)	*2000.00*	
12	"	3p green	2.25	2.25
13	"	5p carmine	2.50	2.75
14	"	10p ultramarine	4.75	5.00
15	"	15p orange & black, *salmon*	5.50	6.00
16	"	20p lake & black	8.50	*18.00*
17	"	25p purple & black, *salmon*	8.00	*18.00*
18	"	40p lake & black, *rose*	13.00	*25.00*

Engraved.

Perf. 14½x14

19	A6	1r claret	30.00	42.50
20	"	2r yellow green	13.50	*55.00*
21	"	3r car. & slate	110.00	165.00
		Nos. 11-21 (11)	200.25	*341.75*

No. 11a was not regularly issued.

Value in Heller.

1905		Typographed	*Perf. 14*	
22	A5	2½h brown	3.25	2.25
23	"	4h green	11.00	2.25
24	"	7½h carmine	11.00	1.65
25	"	15h ultramarine	19.00	5.50
26	"	20h orange & black, *yellow*	13.50	16.50
27	"	30h lake & black	13.50	10.00
28	"	45h purple & black	27.50	32.50
29	"	60h lake & black, *rose*	32.50	*80.00*
		Nos. 22-29 (8)	131.25	*150.65*

1905–16		Wmkd. Lozenges. (125)		
31	A5	2½h brown ('06)	1.10	1.35
32	"	4h green ('06)	1.10	1.10
		a. Booklet pane of 6	8.00	
		b. Booklet pane of 4 + 2 labels	60.00	
		c. Booklet pane of 5 + label	*260.00*	
33	"	7½h carmine ('06)	80	55
		a. Booklet pane of 6	6.50	
		b. Booklet pane of 4 + 2 labels	60.00	
		c. Booklet pane of 5 + label	*325.00*	
34	"	15h ultramarine ('06)	3.00	1.65
35	"	20h orange & black, *yellow* ('11)	2.75	*16.00*
36	"	30h lake & black ('09)	3.00	*8.00*
37	"	45h purple & blk. ('06)	5.50	*32.50*
38	"	60h lake & blk., *rose*	40.00	*135.00*
		Nos. 31-38 (8)	57.25	*196.15*

Engraved

Perf. 14½x14

39	A6	1r red ('16)	9.00	*15,000.00*
40	"	2r yellow green	65.00	
41	"	3r car. & slate ('08)	27.50	*135.00*

No. 40 was never placed in use.

Forged cancellations are found on Nos. 35–39, 41.

OCCUPATION STAMPS.
Issued under Belgian Occupation.

Stamps of Belgian Congo, 1915, Handstamped "RUANDA" in Black or Blue.

1916 *Perf. 13½ to 15.* **Unwmkd.**

N1 A29 5c green & black 20.00 20.00
N2 A30 10c car. & black 20.00 20.00
N3 A21 15c blue green & black 32.50 32.50
N4 A31 25c blue & black 20.00 20.00
N5 A23 40c brn. red & blk. 20.00 20.00
N6 A24 50c brown lake & black 20.00 20.00
N7 A25 1fr olive bistre & black 130.00 130.00
N8 A27 5fr ochre & blk. *1250.00 1250.00*
Nos. N1–N7 (7) 262.50 262.50

Stamps of Belgian Congo, 1915, Handstamped "URUNDI" in Black or Blue.

N9 A29 5c green & black 20.00 20.00
N10 A30 10c car. & black 20.00 20.00
N11 A21 15c blue green & black 32.50 32.50
N12 A31 25c blue & black 20.00 20.00
N13 A23 40c brn. red & blk. 20.00 20.00
N14 A24 50c brown lake & black 20.00 20.00
N15 A25 1fr olive bistre & black 130.00 130.00
N16 A27 5fr ochre & blk. *1250.00 1250.00*
Nos. N9–N15 (7) 262.50 262.50

Stamps of Congo overprinted "Karema", "Kigoma" and "Tabora" were not officially authorized.
Nos. N1–N16 exist with forged overprint.

Stamps of Belgian Congo, 1915, Overprinted in Dark Blue

EST AFRICAIN ALLEMAND
OCCUPATION BELGE.

DUITSCH OOST AFRIKA
BELGISCHE BEZETTING.

1916 *Perf. 12½ to 15.*

N17 A29 5c green & black 40 33
a. "OCOUPATION" 4.00 4.00
b. Inverted overprint 40.00
N18 A30 10c carmine & black 60 55
N19 A21 15c blue green & black 33 33
N20 A31 25c blue & black 2.65 1.85
N21 A23 40c brown red & blk. 7.25 5.75
N22 A24 50c brown lake & black 7.50 5.25
N23 A25 1fr olive bistre & black 90 70
a. "OCOUPATION" 5.00 5.00
N24 A27 5fr ochre & black 1.35 1.30
Nos. N17–N24 (8) 20.98 16.06

Nos. N17–N18, N20–N22 Surcharged in Black or Red **•10c**

1922

N25 A24 5c on 50c brown lake & black 40 38
N26 A29 10c on 5c green & black (R) 50 40
N27 A23 25c on 40c brown red & black (R) 1.65 1.40
N28 A30 30c on 10c carmine & black 33 33
N29 A31 50c on 25c blue & black (R) 40 33
Nos. N25–N29 (5) 3.28 2.84

No. N25 has the surcharge at each side.

SEMI-POSTAL STAMPS.
Issued under Belgian Occupation.

Semi-Postal Stamps of Belgian Congo, 1918, Overprinted **A. O.**

1918 *Perf. 14, 15.* **Unwmkd.**

NB1 A29 5c+10c green & blue 33 33
NB2 A30 10c+15c car. & bl. 33 33
NB3 A21 15c+20c blue green & blue 33 33
NB4 A31 25c+25c deep blue & pale blue 33 33
NB5 A23 40c+40c brown red & blue 50 50
NB6 A24 50c+50c brown lake & blue 50 50
NB7 A25 1fr+1fr olive bistre & blue 2.10 2.10
NB8 A27 5fr+5fr ochre & blue 11.00 7.25
NB9 A28 10fr+10fr green & blue 67.50 60.00
Nos. NB1–NB9 (9) 82.92 71.67

The letters "A.O." are the initials of "Afrique Orientale" (East Africa).

Stamps issued under British occupation are listed in Volume I.

GERMAN NEW GUINEA
(jûr'măn nū gĭn'ĭ)

LOCATION—A group of islands in the west Pacific Ocean, including a part of New Guinea and adjacent islands of the Bismarck Archipelago.

GOVT.—A former German Protectorate.

AREA—93,000 sq. mi.

POP.—601,427 (1913).

CAPITAL — Herbertshöhe (later Kokopo).

The islands were occupied by Australian troops during World War I and renamed "New Britain." By covenant of the League of Nations they were made a mandated territory of Australia in 1920. The old name of "New Guinea" has since been restored. Postage stamps were issued under all regimes. For other listings see New Britain (1914-15), North West Pacific Islands (1915-22) and New Guinea in Vol. I.

100 Pfennig = 1 Mark

A1

A2

Stamps of Germany Overprinted in Black.

1897–99 *Perf. 13½x14½* **Unwmkd.**

1 A1 3pf brown 11.00 12.00
a. 3pf reddish brown ('99) 32.50 38.50
b. 3pf yellow brown ('99) 27.50 32.50
2 A1 5pf green 5.50 5.00
3 A2 10pf carmine 10.00 10.00
4 " 20pf ultramarine 13.50 16.50
5 " 25pf orange ('98) 47.50 52.50
a. Inverted overprint *1000.00*
6 A2 50pf red brown 47.50 52.50

Kaiser's Yacht "Hohenzollern"
A3 A4

1901 Typographed *Perf. 14*

7 A3 3pf brown 1.10 1.35
8 " 5pf green 13.50 1.65
9 " 10pf carmine 50.00 2.75
10 " 20pf ultramarine 1.65 *3.25*
11 " 25pf org. & blk., *yel.* 1.90 *25.00*
12 A3 30pf orange & black, *salmon* 1.90 *27.50*
13 " 40pf lake & black 1.90 *32.50*
14 " 50pf purple & black, *salmon* 2.75 *30.00*
15 " 80pf lake & black, *rose* 4.75 *32.50*

Engraved.
Perf. 14½x14

16 A4 1m carmine 5.50 *67.50*
17 " 2m blue 7.50 *80.00*
18 " 3m black violet 10.00 *165.00*
19 " 5m slate & carmine 190.00 *550.00*
Nos. 7–19 (13) 292.45

Fake cancellations exist on Nos. 10–19.

A5

A6

Wmkd. Lozenges. (125)

1914–19 Typographed *Perf. 14*

20 A3 3pf brown ('19) 1.10
21 A5 5pf green 2.50
22 " 10pf carmine 2.50

Engraved.
Perf. 14½x14

23 A6 5m slate & carmine 27.50

Nos. 20 to 23 were never placed in use.
Nos. 21 to 23 have "NEUGUINEA" as one word without a hyphen.

GERMAN SOUTH-WEST AFRICA
(jûr'măn south'wĕst' ăf'rĭ·kȧ)

LOCATION—In southwest Africa, bordering on the South Atlantic.

GOVT.—A former German Colony.

AREA—322,450 sq. mi. (1913).

POP.—94,372 (1913).

CAPITAL—Windhoek.

The Colony was occupied by British Colonial troops during World War I and in 1920 was mandated to the Union of South Africa by the League of Nations. See South-West Africa in Vol. I.

100 Pfennig = 1 Mark

A1

A2

Stamps of Germany Overprinted "Deutsch- / Südwest-Afrika"

1897 *Perf. 13½x14½* **Unwmkd.**

1 A1 3pf dark brown 10.00 10.00
a. 3pf yel. brown 65.00
2 " 5pf green 5.25 5.50
3 A2 10pf carmine 25.00 25.00
4 " 20pf ultramarine 5.50 6.50
5 " 25pf orange 275.00
6 " 50pf red brown 275.00

Nos. 5 and 6 were prepared for issue but were not set to the Colony.

Overprinted "Deutsch- / Südwestafrika"

1899

7 A1 3pf dark brown 5.00 *32.50*
b. 3pf yel. brown 8.00 8.00
8 " 5pf green 3.25 3.25
9 A2 10pf carmine 3.25 4.75
10 " 20pf ultramarine 19.00 22.50
11 " 25pf orange 450.00 400.00
12 " 50pf red brown 19.00 19.00

Kaiser's Yacht "Hohenzollern"
A3 A4

1900 Typographed *Perf. 14*

13 A3 3pf brown 2.25 1.65
14 " 5pf green 32.50 1.10
15 " 10pf carmine 27.50 1.10
16 " 20pf ultramarine 50.00 1.65
17 " 25pf orange & black, *yellow* 2.50 *6.50*
18 " 30pf orange & black, *salmon* 22.50 3.85
19 " 40pf lake & black 2.50 *4.25*
20 " 50pf purple & black, *salmon* 3.25 3.25
21 " 80pf lake & blk., *rose* 3.25 *8.00*

Engraved.
Perf. 14½x14

22 A4 1m carmine 27.50 30.00
23 " 2m blue 35.00 38.50
24 " 3m black violet 47.50 40.00
25 " 5m slate & car. 275.00 165.00
Nos. 13–25 (13) 531.25 *304.85*

Wmkd. Lozenges. (125)

1906–19 Typo. *Perf. 14*

26 A3 3pf brown ('09) 1.10 1.35
27 " 5pf green 1.10 1.10
a. Booklet pane of 6 10.00
b. Booklet pane of 6 (2 No. 27 & 4 No. 28) 55.00
28 " 10pf carmine 1.10 1.65
a. Booklet pane of 6 10.00
29 " 20pf ultramarine ('11) 1.65 *4.25*
30 " 30pf orange & blk., *buff* ('11) 5.00 *50.00*

Engraved.
Perf. 14½x14

31 A4 1m carmine ('12) 8.00 *22.50*
32 " 2m blue ('11) 8.00 *27.50*
33 " 3m blk. violet ('19) 13.50
34 " 5m slate & car. 30.00 *165.00*
Nos. 26–34 (9) 69.45

No. 33 was never placed in use.
Forged cancellations are found on Nos. 30–32, 34.

GERMAN STATES

BADEN
(bä'dĕn)

LOCATION—In southwestern Germany.

GOVT.—Former Grand Duchy.

AREA—5,817 sq. mi.

POP.—1,432,000 (1864).

CAPITAL—Karlsruhe.

Baden was a member of the German Confederation. In 1870 it became part of the German Empire.

60 Kreuzer = 1 Gulden

Prices for 1-9 unused are for copies without gum. Copies with gum sell for about twice as much. No. 10 and following numbers without gum sell for about half the prices.

A1

Typographed

1851–52 *Imperf.* **Unwmkd.**

1 A1 1kr *dark buff* 325.00 225.00

2 A1 3kr *yellow* 165.00 12.50
3 " 6kr *yellow green* 400.00 47.50
4 " 9kr *lilac rose* 80.00 15.00

Thin Paper (First Printing, 1851)

1a A1 1kr *buff* 775.00 525.00
2a " 3kr *orange* 300.00 35.00
3a " 6kr *blue green* 1550.00 120.00
4a " 9kr *deep rose* 2400.00 220.00
4b " 9kr *blue green* (error) 60,000.00

1853–58

6 A1 1kr black 165.00 20.00
a. Tête bêche gutter pair 12,000.00
7 " 3kr *green* 165.00 6.00
8 " 3kr *blue* ('58) 300.00 20.00
a. Printed on both sides
9 A1 6kr *yellow* 300.00 17.50

Nos. 1–9 with margins all around sell considerably higher.

Reissues (1865) of Nos. 1, 2, 3, 6, 7 and 8 exist on thick paper and No. 9 on thin paper; the color of the last is brighter than that of the original.

Coat of Arms
A2 A3

1860–62 ***Perf. 13½***

10 A2 1kr black 90.00 22.50
12 " 3kr ultramarine('61) 90.00 15.00
a. 3kr Prussian bl. 300.00 16.00
13 " 6kr red org. ('61) 135.00 50.00
a. 6kr yellow orange ('62) 225.00 60.00
14 " 9kr rose ('61) 325.00 125.00

Copies of Nos. 10–14 and 18 with all perforations intact sell considerably higher.

1862 ***Perf. 10***

15 A2 1kr black 40.00 65.00
a. 1kr silver gray 6500.00
16 " 6kr blue 125.00 50.00
17 " 9kr brown 100.00 60.00
a. 9kr bistre 175.00 100.00

Perf. 13½

18 A3 3kr rose 1500.00 260.00

1862–65 ***Perf. 10***

19 A3 1kr black ('64) 45.00 10.00
a. 1kr silver gray 1200.00
20 " 3kr rose 45.00 1.00
a. Imperf. 40,000.00 14,000.00
22 " 6kr ultra. ('65) 10.00 15.00
a. 6kr Prussian blue ('64) 425.00 42.50
23 " 9kr brown ('64) 12.00 17.50
a. 9kr bistre 250.00 17.50
b. Printed on both sides 6000.00
24 " 18kr green 375.00 385.00
25 " 30kr orange 35.00 800.00

Forged cancellations are known on Nos. 25 and 28a.

A4

1868

26 A4 1kr green 3.50 4.00
27 " 3kr rose 2.00 1.25
28 " 7kr dull blue 16.00 20.00
a. 7kr sky blue 50.00 125.00

The postage stamps of Baden were superseded by those of the German Empire on Jan. 1, 1872, but Official stamps were used during the year 1905.

Stamps of the Baden sector of the French Occupation Zone of Germany, issued in 1947–49, are listed under Germany, Occupation Issues.

RURAL POSTAGE DUE STAMPS

RU1

1862 ***Perf. 10*** **Unwmkd.**

Thin Paper

LJ1 RU1 1kr *yellow* 5.00 *225.00*
a. Thick paper 125.00 550.00
LJ2 " 3kr *yellow* 4.00 *90.00*
a. Thick paper 100.00 375.00
LJ3 " 12kr *yellow* 37.50 *13,500.00*
a. Half used as 6kr on cover 20,000.00
b. Quarter used as 3kr on cover 7500.00

On No. LJ3, "LAND-POST" is a straight line.
Paper of Nos. LJ1a and LJ2a is darker yellow.
Forged cancellations abound on Nos. LJ1–LJ3.

OFFICIAL STAMPS.

See Germany Nos. OL16–OL21.

BAVARIA

(bȧ·vâr'ĭ·ȧ)

LOCATION—In southern Germany.
GOVT.—Former Kingdom.
AREA—30,562 sq. mi. (1920).
POP.—7,150,146 (1919).
PRINCIPAL CITY—Munich.

Bavaria was a member of the German Confederation and became part of the German Empire in 1870. After World War I, it declared itself a republic. It lost its postal autonomy on March 31, 1920.

60 Kreuzer = 1 Gulden
100 Pfennig = 1 Mark (1874)

Prices for unused stamps of 1849-78 issues are for copies with original gum. Copies without gum sell for about half the figures quoted.

A1 A1a
Broken Circle.

Typographed

1849 ***Imperf.*** **Unwmkd.**

1 A1 1kr black 650.00 1100.00
a. 1kr deep black 1800.00 1600.00
b. Tête bêche pair 35,000.00

With Silk Thread.

2 A1a 3kr blue 45.00 1.50
a. 3kr greenish blue 60.00 2.00
b. 3kr deep blue 50.00 1.75
3 " 6kr brown *4250.00* 175.00

No. 1 exists with silk thread but only as an essay.

A2 Coat of Arms
Complete circle. A3

1850–58 **With Silk Thread**

4 A2 1kr pink 55.00 22.50
5 A2 6kr brown 45.00 2.25
a. Half used as 3 kr on cover 7000.00
6 " 9kr yellow green 75.00 12.50
a. 9kr blue green 3500.00 85.00
7 " 12kr red ('58) 125.00 150.00
8 " 18kr yellow ('54) 160.00 180.00

1862

9 A2 1kr yellow 70.00 20.00
10 A1a 3kr rose 100.00 1.50
a. 3kr carmine 40.00 4.50
11 A2 6kr blue 60.00 7.00
a. 6kr ultramarine 1600.00
b. Half used as 3 kr on cover 4000.00
12 " 9kr bistre 85.00 12.50
13 " 12kr yellow green 85.00 60.00
a. Half used as 6 kr on cover 14,000.00
14 " 18kr vermilion red 850.00 110.00
a. 18kr pale red 125.00 275.00

No. 11a was not put in use.

1867-68 **Embossed.**

15 A3 1kr yellow green 50.00 4.00
a. 1kr dk. bl. green 185.00 30.00
16 " 3kr rose 42.50 50
a. Printed on both sides
17 " 6kr ultramarine 32.50 15.00
a. Half used as 3 kr on cover 14,000.00
18 " 6kr bistre ('68) 65.00 45.00
a. Half used as 3 kr on cover 14,000.00
19 " 7kr ultramarine ('68) 300.00 12.50
20 " 9kr bistre 45.00 35.00
21 " 12kr lilac 300.00 75.00
22 " 18kr red 100.00 125.00

The paper of the 1867–68 issues often shows ribbed or laid lines.

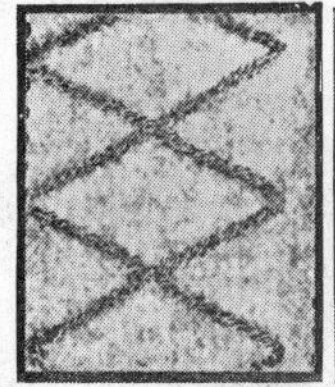

Wmk. 92 Wmk. 93
Lozenge 17mm. wide Lozenge 14mm. wide

Wmkd. Lozenges (92)
Without Silk Thread

1870–72 ***Perf. 11½***

23 A3 1kr green 1.75 75
a. Wmk. 93 60.00 7.00
24 " 3kr rose 4.00 40
a. Wmk. 93 30.00 2.50
25 " 6kr bister 35.00 32.50
a. Wmk. 93 130.00 70.00
26 " 7kr ultramarine 2.00 2.25
a. 7kr Prussian blue 12.00 10.00
b. Wmk. 93 100.00 35.00
27 " 9kr pale brn. ('72) 2.50 2.50
a. Wmk. 93 325.00 450.00
28 " 10kr yellow 6.00 12.00
a. Wmk. 93 275.00 275.00
29 " 12kr lilac, wmk. 93 350.00 *700.00*
a. Wmk. 92 700.00 *1200.00*
30 " 18kr red 10.00 12.50
a. Wmk. 93 225.00 175.00

The paper of the 1870–75 issues frequently appears to be laid with the lines either close or wide apart.

Reprints exist.

A4

Wmk. 94

1874 ***Imperf.*** **Wmk. 92**

31 A4 1m violet (II) 450.00 85.00

1875 ***Perf. 11½***

32 A4 1m violet (II) 150.00 40.00

Wmkd. Horizontal Wavy Lines Wide Apart. (94)

1875

33 A3 1kr green 40 *11.00*
34 " 3kr rose 40 *3.00*
35 " 7kr ultramarine 3.25 *300.00*
36 " 10kr yellow 37.50 *260.00*
37 " 18kr red 27.50 *65.00*

False cancellations exist on Nos. 29, 29a, 33–37.

A5

1876–78 **Embossed** ***Perf. 11½***

38 A5 3pf light green 25.00 30
39 " 5pf dark green 30.00 6.00
40 " 5pf lilac ('78) 125.00 12.50
41 " 10pf rose 10.00 30
42 " 20pf ultramarine 22.50 50
43 " 25pf yellow brown 115.00 2.50
44 " 50pf scarlet 27.50 2.25
45 " 50pf brown ('78) 300.00 22.50
46 A4 1m violet 1450.00 55.00
47 " 2m orange 22.50 4.50

The paper of the 1876–78 issue often shows ribbed lines.

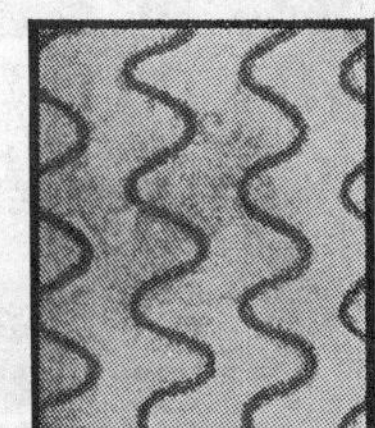

Wmk. 95v

Wmkd. Vertical Wavy Lines Close Together. (95v)

1881–1906 ***Perf. 11½***

48 A5 3pf green 4.50 15
a. Imperf. 125.00 200.00
49 " 5pf lilac 12.00 40
50 " 10pf carmine 3.50 15
a. Imperf. 125.00 175.00
51 " 20pf ultramarine 7.50 50
52 " 25pf yellow brown 75.00 1.00
53 " 50pf deep brown 80.00 1.20
54 A4 1m rose lilac ('00) 2.50 40
a. 1m red lilac, toned paper 27.50 1.25
55 " 2m orange ('01) 3.50 1.75
a. Toned paper ('90) 10.00 1.75
56 " 3m olive gray ('00) 17.50 20.00
a. White paper ('06) 70.00 110.00
57 " 5m yel. grn. ('00) 17.50 20.00
a. White paper ('06) 70.00 110.00

Nos. 56–57 are on toned paper. A 2m lilac was not regularly issued.

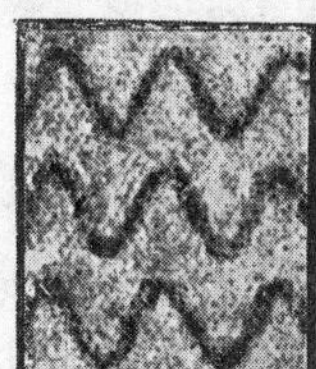

Wmk. 95h

Wmkd. Horizontal Wavy Lines Close Together. (95h)

1888-1900 ***Perf. 14½.***

58 A5 2pf gray ('00) 1.75 20
a. Toned paper ('99) 8.00 1.00

59 A5 3pf green 3.75 20
60 " 3pf brown ('00) 15 10
a. Toned paper ('90) 50 10
61 " 5pf lilac 3.50 1.00
62 " 5pf dark green ('00) 15 10
a. Toned paper ('90) 40 10
63 " 10pf carmine 15 10
a. Toned paper 1.85 10
64 " 20pf ultramarine 15 10
a. Toned paper 2.50 10
65 " 25pf yellow brown 18.50 1.40
66 " 25pf orange ('00) 20 15
a. Toned paper ('90) 4.00 20
67 " 30pf olive green ('00) 18 20
68 " 40pf yellow ('00) 18 20
69 " 50pf deep brown 22.50 75
70 " 50pf maroon ('00) 25 20
a. Toned paper ('90) 10.00 30
71 " 80pf lilac ('00) 1.40 1.80
a. Toned paper ('99) 12.00 3.50

Nos. 59, 61, 65, 69 and 70 are on toned paper; Nos. 67–68 on white.

1911 **Wmk. 95v**

72 A5 5pf dark green 75 2.50

1911 ***Perf. 11½*** **Wmk. 95h**

73 A4 1m rose lilac 6.50 11.00
74 " 2m orange 12.00 16.50
75 " 3m olive gray 12.00 16.50
76 " 5m pale yel. green 18.00 22.50

Prince Regent Luitpold
A6 A7

Prince Regent Luitpold
A8

Lithographed.

1911 ***Perf. 14x14½*** **Wmk. 95h**

77 A6 3pf brn., *gray brown* 30 10
a. "911" for "1911" 150.00 150.00
78 " 5pf dk. green, *green* 25 10
a. Tête bêche pair 4.50 5.00
b. Booklet pane of 4+2 labels 15.00
c. Bklt. pane of 5+label 17.50
d. Bklt. pane of 6 15.00
79 " 10pf scarlet, *buff* 25 10
a. Tête bêche pair 6.00 7.50
b. "911" for "1911" 12.50 12.50
d. Booklet pane of 5+label 20.00
80 " 20pf deep blue, *blue* 1.85 20
81 " 25pf vio. brown, *buff* 2.50 45

Perf. 11½

Wmk. 95v

82 A7 30pf org. buff, *buff* 1.50 20
83 " 40pf olive grn. *buff* 2.00 30
84 " 50pf claret, *gray brown* 2.75 50
84A " 60pf dk. green, *buff* 3.00 50
85 " 80pf violet, *gray brown* 4.50 1.00
86 A8 1m brown, *gray brown* 2.40 1.00
87 " 2m dk. green, *green* 2.40 2.00
88 " 3m lake, *buff* 14.00 14.00
89 " 5m dark blue, *buff* 12.50 15.00
90 " 10m orange, *yellow* 22.50 35.00
91 " 20m blk. brn., *yel.* 20.00 22.50
Nos. 77-91 (16) 92.70 93.05

90th birthday of Prince Regent Luitpold. All values exist in two types except No. 84A.

Nos. 77–84, 85–91 exist imperf.

Prince Regent Luitpold
A9

1911, June 10 **Unwmkd.**

92 A9 5(pf) green, yellow & black 1.00 90
b. Horizontal pair, imperf. between 85.00
93 " 10(pf) rose, yellow & black 1.20 1.20
b. Pair, imperf. between 85.00

Silver Jubilee of Prince Regent Luitpold.

A10 A11

King Ludwig III
A12 A13

Photogravure.

1914-20 ***Perf. 14x14½*** **Wmk. 95h**

94 A10 2pf gray ('18) 15 10
95 " 3pf brown 15 10
96 " 5pf yellow green 15 10
a. 5pf dark green 1.60 30
b. Tête bêche pair 4.00 7.00
c. Booklet pane of 5 + 1 label 20.00
97 " 7½pf deep green ('16) 15 10
a. Tête bêche pair 2.40 4.00
b. Booklet pane of 6 10.00
98 " 10pf vermilion 2.00 30
a. Tête bêche pair 20.00 4.00
b. Booklet pane of 5 + 1 label 15.00
99 " 10pf car. rose ('16) 15 10
100 " 15pf vermilion ('16) 15 10
a. Tête bêche pair 2.40 4.00
b. Booklet pane of 5 + 1 label 12.00
101 " 15pf carmine ('20) 15 15
102 " 20pf blue 15 20
103 " 25pf gray 15 25
104 " 30pf orange 15 25
105 " 40pf olive green 15 25
106 " 50pf red brown 15 25
107 " 60pf blue green 25 30
108 " 80pf violet 25 40

Perf. 11½.

Wmk. 95v

109 A11 1m brown 25 35
110 " 2m violet 50 1.10
111 " 3m scarlet 85 1.75

Wmk. 95h

112 A12 5m deep blue 1.30 3.50
113 " 10m yellow green 2.25 6.50
114 " 20m brown 4.50 12.00
Nos. 94-114 (21) 13.95

Used Prices

of Nos. 94–275 are for postally used stamps. Canceled-to-order stamps, which abound, sell for same prices as unused.

No. 94 Surcharged.

1916 ***Perf. 14x14½*** **Wmk. 95h**

115 A13 2½pf on 2pf gray 15 20
a. Double surcharge

Ludwig III Types of 1914–20.

1916-20 ***Imperf.***

117 A10 2pf gray 15 60
118 " 3pf brown 15 60
119 " 5pf pale yel. green 15 60
120 " 7½pf deep green 15 60
a. Tête bêche pair 2.75
121 " 10pf carmine rose 15 60
122 " 15pf vermilion 15 40
a. Tête bêche pair 2.75
123 " 20pf blue 15 55
124 " 25pf gray 15 55
125 " 30pf orange 15 55
126 " 40pf olive green 15 55
127 " 50pf red brown 15 55
128 " 60pf dark green 15 55
129 " 80pf violet 15 55
130 A11 1m brown 20 2.00
131 " 2m violet 40 3.00
132 " 3m scarlet 60 5.00
133 A12 5m deep blue 1.25 10.00
134 " 10m yellow green 2.00 14.00
135 " 20m brown 3.00 24.00
Nos. 117-135 (19) 9.40

Stamps and Type of 1914–20 Overprinted:

Volksstaat Bayern
a

Volksstaat Bayern
b

Wmk. 95h or 95v

1919 ***Perf. 14x14½***

Overprint "a."

136 A10 3pf brown 15 35
137 " 5pf yellow green 15 20
138 " 7½pf deep green 15 35
139 " 10pf carmine rose 15 20
140 " 15pf vermilion 15 20
141 " 20pf blue 15 35
142 " 25pf gray 15 35
143 " 30pf orange 15 35
144 " 35pf orange 15 65
a. Without ovpt. 125.00
145 " 40pf olive green 15 35
146 " 50pf red brown 15 35
147 " 60pf dark green 15 50
148 " 75pf red brown 15 60
a. Without ovpt. 15.00 140.00
149 " 80pf violet 20 50

Perf. 11½.

Overprint "a."

150 A11 1m brown 35 60
151 " 2m violet 45 1.10
152 " 3m scarlet 65 3.00

Overprint "b."

153 A12 5m deep blue 1.10 4.50
154 " 10m yellow green 1.60 13.50
155 " 20m dark brown 2.75 17.50
Nos. 136-155 (20) 9.05

Inverted overprints exist on Nos. 137–143, 145–147, 149. Price, each $10. Double overprints exist on Nos. 137, 139, 143, 145, 150. Prices, $20–$50.

Imperf.

Overprint "a."

156 A10 3pf brown 20 35
157 " 5pf pale yel. green 20 35
158 " 7½pf deep green 20 35
159 " 10pf carmine rose 20 35
160 " 15pf vermilion 20 35
161 " 20pf blue 20 50
162 " 25pf gray 20 50
163 " 30pf orange 20 50
164 " 35pf orange 20 75
a. Without overprint 8.00
165 " 40pf olive green 20 50
166 " 50pf red brown 20 50
167 " 60pf dark green 20 50
168 " 75pf red brown 20 75
a. Without overprint 125.00
169 " 80pf violet 30 80
170 A11 1m brown 50 1.40
171 " 2m violet 60 1.75
172 " 3m scarlet 80 2.50

Overprint "b."

173 A12 5m deep blue 1.40 6.00
174 " 10m yellow green 1.40 12.00

175 A12 20m brown 3.00 20.00
Nos. 156-175 (20) 10.60

Stamps of Germany 1906-19 Overprinted

Freistaat Bayern

Wmkd. Lozenges. (125)

1919 ***Perf. 14, 14½.***

176 A22 2½pf gray 10 15
177 A16 3pf brown 10 15
178 " 5pf green 10 15
179 A22 7½pf orange 10 15
180 A16 10pf carmine 10 15
181 A22 15pf dark violet 10 15
a. Double ovpt. 120.00 140.00
182 A16 20pf ultramarine 10 15
183 " 25pf orange & black, *yellow* 20 40
184 A22 35pf red brown 20 50
185 A16 40pf lake & black 40 60
186 " 75pf green & black 60 90
187 " 80pf lake & black, *rose* 60 1.40
188 A17 1m carmine rose 1.50 1.65
189 A21 2m dull blue 1.75 2.75
190 A19 3m gray violet 2.00 4.50
191 A20 5m slate & carmine 2.50 3.75
a. Inverted overprint 2000.00
Nos. 176-191 (16) 10.45 17.50

Bavarian Stamps of 1914-16 Overprinted:

Freistaat Bayern
c

Freistaat Bayern
d

1919-20 ***Perf. 14x14½.***

Wmk. 95h or 95v

Overprint "c."

193 A10 3pf brown 10 40
194 " 5pf yellow green 10 20
195 " 7½pf deep green 10 1.20
196 " 10pf carmine rose 10 15
197 " 15pf vermilion 10 15
198 " 20pf blue 10 25
199 " 25pf gray 20 60
200 " 30pf orange 20 60
201 " 40pf olive green 40 1.40
202 " 50pf red brown 15 30
203 " 60pf dark green 40 1.60
204 " 75pf olive bistre 70 2.00
205 " 80pf violet 30 1.60

Perf. 11½.

Overprint "c."

206 A11 1m brown 30 1.40
207 " 2m violet 30 1.75
208 " 3m scarlet 70 3.25

Overprint "d."

209 A12 5m deep blue 1.00 8.00
210 " 10m yellow green 2.00 12.00
211 " 20m dark brown 2.25 15.00
Nos. 193-211 (19) 9.50

Imperf.

Overprint "c."

212 A10 3pf brown 10 60
213 " 5pf pale yel. green 10 60
214 " 7½pf deep green 10 1.25
215 " 10pf carmine rose 10 75
216 " 15pf vermilion 10 60
217 " 20pf blue 10 75
a. Double overprint 55.00
218 " 25pf gray 20 1.50
219 " 30pf orange 20 1.50
220 " 40pf olive green 40 1.50
221 " 50pf red brown 20 1.50
222 " 60pf dark green 40 1.50
223 " 75pf olive bistre 60 2.00
a. Without overprint 8.00
224 " 80pf violet 25 1.50
225 A11 1m brown 30 1.75
226 " 2m violet 30 2.25
227 " 3m scarlet 60 3.00

Overprint "d."

228 A12 5m deep blue 1.00 8.00
229 " 10m yellow green 2.00 12.00
230 " 20m brown 2.50 20.00
Nos. 212-230 (19) 9.55

Ludwig Type of 1914, Printed in Various Colors and Surcharged

1,25 M Freistaat Bayern

1919 *Perf. 11½*
231 A11 1.25m on 1m yel. grn. 15 1.00
232 " 1.50m on 1m orange 15 1.40
233 " 2.50m on 1m gray 25 2.25

1920 *Imperf.*
234 A11 1.25m on 1m yel. grn. 15 3.00
a. Without surcharge 140.00
235 " 1.50m on 1m orange 15 4.00
a. Without surch. 6.00
236 " 2.50m on 1m gray 25 6.00
a. Without surch. 6.00

No. 60 Surcharged in Dark Blue

20 20
20 20

1920 *Perf. 14½*
237 A5 20pf on 3pf brown 10 30
a. Inverted surch. 16.00 25.00
b. Double surcharge 40.00 47.50

Plowman A14

Sower A16

"Electricity" Harnessing Light to a Water Wheel A15

Madonna and Child A17

von Kaulbach's "Genius" A18

Typographed.

1920 *Perf. 14x14½* Wmk. 95h

TWENTY PFENNIG.
Type I. Foot of "2" turns downward.
Type II. Foot of "2" turns upward.

238 A14 5pf yellow green 10 10
a. Imperf., pair 120.00 *450.00*
239 " 10pf orange 10 10
a. Imperf., pair 275.00
240 " 15pf carmine 10 10
241 A15 20pf violet (I) 10 10
a. 20pf violet (II) 17.50 *75.00*
b. Imperf., pair(I)150.00
242 " 30pf deep blue 10 25
243 " 40pf brown 10 40
a. Imperf., pair 240.00
244 A16 50pf vermilion 15 60
a. Imperf., pair 60.00
245 " 60pf blue green 15 75
a. Imperf., pair 65.00
246 " 75pf lilac rose 15 1.30
a. Imperf., pair 65.00

Perf. 12x11½.
Wmk. 95v
247 A17 1m carmine & gray 40 80
a. Imperf., pair 12.00
248 " 1¼m ultramarine & olive bistre 30 1.00
a. Imperf., pair 12.00
249 " 1½m dk. green & gray 30 1.00
a. Imperf., pair 12.00
250 " 2½m black & gray 30 1.25
a. Imperf., pair 20.00

Perf. 11½x12.
Wmk. 95h
251 A18 3m pale blue 40 6.50
a. Imperf., pair 20.00
252 " 5m orange 80 7.00
a. Imperf., pair 20.00
253 " 10m deep green 1.75 8.50
a. Imperf., pair 20.00
254 " 20m black 2.00 12.00
a. Imperf., pair 20.00
Nos. 238-254 (17) 7.30

Perf. 12x11½.
1920 Lithographed Wmk. 95v
255 A17 2½m black & gray 75 *12.00*

On the lithographed 2½m (No. 255), background dots are small, hazy and irregularly spaced. On the typographed 2½m (No. 250), they are large, clear, round, white and regularly spaced in rows. The backs of the typographed stamps usually show a raised impression of parts of the design.

Stamps and Types of Preceding Issue Overprinted — Deutsches Reich

1920
256 A14 5pf yellow green 10 25
a. Inverted ovpt. 15.00
b. Imperf., pair 25.00
257 " 10pf orange 10 25
a. Imperf., pair 25.00
258 " 15pf carmine 10 25
259 A15 20pf violet 10 25
a. Inverted ovpt. 15.00
b. Double ovpt. 15.00
c. Imperf., pair 25.00
260 " 30pf deep blue 10 25
a. Inverted ovpt. 15.00
b. Imperf., pair 35.00
261 " 40pf brown 10 30
a. Inverted ovpt. 20.00
b. Imperf., pair 35.00
262 A16 50pf vermilion 10 30
263 " 60pf blue green 10 30
264 " 75pf lilac rose 35 1.00
265 " 80pf dark blue 15 45
a. Without ovpt. *75.00*
b. Imperf., pair 35.00

Overprinted in Black or Red — Deutsches Reich

266 A17 1m carmine & gray 30 60
a. Imperf., pair 30.00
b. Inverted ovpt. 20.00
267 " 1¼m ultra. & olive bis. 30 60
a. Imperf., pair 30.00
268 " 1½m dark green & gray 30 70
a. Imperf., pair 30.00
269 " 2m vio. & olive bistre 45 85
a. Without ovpt. *45.00*
b. Imperf., pair 30.00
270 " 2½m black & gray (#250) (R) 10 55
c. Imperf., pair 30.00
270A " 2½m black & gray (#255) (R) 1.00 *65.00*
b. Imperf., pair 25.00

Overprinted Deutsches Reich

271 A18 3m pale blue 1.75 3.00
272 " 4m dull red 2.60 4.25
a. Without ovpt. *75.00*
273 " 5m orange 1.75 3.00
274 A18 10m deep green 2.25 4.50
275 " 20m black 4.50 7.50
Nos. 256-275 (21) 16.60

Nos. 256 to 275 were available for postage through all Germany, but were used almost exclusively in Bavaria.

SEMI-POSTAL STAMPS

Regular Issue of 1914-20 Surcharged in Black

5 Pf. für Kriegsbeschädigte Freistaat Bayern

Wmkd. Horizontal Wavy Lines Close Together. (95h)
1919 *Perf. 14x14½.*
B1 A10 10pf+5pf carmine rose 40 50
a. Inverted surcharge 12.00 30.00
b. Surcharge on back 25.00
c. Imperf., pair 325.00 *375.00*
B2 " 15pf+5pf vermilion 40 50
a. Invtd. surcharge 12.00 30.00
b. Imperf., pair 160.00 *575.00*
B3 " 20pf+5pf blue 40 50
a. Invert. surcharge 12.00 30.00
b. Imperf., pair 200.00 *575.00*

Surtax was for wounded war veterans.

POSTAGE DUE STAMPS.

Numeral D1

Arms D2

Typeset
With Silk Thread
1862 *Imperf.* Unwmkd.
J1 D1 3kr black 110.00 240.00
a. "Empfange" 325.00 600.00

Without Silk Thread.
Wmkd. Lozenges. (92)
1870 Typographed *Perf. 11½*
J2 D1 1kr black 20.00 *650.00*
a. Wmk. 93 12.00 *400.00*
J3 " 3kr black 18.00 *450.00*
a. Wmk. 93 12.00 *275.00*

Type of 1876 Regular Issue Overprinted "Vom Empfänger zahlbar" in Red.
Wmkd.
Wavy Lines Wide Apart. (94)
1876
J4 D2 3pf gray 16.00 25.00
J5 " 5pf gray 11.00 25.00
J6 " 10pf gray 3.00 45

Wmkd. Vertical Wavy Lines Close Together. (95v)
1883
J7 D2 3pf gray 100.00 110.00
J8 " 5pf gray 70.00 70.00
J9 " 10pf gray 1.00 40
a. "Empfanper" 100.00 80.00
b. "zahlhar" 90.00 70.00
c. Imperf. 100.00

Wmkd. Horizontal Wavy Lines Close Together. (95h)
1888-95 *Perf. 14½.*
J10 D2 2pf gray ('95) 70 85
a. Rose-toned paper 1.25 1.25
J11 D2 3pf gray ('03) 50 1.00
a. Rose-toned paper 1.25 75
J12 D2 5pf gray ('03) 90 90
a. Rose-toned paper 1.25 60
J13 D2 10pf gray ('03) 60 40
a. Rose-toned paper 1.25 20
b. As "a," double overprint *1200.00*

No. J13b was used at Pirmasens.
Nos. J10-J11 exist with inverted overprint.

Surcharged in Red in Each Corner.
1895
J14 D2 2pf on 3pf gray *25,000.00*

At least six copies exist, all used in Aichach.

OFFICIAL STAMPS.

Nos. 77 to 81, 84, 95, 96, 98, 99 and 102, perforated with a large E were issued for official use in 1912-16.

Regular Issue of 1888-1900 Overprinted — E

Wmkd.
Wavy Lines Close Together. (95h)
1908 *Perf. 14½.*
O1 A5 3pf dark brown (R)1.40 4.50
O2 " 5pf dark green (R) 15 15
O3 " 10pf carmine (G) 15 15
O4 " 20pf ultramarine (R) 40 60
O5 " 50pf maroon (G)5.00 6.50
Nos. O1-O5 (5) 7.10 11.90

Nos. O1 to O5 were issued for the use of railway officials. "E" stands for "Eisenbahn."

Coat of Arms
O1

1916-17 Typographed *Perf. 11½*
O6 O1 3pf bistre brown 10 10
O7 " 5pf yellow green 10 10
O8 " 7½pf green, *green* 10 10
O9 " 7½pf green ('17) 10 10
O10 " 10pf deep rose 10 10
O11 " 15pf red, *buff* 10 10
O12 " 15pf red ('17) 10 10
O13 " 20pf deep blue, *blue* 75 20
O14 " 20pf deep blue ('17) 10 10
O15 " 25pf gray 10 10
O16 " 30pf orange 10 10
O17 " 60pf dark green 20 15
O18 " 1m dull violet, *gray* 80 1.00
O19 " 1m maroon ('17) 4.50 *30.00*
Nos. O6-O19 (14) 7.25

Used Prices
of Nos. O8-O69 are for postally used stamps. Canceled-to-order stamps, which abound, sell for same prices as unused.

1919
Official Stamps and Type of 1916-17 Overprinted — Volksstaat Bayern

O20 O1 3pf bistre brown 10 80
O21 " 5pf yellow green 10 10
O22 " 7½pf gray green 10 20
O23 " 10pf deep rose 10 10
O24 " 15pf red 10 10
O25 " 20pf blue 10 10
a. Imperf.
O26 " 25pf gray 10 10
O27 " 30pf orange 10 10
O28 " 35pf orange 10 10
O29 " 50pf olive gray 10 10
O30 " 60pf dark green 15 80
O31 " 75pf red brown 20 50
O32 " 1m dull violet, *gray* 75 1.25
O33 " 1m maroon 4.50 *30.00*
Nos. O20-O33 (14) 6.60

O2

O3 O4

1920 Typographed. *Perf. 14x14½*

O34	O2	5pf yellow green	10	60
O35	"	10pf orange	10	60
O36	"	15pf carmine	10	60
O37	"	20pf violet	10	60
O38	"	30pf dark blue	10	80
O39	"	40pf bistre	10	80

Perf. 14½x14

Wmk. 95v

O40	O3	50pf vermilion	10	1.20
O41	"	60pf blue green	10	1.20
O42	"	70pf dark violet	10	1.40
		a. Imperf., pair	47.50	
O43	"	75pf deep rose	10	1.40
O44	"	80pf dull blue	10	1.40
O45	"	90pf olive green	10	1.60
O46	O4	1m dark brown	10	1.40
		a. Imperf., pair	80.00	
O47	"	1¼m green	10	1.40
O48	"	1½m vermilion	10	2.25
		a. Imperf., pair	40.00	
O49	"	2½m deep blue	15	2.75
		a. Imperf., pair	80.00	
O50	"	3m dark red	25	5.00
		a. Imperf., pair	35.00	
O51	"	5m black	1.50	*14.00*
		a. Imperf., pair	80.00	
		Nos. O34-O51 (18)	3.40	

Stamps of Preceding Issue Overprinted **Deutsches Reich**

1920, Apr. 1

O52	O2	5pf yellow green	10	25
		a. Imperf., pair		
O53	"	10pf orange	10	15
O54	"	15pf carmine	10	15
O55	"	20pf violet	10	15
O56	"	30pf dark blue	10	15
O57	"	40pf bistre	10	15
O58	O3	50pf vermilion	10	15
		a. Imperf., pair		
O59	"	60pf blue green	10	15
O60	"	70pf dark violet	1.20	75
O61	"	75pf deep rose	40	45
O62	"	80pf dull blue	10	20
O63	"	90pf olive green	1.00	75

Similar Overprint. Words 8mm. apart.

O64	O4	1m dark brown	10	15
		a. Imperf., pair		
O65	"	1¼m green	10	15
O66	"	1½m vermilion	10	15
O67	"	2½m deep blue	20	20
		a. Imperf., pair	75.00	
O68	"	3m dark red	10	25
O69	"	5m black	4.00	*12.50*
		Nos. O52-O69 (18)	8.10	16.85

Nos. O52 to O69 could be used in all parts of Germany, but were almost exclusively used in Bavaria.

BERGEDORF

(bĕr′gĕ·dôrf)

LOCATION—A town in northern Germany.

POP.—2,989 (1861).

Originally Bergedorf belonged jointly to the Free City of Hamburg and the Free City of Lübeck. In 1867 it was purchased by Hamburg.

16 Schillings = 1 Mark

> Prices for unused stamps are for copies with gum. Copies without gum sell for about half the figures quoted.

Combined Arms of Lübeck and Hamburg

A1 A2 A3

A4 A5

Lithographed.

1861-67 *Imperf.* Unwmkd.

1	A1	½s *pale blue*	25.00	*650.00*
		a. ½s *blue* ('67)	60.00	*3850.00*
2	A3	1s *white*	25.00	*325.00*
		a. Tête bêche pair	90.00	
3	A4	1½s *yellow*	12.00	*900.00*
		a. Tête bêche pair	60.00	
4	A2	3s blue, *pink*	15.00	*1850.00*
5	A5	4s *brown*	15.00	*2150.00*

Counterfeit cancellations are plentiful.

The ½s on violet and 3s on rose, listed previously, as well as a 1s and 1½s on thick paper and 4s on light rose brown, come from proof sheets and were never placed in use. A 1½ "SCHILLINGE" (instead of SCHILLING) also exists only as a proof.

Prices:

½s *violet*	325.00
1s *white*	500.00
1½s *yellow*	300.00
3s *rose*	500.00
4s *light rose brown*	1250.00
1½s "SCHILLINGE"	300.00

These stamps were superseded by those of the North German Confederation in 1868.

REPRINTS.

½ SCHILLING.

There is a dot in the upper part of the right branch of "N" of "EIN". The upper part of the shield is blank or almost blank. The horizontal bar of "H" in "HALBER" is generally defective.

1 SCHILLING.

The "1" in the corners is generally with foot. The central horizontal bar of the "E" of "EIN" is separated from the vertical branch by a black line. The "A" of "POSTMARKE" has the horizontal bar incomplete or missing. The horizontal bar of the "H" of "SCHILLING" is separated from the vertical branches by a dark line at each side, sometimes the bar is missing.

1½ SCHILLINGE.

There is a small triangle under the right side of the tower, exactly over the "R" of "POSTMARKE".

3 SCHILLINGE.

The head of the eagle is not shaded. The horizontal bar of the second "E" of "BERGEDORF" is separated from the vertical branch by a thin line. There is generally a colored dot in the lower half of the "S" of "POSTMARKE".

4 SCHILLINGE.

The upper part of the shield is blank or has two or three small dashes. In most of the reprints there is a diagonal dash across the wavy lines of the groundwork at the right of "I" and "E" of "VIER".

Reprints, price $1 each.

BREMEN

(brā′mĕn; brĕm′ĕn)

LOCATION—In northwestern Germany.

AREA—99 sq. mi.

POP.—122,402(1871).

Bremen was a Free City and member of the German Confederation. In 1870 it became part of the German Empire.

22 Grote = 10 Silbergroschen.

> Prices of Bremen stamps vary according to condition. Quotations are for fine copies. Very fine to superb specimens sell at much higher prices, and inferior or poor copies sell at reduced prices, depending on the condition of the individual specimen.
> Prices for unused stamps are for copies with gum. Copies without gum sell for about half the figures quoted.

Coat of Arms

A1

THREE GROTE.

I II III

Type I. The central part of the scroll below the word Bremen is crossed by one vertical line.

Type II. The center of the scroll is crossed by two vertical lines.

Type III. The center of the scroll is crossed by three vertical lines.

Lithographed.

1855 *Imperf.* Unwmkd.

Horizontally Laid Paper

1	A1	3gr *blue*	175.00	285.00

Vertically Laid Paper

1A	A1	3gr *blue*	325.00	600.00

Nos. 1 and 1A can be found with parts of a papermaker's watermark, consisting of lilies. Price: unused, $450; used, $750.

See also Nos. 9-10.

A2 A3

FIVE GROTE.

Type I. The shading at the left of the ribbon containing "funf Grote" runs downward from the shield.

Type II. The shading at the left of the ribbon containing "funf Grote" runs upward from the shield.

1856-60 Wove Paper

2	A2	5gr *rose*	175.00	250.00
		a. Printed on both sides	*300.00*	*350.00*
		b. "Marken" (not issued)	12.00	
3	"	7gr *yellow* ('60)	240.00	*575.00*
4	A3	5sgr green ('59)	120.00	200.00
		a. Chalky paper	45.00	300.00
		b. 5sgr yellow grn.	120.00	225.00

A4 A5

1861-63 *Serpentine Roulette.*

5	A4	2gr orange ('63)	350.00	*1600.00*
		a. 2gr red orange	350.00	*1600.00*
		b. Chalky paper	365.00	*2000.00*
6	A2	5gr *rose* ('62)	130.00	175.00
7	A5	10gr black	325.00	*1000.00*
8	A3	5sgr green ('63)	375.00	200.00
		a. Chalky paper	400.00	300.00
		b. 5sgr yel. green	225.00	175.00

Horizontally (H) or Vertically (V)

1863 Laid Paper.

9	A1	3gr *blue* (V)	*300.00*	*500.00*
		a. 3gr *blue* (H)	1100.00	*1900.00*

1866-67 *Perf. 13*

10	A1	3gr *blue*	85.00	*300.00*

Wove Paper.

11	A4	2gr orange	85.00	*325.00*
		a. 2gr red orange	165.00	*400.00*
		b. Horizontal pair imperf. between		*2000.00*
12	A2	5gr *rose*	135.00	*200.00*
		a. Horizontal pair, imperf. between		
13	"	7gr *yellow* ('67)	135.00	*2500.00*
14	A5	10gr black ('67)	200.00	*1000.00*
15	A3	5sgr green	175.00	*650.00*
		a. 5sgr yellow green	175.00	175.00
		b. As "a," chalky paper	325.00	325.00

The stamps of Bremen were superseded by those of the North German Confederation on Jan. 1, 1868.

BRUNSWICK

(brŭnz′wĭk)

LOCATION—In northern Germany.

GOVT.—Former duchy.

AREA—1,417 sq. mi.

POP.—349,367 (1880).

PRINCIPAL CITY—Brunswick.

Brunswick was a member of the German Confederation and, in 1870 became part of the German Empire.

12 Pfennigs = 1 Gutegroschen

30 Silbergroschen (Groschen) = 24 Gutegroschen = 1 Thaler

> Prices of Brunswick stamps vary according to condition. Quotations for Nos. 1-22 are for fine copies. Very fine to superb specimens sell at much higher prices, and inferior or poor copies sell at reduced prices, depending on the condition of the individual specimen.
> Prices for Nos. 1-3 unused are for copies without gum. Copies with gum sell for about three times the prices quoted. Nos. 4-26 without gum sell for about half the figures quoted.

The "Leaping Saxon Horse"

A1

Typographed.

1852 *Imperf.* Unwmkd.

1	A1	1sgr rose	2250.00	350.00
2	"	2sgr blue	1400.00	250.00
		a. Half used as 1 sgr on cover		
3	"	3sgr vermilion	1400.00	250.00

Wmk. 102

1853-63 Wmkd. Post Horn. (102)

4	A1	¼ggr *brown* ('56)	260.00	180.00
5	"	⅓sgr black ('56)	150.00	350.00
6	"	½gr *green* ('63)	22.50	*200.00*
7	"	1sgr *orange*	150.00	37.50
		a. 1sgr *orange buff*	150.00	37.50
8	"	1sgr *yellow* ('61)	140.00	37.50
9	"	2sgr *blue*	100.00	40.00
		a. Half used as 1 sgr on cover		*3250.00*
10	"	3sgr *rose*	265.00	60.00
11	"	3sgr rose ('62)	275.00	180.00

Nos. 5 and 11 are on white paper.

A3 A4

1857

12	A3	Four ¼ggr *brown* ('57)	30.00	*100.00*
		a. Four ¼ggr *yellow brown*	260.00	225.00

A four ¼ggr bister on white paper was never placed in use. Price $8.

1864 *Serpentine Roulette 16.*

13	A1	⅓sgr black	450.00	*1700.00*
14	"	½gr *green*	300.00	*1250.00*
15	"	1sgr *yellow*	*2500.00*	*1200.00*
16	"	1sgr yellow	160.00	100.00

17 A1 2sgr *blue* 300.00 250.00
a. Half used as 1 sgr on cover *4000.00*
18 " 3sgr rose 1000.00 475.00

Rouletted 12.

20 A1 1sgr *yellow* *2900.00* *2100.00*
21 " 1sgr yellow 325.00 200.00
22 " 3sgr rose *3500.00* *1900.00*

Nos. 13, 16, 18, 21 and 22 are on white paper.
Faked roulettes of Nos. 13–22 exist.

Embossed.
Serpentine Roulette.

1865 **Unwmkd.**
23 A4 ⅓gr black 27.50 *375.00*
a. Imperf., pair 150.00
24 " 1gr carmine 1.75 *32.50*
a. Imperf., pair 45.00
25 " 2gr ultramarine 10.00 *140.00*
a. 2gr gray blue 10.00 *140.00*
b. Imperf., pair 160.00
c. Half used as 1 sgr on cover *8000.00*
26 " 3gr brown 8.00 *160.00*
a. Imperf., pair 190.00

Faked cancellations of Nos. 5–26 exist.
Stamps of Brunswick were superseded by those of the North German Confederation on Jan. 1, 1868.

HAMBURG

(hăm'bûrg)

LOCATION—Northern Germany.
GOVT.—A former Free City.
AREA—160 sq. mi.
POP.—453,869 (1880).
CAPITAL—Hamburg.

Hamburg was a member of the German Confederation and became part of the German Empire in 1870.

16 Schillings = 1 Mark

Prices of unused stamps are for copies without gum. Copies with gum sell for about twice the figures quoted.

A1

Wmk. 128

Wmkd. Wavy Lines. (128)

1859 **Typographed** ***Imperf.***
1 A1 ½s black 55.00 *600.00*
2 " 1s brown 50.00 *80.00*
3 " 2s red 50.00 *100.00*
4 " 3s blue 50.00 *140.00*
5 " 4s yellow green 45.00 *1400.00*
a. 4s green 60.00 *900.00*
6 " 7s orange 50.00 35.00
7 " 9s yellow 120.00 *1600.00*

A2

A3

1864 **Lithographed.**
9 A2 1¼s red lilac 65.00 65.00
a. 1¼s lilac 65.00 65.00
b. 1¼s gray 55.00 55.00
c. 1¼s blue 250.00 *900.00*
d. 1¼s greenish gray 65.00 *100.00*
12 A3 2½s green 80.00 *140.00*

The 1¼s and 2½s have been reprinted on watermarked and unwatermarked paper.

1864-65 Typographed. ***Perf. 13½.***
13 A1 ½s black 3.00 *11.00*
a. Imperf. vert., pair 25.00
14 " 1s brown 6.50 *15.00*
a. Half used as ½s on cover
15 " 2s red 8.00 *22.00*
17 " 3s ultramarine 27.50 *40.00*
a. Imperf., pair 45.00
b. Imperf. vertically
c. 3s blue 27.50 *40.00*
18 " 4s green 5.00 *22.50*
19 " 7s orange 90.00 *120.00*
20 " 7s violet ('65) 6.00 *20.00*
a. Imperf., pair 140.00
21 " 9s yellow 16.50 *1350.00*
a. Vertical pair, imperf. between 400.00

Lithographed

22 A2 1¼s lilac 50.00 9.00
a. 1¼s red lilac 50.00 10.00
b. 1¼s violet 50.00 10.00
23 A3 2½s yellow green 75.00 30.00
a. 2½s blue green 75.00 30.00

The 1¼s has been reprinted on watermarked and unwatermarked paper; the 2½s on unwatermarked paper.

Value Numeral on Arms
A4 A5

Embossed.

1866 ***Rouletted 10*** **Unwmkd.**
24 A4 1¼s violet 22.50 *40.00*
a. 1¼s red violet 40.00 60.00
25 A5 1½s rose 5.00 *145.00*

Reprints:

1¼s: The rosettes between the words of the inscription have a well-defined open circle in the center of the originals, while in the reprints this circle is filled up.

In the upper part of the top of the "g" of "Schilling", there is a thin vertical line which is missing in the reprints.

The two lower lines of the triangle in the upper left corner are of different thicknesses in the originals while in the reprints they are of equal thickness.

The labels at the right and left containing the inscriptions are 2¾mm. in width in the originals while they are 2½mm. in reprints.

1½s: The originals are printed on thinner paper than the reprints. This is easily seen by turning the stamps over, when on the originals the color and impression will clearly show through, which is not the case in the reprints.

The vertical stroke of the upper part of the "g" in Schilling is very short on the originals, scarcely crossing the top line, while in the reprints it almost touches the center of the "g".

The lower part of the "g" of Schilling in the originals, barely touches the inner line of the frame, in some stamps it does not touch it at all, while in the reprints the whole stroke runs into the inner line of the frame.

A6

Wmkd. Wavy Lines. (128)

1867 **Typographed** ***Perf. 13½***
26 A6 2½s dull green 5.00 *80.00*
a. 2½s dark green 15.00 *85.00*
b. Imperf., pair 95.00

Forged cancellations exist on almost all stamps of Hamburg, especially on Nos. 4, 7, 21 and 25.
Nos. 1 to 23 and 26 exist without watermark, but they come from the same sheets as the watermarked stamps.
The stamps of Hamburg were superseded by those of the North German Confederation on Jan. 1, 1868.

HANOVER

(hăn·ō'vẽr ; -ō'fẽr)

LOCATION—Northern Germany
GOVT.—A former Kingdom.
AREA—14,893 sq. mi.
POP.—3,191,000.
CAPITAL—Hanover.

Hanover was a member of the German Confederation and became in 1866 a province of Prussia.

10 Pfennigs = 1 Groschen
24 Gute Groschen = 1 Thaler
30 Silbergroschen = 1 Thaler (1858)

Prices for unused stamps are for copies with gum. Copies without gum sell for about half the prices quoted.

Coat of Arms
A1 A2

Typographed.
Wmkd. Square Frame.

1850 **Rose Gum** ***Imperf.***
1 A1 1g g *gray blue* 2750.00 37.50

The reprints have white gum and no watermark.

Wmk. 130

Wmkd.
Wreath of Oak Leaves. (130)

1851-55
2 A1 1g g *gray green* 32.50 3.75
a. 1g g *yel. green* 240.00 15.00
3 A2 1/30th *salmon* 80.00 35.00
a. 1/30th *crimson* ('55) 75.00 35.00
b. Bisect on cover *1400.00*
5 " 1/15th *gray blue* 100.00 45.00
a. Bisect on cover *3000.00*
6 " 1/10th *yellow* 120.00 50.00
a. 1/10th *orange* 120.00 50.00

Bisects Nos. 3b, 5a, 12a and 13a were used for ½g.

The 1/10th has been reprinted on unwatermarked paper, with white gum.

Crown and Numeral
A3

1853 **Wmk. 130**
7 A3 3pf rose 350.00 325.00

The reprints of No. 7 have white gum.

Fine Network in Second Color

1855 **Unwmkd.**
8 A2 1/10th black & orange 225.00 110.00
a. 1/10th black & yel. 250.00 125.00

No. 8 with olive yellow network and other values with fine network are essays.

Large Network in Second Color

1856-57
9 A3 3pf rose & black 210.00 200.00
a. 3pf rose & gray 265.00 240.00
11 A1 1g g blk. & green 32.50 10.00
12 A2 1/30th blk. & rose 100.00 25.00
a. Bisect on cover *3000.00*
13 " 1/15th black & blue 85.00 45.00
a. Bisect on cover *4750.00*
14 " 1/10th black & orange ('57) 800.00 45.00

The reprints have white gum, and the network does not cover all the outer margin.

Without Network.

1859-63
16 A3 3pf carmine rose 90.00 95.00
a. 3pf pink 75.00 75.00
17 " 3pf green (Drei Zehntel) ('63) 275.00 *700.00*

Copies of No. 25 with rouletting trimmed off sometimes pretend to be No. 17. Minimum size of No. 17 acknowledged as genuine: 21½x24½mm.

The reprints of No. 16 have pink gum instead of red; the extremities of the banderol point downward instead of outward.

Crown and Post Horn
A7

King George V
A8

1859-61 ***Imperf.***
18 A7 ½g black ('60) 80.00 120.00
a. Rose gum 350.00 350.00
19 A8 1g rose 2.75 2.25
a. 1g violet rose 20.00 10.00
b. 1g carmine 3.50 3.00
c. Half used as ½g on cover *3500.00*
20 " 2g ultramarine 22.50 25.00
a. Half used as 1g on cover *4000.00*
22 " 3g yellow 150.00 45.00
a. 3g org. yellow 175.00 45.00
23 " 3g brown ('61) 22.50 27.50
a. One third used as 1g on cover
24 " 10g green ('61) 250.00 *700.00*

Reprints of ½g are on thick toned paper with yellowish gum. Originals are on white paper with rose or white gum. Reprints exist tête bêche.

Reprints of 3g yellow and 3g brown have white or pinkish gum. Originals have rose or orange gum.

White Gum.

1864 ***Percé en Arc 16***
25 A3 3pf green (Drei Zehntel) 35.00 50.00
a. Rose gum 50.00 52.50
26 A7 ½g black 160.00 180.00
a. Rose gum 325.00 375.00
27 A8 1g rose 6.00 2.00
a. Rose gum 22.50 15.00

28 A8 2g ultramarine 75.00 45.00
a. Half used as 1g on cover *4000.00*
29 " 3g brown 65.00 40.00
a. Rose gum *1500.00 1600.00*

Reprints of 3g are percé en arc 13½.

The stamps of Prussia superseded those of Hanover on Oct. 1, 1866.

LUBECK

(lü'běk)

LOCATION—Situated on an arm of the Baltic Sea between the former German States of Holstein and Mecklenburg.

GOVT.—Former Free City and State.

AREA—115 sq. mi.

POP.—136,413.

CAPITAL—Lübeck.

Lubeck was a member of the German Confederation and became part of the German Empire in 1870.

16 Schillings = 1 Mark

Prices of Lubeck stamps vary according to condition. Quotations are for fine copies. Very fine to superb specimens sell at much higher prices, and inferior or poor copies sell at reduced prices, depending on the condition of the individual specimen.

Prices for Nos. 1–7 unused are for copies without gum. Copies with gum sell for about twice the figures quoted. Nos. 8–14 without gum sell for about half the prices quoted.

Coat of Arms
A1

Wmk. 148

Wmkd. Small Flowers. (148)

1859 **Lithographed** ***Imperf.***

1 A1 ½s gray lilac 475.00 *2000.00*
2 " 1s orange 475.00 *2000.00*
3 " 2s brown 17.50 *260.00*
a. Value in words reads "ZWEI EIN HALB" 300.00 *6000.00*
4 " 2½s rose 45.00 *850.00*
5 " 4s green *20.00 600.00*

1862 **Unwmkd.**

6 A1 ½s lilac 16.50 *1350.00*
7 " 1s yellow orange 32.50 *1350.00*

The reprints of the 1859-62 issues are unwatermarked and printed in bright colors.

A2

A3

Eagle Embossed.

1863 ***Rouletted 11½.***

8 A2 ½s green 45.00 *95.00*
9 " 1s orange 135.00 *160.00*
a. Rouletted 10 250.00 *600.00*
10 " 2s rose 25.00 *70.00*
11 " 2½s ultramarine 60.00 *350.00*
12 " 4s bistre 45.00 *125.00*

The reprints are imperforate and without embossing.

1864 **Lithographed** ***Imperf.***

13 A3 1¼s brown 30.00 *65.00*

A4

Eagle Embossed.

1865 ***Rouletted 11½.***

14 A4 1½s red lilac 30.00 *105.00*

The reprints are imperforate and without embossing.

Counterfeit cancellations are found on Nos. 1 to 14.

The stamps of Lübeck were superseded by those of the North German Confederation on Jan. 1, 1868.

MECKLENBURG-SCHWERIN

(měk'lěn-boork-shvå-rēn')

LOCATION—In northern Germany, bordering on the Baltic Sea.

GOVT.—A former Grand Duchy.

AREA—5,065 sq. mi. (approx.).

POP.—674,000 (approx.).

CAPITAL—Schwerin.

Mecklenburg-Schwerin was a member of the German Confederation and became part of the German Empire in 1870.

48 Schillings = 1 Thaler

Prices of Mecklenburg-Schwerin stamps vary according to condition. Quotations are for fine copies. Very fine to superb specimens sell at much higher prices, and inferior or poor copies sell at reduced prices, depending on the condition of the individual specimen.

Prices for unused stamps are for copies with gum. Copies without gum sell for about half the figures quoted.

Coat of Arms
A1 A2

Typographed.

1856 ***Imperf.*** **Unwmkd.**

1 A1 Four ¼s red 175.00 135.00
a. ¼s red 16.50 14.00
2 A2 3s orange yellow 110.00 70.00
3 " 5s blue 285.00 325.00

A3

1864–67 ***Rouletted 11½***

4 A1 Four ¼s red *3000.00 2400.00*
a. ¼s red 185.00 225.00
5 A3 Four ¼s red 85.00 70.00
a. ¼s red 10.00 10.00
6 A2 2s gray lilac ('67) 200.00 *2250.00*
a. 2s red vio. ('66) 300.00 300.00
7 " 3s orange yellow, wide margin ('67) 45.00 *400.00*
a. Narrow margin ('65) 225.00 150.00
8 " 5s bistre brown 200.00 *350.00*
a. Thick paper 300.00 *400.00*

The overall size of No. 7, including margin, is 24½x24½mm. That of No. 7a is 23½x23mm.

Counterfeit cancellations exist on those stamps priced higher used than unused.

These stamps were superseded by those of the North German Confederation on Jan. 1, 1868.

MECKLENBURG-STRELITZ

(měk'lěn-boork-shtrā'lits)

LOCATION—In northern Germany, divided into two parts by Mecklenburg-Schwerin.

GOVT.—A former Grand Duchy.

AREA—1,131 sq. mi.

POP.—106,347.

CAPITAL—Neustrelitz.

Mecklenburg-Strelitz was a member of the German Confederation and became part of the German Empire in 1870.

30 Silbergroschen = 48 Schillings = 1 Thaler

Prices of Mecklenburg-Strelitz stamps vary according to condition. Quotations are for fine copies. Very fine to superb specimens sell at much higher prices, and inferior or poor copies sell at reduced prices, depending on the condition of the individual specimen.

Prices for unused stamps are for copies with gum. Copies without gum sell for about half the figures quoted.

Coat of Arms
A1 A2

Embossed.

1864 ***Rouletted 11½.*** **Unwmkd.**

1 A1 ¼sg orange 185.00 *2500.00*
a. ¼sg yellow orange 450.00 *4750.00*
2 " ⅓sg green 90.00 *1500.00*
a. ⅓sg dk. green 185.00 *2750.00*
3 " 1sch violet 325.00 *4000.00*
4 A2 1sg rose 150.00 225.00
5 " 2sg ultramarine 45.00 *900.00*
6 " 3sg bistre 45.00 *1800.00*

Counterfeit cancellations abound.

These stamps were superseded by those of the North German Confederation in 1868.

OLDENBURG

(ōl'děn-boork)

LOCATION—In northwestern Germany, bordering on the North Sea.

GOVT.—A former Grand Duchy.

AREA—2,482 sq. mi.

POP.—483,042 (1910).

CAPITAL—Oldenburg.

Oldenburg was a member of the German Confederation and became part of the German Empire in 1870.

30 Silbergroschen = 1 Thaler
30 Groschen = 1 Thaler

Prices of Oldenburg stamps vary according to condition. Quotations for Nos. 1–15 are for fine copies. Very fine to superb specimens sell at much higher prices, and inferior or poor copies sell at reduced prices, depending on the condition of the individual specimen.

Prices for Nos. 1–15 unused are for copies without gum. Copies with gum sell for about twice the figures quoted. Nos. 16–25 without gum sell for about half the prices.

Numerals of Value
A1 A2

Lithographed.

1852–55 ***Imperf.*** **Unwmkd.**

1 A1 1/30th *blue* 275.00 25.00
2 " 1/15th *rose* 375.00 100.00
3 " 1/10th *yellow* 375.00 100.00
4 A2 ⅓sgr *green* ('55) 625.00 825.00

There are three types of Nos. 1 and 2.

Coat of Arms
A3 A4

1859

5 A3 ⅓g *green* 2000.00 *3250.00*
6 " 1g *blue* 300.00 45.00
7 " 2g *rose* 600.00 575.00
8 " 3g *yellow* 600.00 525.00
a. "OLBENBURG" 1000.00 *800.00*

1861

9 A4 ¼g orange 225.00 *3250.00*
10 A3 ⅓g green 250.00 *800.00*
a. ⅓g bluish green 275.00 *500.00*
b. ⅓g moss green 850.00 *1750.00*
c. "OLDEIBURG" 375.00 *900.00*
d. "Dritto" 375.00 *900.00*
e. "Drittd" 400.00 *900.00*
f. Printed on both sides *2500.00*
12 A4 ½g reddish brown 325.00 *425.00*
a. ½g dark brown 350.00 *475.00*
13 A3 1g blue 225.00 165.00
a. 1g gray blue 275.00 225.00
b. Printed on both sides *2750.00*
14 " 2g red 385.00 400.00
15 " 3g yellow 450.00 450.00
a. "OLDEIBURG" *475.00* *475.00*
b. Printed on both sides *4000.00*

Forged cancellations are found on Nos. 9, 10, 12 and their minor varieties.

Coat of Arms
A5

Embossed.

1862 ***Rouletted 11½***

16 A5 ⅓g green 225.00 185.00
17 " ⅓g orange 175.00 100.00
a. ⅓g orange red 250.00 110.00
18 " 1g rose 80.00 15.00
19 " 2g ultramarine 185.00 40.00
20 " 3g bistre 185.00 45.00

1867 ***Rouletted 10***

21 A5 ⅓g green 20.00 *475.00*
22 " ⅓g orange 20.00 *350.00*
23 " 1g rose 9.00 *50.00*
a. Half used as ½g on cover *1800.00*
24 " 2g ultramarine 10.00 *300.00*
25 " 3g bistre 27.50 *375.00*

Forged cancellations are found on Nos. 21–25.

The stamps of Oldenburg were replaced by those of the North German Confederation on Jan. 1, 1868.

PRUSSIA

(prŭsh'ȧ)

LOCATION—Prussia formerly comprised the greater part of northern Germany.

GOVT.—A former independent Kingdom.

AREA—134,650 sq. mi.

POP.—40,165,219 (1910).

CAPITAL—Berlin.

Prussia was a member of the German Confederation and became part of the German Empire in 1870.

12 Pfennigs = 1 Silbergroschen
60 Kreuzer = 1 Gulden (1867)

Prices for unused stamps are for copies with gum. Copies without gum sell for about half the figures quoted.

King Frederick William IV
A1 A2

Wmk. 162

Wmkd. Laurel Wreath (162)

1850–56 Engraved *Imperf.*

Background of Crossed Lines

1 A1 4pf yellow green ('56) 110.00 80.00
a. 4pf dark green 135.00 100.00
2 " 6pf (½sg) red orange 90.00 42.50
3 A2 1sg *rose* 75.00 5.00
4 " 2sg *blue* 100.00 12.00
a. Half used as 1 sg on cover
5 " 3sg *yellow* 100.00 10.00
a. 3sg *orange buff* 325.00 27.50

Reprints exist on watermarked and unwatermarked paper.

A3

Solid Background.

1857 Typographed. Unwmkd.

6 A3 1sg rose 300.00 25.00
7 " 2sg blue 1400.00 80.00
a. 2sg dark blue 1750.00 130.00
b. Half used as 1sg on cover 3000.00
8 " 3sg orange 150.00 35.00
a. 3sg yellow 275.00 90.00

The reprints of Nos. 6 to 8 inclusive have a period instead of a colon after "SILBERGR."

A4

1858-60 Typographed.

Background of Crossed Lines.

9 A4 4pf green 80.00 32.50

Engraved.

10 A1 6pf (½sg) orange ('59) 120.00 80.00

Typographed.

11 A2 1sg rose 35.00 3.00
12 " 2sg blue 100.00 20.00
a. 2sg dark blue 165.00 25.00
b. Half used as 1sg on cover
13 " 3sg orange 80.00 16.50
a. 3sg yellow 90.00 18.50

Coat of Arms
A6 A7

Embossed.

1861–65 *Rouletted 11½*

14 A6 3pf red lilac ('65) 16.50 20.00
a. 3pf red violet ('65) 50.00 65.00
15 " 4pf yellow green 10.00 8.00
a. 4pf green 25.00 16.00
16 " 6pf orange 10.00 12.00
a. 6pf vermilion 75.00 37.50
17 A7 1sg rose 3.50 50
18 " 2sg ultramarine 8.00 1.40
a. 2sg blue 375.00 37.50
20 " 3sg bistre 7.50 1.65
a. 3sg gray brn. ('65) 300.00 22.50

A8

A9

Typographed in Reverse on Paper Resembling Goldbeater's Skin

1866 *Rouletted 10*

21 A8 10sg rose 60.00 70.00
22 A9 30sg blue 95.00 180.00

Perfect copies of Nos. 21 and 22 are extremely rare.

A10

1867 Embossed *Rouletted 16*

23 A10 1kr green 25.00 32.50
24 " 2kr orange 37.50 75.00
25 " 3kr rose 22.50 20.00
26 " 6kr ultramarine 22.50 35.00
27 " 9kr bistre brown 27.50 37.50

Imperforate stamps of the above sets are proofs.

The stamps of Prussia were superseded by those of the North German Confederation on Jan. 1, 1868.

OFFICIAL STAMPS.

For stamps formerly listed as Nos. O1-O15, see Germany Nos. OL1-OL15.

SAXONY

(săk'sȏ-nĭ)

LOCATION — In central Germany.

GOVT.—A former kingdom.

AREA—5,787 sq. mi.

POP.—2,500,000 (approx.)

CAPITAL—Dresden.

Saxony was a member of the German Confederation and became a part of the German Empire in 1870.

10 Pfennigs = 1 Neu-Groschen
30 Neu-Groschen = 1 Thaler

Prices of Saxony stamps vary according to condition. Quotations for Nos. 1–14 are for fine copies. Very fine to superb specimens sell at much higher prices, and inferior or poor copies sell at reduced prices, depending on the condition of the individual specimen.

Prices for unused stamps are for copies with gum. Copies without gum sell for about half the figures quoted.

A1

Typographed

1850 *Imperf.* Unwmkd.

1 A1 3pf red *5000.00 5000.00*
a. 3pf dark red *7500.00* 5250.00

Coat of Arms — Frederick Augustus II
A2 A3

1851

2 A2 3pf green 100.00 65.00
a. 3pf yellow green 275.00 225.00

Nos. 2 and 2a with margins all around sell considerably higher.

1851–52 Engraved

3 A3 ½ng *gray* 45.00 12.00
a. ½ng *pale blue* (error) *10,0000.00*
5 " 1ng *rose* 45.00 12.00
6 " 2ng *pale blue* 225.00 47.50
7 " 2ng *dark blue* ('52) 575.00 47.50
8 " 3ng *yellow* 175.00 20.00

King John I
A4

1855–57

9 A4 ½ng *gray* 8.00 2.75
a. "11/22" at left or right 650.00 350.00
10 " 1ng *rose* 8.00 2.50
11 " 2ng *blue* 12.00 22.50
a. 2ng *dark blue* 30.00 9.00
12 " 3ng *yellow* 17.50 5.00
13 " 5ng vermilion ('56) 75.00 45.00
a. 5ng orange brown ('56) 200.00 150.00
b. 5ng dp. brn. ('57) *700.00* 250.00
14 " 10ng blue ('56) 240.00 240.00

The ½ng is found in 3 types, the 1ng in 2.

In 1861 the 5ng and 10ng were printed on hard, brittle, translucent paper.

Coat of Arms
A5 A6

Typo.; Arms Embossed

1863 *Perf. 13*

15 A5 3pf blue green 1.20 *12.00*
a. 3pf yellow green 10.00 *22.50*
16 " ½ng orange 50 1.50
a. ½ng red orange 12.00 5.00
17 A6 1ng rose 50 85
a. Vertical pair, imperf. between *300.00*
b. Horiz. pair, imperf. between *400.00*
18 " 2ng blue 1.75 3.00
a. 2ng dark blue 5.50 7.00
19 " 3ng red brown 1.50 8.00
a. 3ng bistre brown 9.00 3.75
20 " 5ng dull violet 12.00 *25.00*
a. 5ng gray violet 12.00 *65.00*
b. 5ng gray blue 9.00 *24.00*
c. 5ng slate 35.00 *125.00*

The stamps of Saxony were superseded on Jan. 1, 1868, by those of the North German Confederation.

SCHLESWIG-HOLSTEIN

(shläs'vĭk-hōl'shtīn)

LOCATION—In northern Germany, including a part of the Jutland Peninsula.

GOVT.—Former Duchies.

AREA—7,338 sq. mi.

POP.—1,519,000 (approx.).

CAPITAL—Schleswig.

Schleswig-Holstein was an autonomous territory from 1848 to 1851 when it came under Danish rule. In 1864, it was occupied by Prussia and Austria, and in 1866 it became a province of Prussia.

16 Schillings = 1 Mark

Prices of Schleswig-Holstein stamps vary according to condition. Quotations for Nos. 1–2, 15–17 are for fine copies. Very fine to superb specimens sell at much higher prices, and inferior or poor copies sell at reduced prices, depending on the condition of the individual specimen.

Prices for unused stamps are for copies with gum. Copies without gum sell for about half the figures quoted.

Coat of Arms
A1

Typographed; Arms Embossed

1850 *Imperf.* Unwmkd.

With Silk Threads.

1 A1 1s dull blue & greenish bl. 275.00 *2200.00*
a. 1s Prus. blue 600.00
2 " 2s rose & pink 400.00 *4500.00*
a. 2s dp. pink & rose 600.00
b. Dbl. embossing *750.00*

Forged cancellations are found on Nos. 1–2, 5–7, 9, 16 and 19.

A2 A3

Typographed

1865 *Rouletted 11½*

3 A2 ½s rose 35.00 50.00
4 " 1¼s green 14.00 9.00
5 A3 1⅓s red lilac 50.00 *160.00*
6 A2 2s ultramarine 55.00 *325.00*
7 A3 4s bistre 60.00 *1000.00*

Schleswig.

A4

A5

Typographed.

1864 *Rouletted 11½*

8 A4 1¼s green 45.00 12.50
9 " 4s carmine 80.00 *250.00*

1865 *Rouletted 10, 11½*

10 A4 ½s green 35.00 52.50
11 " 1⅓s red lilac 35.00 9.00
a. 1⅓s gray lilac 350.00 90.00
b. Half of #11a used as ⅔s on cover
12 A5 1⅓s rose 37.50 50.00
13 A4 2s ultramarine 25.00 32.50
14 " 4s bistre 37.50 55.00

Holstein.

A6

A7

Type I. Small lettering in frame. Wavy lines in spandrels close together.
Type II. Small lettering in frame. Wavy lines wider apart.
Type III. Larger lettering in frame and no periods after "H R Z G". Wavy lines as type II.

1864 Lithographed. *Imperf.*

15 A6 1¼s blue & gray, type I 55.00 40.00
a. Half used as ⅔s on cover *7250.00*
16 " 1¼s blue & gray, type II 575.00 *2250.00*
a. Half used as ⅔s on cover *24,000.00*
17 " 1¼s blue & gray, type III 50.00 40.00
a. Half used as ⅔s on cover *8000.00*

1864 Typo. *Rouletted 8*

18 A7 1¼s blue & rose 47.50 12.50
a. Half used as ⅔s on cover *1600.00*

A8

1865 *Rouletted 8*

19 A8 ½s green 70.00 120.00
20 " 1¼s red lilac 45.00 16.00
21 " 2s blue 60.00 50.00

A9 A10

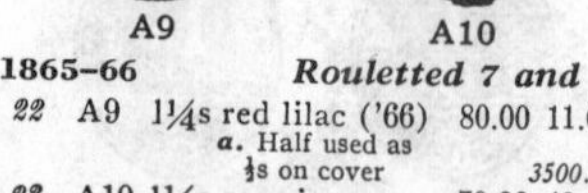

1865-66 *Rouletted 7 and 8*

22 A9 1¼s red lilac ('66) 80.00 11.00
a. Half used as ⅔s on cover *3500.00*
23 A10 1⅓s carmine 70.00 40.00
24 A9 2s blue ('66) 160.00 175.00
25 A10 4s bistre 70.00 55.00

These stamps were superseded by those of North German Confederation on Jan. 1, 1868.

THURN AND TAXIS

(thûrn ănd tăk'sĭs)

A princely house which, prior to the formation of the German Empire, enjoyed the privilege of a postal monopoly. These stamps were superseded on July 1, 1867, by those of Prussia, followed by those of the North German Postal District on Jan. 1. 1868, and later by stamps of the German Empire on Jan. 1, 1872.

30 Silbergroschen or Groschen = 1 Thaler

Prices for unused stamps are for copies with gum. Copies without gum sell for about half the figures quoted.
Prices for the imperforate stamps are for good, average specimens. Stamps with four clear margins are scarce and command much higher prices.

Northern District

Numerals of Value
A1 A2

Typographed.

1852-58 *Imperf.* **Unwmkd.**

1 A1 ¼sgr *red brown* ('54) 180.00 40.00
2 " ⅓sgr *buff* ('58) 90.00 240.00
3 " ½sgr *green* 275.00 22.50
4 " 1sgr *dark blue* 475.00 75.00
5 " 1sgr *lt. blue* ('53) 550.00 12.50
6 " 2sgr *rose* 400.00 16.00
7 " 3sgr *yellow* 375.00 12.50

Reprints of Nos. 1-12, 15-20, 23-24, were made in 1910. They have "ND" in script on the back. Price, $2.75 each.

1859-60

8 A1 ¼sgr red ('60) 42.50 45.00
9 " ½sgr green 200.00 65.00
10 " 1sgr blue 200.00 18.00
11 " 2sgr rose ('60) 100.00 50.00
12 " 3sgr red brn. ('60) 100.00 65.00
13 A2 5sgr lilac 2.00 *275.00*
14 " 10sgr orange 2.00 *575.00*

Excellent forged cancellations exist on Nos. 13 and 14. For reprints, see note after No. 7.

1862-63

15 A1 ¼sgr black ('63) 20.00 *40.00*
16 " ⅓sgr green ('63) 25.00 *225.00*
17 " ½sgr orange yellow 70.00 22.50
18 " 1sgr rose ('63) 40.00 18.00
19 " 2sgr blue ('63) 37.50 *65.00*
20 " 3sgr bistre ('63) 17.50 20.00

For reprints, see note after No. 7.

1865 *Rouletted.*

21 A1 ¼sgr black 12.50 *550.00*
22 " ⅓sgr green 17.50 *325.00*
23 " ½sgr yellow 17.50 *42.50*
24 " 1sgr rose 35.00 20.00
25 " 2sgr blue 2.50 *60.00*
26 " 3sgr bistre 3.00 *30.00*

For reprints, see note after No. 7.

1866

Rouletted in Colored Lines.

27 A1 ¼sgr black 2.00 *1750.00*
28 " ⅓sgr green 2.00 *750.00*
29 " ½sgr yellow 2.00 *165.00*
30 " 1sgr rose 2.00 *75.00*
a. Horizontal pair without rouletting between 100.00
b. Half used as ½sgr on cover *6000.00*
31 A1 2sgr blue 2.00 *700.00*
32 " 3sgr bistre 2.00 *225.00*

Forged cancellations on Nos. 2, 13–14, 15–16, 21–22, 25–32 are plentiful.

Southern District

60 Kreuzer = 1 Gulden

A1

A2

1852-53 *Imperf.* **Unwmkd.**

42 A1 1kr *light green* 120.00 12.50
43 " 3kr *dark blue* 500.00 22.50
44 " 3kr *blue* ('53) 500.00 10.00
45 " 6kr *rose* 500.00 17.50
46 " 9kr *yellow* 475.00 10.00

Reprints of Nos. 42-50, 53-56 were made in 1910. Each has "ND" in script on the back. $2.75 each.

1859

47 A1 1kr green 16.50 8.00
48 " 3kr blue 400.00 16.00
49 " 6kr rose 265.00 50.00
50 " 9kr yellow 400.00 65.00
51 A2 15kr lilac 2.00 *120.00*
52 " 30kr orange 2.00 *450.00*

Forged cancellations exist on Nos. 51 and 52. For reprints, see note after No. 46.

1862

53 A1 3kr rose 37.50 12.50
54 " 6kr blue 10.00 18.00
55 " 9kr bistre 10.00 17.50

For reprints, see note after No. 46.

1865 *Rouletted.*

56 A1 1kr green 15.00 12.50
57 " 3kr rose 20.00 8.50
58 " 6kr blue 2.00 *20.00*
59 " 9kr bistre 2.00 *22.50*

For reprint of No. 56, see note after No. 46.

1867

Rouletted in Colored Lines.

60 A1 1kr green 2.00 *27.50*
61 " 3kr rose 2.00 *22.50*
62 " 6kr blue 2.00 *55.00*
63 " 9kr bistre 2.00 *65.00*

Forged cancellations exist on Nos. 51-52, 58-63.
The Thurn & Taxis Stamps, Northern and Southern Districts, were replaced on July 1, 1867, by those of Prussia.

WURTTEMBERG

(vür'tĕm·bĕrk)

LOCATION—In southern Germany.
GOVT.—A former Kingdom.
AREA—7,530 sq. mi.
POP.—2,580,000 (approx.).
CAPITAL—Stuttgart.

Württemberg was a member of the German Confederation and became a part of the German Empire in 1870. It gave up its postal autonomy on March 31, 1902, but official stamps were issued until 1923.

16 Kreuzer = 1 Gulden
100 Pfennigs = 1 Mark (1875)

Prices of early Wurttemberg stamps vary according to condition. Quotations for Nos. 1–46 are for fine copies. Very fine to superb specimens sell at much higher prices, and inferior or poor copies sell at reduced prices, depending on the condition of the individual specimen.
Prices for Nos. 1–40 unused are for copies without gum. Copies with gum sell for about twice the figures quoted. Nos. 41–54 without gum sell for about half the prices.

A1

A1a

Typographed.

1851-52 *Imperf.* **Unwmkd.**

1 A1 1kr *buff* 275.00 60.00
a. 1kr straw 850.00 350.00
2 " 3kr *yellow* 80.00 4.00
a. 3kr orange 800.00 45.00
4 " 6kr *yellow green* 600.00 22.50
a. 6kr blue green 750.00 35.00
5 " 9kr *rose* *3250.00* 27.50
6 A1a 18kr *dull violet* ('52) 525.00 500.00

On the "reprints" the letters of "Württemberg" are smaller, especially the first "e": the right branch of the "r"s of Württemberg runs upward in the reprints and downward in the originals.

Coat of Arms
A2

Typographed and Embossed With Orange Silk Threads.

1857

7 A2 1kr yellow brown 175.00 50.00
a. 1kr dk. brown 350.00 140.00
9 " 3kr yel. orange 250.00 6.50
10 " 6kr green 275.00 40.00
11 " 9kr carmine rose 475.00 40.00
12 " 18kr blue 750.00 600.00

Copies of Nos. 7-12 with margins all around sell considerably higher.

The reprints have red or yellow silk threads and are printed 2mm. apart, while the originals are ¾mm. apart.

1859 Without Silk Threads.

13 A2 1kr brown 225.00 50.00
a. 1kr dark brown 325.00 100.00
15 " 3kr yel. orange 175.00 4.00
16 " 6kr green *3750.00* 65.00
17 " 9kr carmine rose 750.00 45.00
18 " 18kr dark blue 950.00 850.00

The colors of the reprints are brighter; they are also printed 2mm. apart instead of 1¼mm.

1860 *Perf. 13½.*

19 A2 1kr brown 275.00 65.00
20 " 3kr yel. orange 150.00 6.00
21 " 6kr green 500.00 40.00
22 " 9kr carmine 450.00 65.00

1861 Thin Paper.

23 A2 1kr brown 200.00 85.00
a. 1kr blk. brown 300.00 140.00
25 " 3kr yellow orange 45.00 30.00
26 " 6kr green 65.00 40.00
27 " 9kr rose 275.00 130.00
a. 9kr claret 425.00 200.00
29 " 18kr dark blue 600.00 475.00

Copies of Nos. 23-29 with all perforations intact sell considerably higher.

1862 *Perf. 10.*

30 A2 1kr black brown 200.00 200.00
31 " 3kr yel. orange 80.00 27.50
32 " 6kr green 140.00 90.00
33 " 9kr claret 750.00 375.00

1863

34 A2 1kr yellow green 27.50 6.50
a. 1kr green 145.00 40.00
36 " 3kr rose 15.00 2.00
a. 3kr dark claret 400.00 250.00
37 " 6kr blue 90.00 30.00

39 A2 9kr yellow brown 125.00 35.00
  a. 9kr red brown 85.00 30.00
  b. 9kr black brown 200.00 75.00
40 " 18kr orange 325.00 260.00

1866-68 ***Rouletted 10.***

41 A2 1kr yellow green 20.00 5.00
  a. 1kr dark green 85.00 60.00
42 " 3kr rose 16.00 2.50
  a. 3kr claret 375.00 350.00
43 " 6kr blue 140.00 35.00
44 " 7kr slate bl. ('68) 400.00 85.00
45 " 9kr bistre brown 160.00 65.00
  a. 9kr red brown 140.00 50.00
46 " 18kr orange 575.00 475.00

A3

Typographed and Embossed

1869–73

47 A3 1kr yellow green 12.00 1.75
48 " 2kr orange 45.00 40.00
49 " 3kr rose 12.00 1.00
50 " 7kr blue 40.00 12.50
51 " 9kr lt. brown ('73) 35.00 20.00
52 " 14kr orange 60.00 40.00
  a. 14kr lemon yel. 450.00 200.00

1873 ***Imperf.***

53 A2 70kr red violet 1000.00 1600.00
  a. 70kr violet 1500.00 2250.00

Nos. 53 and 53a have single or double lines of fine black dots printed in the gutters between the stamps.

1874 ***Perf. 11½x11.***

54 A3 1kr yellow green 22.50 15.00

A4

A5

1875–1900 **Typographed**

55 A4 2pf slate gray ('93) 40 25
56 " 3pf green 6.50 1.20
57 " 3pf brown ('90) 25 10
  a. Imperf., pair 75.00
58 " 5pf violet 6.50 45
59 " 5pf green ('90) 60 8
  a. 5pf blue green 45.00 6.00
  b. Imperf., pair 75.00
60 " 10pf carmine 70 8
  a. 10pf rose 22.50 60
  b. Imperf., pair 47.50
61 " 20pf ultramarine 70 20
  a. 20pf dull blue 1.00 20
  b. Imperf., pair 47.50
62 " 25pf red brown 30.00 8.00
63 " 25pf orange ('90) 1.00 70
  a. Imperf., pair 75.00
64 A5 30pf orge. & blk. ('00) 2.00 2.75
65 " 40pf deep rose & black ('00) 2.00 2.75
66 A4 50pf gray 165.00 16.00
67 " 50pf gray green 18.00 2.25
68 " 50pf purple brn. ('90) 90 30
  a. 50pf red brown 55.00 22.50
  b. Imperf., pair 47.50
69 " 2m yellow 650.00 225.00
70 " 2m vermilion, *buff* ('79) 650.00 120.00
71 A5 2m orange & black ('86) 4.50 7.00
  a. 2m yellow & black 65.00 17.50
  b. Imperf., pair 35.00
  Telegraph cancel 1.40
72 " 5m blue & black ('81) 47.50 115.00
  a. Figure of value inverted
  Telegraph cancel 65.00

No. 70 has "Unverkäuflich" (not for sale) printed on its back to remind postal clerks that it, like No. 69, was for their use and not to be sold to the public.

The regular postage stamps of Württemberg were superseded by those of the German Empire in 1902. Official stamps were in use until 1923.

Stamps for the Wurttemberg sector of the French Occupation Zone of Germany, issued 1947–1949, are listed under Germany, Occupation Issues.

OFFICIAL STAMPS.

For the Communal Authorities.

O1

Perf. 11½x11.

1875-1900 Typographed. Unwmkd.

O1 O1 2pf slate gray ('00) 70 70
O2 " 3pf brown ('96) 70 25
O3 " 5pf violet 20.00 1.50
  a. Imperf., pair *1600.00*
O4 " 5pf blue green ('90) 1.20 20
  a. Imperf., pair *40.00*
O5 " 10pf rose 90 20
  a. Imperf., pair *60.00*
O6 " 25pf orange ('00) 9.00 3.50
  Nos. O1-O6 (6) 32.50 6.35

See also Nos. O12–O32.

Used Prices

When italicized, used prices for Nos. O7–O183 are for favor-canceled copies. Postally used copies command a premium.

Stamps of Previous Issues Overprinted in Black

1806 — 1906

1906, Jan. 30

O7 O1 2pf slate gray 27.50 *30.00*
O8 " 3pf dark brown 4.00 *5.00*
O9 " 5pf green 1.25 *1.50*
O10 " 10pf deep rose 1.25 *1.50*
O11 " 25pf orange 30.00 *30.00*
  Nos. O7-O11 (5) 64.00 *68.00*

Centenary of Kingdom of Württemberg.

Nos. O7 to O11 also exist imperforate but it is doubtful if they were ever issued in that condition.

Wmk. 116

1906–21

Wmkd. Crosses and Circles. (116)

O12 O1 2pf slate gray 20 *20*
O13 " 2½pf gray black ('16) 20 10
O14 " 3pf dark brown 20 10
O15 " 5pf green 20 10
O16 " 7½pf orange ('16) 20 10
O17 " 10pf deep rose 20 8
O18 " 10pf orange ('21) 20 *10*
O19 " 15pf yel. brown ('16) 60 *40*
O20 " 15pf purple ('17) 20 30
O21 " 20pf deep ultra. ('11) 20 12
O22 " 20pf deep green ('21) 20 *15*
O23 " 25pf orange 20 12
O24 " 25pf brn. & blk. ('17) 20 15
O25 " 35pf brown ('19) 40 *20*
O26 " 40pf rose red ('21) 20 *10*
O27 " 50pf rose lake ('11) 1.25 *75*
O28 " 50pf violet brn. ('21) 20 *15*
O29 " 60pf olive green ('21) 20 *15*
O30 O1 1.25m emerald ('21) 40 40
O31 " 2m gray ('21) 40 40
O32 " 3m brown ('21) 40 40
  Nos. O12-O32 (21) 6.45 *4.57*

No. O24 contains solid black numerals.

Nos. O12–O32 exist imperf. Price, each pair, $6–$16.

O3

Perf. 14½x14

1916, Oct. 6 Typo. Unwmkd.

O33 O3 2½pf slate 1.50 *1.50*
O34 " 7½pf orange 40 *40*
O35 " 10pf carmine rose 40 *40*
O36 " 15pf yellow brown 40 *40*
O37 " 20pf blue 40 *40*
O38 " 25pf gray black 1.20 *1.20*
O39 " 50pf red brown 2.00 *2.00*
  Nos. O33-O39 (7) 6.30 *6.30*

Nos. O33 to O39 were issued to commemorate the twenty-fifth year of the reign of King Wilhelm II.

Stamps of 1900-06 Surcharged **25 Pf.**

Wmkd. Crosses and Circles. (116)

1916, Sept. 10 ***Perf. 11½x11***

O40 O1 25pf on 25pf orange 2.25 *2.25*
  a. Without wmk. 15.00

No. O13 Surcharged in Blue **2**

1919 **Wmk. 116**

O42 O1 2pf on 2½pf gray black 12 *15*

Volksstaat

Official Stamps of 1906-19 Overprinted

Württemberg

1919

O43 O1 2½pf gray black 20 *30*
O44 " 3pf dark brown 3.00 *2.50*
O45 " 5pf green 20 *10*
O46 " 7½pf orange 40 *30*
O47 " 10pf rose 20 *10*
O48 " 15pf purple 20 *10*
O49 " 20pf ultramarine 20 *15*
O50 " 25pf brown & black 20 *20*
O51 " 35pf brown 50 *40*
O52 " 50pf red brown 1.75 *55*
  Nos. O43-O52 (10) 6.85 *4.70*

Stag

O4

Wmk. 192

Wmkd. Circles. (192)

1920, Mar. 19 Litho. ***Perf. 14½***

O53 O4 10pf maroon 1.40 *1.00*
O54 " 15pf brown 1.40 *1.00*
O55 " 20pf indigo 1.40 *1.00*
O56 " 30pf deep green 1.40 *1.00*
O57 " 50pf yellow 1.40 *1.00*
O58 " 75pf bistre 1.40 *1.00*
  Nos. O53-O58 (6) 8.40 *6.00*

Deutsches

Official Stamps of 1906-19 Overprinted

Reich

Wmkd.

Crosses and Circles. (116)

Perf. 11½x11.

O59 O1 5pf green 3.25 *2.75*
O60 " 10pf deep rose 2.00 *2.00*
O61 " 15pf deep violet 1.50 *1.50*
O62 " 20pf ultramarine 3.25 *3.00*
  a. Wmk. 192 6.00 *4.25*
O63 " 50pf red brown 4.00 *3.25*
  Nos. O59-O63 (5) 14.00 *12.50*

Nos. O59 to O63 were available for official postage throughout all Germany but were used almost exclusively in Württemberg.

Stamps of 1917-21 Surcharged in Black, Red or Blue **10 Mark**

1923

O64 O1 5m on 10pf orange 20 *15*
O65 " 10m on 15pf dp. vio. 20 *12*
O66 " 12m on 40pf rose red 25 *25*
O67 " 20m on 10pf orange 25 *40*
O68 " 25m on 20pf green 20 *10*
O69 " 40m on 20pf green 25 *40*
O70 " 50m on 60pf olive green 20 *15*

Surcharged **60 Mark**

O71 O1 60m on 1.25m emerald 20 *20*
O72 " 100m on 40pf rose red 20 *15*
O73 " 200m on 2m gray (R) 20 *15*
O74 " 300m on 50pf red brown (Bl) 20 *15*
O75 " 400m on 3m brown (Bl) 25 *40*
O76 " 1000m on 60pf olive green 30 *50*
O77 " 2000m on 1.25m emerald 25 *25*
  Nos. O64-O77 (14) 3.15 *3.37*

Abbreviations:

Th = (Tausend) Thousand.
Mil = (Million) Million.
Mlrd = (Milliarde) Billion.

Surcharged **20 Tausend**

1923

O78 O1 5th m on 10pf orange 20 *40*
O79 " 20th m on 40pf rose red 20 *20*
O80 " 50th m on 15pf violet 1.00 *1.50*
O81 " 75th m on 2m gray 2.00 *50*
O82 " 100th m on 20pf green 20 *50*
O83 " 250th m on 3m brown 20 *25*

Surcharged **2 Millionen**

O84 O1 1mil m on 60pf olive green 50 1.50
O85 " 2mil m on 50pf red brown 20 20
O86 " 5mil m on 1.25m emerald 40 60

Surcharged **10 Milliarden**

O87 O1 4 mlrd m on 50pf red brown 3.00 2.50
O88 " 10 mlrd m on 3m brown 1.25 1.75
Nos. O78–O88 (11) 9.15 9.90

No. O23 Surcharged with New Values in Rentenpfennig as **3**

1923, Dec.

O89 O1 3(pf) on 25pf orange 65 50
O90 " 5(pf) on 25pf orange 25 20
O91 " 10(pf) on 25pf orange 25 20
O92 " 20(pf) on 25pf orange 25 75
O93 " 50(pf) on 25pf org. 2.00 1.20
Nos. O89–O93 (5) 3.80 2.85

For the State Authorities.

O6

Perf. 11½x11.

1881–1902 Typographed Unwmkd.

O94 O6 2pf slate gray ('00) 20 40
O95 " 3pf green 5.00 2.75
O96 " 3pf dark brown ('90) 20 10
O97 " 5pf violet 2.40 60
O98 " 5pf green ('90) 20 10
O99 " 10pf rose 1.00 10
O100 " 20pf ultramarine 30 10
O101 " 25pf brown 9.00 3.00
O102 " 25pf orange ('90) 75 20
O103 " 30pf orange & black ('02) 60 1.20
O104 " 40pf deep rose & black ('02) 60 1.20
O105 " 50pf gray green 10.00 7.50
O106 " 50pf maroon ('90) 75 85
a. 50pf red brown 175.00 225.00
O107 " 1m yellow 90.00 180.00
O108 " 1m violet ('90) 12.00 22.50

See also Nos. O119–O135.

Overprinted in Black **1806 – 1906**

1906

O109 O6 2pf slate gray 17.50 17.50
O110 " 3pf dark brown 2.00 1.75
O111 " 5pf green 60 60
O112 " 10pf deep rose 60 60
O113 " 20pf ultramarine 1.50 1.75
O114 " 25pf orange 3.00 2.75
O115 " 30pf orange & black 3.00 2.75
O116 " 40pf deep rose & black 20.00 20.00
O117 " 50pf red brown 20.00 20.00
O118 " 1m purple 35.00 30.00
Nos. O109–O118 (10) 103.20 97.70

Issued to commemorate the centenary of the kingdom of Wüttemberg.

Nos. O109 to O118 are also found imperforate, but it is doubtful if they were ever issued in that condition.

1906-19

Wmkd. Crosses and Circles. (116)

O119 O6 2pf slate gray 10 10
O120 " 2½pf gray black ('16) 10 10
O121 " 3pf dark brown 10 10
O122 " 5pf green 10 10
O123 " 7½pf orange ('16) 10 10
O124 " 10pf deep rose 10 10
O125 " 15pf yellow brown ('16) 10 10
O126 " 15pf purple ('17) 10 10
O127 " 20pf ultramarine 10 10
O128 " 25pf orange 10 10
O129 " 25pf brown & black ('17) 10 10
O130 " 30pf orange & black 10 10
O131 " 35pf brown ('19) 30 40
O132 " 40pf dp. rose & black 10 10
O133 " 50pf red brown 20 15
O134 " 1m purple 1.25 1.00
O135 " 1m slate & black ('17) 70 75
Nos. O119–O135 (17) 3.75 3.60

King Wilhelm II
O8

Typographed.

1916 *Perf. 14.* Unwmkd.

O136 O8 2½pf slate 50 50
O137 " 7½pf orange 20 15
O138 " 10pf carmine 20 30
O139 " 15pf yellow brown 20 15
O140 " 20pf blue 25 30
O141 " 25pf gray black 50 40
O142 " 30pf green 50 40
O143 " 40pf claret 1.00 80
O144 " 50pf red brown 1.25 1.20
O145 " 1m violet 2.00 1.50
Nos. O136–O145 (10) 6.60 5.70

Nos. O136 to O145 were issued to commemorate the 25th year of the reign of King Wilhelm II.

Stamps of 1890-1906 Surcharged **25 Pf.**

Wmkd. Crosses and Circles. (116)

1916-19 *Perf. 11½x11.*

O146 O6 25pf on 25pf orange 50 50
a. Without watermark 14.00 15.00
O147 " 50pf on 50pf red brown 50 50
a. Inverted surch. 40.00

No. O120 Surcharged in Blue **2**

1919 Wmk. 116

O149 O6 2pf on 2½pf gray black 25 20

Volksstaat

Official Stamps of 1890–1919 Overprinted

Württemberg

1919

O150 O6 2½pf gray black 20 15
O151 " 3pf dark brown 2.40 2.00
a. Without watermark 60.00
O152 " 5pf green 15 10
O153 " 7½pf orange 20 40
O154 " 10pf rose 15 10
O155 " 15pf purple 15 10
O156 " 20pf ultramarine 15 10
O157 " 25pf brown & black 15 15
a. Inverted overprint 80.00 90.00
O158 " 30pf orange & blacl: 15 15
a. Inverted ovpt. 140.00 180.00
O159 O6 35pf brown 25 25
O160 " 40pf rose & black 25 30
O161 " 50pf claret 25 30
O162 " 1m slate & black 40 35
Nos. O150–O162 (13) 4.85 4.45

Nos. O151, O151a Surcharged in Carmine **75**

1920 Wmk. 116

O164 O6 75pf on 3pf dark brown 50 60
a. Without watermark 20.00

View of Stuttgart
O9

Designs: 10pf, 50pf, 2.50m, 3m, View of Stuttgart. 15pf, 75pf, View of Ulm. 20pf, 1m, View of Tubingen. 30pf, 1.25m, View of Ellwangen.

Wmkd. Circles. (192)

1920, Mar. 25 Typo. *Perf. 14½*

O166 O9 10pf maroon 60 30
O167 " 15pf brown 60 30
O168 " 20pf indigo 60 30
O169 " 30pf blue green 60 30
O170 " 50pf yellow 60 30
O171 " 75pf bistre 65 60
O172 " 1m orange red 75 60
O173 " 1.25m deep violet 75 60
O174 " 2.50m dark ultra. 2.00 1.20
O175 " 3m yellow green 2.00 1.20
Nos. O166–O175 (10) 9.15 5.70

Deutsches

Official Stamps of 1906–19 Overprinted

Reich

Wmkd. Crosses and Circles. (116)

1920 *Perf. 11½x11*

O176 O6 5pf green 50 75
O177 " 10pf deep rose 10 15
O178 " 15pf purple 12 15
O179 " 20pf ultramarine 12 15
a. Wmk. 192 95.00 95.00
O180 " 30pf orange & black 15 30
O181 " 40pf deep rose & black 25 30
O182 " 50pf red brown 25 35
O183 " 1m slate & black 40 60
Nos. O176–O183 (8) 1.89 2.75

The note after No. O63 will also apply to Nos. O176 to O183.

NORTH GERMAN CONFEDERATION

Northern District
30 Groschen = 1 Thaler

Southern District
60 Kreuzer = 1 Gulden

Hamburg
16 Schillings = 1 Mark

Unused prices for Nos. 1–24 are for copies with original gum. Copies without gum sell for about half the figures quoted.

A1

A2

1868 Typographed. Unwmkd.

Rouletted 8½ to 10, 11 to 12½ and Compound.

1 A1 ¼gr red lilac 24.00 12.00
a. Imperf. 125.00 325.00
2 " ⅓gr green 10.00 2.25
a. Imperf. 57.50 250.00
3 " ½gr orange 17.50 1.20
a. Imperf. 85.00 350.00
4 " 1gr rose 10.00 30
a. Imperf. 40.00 150.00
b. Half used as ½gr on cover 550.00
5 " 2gr ultramarine 50.00 1.20
a. Imperf. 165.00 400.00
6 " 5gr bistre 60.00 6.50
a. Imperf. 165.00 325.00
7 A2 1kr green 20.00 7.50
a. Imperf. 40.00 72.50
8 " 2kr orange 37.50 32.50
a. Imperf. 120.00 52.50
9 " 3kr rose 37.50 1.75
a. Imperf. 47.50 47.50
10 " 7kr ultramarine 140.00 9.00
a. Imperf. 200.00 400.00
11 " 18kr bistre 40.00 55.00
a. Imperf. 200.00 400.00

A3

1868

12 A3 (½s) violet brown 75.00 40.00

1869 *Perf. 13½x14*

13 A1 ¼gr lilac 20.00 12.00
a. ¼gr red violet 37.50 17.50
14 " ⅓gr green 4.00 90
15 " ½gr orange 4.00 65
16 " 1gr rose 3.00 50
17 " 2gr ultramarine 4.00 50
18 " 5gr bistre 9.00 3.50
19 A2 1kr green 14.00 7.00
20 " 2kr orange 42.50 75.00
21 " 3kr rose 6.50 90
22 " 7kr ultramarine 10.00 5.00
23 " 18kr bistre 175.00 950.00

Counterfeit cancels exist on No. 23.

1869

24 A3 (¼s) dull vio. brown 1.85 2.25

A4

A5

Perf. 14x13½.

25 A4 10gr gray 350.00 550.00
Pen cancellation 45.00
26 A5 30gr blue 275.00 800.00
Pen cancellation 100.00

Counterfeit cancels exist on No. 26.

OFFICIAL STAMPS.

O1

Typographed.

1870 *Perf. 14½x14.* Unwmkd.

O1 O1 ¼gr black & flesh 27.50 55.00
O2 " ⅓gr " " 16.50 20.00
O3 " ½gr " " 3.00 4.00
O4 " 1gr " " 3.50 60
O5 " 2gr " " 6.00 3.00
O6 " 1kr black & gray 40.00 240.00
O7 " 2kr " " 100.00 800.00
O8 " 3kr " " 35.00 40.00
O9 " 7kr " " 50.00 240.00

Counterfeit cancels exist on Nos. O6–O9.

The stamps of the North German Confederation were replaced by those of the German Empire on Jan. 1, 1872.

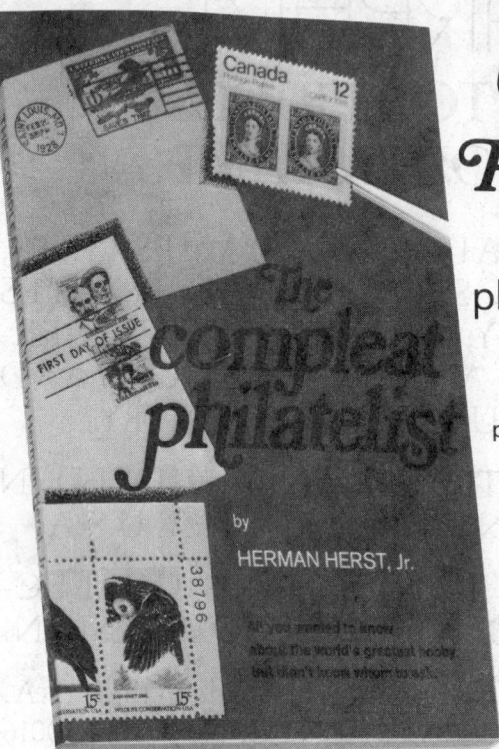

GERMANY

(jûr'mȧ-nĭ)

LOCATION—In northern Europe bordering on the Baltic and North Seas.

AREA—182,104 sq. mi. (until 1945).

POP.—67,032,242 (1946).

CAPITAL—Berlin

30 Silbergroschen or Groschen = 1 Thaler

60 Kreuzer = 1 Gulden

100 Pfennigs = 1 Mark (1875)

100 Pfennigs = 1 Deutsche Mark (1948)

Empire

> Prices of early German Empire stamps vary according to condition. Quotations for Nos. 1–28 are for fine copies. Very fine to superb specimens sell at much higher prices, and inferior or poor copies sell at reduced prices, depending on the condition of the individual specimen.
>
> Unused prices for Nos. 1–13 are for stamps with original gum. Copies without gum sell at lower prices.

Imperial Eagle
A1

Typo., Center Embossed

Eagle with small shield.

1872 *Perf. 13½x14½.* **Unwmkd.**

1 A1 ¼gr violet 160.00 75.00
2 " ⅓gr green 275.00 30.00
a. Imperf.
3 " ½gr red orange 450.00 40.00
a. ½gr orange yellow 550.00 40.00
" 1gr rose 225.00 4.00
a. Imperf.
5 " 2gr ultramarine 425.00 10.00
a. Imperf. *22,500.00*
6 " 5gr bistre 325.00 80.00
a. Imperf. *7500.00*
7 " 1kr green 325.00 50.00
8 " 2kr orange 32.50 *135.00*
a. 2kr red orange 450.00 225.00
9 " 3kr rose 350.00 7.50
10 " 7kr ultramarine 850.00 60.00
11 " 18kr bistre 425.00 300.00

Prices for imperforates are for copies postmarked at Leipzig (1/3gr), Coblenz (1gr), Hoengen (2gr) and Leutersdorf (5gr).

A2

A3

Typographed.

1872 *Perf. 14½x13½*

12 A2 10gr gray 80.00 *750.00*
Pen cancellation 110.00
13 A3 30gr blue 135.00 *1750.00*
Pen cancellation 275.00

A4

A5

Center Embossed.

Eagle with large shield.

1872 *Perf. 13½x14½*

14 A4 ¼gr violet 42.50 60.00
15 " ⅓gr yellow green 27.50 12.50
a. ⅓gr blue green 62.50 60.00
16 A4 ½gr orange 27.50 5.00
a. Imperf.
17 " 1gr rose 27.50 1.50
a. Imperf. *7500.00*
b. Half used as ½ gr on cover *20,000.00*
18 " 2gr ultramarine 18.50 5.00
19 " 2½gr org. brown 1350.00 50.00
a. 2½gr lilac brown *3250.00* 225.00
20 " 5gr bistre 27.50 25.00
a. Imperf. *7500.00*
21 " 1kr yellow green 27.50 22.50
a. 1kr blue green 90.00 100.00
22 " 2kr orange 350.00 *1500.00*
23 " 3kr rose 18.50 5.00
24 " 7kr ultramarine 27.50 50.00
25 " 9kr red brown 200.00 125.00
a. 9kr lilac brn. 850.00 275.00
26 " 18kr bistre 37.50 *1750.00*

Prices for Nos. 17a and 20a are for copies postmarked at Potsdam (1gr), Damgarten or Anklam (5gr).

Nos. 14–26 with embossing inverted are fraudulent.

1874 Brown Surcharge.

27 A5 2½gr on 2½gr brown 30.00 25.00
28 " 9kr on 9kr brown 72.50 *225.00*

A6

A7

"Pfennige"

1875–77 Typographed

29 A6 3pf green 45.00 5.00
30 " 5pf violet 50.00 1.25

Center Embossed.

31 A7 10pf rose 40.00 25
32 " 20pf ultramarine 115.00 1.25
33 " 25pf red brown 385.00 20.00
34 " 50pf gray 500.00 12.50
35 " 50pf slate grn. ('77) 900.00 17.50

A8

1875–81 Typo. *Perf. 14½x13½.*

36 A8 2m rose lilac ('81) 57.50 2.50
a. 2m purple 185.00 10.00
b. 2m dull violet 200.00 35.00
As "b," pen cancel 15.00

Types of 1875–77,
"Pfennig" without final "e"

1880–83 *Perf. 13½x14½*

37 A6 3pf green 1.60 25
a. Imperf.
38 " 5pf violet 1.60 15

Center Embossed

39 A7 10pf rose 8.00 15
a. Imperf. 135.00
40 " 20pf ultramarine 6.00 15
41 " 25pf orange brown 6.00 1.50
a. 25pf red brn.('83) 60.00 2.50
42 " 50pf deep olive green 6.00 1.00
a. 50pf gray green 6.00 1.00

Prices for Nos. 37–42 are for stamps on thin paper. Those on thick paper sell for considerably more.

Numeral of Value
A9

Imperial Eagle
A10

1889-1900 *Perf. 13½x14½*

45 A9 2pf gray ('00) 50 75
a. "REIGHS-POST" 80.00 80.00
46 A9 3pf brown 1.60 12
a. 3pf yellow brown 3.25 50
b. Imperf. 75.00
c. 3pf reddish brn. 32.50 10.00
47 " 5pf green 85 12
48 A10 10pf carmine 2.00 12
a. Imperf. 150.00
49 " 20pf ultramarine 6.00 12
a. 20pf Prussian blue 135.00 15.00
50 " 25pf orange ('90) 32.50 1.25
a. Imperf. 70.00
51 " 50pf chocolate 16.50 15
a. 50pf copper brown 375.00 10.00
b. Imperf. 100.00
Nos. 45–51 (7) 59.95 2.63

Germania
A11

1900, Jan. 1 *Perf. 14*

52 A11 2pf gray 55 22
a. Imperf. 325.00
53 " 3pf brown 55 17
a. Imperf. 325.00
54 " 5pf green 1.35 12
55 " 10pf carmine 2.50 12
a. Imperf. 80.00
56 " 20pf ultramarine 8.00 17
57 " 25pf orange & black, *yellow* 15.00 2.25
a. "REICHSPOST" larger *1000.00 1000.00*
58 A11 30pf orange & black, *salmon* 27.50 80
a. "REICHSPOST" larger *1000.00 1000.00*
59 A11 40pf lake & black 30.00 1.50
a. "REICHSPOST" larger *1000.00 1000.00*
60 A11 50pf purple & black, *salmon* 30.00 1.10
a. "REICHSPOST" larger *1000.00 1000.00*
61 A11 80pf lake & black, *rose* 45.00 2.50
a. "REICHSPOST" larger *1000.00 1000.00*
Nos. 52–61 (10) 160.45 8.95

Early printings of Nos. 57–61 had "REICHSPOST" in taller and thicker letters than on the ordinary stamps.

General Post Office in Berlin
A12

"Union of North and South Germany"
A13

Unveiling Kaiser Wilhelm I Memorial, Berlin—A14

Wilhelm II Speaking at Empire's 25th Anniversary Celebration
A15

Two types of 5m:

I. "5" is thick; "M" has slight serifs.
II. "5" thinner; "M" has distinct serifs.

Engraved *Perf. 14½x14*

62 A12 1m carmine rose 70.00 1.90
a. Imperf. *500.00*
63 A13 2m gray blue 70.00 5.50
64 A14 3m black violet 85.00 50.00
65 A15 5m slate & car., type I 525.00 500.00
d. Inner frame hand painted 300.00 250.00
65A " 5m slate & car., type II 275.00 250.00

No. 65d is the result of a misaligned vignette. White paint was applied to the inner frame. Sometimes red was also used to retouch the vignette.

Nos. 62–65 exist perf. 11½.

Half of No. 54 Handstamp Surcharged in Violet **3PF**

1901 *Perf. 14*

65B A11 3pf on half of 5pf green *11,000.00 10,000.00*

This provisional was produced at New Orleans when the German cruiser Vineta anchored there. The purser, with the ship commander's approval, surcharged and bisected 300 5pf stamps so the ship's post office could meet the need for a 3pf (printed matter rate). The crew wanted to send home newspapers reporting celebrations of the Kaiser's birthday.

A16

1902 Typographed

65C A16 2pf gray 2.50 45
66 " 3pf brown 1.65 27
a. "DFUTSCHES" 16.50 32.50
67 " 5pf green 3.75 17
68 " 10pf carmine 11.00 17
69 " 20pf ultramarine 40.00 33
70 " 25pf orange & black, *yellow* 65.00 2.50
71 " 30pf orange & black, *salmon* 75.00 90
72 " 40pf lake & black 120.00 1.35
73 " 50pf purple & black, *buff* 120.00 2.25
74 " 80pf lake & black, *rose* 250.00 4.00
Nos. 65C–74 (10) 688.90 12.39

Nos. 65C–74 exist imperf. Set price, $1,300.

See also Nos. 80–91, 118–119, 121–132, 169, 174, 210.

A17

A18

A19

A20

Engraved *Perf. 14½*

75 A17 1m carmine rose 200.00 2.50
  a. Imperf. 650.00
76 A18 2m gray blue 75.00 85.00
77 A19 3m black violet 75.00 27.50
  a. Imperf. 650.00
78 A20 5m slate & car. 165.00 27.50
  a. Imperf. 650.00

See also Nos. 92, 94–95, 102, 111–113.

A21

79 A21 2m gray blue 100.00 5.50
  a. Imperf. 650.00

See also Nos. 93, 114.

Wmk. 125

Wmkd. Lozenges. (125)

1905–19 Typographed *Perf. 14*

80 A16 2pf gray 1.65 3.25
81 " 3pf brown 27 27
82 " 5pf green 15 8
  a. Booklet pane of 6 4.00
  b. Bklt. pane 5 + Label 210.00
  c. Bklt. pane 4 + 2 Labels 125.00
  d. Bklt. pane 2 + 4 Labels 125.00
  e. Bklt. pane 6 (1 No. 82 + 5 No. 83) 37.50
  f. Bklt. pane 6 (2 No. 82 + 4 No. 83) 30.00
  g. Bklt. pane 6 (4 No. 82 + 2 No. 83) 15.00
83 " 10pf carmine 38 12
  a. Booklet pane of 6 7.50
  b. Bklt. pane 5 + Label 450.00
  c. Bklt. pane 4 + 2 Labels 210.00
84 " 20pf blue violet ('18) 27 9
  a. 20pf lt. blue 27.50 2.25
  b. 20pf ultra. 1.65 35
  c. Imperf. 325.00 325.00
  d. Half used as 10pf on cover 110.00
  e. Booklet pane of 6 2.50
85 " 25pf orange & black, *yellow* 45 17
86 " 30pf orange & black, *buff* 27 17
  a. 30pf orange & black, *cream* 6.50 6.50
87 " 40pf lake & black 55 12
88 " 50pf purple & black, *buff* 33 22
89 " 60pf magenta ('11) 1.35 38
  a. 60pf red violet 11.00 1.90
90 " 75pf grn. & black ('19) 9 9
91 " 80pf lake & black, *rose* 65 80

Engraved

92 A17 1m carmine rose 3.25 80
  a. 1m carmine red 75.00 5.50
93 A21 2m bright blue 4.25 3.75
  a. 2m gray blue 75.00 7.50
94 A19 3m violet gray 1.65 3.25
  a. 3m black violet ('11) 65.00 42.50
95 A20 5m slate & carmine 1.65 3.75
  a. Center invtd. 7500.00 7500.00
Nos. 80–95 (16) 17.21 17.31

Prewar printings of Nos. 80–95 have brighter colors and white instead of yellow gum. They sell for considerably more than the wartime printings which are priced here.

A22

1916–19 **Typographed**

96 A22 2pf light gray ('18) 9 75
97 " 2½pf light gray 22 17
  a. Bklt. pane of 6 15.00
98 " 7½pf red orange 17 10
  a. Bklt. pane of 6 6.00
  b. Bklt. pane 6 (4 No. 98 + 2 No. 100) 50.00
  c. Bklt. pane 6 (2 No. 98 + 4 No. 99) 50.00
  d. Bklt. pane 6 (2 No. 98 + 4 No. 100) 50.00
  e. Bklt. pane 6 (2 No. 82 + 4 No. 98) 15.00
  f. 7½pf yel. orange 2.75 10
99 " 15pf yellow brown 1.90 22
  a. Bklt. pane of 6 30.00
100 " 15pf dark violet ('17) 9 9
  a. Booklet pane of 6 5.00
  b. Bklt. pane 6 (4 No. 82 + 2 No. 100) 50.00
  c. Bklt. pane 6 (2 No. 83 + 4 No. 100) 10.00
101 " 35pf red brown ('19) 9 9
Nos. 96–101 (6) 2.56 *1.42*

See also No. 120.

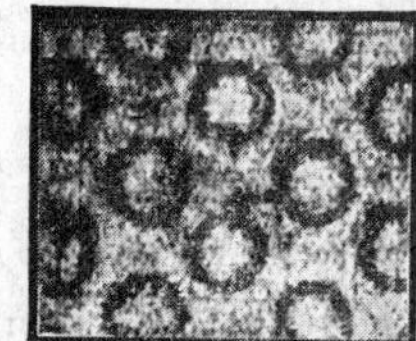

Wmk. 192

Type of 1902.

Wmkd. Circles. (192)

1920 Engraved *Perf. 14½*

102 A19 3m black violet 3500.00 2500.00

Republic

National Assembly Issue.

Live Stump of Tree Symbolizing that Germany will Survive her Difficulties
A23

New Shoots from Oak Stump Symbolical of New Government
A24

Rebuilding Germany
A25

Typographed.

1919–20 *Perf. 13x13½* **Unwmkd.**

105 A23 10pf carmine rose 22 27
106 A24 15pf chocolate & blue 17 27
107 A25 25pf green & red 22 33
108 " 30pf red violet & red ('20) 22 33

Nos. 107–108 exist with date reading "1019" instead of "1919."

Types of 1902

Offset Printing.

Wmkd. Lozenges. (125)

1920 *Perf. 15x14½.*

111 A17 1m red 1.85 55
112 " 1.25m green 1.65 38
113 " 1.50m yellow brown 22 38
114 A21 2.50m lilac rose 17 38
  a. 2.50m magenta 1.90 65
  b. 2.50m brown lilac 80 65

Nos. 111, 112 and 113 differ from the illustration in many minor respects. The numerals of Nos. 75 and 92 are outlined, with shaded background. Those of No. 111 are plain, with solid background and flags have been added to the top of the building, at right and left.

Types of 1902, Engraved, Surcharged

*** 1,25 m. ***

1920 *Perf. 14½.*

115 A17 1.25m on 1m green 45 *2.50*
116 " 1.50m on 1m org. brn. 45 *2.50*
117 A21 2.50m on 2m lilac rose 11.00 *175.00*

Germania Types of 1902–16

1920 Typo. *Perf. 14, 14½*

118 A16 5pf brown 4 17
119 " 10pf orange 5 17
  a. Tête bêche pair 40 *1.75*
  c. Booklet pane of 6 1.00
  d. Bklt. pane 6 (4 No. 119 + 2 No. 123) 2.00
120 A22 15pf violet brown 5 17
  a. Imperf. 125.00
  b. Booklet pane of 6 2.50
  c. Bklt. pane 6 (4 No. 84 + 2 No. 120) 5.50
121 A16 20pf green 5 27
  a. Imperf. 135.00
123 " 30pf dull blue 5 17
  a. Tête bêche pair 40 *1.75*
  c. Booklet pane of 6 1.00
  d. Bklt. pane 6 (2 No. 123 + 4 No. 124) 2.00
124 " 40pf carmine rose 5 17
  a. Tête bêche pair 40 *1.75*
  b. Imperf. 400.00
  c. Booklet pane of 6 1.00
  d. Bklt. pane 6 (2 No. 124 + 4 No. 126) 2.50
125 " 50pf red lilac 70 80
126 " 60pf olive green 9 17
  a. Tête bêche pair 40 *1.75*
  b. Bklt. pane of 6 1.00
  c. Imperf. 400.00
127 " 75pf red violet 9 22
128 " 80pf blue violet 9 22
  a. Imperf. 400.00
129 " 1m violet & green 5 22
  a. Imperf. 175.00
130 " 1¼m vermilion & magenta 5 27
131 " 2m carmine & blue 70 27
132 " 4m black & rose 17 38
Nos. 118–132 (14) 2.23 3.67

Stamps of 1920 Surcharged:

* * * *

1,60 M — *a* 5 Mark — *c*

3 M 3 — *b*

1921, Aug.

133 A16(*a*) 1.60m on 5pf brown 7 20
134 " (*b*) 3m on 1¼m verm. & magenta 7 20
135 A16 (*c*) 5m on 75pf red violet (G) 12 25
136 " (*b*) 10m on 75pf red violet 30 45

In 1920 the current stamps of Bavaria were overprinted "Deutsches Reich". These stamps were available for postage throughout Germany, but because they were used almost exclusively in Bavaria, they are listed among the issues of that state.

Numeral of Value
A26

Iron Workers
A27

Miners
A28

Farmers
A29

Post Horn
A30

Numeral of Value—A31

Plowing—A32

Wmkd. Lozenges. (125)

1921 Typographed *Perf. 14*

137 A26 5pf claret 5 15
138 " 10pf olive green 4 15
  a. Tête bêche pair 75 *5.50*
  b. Bklt. pane 6 (5 No. 138 + 1 No. 141) 3.50
139 " 15pf greenish blue 4 15
140 " 25pf dark brown 8 15
141 " 30pf blue green 6 15
  a. Tête bêche pair 75 *9.00*
  b. Bklt. pane 6 (2 No. 124 + 4 No. 141) 2.50
142 " 40pf red orange 6 15
143 " 50pf violet 40 75
144 A27 60pf red violet 6 20
145 " 80pf carmine rose 5 40
146 A28 100pf yellow green 38 *75*
147 " 120pf ultramarine 10 25
148 A29 150pf orange 25 *75*
149 " 160pf slate green 6 *75*
150 A30 2m dp. violet & rose 20 *75*
151 " 3m red & yellow 25 *3.50*
152 " 4m deep green & yellow green 10 *50*

Engraved.

153 A31 5m brown orange 25 *60*
154 " 10m carmine rose 50 *1.00*
155 A32 20m indigo & green 1.10 1.00
  a. Green background inverted 150.00 *350.00*
Nos. 137–155 (19) 4.03 12.10

1922 Lithographed. *Perf. 14½x14.*

156 A31 100m brown vio., *buff* 27 38
157 " 200m rose, *buff* 14 38
158 " 300m green, *buff* 14 20
159 " 400m bis. brn., *buff* 38 75
160 " 500m orange, *buff* 9 35
Nos. 156-160 (5) 1.02 2.06

Postally Used vs. CTO

Prices quoted for canceled copies of the 1921-1923 issues are for postally used stamps. These bring higher prices than the plentiful canceled-to-order specimens made by applying genuine handstamps to remainders. C.T.O. examples sell for about the same price as unused stamps. Certification of postal usage by competent authorities is necessary.

Wmk. 126

Wmkd. Network. (126)

1921-22 Typographed *Perf. 14, 14½*

161 A26 5pf claret 55 165.00
162 " 10pf olive green 1.65 120.00
163 " 15pf greenish blue 40 135.00
164 " 25pf dark brown 13 1.50
165 " 30pf blue green 70 175.00
166 " 40pf red orange 10 2.50
167 " 50pf violet ('21) 5 20
168 A27 60pf red violet 7 9.00
169 A16 75pf red violet 18 65
170 A26 75pf dp. ultramarine 7 75
171 A27 80pf carmine rose 32 50.00
172 A28 100pf yellow green 5 20
a. Imperf. 110.00
173 " 120pf ultramarine 70 50.00
174 A16 1¼m vermilion & magenta 18 30
175 A29 150pf orange 5 20
a. Imperf. 12.50
176 " 160pf slate green 80 115.00
177 A30 2m violet & rose 12 25
178 " 3m red & yel. ('21) 27 25
a. Imperf. 30.00
179 " 4m deep green & yellow green 9 30
180 " 5m orange & yel. 27 30
a. Imperf. 275.00
181 " 10m car. & pale rose 70 60
a. Pale rose (background) omitted 37.50 225.00
182 A30 20m violet & org. 15 75
a. Imperf. 275.00
183 " 30m brown & yel. 8 20
184 " 50m dk. green & violet 5 20
Nos. 161-184 (24) 7.73

1922-23

SIX MARKS:
Type I. Numerals upright.
Type II. Numerals leaning toward the right and slightly thinner.

EIGHT MARKS:
Type I. Numerals 2½mm. wide with thick strokes.
Type II. Numerals 2 mm. wide with thinner strokes.

185 A30 2m deep violet 5 20
a. Imperf. 200.00
186 " 3m red 5 20
187 " 4m dark green 5 20
a. Imperf. 3.50
188 " 5m orange 5 20
a. Imperf. 200.00
189 " 6m dark blue (II) 5 20
a. 6m dk. blue (I) 15 50
b. Imperf. 200.00
190 " 8m olive green (I) 5 20
a. 8m olive grn. (II) 35 12.50
191 " 20m dark violet ('23) 7 20
192 " 30m deep brown ('23) 25 3.50
193 " 40m light green 5 30

Engraved.

194 A31 5m brown orange 25 30
a. Imperf. 275.00
195 " 10m carmine rose 70 75
196 A32 20m indigo & green 15 75
a. Imperf. 275.00
b. Green background inverted 17.50 25.00
Nos. 185-196 (12) 1.77 7.00

1922-23 Litho. *Perf. 14½x14*

198 A31 50m indigo 22 38
199 " 100m brown violet, *buff* ('23) 30 55
200 " 200m rose, *buff* ('23) 7 17
201 " 300m green, *buff* ('23) 5 15
202 " 400m bistre brown, *buff* ('23) 5 25
203 " 500m orange, *buff* ('23) 6 15
204 " 1000m gray ('23) 7 17
205 " 2000m blue ('23) 12 27
206 " 3000m brown ('23) 12 27
207 " 4000m violet ('23) 13 27
a. Imperf. 30.00
208 " 5000m gray green ('23) 25 50
a. Imperf. 40.00
209 " 100,000m verm. ('23) 18 38
a. Imperf. 100.00
Nos. 198-209 (12) 1.62 3.51

Wmk. 127

Typographed.

1920-22 Wmkd. Quatrefoils. (127)

210 A16 1¼m vermilion & magenta 600.00 450.00
211 A30 50m grn. & vio. ('22) 1.20 325.00

Wmk. 127 was intended for use only in printing revenue stamps.

Arms of Munich
A33

Wmkd. Network. (126)

1922, Apr. 22 Typo. *Perf. 13x13½.*

212 A33 1¼m claret 27 45
213 " 2m dark violet 27 33
214 " 3m vermilion 40 55
215 " 4m deep blue 33 55

Wmkd. Lozenges. (125)

216 A33 10m brown, *buff* 65 1.35
217 " 20m dp. rose, *pink* 2.75 5.00
Nos. 212-217 (6) 4.67 8.23

Munich Industrial Fair.

Miners A34 — Numeral of Value A35

Wmkd. Network. (126)

1922-23 Typographed *Perf. 14*

221 A34 5m orange 10 5.00
222 A29 10m dull blue ('22) 6 20
223 " 12m vermilion ('22) 6 25
224 A34 20m red lilac 6 20
225 A29 25m olive brown 6 20
226 A34 30m olive green 6 20
227 A29 40m green 6 20
228 A34 50m greenish blue 27 60.00
229 A35 100m violet 7 20
230 " 200m carmine rose 6 25
231 " 300m green 6 20
232 " 400m dark brown 6 2.00
233 " 500m red orange 6 85
234 " 1000m slate 5 25
Nos. 221-234 (14) 1.09

The 50m was issued only in vertical coils. Nos. 222-223 exist imperf.

Wartburg Castle A36 — Cathedral of Cologne A37

1923 Engraved.

237 A36 5000m deep blue 27 75
a. Imperf. 400.00
238 A37 10,000m olive green 27 1.00

Abbreviations:

Th = (Tausend) Thousand
Mil = (Million) Million
Mlrd = (Milliarde) Billion

A38

1923 Typographed

238A A38 5th m greenish blue 7 11.00
b. Imperf. 200.00
239 " 50th m bistre 6 12
a. Imperf. 20.00
240 " 75th m dark violet 6 3.00

Stamps and Types of 1922-23 Surcharged in Black, Blue or Green with Bars over Original Value

8
Tausend

Wmkd. Lozenges. (125)

1923 *Perf. 14*

241 A26 8th m on 30pf blue green 5 25
a. "8" inverted 45.00 225.00

Wmkd. Network. (126)

242 A26 5th m on 40pf red orange 5 60
242A " 8th m on 30pf bl. green 30.00 2400.00
243 A29 15th m on 40m grn. 5 25
244 " 20th m on 12m vermilion 5 25
a. Inverted surcharge
245 " 20th m on 25m olive brown 7 75
246 A35 20th m on 200m carmine rose 5 25
a. Inverted surcharge 125.00 185.00
247 A29 25th m on 25m olive brown 5 4.00
248 " 30th m on 10m deep blue 5 25
a. Inverted surcharge 225.00
249 A35 30th m on 200m pale blue (Bl) 5 25
a. Without surcharge 300.00
250 " 75th m on 300m yellow green 8 6.00
a. Imperf. 25.00 25.00
251 " 75th m on 400m yellow green 5 25
252 " 75th m on 1000m yellow green 5 25
a. Without surcharge 300.00
253 " 100th m on 100m violet 5 75
a. Double surcharge 35.00
b. Inverted surcharge 30.00
254 " 100th m on 400m bluish green (G) 5 25
a. Imperf. 100.00
b. Without surcharge 300.00
255 " 125th m on 1000m salmon 5 15
256 " 250th m on 200m carmine rose 10 2.00
a. Inverted surcharge 42.50
b. Double surcharge 100.00
257 " 250th m on 300m deep green 13 5.00
a. Inverted surcharge 42.50
258 " 250th m on 400m dark brown 12 5.00
a. Inverted surcharge 50.00
259 " 250th m on 500m pink 5 25
a. Imperf. 100.00
260 " 250th m on 500m red orange 12 6.00
a. Double surcharge 35.00
b. Inverted surcharge 75.00
261 A26 800th m on 5pf lt. grn. (G) 8 1.50
a. Imperf. 25.00
262 " 800th m on 10pf light green (G) 8 1.50
263 A35 800th m on 200m carmine rose 8 22.50
a. Double surcharge 150.00
b. Inverted surcharge 75.00
264 " 800th m on 300m lt. grn. (G) 8 1.00
a. Black surcharge 40.00
265 " 800th m on 400m dark brown 8 8.00
a. Inverted surcharge 125.00
b. Double surcharge 100.00
c. "800" only
266 " 800th m on 400m light green (G) 8 1.00
267 " 800th m on 500m light green (G) 10 700.00
a. 800th m on 500m red orange (Bk) 40.00
268 " 800th m on 1000m lt. grn. (G) 8 15
269 " 2 mil m on 200m rose red 5 15
b. 2 mil m on 200m car. rose (# 230) 125.00
270 " 2 mil m on 300m deep green 5 60
a. Inverted surcharge 110.00
b. Double surcharge 125.00
271 " 2 mil m on 500m dull rose 5 2.50
272 A38 2 mil m on 5th m dull rose 5 25
b. Imperf. 50.00

Nos. 264a and 267a were not put in use.

Serrate Roulette 13½.

273 A26 400th m on 15pf bistre (Br) 10 *1.50*
a. Imperf. 100.00
274 " 400th m on 25pf bistre (Br) 10 *1.50*
a. Imperf. *400.00*
275 " 400th m on 30pf bistre (Br) 10 *1.50*
a. Imperf. 100.00
276 " 400th m on 40pf bistre (Br) 10 *1.50*
a. Imperf. 75.00
277 A35 2 mil m on 200m rose red 10 *65.00*
278 A38 2 mil m on 5th m dull rose 10 *4.00*
Nos. 273–278 (6) 60

Nos. 273–276 and 278 exist without surcharge. Price, $225–275 each.

Numeral of Value
A39 A39a

The stamps of types A39 and A39a usually have the value darker than the rest of the design.

1923 ***Perf. 14*** **Wmk. 126**

280 A39 500th m brown 7 *1.25*
281 " 1 mil m greenish blue 7 *25*
a. Imperf. 110.00
282 " 2 mil m dull violet 7 *15.00*
284 " 4 mil m yellow green 7 *25*
a. Value double 200.00
b. Imperf. 110.00
285 " 5 mil m rose 7 *25*
286 " 10 mil m red 7 *25*
a. Value doubley 50.00 *200.00*
287 " 20 mil m ultramarine 7 *35*
288 " 30 mil m red brown 7 *5.00*
289 " 50 mil m dull green 7 *25*
a. Imperf. 110.00
b. Value inverted 50.00
290 " 100 mil m gray 7 *25*
291 " 200 mil m bistre brown 7 *25*
a. Imperf. 20.00
293 " 500 mil m olive green 7 *25*
294 A39a 1 mlrd m chocolate 7 *25*
295 " 2 mlrd m pale brown & green 12 *35*
296 " 5 mlrd m yel. & brown 12 *35*
297 " 10 mlrd m apple green & green 12 *35*
a. Imperf. 30.00
298 " 20 mlrd m bluish green & brown 15 *50*
299 " 50 mlrd m blue & deep blue 55 *22.50*
Nos. 280–299 (18) 1.97

The variety "value omitted" exists on Nos. 280–281, 284–287, 290–291, 293–294, 296, 298–299 and 307. Prices $90–$175.

Serrate Roulette 13½

301 A39 10 mil m red 15 *45.00*
302 " 20 mil m ultramarine 15 *150.00*
303 " 50 mil m dull green 15 *3.50*
304 " 200 mil m bistre brown 15 *4.00*
305 A39a 1 mlrd m chocolate 15 *3.50*
306 " 2 mlrd m pale brown & green 15 *2.50*
307 " 5 mlrd m yel. & brn. 15 *1.50*
308 " 20 mlrd m bluish green & brown 45 *8.00*
309 " 50 mlrd m blue & deep blue 1.35 *375.00*
Nos. 301–309 (9) 2.85

Stamps and Types of 1923 Surcharged with New Values.

1923 ***Perf. 14***

310 A35 1 mlrd m on 100m vio. 12 *12.50*
a. Inverted surcharge 75.00
b. 1 mlrd m on 100m deep reddish purple 90.00 *1750.00*
311 A39 5 mlrd m on 2 mil m dull violet 33 *125.00*
a. Inverted surcharge 60.00
b. Dbl. surch. 135.00
312 A39 5 mlrd m on 4 mil m yellow green 22 *20.00*
a. Inverted surcharge 50.00
b. Dbl. surch. 110.00
313 " 5mlrd m on 10 mil m red 22 *1.50*
a. Inverted surcharge 50.00
b. Double surcharge 60.00
314 " 10 mlrd m on 20 mil m ultramarine 33 *1.50*
a. Double surcharge 135.00
b. Inverted surcharge 80.00
315 " 10 mlrd m on 50 mil m dull green 18 *1.50*
a. Inverted surcharge 50.00
b. Double surcharge 110.00
316 " 10 mlrd m on 100 mil m gray 18 *5.00*
a. Inverted surcharge 60.00
b. Double surcharge 135.00
Nos. 310–316 (7) 1.58

No. 310b was issued in Bavaria only and is known as the Hitler provisional. Excellent forgeries exist.

Serrate Roulette 13½

319 A39 5 mlrd m on 10 mil m red 1.10 *175.00*
a. Inverted surcharge 50.00
b. Dbl. surch. 50.00
320 " 10 mlrd m on 20 mil m ultramarine 1.35 *110.00*
321 " 10 mlrd m on 50 mil m dull green 80 *17.50*
a. Inverted surcharge 50.00

A40

1923 ***Perf. 14***

323 A40 3(pf) brown 55 22
a. Imperf. 200.00 150.00
b. Value omitted 200.00
324 " 5(pf) dark green 55 22
a. Imperf. 75.00 50.00
b. Value omitted 200.00
325 " 10(pf) carmine 55 10
a. Imperf. 200.00 150.00
b. Value omitted 200.00
326 " 20(pf) deep ultra. 1.35 22
a. Imperf. 200.00 150.00
b. Value omitted 200.00
327 " 50(pf) orange 2.00 55
a. Imperf. 250.00 175.00
b. Value omitted 200.00
328 " 100(pf) brown violet 7.00 65
a. Imperf. 250.00
b. Value omitted 275.00
Nos. 323–328 (6) 12.00 1.96

German Eagle
A41

1924 **Wmk. 126**

330 A41 3(pf) light brown 30 5
a. Imperf. 225.00 225.00
331 " 5(pf) light green 40 5
a. Imperf. 225.00 225.00
b. Booklet pane of 10 50.00
332 " 10pf vermilion 55 5
a. Imperf. 350.00
b. Booklet pane of 10 125.00
333 " 20pf dull blue 2.00 22
a. Imperf. 350.00
334 " 30pf rose lilac 3.00 33
a. Imperf. 350.00
335 " 40pf olive green 13.50 65
a. Imperf. 325.00
336 " 50pf orange 13.50 1.35
Nos. 330–336 (7) 33.25 2.70

The values above 5pf have "Pf" in the upper right corner.

Rheinstein Castle—A43

View of Cologne—A44

Marienburg Castle—A45

1924 **Engraved** **Wmk. 126**

337 A43 1m green 16.50 3.00
338 A44 2m blue 25.00 3.00
339 A45 3m claret 27.50 5.50

See No. 387.

Dr. Heinrich von Stephan
A46 A47

1924–28 **Typographed**

340 A46 10pf dark green 80 12
341 " 20pf dark blue 1.65 40
342 A47 60(pf) red brown 8.00 33
a. Chalky paper ('28) 32.50 4.75
343 A47 80(pf) slate 13.00 1.90

Universal Postal Union, 50th anniversary. No. 340 exists imperf. Price $300.

Traffic Wheel
A48

German Eagle Watching Rhine Valley
A49

1925, May 30 ***Perf. 13½x13***

345 A48 5(pf) deep green 3.25 3.75
346 " 10(pf) vermilion 4.25 6.50

German Traffic Exhibition, Munich, May 30–Oct. 11, 1925.

1925 ***Perf. 14***

347 A49 5(pf) green 65 25
a. Booklet pane of 10 50.00
348 " 10(pf) vermilion 1.25 25
a. Booklet pane of 10 125.00
349 " 20(pf) deep blue 5.50 1.00

Issued to commemorate 1000 years' union of the Rhineland with Germany.

Speyer Cathedral
A50

Johann Wolfgang von Goethe
A51

1925, Sept. 11 **Engraved**

350 A50 5m dull green 35.00 12.50

1926–27 **Typographed** ***Perf. 14***

Designs: 3pf, 25pf, Goethe. 5pf, Friedrich von Schiller. 8pf, 20pf, Ludwig van Beethoven. 10pf, Frederick the Great. 15pf, Immanuel Kant. 30pf, Gotthold Ephraim Lessing. 40pf, Gottfried Wilhelm Leibnitz. 50pf, Johann Sebastian Bach. 80pf, Albrecht Durer.

351 A51 3(pf) olive brown 55 15
352 " 3(pf) bistre ('27) 1.20 15
353 " 5(pf) dark green 1.20 12
a. Booklet pane of 10 110.00
b. 5 (pf) light green ('27) 1.35 12
354 " 8(pf) blue grn. ('27) 1.35 12
a. Booklet pane of 10 100.00
355 " 10(pf) carmine 1.20 12
a. Booklet pane of 10 110.00
356 " 15(pf) vermilion 2.50 12
a. Booklet pane of 8 + 2 Labels 125.00
357 " 20(pf) myrtle grn. 11.00 75
358 " 25(pf) blue 3.25 40
359 " 30(pf) olive green 6.00 20
360 " 40(pf) deep violet 10.00 40
361 " 50(pf) brown 11.00 3.75
362 " 80(pf) chocolate 32.50 3.75
Nos. 351–362 (12) 81.75 10.03

Nos. 351–354, 356 and 357 exist imperf. Price each $175.

I.A.A.

Nos. 354, 356 and 358 Overprinted

10.-15.10.1927

1927, Oct. 10

363 A51 8(pf) blue green 27.50 30.00
364 " 15(pf) vermilion 27.50 30.00
365 " 25(pf) blue 27.50 32.50

The letters "I.A.A." are the initials of "Internationales Arbeitsamt", i.e. International Labor Bureau, an agency of the League of Nations. The stamps were issued in connection with a meeting of this Bureau in Berlin, Oct. 10–15, 1927. They were also on sale to the public.

President Friedrich Ebert
A60

President Paul von Hindenburg
A61

1928–32 **Typo.** ***Perf. 14***

366 A60 3(pf) bistre 22 15
367 A61 4(pf) light blue ('31) 45 10
a. Tête bêche pair 2.25 2.25
b. Bklt. pane 9 + Label 17.50
368 " 5(pf) light green 38 15
a. Tête bêche pair 3.50 3.50
b. Imperf. 300.00
c. Bklt. pane 6 + 4 Labels 17.50
d. Bklt. pane 10 (4 No. 368 + 6 No. 369) 17.50
369 A60 6(pf) light olive green ('32) 55 10
a. Bklt. pane 10 (2 No. 369 + 8 No. 373) 17.50
370 " 8(pf) dark green 22 15
a. Tête bêche pair 4.00 4.00
b. Booklet pane of 10 17.50
371 " 10(pf) vermilion 1.50 75
372 " 10(pf) red vio. ('30) 1.25 20
373 A61 12(pf) orange ('32) 80 10
a. Tête bêche pair 4.00 4.00
374 " 15(pf) carmine rose 45 15
a. Tête bêche pair 5.50 5.50
b. Bklt. pane 6 + 4 Labels 17.50

375 A60 20(pf) Prus. green 6.50 1.75
a. Imperf. 400.00
376 " 20(pf) gray ('30) 6.00 20
377 A61 25(pf) blue 3.00 35
378 A60 30(pf) olive green 3.25 35
379 A61 40(pf) violet 8.00 45
380 A60 45(pf) orange 6.50 1.00
381 A61 50(pf) brown 6.50 1.00
382 A60 60(pf) orange brn. 12.00 1.50
383 A61 80(pf) chocolate 18.00 4.00
384 " 80(pf) yel. bis. ('30) 6.50 90
Nos. 366-384 (19) 82.07 13.35

Stamps of 1928 Overprinted **30. JUNI 1930**

1930, June 30

385 A60 8(pf) dark green 1.10 12
386 A61 15(pf) carmine rose 1.10 15

Issued in commemoration of the final evacuation of the Rhineland by the Allied forces.

View of Cologne
A63

1930 Engraved Wmk. 126

Inscribed: "Reichsmark".

387 A63 2m dark blue 42.50 17.50

President von Hindenburg
A64

Frederick the Great
A65

Wmkd. Network. (126)

1932, Oct. 1 Typo. *Perf. 14*

391 A64 4(pf) blue 70 25
392 " 5(pf) bright green 70 15
393 " 12(pf) deep orange 7.00 12
394 " 15(pf) dark red 4.00 10.00
395 " 25(pf) ultramarine 1.65 45
396 " 40(pf) violet 16.50 1.00
397 " 50(pf) dark brown 7.00 12.50
Nos. 391-397 (7) 37.55 24.47

Commemorative of the 85th birthday of President von Hindenburg.

1933, Apr. 12 Photogravure.

398 A65 6(pf) dark green 55 75
a. Tête bêche pair 4.00 4.00
b. Booklet pane of 6 10.00
399 " 12(pf) carmine 55 75
a. Tête bêche pair 4.00 4.00
b. Bklt. pane 5 + label 15.00
400 " 25(pf) ultramarine 30.00 22.50

Issued in conjunction with the celebration of Potsdam Day.

Hindenburg Type of 1932.

1933 Typographed

401 A64 3(pf) olive bistre 11.00 60
402 " 4(pf) dull blue 2.50 60
403 " 6(pf) dark green 1.40 25
a. Bklt. pane of 8 55.00
404 " 8(pf) deep orange 4.75 60
a. Bklt. pane 8 (3 No. 404 + 5 No. 406) 75.00
b. Open D 13.50 1.65
405 " 10(pf) chocolate 2.50 60
406 " 12(pf) deep carmine 1.40 25
a. Bklt. pane 8 (4 No. 392 + 4 No. 406) 45.00
407 " 15(pf) maroon 3.50 12.50
408 " 20(pf) bright blue 3.50 75
409 " 30(pf) olive green 5.50 60
410 " 40(pf) red violet 11.00 1.50
411 " 50(pf) dark green & black 11.00 2.50
412 " 60(pf) claret & blk. 16.50 75
413 " 80(pf) dark blue & black 11.00 1.25
414 A64 100(pf) org. & blk. 16.50 10.00
Nos. 401-414 (14) 102.05 32.75

Wmk. 237

Hindenburg Type of 1932.

Wmkd. Swastikas. (237)

1933-36 *Perf. 14*

415 A64 1(pf) black 8 5
a. Bklt. pane 7 (4 No. 415 + 3 No. 417 + Label) 5.00
b. Bklt. pane 8 (3 No. 415 + 3 No. 416 + 2 No. 418) 6.00
c. Bklt. pane 7 (2 No. 415 + 5 No. 420 + Label) 6.00
d. Bklt. pane 8 (4 No. 415 + 4 No. 422) 2.00
416 " 3(pf) olive bistre ('34) 8 5
a. Bklt. pane 8 (4 No. 416 + 4 No. 418) 2.50
b. Bklt. pane 8 (4 No. 416 + 4 No. 419) 2.00
c. Bklt. pane 7 (6 No. 416 + 1 No. 422 + Label) 2.25
417 " 4(pf) dull blue ('34) 8 5
a. Bklt. pane 7 (3 No. 417 + 4 No. 422 + Label) 5.50
418 " 5(pf) bright green ('34) 8 5
a. Bklt. pane 7 (2 No. 418 + 5 No. 419 + Label) 5.50
b. Bklt. pane 8 (2 No. 418 + 3 No. 419 + 3 No. 420) 3.50
c. Bklt. pane 8 (4 No. 418 + 4 No. 420) 5.00
419 " 6(pf) dark green ('34) 8 5
a. Bklt. pane of 8 4.50
b. Bklt. pane 7 + Label 6.00
c. Bklt. pane 7 (1 No. 419 + 6 No. 422 + Label) 15.00
420 " 8(pf) deep orange ('34) 8 5
a. Bklt. pane 7 (3 No. 420 + 4 No. 422 + Label) 5.50
b. Open D 7.50 2.50
421 " 10(pf) chocolate ('34) 8 5
422 " 12(pf) deep carmine ('34) 10 5
a. Bklt. pane 7 +Label 6.00
423 " 15(pf) maroon ('34) 33 5
424 " 20(pf) bright blue ('34) 38 5
425 " 25(pf) ultramarine ('34) 50 5
426 " 30(pf) olive green ('34) 75 5
427 " 40(pf) red violet ('34) 75 5
428 " 50(pf) dark green & black ('34) 1.20 30
429 " 60(pf) claret & black ('34) 1.10 30
430 " 80(pf) dark blue & black ('36) 2.75 60
431 " 100(pf) orange & black ('34) 5.50 60
Nos. 415-431 (17) 13.92 2.45

Franz Adolf E. Lüderitz
A66

Swastika Sun and Nuremberg Castle
A70

Designs: 6pf, Dr. Gustav Nachtigal. 12pf, Karl Peters. 25pf, Hermann von Wissmann.

1934, June 30 *Perf. 13x13½*

432 A66 3(pf) brn. & choc. 3.25 3.75
433 " 6(pf) dark green & chocolate 1.40 1.40
434 " 12(pf) dark carmine & chocolate 1.65 55
435 " 25(pf) bright blue & chocolate 11.00 16.50

Issued in remembrance of the lost colonies of Germany.

Hindenburg Memorial Issue.

Type of 1932.

With Black Border.

1934, Sept. 4 *Perf. 14*

436 A64 3(pf) olive bistre 60 35
437 " 5(pf) bright green 70 50
438 " 6(pf) dark green 1.00 25
439 " 8(pf) vermilion 2.25 35
440 " 12(pf) deep carmine 2.40 25
441 " 25(pf) ultramarine 7.00 6.00
Nos. 436-441 (6) 13.95 7.70

1934, Sept. 1 Photogravure

442 A70 6(pf) dark green 2.50 20
443 " 12(pf) dark carmine 4.50 20

Nazi Congress at Nuremberg.
Imperfs exist. Price, each $400.

Allegory, "Saar Belongs to Germany"
A71

German Eagle
A72

1934, Aug. 26 Typo. Wmk. 237

444 A71 6(pf) dark green 2.50 20
445 A72 12(pf) dark carmine 4.50 20

Issued to mark the Saar Plebiscite.

Friedrich von Schiller
A73

Germania Welcoming Home the Saar
A74

1934, Nov. 5

446 A73 6(pf) green 2.50 20
447 " 12(pf) carmine 4.50 20

175th anniversary of the birth of Friedrich von Schiller.

1935, Jan. 16 Photogravure

448 A74 3(pf) brown 70 80
449 " 6(pf) dark green 1.25 25
450 " 12(pf) lake 1.75 25
451 " 25(pf) dark blue 16.00 6.50

Return of the Saar to Germany.

German Soldier
A75

Wreath and Swastika
A76

1935, Mar. 15

452 A75 6(pf) dark green 1.40 1.10
453 " 12(pf) copper red 1.25 1.10

Issued to commemorate War Heroes' Day.

1935, Apr. 26 Unwmkd.

454 A76 6(pf) dark green 1.40 70
455 " 12(pf) crimson 1.30 70

Issued in connection with the Young Workers' Professional Competitions.

Heinrich Schütz
A77

"The Eagle"
A80

Designs: 12pf, J. S. Bach. 25pf, G. F. Handel.

Wmkd. Swastikas. (237)

1935, June 21 Engr. *Perf. 14*

456 A77 6(pf) dark green 60 35
457 " 12(pf) copper red 95 35
458 " 25(pf) ultramarine 1.20 65

Schutz-Bach-Handel celebration.

1935, July 10 *Perf. 14*

Designs: 12pf, Modern express train. 25pf, "The Flying Hamburger." 40pf, Streamlined locomotive.

459 A80 6(pf) dark green 1.30 55
460 " 12(pf) copper red 1.30 55
461 " 25(pf) ultramarine 8.75 2.25
462 " 40(pf) red violet 11.50 2.25

Centenary of railroad in Germany.
Nos. 459-462 exist imperf. Price, $225 each.

Bugler of Hitler Youth Movement
A84

Eagle and Swastika over Nuremberg
A85

1935, July 25 Photogravure

463 A84 6(pf) deep green 1.90 2.75
464 " 15(pf) brown lake 1.90 2.75

Hitler Youth Meeting.

1935, Aug. 30 Engraved

465 A85 6(pf) gray green 1.15 20
466 " 12(pf) dark carmine 1.65 20

1935 Nazi Congress at Nuremberg.

Nazi Flag Bearer and Feldherrnhalle at Munich
A86

Airplane
A87

1935, Nov. 5 Photo. *Perf. 13½*

467 A86 3(pf) brown 40 25
468 " 12(pf) dark carmine 70 25

Issued to commemorate the 12th anniversary of the first Hitler "Putsch" at Munich, November 9, 1923.

1936, Jan. 6

469 A87 40(pf) sapphire 7.00 1.50

Issued in commemoration of the 10th anniversary of the Lufthansa air service.

Gottlieb Daimler A88 — Carl Benz A89

1936, Feb. 15 *Perf. 14*

470 A88 6(pf) dark green 40 20
471 A89 12(pf) copper red 65 20

The 50th anniversary of the automobile; International Automobile and Motorcycle Show, Berlin.

Otto von Guericke A90 — Symbolical of Municipalities A91

1936, May 4

472 A90 6(pf) dark green 25 20

Issued in commemoration of the 250th anniversary of the death of the German inventor, Otto von Guericke, May 11, 1686.

1936, June 3

473 A91 3(pf) dark brown 20 20
474 " 5(pf) deep green 25 20
475 " 12(pf) lake 50 20
476 " 25(pf) dark ultra. 1.15 80

Sixth International Congress of Municipalities, June 7–13.

Allegory of Recreation Congress A92 — Salute to Swastika A93

1936, June 30

477 A92 6(pf) dark green 50 35
478 " 15(pf) deep claret 80 55

Issued in commemoration of a World Congress for Vacation and Recreation held at Hamburg.

1936, Sept. 3 *Perf. 14*

479 A93 6(pf) deep green 50 22
480 " 12(pf) copper red 90 25

The 1936 Nazi Congress.

Shield Bearer A94 — German and Austrian Carrying Nazi Flag A95

1937, Mar. 3 Engraved. Unwmkd.

481 A94 3(pf) brown 17 20
482 " 6(pf) green 30 16
483 " 12(pf) carmine 60 35

The Reich's Air Protection League.

Wmkd. Swastikas. (237)

1938, Apr. 8 Photo. *Perf. 14x13½*

Size: 23x28 mm.

484 A95 6pf dark green 20 30

Perf. 12½

Unwmkd.

Size: 21½x26 mm.

485 A95 6pf deep green 22 35

Union of Austria and Germany.

Cathedral Island A96 — Hermann Goering Stadium A97

Town Hall, Breslau A98 — Centennial Hall, Breslau A99

1938, June 21 Engraved *Perf. 14*

486 A96 3(pf) dark brown 20 12
487 A97 6(pf) deep green 45 12
488 A98 12(pf) copper red 50 12
489 A99 15(pf) violet brown 1.10 70

Issued to publicize the 16th German Gymnastic and Sports Festival held at Breslau, July 23–31, 1938.

Nazi Emblem A100

1939, Apr. 4 Photo. Wmk. 237

490 A100 6(pf) dark green 1.75 2.75
491 " 12(pf) dp. carmine 1.75 2.75

Young Workers' Professional Competitions.

St. Mary's Church A101 — The Krantor, Danzig A102

1939, Sept. 18

492 A101 6(pf) dark green 20 32
493 A102 12(pf) orange red 30 50

Unification of Danzig with the Reich.

Johannes Gutenberg and Library at Leipzig A103

Designs: 6pf, "High House," Leipzig. 12pf, Old Town Hall, Leipzig. 25pf, View of Leipzig Fair.

Inscribed "Leipziger Messe."

Perf. 10½

1940, Mar. 3 Photo. Unwmkd.

494 A103 3(pf) dark brown 17 25
495 " 6(pf) dark gray green 25 25
496 " 12(pf) henna brown 20 15
497 " 25(pf) ultramarine 38 70

Issued in commemoration of the Leipzig Fair.

House of Nations, Leipzig—A107

Designs: 6pf, Concert Hall, Leipzig. 12pf, Leipzig Fair Office. 25pf, Railroad Terminal, Leipzig.

Inscribed:
"Reichsmesse Leipzig, 1941."

1941, Mar. 1 *Perf. 14x13½*

498 A107 3(pf) brown 25 40
499 " 6(pf) green 25 40
500 " 12(pf) dark red 40 60
501 " 25(pf) bright blue 70 1.00

Issued in commemoration of the Leipzig Fair.

Fashion Allegory A111 — Vienna Fair Hall A112

"Burgtheater" A113 — Monument to Prince Eugene A114

1941, Mar. 8 *Perf. 13½x14*

502 A111 3(pf) dark red brown 20 27
503 A112 6(pf) bright blue green 20 27
504 A113 12(pf) scarlet 35 50
505 A114 25(pf) bright blue 85 1.20

Vienna Fair.

Adolf Hitler
A115 A116

1941–43 Typographed *Perf. 14*

Size: 18½x22½ mm.

506 A115 1(pf) gray black 5 5
  a. Bklt. pane 8 (4 No. 506+4 No. 509) 1.00
507 " 3(pf) light brown 5 5
  a. Bklt. pane 8 (6 No. 507+2 No. 510) 1.00
508 " 4(pf) slate 5 5
  a. Bklt. pane 6 (4 No. 508+2 No. 511)+2 labels 2.00
509 A115 5(pf) deep yellow green 5 5
510 " 6(pf) purple 5 5
  a. Bklt. pane 7+ label 6.00
511 " 8(pf) red 5 5
511A " 10(pf) dk. brn. ('43) 6 22
511B " 12(pf) carmine ('43) 6 12

Engraved.

512 A115 10(pf) dark brown 35 12
513 " 12(pf) bright carmine 28 5
  a. Bklt. pane 6 + 2 labels 3.75
514 " 15(pf) brown lake 5 5
515 " 16(pf) peacock green 12 *50*
516 " 20(pf) blue 5 5
517 " 24(pf) orange brown 8 15

Size: 21½x26 mm.

518 A115 25(pf) bright ultra. 5 5
519 " 30(pf) olive green 5 5
520 " 40(pf) brt. red violet 5 5
521 " 50(pf) myrtle green 7 5
522 " 60(pf) dark red brown 7 5
523 " 80(pf) indigo 8 5

1942–44 Engraved *Perf. 14*

524 A116 1m dk. slate green ('44) 17 6
  a. Perf. 12½ 1.60 6
525 " 2m violet ('44) 35 40
  a. Perf. 12½ 70 1.10
526 " 3m copper red ('44) 90 1.10
  a. Perf. 12½ 70 1.10
527 " 5m dk. blue ('44) 3.25 5.50
  a. Perf. 12½ 2.25 4.50

Nos. 506–527 (24) 6.39 8.92

Nos. 507, 510, 511, 511A, 511B, 520, 524–526 exist imperf.

Storm Trooper Emblem A117 — Adolf Hitler A118

1942, Aug. 8 Photo. *Perf. 14*

528 A117 6(pf) purple 8 18

War Effort Day of the Storm Troopers.

1944 Engraved

529 A118 42(pf) bright green 6 *50*

Exists imperf. Price $140.

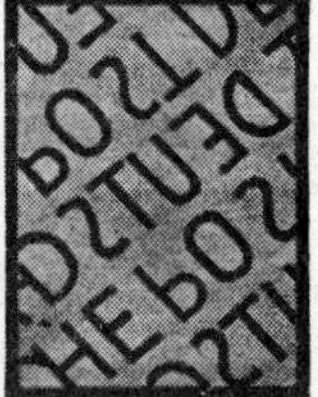

Numeral A119 — Wmk. 284

Wmkd. "DEUTSCHE POST" Multiple. (284)

1946 Typographed. *Perf. 14*

Size: 18x22mm.

530 A119 1pf black 5 10
531 " 2pf black 5 5
532 " 3pf yellow brown 5 15
533 " 4pf slate 5 20
534 " 5pf yellow green 5 5
535 " 6pf purple 5 5
536 " 8pf deep vermilion 5 5
537 " 10pf chocolate 5 5
538 " 12pf bright red 5 5
539 " 12pf slate gray 5 5
  a. Bklt. pane 8 (5 No. 539 + 3 No. 542) 8.50
540 " 15pf violet brown 5 15
541 " 15pf lightyellowgreen 5 5
542 " 16pf slate green 5 5
543 " 20pf light blue 5 5

544 A119 24pf orange brown 5 5
a. Booklet pane of 8 40
545 " 25pf bright ultra. 5 25
546 " 25pf orange yellow 5 10
547 " 30pf olive 5 5
548 " 40pf red violet 5 5
549 " 42pf emerald 45 *1.65*
550 " 45pf bright red 5 5
551 " 50pf dark olive green 5 5
552 " 60pf brown red 5 5
553 " 75pf deep ultramarine 5 5
554 " 80pf dark blue 5 5
555 " 84pf emerald 5 10

Size: 24½x29½mm.

556 A119 1m olive green 5 5
Nos. 530-556 (27) 1.75 *3.65*

Imperforate copies of Nos. 543, 544 and 548 are usually from the souvenir sheet No. B295. Most other denominations exist imperforate.

Planting Olive
A120

Sower
A121

Laborer
A122

16 Pf.
DEUTSCHE POST
Reaping Wheat
A123

Germany Reaching for Peace
A124

Heinrich von Stephan
A125

1947-48 ***Perf. 14.***

557 A120 2pf brown black 5 5
558 " 6pf purple 5 5
559 A121 8pf red 5 5
560 " 10pf yellow green ('48) 5 5
561 A122 12pf gray 5 5
562 A120 15pf chocolate ('48) 5 12
563 A123 16pf dark blue green 5 5
564 A121 20pf blue 5 5
565 A123 24pf brown orange 5 5
566 A120 25pf orange yellow 5 8
567 A122 30pf red ('48) 10 35
568 A121 40pf red violet 5 5
569 A123 50pf ultramarine ('48) 8 35
571 A122 60pf red brown ('48) 5 5
a. 60pf brown red 5 15
572 " 80pf dark blue 5 5
573 A123 84pf emerald 6 25

Engraved.

Perf. 14.

574 A124 1m olive 6 5
575 " 2m dark brown violet 6 10
576 " 3m copper red 12 25
577 " 5m dark blue ('48) 30 1.40
Nos. 557-577 (20) 1.43 3.50

1947, May 15 **Lithographed**

578 A125 24(pf) orange brown 6 10
579 " 75(pf) dark blue 8 25

Issued to commemorate the 50th anniversary of the death of Heinrich von Stephan, first postmaster general of the German Empire.

Leipzig Fair Issues.

Type of
Semi-Postal Stamp of 1947.

Designs: 12pf, Maximilian I granting charter, 1497. 75pf, Estimating and collecting taxes, 1365.

Perf. 13½x13

1947, Sept. 2 **Litho.** **Wmk. 284**

580 SP252 12(pf) carmine 6 15
581 " 75(pf) dk. violet blue 10 20

Type of Semi-Postal Stamp of 1947, Dated 1948.

Designs: 50pf, Merchants at customs barrier, 1388. 84pf, Arranging stocks of merchandise, 1433.

1948, Mar. 2 **Engraved**

582 SP252 50(pf) deep blue 6 15
583 " 84(pf) green 10 20

Exist imperf. Price, each, $400.

Hanover Fair Issue.

Weighing Goods for Export
A126

1948, May 22 **Typo.** ***Perf. 14***

584 A126 24(pf) deep carmine 8 *22*
585 " 50(pf) ultramarine 5 *45*
c. Se-tenant with No. 584 3.25 5.00

For Use in the United States and British Zones

Stamps of Germany 1946-47
Overprinted in Black

a

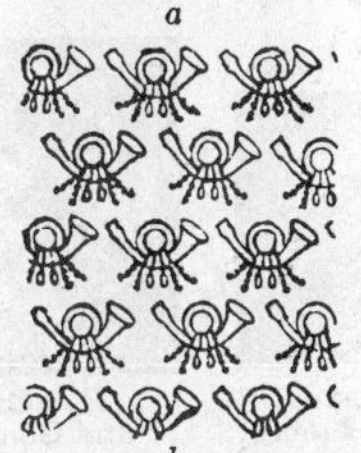
b

Overprint Type "a" on 1946 Numeral Issue.

1948 ***Perf. 14*** **Wmk. 284**

585A A119 2pf black 5.00 11.00
585B " 8pf dp. verm. 11.50 22.00
586 " 10pf chocolate 70 3.00
586A " 12pf bright red 7.75 16.50
586B " 12pf slate gray 140.00 250.00
586C " 15pf violet brown 7.75 16.50
587 " 15pf lt. yel. green 3.00 6.50
587A " 16pf slate green 38.50 82.50
587B " 24pf org. brown 57.50 100.00
587C " 25pf brt. ultra. 14.00 27.50
588 " 25pf org. yellow 1.15 4.75
589 " 30pf olive 1.75 3.50
589A " 40pf red violet 55.00 92.50
590 " 45pf bright red 1.90 4.25
591 " 50pf dk. olive green 1.90 3.75
592 " 75pf dp. ultra. 5.50 9.25
593 " 84pf emerald 5.50 9.25
Nos. 585A-593 (17) 358.40 662.75

Same, Overprinted Type "b".

593A A119 2pf black 16.00 32.50
593B " 8pf dp. verm. 35.00 50.00
593C " 10pf chocolate 28.00 50.00
593D " 12pf bright red 11.50 22.00
593E " 12pf slate gray 300.00 600.00
593F " 15pf violet brown 9.00 19.50
594 " 15pf lt. yel. green 75 3.50
594A A119 16pf slate green 38.50 75.00
594B " 24pf org. brown 50.00 82.50
594C " 25pf brt. ultra. 14.00 25.00
594D " 25pf org. yellow 42.50 75.00
595 " 30pf olive 1.60 3.75
595A " 40pf red violet 60.00 110.00
596 " 45pf bright red 3.00 5.25
597 " 50pf dk. olive grn. 3.00 5.00
598 " 75pf deep ultra. 3.50 6.50
599 " 84pf emerald 3.00 5.25
Nos. 593A-599 (17) 619.35 1170.75

Nine other denominations of type A119—1, 3, 4, 5, 6, 20, 42, 60 and 80pf—were also overprinted with types "a" and "b." These overprints were not authorized, but the stamps were sold at post offices and tolerated for postal use. Forgeries exist.

The overprints on Nos. 585A-599 have been extensively counterfeited.

Overprint Type "a" on Stamps and Types of 1947 Pictorial Issue.

600 A120 2pf brown black 8 10
601 " 6pf purple 8 10
602 A121 8pf deep vermilion 9 9
603 " 10pf yellow green 15 27
604 A122 12pf slate gray 15 7
605 A120 15pf chocolate 4.25 11.00
606 A123 16pf dk. blue green 70 1.10
607 A121 20pf blue 35 80
608 A123 24pf brown orange 10 10
609 A120 25pf orange yellow 35 55
610 A122 30pf red 1.75 3.75
611 A121 40pf red violet 60 95
612 A123 50pf ultramarine 60 95
614 A122 60pf red brown 60 95
a. 60pf brown red 55.00 110.00
615 A122 80pf dark blue 1.00 1.65
616 A123 84pf emerald 3.50 6.50
Nos. 600-616 (16) 14.35 28.93

Same, Overprinted Type "b".

617 A120 2pf brown black 60 1.65
618 " 6pf purple 75 1.90
619 A121 8pf red 75 1.30
620 " 10pf yellow green 8 15
621 A122 12pf gray 70 1.30
622 A120 15pf chocolate 15 30
623 A123 16pf dark blue green 15 20
624 A121 20pf blue 15 20
625 A123 24pf brown orange 50 1.30
626 A120 25pf orange yellow 5.00 11.00
627 A122 30pf red 25 35
628 A121 40pf red violet 25 35
629 A123 50pf ultramarine 30 35
631 A122 60pf red brown 25 42
a. 60pf brown red 2.10 4.00
632 A122 80pf dark blue 42 35
633 A123 84pf emerald 75 1.20
Nos. 617-633 (16) 11.05 22.32

Most of Nos. 585A-633 exist with inverted and double overprints.

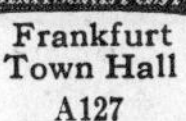

Frankfurt Town Hall
A127

Our Lady's Church, Munich
A128

Cologne Cathedral
A129

Brandenburg Gate, Berlin
A130

Holsten Gate, Lübeck
A131

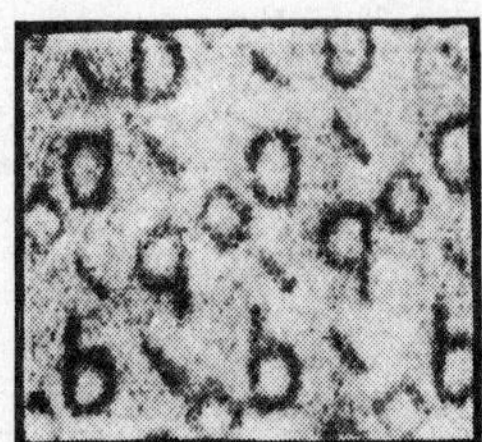
Wmk. 286

Two types of mark values:
I. Four horiz. lines in stairs.
II. Seven horizontal lines.

Wmkd. D P Multiple (286)

1948-51 **Litho.** ***Perf. 11½x11, 11***

634 A127 2(pf) black 10 6
a. Perf. 14 1.40 3.75
635 A128 4(pf) orange brown 20 4
a. Perf. 14 90 4
636 A129 5(pf) blue 20 5
a. Perf. 14 90 5
637 A128 6(pf) orange brown 10 25
638 " 6(pf) orange 15 6
a. Perf. 14 5.25 5.00
639 A127 8(pf) orange yellow 20 55
640 A128 8(pf) dk. slate blue 20 4
641 A129 10(pf) green 25 5
a. Perf. 14 1.40 4
642 A128 15(pf) orange 70 2.75
643 A127 15(pf) violet 45 6
a. Perf. 14 4.50 5
644 A127 16(pf) bluish green 25 60
645 " 20(pf) blue 60 1.65
646 A130 20(pf) carmine 60 5
a. Perf. 14 1.75 5
647 A130 24(pf) carmine 25 25
648 A129 25(pf) vermilion 65 5
a. Perf. 14 12.50 16.50
649 A130 30(pf) blue 90 4
a. Perf. 14 7.00 5
650 A128 30(pf) scarlet 1.20 3.25
651 A129 40(pf) rose lilac 1.50 5
a. Perf. 14 7.00 12
652 A130 50(pf) ultramarine 1.00 1.65
653 A128 50(pf) bluish green 1.35 4
a. Perf. 14 70.00 4
654 A129 60(pf) vio. brown 42.50 4
a. Perf. 14 2.40 6
655 A130 80(pf) red violet 2.75 4
a. Perf. 14 16.00 5
656 A128 84(pf) rose violet 1.10 4.00
657 A129 90(pf) rose lilac 2.25 5
a. Perf. 14 70.00 12

Perf. 11, 11x11½

658 A131 1m yel. grn. (I) 14.00 85
a. Perf. 14 (II) ('51) 52.50 12
b. Perf. 11 (II) 25.00 15
659 A131 2m violet (I) 14.00 85
a. Type II 35.00 25
660 A131 3m car. rose (I) 14.00 2.75
a. Type II 70.00 1.00
661 A131 5m blue (I) 18.50 13.75
a. Type II 125.00 3.25

Imperforates of many values exist.

Specialists collect Nos. 634-661 with watermark in four positions: upright, D's facing left; upright, D's facing right; sideways, D's facing up; sideways, D's facing down.

Two types of perforation: line and comb. Nos. 634-657 are found both perf. 11 and 11½x11.

Herman Hildebrant Wedigh
A132

Wmk. 116

Wmkd. Crosses and Circles. (116)

1949, Apr. 22 **Engraved.** ***Perf. 14***

662 A132 10(pf) green 2.10 1.75
663 " 20(pf) car. rose 2.10 1.75

664 A132 30(pf) blue 3.50 5.00
a. Sheet of 3 80.00 140.00

Hanover Export Fair, 1949.
No. 664a contains one each of Nos. 662 to 664 with inscriptions in carmine rose in upper and lower margins. The sheet was sold for 1 mark.

Federal Republic

AREA—95,520 sq. mi.
POP.—62,040,000 (est. 1974).
CAPITAL—Bonn.

"Reconstruction" A133 — Bavaria Stamp A134

1949, Sept. 7 Litho. Wmk. 286
665 A133 10(pf) blue green 40.00 45.00
666 " 20(pf) rose car. 50.00 47.50

Opening of the first Federal Assembly.
Exist imperf. Price, each $425.

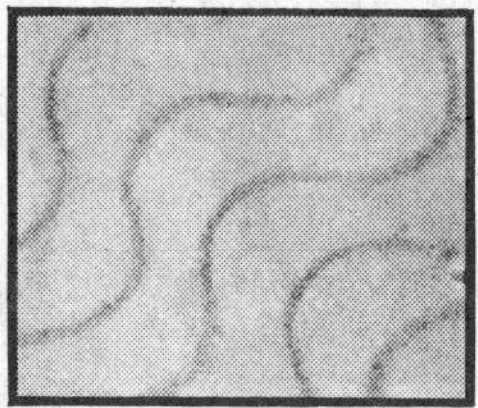

Wmk. 285
Design: 30pf, Bavaria 6kr.

Wmkd. Marbleized Pattern. (285)
1949, Sept. 30 Litho. *Perf. 14*
667 A134 20(pf) red & dull blue 27.50 35.00
668 " 30(pf) dull blue & choc. 42.50 75.00

Issued to commemorate the centenary of German postage stamps. See No. B309.

Heinrich von Stephan, General Post Office and Guild House, Bern—A135

1949, Oct. 9 Wmk. 286
669 A135 30(pf) ultra. 42.50 62.50

Issued to commemorate the 75th anniversary of the formation of the Universal Postal Union.

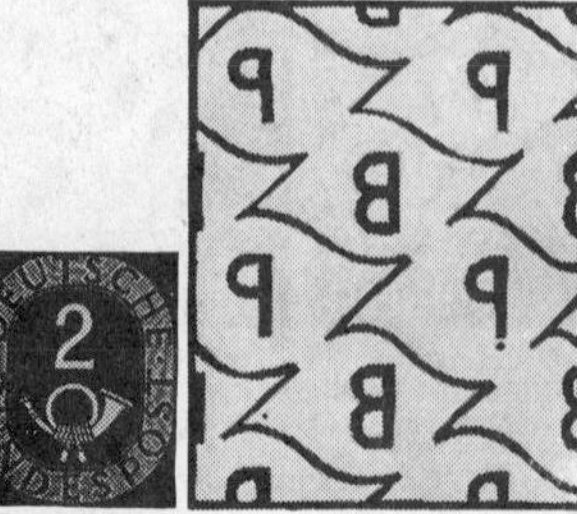

Numeral and Post Horn A136 — Wmk. 295

Wmkd. B P and Zigzag Lines. (295)
1951–52 Typographed
670 A136 2(pf) yellow green 50 55
671 " 4(pf) yellow brown 50 11
a. Booklet pane 10 (3 No. 671 +3 No. 673+4 No. 677) 68.00
672 A136 5(pf) dp. rose vio. 3.00 11
673 " 6(pf) orange 7.00 1.65
674 " 8(pf) gray 14.00 5.50
675 " 10(pf) dark green 1.20 5
a. Booklet pane 9 (4 No. 675 +5 No. 677+label) 90.00
676 A136 15(pf) purple 24.50 80
677 " 20(pf) carmine 1.50 5
678 " 25(pf) dk.rose lake 55.00 2.50

Engraved.
Size: 20x24½mm.
679 A136 30(pf) blue 35.00 20
680 " 40(pf) rose lilac ('52) 75.00 16
681 " 50(pf) blue gray ('52) 100.00 12
682 " 60(pf) brown ('52) 70.00 12
683 " 70(pf) deep yellow ('52) 350.00 7.75
684 " 80(pf) car. ('52) 250.00 1.65
685 " 90(pf) yellow green ('52) 425.00 1.90
Nos. 670–685 (16) 1412.20 23.22

Imperforates exist of Nos. 671, 673, 675, 681 and 684.

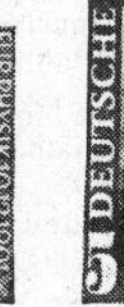

W. K. Roentgen A137 — Mona Lisa A138

1951, Dec. 10
686 A137 30(pf) blue 90.00 30.00

Issued to commemorate the 50th anniversary of the awarding of the Nobel prize in physics to Wilhelm K. Roentgen.

Lithographed
1952, Apr. 15 *Perf. 13½* Wmk. 285
687 A138 5(pf) brown red, dark brown & lt. blue 1.20 85

Issued to commemorate the 500th anniversary of the birth of Leonardo da Vinci.

N. A. Otto A139 — Martin Luther A140

Engraved
1952, July 25 *Perf. 14* Wmk. 295
688 A139 30(pf) deep blue 27.50 22.00

Issued to commemorate the 75th anniversary of the four-cycle gas engine.

1952, July 25
689 A140 10(pf) green 14.00 7.00

Issued to publicize the Lutheran World Federation Assembly, Hanover, 1952.

Freighter Off Heligoland A141 — Carl Schurz A142

1952, Sept. 6
690 A141 20(pf) red 11.50 10.00

Return of Heligoland, Mar. 1, 1952.

Perf. 13½
1952, Sept. 17 Litho. Wmk. 285
691 A142 20(pf) blue, black & brn. org. 21.00 12.00

Issued to commemorate the centenary of Carl Schurz's arrival in America.

Thurn and Taxis Postilion A143 — Philipp Reis A144

1952, Oct. 25
692 A143 10(pf) multi. 4.00 2.75

Issued to commemorate the centenary of the first Thurn and Taxis stamp issue.

1952, Oct. 27 Photo. *Perf. 14*
693 A144 30(pf) blue 40.00 22.00

75 years of telephone service in Germany.

"Prevent Traffic Accidents" A145

1953, Mar. 30 Litho. Wmk. 285
694 A145 20(pf) black, red & bl. green 14.00 5.25

Justus von Liebig A146 — Red Cross and Compass A147

1953, May 12 Engraved Wmk. 295
695 A146 30(pf) dark blue 40.00 30.00

Issued to commemorate the 150th anniversary of the birth of Justus von Liebig, chemist.

Perf. 14x13½
1953, May 8 Litho. Wmk. 285
696 A147 10(pf) deep olive grn.& red 14.00 8.75

Issued to commemorate the 125th anniversary of the birth of Henri Dunant, founder of the Red Cross.

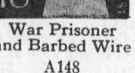

War Prisoner and Barbed Wire A148 — Train and Hand Signal A149

Typographed and Embossed.
1953, May 9 *Perf. 14* Unwmkd.
697 A148 10(pf) gray & blk. 2.75 17

Issued in memory of the prisoners of war.

Engraved
1953, June 20 *Perf. 14* Wmk. 295
Designs: 10(pf), Pigeon and planes. 20(pf), Automobiles and traffic signal. 30(pf), Ship, barges and buoy.
698 A149 4(pf) brown 5.25 9.25
699 " 10(pf) deep green 10.50 16.50
700 " 20(pf) red 14.00 19.00
701 " 30(pf) deep ultra. 35.00 32.50

Exhibition of Transport and Communications, Munich, 1953.

Pres. Theodor Heuss A150

1954–60 Typographed *Perf. 14*
Size: 18½x22mm.
702 A150 2(pf) citron 7 12
a. Booklet pane 9 (5 No. 702, 4 No. 704+label) ('55) 20.00
b. Booklet pane 9 (3 No. 702, 6 No. 704+label) ('56) 4.00
c. Bklt. pane 9 (3 No. 702, 1 No. 707, 5 No. 708+label) ('56) 13.00
703 A150 4(pf) orange brown 7 15
704 " 5(pf) rose lilac 7 10
a. Booklet pane 9 (2 No. 704, 7 No. 708+label) ('55) 20.00
705 A150 6(pf) light brown 9 70
706 " 7(pf) bluish green 35 10
707 " 8(pf) gray 18 70
708 " 10(pf) green 18 9
a. Booklet pane 9 (4 No. 708, 5 No. 710+label) ('55) 20.00
b. Booklet pane of 10 ('60) 7.00
709 A150 15(pf) ultramarine 50 15
710 " 20(pf) dk. car. rose 18 9
711 " 25(pf) red brown 1.00 35

Engraved
Size: 19½x24mm.
712 A150 30(pf) blue 12.50 2.25
713 " 40(pf) red violet 3.00 9
714 " 50(pf) gray 175.00 25
715 " 60(pf) red brown 42.50 15
716 " 70(pf) olive 10.50 80
717 " 80(pf) deep rose 2.00 2.75
718 " 90(pf) deep green 8.75 1.65
Size: 24½x29½mm.
719 A150 1m olive green 1.75 15
720 " 2m lt. violet blue 2.50 1.10
721 " 3m deep plum 4.25 1.65
Nos. 702–721 (20) 265.44 13.39

Coils and sheets of 100 were issued of the 5, 7, 10, 15, 20, 25, 40 and 70pf. Every fifth coil stamp has a control number on the back.
Printings of Nos. 704, 706, 708–711 and 708b were made on fluorescent paper beginning in 1960.
Nos. 702, 709, 714 exist imperf. Price about $375 each.
See also Nos. 737b, 755–761.

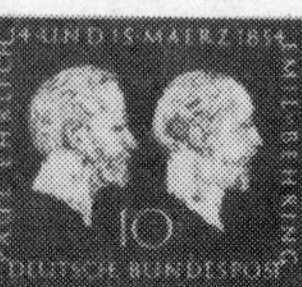

Paul Ehrlich and Emil von Behring A151 — 15th Century Printer A152

Lithographed
1954, Mar. 13 *Perf. 13½* Wmk. 285
722 A151 10(pf) dark green 12.50 5.00

Issued to commemorate the centenary of the births of Paul Ehrlich and Emil von Behring, medical researchers.
Exists imperf. Price $800.

1954, May 5 Typo. Wmk. 295

723 A152 4(pf) chocolate 70 25

Issued to commemorate the 500th anniversary of the publication of Gutenberg's 42-line Bible. Design from woodcut by Jost Amman.

Bishop's Miter and Sword
A153

Carl F. Gauss
A154

Engraved; Center Embossed

Perf. 13½x14

1954, June 5 Unwmkd.

724 A153 20(pf) gray & red 3.85 3.50

Issued to commemorate the 1200th anniversary of the martyrdom of Saint Boniface.

Engraved

1955, Feb. 23 *Perf. 14* Wmk. 295

725 A154 10(pf) deep green 3.00 45

Issued to commemorate the centenary of the death of Carl Friedrich Gauss, mathematician.

Oskar von Miller
A155

Wmk. 304

Wmkd. DBP and Rosettes Multiple. (304)

1955, May 7 Litho. *Perf. 13½*

726 A155 10(pf) green 3.85 2.50

Issued to commemorate the centenary of the birth of Oskar von Miller, electrical engineer.

Friedrich von Schiller
A156

Engraved and Embossed

Perf. 13½x14

1955, May 9 Unwmkd.

727 A156 40(pf) blue 14.50 8.75

Issued to commemorate the 150th anniversary of the death of Friedrich von Schiller, poet.

1906 Automobile
A157

Perf. 13½

1955, June 1 Typo. Wmk. 304

728 A157 20(pf) red & black 11.00 8.75

Issued to commemorate the 50th anniversary of German postal motor-bus service.

Arms of Baden-Württemberg
A158

Globe and Atomic Symbol
A159

Perf. 13x13½

1955, June 15 Litho. Wmk. 295

729 A158 7(pf) lemon, blk. & brown red 3.50 6.50

730 " 10(pf) lemon, black & green 4.50 4.25

a. Value omitted 350.00 350.00

Issued to publicize the Baden-Wurttemberg Exhibition, Stuttgart, 1955.

1955, June 24 Photo. *Perf. 13½x14*

731 A159 20(pf) rose brown 7.00 1.10

Issued to encourage scientific research.

Orb and Symbols of Battle
A160

Photogravure and Embossed

Perf. 14x13½

1955, Aug. 10 Unwmkd.

732 A160 20(pf) red lilac 7.75 4.25

Issued in honor of Augsburg and the millenium of the Battle on the Lechfeld.

Family in Flight
A161

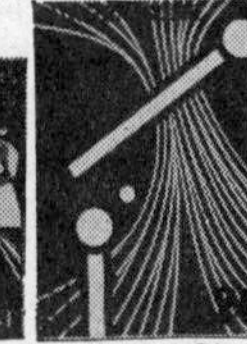

Railroad Signal and Tracks
A162

1955, Aug. 2 Engraved

733 A161 20(pf) brown lake 2.50 40

Issued to commemorate 10 years of German expatriation. See also No. 930.

Perf. 13½x14

1955, Oct. 5 Litho. Wmk. 304

734 A162 20(pf) red & black 7.00 1.40

Issued to commemorate the European Timetable conference at Wiesbaden, Oct. 5–15, 1955.

Stifter Monument and Stylized Trees
A163

United Nations Emblem
A164

1955, Oct. 22 Engraved

735 A163 10(pf) dark green 2.50 2.25

Issued to commemorate the 150th anniversary of the birth of Adalbert Stifter, poet.

Lithographed and Embossed

Perf. 14x13½

1955, Oct. 24 Unwmkd.

736 A164 10(pf) light green & red 1.75 3.50

United Nations Day, Oct. 24, 1955.

Numeral
A165

Numeral and Signature
A166

Typographed.

1955–58 *Perf. 14* Wmk. 304

737 A165 1(pf) gray 5 6

Wmk. 295

737A A165 1(pf) gray ('58) 4.50 8.25

b. Bklt. pane of 10 (2 No. 737A+2 No. 704+1 No. 707+2 No. 708 +3 No. 710) 25.00

No. 737A was issued only in the booklet pane, No. 737b. No. 737 was issued on fluorescent paper in 1963.

1956, Jan. 7 Engraved Wmk. 304

738 A166 20(pf) dark red 6.00 3.25

Issued to commemorate the 125th anniversary of the birth of Heinrich von Stephan, co-founder of the Universal Postal Union.

Clavichord
A167

1956, Jan. 27 Lithographed

739 A167 10(pf) dull lilac 28 25

Issued to commemorate the 200th anniversary of the birth of Wolfgang Amadeus Mozart, composer.

Heinrich Heine
A168

Perf. 13x13½

1956, Feb. 17 Wmk. 295

740 A168 10(pf) olive green & black 2.10 3.25

Centenary of death of Heinrich Heine, poet.

Old Buildings, Lüneburg
A169

Engraved.

1956, May 2 *Perf. 14* Wmk. 304

741 A169 20(pf) dull red 7.00 11.00

Millenary of Lüneburg.

Olympic Rings
A170

Robert Schumann
A171

Perf. 13½x14

1956, June 9 Wmk. 304

742 A170 10pf slate green 28 35

Issued to publicize the Olympic year, 1956.

Perf. 13½x14

1956, July 28 Litho. Unwmkd.

743 A171 10pf citron, black & red 28 25

Issued to commemorate the centenary of the death of Robert Schumann, composer.

Synod Emblem
A172

Thomas Mann
A173

Perf. 13½x13

1956, Aug. 8 Wmk. 304

744 A172 10pf green 1.60 2.50

745 " 20pf brown carmine 2.50 4.00

Issued to honor the meeting of German Protestants (Evangelical Synod), Frankfurt-on-Main, Aug. 8–12.

1956, Aug. 11 Engr. *Perf. 13½x14*

746 A173 20pf pale rose vio. 1.75 2.50

Issued to commemorate the first anniversary of the death of Thomas Mann, novelist.

Maria Laach Abbey
A174

"Rebuilding Europe"
A175

Photogravure

1956, Aug. 24 *Perf. 13x13½*

747 A174 20pf brown lake & gray 1.40 2.25

Issued to commemorate the 800th anniversary of the dedication of the Maria Laach Abbey.

Europa Issue, 1956

1956, Sept. 15 Engraved *Perf. 14*

748 A175 10pf green 65 12

749 " 40pf blue 5.25 1.20

Issued to symbolize the cooperation among the six countries comprising the Coal and Steel Community.

Plan of Cologne Cathedral and Hand
A176

1956, Aug. 29 Litho. *Perf. 13x13½*

750 A176 10pf gray green & red brown 1.40 2.25

Issued to commemorate the 77th meeting of German Catholics, Cologne, Aug. 29.

Map of the World and Policeman's Hand
A177

1956, Sept. 1 *Perf. 13½x13*

751 A177 20pf red orange, grn. & blk. 1.75 2.50

Issued on the occasion of the International Police Show, Essen, Sept. 1-23.

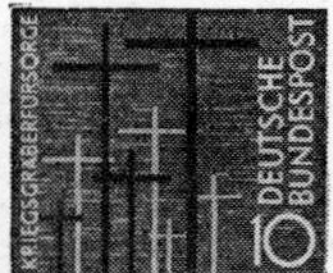

Pigeon Holding Letter
A178

Cemetery Crosses
A179

1956, Oct. 27 Engr. *Perf. 14*

752 A178 10pf green 60 45

Issued to publicize the Day of the Stamp.

1956, Nov. 17 *Perf. 14x13½*

753 A179 10pf slate 60 45

Issued to commemorate the people of Germany who died during World War II and to promote the Society for the Care of Military Cemeteries.

Saar Coat of Arms
A180

1957, Jan. 2 Litho. *Perf. 13x13½*

754 A180 10pf bluish green & brown 30 45

Issued to commemorate the return of the Saar to Germany. See also Saar No. 262.

Heuss Type of 1954.
Engraved.

1956-57 *Perf. 14* Wmk. 304

Size: 18½x22mm.

755 A150 30pf slate green 95 40
756 " 40pf light ultra. 1.75 10
757 " 50pf olive 1.10 6
758 " 60pf light brown 2.50 15
759 " 70pf violet 3.85 6
760 " 80pf red orange 5.00 1.00
761 " 90pf bluish green 15.00 25
Nos. 755-761 (7) 30.15 2.02

Nos. 755-756 were printed on both ordinary and fluorescent paper; Nos. 757-761 only on ordinary paper. Issue dates: 40pf, 1956. Others, 1957.

The 40pf and 70pf were also issued in coils. Every fifth coil stamp has control number on back.

Heinrich Hertz
A181

Paul Gerhardt
A182

1957, Feb. 22 Litho. *Perf. 14*

762 A181 10pf light green & black 50 30

Issued to commemorate the centenary of the birth of Heinrich Hertz, physicist.

1957, May 18 Engraved

763 A182 20pf carmine lake 42 30

Issued to commemorate the 350th anniversary of the birth of Paul Gerhardt, Lutheran clergyman and hymn writer.

Tulip and Post Horn
A183

1957, June 8

764 A183 20pf red orange 42 30

Flora and Philately Exhibition, Cologne, June 8-10.

Arms of Aschaffenburg, 1332
A184

Scholars (Sapiens Manuscript)
A185

Perf. 13x13½

1957, June 15 Wmk. 304

765 A184 20pf deep salmon & black 42 40

Issued to commemorate the 1000th anniversary of the founding of the Abbey and town of Aschaffenburg.

1957, June 24 *Perf. 13½x13*

766 A185 10pf black, blue green & red orange 27 25

Issued to commemorate the 500th anniversary of the founding of Freiburg University.

Modern Passenger Freighter
A186

1957, June 25 *Perf. 13½x14*

767 A186 15pf bright blue, black & red 35 5

Merchant Marine Day, June 25.

Liebig Laboratory
A187

1957, July 3 Engr. *Perf. 14x13½*

768 A187 10pf dark green 27 25

Issued to commemorate the 350th anniversary of the Justus Liebig School at Ludwig University, Giessen.

Albert Ballin
A188

Television Screen
A189

Perf. 13½x14

1957, Aug. 15 Litho. Wmk. 304

769 A188 20pf dark carmine rose & black 50 27

Issued to commemorate the centenary of the birth of Albert Ballin, founder of the Hamburg-America Steamship Line.

1957, Aug. 23 Engr. *Perf. 14x13½*

770 A189 10pf blue violet & green 27 25

Issued to publicize the television industry.

Europa Issue, 1957

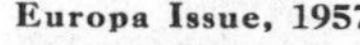

"United Europe"
A190

Lithographed; Tree Embossed

1957-58 *Perf. 14x13½* Unwmkd.

771 A190 10pf yellow green & light blue 22 6
a. Imperf. 300.00 400.00
772 A190 40pf dark blue & light blue 1.90 40

Wmk. 304

772A A190 10pf yellow green & lt. bl. ('58) 3.50 7.00

A united Europe for peace and prosperity. Issue dates: Nos. 771-772, Sept. 16, 1957. No. 772A, August, 1958.

Water Lily
A191

European Robin
A192

Lithographed

1957, Oct. 4 *Perf. 14* Wmk. 304

773 A191 10pf yellow green & orange yellow 25 20
774 A192 20pf multicolored 42 30

Protection of wild animals and plants.

Carrier Pigeons
A193

Baron vom Stein
A194

1957, Oct. 5

775 A193 20pf dp. car. & blk. 42 30

Issued for International Letter Writing Week, Oct. 6-12.

1957, Oct. 26 Engr. *Perf. 13½x14*

776 A194 20pf red 85 45

Issued to commemorate the 200th anniversary of the birth of Baron Heinrich Friedrich vom und zum Stein, Prussian statesman.

Leo Baeck
A195

Landschaft Building, Stuttgart
A196

1957, Nov. 2

777 A195 20pf dark red 85 45

Issued to commemorate the first anniversary of the death of Rabbi Leo Baeck of Berlin.

Perf. 13x13½

1957, Nov. 16 Litho. Wmk. 304

778 A196 10pf dark green & yellow green 42 30

Issued to commemorate the 500th anniversary of the Wurttemberg Landtag (Assembly).

Coach
A197

"Max and Moritz"
A198

1957, Nov. 26 Engraved *Perf. 14*

779 A197 10pf olive green 55 30

Issued to commemorate the centenary of the death of Joseph V. Eichendorff, poet.

1958, Jan. 9 Litho. *Perf. 13½x13*

Design: 20pf, Wilhelm Busch.

780 A198 10pf light olive green & black 22 25
781 " 20pf red & black 55 35

Issued to commemorate the 50th anniversary of the death of Wilhelm Busch, humorist.

"Prevent Forest Fires"
A199

1958, Mar. 5 *Perf. 14*

782 A199 20pf bright red & black 50 30

Rudolf Diesel
A200

1958, Mar. 18 Engraved *Perf. 14*

783 A200 10pf dark blue green 25 25

Issued to commemorate the centenary of the birth of Rudolf Diesel, inventor.

Giraffe and Lion
A201

View of Old Munich
A202

Perf. 13x13½

1958, May 7 Litho. Wmk. 304

784 A201 10pf bright yellow green & black 35 30

Issued to commemorate the centenary of the Zoo at Frankfort on the Main.
Exists imperf. Price $225.

1958, May 22 Engr. *Perf. 14x13½*

785 A202 20pf dark red 35 30

800th anniversary of Munich.

Market Cross, Trier
A203

Heraldic Eagle 5m Coin
A204

1958, June 3

786 A203 20pf dark red & black 35 30

Millennium of the market of Trier (Treves).

1958, June 20 Litho. *Perf. 13x13½*

787 A204 20pf red & black 38 30

Issued to commemorate the 10th anniversary of the German currency reform.
Exists imperf. Price $400.

Turner Emblem and Oak Leaf
A205

Hermann Schulze-Delitzsch
A206

Perf. 13½x14

1958, July 21 Wmk. 304

788 A205 10pf gray, black & dull green 20 20

Issued to commemorate 150 years of German Turners and on the occasion of the 1958 Turner festival.

1958, Aug. 29 Engr. *Perf. 13½x14*

789 A206 10pf yellow green 20 20

Issued to commemorate the 150th anniversary of the birth of Hermann Schulze-Delitzsch, founder of German trade organizations.

Europa Issue, 1958
Common Design Type

1958, Sept. 13 Lithographed

Size: 24½x30mm.

790 CD1 10pf yellow green & blue 40 4
791 " 40pf lt. blue & red 1.40 55

Common Design Types

pictured in section at front of book.

Nicolaus Cusanus (Nikolaus Krebs)
A207

Pres. Theodor Heuss
A208

1958, Dec. 3 Litho. *Perf. 14x13½*

792 A207 20pf dark carmine rose & black 33 20

Issued to commemorate the 500th anniversary of the Cusanus Hospice at Kues, founded by Cardinal Nicolaus (1401–1464).
Exists imperf. Price $250.

1959 *Perf. 14* Wmk. 304

793 A208 7pf blue green 8 5
794 " 10pf green 12 5
795 " 20pf dk. car. rose 27 5

Engraved.

796 A208 40pf blue 1.50 40
797 " 70pf dull purple 1.90 30
Nos. 793-797 (5) 3.87 85

Nos. 793–795 were issued in sheets of 100 and in coils. Every fifth coil stamp has a control number on the back.
An experimental booklet containing one pane of 10 of No. 794 was sold at Darmstadt in 1960. Price $650.

Jakob Fugger
A209

Adam Riese
A210

1959, Mar. 6 *Perf. 13x13½*

798 A209 20pf dark red & black 33 25

500th anniversary of the birth of Jakob Fugger the Rich, businessman and banker.

1959, Mar. 28 *Perf. 13½x13*

799 A210 10pf olive green & black 28 20

Adam Riese (c. 1492–1559), arithmetic teacher, 400th death anniversary.

Alexander von Humboldt
A211

Buildings, Buxtehude
A212

1959, May 6 Engr. *Perf. 13½x14*

800 A211 40pf blue 60 55

Alexander von Humboldt (1769–1859), naturalist and geographer, death centenary.

1959, June 20 Litho. *Perf. 14*

801 A212 20pf lt. bl., verm. & black 27 25

Millennium of town of Buxtehude.

Holy Coat of Trier
A213

Synod Emblem
A214

Lithographed; Coat Embossed

1959, July 18 *Perf. 14* Wmk. 304

802 A213 20pf dull claret, buff & black 27 25

Issued to commemorate the showing of the seamless robe of Christ at the Cathedral of Trier, July 19-Sept. 20.

1959, Aug. 12 Lithographed

803 A214 10pf green, bright violet & black 18 20

Issued to honor the meeting of German Protestants (Evangelical Synod), Munich, Aug. 12–16.

Souvenir Sheet

A215

Portraits: 10pf, George Friedrich Handel. 15pf, Louis Spohr. 20pf, Ludwig van Beethoven. 25pf, Joseph Haydn. 40pf, Felix Mendelssohn-Bartholdy.

Perf. 14x13½

1959, Sept. 8 Engr. Wmk. 304

804 A215 Sheet of five 30.00 82.50
a. 10pf deep green 5.00 10.00
b. 15pf blue 5.00 10.00
c. 20pf dk. carmine 5.00 10.00
d. 25pf brown 5.00 10.00
e. 40pf dark blue 5.00 10.00

Issued to commemorate the opening of Beethoven Hall in Bonn and to honor various anniversaries of German composers. Sheets measure 148x105½mm. with marginal inscription and score from Beethoven's 9th Symphony in light brown.

Europa Issue, 1959
Common Design Type

1959, Sept. 19 Litho. *Perf. 13½x14*

Size: 24 x 29½ mm.

805 CD2 10pf olive green 30 6
806 " 40pf dark blue 90 40

Uprooted Oak Emblem
A216

1960, Apr. 7 *Perf. 13½x13*

807 A216 10pf grn., blk. & lilac 55 20
808 " 40pf blue, black & orange 3.00 1.50

Issued to publicize World Refugee Year, July 1, 1959–June 30, 1960.

Philipp Melanchthon
A217

Symbols of Christ's Sufferings
A218

1960, Apr. 19 *Perf. 13½x14*

809 A217 20pf dark carmine rose & black 1.30 65

400th anniversary of the death of Philipp Melanchthon, co-worker of Martin Luther in the German Reformation.

1960, May 17 *Perf. 14x13½*

810 A218 10pf Prussian green, gray & ochre 20 20

1960 Passion Play, Oberammergau, Bavaria.

Dove, Chalice and Crucifix
A219

1960, July 30 Engr. *Perf. 14x13½*

811 A219 10pf dull green 55 35
812 " 20pf maroon 1.00 95

37th Eucharistic World Congress, Munich.

Wrestlers and Olympic Rings
A220

Hildesheim Cathedral, Miters, Cross and Crosier
A221

Sport scenes from Greek urns: 10pf, Sprinters. 20pf, Discus and Javelin throwers. 40pf, Chariot race.

1960, Aug. 8 Wmk. 304

813 A220 7pf red brown 25 25
814 " 10pf olive green 40 30
815 " 20pf vermilion 75 15
816 " 40pf dark blue 1.25 1.90

Issued to commemorate the 17th Olympic Games, Rome, Aug. 25–Sept. 11.

1960, Sept. 6 Engr. *Perf. 13½x14*

817 A221 20pf claret 90 50

Issued to commemorate the 1000th anniversary of the birth of St. Bernward (960–1022) and St. Godehard (960–1038), bishops.

Europa Issue, 1960
Common Design Type

1960, Sept. 19 Wmk. 304

Size: 30x25mm.

818 CD3 10pf olive green & yel. green 13 15
819 " 20pf bright red & light red 80 20
820 " 40pf blue & light blue 90 1.50

George C. Marshall
A222

Steam Locomotive
A223

1960, Oct. 15 Litho. *Perf. 13x13½*

821 A222 40pf deep blue & black 3.00 2.00

Issued to honor George C. Marshall, U.S. general and statesman.

1960, Dec. 7 *Perf. 13½x14*

822 A223 10pf olive bistre & black 20 20

125th anniversary of German railroads.

St. George
A224

Engraved

1961, Apr. 23 *Perf. 14* Wmk. 304

823 A224 10pf green 20 20

Issued to honor the Boy Scouts of the world on St. George's Day (patron saint of Boy Scouts).

Albrecht Dürer
A225

Portraits: 5pf, Albertus Magnus. 7pf, St. Elizabeth of Thuringia. 8pf, Johann Gutenberg. 15pf, Martin Luther. 20pf, Johann Sebastian Bach. 25pf, Balthasar Neumann. 30pf, Immanuel Kant. 40pf, Gotthold Ephraim Lessing. 50pf, Johann Wolfgang von Goethe. 60pf, Friedrich von Schiller. 70pf, Ludwig van Beethoven. 80pf, Heinrich von Kleist. 90pf, Prof. Franz Oppenheimer. 1m, Annette von Droste-Hülshoff. 2m, Gerhart Hauptmann.

1961–64 Typographed *Perf. 14*

Fluorescent or Ordinary Paper

824 A225 5pf olive 5 5
- *a.* Bklt. pane of 10 ('63) 95
- *b.* Tête bêche pair ('63) 65 65

825 " 7pf dark bistre 11 11
826 " 8pf lilac 11 11
827 " 10pf olive green 10 5
- *a.* Bklt. pane of 10 3.25
- *b.* Tête bêche pair 80 1.25

828 " 15pf blue 15 5
- *a.* Bklt. pane of 10 ('63) 4.50
- *b.* Tête bêche pair ('63) 95 1.35

829 " 20pf dark red 22 5
- *a.* Bklt. pane of 10 ('63) 2.75
- *b.* Tête bêche pair ('63) 1.10 1.35

830 " 25pf orange brown 27 27

Engraved

831 A225 30pf gray 45 4
832 " 40pf blue 45 5
833 " 50pf red brown 80 20
834 " 60pf dk. carmine rose ('62) 65 20
835 " 70pf greenish black 80 5
- *a.* 70pf dp. green 80 20

836 " 80pf brown 80 20
837 " 90pf yel. olive ('64) 1.00 30
838 " 1m violet blue 1.10 25
839 " 2m yel. grn. ('62) 2.25 55
Nos. 824–839 (16) 9.31 2.53

Nos. 824–825, 827–830, 832, 834–835, 835a were issued in coils as well as in sheets. Every fifth coil stamp has a black control number on the back.

Nos. 824–839, including booklet panes and tête bêche pairs, were printed on fluorescent paper. Nos. 824–829 and 832 were also printed on ordinary paper.

Gottlieb Daimler's Car of 1886 and Signature
A226

Design: 20pf, Carl Benz's 3-wheel car of 1886 and signature.

1961, July 3 Lithographed

840 A226 10pf green & black 12 15
841 " 20pf brick red & black 25 25

75 years of motorized traffic.

Messenger, Nuremberg, 18th Century
A227

Cathedral, Speyer
A228

Photogravure and Engraved

1961, Aug. 31 *Perf. 14* Wmk. 304

842 A227 7pf brown red & black 11 11

Issued to publicize the exhibition "The Letter in Five Centuries," Nuremberg.

1961, Sept. 2 Engraved

843 A228 20pf vermilion 27 27

900th anniversary of Speyer Cathedral.

Europa Issue, 1961

Common Design Type

1961, Sept. 18 Lithographed

Size: 28½x18½mm.

844 CD4 10pf olive green 10 9
845 " 40pf violet blue 55 55

No. 84 was printed on both ordinary and fluorescent paper.

Reis Telephone
A229

Engraved

1961, Oct. 26 *Perf. 14* Wmk. 304

846 A229 10pf green 20 20

Issued to commemorate the centenary of the demonstration of the first telephone by Philipp Reis.

Wilhelm Emanuel von Ketteler
A230

1961, Dec. 22 Lithographed

847 A230 10pf olive green & black 20 20

Issued to commemorate the sesquicentennial of the birth of Wilhelm Emanuel von Ketteler, Bishop of Mainz and pioneer in social development.

Fluorescent Paper

was introduced for all stamps, starting with No. 848. Of the stamps before No. 848, those issued on both ordinary and fluorescent paper include Nos. 704, 706, 708–711, 737, 755–756, 824–829, 832, 844. Those issued only on fluorescent paper (up to No. 848) include Nos. 708b, 830–831, 833–839 and 842.

Drusus Stone and Old View of Mainz
A231

Notes and Tuning Fork
A232

1962, May 10 Engraved Wmk. 304

848 A231 20pf deep claret 27 22

The 2000th anniversary of Mainz.

1962, July 12 Litho. *Perf. 14*

849 A232 20pf red & black 22 22

Issued to show appreciation of choral singing. The music is from the choral movement for three voices "In dulci jubilo" from "Musae Sionlae" by Michael Praetorius.

"Faith, Thanksgiving, Service"
A233

1962, Aug. 22 Engr. Unwmkd.

850 A233 20pf magenta 22 22

Issued to commemorate the 79th meeting of German Catholics, Hanover, Aug. 22–29.

Open Bible, Chrismon and Chalice
A234

1962, Sept. 11 Litho. Wmk. 304

851 A234 20pf verm. & blk. 22 22

Issued to commemorate the 150th anniversary of the Württemberg Bible Society.

Europa Issue, 1962

Common Design Type

1962, Sept. 17 Engraved

Size: 28x23mm.

852 CD5 10pf green 10 9
853 " 40pf blue 55 55

"Bread for the World"
A235

Lithographed and Embossed

1962, Nov. 23 *Perf. 14*

854 A235 20pf brn. red & blk. 22 22

Issued in connection with the Advent Collection of the Protestant Church in Germany.

Mother and Child Receiving Gift Parcel—A236

1963, Feb. 9 Engraved

855 A236 20pf dk. carmine 22 22

Issued to express gratitude to the American organizations, CRALOG (Council of Relief Agencies Licensed to Operate in Germany) and CARE (Cooperative for American Remittances to Everywhere), for help during 1946–1962.

Globe, Cross, Seeds and Stalks of Wheat
A237

Checkered Lily
A238

Lithographed and Engraved

1963, Feb. 27 *Perf. 14* Wmk. 304

856 A237 20pf gray, blk. & red 22 22

Issued to publicize the German Catholic "Misereor" (I have compassion) campaign against hunger and illness.

1963, Apr. 28 Litho. Unwmkd.

Flowers: 15pf, Lady's slipper. 20pf, Columbine. 40pf, Beach thistle.

Black Inscription

857 A238 10pf green, lilac & gray 10 10
858 " 15pf multicolored 15 15
859 " 20pf " 27 15
860 " 40pf bl., gray & grn. 65 70

Flora and Philately Exhibition, Hamburg.

Heidelberg Catechism
A239

1963, May 2 Litho. & Engr.

861 A239 20pf deep orange, brn. org. & blk. 22 22

Issued to commemorate the 400th anniversary of the Heidelberg Catechism, containing the doctrine of the reformed church.

Cross of Golgotha, Darkened Sun and Moon—A240

1963, May 4 Litho. Wmk. 304

862 A240 10pf grn., deep car., black & violet 12 12

Issued to commemorate the consecration of the Regina Martyrum Church, Berlin-Plötzensee, in memory of the victims of Nazism.

Arms of 18 Participating Countries, Paris Conference, 1863
A241

Map Showing New Railroad Link, German and Danish Flags
A242

1963, May 7 Engraved

863 A241 40pf violet blue 45 45

Issued to commemorate the centenary of the first International Postal Conference, Paris, 1863.

1963, May 14 Litho. Unwmkd.

864 A242 20pf multicolored 22 22

Issued to commemorate the inauguration of the "Bird Flight Line" railroad link between Germany and Denmark.

Cross

A243

Synod Emblem and Crown of Barbed Wire

A244

Lithographed and Embossed

1963, May 24 *Perf. 14* Unwmkd.

865 A243 20pf magenta, red & yellow 22 22

Issued to commemorate the centenary of the founding of the International Red Cross in connection with the German Red Cross centenary celebrations, Munster, May 24–26.

Perf. 13½x13

1963, July 24 Litho. Wmk. 304

866 A244 20pf dp. orge. & blk. 35 35

Issued to honor the meeting of German Protestants (Evangelical Synod), Dortmund, July 24–28.

Europa Issue, 1963

Common Design Type

1963, Sept. 14 Engr. *Perf. 14*

Size: 28x23½mm.

867 CD6 15pf green 20 25
868 " 20pf red 15 7

Old Town Hall, Hanover

A245

State Capitals: No. 870, Hamburg harbor, 775th anniversary. No. 871, North Ferry pier, Kiel. No. 872, National Theater, Munich. No. 873, Fountain and building, Wiesbaden. No. 874, Reichstag Building, Berlin. No. 875, Gutenberg Museum, Mainz. No. 876, Jan Wellem (Johann Wilhelm II, 1658–1716) statue, Dusseldorf. No. 877, City Hall, Bonn. No. 878, City Hall, Bremen. No. 879, View of Stuttgart. No. 879A, Ludwig's Church, Saarbrucken.

Perf. 14

1964–65 Litho. Unwmkd.

869 A245 20pf gray, blk. & red 30 30
870 " 20pf multicolored 30 30
871 " 20pf " 30 30
872 " 20pf " 30 30
873 " 20pf " 30 30
874 " 20pf bl., blk. & grn. 27 27
875 " 20pf multicolored 27 27
876 " 20pf " 27 27
877 " 20pf " ('65) 27 27
878 " 20pf " ('65) 27 27
879 " 20pf " ('65) 27 27
879A " 20pf " ('65) 27 27
Nos. 869-879A (12) 3.39 3.39

View of Ottobeuren Abbey

A246

Lithographed and Engraved

1964, May 29 *Perf. 14*

880 A246 20pf pink, red & blk. 20 20

Issued to commemorate the 1200th anniversary of the Ottobeuren Benedictine Abbey.

President Heinrich Lübke

A247

Sophie Scholl

A248

1964, July 1 Litho. *Perf. 14*

881 A247 20pf carmine 20 12
882 " 40pf ultramarine 45 25

Issued to honor President Heinrich Lübke on his re-election. See also Nos. 974–975.

1964, July 20 Litho. and Engr.

Designs: No. 884, Ludwig Beck. No. 885, Dietrich Bonhoeffer. No. 886, Alfred Delp. No. 887, Karl Friedrich Goerdeler. No. 888, Wilhelm Leuschner. No. 889, Count James von Moltke. No. 890, Count Claus Schenk von Stauffenberg.

883 A248 20pf bl. gray & blk. 1.65 2.75
884 " 20pf " " " 1.65 2.75
885 " 20pf " " " 1.65 2.75
886 " 20pf " " " 1.65 2.75
887 " 20pf " " " 1.65 2.75
888 " 20pf " " " 1.65 2.75
889 " 20pf " " " 1.65 2.75
890 " 20pf " " " 1.65 2.75
Nos. 883-890 (8) 13.20 22.00

Issued to honor the German resistance to the Nazis, 1943–45. Printed in sheet of eight, containing one each of Nos. 883–890, se-tenant. Size: 148x105mm. The stamps were valid; the sheet was not, though widely used.

John Calvin

A249

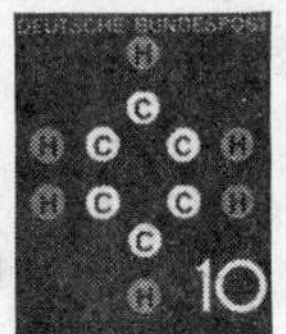

Benzene Ring, Kekulé's Formula

A250

1964, Aug. 3 Litho. *Perf. 14*

891 A249 20pf red & black 20 20

Issued to honor the meeting of the International Union of the Reformed Churches in Germany, Frankfort on the Main, Aug. 3–13.

1964, Aug. 14 *Perf. 14* Unwmkd.

Designs: 15pf, Cerenkov radiation, reactor in operation. 20pf, German gas engine.

892 A250 10pf dark brown, brt. green & black 10 4
893 " 15pf bright green, ultra. & black 15 10
894 " 20pf red, grn. & blk. 20 12

Issued to publicize progress in science and technology: 10pf, centenary of benzene formula by August Friedrich Kekulé; 15pf, 25 years of nuclear fission, Hahn and Strassmann; 20pf, centenary of German internal combustion engine, Nikolaus August Otto and Eugen Langen.

Ferdinand Lasalle

A251

Radiating Sun

A252

1964, Aug. 31 Lithographed

895 A251 20pf slate bl. & blk. 22 22

Issued to commemorate the centenary of the death of Ferdinand Lasalle, a founder of the German Labor Movement.

1964, Sept. 2 Engraved Wmk. 304

896 A252 20pf gray & red 25 30

Issued to commemorate the 80th meeting of German Catholics, Stuttgart, Sept. 2–6. The inscription from Romans 12:2: ". . . be ye transformed through the renewing of your mind."

Europa Issue, 1964

Common Design Type

1964, Sept. 14 Litho. Unwmkd.

Size: 23x29mm.

897 CD7 15pf yel. grn. & lilac 22 25
898 " 20pf rose & lilac 22 7

Judo

A253

Prussian Eagle

A254

1964, Oct. 10

899 A253 20pf multicolored 18 20

18th Olympic Games, Tokyo, Oct. 10–25.

Lithographed and Embossed

1964, Oct. 30 *Perf. 14* Unwmkd.

900 A254 20pf brown orange & black 18 20

Issued to commemorate 250 years of the Court of Accounts in Germany, founded as the Royal Prussian Upper Chamber of Accounts.

John F. Kennedy

A255

Castle Gate, Ellwangen

A256

1964, Nov. 21 Engraved Wmk. 304

901 A255 40pf dark blue 40 45

Issued to commemorate the first anniversary of the death of Pres. John F. Kennedy (1917–1963).

1964–66 Typographed Unwmkd.

Designs: (German buildings through 12 centuries): 10pf, Wall pavilion, Zwinger, Dresden. 15pf, Tegel Castle, Berlin. 20pf, Portico, Lorsch. 40pf, Trifels Fortress, Palatinate. 60pf, Treptow Gate, Neubrandenburg. 70pf, Osthofen Gate, Soest. 80pf, Elling Gate, Weissenburg.

903 A256 10pf brown ('65) 10 5
904 " 15pf dark green ('65) 20 5
a. Booklet pane of 10 ('65) 3.50
b. Tête bêche pair ('65) 1.10 1.10
905 A256 20pf brown red ('65) 22 5
a. Booklet pane of 10 ('66) 3.85
b. Tête bêche pair ('66) 1.00 1.00

Engraved

908 A256 40pf violet blue ('65) 50 5
909 " 50pf olive bister 70 15
910 " 60pf rose red 90 55
911 " 70pf dark green ('65) 90 25
912 " 80pf chocolate 95 35
Nos. 903-912 (8) 4.49 1.50

Nos. 903–905, 908, 910–912 were issued in sheets of 100 and in coils. Every fifth coil stamp has a black control number on the back.

Illustrations from the Works of Matthias Claudius

A257

Otto von Bismarck by Franz von Lenbach

A258

1965, Jan. 21 Engraved *Perf. 14*

917 A257 20pf black & red 20 20

Issued to commemorate the 150th anniversary of the death of Matthias Claudius, poet and editor of the "Wandsbecker Bothe." Exists imperf. Price $350.

1965, Apr. 1 Lithographed *Perf. 14*

918 A258 20pf blk. & dull red 20 20

Issued to commemorate the sesquicentennial of the birth of Prince Otto von Bismarck (1815–1898), Prussian statesman and first chancellor of the German Empire. Exists imperf. Price $250.

Jet Plane and Space Capsule

A259

Bouquet of Flowers

A260

Designs: 5pf, Traffic lights and signs. 10pf, Communications satellite and ground station. 15pf, Old and new post buses. 20pf, Semaphore telegraph and telecommunication tower. 40pf, Old and new railroad engines. 70pf, Sailing ship and ocean liner.

1965

919 A259 5pf gray & multi. 5 5
920 " 10pf multicolored 10 5
921 " 15pf " 15 8
922 " 20pf maroon & multi. 20 8
923 " 40pf dk. bl. & multi. 40 15
924 " 60pf dull vio., yel. & lt. blue 65 55
925 " 70pf multicolored 70 45
Nos. 919-925 (7) 2.25 1.41

Issued to commemorate the International Transport and Communications Exhibition, Munich, June 25–Oct. 30. No. 924 also commemorates the 10th anniversary of the reopening of air service by Lufthansa. Issue dates: No. 924, Apr. 1. Others, June 25.

No. 919 exists imperf.

1965, May 1 Lithographed

926 A260 15pf multicolored 15 17

Issued to commemorate the 75th anniversary of May Day celebration in Germany.

ITU Emblem

A261

Adolph Kolping

A262

1965, May 17 *Perf. 14* Unwmkd.

927 A261 40pf deep bl. & blk. 40 40

Issued to commemorate the centenary of the International Telecommunication Union.

1965, May 26 **Typographed**

928 A262 20pf blk., gray & red 20 20

Issued to commemorate the centenary of the death of Adolph Kolping (1813–1865), founder of the Catholic Unions of Journeymen, the Kolpingwork.

Rescue Ship
A263

1965, May 29 **Litho. & Engr.**

929 A263 20pf red & black 20 20

Issued to commemorate the centenary of the German Sea Rescue Service.

Type of 1955 dated "1945–1965"
Perf. 14x13½

1965, July 28 Engraved Wmk. 304

930 A161 20pf gray 20 20

20 years of German expatriation.

Synod Emblem and Labyrinth
A264

Lithographed and Engraved
Perf. 13½x14

1965, July 28 **Unwmkd.**

931 A264 20pf dp. blue, greenish blue & black 20 20

Issued to honor the 12th meeting of German Protestants (Evangelical Synod), Cologne, July 28–Aug. 1.

Waves and Stuttgart Television Tower
A265

1965, July 28 Litho. *Perf. 13½x13*

932 A265 20pf dp. bl., blk. & bright pink 20 20

Issued to publicize the German Radio Exhibition, Stuttgart, Aug. 27–Sept. 5.

Stamps of Thurn and Taxis, 1852–59—A266

1965, Aug. 28 ***Perf. 14***

933 A266 20pf multicolored 20 20

Issued to commemorate the 125th anniversary of the introduction of postage stamps in Great Britain.

Europa Issue, 1965
Common Design Type
Perf. 14x13½

1965, Sept. 27 Engraved Wmk. 304
Size: 28x23mm.

934 CD8 15pf green 17 25
935 " 20pf dull red 20 10

Nordertor, Flensburg — A267
Brandenburg Gate — A268

Designs: 5pf, Berlin Gate, Stettin. 10pf, Wall Pavilion, Zwinger, Dresden. 20pf, Portico, Lorsch. 40pf, Trifels Fortress, Palatinate. 50pf, Castle Gate, Ellwangen. 60pf, Treptow Gate, Neubrandenburg. 70pf, Osthofen Gate, Soest. 80pf, Elling Gate, Weissenburg. 90pf, Zschocke Ladies' Home, Königsberg. 1m, Melanchthon House, Wittenberg. 1.10m, Trinity Hospital, Hildesheim. 1.30m, Tegel Castle, Berlin. 2m, Löwenberg, Town Hall, interior view.

Engraved

1966–69 ***Perf. 14*** **Unwmkd.**

936	A267	5pf olive	8	5
937	"	10pf dk. brown ('67)	11	5
939	"	20pf dk. green ('67)	27	4
940	"	30pf yellow green	65	5
941	"	30pf red ('67)	50	5
942	"	40pf olive bister ('67)	65	20
943	"	50pf blue ('67)	75	15
944	"	60pf dp. org. ('67)	1.90	65
945	"	70pf slate grn. ('67)	1.65	35
946	"	80pf red brn. ('67)	1.65	65
947	"	90pf black	1.50	35
948	"	1m dull blue	1.50	17
949	"	1.10m red brown	1.80	38
950	"	1.30m green ('69)	1.80	70
951	"	2m purple	2.50	50
		Nos. 936-951 (15)	17.31	4.34

1966–68 **Typographed** ***Perf. 14***

952	A268	10pf chocolate	15	5
		a. Bklt. pane of 10 (4 No. 952, 2 No. 953, 4 No. 954) ('67)	3.85	
		b. Tête bêche pair	35	25
		c. Bklt. pane of 6 (2 No. 952, 4 No. 953)	2.25	
953	A268	20pf deep green	35	4
		a. Tête bêche pair ('68)	80	80
		b. Bklt. pane of 4 (2 No. 953, 2 No. 954)	2.25	
954	A268	30pf red	55	5
		a. Tête bêche pair ('68)	1.20	90
955	A268	50pf dark blue	1.20	45
956	"	100pf dk. blue ('67)	2.25	80
		Nos. 952-956 (5)	4.50	1.39

Nos. 952–956 were issued in sheets of 100 and in coils. Every fifth coil stamp has a black control number on the back.

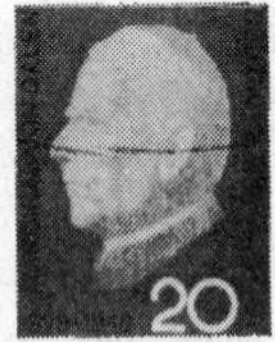

Nathan Söderblom — A269
Cardinal von Galen — A270

1966, Jan. 15 Litho. *Perf. 13x13½*

959 A269 20pf dull lilac & blk. 20 20

Issued to commemorate the centenary of the birth of Nathan Soderblom (1866–1931), Swedish Protestant theologian, who worked for the union of Christian churches and received 1930 Nobel Peace Prize.

1966, Mar. 22 **Litho.** ***Perf. 14***

960 A270 20pf dp. lilac rose, salmon pink & black 20 20

Issued to commemorate the 20th anniversary of the death of Clemens August Cardinal Count von Galen (1878–1946), anti-Nazi Bishop of Munster.

"The Miraculous Draught" — A271
G. W. Leibniz — A272

1966, July 13 **Litho.** ***Perf. 14***

961 A271 30pf dp. org. & blk. 30 20

Issued to commemorate the 81st meeting of German Catholics, Bamberg, July 13–17.

1966, Aug. 24 *Perf. 14* Unwmkd.

962 A272 30pf rose car., pink & black 30 20

Issued to commemorate the 250th anniversary of the death of Gottfried Wilhelm Leibniz (1646–1716), philosopher and mathematician.

Europa Issue, 1966
Common Design Type

1966, Sept. 24 ***Perf. 14***
Size: 23x28½mm.

963 CD9 20pf multicolored 35 35
964 " 30pf " 30 8

Diagram of Three-Phase Transmission — A273
UNICEF Emblem — A274

Design: 30pf, Dynamo.

1966, Sept. 28 **Lithographed**

965 A273 20pf multicolored 20 17
966 " 30pf " 38 17

Issued to publicize progress in science and technology: 20pf, 75th anniversary of three-phase power transmission; 30pf, centenary of discovery by Werner von Siemens of the dynamoelectric principle.

1966, Oct. 24 **Litho.** ***Perf. 14***

967 A274 30pf red, blk. & gray 30 20

Issued to commemorate the awarding of the 1965 Nobel Peace Prize to UNICEF (United Nations International Children's Emergency Fund).

Werner von Siemens
A275

1966, Dec. 13 Engraved *Perf. 14*

968 A275 30pf maroon 30 20

Issued to commemorate the 150th anniversary of the birth of Werner von Siemens (1816–1892), electrical engineer and inventor.

Europa Issue, 1967
Common Design Type

1967, May 2 **Photo.** ***Perf. 14***
Size: 23x28mm.

969 CD10 20pf multicolored 30 30
970 " 30pf " 30 8

Franz von Taxis — A276
"Peace Is Among Us" — A277

Lithographed and Engraved

1967, June 3 ***Perf. 14***

971 A276 30pf dp. org. & blk. 30 20

Issued to commemorate the 450th anniversary of the death of Franz von Taxis, founder of the Taxis (Thurn and Taxis) postal system.

1967, June 21

972 A277 30pf brt. pink & blk. 30 20

Issued to honor the 13th meeting of German Protestants (Evangelical Synod), Hanover, June 21–25.

Friedrich von Bodelschwingh
A278

Perf. 13½x13

1967, July 1 **Litho.** **Unwmkd.**

973 A278 30pf reddish brown & black 30 20

Centenary of Bethel Institution (for the incurable). Friedrich von Bodelschwingh (1877–1946), manager of Bethel (1910–1946) and son of the founder.

Lübke Type of 1964

1967, Oct. 14 **Litho.** ***Perf. 14***

974 A247 30pf carmine 30 25
975 " 50pf ultramarine 55 60

Re-election of President Heinrich Lübke.

The Wartburg, Eisenach
A279

1967, Oct. 31 **Engr.** ***Perf. 14***

976 A279 30pf red 30 20

450th anniversary of the Reformation.

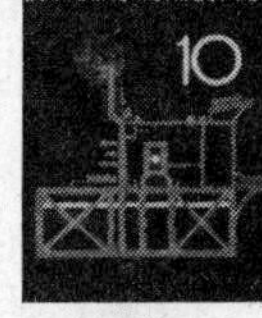

Cross and Map of South America — A280
Koenig Printing Press — A281

1967, Nov. 17 **Photo.** ***Perf. 14***

977 A280 30pf multicolored 30 20

Issued to honor "Adveniat," aid movement of German Catholics for the Latin American church.

1968, Jan. 12 **Litho.** ***Perf. 14***

Designs: 20pf, Zinc sulfide and lead sulfide crystals. 30pf, Schematic diagram of a microscope.

978 A281 10pf multicolored 10 4

979 A281 20pf multicolored 20 12
980 " 30pf " 30 22

Issued to publicize progress in science and technology: 10pf, 150th anniversary of the Koenig printing press; 20pf, 1000th anniversary of mining in the Harz Mountains; 30pf, centenary of scientific microscope construction.

Symbols of Various Crafts
A282

1968, Mar. 8 Litho. ***Perf. 14***
981 A282 30pf multicolored 30 20

Traditions and progress of the crafts. Exists imperf. Price $250.

Souvenir Sheet

Adenauer, Churchill, de Gasperi and Schuman—A283

Portraits: 10pf, Winston S. Churchill. 20pf, Alcide de Gasperi. 30pf, Robert Schuman. 50pf, Konrad Adenauer.

1968, Apr. 19 Litho. ***Perf. 14***
Black Inscriptions
982 A283 Sheet of four 3.25 3.50
a. 10pf dk. red brown 65 70
b. 20pf green 65 70
c. 30pf dark red 65 70
d. 50pf bright blue 65 70

Issued to commemorate the first anniversary of the death of Konrad Adenauer (1876–1967), chancellor of West Germany (1949–63), and to honor leaders in building a united Europe. The sheet has white margin and black inscription. Size: 147x104mm.

Europa Issue, 1968
Common Design Type

1968, Apr. 29 Photogravure
Size: 29x24½mm
983 CD11 20pf grn., yel. & brn. 27 22
984 " 30pf car., yellow & brown 30 7

Karl Marx A284 — Pierre de Coubertin A285

Lithographed and Engraved

1968, Apr. 29 ***Perf. 14***
985 A284 30pf red, blk. & gray 30 20

Issued to commemorate the 150th anniversary of the birth of Karl Marx (1818–1883), political philosopher and writer.

Olympic Games Issue, 1968

1968, June 6 ***Perf. 14*** **Unwmkd.**
986 A285 30pf lilac & dk. pur. 38 9
Nos. 986, B434-B437 (5) 2.93 2.64

Issued to publicize the 19th Olympic Games, Mexico City, Oct. 12–27.

Opening Bars, "Die Meistersinger von Nurnberg," by Wagner—A286

1968, June 21 Litho. and Photo.
987 A286 30pf gray, black & fawn 45 20

Issued to commemorate the centenary of the first performance of Richard Wagner's "Die Meistersinger von Nurnberg."

Konrad Adenauer
A287

1968, July 19 Litho. ***Perf. 14***
988 A287 30pf dp. org. & blk. 45 20

Issued in memory of Konrad Adenauer (1876–1967).

Cross and Dove in Center of Universe
A288

1968, July 19 Litho. and Engr.
989 A288 20pf brt. green, blue black & yel. 45 20

Issued to publicize the 82nd meeting of German Catholics, Essen, Sept. 4–8.

North German Confederation Nos. 4 and 10
A289

1968, Sept. 5 Engraved ***Perf. 14***
990 A289 30pf copper red, gray violet & blk. 40 20

Issued to commemorate the centenary of the stamps of the North German Confederation.

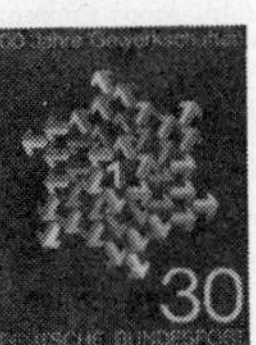

Arrows Symbolizing Determination
A290

Human Rights Flame
A291

1968, Sept. 26 Photo. ***Perf. 14***
991 A290 30pf multicolored 40 20

Centenary of the German trade unions.

1968, Dec. 10 Photo. ***Perf. 14***
992 A291 30pf multicolored 40 20

International Human Rights Year.

Junkers 52
A292

Design: 30pf, Boeing 707.

1969, Feb. 6 Litho. ***Perf. 14***
993 A292 20pf green & multi. 55 17
994 " 30pf red & multi. 75 17

Issued to commemorate the 50th anniversary of German airmail service.

Five-pointed Star
A293

1969, Apr. 28 Litho. ***Perf. 13½x13***
995 A293 30pf red & multi. 40 20

Issued to commemorate the 50th anniversary of the International Labor Organization.

Europa Issue, 1969
Common Design Type

1969, Apr. 28 Photo. ***Perf. 14***
Size: 29x23mm.
996 CD12 20pf grn., bl. & yel. 32 28
997 " 30pf red brown, yel. & black 38 8

Heraldic Eagles of Federal and Weimar Republics
A294

1969, May 23 Photo. ***Perf. 14***
998 A294 30pf red, blk. & gold 45 20

Issued to commemorate the 20th anniversary of the German Basic Law, and the 50th anniversary of the proclamation of the Weimar Constitution.

Crosses
A295

1969, June 4 Litho. and Engr.
999 A295 30pf dk. violet blue & cream 40 20

Issued to commemorate the 50th anniversary of the German War Graves Commission.

Seashore
A296

Designs: 20pf, Foothills. 30pf, Mountains. 50pf, Riverbed.

1969, June 4 ***Perf. 14***
1000 A296 10pf black, gray & bister 15 5
1001 " 20pf black, lt. green & blue 80 35
1002 " 30pf multicolored 38 25
1003 " 50pf " 65 65

Issued to publicize Nature Protection.

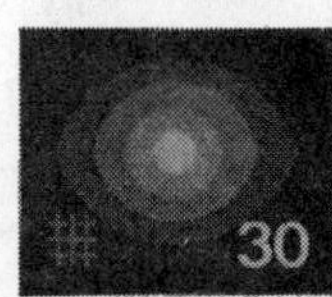

"Hungry for Justice"
A297

1969, July 7 Lithographed ***Perf. 14***
1004 A297 30pf multicolored 40 20

Issued to honor the 14th meeting of German Protestants (Evangelical Synod), Stuttgart, July 16–20.

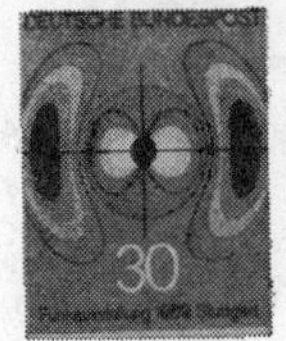

Electromagnetic Field
A298

Maltese Cross
A299

1969, Aug. 11 Litho. ***Perf. 14***
1005 A298 30pf red & multi. 40 20

Issued to publicize the German Radio Exhibition, Stuttgart, Aug. 29–Sept. 7.

1969, Aug. 11 ***Perf. 13x13½***
1006 A299 30pf red & black 40 20

Issued to honor the Maltese Relief Service, founded 1955, for its world-wide activities in social services, first aid and disaster assistance.

Souvenir Sheet

Marie Juchacz, Marie-Elisabeth Lüders and Helene Weber—A300

1969, Aug. 11 Engraved ***Perf. 14***
1007 A300 Sheet of 3 80 80
a. 10pf olive 10 10
b. 20pf dk. green 20 15
c. 30pf lake 30 25

Issued to commemorate the 50th anniversary of universal women's suffrage, Marie Juchacz (1879–1956), Marie-Elisabeth Lüders (1878–1966) and Helene Weber (1881–1962) were members of the German Reichstag. No. 1007 has olive commemorative inscription. Size: 100x60mm.

The lack of a price for a listed item does not necessarily indicate rarity.

Bavaria No. 16 A301 — Brine Pipe Line A302

1969, Sept. 4 **Litho. & Embossed**

1008 A301 30pf gray & rose 40 20

Issued to commemorate the 23rd meeting of the Federation of German Philatelists, Sept. 6, the 70th Philatelists' Day, Sept. 7, and the philatelic exhibition "120 Years of Bavarian Stamps" in Garmish-Partenkirchen, Sept. 4–7.

1969, Sept. 4 Litho. *Perf. 13½x13*

1009 A302 20pf multicolored 27 25

Issued to commemorate the 350th anniversary of the Brine Pipe Line from Traunstein to Bad Reichenhall.

Rothenburg ob der Tauber—A303

Lithographed and Engraved

1969, Sept. 4 ***Perf. 14***

1010 A303 30pf dark red & black 45 20

See also Nos. 1047–1049, 1067–1069A, 1106–1110.

Pope John XXIII A304 — Mahatma Gandhi A305

1969, Oct. 2 Engr. *Perf. 13½x14*

1011 A304 30pf dark red 38 20

Issued in memory of Pope John XXIII (1881–1963).

1969, Oct. 2 **Lithographed**

1012 A305 20pf yel. grn. & blk. 27 25

Issued to commemorate the centenary of the birth of Mohandas K. Gandhi (1869–1948), leader in India's fight for independence.

Ernst Moritz Arndt A306 — Ludwig van Beethoven A307

1969, Nov. 13 **Litho. & Engr.**

1013 A306 30pf gray & maroon 38 20

Issued to commemorate the bicentenary of the birth of Ernst Moritz Arndt (1769–1860), historian, poet and member of German National Assembly.

1970, Mar. 20 ***Perf. 13½x14***

Portraits: 20pf, Georg Wilhelm Hegel (1770–1831), philosopher. 30pf, Friedrich Hölderlin (1770–1843), poet.

1014 A307 10pf pale vio. & blk. 15 9
1015 " 20pf olive & black 25 20
1016 " 30pf rose & black 45 20

Bicentenary of births of Beethoven, Hegel and Hölderlin.

Saar No. 171 A308

1970, Apr. 29 Photo. *Perf. 14x13½*

1017 A308 30pf black, red & gray green 40 20

Issued to publicize the SABRIA National Stamp Exhibition, Saarbrucken, Apr. 29–May 4. No. 1017 was issued Apr. 29 at the SABRIA post office in Saarbrucken, on May 4 throughout Germany.

Europa Issue, 1970

Common Design Type

1970, May 4 Engr. *Perf. 14x13½*

Size: 28x23mm.

1018 CD13 20pf green 27 12
1019 " 30pf red 38 15

Münchhausen on His Severed Horse

A309

1970, May 11 Litho. *Perf. 13½x13*

1020 A309 20pf multicolored 32 17

Issued to commemorate the 250th anniversary of the birth of Count Hieronymus C. F. von Münchhausen (1720–1797), soldier and storyteller.

Seagoing Vessel and Underpass A310 — Nurse Assisting Elderly Woman A311

1970, June 18 **Litho.** ***Perf. 14***

1021 A310 20pf multicolored 30 17

Issued to commemorate the 75th anniversary of the North Sea-Baltic Sea Canal.

1970 **Photogravure**

Designs: 5pf, Welder (industrial protection). 10pf, Mountain climbers (rescuer bringing down casualty). 30pf, Fireman. 50pf, Stretcher bearer, casualty and ambulance. 70pf, Rescuer and drowning boy.

1022 A311 5pf dull bl. & multi. 12 4
1023 " 10pf brown & multi. 16 9
1024 " 20pf grn. & multi. 30 17
1025 " 30pf red & multi. 40 17
1026 " 50pf blue & multi. 70 50
1027 " 70pf green & multi. 1.00 80
Nos. 1022–1027 (6) 2.68 1.77

Honoring various voluntary services.
Issue dates: 20pf, 30pf, June 18. Others, Sept. 21.

Pres. Gustav Heinemann A312 — Cross Seen through Glass A313

1970–73 **Engraved** ***Perf. 14***

1028 A312 5pf dark gray 4 5
1029 " 10pf brown 10 5
1030 " 20pf green 20 5
1030A " 25pf deep yellow grn. ('71) 25 7
1031 " 30pf red brown ('71) 30 5
1032 " 40pf brn. org. ('71) 40 20
1033 " 50pf dk. blue ('71) 50 15
1034 " 60pf blue ('71) 60 22
1035 " 70pf dk. brn. ('71) 70 33
1036 " 80pf slate grn. ('71) 80 45
1037 " 90pf magenta ('71) 1.90 65
1038 " 1m olive 1.00 33
1038A " 1.10m olive gray ('73) 1.10 55
1039 " 1.20m ocher ('72) 1.20 75
1040 " 1.30m ocher ('72) 1.30 55
1040A " 1.40m dk. blue green ('73) 1.40 70
1041 " 1.50m purple ('72) 1.50 65
1042 " 1.60m orange ('72) 1.60 95
1042A " 1.70m orange ('72) 1.70 65
1043 " 1.90m deep claret ('73) 1.90 70
1044 " 2m dp. vio. ('71) 2.00 75
Nos. 1028–1044 (21) 20.49 8.85

1970, Aug. 25 **Lithographed**

1045 A313 20pf emerald & yel. 27 17

Issued to publicize the world mission of Catholic missionaries who bring the Gospel to all peoples.

Cross—A314 — Comenius—A315

1970, Sept. 4 ***Perf. 13x13½***

1046 A314 20pf multicolored 40 17

Issued to publicize the 83rd meeting of German Catholics, Trier, Sept. 9–13.

Town Type of 1969

Designs: No. 1047, View of Cochem and Moselle River. No. 1048, Cathedral and view of Freiburg im Breisgau. No. 1049, View of Oberammergau.

1970 **Litho. & Engr.** ***Perf. 14***

1047 A303 20pf apple green & black 40 17
1048 " 20pf grn. & dk. brn. 35 17
1049 " 30pf dp. org. & blk. 45 20

Issue dates: No. 1047, Sept. 21; No. 1048, Nov. 4; No. 1049, May 11.

1970, Nov. 12 ***Perf. 13½x14***

1050 A315 30pf dk. red & blk. 38 17

Issued to commemorate the 300th anniversary of the death of John Amos Comenius (1592–1670), theologian and educator.

Friedrich Engels A316 — Imperial Eagle, 1872—A317

1970, Nov. 27 **Litho.** ***Perf. 14***

1051 A316 50pf red & vio. blue 65 45

Sesquicentennial of the birth of Friedrich Engels (1820–1895), socialist, collaborator with Karl Marx.

1971, Jan. 18 Litho. *Perf. 13½x14*

1052 A317 30pf multicolored 38 17

Centenary of the German Empire.

Friedrich Ebert (Germany No. 378)—A318 — Molecule Diagram Textile Pattern A319

1971, Jan. 18 ***Perf. 13***

1053 A318 30pf red brown, olive & blk. 38 17

Centenary of the birth of Friedrich Ebert (1871–1925), first President of the German Republic.

1971, Feb. 18 Litho. *Perf. 13½x13*

1054 A319 20pf brt. green, red & black 27 17

Synthetic textile fiber research, 125th anniversary.

School Crossing A320 — Signal to Pass A321

1971, Feb. 18 ***Perf. 14***

Traffic Signs: 20pf, Proceed with caution. 30pf, Stop. 50pf, Pedestrian crossing.

1055 A320 10pf black, ultra. & red 20 9
1056 " 20pf black, red & green 27 12
1057 " 30pf black, gray & red 38 15
1058 " 50pf black, ultra. & red 90 50

New traffic rules, effective Mar. 1, 1971.

1971, Apr. 16 **Photo.** ***Perf. 14***

Traffic Signs: 10pf, Warning signal. 20pf, Drive at right. 30pf, "Observe pedestrian crossings."

1059 A321 5pf blue, black & carmine 9 4
1060 " 10pf multicolored 13 10
1061 " 20pf brt. grn., blk. & carmine 30 17
1062 " 30pf car. & multi. 65 17

New traffic rules, effective Mar. 1, 1971.

Luther Facing Charles V, Woodcut by Rabus—A322 — Thomas à Kempis—A323

1971, March 18 ***Perf. 14***

1063 A322 30pf red & black 38 17

450th anniversary of the Diet of Worms.

Europa Issue, 1971

Common Design Type

1971, May 3 Photo. *Perf. 14*

Size: 28½x23mm.

1064 CD14 20pf green, gold & black 20 12
1065 " 30pf dp. carmine, gold & blk. 45 20

1971, May 3 Engraved

1066 A323 30pf red & black 38 17

500th anniversary of the death of Thomas à Kempis (1379–1471), Augustinian monk, author of "The Imitation of Christ."

Town Type of 1969

Designs: 20pf, View of Goslar. No. 1068, View of Nuremberg. No. 1069, Heligoland. 40pf, Heidelberg.

1971–72 Litho. & Engr. *Perf. 14*

1067 A303 20pf brt. grn. & blk. 35 17
1068 " 30pf verm. & black 45 17
1069 " 30pf lt. green & black ('72) 40 17
1069A " 40pf org. & black ('72) 55 20

Issue dates: 20pf, Sept. 15; No. 1068, May 21; Nos. 1069, 1069A, Oct. 20.

Dürer's Signature
A324

1971, May 21 Engraved

1070 A324 30pf copper red & black 45 17

500th anniversary of the birth of Albrecht Dürer (1471–1528), painter and engraver.

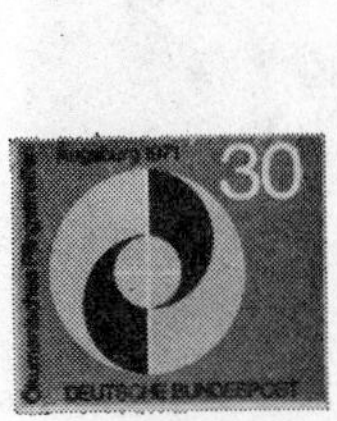

Congress Emblem
A325

Illustration from New Astronomy, by Kepler
A326

1971, May 28 Litho. *Perf. 13½x13*

1071 A325 30pf red, org. & blk. 45 17

Ecumenical Meeting at Pentecost of the German Evangelical and Catholic Churches, Augsburg, June 2–5.

1971, June 25 Photo. *Perf. 14*

1072 A326 30pf brt. carmine, gold & blk. 45 17

400th anniversary of the birth of Johannes Kepler (1571–1630), astronomer.

Dante Alighieri
A327

"Matches Cause Fires"
A328

1971, Sept. 3 Engraved *Perf. 14*

1073 A327 10pf black 16 8

650th anniversary of the death of Dante Alighieri (1265–1321), poet.

1971–74 Typographed *Perf. 14*

Designs: 10pf, Broken ladder. 20pf, Hand and circular saw. 25pf, "Alcohol and automobile." 30pf, Safety helmets prevent injury. 40pf, Defective plug. 50pf, Nail sticking from board. 60pf, 70pf, Traffic safety (ball rolling before car). 1m, Hoisted cargo. 1.50m, Fenced-in open manhole.

1074 A328 5pf orange 10 5
 a. Bklt. pane of 8 (2 each #1074, 1077–1079 ('74) 5.50
1075 A328 10pf dk. brn. ('72) 10 5
 a. Bklt. pane of 6 (4 #1075, 2 #1078) 2.75
 b. Bklt. pane of 8 (2 each # 1075–1076, 1078–1079 ('75) 5.00
 c. Bklt. pane of 8 (2 each # 1079, 1075, 1078, 1076) 1.75
1076 A328 20pf purple ('72) 20 5
1077 " 25pf green 25 5
1078 " 30pf dark red ('72) 30 5
1079 " 40pf rose claret ('72) 40 5
1080 " 50pf Prus. bl. ('73) 50 17
1081 " 60pf violet blue 3.00 1.00
1082 " 70pf green & vio. blue ('73) 75 25
1083 " 100pf olive ('72) 1.00 25
1085 " 150pf red brn. ('72) 1.50 65
 Nos. 1074–1085 (11) 8.10 2.62

Accident prevention.

Issued in sheets of 100 and in coils. Every fifth coil stamp has a control number on the back.

Deaconesses
A329

Senefelder's Lithography Press
A330

1972, Jan. 20 Litho. *Perf. 13x13½*

1087 A329 25pf green, black & gray 32 17

Centenary of the death of Wilhelm Löhe (1808–1872), founder of the Deaconesses Training Institute at Neuendettelsau.

1972, Apr. 14 Litho. *Perf. 13½x13*

1088 A330 25pf multicolored 35 17

175th anniversary of the invention of the lithographic printing process by Alois Senefelder in 1796.

Europa Issue 1972

Common Design Type

1972, May 2 Photo. *Perf. 13½x14*

Size: 23x29mm.

1089 CD15 25pf yel. grn., dk. blue & yel. 30 20
1090 " 30pf pale rose, dk. & light blue 40 25

Lucas Cranach, by Dürer
A331

Archer in Wheelchair
A332

Lithographed and Engraved

1972, May 18 *Perf. 14*

1091 A331 25pf green, buff & black 35 17

500th anniversary of the birth of Lucas Cranach (1472–1553), painter and engraver.

1972, July 18 Litho. *Perf. 14*

1092 A332 40pf yellow, black & red brown 55 20

21st Stoke-Mandeville Games for the Paralyzed, Heidelberg, Aug. 1–10.

Kurt Schumacher
A333

Post Horn and Decree
A334

1972, Aug. 18 Litho. & Engr.

1093 A333 40pf red & black 55 17

20th anniversary of the death of Kurt Schumacher (1895–1952), first chairman of the German Social Democratic Party.

1972, Aug. 18 Photogravure

1094 A334 40pf gold, carmine & black 55 17

Centenary of the German Postal Museum, Berlin. Design shows page from Heinrich von Stephan's decree establishing the museum.

Open Book
A335

Music by Heinrich Schütz
A336

1972, Sept. 11 Photo. *Perf. 13x13½*

1095 A335 40pf red & multi. 55 17

International Book Year 1972.

Lithographed and Engraved

1972, Sept. 29 *Perf. 14*

1096 A336 40pf multicolored 55 17

300th anniversary of the death of Heinrich Schütz (1585–1672), composer.

Carnival Dancers
A337

1972, Nov. 10 Litho. *Perf. 14*

1097 A337 40pf red & multi. 55 17

Cologne Carnival sesquicentennial.

Heinrich Heine
A338

1972, Dec. 13 Litho. *Perf. 14*

1098 A338 40pf rose, black & red 55 17

175th anniversary of the birth of Heinrich Heine (1797–1856), poet.

"Bread for the World"
A339

1972, Dec. 13 Photo. *Perf. 14*

1099 A339 30pf green & red 45 45

14th "Bread for the World-Developing Peace" campaign of the Protestant Church in Germany.

Würzburg Cathedral, 13th Century Seal
A340

1972, Dec. 13 Lithographed

1100 A340 40pf dp. car., lilac rose & blk. 55 17

Synod 72, meeting of Catholic bishoprics, Würzburg.

Colors of France and Germany Interlaced—A340a

1973, Jan. 22 Litho. *Perf. 14*

Size: 51x28mm.

1101 A340a 40pf multicolored 55 35

10th anniversary of the Franco-German Cooperation Treaty.

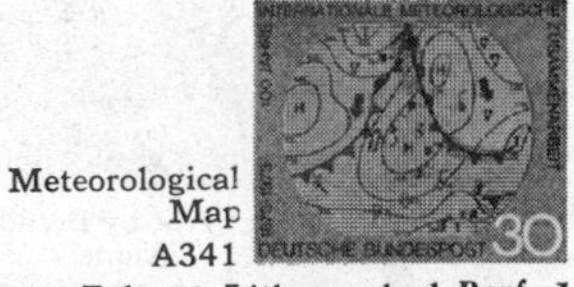

Meteorological Map
A341

1973, Feb. 19 Lithographed *Perf. 14*

1102 A341 30pf multicolored 45 22

Centenary of international meteorological cooperation.

Radio Tower and "Interpol"
A342

1973, Feb. 19 *Perf. 13½x13*

1103 A342 40pf black & red 55 20

50th anniversary of International Criminal Police Organization (INTERPOL).

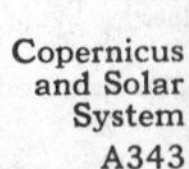

Copernicus and Solar System
A343

1973, Feb. 19 *Perf. 14*

1104 A343 40pf black & red 55 20

500th anniversary of the birth of Nicolaus Copernicus (1473–1543), astronomer.

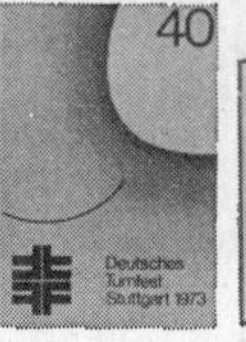

Festival Poster
A344

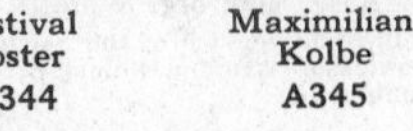

Maximilian Kolbe
A345

1973, Mar. 15 Photo. ***Perf. 14***
1105 A344 40pf multicolored 55 20

German Turner Festival, Stuttgart, June 12–17.

Town Type of 1969

Designs: 30pf, Saarbrücken. No. 1107, Ship in Hamburg Harbor. No. 1108, Rüdesheim. No. 1109, Aachen. No. 1110, Ships, Bremen Harbor.

1973 Litho. and Engr.
1106 A303 30pf yel. grn. & blk. 40 20
1107 " 40pf red & black 55 20
1108 " 40pf org. & black 55 20
1109 " 40pf brn. red & blk. 55 20
1110 " 40pf red & black 55 20
Nos. 1106–1110 (5) 2.60 1.00

Issue dates: Nos. 1107–1108, Mar. 15; Nos. 1106, 1109–1110, Oct. 19.

Europa Issue 1973
Common Design Type

1973, Apr. 30 Photo. ***Perf. 13½x14***
Size: 38½x21mm.
1114 CD16 30pf grn., lt. green & yellow 45 20
1115 " 40pf dp. magenta, lilac & yel. 45 20

1973, May 25 Litho. ***Perf. 14***
1116 A345 40pf red, black & brown 55 20

Maximilian Kolbe (1894–1941), Polish priest who died in Auschwitz and was beatified in 1971.

"R" for Roswitha
A346

"Not by Bread Alone"
A347

1973, May 25
1117 A346 40pf red, blk. & yel. 55 20

Millenary of the death of Roswitha of Gandersheim, Germany's first poetess.

1973, May 25 Photo.
1118 A347 30pf multicolored 38 20

15th meeting of German Protestants (Evangelical Synod), Dusseldorf, June 27–July 1.

Environment Emblem and "Waste"
A348

Designs (Environment Emblem and): 30pf, "Water." 40pf, "Noise." 70pf, "Air."

1973, June 5 Lithographed
1119 A348 25pf multicolored 38 22
1120 " 30pf " 50 25
1121 " 40pf org. & multi. 60 27
1122 " 70pf ultra. & multi. 1.20 55

International environment protection and Environment Day, June 5.

Reconstructed Model of Schickard's Calculator
A349

1973, June 12
1123 A349 40pf org. & multi. 65 65

350th anniversary of the calculator built by Professor Wilhelm Shickard, University of Tubingen.

Otto Wels
A350

1973, Sept. 14 Litho. ***Perf. 14***
1124 A350 40pf magenta & lilac 55 20

Centenary of the birth of Otto Wels (1873–1939), leader of German Social Democratic Party.

Lubeck Cathedral
A351

1973, Sept. 14 Litho. & Engr.
1125 A351 40pf black & multi. 55 20

800th anniversary of Lubeck Cathedral.

Emblems from U.N. and German Flags
A352

1973, Sept. 21 Lithographed
1126 A352 40pf multicolored 55 20

Germany's admission to the United Nations.

Radio and Speaker, 1923
A353

Luise Otto-Peters
A354

1973, Oct. 19 Photo. ***Perf. 14***
1127 A353 30pf brt. green & multi. 38 20

50 years of German broadcasting.

1974, Jan. 15 Litho. & Engr.
Orange & Black
1128 A354 40pf *shown* 65 33
1129 " 40pf *Helene Lange* 65 33
1130 " 40pf *Gertrud Bäumer* 65 33
1131 " 40pf *Rosa Luxemburg* 65 33

Honoring German women writers and leaders in political and women's movements.

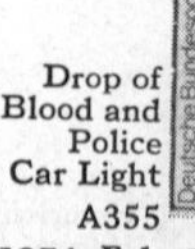

Drop of Blood and Police Car Light
A355

1974, Feb. 15 Photogravure ***Perf. 14***
1132 A355 40pf car. & ultra. 50 20

Blood donor service in conjunction with accident emergency service.

Handicapped People
A356

1974, Feb. 15 Lithographed ***Perf. 14***
1133 A356 40pf red & black 50 20

Rehabilitation of the handicapped.

Thomas Aquinas Teaching
A357

1974, Feb. 15
1134 A357 40pf black & red 50 20

700th anniversary of the death of St. Thomas Aquinas (1225–1274), scholastic philosopher.

Deer in Red, by Franz Marc—A358

Paintings: No. 1136, Girls under Trees, by August Macke, 40pf, Portrait in Blue, by Alexej von Jawlensky (vert.), 50pf, Pechstein (man) Asleep, by Erich Heckel (vert.), 70pf, "Big Still-life," by Max Beckmann. 120pf, Old Farmer, by Ernst Ludwig Kirchner (vert.).

1974 Photogravure
1135 A358 30pf multicolored 38 20
1136 " 30pf " 38 17
1137 " 40pf " 50 20
1138 " 50pf " 70 35
1139 " 70pf " 80 55
1140 " 120pf " 1.35 1.00
Nos. 1135–1140 (6) 4.11 2.47

German expressionist painters.
Issue dates: Nos. 1135 and 1137, Feb. 15. Nos. 1136 and 1138, Aug. 16. Nos. 1139–1140, Oct. 29.

Young Man, by Lehmbruck
A359

Immanuel Kant
A360

Europa Issue 1974

Design: 40pf, Kneeling Woman, by Wilhelm Lehmbruck.

1974, Apr. 17 Lithographed ***Perf. 14***
1141 A359 30pf multicolored 35 17
1142 " 40pf " 45 22

Lithographed and Engraved (#1143), Engraved (#1144)

1974 ***Perf. 14***

Portrait: 40pf, Friedrich Gottlieb Klopstock.

1143 A360 40pf black & red 50 20
1144 " 90pf maroon 90 60

250th anniversaries of the birth of Friedrich Gottlieb Klopstock (1724–1803), poet, and Immanuel Kant (1724–1804), philosopher.
Issue dates: No. 1143, May 15; No. 1144, April 17.

Souvenir Sheet

Federal Eagle and Flag—A361

1974, May 15 Litho. & Embossed
1145 A361 40pf gray & multi. 95 95

25th anniversary of the Federal Republic of Germany. No. 1145 has gray margin with black, red and orange border. Size: 100x70mm.

Soccer and Games Emblem
A362

Design: 40pf, Three soccer players.

1974, May 15 Lithographed
1146 A362 30pf green & multi. 60 20
1147 " 40pf org. & multi. 80 25

World Cup Soccer Championship, Munich, June 13–July 7.

Crowned Cross Emblem of Diaconate
A363

Landscape
A364

1974, May 15
1148 A363 40pf multicolored 50 20

125th anniversary of the Diaconal Association of the German Protestant Church.

1974, May 15
1149 A364 30pf multicolored 38 20

To promote hiking and youth hostels.

Broken Bars of Prison Window
A365

1974, July 16 Litho. ***Perf. 14x13½***
1150 A365 70pf vio. bl. & blk. 80 45

"Amnesty International," an organization for the protection of the rights of political, non-violent, prisoners.

Hans Holbein, Self-portrait
A366

Lithographed and Engraved

1974, July 16 ***Perf. 13½x14***

1151	A366	50pf multicolored	65	27

450th anniversary of the death of Hans Holbein the Elder (c. 1470–1524), painter.

Man and Woman Looking at Moon, by Friedrich—A367

1974, Aug. 16 **Photo.** ***Perf. 14***

1152	A367	50pf multicolored	65	35

200th anniversary of the birth of Caspar David Friedrich (1774–1840), German Romantic painter.

Swiss and German 19th Century Mail Boxes A368

Mothers and Foundation Emblem A369

1974, Oct. 29 **Litho.** ***Perf. 14***

1153	A368	50pf red & multi.	70	65

Centenary of Universal Postal Union.

1975, Jan. 15 Lithographed *Perf. 13*

1154	A369	50pf multicolored	55	22

Convalescent Mothers' Foundation, 25th anniversary.

Annette Kolb (1875–1967), Writer A370

Designs: 40pf, Ricarda Huch (1864–1947), writer. 50pf, Else Lasker-Schüler (1869–1945), poetess. 70pf, Gertrud von Le Fort (1876–1971), writer.

Lithographed and Engraved

1975, Jan. 15 ***Perf. 14***

1155	A370	30pf brn. & multi.	45	20
1156	"	40pf multicolored	45	30
1157	"	50pf claret & multi.	65	30
1158	"	70pf blue & multi.	1.00	80

German women writers.

Albert Schweitzer—A371

Design: 40pf, Hans Böckler.

1975 **Engraved**

1159	A371	40pf green & black	50	22
1160	"	70pf blue & black	85	45

Birth centenaries of Hans Böckler (1875–1951), German Workers' Union leader, and of Dr. Albert Schweitzer (1875–1965), medical missionary. Issue dates: 40pf, Feb. 14; 70pf, Jan. 15.

Head, by Michelangelo A372

Plan of St. Peter's, Rome A373

1975, Feb. 14 **Photo.** ***Perf. 14***

1161	A372	70pf vio. bl. & blk.	1.10	1.10

500th birth anniversary of Michelangelo Buonarroti (1475–1564), Italian sculptor, painter and architect.

1975, Feb. 14

1162	A373	50pf red & multi.	55	25

Holy Year 1975, the "Year of Reconciliation."

Ice Hockey A374

1975, Feb. 14 **Litho.** ***Perf. 14***

1163	A374	50pf blue & multi.	65	25

Ice Hockey World Championship, Munich and Düsseldorf, Apr. 3–19.

Europa Issue 1975

Concentric Group, by Oskar Schlemmer A375

Design: 50pf, Bauhaus Staircase, painting by Oskar Schlemmer (1888–1943) and CEPT emblem.

1975, Apr. 15 **Litho. & Engr.**

1164	A375	40pf gray & multi.	45	25
1165	"	50pf " "	55	30

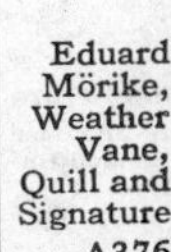

Eduard Mörike, Weather Vane, Quill and Signature A376

1975, May 15

1166	A376	40pf multicolored	50	22

Eduard Mörike (1804–1875), pastor and poet.

Joust, from Jousting Book of William IV A377

1975, May 15 **Photo.** ***Perf. 14***

1167	A377	50pf multicolored	55	22

500th anniversary of the Wedding of Landshut, (last Duke of Landshut married the daughter of King of Poland, now a yearly local festival).

Dome of Mainz A378

1975, May 15 **Litho. & Engr.**

1168	A378	40pf multicolored	50	22

Millennium of the Dome of Mainz.

View of Neuss, Woodcut A379

Space Laboratory A380

1975, May 15

1169	A379	50pf multicolored	55	22

500th anniversary of the unsuccessful siege of Neuss by Duke Charles the Bold of Burgundy.

1975–79 **Engraved** ***Perf. 14***

Designs: 5pf, Symphonie communications satellite. 10pf, Local electric train. 20pf, Old Weser lighthouse. 30pf, Rescue helicopter. 50pf, Radar station. 60pf, X-ray machine. 70pf, Shipbuilding. 80pf, Tractor. 100pf, Bituminous coal excavator. 120pf, Chemical plant, Ludwigshafen. 140pf, Heating plant, Lichterfelde. 160pf, Blast furnace, Rheinhausen. 200pf, Oil drilling platform. 230pf, Frankfurt Airport. 500pf, Effelsberg radio telescope.

1170	A380	5pf olive	5	5
1171	"	10pf rose lilac	10	5
1172	"	20pf red org. ('76)	20	5
1173	"	30pf violet	30	5
1174	"	40pf bluish green	40	13
1175	"	50pf carmine rose	50	13
1176	"	60pf red ('78)	60	15
1177	"	70pf blue	70	22
1178	"	80pf slate green	80	40
1179	"	100pf brown	1.00	40
1180	"	120pf dk. vio. blue	1.20	50
1181	"	140pf dk. carmine	1.40	65
1182	"	160pf green	1.60	60
1183	"	200pf dull purple	2.00	65
1184	"	230pf purple ('79)	2.30	70
1185	"	500pf slate ('76)	5.00	2.25
		Nos. 1170–1185 (16)	18.15	6.98

Market and Town Hall, Alsfeld A381

Designs: No. 1197, Plönlein Corner, Siebers Tower and Kobolzeller Gate, Rothenburg. No. 1198, Town Hall (Steipe), Trier. No. 1199, View of Xanten.

1975, July 15 **Litho. & Engr.**

1196	A381	50pf multicolored	50	25
1197	"	50pf "	50	25
1198	"	50pf "	50	25
1199	"	50pf "	50	25

European Architectural Heritage Year.

Three Stages of Drug Addiction A382

1975, Aug. 14 **Photo.** ***Perf. 14***

1200	A382	40pf multicolored	40	22

Fight against drug abuse.

Matthias Erzberger A383

1975, Aug. 14 **Engraved**

1201	A383	50pf red & black	50	22

Matthias Erzberger (1875–1921), statesman, signer of Compiègne Armistice (1918) at end of World War I.

Sign of Royal Prussian Post, 1776 A384

1975, Aug. 14 **Lithographed**

1202	A384	10pf blue & multi.	10	6

Stamp Day, 1975, and 76th German Philatelists' Day, Sept. 21.

Gustav Stresemann, Ludwig Quidde, Carl von Ossietzky—A385

1975, Nov. 14 **Engr.** ***Perf. 14***

1203	A385	Sheet of 3	1.85	1.85
		a. 50pf, single stamp	60	60

German winners of Nobel Peace Prize. No. 1203 has lithographed marginal inscription and German flag colors. Size: 100x70mm.

Olympic Rings, Symbolic Mountains A386

Konrad Adenauer A387

1976, Jan. 5 **Litho. & Engr.**

1204	A386	50pf red & multi.	50	22

12th Winter Olympic Games, Innsbruck, Austria, Feb. 4–15.

1976, Jan. 5 **Engraved**

1205	A387	50pf dk. slate grn.	50	22

Konrad Adenauer (1876–1967), Chancellor (1949–63), birth centenary.

Books by Hans Sachs A388

1976, Jan. 5 **Lithographed**

1206 A388 40pf multicolored 40 22

Hans Sachs (1494–1576), poet (meistersinger), 400th death anniversary.

Junkers F 13, 1926

A389

German Eagle

A390

1976, Jan. 5

1207 A389 50pf multicolored 50 22

Lufthansa, 50th anniversary.

1976, Feb. 17 **Photo.** ***Perf. 14***

1208 A390 50pf red, black & gold 50 22

Federal Constitutional Court, 25th anniversary.

"EG"

A391

1976, Apr. 6 **Photo.** ***Perf. 14***

1209 A391 40pf red & multi. 40 22

European Coal and Steel Community, 25th anniversary.

Wuppertal Suspension Train

A392

1976, Apr. 6 **Lithographed**

1210 A392 50pf multicolored 50 22

Wuppertal suspension railroad, 75th anniversary.

Europa Issue 1976

Girl Selling Trinkets and Prints

A393

Design: 50pf, Boy selling copperplate prints, and CEPT emblem. Ludwigsburg china figurines, c. 1765.

1976, May 13 **Photogravure**

1211 A393 40pf olive & multi. 40 20

1212 " 50pf scarlet & multi. 50 22

Carl Sonnenschein

A394

1976, May 13 **Lithographed**

1213 A394 50pf car. & multi. 50 22

Dr. Carl Sonnenschein (1876–1929), Roman Catholic clergyman and social reformer.

Weber Conducting "Freischutz" in Covent Garden—A395

1976, May 13

1214 A395 50pf red brown & black 50 22

Carl Maria von Weber (1786–1826), composer, 150th death anniversary.

Hymn, by Paul Gerhardt

A396

1976, May 13 **Engr. & Litho.**

1215 A396 40pf multicolored 32 20

Paul Gerhardt (1607–1676), Lutheran hymn writer, 300th death anniversary.

Carl Schurz, American Flag, Capitol

A397

1976, May 13 **Lithographed**

1216 A397 70pf multicolored 70 35

American Bicentennial.

Modern Stage—A398

1976, July 14 **Litho.** ***Perf. 14***

1217 A398 50pf multicolored 50 22

Bayreuth Festival, centenary.

Bronze Ritual Chariot c. 1000 B.C.

A399

Designs: 40pf, Celtic gold vessel, 5th-4th centuries B.C. 50pf, Celtic silver torque, 2nd–1st centuries B.C. 120pf, Roman cup with masks, 1st century A.D.

1976, July 14

1218 A399 30pf multicolored 30 15

1219 " 40pf " 40 20

1220 " 50pf " 50 22

1221 " 120pf " 1.20 90

Archaeological treasures.

Golden Plover

A400

"Simplicissimus Teutsch"

A401

1976, Aug. 17

1222 A400 50pf multicolored 50 22

Protection of birds.

1976, Aug. 17

1223 A401 40pf multicolored 40 20

Johann Jacob Christoph von Grimmelshausen, 300th birth anniversary; author of the "Adventures of Simplicissimus Teutsch."

Imperial Post Emblem, Höchst am Main, 18th Century

A402

Caroline Neuber as Medea

A403

1976, Oct. 14 **Litho.** ***Perf. 14***

1224 A402 10pf brown & multi. 10 6

Stamp Day.

1976, Nov. 16 **Photogravure**

German Actresses: 40pf, Sophie Schröder (1781–1868) as Sappho. 50pf, Louise Dumont (1862–1932) as Hedda Gabler. 70pf, Hermine Körner (1878–1960) as Lady Macbeth.

1225 A403 30pf multicolored 30 15

1226 " 40pf " 40 20

1227 " 50pf " 50 22

1228 " 70pf " 70 35

Palais de l'Europe, Strasbourg—A404

1977, Jan. 13 **Engr.** ***Perf. 14***

1229 A404 140pf grn. & blk. 1.40 70

Inauguration of the new Council of Europe Headquarters, Jan. 28.

Scenes from Till Eulenspiegel

A405

Marksburg Castle

A406

1977, Jan. 13 **Lithographed**

1230 A405 50pf multicolored 50 22

Till Eulenspiegel (d. 1350), roguish fool and hero, his adventures reported in book of same name.

1977–79 **Typographed** ***Perf. 14***

Castles: 10pf, Glücksburg. 20pf, 190pf, Pfaueninsel. 25pf, Gemen. 30pf, Ludwigstein. 40pf, Eltz. 50pf, Neuschwanstein. 70pf, Mespelbrunn. 90pf, Vischering. 200pf, Bürresheim. 210pf, Schwanenburg. 230pf, Lichtenberg.

1231 A406 10pf gray blue 10 3

a. Booklet pane of 8 (4 #1231, 2 each #1234, 1236) 2.00

1232 A406 20pf red org. ('79) 20 3

1233 " 25pf crimson ('79) 25 3

1234 " 30pf olive 30 3

1235 " 40pf blue green 40 3

1236 " 50pf rose carmine 50 5

1237 " 60pf brown 60 10

1238 " 70pf blue 70 18

1239 " 90pf dk. blue ('79) 90 20

1240 " 190pf red brown 1.90 45

1240A " 200pf green 2.00 50

1241 " 210pf red brn. ('79) 2.10 50

1242 " 230pf dk. grn. ('78) 2.30 60

Nos. 1231–1242 (13) 12.25 2.73

Issued in sheets of 100 and in coils. Every fifth coil stamp has control number on the back.

Souvenir Sheet

German Art Nouveau—A407

Designs: 30pf, Floral ornament. 70pf, Athena, poster by Franz von Stuck. 90pf, Chair, c. 1902.

1977, Feb. 16 **Litho.** ***Perf. 14***

1243 A407 Sheet of 3 2.00 2.00

a. 30pf multicolored 30 30

b. 70pf " 70 70

c. 90pf " 90 90

First German Art Nouveau Exhibition, 75th anniversary. No. 1243 has gold ornamental border. Size: 115x85mm.

Jean Monnet

A408

1977, Feb. 16

1244 A408 50pf blk. & yellow 50 22

Jean Monnet (1888–1979), French proponent of unification of Europe, became first Honorary Citizen of Europe in Apr. 1976.

Flower Show Emblem
A409

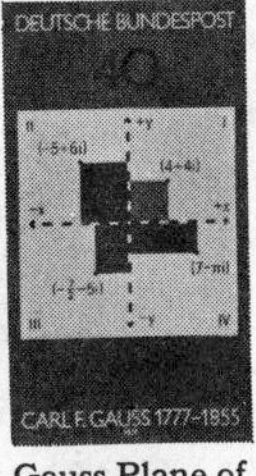

Gauss Plane of Complex Numbers
A410

1977, Apr. 14

1245 A409 50pf grn. & multi. 50 20

25th Federal Horticultural Show, Stuttgart, Apr. 29–Oct. 23.

1977, Apr. 14

1246 A410 40pf silver & multi. 40 20

Carl Friedrich Gauss (1777–1855), mathematician, 200th birth anniversary.

Barbarossa Head, Cappenberg Reliquary
A411

1977, Apr. 14

1247 A411 40pf multicolored 40 20

Staufer Year 1977. "Time of the Hohenstaufen" Exhibition, Stuttgart, Mar. 25–June 5, in connection with the 25th anniversary of Baden-Wurttemberg.

Europa Issue 1977

Rhön Highway—A412

Design: 50pf, Rhine, Siebengebirge and train.

1977, May 7 Litho. & Engr.

1248 A412 40pf brt. grn. & blk. 40 20
1249 " 50pf brt. red & blk. 50 22

P. P. Rubens, Self-portrait
A413

Ulm Cathedral
A414

1977, May 17 Engraved

1250 A413 30pf brown black 30 15

Peter Paul Rubens (1577–1640), Flemish painter, 400th birth anniversary.

1977, May 17 Litho. & Engr.

1251 A414 40pf blue & sepia 40 20

600th anniversary of Ulm Cathedral.

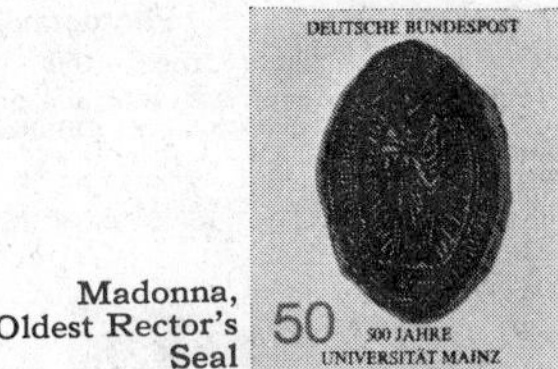

Madonna, Oldest Rector's Seal
A415

Landgrave Philipp, Great Seal of University
A416

1977, May 17 Photogravure

1252 A415 50pf indigo & org. red 50 22
1253 A416 50pf indigo & org. red 50 22

Mainz University, 500th anniversary (No. 1252); Marburg University, 450th anniversary (No. 1253).

Morning, by Runge—A417

1977, July 13 Litho. *Perf. 14*

1254 A417 60pf blue & multi. 60 25

Philipp Otto Runge (1777–1810), painter.

Bishop Ketteler's Coat of Arms
A418

1977, July 13

1255 A418 50pf multicolored 50 22

Wilhelm Emmanuel von Ketteler (1811–1877), Bishop of Mainz, Reichstag member and social reformer, death centenary.

Fritz von Bodelschwingh
A419

1977, July 13 Litho. & Engr.

1256 A419 50pf multicolored 50 22

Pastor Fritz von Bodelschwingh (1877–1946), manager of Bethel Institute (for the incurable sick), birth centenary.

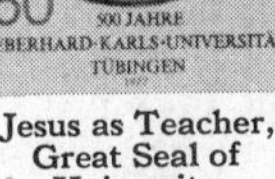

Jesus as Teacher, Great Seal of University
A420

Golden Hat, Schifferstadt, Bronze Age
A421

1977, Aug. 16 Photogravure

1257 A420 50pf multicolored 50 22

Tübingen University, 500th anniversary.

1977, Aug. 16 Lithographed

Designs: 120pf, Gilt helmet, from Prince's Tomb, Krefeld-Gellep. 200pf, Bronze Centaur's head, Schwarzenacker.

1258 A421 30pf multicolored 30 20
1259 " 120pf " 1.20 50
1260 " 200pf " 2.00 90

Archaeological heritage.

Telephone Operator and Switchboard, 1881—A422

1977, Oct. 13 Litho. *Perf. 14*

1261 A422 50pf multicolored 50 22

German telephone centenary.

Arms of Hamburg, Post Emblem, c. 1861
A423

Wilhelm Hauff
A424

1977, Oct. 13

1262 A423 10pf multicolored 10 5

Stamp Day.

1977, Nov. 10 Photo. *Perf. 14*

1263 A424 40pf multicolored 40 20

Wilhelm Hauff (1802–1827), writer and fabulist, 150th death anniversary.

Traveling Surgeon
A425

1977, Nov. 10 Lithographed

1264 A425 50pf multicolored 50 22

Dr. Johann Andreas Eisenbarth (1663–1727), traveling surgeon and adventurer.

Book Cover, by Alexander Schröder
A426

1978, Jan. 12 Litho. *Perf. 14*

1265 A426 50pf multicolored 50 22

Rudolf Alexander Schröder (1878–1962), writer, designer, Lutheran minister.

"Refugees"—A427

1978, Jan. 12 Photogravure

1266 A427 50pf multicolored 50 22

Friedland Aid Society for displaced Germans, 20th anniversary.

Gerhart Hauptmann, Hermann Hesse, Thomas Mann—A428

1978, Feb. 16 Lithographed *Perf. 14*

1267 A428 Sheet of 3 1.70 1.70
 a. 30pf multicolored 30 30
 b. 50pf " 50 50
 c. 70pf " 70 70

German winners of Nobel Literature Prize. Size of No. 1267: 120x70mm.

Martin Buber
A429

1978, Feb. 16

1268 A429 50pf multicolored 50 22

Martin Buber (1878–1965), writer and philosopher.

Museum Tower and Observatory
A430

1978, Apr. 13 **Litho.** ***Perf. 14***

1269 A430 50pf multicolored 50 25

German Museum for Natural Sciences and Technology, Munich, 75th anniversary.

Europa Issue 1978

Old City Hall, Bamberg A431

Old City Halls: 50pf, Regensburg. 70pf, Esslingen on Neckar.

Lithographed and Engraved

1978, May 22 ***Perf. 14***

1270 A431 40pf multicolored 40 20
1271 " 50pf " 50 25
1272 " 70pf " 70 35

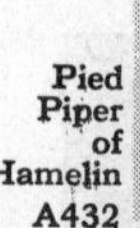

Pied Piper of Hamelin A432

1978, May 22 **Lithographed**

1273 A432 50pf multicolored 50 25

The Pied Piper led 130 children of Hamelin away never to be seen again.

Janusz Korczak A433 **Fossil Bat A434**

1978, July 13 **Litho.** ***Perf. 14***

1274 A433 90pf multicolored 90 45

Dr. Janusz Korczak (1878–1942), physician, educator, proponent of children's rights.

1978, July 13

Design: 200pf, Eohippus (primitive horse; horiz.).

1275 A434 80pf multicolored 80 40
1276 " 200pf " 2.00 1.00

Archaeological heritage from Messel opencast mine, c. 50 million years old.

Parliament, Bonn A435

1978, Aug. 17 **Litho.** ***Perf. 14***

1277 A435 70pf multicolored 70 35

65th Interparliamentary Conference, Bonn, Sept. 3–14.

Rose Window, Freiburg Cathedral A436

1978, Aug. 17

1278 A436 40pf multicolored 40 20

85th Congress of German Catholics, Freiburg, Sept. 13–17.

Brentano as Butterfly, by Luise Duttenhofer A437

1978, Aug. 17

1279 A437 30pf multicolored 30 15

Clemens Brentano (1778–1842), poet.

Inscription A438

1978, Aug. 17

1280 A438 50pf multicolored 50 25

European Human Rights Convention, 25th anniversary.

Bavarian Posthouse Sign, c. 1825 A439 **Saxony No. 1 with "World Philatelic Movement" Cancel A440**

1978, Oct. 12 **Litho.** ***Perf. 14***

1281 A439 40pf multicolored 40 20
1282 A440 50pf " 50 25

Stamp Day and German Philatelists' Meeting, Frankfurt am Main, Oct. 12–15. Nos. 1281–1282 printed se-tenant in sheets of 50.

Easter at Walchensee, by Lovis Corinth—A441

Impressionist Paintings: 70pf, Horseman on Shore, by Max Liebermann (vert.). 120pf, Lady with Cat, by Max Slevogt (vert.).

1978, Nov. 16 **Photo.** ***Perf. 14***

1283 A441 50pf multicolored 50 25
1284 " 70pf " 70 35
1285 " 120pf " 1.20 60

Child and Building A442

1979, Jan. 11 **Photogravure**

1286 A442 60pf black & rose 60 30

International Year of the Child and 20th anniversary of Declaration of Children's Rights.

Agnes Miegel A443 **Film A444**

1979, Feb. 14 **Photo.** ***Perf. 14***

1287 A443 60pf multicolored 60 30

Agnes Miegel (1879–1964), poet.

1979, Feb. 14 **Lithographed**

1288 A444 50pf black & green 50 25

25th German Short-Film Festival, Oberhausen, Apr. 23–28.

Parliament Benches in Flag Colors of Members—A445

1979, Feb. 14

1289 A445 50pf multicolored 50 25

European Parliament, first direct elections, June 7–10, 1979.

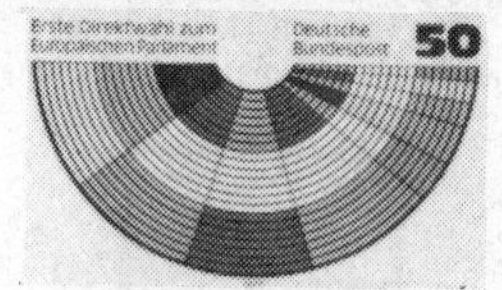

Emblems of Road Rescue Services—A446

1979, Feb. 14

1290 A446 50pf multicolored 50 25

Europa Issue 1979

Telegraph Office, 1863 A447

Design: 60pf, Post Office window, 1854.

1979, May 17 **Litho.** ***Perf. 14***

1291 A447 50pf multicolored 50 25
1292 " 60pf " 60 30

Anne Frank A448

1979, May 17 **Photogravure**

1293 A448 60pf red & black 60 30

Anne Frank (1929–1945), author, Nazi victim.

First Electric Train, 1879 Berlin Exhibition—A449

1979, May 17 **Lithographed**

1294 A449 60pf multicolored 60 30

International Transportation Exhibition, Hamburg.

SEMI-POSTAL STAMPS.
Issues of the Republic.

Regular Issue of 1906-17 Surcharged **5 Pf Für Kriegsbeschädigte**

Wmkd. Lozenges. (125)

1919, May 1 *Perf. 14*

B1 A16 10pf+5pf carmine 15 *3.75*
B2 A22 15pf+5pf dark violet 22 *3.25*

4 Mark für Alters- und Kinderhilfe

"Planting Charity" SP1

Feeding the Hungry SP2

Wmkd. Network. (126)

1922, Dec. 11 Lithographed

B3 SP1 6m+4m ultra. & brn. 18 *12.00*
B4 " 12m+8m red orange & blue gray 18 *12.00*

Nos. 221, 225 and 196 Surcharged **500 M Rhein-Ruhr-Hilfe**

1923, Feb. 19

B5 A34 5m+100m orange 10 *5.50*
B6 A29 25m+500m olive brown 15 *19.00*
a. Inverted surch. 275.00
B7 A32 20m+1000m indigo & green 2.50 *110.00*
a. Inverted surcharge 900.00 900.00
b. Green background inverted 190.00 225.00

Note following No. 160 applies to Nos. B1–B7.

Typographed

1924, Feb. 25 *Perf. 14½x15*

Designs: 10pf+30pf, Giving drink to the thirsty. 20pf+60pf, Clothing the naked. 50pf+1.50m, Healing the sick.

B8 SP2 5(pf)+15pf dark green 1.65 3.00
B9 " 10(pf)+30pf verm. 1.65 2.50
B10 " 20(pf)+60pf dark blue 6.50 8.25
B11 " 50(pf)+1.50m red brown 32.50 60.00

The surtax was used for charity.

Prussia SP6

Coats of Arms: 10pf+10pf, Bavaria. 20pf+20pf, Saxony.

1925, Dec. 15 *Perf. 14*

Inscribed: "1925."

B12 SP6 5pf+5pf dark green, buff & black 55 80
a. Bklt. pane of 4 20.00
B13 " 10pf+10pf brown red, buff & bl. 1.10 1.10
a. Bklt. pane of 4 30.00
B14 " 20pf+20pf dark blue, buff, green & black 8.50 15.00
a. Bklt. pane 2 + 2 Labels 125.00
b. Bklt. pane of 2 175.00

1926, Dec. 1

Coats of Arms: 5pf+5pf, Wurttemberg. 10pf+10pf, Baden. 25pf+25pf, Thuringia. 50pf+50pf, Hesse.

Inscribed: "1926."

B15 SP6 5pf+5pf dark green, buff, red & blk. 1.35 1.35
a. Booklet pane of 8 45.00
B16 " 10pf+10pf deep rose, bistre & red 2.25 2.75
a. Bklt. pane 6 + 2 Labels 75.00
B17 " 25pf+25pf dark blue, buff & red 14.00 16.50
B18 " 50pf+50pf choc., buff, lt. blue & red 60.00 55.00

Pres. Paul von Hindenburg SP13

1927, Sept. 26 Photogravure

B19 SP13 8(pf) dark green 65 1.10
a. Bklt. pane 7 (4 No. B19 + 3 No. B20 + Label) 45.00
B20 " 15(pf) scarlet 95 1.65
B21 " 25(pf) deep blue 11.00 16.50
B22 " 50(pf) bistre brown 15.00 22.50

Issued to commemorate the 80th birthday of President Hindenburg. The stamps were sold at double face value. The surtax was given to a fund for War Invalids.

Arms Type of 1925

Coats of Arms: 5pf+5pf, Hamburg. 8pf+7pf, Mecklenburg-Schwerin. 15pf+15pf, Oldenburg. 25pf+25pf, Brunswick. 50pf+50pf, Anhalt.

1928, Nov. 15 Typographed

Inscribed: "1928."

B23 SP6 5pf+5pf green, yellow & red 65 95
B24 " 8pf+7pf multicolored 65 95
a. Bklt. pane 7 (4 No. B24 + 3 No. B25+Label) 75.00
B25 " 15pf+15pf dp. rose, yellow & blue 1.35 1.90
B26 " 25pf+25pf dk. blue, yellow & red 14.00 19.00
B27 " 50pf+50pf multi. 55.00 70.00
Nos. B23-B27 (5) 71.65 92.80

1929, Nov. 4

Coats of Arms: 5pf+2pf, Bremen. 8pf+4pf, Lippe-Detmold. 15pf+5pf, Lubeck. 25pf+10pf, Mecklenburg-Strelitz. 50pf+40pf, Schaumburg-Lippe.

Inscribed: "1929."

B28 SP6 5pf+2pf green, ochre & red 80 1.35
a. Bklt. pane 6 + 2 Labels 15.00
B29 " 8pf+4pf dark green, ochre & red 80 1.35
a. Bklt. pane 7 (4 No. B29 + 3 No. B30+Label) 45.00
B30 " 15pf+5pf deep rose, ochre & black 1.10 1.90
B31 " 25pf+10pf multi. 16.50 27.50
B32 " 50pf+40pf chocolate, ochre & red 50.00 65.00
a. "PE" for "PF" (error) 275.00 275.00
Nos. B28-B32 (5) 69.20 97.10

International Philatelic Exhibition Issue.

Cathedral of Aachen SP24

Brandenburg Gate, Berlin SP25

Castle of Marienwerder SP26

Statue of St. Kilian and Marienburg Fortress at Würzburg SP27

Wmk. 223

Souvenir Sheet.

SP27a

Wmkd. Eagle. (223)

1930, Sept. 12 Engraved *Perf. 14*

B33 SP27a Sheet of four 350.00 550.00
a. SP24 8(pf)+4pf dark grn. 32.50 45.00
b. SP25 15(pf)+5pf carmine 32.50 45.00
c. SP26 25(pf)+10p dark blue 32.50 45.00
d. SP27 50(pf)+40pf dark brown 32.50 45.00

Issued in sheets measuring 105 x 150mm. containing one each of the four stamps watermarked Eagle on each stamp and "IPOSTA"—"1930" in the margins. Each holder of a ticket of admission to the International Philatelic Exhibition, Berlin, Sept. 12-21, 1930, was entitled to purchase one of these sheets of stamps. The ticket cost 1 m and the sheet cost 1.70 mk. (face value 98pf, charity 59pf, special paper 13pf).

Types of International Philatelic Exhibition Issue.

Wmkd. Network. (126)

1930, Nov. 1

B34 SP24 8(pf)+4pf deep green 45 40
a. Bklt. pane 7 + Label 27.50
b. Bklt. pane 7 (3 No. B34 + 4 No. B35 + Label) 32.50
B35 SP25 15(pf)+5pf carmine 65 60
B36 SP26 25(pf)+10pf dark blue 11.00 19.00
B37 SP27 50(pf)+40pf deep brown 30.00 45.00

The surtax was for charity.

The Zwinger at Dresden SP28

Breslau City Hall SP29

Heidelberg Castle SP30

Holsten Gate, Lübeck SP31

1931, Nov. 1

B38 SP28 8(pf)+4pf dark green 45 70
a. Bklt. pane 7 + Label 27.50
b. Bklt. pane 7 (3 No. B38 + 4 No. B39 + Label) 32.50
B39 SP29 15(pf)+5pf car. 70 1.10
B40 SP30 25(pf)+10pf dark blue 12.00 22.50
B41 SP31 50(pf)+40pf deep brown 37.50 60.00

The surtax was for charity.

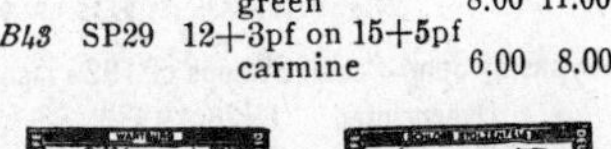

Semi-Postal Stamps of 1931 Surcharged **12+3 Rpf 12 12**

1932, Feb. 2

B42 SP28 6+4pf on 8+4pf green 8.00 11.00
B43 SP29 12+3pf on 15+5pf carmine 6.00 8.00

Wartburg Castle SP32

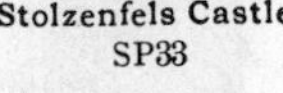

Stolzenfels Castle SP33

Nuremberg Castle SP34

Lichtenstein Castle SP35

Marburg Castle SP36

1932, Nov. 1 Engraved

B44 SP32 4(pf)+2pf light blue 40 40
a. Bklt. pane 10 (5 No. B44 + 5 No. B45) 12.50
B45 SP33 6(pf)+4pf olive green 40 45
B46 SP34 12(pf)+3pf light red 70 1.65
a. Tête bêche pair 3.25 3.75
b. Bklt. pane 8 + 2 Labels 15.00
B47 SP35 25(pf)+10pf deep blue 8.50 14.00
B48 SP36 40(pf)+40pf brn. violet 32.50 60.00
Nos. B44-B48 (5) 42.50 76.50

The surtax was for charity.

"Tannhäuser" SP37

Designs: 4pf+2pf, "Der Fliegende Hollander." 5pf+2pf, "Das Rheingold." 6pf+4pf, "Die Meistersinger." 8pf+4pf, "Die Walkure." 12pf+3pf, "Siegfried." 20pf+10pf, "Tristan und Isolde." 25pf+15pf. "Lohengrin." 40pf+35pf "Parsifal."

Wmkd. Swastikas. (237)

1933, Nov. 1 *Perf. 13½x13*

B49 SP37 3(pf)+2pf bis. brn. 1.65 2.50
B50 " 4(pf)+2pf dk. blue 1.00 80
B51 " 5(pf)+2pf bright green 3.25 3.50
B52 " 6(pf)+4pf gray green 1.10 80
B53 " 8(pf)+4pf dp. org. 1.75 1.65
B54 " 12(pf)+3pf brown red 2.00 75
B55 " 20(pf)+10pf blue 135.00 135.00
B56 " 25(pf)+15pf ultra. 32.50 32.50
B57 " 40(pf)+35pf magenta 110.00 120.00
Nos. B49-B57 (9) 288.25 297.50

Perf. 13½x14

B50a SP37 4(pf)+2pf dk. blue 70 70
b. Bklt. pane 10 (5 No. B50, 5 No. B52) 30.00
B52a " 6(pf)+4pf gray green 70 70
B53a " 8(pf)+4pf dp. orange 1.25 1.65
b. Bklt. pane 9 (5 No. B53, 4 No. B54+ label) 75.00
B54a " 12(pf)+3pf brown red 1.50 1.50
B55a " 20(pf)+10pf blue 95.00 87.50
Nos. B50a-B55a (5) 99.15 92.05

Types of Semi-Postal Stamps of 1924 Issue Overprinted "1923-1933"

Souvenir Sheet.

SP45

1933, Nov. 29 Typo. *Perf. 14½*

B58 SP45 Sheet of four 1500.00 3000.00
a. SP2 5(pf)+15pf dark green 67.50 92.50
b. " 10(pf)+30pf vermilion 67.50 92.50
c. " 20(pf)+60pf dark blue 67.50 92.50
d. " 50(pf)+1.50m dark brown 67.50 92.50

Issued in sheets measuring 208x148mm. containing one each of the four stamps. The Swastika watermark covers the four stamps and above them appears a further watermark "10 Jahre Deutsche Nothilfe" and "1923-1933" below.

Businessman
SP46

Judge
SP54

Designs: 4pf+2pf, Blacksmith. 5pf+2pf, Mason. 6pf+4f, Miner. 8pf+4pf, Architect. 12pf+3pf, Farmer. 20pf+10pf, Agricultural Chemist. 25pf+15pf, Sculptor.

1934, Nov. 5 Engr. *Perf. 13x13½*

B59 SP46 3(pf)+2(pf) brown 90 1.10
B60 " 4(pf)+2(pf) black 65 65
a. Bklt. pane 10 (5 No. B60 + 5 No. B62) 13.50
B61 " 5(pf)+2(pf) green 5.50 6.00
B62 " 6(pf)+4(pf) dull green 45 55
B63 " 8(pf)+4(pf) orange brown 65 75
a. Bklt. pane 9 (5 No. B63 + 4 No. B64 + Label) 20.00
B64 SP46 12(pf)+3(pf) henna brown 45 55
B65 " 20(pf)+10(pf) Prussian bl. 14.00 19.00
B66 " 25(pf)+15(pf) ultramarine 14.00 19.00
B67 SP54 40(pf)+35(pf) plum 40.00 55.00
Nos. B59-B67 (9) 76.60 102.60

Souvenir Sheet.

SP55

Wmk. 241

Wmkd. Cross. (241)

1935, June 23 *Perf. 14*

B68 SP55 Sheet of four 425.00 450.00
a. 3(pf) red brown 18.50 18.50
b. 6(pf) dark green 18.50 18.50
c. 12(pf) dark car. 18.50 18.50
d. 25(pf) dark blue 18.50 18.50

Issued in sheets measuring 148x104 mm. containing one each of the four stamps, watermarked cross on each stamp and "OSTROPA 1935" in the margins of the sheet. 1.70m was the price of a ticket of admission to the International Exhibition, Königsberg, June 23rd to July 3rd, 1935.

Because the gum on No. B68 contains sulphuric acid and tends to damage the sheet, some collectors prefer to remove it. Catalogue unused prices are for sheet and singles without gum.

East Prussia
SP59

Skating
SP69

Designs (Costumes of Various Sections of Germany): 4pf+3pf, Silesia. 5pf+3pf, Rhineland. 6pf+4pf, Lower Saxony. 8pf+4pf, Brandenburg. 12pf+6pf, Black Forest. 15pf+10pf, Hesse. 25pf+15pf, Upper Bavaria. 30pf+20pf, Friesland. 40pf+35pf, Franconia.

Wmkd. Swastikas. (237)

1935, Oct. 4 *Perf. 14x13½*

B69 SP59 3(pf)+2(pf) dark brown 8 12
a. Bklt. pane 9 (4 No. B69 + 5 No. B74 + Label) 10.00
B70 " 4(pf)+3(pf) gray 45 70
B71 " 5(pf)+3(pf) emerald 22 33
a. Bklt. pane 10 (5 No. B71 + 5 No. B72) 4.50
B72 " 6(pf)+4(pf) dark green 8 12
B73 " 8(pf)+4(pf) yellow brown 70 95
B74 " 12(pf)+6(pf) dark carmine 28 45
B75 " 15(pf)+10(pf) red brown 4.25 4.50
B76 " 25(pf)+15(pf) ultramarine 5.25 5.50
B77 " 30(pf)+20(pf) olive brn. 20.00 18.00
B78 SP59 40(pf)+35(pf) plum 10.50 10.00
Nos. B69-B78 (10) 41.81 40.67

1935, Nov. 25 *Perf. 13½*

Designs: 12pf+6pf, Ski jump. 25pf+15pf, Bobsledding.

B79 SP69 6(pf)+4(pf) green 90 65
B80 " 12(pf)+6(pf) car. 2.25 95
B81 " 25(pf)+15(pf) ultramarine 9.50 10.00

Issued in commemoration of the Winter Olympic Games held in Bavaria, Feb. 6th to 16th, 1936.

1936, May 8

Designs:

3pf+2pf, Horizontal bar. 4pf+3pf, Diving. 6pf+4pf, Soccer. 8pf+4pf, Throwing javelin. 12pf+6pf, Torch runner. 15pf+10pf, Fencing. 25pf+15pf, Sculling. 40pf+35pf, Equestrian.

B82 SP69 3(pf)+2(pf) brown 20 25
a. Bklt. pane 10 (5 No. B82 + 5 No. B86) 9.00
B83 " 4(pf)+3(pf) indigo 20 25
a. Bklt. pane 10 (5 No. B83 + 5 No. B84) 9.00
B84 " 6(pf)+4(pf) green 20 25
B85 " 8(pf)+4(pf) red orange 1.10 60
B86 " 12(pf)+6(pf) car. 45 35
B87 " 15(pf)+10(pf) brown violet 7.00 3.75
B88 " 25(pf)+15(pf) ultra. 5.75 4.50
B89 " 40(pf)+35(pf) vio. 12.00 6.50
Nos. B82-B89 (8) 26.90 16.45

Issued in commemoration of the Summer Olympic Games held at Berlin, August 1–16, 1936.

Souvenir Sheet

Horse Race
SP80

1936, June 22 *Perf. 14* **Wmk. 237**

B90 SP80 42(pf) brown 5.25 8.75

Issued in sheets measuring 147x105mm. containing one stamp each. A surtax of 1.08 marks on each stamp was to provide a 100,000 marks sweepstakes prize. Wmk. 237 (Swastikas) appears on the stamp, with "Munchen Riem 1936" watermarked on sheet margin.

Souvenir Sheets

Type of 1935

1936, Aug. 1 *Perf. 14x13½*

B91 SP69 Sheet of 4 37.50 45.00
B92 " Sheet of 4 37.50 45.00

11th Olympic Games, Berlin, Aug. 1–16. No. B91 contains one each of Nos. B82-B84, B89. No. B92 contains one each of Nos. B85-B88.

Wmk. 237 appears on each stamp with "XI Olympische Spiele-Berlin 1936" watermarked on sheet margin. Size: 148x105 mm. Sold for 1m each.

Frontier Highway, Munich
SP81

Designs: 4pf+3pf, Ministry of Aviation. 5pf+3pf, Nuremberg Memorial. 6pf+4pf, Bridge over the Saale, Saxony. 8pf+4pf, Germany Hall, Berlin. 12pf+6pf, German Alpine highway. 15pf+10pf, Fuhrer House, Munich. 25pf+15pf, Bridge over the Mangfall. 40pf+35pf, Museum of German Art, Munich.

Inscribed: "Winterhilfswerk."

Perf. 13½x14

1936, Sept. 21 **Unwmkd.**

B93 SP81 3pf+2pf black brown 12 15
a. Bklt. pane 9 (4 No. B93 + 5 No. B98 + Label) 6.00
B94 SP81 4pf+3pf black 23 30
B95 " 5pf+3pf brt. green 12 15
a. Bklt. pane 10 (5 No. B95 + 5 No. B96) 3.00
B96 " 6pf+4pf dark green 12 15
B97 " 8pf+4pf brown 65 80
B98 " 12pf+6pf brown carmine 15 17
B99 " 15pf+10pf violet brown 4.25 4.50
B100 " 25pf+15pf indigo 3.25 3.75
B101 " 40pf+35pf rose violet 5.25 5.50
Nos. B93-B101 (9) 14.14 15.47

Souvenir Sheets

Adolf Hitler
SP90

Wmkd. Swastikas. (237)

1937, Apr. 5 Photo. *Perf. 14*

B102 SP90 6pf dark green, sheet of four 10.50 6.00
a. Single stamp 90 80

48th birthday of Adolf Hitler, April 5th, 1937. Sold for 1m per sheet. Size: 147x104mm.

1937, Apr. 16 *Imperf.*

B103 SP90 6pf dark green, sheet of four 37.50 16.50
a. Single stamp 3.50 1.65

German National Philatelic Exhibition, Berlin, June 16-18, 1937 and the Philatelic Exhibition of the Stamp Collectors Group of the Strength Through Joy Organization at Hamburg, April 17-20, 1937.

Sold at the Exhibition post offices for 1.50m.

No. B102 with Marginal Inscriptions

Perf. 14 and Rouletted

1937, June 10 **Wmk. 237**

B104 SP90 6pf+25pf dark green, sheet of four 50.00 75.00
a. Single stamp with label 3.50 5.50

No. B104 inscribed in the margin beside each stamp "25 Rpf. einschliesslich Kulturspende" in three lines.

The sheets were rouletted to allow for separation of each stamp with its component label. Sold at the post office as individual stamps with labels attached or in complete sheets.

Souvenir Sheet No. B90.

Overprinted in Red

1937, Aug. 1 *Perf. 14*

B105 SP80 42(pf) brown 50.00 75.00

4th running of the "Brown Ribbon" horse race at the Munich-Riem Race Course, Aug. 1, 1937.

Souvenir Sheet No. B104.
Overprinted in Black on Each Stamp

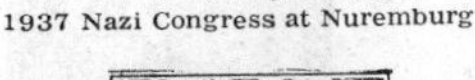

Perf. 14 and Rouletted

1937, Sept. 3 **Wmk. 237**

B106 SP90 6pf+25pf dark green, sheet of four 50.00 30.00
 a. Single stamp 3.50 2.75

1937 Nazi Congress at Nuremburg.

Lifeboat
SP91

Designs: 4pf+3pf, Lightship "Elbe I." 5pf+3pf, Fishing smacks. 6pf+4pf, Steamer. 8pf+4pf, Sailing vessel. 12pf+6pf, The "Tannenberg." 15pf+10pf, Sea-Train "Schwerin." 25pf+15pf, S. S. "Hamburg." 40pf+35pf, S. S. "Bremen."

Perf. 13½

1937, Nov. 4 **Engr.** **Unwmkd.**

Inscribed: "Winterhilfswerk."

B107 SP91 3pf+2pf dk. brn. 17 25
 a. Bklt. pane 9 (4 No. B107+5 No. B112+Label) 7.00
B108 " 4pf+3pf black 50 75
B109 " 5pf+3pf yel. grn. 17 25
 a. Bklt. pane 10 (5 No. B109+5 No. B110) 3.00
B110 " 6pf+4pf bl. green 17 25
B111 " 8pf+4pf orange 1.10 1.00
B112 " 12pf+6pf car. lake 35 20
B113 " 15pf+10pf violet brown 4.25 2.75
B114 " 25pf+15pf ultra. 5.25 2.75
B115 " 40pf+35pf red violet 5.25 5.50
 Nos. B107-B115 (9) 17.21 13.70

Youth Carrying Torch and Laurel
SP100

Adolf Hitler
SP101

Wmkd. Swastikas. (237)

1938, Jan. 28 **Photo.** ***Perf. 14***

B116 SP100 6(pf)+4(pf) dark green 1.10 80
B117 " 12(pf)+8(pf) brt.carmine 1.90 1.35

Issued in commemoration of the fifth anniversary of the assumption of power by the Nazis.

1938, Apr. 13 **Engraved** **Unwmkd.**

B118 SP101 12(pf)+38(pf) copper red 2.25 1.50

Issued to commemorate Hitler's 49th birthday.

Horsewoman—SP102

1938, July 20

B119 SP102 42(pf)+108(pf) deep brown 42.50 30.00

5th "Brown Ribbon" at Munich.

Adolf Hitler
SP103

Theater at Saarbrücken
SP104

1938, Sept. 1

B120 SP103 6(pf)+19(pf) deep green 2.75 3.00

Issued in commemoration of the 1938 Nazi Congress at Nuremberg. The surtax was for Hitler's National Culture Fund.

1938, Oct. 9 **Photo.** **Wmk. 237**

B121 SP104 6(pf)+4(pf) blue green 1.75 1.65
B122 " 12(pf)+8(pf) dark carmine 2.10 2.25

Issued to commemorate the inauguration of the theater of the District of Saarpfalz at Saarbrücken. The surtax was for Hitler's National Culture Fund.

Castle of Forchtenstein—SP105

Designs (scenes in Austria and various flowers): 4pf+3pf, Flexenstrasse in Vorarlberg. 5pf+3pf, Zell am See, Salzburg. 6pf+4pf, Grossglockner. 8pf+4pf, Ruins of Aggstein. 12pf+6pf, Prince Eugene Monument, Vienna. 15pf+10pf, Erzberg. 25pf+15pf, Hall, Tyrol. 40pf+35pf, Braunau.

Engraved.

1938, Nov. 18 ***Perf. 14*** **Unwmkd.**

Inscribed: "Winterhilfswerk."

B123 SP105 3(pf)+2(pf) olive brown 10 12
 a. Bklt. pane 9 (4 No. B123+5 No. B128+Label) 8.50
B124 " 4(pf)+3(pf) indigo 50 65
B125 " 5(pf)+3(pf) emerald 15 20
 a. Bklt. pane 10 (5 No. B125+5 No. B126) 3.50
B126 " 6(pf)+4(pf) dark green 10 9
B127 " 8(pf)+4(pf) red orange 1.00 80
B128 " 12(pf)+6(pf) dark carmine 23 15
B129 " 15(pf)+10(pf) deep claret 4.25 3.50
B130 " 25(pf)+15(pf) dark blue 4.25 3.50
B131 " 40(pf)+35(pf) plum 13.00 5.50
 Nos. B123-B131 (9) 23.58 14.51

The surtax was for "Winter Help."

Sudeten Couple
SP114

Early Types of Automobiles
SP115

1938, Dec. 2 **Photo.** **Wmk. 237**

B132 SP114 6(pf)+4(pf) blue green 1.40 95
B133 " 12(pf)+8(pf) dk. carmine 2.75 2.50

Issued in commemoration of the annexation of the Sudeten Territory. The surtax was for Hitler's National Culture Fund.

1939

Designs: 12pf+8pf, Racing cars. 25pf+10pf, Modern automobile.

B134 SP115 6(pf)+4(pf) dark green 3.00 1.90
B135 " 12(pf)+8(pf) bright carmine 4.75 2.25
B136 " 25(pf)+10(pf) deep blue 14.00 4.50

Berlin Automobile and Motorcycle Exhibition. The surtax was for Hitler's National Culture Fund. See Nos. B141-B143.

Adolf Hitler
SP118

Exhibition Building
SP119

Engraved

1939, Apr. 13 ***Perf. 14*** **Unwmkd.**

B137 SP118 12(pf)+38(pf) carmine 2.50 2.90

Issued to commemorate Hitler's 50th birthday. The surtax was for Hitler's National Culture Fund.

1939, Apr. 22 **Photo.** ***Perf. 12½***

B138 SP119 6(pf)+4(pf) dark green 1.40 2.25
B139 " 15(pf)+5(pf) deep plum 1.40 2.25

Issued in commemoration of the Horticultural Exhibition held at Stuttgart. The surtax was for Hitler's National Culture Fund.

Adolf Hitler
SP120

Perf. 14x13½

1939, Apr. 28 **Wmk. 237**

B140 SP120 6(pf)+19(pf) black brown 2.60 4.00

Issued in commemoration of the Day of National Labor. The surtax was for Hitler's National Culture Fund.
See also No. B147.

Nos. B134-B136 Overprinted in Black Nürburgring-Rennen

1939, May 18 ***Perf. 14***

B141 SP115 6(pf)+4(pf) dark green 30.00 30.00
B142 " 12(pf)+8(pf) brt. carmine 30.00 30.00
B143 " 25(pf)+10(pf) deep blue 30.00 30.00

Issued in commemoration of the Nurburgring Auto Races held May 21 and July 23, 1939.

Racehorse "Investment" and Jockey
SP121

1939, June 18 **Engraved** **Unwmkd.**

B144 SP121 25(pf)+50(pf) ultra. 17.50 14.00

Issued in commemoration of the 70th anniversary of the German Derby. The surtax was divided between Hitler's National Culture Fund and the race promoters.

Man Holding Rearing Horse
SP122

"Venetian Woman" by Albrecht Dürer
SP123

1939, July 12

B145 SP122 42(pf)+108(pf) deep brown 19.00 19.00

6th "Brown Ribbon" at Munich.

1939, July 12 **Photo.** **Wmk. 237**

B146 SP123 6(pf)+19(pf) dark green 4.50 5.00

Issued in commemoration of the day of German Art. The surtax was used for Hitler's National Culture Fund.

Hitler Type of 1939

Inscribed "Reichsparteitag 1939."

1939, Aug. 25 ***Perf. 14x13½***

B147 SP120 6(pf)+19(pf) black brown 4.00 6.25

1939 Nazi Congress at Nuremberg.

Meeting in German Hall, Berlin
SP124

Designs: 4pf+3pf, Meeting of postal and telegraph employees. 5pf+3pf, Professional competitions. 6pf+4pf, 6pf+9pf, Professional camp. 8pf+4pf, 8pf+12pf, Gold flag competitions. 10pf+5pf, Awarding prizes. 12pf+6pf, 12pf+18pf, Automobile race. 15pf+10pf, Sports. 16pf+10pf, 16pf+24pf, Postal police. 20pf+10pf, 20pf+30pf, Glider workshops. 24pf+10pf, 24pf+36pf, Mail coach. 25pf+15pf, Convalescent home, Konigstein.

Photogravure.

1939-41 ***Perf. 13½x14.*** **Unwmkd.**

Inscribed: "Kameradschaftsblock der Deutschen Reichpost."

B148 SP124 3(pf)+2(pf) bistre brown 3.00 4.50
B149 " 4(pf)+3(pf) slate blue 2.75 4.00
B150 " 5(pf)+3(pf) brt. blue grn. 70 1.00
B151 " 6(pf)+4(pf) myrtle green 70 1.00
B151A " 6(pf)+9(pf) dark green ('41) 60 90
B152 " 8(pf)+4(pf) deep orange 70 1.00
B152A " 8(pf)+12(pf) henna brown ('41) 50 70

B153 SP124 10(pf)+5(pf) dark brown 70 1.00
B154 " 12(pf)+6(pf) rose brown 1.10 1.65
B154A " 12(pf)+18(pf) dark carmine rose ('41) 50 75
B155 " 15(pf)+10(pf) dp. red lilac 1.10 1.65
B156 " 16(pf)+10(pf) slate green 1.75 2.50
B156A " 16(pf)+24(pf) black ('41) 1.10 1.75
B157 " 20(pf)+10(pf) ultramarine 1.75 2.50
B157A " 20(pf)+30(pf) ultra. ('41) 1.10 1.75
B158 " 24(pf)+10(pf) olive green 2.50 3.75
B158A " 24(pf)+36(pf) purple ('41) 3.75 6.00
B159 " 25(pf)+15(pf) dark blue 2.50 3.75
Nos. B148-B159 (18) 26.80 40.15

The surtax was used for Hitler's National Culture Fund and the Postal Employees' Fund.

See Nos. B273, B275-B277.

Elbogen Castle
SP136

Buildings: 4pf+3pf, Drachenfels on the Rhine. 5pf+3pf, Kaiserpfalz at Goslar. 6pf+4pf, Clocktower at Graz. 8pf+4pf, Town Hall, Frankfurt. 12pf+6pf, Guild House, Klagenfurt. 15pf+10pf, Ruins of Schreckenstein Castle. 25pf+15pf, Fortress of Salzburg. 40pf+35pf, Castle of Hohentwiel.

Engraved
1939 *Perf. 14.* **Unwmkd.**
Inscribed: "Winterhilfswerk."

B160 SP136 3(pf)+2(pf) dark brown 17 15
a. Bklt. pane 9 (4 No. B160+5 No. B165+Label) 8.50
B161 " 4(pf)+3(pf) gray black 90 1.10
B162 " 5(pf)+3(pf) emerald 22 25
a. Bklt. pane 10 (5 No. B162+5 No. B163) 4.50
B163 " 6(pf)+4(pf) slate green 22 25
B164 " 8(pf)+(4pf) red orange 45 80
B165 " 12(pf)+6(pf) dark carmine 38 25
B166 " 15(pf)+10(pf) brown violet 2.50 3.00
B167 " 25(pf)+15(pf) ultramarine 3.00 3.00
B168 " 40(pf)+35(pf) rose violet 4.50 5.00
Nos. B160-B168 (9) 12.34 13.80

Hall of Honor at Chancellery, Berlin
SP145

Child Greeting Hitler
SP146

1940, Mar. 28
B169 SP145 24(pf) +76(pf) dark green 7.75 12.00

2nd National Stamp Exposition, Berlin.

Perf. 14x13½
1940, Apr. 10 Photo. **Wmk. 237**
B170 SP146 12(pf)+38(pf) copper red 3.00 4.00

51st birthday of Adolf Hitler.

Armed Warrior
SP147

Horseman
SP148

1940, Apr. 30 *Perf. 14* **Unwmkd.**
B171 SP147 6(pf)+4(pf) slate green & light green 35 60

Issued to commemorate May Day.

Perf. 14x13½
1940, June 22 **Wmk. 237**
B172 SP148 25(pf)+100(pf) deep ultra. 4.25 6.50

Issued in commemoration of the Blue Ribbon race held at Hamburg, June 30 1940.
The surtax was for Hitler's National Culture Fund.

Chariot
SP149

Engraved
1940, July 20 *Perf. 14* **Unwmkd.**
B173 SP149 42(pf)+108(pf) brown 19.00 25.00

7th "Brown Ribbon" at Munich.
The surtax was for Hitler's National Culture Fund and the promoters of the race.

View of Malmedy
SP150

Design: 12pf+8pf, View of Eupen.

Perf. 14x13½
1940, July 25 Photo. **Wmk. 237**
B174 SP150 6(pf)+4(pf) dark green 80 1.20
B175 " 12(pf)+8(pf) orange red 80 1.20

Issued on the occasion of the reunion of Eupen-Malmedy with the Reich.

Rocky Cliffs of Heligoland
SP152

Artushof in Danzig
SP153

1940, Aug. 9 **Unwmkd.**
B176 SP152 6(pf)+94(pf) bright blue green & red orange 4.00 6.00

Heligoland's 50th year as part of Germany.

1940, Nov. 5 **Engraved** *Perf. 14*

Buildings: 4pf+3pf, Town Hall, Thorn. 5pf+3pf, Castle at Kaub. 6pf+4pf, City Theater, Poznan. 8pf+4pf, Castle at Heidelberg. 12pf+6pf, Porta Nigra Trier. 15pf+10pf, New German Theater, Prague. 25pf+15pf, Town Hall, Bremen. 40pf+35pf, Town Hall, Munster.

Inscribed: "Winterhilfswerk."

B177 SP153 3(pf)+2(pf) dark brown 8 10
a. Bklt. pane 9 (4 No. B177+5 No. B182)+label 5.50
B178 " 4(pf)+3(pf) bluish black 25 35
B179 " 5(pf)+3(pf) yellow green 8 10
a. Bklt. pane 10 (5 No. B179+5 No. B180 2.75
B180 " 6(pf)+4(pf) dark green 8 10
B181 " 8(pf)+4(pf) deep orange 25 35
B182 " 12(pf)+6(pf) car. 10 15
B183 " 15(pf)+10(pf) dark vio. brown 1.25 1.90
B184 " 25(pf)+15(pf) dp. ultramarine 1.60 2.50
B185 " 40(pf)+35(pf) red lilac 2.75 4.25
Nos. B177-B185 (9) 6.44 9.80

Dr. Emil von Behring
SP162

Postilion
SP163

1940, Nov. 26 **Photogravure**
B186 SP162 6(pf)+4(pf) deep green 55 90
B187 " 25(pf)+10(pf) bright ultra. 95 1.50

Emil von Behring (1854-1917), bacteriologist.

1941, Jan. 12 *Perf. 14x13½*
B188 SP163 6(pf)+24(pf) deep green 60 90

Issued in commemoration of Postage Stamp Day. The surtax was for Hitler's National Culture Fund.

Benito Mussolini and Adolf Hitler
SP164

Perf. 13½x14
1941, Jan. 30 **Wmk. 237**
B189 SP164 12(pf)+38(pf) rose brown 1.40 1.90

Issued as propaganda for the Rome-Berlin Axis. The surtax was for Hitler's National Culture Fund.

Adolf Hitler
SP165

Race Horse
SP166

1941, Apr. 17 *Perf. 14x13½*
B190 SP165 12(pf)+38(pf) dark red 1.40 2.25

Issued in commemoration of the 52nd birthday of Adolf Hitler. The surtax was for Hitler's National Culture Fund.

Perf. 13½x14
1941, June 20 **Engr.** **Unwmkd.**
B191 SP166 25(pf)+100(pf) sapphire 3.75 6.00

Issued in commemoration of the Blue Ribbon race held at Hamburg, June 29, 1941.

Amazons
SP167

1941, July 20 *Perf. 14*
B192 SP167 42(pf)+108(pf) brown 2.75 4.25

8th "Brown Ribbon" at Munich.

Brandenburg Gate, Berlin
SP168

1941, Sept. 9
B193 SP168 25(pf)+50(pf) deep ultra. 1.60 2.50

Issued in honor of the Berlin races.

Marburg
SP169

Veldes
SP170

Pettau
SP171

Triglav
SP172

1941, Sept. 29 **Photogravure**
B194 SP169 3(pf)+7(pf) brn. 35 55
B195 SP170 6(pf)+9(pf) purple 70 1.10
B196 SP171 12(pf)+13(pf) rose brown 1.10 1.65
B197 SP172 25(pf)+15(pf) dark blue 1.90 3.00

Annexation of Styria and Carinthia.

View from Belvedere Palace, Vienna
SP173

Belvedere Gardens, Vienna
SP174

1941, Sept. 16 **Engraved**

B198 SP173 12(pf)+8(pf) deep red 70 1.10
B199 SP174 15(pf)+10(pf) violet 1.00 1.65

Issued to commemorate the Vienna Fair.

Mozart SP175 — Philatelist SP176

1941, Nov. 28

B200 SP175 6(pf)+4(pf) dark rose violet 12 20

To commemorate the 150th anniversary of the death of Wolfgang Amadeus Mozart (1756–91).

1942, Jan. 11 **Photogravure**

B201 SP176 6(pf)+24(pf) deep purple 70 1.20

To commemorate Stamp Day.

Soldier's Head SP177 — Adolf Hitler SP178

1942, Mar. 10 ***Perf. 14x13½***

B202 SP177 12(pf)+38(pf) slate black 45 75

To commemorate Hero Memorial Day.

1942, Apr. 13

B203 SP178 12(pf)+38(pf) lake 1.60 2.50

To commemorate Hitler's 53rd birthday.

Racing Three-year-old
SP179

Engraved

1942, June 16 ***Perf. 14***

B204 SP179 25(pf)+100(pf) dark blue 7.75 12.00

To commemorate the 73rd Hamburg Derby.

Race Horses
SP180

1942, July 14

B205 SP180 42(pf)+108(pf) brown 2.50 4.00

9th "Brown Ribbon" at Munich.

Lüneburg Lion and Nüremberg Betrothal Cup SP181 — Henlein Monument, Nüremberg SP182

Photogravure

1942, Aug. 8 ***Perf. 14x13½***

B206 SP181 6(pf)+4(pf) copper red 35 55
B207 " 12(pf)+88(pf) green 50 80

To commemorate the 10th anniversary of the German Goldsmiths' Society and the first Goldsmiths' Day in Germany.

1942, Aug. 29 ***Perf. 14***

B208 SP182 6(pf)+24(pf) rose violet 40 65

To commemorate the 400th anniversary of the death of Peter Henlein, inventor of the pocket watch.

Postilion and Map of Europe
SP183

Postilion and Globe
SP184

Postilion
SP185

Perf. 13½x14, 14x13½.

1942, Oct. 12 **Photogravure**

B209 SP183 3(pf)+7(pf) dull blue 17 30

Engraved

B210 SP184 6(pf)+14(pf) ultramarine & deep brn. 30 55
B211 SP185 12(pf)+38(pf) rose red & deep brown 60 1.00

European Postal Congress, Vienna.

Nos. B209 to B211 Overprinted in Black ***19.Okt.1942***

1942, Oct. 19

B212 SP183 3(pf)+7(pf) dull blue 90 1.45
B213 SP184 6(pf)+14(pf) ultramarine & deep brown 90 1.45
B214 SP185 12(pf)+38(pf) rose red & dp. brown 90 1.45

To commemorate the signing of the European postal-telegraph agreement at Vienna.

Mail Coach
SP186

1943, Jan. 10 **Engraved**

B215 SP186 6(pf)+24(pf) gray, brown & yellow 15 25

To commemorate Stamp Day. The surtax went to Hitler's National Culture Fund.

Brandenburg Gate SP187 — Nazi Emblem SP188

1943, Jan. 26 **Photogravure**

B216 SP187 54(pf)+96(pf) copper red 40 70

To commemorate the 10th anniversary of the assumption of power by the Nazis.

1943, Jan. 26

B217 SP188 3(pf)+2(pf) olive bistre 8 13

Used to secure special philatelic cancellations.

Submarine
SP189

Designs: 4pf+3pf, Schutz-Staffel Troops. 5pf+4pf, Motorized marksmen. 6pf+9pf, Signal Corps. 8pf+7pf, Engineer Corps. 12pf+8pf, Grenade assault. 15pf+10pf, Heavy artillery. 20pf+14pf, Anti-aircraft units in action. 25pf+15pf, Dive bombers. 30pf+30pf, Paratroops. 40pf+40pf, Tank. 50pf+50pf, Speed boat.

1943, Mar. 21 **Engraved**

B218 SP189 3(pf)+2(pf) dark brown 15 22
B219 " 4(pf)+3(pf) brn. 15 22
B220 " 5(pf)+4(pf) dark green 15 22
B221 " 6(pf)+9(pf) deep violet 15 22
B222 " 8(pf)+7(pf) brown org. 12 20
B223 " 12(pf)+8(pf) carmine lake 17 27
B224 " 15(pf)+10(pf) violet brown 23 38
B225 " 20(pf)+14(pf) slate blue 35 55
B226 " 25(pf)+15(pf) indigo 42 65
B227 " 30(pf)+30(pf) green 65 1.20
B228 " 40(pf)+40(pf) red lilac 65 1.20
B229 " 50(pf)+50(pf) greenish black 1.10 1.90
Nos. B218–B229 (12) 4.29 7.23

Army Day and Hero Memorial Day.
Nos. B220 and B224 exist imperf. Price, each $67.50.

Nazi Flag and Children—SP201

1943, Mar. 26 **Photogravure**

B230 SP201 6(pf)+4(pf) dark green 18 28

To commemorate the Day of Youth Obligation when all German boys and girls had to take an oath of allegiance to Hitler.

Adolf Hitler
SP202

1943, Apr. 13

B231 SP202 3(pf)+7(pf) brown black 45 75
B232 " 6(pf)+14(pf) dark green 45 75
B233 " 8(pf)+22(pf) dark chalky blue 45 75
B234 " 12(pf)+38(pf) copper red 45 75
B235 " 24(pf)+76(pf) violet brown 70 1.20
B236 " 40(pf)+160(pf) dk. olive green 1.10 1.90
Nos. B231–B236 (6) 3.60 6.10

To commemorate Hitler's 54th birthday.
No. B231 exists imperf. Price $100.

Reich Labor Service Corpsmen
SP203 — SP204

Designs: 6pf+14pf, Corpsman chopping. 12pf+18pf, Corpsman with implements.

1943, June 26 **Engraved**

B237 SP203 3(pf)+(7pf) bistre brown 10 20
B238 SP204 5(pf)+10(pf) pale olive green 10 20
B239 " 6(pf)+14(pf) deep blue 10 20
B240 " 12(pf)+18(pf) dark red 25 55

Anniversary of Reich Labor Service.
Nos. B237–B238 exist imperf. Price, each $50.

Rosegger's Birthplace, Upper Styria SP207 — Peter Rosegger SP208

Perf. 13½x14, 14x13½

1943, July 27 **Photogravure**

B241 SP207 6(pf)+4(pf) green 8 15
B242 SP208 12(pf)+8(pf) copper red 10 17

To commemorate the centenary of the birth of Peter Rosegger, Austrian writer.

Hunter
SP209

1943, July 27 Engraved

B243 SP209 42(pf)+108(pf) brown 20 33

10th "Brown Ribbon" at Munich.
No. B243 exists imperf. Price $300.

Race Horse SP210 — Mother and Children—SP211

1943, Aug. 14

B244 SP210 6(pf)+4(pf) violet black 13 25
B245 " 12(pf)+88(pf) dark carmine 16 25

To commemorate the Grand Prize of the Freudenau, the Vienna race track, August 15, 1943.

1943, Sept. 1

B246 SP211 12(pf)+38(pf) dark red 15 25

10th anniversary of Winter Relief.

St. George in Gold SP212 — Ancient Lübeck SP213

1943, Oct. 1

B247 SP212 6(pf)+4(pf) dark olive green 12 17
B248 " 12(pf)+88(pf) violet brown 15 22

German Goldsmiths' Society.

1943, Oct. 24 Photogravure

B249 SP213 12(pf)+8(pf) copper red 15 25

To commemorate the 800th anniversary of the Hanseatic town of Lubeck.
No. B249 exists imperf. Price, $75.

"And Despite All, You Were Victorious" SP214 — Dr. Robert Koch SP215

1943, Nov. 5

B250 SP214 24(pf)+26(pf) henna 15 25

To commemorate the 20th anniversary of the Nazis' Munich beer-hall putsch and to honor those who died for the Nazi movement.

1944, Jan. 25 Engraved Unwmkd.

B251 SP215 12(pf)+38(pf) sepia 15 25

To commemorate the centenary of the birth of the bacteriologist, Robert Koch (1843–1910).

Hitler and Nazi Emblems
SP216

1944, Jan. 29 Photogravure

B252 SP216 54(pf)+96(pf) yellow brown 17 28

To commemorate the 11th anniversary of the assumption of power by the Nazis.

Airport Scene
SP217

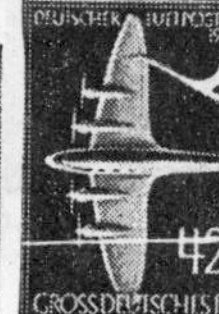

Seaplane SP218 — Plane Seen from Above SP219

Perf. 14x13½, 13½x14.

1944, Feb. 11 Photo. Unwmkd.

B252A SP217 6(pf)+4(pf) dark green 10 18
B252B SP218 12(pf)+8(pf) maroon 10 18
B252C SP219 42(pf)+108(pf) deep slate blue 22 35

To commemorate the 25th anniversary of German air mail. The surtax was for the National Culture Fund.

Infant's Crib SP220 — Assault Boat SP221

Designs: 6pf+4pf, Public nurse. 12pf+8pf, "Mother and Child" clinic. 15pf+10pf, Expectant mothers.

1944, Mar. 2

B253 SP220 3(pf)+2(pf) dark brown 8 14
B254 " 6(pf)+4(pf) dark green 8 14
B255 " 12(pf)+8(pf) deep carmine 8 14
B256 " 15(pf)+10(pf) violet brown 12 20

To commemorate the 10th anniversary of "Mother and Child" aid.

1944, Mar. 11

Inscribed: "Grossdeutsches Reich."

Designs: 4pf+3pf, Chain-wheel vehicle. 5pf+3pf, Paratroops. 6pf+4pf, Submarine officer. 8pf+4pf, Schutz-Staffel grenade throwers. 10pf+5pf, Searchlight. 12pf+6pf, Infantry. 15pf+10pf, Self-propelled gun. 16pf+10pf, Speed boat. 20pf+10pf, Sea raider. 24pf+10pf, Railway artillery. 25pf+15pf, Rockets. 30pf+20pf, Mountain trooper.

B257 SP221 3(pf)+2(pf) yel. brown 15 25
B258 " 4(pf)+3(pf) royal blue 15 25
B259 SP221 5(pf)+3(pf) deep yellow green 15 25
B260 " 6(pf)+4(pf) deep violet 15 25
B261 " 8(pf)+4(pf) org. vermilion 15 25
B262 " 10(pf)+5(pf) choc. 15 25
B263 " 12(pf)+6(pf) car. 15 25
B264 " 15(pf)+10(pf) deep claret 15 25
B265 " 16(pf)+10(pf) dark blue green 22 35
B266 " 20(pf)+10(pf) bright blue 27 50
B267 " 24(pf)+10(pf) dull orange brn. 40 70
B268 " 25(pf)+15(pf) violet blue 60 90
B269 " 30(pf)+20(pf) olive green 50 80
Nos. B257–B269 (13) 3.19 5.25

To commemorate Hero Memorial Day.

Flora Statue in Fulda's Schloss Garden SP234 — Adolf Hitler SP235

1944, Mar. 11

B270 SP234 12(pf)+38(pf) deep brown 12 20

1,200th anniversary of town of Fulda.

1944, Apr. 14 Engraved Unwmkd.

B271 SP235 54(pf)+96(pf) rose carmine 20 38

To commemorate Hitler's 55th birthday.

Type of 1939–41 and

Woman Mail Carrier
SP236

Field Post in the East
SP237

Designs: 8pf+12pf, Mail coach. 16pf+24pf, Automobile race. 20pf+30pf, Postal police. 24pf+36pf, Glider workshops.

1944, May 3 Photogravure

Designs measure 29½x24½ mm.

B272 SP236 6(pf)+9(pf) violet blue 8 15
B273 SP124 8(pf)+12(pf) gray black 8 15
B274 SP237 12(pf)+18(pf) deep plum 8 15
B275 SP124 16(pf)+24(pf) dark green 8 15
B276 " 20(pf)+30(pf) bl. 10 20
B277 " 24(pf)+36(pf) dark purple 10 20
Nos. B272–B277 (6) 52 1.00

The surtax was for the Postal Employees' Fund.

Soldier and Tirolese Rifleman SP238 — Albert I, Duke of Prussia SP239

1944, July

B278 SP238 6(pf)+4(pf) deep green 6 12
B279 " 12(pf)+8(pf) brown lake 10 17

To commemorate the 7th National Shooting Matches at Innsbruck.

1944, July

B280 SP239 6(pf)+4(pf) dark blue green 12 20

To commemorate the 400th anniversary of Albert University, Königsberg.

Labor Corps Girl SP240 — Labor Corpsman SP241

1944, June Engraved

B281 SP240 6(pf)+4(pf) green 8 15
B282 SP241 12(pf)+8(pf) car. 8 15

Issued to honor an exhibit of the Reich Labor Service.

Race Horse and Foal
SP242

1944, July 23 ***Perf. 14x13½***

B283 SP242 42(pf)+108(pf) brown 15 25

11th "Brown Ribbon" at Munich.

Race Horse's Head in Oak Wreath SP243 — Nautilus Cup in Green Vault, Dresden SP244

1944, Aug. Photogravure ***Perf. 14***

B284 SP243 6(pf)+4(pf) Prussian green 7 12
B285 " 12(pf)+88(pf) carmine lake 10 14

To commemorate the Vienna Grand Prize Race.

1944, Sept. 11

B286 SP244 6(pf)+4(pf) dark green 7 12
B287 " 12(pf)+88(pf) carmine brown 10 14

Issued in honor of the German Goldsmiths' Society.
No. B287 exists imperf. Price $175.

Post Horn and Letter
SP245

1944, Oct. 2

B288 SP245 6(pf)+24(pf) dark green 12 20

To commemorate Stamp Day.

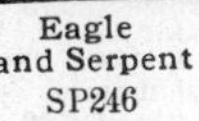

Eagle and Serpent
SP246

Count Anton Günther
SP247

1944, Nov. 9

B289 SP246 12(pf)+8(pf) rose red 12 20

To commemorate the 21st anniversary of the Munich putsch.

1945, Jan. 6 Typo. ***Perf. 13½x14***

B290 SP247 6(pf)+14(pf) brown violet 12 20

To commemorate the 600th anniversary of municipal law in Oldenburg.

People's Army—SP248

1945, Feb. Photo. ***Perf. 14x13½***

B291 SP248 12(pf)+8(pf) rose carmine 17 32

To commemorate the proclamation of the People's Army (Volkssturm) in East Prussia to fight the Russians.

Elite Storm Trooper (S. S.)
SP249

Storm Trooper (S. A.)
SP250

1945, Apr. 21 ***Perf. 13½x14***

B292 SP249 12(pf)+38(pf) bright car. 4.25 7.00

B293 SP250 12(pf)+38(pf) brt. carmine 4.25 7.00

To commemorate the 12th anniversary of the assumption of power by the Nazis. Nos. B292 and B293 were on sale in Berlin briefly before the collapse of that city.

Exist imperf. Price for set, $9.

Souvenir Sheets

SP251

Typographed.

1946, Dec. 8 ***Perf. 14*** **Wmk. 284**

B294 SP251 Sheet of three 35.00 92.50

Imperf.

B295 SP251 Sheet of three 42.50 120.00
- *a.* A119 20pf light blue 4.00 8.25
- *b.* " 24pf orange brown 4.00 8.25
- *c.* " 40pf red violet 4.00 8.25

No. B294 contains one each of Nos. 543, 544 and 548.

Nos. B294–B295 sold for 5 marks each. The surtax was for refugees and the aged. Size: 107x51mm.

Leipzig Proclaimed Market Place, 1160
SP252

Wmk. 48

Design: 60(pf)+40(pf), Foreign merchants displaying their wares, 1268.

Wmkd. Diagonal Zigzag Lines. (48)

1947, Mar. 5 Engraved ***Perf. 13***

B296 SP252 24(pf)+26(pf) chestnut brown 8 20

B297 " 60(pf)+40(pf) dp. violet blue 10 25

1947 Leipzig Fairs.

No. B296 exists imperf. Price $150.

See Nos. 580–583, 10NB1–10NB2, 10NB4–10NB5, 10NB12–10NB13 and German Democratic Republic Nos. B15–B16.

Madonna
SP254

Cathedral Towers
SP255

Designs: 12pf+8pf, Three Kings. 24pf+16pf, Cologne Cathedral.

Typographed.

1948, Aug. 15 ***Perf. 11*** **Wmk. 286**

B298 SP254 6pf+4pf org. brn. 55 1.10
- *a.* "1948-1248" 8.50 11.00

B299 " 12pf+8pf greenish blue 1.00 2.50
- *a.* "1948-1948" 10.00 14.00

B300 " 24pf+16pf car. 1.75 4.25

B301 SP255 50pf+50pf blue 4.50 8.75

Issued to commemorate the 700th anniversary of the laying of the cornerstone of Cologne Cathedral. The surtax was to aid in its reconstruction.

Specialists collect Nos. B298–B301 with watermark in four positions: upright, D's facing left; upright, D's facing right; sideways, D's facing up; sideways, D's facing down. Two types of perforation: line and comb.

Brandenburg Gate, Berlin
SP256

Bicycle Racers
SP257

Perf. 10½x11½, 11.

1948, Dec. **Lithographed**

B302 SP256 10(pf)+5(pf) green 3.25 6.50

B303 " 20(pf)+10(pf) rose carmine 3.25 6.50

The surtax was for aid to Berlin.

Engraved.

1949, May 15 ***Perf. 14*** **Wmk. 116**

B304 SP257 10(pf)+5(pf) grn. 3.50 4.50

B305 " 20(pf)+10(pf) brown orange 8.00 19.00

1949 Bicycle Tour of Germany.

Goethe at Rome
SP258

Johann Wolfgang von Goethe
SP259

Design: 30pf+15pf, Goethe portrait facing left.

1949, Aug. 15

B306 SP258 10(pf)+5(pf) green 2.50 4.00

B307 SP259 20(pf)+10(pf) red 3.25 5.25

B308 " 30(pf)+15(pf) bl. 10.00 22.50

Issued to commemorate the bicentenary of the birth of Johann Wolfgang von Goethe.

The surtax was for the reconstruction of Goethe House, Frankfurt-on-Main.

Federal Republic.

Bavaria Stamp of 1849
SP260

St. Elisabeth
SP261

1949, Sept. 30 Litho. **Wmk. 285**

B309 SP260 10(pf)+2(pf) green & black 10.00 14.00

Centenary of German postage stamps.

1949, Dec. 14 Engraved Wmk. 286

Designs: 10pf+5pf, Paracelsus. 20pf+10pf, F. W. A. Froebel. 30pf+15pf, J. H. Wichern.

B310 SP261 8(pf)+2(pf) brown violet 17.50 22.50

B311 " 10(pf)+5(pf) yellow green 16.00 19.00

B312 " 20(pf)+10(pf) red 17.50 22.50

B313 " 30(pf)+15(pf) violet blue 72.50 115.00

The surtax was for welfare organizations.

Seal of Johann Sebastian Bach
SP262

Frescoes from Marienkirche
SP263

1950, July 28 ***Perf. 14***

B314 SP262 10(pf)+2(pf) dark green 57.50 65.00

B315 " 20(pf)+3(pf) dk. carmine 57.50 65.00

Issued to commemorate the bicentenary of the death of Johann Sebastian Bach, composer.

1951, Aug. 30 Photo. **Wmk. 286**

Center in Gray.

B316 SP263 10(pf)+5(pf) green 72.50 100.00

B317 " 20(pf)+5(pf) brn. lake 72.50 100.00

Issued to commemorate the 700th anniversary of the construction of Marienkirche, Lübeck.

The surtax aided in its reconstruction.

Stamps Under Magnifying Glass
SP264

St. Vincent de Paul
SP265

Typographed.

1951, Sept. 14 ***Perf. 14*** **Wmk. 295**

B318 SP264 10(pf)+2(pf) yellow green, black & yel. 42.50 65.00

B319 " 20(pf)+3(pf) deep magenta, black & yel. 42.50 65.00

Issued to publicize the National Philatelic Exposition, Wuppertal, 1951.

1951, Oct. 23 **Engraved**

Portraits: 10(pf)+3(pf), Friedrich von Bodelschwingh. 20(pf)+5(pf), Elsa Brandstrom. 30(pf)+10(pf), Johann Heinrich Pestalozzi.

B320 SP265 4(pf)+2(pf) brown 7.75 10.00

B321 " 10(pf)+3(pf) green 14.00 12.00

B322 " 20(pf)+5(pf) rose red 14.00 12.00

B323 " 30(pf)+10(pf) deep bl. 90.00 150.00

The surtax was for charitable purposes.

Nuremberg Madonna
SP266

Boy Hikers and Youth Hostel
SP267

1952, Aug. 9

B324 SP266 10(pf)+5(pf) green 21.00 32.50

Issued to commemorate the centenary of the founding of the Germanic National Museum, Nuremberg. The surtax was for the museum.

1952, Sept. 17 ***Perf. 13½x14***

Design: 20(pf)+3(pf). Girls and Hostel.

B325 SP267 10(pf)+2(pf) grn. 17.50 25.00
B326 " 20(pf)+3(pf) deep carmine 19.00 30.00

The surtax was to aid the youth program of the Federal Republic.

Elizabeth Fry SP268 — Owl and Cogwheel SP269

Portraits: 10(pf)+5(pf), Dr. Carl Sonnenschein. 20(pf)+10(pf), Theodor Fliedner. 30(pf)+10(pf), Henri Dunant.

1952, Oct. 1

B327 SP268 4(pf)+2(pf) orange brown 8.00 11.00
B328 " 10(pf)+5(pf) green 6.25 7.75
B329 " 20(pf)+10(pf) brown carmine 17.50 18.00
B330 " 30(pf)+10(pf) deep blue 70.00 100.00

The surtax was for welfare organizations.

1953, May 7 ***Perf. 14*** **Wmk. 295**

B331 SP269 10(pf)+5(pf) deep green 30.00 50.00

Issued to commemorate the 50th anniversary of the founding of the German Museum in Munich.

Thurn and Taxis Palace Gate SP270 — August Hermann Francke SP271

Design: 20(pf)+3(pf), Telecommunications Bldg., Frankfurt-on-Main.

Perf. 13½

1953, July 29 **Litho.** **Wmk. 285**

B332 SP270 10(pf)+2(pf) yellow green, black & terra cotta 22.50 32.50
B333 " 20(pf)+3(pf) terra cotta, blk. & gray 25.00 37.50

The surtax was for the International Stamp Exhibition, Frankfurt-on-Main, 1953.

Engraved.

1953, Nov. 2 ***Perf. 14*** **Wmk. 295**

Designs: 10(pf)+5(pf), Sebastian Kneipp. 20(pf)+10(pf), Dr. Johann Christian Senckenberg. 30(pf)+10(pf), Fridtjof Nansen.

B334 SP271 4(pf)+2(pf) chocolate 5.25 8.25
B335 " 10(pf)+5(pf) bl. green 10.00 10.50
B336 " 20(pf)+10(pf) red 12.00 12.00
B337 " 30(pf)+10(pf) blue 47.50 80.00

The surtax was for welfare organizations.

Käthe Kollwitz SP272 — Carrier Pigeon and Magnifying Glass SP273

Portraits: 10pf+5pf, Lorenz Werthmann. 20pf+10pf, Johann Friedrich Oberlin. 40pf+10pf, Bertha Pappenheim.

1954, Dec. 28 ***Perf. 13½x14***

B338 SP272 7pf+3pf brown 3.50 5.00
B339 " 10pf+5pf green 2.85 2.25
B340 " 20pf+10pf red 8.50 5.50
B341 " 40pf+10pf blue 32.50 55.00

The surtax was for welfare organizations.

1955, Sept. 14 ***Perf. 14*** **Wmk. 304**

Design: 20pf+3pf, Post horn and stamp tongs.

B342 SP273 10pf+2pf green 7.00 11.00
B343 " 20pf+3pf red 10.50 19.00

Issued to commemorate the WESTROPA, 1955, philatelic exhibition at Dusseldorf. The surtax aided the Society of German Philatelists.

Amalie Sieveking SP274

Portraits: 10(pf)+5(pf), Adolph Kolping. 20(pf)+10(pf), Dr. Samuel Hahnemann. 40(pf)+10(pf), Florence Nightingale.

1955, Nov. 15 **Photo. & Litho.**

B344 SP274 7(pf)+3(pf) olive bis. 2.10 3.50
B345 " 10(pf)+5(pf) dk. green 1.60 1.35
B346 " 20(pf)+10(pf) red org. 2.25 1.65
B347 " 40(pf)+10(pf) greenish blue 26.50 45.00

The surtax was for independent welfare organizations.

Boy and Geometrical Designs SP275

Design: 10pf+5pf, Girl playing flute.

Lithographed.

1956, July 21 ***Perf. 14*** **Unwmkd.**

B348 SP275 7pf+3pf red brown, pale gray & blk. 3.00 5.25
B349 " 10pf+5pf light olive green, pale gray & blk. 5.50 10.00

The surtax was for the Youth Hostel Organization.

The Midwife SP276

Designs: 10pf+5pf, Ignaz Philipp Semmelweis. 20pf+10pf, The mother. 40pf+10pf, The children's nurse.

1956, Oct. 1 **Photogravure**

Design and Inscription in Black.

B350 SP276 7pf+3pf orange brown 1.60 2.50
B351 " 10pf+5pf green 1.00 80
B352 " 20pf+10pf bright red 1.10 80
B353 " 40pf+10pf bri ht blue 10.50 19.00

Issued to honor Ignaz Philipp Semmelweis, the discoverer of the cause of puerperal fever. The surtax was for independent welfare organizations.

Children Leaving SP277

Design: 20pf+10pf, Child arriving.

1957, Feb. 1 **Litho.** ***Perf. 13½x13***

B354 SP277 10pf+5pf gray green & red orange 1.40 2.25
B355 " 20pf+10pf red orange & light blue 2.50 4.50

The surtax was for vacations for the children of Berlin.

Young Miner SP278 — "The Fox who Stole the Goose" SP279

Designs: 10pf+5pf, Miner with drill. 20pf+10pf, Miner and conveyor. 40pf+10pf, Miner and coal elevator.

1957, Oct. 1 ***Perf. 14*** **Wmk. 304**

B356 SP278 7pf+3pf bistre brn. & blk. 1.25 1.90
B357 " 10pf+5pf black & yel. grn. 55 45
B358 " 20pf+10pf black & red 1.15 45
B359 " 40pf+10pf black & blue 11.50 22.50

The surtax was for independent welfare organizations.

1958, Apr. 1 **Lithographed**

Design: 20pf+10pf, "A Hunter from the Palatinate."

B360 SP279 10pf+5pf brown red, green & black 80 1.75
B361 " 20pf+10pf multi. 1.20 2.25

The surtax was to finance young peoples' study trips to Berlin.

Friedrich Wilhelm Raiffeisen SP280 — Dairy Maid SP281

Designs: 20pf+10pf, Girl picking grapes. 40pf+10pf, Farmer with pitchfork.

1958, Oct. 1 ***Perf. 14*** **Wmk. 304**

B362 SP280 7pf+3pf golden brown & dark brown 30 65
B363 SP281 10pf+5pf green, red & yellow 35 30
B364 " 20pf+10pf red, yellow & blue 42 35
B365 " 40pf+10pf blue & ochre 3.75 6.50

The surtax was for independent welfare organizations.

Stamp of Hamburg, 1859 SP282

Design: 20pf+10pf, Stamp of Lübeck, 1859.

1959, May 22 **Engr.** **Wmk. 304**

B366 SP282 10pf+5pf green & brown 75 1.45
a. 10pf+5pf yellow green & brown 12 35
B367 " 20pf+10pf maroon & red brown 90 1.65
a. 20pf+10pf red orange & red brown 32 75

Issued to publicize the "Interposta" Philatelic Exhibition, Hamburg, May 22-31, 1959. "Interposta" commemorated the centenary of the first stamps of Hamburg and Lübeck.

The surtax on Nos. B366a and B367a was for vacations for the children of Berlin. Issued Aug. 22, 1959.

Girl Giving Bread to Beggar SP283

Jacob and Wilhelm Grimm SP284

Designs (from "Star Dollars" fairy tale): 10pf + 5pf, Girl giving coat to boy. 20pf + 10pf, Star-Money from Heaven.

1959, Oct. 1 **Litho.** ***Perf. 14***

B368 SP283 7pf+3pf brown & yellow 17 35
B369 " 10pf+5pf green & yellow 27 25
B370 " 20pf+10pf brick red & yellow 38 25
B371 SP284 40pf+10pf blue, black, ochre & emerald 2.10 4.00

The surtax was for independent welfare organizations.

Little Red Riding Hood and the Wolf SP285

Various Scenes from Little Red Riding Hood.

1960, Oct. 1 ***Perf. 14*** **Wmk. 304**

B372 SP285 7pf+3pf brown olive, red & black 20 40
B373 " 10pf+5pf green, red & black 35 20
B374 " 20pf+10pf brick red, emerald & black 55 25
B375 " 40pf+20pf bright blue, red & black 2.25 3.00

The surtax was for independent welfare organizations.

1961, Oct. 2

Various Scenes from Hansel and Gretel.

B376 SP285 7pf+3pf multi. 17 25
B377 " 10pf+5pf " 17 20
B378 " 20pf+10pf " 27 20
B379 " 40pf+20pf " 1.90 2.25

The surtax was for independent welfare organizations.

See Nos. B384–B387, B392–B395, B400–B403.

Fluorescent Paper

was introduced for semipostal stamps, starting with No. B380.

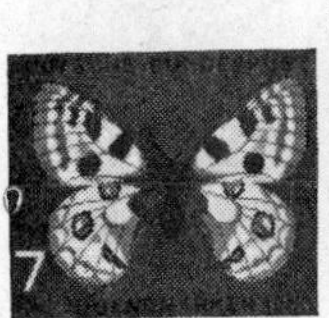

Apollo
SP286

Hoopoe
SP287

Butterflies: 10pf+5pf, Camberwell beauty. 20pf+10pf, Tortoise-shell. 40pf+20pf, Tiger swallowtail.

Lithographed

1962, May 25 ***Perf. 14*** **Wmk. 304**

Butterflies in Natural Colors, Black Inscriptions.

B380 SP286 7pf+3pf bistre brown 32 40
B381 " 10pf+5pf brt. grn. 32 32
B382 " 20pf+10pf deep crimson 50 45
B383 " 40pf+20pf br. bl. 1.65 2.00

Issued for the benefit of young people.

Nos. B381–B383 exist without watermark. Price, each $900 unused, $750 used.

Fairy Tale Type of 1960

Various Scenes from Snow White (Schneewittchen).

1962, Oct. 10 ***Perf. 14***

B384 SP285 7pf+3pf multi. 22 25
B385 " 10pf+5pf " 22 17
B386 " 20pf+10pf " 32 17
B387 " 40pf+20pf " 1.10 1.65

The surtax was for independent welfare organizations.

1963, June 12 ***Perf. 14*** **Unwmkd.**

Birds: 15pf+5pf, European golden oriole. 20pf+10pf, Bullfinch. 40pf+20pf, European kingfisher.

B388 SP287 10pf+5pf multi. 27 32
B389 " 15pf+5pf " 38 45
B390 " 20pf+10pf " 45 45
B391 " 40pf+20pf " 1.45 1.90

Issued for the benefit of young people.

Fairy Tale Type of 1960

Various Scenes from the Grimm Brothers' "The Wolf and the Seven Kids."

1963, Sept. 23 **Lithographed**

B392 SP285 10pf+5pf multi. 15 25
B393 " 15pf+5pf " 15 15
B394 " 20pf+10pf " 18 15
B395 " 40pf+20pf " 1.00 1.35

The surtax was for independent welfare organizations.

Herring
SP288

Woodcock
SP289

Fish: 15pf+5pf, Rosefish. 20pf+10pf, Carp. 40pf+20pf, Cod.

1964, Apr. 10 ***Perf. 14*** **Unwmkd.**

B396 SP288 10pf+5pf multi. 18 35
B397 " 15pf+5pf " 28 32
B398 " 20pf+10pf " 38 32
B399 " 40pf+20pf " 1.35 1.75

Issued for the benefit of young people.

Fairy Tale Type of 1960

Various Scenes from Sleeping Beauty (Dornroschen).

1964, Oct. 6 **Litho.** ***Perf. 14***

B400 SP285 10p+5pf multi. 15 17
B401 " 15pf+5pf " 18 15
B402 " 20pf+10pf " 27 17
B403 " 40pf+20pf " 90 1.50

The surtax was for independent welfare organizations.

1965, Apr. 1 ***Perf. 14*** **Unwmkd.**

Birds: 15pf+5pf, Ring-necked pheasant. 20pf+10pf, Black grouse. 40pf+20pf, Capercaillie.

B404 SP289 10pf+5pf multi. 12 15
B405 " 15pf+5pf " 16 25
B406 " 20pf+10pf " 25 25
B407 " 40pf+20pf " 55 1.25

Issued for the benefit of young people.

Cinderella Feeding Pigeons
SP290

Roe Deer
SP291

Various Scenes from Cinderella.

1965, Oct. 6 **Litho.** ***Perf. 14***

B408 SP290 10pf+5pf multi. 15 25
B409 " 15pf+5pf " 18 20
B410 " 20pf+10pf " 22 20
B411 " 40pf+20pf " 95 1.25

The surtax was for independent welfare organizations.

See also Nos. B418–B421, B426–B429.

1966, Apr. 22 **Litho.** ***Perf. 14***

Designs: 20pf+10pf, Chamois. 30pf+15pf, Fallow deer. 50pf+25pf, Red deer.

B412 SP291 10pf+5pf multi. 15 20
B413 " 20pf+10pf " 28 25
B414 " 30pf+15pf " 55 25
B415 " 50pf+25pf " 1.20 1.90

Issued for the benefit of young people.

See also Nos. B422–B425.

Prussian Letter Carrier
SP292

Design: 30pf+15pf, Bavarian mail coach.

1966 **Lithographed** ***Perf. 14***

B416 SP292 30pf+15pf multi. 75 1.00
B417 " 50pf+25pf multi. 75 1.00

Issued to publicize the meeting of the Federation Internationale de Philatélie (FIP), Munich, Sept. 26–29, and the stamp exhibition, Municipal Museum, Sept. 24–Oct. 1. The surcharge was for the Foundation for the Promotion of Philately and Postal History. Issue dates: No. B416, Sept. 24; No. B417, July 13.

Fairy Tale Type of 1965

Various Scenes from The Princess and the Frog.

1966, Oct. 5 **Litho.** ***Perf. 14***

B418 SP290 10pf+5pf multi. 17 22
B419 " 20pf+10pf " 25 27
B420 " 30pf+15pf " 45 27
B421 " 50pf+25pf " 1.10 1.65

The surtax was for independent welfare organizations.

Animal Type of 1966

Designs: 10pf+5pf, Rabbit. 20pf+10pf, Ermine. 30pf+15pf, Hamster. 50pf+25pf, Red fox.

1967, Apr. 4 **Litho.** ***Perf. 14***

B422 SP291 10pf+5pf multi. 30 35
B423 " 20pf+10pf " 35 35
B424 " 30pf+15pf " 60 50
B425 " 50pf+25pf " 1.55 2.00

Issued for the benefit of young people.

Fairy Tale Type of 1965

Various Scenes from Frau Holle.

1967, Oct. 3 **Litho.** ***Perf. 14***

B426 SP290 10pf+5pf multi. 20 30
B427 " 20pf+10pf " 25 25
B428 " 30pf+15pf " 45 25
B429 " 50pf+25pf " 1.25 1.75

The surtax was for independent welfare organizations.

Wildcat
SP293

Animals: 20pf+10pf, Otter. 30pf+15pf, Badger. 50pf+25pf, Beaver.

1968, Feb. 2 **Photo.** **Unwmkd.**

B430 SP293 10pf+5pf multi. 35 40
B431 " 20pf+10pf " 55 55
B432 " 30pf+15pf " 85 85
B433 " 50pf+25pf " 2.75 3.25

The surtax was for the benefit of young people.

Olympic Games Issue, 1968

Type of Regular Issue

Designs (Olympic Rings and): 10pf+5pf, Karl-Friedrich Freiherr von Langen, equestrian. 20pf+10pf, Rudolf Harbig, runner. 30pf+15pf, Helene Mayer, fencer. 50pf+25pf, Carl Diem, sports organizer.

Lithographed and Engraved

1968, June 6 ***Perf. 14*** **Unwmkd.**

B434 A285 10pf+5pf olive & dark brown 25 25
B435 " 20pf+10pf deep emerald & dark green 50 50
B436 " 30pf+15pf deep rose & dk. red 55 55
B437 " 50pf+25pf brt. bl. & dark blue 1.25 1.25

The surtax was for the Foundation for the Promotion of the 1972 Olympic Games in Munich.

Doll, c. 1878
SP294

Pony
SP295

Designs: Various 19th Century Dolls. Nos. B438–B440 are from Germanic National Museum, Nuremberg; No. B441 is from Altona Museum, Hamburg.

1968, Oct. 3 **Lithographed** ***Perf. 14***

B438 SP294 10pf+5pf multi. 25 30
B439 " 20pf+10pf " 27 25
B440 " 30pf+15pf " 40 38
B441 " 50pf+25pf " 1.20 1.65

The surtax was for independent welfare organizations.

1969, Feb. 6 **Litho.** ***Perf. 14***

Horses: 20pf+10pf, Work horse. 30pf+15pf, Hotblood. 50pf+25pf, Thoroughbred.

B442 SP295 10pf+5pf multi. 45 45
B443 " 20pf+10pf " 50 50
B444 " 30pf+15pf " 1.20 1.20
B445 " 50pf+25pf " 2.75 2.75

The surtax was for the benefit of young people.

Track and Olympic Rings
SP296

Toy Locomotive of Tin
SP297

Designs (Olympic Rings and): 20pf+10pf, Hockey. 30pf+15pf, Archery. 50pf+25pf, Sailing.

1969, June 4 **Photo.** ***Perf. 14***

B446 SP296 10pf+5pf dk. brn. & lemon 25 20
B447 " 20pf+10pf bl. grn. & emerald 50 50
B448 " 30pf+15pf magenta & dp. lilac rose 75 75
B449 " 50pf+25pf dp. bl. & brt. blue 1.75 1.75

Issued to publicize the 1972 Olympic Games in Munich. The surtax was for the German Olympic Committee.

1969, Oct. 2 **Litho.** ***Perf. 13½x14***

Tin Toys: 20pf+10pf, Gardener. 30pf+15pf, Bird seller. 50pf+25pf, Knight on horseback.

B450 SP297 10pf+5pf multi. 15 15
B451 " 20pf+10pf " 30 30
B452 " 30pf+15pf " 50 50
B453 " 50pf+25pf " 1.25 1.25

The surtax was for independent welfare organizations.

Tin Toy Type of 1969 Inscribed: "Weihnachtsmarke 1969"

Design: 10pf+5pf, Jesus in Manger.

1969, Nov. 13 ***Perf. 13½x14***

B454 SP297 10pf+5pf multi. 25 25

Christmas 1969.

Heinrich von Rugge
SP298

Minnesingers: 20pf+10pf, Wolfram von Eschenbach. 30pf+15pf, Walther von Metz. 50pf+25pf, Walther von der Vogelweide.

1970, Feb. 5 **Photo.** ***Perf. 13½x14***

B455 SP298 10pf+5pf multi. 35 35
B456 " 20pf+10pf " 60 60
B457 " 30pf+15pf " 75 75
B458 " 50pf+25pf " 1.75 1.75

Surtax was for benefit of young people.

Residenz (Palace), Munich
SP299

Munich Buildings: 20pf+10pf, Propylaea. 30pf+15pf, Glyptothek. 50pf+25pf, Bavaria Statue and Colonnade.

1970, June 5 Engraved *Perf. 14*

B459	SP299	10pf+5pf olive bister	25	25
B460	"	20pf+10pf dark blue green	55	55
B461	"	30pf+15pf car.	80	80
B462	"	50pf+25pf dk. bl.	1.65	1.65

The surtax was for the Foundation for the Promotion of the 1972 Olympic Games in Munich.

Jester
SP300

King Caspar
SP301

Puppets: 20pf+10pf, "Hanswurst." 30pf+15pf, Clown. 50pf+25pf, Harlequin.

1970, Oct. 6 Litho. *Perf. 13½x14*

B463	SP300	10pf+5pf multi.	17	17
B464	"	20pf+10pf "	30	30
B465	"	30pf+15pf "	50	50
B466	"	50pf+25pf "	1.20	1.20

The surtax was for independent welfare organizations.

1970, Nov. 12

Design: 10pf+5pf, Rococo Angel, from Ursuline Sisters' Convent, Innsbruck.

B467	SP300	10pf+5pf multi.	25	25

Christmas 1970.

1971, Feb. 5 Lithographed *Perf. 14*

Children's Drawings: 20pf+10pf, Flea. 30pf+15pf, Puss-in-Boots. 50pf+25pf, Snake.

B468	SP301	10pf+5pf multi.	22	22
B469	"	20pf+10pf "	45	45
B470	"	30pf+15pf "	65	65
B471	"	50pf+25pf "	1.65	1.65

Surtax for the benefit of young people.

Ski Jump
SP302

Women Churning Butter
SP303

Designs: 20pf+10pf, Figure skating. 30pf+15pf, Downhill skiing. 50pf+25pf, Ice hockey.

"1971" at Lower Right

1971, June 4 Litho. *Perf. 14*

B472	SP302	10pf+5pf brown org. & black	35	35
B473	"	20pf+10pf green & black	75	75
B474	"	30pf+15pf rose red & blk.	1.00	1.00
B475	SP302	50pf+25pf blue & black	2.25	2.25
		a. Souvenir sheet of 4	4.75	4.75
		b. 10pf+5pf brown orange & black	35	35
		c. 20pf+10pf green & black	75	75
		d. 30pf+15pf rose red & black	1.00	1.00
		e. 50pf+25pf blue & black	2.25	2.25

Olympic Games 1972.

No. B475a contains Nos. B475b–B475e which lack the minute date ("1971") at lower right. Gray marginal inscription commemorates the 20th Olympic Games in Munich. Size: 110x66mm.

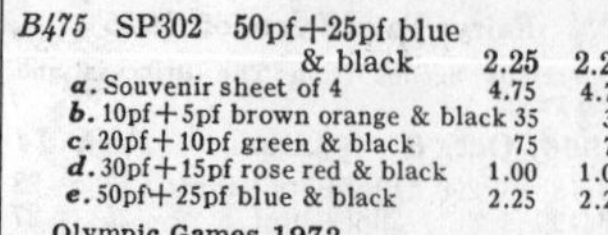

1971, Oct. 5 Lithographed *Perf. 14*

Wooden Toys: 25pf+10pf, Horseback rider. 30pf+15pf, Nutcracker. 60pf+30pf, Dovecot.

B476	SP303	20pf+10pf multi.	28	28
B477	"	25pf+10pf "	30	30
B478	"	30pf+15pf "	40	40
B479	"	60pf+30pf "	1.10	1.10

The surtax was for independent welfare organizations.

1971, Nov. 11

Design: 20pf+10pf, Christmas angel with lights.

B480	SP303	20pf+10pf multi.	35	35

Christmas 1971.

Ducks Crossing Road
SP304

Designs: 25pf+10pf, Hunter chasing deer and rabbits. 30pf+15pf, Girl protecting birds from cat. 60pf+30pf, Boy annoying swans.

1972, Feb. 4 Litho. *Perf. 14*

B481	SP304	20pf+10pf multi.	60	60
B482	"	25pf+10pf "	75	75
B483	"	30pf+15pf "	1.20	1.20
B484	"	60pf+30pf "	2.75	2.75

Animal protection. Surtax for the benefit of young people.

Olympic Rings and Wrestling
SP305

Designs (Olympic Rings and): 25pf+10pf, Sailing. 30pf+15pf, Gymnastics. 60pf+30pf, Swimming.

1972, June 5 Photo. *Perf. 14*

B485	SP305	20pf+10pf multi.	55	55
B486	"	25pf+10pf "	65	65
B487	"	30pf+15pf "	70	70
B488	"	60pf+30pf "	2.50	2.50

20th Olympic Games, Munich, Aug. 26–Sept. 10.

Souvenir Sheet

Olympic Games Site, Munich
SP306

1972, July 5 Litho. *Perf. 14*

Tan, Green, Black and Blue

B489	SP306	Sheet of 4	11.00	11.00
		a. 25pf+10pf *Gymnastics stadium*	2.25	2.25
		b. 30pf+15pf *Soccer stadium*	2.25	2.25
		c. 40pf+20pf *Tent and lake*	2.25	2.25
		d. 70pf+35pf *Television tower* (vert.)	2.25	2.25

20th Olympic Games, Munich, Aug. 26–Sept. 10. Size of No. B489: 147½x105 mm. Surcharge was for the Foundation for the Promotion of the Munich Olympic Games.

Souvenir Sheet

Olympic Games Type of 1972

1972, Aug. 18 Litho. *Perf. 14*

Multicolored

B490	SP305	Sheet of 4	12.00	12.00
		a. 25pf+5pf *Long jump, women's*	2.25	2.25
		b. 30pf+10pf *Basketball*	2.25	2.25
		c. 40pf+10pf *Discus, women's*	2.25	2.25
		d. 70pf+10pf *Canoeing*	2.25	2.25
		e. Booklet pane of 4	25.00	

20th Olympic Games, Munich, Aug. 26–Sept. 11. No. B490 has black marginal inscription. Size: 110x65mm. No. B490e contains one each of Nos. B490a–B490d.

Knight
SP307

Adoration of the Kings
SP308

1972, Oct. 5 Multicolored

B491	SP307	25pf+10pf *shown*	38	38
B492	"	30pf+15pf *Rook*	45	45
B493	"	40pf+20pf *Queen*	60	60
B494	"	70pf+35pf *King*	1.20	1.20

19th century chess pieces made by Faience Works, Gien, France; now in Hamburg Museum. The surtax was for independent welfare organizations.

1972, Nov. 10 Lithographed

B495	SP308	30pf+15pf multi.	55	55

Christmas 1972.

Osprey
SP309

Hesse-Kassel
SP310

Birds of Prey: 30pf+15pf, Buzzard. 40pf+20pf, Red kite. 70pf+35pf, Montagu's harrier.

1973, Feb. 6 Photogravure *Perf. 14*

B496	SP309	25pf+10pf multi.	80	80
B497	"	30pf+15pf "	95	95
B498	"	40pf+20pf "	1.50	1.50
B499	"	70pf+35pf "	2.75	2.75

Surtax was for benefit of young people.

1973, Apr. 5 Litho. *Perf. 14*

Posthouse Signs: No. B501, Prussia. No. B502a, Württemberg. No. B502b, Bavaria.

B500	SP310	40pf+20pf multi.	1.50	1.50
B501	"	70pf+35pf "	1.90	1.90

Souvenir Sheet

B502	SP310	Sheet of 2	5.25	5.25
		a. 40pf+20pf multi.	1.90	1.90
		b. 70pf+35pf "	2.75	2.75

IBRA München 1973 International Philatelic Exhibition, Munich, May 11–20. No. B502 has black inscription. Size: 74x105mm. Sold for 2.20 mark.

French Horn, 19th Century
SP311

Christmas Star
SP312

Musical Instruments: 30pf+15pf, Pedal piano, 18th century. 40pf+20pf, Violin, 18th century. 70pf+35pf, Pedal harp, 18th century.

1973, Oct. 5 Lithographed *Perf. 14*

B503	SP311	25pf+10pf multi.	35	35
B504	"	30pf+15pf "	45	45
B505	"	40pf+20pf "	60	60
B506	"	70pf+35pf "	1.20	1.20

Surtax was for independent welfare organizations.

1973, Nov. 9 Litho. & Engr.

B507	SP312	30pf+15pf multi.	55	50

Christmas 1973.

Young Builder
SP313

Campion
SP314

Designs: 30pf+15pf, Girl in national costume. 40pf+20pf, Boy studying. 70pf+35pf, Girl with microscope.

1974, Apr. 17 Photogravure *Perf. 14*

B508	SP313	25pf+10pf multi.	75	75
B509	"	30pf+15pf "	95	95
B510	"	40pf+20pf "	1.25	1.25
B511	"	70pf+35pf "	2.25	2.25

Surtax was for benefit of young people.

1974, Oct. 15 Lithographed *Perf. 14*

Flowers: 40pf+20pf, Foxglove. 50pf+25pf, Mallow. 70pf+35pf, Bellflower.

B512	SP314	30pf+15pf multi.	45	45
B513	"	40pf+20pf "	60	60
B514	"	50pf+25pf "	75	75
B515	"	70pf+35pf "	1.05	1.05

Surtax was for independent welfare organizations.

1974, Oct. 29

Design: 40pf+20pf, Advent decoration.

B516	SP314	40pf+20pf multi.	65	65

Christmas 1974.

Diesel Locomotive Class 218
SP315

Locomotives: 40pf+20pf, Electric engine Class 103. 50pf+25pf, Electric rail motor train Class 403. 70pf+35pf, Magnetic suspension train "Transrapid" (model).

1975, Apr. 15 Litho. *Perf. 14*

B517	SP315	30pf+15pf multi.	65	65
B518	"	40pf+20pf "	80	80
B519	"	50pf+25pf "	1.10	1.10
B520	"	70pf+35pf "	1.35	1.35

Surtax was for benefit of young people.

Edelweiss
SP316

Alpine Flowers: 40pf+20pf, Trollflower. 50pf+25pf, Alpine rose. 70pf+35pf, Pasqueflower.

1975, Oct. 15 **Litho.** ***Perf. 14***

B521	SP316	30pf+15pf multi.	45	45
B522	"	40pf+20pf "	60	60
B523	"	50pf+25pf "	75	75
B524	"	70pf+35pf "	1.05	1.05

Surtax was for independent welfare organizations.

1975, Nov. 14

Design: 40pf+20pf, Snow rose.

B525	SP316	40pf+20pf multi.	65	65

Christmas 1975.

Basketball
SP317

Designs: 40pf+20pf, Rowing. 50pf+25pf, Gymnastics, women's. 70pf+35pf, Volleyball.

1976, Apr. 6 **Litho.** ***Perf. 14***

B526	SP317	30pf+15pf multi.	55	55
B527	"	40pf+20pf "	75	75
B528	"	50pf+25pf "	95	95
B529	"	70pf+35pf "	1.50	1.50

Youth training for Olympic Games. Surtax was for benefit of young people.

Swimmer and Olympic Rings
SP318

Designs (Olympic Rings and): 30pf+15pf, Hockey. 50pf+25pf, High jump. 70pf+35pf, Rowing, coxed four.

1976, Apr. 6

B530	SP318	40pf+20pf multi.	75	75
B531	"	50pf+25pf "	1.00	1.00

Souvenir Sheet

B532	SP318	Sheet of 2	1.90	1.90
	a.	30pf+15pf multicolored	45	45
	b.	70pf+35pf "	1.30	1.30

21st Olympic Games, Montreal, Canada, July 17–Aug. 1. The surtax was for the German Sports Aid Foundation. No. B532 has black marginal inscription. Size: 110x70mm.

Attractive slip cases are available for most Scott Albums.

The lack of a price for a listed item does not necessarily indicate rarity.

Phlox
SP319

Flowers: 40pf+20pf, Marigolds. 50pf+25pf, Dahlias. 70pf+35pf, Pansies.

1976, Oct. 14 **Litho.** ***Perf. 14***

B533	SP319	30pf+15pf multi.	45	45
B534	"	40pf+20pf "	60	60
B535	"	50pf+25pf "	75	75
B536	"	70pf+35pf "	1.20	1.20

Surtax was for independent welfare organizations.

Souvenir Sheet

Nativity, Window, Frauenkirche, Esslingen—SP320

1976, Nov. 16 **Litho. & Engr.**

B537	SP320	50pf+25pf multi.	75	75

Christmas 1976. No. B537 has multicolored margin and inscription. Size: 70x100mm.

Wapen von Hamburg, c. 1730
SP321

Historic Ships: 40pf+20pf, Preussen, 5-master, 1902. 50pf+25pf, Bremen, 1929. 70pf+35pf, Freighter Sturmfels, 1972.

1977, Apr. 14 **Litho.** ***Perf. 14***

B538	SP321	30pf+15pf multi.	45	45
B539	"	40pf+20pf "	60	60
B540	"	50pf+25pf "	80	80
B541	"	70pf+35pf "	1.20	1.20

Surtax was for benefit of young people.

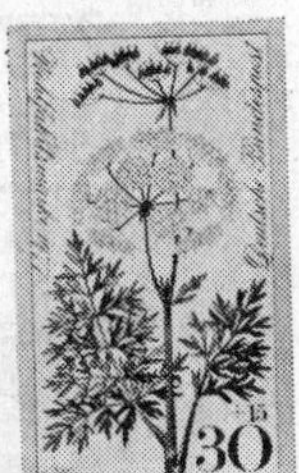

Caraway
SP322

Meadow Flowers: 40pf+20pf, Dandelion. 50pf+25pf, Red clover. 70pf+35pf, Meadow sage.

1977, Oct. 13 **Litho.** ***Perf. 14***

B542	SP322	30pf+15pf multi.	45	45
B543	"	40pf+20pf "	60	60
B544	"	50pf+25pf "	75	75
B545	"	70pf+35pf "	1.05	1.05

Surtax was for independent welfare organizations.
See Nos. B553–B556.

Souvenir Sheet

King Caspar Offering Gold, Window, St. Gereon's, Cologne—SP323

1977, Nov. 10

B546	SP323	50pf+25pf multi.	75	75

Christmas 1977. No. B546 has gray margin and inscription. Size: 70x104mm.

Giant Slalom
SP324

Design: No. B548, Steeplechase.

1978 **Litho.** ***Perf. 14***

B547	SP324	50pf+25pf multi.	75	75
B548	"	70pf+35pf "	1.05	1.05

Issue dates: No. B547, Jan. 12, No. B548, Apr. 13.

Surtax was for the German Sports Foundation.

Balloon Ascent, Oktoberfest, Munich, 1820—SP325

Designs: 40pf+20pf, Airship LZ 1, 1900. 50pf+25pf, Bleriot monoplane, 1909. 70pf+35pf, Grade monoplane, 1909.

1978, Apr. 13 **Litho.** ***Perf. 14***

B549	SP325	30pf+15pf multi.	45	45
B550	"	40pf+20pf "	60	60
B551	"	50pf+25pf "	75	75
B552	"	70pf+35pf "	1.05	1.05

Surtax was for benefit of young people.

Flower Type of 1977

Woodland Flowers: 30pf+15pf, Arum. 40pf+20pf, Weaselsnout. 50pf+25pf, Turk's-cap lily. 70pf+35pf, Liverwort.

1978, Oct. 12 Lithographed ***Perf. 14***

B553	SP322	30pf+15pf multi.	45	45
B554	"	40pf+20pf "	60	60
B555	"	50pf+25pf "	75	75
B556	"	70pf+35pf "	1.05	1.05

Surtax was for independent welfare organizations.

Demand as well as supply determine a stamp's market value. The first is as important as the other.

Souvenir Sheet

Christ Child, Window, Frauenkirche, Munich—SP326

1978, Nov. 16 **Litho.** ***Perf. 14***

B557	SP326	50pf+25pf multi.	75	75

Christmas 1978. No. B557 has multicolored margin and inscription. Size: 65x93mm.

Dornier Wal, 1922
SP327

Airplanes: 50+25pf, Heinkel HE70, 1932. 60+30pf, Junkers W33 Bremen, 1928. 90+45pf, Focke-Wulf FW61, 1936.

1979, Apr. 5 **Litho.** ***Perf. 14***

B558	SP327	40pf+20pf multi.	60	60
B559	"	50pf+25pf "	75	75
B560	"	60pf+30pf "	90	90
B561	"	90pf+45pf "	1.35	1.35

Surtax was for benefit of young people.

Handball
SP328

Design: 90+45pf, Canoeing.

1979, Apr. 5

B562	SP328	60pf+30pf multi.	90	90
B563	"	90pf+45pf "	1.35	1.35

Surtax was for German Sports Foundation.

Questions?
Comment?
Corrections?
Help us serve you better. Let us know what you think by filling out our questionnaire at the front of this book.

AIR POST STAMPS

Issues of the Republic.

Post Horn with Wings
AP1

Biplane—AP2

Perf. 15x14½

1919, Nov. 10 Typo. Unwmkd.

C1 AP1 10pf orange 15 30
C2 AP2 40pf dark green 15 30
a. Imperf. 425.00

No. C2a is ungummed.

Carrier Pigeon AP3 — German Eagle AP4

Wmkd. Network. (126)

1922-23 *Perf. 14, 14½.*

Size: 19x23 mm.

C3 AP3 25(pf) chocolate 55 *10.00*
C4 " 40(pf) orange 55 *17.50*
C5 " 50(pf) violet 27 *3.00*
C6 " 60(pf) carmine 70 *10.00*
C7 " 80(pf) blue green 70 *7.50*

Perf. 13x13½.

Size: 22x28mm.

C8 AP3 1m dark green & pale green 22 *1.50*
C9 " 2m lake & gray 22 *1.50*
C10 " 3m dark blue & gray 22 *1.50*
C11 " 5m red orange & yellow 22 *1.50*
C12 " 10m violet & rose ('23) 22 *4.50*
C13 " 25m brn. & yel. ('23) 22 *3.00*
C14 " 100m olive green & rose ('23) 22 *5.00*
Nos. C3-C14 (12) 4.31

1923

C15 AP3 5m vermilion 15 *22.50*
C16 " 10m violet 15 *5.00*
C17 " 25m dark brown 12 *4.50*
C18 " 100m olive green 12 *3.00*
C19 " 200m deep blue 15 *27.50*
a. Imperf. 85.00
Nos. C15-C19 (5) 69

Issue dates: Nos. C15-C18, June 1. No. C19, July 25.

Note following No. 160 applies to Nos. C1-C19.

1924, Jan. 11 *Perf. 14*

Size: 19x23 mm.

C20 AP3 5(pf) yellow green 1.90 1.65
C21 " 10(pf) carmine 1.90 2.75
C22 " 20(pf) violet blue 4.75 6.00
C23 " 50(pf) orange 13.50 16.50
C24 " 100(pf) dull violet 27.50 35.00
C25 " 200(pf) greenish blue 80.00 80.00
C26 " 300(pf) gray 85.00 110.00
a. Imperf.
Nos. C20-C26 (7) 214.55 251.90

1926-27

C27 AP4 5pf green 70 90
C28 " 10pf rose red 70 90
b. Tête bêche pair 72.50 100.00
c. Bklt. pane of 10 50.00
d. Bklt. pane 10 (6 No. C28 + 4 No. C29) 57.50
C29 AP4 15pf lilac rose ('27) 2.10 1.75
a. Double impression *650.00*
C30 " 20pf dull blue 2.10 1.75
a. Tête bêche pair 72.50 100.00
b. Bklt. pane 4 (4 No. C30 + 6 Labels) 57.50
c. Bklt. pane 5 (5 No. C30 + 5 Labels) 225.00
C31 " 50pf brown orange 22.50 6.00
C32 " 1m blk. & salmon 19.00 6.25
C33 " 2m black & blue 19.00 22.50
C34 " 3m black & olive green 50.00 75.00
Nos. C27-C34 (8) 116.10 115.05

"Graf Zeppelin" Crossing Ocean
AP5

1928-31 Photogravure.

C35 AP5 1m carmine ('31) 32.50 42.50
C36 " 2m ultramarine 60.00 60.00
C37 " 4m black brown 27.50 42.50

Issue dates: 2m, 4m, Oct. 7, 1928. 1m, May 8, 1931.

AP6

1930, Apr. 19 Wmk. 126

C38 AP6 2m ultramarine 225.00 285.00
C39 " 4m black brown 275.00 325.00

First flight of Graf Zeppelin to South America. Nos. C38-C39 exist with watermark vertical or horizontal.

Counterfeits exist of Nos. C38-C45.

Nos. C35-C37 Overprinted in Brown — **POLAR-FAHRT 1931**

1931, July 15

C40 AP5 1m carmine 150.00 100.00
C41 " 2m ultramarine 180.00 260.00
C42 " 4m black brn. 385.00 650.00

Polar flight of Graf Zeppelin.

Nos. C35-C37 Overprinted — Chicagofahrt Weltausstellung 1933

1933, Sept. 25

C43 AP5 1m carmine 450.00 275.00
C44 " 2m ultramarine 62.50 120.00
C45 " 4m black brown 50.00 110.00

Graf Zeppelin flight to Century of Progress International Exhibition, Chicago.

Swastika Sun, Globe and Eagle AP7 — Otto Lilienthal AP8

Design: 3m, Count Ferdinand von Zeppelin.

Typographed
Wmkd. Swastikas. (237)

1934, Jan. 21 *Perf. 14, 13½x13.*

C46 AP7 5(pf) bright green 1.10 38
C47 " 10(pf) brt. carmine 1.10 60
C48 " 15(pf) ultramarine 1.10 60
C49 " 20(pf) dull blue 1.65 1.00
C50 " 25(pf) brown 1.65 75
C51 " 40(pf) red violet 1.65 60
C52 " 50(pf) dark green 4.25 60
C53 " 80(pf) orange yel. 3.25 2.50
C54 " 100(pf) black 3.75 2.25
C55 AP8 2m grn. & blk. 16.50 12.50
C56 " 3m blue & blk. 42.50 30.00
Nos. C46-C56 (11) 78.50 51.78

"Hindenburg"
AP10
Engraved.

1936, Mar. 16 *Perf. 14, 14½x14*

C57 AP10 50pf dark blue 6.50 45
C58 " 75pf dark green 8.00 55

Count Zeppelin AP11 — Airship Gondola AP12

1938, July 5 *Perf. 13½.* Unwmkd.

C59 AP11 25(pf) dull blue 3.50 80
C60 AP12 50(pf) green 5.50 55

Count Ferdinand von Zeppelin (1838-1917), airship inventor and builder.

Federal Republic

Lufthansa Emblem
AP13

Perf. 13½x13

1955, Mar. 31 Litho. Wmk. 295

C61 AP13 5(pf) lilac rose & black 90 1.00
C62 " 10(pf) grn. & black 1.20 1.50
C63 " 15(pf) blue & black 7.00 10.00
C64 " 20(pf) red & black 17.50 12.50

Issued to commemorate the re-opening of the German air service, April 1, 1955.

MILITARY AIR POST STAMPS.

Junkers 52 Transport
MAP1
Typographed.

1942 *Perf. 13½* Unwmkd.

MC1 MAP1 ultramarine 12 12
a. Rouletted 12 40

MILITARY PARCEL POST STAMPS.

Nazi Emblem
MPP1
Typographed

1942 *Perf. 13½.* Unwmkd.

Size: 28x23mm.

MQ1 MPP1 red brown 12 22
a. Rouletted 12 27

Type of 1942.

1944 Size: 22½x18mm. ***Perf. 14.***

MQ2 MPP1 bright green 20 *27.50*

See note "Postally Used vs. CTO" after No. O13.

FELDPOST

No. 520 Overprinted in Black — **2kg**

1944 Engraved

MQ3 A115 On 40(pf) bright red violet 20 *40.00*

See note after No. O13.

OFFICIAL STAMPS.

Issues of the Republic.

In 1920 the Official Stamps of Bavaria and Wurttemberg then current were overprinted "Deutsches Reich" and made available for official use in all parts of Germany. They were, however, used almost exclusively in the two states where they originated and we have listed them among the issues of those states.

O1

O2

O3

O4

O5

O6

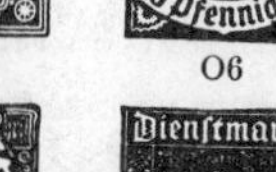

O7

O8

O9

O10

O11

O12

Wmkd. Lozenges. (125)

1920-21 Typographed *Perf. 14*

O1 O1 5pf deep green 80 *2.50*
O2 O2 10pf carmine rose 8 20
O3 " 10pf orange ('21) 55 *150.00*
O4 O3 15pf violet brown 8 20
a. Imperf. ('21) 90.00

O5 O4 20pf dp. ultramarine 8 20
O6 O5 30pf orange, *buff* 8 20
O7 O6 40pf carmine 12 20
O8 O7 50pf violet, *buff* 6 20
O9 O8 60pf red brown ('21) 8 30
O10 O9 1m red, *buff* 6 20
O11 O10 1.25m dark blue, *yellow* 8 30
O12 O11 2m dark blue 5.00 1.00
O13 O12 5m brown, *yellow* 8 20
Nos. O1-O13 (13) 7.15

The price of No. O4a is for a copy postmarked at Bautzen.

Postally Used vs. CTO

Prices quoted for canceled copies of the 1921-23 issues (Nos. O1-O46) are for postally used stamps. These bring higher prices than the plentiful canceled-to-order specimens made by applying genuine handstamps to remainders. C.T.O. examples sell for about the same price as unused stamps. Certification of postal usage by competent authorities is necessary.

O13

O14

O15

1922 **Wmk. 126.**
O14 O13 75pf dark blue 17 *2.50*
O15 O11 2m dark blue 8 20
a. Imperf. 200.00

Wmk. 125
O16 O14 3m brown, *rose* 8 25
O17 O15 10m dark green, *rose* 8 20

1923 **Wmk. 126.**
O18 O15 10m dark green, *rose* 12 *9.00*
O19 " 20m dark blue, *rose* 8 20
O20 " 50m violet, *rose* 8 20
O21 " 100m rose red, *rose* 8 20
Nos. O20-O21 exist imperf.

Regular Issue of 1923 Overprinted

a

1923
O22 A34 20m red lilac 6 *2.50*
O23 " 30m olive green 6 *15.00*
O24 A29 40m green 6 *2.00*
O25 A35 200m carmine rose 6 *25*
O26 " 300m green 6 *30*
O27 " 400m dark brown 6 *30*
O28 " 500m red orange 12 *25*
Nos. O22-O28 (7) 48

Official Stamps of 1920-23 Surcharged with New Values.

Abbreviations:
Th=(Tausend) Thousand
Mil=(Million) Million
Mlrd=(Milliarde) Billion

1923 **Wmk. 125.**
O29 O12 5th m on 5m brown, *yellow* 8 *1.50*
a. Inverted surcharge 140.00
O30 O5 20th m on 30pf orange, *buff* 8 *1.00*
a. Inverted surcharge 140.00
b. Imperf. 140.00
O31 O3 100th m on 15pf violet brown 8 *1.50*
a. Imperf. 140.00
b. Inverted surcharge 140.00
O32 O2 250th m on 10pf carmine rose 15 *1.00*
a. Dbl. surch. 75.00
O33 O5 800th m on 30pf orange, *buff* 70 *250.00*

Official Stamps and Types of 1920-23 Surcharged with New Values.

Wmk. 126
O34 O15 75th m on 50m violet, *rose* 8 *1.00*
a. Invtd.surch. 140.00
O35 O3 400th m on 15pf brown 15 *20.00*
O36 O5 800th m on 30pf orange, *buff* 17 *2.00*
O37 O13 1 mil m on 75pf dark blue 17 *20.00*
O38 O2 2 mil m on 10pf carmine rose 17 *1.50*
a. Imperf. 140.00
O39 O15 5 mil m on 100m rose red, *rose* 17 *4.00*
Nos. O29-O39 (11) 2.00

The 10, 15 and 30 pfennig are not known with this watermark and without surcharge.

Regular Issue of 1923 Overprinted Type "a."

1923
O40 A39 100 mil m gray 22 *110.00*
O41 " 200 mil m bis. brown 22 *100.00*
O42 A39a 2 mlrd m pale brown & green 22 *90.00*
O43 " 5 mlrd m yel. & brn. 22 *30.00*
O44 " 10 mlrd m apple green & green 4.50 *90.00*
O45 " 20 mlrd m bluish green & brown 3.25 *110.00*
O46 " 50 mlrd m blue & deep blue 3.25 *150.00*
Nos. O40-O46 (7) 11.88

Same Overprint on Stamps With Values in Rentenpfennig.

1923
O47 A40 3(pf) brown 27 20
O48 " 5(pf) dark green 27 20
a. Invtd. ovpt. 175.00 150.00
O49 " 10(pf) carmine 40 9
a. Invtd. ovpt. 135.00 150.00
b. Imperf. 75.00
O50 " 20(pf) deep ultra. 90 15
O51 " 50(pf) orange 90 50
O52 " 100(pf) brown violet 3.25 4.50
Nos. O47-O52 (6) 5.99 5.64

Same Overprint On Issues of 1924.

1924
O53 A41 3(pf) light brown 40 25
a. Inverted ovpt. 140.00 225.00
O54 " 5(pf) light green 40 10
a. Imperf. 150.00
b. Inverted ovpt. 225.00
O55 " 10(pf) vermilion 40 10
O56 " 20(pf) blue 40 10
O57 " 30(pf) rose lilac 80 25
O58 " 40(pf) olive green 80 25
O59 " 50pf orange 1.65 1.25
O60 A47 60(pf) red brown 1.50 1.25
O61 " 80(pf) slate 7.50 *20.00*
Nos. O53-O61 (9) 13.85 *23.55*

O16

Swastika
O17

1927-33 ***Perf. 14***
O62 O16 3(pf) bistre 55 15
O63 " 4(pf) light blue ('31) 27 15
O64 " 4(pf) blue ('33) 2.25 2.50
O65 " 5(pf) green 22 10
O66 O16 6(pf) pale olive green ('32) 27 12
O67 " 8(pf) dark green 27 10
O68 " 10(pf) carmine 8.00 5.00
O69 " 10(pf) verm. ('29) 15.00 15.00
O70 " 10(pf) red violet ('30) 45 15
a. Imperf. 150.00
O71 " 10(pf) chocolate ('33) 2.25 2.50
O72 " 12(pf) orange ('32) 33 12
O73 " 15(pf) vermilion 1.65 30
O74 " 15(pf) carmine ('29) 55 15
O75 " 20(pf) Prussian grn. 3.25 1.10
O76 " 20(pf) gray ('30) 80 50
O77 " 30(pf) olive green 1.10 15
O78 " 40(pf) violet 1.10 25
O79 " 60(pf) red brn. ('28) 1.65 50
Nos. O62-O79 (18) 39.96 28.84

1934, Jan. 18 **Wmk. 237**
O80 O17 3(pf) bistre 5 12
O81 " 4(pf) dull blue 5 12
O82 " 5(pf) bright green 5 12
O83 " 6(pf) dark green 7 15
a. Imperf. 110.00
O84 " 8(pf) vermilion 33 15
O85 " 10(pf) chocolate 27 15
O86 " 12(pf) bright carmine 27 12
a. Without wmk. 55 1.00
O87 " 15(pf) claret 80 1.20
O88 " 20(pf) light blue 17 25
O89 " 30(pf) olive green 27 25
O90 " 40(pf) red violet 27 25
O91 " 50(pf) orange yellow 38 30
Nos. O80-O91 (12) 2.98 3.18
O83 exists imperf.

1942 ***Perf. 14*** **Unwmkd.**
O92 O17 3(pf) bistre brown 15 22
O93 " 4(pf) dull blue 15 22
O94 " 5(pf) deep olive 15 22
O95 " 6(pf) deep violet 15 22
O96 " 8(pf) vermilion 30 38
O97 " 10(pf) chocolate 22 30
O98 " 12(pf) rose carmine 35 55
a. Wmk. 237 1.75 3.00
O99 " 15(pf) brown carmine 80 75
O100 " 20(pf) light blue 45 75
O101 " 30(pf) olive green 45 75
O102 " 40(pf) red violet 45 90
O103 " 50(pf) dark green 70 1.10
Nos. O92-O103 (12) 4.32 6.36

LOCAL OFFICIAL STAMPS.

For Use in Prussia.

("Nr. 21" refers to the district of Prussia)
LO1

Typographed.

1903 ***Perf. 14, 14½*** **Unwmkd.**
OL1 LO1 2pf slate 1.35 1.75
OL2 " 3pf bistre brown 1.35 1.75
OL3 " 5pf green 27 12
OL4 " 10pf carmine 27 12
OL5 " 20pf ultramarine 27 12
OL6 " 25pf orange & black, *yellow* 27 12
OL7 " 40pf lake & black 27 1.00
OL8 " 50pf purple & black, *salmon* 55 1.00
Nos. OL1-OL8 (8) 4.60 5.98

LO2 LO3

LO4

LO5

LO6

LO7

LO8

Wmkd. Lozenges. (125)

1920 **Typographed.** ***Perf. 14.***
OL9 LO2 5pf green 25 50
OL10 LO3 10pf carmine 80 70
OL11 LO4 15pf violet brown 20 25
OL12 LO5 20pf deep ultra. 25 30
OL13 LO6 30pf orange, *buff* 15 30
OL14 LO7 50pf brown lilac, *buff* 40 30
OL15 LO8 1m red, *buff* 6.00 2.00
Nos. OL9-OL15 (7) 8.05 4.35

For Use in Baden.

LO9

Typographed.

1905 ***Perf. 14, 14½*** **Unwmkd.**
OL16 LO9 2pf gray blue 57.50 57.50
OL17 " 3pf brown 7.00 7.00
OL18 " 5pf green 3.75 4.25
OL19 " 10pf rose 1.10 1.10
OL20 " 20pf blue 1.90 1.90
OL21 " 25pf orange & blk., *yellow* 35.00 35.00
Nos. OL16-OL21 (6) 106.25 106.75

NEWSPAPER STAMPS.

Newsboy and Globe
N1

Wmkd. Swastikas. (237)

1939, Nov. 1 **Photo.** ***Perf. 14***
P1 N1 5(pf) green 35 65
P2 " 10(pf) red brown 35 65

FRANCHISE STAMPS.

For use by the National Socialist German Workers' Party

Party Emblem
F1

Wmkd. Swastikas. (237)

1938 **Typographed.** ***Perf. 14.***
S1 F1 1(pf) black 28 40
S2 " 3(pf) bistre 28 40
S3 " 4(pf) dull blue 28 40
S4 " 5(pf) bright green 28 40
S5 " 6(pf) dark green 35 55
S6 " 8(pf) vermilion 2.75 55

S7 F1 12(pf) bright carmine 75 40
S8 " 16(pf) gray 75 *3.00*
S9 " 24(pf) citron 1.00 *2.00*
S10 " 30(pf) olive green 1.00 *2.00*
S11 " 40(pf) red violet 1.60 2.50
Nos. S1–S11 (11) 9.32 *12.60*

1942 **Unwmkd.**

S12 F1 1(pf) gray black 15 12
S13 " 3(pf) bistre brown 15 22
S14 " 4(pf) dark gray blue 15 25
S15 " 5(pf) gray green 15 25
S16 " 6(pf) violet 15 25
S17 " 8(pf) deep orange 15 25
a. Imperf. 125.00
S18 " 12(pf) carmine 22 25
S19 " 16(pf) blue green 1.60 85
S20 " 24(pf) yellow brown 25 85
S21 " 30(pf) deep olive green 25 85
S22 " 40(pf) light rose violet 35 85
Nos. S12–S22 (11) 3.57 4.99

OCCUPATION STAMPS.

100 Centimes = 1 Franc
100 Pfennig = 1 Mark

Issued under Belgian Occupation.

Belgian Stamps of 1915–20 Overprinted

ALLEMAGNE

DUITSCHLAND

Perf. 11½, 14, 14½.

1919-21 **Unwmkd.**

1N1 A46 1c orange 35 55
1N2 " 2c chocolate 35 55
1N3 " 3c gray black ('21) 70 80
1N4 " 5c green 1.10 1.65
1N5 " 10c carmine 2.10 2.25
1N6 " 15c purple 1.10 1.65
1N7 " 20c red violet 1.10 1.35
1N8 " 25c blue 1.75 2.25
1N9 A54 25c deep blue ('21) 5.25 8.00

Overprinted **ALLEMAGNE DUITSCHLAND**

1N10 A47 35c brown orange & black 1.10 1.65
1N11 A48 40c green & black 2.10 3.25
1N12 A49 50c carmine rose & black 7.00 10.00
1N13 A56 65c claret & black ('21) 4.25 6.50
1N14 A50 1fr violet 25.00 32.50
1N15 A51 2fr slate 38.50 55.00
1N16 A52 5fr deep blue 9.00 16.50
1N17 A53 10fr brown 57.50 100.00
Nos. 1N1–1N17 (17) 158.25 244.45

Belgian Stamps of 1915 Surcharged

EUPEN & MALMÉDY 5 PF.
a

EUPEN & MALMÉDY 1 MK 25
b

1920 Black Surcharge.

1N18 A46(*a*) 5pf on 5c green 50 80
1N19 " (") 10pf on 10c car. 70 1.10
1N20 " (") 15pf on 15c purple 85 1.35
1N21 " (") 20pf on 20c red violet 1.10 1.65
1N22 " (") 30pf on 25c blue 1.25 1.85

Red Surcharge.

1N23 A49(*b*) 75pf on 50c car. rose & black 22.50 30.00
1N24 A50(") 1m 25(pf) on 1fr violet 25.00 32.50
Nos. 1N18–1N24 (7) 51.90 69.25

EUPEN ISSUE.

Belgian Stamps of 1915-20 Overprinted:

Eupen *a* **Eupen** *b*

1920-21 *Perf. 11½, 14, 14½.*

1N25 A46 (*a*) 1c orange 35 55
1N26 " (") 2c chocolate 35 55
1N27 " (") 3c gray blk. ('21) 60 80
1N28 " (") 5c green 70 1.10
1N29 " (") 10c carmine 90 1.35
1N30 " (") 15c purple 1.20 1.65
1N31 " (") 20c red violet 1.30 1.65
1N32 " (") 25c blue 1.60 2.25
1N33 A54 (") 25c dp. bl. ('21) 5.25 8.00
1N34 A47 (") 35c brown orange & black 1.75 2.50
1N35 A48 (") 40c grn. & black 2.10 2.75
1N36 A49 (") 50c carmine rose & black 7.00 11.00
1N37 A56 (*b*) 65c claret & black ('21) 3.50 5.50
1N38 A50 (") 1fr violet 25.00 32.50
1N39 A51 (") 2fr slate 38.50 55.00
1N40 A52 (") 5fr deep blue 11.00 16.50
1N41 A53 (") 10fr brown 57.50 95.00
Nos. 1N25–1N41 (17) 158.60 238.65

MALMEDY ISSUE.

Belgian Stamps of 1915-20 Overprinted:

Malmédy *d* **Malmédy** *e* **Malmédy** *f*

1920-21

1N42 A46 (*d*) 1c orange 35 55
1N43 " (") 2c chocolate 35 55
1N44 " (") 3c gray blk. ('21) 55 80
1N45 " (") 5c green 70 1.10
1N46 " (") 10c carmine 1.10 1.35
1N47 " (") 15c purple 1.20 1.65
1N48 " (") 20c red violet 1.30 1.85
1N49 " (") 25c blue 1.60 2.25
1N50 A54 (") 25c deep blue ('21) 5.25 8.00
1N51 A47 (*e*) 35c brown orange & black 1.75 2.50
1N52 A48 (") 40c grn. & black 2.10 2.75
1N53 A49 (") 50c carmine rose & black 7.00 11.00
1N54 A56 (*f*) 65c claret & black ('21) 3.50 5.50
1N55 A50 (") 1fr violet 25.00 32.50
1N56 A51 (") 2fr slate 38.50 55.00
1N57 A52 (") 5fr deep blue 12.50 16.50
1N58 A53 (") 10fr brown 57.50 95.00
Nos. 1N42–1N58 (17) 160.25 238.85

OCCUPATION POSTAGE DUE STAMPS.

Belgian Postage Due Stamps of 1919–20, Overprinted **Eupen**

1920 *Perf. 14½.* **Unwmkd.**

1NJ1 D3 5c green 90 1.35
1NJ2 " 10c carmine 1.40 2.25
1NJ3 " 20c gray green 2.50 3.75
1NJ4 " 30c bright blue 2.85 4.25
1NJ5 " 50c gray 14.00 18.50
Nos. 1NJ1–1NJ5 (5) 21.65 30.10

Belgian Postage Due Stamps of 1919-20, Overprinted **Malmédy**

1NJ6 D3 5c green 1.25 1.85
1NJ7 " 10c carmine 1.60 2.25
a. Invtd. ovpt. 30.00
1NJ8 " 20c gray green 10.00 15.00
1NJ9 " 30c bright blue 5.25 6.50
1NJ10 " 50c gray 6.00 10.00
Nos. 1NJ6–1NJ10 (5) 24.10 35.60

A. M. G. ISSUE.

Issued jointly by the Allied Military Government of the United States and Great Britain, for civilian use in areas under Allied occupation.

"M" in Oval
OS1

THREE TYPES:
Type I. Thick paper, white gum.
Type II. Medium paper, yellow gum.
Type III. Medium paper, white gum.

Perf. 11, 11½ and Compound.

1945-46 **Lithographed.** **Unwmkd.**

Type III, Brunswick Printing

Size: 19-19½ x 22-22½ mm.

3N1 OS1 1pf slate gray 5 10
3N2 " 3pf dull lilac 5 10
3N3 " 4pf light gray 5 10
3N4 " 5pf emerald 5 10
3N5 " 6pf yellow 5 10
3N6 " 8pf orange 1.00 1.75
3N7 " 10pf yellow brown 5 10
3N8 " 12pf rose violet 5 10
3N9 " 15pf rose carmine 5 10
3N10 " 16pf dp. Prus. grn. 8 25
3N11 " 20pf blue 5 10
3N12 " 24pf chocolate 20 1.00
3N13 " 25pf bright ultra. 12 25

Size: 21½ x 25 mm.

3N14 OS1 30pf olive 12 20
3N15 " 40pf deep magenta 5 10
3N16 " 42pf green 5 10
3N17 " 50pf slate green 6 20
3N18 " 60pf violet brown 9 20
3N19 " 80pf blue black 8.50 17.50

Size: 25 x 29½ mm.

3N20 OS1 1m dark olive green ('46) 2.35 3.00
Nos. 3N1–3N20 (20) 13.07 25.45

Most of Nos. 3N1–3N20 exist imperforate and part-perforate.

Type I, Washington Printing

Size: 19-19½ x 22-22½ mm.

Perf. 11.

3N2a OS1 3pf lilac 5 10
3N3a " 4pf light gray 8 10
3N4a " 5pf emerald 5 10
3N5a " 6pf yellow 5 10
3N6a " 8pf deep orange 5 5
3N7a " 10pf brown 5 10
3N8a " 12pf rose violet 5 10
3N9a " 15pf cerise 5 10
3N13a " 25pf bright ultramarine 5 10
Nos. 3N2a–3N13a (9) 48 85

Photogravure

Type II, London Printing

Size: 19-19½ x 22-22½ mm.

Perf. 14, 14½ and Compound.

3N2b OS1 3pf lilac 5 10
3N3b " 4pf light gray 5 5
3N4b " 5pf deep emerald 8 30
3N5b " 6pf orange yellow 5 5
3N6b " 8pf dark orange 20 30
3N8b " 12pf rose violet 8 10
Nos. 3N2b–3N8b (6) 51 90

Issued Under French Occupation.

Coats of Arms.

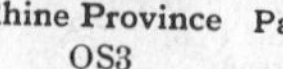

Rhine Province
OS3

Palatinate District
OS4

Saarland
OS5

Württemberg
OS6

Baden
OS7

Johann Wolfgang von Goethe
OS8

Friedrich von Schiller—OS9

Heinrich Heine—OS10

Typographed.

1945-46 *Perf. 14x13½* **Unwmkd.**

4N1 OS3 1pf black, green & lemon 5 5
4N2 OS4 3pf dark red, black & dull yellow 5 5
4N3 OS6 5pf brown, black & orange yellow 5 5
4N4 OS7 8pf brown, yellow & red 5 5
4N5 OS3 10pf brown, green & lemon 2.50 4.50
4N6 OS4 12pf red, black & orange yellow 5 5
4N7 OS5 15pf black, ultra. & red ('46) 5 5
4N8 OS6 20pf red, orange yellow & black 4 4
4N9 OS5 24pf blk., dp. ultra. & red ('46) 4 4
4N10 OS7 30pf black, orange yellow & red 4 4

Engraved

Perf. 13

4N11 OS8 1m lilac brown 1.00 *2.50*
4N12 OS9 2m deep blue ('46) 80 *3.25*
4N13 OS10 5m dull red brown ('46) 1.00 *3.50*
Nos. 4N1–4N13 (13) 5.72 *14.17*

Nos. 4N1–4N13 exist imperf. Price for set, $500.

Baden.

Johann Peter Hebel
OS1

Girl of Constance
OS2

Hans Baldung Grien—OS3

Rastatt Castle—OS4

Black Forest Scene
OS5

Cathedral of Freiburg
OS6

Photogravure

1947 *Perf. 14* **Unwmkd.**

5N1	OS1	2pf gray	5	9
5N2	OS2	3pf brown	5	9
5N3	OS3	10pf slate blue	5	9
5N4	OS1	12pf dark green	5	9
5N5	OS2	15pf purple	5	9
5N6	OS4	16pf olive green	12	55
5N7	OS3	20pf blue	6	9
5N8	OS4	24pf crimson	6	9
5N9	OS2	45pf cerise	6	25
5N10	OS1	60pf deep orange	6	9
5N11	OS3	75pf bright blue	6	45
5N12	OS5	84pf blue green	15	90
5N13	OS6	1m dark brown	15	27
		Nos. 5N1-5N13 (13)	97	3.14

Festival Headdress
OS7

Grand Duchess Stephanie
OS8

1948

5N14	OS1	2pf deep orange	22	30
5N15	OS2	6pf violet brown	22	16
5N16	OS7	8dpf blue green	70	1.50
5N17	OS3	10pf dark brown	30	17
5N18	OS1	12pf crimson	30	17
5N19	OS2	15pf blue	40	35
5N20	OS4	16dpf violet	80	1.50
5N21	OS3	20dpf brown	4.50	1.50
5N22	OS4	24pf dark green	65	17
5N23	OS7	30pf cerise	1.10	75
5N24	OS8	50pf bright blue	1.10	17
5N25	OS1	60dpf gray	4.00	30
5N26	OS5	84dpf rose brown	6.50	3.25
5N27	OS6	1dm bright blue	6.50	3.25
		Nos. 5N14-5N27 (14)	27.29	13.54

Without "PF."

1948-49

5N28	OS1	2(pf) deep orange	65	65
5N29	OS4	4(pf) violet	40	45
5N30	OS2	5(pf) blue	80	65
5N31	"	6(pf) vio. brn.	16.00	8.25
5N32	OS7	8(pf) rose brn.	1.00	65
5N33	OS3	10(pf) dark grn.	1.00	20
5N37	"	20(pf) cerise	1.60	45
5N38	OS4	40(pf) brown	55.00	82.50
5N39	OS1	80(pf) red	10.00	5.50
5N40	OS5	90(pf) rose brn.	40.00	65.00
		Nos. 5N28-5N40 (10)	126.45	164.30

Constance Cathedral and Insel Hotel—OS9

Two types:
I. Frameline thick and straight. Inscriptions thick. Shading dark. Upper part of "B" narrow.
II. Frameline thin and zigzag. Inscriptions fine. Shading light. Upper part of "B" wide.

1949, June 22

5N41	OS9	30(pf) dk. bl. (I)	22.00	*55.00*
		a. Type II	*400.00*	*1300.00*

Issued to publicize the International Engineering Congress, Constance, 1949.

Conradin Kreutzer
OS10

1949, Aug. 27

5N42	OS10	10(pf) dk. green	2.25	3.75

Conradin Kreutzer (1780–1849), composer.

Stagecoach—OS11

Design: 20pf, Post bus, trailer and plane.

1949, Sept. 17

5N43	OS11	10(pf) green	4.00	8.25
5N44	"	20(pf) red brn.	4.00	8.25

Centenary of German postage stamps.

Globe, Olive Branch and Post Horn
OS12

1949, Oct. 4

5N45	OS12	20(pf) dark red	5.00	*15.00*
5N46	"	30(pf) deep blue	5.00	6.50

Issued to commemorate the 75th anniversary of the formation of the Universal Postal Union.

OCCUPATION SEMI-POSTAL STAMPS.

Arms of Baden
OSP1

Cornhouse, Freiburg
OSP2

Perf. 13½x14

1949, Feb. 25 **Photo.** **Unwmkd.**

Cross in Red.

5NB1	OSP1	10(pf)+20(pf) green	17.50	*85.00*
5NB2	"	20(pf)+40(pf) lilac	17.50	*85.00*
5NB3	"	30(pf)+60(pf) blue	17.50	*85.00*
5NB4	"	40(pf)+80(pf) gray	17.50	*85.00*
		a. Sheet of 4, imperf.	125.00	*1200.00*

The surtax was for the Red Cross.

No. 5NB4a measures 90x101mm. and contains one each of Nos. 5NB1 to 5NB4, with red inscription in upper margin and no gum.

1949, Feb. 24 *Perf. 14*

Designs: 10pf+20pf, Cathedral tower. 20pf+30pf, Trumpeting angel. 30pf+50pf, Fish pool.

5NB5	OSP2	4(pf)+16(pf) dark violet	6.75	*18.50*
5NB6	"	10(pf)+20(pf) dark green	8.75	*25.00*
5NB7	"	20(pf)+30(pf) carmine	11.00	*25.00*
5NB8	"	30(pf)+50(pf) blue	14.00	*25.00*
		a. Sheet of 4	*100.00*	*550.00*
		b. Same imperf.	*87.50*	*550.00*

The surtax was for the reconstruction of historical monuments in Freiburg.

Nos. 5NB8a, 5NB8b contain one each of Nos. 5NB5–5NB8, with black inscription in lower margin. Size: No. 5NB8a, 69x78mm, No. 5NB8b, 65x77mm.

Carl Schurz at Rastatt
OSP3

Johann Wolfgang von Goethe
OSP4

1949, Aug. 23

5NB9	OSP3	10(pf)+5(pf) green	8.50	*27.50*
5NB10	"	20(pf)+10(pf) cerise	8.50	*27.50*
5NB11	"	30(pf)+15(pf) blue	8.50	*27.50*

Centenary of the surrender of Rastatt.

1949, Aug. 12 **Various Portraits**

5NB12	OSP4	10(pf)+5(pf) green	10.00	*22.00*
5NB13	"	20(pf)+10(pf) cerise	10.00	*22.00*
5NB14	"	30(pf)+15(pf) blue	12.00	*50.00*

Johann Wolfgang von Goethe (1749–1832).

Rhine Palatinate.

Ludwig van Beethoven
OS1

Wilhelm E. F. von Ketteler
OS2

Girl Carrying Grapes
OS3

Porta Nigra, Trier
OS4

Karl Marx
OS5

"Devil's Table", Near Pirmasens
OS6

Street Corner, St. Martin
OS7

Cathedral of Worms
OS8

Cathedral of Mainz
OS9

Statue of Johann Gutenberg
OS10

Gutenfels and Pfalzgrafenstein Castles on Rhine—OS11

Statue of Charlemagne
OS12

Photogravure.

1947-48 *Perf. 14* **Unwmkd.**

6N1	OS1	2pf gray	5	7
6N2	OS2	3pf dark brown	5	7
6N3	OS3	10pf slate blue	5	9
6N4	OS4	12pf green	5	7
6N5	OS5	15pf purple	5	7
6N6	OS6	16pf light olive green	5	9
6N7	OS7	20pf bright blue	5	9
6N8	OS8	24pf crimson	5	7
6N9	OS10	30pf cerise ('48)	6	55
6N10	OS9	45pf cerise	6	20
6N11	"	50pf blue ('48)	6	65
6N12	OS1	60pf deep orange	5	6
6N13	OS10	75pf blue	6	12
6N14	OS11	84pf green	15	70
6N15	OS12	1m brown	15	25
		Nos. 6N1-6N15 (15)	99	3.15

Nos. 6N1–6N15 exist imperf. Price for set, $600.

1948

6N16	OS1	2pf deep orange	20	25
6N17	OS2	6pf violet brown	20	25
6N18	OS4	8dpf blue green	50	1.65
6N19	OS3	10pf dark brown	50	9
6N20	OS4	12pf crimson rose	45	10
6N21	OS5	15pf blue	1.00	55
6N22	OS6	16dpf dark violet	55	1.10
6N23	OS7	20dpf brown	1.40	90
6N24	OS8	24pf green	45	15
6N25	OS9	30pf cerise	1.00	25
6N26	OS10	50pf bright blue	1.40	25
6N27	OS1	60dpf gray	8.75	35
6N28	OS11	84dpf rose brown	4.00	3.50
6N29	OS12	1dm bright blue	4.00	3.50
		Nos. 6N16-6N29 (14)	24.40	12.89

No. 6N16–6N29 exist imperf. Price for set, $600.

Types of 1947.

1948-49 Without "PF."

6N30 OS1 2(pf) deep orange 22 25
6N31 OS6 4(pf) violet ('49) 45 25
6N32 OS5 5(pf) blue ('49) 65 35
6N33 OS2 6(pf) vio. brn. 25.00 11.00
6N33A OS4 8(pf) rose brown ('49) 55.00 *110.00*
6N34 OS3 10(pf) dark green 85 25
a. Imperf., pair 350.00
6N35 OS7 20(pf) cerise 85 25
6N36 OS8 40(pf) brn. ('49) 2.00 2.25
6N37 OS4 80(pf) red ('49) 2.50 3.25
6N38 OS11 90(pf) rose brown ('49) 4.00 14.00
Nos. 6N30-6N38 (10) 91.52 *141.85*

Type of Baden, 1949.
Designs as in Baden.

1949, Sept. 17
6N39 OS11 10pf green 8.75 19.00
6N40 " 20pf red brn. 8.75 19.00

Centenary of German postage stamps.

UPU Type of Baden, 1949.

1949, Oct. 4
6N41 OS12 20pf dark red 4.75 *12.00*
6N42 " 30pf deep blue 4.75 6.50

Issued to commemorate the 75th anniversary of the formation of the Universal Postal Union.

OCCUPATION SEMI-POSTAL STAMPS.

St. Martin
OSP1

Photogravure.
Design: 30pf+50pf, St. Christopher.

1948 *Perf. 14* Unwmkd.
6NB1 OSP1 20pf+30pf deep claret 1.00 2.25
6NB2 " 30pf+50pf deep blue 1.00 2.25

The surtax was to aid victims of an explosion at Ludwigshafen.

Type of Baden, 1949, Showing Arms of Rhine Palatinate.

1949, Feb. 25 *Perf. 13½x14*
Cross in Red.
6NB3 OSP1 10pf+20pf green 15.00 *87.50*
6NB4 " 20pf+40pf lilac 15.00 *87.50*
6NB5 " 30pf+60pf blue 15.00 *87.50*
6NB6 " 40pf+80pf gray 15.00 *87.50*
a. Sheet of 4 imperf. 110.00 *1200.00*

The surtax was for the Red Cross.
No. 6NB6a measures 90x100mm. and contains one each of Nos. 6NB3 to 6NB6, with red inscription in upper margin and no gum.

Goethe Type of Baden, 1949.

1949, Aug. 12 Various Portraits
6NB7 OSP4 10pf+5pf green 4.25 8.25
6NB8 " 20pf+10pf cerise 4.25 8.25
6NB9 " 30pf+15pf blue 9.25 *19.00*

Johann Wolfgang von Goethe (1749–1832).

Saar.

See Volume IV.

Württemberg.

Friedrich von Schiller
OS1

Castle of Bebenhausen, near Tübingen
OS2

Friedrich Hölderlin
OS3

Town Gate of Wangen (Allgäu)
OS4

Lichtenstein Castle
OS5

Zwiefalten Church
OS6

Photogravure.

1947–48 *Perf. 14.* Unwmkd.
8N1 OS1 2pf gray ('48) 5 7
8N2 OS3 3pf brown ('48) 5 7
8N3 OS4 10pf slate blue('48) 5 7
8N4 OS1 12pf dark green 5 7
8N5 OS3 15pf purple ('48) 6 10
8N6 OS2 16pf olive green ('48) 6 30
8N7 OS4 20pf blue ('48) 6 15
8N8 OS2 24pf crimson 6 7
8N9 OS3 45pf cerise 10 15
8N10 OS1 60pf dp. org. ('48) 10 55
8N11 OS4 75pf bright blue 10 55
8N12 OS5 84pf blue green 14 80
8N13 OS6 1m dark brown 20 55
Nos. 8N1-8N13 (13) 1.08 3.50

The 12pf and 60pf exist imperf. Price, each $35.

Waldsee
OS7

Ludwig Uhland
OS8

1948
8N14 OS1 2pf deep orange 25 65
8N15 OS3 6pf violet brown 25 15
8N16 OS7 8dpf blue green 80 1.90
8N17 OS4 10pf dark brown 20 35
8N18 OS1 12pf crimson 25 15
8N19 OS3 15pf blue 50 30
8N20 OS2 16dpf dark violet 80 1.90
8N21 OS4 20dpf brown 1.50 1.25
8N22 OS2 24pf dark green 80 15
8N23 OS7 30pf cerise 1.25 35
8N24 OS8 50pf dull blue 2.00 35
8N25 OS1 60dpf gray 9.50 35
8N26 OS5 84dpf rose brown 4.75 3.25
8N27 OS6 1dm bright blue 4.75 2.75
Nos. 8N14-8N27 (14) 27.60 13.85

The 2pf, 10pf, 24pf and 30pf exist imperf. Price, each $35.

1948-49 Without "PF."
8N28 OS1 2(pf) dp. orange 1.25 55
8N29 OS2 4(pf) violet 1.25 55
8N30 OS3 5(pf) blue 2.00 1.25
8N31 " 6(pf) violet brn. 4.25 4.50
8N32 OS7 8(pf) rose brown 4.75 1.65
8N33 OS4 10(pf) dark green 4.75 15
8N34 " 20(pf) cerise 4.75 20
8N35 OS2 40(pf) brown 25.00 32.50
8N36 OS1 80(pf) red 55.00 27.50
8N37 OS5 90(pf) rose brn. 65.00 *100.00*
Nos. 8N28-8N37 (10) 168.00 *168.85*

The 4pf and 6pf exist imperf. Price, respectively $100 and $37.50.

Type of Baden, 1949.
Designs as in Baden.

1949, Sept. 17
8N38 OS11 10(pf) green 6.75 12.00
8N39 " 20(pf) red brn. 7.25 14.00

Centenary of German postage stamps.

UPU Type of Baden, 1949.

1949, Oct. 4
8N40 OS12 20(pf) dark red 5.25 *14.00*
8N41 " 30(pf) deep blue 5.25 5.50

Issued to commemorate the 75th anniversary of the formation of the Universal Postal Union.

OCCUPATION SEMI-POSTAL STAMPS.

Type of Baden, 1949.
Design: Arms of Württemberg.

Perf. 13½x14

1949, Feb. 25 Photo. Unwmkd.
Cross in Red.
8NB1 OSP1 10(pf)+20(pf) green 35.00 *130.00*
8NB2 " 20(pf)+40(pf) lilac 35.00 *130.00*
8NB3 " 30(pf)+60(pf) blue 35.00 *130.00*
8NB4 " 40(pf)+80(pf) gray 35.00 *130.00*
a. Sheet of 4 imperf. 160.00 *1900.00*

The surtax was for the Red Cross.
No. 8NB4a measures 90x100mm. and contains one each of Nos. 8NB1 to 8NB4, with red inscription in upper margin and no gum.

View of Isny
OSP1

Design: 20pf+6pf, Skier and village.

Perf. 14

1949, Feb. 11 Typo. Wmk. 116
8NB5 OSP1 10(pf)+4(pf) dull green 3.25 6.50
8NB6 " 20(pf)+6(pf) red brown 3.25 6.50

Issued to commemorate the 1948–49 German Ski Championship at Isny im Allgau.

Gustav Werner
OSP2

1949, Sept. 4
8NB7 OSP2 10(pf)+5(pf) blue green 3.75 *11.00*
8NB8 " 20(pf)+10(pf) claret 3.75 *11.00*

Issued to commemorate the centenary of the founding of Gustav Werner's "Christianity in Action" and "House of Brotherhood."

Goethe Type of Baden, 1949.

1949, Aug. 12 Various Portraits
8NB9 OSP4 10(pf)+5(pf) green 8.00 12.00
8NB10 " 20(pf)+10(pf) cerise 9.50 17.50
8NB11 " 30(pf)+15(pf) blue 11.00 *25.00*

Issued to commemorate the bicentenary of the birth of Johann Wolfgang von Goethe.

Berlin.

Issued for Use in the American, British and French Occupation Sectors of Berlin.

Germany, Nos. 557-569, 571-573 Overprinted Diagonally in Black

BERLIN
a

Perf. 14

1948, Sept. 1 Typo. Wmk. 284
9N1 A120 2pf brn. black 1.10 *4.00*
9N2 " 6pf purple 55 1.25
9N3 A121 8pf red 65 1.25
9N4 " 10pf yellow green 45 25
9N5 A122 12pf gray 45 1.35
9N6 A120 15pf chocolate 11.50 *50.00*
9N7 A123 16pf dk. blue grn. 70 1.65
9N8 A121 20pf blue 2.10 5.00
9N9 A123 24pf brn. orange 55 80
9N10 A120 25pf org. yel. 19.00 *65.00*
9N11 A122 30pf red 3.00 5.00
9N12 A121 40pf red violet 2.10 2.75
9N13 A123 50pf ultramarine 6.25 *32.50*
9N14 A122 60pf red brown 2.65 35
9N15 " 80pf dark blue 6.25 *22.50*
9N16 A123 84pf emerald 12.50 *92.50*

Germany, Nos. 574-577 Overprinted Diagonally in Black

BERLIN
b

Engraved.
9N17 A124 1m olive 27.50 *130.00*
9N18 " 2m dark brown violet 42.50 *465.00*
9N19 " 3m copper red 60.00 *650.00*
9N20 " 5m dark blue 60.00 *775.00*
Nos. 9N1-9N20 (20) 259.80

Forged overprints and cancellations are found on Nos. 9N1–9N20.

Stamps of Germany, 1947-48, with "a" Overprint in Red.

Typographed.

1948-49 *Perf. 14.* Wmk. 284
9N21 A120 2pf brn.blk.('49) 2.65 2.25
9N22 " 6pf purple ('49) 11.50 2.25
9N23 A121 8pf red ('49) 35.00 4.00
9N24 " 10pf yellow green 2.25 40
9N25 A120 15pf chocolate 5.25 2.50
9N26 A121 20pf blue 2.65 80
9N27 A120 25pf orange yellow ('49) 100.00 45.00
9N28 A122 30pf red ('49) 42.50 6.50
9N29 A121 40pf red violet ('49) 42.50 8.75
9N30 A123 50pf ultra. ('49) 60.00 6.50
9N31 A122 60pf red brown 7.00 40
9N32 " 80pf dark blue ('49) 100.00 8.25

With "b" Overprint in Red.

Engraved
9N33 A124 1m olive 450.00 310.00
9N34 " 2m dark brown violet 250.00 145.00
Nos. 9N21-9N34 (14) 1111.30 542.60

Forgeries exist of the overprints on Nos. 9N21–9N34. No. 9N33 exists imperf.

Statue of Heinrich von Stephan
OS1 OS2

1949, Apr. 9 Litho. *Perf. 14*

9N35 OS1 12(pf) gray 5.25 6.50
9N36 " 16(pf) bl. green 14.00 7.75
9N37 " 24(pf) org. brn. 10.50 40
9N38 " 50(pf) brown olive 95.00 16.50
9N39 " 60(pf) brn. red 95.00 16.50
9N40 OS2 1m olive 45.00 65.00
9N41 " 2m brown violet 52.50 37.50
Nos. 9N35-9N41 (7) 317.25 150.15

Issued to commemorate the 75th anniversary of the formation of the Universal Postal Union.

Brandenburg Gate, Berlin — OS3
Tempelhof Airport — OS4

Designs: 4pf, 8pf, 40pf, Schoeneberg, Rudolf Wilde Square. 5pf, 25pf, 5m, Tegel Castle. 6pf, 50pf, Reichstag Building. 10pf, 30pf, Cloisters, Kleist Park. 15pf, Tempelhof Airport. 20pf, 80pf, 90pf, Polytechnic College, Charlottenburg. 60pf, National Gallery. 2m, Gendarmen Square. 3m, Brandenburg Gate.

1949 Typographed **Wmk. 284**

Size: 22x18mm.

9N42 OS3 1pf black 8 4
  a. Bklt. pane 5 + label 7.50
  b. Tête bêche 45 55
9N43 " 4pf yellow brown 25 5
  a. Bklt. pane 5 + label 7.50
  b. Tête bêche 1.35 1.90
  c. Imperf. 1000.00
9N44 " 5pf blue green 42 5
9N45 " 6pf red violet 55 75
9N46 " 8pf red orange 1.00 75
9N47 " 10pf yellow green 90 5
  a. Bklt. pane 5 + label 32.50
9N48 OS4 15pf chocolate 4.50 38
9N49 OS3 20pf red 3.50 5
  a. Bklt. pane 5 + label 42.50
9N50 " 25pf orange 16.00 45
9N51 " 30pf violet blue 4.50 40
  a. Imperf. 1000.00
9N52 " 40pf lake 7.00 15
9N53 " 50pf olive 8.50 15
9N54 " 60pf red brown 32.50 7
9N55 " 80pf dark blue 7.00 1.00
9N56 " 90pf emerald 7.00 60

Engraved.

Size: 29¼-29¾ x 24-24½mm.

9N57 OS4 1m olive 14.00 60
9N58 " 2m brown violet 26.50 80
9N59 " 3m henna brown 160.00 5.50
9N60 " 5m deep blue 77.50 7.75
Nos. 9N42-9N60 (19) 371.70 19.59

See also Nos. 9N101-102, 9N108-110.

Goethe and "Iphigenie" — **OS5**
Statue of Atlas, New York — **OS6**

Designs (Goethe and scenes from his works): 20pf, "Reineke Fuchs." 30pf, "Faust."

1949, July 29 Litho. ***Perf. 14***

9N61 OS5 10(pf) green 92.50 50.00
9N62 " 20(pf) carmine 92.50 60.00
9N63 " 30(pf) ultramarine 12.50 19.00

Issued to commemorate the bicentenary of the birth of Johann Wolfgang von Goethe.

Germany Nos. 550, 565, 572 and 576 Surcharged "BERLIN" and New Value in Dark Green.

1949, Aug. 1 Typographed

9N64 A119 5(pf) on 45pf bright red 2.10 20
9N65 A123 10(pf) on 24pf brn. orange 5.00 30
9N66 A122 20(pf) on 80pf dark blue 22.50 18.00

Engraved

9N67 A124 1(m) on 3m copper red 85.00 15.00

1950, Oct. 1 Engraved **Wmk. 116**

9N68 OS6 20(pf) dk. car. 52.50 55.00

Issued to publicize the European Recovery Plan.

Albert Lortzing — OS7
Freedom Bell, Berlin — OS8

1951, Apr. 22

9N69 OS7 20(pf) red brown 42.50 55.00

Issued to commemorate the centenary of the death of Albert Lortzing, composer.

1951 ***Perf. 14***

9N70 OS8 5(pf) chocolate 2.85 4.50
9N71 " 10(pf) deep green 9.00 13.50
9N72 " 20(pf) rose red 3.50 6.50
9N73 " 30(pf) blue 25.00 40.00
9N74 " 40(pf) rose violet 16.00 35.00
Nos. 9N70-9N74 (5) 56.35 99.50

1951-52 Re-engraved

9N75 OS8 5(pf) olive bister ('52) 1.60 1.25
9N76 " 10(pf) yellow green 4.00 5.50
9N77 " 20(pf) bright red 16.00 22.50
9N78 " 30)pf) blue ('52) 30.00 37.50
9N79 " 40(pf) dp. car. ('52) 14.00 16.50
Nos. 9N75-9N79 (5) 65.60 83.25

Bell clapper moved from left to right. Imprint "L. Schnell" in lower margin.
No. 9N76 exists imperf. Price $900.
See also Nos. 9N94-9N98.

Ludwig van Beethoven — OS9
Olympic Symbols — OS10

1952, Mar. 26 Engr. **Unwmkd.**

9N80 OS9 30(pf) blue 35.00 40.00

Issued to commemorate the 125th anniversary of the death of Ludwig van Beethoven.

1952, June 20 Litho. **Wmk. 116**

9N81 OS10 4(pf) yel. brown 80 1.25
9N82 " 10(pf) green 6.00 10.00
9N83 " 20(pf) rose red 9.50 16.50

Issued to publicize the pre-Olympic Festival Day, June 20, 1952.

Carl Friedrich Zelter — OS11
Arms Breaking Chains — OS12

Portraits: 5(pf), Otto Lilienthal. 6(pf), Walter Rathenau. 8(pf), Theodor Fontane. 10(pf), Adolph von Menzel. 15(pf), Rudolf Virchow. 20(pf), Werner von Siemens. 25(pf), Karl Friedrich Schinkel. 30(pf), Max Planck. 40(pf), Wilhelm von Humboldt.

1952-53 Engraved. **Wmk. 284**

9N84 OS11 4(pf) brown 35 20
9N85 " 5(pf) deep blue ('53) 50 50
9N86 " 6(pf) choc. ('53) 4.50 8.75
9N87 " 8(pf) henna brown ('53) 1.60 2.75
9N88 " 10(pf) deep green 1.75 65
9N89 " 15(pf) purple ('53) 8.00 12.00
9N90 " 20(pf) brown red 2.25 80
9N91 " 25(pf) deep olive ('53) 26.50 6.50
9N92 " 30(pf) brown violet ('53) 9.00 7.75
9N93 " 40(pf) black ('53) 14.00 4.00
Nos. 9N84-9N93 (10) 68.45 43.90

Bell Type of 1951-1952
Second Re-engraving.

1953 ***Perf. 14.*** **Wmk. 284**

9N94 OS8 5(pf) brown 85 1.10
9N95 " 10(pf) deep green 2.10 2.25
9N96 " 20(pf) bright red 5.00 5.00
9N97 " 30(pf) blue 9.75 13.50
9N98 " 40(pf) rose violet 35.00 30.00
Nos. 9N94-9N98 (5) 52.70 51.85

Bell clapper hangs straight down. Marginal imprint omitted.

1953, Aug. 17 Typographed

Design: 30(pf), Brandenburg Gate.

9N99 OS12 20(pf) black 3.00 1.90
9N100 " 30(pf) deep car. 19.00 30.00

Issued to commemorate the strike of East German workers, June 17, 1953.

Similar to Type of 1949.

Designs: 4pf, Exposition halls. 20pf, Olympic Stadium, Berlin.

1953-54 ***Perf. 14.*** **Wmk. 284**

9N101 OS3 4pf yel. brn. ('54) 1.75 1.75
9N102 " 20pf red 42.50 38

Allied Council Building
OS13

1954, Jan. 25 Lithographed

9N103 OS13 20(pf) red 6.00 5.00

Issued to publicize the Four Power Conference, Berlin, 1954.

Ernst Reuter
OS14

1954, Jan. 18 Engr. **Wmk. 284**

9N104 OS14 20(pf) choc. 6.00 1.30

Prof. Ernst Reuter (1889-1953), mayor of Berlin, 1948-1953.
See also No. 9N174.

Ottmar Mergenthaler and Linotype
OS15

1954, May 11

9N105 OS15 10(pf) dark blue green 1.40 2.25

Issued to commemorate the centenary of the birth of Ottmar Mergenthaler.

No. 9N96 Overprinted in Black

Wahl des Bundespräsidenten in Berlin 17. Juli 1954

1954, July 17 ***Perf. 13½x14***

9N106 OS8 20(pf) bright red 2.50 4.75

Issued to publicize the West German presidential election held in Berlin July 17, 1954.

Germany in Bondage — OS16
Richard Strauss — OS17

1954, July 20 Typographed

9N107 OS16 20(pf) carmine & gray 4.00 6.00

Issued to commemorate the 10th anniversary of the attempted assassination of Adolf Hitler.

Similar to Type of 1949

Designs: 7pf, Exposition halls. 40pf, Memorial library. 70pf, Hunting lodge, Grunewald.

1954 ***Perf. 14*** **Wmk. 284**

9N108 OS3 7pf aquamarine 3.50 25
9N109 " 40pf rose lilac 11.00 3.25
9N110 " 70pf olive green 65.00 16.50

1954, Sept. 18 Engraved

9N111 OS17 40(pf) vio. blue 9.75 2.65

Issued to commemorate the fifth anniversary of the death of Richard Strauss, composer.

Early Forge
OS18

1954, Sept. 25

9N112 OS18 20(pf) reddish brown 7.00 1.80

Issued to commemorate the centenary of the death of August Borsig, industrial leader.

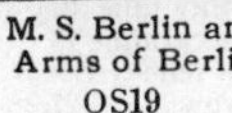

M. S. Berlin and Arms of Berlin — OS19
Wilhelm Furtwängler — OS20

1955, Mar. 12 **Wmk. 284**

9N113 OS19 10(pf) Prussian green 70 55
9N114 " 25(pf) vio. blue 4.25 4.75

Issued to publicize the resumption of shipping under West German ownership.

Perf. 13½x14

1955, Sept. 17 **Unwmkd.**

9N115 OS20 40(pf) ultra 10.50 16.50

Issued to honor the conductor Wilhelm Furtwangler and to publicize the Berlin Music Festival, September 1955.

Arms of Berlin

OS21 OS22

1955, Oct. 17 **Litho.** **Wmk. 304**

9N116 OS21 10(pf) red, orange yellow & black 18 25
9N117 " 20(pf) red, orange yellow & black 3.50 7.00

Issued to commemorate the meeting of the German Bundestag in Berlin, Oct. 17–22, 1955.

1956, Mar. 16

9N118 OS22 10(pf) red, ochre & black 75 55
9N119 " 25(pf) red, ochre & black 2.65 4.00

Issued to commemorate the meeting of the German Bundesrat in Berlin March 16, 1956.

(No top inscription) (Top inscription)

Radio Station, Berlin

OS23 OS24

Free University OS25

Monument of the Great Elector Frederick William OS26

Designs: 1pf, 3pf, Brandenburg Gate. 5pf, General Post Office. 8pf, City Hall, Neukölln. 10pf, Kaiser Wilhelm Memorial Church. 15pf, Airlift memorial. 25pf, Lilienthal Monument. 30pf, Pfaueninsel Castle. 40pf, Charlottenburg Castle. 50pf, Reuter power plant. 60pf, Chamber of Commerce and Industry and Stock Exchange. 70pf, Schiller Theater. 3m, Congress Hall.

Typo.; Litho. (3pf, 9N122)

1956-63 ***Perf. 14*** **Wmk. 304**

9N120 OS25 1pf gray ('57) 5 5
9N120A " 3pf bright purple ('63) 5 5
9N121 " 5pf rose lilac ('57) 12 7
9N122 OS23 7pf blue green 4.00 2.25
9N123 OS24 7pf blue green 18 12
9N124 " 8pf gray 28 75
9N125 " 8pf red orange ('59) 12 17
9N126 " 10pf emerald 12 7
9N127 " 15pf chalky blue 27 25
9N128 OS25 20pf rose carmine 18 7
9N129 OS24 25pf dull red brown 27 65

Engraved.

9N130 OS24 30pf gray green ('57) 28 1.10
9N131 OS25 40pf light ultra. ('57) 5.25 4.25
9N132 OS24 50pf olive 65 1.25
9N133 OS25 60pf light brown ('57) 90 1.35
9N134 " 70pf violet 16.00 11.00
9N135 OS26 1m olive 1.40 1.80

Size: 29 x 24½ mm.

9N136 OS25 3m rose claret ('58) 4.50 10.00

Nos. 9N120-9N136 (18) 34.62 35.25

No. 9N120 exists on both ordinary and fluorescent paper; No. 9N120A on fluorescent paper only; others on ordinary paper.

Engineers' Society Emblem OS27

Paul Lincke OS28

1956, May 12 **Engraved** ***Perf. 14***

9N140 OS27 10pf dark green 90 55
9N141 " 20pf dark red 3.25 5.50

Centenary of Society of German Civil Engineers.

1956, Sept. 3

9N142 OS28 20pf dark red 85 1.65

Issued to commemorate the 10th anniversary of the death of Paul Lincke, composer.

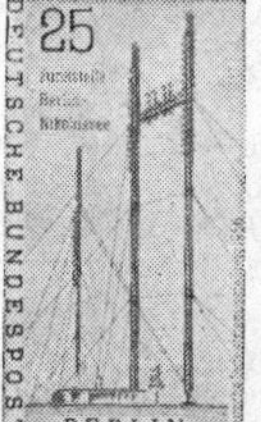

Radio Station, Berlin-Nikolassee OS29

Spandau, 1850 OS30

1956, Sept. 15

9N143 OS29 25pf brown 4.00 6.50

Issued to publicize the German Industrial Fair, Berlin, Sept. 15–30.

1957, Mar. 7

9N144 OS30 20pf gray olive & brown red 17 45

725th anniversary of Spandau.

Hansa Model Town and "B"

OS31

Designs: 20pf, View of exposition grounds and "B." 40pf, Auditorium and "B."

1957 **Engraved**

9N145 OS31 7pf violet brown 10 10
9N146 " 20pf carmine 22 25
9N147 " 40pf violet blue 50 1.40

Issued to publicize the International Building Show, Berlin, July 6–Sept. 29, 1957.

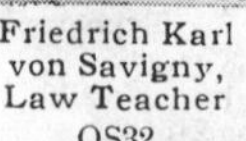

Friedrich Karl von Savigny, Law Teacher OS32

Uta Statue, Naumburg Cathedral OS33

Portraits: 7pf, Theodor Mommsen, historian. 8pf, Heinrich Zille, painter. 10pf, Ernst Reuter, mayor of Berlin. 15pf, Fritz Haber, chemist. 20pf, Friedrich Schleiermacher, theologian. 25pf, Max Reinhardt, theatrical director. 40pf, Alexander von Humboldt, naturalist and geographer. 50pf, Christian Daniel Rauch, sculptor.

1957-59 ***Perf. 14*** **Wmk. 304**

Portraits in Brown.

9N148 OS32 7pf blue green ('58) 5 7
9N149 " 8pf gray ('58) 7 9
9N150 " 10pf green ('58) 8 10
9N151 " 15pf dark blue 50 70
9N152 " 20pf carmine ('58) 18 20
9N153 " 25pf magenta 55 1.10
9N154 " 30pf olive green 80 1.50
9N155 " 40pf blue ('59) 32 55
9N156 " 50pf olive 1.90 3.25

Nos. 9N148-9N156 (9) 4.45 7.56

Issued to honor famous men of Berlin. See also No. 9NB19.

1957, Aug. 6

9N157 OS33 25pf brown red 28 70

Issued to publicize the annual meeting of the East German Culture Society in Berlin.

"Unity and Justice and Liberty" OS34

Postilion 1897-1925 OS35

1957, Oct. 15 **Lithographed**

9N158 OS34 10pf red, ochre & black 25 38
9N159 " 20pf red, ochre & black 1.00 2.25

Issued to commemorate the first meeting of the third German Bundesrat, Berlin, Oct. 15.

1957, Oct. 23 ***Perf. 14*** **Wmk. 304**

9N160 OS35 20pf multi. 45 75

Issued for Stamp Day and BEPHILA stamp exhibition, Berlin, Oct. 23–27.

World Veterans' Federation Emblem OS36

Christ and the Cosmos OS37

1957, Oct. 28

9N161 OS36 20pf bl. grn., olive grn. & yel. 42 75

Issued to publicize the 7th General Assembly of the World Veterans' Federation, Berlin, Oct. 24–Nov. 1.

1958, Aug. 13

9N162 OS37 10pf light blue green & black 15 25
9N163 " 20pf rose lilac & black 35 90

Issued in honor of the 78th German Catholics Meeting, Berlin, Aug. 13-17.

Otto Suhr OS38

1958, Aug. 30 **Engraved** ***Perf. 14***

9N164 OS38 20pf rose red 38 75

Prof. Otto Suhr (1894–1957), mayor of Berlin, 1955–1957.

Pres. Heuss Type of Germany, 1959

1959 **Litho., Engr. (40pf, 70pf)**

9N165 A208 7pf blue green 8 7
9N166 " 10pf green 15 7
9N167 " 20pf dk. car. rose 28 15
9N168 " 40pf blue 1.15 1.60
9N169 " 70pf dull purple 2.50 3.75

Nos. 9N165-9N169 (5) 4.16 5.64

Nos. 9N168–9N169 were issued in sheets of 100 and in coils. Every fifth coil stamp has a control number on the back.

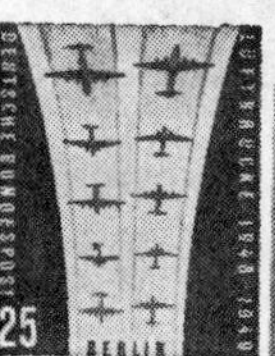

Aerial Bridge to Berlin OS39

Globe and Brandenburg Gate OS40

1959, May 12 **Engraved**

9N170 OS39 25pf maroon & black 22 45

10th anniversary of Berlin Airlift.

1959, June 18 **Litho.** ***Perf. 14***

9N171 OS40 20pf light blue & red 25 45

Issued to publicize the 14th International Municipal Congress, Berlin, June 18–23.

Friedrich von Schiller—OS41

1959, Nov. 10 **Engraved** **Wmk. 304**

9N172 OS41 20pf dull red & brown 15 25

Issued to commemorate the 200th anniversary of the birth of Friedrich von Schiller, poet.

Robert Koch OS42

Hans Böckler OS43

1960, May 27 ***Perf. 14***

9N173 OS42 20pf rose lake 15 25

Dr. Robert Koch (1843–1910), bacteriologist, 50th death anniversary.

Mayor Type of 1954.

Portrait: Walther Schreiber.

1960, June 30 ***Perf. 14*** **Wmk. 304**

9N174	OS14	20pf brn. car.	25	45

Issued to honor Dr. Walther Carl Rudolf Schreiber, Mayor of Berlin, 1953–1954.

1961, Feb. 16 **Litho.** ***Perf. 14***

9N175	OS43	20pf dk. brick red & black	15	20

Issued to honor Hans Böckler (1875–1951), labor leader, on the 10th anniversary of his death, Feb. 26, 1961.

Fluorescent Paper

was introduced for all stamps, starting with No. 9N176, and including Nos. 9N120 and 9N120A.

Albrecht Dürer OS44 — Louise Schroeder OS45

Portraits: 5pf, Albertus Magnus. 7pf, St. Elizabeth of Thuringia. 8pf, Johann Gutenberg. 15pf, Martin Luther. 20pf, Johann Sebastian Bach. 25pf, Balthasar Neumann. 30pf, Immanuel Kant. 40pf, Gotthold Ephraim Lessing. 50pf, Johann Wolfgang von Goethe. 60pf, Friedrich von Schiller. 70pf, Ludwig van Beethoven. 80pf, Heinrich von Kleist. 1m, Annette von Droste-Hülshoff. 2m, Gerhart Hauptmann.

1961–62 **Typographed** **Wmk. 304**

Fluorescent Paper

9N176	OS44	5pf olive	7	7
9N177	"	7pf dark bistre	30	25
9N178	"	8pf lilac	25	25
9N179	"	10pf olive green	12	7
		a. Bklt. pane of 10	3.00	
		b. Tête bêche pair	80	1.25
9N180	"	15pf blue	35	35
9N181	"	20pf dark red	22	5
9N182	"	25pf orange brn.	35	35
		Engraved		
9N183	OS44	30pf gray	45	70
9N184	"	40pf blue	55	70
9N185	"	50pf red brown	60	75
9N186	"	60pf dk. carmine rose ('62)	70	80
9N187	"	70pf green	80	80
9N188	"	80pf brown	1.90	2.00
9N189	"	1m violet blue	1.65	1.10
9N190	"	2m yellow green ('62)	2.50	1.90
		Nos. 9N176–9N190 (15)	10.81	10.14

Nos. 9N176–9N182, 9N184 and 9N187 were issued in sheets and in coils. Every fifth coil stamp has a black control number on the back.

1961, June 3 **Engr.** ***Perf. 14***

9N192	OS45	20pf dark brown	15	25

Issued to honor Louise Schroeder, acting mayor of Berlin (1947–1948).

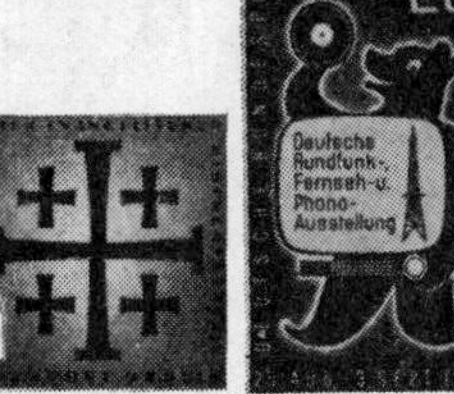

Synod Emblem and St. Mary's Church OS46 — Berlin Bear with Record, TV Set and Radio Tower OS47

Design: 20pf, Emblem and Kaiser Wilhelm Memorial Church.

1961, July 19 **Litho.** **Wmk. 304**

9N193	OS46	10pf green & vio.	10	12
9N194	"	20pf rose claret & violet	25	25

Issued to honor the 10th meeting of German Protestants (Evangelical Synod), Berlin, July 19–23.

1961, Aug. 3 **Engraved**

9N195	OS47	20pf brown red & dark brown	15	20

Issued to publicize the German Radio, Television and Phonograph Exhibition, Berlin, Aug. 25–Sept. 3.

Berlin, 1650
OS48

Views of Old Berlin: 10pf, Spree and Waisenbrücke (Orphans' Bridge). 15pf, Mauer Street, 1780. 20pf, Berlin Palace, 1703. 25pf, Potsdam Square, 1825. 40pf, Bellevue Palace, 1800. 50pf, Fischer Bridge, 1830. 60pf, Halle Gate, 1880. 70pf, Parochial Church, 1780. 80pf, University, 1825. 90pf, Opera House, 1780. 1m, Grunewald Lake, 1790.

1962–63 ***Perf. 14*** **Wmk. 304**

9N196	OS48	7pf dk. gray & golden brn.	8	8
9N197	"	10pf green & dark gray	10	8
9N198	"	15pf bluish gray & dk. blue ('63)	15	8
9N199	"	20pf orge. brown & sepia	20	10
9N200	"	25pf olive & gray ('63)	20	20
9N201	"	40pf bluish gray & ultra.	40	25
9N202	"	50pf gray & dark brn. ('63)	50	35
9N203	"	60pf gray & car. rose ('63)	60	55
9N204	"	70pf dark gray & lilac	70	60
9N205	"	80pf dk. gray & dark red ('63)	80	80
9N206	"	90pf sepia & brn. orge. ('63)	90	1.00
9N207	"	1m olive gray & dp. grn.	1.00	1.30
		Nos. 9N196–9N207 (12)	5.63	5.39

Gelber Hund, 1912, and Boeing 707 OS49 — Berlin Bear and Radio Tower OS50

1962, Sept. 12 **Lithographed**

9N208	OS49	60pf bright blue & black	60	75

Issued to commemorate the 50th anniversary of German airmail service.

1963, July 24 ***Perf. 14*** **Unwmkd.**

9N209	OS50	20pf blue, violet bl. & gray	20	28

Issued to publicize the German Radio, Television and Phonograph Exhibition, Berlin, Aug. 30–Sept. 8.

Schöneberg City Hall, John F. Kennedy Place, Berlin
OS51

1964, May 30 **Engr.** **Wmk. 304**

9N210	OS51	20pf dk. brn., *cream*	20	28

Issued to commemorate the 700th anniversary of the Schöneberg district of Berlin. The Senate and House of Representatives of West Berlin meet at Schöneberg City Hall.

Lübke Type of Germany, 1964,

1964, July 1 **Litho.** **Unwmkd.**

9N211	A247	20pf carmine	20	20
9N212	"	40pf ultramarine	45	45

Re-election of Pres. Heinrich Lübke. See also Nos. 9N263–9N264.

Capitals Type of Germany

Design: Reichstag Building, Berlin.

1964, Sept. 14 **Litho.** ***Perf. 14***

9N213	A245	20pf bl., blk. & grn.	20	25

Kennedy Type of Germany

1964, Nov. 21 **Engr.** **Wmk. 304**

9N214	A255	40pf dark blue	40	45

Issued to commemorate the first anniversary of the death of Pres. John F. Kennedy (1917–1963).

Castle Gate, Ellwangen
OS52

Designs (German buildings through 12 centuries): 10pf, Wall pavilion, Zwinger, Dresden. 15pf, Tegel Castle, Berlin. 20pf, Portico, Lorsch. 40pf, Trifels Fortress, Palatinate. 60pf, Treptow Gate, Neubrandenburg. 70pf, Osthofen Gate, Soest. 80pf, Elling Gate, Weissenburg.

1964–65 **Typographed** **Unwmkd.**

9N215	OS52	10pf brown ('65)	10	5
		a. Bklt. pane of 10 ('65)	1.20	
		b. Tête bêche pair	25	25
9N216	"	15pf dk. grn. ('65)	15	9
9N217	"	20pf brn. red ('65)	20	7
		Engraved		
9N218	OS52	40pf vio. bl. ('65)	40	30
9N219	"	50pf olive bister	3.00	3.00
9N220	"	60pf rose red	65	65
9N221	"	70pf dk. green ('65)	1.35	1.35
9N222	"	80pf chocolate	80	80
		Nos. 9N215–9N222 (8)	6.65	6.31

Nos. 9N215–9N218, 9N221 were issued in sheets of 100 and in coils. Every fifth coil stamp has a black control number on the back.

Kaiser Wilhelm Memorial Church OS53 — Nordertor, Flensburg OS54

The New Berlin: 15pf, German Opera House (horiz.). 20pf, Philharmonic Hall (horiz.). 30pf, Jewish Community Center (horiz.). 40pf, Regina Martyrum Memorial (horiz.). 50pf, Ernst Reuter Square (horiz.). 60pf, Europa Center. 70pf, School of Engineering (horiz.). 80pf, City Highway. 90pf, Planetarium and observatory (horiz.). 1m, Schaeferberg radio tower, Wannsee. 1.10m, University clinic, Steglitz (horiz.).

Engraved and Lithographed

1965–66 ***Perf. 14*** **Unwmkd.**

9N223	OS53	15pf multi.	15	5
9N224	"	15pf "	15	5
9N225	"	20pf "	20	7
9N226	"	30pf " ('66)	30	12
9N227	"	40pf "	40	17
9N228	"	50pf "	50	38
9N229	"	60pf " ('66)	60	38
9N230	"	70pf " ('66)	70	50
9N231	"	80pf "	80	50
9N232	"	90pf " ('66)	90	55
9N233	"	1m " ('66)	1.00	75
9N234	"	1.10m " ('66)	1.10	90
		Nos. 9N223–9N234 (12)	6.80	4.42

1966–69 **Engraved** ***Perf. 14***

Designs: 5pf, Berlin Gate, Stettin. 8pf, Castle, Kaub on the Rhine. 10pf, Wall Pavilion, Zwinger, Dresden. 20pf, Portico, Lorsch. 40pf, Trifels Fortress, Palatinate. 50pf, Castle Gate, Ellwangen. 60pf, Treptow Gate, Neubrandenburg. 70pf, Osthofen Gate, Soest. 80pf, Elling Gate, Weissenburg. 90pf, Zschocke Ladies' Home, Königsberg. 1m, Melanchthon House, Wittenberg. 1.10m, Trinity Hospital, Hildesheim. 1.30m, Tegel Castle, Berlin. 2m, Löwenberg Town Hall, interior view.

9N235	OS54	5pf olive	6	5
9N236	"	8pf carmine rose	38	38
9N237	"	10pf dk. brn. ('67)	10	5
9N238	"	20pf dk. grn. ('67)	25	8
9N239	"	30pf yel. green	45	45
9N240	"	30pf red ('67)	45	7
9N241	"	40pf olive bister ('67)	80	80
9N242	"	50pf blue ('67)	80	55
9N243	"	60pf dp. org. ('67)	1.10	1.00
9N244	"	70pf slate green ('67)	1.20	1.00
9N245	"	80pf red brown ('67)	1.50	1.00
9N246	"	90pf black	1.40	1.10
9N247	"	1m dull blue	1.40	55
9N248	"	1.10m red brown	1.65	90
9N249	"	1.30m grn. ('69)	1.90	1.90
9N250	"	2m purple	2.25	1.30
		Nos. 9N235–9N250 (16)	15.69	11.18

Brandenburg Gate Type of Germany

1966–70 **Typographed** ***Perf. 14***

9N251	A268	10pf chocolate	12	4
		a. Bklt. pane of 10 (4 No. 9N251, 2 No. 9N252, 4 No. 9N253)	3.25	
		b. Tête bêche pair	30	30
		c. Bklt. pane of 6 (4 No. 9N251, 2 No. 9N253) ('70)	1.75	
9N252	"	20pf deep green	20	8
		a. Bklt. pane of 4 (2 No. 9N252, 2 No. 9N253) ('70)	1.65	
9N253	"	30pf red	35	4
		a. Tête bêche pair	1.20	1.20
9N254	"	50pf dark blue	85	60
9N255	"	100pf dk. bl. ('67)	1.90	1.90
		Nos. 9N251–9N255 (5)	3.42	2.66

Nos. 9N251–9N255 were issued in sheets of 100 and in coils. Every fifth coil stamp has a black control number on the back.

Young Man, by Conrat Meit, 1520
OS55

Designs: 20pf, The Great Elector Friedrich Wilhelm (1640–88), head from monument by Andreas Schlüter. 30pf, The Evangelist Mark, by Tilman Riemenschneider. 50pf, Head of "Victory" from Brandenburg Gate, by Gottfried Schadow, 1793. 1m, Madonna, by Joseph Anton Feuchtmayer. 1.10m, Jesus and John, wood sculpture, anonymous, c. 1320.

1967 Engraved *Perf. 14*

9N256 OS55 10pf sepia & lemon 12 10
9N257 " 20pf slate green & bluish gray 25 17
9N258 " 30pf brn. & olive 30 27
9N259 " 50pf blk. & gray 60 65
9N260 " 1m blk. & chalky blue 1.20 1.20

Size: 22x40mm.

9N261 OS55 1.10m brn. & buff 1.35 1.35
Nos. 9N256–9N261 (6) 3.82 3.74

Issued to publicize Berlin art treasures.

Berlin Radio Tower and Television Screens
OS56

Lithographed and Engraved

1967, July 19 *Perf. 14* Unwmkd.

9N262 OS56 30pf multi. 30 35

Issued to publicize the 25th German Radio, Television and Phonograph Exhibition, Berlin, Aug. 25–Sept. 3.

Lübke Type of Germany, 1964,

1967, Oct. 14 Lithographed

9N263 A247 30pf carmine 30 25
9N264 " 50pf ultramarine 55 55

Re-election of Pres. Heinrich Lübke.

Old Court Building (Berlin Museum)
OS57

Turners' Emblem
OS58

1968, Mar. 16 Engr. *Perf. 14*

9N265 OS57 30pf black 35 40

Issued to commemorate the 500th anniversary of the Berlin Court of Appeal.

1968, Apr. 29 Litho. *Perf. 14*

9N266 OS58 20pf gray, black & red 25 27

Issued to publicize the German Turner Festival, Berlin, May 28–June 3.

Newspaper Vendor by Christian Wilhelm Allers
OS59

19th Century Berliners: 5pf, Hack, by Heinrich Zille (horiz.). No. 9N269, Horse omnibus, coachman and passengers, 1890, by C. W. Allers. No. 9N270, Cobbler's apprentice, by Franz Kruger. No. 9N271, Cobbler, by Adolph von Menzel. No. 9N272, Blacksmiths, by Paul Meyerheim. No. 9N273, Three Ladies, by Franz Kruger. 50pf, Strollers at Brandenburg Gate, by Christian W. Allers.

1969 Engraved *Perf. 14*

9N267 OS59 5pf black 6 6
9N268 " 10pf deep brown 12 12
9N269 OS59 10pf brown 10 10
9N270 " 20pf dk. olive grn. 22 22
9N271 " 20pf green 22 22
9N272 " 30pf dk. red brown 40 40
9N273 " 30pf red brown 30 30
9N274 " 50pf ultramarine 1.00 1.00
Nos. 9N267–9N274 (8) 2.42 2.42

Souvenir Sheet

Berlin Zoo Animals—OS60

Designs: 10pf, Orangutan family. 20pf, White pelicans. 30pf, Gaur and calf. 50pf, Zebra and foal.

Engraved and Lithographed

1969, June 4 *Perf. 14*

9N275 OS60 Sheet of 4 2.65 2.65
a. 10pf bis. & blk. 20 20
b. 20pf lt. green & black 40 40
c. 30pf lilac rose & black 55 55
d. 50pf blue & blk. 90 90

Issued to commemorate the 125th anniversary of the Berlin Zoo. The sheet was sold with a 20pf surtax for the benefit of the Zoo.

Australian Postman—OS61

Joseph Joachim
OS62

Designs: 20pf, African telephone operator. 30pf, Middle East telecommunications engineer. 50pf, Loading mail on plane.

1969, July 21 Litho. *Perf. 14*

9N276 OS61 10pf olive & apple grn. 10 8
9N277 " 20pf dark brown, bister & brown 22 22
9N278 " 30pf violet black & bister 30 30
9N279 " 50pf dk. bl. & bl. 60 60

Issued to commemorate the 20th Congress of the Post Office Trade Union Federation, Berlin, July 7–11.

1969, Sept. 12 Photo. *Perf. 14*

Design: 50pf, Alexander von Humboldt, painting by Joseph Stieler.

9N280 OS62 30pf multicolored 40 40
9N281 " 50pf multicolored 60 60

Issued (30pf) to commemorate the centenary of the Berlin Music School and to honor its first director Joseph Joachim (1831–1907), violinist, conductor and composer; (50pf), bicentenary of the birth of Alexander von Humboldt (1769–1859), naturalist and explorer.

1970, Jan. 7

Design: 20pf, Theodor Fontane, painting by Hanns Fechner.

9N282 OS62 20pf multicolored 30 30

Issued to commemorate the 150th anniversary of the birth of Theodor Fontane (1819–1898), poet and writer.

See also No. 9N303.

Film Frame
OS63

Symbols of Dance, Theater and Art—OS64

1970, June 18 Photo. *Perf. 14*

9N283 OS63 30pf multicolored 40 40

20th International Film Festival.

President Heinemann Type of Germany Inscribed "Berlin"

1970–73 Engraved *Perf. 14*

9N284 A312 5pf dark gray 5 5
9N285 " 8pf olive bister ('71) 1.20 1.20
9N286 " 10pf brown 10 5
9N286A " 15pf olive ('72) 17 10
9N287 " 20pf green 17 5
9N288 " 25pf dp. yellow grn. ('71) 1.10 1.00
9N289 " 30pf red brn. ('71) 28 9
9N290 " 40pf brn. org. ('71) 40 20
9N291 " 50pf dk. blue ('71) 50 15
9N292 " 60pf blue ('71) 60 30
9N293 " 70pf dk. brn. ('71) 70 35
9N294 " 80pf slate grn. ('71) 80 40
9N295 " 90pf magenta ('71) 1.50 1.00
9N296 " 1m olive 1.00 28
9N296A " 1.10m olive gray ('73) 1.10 55
9N297 " 1.20m ocher ('72) 1.20 70
9N298 " 1.30m ocher ('72) 1.30 60
9N298A " 1.40m dk. bl. grn. ('73) 1.40 65
9N299 " 1.50m purple ('72) 1.50 70
9N300 " 1.60m orange ('72) 1.60 80
9N300A " 1.70m orange ('72) 1.70 75
9N300B " 1.90m dp. claret ('73) 1.90 90
9N301 " 2m dp. vio. ('71) 2.00 1.00
Nos. 9N284–9N301 (23) 22.27 11.87

1970, Sept. 4 Litho. *Perf. 13½x14*

9N302 OS64 30pf gray & multi. 40 40

20th Berlin Festival Weeks.

Portrait Type of 1969

Design: 30pf, Leopold von Ranke, by Julius Schrage.

1970, Oct. 23 Photo. *Perf. 13½x14*

9N303 OS62 30pf multi. 40 40

Issued to commemorate the 175th anniversary of the birth of Leopold von Ranke (1795–1886), historian.

Imperial Eagle Type of Germany

1971, Jan. 18 Litho. *Perf. 13½x14*

9N304 A317 30pf orange, red, gray & blk. 40 40

Centenary of the founding of the German Empire.

Metropolitan Train, 1932
OS65

Designs: 5pf, Suburban train, 1925. 10pf, Street cars, 1890. 20pf, Horsedrawn trolley. 50pf, Street car, 1950. 1m, Subway train, 1971.

1971 Lithographed *Perf. 14*

9N305 OS65 5pf multi. 10 10
9N306 " 10pf " 17 17
9N307 " 20pf " 50 50
9N308 " 30pf " 60 60
9N309 " 50pf " 1.20 1.20
9N310 " 1m " 1.80 1.80
Nos. 9N305–9N310 (6) 4.37 4.37

Issue dates: 30pf, 1m, Jan. 18. Others, May 3.

Bagpipe Player, by Dürer
OS66

1971, May 21 Engraved *Perf. 14*

9N311 OS66 10pf blk. & brown 18 18

500th anniversary of the birth of Albrecht Dürer (1471–1528), painter and engraver.

Score from 2nd Brandenburg Concerto and Bach—OS67

1971, July 14 Litho. *Perf. 14*

9N312 OS67 30pf buff, brown & slate 38 38

250th anniversary of first performance of Johann Sebastian Bach's 2nd Brandenburg Concerto.

Telecommunications Tower, Berlin
OS68

1971, July 14 Photogravure

9N313 OS68 30pf dk. blue, blk. & carmine 38 38

International Broadcasting Exhibition, Berlin.

Hermann von Helmholtz—OS69

1971, Aug. 27

9N314 OS69 25pf multicolored 35 35

Sesquicentennial of the birth of Hermann von Helmholtz (1821–1894), scientist. See Nos. 9N332–9N333, 9N341.

Souvenir Sheet

Racing Cars—OS70

1971, Aug. 27 Litho. *Perf. 14*

9N315 OS70 Sheet of 4, multicolored 1.90 1.90
a. 10pf *Opel racer* 9 9
b. 25pf *Auto Union racer* 25 25
c. 30pf *Mercedes-Benz SSKL, 1931* 30 30
d. 60pf *Mercedes and Auto Union cars racing on North embankment* 60 60

50th anniversary of Avus Race Track. No. 9N315 has blue marginal inscription. Size: 98x74mm.

Accident Prevention Type of Germany

Designs: 5pf, "Matches cause fires." 10pf, Broken ladder. 20pf, Hand and circular saw. 25pf, "Alcohol and automobile." 30pf, Safety helmets prevent injury. 40pf, Defective plug. 50pf, Nail sticking from board. 60pf, 70pf, Traffic safety (ball rolling before car). 100pf, Hoisted cargo. 150pf, Fenced-in open manhole.

1971-73 Typographed Perf. 14

9N316 A328 5pf orange 50 25
9N317 " 10pf dk. brown ('72) 10 5
a. Bklt. pane of 8 (2 each #9N317-9N318, 9N320-9N321) ('74) 5.50
9N318 A328 20pf purple ('72) 20 9
9N319 " 25pf green 25 10
9N320 " 30pf dk. red ('72) 30 5
9N321 " 40pf rose claret ('72) 40 12
9N322 " 50pf Prus. bl. ('73) 50 25
9N323 " 60pf violet blue 2.25 1.00
9N323A " 70pf green & violet blue ('73) 70 50
9N324 " 100pf olive ('72) 1.00 40
9N325 " 150pf red brn. ('72) 1.50 85
Nos. 9N316-9N325 (11) 7.70 3.66

Accident prevention.

Issued in sheets of 100 and coils. Every fifth coil stamp has a control number on the back.

Microscope and Metal Slide
OS71

Friedrich Gilly, by Gottfried Schadow
OS72

1971, Oct. 26 Photo. Perf. 14

9N326 OS71 30pf multi. 40 40

Materials Testing Laboratory centenary.

1972, Feb. 4 Engraved Perf. 14

9N327 OS72 30pf black & blue 40 40

Bicentenary of the birth of Friedrich Gilly (1772-1800), sculptor.

Grunewaldsee, by Alexander von Riesen
OS73

Paintings of Berlin Lakes: 25pf, Wannsee, by Max Liebermann. 30pf, Schlachtensee, by Walter Leistikow.

1972, Apr. 14 Photo. Perf. 14

9N328 OS73 10pf blue & multi. 15 15
9N329 " 25pf grn. & multi. 40 35
9N330 " 30pf blk. & multi. 55 55

E. T. A. Hoffmann
OS74

Stamp-Printing Press
OS75

1972, May 18

9N331 OS74 60pf vio. & blk. 75 75

Sesquicentennial of the death of E. T. A. Hoffmann (1776-1822), writer and composer. (Portrait by Wilhelm Hensel.)

Portrait Type of 1971

Designs: No. 9N332, Max Liebermann, self-portrait. No. 9N333, Duke of Hardenberg, by J. H. W. Tischbein.

1972 Photo. Perf. 14

9N332 OS69 40pf multi. 50 50
9N333 " 40pf " 45 45

125th anniversary of the birth of Max Liebermann (1847-1935), painter (9N332).

Sesquicentennial of the death of Karl August, Duke of Hardenberg (1750-1822), Prussian statesman (9N333).

Issue dates: No. 9N332, July 18; No. 9N333, Nov. 10.

1972, Oct. 20 Engr. & Litho.

9N334 OS75 20pf dk. red, blk. & lt. blue 25 25

Stamp Day 1972, and for the 5th National Youth Philatelic Exhibition, Berlin, Oct. 26-29.

Streetcar, 1907
OS76

Designs: No. 9N336, Double-decker bus, 1919. No. 9N337, Double-decker bus, 1925. No. 9N338, Electrobus, 1933. No. 9N339, Double-decker bus, 1970. No. 9N340, Elongated bus, 1973.

1973, Apr. 30 Litho. Perf. 14

9N335 OS76 20pf gray & multi. 35 35
9N336 " 30pf " " 55 55
9N337 " 40pf " " 75 75

1973, Sept. 14

9N338 OS76 20pf gray & multi. 35 35
9N339 " 30pf " " 55 55
9N340 " 40pf " " 75 75
Nos. 9N335-9N340 (6) 3.30 3.30

Public transportation in Berlin.

Portrait Type of 1971

Design: 40pf, Ludwig Tieck, by Carl Christian Vogel von Vogelstein.

1973, May 25 Photo. Perf. 14

9N341 OS69 40pf multicolored 55 55

Bicentenary of the birth of Ludwig Tieck (1773-1853), poet and writer.

Johann J. Quantz
OS77

1973, June 12 Engr. Perf. 14

9N342 OS77 40pf black 45 45

Bicentenary of the death of Johann Joachim Quantz (1697-1773), flutist and composer.

Souvenir Sheet

50 Years of Broadcasting—OS78

1973, Aug. 23 Litho. Perf. 14

9N343 OS78 Sheet of 4, multicolored 4.85 4.85
a. 20pf *Speaker, set, 1926* 55 55
b. 30pf *Hans Bredow* 80 80
c. 40pf *Girl, TV, tape recorder* 1.10 1.10
d. 70pf *TV camera* 1.90 1.90

50 years of German broadcasting. No. 9N343 has light gray margin with gray inscription and drawings of VOX House and General Post Office. Size: 148x105mm. Sold for 1.80m.

Georg W. von Knobelsdorff
OS79

Gustav R. Kirchhoff
OS80

1974, Feb. 15 Engraved Perf. 14

9N344 OS79 20pf chocolate 25 25

275th anniversary of the birth of Georg Wenzelslaus von Knobelsdorff (1699-1753), architect.

1974, Feb. 15 Litho. & Engr.

9N345 OS80 30pf gray & dark green 38 38

Sesquicentennial of the birth of Gustav Robert Kirchhoff (1824-1887), physicist.

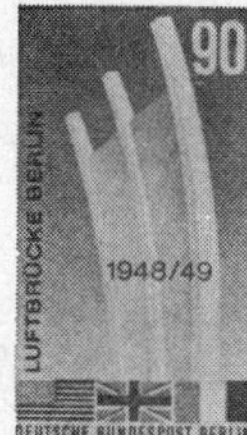

Airlift Memorial, Allied Flags
OS81

Adolf Slaby and Waves
OS82

1974, Apr. 17 Photogravure Perf. 14

9N346 OS81 90pf multi. 1.10 1.10

25th anniversary of the end of the Allied airlift into Berlin.

1974, Apr. 17 Lithographed Perf. 14

9N347 OS82 40pf blk. & red 45 45

125th anniversary of the birth of Adolf Slaby (1849-1913), radio pioneer.

School Seal Showing Athena and Hermes
OS83

1974, July 13 Photogravure Perf. 14

9N348 OS83 50pf multicolored 50 50

400th anniversary of the Gray Brothers' School, a secondary Franciscan school.

Berlin-Tegel Airport
OS84

Lithographed and Engraved

1974, Oct. 15 Perf. 14

9N349 OS84 50pf multicolored 50 50

Opening of Berlin-Tegel Airport and Terminal, Nov. 1, 1974.

Venus, by F. E. Meyer, c. 1775
OS85

Gottfried Schadow
OS86

Berlin Porcelain: 40pf, "Astronomy," by W. C. Meyer, c. 1772. 50pf, "Justice," by J. G. Müller, c. 1785.

1974, Oct. 29 Litho. Perf. 14

9N350 OS85 30pf car. & multi. 45 45
9N351 " 40pf " " 55 55
9N352 " 50pf " " 75 75

1975, Jan. 15 Engraved Perf. 14

9N353 OS86 50pf maroon 50 50

Johann Gottfried Schadow (1764-1850), sculptor.

S.S. Princess Charlotte—OS87

Ships: 40pf, S.S. Siegfried. 50pf, S.S. Sperber. 60pf, M.S. Vaterland. 70pf, M.S. Moby Dick.

1975, Feb. 14 Litho. Perf. 14

9N354 OS87 30pf gray & multi. 65 55
9N355 " 40pf olive & multi. 80 70
9N356 " 50pf ultra. & multi. 80 80
9N357 " 60pf red brown & multi. 1.00 1.00
9N358 " 70pf dk. blue & multi. 1.10 1.10
Nos. 9N354-9N358 (5) 4.35 4.15

Berlin passenger ships.

Industry and Technology Type of 1975

Designs: 5pf, Symphonie communications satellite. 10pf, Local electric train. 20pf, Old Weser Lighthouse. 30pf, Rescue helicopter. 40pf, Space. 50pf, Radar station. 60pf, X-ray machine. 70pf, Shipbuilding. 80pf, Tractor. 100pf, Bituminous coal excavator. 120pf, Chemical plant, Ludwigshafen. 140pf, Heating plant, Lichterfelde. 160pf, Blast furnace, Rheinhausen. 200pf, Oil drilling platform. 230pf, Frankfurt Airport. 500pf, Effelsberg radio telescope.

1975-79 Engraved Perf. 14

9N359 A380 5pf olive 5 5
9N360 " 10pf rose lilac 10 5
9N361 " 20pf red orange ('76) 20 10
9N362 " 30pf violet 30 15
9N363 " 40pf bluish grn. 40 20
9N364 " 50pf car. rose 50 20
9N365 " 60pf red ('78) 60 15
9N366 " 70pf blue 70 35
9N367 " 80pf slate green 80 40
9N368 " 100pf bis. brown 1.00 45
9N369 " 120pf dk. vio. bl. 1.20 60
9N370 " 140pf dk. car. 1.40 80
9N371 " 160pf green 1.60 80
9N372 " 200pf dull pur. 2.00 90
9N373 " 230pf pur. ('79) 2.30 1.00
9N374 " 500pf slate ('76) 5.00 4.25
Nos. 9N359-9N374 (16) 18.15 10.45

Ferdinand Sauerbruch
OS88

Gymnasts' Emblem
OS89

Lithographed and Engraved

1975, May 15 *Perf. 13½x14*

9N379 OS88 50pf dull red & dk. brn. 50 50

Ferdinand Sauerbruch (1875–1951) surgeon, birth centenary.

1975, May 15 Photo. *Perf. 14*

9N380 OS89 40pf grn., gold & black 50 50

6th Gymnaestrada, Berlin, July 1–5.

Lovis Corinth, Self-portrait, 1900
OS90

1975, July 15 Photo. *Perf. 14*

9N381 OS90 50pf multicolored 50 50

Lovis Corinth (1858–1925), painter and graphic artist, 50th death anniversary.

Architecture Type of 1975

Design: Houses, Naunynstrasse, Berlin-Kreuzberg.

1975, July 15 Litho. & Engr.

9N382 A381 50pf multicolored 50 50

European Architectural Heritage Year.

Paul Löbe and Reichstag
OS92

1975, Nov. 14 Engr. *Perf. 14*

9N383 OS92 50pf copper red 50 50

Paul Löbe (1875–1967), president of German Parliament 1920–1932, birth centenary.

Grain
OS93

1976, Jan. 5 Photo. *Perf. 14*

9N384 OS93 70pf grn. & yel. 75 75

Green Week International Agricultural Exhibition, Berlin, 50th anniversary.

Hockey
OS94

1976, May 13 Engr. *Perf. 14*

9N385 OS94 30pf green 35 35

Women's World Hockey Championships.

Treble Clef
OS95

Berlin Fire Brigade Emblem
OS96

1976, May 13 Photogravure

9N386 OS95 40pf multicolored 45 45

German Choir Festival.

1976, May 13 Lithographed

9N387 OS96 50pf red & multi. 55 55

Berlin Fire Brigade, 125th anniversary.

Sailboat on Havel River
OS97

Berlin Views: 40pf, Spandau Castle. 50pf, Tiergarten.

1976, Nov. 16 Engr. *Perf. 14*

9N388	OS97	30pf bl. & black	30	30
9N389	"	40pf brn. & blk.	40	40
9N390	"	50pf grn. & blk.	60	60

See Nos. 9N422–9N424.

Castle Type of Germany

1977–79 Typographed *Perf. 14*

Castles: 10pf, Glücksburg. 20pf, 190pf, Pfaueninsel. 25pf, Gemen. 30pf, Ludwigstein. 40pf, Eltz. 50pf, Neuschwanstein. 60pf, Marksburg. 70pf, Mespelbrunn. 90pf, Vischering. 200pf, Bürresheim. 210pf, Schwanenburg. 230pf, Lichtenberg.

9N391	A406	10pf gray blue	10	3
		a. Booklet pane of 8 (4 #9N391, 2 each #9N394, 9N396)	2 00	
9N392	A406	20pf orange	20	3
9N393	"	25pf crimson ('79)	25	3
9N394	"	30pf olive	30	3
9N395	"	40pf blue green	40	3
9N396	"	50pf rose car.	50	5
9N397	"	60pf brown	60	10
9N398	"	70pf blue	70	18
9N399	"	90pf dark blue ('79)	90	20
9N400	"	190pf red brn.	1.90	58
9N401	"	200pf green	2.00	60
9N402	"	210pf red brown ('79)	2.10	50
9N403	"	230pf dark green ('78)	2.30	60
		Nos. 9N391-9N403 (13)	12.25	2.96

Issued in sheets of 100 and coils. Every fifth coil stamp has a control number on the back.

Eugenie d'Alton, by Rausch
OS98

Eduard Gaertner
OS99

1977, Jan. 13 Photo. *Perf. 14*

9N404 OS98 50pf violet black 55 55

Christian Daniel Rausch (1777–1857), sculptor, birth bicentenary.

1977, Feb. 16 Litho. & Engr.

9N405 OS99 40pf lt. grn., grn. & black 45 45

Eduard Gaertner (1801–1877), painter.

Fountain, by Georg Kolbe
OS100

"Bear each other's burdens"
OS101

1977, Apr. 14 Photo. *Perf. 14*

9N406 OS100 30pf dark olive 30 30

Georg Kolbe (1877–1947), sculptor.

1977, May 17 Litho. *Perf. 14*

9N407 OS101 40pf green, blk. & yel. 45 45

17th meeting of German Protestants (Evangelical Synod), Berlin.

Patent Office, Berlin-Kreuzberg
OS102

Lithographed and Engraved

1977, July 13 *Perf. 14*

9N408 OS102 60pf gray & red 60 60

Centenary of German patent laws.

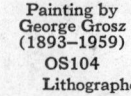

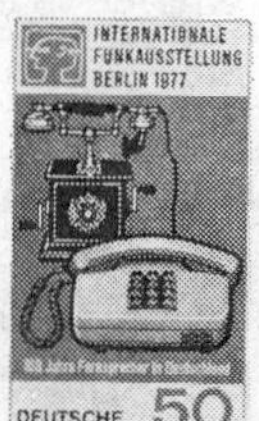
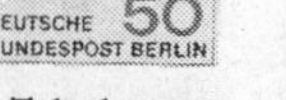
Telephones, 1905 and 1977
OS103

Painting by George Grosz (1893–1959)
OS104

1977, July 13 Lithographed

9N409 OS103 50pf multicolored 55 55

International Broadcasting Exhibition, Berlin, Aug. 26–Sept. 4, and centenary of telephone in Germany.

1977, July 13

9N410 OS104 70pf multicolored 70 70

15th European Art Exhibition, Berlin, Aug. 14–Oct. 16.

Rhinecanthus Aculeatus—OS105

Designs: 30pf, Paddlefish. 40pf, Tortoise. 50pf, Rhinoceros iguana. Designs include statue of iguanodon from Aquarium entrance.

1977, Aug. 16 Photo. *Perf. 14*

9N411	OS105	20pf multi.	20	20
9N412	"	30pf "	30	30
9N413	"	40pf "	45	45
9N414	"	50pf "	55	55

25th anniversary of the reopening of Berlin Aquarium.

Walter Kollo
OS106

1978, Jan. 12 Engr. *Perf. 14*

9N415 OS106 50pf brn., red & dk. brn. 50 25

Walter Kollo (1878–1940), composer.

Chamber of Commerce Emblem
OS107

1978, Apr. 13 Engr. *Perf. 14*

9N416 OS107 90pf dark blue & red 90 45

American Chamber of Commerce in Germany, 75th anniversary.

Albrecht von Graefe
OS108

Friedrich Ludwig Jahn
OS109

1978, May 22 Engr. *Perf. 14*

9N417 OS108 30pf red brown & black 30 15

Dr. Albrecht von Graefe (1828–1870) ophthalmologist.

1978, July 13 Engr. *Perf. 14*

9N418 OS109 50pf dk. car. 50 25

Friedrich Ludwig Jahn (1778–1852), founder of organized gymnastics.

Swimmers
OS110

1978, Aug. 17 Litho. *Perf. 14*

9N419	OS110	40pf multi.	40	20

3rd World Swimming Championships, Berlin, Aug. 18–28.

The Boat, by Karl Hofer—OS111

1978, Oct. 12 Photo. *Perf. 14*

9N420	OS111	50pf multi.	50	25

Karl Hofer (1878–1955), painter.

National Library OS112

1978, Nov. 16 Engr. *Perf. 14*

9N421	OS112	90pf red & olive	90	22

Opening of new National Library building.

Views Type of 1976

Berlin Views: 40pf, Belvedere, Charlottenburg Castle. 50pf, Shell House on Landwehr Canal. 60pf, Village Church, Alt-Lichtenrade.

1978, Nov. 16

9N422	OS97	40pf grn. & blk.	40	35
9N423	"	50pf lilac & blk.	50	45
9N424	"	60pf brn. & blk.	60	55

International Conference Center OS113

Photogravure and Engraved

1979, Feb. 14 *Perf. 14*

9N425	OS113	60pf multi.	60	55

Opening of International Conference Center in Berlin.

Prussian and German Eagles OS114

1979, May 17 Litho. *Perf. 14*

9N426	OS114	60pf multi.	60	55

Centenary of German National Printing Bureau.

OCCUPATION SEMI-POSTAL STAMPS.

Offering Plate and Berlin Bear
OSP1

Lithographed.

1949, Dec. 1 *Perf. 14* **Wmk. 284**

9NB1 OSP1 10(pf)+5(pf) green 72.50 160.00
9NB2 " 20(pf)+5(pf) carmine 72.50 160.00
9NB3 " 30(pf)+5(pf) blue 72.50 160.00
a. Souvenir sheet 700.00 2200.00

The surtax was for Berlin victims of currency devaluation.
No. 9NB3a contains one each of Nos. 9NB1 to 9NB3, with marginal inscriptions in carmine. Size: 110x66mm.

Harp and Laurel Branch
OSP2

"Singing Angels"
OSP3

1950, Oct. 29 Engr. **Wmk. 116**

9NB4 OSP2 10(pf)+5(pf) green 27.50 45.00
9NB5 OSP3 30(pf)+5(pf)dk. slate blue 55.00 82.50

The surtax was to aid in reestablishing the Berlin Philharmonic Orchestra.

Young Stamp Collectors
OSP4

Reconstructed Kaiser Wilhelm Memorial Church
OSP5

1951, Oct. 7 *Perf. 14*

9NB6 OSP4 10(pf)+3(pf) green 12.00 25.00
9NB7 " 20(pf)+2(pf) brown red 17.50 27.50

Stamp Day, Berlin, Oct. 7, 1951.

1953, Aug. 9 **Wmk. 284**

Design: 20(pf)+10(pf), 30(pf)+15(pf), Ruins of Kaiser Wilhelm Memorial Church.

9NB8 OSP5 4(pf)+1(pf) chocolate 21 38
9NB9 " 10(pf)+5(pf) green 1.75 3.50
9NB10 " 20(pf)+10(pf) carmine 85 1.30
9NB11 " 30(pf)+15(pf) deep blue 22.50 45.00

The surtax was to aid in reconstructing the church.

Prussian Postilion
OSP6

1954, Aug. 4 Litho. **Wmk. 284**

9NB12 OSP6 20(pf)+10(pf) multi. 11.50 23.00

National Stamp Exhibition, Berlin, Aug. 4–8.

Prussian Field Postilion
OSP7

Perf. 13½x14

1955, Oct. 27 **Wmk. 304**

9NB13 OSP7 25(pf)+10(pf) multicolored 5.00 9.00

The surtax was for the benefit of philately.

St. Otto, Bishop of Bamberg
OSP8

Statues: 10(pf)+5(pf), St. Hedwig, Duchess of Silesia. 20(pf)+10(pf), St. Peter.

1955, Nov. 26 Engraved *Perf. 14*

9NB14 OSP8 7(pf)+3(pf) brown 55 1.10
9NB15 " 10(pf)+5(pf) gray green 42 80
9NB16 " 20(pf)+10(pf) rose lilac 70 1.35

Issued to commemorate the 25th anniversary of the Bishopric of Berlin.
The surtax was for the reconstruction of destroyed churches throughout the bishopric.

Bell Type of 1951 Surcharged

+10
Berlinhilfe
für die
Hochwassergeschädigten

DEUTSCHE BUNDESPOST·BERLIN

Perf. 13½x14

1956, Aug. 9 **Wmk. 284**

9NB17 OS8 20pf+10pf citron 1.40 2.75

The surtax was for help for flood victims.

Postrider of Brandenburg, 1700
OSP9

Ludwig Heck
OSP10

Perf. 14

1956, Oct. 26 Litho. **Wmk. 304**

9NB18 OSP9 25pf+10pf multi. 1.10 2.00

The surtax was for the benefit of philately.

1957, Sept. 7 Engr. *Perf. 13½x14*

9NB19 OSP10 20pf+10pf red & dark brown 25 50

Issued in honor of Dr. Ludwig Heck, zoologist and long-time director of the Berlin Zoo. The surtax was for the Zoo.

Elly Heuss-Knapp and Relaxing Mothers
OSP11

Boy at Window
OSP12

1957, Nov. 30 *Perf. 14*

9NB20 OSP11 20pf+10pf dark red 55 1.10

The surtax was for welfare work among mothers.

1960, Sept. 15 Litho. **Wmk. 304**

Designs: 10pf+5pf, Girl going to school. 20pf+10pf, Girl with flower and mountains. 40pf+20pf, Girls at seashore.

9NB21 OSP12 7pf+3pf dark brown & brown 20 22
9NB22 " 10pf+5pf olive green & slate green 15 22
9NB23 " 20pf+10pf dark carmine & brown black 28 30
9NB24 " 40pf+20pf blue & indigo 90 1.60

The surtax was for vacations for the children of Berlin.

Fluorescent Paper

was introduced for semipostal stamps, starting with Nos. 9NB25–9NB28.

Fairy Tale Type of 1960

Various Scenes from Sleeping Beauty

1964, Oct. 6 *Perf. 14* **Unwmkd.**

9NB25 SP285 10pf+5pf multi. 17 20
9NB26 " 15pf+5pf " 17 17
9NB27 " 20pf+10pf " 33 17
9NB28 " 40pf+20pf " 80 1.40

The surtax was for independent welfare organizations.

Beginning with 9NB25–9NB28 semipostals are types of Germany inscribed "Berlin" unless otherwise noted.

Bird Type of 1965

Birds: 10pf+5pf, Woodcock. 15pf+5pf, Ring-necked pheasant. 20pf+10pf, Black grouse. 40pf+20pf, Capercaillie.

1965, Apr. 1 Litho. *Perf. 14*

9NB29 SP289 10pf+5pf multi. 15 20
9NB30 " 15pf+5pf " 20 25
9NB31 " 20pf+10pf " 28 33
9NB32 " 40pf+20pf " 75 90

Issued for the benefit of young people.

Fairy Tale Type of 1965

Various Scenes from Cinderella

1965, Oct. 6 Litho. *Perf. 14*

9NB33 SP290 10pf+5pf multi. 20 22
9NB34 " 15pf+5pf " 17 17
9NB35 " 20pf+10pf " 30 22
9NB36 " 40pf+20pf " 90 1.25

The surtax was for independent welfare organizations.

Animal Type of 1966

Designs: 10pf+5pf, Roe deer. 20pf+10pf, Chamois. 30pf+15pf, Fallow deer. 50pf+25pf, Red deer.

1966, Apr. 22 Litho. *Perf. 14*

9NB37 SP291 10pf+5pf multi. 15 25
9NB38 " 20pf+10pf " 25 30
9NB39 " 30pf+15pf " 40 45
9NB40 " 50pf+25pf " 1.00 1.50

Issued for the benefit of young people.

Fairy Tale Type of 1965

Various Scenes from The Princess and the Frog.

1966, Oct. 5 Litho. *Perf. 14*

9NB41 SP290 10pf+5pf multi. 22 20
9NB42 " 20pf+10pf " 25 25
9NB43 " 30pf+15pf " 40 40
9NB44 " 50pf+25pf " 1.10 1.50

The surtax was for independent welfare organizations.

Animal Type of 1966

Designs: 10pf+5pf, Rabbit. 20pf+10pf, Ermine. 30pf+15pf, Hamster. 50pf+25pf, Red fox.

1967, Apr. 4 **Unwmkd.**

9NB45 SP291 10pf+5pf multi. 20 25
9NB46 " 20pf+10pf " 35 32
9NB47 " 30pf+15pf " 50 50
9NB48 " 50pf+25pf " 1.35 1.75

Issued for the benefit of young people.

Fairy Tale Type of 1965

Various Scenes from Frau Holle.

1967, Oct. 3 Litho. *Perf. 14*

9NB49 SP290 10pf+5pf multi. 30 38
9NB50 " 20pf+10pf " 30 25
9NB51 " 30pf+15pf " 45 35
9NB52 " 50pf+25pf " 1.10 1.50

The surtax was for independent welfare organizations.

Animal Type of 1968

Animals: 10pf+5pf, Wildcat. 20pf+10pf, Otter. 30pf+15pf, Badger. 50pf+25pf, Beaver.

1968, Feb. 2 Photo. *Perf. 14*

9NB53 SP293 10pf+5pf multi. 35 40
9NB54 " 20pf+10pf " 50 55
9NB55 " 30pf+15pf " 75 85
9NB56 " 50pf+25pf " 2.10 2.65

Surtax for benefit of young people.

Doll Type of 1968

Designs: Various 19th century dolls in sitting position (same dolls as on Germany B438–B441).

1968, Oct. 3 Lithographed *Perf. 14*

9NB57 SP294 10pf+5pf multi. 25 38
9NB58 " 20pf+10pf " 30 22
9NB59 " 30pf+15pf " 45 35
9NB60 " 50pf+25pf " 1.10 1.50

The surtax was for independent welfare organizations.

Horse Type of 1969

Horses: 10pf+5pf, Pony. 20pf+10pf, Work horse. 30pf+15pf, Hotblood. 50pf+25pf, Thoroughbred.

1969, Feb. 6 Litho. *Perf. 14*

9NB61 SP295 10pf+5pf multi. 38 38
9NB62 " 20pf+10pf " 50 50
9NB63 " 30pf+15pf " 75 75
9NB64 " 50pf+25pf " 2.00 2.00

Surtax for benefit of young people.

Tin Toy Type of 1969

Tin Toys: 10pf+5pf, Coach. 20pf+10pf, Woman feeding chickens. 30pf+15pf, Woman grocer. 50pf+25pf, Postilion on horseback.

1969, Oct. 2 Litho. *Perf. 13½x14*

9NB65 SP297 10pf+5pf multi. 15 15
9NB66 " 20pf+10pf " 30 30
9NB67 " 30pf+15pf " 50 50
9NB68 " 50pf+25pf " 1.10 1.10

The surtax was for independent welfare organizations.

1969, Nov. 13 Litho. *Perf. 13½x14*

Design: 10pf+5pf, The Three Kings.

9NB69 SP297 10pf+5pf multi. 25 25

Christmas 1969.

Minnesinger Type of 1970

Minnesingers (and their Ladies): 10pf+5pf, Heinrich von Stretlingen. 20pf+10pf, Meinloh von Sevelingen. 30pf+15pf, Burkhart von Hohenfels. 50pf+25pf, Albrecht von Johansdorf.

1970, Feb. 5 Photo. *Perf. 13½x14*

9NB70 SP298 10pf+5pf multi. 28 28
9NB71 " 20pf+10pf " 55 55

9NB72 SP298 30pf+15pf multi. 75 75
9NB73 " 50pf+25pf " 1.65 1.65

Surtax for benefit of young people.

Puppet Type of 1970

Puppets: 10pf+5pf, "Kasperl." 20pf+10pf, Polichinelle. 30pf+5pf, Punch. 50pf+25pf, Pulcinella.

1970, Oct. 6 Litho. *Perf. 13½x14*

9NB74 SP300 10pf+5pf multi. 15 15
9NB75 " 20pf+10pf " 30 35
9NB76 " 30pf+15pf " 45 45
9NB77 " 50pf+25pf " 1.10 1.10

The surtax was for independent welfare organizations.

1970, Nov. 12

Design: 10pf+5pf, Rococo angel, from Ursuline Sisters' Convent, Innsbruck.

9NB78 SP300 10pf+5pf multi. 25 25

Christmas 1970.

Drawings Type of 1971

Children's Drawings: 10pf+5pf, Fly. 20pf+10pf, Fish. 30pf+15pf, Porcupine. 50pf+25pf, Cock. All stamps horizontal.

1971, Feb. 5 Lithographed *Perf. 14*

9NB79 SP301 10pf+5pf multi. 17 17
9NB80 " 20pf+10pf " 35 35
9NB81 " 30pf+15pf " 60 60
9NB82 " 50pf+25pf " 1.35 1.35

Surtax for the benefit of young people.

Wooden Toy Type of 1971

Wooden Toys: 10pf+5pf, Movable dolls in box. 25pf+10pf, Knight on horseback. 30pf+15pf, Jumping jack. 60pf+30pf, Nurse rocking babies.

1971, Oct. 5

9NB83 SP303 10pf+5pf multi. 15 15
9NB84 " 25pf+10pf " 30 30
9NB85 " 30pf+15pf " 45 45
9NB86 " 60pf+30pf " 1.10 1.10

1971, Nov. 11

Design: 10pf+5pf, Christmas angel with candles.

9NB87 SP303 10pf+5pf multi. 20 20

Christmas 1971.

Animal Protection Type of 1972

Designs: 10pf+5pf, Boy trying to rob bird's nest. 25pf+10pf, Girl with kittens to be drowned. 30pf+15pf, Watch dog and man with whip. 60pf+30pf, Hedgehog and deer passing before car at night.

1972, Feb. 4

9NB88 SP304 10pf+5pf multi. 35 35
9NB89 " 25pf+10pf " 50 50
9NB90 " 30pf+15pf " 1.00 1.00
9NB91 " 60pf+30pf " 2.60 2.60

Animal protection. Surtax for the benefit of young people.

Chess Type of 1972

1972, Oct. 5 Litho. *Perf. 14*

Multicolored

9NB92 SP307 20pf+10pf *Knight* 30 30
9NB93 " 30pf+15pf *Rook* 45 45
9NB94 " 40pf+20pf *Queen* 60 60
9NB95 " 70pf+35pf *King* 1.15 1.15

19th century chess pieces made by Faience Works, Gien, France; now in Hamburg Museum. The surtax was for independent welfare organizations.

Christmas Type of 1972

Design: 20pf+10pf, Holy Family.

1972, Nov. 10 Litho. *Perf. 14*

9NB96 SP308 20pf+10pf multi. 35 35

Bird Type of 1973

Birds of Prey: 20pf+10pf, Goshawk. 30pf+15pf, Peregrine falcon. 40pf+20pf, Sparrow hawk. 70pf+35pf, Golden eagle.

1973, Feb. 6 Photogravure *Perf. 14*

9NB97 SP309 20pf+10pf multi. 60 60
9NB98 " 30pf+15pf " 75 75
9NB99 " 40pf+20pf " 1.30 1.30
9NB100 " 70pf+35pf " 2.15 2.15

Surtax was for benefit of young people.

Instrument Type of 1973

Musical Instruments: 20pf+10pf, Hurdy-gurdy, 17th century. 30pf+15pf, Drum, 16th century. 40pf+20pf, Archlute, 18th century. 70pf+35pf, Organ, 16th century.

1973, Oct. 5 Litho. *Perf. 14*

9NB101 SP311 20pf+10pf multi. 32 32
9NB102 " 30pf+15pf " 50 50
9NB103 " 40pf+20pf " 65 65
9NB104 " 70pf+35pf " 1.10 1.10

Surtax was for independent welfare organizations.

Star Type of 1973

Design: 20pf+10pf, Christmas star.

1973, Nov. 9 Litho. & Engr.

9NB105 SP312 20pf+10pf multi. 35 35

Christmas 1973.

Youth Type of 1974

Designs: 20pf+10pf, Boy photographing. 30pf+15pf, Boy athlete. 40pf+20pf, Girl violinist. 70pf+35pf, Nurse's aid.

1974, Apr. 17 Photogravure *Perf. 14*

9NB106 SP313 20pf+10pf multi. 55 55
9NB107 " 30pf+15pf " 75 75
9NB108 " 40pf+20pf " 90 90
9NB109 " 70pf+35pf " 1.80 1.80

Surtax was for benefit of young people.

Flower Type of 1974

Designs: 30pf+15pf, Spring bouquet. 40pf+20pf, Autumn bouquet. 50pf+25pf, Roses. 70pf+35pf, Winter flowers. All horizontal.

1974, Oct. 15 Lithographed *Perf. 14*

9NB110 SP314 30pf+15pf multi. 45 45
9NB111 " 40pf+20pf " 60 60
9NB112 " 50pf+25pf " 75 75
9NB113 " 70pf+35pf " 1.10 1.10

Surtax was for independent welfare organizations.

1974, Oct. 29

Design: 30pf+15pf, Christmas bouquet (horiz.).

9NB114 SP314 30pf+15pf multi. 50 50

Christmas 1974.

Locomotive Type of 1975

Steam Locomotives: 30pf+15pf, Dragon. 40pf+20pf, Class 89 (70–75). 50pf+25pf, Class O50. 70pf+35pf, Class O10.

1975, Apr. 15 Litho. *Perf. 14*

9NB115 SP315 30pf+15pf multi. 50 50
9NB116 " 40pf+20pf " 65 65
9NB117 " 50pf+25pf " 95 95
9NB118 " 70pf+35pf " 1.50 1.50

Surtax was for benefit of young people.

Flower Type of 1975.

Alpine Flowers: 30pf+15pf, Yellow gentian. 40pf+20pf, Arnica. 50pf+25pf, Cyclamen. 70pf+35pf, Blue gentian.

1975, Oct. 15 Litho. *Perf. 14*

9NB119 SP316 30pf+15pf multi. 45 45
9NB120 " 40pf+20pf " 60 65
9NB121 " 50pf+25pf " 75 75
9NB122 " 70pf+35pf " 1.10 1.10

Surtax was for independent welfare organizations.

1975, Nov. 14

Design: 30pf+15pf, Snow heather.

9NB123 SP316 30pf+15pf multi. 45 45

Christmas 1975.

Sports Type of 1976

Designs: 30pf+15pf, Shot put, women's. 40pf+20pf, Hockey. 50pf+25pf, Handball. 70pf+35pf, Swimming.

1976, Apr. 6 Litho. *Perf. 14*

9NB124 SP317 30pf+15pf multi. 50 50
9NB125 " 40pf+20pf " 65 65
9NB126 " 50pf+25pf " 85 85
9NB127 " 70pf+35pf " 1.25 1.25

Youth training for Olympic Games. The surtax was for the benefit of young people.

Iris
OSP13

Flowers: 40pf+20pf, Wallflower. 50pf+25pf, Dahlia. 70pf+35pf, Larkspur.

1976, Oct. 14 Litho. *Perf. 14*

Multicolored

9NB128 OSP13 30pf+15pf 45 45
9NB129 " 40pf+20pf 60 60
9NB130 " 50pf+25pf 75 75
9NB131 " 70pf+35pf 1.10 1.10

Surtax was for independent welfare organizations.

Souvenir Sheet

Christmas Type of 1976

Design: 30pf+15pf, Annunciation to the Shepherds, stained-glass window, Frauenkirche, Esslingen.

1976, Nov. 16 Litho. & Engr.

9NB132 SP320 30pf+15pf multi. 55 55

Christmas 1976. No. 9NB132 has multicolored margin and inscription. Size: 70x100mm.

Ship Type of 1977

Historic Ships: 30pf+15pf, Bremer Kogge, c. 1380. 40pf+20pf, Helena Sloman, 1850. 50pf+25pf, Passenger ship, Cap Polonio, 1914. 70pf+35pf, Freighter Widar, 1971.

1977, Apr. 14 Litho. *Perf. 14*

Multicolored

9NB133 SP321 30pf+15pf 45 45
9NB134 " 40pf+20pf 60 60
9NB135 " 50pf+25pf 75 75
9NB136 " 70pf+35pf 1.10 1.10

Surtax was for benefit of young people.

Flower Type of 1977

Meadow Flowers: 30pf+15pf, Daisy. 40pf+20pf, Cowslip. 50pf+25pf, Sainfoin. 70pf+35pf, Forget-me-not.

1977, Oct. 13 Litho. *Perf. 14*

Multicolored

9NB137 SP322 30pf+15pf 45 45
9NB138 " 40pf+20pf 60 60
9NB139 " 50pf+25pf 75 75
9NB140 " 70pf+35pf 1.10 1.10

Surtax was for independent welfare organizations.

See Nos. 9NB148–9NB151.

Souvenir Sheet

Christmas Type of 1977

Design: 30pf+15pf, Virgin and Child, stained-glass window, Sacristy of St. Gereon Basilica, Cologne.

1977, Nov. 10

9NB141 SP323 30pf+15pf multi. 50 50

Christmas 1977. No. 9NB141 has gray margin and inscription. Size: 70x104mm.

Aviation Type of 1978

Designs: 30pf+15pf, Montgolfier balloon, 1783. 40pf+20pf, Lilienthal's glider, 1891. 50pf+25pf, Wright brothers' plane, 1909. 70pf+35pf, Etrich/Rumpler Taube, 1910.

1978, Apr. 13 Litho. *Perf. 14*

Multicolored

9NB142 SP325 30pf+15pf 45 45
9NB143 " 40pf+20pf 60 60
9NB144 " 50pf+25pf 75 75
9NB145 " 70pf+35pf 1.05 1.05

Surtax was for benefit of young people.

Sports Type of 1978

Designs: 50pf+25pf, Bicycling. 70pf+35pf, Fencing.

1978, Apr. 13 Litho. *Perf. 14*

Multicolored

9NB146 SP324 50pf+25pf 75 75
9NB147 " 70pf+35pf 1.05 1.05

Surtax was for German Sports Foundation.

Flower Type of 1977

Woodland Flowers: 30pf+15pf, Solomon's-seal. 40pf+20pf, Wood primrose. 50pf+25pf, Cephalanthera rubra (orchid). 70pf+35pf, Bugle.

1978, Oct. 12 Litho. *Perf. 14*

Multicolored

9NB148 SP322 30pf+15pf 45 45
9NB149 " 40pf+20pf 60 60
9NB150 " 50pf+25pf 75 75
9NB151 " 70pf+35pf 1.05 1.05

Surtax was for independent welfare organizations.

Souvenir Sheet

Christmas Type of 1978

Design: 30pf+15pf, Adoration of the Kings, stained glass window, Frauenkirche, Munich.

1978, Nov. 16 Litho. *Perf. 14*

9NB152 SP326 30pf+15pf multi. 45 45

Christmas 1978. No. 9NB152 has multicolored margin and inscription. Size: 65x93mm

Aviation Type of 1979

Airplanes: 40+20pf, Vampyr, 1921. 50+25pf, Junkers JU52/3M, 1932. 60+30pf, Messerschmitt BF/ME 108, 1934. 90+45pf, Douglas DC3, 1935.

1979, Apr. 5 Litho. *Perf. 14*

Multicolored

9NB153 SP327 40pf+20pf 60 60
9NB154 " 50pf+25pf 75 75
9NB155 " 60pf+30pf 90 90
9NB156 " 90pf+45pf 1.35 1.35

Surtax was for benefit of young people.

Sports Type of 1979

Designs: 60+30pf, Runners. 90+45pf, Archers.

1979, Apr. 5

Multicolored

9NB157 SP328 60pf+30pf 90 90
9NB158 " 90pf+45pf 1.35 1.35

Surtax was for German Sports Foundation.

Issued Under Russian Occupation.

(For Use in All Provinces in the Russian Zone.)

When the mark was revalued in June, 1948, a provisional overprint, consisting of various city and town names and post office or zone numerals, was applied by hand in black, violet or blue at innumerable post offices to their stocks.

Germany Nos. 557 to 573 Overprinted in Black **Sowjetische Besatzungs Zone**

1948, July 3 *Perf. 14* Wmk. 284

10N1	A120	2pf brown black	6	9
10N2	"	6pf purple	6	9
10N3	A121	8pf red	6	9
10N4	"	10pf yellow green	6	9
10N5	A122	12pf gray	6	9
10N6	A120	15pf chocolate	6	15
10N7	A123	16pf dk. bl. green	6	15
10N8	A121	20pf blue	6	9
10N9	A123	24pf brown orange	6	9
10N10	A120	25pf orange yellow	6	20
10N11	A122	30pf red	12	15
10N12	A121	40pf red violet	12	15
10N13	A123	50pf ultramarine	20	25
10N14	A122	60pf red brown	27	12
		a. 60pf brown red	12.00	16.50
10N15	"	80pf dark blue	30	50
10N16	"	84pf emerald	30	50
		Nos. 10N1-10N16 (16)	1.91	2.80

Same Overprint on Numeral Stamps of Germany, 1946.

1948, Sept.

10N17	A119	5pf yellow green	6	7
10N18	"	30pf olive	20	55
10N19	"	45pf bright red	8	25
10N20	"	75pf deep ultra.	8	25
10N21	"	84pf emerald	20	25
		Nos. 10N17-10N21 (5)	62	1.37

Nos 10N1-10N21 all exist with inverted overprint, and majority with double overprint.

Bear from Berlin Arms

OS1

Design differs for each stamp.

All inscribed: "Stadt Berlin"

Overprint in Black.

Lithographed

1948, Sept. *Perf. 14* Unwmkd.

10N22	OS1	5(pf) green	6	10
		a. Serrate roulette	6	12
10N23	"	6pf violet	6	7
10N24	"	8(pf) red	6	10
10N25	"	10pf brown	6	10
10N26	"	12pf rose	15	33
10N27	"	20(pf) blue	10	22
10N28	"	30(pf) olive	10	28
		Nos. 10N22-10N28 (7)	59	1.20

The overprint made Nos. 10N22 to 10N28 valid for postage throughout the Russian Zone.

Käthe Kollwitz

OS2

Wmk. 292

Designs: 6pf, 40pf, Gerhard Hauptmann. 8pf, 50pf, Karl Marx. 10pf, 84pf, August Bebel. 12pf, 30pf, Friedrich Engels. 15pf, 60pf, G. W. F. Hegel. 16pf, 25pf, Rudolf Virchow. 20pf, Käthe Kollwitz. 24pf, 80pf, Ernst Thälmann.

Wmkd. Flowers, Multiple. (292)

1948 Typographed *Perf. 13x12½*

10N29	OS2	2(pf) gray	10	10
10N30	"	6(pf) violet	10	10
10N31	"	8(pf) red brown	18	15
10N32	"	10(pf) blue green	18	15
10N33	"	12(pf) blue	2.50	20
10N34	"	15(pf) brown	30	60
10N35	"	16(pf) turquoise	30	22
10N36	"	20(pf) maroon	30	38
10N37	"	24(pf) carmine	2.75	20
10N38	"	25(pf) olive green	45	75
10N39	"	30(pf) red	35	30
10N40	"	40(pf) red violet	45	35
10N41	"	50(pf) dark ultra.	45	22
10N42	"	60(pf) dull green	1.25	22
10N43	"	80(pf) dark blue	90	22
10N44	"	84(pf) brn. lake	1.25	60
		Nos. 10N29-10N44 (16)	11.81	4.76

See also German Democratic Republic Nos. 122-136.

Karl Liebknecht and Rosa Luxemburg

OS3

Perf. 13½x13

1949, Jan. 15 Litho. Wmk. 292

10N45	OS3	24pf rose	20	38

Issued to commemorate the 30th anniversary of the death of Karl Liebknecht and Rosa Luxemburg, German socialists.

Dove and Laurel

OS4

1949

10N46	OS4	24pf carmine rose	35	85

Overprinted in Black:

"3. Deutscher Volkskongress 29.-30. Mai 1949."

1949, May 29

10N47	OS4	24pf carmine rose	35	65

Nos. 10N46 and 10N47 were issued to commemorate the 3rd German People's Congress.

For succeeding issues see German Democratic Republic.

OCCUPATION SEMI-POSTAL STAMPS.

Leipzig Fair Issue.

Type of German Semi-Postal Stamps of 1947.

Designs: 16pf+9pf, First New Year's Fair, 1459. 50pf+25pf, Arrival of clothmakers from abroad, 1469.

Perf. 13½

1948, Aug. 29 Litho. Wmk. 292

10NB1	SP252	16(pf)+9(pf) dark violet brown	15	15
10NB2	SP252	50(pf)+25(pf) dull vio. bl.	20	22

The 1948 Leipzig Autumn Fair.

Emblem of Philatelic Institute

OSP1

1948, Oct. 23 *Perf. 13x13½*

10NB3	OSP1	12pf+3pf red	12	17

Issued to commemorate Stamp Day, Oct. 26, 1948.

Leipzig Fair Issue.

Type of German Semi-Postal Stamps of 1947.

Designs: 30pf+15pf, First fair in newly built Town Hall, 1556. 50pf+25pf, Italians at the Fair, 1536.

1949, Mar. 6 Litho. *Perf. 13½*

10NB4	SP252	30(pf)+15(pf) red	90	1.75
10NB5	"	50(pf)+25(pf) blue	1.50	2.75

Issued to publicize the 1949 Leipzig Spring Fair.

Johann Wolfgang von Goethe

OSP2

Designs: Different Goethe portraits.

1949, July 20 *Perf. 13* Wmk. 292

10NB6	OSP2	6(pf)+4(pf) dull violet	90	1.10
10NB7	"	12(pf)+8(pf) dull brown	70	85
10NB8	"	24(pf)+16(pf) red brown	60	75
10NB9	"	50(pf)+25(pf) dark blue	70	85
10NB10	"	84(pf)+36(pf) olive gray	1.20	1.50
		Nos. 10NB6-10NB10 (5)	4.10	5.05

Issued to commemorate the bicentenary of the birth of Johann Wolfgang von Goethe.

Souvenir Sheet.

Profile of Goethe

OSP3

1949, Aug. 22 Engraved *Perf. 14*

10NB11	OSP3	50pf+4.50m blue	150.00	185.00

The sheet measures 106x105mm. The surtax was for the reconstruction of Weimar.

Leipzig Fair Issue.

Type of German Semi-Postal Stamps of 1947.

Designs: 12pf+8pf, Russian merchants at the Fair, 1650. 24pf+16pf, Young Goethe at the Fair, 1765.

1949, Aug. 30 Litho. *Perf. 13½*

10NB12	SP252	12(pf)+8(pf) gray	1.50	1.90
10NB13	"	24(pf)+16(pf) lake brown	1.75	2.10

The 1949 Leipzig Autumn Fair.

GERMAN DEMOCRATIC REPUBLIC

LOCATION—Eastern Germany.
GOVT.—Republic.
AREA—41,659 sq. mi.
POP.—16,770,000 (est. 1977).
CAPITAL—Berlin (Soviet sector).

100 Pfennigs = 1 Deutsche Mark (East)

100 Pfennigs = 1 Mark of the Deutsche Notenbank (MDN) (1965)

100 Pfennigs = 1 Mark of the National Bank (M) (1969)

Pigeon, Letter and Globe—A5

Wmkd. Flowers Multiple. (292)

1949, Oct. 9 Litho. *Perf. 13½*

48	A5	50pf light blue & dark blue	2.75	2.75

Issued to commemorate the 75th anniversary of the formation of the Universal Postal Union.

Letter Carriers

A6

Skier

A7

1949, Oct. 27 *Perf. 13*

49	A6	12(pf) blue	1.00	1.00
50	"	30(pf) red	4.00	4.00

Issued to commemorate the "Day of the International Postal Workers' Trade Union," October 27-29, 1949.

1950, Mar. 2 *Perf. 13*

51	A7	12(pf) dp. blue violet	1.50	1.50
52	"	24(pf) blue (*Skater*)	1.75	1.75

Issued to publicize the first German Winter Sport Championship Matches, Schierke, 1950.

Globe and Sun

A8

1950, May 1 Typographed

53	A8	30(pf) deep carmine	3.50	3.75

Issued to commemorate the 60th anniversary of Labor Day, May 1, 1950.

Pres. Wilhelm Pieck
A9 A10

1950–51 *Perf. 13x12½* **Wmk. 292**

54 A9 12(pf) dark blue 4.50 50
55 " 24(pf) red brown 7.25 25

Perf. 13x13½

56 A10 1m olive green 6.00 1.10

Lithographed

57 A10 2m red brown 3.25 1.50

Engraved

57A A10 5m deep blue ('51) 1.50 40
Nos. 54-57A (5) 22.50 3.75

See also Nos. 113-117, 120-121.

Leonhard Euler A11
Miner A12

Portraits: 5pf, Alexander von Humboldt. 6pf, Theodor Mommsen. 8pf, Wilhelm von Humboldt. 10pf, H. L. F. von Helmholtz. 12pf, Max Planck. 16pf, Jacob Grimm. 20pf, W. H. Nernst. 24pf, Gottfried von Leibnitz. 50pf, Adolf von Harnack.

Perf. 12½

1950, July 10 **Litho.** **Wmk. 292**

58 A11 1(pf) gray 90 90
59 " 5(pf) deep green 2.25 2.25
60 " 6(pf) purple 4.50 3.50
61 " 8(pf) orange brown 5.25 4.75
62 " 10(pf) dk. gray green 3.25 3.50
63 " 12(pf) dark blue 1.00 1.00
64 " 16(pf) Prussian blue 5.00 7.00
65 " 20(pf) violet brown 4.50 5.00
66 " 24(pf) red 6.50 1.50
67 " 50(pf) deep ultra. 7.50 7.00
Nos. 58-67 (10) 40.65 36.40

Issued to commemorate the 250th anniversary of the founding of the Academy of Science, Berlin.

See also Nos. 352-354.

Canceled to Order

The government stamp agency started about 1950 to sell canceled sets of new issues.

1950, Sept. 1 *Perf. 13*

Design: 24pf, Smelting copper.

68 A12 12(pf) blue 65 80
69 " 24(pf) dark red 1.25 1.25

Issued to commemorate the 750th anniversary of the opening of the Mannsfeld copper mines.

Symbols of a Democratic Vote
A13

Hand Between Dove and Tank
A14

1950, Sept. 28

70 A13 24(pf) brown red 1.00 1.00

Issued to publicize the election of October 15, 1950.

1950, Dec. 15 **Litho.** *Perf. 13*

Designs show hand shielding dove from: 8pf, Exploding shell; 12pf, Atomic explosion; 24pf, Cemetery.

71 A14 6(pf) violet blue 1.65 2.00
72 " 8(pf) brown 1.25 1.00
73 A14 12(pf) blue 2.00 2.00
74 " 24(pf) red 1.75 1.00

Issued to publicize the "Fight for Peace."

Tobogganing
A15

Design: 24pf, Ski jump.

1951, Feb. 3 **Litho.** *Perf. 13*

76 A15 12(pf) blue 2.25 2.25
77 " 24(pf) rose 2.75 2.75

Issued to publicize the second Winter Sports Championship Matches at Oberhof.

A16

1951, Mar. 4 *Perf. 13* **Wmk. 292**

78 A16 24(pf) rose carmine 6.00 7.50
79 " 50(pf) violet blue 6.00 4.50

Issued to publicize the 1951 Leipzig Fair.

Pres. Wilhelm Pieck and Pres. Boleslaw Bierut Shaking Hands Across Oder-Neisse Frontier
A17

1951, Apr. 22 *Perf. 13*

80 A17 24(pf) scarlet 7.50 7.50
81 " 50(pf) blue 7.50 7.50

Issued to commemorate the visit of Pres. Boleslaw Bierut of Poland to the Russian Zone of Germany.

Mao Tse-tung
A18

Redistribution of Chinese Land
A19

1951, June 22 *Perf. 13*

82 A18 12(pf) dark green 16.50 13.50
83 A19 24(pf) dp. carmine 24.00 19.50
84 A18 50(pf) violet blue 15.00 10.00

Issued to publicize East Germany's friendship toward Communist China.

Boy Raising Flag
A20

5-Year Plan Symbolism
A21

Design: 24(pf), 50(pf), Girls dancing.

Grayish Paper, Except 30(pf).

1951, Aug. 3

85 A20 12(pf) chocolate & orange brown 3.50 4.00
86 " 24(pf) dark carmine & yellow green 4.50 2.50
87 " 30(pf) dark blue green & orange brown, *citron* 6.00 4.00
88 " 50(pf) violet blue & dark carmine 4.50 3.25

3rd World Youth Festival, Berlin, 1951.

1951, Sept. 2 **Typo.** **Wmk. 292**

89 A21 24(pf) multicolored 70 70

East Germany's Five-Year Plan.

Karl Liebknecht
A22

Father and Children with Stamp Collection
A23

1951, Oct. 7 **Litho.** *Perf. 13½x13*

90 A22 24(pf) red & bl. gray 85 85

Issued to commemorate the 80th anniversary of the birth of Karl Liebknecht, socialist.

1951, Oct. 28 *Perf. 13*

91 A23 12(pf) deep blue 60 60

Issued to publicize Stamp Day, Oct. 28, 1951.

Stalin and Wilhelm Pieck—A24

Design: 12(pf), Pavel Bykov and Erich Wirth.

1951–52

92 A24 12(pf) dp. blue ('52) 1.25 1.25
93 " 24(pf) red 1.50 1.50

Month of East German-Soviet friendship.

Skier
A25

Beethoven
A26

Design: 24(pf), Ski jump.

1952, Jan. 12 **Wmk. 292**

94 A25 12(pf) blue green 80 80
95 " 24(pf) deep blue 1.00 1.20

Winter Sports Championship Matches, Oberhof, 1952.

1952, Mar. 26 *Perf. 13½*

Design: 12(pf), Beethoven full face.

96 A26 12(pf) blue gray & violet blue 30 8
97 " 24(pf) gray & red brown 50 12

125th anniversary of the death of Ludwig van Beethoven.

See also Nos. 100-102.

Cyclists
A27

1952, May 5 **Photo.** *Perf. 13x13½*

98 A27 12(pf) blue 30 35

Issued to publicize the 5th International Bicycle Peace Race, Warsaw-Berlin-Prague.

Klement Gottwald
A28

1952, May 1

99 A28 24(pf) violet blue 50 60

Issued to publicize the friendship between German Democratic Republic and Czechoslovakia.

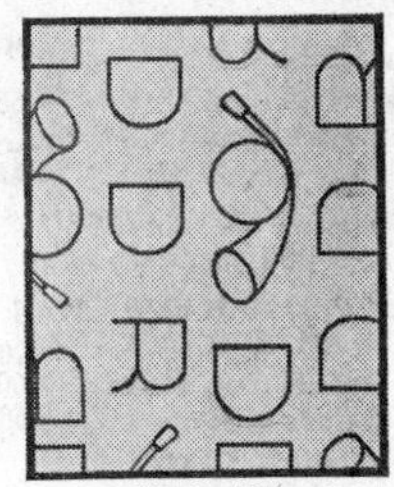

Wmk. 297

Similar to A26.

Portraits: 6(pf), G. F. Handel. 8(pf), Albert Lortzing. 50(pf), C. M. von Weber.

Wmkd. DDR and Post Horn. (297)

1952, July 5 **Lithographed**

100 A26 6(pf) brown buff & chocolate 60 50
101 " 8(pf) pink & deep rose pink 60 50
102 " 50(pf) blue gray & deep blue 1.00 75

Victor Hugo
A29

Portraits: 20(pf), Leonardo da Vinci. 24(pf), Nicolai Gogol. 35(pf), Avicenna.

Photogravure.

1952, Aug. 11 *Perf. 13* **Wmk. 292**

103 A29 12(pf) brown 80 80
104 " 20(pf) green 80 80
105 " 24(pf) rose 80 80
106 " 35(pf) blue 1.25 1.25

Machine, Globe and Dove
A30

Friedrich Ludwig Jahn
A31

1952, Sept. 7 *Perf. 13* Wmk. 297

108	A30	24(pf) red	60	25
109	"	35(pf) deep blue	65	90

Issued to publicize the 1952 Leipzig Fair.

1952, Oct. 15 Lithographed

110	A31	12(pf) blue	18	18

Issued to commemorate the centenary of the death of F. L. Jahn (1778–1852), who introduced gymnastics to Germany, and also was a politician.

Halle University
A32

Stamp, Flags, Wreath, Dove and Hammer
A33

1952, Oct. 18 Photogravure

111	A32	24(pf) green	15	15

Issued to commemorate the 450th anniversary of the founding of Halle University, Wittenberg.

1952, Oct. 26

112	A33	24(pf) red brown	35	35

Stamp Day, Oct. 26, 1952.

Pieck Types of 1950.
Typographed

1952–53 *Perf. 13x13½* Wmk. 297

113	A9	5(pf) blue green	1.20	60
114	"	12(pf) dark blue	7.00	30
115	"	24(pf) red brown	3.50	30

Perf. 13x13½.

116	A10	1m olive green	4.50	4.50

Lithographed
Perf. 13

117	A10	2m red brown ('53)	4.00	1.50
		Nos. 113–117 (5)	20.20	7.20

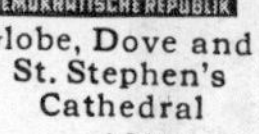

Globe, Dove and St. Stephen's Cathedral
A34

Pres. Wilhelm Pieck
A35

1952, Dec. 8 Photo. *Perf. 13*

118	A34	24(pf) bright carmine	40	30
119	"	35(pf) deep blue	60	75

Issued to publicize the Congress of Nations for Peace, Vienna, Dec. 12-19, 1952.

1953 *Perf. 13x13½* Wmk. 297

120	A35	1m olive	4.75	10
	a.	1m dark olive ('55)	7.50	10
121	A35	2m red brown	4.75	18

See also Nos. 339–340, 532.

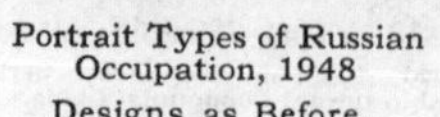

Portrait Types of Russian Occupation, 1948
Designs as Before.

1953 Typo. *Perf. 13x12½*

122	OS2	2(pf) gray	35	30
123	"	6(pf) purple	35	30
124	"	8(pf) red brown	35	45
125	"	10(pf) blue green	70	30
126	"	15(pf) brown	2.75	3.00
127	"	16(pf) turquoise	70	60
128	"	20(pf) maroon	70	60
129	"	25(pf) olive green	10.50	10.50
130	"	30(pf) red	1.40	1.40
131	"	40(pf) red violet	70	70
132	"	50(pf) dk. ultra.	10.50	10.50
133	"	60(pf) dull green	70	70
134	"	80(pf) dark blue	70	70
		a. Varnish coating	2.10	3.50
135	"	80(pf) crimson	4.25	4.25
136	"	84(pf) brown lake	9.00	9.00
		Nos. 122–136 (15)	43.65	43.30

"Industry" and Red Flag
A36

Karl Marx Speaking
A38

Marx and Engels
A37

Karl Marx Medallion
A39

Designs: 12(pf), Spasski tower and communist flag. 16(pf), Marching workers. 24pf, Portrait of Karl Marx. 35(pf), Marx addressing audience. 48(pf), Karl Marx and Friedrich Engels. 60(pf). Red banner above heads and shoulders of workers.

1953 Photogravure. *Perf. 13.*

137	A36	6(pf) greenish gray & red	20	8
138	A37	10(pf) greenish gray & dk. brn.	1.50	30
139	A36	12(pf) grn., dp. plum & dark green	24	12
140	A37	16(pf) violet blue & dk. carmine	85	85
141	A38	20(pf) brown & buff	30	35
142	"	24(pf) brown & red	75	5
143	A36	35(pf) deep purple & cream	1.00	1.00
144	"	48(pf) dark olive green & red brown	30	30
		a. Souvenir sheet of 6	30.00	30.00
145	A37	60(pf) violet brown & red	1.20	1.20
146	A39	84(pf) blue & brown	60	65
		a. Souvenir sheet of 4	30.00	30.00
		Nos. 137–146 (10)	6.94	4.90

No. 144a measures 148 x 105mm., and contains one each of the denominations in types A36 and A38, with inscriptions and flags in greenish gray, black, red and yellow. Perforate and imperforate.

No. 146a measures 148 x 105mm., and contains one each of the denominations in types A37 and A39, with inscriptions, decorative panels and medallions in greenish gray and brown. Perforate and imperforate.

Maxim Gorky
A40

Bicycle Racers
A41

1953, Mar. 28

147	A40	35(pf) brown	8	6

1953, May 2 *Perf. 13* Wmk. 297

Designs: 35pf, 60pf, Different views of bicycle race.

148	A41	24(pf) bluish green	40	32
149	"	35(pf) deep ultra.	30	32
150	"	60(pf) chocolate	55	45

6th International Bicycle Peace Race.

Heinrich von Kleist
A42

Coal Miner
A43

Designs: 20(pf), Evangelical Marienkirche. 24(pf), Sailboat on Oder River. 35(pf), City Hall, Frankfurt-on-Oder.

1953, July 6 Lithographed

151	A42	16(pf) chocolate	30	40
152	"	20(pf) blue green	18	20
153	"	24(pf) rose red	30	15
154	"	35(pf) violet blue	35	35

Issued to commemorate the 700th anniversary of the founding of Frankfurt-on-Oder.

1953 Litho. *Perf. 13x12½*

Designs: 5(pf), Woman mariner. 6(pf), German and Soviet workers. 8(pf), Mother teaching Marxist principles. 10(pf), Machinists. 12(pf), Worker, peasant and intellectual. 15(pf), Teletype operator. 16(pf), Steel worker. 20(pf), Bad Elster. 24(pf), Stalin Boulevard. 25(pf), Locomotive building. 30(pf), Dancing couple. 35(pf), Sports Hall, Berlin. 40(pf), Laboratory worker. 48(pf), Zwinger Castle, Dresden. 60(pf), Launching ship. 80(pf), Agricultural workers. 84(pf), Dove and East German family.

155	A43	1(pf) black brown	20	3
156	"	5(pf) emerald	45	3
157	"	6(pf) violet	40	3
158	"	8(pf) orange brown	65	3
159	"	10(pf) blue green	45	3
160	"	12(pf) blue	60	3
161	"	15(pf) purple	90	3
162	"	16(pf) dark violet	1.00	3
163	"	20(pf) olive	1.00	3
163A	"	24(pf) carmine	1.00	3
164	"	25(pf) dark green	1.35	3
165	"	30(pf) deep carmine	1.35	3
166	"	35(pf) violet blue	2.25	3
167	"	40(pf) rose red	3.00	3
168	"	48(pf) rose violet	2.50	3
169	"	60(pf) deep blue	2.50	3
170	"	80(pf) aquamarine	4.50	3
171	"	84(pf) chocolate	4.50	3
		Nos. 155–171 (18)	28.60	54

See also Nos. 187–204, 216–223A, 227–230, 330–338, 476–482.

Used prices of Nos. 155–171 are for canceled-to-order reprints with printed cancellations. The reprints differ slightly from originals in design and shade.

Power Shovel
A44

Design: 35(pf), Road-building machine.

1953, Aug. 29 Photo. *Perf. 13*

172	A44	24(pf) red brown	45	25
173	"	35(pf) deep green	80	75

The 1953 Leipzig Fair.

G. W. von Knobelsdorff and Berlin State Opera House—A45

Design: 35(pf), Balthasar Neumann and Wurzburg bishop's palace.

1953, Sept. 16 *Perf. 13x12½*

174	A45	24(pf) cerise	30	15
175	"	35(pf) dark slate blue	70	85

Issued to commemorate the 200th anniversary of the deaths of G. W. von Knobelsdorff and Balthasar Neumann, architects.

Lucas Cranach
A46

Nurse Applying Bandage
A47

1953, Oct. 16 *Perf. 13x13½*

176	A46	24(pf) brown	40	45

400th anniversary of the death of Lucas Cranach (1472–1553), painter.

Perf. 13½x13

1953, Oct. 23 Wmk. 297

177	A47	24(pf) brown & red	32	12

Issued to honor the Red Cross.

Mail Delivery
A48

Lion and Lioness
A49

1953, Oct. 25 Photogravure

178	A48	24(pf) blue gray	40	15

Issued to publicize Stamp Day, October 24, 1953.

1953, Nov. 2 *Perf. 13x13½*

179	A49	24(pf) olive brown	40	12

75th anniversary of Leipzig Zoo.

Thomas Muntzer and Attackers
A50

Designs: 16(pf), H. F. K. vom Stein. 20(pf), Ferdinand von Schill leading cavalry. 24(pf), G. L. Blucher and battle scene. 35(pf), Students fighting for National Unity. 48(pf), Revolution of 1848.

1953, Nov. Photo. *Perf. 13x12½*

180	A50	12(pf) brown	45	15
181	"	16(pf) deep brown	45	10
182	"	20(pf) dark carmine rose	30	10
183	"	24(pf) deep blue	35	10
184	"	35(pf) dark green	75	50
185	"	48(pf) dark brown	75	35
		Nos. 180-185 (6)	3.05	1.30

Issued to honor German patriots.

Franz Schubert
A51

Gotthold E. Lessing
A52

1953, Nov. 13 ***Perf. 13½x13***

186	A51	48(pf) brt. org. brown	40	45

Issued to commemorate the 125th anniversary of the death of Franz Schubert.

Types of 1953 Redrawn.
Designs as Before.

1953-54 Typographed. ***Perf. 13x12½***

187	A43	1(pf) black brown	24	3
188	"	5(pf) emerald	60	3
		a. Bklt. pane 6 (3 No. 188 + 3 No. 227)	3.50	
		b. Bklt. pane 6 (3 No. 188 + 3 No. 228)	4.00	
189	"	6(pf) purple	45	3
190	"	8(pf) orange brown	60	3
191	"	10(pf) blue green	2.25	3
192	"	12(pf) greenish blue	90	3
193	"	15(pf) brt. vio. ('54)	1.75	3
194	"	16(pf) dark purple	1.20	3
195	"	20(pf) olive ('54)	1.50	3
196	"	24(pf) carmine	1.75	3
197	"	25(pf) dk. blue green	1.50	3
198	"	30(pf) deep carmine	2.25	3
199	"	35(pf) dp. violet blue	1.50	3
200	"	40(pf) rose red ('54)	2.25	3
201	"	48(pf) rose violet	3.50	3
202	"	60(pf) blue	3.00	3
203	"	80(pf) aquamarine	3.50	3
204	"	84(pf) chocolate	5.50	3
		Nos. 187-204 (18)	34.24	54

Nos. 155–171 were printed from screened halftones, and shading consists of dots. Shading in lines without screen on Nos. 187–204. Designers' and engravers' names added below design on all values except 6, 12, 16 and 35pf. There are many other minor differences.

See note on used prices after No. 171.

1954, Jan. 20 Photo. ***Perf. 13***

205	A52	20(pf) dark green	25	12

Issued to commemorate the 225th anniversary of the birth of G. E. Lessing, dramatist.

Dove Over Conference Table
A53

Joseph V. Stalin
A54

1954, Jan. 25 ***Perf. 12½x13***

206	A53	12(pf) blue	15	12

Four Power Conference, Berlin, 1954.

1954, Mar. 5 Typo. ***Perf. 13x12½***

207	A54	20pf gray, dark brown & red orange	30	20

Issued to commemorate the first anniversary of the death of Joseph V. Stalin.

Cyclists
A55

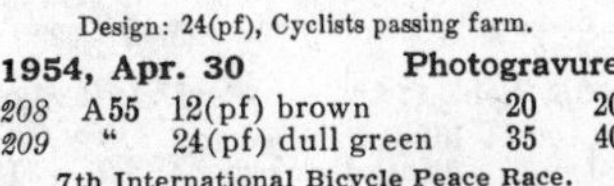

Design: 24(pf), Cyclists passing farm.

1954, Apr. 30 **Photogravure**

208	A55	12(pf) brown	20	20
209	"	24(pf) dull green	35	40

7th International Bicycle Peace Race.

Dancers
A56

Fritz Reuter
A57

Design: 24(pf), Boy, two girls and flag.

1954, June 3 ***Perf. 13***

210	A56	12(pf) emerald	15	15
211	"	24(pf) rose brown	20	18

Issued to publicize the 2nd German youth meeting for peace, unity and freedom.

1954, July 12

212	A57	24(pf) sepia	24	15

Issued to commemorate the 80th anniversary of the death of Fritz Reuter, writer.

Ernst Thälmann
A58

Hall of Commerce, Leipzig Fair
A59

1954, Aug. 18 ***Perf. 13½x13***

213	A58	24(pf) red orange & indigo	15	12

Issued to commemorate the 10th anniversary of the death of Ernst Thälmann (1886–1944), Communist leader.

1954, Sept. 4 ***Perf. 13x13½***

214	A59	24(pf) dark red	12	8
215	"	35(pf) gray blue	20	10

Issued to publicize the 1954 Leipzig Fair.

Redrawn Types of 1953-54 Surcharged with New Value and "X" in Black

1954 **Typographed** ***Perf. 13x12½***

216	A43	5(pf) on 6(pf) purple	5	3
217	"	5(pf) on 8(pf) orange brown	8	3
218	"	10(pf) on 12(pf) greenish blue	15	3
219	"	15(pf) on 16(pf) dark purple	10	3
220	"	20(pf) on 24(pf) car.	15	3
221	"	40(pf) on 48(pf) rose violet	50	3
222	"	50(pf) on 60(pf) blue	50	3
223	"	70(pf) on 84(pf) chocolate	72	3
		Nos. 216-223 (8)	2.25	24

See note on used prices after No. 171.

No. 163A Surcharged with New Value and "X" in Black.

1955 **Lithographed.**

223A	A43	20(pf) on 24(pf) carmine	18	3

Counterfeit surcharges exist on other values of the lithographed set (Nos. 155–171).

Pres. Wilhelm Pieck and Flags
A60

1954, Oct. 6 **Photogravure**

224	A60	20(pf) brown	15	10
225	"	35(pf) greenish blue	25	20

Issued to commemorate the fifth anniversary of the founding of the German Democratic Republic.

Cologne Cathedral, Leipzig Monument and Unissued Stamp Design—A61

1954, Oct. 23 ***Perf. 13x13½***

226	A61	20pf bright carmine rose	25	10
		a. Souvenir sheet	12.00	12.00

Stamp Day. No. 226a contains one imperforate copy of No. 226 with frame and inscription in blue. Size: 60x80mm.

Redrawn Types of 1953-54.

Designs: 10(pf), Worker, peasant and intellectual. 15(pf), Steelworker. 20(pf), Stalin Boulevard. 40(pf), Zwinger Castle, Dresden. 50(pf), Launching ship. 70(pf), Dove and East German family.

1955 Typographed. ***Perf. 13x12½***

227	A43	10(pf) blue	45	3
		a. Bklt. pane 6 (4 No. 227+2 No. 228)	3.20	
227B	"	15(pf) violet	80	3
228	"	20(pf) carmine	60	3
229	"	40(pf) rose violet	1.00	3
230	"	50(pf) deep blue	1.00	3
230A	"	70(pf) chocolate	2.50	3
		Nos. 227-230A (6)	6.35	18

See note on used prices after No. 171.

Soviet Pavilion, Leipzig Spring Fair
A62

Women of Three Nations
A63

Design: 35(pf), Chinese pavilion.

Perf. 13x13½

1955, Feb. 21 Photo. **Wmk. 297**

231	A62	20(pf) rose violet	10	6
232	"	35(pf) violet blue	25	20

Issued to publicize the Leipzig Spring Fair.

1955, Mar. 1 ***Perf. 13x13½***

233	A63	10(pf) green	16	8
234	"	20(pf) red	20	16

International Women's Day, 45th year.

Workers' Demonstration—A64

1955, Mar. 15 ***Perf. 13x12½***

235	A64	10(pf) black & red	12	10

Issued to publicize the International Trade Union Conference, April, 1955.

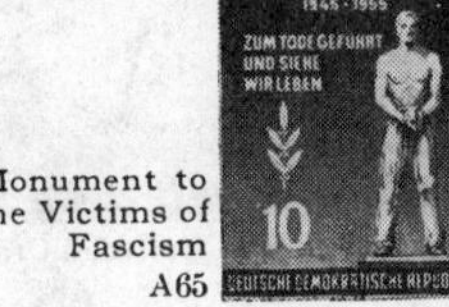

Monument to the Victims of Fascism
A65

1955, Apr. 9 ***Perf. 13½x13***

236	A65	10(pf) violet blue	16	8
237	"	20(pf) cerise	20	12
		a. Souvenir sheet	3.50	4.25

No. 237a measures 73x100mm. and contains one each, imperforate, of Nos. 236-237 with inscriptions in dark violet blue. Issued for reconstruction of national memorial sites. Sold for 50pf.

Russian War Memorial, Berlin
A66

1955, Apr. 15 ***Perf. 12½x13***

238	A66	20(pf) lilac rose	12	12

Nos. 236-238 were issued to commemorate the 10th anniversary of liberation.

Cyclists
A67

Friedrich von Schiller
A68

1955 ***Perf. 13½x13*** **Wmk. 297**

239	A67	10(pf) blue green	8	8
240	"	20(pf) carmine rose	12	12

Issued to publicize the 8th International Bicycle Peace Race, Prague-Berlin-Warsaw.

Starting with the 1955 issues, commemorative stamps which are priced in italics were sold on a restricted basis.

Various Portraits of Schiller.

1955, Apr. 20

241	A68	5(pf) dark gray green	*50*	*50*
242	"	10(pf) bright blue	5	5
243	"	20(pf) chocolate	4	4
		a. Souvenir sheet	*4.25*	*5.25*

Issued to commemorate the 150th anniversary of the death of Friedrich von Schiller, poet.

No. 243a measures 73x100mm. and contains one each, imperforate, of Nos. 241-243 with inscriptions in dark greenish blue. Sold for 50pf.

Karl Liebknecht—A69

Portraits: 10(pf), August Bebel. 15(pf), Franz Mehring. 20(pf), Ernst Thälmann. 25(pf), Clara Zetkin. (40pf), Wilhelm Liebknecht. 60(pf), Rosa Luxemburg.

1955, June 20 Photo. ***Perf. 13x12½***

244	A69	5(pf) blue green	5	3
245	"	10(pf) deep blue	5	3
246	"	15(pf) violet	*1.50*	*75*
247	"	20(pf) red	9	4
248	"	25(pf) slate	12	6
249	"	40(pf) rose carmine	12	6
250	"	60(pf) dark brown	18	8
		Nos. 244-250 (7)	*2.11*	*1.05*

Issued to honor German communists.

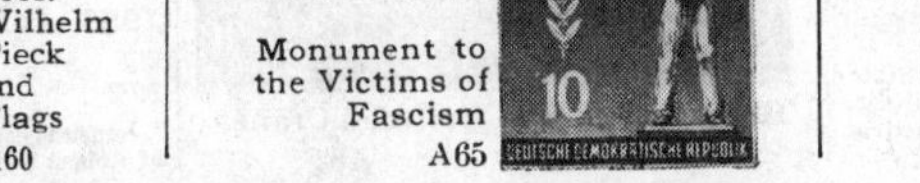

Optical Goods
A70

Design: 20(pf), Pottery and china.

1955, Aug. 29 Photo. *Perf. 13x13½*

253	A70	10(pf) dark blue	7	7
254	"	20(pf) slate green	8	8

Issued to publicize the 1955 Leipzig Fair.

Farmer Receiving Deed
A71

Harvesters
A72

Design: 10(pf), Construction of new farm community.

Perf. 13½x13, 13x13½

1955, Sept. 3

Inscribed: "1945 Bodenreform 1955"

255	A71	5(pf) dull green	*80*	*85*
256	"	10(pf) ultramarine	10	6
257	A72	20(pf) lake	10	6

Issued to commemorate the tenth anniversary of the Land-Reform Program.

Man Holding Badge of Peoples' Solidarity
A73

Engels at "First International," 1864
A74

Perf. 13½x13

1955, Oct. 10 Wmk. 297

258	A73	10(pf) dark blue	10	8

Issued to commemorate the tenth anniversary of the "Peoples' Solidarity."

1955, Nov. 7 *Perf. 13½x13*

Designs: 10(pf), Marx and Engels writing the Communist Manifesto. 15(pf), Engels as newspaper editor. 20(pf), Friedrich Engels. 30(pf), Friedrich Engels. 70(pf), Engels on the barricades in 1848.

259	A74	5(pf) Prussian blue & olive	10	10
260	"	10(pf) dark blue & yellow	10	10
261	"	15(pf) dark green & olive	10	10
262	"	20(pf) brown violet & orange	30	30
263	"	30(pf) orange brown & light blue	*2.25*	*2.25*
264	"	70(pf) gray green & rose carmine	45	45
		a. Souvenir sheet of six	*30.00*	*30.00*
		Nos. 259-264 (6)	*3.30*	*3.30*

Issued to commemorate the 135th anniversary of the birth of Friedrich Engels.

No. 264a contains one each of Nos. 259-264 and measures 148x105 mm. Marginal inscription and flags.

Cathedral at Magdeburg
A75

Georgius Agricola
A76

German Buildings: 10(pf), German State Opera. 15(pf), Old City Hall, Leipzig. 20(pf), City Hall, Berlin. 30(pf), Cathedral at Erfurt. 40(pf), Zwinger at Dresden.

1955, Nov. 14

265	A75	5(pf) black brown	15	15
266	"	10(pf) gray green	15	15
267	"	15(pf) purple	15	15
268	"	20(pf) carmine	18	18
269	"	30(pf) dk. red brn.	*2.50*	*2.50*
270	"	40(pf) indigo	20	20
		Nos. 265-270 (6)	*3.33*	*3.33*

1955, Nov. 21 Wmk. 297

271	A76	10(pf) brown	10	10

Issued to commemorate the 400th anniversary of the death of Georgius Agricola, mineralogist and scholar.

Portrait of a Young Man, by Dürer
A77

Wolfgang Amadeus Mozart
A78

Famous Paintings: 10(pf), Chocolate Girl, Liotard. 15(pf), Portrait of a Boy, Pinturicchio. 20(pf), Self-portrait with Saskia, Rembrandt. 40(pf), Girl with Letter, Vermeer. 70(pf), Sistine Madonna, Raphael.

1955, Dec. 15 *Perf. 13½x13*

272	A77	5(pf) dk. red brown	18	7
273	"	10(pf) chestnut	18	10
274	"	15(pf) pale purple	*6.50*	*4.00*
275	"	20(pf) brown	24	7
276	"	40(pf) olive green	30	15
277	"	70(pf) deep blue	60	24
		Nos. 272-277 (6)	*8.00*	*4.63*

Issued to publicize the return of famous art works to the Dresden Art Gallery.

See also Nos. 355-360, 439-443.

1956, Jan. 27 Photogravure

Designs: 20(pf), Portrait facing left.

278	A78	10(pf) gray green	75	*80*
279	"	20(pf) copper brown	45	30

Issued to commemorate the 200th anniversary of the birth of Wolfgang Amadeus Mozart, composer.

Flag and Schoenefeld Airport, Berlin—A79

Lufthansa Plane—A80

Designs: 15(pf), Plane facing right. 20(pf), Plane facing down and left.

1956, Feb. 1 *Perf. 13x12½*

280	A79	5(pf) multicolored	*1.50*	*1.50*
281	A80	10(pf) gray green	4	4
282	"	15(pf) dull blue	6	6
283	"	20(pf) brown red	6	6

Issued to commemorate the opening of passenger service of the German Lufthansa.

Heinrich Heine
A81

Railroad Cranes
A82

Design: 20(pf), Heine (different portrait.)

1956, Feb. 17 *Perf. 13½x13*

284	A81	10(pf) Prus. green	*80*	*80*
285	"	20(pf) dark red	30	30

Centenary of the death of Heinrich Heine, poet.

1956, Feb. 26 *Perf. 13x13½*

286	A82	20(pf) brown red	8	6
287	"	35(pf) violet blue	12	15

Issued to publicize the Leipzig Spring Fair.

Ernst Thälmann
A83

1956, Apr. 16 Litho. *Perf. 13x13½*

288	A83	20(pf) black olive & red	10	8
		a. Souvenir sheet.	*1.75*	*2.25*

Issued to commemorate the 70th anniversary of the birth of Ernst Thälmann.

No. 288a measures 74x100mm. and contains one imperforate copy of No. 288. Marginal inscription in black. It was sold at double face value. The proceeds were used for national memorials at former concentration camps.

Wheel, Hand and Olive Branch
A84

City Hall and Old Market
A85

Design: 20pf, Wheel and coats of arms of Warsaw, Berlin, Prague.

Perf. 13½x13

1956, Apr. 30 Wmk. 297

289	A84	10pf light green	7	5
290	"	20pf bright carmine	10	10

Issued to commemorate the 9th International Bicycle Peace Race, Warsaw-Berlin-Prague, May 1-15, 1956.

1956, June 1

Designs: 20pf, Hofkirche and Elbe Bridge. 40pf, Technical College.

291	A85	10pf green	4	3
292	"	20pf carmine rose	4	4
293	"	40pf bright purple	*30*	*30*

750th anniversary of Dresden.

Worker Holding Cogwheel Emblem
A86

Robert Schumann (Music by Schubert)
A87

1956, June 30 *Perf. 13½x13*

294	A86	20pf rose red	8	5

Issued to commemorate the 10th anniversary of nationalized industry.

1956, July 20 *Perf. 13x13½*

295	A87	10pf bright green	*35*	*35*
296	"	20pf rose red	5	5

Issued to commemorate the centenary of the death of Robert Schumann, composer. See Nos. 303-304.

Soccer Players
A88

Thomas Mann
A89

Designs: 10pf, Javelin Thrower. 15pf, Women Hurdlers. 20pf, Gymnast.

1956, July 25 *Perf. 13½x13*

297	A88	5pf green	4	4
298	"	10pf dark violet blue	4	4
299	"	15pf red violet	*45*	*30*
300	"	20pf rose red	4	4

Second Sports Festival, Leipzig, Aug. 2-5.

1956, Aug. 13 Wmk. 297

301	A89	20pf bluish black	8	6

Issued to commemorate the first anniversary of the death of Thomas Mann, novelist.

Jakub Bart Cisinski
A90

Robert Schumann (Music by Schumann)
A91

1956, Aug. 20 Photogravure

302	A90	50pf claret	10	10

Birth centenary of Jakub Bart Cisinski, poet.

1956, Oct. 8 *Perf. 13x13½*

303	A91	10pf bright green	*25*	*25*
304	"	20pf rose red	10	5

See Nos. 295, 296.

Lace
A92

Olympic Rings, Laurel and Torch
A93

Design: 20pf, Sailboat.

1956, Sept. 1 Typo. *Perf. 13½x13*

305	A92	10pf green & black	8	6
306	"	20pf rose red & black	8	12

Leipzig Fair, Sept. 2-9.

1956, Sept. 28 Lithographed

Design: 35pf, Classic javelin thrower.

307	A93	20pf brown red	6	3
308	"	35pf slate blue	9	6

Issued to publicize the 16th Olympic Games at Melbourne, Nov. 22-Dec. 8, 1956.

Post Runner of 1450
A94

Greifswald University Seal
A95

1956, Oct. 27

309	A94	20pf red	10	10

Issued to publicize the Day of the Stamp.

1956, Oct. 17 ***Perf. 13x13½***
310 A95 20pf magenta 10 10

Issued to commemorate the 500th anniversary of Greifswald University.

Ernst Abbe
A96

Zeiss Works, Jena
A97

Portrait: 25pf, Carl Zeiss.

Perf. 12½x13, 13x12½

1956, Nov. 9 **Photo.** **Wmk. 297**
311 A96 10pf dark green 3 3
312 A97 20pf brown red 4 3
313 A96 25pf bluish black 5 3

Issued to commemorate the 110th anniversary of the Carl Zeiss Optical Works in Jena.

Chinese Girl with Flowers
A98

Designs: 10pf, Negro woman and child. 25pf, European man and dove.

1956, Dec. 10 **Litho.** ***Perf. 13***
314 A98 5pf olive, *pale lemon* 20 18
315 " 10pf brown, *pink* 4 3
316 " 25pf violet blue, *pale violet blue* 6 4

Issued for Human Rights Day.

Elephants—A99

Animals: 10pf, Flamingoes. 15pf, White rhinoceros. 20pf, Mouflon. 25pf, Bison. 30pf, Polar bear.

1956, Dec. 17 Photo. ***Perf. 13x12½***

Design in Gray.

317 A99 5pf black 3 3
318 " 10pf dark green 3 3
319 " 15pf purple 60 45
320 " 20pf henna brown 6 3
321 " 25pf dark brown 9 4
322 " 30pf dark blue 12 8
Nos. 317-322 (6) *93* *66*

Issued to publicize the Berlin Zoo.

Freighter
A100

Design: 25pf, Electric Locomotive.

Wmkd. Quatrefoil and DDR (313)

1957, Mar. 1 **Litho.** ***Perf. 13x12½***
323 A100 20pf rose red 7 3
324 " 25pf bright blue 8 4

Leipzig Spring Fair.

Silver Thistle
A101

Designs: 10pf, Emerald lizard. 20pf, Lady's-slipper.

1957, Apr. 12 **Photo.** **Wmk. 313**
325 A101 5pf chocolate 3 3
326 " 10pf dark slate green *30* *15*
327 " 20pf red brown 5 3

Issued for Nature Conservation Week, April 14-20.

Children at Play
A102

Design: 20pf, Friedrich Froebel and Children.

1957, Apr. 18 **Litho.** ***Perf. 13***
328 A102 10pf dark slate green & olive *20* *15*
329 " 20pf blk. & brn. red 8 4

Issued to commemorate the 175th anniversary of the birth of Friedrich Froebel, educator.

Redrawn Types of 1953

Designs: 5pf, Woman mariner. 10pf, Worker, peasant and intellectual. 15pf, Steel worker. 20pf, Stalin Boulevard. 25pf, Locomotive building. 30pf, Dancing couple. 40pf, Zwinger Castle, Dresden. 50pf, Launching ship. 70pf, Dove and East German family.

Imprint: "E. Gruner K. Wolf".
No imprint on 10pf, 15pf.

Perf. 13x12½

1957-58 **Typographed.** **Wmk. 313**
330 A43 5pf emerald 5 3
a. Booklet pane 6 (3 No. 330 + 3 No. 331) 4.00
b. Booklet pane 6 (3 No. 330 + 3 No. 333) 4.00
c. Booklet pane 6 30
331 " 10pf blue 25 3
a. Booklet pane 6 (4 No. 331 + 2 No. 333) 4.00
b. Perf. 14 ('58) 12 3
332 " 15pf violet 10 3
a. Perf. 14 ('58) 4 3
333 " 20pf carmine 4 3
a. Booklet pane (5 No. 333 + 1 No. 477) 35
334 " 25pf bluish green 10 3
335 " 30pf dull red 20 3
336 " 40pf rose violet 30 3
337 " 50pf bright blue 40 5
338 " 70pf chocolate 45 10

See also Nos. 476-482.

Pieck Type of 1953.

Photogravure.

Perf. 13x13½

339 A35 1m dark olive green ('58) 60 5
340 " 2m red brown ('58) 1.30 10
Nos. 330-340 (11) 3.79 51

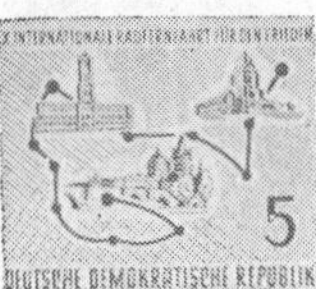

Bicycle Race Route
A103

Perf. 13x13½

1957, Apr. 30 **Litho.** **Wmk. 313**
346 A103 5pf orange 5 3

Issued to publicize the 10th International Bicycle Peace Race, Prague-Berlin-Warsaw.

Steam Shovel
A104

Miner
A105

Design: 20pf, Coal conveyor.

Perf. 13x12½, 13½x13 (25pf)

1957, May 3
347 A104 10pf green 4 3
348 " 20pf reddish brown 8 3
349 A105 25pf blue violet *30* *20*

Issued in honor of the coal mining industry.

Henri Dunant and Globe
A106

Design: 25pf, Henri Dunant facing right and globe.

1957, May 7 **Photo.** ***Perf. 13x12½***
350 A106 10pf green, red & black 3 3
351 " 25pf bright blue, red & black 8 4

Tenth Red Cross world conference.

Portrait Type of 1950, Redrawn.

Portraits: 5pf, Joachim Jungius. 10pf, Leonhard Euler. 20pf, Heinrich Hertz.

1957, June 7 **Lithographed**
352 A11 5pf brown *20* *20*
353 " 10pf green 4 3
354 " 20pf henna brown 8 3

Issued to honor famous German scientists.

Painting Type of 1955.

Famous Paintings: 5pf, Holy Family, Mantegna. 10pf, The Dancer Campani, Carriera. 15pf, Portrait of Morette, Holbein. 20pf, The Tribute Money, Titian. 25pf, Saskia with Red Flower, Rembrandt. 40pf, Young Standard Bearer, Piazetta.

Perf. 13½x13

1957, June 26 **Photo.** **Wmk. 313**
355 A77 5pf dark brown 3 3
356 " 10pf light yellow green 3 3
357 " 15pf brown olive 6 3
358 " 20pf rose brown 8 4
359 " 25pf deep claret 10 4
360 " 40pf dark blue gray *75* *50*
Nos. 355-360 (6) *1.05* 67

Clara Zetkin
A107

Bertolt Brecht
A108

1957, July 5 ***Perf. 13x13½***
361 A107 10pf dark green & red 5 3

Issued to commemorate the centenary of the birth of Clara Zetkin, politician and founder of the socialist women's movement.

1957, Aug. 14 ***Perf. 13½x13***
362 A108 10pf dark green 4 3
363 " 25pf deep blue 8 4

Issued to honor Bertolt Brecht (1898-1956), playwright and poet, on the first anniversary of his death.

Congress Emblem
A109

Fair Emblem
A110

1957, Aug. 23 **Lithographed**
364 A109 20pf bright red & black 7 5

Issued to publicize the fourth International Trade Union Congress, Leipzig, Oct. 4-15.

1957, Aug. 30 **Wmk. 313**
365 A110 20pf crimson & vermilion 6 3
366 " 25pf bright blue & light blue 6 3

Issued to publicize the 1957 Leipzig Fair.

Savings Book
A111

Postrider, 1563
A112

1957, Oct. 10 ***Perf. 13½x13***
367 A111 10pf green & black, *gray* *25* *25*
368 " 20pf rose carmine & black, *gray* 5 3

Issued to publicize "Savings Weeks."

1957, Oct. 25 **Wmk. 313**
369 A112 5pf *pale sepia* 5 5

Issued for the Day of the Stamp.

Sputnik I
A113

Storming of the Winter Palace
A114

Designs: 20pf, Stratospheric balloon above clouds. 25pf, Ship with plumb line exploring deep sea.

1957–58 *Perf. 12½x13*

370 A113 10pf blue black 4 3
371 " 20pf carmine rose ('58) 5 3
372 " 25pf bright blue ('58) 40 30

Issued for the International Geophysical Year. The 10pf also commemorates the launching of the first artificial satellite.

1957, Nov. 7 **Photogravure**

373 A114 10pf yel. grn. & red 5 3
374 " 25pf bright blue & red 9 3

Issued to commemorate the 40th anniversary of the Russian Revolution.

Guenther Ramin A115 — Dove and Globe A116

Portrait: 20pf, Hermann Abendroth.

Perf. 13½x13

1957, Nov. 22 **Litho.** **Wmk. 313**

375 A115 10pf yel. grn. & blk. 25 15
376 " 20pf red orange & black 5 4

Issued to honor Guenther Ramin (1898–1956) and Hermann Abendroth (1883–1956), musicians, on the first anniversary of their death.

1958, Feb. 27 *Perf. 13x13½*

377 A116 20pf rose red 5 3
378 " 25pf blue 8 4

Issued to publicize the 1958 Leipzig Fair.

Radio Tower, Morse Code and Post Horn—A117

Design: 20pf, Radio tower and small post horn.

1958, Mar. 6 *Perf. 13x12½*

379 A117 5pf gray & black 25 20
380 " 20pf crimson rose & dark red 5 4

Issued to commemorate the Conference of Postal Ministers of Communist countries, Moscow, Dec. 3–17, 1957.

Sketch by Zille A118 — Symbolizing Quantum Theory A119

Design: 20pf, Self-portrait of Zille.

1958, Mar. 20 *Perf. 13½x13*

381 A118 10pf green & gray 25 20
382 " 20pf dp. car. & gray 9 3

Issued to commemorate the centenary of the birth of Heinrich Zille, artist.

1958, Apr. 23 **Lithographed**

Design: 20pf, Max Planck.

383 A119 10pf gray green 25 20
384 " 20pf magenta 6 3

Issued to commemorate the centenary of the birth of Max Planck, physicist.

Prize Cow A120 — Charles Darwin A121

Designs: 10pf, Mowing machine. 20pf, Beet harvester.

Perf. 13x13½

1958, June 4 **Wmk. 313**

Size: 28x23mm.

385 A120 5pf gray & black 35 35

Perf. 13x12½

Size: 39x22mm.

386 A120 10pf bright green 4 3
387 " 20pf rose red 8 3

6th Agricultural Show, Markkleeberg.

1958, June 19 *Perf. 13x13½*

Portrait: 20pf, Carl von Linné.

388 A121 10pf green & black 20 15
389 " 20pf dark red & black 5 3

Issued to commemorate the centenary of Darwin's theory of evolution and the bicentenary of Linné's botanical system.

Seven Towers of Rostock and Ships A122 — Congress Emblem A123

Designs: 10pf, Ship at pier. 25pf, Ships in harbor.

1958 *Perf. 13½x13*

390 A122 10pf emerald 4 3
391 " 20pf red orange 5 3
392 " 25pf light blue 30 25

Establishment of Rostock as a seaport. Issue dates: 20pf, July 5; 10pf and 25pf, Nov. 24.

1958, June 25 *Perf. 13x13½*

393 A123 10pf rose red 8 3

Issued to commemorate the fifth congress of the Socialist Party of the German Democratic Republic (SED).

Mare and Foal A124

Designs: 10pf, Trotter. 20pf, Horse race.

1958, July 22 **Photo.** *Perf. 13x12½*

394 A124 5pf black brown 40 40
395 " 10pf dark olive green 4 3
396 " 20pf dark red brown 6 3

Issued to publicize the Grand Prize of the DDR, 1958.

Jan A. Komensky A125

Design: 20pf, Teacher and pupils, 17th century.

1958, Aug. 7 **Litho.** *Perf. 13x13½*

397 A125 10pf bright blue green & black 25 25
398 " 20pf orange brown & black 5 3

Issued in honor of Jan Amos Komensky (Comenius).

University Seal—A126

Design: 20pf, Schiller University, Jena.

1958, Aug. 19 *Perf. 13x12½*

399 A126 5pf gray & black 25 15
400 " 20pf dark red & gray 5 3

Issued to commemorate the 400th anniversary of Friedrich Schiller University in Jena.

Soldier on Obstacle Course A127 — Arms Breaking A-Bomb A128

Designs: 20pf, Spartacist emblem. 25pf, Marching athletes, map and flag.

Perf. 13½x13

1958, Sept. 19 **Litho.** **Wmk. 313**

401 A127 10pf emerald & brown 30 30
402 " 20pf brown red & yellow 4 3
403 " 25pf light blue & red 6 3

Issued to publicize the first Spartacist Sports Meet of Friendly Armies, Leipzig, Sept. 20-28.

1958, Sept. 19 *Perf. 13x13½*

404 A128 20pf rose red 5 3
405 " 25pf blue 8 3

Issued to publicize the people's fight against atomic death.

Woman and Leipzig Railroad Station—A129

Design: 25pf, Woman in Persian lamb coat and old City Hall, Leipzig.

1958, Aug. 29 *Perf. 13x12½*

406 A129 10pf green, brown & black 5 3
407 " 25pf blue & black 5 3

Issued to publicize the 1958 Leipzig Fair.

Post Wagon, 17th Century A130

Design: 20pf, Mail train and plane.

1958, Oct. 23 **Wmk. 313**

408 A130 10pf green 25 20
409 " 20pf lake 5 3

Issued for the Day of the Stamp.

Brandenburg Gate, Berlin A131 — Head from Greek Tomb A132

1958, Nov. 29 *Perf. 13x13½*

410 A131 20pf rose red 5 3
411 " 25pf dark blue 30 30

Issued to commemorate 10 years of democratic city administration of Berlin.

1958, Dec. 2 *Perf. 13½x13*

Design: 20pf, Giant's head from Pergamum frieze.

412 A132 10pf blue green & black 35 30
413 " 20pf deep rose & black 6 3

Issued to commemorate the return of art treasures from Russia. See also Nos. 484–486.

Negro and Caucasian Men—A133

Design: 25pf, Chinese and Caucasian girls.

1958, Dec. 10 *Perf. 13x12½*

414 A133 10pf bright blue green & black 5 3
415 " 25pf blue & black 30 30

Issued to commemorate the tenth anniversary of the signing of the Universal Declaration of Human Rights.

Worker and Soldier A134 — Otto Nuschke A135

1958, Nov. 7 *Perf. 12½x13*

416 A134 20pf black, vermilion & dull purple 4.50 5.00

Issued to commemorate the 40th anniversary of the Revolution of Nov. 7. (Stamp inscribed Nov. 9.) Withdrawn from sale on day of issue.

Perf. 13½x13

1958, Dec. 27 **Wmk. 313**

417 A135 20pf red 8 6

Issued to commemorate the first anniversary of the death of Otto Nuschke, vice president of the republic.

Communist Newspaper, "The Red Flag" A136

1958, Dec. 30 *Perf. 13x12½*

418 A136 20pf red 7 5

Issued to commemorate the 40th anniversary of the German Communist Party.

Rosa Luxemburg Addressing Crowd
A137

Design: 20pf, Karl Liebknecht addressing crowd.

Perf. 13x13½

1959, Jan. 15 Wmk. 313

419 A137 10pf blue green *30* *30*
420 " 20pf henna brown & black 5 5

Issued to commemorate the 40th anniversary of the death of Rosa Luxemburg and Karl Liebknecht.

Gewandhaus, Leipzig
A138

President Wilhelm Pieck
A139

Design: 25pf, Opening theme of Mendelssohn's A Major symphony.

1959, Feb. 28 Engr. *Perf. 14*

421 A138 10pf green, *greenish* 4 3
422 " 25pf blue, *bluish* *35* *25*

Issued to commemorate the 150th anniversary of the birth of Felix Mendelssohn-Bartholdy, composer.

1959, Jan. 3 Photo. *Perf. 13½x13*

423 A139 20pf henna brown 5 3

Issued to commemorate the 83rd birthday of President Wilhelm Pieck. See also No. 511.

"Black Pump" Plant
A140

Design: 25pf, Photographic equipment.

1959, Feb. 28 Litho. *Perf. 13x12½*

424 A140 20pf carmine rose 4 3
425 " 25pf light ultra. 6 3

Issued to publicize the 1959 Leipzig Spring Fair.

Boy and Girl
A141

Statue of Handel, Halle
A142

1959, Apr. 2 *Perf. 13½x13*

426 A141 10pf *light green* *30* *30*
427 " 20pf *salmon* 5 3

Issued to commemorate five years of the Youth Consecration ceremony.

1959, Apr. 27 Wmk. 313

Design: 20pf, Handel by Thomas Hudson, 1749.

428 A142 10pf bluish green & black *30* *30*
429 " 20pf rose & black 5 3

Issued to commemorate the bicentenary of the death of George Frederick Handel, composer.

Alexander von Humboldt and Central American View
A143

Post Horn
A144

Design: 20pf, Portrait and Siberian view.

1959, May 6

430 A143 10pf bluish green *30* *30*
431 " 20pf rose 5 3

Issued to commemorate the centenary of the death of Alexander von Humboldt, naturalist and geographer.

1959, May 30 *Perf. 13½x13*

432 A144 20pf scarlet, yellow & black 5 3
433 " 25pf light blue, yel. & black *45* *35*

Conference of socialist postal ministers.

Gray Heron
A145

Designs: 10pf, Bittern. 20pf, Lily of the valley and butterfly. 25pf, Beaver. 40pf, Pussy willows and bee.

1959, June 26 *Perf. 13x12½*

434 A145 5pf light blue, black & lilac 5 5
435 " 10pf greenish blue, dk. brn. & org. 5 3
436 " 20pf orange red, green & violet 5 3
437 " 25pf lilac, yel. & blk. 8 6
438 " 40pf gray blue, yel. & black *1.25* *80*
Nos. 434-438 (5) *1.48* *97*

Issued to publicize wildlife protection.

Painting Type of 1955.

Famous Paintings: 5pf, Portrait, Angelica Kauffmann. 10pf, The Lady Lace Maker, Gabriel Metsu. 20pf, Mademoiselle Lavergne, Liotard. 25pf, Old Woman with Brazier, Rubens. 40pf, Young Man in Black Coat, Hals.

Perf. 13½x13

1959, June 29 Photogravure

439 A77 5pf olive 3 3
440 " 10pf green 4 3
441 " 20pf deep orange 8 3
442 " 25pf chestnut 10 6
443 " 40pf deep magenta *1.05* *70*
Nos. 439-443 (5) *1.30* *85*

Great Cormorant
A146

Youths of Three Races
A147

Birds: 10pf, Black Stork. 15pf, Eagle owl. 20pf, Black grouse. 25pf, Hoopoe. 40pf, Peregrine falcon.

Perf. 13x13½

1959, July 2 Litho. Wmk. 313

Designs in Black.

444 A146 5pf yellow 5 3
445 " 10pf light green 5 3
446 " 15pf pale violet *1.00* *60*
447 " 20pf deep pink 5 3
448 " 25pf blue 8 5
449 " 40pf vermilion 10 7
Nos. 444-449 (6) *1.33* *81*

Protection of native birds.

Perf. 12½x13, 13x12½

1959, July 25

Design: 25pf, Swedish girl kissing African girl (horiz.).

450 A147 20pf crimson 5 3
451 " 25pf bright blue *35* *30*

Issued to publicize the 7th World Youth Festival, Vienna, July 26-Aug. 14.

Glass Tea Service
A148

Design: 25pf, Distilling apparatus (vert.).

Perf. 13x12½, 12½x13

1959, Sept. 1

452 A148 10pf bluish green 4 3
453 " 25pf bright blue *35* *30*

Issued to commemorate 75 years of Jena glassware.

Lunik 2 Hitting Moon
A149

1959, Sept. 21 *Perf. 13½x13*

454 A149 20pf rose red 10 5

Issued to commemorate the landing of the Soviet rocket Lunik 2 on the moon, Sept. 13, 1959.

New Buildings, Leipzig, Globe and Fair Emblem
A150

1959, Aug. 17 *Perf. 13x12½*

455 A150 20pf gray & rose 10 5

Issued to publicize the 1959 Leipzig Fall Fair.

Flag and Harvester
A151

Johannes R. Becher
A152

Designs (Flag and): 10pf, Fritz Heckert rest home. 15pf, Zwinger, Dresden. 20pf, Steelworker. 25pf, Chemist. 40pf, Central Stadium, Leipzig. 50pf, Woman tractor driver. 60pf, Airplane. 70pf, Merchant ship. 1m, First atomic reactor of the DDR.

1959, Oct. 6 *Perf. 13½x13*

Flag in Black, Red & Orange Yellow Inscription and Design in Black&Red.

456 A151 5pf yellow 3 3
457 " 10pf gray 4 3
458 " 15pf citron 6 3
459 " 20pf gray 6 3
460 " 25pf light gray olive 12 3
461 " 40pf citron 12 3
462 " 50pf salmon 16 4
463 " 60pf pale bluish green 12 3
464 " 70pf pale greenish yellow 16 3
465 " 1m bistre brown 24 3
Nos. 456-465 (10) 1.11 31

Issued to commemorate the 10th anniversary of the German Democratic Republic.

1959, Oct. 28 Litho. *Perf. 13x13½*

466 A152 20pf red & slate 15 7

Issued to commemorate the first anniversary of the death of Johannes R. Becher, writer.

Printed with alternating yellow labels. The label carries in blue a verse from the national anthem and Becher's signature.

Schiller's Home, Weimar
A153

Post Rider and Mile Stone, 18th Century
A154

Design: 20pf, Friedrich von Schiller.

1959, Nov. 10 Engr. *Perf. 14*

467 A153 10pf dull green, *greenish* *50* *30*
468 " 20pf lake, *pink* 8 5

Issued to commemorate the 200th anniversary of the birth of Friedrich von Schiller.

1959, Nov. 17 Litho. *Perf. 13½x13*

Design: 20pf, Motorized mailman.

469 A154 10pf green *30* *20*
470 " 20pf dark carmine rose 5 3

Issued for the Day of the Stamp.

Red Squirrels
A155

Animals: 10pf, Hares. 20pf, Roe deer. 25pf, Red deer. 40pf, Lynx.

1959, Nov. 27 *Perf. 13x12½*

471 A155 5pf gray, red brown & olive gray 3 3
472 " 10pf bright green & yellow brown 4 3
473 " 20pf vermilion, brown & olive gray 8 3
474 " 25pf blue, brown & green 10 3
475 " 40pf brt. vio., bister & olive gray *2.00* *90*
Nos. 471-475 (5) *2.25* *1.02*

Redrawn Types of 1953.
Without Imprint.
Typographed

1959-60 *Perf. 14* Wmk. 313

476 A43 5pf emerald 4 3
477 " 10pf light blue green (*Machinists*) 18 3
a. Perf. 13x12½ 9 3
b. As "a," bklt. pane of 6 55
478 A43 20pf carmine 6 3
a. Se-tenant with DEBRIA label 40 10
479 A43 30pf dull red 5 3

480 A43 40pf rose violet 10 4
481 " 50pf bright blue 15 5
482 " 70pf chocolate ('60) 20 8
Nos. 476-482 (7) 78 29

No. 478a was issued Sept. 3, 1959, to commemorate the 2nd German Stamp Exhibition, Berlin. Sheet contains 60 stamps, 40 labels.

Two other stamps without imprint are Nos. 331-332.

Type of 1958 and

Pergamum Altar of Zeus
A156

Designs: 5pf, Head of an Attic goddess, 580 B.C. 10pf, Head of a princess from Tell el Amarna, 1360 B.C. 20pf, Bronze figure from Toprak-Kale (Armenia), 7th century B.C.

1959, Dec. 29 Litho. *Perf. 13½x13*
484 A132 5pf yellow & black 3 3
485 " 10pf bluish green & black 4 3
486 " 20pf rose & black 8 3
487 A156 25pf light blue & black *95* *40*

Boxing
A157

Designs: 10pf, Sprinters. 20pf, Ski jump. 25pf, Sailboat.

Perf. 13x13½
1960, Jan. 27 Wmk. 313
488 A157 5pf brown & ochre *2.25* *80*
489 " 10pf green & ochre 4 3
490 " 20pf carmine & ochre 10 4
491 " 25pf ultramarine & ochre 15 5

Issued to publicize the 1960 Winter and Summer Olympic Games.

Technical Fair, North Entrance
A158

Design: 25pf, "Ring" Fair building.

1960, Feb. 17 *Perf. 13x12½*
492 A158 20pf red & gray 5 5
493 " 25pf light blue & gray 8 5

Issued to publicize the 1960 Leipzig Spring Fair.

Purple Foxglove
A159

Lenin
A160

Medicinal Plants: 10pf, Camomile. 15pf, Peppermint. 20pf, Poppy. 40pf, Dog rose.

1960, Apr. 7 *Perf. 12½x13*
494 A159 5pf green, gray & carmine rose 4 4
495 " 10pf citron, gray & green 4 3
496 " 15pf terra cotta, gray & green 8 8
497 " 20pf greenish blue, gray & violet 8 5
498 " 40pf brown, gray, green & red *2.00* *65*
Nos. 494-498 (5) *2.24* *85*

1960, Apr. 22 Engr. *Perf. 14*
499 A160 20pf lake 10 5

90th anniversary of the birth of Lenin.

No. 390 Overprinted:
"Inbetriebnahme des Hochseehafens
1.Mai 1960"

1960, Apr. 28 Litho. *Perf. 13½x13*
500 A122 10pf emerald 10 5

Inauguration of the seaport Rostock.

Russian Soldier and Liberated Prisoner—A161

1960, May 5 Litho. *Perf. 13x13½*
501 A161 20pf rose red 10 5

Issued to commemorate the 15th anniversary of Germany's liberation from fascism.

Model of Vacation Ship—A162

Designs: 25pf, Ship before Leningrad.

Perf. 13½x13
1960, June 23 Wmk. 313
502 A162 5pf slate, citron & black 3 3
503 " 25pf black, yellow & ultra. *1.15* *1.00*

Issued to commemorate the launching of the trade union (FDGB) vacation ship, June 25, 1960. See also Nos. B58-B59.

Masked Dancer in Porcelain
A163

Lenin Monument, Eisleben
A164

Meissen porcelain: 10pf, Plate with Meissen mark and date. 15pf, Otter. 20pf, Potter. 25pf, Coffee pot.

1960, July 28 *Perf. 12½x13*
504 A163 5pf blue & orange 3 3
505 " 10pf blue & emerald 4 3
506 " 15pf blue & purple *1.25* *1.50*
507 " 20pf blue & org. red 8 3
508 " 25pf blue & apple green 10 3
Nos. 504-508 (5) *1.50* *1.62*

Issued to commemorate the 250th anniversary of the Meissen porcelain works.

Perf. 13x13½
1960, July 2 Wmk. 313

Design: 20pf, Thälmann monument, gift for Pushkin, USSR.

509 A164 10pf dark green 6 3
510 " 20pf bright red 10 5

Pieck Type of 1959

1960, Sept. 10 Litho. *Perf. 13½x13*
511 A139 20pf black 10 5
a. Souvenir sheet 20 20

Issued in memory of Pres. Wilhelm Pieck (1876-1960). No. 511a contains one imperf. copy of No. 511 with black marginal inscription and border. Size: 89x107mm.

Modern Postal Trucks—A165

Design: 25pf, Railroad mail car, 19th century.

1960, Oct. 6 *Perf. 13x12½*
512 A165 20pf carmine rose, black & yel. 8 3
513 " 25pf blue, gray & black *65* *55*

Issued for the Day of the Stamp, 1960.

New Opera House, Leipzig—A166

Design: 25pf, Car, sailboat, tent, campers.

1960, Aug. 29 Wmk. 313
514 A166 20pf rose brown & gray 8 5
515 " 25pf blue & grayish brown 12 5

Issued to publicize the 1960 Leipzig Fall Fair.

Hans Burkmair Medal, 1518
A167

Neidhardt von Gneisenau
A168

Design: 25pf, Dancing Peasants by Albrecht Dürer.

1960, Oct. 20 Litho. *Perf. 12½x13*
516 A167 20pf buff, green & ochre 8 5
517 " 25pf lt. blue & blk. *75* *75*

Issued to commemorate the 400th anniversary of the Dresden Art Gallery.

Perf. 13x12½, 12½x13
1960, Oct. 27

Design: 20pf, Neidhardt von Gneisenau (horiz.).

518 A168 20pf dk. car. & blk. 8 5
519 " 25pf ultramarine *70* *70*

Issued to commemorate the 200th anniversary of the birth of Count August Neidhardt von Gneisenau, Prussian Field Marshal.

Rudolf Virchow
A169

Humboldt University, Berlin
A170

Designs: 10pf, Robert Koch. 25pf, Wilhelm and Alexander von Humboldt medal. 40pf, Wilhelm Griesinger.

1960, Nov. 4 Litho. *Perf. 13x12½*
520 A169 5pf ochre & black 3 3
521 " 10pf green & black 4 3
522 A170 20pf copper red, gray & black 6 3
523 " 25pf bright blue & black 7 5
524 A169 40pf carmine rose & black *1.00* *70*
Nos. 520-524 (5) *1.20* *84*

Nos. 520, 521, 524 issued to commemorate the 250th anniversary of the Charité (hospital), Berlin; Nos. 522-523 commemorate the 150th anniversary of Humboldt University, Berlin.

Nos. 520 and 523, and Nos. 521 and 522 are printed se-tenant.

Scientist and Chemical Formula
A171

"Young Socialists' Express"
A172

Designs: 10pf, Chemistry worker (fertilizer). 20pf, Woman worker (automobile). 25pf, Laboratory assistant (synthetic fabrics).

Perf. 13x13½
1960, Nov. 10 Wmk. 313
525 A171 5pf dark red & gray 3 3
526 " 10pf orange & bright green 4 3
527 " 20pf blue & red 8 3
528 " 25pf yellow & ultra. *70* *55*

Day of the Chemistry Worker.

Perf. 13x13½; 13x12½ (20pf)
1960, Dec. 5

Designs: 20pf, Sassnitz Harbor station and ferry. 25pf, Diesel locomotive and 1835 "Adler."

Sizes: 10pf, 25pf, 28x23mm.
20pf, 38½x22mm.

529 A172 10pf emerald & black 5 5
530 " 20pf red & black 5 5
531 " 25pf blue & black *3.00* *3.50*

Issued to commemorate the 125th anniversary of German railroads. No. 530 exists imperf. Price 25 cents.

Pieck Type of 1953 with Dates Added.

1961, Jan. 3 Photo. ***Perf. 13x13½***

532 A35 20pf henna brown & black 10 5

Issued on the 85th anniversary of the birth of Pres. Wilhelm Pieck (1876–1960).

380 Kilovolt Switch
A173

Lilienstein
A174

Design: 25pf, Leipzig Press Center.

1961, Mar. 3 Litho. ***Perf. 13½x13***

533 A173 10pf bright green & dark gray 4 3
534 " 25pf violet blue & dark gray 10 5

Leipzig Spring Fair of 1961.

1961 Typographed ***Perf. 14***

Designs: 5pf, Rudelsburg on Saale. 10pf, Wartburg. No. 538, City Hall, Wernigerode. 25pf, Brocken, Harz Mts. (horiz.).

535 A174 5pf gray 4 3
536 " 10pf blue green 6 3
537 " 20pf red brown 10 3
538 " 20pf dull red 10 3
539 " 25pf dark blue 10 4
Nos. 535–539 (5) 40 16

Trawler
A176

Designs: 20pf, Fishermen. 25pf, S.S. Robert Koch. 40pf, Cannery worker.

1961, Apr. 4 Engr. **Wmk. 313**

545 A176 10pf gray green 4 3
546 " 20pf claret 5 3
547 " 25pf slate 5 3
548 " 40pf dull violet *1.35* *1.00*

Deep-sea fishing industry.

Vostok 1 Leaving Earth
A177

Designs: 20pf, Astronaut in capsule. 25pf, Parachute landing of capsule.

Lithographed

1961, Apr. ***Perf. 13x12½***

549 A177 10pf light blue green & red 20 8
550 " 20pf red 25 8
551 " 25pf light blue *2.25* *2.50*

Issued to commemorate the first man in space, Yuri A. Gagarin, Apr. 12, 1961.

Issue dates: 10pf, Apr. 18; others, Apr. 20.

Engels, Marx, Lenin and Crowd
A179

Design: 20pf, Black-and-white colobus monkeys.

1961, May 9

552 A178 10pf green & black *1.40* *1.00*
553 " 20pf lilac rose & black 8 5

Centenary of the Dresden Zoo.

1961, April 20 Litho. ***Perf. 13½x13***

554 A179 20pf red 10 5

15th anniversary of Socialist Unity Party of Germany (SED).

Stag Leap—A180

Designs: 20pf, Arabesque. 25pf, Exercise on parallel bars (horiz.).

Perf. 13½x13, 13x13½

1961, June 3

555 A180 10pf blue green 5 3
556 " 20pf rose pink 10 4
557 " 25pf bright blue *1.75* *1.75*

3rd Europa Cup for Women's Gymnastics.

Salt Miners and Castle Giebichenstein
A181

Design: 20pf, Chemist and "Five Towers" of Halle.

1961, June 22 ***Perf. 13x12½***

558 A181 10pf black, green & yellow *50* *50*
559 " 20pf black, dk. red & yellow 8 5

Issued to commemorate the 1000th anniversary of the founding of Halle.

Kayak Slalom
A182

Designs: 10pf, Canoe. 20pf, Two-seater canoe.

1961, July 6 Litho. **Wmk. 313**

560 A182 5pf gray & Pruss. blue *1.25* *1.25*
561 " 10pf gray & slate green 5 3
562 " 20pf gray & dark carmine rose 5 5

Issued to commemorate the Canoe Slalom and Rapids World Championships.

Target Line Casting
A183

Design: 20pf, River fishing.

1961, July 21

563 A183 10pf green & blue *1.35* *1.35*
564 " 20pf dk. red brown & blue 10 5

World Fishing Championships, Dresden.

Tulip
A184

"Alte Waage," Historical Building, Leipzig
A185

Designs: 20pf, Dahlia. 40pf, Rose.

Photogravure

1961, Sept. 13 ***Perf. 14***

565 A184 10pf green, red & yellow 5 5
566 " 20pf brown, red & yellow 10 8
567 " 40pf blue, pink, yel. & green *2.25* *2.25*

Issued to commemorate the International Horticulture Exhibition, Erfurt.

Perf. 13½x13

1961, Aug. 23 Litho. **Wmk. 313**

Design: 25pf, Old Exchange Building.

568 A185 10pf citron & blue green 5 3
569 " 25pf light blue & ultramarine 25 5

Issued to publicize the 1961 Leipzig Fall Fair. See also Nos. 595–597.

Liszt's Hand, French Sculpture
A186

Television Camera and Screen
A187

Designs: 5pf, Liszt and Hector Berlioz. 20pf, Franz Liszt, medallion by Ernst Rietschel, 1852. 25pf, Liszt and Frederic Chopin.

1961, Oct.-Nov. Engr. ***Perf. 14***

570 A186 5pf gray 4 3
571 " 10pf blue green *40* *40*
572 " 20pf dull red 12 8
573 " 25pf chalky blue *60* *60*

Issued to commemorate the 150th anniversary of the birth of Franz Liszt, composer.

1961, Oct. 25 ***Perf. 13x13½***

Design: 20pf, Microphone and radio dial.

574 A187 10pf brt. grn. & blk. *50* *50*
575 " 20pf brick red & black 5 5

Issued for Stamp Day, 1961.

Maj. Gherman Titov and Young Pioneers—A188

Designs: 10pf, Titov in Leipzig (vert.). 15pf, Titov in spaceship. 20pf, Titov and Walter Ulbricht. 25pf, Spaceship Vostok 2. 40pf, Titov and Ulbricht in Berlin.

1961, Dec. 11 Litho. ***Perf. 13½***

576 A188 5pf carmine & vio. 8 8
577 " 10pf olive green & carmine 10 10
578 " 15pf blue & lilac *3.00* *4.00*
579 " 20pf blue & car. rose 12 10
580 " 25pf car. & blue 10 10
581 " 40pf carmine & dark blue 30 10
Nos. 576–581 (6) *3.70* *4.48*

Issued to commemorate the visit of Russian Maj. Gherman Titov to the German Democratic Republic.

Chairman Walter Ulbricht
A189

Red Ants
A190

Typographed

1961-67 ***Perf. 14*** **Wmk. 313**

Size: 17x21mm.

582 A189 5pf slate 4 3
a. Bklt. pane of 8 32
583 " 10pf bright green 6 3
a. Bklt. pane of 8 48
584 " 15pf red lilac 8 3
585 " 20pf dark red 10 3
586 " 25pf dull blue ('63) 16 3
587 " 30pf car. rose ('63) 20 3
588 " 40pf brt. vio. ('63) 20 3
589 " 50pf ultra. ('63) 32 3
589A " 60pf dp. yel. green ('64) 40 3
590 " 70pf red brown ('63) 48 3
590A " 80pf brt. bl. ('67) 60 3

Engraved

Size: 24x28½mm.

590B A189 1dm dull grn. ('63) 60 4
590C " 2dm brown ('63) 1.25 5
Nos. 582–590C (13) 4.49 42

See also Nos. 751–752, 1112A–1114A, 1483. Currency abbreviation is "DM" on Nos. 590B–590C, "MDN" on Nos. 751–752, and "M" on Nos. 1113–1114A.

1962, Feb. 16 Photogravure

Designs: 10pf, Weasels. 20pf, Shrews. 40pf, Bat.

591 A190 5pf yellow, black & brown *1.20* *1.00*
592 " 10pf br. green & red brown 10 5
593 " 20pf dark carmine & dp. brown 15 8
594 " 40pf violet, gray & yellow 35 12

See also Nos. 663–667.

Type of 1961

Buildings: 10pf, "Coffee Tree House." 20pf, Gohlis Castle. 25pf, Romanus House.

1962, Feb. 22 Litho. ***Perf. 13x13½***

595 A185 10pf olive green & brown 10 5
596 " 20pf org. red & blk. 20 12
597 " 25pf bright blue & brown 35 24

Leipzig Spring Fair of 1962.

Air Defense
A191

Designs: 10pf, Motorized infantry. 20pf, Soldier and worker as protectors. 25pf, Sailor and destroyer escort. 40pf, Tank and tankman.

1962, March 1 *Perf. 13x12½*

598 A191 5pf light blue 6 3
599 " 10pf bright green 8 4
600 " 20pf red 16 8
601 " 25pf ultramarine 20 20
602 " 40pf brown *90* *1.00*
Nos. 598-602 (5) *1.40* *1.35*

Issued to commemorate the 6th anniversary of the National People's Army.

Cyclists and Hradcany, Prague
A192

Design: 25pf, Cyclist, East Berlin City Hall and dove.

1962, Apr. 26 Litho. Wmk. 313

603 A192 10pf multicolored 10 8
604 " 25pf " *1.10* 70

Issued to commemorate the 15th International Bicycle Peace Race, Berlin-Warsaw-Prague. See also No. B89.

Johann Gottlieb Fichte
A193

Design: 10pf, Fichte's birthplace in Rammenau.

1962, May 17 *Perf. 13x13½*

605 A193 10pf bright green & black *50* *50*
606 " 20pf verm. & black 10 10

Issued to commemorate bicentenary of the birth of Johann Gottlieb Fichte, philosopher.

Cross, Crown of Thorns and Rose
A194

George Dimitrov at Reichstag Trial, Leipzig
A195

1962, June 7 *Perf. 12½x13*

607 A194 20pf red & black 5 10
608 " 25pf brt. blue & blk. *70* *70*

Issued to commemorate the 20th anniversary of the destruction of Lidice in Czechoslovakia by the Nazis.

1962, June 18 Photo. *Perf. 14*

Design: 20pf, Dimitrov as Premier of Bulgaria.

609 A195 5pf blue grn. & blk. *45* *40*
610 " 20pf car. rose & blk. 5 5

Issued to commemorate the 80th anniversary of the birth of George Dimitrov, (1882–1949), communist leader and premier of the Bulgarian Peoples' Republic.

Nos. 609–610 are printed se-tenant, divided by a label inscribed with a Dimitrov quotation.

Corn Planter
A196

Designs: 20pf, Milking machine. 40pf, Combine harvester.

1962, June 26 Litho. *Perf. 13x12½*

611 A196 10pf multicolored 5 5
612 " 20pf " 10 5
613 " 40pf yellow, green & dark red *85* *85*

10th Agricultural Exhibition, Markkleeberg.

Map of Baltic Sea and Emblem
A197

Brandenburg Gate, Berlin
A198

Designs: 20pf, Hotel, Rostock (vert.). 25pf, Cargo ship "Frieden" in Rostock harbor.

Perf. 13x13½, 13½x13 (20pf)

1962, July 2 Wmk. 313

614 A197 10pf bluish green & ultra. 6 3
615 " 20pf dk. red & yel. 10 10
616 " 25pf blue & bistre *80* *80*

Issued to commemorate the Fifth Baltic Sea Week, Rostock, July 7–15.

1962, July 17 *Perf. 13½x13*

Designs: No. 618, Heads of youths of three races. No. 619, Peace dove. No. 620, National Theater, Helsinki.

617 A198 5pf multicolored *30* *35*
618 " 5pf " *30* *35*
619 " 20pf " *30* *35*
620 " 20pf " *30* *35*

Issued to publicize the 8th Youth Festival for Peace and Friendship, Helsinki, July 28–Aug. 6, 1962.

Printed in sheets of 60 incorporating all four designs arranged in blocks to form the festival flower emblem. See Nos. B90–B91.

Free Style Swimming
A199

Municipal Store, Leipzig
A200

Designs: 10pf, Back stroke. 25pf, Butterfly stroke. 40pf, Breast stroke. 70pf, Water polo.

1962, Aug. 7 Litho. *Perf. 13x13½*

Design in Greenish Blue

621 A199 5pf orange 5 4
622 " 10pf greenish blue 5 3
623 " 25pf ultramarine 5 3
624 " 40pf bright violet *2.00* *2.00*
625 " 70pf red brown 15 10
Nos. 621-625, B92 (6) *2.35* *2.25*

Issued to publicize the 10th European Swimming Championships, Leipzig, Aug. 18–25.

Nos. 621–625 and B92 were also printed in the same sheet, arranged in se-tenant blocks of six.

Engraved and Photogravure

1962, Aug. 28 *Perf. 14* Wmk. 313

Buildings: 20pf, Mädler Passage. 25pf, Leipzig Air Terminal and plane.

626 A200 10pf blk. & emerald 10 5
627 " 20pf black & red 25 5
628 " 25pf black & blue 30 20

Leipzig Fall Fair of 1962.

"Transportation and Communication"
A201

1962, Oct. 3 Litho. *Perf. 13½x13*

629 A201 5pf lt. blue & blk. 10 6

Issued to commemorate the 10th anniversary of the Friedrich List Transportation College.

Souvenir Sheet

WOSTOK III 11.8.1962, 9.30 Uhr, bis 15.8.1962, 7.55 Uhr (MEZ)
WOSTOK IV 12.8.1962, 9.02 Uhr, bis 15.8.1962, 8.01 Uhr (MEZ)

Pavel R. Popovich, Andrian G. Nikolayev and Space Capsules
A202

1962, Sept. 13 *Imperf.* Wmk. 313

630 A202 70pf dk. blue, light green & yel. *1.50* *1.50*

Issued to commemorate the first Russian group space flight of Vostoks III and IV, Aug. 11–13, 1962. Sheet has dark blue marginal inscription and two red stars. Size: 88x106mm.

DDR Television Signal
A203

Young Collectors and World Map
A204

1962, Oct. 25 *Perf. 13½x13*

631 A203 20pf green & gray 18 3
632 A204 40pf brt. pink & blk. *75* *85*

No. 631 commemorates the 10th anniversary of television in the German Democratic Republic; No. 632 is for Stamp Day.

Gerhart Hauptmann—A205

1962, Nov. 15 *Perf. 13x13½*

633 A205 20pf red & black 25 5

Issued to commemorate the centenary of the birth of Gerhart Hauptmann, playwright.

Souvenir Sheet

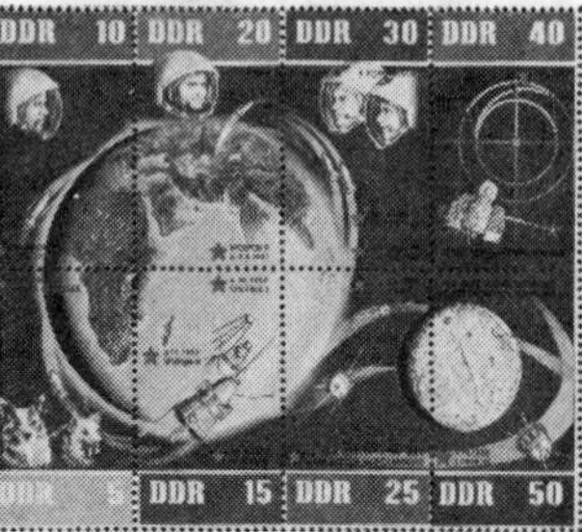

Russian Space Flights and Astronauts—A206

1962, Dec. 28 Litho. *Perf. 12½x13*

634 A206 Sheet of 8, multi. *9.00* *10.50*
a. 5pf yellow 75
b. 10pf emerald 75
c. 15pf magenta 75
d. 20pf red 75
e. 25pf greenish blue 75
f. 30pf red brown 75
g. 40pf crimson 75
h. 50pf ultramarine 75

Issued to show the development of Russian space flights from Sputnik 1 to Vostoks 3 and 4, and to honor the Russian astronauts Gagarin, Titov, Nikolayev and Popovich. Size: 127x107mm.

Pierre de Coubertin
A207

Congress Emblem, Flag with Marx, Engels and Lenin
A208

Design: 25pf, Stadium and Olympic rings.

1963, Jan. 2 *Perf. 13½x13*

635 A207 20pf carmine & gray 10 5
636 " 25pf blue & bister *60* *50*

Issued to commemorate the centenary of the birth of Baron Pierre de Coubertin, organizer of the modern Olympic Games.

1963, Jan. 15 *Perf. 13x13½*

637 A208 10pf yellow, orange, red & black 12 5

6th congress of Socialist Unity Party of Germany (SED).

World Map and Exterminator
A209

Designs: 25pf, Map, cross and staff of Aesculapius. 50pf, Map, cross, mosquito.

1963, Feb. 6 *Perf. 13x12½*

638 A209 20pf deep orange, dk. red & blk. 5 5

639 A209 25pf multicolored 10 5
640 " 50pf " 1.25 1.25

Issued for the World Health Organization drive to eradicate malaria.

Silver Fox
A210

Design: 25pf, Karakul.

1963, Feb. 14 Photo. *Perf. 14*

641 A210 20pf rose & black 10 5
642 " 25pf blue & black 60 60

Issued to publicize the International Fur Auctions. Leipzig, Feb. 14–15, Apr. 21–24.

Barthels House, Leipzig
A211

Designs: 20pf, New Leipzig City Hall. 25pf, Belltower Building.

Engraved and Photogravure

1963, Feb. 26 *Perf. 14* Wmk. 313

643 A211 10pf black & citron 8 5
644 " 20pf blk. & red orge. 12 10
645 " 25pf black & blue 35 35

1963 Leipzig Spring Fair.

Souvenir Sheet

On March 12, 1963, a souvenir sheet publicizing "Chemistry for Peace and Socialism" was issued. It contains two imperforate stamps, 50pf and 70pf, printed on ungummed synthetic tissue. Size: 105x74mm. Price $2.

Richard Wagner and "The Flying Dutchman"
A213

Designs (Portrait and Scene from Play): 5pf, Johann Gottfried Seume (1763–1810). 10pf, Friedrich Hebbel (1813–1863). 20pf, Georg Büchner (1813–1837).

1963, Apr. 9 Litho. *Perf. 13x12½*

647 A213 5pf bright citron & black 5 3
648 " 10pf brt. grn. & blk. 5 3
649 " 20pf orange & blk. 5 5
650 " 25pf dull bl. & blk. 1.00 90

Issued to commemorate anniversaries of German dramatists and the 150th anniversary of the birth of Richard Wagner, composer.

First Aid Station
A214

Design: 20pf, Ambulance and hospital.

1963, May 14 Wmk. 313

651 A214 10pf multicolored 65 65
652 " 20pf red, blk. & gray 5 5

Centenary of International Red Cross.

Eugene Pottier, Writer—A215

Design: 25pf, Pierre-Chretien Degeyter, composer.

1963, June 18 *Perf. 13x13½*

653 A215 20pf verm. & black 8 5
654 " 25pf vio. bl. & blk. 65 65

Issued to commemorate the 75th anniversary of the communist song "The International."

Valentina Tereshkova and Vostok 6
A216

Motorcyclist in "Motocross" at Apolda
A217

Design: No. 656, Valeri Bykovski and Vostok 5.

1963, July 18 Photo. *Perf. 13½*

655 A216 20pf blue, black & gray blue 20 5
656 " 20pf blue, black & gray blue 20 5

Issued to commemorate the space flights of Valeri Bykovski, June 14–19, and Valentina Tereshkova, first woman cosmonaut, June 16–19, 1963.

Nos. 655–656 printed se-tenant. Each sheet contains 40 se-tenant pairs.

Engraved & Photogravure

1963, July 30 *Perf. 14*

Designs: 20pf, Motorcyclist at Sachsenring (horiz.). 25pf, Two motorcyclists at Sachsenring (horiz.).

Size: 23x28mm.

657 A217 10pf lt. grn. & dk. grn. 1.35 1.35

Size: 48½x21mm.

658 A217 20pf rose & dk. red 5 3
659 " 25pf lt. bl. & dk. bl. 8 4

Motorcycle World Championships.

Monument at Treblinka
A218

Globe, Car and Train
A219

Perf. 13x13½

1963, Aug. 20 Litho. Wmk. 313

660 A218 20pf brick red & dark blue 18 3

Issued to commemorate the erection of a memorial at Treblinka (Poland) concentration camp.

1963, Aug. 27 *Perf. 13½x13*

Design: No. 662, Globe, plane and bus.

661 A219 10pf multicolored 15 3
662 " 10pf " 15 3

Issued to publicize the 1963 Leipzig Fall Fair. Nos. 661–662 printed se-tenant.

Fauna Type of 1962

Designs: 10pf, Stag beetle. 20pf, Fire salamander. 30pf, Pond turtle. 50pf, Green toad. 70pf, Hedgehogs.

1963, Sept. 10 Photo. *Perf. 14*

663 A190 10pf emerald, brown & black 3 3
664 " 20pf crimson, black & yellow 5 3
665 " 30pf multicolored 10 4
666 " 50pf " 1.85 1.50
667 " 70pf claret brown, brown & bister 22 8
Nos. 663–667 (5) 2.25 1.68

Neidhardt von Gneisenau and Gebhard Leberecht von Blücher
A220

Designs: 10pf, Cossacks and home guard, Berlin. 20pf, Ernst Moritz Arndt and Baron Heinrich vom Stein. 25pf, Lützow's volunteers before battle. 40pf, Gerhard von Scharnhorst and Prince Mikhail I. Kutuzov.

1963, Oct. 10 Litho. *Perf. 13½x13*

Center in Tan and Black

668 A220 5pf bright yellow 4 3
669 " 10pf emerald 5 3
670 " 20pf deep orange 10 5
671 " 25pf dp. ultramarine 10 8
672 " 40pf dark red 1.00 1.00
Nos. 668–672 (5) 1.29 1.19

150th anniversary of War of Liberation.

Valentina Tereshkova and Space Craft
A221

Burning Synagogue and Star of David in Chains
A222

Designs: No. 674, Tereshkova and map of DDR (vert.). No. 675, Yuri A. Gagarin and map of DDR (vert.). 25pf, Tereshkova in space capsule.

1963 *Perf. 13½x13, 13x13½*

Size: 28x28mm. (10pf, 25pf); 28x37mm. (20pf)

673 A221 10pf ultra. & green 5 5
674 " 20pf red, black & ocher 10 5
675 " 20pf red, green & ocher 10 5
676 " 25pf orange & blue 90 90

Issued to commemorate the visit of astronauts Valentina Tereshkova and Yuri A. Gagarin to the German Democratic Republic.

Perf. 13½x13

1963, Nov. 8 Wmk. 313

677 A222 10pf multicolored 12 3

Issued to mark the 25th anniversary of the "Crystal Night," the start of the systematic persecution of the Jews in Germany. Inscribed: "Never again Crystal Night."

Letter Sorting Machine—A223

Design: 20pf, Mechanized mail loading.

1963, Nov. 25 *Perf. 13x12½*

678 A223 10pf multicolored 40 40
679 " 20pf " 10 5

Issued for Stamp Day.

Ski Jump and Olympic Rings
A224

Designs (ski jumps): 10pf, Start. 25pf, Landing.

1963, Dec. 16 Litho. *Perf. 13½x13*

Rings in Blue, Yellow, Black, Emerald & Carmine

680 A224 5pf brt. yel. & blk. 5 3
681 " 10pf emerald & blk. 5 3
682 " 25pf blue & back 1.00 1.00

Issued to publicize the 9th Winter Olympic Games, Innsbruck, Jan. 29–Feb. 9, 1964. See also No. B111.

Admiral—A225

Butterflies: 15pf, Alpine Apollo. 20pf, Swallowtail. 25pf, Postillon. 40pf, Great fox.

Photogravure

1964, Jan. 15 *Perf. 14* Wmk. 313

Butterflies in Natural Colors

683 A225 10pf citron & black 5 3
684 " 15pf pale violet & black 8 5
685 " 20pf light brick red & black 8 3
686 " 25pf light blue & dark brown 10 10
687 " 40pf light ultra. & black 1.20 1.00
Nos. 683–687 (5) 1.51 1.21

William Shakespeare
A226

Designs: 20pf, Quadriga, Brandenburg Gate, Berlin. 25pf, Keystone, History Museum (Zeughaus), Berlin.

1964, Feb. 6 Litho. *Perf. 13x12½*

688 A226 20pf rose & dk. bl. 10 3
689 " 25pf light blue & magenta 10 10
690 " 40pf light violet & dk. bl. grn. 1.25 90

Issued to commemorate the 200th anniversary of the birth of the sculptor Johann Gottfried Schadow (20pf); the 300th anniversary of the birth of the sculptor Andreas Schlüter (25pf), and the 400th anniversary of the birth of William Shakespeare, dramatist (40pf).

Electrical Engineering Exhibit
A227

Design: 20pf, Bräunigkes Court, exhibition hall, 1700.

Perf. 13x13½

1964, Feb. 26 **Wmk. 313**

691	A227	10pf brt. grn. & blk.	55	3
692	"	20pf red & black	90	5

Issued to publicize the Leipzig Spring Fair, March 1–10, 1964. Nos. 691–692 printed in same sheet with alternating yellow and black label.

Khrushchev and Inventors
A228

Youth Training for Leadership
A229

Design: 40pf, Khrushchev, Tereshkova and Bykovski.

1964, May 15 ***Perf. 13x13½***

693	A228	25pf blue	10	5
694	"	40pf lilac & greenish black	2.00	1.10

Issued in honor of Premier Nikita S. Khrushchev of the Soviet Union.

1964, May 13 **Lithographed**

Designs: 20pf, Young athletes. 25pf, Accordion player and girl with flowers.

Center in Black

695	A229	10pf ultra., magenta & emerald	5	3
696	"	20pf emerald, ultra. & magenta	10	5
697	"	25pf magenta, emerald & ultra.	85	65

German Youth Meeting, Berlin.

Television Antenna and Puppets
A230

Designs: Various characters from children's television programs.

1964, June 1 ***Perf. 13x13½***

Black Background

698	A230	5pf multicolored	5	3
699	"	10pf "	5	5
700	"	15pf "	8	8
701	"	20pf "	10	5
702	"	40pf "	1.60	1.10
		Nos. 698-702 (5)	1.88	1.31

Issued for Children's Day.

Woman as Educator and Portrait of Jenny Marx
A231

Designs: 25pf, Women in industry and transistor diagram. 70pf, Women in agriculture.

Perf. 13½x13

1964, June 26 Litho. Wmk. 313

703	A231	20pf crimson, gray & yellow	5	4
704	"	25pf lt. bl., gray & red	1.40	1.00
705	"	70pf emerald, gray & yellow	18	10

Issued to commemorate the Congress of Women of the German Democratic Republic, June 25–27.

Bicycling
A232

Diving
A233

Designs: 10pf, Volleyball. 20pf, Judo. 25pf, Woman diver. 70pf, Equestrian.

Lithographed and Engraved

1964, July 15 ***Perf. 14***

Olympic Rings in Blue, Yellow, Black, Green and Red

706	A232	5pf green & black	5	3
707	"	10pf yel. grn. & blk.	5	3
708	"	20pf red & black	5	3
709	"	25pf dark bl. & blk.	10	4
710	"	70pf bister & blk.	1.80	1.50
		Nos. 706-710, B118 (6)	2.40	1.73

Lithographed

Perf. 13x13½

Designs: No. 712, Volleyball. No. 713, Bicycling. No. 714, Judo.

711	A233	10pf multicolored	75	75
712	"	10pf "	75	75
713	"	10pf "	75	75
714	"	10pf "	75	75
		a. Block of six (Nos. 711-714 and B119-B120)	5.00	5.00

Nos. 706–714 commemorate the 18th Olympic Games, Tokyo, Oct. 10–25, 1964. See also Nos. B118–B120. No. 714a printed in 2 horizontal rows: (first row: No. 711, No. B119, No. 712. Second row: No. 713, No. B120, No. 714). The Olympic rings extend over the six stamps.

Monument, Leningrad
A234

1964, Aug. 8 Litho. ***Perf. 13x13½***

715	A234	25pf bright blue, blk. & yellow	30	6

Issued to honor the victims of the siege of Leningrad, Sept. 1941–Jan. 1943.

Bertha von Suttner
A235

Medieval Glazier and Goblet
A236

Designs: 20pf, Frederic Joliot Curie. 50pf, Carl von Ossietzky.

1964, Sept. 1 ***Perf. 14***

716	A235	20pf red & black	12	3
717	"	25pf ultra. & black	15	5
718	"	50pf lilac & black	1.10	90

Issued to promote World Peace.

1964, Sept. 3 ***Perf. 14***

Design: 15pf, Jena glass for chemical industry.

719	A236	10pf lt. ultra. & multi.	22	3
720	"	15pf red & multi.	22	3

Issued for the Leipzig Fall Fair, 1964. Nos. 719–720 printed as triptychs with label inscribed "800 years Leipzig Fair" between.

Handstamp of First Socialist International, 1864
A237

1964, Sept. 16 Photo. Wmk. 313

721	A237	20pf orge. red & blk.	12	5
722	"	25pf dull bl. & black	60	55

Centenary of First Socialist International.

Stamp of 1955 (Dürer's Portrait of Young Man)
A238

1964, Sept. 23 Litho. ***Perf. 13x13½***

723	A238	50pf gray & dark red brown	1.10	90

Issued to publicize the National Stamp Exhibition, Berlin, Oct. 3–18. See also Nos. B124–B125.

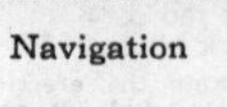

Navigation
A239

Man from Mönchgut, Rügen
A240

Designs: No. 725, Flag and new Berlin buildings. No. 726, Bituminous coal transport and surveyors level. No. 727, Chemist. No. 728, Soldier. No. 729, Farm woman and cows. No. 730, Steel worker. No. 731, Woman scientist and lecture hall. No. 732, Heavy industry. No. 733, Optical industry. No. 734, Consumer goods (woman examining cloth). No. 735, Foreign trade, Leipzig fair emblem. No. 736, Buildings industry. No. 737, Sculptor. No. 738, Woman skier.

Perf. 13½x13

1964, Oct. 6 Litho. Wmk. 313

724	A239	10pf blue & multi.	12	3
725	"	10pf blue & multi.	12	3
726	"	10pf gray & multi.	12	3
727	"	10pf red & multi.	12	3
728	"	10pf red & multi.	12	3
729	"	10pf yellow green & multi.	12	3
730	"	10pf red & multi.	12	3
731	"	10pf red & multi.	12	3
732	"	10pf gray & multi.	12	3
733	"	10pf gray & multi.	12	3
734	"	10pf blue & multi.	12	3
735	"	10pf blue & multi.	12	3
736	"	10pf yellow green & multi.	12	3
737	"	10pf yellow green & multi.	12	3
738	"	10pf blue & multi.	12	3
		Nos. 724-738 (15)	1.80	45

Issued to commemorate the 15th anniversary of the German Democratic Republic. A souvenir sheet contains 15 imperf. stamps similar to Nos. 724–738; map of Republic in background, inscription and coat of arms in margin. Size: 210x287mm. Price $11.

1964, Nov. 25 Photo. ***Perf. 14***

Regional Costumes: No. 740, Woman from Mönchgut, Rügen. No. 741, Man from Spreewald. No. 742, Woman from Spreewald. No. 743, Man from Thuringia. No. 744, Woman from Thuringia.

739	A240	5pf multicolored	2.25	2.25
740	"	5pf "	2.25	2.25
741	"	10pf "	10	6
742	"	10pf "	10	6
743	"	20pf "	20	10
744	"	20pf "	20	10
		Nos. 739-744 (6)	5.10	4.82

The male and female costume stamps of the same denomination are printed se-tenant in checkerboard arrangement.

See also Nos. 859–864.

Souvenir Sheets

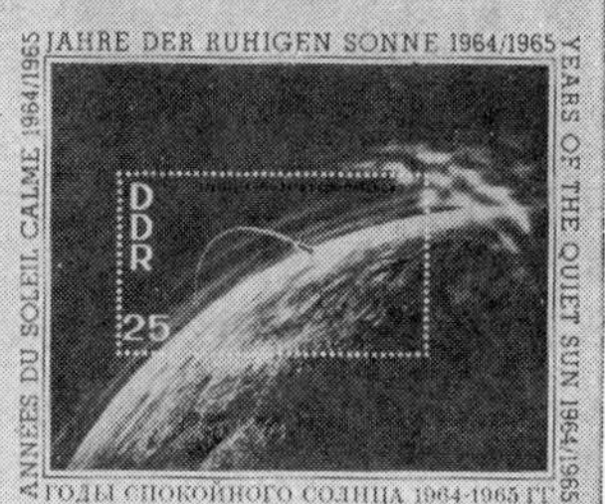

Exploration of Ionosphere
A241

Designs: 40pf, Exploration of sun activities. 70pf, Exploration of radiation belt.

1964, Dec. 29 Litho. ***Perf. 13½x13***

745	A241	25pf vio. bl. & yel.	2.50	2.50
746	"	40pf vio. blue, yel. & red	60	60
747	"	70pf dp. green, vio. blue & yel.	80	80

Issued to publicize the International Quiet Sun Year, 1964–65. Nos. 745–747 contain one stamp. Size of stamp: 54x30 mm.; size of sheet: 107x90mm.

Albert Schweitzer as Physician
A242

August Bebel
A243

Designs (Schweitzer): 20pf, As fighter against war and atom bomb. 25pf, At the organ with score of Organ Prelude by Bach.

Photogravure

1965, Jan. 14 ***Perf. 14*** **Wmk. 313**

748 A242 10pf emerald, blk. & bister 5 5
749 " 20pf crimson, blk. & bister 10 5
750 " 25pf blue, black & bister *1.75* *1.35*

Issued to commemorate the 90th birthday of Dr. Albert Schweitzer, medical missionary.

Ulbricht Type of 1961–63
Currency in "Mark of the Deutsche Notenbank" (MDN)

1965, Feb. 10 Engraved

Size: 24x28½mm.

751 A189 1mdn dull green 80 5
752 " 2mdn brown 1.20 8

See note below Nos. 590B–590C.

1965 **Photogravure** ***Perf. 14***

Portraits: 10pf, Wilhelm Conrad Röntgen. No. 753A, Adolph von Menzel. 25pf, Wilhelm Külz. 40pf, Erich Weinert. 50pf, Dante Alighieri.

753 A243 10pf dk. brn., yel. & emerald 10 3
753A " 10pf dk. brn., yel. & orange 10 3
754 " 20pf olive brown, red & buff 20 3
754A " 25pf olive brown, yel. & blue 25 3
754B " 40pf olive brn., buff & car. rose 45 4
755 " 50pf dk. brown, yel. & org. 65 4
Nos. 753-755 (6) 1.75 20

No. 753 commemorates the 120th anniversary of the birth of Wilhelm Conrad Röntgen (1845–1923), physicist, discoverer of X-rays. No. 753A, the sesquicentennial of the birth of Adolph von Menzel, painter and graphic artist. No. 754, the 125th anniversary of the birth of August Bebel, labor leader (1840–1913). No. 754A, the 90th anniversary of the birth of Wilhelm Külz, politician. No. 754B, the 75th anniversary of the birth of Erich Weinert, poet. No. 755, the 700th anniversary of the birth of Dante Alighieri (1265–1321), Italian poet.

Issue dates: No. 753, Mar. 24; No. 753A, Dec. 8; 20pf, Feb. 22; 25pf, July 5; 40pf, July 28; 50pf, Apr. 15.

Gold Medal, Leipzig Fair
A244

Designs: 15pf, Obverse of medal, arms of German Democratic Republic. 25pf, Chemical plant.

1965, Feb. 25 **Wmk. 313**

756 A244 10pf lilac rose & gold 10 8
757 " 15pf lilac rose & gold 15 12
758 " 25pf bright blue, yellow & gold 25 12

Issued to publicize the 1965 Leipzig Spring Fair and to commemorate the 800th anniversary of the Fair.

Giraffe—A245

Designs: 25pf, Common iguana (horiz.). 30pf, White-tailed gnu.

1965, Mar. 24

759 A245 10pf green & gray 8 3
760 " 25pf dark violet blue & gray 20 4
761 " 30pf brown & gray 80 80

10th anniversary of Berlin Zoo.

Col. Pavel Belyayev and Lt. Col. Alexei Leonov
A246

Boxing Glove and Laurel Wreath
A247

Design: 25pf, Lt. Col. Leonov floating in space.

Perf. 13½x13

1965, Apr. 15 **Litho.** **Wmk. 313**

762 A246 10pf red 8 3
763 " 25pf dark ultra. *65* *65*

Issued to commemorate the space flight of Voskhod 2 and the first man walking in space, Lt. Col. Alexei Leonov.

1965, Apr. 27 **Photo.** ***Perf. 14***

764 A247 20pf blk., red & gold *60* *60*

Issued to publicize the 16th European Boxing Championship, Berlin, May, 1965. See also No. B126.

Walter Ulbricht and Erich Weinert Distributing "Free Germany" Leaflets on the Eastern Front
A248

Designs: 50pf, Liberation of concentration camps. 60pf, Russian soldiers raising flag on Reichstag, Berlin. 70pf, Political demonstration.

1965, May 5 Photogravure ***Perf. 14***

Flags in Red, Black & Yellow

765 A248 40pf bl. grn. & red 15 15
766 " 50pf dull blue & red 18 18
767 " 60pf brown & red *3.50* *3.00*
768 " 70pf vio. blue & red 18 18
Nos. 765-768, B127-B131 (9) *4.49* *3.99*

Issued to commemorate the 20th anniversary of liberation from fascism.

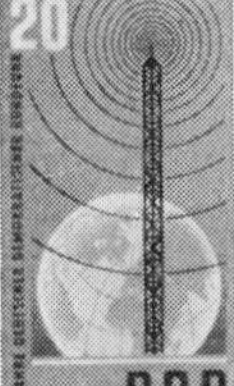

Radio Tower and Globe
A249

ITU Emblem and Frequency Diagram
A250

Design: 40pf, Workers and broadcasting equipment.

1965, May 12 Litho. ***Perf. 12½x13***

769 A249 20pf dk. carmine rose & black 5 5
770 " 40pf vio. bl. & blk. *75* *60*

Issued to commemorate the 20th anniversary of the German Democratic broadcasting system.

1965, May 17

Design: 25pf, ITU emblem and telephone diagram.

771 A250 20pf olive, yellow & black 5 5
772 " 25pf vio., pale violet & black *65* *50*

Issued to commemorate the centenary of the International Telecommunication Union.

Emblem of Free German Trade Union
A251

Hemispheres with Crowd of Workers—A252

1965, June 10 **Photo.** ***Perf. 14***

773 A251 20pf red & gold 5 5
774 A252 25pf gold, bl. & blk. *65* *50*

Issued to commemorate the 20th anniversary of the Free German Trade Union (FDGB) and of the World Organization of Trade Unions.

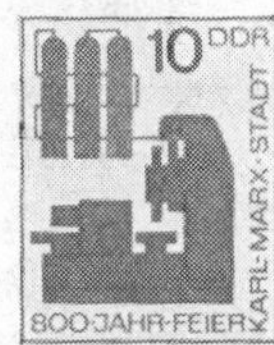

Symbols of Industry
A253

Marx and Lenin
A254

Designs: 20pf, Red Tower. 25pf, City Hall.

1965, June 16

775 A253 10pf gold & emerald 5 4
776 " 20pf gold & crimson 10 5
777 " 25pf gold & brt. bl. *70* *70*

Issued to commemorate the 800th anniversary of Chemnitz (Karl Marx City).

1965, June 21 Litho. ***Perf. 13½x13***

778 A254 20pf red, blk. & buff 20 5

Issued to commemorate the 6th Conference of Postal Ministers of Communist Countries, Peking, June 21–July 15.

"Alte Waage" and New Building, Leipzig
A255

Designs: 25pf, Old City Hall. 40pf, Opera House and General Post Office. 70pf, Hotel "Stadt Leipzig."

Perf. 14

1965, Aug. 25 **Photo.** **Unwmkd.**

781 A255 10pf gold, claret brn. & ultra. 5 4
a. Souv. sheet of 2 1.80 1.80
782 " 25pf gold, brown, & ocher 8 10
a. Souv. sheet of 2 90 90
783 " 40pf gold, brown, ocher & yel. green 10 15
784 " 70pf gold & ultra. *1.75* *1.75*

Issued to commemorate the 800th anniversary of the City of Leipzig. No. 781a contains one each of Nos. 781 and 784; No. 782a contains Nos. 782–783. Marginal inscription in gold: "INTERMESS III / LEIPZIG 1965" No. 781a sold for 90pf; No. 782a for 80pf. Size: 138x98mm. The souvenir sheets were issued Sept. 4, 1965.

Cameras
A256

Equestrian
A257

Designs: 15pf, Electric guitar and organ. 25pf, Microscope.

1965, Sept. 9 ***Perf. 14***

785 A256 10pf green, black & gold 5 5
786 " 15pf multicolored 10 5
787 " 25pf " 45 15

Leipzig Fall Fair, 1965.

Perf. 13½x13

1965, Sept. 15 **Litho.** **Unwmkd.**

Sport: No. 790, Swimmer. No. 791, Runner.

789 A257 10pf multicolored 5 4
790 " 10pf " 5 4
791 " 10pf " *70* *70*
Nos. 789-791, B135-B136 (5) *1.00* 88

Issued to commemorate the International Modern Pentathlon Championships, Leipzig.

Alexei Leonov and Brandenburg Gate
A258

Memorial Monument, Putten
A259

Designs: No. 793, Pavel Belyayev and Berlin City Hall. 25pf, Leonov floating in space and space ship.

Lithographed

1965, Nov. 1 *Perf. 14* Wmk. 313

Size: 23½x28½mm.

792 A258 20pf bl., silver & red *30* *30*
793 " 20pf " " " " *30* *30*

Size: 51x28½mm.

794 A258 25pf bl., silver & red *45* *45*

Issued to commemorate the visit of the Russian astronauts to the German Democratic Republic. Nos. 792–794 printed se-tenant. Each sheet contains ten strips of three.

1965, Nov. 19 *Perf. 13x13½*

795 A259 25pf bright blue, pale yel. & black 25 3

Issued in memory of the victims of a Nazi attack on Putten, Netherlands, Sept. 30, 1944.

Furnace
A260

Designs (after old woodcuts): 15pf, Ore miners. 20pf, Proustite crystals. 25pf, Sulphur crystals.

Perf. 13x12½

1965, Nov. 11 Litho. Unwmkd.

796 A260 10pf black & multi. 5 4
797 " 15pf " " *80* *70*
798 " 20pf " " 10 8
799 " 25pf " " 20 15

Issued to commemorate the bicentenary of the Mining Academy in Freiberg.

Red Kite A261 | Otto Grotewohl A262

Birds: 10pf, Lammergeier. 20pf, Buzzard. 25pf, Kestrel. 40pf, Northern goshawk. 70pf, Golden eagle.

1965, Dec. 8 Photo. *Perf. 14*

Gold Frame

800 A261 5pf orange & black 5 3
801 " 10pf emerald, brn. & black 5 5
802 " 20pf car., red brown & black 5 5
803 " 25pf blue, red brown & black 8 5
804 " 40pf lilac, black & dark red 10 8
805 " 70pf brn., blk. & yel. *2.00* *1.50*
Nos. 800–805 (6) *2.33* *1.76*

1965, Dec. 14 Photo. Wmk. 313

806 A262 20pf black 25 3

Issued in memory of Otto Grotewohl (1894–1964), prime minister (1949–1964).

Souvenir Sheet

Spartacus Letter, Karl Liebknecht and Rosa Luxemburg—A263

1966, Jan. 3 Unwmkd.

807 A263 Sheet of 2 *80* *80*
a. 20pf red & black *25* *25*
b. 50pf red & black *25* *25*

Issued to commemorate the 50th anniversary of the national conference of the Spartacus organization. No. 807 has gray and red marginal inscription. Size of stamps: 50x28½mm. Size of sheet: 136½x98mm.

Tobogganing, Women's Singles
A264

Tobogganing: 20pf, Men's doubles. 25pf, Men's singles.

Perf. 13½x13

1966, Jan. 25 Litho. Unwmkd.

808 A264 10pf citron & dp. grn. 10 6
809 " 20pf car. rose & dk. violet blue 25 10
810 " 25pf bl. & dk. bl. *1.00* *1.00*

Issued to commemorate the 10th International Tobogganing Championships, Friedrichroda, Feb. 8–13.

Electronic Computer
A265

Design: 15pf, Drill and milling machine.

1966, Feb. 24 *Perf. 13x12½*

811 A265 10pf multicolored 15 8
812 " 15pf " 20 10

Leipzig Spring Fair, 1966.

Jan Arnost Smoler and Linden Leaf A266 | Soldier and National Gallery, Berlin A267

Design: 25pf, House of the Sorbs, Bautzen, Saxony.

1966, March 1 *Perf. 13x13½*

813 A266 20pf brt. blue, blk. & brt. red 16 8
814 " 25pf brt. red, black & bright blue *55* *50*

Issued to commemorate the sesquicentennial of the birth of Jan Arnost Smoler (1816–1884), philologist of the Sorbian language. The Sorbs are a small group of slavic people in Saxony.

Perf. 14

1966, March 1 Photo. Wmk. 313

Designs (Soldier and): 10pf, Brandenburg Gate. 20pf, Factory. 25pf, Combine.

815 A267 5pf olive gray, black & yel. 4 3
816 " 10pf olive gray, black & yel. 8 3
817 " 20pf olive gray, black & yel. 15 8
818 " 25pf olive gray, black & yel. *70* *70*

National People's Army, 10th anniversary.

Luna 9 on Moon A268 | Medal for Scholarship A269

1966, Mar. 7 Unwmkd.

819 A268 20pf multicolored 30 5

Issued to commemorate the first soft landing on the moon by Luna 9, Feb. 3, 1966.

1966, Mar. 7 Litho. *Perf. 13½x13*

820 A269 20pf multicolored 20 5

Issued to commemorate the 20th anniversary of the State Youth Organization.

Traffic Signs
A270

Designs: 15pf, Automobile and child with scooter. 25pf, Bicyclist and signalling hand. 50pf, Motorcyclist, ambulance and glass of beer.

1966, Mar. 28 Litho. *Perf. 13*

821 A270 10pf dk. & lt. blue, red & black 5 4
822 " 15pf brt. grn., citron & black 5 6
823 " 25pf olive bister, brt. blue & black 10 10
824 " 50pf car., yellow, gray & blk. *1.50* *1.20*

Issued to publicize traffic safety.

Marx, Lenin and Crowd—A271

Designs: 5pf, Party emblem and crowd (vert.). 15pf, Marx, Engels and title page of Communist Manifesto (vert.). 20pf, Otto Grotewohl and Wilhelm Pieck shaking hands, and Party emblem (vert.). 25pf, Chairman Walter Ulbricht receiving flowers.

1966, Mar. 31 Photo. *Perf. 14*

825 A271 5pf multicolored 5 4
826 " 10pf " 8 6
827 " 15pf green & black 10 7
828 " 20pf dk. car. & black 17 13
829 " 25pf multicolored *70* *70*
Nos. 825–829 (5) *1.10* *1.00*

20th anniversary of Socialist Unity Party of Germany (SED).

WHO Headquarters, Geneva—A272

Perf. 13x12½

1966, Apr. 26 Litho. Unwmkd.

830 A272 20pf multicolored 25 3

Issued to commemorate the inauguration of the World Health Organization Headquarters, Geneva.

Rügen Island, Königsstuhl—A273

National Parks: 10pf, Spree River woodland. 20pf, Saxon Switzerland. 25pf, Dunes at Westdarss. 30pf, Thale in Harz, Devil's Wall. 50pf, Feldberg Lakes, Mecklenburg.

Perf. 13x12½

1966, May 17 Litho. Unwmkd.

831 A273 10pf multicolored 5 4
832 " 15pf " 5 5
833 " 20pf " 8 5
834 " 25pf " 8 8
835 " 30pf " 10 10
836 " 50pf " *1.60* *1.55*
Nos. 831–836 (6) *1.96* *1.87*

Plauen Lace
A274

Various Lace Designs

1966, May 26 *Perf. 13x13½*

837 A274 10pf grn. & lt. green 8 4
838 " 20pf dk. bl. & lt. bl. 16 8
839 " 25pf brown red & vermilion 20 10
840 " 50pf dark violet & bluish lilac *1.20* *1.20*

Rhododendron A275 | Parachutist Landing on Target A276

Flowers: 20pf, Lilies of the Valley. 40fr, Dahlias. 50 pf, Cyclamen.

Photogravure and Engraved

1966 *Perf. 14x13½* Unwmkd.

841 A275 20pf multicolored 4 4
842 " 25pf " 8 6
843 " 40pf " 8 8
844 " 50pf " *1.80* *1.35*

Issued to commemorate the International Flower Show, Erfurt. Issue dates: 20pf, Aug. 16; others, June 28.

1966, July 12 Litho. *Perf. 12½x13*

Designs: 15pf, Group parachute jump. 20pf, Free fall.

845 A276 10pf bl., blk. & olive 5 3
846 " 15pf multicolored *60* *60*
847 " 20pf sky blue, black & olive 10 5

Issued to publicize the 8th International Parachute Championships, Leipzig.

Hans Kahle, Song of German Fighters and Medal of Spanish Republic—A277

Design: 15pf, Hans Beimler and street fighting in Madrid.

1966, July 15 Photo. *Perf. 14*

Frame and Flags in Red, Yellow and Lilac

848	A277	5pf black	3	3
849	"	15pf "	4	4
		Nos. 848-849, B137-B140 (6)	*2.12*	*1.98*

Issued to honor the German fighters in the Spanish Civil War.

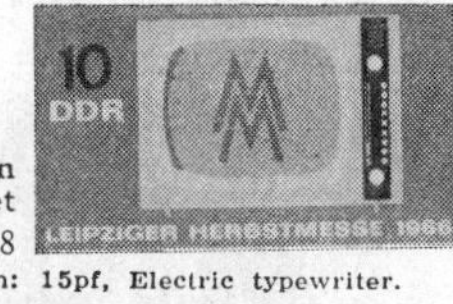

Television Set
A278

Design: 15pf, Electric typewriter.

Perf. 13x12½

1966, Aug. 29 Litho. Unwmkd.

850	A278	10pf brt. grn., blk. & gray	12	6
851	"	15pf red, blk. & gray	20	8

1966 Leipzig Fall Fair.

Women's Doubles Kayak Race
A279

1966, Aug. 16

852	A279	15pf brt. bl. & multi.	*50*	*50*

Issued to commemorate the 7th Canoe World Championships, Berlin. See also No. B141.

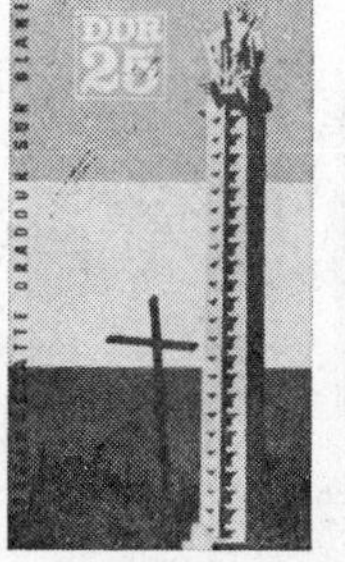

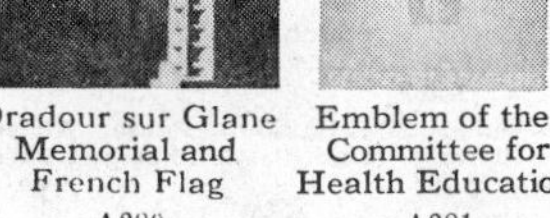

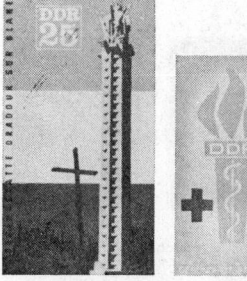

Oradour sur Glane Memorial and French Flag
A280

Emblem of the Committee for Health Education
A281

Perf. 13x13½

1966, Sept. 9 Wmk. 313

853	A280	25pf ultramarine, black & red	25	5

Issued in memory of the victims of the Nazi attack on Oradour, France, June 10, 1944.

1966, Sept. 13 *Perf. 14*

Designs: 5pf, Symbolic blood donor and recipient (horiz.).

854	A281	5pf brt. grn. & red	4	3
855	"	40pf brt. blue & red	*90*	*90*

Issued to publicize blood donations and health education. See also No. B142.

Weight Lifter
A282

Perf. 13½x13

1966, Sept. 22 Litho. Unwmkd.

856	A282	15pf lt. brn. & blk.	*50*	*50*

Issued to commemorate the International and European Weight Lifting Championships, Berlin. See also No. B143.

Congress Hall
A283

Emblem
A284

1966, Oct. 10 *Perf. 13*

857	A283	10pf multicolored	*50*	*40*
858	A284	20pf dk. bl. & yellow	10	5

Issued to commemorate the 6th Congress of the International Organization of Journalists, Berlin.

Costume Type of 1964

Regional Costumes: 5pf, Woman from Altenburg. No. 860, Man from Altenburg. No. 861, Woman from Mecklenburg. 15pf, Man from Mecklenburg. 20pf, Woman from Magdeburg area. 30pf, Man from Magdeburg area.

1966, Oct. 25 Photo. *Perf. 14*

859	A240	5pf multicolored	4	3
860	"	10pf "	7	3
861	"	10pf lt. grn. & multi.	7	3
862	"	15pf " " "	12	3
863	"	20pf yellow & multi.	*75*	*75*
864	"	30pf " "	*75*	*75*
		Nos. 859-864 (6)	*1.80*	*1.62*

The male and female costume designs of the same region are printed se-tenant in checkerboard arrangement.

Megalamphodus Megalopterus
A285

Various Tropical Fish in Natural Colors.

1966, Nov. 8 Litho. *Perf. 13x12½*

865	A285	5pf lt. blue & gray	4	3
866	"	10pf blue & indigo	6	3
867	"	15pf citron & black	*1.20*	*1.10*
868	"	20pf green & black	12	6
869	"	25pf ultra. & black	18	8
870	"	40pf emerald & black	25	10
		Nos. 865-870 (6)	*1.85*	*1.40*

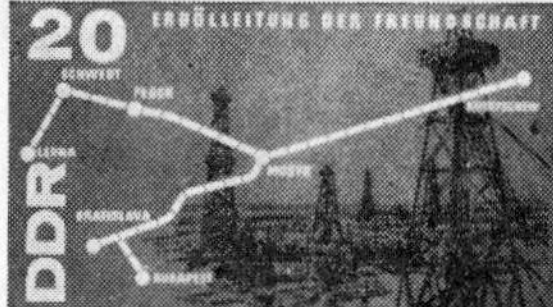

Map of Oil Pipeline and Oil Field
A286

Design: 25pf, Map of oil pipelines and "Walter Ulbricht" Leuna chemical factory.

1966, Nov. 8 *Perf. 13½x13*

871	A286	20pf red & black	10	3
872	"	25pf blue & black	*65*	*65*

Chemical industry.

Detail from Ishtar Gate, Babylon, 580 B.C.—A287

Designs from Babylon c. 580 B.C.: 20pf, Mythological animal from Ishtar Gate. 25pf, Lion facing right and ornaments (vert.). 50pf, Lion facing left and ornaments (vert.).

Perf. 13½x14, 14x13½

1966, Nov. 23 Photogravure

873	A287	10pf multicolored	5	5
874	"	20pf "	5	5
875	"	25pf "	10	10
876	"	50pf "	*1.50*	*1.25*

Near East Museum, Berlin.

Wartburg, Thuringia
A288

Gentian
A289

Design: 25pf, Wartburg, Palace.

1966, Nov. 23 Litho. *Perf. 13x13½*

877	A288	20pf olive	10	5
878	"	25pf violet brown	*75*	*75*

Issued to commemorate the 900th anniversary (in 1967) of the Wartburg (castle) near Eisenach, Thuringia. See also No. B145.

1966, Dec. 8 Litho. *Perf. 12½x13*

Protected Flowers: 20pf, Cephalanthera rubra (orchid). 25pf, Mountain arnica.

Black Background

879	A289	10pf yel., grn. & bl.	10	5
880	"	20pf yel., grn. & red	10	8
881	"	25pf red, yel. & grn.	*80*	*80*

Son Leaving Home
A290

City Hall, Stralsund
A291

Various Scenes from Fairy Tale "The Table, the Ass and the Stick."

1966, Dec. 8 *Perf. 13½x13*

882	A290	5pf multicolored	30	30
883	"	10pf "	30	30
884	"	20pf "	30	30
885	"	25pf "	30	30
886	"	30pf "	30	30
887	"	50pf "	30	30
		a. Sheet of 6 (#882-887)	2.25	2.25
		Nos. 882-887 (6)	1.80	1.80

Nos. 882-887 printed together in sheets of six. See also Nos. 968-973, 1063-1068, 1339-1344.

Perf. 14x13½, 13½x14

1967, Jan. 24 Photogravure

Buildings: 5pf, Wörlitz Castle (horiz.). 15pf, Chorin Convent. 20pf, Ribbeck House, Berlin (horiz.). 25pf, Moritzburg, Zeitz. 40pf, Old City Hall, Potsdam.

888	A291	5pf multicolored	4	3
889	"	10pf "	7	3
890	"	15pf "	9	3
891	"	20pf "	15	3
892	"	25pf "	20	3
893	"	40pf "	*1.35*	*1.35*
		Nos. 888-893 (6)	*1.90*	*1.50*

See also Nos. 1018, 1020, 1071-1076.

Rifle Shooting, Prone—A292

Designs: 20pf, Shooting on skis. 25pf, Relay race with rifles on skis.

1967, Feb. 15 Litho. *Perf. 13x12½*

894	A292	10pf Prus. bl., gray & brt. pink	7	5
895	"	20pf slate grn., brt. blue & grn.	15	10
896	"	25pf olive grn., olive & greenish bl.	*60*	*60*

Issued to commemorate the World Biathlon Championships (skiing and shooting), Altenberg, Feb. 15-19.

Circular Knitting Machine
A293

Mother and Child
A294

Design: 15pf, Zeiss telescope and galaxy.

1967, Mar. 2 *Perf. 13½x13*

897	A293	10pf dull magenta & brt. green	10	5
898	"	15pf ultra. & gray	20	15

Leipzig Spring Fair of 1967.

1967, Mar. 7 *Perf. 13x13½*

Design: 25pf, Working women.

899	A294	20pf rose brown, red & gray	12	3
900	"	25pf dk. blue, brt. bl. & brown	*60*	*55*

Issued to commemorate the 20th anniversary of the Democratic Women's Federation of Germany.

Marx, Engels, Lenin and Electronic Control Center—A295

Designs (Portraits and): 5pf, Farmer driving combine. No. 903, Students and teacher. 15pf, Family. No. 905, Soldier, sailor and aviator. No. 906, Ulbricht among workers. 25pf, Soldier, sailor, aviator and factories. 40pf, Farmers with modern equipment. Nos. 901, 903-905 are vertical.

1967 Photogravure *Perf. 14*

901	A295	5pf multicolored	3	3
902	"	10pf "	6	5

903	A295	10pf multicolored	6	5
904	“	15pf “	50	50
905	“	20pf “	15	5
906	“	20pf “	15	5
907	“	25pf “	15	8
908	“	40pf “	90	90
		Nos. 901–908 (8)	2.00	1.71

7th congress of Socialist Unity Party of Germany (SED), Apr. 17.

Nos. 902, 906–908 issued Mar. 22; Nos. 901, 903–905, Apr. 6.

Tahitian Women, by Paul Gauguin

A296

Paintings from Dresden Gallery: 20pf, Young Woman, by Ferdinand Hodler. 25pf, Peter in the Zoo, by H. Hakenbeck. 30pf, Venetian Episode (woman feeding pigeons), by R. Bergander. 50pf, Grandmother and Granddaughter, by J. Scholtz. 70pf, Cairn in the Snow, by Caspar David Friedrich. 20pf, 25pf, 30pf, 50pf are vertical.

1967, March 29

909	A296	20pf multicolored	5	5
910	“	25pf “	8	8
911	“	30pf “	10	10
912	“	40pf “	15	15
913	“	50pf “	2.75	2.75
914	“	70pf “	15	15
		Nos. 909–914 (6)	3.28	3.28

Barn Owl

A297

Protected Birds: 10pf, Eurasian crane. 20pf, Peregrine falcon. 25pf, Bullfinches. 30pf, European kingfisher. 40pf, European roller.

1967, Apr. 27 Photogravure *Perf. 14*

Birds in Natural Colors

915	A297	5pf gray blue	3	3
916	“	10pf “ “	5	3
917	“	20pf “ “	5	5
918	“	25pf “ “	8	5
919	“	30pf “ “	1.75	1.50
920	“	40pf “ “	10	10
		Nos. 915–920 (6)	2.06	1.76

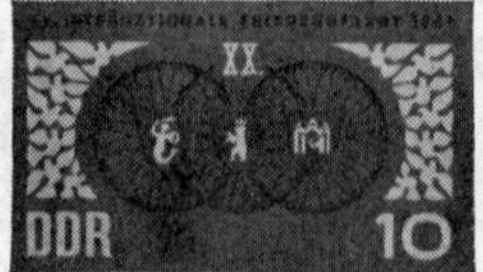

Arms of Warsaw, Berlin and Prague—A298

Design: 25pf, Bicyclists and doves.

Perf. 13x12½

1967, May 10 Litho. Wmk. 313

921	A298	10pf org., blk. & lilac	10	3
922	“	25pf lt. bl. & dk. car.	50	50

Issued to commemorate the 20th International Bicycle Peace Race, Berlin-Warsaw-Prague.

Cat

A299

Children's Drawings: 10pf, Snow White and the Seven Dwarfs. 15pf, Fire truck. 20pf, Cock. 25pf, Flowers in vase. 30pf, Children playing ball.

1967, June 1 Unwmkd.

923	A299	5pf multicolored	4	3
924	“	10pf black & multi.	6	5
925	“	15pf dk. bl. & multi.	10	5
926	“	20pf org. & multi.	15	5
927	“	25pf multicolored	20	12
928	“	30pf “	1.00	1.00
		Nos. 923–928 (6)	1.55	1.30

Issued for International Children's Day.

Girl with Straw Hat, by Salomon Bray

A300

Exhibition Emblem and Map of DDR

A301

Paintings: 5pf, Three Horsemen, by Rubens (horiz.). 10pf, Girl Gathering Grapes, by Gerard Dou. 20pf, Spring Idyl, by Hans Thoma (horiz.). 25pf, Wilhelmine Schroder-Devrient, by Karl Begas. 50pf, The Four Evangelists, by Jacob Jordaens.

1967, June 7 Photo. *Perf. 14*

929	A300	5pf lt. & dark blue	3	3
930	“	10pf lt. red brown & red brown	6	5
931	“	20pf lt. & dp. yellow green	10	5
932	“	25pf pale rose & rose lilac	10	10
933	“	40pf pale grn. & olive green	15	15
934	“	50pf tan & sepia	1.65	1.65
		Nos. 929–934 (6)	2.09	2.03

Issued to publicize paintings missing from museums since World War II.

Perf. 12½x13

1967, June 14 Litho. Unwmkd.

935	A301	20pf dark green, ocher & red	20	5

Issued to commemorate the 15th Agricultural Exhibition, Markkleeberg.

Marie Curie

A302

German Playing Cards

A303

Portraits: 5pf, Georg Herwegh, poet. 20pf, Käthe Kollwitz. 25pf, Johann J. Winckelmann, archaeologist. 40pf, Theodor Storm, writer.

1967 Engraved *Perf. 14*

936	A302	5pf brown	5	3
937	“	10pf dark blue	6	3
938	“	20pf dull red	8	5
939	“	25pf gray	16	10
940	“	40pf slate green	1.00	1.00
		Nos. 936–940 (5)	1.35	1.21

Issued to commemorate the 150th anniversary of the birth of Herwegh, Winckelmann and Storm, and the birth centenaries of Curie and Kollwitz.

1967, July 18 Photogravure

Designs: Various German playing cards.

941	A303	5pf red & multi.	3	3
942	“	10pf green & multi.	6	5
943	“	20pf multicolored	10	10
944	“	25pf “	90	75

Mare and Foal

A304

Horses: 10pf, Stallion. 20pf, Horse race finish. 50pf, Colts (vert.).

Perf. 13½x13, 13x13½

1967, Aug. 15 Litho. Unwmkd.

945	A304	5pf multicolored	3	3
946	“	10pf orange, black & dark brown	6	5
947	“	20pf blue & multi.	10	8
948	“	50pf multicolored	1.20	1.10

Issued to publicize the Thoroughbred Horseshow of Socialist Countries, Hoppegarten, Berlin.

Small Electrical Appliances

A305

Design: 15pf, Woman's fur coat and furrier's trademark.

Perf. 14x13½

1967, Aug. 8 Photo. Unwmkd.

949	A305	10pf brt. blue, black & yellow	10	3
950	“	15pf yellow, brown & black	15	12

Leipzig Fall Fair, 1967.

Max Reichpietsch and Warship

A306

Designs: 15pf, Albin Köbis and warship. 20pf, Sailors marching with red flag, and warship.

1967, Sept. 5 Litho. *Perf. 13½x13*

951	A306	10pf dk. blue, gray & red, *bluish*	5	3
952	“	15pf dk. blue, gray & red, *bluish*	45	45
953	“	20pf dk. blue, gray & red, *bluish*	10	3

Issued to commemorate the 50th anniversary of the sailors' uprising at Kiel.

Monument at Kragujevac

A307

1967, Sept. 20 *Perf. 13x13½*

954	A307	25pf dk. red, yellow & black	25	5

Issued in memory of the victims of the Nazis at Kragujevac, Jugoslavia, Oct. 21, 1941.

Worker and Symbols of Electrification—A308

Designs (Communist Emblem and): 5pf, Worker, and Communist newspaper masthead. 15pf, Russian War Memorial, Berlin-Treptow. 20pf, Russian and German soldiers, and coat of arms. 40pf, Lenin and cruiser Aurora.

1967, Oct. 6 Photo. *Perf. 14x14½*

955	A308	5pf multicolored	3	3
956	“	10pf “	6	3
957	“	15pf “	9	3
958	“	20pf “	12	3
959	“	40pf “	1.00	1.00
		a. Souv. sheet of 2	1.20	1.20
		Nos. 955–959 (5)	1.30	1.12

Issued to commemorate the 50th anniversary of the Russian October Revolution. No. 959a contains 2 imperf. stamps similar to Nos. 958–959 with simulated perforations. Gray and dark red marginal inscription; it commemorates the Red October Jubilee Stamp Exhibition, Karl-Marx-Stadt, Oct. 6–15. Size: 129x83mm. Sold for 85pf.

Martin Luther, by Lucas Cranach

A309

Young Inventors and Fair Emblem

A310

Designs: 25pf, Luther's House, Wittenberg (horiz.). 40pf, Castle Church, Wittenberg.

Engraved and Photogravure

1967, Oct. 17 *Perf. 14*

960	A309	20pf blk. & rose lilac	5	5
961	“	25pf black & blue	10	10
962	“	40pf black & lemon	95	95

450th anniversary of the Reformation.

Engraved and Photogravure

1967, Nov. 15 *Perf. 14* Unwmkd.

Designs: No. 964, Boy's and girl's heads and emblem of the Free German Youth Organization. 25pf, Young workers receiving awards, and medal.

Size: 23x28½mm.

963	A310	20pf multicolored	30	25
964	“	20pf “	30	25

Size: 51x28½mm.

965 A310 25pf multicolored 30 25
Strip of 3 1.00 80

Issued to publicize the 10th Masters of Tomorrow Fair, Leipzig, Nov. 15–26. Nos. 963–965 printed se-tenant. Each sheet contains ten strips of three.

Goethe House, Weimar—A311

Design: 25pf, Schiller House, Weimar.

1967, Nov. 27 Litho. *Perf. 13x12½*

966 A311 20pf gray, blk. & brn. 10 5
967 " 25pf citron, dark green & brn. 55 55

Issued to honor German classical humanism.

Fairy Tale Type of 1966

Various Scenes from King Drosselbart.

1967, Nov. 27 *Perf. 13½x13*

968 A290 5pf multicolored 30 30
969 " 10pf " 30 30
970 " 15pf " 30 30
971 " 20pf " 30 30
972 " 25pf " 30 30
973 " 30pf " 30 30
Sheet of 6 (#968-973) 1.80 1.80

Nos. 968–973 printed together in sheets of 6.

Farmers, Stables and Silos—A312

Perf. 13x12½

1967, Dec. 6 Litho. Unwmkd.

974 A312 10pf multicolored 12 5

Issued to publicize the 15th anniversary of the first agricultural co-operatives.

Nutcracker and Figurines
A313

Speed Skating
A314

Design: 20pf, Candle holders: angel and miner.

1967, Dec. 6 Photo. *Perf. 13½x14*

975 A313 10pf green & multi. *30* *25*
976 " 20pf red & multi. 10 7

Issued to publicize local handicrafts of the Erzgebirge in Saxony (Ore Mountains).

Perf. 13½x13

1968, Jan. 17 Litho. Unwmkd.

Sport and Olympic Rings: 15pf, Slalom. 20pf, Ice hockey. 25pf, Figure skating, pair. 30pf, Long-distance skiing.

977 A314 5pf bl., dk. bl. & red 3 3
978 " 15pf multicolored 7 5
979 " 20pf greenish bl., dk. blue & red 12 5
980 " 25pf multicolored 16 10
981 " 30pf greenish blue, vio. bl. & red *1.25* *1.25*
Nos. 977-981, B146 (6) *1.68* *1.53*

10th Winter Olympic Games, Grenoble, France, Feb. 6–18.

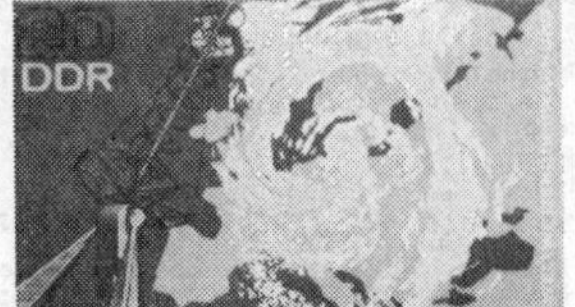

Antenna, Cloud Formation and Map of Europe—A315

Designs: 10pf, Actinometer, Sun and Potsdam Meteorological Observatory. 25pf, Weather influence on farming (fields by day and night, produce).

Perf. 13½x13

1968, Jan. 24 Unwmkd.

Size: 23x28mm.

982 A315 10pf brt. magenta, org. & black 35 30

Size: 50x28mm.

983 A315 20pf multicolored 35 30

Size: 23x28mm.

984 A315 25pf olive, black & yellow 35 30
Strip of 3 (#982-984) 1.10 1.00

Issued to commemorate the 75th anniversary of the Meteorological Observatory in Potsdam. Nos. 982–984 printed se-tenant.

Venus 4 Interplanetary Station
A316

Design: 25pf, Earth satellites Kosmos 186 and 188 orbiting earth.

1968, Jan. 24 Photo. *Perf. 14*

985 A316 20pf multicolored 10 10
986 " 25pf " *55* *55*

Russian space explorations.

Fighters of The Underground
A317

Designs: 20pf, "The Liberation." 25pf, "The Partisans."

1968, Feb. 21 Photo. *Perf. 14x13½*

987 A317 10pf blk. & multi. 5 5
988 " 20pf " " 10 10
989 " 25pf " " *70* *70*

The designs are from the stained glass window triptych by Walter Womacka in the Sachsenhausen Memorial Museum.

Diesel Locomotive—A318

Design: 15pf, Refrigerator fishing ship.

1968, Feb. 29 *Perf. 14*

990 A318 10pf multicolored 10 5
991 " 15pf " 25 15

The 1968 Leipzig Spring Fair.

Woman from Hoyerswerda
A319

Maxim Gorky and View of Gorky
A320

Sorbian Regional Costumes: 20pf, Woman from Schleife. 40pf, Woman from Crostwitz. 50pf, Woman from Spreewald.

1968, Mar. 14

992 A319 10pf citron & multi. 3 3
993 " 20pf lawn & multi. 8 5
994 " 40pf bl. grn. & multi. 15 12
995 " 50pf green & multi. *1.50* *1.50*

1968, Mar. 14 Engraved

Design: 25pf, Stormy petrel and toppling towers.

996 A320 20pf brn. & rose car. 10 3
997 " 25pf " " *50* *50*

Issued to commemorate the centenary of the birth of Maxim Gorky (1868–1936), Russian writer.

Ring-necked Pheasants
A321

Designs: 15pf, Gray partridges. 20pf, Mallards. 25pf, Graylag geese. 30pf, Wood pigeons. 40pf, Hares.

1968, Mar. 26 Litho. *Perf. 13½x13*

998 A321 10pf gray & multi. 5 5
999 " 15pf " " 8 8
1000 " 20pf " " 10 5
1001 " 25pf " " 12 10
1002 " 30pf " " 15 12
1003 " 40pf " " *1.60* *1.60*
Nos. 998-1003 (6) *2.10* *2.00*

Karl Marx
A322

Fritz Heckert
A323

Designs: 10pf, Title page of the "Communist Manifesto." 25pf, Title page of "Das Kapital."

1968, Apr. 25 Photo. *Perf. 14*

1004 A322 10pf yel. green & black 30 25
1005 " 20pf magenta, yel. & black 30 25
1006 " 25pf lemon, black & red brn. 30 25
a. Souv. sheet of 3 1.00 1.00

Issued to commemorate the 150th anniversary of the birth of Karl Marx (1818–1883). Nos. 1004–1006 are printed se-tenant. No. 1006a contains 3 imperf. stamps similar to Nos. 1004–1006 with simulated perforations. Magenta marginal inscription. Size: 125½x86mm.

1968, Apr. 25

Design: 20pf, Young workers, new apartment buildings and Congress emblem.

1007 A323 10pf multicolored 15 3
1008 " 20pf " 25 18

Issued to publicize the 7th Congress of the Free German Trade Unions.

"Right to Work"
A324

Designs: 10pf, "Right to Live," tree and globe. 25pf, "Right for Peace," dove and sun.

1968, May 8 Litho. *Perf. 13½x13*

1009 A324 5pf maroon & pink 5 5
1010 " 10pf brown olive & olive bister 5 5
1011 " 25pf Prus. blue & light blue *50* *50*

International Human Rights Year.

Angler
A325

Designs: No. 1013, Rowing (woman). No. 1014, High jump (woman).

Photogravure

1968, June 6 *Perf. 14* Unwmkd.

1012 A325 20pf olive grn., slate bl. & dk. red 10 3
1013 " 20pf Prus. blue, dk. blue & olive 10 3
1014 " 20pf copper red, deep claret & blue *60* *60*

Issued to publicize: World angling championships, Gustrow (No. 1012); European women's rowing championships, Berlin (No. 1013); second European youth athletic competition, Leipzig (No. 1014).

Brandenburg Gate, Torch
A326

Youth Festival Emblem
A327

Design: 25pf, Stadium and torch.

1968, June 20 Litho. *Perf. 13½x13*

1015 A326 10pf multicolored 8 5
1016 " 25pf " *45* *45*

Issued to publicize the 2nd Children's and Youths' Spartakiad, Berlin.

1968, June 20

1017 A327 25pf multicolored *70* *70*

Issued to publicize the 9th Youth Festival for Peace and Friendship, Sofia. See No. B148.

Type of 1967 and

Moritzburg Castle, Dresden—A328

Buildings: 10pf, City Hall, Wernigerode. 25pf, City Hall, Greifswald. 30pf, Sanssouci Palace, Potsdam.

1968, June 25 Photo. ***Perf. 13½x14***

1018	A291	10pf	multicolored	5	3
1019	A328	20pf	"	10	5
1020	A291	25pf	"	15	5
1021	A328	30pf	"	*95*	*95*

Walter Ulbricht and Arms of Republic
A329

Photogravure and Engraved

1968, June 27 ***Perf. 14***

1022	A329	20pf	orange, deep car. & black	22	5

Issued to commemorate the 75th birthday of Walter Ulbricht, chairman of the Council of State, Communist party secretary and deputy prime minister.

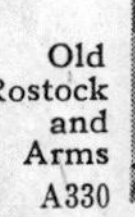

Old Rostock and Arms
A330

Design: 25pf, Historic and modern buildings, 1968, and arms of Rostock.

1968, July 9 **Photogravure**

1023	A330	20pf	multicolored	10	10
1024	"	25pf	"	60	60

Issued to commemorate the 750th anniversary of Rostock and to publicize the 11th Baltic Sea Week.

Karl Landsteiner, M.D. (1868–1943)
A331

"Trener" Stunt Plane
A332

Portraits: 15pf, Emanuel Lasker (1868–1941), chess champion and writer. 20pf, Hanns Eisler (1898–1962), composer. 25pf, Ignaz Semmelweis, M.D. (1818–1865). 40pf, Max von Pettenkofer (1818–1901), hygienist.

1968, July 17 **Engr.** ***Perf. 14***

1025	A331	10pf	gray green	5	3
1026	"	15pf	black	7	7
1027	"	20pf	brown	10	5
1028	"	25pf	gray blue	13	10
1029	"	40pf	rose lake	*1.10*	*1.10*
			Nos. 1025–1029 (5)	*1.45*	*1.35*

Birth anniversaries.

1968, Aug. 13 Litho. ***Perf. 12½x13***

Design: 25pf, Two "Trener" stunt planes in parallel flight.

1030	A332	10pf	multicolored	5	3
1031	"	25pf	blue & multi.	*55*	*55*

Peasant Woman, by Wilhelm Leibl
A333

Paintings from Dresden Gallery: 10pf, "On the Beach," by Walter Womacka (horiz.). 15pf, Mountain Farmers Mowing, by Albin Egger-Lienz (horiz.). 40pf, The Artist's daughter, by Venturelli. 50pf, High School Girl, by Michaelis. 70pf, Girl with Guitar, by Castelli.

Perf. 14x13½, 13½x14

1968, Aug. 20 Photogravure

1032	A333	10pf	multicolored	5	5
1033	"	15pf	"	5	5
1034	"	20pf	"	5	5
1035	"	40pf	"	15	15
1036	"	50pf	"	20	20
1037	"	70pf	"	*2.00*	*2.00*
			Nos. 1032–1037 (6)	*2.50*	*2.50*

Model Trains
A334

1968, Aug. 29 ***Perf. 14x13½***

1038	A334	10pf	light ultra., red & black	13	5

The 1968 Leipzig Fall Fair.

Spremberg Dam
A335

Designs: 10pf, Pöhl Dam (vert.). 15pf, Ohra Dam (vert.). 20pf, Rappbode Dam.

Perf. 13x12½, 12½x13

1968, Sept. 11 **Lithographed**

1039	A335	5pf	multicolored	3	3
1040	"	10pf	"	5	5
1041	"	15pf	"	*60*	*60*
1042	"	20pf	"	10	5

Issued to publicize dams built since 1945.

Runner
A336

Designs: 25pf, Woman gymnast (vert.). 40pf, Water polo (vert.). 70pf, Sculling.

1968, Sept. 18 Photo. ***Perf. 14***

1043	A336	5pf	multicolored	3	3
1044	"	25pf	"	5	5
1045	"	40pf	"	15	15
1046	"	70pf	blue & multi.	*2.25*	*2.25*

Issued to publicize the 19th Olympic Games, Mexico City, Oct. 12–27. See also Nos. B149–B150.

Monument, Fort Breendonk, Belgium
A337

Tiger Beetle
A338

1968, Oct. 10 Litho. ***Perf. 13x13½***

1047	A337	25pf	multicolored	25	3

Issued in memory of the victims of the Nazis at the Fort Breendonk Concentration Camp.

1968, Oct. 16 ***Perf. 13½x13***

Insects: 15pf, Ground beetle (Cychrus caraboides). 20pf, Ladybug. 25pf, Ground beetle (Carabus arcensis hrbst.). 30pf, Hister beetle. 40pf, Checkered beetle.

1048	A338	10pf	yel. & multi.	5	3
1049	"	15pf	bluish lilac & black	7	5
1050	"	20pf	multicolored	10	5
1051	"	25pf	light lilac & black	*1.75*	*1.75*
1052	"	30pf	light green, blk. & red	13	10
1053	"	40pf	pink & black	20	12
			Nos. 1048–1053 (6)	*2.30*	*2.10*

Lenin and Letter to Spartacists
A339

Designs: 20pf, Workers, soldiers and sailors with masthead and slogans. 25pf, Karl Liebknecht and Rosa Luxemburg.

1968, Oct. 29 Litho. ***Perf. 13x12½***

1054	A339	10pf	lemon, red & black	5	5
1055	"	20pf	lemon, red & black	10	8
1056	"	25pf	lemon, red & black	*65*	*65*

Issued to commemorate the 50th anniversary of the November Revolution in Germany.

Cattleya
A340

Orchids: 10pf, Paphiopedilum albertianum. 15pf, Cattleya fabia. 20pf, Cattleya aclandiae. 40pf, Sobralia macrantha. 50pf, Dendrobium alpha.

1968, Nov. 12 Photo. ***Perf. 13***

Flowers in Natural Colors

1057	A340	5pf	bluish lilac	3	3
1058	"	10pf	green	5	5
1059	"	15pf	bister	7	7
1060	"	20pf	green	7	7
1061	"	40pf	lt. brown	15	12
1062	"	50pf	gray	*2.00*	*2.00*
			Nos. 1057–1062 (6)	*2.37*	*2.34*

Fairy Tale Type of 1966

Various Scenes from Puss in Boots.

1968, Nov. 27 Litho. ***Perf. 13½x13***

1063	A290	5pf	multicolored	30	30
1064	"	10pf	"	30	30
1065	"	15pf	"	30	30
1066	"	20pf	"	30	30
1067	"	25pf	"	30	30
1068	"	30pf	"	30	30
			Sheet of 6 (#1063–1068)	1.80	1.80

Nos. 1063–1068 printed together in sheets of six.

Young Pioneers
A341

Design: 15pf, Five Young Pioneers.

1968, Dec. 3 ***Perf. 13x13½***

1069	A341	10pf	blue & multi.	5	3
1070	"	15pf	multicolored	*35*	*35*

Issued to commemorate the 20th anniversary of the founding of the Ernst Thalmann Young Pioneers' organization.

Buildings Type of 1967

Buildings: 5pf, City Hall, Tangermunde. 10pf, German State Opera, Berlin (horiz.). 20pf, Wall Pavilion, Dresden. 25pf, Burgher's House, Luckau. 30pf, Rococo Palace, Dornburg (horiz.). 40pf, "Stockfish" House, Erfurt.

1969, Jan. 1 Photogravure ***Perf. 14***

1071	A291	5pf	multicolored	3	3
1072	"	10pf	"	5	3
1073	"	20pf	"	10	3
1074	"	25pf	"	*1.25*	*1.25*
1075	"	30pf	"	15	15
1076	"	40pf	"	20	20
			Nos. 1071–1076 (6)	*1.78*	*1.69*

Martin Andersen Nexö, Danish Writer—A342

Portraits: 20pf, Otto Nagel (1894–1967), painter. 25pf, Alexander von Humboldt (1769–1859), naturalist, traveler, statesman. 40pf, Theodor Fontane (1819–1898), writer.

1969, Feb. 5 Engraved ***Perf. 14***

1077	A342	10pf	greenish black	5	3
1078	"	20pf	deep brown	10	5
1079	"	25pf	violet blue	*1.00*	*1.00*
1080	"	40pf	brown	20	15

Issued to honor famous men.

Be Attentive and Considerate!
A343

Designs: 10pf, Watch ahead! (car, truck and traffic signal). 20pf, Watch railroad crossings! (train and car at crossing). 25pf, If in doubt don't pass! (cars and truck).

1969, Feb. 18 Litho. ***Perf. 13x13½***

1081	A343	5pf	lt. blue & multi.	3	3
1082	"	10pf	yellow & multi.	5	5
1083	"	20pf	pink & multi.	10	10
1084	"	25pf	multicolored	*60*	*60*

Traffic safety campaign.

Combine
A344

Design: 15pf, Planeta-Variant offset printing press.

1969, Feb. 26 Photo. ***Perf. 14***

1085	A344	10pf	multicolored	7	5
1086	"	15pf	crimson, black & blue	22	12

The 1969 Leipzig Spring Fair.

Jorinde and Joringel
A345

Various Scenes from Fairy Tale "Jorinde and Joringel."

1969, Mar. 18 Litho. *Perf. 13½x13*

1087	A345	5pf black & multi.	30	30
1088	"	10pf " "	30	30
1089	"	15pf " "	30	30
1090	"	20pf " "	30	30
1091	"	25pf " "	30	30
1092	"	30pf " "	30	30
		Sheet of 6 (#1087-1092)	1.80	1.80

Nos. 1087-1092 printed together in sheets of six.

Spring Snowflake
A346

Red Cross, Crescent, Lion and Sun Emblems
A347

Protected Plants: 10pf, Adonis. 15pf, Globeflowers. 20pf, Garden Turk's-cap. 25pf, Button snakeroot. 30pf, Dactylorchis latifolia.

1969, Apr. 4 Photo. *Perf. 14*

1093	A346	5pf green & multi.	5	5
1094	"	10pf " "	5	5
1095	"	15pf " "	8	5
1096	"	20pf " "	14	5
1097	"	25pf " "	1.25	1.25
1098	"	30pf " "	15	10
		Nos. 1093-1098 (6)	1.72	1.55

1969, Apr. 23 Litho. *Perf. 12½x13*

Design: 15pf, Large Red Cross, Red Crescent and Lion and Sun Emblems.

1099	A347	10pf gray, red & yel.	7	3
1100	"	15pf multicolored	35	35

Issued to commemorate the 50th anniversary of the League of Red Cross Societies.

Conifer Nursery
A348

Erythrite from Schneeberg
A349

Designs: 10pf, Forests as natural resources (timber and resin). 20pf, Forests as regulators of climate. 25pf, Forests as recreation areas (tents along lake).

1969, Apr. 23

1101	A348	5pf multicolored	3	3
1102	"	10pf "	5	3
1103	"	20pf "	10	3
1104	"	25pf "	75	75

Prevention of forest fires.

1969, May 21 Photo. *Perf. 13½x14*

Minerals: 10pf, Fluorite from Halsbrücke. 15pf, Galena from Neudorf. 20pf, Smoky quartz from Lichtenberg. 25pf, Calcite from Niederrabenstein. 50pf, Silver from Freiberg.

1105	A349	5pf tan & multi.	3	3
1106	"	10pf multicolored	5	3
1107	"	15pf gray & multi.	8	3
1108	"	20pf lemon & multi.	10	3
1109	"	25pf multicolored	1.50	1.50
1110	"	50pf lt. bl. & multi.	25	7
		Nos. 1105-1110 (6)	2.01	1.69

Women and Symbols of Agriculture, Science and Industry—A350

Design: 25pf, Woman's head and symbols.

1969, May 28 Engraved *Perf. 14*

1111	A350	20pf dk. red & blue	15	3
1112	"	25pf blue & dk. red	60	60

2nd Women's Congress of the German Democratic Republic.

Ulbricht Type of 1961-67
Typographed

1969-71 *Perf. 14* Wmk. 313

Size: 17x21mm.

1112A	A189	35pf Prus. bl. ('71)	35	3

Engraved Unwmkd.

Size: 24x28½mm.

1113	A189	1m dull green	60	35
1114	"	2m brown	1.20	75

See note below Nos. 590B-590C.

Coil Stamp

1970, Jan. 20 Typo. Wmk. 313

Size: 17x21mm.

1114A	A189	1m olive	75	5

Emblem of DDR Philatelic Society
A351

Worker Protecting Children
A352

1969, June 4 Photo. Unwmkd.

1115	A351	10pf red, gold & ultramarine	12	3

Issued to publicize the National Philatelic Exhibition "20 Years DDR," Magdeburg, Oct. 31-Nov. 9.

1969, June 4 Litho. *Perf. 13*

Designs: 25pf, Workers of various races. 20pf+5pf, Berlin buildings: Brandenburg Gate, Council of State, Soviet Cenotaph, Town Hall Tower, Television Tower, Teachers' Building and Hall.

Size: 23x28mm.

1116	A352	10pf lemon & multi.	30	30

Size: 50x28mm.

1117	A352	20pf+5pf multi.	30	30

Size: 23x28mm.

1118	A352	25pf lemon & multi.	30	30
		Strip of 3 (#1116-1118)	95	95

Issued to publicize the International Peace Meeting, Berlin. Nos. 1116-1118 printed se-tenant. The surtax on No. 1117 was for the Peace Council of the German Democratic Republic.

Opening Ceremony before Battle of Leipzig Monument—A353

Designs: 15pf, Parading athletes and stadium. 25pf, Running, hurdling, javelin and flag waving. 30pf, Presentation of colors before old Leipzig Town Hall.

Photogravure and Engraved

1969, June 18 *Perf. 14*

1119	A353	5pf multi. & black	3	3
1120	"	15pf " "	8	3
1121	"	25pf " "	1.25	1.25
1122	"	30pf " "	15	15
		Nos. 1119-1122, B152-B153 (6)	1.73	1.56

Issued to publicize the 5th German Gymnastic and Sports Festival, Leipzig.

Pierre de Coubertin, by Wieland Forster
A354

Knight
A355

Design: 25pf, Coubertin column, Memorial Grove, Olympia.

1969, June 6 *Perf. 14x13½*

1123	A354	10pf blk. & lt. blue	5	3
1124	"	25pf blk. & sal. pink	50	50

Issued to commemorate the 75th anniversary of the revival of the Olympic Games.

1969, July 29 Photo. *Perf. 14*

Designs: No. 1126, Bicycle wheel. No. 1127, Volleyball.

1125	A355	20pf red, gold & dark brown	20	12
1126	"	20pf green, gold & red	20	12
1127	"	20pf multicolored	20	12

Issued to publicize: 16th Students' Chess World Championships, Dresden (No. 1125); Indoor Bicycle World Championships, Erfurt (No. 1126); 2nd Volleyball World Cup (No. 1127).

Merchandise
A356

1969, Aug. 27 Litho. *Perf. 12½x13*

1128	A356	10pf multicolored	18	5

Leipzig Fall Fair, Aug. 31-Sept. 7, 1969.

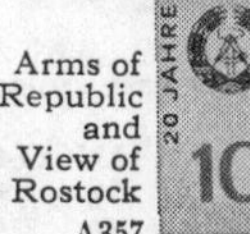

Arms of Republic and View of Rostock
A357

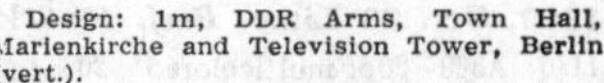

Design: 1m, DDR Arms, Town Hall, Marienkirche and Television Tower, Berlin (vert.).

1969, Sept. 23 Photo. *Perf. 14*

Multicolored

1129	A357	10pf (Rostock)	10	3
1130	"	10pf (Neubrandenburg)	10	3
1131	"	10pf (Potsdam)	10	3
1132	"	10pf (Eisenhüttenstadt)	10	3
1133	"	10pf (Hoyerswerda)	10	3
1134	"	10pf (Magdeburg)	10	3
1135	"	10pf (Halle-Neustadt)	10	3
1136	"	10pf (Suhl)	10	3
1137	"	10pf (Dresden)	10	3
1138	"	10pf (Leipzig)	10	3
1139	"	10pf (Karl-Marx-Stadt)	10	3
1140	"	10pf (Berlin)	10	3
		Nos. 1129-1140 (12)	1.20	36

Souvenir Sheet

1141	A357	1m multicolored	1.25	1.25

Nos. 1129-1141 and 1142-1145 were issued to commemorate the 20th anniversary of the German Democratic Republic.

No. 1141 contains one vertical stamp (size: 29x52mm.). Sheet has black, red & yellow frame and gold inscription. Size: 88x52mm.

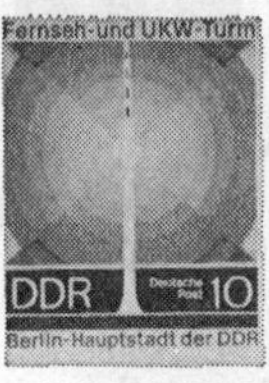

Television Tower, Berlin
A358

People and Flags
A359

Designs: 20pf, Sphere of Television Tower and TV test picture. No. 1144, Television Tower and TV test picture.

1969, Oct. 6 *Perf. 14*

1142	A358	10pf multicolored	10	5
1143	"	20pf "	20	12

Souvenir Sheets

1144	A358	1m dark blue & multi.	1.80	1.75

Perf. 13x12½

1145	A359	1m red & multi.	1.20	1.20

No. 1144 contains one vertical stamp (size: 21½x60mm.). Dark blue margin and inscription with radio waves and Berlin buildings. Size: 85x103½mm.

No. 1145 contains one stamp (size: 81x71mm.). Sheet has black, red and yellow frame, red inscription and coat of arms in margin. Size: 100x143mm.

Cathedral, Otto von Guericke Monument and Hotel International, Magdeburg—A360

1969, Oct. 28 Litho. *Perf. 13x12½*

1146 A360 20pf multicolored 20 3

Issued to publicize the National Postage Stamp Exhibition in honor of the 20th anniversary of the German Democratic Republic, Magdeburg, Oct. 31–Nov. 9. See No. B154.

UFI Emblem
A361

1969, Oct. 28 *Perf. 13x13½*

1147 A361 10pf multicolored 5 3
1148 " 15pf " *32* *32*

Issued to commemorate the 36th UFI Congress (Union des Foires Internationales), Leipzig, Oct. 28–30.

Memorial Monument, Copenhagen-Ryvangen
A362

Rostock University Seal and Building
A363

1969, Oct. 28 *Perf. 13*

1149 A362 25pf multicolored 28 3

Issued in memory of the victims of the Nazis in Denmark.

1969, Nov. 12 *Perf. 12½x13*

Design: 15pf, Steam turbine, curve and Rostock University emblem.

1150 A363 10pf brt. bl. & multi. 5 3
1151 " 15pf violet & multi. *32* *32*

550th anniversary of Rostock University.

ILO Emblem
A364

Mold for Christmas Cookies
A365

1969, Nov. 12 *Perf. 13½x14*

1152 A364 20pf deep green & silver 5 3
1153 " 25pf lilac rose & silver *65* *65*

Issued to commemorate the 50th anniversary of the International Labor Organization.

1969, Nov. 25 Litho. *Perf. 13½x13*

Design: 50pf, Negro couple, shaped spice cookie.

1154 A365 10pf dull org., black & red brown 15 15
1155 " 50pf lt. bl. & multi. 85 85

Issued to publicize folk art of Lusatia. Nos. 1154–1155 printed se-tenant. See No. B155.

Antonov An-24
A366

Planes: 25pf, Ilyushin Il-18. 30pf, Tupolev Tu-134. 50pf, Mi-8 helicopter.

1969, Dec. 2 *Perf. 13x12½*

1156 A366 20pf bl., red & blk. 10 3
1157 " 25pf vio., red & blk. *1.50* *1.50*
1158 " 30pf ultra., red & black 15 5
1159 " 50pf olive, red & black 25 10

Siberian Teacher, by D. K. Sveshnikov
A367

Russian Paintings from Dresden Gallery of Modern Masters: 10pf, Steelworker, by V. A. Serov. 20pf, Still Life, by E. A. Aslamasjan. 25pf, Hot Day (boats on river), by J. D. Romas. 40pf, Spring is Coming (young woman and snow-covered street), by L. V. Kabatchek. 50pf, Man on River Bank, by V. J. Makovskij.

1969, Dec. 10 Photo. *Perf. 13*

1160 A367 5pf gray & multi. 3 3
1161 " 10pf " " 10 3
1162 " 20pf " " 5 3
1163 " 25pf " " *1.75* *1.75*
1164 " 40pf " " 20 12
1165 " 50pf " " 25 18
Nos. 1160–1165 (6) *2.38* *2.14*

Ernst Barlach (1870–1938), Sculptor and Writer
A368

Portraits: 10pf, Johann Gutenberg (1400–1468). 15pf, Kurt Tucholsky (1890–1935), writer. 20pf, Ludwig van Beethoven (1770–1827). 25pf, Friedrich Hölderlin (1770–1843), poet. 40pf, Georg Wilhelm Friedrich Hegel (1770–1831), philosopher.

1970, Jan. 20 Engraved *Perf. 14*

1166 A368 5pf blue violet 3 3
1167 " 10pf gray brown 5 3
1168 " 15pf violet blue 7 4
1169 " 20pf rose lilac 10 4
1170 " 25pf blue green *1.20* *1.20*
1171 " 40pf rose claret 20 10
Nos. 1166–1171 (6) *1.65* *1.44*

Rabbit—A369

Designs: 20pf, Red fox. 25pf, Mink. 40pf, Hamster.

1970, Feb. 5 Photo. *Perf. 13½x14*

1172 A369 10pf multicolored 5 5
1173 " 20pf " 10 5
1174 A369 25pf multicolored *1.10* *1.10*
1175 " 40fp " 20 15

Issued to publicize the 525th International Fur Auctions, Leipzig.

Fairy Tale Type of 1969

Various Scenes from Fairy Tale "Little Brother and Sister."

1970, Feb. 17 Litho. *Perf. 13½x13*

1176 A345 5pf lilac & multi. 30 30
1177 " 10pf " " 30 30
1178 " 15pf " " 30 30
1179 " 20pf " " 30 30
1180 " 25pf " " 30 30
1181 " 30pf " " 30 30
Sheet of 6 (#1176–1181) 1.80 1.80

Nos. 1176–1181 printed together in sheets of 6.

Telephone Coordinating Station
A370

Design: 15pf, High voltage testing transformer (vert.).

Perf. 13x12½, 12½x13

1970, Feb. 24

1182 A370 10pf multicolored 7 5
1183 " 15pf " 22 10

Leipzig Spring Fair, Mar. 1–10, 1970.

Horseman's Tombstone (700 A.D.)
A371

Treasures from the Halle Museum: 20pf, Helmet (500 A.D.). 25pf, Bronze basin (1000 B.C.). 40pf, Clay drum (2500 B.C.).

1970, Mar. 3 Photo. *Perf. 13*

1184 A371 10pf dp. green, gray & dk. brown 5 3
1185 " 20pf multicolored 8 3
1186 " 25pf yel. & multi. *1.10* *1.10*
1187 " 40pf multicolored 15 10

Lenin and Clara Zetkin—A372

Designs: 10pf, Lenin, "ISKRA" (newspaper's name), composing frame and printing press. 25pf, Lenin and title page of German edition of "State and Revolution." 40pf, Lenin statue, Eisleben. 70pf, Lenin monument and Lenin Square, Berlin. 1m, Lenin portrait (vert.).

Photogravure and Engraved

1970, Apr. 16 *Perf. 14*

1188 A372 10pf multicolored 5 3
1189 " 20pf " 10 5
1190 " 25pf " *1.75* *1.75*
1191 " 40pf " 20 10
1192 " 70pf " 28 20
Nos. 1188–1192 (5) *2.38* *2.13*

Souvenir Sheet

1193 A372 1m dark carmine & multicolored 1.50 1.50

Issued to commemorate the centenary of the birth of Lenin (1870–1924), Russian communist leader. No. 1193 contains one vertical stamp. Deep carmine margin with gold medallions of Marx and Engels. Size: 118x83mm.

Sea Kale
A373

Red Army Soldier Raising Flag over Berlin Reichstag
A374

Protected Plants: 20pf, European pasqueflower. 25pf, Fringed gentian. 30pf, Galeate orchis. 40pf, Marsh tea. 70pf, Round-leaved wintergreen.

1970, Apr. 28 Photogravure

1194 A373 10pf multicolored 5 3
1195 " 20pf violet & multi. 5 5
1196 " 25pf multicolored *2.25* *2.25*
1197 " 30pf " 8 8
1198 " 40pf " 10 10
1199 " 70pf " 15 15
Nos. 1194–1199 (6) *2.68* *2.66*

1970, May 5 Litho. *Perf. 13x13½*

Designs: 20pf, Spasski Tower, Kremlin; State Council Building, Berlin; coats of arms of USSR and German Democratic Republic, and newspaper clipping about friendship treaty with USSR. 25pf, Mutual Economic Aid Building, Moscow, and flags of member countries. 70pf, Memorial monument, Buchenwald (horiz.).

1200 A374 10pf multicolored 5 3
1201 " 20pf " 10 3
1202 " 25pf " *70* *70*

Souvenir Sheet

1203 A374 70pf multicolored 1.10 1.10

Issued to commemorate the 25th anniversary of liberation from Fascism. No. 1203 contains one stamp, marginal inscription with quotation from an oath for liberty given at Buchenwald Concentration Camp Memorial, Apr. 11, 1954. Size: 135x105mm.

Shortwave Antenna, RBI Emblem and Globe
A375

Grain and Globe
A376

Designs: 15pf, Berlin Radio Station, emblems of Radio Berlin International (RBI), Radio DDR and Radio Germany.

1970, May 13 Litho. *Perf. 13½x13*

Size: 23x28mm.

1204 A375 10pf apple green, vio. bl. & bl. 20 18

Size: 50x28mm.

1205 A375 15pf vio. bl., dp. rose & apple green 30 30

Issued to commemorate the 25th anniversary of the German Democratic Republic broadcasting system. Nos. 1204–1205 printed se-tenant.

1970, May 19

Design: 25pf, House of Culture, Dresden, and grain.

1206 A376 20pf violet blue, yel. & blue 35 35

1207 A376 25pf vio. bl., yel. & bl. 40 40
Strip of 2 (#1206–1207) + label 80 80

Issued to publicize the 5th World Cereal and Bread Congress, Dresden, May 24–29. Nos. 1206–1207 printed se-tenant with label in between carrying name of congress in German, English, French and Russian.

Fritz Heckert Medal
A377

Design: 25pf, Globes and "FSM."

1970, June 9 ***Perf. 13x12½***

1208 A377 20pf red, yellow & brown 10 6
1209 " 25pf red, bl. & yel. *60 60*

Issued to commemorate the 25th anniversary of the Free German Trade Union and of the World Organization of Trade Unions.

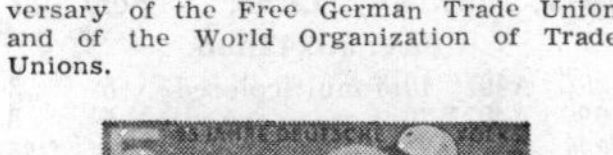

Traffic Policeman
A378

Designs: 10pf, Young Pioneers congratulating police woman. 15pf, Volga police car. 20pf, Railroad policeman with radiotelephone. 25pf, River police in Volga wing-type boat.

1970, June 23 Litho. ***Perf. 13x12½***

1210 A378 5pf ocher & multi. 3 3
1211 " 10pf green & multi. 5 3
1212 " 15pf ultra. & multi. 8 3
1213 " 20pf multicolored 10 6
1214 " 25pf " *1.00 1.00*
Nos. 1210–1214 (5) *1.26 1.15*

25th anniversary of the People's Police.

Gods Amon, Shu and Tefnut—A379

Designs from Lion Temple in Musawwarat: 15pf, Head of King Arnekhamani. 20pf, Cow from cattle frieze. 25pf, Head of Prince Arka. 30pf, Head of God Arensnuphis (vert.). 40pf, Elephants and prisoners of war. 50pf, Lion God Apedemak.

Perf. 13½x14, 14x13½

1970, June 23 Photogravure

1215 A379 10pf multicolored 5 3
1216 " 15pf " 5 3
1217 " 20pf " 5 3
1218 " 25pf " *2.25 2.25*
1219 " 30pf " 7 5
1220 " 40pf " 10 8
1221 " 50pf " 12 8
Nos. 1215–1221 (7) *2.69 2.55*

Issued to publicize the archaeological work in the Sudan by the Humboldt University, Berlin.

Arms and Flags of DDR and Poland—A380

1970, July 1 Litho. ***Perf. 13x12½***

1222 A380 20pf multicolored 25 5

Issued to commemorate the 20th anniversary of the Görlitz Agreement concerning the Oder-Neisse border.

Culture Association Emblem
A381

Athlete on Vaulting Horse
A382

Design: 25pf, Johannes R. Becher medal.

1970, July 1 Photo. ***Perf. 14***

1223 A381 10pf ultra., silver & brown 30 30
1224 " 25pf ultra., gold & brown 30 30
Strip of 2 (#1223–1224) + label 70 70

Issued to commemorate the 25th anniversary of the German Kulturbund. Nos. 1223–1224 printed se-tenant with gray and gold label with commemorative inscription.

1970, July 1 ***Perf. 14x13½***

1225 A382 10pf black, yellow & brn. red 10 3

Issued to publicize the 3rd Children's and Youths' Spartakiad. See No. B156.

Meeting of the American, British and Russian Delegations—A383

Designs: 10pf, Cecilienhof Castle. 25pf, "Potsdam Agreement" in German, English, French and Russian.

1970, July 28 Litho. ***Perf. 13***

Size: 23x28mm.

1226 A383 10pf black, citron & red 28 28
1227 " 20pf black, citron & red 28 28

Size: 77x28mm.

1228 A383 25pf red & black 28 28
Strip of 3 (#1226–1228) 90 90

Issued to commemorate the 25th anniversary of the Potsdam Agreement among the Allies concerning Germany at the end of World War II. Printed se-tenant in sheets of 30 (3x10).

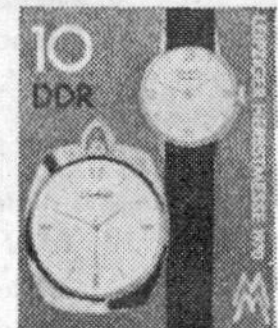

Men's Pocket and Wrist Watches
A384

1970, Aug. 25 Photo. ***Perf. 13½x14***

1229 A384 10pf ultramarine, black & gold 13 3

Leipzig Fall Fair, 1970.

Theodor Neubauer and Magnus Poser
A385

"Homeland" from Soviet Cenotaph, Berlin-Treptow
A386

1970, Sept. 2 ***Perf. 13x12½, 12½x13***

1230 A385 20pf dk. blue, car. & pale grn. 20 20
1231 A386 25pf deep carmine, pale blue 35 35

Issued in memory of fighters against "fascism and imperialistic wars."

Competition Map and Compass
A387

Design: 25pf, Competition map and runner at 3 different stations.

1970, Sept. 15 Litho. ***Perf. 13x12½***

1232 A387 10pf yel. & multi. 5 3
1233 " 25pf " " *55 55*

World Orienting Championships.

Mother and Child, by Käthe Kollwitz
A388

"The Little Trumpeter"
A389

Works of Art: 10pf, "Forest Worker Scharf's Birthday," by Otto Nagel. 20pf, Portrait of a Girl, by Otto Nagel. 25pf, "No More War," (Woman with raised arm) by Käthe Kollwitz. 40pf, Head from Gustrow Memorial, by Ernst Barlach. 50pf, The Flutist, by Ernst Barlach.

Photo.; Litho. (25pf, 30pf)

1970, Sept. 22 ***Perf. 14x13½***

1234 A388 10pf multicolored 5 5
1235 " 20pf " 5 5
1236 " 25pf pink & dark brown *2.00 2.00*
1237 " 30pf salmon & blk. 8 8
1238 " 40pf yellow & blk. 10 10
1239 " 50pf " " 12 12
Nos. 1234–1239 (6) *2.40 2.40*

Issued in memory of the artists Otto Nagel, Käthe Kollwitz and Ernst Barlach.

1970, Oct. 1 Photogravure

1240 A389 10pf dp. ultra., brn. & orange 13 10

Issued to publicize the 2nd National Youth Stamp Exhibition, Karl-Marx-Stadt, Oct. 4–11. The design shows the memorial in Halle for Fritz Weineck, trumpeter for the Red War Veterans' Organization. See No. B160.

Emblem with Flags of East Block Nations—A390

1970, Oct. 1 Litho. ***Perf. 13x12½***

1241 A390 10pf car. & multi. 13 6
1242 " 20pf multicolored 25 18

Issued to publicize the Brothers in Arms maneuvers of the East Bloc countries in the territory of the German Democratic Republic.

Musk Ox
A391

Designs: 15pf, Shoebill. 20pf, Addax. 25pf, Malayan sun bear.

1970, Oct. 6 Photo. ***Perf. 14***

1243 A391 10pf blue & multi. 5 3
1244 " 15pf grn. & multi. 5 3
1245 " 20pf org. & multi. 8 5
1246 " 25pf multicolored *1.00 1.00*

Issued to publicize the Berlin Zoo.

U.N. Headquarters and Emblem
A392

1970, Oct. 20 Photo. ***Perf. 13***

1247 A392 20pf ultra. & multi. 25 3

25th anniversary of the United Nations.

Friedrich Engels
A393

Epiphyllum
A394

Designs: 20pf, Friedrich Engels and Karl Marx. 25pf, Engels and title page of his polemic against Dühring.

Photogravure and Engraved

1970, Nov. 24 ***Perf. 14***

1248 A393 10pf vermilion, gray & black 5 5
1249 " 20pf verm., dk. grn. & black 5 5
1250 " 25pf verm., dk. car. rose & blk. *75 75*

Issued to commemorate the 150th anniversary of the birth of Friedrich Engels (1820–1895), socialist, collaborator with Karl Marx.

1970, Dec. 2 Photo. *Perf. 14*

Flowering Cactus Plants: 10pf, Astrophytum myriostigma. 15pf, Echinocereus salm-dyckianus. 20pf, Selenicereus grandiflorus. 25pf, Hamatocactus setispinus. 30pf, Mamillaria boolii.

1251	A394	5pf multicolored	5	5
1252	"	10pf dk. bl. & multi.	5	5
1253	"	15pf multicolored	5	5
1254	"	20pf "	5	5
1255	"	25pf dk. bl. & multi.	*1.25*	*1.25*
1256	"	30pf purple & multi.	7	7
		Nos. 1251-1256 (6)	*1.52*	*1.52*

Souvenir Sheet

Ludwig van Beethoven—A395

1970, Dec. 10 Engraved *Perf. 14*

1257	A395	1m gray	1.50	1.50

Bicentenary of the birth of Ludwig van Beethoven (1770–1827), composer.

Dancer's Mask, South Seas
A396

Works from Ethnological Museum, Leipzig: 20pf, Bronze head, Africa. 25pf, Tea pot, Asia. 40pf, Clay figure (jaguar), Mexico.

1971, Jan. 12 Photo. *Perf. 13*

1258	A396	10pf multicolored	5	5
1259	"	20pf "	5	5
1260	"	25pf "	*1.40*	*1.40*
1261	"	40pf "	10	5

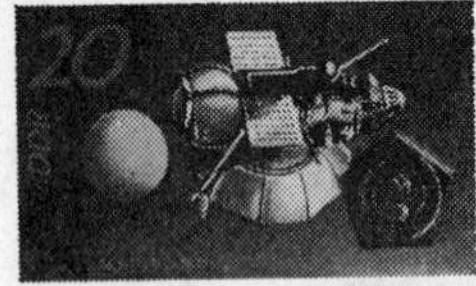

Venus 5, Soft-landing on Moon
A397

Designs: No. 1263, Model of space station. No. 1264, Luna 16 and Luna 10 satellites. No. 1265, Group flight of Soyuz 6, 7 and 8. No. 1266, Proton 1, radiation measuring satellite. No. 1267, Communications satellite Molniya 1. No. 1268, Yuri A. Gagarin, first flight of Vostok 1. No. 1269, Alexei Leonov walking in space, Voskhod 2.

1971, Feb. 11 Litho. *Perf. 13x12½*

1262	A397	20pf dk. bl. & multi.	50	50
1263	"	20pf " "	50	50
1264	"	20pf " "	50	50
1265	"	20pf " "	50	50
1266	"	20pf " "	50	50
1267	"	20pf " "	50	50
1268	"	20pf " "	50	50
1269	"	20pf " "	50	50
		Min. sheet of 8 (#1262-1269)	4.00	4.00

Soviet space research. Nos. 1262–1269 printed together in sheets of eight.

Johannes R. Becher—A398 Karl Liebknecht A399

Portraits: 10pf, Heinrich Mann. 15pf, John Heartfield. 20pf, Willi Bredel. 25pf, Franz Mehring. 40pf, Rudolf Virchow. 50pf, Johannes Kepler.

1971 Engraved *Perf. 14*

1270	A398	5pf brown	5	3
1271	"	10pf violet blue	5	3
1272	"	15pf black	6	3
1273	"	20pf rose lake	6	3
1274	"	25pf green	*1.60*	*1.60*
1274A	"	40pf pale purple	32	3
1275	"	50pf deep black	12	5
		Nos. 1270-1275 (7)	*2.26*	*1.80*

Honoring prominent Germans. See Nos. 1349–1353.

1971, Feb. 23 Photogravure

Design: 25pf, Rosa Luxemburg.

1276	A399	20pf gold, magenta & black	35	30
1277	"	25pf gold, magenta & black	35	30

Centenary of the births of Karl Liebknecht (1871–1919) and Rosa Luxemburg (1871–1919), leaders of Spartacist Movement. Printed se-tenant.

Soldier and Army Emblem—A400

1971, Mar. 1 *Perf. 13½x14*

1278	A400	20pf gray & multi.	25	5

15th anniversary of the National People's Army.

Crushing and Conveyor Plant, Magdeburg
A401

Design: 15pf, Dredger for low temperature work.

1971, March 9 Litho. *Perf. 13x12½*

1279	A401	10pf grn. & multi.	13	3
1280	"	15pf multicolored	18	12

Leipzig Spring Fair, 1971.

Proclamation of the Commune, Town Hall, Paris
A402

Designs: 20pf, Barricade at Place Blanche, defended by women. 25pf, Illustration by Theophile A. Steinlen for the International. 30pf, Title page for "The Civil War in France," by Karl Marx.

1971, March 9 *Perf. 13*

1281	A402	10pf red, bister & black	5	3
1282	"	20pf red, bister & black	5	4
1283	"	25pf red, buff & blk.	*1.30*	*1.30*
1284	"	30pf red, gray & blk.	8	6

Centenary of the Paris Commune.

Lunokhod 1 on Moon—A403

1971, March 30 Photo. *Perf. 14*

1285	A403	20pf vio. bl., brt. rose & lt. bl.	25	10

Luna 17 unmanned, automated moon mission, Nov. 10–17, and to commemorate the 24th Communist Party Congress of the Soviet Union.

Discobolus—A404

1971, Apr. 6 Litho. *Perf. 13½x13*

1286	A404	20pf dull blue, lt. blue & buff	25	6

20th anniversary of the Olympic Committee of German Democratic Republic.

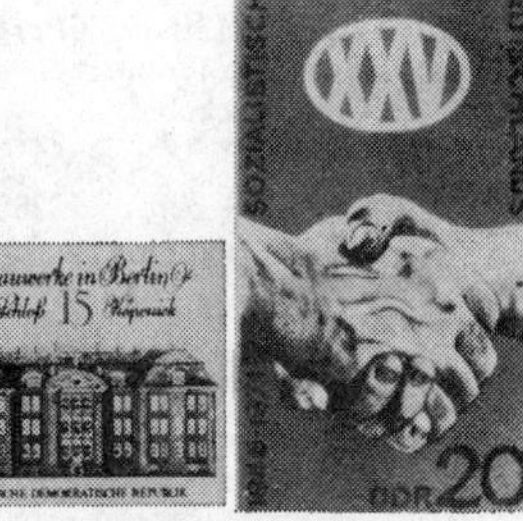

Köpenick Castle A405 Clasped Hands A406

Berlin Buildings: 10pf, St. Mary's Church (vert.). 20pf, Old Library. 25pf, Ermeler House (vert.). 50pf, New Guard Memorial. 70pf, National Gallery of Art.

Perf. 13½x14, 14x13½

1971, Apr. 6 Photogravure

1287	A405	10pf multicolored	5	5
1288	"	15pf "	5	5
1289	"	20pf "	5	5
1290	"	25pf "	*2.75*	*2.75*
1291	"	50pf "	12	8
1292	"	70pf "	25	12
		Nos. 1287-1292 (6)	*3.27*	*3.10*

Lithographed and Embossed

1971, Apr. 20 *Perf. 13x13½*

1293	A406	20pf red, black & gold	25	4

25th anniversary of Socialist Unity Party of Germany (SED).

The lack of a price for a listed item does not necessarily indicate rarity.

Dance Costume, Schleife A407 Self-Portrait, by Dürer A408

Sorbian Dance Costumes from: 20pf, Hoyerswerda. 25pf, Cottbus. 40pf, Kamenz.

1971, May 4 Litho. *Perf. 13*

Size: 33x42mm.

1294	A407	10pf multicolored	5	3
1295	A407	20pf green & multi.	5	3
1296	A407	25pf blue & multi.	*1.50*	*1.35*
1297	"	40pf multicolored	10	5

1971, Nov. 23 *Perf. 13½x13*

Size: 23x28mm.

1297A	A407	10pf multicolored	8	5
		c. Booklet pane of 4	35	
		d. Booklet pane of 4 (2 #1297A, 2 #1297B)	1.25	
1297B	A407	20pf multicolored	50	35

Nos. 1297A–1297B were issued only in booklets.

1971, May 18 *Perf. 12½x13*

Art Works by Dürer: 40pf, Three Peasants. 70pf, Portrait of Philipp Melanchthon.

1298	A408	10pf multicolored	5	5
1299	"	40pf brn. & multi.	10	10
1300	"	70pf gray & multi.	*1.90*	*1.90*

500th anniversary of the birth of Albrecht Dürer (1471–1528), painter and engraver.

Building Industry A409 Congress Emblem A410

Designs: 10pf, Science and technology. No. 1303, Farming. 25pf, Civilian defense.

1971, June 9 Photo. *Perf. 14*

1301	A409	5pf cream, red & black	3	3
1302	"	10pf cream, red & black	5	3
1303	"	20pf cream, red, bl. & black	5	3
1304	A410	20pf gold, deep car. & red	25	3
1305	A409	25pf cream, red & black	*1.00*	*1.00*
		Nos. 1301-1305 (5)	*1.38*	*1.12*

8th Congress of Socialist Unity Party of Germany (SED).

Golden Fleece, 1730
A411

Treasures from the Green Vault, Dresden: 5pf, Cherry stone with 180 heads carved on it, 1590. 15pf, Tankard, Nuremberg, 1530. 20pf, Moor with drums on horseback, 1720. 25pf, Decorated writing box, 1562. 30pf, St. George pendant, 1570.

1971, June 22 *Perf. 13*

1306 A411 5pf dp. car. & multi. 5 5
1307 " 10pf green & multi. 5 5
1308 " 15pf violet & multi. 5 5
1309 " 20pf multicolored 5 5
1310 " 25pf " *1.75* *1.50*
1311 " 30pf " 10 10
Nos. 1306-1311 (6) *2.05* *1.80*

Prisoners, by Fritz Cremer
A412

Design: 25pf, Brutality in Buchenwald Concentration Camp, by Fritz Cremer.

1971, June 22 Litho. *Perf. 13*

1312 A412 20pf bister & black 45 40
1313 " 25pf lt. bl. & black 45 40

International Federation of Resistance Fighters (FIR), 20th anniversary. Nos. 1312-1313 printed se-tenant with embossed label with commemorative inscription in between.

Coat of Arms of Mongolia
A413

1971, July 6 Lithographed *Perf. 13*

1314 A413 20pf dk. red, yellow & black 24 12

50th anniversary of the Mongolian People's Revolution.

Child's Head, UNICEF Emblem
A414

1971, July 13 Photogravure

1315 A414 20pf multicolored 24 12

25th anniversary of UNICEF (United Nations International Children's Fund).

Militiaman, Soldier and Brandenburg Gate
A415

Design: 35pf, Brandenburg Gate and new buildings in East Berlin.

1971, Aug. 12

1316 A415 20pf red & multi. 24 12
1317 " 35pf yellow & multi. 45 25

10 years of Berlin Wall.

Passenger Ship Iwan Franko—A416

Ships: 15pf, Freighter, type 17. 20pf, Freighter Rostock, type XD. 25pf, Fish processing ship "Junge Welt." 40pf, Container cargo ship. 50pf, Explorer ship Akademik Kurtschatow.

1971, Aug. 24 Engraved

1318 A416 10pf pale purple 5 5
1319 " 15pf pale brown & indigo 5 5
1320 " 20pf gray green 5 5
1321 " 25pf slate *2.75* *2.40*
1322 " 40pf maroon 10 10
1323 " 50pf grayish blue 15 15
Nos. 1318-1323 (6) *3.15* *2.80*

Shipbuilding industry.

Butadiene Plant
A417

Design: 25pf, Refinery.

1971, Sept. 2 Photogravure *Perf. 13*

1324 A417 10pf olive, violet & magenta 12 3
1325 " 25pf blue, violet & olive 30 20

Leipzig Fall Fair, 1971.

Raised Fists, Photo Montage by John Heartfield, 1937
A418

1971, Sept. 23

1326 A418 35pf greenish blue, blk. & silver 45 5

International Year Against Racial Discrimination.

Karl Marx Monument
A419

1971, Oct. 5 Photo. *Perf. 14x13½*

1327 A419 35pf vio. brn., pink & buff 45 5

Unveiling of Karl Marx memorial at Karl-Marx-Stadt (Chemnitz).

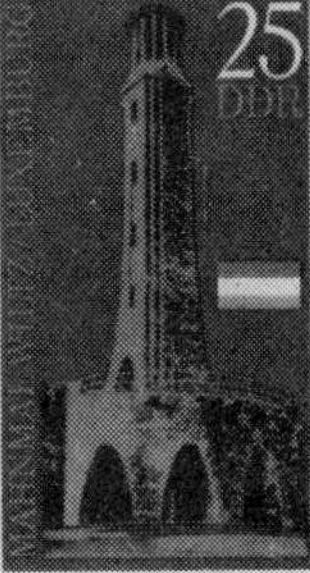

Wiltz Memorial, Flag of Luxembourg
A420

1971, Oct. 5

1328 A420 25pf multicolored 30 5

Memorial for victims of the Nazis, Wiltz, Luxembourg.

Postal Milestones, Saxony, and Zürner's Surveyor Carriage—A421

Photogravure and Engraved

1971, Oct. 5 *Perf. 14*

1329 A421 25pf blue, olive & lilac *70* *70*

Philatelists' Day 1971. See No. B162.

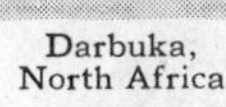

Darbuka, North Africa
A422

Geodetic Apparatus
A423

Musical Instruments: 15pf, Two morin chuur, Mongolia. 20pf, Violin, Germany. 25pf, Mandolin, Italy. 40pf, Bagpipes, Bohemia. 50pf, Kasso, Sudan.

1971, Oct. 26 Photo. *Perf. 14x13½*

1330 A422 10pf multicolored 5 5
1331 " 15pf " 5 5
1332 " 20pf ocher & multi. 5 5
1333 " 25pf blue & multi. 10 8
1334 " 40pf gray & multi. 15 15
1335 " 50pf multicolored *2.75* *2.50*
Nos. 1330-1335 (6) *3.75* *2.88*

Instruments from the Music Museum in Markneukirchen.

1971, Nov. 9 Photo. *Perf. 13½x14*

Designs: 20pf, Ergaval microscope. 25pf, Planetarium.

Size: 23½x28½mm.

1336 A423 10pf bl., blk. & red 45 40
1337 " 20pf " " 45 40

Size: 50½x28½mm.

1338 A423 25pf blue, violet bl. & yellow 45 40
Strip of 3 (# 1336-1338) 1.35 1.20

125th anniversary of the Carl Zeiss optical works in Jena.

Fairy Tale Type of 1966

Designs: Various Scenes from Fairy Tale "The Bremen Town Musicians."

1971, Nov. 23 Litho. *Perf. 13½x13*

1339 A290 5pf multicolored 40 40
1340 " 10pf ocher & multi. 40 40
1341 A290 15pf gray & multi. 40 40
1342 " 20pf verm. & multi. 40 40
1343 " 25pf vio. & multi. 40 40
1344 " 30pf yel. & multi. 40 40
Sheet of 6 (#1339-1344) 2.40 2.40

Nos. 1339-1344 printed together in sheets of 6.

Olympic Rings and Sledding—A424

Olympic Rings and: 20pf, Long-distance skiing. 25pf, Biathlon. 70pf, Ski jump.

1971, Dec. 7 Photo. *Perf. 13½x14*

1345 A424 5pf grn., car. & blk. 5 5
1346 " 20pf car. rose, violet & black 5 5
1347 " 25pf vio., car. & blk. *2.75* *2.75*
1348 " 70pf vio. bl., violet & black 25 25
Nos. 1345-1348, B163-B164 (6) *3.20* *3.20*

11th Winter Olympic Games, Sapporo, Japan, Feb. 3-13, 1972.

Portrait Type of 1971.

Portraits: 10pf, Johannes Tralow (1882-1968), playwright. 20pf, Leonhard Frank (1882-1961), writer. 25pf, K. A. Kocor (1822-1904), composer. 35pf, Heinrich Schliemann (1822-1890), archaeologist. 50pf, F. Caroline Neuber (1697-1760), actress.

1972, Jan. 25 Engraved *Perf. 14*

1349 A398 10pf green 3 3
1350 " 20pf rose claret 3 3
1351 " 25pf dark blue 5 5
1352 " 35pf brown 5 5
1353 " 50pf rose violet *2.50* *2.25*
Nos. 1349-1353 (5) *2.66* *2.41*

Honoring famous personalities.

Gypsum, Eisleben
A425

Minerals found in East Germany: 10pf, Zinnwaldite, Zinnwald. 20pf, Malachite, Ullersreuth. 25pf, Amethyst, Wiesenbad. 35pf, Halite, Merkers. 50pf, Proustite, Schneeberg.

1972, Feb. 22 Photo. *Perf. 13*

1354 A425 5pf greenish blue & brn. black 5 5
1355 " 10pf citron, brown & black 5 5
1356 " 20pf multicolored 5 5
1357 " 25pf " 5 5
1358 " 35pf lt. green, indigo & black 5 5
1359 " 50pf gray & multi. *2.75* *2.50*
Nos. 1354-1359 (6) *3.00* *2.75*

Russian Pavilion and Fair Emblem
A426

Design: 25pf, Flags of East Germany and Russia, and Fair emblem.

1972, Mar. 3 Photo. *Perf. 14*

1360 A426 10pf vio. bl. & multi. 13 3
1361 " 25pf claret & multi. 35 24

50 years of Russian participation in the Leipzig Fair.

Miniature Sheets

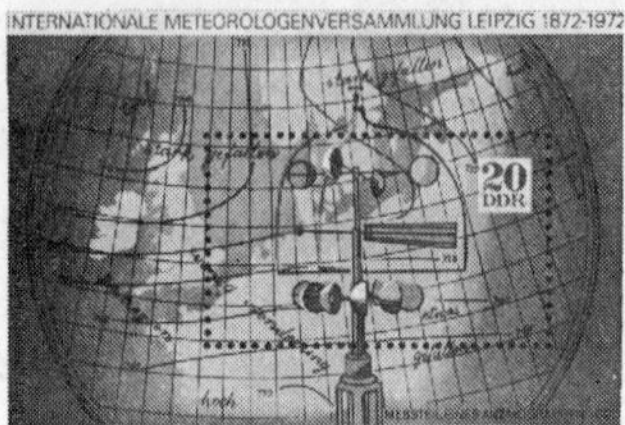

Anemometer, 1896, and Meteorological Chart, 1876—A427

Designs: 35pf, Dipole and cloud photograph taken by satellite. 70pf, Meteor weather satellite and weather map.

1972, Mar. 23 Litho. *Perf. 13x12½*

1362 A427 20pf multicolored 1.00 1.00
1363 " 35pf " 1.00 1.00
1364 " 70pf grn. & multi. 1.00 1.00

International Meteorologists' Centenary Meeting, Leipzig. Size of Nos. 1362–1364: 85x57mm.

World Health Organization Emblem A428

1972, Apr. 4 Photo. *Perf. 13*

1365 A428 35pf lt. blue, vio. blue & silver 50 5

World Health Day.

Kamov Helicopter A429

Aircraft: 10pf, Agricultural spray plane. 35pf, Ilyushin jet. 1m, Jet and tail with Interflug emblem.

1972, Apr. 25 *Perf. 14*

1366 A429 5pf blue & multi. 5 5
1367 " 10pf multicolored 5 5
1368 " 35pf bl. grn. & multi. 5 5
1369 " 1m multicolored *3.00* *2.75*

Wrestling and Olympic Rings—A430

Sport and Olympic Rings: 20pf, Pole vault. 35pf, Volleyball. 70pf, Women's gymnastics.

1972, May 16 Photo. *Perf. 13½x14*

1370 A430 5pf bl., gold & blk. 5 5
1371 " 20pf magenta, gold & black 5 5
1372 " 35pf olive bister, gold & black 10 5
1373 " 70pf yel. grn., gold & black *3.50* *3.25*
Nos. 1370-1373, B166-B167 (6) *3.85* *3.55*

20th Olympic Games, Munich, Aug. 26–Sept. 11.

Flags of USSR and German Democratic Republic—A431

Design: 20pf, Flags, Leonid Brezhnev and Erich Honecker.

1972, May 24 Engr. & Photo.

1374 A431 10pf red, yel. & blk. 18 15
1375 " 20pf " " " 25 20

Society for German-Soviet Friendship, 25th anniversary.

Workers A432

Design: 35pf, Students.

1972, May 24 Litho. *Perf. 13*

1376 A432 10pf dull yel., org. & magenta 48 45
1377 " 35pf dull yellow & ultra. 48 45
a. Strip of 2 (#1376–1377) + label 1.00 1.00

8th Congress of Free German Trade Unions, Berlin. Nos. 1376–1377 printed se-tenant with label between carrying Congress emblem and inscription.

Karneol Rose A433

1972, June 13 Photo. *Perf. 13*

Size: 36x36mm.

Roses in Natural Colors

1378 A433 5pf *shown* 5 5
1379 " 10pf *Berger's Erfurt rose* 5 5
1380 " 15pf *Charme* *2.25* *2.25*
1381 " 20pf *Izetka Spree-Athens* 8 8
1382 " 25pf *Köpenick summer* 10 10
1383 " 35pf *Prof. Knöll* 12 12
Nos. 1378–1383 (6) *2.65* *2.65*

International Rose Exhibition.

Redrawn

1972, Aug. 22 *Perf. 13½x13*

Size: 23x28mm.

1383A A433 10pf multicolored 10 5
d. Booklet pane of 4 50
1383B A433 25pf multicolored 50 25
e. Booklet pane of 4 (2 #1383B, 2 #1383C) 2.25
1383C A433 35pf multicolored 50 25

International Rose Exhibition. Nos. 1383A–1383C were issued only in booklets.

Young Mother and Child, by Cranach A434

Paintings by Lucas Cranach: 5pf, Young man. 35pf, Margarete Luther (Martin's mother). 70pf, Reclining nymph (horiz.).

1972, July 4 *Perf. 14x13½, 13½x14*

1384 A434 5pf gold & multi. 5 5
1385 " 20pf " " 8 5
1386 " 35pf " " 12 5
1387 " 70pf " " *2.75* *2.75*

500th anniversary of the birth of Lucas Cranach (1472–1553), painter.

Compass and Motorcyclist A435

Designs: 10pf, Parachute and light plane. 20pf, Target and military obstacle race. 25pf, Amateur radio transmitter, Morse key and tape. 35pf, Propeller and sailing ship.

1972, Aug. 8 Photo. *Perf. 14*

1388 A435 5pf multicolored 5 5
1389 " 10pf " 5 5
1390 " 20pf " 5 5
1391 " 25pf " *1.75* *1.75*
1392 " 35pf " 12 5
Nos. 1388–1392 (5) *2.02* *1.95*

Society for Sport and Technology.

Young Worker Reading, by Jutta Damme—A436

1972, Aug. 22 Photo. *Perf. 13½x14*

1393 A436 50pf multicolored 80 35

International Book Year 1972.

Polylux Writing Projector A437

George Dimitrov A438

Design: 25pf, Pentacon-audiovision projector (horiz.).

Perf. 12½x13, 13x12½

1972, Aug. 29 Lithographed

1394 A437 10pf crimson & blk. 15 6
1395 " 25pf brt. grn. & blk. 35 20

Leipzig Fall Fair, 1972.

1972, Sept. 19 *Perf. 13x13½*

1396 A438 20pf rose red & blk. 32 18

90th anniversary of the birth of George Dimitrov (1882–1949), Bulgarian Communist party leader.

Bird Catchers, Egypt, c. 2400 B.C. A439

Red Cross Trainees and Red Cross A440

Design: 20pf, Rug with animal design, Anatolia, c. 1400 A.D.

1972, Sept. 19 Photo. *Perf. 14*

1397 A439 10pf multicolored 10 5
1398 " 20pf " 20 5

Interartes Philatelic Exhibition, Berlin, Oct. 4–Nov. 11. See Nos. B168–B169.

1972, Oct. 3 Litho. *Perf. 13*

Designs: 15pf, Red Cross rescue launch in the Baltic. 35pf, Red Cross with world map, ship, plane and vehicles.

Size: 23x28mm.

1399 A440 10pf greenish blue, dk. bl. & red 20 18
1400 " 15pf greenish blue, dk. bl. & red 35 30

Size: 50x28mm.

1401 A440 35pf greenish blue, dk. bl. & red 80 80

Red Cross at work in the German Democratic Republic. Nos. 1399–1401 printed se-tenant.

Arab Celestial Globe, 1279 A441

Anti-Fascists Monument A442

Designs: 10pf, Globe, by Joachim R. Praetorius, 1568. 15pf, Globe clock, by Reinhold and Roll, 1586. 20pf, Globe clock, by J. Bürgi, c. 1590. 25pf, Armillary sphere, by J. Moeller, 1687. 35pf, Heraldic celestial globe, 1690.

1972, Oct. 17 Photo. *Perf. 14x13½*

1402 A441 5pf gray & multi. 5 5
1403 " 10pf " " 5 5
1404 " 15pf " " *2.25* *2.25*
1405 " 20pf " " 5 5
1406 " 25pf " " 10 8
1407 " 35pf " " 20 12
Nos. 1402–1407 (6) *2.70* *2.60*

Celestial and terrestrial globes from the National Mathematical and Physics Collection, Dresden.

1972, Oct. 24 Litho. *Perf. 12½x13*

1408 A442 25pf multicolored 35 18

Monument for Polish soldiers and German anti-Fascists, unveiled in Berlin, May 14, 1972.

Young Workers Receiving Technical Education—A443

Design: 25pf, Workers with modern welding machine.

1972, Nov. 2 Photo. *Perf. 13½x14*

1409 A443 10pf blue & multi. 35 35

1410 " 25pf " " 35 35

Strip of 2 (#1409-1410)+label 75 75

15th Central Fair of Masters of Tomorrow. Nos. 1409-1410 printed se-tenant with label showing emblems of Fair and German Youth Organization.

Mauz and Hoppel

A444

Designs: Children's television characters.

1972, Nov. 28 Litho. *Perf. 13½x13*

Blue and Multicolored

1411 A444 5pf *shown* 50 50

1412 " 10pf *Fox and magpie* 50 50

1413 " 15pf *Mr. Owl* 50 50

1414 " 20pf *Mrs. Hedgehog and Borstel* 50 50

1415 " 25pf *Schnuffel and Pieps* 50 50

1416 " 35pf *Paul from the Library* 50 50

Nos. 1411-1416 (6) 3.00 3.00

Nos. 1411-1416 printed together in sheets of 6.

Grandmother, Children, Magic Mirror

A445

Scenes from Hans Christian Andersen's "Snow Queen": 10pf, Kay and Snow Queen. 15pf, Gerda in magic garden. 20pf, Gerda and crows at palace. 25pf, Gerda and reindeer in Lapland. 35pf, Gerda and Kay at Snow Queen's palace.

1972, Nov. 28 *Perf. 13x13½*

1417 A445 5pf multicolored 50 50

1418 " 10pf " 50 50

1419 " 15pf " 50 50

1420 " 20pf " 50 50

1421 " 25pf " 50 50

1422 " 35pf " 50 50

Nos. 1417-1422 (6) 3.00 3.00

Nos. 1417-1422 printed together in sheets of 6.

Souvenir Sheet

Heinrich Heine—A446

1972, Dec. 5 *Perf. 12½x13*

1423 A446 1m brown olive, black & red *2.25* *2.25*

150th anniversary of the birth of Heinrich Heine (1797-1856), poet.

No. 1423 has buff margin with black and red inscription. Size: 61½x85mm.

Coat of Arms of USSR A447

Michelangelo da Caravaggio A448

1972, Dec. 5 Photo. *Perf. 13½x14*

1424 A447 20pf red & multi. 35 18

50th anniversary of the Soviet Union.

1973 Lithographed *Perf. 13½x13*

1425 A448 5pf brown *1.50* *1.50*

1426 " 10pf dull green 5 5

1427 " 20pf rose lilac 10 5

1428 " 25pf blue 15 10

1429 " 35pf brown red 20 10

1429A " 40pf rose claret 50 20

Nos. 1425-1429A (6) *2.50* *2.00*

Famous Men: Michelangelo da Caravaggio (1565(?)-1609), Italian painter (5pf). Friedrich Wolf (1888-1953), writer (10pf). Max Reger (1873-1916), composer (20pf). Max Reinhardt (1873-1943), Austrian theatrical director (25pf). Johannes Dieckmann (1893-1969), member and president of People's Chamber (35pf). Hermann Matern (1893-1971), vice-president of DDR (40pf).

Lenin Square, Berlin

A449

Coat of Arms of DDR

A449a

1973-74 Engraved *Perf. 14x13½*

Designs: 5pf, Pelican, Berlin Zoo. 10pf, Neptune Fountain, City Hall Street. 15pf, Fisherman's Island, Berlin. 25pf, World clock, Alexander Square, Berlin. 30pf, Workers' Memorial, Halle. 35pf, Marx monument, Karl-Marx-Stadt. 40pf, Brandenburg Gate, Berlin. 50pf, New Guardhouse, Berlin. 60pf, Zwinger, Dresden. 70pf, Old Town Hall, Office Building, Leipzig. 80pf, Old and new buildings, Rostock-Warnemunde. 1m, Soviet War Memorial, Treptow.

Size: 29x23½mm.

1430 A449 5pf blue green 8 3

1431 " 10pf emerald 15 3

1432 " 15pf rose lilac 17 3

1433 " 20pf rose magenta 28 3

1434 " 25pf greenish blue 32 3

1435 " 30pf orange 35 4

1436 " 35pf greenish blue 42 4

1437 " 40pf dull violet 48 5

1438 " 50pf blue, *bluish* 60 5

1439 " 60pf lilac ('74) 70 6

1440 " 70pf reddish brown 85 8

1441 " 80pf vio. blue ('74) 95 8

1442 " 1m olive 1.20 8

1443 A449a 2m lake 2.40 10

1443A " 3m rose lilac ('74) 3.60 30

Nos. 1430-1443A (15) 12.55 1.03

For coil stamps see Nos. 1610-1617.

Lebachia Speciosa (Oldest Conifer)

A450

Fossils from Natural History Museum, Berlin: 15pf, Sphenopteris hollandica (carbon fern). 20pf, Pterodactylus kochi (flying reptile). 25pf, Botryopteris (permian fern). 35pf, Archaeopteryx lithographica (primitive reptile-like bird). 70pf, Odontopleura ovata (trilobite).

1973, Feb. 6 Photogravure *Perf. 13*

1444 A450 10pf multicolored 5 5

1445 " 15pf ultra., gray & black 10 5

1446 " 20pf yel. & multi. 15 5

1447 " 25pf emerald, blk. & brown 20 10

1448 " 35pf ocher & multi. 25 15

1449 " 70pf indigo, black & yellow *3.00* *3.00*

Nos. 1444-1449 (6) *3.75* *3.40*

Bobsled Track, Oberhof

A451

1973, Feb. 13 Litho. *Perf. 12½x13*

1450 A451 35pf dk. blue, blue & orange 60 35

15th Bobsledding Championships, Oberhof.

Combines

A452

Design: 25pf, Computerized threshing and silage producing machine.

1973, Mar. 6 Litho. *Perf. 13x12½*

1451 A452 10pf olive & multi. 15 3

1452 " 25pf blue & multi. 40 24

Leipzig Spring Fair.

Firecrests

A453

Songbirds: 10pf, White-winged crossbill. 15pf, Waxwing. 20pf, White-spotted and red-spotted bluethroats. 25pf, Goldfinch. 35pf, Golden oriole. 40pf, Gray wagtail. 50pf, Wall creeper.

1973, Mar. 20 Photo. *Perf. 14x13½*

1453 A453 5pf multicolored 5 3

1454 " 10pf " 10 5

1455 " 15pf " 15 5

1456 " 20pf " 20 8

1457 " 25pf " 25 10

1458 " 35pf " 35 12

1459 " 40pf " 40 15

1460 " 50pf ocher & multi. *3.50* *3.50*

Nos. 1453-1460 (8) *5.00* *4.08*

Copernicus and Title Page—A454

1973, Feb. 13 Litho. *Perf. 13½x13*

1461 A454 70pf multicolored 1.10 50

500th anniversary of the birth of Nicolaus Copernicus (1473-1543), astronomer.

Electric Locomotive—A455

Railroad Cars Manufactured in DDR: 10pf, Refrigerator car. 20pf, Long-distance coach. 25pf, Multiple tank car with pneumatic filling device. 35pf, Two-story coach. 85pf, International coaches.

1973, May 22 Litho. *Perf. 13x12½*

1462 A455 5pf gray & multi. 10 5

1463 " 10pf brt. bl. & multi. 10 5

1464 " 20pf dk. bl. & multi. 20 8

1465 " 25pf gray & multi. 25 10

1466 " 35pf multicolored 35 12

1467 " 85pf grn. & multi. *3.25* *3.25*

Nos. 1462-1467 (6) *4.25* *3.65*

King Lear, Staged by Wolfgang Langhoff

A456

Great Theatrical Productions: 25pf, Midsummer Marriage, staged by Walter Felsenstein. 35pf, Mother Courage, staged by Bertolt Brecht.

1973, May 29 Photo. *Perf.13*

1468 A456 10pf maroon, rose & yellow 12 5

1469 " 25pf vio. blue, lt. blue & rose 30 10

1470 " 35pf dark gray, bis. & blue *1.60* *1.60*

Goethe and his Home in Weimar
A457

Fireworks, TV Tower, World Clock
A458

Designs (Portraits and Houses): 15pf, Christoph Martin Wieland. 20pf, Friedrich von Schiller. 25pf, Johann Gottfried Herder. 35pf, Lucas Cranach, the Elder. 50pf, Franz Liszt.

1973, June 26 Litho. *Perf. 12½x13*

1471 A457 10pf blue & multi. 5 5
1472 " 15pf multicolored 8 5
1473 " 20pf " 8 6
1474 " 25pf " 10 6
1475 " 35pf grn. & multi. 15 6
1476 " 50pf multicolored 3.00 3.00
Nos. 1471-1476 (6) 3.46 3.28

Famous men and their homes in Weimar.

1973

Designs (Festival Emblem and): 15pf, Vietnamese and European men, book and girder. 20pf, Construction workers and valve. 30pf, Negro and European students, dam and retort. 35pf, Emblems of World Federation of Democratic Youth and International Students Union. 50pf, Brandenburg Gate.

1477 A458 5pf vio. bl. & multi. 5 5
a. Bklt. pane of 4 60
1478 A458 15pf olive & multi. 8 5
1479 " 20pf multicolored 10 5
a. Bklt. pane of 4 1.25
1480 A458 30pf blue & multi. 1.80 1.80
1481 " 35pf green & multi. 15 10
Nos. 1477-1481 (5) 2.18 2.05

Souvenir Sheet

1482 A458 50pf aqua. & multi. 85 80

10th Festival of Youths and Students, Berlin, July 1973. No. 1482 contains one stamp. Aquamarine margin with white inscription. Size: 86x107mm.

Issue dates: Nos. 1477-1481, July 3; No. 1482, July 26.

Ulbricht Type of 1961-67

1973, Aug. 8 Engr. *Perf. 14*

Size: 24x28½mm.

1483 A189 20pf black 36 18

In memory of Walter Ulbricht (1893-1973), chairman of Council of State.

Pylon, Map of Electric Power System
A459

1973, Aug. 14 Photo. *Perf. 14*

1484 A459 35pf magenta, org. & light blue 55 32

10th anniversary of the united East European electric power system "Peace."

Sports Equipment
A460

Design: 25pf, Sailboat, guitar, electric drill.

1973, Aug. 28 Photo. *Perf. 14*

1485 A460 10pf multicolored 12 8
1486 " 25pf " 40 20

Leipzig Fall Fair and EXPOVITA exhibition for leisure time equipment.

Militia-man and Emblem
A461

Designs: 20pf, Militia guarding border at Brandenburg Gate. 50pf, Representatives of Red Veterans' League, International Brigade in Spain and Workers' Militia in DDR (vert.).

1973, Sept. 11 Litho. *Perf. 13x12½*

1487 A461 10pf multicolored 12 8
1488 " 20pf tan, red & blk. 35 20

Souvenir Sheet

Perf. 12½x13

1489 A461 50pf multicolored 85 80

20th anniversary of Workers' Militia of the German Democratic Republic. No. 1489 contains one stamp; marginal design shows hand holding gun with red flag. Size: 61x85mm.

Globe and Red Flag Emblem
A462

1973, Sept. 11 Photo. *Perf. 13½x14*

1490 A462 20pf gold & red 35 18

15th anniversary of the review "Problems of Peace and Socialism," published in Prague in 28 languages.

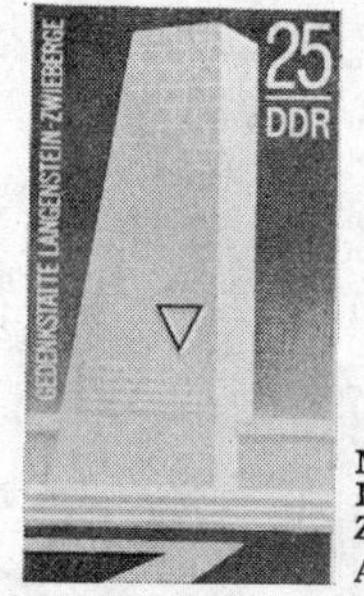

Memorial, Langenstein-Zwieberge
A463

1973, Sept. 18 *Perf. 14x13½*

1491 A463 25pf multicolored 45 20

In memory of the workers who perished in the subterranean munitions works at Langenstein-Zwieberge.

UN Headquarters, N.Y., UN and DDR Emblems
A464

1973, Sept. 21 *Perf. 13*

1492 A464 35pf multicolored 50 35

Admission of the German Democratic Republic to the United Nations.

Union Emblem
A465

Rocket Launching
A466

1973, Oct. 11 Photo. *Perf. 14x13½*

1493 A465 35pf silver & multi. 50 35

8th Congress of the World Federation of Trade Unions, Varna, Bulgaria.

1973, Oct. 23 *Perf. 14*

Designs: 20pf, Emblem with map of Russia and hammer and sickle (horiz.). 25pf, Oil refinery, Ryazan.

1494 A466 10pf vio. bl. & multi.
1495 " 20pf vio. blue, red & silver 10 10
20 20
1496 " 25pf multicolored 1.25 1.25

Soviet Science and Technology Days in German Democratic Republic.

Child with Doll, by Christian L. Vogel
A467

Paintings: 15pf, Madonna with the Rose, by Parmigianino. 20pf, Woman with Plaited Blond Hair, by Rubens. 25pf, Lady in White, by Titian. 35pf, Archimedes, by Domenico Fetti. 70pf, Bouquet with Blue Iris, by Jan D. de Heem.

1973, Nov. 13 Photo. *Perf. 14*

1497 A467 10pf gold & multi. 5 5
1498 " 15pf " " 8 5
1499 " 20pf " " 10 5
1500 " 25pf " " 15 8
1501 " 35pf " " 20 12
1502 " 70pf " " 3.50 3.50
Nos. 1497-1502 (6) 4.08 3.85

Human Rights Flame
A468

1973, Nov. 20 *Perf. 13*

1503 A468 35pf dp. rose, dk. car. & silv. 60 35

25th anniversary of the Universal Declaration of Human Rights.

Boy Holding Pike
A469

Designs: Various scenes from Russian Folktale "At the Bidding of the Pike."

1973, Dec. 4 Litho. *Perf. 13x13½*

1504 A469 5pf multicolored 65 65
1505 " 10pf " 65 65
1506 " 15pf " 65 65
1507 " 20pf " 65 65
1508 " 25pf " 65 65
1509 " 35pf " 65 65
Nos. 1505-1509 (6) 3.90 3.90

Nos. 1504-1509 printed together in sheets of 6.

Edwin Hoernle
A470

Portraits: No. 1511, Etkar Andre. No. 1512, Paul Merker. No. 1513, Hermann Duncker. No. 1514, Fritz Heckert. No. 1515, Otto Grotewohl. No. 1516, Wilhelm Florin. No. 1517, Georg Handke. No. 1518, Rudolf Breitscheid. No. 1519, Kurt Bürger. No. 1519A Carl Moltmann.

1974 Lithographed *Perf. 13½x13*

1510 A470 10pf gray green 20 15
1511 " 10pf rose violet 20 15
1512 " 10pf dark blue 20 15
1513 " 10pf brown 20 15
1514 " 10pf dull green 20 15
1515 " 10pf red brown 20 15
1516 " 10pf violet blue 20 15
1517 " 10pf olive brown 20 15
1518 " 10pf slate green 20 15
1519 " 10pf dull violet 20 15
1519A " 10pf brown 20 15
Nos. 1510-1519A (11) 2.20 1.65

Leaders of German labor movement.

Issue dates: Nos. 1510-1517, Jan. 8; others July 9.

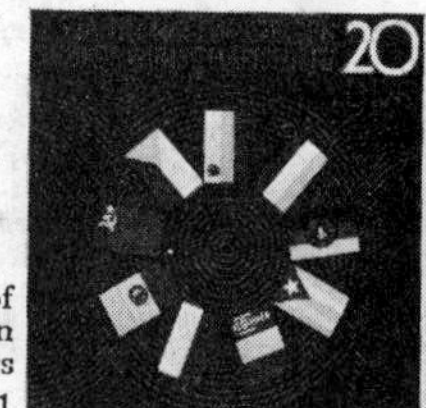

Flags of Comecon Members
A471

1974, Jan. 22 Photo. *Perf. 13*

1520 A471 20pf red & multi. 35 20

25th anniversary of the Council of Mutual Economic Assistance (Comecon).

Pablo Neruda and Chilean Flag
A472

1974, Jan. 22 *Perf. 14*

1521 A472 20pf multicolored 35 20

Pablo Neruda (Neftali Ricardo Reyes, 1904-1973), Chilean poet.

Echinopsis Multiplex
A473

Field Ball
A474

Various Flowering Cacti: 10pf, Lobivia haageana. 15pf, Parodia sanguiniflora. 20pf, Gymnocal. monvillei. 25pf, Neoporteria rapifera. 35pf, Notocactus concinnus.

1974, Feb. 12 Photogravure *Perf. 14*

No.	Type	Description	Unused	Used
1522	A473	5pf multicolored	5	5
1523	"	10pf tan & multi.	8	5
1524	"	15pf green & multi.	3.00	3.00
1525	"	20pf multicolored	15	10
1526	"	25pf vio. & multi.	25	20
1527	"	35pf multicolored	35	30
		Nos. 1522–1527 (6)	3.88	3.70

1974, Feb. 26 Lithographed *Perf. 13*

Design: Various fieldball scenes.

No.	Type	Description	Unused	Used
1528	A474	5pf green & multi.	20	20
1529	"	10pf " "	35	35
1530	"	35pf " "	1.20	1.20
		Strip of 3, #1528–1530	1.75	1.75

8th World Fieldball Championships for Men. Nos. 1528–1530 printed se-tenant.

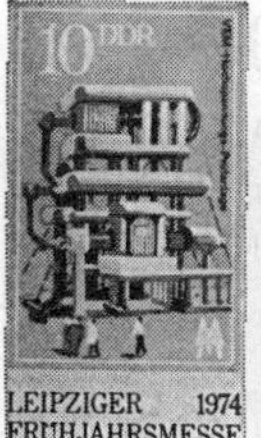

Power Testing Station A475

Rhodophyllus Sinuatus A476

Design: 25pf, Robotron EC 2040 data processer (horiz.).

1974, Mar. 5 Photo. *Perf. 14*

No.	Type	Description	Unused	Used
1531	A475	10pf multicolored	15	8
1532	"	25pf "	38	24

Leipzig Spring Fair.

1974, Mar. 19 Litho. *Perf. 13x13½*

European Poisonous Mushrooms: 10pf, Boletus satanas. 15pf, Amanita pantherina. 20pf, Amanita muscaria. 25pf, Gyromitra esculenta. 30pf, Inocybe patouillardii. 35pf, Amanita phalloides. 40pf, Clitocybe dealbata.

No.	Type	Description	Unused	Used
1533	A476	5pf buff & multi.	5	5
1534	"	10pf " "	8	5
1535	"	15pf " "	12	10
1536	"	20pf " "	15	8
1537	"	25pf " "	25	18
1538	"	30pf " "	30	25
1539	"	35pf " "	35	30
1540	"	40pf " "	3.25	3.25
		Nos. 1533–1540 (8)	4.55	4.26

Gustav Robert Kirchhoff A477

Portraits: 10pf, Immanuel Kant. 20pf, Ehm Welk. 25pf, Johann Gottfried Herder. 35pf, Lion Feuchtwanger.

1974, Mar. 26 Litho. *Perf. 13½x13*

No.	Type	Description	Unused	Used
1541	A477	5pf black & gray	5	5
1542	"	10pf vio. bl. & dull bl.	10	5
1543	"	20pf maroon & rose	20	10
1544	"	25pf slate grn. & grn.	25	15
1545	"	35pf brn. & lt. brn.	1.35	1.35
		Nos. 1541–1545 (5)	1.95	1.70

"Peace" A477a

1974, Apr. 16 *Perf. 13*

No.	Type	Description	Unused	Used
1548	A477a	35pf silver & multi.	50	35

25th anniversary of the First World Peace Congress.

Truck Driver and Arms of DDR A477b

Designs: 20pf, Students. 25pf, Woman worker. 35pf, Family.

1974, Apr. 30 Photo. *Perf. 13*

No.	Type	Description	Unused	Used
1549	A477b	10pf multicolored	8	5
1550	"	20pf gold & dark carmine rose	15	10
1551	"	25pf gold & multi.	20	15
1552	"	35pf grn. & multi.	1.85	1.75

25th anniversary of the German Democratic Republic.

Buk Lighthouse, 1878, and Map A478

Lighthouses, Maps and Nautical Charts: 15pf, Warnemünde, 1898. 20pf, Darsser Ort, 1848. 35pf, Arkona, 1827 and 1902. 40pf, Greifswalder Oie, 1855.

1974, May 7 Litho. *Perf. 14*

No.	Type	Description	Unused	Used
1553	A478	10pf multicolored	15	10
1554	"	15pf "	25	15
1555	"	20pf "	30	15
1556	"	35pf "	50	35
1557	"	40pf "	2.25	2.25
		Nos. 1553–1557 (5)	3.45	3.00

Hydrographic Service of German Democratic Republic. See Nos. 1645–1649.

The Ages of Man, by C. D. Friedrich—A479

C. D. Friedrich, Self-portrait—A480

Paintings by Friedrich: 10pf, Two Men Observing Moon. 25pf, The Heath near Dresden. 35pf, View of Elbe Valley.

1974, May 21 Photo. *Perf. 13½*

No.	Type	Description	Unused	Used
1558	A479	10pf gold & multi.	10	5
1559	"	20pf " "	20	8
1560	"	25pf " "	1.80	1.80
1561	"	35pf " "	35	10

Souvenir Sheet

Engraved

Perf. 14x13½

No.	Type	Description	Unused	Used
1562	A480	70pf sepia	1.85	1.85

200th anniversary of the birth of Caspar David Friedrich (1774–1840), German Romantic painter. No. 1562 has sepia margin and inscription. Size: 80x55mm.

Plauen Lace A481

Designs: Various Plauen lace patterns.

1974, June 11 Litho. *Perf. 13*

No.	Type	Description	Unused	Used
1563	A481	10pf violet, lilac & black	6	4
1564	"	20pf brn., ol. & blk.	10	6
1565	"	25pf bl., lt. bl. & black	1.80	1.50
1566	"	35pf lilac rose, rose & black	24	12

Trotter—A482

Designs: 10pf, Thoroughbred hurdling (vert.). 25pf, Haflinger breed horses. 35pf, British thoroughbred race horse.

Perf. 14x13½, 13½x14

1974, Aug. 13 Photographed

No.	Type	Description	Unused	Used
1570	A482	10pf olive & multi.	6	4
1571	"	20pf multicolored	12	6
1572	"	25pf lt. bl. & multi.	1.25	1.00
1573	"	35pf ocher & multi.	30	20

International Horse Breeders' of Socialist Countries Congress, Berlin.

Crane Lifting Diesel Locomotive A483

Design: 25pf, Sugar beet harvester, type KS6.

1974, Aug. 27 Litho. *Perf. 13x12½*

No.	Type	Description	Unused	Used
1574	A483	10pf multicolored	12	5
1575	"	25pf org. & multi.	35	20

Leipzig Fall Fair.

Miniature China and Mirror Exhibits A484

Designs: Scenes from 18th century Thuringia, Dolls' Village, Arnstadt Castle Museum.

1974, Sept. 10 Photo. *Perf. 14x13½*

Multicolored

No.	Type	Description	Unused	Used
1576	A484	5pf *shown*	4	4
1577	"	10pf *Harlequin barker at Fair*	6	4
1578	"	15pf *Wine tasters*	10	8
1579	"	20pf *Cooper and apprentice*	12	8
1580	"	25pf *Bagpiper*	2.25	2.00
1581	"	35pf *Butcher and beggar, women*	30	20
		Nos. 1576–1581 (6)	2.87	2.44

Bound Guerrillas, Ardeatine Caves, Rome—A485

Design: No. 1583, Resistance Fighters, monument near Chateaubriant, France.

1974, Sept. 24 *Perf. 13½x14*

No.	Type	Description	Unused	Used
1582	A485	35pf grn., blk. & red	55	45
1583	"	35pf bl., blk. & red	55	45

International war memorials.

Souvenir Sheet

Family and Flag—A486

1974, Oct. 3 Photogravure *Perf. 13*

No.	Type	Description	Unused	Used
1584	A486	1m multicolored	2.00	1.75

25th anniversary of the German Democratic Republic. No. 1584 has multicolored margin showing stylized "25" and gold inscription. Size: 90x108mm.

Freighter and Paddle Steamer A487

"In Praise of Dialectics" A488

Designs (UPU Emblem and): 20pf, Old steam locomotive and modern Diesel. 25pf, Bi-plane and jet. 35pf, Mail coach and truck.

1974, Oct. 9 *Perf. 14*

No.	Type	Description	Unused	Used
1585	A487	10pf grn. & multi.	6	4
1586	"	20pf multicolored	12	5

1587 A487 25pf blue &multi. 18 12
1588 " 35pf multicolored *1.25* *1.00*

Centenary of Universal Postal Union.

1974, Oct. 24 Litho. *Perf. 13x13½*

Designs: 10pf+5pf, "Praise to the Revolutionaries." 25pf, "Praise to the Party." Designs are from bas-reliefs by Rossdeutscher, Jastram and Wetzel, illustrating poems by Bertholt Brecht.

1589 A488 10pf+5pf multi. *30* *25*
1590 " 20pf " *40* *35*
1591 " 25pf " *50* *45*
Strip of 3 (#1589–1591) *1.25* *1.10*

DDR '74 National Stamp Exhibition, Karl-Marx-Stadt. Nos. 1589–1591 printed se-tenant in sheets of 45.

Souvenir Sheet

Drawings by Young Pioneers—A489

1974, Nov. 26 Litho. *Perf. 14*

1592 A489 Souvenir sheet of 4, multi. *2.00* *1.75*
a. 20pf *Sun shines on everybody* 45 35
b. 20pf *My Friend Sascha* 45 35
c. 20pf *Carsten, the Best Swimmer* 45 35
d. 20pf *Me at the Blackboard* 45 35

Young Pioneers' drawings (7–10 years old). The center label shows Young Pioneers' orchestra. Size of sheet: 138x95 mm.

Man Cutting Tree, and Bird A490

Meditating Girl, by Wilhelm Lachnit A491

1974, Dec. 3 *Perf. 13x13½*

Designs: Various scenes from Russian folktale "Twittering To and Fro."

1593 A490 10pf multicolored *60* *50*
1594 " 15pf " *60* *50*
1595 " 20pf " *60* *50*
1596 " 30pf " *60* *50*
1597 " 35pf " *60* *50*
1598 " 40pf " *60* *50*
Nos. 1593–1598 (6) *3.60* *3.00*

Nos. 1593–1598 printed together in sheets of 6.

Perf. 13½x14, 14x13½

1974, Dec. 10

Paintings: 10pf, Still Life, by Ronald Paris (horiz.). 20pf, Fisherman's House, Vitte, by Harald Hakenbeck. 35pf, Girl in Red, by Rudolf Bergander (horiz.). 70pf, The Artist's Parents, by Willi Sitte.

1599 A491 10pf multicolored 6 4
1600 " 15pf " 12 5
1601 " 20pf " 12 5
1602 " 35pf " 25 10
1603 " 70pf " *2.75* *2.25*
Nos. 1599–1603 (5) *3.30* *2.49*

Paintings in Berlin Museums.

Banded Jasper A492

Minerals: 15pf, Smoky quartz. 20pf, Topaz. 25pf, Amethyst. 35pf, Aquamarine. 70pf, Agate.

1974, Dec. 17 Photogravure *Perf. 14*

1604 A492 10pf lt. yel. & multi. 6 4
1605 " 15pf " " 12 5
1606 " 20pf " " 12 5
1607 " 25pf " " 18 8
1608 " 35pf " " 25 12
1609 " 70pf " " *2.75* *2.25*
Nos. 1604–1609 (6) *3.48* *2.59*

Minerals from the collection of the Mining Academy in Freiberg.

Coil Stamps

Type of 1973

1974–75 Photogravure *Perf. 14*

Designs: 5pf, Pelican. 10pf, Neptune Fountain. 20pf, Lenin Square. 25pf, World clock. 50pf, New Guard House. 1m, Soviet War Memorial.

Size: 21x17½mm.

1610 A449 5pf blue green ('74) 6 4
1611 " 10pf emerald 12 4
1612 " 20pf rose magenta 24 4
1613 " 25pf green ('75) 30 5
1615 " 50pf blue ('74) 60 10
1617 " 1m olive ('74) 1.20 20
Nos. 1610–1617 (6) 2.52 47

Black control number on back of every fifth stamp.

The 20pf was issued in sheets of 100 in 1975.

Martha Arendsee A493

1975, Jan. 14 Litho. *Perf. 13½x13*

1618 A493 10pf dull red 15 6

90th birth anniversary of Martha Arendsee (1885–1953), communist politician.

Souvenir Sheet

Peasants' War, Contemporary Woodcuts—A494

1975, Feb. 11 *Perf. 12½x13*

Gray and Multicolored

1619 A494 Sheet of 6+label *3.00* *2.50*
a. 5pf *Forced labor*
b. 10pf *Peasant paying tithe*
c. 20pf *Thomas Münzer*
d. 25pf *Armed peasants*
e. 35pf *Peasant with "Liberty" flag*
f. 50pf *Peasant on trial*

Peasants' War, 450th anniversary. Yellow label with black inscription shows title page of 12 demands submitted by the peasants. Size: 128x113mm.

Black Women A495

Designs: 20pf, Caucasian women. 25pf, Indian woman and child.

1975, Feb. 25 Litho. *Perf. 13*

1620 A495 10pf red & multi.
1621 " 20pf " "
1622 " 25pf " "
Strip of 3, #1620–1622 *1.25* *1.00*

International Women's Year 1975. Nos. 1620–1622 printed se-tenant.

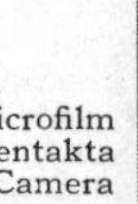

Microfilm Pentakta Camera A496

Design: 25pf, Sket cement plant.

1975, Mar. 4 Photo. *Perf. 14*

1623 A496 10pf ultra. & multi. 25 12
1624 " 25pf org. & multi. 50 25

Leipzig Spring Fair.

Hans Otto (1900–33) Actor A497

Portraits: 10pf, Thomas Mann (1875–1955), writer. 20pf, Albert Schweitzer (1875–1965), medical missionary. 25pf, Michelangelo (1475–1564), painter and sculptor. 35pf, André Marie Ampère (1775–1836), scientist.

1975, Mar. 18 Litho. *Perf. 13½x13*

1625 A497 5pf dark blue 4 4
1626 " 10pf dk. car. rose 6 4
1627 " 20pf dark green 10 4
1628 " 25pf sepia 16 10
1629 " 35pf violet blue *1.50* *1.25*
Nos. 1625–1629 (5) *1.86* *1.47*

Famous men, birth anniversaries.

Blue and Yellow Macaws, Magdeburg Zoo A498

Designs: 10pf, Orangutan family, Dresden. 15pf, Siberian chamois, Halle. 20pf, Rhinoceros, Berlin. 25pf, Dwarf hippopotamus, Erfurt. 30pf, Baltic seal and pup, Rostock. 35pf, Siberian tiger, Leipzig. 50pf, Boehm's zebra, Cottbus. 20pf, 25pf, 30pf, 35pf are horiz.

Perf. 13½x13, 13x13½

1975, Mar. 25

1630 A498 5pf multicolored 4 4
1631 " 10pf " 6 4
1632 " 15pf " 8 4
1633 " 20pf " 10 5
1634 " 25pf " 16 10
1635 " 30pf " 20 12
1636 " 35pf " 25 15
1637 " 50pf " *2.75* *2.50*
Nos. 1630–1637 (8) *3.64* *3.04*

German Zoological Gardens.

Soldiers, Industry and Agriculture—A499

1975, May 6 Photo. *Perf. 13½x14*

1638 A499 20pf multicolored 30 20

20th anniversary of the signing of the Warsaw Treaty (Bulgaria, Czechoslovakia, German Democratic Rep., Hungary, Poland, Romania, USSR).

Soviet War Memorial, Berlin-Treptow A500

Ribbons, Youth Organization Emblems of DDR and USSR A501

Designs (Arms of German Democratic Rep. and): 20pf, Buchenwald Memorial (detail). 25pf, Woman reconstruction worker. 35pf, Skyscraper and statue at Orenburg (economic integration). 50pf, Soldier raising Red Flag on Reichstag Building, Berlin.

1975, May 6 *Perf. 14x13½*

1639 A500 10pf red & multi. 6 4
1640 " 20pf " " 12 5
1641 " 25pf " " 18 12
1642 " 35pf " " *1.35* *1.25*

Souvenir Sheet

Imperf.

1643 A500 50pf red & multi. 1.00 75

30th anniversary of liberation from fascism. No. 1643 contains one stamp with design extending into red margin; black and white marginal inscription. Size: 108 x90mm.

1975, May 13 *Perf. 14*

1644 A501 10pf multicolored 15 12

Third Friendship Festival of Russian and German Youths, Halle, 1975.

Lighthouse Type of 1974

Lighthouses, Maps and Nautical Charts: 5pf, Timmendorf, 1872. 10pf, Gellen, 1905. 20pf, Sassnitz, 1904. 25pf, Dornbush, 1888. 35pf, Peenemünde, 1954.

1975, May 13 Litho. *Perf. 14*

1645 A478 5pf multicolored 4 4
1646 " 10pf " 6 4
1647 " 20pf " 10 4
1648 " 25pf " 16 10
1649 " 35pf " *1.60* *1.35*
Nos. 1645–1649 (5) *1.96* *1.57*

Hydrographic Service of German Democratic Republic.

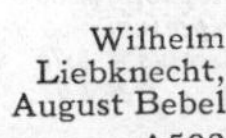

Wilhelm Liebknecht, August Bebel
A502

Designs: 20pf, Tivoli House and front page of Protocol of Gotha. 25pf, Karl Marx and Friedrich Engels.

1975, May 21 Photogravure

1650 A502 10pf buff, brn. & red *22* 18
1651 " 20pf sal., brn. & red *45* 35
1652 " 25pf buff, brn. & red *55* 50

Centenary of the Congress of Gotha, the beginning of German Socialist Workers' Party. Nos. 1650–1652 printed se-tenant in sheets of 45.

Construction Workers, Union Emblem—A503

1975, June 10 Photo. ***Perf. 14***

1653 A503 20pf red & multi. 40 20

Free German Association of Trade Unions (FDGB), 30th anniversary.

"Socialist Scientific Cooperation" Mosaic by Walter Womacka
A504

1975, June 10 Litho. ***Perf. 13***

1654 A504 20pf multicolored 25 20

Eisenhüttenstadt, first socialist city of DDR, 25th anniversary.

Automatic Clock by Paulus Schuster, 1585
A505

Clocks, Dresden Museums: 10pf, Astronomical table clock, Augsburg, c. 1560. 15pf, Automatic clock, Hans Schlottheim, c. 1600. 20pf, Table clock, Johann Heinrich Köhler, c. 1720. 25pf, Table clock, Köhler, c. 1700. 35pf, Astronomical clock, Johannes Klein, 1738.

1975, June 24 Photo. ***Perf. 14***

1655 A505 5pf multicolored 4 4
1656 " 10pf ultra. & multi. 6 4
1657 " 15pf red & multi. *2.75* *2.50*
1658 " 20pf olive & multi. 10 4
1659 " 25pf multicolored 15 9
1660 " 35pf ocher & multi. 25 15
Nos. 1655–1660 (6) *3.35* *2.86*

Dictionary, Compiled by Jacob and Wilhelm Grimm—A506

Designs: 20pf, Karl-Schwarzschild Observatory, Tautenburg near Jena. 25pf, Electron microscope and chemical plant (scientific and practical cooperation). 35pf, Intercosmos 10 satellite.

1975, July 2 Litho. ***Perf. 13½x13***

1661 A506 10pf plum, olive & black 8 4
1662 " 20pf vio. bl. & blk. 12 4
1663 " 25pf green, yellow & black 18 6
1664 " 35pf bl. & multi. *1.50* *1.25*

German Academy of Sciences, 275th anniversary.

Torch Bearer
A507

Designs: 20pf, Hurdling. 25pf, Diving. 35pf, Gymnast on bar.

1975, July 15 ***Perf. 13½x13***

1665 A507 10pf sal. rose & blk. 8 4
1666 " 20pf yel. & black 12 4
1667 " 25pf ultra. & blk. 18 6
1668 " 35pf yel. grn. & black *1.50* *1.25*

5th Children and Youths Spartakiad.

Map of Europe
A508

1975, July 30 Photo. ***Perf. 13***

1669 A508 20pf multicolored 40 30

European Security and Cooperation Conference, Helsinki, July 30–Aug. 1.

China Aster
A509

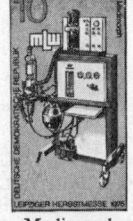

Medimorph Anesthesia Unit
A510

1975, Aug. 19 Photo. ***Perf. 13½x14***

Multicolored

1670 A509 5pf *shown* 4 4
1671 " 10pf *Geranium* 6 4
1672 " 20pf *Transvaal daisies* 10 5
1673 " 25pf *Carnation* 16 10
1674 " 35pf *Chrysanthemum* 22 18
1675 " 70pf *Pansies* *3.50* *3.00*
Nos. 1670–1675 (6) *4.08* *3.41*

1975, Aug. 28 ***Perf. 14***

Design: 25pf, Motorcycle, type MZ TS 250 (horiz.).

1676 A510 10pf multicolored 20 12
1677 " 25pf yel. & multi. 50 30

Leipzig Fall Fair.

Children and Child Crossing Guard
A511

Designs: 15pf, Traffic policewoman. 20pf, Policeman helping, motorist. 25pf, Motor vehicle inspection. 35pf, Volunteer instructor.

1975, Sept. 9 Litho. ***Perf. 13x12½***

1678 A511 10pf multicolored 6 4
1679 " 15pf green & multi. *2.00* *1.75*
1680 " 20pf brn. & multi. 10 4
1681 " 25pf vio. & multi. 16 10
1682 " 35pf multicolored 25 12
Nos. 1678–1682 (5) *2.57* *2.05*

Traffic police serving and instructing the public.

Soyuz Take-off
A512

Designs: 20pf, Soyuz and Apollo in space. 70pf, Spacecraft after link-up (horiz.; 79x28mm.).

Perf. 14x13½, 13½x14

1975, Sept. 15 Photogravure

1683 A512 10pf multicolored 6 4
1684 " 20pf " 10 4
1685 " 70pf " *2.25* *2.00*

Apollo Soyuz space test project (Russo-American space cooperation), launching July 15; link-up, July 17.

Weimar, 1630, after Merian—A513

Designs: 20pf, Buchenwald Liberation Monument (vert.). 35pf, Composite view of old and new buildings in Weimar.

1975, Sept. 23 Litho. ***Perf. 13½x13***

1686 A513 10pf grn., gray & black 6 4
1687 " 20pf red & multi. 10 4
1688 " 35pf ultra. & multi. *1.00* 75

Millennium of Weimar.

Monument, Vienna
A514

Louis Braille and Dots
A515

1975, Oct. 14 Photo. ***Perf. 14x13½***

1689 A514 35pf red & multi. 40 20

Memorial for the victims of the struggle for a free Austria, 1934–1945.

1975, Oct. 14

Designs: 35pf, Hands reading Braille. 50pf, Eyeball and protective glasses.

1690 A515 20pf gray & multi. 10 4
1691 " 35pf multicolored 22 10
1692 " 50pf " *1.75* *1.50*

World Braille Year 1975. Sesquicentennial of the invention of Braille system of writing for the blind, by Louis Braille (1809–1852).

Post Office Bärenfels
A516

1975, Oct. 21 Photo. ***Perf. 14***

1693 A516 20pf multicolored 30 18

Philatelists' Day 1975. See No. B177.

Emperor Ordering Clothes—A517

Designs: Scenes from "The Emperor's New Clothes," by Hans Christian Andersen and Andersen portrait.

1975, Nov. 18 Litho. ***Perf. 14x13***

1694 A517 20pf ocher & multi.
1695 " 35pf " "
1696 " 50pf " "
Sheet of 3, #1694–1696 *2.50* *2.00*

Nos. 1694–1696 issued in sheet of 3.

Tobogganing and Olympic Rings—A518

Designs (Olympic Rings and): 20pf, Speed-skating Rink, Berlin. 35pf, Figure-skating Hall, Karl-Marx Stadt. 70pf, Mass skiing at Schmiedefeld. 1m, Innsbruck and surrounding mountains.

1975, Dec. 2 Photo. ***Perf. 14***

1697 A518 5pf multicolored 4 4
1698 " 20pf olive & multi. 14 10
1699 " 35pf multicolored 22 18
1700 " 70pf " *3.00* *2.50*
Nos. 1697–1700, B178–B179 (6) *3.76* *3.00*

Souvenir Sheet

1701 A518 1m ultra. & multi. 2.50 2.00

12th Winter Olympic Games, Innsbruck, Austria, Feb. 4–15, 1976. No. 1701 contains one stamp (size: 32x27mm.). Multicolored margin with continuation of stamp design and Innsbruck Olympic Games emblem. Size: 79x55mm.

Wilhelm Pieck A519

Ernst Thälmann (1886–1944) A520

1975, Dec. 30 Litho. *Perf. 13½x13*

1702 A519 10pf lt. ultra. & black 15 10

President Wilhelm Pieck (1876–1960), birth centenary.

1976, Jan. 13 *Perf. 13½x13*

Labor Leaders: No. 1704, Georg Schumann (1886–1945). No. 1705, Wilhelm Koenen (1886–1963). No. 1706, John Schehr (1896–1934).

1703 A520 10pf rose & black 12 12
1704 " 10pf emerald & black 12 12
1705 " 10pf ocher & blk. 12 12
1706 " 10pf vio. & black 12 12

See Nos. 1852–1854.

Silbermann Organ, Rötha A521

Silbermann Organs: 20pf, Freiberg. 35pf, Fraureuth. 50pf, Dresden.

1976, Jan. 27 Photo. *Perf. 14*

1707 A521 10pf grn. & multi. 6 4
1708 " 20pf red & multi. 14 6
1709 " 35pf multicolored 22 14
1710 " 50pf brn. & multi. 2.00 1.75

Organs built by Gottfried Silbermann (1683–1753).

Souvenir Sheet

Richard Sorge—A522

1976, Feb. 3 Litho. *Imperf.*

1711 A522 1m multicolored 2.25 2.00

Dr. Richard Sorge (1895–1944), Soviet intelligence agent. No. 1711 contains one stamp with simulated perforations; yellow Hero of the Soviet Union medal in dark red margin. Size: 81x65mm.

Military Flag, Sailor, Soldier, Aviator—A523

Design: 20pf, Military flag, ships, tanks, missile and planes.

1976, Feb. 24 Litho. *Perf. 13½x14*

1712 A523 10pf multicolored 15 8
1713 " 20pf " 30 20

National People's Army, 20th anniversary.

Telephone A524

Apartment House, Leipzig A525

1976, Mar. 2 *Perf. 13*

1714 A524 20pf light blue 25 5

Centenary of first telephone call by Alexander Graham Bell, March 10, 1876.

1976, Mar. 9 Photo. *Perf. 14*

Design: 25pf, Ocean super trawler (horiz.).

1715 A525 10pf grn. & multi. 15 8
1716 " 25pf viol. bl., blk. & green 40 22

Leipzig Spring Fair.

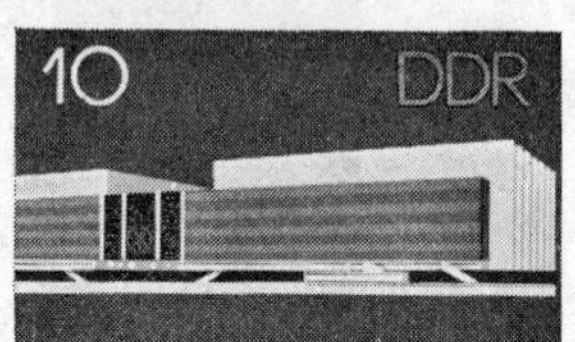

Palace of the Republic—A526

1976, Apr. 22 Photo. *Perf. 14*

1717 A526 10pf violet blue & multi. 15 5

Inauguration of Palace of the Republic, Berlin. See No. 1721.

Post Office Radar Station A527

Marx, Engels, Lenin and Party Flag A528

1976, Apr. 27 Photo. *Perf. 13½x14*

1718 A527 20pf multicolored 30 15

Intersputnik 1976.

Perf. 14x13½, 13½x14

1976, May 11

Designs: 20pf, New factories and apartment houses, party flag (horiz.). 1m, Palace of the Republic.

1719 A528 10pf dp. magenta, gold & red 20 10
1720 " 20pf multicolored 45 25

Souvenir Sheet

Perf. 14

1721 A526 1m multicolored 2.25 2.00

9th Congress of Unity Party (SED). No. 1721 contains one stamp; ocher and multicolored margin showing young worker, people and party flag. Size: 110x90mm.

Peace Bicycle Race and Olympic Rings—A529

Designs: 20pf, Town and sport halls, Suhl. 25pf, Regatta course, Brandenburg. 70pf, 1500-meter race. 1m, Central Stadium, Leipzig.

1976, May 18 Photo. *Perf. 13½x14*

1722 A529 5pf grn. & multi. 5 4
1723 " 20pf blue & multi. 12 6
1724 " 25pf multicolored 20 14
1725 " 70pf ultra. & multi. 3.50 3.00
Nos. 1722–1725, B180–B181 (6) 4.25 3.47

Souvenir Sheet

Perf. 14

1726 A529 1m multicolored 2.50 2.25

21st Olympic Games, Montreal, Canada, July 17–Aug. 1. No. 1726 contains one stamp (32x27mm.). Multicolored margin with continuation of stamp design. Size: 80x55mm.

Ribbons and Emblem A530

Design: 20pf, Young man and woman, industrial installations.

1976, May 25 *Perf. 14*

1727 A530 10pf blue & multi. 15 10
1728 " 20pf multicolored 30 20

10th Parliamentary Meeting of the Free German Youth Organization.

Himantoglossum Hircinum A531

Dancer at Rest, by Walter Arnold A532

Designs: European orchids.

1976, June 15 Litho. *Perf. 12½x13*

Multicolored

1729 A531 10pf *shown* 6 4
1730 " 20pf *Dactylorhiza incarnata* 18 8
1731 A531 25pf *Anacamptis pyramidalis* 20 10
1732 " 35pf *Dactylorhiza sambucina* 28 18
1733 " 40pf *Orchis coriophora* 30 20
1734 " 50pf *Cypripedium calceolus* 3.75 3.25
Nos. 1729–1734 (6) 4.77 3.85

1976, June 22 Photo. *Perf. 14*

Small Sculptures: 10pf, Shetland Pony, by Heinrich Drake (horiz.). 25pf, "At the Beach," by Ludwig Engelhardt. 35pf, Hermann Duncker, by Walter Howard. 50pf, "The Conversation," by Gustav Weidanz.

1735 A532 10pf blk. & bl. grn. 6 4
1736 " 20pf ocher & black 14 6
1737 " 25pf " " 16 8
1738 " 35pf yel. green & black 22 12
1739 " 50pf brick red & black 2.50 2.25
Nos. 1735–1739 (5) 3.08 2.55

Marx, Engels, Lenin, Red Flags, Berlin Buildings A533

1976, June 29 Photo. *Perf. 14*

1740 A533 20pf blue, red & dark red 22 15

European Communist Workers' Congress, Berlin.

Coronation Coach, 1790 A534

Historic Coaches: 20pf, Open carriage, Russia, 1800. 25pf, Court landau, Saxony, 1840. 35pf, State carriage, Saxony, 1860. 40pf, Mail coach, 1850. 50pf, Town carriage, Saxony, 1889.

1976, July 27

1741 A534 10pf multicolored 6 4
1742 " 20pf " 10 5
1743 " 25pf " 14 10
1744 " 35pf " 18 12
1745 " 40pf " 20 13
1746 " 50pf " 3.25 2.75
Nos. 1741–1746 (6) 3.93 3.19

View of Gera A535

Design: 10pf+5pf, View of Gera, c. 1652.

1976, Aug. 5 Litho. *Perf. 13*

1747 A535 10pf+5pf multi.
1748 " 20pf "
Strip of 2 (#1747–1748) + label 85 60

4th German Youth Philatelic Exhibition, Gera. Nos. 1747–1748 printed se-tenant with label showing arms of Gera.

Boxer A536

Dogs: 10pf, Airedale terrier. 20pf, German shepherd. 25pf, Collie. 35pf, Giant schnauzer. 70pf, Great Dane.

1976, Aug. 17 ***Perf. 14***

1749 A536 5pf multicolored 4 4
1750 " 10pf " 6 4
1751 " 20pf " 10 5
1752 " 25pf " 16 10
1753 " 35pf " 18 12
1754 " 70pf " *3.25* *2.75*
Nos. 1749-1754 (6) *3.79* *3.10*

Oil Distillery
A537

Design: 25pf, German Library, Leipzig.

1976, Sept. 1 ***Perf. 13x12½***

1755 A537 10pf multicolored 15 8
1756 " 25pf " 35 20

Leipzig Fall Fair.

Templin Lake Bridge—A538

Designs: 15pf, Overpass, Berlin-Adlergestell. 20pf, Elbe River Bridge, Rosslau. 25pf, Göltzschtal Viaduct. 35pf, Elbe River Bridge, Magdeburg. 50pf, Grosser Dreesch Overpass, Schwerin.

1976, Sept. 21 **Photo.** ***Perf. 14***

1757 A538 10pf multicolored 6 4
1758 " 15pf " 8 5
1759 " 20pf " 10 5
1760 " 25pf " 16 10
1761 " 35pf " 18 12
1762 " 50pf " *3.00* *2.50*
Nos. 1757-1762 (6) *3.58* *2.86*

Memorial Monument (detail), Budapest—A539

1976, Oct. 5 **Photo.** ***Perf. 14***

1763 A539 35pf tan & multi. *50* *25*

Memorial to World War II victims.

Brass Jug, c. 1500
A540

Guppy
A541

Artistic Handicraft Works: 20pf, Faience vase with lid, c. 1710. 25pf, Porcelain centerpiece (woman carrying bowl), c. 1768. 35pf, Porter, gilded silver, c. 1700. 70pf, Art Nouveau glass vase, c. 1900.

1976, Oct. 19

1764 A540 10pf dark carmine multi. 6 4
1765 " 20pf ultra. & multi. 10 5
1766 " 25pf green & multi. 14 6
1767 " 35pf violet blue & multi. 18 10
1768 A540 70pf red brn. & multi. *3.00* *2.50*
Nos. 1764-1768 (5) *3.48* *2.75*

1976, Nov. 9 **Litho.** ***Perf. 13½x13***

Designs: Various guppies.

1769 A541 10pf multicolored 6 4
1770 " 15pf " 8 5
1771 " 20pf " 10 5
1772 " 25pf " 16 7
1773 " 35pf " 18 10
1774 " 70pf " *3.00* *2.50*
Nos. 1769-1774 (6) *3.58* *2.81*

Vessels, c. 3000 B.C.
A542

Designs: 20pf, Cult cart, c. 1300 B.C. 25pf, Roman gold coin, 270-273 A.D. 35pf, Gold pendant, 950 A.D. 70pf, Glass cup, 3rd century A.D.

1976, Nov. 23 **Photo.** ***Perf. 13***

1775 A542 10pf multicolored 6 4
1776 " 20pf " 10 5
1777 " 25pf " 16 7
1778 " 35pf " 18 10
1779 " 70pf " *3.00* *2.50*
Nos. 1775-1779 (5) *3.50* *2.76*

Archaeological finds in German Democratic Republic.

"Air," by Rosalba Carriera
A543

Rumpelstiltskin and King
A544

Paintings, Dresden Museum: 15pf, Virgin and Child, by Murillo. 20pf, Woman Viola da Gamba Player, by Bernardo Strozzi. 25pf, Ariadne Forsaken, by Angelica Kauffmann. 35pf, Old Man with Black Cap, by Bartolomeo Nazzari. 70pf, Officer Reading a Letter, by Gerard Terborch.

1976, Dec. 14 **Photo.** ***Perf. 13½x14***

1780 A543 10pf multicolored 4 4
1781 " 15pf " 8 4
1782 " 20pf " 8 5
1783 " 25pf " 14 7
1784 " 35pf " 18 10
1785 " 70pf " *3.00* *2.50*
Nos. 1780-1785 (6) *3.52* *2.80*

1976, Dec. 14 **Litho.** ***Perf. 13***

Designs: Scenes from fairy tale "Rumpelstiltskin."

1786 A544 5pf multicolored *55* *40*
1787 " 10pf " *55* *40*
1788 " 15pf " *55* *40*
1789 " 20pf " *55* *40*
1790 " 25pf " *55* *40*
1791 " 30pf " *55* *40*
Sheet of 6 (#1786-1791) *3.30* *2.40*

Nos. 1786-1791 printed se-tenant in sheet of 6.

Arnold Zweig and Quotation
A545

Designs: 20pf, Otto von Guericke and Magdeburg hemispheres. 35pf, Albrecht D. Thaer, wheat, plow and sheep. 40pf, Gustav Hertz and diagram of separation of isotopes.

1977, Feb. 8 **Litho.** ***Perf. 13x12½***

1792 A545 10pf rose & black 6 4
1793 " 20pf gray & black 10 5
1794 " 35pf lt. grn. & blk. 18 10
1795 " 40pf blue & black *1.35* *1.00*

Honoring Arnold Zweig (1887-1968), novelist; Otto von Guericke (1602-1686), physicist; Albrecht D. Thaer (1752-1828), agronomist and physician; Gustav Hertz (1887-1975), physicist.

Spring near Plaue
A546

Natural Monuments: 20pf, Small Organ, Johnsdorf. 25pf, Ivenacker Oaks, Reuterstadt. 35pf, Stone Rose, Saalburg. 50pf, Rauenscher Stein (boulder), Furstenwalde.

1977, Feb. 24 **Litho.** ***Perf. 12½x13***

1796 A546 10pf multicolored 4 4
1797 " 20pf " 8 5
1798 " 25pf " 14 7
1799 " 35pf " 18 10
1800 " 50pf " *2.10* *1.75*
Nos. 1796-1800 (5) *2.54* *2.01*

Fair Building, Book Fair
A547

Design: 25pf, Wide aluminum roll casting machine, Nachterstedt factory.

1977, Mar. 8 **Photo.** ***Perf. 14***

1801 A547 10pf multicolored 15 6
1802 " 25pf " 35 20

Leipzig Spring Fair.

Costume Senftenberg
A548

Start after Wheel Change
A549

Sorbian Costumes from: 20pf, Bautzen. 25pf, Klitten. 35pf, Nochten. 70pf, Muskau.

1977, Mar. 22

1803 A548 10pf multicolored 6 4
1804 " 20pf " 10 5
1805 " 25pf " 14 6
1806 " 35pf " 18 10
1807 " 70pf " *2.75* *2.25*
Nos. 1803-1807 (5) *3.23* *2.50*

1977, Apr. 19 **Photo.** ***Perf. 14***

Designs: 20pf, Sprint. 35pf, At finish line.

1808 A549 10pf multicolored *15* *15*
1809 " 20pf " *35* *35*
1810 " 35pf " *90* *90*

30th International Peace Bicycling Race. Nos. 1808-1810 printed se-tenant.

Carl Fried-rich Gauss
A550

1977, Apr. 19 **Litho.** ***Perf. 13x12½***

1811 A550 20pf lt. ultra. & black 30 4

Carl Friedrich Gauss (1777-1855), mathematician, 200th birth anniversary.

Flags and Hand-shake
A551

1977, May 3 **Photo.** ***Perf. 13***

1812 A551 20pf violet blue & multicolored 30 4

9th German Trade Union Congress, Berlin.

VKM Channel Converter, Filter and ITU Emblem
A552

1977, May 17 **Litho.** ***Perf. 14***

1813 A552 20pf multicolored 30 4

International Telecommunications Day.

Pistol Shooting
A553

Designs: 20pf, Deep-sea diver. 35pf, Radio controlled model boat.

1977, May 17 **Photogravure**

1814 A553 10pf light green & multi. 4 4
1815 " 20pf light blue & multi. 6 4
1816 " 35pf sal. & multi. *1.30* *1.10*

Organization for Physical and Technical Training.

Accordion, c. 1900
A554

Designs: 20pf, Treble viola da gamba, 1747. 25pf, Oboe, 1785, Clarinet, 1830 and flute, 1817. 35pf, Concert zither, 1891. 70pf, Trumpet, 1860.

1977, June 14

1817	A554	10pf multicolored	4	4
1818	"	20pf "	7	4
1819	"	25pf "	10	6
1820	"	35pf "	13	10
1821	"	70pf "	*3.00*	*2.50*
		Nos. 1817-1821 (5)	*3.34*	*2.74*

Vogtland musical instruments from Markneukirchen Museum.

Mercury and Argus, by Rubens—A555

Rubens Paintings in Dresden Gallery: 10pf, Bath of Bathsheba (vert.). 20pf, The Drunk Hercules (vert.). 25pf, Diana Returning from the Hunt. 35pf, Old Woman with Brazier (vert.). 50pf, Leda and the Swan.

1977, June 28 Photo. *Perf. 14*

1822	A555	10pf multicolored	4	4
1823	"	15pf "	6	4
1824	"	20pf "	7	4
1825	"	25pf "	10	6
1826	"	35pf "	13	10
1827	"	50pf "	*3.00*	*2.50*
		Nos. 1822-1827 (6)	*3.40*	*2.78*

Peter Paul Rubens (1577-1640), Flemish painter, 400th birth anniversary.

Souvenir Sheet

Wreath, Flags of USSR and DDR—A556

1977, June 28

1828	A556	50pf multicolored	*1.50*	*1.25*

Society for German-Soviet Friendship, 30th anniversary. No. 1828 has red border and marginal inscription. Size: 82½x55 mm.

Tractor with Plow—A557

Designs: 20pf, Fertilizer-spreader. 25pf, Potato digger and loader. 35pf, High-pressure harvester. 50pf, Rotating milking machine.

1977, July 12 Litho. *Perf. 13x12½*

1829	A557	10pf multicolored	4	4
1830	"	20pf "	7	4
1831	"	25pf "	10	6
1832	"	35pf "	13	10
1833	"	50pf "	*2.75*	*2.40*
		Nos. 1829-1833 (5)	*3.09*	*2.64*

Motorized modern agriculture.

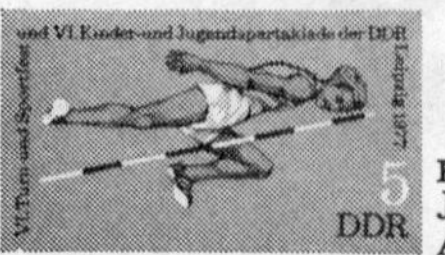

High Jump A558

Designs: 20pf, Hurdles, girls. 35pf, Dancing. 40pf, Torch bearer and flags.

1977, July 19

1834	A558	5pf red & multi.		
1835	"	20pf lt. grn. & multi.		
1836	"	35pf grn. & multi.		
1837	"	40pf blue & multi.		
		Nos. 1834-1837, B183-B184 (6)	*3.00*	

6th Gymnastics and Sports Festival and 6th Children's and Youth Spartacist Games.

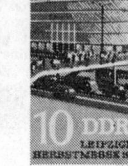

"Bread for all . . ." by Wolfram Schubert A559

Konsument Department Store, Leipzig A560

Design: 25pf, "When Communists Dream," by Walter Womacka (detail) and Sozphilex emblem.

1977, Aug. 16 Photo. *Perf. 14*

1838	A559	10pf multicolored	25	15
	a.	Souvenir sheet of 4	1.00	
1839	A559	25pf multicolored	62	35
	a.	Souvenir sheet of 4	2.50	

SOZPHILEX '77 Philatelic Exhibition, Berlin, Aug. 19-28. Nos. 1838a and 1839a have pink and black border. Size: 76x110mm. See No. B185.

1977, Aug. 30

Design: 25pf, Glasses and wooden plate.

1840	A560	10pf blue & multi.	25	6
1841	"	25pf multicolored	62	15

Leipzig Fall Fair.

Souvenir Sheet

Dzerzhinski and Quotation from Mayakovsky—A561

1977, Sept. 6 Litho. *Perf. 12½x13*

1842	A561	Sheet of 2	1.40	1.10
	a.	20pf multicolored	50	35
	b.	35pf "	70	60

Feliks E. Dzerzhinski (1877-1926), organizer and head of Russian Secret Police (Cheka), birth centenary. No. 1842 has blue marginal inscription. Size: 127x70 mm.

Muldenthal Locomotive, 1861 A562

Designs: 10pf, Trolley car, Dresden, 1896. 20pf, First successful German plane, 1909. 25pf, 3-wheel car "Phänomobile," 1924. 35pf, Passenger steamship on the Elbe, 1837.

1977, Sept. 13 Photo. *Perf. 14*

1843	A562	5pf grn. & multi.	4	4
1844	"	10pf " "	4	4
1845	"	20pf " "	7	4
1846	"	25pf " "	9	6
1847	"	35pf " "	*2.00*	*1.50*
		Nos. 1843-1847 (5)	2.24	1.68

Transportation Museum, Dresden.

Cruiser "Aurora" A563

Designs: 25pf, Storming of the Winter Palace. 1m, Lenin (vert.).

1977, Sept. 20

1848	A563	10pf multicolored	*15*	*10*
1849	"	25pf "	*60*	*40*

Souvenir Sheet

Perf. 12½x13

1850	A563	1m car. & black	*2.25*	*2.00*

60th anniversary of the Russian Revolution. No. 1850 has multicolored margin showing Red flag and front page of Izvestia, Oct. 27, 1917. Size: 55x86mm.

Mother Russia and Obelisk A564

1977, Sept. 20 Litho. *Perf. 14*

1851	A564	35pf multicolored	50	4

Soviet soldiers' memorial, Berlin-Schönholz.

Labor Leaders Type of 1976

Portraits: No. 1852, Ernst Meyer (1887-1930). No. 1853, August Fröhlich (1877-1966). No. 1854, Gerhart Eisler (1897-1968).

1977, Oct. 18 Litho. *Perf. 14*

1852	A520	10pf olive & brown	12	12
1853	"	10pf rose & brown	12	12
1854	"	10pf lt. blue & blk. brown	12	12

Souvenir Sheet

Heinrich von Kleist, by Peter Friedl, 1801—A565

1977, Oct. 18

1855	A565	1m multicolored	*3.00*	*2.50*

Heinrich von Kleist (1777-1811), poet and playwright, birth bicentenary. Margin design of No. 1855 shows characters from plays. Size: 82x54mm.

Rocket A566

Design: 20pf, as 10pf, design reversed.

1977, Nov. 8 Photo. *Perf. 14*

1856	A566	10pf red, blk. & silver	*20*	*15*
1857	A566	20pf ultra., black & gold	*60*	*50*
		Strip of 2 (#1856-1857) + label	*80*	*65*

20th Central Young Craftsmen's Exhibition (Masters of Tomorrow). Nos. 1856-1857 printed se-tenant with label showing exhibition emblem.

Mouflons A567

Children Visiting Firehouse A568

Designs: 15pf, Red deer. 20pf, Retriever with pheasant, hunter. 25pf, Red fox, wild duck. 35pf, Tractor driver saving fawn. 70pf, Wild boars.

1977, Nov. 15

1858	A567	10pf multicolored		
1859	"	15pf "		
1860	"	20pf "		
1861	"	25pf "		
1862	"	35pf "		
1863	"	70pf "		
		Nos. 1858-1863 (6)	*3.50*	*3.00*

Hunting in East Germany.

1977, Nov. 22 Litho. *Perf. 14*

Firemen's Activities: 10pf, Firemen racing with ladders (horiz.). 25pf, Fire engines fighting forest and brush fires (horiz.). 35pf, Artificial respiration. 50pf, Fireboat alongside freighter (horiz.).

1864	A568	10pf multicolored		
1865	"	20pf "		
1866	"	25pf "		
1867	"	35pf "		
1868	"	50pf "		
		Nos. 1864-1868 (5)	*3.25*	

Knight and King—A569

1977, Nov. 22 *Perf. 13x13½*

Designs: Various scenes from fairytale: "Six Men Around the World."

1869	A569	5pf black & multi.		
1870	"	10pf " "		
1871	"	20pf " "		
1872	"	25pf " "		
1873	"	35pf " "		
1874	"	60pf " "		
		Nos. 1869-1874 (6)	*4.00*	

Nos. 1869-1874 printed together in sheets of 6.

Hips and Dog Rose A570

Medicinal Plants: 15pf, Birch. 20pf, Camomile. 25pf, Coltsfoot. 35pf, Linden. 50pf, Elder.

1978, Jan. 10 Photo. *Perf. 14*

1875	A570	10pf multicolored		
1876	"	15pf "		
1877	"	20pf "		
1878	"	25pf "		
1879	"	35pf "		
1880	"	50pf "		
		Nos. 1875-1880 (6)	*3.50*	

Amilcar Cabral
A571

Town Hall, Suhl-Heinrichs
A572

1978, Jan. 17 Litho. ***Perf. 14***

1881 A571 20pf multicolored 25 4

Amilcar Cabral (1924–1973), freedom movement leader from Guinea-Bissau.

1978, Jan. 24 Photo. ***Perf. 14***

Half-timbered Buildings, 17th–18th Centuries: 20pf, Farmhouse, Niederoderwitz. 25pf, Farmhouse, Strassen. 35pf, Townhouse, Quedlinburg. 40pf, Townhouse, Eisenach.

1882 A572 10pf multicolored
1883 " 20pf "
1884 " 25pf "
1885 " 35pf "
1886 " 40pf "
Nos. 1882–1886 (5) 2.40

Mail Truck, 1921
A573

Past and Present Mail Transport: 20pf, Mail truck, 1978. 25pf, Railroad mail car, 1896. 35pf, Railroad mail car, 1978.

1978, Feb. 9 Litho. ***Perf. 13x12½***

1887 A573 10pf brn. & multi.
1888 " 20pf " "
1889 " 25pf " "
1890 " 35pf " "
Nos. 1887–1890 (4) 2.50

Nos. 1887–1890 printed se-tenant in blocks of 4.

Earring, 11th Century
A574

Royal House, Leipzig
A575

Archaeological Artifacts: 20pf, Earring, 10th century. 25pf, Bronze sheath, 10th century. 35pf, Bronze horse, 8th century. 70pf, Arabian coin, 8th century.

1978, Feb. 21 Photo. ***Perf. 14***

1891 A574 10pf multicolored
1892 " 20pf "
1893 " 25pf "
1894 " 35pf "
1895 " 70pf "
Nos. 1891–1895 (5) 3.30

Treasures found on Slavic sites.

1978, Mar. 7

Design: 25pf, Universal measuring instrument by Carl Zeiss.

1896 A575 10pf multicolored 15 6
1897 " 25pf " 30 15

Leipzig Spring Fair.

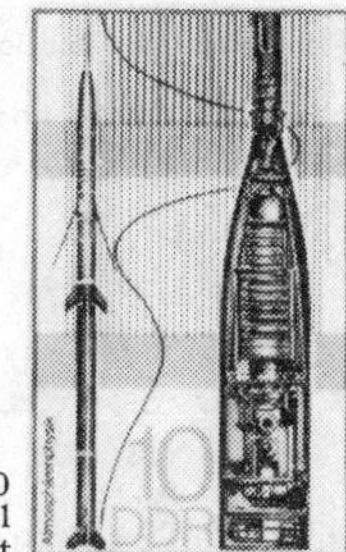

M-100 Meteorological Rocket
A576

Designs: 20pf, Intercosmos I satellite. 35pf, Meteor satellite with spectometric complex. 1m, MFK-6 multi-spectral camera over city.

1978, Mar. 21 Photo. ***Perf. 14x13½***

1898 A576 10pf multicolored
1899 " 20pf "
1900 " 35pf "
Nos. 1898–1900 (3) 1.50

Souvenir Sheet

1901 A576 1m multicolored 3.00

Achievements in atmospheric and space research. No. 1901 contains one stamp, multicolored margin shows city and surrounding countryside. Size: 90x109mm.

Samuel Heinicke, Leipzig, c. 1800
A577

Design: 25pf, Deaf child learning sign language.

1978, Apr. 4 Litho. ***Perf. 13x12½***

1902 A577 20pf multicolored
1903 " 25pf "
Nos. 1902–1903 (2) 1.00

National Institute for the Education of the Deaf, established by Samuel Heinicke, 200th anniversary.

Radio Tower, Dequede, TV Truck
A578

Saxon Miner, 19th Century
A579

Design: 20pf, TV equipment and tower (vert.).

Perf. 13½x14, 14x13½

1978, Apr. 25

1904 A578 10pf multicolored
1905 " 20pf "
Nos. 1904–1905 (2) 45

World Telecommunications Day.

1978, May 9 ***Perf. 12½x13***

Dress Uniforms, 19th Century: 20pf, Foundry worker, Freiberg. 25pf, Mining Academy student. 35pf, Chief Inspector of Mines.

1906 A579 10pf silv. & multi.
1907 " 20pf " "
1908 " 25pf " "
1909 " 35pf " "
Nos. 1906–1909 (4) 2.50

Lion Cub
A580

Young Animals: 20pf, Leopard. 35pf, Tiger. 50pf, Snow leopard.

1978, May 23 Photo. ***Perf. 14***

1910 A580 10pf multicolored
1911 " 20pf "
1912 " 35pf "
1913 " 50pf "
Nos. 1910–1913 (4) 2.80

Centenary of Leipzig Zoo.

Loading Container
A581

Ceramic Bull
A582

Designs: 20pf, Loading container on flatbed truck. 35pf, Container trains in terminal. 70pf, Loading container on ship.

1978, June 13 Litho. ***Perf. 12½x13***

1914 A581 10pf multicolored
1915 " 20pf "
1916 " 35pf "
1917 " 70pf "
Nos. 1914–1917 (4) 3.50

Perf. 14x13½, 13½x14

1978, June 20 Photogravure

Designs: 10pf, Woman's head, ceramic. 20pf, Gold armband (horiz.). 25pf, Animal head, gold ring. 35pf, Seated family from signet ring. 40pf, Necklace (horiz.).

1918 A582 5pf multicolored
1919 " 10pf "
1920 " 20pf "
1921 " 25pf "
1922 " 35pf "
1923 " 40pf "
Nos. 1918–1923 (6) 3.40

African art from 1st and 2nd centuries in Berlin and Leipzig Egyptian museums.

Old and New Buildings, Cottbus
A583

Design: 10pf+5pf, View of Cottbus, 1730.

1978, July 18 Litho. ***Perf. 13x12½***

1924 A583 10pf+5pf multi.
1925 " 20pf "
Strip of 2 + label 1.10

5th Youth Philatelic Exhibition, Cottbus. Nos. 1924–1925 printed se-tenant with label between showing arms of Cottbus and inscription.

Justus von Liebig, Wheat and Retort
A584

Famous Germans: 10pf, Joseph Dietzgen (1828–1888) and title page. 15pf, Alfred Döblin (1878–1957) and title page. 20pf, Hans Loch (1898–1960) and signature, president of Liberal Democratic Party. 25pf, Dr. Theodor Brugsch (1878–1963), and blood circulation. 35pf, Friedrich Ludwig Jahn (1778–1852) and gymnast. 70pf, Dr. Albrecht von Graefe (1828–1870) and ophthalmological instruments.

1978, July 18

1926 A584 5pf yellow & blk.
1927 " 10pf gray & blk.
1928 " 15pf yel. grn. & blk.
1929 " 20pf ultra. & blk.
1930 " 25pf sal. & blk.
1931 " 35pf lt. grn. & blk.
1932 " 70pf olive & blk.
Nos. 1926–1932 (7) 4.00

Festival Emblem and New Buildings, Havana—A585

Design: 35pf, Balloons and new buildings, Berlin.

1978, July 25 Litho. ***Perf. 13x12½***

1933 A585 20pf multicolored
1934 " 35pf "
Strip of 2 + label 1.60

11th World Youth Festival, Havana, July 28–Aug. 5. Nos. 1933–1934 printed se-tenant with label between inscribed in 5 languages.

Foot Soldier, by Hans Schäufelein
A586

Fair Building "Three Kings," Leipzig
A587

Etchings: 20pf, Woman Reading Letter, by Jean Antoine Watteau. 25pf, Seated Boy, by Gabriel Metsu. 30pf, Seated Young Man, by Cornelis Saftleven. 35pf, St. Anthony, by Matthias Grunewald. 50pf, Seated Man, by Abraham van Diepenbeeck.

1978, July 25 ***Perf. 13½x14***

1935 A586 10pf lemon & black
1936 " 20pf " "
1937 " 25pf " "
1938 " 30pf " "
1939 " 35pf " "
1940 " 50pf " "
Nos. 1935–1940 (6) 5.00

Etchings from Berlin Museums. Nos. 1935–1940 printed together in sheets of 6.

1978, Aug. 29 Photo. ***Perf. 14***

Design: 10pf, IFA Multicar 25 truck (horiz.).

1941 A587 10pf multicolored
1942 " 25pf "
Nos. 1941–1942 (2) 60

Leipzig Fall Fair.

Mauthausen Memorial—A588

1978, Sept. 5 ***Perf. 13½x14***

1943 A588 35pf multicolored 55

International war memorials.

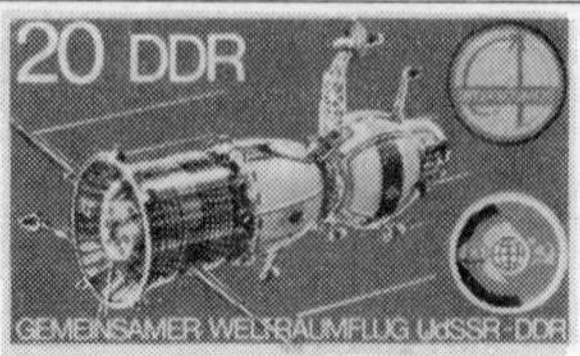

Soyuz, Intercosmos and German-Soviet Space Flight Emblems—A589

Soyuz, Camera and Space Complex
A590

Designs: 10pf, Soyuz and Albert Einstein. 20pf, Sigmund Jähn, 1st German cosmonaut (vert.). 35pf, Salyut-Soyuz space station, Otto Lilienthal and his glider. 1m, Cosmonauts Bykovsky and Jähn and space ships.

1978, Sept. Photo. *Perf. 14*

1944 A589 20pf multicolored *45*

Lithographed

Perf. 13½x13

1945 A590 5pf multicolored
1946 " 10pf "
1947 " 20pf "
1948 " 35pf "
Nos. 1945-1948 (4) *1.90*

Souvenir Sheet

Perf. 13½x14

1949 A590 1m multicolored *3.00*

First German cosmonaut on Russian space mission. No. 1949 contains one stamp (54x33mm.); multicolored margin. Size: 110x90mm.

Issue dates: No. 1944, Sept. 4; others, Sept. 21.

Marching Soldiers, Tractor, Factory
A591

Design: 35pf, Russian and German Soldiers, Communist war veteran, 1933.

1978, Sept. 19 Photo. *Perf. 14*

1950 A591 20pf multicolored
1951 " 35pf "
Strip of 2 + label *1.75*

Workers' military units, 25th anniversary. Nos. 1950-1951 printed se-tenant with label between showing emblem.

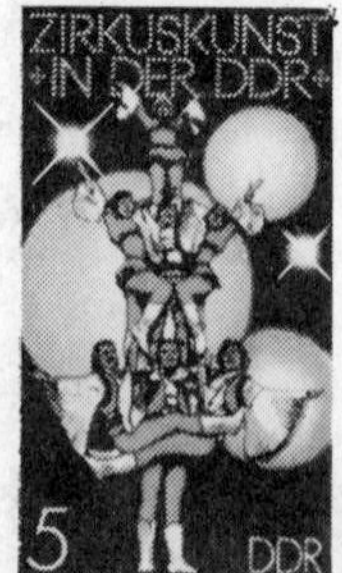

Seven-person Pyramid
A592

Designs: 10pf, Elephant on tricycle. 20pf, Dressage. 35pf, Polar bear kissing woman trainer.

1978, Sept. 26 Photo. *Perf. 14*

1952 A592 5pf blk. & multi.
1953 " 10pf " "
1954 " 20pf " "
1955 " 35pf " "
Nos. 1952-1955 (4) *1.90*

Circus in German Democratic Republic. Nos. 1952-1955 printed se-tenant in blocks of four in sheets of 16 (4x4).

Construction of Gas Pipe Line, Drushba Section—A593

1978, Oct. 3 Litho. *Perf. 13x12½*

1956 A593 20pf multicolored *60*

German youth helping to build gas pipe line from Orenburg to Russian border.

African Behind Barbed Wire
A594

Papilio Hahneli
A595

1978, Oct. 3 Litho. *Perf. 12½x13*

1957 A594 20pf multicolored *60*

Anti-Apartheid Year.

1978, Oct. 24 Photo. *Perf. 14*

Designs: 20pf, Agama lehmanni (lizards). 25pf, Agate from Wiederau. 35pf, Paleobatrachus diluvianus. 40pf, Clock, 1720. 50pf, Table telescope, 1750.

1958 A595 10pf multicolored
1959 " 20pf "
1960 " 25pf "
1961 " 35pf "
1962 " 40pf "
1963 " 50pf "
Nos. 1958-1963 (6) *4.75*

Dresden Museum of Natural History, 250th anniversary.

Wheel Lock Gun, 1630—A596

Hunting Guns: 10pf, Double-barreled gun, 1978. 20pf, Spring-cock gun, 1780. 25pf, Superimposed double-barreled gun, 1978. 35pf, Percussion gun, 1850. 70pf, Three-barreled gun, 1978.

1978, Nov. 1 Photo. *Perf. 14*

1964 A596 5pf silver & multi.
1965 " 10pf " "
1966 " 20pf " "
1967 " 25pf " "
1968 " 35pf " "
1969 " 70pf " "
Nos. 1964-1969 (6) *5.40*

5pf, 20pf, 35pf printed se-tenant in sheets of 9, as are 10pf, 25pf, 70pf.

Rapunzel's Rescuer and Witch
A597

Designs: Scenes from fairy tale "Rapunzel."

1978, Nov. 21 Litho. *Perf. 13*

1970 A597 10pf multicolored
1971 " 15pf "
1972 " 20pf "
1973 " 25pf "
1974 " 35pf "
1975 A597 50pf multicolored
Nos. 1970-1975 (6) *4.80*

Nos. 1970-1975 printed se-tenant in sheets of 6.

Chaffinches
A598

Song Birds: 10pf, Nuthatch. 20pf, Robin. 25pf, Bullfinches. 35pf, Blue tit. 50pf, Red linnets.

1979, Jan. 9 Photo. *Perf. 13½x14*

1976 A598 5pf multicolored
1977 " 10pf "
1978 " 20pf "
1979 " 25pf "
1980 " 35pf "
1981 " 50pf "
Nos. 1976-1981 (6) *4.00*

Chabo Cock
A599

German Cocks: 15pf, Kraienkopp. 20pf, Porcelain-colored bantam. 25pf, Saxonian. 35pf, Phoenix. 50pf, Striped Italian.

1979, Jan. 23 *Perf. 14x13½*

1982 A599 10pf multicolored
1983 " 15pf "
1984 " 20pf "
1985 " 25pf "
1986 " 35pf "
1987 " 50pf "
Nos. 1982-1987 (6) *4.25*

Telephone Operators, 1900 and 1979—A600

Design: 35pf, Telegraph operators, 1880 and 1979.

1979, Feb. 6 Photo. *Perf. 13½x14*

1988 A600 20pf multicolored
1989 " 35pf "
Nos. 1988-1989 (2) *1.50*

Development of German postal telephone and telegraph service.

Souvenir Sheet

Albert Einstein—A601

1979, Feb. 20 Litho. *Perf. 14*

1990 A601 1m multicolored *3.50*

Albert Einstein (1879-1955), theoretical physicist. No. 1990 has lt. & dk. green and brown margin showing formula of relativity and Einstein Tower, Potsdam. Size: 55x87mm.

Max Klinger House, Leipzig
A602

Design: 25pf, Horizontal drilling and milling machine (horiz.).

1979, Mar. 6 Litho. *Perf. 14*

1991 A602 10fr multicolored .
1992 " 25pf "
Nos. 1991-1992 (2) *68*

Leipzig 1979 Spring Fair.

Container Ship, Tug, World Map and IMCO Emblem—A603

1979, Mar. 20 Photogravure

1993 A603 20pf multicolored *35*

World Navigation Day.

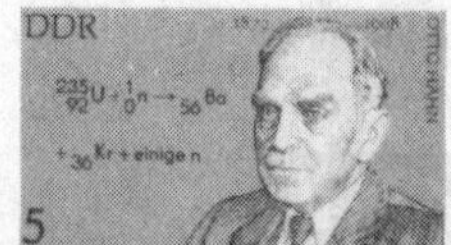

Otto Hahn and Equation of Nuclear Fission—A604

Famous Germans: 10pf, Max von Laue (1879-1969) and diagram of sulphide zinc. 20pf, Arthur Scheunert (1879-1957), symbol of nutrition and health. 25pf, Friedrich August Kekulé (1829-1896), and benzene ring. 35pf, George Forster (1754-1794) and Capt. Cook's ship Resolution. 70pf, Gotthold Ephraim Lessing (1729-1781) and title page for Nathan the Wise.

1979, Mar. 20 Litho. *Perf. 13x12½*

1994 A604 5pf pale salmon & blk.
1995 " 10pf bl. gray & blk.
1996 " 20pf lemon & blk.
1997 " 25pf lt. grn. & blk.
1998 " 35pf lt. bl. & blk.
1999 " 70pf pink & blk.
Nos. 1994-1999 (6) *3.75*

SEMI-POSTAL STAMPS

Some se-tenant issues include a semi-postal stamp. To avoid splitting the se-tenant piece the semipostal is listed with the regular issue.

Bavaria No. 1 and Magnifier SP4

Perf. 14

1949, Oct. 30 Litho. Wmk. 292

B14 SP4 12(pf)+3(pf) gray black 80 80

Stamp Day, 1949. See No. B21a.

Leipzig Fair Issue.

Type of German Semi-Postal Stamps of 1947.

Inscribed: "Deutsche Demokratische Republik."

Designs: 24pf+12pf, First porcelain at Fair, 1710. 30pf+14pf, First Fair at Municipal Store, 1894.

1950, Mar. 5 ***Perf. 13***

B15 SP252 24(pf)+12(pf) red violet 2.00 2.25
B16 " 30(pf)+14(pf) rose carmine 2.50 2.75

Issued to publicize the 1950 Leipzig Spring Fair.

Shepherd Boy with Double Flute SP5

Designs: 24pf+6pf, Girl with hand organ. 30pf+8pf, Johann Sebastian Bach. 50pf+16pf, Chorus.

1950, June 14 ***Perf. 14***

B17 SP5 12(pf)+4(pf) blue green 1.25 1.25
B18 " 24(pf)+6(pf) olive 1.25 1.25
B19 " 30(pf)+8(pf) dark red 3.00 3.00
B20 " 50(pf)+16(pf) bl. 3.50 3.50

Issued to publicize "Bach Year," 1950.

Saxony No. 1, Globe and Dove SP6

1950, July 1 Photo. Wmk. 292

B21 SP6 84(pf)+41(pf) brown red 3.25 3.25
a. Souv. sheet of 2 40.00 40.00

German Stamp Exhibition (DEBRIA) held at Leipzig to commemorate the centenary of Saxony's first postage stamp.

No. B21a contains imperf. examples of Nos. B14 and B21, with colorless marginal inscriptions on orange yellow background. Size: 92x52½mm.

Clearing Land SP7

Designs: 24(pf)+6(pf), Bricklaying. 30(pf)+10(pf), Carpentry. 50(pf)+10(pf), Inspecting plans.

1952, May 1 Lithographed

B22 SP7 12(pf)+3(pf) bright violet 15 15
B23 " 24(pf)+6(pf) henna brown 18 18
B24 " 30(pf)+10(pf) deep green 18 18
B25 SP7 50(pf)+10(pf) violet blue 25 25

Reconstruction program.

Dam SP8

1954, Aug. 16 Unwmkd.

B26 SP8 24(pf)+6(pf) green 15 15

The surtax was for flood victims.

No. B26 Surcharged with New Value and "X" in Black

1955, Feb. 25

B27 SP8 20(pf)+5(pf) on 24(pf)+6(pf) green 15 15

The surtax was for flood victims.

Buchenwald Memorial—SP9

Perf. 13½x13

1956, Sept. 8 Wmk. 297

B28 SP9 20pf+80pf rose red 75 75

The surtax was for the erection of national memorials at the concentration camps of Buchenwald, Ravensbruck and Sachsenhausen. See also No. B43.

Type of 1955 Surcharged "HELFT AGYPTEN +10"

Wmk. 313

Wmkd. Quatrefoil and DDR. (313)

1956, Dec. 20 ***Perf. 13½x13***

B29 A75 20pf+10pf carmine 6 6

Type of 1955 Surcharged "HELFT DEM SOZIALISTISCHEN UNGARN +10"

B30 A75 20pf+10pf carmine 6 6

Monument to Ravensbrück SP10

Memorial Park and Lake—SP11

Perf. 13x13½, 13½x13

1957, Apr. 25 Lithographed

B31 SP10 5pf+5pf green 8 10
B32 SP11 20pf+10pf rose red 20 25

Issued for the International Day of Liberation. See also Nos. B54, B70.

Ernst Thälmann SP12

Bugler, Flag and Camp SP13

Portraits: 25pf+15pf, Rudolf Breitscheid. 40pf+20pf, Rev. Paul Schneider.

1957, Dec. 3 Photo. ***Perf. 13***

Portraits in Gray

B33 SP12 20pf+10pf deep plum 10 5
B34 " 25pf+15pf dk. bl. 12 10
B35 " 40pf+20pf violet 20 12
a. Souvenir sheet of 3, imperf. ('58) 16.50 19.50

No. B35a measures 139x94mm. and contains one each of Nos. B33–B35. Black marginal inscription.

1958, July 11 ***Perf. 13*** **Wmk. 313**

Portraits: 5pf+5pf, Albert Kuntz. 10pf+5pf, Rudi Arndt. 15pf+10pf, Kurt Adams. 20pf+10pf, Rudolf Renner. 25pf+15pf, Walter Stoecker.

Portraits in Gray

B36 SP12 5pf+5pf brn. blk. 10 10
B37 " 10pf+5pf dark slate green 10 10
B38 " 15pf+10pf dp. vio. 20 35
B39 " 20pf+10pf dark red brown 25 25
B40 " 25pf+15pf bl. blk. 40 60
Nos. B36–B40 (5) 1.05 1.40

Issued to honor the murdered victims of the Nazis at Buchenwald. The surtax was for the erection of national memorials.

See also Nos. B49–B53, B55–B57, B60–B64, B71–B75, B79–B81.

1958, Aug. 7 Litho. ***Perf. 12½***

Design: 20pf+10pf, Pioneers and flag.

B41 SP13 10pf+5pf green 8 8
B42 " 20pf+10pf red 15 12

Pioneer organization, 10th anniversary.

Type of 1956 Overprinted in Black "14. September 1958."

Perf. 13½x13

1958, Sept. 15 Unwmkd.

B43 SP9 20pf+20pf rose red 30 30

Issued for the dedication of the memorial at Buchenwald concentration camp, Sept. 14, 1958.

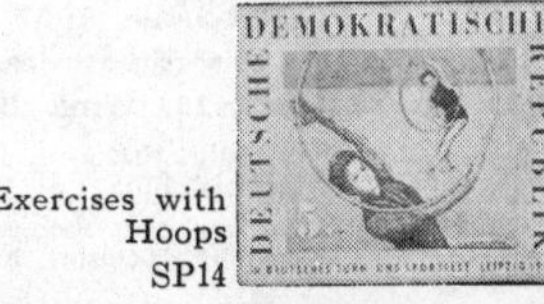

Exercises with Hoops SP14

Designs: 10pf+5pf, High jump. 20pf+10pf Vaulting. 25pf+10pf, Girl gymnasts. 40pf+20pf, Leipzig stadium and fireworks.

Perf. 13x13½

1959, Aug. 10 Litho. Wmk. 313

B44 SP14 5pf+5pf orange 5 5
B45 " 10pf+5pf green 5 5
B46 " 20pf+10pf bright carmine 5 5
B47 " 25pf+10pf brt. bl. 8 10
B48 " 40pf+20pf red vio. 1.00 60
Nos. B44–B48 (5) 1.23 85

3rd German Sports Festival, Leipzig.

Portrait Type of 1957–58.

Portraits: 5pf+5pf, Tilde Klose. 10pf+5pf, Kathe Niederkirchner. 15pf+10pf, Charlotte Eisenblatter. 20pf+10pf, Olga Benario-Prestes. 25pf+15pf, Maria Grollmuss.

1959, Sept. 3 Photo. ***Perf. 13***

Portraits in Gray.

B49 SP12 5pf+5pf sepia 4 4
B50 " 10pf+5pf deep green 4 4
B51 " 15pf+10pf dp. vio. 7 7
B52 " 20pf+10pf magenta 4 4
B53 " 25pf+15pf dark blue 50 65
Nos. B49–B53 (5) 69 84

Issued to honor women murdered by the Nazis at Buchenwald.

Ravensbrück Type of 1957 Dated: "12. September 1959"

Perf. 13½x13

1959, Sept. 11 Litho. Wmk. 313

B54 SP11 20pf+10pf deep carmine & blk. 15 5

Portrait Type of 1957–58.

Portraits: 5pf+5pf, Lothar Erdmann. 10pf+5pf, Ernst Schneller. 20pf+10pf, Lambert Horn.

Perf. 13½x13

1960, Feb. 25 Photogravure

Portraits in Gray.

B55 SP12 5pf+5pf olive bistre 8 5
B56 " 10pf+5pf dark green 8 5
B57 " 20pf+10pf dull magenta 8 5

Issued to honor murdered victims of the Nazis at Sachsenhausen.

Type of Regular Issue, 1960.

Designs: 10pf+5pf, Vacation ship under construction, Wismar. 20pf+10pf, Ship before Stubbenkammer and sailboat.

Perf. 13

1960, June 23 Litho. Wmk. 313

B58 A162 10pf+5pf black, yellow & red 5 5
B59 " 20pf+10pf black, red & blue 5 6

Issued to commemorate the launching of the trade union (FDGB) vacation ship, June 25, 1960.

Portrait Type of 1957–58.

Portraits: 10pf+5pf, Max Lademann. 15pf+5pf, Lorenz Breunig. 20pf+10pf, Mathias Thesen. 25pf+10pf, Gustl Sandtner. 40pf+20pf, Hans Rothbarth.

1960 ***Perf. 13½x13*** **Wmk. 313**

Portraits in Gray

B60 SP12 10pf+5pf green 10 5
B61 " 15pf+5pf dp. vio. 60 60
B62 " 20pf+10pf maroon 15 6
B63 " 25pf+10pf dk. blue 10 10
B64 " 40pf+20pf light red brown 1.50 75
Nos. B60–B64 (5) 2.45 1.56

Issued to honor the murdered victims of the Nazis at Sachsenhausen.

Bicyclist SP15

Design: 25pf+10pf, Bicyclists and spectators.

1960, Aug. 3 *Perf. 13x13½, 13x12½*

Size: 28x23mm.

B65 SP15 20pf+10pf multi. 5 5

Size: 38½x21mm.

B66 SP15 25pf+10pf blue, gray & brown *75* *50*

Issued to publicize the Bicycling World Championships, Aug. 3–14.

Rook and Congress Emblem
SP16

Designs: 20pf+10pf, Knight. 25pf+10pf, Bishop.

Perf. 14x13½

1960, Sept. 19 Engr. Wmk. 313

B67 SP16 10pf+5pf bl. grn. 3 3
B68 " 20pf+10pf rose claret 3 3
B69 " 25pf+10pf blue *1.15* *95*

14th Chess Championships, Leipzig.

Type of 1957

Design: Monument and memorial wall of Sachsenhausen National Memorial.

1960, Sept. 8 Litho. *Perf. 13x13½*

B70 SP10 20pf+10pf deep carmine 15 4

No. B70 was re-issued Apr. 20, 1961, with gray label adjoining each stamp in sheet, to commemorate the dedication of Sachsenhausen National Memorial.

Type of 1957

Portraits: 5pf+5pf, Werner Kube. 10pf+5pf, Hanno Gunther. 15pf+5pf, Elvira Eisenschneider. 20pf+10pf, Hertha Lindner. 25pf+10pf, Herbert Tschäpe.

1961, Feb. 6 *Perf. 13½x13*

Portraits in Black

B71 SP12 5pf+5pf brt. brn. 5 5
B72 " 10pf+5pf blue green 5 5
B73 " 15pf+5pf bright lilac *1.25* *1.25*
B74 " 20pf+10pf deep rose 10 7
B75 " 25pf+10pf brt. bl. 10 8
Nos. B71-B75 (5) *1.55* *1.50*

The surtax was for the erection of national memorials.

Pioneers Playing Volleyball
SP17

Designs: 20+10pf, Folk dancing. 25+10pf, Building model airplanes.

1961, May 25 *Perf. 13x12½*

B76 SP17 10pf+5pf multi. 5 4
B77 " 20pf+10pf " 8 5
B78 " 25pf+10pf " *1.50* *1.35*

Young Pioneers' meeting, Erfurt.

Type of 1957 and

Sophie and Hans Scholl
SP18

Portraits: 5pf+5pf, Carlo Schönhaar. 10pf+5pf, Herbert Baum. 20pf+10pf, Liselotte Herrmann. 40pf+20pf, Hilde and Hans Coppi.

Perf. 13½x13, 13x13½

1961, Sept. 7 Litho. Wmk. 313

Portraits in Black

B79 SP12 5pf+5pf green 5 5
B80 " 10pf+5pf bl. green 8 8
B81 " 20pf+10pf rose carmine 15 5
B82 SP18 25pf+10pf blue 20 10
B83 " 40pf+20pf rose brown *1.40* *1.40*
Nos. B79-B83 (5) *1.88* *1.68*

The surtax was for the support of national memorials at Buchenwald, Ravensbrück and Sachsenhausen.

Danielle Casanova of France
SP19

Portraits: 10pf+5pf, Julius Fucik, Czechoslovakia. 20pf+10pf, Johanna Jannetje Schaft, Netherlands. 25pf+10pf, Pawel Finder, Poland. 40pf+20pf, Soya Anatolyevna Kosmodemyanskaya, Russia.

1962, March 22 Engr. *Perf. 13½*

B84 SP19 5pf+5pf gray 5 5
B85 " 10pf+5pf green 5 5
B86 " 20pf+10pf maroon 8 8
B87 " 25pf+10pf dp. blue 20 20
B88 " 40pf+20pf sepia *2.00* *1.50*
Nos. B84-B88 (5) *2.38* *1.88*

Issued in memory of foreign victims of the Nazis.

Type of Regular Issue, 1962

Design: 20pf++10pf, Three cyclists and Warsaw Palace of Culture and Science.

Perf. 13x12½

1962, Apr. 26 Litho. Wmk. 313

B89 A192 20pf+10pf vermilion, blue, black & yel. 15 5

Issued to commemorate the 15th International Peace Bicycle Race, Berlin-Warsaw-Prague.

Folk Dance
SP20

Design: 15pf+5pf, Youths of three nations parading.

1962, July 17 *Perf. 14* Wmk. 313

B90 SP20 10pf+5pf multi. 15 10
B91 " 15pf+5pf " 15 10

Issued to publicize the 8th Youth Festival for Peace and Friendship, Helsinki, July 28–Aug. 6, 1962.

Nos. B90-B91 are printed se-tenant forming the festival emblem. Each sheet of 80 contains 40 se-tenant pairs.

Type of Regular Issue, 1962

Design: 20pf+10pf, Springboard diving.

1962, Aug. 7 *Perf. 13* Wmk. 313

B92 A199 20pf+10pf lilac rose & greenish blue 5 5

Issued to publicize the 10th European Swimming Championships, Leipzig, Aug. 18–25.

René Blieck of Belgium
SP21

Seven Cervi Brothers of Italy
SP22

Portraits: 10pf+5pf, Dr. Alfred Klahr, Austria. 15pf+5pf, José Diaz, Spain. 20pf+10pf, Julius Alpari, Hungary.

1962, Oct. 4 Engraved *Perf. 14*

B93 SP21 5pf+5pf dk. blue gray 5 5
B94 " 10pf+5pf green 8 8
B95 " 15pf+5pf brt. vio. 8 8
B96 " 20pf+10pf dull red brown 12 12
B97 SP22 70pf+30pf sepia *2.00* *1.75*
Nos. B93-B97 (5) *2.33* *2.08*

Issued to commemorate foreign victims of the Nazis.

Walter Bohne, Runner
SP23

Gymnasts
SP24

Portraits: 10pf+5pf, Werner Seelenbinder, wrestler. 15pf+5pf, Albert Richter, bicyclist. 20pf+10pf, Heinz Steyer, soccer player. 25pf+10pf, Kurt Schlosser, mountaineer.

Engraved and Photogravure

1963, May 27 *Perf. 14* Wmk. 313

B98 SP23 5pf+5pf yellow & black 7 5
B99 " 10pf+5pf pale yellow green & black 8 5
B100 " 15pf+5pf rose lilac & black 15 10
B101 " 20pf+10pf pink & black 20 15
B102 " 25pf+10pf pale blue & black *1.50* *1.50*
Nos. B98-B102 (5) *2.00* *1.85*

Issued to commemorate sportsmen victims of the Nazis. Each stamp printed with alternating label showing sporting events connected with each person honored. The surtax went for the maintenance of national memorials See also Nos. B106-B110.

1963, June 13 Litho. *Perf. 12½x13*

Designs: 20pf+10pf, Women gymnasts. 25pf+10pf, Relay race.

B103 SP24 10pf+5pf blk., yel. grn. & lemon 5 3
B104 " 20pf+10pf black, red & violet 8 5
B105 " 25pf+10pf black, blue & gray *1.20* *1.00*

Issued to commemorate the 4th German Gymnastic and Sports Festival, Leipzig. The surtax went to the festival committee.

Type of 1963

Portraits: 5pf+5pf, Hermann Tops, gymnastics instructor. 10pf+5pf, Käte Tucholla, field hockey players. 15pf+5pf, Rudolph Seiffert, long-distance swimmers. 20pf+10pf, Ernst Grube, sportsmen demonstrating for peace. 40pf+20pf, Kurt Biedermann, kayak in rapids.

Engraved and Photogravure

1963, Sept. 24 *Perf. 14* Wmk. 313

B106 SP23 5pf+5pf yel. & blk. 5 3
B107 " 10pf+5pf grn. & blk. 5 3
B108 " 15pf+5pf lilac & blk. 10 7
B109 " 20pf+10pf pale pink & black 20 7
B110 " 40pf+20pf light blue & black *2.00* *1.75*
Nos. B106-B110 (5) *2.40* *1.95*

See note after No. B102.

Type of Regular Issue, 1963

Design: 20pf+10pf, Ski jumper in mid-air.

Perf. 13½x13

1963, Dec. 16 Litho. Wmk. 313

B111 A224 20pf+10pf multi. 15 5

Issued to publicize the 9th Winter Olympic Games, Innsbruck, Jan. 29–Feb. 9, 1964. The surtax was for the National Olympic Committee.

Anton Saefkow—SP25

Designs: 10pf+5pf, Franz Jacob. 15pf+5pf, Bernhard Bästlein. 20pf+5pf, Harro Schulze-Boysen. 25pf+10pf, Adam Kuckhoff. 40pf+10pf, Mildred and Arvid Harnack. Nos. B112-B114 show group posting anti-Hitler and pacifist posters. Nos. B115-B117 show production of anti-fascist pamphlets.

1964, Mar. 24 *Perf. 13* Wmk. 313

Size: 41x32mm.

B112 SP25 5pf+5pf dark red brown & chalky blue 10 5
B113 " 10pf+5pf dark red brown & gray olive 10 5
B114 " 15pf+5pf dark red brn. & lt. vio. 10 10
B115 " 20pf+5pf car. rose & gray olive 20 10
B116 " 25pf+10pf bright bl. & gray olive 30 20

Size: 48½x28mm.

B117 SP25 40pf+10pf dull red brown & gray olive *1.85* *1.40*
Nos. B112-B117 (6) *2.65* *1.90*

The surtax was for the support of national memorials for victims of the Nazis.

Olympic Types of Regular Issues

Design: 40pf+20pf, Two runners.

Lithographed and Engraved

1964, July 15 *Perf. 14* Wmk. 313

B118 A232 40pf+20pf multi. 35 10

Lithographed

Perf. 13

Designs: No. B119, Equestrian. No. B120, Three runners.

B119 A233 10pf+5pf multi. 75 75
B120 " 10pf+5pf " 75 75

See note after No. 714.

Pioneers Studying—SP26

Designs: 20pf+10pf, Pioneers planting tree. 25pf+10pf, Pioneers playing.

1964, July 29

B121 SP26 10pf+5pf multi. 5 5
B122 " 20pf+10pf " 15 5
B123 " 25pf+10pf " *1.25* *80*

Issued to commemorate the Fifth Young Pioneers Meeting, Karl-Marx-Stadt.

Stamp Exhibition Type of 1964

Designs: 10pf+5pf, Stamp of 1958 (No. 390). 20pf+10pf, Stamp of 1950 (No. 73).

Perf. 13x13½

1964, Sept. 23 Litho. Wmk. 313

B124 A238 10pf+5pf orange & emerald 10 3
B125 " 20pf+10pf bright pink & blue 20 6

Issued to publicize the National Stamp Exhibition, Berlin, Oct. 3–18.

Boxing Type of Regular Issue

Design: 10pf+5pf, Two boxing gloves and laurel.

Perf. 13½x14

1965, Apr. 27 Photo. Wmk. 313

B126 A247 10pf+5pf black, gold, red & bl. 8 8

Issued to publicize the 16th European Boxing Championship, Berlin, May, 1965. The surtax went to the German Turner and Sport Organization.

Type of Regular Issue, 1965

1965, May 5 *Perf. 14* Wmk. 313

Designs: 5pf+5pf, George Dimitrov at Leipzig trial and communist newspaper. 10pf+5pf, Anti-fascists clandestinely distributing leaflets. 15pf+5pf, Fighting in Spanish Civil War. 20pf+10pf, Ernst Thalman behind bars and demonstration for his release. 25pf+10pf, Founding of National Committee for Free Germany and signatures.

Photogravure

Flags in Red, Black and Yellow

B127 A248 5pf+5pf black, orange & red 5 5
B128 " 10pf+5pf green & red 8 8
B129 " 15pf+5pf lilac, red & yellow 10 10
B130 " 20pf+10pf black & red 10 10
B131 " 25pf+10pf olive grn., yel. & blk. 15 15
Nos. B127-B131 (5) 48 48

Issued to commemorate the 20th anniversary of liberation from fascism. The surtax went for the maintenance of national memorials.

Doves, Globe and Finnish Flag
SP27

1965, July 5 Litho. *Perf. 13x13½*

B132 SP27 10pf+5pf vio. blue & emerald 10 8
B133 " 20pf+5pf red & violet blue *60* *50*

Issued to publicize the World Peace Congress, Helsinki, July 10–17. The surtax went to the peace council of the German Democratic Republic.

Hilfe für VIETNAM

No. 725 Surcharged

+10

Perf. 13½x13

1965, Aug. 23 Wmk. 313

B134 A239 10pf+10pf multi. 20 5

Surtax was for North Viet Nam.

Sports Type of Regular Issue

Sport: No. B135, Fencer. No. B136, Pistol shooter.

Perf. 13½x13

1965, Sept. 15 Litho. Unwmkd.

B135 A257 10pf+5pf vio. blue & greenish bl. 10 5
B136 " 10pf+5pf dk. car. rose, gray & black 10 5

International Modern Pentathlon Championships, Leipzig.

Type of Regular Issue

Designs: 10pf+5pf, Willi Bredel and instruction of International Brigade. 20pf +10pf, Heinrich Rau and parade after battle of Brunete. 25pf+10pf, Hans Marchwitza, international fighters and globe. 40pf+10pf, Artur Becker and battle on the Ebro.

1966, July 15 Photo. *Perf. 14*

Frame and Flags in Red, Yellow and Lilac

B137 A277 10pf+5pf black 5 5
B138 " 20pf+10pf " 12 12
B139 " 25pf+10pf " 28 14
B140 " 40pf+10pf " *1.60* *1.60*

Issued to honor the German fighters in the Spanish Civil War. The surtax was for the maintenance of national memorials.

Canoe Type of Regular Issue

Design: 10pf+5pf, Men's single canoe race.

Perf. 13x12½

1966, Aug. 16 Litho. Unwmkd.

B141 A279 10pf+5pf multi. 5 5

7th Canoe World Championships, Berlin.

Red Cross Type of Regular Issue

Design: 20pf+10pf, ICY Red Crescent, Red Cross, and Red Lion and Sun emblems (horiz.).

1966, Sept. 13 *Perf. 14* Wmk. 313

B142 A281 20pf+10pf violet & red 5 5

International health cooperation. Surtax for German Red Cross.

Sports Type of Regular Issue

Design: 20pf+5pf, Weight lifter.

Perf. 13½x13

1966, Sept. 22 Litho. Unwmkd.

B143 A282 20pf+5pf ultra. & black 12 10

Issued to commemorate the International and European Weight Lifting Championships, Berlin.

Armed Woman Planting Flower
SP28

1966, Oct. 25 *Perf. 13½x13*

B144 SP28 20pf+5pf black & pink 30 5

Surtax was for North Viet Nam.

Wartburg Type of Regular Issue

Design: 10pf+5pf, Wartburg, view from the East.

1966, Nov. 23 *Perf. 13x13½*

B145 A288 10pf+5pf slate 10 3

See note after No. 878.

Olympic Type of Regular Issue

Design: 10pf+5pf, Tobogganing.

1968, Jan. 17 Litho. *Perf. 13½x13*

B146 A314 10pf+5pf greenish blue, vio. blue & red 5 5

Issued to commemorate the 10th Winter Olympic Games, Grenoble, France, Feb. 6–18. The surtax was for the Olympic Committee of the German Democratic Republic.

Armed Mother and Child
SP29

Armed Vietnamese Couple
SP30

1968, May 8 *Perf. 13½x13*

B147 SP29 10pf+5pf yellow & multicolored 20 5

Surtax was for North Viet Nam.

Festival Type of Regular Issue

1968, June 20 Litho. *Perf. 13½x13*

B148 A327 20pf+5pf multi. 10 5

Issued to publicize the 9th Youth Festival for Peace and Friendship, Sofia.

Olympic Games Type of Regular Issue, 1968

Designs: 10pf+5pf, Pole vault (vert.). 20pf+10pf, Soccer (vert.).

1968, Sept. 18 Photo. *Perf. 14*

B149 A336 10pf+5pf multi. 5 5
B150 " 20pf+10pf " 10 10

Issued to publicize the 19th Olympic Games, Mexico City, Oct. 12–27. The surtax was for the Olympic Committee.

1969, June 4

B151 SP30 10pf+5pf multi. 15 5

Surtax was for North Viet Nam.

Sports Type of Regular Issue, 1969

Designs: 10pf+5pf, Gymnastics. 20pf+5pf, Art Exhibition with sports motifs.

Photogravure and Engraved

1969, June 18 *Perf. 14*

B152 A353 10pf+5pf multi. 8 4
B153 " 20pf+5pf " 14 6

Issued to publicize the 5th German Gymnastic and Sports Festival, Leipzig. The surtax was for the German Gymnastic and Sports League.

Otto von Guericke's Vacuum Test with Magdeburg Hemispheres
SP31

1969, Oct. 28 Litho. *Perf. 13x12½*

B154 SP31 40pf+10pf multi. *1.00* *1.00*

See note after No. 1146.

Folk Art Type of Regular Issue

Design: 20pf+5pf, Decorative plate.

1969, Nov. 25 Litho. *Perf. 13½x13*

B155 A365 20pf+5pf yellow, blk. & ultra. 60 55

Issued to publicize folk art of Lusatia.

Sports Type of Regular Issue

Design: 20pf+5pf, Children hurdling.

1970, July 1 Photo. *Perf. 14x13½*

B156 A382 20pf+5pf multi. 35 20

Third Children's and Youths' Spartakiad.

Pioneer Waving Kerchief, and Pioneer Activities—SP32

Design: 25pf+5pf, Girl Pioneer holding kerchief, and Pioneer activities.

1970, July 28 Litho. *Perf. 13x12½*

B157 SP32 10pf+5pf multi. 35 35
B158 " 25pf+5pf " 35 35

Issued to commemorate the 6th Youth Pioneer Meeting, Cottbus. Printed setenant in sheets of 20 (2x10) with continuous design.

Ho Chi Minh
SP33

German Democratic Republic No. 460
SP34

1970, Sept. 2 *Perf. 13x13½*

B159 SP33 20pf+5pf rose, black & red 35 5

Surtax was for North Viet Nam.

1970, Oct. 1 Photo. *Perf. 14x13½*

B160 SP34 15pf+5pf multi. 28 15

Issued to publicize the 2nd National Youth Philatelic Exhibition, Karl-Marx-Stadt, Oct. 4–11.

Mother and Child
SP35

Vietnamese Farm Woman
SP36

Photogravure & Engraved

1971, Sept. 2 *Perf. 14*

B161 SP35 10pf+5pf multi. 20 5

Surtax was for North Viet Nam.

Type of Regular Issue

Design: 10pf+5pf, Loading and unloading mail at airport.

Photogravure and Engraved

1971, Oct. 5 *Perf. 14*

B162 A421 10pf+5pf multi. 8 8

Olympic Games Type of Regular Issue

Olympic Rings and: 10pf+5pf, Figure skating, pairs. 15pf+5pf, Speed skating.

1971, Dec. 7 Photo. *Perf. 13½x14*

B163 A424 10pf+5pf blue, car. & black 5 5
B164 " 15pf+5pf green, black & blue 5 5

11th Winter Olympic Games, Sapporo, Japan, Feb. 3–13, 1972.

1972, Feb. 22 Litho. *Perf. 13½x13*

B165 SP36 10pf+5pf multi. 20 5

Surtax was for North Viet Nam.

Olympic Games Type of Regular Issue

Sport and Olympic Rings: 10pf+5pf, Diving. 25pf+10pf, Rowing.

1972, May 16 Photo. *Perf. 13½x14*

B166 A430 10pf+5pf greenish bl., gold & blk. 5 5

B167	A430	25pf+10pf multi.	10	10

20th Olympic Games, Munich, Aug. 26–Sept. 11.

Interartes Type of Regular Issue

Designs: 15pf+5pf, Spear carrier, Persia, 500 B.C. 35pf+5pf, Grape Sellers, by Max Lingner, 1949 (horiz.).

1972, Sept. 19 Photo. ***Perf. 14***

B168	A439	15pf+5pf multi.	*2.00*	*1.75*
B169	"	35pf+5pf "	15	5

Interartes Philatelic Exhibition, Berlin, Oct. 4–Nov. 11.

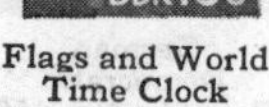

Flags and World Time Clock

SP37

Young Couple, by Günter Glombitza

SP38

Design: 25pf+5pf, Youth group with guitar and dove.

1973, Feb. 13 Litho. ***Perf. 12½x13***

B170	SP37	10pf+5pf multi.	25	15
B171	"	25pf+5pf "	50	30

10th World Youth Festival, Berlin.

1973, Oct. 4 Photo. ***Perf. 13½x14***

B172	SP38	20pf+5pf multi.	40	20

Philatelists' Day and for the 3rd National Youth Philatelic Exhibition, Halle.

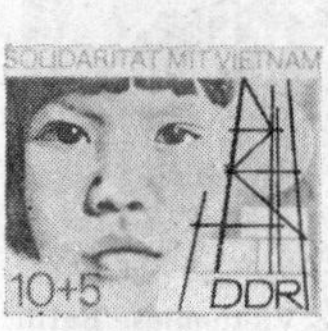

Child, Symbols of Reconstruction

SP39

Luis Corvalan, Red Flag

SP40

1973, Oct. 11 ***Perf. 14x13½***

B173	SP39	10pf+5pf multi.	20	18

Surtax was for North Viet Nam.

1973, Nov. 5 ***Perf. 13½x14***

Design: 25pf+5pf, Salvador Allende and Chilean flag.

B174	SP40	10pf+5pf multi.	*35*	*35*
B175	"	25pf+5pf "	*70*	*70*

Solidarity with the people of Chile.

Raised Fist and Star

SP41

Restored Post Gate, Wurzen, 1734

SP42

1975, Sept. 23 Litho. ***Perf. 13x13½***

B176	SP41	10pf+5pf multi.	20	18

Surtax was for the Solidarity Committee of the German Democratic Republic.

1975, Oct. 21 Photo. ***Perf. 14***

B177	SP42	10pf+5pf multi.	*50*	*40*

Philatelists' Day 1975.

Olympic Games Type of 1975

Designs: 10pf+5pf, Luge run, Oberhof. 25pf+5pf, Ski jump, Rennsteig at Oberhof.

1975, Dec. 2 Photo. ***Perf. 14***

B178	A518	10pf+5pf multi.	14	5
B179	"	25pf+5pf "	22	13

12th Winter Olympic Games, Innsbruck, Austria, Feb. 4–15, 1976.

Olympic Games Type of 1976

Designs: 10pf+5pf, Swimming pool, High School for Physical Education, Leipzig. 35pf+10pf, Rifle range, Suhl.

1976, May 18 Photo. ***Perf. 13½x14***

B180	A529	10pf+5pf multi.	8	5
B181	"	35pf+10pf "	30	18

21st Olympic Games, Montreal, Canada, July 17–Aug. 1.

TV Tower, Berlin, and Perforations

SP43

Hand Holding Torch

SP44

1976, Oct. 19 Litho. ***Perf. 13***

B182	SP43	10pf+5pf orange & blue	20	18

Surtax was for Sozphilex 77, Philatelic Exhibition of Socialist Countries, in connection with 60th anniversary of October Revolution.

Sports Type of 1977

Designs: 10pf+5pf, Young milers. 25pf+5pf, Girls artistic gymnastic performance.

1977, July 19 Litho. ***Perf. 13x12½***

B183	A558	10pf+5pf multi.		
B184	"	25pf+5pf "		

6th Gymnastics and Sports Festival and 6th Children's and Youth Spartacist Games.

Sozphilex Type of 1977

Design: 50pf+20pf, World Youth Song, by Lothar Zitzmann (horiz.).

1977, Aug. 16 Photo. ***Perf. 13***

B185	A559	50pf+20pf multi.	*1.75*	

SOZPHILEX '77 Philatelic Exhibition, Berlin, Aug. 19–28. No. B185 has maroon marginal inscription and Sozphilex emblem. Size: 85x55mm.

1977, Oct. 18 Litho. ***Perf. 14***

B186	SP44	10pf+5pf multi.	18	18

Surtax was for East German Solidarity Committee.

AIR POST STAMPS

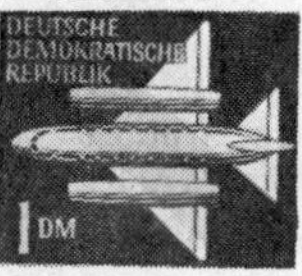

Stylized Plane

AP1 AP2

Perf. 13x12½, 13x13½ (AP2)

1957, Dec. 13 Litho. **Wmk. 313**

C1	AP1	5pf gray & black	3	3
C2	"	20pf bright carmine & black	8	3
C3	"	35pf violet & black	15	5
C4	"	50pf maroon & black	18	5
C5	AP2	1m olive & yellow	50	7
C6	"	3m choc. & yellow	1.75	7
C7	"	5m dk. bl. & yellow	3.00	10
		Nos. C1–C7 (7)	5.69	40

Used prices of Nos. C1–C7 are for canceled-to-order copies.

OFFICIAL STAMPS

While valid, these Official stamps were not sold to the public unused. After their period of use, some sets were sold abroad by the government stamp sales agency.

Used prices of Official stamps are for canceled-to-order copies.

Reprints of type O1 stamps have printed cancellations.

Arms of Republic

O1

Numeral

O2

Lithographed.

1954 ***Perf. 13x12½*** **Wmk. 297**

O1	O1	5(pf) emerald	2.25	3
O2	"	6(pf) violet	1.00	3
O3	"	8(pf) org. brown	2.25	3
O4	"	10(pf) lt. bl. green	2.25	3
O5	"	12(pf) blue	2.25	3
O6	"	15(pf) dark violet	2.25	3
O7	"	16(pf) dark violet	1.10	3
O8	"	20(pf) olive	1.00	3
O9	"	24(pf) brown red	1.00	3
O10	"	25(pf) sage green	1.50	3
O11	"	30(pf) brown red	60	3
O12	"	40(pf) red	1.50	3
O13	"	48(pf) rose lilac	75	75
O14	"	50(pf) rose lilac	75	3
O15	"	60(pf) bright blue	75	3
O16	"	70(pf) brown	75	3
O17	"	84(pf) brown	75	1.35
		Nos. O1–O17 (17)	22.70	2.55

Type of 1954 Redrawn

Arc of compass projects at right.

1954–56 **Typographed**

O18	O1	5(pf) emerald ('54)	75	4
O19	"	10(pf) blue green	75	4
O20	"	12(pf) dk. blue ('54)	60	4
O21	"	15(pf) dark violet	75	4
O22	"	20(pf) olive ('56)	*175.00*	4
		a. Arc of compass projects at left	5.00	4
O23	"	25(pf) dark green	35	4
O24	"	30(pf) brown red	1.00	4
O25	"	40(pf) red	60	4
O26	"	50(pf) rose lilac	50	4
O27	"	70(pf) brown	60	4
		Nos. O18–O21, O22a, O23–O27 (9)	10.90	40

Shaded background of emblem consists of vertical lines; on Nos. O1–O17 it consists of dots.

Granite paper was used for a 1956 printing of the 5pf, 10pf, 15pf, 20pf and 40pf. Price for set unused $300, used 30 cents.

1956 ***Perf. 13x12½*** **Wmk. 297**

O28	O2	5(pf) black	5	5
O29	"	10(pf) "	10	5
O30	"	20(pf) "	15	5
O31	"	40(pf) "	30	5
O32	"	70(pf) "	50	5
		Nos. O28–O32 (5)	1.10	25

O3

1956 **Lithographed** **Wmk. 297**

O33	O3	10pf lilac & black	25	20
O34	"	20pf " "	*30.00*	15
O35	"	40pf " "	25	25
O36	"	70pf " "	75	65

Nos. O33–O36 exist also with black or violet overprint of 4-digit control number.

No. O34 was reprinted with watermark sideways ("DDR" vertical). Price $2.

Redrawn Type of 1954–56

Perf. 13x12½, 14

1957–60 Typo. **Wmk. 313**

Granite Paper.

O37	O1	5pf emerald	5	3
O38	"	10pf blue green	5	3
O39	"	15pf dark violet	5	6
O40	"	20pf olive	5	3
O41	"	30pf dark red ('58)	18	6
O42	"	40pf red	8	6
O42A	"	50pf rose lilac ('60)	40	10
O43	"	70pf brown ('58)	40	12
		Nos. O37–O43 (8)	1.26	49

Nos. O37–O43 were all issued in perf. 13x12½. Nos. O37–O40 were also issued perf. 14. Prices are the same.

Type of 1956.

1957 **Lithographed** ***Perf. 13x12½***

O44	O3	10pf lilac & black	30	25
O45	"	20pf " "	30	25

Nos. O44–O45 have black or violet overprint of four-digit control number.

Stamps similar to type O3 were issued later, with denomination expressed in dashes: one for 10pf, two for 20pf.

GERMAN OFFICES ABROAD.

OFFICES IN CHINA

100 Pfennigs = 1 Mark
100 Cents = 1 Dollar (1905)

Stamps of Germany, 1889-90, Overprinted in Black at 56° Angle

1898 ***Perf. 13½x14½.*** **Unwmkd.**

1 A9 3pf dark brown 4.50 4.50
  a. 3pf yellow brn. 8.50 8.50
  b. 3pf reddish brn. 32.50 37.50
2 " 5pf green 3.25 3.25
3 A10 10pf carmine 6.00 6.00
4 " 20pf ultramarine 17.50 20.00
5 " 25pf orange 30.00 32.50
6 " 50pf red brown 12.50 10.00

Overprinted at 48° Angle.

1c A9 3pf yellow brown 140.00 *8500.00*
1d " 3pf reddish brown 190.00
2a " 5pf green 16.50 16.50
3a A10 10pf carmine 22.50 14.00
4a " 20pf ultramarine 19.00 11.00
5a " 25pf orange 70.00 70.00
6a " 50pf red brown 27.50 14.00

Foochow Issue.

Nos. 3 and 3a Handstamp Surcharged **5 pf**

16 A10 5pf on 10pf carmine (on #3) 650.00 725.00
  a. On No. 3a 550.00 650.00

For similar 5pf surcharges on 10pf carmine, see Tsingtau Issue, Kiauchau.

Tientsin Issue.

German Stamps of 1900 Issue Handstamped

1900

17 A11 3pf brown 600.00 600.00
18 " 5pf green 325.00 325.00
19 " 10pf carmine 725.00 650.00
20 " 20pf ultramarine 800.00 800.00
21 " 30pf orange & black, *salmon* *4750.00* *4750.00*
22 " 50pf purple & blk., *salmon* *15,000.00* *13,500.00*
23 " 80pf lake & black, *rose* *4250.00* *4000.00*

This handstamp is known inverted and double on most values.
Excellent faked handstamps are plentiful.

Regular Issue.

A3

A4

A5

A6

A7

Overprinted Horizontally in Black.

1901 ***Perf. 14, 14½.***

24 A3 3pf brown 2.25 2.25
  a. 3pf lt. red brown 110.00 65.00
25 A3 5pf green 2.25 1.40
26 " 10pf carmine 3.25 1.10
27 " 20pf ultramarine 4.25 1.90
28 " 25pf orange & black, *yellow* 14.00 16.50
29 " 30pf orange & black, *salmon* 14.00 14.00
30 " 40pf lake & black 14.00 10.00
31 " 50pf purple & black, *salmon* 14.00 10.00
32 " 80pf lake & black, *rose* 16.50 14.00

Overprinted in Black or Red.

33 A4 1m carmine rose 38.50 38.50
34 A5 2m gray blue 35.00 35.00
35 A6 3m black violet (R) 55.00 65.00
36 A7 5m slate & carmine, type I 325.00 450.00
36A " 5m slate & carmine, type II 275.00 375.00
Nos. 24-36A (14) 813.00 1034.65

Surcharged on German Stamps of 1902 in Black or Red

a

* 1 Dollar *

China

b

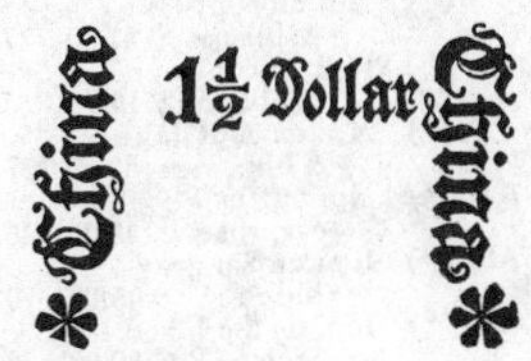

c

1905

37 A16 (*a*) 1c on 3pf brown 4.50 4.50
38 " (") 2c on 5pf green 4.50 1.40
39 " (") 4c on 10pf car. 9.50 1.40
40 " (") 10c on 20pf ultramarine 4.25 2.25
41 " (") 20c on 40pf lake & black 22.50 7.25
42 " (") 40c on 80pf lake & black, *rose* 50.00 16.50
43 A17 (*b*) ½d on 1m car. rose 22.50 22.50
44 A21 (*b*) 1d on 2m gray blue 27.50 25.00
45 A19 (*c*) 1½d on 3m black vio. (R) 19.00 *50.00*
46 A20 (*b*) 2½d on 5m slate & carmine 160.00 275.00
Nos. 37-46 (10) 324.25 *405.80*

Surcharged on German Stamps of 1905 in Black or Red

1906-13 **Wmk. 125**

47 A16 (*a*) 1c on 3pf brown 55 1.10
48 " (") 2c on 5pf green 55 90
49 " (") 4c on 10pf car. 55 90
50 " (") 10c on 20pf ultra. 1.20 *9.00*
51 " (") 20c on 40pf lake & black 1.65 3.25
52 " (") 40c on 80pf lake & black, *rose* 1.65 *38.50*
53 A17 (*b*) ½d on 1m carmine rose 3.25 *25.00*
54 A21 (") 1d on 2m gray blue 6.00 *32.50*
55 A19 (*c*) 1½d on 3m black violet (R) 9.00 *100.00*
56 A20 (*b*) 2½d on 5m slate & carmine 19.00 *75.00*
Nos. 47-56 (10) 43.40

Forged cancellations exist.

OFFICES IN MOROCCO

100 CENTIMOS=1 PESETA

A1

A2

Stamps of Germany Surcharged in Black.

1899 ***Perf. 13½x14½*** **Unwmkd.**

1 A1 3c on 3pf dark brown 2.50 2.50
2 " 5c on 5pf green 2.75 2.75
3 A2 10c on 10pf carmine 9.00 9.00
4 " 25c on 20pf ultra. 16.50 16.50
5 " 30c on 25pf orange 32.50 38.50
6 " 60c on 50pf red brn. 30.00 32.50

Before Nos. 1–6 were issued, the same six basic stamps of Germany's 1889–1900 issue were overprinted "Marocco" diagonally without the currency-changing surcharge line, but were not issued. Price, $1,200.

A3

A4

A5

A6

A7

Black or Red Surcharge.

1900 ***Perf. 14, 14½.***

7 A3 3c on 3pf brown 2.25 1.90
8 " 5c on 5pf green 2.25 1.40
9 " 10c on 10pf carmine 3.25 1.40
10 " 25c on 20pf ultra. 4.50 3.25
11 " 30c on 25pf org. & black, *yellow* 12.00 16.50
12 " 35c on 30pf org. & blk., *salmon* 12.00 9.00
13 " 50c on 40pf lake & black 12.00 9.00
14 " 60c on 50pf purple & black, *salmon* 27.50 45.00
15 " 1p on 80pf lake & black, *rose* 19.00 16.50
16 A4 1p 25c on 1m carmine rose 50.00 55.00
17 A5 2p 50c on 2m gray blue 50.00 65.00
18 A6 3p 75c on 3m blk. violet (R) 65.00 75.00
19 A7 6p 25c on 5m slate & carmine, type I 325.00 450.00
19A " 6p 25c on 5m slate & carmine, type II 300.00 325.00
Nos. 7-19A (14) 884.75 1073.95

A 1903 printing of Nos. 8, 16–18 and 19A differs in the "M" and "t" of the surcharge. These sell for more than the 1900 printing.

German Stamps of 1902 Surcharged in Black or Red

Marocco
3 Centimos
a

Marocco 1 Pes. 25 Cts. Marocco
b

Marocco 3 Pes. 75 Cts.
c

1905

20 A16 (*a*) 3c on 3pf brown 4.50 3.85
21 " (") 5c on 5pf green 8.50 1.65
22 " (") 10c on 10pf car. 16.50 1.10
23 " (") 25c on 20pf ultramarine 32.50 4.50
24 " (") 30c on 25pf orange & black, *yellow* 9.50 7.25
25 " (") 35c on 30pf orange & black, *buff* 16.50 8.50
26 " (") 50c on 40pf lake & black 14.00 10.00
27 " (") 60c on 50pf purple & black, *buff* 22.50 32.50
28 " (") 1p on 80pf lake & black, *rose* 21.00 22.50
29 A17 (*b*) 1p 25c on 1m carmine rose 55.00 42.50
30 A21 (") 2p 50c on 2m gray blue 140.00 165.00

31 A19 (c) 3p 75c on 3m black violet (R) 47.50 70.00
32 A20 (b) 6p 25c on 5m slate & carmine 190.00 190.00
Nos. 20-32 (13) 578.00 559.35

Surcharged on Germany No. 54

32A A11(a) 5c on 5pf grn. 9.00 22.50

German Stamps of 1905 Surcharged

1906-11 **Wmk. 125**

33 A16 (a) 3c on 3pf brown 11.00 2.25
34 " (") 5c on 5pf green 4.50 1.40
35 " (") 10c on 10pf car. 4.50 1.40
36 " (") 25c on 20pf ultra. 5.50 3.25
37 " (") 30c on 25pf orange & black, *yellow* 16.50 11.00
38 " (") 35c on 30pf orange & black, *buff* 14.00 12.00
39 " (") 50c on 40pf lake & black 40.00 *140.00*
40 " (") 60c on 50pf purple & black, *buff* 27.50 19.00
41 " (") 1p on 80pf lake & black, *rose* 165.00 225.00
42 A17 (b) 1p 25c on 1m carmine rose 85.00 *150.00*
43 A21 (") 2p 50c on 2m gray blue 85.00 *190.00*
44 A20 (") 6p 25c on 5m slate & carmine 190.00 250.00
Nos. 33-44 (12) 648.50 1005.30

Excellent forgeries exist of No 41.

Surcharge Spelled "Marokko" in Black or Red

1911

45 A16 (a) 3c on 3pf brown 85 85
46 " (") 5c on 5pf green 85 1.10
47 " (") 10c on 10pf carmine 85 1.40
48 " (") 25c on 20pf ultramarine 1.10 1.65
49 " (") 30c on 25pf orange & blk., *yellow* 1.90 *22.50*
50 " (") 35c on 30pf orange & black, *buff* 1.90 *11.00*
51 " (") 50c on 40pf lake & black 1.90 *6.50*
52 " (") 60c on 50pf purple & black, *buff* 2.75 *38.50*
53 " (") 1p on 80pf lake & black, *rose* 2.75 *22.50*
54 A17 (b) 1p 25c on 1m carmine rose 3.85 *55.00*
55 A21 (") 2p 50c on 2m gray blue 5.00 *55.00*
56 A19 (c) 3p 75c on 3m black violet (R) 11.00 *190.00*
57 A20 (b) 6p 25c on 5m slate & carmine 25.00 *300.00*
Nos. 45-57 (13) 59.70

Forged cancellations exist.

OFFICES IN THE TURKISH EMPIRE

40 PARAS=1 PIASTRE

> Unused prices for Nos. 1-6 are for stamps with original gum. Copies without gum sell for about one-third of the figures quoted.

A1

A2

German Stamps of 1880-83 Surcharged in Black or Blue.

1884 ***Perf. 13½x14½*** **Unwmkd.**

1 A1 10pa on 5pf violet 32.50 27.50
2 A2 20pa on 10pf rose 42.50 27.50
3 " 1pi on 20pf ultra. (Bk) 75.00 2.25
4 " 1pi on 20pf ultra. (Bl) *800.00* 50.00
5 A2 1¼pi on 25pf brown 165.00 165.00
6 " 2½pi on 50pf gray green 140.00 110.00
a. 2½pi on 50pf dp. olive green 325.00 275.00

There are two types of the surcharge on the 1¼pi and 2½pi stamps, the difference being in the spacing between the figures and the word "PIASTER".

There are re-issues of these stamps which vary only slightly from the originals in overprint measurements.

A3

A4

A5

German Stamps of 1889-1900 Surcharged in Black.

1889

8 A3 10pa on 5pf green 2.25 55
9 A4 20pa on 10pf carmine 5.50 1.40
10 " 1pi on 20pf ultra. 6.50 85
11 A5 1¼pi on 25pf orange 32.50 16.50
12 " 2½pi on 50pf choc. 38.50 27.50
a. 2½pi on 50pf copper brown 250.00 165.00

A6

A7

A8

A9

A10

A11

1900 ***Perf. 14, 14½***

Black or Red Surcharge.

13 A6 10pa on 5pf green 2.50 2.75
14 " 20pa on 10pf carmine 2.75 2.75
15 A6 1pi on 20pf ultra. 5.50 2.25
16 A7 1¼pi on 25pf orange & black, *yellow* 11.00 6.50
17 " 1½pi on 30pf orange & black, *salmon* 11.00 6.50
18 A6 2pi on 40pf lake & black 11.00 6.50
19 A7 2½pi on 50pf purple & black, *salmon* 19.00 22.50
20 A6 4pi on 80pf lake & black, *rose* 22.50 22.50
21 A8 5pi on 1m carmine rose 50.00 55.00
22 A9 10pi on 2m gray bl. 50.00 52.50
23 A10 15pi on 3m black violet (R) 85.00 90.00
24 A11 25pi on 5m slate & car., type I 300.00 275.00
a. Double surcharge *2250.00*
24B " 25pi on 5m slate & car., type II 275.00 350.00
c. Double surch. *3000.00 2250.00*
Nos. 13-24B (13) 845.25 894.75

German Stamps of 1900 Surcharged in Black

1 PIASTER 1

1903-05

25 A11 10pa on 5pf green 11.00 6.50
26 " 20pa on 10pf car. 50.00 16.50
27 " 1pi on 20pf ultra. 11.00 1.65

5 PIASTER 5

28 A12 5pi on 1m carmine rose 100.00 50.00
29 A13 10pi on 2m blue ('05) 200.00 225.00
30 A15 25pi on 5m slate & carmine 325.00 450.00
a. Double surch. *2650.00*
Nos. 25-30 (6) 697.00 749.65

The 1903-05 surcharges may be easily distinguished from those of 1900 by the added bar at the top of the letter "A".

German Stamps of 1902 Surcharged in Black or Red

10 10
Para
a

5 Piaster 5
b

1905 **Unwmkd.**

31 A16 (a) 10pa on 5pf grn. 4.75 3.25
32 " (") 20pa on 10pf carmine 14.00 4.50
33 " (") 1pi on 20pf ultramarine 15.00 3.25
34 " (") 1¼pi on 25pf org. & blk., *yel.* 15.00 12.00
35 " (") 1½pi on 30pf org. & blk., *buff* 27.50 27.50
36 " (") 2pi on 40pf lake & black 47.50 27.50
37 " (") 2½pi on 50pf pur. & blk., *buff* 16.50 *45.00*
38 " (") 4pi on 80pf lake & blk., *rose* 50.00 27.50
39 A17 (b) 5pi on 1m car. rose 45.00 40.00
40 A21 (") 10pi on 2m gray blue 65.00 70.00
41 A19 (") 15pi on 3m blk. violet (R) 80.00 75.00
42 A20 (") 25pi on 5m slate & carmine 325.00 375.00
Nos. 31-42 (12) 705.25 710.50

German Stamps of 1905 Surcharged in Black or Red

1906-12 **Wmk. 125**

43 A16 (a) 10pa on 5pf green 3.25 85
44 " (") 20pa on 10pf car. 3.85 90
45 " (") 1pi on 20pf ultra. 6.00 85
46 " (") 1¼pi on 25pf orange & blk., *yel.* 22.50 16.50
47 A16 (a) 1½pi on 30pf orange & black, *buff* 15.00 6.50
48 " (") 2pi on 40pf lake & black 7.50 2.00
49 " (") 2½pi on 50pf purple & black, *buff* 16.50 14.00
50 " (") 4pi on 80pf lake & black, *rose* 16.50 16.50
51 A17 (b) 5pi on 1m carmine rose 32.50 27.50
52 A21 (") 10pi on 2m gray blue 32.50 32.50
53 A19 (") 15pi on 3m black violet (R) 40.00 *425.00*
54 A20 (") 25pi on 5m slate & carmine 40.00 *90.00*
Nos. 43-54 (12) 236.10 *633.10*

German Stamps of 1905 Surcharged Diagonally in Black

10 Centimes

1908

55 A16 5c on 5pf green 1.90 2.25
56 " 10c on 10pf carmine 4.25 5.00
57 " 25c on 20pf ultra. 11.00 *35.00*
58 " 50c on 40pf lake & black 50.00 *85.00*
59 " 100c on 80pf lake & black, *rose* 100.00 *125.00*
Nos. 55-59 (5) 167.15 *252.25*

Forged cancellations exist on Nos. 37, 53-54, 57-59.

GHADAMES

See Libya, Occupation Stamps.

GRAND COMORO

(grănd kŏm'ō-rō)

LOCATION—One of the Comoro Islands in the Mozambique Channel between Madagascar and Mozambique.
GOVT.—Former French Colony.
AREA—385 sq. mi. (approx.)
POP.—50,000 (approx.)
CAPITAL—Moroni.

See Comoro Islands.

100 Centimes = 1 Franc

Navigation and Commerce
A1

Perf. 14x13½.

1897-1907 **Typographed.** **Unwmkd.**

Name of Colony in Blue or Carmine.

1 A1 1c *lilac blue* 30 30
2 " 2c brown, *buff* 50 50
3 " 4c claret, *lavender* 70 70
4 " 5c green, *greenish* 1.00 1.00
5 " 10c *lavender* 2.00 1.75
6 " 10c red ('00) 4.00 4.00
7 " 15c blue, quadrille paper 4.50 3.00
8 " 15c gray, *light gray* ('00) 4.00 4.00
9 " 20c red, *green* 4.50 3.50
10 " 25c *rose* 4.50 3.25
11 " 25c blue ('00) 6.00 3.00
12 " 30c brown, *bistre* 5.50 3.50
13 " 35c *yellow* ('06) 6.00 4.00
14 " 40c red, *straw* 5.50 4.00
15 " 45c *gray green* ('07) 28.50 25.00
16 " 50c carmine, *rose* 9.00 5.50
17 " 50c brown, *bluish* ('00) 12.00 11.00

18 A1 75c deep violet *orange* 13.50 9.00
19 " 1fr bronze green, *straw* 9.00 6.00
Nos. 1–19 (19) 121.00 93.00

Issues of 1897–1907 Surcharged in Black or Carmine **05** *a* **10** *b*

1912

Surcharged Type "a"

20 A1 5c on 2c brown, *buff* 30 30
a. Inverted surcharge 55.00
21 " 5c on 4c claret, *lavender* (C) 25 25
22 " 5c on 15c blue (C) 20 20
23 " 5c on 20c red, *green* 25 25
24 " 5c on 25c *rose* (C) 30 30
25 " 5c on 30c brown, *bistre* (C) 35 35

Surcharged Type "b"

26 A1 10c on 40c red, *straw* 30 30
27 " 10c on 45c *gray green* (C) 35 35
28 " 10c on 50c car., *rose* 45 45
29 " 10c on 75c deep violet, *orange* 45 45
Nos. 20–29 (10) 3.20 3.20

Two spacings between the surcharged numerals are found on Nos. 20 to 29.

Nos. 20 to 29 were available for use in Madagascar and the entire Comoro archipelago.

Stamps of Grand Comoro were superseded by those of Madagascar, and in 1950 by those of Comoro Islands.

GREECE

(grēs)

(Hellas)

LOCATION — Occupying the southern part of the Balkan Peninsula in southeastern Europe and bordering on the Ionian, Aegean and Mediterranean Seas.

GOVT.—Republic.

AREA—50,942 sq. mi.

POP.—9,050,000 (est. 1975).

CAPITAL—Athens.

In 1923 the reigning king was forced to abdicate his throne and the following year Greece was declared a republic. In 1935 the king was recalled by a "plebiscite" of the people. Greece became a republic in June 1973. The country today includes the Aegean Islands of Chios, Mytilene (Lesbos), Samos, Icaria (Nicaria) and Lemnos, the Ionian Islands (Corfu, etc.), Crete, Macedonia, Western Thrace and part of Eastern Thrace, the Mount Athos District, Epirus and the Dodecanese Islands.

100 Lepta = 1 Drachma

Prices of early Greek stamps vary according to condition. Quotations for Nos. 1–58 are for fine copies. Very fine to superb specimens sell at much higher prices, and inferior or poor copies sell at reduced prices, depending on the condition of the individual specimen.

Prices for Nos. 1–7 unused are for specimens without gum. Stamps with original gum are worth considerably more.

Hermes (Mercury)
A1

Paris Print, Fine Impression.

The enlarged illustrations show the head in various states of the plates. The differences are best seen in the shading lines on the cheek and neck.

Typographed.

1861 *Imperf.* **Unwmkd.**

Without Figures on Back

1 A1 1 l chocolate, *cream* 375.00 250.00
a. 1 l red brown, *cream* 400.00 250.00
2 " 2 l olive bistre, *straw* 35.00 37.50
a. 2 l brown buff, *buff* 35.00 37.50
3 " 5 l emerald, *greenish* 450.00 100.00
4 " 20 l blue, *bluish* 525.00 50.00
a. 20 l deep blue, *bluish* 600.00 150.00
b. On pelure paper 275.00
5 " 40 l violet, *blue* 250.00 100.00
6 " 80 l rose, *pink* 200.00 80.00
a. 80 l carmine, *pink* 200.00 80.00

Large Figures, 8mm. high, on Back.

7 A1 10 l red orange, *blue* 675.00 325.00
a. "01" on back
b. Without "10" on back 600.00
c. "0" of "10" inverted on back 700.00
d. "1" of "10" inverted on back 800.00

No. 7b was not regularly issued.

Trial impressions of Paris prints exist in many shades, some being close to those of the issued stamps. The gum used was thin and smooth instead of thick, brownish and crackly as on the issued stamps.

Athens Print, Clear Impression

1861–62

Without Figures on Back.

8 A1 1 l chocolate, *cream* ('62) 200.00 125.00
a. 1 l dark chocolate, *cream* 400.00 275.00
9 " 2 l bis. brn., *cream* 42.50 55.00
a. 2 l dark brown, *straw* 2000.00
10 " 20 l dark blue, *bluish* (coarse print) 7000.00

No. 10 often shows a quadrille appearance in the background.

With Figures on Back.

a *b*

11 A1(*a*) 5 l green, *greenish* 175.00 70.00
a. 5 l green, *greenish with yellow cast* 210.00 70.00
b. Double "5" on back 500.00

12 A1 10 l orange, *greenish* 450.00 75.00
a. 10 l orange, *greenish with yellow cast* 675.00 100.00
13 " 20 l dark blue, *bluish* 1750.00 60.00
a. 20 l dull blue, *bluish with gray cast* 2000.00 90.00
14 " 40 l red vio., *blue* 1350.00 90.00
a. 40 l red violet, *blue with yellow cast* 1500.00 200.00
15 " 80 l dull rose, *pink* ('62) 450.00 100.00
a. 80 l carmine, *pink* ('62) 450.00 100.00

Nos. 9a and 11-14 may be divided into two groups, the first rather poorly printed and the second very finely executed. These stamps can be distinguished by the delicate lines of the numerals on the back as compared with the coarser ones of later printings.

Nos. 15 and 15a have vermilion figures on the back, while those of all later printings are carmine.

Athens Print, Coarse Impression

1862–67

With Figures on Back, Except 1L and 2L.

16 A1 1 l chocolate, *cream* 40.00 30.00
a. 1 l red brown, *cream* (poor print) 125.00 70.00
b. 1 l brown, *cream* (poor print) 52.50 27.50
17 " 2 l brownish bistre, *cream* 8.00 7.00
a. 2 l bistre, *cream* 8.00 7.00
18 " (*b*) 5 l grn., *greenish* 125.00 10.00
a. 5 l yellowish green, *greenish* 125.00 10.00
19 " 10 l yellow orange, *bluish* 140.00 11.00
a. 10 l orange, *blue* (1864) 325.00 12.00
b. "10" on face instead of back (No. 19a) 2250.00
c. 10 l red orange, *blue* (Dec. 1865) 300.00 12.00
d. "01" on back 1000.00 110.00
20 " 20 l blue, *bluish* 120.00 5.50
a. 20 l light blue, *bluish* (fine print) 185.00 15.00
b. 20 l dark blue, *bluish* 375.00 17.50
c. 20 l bl., *greenish* 950.00 12.00
d. "80" on back 500.00
e. Double "20" on back 135.00
f. Without "20" on back 1400.00
21 " 40 l red violet, *blue* 185.00 12.50
a. 40 l brown violet, *blue* 185.00 12.50
b. 40 l lilac brown, *lilac gray* 850.00 14.00
c. Double "40" on back 250.00
22 " 80 l carmine, *pale rose* 75.00 20.00
a. 80 l rose, *pale rose* 80.00 20.00
b. "8" on back inverted 900.00 200.00
c. "80" on back inverted 250.00
d. "8" only on back 210.00

Faint vertical lines are visible in the background of Nos. 16, 16a and 16b.

Many stamps of this and succeeding issues which are normally imperforate are known rouletted, pin-perforated, percé en scie, etc., all of which are unofficial.

1868-69

Athens Print, From Cleaned Plates.

23 A1 1 l reddish brown, *cream* 22.50 22.50
a. 1 l dark reddish brown, *cream* 25.00 32.50
24 A1 2 l gray bister, *cream* 20.00 20.00
25 " (*b*) 5 l grn., *greenish* 225.00 17.50
26 " 10 l pale orange, *bluish* 225.00 8.50
a. "10" on back inverted 150.00
27 " 20 l pale blue, *bluish* 210.00 6.50
a. Double "20" on back 200.00
28 " 40 l rose vio., *blue* 175.00 17.50
a. "20" on back, corrected to "40" 1250.00 650.00
29 " 80 l rose carmine, *pale rose* 110.00 75.00

The "0" on the back of No. 29 is printed more heavily than the "8".

1870

Special Athens Printing Made Under Supervision of German Workmen.

Good Impression.

30 A1 1 l reddish brown, *cream* 150.00 125.00
a. 1 l deep reddish brown, *cream* 150.00 150.00
31 " 20 l light blue, *bluish* 1500.00 12.50
a. 20 l blue, *bluish* 1650.00 15.00
b. "02" on back 250.00
c. "20" on back inverted 210.00

Nos. 30 and 30a have short lines of shading on cheek. The spandrels of No. 31 are very pale with the lines often broken or missing.

1870-71

Medium to Thin Paper Without Mesh.

32 A1 1 l brown, *cream* 40.00 32.50
a. 1 l purple brown, *cream* 42.50 35.00
33 " 2 l salmon bistre, *cream* 8.00 8.00
34 " (*b*) 5 l grn., *greenish* 250.00 15.00
35 " 10 l light red orange, *greenish* 225.00 15.00
36 " 20 l blue, *bluish* 300.00 6.50
a. "02" on back 210.00
b. Double "20" on back 225.00
37 " 40 l salmon, *greenish* 450.00 85.00
a. 40 l lilac, *greenish* 6000.00

The stamps of this issue have rather coarse figures on back.

No. 37a is printed in the exact shade of the numerals on the back of No. 37.

1872-75

Thin Transparent Paper Showing Mesh.

38 A1 1 l red brown, *yellowish* 30.00 20.00
a. 1 l grayish brown, *straw* 37.50 32.50
39 A1(*b*) 5 l green, *greenish* 175.00 15.00
a. 5 l dark green, *greenish* 225.00 25.00
b. Double "5" on back 110.00
40 A1 10 l red orange, *greenish* 175.00 10.00
a. 10 l red orange, *pale lilac* 900.00 40.00
b. "10" on back inverted (No. 40) 375.00 65.00
c. Double "10" on back (No. 40) 175.00
d. "0" on back 75.00
41 A1 20 l dark blue, *bluish* 300.00 7.00
a. 20 l blue, *bluish* 300.00 7.00
b. 20 l dark blue, *blue* 575.00 22.50
42 A1 40 l brown, *blue* 20.00 15.00
a. 40 l olive brown, *blue* 20.00 15.00
b. 40 l red violet, *blue* 200.00 20.00
c. 40 l gray violet, *blue* 200.00 15.00
d. Figures on back bister 70.00 15.00
e. Double "40" on back 275.00

The mesh is not apparent on Nos. 38 and 38a.

1875-80

On Cream Paper Unless Otherwise Stated.

43 A1 1 l gray brown 7.00 5.00
a. 1 l dark gray brown 6.00 5.00
b. 1 l black brown 15.00 12.50
c. 1 l red brown 12.00 7.50
d. 1 l dark red brown 15.00 10.00
e. 1 l purple brown 17.50 10.00
44 " 2 l bistre 15.00 12.50

45 A1 (b) 5 l dark yellow green 90.00 15.00
a. 5 l pale yellow green 90.00 15.00
46 " 10 l orange 100.00 10.00
a. 10 l orange, *yellow* 110.00 12.50
b. Double impression (No. 46a) 250.00
c. "00" on back 135.00 70.00
d. "1" on back 150.00 75.00
e. "0" on back 140.00 75.00
f. "01" on back 75.00
g. Double "10" on back 150.00
47 " 20 l ultramarine 125.00 7.00
a. 20 l blue 140.00 8.00
b. 20 l dull blue 300.00 12.50
c. "02" on back 135.00
d. "20" on back inverted 250.00
e. "50" on back 135.00
f. Double "20" on back 135.00
48 " 40 l salmon 20.00 17.50

The back figures are found in many varieties, including "1" and "0" inverted in "10."

1876

Without Figures on Back.

Paris Print. Clear Impression.

49 A1 30 l olive brown, *yellowish* 225.00 60.00
a. 30 l brn., *yellowish* 325.00 70.00
50 " 60 l green, *greenish* 30.00 47.50

Athens Print. Coarse Impression.

Yellowish Paper.

51 A1 30 l dark brown 40.00 5.00
a. 30 l black brown 45.00 6.00
52 " 60 l green 375.00 85.00

1880-82 Cream Paper.

53 A1 5 l green 6.50 2.00
54 " 10 l orange 9.00 2.50
a. 10 l yellow 9.00 2.50
b. 10 l red orange 650.00 45.00
55 " 20 l ultramarine 250.00 65.00
56 " 20 l rose (aniline ink) ('82) 8.00 2.00
a. 20 l pale rose (aniline ink) ('82) 4.00 2.00
b. 20 l deep carmine 100.00 10.00
57 " 30 l ultramarine ('82) 85.00 12.50
a. 30 l slate blue 90.00 15.00
58 " 40 l lilac 85.00 12.50
a. 40 l violet 90.00 15.00

Stamps of type A1 were not regularly issued with perf. 11½.

Hermes
A2

Lepta denominations have white numeral tablets.

Belgian Print, Clear Impression.

1886-88 *Imperf.*

64 A2 1 l brown ('88) 1.20 1.20
65 " 2 l bistre ('88) 8.50 8.50
66 " 5 l yel. green ('88) 12.00 2.50
67 " 10 l yellow ('88) 17.50 3.50
68 " 20 l carmine rose ('88) 30.00 1.35
69 " 25 l blue 125.00 3.00
70 " 40 l violet ('88) 90.00 25.00
71 " 50 l gray green 7.00 6.00
72 " 1 d gray 135.00 4.25

1891 *Perf. 11½.*

81 A2 1 l brown 2.25 2.25
82 " 2 l bistre 11.00 10.00
83 " 5 l yellow green 14.00 7.25
84 " 10 l yellow 18.50 7.25
85 " 20 l carmine rose 32.50 13.00
86 " 25 l blue 125.00 30.00
87 " 40 l violet 110.00 25.00
88 " 50 l gray green 9.00 7.25
89 " 1 d gray 135.00 5.00

The Belgian Printings perf. 13½ and most of the values perf. 11½ (Nos. 82-86) were perforated on request of philatelists at the main post office in Athens, but were not regularly issued.

Wmkd. Greek Words in Some Sheets.

Athens Print. Poor Impression.

1889-95 *Imperf.*

90 A2 1 l black brown 1.00 40
a. 1 l brown 60 30
91 " 2 l pale bister 1.00 1.00
a. 2 l buff 1.00 1.00
92 " 5 l green 3.00 20
a. Double impression
b. 5 l deep green 4.00 30
93 " 10 l yellow 8.00 30
a. 10 l orange 40.00 50
b. 10 l dull yellow 15.00 50
94 " 20 l carmine 4.00 15
a. 20 l rose 4.00 15
95 " 25 l bright blue 45.00 1.00
a. 25 l indigo 60.00 5.00
b. 25 l ultramarine 75.00 5.00
c. 25 l dull blue 45.00 3.00
96 " 25 l red violet ('93) 3.00 50
a. 25 l lilac 3.00 50
97 " 40 l red violet ('91) 75.00 27.50
98 " 40 l blue ('93) 7.00 2.50
99 " 1 d gray ('95) 135.00 9.00

Perf. 13½.

100 A2 1 l brown 6.00 6.00
101 " 2 l buff 2.50 2.50
103 " 10 l orange 40.00 10.00
104 " 20 l carmine 8.50 8.50
a. 20 l rose 8.50 8.50
105 " 40 l red violet 85.00 25.00

Other denominations of type A2 were not officially issued with perf. 13½.

Perf. 11½.

107 A2 1 l brown 80 70
a. 1 l black brown 3.00 2.00
108 " 2 l pale bistre 1.25 1.00
a. 2 l buff 1.25 1.00
109 " 5 l pale green 4.00 80
a. 5 l deep green 6.00 90
110 " 10 l yellow 10.00 1.50
a. 10 l dull yellow 20.00 1.75
b. 10 l orange 50.00 3.00
111 " 20 l carmine 4.50 1.00
a. 20 l rose 4.50 1.00
112 " 25 l dull blue 45.00 5.00
a. 25 l indigo 75.00 11.00
b. 25 l ultramarine 90.00 15.00
c. 25 l bright blue 45.00 3.50
113 " 25 l red violet 4.00 1.00
a. 25 l lilac 4.00 1.00
114 " 40 l red violet 70.00 22.50
115 " 40 l blue 10.00 5.00
116 " 1 d gray 140.00 25.00

Partly-perforated varieties sell for about twice as much as normal copies.

The watermark on Nos. 90-116 consists of three Greek words meaning Paper for Public Service. It is in double-lined capitals, measures 270x35mm., and extends across three panes.

Wrestlers
A3

Discobolus by Myron
A4

Vase Depicting Pallas Athene (Minerva)
A5

Chariot Driving
A6

Stadium and Acropolis
A7

Statue of Hermes by Praxiteles
A8

Statue of Victory by Paeonius
A9

Acropolis and Parthenon—A10

Perf. 14x13½, 13½x14

1896 **Unwmkd.**

117 A3 1 l ochre 60 40
118 " 2 l rose 60 40
a. Without engraver's name 6.00 5.00
119 A4 5 l lilac 2.00 80
120 " 10 l slate gray 2.50 80
121 A5 20 l red brown 9.00 40
122 A6 25 l red 25.00 2.00
123 A5 40 l violet 6.00 4.00
124 A6 60 l black 20.00 18.00
125 A7 1 d blue 70.00 6.00
126 A8 2 d bistre 100.00 32.50
a. Horiz. pair, imperf. between
127 A9 5 d green 300.00 185.00
128 A10 10 d brown 375.00 225.00
Nos. 117-128 (12) 910.70 475.30

Issued to commemorate the first international Olympic Games of the modern era, held at Athens. Counterfeits of Nos. 123-124 and 126-128 exist.

Preceding Issues Surcharged

ΛΕΠΤΑ
20

1900 *Imperf.*

129 A2 20 l on 25 l dull blue (No. 95c) 1.20 75
a. 20 l on 25 l indigo (No. 95a) 37.50 3.50
b. 20 l on 25 l ultramarine (No. 95 b) 47.50 20.00
c. Double surcharge 8.50 7.00
d. Triple surcharge 11.00
e. Inverted surcharge 8.00 7.00
f. "20" above word 11.00 7.00
g. Pair, one without surcharge 20.00
h. "20" without word
130 A1 30 l on 40 l violet, *cream* (No. 58a) 5.00 2.75
a. 30 l on 40 l lilac (No. 58) 6.75 5.25
b. Broad "0" in "30" 6.00 4.00
c. First letter of word is "A" 11.00 11.00
d. Double surcharge 13.50
132 " 40 l on 2 l bistre, *cream* (No. 44) 5.00 4.00
a. Broad "0" in "40" 5.25 5.25
b. First letter of word is "A" 11.00 11.00
133 " 50 l on 40 l salmon, *cream* (No. 48) 5.50 4.00
a. Broad "0" in "50" 6.50 5.25
b. First letter of word is "A" 11.00 11.00
c. "50" without word
d. "50" above word
134 A2 1 d on 40 l red violet (No. 97) 12.50 10.00
137 A1 3 d on 10 l orange, *cream* (No. 54) 15.00 11.00
a. 3 d on 10 l yellow (No. 54a) 15.00 11.00
138 " 5 d on 40 l red violet, *blue* (No. 21) 40.00 37.50
a. 5 d on 40 l red violet, *blue* (No. 28) 40.00 37.50
b. "20" on back corrected to "40"
139 " 5 d on 40 l red violet, *blue* (No. 42) 350.00

Perf. 11½.

140 A2 20 l on 25 l dull blue (No. 112) 2.75 1.00
a. 20 l on 25 l indigo (No. 112a) 45.00 10.00
b. 20 l on 25 l ultra. (No. 112b) 55.00 20.00
c. Double surcharge 10.00 10.00
d. Triple surcharge 13.50 11.00
e. Inverted surcharge 11.00 10.00
f. "20" above word 13.50 8.50
141 A1 30 l on 40 l violet, *cream* (No. 58a) 6.00 5.00
a. 30 l on 40 l lilac (No. 58) 7.00 7.00
b. Broad "0" in "30" 9.00 9.00
c. First letter of word "A" 13.50 13.50
d. Double surcharge
142 " 40 l on 2 l bistre, *cream* (No. 44) 7.00 7.00
a. Broad "0" in "40" 9.00 9.00
b. First letter of word "A" 13.50 13.50
143 " 50 l on 40 l salmon, *cream* (No. 48) 7.00 7.00
a. Broad "0" in "50" 9.00 9.00
b. First letter of word "A" 13.50 13.50
c. "50" without word
d. "50" above word
144 A2 1 d on 40 l red violet (No. 114) 16.50 11.00
147 A1 3 d on 10 l orange, *cream* (No. 54) 17.50 17.50
a. 3 d on 10 l yel., *cream* (No. 54a) 17.50 17.50
148 " 5 d on 40 l red violet, *blue* (No. 21) 40.00 37.50
a. 5 d on 40 l red violet, *blue* (No. 28) 40.00 37.50
149 " 5 d on 40 l red violet, *blue* (No. 42) 450.00

Perf. 13½.

150 A2 2 d on 40 l red violet (No. 105) 8.00 8.00

The 1 d on 40 l perf. 13½ and the 2 d on 40 l, both imperf. and perf. 13½, were not officially issued.

Surcharge Including "A M"

"A M" = "Axia Metalliki" or "Value in Metal (gold)."

1900 *Imperf.*

151 A2 25 l on 40 l violet (No. 70) 14.00 12.00
152 " 50 l on 25 l blue (No. 69) 15.00 15.00
153 A1 1 d on 40 l brown, *blue* (No. 42b) 55.00 50.00
154 " 2 d on 5 l green, *cream* (No. 53) 13.50 13.50

Perf. 11½.

155 A2 25 l on 40 l violet (No. 87) 15.00 13.00
156 " 50 l on 25 l blue (No. 69) 18.00 18.00
157 A1 1 d on 40 l brown, *blue* (No. 42b) 60.00 60.00
158 " 2 d on 5 l green, *cream* (No. 53) 14.00 14.00

Partly-perforated varieties of Nos. 129-158 sell for about two to three times as much as normal copies.

Surcharge Including "A M" on Olympic Issue in Red

1900-01 *Perf. 14x13½*

159 A7 5 l on 1 d blue 5.00 5.00
a. Wrong font "M" with serifs 9.00 9.00
b. Double surcharge 175.00 175.00
160 A5 25 l on 40 l violet 60.00 45.00
161 A8 50 l on 2 d bistre 60.00 55.00
a. Broad "0" in "50" 70.00 65.00

162 A9 1d on 5d grn. ('01) 200.00 175.00
a. Greek "D" instead of "A" as 3rd letter 400.00 400.00
163 A10 2d on 10d brn. ('01) 55.00 50.00
a. Greek "D" instead of "A" as 3rd letter 150.00 150.00
Nos. 159-163 (5) 380.00 330.00

Black Surcharge on No. 160.

164 A5 50 l on 25 l on 40 l vio. (R+Bk) 375.00 500.00
a. Broad "0" in "50" 450.00 525.00

Nos. 151-164 and 179-183, gold currency stamps, were generally used for parcel post and foreign money orders. They were also available for use on letters, but cost about 20 per cent more than the regular stamps of the same denomination.

Counterfeit surcharges exist of Nos. 159-164.

Giovanni da Bologna's Hermes
A11 A12

A13

Wmk. 129

FIVE LEPTA.

Type I. Letters of "ELLAS" not outlined at top and left. Only a few faint horizontal lines between the outer vertical lines at sides.

Type II. Letters of "ELLAS" fully outlined. Heavy horizontal lines between the vertical frame lines.

Engraved.

Wmkd. Crown and ET. (129)

1901 ***Perf. 11½, 12½, 13½.***

165 A11 1 l yellow brown 25 15
a. Imperf., pair 8.00
166 " 2 l gray 25 15
a. Imperf., pair 8.00
167 " 3 l orange 40 18
a. Imperf., pair 10.00
168 A12 5 l green, type I 40 15
a. 5 l yellow green, type I 40 15
b. 5 l yellow green, type II 40 15
c. Imperf., pair 8.00
169 " 10 l rose 40 25
a. Imperf., pair 10.00
170 A11 20 l red lilac 50 25
a. Imperf., pair 10.00
171 A12 25 l ultramarine 80 25
a. Imperf., pair 10.00
172 A11 30 l dull violet 7.50 3.00
a. Imperf., pair 25.00
173 " 40 l dark brown 3.75 1.75
a. Imperf., pair 30.00
174 " 50 l brown lake 3.75 75
a. Imperf., pair 25.00

Perf. 12½, 14 and Compound.

175 A13 1d black 37.50 2.00
a. Horizontal pair, imperf. between 125.00
b. Imperf., pair 125.00
c. Imperf. vertically, pair 125.00
d. Imperf. horizontally, pair 125.00

Lithographed.

Perf. 12½.

176 A13 2d bronze 8.50 5.00
177 " 3d silver 10.00 8.00
a. Horizontal pair, imperf. between 300.00 300.00
178 " 5d gold 15.00 13.50
Nos. 165-178 (14) 89.00 35.38

Hermes
A14

1902, Jan. 1 **Engr.** ***Perf. 13½***

179 A14 5 l deep orange 2.50 1.00
a. Imperf., pair 40.00
180 " 25 l emerald 10.00 2.00
181 " 50 l ultramarine 10.00 2.00
a. Imperf., pair 300.00
182 " 1d rose red 20.00 10.00
183 " 2d orange brown 40.00 22.50
Nos. 179-183 (5) 82.50 37.50

See note after No. 164. In 1913 remainders of Nos. 179-183 were used as postage dues.

Apollo Throwing Discus
A15

Jumper, with Jumping Weights
A16

Victory
A17

Atlas and Hercules
A18

Struggle of Hercules and Antaeus
A19

Wrestlers
A20

Daemon of the Games
A21

Foot Race
A22

Nike, Priest and Athletes in Pre-Games Offering to Zeus
A23

Wmkd. Crown and ET. (129)

1906, Mar. **Engr.** ***Perf. 13½, 14***

184 A15 1 l brown 2.50 60
a. Imperf., pair 50.00 50.00
185 " 2 l gray 3.00 60
a. Imperf., pair 50.00
186 A16 3 l orange 3.00 2.00
a. Imperf., pair 60.00
187 " 5 l green 5.00 60
a. Imperf., pair 50.00 40.00
188 A17 10 l rose red 7.50 60
a. Imperf., pair 50.00
189 A18 20 l magenta 8.00 40
a. Imperf., pair 75.00
190 A19 25 l ultramarine 17.50 1.50
a. Imperf., pair 75.00
191 A20 30 l dull purple 20.00 5.00
a. Double impression 700.00
192 A21 40 l dark brown 8.00 4.00
193 A18 50 l brown lake 20.00 2.00
194 A22 1d gray black 60.00 15.00
a. Imperf., pair 350.00 350.00
195 " 2d rose 100.00 30.00
196 " 3d olive yellow 200.00 125.00
197 A23 5d dull blue 185.00 110.00
Nos. 184-197 (14) 639.50 297.30

Issued to commemorate the Greek Special Olympic Games of 1906 at Athens, celebrating the 10th anniversary of the modern Olympic Games.

Hermes, from Old Cretan Coin
A24

Iris Holding Caduceus
A25

Hermes Donning Sandals
A26

Hermes Carrying Infant Arcas
A27

A28

Designs A24 to A28 are from Cretan and Arcadian coins of the 4th Century, B.C.

Serrate Roulette 13½.

1911-21 **Engraved** **Unwmkd.**

198 A24 1 l green 30 10
a. Imperf., pair 17.50
199 A25 2 l carmine rose 30 10
200 A24 3 l vermilion 20 10
a. Imperf., pair 25.00 25.00
201 A26 5 l green 2.00 10
a. Imperf., pair 17.50
202 A24 10 l carmine rose 5.00 10
a. Imperf., pair 25.00
203 A25 20 l gray lilac 2.00 40
a. Imperf., pair 25.00
204 " 25 l ultramarine 20.00 20
a. Rouletted in black 50.00
b. Imperf., pair 70.00
205 A26 30 l carmine rose 3.00 30
206 A25 40 l deep blue 10.00 2.00
a. Imperf., pair 60.00
207 A26 50 l dull violet 15.00 40
a. Imperf., pair 75.00
208 A27 1d ultramarine 12.00 20
a. Imperf., pair 125.00
209 " 2d vermilion 17.50 1.00
a. Imperf., pair 75.00
210 A27 3d carmine rose 14.00 1.50
a. Size 20¼x25½mm. ('21) 60.00 12.00
b. Imperf., pair 75.00
211 " 5d ultramarine 17.50 2.50
a. Size 20¼x25½ mm. ('21) 70.00 4.00
b. Imperf., pair 90.00
212 " 10d deep blue, 20¼x25½mm. ('21) 20.00 17.50
a. Size 20x26½ mm. ('11) 210.00 100.00
b. As "a," imperf., pair 450.00
213 A28 25d deep blue 35.00 32.50
a. Imperf., pair 225.00
Nos. 198-213 (16) 173.80 59.00

The 1921 reissues of the 3d, 5d and 10d measure 20 1/4x25 1/2mm., instead of 20x26 1/2mm.

Serrate Roulette
10½x13½, 13½.

1913-23 **Lithographed**

214 A24 1 l green 12 6
a. Without period after "Ellas" 35.00 35.00
b. Imperf., pair 20.00
215 A25 2 l rose 12 10
a. Imperf., pair 20.00
216 A24 3 l vermilion 12 10
a. Imperf., pair 22.00
217 A26 5 l green 10 3
a. Imperf., pair 15.00
218 A24 10 l carmine 10 3
a. Imperf., pair 15.00
219 A25 15 l dull blue ('18) 12 6
220 " 20 l slate 30 3
a. Imperf., pair 30.00
221 " 25 l ultramarine 1.00 6
a. 25 l blue 4.00 6
b. Imperf., pair 35.00
c. Double impression 25.00
222 A26 30 l rose ('14) 1.00 12
a. Imperf., pair 40.00
223 A25 40 l indigo ('14) 3.00 7
224 A26 50 l vio. brown ('14) 1.00 10
a. Imperf., pair 50.00
b. Vertical pair, imperf. between 50.00
c. Double impression 25.00
225 " 80 l violet brn. ('23) 1.25 8
b. Imperf., pair 50.00
c. Double impression 25.00
226 A27 1d ultra. ('19) 4.00 6
227 " 2d vermilion ('19) 5.00 15
a. Imperf., pair 60.00
b. Imperf. vertically, pair 60.00
228 " 3d car. rose ('20) 8.00 15
b. Imperf., pair 60.00
c. Imperf. vertically, pair 50.00
229 " 5d ultra. ('22) 17.50 15
a. Imperf., pair 80.00
b. Vertical pair, imperf. between 70.00
230 " 10d deep blue ('22) 8.00 1.00
231 A28 25d indigo ('22) 20.00 4.00
Nos. 214-231 (18) 70.73 6.35

Nos. 221, 223 and 226 were re-issued in 1926, printed in Vienna from new plates. There are slight differences in minor details.

The 10 lepta brown, on thick paper, type A28, is not a postage stamp. It was issued in 1922 to replace coins of this denomination during a shortage of copper.

Raising Greek Flag at Suda Bay, Crete
A29

1913, Dec. 1 Engr. ***Perf. 14½***

232 A29 25 l blue & black 6.00 2.50
a. Imperf., pair 110.00

No. 232 was issued to commemorate the union of Crete with Greece. It was used only in Crete.

Stamps of 1911-14 Overprinted in Red or Black

Serrate Roulette 13½

1916, Nov. 1 Lithographed

233 A24 1 l green (R) 15 15
234 A25 2 l rose 15 15
235 A24 3 l vermilion 15 15
236 A26 5 l green (R) 50 15
237 A24 10 l carmine 15 10
238 A25 20 l slate (R) 75 20
239 " 25 l blue (R) 60 10
a. 25 l ultramarine 35.00 3.00
240 A26 30 l rose 60 20
a. Pair, one without overprint
241 A25 40 l indigo (R) 5.00 40
242 A26 50 l violet brown (R) 20.00 30

Engraved.

243 A24 3 l vermilion 65 60
244 A26 30 l carmine rose 3.00 1.50
245 A27 1d ultra. (R) 25.00 30
a. Rouletted in black 60.00
246 A27 2d vermilion 12.00 85
247 " 3d carmine rose 5.50 1.00
248 " 5d ultra. (R) 40.00 3.00
248B " 10d deep blue (R) 10.00 10.00
Nos. 233-248B (17) 124.20 19.15

Most of Nos. 233-248B exist with overprint double, inverted, etc. Prices two to three times those of normal examples, minimum, $1.50. Excellent counterfeits of the inverted overprint varieties exist.

Issued by the Venizelist Provisional Government.

Iris
A32

1917, Feb. 5 Litho. ***Perf. 14***

249 A32 1 l deep green 20 15
a. Imperf., pair 10.00
250 " 5 l yellow green 50 40
a. Imperf., pair 10.00
251 " 10 l rose 40 35
a. Imperf., pair 10.00
252 " 25 l light blue 90 70
a. Imperf., pair 8.00
253 " 50 l gray violet 2.00 50
a. Imperf., pair 10.00
254 " 1d ultramarine 2.00 40
a. Imperf., pair 10.00
255 " 2d light red 4.00 50
a. Imperf., pair 15.00
256 " 3d claret 15.00 4.00
a. Imperf., pair 45.00
257 " 5d gray blue 6.00 1.00
a. Imperf., pair 20.00
258 " 10d dark blue 35.00 6.50
a. Imperf., pair 90.00
259 " 25d slate 75.00 65.00
a. Imperf., pair 185.00
Nos. 249-259 (11) 141.00 79.50

The 4d, type A32, was used only as a revenue stamp.

Stamps of 1917 Surcharged

ΕΠΑΝΑΣΤΑΣΙΣ
1922
ΛΕΠΤΑ 10

1923

260 A32 5 l on 10 l rose 18 18
a. Inverted surcharge 3.00
261 A32 50 l on 50 l gray violet 25 25
262 " 1d on 1d ultramarine 25 25
a. 1d on 1d gray blue 50 50
263 " 2d on 2d light red 50 50
264 " 3d on 3d claret 3.75 3.75
265 " 5d on 5d dark blue 2.50 2.50
266 " 25d on 25d slate 18.50 18.50

Same Surcharge on Occupation of Turkey Stamps, 1913.

Perf. 13½.

267 O2 5 l on 3 l orange 15 15
a. Inverted surcharge 6.00
268 O1 10 l on 20 l violet 25 25
a. Invtd., surcharge 12.50
269 O2 10 l on 25 l pale blue 15 15
270 O1 10 l on 30 l gray green 40 40
271 O2 10 l on 40 l indigo 40 40
272 O1 50 l on 50 l dark blue 40 40
a. Invtd. surch. 10.00
273 " 2d on 2d gray brn. 50.00 50.00
274 O2 3d on 3d dull blue 4.00 4.00
a. Imperf., pair 150.00
275 O1 5d on 5d gray 4.00 4.00
276 O2 10d on 1d vio. brn. 4.00 4.00
276A " 10d on 10d car. 1100.00

Dangerous counterfeits of No. 276A exist.

Same Surcharge on Stamps of Crete.

Perf. 14.

On Stamps of 1900.

276B A6 5 l on 1 l red brown 32.50 32.50
277 A8 10 l on 10 l red 20 20
277B " 10 l on 25 l blue (No. 59) 65.00

On Stamps of 1901.

278 A8 10 l on 25 l blue 40 40
279 A6 50 l on 50 l lilac 40 40
279A " 50 l on 50 l ultra. 1.15 1.15
280 A9 50 l on 1d gray violet 80 80
280A A11 50 l on 5d green & black 20.00

On Stamps of 1905.

281 A15 10 l on 20 l blue green 60.00 55.00
282 A16 10 l on 25 l ultra. 1.00 1.00
a. Double surcharge 8.00
283 A17 50 l on 50 l yel. brn. 60 60
284 A18 50 l on 1d rose carmine & brown 2.75 2.75
a. Imperf., pair
285 A19 3d on 3d orange & black 8.00 8.00
286 A20 5d on 5d olive green & black 7.00 7.00

On Stamps of 1907.

287 A21 10 l on 25 l blue & black 1.00 1.00
a. Imperf., pair
287B A22 50 l on 1d green & black 3.00 3.00

On Stamp of 1908.

288 A23 10 l on 10 l brown red 15 15
a. Invtd. surcharge 3.00

On Stamp of 1908 with Overprint ΕΛΛΑΣ

288B A17 50 l on 50 l yellow brown 60.00

Dangerous counterfeits of No. 288B are plentiful.

On Stamp of 1909 with Overprint ΕΛΛΑΣ

289 A19 3d on 3d orange & black 15.00 15.00

On Stamps of 1909-10 with Overprint ΕΛΛΑΣ

290 A6 5 l on 1 l violet brown 20 20
a. Inverted surcharge 7.50 7.50
291 A13 5 l on 5 l green 20 20
a. Inverted surcharge 7.50
292 A23 10 l on 10 l brown red 20 20
a. Inverted surcharge 7.50
293 A15 10 l on 20 l blue green 20 20
a. Inverted surcharge 7.50
294 A16 10 l on 25 l ultra. 20 20
a. Inverted surcharge 10.00 10.00
295 A17 50 l on 50 l yel. brn. 40 40
296 A18 50 l on 1d rose carmine & brown 5.00 5.00
a. Inverted surcharge
b. Double surcharge 50.00
c. Double surcharge, one inverted
d. Imperf., pair
297 A19 3d on 3d orange & black 9.00 9.00
298 A20 5d on 5d olive green & black 150.00 140.00

Dangerous counterfeits of No. 298 exist.

Same Surcharge on Postage Due Stamps of Crete.

On Stamps of 1901.

299 D1 5 l on 5 l red 35 35
a. Inverted surcharge 5.00 5.00
300 " 5 l on 10 l red 35 35
301 " 10 l on 20 l red 27.50 27.50
a. Inverted surcharge
302 " 10 l on 40 l red 35 35
303 " 50 l on 50 l red 35 35
304 " 50 l on 1d red 35 35
a. Double surcharge
305 " 50 l on 1d on 1d red 3.00 3.00
306 " 2d on 2d red 40 40

On Stamps of 1908 with Overprint ΕΛΛΑΣ

307 D1 5 l on 5 l red 1.25 1.25
308 " 5 l on 10 l red 1.25 1.25
a. "Ellas" inverted 3.00
309 " 10 l on 20 l red 30.00 30.00

On Stamps of 1910 with Overprint ΕΛΛΑΣ

310 D1 5 l on 5 l red 75 75
311 " 5 l on 10 l red 75 75
a. Inverted surcharge 7.50
312 " 10 l on 20 l red 75 75
313 " 50 l on 50 l " 1.85 1.85
314 " 50 l on 1d " 3.75 3.75
315 " 2d on 2d " 9.00 9.00

These surcharged Postage Due stamps were intended for the payment of ordinary postage.
Nos. 260 to 315 were surcharged in commemoration of the revolution of 1922.

Issues of the Republic.

Lord Byron
A33

Byron at Missolonghi—A34

1924, Apr. 16 Engraved ***Perf. 12***

316 A33 80 l dark blue 1.00 40
317 A34 2d dull violet & black 3.00 1.50

Issued to commemorate the centenary of the death of Lord Byron (1788-1824) at Missolonghi.

Tomb of Markos Botsaris
A35

Serrate Roulette 13½

1926, Apr. 24 Lithographed

318 A35 25 l lilac 1.50 25

Issued to commemorate the centenary of the defense of Missolonghi against the Turks.

Corinth Canal
A36

Dodecanese Costume
A37

Macedonian Costume
A38

Monastery of Simon Peter on Mt. Athos
A39

White Tower of Salonika
A40

Temple of Hephaestus
A41

The Acropolis
A42

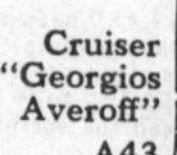

Cruiser "Georgios Averoff"
A43

Academy of Sciences, Athens
A44

Temple of Hephaestus
A45

Acropolis
A46

Perf. 12½x13, 13, 13x12½, 13½, 13½x13

1927, Apr. 1 Engraved

321 A36 5 l dark green 6 6
a. Vert. pair, imperf. horiz. 30.00
322 A37 10 l orange red 6 6
a. Horizontal pair, imperf. between 30.00
c. Dble. impression 10.00
323 A38 20 l violet 10 6
324 A39 25 l slate blue 15 6
a. Imperf., pair 50.00 50.00
b. Vertical pair, imperf. between 50.00

325 A40 40 l slate blue 40 6
326 A36 50 l violet 2.00 6
327 " 80 l dark blue & black 90 5
a. Imperf., pair 65.00
328 A41 1d dark blue & bistre brown (I) 3.50 7
a. Imperf., pair 175.00
b. Center inverted 5000.00
c. Double impression of center
d. Double impression of frame 75.00
329 A42 2d dark green & black 7.00 8
a. Imperf., pair 100.00
330 A43 3d dp. vio. & blk. 8.00 10
a. Double impression of center 125.00
b. Center inverted 1500.00
331 A44 5d yellow & black 13.50 55
a. Imperf., pair 225.00
b. Center inverted 1000.00
c. 5d yellow & green 100.00 30.00
332 A45 10d brown carmine & black 55.00 1.00
333 A44 15d brt. yel. green & black 65.00 8.00
334 A46 25d green & black 72.50 8.00
a. Double impression 100.00
Nos. 321-334 (14) 228.17 18.21

See notes preceding No. 364.

This series, as prepared, included a 1 lepton dark brown, type A37, but that value was never issued and most copies were burned. Price $25.

Gen. Charles N. Fabvier and Acropolis—A47

1927, Aug. 1 *Perf. 12*

335 A47 1d red 2.00 40
336 " 3d dark blue 9.00 80
337 " 6d green 25.00 16.50

Issued to commemorate the centenary of the liberation of Athens from the Turks in 1826.

Bay of Navarino and Pylos A48

Battle of Navarino A49

"Edward" omitted. "Edward" added.
Sir Edward Codrington
A50 A51

Admiral de Rigny A52 Admiral van der Heyden A53

Perf. 13½x12½, 12½x13½, 13x12½, 12½x13.

1927-28 **Lithographed.**

338 A48 1.50d gray green 4.50 30
a. Imperf., pair 100.00
b. Horizontal pair, imperf. between 100.00
c. Imperf. vertically (pair) 100.00
339 A49 4d dark gray blue ('28) 25.00 90
340 A50 5d dark brown & gray 15.00 3.00
a. 5d black brown & black ('28) 15.00 3.00
341 A51 5d dark brown & black ('28) 60.00 22.50
342 A52 5d violet blue & black ('28) 40.00 5.25
343 A53 5d lake & black ('28) 22.50 3.75
Nos. 338-343 (6) 167.00 35.70

Centenary of the naval battle of Navarino.

Independence Centenary Issue.

Admiral Lascarina Bouboulina A54 Athanasios Diakos A55

Map of Greece in 1830 and 1930 A56 Sortie from Missolonghi A58

Patriots Declaring Independence A57

Portraits: 10 l, Constantine Rhigas Ferreos. 20 l, Gregorios V. 40 l, Prince Alexandros Ypsilantis. No. 345, Bouboulina. No. 355, Diakos. No. 346, Theodoros Kolokotronis. No.356, Konstantinos Kanaris. No.347, Georgios Karaiskakis. No. 357, Markos Botsaris. 2d, Andreas Miaoulis. 3d, Lazaros Koundouriotis. 5d, Count John Capo d'Istria (Capodistria). 10d, Petros Mavromichalis. 15d, Dionysios Solomos. 20d, Adamantios Korais.

Various Frames

1930, Apr. 1 Engr. *Perf. 13½, 14*

Imprint of Perkins, Bacon & Co.

344 A55 10 l brown 5 5
345 A54 50 l red 10 10
346 " 1d carmine rose 25 20
347 A55 1.50d light blue 20 8
348 " 2d orange 30 18
349 " 5d purple 3.00 25
350 A54 10d gray black 12.00 4.00
351 " 15d yellow green 15.00 9.00
352 A55 20d blue black 22.50 9.00

Imprint of Bradbury, Wilkinson & Co.

Perf. 12.

353 A55 20 l black 10 8
354 " 40 l blue green 15 10
355 " 50 l bright blue 20 15
356 " 1d brown orange 30 18
357 " 1.50d dark red 25 8
358 " 3d dark brown 1.00 25
359 A56 4d dark blue 5.00 40
360 A57 25d black 22.50 7.50
361 A58 50d red brown 80.00 50.00
Nos. 344-361 (18) 162.90 81.60

Nos. 344 to 361 were issued to commemorate the centenary of Greek independence. Nos. 344-352 exist imperf.

Arcadi Monastery and Abbot Gabriel (Mt. Ida in Background)—A60

1930, Nov. 8 *Perf. 12*

363 A60 8d deep violet 27.50 1.00

Issue of 1927 Re-engraved

50 l: Design is clearer, especially "50" and the 10 letters.

1 ΔΡΑΧΜΗ 1

Type I 1927

1 ΔΡΑΧΜΗ 1

Type II 1931.

1d. Type I. Greek letters "L", "A", "D" have sharp pointed tops; numerals "1" are 1½ mm. wide at the foot, and have a straight slanting serif at top.

1d. Type II. Greek letters "L", "A", "D" have flat tops; numerals "1" are 2mm. wide at foot and the serif at top is slightly curved. Perf. 14.

There are many minor differences in the lines of the two designs.

1d. Type III. The "1" in lower left corner has no serif at left of foot. Lines of temple have been deepened, so details stand out more clearly.

2d. On 1927 stamp the Parthenon is indistinct and blurred. On 1933 stamp it is strongly outlined and clear. Between the two pillars at lower right are four blocks of marble. These blocks are clear and distinct on the 1933 stamp but run together on the 1927 issue.

3d. Design is clearer, especially vertical lines of shading in smoke stacks and reflections in the water. Two or more sides perf. 11½.

10d. Background and shading of entire stamp have been lightened. Detail of frame is clearer and more distinct.

15d. Many more lines of shading in sky and foreground. Engraving is sharp and clear, particularly in frame. Two or more sides perf. 11½.

25d. Background has been lightened and foreground reduced until base of larger upright column is removed and fallen column appears nearly submerged.

Sizes in millimeters:

50 l, 1927, 18x24¾. 1933, 18½x24½.
1d, 1927, 24¾x17¾. 1931, 24¾x17¼. 1933, 24½x18¼.
2d, 1927, 24½x17¾. 1933, 24½x18½.

Perf. 11½, 11½x12½, 12½x10, 13, 13x12½, 14.

1931-35

364 A36 50 l dark violet ('33) 8.00 3
365 A41 1d dark blue & orange brown, type II 8.00 3
366 " 1d dark blue & orange brown, type III ('33) 3.50 3
367 A42 2d dark green & black ('33) 5.00 3
368 A43 3d red violet & black ('34) 7.00 6
a. Imperf., pair
369 A45 10d brown carmine & blk. ('35) 70.00 1.00
370 A44 15d pale yel. green & black ('34) 75.00 7.00
a. Imperf., pair
371 A46 25d dark green & black ('35) 30.00 5.00
Nos. 364-371 (8) 206.50 13.18

Stamps of 1927-28 and 1927 Surcharged in Red **ΔΡ.1.50**

1932 *Perf. 12½x13½, 12½x13*

372 A52 1.50d on 5d dark blue & black 3.00 15
373 A53 1.50d on 5d lake & black 4.50 15
a. Dbl. surcharge 35.00
374 A50 2d on 5d black brown & black 5.00 15
375 A51 2d on 5d black brown & black 12.00 15

Perf. 12.

376 A47 2d on 3d dark blue 6.50 25
a. Double surcharge 25.00
377 " 4d on 6d green 8.00 1.00
Nos. 372-377 (6) 39.00 1.85

Adm. Pavlos Koundouriotis and Cruiser "Averoff" A61

Pallas Athene A62 Youth of Marathon A63

1933 *Perf. 13½x13, 13x13½*

378 A61 50d blk. & indigo 135.00 2.50
379 A62 75d black & violet brown 200.00 190.00
a. Imperf. (pair) 550.00
380 A63 100d brown & dull green 800.00 27.50

Approach to Athens Stadium—A64

Perf. 11½, 11½x10, 13½x11½

1934, Dec. 10

381 A64 8d blue 110.00 80

Perforations on No. 381 range from 10½ to 13, including compounds.

Church of Pantanassa, Mistra A65

1935, Nov. 1 *Perf. 13x12½*

382 A65 4d brown 30.00 30
a. Horizontal pair, imperf. between 150.00
b. Imperf. (pair) 150.00

Issues of the Monarchy.

Postage Due Stamp and Type of 1913 Surcharged in Red or Blue

Serrate Roulette 13½

1935, Nov. 24 Lithographed

383 D3 50 l on 40 l indigo (R) 1.50 5
a. Double surcharge 25.00
384 " 3d on 3d verm. (Bl) 4.00 1.00

Surcharged on No. J 82.

Perf. 13.

385 D3 3d on 3d rose red (Bl) 20.00 1.00

Nos. 380, 379 Surcharged in Red or Blue

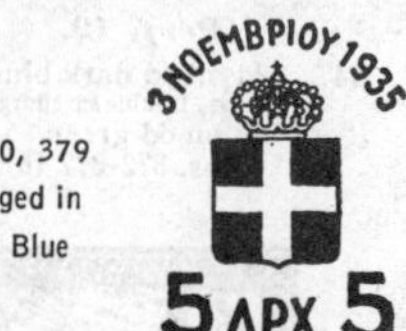

Perf. 13x13½

386 A63 5d on 100d brown & dull green (R) 7.00 60
387 A62 15d on 75d black & violet brn. (Bl) 40.00 6.00

King Constantine A66

Wmk. 252

Center Engr., Frame Litho.
Wmkd. Crowns. (252)

1936, Nov. 18 *Perf. 12x13½*

389 A66 3d black & brown 3.00 40
a. Pair with printer's name in Greek 20.00
b. Pair with printer's name in English 20.00
390 " 8d black & blue 4.00 3.00
a. Pair with printer's name in Greek 20.00
b. Pair with printer's name in English 20.00

Issued in commemoration of the re-burial of the remains of King Constantine and Queen Sophia.

Two printings exist, the first containing varieties "a" and "b" with gray border; second with black border.

King George II A67

Pallas Athene A68

Perf. 12½x12

1937, Jan. 24 Engraved

391 A67 1d green 25 5
392 " 3d red brown 30 5
393 " 8d deep blue 1.50 15
394 " 100d carmine lake 25.00 20.00

1937, Apr. 17 *Perf. 11½* **Unwmkd.**

395 A68 3d yellow brown 80 12

Centenary of the University of Athens.

Contest with Bull A69

Lady of Tiryns A70

Zeus of Dodona A71

Coin of Amphictyonic League A72

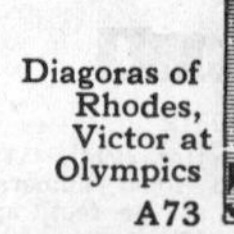

Diagoras of Rhodes, Victor at Olympics A73

Venus of Melos A74

Allegorical Figure of Glory A81

Battle of Salamis A75

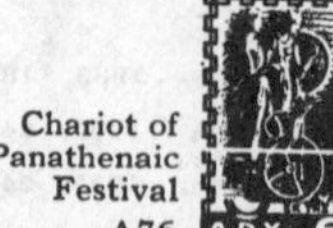

Chariot of Panathenaic Festival A76

Alexander the Great at Battle of Issos A77

St. Paul Preaching to Athenians A78

St. Demetrius' Church at Salonika A79

Leo III Victory over Arabs A80

Perf. 13½x12, 12x13½.

1937, Nov. 1 Litho. **Wmk. 252**

396 A69 5 l brown red & blue 7 7
a. Double impression of frame 75.00
397 A70 10 l blue & brown red 7 7
a. Double impression of frame 18.00
398 A71 20 l black & green 7 7
399 A72 40 l green & black 7 7
a. Green impression doubled 22.50
400 A73 50 l brown & black 7 7
401 A74 80 l indigo & yellow brown 7 7

Engraved.

402 A75 2d ultramarine 6 6
403 A76 5d red 7 7
a. Printer's name omitted 5.00 5.00
404 A77 6d olive brown 80 40
405 A78 7d dark brown 1.00 35
406 A79 10d red brown 7 7
407 A80 15d green 15 15
408 A81 25d dark blue 15 15
Nos. 396-408 (13) 2.72 1.67

See also Nos. 413, 459-466.

Cerigo, Paxos, Lefkas

Greek stamps with Italian overprints for the islands of Cerigo (Kithyra), Paxos and Lefkas (Santa Maura) are fraudulent.

Royal Wedding Issue.

Princess Frederika-Louise and Crown Prince Paul—A82

1938 *Perf. 13½x12* **Wmk. 252**

409 A82 1d green 15 20
410 " 3d orange brown 2.00 40
411 " 8d dark blue 4.00 3.00

Arms of Greece, Romania, Jugoslavia and Turkey A83

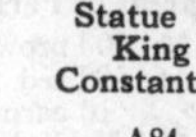

Statue of King Constantine A84

Perf. 12x12½

1938, Feb. 8 Litho. **Unwmkd.**

412 A83 6d blue 16.00 5.50

Issued in commemoration of the "Balkan Entente."

Tiryns Lady Type of 1937.
Corrected Inscription.

1938 *Perf. 12x13½.* **Wmk. 252**

413 A70 10 l blue & brown red 50 40

The first four letters of the third word of the inscription read "TIPY" instead of "TYPI".

Perf. 12x13½

1938, Oct. 8 Engr. **Unwmkd.**

414 A84 1.50d green 65 20
415 " 30d orange brown 6.00 4.50

Coats of Arms of Ionian Islands A85

Fort at Corfu A86

King George I of Greece and Queen Victoria of England—A87

Perf. 12½x12, 13½x12.

1939, May 21 Engr. **Unwmkd.**

416 A85 1d dark blue 75 20
417 A86 4d green 8.00 1.50
418 A87 20d yellow orange 50.00 37.50
419 " 20d dull blue 50.00 37.50
420 " 20d carmine lake 50.00 37.50
Nos. 416-420 (5) 158.75 114.20

Issued to commemorate the 75th anniversary of the union of the Ionian Islands with Greece.

Pan-Balkan Games Issue.

Runner with Shield A88

Javelin Thrower A89

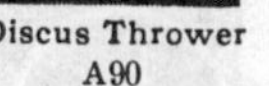

Discus Thrower A90

Jumper A91

Perf. 12x13½

1939, Oct. 1 Litho. **Unwmkd.**

421 A88 50 l slate grn. & grn. 40 25
422 A89 3d henna brown & dull rose 5.00 50
423 A90 6d copper brown & dull orange 6.00 6.00
424 A91 8d ultra. & gray 7.00 6.00

The 10th Pan-Balkan Games.

Arms of Greece, Romania, Turkey and Jugoslavia
A92

Perf. 13x12½

1940, May 27 **Wmk. 252**

No.	Type	Description	Unused	Used
425	A92	6d blue	7.50	50
426	"	8d blue gray	8.50	1.00

Issued in commemoration of the Balkan Entente.

Emblem of Youth Organization
A93

Boy Member
A94

Designs: 3d, 100d, Emblem of Greek Youth Organization. 10d, Girl member. 15d, Javelin Thrower. 20d, Column of members. 25d, Flag bearers and buglers. 30d, Three youths. 50d, Line formation. 75d, Coat of arms.

Perf. 12½, 13½x12½.

1940, Aug. 3 **Litho.** **Wmk. 252**

No.	Type	Description	Unused	Used
427	A93	3d silver, deep ultra. & red	1.65	1.65
428	A94	5d dark blue & black	12.00	11.00
429	"	10d red orange & black	15.00	13.50
430	"	15d dark green & black	100.00	80.00
431	"	20d lake & black	32.50	30.00
432	"	25d dark blue & black	40.00	35.00
433	"	30d rose violet & black	42.50	35.00
434	"	50d lake & black	42.50	35.00
435	"	75d dark blue, brn. & gold	50.00	45.00
436	A93	100d silver, deep ultra. & red	62.50	50.00
		Nos. 427-436 (10)	398.65	336.15

Issued in commemoration of the 4th anniversary of the founding of the Greek Youth Organization. The stamps were good for postal duty on August 3-4-5, 1940, only. They remained on sale until February 3, 1941.

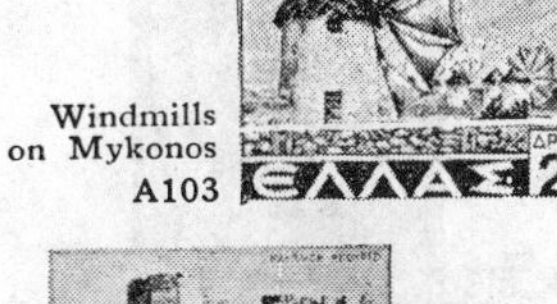

Windmills on Mykonos
A103

Bourtzi Fort
A104

Aspropotamos River
A105

Candia Harbor, Crete
A106

Houses at Hydra
A107

Meteora Monasteries
A108

Edessa
A109

Pantokratoros Monastery and Port
A110

Bridge at Konitsa
A111

Ekatontapiliani Church, Paros
A112

Ponticonissi, Corfu (Mouse Island)—A113

Perf. 12½, 13½x12½.

1942-44 **Lithographed** **Wmk. 252**

No.	Type	Description	Unused	Used
437	A103	2d red brown	4	4
438	A104	5d lt. bl. green	3	3
439	A105	10d light blue	3	3
		a. Imperf., pair	70.00	
440	A106	15d red violet	10	10
		a. Imperf., pair	70.00	
441	A107	25d orange red	3	3
		a. Imperf., pair	70.00	
442	A108	50d sapphire	3	3
		a. Imperf., pair	50.00	
443	A109	75d deep rose	4	4
444	A110	100d black	3	3
445	"	200d ultramarine	4	4
		a. Imprint omitted	2.00	2.00
446	A111	500d dk. olive ('44)	3	3
		a. Imperf., pair	70.00	
447	A112	1,000d org. brn. ('44)	3	3
		a. Imperf., pair	70.00	
448	A113	2,000d deep blue ('44)	3	3
		a. Imperf., pair	70.00	
449	A111	5,000d rose red ('44)	8	8
		a. Imperf., pair	70.00	
450	A112	15,000d rose lilac ('44)	20	20
		a. Imperf., pair	70.00	
451	A113	25,000d green ('44)	5	5
		a. Imperf., pair	70.00	
452	A105	500,000d blue ('44)	50	50
		a. Imperf., pair	90.00	
453	A103	2,000,000d turquoise grn. ('44)	50	50
454	A104	5,000,000d rose brown ('44)	50	50
		a. Imperf., pair		
		Nos. 437-454 (18)	2.29	2.29

Double impressions exist of 10d, 25d, 50d, 100d, 200d, 1,000d and 2,000d. Price, each $30.

Nos. 400 402, 403 and 404 Surcharged in Blue Black **ΔΡΑΧΜΑΙ ΝΕΑΙ**

1944-45 *Perf. 13½x12*

No.	Type	Description	Unused	Used
455	A73	50 l brown & black	10	10
		a. Double surcharge	4.00	4.00
456	A75	2d ultramarine	10	10
457	A76	5d red	25	25
		a. Invtd. surch.	10.00	
		b. Double surcharge	10.00	
		c. Printer's name omitted (on 403a)	6.00	6.00
		d. Pair, one without surcharge	8.00	
458	A77	6d olive brown ('45)	80	70

Glory Type of 1937.

Perf. 12½x13½

1945 **Lithographed** **Wmk. 252**

No.	Type	Description	Unused	Used
459	A81	1d dull rose violet	5	5
460	"	3d rose brown	5	5
		a. Imperf., pair	50.00	
461	A81	5d ultramarine	5	5
		a. Imperf., pair	50.00	
462	A81	10d dull brown	6	5
463	"	20d dull violet	15	10
464	"	50d olive black	15	10
465	"	100d pale blue	14.00	12.00
		a. Imperf., pair	175.00	
466	A81	200d slate	2.25	85
		Nos. 459-466 (8)	16.76	13.25

1945, Oct. 28 **Unwmkd.**

No.	Type	Description	Unused	Used
467	A114	20d orange brown	20	20
468	"	40d blue	30	30
		a. Dbl. impression	20.00	

Vote of Oct. 28, 1940, refusing Italy's ultimatum. "OXI" means "No."
Exist imperf.

1945, Dec. 21 **Unwmkd.**

No.	Type	Description	Unused	Used
469	A115	30d blk. & red brn.	20	20
		a. Center double	65.00	65.00
		c. Inverted frame	65.00	
		d. Imperf., pair	70.00	
470	A115	60d black & slate gray	40	40
		a. Center double	60.00	60.00
		b. 60d black & blue gray	10.00	8.00
		c. Imperf., pair	100.00	
		d. Inverted frame	60.00	
471	A115	200d blk. & vio. brn.	50	50
		a. Center double	70.00	70.00
		b. Imperf., pair	125.00	

Issued to mourn the death of Pres. Franklin D. Roosevelt.

Nos. C61, C63, 447-451, 453, 398, 401, 454 and 452 Surcharged in Black or Carmine **ΔΡΧ. 10**

Perf. 12½, 12x13½, 13½x12½

1946 **Wmk. 252**

No.	Type	Description	Unused	Used
472	AP35	10d on 10d rose red	5	5
		a. Inverted surcharge	22.50	22.50
		b. Double surcharge	12.50	
472C	A113	10d on 2,000d deep blue (C)	5	5
473	AP35	20d on 50d violet blue (C)	10	10
		a. Inverted surcharge	20.00	
473B	A112	20d on 1,000d orange brown	20	10
474	A113	50d on 25,000d green (C)	20	10
475	A103	100d on 2,000,000d turquoise green (C)	25	10
476	A71	130d on 20 l black & green (C)	40	15
		b. Double surcharge	20.00	
476A	"	250d on 20 l black & green (C)	1.00	10
		c. Dbl. surch.	25.00	
477	A74	300d on 80 l indigo & yel. brn.	1.00	20
		a. Purple brown surcharge	7.00	4.00
		b. Double surcharge	30.00	
478	A104	500d on 5,000,000d rose brown	4.00	10
		a. Inverted surcharge	35.00	
		b. Dbl. surch.	25.00	
479	A105	1000d on 500,000d blue (C)	11.00	20
		a. Double surcharge	30.00	
480	A111	2000d on 5000d rose red	35.00	1.75
481	A112	5000d on 15,000d rose lilac	90.00	14.00
		a. Blue surch.	90.00	90.00
		Nos. 472-481 (13)	143.25	17.00

The surcharge exists in various shades on most denominations. A 150d on 20 l is fraudulent.

Doric Column and Greek Flag
A114

Franklin D. Roosevelt
A115

Eleutherios K. Venizelos
A116

Panaghiotis Tsaldaris
A117

Perf. 12x13½

1946, Mar. 25 Litho. Wmk. 252

482 A116 130d brown olive & buff 20 20
 a. Double impression of brown olive 15.00
483 " 300d red brown & pale brown 40 35
 a. Double impression of red brown 15.00

Issued to commemorate the 10th anniversary of the death of Eleutherios K. Venizelos (1864–1936), statesman.

Nos. 391 to 394 Surcharged in Blue Black

1-9-1946

1946, Sept. 28 *Perf. 12½x12*

484 A67 50d on 1d green 20 4
485 " 250d on 3d red brown 50 5
 a. Date omitted 25.00
 b. Invtd. surch. 20.00 20.00
486 " 600d on 8d deep blue 2.50 75
 a. Additional surcharge on back, inverted 25.00
 b. Carmine surcharge 85.00
487 " 3000d on 100d carmine lake 12.00 70

Issued to commemorate the plebiscite of September 1, 1946, which resulted in the return of King George II to Greece.

Perf. 12½x13½

1946, Nov. 15 Litho. Unwmkd.

488 A117 250d red brown & buff 2.00 25
489 " 600d deep blue & pale blue 5.00 4.00
 a. Double impression 75.00

Naval Convoy—A118

Torpedoing of Cruiser Helle A119

Campaign of Greek Troops in Italy A122

Women Carrying Ammunition in Pindus Mountains
A120

Troops in Albania—A121

Allegory of Flight
A123

Greek Torpedo Boat Towing Captive Submarine
A124

Design: 5000d, Memorial Tomb, El Alamein.

Engraved.

1946–47 *Perf. 13* **Unwmkd.**

490 A118 50d dark blue green 22 10
491 A119 100d deep ultramarine 22 10
492 A120 250d yellow green ('46) 30 8
493 A121 500d yellow brown 1.50 12
494 A122 600d dark brown 3.00 80
495 A123 1000d dull lilac 4.00 20
496 A124 2000d deep ultra. 15.00 8.00
497 A119 5000d dark carmine 30.00 75
 a. Imperf., pair 250.00
 Nos. 490-497 (8) 54.24 10.15

King George II Memorial Issue.

Nos. 391 to 393 Surcharged in Black

Perf. 12½x12

1947, Apr. 15 Wmk. 252

498 A67 50d on 1d green 50 15
 a. Double surcharge 8.00
499 " 250d on 3d red brown 1.00 15
 a. Double surcharge 8.00
 b. Pair, one without surcharge 12.50
500 " 600d on 8d deep blue 3.00 2.00
 a. Double surcharge 8.00

Nos. 446, 438, 442, 439 and 443 Surcharged in Carmine or Black

1947 *Perf. 12½*

501 A111 20d on 500d dark olive 8 5
 a. Dble. surcharge 12.00
502 A104 30d on 5d light blue green 8 5
503 A108 50d on 50d sapphire 10 5
504 A105 100d on 10d light blue 50 5
505 A109 450d on 75d deep rose (Bk) 2.00 40
 Nos. 501-505 (5) 2.76 60

Castellorizo Castle
A126

Dodecanese Vase
A127

Dodecanese Costume
A128

Monastery where St. John Preached, Patmos
A129

Emanuel Xanthos
A130

Sailing Vessel of 1824
A131

Revolutionary Stamp of 1912
A132

Statue of Hippocrates
A133

Colossus of Rhodes—A134

Perf. 12½x13½, 13½x12½.

1947–48 Lithographed Wmk. 252

506 A126 20d ultramarine 5 5
507 A127 30d black brown & buff 5 5
508 A128 50d chalky blue 20 15
509 A129 100d black green & pale green 20 5
510 A130 250d gray green & pale green 50 15
511 A132 450d dp. blue ('48) 2.00 10
512 A131 450d deep blue & pale bl. ('48) 2.00 10
 a. Imperf., pair 100.00
513 A132 500d red 80 10
514 A133 600d violet brown & pale pink 2.00 20
515 A134 1000d brn. & cream 3.00 10
 a. Imperf., pair 100.00
 Nos. 506-515 (10) 10.80 1.05

Issued to commemorate the return of the Dodecanese to Greece. See also Nos. 520–522, 525–534.

Battle of Crete
A135

1948, Sept. 15 Engr. *Perf. 13x13½*

516 A135 1000d dark green 8.50 20

Battle of Crete, 7th anniversary.

Abduction of Children
A136

Concentration Camp
A137

Protective Mother
A138

Perf. 13½x12½, 12½x13½.

1949, Feb. 1 Lithographed Wmk. 252

517 A136 450d dk. & lt. vio. 2.50 2.00
518 A137 1000d dk. & lt. brn. 5.50 40
519 A138 1800d dark red & cream 7.50 60

Types of 1947.

1950, Apr. 5 *Perf. 12½x13½*

520 A127 2000d orange brown & salmon 20.00 20
 a. Imperf., pair 65.00
521 A133 5000d rose violet 40.00 15
522 A134 10,000d ultramarine 22.50 30

Map of Crete and Flags
A139

Perf. 13½x13

1950, Apr. 28 Engr. Wmk. 252

523 A139 1000d deep blue 10.00 50
 a. Imperf., pr. 375.00

Battle of Crete, 9th anniversary.

Youth of Marathon
A140

Engraved and Lithographed.

1950, May 21 *Perf. 13x13½*

No.	Type	Description	Unused	Used
524	A140	1000d cream & deep green	1.35	35
		a. Without dates	90.00	
		b. "1949" only	80.00	
		c. Dates inverted	80.00	
		d. Dates doubled	80.00	

Issued to commemorate the 75th anniversary (in 1949) of the formation of the Universal Postal Union.

Types of 1947-48.

Perf. 12½x13½, 13½x12½.

1950 Lithographed Wmk. 252

No.	Type	Description	Unused	Used
525	A130	200dr orange	65	3
526	A128	300dr orange	65	3
527	A129	400dr blue	1.25	4
528	A133	700dr lilac rose	3.75	6
529	"	700dr blue green	5.00	8
		a. Imperf., pr.	90.00	
530	A131	800dr purple & pale green	2.50	10
531	A132	1300dr carmine	18.50	18
532	A126	1500dr brn. org.	25.00	18
533	A127	1600dr ultramarine & bl. gray	6.25	15
534	A134	2600dr emerald & pale grn.	14.00	50
		Nos. 525-534 (10)	77.55	1.35

Altar and Sword A141

St. Paul A142

St. Paul by El Greco A143

Preaching to Athenians A144

Perf. 13½x12, 12x13½.

1951, June 15 Engr. Unwmkd.

No.	Type	Description	Unused	Used
535	A141	700d red violet	1.50	40
536	A142	1600d light blue	10.00	2.00
537	A143	2600d dark olive bistre	20.00	5.00
538	A144	10,000d red brn.	160.00	75.00

Issued to commemorate the 1900th anniversary of St. Paul's visit to Athens.

Industrialization A145

Designs: 800d, Fishing. 1300d, Rebuilding. 1600d, Farming. 2600d, Home Industries. 5000d, Electrification and map of Greece.

Perf. 12½x13½

1951, Sept. 20 Wmk. 252

Inscribed: ERP Monogram in Circle.

No.	Type	Description	Unused	Used
539	A145	700d red orange	7.50	10
540	"	800d aquamarine	12.50	1.00
541	"	1300d greenish blue	21.00	20
542	"	1600d olive green	42.50	50
543	"	2600d violet gray	125.00	4.00
544	"	5000d deep plum	135.00	1.00
		Nos. 539-544 (6)	343.50	6.80

Issued to publicize Greek recovery under the Marshall Plan.

King Paul I A146

Allegorical Figure and Medal A147

1952, Dec. 14 Engr. *Perf. 12½x12*

No.	Type	Description	Unused	Used
545	A146	200d deep green	75	15
546	"	1000d red	2.25	15
547	A147	1400d blue	13.50	1.00
548	A146	10,000d dk. red lilac	85.00	20.00

50th birthday of King Paul I.

Oranges A148

Tobacco A149

National Products: 1000d, Olive oil, Pallas Athene. 1300d, Wine. 2000d, Figs. 2600d, Grapes and bread. 5000d, Bacchus holding grapes.

Perf. 13½x13, 13x13½

1953, July 1

No.	Type	Description	Unused	Used
549	A148	500d deep carmine & orange	1.00	15
550	A149	700d dark brown & orange yel.	1.80	8
551	A148	1000d blue & light olive green	2.00	12
		a. Imperf., pair	65.00	
552	A149	1300d deep plum & org. brn.	11.00	15
553	"	2000d dark brown & lt. green	15.00	25
554	"	2600d violet & olive bistre	27.50	1.50
555	"	5000d dark brown & yel. green	27.50	40
		Nos. 549-555 (7)	85.80	2.65

Pericles A150

Homer A151

Hunting Wild Boar A152

Shepherd Carrying Calf A152a

Designs: 200d, Mycenaean oxhead vase. 500d, Zeus of Istiaea. 600d, Head of a youth. 1000d, Alexander the Great. 1200d, Charioteer of Delphi. 2000d, Vase of Dipylon. 4000d, Voyage of Dionysus. 20,000d, Pitcher bearers.

Perf. 13½x13, 12½x12, 13x13½.

1954, Jan. 15 Lithographed

No.	Type	Description	Unused	Used
556	A150	100d red brown	25	15
557	"	200d black	35	5
558	A151	300d blue violet	1.75	5
559	"	500d green	1.75	4
560	"	600d rose pink	2.50	5
561	"	1000d dull blue & black	2.50	10
562	A150	1200d olive green	2.50	10
563	"	2000d red brown	7.00	15
564	A152	2400d greenish bl.	15.00	35
		a. Double impression	125.00	
565	A152a	2500d dk. bl. grn.	15.00	25
566	A151	4000d dk. car.	15.00	30
567	A150	20,000d rose lilac	150.00	3.00
		Nos. 556-567 (12)	213.60	4.59

See Nos. 574-581, 632-638, and 689.

British Parliamentary Debate and Ink Blot A153

1954, Sept. *Perf. 12½*

Center in Black

No.	Type	Description	Unused	Used
568	A153	1.20d cream	5.00	15
569	"	2d orange	16.50	6.00
570	"	2d light blue	16.50	6.00
571	"	2.40d lilac	16.50	1.25
572	"	2.50d pink	16.50	1.25
573	"	4d citron	28.50	2.50
		Nos. 568-573 (6)	99.50	17.15

Document in English on Nos. 569, 572, 573; in French on Nos. 570, 571 and in Greek on No. 568.

Issued to promote the proposed union between Cyprus and Greece.

Types of 1954

Perf. 13½x13, 12½x12, 13x13½

1955 Lithographed. Wmk. 252

Designs: 20 l, Mycenaean oxhead vase. 30 l, Pericles. 50 l, Zeus of Istiaea. 1d, Head of a youth. 2d, Alexander the Great. 3d, Hunting wild boar. 3.50d, Homer. 4d, Voyage of Dionysus.

No.	Type	Description	Unused	Used
574	A150	20 l dark green	90	15
575	"	30 l yellow brown	1.20	5
576	A151	50 l carmine lake	2.40	5
577	"	1d blue green	3.00	3
578	"	2d brn. & black	9.00	3
579	A152	3d red orange	11.00	10
580	A151	3.50d rose crimson	20.00	30
581	"	4d violet blue	35.00	20
		Nos. 574-581 (8)	82.50	91

Samos Coin Picturing Pythagoras A154

Pythagorean Theorem A155

Samos Mapped in Antique Style A156

1955, Aug. 20 *Perf. 12x13½*

No.	Type	Description	Unused	Used
582	A154	2d green	8.00	50
583	A155	3.50d intense black	22.50	2.00
584	A154	5d plum	50.00	2.00
585	A156	6d blue	22.50	22.50

Issued to commemorate the 2500th anniversary of the founding of the first School of Philosophy by Pythagoras on Samos.

Globe and Rotary Emblem A157

Perf. 12x13½

1956, May 15 Litho. Wmk. 252

No.	Type	Description	Unused	Used
586	A157	2d ultramarine	10.00	1.00

Issued to commemorate the 50th anniversary of Rotary International (in 1955).

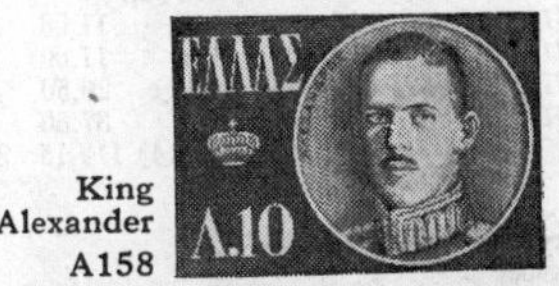

King Alexander A158

Crown Prince Constantine A159

Portraits: 30 l, George I. 50 l, Queen Olga. 70 l, King Otto. 1d, Queen Amalia. 1.50d, King Constantine. 2d, 7.50d, King Paul. 3d, George II. 3.50d, Queen Sophia. 4d, Queen Frederica. 5d, King Paul and Queen Frederica. 10d, King, Queen and Crown Prince.

Perf. 13½x12, 12x13½

1956, May 21 Engraved

No.	Type	Description	Unused	Used
587	A158	10 l blue violet	65	10
588	A159	20 l dull purple	65	5
589	"	30 l sepia	65	5
590	"	50 l red brown	65	5
591	"	70 l light ultra.	1.35	7
592	"	1d greenish blue	1.35	4
593	"	1.50d gray blue	2.00	10
594	"	2d black	2.00	3
595	"	3d brown	3.25	15
596	"	3.50d copper brown	8.00	20
597	"	4d gray green	8.00	15
598	A158	5d rose carmine	8.00	11
599	A159	7.50d ultramarine	21.50	1.00
600	A158	10d dark blue	30.00	85
		Nos. 587-600 (14)	88.05	2.95

See also Nos. 604-617.

Dionysios Solomos and Nicolaos Mantzaros—A160

Dionysios Solomos
A161

Design: 5d, View on Zante and bust of Solomos.

Perf. 13½x12, 12x13½

1957, Mar. 26 Litho. Wmk. 252

601 A160 2d red brown & ochre 7.00 10
602 A161 3.50d blue & gray 17.50 11.00
603 A160 5d dark green & olive bistre 20.00 16.00

Issued to commemorate the centenary of the death of Dionysios Solomos, composer of the Greek national anthem.

Types of 1956. Designs as Before.

Engraved.

1957 *Perf. 13½x12* Wmk. 252

604 A158 10 l rose lake 75 10
605 A159 20 l orange 75 5
606 " 30 l gray black 75 5
607 " 50 l greenish black 75 3
608 " 70 l rose lilac 1.90 80
609 " 1d rose red 1.60 3
610 " 1.50d lt. olive green 2.40 8
611 " 2d carmine 2.40 3
612 " 3d dark blue 3.85 15
613 " 3.50d black violet 11.00 25
a. Imperf., pair
614 " 4d red brown 11.00 15
615 A158 5d gray blue 11.00 13
616 A159 7.50d yel. orange 26.50 90
617 A158 10d green 37.50 40
Nos. 604-617 (14) 112.15 3.15

Oil Tanker
A162

Ships: 1d, Ocean liner. 1.50d, Sailing ship, 1820. 2d, Byzantine vessel. 3.50d, Ship from 6th century B. C. 5d, "Argo."

Perf. 13½x12

1958, Jan. 30 Litho. Wmk. 252

618 A162 50 l multicolored 13 10
619 " 1d ultramarine, black & bistre 33 15
620 " 1.50d blk. & car. 40 30
a. Dbl. impression of black 70.00
621 " 2d violet blue, black & red brown 65 15
622 " 3.50d light blue, black & red 2.00 75
a. Double impression of black 150.00 75.00
623 " 5d blue green, black & carmine 16.50 16.00
Nos. 618-623 (6) 20.01 17.45

Issued to honor the Greek merchant marine.

Narcissus
A163

Designs: 30 l, Daphne (laurel) and Apollo. 50 l, Adonis (hibiscus) and Aphrodite. 70 l, Pitys (pine) and Pan. 1d, Crocus. 2d, Iris. 3.50d, Tulips. 5d, Cyclamen.

1958, Sept. 15 *Perf. 13* Wmk. 252

Size: 22½x38mm.

624 A163 20 l multicolored 10 10
625 " 30 l " 15 15
626 " 50 l " 15 15
627 " 70 l " 20 15

Perf. 12½x12

Size: 21½x26mm.

628 A163 1d multicolored 30 10

Perf. 12x13½

Size: 22x32mm.

629 A163 2d multicolored 30 10
630 " 3.50d " 2.00 2.00
a. Imperf., pair 250.00
631 " 5d multicolored 5.00 5.00
Nos. 624-631 (8) 8.20 7.75

Issued to commemorate the International Congress for the Protection of Nature, held in Athens.

Types of 1954.

Designs: 10 l, Pericles. 20 l, Mycenaean oxhead vase. 50 l, Zeus of Istiaea. 70 l, Charioteer of Delphi. 1d, Head of a youth. 1.50d, Pitcher bearers. 2.50d, Alexander the Great.

Two types of 2.50d:
I. Nine dots in upper half of right border.
II. Ten dots.

Perf. 13½x13, 12½x12

1959 Lithographed. Wmk. 252

632 A150 10 l emerald 60 15
633 " 20 l magenta 40 10
634 A151 50 l lt. blue green 2.00 5
635 A150 70 l red orange 40 10
636 A151 1d reddish brown 6.00 5
637 A150 1.50d bright blue 14.00 6
638 A151 2.50d magenta & black (II) 25.00 3
a. Type I 37.50 50
Nos. 632-638 (7) 48.40 54

Zeus-Eagle Coin
A164

Helios-Rose Coin
A165

Ancient Greek Coins: 20 l, Athena & Owl. 50 l, Nymph Arethusa & Chariot. 70 l, Hercules & Zeus. 1.50d, Griffin & Square. 2.50d, Apollo & Lyre. 4.50d, Apollo & Labyrinth. 6d, Aphrodite & Apollo. 8.50d, Ram's Head & Incuse Squares.

1959, Mar. 24 *Perf. 14* Wmk. 252

Coins in Various Shades of Gray

639 A164 10 l red brn. & blk. 40 20
640 " 20 l deep blue & black 40 10
641 " 50 l plum & black 1.00 10
642 " 70 l ultra. & black 1.00 10
643 A165 1d dark carmine rose & black 2.00 10
644 A164 1.50d ochre & black 2.00 10
645 " 2.50d deep magenta & black 3.50 10
646 A165 4.50d Prussian green & black 6.00 50
647 " 6d olive green & black 9.00 40
648 " 8.50d deep carmine & black 7.00 2.00
Nos. 639-648 (10) 32.30 3.70

See also Nos. 750-758.

Audience, Vase 580 B. C.
A166

Theater, Delphi
A167

Designs: 50 l, Clay tragedy mask, 3rd century B. C. 1d, Flute, drum and lyre. 2.50d, Clay statue of an actor, 3rd century B. C. 4.50d, Andromeda, vase, 4th century B. C. 6d, Actors, bowl 410 B. C.

1959, June 20 Litho. Wmk. 252

Perf. 13x13½, 13½x13

649 A166 20 l black, terra cotta & gray 15 10
650 " 50 l dark red brown & olive bistre 35 15
651 " 1d green, brown & ochre 35 20
652 " 2.50d brown & blue 55 15
653 A167 3.50d red brown, green & sepia 10.00 10.00
654 " 4.50d black & terra cotta 2.50 1.00
655 A166 6d black, terra cotta & gray 2.50 1.00
Nos. 649-655 (7) 16.40 12.60

Ancient Greek theater.

"Victory" and Soldiers
A168

Perf. 13x13½

1959, Aug. 29 Wmk. 252

656 A168 2.50d red brown, ultra. & blk. 4.00 50

10th anniversary of civil war.

Aesculapius
A169

The Good Samaritan
A170

Designs: 20 l, Plane tree of Hippocrates. 70 l, St. Basil. 2.50d, Achilles and Patroclus. 3d, Globe and Red Cross over people receiving help. 4.50d, Henri Dunant.

Perf. 13½x12, 12x13½.

1959, Sept. 21 Lithographed

657 A170 20 l multicolored 10 10
658 A169 50 l " 20 15
659 " 70 l " 30 30
660 " 2.50d " 40 5
661 " 3d " 12.00 12.00
662 A169 4.50d multicolored 1.00 45
663 A170 6d " 1.25 35
Nos. 657-663 (7) 15.25 13.40

Issued to commemorate the centenary of the Red Cross idea. Nos. 658-660, 662 measure 24½x32mm., No. 661 measures 32x47mm.

Imre Nagy
A171

Costis Palamas
A172

Perf. 13x13½

1959, Dec. 8 Wmk. 252

664 A171 4.50d orange brown & dk. brown 2.00 2.00
665 " 6d bright blue, blue & black 2.00 2.00

Issued to commemorate the third anniversary of the crushing of the 1956 Hungarian Revolution, and to honor Premier Imre Nagy, its leader.

1960, Jan. 25 *Perf. 12x13½*

666 A172 2.50d multicolored 5.00 35

Issued to commemorate the centenary of the birth of Costis Palamas (1859-1943), poet.

Ship Battling Storm
A173

Design: 4.50d, Ship in calm sea and rainbow.

Perf. 13½x13

1960, Apr. 7 Wmk. 252

667 A173 2.50d multicolored 50 20
668 " 4.50d " 1.75 1.75

Issued to publicize World Refugee Year, July 1, 1959–June 30, 1960.

Boy Scout on Horseback, St. George and Dragon
A174

Scouts Planting Tree
A175

Designs: 30 l, Scout taking oath and boy of ancient Athens. 40 l, Scouts helping in disaster. 70 l, Scouts reading map and tent. 1d, Boy Scout, Sea Scout and Air Scout. 2.50d, Crown Prince Constantine. 6d, Scout flag of Greece and Military Merit medal.

Perf. 13x13½, 13½x13

1960, Apr. 23 Lithographed

669 A174 20 l multicolored 15 15
670 " 30 l " 20 20
671 " 40 l " 20 20

672 A175 50 l multicolored 35 35
673 " 70 l " 40 40
674 " 1d " 40 20
675 A174 2.50d " 85 30
676 A175 6d " 6.50 6.50
Nos. 669-676 (8) 9.05 8.30

Issued to commemorate the 50th anniversary of the Greek Boy Scout Organization.

Greek Holding Sacred Disk Proclaiming Armistice During Games
A176

Lighting Olympic Flame
A177

Designs: 70 l, Youth taking oath. 80 l, Boy cutting olive branches for Olympic prizes. 1d, Judges entering stadium. 1.50d, Long jump. 2.50d, Discus thrower. 4.50d, Sprinters. 5d, Javelin thrower. 6d, Crowning the victors. 12.50d, Victor in chariot entering home town.

Perf. 13x13½, 13½x13

1960, Aug. 12 Wmk. 252

677 A176 20 l multicolored 15 15
678 A177 50 l " 30 15
679 A176 70 l " 30 30
680 A177 80 l " 30 30
a. Imperf., pair 200.00
681 " 1d multicolored 30 15
682 " 1.50d " 30 30
683 A176 2.50d " 75 20
684 A177 4.50d " 1.25 1.00
a. Dbl. impression of black 175.00 135.00
685 A176 5d multicolored 1.75 1.50
686 A177 6d " 1.60 1.00
687 " 12.50d " 17.50 17.50
Nos. 677-687 (11) 24.50 22.55

Issued to commemorate the 17th Olympic Games, Rome, Aug. 25—Sept. 11.

Europa Issue, 1960
Common Design Type
Perf. 13½x12

1960, Sept. 19 Litho. Wmk. 252
Size: 33x23mm.

688 CD3 4.50d ultramarine 9.00 5.00
a. Double impression 60.00

Shepherd Type of 1954

1960, Sept. 1 *Perf. 13* Wmk. 252

689 A152a 3d ultramarine 5.00 50

Crown Prince Constantine and Yacht—A178

1961, Jan. 18 *Perf. 13½x13*

690 A178 2.50d multicolored 1.00 80

Issued to commemorate the victory of Crown Prince Constantine and his crew at the 17th Olympic Games, Rome (Gold medal, Yachting, Dragon class).

Common Design Types
pictured in section at front of book.

Castoria
A179

Delphi
A180

Landscapes and Ancient Monuments: 20 l, Meteora. 50 l, Hydra harbor. 70 l, Acropolis, Athens. 80 l, Mykonos. 1d, St. Catherine's Church, Salonika. 1.50d, Olympia. 2.50d, Knossos. 3.50d, Rhodes. 4d, Epidauros amphitheater. 4.50d, Temple of Poseidon, Sounion. 5d, Temple of Zeus, Athens. 7.50d, Aslan's mosque, Ioannina. 8d, Mount Athos. 8.50d, Santorini. 12.50d, Marble lions, Delos.

Perf. 13½x12½, 12½x13½

1961, Feb. 15 Engr. Wmk. 252

691 A179 10 l dark gray blue 25 8
692 " 20 l dark purple 25 5
693 " 50 l blue 25 5
694 " 70 l dark purple 50 10
695 " 80 l bright ultra. 30 10
696 " 1d red brown 55 5
697 " 1.50d bright green 90 6
698 " 2.50d carmine 7.00 3
699 " 3.50d purple 1.35 20
700 " 4d slate green 1.35 10
701 " 4.50d dark blue 1.35 10
702 " 5d claret 3.50 10
703 A180 6d slate green 4.00 15
704 A179 7.50d black 4.00 60
705 A180 8d dk. violet blue 6.00 80
706 " 8.50d orange verm. 7.50 90
707 A179 12.50d dark brown 9.00 1.85
Nos. 691-707 (17) 48.05 5.32

Issued for tourist publicity.

Lily Vase
A181

Partridge and Fig Pecker—A182

Minoan Art: 1d, Fruit dish. 1.50d, Rhyton bearer. 2.50d, Ladies of Knossos Palace. 4.50d, Sarcophagus of Hagia Trias. 6d, Dancer. 10d, Two vessels with spouts.

Perf. 13x13½, 13½x13

1961, June 30 Lithographed

708 A181 20 l multicolored 50 50
709 A182 50 l " 70 50
710 " 1d " 1.20 35
711 A181 1.50d " 1.40 40
712 A182 2.50d " 1.90 25
713 A181 4.50d " 4.75 4.00
714 A182 6d " 6.00 4.00
715 " 10d " 24.00 22.50
Nos. 708-715 (8) 40.45 32.50

Democritus Nuclear Research Center
A183

Democritus—A184

1961, July 31 *Perf. 13½x13*

716 A183 2.50d dp. lilac rose & rose lilac 80 15
717 A184 4.50d violet blue & pale violet blue 2.00 2.00

Issued to commemorate the inauguration of the Democritus Nuclear Research Center at Aghia Paraskevi.

Europa Issue, 1961
Common Design Type

1961, Sept. 18 *Perf. 13½x12*
Size: 32½x22mm.

718 CD4 2.50d vermilion & pink 30 30
a. Inscriptions white (pink omitted) 30.00 30.00
719 CD4 4.50d ultramarine & lt. ultra. 55 55

Nicephoros Phocas
A185

Hermes Head of 1861
A186

1961, Sept. 22 Wmk. 252

720 A185 2.50d multicolored 1.50 1.00

Issued to commemorate the 1000th anniversary of the liberation of Crete from the Saracens under the Byzantine general (later emperor) Phocas.

Lithographed

1961, Dec. 20 *Perf. 13x13½*

Each denomination shows a different stamp of 1861 issue.

721 A186 20 l brown, red brn. & cream 33 33
722 " 50 l brown, bistre & straw 40 40
723 " 1.50d emerald & gray 50 50
724 " 2.50d red orange & olive bistre 55 22
725 " 4.50d dk. blue, blue & gray 65 65
726 " 6d rose lilac, pale rose & blue 1.10 70
727 " 10d carmine, rose & cream 6.00 6.00
Nos. 721-727 (7) 9.53 8.80

Centenary of Greek postage stamps.

Tauropos Dam and Lake
A187

Ptolemais Power Station
A188

Designs: 50 l, Ladhon river hydroelectric plant. 1.50d, Louros river dam. 2.50d, Aliverion power plant. 4.50d, Salonika hydroelectric sub-station. 6d, Agra river hydroelectric station, interior.

Perf. 13x13½, 13½x13

1962, Apr. 14 Wmk. 252

728 A187 20 l multicolored 10 10
729 " 50 l " 10 10
730 A188 1d " 40 20
731 " 1.50d " 40 15
732 " 2.50d " 50 20
733 " 4.50d " 2.00 2.00
734 " 6d " 4.00 4.00
Nos. 728-734 (7) 7.50 6.75

National electrification project.

Youth with Shield and Helmet from Ancient Vase
A189

Designs: 2.50d, Zappion hall (horiz.). 4.50d, Kneeling soldier from Temple of Aphaea, Aegina. 6d, Standing soldier from stele of Ariston.

Perf. 13½x12, 12x13½

1962, May 3 Litho. Wmk. 252
Sizes: 22x33mm., 33x22mm.

735 A189 2.50d green, blue, red & brown 50 15
736 " 3d brown, buff & red brn. 1.00 50
737 " 4.50d blue & gray 1.50 1.25

Size: 21x37mm.

738 A189 6d brown red & black 1.50 75

Issued to commemorate the ministerial congress of NATO countries (North Atlantic Treaty Organization), Athens, May 3-5.

Europa Issue, 1962
Common Design Type

1962, Sept. 17 *Perf. 13½x12*
Size: 33x23mm.

739 CD5 2.50d verm. & blk. 65 35
740 " 4.50d ultra. & blk. 2.75 2.75

The lack of a price for a listed item does not necessarily indicate rarity.

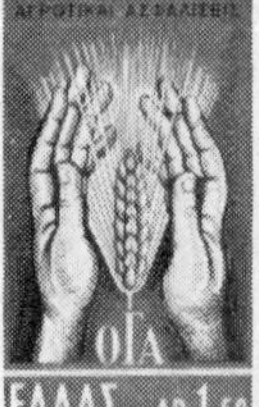

Hands and Grain
A190

Demeter
A191

1962, Oct. 30 *Perf. 13x13½*

741 A190 1.50d dp. carmine, blk. & brn. 60 25
742 " 2.50d bright green, blk. & brn. 1.35 40

Agricultural Insurance Program.

Perf. 12x13½

1963, Apr. 25 **Wmk. 252**

Design: 4.50d, Wheat and globe.

743 A191 2.50d brn. carmine, gray & blk. 60 15
744 " 4.50d multicolored 1.35 1.00

Issued for the "Freedom from Hunger" campaign of the U.N. Food and Agriculture Organization.

George I, Constantine XII, Alexander I, George II and Paul I—A192

Engraved

1963, June 29 *Perf. 13½x12½*

745 A192 50 l rose carmine 38 20
746 " 1.50d green 80 35
747 " 2.50d reddish brn. 1.25 25
748 " 4.50d dark blue 10.00 3.00
749 " 6d violet 6.75 1.50
Nos. 745-749 (5) 19.18 5.30

Centenary of the Greek dynasty.

Coin Types of 1959

Ancient Greek Coins: 50 l, Nymph Arethusa & Chariot. 80 l, Hercules & Zeus. 1d, Helios & Rose. 1.50d, Griffin & Square. 3d, Zeus & Eagle. 3.50d, Athena & Owl. 4.50d, Apollo & Labyrinth. 6d, Aphrodite & Apollo. 8.50d, Ram's head & Incuse Squares.

Perf. 13½x13, 13x13½

1963, July 5 **Litho.** **Wmk. 252**

Coins in Various Shades of Gray

750 A164 50 l violet blue 10 10
751 " 80 l dp. magenta 35 35
752 A165 1d emerald 60 4
753 A164 1.50d lilac rose 60 10
754 " 3d olive 1.00 10
755 " 3.50d vermilion 1.50 20
756 A165 4.50d reddish brn. 2.00 40
757 " 6d blue green 3.00 30
758 " 8.50d bright blue 4.00 75
Nos. 750-758 (9) 13.15 2.34

"Acropolis at Dawn" by Lord Baden-Powell
A193

Jamboree Badge (Boeotian Shield)
A194

Athenian Treasury, Delphi
A195

Designs: 2.50d, Crown Prince Constantine, Chief Scout. 3d, Athanassios Lefkadites (founder of Greek Scouts) and Lord Baden-Powell. 4.50d, Scout bugling with conch shell.

1963, Aug. 1

759 A193 1d bl., sal. & olive 25 25
760 A194 1.50d dk. bl., org. brn. & brn. 20 15
761 " 2.50d multicolored 30 10
762 A193 3d " 75 35
763 A194 4.50d " 3.50 3.50
Nos. 759-763 (5) 5.00 4.35

11th Boy Scout Jamboree, Marathon, July 29–Aug. 16, 1963.

1963, Sept. 16 *Perf. 12x13½*

Designs: 2d, Centenary emblem. 2.50d, Queen Olga, founder of Greek Red Cross. 4.50d, Henri Dunant.

Cross in Red

764 A195 1d multicolored 20 20
765 " 2d " 25 20
766 " 2.50d " 30 10
767 " 4.50d " 1.35 1.35

International Red Cross Centenary.

Europa Issue, 1963

Common Design Type

1963, Sept. 16 *Perf. 13½x12*

Size: 33x23mm.

768 CD6 2.50d green 3.00 75
769 " 4.50d brt. magenta 7.50 5.00

Vatopethion Monastery
A196

King Paul I (1901–1964)
A197

Designs: 80 l, St. Denys' Monastery. 1d, "Protaton" (Founder's) Church (horiz.). 2d, Stavronikita Monastery. 2.50d, Jeweled cover of Nicephoros Phocas Gospel. 3.50d, Fresco of St. Athanassios, founder of community. 4.50d, Presentation of Christ, 11th century manuscript. 6d, Great Lavra Church (horiz.).

Stamps Inscribed: ΑΓ. ΟΡΟΣ 963-1963

Perf. 13x13½, 13½x13

1963, Dec. 5 **Litho.** **Wmk. 252**

770 A196 30 l multicolored 15 15
771 " 80 l " 25 25
772 " 1d " 75 25
773 " 2d " 1.00 25
774 " 2.50d " 1.00 25
775 " 3.50d " 2.00 1.75
776 " 4.50d " 3.00 2.50
777 " 6d " 3.50 1.50
Nos. 770-777 (8) 11.65 6.90

Issued to commemorate the millennium of the founding of the monastic community on Mt. Athos.

1964, May 6 *Perf. 12x13½*

778 A197 30 l brown 15 5
779 " 50 l purple 30 3
780 A197 1d green 30 5
781 " 1.50d orange 50 8
782 " 2d blue 65 8
783 " 2.50d chocolate 1.00 3
784 " 3.50d red brown 2.00 30
785 " 4d ultramarine 2.00 30
786 " 4.50d bluish black 3.00 40
787 " 6d rose pink 5.00 50
Nos. 778-787 (10) 14.90 1.82

Archangel Michael
A198

Designs: 1d, Bulgaroctonus coin of Emperor Basil II. 1.50d, Two armed saints from ivory triptych by Harbaville, Louvre. 2.50d, Lady, fresco by Panselinos, Protaton Church, Mt. Athos. 4.50d, Angel, mosaic, Daphni Church, Athens.

1964, June 10 *Perf. 12x13½*

788 A198 1d multicolored 40 15
789 " 1.50d " 40 15
790 " 2d " 60 20
791 " 2.50d " 1.00 15
792 " 4.50d " 5.00 4.00
Nos. 788-792 (5) 7.40 4.65

Issued to commemorate Byzantine Art and in connection with the Byzantine Art Exhibition, Athens, April–June, 1964.

Birth of Aphrodite, Emblem of Kythera
A199

Designs (emblems of islands): 20 l, Trident, Paxos. 1d, Head of Ulysses, Ithaca. 2d, St. George slaying dragon, Lefkas. 2.50d, Zakyntnos, Zante. 4.50d, Cephalus, dog and spear, Cephalonia. 6d, Trireme, Corfu.

Perf. 13½x12

1964, July 20 **Litho.** **Wmk. 252**

793 A199 20 l multicolored 12 12
794 " 30 l " 12 12
795 " 1d " 12 12
796 " 2d " 25 18
797 " 2.50d slate green & dull green 30 12
798 " 4.50d multicolored 1.60 1.20
799 " 6d " 1.60 80
Nos. 793-799 (7) 4.11 2.66

Centenary of the union of the Ionian Islands with Greece.

Child and Sun
A200

1964, Sept. 10 **Wmk. 252**

800 A200 2.50d multicolored 40 20

Issued to commemorate the 50th anniversary of the National Institute of Social Welfare for the Protection of Children and Mothers (P.I.K.P.A.).

Europa Issue, 1964

Common Design Type

1964, Sept. 14 Litho. *Perf. 13x13½*

Size: 23x39mm.

801 CD7 2.50d light green & dark red 1.00 40
802 " 4.50d gray & brn. 2.00 2.00

King Constantine II and Queen Anne-Marie
A201

Peleus and Atalante Fighting, 6th Century B.C. Vase
A202

1964, Sept. 18 Engr. *Perf. 13½x14*

803 A201 1.50d green 30 25
804 " 2.50d rose carmine 40 20
805 " 4.50d bright ultra. 1.85 1.85

Issued to commemorate the wedding of King Constantine II and Princess Anne-Marie of Denmark, Sept. 18, 1964.

Perf. 12x13½, 13½x12

1964, Oct. 24 **Litho.** **Wmk. 252**

Designs: 1d, Runners on amphora (horiz.). 2d, Athlete on vase (horiz.). 2.50d, Discus thrower and judge, pitcher. 4.50d, Charioteer, sculpture (horiz.). 6d, Boxers, vase (horiz.). 10d, Apollo, frieze from Zeus Temple at Olympia.

806 A202 10 l multicolored 12 12
807 " 1d " 12 12
808 " 2d " 22 22
809 " 2.50d " 30 18
810 " 4.50d " 1.00 1.00
811 " 6d " 1.00 75
812 " 10d " 2.50 2.50
Nos. 806-812 (7) 5.26 4.89

18th Olympic Games, Tokyo, Oct. 10–25.

Detail from "Christ Stripped of His Garments" by El Greco
A203

Aesculapius Theatre, Epidauros
A204

Paintings by El Greco: 1d, Concert of the Angels. 1.50d, El Greco's painted signature (horiz.). 2.50d, Self-portrait. 4.50d, Storm-lashed Toledo.

Perf. 12x13½, 13½x12

1965, Mar. 6 **Litho.** **Wmk. 252**

813 A203 50 l sepia & multi. 25 25
814 " 1d gray & multi. 30 30
a. Dbl. impression of black
815 A203 1.50d multicolored 30 30
816 " 2.50d slate & multi. 60 50
817 " 4.50d multicolored 1.35 1.35
Nos. 813-817 (5) 2.80 2.70

Issued to commemorate the 350th anniversary of the death of Domenico Theotocopoulos, El Greco (1541–1614).

1965, Apr. 30 Litho. *Perf. 12x13½*

Design: 4.50d, Herod Atticus Theatre, and Acropolis, Athens.

818 A204 1.50d multicolored 30 20
819 " 4.50d " 65 65

Epidauros and Athens theatrical festivals.

ITU Emblem, Old and New Telecommunication Equipment
A205

1965, Apr. 30 *Perf. 13½x12*

820 A205 2.50d dk. bl., bluish gray & red 45 30

Issued to commemorate the centenary of the International Telecommunication Union.

Swearing-in Ceremony
A206

Flag of Philiki Hetaeria, the Friends' Society—A207

Perf. 13½x12

1965, May 31 Litho. Wmk. 252

821 A206 1.50d multicolored 30 15
822 A207 4.50d gray & multi. 60 60

Issued to commemorate the 150th anniversary of the Friends' Society, a secret organization for the liberation of Greece from Turkey.

Emblem of A.H.E.P.A.
A208

Eleutherios Venizelos, Therissos, 1905
A209

1965, June 30

823 A208 6d light blue, black & olive 1.00 55

Issued to publicize the Congress of the American Hellenic Educational Progressive Association, Athens.

1965, June 30 Engr. *Perf. 12½x13*

Designs: 2d, Venizelos signing Treaty of Sevres, 1920. 2.50d, Venizelos portrait.

824 A209 1.50d green 20 12
825 " 2d dark blue 32 25
826 " 2.50d brown 65 12

Issued to commemorate the centenary of the birth of Eleutherios Venizelos (1864–1963), statesman and prime minister.

Symbols of Planets
A210

Astronaut in Space
A211

Design: 6d, Two space ships over globe.

Perf. 12½x13½

1965, Sept. 11 Litho. Wmk. 252

827 A210 50 l multicolored 15 15
828 A211 2.50d " 30 25
829 " 6d " 70 65

Issued to commemorate the 16th Astronautical Congress, Athens, Sept. 12–18.

Victory Medal
A212

Stadium, Phaleron
A213

Design: 1d, Games' emblem and "JBA."

Perf. 13½x13, 13x13½

1965, Sept. 11

830 A213 1d multicolored 10 10
831 A212 2d " 20 15
832 A213 6d " 70 70

24th Balkan Games, Sept. 1–10.

Europa Issue, 1965
Common Design Type

1965, Oct. 21 *Perf. 13½x12*

Size: 33x23mm.

833 CD8 2.50d blue gray, blk. & dark blue 1.00 40
834 " 4.50d olive, black & green 2.00 2.00

Hipparchus and Astrolabe
A214

1965, Oct. 21 Litho. Wmk. 252

835 A214 2.50d blue grn., blk. & dark red 50 20

Issued to commemorate the opening of the Evghenides Planetarium, Athens.

St. Andrew's Church, Patras
A215

St. Andrew
A216

1965, Nov. 30 *Perf. 12x13½*

836 A215 1d multicolored 15 15
837 A216 5d " 30 30

Issued to commemorate the return of the head of St. Andrew from St. Peter's, Rome to St. Andrew's, Patras. The design of the 5d is from an 11th century mosaic at St. Luke's Monastery, Boeotia.

Ants and Anthill
A217

Savings Bank and Book
A218

1965, Nov. 30 Litho. Wmk. 252

838 A217 10 l green, black & bister 10 10
839 A218 2.50d multicolored 25 20

Issued to commemorate the 50th anniversary of the Post Office Savings Bank.

Theodore Brysakes
A219

Jean Gabriel Eynard
A220

Banknote of 1867—A221

Painters: 1d, Nikeforus Lytras. 2.50d, Constantin Volonakes. 4d, Nicolas Gyses. 5d, George Jacobides.

Perf. 13x13½

1966, Feb. 28 Litho. Wmk. 252

840 A219 80 l multicolored 20 15
841 " 1d " 20 10
842 " 2.50d " 33 10
843 " 4d " 40 30
844 " 5d " 60 30
Nos. 840-844 (5) 1.73 95

Issued to honor Greek painters.

Perf. 12x13½

1966, Mar. 30 Engraved Wmk. 252

Designs: 2.50d, Georgios Stavros. 4d, Bank's first headquarters, etching by Yannis Kefallinos.

845 A220 1.50d gray green 10 10
846 " 2.50d brown 20 15
847 A221 4d ultramarine 40 30
848 " 6d black 80 60

Issued to commemorate the 125th anniversary of the National Bank of Greece.

Symbolic Water Cycle
A222

UNESCO Emblem
A223

WHO Headquarters, Geneva
A224

Perf. 12x13½, 13½x12

1966, Apr. 18 Lithographed

849 A222 1d multicolored 12 8
850 A223 3d " 25 15
851 A224 5d " 80 70

Issued to publicize the Hydrological Decade (UNESCO), 1965–74, (1d); to commemorate the 20th anniversary of UNESCO (3d); and to commemorate the inauguration of the World Health Organization Headquarters, Geneva (5d).

Geannares Michael (Hatzes)
A225

Explosion at Arkadi Monastery
A226

Map of Crete
A227

1966, Apr. 18

852 A225 2d multicolored 15 10
853 A226 2.50d " 20 10
854 A227 4.50d " 80 80

Issued to commemorate the centenary of the Cretan revolt against the Turks. Geannares Michael (Hatzes), the leader of the revolt, was a member of Cretan government and a writer.

Copper Mask, 4th Century, B.C.
A228

Dionysus on a Thespian Ship-Chariot
A229

Designs: 2.50d, Old Theater of Dionysus, Athens, 6th Century B.C. 4.50d, Dancing Dionysus, from vase by Kleophrades, c. 500 B.C.

Perf. 12x13½, 13½x12

1966, May 26 Litho. Wmk. 252

855 A228 1d multicolored 10 10
856 A229 1.50d " 15 10
857 " 2.50d " 25 10
858 A228 4.50d " 75 75

2500th anniversary of Greek theater.

Boeing 707-320 over New York Buildings and Greek Column—A230

1966, May 26 *Perf. 13x12½*

859 A230 6d blue & dk. blue 75 60

Issued to commemorate the inauguration of transatlantic flights of Olympic Airways.

Tobacco Worker
A231

Design: 5d, Woman sorting tobacco leaves.

Perf. 12½x13½

1966, Sept. 19 Litho. Wmk. 252

860 A231 1d multicolored 15 10
861 " 5d " 45 40

Issued to publicize the Greek tobacco industry, in connection with the 4th International Scientific Tobacco Congress, Athens, Sept. 19–26.

Europa Issue, 1966
Common Design Type

1966, Sept. 19 Litho. Wmk. 252
Size: 23x33mm.

862 CD9 1.50d olive 1.00 40
863 " 4.50d lt. red brn. 2.00 2.00

Carved Cases for Knitting Needles
A232

Bridegroom, Embroidery from Epirus
A233

Designs (Popular Art): 50 l, Lyre, Crete. 1d, Massa (stringed instrument). 1.50d, Bas-relief (cross and angels). 2d, Icon (Sts. Constantine and Helena). 2.50d, Virgin (wood carving, Church of St. Nicholas, Galaxeidon). 3d, Embroidery (sailing ship from Skyros). 4d, Embroidery (wedding parade). 4.50d, Carved wooden distaff (Sts. George and Barbara). 5d, Silver and agate necklace and earrings. 20d, Handwoven cloth, Cyprus.

Perf. 12x13½, 13½x12

1966, Nov. 21 Litho. Wmk. 252

864 A232 10 l tan, dk. blue & orange 3 3
865 A233 30 l multicolored 3 3
866 A232 50 l " 4 4
867 " 1d " 12 3
868 " 1.50d " 12 5
869 " 2d " 20 4
870 " 2.50d " 25 4
871 A233 3d " 30 10
872 " 4d " 35 15
873 A232 4.50d grn. & multi. 1.00 40
874 " 5d multicolored 1.00 20
875 A233 20d " 16.50 2.75
Nos. 864-875 (12) 19.94 3.86

King Constantine II, Queen Anne-Marie and Princess Alexia
A234

Designs: 2d, Princess Alexia. 3.50d, Queen Anne-Marie and Princess Alexia.

Perf. 13½x14

1966, Dec. 19 Engr. Wmk. 252

876 A234 2d green 20 20
877 " 2.50d brown 40 40
878 " 3.50d ultramarine 80 80

Issued to honor Princess Alexia, successor to the throne of Greece.

"Night" by John Cossos (1830–1873)
A235

Sculptures: 50 l, Penelope by Leonides Drosses (1836–1882). 80 l, Shepherd by George Fytales. 2d, Woman's torso by Constantine Demetriades (1881–1943). 2.50d, "Colocotrones" (equestrian statue) by Lazarus Sochos (1862–1911). 3d, Sleeping Young Lady by John Halepas (1851–1938) (horiz.). 10d, Woodcutter by George Filippotes (1839–1919; horiz.).

Perf. 12x13½, 13½x12

1967, Feb. 28 Litho. Wmk. 252

879 A235 20 l Prus. bl., gray & black 7 5
880 " 50 l brown, gray & black 12 7
881 " 80 l brn. red, gray & black 40 20
882 " 2d vio. blue, gray & black 35 15
883 " 2.50d ultra., black & green 40 10
884 " 3d blue, lt. blue, gray & black 90 70
885 " 10d blue & multi. 1.10 60
Nos. 879-885 (7) 3.34 1.87

Issued to honor modern Greek sculptors.

World Map and Olympic Rings
A236

Discus Thrower by C. Demetriades
A237

Designs: 1.50d, Runners on ancient clay vessel. 2.50d, Hurdler and map of Europe and Near East. 6d, Rising sun over Altis ruins at Olympia.

Perf. 13½x12, 12x13½

1967, Apr. 6 Litho. Wmk. 252

886 A236 1d multicolored 15 15
887 " 1.50d " 20 15
888 " 2.50d " 30 10
889 A237 5d " 85 70
890 A236 6d " 95 65
Nos. 886-890 (5) 2.45 1.75

Issued to commemorate Olympic Games Day, Apr. 6 (1d); to commemorate the Classic Marathon Race, Apr. 6 (1.5d); to publicize the athletic qualifying rounds for the Cup of Europe, June 24–25 (2.50d); to publicize the 9th contest for the European Athletic Championships, 1969 (5d); to publicize the founding of the International Academy at Olympia and the 7th meeting of the Academy, July 29–Aug. 14, 1967 (6d).

Europa Issue, 1967
Common Design Type

Perf. 12x13½

1967, May 2 Litho. Wmk. 252
Size: 23x33½mm.

891 CD10 2.50d buff, lt. & dk. brown 1.00 40
892 " 4.50d green, light & dk. grn. 2.00 2.00

Chapel, Skopelos Island
A238

Plaka District, Athens
A239

Perf. 13½x12, 12x13½

1967, June 26 Litho. Wmk. 252

Design: 4.50d, Doric Temple of Epicurean Apollo, by Itkinus, c. 430 B.C.

893 A238 2.50d multicolored 30 10
894 " 4.50d " 65 65
a. Dbl. impression of black
895 A239 6d multicolored 85 65

International Tourist Year 1967.

Destroyer and Sailor
A240

Training Ship, Merchant Marine Academy
A241

Designs: 2.50d, Merchant Marine Academy, Aspropyrgos, Attica, and rowing crew. 3d, Cruiser Georgios Averoff and Naval School, Poros. 6d, Merchant ship and bearded figurehead.

1967, June 26

896 A240 20 l multicolored 10 10
897 A241 1d " 10 10
898 A240 2.50d " 30 10
899 " 3d " 1.00 1.00
900 " 6d " 1.00 1.00
Nos. 896-900 (5) 2.50 2.30

Issued to publicize Maritime Week.

Soldier and Rising Phoenix
A242

Blast Furnaces
A243

Perf. 12x13½

1967, Aug. 30 Litho. Wmk. 252

901 A242 2.50d blue & multi. 50 20
902 " 3d org. & multi. 50 30
903 " 4.50d multicolored 2.00 2.00

Revolution of Apr. 21, 1967.

1967, Nov. 29 *Perf. 13x14*

904 A243 4.50d brt. bl. & dk. violet blue 1.50 90

Issued to publicize the first meeting of the United Nations Industrial Development Organization, Athens, Nov. 29–Dec. 20.

Sailboats
A244

Children's Drawings: 1.50d, Steamship and island. 3.50d, Farmhouse. 6d, Church on hill.

1967, Dec. 20 *Perf. 13½x12½*

905 A244 20 l multicolored 10 10
906 " 1.50d green, dark blue & black 30 12
907 " 3.50d multicolored 85 45
908 " 6d " 1.10 50

Javelin
A245

Apollo, Olympic Academy Seal
A246

Discus Thrower by Demetriades
A247

Designs: 1d, Jumping. 2.50d, Attic vase showing lighting of Olympic torch. 4d, Olympic rings and map of Europe (horiz.). 6d, Long-distance runners (vert.).

Lithographed

1968, Feb. 28 *Perf. 12½* **Wmk. 252**

909 A245 50 l ultra. & bister 10 10
910 " 1d green, yellow, black & gray 15 10
911 A246 1.50d blk., bl. & buff 20 15
912 " 2.50d olive grn., blk. & org. brn. 30 12
913 " 4d gray & multi. 1.00 40
914 A247 4.50d blue, green, yel. & blk. 2.50 2.50
915 A245 6d brn., red & bl. 85 60
Nos. 909-915 (7) 5.10 3.97

Issued to publicize: 50 l, 1d, 6d, 27th Balkan Games, Athens, Aug. 29–Sept. 1; 1.50d, Meeting of the International Olympic Academy; 2.50d, Lighting of the Olympic torch for 19th Olympic Games, Mexico City; 4d, Olympic Day, Apr. 6; 4.50d, 9th European Athletic Championships, 1969.

Europa Issue, 1968
Common Design Type

Perf. 13½x12

1968, Mar. 29 Litho. Wmk. 252
Size: 33x23mm.

916 CD11 2.50d copper red, bister & black 1.00 40
917 " 4.50d violet, bister & black 2.00 2.00

Emblems of Greek and International Automobile Clubs
A248

1968, Mar. 29 *Perf. 13x14*

918	A248	5d ultra.& org. brn.	1.50	1.00

Issued to publicize the General Assembly of the International Automobile Federation, Athens, Apr. 8–14.

Athena Defeating Alkyoneus, from Pergamos Altar, 180 B.C.—A249

Athena, 2nd Century, B.C.
A250

Winged Victory of Samothrace, c. 190 B.C.
A251

Designs: 50 l, Alexander the Great on horseback, from sarcophagus, c. 310 B.C. 1.50d, Emperors Constantine and Justinian bringing offerings to Virgin Mary, Byzantine mosaic. 2.50d, Emperor Constantine Paleologos, lithograph by D. Tsokos, 1859. 3d, Greece in Missolonghi, by Delacroix. 4.50d, Greek Soldier (evzone), by G. B. Scott.

Perf. 13½x13, 13x13½, 13½x14 (A249)

1968, Apr. 27

919	A249	10 l gray & multi.	7	5
920	A250	20 l green & multi.	7	5
921	"	50 l pur. & multi.	13	8
922	A249	1.50d gray & multi.	20	10
923	A250	2.50d multicolored	25	10
924	A251	3d "	50	30
925	"	4.50d "	1.35	1.35
926	"	6d "	3.00	2.85
		Nos. 919-926 (8)	5.57	4.88

Issued to publicize an exhibition "The Hellenic Fight for Civilization."

Monument to the Unknown Priest and Teacher, Rhodes
A252

Map and Flag of Greece
A253

Cross and Globe
A254

Perf. 14x13½, 13½x14

1968, July 11 Litho. **Wmk. 252**

927	A252	2d multicolored	75	15
928	A253	5d "	1.25	1.25

Issued to commemorate the 20th anniversary of the union of the Dodecanese Islands with Greece.

1968, July 11 *Perf. 13½x14*

929	A254	6d multicolored	1.50	65

Issued to commemorate the 19th Biennial Congress of the Greek Orthodox Archdiocese of North and South America.

Antique Lamp (GAPA Emblem)
A255

1968, July 11 *Perf. 14x13½*

930	A255	6d multicolored	1.50	65

Issued to publicize the Regional Congress of the Greek-American Progressive Association, G.A.P.A.

Fragment of Bas-relief, Temple of Aesculapius, Athens
A256

Perf. 13½x14

1968, Sept. 8 Litho. **Wmk. 252**

931	A256	4.50d blk., car. lake, gray & org.	6.00	3.50

Issued to publicize the 5th European Cardiology Congress, Athens, Sept. 8–14.

View of Olympia, Site of Ancient Games
A257

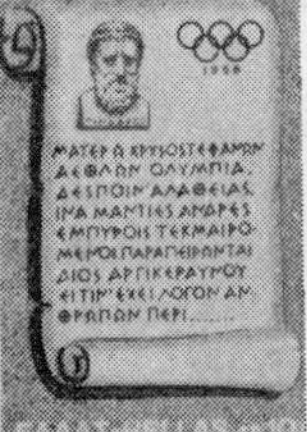

Pindar and Olympic Ode
A258

Hygeia and WHO Emblem
A259

Design: 2.50d, Panathenaic Stadium, site of 1896 Olympic Games.

Perf. 14x13½, 13x13½

1968, Sept. 25 Litho. **Wmk. 252**

932	A257	2.50d multicolored	25	15
933	"	5d green & multi.	40	25
934	A258	10d blue, yellow & brown	3.50	2.50

Issued to publicize the 19th Olympic Games, Mexico City, Oct. 12–27.

On 10d, hyphen is omitted at end of 5th line of ode on 5 of 50 stamps in each sheet.

1968, Nov. 8 *Perf. 13½x14*

935	A259	5d gray & multi.	1.25	1.00

Issued to commemorate the 20th anniversary of the World Health Organization.

Mediterranean, Breguet 19 and Flight Route, 1928
A260

Farman, 1912, Plane and F-104G Jet
A261

St. Zeno, The Letter Bearer
A262

Design: 2.50d, Greek air force pilot ramming enemy plane over Langada.

1968, Nov. 8 *Perf. 14x13½, 13½x14*

936	A260	2.50d ultra., black & yellow	25	15
937	"	3.50d multicolored	40	40
938	A261	8d "	3.00	3.00

Exploits of Royal Hellenic Air Force.

Perf. 13½x14

1969, Feb. 10 Litho. **Wmk. 252**

939	A262	2.50d multicolored	90	50

Issued to commemorate the establishment of the feast day of St. Zeno as the day of Greek post office personnel.

Hephaestus and Cyclops, Bas-relief
A263

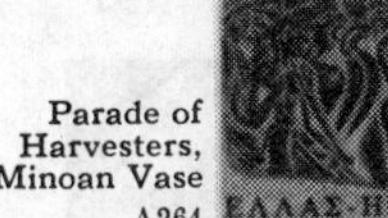

Parade of Harvesters, Minoan Vase
A264

1969, Feb. 10 *Perf. 13½x12½*

940	A263	1.50d multicolored	55	20
941	A264	10d "	2.10	1.85

Issued for the 50th anniversary of the International Labor Organization.

Yachts in Vouliagmeni Harbor
A265

Athens Festival, Chorus of Elders
A266

View of Astypalaia
A267

Perf. 13½x12½, 12½x13½

1969, Mar. 3

942	A265	1d multicolored	20	10
943	A266	5d "	1.80	1.80
944	A267	6d "	90	40

Issued for tourist publicity.

Attic Shield and Helmet on Greek Coin, 461–450 B.C.
A268

Hoplites and Flutist, from Proto-Corinthian Pitcher, 640–630 B.C.
A269

Perf. 12½x13½, 13½x12½

1969, Apr. 4 Litho. **Wmk. 252**

945	A268	2.50d rose red, black & slate	70	40
946	A269	4.50d multicolored	2.00	2.00

Issued to commemorate the 20th anniversary of NATO (North Atlantic Treaty Organization).

Europa Issue, 1969
Common Design Type

1969, May 5 *Perf. 13½x12½*

Size: 33x23mm.

947	CD12	2.50d multicolored	1.00	40
948	"	4.50d "	2.50	2.50

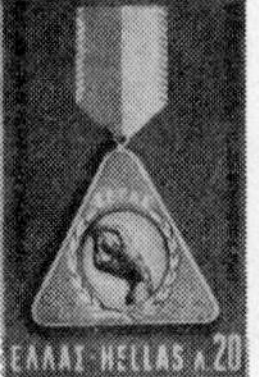

Victory Medal
A270

Pole Vault and Pentathlon (from Panathenaic Amphora)
A271

Designs: 5d, Relay race and runners from amphora, 525 B.C. (horiz.). 8d, Modern and ancient (Panathenaic amphora, c. 480 B.C.) discus throwers.

Perf. 12½x13½, 13½x12½

1969, May 5

949	A270	20 l red & multi.	10	10
950	A271	3d gray & multi.	30	25
951	"	5d multicolored	30	20
952	"	8d "	3.00	3.00

Issued to publicize the 9th European Athletic Championships, Athens, Sept. 16–21.

Greece and the Sea Issue

Oil Tanker
A272

Merchant Vessels and Warships, 1821
A273

Designs: 80 l, Brig and steamship, painting by Ioannis Poulakas (vert.). 4.50d, Warships on maneuvers. 6d, Battle of Salamis, 480 B.C., painting by Constantine Volonakis.

Perf. 12½x13½, 13½x12½, 13½x13

1969, June 28 Litho. Wmk. 252

953	A272	80 l multicolored	40	40
954	"	2d blk., bl. & gray	20	15
955	A273	2.50d dk. bl. & multi.	20	10
956	A272	4.50d brown, gray & blue	3.00	3.00
957	A273	6d multicolored	3.50	3.50
		Nos. 953-957 (5)	7.30	7.15

Raising Greek Flag
A274

1969, Aug. 31 ***Perf. 13x13½***

958	A274	2.50d blue & multi.	1.00	40

Issued to commemorate the 20th anniversary of the Grammos-Vitsi victory.

Athena Promachos and Map of Greece
A275

"National Resistance"
A276

Greek Participation in World War II
A277

Perf. 13x13½, 13½x14

1969, Oct. 12 Litho. Wmk. 252

959	A275	4d multicolored	20	15
960	A276	5d "	2.00	2.00
961	A277	6d "	1.20	50

Issued to commemorate the 25th anniversary of the liberation of Greece in World War II.

Demetrius Tsames Karatasios, by G. Demetriades
A278

Pavlos Melas, by P. Mathiopoulos
A279

Designs: 2.50d, Emmanuel Pappas, statue by Nicholas Perantinos. 4.50d, Capetan Kotas.

Perf. 12x13½

1969, Nov. 12 Litho. Wmk. 252

962	A278	1.50d multicolored	12	10
963	"	2.50d blue & multi.	15	10
964	A279	3.50d gray & multi.	30	25
965	"	4.50d multicolored	3.00	3.00

Issued to honor Greek heroes in Macedonia's struggle for liberation.

Angel of the Annunciation, Daphni Church, 11th Century
A280

Christ's Descent into Hell, Nea Moni Church, 11th Century
A282

Dolphins, Delos, 110 B.C.—A281

Greek Mosaics: 1.50d, The Holy Ghost (dove), Hosios Loukas Monastery, 11th century. 2d, The Hunter, Pella, 4th century B.C. 5d, Bird, St. George's Church, Salonica, 5th century.

Perf. 12x13½, 13½x12 (1d), 13x13½ (6d)

1970, Jan. 16 Litho. Wmk. 252

966	A280	20 l multicolored	20	20
967	A281	1d "	20	20
968	A280	1.50d blue & multi.	25	15
969	"	2d gray & multi.	15	10
970	"	5d bis. & multi.	1.00	35
971	A282	6d multicolored	5.00	5.00
		Nos. 966-971 (6)	6.80	6.00

Hercules and the Cretan Bull
A283

Hercules and the Erymanthian Boar
A284

Labors of Hercules: 30 l, Capture of Cerberus. 1d, Capture of the golden apples of the Hesperides. 1.50d, Lernean Hydra. 2d, Slaying of Geryon. 3d, Centaur Nessus. 4.50d, Fight with the river god Achelos. 5d, Nemean lion. 6d, Stymphalian birds. 20d, Giant Antaeus. Designs of 20 l and 1d are from Temple of Zeus, Olympia; others from various vessels; all from 7th–5th centuries B.C.

Perf. 13½x12, 12x13½

1970, Mar. 16 Litho. Wmk. 252

972	A283	20 l gray, black & yellow	8	3
973	"	30 l ocher & multi.	8	3
974	A284	1d bl. gray, black & blue	20	6
975	A283	1.50d dk. brn., bister & slate grn.	25	6
976	"	2d ocher & multi.	75	6
977	A284	2.50d ocher, dk. brn. & dull red	45	5
978	"	3d multicolored	55	10
979	A283	4.50d dk. bl. & multi.	1.20	30
980	"	5d multicolored	2.00	15
981	"	6d "	2.00	15
982	"	20d blk. & multi.	12.50	2.75
		Nos. 972-982 (11)	20.06	3.74

Satellite, Earth Station and Hemispheres
A285

1970, Apr. 21 ***Perf. 13½x12***

983	A285	2.50d bl., gray & yel.	1.00	40
984	"	4.50d brown, olive & blue	3.00	3.00

Issued to publicize the opening of the Earth Satellite Telecommunications Station "Thermopylae," Apr. 21, 1970.

Europa Issue, 1970

Common Design Type and

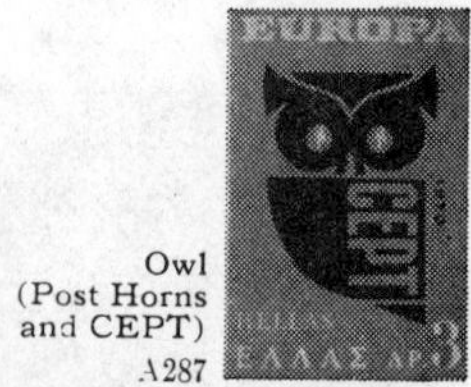

Owl (Post Horns and CEPT)
A287

Perf. 13½x12, 12x13½

1970, Apr. 21

985	CD13	2.50d rose red & org.	1.00	40
986	A287	3d brt. bl., gray & vio. blue	1.50	1.00
987	CD13	4.50d ultra. & org.	3.00	3.00

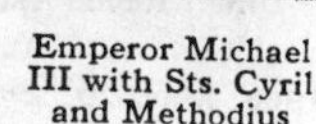

St. Demetrius with Cyril and Methodius as Children
A288

Emperor Michael III with Sts. Cyril and Methodius
A290

St. Cyril
A289

St. Methodius
A291

Perf. 13½x14 (50 l); 12x13½ (2d, 10d); 13x13½ (5d).

1970, Apr. 17 Litho. Wmk. 252

988	A288	50 l multicolored	15	15
989	A289	2d "	1.00	75
990	A290	5d "	1.00	75
991	A291	10d "	3.00	3.00

Issued to commemorate Sts. Cyril and Methodius who translated the Bible into Slavonic. No. 989 and 991 printed se-tenant.

Greek Fir
A292

Jankaea Heldreichii
A293

Designs: 6d, Rock partridge (horiz.). 8d, Wild goat.

Perf. 13x14, 14x13, 12x13½ (2.50d)

1970, June 16 Litho. Wmk. 252

992	A292	80 l multicolored	22	15
993	A293	2.50d "	30	10
994	A292	6d "	3.00	1.00
995	"	8d "	5.25	4.75

European Nature Conservation Year, 1970.

Map Showing Link Between AHEPA Members and Greece
A294

1970, Aug. 1 ***Perf. 13½x13***

996 A294 6d blue & multi. 2.00 90

Issued to publicize the 48th annual AHEPA (American Hellenic Educational Progressive Association) Congress, Athens, Aug. 1970.

U.P.U. Headquarters, Bern
A295

Education Year Emblem
A296

Mahatma Gandhi
A297

United Nations Emblem
A298

Ludwig van Beethoven
A299

Perf. 13½x12, 13x14, 12x13½

1970, Oct. 7 Litho. **Wmk. 252**

997 A295 50 l bister & multi. 5 5
998 A296 2.50d blue & multi. 20 10
999 A297 3.50d multi. 1.50 1.00
1000 A298 4d blue & multi. 90 40
1001 A299 4.50d blk. & multi. 3.00 3.00
Nos. 997-1001 (5) 5.65 4.55

Issued to commemorate: Inauguration of the Universal Postal Union Headquarters, Bern (50 l); International Education Year (2.50d); centenary of the birth of Mohandas K. Gandhi (1869–1948), leader in India's struggle for independence (3.50d); 25th anniversary of the United Nations (4d); bicentenary of the birth of Ludwig van Beethoven (1770–1827), composer (4.50d).

The Shepherds (Mosaic)
A300

Designs (from Mosaic in the Monastery of Hosios Loukas, Boetia, 11th century): 4.50d, The Three Kings and Angel. 6d, Nativity (horiz.).

1970, Dec. 5 ***Perf. 13x14, 14x13***

1002 A300 2d bister & multi. 50 40
1003 " 4.50d " " 1.50 1.35
1004 " 6d " " 2.50 2.50

Christmas 1970.

"Leonidas"
A301

Priest Sworn in as Fighter, from Commemorative Medal
A302

Eugenius Voulgaris (1716–1806)
A303

Battle of Corinth
A304

Kaltetsi Monastery, Seal of Peloponnesian Senate—A305

Death of Bishop Isaias, Battle of Alamana—A306

1971 **Litho.** **Wmk. 252**

Multicolored

1005 A301 20 l *shown* 18 17
1006 A302 50 l *shown* 18 17
1007 A303 50 l *shown* 18 17
1008 A304 50 l *shown* 18 17
1009 A301 1d *"Pericles"* 45 35
1010 A304 1d *Sacrifice of Kapsalis* 27 20
1011 A301 1.50d *"Terpsichore"* 45 35
1012 A302 2d *Patriarch Grigorius IV* 45 35
1013 A304 2d *Suliot women in battle* (horiz.) 45 35
1014 A305 2d *shown* 45 35
1015 A301 2.50d *"Karteria"* 90 35
1016 A303 2.50d *Adamantios Korais, M.D.* 3.25 3.25
1017 A305 2.50d *Memorial column, provincial administrative seal of Epidaurus* 45 35
1018 A304 3d *Naval battle, Samos* (horiz.) 90 70
1019 A306 4d *shown* 70 42
1020 A304 5d *Battle of Athens* 1.35 85
1021 A301 6d *Naval battle, Yeronda* 1.80 1.45
1022 " 6.50d *Battle of Maniaki* 2.00 1.50
1023 " 9d *Battle of Karpenisi, death of Marcos Botsaris* 2.00 2.00
1024 A306 10d *Bishop Germanos blessing flag* 2.65 2.65
1025 " 15d *"Secret School"* 4.00 4.00
1026 A305 20d *John Capodistrias' signature and seal* 4.50 3.00
Nos. 1005-1026 (22) 27.74 23.15

Sesquicentennial of Greece's uprising against the Turks. Emphasize role of Navy (Nos. 1005, 1009, 1011, 1015, 1018, 1021), issued Mar. 15; Church (Nos. 1006, 1012, 1019, 1024), Feb. 8; Instructors (Nos. 1007, 1016, 1025), June 21; Land Forces (Nos. 1008, 1010, 1013, 1020, 1022–1023), Sept. 21; Provincial Administrations (Nos. 1014, 1017, 1026), Oct. 19.

Sizes: 37x24 mm.: (Nos. 1005, 1009, 1011, 1015); 40x27½ mm. (No. 1021); 48x33mm. (Nos. 1022, 1023).

Perfs.: 14x13 (Nos. 1005, 1009, 1011, 1013, 1015, 1018); 13½x14 (Nos. 1006, 1012); 12x13½ (Nos. 1007, 1016, 1019, 1022–1025); 13x14 (Nos. 1008, 1010, 1020); 13½x13 (Nos. 1014, 1017, 1021, 1026).

Spyridon Louis, Winner of 1896 Marathon Race, Arriving at Stadium—A307

Pierre de Coubertin and Memorial Column
A308

Perf. 13½x13, 13x13½

1971, Apr. 10 Litho. **Wmk. 252**

1027 A307 3d multicolored 1.00 80
1028 A308 8d " 1.50 1.50

75th anniversary of the revival of the Olympic Games.

Europa Issue, 1971
Common Design Type

1971, May 18 ***Perf. 13½x12***

Size: 33x22½mm.

1029 CD14 2.50d green, yellow & black 1.00 40
1030 " 5d org., yellow & black 2.00 2.00

Hosios Lukas Monastery
A309

Monasteries and Churches: 1d, Daphni Church. 2d, St. John the Divine, Patmos. 2.50d, Koumbelidiki Church, Kastoria. 4.50d, Chalkeon Church, Thessalonica. 6.50d, Paregoritissa Church, Arta. 8.50d, St. Paul's Monastery, Mt. Athos.

1972, Jan. 17 ***Perf. 14x13***

1031 A309 50 l multicolored 10 10
1032 " 1d " 10 10
1033 A309 2d multicolored 15 12
1034 " 2.50d " 20 9
1035 " 4.50d " 1.00 90
1036 " 6.50d " 1.50 50
1037 " 8.50d " 3.00 2.75
Nos. 1031-1037 (7) 6.05 4.56

Cretan Costume
A310

Designs: Greek regional costumes.

1972, Mar. 1 ***Perf. 12½x13½***

Costumes in Original Colors; Dull Yellow Frame

1038 A310 50 l *shown* 10 5
1039 " 1d *Woman, Pindus* 18 8
1040 " 2d *Man, Missolonghi* 35 8
1041 " 2.50d *Woman, Sarakatsan, Attica* 50 8
a. "1972" omitted 1.25 1.25
1042 A310 3d *Woman, Island of Nisyros* 55 10
1043 " 4.50d *Woman, Megara* 2.50 25
1044 " 6.50d *Woman, Trikeri* 3.50 25
1045 " 10d *Woman, Pylaia, Macedonia* 5.00 1.50
Nos. 1038-1045 (8) 12.68 2.39

See Nos. 1073–1089, 1121–1135.

Memorial Medal, Science and Industry
A311

Flag and Map of Greece
A312

Honeycomb, Transportation and Industry
A313

Perf. 13½x13, 13x13½

1972, Apr. 21 **Wmk. 252**

1046 A311 2.50d blue & multi. 18 10
1047 A312 4.50d ocher & multi. 80 80
1048 A313 5d multicolored 1.00 1.00

5th anniversary of the revolution.

Europa Issue 1972
Common Design Type

1972, May 2 ***Perf. 12x13½***

Size: 23x33mm.

1049 CD15 3d multi. 1.00 50
1050 " 4.50d blue & multi. 2.00 2.00

Acropolis and Car
A314

Route of Automobile Rally
A315

1972, May 26 *Perf. 13½x12*

1051 A314 4.50d multi. 1.00 1.00
1052 A315 5d bl. & multi. 1.00 1.00

20th Acropolis Automobile Rally, May 26–29.

Gaia Handing Erecthonius to Athena, Cecrops—A316

Designs: 2d, Uranus, from altar of Zeus at Pergamum. 2.50d, Gods defeating the Giants, Treasury of Siphnos. 5d, Zeus of Dodona.

1972, June 26 Litho. *Perf. 14x13½*

1053 A316 1.50d yellow green & black 15 15
1054 " 2d dk. bl. & blk. 20 15
1055 " 2.50d org. brn. & blk. 30 15
1056 " 5d dark brown & black 1.75 1.75

Greek mythology. No. 1056 issued only se-tenant with Nos. 1053–1055 in sheets of 40 (4x10). Nos. 1053–1055 issued also in sheets of 50 each.

Olympic Rings, Wrestlers—A317

Designs: 50 l, Young athlete, crowning himself, c. 480 B.C. (vert.). 3.50d, Spartan woman running, Archaic period (vert.). 4.50d, Episkyros ball game, 6th century B.C. 10d, Running youths, from Panathenaic amphora.

Perf. 13½x14, 14x13½

1972, July 28 Litho. Wmk. 252

1057 A317 50 l maroon, black & gray 10 10
1058 " 1.50d brown, gray & black 20 15
1059 " 3.50d ocher & multi. 40 40
1060 " 4.50d green, buff & black 1.00 1.00
1061 " 10d black & terra cotta 2.00 2.00
Nos. 1057–1061 (5) 3.70 3.65

20th Olympic Games, Munich, Aug. 26–Sept. 11.

Young Stamp Collector A318

Three Kings and Angels A319

1972, Nov. 15 *Perf. 13x14*

1062 A318 2.50d multicolored 50 50

Stamp Day.

1972, Nov. 15

Design: 4.50d, Nativity.

1063 A319 2.50d multicolored 45 45
1064 " 4.50d " 75 75

Christmas 1972. Printed se-tenant in sheets of 50.

Technical University, 1885, by Luigi Lanza—A320

1973, Mar. 30 *Perf. 13½x13*

1065 A320 2.50d multicolored 60 50

Centenary of the Metsovion National Technical University.

"Spring," Fresco A321

Breast-form Jug A322

"Wooing and Twittering Swallows" Fresco A323

Designs: 30 l, "Blue Apes" fresco. 1.50d, Jug decorated with birds. 5d, "Wild Goats" fresco. 6.50d, Wrestlers, fresco.

Perf. 13x13½, 13½x13

1973, Mar. 30

1066 A321 10 l multicolored 10 10
1067 A322 20 l " 10 10
1068 A323 30 l " 10 10
1069 A322 1.50d grn. & multi. 20 15
1070 A323 2.50d multicolored 30 20
1071 " 5d " 75 75
1072 " 6.50d " 3.00 3.00
Nos. 1066–1072 (7) 4.55 4.40

Archaeological treasures from Santorini Island (Thera).

Costume Type of 1972

1973, Apr. 18 *Perf. 12½x13½*

Costumes in Original Colors; Dull Yellow Frame

1073 A310 10 l *Man, Peloponnesus* 5 3
1074 " 20 l *Man, Central Greece* 5 3
1075 " 30 l *Woman, Locris* 5 3
1076 " 50 l *Man, Skyros* 5 3
1077 " 1d *Woman, Spetsai* 12 3
1078 " 1.50d *Woman, Almyros* 15 3
1079 " 2.50d *Woman, Macedonia* 28 3
1080 " 3.50d *Woman, Salamis* 37 11
1081 " 4.50d *Woman, Epirus* 50 20
1082 " 5d *Man, Lefkas* 55 10
1083 " 6.50d *Woman, Skyros* 65 25
1084 " 8.50d *Woman, Corinth* 90 60
1085 " 10d *Woman Corfu* 1.10 30
1086 " 15d *Man, Epirus* 2.25 40
1087 " 20d *Woman, Thessaly* 3.00 1.50
1088 A310 30d *Woman, Macedonia* 4.25 2.00
1089 " 50d *Woman, Thrace* 7.00 4.00
Nos. 1073–1089 (17) 21.32 9.67

Europa Issue 1973

Common Design Type

1973, May 2 *Perf. 13½x12½*

Size: 35x22mm.

1090 CD16 2.50d deep blue & light blue 30 20
1091 " 3d dp. carmine & dp. org. 50 40
1092 " 4.50d olive green & yellow 1.35 1.35

Zeus Battling Typhoeus, from Amphora A324

Designs: 1d, Mount Olympus, after photograph. 2.50d, Zeus battling Giants, from Pergamum Altar. 4.50d, Punishment of Atlas and Prometheus, from vase.

1973, June 25 Wmk. 252

Perf. 14x13½

1093 A324 1d gray & black 10 10
1094 " 2d multicolored 20 18
1095 " 2.50d gray, black & buff 60 60
1096 " 4.50d ocher & multi. 1.00 1.00
Strip of 4, # 1093–1096 2.25 2.25

Greek mythology. Nos. 1093–1096 printed se-tenant in sheets of 40 (4x10).

Dr. George Papanicolaou A325

Icon, The Annunciation A326

Perf. 13x13½

1973, Aug. 10 Litho. Wmk. 252

1097 A325 2.50d multicolored 1.50 1.50
1098 " 6.50d " 1.50 1.50

Dr. George Papanicolaou (1883–1962), cytologist and cancer researcher.

1973, Aug. 10

1099 A326 2.50d multicolored 85 60

Miraculous icon of Our Lady of the Annunciation found on Tinos, 1823.

Triptolemus Holding Wheat on Chariot A327

Perf. 13x14

1973, Oct. 22 Litho. Wmk. 252

1100 A327 4.50d buff, dk. brn. & red 1.00 1.00

5th Symposium of the European Conference of Transport Ministers, Athens, Oct. 22–25.

Georgios Averoff A328

National Benefactors: 2d, Apostolos Arsakis. 2.50d, Constantine Zappas. 4d, Andrea Sygros. 6.50d, John Varvakis.

1973, Nov. 15 Engraved

1101 A328 1.50d dk. red brown 18 10
1102 " 2d carmine rose 22 12
1103 " 2.50d slate green 27 15
1104 " 4d purple 45 30
1105 " 6.50d black 2.00 1.80
Nos. 1101–1105 (5) 3.12 2.47

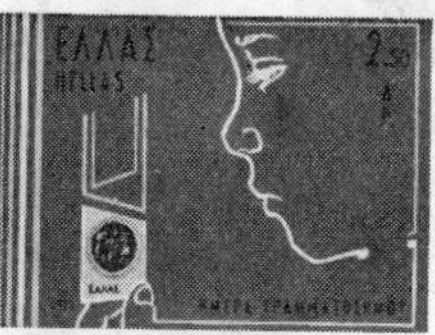

Child Examining Stamp A329

1973, Nov. 15 Litho. *Perf. 14x13*

1106 A329 2.50d multicolored 50 50

Stamp Day.

Lord Byron in Souliot Costume A330

Byron Taking Oath at Grave of Botsaris A331

Lithographed

1974, Apr. 4 *Perf. 13x14* **Wmk. 252**

1107 A330 2.50d multicolored 25 25
1108 A331 4.50d " 50 50

Sesquicentennial of the death of George Gordon, Lord Byron (1788–1824), English poet involved in Greek struggle for independence.

Europa Issue 1974

Harpist of Keros, c. 2800–2200 B.C. A332

Designs: 4.50d, Statue of Young Women, c. 510 B.C. 6.50d, Charioteer of Delphi, c. 480–450 B.C.

1974, May 10 *Perf. 13x14*

1109 A332 3d dp. bl. & multi. 50 45
1110 " 4.50d dull red & multi. 75 60
1111 " 6.50d yel. & multi. 1.25 1.25

Zeus and Hera Enthroned, and Iris
A333

Design from Mycenean Vase and UPU Emblem
A334

Designs (from Vases, 5th Century B.C.): 2d, Birth of Athena (horiz.). 2.50d, Artemis, Apollo, Leto (horiz.). 10d, Hermes, the messenger.

1974, June 24 ***Perf. 13x14, 14x13***

1112 A333 1.50d ocher, black & brown 10 10
1113 " 2d black, ocher & brown 20 18
1114 " 2.50d black, ocher & brown 30 15
1115 " 10d ocher, black & brown 1.50 1.50

Greek mythology.

1974, Sept. 14 ***Perf. 12½x13½***

Designs (UPU Emblem and): 4.50d, Hermes on the Move (horiz.). 6.50d, Woman reading letter.

1116 A334 2d violet & black 40 35
1117 " 4.50d " " 60 60
1118 " 6.50d " " 1.25 1.25

Centenary of Universal Postal Union.

Crete No. 80
A335

1974, Nov. 15 Litho. ***Perf. 13½x13***

1119 A335 2.50d multicolored 75 75

Stamp Day.

Flight into Egypt—A336

1974, Nov. 15 ***Perf. 13½x14***

1120 A336 Strip of 3 2.50 2.50
a. 2d ocher & multi. 25 8
b. 4.50d " " 30 30
c. 8.50d " " 1.75 1.75

Christmas 1974. Printed in sheets of 36 containing 12 triptychs. Design is from 11th century Codex of Dionysos Monastery on Mount Athos.

Costume Type of 1972

Perf. 12½x13½

1974, Dec. 5 Litho. Wmk. 252

Designs: Women's costumes, except 1.50d.

Costumes in Original Colors, Dull Yellow Frame

1121 A310 20 l *Megara* 3 3
1122 " 30 l *Salamis* 3 3
1123 " 50 l *Edipsos* 3 3
1124 " 1d *Kyme* 7 3
1125 " 1.50d *Sterea Hellas* 10 3
1126 " 2d *Desfina* 14 4
1127 " 3d *Epirus* 20 10
1128 " 3.50d *Naousa* 25 15
1129 " 4d *Hasia* 28 15
1130 " 4.50d *Thasos* 32 20
1131 " 5d *Skopelos* 35 20
1132 A310 6.50d *Epirus* 45 40
1133 " 10d *Pelion* 70 40
1134 " 25d *Kerkyra* 1.75 1.00
1135 " 30d *Boeotia* 2.10 1.10
Nos. 1121-1135 (15) 6.80 3.89

Secret Vostitsa Assembly, 1821
A337

Grigorios Dikeos-Papaflessas
A338

Aghioi Apostoli Church, Kalamata
A339

Perf. 13½x12½, 12½x13½

1975, Mar. 24

1136 A337 4d multicolored 28 20
1137 A338 7d " 48 45
1138 A339 11d " 78 75

Grigorios Dikeos-Papaflessas (1788–1825), priest and leader in Greece's uprising against the Turks, sesquicentennial of death.

Vase with Flowers
A340

Erotokritos and Aretussa
A341

Design: 11d, Girl with Hat. All designs are after paintings by Theophilos Hatzimichael (d. 1934).

Perf. 12½x13½

1975, May 10 Litho. Wmk. 252

1139 A340 4d multicolored 60 40
1140 A341 7d " 1.00 1.00
1141 A340 11d " 1.85 1.50

House, Kastoria
A342

Greek Houses, 18th Century: 40 l, Arnea, Halkidiki. 4d, Veria. 6d, Siatista. 11d, Ambelakia, Thessaly.

Perf. 13½x12½

1975, June 26 Wmk. 252

1142 A342 10 l brt. bl. & blk. 10 10
1143 " 40 l red org. & blk. 15 15
1144 " 4d bister & black 55 40
1145 " 6d ultra. & multi. 85 60
1146 " 11d org. & black 2.50 2.00
Nos. 1142-1146 (5) 4.15 3.25

IWY Emblem, Neolithic Goddess
A343

"Looking to the Future"
A344

Design: 8.50d, Confrontation between Antigone and Creon.

Perf. 12½x13½

1975, Sept. 29 Litho. Wmk. 252

1147 A343 1.50d lilac & dark brown 20 10
1148 " 8.50d bister, black & brown 1.20 1.00
1149 A344 11d blue & black 1.50 1.50

International Women's Year 1975.

Papanastasiou and University Buildings
A345

First University Building
A346

University City Plan
A347

1975, Sept. 29 ***Perf. 14x13½***

1150 A345 1.50d tan & sepia 15 10
1151 A346 4d multicolored 42 20
1152 A347 11d " 1.15 1.00

Thessaloniki University, 50th anniversary. Alexandros Papanastasiou (1876–1936), founded University while Prime Minister.

Evangelos Zappas and Zappeion Building—A348

National Benefactors: 4d, Georgios Rizaris and Rizarios Ecclesiastical School. 6d, Michael Tositsas and Metsovion Technical University. 11d, Nicolaos Zosimas and Zosimea Academy.

Perf. 14x13

1975, Nov. 15 Litho. Wmk. 252

1153 A348 1d black & green 10 6
1154 " 4d blk. & brown 40 15
1155 " 6d blk. & orange 65 50
1156 " 11d black & brick red 1.35 1.35

Greece No. 380
A349

1975, Nov. 15 ***Perf. 13x14***

1157 A349 11d dull green & brown 78 75

Stamp Day 1975.

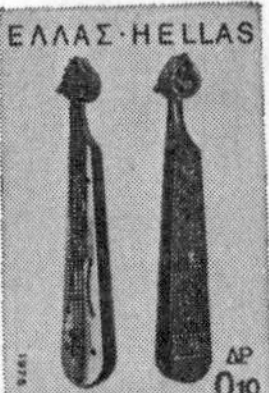

Pontos Lyre
A350

Musicians, Byzantine Mural
A351

Designs: 1d, Cretan lyre. 1.50d, Tambourine. 4d, Guitarist, from amphora (horiz.). 6d, Bagpipes. 7d, Lute. 10d, Barrel organ. 11d, Pipes and zournadas. 20d, Musicians and singers praising God, Byzantine mural (horiz.). 25d, Drums. 30d, Kanonaki (horiz.).

Perf. 12½x13½, 13½x12½

1975, Dec. 15 Litho. Wmk. 252

1158 A350 10 l multicolored 5 5
1159 A351 20 l " 5 5
1160 A350 1d ultra. & multi. 9 5
1161 " 1.50d multicolored 12 5
1162 A351 4d " 35 10
1163 A350 6d " 50 40
1164 " 7d " 60 40
1165 " 10d " 85 70
1166 " 11d red & multi. 95 75
1167 A351 20d multicolored 1.75 1.20
1168 A350 25d " 2.10 1.50
1169 " 30d " 2.50 1.85
Nos. 1158-1169 (12) 9.91 7.10

Popular musical instruments.

Early Telephone, Globe, Waves
A352

Design: 11d, Globe, waves, telephone 1976.

Perf. 13½x12½

1976, Mar. 23 Litho. Wmk. 252

1170 A352 7d black & multi. 60 60
1171 " 11d " " 1.00 1.00
Pair #1170-1171 2.00 2.00

Centenary of first telephone call by Alexander Graham Bell, Mar. 10, 1876. Nos. 1170–1171 printed se-tenant in sheets of 50.

Sortie of Missolonghi
A353

1976, Mar. 23 ***Perf. 13½x13***

1172 A353 4d multicolored 40 40

Sortie of the garrison of Missolonghi, sesquicentennial.

Europa Issue 1976

Florina Jug A354 — Avramidis Plate A355

Design: 11d, Egina pitcher with Greek flags.

Perf. 13x14, 12½x12 (A355)

1976, May 10 Litho. Wmk. 252

1173	A354	7d buff & multi.	70	65
1174	A355	8.50d blk. & multi.	85	85
1175	A354	11d gray & multi.	1.50	1.40

Lion Attacking Bull A356 — Head of Silenus A357

Designs: 4.50d, Flying aquatic birds. 7d, Wounded bull. 11d, Cow feeding calf (horiz.). Designs from Creto-Mycenaean engraved seals, c. 1400 B.C.

Perf. 13x12½, 13½x14, 14x13½

1976, May 10

1176	A356	2d bis. & multi.	20	18
1177	"	4.50d multicolored	45	42
1178	"	7d "	70	70
1179	A357	8.50d pur. & multi.	85	85
1180	"	11d brown & multi.	1.10	1.10
		Nos. 1176-1180 (5)	3.30	3.25

Long Jump A358

Montreal and Athens Stadiums—A359

Designs (Classical and Modern Events): 2d, Basketball. 3.50d, Wrestling. 4d, Swimming. 25d, Lighting Olympic flame and Montreal Olympic Games torch.

Perf. 14x13½, 12½x13½ (A359)

1976, June 25 Litho. Wmk. 252

1181	A358	50 l org. & multi.	4	3
1182	"	2d " "	20	20
1183	"	3.50d " "	25	20
1184	"	4d bl. & multi.	40	25
1185	A359	11d multi.	1.10	1.10
1186	A358	25d org.& multi.	3.00	3.00
		Nos. 1181-1186 (6)	4.99	4.78

21st Olympic Games, Montreal, Canada, July 17–Aug. 1.

Lesbos, View and Map A360

Designs (Views and Maps): 30d, Lemnos (vert.). 75d, Chios. 100d, Samos.

Perf. 13½x14, 14x13½

1976, July 26 Litho. Wmk. 252

1187	A360	30d blue & multi.	2.25	1.40
1188	"	50d " "	3.75	2.50
1189	"	75d " "	5.75	3.75
1190	"	100d " "	7.50	4.75

Greek Aegean Islands.

Three Kings Speaking to the Jews A361

Design: 7d, Nativity. Designs from manuscripts in Esfigmenou Monastery, Mount Athos.

Perf. 13½x14

1976, Dec. 8 Litho. Wmk. 252

1191	A361	4d yel. & multi.	28	25
1192	"	7d " "	42	35

Christmas 1976.

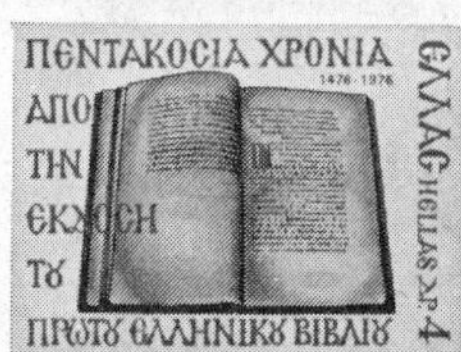

Greek Grammar of 1478 A362

1976, Dec. 8 *Perf. 14x13*

1193	A362	4d multicolored	28	25

500th anniversary of printing of first Greek book by Constantin Lascaris, Milan.

Heinrich Schliemann A363 — Brooch with Figure of Goddess A364

Designs: 4d, Gold bracelet (horiz.). 7d, Gold diadem (horiz.). 11d, Gold mask (Agamemnon). Treasures from Mycenaean tombs.

1976, Dec. 8 *Perf. 13x14, 14x13*

1194	A363	2d multicolored	28	25
1195	A364	4d "	55	50
1196	"	5d green & multi.	70	70
1197	"	7d multicolored	85	70
1198	A364	11d multicolored	1.50	1.20
		Nos. 1194-1198 (5)	3.88	3.35

Centenary of the discovery of the Mycenaean royal shaft graves by Heinrich Schliemann.

Aesculapius with Patients A365 — Patient in Clinic A366

Designs: 1.50d, Aesculapius curing young man. 2d, Young Hercules with old nurse. 20d, Old man with votive offering of large leg.

Perf. 12½x13½ (A365); 13x12 (A366)

1977, Mar. 15 Litho. Wmk. 252

1199	A365	50 l multicolored	4	4
1200	A366	1d "	7	7
1201	"	1.50d "	10	10
1202	"	2d "	14	14
1203	A365	20d "	2.00	2.00
		Nos.1199-1203 (5)	2.35	2.35

International Rheumatism Year.

Winged Wheel, Modern Transportation A367

1977, May 16 Litho. *Perf. 14x13½*

1204	A367	7d multicolored	60	60

European Conference of Ministers of Transport (E.C.M.T.), Athens, June 1–3.

Europa Issue 1977

Mani Castle, Vathia A368

Designs: 7d, Santorini (vert.). 15d, Windmills on Lasithi plateau.

Perf. 14x13½, 13½x14

1977, May 16 Litho. Wmk. 252

1205	A368	5d multicolored	50	45
1206	"	7d "	65	60
1207	"	15d "	1.50	1.50

Alexandria Lighthouse, from Roman Coin A369

Designs: 1d, Alexander places Homer's works into Achilles' tomb, fresco by Raphael. 1.50d, Alexander descends to the bottom of the sea, Flemish miniature. 3d, Alexander searching for water of life, Hindu plate. 7d, Alexander on horseback, Coptic carpet. 11d, Alexander hearing oracle that his days are numbered, Byzantine manuscript. 30d, Death of Alexander, Persian miniature. All designs include gold coin of Lysimachus with Alexander's head.

Perf. 14x13

1977, July 23 Wmk. 252

1208	A369	50 l silv. & multi.	4	4
1209	"	1d " "	7	7
1210	"	1.50d " "	10	10
1211	"	3d " "	20	20
1212	A369	7d silv. & multi.	50	50
1213	"	11d " "	78	78
1214	"	30d " "	2.10	2.10
		Nos. 1208-1214 (7)	3.79	3.79

Cultural influence of Alexander the Great (356–323 B.C.), King of Macedonia.

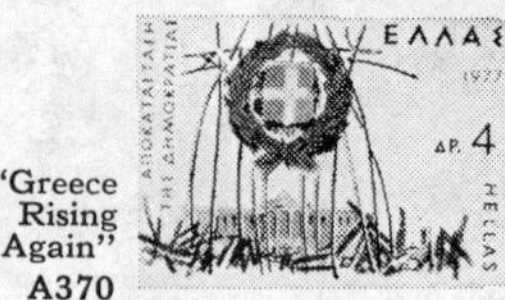

"Greece Rising Again" A370

People in Front of University A371 — Greek Flags, Laurel, University A372

Perf. 13½x12½, 12x12½, 12½x12

1977, July 23 Unwmkd.

1215	A370	4d multicolored	28	20
1216	A371	7d "	50	50
1217	A372	20d "	1.40	1.40

Restoration of Democracy in Greece.

Archbishop Makarios, Map of Cyprus—A373

Design: 4d, Archbishop Makarios (vert.).

Perf. 13x13½, 13½x13

1977, Sept. 10 Litho. Unwmkd.

1218	A373	4d sepia & black	28	28
1219	"	7d buff, brown & black	80	80

Archbishop Makarios (1913–1977), President of Cyprus.

Old Athens Post Office A374

Buildings: 1d, Institution for the Blind, Salonika. 1.50d, Townhall, Syros. 2d, National Bank of Greece, Piraeus. 5d, Byzantine Museum, Athens. 50d, Municipal Theater, Patras.

Unwmkd.

1977, Sept. 22 Litho. *Perf. 13½x13*

1220	A374	50 l multicolored	4	4
1221	"	1d "	7	7
1222	"	1.50d "	10	10
1223	"	2d "	14	14
1224	"	5d "	35	35
1225	"	50d "	3.50	3.50
		Nos. 1220-1225 (6)	4.20	4.20

Neo-Hellenic architecture.

Battle of Navarino, Lithograph—A375

Adm. Van Heyden, Sir Edward Codrington, Count de Rigny—A376

Perf. 13½x13

1977, Oct. 20 Litho. Unwmkd.

1226	A375	4d brown, buff & black	28	28
1227	A376	7d multicolored	50	50

150th anniversary of Battle of Navarino.

Parthenon and Refinery A377

Caryatid and Factories A379

Fish and Birds Suffering from Pollution A378

Design: 7d, Birds and trees in polluted air.

Perf. 13½x14, 14x13½

1977, Oct. 20

1228	A377	3d org. & black	22	22
1229	A378	4d multicolored	28	28
1230	"	7d "	50	50
1231	A379	30d black, gray & slate	2.20	2.20

Protection of the environment.

Map of Greece and Ships A380

Globe and Swallows A381

Letter with Flags, Swallow A382

Designs: 5d, Globe with Greek flag. 13d, World map showing dispersion of Greeks abroad.

1977, Dec. 15 Litho. *Perf. 13½x12½*

1232	A380	4d multicolored	28	28
1233	"	5d "	35	35
1234	A381	7d "	50	50
1235	A382	11d "	80	80
1236	A380	13d "	90	90
		Nos. 1232-1236 (5)	2.83	2.83

Greeks living abroad.

Kalamata Harbor, by Constantine Parthenis A383

Greek Paintings: 2.50d, Boats, Arsanas, by Spyros Papaloucas (vert.). 4d, Santorini, by Constantine Maleas. 7d, The Engagement, by Nicolaus Gyzis. 11d, Woman with Straw Hat, by Nicolaus Lytras (vert.). 15d, "Spring" (nude), by Georgio Iacovidis.

Perf. 13½x13, 13x13½

1977, Dec. 15

1237	A383	1.50d yel. & multi.	10	10
1238	"	2.50d " "	18	18
1239	"	4d " "	28	28
1240	"	7d " "	50	50
1241	"	11d " "	80	80
1242	"	15d " "	1.05	1.05
		Nos. 1237-1242 (6)	2.91	2.91

Ebenus Cretica A384

Greek Flora: 2.50d, Dwarf lily. 3d, Campanula oreadum. 4d, Tiger lily. 7d, Viola delphinantha. 25d, Paeonia rhodia.

1978, Mar. 30 Litho. *Perf. 13x13½*

1243	A384	1.50d multicolored	10	10
1244	"	2.50d "	18	18
1245	"	3d "	22	22
1246	"	4d "	28	28
1247	"	7d "	50	50
1248	"	25d "	1.75	1.75
		Nos. 1243-1248 (6)	3.03	3.03

Postrider, Cancellation A385

Designs: 5d, S.S. Maximilianos and Hermes Head. 7d, 19th century mail train and No. 122. 30d, Mailmen on motorcycles and No. 1062.

1978, May 15 Litho. *Perf. 13½x12½*

1249	A385	4d buff & multi.	40	40
1250	"	5d " "	50	50
1251	"	7d " "	70	70
1252	"	30d " "	3.00	3.00
		a. Souvenir sheet of 4	5.25	5.25

150th anniversary of Greek postal service.

No. 1252a issued Sept. 25, contains Nos. 1249-1252 in slightly changed colors; gray margin with black inscription. Size: 101x92mm. Sold for 60d.

Lighting Olympic Flame, Olympia A386

Start of 100-meter Race A387

1978, May 15 *Perf. 13x14*

1253	A386	7d multicolored	35	35
1254	A387	13d "	65	65

80th session of International Olympic Committee, Athens, May 10-21.

Europa Issue 1978

St. Sophia, Salonica A388

Lysicrates Monument, Athens A389

1978, May 15 *Perf. 13x14, 14x13*

1255	A388	4d multicolored	30	20
1256	A389	7d "	50	50

Aristotle, Roman Bust A390

School of Athens, by Raphael A391

Map of Chalcidice, Base of Statue from Attalus Arcade A392

Aristotle the Wise, Byzantine Fresco, St. George's Church, Ioannina A393

Perf. 13x13½, 13½x14 (20d)

1978, July 10 Lithographed

1257	A390	2d multicolored	10	10
1258	A391	4d "	20	20
1259	A392	7d "	35	35
1260	A393	20d "	1.00	1.00

Aristotle (384-322 B.C.), systematic philosopher.

Rotary Emblem A394

Surgeons Operating A395

Ugo Foscolo, View of Zante A396

Hellenistic Bronze Head A397

Charioteer's Hand, Delphi A398

Wright Brothers' Plane, Daedalus and Icarus A399

1978, Sept. 21 Litho. *Perf. 12½*

1261	A394	1d multicolored	*35*	*35*
1262	A395	1.50d "	8	8
1263	A396	2.50d "	12	12
1264	A397	5d "	25	25
1265	A398	7d "	35	35
1266	A399	13d "	65	65
		Nos. 1261-1266 (6)	*1.80*	*1.80*

Rotary in Greece, 50th anniversary (1d); 11th Greek Surgery Congress, Salonica (1.50d); Ugo Foscolo (1778-1827), Italian writer (2.50d); European Convention on Human Rights, 25th anniversary (5d); 2nd Conference of Ministers of Culture of the Council of Europe member countries, Athens, Oct. 23-27 (7d); 75th anniversary of first powered flight (13d).

Poor Woman and her 5 Children A400

Scenes from Fairy Tale "The 12 Months": 3d, The poor woman and the 12 months. 4d, The poor woman and the gold coins. 20d, Punishment of the greedy woman.

1978, Nov. 6 Litho. *Perf. 13½x13*

1267	A400	2d multicolored	10	10
1268	"	3d "	15	15
1269	"	4d "	20	20
1270	"	20d "	1.00	1.00

See "Special Notices" at the front of this volume for data on the listing methods of this Catalogue, abbreviations, condition, prices and examination.

"Transplants"
A401

The Miracle of St. Anarghiri
A402

1978, Nov. 6 ***Perf. 12½x13½***

1271	A401	4d multicolored		20	20
1272	A402	10d	"	50	50

Advancements in organ transplants.

Cruiser
A403

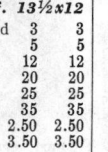

New and Old Greek Naval Ships: 1d, Torpedo boats. 2.50d, Submarine Papanicolis. 4d, Battleship Psara. 5d, Sailing ship "Madonna of Hydra." 7d, Byzantine corvette. 50d, Archaic trireme.

1978, Dec. 15 Litho. ***Perf. 13½x12***

1273	A403	50 l	multicolored	3	3
1274	"	1d	"	5	5
1275	"	2.50d	"	12	12
1276	"	4d	"	20	20
1277	"	5d	"	25	25
1278	"	7d	"	35	35
1279	"	50d	"	2.50	2.50
	Nos. 1273-1279 (7)			3.50	3.50

Cadet Officer, Military School, Nauplia
A404

Cadet Officers' School Emblem
A405

Design: 10d, Cadet Officers Military School, Athens, Cadet's uniform, 1978.

Perf. 13½x12, 12x13½

1978, Dec. 15

1280	A404	1.50d multicolored		8	8
1281	A405	2d	"	10	10
1282	A404	10d	"	50	50

Cadet Officers Military School, 150th anniversary.

Virgin and Child
A406

Baptism of Christ
A407

Designs from 16th century icon stands in Stavronikita Monastery.

1978, Dec. 15 ***Perf. 13x13½***

1283	A406	4d multicolored		20	20
1284	A407	7d	"	35	35

Christmas 1978.

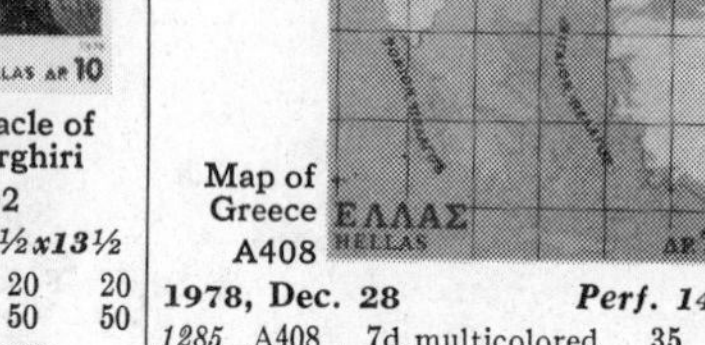

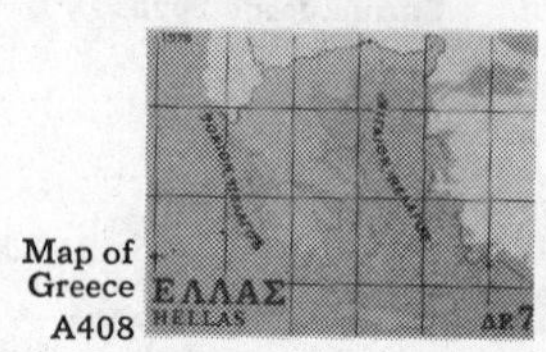

Map of Greece
A408

1978, Dec. 28 ***Perf. 14x13***

1285	A408	7d	multicolored	35	35
1286	"	11d	"	55	55
1287	"	13d	"	65	65

Kitsos Tzavellas
A409

Souli Castle
A410

Designs: 10d, Fighting Souliots. 20d, Fight of Zalongo.

Perf. 12½x13½, 13½x12½

1979, Mar. 12 **Lithographed**

1288	A409	1.50d buff, black & brown		8	8
1289	A410	3d multicolored		15	15
1290	"	10d	"	50	50
1291	A409	20d buff, black & brown		1.00	1.00

Struggle of the Souliots, 18th century fighters for freedom from Turkey.

Cycladic Figure from Amorgos
A411

Mailmen from Crete
A412

1979, Apr. 26 Litho. ***Perf. 12x13½***

1292	A411	20d multicolored		1.00	1.00

Aegean art.

Europa Issue 1979

Design: 7d, Rural mailman on horseback, Crete.

1979, May 11 ***Perf. 13½x14***

1293	A412	4d multicolored		20	20
1294	"	7d	"	35	35

Nos. 1293-1294 printed se-tenant in sheets of 50.

Unused prices are for stamps that have been hinged.

Nicolas Scoufas
A413

Basketball
A415

Locomotives
A414

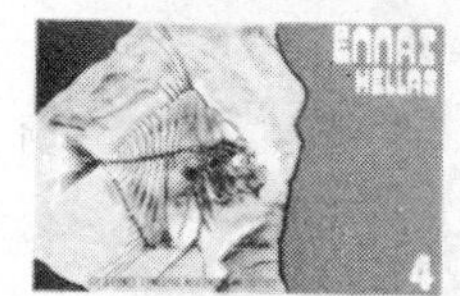

Mene Psarianosi Symeonidis Fossil
A416

Greek Temple and Byzantine Church
A417

Victory of Paeonius Statue, Flags of Balkan Countries
A418

1979, May 12 ***Perf. 13x14, 14x13***

1295	A413	1.50d	multicolored	8	8
1296	A414	2d	"	10	10
1297	A415	3d	"	15	15
1298	A416	4d	"	20	20
1299	A417	10d	"	50	50
1300	A418	20d	"	1.00	1.00
	Nos. 1295-1300 (6)			2.03	2.03

Nicolas Scoufas (1779-1818), founder of (patriotic) Friendly Society; Piraeus-Athens-to-the-frontier railroad, 75th anniversary; European Basketball Championship; 7th International Congress for the Study of the Neocene Period in the Mediterranean; Balkan Tourist Year 1979; 50 years of track and field competitions in Balkan countries.

SEMI-POSTAL STAMPS.

Greece, Nos. 440 - 444
Surcharged in Blue

1944 *Perf. 12½.* **Wmk. 252**

B1	A106	100,000d on 15d red violet	70	75
B2	A107	100,000d on 25d orange red	70	75
B3	A108	100,000d on 50d sapphire	70	75
B4	A109	100,000d on 75d deep rose	70	75
B5	A110	100,000d on 100d black	70	75
		Nos. B1-B5 (5)	3.50	3.75

The proceeds aided victims of the Piraeus bombing, January 11, 1944. The exceptionally high face value discouraged the use of these stamps.

Nos. 437 to 441 Surcharged in Blue

ΠΑΙΔΙΚΑΙ ΕΞΟΧΑΙ
ΔΡΧ.
50,000+450,000

1944, July 20

B11	A103	50,000d+450,000d on 2d red brown	85	90
B12	A104	50,000d+450,000d on 5d light blue green	85	90
B13	A105	50,000d+450,000d on 10d light blue	85	90
B14	A106	50,000d+450,000d on 15d red violet	85	90
		a. Pair, one without surch.	50.00	
B15	A107	50,000d+450,000d on 25d orange red	85	90
		Nos. B11-B15 (5)	4.25	4.50

The surtax aided children's camps.

AIR POST STAMPS

Italy-Greece-Turkey-Rhodes Service.

Flying Boat off Phaleron Bay—AP1

Flying Boat over Acropolis—AP2

Flying Boat over Map of Southern Europe—AP3

Flying Boat Seen through Colonnade
AP4

Lithographed.

1926, Oct. 20 *Perf. 11½* **Unwmkd.**

C1	AP1	2d multicolored	75	75
		a. Imperf. vertically (pair)	90.00	
C2	AP2	3d multicolored	12.50	8.00
C3	AP3	5d "	1.00	1.00
C4	AP4	10d "	10.00	10.00

Graf Zeppelin Issue.

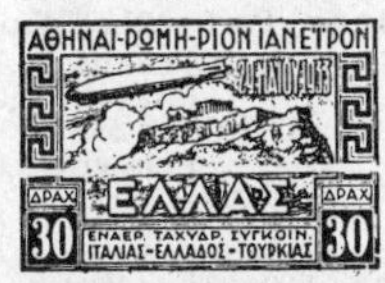

Zeppelin over Acropolis—AP5

1933, May 2 *Perf. 13½x12½*

C5	AP5	30d rose red	15.00	15.00
C6	"	100d deep blue	65.00	60.00
C7	"	120d dark brown	70.00	60.00

Propeller and Pilot's Head—AP6

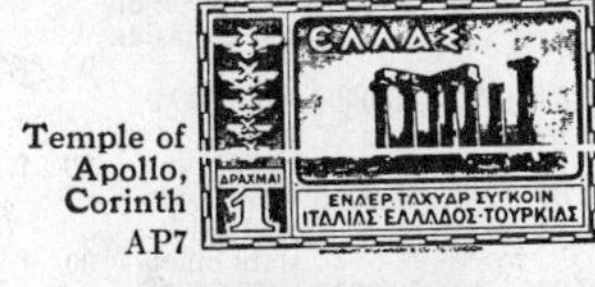

Temple of Apollo, Corinth
AP7

Plane over Hermoupolis, Syros
AP8

Allegory of Flight
AP9

Map of Italy-Greece-Turkey-Rhodes Airmail Route—AP10

Head of Hermes and Airplane
AP11

Allegory of Flight
AP12

1933, Oct. 10 **Engraved** *Perf. 12*

C8	AP6	50l green & orange	40	40
C9	AP7	1d bl. & brn. org.	40	40
C10	AP8	3d dark violet & org. brown	1.00	1.00
C11	AP9	5d brn. orange & dark blue	3.00	3.00
C12	AP10	10d deep red & blk.	2.00	2.00
C13	AP11	20d black & green	5.00	5.00
C14	AP12	50d deep brown & deep blue	100.00	100.00
		Nos. C8-C14 (7)	111.80	111.80

By error the 1d stamp is inscribed in the plural "Draxmai" instead of the singular "Draxmh." This stamp exists bisected, used as a 50 lepta denomination.

All values of this set exist imperforate but were not regularly issued.

For General Air Post Service.

Airplane over Map of Greece
AP13

Airplane over Map of Icarian Sea
AP14

Airplane over Acropolis
AP15

Perf. 13 x13½, 13 x12½, 13½ x13, 12½ x13.

1933, Nov. 2

C15	AP13	50l green	30	30
C16	"	1d red brown	90	70
C17	AP14	2d light violet	1.20	1.20
C18	AP15	5d ultramarine	9.50	7.25
		a. Imperf. (pair)	250.00	250.00
		b. Imperf. vertically (pair)	200.00	
C19	AP14	10d carmine rose	30.00	27.50
C20	AP13	25d dark blue	47.50	42.50
C21	AP15	50d dark brown	60.00	55.00
		a. Imperf. (pair)	375.00	375.00
		Nos. C15-C21 (7)	149.40	134.45

Helios Driving the Sun Chariot
AP16

Iris
AP17

Daedalus Preparing Icarus for Flying
AP18

Pallas Athene Holding Pegasus
AP19

Hermes
AP20

Zeus Carrying off Ganymede
AP21

Triptolemos, King of Eleusis
AP22

Bellerophon and Pegasus
AP23

Phrixos and Helle on the Ram Flying over the Hellespont
AP24

Perf. 13x12½, 12½x13

1935, Nov. 10 **Engraved**

Grayish Paper

Size: 34x23½mm., 23½x34mm.

C22	AP16	1d deep red	37	25
C23	AP17	2d dull blue	1.85	50
C24	AP18	5d dark violet	11.00	1.20
C25	AP19	7d blue violet	21.50	6.00
C26	AP20	10d bistre brown	12.00	1.85
C27	AP21	25d rose	18.00	18.00
C28	AP22	30d dark green	90	90
C29	AP23	50d violet	4.75	4.75
C30	AP24	100d brown	3.00	3.00
		Nos. C22-C30 (9)	73.37	36.45

1937-39 **Re-engraved**

White Paper

Size: 34¼x24mm., 24x34¼mm.

C31	AP16	1d red	15	15
C32	AP17	2d gray blue	10	10
C33	AP18	5d violet	10	10
C34	AP19	7d deep ultramarine	10	10

C35 AP20 10d brown orange ('39) 2.00 2.00
Nos. C31-C35 (5) 2.45 2.45

Postage Due Stamp, 1913, Overprinted in Red

Serrate Roulette 13½.

1938, Aug. 8 Litho. Unwmkd.

C36 D3 50 l violet brown 10 10
a. "O" for "P" in word at foot 17.50 17.50

Same Overprint on No. J79 in Red

1939, June 26 *Perf. 13½x12½*

C37 D3 50 l dark brown 10 10

National Youth Issue.

Meteora Monasteries, near Trikkala
AP25

Designs: 4d, Simon Peter Monastery. 6d, View of Santorin. 8d, Church of Pantanassa. 16d, Santorin view. 32d, Ponticonissi, Corfu. 45d, Acropolis, Athens. 55d, Erechtheum. 65d, Temple of Nike Apteros. 100d, Temple of the Olympian Zeus, Athens.

Wmkd. Crowns. (252)

1940, Aug. 3 Litho. *Perf. 12½*

C38 AP25 2d red orange & black 2.50 2.50
C39 " 4d dk. grn. & blk. 21.50 25.00
C40 " 6d lake & black 21.50 25.00
C41 " 8d dark blue & black 37.50 40.00
C42 " 16d rose violet & black 37.50 40.00
C43 " 32d red orange & black 42.50 45.00
C44 " 45d dk. grn. & blk. 50.00 50.00
C45 " 55d lake & black 57.50 57.50
C46 " 65d dark blue & black 57.50 57.50
C47 " 100d rose violet & black 57.50 57.50
Nos. C38-C47 (10) 385.50 400.00

Issued in commemoration of the 4th anniversary of the founding of the Greek Youth Organization. The stamps were good for postal duty on August 3-4-5, 1940, only. They remained on sale until February 3, 1941.

Postage Due Stamps Nos. J81 and J75 Surcharged in Red

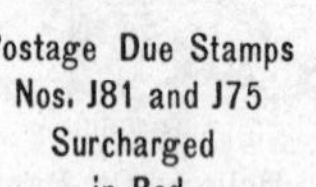

1941-42 *Perf. 13x12½* Unwmkd.

C48 D3 1d on 2d light red 20 20
a. Inverted surcharge 11.50

Serrate Roulette 13½

C49 D3 1d on 2d verm. ('42) 20 20
a. Inverted surcharge 12.50
b. Double surcharge 11.50

Nos. J83, J84, J86, J87 Overprinted in Red

1941-42 *Perf. 13, 12½x13*

C50 D3 5d gray blue ('42) 30 30
a. Inverted overprint 10.00
b. Double overprint 10.00
c. Pair, one without overprint 15.00
d. Surcharge on back 20.00
C51 " 10d gray green 30 30
a. Inverted overprint 15.00
b. Vertical pair, imperf. between 100.00
C52 " 25d light red 1.50 1.50
a. Inverted overprint 25.00
C53 " 50d orange 2.00 2.00

Same Overprint on No. J78.
Serrate Roulette 13½

1942, Mar. 15

C54 D3 5d gray blue 85.00 100.00

Some specialists question the status of No. C54. Counterfeits exist.

Boreas, North Wind
AP35

Winds: 5d, Notus, South. 10d, Apeliotes, East. 20d, Lips, Southwest. 25d, Zephyrus, West. 50d, Kaikias, Northeast.

Lithographed.

1942, Aug. 15 *Perf. 12½* Wmk. 252

C55 AP35 2d emerald 15 15
C56 " 5d red orange 15 15
a. Imperf. (pair) 125.00
b. Double impression 20.00 20.00
C57 " 10d red brown 15 15
C58 " 20d bright blue 15 15
C59 " 25d dark red orange 15 15
C60 " 50d gray black 2.00 2.00
a. Double impression 85.00
Nos. C55-C60 (6) 2.75 2.75

1943, Sept. 15

Winds: 10d, Apeliotes, East. 25d, Zephyrus, West. 50d, Kaikias, Northeast. 100d, Boreas, North. 200d, Eurus, Southeast. 400d, Skiron, Northwest.

C61 AP35 10d rose red 12 12
a. Imperf., pair 85.00
C62 " 25d Prussian green 12 12
a. Imperf., pair 75.00
C63 " 50d violet blue 12 12
a. Imperf., pair 75.00
C64 " 100d slate black 12 12
a. Imperf., pair 80.00
C65 " 200d claret 12 12
a. Imperf., pair 90.00
C66 " 400d steel blue 25 25
a. Imperf., pair 90.00
Nos. C61-C66 (6) 85 85

Double impressions exist of 10d and 400d. Price, each $30.

Priest Blessing Troops on Summit of Mt. Grammos
AP36

Torchbearer
AP37

Designs: 1700d, Victory above Mt. Vitsi. 2700d, Battle Scene. 7000d, Victory leading infantry.

1952, Aug. 29 Engr. *Perf. 12x13½*

C67 AP36 1000d deep blue 4.00 15
C68 " 1700d dp. bl. grn. 5.25 75
C69 " 2700d brown 13.50 4.00
C70 " 7000d olive grn. 25.00 7.00

Issued to publicize the Greek army's struggle against communism.

1954, May 15 *Perf. 13*

Designs: 2400dr, Coin of Amphictyonic League. 4000dr, Pallas Athene.

C71 AP37 1200d deep orge. 35.00 30
C72 " 2400d dark green 45.00 7.00
C73 " 4000d dp. ultra. 45.00 10.00

Issued to commemorate the fifth anniversary of the signing of the North Atlantic Treaty.

Piraeus
AP38

Harbors: 15d, Salonika. 20d, Patras. 25d, Hermoupolis (Syra). 30d, Volos. 50d, Cavalla. 100d, Herakleion (Candia).

Lithographed.

1958, July 1 *Perf. 13½x13* Wmk. 252

C74 AP38 10d multicolored 2.15 15
C75 " 15d " 2.25 45
C76 " 20d " 4.25 25
C77 " 25d " 3.50 85
C78 " 30d " 4.25 35
C79 " 50d " 9.00 50
C80 " 100d " 21.50 3.75
Nos. C74-C80 (7) 46.90 6.30

AIR POST SEMI-POSTAL STAMPS.

Nos. C61 to C65 Surcharged in Blue

ΒΟΜΒΑΡΔΙΣΜΟΣ
ΠΕΙΡΑΙΩΣ
11-1-1944
ΔΡ. 100.000

1944, June *Perf. 12½* Wmk. 252

CB1 AP35 100,000d on 10d rose red 1.00 1.10
CB2 " 100,000d on 25d Prus. grn. 1.00 1.10
CB3 " 100,000d on 50d violet blue 1.00 1.10
a. Inverted ovpt. 50.00
CB4 " 100,000d on 100d slate blk. 1.00 1.10
CB5 " 100,000d on 200d claret 1.00 1.10
Nos. CB1-CB5 (5) 5.00 5.50

The exceptionally high face value discouraged the use of these stamps.
The proceeds aided victims of the Piraeus bombing, January 11, 1944.

Nos. C61 to C65 Surcharged in Blue

1944, July

CB6 AP35 50,000d+450,000d on 10d rose red 90 1.10
CB7 " 50,000d+450,000d on 25d Prussian green 90 1.10
CB8 " 50,000d+450,000d on 50d violet blue 90 1.10
CB9 " 50,000d+450,000d on 100d slate black 90 1.10
CB10 " 50,000d+450,000d on 200d claret 90 1.10
Nos. CB6-CB10 (5) 4.50 5.50

The surtax aided children's camps.
Surcharge on Nos. CB6-CB10 exists inverted or double. Price, each $45.

POSTAGE DUE STAMPS

D1

D2

1875 Lithographed Unwmkd.

Perf. 9, 9½, and 10, 10½ and Compound

J1 D1 1 l green & black 1.00 1.00
J2 " 2 l " " 1.00 1.00
J3 " 5 l " " 2.00 1.50
J4 " 10 l " " 2.00 1.50
J5 " 20 l " " 55.00 40.00
J6 D1 40 l green & black 10.00 7.00
a. Imperf., pair 45.00 45.00
J7 " 60 l green & black 60.00 30.00
J8 " 70 l " " 5.00 5.00
J9 " 80 l " " 10.00 9.00
J10 " 90 l " " 7.00 6.00
J11 " 1d green & black 7.00 6.00
a. Imperf.
b. Center inverted 200.00
J12 " 2d green & black 8.00 8.00
a. Center inverted 140.00

Imperforate and part perforated, double and inverted center varieties of Nos. J1-J12 are believed to be printers' waste.

Perf. 12, 13 and 10½ x13.

J13 D1 1 l green & black 1.50 1.50
J14 " 2 l " " 1.50 1.50
J15 " 5 l " " 3.00 3.00
J16 " 10 l " " 3.00 2.50
J17 " 20 l " " 70.00 50.00
J18 " 40 l " " 10.00 8.00
J19 " 60 l " " 75.00 60.00
J20 " 70 l " " 6.50 6.50
J21 " 80 l " " 10.00 9.00
J22 " 90 l " " 8.00 7.00
J23 " 1d " " 8.00 7.00
J24 " 2d " " 10.00 10.00

1876 Redrawn

"Lepton" or "Lepta" in Larger Greek Letters.

Perf. 9, 9½, and 10, 10½.

J25 D2 1 l green & black 1.00 1.00
J26 " 2 l dk. green & black 3.00 3.00
J27 " 5 l dk. grn. & blk. 225.00 175.00
a. Imperf., pair
J28 " 10 l green & black 2.00 2.00
J29 " 20 l green & black 2.00 2.00
a. Imperf. vertically
J30 " 40 l green & black 12.00 12.00
a. Imperf., pair
J31 " 60 l green & black 10.00 10.00
J32 " 70 l " " 20.00 20.00
J33 " 80 l " " 20.00 20.00
J34 " 90 l " " 10.00 10.00
J35 " 100 l " " 15.00 15.00
J36 " 200 l " " 15.00 15.00

Perf. 11½ to 13

J37 D2 1 l yel. grn. & blk. 40 40
J38 " 2 l " " " 40 40
J39 " 5 l " " " 50 50
J40 " 10 l " " " 50 50
a. Perf. 10-10½x11½-13 2.00
J41 " 20 l yel. grn. & blk. 70 70
J42 " 40 l " " " 7.50 7.50
J43 " 60 l " " " 7.50 7.50
J47 " 100 l " " " 10.00 10.00
J48 " 200 l " " " 10.00 10.00

Footnote below No. J12 applies also to Nos. J25-J48.

D3

Wmkd. Crown and E. T. (129)

1902 Engraved *Perf. 13½.*

J49 D3 1 l chocolate 25 25
J50 " 2 l gray 15 15
a. Imperf., pair 15.00
J51 " 3 l orange 15 15
a. Imperf., pair 15.00
J52 " 5 l yellow green 30 15
a. Imperf., pair 15.00
J53 " 10 l scarlet 30 15
J54 " 20 l lilac 30 15
J55 " 25 l ultramarine 3.00 80
a. Imperf., pair 15.00
J56 " 30 l deep violet 25 10
a. Imperf., pair 25.00
J57 " 40 l dark brown 45 45
J58 " 50 l red brown 30 30
a. Imperf., pair 20.00
J59 " 1d black 1.00 75
a. Imperf., pair 25.00

Lithographed.

J60 D3 2d bronze 2.25 1.75
J61 " 3d silver 3.00 3.00
J62 " 5d gold 22.50 17.50
Nos. J49-J62 (14) 34.20 25.65

Serrate Roulette 13½.

1913-26 Unwmkd.

J63 D3 1 l green 5 5
J64 " 2 l carmine 5 5
J65 " 3 l vermilion 5 5
J66 " 5 l green 5 5
 a. Imperf., pair 10.00
 b. Double impression 15.00
 c. "o" for "p" in lowest word 1.00 50
J67 " 10 l carmine 5 5
J68 " 20 l slate 20 5
J69 " 25 l ultramarine 5 5
J70 " 30 l carmine 5 5
J71 " 40 l indigo 50 8
J72 " 50 l violet brown 30 7
 a. "o" for "p" in lowest word 15.00 10.00
J73 " 80 l lilac brown ('24) 1.00 1.00
J74 " 1d blue 3.00 20
 a. 1d ultramarine 10.00 1.00
J75 " 2d vermilion 50 20
J76 " 3d carmine 5.00 3.00
J77 " 5d ultramarine 18.00 3.00
J78 " 5d gray blue ('26) 6.00 3.50
 Nos. J63-J78 (16) 34.85 11.45

In 1922-23 and 1941-42 some postage due stamps were used for ordinary postage.

In 1916 Nos. J52, and J63 to J75 were surcharged for the Mount Athos District (see note after No. N166) but were never issued there. By error some of them were put in use as ordinary postage due stamps in Dec., 1924. In 1932 the balance of the stamps was burned.

Type of 1902 Issue.

Perf. 13, 13½x12½, 13½x13.

1930 Lithographed.

J79 D3 50 l dark brown 10 10
J80 " 1d light blue 2.00 10
J81 " 2d light red 10 10
J82 " 3d rose red 20.00 18.00
J83 " 5d gray blue 10 10
J84 " 10d gray green 12 12
J85 " 15d red brown 12 12
J86 " 25d light red 18 18
 Nos. J79-J86 (8) 22.72 18.82

Type of 1902 Issue.

1935 Engraved. *Perf. 12½x13.*

J87 D3 50d orange 20 20
J88 " 100d slate green 30 30

No. J70 Surcharged with New Value in Black.

1942

J89 D3 50 (l) on 30 l carmine 40 40

Type of 1902.
Lithographed.

1943 *Perf. 12½.* Wmk. 252

J90 D3 10d red orange 10 10
J91 " 25d ultramarine 10 10
J92 " 100d black brown 10 10
J93 " 200d violet 10 10

POSTAL TAX STAMPS.

"The Tragedy of War"
PT1

Red Cross, Nurses, Wounded and Bearers
PT1a

1914 Lithographed Unwmkd.

Serrate Roulette 13½

RA1 PT1 2 l carmine 5 5
 a. 2 l red 5 5
 b. Imperf., pair 30.00
RA2 " 5 l blue 30 15
 a. Imperf., pair

1915 *Serrate Roulette 13*

RA2B PT1a (5 l) dk. blue & red 8.00 50

The tax was for the Red Cross.

Women's Patriotic League Badge
PT1b

1915, Nov. *Perf. 11½*

RA2C PT1b (5 l) dk. blue & car. 3.00 40
 d. Horiz. pair, imperf. between 60.00

The tax was for the Greek Women's Patriotic League.

Regular Issue of 1901
Surcharged in Black or Brown:

Κ.Π. λεπτοῦ 1 (a)   Κ. Π. λεπτοῦ 1 (b)

In type "b" the letters, especially those in the first line, are thinner than in type "a", making them appear taller.

Perf. 11½, 12½, 13½ and Compound.

1917 Engraved. Wmk. 129

RA3 A11 (a) 1 l on 1 l brown 90 90
 a. Double surcharge 3.00
RA4 " (") 1 l on 1 l brown (Br) 18.50 18.50
RA5 " (") 1 l on 3 l orange 15 15
RA6 " (b) 1 l on 3 l orange 5 5
 a. Triple surcharge 3.00
 b. Double surcharge, one inverted 3.00
 c. "K.M." for "K.Π." 5.00 5.00
RA7 " (a) 5 l on 1 l brown 1.50 1.25
 a. Double surcharge 3.00
 b. Double surcharge, one inverted 3.00
 c. Inverted surcharge 3.00
RA8 " (") 5 l on 20 l red lilac 45 45
 a. Double surcharge 3.00
 b. Double surcharge, one inverted 3.00
RA9 " (b) 5 l on 40 l drak brown 50 50
 a. Imperf.
RA10 " (") 5 l on 50 l brown lake 38 38
 a. Double surcharge 3.00
 b. Double surcharge, one inverted 3.00
RA11 A13 (") 5 l on 1d black 75 75
 a. Imperf.
 b. Inverted surcharge 10.00
RA12 A11 (a) 10 l on 30 l dull violet 45 45
 a. Imperf.
 b. Dbl. surch. 3.00
RA13 " (") 30 l on 30 l dull violet 1.10 1.10
 a. Dbl. surch. 4.00
 Nos. RA3-RA13 (11) 24.73 24.48

Same Surcharge
On Occupation Stamps of 1912.

Serrate Roulette 13½.

1917 Lithographed. Unwmkd.

RA14 O2 (b) 5 l on 25 l pale blue 30 30
 a. Triple surcharge, one inverted 4.00
 b. Double surcharge 3.00
RA15 " (") 5 l on 40 l indigo 30 30
 a. Double surcharge, one inverted 3.00
 b. Double surcharge 3.00

RA16 O1 (b) 5 l on 50 l dark blue 22 22
 a. Double surcharge 3.00
 b. Inverted surcharge 3.00

There are many wrong font, omitted and misplaced letters and punctuation marks and similar varieties in the surcharges on Nos. RA3 to RA16.

"Victory"
R1

Revenue Stamps Surcharged in Brown

Κ. Π. λεπτοῦ 1

1917

RA17 R1 1 l on 10 l blue 3.00 3.00
RA18 " 1 l on 80 l blue 1.00 1.00
RA19 " 5 l on 10 l blue 10.00 6.00
RA20 " 5 l on 60 l blue 9.00 7.00
 a. Perf. vertically through middle 9.00 7.00
RA21 " 5 l on 80 l blue 9.00 7.00
 a. Perf. vertically through middle 9.00 7.00
 b. Inverted surcharge
RA22 " 10 l on 70 l blue 20.00 15.00
 a. Perf. vertically through middle 4.00 3.00
RA23 " 10 l on 90 l blue 10.00 8.00
 a. Perf. vertically through middle 15.00 15.00
RA24 " 20 l on 20 l blue 275.00 150.00
RA25 " 20 l on 30 l blue 7.00 4.00
RA26 " 20 l on 40 l blue 27.50 20.00
RA27 " 20 l on 50 l blue 10.00 6.00
RA28 " 20 l on 60 l blue 100.00 80.00
RA29 " 20 l on 80 l blue 50.00 40.00
RA30 " 20 l on 90 l blue 8.00 4.00
 a. Invtd. surch. 35.00
 Nos. RA17-RA30 (14) 539.50 351.00

No. RA19 is known only with vertical perforation through the middle.

Surcharged in Brown or Black

Κ. Π. 5 λεπτ. 5

RA31 R1 1 l on 50 l violet (Bk) 40 40
RA32 " 5 l on 10 l blue (Br) 80 30
 a. Inverted surcharge 10.00
 b. Left "5" invert. 10.00
RA33 " 5 l on 10 l vio. (Br) 60 25
RA34 " 10 l on 50 l vio. (Br) 1.40 30
RA35 " 10 l on 50 l violet (Bk) 10.00 5.00
RA36 " 20 l on 2d blue (Bk) 6.00 2.00
 a. Surcharged "20 lept. 30" 20.00 15.00
 b. Horizontal pair, imperf. between
 Nos. RA31-RA36 (6) 19.20 8.25

The "t," fourth Greek letter of the denomination in the surcharge ("Lept."), is normally omitted on Nos. RA31, RA34-RA36.

Corfu Issue.

Surcharged in Black

Κ.Π. 1 ΛΕΠΤΟΝ 1

1917

RA37 R1 1 l on 10 l blue 2.00 1.00
RA38 " 5 l on 50 l blue 35.00 16.50
RA39 " 10 l on 50 l blue 200.00 175.00
RA40 " 20 l on 50 l blue 225.00 200.00

Surcharged in Black

Κ.Π. 20 ΛΕΠΤΑ 20

RA41 R1 10 l on 50 l blue 7.50 5.00
RA42 " 20 l on 50 l blue 15.00 12.00
RA43 " 30 l on 50 l blue 15.00 12.00

Surcharged in Black

Κ. Π. 5 Λεπτὰ 5

RA44 R1 5 l on 10 l vio. & red 4.00 1.00
 a. "K" with serifs 5.00 1.50

Counterfeits exist of Nos. RA17-RA44.

Similar stamps with denominations higher than 30 lepta were for revenue use.

Wounded Soldier
PT2

1918 *Serrate Roulette 13½, 11½*

RA45 PT2 5 l blue, yellow & red 5.00 80

Overprinted Π.Ι.Π.

RA46 PT2 5 l blue, yellow & red 5.00 80

The letters are the initials of Greek words equivalent to "Patriotic Relief Institution". The proceeds were given to the Patriotic League, for the aid of disabled soldiers.

Counterfeits exist of Nos. RA45-RA46.

PT3

Surcharge in Red.

1922 Lithographed. *Perf. 11½*

RA46A PT3 5 l on 10 l dark blue & red 125.00 3.00
RA46B " 5 l on 20 l dark blue & red 25.00 22.50
RA46C " 5 l on 50 l dark blue & red 90.00 70.00
RA46D " 5 l on 1d dark blue & red 5.00 5.00

Nos. RA46A-RA46C exist without surcharge (not issued). Price, 20 cents each. Counterfeits of the surcharge exist on Nos. RA46A-RA46C.

Red Cross Help to Soldier and Family
PT3a

St. Demetrius
PT4

1924 ***Perf. 11½, 13½x12½.***

RA47 PT3a 10 l blue, buff & red 5 5
- *a.* Imperf., pair 10.00
- *b.* Horizontal pair, imperf. between 10.00
- *c.* Double impression of cross 10.00

Proceeds were given to the Red Cross.

1934 ***Perf. 11½.***

RA48 PT4 20 l brown 12 12
- *a.* Horizontal pair, imperf. between 10.00
- *b.* Vertical pair, imperf. between 10.00
- *c.* Imperf., pair 10.00

No. RA48 was obligatory as a tax on all interior mail, including air post, mailed from Salonika.

"Health"

PT5 PT6

1934, Dec. 28 ***Perf. 13, 13x13½***

RA49 PT5 10 l blue green, orange & buff 15 15
- *a.* Imperf. horiz.

RA50 " 20 l ultramarine, orange & buff 40 40

RA51 " 50 l green, orange & buff 75 50

1935

RA52 PT6 10 l yellow green, orange & buff 10 10

RA53 " 20 l ultramarine, orange & buff 20 20

RA54 " 50 l green, orange & buff 50 25

The use of Nos. RA49 to RA54 was obligatory on all mail during four weeks each year including Christmas, the New Year and Easter, and on parcel post packages at all times. For the benefit of the tubercular clerks and officials of the Post, Telephone and Telegraph Serice.

No. 364 Overprinted in Red

ΠΡΟΝΟΙΑ

1937, Jan. 20 **Engr.** ***Perf. 13x12½***

RA55 A36 50 l violet 50 10

Overprint Inverted.

RA55A A36 50 l violet 50 10

No. RA55A first appeared as an error, then was issued deliberately in quantity to avoid speculation.

Same Overprint in Blue on No. J67.

Lithographed

Serrate Roulette 13½.

RA56 D3 10 l carmine 15 15
- *a.* Invtd. overprint 20.00

No. RA56 with blue overprint double exists only with additional black overprint of Ionian Islands No. NRA1a.

Same Overprint in Green on No. 364.

1937 **Engraved** ***Perf. 13x12½***

RA57 A36 50 l violet 75 15

Same Overprint, with Surcharge of New Value, on Nos. J66, J68 and 323 in Blue or Black.

Serrate Roulette 13½.

1938 **Lithographed** **Unwmkd.**

RA58 D3 50 l on 5 l green 75 15
- *a.* "o" for "p" in lowest word 3.50 3.50
- *b.* Imperf. horiz., pair 15.00

RA59 " 50 l on 20 l slate 75 15

Engraved

Perf. 13x12½

RA60 A38 50 l on 20 l violet (Bk) 75 10

Surcharge on No. RA60 measures 14½x16½mm.

Queens Olga and Sophia—PT7

1939, Feb. 1 **Litho.** ***Perf. 13½x12***

RA61 PT7 10 l bright rose, *pale rose* 5 5

RA62 " 50 l gray green, *pale green* 10 10

RA63 " 1d dull blue, *light blue* 40 40

"Health" Type of 1935.

1939 ***Perf. 12½***

RA64 PT6 50 l brown & buff 40 25

No. RA62 Overprinted in Red

ΠΡΟΣΤΑΣΙΑ ΦΥΜΑΤΙΚΩΝ ΤΤΤ

1940 ***Perf. 13½x12.***

RA65 PT7 50 l gray green, *pale green* 20 20
- *a.* Inverted overprint 20.00
- *b.* Pair, one without surcharge 15.00

Proceeds of Nos. RA64 and RA65 were used for the benefit of tubercular clerks and officials of the Post, Telephone and Telegraph Service. No. RA65 was used in Albania during the Greek occupation, 1940-41 without additional overprint.

No. 321 Surcharged in Carmine

Κ.Π. λεπτῶν 50

Engraved

1941 ***Perf. 13½x13*** **Unwmkd.**

RA66 A36 50 l on 5 l dark green 10 10
- *a.* Inverted surch. 10.00

No. RA49 and Type of 1935 Surcharged with New Value in Black.

Lithographed

Perf. 12½x13, 13x13½.

RA67 PT5 50 l on 10 l blue green, dull orange & buff 5.00 5.00

RA68 PT6 50 l on 10 l deep blue green, dull orange & buff 30 30
- *a.* Inverted surcharge 15.00
- *b.* Double surch. 15.00

No. RA48 Surcharged in Green

ΔΡ. 1

1942 ***Perf. 11½.***

RA69 PT4 1d on 20 l brown 15 15
- *a.* Pair, one without surcharge 10.00
- *b.* Imperf. (pair) 12.50
- *c.* Dbl. surch. 15.00

Nos. 321, 324 Surcharged in Red or Carmine

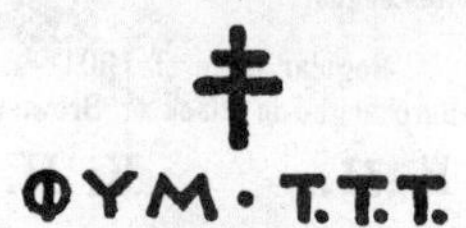

1942–43 **Engraved** ***Perf. 13½x13***

RA70 A36 10d on 5 l dark green (R) ('43) 10 10
- *a.* Double surcharge 10.00

RA71 A39 10d on 25 l slate blue (C) 15 15
- *a.* Inverted surch. 10.00

No 444 Overprinted in Red

ΦΥΜ·Τ.Τ.Τ.

Lithographed

1944 ***Perf. 12½.*** **Wmk. 252**

RA72 A110 100d black 10 10
- *a.* Double overprint 5.00
- *b.* Inverted overprint 5.00

No. 443 Surcharged in Blue

ΦΥΜ·Τ.Τ.Τ.
ΔΡ. 5000

RA73 A109 5,000d on 75d deep rose 10 10
- *a.* Double surcharge 15.00

No. 437 Surcharged in Blue

ΥΠΕΡ ΤΩΝ ΦΥΜΑΤΙΚΩΝ Τ.Τ.Τ. ΔΡΧ. 25.000

RA74 A103 25,000d on 2d red brown 10 10
- *a.* Double surcharge 10.00
- *b.* Additional surcharge on back 12.50

No. 399 Surcharged in Blue or Carmine

ΥΠΕΡ ΤΩΝ ΦΥΜΑΤΙΚΩΝ Τ.Τ.Τ. ΔΡΑΧΜΗ 1

1945 ***Perf. 13½x12.***

RA75 A72 1d on 40 l green & black 10 10
- *a.* Double surcharge 6.00

RA76 " 2d on 40 l green & black (C) 10 10
- *a.* Vertical pair, one without surcharge 6.00
- *b.* Surcharged on back 8.00
- *c.* Inverted surcharge 6.00

The tax on Nos. RA67, RA68 and RA70 to RA76 aided the postal clerks' tuberculosis fund.

Nos. 396 and 399 Surcharged in Carmine

ΠΡΟΝΟΙΑ ΠΡΟΣΩΠΙΚΟΥ Τ.Τ.Τ. ΔΡΑΧΜΑΙ 20

1946

RA77 A72 20d on 40 l green & black 20 15
- *a.* Pair, one without surcharge 10.00

RA78 A69 20d on 5 l brown red & blue 35 35

Same Surcharge in Carmine on Nos. RA62 and RA63.

1946-47 ***Perf. 13½x12.*** **Unwmkd.**

RA79 PT7 50d on 50 l gray green, *pale green* ('47) 30 10
- *a.* Inverted surch. 15.00

RA80 " 50d on 1d dull blue, *light blue* 30 10
- *a.* Violet black surcharge 4.00 1.00

The tax on Nos. RA77 to RA80 was for the Postal Clerks' Welfare Fund.

Nos. RA65 and RA62 Surcharged in Carmine

ΔΡ. — 50

1947

RA81 PT7 50d on 50 l gray green, *pale green* (#RA65) 25 20

RA81A " 50d on 50 l gray green, *pale green* (#RA62) 15.00 15.00

The tax was for the postal clerks' tuberculosis fund.

St. Demetrius—PT8

1948 **Lithographed** ***Perf. 12x13½***

RA82 PT8 50d yellow brown 50 10

Obligatory on all domestic mail. The tax was for restoration of historical monuments and churches destroyed during World War II.

Nos. 397 and 413 Surcharged in Blue

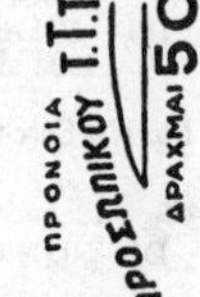

1950 **Wmk. 252**

RA83 A70 50d on 10 l (#397) 30 20
- *a.* Stamp with double frame 8.00
- *b.* Surcharge reading down 15.00 15.0

RA84 " 50d on 10 l (#413) 30 20
- *a.* Surcharge reading down 12.50 12.50

The tax was for the Postal Clerks' Welfare Fund.

No. 396 Surcharged in Carmine

ΠΡΟΝΟΙΑ ΤΑΧ. ΥΠΑΛΛΗΛΩΝ ΔΡΑΧΜΑΙ 50

1951 ***Perf. 13½x12***

RA85 A69 50d on 5 l brown red & blue 35 20

The tax was for the Postal Employees' Welfare Fund.

No. 392 Surcharged in Black

50

1951 ***Perf. 12½x12*** **Wmk. 252**

RA86 A67 50(d) on 3d red brown 30 20
- *a.* Pair, one without surcharge 10.00
- *b.* "50" omitted 12.00

The tax was for the postal clerks' tuberculosis fund.

No. 393 Surcharged in Carmine

ΠΡΟΣΘΕΤΟΝ ΔΡ. 100

1952

RA87 A67 100d on 8d deep blue 35 25

The tax was for the State Welfare Fund.

Ruins of Church of Phaneromeni, Zante

PT9

Zeus on Macedonian Coin of Philip II

PT10

Design: 500dr, Map and scene of destruction, Argostoli.

Lithographed.

1953 *Perf. 12½.* **Wmk. 252**

RA88 PT9 300d indigo & pale green 1.20 20

RA89 " 500d dark brown & buff 1.50 30

The tax was for the reconstruction of Cephalonia, Ithaca, and Zante, Ionian Islands destroyed by earthquake.

1956 *Perf. 13½*

Design: 1d, Aristotle.

RA90 PT10 50l dark carmine rose 1.20 25

a. Imperf., pair 40.00

RA91 " 1d bright blue 1.85 50

The tax was for archaeological research in Macedonia. The coin on No. 90 portrays Zeus despite inscription of Philip's name.

POSTAL TAX SEMI-POSTAL STAMPS.

Child

PTSP1

Mother and Child

PTSP2

Virgin and Christ Child

PTSP3

Lithographed.

1943 *Perf. 12x13½* **Wmk. 252**

RAB1 PTSP1 25d+25d blue green 15 15

RAB2 PTSP2 100d+50d rose violet 15 15

RAB3 PTSP3 200d+100d red brown 35 35

The surtax aided needy children. These stamps were compulsory on domestic mail in October 1943.

OCCUPATION AND ANNEXATION STAMPS.

During the Balkan wars, 1912-13, Greece occupied certain of the Aegean Islands and part of Western Turkey. She subsequently acquired these territories and they were known as the New Greece.

Most of the special issues for the Aegean Islands were made by order of the military commanders.

For Use in the Aegean Islands Occupied by Greece.

CHIOS.

Greece No. 221a Overprinted in Red

Ε*Δ

Serrate Roulette 13½.

1913 **Lithographed** **Unwmkd.**

N1 A25 25l ultramarine 40.00 35.00

a. Inverted overprint 90.00 90.00

b. Greek "L" instead of "D" 75.00 75.00

ICARIA (NICARIA).

Penelope

I1

Lithographed.

1912 *Perf. 11½.* **Unwmkd.**

N2 I1 2l orange 1.25 1.50

N3 " 5l blue green 1.25 1.50

N4 " 10l rose 1.25 1.50

N5 " 25l ultramarine 1.25 1.50

N6 " 50l gray lilac 1.25 1.50

N7 " 1d dark brown 3.75 *5.00*

N8 " 2d claret 3.75 *5.00*

N9 " 5d slate 3.75 *8.00*

Nos. N2-N9 (8) 17.50 *25.50*

Counterfeits of Nos. N1-N15 are plentiful.

Stamps of Greece, 1911-23, Overprinted

ΕΛΛΗΝΙΚΗ ΔΙΟΙΚΗΣΙΣ

1913 **Engraved**

On Issue of 1911-21.

N10 A25 2l carmine rose 12.00 10.00

N11 A24 3l vermilion 12.00 10.00

Lithographed

On Issue of 1912-23.

N12 A24 1l green 12.00 10.00

N13 " 3l vermilion 12.00 10.00

N14 A26 5l green 12.00 10.00

N15 A24 10l carmine 12.00 10.00

Nos. N10-N15 (6) 72.00 60.00

LEMNOS.

Regular Issues of Greece Overprinted in Black

ΛΗΜΝΟΣ

On Issue of 1901.

Engraved

1912 *Perf. 13½.* **Wmk. 129**

N16 A11 20l red lilac 3.00 2.00

On Issue of 1911-21.

Unwmkd.

Serrate Roulette 13½.

N17 A24 1l green 55 55

N18 A25 2l carmine rose 55 55

N19 A24 3l vermilion 55 55

N20 A26 5l green 1.10 1.10

N21 A24 10l carmine rose 1.10 85

N22 A25 20l gray lilac 1.65 1.10

N23 " 25l ultramarine 3.75 3.25

N24 A26 30l carmine rose 1.65 1.65

N25 A25 40l deep blue 11.00 9.00

N26 A26 50l dull violet 11.00 9.00

N27 A27 1d ultramarine 11.00 9.00

N28 " 2d vermilion 16.50 13.50

N29 " 3d carmine rose 22.50 13.50

N30 " 5d ultramarine 27.50 27.50

N31 " 10d deep blue 200.00 200.00

N32 A28 25d deep blue 85.00 75.00

On Issue of 1912-23.

Lithographed

N33 A24 1l green 35 35

a. Without period after "Ellas" 60.00 60.00

N34 A26 5l green 45 35

N35 A24 10l carmine 2.00 2.00

N36 A25 25l ultramarine 9.00 3.25

Nos. N16-N36 (21) 410.20 374.05

Red Overprint.

On Issue of 1911-21.

Engraved

N37 A25 2l carmine rose 1.65 1.65

N38 A24 3l vermilion 1.65 1.65

N39 A25 20l gray lilac 5.50 5.50

N40 A26 30l carmine rose 7.25 7.25

N41 A25 40l deep blue 10.00 9.00

N42 A26 50l dull violet 11.00 9.00

N43 A27 1d ultramarine 11.00 9.00

N44 " 2d vermilion 25.00 25.00

N45 " 3d carmine rose 16.50 16.50

N46 " 5d ultramarine 65.00 65.00

N47 " 10d deep blue 95.00 95.00

N48 A28 25d deep blue 75.00 75.00

On Issue of 1912-23.

Lithographed

N49 A24 1l green 85 85

a. Without period after "Ellas" 85.00 85.00

N50 A26 5l green 55 55

N51 A24 10l carmine 10.00 10.00

N52 A25 25l ultramarine 2.00 2.00

Nos. N37-N52 (16) 337.95 332.95

The overprint is found inverted or double on many of Nos. N16-N52. There are several varieties in the overprint: Greek "D" for "L", large Greek "S" or "O", and small "O".

No. N49 with Added 'Greek Administration' Overprint, as on Nos. N109-N148, in Black.

1913

N52A A24 1l green 5.50 5.50

Counterfeits of Nos. N16-N52A are plentiful.

MYTILENE (LESBOS).

Turkey Nos. 162, 158 Overprinted in Blue

Ἑλληνικὴ Κατοχὴ Μυτιλήνης

Perf. 12, 13½ and Compound

1912 **Typographed** **Unwmkd.**

N53 A21 20pa rose 85.00 75.00

N54 " 10pi dull red 120.00 95.00

On Turkey Nos. P68, 151-155, 137, 157-158 in Black

N55 A21 2pa olive green 2.00 2.00

N56 " 5pa ochre 2.00 2.00

N57 " 10pa blue green 2.00 2.00

N58 " 20pa rose 1.50 1.50

N59 " 1pi ultramarine 3.00 3.00

N60 " 2pi blue black 15.00 15.00

N61 A19 2½pi dark brown 5.00 5.00

N62 A21 5pi dark violet 17.50 17.50

N63 " 10pi dull red 40.00 40.00

Nos. N55-N63 (9) 88.00 88.00

On Turkey Nos. 161-163, 145 in Black

N64 A21 10pa blue green 6.00 5.00

a. Dbl. overprint 10.00

N65 " 20pa rose 6.00 5.00

N66 " 1pi ultra. 5.00 5.00

N67 A19 2pi blue black 35.00 35.00

Nos. N55, N58, N65, N59 Surcharged in Blue or Black

N68 A21 25l on 2pa olive green (Bl) 7.50 7.50

a. New value inverted 15.00

N69 " 50l on 20pa rose (Bl) 8.00 8.00

a. New value inverted 15.00

N70 " 1d on 20pa rose (Bk) 12.50 12.50

a. New value inverted 30.00

N71 " 2d on 1pi ultramarine (Bk) 12.50 12.50

a. New value inverted

Same Overprint on Turkey No. J49

N72 A19 1pi *deep rose* 50.00 45.00

The overprint is found on all values reading up or down with inverted "l" in the first word and inverted "e" in the third word. Counterfeits of Nos. N53-N72 are plentiful.

SAMOS.

Issues of the Provisional Government.

Map of Samos

OS1

Typographed.

1912 *Imperf.* **Unwmkd.**

N73 OS1 5l gray green 60.00 12.50

N74 " 10l red 60.00 12.50

N75 " 25l blue 60.00 12.50

a. 25l green (error) *300.00 500.00*

Nos. N73-N75 exist in tête bêche pairs. Price per set, $400 unused, $165 used. Counterfeits exist of Nos. N73 to N75.

Hermes

OS2

1912 **Lithographed** *Perf. 11½*

Without Overprint.

N76 OS2 1l gray 3.00 2.00

a. Imperf., pair 12.00 12.00

N77 " 5l light green 3.00 2.00

a. Imperf., pair 12.00 12.00

N78 " 10l rose 3.00 2.00

a. Imperf., pair 12.00 12.00

b. Half used as 5 on cover 15.00

N79 " 25l light blue 3.00 2.00

a. Imperf., pair 12.00 12.00

N80 " 50l violet brown 3.00 2.00

a. Imperf., pair 12.00 12.00

With Overprint.

N81 OS2 1l gray 2.50 1.65

a. Imperf., pair 35.00 30.00

N82 " 5l blue green 2.50 1.65

a. Imperf., pair 35.00 30.00

N83 " 10l rose 2.50 1.65

a. Imperf., pair 35.00 30.00

b. Half used as 5l on cover 15.00

N84 " 25l blue 3.00 1.75

N85 " 50l violet brown 4.00 2.00

a. Imperf., pair 40.00 30.00

N86 " 1d orange 15.00 9.00

Nos. N76-N86 (11) 44.50 27.70

Church in Savior's Name and Fort Ruins
OS3

Manuscript Initials in Red or Black

1913

N87 OS3 1d brown (R) 35.00 30.00
N88 " 2d deep blue (R) 35.00 30.00
N89 " 5d gray green (R) 35.00 25.00
N90 " 10d yellow green (R) 200.00 200.00
a. Black initials 300.00
N91 " 25d red (Bk) 150.00 150.00
a. Red initials 185.00
Nos. N87–N91 (5) 455.00 435.00

Nos. N87–N91 were issued to commemorate the victory of the Greek fleet in 1824 and the capture of Samos in 1912. The manuscript initials are those of Pres. Themistokles Sofulis.

Counterfeits of Nos. N87–N91 are plentiful.

Nos. N76 to N80 Overprinted ΕΛΛΑΣ

1914

N92 OS2 1 l gray 8.00 6.00
N93 " 5 l light green 8.00 6.00
N94 " 10 l rose 8.00 6.00
a. Double overprint 50.00
N95 " 25 l light blue 8.00 6.00
N96 " 50 l violet brown 8.00 6.00
a. Double overprint 50.00
Nos. N92–N96 (5) 40.00 30.00

Charity Issues of Greek Administration.

Nos. N81 to N86 Overprinted in Red or Black

1915

N97 OS2 1 l gray (R) 25.00 25.00
a. Black overprint 75.00
b. Without ovpt. 45.00
N98 " 5 l blue green (Bk) 5.50 5.50
a. Red overprint 65.00
b. Double overprint 60.00
N99 " 10 l rose (Bk) 5.50 5.50
a. Red overprint 70.00
b. Inverted ovpt. 60.00
N100 " 25 l blue (Bk) 5.50 5.50
a. Red overprint 70.00
N101 " 50 l violet brn. (Bk) 5.50 5.50
a. Red overprint 65.00
N102 " 1d orange (R) 6.25 6.25
a. Invtd. ovpt. 75.00
b. Black overprint 80.00
c. Double black overprint 75.00

No. N102 With Additional Surcharge in Black ΛΕΠΤΟΝ

N103 OS2 1 l on 1d orange (R+Bk) 7.50 7.50
a. Black surcharge double 70.00
b. Black surcharge inverted 75.00
Nos. N97–N103 (7) 60.75 60.75

Issue of 1913 Overprinted in Red or Black

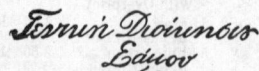

Γενική Διοίκησις Σάμου

1915

N104 OS3 1d brown (R) 35.00 30.00
N105 " 2d deep blue (R) 35.00 30.00
a. Dbl. overprint 200.00 250.00
N106 " 5d gray grn. (R) 30.00 25.00
N107 " 10d yel. grn. (Bk) 75.00 65.00
a. Inverted ovpt. 225.00 225.00
N108 OS3 25d red (Bk) 750.00 700.00
Nos. N104–N108 (5) 925.00 850.00

Nos. N97 to N108 inclusive have an embossed control mark, consisting of a cross encircled by a Greek inscription.

Most copies of Nos. N104–N108 lack the initials.

Counterfeits of Nos. N104–N108 are plentiful.

FOR USE IN PARTS OF TURKEY OCCUPIED BY GREECE, (NEW GREECE).

Regular Issues of Greece Overprinted

ΕΛΛΗΝΙΚΗ ΔΙΟΙΚΗΣΙΣ

Black Overprint Meaning "Greek Administration"

On Issue of 1901.

Engraved

1912 *Perf. 13½.* **Wmk. 129**

N109 A11 20 l red lilac 3.00 1.00

On Issue of 1911-21.

Unwmkd.

Serrate Roulette 13½.

N110 A24 1 l green 50 50
N111 A25 2 l carmine rose 50 50
N112 A24 3 l vermilion 50 50
N113 A26 5 l green 1.20 50
N114 A24 10 l carmine rose 40 30
N115 A25 20 l gray lilac 1.60 70
N116 " 25 l ultramarine 4.00 1.50
N117 A26 30 l carmine rose 1.60 85
N118 A25 40 l deep blue 6.25 4.25
N119 A26 50 l dull violet 6.25 4.25
N120 A27 1d ultramarine 4.75 85
N121 " 2d vermilion 18.50 11.50
N122 " 3d carmine rose 23.50 14.00
N123 " 5d ultramarine 12.50 8.50
N124 " 10d deep blue 150.00 140.00
N125 A28 25d deep blue, ovpt. horiz. 80.00 70.00

On Issue of 1912-23.

Lithographed

N126 A24 1 l green 20 18
b. Without period after "Ellas" 50.00 50.00
N127 A26 5 l green 50 50
N128 A24 10 l carmine 65 50
N129 A25 25 l blue 11.50 2.40
Nos. N109–N129 (21) 327.90 263.28

Red Overprint.

On Issue of 1911-21.

Engraved

N130 A24 1 l green 1.15 85
N131 A25 2 l carmine rose 2.35 2.10
N132 A24 3 l vermilion 2.35 2.10
N133 A26 5 l green 90 60
N134 A25 20 l gray lilac 3.00 2.10
N135 " 25 l ultramarine 20.00 15.00
N136 A26 30 l carmine rose 12.50 8.50
N137 A25 40 l deep blue 3.00 2.10
N138 A26 50 l dull violet 3.00 1.85
N139 A27 1d ultramarine 9.50 4.25
N140 " 2d vermilion 30.00 21.00
N141 " 3d carmine rose 9.50 7.25
N142 " 5d ultramarine 150.00 140.00
N143 " 10d deep blue 57.50 50.00
N144 A28 25d deep blue, ovpt. horiz. 30.00 30.00
a. Vertical ovpt. 110.00 110.00

On Issue of 1912-23.

Lithographed

N145 A24 1 l green 1.00 95
a. Without period after "Ellas" 65.00
N146 A26 5 l green 65 50
N147 A24 10 l carmine 20.00 15.00
N148 A25 25 l blue 1.00 50
Nos. N130–N148 (19) 357.40 304.65

The normal overprint is vertical, reading upward on N109–N124, N126–N143, N145–N148. It is often inverted or double. There are numerous broken, missing and wrong font letters with a Greek "L" instead of "D" as the first letter of the second word.

Counterfeits exist of Nos. N109–N148.

Cross of Constantine
O1

Eagle of Zeus
O2

1912 **Lithographed**

N150 O1 1 l brown 22 22
a. Imperf., pair 25.00
N151 O2 2 l red 30 25
a. 2 l rose 30 22
b. Imperf., pair 25.00
N153 " 3 l orange 30 22
a. Imperf., pair 20.00
N154 O1 5 l green 1.50 22
a. Imperf., pair 20.00
N155 " 10 l rose red 2.25 20
a. Imperf., pair 25.00
N156 " 20 l violet 2.00 70
a. Imperf., pair 25.00
N157 O2 25 l pale blue 2.00 35
a. Imperf., pair 25.00
N158 O1 30 l gray green 20.00 75
a. Imperf., pair 175.00
N159 O2 40 l indigo 5.75 4.25
a. Imperf., pair 45.00
N160 O1 50 l dark blue 1.50 1.50
N161 O2 1d violet brown 1.65 75
N162 O1 2d gray brown 22.50 3.00
N163 O2 3d dull blue 85.00 10.00
a. Imperf., pair 375.00
N164 O1 5d gray 85.00 25.00
N165 O2 10d carmine 110.00 100.00
N166 O1 25d gray black 75.00 75.00
Nos. N150–N166 (16) 414.97 222.41

Issued in commemoration of the occupation of Macedonia, Epirus and some of the Aegean Islands.

These stamps were sold only in New Greece.

Dangerous forgeries of Nos. N165–N166 exist.

In 1916 some stamps of this issue were overprinted in Greek: "I (era) Koinotis Ag (iou) Orous" for the Mount Athos Monastery District. They were never placed in use and most of them were destroyed.

CAVALLA.

Stamps of Bulgaria of 1911 Surcharged

ΕΛΛΗΝΙΚΗ
ΔΙΟΙΚΗΣΙΣ

25 ΛΕΠΤΑ 25

Engraved

1913 *Perf. 12* **Unwmkd.**

Red Surcharge.

N167 A20 5 l on 1s myrtle green *13.50 13.50*
N169 A25 10 l on 15s brown bistre *50.00 50.00*
N170 A26 10 l on 25s ultramarine & black *15.00 15.00*
N171 A21 15 l on 2s carmine & black *25.00 25.00*
N172 A22 20 l on 3s lake & black *18.00 18.00*
N173 A23 25 l on 5s green & black *10.50 8.50*
N174 A24 50 l on 10s red & black *13.50 8.50*
N175 A25 1d on 15s brown bistre *30.00 25.00*
N176 A27 1d on 30s blue & black *60.00 30.00*
N177 A28 1d on 50s ochre & black *100.00 50.00*

Blue Surcharge.

N178 A24 50 l on 10s red & black *13.50 9.00*
Nos. N167–N178 (11) *348.50 252.50*

The counterfeits and reprints of Nos. N167–N178 are difficult to distinguish from originals. Many overprint varieties exist.

Some specialists question the status of Nos. N167–N178.

DEDEAGATCH.
(Alexandroupolis)

ΕΛΛΗΝΙΚΗ
ΔΙΟΙΚΗΣΙΣ
ΔΕΔΕΑΓΑΤΣ
ΔΕΚΑ ΛΕΠΤΑ
(10 lepta)
D1

Typeset. Control Mark in Red.

1913 *Perf. 11½* **Unwmkd.**

N179 D1 5 l black 30.00 25.00
N180 " 10 l black 2.25 2.00
N181 " 25 l black 4.00 3.50
Sheet of 8 100.00 90.00

Nos. N179–N181 were issued without gum in sheets of eight, consisting of one 5 l, three 10 l in normal position, one 10 l inverted, three 25 l and one blank square. The sheet yields se-tenant pairs of 5 l+10 l and 5 l +25 l; tete beche pairs of 5 l +10 l, 10 l+25 l, and 10 l+10 l. Some sheets were issued imperforate; price, $125 unused, $110 canceled.

The 5 l reads "PENTE LEPTA" in Greek letters; the 10 l is illustrated; the 25 l carries the numeral "25."

Stamps of Bulgaria of 1911 Surcharged

ΕΛΛΗΝΙΚΗ
ΔΙΟΙΚΗΣΙΣ
ΔΕΔΕΑΓΑΤΣ
10
ΛΕΠΤΑ

Red Surcharge.

1913 *Perf. 12*

N182 A20 5 l on 1s myrtle green 52.50 35.00
N183 A26 1d on 25s ultramarine & black 52.50 40.00

Blue Surcharge.

N184 A24 10 l on 10s red & black 20.00 20.00
N185 A23 25 l on 5s green & black 35.00 28.50
N187 A21 50 l on 2s carmine & black 57.50 45.00
Nos. N182–N185, N187 (5) 217.50 168.50

The surcharges on Nos. N182 to N187 are printed from a setting of eight, which was used for all, with the necessary changes of value. No. 6 in the setting has a Greek "L" instead of "D" for the third letter of the third word of the surcharge.

The 25 L surcharge also exists on 8 copies of the 25s, Bulgaria No. 95.

ΠΡΟΣΩΡΙΝΟΝ
ΕΛΛΗΝΙΚΗ
ΔΙΟΙΚΗΣΙΣ
ΔΕΔΕΑΓΑΤΣ
1 ΛΕΠΤΟΝ 1
D2

Type-set. Control Mark in Blue.

1913, Sept. 15 *Perf. 11½*

N188 D2 1 l blue 75.00
N189 " 2 l " 75.00
N190 " 3 l " 75.00
N191 " 5 l " 75.00
N192 " 10 l " 75.00
N193 " 25 l " 75.00
N194 " 40 l " 75.00
N195 " 50 l " 75.00

Nos. N188 to N195 were issued without gum in sheets of eight containing all values.

ΠΡΟΣΩΡΙΝΟΝ
ΕΛΛΗΝΙΚΗ
ΔΙΟΙΚΗΣΙΣ
ΔΕΔΕΑΓΑΤΣ
5 ΛΕΗΤΑ 5

D3

Type-set. Control Mark in Blue.

1913, Sept. 25

N196 D3 1 l blue, *gray blue* 90.00
N197 " 5 l " " 90.00
N198 " 10 l " " 90.00
N199 " 25 l " " 90.00
N200 " 30 l " " 90.00
N201 " 50 l " " 90.00

Nos. N196 to N201 were issued without gum in sheets of six containing all values.
Counterfeits of Nos. N182-N201 are plentiful.

FOR USE IN NORTH EPIRUS. (ALBANIA)

Greek Stamps of 1937-38 Overprinted in Black

ЄΛΛΗΝΙΚΗ
ΔΙΟΙΚΗCIC

Perf. 13½x12, 12x13½

1940 Lithographed **Wmk. 252**

N202 A69 5 l brown red & blue 5 5
a. Inverted ovpt. 15.00
N203 A70 10 l blue & brown red (*No. 413*) 5 5
a. Double impression of frame 10.00
N204 A71 20 l black & green 5 5
a. Inverted ovpt. 25.00
N205 A72 40 l green & black 5 5
a. Invtd. ovpt. 25.00
N206 A73 50 l brown & black 5 5
N207 A74 80 l indigo & yellow brown 5 5
N208 A67 1d green 15 15
a. Inverted ovpt. 25.00
N209 A75 2d ultramarine 15 15
N210 A67 3d red brown 15 15
N211 A76 5d red 25 25
N212 A77 6d olive brown 30 30
N213 A78 7d dark brown 50 50
N214 A67 8d deep blue 75 75
N215 A79 10d red brown 75 75
N216 A80 15d green 1.50 1.50
N217 A81 25d dark blue 1.50 1.50
a. Inverted ovpt. 45.00

Engraved
Unwmkd.

N218 A84 30d orange brown 3.75 3.75
Nos. N202-N218 (17) 10.05 10.05

Same Overprinted in Carmine on National Youth Issue.

Lithographed

1941 *Perf. 12½, 13½x12½.*

N219 A93 3d silver, deep ultra. & red 1.85 1.85
N220 A94 5d dark blue & black 2.50 2.50
N221 " 10d red orange & black 3.00 3.00
N222 " 15d dark green & black 50.00 50.00
N223 " 20d lake & black 5.75 5.75
N224 " 25d dark blue & black 12.00 12.00
N225 " 30d rose violet & black 12.50 12.50
N226 A94 50d lake & black 12.50 12.50
N227 " 75d dark blue, brn. & gold 12.50 12.50
N228 A93 100d silver, deep ultra. & red 12.50 12.50
a. Inverted overprint 100.00
Nos. N219-N228 (10) 125.10 125.10

Same Overprint in Carmine on National Youth Air Post Stamps.

N229 AP25 2d red orange & black 1.15 70
N230 " 4d dark green & black 5.75 5.50
a. Inverted overprint 60.00
N231 " 6d lake & black 5.75 5.75
a. Inverted overprint 60.00
N232 " 8d dark blue & black 5.75 5.75
N233 " 16d rose violet & black 9.50 9.50
N234 " 32d red orange & black 9.50 9.50
N235 " 45d dark green & black 12.50 12.50
N236 " 55d lake & black 12.50 12.50
N237 " 65d dark blue & black 12.50 12.50
N238 " 100d rose violet & black 12.50 12.50
Nos. N229-N238 (10) 87.40 86.70

Some specialists have questioned the status of Nos. N230a and N231a.

For other stamps issued by Greece for use in occupied parts of Epirus and Thrace, see the catalogue listings of those countries.

FOR USE IN THE DODECANESE ISLANDS

Greece, No. 472C, with Additional Overprint in Carmine or Silver

Σ. Δ. Δ.

Lithographed

1947 *Perf. 12½.* **Wmk. 252**

N239 A113 10d on 2,000d deep blue (C) 30 30
N240 " 10d on 2,000d deep blue (S) 30 30

These stamps sold for 5 lire (100 drachmas) and paid postage for that amount.

King George II Memorial Issue.

Greece, Nos. 484 and 485, With Additional Overprint in Black

Σ
Δ
Δ

1947 Engraved *Perf. 12½x12*

N241 A67 50d on 1d green 15 20
N242 " 250d on 3d red brown 25 30

The letters are initials of the Greek words for "Military Administration of the Dodecanese."

Greece, Nos. 501 and 502 Overprinted in Carmine

Σ. Δ. Δ.

Lithographed

1947 *Perf. 12½.* **Wmk. 252**

N243 A111 20d on 500d dark olive 35 35
N244 A104 30d on 5d light blue green 35 35

Greece, Nos. 437, 406, 407 and 445, Surcharged in Black or Carmine

1947 *Perf. 12½, 13½x12*

N245 A103 50d on 2d red brown 1.00 1.00

Engraved

N246 A79 250d on 10d red brown 2.00 2.00
N247 A80 400d on 15d green (C) 3.00 3.00
a. Invtd. surcharge 150.00

Lithographed

N248 A110 1000d on 200d ultramarine (C) 3.00 3.00
a. Imprint omitted 70.00

POSTAGE DUE STAMPS. FOR USE IN PARTS OF TURKEY OCCUPIED BY GREECE. (NEW GREECE)

Postage Due Stamps of Greece, 1902, Overprinted

ΕΛΛΗΝΙΚΗ
ΔΙΟΙΚΗΣΙΣ

Engraved

1912 *Perf. 13½.* **Wmk. 129**

Black Overprint.

NJ1 D3 1 l chocolate 45 45
NJ2 " 2 l gray 45 45
NJ3 " 3 l orange 45 45
NJ4 " 5 l yellow green 1.00 1.00
NJ5 " 10 l scarlet 70 70
NJ6 " 20 l lilac 1.00 1.00
NJ7 " 30 l deep violet 1.65 1.65
NJ8 " 40 l dark brown 1.75 1.50
NJ9 " 50 l red brown 3.00 3.00
NJ10 " 1d black 10.00 10.00
NJ11 " 2d bronze 20.00 20.00
NJ12 " 3d silver 42.50 32.50
NJ13 " 5d gold 85.00 70.00
Nos. NJ1-NJ13 (13) 167.95 142.70

Red Overprint.

NJ14 D3 1 l chocolate 70 70
NJ15 " 2 l gray 70 70
NJ16 " 3 l orange 7.00 7.00
NJ17 " 5 l yellow green 70 70
NJ18 " 10 l scarlet 11.00 11.00
NJ19 " 20 l lilac 1.30 1.30
NJ20 " 30 l deep violet 1.50 1.50
NJ21 " 40 l dark brown 1.10 1.10
NJ22 " 50 l red brown 1.00 1.00
NJ23 " 1d black 5.75 5.75
NJ24 " 2d bronze 9.00 9.00
NJ25 " 3d silver 22.50 22.50
NJ26 " 5d gold 60.00 60.00
Nos. NJ14-NJ26 (13) 122.25 122.25

The normal position of the overprint is reading upward but it is often reversed. On Nos. NJ16 and NJ18 the overprint always reads downward. Some of the varieties of lettering which occur on the postage stamps are also found on the postage due stamps. Double overprints exist on some denominations.

FOR USE IN NORTH EPIRUS. (ALBANIA)

Postage Due Stamps of Greece, 1930, Surcharged or Overprinted in Black:

ЄΛΛΗΝΙΚΗ
ΔΙΟΙΚΗCIC
50
ΛΕΠΤΑ
a

ЄΛΛΗΝΙΚΗ
ΔΙΟΙΚΗCIC
b

Perf. 13, 13x12½

1940 Lithographed **Unwmkd.**

NJ27 D3 (*a*) 50 l on 25d lt. red 20 20
NJ28 " (*b*) 2d light red 35 40
a. Inverted overprint 20.00
NJ29 " (") 5d blue gray 45 45
NJ30 " (") 10d green 60 60
NJ31 " (") 15d red brown 1.00 1.00
Nos. NJ27-NJ31 (5) 2.60 2.65

POSTAL TAX STAMPS. FOR USE IN NORTH EPIRUS. (ALBANIA)

Postal Tax Stamps of Greece, 1939, Overprinted in Black

ЄΛΛΗΝΙΚΗ
ΔΙΟΙΚΗCIC

Lithographed

1940 *Perf. 13½x12.* **Unwmkd.**

NRA1 PT7 10 l bright rose, *pale rose* 10 10
NRA2 " 50 l gray green, *pale green* 10 10
a. Inverted overprint 25.00
NRA3 " 1d dull blue, *light blue* 30 30

GREENLAND

(grēn′lănd)

LOCATION—North Atlantic Ocean
GOVT.—Danish.
AREA—827,300 sq. mi.
POP.—49,666 (est. 1976).
CAPITALS—Godthaab, for South Greenland Inspectorate; Godhavn, for North Greenland Inspectorate. In 1953 the colony of Greenland became an integral part of Denmark.

100 Ore = 1 Króne

King Christian X
A1

Polar Bear
A2

Engraved.

1938-46 *Perf. 13x12½* **Unwmkd.**

1 A1 1ö olive black 30 25
2 " 5ö rose lake 2.25 70
3 " 7ö yellow green 2.50 2.50
4 " 10ö purple 1.50 70
5 " 15ö red 1.40 70
5A " 20ö red ('46) 2.25 75
6 A2 30ö blue 7.50 7.50
6A " 40ö blue ('46) 22.50 8.50
7 " 1k light brown 8.50 8.50
Nos. 1-7 (9) 48.70 30.10

Harp Seal
A3

King Christian X
A4

Dog Team
A5

Designs: 1k, Polar bear. 2k, Eskimo in kayak. 5k, Eider duck.

1945, Feb. 1 *Perf. 12*

8 A3 1ö olive blk. & vio. 27.50 27.50
9 " 5ö rose lake & olive bistre 27.50 27.50

10 A3 7ö green & black 27.50 27.50
11 A4 10ö purple & olive 27.50 27.50
12 " 15ö red & bright ultramarine 27.50 27.50
13 A5 30ö dark blue & red brown 27.50 27.50
14 " 1k brown & gray black 27.50 27.50
15 " 2k sepia & dp. grn. 27.50 27.50
16 " 5k dark purple & dull brown 27.50 27.50
Nos. 8-16 (9) 247.50 247.50

Nos. 8 to 16 Overprinted in Carmine or Blue

DANMARK
BEFRIET
5 MAJ 1945

1945

17 A3 1ö olive black & violet (C) 30.00 32.50
18 " 5ö rose lake & olive bistre (Bl) 30.00 32.50
19 " 7ö green & black (C) 30.00 32.50
20 A4 10ö purple and olive (Bl) 55.00 47.50
a. Overprint in carmine 240.00 260.00
21 " 15ö red & bright ultra. (C) 45.00 47.50
a. Overprint in blue 75.00 80.00
22 A5 30ö dark blue & red brown (Bl) 45.00 47.50
a. Overprint in carmine 75.00 80.00
23 " 1k brown & gray black (C) 45.00 47.50
a. Overprint in blue 75.00 80.00
24 " 2k sepia & deep green (C) 45.00 47.50
a. Overprint in blue 75.00 80.00
25 " 5k dark purple & dull brn. (Bl) 45.00 47.50
a. Overprint in carmine 5.00 80.00
Nos. 17-25 (9) 370.00 382.50
Nos. 20a-25a (6) 615.00 660.00

The liberation of Denmark from the Germans.

Overprint illustrated as on Nos. 17-19. Larger type and different settings used for types A4 and A5. Overprint often smudged.

Nos. 17-25 exist with overprint inverted. Price, each $450.

King Frederik IX
A9

Polar Ship "Gustav Holm"
A10

Engraved.

1950-60 *Perf. 13* **Unwmkd.**

26 A9 1ö dark olive green 10 10
27 " 5ö deep carmine 20 15
28 " 10ö green 35 20
29 " 15ö purple ('60) 75 55
a. 15ö dull pur. 2.50 75
30 " 25ö vermilion 1.25 1.00
31 " 30ö dark blue ('53) 11.00 3.50
31A " 30ö vermilion ('59) 60 45
32 A10 50ö deep blue 14.00 10.00
33 " 1k brown 7.50 1.50
34 " 2k dull red 5.00 1.75
35 " 5k gray ('58) 3.50 2.25
Nos. 26-35 (11) 44.25 21.45

Nos. 6A and 7 Surcharged

60
ØRE

1956, Mar. 8

36 A2 60ö on 40ö blue 7.00 4.00
37 " 60ö on 1k lt. brown 37.50 14.00

"The Mother of the Sea"
A11

Hans Egede
A12

1957, May 2 Engr. *Perf. 13*
38 A11 60ö blue 2.50 1.40

1958, Nov. 5
39 A12 30ö henna brown 8.50 2.50

Issued to commemorate the 200th anniversary of the death of Hans Egede, missionary to the Eskimos in Greenland.

Knud Rasmussen
A13

Drum Dancer
A14

1960, Nov. 24 *Perf. 13*
40 A13 30ö dull red 2.00 1.00

Issued to commemorate the 50th anniversary of the establishment by Knud Rasmussen of the mission and trading station at Thule (Dundas).

1961, March 16 **Unwmkd.**
41 A14 35ö gray olive 1.40 85

Northern Lights and Crossed Anchors
A15

King Frederick IX
A16

Polar Bear
A17

1963-68 Engraved *Perf. 13*

42 A15 1ö gray 10 10
43 " 5ö rose claret 6 6
44 " 10ö green 55 35
45 " 12ö yellow green 55 50
46 " 15ö rose violet 75 75
47 A16 20ö ultramarine 2.50 2.25
48 " 25ö light brown ('64) 50 50
48A " 30ö green ('68) 30 30
49 " 35ö dull red ('64) 30 30
50 " 40ö gray ('64) 60 60
51 " 50ö greenish bl. ('64) 4.00 3.50
51A " 50ö dark red ('65) 40 25
51B " 60ö rose claret ('68) 80 50
52 " 80ö orange 75 50
53 A17 1k brown 65 20
54 " 2k dull red 2.25 55
55 " 5k dark blue 3.75 1.10
56 " 10k dull slate green 3.50 85
Nos. 42-56 (18) 22.31 13.16

Niels Bohr and Atom Diagram
A18

1963, Nov. 21 **Unwmkd.**
57 A18 35ö red brown 45 35
58 " 60ö dark blue 2.50 2.50

Issued to commemorate the 50th anniversary of the atom theory of Prof. Niels Bohr (1885-1962).

Samuel Kleinschmidt
A19

"The Boy and the Fox"
A20

1964, Nov. 26 **Engraved**
59 A19 35ö brown red 70 55

Issued to commemorate the 150th anniversary of the birth of Samuel Kleinschmidt (1814-86), philologist.

1966-67 **Engraved** *Perf. 13*

Design: 90ö, "The Great Northern Diver and The Raven."

60 A20 50ö brown red 1.00 1.00
61 " 90ö dark blue ('67) 1.75 1.75

Issues dates: 50ö, Sept. 22, 1966; 90ö, Nov. 23, 1967.

Princess Margrethe and Prince Henri
A21

1967, June 10 Engr. *Perf. 13*
62 A21 50ö red 3.25 3.25

Issued to commemorate the wedding of Crown Princess Margrethe and Prince Henri de Monpezat.

Frederik IX and Map of Greenland
A22

"The Girl and the Eagle"
A23

1969, Mar. 11 Engr. *Perf. 13*
64 A22 60ö dull red 1.75 1.75

70th birthday of King Frederik IX.

1969, Sept. 18
65 A23 80ö light brown 1.50 1.50

Musk Ox
A24

Liberation Celebration at Jakobshaven
A25

Designs: 1k, Right whale diving off Disko Island. 2k, Narwhal. 5k, Polar bear. 10k, Walruses.

1969-76 Engraved *Perf. 13*

68 A24 1k dark blue ('70) 60 35
69 " 2k gray green ('75) 80 80
73 " 5k blue ('76) 2.00 2.00
74 " 10k sepia ('73) 4.00 2.50
75 " 25k greenish gray 10.00 3.50
Nos. 68-75 (5) 17.40 9.15

1970, May 4
76 A25 60ö red brown 1.75 1.75

The 25th anniversary of Greenland's liberation from the Germans.

Hans Egede and Gertrude Rask on the Haabet
A26

1971, May 6 Engraved *Perf. 13*
77 A26 60ö brown red 1.50 1.50

250th anniversary of arrival of Hans Egede in Greenland and the beginning of its colonization.

Mail-carrying Kayaks
A27

Designs: 70ö, Umiak (women's rowboat). 80ö, Catalina seaplane dropping mail by parachute. 90ö, Dog sled. 1k, Coaster Kununguak and pilot boat. 1.30k, Schooner Sokongen. 1.50k, Longboat off Greenland coast. 2k, Helicopter over mountains.

1971-77 Engraved *Perf. 13*

80 A27 50ö green 35 30
81 " 70ö dull red ('72) 25 25
82 " 80ö black ('76) 30 30
83 " 90ö blue ('72) 35 35
84 " 1k red ('76) 65 60
85 " 1.30k dull blue ('75) 50 50
86 " 1.50k gray green ('74) 60 60
87 " 2k blue ('77) 80 80
Nos. 80-87 (8) 3.80 3.70

Queen Margrethe
A28

1973-78 Engraved *Perf. 13*

92 A28 5ö car. rose ('78) 3 3
93 " 10ö slate green 4 4
96 " 60ö sepia 30 25
99 " 90ö red brn. ('74) 50 35
100 " 1k dark red ('77) 40 40
101 " 1.20k dk. blue ('74) 75 70
102 " 1.20k maroon ('78) 50 50
103 " 1.30k dk. blue ('77) 50 50
105 " 1.80k dull green ('78) 70 70
Nos. 92-105 (9) 3.72 3.47

Nos. 93 and 96 were printed on both ordinary and fluorescent paper.

Trawler and Kayaks
A29

Design: 2k, Old Trade Buildings, Copenhagen (vert.).

1974, May 16 Engraved *Perf. 13*
112 A29 1k light red brown 85 75
113 " 2k sepia 1.10 90

Bicentenary of Royal Greenland Trade Department.

Falcon and Radar
A30

1975, Sept. 4 Engr. *Perf. 13*
114 A30 90ö red 35 35

50th anniversary of Greenland's telecommunications system.

Sirius Sled Patrol—A31

1975, Oct. 16 **Engr.** ***Perf. 13***

115 A31 1.20k sepia 60 60

Sirius sled patrol in northeast Greenland, 25th anniversary.

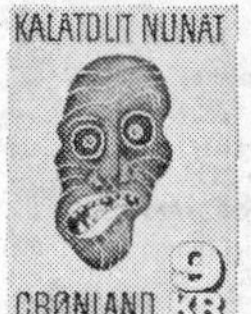

Inuit Cult Mask

A36

Jorgen Bronlund, Jakobshavn, Disko Bay

A37

Design: 6k, Tupilac, a magical creature, carved whalebone.

1977–78 **Engr.** ***Perf. 12½x13***

118 A36 6k deep rose lilac 2.40 2.40
120 " 9k black 3.60 3.60

Issue dates: 9k, Sept. 6, 1977; 6k, Oct. 5, 1978.

1977, Oct. 20 **Engr.** ***Perf. 13***

121 A37 1k red brown 40 45

Jorgen Bronlund, arctic explorer, birth centenary.

Meteorite

A38

1978, Jan. 20 **Engr.** ***Perf. 13***

122 A38 1.20k dull red 50 50

Scientific Research Commission, centenary.

Sun Rising over Mountains

A39

1978, June 5 **Engr.** ***Perf. 13***

123 A39 1.50k dark blue 60 60

25th anniversary of Constitution.

Hans Egede, Settlers, Troops and Drummer—A40

1978, Aug. 29 **Engr.** ***Perf. 13***

124 A40 2.50k red brown 1.00 90

Founding of Godthaab, 250th anniversary.

SEMI-POSTAL STAMPS

No. 32 Surcharged in Red

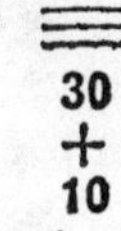

30 + 10

1958, May 22 **Engr.** ***Perf. 13***

B1 A10 30+10 on 50(ö) deep blue 3.25 2.75

The surtax was for the campaign against tuberculosis in Greenland.

No. 30 Surcharged:

"Gronlandsfonden 30 + 10" and Bars.

1959, Feb. 23 **Unwmkd.**

B2 A9 30+10ö on 25ö verm. 4.75 4.75

The surtax was for the benefit of the Greenland Fund.

Two Greenland Boys in Round Tower

SP1

1968, Sept. 12 **Engraved** ***Perf. 13***

B3 SP1 60ö+10ö dark red 1.75 1.75

The surcharge was for child welfare work in Greenland.

Hans Egede Explaining Bible to Natives

SP2

1971, July 3 **Engraved** ***Perf. 13***

B4 SP2 60ö+10ö red brown 1.75 1.75

250th anniversary of arrival of Hans Egede in Greenland and the beginning of its colonization.

Frederik IX, "Dannebrog" off Umanak

SP3

1972, Apr. 20

B5 SP3 60ö+10ö dull red 1.60 1.60

In memory of King Frederik IX (1899–1972). The surtax was for humanitarian and charitable purposes.

Heimaey Town and Volcano

SP4

1973, Oct. 18 **Engr.** ***Perf. 13***

B6 SP4 70ö+20ö gray & red 1.75 1.75

The surtax was for the victims of the eruption of Heimaey Volcano.

Arm Pulling, by Hans Egede

SP5

1976, Apr. 8 **Engr.** ***Perf. 12½***

B7 SP5 100ö+20ö multi. 80 80

The surtax was for the Greenland Athletic Union.

PARCEL POST STAMPS

Arms of Greenland

PP1

Typographed

1905–37 ***Perf. 11, 11½*** **Unwmkd.**

Q1	PP1	1ö olive grn. ('16)	32.50	32.50
	a.	Perf. 12½ ('05)	325.00	325.00
Q2	PP1	2ö yellow ('16)	85.00	75.00
Q3	"	5ö brown ('16)	75.00	75.00
	a.	Perf. 12½ ('05)	325.00	325.00
Q4	PP1	10ö blue ('37)	25.00	37.50
	a.	Perf. 12½ ('05)	325.00	325.00
	b.	Perf. 11½ ('16)	25.00	32.50
Q5	PP1	15ö violet ('16)	110.00	100.00
Q6	"	20ö red ('16)	15.00	13.00
	a.	Perf. 11 ('37)	32.50	40.00
Q7	PP1	70ö violet ('37)	25.00	*80.00*
	a.	Perf. 11½ ('30)	65.00	60.00
Q8	PP1	1kr yellow ('37)	25.00	*67.50*
	a.	Perf. 11½ ('30)	42.50	30.00
Q9	PP1	3kr brown ('30)	100.00	110.00

1937 **Lithographed** ***Perf. 11***

Q10	PP1	70ö pale violet	27.50	*55.00*
Q11	"	1kr yellow	25.00	*50.00*

On lithographed stamps, PAKKE-PORTO is slightly larger, hyphen has rounded ends and lines in shield are fine, straight and evenly spaced.

On typographed stamps, hyphen has squared ends and shield lines are coarse, uneven and inclined to be slightly wavy.

Used prices are for postally used stamps. Numeral cancels indicate use as postal savings stamps.

Sheets of 25. Certain printings of Nos. Q1–Q2, Q3a, Q4a, and Q5–Q6 were issued without sheet margins. Stamps from the outer rows are straight edged.

GUADELOUPE

(gwȧ'dē-lōōp')

LOCATION — In the West Indies lying between Montserrat and Dominica.

GOVT.—Former French colony

AREA—688 sq. mi.

POP.— 271,262 (1946).

CAPITAL—Basse-Terre.

Guadeloupe consists of two large islands, Guadeloupe proper and Grande-Terre, together with five smaller dependencies. Guadeloupe became an overseas department of France in 1946.

100 Centimes = 1 Franc

Stamps of French Colonies Surcharged

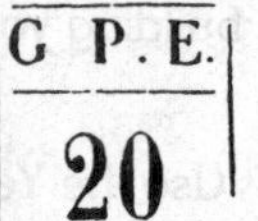

1884 *Imperf.* **Unwmkd.**

1 A8 20c on 30c brown, *bistre* 17.50 15.00
 a. Large "2" 65.00 60.00
 b. "20" double 50.00
2 " 25c on 35c *orange* 17.50 15.00
 a. Large "2" 60.00 50.00
 b. Large "5" 55.00 45.00

The 5c on 4c (French Colonies No. 40) was not regularly issued. Price $225.

c

d

1889 *Perf. 14x13½*

Surcharged Type c

3 A9 3c on 20c red, *green* 1.00 1.00
4 " 15c on 20c red, *green* 10.00 9.00
5 " 25c on 20c red, *green* 9.00 7.00

Surcharged Type d

6 A9 5c on 1c *lilac blue* 4.00 4.00
 a. Inverted surcharge 175.00 175.00
 b. Double surch. 70.00 70.00
 c. Surcharged "5" only 50.00
7 " 10c on 40c red, *straw* 9.00 8.00
 a. Dbl. surch. 125.00
8 " 15c on 20c red, *green* 8.00 6.00
 a. Dbl. surch. 125.00
9 " 25c on 30c brown, *bistre* 13.50 10.00
 a. Double surch. 125.00

The word "centimes" in surcharges "b" and "c" varies from 10 to 12½mm.

5 C.
GPE

1891

10 A9 5c on 10c *lavender* 4.00 3.00
11 " 5c on 1fr bronze green, *straw* 4.00 3.00

Stamps of French Colonies Overprinted in Black

GUADELOUPE

1891 *Imperf.*

12 A7 30c brown, *yellowish* 125.00 125.00
13 " 80c carmine, *pinkish* 350.00 350.00

Same Overprint

1891 *Perf. 14x13½.*

14 A9 1c *lilac blue* 50 50
 a. Double ovpt. 8.00 7.00
 b. Inverted ovpt. 30.00 30.00
15 " 2c brown, *buff* 60 40
 a. Double overprint 8.00 7.00
16 " 4c claret, *lavender* 1.40 1.40
17 " 5c green, *greenish* 2.00 2.00
 a. Double ovpt. 11.00 6.00
 b. Inverted ovpt. 45.00 45.00
18 " 10c *lavender* 4.50 3.75
19 " 15c blue 11.00 1.00
 a. Double ovpt. 30.00 30.00
20 " 20c red, *green* 11.00 8.00
 a. Double ovpt. 70.00 50.00
21 " 25c *rose* 11.00 1.00
 a. Double ovpt. 70.00 50.00
 b. Inverted ovpt. 50.00 50.00
22 " 30c brown, *bistre* 11.00 10.00
 a. Double ovpt. 70.00 60.00
23 " 35c deep violet, *orange* 22.50 20.00
24 " 40c red, *straw* 14.00 13.00
 a. Double ovpt. 225.00 225.00
25 " 75c carmine, *rose* 45.00 40.00
26 " 1fr bronze green, *straw* 25.00 22.50

The following errors may be found in all values of Nos. 12–26: "GNADELOUPE", "GUADELOUEP", "GUADELONPE" and "GUADBLOUPE".

Navigation and Commerce
A7

1892–1901 **Typo.** **Unwmkd.**

Colony Name in Blue or Carmine

27 A7 1c *lilac blue* 40 20
28 " 2c brown, *buff* 40 20
29 " 4c claret, *lavender* 40 20
30 " 5c green, *greenish* 1.25 20
31 " 5c yellow green ('01) 1.00 40
32 " 10c *lavender* 3.75 60
33 " 10c red ('00) 1.85 60
 a. Imperf. 35.00
34 " 15c blue, quadrille paper 3.00 20
35 " 15c gray, *light gray* ('00) 3.25 20
36 " 20c red, *green* 2.00 1.25
37 " 25c *rose* 2.00 40
38 " 25c blue ('00) 35.00 35.00
39 " 30c brown, *bistre* 6.00 4.75
40 " 40c red, *straw* 6.00 3.00
41 " 50c carmine *rose* 11.00 6.00
42 " 50c brn., *azure* ('00) 14.00 9.00
43 " 75c dp. vio., *orange* 9.00 8.00
44 " 1fr bronze green, *straw* 10.00 10.00
 Nos. 27–44 (18) 110.30 80.20

Stamps of 1892 Surcharged in Black:

G & D 5 f   **GetD 10** g   **G & D 1fr.** h

1903

45 A7 (*f*) 5c on 30c brown, *bistre* 1.25 1.25
 a. "C" instead of "G" 6.00 6.00
 b. Inverted surcharge 10.00 10.00
 c. Double surcharge 35.00 35.00
 d. Double surcharge, inverted 40.00
46 " (*g*) 10c on 40c red, *straw* 1.75 1.75
 a. "C" instead of "G" 7.00 7.00
 b. "1" inverted 12.00 12.00
 c. Inverted surcharge 12.00 12.00
47 " (*f*) 15c on 50c carmine, *rose* 2.75 2.75
 a. "C" instead of "G" 8.00 8.00
 b. Inverted surcharge 25.00 25.00
 c. "15" inverted 100.00 100.00
48 " (*g*) 40c on 1fr bronze green, *straw* 3.00 3.00
 a. "C" instead of "G" 9.00 9.00
 b. "4" inverted 27.50 27.50
 c. Inverted surcharge 32.50 32.50
 d. Double surcharge 55.00 55.00
49 A7 (*h*) 1fr on 75c deep violet, *orange* 12.00 12.00
 a. "C" instead of "G" 27.50 27.50
 b. "1" inverted 40.00 40.00
 c. Value above "G & D" 90.00 90.00
 d. Invtd. surcharge 27.50 27.50
 Nos. 45–49 (5) 20.75 20.75

Letters and figures from several fonts were used for these surcharges, resulting in numerous minor varieties.

With Additional Overprint "1903" in a Frame.

1904 Black and Red Surcharges.

50 A7 (*g*) 40c on 1fr bronze green, *straw* 17.50 17.50
 a. Inverted surcharge 35.00
 b. Black surcharge omitted
51 " (*h*) 1fr on 75c deep violet, *orange* 25.00 25.00
 a. Double surcharge 30.00

Black and Blue Surcharges.

52 A7 (*g*) 40c on 1fr bronze grn., *straw* 12.50 12.50
53 " (*h*) 1fr on 75c deep violet, *org.* 25.00 25.00

The date "1903" may be found at top, bottom or sides of the frame, in many type faces. These stamps may also be found with the minor varieties of Nos. 48–49.

Harbor at Basse-Terre
A8

View of La Soufrière
A9

Pointe-à-Pitre, Grand-Terre
A10

1905–27 **Typo.** *Perf. 14x13½*

54 A8 1c *bluish* 4 4
55 " 2c violet brown, *straw* 6 6
56 " 4c bistre brown, *azure* 8 8
57 " 5c green 20 15
 a. Booklet pane of 4
58 " 5c deep blue ('22) 6 6
59 " 10c rose 20 6
60 " 10c green ('22) 8 8
61 " 10c red, *bluish* ('25) 10 10
62 " 15c violet 10 8
63 A9 20c red, *green* 5 5
64 " 20c blue green ('25) 6 6
65 " 25c blue 8 8
66 " 25c olive green ('22) 8 8
 a. Booklet pane of 4
67 " 30c black 1.10 60
68 " 30c rose ('22) 10 10
69 " 30c brown olive, *lavender* ('25) 8 8
70 " 35c *yellow* ('06) 8 8
71 " 40c red, *straw* 15 10
72 " 45c olive gray, *lilac* ('07) 10 10
73 " 45c rose ('25) 10 10
74 " 50c gray grn., *straw* 1.35 90
75 " 50c deep blue ('22) 18 18
76 " 50c violet ('25) 10 10
77 " 65c blue ('27) 10 10
78 " 75c carmine, *blue* 20 18
79 A10 1fr *green* 40 40
80 " 1fr light blue ('25) 12 12
81 " 2fr carmine, *orange* 45 45
82 " 5fr dp. blue, *orange* 1.85 1.85
 Nos. 54–82 (29) 7.65 6.42

Nos. 29, 39 and 40 Surcharged in Carmine or Black

05 a   **10** b

1912

83 A7 (*a*) 5c on 4c claret, *lavender* (C) 20 20
84 " (") 5c on 30c brown, *bistre* (C) 25 25
85 " (*b*) 10c on 40c red, *straw* 50 50

Two spacings between the surcharged numerals are found on Nos. 83 to 85.

Stamps and Types of 1905-27 Surcharged with New Value and Bars.

1924-27

86 A10 25c on 5fr deep blue, *orange* ('24) 10 10
87 " 65c on 1fr gray green ('25) 20 20
88 " 85c on 1fr gray green ('25) 22 22
89 A9 90c on 75c dull red ('27) 25 25
90 A10 1.05fr on 2fr vermilion (Bl) ('26) 13 13
91 " 1.25fr on 1fr light blue (R) ('26) 10 10
92 " 1.50fr on 1fr dk. bl. ('27) 25 25
93 " 3fr on 5fr orange brown ('27) 25 25
94 " 10fr on 5fr violet rose, *orange* ('27) 3.00 3.00
95 " 20fr on 5fr rose lilac, *pinkish* ('27) 3.00 3.00
 Nos. 86–95 (10) 7.50 7.50

Sugar Mill
A11

Saints Roadstead
A12

Harbor Scene
A13

Typographed

1928–40 *Perf. 14x13½* **Unwmkd.**

96 A11 1c yellow & violet 5 5
97 " 2c black & light red 6 6
98 " 3c yellow & red violet ('40) 6 6
99 " 4c yel. grn. & orange brown 6 6
100 " 5c vermilion & green 6 6
101 " 10c bistre brown & deep blue 6 6
102 " 15c brown red & black 5 5
103 " 20c lilac & olive brn. 6 6
104 A12 25c greenish blue & olivine 6 6
105 " 30c gray green & yellow green 6 6
106 " 35c blue green ('38) 10 10
107 " 40c yellow & violet 6 5
108 " 45c violet brown & slate 13 12
109 " 45c blue green & dull green ('40) 12 12
110 " 50c dull green & orange 5 5
111 " 55c ultramarine & carmine ('38) 10 8
112 " 60c ultramarine & carmine ('40) 10 10
113 " 65c gray black & vermilion 10 10
114 " 70c gray black & vermilion ('40) 10 10

115 A12 75c dull red & blue green 12 12
116 " 80c carmine & brown ('38) 10 10
117 " 90c dull red & dull rose 65 60
118 " 90c rose red & blue ('39) 20 20
119 A13 1fr light rose & light blue 1.35 60
120 " 1fr rose red & orange ('38) 20 20
121 " 1fr blue gray & black brown ('40) 10 10
122 " 1.05fr light blue&rose 35 35
123 " 1.10fr light red & green 90 80
124 " 1.25fr blue gray & blk. brn. ('33) 7 7
125 " 1.25fr bright rose & red orange('39) 15 15
126 " 1.40fr light blue & lilac rose ('40) 12 12
127 " 1.50fr dull blue & blue 8 8
128 " 1.60fr lilac rose & yellow brown ('40) 10 10
129 " 1.75fr lilac rose & yel. brn. ('33) 1.25 85
130 " 1.75fr violet blue ('38) 1.50 1.25
131 " 2fr blue green & dark brown 10 10
132 " 2.25fr violet blue ('39) 13 13
133 " 2.50fr pale orange & green ('40) 12 12
134 " 3fr orange brown & slate 8 8
135 " 5fr dull blue & orange 10 10
136 " 10fr violet & olive brown 17 15
137 " 20fr green & magenta 30 30
Nos. 96-137 (42) 9.68 8.07

Colonial Exposition Issue.

Common Design Types

1931 Engraved. *Perf. 12½.*

Name of Country in Black

138 CD70 40c deep green 85 85
139 CD71 50c violet 85 85
140 CD72 90c red orange 1.65 1.65
141 CD73 1.50fr dull blue 1.35 1.35

Cardinal Richelieu Establishing French Antilles Co., 1635—A14

Victor Hugues and his Corsairs

A15

1935 *Perf. 13*

142 A14 40c gray brown 3.00 3.00
143 " 50c dull red 3.00 3.00
144 " 1.50fr dull blue 3.00 3.00
145 A15 1.75fr lilac rose 3.00 3.00
146 " 5fr dark brown 3.00 3.00
147 " 10fr blue green 3.00 3.00
Nos. 142-147 (6) 18.00 18.00

Issued in commemoration of the tercentenary of the establishment of the French colonies in the West Indies.

Common Design Types pictured in section at front of book.

Paris International Exposition Issue.

Common Design Types

1937 *Perf. 13*

148 CD74 20c deep violet 30 30
149 CD75 30c dark green 30 30
150 CD76 40c carmine rose 30 30
151 CD77 50c dk. brn. & blk. 30 30
152 CD78 90c red 30 30
153 CD79 1.50fr ultramarine 30 30
Nos. 148-153 (6) 1.80 1.80

Colonial Arts Exhibition Issue.

Souvenir Sheet

Common Design Type

1937 *Imperf.*

154 CD75 3fr dark blue 1.50 1.50

Size of sheet: 118x99mm.

New York World's Fair Issue.

Common Design Type

1939 Engraved *Perf. 12½x12*

155 CD82 1.25fr carmine lake 25 25
156 " 2.25fr ultramarine 25 25

La Soufrière View and Marshal Pétain

A16

1941 Engraved *Perf. 12½x12*

157 A16 1fr lilac 15
158 " 2.50fr blue 15

Nos. 157-158 were issued by the Vichy government and were not placed on sale in Guadeloupe. This is also true of a 10c stamp, type A11 without "RF," released in 1944.

Nos. 155, 156, 113, 117 and 118 Surcharged with New Values in Black.

1943 *Perf. 14x13½, 12½x12.*

159 A18 40c on 1.25fr carmine lake 25 25
160 " 40c on 2.25fr ultra. 45 35
161 A12 50c on 65c gray black & vermilion 20 20
162 " 1fr on 90c dull red & dull rose 35 35
163 " 1fr on 90c rose red & blue 25 20
Nos. 159-163 (5) 1.50 1.35

Nos. 104, 106, 113 and 90 Surcharged with New Values in Black.

1944 *Perf. 14x13½*

164 A12 40c on 35c blue green 20 15
165 " 50c on 25c greenish blue & olivine 10 10
166 " 1fr on 65c gray black & vermilion 10 10
a. Double surch. 25.00
167 A10 4fr on 1.05fr on 2fr vermilion 50 50

Dolphins—A17

Photogravure

1945 *Perf. 11½* Unwmkd.

168 A17 10c chalky blue & red orange 5 5
169 " 30c light yellow green & red 8 8
170 " 40c lt. blue & car. 10 10
171 A17 50c red orange & yellow green 8 5
172 " 60c olive bistre & light blue 8 8
173 " 70c light gray & yellow green 10 12
174 " 80c light blue green & yellow 10 10
175 " 1fr brn. vio. & grn. 10 10
176 " 1.20fr bright red violet & yel. grn. 10 10
177 " 1.50fr dull brown & carmine 15 10
178 " 2fr cerise & blue 15 10
179 " 2.40fr salmon & yellow green 35 25
180 " 3fr gray brown & blue violet 10 10
181 " 4fr ultra. & buff 10 10
182 " 4.50fr brn. org. & grn. 10 10
183 " 5fr dk. vio. & green 10 10
184 " 10fr gray green & red violet 15 15
185 " 15fr slate gray & orange 20 20
186 " 20fr pale gray & dull orange 30 20
Nos. 168-186 (19) 2.49 2.18

Eboue Issue.

Common Design Type

1945 Engraved *Perf. 13*

187 CD91 2fr black 10 10
188 " 25fr Prussian green 20 20

Basse-Terre Harbor and Woman

A18

Cutting Sugar Cane

A19

Pineapple Bearer

A20

Guadeloupe Woman

A21

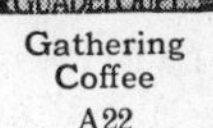

Gathering Coffee

A22

Guadeloupe Woman

A23

Engraved

1947 *Perf. 13* Unwmkd.

189 A18 10c red brown 6 6
190 " 30c sepia 5 5
191 " 50c blue green 7 7
192 A19 60c black brown 8 6
193 " 1fr deep carmine 10 10
194 " 1.50fr dark gray blue 20 20
195 A20 2fr blue green 40 35
196 " 2.50fr deep carmine 25 25
197 " 3fr deep blue 40 30
198 A21 4fr violet 30 30
199 " 5fr blue green 30 25
200 " 6fr red 30 25
201 A22 10fr deep blue 30 25
202 " 15fr dk. vio. brown 60 50
203 " 20fr rose red 80 50
204 A23 25fr blue green 90 80
205 " 40fr red 1.10 1.00
Nos. 189-205 (17) 6.21 5.29

SEMI-POSTAL STAMPS.

Nos. 59 and 62 Surcharged in Red ✚ 5c

1915-17 *Perf. 14x13½.* Unwmkd.

B1 A8 10c+5c rose 1.40 60
B2 " 15c+5c violet 85 60
a. Double surcharge 25.00 25.00

Curie Issue

Common Design Type

1938 *Perf. 13.*

B3 CD80 1.75fr+50c bright ultramarine 3.25 3.25

French Revolution Issue

Common Design Type

Name and Value Typo. in Black.

1939 Photogravure. *Perf. 13.*

B4 CD83 45(c)+25(c) green 2.25 2.25
B5 " 70(c)+30(c) brown 2.25 2.25
B6 " 90(c)+35(c) red orange 2.25 2.25
B7 " 1.25fr+1fr rose pink 2.25 2.25
B8 " 2.25fr+2fr blue 2.25 2.25
Nos. B4-B8 (5) 11.25 11.25

Common Design Type and

Colonial Artillery

SP1

Colonial Infantry

SP2

1941 Photogravure *Perf. 13½*

B9 SP1 1fr+1fr red 25
B10 CD86 1.50fr+3fr maroon 25
B11 SP2 2.50fr+1fr blue 25

Nos. B9-B11 were issued by the Vichy government, and were not placed on sale in Guadeloupe.

Nos. 157-158 were surcharged "OEUVRES COLONIALES" and surtax (including change of denomination of the 2.50fr to 50c). These were issued in 1944 by the Vichy government, and not placed on sale in Guadeloupe.

Red Cross Issue

Common Design Type

1944 *Perf. 14½x14.*

B12 CD90 5fr+20fr ultra. 25 25

The surtax was for the French Red Cross and national relief.

AIR POST STAMPS.

Common Design Type

Photogravure.

1945 *Perf. 14½x14.* **Unwmkd.**

C1 CD87 50fr green 35 35
C2 " 100fr deep plum 50 50

Victory Issue

Common Design Type

1946 Engraved *Perf. 12½*

C3 CD92 8fr reddish brown 30 30

Issued to commemorate the European victory of the Allied Nations in World War II.

Chad to Rhine Issue

Common Design Types

1946, June 6

C4 CD93 5fr dark slate green 40 40
C5 CD94 10fr deep blue 40 40
C6 CD95 15fr bright violet 40 40
C7 CD96 20fr brown carmine 40 40
C8 CD97 25fr black 40 40
C9 CD98 50fr red brown 40 40
Nos. C4-C9 (6) 2.40 2.40

Gathering Bananas—AP1

Seaplane at Roadstead—AP2

Pointe-a-Pitre Harbor and Guadeloupe Woman—AP3

1947 *Perf. 13* **Unwmkd.**

C10 AP1 50fr dk. brn. vio. 2.50 1.85
C11 AP2 100fr deep blue 2.50 1.85
C12 AP3 200fr red 3.00 2.25

AIR POST SEMI-POSTAL STAMPS.

Stamps of the design shown above and stamp of Cameroun type V10 inscribed "Guadeloupe" were issued in 1942 by the Vichy Government, but were not placed on sale in Guadeloupe.

POSTAGE DUE STAMPS.

D1  D2  D3

Typeset

1876 *Imperf.* **Unwmkd.**

J1 D1 25c black 325.00 250.00
J2 D2 40c *blue* 11,000.00
J3 D3 40c black 375.00 325.00

Twenty varieties of each.

Nos. J1 and J3 have been reprinted on thinner and whiter paper than the originals.

D4 D5

1879

J4 D4 15c *blue* 12.00 9.00
a. Period after "c" omitted 45.00 40.00
J5 D4 30c black 30.00 20.00
a. Period after "c" omitted 75.00 55.00

Twenty varieties of each.

1884

J6 D5 5c black 6.00 6.00
J7 " 10c *blue* 17.50 12.00
J8 " 15c *violet* 30.00 15.00
a. Printed on both sides
J9 " 20c *rose* 45.00 35.00
a. Italic "2" in "20" 275.00 250.00
J10 " 30c *yellow* 45.00 40.00
a. Printed on both sides
J11 " 35c *gray* 13.50 10.00
J12 " 50c *green* 6.00 5.00
a. Printed on both sides

There are ten varieties of the 35c, and fifteen of each of the other values, also numerous wrong font and missing letters.

Postage Due Stamps of French Colonies Surcharged in Black

G & D 30

1903

J13 D1 30c on 60c brown, *cream* 125.00 125.00
a. "3" with flat top 200.00 200.00
b. Inverted surcharge 200.00 200.00
c. As "a," inverted 450.00 450.00
J14 " 30c on 1fr rose, *cream* 135.00 135.00
a. Inverted surcharge 275.00 275.00
b. "3" with flat top 265.00 265.00
c. As "b," inverted 500.00 500.00

Gustavia Bay

D6

Avenue of Royal Palms

D7

1905-06 Typo. *Perf. 14x13½*

J15 D6 5c blue 5 5
J16 " 10c brown 10 10
J17 " 15c green 10 10
J18 " 20c *yellow* ('06) 10 10
J19 " 30c rose 12 12
J20 " 50c black 70 70
J21 " 60c brown orange 22 22
J22 " 1fr violet 60 60
Nos. J15-J22 (8) 1.99 1.99

Type of 1905-06 Issue Surcharged

2 francs à percevoir

1926

J23 D6 2fr on 1fr gray 25 25
J24 " 3fr on 1fr ultramarine 65 65

1928

J25 D7 2c olive brown & lilac 4 4
J26 " 4c blue & orange brown 5 5
J27 " 5c gray green & dark brown 5 5
J28 " 10c dull violet & yellow 6 6
J29 " 15c rose & olive green 6 6
J30 " 20c brown orange & olive green 6 6
J31 " 25c brown red & blue green 5 5
J32 " 30c slate & olivine 7 7
J33 " 50c olive brown & light red 10 10
J34 " 60c deep blue & black 25 25
J35 " 1fr green & orange 65 65
J36 " 2fr bistre brown & light red 40 40
J37 " 3fr violet & blue black 25 25
Nos. J25-J37 (13) 2.09 2.09

Stamps of type D7 without "RF" monogram were issued in 1944 by the Vichy Government, but were not placed on sale in Guadeloupe.

D8

Engraved.

1947 *Perf. 14x13.* **Unwmkd.**

J38 D8 10c black 5 5
J39 " 30c dull blue green 5 5
J40 " 50c bright ultramarine 5 5
J41 " 1fr dark green 8 8
J42 " 2fr dark blue 15 15
J43 " 3fr black brown 15 15
J44 " 4fr lilac rose 30 30
J45 " 5fr purple 35 35
J46 " 10fr red 40 40
J47 " 20fr dark violet 45 45
Nos. J38-J47 (10) 2.03 2.03

GUATEMALA

(gwä'tȧ-mä'lä)

LOCATION—Central America, bordering on Atlantic and Pacific Oceans.

GOVT.—Republic.

AREA—42,042 sq. mi.

POP.—6,440,000 (est. 1977).

CAPITAL—Guatemala City.

100 Centavos = 8 Reales = 1 Peso

100 Centavos de Quetzal = 1 Quetzal (1927)

Coat of Arms

A1 A2

Two types of 10c:
Type I—Both "O"s in "10" are wide.
Type II—Left "O" narrow.

Perf. 14x13½

1871, Mar. 1 Typo. **Unwmkd.**

1 A1 1c ochre 1.00 *15.00*
a. Imperf., pair 3.00
b. Printed on both sides, imperf. 45.00
2 " 5c lt. bister brown 4.00 *10.00*
a. Imperf., pair 25.00
b. Tête bêche pair 150.00
c. Tête bêche pair imperf. 2000.00
3 " 10c blue (I) 6.00 *10.00*
a. Imperf., pair (I) 30.00
b. Type II 12.00 *15.00*
c. Imperf., pair (II) 50.00
4 A1 20c rose 5.00 *12.00*
a. Imperf., pair 30.00
b. 20c blue (error) 100.00 125.00
c. As "b," imperf. *750.00*

Forgeries exist. Forged cancellations abound. See No. C458.

1873 Lithographed *Perf. 12*

5 A2 4r dull red violet 300.00 65.00
6 " 1p dull yellow 125.00 100.00

Forgeries exist.

Liberty

A3 A4

A5 A6

1875, Apr. 15 **Engraved**

7 A3 ¼r black 1.50 *7.50*
8 A4 ½r blue green 1.50 *4.00*
9 A5 1r blue 1.50 *4.00*
a. Half used as ½r on cover *1250.00*
10 A6 2r dull red 1.50 *4.00*

Nos. 7-10 normally lack gum.
Forgeries and forged cancellations exist.

Indian Woman

A7

Quetzal

A8

Typographed on Tinted Paper.

1878, Jan. 10 *Perf. 13*

11 A7 ½r yellow green 1.25 *5.00*
a. Imperf., pair 75.00
12 " 2r carmine rose 2.00 *6.00*
a. Imperf., pair 75.00
13 " 4r violet 2.00 *7.00*
a. Imperf., pair 75.00
14 " 1p yellow 3.00 *15.00*
a. Imperf., pair 75.00
c. Half used as 4r on cover *1750.00*

Some sheets of Nos. 11-14 have papermaker's watermark, "LACROIX FRERES," in double-lined capitals appearing on six stamps.

Part perforate pairs of Nos. 11, 12 and 14 exist. Price for each, about $100.

Forgeries of Nos. 11-14 are plentiful. Forged cancellations exist.

1879 Engraved *Perf. 12*

15 A8 ¼r brown & green 4.00 5.00
16 " 1r black & green 5.00 6.00
a. Half used as ½r on cover *1500.00*

Nos. 11, 12, 15, 16 Surcharged in Black

1 centavo.

1881 *Perf. 12 and 13*

17 A8 1c on ¼r brown & green 8.00 9.00
a. "ecntavo." 30.00 30.00
b. Pair, one without surch. 200.00
18 A7 5c on ½r yel. grn. 8.50 9.00
a. "ecntavos." 30.00 30.00
b. "5" omitted 100.00
c. Double surcharge 75.00 80.00

19 A8 10c on 1r black & green 12.00 15.00
a. "s" of "centavos" missing 75.00 80.00
b. "ecntavos." 45.00 50.00

20 A7 20c on 2r carmine rose 45.00 50.00
a. Horiz. pr., imperf. between 250.00

The 5c had two settings.

Surcharge varieties found on Nos. 17–20 include: Period omitted; comma instead of period; "ecntavo." or "ecntavos."; "c" or "s" omitted; spaced "centavos."; wider "0" in "20".

Counterfeits of Nos. 17–20 are plentiful.

Quetzal
A11

1881, Nov. 7 Engraved *Perf.* 12

21	A11	1c black & green	1.00	1.00
22	"	2c brown & green	1.00	1.00
		a. Center inverted	100.00	100.00
23	"	5c red & green	2.50	1.50
		a. Center inverted	2000.00	600.00
24	"	10c gray violet & green	1.00	1.00
25	"	20c yellow & green	1.00	1.50
		a. Center inverted	150.00	150.00
		Nos. 21-25 (5)	6.50	6.00

Gen. Justo Rufino Barrios
A12

Black Surcharge

Correos Nacionales
25 c. 25 c.
Guatemala.
25 c. 25 c.
25 centavos.

1886, Mar. 6

26 A12 25c on 1p vermilion 65 65
a. "centovos." 2.00
b. "centaños." 2.00
c. "255" instead of "25" 40.00
d. Inverted "S" in "Nacionales." 2.00
f. "cen avos" 25.00
h. "Corre cionales" 20.00

27 50c on 1p vermilion 65 65
a. "centovos." 2.00
b. "centaños." 2.00
c. "Carreos" 2.00
d. Inverted surcharge 50.00
e. Double surcharge 75.00
f. Inverted "S" in "Nacionales" 2.00
g. "centavo" 2.00
h. "cen avos" 20.00

28 " 75c on 1p vermilion 65 65
a. "centovos." 2.00
b. "centaños." 2.00
c. "Carreos" 2.50
d. "50" for "75" at upper right 3.00
e. Inverted "S" in "Nacionales" 2.00
f. Double surcharge 75.00
g. "ales" inverted 50.00

29 " 100c on 1p vermilion 75 75
a. "110" at upper left and "400" at lower left, instead of "100" 7.50
b. Inverted surcharge 75.00
c. "Guatemala." bolder; 23 mm. instead of 18½ mm. wide 3.00
d. Double surch., one diagonal 85.00

30 A12 150c on 1p vermilion 75 75
a. Inverted "G" 7.50
b. "Guetemala" and italic "5" in upper 4 numerals 7.50
d. Inverted surcharge 75.00
e. Pair, one without surcharge 100.00
f. Double surcharge 75.00
Nos. 26-30 (5) 3.45 3.45

There are many other minor varieties, such as wrong font letters, etc. The surcharge on Nos. 29 and 30 has different letters and ornaments. On No. 29, "Guatemala," normally is 18½mm. wide.

Used prices of Nos. 26–30 are for canceled to order stamps. Postally used sell for much more.

National Emblem
A13

1886, July 1 Litho. *Perf.* 12

31	A13	1c dull blue	7.50	3.50
32	"	2c brown	7.50	5.00
33	"	5c purple	50.00	2.00
34	"	10c red	30.00	2.50
35	"	20c emerald	30.00	2.50
36	"	25c orange	30.00	2.50
37	"	50c olive green	15.00	5.00
38	"	75c carmine rose	15.00	5.00
39	"	100c red brown	15.00	5.00
40	"	150c dark blue	18.50	6.00
41	"	200c orange yellow	18.50	6.00
		Nos. 31-41 (11)	237.00	45.00

Used prices of Nos. 38–41 are for canceled to order stamps. Postally used sell for more.

See also Nos. 43–50, 99–107.

No. 32 Surcharged in Black

PROVISIONAL.
1886
1
UN CENTAVO

1886, Nov. 12

Two settings:
I. "1886" (no period).
II. "1886." (period).

42 A13 1c on 2c brown, I 3.50 4.00
a. Date inverted, I 60.00
b. Date double, I 60.00
c. Date omitted, I 60.00
d. Date double, one invtd., I 75.00
e. Date triple, one inverted, I 75.00
f. Setting II 2.00 3.00
g. Invtd. surch., II 6.00
h. Double surch., II 75.00

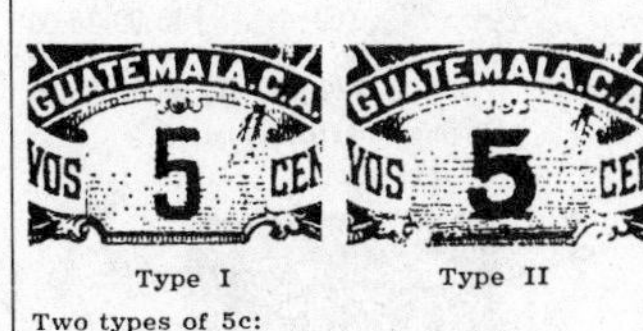

Type I Type II

Two types of 5c:
I. Thin "5."
II. Larger, thick "5."

1886-95 Engraved *Perf.* 12

43	A13	1c blue	1.00	30
44	"	2c yellow brown	2.00	40
		a. Half used as 1c on cover		100.00
45	A13	5c purple (I)	100.00	2.00
46	"	5c violet (II) ('88)	2.00	50
47	"	6c lilac ('95)	2.00	60
48	"	10c red ('90)	2.00	60
49	"	20c green ('93)	4.00	1.50
50	A13	25c red orange ('93)	7.50	2.00
		Nos. 43-44, 46-50 (7)	20.50	5.90

The impression of the engraved stamps is sharper than that of the lithographed. On the engraved stamps the top four lines at left are heavier than those below them. (This is also true of the 1c litho., which is distinguished from the engraved only by a slight color difference and the impression.) The "2" and "5" (I) are more open than the litho. numerals. The "10" of the engraved is wider. The 20c and 25c of the engraved have a vertical line at right end of the "centavos" ribbon.

No. 38 Surcharged in Blue Black

1894
2
CENTAVOS
a

"1894" 14½mm. wide.

1894, Apr. 25

51 A13 10c on 75c carmine rose (BlBk) 7.50 7.50
a. Double surcharge 100.00

Nos. 39-41 with Surcharge "a" in Blue or Red

"1894" 14mm. wide.

1894, June 13

52 A13 2c on 100c red brown (Bl) 6.00 6.00
53 " 6c on 150c dark blue (R) 6.00 6.00
54 " 10c on 75c carmine rose (Bl) 400.00 400.00
55 " 10c on 200c orange yellow (Bl) 6.00 6.00
b. Double surcharge 100.00
c. Inverted surcharge 75.00

Nos. 54–55 exist with thick or thin "1" in new value.

Nos. 39-41 with Surcharge "a" in Black or Red

"1894" 12mm. wide.

1894, July 14

52a A13 2c on 100c red brn. (Bk) 6 00 6.00
b. Vert. pair, one without surch. 125.00
53a A13 6c on 150c dk. blue (R) 6.00 6.00
55a " 10c on 200c org. yel. (Bk) 6.00 6.00

Nos. 44 and 46 Surcharged in Black, Blue Black, or Red:

1894 1 CENTAVO *b*

1895 1 CENTAVO *c*

1 CENTAVO 1895 *d*

1 CENTAVO 1895 *e*

1894-96

56 A13 (*b*) 1c on 2c yellow brown (Bk) 1.10 1.00
a. "Centav" 10.00 10.00
b. Dbl. surch. 75.00
c. As "a", dbl. surcharge 150.00
d. Blue black surcharge 10.00 10.00
e. Dbl. surch., one inverted 150.00

57 " (*c*) 1c on 5c violet (R) ('95) 75 50
a. Invtd. surch. 5.00 5.00
b. "1894" instead of "1895" 5.00 5.00
c. Double surch. 50.00

58 A13 (*d*) 1c on 5c violet (R) ('95) 75 50
a. Invtd. surch. 50.00 50.00
b. Double surch. 50.00

59 " (*e*) 1c on 5c violet (R) ('96) 1.50 90
a. Invtd. surch. 50.00
b. Double surch. 50.00

Nos. 56–58 may be found with thick or thin "1" in the new value.

National Arms and President J. M. Reyna Barrios
A21

1897, Jan. 1 Engraved Unwmkd.

60	A21	1c *lilac gray*	75	75
61	"	2c *greenish gray*	75	75
62	"	6c *brown orange*	75	75
63	"	10c *dull blue*	1.00	1.00
64	"	12c *rose red*	1.00	1.00
65	"	18c *grayish white*	12.00	12.00
66	"	20c *scarlet*	1.50	1.25
67	"	25c *bistre brown*	1.50	1.25
68	"	50c *reddish brown*	1.50	1.25
69	"	75c *gray*	75.00	75.00
70	"	100c *blue green*	1.50	1.25
71	"	150c *dull rose*	125.00	125.00
72	"	200c *magenta*	1.50	1.25
73	"	500c *yellow green*	1.50	1.25
		Nos. 60-73 (14)	225.25	223.75

Issued for Central American Exposition.

Stamps often sold as Nos. 65, 69 and 71 are copies with telegraph overprint removed.

Used prices for Nos. 60–73 are for canceled-to-order copies. Postally used examples are worth more.

The paper of Nos. 64 and 66 was originally colored on one side only, but has "bled through" on some copies.

No. 64 Surcharged in Violet

UN
CENTAVO
1898

1897, Nov.

74 A21 1c on 12c *rose red* 1.25 1.25
a. Inverted surch. 30.00 30.00
b. Pair, one without surch. 75.00

Stamps of 1886–93 Surcharged in Red

1898 1 centavo *f*

1898 10 centavos *g*

1898

75	(*f*)	1c on 5c violet	1.50	1.50
76	(")	1c on 50c olive green	3.00	3.00
		a. Inverted surcharge		100.00
77	(")	6c on 5c violet	6.00	4.00
78	(")	6c on 150c dark blue	6.00	6.00
79	(*g*)	10c on 20c emerald	6.00	6.00
		a. Double surch., one inverted	100.00	100.00
		Nos. 75-79 (5)	22.50	20.50

Black Surcharge.

80	(*f*)	1c on 25c red orange	4.00	4.00
81	(")	1c on 75c car. rose	3.00	3.00
82	(")	6c on 10c red	15.00	15.00
83	(")	6c on 20c emerald	6.00	6.00
84	(")	6c on 100c red brown	6.00	6.00
85	(")	6c on 200c org. yel.	6.00	6.00
		a. Invtd. surcharge	45.00	45.00
		Nos. 80-85 (6)	40.00	40.00

National Emblem
A24 A25

Revenue Stamp Overprinted or Surcharged in Carmine

Perf. 12, 12x14, 14x12

1898, Oct. 8 **Lithographed**

86 A24 1c dark blue 1.50 1.50
a. Inverted overprint 25.00 25.00
87 " 2c on 1c dark blue 2.00 2.00
a. Inverted surcharge 25.00 25.00

Counterfeits exist of Nos. 86a, 87a.

Revenue Stamps Surcharged in Carmine.

1898 **Engraved** ***Perf. 12½ to 16***

88 A25 1c on 10c blue gray 1.00 1.00
a. "ENTAVO" 7.50 7.50
89 A25 2c on 5c purple 1.50 1.50
90 " 2c on 10c blue gray 7.50 7.50
a. Double surch., car. & black 75.00 75.00
91 A25 2c on 50c deep blue 12.50 12.50
a. Double surch., car. & black 100.00 100.00

Black Surcharge.

92 A25 2c on 1c lilac rose 5.00 4.00
93 " 2c on 25c red 10.00 10.00
94 " 6c on 1p purple 5.00 4.00
95 " 6c on 5p gray violet 8.50 8.50
96 " 6c on 10p emerald 8.50 8.50
Nos. 92-96 (5) 37.00 35.00

Nos. 88 and 90 are found in shades ranging from Prussian blue to slate blue.
Varieties other than those listed are bogus. Counterfeits exist of No. 92.
Soaking in water causes marked fading.

No. 46 Surcharged in Red

Un I Centavo

1899

1899, Sept. ***Perf. 12***

97 A13 1c on 5c violet 50 40
a. Inverted surcharge 8.00 8.00
b. Double surcharge 15.00 15.00
c. Double surcharge, one inverted 15.00 15.00

No. 48 Surcharged in Black

1900
1
CENTAVO

1900, Jan.

98 A13 1c on 10c red 60 60
a. Inverted surcharge 15.00 15.00
b. Double surcharge 75.00 75.00

Quetzal Type of 1886

1900-02 **Engraved.**

99 A13 1c dark green 60 40
100 " 2c carmine 60 40
101 " 5c blue (II) 2.00 65
102 " 6c light green 75 40
103 " 10c bistre brown 3.00 60
104 " 20c purple 6.00 6.00
105 " 20c bistre brown ('02) 7.50 7.50
106 " 25c yellow 6.00 6.00
107 " 25c blue green ('02) 7.50 7.50
Nos. 99-107 (9) 33.95 29.45

Canceled-to-order stamps are often from remainders. Most collectors of canceled stamps prefer postally used specimens.

No. 49 Surcharged in Black

1901
1
CENTAVO

1901, May

108 A13 1c on 20c green 1.35 1.35
a. Inverted surcharge 20.00 20.00
b. Double surch., one diagonal 45.00
109 A13 2c on 20c green 2.75 2.75

No. 50 Surcharged in Black

UN
1
CENTAVO
1901

1901, Apr.

110 A13 1c on 25c red orange 1.00 1.00
a. Inverted surcharge 30.00 30.00
b. Double surcharge 40.00 40.00

A26 A27

Revenue Stamps Surcharged in Carmine or Black

1902, July ***Perf. 12, 14x12, 12x14***

111 A26 1c on 1c dark blue 2.00 2.00
a. Double surcharge 30.00
b. Invtd. surcharge 30.00
112 " 2c on 1c dark blue 2.00 2.00
a. Double surch. 100.00
b. Invtd. surcharge 30.00

Perf. 14, 15.

113 A27 6c on 25c red (B) 3.00 3.00
a. Double surcharge, one inverted 60.00 60.00

National Emblem
A28

Statue of Justo Rufino Barrios
A29

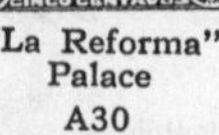

"La Reforma" Palace
A30

Temple of Minerva
A31

Lake Amatitlán
A32

Cathedral in Guatemala
A33

Columbus Theater
A34

Artillery Barracks
A35

Monument to Columbus
A36

School for Indians
A37

1902 **Engraved.** ***Perf. 12 to 16.***

114 A28 1c green & claret 30 15
a. Imperf. vert., pr. 75.00
115 A29 2c lake & black 30 15
a. Horiz. or vert. pair, imperf. between 150.00
116 A30 5c blue & black 30 15
a. 5c ultramarine & black 45 15
b. Imperf., pair 100.00 100.00
c. Horiz. pair, imperf. vert. 90.00
117 A31 6c bistre & green 30 15
a. Horiz. pair, imperf. between 150.00
118 A32 10c orange & blue 30 15
119 A33 20c rose lilac & black 60 25
a. Horiz. pair, imperf. vert. 100.00
120 A34 50c red brown & blue 45 20
121 A35 75c gray lilac & black 65 25
a. Horizontal pair, imperf. between 125.00
122 A36 1p brown & black 75 25
a. Horizontal pair, imperf. btwn. 125.00
123 A37 2p verm. & black 1.00 50
Nos. 114-123 (10) 4.95 2.20

See also Nos. 210, 212-214, 219, 223, 239-241, 243.

Issues of 1886-1900 Surcharged in Black or Carmine

1903
25
CENTAVOS

1903, Apr. 18 ***Perf. 12***

124 A13 25c on 1c dark green 1.50 75
a. Inverted surcharge 50.00 50.00
125 " 25c on 2c carmine 2.00 75
126 " 25c on 6c light green 3.00 3.00
a. Invtd. surcharge 50.00 50.00
127 " 25c on 10c bis. brn. 12.50 6.00
128 " 25c on 75c rose 15.00 15.00
129 " 25c on 150c dk. blue. (C) 15.00 15.00
130 " 25c on 200c yellow 17.50 17.50
Nos. 124-130 (7) 66.50 58.00

Bogus varieties exist.

Declaration of Independence
A38

1907, Jan. 1 ***Perf. 13½ to 15***

132 A38 12½c ultra. & black 40 30
a. Horiz. pair, imperf. btwn. 125.00

Nos. 118, 119 and 132 Surcharged in Black or Red

1908
UN 1 UN
CENTAVO

1908, May

133 A32 1c on 10c orange & blue (Bk) 60 60
a. Double surcharge 35.00
b. Invtd. surch. 15.00
c. Pair, one without surcharge 50.00
134 A38 2c on 12½c ultra. & black (R) 60 60
a. Horiz. or vert. pair, imperf. between 100.00
b. Inverted surcharge 20.00 7.50
c. Dbl. surch. 35.00
135 A33 6c on 20c rose lilac & black (Bk) 50 50
a. Invtd. surch. 20.00

Similar Surcharge, Dated 1909, in Red or Black on Nos. 121 and 120.

1909, Apr.

136 A35 2c on 75c gray lilac & blk. (R) 1.00 1.00
137 A34 6c on 50c red brown & blue (R) 30.00 30.00
a. Double surcharge 75.00 75.00
138 " 6c on 50c red brown & blue (Bk) 50 50

Counterfeits exist of Nos. 137, 137a.

No. 123 Surcharged in Black

12½
CENTAVOS
1909.

139 A37 12½c on 2p vermilion & black 1.00 1.00
a. Inverted surcharge 35.00 35.00
b. Period omitted after "1909" 10.00 10.00

Gen. Miguel García Granados
A39

1910, Feb. 11 ***Perf. 14***

140 A39 6c bistre & indigo 1.00 50
a. Imperf., pair 60.00

Commemorative of the centenary of the birth of President Miguel Garcia Granados.

General Post Office—A40

President Manuel Estrada Cabrera
A41

1911, June ***Perf. 12***

141 A40 25c blue & black 1.00 25
a. Center invtd. 2000.00 750.00
142 A41 5p red & black 1.35 1.35
a. Center inverted 35.00 30.00

Nos. 116, 118 and 140
Surcharged in Black or Red:

1911

Un Centavo

h

DOS
CENTAVOS
Correos de Guatemala
1911

i

SEIS
CENTAVOS
Correos de Guatemala
1911

j

1911 *Perf. 14*

143 A39 (*h*) 1c on 6c bistre & indigo (Bk) 20.00 8.00
a. Dbl. surch. 75.00
144 A30 (*i*) 2c on 5c blue & black (R) 3.00 1.50
145 A32 (*j*) 6c on 10c orange & blue (Bk) 2.00 2.00
a. Dbl. surch. 45.00

Nos. 119–121 Surcharged in Black:

1912

1 UN CENTAVO 1

k

1912 1912

2 CENTAVOS 2

l

5 5

CINCO CENTAVOS 1912

m

1912, Sept.

147 A33 (*k*) 1c on 20c rose lilac & black (Bk) 65 65
a. Inverted surcharge 15.00 15.00
b. Double surcharge 20.00 20.00
148 A34 (*l*) 2c on 50c red brown & blue (Bk) 65 65
a. Inverted surcharge 15.00 15.00
b. Double surcharge 15.00
c. Double inverted surcharge 20.00
149 A35 (*m*) 5c on 75c gray lilac & blk. (Bk) 1.50 1.50
a. "191" for "1912" 12.50 12.50
b. Double surcharge 20.00 20.00
c. Inverted surcharge 18.50

Nos. 120, 122 and 123
Surcharged in Blue, Green or Black:

1913

UN CENTAVO

n

1913

Seis centavos

o

1913

12½ CENTAVOS

p

1913, July

151 A34 (*n*) 1c on 50c red brown & blue (Bl) 50 50
a. Inverted surcharge 12.50
b. Double surcharge 20.00
c. Horiz. pair, imperf. btwn. 100.00
152 A36 (*o*) 6c on 1p brown & black (G) 75 75
153 A37 (*p*) 12½c on 2p vermilion & black (Bk) 60 60
a. Inverted surcharge 25.00 25.00
b. Dbl. surch. 45.00

Nos. 114 and 115 Surcharged in Black:

DOS
CENTAVOS

q

SEIS
CENTAVOS

r

12½
CENTAVOS

s

VEINTICINCO
CENTAVOS

t

1916–17

154 A28 (*q*) 2c on 1c green & claret ('17) 60 40
a. Inverted surcharge 20.00
b. Double surcharge 25.00
155 " (*r*) 6c on 1c green & claret 60 40
156 " (*s*) 12½c on 1c green & claret 60 40
157 A29 (*t*) 25c on 2c lake & black 45 35

Numerous errors of value and color, inverted and double surcharges and similar varieties are in the market. They were not regularly issued, but were surreptitiously made and sold.
Counterfeit surcharges abound.

"Liberty" and President Estrada Cabrera
A51

Estrada Cabrera and Quetzal
A52

1917, Mar. 15 *Perf. 14, 15*

158 A51 25c deep blue & brown 65 40
Re-election of President Estrada Cabrera.

1918 *Perf. 12*

161 A52 1.50p dark blue 60 40

Radio Station
A54

"Joaquina" Maternity Hospital
A55

"Estrada Cabrera" Vocational School
A56

National Emblem
A57

1919, May 3 *Perf. 14, 15*

162 A54 30c red & black 5.50 90
163 A55 60c olive grn. & blk. 1.25 65
164 A56 90c red brn & black 1.00 1.00
165 A57 3p deep grn. & blk. 3.00 65
See also Nos. 215, 227.

No. 162 Surcharged

1920
2 centavos

Blue Overprint and Black Surcharge.

1920, Jan. **Unwmkd.**

166 A54 2c on 30c red & black 60 60
a. Inverted surcharge 15.00 15.00
b. "1920" double 12.50 12.50
c. "1920" omitted 20.00 20.00
d. "2 centavos" omitted 20.00

Nos. 123 and 163 Surcharged:

2 centavos

1920

u

25

Centavos

v

1920

167 A55 (*u*) 2c on 60c olive green & black (Bk & R) 60 60
a. Inverted surcharge 12.50 12.50
b. "1920" inverted 12.50 12.50
c. "1920" omitted 12.50 12.50
d. "1920" only 12.50

168 A37 (*v*) 25c on 2p vermilion & black (Bk) 65 50
a. "35" for "25" 10.00 10.00
b. Large "5" in "25" 7.50 7.50
c. Inverted surcharge 15.00 15.00
d. Double surch. 25.00

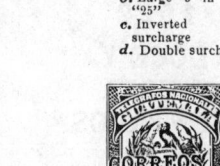

A61

1920

169 A61 25c green 65 50
a. Double overprint 50.00

No. 119 Surcharged

1921
Doce y medio
centavos

1921, Apr.

170 A33 12½c on 20c rose lilac & black 65 40
a. Double surcharge 17.50
b. Inverted surcharge 20.00

No. 121 Surcharged

1921
Cincuenta
centavos

1921, Apr.

171 A35 50c on 75c lilac & black 90 50
a. Dbl. surcharge 15.00
b. Invtd. surcharge 25.00

Mayan Stele at Quiriguá
A62

Monument to President Granados
A63

"La Penitenciaria" Bridge
A64

1921, Sept. 1 *Perf. 13½, 14, 15*

172 A62 1.50p blue & orange 65 50
173 A63 5p brown & green 3.00 1.50
174 A64 15p black & verm. 10.00 6.00
See also Nos. 216, 228, 229.

A65

A66

Telegraph Stamps Overprinted or Surcharged in Black or Red

1921 *Perf. 14*

175 A65 25c green 65 40
176 A66 12½c on 25c green (R) 50 40
a. Inverted overprint 25.00
177 A66 12½c on 25c green 5.00 5.00

Nos. 119, 163 and 164
Surcharged in Black or Red:

1922
DOCE Y
MEDIO
CENTAVOS
w

1922
25
CENTAVOS
x

1922, Mar.

178 A33 (*w*) 12½c on 20c rose lilac & black 65 65
a. Invtd. surch. 6.00
179 A55 (") 12½c on 60c olive green & black (R) 1.50 1.50
a. Invtd. surch. 20.00
180 A56 (") 12½c on 90c red brn. & black 1.50 1.50
181 A55 (*x*) 25c on 60c olive grn. & black 1.50 1.50
a. Invtd. surch. 5.00
182 " (") 25c on 60c olive green & black (R) 100.00
183 A56 (") 25c on 90c red brn. & black 1.50 1.50
a. Invtd. surch. 6.00
184 " (") 25c on 90c red brown & black (R) 6.00 6.00
Nos. 178-181, 183-184 (6) 12.65 12.65
Counterfeits of No. 182 exist.

Stamps of 1919-21 Surcharged in Red or Dark Blue

1922
DOCE
Y MEDIO
CENTAVOS

1922

185 A57 12½c on 3p green & black (R) 60 50
186 A63 12½c on 5p brown & green 1.00 90
187 A64 12½c on 15p black & vermilion 1.00 90

Surcharged in Red or Black

1922
25
CENTAVOS

25 (I) 25 (II) 25 (III) 25 (IV)

1922

188 A57 25c on 3p green & black (I) (R) 65 65
a. Type II 1.35 1.35
b. Type III 1.35 1.35
c. Type IV 1.00 1.00
d. Inverted surcharge 30.00
e. Horiz. or vert. pair, imperf. between (I) 125.00
189 A63 25c on 5p brown & green (I) 1.50 1.50
a. Type II 3.00 2.00
b. Type III 3.00 2.00
c. Type IV 1.50 1.50
190 A64 25c on 15p black & vermilion (I) 1.50 1.50
a. Type II 3.00 2.00
b. Type III 3.00 2.00
c. Type IV 1.50 1.50
191 " 25c on 15p black & vermilion (I) (R) 35.00 35.00
a. Type II 60.00 45.00
b. Type III 60.00 45.00
c. Type IV 50.00 40.00

Stamps of 1902-21 Surcharged in Dark Blue or Red

1922
25
CENTAVOS

25 (V) 25 (VI) 25 (VII)
25 (VIII) 25 (IX)

1922, Aug. On Stamps of 1902.

192 A35 25c on 75c gray lilac & black (V) 65 65
a. Type VI 65 65
b. Type VII 3.00 3.00
c. Type VIII 8.00 5.00
d. Type IX 9.00 6.00
193 A36 25c on 1p brown & black (V) 50 50
a. Type VI 50 50
b. Type VII 2.00 2.00
c. Type VIII 4.00 4.00
d. Type IX 6.00 5.00
e. Inverted surcharge
194 A37 25c on 2p vermilion & black (V) 75 75
a. Type VI 75 75
b. Type VII 2.00 2.00
c. Type VIII 6.00 5.00
d. Type IX 9.00 9.00

On Stamps of 1919.

195 A54 25c on 30c red & black (V) 75 75
a. Type VI 75 75
b. Type VII 2.00 2.00
c. Type VIII 8.00 8.00
d. Type IX 9.00 9.00
196 A55 25c on 60c olive green & black (V) 2.00 2.00
a. Type VI 2.00 2.00
b. Type VII 8.00 8.00
c. Type VIII 12.00 12.00
d. Type IX 15.00 15.00
197 A56 25c on 90c red brown & black (V) 2.00 2.00
a. Type VI 3.00 3.00
b. Type VII 8.00 8.00
c. Type VIII 12.50 12.50
d. Type IX 15.00 15.00
198 A57 25c on 3p green & black (R) (V) 65 65
a. Type VI 65 65
b. Type VII 2.00 2.00
c. Type VIII 8.00 5.00
d. Type IX 9.00 9.00
e. Invtd. surch. 30.00

On Stamps of 1921.

199 A62 25c on 1.50p blue & orange (V) 50 50
a. Type VI 50 50
b. Type VII 1.75 1.75
c. Type VIII 4.00 4.00
d. Type IX 6.00 6.00
e. Invtd. surch. 45.00
200 A63 25c on 5p brown & green (V) 1.50 1.50
a. Type VI 1.65 1.65
b. Type VII 5.00 5.00
c. Type VIII 10.00 10.00
d. Type IX 12.00 12.00
201 A64 25c on 15p black & verm. (V) 1.65 1.65
a. Type VI 2.50 2.50
b. Type VII 7.50 7.50
c. Type VIII 10.00 10.00
d. Type IX 15.00 15.00

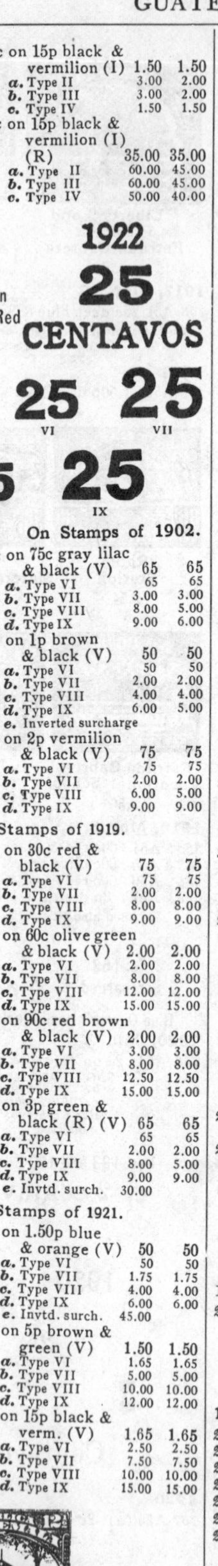

Centenary Palace
A69

National Palace at Antigua
A70

Printed by Waterlow & Sons.

1922 ***Perf. 14, 14½.***

202 A69 12½c green 35 20
a. Horiz. or vert. pair, imperf. between 100.00
203 A70 25c brown 35 20
See also Nos. 211, 221, 234.

Columbus Theater
A71

Quetzal
A72

Granados Monument
A73

Lithographed by Castillo Bros.

1924, Feb. Lithographed ***Perf. 12***

204 A71 50c rose 65 40
a. Imperf., pair 12.50
b. Horiz. or vert. pair, imperf. between 20.00
205 A72 1p dark green 65 40
a. Imperf. vertically 15.00
b. Vertical pair, imperf. between 20.00
c. Imperf., pair 12.50
206 A73 5p orange 2.00 75
a. Imperf., pair 12.50
b. Horizontal pair, imperf. between 17.50

Nos. 172 and 206 Surcharged

1924
UN PESO
25 Cents.

1924, July

207 A62 1p on 1.50p blue & orange 50 40
208 A73 1.25p on 5p orange 75 60
a. "UN PESO 25 Cents." omitted 45.00
b. Vert. or horiz. pair, imperf. between 30.00

No. 208 with two bars over "25 Cents."

1924

209 A73 1p on 5p orange 75 60
a. Bars at top and bottom 20.00

Engraved by Perkins Bacon & Co.

Types of 1902-22 Issues.

1924, Aug. Re-engraved ***Perf. 14***

210 A31 6c bistre 40 20
211 A70 25c brown 35 20
212 A34 50c red 35 20
213 A36 1p orange brown 40 20
214 A37 2p orange 65 40
215 A57 3p deep green 4.00 75
216 A64 15p black 5.00 1.50
Nos. 210-216 (7) 11.15 3.45

The designs of the stamps of 1924 differ from those of the 1902-22 issues in many details which are too minute to illustrate. The re-engraved issue may be readily distinguished by the imprint "Perkins Bacon & Co. Ld. Londres".

President Justo Rufino Barrios
A74

Lorenzo Montúfar
A75

1924, Aug.

217 A74 1.25p ultramarine 50 20
218 A75 2.50p dark violet 75 30
See also Nos. 224, 226.

Aurora Park
A76

National Post Office
A77

National Observatory
A78

Engraved by Waterlow & Sons, Ltd.

Types of 1921-24
Re-engraved and New Designs
Dated 1926.

1926, July-Aug. ***Perf. 12½***

219 A31 6c ochre 30 25
220 A76 12½c green 30 25
221 A70 25c brown 30 25
222 A77 50c red 30 25
223 A36 1p orange brown 45 30
224 A74 1.50p dark blue 30 25
225 A78 2p orange 3.75 65
226 A75 2.50p dark violet 3.75 1.00
227 A57 3p dark green 75 40
228 A63 5p brown violet 2.00 65
229 A64 15p black 4.00 1.50
Nos. 219-229 (11) 16.20 5.75

These stamps may be distinguished from those of the same designs in preceding issues by the imprint "Waterlow & Sons, Limited, Londres", the date, "1926", and the perforation.
See also Nos. 233, 242.

Stamps of 1926 Surcharged in Various Colors

1928
½ CENTAVO
DE QUETZAL

1928

230 A78 ½c on 2p org. (Bl) 1.50 1.00
a. Invtd. surcharge 15.00
231 A63 ½c on 5p brown violet (Bk) 65 40
a. Invtd. surcharge 12.50 12.50
b. Double surcharge 25.00
c. Blue surcharge 25.00 25.00
d. Blue and black surcharge 50.00 50.00
232 A75 1c on 2.50p dark violet (R) 65 40
a. Inverted surcharge 50.00
b. Double surcharge 50.00

Barrios
A79

Montúfar
A80

Granados
A81

General Orellana
A82

Coat of Arms of Guatemala City
A83

Engraved by T. De la Rue & Co.

1929, Jan. ***Perf. 14***

233	A78	½c yellow green	1.50	40
234	A70	1c dark brown	25	20
235	A79	2c deep blue	25	20
236	A80	3c dark violet	25	20
237	A81	4c orange	30	25
238	A82	5c dark carmine	45	20
239	A31	10c brown	60	20
240	A36	15c ultramarine	75	20
241	A29	25c brown orange	1.50	40
242	A76	30c green	2.00	75
243	A32	50c pale rose	3.00	75
244	A83	1q black	6.00	1.00
		Nos. 233-244 (12)	16.85	4.75

Nos. 233, 234 and 239 to 243 differ from the illustrations in many minor details, particularly in the borders. See No. 300 for bisect of No. 235.

No. 227 Surcharged in Black or Red

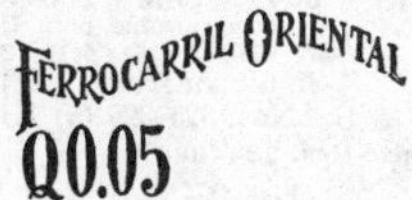

1929, Dec. 28 ***Perf. 12½, 13***

245	A57	3c on 3p dk. grn. (Bk)	2.50	2.50
		a. Inverted surcharge	17.50	17.50
246	"	5c on 3p dk. green (R)	2.50	2.50
		a. Inverted surcharge	15.00	15.00

Issued in commemoration of the inauguration of the Eastern Railroad connecting Guatemala and El Salvador.

No. 229 Surcharged in Red

FERROCARRIL
DE LOS ALTOS
Inaugurado en 1929
2 CENTAVOS
DE QUETZAL

1930, Mar. 30 **Unwmkd.**

247	A64	1c on 15p black	1.00	1.00
248	"	2c on 15p black	1.00	1.00
249	"	3c on 15p black	1.00	1.00
250	"	5c on 15p black	1.00	1.00
251	"	15c on 15p black	1.00	1.00
		Nos. 247-251 (5)	5.00	5.00

Opening of Los Altos electric railway.

Hydroelectric Dam
A85

Los Altos Railway
A86

Railroad Station
A87

1930, Mar. 30 **Typo.** ***Perf. 12***

252	A85	2c brown violet & black	1.50	1.50
		a. Horizontal pair imperf. between	125.00	
253	A86	3c deep red & black	2.75	2.75
254	A87	5c buff & dark blue	2.75	2.75

Opening of Los Altos electric railway. Exist imperf.

Mayan Stele at Quiriguá
A91

1932, Apr. 8 **Engraved**

258	A91	3c carmine rose	1.00	25

See also Nos. 302-303.

Day of the Race Issue.

Flag of the Race, Columbus and Tecum Uman
A92

1933, Aug. 3 **Litho.** ***Perf. 12½***

259	A92	½c dark green	1.00	1.00
260	"	1c dull brown	2.00	2.00
261	"	2c deep blue	2.00	2.00
262	"	3c dull violet	1.50	1.50
263	"	5c rose	2.00	2.00
		Nos. 259-263 (5)	8.50	8.50

Commemorating the Day of the Race and the 441st anniversary of the sailing of Columbus from Palos, Spain, August 3rd, 1492, on his first voyage to the New World. The 3c and 5c exist imperf.

Birthplace of Barrios
A93

View of San Lorenzo
A94

Justo Rufino Barrios
A95

National Emblem and Locomotive
A96

General Post Office
A97

Telegraph Building and Barrios
A98

Military Academy
A99

National Police Headquarters
A100

Jorge Ubico and J. R. Barrios
A101

1935, July 19 **Photogravure**

264	A93	½c yellow green & magenta	1.00	1.00
265	A94	1c orange red & peacock blue	1.00	1.00
266	A95	2c orange & black	1.00	1.00
267	A96	3c carmine rose & peacock blue	1.00	1.00
268	A97	4c peacock blue & orange red	7.50	7.50
269	A98	5c blue green & brown	5.00	5.00
270	A99	10c slate green & rose lake	7.50	7.50
271	A100	15c olive green & orange brown	7.50	7.50
272	A101	25c scarlet & black	7.50	7.50
		Nos. 264-272 (9)	39.00	39.00

Issued to commemorate the birth of General Barrios. See also Nos. C29-C31.

Lake Atitlán
A102

Quetzal
A103

Legislative Building
A104

1935, Oct. 10

273	A102	1c brown & crimson	40	25
274	A103	3c rose carmine & peacock green	1.25	25
275	"	3c red orange & peacock green	1.25	25
276	A104	4c bright blue & deep rose	75	35

No. 273 perforated diagonally through the center.

1935, July ***Perf. 12½x12***

277	A102	(½c) brown & crimson	50	20
		a. Unsevered pair	1.00	1.00

Bureau of Printing
A105

Map of Guatemala
A106

1936, Sept. 24 ***Perf. 12½***

278	A105	½c green & purple	25	15
279	A106	5c blue & dark brown	75	35

Quetzal
A107

Gen. Jorge Ubico on Horseback
A109

Union Park, Quezaltenango
A108

Designs: 1c, Tower of the Reformer. 3c, National Post Office. 4c, Government Building, Retalhuleu. 5c, Legislative Palace entrance. 10c, Custom House. 15c, Aurora Airport Custom House. 25c, National Fair. 50c, Residence of Presidential Guard. 1.50q, General Ubico, portrait standing, no cap.

1937, May 20

280 A107 ½c peacock blue & carmine rose 50 50
281 " 1c olive gray & red brown 60 60
282 A108 2c vio. & car. rose 65 65
283 " 3c brown violet & bright blue 45 45
284 " 4c yellow & dull olive green 3.50 3.50
285 A107 5c crimson & bright violet 3.00 3.00
286 " 10c magenta & brown black 4.00 4.00
287 A108 15c ultramarine & copper red 4.50 4.50
288 " 25c red orange & violet 6.00 6.00
289 " 50c dark green & orange red 7.50 7.50
290 A109 1q magenta & black 35.00 35.00
291 " 1.50q red brown & black 35.00 35.00
Nos. 280-291 (12) 100.70 100.70

Second term of President Ubico.

Mayan Calendar
A119

National Flower (White Nun Orchid)
A120

Quetzal
A121

Map of Guatemala—A122

1939, Sept. 7 *Perf. 13x12, 12½*

292 A119 ½c grn. & red brn. 30 30
293 A120 2c blue & gray blk. 3.00 75
294 A121 3c red orange & turquoise grn.. 1.25 60
295 " 3c olive bistre & turquoise grn. 1.25 60
296 A122 5c blue & red 3.50 1.00
Nos. 292-296 (5) 9.30 3.25

No. 235 Surcharged with New Value in Red.

1939, Sept. *Perf. 14*

297 A79 1c on 2c deep blue 60 30

Stamps of 1929 Surcharged in Blue:

1 1
UN CENTAVO
y
5 5
z

1940, June

298 A29 (y) 1c on 25c brn. org. 45 20
299 A32 (z) 5c on 50c pale rose (bar 10x¾mm) 60 40
a. Bar 12½x2mm. 75 40
b. Bar 12½x1mm. 85.00 12.00

No. 235 perforated diagonally through the center.

1941, Aug. 16 *Perf. 14x11½*

300 A79 (1c) deep blue 35 20
a. Unsevered pair 75 75

No. 241 Surcharged in Black

½ ½
MEDIO CENTAVO

1941, Dec. 24 *Perf. 14*

301 A29 ½c on 25c brn. orange 35 35

Type of 1932 Inscribed "1942".

1942 Engraved. *Perf. 12.*

302 A91 3c green 75 30
303 " 3c deep blue 75 30

Issued to publicize the coffee of Guatemala.

Vase of Guastatoya
A123

Home for the Aged
A124

1942, July 13 **Unwmkd.**

304 A123 ½c red brown 50 25
305 A124 1c carmine rose 50 25

National Printing Works
A125

Rafael Maria Landivar
A126

1943, Jan. 25 Engr. *Perf. 11, 12*

307 A125 2c scarlet 40 20
a. Vert. pair, imperf. horiz. 35.00

1943, Aug. *Perf. 11*

308 A126 5c bright ultramarine 45 40

Issued to commemorate the 150th anniversary of the death of Rafael Landivar, poet.

National Palace—A127

1944, June 30 *Perf. 11*

309 A127 3c dark blue green 25 15

Issued to commemorate the inauguration of the National Palace, November 10, 1943.

Ruins of Zakuleu
A128

1945, Jan. 6

310 A128 ½c black brown 20 12

Type of 1944 Overprinted in Blue

25 de junio de 1944
PALACIO NACIONAL

1945, Jan. 15

311 A127 3c deep blue 35 20

Overprint Bar 1mm. Thick.

311A A127 3c deep blue 1.25 1.00

Allegory of the Revolution
A129

Torch
A130

1945, Feb. 20

312 A129 3c grayish blue 20 15

Issued to commemorate the Revolution of Oct. 20, 1944. See also Nos. C128–C131.

1945, Oct. 20

313 A130 3c deep blue 25 15

Issued to commemorate the first anniversary of the Revolution of Oct. 20, 1944. See No. C135–C136.

José Milla y Vidaurre
A131

Payo Enriquez de Rivera
A132

1945 *Perf. 11, 12½*

314 A131 1c deep green 20 15
315 A132 2c dull lilac 20 15

See also Nos. 343–346, 379, C134–C134A, C137, C269, C311–C315.

José Batres y Montufar
A133

U. P. U. Monument Bern, Switzerland
A134

1946 **Unwmkd.**

316 A133 ½c sepia 15 12
317 " 3c deep blue 20 12
a. Booklet pane of 9

See also Nos. 319, C142.

1946, Aug. 5 Photo. *Perf. 14x13*

318 A134 1c violet & gray brown 50 40

Issued to commemorate the centenary of the first postage stamp. See Nos. C140–C141.

Batres Type of 1946.

1947, Nov. 11 Engr. *Perf. 11, 12½*

319 A133 3c dull green 25 20
a. Booklet pane of 9

Symbolical of Labor
A135

Bartolomé de las Casas and Indian
A136

1948, May 14 **Unwmkd.**

320 A135 1c deep green 25 15
321 " 2c sepia 25 15
322 " 3c deep ultra. 25 15
323 " 5c rose carmine 30 20

Labor Day, May 1, 1948.

No. 296 Overprinted "1948" in Carmine at Lower Right.

1948, May 14 *Perf. 12½*

324 A122 5c blue & red 25 20

1949, Oct. 8 Engr. *Perf. 12½, 13½*

325 A136 ½c red 25 20
326 " 1c black brown 25 20
327 " 2c dark blue green 25 20
a. 2c green, perf. 11, 11½ ('60) 25 20
328 " 3c rose pink 30 25
a. 3c carmine, perf. 11, 12½, 13½ ('64) 30 25
329 " 4c ultramarine 40 30
Nos. 325-329 (5) 1.45 1.15

See also Nos. 384–386.

Gathering Coffee
A137

Designs: 1c, Poptun Agricultural Colony. 2c, Banana trees. 3c, Sugar cane field. 6c, International Bridge.

1950, Feb. Photo. *Perf. 14*

330 A137 ½c violet blue, pink & olive gray 40 15
331 " 1c red brown, yellow & greenish gray 40 15
332 " 2c olive green, pink & blue gray 40 15
333 " 3c purple, blue & orange brown 40 15
334 " 6c deep orange, aqua. & violet 60 20
Nos. 330-334 (5) 2.20 80

See also Nos. 347–349.

Badge of Public and Social Assistance Ministry
A138

Nurse A139 — Map Showing Hospitals A140

1950-51 Litho. *Perf. 12, 12½x12*

335 A138 1c car. rose & blue 30 20
336 A139 3c dull green & rose red 50 30

Perf. 12

337 A140 5c dark blue & choc. ('51) 75 50
a. Souv. sheet ('51) 5.00 5.00

Issued to publicize the National Hospitals Fund. See Nos. C177-C180a.

No. 337a measures 130x79½mm., and contains one each of Nos. 335 to 337, with marginal inscriptions in brown. It exists both perforated and imperforate.

A perforated souvenir sheet is known which is similar to No. 337a, but with the 5c stamp like the basic stamp of No. C232 (with "BRITISH HONDURAS" inscription).

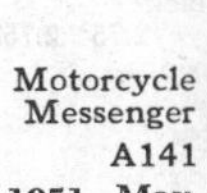

Motorcycle Messenger
A141

1951, May 22 *Perf. 14x12½*

337B A141 4c blue green & gray black 60 40

Issued for regular postage, although inscribed "Expreso." See No. E2.

Souvenir Sheet.

A142

Typographed and Engraved

1951, Oct. 22 *Imperf.*

338 A142 Sheet of two 75 75
a. 1c rose carmine 30 30
b. 10c deep ultramarine 30 30

Issued in sheets measuring 114x69mm., with marginal inscriptions and ornaments in light blue, to commemorate the 75th anniversary (in 1949) of the formation of the Universal Postal Union.

A143

Modern Model Schools—A144

1951, Oct. 22 Photo. *Perf. 13½x14*

339 A143 ½c purple & sepia 30 20
340 A144 1c brown carmine & dull green 30 20
341 A143 2c greenish blue & red brown 30 25
342 A144 4c black brown & rose violet 40 25

Enriquez de Rivera Type of 1945
Re-engraved.

1952, June 4 *Perf. 12½*

343 A132 ½c violet 15 12
344 " 1c rose carmine 15 12
345 " 2c green 15 12
346 " 4c orange 30 15

A panel containing the dates "1660-1951" has been added below the portrait.

Produce Type of 1950.

Designs: ½c, Sugar cane field. 1c, Banana trees. 2c, Poptun Agricultural Colony.

1953, Feb. 11 Photo. *Perf. 13½*

347 A137 ½c dark brown & deep blue 25 20
348 " 1c red orange & olive green 25 20
349 " 2c dark carmine & gray black 25 20

Issued to publicize farming.

Rafael Alvarez Ovalle and José Joaquin Palma—A145

1953, May 13

350 A145 ½c purple & black 35 20
351 " 1c dark green & orange brown 40 20
352 " 2c orange brown & olive green 40 25
353 " 3c dark blue & olive brown 40 25

Issued to honor the authors of Guatemala's national anthem.

Quetzal
A146

Engraved

1954, Sept. 27 *Perf. 12½, 11*

354 A146 1c deep violet blue 20 15

See also Nos. 367-373, 380-382A.

Mario Camposeco A147 — Globe and Red Cross A148

Designs: 10c, Carlos Aguirre Matheu. 15c, Goalkeeper.

1955-56 *Perf. 12½* Unwmkd.

355 A147 4c violet 2.00 60
356 " 4c carmine ('56) 2.00 60
357 " 4c blue green ('56) 2.00 60
358 " 10c bluish green 5.00 75
359 " 15c dark blue 6.00 4.00
Nos. 355-359 (5) 17.00 6.55

Issued to commemorate 50 years of Soccer in Guatemala.

1956, May 23 *Perf. 13x12½*

Designs: 3c, Red Cross, Telephone and "5110." 4c, Nurse, patient and Red Cross flag.

360 A148 1c brown & carmine 25 25
361 A148 3c dark green & red 30 25
362 " 4c dark slate green & red 30 25

Red Cross. See Nos. B5-B7.

Dagger-Cross of the Liberation
A149

Designs: 1c, Map showing 2,000km. (1,243 miles) of new roads. 3c, Oil production.

1956 Engraved. *Perf. 12½*

363 A149 ½c violet 15 12
364 " 1c dark blue green 15 12

Perf. 11

365 A149 3c sepia 20 15

Issued to commemorate the Liberation of 1954-55. Issue dates: ½c, 1c, July 27; 3c, Oct. 31. See Nos. C210-C218.

Quetzal Type of 1954.

1957-58 *Perf. 11, 12½.*

367 A146 2c violet 10 10
368 " 3c carmine rose 15 10
369 " 3c ultramarine 15 10
a. 3c dark blue, perf. 11½ ('72) 10 10
370 A146 4c orange 20 10
371 " 5c brown 30 15
372 " 5c org. verm. ('58) 30 15
373 " 6c yellow green 35 20
Nos. 367-373 (7) 1.55 90

No. 368 is only perf. 12½. The 2c, 4c and No. 369 are found in perf. 11 and 12½. Other values are only perf. 11.

No. 350 Overprinted in Blue, Black, Carmine, Red Orange or Green:

1858 1958

CENTENARIO

1958, Nov.-Dec. Photo. *Perf. 13½*

374 A145 ½c pur. & blk. (Bl) 40 40
375 " ½c pur. & blk. (Bk) 40 40
376 " ½c pur. & blk. (C) 40 40
377 " ½c pur. & blk. (RO) 40 40
378 " ½c pur. & blk. (G) 40 40
Nos. 374-378 (5) 2.00 2.00

Issued to commemorate the centenary of the birth of Rafael Alvarez Ovalle, composer of Guatemala's national anthem.

Re-engraved Rivera Type of 1945.

1959, Sept. 12 Engr. *Perf. 11, 12½*

379 A132 4c gray blue 20 8

See note after No. 346.

Quetzal Type of 1954.

1960-63 *Perf. 11* Unwmkd.

380 A146 2c brown ('61) 12 10
381 " 4c light violet 20 10
382 " 5c blue green 30 15

Perf. 12½

382A A146 5c slate gray ('63) 50 15

Romulus and Remus Statue, Rome
A150

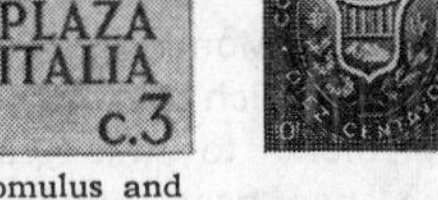

Stamp of 1871
A151

1961 Photogravure *Perf. 14*

383 A150 3c blue 20 15

Inauguration of the Plaza Italia.

Las Casas Type of 1949
Engraved

1962-64 *Perf. 11, 11½, 12½, 13½*

384 A136 ½c blue 15 12
385 " 1c brt. violet ('64) 15 12
386 " 4c brown ('64) 20 15

1963-66 *Perf. 11* Unwmkd.

387 A151 10c carmine 40 15
388 " 10c slate ('64) 30 15

Perf. 11½

389 A151 10c olive brn. ('66) 30 15
390 " 20c deep pur. ('64) 65 25
391 " 20c dark blue ('65) 65 25
Nos. 387-391 (5) 2.30 95

For souvenir sheet, see No. C310.

Pedro Bethancourt Comforting Sick Man
A152

1964, Jan. 6 Engraved *Perf. 11*

394 A152 2½c olive bister 15 8

Issued to commemorate the beatification (1962-63) of Pedro Bethancourt (1626-1667). See also Nos. C319-C322.

Quetzal Type of 1957-58 Overprinted in Blue:

**HOMENAJE
A LA
"I. S. G. C."
1948—1963**

1964, Dec. 29 Engraved *Perf. 12½*

395 A146 4c orange 20 20

Issued to commemorate the 15th anniversary (in 1963) of the International Society of Guatemala Collectors.

Map of Guatemala and British Honduras A153 — Quetzal, Mayan Ball Game Goal A154

1967, Apr. 28 Litho. *Perf. 14x13½*

396 A153 4c olive, vio. blue & deep rose 15 10
397 " 5c ocher, vio. blue & deep orange 20 12
398 " 6c dp. orange, violet blue & gray 25 15

Issued to state Guatemala's claim to British Honduras.

Lithographed and Engraved

1968, Oct. 15 *Perf. 11½*

399 A154 1c black, light green & red 20 15
400 " 5c yellow, light green & red 25 15
401 " 8c orange, light green & red 30 20
402 " 15c blue, light green & red 60 35

403 A154 30c light violet, light green & red 1.10 1.10
Nos. 399-403 (5) 2.45 1.95

Issued to commemorate the 19th Olympic Games, Mexico City, Oct. 12–27. See also Nos. 412–415.

Child and Poinsettia
A155

1968–70 Typographed *Perf. 13½*

404 A155 2½c green, dp. bister & carmine 20 15
405 " 2½c green, orange & carmine ('70) 20 15
406 " 5c green, gray & carmine 30 15
407 " 21c green, lilac & carmine 75 75

Issued to help abandoned children.

Type of 1968 Overprinted in Black or Red

Cincuentenario O. I. T.

1970, Mar. 19 Litho. *Perf. 13½*

408 A154 8c orange, light green & red (B) 30 15
409 " 8c orange, light green & red (R) 30 15

Perf. 12½

410 A154 15c blue, lt. green & red (B) 50 25
411 " 15c blue, lt. green & red (R) 50 25

50th anniversary of International Labor Organization. Gold overprint believed to be a trial color.

Type of 1968

1971 *Perf. 11½* Typo. & Engr.

412 A154 1c gray, yel. green & red 25 15

Typographed

413 A154 5c bright pink, yel. green & red 20 15
414 " 5c brn., green & red 20 15
415 " 5c dk. bl., grn. & red 20 15

Mayas and CARE Package
A156

1971–72 Typographed *Perf. 13½*

416 A156 1c black & multi. 15 10

Perf. 11½

417 A156 1c vio. & multi. ('72) 15 10
418 " 1c brn. & " ('72) 15 10

10th anniversary of CARE in Guatemala, a U.S.-Canadian Cooperative for American Relief Everywhere. Nos. 417–418 exist imperf. See No. C459.

No. 338 (trimmed) Overprinted in Orange with Olympic Rings and: "JUEGOS OLIMPICOS / MUNICH 1972"

Souvenir Sheet

Typographed and Engraved

1972, Oct. 23 *Imperf.*

419 A142 Sheet of two 60 60
a. 1c rose carmine ("MUNICH") 10 10
b. 10c deep ultramarine ("1972") 40 40

20th Olympic Games, Munich, Aug. 26–Sept. 11. Commemorative inscriptions on No. 338 at left, top and right have been trimmed off. Size: 61x45mm. (approximately). Many varieties exist.

Pres. Carlos Arana Osorio
A157

Designs: 3c, 5c, President Osorio seated (vert.). 8c, Pres. Osorio standing (vert.).

1973–74 Typographed *Perf. 12½*

420 A157 2c blue & black 10 6
421 " 3c orange & brown 12 8
422 " 5c rose car. & black 20 10
423 " 8c blk. & brt. green 32 10
a. Litho ('74) 30 8

8th population and 3rd dwellings census, Mar. 26–Apr. 7, 1973.

Francisco Ximenez
A158

Typo., Litho. (#426)

1973–77 *Perf. 11½, 13½ (#426)*

424 A158 2c black & emerald 6 5
425 " 3c dk. brn. & orange 10 6
426 " 3c black & yellow 6 3
427 " 6c black & brt. blue 25 10

Brother Francisco Ximenez, discoverer and translator of National Book of Guatemala. No. 427 issued for International Book Year 1972.

Issue dates: 6c, Aug. 2, 1973; 2c, Jan. 14, 1975; No. 425, Mar. 5, 1975; No. 426, Sept. 26, 1977.

Sculpture of Christ, by Pedro de Mendoza, 1643—A159

Design: 8c, Sculpture by Lanuza Brothers, 18th century.

1977, Apr. 4 Litho. *Perf. 11*

428 A159 6c purple & multi. 12 5
429 " 8c " " 16 8
Nos. 428-429, C614-C619 (8) 1.66 82

Holy Week 1977.

INTERFER 77 Emblem
A160

1977, Oct. 31 Litho. *Perf. 11½*

430 A160 7c black & multi. 14 6

INTERFER 77, 4th International Fair, Guatemala, Oct. 31–Nov. 13.

SEMI-POSTAL STAMPS.

Regular Issues of 1935–36 Surcharged in Blue or Red similar to illustration

EXPOSICION 1937 FILATELICA +1

1937, Mar. 15 *Perf. 12½* Unwmkd.

B1 A102 1c+1(c) brown & crimson (Bl) 50 50
B2 A103 3c+1(c) rose carmine & peacock green (Bl) 50 50
B3 " 3c+1(c) red orange & peacock green (Bl) 50 50
B4 A106 5c+1(c) blue & dark brown (R) 50 50

Issued to commemorate the first Philatelic Exhibition held in Guatemala, March 15–20, 1937.

Type of Regular Issue, 1956.

Designs: 5c+15c, Nurse, Patient and Red Cross Flag. 15c+50c, Red Cross, telephone and "5110." 25c+50c, Globe and Red Cross.

Engraved

1956, June 19 *Perf. 13x12½*

B5 A148 5c+15c ultramarine & red 1.10 1.10
a. Imperf., pair 50.00
B6 A148 15c+50c dark violet & red 2.75 2.75
B7 " 25c+50c bluish black & carmine 2.75 2.75

The surtax was for the Red Cross.

Jesus and Esquipulas Cathedral
SP1

1957, Oct. 29 *Perf. 13*

B8 SP1 1½c+½c black & brown 1.00 60

The tax was for the Esquipulas highway.

Type of Air Post Semi-Postal Stamps and

Arms
SP2

Design: 3c+3c, Wounded man, Battle of Solferino.

1960, Apr. 9 Photo. *Perf. 13½x14*

Cross in Rose Red

B9 SP2 1c+1c red brown & blue 40 30
B10 SPAP2 3c+3c lilac, blue & pink 40 30
B11 SP2 4c+4c black & blue 40 40

Issued to commemorate the centenary (in 1959) of the Red Cross idea. The surtax went to the Red Cross. Exist imperf. See Nos. CB15–CB21.

AIR POST STAMPS.

AP1

AP2

Surcharged in Red on No. 229.
Imprint: "Waterlow & Sons Limited, Londres"
Perf. 12½

1929, May 20 **Unwmkd.**
C1 AP1 3c on 15p black 1.00 1.00
C2 " 5c on 15p " 50 30
C3 " 15c on 15p black 1.25 50
a. Double surcharge (G & R) 100.00
C4 " 20c on 15p black 2.00 2.00
a. Invtd. surcharge 100.00
b. Double surcharge 100.00

Surcharged in Red on No. 216.
Imprint: "Perkins Bacon & Co. Ld. Londres"

1929, May 20 *Perf. 14*
C5 AP1 5c on 15p black 3.00 3.00

Surcharged in Black on No. 218.

1929, Oct. 9
C6 AP2 3c on 2.50p dk. vio. 2.00 2.00

Airplane and Mt. Agua
AP3

1930, June 4 **Litho.** *Perf. 12½*
C7 AP3 6c rose red 1.50 1.00
a. Double impression 25.00 20.00
b. Imperf. (pair) 400.00

Nos. 227, 229 Surcharged in Black or Red

SERVICIO
AEREO INTERIOR
10 Centavos
DE QUETZAL
1930

1930, Dec. 9 *Perf. 12½*
C8 A57 1c on 3p green (Bk) 75 75
a. Double surch. 100.00
C9 " 2c on 3p grn. (Bk) 1.75 1.75
C10 " 3c on 3p grn. (R) 1.75 1.75
C11 " 4c on 3p " (R) 1.00 1.00
C12 A64 10c on 15p blk. (R) 2.50 2.50
a. Dbl. surcharge 125.00
Nos. C8-C12 (5) 7.75 7.75

No. 237 Overprinted

AEREO
EXTERIOR
1931

1931, May 19 *Perf. 14*
C13 A81 4c orange 75 40
a. Double overprint 50.00 50.00

No. C7 Overprinted

EXTERIOR - 1931

Perf. 12½.
C14 AP3 6c rose red 1.75 1.75
a. On C7a 30.00 25.00
b. Invtd. overprint 12.00 12.00

AP4

AP5

Red Overprint.

1931, Oct. 21 *Perf. 14*
C15 AP4 15c ultramarine 2.50 50
a. Double ovpt. 125.00 125.00
C16 AP5 30c green 4.50 2.00
a. Double ovpt. 125.00 125.00

Nos. 235–236 Overprinted in Red or Green

Primer Vuelo
Postal
BARRIOS-
MIAMI
1931

1931, Dec. 5
C17 A79 2c deep blue (R) 5.00 4.50
C18 A80 3c dark violet (G) 5.00 4.50

No. 240 Overprinted

Primer Vuelo Postal
BARRIOS-MIAMI
1931

C19 A36 15c ultramarine (R) 5.00 4.50

Nos. C17 to C19 were issued in connection with the first postal flight from Barrios to Miami.

No. 224 Surcharged in Red

SERVICIO
AEREO
INTERIOR
1932
Q0.02

1932–33 *Perf. 12½*
C20 A74 2c on 1.50p dark blue (R) 2.00 1.50

Nos. 227, 229 Surcharged in Violet, Red or Blue

SERVICIO AEREO
INTERIOR — 1932
Q0.03

C21 A57 3c on 3p green (V) 1.00 30
a. Invtd. surcharge 65.00 65.00
b. Imperf. horiz., pair 1000.00
C22 " 3c on 3p green (R) 1.25 50
C23 A64 10c on 15p black (R) 12.00 10.00
b. First "I" of "Interior" missing 35.00 35.00
C24 " 15c on 15p blk. (Bl) 17.50 15.00
a. First "I" of "Interior" missing 45.00 45.00
Nos. C20-C24 (5) 33.75 27.30

Issue dates: No. C22, Jan. 1, 1933; others, Feb. 11, 1932.

AP6

Green Overprint.

1933, Jan. 1 *Perf. 14*
C25 AP6 4c orange 75 25
a. Double ovpt. 60.00 60.00

Nos. 235, 238 and 240 Overprinted in Red or Black

AEREO
EXTERIOR
1934

1934, Aug. 7
C26 A82 5c dark car. (Bk) 2.50 20
C27 A36 15c ultramarine (R) 2.50 50

Overprinted

AEREO
INTERIOR
1934

C28 A79 2c deep blue (R) 1.00 30

View of Port Barrios
AP7

Designs: 15c, Tomb of Barrios. 30c, Equestrian Statue of Barrios.

1935, July 19 **Photo.** *Perf. 12½*
C29 AP7 10c yel. brown & peacock grn. 3.50 3.00
C30 " 15c gray & brown 3.50 3.00
C31 " 30c carmine rose & blue violet 3.50 2.00

Birth centenary of Gen. Justo Rufino Barrios.

Lake Amatitlán—AP10

Designs: Nos. C36, C37, C45, C46. Different views of Lake Amatitlan. 3c, Port Barrios. No. C34, C35, Ruins of Port San Felipe. 10c, Port Livingston. No. C39, C40, Port San Jose. No. C41, C42, View of Atitlan. No. C43, C44, Aurora Airport.

Overprinted with Quetzal in Green.

1935–37 Size: 37x17mm.
C32 AP10 2c orange brown 15 15
C33 " 3c blue 35 25
C34 " 4c black 50 12
C35 " 4c ultramarine ('37) 40 10
C36 " 6c yellow green 45 18
C37 " 6c black vio. ('37) 5.00 15
C38 " 10c claret 1.00 50
C39 " 15c red orange 1.25 75
C40 " 15c yel. green ('37) 1.25 90
C41 " 30c olive green 10.00 10.00
C42 " 30c olive bistre ('37) 1.25 1.25
C43 " 50c rose violet 25.00 25.00
C44 " 50c Prussian blue ('36) 7.50 5.00
C45 " 1q scarlet 25.00 25.00
C46 " 1q carmine ('36) 7.50 6.00
Nos. C32-C46 (15) 86.60 75.35

Central Park, Antigua—AP11

Designs: 1c, Guatemala City. 2c, Central Park, Guatemala City. 3c, Monastery. Nos. C50–C51, Mouth of Dulce River. Nos. C52–C53, Plaza Barrios. Nos. C54–C55, Los Proceres Monument. No. C56, Central Park, Antigua. No. C57, Dulce River. Nos. C58–C59, Quezaltenango. Nos. C60–C61, Ruins at Antigua. Nos. C62–C63, Dock at Port Barrios. Nos. C64–C65, Port San Jose. Nos. C66–C67, Aurora Airport. 2.50q, Island off Atlantic Coast. 5q, Atlantic Coast view.

Overprinted with Quetzal in Green.

Size: 34x15mm.
C47 AP11 1c yellow brown 15 10
C48 " 2c vermilion 25 25
C49 " 3c magenta 1.00 50
C50 " 4c org. yel. ('36) 3.00 2.50
C51 " 4c carmine lake ('37) 2.00 1.50
C52 " 5c dull blue 40 20
C53 " 5c orange ('37) 20 10
C54 " 10c red brown 1.00 70
C55 " 10c olive green ('37) 1.00 75
C56 " 15c rose red 50 15
C57 " 15c vermilion ('37) 45 15
C58 " 20c ultramarine 4.00 4.00
C59 " 20c deep claret ('37) 1.00 75
C60 AP11 25c gray black 5.00 5.00
C61 " 25c blue green ('37) 90 50
a. Quetzal omitted 2000.00
C62 AP11 30c yellow green 2.25 2.25
C63 " 30c rose red ('37) 1.00 20
C64 " 50c carmine rose 12.00 12.00
C65 " 50c purple ('36) 11.00 11.00
C66 " 1q dark blue 40.00 40.00
C67 " 1q dk. grn. ('36) 11.00 11.00

Size: 46x20mm.
C68 AP11 2.50q rose red & olive green ('36) 7.50 6.00
C69 " 5q orange & indigo ('36) 10.00 10.00
a. Quetzal omitted 1000.00 700.00
Nos. C47-C69 (23) 115.60 109.60

Issue dates of Nos. C32–C69: Nov. 1, 1935; Oct. 1, 1936; Jan. 1, 1937.

Types of Air Post Stamps, 1935.

1937, May 18

Overprinted with Airplane in Blue.

Designs: 2c, Quezaltenango. 3c, Lake Atitlan. 4c, Progressive Colony, Lake Amatitlan. 6c, Carmen Hill. 10c, Relief map. 15c, National University. 30c, Espana Plaza. 50c, Police Station, Aurora Airport. 75c, Amphitheater, Aurora Airport. 1q, Aurora Airport.

Center in Brown Black.
C70 AP10 2c carmine 30 15
C71 " 3c blue 1.50 1.50
C72 " 4c citron 25 20
C73 " 6c yellow green 70 50
C74 " 10c red violet 3.00 3.00
C75 " 15c orange 3.00 2.00
C76 " 30c olive green 6.50 6.00
C77 " 50c peacock blue 6.50 6.00
C78 " 75c dark violet 15.00 15.00
C79 " 1q deep rose 15.00 15.00
Nos. C70-C79 (10) 51.75 49.35

Overprinted with Airplane in Black.

Designs: 1c, 7th Ave., Guatemala City. 2c, Los Proceres Monument. 3c, National Printing Office. 5c, National Museum. 10c, Central Park. 15c, Escuintla. 20c, Motorcycle Police. 25c, Slaughterhouse, Escuintla. 30c, Exhibition Hall. 50c, Barrios Plaza. 1q, Polytechnic School. 1.50q, Aurora Airport.

Size: 33x15mm.
C80 AP11 1c yellow brown & bright blue 20 18
C81 " 2c crimson & deep violet 30 25
C82 " 3c red violet & red brown 1.00 1.00
C83 " 5c peacock green & copper red 6.00 6.00
C84 " 10c carmine & green 2.00 1.50
C85 " 15c rose & dull olive green 75 50
C86 " 20c ultra. & black 2.00 1.50
C87 " 25c dark gray & scarlet 3.50 3.50
C88 " 30c green & dp. vio. 2.00 2.00
C89 " 50c magenta & ultramarine 15.00 15.00

Size: 42x19mm.
C90 AP11 1q olive green & red violet 16.00 16.00
C91 " 1.50q scarlet & olive brown 17.00 17.00
Nos. C80-C91 (12) 65.75 64.43

Second term of President Ubico.

Souvenir Sheet.

AP12

1938, Jan. 10 *Perf. 12½*

C92 AP12 Sheet of four 3.00 3.00
- *a.* 15c dark blue & sepia (*Pres. George Washington*) 65 65
- *b.* 4c carmine & sepia (*Pres. Franklin D. Roosevelt*) 65 65
- *c.* 4c carmine & dark blue (*Map of the Americas*) 65 65
- *d.* 15c dark blue & sepia (*Pan American Union Building, Washington, D. C.*) 65 65

150th anniversary of U.S. Constitution. Sheet size: 104x112½mm.

President Arosemena, Panama
AP13

Designs: 2c, Pres. Cortés Castro, Costa Rica. 3c, Pres. Somoza, Nicaragua. 4c, Pres. Carias Andino, Honduras. 5c, Pres. Martinez, El Salvador. 10c, Pres. Ubico, Guatemala.

1938, Nov. 20 **Unwmkd.**

C93	AP13	1c orange & olive brown	30	30
C94	"	2c scarlet, pale pink & slate green	35	35
C95	"	3c green, buff & olive brown	55	55
C96	"	4c dark claret, pale lilac & brown	65	65
C97	"	5c bistre, pale green & olive brown	85	85
C98	"	10c ultramarine, pale blue & brown	1.50	1.50
		Nos. C93-C98 (6)	4.20	4.20

First Central American Philatelic Exhibition, Guatemala City, Nov. 20–27, 1938.

Souvenir Sheet.

Flags of Central American Countries—AP19
Multicolored

C99 AP19 Sheet of six 2.00 2.00
- *a.* 1c *Guatemala* 30 30
- *b.* 2c *El Salvador* 30 30
- *c.* 3c *Honduras* 30 30
- *d.* 4c *Nicaragua* 30 30
- *e.* 5c *Costa Rica* 30 30
- *f.* 10c *Panama* 30 30

First Central American Philatelic Exhibition, Guatemala City, Nov. 20–27, 1938. Sheet size: 145x95mm.

La Merced Church, Antigua—AP20

Designs: 2c, Ruins of Christ School, Antigua. 3c, Aurora Airport. 4c, Drill ground, Guatemala City. 5c, Cavalry barracks. 6c, Palace of Justice. 10c, Customhouse, San José. 15c, Communications Building, Retalhuleu. 30c, Municipal Theater, Quezaltenango. 50c, Customhouse, Retalhuleu. 1q, Departmental Building.

Inscribed "Aéreo Interior"
Overprinted with Quetzal in Green.

1939, Feb. 14

C100	AP20	1c olive bistre & chestnut	20	12
C101	AP20	2c rose red & slate green	25	18
C102	"	3c dull blue & bistre	30	25
C103	"	4c rose pink & yellow green	25	8
C104	"	5c brown lake & bright ultra.	35	30
C105	"	6c orange & gray brown	50	30
C106	"	10c bistre brown & gray black	75	40
C107	"	15c dull violet & black	75	45
C108	"	30c deep blue & dark carmine	1.25	50
C109	"	50c orange & brt. violet	1.75	75
		a. Quetzal omitted	*2000.00*	
C110	"	1q yellow green & bright ultra.	2.75	2.00
		Nos. C100-C110 (11)	9.10	5.33

1939, Feb. 14

Designs: 1c, Mayan Altar, Aurora Park. 2c, Sanitation Building. 3c, Lake Amatitlan. 4c, Lake Atitlan. 5c, Tamazulapa River bridge. 10c, Los Proceres Monument. 15c, Palace of Captains General. 20c, Church on Carmen Hill. 25c, Barrios Park. 30c, Mayan Altar. 50c, Charles III fountain. 1q, View of Antigua.

Inscribed "Aéreo International" or "Aérea Exterior"
Overprinted with Quetzal in Green.

C111	AP20	1c olive green & golden brown	20	12
C112	"	2c lt. grn. & black	35	35
C113	"	3c ultramarine & cobalt blue	25	18
C114	"	4c orange brown & yellow green	25	15
C115	"	5c sage green & red orange	50	12
C116	"	10c lake & slate black	2.00	12
C117	"	15c ultramarine & bright rose	2.25	8
C118	"	20c yellow green & apple green	60	35
C119	"	25c dull violet & light olive green	70	30
C120	"	30c dull rose & black	90	10
C121	"	50c scarlet & bright yellow	1.65	30
C122	"	1q orange & yellow green	2.50	50
		Nos. C111-C122 (12)	12.15	2.67

No. 240 Overprinted in Carmine

UNION PANAMERICANA
1890-1940
CORREO AEREO

1940, Apr. 14 *Perf. 14*

C123 A36 15c ultramarine 75 30

Pan American Union, 50th anniversary.

No. C112 Overprinted in Carmine

DICIEMBRE 2
1941
SEGUNDO DIA PAN-
AMERICANO DE LA SALUD

1941, Dec. 2 *Perf. 12½*

C124 AP20 2c lt. green & blk. 60 40

Second Pan American Health Day.

San Carlos University, Antigua
AP21

1943, June 25 Engraved *Perf. 11*

C125 AP21 15c dk. red brown 60 20
- *a.* Imperf., pair 80.00

Don Pedro de Alvarado—AP22

Type I. Diagonal shading lines at inner edges of commemorative tablet.
Type II. Overall shading added to tablet.

1943, Mar. 10 *Perf. 11½* **Unwmkd.**

C126 AP22 15c deep ultramarine (II) 65 20
- *a.* Type I 27.50 18.50

Issued to commemorate the 400th anniversary of the founding of Antigua.

National Police Building—AP23

1943, Aug. 3 *Perf. 11*

C127 AP23 10c deep rose violet 70 20

Allegory of 1944 Revolution
AP24

1945, Apr. 27 Engraved

C128	AP24	5c deep rose	60	40
C129	"	6c dark blue green	60	40
		a. Imperf., pair	175.00	
C130	"	10c violet	60	40
C131	"	15c aquamarine	60	40

Revolution of October 20, 1944.

No. C113 Surcharged in Red

1945
FERIA DEL LIBRO
2½ CENTAVOS

1945, July 25 *Perf. 12½*

C132 AP20 2½c on 3c ultramarine & cobalt blue 3.50 3.50

The 1945 Book Fair.

National Palace—AP25
Carmine Overprint.

1945, Aug. Engraved *Perf. 11*

C133 AP25 5c rose carmine 40 25
- *a.* Triple overprint, one inverted 65.00 30.00
- *b.* Double ovpt., one inverted 70.00

See also Nos. C137A-C139.

José Milla y Vidaurre
AP26

Torch
AP27

AP28

1945

C134	AP26	7½c sepia	1.50	1.50
C134A	"	7½c dark blue	1.00	1.00

Issue dates: No. C134, Sept. 28. No. C134A, Dec. 6.

1945, Oct. 19

C135 AP27 5c bright red violet 60 40

Souvenir Sheet.
Imperf.

C136 AP28 Sheet of two 2.25 2.25
- *a.* 5c brt. red violet 1.00 1.00

Nos. C135–C136 were issued to commemorate the 1st anniversary of the Revolution of October 20, 1944. No. C136 measures 90x70½mm.

See also Nos. C147–C150.

Payo Enriquez de Rivera
AP29

1946, Jan. 22 *Perf. 11* **Unwmkd.**

C137 AP29 5c rose pink 50 30

See also Nos. C269, C311–C315.

Palace Type of 1945.
1946-47 Without Overprint.

C137A	AP25	5c rose carmine ('47)	50	15
C138	"	10c deep lilac	50	20
		a. Imperf., pair	100.00	
C139	"	15c blue	85	40
		a. Imperf., pair	100.00	

Sir Rowland Hill
AP30

Globes, Quetzal
AP31

1946, Aug. 5 Photo. *Perf. 14x13*

C140 AP30 5c slate & brown (blk. ovpt.) 85 25
- *a.* Without "AEREO" overprint 600.00 600.00

C141 AP31 15c carmine lake, ultramarine & emerald 1.10 50

Centenary of the first postage stamp.

José Batres y Montufar
AP32

Signing the Declaration of Independence
AP33

1946, Sept. 16 Engraved *Perf. 11*

C142 AP32 10c Prussian green 50 15
- *a.* Perf. 12½ 10.00 15

1946, Dec. 19 *Perf. 11*

C143	AP33	5c rose carmine	15	10
		a. Booklet pane of 6	25.00	
C144	"	6c olive brown	25	20
C145	"	10c violet	35	25
C146	"	20c blue	65	60

Issued to commemorate the 125th anniversary of the signing of the Declaration of Independence.

Torch Type of 1945.

Dated 1944-1946.

1947, Feb. 3 Engraved

C147	AP27	1c green	25	15
C148	"	2c carmine	30	15
C149	"	3c violet	30	15
C150	"	5c deep blue	35	15

Inscribed "II Aniversario de la Revolucion." "Aereo" in color on a white background.

Issued to commemorate the second anniversary of the Revolution of October 20, 1944.

Franklin D. Roosevelt
AP34

1947, June 6

C151	AP34	5c rose carmine	30	20
C152	"	6c blue	35	20
C153	"	10c deep ultra.	75	25
C154	"	30c gray black	2.50	2.00
C155	"	50c light violet	5.00	5.00
		a. Imperf., pair	150.00	
C156	AP34	1q gray green	7.50	7.50
		a. Imperf., pair	150.00	
		Nos. C151-C156 (6)	16.40	15.15

1948

No. 296 Overprinted in Carmine

AEREO

1948, May 14 *Perf. 12½*

C157	A122	5c blue & red	30	15

Soccer Game AP35 — Seal, University of Guatemala AP36

1948, Aug. 31 Engraved

Center in Black.

C158	AP35	3c brt. carmine	1.50	75
C159	"	5c blue green	1.75	1.00
C160	"	10c dark violet	2.00	1.00
C161	"	30c deep blue	8.00	5.00
C162	"	50c bistre	8.50	5.00
		Nos. C158-C162 (5)	21.75	12.75

Issued to commemorate the Fourth Central American and Caribbean Soccer Championship, March, 1948.

1949, Nov. 29 *Perf. 12½*

Center in Blue.

C163	AP36	3c carmine	70	50
C164	"	10c green	1.25	75
C165	"	50c yellow	5.00	5.00

Issued to publicize the first Latin American Congress of Universities.

Lake Atitlan AP37 — Tecum Uman Monument AP38

Designs: 8c, San Cristobal Church. 13c, Weaver. 35c, Momostenango Cliffs.

1950, Feb. 17 Photo. *Perf. 14*

Multicolored Centers.

C166	AP37	3c carmine rose	60	15
C167	AP38	5c red brown	60	20
C168	AP37	8c dk. slate green	70	25
C169	AP38	13c brown	1.00	50
C170	AP37	35c purple	4.00	4.00
		Nos. C166-C170 (5)	6.90	5.10

See also No. C181.

Soccer AP39 — Pole Vault AP40

Designs: 3c, Foot race. 8c, Tennis. 35c, Diving. 65c, Stadium.

1950, Feb. 25 Engr. *Perf. 12½*

Center in Black

C171	AP39	1c purple	1.25	75
C172	"	3c carmine	1.35	75
C173	AP40	4c orange brn.	1.50	1.00
C174	AP39	8c red violet	1.65	1.00
C175	AP40	35c light blue	7.50	6.50

Center in Green.

C176	AP40	65c dk. slate grn.	11.00	9.00
		Nos. C171-C176 (6)	24.25	19.00

6th Central American and Caribbean Games.

Nurse and Patient
AP41

Designs: 10c, School of Nurses. 50c, Zacapa Hospital. 1q, Roosevelt Hospital.

1950, Sept. 6 Litho. *Perf. 12*

Quetzal in Blue Green.

C177	AP41	5c rose vio. & car.	35	25
		a. Double impression (frame)	35.00	
C178	AP41	10c olive brown & emerald	75	45
C179	"	50c vermilion & red violet	3.75	3.00
C180	"	1q orange yellow & sage green	3.75	3.75
		a. Souvenir sheet	9.00	9.00

Issued to publicize the National Hospital Fund.

Nos. C177-C180 exist with colors reversed, perf. and imperf.

No. C180a measures 149½x100mm., and contains one each of Nos. C177 to C180, with marginal inscriptions in brown.

No. C168 perf. 12½ or 12 diagonally through center.

1951, Apr. *Perf. 14*

Multicolored Center.

C181	AP37	(4c) dark slate green	15.00	11.00
		a. Unsevered pair	35.00	30.00

Counterfeits of diagonal perforation exist.

Ceremonial Stone Ax AP42 — National Flag and Emblem AP43

1953, Feb. 11 Photo. *Perf. 14x13½*

C182	AP42	3c dark blue & olive gray	28	25
C183	"	5c dark gray & henna brown	33	30
C184	"	10c dark purple & slate	60	45

1953, Mar. 14 *Perf. 13½*

Multicolored Center

C185	AP43	1c maroon	40	30
C186	"	2c slate green	50	40
C187	"	4c dark brown	65	50

Issued to mark the passing of the presidency from J. J. Arevalo to Col. Jacobo Arbenz Guzman.

Regional Dance
AP44

Horse Racing
AP45

Designs: 4c, White nun — national flower. 5c, Allegory of the fair. 20c, Zakuleu ruins. 30c, Symbols of Agriculture. 50c, Champion bull. 65c, Bicycle racing. 1q, Quetzal.

1953, Dec. 18 Engr. *Perf. 12½*

C188	AP44	1c deep ultramarine & carmine	25	15
C189	"	4c orange & grn.	1.25	30
C190	"	5c emerald & chocolate	75	40
C191	AP45	15c chocolate & dark purple	2.50	1.50
C192	"	20c car. & ultra.	3.00	1.50
C193	AP44	30c deep ultra. & chocolate	3.00	2.00
C194	AP45	50c purple & blk.	5.00	5.00
C195	"	65c light blue & dark green	7.50	7.50
C196	AP44	1q dark blue green & dark red	15.00	15.00
		Nos. C188-C196 (9)	38.25	33.35

National Fair, Oct. 20, 1953.

Indian
AP46

Perf. 12½

1954, Apr. 21 Unwmkd.

C197	AP46	1c carmine	30	25
C198	"	2c deep blue	40	30
C199	"	4c yellow green	40	35
C200	"	5c aquamarine	50	40
C201	"	6c orange	60	40
C202	"	10c violet	75	60
C203	"	20c black brown	3.50	3.00
		Nos. C197-C203 (7)	6.45	5.30

Guatemala and ODECA Flags AP47 — Rotary Emblem, Map of Guatemala AP48

1954, Oct. 13 Photo. *Perf. 14x13½*

C204	AP47	1c multicolored	25	20
C205	"	2c "	30	20
C206	"	4c "	40	25

Issued to commemorate the third anniversary of the formation of the Organization of Central American States.

1956, Sept. 8 Engraved

C207	AP48	4c bl. & dull yel.	40	30
C208	"	6c light blue green & dull yellow	40	30
C209	"	35c purple & dull yellow	2.50	2.50

Issued to commemorate the 50th anniversary of Rotary International (in 1955).

Mayan Warrior Holding Dagger Cross of the Liberation—AP49

Designs: 4c, Family looking into the sun. 5c, The dagger of the Liberation destroying communist symbols. 6c, Hands holding cogwheel and map of Guatemala. 20c, Monument to the victims of communism and flag. 30c, Champerico harbor. 65c, Radio tower, Mercury and map of Guatemala. 1q, Flags of the American nations. 5q, Pres. Carlos Castillo Armas.

1956, Oct. 10 Photo. *Perf. 14x13½*

C210	AP49	2c deep green, red, blue & brown	30	20
C211	"	4c deep carmine & gray black	30	30
C212	"	5c blue & red brown	40	40
C213	"	6c dark brown & dp. ultra.	30	25
C214	"	20c violet, brown & blue	3.00	2.00
C215	"	30c deep blue & olive	3.00	2.00
C216	"	65c chestnut brown & green	6.00	6.00
C217	"	1q dark brown & multicolored	7.50	7.50
C218	"	5q multicolored	15.00	15.00
		Nos. C210-C218 (9)	35.80	33.65

Issued to commemorate the Liberation of 1954-55.

Red Cross, Map and Quetzal
AP50

Designs: 2c, José Ruiz Angulo and woman with child (vert.) 3c, Pedro de Bethancourt with sick man. 4c, Rafael Ayau.

Perf. 13½x14, 14x13½

1958, May 13 **Unwmkd.**

C219	AP50	1c multicolored	45	20
C220	"	2c "	45	20
C221	"	3c "	50	20
C222	"	4c "	50	20

Issued in honor of the Red Cross.

Col. Carlos Castillo Armas AP51

Galleon of 1532 and Freighter "Quezaltenango" AP52

1959, Feb. 27 ***Perf. 14x13½***

Center in Dark Blue and Yellow

C223	AP51	1c black	20	15
C224	"	2c rose red	20	15
C225	"	4c brown	20	15
C226	"	6c dark blue green	20	15
C227	"	10c dark purple	45	30
C228	"	20c blue green	1.20	90
C229	"	35c gray	1.85	1.35
		Nos. C223-C229 (7)	4.30	3.15

Issued in memory of Pres. Carlos Castillo Armas (1914-1957).

No. C134A Overprinted in Carmine: "HOMENAJE A LAS NACIONES UNIDAS"

1959, Mar. 4 **Engraved.** ***Perf. 11***

C230	AP26	7½c dark blue	2.25	2.25

Issued to honor the United Nations.

1959, May 15 **Litho.** ***Perf. 11***

C231	AP52	6c ultramarine & rose red	40	20

Issued to honor the formation of the Guatemala-Honduras merchant fleet.

Type of 1950 Overprinted in Dark Blue

BELICE ES NUESTRO / AEREO

1959, Oct. 9 ***Perf. 12***

C232	A140	5c dark blue & lt. brown	50	25
		a. Invtd. ovpt.	275.00	45.00

Issued to state Guatemala's claim to British Honduras. Overprint reads: "Belize is ours." Map includes "BRITISH HONDURAS" and its borderline, and excludes bit extending above "A" of "GUATEMALA" on No. 337.

No. C232 is known without overprint in multiples.

No. C213 Overprinted in Red: "1859 Centenario Primera Exportacion de Cafe 1959." Photogravure.

1959, Oct. 26 ***Perf. 14x13½***

C233	AP49	6c dark brown & deep ultramarine	75	30

Centenary of coffee export.

Pres. and Mrs. Villeda of Honduras—AP53

1959, Nov. 3 **Lithographed** ***Perf. 11***

C234	AP53	6c pale brown	25	20

Issued to commemorate the visit of President Ramon Villeda Morales of Honduras, Oct. 12, 1958.

Nos. C219-C222 Overprinted: "AÑO MUNDIAL DE REFUGIADOS" in Green, Violet, Blue or Brown.

Perf. 13½x14, 14x13½

1960, Apr. 23 **Photo.** **Unwmkd.**

C235	AP50	1c multicolored	2.00	1.50
C236	"	2c "	2.00	1.50
C237	"	3c "	2.00	2.00
C238	"	4c "	2.00	2.00

Nos. C219-C222 Overprinted as Above and Surcharged with New Value.

C239	AP50	6c on 1c multi.	5.00	3.00
C240	"	7c on 2c "	5.00	3.00
C241	"	10c on 3c "	6.00	3.00
C242	"	20c on 4c "	7.00	4.00
		Nos. C235-C242 (8)	31.00	20.00

Nos. C235-C242 issued to publicize World Refugee Year, July 1, 1959-June 30, 1960.

No. C213 Overprinted in Red: "Fundacion de la ciudad Melchor de Mencos, 30-IV-1960"

1960, Apr. 30 ***Perf. 14x13½***

C243	AP49	6c dark brown & deep ultra.	2.00	2.00

Founding of the city of Melchor de Mencos.

UNESCO and Eiffel Tower, Paris AP54

1960, Nov. 4 **Photo.** ***Perf. 12½***

C244	AP54	5c deep magenta & violet	20	15
C245	"	6c ultra. & vio. brown	30	18
C246	"	8c emerald & magenta	50	25
C247	"	20c red brown & dull blue	2.00	1.25

Issued to honor UNESCO (U.N. Educational, Scientific and Cultural Organization).

Abraham Lincoln AP55

1960, Oct. 29 **Engraved** ***Perf. 11***

C248	AP55	5c violet blue	40	30
C249	"	30c violet	3.50	3.00
C250	"	50c gray	12.00	12.00

Issued to commemorate the sesquicentenary of the birth of Abraham Lincoln.

An 8c was also printed, but was not issued and all copies were destroyed.

Nos. C219-C222 Overprinted "Mayo de 1960" in Green, Blue or Brown

Perf. 13½x14, 14x13½

1961, Apr. 20 **Photo.** **Unwmkd.**

C251	AP50	1c multi. (G)	60	40
C252	"	2c " (Bl)	60	40
C253	"	3c " (Bl)	60	40
C254	"	4c " (Br)	60	40

Issued to honor the Red Cross.

Proclamation of Independence AP56

1962 **Engraved** ***Perf. 11***

C255	AP56	4c sepia	20	15
C256	"	5c violet blue	25	15
C257	"	15c bright violet	75	50

Issued to commemorate the 140th anniversary of Independence (in 1961). Nos. 255-256 were issued May 23; No. 257, Aug. 10.

No. C245 Overprinted in Red: "1962 / EL MUNDO UNIDO / CONTRA LA MALARIA"

1962, Oct. 4 **Photo.** ***Perf. 12½***

C258	AP54	6c ultramarine & violet brown	2.00	2.00

Issued for the World Health Organization drive to eradicate malaria.

Dr. José Luna AP57

Physicians: 4c, Rodolfo Robles. 5c, Narciso Esparragoza y Gallardo. 6c, Juan J. Ortega. 10c, Dario Gonzalez. 20c, José Felipe Flores.

1962, Dec. 12 **Photo.** ***Perf. 14x13½***

C259	AP57	1c olive bister & dull purple	50	18
C260	"	4c orange yellow & gray olive	50	18
C261	"	5c pale blue & red brown	50	18
C262	"	6c salmon & blk.	50	18
C263	"	10c pale green & red brown	60	30
C264	"	20c pale pink & bl.	1.00	60
		Nos. C259-C264 (6)	3.60	1.62

Issued to honor Guatemalan physicians.

No. C213 Overprinted in Red: "PRESIDENTE/YDIGORAS/FUENTES/ RECORRE POR TIERRA/CENTRO AMERICA/14 A 20 DIC. 1962"

1962, Dec. **Photo.** ***Perf. 14x13½***

C265	AP49	6c dk. brown & deep ultra.	75	50

Issued to commemorate Pres. Ydigoras' tour of Central America, Dec. 14-20, 1962.

No. C213 Overprinted in Vermilion: "Reunion Presidentes: Kennedy, EE. UU. —Ydigoras F., Guat.—Rivera. Salv.— Villeda M., Hond.—Somoza, Nic.—Orlich, C. R.—Chiari, Panama—San Jose, Costa Rica, 18 A 21 de Marzo de 1963"

Perf. 14x13½

1963, Mar. 18 **Unwmkd.**

C266	AP49	6c dark brown & deep ultra.	15.00	7.00

Issued to commemorate the meeting of President John F. Kennedy with the Presidents of the Central American Republics, San Jose, Costa Rica, March 18-21.

Nos. C245-C246 Overprinted "CONMEMORA / CION FIRMA / NUEVA CARTA / ODECA.—1962" in Magneta or Black

1963, Mar. 14 ***Perf. 12½***

C267	AP54	6c ultra. & violet brown (M)	40	20
C268	AP54	8c emerald & magenta	50	20

Issued to commemorate the signing of the new charter of the Organization of Central American States (ODECA).

Enriquez de Rivera Type of 1946 Engraved

1963, Mar. 26 ***Perf. 11, 11½, 12½***

C269	AP29	5c olive bister	20	15

Woman Carrying Fruit Basket AP58

Lithographed

1963, Mar. 14 ***Perf. 11, 12½***

C270	AP58	1c multicolored	15	10

Spring Fair, 1960.

Reaper AP59

Ceiba Tree AP60

1963, July 25 **Photo.** ***Perf. 14***

C271	AP59	5c Prussian grn.	30	20
C272	"	10c dark blue	50	30

Issued for the "Freedom from Hunger" campaign of the U.N. Food and Agriculture Organization.

1963 ***Perf. 12*** **Unwmkd.**

C273	AP60	4c brown & green	20	15

Patzun Palace—AP61

Buildings: 3c, Coban. 4c, Retalhuleu. 5c, San Marcos. 6c, Captains General of Antigua.

1964, Jan. 15 ***Perf. 13½x14***

C274	AP61	1c rose red & brn.	20	15
C275	"	3c rose claret & Pruss. grn.	25	15
C276	"	4c violet blue & rose lake	25	20
C277	"	5c brown & blue	35	20
C278	"	6c green & slate	35	20
		Nos. C274-C278 (5)	1.40	90

City Hall, Guatemala City AP62

Design: 4c, Social Security Institute.

1964, Jan. 15 **Photo.** ***Perf. 12x11½***

C279	AP62	3c brt. bl. & brn.	20	15
C280	"	4c brn. & brt. bl.	25	20

1964–65 Engraved *Perf. 11½*

Designs: 3c, Social Security Institute. 4c, University administration building. No. C282, City Hall, Guatemala City. No. C282A, Engineering School.

Different Frames

C281	AP62	3c dull green	25	15
C281A	"	4c gray ('65)	25	15
C282	"	7c blue	30	18
C282A	"	7c olive bister ('65)	30	18

Nos. C219–C222 Overprinted in Green, Blue or Black with Olympic Rings and: "OLIMPIADAS / TOKIO—1964"

Photogravure

1964 *Perf. 13½x14, 14x13½*

C283	AP50	1c multi. (G)	1.20	1.20
C284	"	2c " (Bl)	1.20	1.20
C285	"	3c " (G)	1.20	1.20
C286	"	4c " (Bk)	1.20	1.20

Issued to publicize the 18th Olympic Games, Tokyo, Oct. 10–25, 1964.

Nos. C219–C222 Surcharged in Green, Blue or Black with New Value and: "HABILITADA—1964"

1964

C287	AP50	7c on 1c multi. (G)	30	30
C288	"	9c on 2c " (Bl)	40	40
C289	"	13c on 3c " (Bl)	50	50
C290	"	21c on 4c " (Bk)	1.00	1.00

Nos. C219–C222 Overprinted "FERIA MUNDIAL / DE NEW YORK" in Green, Blue or Black.

1964, June 25

C291	AP50	1c multi. (G)	1.00	1.00
C292	"	2c " (Bl)	1.00	1.00
C293	"	3c " (G)	1.00	1.00
C294	"	4c " (Bk)	1.00	1.00

New York World's Fair.

Nos. C219–C222 Overprinted in Green, Blue or Black: "VIII VUELTA / CICLISTICA"

1964

C295	AP50	1c multi. (G)	1.75	1.75
C296	"	2c " (Bl)	1.75	1.75
C297	"	3c " (G)	1.75	1.75
C298	"	4c " (Bk)	1.75	1.75

Eighth Bicycle Race.

Pres. John F. Kennedy
AP63

Centenary Emblem
AP64

1964 Engraved *Perf. 11½*

C299	AP63	1c violet	1.00	75
C300	"	2c yellow green	1.00	75
C301	"	3c brown	1.00	75
C302	"	7c deep blue	1.00	75
C303	"	50c dark gray	20.00	17.50
		Nos. C299–C303 (5)	24.00	20.50

Issued in memory of U.S. President John F. Kennedy (1917–1963). Minute letters "TEOK" are in lower right corner of 1c, 2c, 3c and 50c.

Issue dates: 7c, July 10; others, Aug. 21.

Photogravure

1964, Sept. 9 *Perf. 11x12* Unwmkd.

C304	AP64	7c ultra., silver & red	75	50
C305	"	9c orange, silver & red	75	50
C306	"	13c purple, silver & red	1.00	1.00
C307	"	21c brt. grn., silver & red	1.50	1.50
C308	"	35c brown, silver & red	1.50	1.50
C309	AP64	1q lemon, silver & red	7.50	7.50
		Nos. C304–C309 (6)	13.00	12.50

Issued to commemorate the centenary (in 1963) of the International Red Cross.

Souvenir Sheet

Type of Regular Issue 1963

1964 Engraved *Imperf.*

C310	A151	Souv. sheet of 2	5.00	5.00
		a. 10c violet blue	2.00	2.00
		b. 20c carmine	2.00	2.00

Issued to honor the 15th Universal Postal Union Congress, Vienna, May–June, 1964. Typographed violet blue inscription: "CORREOS DE GUATEMALA / AEREO / HOMENAJE AL XV CONGRESO DE / LA UNION POSTAL UNIVERSAL" Size: 85x59mm.

Enriquez de Rivera Type of 1946

1964, Dec. 18 Engraved *Perf. 11½*

C311	AP29	5c gray	20	15
C312	"	5c orange	20	15
C313	"	5c light green	20	15
C314	"	5c light ultra.	20	15
C315	"	5c dull violet	20	15
		Nos. C311–C315 (5)	1.00	75

Bishop Francisco Marroquin
AP65

Guatemalan Boy Scout Emblem
AP66

1965, Jan. 21 Photo. Unwmkd.

C316	AP65	4c lilac & brown	20	12
C317	"	7c gray & sepia	35	18
C318	"	9c vio. bl. & blk.	40	20

Issued to honor Bishop Francisco Marroquin.

Bethancourt Type of Regular Issue, 1964

1965, Apr. 20 Engraved *Perf. 11½*

C319	A152	2½c violet blue	15	12
C320	"	3c orange	15	12
C321	"	4c purple	20	12
C322	"	5c yellow green	25	15

Nos. C304–C308 Overprinted in Red: "AYUDENOS / MAYO 1965"

1965, June 18 Photo. *Perf. 11x12*

C323	AP64	7c ultramarine, silver & red	40	40
C324	"	9c orange, silver & red	50	50
C325	"	13c purple, silver & red	60	60
C326	"	21c bright green, silver & red	85	85
C327	"	35c brown, silver & red	1.35	1.35
		Nos. C323–C327 (5)	3.70	3.70

1966, Mar. 3 Photo. *Perf. 14x13½*

Designs: 9c, Campfire and Scouts. 10c, Scout emblem and Scout carrying torch and flag. 15c, Scout emblem, flags and Scout giving Scout sign. 20c, Lord Baden-Powell.

C328	AP66	5c multicolored	30	20
C329	"	9c "	50	35
C330	"	10c "	60	40
C331	"	15c "	85	60
C332	"	20c "	1.00	1.00
		Nos. C328–C332 (5)	3.25	2.55

Issued to commemorate the Fifth Inter-american Regional Training Conference, Guatemala City, March 1–3.

Central American Independence Issue

Flags of Central American States
AP67

1966, March 9 *Perf. 12½x13½*

C333	AP67	6c multicolored	30	15

Queen Nefertari Temple, Abu Simbel
AP68

1966, Oct. 3 Photo. *Perf. 12*

C334	AP68	21c vio. & ocher	80	45

Issued to publicize the UNESCO world campaign to save historic monuments in Nubia.

Coat of Arms
AP69

1966–70 Engraved *Perf. 13½*

C335	AP69	5c orange	20	15
C336	"	5c green	20	15
		a. 5c yellow green, perf. 11½ ('69)	10	12

Perf. 11½, 12½

C337	AP69	5c blue ('67)	20	15
		a. 5c dark blue, perf. 12½ ('69)	20	15
C338	AP69	5c gray ('67)	20	15
C339	"	5c purple ('67)	20	15
		a. 5c bright violet, perf. 12½ ('69)	20	15
C339B	AP69	5c dp. magenta ('70)	15	15
C339C	"	5c green, *yellow* ('70)	15	15
		Nos. C335–C339C (7)	1.30	1.05

Issued dates: No. C335, Oct. 3; No. C336, Dec. 15, 1966; No. C337, Feb. 9, 1967; Nos. C338–C339, Apr. 28, 1967. No. C339B, July 8, 1970; No. C339C, Oct. 16, 1970.

Msgr. Mariano Rossell y Arellano
AP70

1966, Nov. 3 Engraved *Perf. 13½*

C340	AP70	1c deep violet	20	15
C341	"	2c green	25	12
C342	"	3c brown	25	15
C343	"	7c blue	35	30
C344	"	50c gray	1.65	1.65
		Nos. C340–C344 (5)	2.70	2.37

Issued to honor Msgr. Mariano Rossell y Arellano, apostolic delegate.

Mario Mendez Montenegro
AP71

Morning Glory and Map of Guatemala
AP72

1966–67 *Perf. 13½*

C345	AP71	2c rose red ('67)	15	10
C346	"	3c orange ('67)	20	15
C347	"	4c rose claret ('67)	25	15
C348	"	5c gray	30	15
C349	"	5c lt. ultra. ('67)	30	15
C350	"	5c green ('67)	30	15
C351	"	5c bluish black ('67)	30	15
		Nos. C345–C351 (7)	1.80	1.00

Issued in memory of Mario Mendez Montenegro (1910–1965), founder of the Revolutionary Party.

1967, Jan. 12 Photo. *Perf. 12*

Flowers: 8c, Bird of paradise (horiz.). 10c, White nun orchid, national flower (horiz.). 20c, Nymphs of Amatitlan.

Flowers in Natural Colors

C352	AP72	4c orange	40	20
C353	"	8c green	40	20
C354	"	10c dark blue	60	30
C355	"	20c dark red	1.00	50

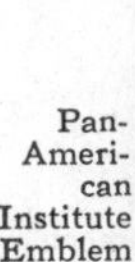

Pan-American Institute Emblem
AP73

1967, Apr. 13 Photo. *Perf. 13½*

C356	AP73	4c lt. brown, lilac & black	20	15
C357	"	5c olive, bl. & blk.	30	18
C358	"	7c orange yellow, blue & black	40	20

Issued to commemorate the 8th General Assembly of the Pan-American Geographical and Historical Institute in 1965.

No. C281 Overprinted

GUATEMALA
CAMPEON
III Norceca Foot-Ball

1967, Apr. 28 Engraved *Perf. 11½*

C360	AP62	3c dull green	2.25	2.25

Issued to commemorate Guatemala's victory in the 3rd Norceca Soccer Games (Caribbean, Central and North American).

No. C281A Overprinted in Red: "REUNION JEFES DE ESTADO / AMERICANO, PUNTA DEL ESTE, / MONTEVIDEO, URUGUAY 1967."

1967, June 28 Engraved *Perf. 11½*

C361	AP62	4c gray	1.00	75

Meeting of American Presidents, Punta del Este, Apr. 10–12.

Handshake
AP74

1967, June 28 Photo. *Perf. 12*
C362 AP74 7c pink, brown & green 30 20
C363 " 21c lt. blue, green & brown 75 45

Issued to publicize "Peace and Progress through Cooperation."

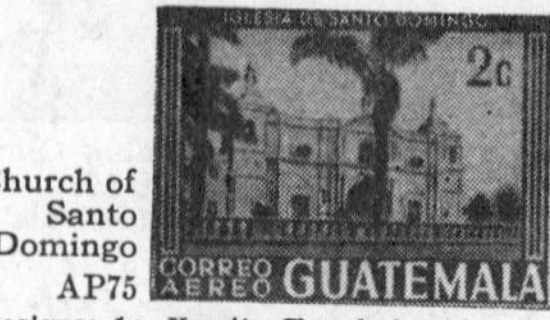

Church of Santo Domingo
AP75

Designs: 1c, Yurrita Church (vert.). 3c, Church of St. Francis. 4c, Antonio José de Irisarri (vert.). 5c, Church of the Convent (vert.). 7c, Mercy Church, Antigua. 10c, Metropolitan Cathedral.

1967, Aug. *Perf. 11½x12, 12x11½*
C364 AP75 1c grn., lt. blue & dark brown 20 12
C365 " 2c plum, salmon pink & brown 25 12
C366 " 3c bright rose, gray & black 25 12
C367 " 4c maroon, slate green & org. 25 12
C368 " 5c lilac, pale grn. & dark brn. 25 15
C369 " 7c ultra., lilac rose & black 35 20
C370 " 10c pur., yel. & blk. 50 25
Nos. C364-C370 (7) 2.05 1.08

Abraham Lincoln
AP76

1967 Engr. *Perf. 13½, 11½* (9c)
C371 AP76 7c gray & dp. org. 40 30
C372 " 9c dk. grn. & gray 45 35
C373 " 11c brown orange & slate 45 35
C374 " 15c ultra. & violet brown 75 50
C375 " 30c magenta & green 2.00 1.50
Nos. C371-C375 (5) 4.05 3.00

Issued to commemorate the centenary of the death of Abraham Lincoln (1809-1865).

Issue dates: 7c, 9c, Oct. 9. Others, Dec. 12.

Nos. C328-C332 Overprinted: "VIII Camporee Scout / Centroamericano / Diciembre 1-8/1967"

1967, Dec. 1 Photo. *Perf. 14x13½*
C376 AP66 5c multicolored 50 50
C377 " 9c " 85 85
C378 " 10c " 1.00 1.00
C379 " 15c " 1.35 1.35
C380 " 20c " 1.65 1.65
Nos. C376-C380 (5) 5.35 5.35

Issued to commemorate the 8th Central American Boy Scout Camporee, Dec. 1-8.

Nos. C320-C321 Overprinted in Four Lines: "Premio Nóbel de Literatura — 10 diciembre 1967 — Miguel Angel Asturias"

1967, Dec. 11 Engraved *Perf. 11½*
C381 A152 3c orange 40 40
C382 " 4c purple 40 40

Issued to commemorate the awarding of the Nobel Prize for Literature to Miguel Angel Asturias, Guatemalan writer.

Institute Emblem
AP77

1967, Dec. 12 Engraved *Perf. 11½*
C383 AP77 9c black & green 50 50
C384 " 25c car. & brown 1.25 1.25
C385 " 1q ultra. & blue 5.00 5.00

Issued to commemorate the 25th anniversary of the Inter-American Agriculture Institute.

UNESCO Emblem and Children
AP78

1967, Dec. 12
C386 AP78 4c blue green 15 10
C387 " 5c blue 20 12
C388 " 7c gray 27 20
C389 " 21c brt. rose lilac 85 85

Issued to commemorate the 20th anniversary (in 1966) of UNESCO (United Nations Educational, Scientific and Cultural Organization).

Nos. C219-C221 and C304-C308 Overprinted in Black or Yellow Green: "III REUNION DE / PRESIDENTES / Nov. 15-18, 1967"

Perf. 13½x14, 14x13½, 11x12

1968, Jan. 23 Photogravure
C390 AP50 1c multi. (Bk) 1.00 1.00
C391 " 1c " (G) 1.00 1.00
C392 " 2c " (Bk) 1.00 1.00
C393 " 2c " (G) 1.00 1.00
C394 " 3c " (Bk) 1.00 1.00
C395 " 3c " (G) 1.00 1.00
C396 AP64 7c " (Bk) 1.00 1.00
C397 " 9c " (") 1.25 1.25
C398 " 13c " (") 1.25 1.25
C399 " 21c " (") 1.25 1.25
C400 " 35c " (") 2.50 2.50
Nos. C390-C400 (11) 13.25 13.25

Issued to commemorate the 3rd meeting of Central American Presidents, Nov. 15-18, 1967.

Our Lady of the Coro
AP79

Miguel Angel Asturias, Flags of Guatemala and Sweden
AP80

1968-74 Engr. *Perf. 13½, 11½*
C403 AP79 4c ultramarine 50 20
C404 " 7c slate 30 20
C405 " 9c green 60 20
C406 " 9c lilac ('73) 18 13
C407 " 10c brick red 60 20
C408 " 10c gray 40 20
C408A " 10c vio. bl. ('74) 20 10
C409 " 1q violet brown 3.25 2.00
C410 " 1q org. yellow 3.25 2.00
Nos. C403-C410 (9) 9.28 5.23

Perf. 13½ applies to 4c and Nos. C407, C409-C410; perf. 11½ to 4c, 7c, 9c and Nos. C408, C408A.

Nos. 396-398 Overprinted: "AEREO / XI VUELTA / CICLISTICA / 1967"

1968, Mar. 25 Litho. *Perf. 14x13½*
C411 A153 4c multicolored 75 75
C412 " 5c " 75 75
C413 " 6c " 60 60

The 11th Bicycle Race.

1968, June 18 Engraved *Perf. 11½*
C414 AP80 20c ultramarine 60 50

Issued to commemorate the awarding of the Nobel Prize for Literature to Miguel Angel Asturias.

No. C234 Overprinted in Carmine: "1968.—AÑO INTERNACIONAL / DERECHOS HUMANOS.—ONU"

1968, July 18 Litho. *Perf. 11*
C415 AP53 6c pale brown 75 40

International Human Rights Year.

No. C362 Overprinted: "AYUDA A CONSERVAR / LOS BOSQUES.—1968"

1968, July 18 Photo. *Perf. 12*
C416 AP74 7c pink, brown & green 40 20

Issued to publicize forest conservation.

No. C213 Overprinted in Brown: "Expedición / Científica / Nahakín / Guatemala-Peru / Ruta de los / Mayas"

1968, Aug. 23 Photo. *Perf. 14x13½*
C417 AP49 6c dark brown & deep ultra. 40 25

Issued to commemorate the Nahakin scientific expedition along the route of the Mayas undertaken jointly with Peru.

Views, Quetzal and White Nun Orchid
AP81

1968, Aug. 23 Engraved *Perf. 13½*
C418 AP81 10c deep claret & green 30 15
C419 " 20c deep orange & black 60 45
C420 " 50c ultra. & car. 1.50 1.50

Issued for tourist publicity.

No. C281A Overprinted in Carmine: "CONFEDERACION / DE UNIVERSIDADES / CENTROAMERICANAS / 1948 1968"

1968, Nov. 4 *Perf. 11½*
C421 AP62 4c gray 40 20

Issued to commemorate the 20th anniversary of the Federation of Central American Universities.

Presidents Gustavo Diaz Ordaz and Julio Cesar Mendez Montenegro
AP82

1968, Dec. 3 Litho. *Perf. 14x13½*
C422 AP82 5c emerald, ocher, red & dull blue 20 12
C423 " 10c brt. bl., ocher & dull blue 40 20
C424 AP82 25c brt. bl., ocher & dull blue 85 50

Mutual visits of the Presidents of Mexico and Guatemala.

ITU Emblem, Old and New Communication Equipment—AP83

Engr. & Photo.

1968-74 *Perf. 11½, 12½* (21c)
C425 AP83 7c violet blue 25 15
C426 " 15c gray & emerald 45 20
C426A " 15c vio. brown & org. ('74) 55 20
C427 " 21c magenta 60 50
C428 " 35c rose red & emerald 1.00 50
C429 " 75c green & red 2.50 2.50
C430 " 3q brown & red 8.00 8.00
Nos. C425-C430 (7) 13.35 12.05

Issued to commemorate the centenary (in 1965) of the International Telecommunication Union.

Nos. C425 and C427 are engraved only; on others denominations are photogravure. No. C426A is on thin, toned paper.

Dates of issue: No: C426A, Feb. 18, 1974; others Dec. 13, 1968.

Nos. 399-403 Overprinted in Red, Black or Gold: AEREO

Lithographed and Engraved

1969 *Perf. 11½, 13½* (1c)
C431 A154 1c black, lt. green & red (R) 75 35
C432 " 5c yellow, lt. green & red 1.00 50
C433 " 8c orange, lt. green & red 1.25 85
C434 " 15c blue, lt. green & red 1.50 1.00
C435 " 30c lt. violet, lt. grn. & red (G) 1.50 1.00
Nos. C431-C435 (5) 6.00 3.70

Dante Alighieri
AP84

1969, July 17 Engraved *Perf. 12½*
C436 AP84 7c rose violet & ultra. 25 12
C437 " 10c dark blue 30 12
C438 " 20c green 50 22
C439 " 21c gray & brown 75 35
C440 " 35c pur. & brt. grn. 1.50 75
Nos. C436-C440 (5) 3.30 1.56

Issued to honor Dante Alighieri (1265-1321), Italian poet.

Map of Latin America—AP85

Design: 9c, Seal of University.

1969, Oct. 29 Typo. *Perf. 13*
Size: 44x27mm.
C441 AP85 2c brt. pink & blk. 15 12

Size: 35x27mm.

C442 AP85 9c gray & black 35 15

Souvenir Sheet

Imperf.

C443 AP85 Sheet of 2 75 75
a. 2c lt. blue & black 30 30
b. 9c orange & black 30 30

Issued to commemorate the 20th anniversary of the Union of Latin American Universities.

No. C443 has light violet margin with black inscription. Size: 117x74mm.

Moon Landing Issue

Moon Landing AP86

1969–70 Engraved *Perf. 11½*

C444 AP86 50c maroon & black 5.00 4.00
C445 " 1q ultra. & blk. 6.50 6.50

Souvenir Sheet

Imperf.

C446 AP86 1q yel. green & ultramarine 5.50 5.50

See note after U.S. No. C76. No. C446 contains one stamp with simulated perforations, ultramarine marginal inscription. Size: 110x80mm.

Issue dates: Nos. C445–C446, Dec. 19, 1969; No. C444, Jan. 6, 1970.

Giant Grebe Family on Lake Atitlan AP87

Designs: 4c, Lake Atitlan. 20c, Grebe chick, eggs atop floating nest (vert.).

1970, Mar. 31 Litho. *Perf. 13½*

C447 AP87 4c red & multi. 12 8
C448 " 9c " " 30 20
a. Souv. sheet of 2 1.00 1.00
C449 AP87 20c red & multi. 60 40

Issued to publicize protection of zambullidor ducks. No. C448a contains one each of Nos. C447–C448 with blue border and black marginal inscription. Size: 120x75mm.

Dr. Victor Manuel Calderon—AP88

Hand Holding Bible—AP89

1970 Litho. & Engr. *Perf. 13*

C450 AP88 1c lt. bl. & black 15 10
C451 " 2c pale grn. & blk. 20 10
C452 " 9c yellow & black 25 15

Issued in memory of Dr. Victor Manuel Calderon (1889–1969), who described microfilaria, a blood parasite.

1970 Litho. & Typo. *Perf. 13x13½*

C453 AP89 5c red & multi. 12 8

Fourth centenary of the Bible in Spanish.

No. C430 Surcharged

VALE Q0.50

1971, Mar. 11 Engraved *Perf. 11½*

C454 AP83 50c on 3q brown & red 1.50 1.50

Arms of Guatemala, Newspapers AP90

Official Decree of First Issue AP91

1971 Litho. *Perf. 11½, 12½*

C455 AP90 2c dark blue & red 10 5
C456 " 5c brown & red 25 10
C457 " 25c brt. blue & red 75 50

Souvenir Sheet

Lithographed and Engraved

Imperf.

C458 AP91 Sheet of 5 (40c) black & multi. 1.50 1.50

Nos. C455–C458 issued for centenary of Guatemala's postage stamps.

Nos. C456–C457 have white value tablet.

No. C458 contains a lithographed 4c black and engraved reproductions of Nos. 1–4 in colors similar to 1871 issue. Simulated perforations. Black marginal inscription. Size: 139x109mm.

In 1974 No. C458 was overprinted "Conmemorativa / al Campeonato Mundial de Foot Ball / Munich 1974" and Munich Games emblem in black. Overprint in gold or other colors was not authorized.

See Nos. C569–C570.

Mayas with CARE Package—AP92

1971 Typographed *Perf. 11½*

C459 AP92 5c multicolored 20 10
a. Souv. sheet of 2 2.00 2.00

25th anniversary of CARE, a U.S.-Canadian Cooperative for American Relief Everywhere.

No. C459a contains imperf. stamps similar to Nos. 416 and C459. Dark blue border and commemorative inscription. Size: 140x97mm.

J. Rufino Barrios, M. Garcia Granados, Map of Guatemala, Quetzal—AP93

1971, June 30 *Perf. 11½*

Value in Red

C460 AP93 2c black & multi. 10 3
a. Value in pink ('72) 4 3
C461 AP93 10c green & multi. 30 15
a. Value in pink, perf. 12½ ('72) 25 15
C462 AP93 50c brn. & multi. 1.50 80
C463 " 1q vio. & multi. 3.00 2.00

Centenary of the liberal revolution of 1871.

Chavarry Arrué and León Bilak AP94

Perf. 11½, 11x12½, 12½

1971–72 Engraved

C464 AP94 1c green & black ('72) 10 8
C465 " 2c lt. brn. & black ('72) 15 10
C466 " 5c org. & black 20 15

Honoring J. Arnoldo Chavarry Arrué, stamp engraver; León Bilak, philatelist.

FERIA INTERNACIONAL

No. C231 Overprinted

"INTERFER—71"

30 Oct. al 21 Nov.

1971, Oct. 25 Lithographed *Perf. 11*

C467 AP52 6c ultra. & rose red 25 15

INTERFER 71, International Fair, Guatemala, Oct. 30–Nov. 21.

Flag and Map of Guatemala AP95

UNICEF Emblem and Mayan Figure AP96

Perf. 13½ (1c), 12½ (3c, 9c), 11 (5c)

1971–75 Typographed

C468 AP95 1c blk., bl. & lilac 10 10
a. Litho ('75) 10 8
C469 AP95 3c brown, brt. pink & blue ('72) 10 8
C470 " 5c brown, orange & blue ('72) 15 10
a. Litho., perf. 12½ ('74) 12 10
C471 AP95 9c black, emerald & blue ('72) 30 15

Sesquicentennial of Central American independence.

Date of issue: Nos. C469–C471, July 10, 1972.

1971–75 Engraved *Perf. 11½*

C472 AP96 1c yellow green 8 8
C472A " 2c purple 10 10
C473 " 50c violet brown 1.25 90
C474 " 1q ultramarine 2.50 1.75

25th anniversary of the United Nations International Children's Fund (UNICEF).

Issue dates: 2c, Feb. 24, 1975, others, Nov. 1971.

Early Boeing Planes—AP97

Design: 10c, Bleriot's plane.

1972 Typographed *Perf. 11½*

C475 AP97 5c light brown & bright blue 15 12
C476 " 10c dark blue 40 20

50th anniversary of military aviation in Guatemala.

Arches, Antigua—AP98

1972–73 Typographed *Perf. 11½*

Dark and Light Blue

C480 AP98 1c *shown* 10 3
C481 " 1c *Cathedral* 10 3
C482 " 1c *Fountain, Central Park* 10 3
C483 " 1c *Capuchin Monastery* 10 3
C484 " 1c *Fountain and Santa Clara* 10 3
C485 " 1c *Portal of San Francisco* 10 3
Nos. C480–C485 (6) 60 18

Black, Lilac Rose, and Silver

C486 AP98 2½c *shown* 20 3
C487 " 2½c *Cathedral* 20 3
C488 " 2½c *Fountain and St. Clara* 20 3
C489 " 2½c *Portal of San Francisco* 20 3
C490 " 2½c *Fountain* 20 3
C491 " 2½c *Capuchin Monastery* 20 3
Nos. C486–C491 (6) 1.20 18

Blue, Orange and Black

C492 AP98 5c *shown* 40 7
C493 " 5c *Cathedral* 40 7
C494 " 5c *Fountain and St. Clara* 40 7
C495 " 5c *Portal of San Francisco* 40 7
C496 " 5c *Fountain* 40 7
C497 " 5c *Capuchin Monastery* 40 7
Nos. C492–C497 (6) 2.40 42

Perf. 12½

Red, Blue and Black

C498 AP98 1q *Fountain* 2.50 1.40
C499 " 1q *Capuchin Monastery* 2.50 1.40
C500 " 1q *shown* 2.50 1.40
C501 " 1q *Cathedral* 2.50 1.40

C502 AP98 1q *Fountain and Santa Clara* 2.50 1.40
C503 " 1q *Portal of San Francisco* 2.50 1.40
Nos. C498–C503 (6) 15.00 8.40

Earthquake ruins of Antigua. Nos. C480–C485 printed se-tenant in sheets of 90 (10x9); Nos. C486–C491 and C492–C497 each group printed se-tenant in sheets of 30 (5x6); Nos. C498–C503 se-tenant in sheets of 6 (3x2).

On Nos. C498–C503 the inks were applied by a thermographic process giving a shiny raised effect.

Issue dates: Nos. C480–C485, Dec. 14, 1972; Nos. C486–C491, Jan. 22, 1973; Nos. C492–C497, Mar. 12, 1973; Nos. C498–C503, Aug. 22, 1973.

Nos. C480–C485 were overprinted "'II Feria Internacional' / INTERFER/73 / 31 Octubre—Noviembre 18 / 1973 / GUATEMALA" in lilac rose and issued Nov. 3, 1973. Price $3.

The Interfer overprint exists in black on Nos. C480–C485, but these stamps were not decreed or issued.

See Nos. C528–C551.

Simon Bolivar and Map of Americas AP99

1973–74 ***Perf. 11½***

C504 AP99 3c brt. lilac rose & black 8 6
C505 " 3c org. & dk. blue ('74) 8 6
C506 " 5c yel. & multi. 15 10
C507 " 5c brt. grn. & blk. 15 10

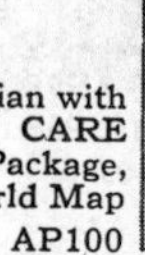

Indian with CARE Package, World Map AP100

CARE Package AP101

1973, June 14 **Typo.** ***Perf. 12½***

C508 AP100 2c blk. & multi. 15 15
C509 AP101 10c " " 40 30
a. Souvenir sheet of 2 1.00 1.00

25th anniversary of CARE (in 1971), a US-sponsored relief organization and 10th anniversary of its work in Guatemala.

No. C509a contains 2 stamps similar to Nos. C508–C509 with simulated perforations. Black marginal inscription and design. Size: 130x86mm.

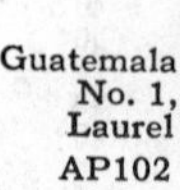

Guatemala No. 1, Laurel AP102

Perf. 12½, 11½ (1q)

1973–74 **Engraved**

C510 AP102 1c yel. brn. ('74) 15 10
C511 " 1q rose claret 2.50 1.40

Centenary (in 1971) of Guatemala postage stamps. See Nos. C574–C576A.

Oak Wreath and Star AP103

1973, Aug. 22 **Typo.** ***Perf. 12½***

C512 AP103 5c brn., yel. & bl. 10 8

Centenary of Escuela Politecnica, Guatemala's military academy.

See Nos. C552–C553.

Eleanor Roosevelt AP104

1973, Sept. 11 Engraved ***Perf. 12½***

C513 AP104 7c blue 14 9

Eleanor Roosevelt (1884–1962), wife of Franklin D., lecturer, writer. United Nations delegate.

Boys' School, Chiquimula AP105

1973–74 **Typographed** ***Perf. 12½***

C514 AP105 3c black & blue 8 6
C515 " 5c black & deep lilac rose 12 10

Centenary of the Instituto Varones in Chiquimula.

Issue dates: 5c, Dec. 5, 1973, 3c, June 13, 1974.

No. C430 Surcharged in Red: "Desvalorizadas a Q0.50" and Ornamental Obliteration of Old Denomination.

1974 **Engr. & Photo.** ***Perf. 11½***

C516 AP83 50c on 3q brown & red 1.00 70

Nos. C480–C485 and C509a Overprinted with UPU Emblem, "UPU / HOMENAJE CENTENARIO / 1874 1974"

1974, June 13 **Typo.** ***Perf. 11½***

C517 AP98 1c dk. & lt. blue 30 30
C518 " 1c " " " 30 30
C519 " 1c " " " 30 30
C520 " 1c " " " 30 30
C521 " 1c " " " 30 30
C522 " 1c " " " 30 30
Nos. C517–C522 (6) 1.80 1.80

Souvenir Sheet

C523 Sheet of 2 7.50

Centenary of Universal Postal Union.

No. C523 consists of an overprint on No. C509a, including "UNIVERSAL POSTAL UNION" instead of "UPU."

The overprint on No. C523 in red was not authorized by the Post Office.

Antigua Type of 1972–73

1974, Oct. 8 **Typo.** ***Perf. 11½***

Black and Light Brown

C528 AP98 2c *Capuchin Monastery* 5 3
C529 " 2c *Arches* 5 3
C530 " 2c *Cathedral* 5 3
C531 " 2c *Fountain and Santa Clara* 5 3
C532 AP98 2c *Portal of San Francisco* 5 3
C533 " 2c *Fountain* 5 3
Nos. C528–C533 (6) 30 18

1974, Sept. 24

Black and Yellow

C540 AP98 20c *Capuchin Monastery* 40 28
C541 " 20c *Arches* 40 28
C542 " 20c *Cathedral* 40 28
C543 " 20c *Fountain and Santa Clara* 40 28
C544 " 20c *Portal of San Francisco* 40 28
C545 " 20c *Fountain* 40 28
Nos. C540–C545 (6) 2.40 1.68

Earthquake ruins of Antigua. Each group of six printed se-tenant in sheets of 30 (5x6).

Nos. C528–C533 were printed in 1975 in black and bister se-tenant in sheets of 24 (4x6) on whiter paper.

Generals Justo Rufino Barrios and M. Garcia Granados AP106

Polytechnic School AP107

Perf. 12½, 11½(25c)

1974–75 **Typographed**

C552 AP106 6c red, gray & bl. 12 8
C553 AP107 25c multicolored 50 25

Centenary (in 1973) of Escuela Politecnica, Guatemala's military academy.

Issue dates: 6c, Sept. 17, 1974; 25c, Jan. 14, 1975.

No. C373 Surcharged in Black and Green

1974, Dec. 3 **Engraved** ***Perf. 13½***

C554 AP76 10c on 11c multi. 20 10

Nature protection. The quetzal, Guatemala's national bird.

Costume San Martin Sacatepequez AP108

Costumes of Women: 2c, Solola. 9c, Coban. 20c, Chichicastenango.

1974–75 **Typographed** ***Perf. 12½***

C556 AP108 2c car. & multi. 4 3
C557 " 2½c blue, car. & brown 5 3
C559 " 9c blue & multi. 18 5
a. Perf. 12½x13½ 18 5
C561 AP108 20c red & multi. 40 20

Issue dates: 2½c, Dec. 16, 1974; 20c, Jan. 14, 1975; 2c, 9c, May 19, 1975.

Quetzals and Maya Quekchi Woman Wearing Huipil—AP109

1975, June 25 **Litho.** ***Perf. 13½***

C565 AP109 8c blue & multi. 16 10
C566 " 20c red & multi. 40 20

International Women's Year 1975.

Rotary Emblem—AP110

1975–76 **Typo.** ***Perf. 13½***

C567 AP110 10c bl. & multi. 20 10

Perf. 11½

C568 AP110 15c bl. & multi. 30 15

Guatemala City Rotary Club, 50th anniversary. Issue dates: 10c, Oct. 1, 1975; 15c, Dec. 21, 1976.

Gaceta Type of 1971 Redrawn

1975–76 **Typo.** ***Perf. 12½***

C569 AP90 5c brown & red 10 5
C570 " 50c brt. rose & brn. 1.00 50

The white background around numeral and on right of arms has been filled in.

Issue dates: 5c, Dec. 12, 1975; 50c, Dec. 1, 1976.

IWY Emblem and White Nun Orchid AP111

1975–76 ***Perf. 12½x13½***

C571 AP111 1c multicolored 3 3
C572 " 8c yel. & multi. 16 8
C573 " 26c rose & multi. 52 26

International Women's Year 1975.

Issue dates: 1c, Dec. 19; 8c, Dec. 12; 26c, May 10, 1976.

Stamp Centenary Type of 1973

1975–77 **Engraved** ***Perf. 11½***

C574 AP102 6c orange 12 6
C575 " 6c green 12 6
C576 " 6c gray 12 6
C576A " 6c violet blue 12 6

Centenary (in 1971) of Guatemala's postage stamps.

Issue dates: No. C574, Dec. 31, 1975. No. C575, May 10, 1976. Nos. C576–C576A, Aug. 10, 1977.

Destroyed Joyabaj Village—AP112

Designs (Guatemala Flag and): 3c, Emergency food distribution. 5c, Jaguar Temple, Tikal. 10c, Destroyed bridge. 15c, Outdoors emergency hospital. 20c, Sugar cane harvest. 25c, Destroyed house. 30c, New building, Tecpan. 50c, Destroyed Cerrodel Carmen church. 75c, Cleaning up debris. 1q, Military help. 2q, Lake Atitlan.

1976, June 4 Litho. *Perf. 12½*

C577	AP112	1c red & multi.	3	3
C578	"	3c multicolored	6	3
C579	"	5c pink & multi.	10	5
C580	"	10c red & multi.	20	10
C581	"	15c multicolored	30	15
C582	"	20c pink & multi.	40	20
C583	"	25c red & multi.	50	25
C584	"	30c multicolored	60	30
C585	"	50c red & multi.	1.00	50
C586	"	75c multi.	1.50	75
C587	"	1q "	2.00	1.00
C588	"	2q "	4.00	2.00
		Nos. C577-C588 (12)	10.69	5.36

Earthquake of Feb. 4, 1976, and gratitude for foreign help. Inscriptions in colored panels vary. 3 imperf. souvenir sheets exist (50c, 1q, 2q). Size: 112x83 mm.

Allegory of Independence—AP113

Designs: 2c, Boston Tea Party. 3c, Thomas Jefferson (vert.). 4c, 20c, 35c, Allegory of Independence (each different; 4c, 35c, vert.). 5c, Warren's Death at Bunker Hill. 10c, Washington at Valley Forge. 15c, Washington at Monmouth. 25c, The Generals at Yorktown. 30c, Washington Crossing the Delaware. 40c, Declaration of Independence. 45c, Patrick Henry (vert.). 50c, Congress Voting Independence. 1q, Washington (vert.). 2q, Lincoln (vert.). 3q, Franklin (vert.). 5q, John F. Kennedy (vert.). The historical designs and portraits are after paintings.

1976, July 4 Litho. *Perf. 12½*

Size: 46x27, 27x46mm.

C592	AP113	1c multicolored	3	3
C593	"	2c "	4	3
C594	"	3c "	6	3
C595	"	4c "	8	4
C596	"	5c "	10	5
C597	"	10c "	20	10
C598	"	15c "	30	15
C599	"	20c "	40	20
C600	"	25c "	50	25
C601	"	30c "	60	30
C602	"	35c "	70	35
C603	"	40c "	80	40
C604	"	45c "	90	45
C605	"	50c "	1.00	50
C606	"	1q "	2.00	1.00
	a.	Souvenir sheet	2.20	
C607	AP113	2q multicolored	4.00	2.00
	a.	Souvenir sheet	4.40	
C608	AP113	3q multicolored	6.00	3.00
	a.	Souvenir sheet	6.60	

Size: 35x55mm.

C609	AP113	5q multi.	10.00	5.00
	a.	Souvenir sheet	11.00	
		Nos. C592-C609 (18)	27.71	13.88

American Bicentennial. Souvenir sheets contain one imperf. stamp each. Multicolored margins with U.S. patriotic designs. Size: 146x107mm.

1974 Quetzal Coin
AP114

Lithographed and Engraved

1976, Dec. 1 *Perf. 11½*

C610	AP114	8c orange, black & blue	16	8

Perf. 13½

C611	AP114	20c brt. rose, blue & black	40	20

50th anniversary of introduction of Quetzal currency.

Engineers at Work—AP115

1976, Dec. 21 Engr. *Perf. 11½*

C612	AP115	9c ultramarine	18	10
C613	"	10c green	20	10

School of Engineering, Guatemala City, centenary.

Holy Week Type of 1977

Designs: Sculptures of Christ from various Guatemalan churches. 4c, 7c, 9c, 20c, vertical.

1977, Apr. 4 Litho. *Perf. 11*

C614	A159	3c purple & multi.	6	3
C615	"	4c " "	8	4
C616	"	7c " "	14	6
C617	"	9c " "	18	10
C618	"	20c " "	40	20
C619	"	26c " "	52	26
		Nos. C614-C619 (6)	1.38	69

Souvenir Sheet

Roulette 7½

C620	A159	30c pur. & multi.	75	

Holy Week 1977. No. C620 has blue and deep rose margin showing Easter Procession in Antigua. Size: 100x70mm.

City Hall and Bank of Guatemala
AP116

Designs: 6c, Deed to original site (vert.). 8c, Church and farm house, site of first legislative session. 9c, Coat of arms of Pedro Cortes, first archbishop. 22c, Arms of Guatemala City (vert.).

Perf. 13½ (6c); 11½ (others)

1977, Aug. 10 Lithographed

C621	AP116	6c multicolored	12	6
C622	"	7c "	14	7
C623	"	8c "	16	8
C624	"	9c "	18	9
	a.	Souvenir sheet	25	
C625	AP116	22c multicolored	44	22
	a.	Souvenir sheet	60	
		Nos. C621-C625 (5)	1.04	52

Bicentenary of the founding of Nueva Guatemala de la Asuncion (Guatemala City. Nos. C624a-C625a contain one stamp each with simulated perforations. Margins show views of Guatemala City. Size: 110x80mm.

Arms of Quetzaltenango
AP117

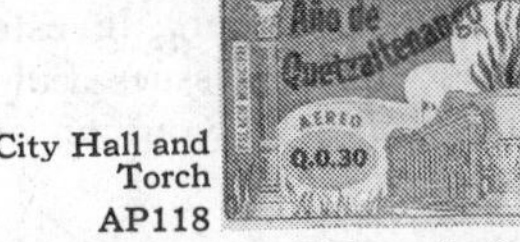

City Hall and Torch
AP118

1977, Sept. 11 Litho. *Perf. 11½*

C626	AP117	7c blk. & silver	14	7
C627	AP118	30c bl. & yellow	60	30

150th anniversary of the founding of Quetzaltenango.

Mayan Bas-relief
AP119

1977, Nov. 7

C628	AP119	10c brt. car. & black	20	10

14th International Congress of Latin Notaries.

Children Bringing Gifts to Christ Child
AP120

Designs: 1c, Mother and children (horiz.). 4c, Guatemalan children's Nativity scene.

1977, Dec. 16 Litho. *Perf. 11½*

C629	AP120	1c multicolored	3	3
C630	"	2c "	4	3
C631	"	4c "	8	4

Christmas 1977.

Almolonga Costume, Cancer League Emblem
AP121

Virgin of Sorrows, Antigua
AP122

Regional Costumes after Paintings by Carlos Mérida and Cancer League Emblem: 2c, Nebaj woman. 5c, San Juan Cotzal couple. 6c, Todos Santos couple. 20c, Regidores men. 30c, San Cristobal woman.

Perf. 14 (1c, 5c, No. C636);
Perf. 12, (2c, 6c, No. C636a, 30c).

1978, Apr. 3 Lithographed

C632	AP121	1c gold & multi.	3	3
C633	"	2c " "	4	3
C634	"	5c " "	10	5
C635	"	6c " "	12	6
C636	AP121	20c gold & multi.	40	20
	a.	Souvenir sheet	45	
C637	AP121	30c gold & multi.	60	30
		Nos. C632-C637 (6)	1.29	67

No. C636a contains one No. C636; light blue, black and rose margin shows crab and Mayan warrior holding caduceus. Size: 70x90mm.

Part of proceeds from sale of stamps went to National League to Fight Cancer.

1978 Litho. *Perf. 11½*

Statues from Various Churches: 4c, Virgin of Mercy, Antigua. 5c, Virgin of Anguish, Yurrita. 6c, Virgin of the Rosary, Santo Domingo. 8c, Virgin of Sorrows, Santo Domingo. 9c, Virgin of the Rosary, Quetzaltenango. 10c, Virgin of the Immaculate Conception, Church of St. Francis. 20c, Virgin of the Immaculate Conception, Cathedral Church.

C638	AP122	2c multicolored	4	3
C639	"	4c "	8	4
C640	"	5c "	10	5
C641	"	6c "	12	6
C642	"	8c "	16	8
C643	"	9c "	18	9
C644	"	10c "	20	10
C645	"	20c "	40	20
		Nos. C638-C645 (8)	1.28	65

Holy Week 1978. A 30c imperf. souvenir sheet shows the Pietà from Calvary Church, Antigua. Size: 71x101mm.

Issue dates: 6c, 10c, 20c, Sept. 28. Others, May 22.

Soccer Player, Argentina '78 Emblem
AP123

Gymnastics
AP124

1978, July 3 Litho. *Perf. 12*

C646	AP123	10c multicolored	20	10

11th World Cup Soccer Championship, Argentina, June 1-25.

1978, Sept. 4 *Perf. 12*

Multicolored

C647	AP124	6c *shown*	12	6
C648	"	6c *Volleyball*	12	6
C649	"	6c *Target shooting*	12	6
C650	"	6c *Weight lifting*	12	6
C651	"	8c *Soccer*	16	10
		Nos. C647-C651 (5)	64	34

13th Central American and Caribbean Games, Medellin, Colombia. Nos. C647-C650 printed se-tenant in panes of 50.

Cattleya Pachecoi
AP125

Designs: Orchids.

1978, Dec. 7 Litho. *Perf. 12*

Multicolored

C652	AP125	1c *shown*	3	3
C653	"	1c *Sobralia*	3	3
C654	"	1c *Cypripedium*	3	3
C655	"	1c *Oncidium*	3	3
C656	"	3c *Cattleya bowrigiana*	6	3
C657	"	3c *Encyclia*	6	3
C658	"	3c *Epidendrum*	6	3
C659	"	3c *Barkenia*	6	3
C660	"	8c *Spiranthes*	16	4
C661	"	20c *Lycaste*	40	10
		Nos. C652-C661 (10)	92	38

Stamps of same denomination printed se-tenant. Sheets of 60.

Seal of University

AP126

Students of Different Departments

AP127

Designs: 12c, Student in 17th century clothes. 14c, Students, 1978, and molecular model.

1978, Dec. 7

C662	AP126	6c multicolored		12	3
C663	AP127	7c	"	14	4
C664	AP126	12c	"	24	6
C665	"	14c	"	28	7

San Carlos University of Guatemala, tercentenary.

Brown and White Children

AP128

A Helping Hand

AP129

Designs: 7c, Child at play. 14c, Hands sheltering Indian girl.

1978, Dec. 7

C666	AP128	6c multicolored		12	3
C667	"	7c	"	14	4
C668	AP129	12c	"	24	6
C669	"	14c	"	28	7

Year of the Children of Guatemala.

AIR POST SEMI-POSTAL STAMPS.

Air Post Stamps of 1937 Surcharged in Red or Blue

1937

EXPOSICION FILATELICA

+1

1937, Mar. 15 *Perf. 12½.* **Unwmkd.**

CB1 AP10 4c+1(c) ultramarine (R) 1.25 1.25
CB2 " 6c+1(c) black violet (R) 1.25 1.25
CB3 AP11 10c+1(c) olive green (Bl) 1.25 1.25
CB4 " 15c+1(c) vermilion (Bl) 1.25 1.25

Issued to commemorate the first Philatelic Exhibition held in Guatemala March 15-20, 1937.

Type of Regular Issue, 1956.

Designs: 35c+1q, Red Cross, Ambulance and Volcano. 50c+1q, Red Cross, Hospital and Nurse. 1q+1q, Nurse and Red Cross.

Perf. 13x12½

1956, June 19 Engraved. **Unwmkd.**

CB5 A148 35c+1q red & olive green 10.00 8.50
CB6 " 50c+1q ultramarine & red 10.00 8.50
CB7 " 1q+1q dark green & dark red 10.00 8.50

The surtax was for the Red Cross.

Nos. B5-B7 Overprinted **AEREO - 1957**

1957, May 11

CB8 A148 5c+15c ultramarine & red 15.00 15.00
a. Imperf., pair 350.00
CB9 " 15c+50c dark violet & red 15.00 15.00
a. Overprint inverted 150.00
CB10 " 25c+50c bluish black & car. 15.00 15.00

The surtax was for the Red Cross.

Type of Semi-Postal Stamps, 1957 and

Esquipulas Cathedral
SPAP1

Designs: 15c+1q, Cathedral and crucifix. 20c+1q, Christ with crown of thorns and part of globe. 25c+1q, Archbishop Mariano Rossell y Arellano.

Perf. 13½x14½, 13

1957, Oct. 29 Engraved. **Unwmkd.**

CB11 SPAP1 10c+1q choc. & emerald 12.50 11.00
CB12 SP1 15c+1q dull grn. & sepia 12.50 11.00
CB13 " 20c+1q bl. gray & brown 14.00 12.00
CB14 " 25c+1q lt. vio. & carmine 14.00 12.00

The tax was for the Esquipulas highway.

Wounded Man, Battle of Solferino
SPAP2

Designs: 6c+6c, 20c+20c, Flood disaster. 10c+10c, 25c+25c, Earth, moon and stars. 15c+15c, 30c+30c, Red Cross headquarters.

1960, Apr. 9 Photo. *Perf. 13½x14*

Cross in Rose Red

CB15 SPAP2 5c+5c deep carmine, blue & pink 5.00 5.00
CB16 " 6c+6c brown red, green & pink 5.00 5.00
CB17 " 10c+10c blue & pink 5.00 5.00
CB18 " 15c+15c red brown & blue 5.00 5.00
CB19 " 20c+20c lilac & green 5.00 5.00
CB20 " 25c+25c gray, dark blue & pink 5.00 5.00
CB21 " 30c+30c green, salmon & blue 5.00 5.00
Nos. CB15-CB21 (7) 35.00 35.00

Issued to commemorate the centenary (in 1959) of the Red Cross idea. The surtax went to the Red Cross. Exist imperf.

AIR POST OFFICIAL STAMPS.

Air Post Stamps of 1938 Overprinted in Black

OFICIAL **OFICIAL**

1939, Apr. 29 *Perf. 12½* **Unwmkd.**

CO1 AP13 1c orange & olive brown 1.50 1.25
CO2 " 2c scarlet, pale pink & slate green 1.50 1.25
CO3 " 3c green, buff & olive brown 1.50 1.25
CO4 " 4c dark claret, pale lilac & brown 1.50 1.25
CO5 " 5c bistre, pale green & olive brown 1.50 1.25
CO6 " 10c ultramarine, pale blue & brown 1.50 1.25
Nos. CO1-CO6 (6) 9.00 7.50

Air Post Souvenir Sheet of 1938 with Same Overprint on each Stamp.

1939, Nov. 20

CO7 AP19 Sheet of six 3.00 2.25
a. 1c yellow orange, blue & black 40 30
b. 2c lake, orange, blue & black 40 30
c. 3c olive, blue & orange 40 30
d. 4c dark claret, blue, orange & black 40 30
e. 5c greenish blue, blue, red, orange & black 40 30
f. 10c olive bistre, red & orange 40 30

SPECIAL DELIVERY STAMPS.

No. 237 Overprinted in Red **EXPRESO**

1940, June *Perf. 14* **Unwmkd.**

E1 A81 4c orange 1.50 50

No. E1 paid for express service by motorcycle messenger between Guatemala City and Coban.

Motorcycle Messenger
SD1

Black Surcharge.

1948, Sept. 3 Photo. *Perf. 14x12½*

E2 SD1 10c on 4c blue green & gray black 2.00 1.50

No. E2 without surcharge was issued for regular postage, not special delivery. See No. 337B.

OFFICIAL STAMPS.

O1

National Emblem
O2

Typeset.

1902, Dec. 18 *Perf. 12* **Unwmkd.**

O1 O1 1c green 5.00 3.00
O2 " 2c carmine 5.00 3.00
O3 " 5c ultramarine 5.00 2.25
O4 " 10c brown violet 7.00 2.25
O5 " 25c orange 7.00 2.25
a. Horiz. pair imperf. between 100.00
Nos. O1-O5 (5) 29.00 12.75

Counterfeits of Nos. O1-O5 exist.

During the years 1912 to 1926 the Post Office Department perforated the word "OFICIAL" on limited quantities of the following stamps: Nos. 114-123, 132, 141-149, 151-153, 158, 202, 210-229 and RA2. The perforating was done in blocks of four stamps at a time and was of two types.

A rubber handstamp "OFICIAL" was also used during the same period and was applied in violet, red, blue or black to stamps Nos. 117-118, 121-123, 163-165, 172 and 202-218.

Both perforating and handstamping were done in the post office at Guatemala City and use of the stamps was limited to that city.

1929, Jan. Engraved *Perf. 14*

O6 O2 1c pale greenish blue 30 30
O7 " 2c dark brown 30 30
O8 " 3c green 30 30
O9 " 4c deep violet 35 35
O10 " 5c brown carmine 40 40
O11 " 10c brown orange 75 75
O12 " 25c dark blue 1.50 1.00
Nos. O6-O12 (7) 3.90 3.40

POSTAL TAX STAMPS.

National Emblem
PT1

Perf. 13½, 14, 15

1919, May 3 Engraved **Unwmkd.**

RA1 PT1 12½c carmine 40 25

No. RA1 represented a postal tax for rebuilding post offices.

G. P. O. and Telegraph Building
PT2

1927, Nov. 10 Typo. *Perf. 14*

RA2 PT2 1c olive green 25 15

This stamp was intended to provide a fund for building a post office in Guatemala City. A copy of this stamp had to be affixed, in addition to the regular postage, to every letter and parcel sent through the post.

No. RA2 Overprinted in Green **1871 30 DE JUNIO 1936**

1936, June 30

RA3 PT2 1c olive green 75 40

Liberal revolution, 65th anniversary.

No. RA2 Overprinted in Blue **1821 15 de SEPTIEMBRE 1936**

1936, Sept. 15

RA4 PT2 1c olive green 50 30

Issued in commemoration of the 115th anniversary of the Independence of Guatemala.

No. RA2 Overprinted in Red Brown **FERIA NACIONAL 1936**

1936, Nov. 15

RA5 PT2 1c olive green 60 60

Issued in commemoration of the National Fair.

No. RA2 Overprinted in Red **EXPOSICION FILATELICA 1937**

1937, Mar. 15

RA6 PT2 1c olive green 50 50

No. RA2 Overprinted in Blue **1787-1789 CL ANIVERSARIO DE LA CONSTITUCION EE. UU. 1937-1939**

1938, Jan. 10 *Perf. 14x14½*

RA7 PT2 1c olive green 30 20
a. "1937-1939" omitted 125.00

Issued in commemoration of the 150th anniversary of the Constitution of the United States of America.

No. RA2 Overprinted in Blue or Red **1938**

1938 *Perf. 14.*

RA8 PT2 1c olive green (Bl) 30 30
RA9 " 1c " (R) 30 20

No. RA2 Overprinted in Violet **Primera Exposicion Filatélica Centroamericana 1938**

1938, Nov. 20

RA10 PT2 1c olive green 30 20

Issued in commemoration of the First Central American Philatelic Exposition.

No. RA2 Overprinted in Green or Black **1939**

1939

RA11 PT2 1c olive green (G) 30 20
RA12 " 1c " (Bk) 20 20

No. RA2 Overprinted in Violet or Brown **1940**

1940

RA13 PT2 1c olive green (V) 30 20
RA14 " 1c " (Br) 30 20

No. RA2 Overprinted in Red **Conmemorativo Unión Panamericana 1890-1940**

1940, Apr. 14

RA15 PT2 1c olive green 30 20

Pan American Union, 50th anniversary.

No. RA2 Overprinted in Red **1941**

1941

RA16 PT2 1c olive green 30 20

No. 235 Surcharged in Red

CONSTRUCCION CONSTRUCCION
UN CENTAVO

RA17 A79 1c on 2c deep blue 30 20

No. 235 Surcharged in Carmine

CONSTRUCCION
1942
UN CENTAVO

1942, Jan.

RA18 A79 1c on 2c deep blue 30 20

Arch of Communications Building
PT3 PT4

With Imprint Below Design.
Perf. 11, 12x11

1942, June 3 Engraved

RA19 PT3 1c black brown 5.00 1.50

No imprint; Thin Paper.
Perf. 11, 12x11, 11x12, 11 (3 sides)x12 (rt. side)

1942, July 18

RA20 PT3 1c black brown 30 20

1943 *Perf. 11, 12x11, 12*

RA21 PT4 1c orange 30 20

PT5

Perf. 11, 12½ and Compound

1945, Feb. Unwmkd.

RA22 PT5 1c orange 30 20
a. Booklet pane of 9

1949 *Perf. 12½.*

RA23 PT5 1c dp. ultramarine 30 20

Stamps not listed in this Catalogue or mentioned in "For the Record" (unless recent issues) usually are revenues, locals or labels.

GUINEA

(gĭn'ĭ)

LOCATION—Coast of West Africa, between Guinea-Bissau and Sierra Leone.
GOVT.—Republic.
AREA—94,925 sq. mi.
POP.—4,650,000 (est. 1977).
CAPITAL—Conakry.

This former French Overseas Territory of French West Africa proclaimed itself an independent republic Oct. 2, 1958. For earlier stamps of this area, see French West Africa and French Guinea.

100 Centimes = 1 Franc
100 Caury = 1 Syli (1973)

French West Africa No. 79 Overprinted

REPUBLIQUE
DE GUINEE

Photogravure.

1959 *Perf. 12x12½* **Unwmkd.**

168 CD104 10fr multicolored 1.50 1.65

French West Africa No. 78 Surcharged in Red

45F =
REPUBLIQUE
DE GUINEE

Engraved.
Perf. 13

169 A33 45fr on 20fr multi. 1.50 1.65

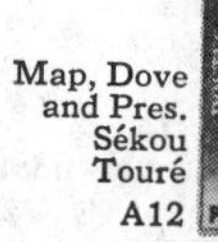

Map, Dove and Pres. Sékou Touré
A12

Engraved.

1959 *Perf. 13* **Unwmkd.**

170 A12 5fr rose carmine 18 12
171 " 10fr ultramarine 30 18
172 " 20fr orange 55 38
173 " 65fr slate green 1.50 1.00
174 " 100fr violet 2.75 2.00
Nos. 170-174 (5) 5.28 3.68

Issued to commemorate the proclamation of independence, Oct. 2, 1958.

Bananas
A13

Fruits: 15fr, Grapefruit. 20fr, Lemons. 25fr, Avocados. 50fr, Pineapple.

1959 Lithographed. *Perf. 11½*

Fruits in Natural Colors.

175 A13 10fr red 12 8
176 " 15fr green & pink 18 15
177 " 20fr red brown & blue 30 18
178 A13 25fr blue & yellow 38 30
179 " 50fr dark violet blue 65 33
Nos. 175-179 (5) 1.63 1.04

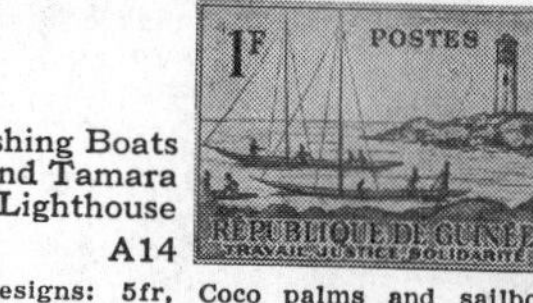

Fishing Boats and Tamara Lighthouse
A14

Designs: 5fr, Coco palms and sailboat (vert.). 10fr, Launching fishing pirogue. 15fr, Elephant's head. 20fr, Pres. Sékou Touré and torch (vert.). 25fr, Elephant.

1959 Engraved. *Perf. 13½*

180 A14 1fr rose 5 3
181 " 2fr green 5 3
182 " 3fr brown 5 3
183 " 5fr blue 6 6
184 " 10fr claret 8 6
185 " 15fr light brown 40 22
186 " 20fr claret 55 13
187 " 25fr red brown 60 18
Nos. 180-187 (8) 1.84 74

Flag Raising, Labé
A15

1959 Lithographed *Perf. 12*

188 A15 50fr multicolored 65 30
189 " 100fr " 1.30 75

U.N. Headquarters, New York, and People of Guinea—A16

1959 *Perf. 12*

Size: 40x23mm.

190 A16 1fr violet blue & orange 6 5
191 " 2fr red lilac & emerald 6 5
192 " 3fr brown & crimson 7 6
193 " 5fr brown & greenish blue 10 8
Nos. 190-193, C22-C23 (6) 1.99 1.59

Issued to commemorate the first anniversary of Guinea's admission to the United Nations.

Uprooted Oak Emblem
A17

1960 Photogravure *Perf. 11½*

Granite Paper

194 A17 25fr multicolored 45 38
195 " 50fr " 65 45

Issued to publicize World Refugee Year, July 1, 1959–June 30, 1960.

Common Design Types

pictured in section at front of book.

UPU Monument, Bern
A18

1960 Granite Paper **Unwmkd.**

196 A18 10fr gray brown & black 15 8
197 " 15fr lilac & purple 18 10
198 " 20fr ultramarine & dark blue 25 13
199 " 25fr yellow green & slate green 38 15
200 " 50fr red orange & brown 70 30
Nos. 196-200 (5) 1.66 76

Nos. 199-200 are vertical.

Issued to commemorate the first anniversary of Guinea's admission to the UPU.

Nos. 188-189 Overprinted in Black, Orange or Carmine: "Jeux Olympiques Rome 1960" and Olympic Rings.

1960 Lithographed *Perf. 12*

201 A15 50fr multi. (Bk) 4.00 4.00
202 " 100fr " (O or C) 6.00 6.00
Nos. 201-202, C24-C26 (5) 42.00 38.00

Issued to commemorate the 17th Olympic Games, Rome, Aug. 25-Sept. 11.

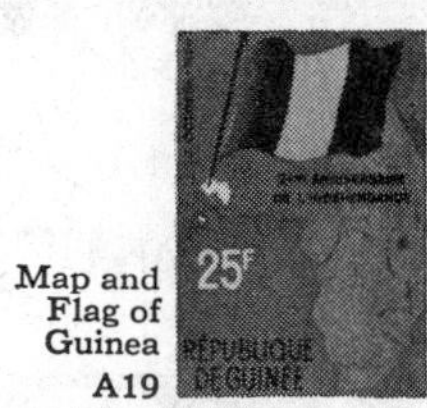

Map and Flag of Guinea
A19

1960 Photogravure *Perf. 11½*

203 A19 25fr multicolored 30 25
204 " 30fr " 38 33

Second anniversary of independence.

Nos. 190-193 Overprinted

XVÈME
ANNIVERSAIRE
DES NATIONS UNIES

1961 Lithographed *Perf. 12*

205 A16 1fr vio. blue & org. 10 10
206 " 2fr red lilac & emerald 10 10
207 " 3fr brown & crimson 10 10
208 " 5fr brown & greenish blue 10 10

Nos. 175-179 Overprinted in Black or Orange

XVEME
ANNIVERSAIRE

DES
NATIONS UNIES

Perf. 11½

Fruits in Natural Colors

209 A13 10fr red 13 13
210 " 15fr green & pink 25 22
211 " 20fr red brn. & blue 33 30
212 " 25fr bl. & yellow (O) 40 35
213 " 50fr dark violet blue 75 70
Nos. 205-213, C27-C28 (11) 3.96 3.45

Nos. 205-213 issued to commemorate 15th anniversary of United Nations.

Defassa Waterbuck—A20

Photogravure

1961, Sept. 1 ***Perf. 11½*** **Unwmkd.**

Multicolored Design; Granite Paper

214 A20 5fr bright green 8 4
215 " 10fr emerald 12 4
216 " 25fr lilac 27 15
217 " 40fr orange 45 22
218 " 50fr red orange 60 25
219 " 75fr ultramarine 1.00 40
Nos. 214-219 (6) 2.52 1.10

Exhibition Hall
A21

1961, Oct. 2 ***Perf. 11½***

Flag in Red, Yellow & Green.

Granite Paper

220 A21 5fr ultra. & red 6 6
221 " 10fr brown & red 10 10
222 " 25fr gray grn. & red 22 22

First Three-Year Plan.

Gray-breasted Helmet Guinea Fowl
A22

1961 ***Perf. 13x14*** **Unwmkd.**

223 A22 5fr rose lilac, sepia & blue 12 4
224 " 10fr deep orange, sepia & blue 18 6
225 " 25fr cerise, sepia & blue 18 10
226 " 40fr ochre, sepia & blue 40 15
227 " 50fr lemon, sepia & blue 50 25
228 " 75fr apple green, sepia & blue 1.10 45
Nos. 223-228 (6) 2.48 1.05

Patrice Lumumba and Map of Africa
A23

1962, Feb. 13 Photo. ***Perf. 11½***

229 A23 10fr multicolored 55 38
230 " 25fr " 75 38
231 " 50fr " 45 38

Issued to commemorate the anniversary of the death, on Feb. 12, 1961, of Patrice Lumumba, Premier of the Congo Republic.

King Mohammed V of Morocco and Map of Africa
A24

1962, Mar. 15 Litho. ***Perf. 13***

232 A24 25fr multicolored 65 25
233 " 75fr " 1.35 45

Issued to commemorate the first anniversary of the conference of African heads of state at Casablanca.

African Postal Union Issue

Map of Africa and Post Horn
A24a

1962, Apr. 23 Photo. ***Perf. 13½x13***

234 A24a 25fr orange, black & green 75 15
235 " 100fr deep brown & orange 1.85 40

Establishment of African Postal Union.

Boté Player
A25

Bolon Player
A26

Musical Instruments: 1fr, 10fr, Flute. 1.50fr, 3fr, Koni. 2fr, 20fr, Kora. 25fr, 50fr, Boté. 40fr, 75fr, Bolon.

Perf. 13½x13, 13x13½

1962, June 15 Photogravure

236 A25 30c blue, dark green & red 3 3
237 A26 50c salmon, brn. & br. grn. 3 3
238 A25 1fr yel. grn., grn. & lilac 3 3
239 A26 1.50fr yellow, red & blue 4 4
240 " 2fr rose lilac, red lilac & grn. 4 4
241 " 3fr br. grn., grn. & lilac 4 4
242 A25 10fr org., brn. & blue 8 4
243 A26 20fr olive, dk. olive & carmine 18 8
244 A25 25fr olive, dark olive & lilac 30 17
245 A26 40fr blue, green & red lilac 45 30
246 A25 50fr rose, dp. rose & Prus. blue 60 38
247 A26 75fr dull yel., brn. & Prus. blue 75 50
Nos. 236-247, C32-C34 (15) 9.57 6.18

Hippopotamus
A27

Designs: 25fr, 75fr, Lion. 30fr, 100fr, Leopard.

1962, Aug. 25 Litho. ***Perf. 13x13½***

248 A27 10fr org., grn. & brn. 18 8
249 " 25fr emerald, black & brown 38 15
250 " 30fr yel. green, dk. brown & yel. 45 18
251 " 50fr vio. blue, dk. brn. & green 65 38
252 " 75fr lilac, lt. lilac & red brown 80 50
253 " 100fr greenish blue, dk. brn. & yel. 1.00 75
Nos. 248-253 (6) 3.46 2.04

See also Nos. 340-345.

Child at Blackboard
A28

Alfa Yaya
A29

Designs: 10fr, 20fr, Adult class.

Photogravure

1962, Sept. 19 ***Perf. 13½x13***

254 A28 5fr yellow, dark brown & org. 6 5
255 " 10fr org. & dk. brn. 10 5
256 " 15fr yel. green, dark brown & red 22 8
257 " 20fr blue & dk. brown 30 18

Campaign against illiteracy.

Imperforates

From late 1962 onward, most Guinea stamps exist imperforate.

1962, Oct. 2 ***Perf. 13½***

Portraits: 30fr, King Béhanzin. 50fr, King Ba Bemba. 75fr, Almamy Samory. 100fr, Tierno Aliou.

Gold Frame

258 A29 25fr brt. bl. & sepia 33 15
259 " 30fr yellow & sepia 50 25
260 " 50fr bright pink & sepia 65 33
261 " 75fr yellow green & sepia 1.50 60
262 " 100fr orange, red & sepia 1.85 90
Nos. 258-262 (5) 4.83 2.23

Heroes and martyrs of Africa.

Gray Parrot
A30

Birds: 30c, 3fr, 50fr, Crowned crane (vert). 1fr, 20fr, Abyssinian ground hornbill. 1.50fr, 25fr, White spoonbill. 2fr, 40fr, Bateleur eagle.

Perf. 13½x13, 13x13½

1962, Dec. **Unwmkd.**

263 A30 30c multicolored 5 3
264 " 50c " 5 3
265 " 1fr " 7 3
266 " 1.50fr " 7 3
267 " 2fr " 7 3
268 " 3fr slate, yel. & pink 7 3
269 A30 10fr multicolored 18 6
270 " 20fr " 25 15
271 " 25fr " 30 18
272 " 40fr " 45 30
273 " 50fr " 60 38
274 " 75fr bright yellow, gray & brn. 75 50
Nos. 263-274, C41-C43 (15) 11.76 6.45

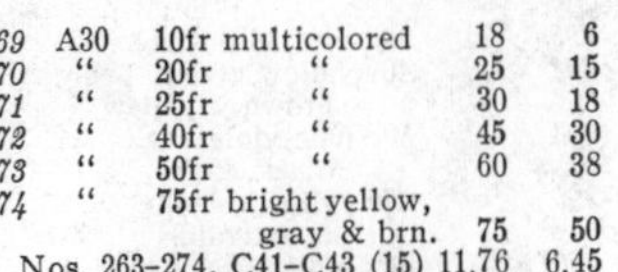

Wheat Emblem and Globe
A31

1963, Mar. 21 Photo. ***Perf. 13x14***

275 A31 5fr red & yellow 5 5
276 " 10fr emerald & yellow 10 6
277 " 15fr brown & yellow 13 10
278 " 25fr dk. olive & yel. 30 15

Issued for the "Freedom from Hunger" campaign of the U.N. Food and Agriculture Organization.

Basketball—A32

Designs: 50c, 4fr, 30fr, Boxing. 1fr, 5fr, Running. 1.50fr, 10fr, Bicycling. 2fr, 20fr, Single sculls.

1963, Mar. 16 ***Perf. 14*** **Unwmkd.**

279 A32 30c vermilion, dp. claret & grn. 3 3
280 " 50c lilac & blue 3 3
281 " 1fr dull orange, sepia & green 3 3
282 " 1.50fr orange, ultra. & magenta 5 3
283 " 2fr aquamarine, dark blue & magenta 5 5
284 " 3fr olive, dp. claret & green 5 5
285 " 4fr carmine rose, purple & blue 6 5
286 " 5fr brt. grn., olive & magenta 8 6
287 " 10fr lilac rose, ultra. & magenta 20 5
288 " 20fr red orge., dk. bl. & crimson 22 6
289 " 25fr emerald, deep claret & dark green 38 15
290 " 30fr gray, pur. & bl. 45 30
Nos. 279-290, C44-C46 (15) 9.38 5.19

A33

Various Butterflies.

1963, May 10 Photo. ***Perf. 12***

291 A33 10c deep rose black & gray 5 5

292 A33 30c rose, blk. & yel. 5 5
293 " 40c yellow green, brown & yellow 5 5
294 " 50c pale violet, black & grn. 7 5
295 " 1fr yellow, black & emerald 7 5
296 " 1.50fr bluish green, black & sepia 10 5
297 " 2fr multicolored 10 5
298 " 3fr " 10 6
299 " 10fr rose lilac, black & green 10 6
300 " 20fr gray, blk. & grn. 30 10
301 " 25fr yellow green, black & gray 45 12
302 " 40fr multicolored 60 25
303 " 50fr ultramarine, black & yellow 75 30
304 " 75fr yel., blk. & grn. 90 50
Nos. 291-304, C47-C49 (17) 12.69 5.79

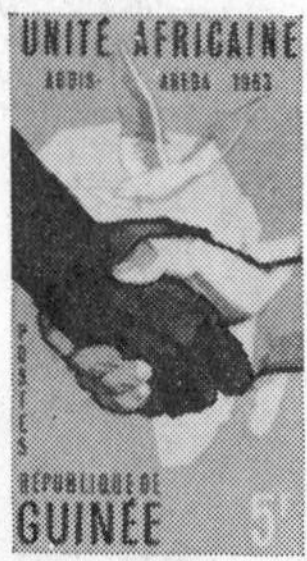

Handshake, Map and Dove
A34

1963, May 22 ***Perf. 13½x14***

305 A34 5fr bluish green & dark brown 5 5
306 " 10fr orange yellow & dark brown 8 5
307 " 15fr olive & dk. brn. 18 10
308 " 25fr bister brown & dark brown 27 18

Issued to commemorate the conference of African heads of state for African Unity, Addis Ababa.

Globe Encircled by Satellite—A35

Engraved

1963, July 25 ***Perf. 10½*** **Unwmkd.**

309 A35 5fr green & carmine 8 5
310 " 10fr vio. bl. & carm. 12 10
311 " 15fr yellow & carm. 18 15

Issued to commemorate the centenary of the International Red Cross. See Nos. C50-C51.

Nos. 279-281 Surcharged in Carmine, Yellow or Orange:
"COMMISSION PRÉPARATOIRE AUX JEUX OLYMPIQUES À CONAKRY,"
New value and Olympic Rings.

1963, Nov. 20 **Photo.** ***Perf. 14***

312 A32 40fr on 30c verm., dp. claret & green (C or Y) 1.10 1.00
313 " 50fr on 50c lilac & blue (C or O) 1.50 1.35
314 " 75fr on 1fr dull orange, sepia & green (C or O) 2.50 2.10
Nos. 312-314, C58-C60 (6) 15.10 12.65

Issued to publicize the meeting of the Olympic Games Preparatory Commission at Conakry. The overprint is in a circular line on No. 312, in three lines on each side on Nos. 313-314.

Jewelfish—A36

Fish: 40c, 30fr, Golden pheasant. 50c, 40fr, Blue gularis. 1fr, 75fr, Banded Jewelfish. 1.50fr, African lyretail. 2fr, Six-barred epiplatys. 5fr, Jewelfish.

1964, Feb. 15 **Litho.** ***Perf. 14x13½***

315 A36 30c car. rose & multi. 3 3
316 " 40c purple & multi. 3 3
317 " 50c car. rose & multi. 3 3
318 " 1fr blue & multi. 3 3
319 " 1.50fr blue & multi. 3 3
320 " 2fr purple & multi. 4 3
321 " 5fr blue & multi. 6 5
322 " 30fr green & multi. 27 18
323 " 40fr purple & multi. 75 33
324 " 75fr multicolored 1.00 50
Nos. 315-324, C54-C55 (12) 6.37 3.34

John F. Kennedy
A37

1964, March 5 **Engraved** ***Perf. 10½***

Flag in Red and Blue

325 A37 5fr black & purple 8 6
326 " 25fr green & purple 25 18
327 " 50fr brown & purple 60 38

Issued in memory of John F. Kennedy. Issued in sheets of 20 with marginal quotations in English and French. Two sheets for each denomination. See No. C56.

Workers Welding Pipe
A38

Designs: 5fr, Pipe line over mountains (vert.). 10fr, Waterworks. 30fr, Transporting pipe. 50fr, Laying pipe.

Photogravure

1964, May 1 ***Perf. 11½*** **Unwmkd.**

328 A38 5fr deep magenta 5 5
329 " 10fr bright purple 8 5
330 " 20fr orange red 15 10
331 " 30fr ultramarine 27 18
332 " 50fr yellow green 55 32
Nos. 328-332 (5) 1.10 70

Issued to commemorate the completion of the water-supply pipe line to Conakry, March 1964.

Ice Hockey
A39

Sport: 25fr, Ski jump. 50fr, Slalom.

1964, May 15 ***Perf. 13x12½***

333 A39 10fr gold, emerald & slate green 15 12
334 " 25fr gold, lilac & dark violet 45 18
335 A39 50fr gold, blue & slate blue 90 50

Issued to commemorate the 9th Winter Olympic Games, Innsbruck, Jan. 29-Feb. 9, 1964. See also No. C57.

Eleanor Roosevelt Reading to Children—A40

1964, June 1 **Engraved** ***Perf. 10½***

336 A40 5fr green 8 5
337 " 10fr red orange 12 5
338 " 15fr bright blue 22 12
339 " 25fr carmine rose 27 15
Nos. 336-339, C61 (5) 1.29 77

Issued to honor Eleanor Roosevelt on the 15th anniversary of the Universal Declaration of Human Rights (in 1963).

Animal Type of 1962

Designs: 5fr, 30fr, Striped hyenas. 40fr, 300fr, Black buffaloes. 75fr, 100fr, Elephants.

Perf. 13x13½

1964, Oct. 8 **Litho.** **Unwmkd.**

340 A27 5fr yellow & black 8 3
341 " 30fr lt. blue & black 27 18
342 " 40fr lilac rose & blk. 40 22
343 " 75fr yel. grn. & blk. 80 33
344 " 100fr bister & black 1.00 55
345 " 300fr orange & black 2.75 1.65
Nos. 340-345 (6) 5.30 2.96

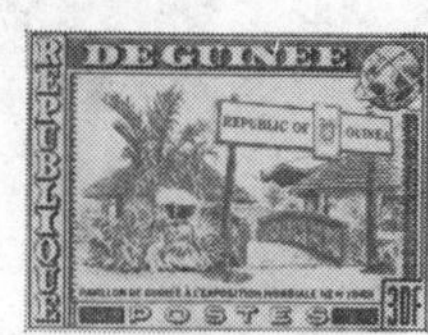

Guinea Exhibit, World's Fair—A41

1964, Oct. 26 **Engraved** ***Perf. 10½***

346 A41 30fr vio. & emerald 30 18
347 " 40fr red lilac & emerald 45 22
348 " 50fr sepia & emerald 60 27
349 " 75fr rose red & dk. bl. 90 38

New York World's Fair, 1964-65.

Queen Nefertari Crowned by Isis and Hathor
A42

Weight Lifter and Caucasian, Japanese and Negro Children
A43

Designs: 25fr, Ramses II in battle. 50fr, Submerged sphinxes, sailboat, Wadi-es-Sebua. 100fr, Ramses II holding crook and flail, Abu Simbel. 200fr, Feet and legs of Ramses statues, Abu Simbel.

1964, Nov. 19 **Photo.** ***Perf. 12***

350 A42 10fr dk. bl., red brn. & citron 12 6
351 " 25fr black, dull red & brown 18 13
352 " 50fr dk. brown, blue & violet 45 18
353 " 100fr dk. brown, yel. & purple 75 55
354 A42 200fr purple, dull green & buff 1.65 1.10
Nos. 350-354, C64 (6) 7.15 4.27

UNESCO world campaign to save historic monuments in Nubia.

1965, Jan. 18 **Photo.** ***Perf. 13x12½***

Designs: 10fr, Runner carrying torch. 25fr, Pole vaulting and flags. 40fr, Runners. 50fr, Judo. 75fr, Japanese woman, flags and stadium.

355 A43 5fr gold, claret & blk. 5 4
356 " 10fr gold, black, verm. & blue 10 6
357 " 25fr gold, black, yel. green & red 22 15
358 " 40fr gold, black, brown & yel. 30 22
359 " 50fr gold, blk. & grn. 50 33
360 " 75fr gold & multi. 85 50
Nos. 355-360, C65 (7) 3.52 1.80

Issued to commemorate the 18th Olympic Games, Tokyo, Oct. 10-25, 1964. Exist imperf.

Doudou Mask, Boké
A44

Designs: 40c, 1fr, 15fr, Various Niamou masks, N'Zérékoré region. 60c, "Yoki," woodcarved statuette of a girl, Boke. 80c, Masked woman dancer from Guekedou. 2fr, Masked dancer from Macenta. 20fr, Beater from Tamtam. 60fr, Bird dancer from Macenta. 80fr, Bassari dancer from Koundara. 100fr, Sword dancer from Karana.

1965, Feb. 15 ***Perf. 14*** **Unwmkd.**

361 A44 20c multicolored 3 3
362 " 40c " 3 3
363 " 60c " 3 3
364 " 80c " 3 3
365 " 1fr " 5 5
366 " 2fr " 10 8
367 " 15fr " 15 10
368 " 20fr " 30 15
369 " 60fr " 75 50
370 " 80fr " 75 55
371 " 100fr " 1.10 80
Nos. 361-371, C68 (12) 6.82 3.70

World's Fair Type of 1964
Inscribed "1965"

1965, Mar. 24 **Engraved** ***Perf. 10½***

372 A41 30fr green & orange 22 15
373 " 40fr car. & brt. grn. 33 22
374 " 50fr brt. grn. & vio. 50 38
375 " 75fr brown & violet 75 55

See also Nos. C69-C70.

Blacksmith
A45

Handicrafts: 20fr, Potter. 60fr, Cloth dyers. 80fr, Basketmaker.

1965, May 1 Photo. *Perf. 14*

376 A45 15fr multicolored 12 8
377 " 20fr " 18 12
378 " 60fr " 55 38
379 " 80fr " 70 50
Nos. 376-379, C71-C72 (6) 5.45 2.78

ITU Emblem, Old and New Communication Equipment—A46

1965, May 17 Unwmkd.

380 A46 25fr yellow, gray, gold & black 22 18
381 " 50fr yellow, green, gold & black 45 33

Issued to commemorate the centenary of the International Telecommunication Union. Exist imperf. See also Nos. C73-C74.

Maj. Virgil I. Grissom A47

Moon from 258mi. A48

Sputnik Over Earth A49

1965, July 19 Photo. *Perf. 13*

American Achievements in Space: 10fr, Lt. Com. John W. Young. 25fr, Moon from 115mi. 30fr, Moon from 58mi. 100fr, Grissom and Young in Gemini 2 spaceship.

Size: 21x29mm.

382 A47 5fr dk. red & multi. 5 3
383 " 10fr " " " 9 6
384 A48 15fr gold, bl. & dk. bl. 12 8

Size: 39x28mm.

385 A48 25fr gold, bl. & dk. bl. 20 15

Size: 21x29mm.

386 A48 30fr gold, bl. & dk. bl. 25 18

Size: 39x28mm.

387 A47 100fr multi. & dk. red 85 60
a. Sheet of 15 6.00

Russian Achievements in Space: 5fr, Col. Pavel Belyayev. 10fr, Lt. Col. Alexei Leonov. 15fr, Vostoks 3 & 4 in space. 30fr, Vostoks 5 & 6 over Earth. 100fr, Leonov floating in space.

Size: 21x29mm.

388 A47 5fr blue & multi. 5 3
389 " 10fr " " 9 6
390 A49 15fr " " 12 8

Size: 39x28mm.

391 A49 25fr blue & multi. 20 15

Size: 21x29mm.

392 A49 30fr blue & multi. 25 18

Size: 39x28mm.

393 A47 100fr black, dk. red & gold 85 60
a. Sheet of 15 6.00
Nos. 382-393 (12) 3.12 2.20

Issued to honor American and Russian achievements in space. Nos. 387a and 393a contain five triptychs each: four rows with 5fr, 100fr and 10fr, and a center row with 15fr, 25fr and 30fr stamps each. No. 387a contains Nos. 382-387, No. 393a, Nos. 388-393. Margins inscribed in gold: "REPUBLIQUE DE GUINEE" and stars. Size: 145x213mm. Exist imperf.

ICY Emblem, U.N. Headquarters and Skyline, New York—A50

1965, Sept. 8 *Perf. 10½*

394 A50 25fr yel. grn. & verm. 22 15
395 " 45fr violet & orange 38 27
396 " 75fr red brn. & org. 60 40

Issued for the International Cooperation Year, 1965. See also No. C75.

Polytechnic Institute, Conakry A51

New Projects, Conakry: 30fr, Hotel Camayenne. 40fr, Gbessia Airport. 75fr, Stadium "28 September."

1965, Oct. 2 Photo. *Perf. 13½*

397 A51 25fr multicolored 25 15
398 " 30fr " 35 18
399 " 40fr " 65 38
400 " 75fr " 85 50
Nos. 397-400, C76-C77 (6) 10.85 5.41

Seventh anniversary of independence.

Photographing Far Side of Moon A52

Designs: 10fr, Trajectories of Ranger VII on flight to moon. 25fr, Relay satellite. 45fr, Vostoks I & II and globe.

1965, Nov. 15 Litho. *Perf. 14x13½*

401 A52 5fr black, purple & ocher 4 3
402 " 10fr red brown, light grn. & yellow 10 5
403 " 25fr blk., bl. & bister 30 18
404 " 45fr blk., lt. ultra. & bister 55 30
Nos. 401-404, C78-C79 (6) 4.49 1.91

Issued to publicize the efforts to reach the moon.

Sword Dance, Karana A53

Designs: 30c, Dancing girls, Lower Guinea. 50c, Behore musicians of Tiekere playing "Eyoro" (horiz.). 5fr, Doundouba dance of Kouroussa. 40fr, Bird man's dance of Macenta.

1966, Jan. 5 Photo. *Perf. 13½*

Size: 26x36mm.

405 A53 10c multicolored 5 5
406 " 30c " 5 5

Size: 36x28½mm.

407 A53 50c multicolored 5 5

Size: 26x36mm.

408 A53 5fr multicolored 6 5
409 " 40fr " 50 28
Nos. 405-409, C80 (6) 1.81 98

Festival of African Art and Culture. See No. 436-441.

Engraved Overprint in Red or Orange on Nos. 355-356 and Nos. 358-360

1966, March 14 *Perf. 13x12½*

410 A43 5fr multi. (R) 8 6
411 " 10fr " (R) 12 10
412 " 40fr " (O) 50 38
413 " 50fr " (R) 70 50
414 " 75fr " (R) 1.20 85
Nos. 410-414, C81 (6) 3.80 2.44

Issued to commemorate the Fourth Pan Arab Games, Cairo, Sept. 2-11, 1965. The same overprint was also applied to imperf. sheets of No. 357.

Engraved Red Orange Overprint on No. 352: "CENTENAIRE DU TIMBRE CAIRE 1966"

1966, March 14 *Perf. 12*

415 A42 50fr dk. brown, blue & violet 50 50

Issued to commemorate the centenary of the first Egyptian postage stamps. See also No. C82.

Vonkou Rock, Teliméle A54

Views: 25fr, Artificial lake, Coyah. 40fr, Kalé waterfalls. 50fr, Forécariah bridge. 75fr, Liana bridge.

1966, Apr. 4 Photo. *Perf. 13½*

416 A54 20fr multicolored 15 8
417 " 25fr " 22 12
418 " 40fr " 30 15
419 " 50fr " 45 22
420 " 75fr " 65 40
Nos. 416-420, C83 (6) 2.87 1.47

See also Nos. 475-478, C83, C90-C91.

UNESCO Emblem A55

1966, May 2 Photo. Unwmkd.

421 A55 25fr multicolored 32 18

Issued to commemorate the 20th anniversary of UNESCO (United Nations Educational, Scientific and Cultural Organization). See also Nos. C84-C85.

Woman of Guinea and Morning-glory A56

Symbolic Water Cycle and UNESCO Emblem A57

Designs: Women and Flowers of Guinea.

1966, May 30 Photo. *Perf. 13½*

Size: 23x34mm.

422 A56 10c multicolored 5 3
423 " 20c " 5 3
424 " 30c " 5 3
425 A56 40c multicolored 5 3
426 " 3fr " 5 3
427 " 4fr " 5 3
428 " 10fr " 10 4
429 " 25fr " 38 12

Size: 28x43mm.

430 A56 30fr multicolored 45 18
431 " 50fr " 60 33
432 " 80fr " 85 45
Nos. 422-432, C86-C87 (13) 9.18 3.85

1966, Sept. 26 Engraved *Perf. 10½*

433 A57 5fr blue & dp. org. 6 5
434 " 25fr grn. & dp. org. 18 12
435 " 100fr brt. rose lilac & dp. orange 85 50

Hydrological Decade (UNESCO), 1965-74.

Dance Type of 1966

Designs: Various folk dances. 25fr, 75fr, horizontal.

1966, Oct. 24 Photo. *Perf. 13½*

Sizes: 26x36mm. (vert.); 36x28½mm. (horiz.)

436 A53 60c multicolored 3 3
437 " 1fr " 3 3
438 " 1.50fr " 4 4
439 " 25fr " 22 13
440 " 50fr " 50 27
441 " 75fr " 70 50
Nos. 436-441 (6) 1.52 1.00

Issued to publicize the Guinean National Dancers.

Child's Drawing and UNICEF Emblem A58

Children's Drawings: 2fr, Elephant. 3fr, Girl. 20fr, Village (horiz.). 25fr, Boy playing soccer. 40fr, Still life. 50fr, Bird in a tree.

1966, Dec. 12 Photo. *Perf. 13½*

442 A58 2fr multicolored 5 3
443 " 3fr " 5 3
444 " 10fr " 8 6
445 " 20fr " 13 8
446 " 25fr " 25 12
447 " 40fr " 38 22
448 " 50fr " 50 30
Nos. 442-448 (7) 1.44 84

Issued to commemorate the 20th anniversary of UNICEF (United Nations International Children's Emergency Fund). Printed in sheets of 10 stamps and 2 labels with ornamental borders and inscriptions.

Laboratory Technician A59

Designs (World Health Organization Emblem and): 50fr, Physician examining infant. 75fr, Pre-natal care and instruction. 80fr, World Health Organization Headquarters, Geneva.

1967, Jan. 20 Photo. *Perf. 13½*

449 A59 30fr multicolored 22 12
450 " 50fr " 38 22
451 " 75fr " 55 33
452 " 80fr " 70 50

Issued to commemorate the inauguration (in 1966) of World Health Organization Headquarters, Geneva.

Niamou Mask, N'Zerekore
A60

Designs: 10c, 1fr, 30fr, Small Banda mask, Kanfarade, Boké region. 1.50fr. 50fr, Like 30c. 50c, 5fr, 75fr, Bearded Niamou mask. 60c, 25fr, 100fr, Horned Yinadjinkele mask, Kankan region.

1967, March 25 Photo. *Perf. 14x13*

453	A60	10c org. & multi.	5	3
454	"	30c citron & brown black	5	3
455	"	50c deep lilac rose, black & red	5	3
456	"	60c deep orange, black & bister	5	3
457	"	1fr yel. grn. & multi.	5	3
458	"	1.50fr salmon pink & brown black	5	3
459	"	5fr apple green, black & red	15	5
460	"	25fr red lilac, black & bister	25	8
461	"	30fr bister & multi.	40	12
462	"	50fr greenish blue & brn. black	60	22
463	"	75fr yel., blk., & red	90	40
464	"	100fr lt. ultra., black & bister	1.40	60
		Nos. 453-464 (12)	4.00	1.65

Ball Python
A61

Designs: 20c, Pastoria Research Institute. 50c, 75fr, Extraction of snake venom. 1fr, 50fr, Rock python. 2fr, Men holding rock python. 5fr, 30fr, Gaboon viper. 20fr, West African mamba.

1967, May 15 Litho. *Perf. 13½*

Size: 43½x20mm.

465	A61	20c multicolored	5	3
466	"	30c "	5	3
467	"	50c "	5	3
468	"	1fr "	5	3
469	"	2fr "	5	3
470	"	5fr "	7	3

Size: 56x26mm.

471	A61	20fr multicolored	22	12
472	"	30fr "	50	10
473	"	50fr "	65	18
474	"	75fr "	1.00	30
		Nos. 465-474, C88-C89 (12)	8.19	3.58

Issued to publicize the Research Institute for Applied Biology of Guinea (Pastoria). For souvenir sheet see No. C88a.

Scenic Type of 1966

Views: 5fr, Loos Island. 30fr, Tinkisso Waterfalls. 70fr, "The Elephant's Trunk" Hotel, Mt. Kakoulima. 80fr, Evening at the shore, Ratoma.

1967, June 20 Photo. *Perf. 13½*

475	A54	5fr multicolored	4	3
476	"	30fr "	25	7
477	"	70fr "	65	10
478	"	80fr "	85	22
		Nos. 475-478, C90-C91 (6)	4.69	2.12

People's Palace, Conakry—A62

Elephant
A63

1967, Sept. 28 Photo. *Perf. 13½*

479	A62	5fr silver & multi.	4	3
480	A63	30fr silver & multi.	35	25
481	A62	55fr gold & multi.	60	30

Issued to commemorate the 20th anniversary of the Democratic Party of Guinea and the opening of the People's Palace, Conakry. See also No. C92.

Nos. 418-420 and 475-478 Overprinted with Lions Emblem and: "AMITIE DES PEUPLES GRACE AU TOURISME 1917-1967"

1967, Nov. 6

482	A54	5fr multicolored	25	8
483	"	30fr "	55	22
484	"	40fr "	50	22
485	"	50fr "	70	30
486	"	70fr "	85	38
487	"	75fr "	1.20	55
488	"	80fr "	1.50	55
		Nos. 482-488, C93-C95 (10)	10.20	4.65

50th anniversary of Lions International.

WHO Office for Africa
A64

1967, Dec. 4 Photo. *Perf. 13½*

489	A64	30fr lt. olive green, bister & dark green	40	15
490	"	75fr red org., bister & dark blue	80	38

Issued to commemorate the inauguration of the World Health Organization Regional Office for Africa in Brazzaville, Congo.

Human Rights Flame
A65

1968, Jan. 15 Photo. *Perf. 13½*

491	A65	30fr ocher, green & dk. carmine	35	15
492	"	40fr vio., grn. & car.	45	18

International Human Rights Year, 1968.

Coyah, Dubréka Region
A66

Homes and People: 30c, 30fr, Kankan Region. 40c, Kankan, East Guinea. 50c, 15fr, Woodlands Region. 60c, Fulahmori, Gaoual Region. 5fr, Cognagui, Kundara Region. 40fr, Fouta Djallon, West Guinea. 100fr, Labé, West Guinea.

1968, Apr. 1 Photo. *Perf. 13½x14*

Size: 36x27mm.

493	A66	20c gold & multi.	3	3
494	"	30c " "	3	3
495	"	40c " "	3	3
496	"	50c " "	3	3

Perf. 14x13½

Size: 57x36mm.

497	A66	60c gold & multi.	3	3
498	"	5fr " "	4	3
499	"	15fr " "	15	5
500	"	20fr " "	25	12
501	"	30fr " "	40	15
502	"	40fr " "	55	22
503	"	100fr " "	1.40	33
		Nos. 493-503, C100 (12)	5.94	2.25

The Storyteller—A67

African Legends: 15fr, The Little Genie of Mt. Nimba. No. 506, The Legend of the Moons and the Stars. No. 507, Lan, the Child Buffalo (vert.). 40fr, Nianablas and the Crocodiles. 50fr, Leuk the Hare Playing the Drum (vert.). 75fr, Leuk the Hare Selling his Sister (vert.). 80fr, The Hunter and the Antelope-woman. The designs are from paintings by students of the Academy of Fine Arts in Bellevue.

1968 Photogravure *Perf. 13½*

504	A67	15fr multicolored	10	5
505	"	25fr "	20	6
506	"	30fr "	20	10
507	"	30fr "	30	12
508	"	40fr "	45	18
509	"	50fr "	60	22
		a. Souv. sheet of 4	5.50	5.50
510	"	75fr multicolored	65	38
511	"	80fr "	1.00	40
		Nos. 504-511, C101-C104 (12)	11.45	3.79

Issued in sheets of 10 plus 2 labels. No. 509a contains 4 imperf. stamps similar to Nos. 508-509, C101 and C104. "Poste Aerienne" omitted on the 70fr and 300fr of the souvenir sheet.

Issue dates: May 16, Nos. 505-506, 510-511. Sept. 16, Nos. 504, 507-509.

Anubius Baboon
A68

African Animals: 10fr, Leopards. 15fr, Hippopotami. 20fr, Nile crocodile. 30fr, Ethiopian wart hog. 50fr, Defassa waterbuck. 75fr, Cape buffaloes.

1968, Nov. 25 Photo. *Perf. 13½*

Size: 44x31mm.

512	A68	5fr gold & multi.	5	4
513	"	10fr " "	12	6
514	"	15fr " "	18	5
		a. Souv. sheet of 3	45	45
515	"	20fr gold & multi.	32	6
516	"	30fr " "	45	10
517	A68	50fr gold & multi.	60	18
		a. Souv. sheet of 3	1.35	1.35
518	"	75fr gold & multi.	90	38
		a. Souv. sheet of 3	4.75	4.75
		Nos. 512-518, C105-C106 (9)	6.22	2.22

No. 514a contains one each of Nos. 512-514, No. 517a one each of Nos. 515-517; No. 518a contains one No. 518 and one each similar to Nos. C105-C106 without "POSTE AERIENNE" inscription. The sheets contain 3 stamps and one green and gold label inscribed "FAUNE AFRICAINE," buff and gold decorative margins and carmine inscriptions. Size: 118x100mm.

Senator Robert F. Kennedy
A69

Portraits: 75fr, Rev. Martin Luther King, Jr. 100fr, Pres. John F. Kennedy.

1968, Dec. 16

519	A69	30fr yellow & multi.	25	8
520	"	75fr multicolored	75	18
521	"	100fr "	1.00	40
		Nos. 519-521, C107-C109 (6)	6.00	1.81

Issued to honor Robert F. Kennedy, John F. Kennedy and Martin Luther King, Jr. as martyrs for freedom.

The stamps are printed in sheets of 15 (3x5) containing 10 stamps and five yellow-green and gold center labels. Sheets come either with English or French inscriptions on label.

Sculpture and Runner
A70

Sculpture and Soccer—A71

Designs (Sculpture and): 10fr, Boxing. 15fr, Javelin. 30fr, Hurdling. 50fr, Hammer throw. 75fr, Bicycling.

1969, Feb. 18 Photo. *Perf. 13½*

522	A70	5fr multicolored	4	3
523	"	10fr "	8	6
524	"	15fr "	12	8
525	A71	25fr "	35	10
526	A70	30fr "	40	10
527	"	50fr "	65	22
528	"	75fr "	85	27
		Nos. 522-528, C110-C112 (10)	8.99	2.74

Issued to commemorate the 19th Olympic Games, Mexico City, Oct. 12-27.

No. 404 Surcharged and Overprinted in Red

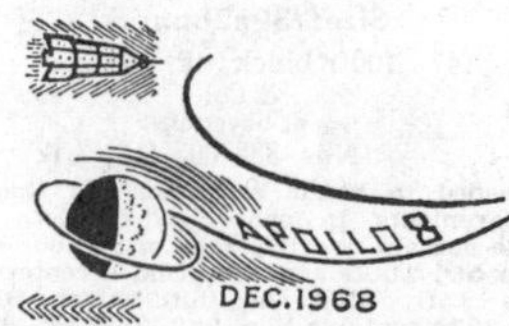

1969, Mar. 17 Litho. *Perf. 14x13½*

529	A52	30fr on 45fr multi.	50	50

530 A52 45fr multicolored 50 50
Nos. 529-530, C113-C115 (5) 5.40 3.70

Issued to commemorate the U.S. Apollo 8 mission, the first men in orbit around the moon, Dec. 21–27, 1968.

Nos. 529–530 also exist with surcharge and overprint in black. These sell for about 10% more.

Tarzan
A72

Designs: 30fr, Tarzan sitting in front of Pastoria Research Institute gate. 75fr, Tarzan and his family. 100fr, Tarzan sitting in a tree.

1969, June 6 Photo. *Perf. 13½*

531	A72	25fr org. & multi.	25	12
532	"	30fr bl. grn. & multi.	35	15
533	"	75fr yel. grn. & multi.	75	27
534	"	100fr yellow & multi.	1.20	45

Tarzan was a Guinean chimpanzee with superior intelligence and ability.

Campfire
A73

Designs: 25fr, Boy Scout and tents. 30fr, Marching Boy Scouts. 40fr, Basketball. 45fr, Senior Scouts, thatched huts and mountain. 50fr, Guinean Boy Scout badge.

1969, July 1

535	A73	5fr gold & multi.	10	3
536	"	25fr " "	25	8
537	"	30fr " "	30	10
538	"	40fr " "	45	18
539	"	45fr " "	50	17
540	"	50fr " "	60	27
		a. Min. sheet of 6	3.00	3.00
		Nos. 535-540 (6)	2.20	83

Issued to honor the Boy Scouts of Guinea. No. 540a contains one each of Nos. 535–540. Gold decorative margin with black inscription. Size: 120x136mm.

Launching Apollo 11
A74

Designs: 30fr, Earth showing Africa as seen from moon. 50fr, Separation of lunar landing module and spaceship. 60fr, Astronauts and module on moon. 75fr, Module on moon and earth. 100fr, Module leaving moon. 200fr, Splashdown.

1969, Aug. 20 Photo. *Perf. 13½*

Size: 34x55mm.

541	A74	25fr gold & multi.	20	8
		a. Pair	40	
542	"	30fr gold & multi.	30	10
		a. Pair	60	
543	A74	50fr gold & multi.	40	13
		a. Pair	80	
544	"	60fr gold & multi.	65	22
		a. Pair	1.30	
545	"	75fr gold & multi.	75	27
		a. Pair	1.50	

Size: 34x71mm.

546	A74	100fr gold & multi.	1.20	40
		a. Pair	2.40	

Size: 34x55mm.

547	A74	200fr gold & multi.	2.50	90
		a. Pair	5.00	
		Nos. 541-547 (7)	6.00	2.10
		Nos. 541a-547a (7)	12.00	6.82

Issued to commemorate man's first landing on the moon, July 20, 1969. U.S. astronauts Neil A. Armstrong and Col. Edwin E. Aldrin, Jr., with Lieut. Col. Michael Collins piloting Apollo 11.

The commemorative inscription on Nos. 541–547 is printed in French or English alternating in the sheet. Nos. 541a–547a are for se-tenant French and English inscribed stamps.

Harvest and ILO Emblem
A75

Designs (ILO Emblem and): 25fr, Power lines and blast furnaces. 30fr, Women in broadcasting studio. 200fr, Potters.

1969, Oct. 28 Photo. *Perf. 13½*

548	A75	25fr gold & multi.	25	8
549	"	30fr " "	30	8
550	"	75fr " "	75	22
551	"	200fr " "	2.25	75

Issued to commemorate the 50th anniversary of the International Labor Organization.

Mother and Sick Child
A76

Designs: 25fr, Sick child. 40fr, Girl receiving vaccination. 50fr, Boy receiving vaccination. 60fr, Mother receiving vaccination. 200fr, Edward Jenner, M.D.

1970, Jan. 15 Photo. *Perf. 13½*

552	A76	25fr multicolored	20	10
553	"	30fr "	30	13
554	"	40fr "	40	15
555	"	50fr "	60	27
556	"	60fr "	70	27
557	"	200fr "	2.25	1.15
		Nos. 552-557 (6)	4.45	2.07

Campaign against smallpox and measles.

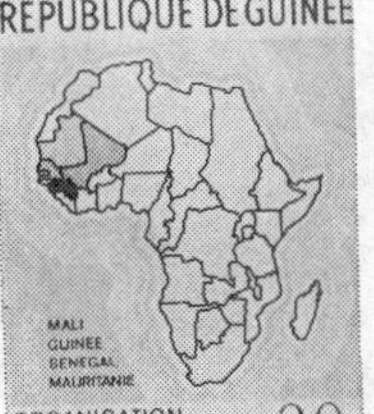

Map of Africa
A77

1970, Feb. 3 Litho. *Perf. 14½x14*

558	A77	30fr lt. blue & multi.	30	15
559	"	200fr lt. vio. & multi.	2.00	1.15

Meeting of statesmen of countries bordering on Senegal River: Mali, Guinea, Senegal and Mauritania.

Open Book and Radar—A78

1970, July 6 Litho. *Perf. 14*

560	A78	5fr lt. blue & black	5	3
561	"	10fr rose & black	10	5
562	"	50fr yellow & black	55	6
563	"	200fr lilac & black	2.00	1.10

International Telecommunications Day.

Lenin
A79

Designs: 20fr, Meeting with Lenin, by V. Serov. 30fr, Lenin Addressing Workers, by V. Serov. 40fr, Lenin with Red Guard Soldier and Sailor, by P. V. Vasiliev. 100fr, Lenin Speaking from Balcony, by P. V. Vasiliev. 200fr, Like 5fr.

1970, Nov. 16 Photo. *Perf. 13*

564	A79	5fr gold & multi.	5	5
565	"	20fr " "	25	10
566	"	30fr " "	35	13
567	"	40fr " "	55	15
568	"	100fr " "	1.25	40
569	"	200fr " "	2.50	1.00
		Nos. 564-569 (6)	4.95	1.83

Issued to commemorate the centenary of the birth of Lenin (1870–1924), Russian communist leader.

Phenecogrammus Interruptus—A80

Designs: Various fish from Guinea.

1971, Apr. 1 Photo. *Perf. 13*

570	A80	5fr gold & multi.	7	3
571	"	10fr " "	12	5
572	"	15fr " "	15	8
573	"	20fr " "	22	12
574	"	25fr " "	30	12
575	"	30fr " "	38	13
576	"	40fr " "	40	18
577	"	45fr " "	45	27
578	"	50fr " "	50	27
579	"	75fr " "	90	38
580	"	100fr " "	1.15	50
581	"	200fr " "	2.10	1.20
		Nos. 570-581 (12)	6.74	3.33

Violet-crested Touraco—A81

Birds: 20fr, European golden oriole. 30fr, Blue-headed coucal. 40fr, Northern shrike. 75fr, Vulturine guinea fowl. 100fr, Southern ground hornbill.

1971, June 18 Photo. *Perf. 13*

Size: 34x34mm.

582	A81	5fr gold & multi.	5	3
583	"	20fr " "	17	12
584	"	30fr " "	25	15
585	"	40fr " "	45	18
586	"	75fr " "	1.10	33
587	"	100fr " "	1.40	50
		Nos. 582-587, C116-C118 (9)	7.92	2.81

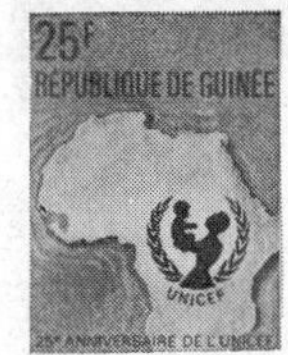

UNICEF Emblem, Map of Africa
A82

1971, Dec. 24 *Perf. 12x12½*

Map in Olive

588	A82	25fr orange & black	20	8
589	"	30fr pink & black	25	12
590	"	50fr gray grn. & blk.	50	15
591	"	60fr gray blue & blk.	65	22
592	"	100fr lilac rose & blk.	1.10	40
		Nos. 588-592 (5)	2.70	97

25th anniversary of the United Nations International Children's Fund (UNICEF).

Certain unlisted issues of Guinea, starting in 1972, are mentioned and briefly described in "For the Record" at the back of this volume.

Imaginary Prehistoric Space Creature—A83

Designs: Various imaginary prehistoric space creatures.

1972, Apr. 1 *Perf. 13½x13*

593	A83	5fr multicolored	5	3
594	"	20fr "	18	8
595	"	30fr "	22	12
596	"	40fr "	38	15
597	"	100fr "	90	45
598	"	200fr "	1.65	85
		Nos. 593-598 (6)	3.38	1.68

Black Boy, Men of 4 Races, Emblem—A84

Designs: 20fr, Oriental boy. 30fr, Indian youth. 50fr, Caucasian girl. 100fr, Men of 4 races and Racial Equality emblem.

1972, May 14 **Perf. 13x13½**

599	A84	15fr gold & multi.	12	6
600	"	20fr " "	15	10
601	"	30fr " "	22	12
602	"	50fr " "	40	18
603	"	100fr " "	75	38
		Nos. 599-603, C119 (6)	2.54	1.34

International Year Against Racial Discrimination, 1971.

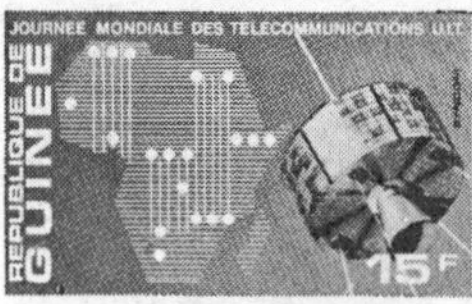

Map of Africa, Syncom Satellite
A85

Designs (Map of Africa and Satellites): 30fr, Relay. 75fr, Early Bird. 80fr, Telstar.

1972, May 17 **Litho.** **Perf. 13**

604	A85	15fr multicolored	12	8
605	"	30fr red org. & multi.	18	12
606	"	75fr green & multi.	55	30
607	"	80fr multicolored	70	45
		Nos. 604-607, C120-C121 (6)	3.80	2.08

4th World Telecommunications Day.

Carrier Pigeon, UPAF Emblem
A86

1972, July 10

608	A86	15fr brt. bl. & multi.	12	8
609	"	30fr multicolored	18	12
610	"	75fr lilac & multi.	55	30
611	"	80fr multicolored	70	45
		Nos. 608-611, C122-C123 (6)	4.25	2.30

10th anniversary of African Postal Union (UPAF).

Book Year Emblem, Reading Child
A87

Designs (Book Year Emblem and): 15fr, Book as sailing ship. 40fr, Young woman with flower and book. 50fr, Book as key. 75fr, Man reading and globe. 200fr, Book and laurel.

1972, Aug. 2 **Photo.** **Perf. 14x13½**

612	A87	5fr red & multi.	5	3
613	"	15fr multicolored	12	5
614	"	40fr yellow & multi.	30	12
615	"	50fr blue & multi.	45	18
616	"	75fr dk. red & multi.	75	45
617	"	200fr orange & multi.	1.35	85
		Nos. 612-617 (6)	3.02	1.68

International Book Year 1972.

Javelin, Olympic Emblems, Arms of Guinea
A88

1972, Aug. 26 **Photo.** **Perf. 13**

Multicolored

618	A88	5fr *shown*	5	3
619	"	10fr *Pole vault*	7	5
620	"	25fr *Hurdles*	18	10
621	"	30fr *Hammer throw*	22	12
622	"	40fr *Boxing*	38	15
623	"	50fr *Vaulting*	40	22
624	"	75fr *Running*	60	38
		Nos. 618-624, C124-C125 (9)	4.55	2.40

20th Olympic Games, Munich, Aug. 26–Sept. 11.

Nos. 588–592 Overprinted

1972, Sept. 28 **Photo.** **Perf. 12x12½**

Map in Olive

625	A82	25fr orange & black	18	8
626	"	30fr pink & black	22	12
627	"	50fr gray grn. & black	40	15
628	"	60fr gray blue & black	55	22
629	"	100fr lilac rose & black	70	40
		Nos. 625-629 (5)	2.05	97

U.N. Conference on Human Environment, Stockholm, June 5–16.

Dimitrov at Leipzig Trial
A89

1972, Sept. 28 **Perf. 13**

Gold, Dark Green & Black

630	A89	5fr *shown*	5	3
631	"	25fr *In Moabit Prison, 1933*	15	8
632	"	40fr *Writing his memoirs*	30	22
633	"	100fr *Portrait*	85	40

90th anniversary of the birth of George Dimitrov (1882–1949), Bulgarian Communist party leader and Premier.

Emperor Haile Selassie
A90

Syntomeida Epilais
A91

Design: 200fr, Emperor facing right.

1972, Oct. 2

634	A90	40fr black & multi.	33	27
635	"	200fr multicolored	1.65	1.00

80th birthday of Emperor Haile Selassie of Ethiopia.

1973, Mar. 5 **Photo.** **Perf. 14x13½**

Designs: Various insects.

Multicolored

636	A91	5fr *shown*	5	4
637	"	15fr *Ladybugs*	12	5
638	"	30fr *Green locust*	22	12
639	"	40fr *Honey bee*	30	18
640	"	50fr *Photinus pyralis*	38	22
641	"	200fr *Ancyluris formosissima*	1.65	1.10
		Nos. 636-641 (6)	2.72	1.71

Kwame Nkrumah
A92

Designs: Various portraits of Kwame Nkrumah.

1973, May 25 **Photo.** **Perf. 13½**

642	A92	1.50s lt. green, gold & brown	12	8
643	"	2.50s lt. green, gold & brown	22	12
644	"	5s lt. green, gold & brown	40	30
645	"	10s gold & dk. vio.	75	50

Organization for African Unity, 10th anniversary.

Institute for Applied Biology, Kindia—A93

Designs (WHO Emblem and): 2.50s, Technicians inoculating egg. 3s, Filling vaccine into ampules. 4s, Sterilization of vaccine. 5s, Assembling of vaccine and vaccination gun. 10s, Inocculation of steer. 20s, Vaccination of woman.

1973, Nov. 16 **Photo.** **Perf. 13½**

Size: 40x36mm.

646	A93	1s gold & multi.	8	8
647	"	2.50s " "	22	12
648	"	3s " "	30	18
649	"	4s " "	33	22

Size: 47½x31mm.

650	A93	5s gold & multi.	50	27
651	"	10s " "	75	40
652	"	20s " "	1.80	85
		Nos. 646-652 (7)	3.98	2.12

25th anniversary of World Health Organization.

Copernicus, Heliocentric System, Primeval Landscape—A94

Nicolaus Copernicus
A95

Designs (Copernicus and): 2s, Sun rising over volcanic desert, and spacecraft. 4s, Earth, moon and spacecraft. 5s, Moon scape and spacecraft. 10s, Jupiter and spacecraft. 20s, Saturn and heliocentric system.

1973, Dec. 17 **Photo.** **Perf. 13½**

653	A94	50c gold & multi.	5	4
654	"	2s " "	15	10
655	"	4s " "	27	12
656	"	5s " "	45	18
657	"	10s " "	90	40
658	"	20s " "	1.80	95
		Nos. 653-658 (6)	3.62	1.79

Souvenir Sheet

659	A95	Sheet of 4, multi.	10.00	10.00
	a.	20s Single stamp	2.00	1.50

500th anniversary of the birth of Nicolaus Copernicus (1473–1543), Polish astronomer. No. 659 contains 4 No. 659a; center label showing rocket and heliocentric system in gold margin. Size: 133x133mm.

Loading Bauxite on Freighter—A96

1974, Mar. 1 **Litho.** **Perf. 13½**

Multicolored

660	A96	4s *shown*	30	15
661	"	6s *Freight train*	45	30
662	"	10s *Mining*	75	45

Bauxite mining, Boke.

Clappertonia Ficifolia
A97

1974, May 20 **Photo.** **Perf. 13**

Size: 25x36mm.

Multicolored

663	A97	50c *shown*	5	4
664	"	1s *Rothmannia longiflora*	6	5
665	"	2s *Oncoba spinosa*	13	6
666	"	3s *Venidium fastuosum*	18	10

Size: 31x42mm.

667	A97	4s *Bombax costatum*	27	12
668	"	5s *Clerodendrum splendens*	38	18
669	"	7.50s *Combretuni grandiflorum*	55	30
670	"	10s *Mussaendra erythrophylla*	85	45

Size: 38x38mm. (Diamond)

671	A97	12s *Argemone mexicana*	1.00	60
		Nos. 663-671, C127-C129 (12)	9.97	5.30

Drummers, Pigeon, UPAF and UPU Emblems—A98

Designs (Carrier Pigeon, African Postal Union and UPU Emblems): 6s, Runner with letter stick. 7.50s, Monorail and mail truck. No. 675, Jet and ocean liner. No. 676, Balloon and dugout canoe. 20s, Satellites over earth.

1974, Oct. 16 Photo. *Perf. 13½x14*

672 A98 5s magenta & multi. 38 22
673 " 6s grn. & multi. 50 30
674 " 7.50s verm. & multi. 70 40
675 " 10s Prussian blue & multi. 85 70

Souvenir Sheets

Perf. 13½

676 A98 10s ocher & multi. 5.00
677 " Sheet of 4, multi. 8.50
a. 20s Single stamp 2.00 1.50

Centenary of Universal Postal Union. No. 676 contains one stamp; Size: 70x60mm. No. 677 contains 4 No. 677a. Size: 112x96mm. Both sheets have dark violet, gold and blue margins.

Rope Bridge A99

Designs (Pioneers): 2s, Field observation. 4s, Communication. 5s, Cooking in camp. 7.50s, Salute. 10s, Basketball.

1974, Nov. 22 Photo. *Perf. 14x13½*

678 A99 50c multicolored 5 4
679 " 2s " 15 8
680 " 4s " 27 12
681 " 5s " 38 15
682 " 7.50s " 55 30
683 " 10s " 75 45
a. Souvenir sheet of 2 2.50 2.50
Nos. 678-683 (6) 2.15 1.14

National Pioneer Movement. No. 683a contains one each of Nos. 682-683, violet and gold margin. Size: 77x60mm.

Souvenir Sheet

Fruit—A100

1974, Nov. 22 Photo. *Perf. 13x14*

684 A100 Sheet of 5, multi. 5.00
a. 4s *Limes* 40
b. 4s *Oranges* 40
c. 5s *Bananas* 50
d. 5s *Mangos* 50
e. 12s *Pineapple* 1.20

No. 684 has gold and green margin and black control number. Size: 127x113mm.

Chimpanzee A101

1975, May 14 Photo. *Perf. 13½*

Multicolored

685 A101 1s *shown* 6 5
686 " 2s *Impala* 12 8
687 " 3s *Wart hog* 20 12
688 " 4s *Kobus defassa* 27 18
a. Souvenir sheet of 4 1.00 1.00
689 A101 5s *Leopard* 30 22
690 " 6s *Greater kudu* 40 30
691 " 6.50s *Zebra* 45 33
692 " 7.50s *Cape buffalo* 50 38
a. Souvenir sheet of 4, air post 2.00 2.00
693 A101 8s *Hippopotamus* 55 40
694 " 10s *Lion* 65 45
695 " 12s *Black rhinoceros* 75 50
696 " 15s *Elephant* 1.00 75
a. Souvenir sheet of 4, air post 3.50 3.50
Nos. 685-696 (12) 5.25 3.76

No. 688a contains one each of Nos. 685-688; No. 692a four stamps similar to Nos. 689-692, inscribed "Poste Aerienne." Same inscription on Nos. 693-696 contained in sheet No. 696a. Sheets exist perf. and imperf., have gold and black margins. Size: 96x96mm.

Lions, Pipe Line and ADB Emblem A102

Designs (African Development Bank Emblem, Pipe Line and): 7s, Elephants. 10s, Male lions. 20s, Elephant and calf.

1975, June 16 Photo. *Perf. 13½*

697 A102 5s gold & multi. 38 22
698 " 7s " " 45 25
699 " 10s " " 70 38
700 " 20s " " 1.50 90

African Development Bank, 10th anniversary.

Women Musicians, IWY Emblem A103

Designs (IWY Emblem and): 7s, Women banjo and guitar players. 9s, Woman railroad shunter and train. 15s, Woman physician examining infant. 20s, Male and female symbols.

1976, Apr. 12 Photo. *Perf. 13½*

701 A103 5s multicolored 38 22
702 " 7s " 55 30
703 " 9s blue & multi. 70 45
704 " 15s multicolored 1.15 75
a. Souvenir sheet 1.25 1.25
705 A103 20s vio. bl. & multi. 1.50 1.10
a. Souvenir sheet of 4 6.50 6.50
Nos. 701-705 (5) 4.28 2.82

International Women's Year 1975. No. 704a contains one stamp similar to No. 704 with gold frame. Size: 70x82mm. No. 705a contains 4 stamps similar to No. 705 with gold frame. Size: 89x125mm. Both sheets have bluish gray margins with gold ornaments, IWY emblem and commemorative inscriptions in black or gold.

Woman Gymnast A104

Designs (Montreal Olympic Games Emblem and): 4s, Long jump. 5s, Hammer throw. 6s, Discus. 6.50s, Hurdles. 7s, Javelin. 8s, Running. 8.50s, Bicycling. 10s, High jump. 15s, Shot put. 20s, Pole vault. No. 717, Soccer. No. 718, Swimming.

1976, May 17 Photo. *Perf. 13½*

Size: 38x38mm.

706 A104 3s multicolored 22 12
707 " 4s grn. & multi. 30 15
708 " 5s yel. & multi. 38 22
709 " 6s multicolored 45 30
710 " 6.50s plum & multi. 50 30
711 " 7s blue & multi. 55 33
712 " 8s ultra. & multi. 60 38
713 " 8.50s org. & multi. 65 38
714 " 10s multicolored 75 45
715 " 15s " 1.15 75
716 " 20s " 1.50 1.10
717 " 25s grn. & multi. 2.00 1.20
Nos. 706-717 (12) 9.05 5.68

Souvenir Sheet

718 A104 25s multicolored 2.25 2.25

21st Olympic Games, Montreal, Canada, July 17-Aug. 1. No. 718 contains one stamp (32x32mm.); black and gray marginal inscription, lilac rose games emblem and black control number. Size: 82x62 mm. See No. C130.

A. G. Bell, Telephone, 1900 A105

Designs: 7s, Wall telephone, 1910. 12s, Syncom telecommunications satellite. No. 722, Telstar satellite. No. 723, Telephone switchboard operator, 1914.

1976, Nov. 15 Photo. *Perf. 13*

719 A105 5s multicolored 38 22
720 " 7s " 55 30
721 " 12s " 1.00 60
722 " 15s " 1.20 75
a. Souvenir sheet of 4 3.50 3.50

Souvenir Sheet

723 A105 15s multicolored 1.50 1.50

Centenary of first telephone call by Alexander Graham Bell, Mar. 10, 1876. No. 722a contains one each of Nos. 719-722. Size: 111x93mm. No. 723 contains one stamp; multicolored margin. Size: 70x59 mm.

Collybia Fusipes—A106

Mushrooms: 7s, Lycoperdon perlatum. 9s, Boletus edulis. 9.50s, Lactarius deliciosus. 11.50s, Agaricus campestris.

1977, Feb. 6 Photo. *Perf. 13*

Size: 48x26mm.

724 A106 5s multicolored 38 22
725 " 7s " 55 27
726 " 9s " 70 33
a. Souvenir sheet of 2 1.50 1.50
727 A106 9.50s multicolored 85 45

Size: 48x31mm.

728 A106 11.50s multi. 1.00 60
Nos. 724-728, C131-C133 (8) 6.53 3.57

No. 726a contains one each of Nos. 724 and 726; gold and multicolored margin shows morchella, black control number. Size: 116x87mm.

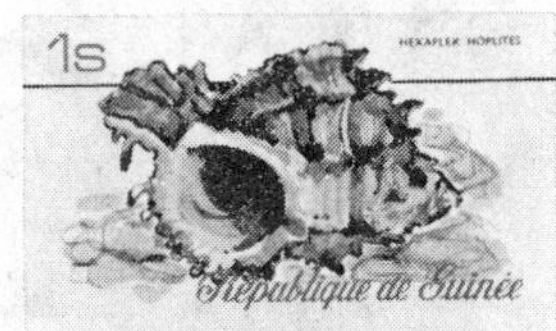

Hexaplex Hoplites—A107

Sea Shells: 2s, Perrona lineata. 4s, Marginella pseudofaba. 5s, Tympanotonos radula. 7s, Marginella strigata. 8s, Harpa doris. 10s, Demoulia pinguis. 20s, Bursa scrobiculator. 25s, Marginella adansoni.

1977, Apr. 25 Photo. *Perf. 13*

Size: 50x25mm.

729 A107 1s gold & multi. 10 6
730 " 2s " " 20 12
731 " 4s " " 40 25
732 " 5s " " 50 30
733 " 7s " " 70 42
734 " 8s " " 80 48

Size: 50x30mm.

735 A107 10s gold & multi. 1.00 60
736 " 20s " " 2.00 1.20
737 " 25s " " 2.50 1.50
Nos. 729-737 (9) 8.20 4.93

Farmers and Ox Plow A108

Designs: 5s, Pres. Touré addressing rally. 20s, Soldier driving farm tractor. 25s, Pres. Touré addressing U.N. General Assembly. 30s, 40s, Pres. Sékou Touré (vert.).

Perf. 13½x13, 13x13½

1977, May 14 Photogravure

738 A108 5s gold & multi. 50 30
739 " 10s " " 1.00 60
740 " 20s " " 2.00 1.20
741 " 25s " " 2.50 1.50
a. Souvenir sheet of 4 6.50 5.00
742 A108 30s gold & dk. brn. 3.00 1.80
743 " 40s gold & slate green 4.00 2.40
a. Souvenir sheet of 2 7.50 6.00
Nos. 738-743 (6) 13.00 7.80

Democratic Party of Guinea, 30th anniversary. No. 741a contains one each of Nos. 738-741; green and gold margin. Size: 122x97mm. No. 743a contains one each of Nos. 742-743; green and gold margins. Size: 97x77mm.

Nile Monitor—A109

Reptiles and Snakes: 4s, Frogs. 5s, Lizard (uromastix). 6s, Sand skink. 6.50s, Agama. 7s, Black-lipped spitting cobra. 8.50s, Ball python. 20s, Toads.

1977, Oct. 10 Photo. *Perf. 13½*

Size: 46x20mm.

744	A109	3s multicolored	30	18
745	"	4s "	40	25
746	"	5s "	50	30

Size: 46x30mm.

747	A109	6s multicolored	60	35
748	"	6.50s "	65	40
749	"	7s "	70	42
750	"	8.50s "	85	50
751	"	20s "	2.00	1.20
		Nos. 744-751, C134-C136 (11)	11.00	6.60

Eland—A110

Endangered Animals: 2s, Chimpanzee. 2.50s, Pygmy elephant. 3s, Lion. 4s, Palm squirrel. 5s, Hippopotamus. Each animal shown male, female and young.

1977, Dec. 12 Photo. *Perf. 14x13½*

Multicolored

752	A110	1s Strip of three	30	18
		a. Single stamp	10	
753	A110	2s Strip of three	60	35
		a. Single stamp	20	
754	A110	2.50s Strip of three	75	45
		a. Single stamp	25	
755	A110	3s Strip of three	90	55
		a. Single stamp	30	
756	A110	4s Strip of three	1.20	75
		a. Single stamp	40	
757	A110	5s Strip of three	1.50	90
		a. Single stamp	50	
		Nos. 752-757, C137-C142 (12 strips of 3)	22.35	13.33

Lenin Speaking, 1917 A111

Designs: 2.50s, First Lenin debate, Moscow. 7.50s, Lenin and people. 8s, Lenin in first parade on Red Square.

1978, Feb. 27 Photo. *Perf. 14*

758	A111	2.50s gold & multi.	25	15
759	"	5s " "	50	30
760	"	7.50s " "	75	45
761	"	8s " "	80	50
		Nos. 758-761, C143-C144 (6)	6.30	3.80

60th anniversary of Russian October Revolution.

SEMI-POSTAL STAMPS

Eye Examination
SP1

Microscopic Examination
SP2

Designs: 30fr+20fr, Medical laboratory. 40fr+20fr, Insect control. 100fr+100fr, Surgical operation.

Engraved and Lithographed.

1960 *Perf. 11½* **Unwmkd.**

B12	SP1	20fr+10fr ultra. & carmine	70	70
B13	"	30fr+20fr brown orange & vio.	70	70
B14	"	40fr+20fr rose lilac & blue	80	80
B15	SP2	50fr+50fr green & brown	1.35	1.35
B16	"	100fr+100fr lilac & green	1.75	1.75
		Nos. B12-B16 (5)	5.30	5.30

Issued for national health propaganda.

Nos. 194-195 Surcharged "1961" and New Value in Red or Orange.

1961, June 6 Photogravure

B17	A17	25fr+10fr multi. (R or O)	4.25	4.25
B18	"	50fr+20fr multi. (R or O)	4.25	4.25

Nos. B17-B18 exist with orange surcharges transposed: "1961 + 10FRS." on 50fr and "1961 + 20FRS." on 25fr.

Nos. 214-219 Surcharged in Green, Lilac, Orange or Blue: "POUR LA PROTECTION DE NOS ANIMAUX +5 FRS."

Photogravure, Surcharge Engraved

1961, Dec. 8

Multicolored Design; Granite Paper

B19	A20	5fr+5fr brt. green (G)	10	10
B20	"	10fr+5fr emerald (G)	15	10
B21	"	25fr+5fr lilac (L)	48	27
B22	"	40fr+5fr orange (O)	60	35
B23	"	50fr+5fr red org. (O)	80	50
B24	"	75fr+5fr ultra. (B)	1.20	70
		Nos. B19-B24 (6)	3.33	2.02

The surtax was for animal protection.

Nos. B12-B16 Overprinted in Red or Orange

Engraved and Lithographed

1962, Feb. *Perf. 11½* **Unwmkd.**

B25	SP1	20fr+10fr ultra. & carmine (R or O)	38	38
B26	"	30fr+20fr brown orange & violet (R or O)	50	50
B27	"	40fr+20fr rose lilac & blue (R or O)	55	55
B28	SP2	50fr+50fr green & brown (R or O)	1.20	1.20
B29	"	100fr+100fr lilac & green (R or O)	2.40	2.40
		Nos. B25-B29 (5)	5.03	5.03

Issued for the World Health Organization's drive to eradicate malaria.
No. B25 also exists with black overprint.

Nos. 223-228 Surcharged in Red: "POUR LA PROTECTION DE NOS OISEAUX + 5 FRS."

Photogravure, Surcharge Engraved

1962, May 14 *Perf. 13x14*

B30	A22	5fr+5fr rose lilac, sepia & blue	18	8
B31	"	10fr+5fr dp. orange, sepia & blue	18	12
B32	"	25fr+5fr cerise, sepia & blue	33	25
B33	"	40fr+5fr ochre, sepia & blue	50	35
B34	"	50fr+5fr lemon, sepia & blue	95	55
B35	"	75fr+5fr apple grn., sepia & bl.	2.00	1.10
		Nos. B30-B35 (6)	4.14	2.45

The surtax was for bird protection.

Nos. 232-233 Surcharged in Orange or Red and Overprinted: "Aide aux Réfugiés Algeriens"

1962, Nov. 1 Litho. *Perf. 13*

B36	A24	25fr+15fr multi.	60	60
B37	"	75fr+25fr "	1.20	1.20

Issued to help Algerian refugees.

AIR POST STAMPS

Lockheed Constellation—AP1

Design: 500fr, Plane on ground.

Lithographed and Engraved

1959, July 13 *Perf. 11½* **Unwmkd.**

Size: 52½x24mm.

C14	AP1	100fr deep carmine, ultramarine & emerald	1.50	1.00
C15	"	200fr emerald, brn. & lilac	2.10	1.50

Size: 56½x26mm.

C16	AP1	500fr multicolored	5.25	3.00

Doves with Letter and Olive Twig
AP2

1959, Oct. 16 Engraved *Perf. 13½*

C17	AP2	40fr blue	30	30
C18	"	50fr emerald	55	45
C19	"	100fr dk. car. rose	1.10	75
C20	"	200fr rose red	1.85	1.50
C21	"	500fr red orange	5.00	3.75
		Nos. C17-C21 (5)	8.80	6.75

Type of Regular Issue, 1959.

Engraved and Lithographed.

1959, Dec. 12 *Perf. 12*

Size: 44 x 26 mm.

C22	A16	50fr multicolored	70	60
C23	"	100fr "	1.00	75

Issued to commemorate the first anniversary of Guinea's admission to the United Nations.

Nos. C14–C16 Overprinted in Carmine, Orange or Blue: "Jeux Olympiques Rome 1960" and Olympic Rings.

1960 Litho. & Engr. *Perf. 11½*

Size: 52½x24mm.

C24 AP1 100fr multicolored (C or O) 4.00 3.00
C25 " 200fr multi. (Bl) 8.00 5.00

Size: 56½x26mm.

C26 AP1 500fr multicolored (C or O) 20.00 20.00

Issued to commemorate the 17th Olympic Games, Rome, Aug. 25–Sept. 11.

Nos. C22–C23 Overprinted XVème ANNIVERSAIRE DES NATIONS UNIES

Engraved & Lithographed

1961, Oct. 24 *Perf. 12*

C27 A16 50fr multicolored 70 55
C28 " 100fr " 1.00 80

United Nations, 15th anniversary.

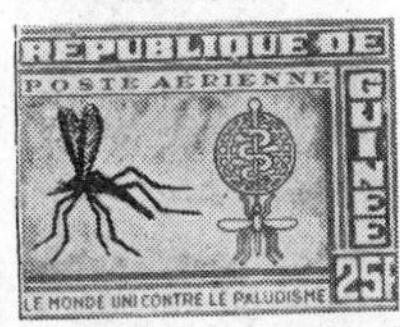

Mosquito and Malaria Eradication Emblem AP3

Engraved

1962, Apr. 7 *Perf. 10½* Unwmkd.

C29 AP3 25fr orange & black 40 22
C30 " 50fr carmine rose & black 55 38
C31 " 100fr green & black 1.10 70

Issued for the World Health Organization drive to eradicate malaria.

A souvenir sheet exists containing a 100fr green & sepia stamp, imperf. Sepia coat of arms in margin. Size: 102x76mm.

Musician Type of Regular Issue

Musical Instruments: 100fr, 200fr, Kora. 500fr, Balafon.

1962, June 15 Photo. *Perf. 13x13½*

C32 A26 100fr brt. pink, dk. carmine & Prussian blue 75 60
C33 " 200fr lt. & dk. ultra. & car. rose 1.50 90
C34 " 500fr dull orange, purple & Prus. blue 4.75 3.00

Nos. C17–C20 Overprinted in Carmine, Orange or Black: "La Conquête De L'Espace"

Engraved

1962, Nov. 15 *Perf. 13½* Unwmkd.

C35 AP2 40fr blue (C or O) 60 35
C36 " 50fr emerald (C or O) 60 35
C37 " 100fr dark carmine rose (B) 1.00 70
C38 " 200fr rose red (B) 1.85 1.40

Issued to commemorate the conquest of space. Two types of overprint: Straight lines on 40fr and 50fr in carmine, 100fr (black). Curved lines on 40fr and 50fr in orange, 200fr (black).

Bird Type of Regular Issue

Birds: 100fr, Hornbill. 200fr, White spoonbill. 500fr, Bateleur eagle.

1962, Dec. Photo. *Perf. 13x13½*

C41 A30 100fr multicolored 1.35 60
C42 " 200fr " 2.25 1.10
C43 " 500fr " 5.25 3.00

Sports Type of Regular Issue, 1963

Designs: 100fr, Running. 200fr, Bicycling. 500fr, Single sculls.

1963, Mar. 16 *Perf. 14*

C44 A32 100fr deep rose, sepia & grn. 1.00 45
C45 A32 200fr olive bister, ultra. & magenta 2.25 1.10
C46 " 500fr ocher, dk. blue & red 4.50 2.75

Butterfly Type of Regular Issue, 1963

Various Butterflies

1963, May 10 *Perf. 12* Unwmkd.

C47 A33 100fr citron, dark brown & gray 1.00 45
C48 " 200fr salmon pink, black & green 2.75 1.10
C49 " 500fr multicolored 5.25 2.50

Red Cross Type of Regular Issue

1963, July 25 Engraved *Perf. 10½*

C50 A35 25fr blk. & carmine 38 18

Centenary of International Red Cross.

Souvenir Sheet

Imperf.

C51 A35 100fr green & car. 2.25 2.25

No. C51 measures 102x76mm. and has green coat of arms in margin.

Nos. C14–C15 Overprinted:

PREMIER SERVICE DIRECT
CONAKRY-NEW YORK
PAN AMERICAN
30, JUILLET 1963

Lithographed and Engraved

1963, Oct. 28 *Perf. 11½* Unwmkd.

C52 AP1 100fr dp. carmine, ultra. & emerald 1.75 1.10
C53 " 200fr emerald, brn. & lilac 3.75 1.80

Issued to commemorate the first Pan American air service from Conakry to New York, July 30, 1963.

Fish Type of Regular Issue, 1964.

Designs: 100fr, African lyretail. 300fr, Six-barred epiplatys.

1964, Feb. 15 Litho. *Perf. 14x13½*

C54 A36 100fr green & multi. 1.10 60
C55 " 300fr brn. & multi. 3.00 1.50

Kennedy Type of Regular Issue, 1964

1964, Mar. 5 Engraved *Perf. 10½*

C56 A37 100fr multicolored 1.20 1.20

Issued in memory of John F. Kennedy. See note after No. 327.

Olympic Type of Regular Issue

Design: 100fr, Women's ice skating.

1964, May 15 Photo. *Perf. 13x12½*

C57 A39 100fr gold, brown org. & indigo 1.00 65

See note after No. 335.

Nos. C44–C46 Overprinted in Carmine or Orange: "Jeux Olympiques Tokyo 1964" and Olympic Rings.

1964, May 15 *Perf. 14* Unwmkd.

C58 A32 100fr deep rose, sepia & grn. (C or O) 1.75 1.35
C59 " 200fr olive bister, ultra. & magenta (C or O) 2.50 2.10
C60 " 500fr ocher, dark blue & red (C or O) 5.75 4.75

18th Olympic Games, Tokyo, Oct. 10–25.

Mrs. Roosevelt Type of Regular Issue, 1964

1964, June 1 Engraved *Perf. 10½*

C61 A40 50fr violet 60 40

See note after No. 339.

Souvenir Sheets

Unisphere, "Rocket Thrower" and Guinea Pavilion—AP4

Engraved

1964, Oct. 26 *Imperf.* Unwmkd.

C62 AP4 100fr dk. bl. & orge. 1.50 1.50
C63 " 200fr rose red & emerald 3.00 3.00

Issued to commemorate the New York World's Fair, 1964–65. Nos. C62–C63 contain one stamp each. Arms of Guinea and inscription in margin, orange on No. C62, emerald on No. C63. Size: 102x77mm. See Nos. C69–C70.

Nubian Monuments Type of Regular Issue, 1964

Design: 300fr, Queen Nefertari, Abu Simbel.

1964, Nov. 19 Photo. *Perf. 12*

C64 A42 300fr gold, dull red brn. & sal. 4.00 2.25

See note after No. 354.

Japanese Hostess, Plane and Map of Africa—AP5

1965, Jan. 18 *Perf. 12½x13*

C65 AP5 100fr gold, black & red lilac 1.50 50

Issued to commemorate the 18th Olympic Games, Tokyo, Oct. 10–25, 1964. Two multicolored souvenir sheets (200fr vert. and 300fr horiz.) exist, showing different views of Mt. Fuji. Sizes: 86x119mm., 119x86mm.

Mask Type of Regular Issue

Design: 300fr, Niamou mask from N'Zérékoré.

1965, Feb. 15 Photo. *Perf. 14*

C68 A44 300fr multicolored 3.50 1.35

World's Fair Type of 1964 Souvenir Sheets

1965, Mar. 24 Engraved *Imperf.*

C69 AP4 100fr grn. & brown 1.50 1.50
C70 " 200fr grn. & carm. rose 3.00 3.00

Nos. C69–C70 contain one stamp each; coat of arms and inscription in brown in margin of 100fr, in carmine rose in margin of 200fr. "1965" in green inscribed in margin of both sheets.

Handicraft Type of Regular Issue

Handicrafts: 100fr, Cabinetmaker. 300fr, Ivory carver.

1965, May 1 Photo. *Perf. 14*

C71 A45 100fr multicolored 90 50
C72 " 300fr " 3.00 1.20

ITU Type of Regular Issue, 1965

1965, May 17 Unwmkd.

C73 A46 100fr multicolored 1.00 45
C74 " 200fr " 2.50 75

Issued to commemorate the centenary of the International Telecommunication Union. Exist imperf.

ICY Type of Regular Issue, 1965

1965, Sept. 8 Engraved *Perf. 10½*

C75 A50 100fr bl. & yel. org. 1.25 50

International Cooperation Year, 1965.

West Facade, Polytechnic Institute AP6

Design: 200fr, North facade.

1965, Oct. 2 Photo. *Perf. 13½*

C76 AP6 200fr gold & multi. 2.25 1.20
C77 " 500fr " " 6.50 3.00

Seventh anniversary of independence.

Type of Regular Issue, 1965

Designs: 100fr, Ranger VII approaching moon (vert.). 200fr, Launching of Ranger VII, Cape Kennedy (vert.).

1965, Nov. 15 Litho. *Perf. 13½x14*

C78 A52 100fr rose red, yellow & dk. brown 1.00 45
C79 " 200fr multicolored 2.50 90

Issued to publicize the efforts to reach the moon.

Dancer Type of Regular Issue, 1966

Design: 100fr, Kouyate Kandia, national singer (horiz.).

1966, Jan. 5 Photo. *Perf. 13½*

Size: 36x28½mm.

C80 A53 100fr multicolored 1.10 50

Festival of African Art and Culture.

Engraved Overprint on No. C65

1966, Mar. 14 Photo. *Perf. 12½x13*

C81 AP5 100fr gold, black & red lilac 1.20 55

Issued to commemorate the Fourth Pan Arab Games, Cairo, Sept. 2–11, 1965. The same overprint was applied to two souvenir sheets noted after No. C65 (red ovpt. on 200fr, black ovpt. on 300fr).

Engraved Dark Blue Overprint on No. C64: "CENTENAIRE DU TIMBRE / CAIRE 1966"

1966, March 14 *Perf. 12*

C82 A42 300fr gold, dull red brn. & sal. 3.00 1.80

Centenary of first Egyptian postage stamp.

Scenic Type of Regular Issue

View: Boulbinet Lighthouse.

1966, Apr. 4 *Perf. 13½*

C83 A54 100fr multicolored 1.10 50

See also Nos. C90–C91.

Nos. C76–C77 Overprinted in Blue or Yellow

1966, May 2 Photo. *Perf. 13½*

C84 AP6 200fr multi. (Bl) 2.00 1.35
C85 " 500fr " (Y) 4.75 3.00

See note after No. 421.

Woman-Flower Type of Regular Issue

Designs: Women and flowers of Guinea.

1966, May 30 Photo. *Perf. 13½*

Size: 28x34mm.

C86 A56 200fr multicolored 2.50 90
C87 " 300fr " 4.00 1.65

Snake Type of Regular Issue

Designs: 200fr, Pastoria Research Institute. 300fr, Men holding rock python.

1967, May 15 Litho. *Perf. 13½*

Size: 56x20mm.

C88 A61 200fr multicolored 2.00 1.10
a. Souv. sheet of 3 6.00 5.00
C89 " 300fr multicolored 3.50 1.60

Issued to publicize the Research Institute for Applied Biology (Pastoria). No. C88a contains one each of Nos. 471, 474 and C88. Yellow margin with black inscription. Size: 105x125mm.

Scenic Type of Regular Issue

Views: 100fr, House of explorer Olivier de Sanderval. 200fr, Conakry.

1967, June 20 Photo. *Perf. 13½*

C90 A54 100fr multicolored 90 60
C91 " 200fr " 2.00 1.10

Elephant Type of Regular Issue, 1967

1967, Sept. 28 Photo. *Perf. 13½*

C92 A63 200fr gold & multi. 2.00 1.00

Issued to commemorate the 20th anniversary of the Democratic Party of Guinea.

Nos. C83 and C90–C91 Overprinted with Lions Emblem and: "AMITIE DES PEUPLES GRACE AU TOURISME 1917–1967"

1967, Nov. 6

C93 A54 100fr multi. (#C83) 1.20 60
C94 " 100fr " (#C90) 1.20 60
C95 " 200fr " (#C91) 2.25 1.15

50th anniversary of Lions International.

Detail from Mural by José Vela Zanetti—AP7

Family, Mural by Per Krohg AP8

The Designs of the 30fr, 50fr and 200fr show mankind's struggle for a lasting peace after the mural in the lobby of the U.N. Conference Building, N.Y. The designs of the 100fr and of Nos. C98a–C98b show mankind's hope for the future after a mural in the U.N. Security Council Chamber.

1967, Nov. 11

C96 AP7 30fr multicolored 35 15
C97 " 50fr " 45 22
C98 AP8 100fr multicolored 1.00 45
a. Souv. sheet of 3, English inscription 2.25 2.25
b. Souv. sheet of 3, French inscription 2.25 2.25
C99 AP7 200fr multicolored 2.00 70

Nos. C98a and C98b each contain a 100fr stamp similar to No. C98 and two 50fr stamps showing festival scenes. The 50fr stamps have not been issued individually. Size: 126x84mm.

People and Dwellings Type of Regular Issue

Design: 300fr, People and village of Les Bassari, Kundara Region.

1968, Apr. 1 Photo. *Perf. 14x13½*

Size: 57x36mm.

C100 A66 300fr gold & multi. 3.00 1.20

Legends Type of Regular Issue

Designs: 70fr, The Girl and the Hippopotamus. 100fr, Old Faya's Inheritance (vert.). 200fr, Soumangourou Kante Killed by Djegue (woman on horseback). 300fr, Little Gouné, Son of the Lion (vert.).

1968 Photogravure *Perf. 13½*

C101 A67 70fr multicolored 75 18
C102 " 100fr multicolored 1.20 30
C103 " 200fr multicolored 2.50 55
a. Souv. sheet of 4 5.50 5.50
C104 " 300fr multicolored 3.50 1.25

Issued in sheets of 10 plus 2 labels. No. C103a contains 4 imperf. stamps similar to Nos. 510–511 and C102–C103; yellow and gray label, blue border and black commemorative inscription. Size: 105x140mm.

For souvenir sheet see No. 509a.

Issue dates: May 16, Nos. C102–C103. Sept. 16, Nos. C101, C104.

Animal Type of Regular Issue

African Animals: 100fr, Lions. 200fr, Elephant.

1968, Nov. 25 Photo. *Perf. 13½*

Size: 49x35mm.

C105 A68 100fr gold & multi. 1.35 45
C106 " 200fr " " 2.25 90

For souvenir sheet see No. 518a.

Robert F. Kennedy Type of Regular Issue, 1968

Portraits: 50fr, Senator Robert F. Kennedy. 100fr, Rev. Martin Luther King, Jr. 200fr, Pres. John F. Kennedy.

1968, Dec. 16

C107 A69 50fr yel. & multi. 50 15
C108 " 100fr multicolored 1.10 30
C109 " 200fr " 2.40 70

Issued to honor Robert F. Kennedy, John F. Kennedy and Martin Luther King, Jr. as martyrs of liberty.

The stamps are printed in sheets of 15 (3x5) containing 10 stamps and five green and gold center labels. Sheets come either with English or French inscriptions on label.

Olympic Type of Regular Issue

Designs (Sculpture and): 100fr, Gymnast on vaulting horse. 200fr, Gymnast on rings. 300fr, High jump.

1969, Feb. 1 Photo. *Perf. 13½*

C110 A71 100fr multicolored 1.00 38
C111 " 200fr " 2.00 60
C112 " 300fr " 3.50 90

Issued to commemorate the 19th Olympic Games, Mexico City, Oct. 12–27.

Nos. C78–C79 Surcharged and Overprinted in Red

1969, Mar. 17 Litho. *Perf. 13½x14*

C113 A52 25fr on 200fr multi. 50 20
C114 " 100fr multicolored 1.40 1.00
C115 " 200fr multicolored 2.50 1.50

See note after No. 530.

Nos. C113–C115 also exist with surcharge and overprint in orange (25fr, 200fr) or black (100fr). These sell for a small premium.

Bird Type of Regular Issue

Birds: 50fr, Violet-crested touraco. 100fr, European golden oriole. 200fr, Vulturine guinea fowl.

1971, June 18 Photo. *Perf. 13*

Size: 41x41mm.

C116 A81 50fr gold & multi. 80 30
C117 " 100fr " " 1.20 45
C118 " 200fr " " 2.50 75

Racial Equality Year Type of Regular Issue

Design: 100fr, Men of 4 races and racial equality emblem (like No. 603).

1972, May 14 Photo. *Perf. 13x13½*

C119 A84 100fr gold & multi. 90 50

International Year Against Racial Discrimination.

Satellite Type of Regular Issue

Designs: 100fr, Map of Africa and Relay. 200fr, Map of Africa and Early Bird.

1972, May 17 Litho. *Perf. 13*

C120 A85 100fr yel. & multi. 75 38
C121 " 200fr multicolored 1.50 75

4th World Telecommunications Day.

Postal Union Type of Regular Issue

Designs: 100fr, 200fr, Air mail envelope and UPAF emblem.

1972, July 10

C122 A86 100fr multicolored 90 45
C123 " 200fr " 1.80 90

10th anniversary of African Postal Union (UPAF).

Olympic Type of Regular Issue

1972, Aug. 26 Photo. *Perf. 13*

Multicolored

C124 A88 100fr *Gymnast on rings* 1.00 45
C125 " 200fr *Bicycling* 1.65 90

Souvenir Sheet

C126 A88 300fr *Soccer* 2.75 2.75

20th Olympic Games, Munich, Aug. 26–Sept. 11. No. C126 contains one stamp and has multicolored margin. Size: 110x74½mm.

Flower Type of 1974

1974, May 20 Photo. *Perf. 13*

Multicolored

Size: 38x38mm. (Diamond)

C127 A97 20s *Thunbergia alata* 1.35 70
C128 " 25s *Diascia barberae* 1.65 90
C129 " 50s *Kigelia africana* 3.50 1.80

Two air post souvenir sheets, type A101, are listed as Nos. 692a and 696a.

Olympic Games Type of 1976

Souvenir Sheet

Design: 25s, Soccer.

1976, May 17 Photo. *Perf. 13½*

C130 A104 Souvenir sheet of 4, multicolored 10.00 10.00

21st Olympic Games, Montreal, Canada, July 17–Aug. 1. No. C130 contains four 25s stamps (32x32mm.); black and gray marginal inscription, lilac rose games emblem and black control number. Size: 82x112½mm.

Mushroom Type of 1977

Mushrooms: 10s, Morchella esculenta. 12s, Lepiota procera. 15s, Cantharellus cibarius.

1977, Feb. 6 Photo. *Perf. 13*

Size: 48x31mm.

C131 A106 10s multicolored 85 45
C132 " 12s " 1.00 55
C133 " 15s " 1.20 70

Reptile Type of 1977

Reptiles: 10s, Flap-necked chameleon. 15s, Nile crocodiles. 25s, Painted tortoise.

1977, Oct. 10 Photo. *Perf. 13½*

Size: 46x30mm.

C134 A109 10s multicolored 1.00 60
C135 " 15s " 1.50 90
C136 " 25s " 2.50 1.50

Animal Type of 1977

Endangered Animals: 5s, Eland. 8s, Pygmy elephant. 9s, Hippopotamus. 10s, Chimpanzee. 12s, Palm squirrel. 13s, Lion. Male, female and young of each animal shown.

1977, Dec. 12 Photo. *Perf. 14x13½*

Gold & Multicolored

C137 A110 5s Strip of three 1.50 90
a. Single stamp 50
C138 A110 8s Strip of three 2.40 1.40
a. Single stamp 80
C139 A110 9s Strip of three 2.70 1.60
a. Single stamp 90
C140 A110 10s Strip of three 3.00 1.80
a. Single stamp 1.00
C141 A110 12s Strip of three 3.60 2.10
a. Single stamp 1.20
C142 A110 13s Strip of three 3.90 2.35
a. Single stamp 1.30
Nos. C137–C142 (6 strips of 3) 17.10 10.15

Russian Revolution Type, 1978

Designs: 10s, Russian ballet. 30s, Pushkin Monument.

1978, Feb. 27 Photo. *Perf. 14*

C143 A111 10s gold & multi. 1.00 60
C144 " 30s " 3.00 1.80

60th anniversary of Russian October Revolution.

POSTAGE DUE STAMPS

D5

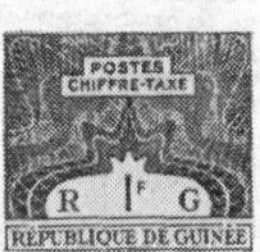

D6

Lithographed.

1959 *Perf. 11½* Unwmkd.

J36 D5 1fr emerald 5 5
J37 " 2fr lilac rose 6 6
J38 " 3fr brown 10 10
J39 " 5fr blue 25 25
J40 " 10fr orange 90 90
J41 " 20fr rose lilac 1.65 1.65
Nos. J36–J41 (6) 3.01 3.01

1960 Engraved. *Perf. 13½*

J42 D6 1fr dark carmine 20 20
J43 " 2fr brown orange 20 20
J44 " 3fr dark carmine rose 40 30
J45 " 5fr bright green 70 60
J46 " 10fr dark brown 1.35 1.00
J47 " 20fr dull blue 2.75 2.25
Nos. J42–J47 (6) 5.60 4.55

GUINEA-BISSAU

LOCATION—West coast of Africa between Senegal and Guinea.
GOVT.—Republic.
AREA—13,948 sq. mi.
POP.—540,000 (est. 1977).
CAPITAL—Bissau.

Guinea-Bissau, the former Portuguese Guinea, attained independence Sept. 10, 1974. The state includes the Bissagos Islands.

100 Centavos = 1 Escudo
100 Centavos = 1 Peso

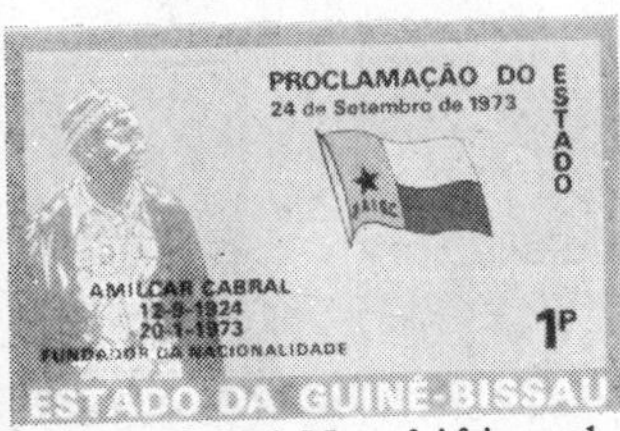

Amilcar Cabral, Map of Africa and Flag—A27

Design: Flag of the PAIGC (African Party of Independence of Guinea-Bissau and Cape Verde) shows location of Guinea-Bissau on map of Africa.

1974, Sept. 10 Litho. ***Perf. 11x10½***

345 A27 1p brn. & multi.
346 " 2.50p " "
347 " 5p " "
348 " 10p " "
Nos. 345-348 (4) *20.00*

First anniversary of Proclamation of Independence, Sept. 24, 1973.

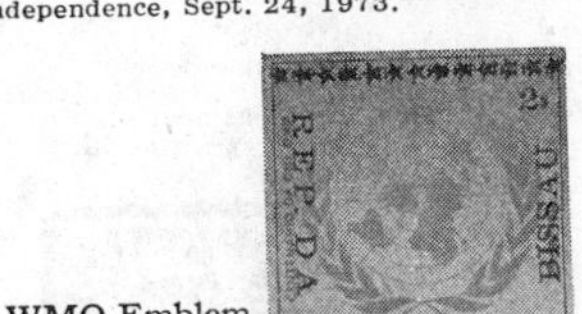

WMO Emblem A28

Portuguese Guinea No. 344 Overprinted in Black

1975 Lithographed ***Perf. 13***

349 A28 2e brown & multi. 30 25

No. 349 exists with overprint in brown.

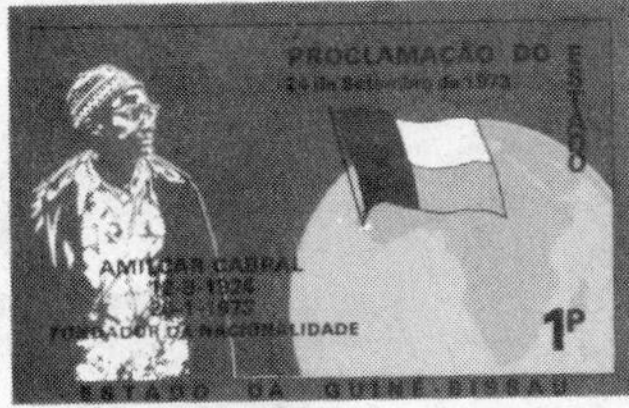

Amilcar Cabral, Map of Africa, Flag A29

1975 Lithographed ***Perf. 11***

350 A29 1p brn. & multi.
351 " 2.50p " "
352 " 5p " "
353 " 10p " "
Nos. 350-353 (4) *10.00*

Flag and Arms of Guinea-Bissau and Amilcar Cabral—A30

Designs: (Flag, Arms and): 2e, No. 358, Family. 3e, 5e, Pres. Luiz Cabral. No. 359, like 1e.

1975, Sept. ***Perf. 14***

354 A30 1e yellow & multi. 8
355 " 2e multicolored 12
356 " 3e red & multi. 20
357 " 5e yellow & multi. 40
358 " 10e red & multi. 75
359 " 10e bright green & multicolored 75
Nos. 350-355 (6) 2.30

Amilcar Cabral's 51st birth anniversary (1e, No. 359); African Party of Independence of Guinea-Bissau and Cape Verde, 19th anniversary (2e, No. 358); Proclamation of Independence, 2nd anniversary (3e, 5e).

Cabral, Guinean Mother and Children A31

1976, Aug. Litho. ***Perf. 13½***

360 A31 3p multicolored 20 12
361 " 5p " 32 18
362 " 6p " 40 25
363 " 10p " 65 40

3rd anniversary of assassination of Amilcar Cabral (1924-1973), revolutionary leader.

Cabral Addressing U.N. General Assembly A32

Design: 50c, Cabral and guerrilla fighters.

1977, July Litho. ***Perf. 13½***

364 A32 50c multicolored 6
365 " 3.50p " 42

Torch and Party Emblem A33

Congress Emblem A34

1977, Sept. Litho. ***Perf. 14***

366 A33 3p yellow & multi. 36
367 " 15p sal. & multi. 1.80
368 " 50p light green & multicolored 6.00

African Party of Independence of Guinea-Bissau and Cape Verde, 20th anniversary.

1977, Nov. 15 Litho. ***Perf. 14***

369 A34 3.50p multicolored 50

3rd PAIGC Congress (Party of International Action), Bissau, Nov. 15-20.

Antenna, ITU Emblem A35

1978, May 17 Litho. ***Perf. 13½***

370 A35 3.50p silver & multi. 42
371 " 10p gold & multi. 1.20

10th World Telecommunications Day.

Boy A36

Designs: 3p, Infant and grandfather. 5p, Boys. 30p, Girls.

1978 ***Perf. 14***

372 A36 50c yel. grn. & dk. bl. 6
373 " 3p claret & car. rose 36
374 " 5p ocher & brown 60
375 " 30p car. & ocher 3.60

Children's Day.

AIR POST STAMPS

Nos. 364-365 Surcharged with New Value and "CORREIO AEREO" in Black on Silver Panels

1978 Litho. ***Perf. 13½***

C10 A32 15p on 3.50p multi. 1.80
C11 " 30p on 50c " 3.60

HAITI

(hä'tĭ)

LOCATION – In the western part of Hispaniola, West Indies.
GOVT.—Republic.
AREA—10,714 sq. mi.
POP.—4,750,000 (est. 1977).
CAPITAL—Port-au-Prince.

100 Centimes = 1 Piastre (1906)
100 Centimes = 1 Gourde

Liberty Head
A1 A2

Typographed.

1881 *Imperf.* **Unwmkd.**

1	A1	1c vermilion, *yellowish*	3.50	2.50
2	"	2c dark violet, *pale lilac*	5.00	3.50
3	"	3c bistre, *pale bistre*	9.00	4.00
4	A2	5c green, *greenish*	15.00	7.00
5	A1	7c blue, *grayish*	10.00	2.00
6	"	20c red brown, *yellowish*	40.00	17.50

Nos. 1–6 were printed from plate I, Nos. 7–13 from plates II and III.

1882 *Perf. 13½.*

7	A1	1c vermilion, *yellowish*	3.00	1.00
		a. Vert. pair, imperf. horiz.		
		b. Horiz. pair, imperf. vert.	70.00	
		c. Horiz. pair, imperf. btwn.	70.00	
		d. Vert. pair imperf. btwn.	60.00	60.00
8	A1	2c dark violet, *pale lilac*	5.00	1.75
		a. 2c dark violet	6.50	4.50
		b. 2c red violet, *pale lilac*	5.00	2.00
		c. Horiz. or vert. pair, imperf. vert.	65.00	
		e. Horiz. or vert. pair, imperf. between	75.00	75.00
9	A1	3c bistre, *pale bistre*	6.00	3.00
		a. Horiz. pair, imperf. vert.		
10	A2	5c green, *greenish*	4.00	1.00
		a. 5c yellow green, *greenish*	4.00	1.00
		b. 5c deep green, *greenish*	4.00	1.00
		c. Horiz. pair, imperf. vert.	60.00	
		d. Horiz. or vert. pr., imperf. btwn.		80.00
11	A1	7c blue, *grayish*	6.00	1.50
		a. Horiz. pair, imperf. between		
12	A1	7c ultra., *grayish*	8.00	2.00
		a. Vert. pair, imperf. between		
		b. Horiz. pair, imperf. vert.		
13	A1	20c pale brown, *yellowish*	4.50	1.25
		a. 20c red brown, *yellowish*	10.00	2.50
		b. Horiz. pair, imperf. vert.		55.00
		c. Vert. pair, imperf. horiz.		65.00
		d. Horiz. or vert. pair, imperf. between	70.00	65.00

A3 A4

1886–87 *Perf. 13½*

18	A3	1c vermilion, *yellowish*	3.50	1.25
		a. Horiz. pair, imperf. vert.		80.00
		b. Horiz. pair, imperf. between	75.00	75.00
		c. Vert. pair, imperf. between	135.00	
19	A3	2c dark violet, *lilac*	30.00	5.00
20	A4	5c green ('87)	12.00	1.50

Differences between Nos. 18–20 (which were printed from new dies) and the preceding issues are too small to illustrate clearly. These stamps can be identified by the numerals of value, which are larger than the earlier ones and differ slightly in shape. Nos. 18 and 19 show crossed lines of dots on face.

Stamps perf. 14, 16 are forgeries which were made to defraud the government and used freely in the mails.

General Louis Etienne Félicité Salomon
A5

1887 **Engraved.** ***Perf. 14***

21	A5	1c lake	35	35
22	"	2c violet	75	60
23	"	3c blue	60	40
24	"	5c green	2.50	40

Some experts believe the imperfs. of Nos. 21–24 are probably plate proofs. Price per pair, $15.

No. 23 Handstamp Surcharged in Red

a

1890

25	A5	2c on 3c blue	50	40

This surcharge being handstamped is to be found double, inverted, etc. This applies to succeeding surcharged issues.

Coat of Arms — A7
Coat of Arms (Leaves Drooping) — A9

1891 ***Perf. 13.***

26	A7	1c violet	30	25
27	"	2c blue	60	30
28	"	3c gray lilac	70	35
		a. 3c slate	75	40
29	"	5c orange	2.50	30
30	"	7c red	5.00	2.50
		Nos. 26–30 (5)	9.10	3.70

Nos. 26–30 exist imperf. Price of unused pairs, each $20.
The 2c, 3c and 7c exist imperf. vertically.

No. 28 Surcharged type "a" in Red.

1892

31	A7	2c on 3c gray lilac	1.00	90
		a. 2c on 3c slate	1.00	90

1893–95 ***Perf. 14x13½***

32	A9	1c lilac	18	12
33	"	2c deep blue	18	12
		a. Imperf., pair	4.50	
34	"	3c gray	50	40
		b. Imperf., pair	4.50	
35	"	5c orange	1.75	25
36	"	7c red	25	25
		a. Imperf., pair	4.50	
37	"	20c brown	70	50
		Nos. 32–37 (6)	3.56	1.64

1896 **Re-engraved.** ***Perf. 13½.***

38	A9	1c light blue	15	15
39	"	2c red brown	30	20
40	"	3c lilac brown	20	15
41	"	5c slate green	20	15
42	"	7c dark gray	20	20
43	"	20c orange	25	25
		Nos. 38–43 (6)	1.30	1.10

The stamps of 1893–95 are 24¼mm. high, those of 1896 are 23½mm. On the 1893–95 stamps the letters of "REPUBLIQUE D'HAITI" are 1¾mm. high; on the 1896 stamps they are 1½mm. high. The stamps of the two issues may be readily distinguished by their colors.

Nos. 38–43 exist imperf. Price of unused pairs, each $3.

Nos. 37 and 43 Surcharged type "a" in Red.

1898

44	A9	2c on 20c brown	75	50
45	"	2c on 20c orange	45	35

Coat of Arms
A11

Wmk. 131

1898 ***Perf. 11*** **Wmkd. RH. (131)**

46	A11	1c ultramarine	1.25	1.00
47	"	2c brown carmine	35	20
48	"	3c dull violet	1.00	75
49	"	5c dark green	35	20
50	"	7c gray	2.50	2.00
51	"	20c orange	2.50	2.00
		Nos. 46–51 (6)	7.95	6.15

All values exist imperforate.

Pres. T. Augustin Simon Sam — A12
Coat of Arms — A13

1898–99 ***Perf. 12*** **Unwmkd.**

52	A12	1c ultramarine	12	12
53	A13	1c yel. green ('99)	12	12
54	A12	2c deep orange	12	12
55	A13	2c car. lake ('99)	12	12
56	A12	3c green	15	12
57	A13	4c red	20	12
58	A12	5c red brown	15	12
59	A13	5c pale blue ('99)	12	8
60	A12	7c gray	15	12
61	A13	8c carmine	20	12
62	"	10c orange red	18	12
63	"	15c olive green	65	40
64	A12	20c black	60	45
65	"	50c rose brown	70	45
66	"	1g red violet	2.00	2.00
		Nos. 52–66 (15)	5.58	4.58

Stamps of 1898–99 Handstamped in Black

MAI
G^t P^re
1902

1902

67	A12	1c ultramarine	50	50
68	A13	1c yellow green	40	20
69	A12	2c deep orange	75	75
70	A13	2c carmine lake	40	15
71	A12	3c green	40	40
72	A13	4c red	50	50
73	A12	5c red brown	1.50	1.50
74	A13	5c pale blue	40	40
75	A12	7c gray	75	75
76	A13	8c carmine	75	75
77	"	10c orange red	75	75
78	"	15c olive green	3.75	2.75
79	A12	20c black	3.75	3.50
80	"	50c rose brown	10.00	5.00
81	"	1g red violet	17.50	15.00
		Nos. 67–81 (15)	42.10	32.90

Many excellent forgeries exist of this overprint.

Centenary of Independence Issues.

Coat of Arms — A14
Pierre D. Toussaint L'Ouverture — A15

Emperor Jean Jacques Dessalines — A16
President Alexandre Sabes Pétion — A17

1904 **Engraved** ***Perf. 13½, 14***

82	A14	1c green	20	15

Center Engr., Frame Litho.

83	A15	2c rose & black	20	15
84	"	5c dull blue & black	20	15
85	A16	7c plum & black	20	15
86	"	10c yellow & black	20	15
87	A17	20c slate & black	20	15
88	"	50c olive & black	20	15
		Nos. 82–88 (7)	1.40	1.05

Nos. 82 to 88 exist imperforate.
Nos. 83–88 exist with centers inverted. Some are known with head omitted.

Same Handstamped in Blue

1904

89	A14	1c green	25	25
90	A15	2c rose & black	30	30
91	"	5c dull bl. & black	30	30
92	A16	7c plum & black	35	35
93	"	10c yellow & black	35	35
94	A17	20c slate & black	35	35
95	"	50c olive & black	35	35
		Nos. 89–95 (7)	2.25	2.25

Two dies were used for the handstamped overprint on Nos. 89–95. Letters and figures are larger on one than on the other. All values exist imperforate.

President Pedro Nord-Alexis
A18

1904 **Engraved**

96	A18	1c green	5	5
97	"	2c carmine	5	5
98	"	5c dark blue	5	5
99	"	10c orange brown	6	6
100	"	20c orange	6	10
101	"	50c claret	12	12
		a. Tête bêche pair	10.00	
		Nos. 96–101 (6)	39	43

Nos. 96 to 101 exist imperforate.

Reprints or very accurate imitations of this issue exist, including No. 101a. They are printed in very bright colors on very white paper and are found both perforated and imperforate.

Same Handstamped in Blue

1904

No.	Type	Description	Unused	Used
102	A18	1c green	50	35
103	"	2c carmine	50	35
104	"	5c dark blue	50	35
105	"	10c orange brown	50	35
106	"	20c orange	50	45
107	"	50c claret	50	45
		Nos. 102-107 (6)	3.00	2.30

The note after No. 95 applies also to Nos. 102–107 inclusive. All values exist imperforate.

Regular Issue of 1904 Handstamp Surcharged in Black:

1906

No.	Type	Description	Unused	Used
108	A18	1c on 20c orange	20	15
108C	"	1c on 50c claret	800.00	
109	"	2c on 50c claret	20	15

No. 108C is known only with inverted surcharge.

Stamps of 1898–99 Handstamped in Red

1906

No.	Type	Description	Unused	Used
110	A12	1c ultramarine	1.00	75
111	A13	1c yellow green	60	60
112	A12	2c deep orange	2.00	2.00
113	A13	2c carmine lake	1.25	1.25
114	A12	3c green	1.25	1.25
115	A13	4c red	6.00	5.00
116	A12	5c red brown	6.00	5.00
117	A13	5c pale blue	75	50
118	A12	7c gray	4.00	4.00
119	A13	8c carmine	75	75
120	"	10c orange red	1.50	1.00
121	"	15c olive green	1.75	1.25
122	A12	20c black	5.00	4.00
123	"	50c rose brown	5.00	3.50
124	"	1g red violet	9.00	7.50
		Nos. 110-124 (15)	45.85	38.35

Forgeries of this overprint are plentiful.

Coat of Arms
A19

President Nord-Alexis
A20

Market at Port-au-Prince
A21

Sans Souci Palace
A22

Independence Palace at Gonaives
A23

Entrance to Catholic College at Port-au-Prince
A24

Monastery and Church at Port-au-Prince
A25

Seat of Government at Port-au-Prince
A26

Presidential Palace at Port-au-Prince—A27

For Foreign Postage.
(centimes de piastre)

1906–13 *Perf. 12*

No.	Type	Description	Unused	Used
125	A19	1c de p green	20	15
126	A20	2c de p vermilion	40	20
127	A21	3c de p brown	60	20
128	"	3c de p orange yellow ('11)	3.50	3.00
129	A22	4c de p carmine lake	60	30
130	"	4c de p light olive green ('13)	6.00	5.00
131	A20	5c de p dark blue	2.00	20
132	A23	7c de p gray	1.25	75
133	"	7c de p orange red ('13)	20.00	17.50
134	A24	8c de p car. rose	1.50	70
135	"	8c de p olive green ('13)	12.50	10.00
136	A25	10c de p orange red	1.00	20
137	"	10c de p red brown ('13)	12.00	10.00
138	A26	15c de p slate green	2.00	75
139	"	15c de p yellow ('13)	5.00	3.50
140	A20	20c de p blue green	1.75	75
141	A19	50c de p red	3.00	2.50
142	"	50c de p orange yellow ('13)	6.00	5.00
143	A27	1 pi claret	5.50	4.50
144	"	1 pi red ('13)	6.00	6.00
		Nos. 125-144 (20)	90.80	71.20

Nord-Alexis
A28

Coat of Arms
A29

For Domestic Postage.
(centimes de gourde)

1906-11

No.	Type	Description	Unused	Used
145	A28	1c de g blue	20	12
146	A29	2c de g org. yellow	30	10
147	"	2c de g lemon ('11)	60	15
148	A28	3c de g slate	30	10
149	A29	7c de g green	1.00	40
		Nos. 145-149 (5)	2.40	87

Regular Issue of 1904 Handstamp Surcharged in Red:

1907

No.	Type	Description	Unused	Used
150	A18	1c on 5c dark blue	30	25
151	"	1c on 20c orange	20	15
152	"	2c on 10c org. brn.	25	18
153	"	2c on 50c claret	40	25

Black Surcharge.

No.	Type	Description	Unused	Used
154	A18	1c on 5c dark blue	40	20
155	"	1c on 10c org. brn.	25	12
156	"	2c on 20c orange	20	20

Brown Surcharge.

No.	Type	Description	Unused	Used
157	A18	1c on 5c dark blue	40	40
158	"	1c on 10c org. brn.	65	40
159	"	2c on 20c orange	1.75	1.75
160	"	2c on 50c claret	18.50	18.50

Violet Surcharge.

No.	Type	Description	Unused	Used
161	A18	1c on 20c orange	75.00	

The handstamps are found sideways, diagonal, inverted and double.

President Antoine T. Simon
A30 A31

For Foreign Postage.

1910

No.	Type	Description	Unused	Used
162	A30	2c de p rose red & black	60	40
163	"	5c de p blue & blk.	10.00	60
164	"	20c de p yellow green & black	7.50	7.00

For Domestic Postage.

No.	Type	Description	Unused	Used
165	A31	1c de g lake & black	15	15

Pres. Cincinnatus Leconte
A32 A33

A34

1912

No.	Type	Description	Unused	Used
166	A32	1c de g carmine lake	20	18
167	A33	2c de g deep orange	25	20

For Foreign Postage.

No.	Type	Description	Unused	Used
168	A34	5c de p deep blue	50	20

Stamps of Preceding Issues Handstamped Vertically

Gl O.Z.
7 Fév. 1914

1914 On Stamp of 1898-99.

No.	Type	Description	Unused	Used
169	A13	8c carmine	10.00	8.50

On Regular Issue of 1904.

No.	Type	Description	Unused	Used
170	A18	1c green	30.00	27.50
171	"	2c carmine	30.00	27.50
172	"	5c dark blue	50	30
173	"	10c orange brown	50	30
174	"	20c orange	75	35
175	"	50c claret	2.25	1.00

Perforation varieties of Nos. 172–175 exist.

On Stamp of 1904.
With "Poste Paye" Handstamp.

No.	Type	Description	Unused	Used
176	A18	50c claret	2500.00	2500.00

Horizontally on Stamps of 1906–13.

No.	Type	Description	Unused	Used
177	A19	1c de p green	40	30
178	A20	2c de p vermilion	60	30
179	A21	3c de p brown	75	60
180	"	3c de p orange yellow	40	30
181	A22	4c de p carmine lake	75	75
182	"	4c de p lt. olive grn.	1.25	75
183	A23	7c de p gray	3.00	3.00
184	"	7c de p orange red	3.00	3.00
185	A24	8c de p carmine rose	3.50	3.50
186	"	8c de p olive green	4.00	4.00
187	A25	10c de p orange red	1.00	60
188	"	10c de p red brown	1.50	1.00
189	A26	15c de p slate green	3.00	3.00
190	"	15c de p yellow	1.25	75
191	A20	20c de p blue green	2.50	1.00
192	A19	50c de p red	5.00	5.00
193	"	50c de p org. yellow	5.00	5.00
194	A27	1pi claret	5.00	5.00
195	"	1pi red	5.00	5.00
196	A29	2c de g lemon	40	20
197	A28	3c de g slate	40	25
		Nos. 177-197 (21)	47.70	43.30

On Stamp of 1910.

No.	Type	Description	Unused	Used
198	A30	20c de p yellow green & black	3.50	3.50

Vertically on Stamps of 1912.

No.	Type	Description	Unused	Used
199	A32	1c de g carmine lake	25	20
200	A33	2c de g deep orange	50	35
201	A34	5c de p deep blue	75	25

Two handstamps were used for the overprints on Nos. 169 to 201. They may be distinguished by the short and long foot of the "L" of "GL" and the position of the first "1" in "1914" with regard to the period above it. Both handstamps are found on all these stamps.

Handstamp Surcharged

Gl O.Z.
1 Cent de Piastre
7 Fév. 1914

On Nos. 141 and 143.

No.	Type	Description	Unused	Used
213	A19	1c de p on 50c de p red	30	25
214	A27	1c de p on 1 pi claret	50	50

On Nos. 142 and 144.

No.	Type	Description	Unused	Used
215	A19	1c de p on 50c de p orange yellow	50	40
216	A27	1c de p on 1 pi red	60	50

Handstamp Surcharged

On Nos. 100 and 101.

217 A18 7c on 20c orange 50 25

218 " 7c on 50c claret 40 25

The initials on the preceding handstamps are those of Gen. Oreste Zamor; the date is that of his triumphal entry into Port-au-Prince.

President Oreste Zamor
A35

Coat of Arms
A36

President Tancrède Auguste
A37

Coat of Arms A38 — Zamor A39

For Foreign Postage.

1915-16

219 A35 1c de p dark green & black 1.50

221 A36 3c de p dull green & black 15

223 A35 5c de p blue & black 25

224 A37 7c de p org. & black 65

226 A35 10c de p black brown & black 20

227 " 15c de p olive gray & black 25

228 A36 20c de p yellow brown & black 25

For Domestic Postage.

230 A39 2c de g yellow & black 50

231 A38 5c de g yellow green & black 75

232 A39 7c de g rose & black 45

Nos. 219-232 (10) 4.95

Owing to the theft of a large quantity of Nos. 219-232 while in transit from the printers, the stamps were never placed on sale at post offices. A few copies have been cancelled through carelessness or favor.

Preceding Issues Handstamp Surcharged in Carmine or Blue

On Nos. 98-101.

1915-16

235 A18 1c on 5c dark blue (C) 1.50 1.50

236 " 1c on 10c org. brn. 15 15

237 " 1c on 20c orange 45 40

238 " 1c on 50c claret 15 10

On No. 132.

239 A23 1c on 7c de p gray (C) 10 10

On Nos. 106-107.

240 A18 1c on 20c orange 50 1.00

241 " 1c on 50c claret 2.00 60

242 " 1c on 50c claret (C) 30.00 25.00

Nos. 240-242 are known with two types of the "Post Paye" overprint. No. 237 with red surcharge and any stamps with violet surcharge are unofficial.

No. 143 Handstamp Surcharged in Red

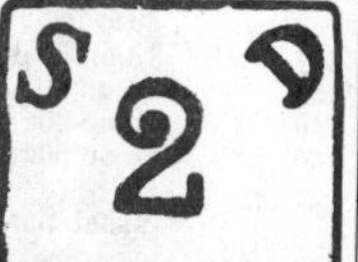

1917-19

245 A27 2c on 1pi claret 20 15

Stamps of 1906-14 Handstamp Surcharged in Various Colors

a

2 cts. GOURDE

b

On Stamps of 1906.
With Oval Surcharge.

247 A12 (a) 1c on 50c rose brown(R) 20.00 15.00

248 " (") 1c on 1g red violet(R) 22.50 20.00

On Regular Issue of 1905.

249 A22 (a) 1c on 4c de p carmine lake (Br) 15 15

250 A25 (") 1c on 10c de p orange red(Bl) 10 10

251 " (") 1c on 10c de p orange red (Bk) 75 75

252 A20 (") 1c on 20c de p blue green (R) 20 15

253 " (") 1c on 20c de p blue green (Bk) 25 15

254 A19 (") 1c on 50c de p red (R) 20 15

255 " (") 1c on 50c de p red (Bk) 25 15

256 A21 (b) 2c on 3c de p brown (R) 30 20

257 A24 (") 2c on 8c de p carmine rose(R) 20 15

258 " (") 2c on 8c de p carmine rose (Bk) 25 15

259 A26 (b) 2c on 15c de p slate green(R) 20 12

260 A20 (") 2c on 20c de p blue green(R) 25 15

Nos. 249-260 (12) 3.35 2.62

On Stamps of 1910-11.

262 A30 (a) 1c on 20c de p yellow green & black (Bk) 3.50 3.50

263 A21 (b) 2c on 3c de p org. yellow (R) 40 30

On Stamps of 1913.

265 A22 (a) 1c on 4c de p light olive green (R) 30 30

266 A23 (") 1c on 7c de p orange red(Br) 40 30

267 A26 (") 1c on 15c de p yellow (R) 40 30

268 A19 (") 1c on 50c de p orange yellow (Bk) 1.25 1.25

269 A27 (") 1c on 1pi red (Bk) 1.25 1.25

270 A24 (b) 2c on 8c de p olive green(R) 40 40

271 A25 (") 2c on 10c de p red brown (Br) 35 15

272 A26 (") 2c on 15c de p yellow (R) 50 50

273 A25 (a) 5c on 10c de p red brown(Bl) 80 80

274 " (") 5c on 10c de p red brown(VBk) 50 50

275 A26 (") 5c on 15c de p yellow (R) 4.00 4.00

Nos. 265-275 (11) 10.00 9.50

"O. Z." Stamps of 1914 Handstamp Surcharged

1CT GOURDE

c

276 A26 (c) 1c on 15c de p slate green(R) 20 20

277 A20 (") 1c on 20c de p blue green(R) 20 20

278 A30 (") 1c on 20c de p yellow green & black (R) 40 40

279 A27 (") 1c on 1pi claret (Br) 20 15

280 " (") 1c on 1 pi claret (R) 1.25 1.25

281 " (") 5c on 1pi red (Br) 40 40

Nos. 276-281 (6) 2.65 2.60

"O. Z." Stamps of 1914 Handstamp Surcharged as in 1917-19 and

d

1919-20

282 A22 (b) 2c on 4c de p carmine lake (V) 35 35

283 A24 (") 2c on 8c de p carmine rose (G) 30 15

284 " (") 2c on 8c de p olive green (R) 20 15

285 A30 (") 2c on 20c de p yellow green & black (R) 30 15

286 A19 (") 2c on 50c de p red (G) 15 8

287 " (") 2c on 50c de p red (Bk) 7.50 7.50

288 " (") 2c on 50c de p red (R) 50 40

289 A19 (b) 2c on 50c de p orange yellow (R) 25 20

290 A27 (") 2c on 1pi claret (R) 2.50 2.25

291 " (") 2c on 1pi red (R) 1.75 1.75

292 A21 (d) 3c on 3c de p brown (R) 40 40

293 A23 (") 3c on 7c de p orange red (R) 35 20

294 A21 (a) 5c on 3c de p brown (R) 40 20

295 " (") 5c on 3c de p org. yellow (R) 1.50 1.50

296 A22 (") 5c on 4c de p carmine lake (R) 50 50

297 " (") 5c on 4c de p olive green (R) 25 25

298 A23 (") 5c on 7c de p gray (V) 30 30

299 " (") 5c on 7c de p orange red (V) 40 40

300 A25 (") 5c on 10c de p orange red (V) 25 25

301 A26 (") 5c on 15c de p yellow (M) 40 40

Nos. 282-301 (20) 18.55 17.38

Nos. 217 and 218 Handstamp Surcharged with New Value.

302 A18 (a) 5c on 7c on 20c orange (M) 40 40

303 " (") 5c on 7c on 50c claret (M) 3.00 3.00

No. 187 Handstamp Surcharged

304 A25 5c de p on 10c de p orange red (M) 50 50

Postage Due Stamps of 1906-14 Handstamp Surcharged

On Stamp of 1906.

305 D2 5c on 50c olive gray (Bk) 12.00 10.00

On Stamps of 1914.

306 D2 5c on 10c violet (Bk) 40 40

307 " 5c on 50c olive gray (Bk) 50 50

308 " 5c on 50c olive gray (M) 2.00 2.00

Nos. 299 with red surcharge and 306 and 307 with violet surcharge are trial colors or essays.

Allegory of Agriculture
A40

Allegory of Commerce
A41

1920 Engraved. *Perf. 12.*

No.	Type	Description	Unused	Used
310	A40	3c deep orange	20	20
311	"	5c green	20	20
312	A41	10c vermilion	50	35
313	"	15c violet	40	30
314	"	25c deep blue	50	20
		Nos. 310-314 (5)	1.80	1.25

Stamps of this issue overprinted "T. M." are revenue stamps. The letters are the initials of "Timbre-Mobile".

President Louis J. Borno
A42

Christophe's Citadel
A43

Old Map of West Indies
A44

Borno
A45

National Capitol
A46

1924, Sept. 3

No.	Type	Description	Unused	Used
315	A42	5c deep green	18	12
316	A43	10c carmine	30	12
317	A44	20c violet blue	60	20
318	A45	50c orange & black	65	25
319	A46	1g olive green	1.50	35
		Nos. 315-319 (5)	3.23	1.04

Coffee Beans and Flowers—A47

1928, Feb. 6

No.	Type	Description	Unused	Used
320	A47	35c deep green	4.00	75

Pres. Louis Borno—A48

1929, Nov. 4

No.	Type	Description	Unused	Used
321	A48	10c carmine rose	45	25

Issued in commemoration of the signing of the "Frontier" treaty between Haiti and the Dominican Republic.

Presidents Salomon and Vincent
A49

Pres. Sténio Vincent—A50

1931

No.	Type	Description	Unused	Used
322	A49	5c deep green	1.00	50
323	A50	10c carmine rose	1.00	50

Issued in commemoration of the fiftieth anniversary of Haiti's joining the Universal Postal Union.

President Vincent
A52

Aqueduct at Port-au-Prince
A53

Fort National
A54

Palace of Sans Souci
A55

Christophe's Chapel at Milot
A56

King's Gallery Citadel
A57

Vallières Battery
A58

1933-40

No.	Type	Description	Unused	Used
325	A52	3c orange	12	10
326	"	3c deep olive green ('39)	15	10
327	A53	5c green	15	8
328	"	5c olive green ('40)	45	10
329	A54	10c rose carmine	35	12
		a. 10c vermilion	50	12
330	"	10c red brown ('40)	30	15
331	A55	25c blue	60	25
332	A56	50c brown	2.25	70
333	A57	1g dark green	2.25	70
334	A58	2.50g olive bistre	3.00	1.00
		Nos. 325-334 (10)	9.62	3.30

Alexandre Dumas, His Father and Son—A59

1935, Dec. 29 Litho. *Perf. 11½*

No.	Type	Description	Unused	Used
335	A59	10c rose pink & chocolate	75	40
336	"	25c blue & chocolate	1.50	50

Issued in honor of the visit of a delegation from France to Haiti. See No. C10.

No. 320 Surcharged in Red

25c
= =

1939, Jan. 24 *Perf. 12*

No.	Type	Description	Unused	Used
337	A47	25c on 35c deep green	75	30

Statue of Liberty, Map of Haiti and Flags of American Republics
A60

1941, June 30 Engraved *Perf. 12*

No.	Type	Description	Unused	Used
338	A60	10c rose carmine	1.00	30
339	"	25c dark blue	75	60

Issued in commemoration of the Third Inter-American Caribbean Conference, held at Port-au-Prince. See Nos. C12-C13.

Patroness of Haiti, Map and Coat of Arms
A61

1942, Dec. 8 Size: 26x36¼mm.

No.	Type	Description	Unused	Used
340	A61	3c dull violet	50	40
341	"	5c bright green	75	40
342	"	10c rose carmine	75	40
343	"	15c orange	1.00	75
344	"	20c brown	1.00	80
345	"	25c deep blue	2.00	80
346	"	50c red orange	2.50	1.25
347	"	2.50g olive black	10.00	2.50

Size: 32x45mm.

No.	Type	Description	Unused	Used
348	A61	5g purple	20.00	5.00
		Nos. 340-348 (9)	38.50	12.30

Issued in honor of Our Lady of Perpetual Help, patroness of Haiti. See Nos. C14-C21.

Adm. Hammerton Killick and Destruction of "La Crête-à-Pierrot"
A62

1943, Sept. 6

No.	Type	Description	Unused	Used
349	A62	3c orange	40	20
350	"	5c turquoise green	50	25
351	"	10c carmine rose	50	20
352	"	25c deep blue	70	30
353	"	50c olive	1.50	45
354	"	5g brown black	7.50	4.50
		Nos. 349-354, C22-C23 (8)	14.60	8.85

Nos. 343 and 345 Surcharged with New Value and Bars in Red.

1944, July 19

No.	Type	Description	Unused	Used
355	A61	10c on 15c orange	50	40
356	"	10c on 25c deep blue	50	40

Nos. 319, 326 and 334 Surcharged with New Values and Bars in Red.

1944-45

No.	Type	Description	Unused	Used
357	A52	2c on 3c dp. olive grn.	18	18
358	"	5c on 3c dp. olive grn.	30	25
359	A46	10c on 1g olive green	50	20
		a. Surcharged 01.0		
360	A58	20c on 2.50g olive bistre	50	40

Nurse and Wounded Soldier on Battlefield
A63

1945, Feb. 20 Cross in Rose

No.	Type	Description	Unused	Used
361	A63	3c gray black	10	10
362	"	5c dark blue green	20	10
363	"	10c red orange	30	12
364	"	20c black brown	20	10
365	"	25c deep blue	40	15
366	"	35c orange	40	30
367	"	50c carmine rose	1.00	40
368	"	1g olive green	1.25	50
369	"	2.50g pale violet	4.00	1.00
		Nos. 361-369 (9)	7.85	2.77

Issued to honor the International Red Cross. See Nos. C25-C32.

Col. François Capois
A64

Jean Jacques Dessalines
A65

Engraved

1946 *Perf. 12* Unwmkd.

No.	Type	Description	Unused	Used
370	A64	3c red orange	10	10
371	"	5c Prussian green	10	10
372	"	10c red	10	10
373	"	20c olive black	15	10
374	"	25c deep blue	15	12
375	"	35c orange	25	25
376	"	50c red brown	35	25
377	"	1g olive brown	50	15
378	"	2.50g gray	2.00	60
		Nos. 370-378 (9)	3.70	1.77

See also Nos. C35-C42.

1947-54

No.	Type	Description	Unused	Used
379	A65	3c orange yellow	8	5
380	"	5c green	8	5
380A	"	5c deep violet ('54)	60	10
381	"	10c carmine rose	10	6
382	"	25c deep blue	25	10
		Nos. 379-382, C46 (6)	1.36	44

No. 375 Surcharged with New Value and Rectangular Block in Black.

1948

No.	Type	Description	Unused	Used
383	A64	10c on 35c orange	25	15

Arms of Port-au-Prince
A66

Engraved and Lithographed.

1950, Feb. 12 *Perf. 12½*

384 A66 10c multicolored 30 20

Issued to commemorate the 200th anniversary (in 1949) of the founding of Port-au-Prince. See Nos. C47–C48.

Nos. RA10-RA12 and RA16 Surcharged or Overprinted in Black

U P U

1874 1949

0.03

1950, Oct. 4 *Perf. 12* **Unwmkd.**

385 PT2 3c on 5c olive gray 12 10
386 " 5c green 40 30
387 " 10c on 5c carmine rose 40 40
388 " 20c on 5c blue 50 50
Nos. 385-388, C49-C51 (7) 4.57 4.05

Issued to commemorate the 75th anniversary (in 1949) of the Universal Postal Union.

Cacao
A67

Pres. Paul E. Magloire and Day Nursery, Saline
A68

1951, Sept. 3 Photo. *Perf. 12½*

389 A67 5c dark green 40 15

See also Nos. C52–C54.

1953, May 4 Engraved *Perf. 12*

Design: 10c, Applying asphalt.

390 A68 5c green 15 6
391 " 10c rose carmine 20 12
Nos. 390-391, C57-C60 (6) 4.85 2.86

No. 375 Surcharged in Black

7 AVRIL

1803 - 1953

50

1953, May 13

392 A64 50c on 35c orange 50 30

Issued to commemorate the 150th anniversary of the death of Gen. Pierre Dominique Toussaint L'Ouverture (1743–1803), liberator.

J. J. Dessalines and Paul E. Magloire
A69

Alexandre Sabes Pétion
A70

Battle of Vertieres
A71

Design: No. 401, Marie Jeanne and Lamartiniere leading attack.

1954, Jan. 1 Photo. *Perf. 11½*

Portraits in Black.

393 A69 3c blue gray 10 6
394 A70 5c yellow green 25 12
395 " 5c yellow green (*Lamartiniere*) 20 12
396 " 5c yellow green (*Boisrond-Tonnerre*) 25 12
397 " 5c yellow green (*Toussaint L'Ouverture*) 20 12
398 A69 10c crimson 20 12
399 A70 15c rose lilac (*Capois*) 30 20

Perf. 12½

400 A71 25c dark gray 30 15
401 " 25c deep orange 30 15
Nos. 393-401 (9) 2.10 1.16

Nos. 393 to 401 were issued to commemorate the 150th anniversary of Haitian independence.
See also Nos. C63–C74, C95–C96.

Mme. Yolette Magloire
A72

1954, Jan. 1 *Perf. 11½*

402 A72 10c orange 20 15
403 " 10c blue 18 12

See also Nos. C75–C80.

Henri Christophe, Paul Magloire and Citadel—A73

Tomb and Arms of Henri Christophe
A74

Perf. 13½x13

1954, Dec. 6 Litho. **Unwmkd.**

404 A73 10c carmine 20 12

Perf. 13

405 A74 10c red, blk. & carmine 20 15

Nos. 404 and 405 were issued to publicize the restoration of Christophe's Citadel.
See also Nos. C81–C90.

J. J. Dessalines
A75

Pres. Magloire and Dessalines Memorial, Gonaives
A76

1955–57 Photogravure. *Perf. 11½*

406 A75 3c ochre & black 10 5
407 " 5c pale violet & black ('56) 8 5
408 " 10c rose & black 15 5
a. 10c salmon pink & black ('57) 12 5
409 " 25c chalky blue & black ('56) 30 12
a. 25c bl. & blk. ('57) 30 12
Nos. 406-409, C93-C94 (6) 93 51

1955, Aug. 1

410 A76 10c deep blue & black 45 40
411 " 10c crimson & black 45 40

Issued to commemorate the 21st anniversary of the new Haitian army.

Nos. 410-411 were printed in a single sheet of 20 (5x4). The two upper rows are of No. 410, the two lower No. 411, providing five se-tenant pairs.
See also Nos. C97–C98.

Flamingo
A77

Mallard
A78

Granite Paper

1956, Apr. 14 Photo. *Perf. 11½*

412 A77 10c blue & ultra. 40 25
413 A78 25c dark green & bluish green 1.00 50

See also Nos. C99–C104.

Immanuel Kant—A79

1956, July 19 Granite Paper *Perf. 12*

414 A79 10c bright ultra. 20 15

Issued to commemorate the tenth anniversary of the first Inter-American Philosophical Congress. See also Nos. C105–C107a.

Zim Waterfall
A80

J. J. Dessalines and Dessalines Memorial, Gonaives
A81

Granite Paper.

1957, Dec. 16 *Perf. 11½* **Unwmkd.**

415 A80 10c orange & blue 20 5

See also Nos. C108–C111.

1958, July 1 **Photogravure**

416 A81 5c yellow green & black 12 5

Bicentenary of birth of J. J. Dessalines. See also Nos. 470–471, C112, C170.

"Atomium"—A82

View of Brussels Exposition
A83

Perf. 13x13½, 13½x13

1958, July 22 Litho. **Unwmkd.**

417 A82 50c brown 50 25
418 A83 75c bright green 50 30
419 A82 1g purple 1.20 40
420 A83 1.50g red orange 80 45
Nos. 417-420, C113-C114 (6) 6.50 3.90

Issued for the Universal and International Exposition at Brussels.

Sylvio Cator
A84

U. S. Satellite
A85

1958, Aug. 16 Photo. *Perf. 11½*

Granite Paper

421 A84 5c green 12 5
422 " 10c brown 18 6
423 " 20c lilac 24 8
Nos. 421-423, C115-C118 (7) 5.14 1.89

Issued to commemorate the 30th anniversary of the world championship record broad jump of Sylvio Cator.

1958, Oct. 8 *Perf. 14x13½*

Designs: 20c, Emperor penguins. 50c, Modern observatory. 1g, Ocean exploration.

424 A85 10c bright blue & brown red 25 6
425 " 20c black & dp. org. 75 40
426 " 50c grn. & rose brn. 1.00 40
427 " 1g black & blue 1.25 30
Nos. 424-427, C119-C121 (7) 9.50 2.71

Issued for the International Geophysical Year 1957–58. See No. C121a.

President François Duvalier
A86

Engraved and Lithographed.

1958, Oct. 22 ***Perf. 11½*** **Unwmkd.**

Commemorative Inscription in Ultramarine.

428 A86 10c black & deep pink 15 5
429 " 50c black & light green 50 18
430 " 1g black & brick red 75 40
431 " 5g black & salmon 4.00 3.00
Nos. 428–431, C122–C125 (8) 16.90 11.28

Issued to commemorate the first anniversary of the inauguration of Pres. Dr. François Duvalier. See note on souvenir sheets after No. C125.

Regular Issue.

Without Commemorative Inscription.

1958, Nov. 20

432 A86 5c black & light violet blue 5 3
433 " 10c black & deep pink 5 4
434 " 20c black & yellow 15 15
435 " 50c black & lt. green 35 20
436 " 1g black & brick red 50 30
437 " 1.50g black & rose pink 75 55
438 " 2.50g black & gray violet 1.25 1.00
439 " 5g black & salmon 2.50 2.00
Nos. 432–439 (8) 5.60 4.27

See Nos. C126–C132.

Map of Haiti—A87

1958, Dec. 5 **Photo.** ***Perf. 11½***

Granite Paper

440 A87 10c rose pink 15 10
441 " 25c green 30 15
Nos. 440–441, C133–C135 (5) 1.85 90

Issued in tribute to the United Nations. See also No. C135a.

Nos. 440–441 Overprinted "10th ANNIVERSARY OF THE / UNIVERSAL DECLARATION / OF HUMAN RIGHTS" in English, French, Spanish or Portuguese.

1959, Jan. 28

442 A87 10c rose pink 10 10
a. Block of four 50 50
443 " 25c green 40 30
a. Block of four 1.75 1.25
Nos. 442–443, C136–C138 (5) 5.50 5.40
Nos. 442a–443a, C136a–C138a (5) 22.25 21.75

Nos. 442a and 443a contain overprints in English, French, Spanish and Portuguese.

Issued to commemorate the tenth anniversary of the signing of the Universal Declaration of Human Rights.

Pope Pius XII and Children

A88

Designs: 50c, Pope praying. 2g, Pope on throne.

1959, Feb. 28 **Photo.** ***Perf. 14x13½***

444 A88 10c violet blue & olive 12 4
445 " 50c green & deep brown 35 20
446 " 2g deep claret & dark brown 1.25 60
Nos. 444–446, C139–C141 (6) 4.52 1.59

Issued in memory of Pope Pius XII.

Abraham Lincoln—A89

1959, May 12 **Photo.** ***Perf. 12***

447 A89 50c light blue & deep claret 50 25

Issued to commemorate the sesquicentennial of the birth of Abraham Lincoln. See Nos. C142–C144a.

Chicago's Skyline and Dessables House—A90

Jean Baptiste Dessables and Map of American Midwest, c. 1791

A91

Design: 50c, Discus thrower and flag of Haiti.

1959, Aug. 27 ***Perf. 14*** **Unwmkd.**

448 A90 25c black brown & light blue 50 30
449 " 50c multicolored 1.00 75
450 A91 75c brown & blue 1.25 1.00
Nos. 448–450, C145–C147 (6) 7.50 3.80

Issued to commemorate the 3rd Pan American Games, Chicago, Aug. 27–Sept. 7.

No. 449 Overprinted

1960, Feb. 29

451 A90 50c multicolored 2.50 2.00

Issued to commemorate the 8th Olympic Winter Games, Squaw Valley, Calif., Feb. 18–29, 1960. See Nos. C148–C150.

Uprooted Oak Emblem and Hands

A92

1960, Apr. 7 **Litho.** ***Perf. 12½x13***

452 A92 10c salmon & green 15 10
453 " 50c violet & magenta 40 30

Issued to publicize World Refugee Year, July 1, 1959–June 30, 1960. See also Nos. 489–490, C151–C152a, C191–C192.

No. 406 Surcharged with New Values.

1960, Apr. 27 **Photo.** ***Perf. 11½***

454 A75 5c on 3c ochre & black 10 5
455 " 10c on 3c ochre & black 20 8

No. 369 Surcharged or Overprinted in Red: "28eme ANNIVERSAIRE."

1960, May 8 **Engraved** ***Perf. 12***

Cross in Rose.

456 A63 1g on 2.50g pale vio. 1.25 60
457 " 2.50g pale violet 1.75 1.50

Issued to commemorate the 28th anniversary of the Haitian Red Cross. See also Nos. C153–C160.

Claudinette Fouchard, Miss Haiti, Sugar Queen—A93

Sugar Queen and: 20c, Sugar harvest. 50c, Beach. 1g, Sugar plantation.

Perf. 11½

1960, May 30 **Photo.** **Unwmkd.**

Granite Paper

458 A93 10c olive bis. & vio. 12 5
459 " 20c red brn. & black 20 8
460 " 50c brt. blue & brown 40 15
461 " 1g green & brown 75 30
Nos. 458–461, C161–C162 (6) 2.87 1.23

Haitian sugar industry.

Olympic Victors, Athens, 1896, Melbourne Stadium and Olympic Torch—A94

Designs: 20c, Discus thrower and Rome stadium. 50c, Pierre de Coubertin and victors, Melbourne, 1956. 1g, Athens stadium, 1896.

1960, Aug. 18 **Photo.** ***Perf. 12***

462 A94 10c black & orange 10 8
463 " 20c dark blue & crimson 15 10
464 " 50c green & ochre 35 15
465 " 1g dark brown & greenish blue 65 20
Nos. 462–465, C163–C165 (7) 4.05 1.73

Issued to commemorate the 17th Olympic Games, Rome, Aug. 25–Sept. 11. See also No. C165a.

Occide Jeanty and Score from "1804"—A95

Designs: 20c, Occide Jeanty and National Capitol.

1960, Oct. 19 ***Perf. 14x14½***

466 A95 10c orange & red lilac 20 8
467 " 20c blue & red lilac 45 18
468 A95 50c green & sepia 90 30
Nos. 466–468, C166–C167 (5) 3.55 1.11

Issued to commemorate the centenary of the birth of Occide Jeanty, composer. Printed in sheets of 12 (3x4) with commemorative inscription and opening bars of "1804," Jeanty's military march, in top margin.

U.N. Headquarters, New York

A96

Alexandre Dumas Père and Musketeer

A97

1960, Nov. 25 **Engraved** ***Perf. 10½***

469 A96 1g green & black 65 35

Issued to commemorate the 15th anniversary of the United Nations. See also Nos. C168–C169a.

Dessalines Type of 1958

Photogravure

1960 ***Perf. 11½*** **Unwmkd.**

Granite Paper

470 A81 10c red org. & blk. 15 4
471 " 25c ultra. & black 30 8

See also No. C170.

1961, Feb. 10 ***Perf. 11½***

Granite Paper

Designs: 5c, Map of Haiti and birthplace of General Alexandre Dumas (horiz.) 50c, Alexandre Dumas, father and son and French and Haitian flags (horiz.)

472 A97 5c lt. blue & choc. 5 4
473 " 10c rose, black & sepia 12 8
474 " 50c dark blue & crimson 45 25
Nos. 472–474, C177–C179 (6) 2.57 1.57

Issued to commemorate General Dumas (Alexandre Davy de la Pailleterie), born in Jeremie, Haiti, and his son and grandson, French authors.

Privateer in Battle—A98

Designs: 5c, Map of Tortuga. 10c, Three Pirates. 15c, Pirates. 50c, Pirate with cutlass in rigging.

1961, Apr. 4 **Litho.** ***Perf. 12***

475 A98 5c blue & yellow 6 4
476 " 10c lake & yellow 8 5
477 " 15c olive grn. & org. 15 8
478 " 20c choc. & orange 20 15
479 " 50c violet blue & orange 40 25
Nos. 475–479, C180–C182 (8) 2.09 1.18

Issued as tourist publicity.

Nos. 416, 470–471 and 378 Overprinted: "Dr. F. Duvalier / Président / 22 Mai 1961"

1961, May 22 Photo. ***Perf. 11½***

480 A81 5c yel. green & black 5 4
481 " 10c red org. & blk. 10 8
482 " 25c ultra. & black 25 20

Engraved

Perf. 12

483 A64 2.50g gray 1.75 1.25
Nos. 480–483, C183–C185 (7) 3.10 2.27

Issued to commemorate the re-election of Pres. Francois Duvalier.

No. 475 Surcharged: "EXPLORATION SPATIALE JOHN GLENN," Capsule and New Value

1962, May 10 **Lithographed**

484 A98 50c on 5c bl. & yel. 75 50
485 " 1.50g on 5c bl. & yel. 2.25 1.75

Issued to honor the United States' achievement in space exploration and to commemorate the first orbital flight of a U.S. astronaut, Lt. Col. John H. Glenn, Jr., Feb. 20, 1962. See Nos. C186–C187.

Malaria Eradication Emblem—A99

Design: 10c, Triangle pointing down.

Lithographed

1962, May 30 ***Perf. 12*** **Unwmkd.**

486 A99 5c crimson & dp. blue 8 4
487 " 10c red brown & emerald 10 8
488 " 50c blue & crimson 40 20
Nos. 486–488, C188–C190 (6) 1.68 1.02

Issued for the World Health Organization drive to eradicate malaria.

Printed in sheets of 12 with marginal inscription.

WRY Type of 1960 Dated "1962"

1962, June 22 ***Perf. 12½x13***

489 A92 10c lt. blue & orange 6 4
490 " 50c rose lilac & olive green 35 25

Issued to publicize the plight of refugees. For souvenir sheet see note after Nos. C191–C192.

Haitian Scout Emblem
A100

Designs: 5c, 50c, Scout giving Scout sign. 10c, Lord and Lady Baden-Powell (horiz.).

Perf. 14x14½, 14½x14

1962, Aug. 6 **Photogravure**

491 A100 3c black, ochre & purple 5 4
492 " 5c citron, red brown & blk. 5 4
493 " 10c ochre, black & green 10 5
494 " 25c maroon, olive & blue 20 10
495 " 50c violet, green & red 40 20
Nos. 491–495, C193–C195 (8) 2.15 1.31

Issued to commemorate the 22nd anniversary of the Haitian Boy Scouts.

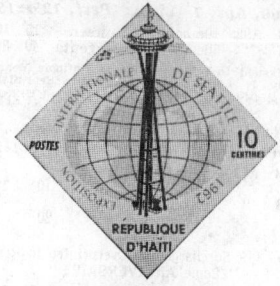

Space Needle, Space Capsule and Globe—A101

1962, Nov. 19 Litho. ***Perf. 12½***

496 A101 10c red brn. & lt. bl. 8 4
497 " 20c vio. blue & pink 18 8
498 " 50c emerald & yel. 60 15
499 " 1g carmine & light green 90 35
Nos. 496–499, C200–C202 (7) 3.86 1.22

Issued to commemorate the "Century 21" International Exposition, Seattle, Wash., Apr. 21–Oct. 21.

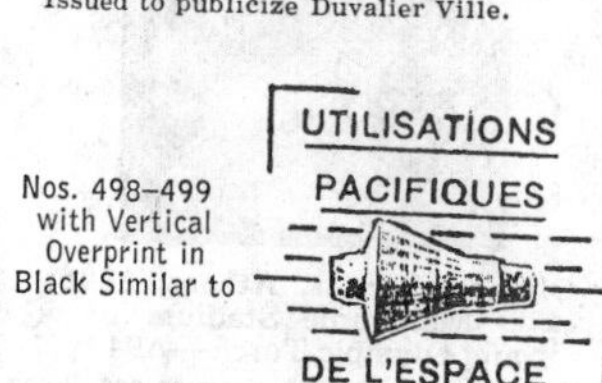

Plan of Duvalier Ville and Stamp of 1904—A102

1962, Dec. 10 Photo. ***Perf. 14x14½***

500 A102 5c violet, yellow & black 8 5
501 " 10c carmine rose, yellow & blk. 15 10
502 " 25c blue gray, yellow & blk. 25 20
Nos. 500–502, C203–C205 (6) 2.03 1.55

Issued to publicize Duvalier Ville.

Nos. 498–499 with Vertical Overprint in Black Similar to

UTILISATIONS
PACIFIQUES
DE L'ESPACE

1963, Jan. 23 Litho. ***Perf. 12½***

503 A101 50c emerald & yel. 60 50
a. Claret ovpt., horiz. 75 50
504 A101 1g car. & lt. green 1.00 75
a. Claret ovpt., horiz. 1.20 85

Issued to publicize "Peaceful Uses of Outer Space." The black vertical overprint has no outside frame lines and no broken shading lines around capsule. Nos. 503a and 504a were issued Feb. 20.
See Nos. C206–C207a.

Symbolic Harvest
A103

1963, July 12 Photo. ***Perf. 13x14***

505 A103 10c orange & black 10 8
506 " 20c bluish grn. & blk. 15 12

Issued for the "Freedom from Hunger" campaign of the U.N. Food and Agriculture Organization. See Nos. C208–C209.

J. J. Dessalines **Weight Lifter**
A104 **A105**

Perf. 14x14½

1963, Oct. 17 **Unwmkd.**

507 A104 5c tan & vermilion 5 3
508 " 10c yellow & blue 5 3

See also Nos. C214–C215.

No. 508 Overprinted: "FETE DES MERES / 1964"

1964, July 22

509 A104 10c yellow & blue 10 10

Issued for Mother's Day, 1964. See Nos. C216–C218.

1964, Nov. 12 Photo. ***Perf. 11½***

Granite Paper

Design: 50c, Hurdler.

510 A105 10c lt. bl. & dk. brn. 8 5
511 " 25c salmon & dark brown 15 10
512 " 50c pale rose lilac & dk. brown 25 20
Nos. 510–512, C223–C226 (7) 1.98 1.36

Issued to commemorate the 18th Olympic Games, Tokyo, Oct. 10–25. Printed in sheets of 50 (10x5), with map of Japan in background extending over 27 stamps.

Madonna of Haiti and International Airport, Port-au-Prince
A106

Unisphere, New York World's Fair
A107

1964, Dec. 15 ***Perf. 14½x14***

513 A106 10c org. yel. & black 15 8
514 " 25c bl. grn. & black 25 15
515 " 50c brt. yel. green & black 40 20
516 " 1g verm. & black 60 40
Nos. 513–516, C227–C229 (7) 4.20 1.98

Issued to commemorate the opening of the International Airport in Port-au-Prince.

Same Overprinted "1965"

1965, Feb. 11

517 A106 10c orge. yel. & blk. 15 10
518 " 25c bl. grn. & black 30 15
519 " 50c bright yellow grn. & black 40 20
520 " 1g verm. & black 60 40
Nos. 517–520, C230–C232 (7) 4.35 2.60

1965, Mar. 22 Photo. ***Perf. 13½***

Design: 20c, "Rocket Thrower" by Donald De Lue.

521 A107 10c grn., yel. olive & dark red 12 10
522 " 20c plum & orange 20 15
523 " 50c dk. brn., dk. red, yel. & green 40 25
Nos. 521–523, C233–C235 (6) 5.37 3.60

New York World's Fair, 1964–65.

Merchantmen—A108

1965, May 13 ***Perf. 11½*** **Unwmkd.**

524 A108 10c blk., lt. grn. & red 5 3
525 " 50c blk., lt. bl. & red 20 15

Issued to honor the merchant marine. See also Nos. C236–C237.

ITU Emblem, Old and New Communication Equipment—A109

1965, Aug. 16 Litho. ***Perf. 13½***

526 A109 10c gray & multi. 10 5
527 " 25c multicolored 20 10
528 " 50c " 40 20
Nos. 526–528, C242–C245 (7) 2.80 2.05

Issued to commemorate the centenary of the International Telecommunication Union.

Statue of Our Lady of the Assumption
A110

Passionflower
A111

Designs: 5c, Cathedral of Port-au-Prince (horiz.). 10c, High altar.

Photogravure

1965, Nov. 19 ***Perf. 14x13, 13x14***

Size: 39x29, 29x39mm.

529 A110 5c multicolored 5 3
530 " 10c " 10 8
531 " 25c " 15 12
Nos. 529–531, C246–C248 (6) 4.00 3.23

Issued to commemorate the 200th anniversary of the Metropolitan Cathedral of Port-au-Prince.

1965, Dec. 20 Photo. ***Perf. 11½***

Flowers: 5c, 15c, American elder. 10c, Okra.

Granite Paper

532 A111 3c dk. vio., lt. vio. blue & green 4 4
533 " 5c grn., lt. bl. & yel. 5 4
534 " 10c multicolored 10 5
a. "0.10" omitted
535 A111 15c grn., pink & yel. 12 10
536 " 50c dark violet, yellow & green 40 20
Nos. 532–536, C249–C254 (11) 4.51 3.63

Nos. 526–528 Overprinted in Red: "20e. Anniversaire / UNESCO"

1965, Aug. 27 Litho. ***Perf. 13½***

537 A109 10c gray & multi. 30 30
538 " 25c yel. brn. & multi. 75 75
539 " 50c pale grn. & multi. 1.50 1.50
Nos. 537–539, C255–C256 (5) 7.05 4.05

20th anniversary of UNESCO.

Amulet
A112

Ceremonial Stool
A113

Perf. 14½x14, 14x14½

1966, March 14 Photo. **Unwmkd.**

540 A112 5c greenish blue, blk. & yellow 5 4
541 A113 10c multicolored 6 5
542 A112 50c scarlet, yellow & black 25 20
Nos. 540-542, C257-C259 (6) 2.66 1.79

No. 541 Overprinted in Red: "Hommage / a Hailé Sélassié Ier / 24-25 Avril 1966"

1966, Apr. 24

543 A113 10c multicolored 25 25

Issued to commemorate the visit of Emperor Haile Selassie of Ethiopia, Apr. 24-25. See also Nos. C260-C262.

Walter M. Shirra, Thomas P. Stafford, Frank A. Borman, James A. Lovell and Gemini VI
A114

1966, May 3 ***Perf. 13½***

544 A114 5c violet blue, brn. & light blue 5 3
545 " 10c purple, brown & light blue 10 6
546 " 25c green, brown & & light blue 18 10
547 " 50c dk. red, brown & light blue 35 18
Nos. 544-547, C263-C265 (7) 2.23 1.57

Rendezvous in space of U.S. spacecraft Gemini VI and VII, Dec. 15, 1965.

Soccer Ball within Wreath and Pres. Duvalier
A115

Design: 10c, 50c, Soccer player within wreath and Duvalier.

Lithographed and Photogravure

1966, June 16 ***Perf. 13x13½***

Portrait in Black; Gold Inscription; Green Commemorative Inscription in Two Lines

548 A115 5c pale sal. & green 8 4
549 " 10c lt. ultra. & green 10 5
550 " 15c lt. green & green 15 6
551 " 50c pale lilac rose & green 35 18

Green Commemorative Inscription in 3 Lines; Gold Inscription Omitted

552 A115 5c pale sal. & green 8 4
553 " 10c lt. ultra. & green 10 5
554 " 15c lt. green & green 15 6
555 " 50c pale lilac rose & green 35 18
Nos. 548-555, C266-C269 (12) 3.26 2.26

Issued to commemorate the Caribbean Soccer Festival, June 10-22. Nos. 548-551 also commemorate the National Soccer Championships, May 8-22.

"ABC," Boy and Girl
A116

Designs: 10c, Scout symbols. 25c, Television set, book and communications satellite (horiz.).

Perf. 14x13½, 13½x14

1966, Oct. 18 Litho. and **Engraved**

556 A116 5c green, sal. pink & brown 5 4
557 " 10c red brn., lt. brn. & black 6 5
558 " 25c green, blue & dk. violet 10 8
Nos. 556-558, C270-C272 (6) 1.41 1.37

Issued to publicize education through literacy, Scouting and by audio-visual means.

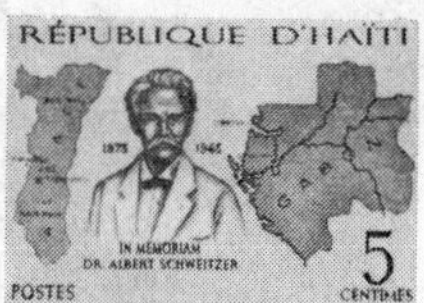

Dr. Albert Schweitzer, Maps of Alsace and Gabon—A117

Designs: 10c, Dr. Schweitzer and pipe organ. 20c, Dr. Schweitzer and Albert Schweitzer Hospital, Deschapelles, Haiti.

Perf. 12½x13

1967, Apr. 20 Photo. **Unwmkd.**

559 A117 5c pale lilac & multi. 5 5
560 " 10c buff & multi. 10 5
561 " 20c gray & multi. 20 10
Nos. 559-561, C273-C276 (7) 2.70 2.20

Issued in memory of Dr. Albert Schweitzer (1875-1965), medical missionary to Gabon, theologian and musician.

Watermelon and J. J. Dessalines
A118

Designs (Dessalines and): 10c, Cabbage. 20c, Tangerine. 50c, Chayote.

1967, July 4 Photo. ***Perf. 12½***

562 A118 5c multicolored 5 4
563 " 10c " 6 5
564 " 20c " 10 8
565 " 50c " 25 18
Nos. 562-565, C277-C279 (7) 1.66 1.30

No. 532 Surcharged

12e Jamborée Mondial 1967

1967, Aug. 21 Photo. ***Perf. 11½***

566 A111 50c on 3c multi. 25 20
Nos. 566, B38-B40, CB55-CB56 (6) 1.85 1.70

Issued to commemorate the 12th Boy Scout World Jamboree, Farragut State Park, Idaho, Aug. 1-9.

Nos. 540-542 Overprinted and Surcharged

Perf. 14½x14, 14x14½

1967, Aug. 30 Photogravure

567 A112 5c greenish blue, black & yellow 5 4
568 A113 10c multicolored 6 5
569 A112 50c scarlet, yellow & black 25 20
570 " 1g on 5c greenish bl., blk. & yel. 50 40
Nos. 567-570, C280-C281 (6) 2.61 2.09

Issued to commemorate EXPO '67 International Exhibition, Montreal, Apr. 28-Oct. 27.

Pres. Duvalier and Brush Turkey
A119

1967, Sept. 22 Photo. ***Perf. 14x13***

571 A119 5c car. rose & gold 5 4
572 " 10c ultra. & gold 6 5
573 " 25c dk. red brown & gold 15 12
574 " 50c deep red lilac & gold 25 20
Nos. 571-574, C282-C284 (7) 2.76 2.21

10th anniversary of Duvalier revolution.

Writing Hands
A120

Designs: 10c, Scout emblem and Scouts (vert.). 25c, Audio-visual teaching of algebra.

1967, Dec. 11 Litho. ***Perf. 11½***

575 A120 5c multicolored 5 4
576 " 10c " 8 5
577 " 25c dk. green, lt. blue & yellow 20 10
Nos. 575-577, C285-C287 (6) 1.53 1.19

Issued to publicize the importance of education.

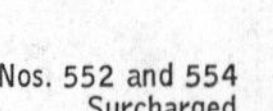

Nos. 552 and 554 Surcharged

Lithographed and Photogravure

1968, Jan. 18 ***Perf. 13x13½***

578 A115 50c on 15c lt. green & green 25 20
579 " 1g on 5c pale sal. & green 40 35

Issued to publicize the 19th Olympic Games, Mexico City, Oct. 12-27. See No. C288, CB57.

The 1968 date is missing on 2 stamps in every sheet of 50.

Caïman Woods, by Raoul Dupoux
A121

1968, Apr. 22 Photo. ***Perf. 12***

Size: 36x26mm.

580 A121 5c multicolored 6 4
581 " 10c rose red & multi. 8 5
582 " 25c multicolored 12 10
583 " 50c dull lilac & multi. 25 20
Nos. 580-583, C289-C295 (11) 5.31 4.39

Issued to commemorate the Caïman Woods ceremony during the Slaves' Rebellion, Aug. 14, 1791.

No. 547 Overprinted

Xème JEUX OLYMPIQUES D'HIVER-GRENOBLE 1968

1968, Apr. 19 Photo. ***Perf. 13½***

584 A114 50c dk. red, brown & light blue 1.00 1.00

Issued to commemorate the 10th Winter Olympic Games, Grenoble, France, Feb. 6-18, 1968. See also Nos. C296-C298.

Certain unlisted issues of Haiti, starting in 1968, are mentioned and briefly described in "For the Record" at the back of this volume.

Monument to the Unknown Maroon
A122

Palm Tree and Provincial Coats of Arms
A123

Madonna, Papal Arms and Arms of Haiti—A124

1968, May 22 *Perf. 11½*

Granite Paper

585 A122 5c blue & black 6 4
586 " 10c rose brn. & black 10 6
587 " 20c violet & black 20 12
588 " 25c lt. ultra. & black 25 15
589 " 50c brt. blue green & black 45 20
Nos. 585-589, C299-C301 (8) 2.61 1.60

Issued to commemorate the unveiling of the monument to the Unknown Maroon, Port-au-Prince.

Perf. 13x14, 12½x13½

1968, Aug. 16 Photogravure

Design: 25c, Cathedral, arms of Pope Paul VI and arms of Haiti.

590 A123 5c green & multi. 10 6
591 A124 10c brown & multi. 12 10
592 " 25c multicolored 25 18
Nos. 590-592, C302-C305 (7) 2.67 2.24

Issued to commemorate the consecration of the Bishopric of Haiti, Oct. 28, 1966.

Air Terminal, Port-au-Prince A125

1968, Sept. 22 Photo. *Perf. 11½*

Portrait in Black

593 A125 5c brown & light ultramarine 4 3
594 " 10c brown & lt. blue 8 6
595 " 25c brn. & pale lilac 15 12
Nos. 593-595, C306-C308 (6) 2.07 1.76

Issued to commemorate the inauguration of the Francois Duvalier Airport in Port-au-Prince.

Slave Breaking Chains, Map of Haiti, Torch, Conch A126

1968, Oct. 28 Litho. *Perf. 14½x14*

596 A126 5c brown, light blue & bright pink 6 3
597 " 10c brown, lt. olive & bright pink 8 4
598 " 25c brown, bister & bright pink 12 8
Nos. 596-598, C310-C313 (7) 2.26 1.80

Slaves' Rebellion, of 1791.

Children Learning to Read—A127

Designs: 10c, Children watching television. 50c, Hands throwing ball, and sports medal.

1968, Nov. 14 *Perf. 11½*

599 A127 5c multicolored 6 3
600 " 10c " 8 4
601 " 50c " 20 15
Nos. 599-601, C314-C316 (6) 1.69 1.22

Issued to publicize education through literacy, audio-visual means and sport.

Winston Churchill—A128

Churchill: 5c, as painter. 10c, as Knight of the Garter. 15c, and soldiers at Normandy. 20c, and early seaplane. 25c, and Queen Elizabeth II. 50c, and Big Ben, London.

1968, Dec. 23 Photo. *Perf. 13*

602 A128 3c gold & multi. 3 3
603 " 5c " " 5 3
604 " 10c " " 6 4
605 " 15c " " 8 5
606 " 20c " " 10 6
607 " 25c " " 12 8
608 " 50c " " 25 15
Nos. 602-608, C319-C322 (11) 2.19 1.69

Issued in memory of Sir Winston Spencer Churchill (1874-1965), statesman and World War II leader. Exist imperforate.

No. 589 Surcharged with New Value and Rectangle.

1969, Feb. 21 Photo. *Perf. 11½*

609 A122 70c on 50c brt. blue green & black 45 30

See Nos. C324-C325.

Blue-headed Euphonia A129

Power Lines and Light Bulb A131

Birds of Haiti: 10c, Hispaniolan trogon. 20c, Palm chat. 25c, Stripe-headed tanager. 50c, Like 5c.

1969, Feb. 26 *Perf. 13½*

610 A129 5c lt. green & multi. 6 3
611 " 10c yellow & multi. 8 4
612 " 20c cream & multi. 15 7
613 " 25c lt. lilac & multi. 20 8
614 " 50c lt. gray & multi. 35 15
Nos. 610-614, C326-C329 (9) 2.84 2.10

1969, May 22 Litho. *Perf. 13x13½*

623 A131 20c lilac & blue 12 10

Issued to publicize the Duvalier Hydroelectric Station. See Nos. C338-C340.

Learning to Write A132

Designs: 10c, children playing (vert.). 50c, Peace poster on educational television (vert.).

1969, Aug. 12 Litho. *Perf. 13½*

624 A132 5c multicolored 5 5
625 " 10c " 8 6
626 " 50c " 20 15
Nos. 624-626, C342-C344 (6) 1.78 1.16

Issued to publicize national education.

ILO Emblem A133

1969, Sept. 22 *Perf. 14*

627 A133 5c bl. green & black 5 3
628 " 10c brown & black 8 4
629 " 20c vio. blue & blk. 15 8
Nos. 627-629, C345-C347 (6) 1.78 1.03

Issued to commemorate the 50th anniversary of the International Labor Organization.

Papilio Zonaria A134

Butterflies: 20c, Zerene cesonia cynops. 25c, Papilio machaonides.

1969, Nov. 14 Photo. *Perf. 13½*

630 A134 10c pink & multi. 8 4
631 " 20c gray & multi. 14 6
632 " 25c lt. blue & multi. 18 8
Nos. 630-632, C348-C350 (6) 2.00 1.53

Martin Luther King, Jr. A135

Lithographed

1970, Jan. 12 *Perf. 12½x13½*

633 A135 10c bister, red & blk. 4 4
634 " 20c greenish blue, red & black 10 8
635 " 25c brt. rose, red & black 12 10
Nos. 633-635, C351-C353 (6) 1.76 1.22

Issued in memory of the Rev. Dr. Martin Luther King, Jr. (1929-1968), American civil rights leader.

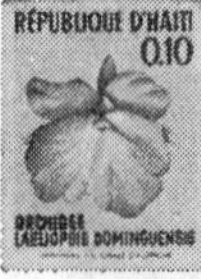

Laeliopsis Dominguensis A136

U.P.U. Monument and Map of Haiti A137

Haitian Orchids: 20c, Oncidium Haitiense. 25c, Oncidium calochilum.

1970, Apr. 3 Litho. *Perf. 13x12½*

636 A136 10c yel., lilac & blk. 10 6
637 " 20c lt. blue green, yel. & brown 30 15
638 " 25c blue & multi. 40 20
Nos. 636-638, C354-C356 (6) 2.50 1.76

1970, June 23 Photo. *Perf. 11½*

Designs: 25c, Propeller and U.P.U. emblem (vert.). 50c, Globe and doves.

639 A137 10c blk., brt. green & olive bister 10 6
640 " 25c blk., brt. rose & olive bister 25 18
641 " 50c black & blue 50 35
Nos. 639-641, C357-C359 (6) 2.85 1.94

Issued to commemorate the 16th Congress of the Universal Postal Union, Tokyo, Oct. 1-Nov. 16, 1970.

Map of Haiti, Dam and Generator A138

Design: 25c, Map of Haiti, dam and pylon.

1970, Litho. *Perf. 14x13½*

642 A138 20c lt. green & multi. 20 10
643 " 25c lt. blue & multi. 25 15

Issued to publicize the François Duvalier Central Hydroelectric Plant.

No. 641 Overprinted in Red with U.N. Emblem and: "XXVe ANNIVERSAIRE / O.N.U."

1970, Dec. 14 Photo. *Perf. 11½*

644 A137 50c black & blue 30 20

United Nations, 25th anniversary. See Nos. C360-C362.

Fort Nativity, Drawing by Columbus—A139

Ascension, by Castera Bazile—A140

1970, Dec. 22

645 A139 3c dk. brown & buff 5 5
646 " 5c dk. grn. & pale grn. 25 20

Christmas 1970.

1971, Apr. 29 Litho. *Perf. 12x12½*

Paintings: 5c, Man with Turban, by Rembrandt. 20c, Iris in a Vase, by Van Gogh. 50c, Baptism of Christ, by Castera Bazile. No. 651, Young Mother Sewing, by Mary Cassatt. No. 652, The Card Players, by Cezanne.

Size: 20x40mm.

647 A140 5c multicolored 5 3
648 " 10c " 8 3

Perf. 13x12½ Size: 25x37mm.

649 A140 20c multicolored 18 8

Perf. 12x12½ Size: 20x40mm.

650 A140 50c multicolored 40 20
Nos. 647-650, C366-C368 (7) 2.21 1.54

Souvenir Sheets

Imperf.

651 A140 3g multicolored 1.50
652 " 3g " 1.50

No. 651 contains one stamp, size: 20x40mm., No. 652 contains one stamp, size: 25x37mm. Sheets have blue inscription and magenta border. Size: 65x85mm.

Soccer Ball
A141

Design: No. 655, 1g, 5g, Jules Rimet cup.

1971, June 14 Photo. *Perf. 11½*

653 A141 5c salmon & black 5 3
654 " 50c tan & black 30 20
655 " 50c rose pink, black & gold 30 20
656 " 1g lilac, black & gold 55 40
657 " 1.50g gray & black 75 60
658 " 5g gray, black & gold 2.50 2.25
Nos. 653-658 (6) 4.45 3.68

Souvenir Sheet
Imperf.

659 A141 Sheet of 2 12.00 10.00
a. 70c light violet & black
b. 1g light green, blue & gold

9th World Soccer Championships for the Jules Rimet Cup, Mexico City, May 30–June 21, 1970. The surface tint of the sheets of 50 (10x5) of Nos. 653-658 includes a map of Brazil covering 26 stamps. Positions 27, 37 and 38 inscribed "Brasilia," "Santos," "Rio de Janeiro" respectively. On soccer ball design the 4 corner stamps are inscribed "Pele."

No. 659 has black marginal inscription and control number. Nos. 659a and 659b have portions of map of Brazil in background; No. 659a inscribed "Pele" and "Santos," No. 659b "Brasilia." Size of No. 659: 84x66mm.

J. J. Dessalines — A142

"Sun" and EXPO '70 Emblem — A143

1972, Apr. 28 Photo. *Perf. 11½*

660 A142 5c green & black 5 3
661 " 10c brt. blue & black 10 3
662 " 25c orange & black 12 8
Nos. 660-662, C378-C379 (5) 1.77 1.04

See Nos. 697-700, C448-C458.

1972, Oct. 27 Photo. *Perf. 11½*

663 A143 10c ocher, brown & green 6 3
664 " 25c ocher, brown & maroon 15 12
Nos. 663-664, C387-C390 (6) 2.76 1.80

EXPO '70 International Exposition, Osaka, Japan, Mar. 15–Sept. 13, 1970.

Basket Vendors
A144

Designs: 80c, 2.50g, Postal bus.

1973, Jan. Photo. *Perf. 11½*

665 A144 50c black & multi. 25 15
666 " 80c " " 40 24
667 " 1.50g " " 75 45
668 " 2.50g " " 1.75 75

20th anniversary of Caribbean Travel Association.

Micromelo Undata
A145

Designs: Marine life; 50c horizontal.

1973, Sept. 4 Lithographed *Perf. 14*

Multicolored

669 A145 5c *shown* 3 3
670 " 10c *Nemaster rubiginosa* 4 3
671 " 25c *Cyerce cristallina* 10 8
672 " 50c *Desmophyllum riisei* 20 15
Nos. 669-672, C395-C398 (8) 2.32 1.76

Gramma Loreto—A146

1973 *Perf. 13½*

Multicolored

673 A146 10c *shown* 4 3
674 " 50c *Acanthurus coeruleus* 25 15
Nos. 673-674, C399-C402 (6) 3.44 2.55

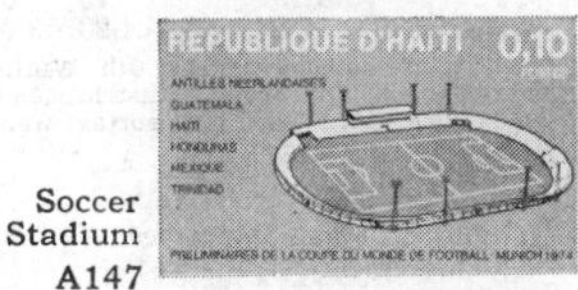

Soccer Stadium
A147

Design: 20c, Haiti No. 654.

1973, Nov. 29 *Perf. 14x13*

675 A147 10c bister, black & emerald 4 3
676 " 20c rose lilac, black & tan 8 7
Nos. 675-676, C407-C410 (6) 5.34 4.00

Caribbean countries preliminary games of the World Soccer Championships, Munich, 1974.

Jean Jacques Dessalines — A148

Nicolaus Copernicus — A149

1974, Apr. 22 Photo. *Perf. 14*

677 A148 10c lt. bl. & emerald 4 3
678 " 20c rose & black 8 7
679 " 25c yellow & violet 10 8
Nos. 677-679, C411-C414 (7) 1.84 1.38

1974, May 24 Litho. *Perf. 14x13½*

Design: 10c, Symbol of heliocentric system.

680 A149 10c multicolored 4 3
681 " 25c brt. grn. & multi. 10 8
Nos. 680-681, C415-C419 (7) 1.96 1.46

500th anniversary of the birth of Nicolaus Copernicus (1473-1543), Polish astronomer.

Pres. Jean-Claude Duvalier
A151

1974 Photo. *Perf. 14x13½*

689 A151 10c green & gold 4 3
690 " 20c car. rose & gold 8 7
691 " 50c blue & gold 20 16
Nos. 689-691, C421-C426 (9) 4.54 3.42

Nos. 662, 673 and 679-680 Surcharged with New Value and Bar

Photo.; Litho.

1976 *Perf. 11½, 13½, 14, 14x13½*

692 A142 80c on 25c 50 28
693 A146 80c on 10c 50 28
694 A148 80c on 25c 50 28
695 A149 80c on 10c 50 28

Haiti No. C11 and Bicentennial Emblem—A152

1976, Apr. 22 Photo. *Perf. 11½*

Granite Paper

696 A152 10c multicolored 4 3
Nos. 696, C434-C437 (5) 4.16 3.12

American Bicentennial.

Dessalines Type of 1972

1977 Photogravure *Perf. 11½*

697 A142 10c rose & black 4 3
698 " 20c lemon & black 8 5
699 " 50c violet & black 20 15
700 " 50c tan & black 20 15

Dessalines Type of 1972 Surcharged in Black or Red

1978 Photo. *Perf. 11½*

705 A142 1g on 20c (#698) 40 30
706 " 1g on 1.75g (#C454) 40 30
707 " 1.25g on 75c (#C448) 50 38
708 " 1.25g on 1.50g (#C453) 50 38
709 " 1.25g on 1.50g (#C453; R) 50 38
Nos. 705-709 (5) 2.30 1.74

Rectangular bar obliterates old denomination on Nos. 705-709 and "Par Avion" on Nos. 706-709.

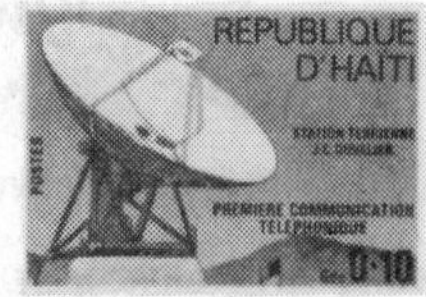

J. C. Duvalier Earth Telecommunications Station—A153

Designs: 20c, Video telephone. 50c, Alexander Graham Bell (vert.).

1978, June 19 Litho. *Perf. 13½*

710 A153 10c multicolored 4 3
711 " 20c " 8 6
712 " 50c " 20 15
Nos. 710-712, C466-C468 (6) 2.02 1.52

Centenary of first telephone call by Alexander Graham Bell, March 10, 1876.

Athletes' Inaugural Parade
A154

Designs (Montreal Olympic Games' Emblem and): 25c, Bicyclists. 50c, High jump.

1978, Sept. 4 Litho. *Perf. 13½x13*

713 A154 5c multicolored 3 3
714 " 25c " 10 8
715 " 50c " 20 15
Nos. 713-715, C469-C471 (6) 3.83 2.89

21st Olympic Games, Montreal, July 17–Aug. 1, 1976.

Mother Nursing Child
A155

1979, Jan. 15 Photo. *Perf. 14x14½*

716 A155 25c multicolored 10 8

Inter-American Children's Institute, 50th anniversary. See Nos. C472-C473.

SEMI-POSTAL STAMPS

Pierre de Coubertin—SP1

Engraved

1939, Oct. 3 ***Perf. 12*** **Unwmkd.**

B1 SP1 10c+10c multi. 35.00 35.00

Issued to honor Pierre de Coubertin, organizer of the modern Olympic Games. The surtax was used to build a Sports Stadium at Port-au-Prince.
See also Nos. CB1–CB2.

Nos. 419-420 Surcharged in Deep Carmine

+ 50 CENTIMES

e

Perf. 13x13½, 13½x13

1958, Aug. 30 Litho. **Unwmkd.**

B2 A82 1g+50c purple 4.00 4.00

B3 A83 1.50g+50c red orange 4.50 4.50

The surtax was for the Red Cross. Overprint arranged horizontally on No. B3. See also No. CB9.

Similar Surcharge in Red on One Line on Nos. 440-441.

1959, Apr. 7 Photo. ***Perf. 11½***

Granite Paper

B4 A87 10c+25c rose pink 40 35

B5 " 25c+25c green 60 50

Nos. 444-446 Surcharged Type "e" in Red

Perf. 14x13½

B6 A88 10c+50c violet blue & olive 1.25 80

B7 " 50c+50c green & deep brown 1.25 90

B8 " 2g+50c deep claret & dark brown 1.75 1.50

Nos. B4-B8 (5) 5.25 4.05

The surtax from Nos. B4–B8 was for the Red Cross. See also Nos. CB10–CB15.

No. 447 Surcharged Diagonally

Nations Unies
ANNEE DES REFUGIES
1959-1960
+ 20
Centimes

Photogravure.

1959, July 23 ***Perf. 12*** **Unwmkd.**

B9 A89 50c + 20c light blue & deep claret 1.25 1.25

Issued for the World Refugee Year, July 1, 1959–June 30, 1960. See Nos. CB16–CB18.

Nos. 448-450 Surcharged in Dark Carmine

POUR LE SPORT
+ 0.75
CENTIMES

1959, Oct. 30 ***Perf. 14***

B10 A90 25c+75c black brown & light blue 1.25 1.00

B11 " 50c+75c multi. 1.50 1.00

B12 A91 75c+75c brn. & blue 1.50 1.00

Nos. B10-B12, CB19-CB21 (6) 8.75 6.75

The surtax was for Haitian athletes.
On No. B12, surcharge lines are spaced to total depth of 16mm.

No. 436 Surcharged in Red:
"Hommage a l' UNICEF +G. 0,50"

Engraved and Lithographed

1960, Feb. 2 ***Perf. 11½***

B13 A86 1g+50c black & brick red 1.50 1.50

Issued to honor the United Nations International Children's Emergency Fund. See Nos. CB22–CB23.

Nos. 452-453 Surcharged with Additional Value and Overprinted "ALPHABETISATION" in Red or Black.

Perf. 12½x13

1960, July 12 Litho. **Unwmkd.**

B14 A92 10c+20c salmon & green (R) 40 30

B15 " 10c+30c salmon & green 50 40

B16 " 50c+20c violet & magenta (R) 75 60

B17 " 50c+30c violet & magenta 1.00 80

Nos. B14-B17, CB24-CB27 (8) 7.40 5.60

Olympic Games Issue.

Nos. 464-465 Surcharged with Additional Value.

1960, Sept. 9 Photo. ***Perf. 12***

B18 A94 50c+25c green & ochre 60 40

B19 " 1g+25c dark brown & greenish blue 75 50

See Nos. CB28–CB29.

No. 469 Surcharged
"UNICEF +25 centimes"

1961, Jan. 14 Engraved ***Perf. 10½***

B20 A96 1g+25c grn. & blk. 75 50

Issued for the United Nations International Children's Emergency Fund. See Nos. CB30–CB31.

No. 469 Surcharged:
"OMS SNEM +20 CENTIMES"

1961, Dec. 11

B21 A96 1g+20c grn. & blk. 1.25 1.00

Issued to publicize Haiti's participation in the U.N. malaria eradication drive. See Nos. CB35–CB36.

Nos. 434, 436 and 438 Surcharged in Black or Red:

Duvalier-Ville
+25
CENTIMES

(Surcharge arranged to fit shape of stamp.)

1961-62 Engr. & Litho. ***Perf. 11½***

B22 A86 20c+25c black & yellow 50 40

B23 " 1g+50c black & brick red (R) ('62) 1.00 75

B24 " 2.50g+50c black & gray violet (R) ('62) 1.50 1.20

Nos. B22-B24, CB37-CB41 (8) 11.60 9.95

The surtax was for the benefit of the urban rehabilitation program in Duvalier Ville.

Nos. 486–488 Surcharged:
"+25 centimes"

1962, Sept. 13 Litho. ***Perf. 12***

B25 A99 5c+25c crimson & deep blue 30 20

B26 " 10c+25c red brown & emerald 40 25

B27 " 50c+25c blue & crimson 50 35

Nos. B25-B27, CB42-CB44 (6) 2.50 1.80

Nos. 489–490 Surcharged in Red:
"+0.20"

1962 ***Perf. 12½x13*** **Unwmkd.**

B28 A92 10c+20c blue & org. 25 20

B29 " 50c+20c rose lilac & olive green 40 30

See also Nos. CB45–CB46.

No. 502 Surcharged:
"ALPHABETISATION" and "+0,10"

1963, Mar. 15 Photo. ***Perf. 14x14½***

B30 A102 25c+10c bl. gray, yel. & blk. 20 15

See also Nos. CB47–CB48.

Nos. 491–494 Surcharged and Overprinted in Black or Red With Olympic Emblem and: "JEUX OLYMPIQUES / D'HIVER / INNSBRUCK 1964"

Perf. 14x14½, 14½x14

1964, July 27 **Unwmkd.**

B31 A100 50c+10c on 3c multi. (R) 75 50

B32 " 50c+10c on 5c multi. 75 50

B33 " 50c+10c on 10c multi. (R) 75 50

B34 " 50c+10c on 25c multi. 75 50

Nos. B31-B34, CB49 (5) 4.20 3.00

Issued to commemorate the 9th Winter Olympic Games, Innsbruck, Austria, Jan. 20–Feb. 9, 1964. The 10c surtax went for charitable purposes.

Nos. 510-512 Surcharged:
"+ 5c." in Black

1965, Mar. 15 Photo. ***Perf. 11½***

Granite Paper

B35 A105 10c+5c light blue & dark brown 12 6

B36 " 25c+5c salmon & dark brown 25 16

B37 " 50c+5c pale rose lilac & dk. brn. 50 40

Nos. B35-B37, CB51-CB54 (7) 3.47 3.22

Nos. B35–B37 and CB51–CB54 also exist with this surcharge (with period after "c") in red or green. They also exist with a similar black surcharge which lacks the period and is in a thinner, lighter type face.

Nos. 533 and 535–536 Surcharged and Overprinted with Haitian Scout Emblem and "12e Jamboree / Mondial 1967" Like Regular Issue

1967, Aug. 21 Photo. ***Perf. 11½***

B38 A111 10c+10c on 5c multi. 10 10

B39 " 15c+10c multi. 15 15

B40 " 50c+10c " 30 30

Issued to commemorate the 12th Boy Scout World Jamboree, Farragut State Park, Idaho, Aug. 1–9. The surcharge on No. B38 includes 2 bars through old denomination. See Nos. CB55–CB56.

Nos. 600–601 Surcharged in Red with New Value, Red Cross and:
"50ème. Anniversaire / de la Ligue des / Sociétés de la / Croix Rouge"

1969, June 25 Litho. ***Perf. 11½***

B41 A127 10c+10c multi. 10 10

B42 " 50c+20c " 35 35

Issued to commemorate the 50th anniversary of the League of Red Cross Societies. See Nos. CB61–CB62.

Nos. 642–643 Surcharged with New Value and:
"INAUGURATION / 22-7-71"

1971, Aug. 3 Litho. ***Perf. 14x13½***

B43 A138 20c+50c multi. 40 35

B44 " 25c+1.50g " 1.00 75

Inauguration of the François Duvalier Central Hydroelectric Plant, July 22, 1971.

AIR POST STAMPS.

Plane over Port-au-Prince—AP1

Engraved.

1929-30 ***Perf. 12.*** **Unwmkd.**

C1 AP1 25c deep green ('30) 40 30

C2 " 50c deep violet 60 25

C3 " 75c red brown ('30) 1.75 1.50

C4 " 1g deep ultramarine 2.00 1.65

AP2a

Red Surcharge.

1933, July 6

C4A AP2a 60c on 20c blue 50.00 50.00

Issued to commemorate the non-stop flight of Capt. J. Errol Boyd and Robert G. Lyon from New York to Port-au-Prince.

Plane over Christophe's Citadel

AP2

1933–40

C5 AP2 50c orange brown 5.00 75

C6 " 50c olive green ('35) 3.50 75

C7 " 50c car. rose ('37) 2.50 1.50

C8 " 50c black ('38) 2.00 75

C8A " 60c chocolate ('40) 90 10

C9 " 1g ultramarine 1.50 40

Nos. C5-C9 (6) 15.40 4.25

Alexandre Dumas, His Father and Son—AP3

1936, Mar. 1 Litho. ***Perf. 11½***

C10 AP3 60c bright violet & chocolate 5.00 3.00

Visit of delegation from France to Haiti.

Arms of Haiti and Portrait of George Washington—AP4

1938, Aug. 29 Engraved. *Perf. 12*

C11	AP4	60c deep blue	75	35

Issued in commemoration of the 150th anniversary of the Constitution of the United States of America.

Caribbean Conference Type of Regular Issue

1941, June 30

C12	A60	60c olive	5.00	1.00
C13	"	1.25g purple	4.00	75

Issued to commemorate the Third Inter-American Caribbean Conference, held at Port-au-Prince.

Madonna Type of Regular Issue and

AP7

1942, Dec. 8 *Perf. 12*

C14	A61	10c dark olive	40	20
C15	"	25c bright ultra.	60	50
C16	"	50c turq. green	1.00	40
C17	"	60c rose carmine	1.50	75
C18	"	1.25g black	3.00	75
		Nos. C14–C18 (5)	6.50	2.60

Souvenir Sheets.

Perf. 12, Imperf.

C19	AP7	Sheet of 2, #C14 & C16	4.00	4.00
C20	"	Sheet of 2, #C15 & C17	4.00	4.00
C21	"	Sheet of 1, #C18	4.00	4.00

Issued in honor of Our Lady of Perpetual Help, patroness of Haiti. Sheet size: 140x128mm.

Killick Type of Regular Issue.

1943, Sept. 6

C22	A62	60c purple	75	45
C23	"	1.25g black	2.75	2.50

No. C8A Surcharged with New Value and Bars in Red.

1944, Nov. 25

C24	AP2	10c on 60c chocolate	75	45
		a. Bars at right vertical	2.50	
		b. Double surcharge	75.00	

Red Cross Type of Regular Issue.

1945 Cross in Rose.

C25	A63	20c yellow orange	20	15
C26	"	25c bright ultra.	20	10
C27	"	50c olive black	25	10
C28	"	60c dull violet	35	15
C29	"	1g yellow	1.75	20
C30	"	1.25g carmine	1.25	40
C31	"	1.35g green	1.25	80
C32	"	5g black	7.50	4.50
		Nos. C25–C32 (8)	12.75	6.40

International Red Cross.

Issue dates: 1g, Aug. 14; others, Feb. 20.

Franklin D. Roosevelt
AP11

1946, Feb. 5 *Perf. 12* Unwmkd.

C33	AP11	20c black	20	10
C34	"	60c "	30	15

Capois Type of Regular Issue

1946, July 18 Engraved.

C35	A64	20c carmine rose	10	10
C36	"	25c dark green	15	15
C37	"	50c orange	25	18
C38	"	60c purple	30	18
C39	"	1g gray black	50	15
C40	"	1.25g red violet	1.00	60
C41	"	1.35g black	1.25	1.00
C42	"	5g rose carmine	3.50	2.50
		Nos. C35–C42 (8)	7.05	4.86

Nos. C37 and C41 Surcharged with New Value and Bar or Block in Red or Black.

1947-48

C43	A64	5c on 1.35g black (R) ('48)	80	25
C44	"	30c on 50c orange	60	45
C45	"	30c on 1.35g black (R)	60	55

Dessalines Type of 1947–54 Regular Issue.

1947, Oct. 17 Engraved.

C46	A65	20c chocolate	25	8

Christopher Columbus and Fleet
AP14

Pres. Dumarsais Estimé and Exposition Buildings
AP15

1950, Feb. 12 *Perf. 12½*

C47	AP14	30c ultra. & gray	1.00	50
C48	AP15	1g black	1.00	40

Issued to commemorate the 200th anniversary (in 1949) of the founding of Port-au-Prince.

Nos. C36, C39 and C41 Surcharged or Overprinted in Carmine

UPU
1874 1949
30

1950, Oct. 4 *Perf. 12*

C49	A64	30c on 25c dk. grn.	50	50
		a. 30c on 1g gray black	100.00	
C50	A64	1g gray black	1.00	90
		a. "P" of ovpt. omitted	60.00	60.00
C51	A64	1.50g on 1.35g black	1.65	1.35

Issued to commemorate the 75th anniversary (in 1949) of the formation of the Universal Postal Union.

Bananas
AP16

Coffee
AP17

Sisal
AP18

1951, Sept. 3 Photo. *Perf. 12½*

C52	AP16	30c deep orange	80	35
C53	AP17	80c dark green & salmon pink	2.00	1.00
C54	AP18	5g gray	7.00	4.00

Queen Isabella I
AP19

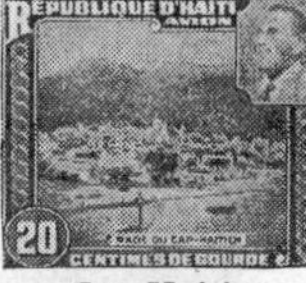

Cap Haitien Roadstead
AP20

1951, Oct. 12 *Perf. 13*

C55	AP19	15c brown	40	20
C56	"	30c dull blue	75	30

Issued to commemorate the 500th anniversary of the birth of Queen Isabella I of Spain.

1953, May 4 Engr. *Perf. 12*

Designs: 30c, Workers' housing, St. Martin. 1.50g, Restored cathedral. 2.50g, School lunchroom.

C57	AP20	20c deep blue	25	18
C58	"	30c red brown	50	25
C59	"	1.50g gray black	1.25	75
C60	"	2.50g violet	2.50	1.50

Nos. C38 and C41 Surcharged in Black

18 MAI
1803 - 1953
50

1953, May 18

C61	A64	50c on 60c purple	60	20
		a. Dble. surch.	20.00	20.00
C62	"	50c on 1.35g black	60	30
		a. Double surcharge	20.00	

Issued to commemorate the 150th anniversary of the adoption of the national flag.

Henri Christophe
AP21

J. J. Dessalines and Paul E. Magloire
AP22

1954, Jan. 1 Photo. *Perf. 11½*

Portraits in Black.

C63	AP21	50c salmon	60	30
C64	"	50c olive green (*Toussaint L'Ouverture*)	60	30
C65	"	50c olive green (*Dessalines*)	60	30
C66	AP21	50c blue (*Petion*)	60	30
C67	"	50c brown (*Boisrond-Tonerre*)	60	30
C68	"	1g gray (*Petion*)	1.00	65
C69	"	1.50g rose pink (*Lamartiniere*)	2.00	1.50
C70	AP22	7.50g orange	7.00	7.00
		Nos. C63–C70 (8)	13.00	10.65

See also Nos. C95–C96.

Marie Jeanne and Lamartinière Leading Attack—AP23

Design: Nos. C73 & C74, Battle of Vertieres.

1954, Jan. 1 *Perf. 12½*

C71	AP23	50c black	45	15
C72	"	50c carmine	40	15
C73	"	50c ultramarine	40	15
C74	"	50c salmon pink	40	15

Nos. C63 to C74 were issued to commemorate the 150th anniversary of Haitian independence.

Mme. Magloire Type of Regular Issue.

1954, Jan. 1 *Perf. 11½*

C75	A72	20c red orange	15	15
C76	"	50c brown	35	35
C77	"	1g gray green	75	60
C78	"	1.50g crimson	1.00	90
C79	"	2.50g blue green	1.75	1.35
C80	"	5g gray	4.00	3.25
		Nos. C75–C80 (6)	8.00	6.60

Christophe Types of Regular Issue

1954, Dec. 6 Litho. *Perf. 13½x13*

Portraits in Black

C81	A73	50c orange	60	30
C82	"	1g blue	1.00	90
C83	"	1.50g green	1.50	1.35
C84	"	2.50g gray	2.50	1.75
C85	"	5g rose carmine	5.00	3.00

Perf. 13

Flag in Black and Carmine

C86	A74	50c orange	60	30
C87	"	1g deep blue	1.00	90
C88	"	1.50g blue green	1.50	1.35
C89	"	2.50g gray	2.50	1.75
C90	"	5g red orange	4.50	3.25
		Nos. C81–C90 (10)	20.70	14.85

Nos. C81 to C90 were issued to publicize the restoration of Christophe's Citadel.

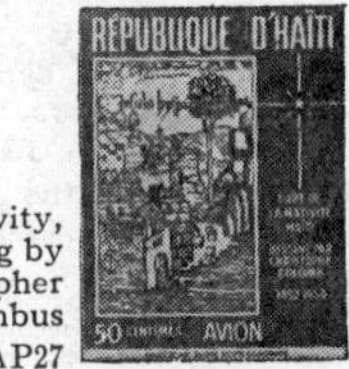

Fort Nativity, Drawing by Christopher Columbus
AP27

1954, Dec. 14 Engraved *Perf. 12*

C91	AP27	50c dark rose car.	1.00	40
C92	"	50c dark gray	1.00	40

Dessalines Type of 1955–57 Issue.

Photogravure.

1955, July 14 *Perf. 11½* Unwmkd.

C93	A75	20c orange & black	15	12
C94	"	20c yellow green & black	15	12

Portrait Type of 1954

Design: J. J. Dessalines.

1955, July 19

Dates omitted. Portrait in black.

C95	AP21	50c gray	50	18
C96	"	50c blue	50	20

Dessalines Memorial Type of Regular Issue.

1955, Aug. 1

C97 A76 1.50g gray & black 1.00 35
C98 " 1.50g green & black 1.25 50

21st anniversary of new Haitian army.

Types of 1956 Regular Issue and

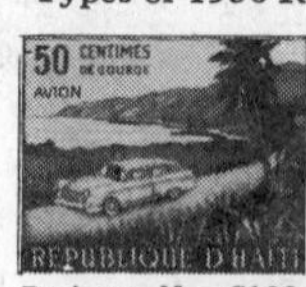

Car and Coastal View
AP30

Designs: No. C100, 75c, Plane, steamship and Haiti map. 1g, Car and coastal view. 2.50g, Flamingo. 5g, Mallard.

Granite Paper.

1956, Apr. 14 *Perf. 11½* Unwmkd.

C99 AP30 50c henna brown & light blue 45 20
C100 " 50c black & gray 45 20
C101 " 75c deep green & blue green 90 70
C102 " 1g olive green & light blue 90 50
C103 A77 2.50g deep orange & orange 5.00 1.85
C104 A78 5g red & buff 7.50 3.75
Nos. C99-C104 (6) 15.20 7.20

Kant Type of Regular Issue.

1956, July 19 Photo. *Perf. 12*

Granite Paper.

C105 A79 50c chestnut 40 25
C106 " 75c dp. yel. green 60 35
C107 " 1.50g dp. magenta 2.00 75
a. Miniature sheet of 3 6.00 4.00

Issued to commemorate the tenth anniversary of the first Inter-American Philosophical Congress.
No. C107a exists both perf. and imperf., measuring 154x50mm. Each sheet contains Nos. C105, C106 and a 1.25g gray black of same design.

Waterfall Type of Regular Issue.

1957, Dec. 16 *Perf. 11½*

Granite Paper.

C108 A80 50c green & greenish blue 30 20
C109 " 1.50g olive green & greenish blue 90 80
C110 " 2.50g dark blue & bright blue 1.50 1.10
C111 " 5g bluish black & sapphire 3.50 2.75

Dessalines Type of Regular Issue.

1958, July 2

C112 A81 50c orange & black 40 25

Issued to commemorate the bicentenary of the birth of J. J. Dessalines.

Brussels Fair Types of Regular Issue, 1958.

Perf. 13x13½, 13½x13

1958, July 22 Litho. Unwmkd.

C113 A82 2.50g pale carmine rose 1.50 1.00
C114 A83 5g bright blue 2.00 1.50
a. Souvenir sheet, imperf. 6.00 6.00

Issued for the Universal and International Exposition at Brussels.
No. C114a measures 70x108mm. and contains one each of Nos. C113-C114. Marginal inscription in bright blue: "Progres, Prosperite et Paix par le Commerce International."

Sylvio Cator
AP33

1958, Aug. 16 Photo. *Perf. 11½*

Granite Paper

C115 AP33 50c green 25 10
C116 " 50c black brown 25 10
C117 AP33 1g orange brown 60 25
C118 " 5g gray 3.50 1.25

Issued to commemorate the 30th anniversary of the world championship record broad jump of Sylvio Cator.

IGY Type of Regular Issue, 1958.

Designs: 50c, U. S. Satellite. 1.50g, Emperor penguins. 2g, Modern observatory.

1958, Oct. 8 *Perf. 14x13½*

C119 A85 50c deep ultramarine & brown red 75 30
C120 " 1.50g brown & crimson 2.50 75
C121 " 2g dark blue & crimson 3.00 50
a. Souvenir sheet of 4, imperf. 10.00 9.00

International Geophysical Year 1957-58.
No. C121a contains one each of Nos. C119-C121 and No. 427. Black marginal inscription. Size: 82½x112mm.

President Francois Duvalier
AP34

Engraved and Lithographed.

1958, Oct. 22 *Perf. 11½* Unwmkd.

Commemorative Inscription in Ultramarine.

C122 AP34 50c black & rose 1.50 25
C123 " 2.50g black & ochre 2.00 90
C124 " 5g black & rose lilac 3.00 2.50
C125 " 7.50g black & light blue green 5.00 4.00

See note after No. 431.
Souvenir sheets of 3 exist, perf. and imperf., containing one each of Nos. C124-C125 and No. 431. Sheets measure 132x77mm. with marginal inscription in ultramarine. Price, $9 each.

Same Without Commemorative Inscription.

1958, Nov. 20

C126 AP34 50c black & rose 40 20
C127 " 1g black & violet 75 40
C128 " 1.50g black & pale brown 1.00 60
C129 " 2g black & rose pink 1.50 80
C130 " 2.50g black & ochre 1.50 1.00
C131 " 5g black & rose lilac 3.00 2.25
C132 " 7.50g black & light blue green 4.50 3.25
Nos. C126-C132 (7) 12.65 8.50

Type of Regular Issue and

Flags of Haiti and U.N.
AP35

Photogravure.

1958, Dec. 5 *Perf. 11½* Unwmkd.

Granite Paper

C133 AP35 50c pink, carmine & ultramarine 30 15
C134 A87 75c bright blue 45 20
C135 " 1g brown 65 30
a. Souvenir sheet 7.00 7.00

Issued in tribute to the United Nations.
No. C135a contains one each of Nos. C133 and C135, imperf. Size: 108x67mm. Brown marginal inscription and U. N. Emblem.

Nos. C133-C135 Overprinted: "10th ANNIVERSARY OF THE UNIVERSAL DECLARATION OF HUMAN RIGHTS," in English, French, Spanish or Portuguese.

1959, Jan. 28

C136 AP35 50c pink, carmine & ultra. 1.00 1.00
a. Block of four 4.00 4.00
C137 A87 75c bright blue 1.50 1.50
a. Block of four 6.00 6.00
C138 " 1g brown 2.50 2.50
a. Block of four 10.00 10.00

Nos. C136a, C137a and C138a contain overprints in English, French, Spanish and Portuguese. See note after No. 443.

Pope Pius XII
AP36

Designs: 1.50g, Pope praying. 2.50g, Pope on throne.

1959, Feb. 28 Photo. *Perf. 14x13½*

C139 AP36 50c green & lilac 30 10
C140 " 1.50g olive & red brown 1.00 20
C141 " 2.50g purple & dark blue 1.50 45

Issued in memory of Pope Pius XII.

Abraham Lincoln Issue

Type of Regular Issue, 1959.

Designs: Various Portraits of Lincoln.

1959, May 12 *Perf. 12*

C142 A89 1g light green & chestnut 50 25
C143 " 2g pale lemon & slate green 1.00 30
C144 " 2.50g buff & violet blue 1.10 50
a. Miniature sheet of 4 5.00 5.00

Issued to commemorate the sesquicentennial of the birth of Abraham Lincoln.
No. C144a measures 120x105mm. and contains one each of Nos. 447 and C142-C144, imperforate.

Pan American Games Types of Regular Issue.

Designs: 50c, Jean Baptiste Dessables and map of American Midwest, c. 1791. 1g, Chicago's skyline and Dessables house. 1.50g, Discus thrower and flag of Haiti.

Photogravure.

1959, Aug. 27 *Perf. 14* Unwmkd.

C145 A91 50c henna brown & aquamarine 1.25 40
C146 A90 1g lilac & aqua. 1.50 60
C147 " 1.50g multicolored 2.00 75

Issued to commemorate the 3rd Pan American Games, Chicago, Aug. 27-Sept. 7.

Nos. C145-C147 Overprinted

1960, Feb. 29

C148 A91 50c henna brown & aquamarine 2.00 2.00
C149 A90 1g lilac & aqua. 3.00 3.00
C150 " 1.50g multicolored 4.00 4.00

Issued to commemorate the 8th Olympic Winter Games, Squaw Valley, Calif., Feb. 18-29, 1960.

WRY Type of Regular Issue, 1960.

1960, Apr. 7 Litho. *Perf. 12½x13*

C151 A92 50c blue & black 35 25
C152 A92 1g light green & maroon 75 50
a. Souvenir sheet of 4 9.00 9.00

Issued to publicize World Refugee Year, July 1, 1959-June 30, 1960.
No. C152a contains one each of Nos. 452-453 and C151-C152, imperf. Black marginal inscription. Size: 133x76mm.
See also Nos. C191-C192.

Nos. C31, C28 and 369 Surcharged or Overprinted in Red: "28ème ANNIVERSAIRE"

1960, May 8 Engraved *Perf. 12*

Cross in Rose.

C153 A63 20c on 1.35g green 25 12
C154 " 50c on 60c dull violet 40 30
C155 " 50c on 1.35g green 40 35
C156 " 50c on 2.50g pale violet 40 35
C157 " 60c dull violet 50 35
C158 " 1g on 1.35g green 65 60
C159 " 1.35g green 90 80
C160 " 2g on 1.35g green 1.50 1.35
Nos. C153-C160 (8) 5.00 4.22

Issued to commemorate the 28th anniversary of the Haitian Red Cross. Additional overprint "Avion" on No. C156.

Sugar Type of Regular Issue

Designs (Miss Fouchard and): 50c, Harvest. 2.50g, Beach.

Photogravure

1960, May 30 *Perf. 11½* Unwmkd.

Granite Paper

C161 A93 50c lilac rose & brown 40 15
C162 " 2.50g ultramarine & brown 1.00 50

Haitian sugar industry.

Olympic Type of Regular Issue

Designs: 50c, Pierre de Coubertin, Melbourne stadium and torch. 1.50g, Discus thrower and Rome stadium. 2.50g, Victors' parade, Athens, 1896, and Melbourne, 1956.

1960, Aug. 18 *Perf. 12*

C163 A94 50c maroon & bistre 30 20
C164 " 1.50g rose carmine & yellow grn. 1.00 40
C165 " 2.50g slate green & magenta 1.50 60
a. Souv. sheet of 2 5.00 5.00

Issued to commemorate the 17th Olympic Games, Rome, Aug. 25-Sept. 11.
No. C165a contains one each of Nos. 465 and C165, imperf. with marginal inscription in bister & slate green. Size: 104½x57mm.

Jeanty Type of Regular Issue

Designs: 50c, Occide Jeanty and score from "1804." 1.50g, Occide Jeanty and National Capitol.

1960, Oct. 19 *Perf. 14x14½*

C166 A95 50c yellow & blue 75 15
C167 " 1.50g lilac rose & slate green 1.25 40

Issued to commemorate the centenary of the birth of Occide Jeanty, composer.
Printed in sheets of 12 (3x4) with commemorative inscription and opening bars of "1804." Jeanty's military march, in top margin.

UN Type of Regular Issue, 1960

1960, Nov 25 Engr. *Perf. 10½*

C168 A96 50c red orange & black 30 12
C169 " 1.50g dark blue & black 80 40
a. Souvenir sheet of 3 4.50 4.50

United Nations, 15th anniversary.
No. 169a contains one each of Nos. 469, C168-169, imperf. Black marginal inscription. Size: 106x77mm.

Type of Regular Issue, 1958 (Dessalines)

1960, Nov. 5 Photo. *Perf. 11½*

Granite Paper

C170 A81 20c gray & black 15 8

Sud-Caravelle Jet Airliner and Orchid—AP37

Designs: 50c, Boeing 707 jet airliner, facing left, and Kittyhawk. 1g, Sud-Caravelle jet airliner and Orchid. 1.50g, Boeing 707 jet airliner and air post stamp of 1933.

1960, Dec. 17 Photo. Unwmkd.

Granite Paper

C171 AP37 20c deep ultra. & carmine 10 8
C172 " 50c rose brown & green 40 25
C173 " 50c brt. greenish blue & olive grn. 40 25
C174 " 50c gray & green 40 25
C175 " 1g gray olive & vermilion 50 40
C176 " 1.50g bright pink & dark blue 1.00 60
a. Souvenir sheet of 3 2.50 2.25
Nos. C171-C176 (6) 2.80 1.83

Issued for Aviation Week, Dec. 17–23.

Nos. C172–C174 are dated 17 Decembre 1903.

No. C176a contains one imperf. copy each of Nos. C174–C176 with olive green marginal inscription: "Aéroport International, Port-au-Prince, Republique d'Haiti." Size: 80x124mm.

Dumas Type of Regular Issue.

Designs: 50c, The Three Musketeers and Dumas père (horiz.) 1g, The Lady of the Camellias and Dumas fils. 1.50g, The Count of Monte Cristo and Dumas père.

1961, Feb. 10 Photo. *Perf. 11½*

Granite Paper

C177 A97 50c bright blue & black 45 20
C178 " 1g black & red 60 40
C179 " 1.50g bright green & blue black 90 60

See note after No. 474.

Type of Regular Issue, 1961.

Designs: 20c, Privateer in Battle. 50c, Pirate with cutlass in rigging. 1g, Map of Tortuga.

1961, Apr. 4 Litho. *Perf. 12*

C180 A98 20c dk. blue & yel. 20 8
C181 " 50c bright purple & orange 40 18
C182 " 1g Prussian green & yellow 60 35

Issued as tourist publicity.

Nos. C170, C112 and C101 Overprinted: "Dr. F. Duvalier Président 22 Mai 1961"

1961, May 22 Photo. *Perf. 11½*

C183 A81 20c gray & black 15 10
C184 " 50c orange & black 30 20
C185 AP30 75c deep green & blue green 50 40

Re-election of Pres. Francois Duvalier.

No. C182 Overprinted or Surcharged: "EXPLORATION SPATIALE JOHN GLENN" and Capsule

1962, May 10 Litho. *Perf. 12*

C186 A98 1g Prussian green & yellow 1.25 1.00
C187 " 2g on 1g Prussian green & yellow 2.25 2.00

See note after No. 485.

Malaria Type of Regular Issue.

Designs: 20c, 1g, Triangle pointing down. 50c, Triangle pointing up.

1962, May 30 Unwmkd.

C188 A99 20c lilac & red 15 10
C189 " 50c emerald & rose carmine 35 20
C190 " 1g org. & dk. violet 60 40
a. Souv. sheet of 3 3.00 3.00

Issued for the World Health Organization drive to eradicate malaria. Printed in sheets of 12 with marginal inscription.

No. C190a contains stamps similar to Nos. 488 and C189–C190 in changed colors and imperf. Maroon inscription, "Contribution d'Haiti a l'OMS," in bottom margin; "Republique d'Haiti" in top margin. Size: 140x70mm. Issued July 16.

A similar sheet without the "Contribution . . ." inscription was issued May 30.

WRY Type of 1960 Dated "1962"

1962, June 22 *Perf. 12½x13*

C191 A92 50c light blue & red brown 20 20
C192 " 1g bistre & black 45 40

Issued to publicize the plight of refugees. A souvenir sheet exists containing one each of Nos. 489–490 and C191–C192, imperf. with brown border and marginal inscription. Size: 132x76 mm. Price, $5.

Boy Scout Type of 1962.

Designs: 20c, Scout giving Scout sign. 50c, Haitian Scout emblem. 1.50g, Lord and Lady Baden-Powell (horiz.).

Perf. 14x14½, 14½x14

1962, Aug. 6 Photo. Unwmkd.

C193 A100 20c multicolored 20 8
C194 " 50c " 40 20
C195 " 1.50g " 75 60

Issued to commemorate the 22nd anniversary of the Haitian Boy Scouts. A souvenir sheet contains one each of Nos. C194–C195 imperf. with dark green marginal inscription. Size: 101x60mm. Price, $1.25.

Nos. 495 and C193–C195 Overprinted: "AÉROPORT INTERNATIONAL 1962"

1962, Oct. 26 *Perf. 14x14½, 14½x14*

C196 A100 20c multi., #C193 20 10
C197 " 50c " #495 40 20
C198 " 50c " #C194 40 20
C199 " 1.50g " #C195 70 60

Proceeds from the sale of Nos. C196–C199 were for the construction of new airport at Port-au-Prince. The overprint on No. C197 has "Poste Aérienne" added.

Seattle Fair Type of 1962

Design: Denomination at left, "Avion" at right.

1962, Nov. 19 Litho. *Perf. 12½*

C200 A101 50c black & pale lilac 40 10
C201 " 1g orange brown & gray 80 20
C202 " 1.50g red lilac & orange 90 30

Issued to commemorate the "Century 21" International Exposition, Seattle, Wash., Apr. 21–Oct. 21. An imperf. sheet of two exists containing one each of Nos. C201–C202 with simulated gray perforations. Size: 133x82mm. Price, $3.50.

Street in Duvalier Ville and Stamp of 1881—AP38

1962, Dec. 10 Photo. *Perf. 14x14½*

Stamp in Dark Brown

C203 AP38 50c orange 30 20
C204 " 1g blue 50 40
C205 " 1.50g green 75 60

Issued to publicize Duvalier Ville.

Nos. C201–C202 with Vertical Overprint in Black Similar To

1963, Jan. 23 Litho. *Perf. 12½*

C206 A101 1g orange brown & gray 1.00 75
a. Claret ovpt., horiz. 1.25 85
C207 A101 1.50g red lilac & orange 1.50 1.50
a. Claret ovpt., horiz. 1.65 1.65

Issued to publicize "Peaceful Uses of Outer Space." The black vertical overprint has no outside frame lines and no broken shading lines around capsule. Nos. C206a and C207a were issued Feb. 20.

Hunger Type of Regular Issue

Photogravure

1963, July 12 *Perf. 13x14* Unwmkd.

C208 A103 50c lilac rose & black 20 12
C209 " 1g lt. olive green & black 45 25

Issued for the "Freedom from Hunger" campaign of the U.N. Food and Agriculture Organization.

Dag Hammarskjold and U.N. Emblem—AP39

Lithographed and Photogravure

1963, Sept. 28 *Perf. 13½x14*

Portrait in Slate

C210 AP39 20c buff & brown 15 10
C211 " 50c lt. bl. & car. 30 25
a. Souvenir sheet of 2 2.00 2.00
C212 " 1g pink & blue 50 40
C213 " 1.50g gray & grn. 80 60

Issued in memory of Dag Hammarskjold, Secretary General of the United Nations, 1953–61. Printed in sheets of 25 (5x5) with map of Sweden extending over 9 stamps in second and third vertical rows. No. C211a contains 2 imperf. stamps: 50c blue and carmine and 1.50g ocher and brown with map of southern Sweden in background. Red marginal inscription. Size: 110x65mm.

Dessalines Type of Regular Issue, 1963

1963, Oct. 17 Photo. *Perf. 14x14½*

C214 A104 50c blue & lilac rose 30 15
C215 " 50c orange & green 30 15

Nos. C214–C215 and C53 Overprinted in Black or Red: "FETE DES MERES / 1964"

1964, July 22 *Perf. 14x14½, 12½*

C216 A104 50c bl. & lilac rose 40 20
C217 " 50c orange & grn. 40 20
C218 AP17 1.50g on 80c dark grn. & salmon pink (R) 75 30

Issued for Mother's Day, 1964.

Nos. C210–C213 Overprinted in Red

1863 1963

Lithographed and Photogravure

1964, Oct. 2 *Perf. 13½x14*

Portrait in Slate

C219 AP39 20c buff & brown 50 10
C220 AP39 50c lt. bl. & carm. 40 18
C221 " 1g pink & blue 60 40
C222 " 1.50g gray & green 85 55
Nos. C219–C222, CB50 (5) 4.35 2.98

Issued to commemorate the centenary (in 1963) of the International Red Cross.

Olympic Type of Regular Issue

1964, Nov. 12 Photo. *Perf. 11½*

Granite Paper

Designs: No. C223, Weight lifter. Nos. C224–C226, Hurdler.

C223 A105 50c pale lilac & dark brown 25 18
C224 " 50c pale green & dark brown 25 18
C225 " 75c buff & dk. brn. 35 30
C226 " 1.50g gray & dk. brn. 65 35
a. Souv. sheet of 4 1.75 1.75

Issued to commemorate the 18th Olympic Games, Tokyo, Oct. 10–25. Printed in sheets of 50 (10x5), with map of Japan in background extending over 27 stamps.

No. C226a contains four imperf. stamps similar to Nos. C223–C226 in changed colors and with map of Tokyo area in background. Black brown marginal inscription. Size: 74x90mm.

Airport Type of Regular Issue, 1964

1964, Dec. 15 *Perf. 14½x14*

C227 A106 50c org. & black 40 10
C228 " 1.50g brt. lilac rose & black 90 30
C229 " 2.50g lt. violet & black 1.50 75

Issued to commemorate the opening of the International Airport in Port-au-Prince.

Same Overprinted "1965"

1965, Feb. 11 Photogravure

C230 A106 50c orge. & black 40 15
C231 " 1.50g brt. lilac rose & black 1.00 60
C232 " 2.50g lt. vio. & blk. 1.50 1.00

World's Fair Type of Regular Issue, 1965

Designs: 50c, 1.50g, "Rocket Thrower" by Donald De Lue. 5g, Unisphere, N.Y. World's Fair.

1965, Mar. 22 *Perf. 13½* Unwmkd.

C233 A107 50c dp. bl. & orge. 40 15
C234 " 1.50g gray & orange 75 45
C235 " 5g multicolored 3.50 2.50

New York World's Fair, 1964–65.

Merchant Marine Type of Regular Issue, 1965

1965, May 13 Photo. *Perf. 11½*

C236 A108 50c blk., lt. greenish blue & red 20 15
C237 " 1.50g blk., lt. vio. & red 60 45

Issued to honor the merchant marine.

O. N. U.

Nos. C210–C213 Overprinted

1945-1965

Lithographed and Photogravure

1965, June 26 *Perf. 13½x14*

Portrait in Slate

C238 AP39 20c buff & brown 12 8
C239 " 50c lt. bl. & car. 25 15
C240 " 1g pink & blue 40 35
C241 " 1.50g gray & green 60 50

20th anniversary of the United Nations.

ITU Type of Regular Issue

Lithographed

1965, Aug. 16 *Perf. 13½* Unwmkd.

C242 A109 50c multicolored 20 15
C243 " 1g " 40 35

C244	A109	1.50g blue & multi.	60	50
C245	"	2g pink & multi.	90	70

Issued to commemorate the centenary of the International Telecommunication Union.

A souvenir sheet, released in 1966, contains 50c and 2g stamps resembling Nos. C242 and C245, with simulated perforations. Margins in tan with brown inscriptions. Size: 117x67½mm.

Cathedral Type of Regular Issue, 1965

Designs: 50c, Cathedral, Port-au-Prince (horiz.). 1g, High Altar. 7.50g, Statue of Our Lady of the Assumption.

Photogravure

1965, Nov. 19 ***Perf. 14x13, 13x14***

Size: 39x29, 29x39mm.

C246	A110	50c multicolored	30	10
C247	"	1g "	40	25

Size: 38x52mm.

C248	A110	7.50g multi.	3.00	2.50

Issued to commemorate the 200th anniversary of the Metropolitan Cathedral of Port-au-Prince.

Flower Type of Regular Issue

Flowers: No. C249, 5g, Passionflower. Nos. C250, C252, Okra. Nos. C251, C253, American elder.

1965, Dec. 20 Photo. ***Perf. 11½***

Granite Paper

C249	A111	50c dark violet, yel. & green	20	15
C250	"	50c multicolored	20	15
C251	"	50c green, gray & yellow	20	15
C252	"	1.50g multicolored	60	50
C253	"	1.50g grn., tan & yel.	60	50
C254	"	5g dark vio., yel. grn. & grn.	2.00	1.75
		Nos. C249-C254 (6)	3.80	3.20

Nos. C242-C243 Overprinted in Red: "20e. Anniversaire / UNESCO"

1965, Aug. 27 Litho. ***Perf. 13½***

C255	A109	50c lt. vio. & multi.	1.50	50
C256	"	1g citron & multi.	3.00	1.00

20th anniversary of UNESCO.

The souvenir sheet noted below No. C245 was also overprinted "20e. Anniversaire / UNESCO" in red.

Culture Types of Regular Issue and

Modern Painting—AP40

Designs: 50c, Ceremonial stool. 1.50g, Amulet.

Perf. 14x14½, 14½x14, 14

1966, March 14 Photo. **Unwmkd.**

C257	A113	50c lilac, brown & bronze	30	15
C258	A112	1.50g brt. rose lilac, yel. & blk.	75	50
C259	AP40	2.50g multi.	1.25	85

Nos. C257-C259 Overprinted in Black or Red: "Hommage / a Hailé Sélassié Ier / 24-25 Avril 1966"

1966, Apr. 24

C260	A112	50c lilac, brown & bronze (R)	30	20
C261	A113	1.50g brt. rose lilac, yel. & blk. (vert. ovpt.)	75	60
C262	AP40	2.50g multi. (R)	1.25	1.00

See note after No. 543.

Walter M. Schirra, Thomas P. Stafford, Frank A. Borman, James A. Lovell and Gemini VI and VII—AP41

1966, May 3 ***Perf. 13½***

C263	AP41	50c vio. bl., brn. & lt. blue	30	20
C264	"	1g grn., brn. & light blue	50	40
C265	"	1.50g carmine, brn. & blue	75	60

See note after No. 547.

Soccer Type of Regular Issue

Designs: 50c, Pres. Duvalier and soccer ball within wreath. 1.50g, President Duvalier and soccer player within wreath.

Lithographed and Photogravure

1966, June 16 ***Perf. 13x13½***

Portrait in Black; Gold Inscription; Green Commemorative Inscription in Two Lines

C266	A115	50c lt. olive green & plum	20	20
C267	"	1.50g rose & plum	75	60

Green Commemorative Inscription in 3 Lines; Gold Inscription Omitted

C268	A115	50c lt. olive green & plum	20	20
C269	"	1.50g rose & plum	75	60

Issued to commemorate the Caribbean Soccer Festival, June 10-22. Nos. C266-C267 also commemorate the National Soccer Championships, May 8-22.

Education Type of Regular Issue

Designs: 50c, "ABC", boy and girl. 1g, Scout symbols. 1.50g, Television set, book and communications satellite (horiz.).

Perf. 14x13½, 13½x14

1966, Oct. 18 Litho. and Engraved

C270	A116	50c green, yellow & brown	20	20
C271	"	1g dk. brown, org. & black	40	40
C272	"	1.50g green, bl. grn. & dk. blue	60	60

Issued to publicize education through literacy, Scouting and by audio-visual means.

Schweitzer Type of Regular Issue

Designs (Schweitzer and): 50c, 1g, Albert Schweitzer Hospital, Deschapelles, Haiti. 1.50g, Maps of Alsace and Gabon. 2g, Pipe organ.

Perf. 12½x13

1967, Apr. 20 Photo. **Unwmkd.**

C273	A117	50c multicolored	25	20
C274	"	1g "	50	40
C275	"	1.50g lt. bl. & multi.	70	60
C276	"	2g multicolored	90	80

See note after No. 561.

Fruit-Vegetable Type of Regular Issue, 1967

Designs (J. J. Dessalines and): 50c, Watermelon. 1g, Cabbage. 1.50g, Tangerine.

1967, July 4 Photo. ***Perf. 12½***

C277	A118	50c multicolored	20	15
C278	"	1g "	40	30
C279	"	1.50g "	60	50

No. C258 Overprinted and Surcharged Like EXPO '67 Regular Issue

1967, Aug. 30 Photo. ***Perf. 14½x14***

C280	A112	1.50g multicolored	75	60
C281	"	2g on 1.50g "	1.00	80

Issued to commemorate EXPO '67 International Exhibition, Montreal, Apr. 28-Oct. 27.

Duvalier Type of Regular Issue, 1967

1967, Sept. 22 Photo. ***Perf. 14x13***

C282	A119	1g bright green & gold	50	40
C283	"	1.50g violet & gold	75	60
C284	"	2g orange & gold	1.00	80

10th anniversary of Duvalier revolution.

Education Type of Regular Issue, 1967

Designs: 50c, Writing hands. 1g, Scout emblem and Scouts (vert.). 1.50g, Audio-visual teaching of algebra.

1967, Dec. 11 Litho. ***Perf. 11½***

C285	A120	50c multicolored	20	15
C286	"	1g "	40	35
C287	"	1.50g "	60	50

Issued to publicize the importance of education.

No. C269 Overprinted MEXICO 1968 (Olympic rings)

Lithographed and Photogravure

1968, Jan. 18 ***Perf. 13x13½***

C288	A115	1.50g rose & plum	75	60

Issued to publicize the 19th Olympic Games, Mexico City, Oct. 12-27.

See note after No. 579.

Caïman Woods Type of Regular Issue

1968, Apr. 22 Photo. ***Perf. 12***

Size: 36x26mm.

C289	A121	50c multicolored	20	20
C290	"	1g "	40	40

Perf. 12½x13½

Size: 49x36mm.

C291	A121	50c multicolored	20	15
C292	"	1g "	40	35
C293	"	1.50g "	60	60
C294	"	2g gray & multi.	1.00	80
C295	"	5g multicolored	2.00	1.50
		Nos. C289-C295 (7)	4.80	4.00

Issued to commemorate the Caïman Woods ceremony during the Slaves' Rebellion, Aug. 14, 1791.

Xème JEUX OLYMPIQUES D'HIVER-GRENOBLE 1968

Nos. C263-C265 Overprinted

1968, Apr. 19 ***Perf. 13½***

C296	AP41	50c multicolored	75	35
C297	"	1g "	1.50	75
C298	"	1.50g "	2.50	1.25

Issued to commemorate the 10th Winter Olympic Games, Grenoble, France, Feb. 6-18, 1968.

Monument Type of Regular Issue

1968, May 22 ***Perf. 11½***

Granite Paper

C299	A122	50c olive bister & black	30	18
C300	"	1g bright rose & black	50	35
C301	"	1.50g orange & blk.	75	50

Issued to commemorate the unveiling of the monument to the Unknown Maroon, Port-au-Prince.

Types of Regular Bishopric Issue

Designs: 50c, Palm tree and provincial coats of arms. 1g, 2.50g, Madonna, papal arms and arms of Haiti. 1.50g, Cathedral, arms of Pope Paul VI and arms of Haiti.

Perf. 13x14, 12½x13½

1968, Aug. 16 Photogravure

C302	A123	50c lilac & multi.	20	15
C303	A124	1g multicolored	40	35
C304	A124	1.50g multicolored	60	50
C305	"	2.50g "	1.00	90

Issued to commemorate the consecration of the Bishopric of Haiti, Oct. 28, 1966.

Airport Type of Regular Issue

Design: 50c, 1.50g, 2.50g, Front view of air terminal.

1968, Sept. 22 Photo. ***Perf. 11½***

Portrait in Black

C306	A125	50c rose lake & pale violet	20	15
C307	"	1.50g rose lake & blue	60	50
C308	"	2.50g rose lake & lt. greenish blue	1.00	90

Issued to commemorate the inauguration of the Francois Duvalier Airport in Port-au-Prince.

Freed Slaves' Type of Regular Issue

1968, Oct. 28 Litho. ***Perf. 14½x14***

C310	A126	50c brn., lilac & brt. pink	20	15
C311	"	1g brn., yel. grn. & brt. pink	40	35
C312	"	1.50g brown, lt. vio. blue & brt. pink	60	50
C313	"	2g brn., lt. grn. & brt. pink	80	65

Slaves' Rebellion of 1791.

Education Type of Regular Issue, 1968

Designs: 50c, 1.50g, Children watching television. 1g, Hands throwing ball, and sports medal.

1968, Nov. 14 ***Perf. 11½***

C314	A127	50c multicolored	20	15
C315	"	1g "	40	35
C316	"	1.50g "	75	50

Issued to publicize education through literacy, audio-visual means and sport.

Jan Boesman and his Balloon AP43

Cachet of May 2, 1925 Flight AP44

1968, Nov. 28 Litho. ***Perf. 13½***

C317	AP43	70c lt. yel. green & sepia	50	40
C318	"	1.75g greenish blue & sepia	1.25	1.00

Issued to commemorate Dr. Jan Boesman's balloon flight at Mexico City in November, 1968.

Miniature Sheet

1968, Nov. 28 Litho. ***Perf. 13½x14***

Black Cachets, Magenta Inscriptions and Rose Lilac Background

C318A	AP44	Sheet of 12	8.00	8.00
		b. 70c (*2 Mai 1925*)	50	50
		c. 70c (*2 Septembre 1925*)	50	50
		d. 70c (*28 Mars 1927*)	50	50
		e. 70c (*12 Juillet 1927*)	50	50
		f. 70c (*13 Septembre 1927*)	50	50
		g. 70c (*6 Fevrier 1928*)	50	50

Issued to commemorate Galiffet's 1784 balloon flight and pioneer flights of the 1920's. No. C318A contains 2 each of Nos. C318b-C318g. The background of the sheet shows in white outlines a balloon and the inscription "BALLON GALIFFET 1784." The design of each stamp shows a different airmail cachet, date of a special flight and part of the white background design. Size of sheet: 120x149mm.

Churchill Type of Regular Issue

Churchill: 50c, and early seaplane. 75c, and soldiers at Normandy. 1g, and Queen Elizabeth II. 1.50g, and Big Ben, London. 3g, and coat of arms (horiz.)

1968, Dec. 23 Photo. *Perf. 13*

C319 A128 50c gold & multi. 20 15
C320 " 75c " " 30 25
C321 " 1g " " 40 35
C322 " 1.50g " " 60 50

Souvenir Sheet

Perf. 12½x13, Imperf.

C323 A128 3g silver, black & red 1.50 1.50

Issued in memory of Sir Winston Spencer Churchill (1874–1965), statesman and World War II leader. Nos. C319–C322 exist imperf.

No. C323 contains one horizontal stamp (size: 38x25½mm.) arms of Haiti, commemorative inscription and control number in margin. Size: 101x75mm.

Nos. C299–C300 Surcharged with New Value and Rectangle

1969, Feb. 21 Photo. *Perf. 11½*

C324 A122 70c on 50c olive bister & black 30 25
C325 " 1.75g on 1g bright rose & black 75 60

Bird Type of Regular Issue

Birds of Haiti: 50c, Hispaniolan trogon. 1g, Black-cowled oriole. 1.50g, Stripe-headed tanager. 2g, Striated woodpecker.

1969, Feb. 26 *Perf. 13½*

C326 A129 50c multicolored 20 18
C327 " 1g lt. bl. & multi. 40 35
C328 " 1.50g multicolored 60 50
C329 " 2g gray & multi. 80 70

Electric Power Type of 1969

1969, May 22 Litho. *Perf. 13x13½*

C338 A131 20c dk. blue & lilac 10 8
C339 " 25c grn. & rose red 10 10
C340 " 25c rose red & grn. 20 15

Issued to publicize the Duvalier Hydroelectric Station.

Education Type of 1969

Designs: 50c, Peace poster on educational television (vert.). 1g, Learning to write. 1.50g, Playing children (vert.).

1969, Aug. 12 Litho. *Perf. 13½*

C342 A132 50c multicolored 20 15
C343 " 1g " 50 25
C344 " 1.50g " 75 50

Issued to publicize national education.

ILO Type of Regular Issue

1969, Sept. 22 *Perf. 14*

C345 A133 25c red & black 20 8
C346 " 70c org. & black 35 20
C347 " 1.75g brt. pur. & blk. 95 60

Issued to mark the 50th anniversary of the International Labor Organization.

Butterfly Type of Regular Issue

Butterflies: 50c, Danaus eresimus kaempfferi. 1.50g, Anaea marthesia nemesis. 2g, Prepona antimache.

1969, Nov. 14 Photo. *Perf. 13½*

C348 A134 50c multicolored 20 15
C349 " 1.50g " 60 50
C350 " 2g yel. & multi. 80 70

King Type of Regular Issue

Lithographed

1970, Jan. 12 *Perf. 12½x13½*

C351 A135 50c emerald, red & black 25 15
C352 " 1g brick red, red & black 50 35
C353 " 1.50g brt. blue, red & black 75 50

Orchid Type of Regular Issue

Haitian Orchids: 50c, Tetramicra elegans. 1.50g, Epidendrum truncatum. 2g, Oncidium desertorum.

1970, Apr. 3 Litho. *Perf. 13x12½*

C354 A136 50c buff, brown & magenta 20 15
C355 A136 1.50g multicolored 60 50
C356 " 2g lilac & multi. 90 70

U.P.U. Type of Regular Issue

Designs: 50c, Globe and doves. 1.50g, Propeller and U.P.U. emblem (vert.). 2g, U.P.U. Monument and map of Haiti.

1970, June 23 Photo. *Perf. 11½*

C357 A137 50c blk. & violet 25 15
C358 " 1.50g multicolored 75 50
C359 " 2g " 1.00 70
a. Souvenir sheet of 3 2.25

Issued to commemorate the 16th Congress of the Universal Postal Union, Tokyo, Oct. 1–Nov. 16, 1969. No. C359a contains 3 imperf. stamps similar to Nos. C357–C359. Black marginal inscription. Size: 129x72½mm.

Nos. C357–C359a Overprinted in Red with U.N. Emblem and: "XXVe ANNIVERSAIRE / O.N.U."

1970, Dec. 14 Photo. *Perf. 11½*

C360 A137 50c blk. & violet 25 15
C361 " 1.50g multicolored 75 50
C362 " 2g " 1.00 70
a. Souvenir sheet of 3 2.75

United Nations, 25th anniversary. No. C362a also has a red control number.

Haitian Nativity AP45

1970, Dec. 22

C363 AP45 1.50g sepia & multi. 75 50
C364 " 1.50g ultramarine & multi. 75 50
C365 " 2g multi. 1.25 70

Christmas 1970.

Painting Type of Regular Issue

Paintings: 50c, Nativity, by Rigaud Benoit. 1g, Head of a Negro, by Rubens. 1.50g, Ascension, by Castera Bazile (like No. 648).

1971, Apr. 29 Litho. *Perf. 12x12½*

Size: 20x40mm.

C366 A140 50c multicolored 25 20
C367 " 1g " 50 40
C368 " 1.50g " 75 60

Balloon and Haiti No. C2—AP46

Designs: No. C370, as No. C369. No. C373, Haiti No. C2. 1g, 1.50g, Supersonic transport and Haiti No. C2.

1971, Dec. 22 Photo. *Perf. 11½*

C369 AP46 20c blue, red orange & black 15 5
C370 " 50c ultra., red org. & black 30 15
C371 " 1g orange & black 60 30
C372 " 1.50g lilac rose & black 1.00 45

Souvenir Sheet

Imperf.

C373 AP46 50c brt. green & black 5.00

40th anniversary (in 1969) of air post service in Haiti. No. C373 contains one stamp. Black marginal inscription. Size: 85x70mm.

Nos. C369–C372 Overprinted

INTERPEX 72 AFA

1972, Mar. 17 *Perf. 11½*

C374 AP46 20c multicolored 10
C375 " 50c " 25
C376 " 1g orange & black 50
C377 " 1.50g lilac rose & blk. 75

14th International Stamp Exhibition (INTERPEX), New York City, Mar. 17–19.

Dessalines Type of Regular Issue.

1972, Apr. 28 Photo. *Perf. 11½*

C378 A142 50c yel. grn. & blk. 25 15
C379 " 2.50g lilac & black 1.25 75

See Nos. C450–C453.

Nos. C369–C372 Overprinted

HAIPEX 5ème. CONGRES

1972, May 4

C380 AP46 20c multicolored 10 6
C381 " 50c " 25 15
C382 " 1g org. & black 50 30
C383 " 1.50g lilac rose & black 75 40

HAIPEX, 5th Congress.

Nos. C370–C372 Overprinted

1972, July

C384 AP46 50c multicolored 25 15
C385 " 1g orange & blk. 50 30
C386 " 1.50g lilac rose & black 75 45

Belgica '72, International Philatelic Exhibition, Brussels, June 24–July 9.

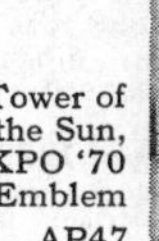

Tower of the Sun, EXPO '70 Emblem AP47

1972, Oct. 27

C387 AP47 50c blue, plum & dark blue 20 15
C388 " 1g blue, plum & red 50 30
C389 " 1.50g blue, plum & black 60 45
C390 " 2.50g blue, plum & green 1.25 75

EXPO '70 International Exposition, Osaka, Japan, Mar. 15–Sept. 13, 1970.

Headquarters and Map of Americas AP48

1973, Aug. Lithographed *Perf. 14½*

C391 AP48 50c dk. bl. & multi. 20 15
C392 " 80c multicolored 32 25
C393 " 1.50g violet & multi. 60 45
C394 " 2g brown & multi. 80 60

70th anniversary (in 1972) of the Pan-american Health Organization.

Marine Life Type of Regular Issue

Designs: Marine life; 50c, 1.50g horizontal.

1973, Sept. 4 *Perf. 14*

Multicolored

C395 A145 50c *Platypodia spectabilis* 20 15
C396 " 85c *Goniaster tessellatus* 35 27
C397 " 1.50g *Stephanocyathus diadema* 60 45
C398 " 2g *Phyllangia americana* 80 60

Fish Type of Regular Issue

Designs: Tropical fish.

1973 *Perf. 13½*

Multicolored

C399 A146 50c *Gramma melacara* 20 15
C400 " 85c *Holacanthus tricolor* 35 27
C401 " 1.50g *Liopropoma rubre* 60 45
C402 " 5g *Clepticus parrai* 2.00 1.50

Haitian Flag AP49

Designs: Nos. C404, C405, Haitian flag and coat of arms. No. C406, Flag and Pres. Jean-Claude Duvalier.

1973, Nov. 18 *Perf. 14½x14*

Size: 35x22½mm.

C403 AP49 80c black & red 32 25
C404 " 80c red & black 32 25

Perf. 14x13½

Size: 42x27mm.

C405 AP49 1.85g black & red 75 45
C406 " 1.85g red & black 75 45

Soccer Type of Regular Issue

Designs: 50c, 80c, Soccer Stadium. 1.75g, 10g, Haiti No. 654.

1973, Nov. 29 *Perf. 14x13*

C407 A147 50c red, black & emerald 20 15
C408 " 80c ultra., black & emerald 32 25
C409 " 1.75g emerald, black & tan 70 50
C410 " 10g ocher, black, & tan 4.00 3.00

Caribbean countries preliminary games of the World Soccer Championships, Munich, 1974.

Dessalines Type of 1974

1974, Apr. 22 Photo. *Perf. 14*

C411 A148 50c brown & greenish bl. 20 15
C412 " 80c gray & brown 32 25
C413 " 1g light green & maroon 40 30
C414 " 1.75g lilac & olive brown 70 50

Copernicus Type of 1974

Designs: No. C415, 80c, 1.50g, 1.75g, Symbol of heliocentric system. No. C416, 1g, 2.50g, Nicolaus Copernicus.

1974, May 24 Litho. *Perf. 14x13½*

C415 A149 50c org. & multi. 20 15
C416 " 50c yel. & multi. 20 15
C417 " 80c multicolored 32 25
C418 " 1g " 40 30
C419 " 1.75g brn. & multi 70 50

Souvenir Sheet

Imperf.

C420 A149 Sheet of 2 1.75
a. 1.50g lt. green & multicolored 60
b. 2.50g dp. org. & multicolored 1.00

500th anniversary of the birth of Nicolaus Copernicus (1473–1543), Polish astronomer. No. C420 has black marginal inscription and deep orange border. Size: 95x65mm.

Pres. Duvalier Type of 1974

1974 Photogravure *Perf. 14x13½*

C421 A151 50c violet brown & gold 20 16
C422 " 80c rose red & gold 32 25
C423 " 1g red lilac & gold 40 30
C424 " 1.50g Prussian blue & gold 60 45
C425 " 1.75g brt. violet & gold 70 50
C426 " 5g olive green & gold 2.00 1.50
Nos. C421-C426 (6) 4.22 3.16

Nos. C405–C406 Surcharged in Violet Blue

G. 0.80

1975, July 15 Litho. *Perf. 14x13½*

C427 AP49 80c on 1.85g, #C405 (VB)
C428 " 80c on 1.85g, #C406 (VB)

Nos. C405–C406 Overprinted in Blue

1874 UPU 1974

100 ANS

1975, July 15 Litho. *Perf. 14x13½*

C432 AP49 1.85g black & red 75 45
C433 " 1.85g red & black 75 45

Centenary of Universal Postal Union. "100 ANS" in 2 lines on No. C433.

Names of Haitian Participants at Siege of Savannah—AP50

1976, Apr. 22 Photo. *Perf. 11½*

Granite Paper

C434 AP50 50c multicolored 20 15
C435 " 80c " 32 24
C436 " 1.50g " 60 45
C437 " 7.50g " 3.00 2.25

American Bicentennial.

Stamps of 1972–74 Surcharged with New Value and Bar in Black or Violet Blue

Photogravure; Lithographed

1976 *Perf. 11½, 13½, 14x13½, 14*

C438 A142 80c on 2.50g, #C379 32 24
C439 A145 80c on 85c, #C396 32 24
C440 A146 80c on 85c, #C400 32 24
C441 AP49 80c on 1.85g, #C405 32 24
C442 " 80c on 1.85g, #C406 32 24
C443 A148 80c on 1.75g, #C414 (VB) 32 24
C444 A149 80c on 1.75g, #C419 (VB) 32 24
C445 A151 80c on 1.75g, #C425 32 24
C446 AP50 80c on 1.50g, #C436 32 24
C447 AP47 80c on 1.50g, #C389
Nos. C438-C446 (9) 2.88 2.16

Black surcharge of Nos. C441–C442 differs from the violet blue surcharge of Nos. C427–C428 in type face, arrangement of denomination and bar, and size of bar (10x6mm.).

Dessalines Type of 1972

1976–77 Photo. *Perf. 11½*

Granite Paper

C448 A142 75c yel. & black ('77) 30 25
C449 " 80c emerald & black ('77) 32 22
C450 " 1g blue & black 40 30
C451 " 1g red brown & black ('77) 40 30
C452 " 1.25g yellow green & black 50 38
C453 " 1.50g blue gray & black 60 45
C454 " 1.75g rose & black ('77) 70 55
C455 " 2g yel. & black 80 60
C457 " 5g blue green & blk. ('77) 2.00 1.50
C458 " 10g ocher & blk. ('77) 4.00 3.00
Nos. C448-C458 (10) 10.02 7.55

Nos. C415–C416, C418–C419 Overprinted or Surcharged in Black, Dark Blue or Green

G. 1.25

1977, July 6 Litho. *Perf. 14x13½*

C460 A149 1g multi. (Bk) 40 30
C461 " 1.25g on 50c multi. (DB) 50 38
C462 " 1.25g on 50c multi. (G) 50 38
C463 " 1.25g on 1.75g multi. (Bk) 50 38

Charles A. Lindbergh's solo transatlantic flight from New York to Paris, 50th anniversary.

Telephone Type of 1978

Designs: 1g, Telstar over globe. 1.25g, Duvalier Earth Telecommunications Station. 2g, Wall telephone, 1890 (vert.).

1978, June 19 Litho. *Perf. 13½*

C466 A153 1g multicolored 40 30
C467 " 1.25g " 50 38
C468 " 2g " 80 60

Centenary of first telephone call by Alexander Graham Bell, March 10, 1876.

Olympic Games Type of 1978

Designs (Montreal Olympic Games' Emblem and): 1.25g, Equestrian. 2.50g, Basketball. 5g, Yachting.

1978, Sept. 4 Litho. *Perf. 13½x13*

C469 A154 1.25g multicolored 50 38
C470 " 2.50g " 1.00 75
C471 " 5g " 2.00 1.50

21st Olympic Games, Montreal, July 17–Aug. 1, 1976.

Children's Institute Type, 1979

Designs: 1.25g, Mother nursing child. 2g, Nurse giving injection.

1979, Jan. 15 Photo. *Perf. 14x14½*

C472 A155 1.25g multicolored 50 38
C473 " 2g " 80 60

Inter-American Children's Institute, 50th anniversary.

AIR POST SEMI-POSTAL STAMPS

Coubertin Semipostal Type of 1939

Engraved

1939, Oct. 3 *Perf. 12* Unwmkd.

CB1 SP1 60c+40c multi. 30.00 30.00
CB2 " 1.25g+60c multi. 30.00 30.00

Issued to honor Pierre de Coubertin, organizer of the modern Olympic Games. The surtax was used to build a Sports Stadium at Port-au-Prince.

Mosquito and National Sanatorium

SPAP2

1949, July 22 Cross in Carmine

CB3 SPAP2 20c+20c sepia 15.00 9.00
CB4 " 30c+30c deep green 15.00 9.00
CB5 " 45c+45c light red brown 15.00 9.00
CB6 " 80c+80c purple 15.00 9.00
CB7 " 1.25g+1.25g car. rose 15.00 9.00
a. Souvenir sheet 40.00 35.00
CB8 " 1.75g+1.75g blue 15.00 9.00
a. Souvenir sheet 40.00 35.00
Nos. CB3-CB8 (6) 90.00 54.00

The surtax was used for fighting tuberculosis and malaria.

Nos. CB7a and CB8a measure 120 x 80 mm., and contain arms and inscription in the color of the stamp.

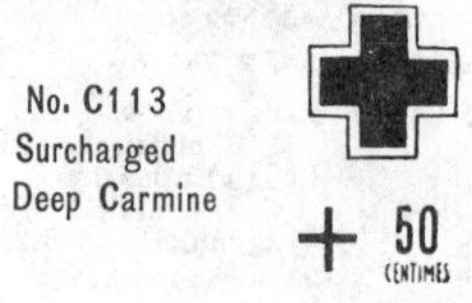

No. C113 Surcharged in Deep Carmine

+ 50 CENTIMES

e

1958, Aug. 30 Litho. *Perf. 13x13½*

CB9 A82 2.50g+50c pale carmine rose 4.50 4.50

The surtax was for the Red Cross.

Similar Surcharge in Red on One Line on Nos. C133-C135.

1959, Apr. 7 Photo. *Perf. 11½*

Granite Paper

CB10 AP35 50c+25c pink, car. & ultramarine 60 50
CB11 A87 75c+25c bright blue 75 60
CB12 " 1g+25c brown 1.00 90

Nos. C139-C141 Surcharged Type "e" in Red

CB13 AP36 50c+50c green & lilac 1.50 1.50
CB14 " 1.50g+50c olive, & red brown 1.50 1.50
CB15 " 2.50g+50c purple & dark blue 1.50 1.50
Nos. CB10-CB15 (6) 6.85 6.50

The surtax from Nos. CB10-CB15 was for the Red Cross.

Nos. C142–C144 Surcharged Diagonally

Nations Unies
ANNEE DES REFUGIES
1959-1960
+ 20
Centimes

1959, July 23 *Perf. 12* Unwmkd.

CB16 A89 1g+20c light green & chestnut 1.50 1.00
CB17 " 2g+20c pale lemon & slate green 1.50 1.50
CB18 A89 2.50g+20c buff & violet blue 1.50 1.50

Issued for the World Refugee Year, July 1, 1959–June 30, 1960. A similar surcharge of 50c was applied horizontally to stamps in No. C144a. Price $25.

C145–C147 Surcharged in Dark Carmine

POUR LE SPORT
+ 0.75
CENTIMES

1959, Oct. 30 Photo. *Perf. 14*

CB19 A91 50c+75c henna brown & aquamarine 1.50 1.00
CB20 A90 1g+75c lilac & aquamarine 1.50 1.25
CB21 " 1.50g+75c multi. 1.50 1.50

The surtax was for Haitian athletes.

On No. CB19, surcharge lines are spaced to total depth of 16mm.

Nos. C129-C130 Surcharged in Red: "Hommage a l'UNICEF +G. 0,50"

Engraved and Lithographed

1960, Feb. 2 *Perf. 11½*

CB22 AP34 2g+50c black & rose pink 2.00 2.00
CB23 " 2.50g+50c black & ochre 3.00 3.00

Issued to honor the United Nations International Children's Emergency Fund.

Nos. C151–C152 Surcharged and Overprinted: "ALPHABETISATION" in Red or Black.

1960, July 12 Litho. *Perf. 12½x13*

CB24 A92 50c+20c blue & black (R) 75 60
CB25 " 50c+30c blue & black 1.00 70
CB26 " 1g+20c lt. green & maroon (R) 1.50 1.10
CB27 " 1g+30c lt. green & maroon 1.50 1.10

Olympic Games Issue.

Nos. C163–C164 Surcharged.

1960, Sept. 9 Photo. *Perf. 12*

CB28 A94 50c+25c maroon & bistre 40 35
CB29 " 1.50g+25c rose car. & yellow green 90 75

Nos. C168–C169 Surcharged: "UNICEF +25 centimes"

1961, Jan. 14 Engr. *Perf. 10½*

CB30 A96 50c+25c red org. & black 50 20
CB31 " 1.50g+25c dark blue & black 90 50

Issued for the United Nations International Children's Emergency Fund.

Nos. C171, C175–C176 Surcharged with Additional Value, Scout Emblem and: "18e Conference Internationale du Scoutisme Mondial Lisbonne Septembre 1961"

1961, Sept. 30 Photo. *Perf. 11½*

CB32 AP37 20c+25c deep ultra. & car. 50 25
CB33 " 1g+25c gray olive & verm. 75 60
CB34 " 1.50g+25c brt. pink & dk. blue 90 90

Issued to commemorate the 18th Boy Scout World Conference, Lisbon, Sept. 19–24, 1961.

The surtax was for the Red Cross. Additional proceeds from the sale of Nos. CB32–CB34 benefited the Port-au-Prince airport project.

The same surcharge was also applied to No. C176a.

Nos. C168–C169 Surcharged: "OMS SNEM +20 CENTIMES"

1961, Dec. 11 Engraved *Perf. 10½*

CB35 A96 50c+20c red orge. & black 2.00 2.00
CB36 " 1.50g+20c dk. blue & black 3.00 3.00

Issued to publicize Haiti's participation in the U.N. malaria eradication drive.

Nos. C123, C126–C127 and C131–C132. Surcharged in Black or Red:

Duvalier-Ville
+25
CENTIMES

Engraved and Lithographed

1961–62 ***Perf. 11½***

CB37	AP34	50c+25c black & rose	35	30
CB38	"	1g+50c black & violet	75	60
CB39	"	2.50g+50c black, ochre & ultra. (R) ('62)	1.50	1.20
CB40	"	5g+50c black & rose lilac	2.50	2.50
CB41	"	7.50g+50c black & lt. blue green (R) ('62)	3.50	3.00
		Nos. CB37–CB41 (5)	8.60	7.60

The surtax was for the benefit of the urban rehabilitation program in Duvalier Ville.

Nos. C188–C190 Surcharged: "+25 centimes"

1962, Sept. 13 **Litho.** ***Perf. 12***

CB42	A99	20c+25c lilac & red	30	20
CB43	"	50c+25c emerald & rose carmine	40	30
CB44	"	1g+25c orange & dark violet	60	50

Nos. C191–C192 Surcharged in Red: "+0.20"

1962 ***Perf. 12½x13***

CB45	A92	50c+20c light blue & red brown	40	30
CB46	"	1g+20c bistre & black	60	50

Nos. C203 and C205 Surcharged: "ALPHABETISATION" and "0, 10"

1963, Mar. 15 Photo. ***Perf. 14x14½***

CB47	AP38	50c+10c orge. & dark brown	40	25
CB48	"	1.50g+10c green & dark brown	65	65

No. C110 Surcharged in Red with Olympic Emblem and: "JEUX OLYMPIQUES / D'HIVER / INNSBRUCK 1964"

1964, July 27 **Photo.** ***Perf. 11½***

CB49	A80	2.50g+50c+10c dark blue & bright blue	1.20	1.00

Issued to commemorate the 9th Winter Olympic Games, Innsbruck, Austria, Jan. 20–Feb. 9, 1964. The 50c+10c surtax went for charity.

No. C213 Surcharged in Red

Lithographed and Photogravure

1964, Oct. 2 ***Perf. 13½x14***

CB50	AP39	2.50g+1.25g on 1.50g gray, slate & grn.	2.00	1.75

Issued to commemorate the centenary (in 1963) of the International Red Cross.

Nos. C223–C226 Surcharged: "+ 5c." in Black

1965, Mar. 15 **Photo.** ***Perf. 11½***

CB51	A105	50c+5c pale lilac & dark brown	40	40
CB52	"	50c+5c pale grn. & dk. brown	40	40
CB53	"	75c+5c buff & dark brown	60	60
CB54	"	1.50g+5c gray & dark brown	1.20	1.20

The souvenir sheet No. C226a was surcharged "+25c."
See note following No. B37.

Nos. C251 and C253 Surcharged and Overprinted with Haitian Scout Emblem and "12e Jamboree / Mondial 1967" Like Regular Issue

1967, Aug. 21 **Photo.** ***Perf. 11½***

CB55	A111	50c+10c multi.	25	25
CB56	"	1.50g+50c "	80	70

Issued to commemorate the 12th Boy Scout World Jamboree, Farragut State Park, Idaho, Aug. 1–9.

No. C269 Surcharged Like Regular Issue

Lithographed and Photogravure

1968, Jan. 18 ***Perf. 13x13½***

CB57	A115	2.50g+1.25g on 1.50g rose & plum	1.75	1.40

Issued to publicize the 19th Olympic Games, Mexico City, Oct. 12–27.
See note after No. 579.

Nos. C285–C287 Surcharged "CULTURE + 10"

1968, July 4 **Litho.** ***Perf. 11½***

CB58	A120	50c+10c multi.	25	25
CB59	"	1g+10c "	45	45
CB60	"	1.50g+10c "	65	65

Nos. C314 and C316 Surcharged in Red with New Value, Red Cross and: "50ème. Anniversaire / de la Ligue des / Sociétés de la / Croix Rouge"

1969, June 25 **Litho.** ***Perf. 11½***

CB61	A127	50c+20c multi.	40	28
CB62	"	1.50g+25c "	1.00	70

Issued to commemorate the 50th anniversary of the League of Red Cross Societies.

AIR POST OFFICIAL STAMPS

Nos. C172–C176 and C176a Overprinted: "OFFICIEL"

Photogravure

1961, March ***Perf. 11½*** **Unwmkd.**

CO1	AP37	50c rose brn. & grn.		35
CO2	"	50c brt. greenish blue & olive green		35
CO3	"	50c gray & green		35
CO4	"	1g gray olive & vermilion		50
CO5	"	1.50g bright pink & dark blue		75
		a. Sheet of 3		2.50
		Nos. CO1–CO5 (5)		2.30

Nos. CO1–CO5a only available cancelled.

Jean Jacques Dessalines
OA1

1962, Mar. 7 **Photo.** ***Perf. 14x14½***

Size: 20½x38mm.

CO6	OA1	50c dk. blue & sepia	30	20
CO7	OA1	1g light blue & maroon	50	40
CO8	"	1.50g bistre & blue	75	60

Size: 30x40mm.

CO9	OA1	5g rose & olive green	2.25	2.00

Inscription at bottom of No. CO9 is in 2 lines.

AIR POST PARCEL POST STAMPS

Nos. C112 and C111 Overprinted in Red

COLIS
POSTAUX

Photogravure

1960, Nov. 21 ***Perf. 11½*** **Unwmkd.**

CQ1	A81	50c orange & black	35	25
CQ2	A80	5g bluish black & sapphire	3.00	2.50

Type of Parcel Post Stamps, 1961 Inscribed "Poste Aerienne"

1961, Mar. 24 ***Perf. 14***

CQ3	PP1	2.50g yellow green & maroon	1.50	1.00
CQ4	"	5g org. & green	3.00	2.00

SPECIAL DELIVERY STAMP.

Postal Administration Building
SD1

Engraved.

1953, May 4 ***Perf. 12*** **Unwmkd.**

E1	SD1	25c vermilion	75	75

POSTAGE DUE STAMPS.

D1

Engraved

1898, May ***Perf. 12*** **Unwmkd.**

J1	D1	2c black	25	20
J2	"	5c red brown	35	25
J3	"	10c brown orange	50	30
J4	"	50c slate	1.25	60

Stamps of 1898 Handstamped

MAI
Gt Pre
1902

1902 Black Overprint.

J5	D1	2c black	75	50
J6	"	5c red brown	75	50
J7	"	10c brown orange	1.00	50
J8	"	50c slate	4.00	2.50

Red Overprint.

J9	D1	2c black	1.00	1.00
		Nos. J5–J9 (5)	7.50	5.00

D2

1906

J10	D2	2c dull red	75	50
J11	"	5c ultramarine	2.25	2.25
J12	"	10c violet	2.50	2.25
J13	"	50c olive gray	7.00	5.00

Preceding Issues Handstamped

Gl O.Z.
7 Fév. 1914

1914 **On Stamps of 1898.**

J14	D1	5c red brown	75	60
J15	"	10c brown orange	60	60
J16	"	50c slate	3.50	3.00

On Stamps of 1906.

J17	D2	2c dull red	50	40
J18	"	5c ultramarine	90	60
J19	"	10c violet	4.00	3.00
J20	"	50c olive gray	6.00	5.00

The note after No. 201 applies to Nos. J14–J20 also.

Unpaid Letter
D3

1951, July **Litho.** ***Perf. 11½***

J21	D3	10c carmine	12	12
J22	"	20c red brown	20	20
J23	"	40c green	35	35
J24	"	50c orange yellow	50	50

PARCEL POST STAMPS

Nos. 416, 470–471 and 378 Overprinted in Red

COLIS
POSTAUX

Photogravure, Engraved

Perf. 11½, 12

1960, Nov. 21 **Unwmkd.**

Q1	A81	5c yel. grn. & black	5	5
Q2	"	10c red org. & black	8	8
Q3	"	25c ultra. & black	20	20
Q4	A64	2.50g gray	1.50	1.50

Coat of Arms
PP1

Photogravure

1961, Mar. 24 ***Perf. 14*** **Unwmkd.**

Q5	PP1	50c bistre & purple	50	20
Q6	"	1g pink & dark blue	75	40

See Nos. CQ3–CQ4.

POSTAL TAX STAMPS.

Haitian Woman, War Invalids and Ruined Buildings—PT1

Engraved.

1944, Aug. 16 Perf. 12 Unwmkd.

RA1	PT1	5c dull purple	1.50	75
RA2	"	5c dark blue	1.50	75
RA3	"	5c olive green	1.50	75
RA4	"	5c black	1.50	75

1945, Dec. 17

RA5	PT1	5c dark green	1.50	75
RA6	"	5c sepia	1.50	75
RA7	"	5c red brown	1.50	75
RA8	"	5c rose carmine	1.50	75

The proceeds from the sale of Nos. RA1 to RA8 were for United Nations Relief.

George Washington, J. J. Dessalines and Simón Bolivar—PT2

1949, Sept. 20

RA9	PT2	5c red brown	30	20
RA10	"	5c olive gray	30	20
RA11	"	5c blue	30	20
RA12	"	5c green	30	20
RA13	"	5c violet	30	20
RA14	"	5c black	30	20
RA15	"	5c orange	30	20
RA16	"	5c carmine rose	30	20
		Nos. RA9-RA16 (8)	2.40	1.60

Bicentenary of Port-au-Prince.

Helicopter Inspection of Cyclone Damage PT3 — Helicopter PT4

1955, Jan. 3 Photo. Perf. 11½

RA17	PT3	10c bright green	12	6
RA18	"	10c bright blue	12	6
RA19	"	10c gray black	12	6
RA20	"	10c orange	12	6
RA21	"	20c rose carmine	20	6
RA22	"	20c deep green	20	6
		Nos. RA17-RA22 (6)	88	36

1955, May 3

RA23	PT4	10c black, *gray*	15	6
RA24	"	20c violet blue, *blue*	20	6

The surface tint of the sheets of 50 (10x5) of Nos. RA23-RA24 and RAC1-RAC2 includes a map of Haiti's southern peninsula which extends over the three center rows of stamps.

The tax was for reconstruction.

PT5 — "CA" PT6

Photogravure

1959-60 Perf. 11½ Unwmkd.

Size: 38x22½mm.

RA25	PT5	5c green	6	5
RA26	"	5c black ('60)	6	5
RA27	"	10c red	8	6

1960-61 Size: 28x17mm.

RA28	PT5	5c green	6	5
RA29	"	10c red	8	5
RA30	"	10c blue ('61)	8	5

1963, Sept. Perf. 14½x14

Size: 13½x21mm.

RA31	PT6	10c red orange	8	5
RA32	"	10c bright blue	8	5
RA33	"	10c olive	8	5
		Nos. RA31-RA33, RAC6-RAC8 (6)	42	30

1966-69 Photo. Perf. 14x14½

Size: 17x25mm.

RA34	PT6	10c bright green	8	5
RA35	"	10c violet	8	5
RA36	"	10c violet blue	4	3
RA37	"	10c brown ('69)	4	3
		Nos. RA34-RA37, RAC9-RAC15 (11)	74	39

Nos. RA25-RA37 represent a tax for a literacy campaign.

See Nos. RA42-RA45, RAC20-RAC21.

Duvalier de Peligre Hydroelectric Works PT7

1970-72

RA38	PT7	20c vio. & olive	16	10
RA39	"	20c ultra. & blk. ('72)	8	5

See Nos. RAC16-RAC19.

Nos. 642-643 Surcharged: "ALPHABETISATION +10"

1971, Dec. 23 Litho. Perf. 14x13½

RA40	A138	20c+10c multi.	12	6
		a. Inverted surcharge		2.00
RA41	A138	25c+10c "	14	8

Tax was for the literacy campaign.

"CA" Type of 1963

1972-74 Photo. Perf. 14x14½

Size: 17x25mm.

RA42	PT6	5c violet blue	3	3
RA43	"	5c deep carmine	3	3
RA44	"	5c ultra. ('74)	3	3
RA45	"	5c car. rose ('74)	3	3

Tax was for literacy campaign.

AIR POST POSTAL TAX STAMPS

Helicopter PTAP1

Photogravure.

1955 Perf. 11½ Unwmkd.

RAC1	PTAP1	10c red brown, *pale salmon*	20	8
RAC2	"	20c rose pink, *pink*	20	8

See note after RA24.

Type of Postal Tax Stamps, 1960-61

1959 Size: 28x17mm.

RAC3	PT5	5c yellow	6	5
RAC4	"	10c dull salmon	8	6
RAC5	"	10c blue	8	6

Type of Postal Tax Stamps, 1963

1963, Sept. Perf. 14½x14

Size: 13½x21mm.

RAC6	PT6	10c dark gray	6	5
RAC7	"	10c violet	6	5
RAC8	"	10c brown	6	5

1966-69 Perf. 14x14½

Size: 17x25mm.

RAC9	PT6	10c orange	5	4
RAC10	"	10c sky blue	5	4
RAC11	"	10c yellow ('69)	8	3
RAC12	"	10c carmine ('69)	8	3
RAC13	"	10c gray grn. ('69)	8	3
RAC14	"	10c lilac ('69)	8	3
RAC15	"	10c dp. claret ('69)	8	3
		Nos. RAC9-RAC15 (7)	50	23

Nos. RAC3-RAC15, RAC20-RAC21 represent a tax for a literacy campaign.

Hydroelectric Type of 1970

1970-74

RAC16	PT7	20c tan & slate	16	10
RAC17	"	20c brt. blue & dull violet	16	10
RAC18	"	25c sal. & bluish black ('74)	25	6
RAC19	"	25c yel. olive & bluish black ('74)	25	6

"CA" Type of 1963

1973 Photo. Perf. 14x14½

Size: 17x26mm.

RAC20	PT6	10c brown & blue	20	5
RAC21	"	10c brn. & green	20	5
RAC22	"	10c brown & org.	20	5

Prices of premium quality never hinged stamps will be in excess of catalogue price.

HAMBURG
HANOVER

See German States group preceding Germany.

HATAY

(hä'tä'ĭ)

(Formerly Alexandretta.)

LOCATION — Northwest of Syria, bordering on Mediterranean Sea.
GOVT.—Former semi-independent republic.
AREA—10,000 sq. mi. (approx.).
POP.—273,350 (1939).
CAPITAL—Antioch.

Alexandretta, a semi-autonomous district of Syria under French mandate, was renamed Hatay in 1938 and transferred to Turkey in 1939.

100 Santims = 1 Kurush
40 Paras = 1 Kurush (1939)

Stamps of Turkey, 1931-38, Surcharged in Black:

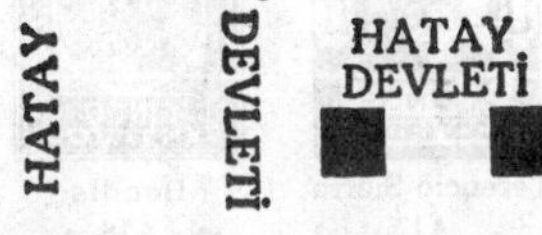

a b

1939 *Perf. 11½x12.* **Unwmkd.**

No.	Type	Description	Unused	Used
1	A77 (a)	10s on 20pa deep orange	25	25
a.		"Sent" instead of "Sant"	2.50	2.50
2	A78 (b)	25s on 1ku dark slate green	25	25
a.		Small "25"	35	35
3	" (")	50s on 2ku dark violet	25	25
a.		Small "50"	35	35
4	A77 (a)	75s on 2½ku green	25	25
5	A78 (b)	1ku on 4ku slate	30	30
6	" (")	1ku on 5ku rose red	35	35
7	" (")	1½ku on 3ku brown orange	50	50
8	" (")	2½ku on 4ku slate	50	50
9	" (")	5ku on 8ku bright blue	1.50	1.50
10	A77 (a)	12½ku on 20ku olive green	2.25	2.25
11	" (")	20ku on 25ku Prus. blue	2.50	2.50
		Nos. 1-11 (11)	8.90	8.90

Map of Hatay
A1

Lions of Antioch—A2

Flag of Hatay—A3

Post Office—A4

Typographed.

1939 *Perf. 12.* **Unwmkd.**

No.	Type	Description	Unused	Used
12	A1	10p orange & aqua.	20	20
13	"	30p light violet & aquamarine	30	30
14	"	1½ku olive & aqua.	35	35
15	A2	2½ku turquoise green	40	40
16	"	3ku light blue	50	50
17	"	5ku chocolate	60	60
18	A3	6ku bright blue & carmine	60	60
19	"	7½ku deep green & carmine	75	75
20	"	12ku violet & carmine	1.00	1.00
21	"	12½ku dark blue & carmine	1.20	1.20
22	A4	17½ku brown carmine	1.50	1.50
23	"	25ku olive brown	2.25	2.25
24	"	50ku slate blue	4.50	4.50
		Nos. 12-24 (13)	14.15	14.15

Stamps of 1939 Overprinted in Black

T. C.
ilhak tarihi
30-6-1939

1939

No.	Type	Description	Unused	Used
25	A1	10p orange & aqua.	20	20
a.		Overprint reading up		
26	"	30p light violet & aquamarine	30	30
27	"	1½ku olive & aqua.	35	35
28	A2	2½ku turquoise green	40	40
29	"	3ku light blue	50	50
30	"	5ku chocolate	55	55
a.		Overprint inverted		
31	A3	6ku bright blue & carmine	60	60
32	"	7½ku deep green & carmine	60	60
33	"	12ku violet & carmine	70	70
34	"	12½ku dark blue & carmine	80	80
35	A4	17½ku brown carmine	1.40	1.40
a.		Overprint inverted		
36	"	25ku olive brown	2.25	2.25
37	"	50ku slate blue	4.50	4.50
		Nos. 25-37 (13)	13.15	13.15

The overprint reads "Date of annexation to the Turkish Republic, June 30, 1939."

On Nos. 25-27, the overprint reads down. On Nos. 28-37, it is horizontal.

POSTAGE DUE STAMPS.

Postage Due Stamps of Turkey, 1936, Surcharged or Overprinted in Black

HATAY 1
DEVLETİ Krş

1939 *Perf. 11½.* **Unwmkd.**

No.	Type	Description	Unused	Used
J1	D6	1ku on 2ku light blue	40	40
J2	"	3ku bright violet	60	60
J3	"	4ku on 5ku Prus. blue	80	80
J4	"	5ku on 12ku brt. rose	1.25	1.25
J5	"	12ku bright rose	4.00	4.00
		Nos. J1-J5 (5)	7.05	7.05

Castle at Antioch—D1

1939 Typographed *Perf. 12*

No.	Type	Description	Unused	Used
J6	D1	1ku red orange	50	50
J7	"	3ku dark olive brown	60	60
J8	"	4ku turquoise green	80	80
J9	"	5ku slate black	1.00	1.00

Nos. J6–J9 Overprinted in Black

T. C.
ilhak tarihi
30-6-1939

1939

No.	Type	Description	Unused	Used
J10	D1	1ku red orange	50	50
J11	"	3ku dark olive brown	60	60
J12	"	4ku turquoise green	75	75
J13	"	5ku slate black	90	90
a.		Overprint inverted	5.00	

HEJAZ

See Saudi Arabia, Vol. IV.

HONDURAS

(hŏn-dōō'răs)

LOCATION — In Central America, between Guatemala on the north and Nicaragua on the south.
GOVT.—Republic.
AREA—43,277 sq. mi.
POP.—2,830,000 (est. 1976).
CAPITAL—Tegucigalpa.

8 Reales = 1 Peso
100 Centavos = 1 Peso (1878)
100 Centavos = 1 Lempira (1933)

Coat of Arms
A1

Lithographed.

1866 *Imperf.* **Unwmkd.**

No.	Type	Description	Unused
1	A1	2r *green*	50
2	"	2r *pink*	50

Comayagua Issue.

A2

1877 Red Surcharge

No.	Type	Description	Unused
3	A2	½r on 2r *green*	80.00
4	"	1r on 2r *green*	300.00

Blue Surcharge.

No.	Type	Description	Unused
5	A2	2r on 2r *green*	120.00
6	"	2r on 2r *pink*	120.00

Black Surcharge.

No.	Type	Description	Unused
7	A2	1r on 2r *green*	60.00
8	"	1r on 2r *pink*	300.00
9	"	2r on 2r *pink*	120.00
10	"	2r on 2r *green*	300.00

Tegucigalpa Issue.

A3

1877 Black Surcharge.

No.	Type	Description	Unused
11	A3	½r on 2r *green*	17.50
12	"	½r on 2r *pink*	17.50
13	"	1r on 2r *green*	17.50
14	"	1r on 2r *pink*	20.00
16	"	2r on 2r *pink*	17.50
17	"	2r on 2r *green*	30.00

Blue Surcharge.

No.	Type	Description	Unused
18	A3	½r on 2r *green*	17.50
19	"	½r on 2r *pink*	17.50
20	"	1r on 2r *pink*	20.00
21	"	1r on 2r *green*	175.00
22	"	2r on 2r *green*	75.00
23	"	2r on 2r *pink*	17.50

Red Surcharge

No.	Type	Description	Unused
24	A3	½r on 2r *green*	17.50
25	"	½r on 2r *pink*	20.00
26	"	1r on 2r *green*	30.00
27	"	1r on 2r *pink*	25.00
28	"	2r on 2r *pink*	20.00
29	"	2r on 2r *green*	22.50

Nos. 3 to 29 have been extensively counterfeited.

Regular Issue.

President Francisco Morazán
A4

Thin, hard paper, colorless gum.
Various Frames.
Printed by
National Bank Note Co. of N. Y.

1878 Engraved. *Perf. 12.*

No.	Type	Description	Unused	Used
30	A4	1c violet	35	50
31	"	2c brown	35	60
32	"	½r black	40	60
33	"	1r green	1.00	1.25
34	"	2r deep blue	2.00	2.25
35	"	4r vermilion	2.50	2.25
36	"	1p orange	3.00	4.00
		Nos. 30-36 (7)	9.60	11.45

Various counterfeit cancellations exist on Nos. 30–36.

Re-Issue.
Soft paper, yellowish gum.
Various Frames.
Printed by
American Bank Note Co. of N. Y.

1889

No.	Type	Description	Unused
30a	A4	1c deep violet	15
31a	"	2c red brown	18
32a	"	½r black	18
33a	"	1r blue green	20
34a	"	2r ultramarine	20
35a	"	4r scarlet vermilion	25
36a	"	1p orange yellow	30
		Nos. 30a-36a (7)	1.46

Arms of Honduras
A5

1890, Jan. 6

No.	Type	Description	Unused	Used
40	A5	1c yellow green	15	18
41	"	2c red	15	18
42	"	5c blue	15	18
43	"	10c orange	15	20
44	"	20c ochre	15	25
45	"	25c rose red	15	30
46	"	30c purple	15	35

47	A5	40c dark blue	15	*50*
48	"	50c brown	15	*50*
49	"	75c blue green	15	*1.50*
50	"	1p carmine	15	*2.25*
		Nos. 40–50 (11)	1.65	*6.39*

The tablets and numerals of Nos. 40 to 50 differ for each denomination.

Used prices of Nos. 40–94 are for stamps with genuine cancellations applied while the stamps were valid. Various counterfeit cancellations exist.

President Luis Bográn

A6 A7

1891, July 31

51	A6	1c dark blue	20	20
52	"	2c yellow brown	20	20
53	"	5c blue green	20	20
54	"	10c vermilion	20	25
55	"	20c brown red	20	30
56	"	25c magenta	20	35
57	"	30c slate	20	35
58	"	40c blue green	20	*40*
59	"	50c black brown	20	*50*
60	"	75c purple	20	*75*
61	"	1p brown	20	*1.25*
62	A7	2p brown & black	25	*4.00*
		a. Head inverted	150.00	
63	"	5p purple & black	25	*5.00*
		a. Head inverted	50.00	
64	"	10p green & black	25	*5.00*
		a. Head inverted	50.00	
		Nos. 51–64 (14)	2.95	*18.75*

Nos. 62 and 64 exist with papermakers watermark.

Columbus Sighting Honduran Coast — General Trinidad Cabanas

A8 A9

1892, July 31

65	A8	1c slate	15	20
66	"	2c deep blue	15	20
67	"	5c yellow green	15	20
68	"	10c blue green	15	25
69	"	20c red	15	25
70	"	25c orange brown	15	30
71	"	30c ultramarine	15	35
72	"	40c orange	15	*60*
73	"	50c brown	15	*75*
74	"	75c lake	15	*1.25*
75	"	1p purple	15	*1.50*
		Nos. 65–75 (11)	1.65	*5.85*

Commemorative of the fourth centenary of the discovery of America by Christopher Columbus.

1893

76	A9	1c green	15	20
77	"	2c scarlet	15	20
78	"	5c dark blue	15	20
79	"	10c orange brown	15	20
80	"	20c brown red	15	25
81	"	25c dark blue	15	30
82	"	30c red orange	15	*60*
83	"	40c black	15	*90*
84	"	50c olive brown	15	*1.25*
85	"	75c purple	15	*1.75*
86	"	1p deep magenta	15	*2.25*
		Nos. 76–86 (11)	1.65	*8.10*

"Justice" — President Celio Arias

A10 A11

1895, Jan. 25

87	A10	1c vermilion	15	15
88	"	2c deep blue	15	15
89	"	5c slate	15	20
90	"	10c brown rose	15	20
91	"	20c violet	15	30
92	"	30c deep violet	15	*85*
93	"	50c olive brown	15	*1.50*
94	"	1p dark green	15	*2.00*
		Nos. 87–94 (8)	1.20	*5.35*

The tablets and numerals of Nos. 76–94 differ for each denomination.

1896 Lithographed. *Perf. 11½.*

95	A11	1c dark blue	20	20
96	"	2c yellow brown	20	20
97	"	5c purple	20	20
		a. 5c red violet	50	50
98	"	10c vermilion	25	20
99	"	20c emerald	35	25
		a. 20c deep green		
100	"	30c ultramarine	50	60
101	"	50c rose	50	90
102	"	1p black brown	50	*1.75*
		Nos. 95–102 (8)	2.70	*4.30*

Nos. 95–102 exist imperf.
Counterfeits of Nos. 95–102 are plentiful.

Originals of Nos. 95 to 102 are on both thin, semi-transparent paper and opaque paper; reprints are on thicker, opaque paper and usually have a black cancellation "HONDURAS" between horizontal bars.

Railroad Train
A12

1898, Aug. 1

103	A12	1c brown	15	10
		a. Laid paper	35	30
104	"	2c rose	20	10
		a. Laid paper	50	35
105	"	5c dull ultramarine	50	20
		a. Laid paper	50	35
		b. 5c red vio. (error)	1.00	1.00
106	"	6c red violet	30	25
		a. Laid paper	50	50
		b. 6c dull rose (error)		
107	"	10c dark blue	35	30
		a. Laid paper	60	60
108	"	20c dull orange	60	60
109	"	50c orange red	1.00	1.50
110	"	1p blue green	1.25	1.75
		Nos. 103–110 (8)	4.35	4.80

Excellent counterfeits of Nos. 103 to 110 exist.

General Santos Guardiola — President José Medina

A13 A14

1903, Jan. 1 Engraved *Perf. 12*

111	A13	1c yellow green	15	15
112	"	2c carmine rose	15	15
113	"	5c blue	15	15
114	"	6c dark violet	20	15
115	"	10c brown	20	20
116	"	20c dull ultramarine	25	25
117	A13	50c vermilion	60	60
118	"	1p orange	75	75
		Nos. 111–118 (8)	2.45	2.40

Nos. 111–118 exist imperf.

"PERMITASE" handstamped on stamps of 1896–1903 was applied as a control mark by the isolated Pacific Coast post office of Amapala to prevent use of stolen stamps.

1907, Jan. 1 *Perf. 14*

119	A14	1c dark green	12	12
120	"	2c scarlet	15	15
120A	"	2c carmine	90	50
121	"	5c blue	15	12
122	"	6c purple	20	12
		a. 6c dark violet	15	15
123	"	10c gray brown	25	25
124	"	20c ultramarine	35	35
		a. 20c blue violet	75.00	75.00
125	"	50c deep lake	45	50
126	"	1p orange yellow	60	75
		Nos. 119–126 (9)	3.17	2.86

All values of the above set exist imperforate, imperforate horizontally and in horizontal pairs imperforate between.

1909 Lithographed *Perf. 11½*

127	A14	1c green	75	75
		a. Imperf., pair	2.00	2.00
		b. Printed on both sides	5.00	3.00

The 1909 issue is roughly lithographed in imitation of the 1907 design. It exists pin perf. 8, 13, etc.

No. 124 Surcharged in Black, Green or Red:

1 *a* **5** *b* **10** *c*

1910, Dec. *Perf. 14*

128	A14 (*a*)	1c on 20c ultra.	2.25	2.25
		a. Double surcharge		
129	" (*b*)	5c on 20c ultra. (G)	2.25	2.25
		a. Double surcharge		
		b. Inverted surcharge		
130	" (*c*)	10c on 20c ultra. (R)	2.25	2.25
		a. Double surcharge		

Honduran Scene
A15

1911, Jan. Litho. *Perf. 14, 12 (1p)*

131	A15	1c violet	12	12
132	"	2c green	12	12
		a. Perf. 12	20	20
133	"	5c carmine	12	12
		a. Perf. 12	75	75
134	"	6c ultramarine	25	25
135	"	10c blue	35	35
136	"	20c yellow	40	40
137	"	50c brown	1.00	1.00
138	"	1p olive green	1.75	1.50
		Nos. 131–138 (8)	4.11	3.86

No. 132a Overprinted in Red

XC
Aniversario de la
Independencia

1911, Sept. *Perf. 12*

139	A15	2c green	10.00	10.00
		a. Inverted overprint	20.00	20.00

90th anniversary of Independence.

President Manuel Bonilla
A16

1912, Feb. Litho. *Perf. 11½*

140	A16	1c orange red	12.50	12.50

Election of Pres. Manuel Bonilla.

Stamps of 1911 Surcharged in Black, Red or Blue:

2 CENTAVOS *a* 5 cts. *b*

1913 *Perf. 14.*

141	A15 (*a*)	2c on 1c violet	50	50
		a. Dbl. surch.		4.00
		b. Invtd. surch.	4.00	
		c. Double surch., one invtd.	6.00	
		d. Red surcharge	50.00	50.00
142	" (*b*)	2c on 1c violet	6.00	6.00
		a. Invtd. surch.	15.00	
143	" (")	2c on 10c blue	85	85
		a. Double surch.	5.00	5.00
		b. Invtd. surch.		
144	" (")	2c on 20c yellow	4.00	4.00
145	" (")	5c on 1c violet	1.00	50
146	" (")	5c on 10c bl. (Bl)	1.25	1.00
147	" (")	6c on 1c violet	1.25	1.00
		Nos. 141–147 (7)	14.85	13.85

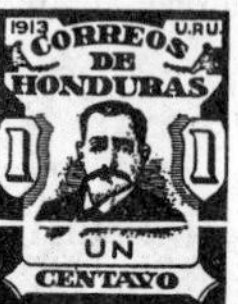

Terencio Sierra — Bonilla

A17 A18

ONE CENTAVO:
Type I. Solid border at sides below numerals.
Type II. Border of light and dark stripes.

1913–14 Lithographed. *Perf. 11½.*

151	A17	1c dark brown, I	15	12
		a. 1c brown, type II	15	15
152	"	2c carmine	18	18
153	A18	5c blue	20	20
154	"	5c ultramarine ('14)	20	20
155	"	6c gray violet	25	25
156	"	6c purple ('14)	15	8
		a. 6c red lilac	30	30
157	A17	10c blue	40	40
158	"	10c brown ('14)	80	40
159	"	20c brown	50	50
160	A18	50c rose	1.25	1.25
161	"	1p gray green	1.50	1.35
		Nos. 151–161 (11)	5.58	4.96

Surcharged in Black or Carmine **1 cent.**

1914

162	A17	1c on 2c carmine	40	40
163	"	5c on 2c carmine	75	75
164	A18	5c on 6c gray vio.	1.50	1.50
165	A17	10c on 2c carmine	2.00	2.00
166	A18	10c on 6c gray vio.	2.00	2.00
		a. Double surch.	10.00	
167	"	10c on 6c gray violet (C)	2.00	2.00
168	"	10c on 50c rose	5.00	3.75
		Nos. 162–168 (7)	13.65	12.40

No. 158 Surcharged with New Value.

1915

173	A17	5c on 10c brown	2.00	1.25

Ulua Bridge — Bonilla Theater

A19 A20

1915-16 Lithographed.

174	A19	1c chocolate	10	10
		a. Imperf., pair	2.00	2.00
175	"	2c carmine	12	10
		a. Tête bêche pair	1.00	1.00
		b. Imperf., pair	2.00	2.00
176	A20	5c bright blue	15	10
		a. Imperf., pair	4.00	
177	"	6c deep purple	18	15
178	A19	10c dull blue	20	18
		a. Imperf., pair	4.00	

179 A19 20c red brown 60 60
a. Tête bêche pair 2.50 2.50
b. Imperf., pair 6.00
180 A20 50c red 60 60
a. Imperf., pair 7.50
181 " 1p yellow green 1.35 1.25
a. Imperf., pair 10.00 10.00
Nos. 174–181 (8) 3.30 3.08

Francisco Bertrand
A21

Statue to Francisco Morazán
A22

1916, Feb. 1

182 A21 1c orange 3.50 3.50

Election of Pres. Francisco Bertrand.
Counterfeits exist.

Official Stamp No. 060 Overprinted **CORRIENTE**

1918

183 A20 5c bright blue 2.50 2.00
a. Inverted ovpt. 7.00 7.00

1919

184 A22 1c brown 8 8
a. Printed on both sides 3.00
b. Imperf., pair 1.00
185 " 2c carmine 12 10
186 " 5c lilac rose 12 10
187 " 6c bright violet 20 12
188 " 10c dull blue 25 25
189 " 15c light blue 50 25
190 " 15c dark violet 35 25
191 " 20c orange brown 40 25
a. 20c gray brown 40 25
b. Imperf., pair 3.00
192 " 50c light brown 85 85
a. Imperf., pair 6.00
193 " 1p yellow green 1.25 1.25
a. Imperf., pair 6.00
b. Printed on both sides 6.00
c. Tête bêche pair 7.00
Nos. 184–193 (10) 4.12 3.50

Counterfeits exist.

"Dawn of Peace"
A23

1920 Size: 27x21mm.

194 A23 2c rose 2.00 2.00
a. Tête bêche pair 10.00 10.00
b. Imperf., pair 10.00 10.00

Size: 51x40mm.

195 A23 2c gold 6.00 6.00
196 " 2c silver 6.00 6.00
197 " 2c bronze 7.50 7.50
198 " 2c red 6.00 6.00
Nos. 194–198 (5) 27.50 27.50

Assumption of power by Gen. Rafael Lopez Gutierrez.
Nos. 195–198 exist imperf.
Counterfeits of Nos. 195–198 exist.

Type of 1919, Dated "1920"

1921

201 A22 6c dark violet 5.00 5.00
a. Tête bêche pair 15.00
b. Imperf., pair 15.00
c. Invtd. ovpt. 15.00 12.50

Counterfeits exist.

No. 185 Surcharged in Antique Letters **VALE SEIS CTS.**

1922

202 A22 6c on 2c carmine 35 25
a. "ALE" for "VALE" 3.00 3.00
b. Comma after "CTS" 3.00 3.00
c. Without period after "CTS" 3.00 3.00
d. "CT" for "CTS" 3.00 3.00
e Double surcharge 6.00
f. Inverted surcharge 6.00

Stamps of 1919 Surcharged in Roman Figures and Antique Letters in Green **$ 0.50 HABILITADO VALE CTA. CTS.**

1923

203 A22 10c on 1c brown 25 30
204 " 50c on 2c carmine 75 60
a. Invtd. surcharge 5.00 5.00
b. "HABILTADO" 5.00 5.00

Surcharged in Black or Violet Blue **$ 1.00 HABILITADO VALE UN PESO**

205 A22 1p on 5c lilac rose (Bk) 3.50 3.50
a. "PSEO" 20.00 20.00
b. Invtd. surch. 20.00 20.00
206 " 1p on 5c lilac rose (Bl) 20.00 20.00
a. "PSEO" 100.00

On Nos. 205–206, "Habilitado Vale" is in Antique letters, "Un Peso" in Roman.

No. 185 Surcharged in Roman Letters in Green **VALE SEIS CTS**

207 A22 6c on 2c carmine 3.00 3.00

Nos. 184–185 Surcharged in Roman Letters in Green **$ 0.50 HABILITADO VALE CTA CTS**

208 A22 10c on 1c brown 1.00 75
a. "DIES" 4.00
b. "DEIZ" 4.00
c. "DEIZ CAS" 4.00
d. "TTS" for "CTS" 4.00
e. "HABILTADO" 4.00
f. "HABILITAD" 4.00
g. "HABILITA" 4.00
h. Inverted surcharge 15.00
209 " 50c on 2c carmine 1.50 1.00
a. "CAT" for "CTA" 7.50
b. "TCA" for "CTA" 7.50
c. "TTS" for "CTS" 7.50
d. "CAS" for "CTS" 7.50
e. "HABILTADO" 7.50

Surcharge on No. 209 is found in two spacings between value and HABILITADO: 5mm. (illustrated) and 1½mm.

No. 186 Surcharged in Antique Letters in Black **$ 1.00 HABILITADO VALE UN PESO**

210 A22 1p on 5c lilac rose 17.50 17.50
a. "PFSO" 75.00

In the surcharges on Nos. 202 to 210 there are various wrong font, inverted and omitted letters.

No. 184 Surcharged in Large Antique Letters in Green **$ 0.10 HABILITADO VALE DIEZ CTS**

210C A22 10c on 1c brown 18.00 18.00
d. "DIFZ" 65.00 65.00

Dionisio de Herrera
A24

1924 Lithographed. *Perf. 11, 11½.*

211 A24 1c olive green 20 10
212 " 2c deep rose 20 10
213 " 6c red violet 30 12
214 " 10c blue 30 15
215 " 20c yellow brown 60 20
216 " 50c vermilion 1.25 60
217 " 1p emerald 2.50 75
Nos. 211–217 (7) 5.35 2.02

In 1924 a facsimile of the signature of Santiago Herrera, covering four stamps, was handstamped in violet to prevent the use of stamps that had been stolen during a revolution.

Pres. Miguel Paz Baraona
A25

1925, Feb. 1 *Perf. 11½*

218 A25 1c dull blue 3.00 3.00
a. 1c dark blue 3.00 3.00
219 " 1c carmine rose 6.50 6.50
a. 1c brown carmine 6.50 6.50
220 " 1c olive brown 17.50 17.50
a. 1c orange brown 17.50 17.50
b. 1c dark brown 17.50 17.50
c. 1c black brown 18.50 17.50
221 " 1c buff 15.00 15.00
222 " 1c red 45.00 45.00
223 " 1c green 45.00 45.00
Nos. 218–223 (6) 132.00 132.00

Imperf.

225 A25 1c dull blue 7.00 7.00
a. 1c dark blue 7.00 7.00
226 " 1c carmine rose 10.00 10.00
a. 1c brown carmine 10.00 10.00
227 " 1c olive brown 10.00 10.00
a. 1c orange brown 10.00 10.00
b. 1c deep brown 10.00 10.00
c. 1c black brown 10.00 10.00
228 " 1c buff 10.00 10.00
229 " 1c red 45.00 45.00
229A " 1c green 45.00 45.00
Nos. 225–229A (6) 127.00 127.00

Inauguration of President Barano.
Counterfeits exist.

No. 187 Overprinted n Black and Red **Acuerdo Mayo 3 de 1926 HABILITADO**

1926, June *Perf. 11½*

230 A22 6c bright violet 1.25 1.25

Many varieties of this two-part overprint exist: one or both inverted or double, and various combinations. Price, each $4.

Nos. 177 and 187 Overprinted in Black or Red **1926**

1926

231 A20 6c dp. purple (Bk) 2.00 2.00
a. Inverted ovpt. 5.00 5.00
b. Double overprint 5.00 5.00
232 " 6c deep purple (R) 2.50 2.50
a. Double overprint 5.00 5.00
233 A22 6c violet (Bk) 60 60
a. 6c lilac 60 60
b. Inverted overprint 5.00 4.00
c. Double overprint 5.00 4.00
d. Double, ovpt., one inverted 5.00 5.00
e. "192" 7.50 7.50
f. Double overprint, both inverted 7.50 7.50

Same Overprint on No. 201.

234 A22 6c dark violet 5.00 5.00
a. Double overprint
b. Inverted overprint

Same Overprint on No. 230.

235 A22 6c violet 7.50 7.50
a. "1926" inverted 10.00 10.00
b. "Habilitado" triple, one inverted 10.00 10.00

No. 188 Surcharged in Red or Black **Vale 6 Cts. 1926**

236 A22 6c on 10c blue (R) 35 20
c. Double surcharge 2.00 2.00
d. Without bar
e. Invtd. surcharge 3.00 3.00
f. "Vale" omitted
g. "6 cts" omitted
h. "cts" omitted
236K " 6c on 10c blue (Bk) 40.00 40.00

Nos. 175 and 185 Overprinted in Green **HABILITADO 1926**

237 A19 2c carmine 25 25
a. Tête bêche pair 1.00 1.00
b. Double overprint 3.00 2.00
c. "HARILITADO" 3.00 2.00
d. "1926" only 4.00 4.00
e. Double overprint, one inverted 4.00 4.00
f. "1926" omitted 5.00 5.00
g. Triple overprint, two inverted 7.50 7.50
h. Double on face, one on back 7.50 7.50
238 A22 2c carmine 25 25
a. HARILITADO 1.25 1.25
b. Double overprint 2.00 2.00
c. Inverted overprint 3.00 3.00

No. 177 Overprinted in Red **1926**
Large Numerals, 12x5 mm.

1927

239 A20 6c deep purple 10.00 10.00
a. "1926" over "1927" 17.50 17.50
b. Inverted overprint on face of stamp, normal overprint on back 20.00

No. 179 Surcharged **vale 6 cts. 1927**

1927

240 A19 6c on 20c brown 75 75
a. Tête bêche pair 4.00 4.00
c. Inverted surcharge 3.00 3.00
d. Double surcharge 12.00 12.00

Nos. 8 and 10 in the setting have no period after "cts" and No. 50 has the "t" of "cts" inverted.

Same Surcharge on Nos. 189-191.

241 A22 6c on 15c blue 35.00 35.00
a. "c" of "cts" omitted
242 " 6c on 15c violet 75 75
a. Double surcharge 2.50 2.50
b. Double surcharge, one inverted 3.00 3.00
c. "L" of "Vale" omitted
243 " 6c on 20c yel. brown 60 50
a. 6c on 20c deep brown
b. "6" omitted 2.50 2.50
c. "Vale" and "cts" omitted 5.00 5.00

On Nos. 242 and 243 stamps Nos. 12, 16 and 43 in the setting have no period after "cts" and No. 34 often lacks the "s". On No. 243 the "c" of "cts" is missing on stamp No. 38. On No. 241 occur the varieties "ct" or "ts" for "cts." and no period.

Southern Highway
A26

Ruins of Copán
A27

Pine Tree
A28

Presidential Palace
A29

Ponciano Leiva
A30

Pres. M.A. Soto
A31

Lempira
A32

Map of Honduras
A33

President Juan Lindo
A34

Statue of Columbus
A35

Wmk. 209

Wmkd. Multiple Ovals. (209).

1927–29

244	A26	1c ultramarine	20	20
		a. 1c blue	25	25
245	A27	2c carmine	20	15
246	A28	5c dull violet	25	15
247	"	5c blue gray ('29)	3.00	1.75
248	A29	6c blue black	35	35
		a. 6c gray black	75	75
249	"	6c dark blue ('29)	25	15
		a. 6c light blue	25	15
250	A30	10c blue	35	20
251	A31	15c deep blue	50	25
252	A32	20c dark blue	75	40
253	A33	30c dark brown	1.25	75
254	A34	50c light blue	1.75	1.00
255	A35	1p red	3.50	1.50
		Nos. 244–255 (12)	12.35	6.85

In 1929 a quantity of imperforate sheets of No. 249 were stolen from the Litografia Nacional. Some of them were perforated by sewing machine and a few copies were passed through the post. To prevent the use of stolen stamps of the 1927-29 issues they were declared invalid and the stock on hand was overprinted "1929 a 1930".

Pres. Vicente Mejia Colindres and Vice-Pres. Rafael Diaz Chávez
A36

President Mejia Colindres
A37

1929, Feb. 25

256	A36	1c dark carmine	1.75	1.75
257	A37	2c emerald	1.75	1.75

Issued to commemorate the installation of Pres. Vicente Mejia Colindres. Printed in sheets of ten.

Nos. 256 and 257 were surreptitiously printed in transposed colors. They were not regularly issued.

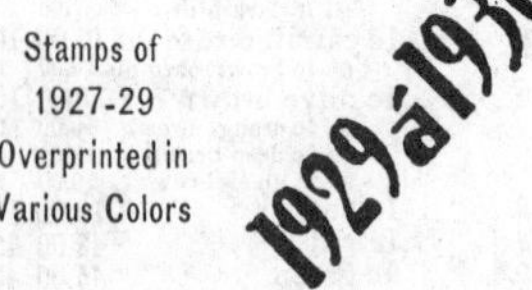

Stamps of 1927-29 Overprinted in Various Colors

1929 á 1930

1929, Oct.

259	A26	1c blue (R)	15	15
		a. 1c ultramarine (R)	50	20
		b. Double overprint	2.00	2.00
		c. As "a," double overprint	2.00	2.00
260	"	1c blue (Bk)	6.00	6.00
		a. 1c ultramarine (Bk)		
261	A27	2c carmine (R. Br)	3.00	3.00
		a. Double overprint		
262	"	2c carmine (Bl Gr)	75	75
		a. Double overprint		
263	"	2c carmine (Bk)	25	25
264	"	2c carmine (V)	75	75
		a. Double ovpt.		
		b. Double ovpt., one inverted		
265	"	2c orange red (V)	1.00	
266	A28	5c dull violet (R)	35	25
		a. Double overprint (R+V)		
267	"	5c blue gray (R)	85	75
		a. Double overprint (R+Bk)		
269	A29	6c gray black (R)	2.50	2.00
		a. Dbl. ovpt.	6.00	6.00
272	"	6c dark blue (R)	30	20
		a. 6c light blue (R)	30	20
		b. Dbl. ovpt.	2.00	2.00
		c. Double overprint (R+V)		
273	A30	10c blue (R)	35	20
		a. Dbl. ovpt.	2.50	2.50
274	A31	15c deep blue (R)	40	25
		a. Double overprint	3.50	3.50
275	A32	20c dark blue (R)	40	30
276	A33	30c dark brown (R)	60	60
		a. Dbl. ovpt.	3.50	3.50
277	A34	50c light blue (R)	1.00	1.00
278	A35	1p red (V)	2.75	2.75

Nos. 259 to 278 exist in numerous shades. There are also various shades of the red and violet overprints. The overprint may be found reading upwards, downwards, inverted, double, triple, tête bêche or combinations.

Status of both 6c stamps with overprint in black is questioned.

A38

1929, Dec. 10

279	A38	1c on 6c lilac rose	75	75
		a. "1992" for "1929"		
		b. "9192" for "1929"		
		c. Surch. reading down		
		d. Double surcharge, one reading down		

Varieties include "1992" reading down and pairs with one surcharge reading down, double or with "1992".

No. 214 Surcharged in Red

Vale 2 cts. 1930

1930 ***Perf. 11, 11½.*** **Unwmkd.**

280	A24	1c on 10c blue	30	30
		a. "1093" for "1930"	2.00	
		b. "tsc" for "cts"	2.00	
281	"	2c on 10c blue	30	30
		a. "tsc" for "cts"	3.00	
		b. "Vale 2" omitted		

Official Stamps of 1929 Overprinted in Red or Violet

Habilitado para el servicio públi- co. 1930

Wmkd. Multiple Ovals. (209)

Perf. 11½.

282	O1	1c blue (R)	50	50
		a. Double overprint	3.00	3.00
284	"	2c carmine (V)	1.00	1.00

Stamps of 1915-26 Overprinted in Blue

Habilitado julio.—1930

On Stamp No. 174.

1930 **Unwmkd.**

285	A19	1c chocolate	25	25
		a. Double overprint	1.25	1.25
		b. Inverted overprint	1.50	1.50
		c. Double overprint, one inverted	1.50	1.50
		d. "juiio"	2.25	2.25

On Stamps Nos. 184 and 191

287	A22	1c brown	6.00	6.00
		a. Double overprint		
		b. "juiio"		
		c. Invtd. ovpt.		
288	"	20c brown	12.00	12.00
		a. "juiio"		

On Stamp No. 204.

289	A22	50c on 2c car.	100.00	100.00
		a. "juiio"		
		b. Invtd. surch.	100.00	100.00
		c. As "a" and "b"		

On Stamps Nos. 211 and 212.

290	A24	1c olive green	25	20
		a. Double overprint	2.50	2.50
		b. Invtd. overprint	2.50	2.50
		c. "juiio"	3.00	3.00
		d. On No. O75	17.50	
291	"	2c carmine rose	30	30
		a. Double overprint	2.50	2.50
		b. Invtd. overprint	2.50	2.50
		c. "juiio"		

On Stamp No. 237.

292	A19	2c carmine (G & Bl)	50.00	50.00

From Title Page of Government Gazette, First Issue
A39

Wmkd. Multiple Ovals. (209)

1930, Aug. 11

295	A39	2c orange	65	50
296	"	2c ultramarine	65	50
297	"	2c red	65	50

Issued in commemoration of the publication of the first newspaper in Honduras. The stamps were on sale and available for postage on August 11th, 1930, only. Not more than five copies of each color could be purchased by an applicant.

Nos. 295-297 exist imperf. and part-perforate.

Paz Baraona
A40

Manuel Bonilla
A41

Lake Yojoa
A42

View of Palace at Tegucigalpa
A43

City of Amapala—A44

Mayan Stele at Copán
A45

Christopher Columbus
A46

Discovery of America—A47

Loarque Bridge—A48

Engraved.

1931, Jan. 2 *Perf. 12* **Unwmkd.**

298 A40 1c black brown 15 12
299 A41 2c carmine rose 15 12
300 A42 5c dull violet 25 15
301 A43 6c deep green 25 15
302 A44 10c brown 35 20
303 A45 15c dark blue 35 20
304 A46 20c black 60 30
305 A47 50c olive green 1.50 85
306 A48 1p slate black 3.00 1.50
Nos. 298-306 (9) 6.60 3.59

Regular Issue of 1931 Overprinted **T.S.de C.** in Black or Various Colors.

1931

307 A40 1c black brown 20 20
308 A41 2c carmine rose 25 20
309 A45 15c dark blue 40 30
310 A46 20c black 50 35

Overprinted **T. S. de C.**

311 A42 5c dull violet 25 25
312 A43 6c deep green 25 20
315 A44 10c brown 40 40
316 A47 50c olive green 3.00 2.50
317 A48 1p slate black 4.00 3.50
Nos. 307-317 (9) 9.25 7.90

The overprint is a control mark. It stands for "Tribunal Superior de Cuentas" (Superior Tribunal of Accounts).

Overprint varieties include: inverted; double; double, one or both inverted; on back; pair, one without overprint differing colors (6c exists with overprint in orange, yellow and red).

See also Nos. C51–C55.

President Carías and Vice-President Williams

A49

1933, Apr. 29

318 A49 2c carmine rose 30 30
319 " 6c deep green 35 35
320 " 10c deep blue 40 40
321 " 15c red orange 50 50

Issued to commemorate the inauguration of President Tiburico Carias Andino and Vice-President Abraham Williams, February 1, 1933.

Columbus' Fleet and Flag of the Race—A50

Perf. 11½

1933, Aug. 3 Litho. Wmk. 209

322 A50 2c ultramarine 45 45
323 " 6c yellow 50 50
324 " 10c lemon 60 60

Perf. 12

325 A50 15c violet 85 85
326 " 50c red 2.25 2.25
327 A50 1 l emerald 4.50 4.50
Nos. 322-327 (6) 9.15 9.15

Commemorating the "Day of the Race", an annual holiday throughout Spanish-American countries. Also commemorating the 441st anniversary of the sailing of Columbus to the New World, August 3rd, 1492.

Masonic Temple, Tegucigalpa

A51

Designs: 2c, President Carias. 5c, Flag. 6c, Tomás Estrada Palma.

Engraved.

1935, Jan. 12 *Perf. 12* **Unwmkd.**

328 A51 1c green 20 15
329 " 2c carmine 20 20
330 " 5c dark blue 25 35
331 " 6c black brown 30 35
a. Vert. pair, imperf. btwn. 17.50 17.50

See also Nos. C77–C83.

Gen. Carías Bridge

A55

1937

332 A55 6c car. & olive grn. 50 50
333 " 21c green & violet 60 60
334 " 46c orange & brown 1.25 85
335 " 55c ultra. & black 1.50 1.25

Issued in commemoration of the prolongation of the Presidential term to January 19th, 1943.

Seal of Honduras

A56

Central District Palace

A57

Designs: 3c, Map of Honduras. 5c, Bridge of Choluteca. 8c, Flag.

1939, Mar. 1 *Perf. 12½*

336 A56 1c orange yellow 10 10
337 A57 2c red orange 12 10
338 " 3c carmine 15 10
339 " 5c orange 20 12
340 A56 8c dark blue 25 15
Nos. 336-340 (5) 82 57

Nos. 336–340 exist imperf.

See also Nos. C89–C98.

Nos. 336 and 337 Overprinted in Green **HABILITADO 1944-45**

1944 *Perf. 12½.*

342 A56 1c orange yellow 30 30
a. Inverted ovpt. 6.00 6.00
343 A57 2c red orange 55 55
a. Inverted ovpt. 6.00 6.00

AIR POST STAMPS.

Regular Issue of 1915-16 Overprinted in Black, Blue or Red

AERO
CORREO

1925 *Perf. 11½.* **Unwmkd.**

C1 A20 5c light blue (Bk) 85.00 85.00
C2 " 5c light blue (Bl) 300.00 300.00
a. Inverted overprint 400.00
b. Vertical overprint 600.00
c. Double overprint 750.00
C3 " 5c lt. blue (R) 10,000.00
C4 A19 10c dark blue (R) 150.00 150.00
a. Inverted overprint 350.00
b. Overprint tête bêche (pair) 800.00
C5 " 10c dark blue (Bk) 2500.00
C6 " 20c red brn. (Bk) 175.00 175.00
a. Inverted ovpt. 225.00
b. Tête bêche pair 400.00
c. Overprint tête bêche (pair) 750.00
d. "AFRO" 1500.00
e. Double overprint 600.00
C7 " 20c red brown (Bl) 175.00 175.00
a. Inverted overprint 450.00
b. Tête bêche pair 800.00
c. Vertical overprint 650.00
C8 A20 50c red (Bk) 350.00 350.00
a. Inverted overprint 600.00
b. Overprint tête bêche (pair) 800.00
C9 " 1p yellow green (Bk) 1100.00 1100.00

Surcharged

AERO
CORREO
25

C10 A19 25c on 1c chocolate (Bk) 125.00 125.00
a. Inverted surcharge 350.00
C11 A20 25c on 5c light blue (Bl) 225.00 225.00
a. Inverted surcharge 425.00
b. Double inverted surcharge 550.00
C12 A19 25c on 10c dark blue (Bk) 60,000.00
C13 " 25c on 20c brown (Bl) 250.00 250.00
a. Inverted surcharge 325.00
b. Tête bêche pair 525.00

Counterfeits of Nos. C1–C13 are plentiful.

Monoplane and Lisandro Garay

AP1

Typographed

1929, June 5 *Perf. 12* **Unwmkd.**

C13C AP1 50c carmine 3.00 3.00

No. 216 Surcharged in Blue

Servicio aéreo
Vale 25 centa-
vos oro.—1929.

1929 *Perf. 11, 11½.*

C14 A24 25c on 50c vermilion 6.00 6.00

In the surcharges on Nos. C14 to C40 there are various wrong font and defective letters and numerals, also periods omitted.

AP2

Surcharged in Green, Black or Red.

1929, Oct.

C15 AP2 5c on 20c yellow brown (G) 1.50 1.50
a. Double surcharge (R+G) 60.00
C16 " 10c on 50c vermilion (Bk) 2.50 2.00
C17 " 15c on 1p emerald (R) 4.00 4.00

Nos. 214 and 216 Surcharged Vertically in Red or Black

Servicio Aéreo Internacional Vale 5 cts. oro 1929
a

Servicio Aéreo Internacional.—Vale 20.cts. oro.—1929
b

1929, Dec. 10

C18 A24 (*a*) 5c on 10c blue (R) 60 60
C19 " (*b*) 20c on 50c verm. (Bk) 1.25 1.25
a. "1299" for "1929" 275.00
b. "cts. cts." for "cts. oro." 275.00
c. "r" of "Aereo" omitted 3.00
d. Horizontal pair, imperf. between 30.00

Nos. 214, 215 and 180 Surcharged in Various Colors

Servicio Aéreo Internacional Vale 25 cts. oro 1930

1930

C20 A24 5c on 10c blue (R) 60 60
a. "1930" reading down 5.00
b. "1903" for "1930" 5.00
c. Surcharge reading down 14.00
d. Double surcharge 20.00
e. Double surcharge, one downward 20.00
C21 " 5c on 10c blue (Y) 900.00 900.00
C22 " 5c on 20c yellow brown (Bl) 150.00 150.00
C23 " 10c on 20c yellow brown (Bk) 1.00 1.00
a. "0" for "10" 5.00
b. Double surcharge 12.50
c. Double surcharge, one downward 17.50
d. Horizontal pair, imperf. between 100.00
C24 " 10c on 20c yellow brown (V) 900.00 900.00
a. "0" for "10" 1100.00
C25 A20 25c on 50c red (Bk) 1.25 1.25
a. "Internaoicnal" 5.00
b. "o" for "oro" 5.00
c. Inverted surcharge 25.00
d. As "a," invtd. surch. 250.00
e. As "b," invtd. surch. 250.00

Surcharge on No. C25 is horizontal.

Nos. 214, 215 and 180 Surcharged

Servicio aéreo
Vale 15 centa-
vos oro.—Mar
zo —1930

1930, Mar.

C26 A24 5c on 10c blue 55
a. Dbl. surcharge 13.50
b. "Servicioa" 5.00

C27 A24 15c on 20c yel. brn. 75 75
a. Double surcharge 10.00
C28 A20 20c on 50c red, surch. reading down 1.25 1.25
a. Surcharge reading up 10.00

Nos. C22 and C23 Surcharged Vertically in Red

Vale 10 cts. oro

1930
C29 A24 10c on 5c on 20c yellow brn. (Bl+R) 1.00 1.00
a. "1930" reading down 13.00 13.00
b. "1903" for "1930" 13.00 13.00
c. Red surcharge reading down 20.00
C30 " 10c on 10c on 20c yellow brown (Bk+R) 125.00 125.00
a. "0" for "10" 275.00

No. 181 Surcharged as No. C25 and Re-surcharged

Vale 50 cts. oro

C31 A20 50c on 25c on 1p green 3.00 3.00
a. "Internaoicnal" 8.00
b. "o" for "oro" 8.00
c. 25c surch. invtd. 25.00 25.00
d. 50c surch. invtd. 25.00 25.00
e. As "a" and "c"
f. As "a" and "d"
g. As "b" and "c"
h. As "b" and "d"

No. 215 Surcharged in Dark Blue

Servicio aéreo Vale 5 centavos oro. Mayo.

1930, May 19
C32 A24 5c on 20c yellow brown 1.25 1.25
a. Double surcharge 7.50 7.50
b. Horizontal pair, imperf. between 60.00 60.00
c. Vertical pair, imperf. between 30.00 30.00

Official Stamps Nos. O78-O80 Surcharged like Nos. C20 to C25 in Various Colors.

1930
C33 A24 5c on 10c blue (R) 400.00 400.00
a. "1930" reading down *1000.00*
b. "1903" for "1930" *1000.00*
C34 " 5c on 20c yellow brown (Bl) 500.00 500.00
C35 " 25c on 50c vermilion (Bk) 200.00 200.00
a. 55c on 50c verm. 350.00 350.00

No. C35 exists with inverted surcharge.

Official Stamp No. O64 Surcharged like No. C28

C36 A20 20c on 50c red (dbl. surch., reading up) *1150.00 1150.00*
a. Dbl. surch. reading down *1150.00 1150.00*

Official Stamp No. O87 Overprinted

HABILITADO Servicio Aéreo Internacional 1930

Wmkd. Multiple Ovals. (209)
Perf. 11½.
C37 O1 50c yel., grn. & bl. 1.75 1.75
a. "Internacional" 6.00
b. "Iuternacional" 6.00
c. Double overprint 6.00

Official Stamps Nos. O86-O88 Overprinted in Various Colors

HABILITADO Servicio Aéreo MAYO 1930

1930, May 23
C38 O1 20c dark blue (R) 1.00 1.00
a. Double overprint 10.00
b. Triple ovpt. 15.00
C39 " 50c orange, green & blue (Bk) 1.50 1.25
C40 " 1p buff (Bl) 1.50 1.50
a. Dbl. ovpt. 12.50

National Palace
AP3

Engraved.

1930, Oct. 1 ***Perf. 12*** **Unwmkd.**
C41 AP3 5c yellow orange 50 35
C42 " 10c carmine 75 65
C43 " 15c green 1.00 80
C44 " 20c dull violet 1.25 80
C45 " 1p light brown 4.50 4.50
Nos. C41-C45 (5) 8.00 7.10

Same Overprinted in Various Colors

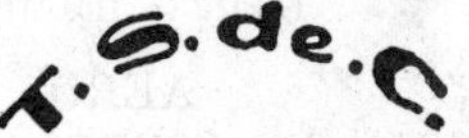

T. S. de C.

1931 ***Perf. 12***
C51 AP3 5c yel. orange (R) 1.00 1.00
C52 " 10c carmine (Bk) 3.00 3.00
C53 " 15c green(Br) 3.00 3.00
C54 " 20c dull violet (O) 5.00 5.00
C55 " 1p lt. brown (G) 11.00 11.00
Nos. C51-C55 (5) 23.00 23.00

See note after No. 317.

Stamps of Various Issues Surcharged

Servicio aéreo interior. Vale 15 cts. Octubre 1931.

Blue Surcharge.

1931, Oct. ***Perf. 11½.***

On Stamp No. 215.

C56 A24 15c on 20c yellow brown 3.50 3.50
a. Horizontal pair, imperf. between 50.00
b. Green surcharge 15.00 15.00

On Official Stamp No. O64.

C57 A20 15c on 50c red 5.00 5.00
a. Inverted surcharge 12.00 12.00

On Official Stamp No. O72.

C58 A22 15c on 20c brown 5.00 5.00
a. Vert. pair, imperf. between 15.00

On Nos. C57 and C58 the word "OFICIAL" is cancelled by two bars.

Black Surcharge.

On Official Stamp No. O88.

Wmkd. Multiple Ovals. (209)
C59 O1 15c on 1p buff 5.00 5.00
a. Imperf. horizontally (pair) 10.00
b. "Sevricio" 17.50 17.50

The varieties "Vaie" for "Vale", "aereo" with circumflex accent on the first "e" and "Interior" with initial capital "I" are found on Nos. C56, C58 and C59. No. C57 is known with initial capital in "Interior."

A similar surcharge, in slightly larger letters and with many minor varieties, exists on Nos. 215, O63, O64 and O73. The authenticity of this surcharge is questioned.

Various Designs Surcharged in Green, Red or Black

S.—Aéreo VI. 15 cts. XI 1931.

1931, Nov. **Unwmkd.**

On Stamp No. 215.

C60 A24 15c on 20c yellow brown(G) 4.00 4.00
a. Inverted surcharge 7.50
b. "XI" omitted 7.50
c. "X" for "XI" 7.50
d. "PI" for "XI" 7.50

On Official Stamp No. O73.

C61 A22 15c on 50c light brown (R) 4.00 4.00
a. "XI" omitted 7.50
b. "PI" for "XI" 7.50
c. Double surcharge 25.00 25.00

On No. C61 the word "OFICIAL" is not barred out.

On Official Stamps Nos. O87 and O88
Wmkd. Multiple Ovals. (209)

C62 O1 15c on 50c orange, green & blue (Bk) 4.00 4.00
a. "1391" for "1931" 12.50 12.50
b. Double surcharge 10.00 10.00
C63 " 15c on 1p buff (Bk) 4.00 4.00
a. "1391" for "1931" 12.50
b. Surcharged on both sides 10.00

Official Stamps Nos. O76-O78 Surcharged in Black or Red

Aéreo interior VALE 15 Cts. 1932

1932 ***Perf. 11, 11½*** **Unwmkd.**
C73 A24 15c on 2c deep rose 50 50
a. Double surcharge 8.00
b. Inverted surcharge 5.00
c. "Ae" of "Aero" omitted 1.00
d. On No. 212 (no 'Oficial')
C74 " 15c on 6c red violet 50 50
a. Double surcharge 5.00
b. Horizontal pair, imperf. between 25.00
c. "Aer'" omitted
d. "A" omitted 1.00
e. Inverted surcharge 5.00
C75 " 15c on 10c deep blue (R) 50 50
a. Double surcharge 8.00
b. Inverted surcharge 5.00
c. "r" of "Aereo" omitted 1.00

Same Surcharge on No. 214 in Red.

C76 A24 15c on 10c deep blue *125.00 125.00*

There are various broken and missing letters in the setting.

Post Office and National Palace
AP4

View of Tegucigalpa—AP5

Designs: 15c, Map of Honduras. 20c, Mayo Bridge. 40c, View of Tegucigalpa. 50c, Owl. 1 l, Coat of Arms.

1935, Jan. 10 ***Perf. 12***
C77 AP4 8c blue 12 10
C78 AP5 10c gray 20 12
C79 " 15c olive gray 30 20
C80 " 20c dull green 30 15
C81 " 40c brown 55 30
C82 AP4 50c yellow 3.00 2.00
C83 " 1 l green 2.00 2.00
Nos. C77-C83 (7) 6.47 4.87

Flags of U. S. and Honduras
AP11

Engraved and Lithographed.

1937, Sept. 17 **Unwmkd.**
C84 AP11 46c multicolored 2.50 2.00

Issued in commemoration of the 150th anniversary of the Constitution of the United States of America.

Comayagua Cathedral
AP12

Founding of Comayagua
AP13

Alonzo Cáceres and Pres. Carías
AP14

Lintel of Royal Palace
AP15

1937, Dec. 7 **Engraved**
C85 AP12 2c copper red 20 12
C86 AP13 8c dark blue 25 15
C87 AP14 15c slate black 50 40
C88 AP15 50c dark brown 1.25 1.25

Issued in commemoration of the 400th anniversary of the founding of the city of Comayagua.

Mayan Stele at Copán
AP16

Mayan Temple, Copán
AP17

Designs: 15c, President Carias. 30c, José C. de Valle. 40c, Presidential House. 46c, Lempira. 55c, Church of Our Lady of Suyapa. 66c, J. T. Reyes. 1 l, Hospital at Choluteca. 2 l, Ramón Rosa.

1939, Mar. 1 ***Perf. 12½***

C89	AP16	10c orange brown	15	10
C90	"	15c greenish blue	20	10
C91	AP17	21c gray	30	10
C92	AP16	30c dark blue green	40	15
C93	AP17	40c dull violet	60	20
C94	AP16	46c dark gray brn.	70	65
C95	"	55c green	90	85
		a. Imperf., pair	25.00	
C96	"	66c black	1.50	1.15
C97	"	1 l olive green	2.25	80
C98	"	2 l henna red	4.00	3.00
		Nos. C89-C98 (10)	11.00	7.10

Souvenir Sheets.

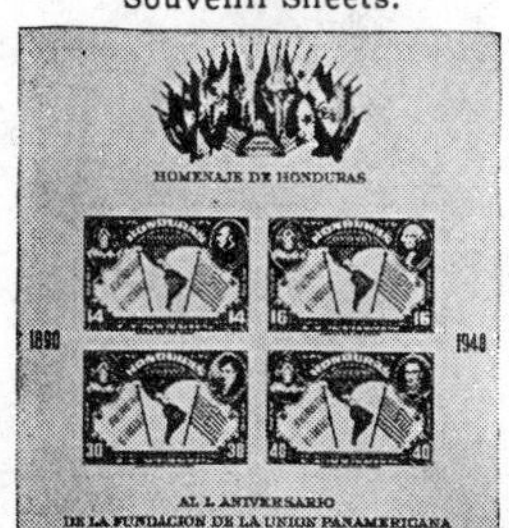

AP26

Engraved.

Designs: 14c, Francisco Morazan. 16c, George Washington. 30c, J. C. de Valle. 40c, Simon Bolivar.

Centers of Stamps Lithographed.

1940, Apr. 13 ***Perf. 12*** **Unwmkd.**

C99	AP26	Sheet of four	3.50	3.50
		a. 14c black, yellow, ultramarine & rose	50	50
		b. 16c black, yellow, ultramarine & rose	60	60
		c. 30c black, yellow, ultramarine & rose	90	90
		d. 40c black, yellow, ultramarine & rose	1.25	1.25
		Imperf.		
C100	AP26	Sheet of four	3.50	3.50
		a. 14c black, yellow, ultramarine & rose	50	50
		b. 16c black, yellow, ultramarine & rose	60	60
		c. 30c black, yellow, ultramarine & rose	90	90
		d. 40c black, yellow, ultramarine & rose	1.25	1.25

Issued to commemorate the 50th anniversary of the Pan American Union. Sheet size: 103x114mm.

Air Post Official Stamps of 1939 Overprinted in Red

Correo Aéreo
Habilitado para
Servicio Publico
Pro-Faro Colon-1940

1940, Oct. 12 ***Perf. 12½***

C101	OA2	2c dp. blue & grn.	25	20
C102	"	5c dp. blue & org.	30	30
C103	"	8c dp. blue & brn.	30	30
C104	"	15c dp. blue & car.	50	50
C105	"	46c deep blue & olive green	1.00	1.00
C106	"	50c dp. blue & vio.	1.00	1.00
C107	"	1 l deep blue & red brown	3.50	3.50
C108	"	2 l deep blue & red orange	7.50	7.50
		Nos. C101-C108 (8)	14.35	14.30

Issued in conjunction with the erection and dedication of the Columbus Memorial Lighthouse.

Air Post Official Stamps of 1939 Overprinted in Black

Habilitada para el
Servicio Público
1941

1941, Aug. 2

C109	OA2	5c deep blue & orange	3.00	30
C110	"	8c deep blue & brown	4.50	30
		a. Overprint inverted	*250.00*	

Air Post Official Stamps of 1939 Surcharged in Black

Rehabilitada para
el Servicio Público
1941
Vale tres cts.

1941, Oct. 28

C111	OA2	3c on 2c deep blue & green	40	25
C112	"	8c on 2c deep blue & green	50	45
C113	"	8c on 15c deep blue & carmine	50	30
C114	"	8c on 46c deep blue & olive green	75	60
C115	"	8c on 50c deep blue & violet	85	60
C116	"	8c on 1 l deep blue & red brown	1.25	75
C117	"	8c on 2 l deep blue & red orange	1.50	1.00
		Nos. C111-C117 (7)	5.75	3.95

Once in each sheet a large "h" occurs in "ocho" on Nos. C112-C117.

Nos. C90 and C94 Surcharged in Red

Correo Aéreo
L 0.08

1942, July 14

C118	AP16	8c on 15c greenish blue	1.00	35
		a. "Cerreo"	3.00	3.00
		b. Dbl. surch.	35.00	35.00
		c. As "a," dbl. surch.	*250.00*	
C119	"	16c on 46c dark gray brown	1.00	35
		a. "Cerreo"	3.00	3.00

Commemorative Plaque
AP27

Morazán's Tomb, San Salvador
AP28

Designs: 5c, Battle of La Trinidad. 8c, Morazán's birthplace. 16c, Statue of Morazán. 21c, Church where Morazán was baptized. 1 l, Arms of Central American Federation. 2 l, Gen. Francisco Morazán.

1942, Sept. 15 ***Perf. 12***

C120	AP27	2c red orange	10	10
C121	"	5c turquoise green	15	10
C122	"	8c sepia	20	10
C123	AP28	14c black	45	40
C124	AP27	16c olive gray	30	30
C125	"	21c light blue	1.10	90
C126	"	1 l bright ultra.	3.50	3.00
C127	AP28	2 l dk. olive brn.	10.00	8.50
		Nos. C120-C127 (8)	15.80	13.40

Issued in honor of General Francisco Morazán.

Coat of Arms
AP35

Cattle
AP36

Bananas
AP37

Pine Tree
AP38

Tobacco Plant
AP39

Orchid
AP40

Coco Palm
AP41

Map of Honduras
AP42

Designs: 2c, Flag. 8c, Rosario. 16c, Sugar cane. 30c, Oranges. 40c, Wheat. 1 l, Corn. 2 l, Map of Americas.

1943, Sept. 14 ***Perf. 12½***

C128	AP35	1c light green	10	10
C129	"	2c blue	10	10
C130	AP36	5c green	25	10
C131	AP37	6c dark blue grn.	25	10
C132	AP36	8c lilac	30	10
C133	AP38	10c light brown	30	10
C134	AP39	15c deep claret	35	10
C135	AP38	16c dark red	35	12
C136	AP40	21c deep blue	50	10
C137	AP39	30c orange brown	65	12
C138	AP40	40c red orange	65	12
C139	AP41	55c black	85	60
C140	"	1 l dark olive	1.35	1.25
C141	AP37	2 l brown red	5.50	3.85
C142	AP42	5 l orange	15.00	13.00
		a. Vert. pair, imperf. btwn.	160.00	
		Nos. C128-C142 (15)	26.50	19.86

Pan-American School of Agriculture
AP50

1944, Oct. 12 ***Perf. 12***

C143	AP50	21c dark blue green	45	25

Issued to commemorate the inauguration of the Pan-American School of Agriculture at Tegucigalpa.

Air Post Stamps of 1937-39 Surcharged in Red or Green

Correo. Aéreo
HABILITADO
Acd. No 798-1945
L 0.01

1945, Mar. 13 ***Perf. 11, 12½***

C144	AP15	1c on 50c dark brown	15	12
C145	AP12	2c on 2c copper red	20	15
C146	AP14	8c on 15c slate black	25	25
C147	AP16	10c on 10c orange brown (G)	50	45
C148	"	15c on 15c greenish blue (G)	30	30
C149	AP17	30c on 21c gray (G)	4.50	4.50
C150	"	40c on 40c dull violet (G)	2.00	1.65
C151	AP16	1 l on 46c dark gray brown (G)	2.00	1.75
C152	"	2 l on 66c black (G)	4.00	4.00
		Nos. C144-C152 (9)	13.90	13.17

Souvenir Sheets.

Nos. C99 and C100 Overprinted in Red "VICTORIA DE LAS NACIONES UNIDAS. ALEMANIA SE RINDE INCONDICIONALMENTE 8 DE MAYO DE 1945. ACDO. No. 1231 QUE AUTORIZA LA CONTRAMARCA"

1945, Oct. 1 ***Perf. 12***

C153	AP26	Sheet of four	2.75	2.75
		Imperf.		
C154	AP26	Sheet of four	5.00	5.00

Issued to commemorate the Allied Nations' victory and Germany's unconditional surrender, May 8, 1945.

Seal of Honduras
AP51

Arms of Gracias and Trujillo
AP52

Franklin D. Roosevelt ("F.D.R." under Column)
AP53

Arms of San Miguel de Heredia de Tegucigalpa
AP54

Designs (Coats of Arms): 5c, Comayagua and San Jorge de Olancho. 15c, Province of Honduras and San Juan de Puerto Caballas. 21c, Comayagua and Tencoa. 1 l, Jerez de la Frontera de Choluteca and San Pedro de Zula.

Engraved.

1946, Oct. 15 ***Perf. 12½*** **Unwmkd.**

C155 AP51 1c red 8 5
a. Vert. pair, imperf. between 25.00
b. Imperf., pr. 100.00
C156 AP52 2c red orange 10 8
a. Imperf., pr. 100.00
C157 " 5c violet 25 18
C158 AP53 8c brown 1.00 75
a. Horiz. pair, imperf. between 100.00
C159 AP52 15c sepia 50 25
C160 " 21c deep blue 50 40
a. Horiz. pair, imperf. between 27.50
b. Imperf., pr. 100.00
C161 " 1 l green 1.50 1.25
C162 AP54 2 l dark green 2.50 2.25
Nos. C155–C162 (8) 6.43 5.21

No. C158 commemorates the death of Franklin D. Roosevelt and the Allied victory over Japan in World War II.

Type AP53 Redrawn ("Franklin D. Roosevelt" under Column)
AP59

1947, Oct. ***Perf. 12½***

C163 AP59 8c brown 1.00 75
a. Vert. pair, imperf. between 125.00
b. Horiz. pair, imperf. between
c. Perf. 12x6 *250.00*

Map, Ancient Monuments and Conference Badge
AP60

1947, Oct. 20 ***Perf. 11x12½***

Various Frames

C164 AP60 16c green 35 20
C165 " 22c orange yellow 30 25
C166 " 40c orange 55 45
C167 " 1 l deep blue 1.25 1.10
C168 " 2 l lilac 4.00 3.75
C169 " 5 l brown 10.00 10.00
Nos. C164–C169 (6) 17.45 15.75

First International Archeological Conference of the Caribbean.

Flag and Arms of Honduras
AP61

Juan Manuel Galvez
AP62

J. M. Galvez, Gen. Tiburcio Carias A. and Julio Lozano—AP63

National Stadium
AP64

Designs: 5c, 15c, Julio Lozano. 9c, Juan Manuel Galvez. 40c, Custom House. 1 l, Recinto Hall. 2 l, Gen. Tiburcio Carias A. 5 l, Galvez and Lozano.

Various Frames.

Inscribed:
"Conmemorativa de la Sucesion Presidencial para el Periodo de 1949-1955."

1949, Sept. 17 **Engr.** ***Perf. 12***

C170 AP61 1c deep blue 10 10
C171 AP62 2c rose carmine 10 10
C172 " 5c deep blue 10 10
C173 " 9c sepia 15 12
C174 " 15c red brown 20 12
C175 AP63 21c gray black 30 15
C176 AP64 30c olive gray 60 20
C177 " 40c slate gray 75 25
C178 AP61 1 l red brown 1.25 50
C179 AP62 2 l violet 3.00 2.00
C180 AP64 5 l rose carmine 8.50 8.00
Nos. C170–C180 (11) 15.05 11.64

Issued to commemorate the presidential succession for the 1949–1955 term.

Nos. C164–C169 Overprinted in Carmine

U. P. U.
75 Aniversario
1874-1949

1951, Feb. 26 ***Perf. 11x12½***

C181 AP60 16c green 70 70
a. Invtd. ovpt. 65.00
C182 " 22c orange yellow 70 70
a. Invtd. ovpt. 65.00
C183 " 40c orange 90 90
C184 " 1 l deep blue 2.50 2.50
C185 " 2 l lilac 4.00 4.00
a. Invtd. ovpt. 90.00
C186 " 5 l brown 35.00 35.00
Nos. C181–C186 (6) 43.80 43.80

Souvenir Sheets.

Same Overprint in Carmine on Nos. C99 and C100.

Perf. 12.

C187 AP26 Sheet of four 5.00 5.00
a. Imperf. 100.00 100.00

Issued to commemorate the 75th anniversary (in 1949) of the formation of the Universal Postal Union.

Nos. C170 to C179 Overprinted in Carmine

Conmemorativa
Fundación
Banco Central
Administración
Gálvez—Lozano
Julio 1º. de 1950

1951, Feb. 27 ***Perf. 12***

C188 AP61 1c deep blue 10 10
C189 AP62 2c rose carmine 12 10
C190 " 5c deep blue 15 12
C191 " 9c sepia 18 15
C192 " 15c red brown 20 15
C193 AP63 21c gray black 35 35
C194 AP64 30c olive gray 65 50
C195 " 40c slate gray 1.00 90
C196 AP61 1 l red brown 2.00 1.75
C197 AP62 2 l violet 6.00 5.50
Nos. C188–C197 (10) 10.75 9.62

Founding of Central Bank, July 1, 1950.

Discovery of America
AP65

Queen Isabella I
AP66

Designs: 2c, 1 l, Columbus at court. 8c, Surrender of Granada. 30c, Queen Isabella offering her jewels.

Perf. 13½x14, 14x13½.

1952, Oct. 11 **Engr.** **Unwmkd.**

C198 AP65 1c red orange & black 10 10
C199 " 2c blue & red brown 10 10
C200 " 8c dark green & dark brown 25 15
C201 AP66 16c dark blue & black 40 25
C202 AP65 30c purple & dark green 75 75
C203 " 1 l deep carmine & black 2.00 1.50
C204 " 2 l brn. & vio. 4.00 4.00
C205 AP66 5 l rose lilac & olive 10.00 10.00
Nos. C198–C205 (8) 17.60 16.85

Issued to commemorate the 500th anniversary of the birth of Queen Isabella I of Spain.

No. C175 Surcharged in Carmine

HABILITADO 1953
L 0.05

1953, May 13 ***Perf. 12***

C206 AP63 5c on 21c gray black 12 12
C207 " 8c on 21c " 25 15
C208 " 16c on 21c " 50 25

Nos. CO52–CO54 Surcharged "HABILITADO 1953" and New Value in Red.

1953, Dec. 8 ***Perf. 13½x14, 14x13½.***

C209 AP65 10c on 1c rose lilac & olive 10 10
a. Invtd. surch. 65.00 65.00
C210 " 12c on 1c rose lilac & olive 12 12
C211 AP65 15c on 2c brown & violet 20 20
C212 " 20c on 2c brown & violet 30 30
C213 " 24c on 2c brown & violet 30 30
a. Invtd. surch. 65.00 65.00
C214 " 25c on 2c brown & violet 35 35
C215 " 30c on 8c deep car. & black 35 35
C216 " 35c on 8c deep car. & black 45 45
C217 " 50c on 8c deep car. & blk. 60 60
C218 " 60c on 8c deep car. & blk. 80 80

Same Overprint on Nos. CO57–CO59.

C219 AP65 1 l dark green & dark brown 1.50 1.35
C220 " 2 l blue & red brown 3.75 3.50
C221 AP66 5 l red orange & black 10.00 10.00
a. Date inverted 175.00
Nos. C209–C221 (13) 18.82 18.42

Flags of UN and Honduras
AP67

Designs: 2c, UN emblem. 3c, UN building. 5c, Shield. 15c, Juan Manuel Galvez. 30c, UNICEF. 1 l, UNRRA. 2 l, UNESCO. 5 l, FAO.

Engraved; Center of 1c Litho.

1953, Dec. 18 ***Perf. 12½.***

Frames in Black.

C222 AP67 1c ultramarine & violet blue 10 10
C223 " 2c blue 12 12
C224 " 3c rose lilac 25 15
C225 " 5c green 20 15
C226 " 15c red brown 50 45
C227 " 30c brown 1.25 1.10
C228 " 1 l deep carmine 9.00 8.00
C229 " 2 l orange 10.00 9.00
C230 " 5 l blue green 27.50 26.50
Nos. C222–C230 (9) 48.92 45.57

Issued to honor the United Nations.

Nos. CO60–CO66 Overprinted in Red

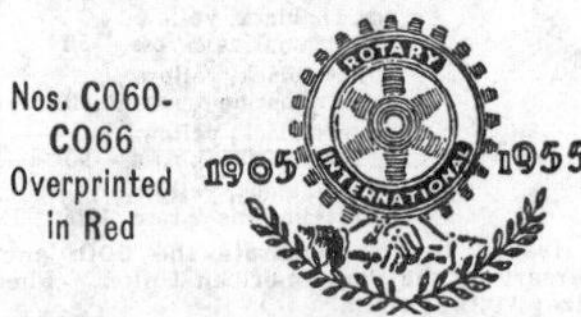

1955, Feb. 23 ***Perf. 12½*** **Unwmkd.**

Frames in Black

C231 AP67 1c ultramarine & violet blue 20 20
C232 " 2c deep blue green 20 20
C233 " 3c orange 25 25
C234 " 5c deep carmine 30 30
C235 " 15c dark brown 50 50
C236 " 30c purple 1.50 1.50
C237 " 1 l olive gray 30.00 30.00

Overprint exists inverted on 1c, 3c.

Nos. C231 to C233 Surcharged with New Value in Black

Frames in Black

C238 AP67 8c on 1c ultramarine & violet blue 18 18
C239 " 10c on 2c deep blue green 25 25
C240 " 12c on 3c orange 25 35
Nos. C231–C240 (10) 33.73 33.73

Nos. C231 to C240 were issued to commemorate the 50th anniversary of the founding of Rotary International.

Nos. C060-C063, C226-C230 Overprinted — **ONU X ANIVERSARIO 1945 · 1955**

1956, July 14 *Perf. 12½* **Unwmkd.**

Frames in Black.

No.	Type	Description	Unused	Used
C241	AP67	1c ultramarine & violet blue	25	25
C242	"	2c deep blue green	25	25
C243	"	3c orange	35	35
C244	"	5c deep carmine	40	40
C245	"	15c red brown	50	50
C246	"	30c brown	80	80
C247	"	1 l deep carmine	5.00	5.00
C248	"	2 l orange	7.00	7.00
C249	"	5 l blue green	19.00	19.00
		Nos. C241-C249 (9)	33.55	33.55

United Nations' 10th anniversary (in 1955). The red "OFICIAL overprint was not obliterated.

The "ONU" overprint exists inverted on 1c, 3c, 5c and 1-lempira.

Basilica of Suyapa
AP68

Pres. Julio Lozano Diaz
AP69

Designs: 3c, Southern Highway. 4c, Genoveva Guardiola de Estrada Palma. 5c, Maria Josefa Lastiri de Morazan. 8c, Landscape and cornucopia (5-Year Plan). 10c, National Stadium. 12c, U. S. School. 15c, Central Bank. 20c, Legislative Palace. 25c, Development Bank (projected). 30c, Toncontin Airport. 40c, Juan Ramon Molina Bridge. 50c, Peace Monument. 60c, Treasury Palace. 1 l, Blood bank. 2 l, Communications Building. 5 l, Presidential Palace.

Engraved; ※C255 Lithographed.

1956, Oct. 3 *Perf. 13x12½, 12½x13*

No.	Type	Description	Unused	Used
C250	AP68	1c black & violet blue	10	10
C251	AP69	2c blk. & dk. blue	10	10
C252	AP68	3c black & brown	10	10
C253	AP69	4c black & lilac	10	10
C254	"	5c black & dark red	10	10
C255	AP68	8c brn. & multi.	15	10
C256	"	10c black & emerald	20	10
C257	"	12c black & green	20	10
C258	"	15c dark red & black	25	18
C259	"	20c black & ultra.	25	20
C260	AP69	24c black & lilac	35	25
C261	AP68	25c black & green	40	35
C262	"	30c black & carmine rose	45	35
C263	"	40c black & red brown	50	40
C264	AP69	50c black & blue green	60	50
C265	AP68	60c black & orange	75	60
C266	"	1 l black & rose violet	1.50	1.00
C267	AP69	2 l black & magenta	3.00	2.00
C268	"	5 l black & brown carmine	7.50	5.00
		Nos. C250-C268 (19)	16.60	11.63

Issued to publicize the Five-Year Plan.

Flag of Honduras
AP70

Designs: 2c, 8c, Monument and mountains. 10c, 15c, 1 l, Lempira. 30c, 2 l, Coat of arms.

Lithographed.

1957, Oct. 21 *Perf. 13* **Unwmkd.**

Frames in Black.

No.	Type	Description	Unused	Used
C269	AP70	1c buff & ultra.	10	10
C270	"	2c orange, purple & emerald	15	10
C271	AP70	5c pink & ultra.	20	10
C272	"	8c orange, violet & olive	25	10
C273	"	10c violet & brn.	25	12
C274	"	12c light green & ultramarine	35	25
C275	"	15c green & brn.	45	30
C276	"	30c pink & slate	60	35
C277	"	1 l blue & brown	1.75	1.75
C278	"	2 l light green & slate	3.00	3.00
		Nos. C269-C278 (10)	7.10	6.17

Issued to commemorate the first anniversary of the October revolution.

Control marks were handstamped in violet on many current stamps in July and August, 1958, following fire and theft of stamps at Tegucigalpa in April. All post offices were ordered to honor only stamps overprinted with the facsimile signature of their departmental revenue administrator. Honduras has 18 departments.

Flags of Honduras and U. S.
AP71

1958, Oct. 2 Engraved. *Perf. 12*

Flags in National Colors.

No.	Type	Description	Unused	Used
C279	AP71	1c light blue	15	12
C280	"	2c red	15	12
C281	"	5c green	15	15
C282	"	10c brown	25	25
C283	"	20c orange	50	35
C284	"	30c deep rose	50	45
C285	"	50c gray	60	55
C286	"	1 l orange yellow	1.50	1.35
C287	"	2 l gray olive	3.50	3.25
C288	"	5 l violet blue	7.50	7.50
		Nos. C279-C288 (10)	14.80	14.09

Issued to publicize the Honduras Institute of Inter-American Culture. The proceeds were intended for the Binational Center, Tegucigalpa.

Abraham Lincoln
AP72

Lincoln's Birthplace
AP73

Designs: 3c, 50c, Gettysburg Address. 5c, 1 l, Freeing the slaves. 10c, 2 l, Assassination. 12c 5 l, Memorial, Washington.

1959, Feb. 12 *Perf. 13½* **Unwmkd.**

Flags in National Colors.

No.	Type	Description	Unused	Used
C289	AP72	1c green	20	20
C290	AP73	2c dark blue	20	20
C291	"	3c purple	25	25
C292	"	5c dark carmine	25	25
C293	"	10c black	35	25
C294	"	12c dark brown	35	25
C295	AP72	15c red orange	50	25
C296	AP73	25c dull purple	75	40
C297	"	50c ultramarine	1.00	75
C298	"	1 l red brown	2.00	1.75
C299	AP73	2 l gray olive	3.25	2.00
C300	"	5 l ochre	7.00	5.50
		a. Miniature sheet	9.00	9.00
		Nos. C289-C300 (12)	16.10	12.05

Issued to commemorate the sesquicentennial of the birth of Abraham Lincoln.

No. C300a contains one each of the 1c, 3c, 10c, 25c, 1 l and 5 l, imperf. No marginal inscription. Size 178½x140½mm.

Constitution
AP74

Designs: 2c, 12c, Inauguration of Pres. Villeda Morales (horiz.). 3c, 25c, Pres. Ramon Villeda Morales. 5c, 50c, Allegory of Second Republic (Torch and olive branches).

Engraved; Seal Litho. on 1c, 10c.

1959, Dec. 21 *Perf. 13½*

No.	Type	Description	Unused	Used
C301	AP74	1c red brown, carmine & ultramarine	10	10
C302	"	2c bistre brown	10	10
C303	"	3c ultramarine	10	10
C304	"	5c orange	15	15
C305	"	10c dull green, car. & ultra.	20	15
C306	"	12c rose red	30	25
C307	"	25c dull lilac	60	30
C308	"	50c dark blue	1.10	50
		Nos. C301-C308 (8)	2.65	1.65

Issued to commemorate the second anniversary of the Second Republic of Honduras.

King Alfonso XIII and Map
AP75

Designs: 2c, 1906 award of King Alfonso XIII of Spain. 5c, Arbitration commission delivering its award, 1907. 10c, Int. Court of Justice. 20c, Verdict of the Court, 1960. 50c, Pres. Morales, Foreign Minister Puerto and map. 1 l, Pres. Davila and Pres. Morales.

1961, Nov. 18 Engr. *Perf. 14½x14*

No.	Type	Description	Unused	Used
C309	AP75	1c dark blue	10	10
C310	"	2c magenta	10	10
C311	"	5c deep green	10	10
C312	"	10c brown orange	20	15
C313	"	20c vermilion	40	25
C314	"	50c brown	75	55
C315	"	1 l violet black	1.35	1.10
		Nos. C309-C315 (7)	3.00	2.35

Issued to commemorate the judgment of the International Court of Justice at The Hague, Nov. 18, 1960, returning a disputed territory to Honduras from Nicaragua.

Nos. C295-C297 and C0105 Surcharged: **L 0.06**

1964, Apr. 7 *Perf. 13½*

Flags in National Colors

No.	Type	Description	Unused	Used
C316	AP72	6c on 15c red orge.	15	15
C317	AP73	8c on 25c dull pur.	15	15
C318	"	10c on 50c ultra.	25	25
C319	"	20c on 25c black	50	50

The red "OFICIAL" overprint on No. C319 was not obliterated.

See also Nos. C345-C355, C419-C421.

Nos. C279-C281, C284 and C287 Overprinted: "FAO/Lucha Contra/el Hambre"

1964, March 23 *Perf. 12* **Unwmkd.**

Flags in National Colors

No.	Type	Description	Unused	Used
C320	AP71	1c light blue	25	25
C321	"	2c red	25	25
C322	"	5c green	30	30
C323	AP71	30c deep rose	1.00	1.00
C324	"	2 l gray olive	7.00	7.00
		Nos. C320-C324 (5)	8.80	8.80

Issued for the "Freedom from Hunger Campaign" (in 1963) of the U.N. Food and Agriculture Organization.

Nos. C098-C0101, C0104 and C0106 Overprinted in Blue or Black: "IN MEMORIAM/JOHN F. KENNEDY/ 22 NOVEMBRE 1963"

1964, May 29 *Perf. 13½*

Flags in National Colors

No.	Type	Description	Unused	Used
C325	AP72	1c ochre (Bl)	20	20
C326	AP73	2c gray olive (Bl)	25	25
C327	"	3c red brown (Bl)	30	30
C328	"	5c ultra. (Bk)	50	50
C329	AP72	15c dk. brn. (Bl)	1.50	1.50
C330	AP73	50c dk. car. (Bl)	8.00	8.00
		Nos. C325-C330 (6)	10.75	10.75

Issued in memory of President John F. Kennedy (1917-63). The red "OFICIAL" overprint was not obliterated. The same overprint was applied to the stamps in miniature sheet No. C300a and seal of Honduras and Alliance for Progress emblem added in margin.

Nos. C222-C224, C226 and C067 Overprinted with Olympic Rings and "1964"

Engraved; Center of 1c Litho.

1964, July 23 *Perf. 12½*

Frames in Black

No.	Type	Description	Unused	Used
C331	AP67	1c ultra. & vio. bl.	20	20
C332	"	2c blue	30	30
C333	"	3c rose lilac	40	40
C334	"	15c red brown	75	75
C335	"	2 l lilac rose	8.00	8.00
		Nos. C331-C335 (5)	9.65	9.65

Issued to commemorate the 18th Olympic Games, Tokyo, Oct. 10-25. The red "OFICIAL" overprint on No. C335 was not obliterated.

The same overprint was applied in black to the six stamps in No. CO108a, with additional rings and "1964" in margins of souvenir sheet. Price $55.

View of Copan
AP76

Designs: 2c, 12c, Stone marker from Copan. 5c, 1 l, Mayan ball player (stone). 8c, 2 l, Olympic Stadium, Tokyo.

Photogravure

1964, Nov. 27 *Perf. 14* **Unwmkd.**

Black Design and Inscription

No.	Type	Description	Unused	Used
C336	AP76	1c yellow green	10	10
C337	"	2c pale rose lilac	10	10
C338	"	5c lt. ultramarine	18	18
C339	"	8c bluish green	35	35
C340	"	10c buff	50	40
C341	"	12c lemon	60	50
C342	"	1 l light ocher	1.50	1.25
C343	"	2 l pale olive grn.	4.00	3.00
C344	"	3 l rose	6.00	4.50
		Nos. C336-C344 (9)	13.33	10.38

Issued to commemorate the 18th Olympic Games, Tokyo, Oct. 10-25. Perf. and imperf. souvenir sheets of four exist containing one each of Nos. C338-C339, C341 and C344. Size: 129x110mm.

Nos. C292, C174, C0106, C0104, C124-C125, C165, C0105, C167-C168 and C178 Surcharged **L. 0.12**

1964-65

No.	Type	Description	Unused	Used
C345	AP73	4c on 5c dk. car., blue & red	10	10
C346	AP62	10c on 15c red brn.	12	10
C347	AP73	10c on 50c dk. car., blue & red	12	10
C348	AP72	12c on 15c dk. brn., blue & red	15	12
C349	AP27	12c on 16c olive gray	15	12
C350	"	12c on 21c lt. blue	15	12
C351	AP60	12c on 22c org. yel.	15	12

No.	Type	Description	Unused	Used
C352	AP73	12c on 25c black, blue & red	15	12
C353	AP60	30c on 1 l dp. blue	35	30
C354	"	40c on 2 l lilac ('65)	65	40
C355	AP61	40c on 1 l red brown ('65)	65	40
		Nos. C345-C355 (11)	2.74	2.00

The red "OFICIAL" overprint on Nos. C347-C348 and C352 was not obliterated.

Nos. C289, C099, C291-C292, C295-C296, C0106 and C299-C300 Overprinted in Black or Green: "Toma de Posesión / General / Oswaldo López A. / Junio 6, 1965"

1965 Engraved *Perf. 13½*

Flags in National Colors

No.	Type	Description	Unused	Used
C356	AP72	1c green	10	10
C357	AP73	2c gray olive (G)	10	10
C358	"	3c purple (G)	15	15
C359	"	5c dk. car. (G)	15	15
C360	AP72	15c red orange	25	18
C361	AP73	25c dull pur. (G)	40	25
C362	"	50c dk. car. (G)	70	50
C363	"	2 l gray olive (G)	3.00	2.00
C364	"	5 l ocher (G)	7.50	6.00
		Nos. C356-C364 (9)	12.35	9.43

Issued to commemorate the inauguration of Gen. Oswaldo López Arellano as president. The red "OFICIAL" overprint on Nos. C358 and C362 was not obliterated.

Ambulance and Maltese Cross
AP77

Designs (Maltese Cross and): 5c, Hospital of Knights of Malta. 12c, Patients treated in village. 1 l, Map of Honduras.

1965, July 27 Litho. *Perf. 12x11*

No.	Type	Description	Unused	Used
C365	AP77	1c ultramarine	15	15
C366	"	5c dark green	25	25
C367	"	12c dark brown	35	35
C368	"	1 l brown	1.50	1.50

Issued to honor the Knights of Malta and to publicize the campaign against leprosy.

Father Manuel de Jesus Subirana
AP78

Designs: 1c, Jicaque Indian. 2c, Preaching to the Indians. 10c, Msgr. Juan de Jesus Zepeda. 12c, Pope Pius IX. 20c, Tomb of Father Subirana, Yore. 1 l, Mission church. 2 l, Jicaque mother and child.

Perf. 13½x14

1965, July 27 Litho. Unwmkd.

No.	Type	Description	Unused	Used
C369	AP78	1c blk., vio. & gold	10	10
C370	"	2c black, salmon & gold	10	10
C371	"	8c black, salmon pink & gold	15	15
C372	"	10c black, lilac rose & gold	15	15
C373	"	12c blk., tan & gold	20	20
C374	"	20c black, emerald & gold	40	40
C375	"	1 l black, yellow grn. & gold	1.50	1.00
C376	AP78	2 l black, bright blue & gold	3.00	3.00
		a. Souvenir sheet of 4	22.00	
		Nos. C369-C376 (8)	5.60	5.10

Issued to commemorate the centenary (in 1964) of the death of Father Manuel de Jesus Subirana (1807-64), Spanish missionary to the Central American Indians. No. C376a contains one each of Nos. C371, C373 and C375-C376. Black and blue inscriptions, red control number. Size: 99x148mm.

Nos. C198-C199 and C168 Overprinted: "IN MEMORIAM / Sir Winston Churchill / 1874-1965."

1965, Dec. 20 Engr. *Perf. 13½x14*

No.	Type	Description	Unused	Used
C377	AP65	1c red org. & blk.	50	50
C378	"	2c bl. & red brn.	1.00	1.00
C379	AP60	2 l lilac	8.50	8.50

Issued in memory of Sir Winston Spencer Churchill (1874-1965), statesman and World War II leader.

Nos. C369-C375 Overprinted

CONMEMORATIVA
Visita S. S.
Pablo VI
a la ONU.
4-X-1965

1966, Mar. 12 Litho. *Perf. 13½x14*

No.	Type	Description	Unused	Used
C380	AP78	1c multicolored	12	12
C381	"	2c "	12	12
C382	"	8c "	18	18
C383	"	10c "	18	18
C384	"	12c "	22	18
C385	"	20c "	30	25
C386	"	1 l "	2.25	1.50
		Nos. C380-C386 (7)	3.37	2.53

Issued to commemorate the visit of Pope Paul VI to the United Nations, New York City, Oct. 4, 1965.

Stamp of 1866, No. 1
AP79

Tomas Estrada Palma
AP80

Post Office, Tegucigalpa
AP81

Designs: 2c, Air post stamp of 1925, No. C1. 5c, Locomotive. 6c, 19th century mail transport with mules. 7c, 19th century mail room. 8c, Sir Rowland Hill. 9c, Modern mail truck. 10c, Gen. Oswaldo Lopez Arellano. 12c, Postal emblem. 15c, Heinrich von Stephan. 20c, Mail plane. 30c, Flag of Honduras. 40c, Coat of Arms. 1 l, U.P.U. monument, Bern. 2 l, José Maria Medina.

Perf. 14½x14, 14x14½

1966, May 31 Litho. Unwmkd.

No.	Type	Description	Unused	Used
C387	AP79	1c gold, black & greenish gray	10	10
C388	"	2c orange, blk. & light blue	12	12
C389	AP80	3c brt. rose, gold & dp. plum	15	15
C390	AP81	4c bl., gold & blk.	15	15
C391	"	5c pink, gold & black	15	15
C392	AP81	6c lilac, gold & black	15	15
C393	"	7c lt. blue green, gold & blk.	15	15
C394	AP80	8c light blue, gold & black	18	18
C395	AP81	9c lt. ultra., gold & black	20	20
C396	AP80	10c citron, gold & black	20	20
C397	AP79	12c gold, blk., yel. & emerald	20	20
C398	AP80	15c brt. pink, gold & dp. claret	35	35
C399	AP81	20c orange, gold & black	45	45
C400	AP79	30c gold & blue	50	50
C401	"	40c multicolored	75	75
C402	"	1 l emerald, gold & dk. grn.	1.85	1.50
C403	AP80	2 l gray, gold & black	3.75	3.00
		a. Souv. sheet of 6	5.00	5.00
		Nos. C387-C403 (17)	9.40	8.30

Issued to commemorate the centenary of the first Honduran postage stamp. No. C403a exists perf. and imperf. and contains one each of Nos. C387-C388, C396-C397, and C402-C403. Marginal inscription in gold. Size: 139x120mm. See also No. CE3.

Nos. C053, C201 and C204 Overprinted: "CAMPEONATO DE FOOTBALL Copa Mundial 1966 Inglaterra-Alemania Wembley, Julio 30"

Engraved

1966 *Perf. 13½x14, 14x13½*

No.	Type	Description	Unused	Used
C404	AP65	2c brown & vio.	25	25
C405	AP66	16c dk. bl. & blk.	50	50
C406	AP65	2 l brn. & vio.	10.00	10.00

Issued to commemorate the final game between England and Germany in the World Soccer Cup Championship, Wembley, July 30, 1966. The overprint on the 2c and 2 l is in 5 lines, it is in 8 lines on the 16c. There is no hyphen between "Inglaterra" and "Alemania" on the 16c.

Nos. C369-C371 and C373-C376 Overprinted in Red: "CONMEMORATIVA / del XX Aniversario / ONU 1966"

1966 Lithographed *Perf. 13½x14*

No.	Type	Description	Unused	Used
C407	AP78	1c blk., vio. & gold	25	25
C408	"	2c blk., sal. & gold	30	30
C409	"	8c blk., sal. pink & gold	50	50
C410	"	12c blk., tan & gold	65	65
C411	"	20c blk., emerald & gold	85	85
C412	"	1 l blk., yel. grn. & gold	2.00	2.00
C413	"	2 l blk., brt. blue & gold	4.50	4.50
		Nos. C407-C413 (7)	9.05	9.05

Issued to commemorate the 20th anniversary of the United Nations.

Nos. C250, C252, C258, C261 and C267 Overprinted in Red: "Siméon Cañas y Villacorta / Libertador de los esclavos / en Centro America / 1767-1967"

1967 Engr. *Perf. 13x12½, 12½x13*

No.	Type	Description	Unused	Used
C414	AP68	1c blk. & vio. bl.	20	20
C415	"	3c black & brown	35	35
C416	"	15c dk. red & blk.	50	50
C417	"	25c black & green	75	75
C418	AP69	2 l black & magenta	3.00	3.00
		Nos. C414-C418 (5)	4.80	4.80

Issued to commemorate the bicentenary of the birth of Father José Siméon Cañas y Villacorta, D.D. (1767-1838), emancipator of the Central American slaves. The overprint is in 6 lines on the 2 l, in 4 lines on all others.

Nos. C178-C179 and CE2 Surcharged

L. 0.10

1967

No.	Type	Description	Unused	Used
C419	AP61	10c on 1 l red brn.	15	12
C420	AP62	10c on 2 l violet	15	12
C421	APSD1	10c on 20c black & red	15	12

José Cecilio del Valle, Honduras
AP82

Designs: 12c, Ruben Dario, Nicaragua. 14c, Batres Montufar, Guatemala. 20c, Francisco Antonio Gavidia, El Salvador. 30c, Juan Mora Fernandez, Costa Rica. 40c, Federation Emblem with map of Americas. 50c, Map of Central America.

1967, July Litho. *Perf. 13*

No.	Type	Description	Unused	Used
C422	AP82	11c gold, ultra. & black	12	10
C423	"	12c lt. blue, yel. & black	15	10
C424	"	14c silver, green & black	18	15
C425	"	20c pink, green & black	25	18
C426	"	30c bluish lilac, yel. & blk.	35	30
C427	"	40c purple, light blue & gold	1.00	1.00
C428	"	50c lemon, grn. & car. rose	1.00	1.00
		Nos. C422-C428 (7)	3.05	2.83

Issued to publicize the founding of the Federation of Central American Journalists.

Olympic Rings, Flags of Mexico and Honduras
AP83

Olympic Rings and Winners of 1964 Olympics: 2c, Like 1c. 5c, Italian flag and boxers. 10c, French flag and women skiers. 12c, German flag and equestrian team. 50c, British flag and women runners. 1 l, U.S. flag and runners (Bob Hayes).

1968, Mar. 4 Litho. *Perf. 14x13½*

No.	Type	Description	Unused	Used
C429	AP83	1c gold & multi.	20	20
C430	"	2c " "	30	30
C431	"	5c " "	40	40
C432	"	10c " "	50	50
C433	"	12c " "	75	75
C434	"	50c " "	3.00	3.00
C435	"	1 l " "	6.00	6.00
		Nos. C429-C435 (7)	11.15	11.15

Issued to publicize the 19th Olympic Games, Mexico City, Oct. 12-27. Perf. and imperf. souvenir sheets of 2 exist containing 20c and 40c stamps in design of 1c. Price $4.50 each.

John F. Kennedy, Rocket at Cape Kennedy
AP84

Designs ITU Emblem and: 2c, Radar and telephone. 3c, Radar and television set. 5c, Radar and globe showing Central America. 8c, Communications satellite. 10c, 20c, like 1c.

1968, Nov. 28 *Perf. 14x13½*

No.	Type	Description	Unused	Used
C436	AP84	1c violet & multi.		
C437	"	2c silver & multi.		
C438	"	3c multicolored		
C439	"	5c org. & multi.		
C440	"	8c multicolored		
C441	"	10c olive & multi.		

C442 AP84 20c multicolored

Centenary of International Telecommunications Union. A 30c in design of 2c, a 1 l in design of 5c and a 1.50 l in design of 1c exist; also two souvenir sheets, one containing 10c, 50c and 75c, the other one 1.50 l.

Nos. C436, C441–C442 Overprinted:
"In Memoriam /
Robert F. Kennedy / 1925–1968"

1968, Dec. 23

C446 AP84 1c violet & multi.
C447 " 10c olive & multi.
C448 " 20c multicolored

In memory of Robert F. Kennedy. Same overprint was also applied to a 1.50 l and to a souvenir sheet containing one 1.50 l.

Nos. C437–C440 Overprinted in Blue or Red with Olympic Rings and:
"Medallas de Oro / Mexico 1968"

1969, Jan.

C450 AP84 2c multi. (Bl)
C451 " 3c " (Bl)
C452 " 5c " (Bl)
C453 " 8c " (R)

Gold medal winners in 19th Olympic Games, Mexico City. The same red overprint was also applied to a 30c and a 1 l. The souvenir sheet of 3 noted after No. C442 exists with this overprint in black.

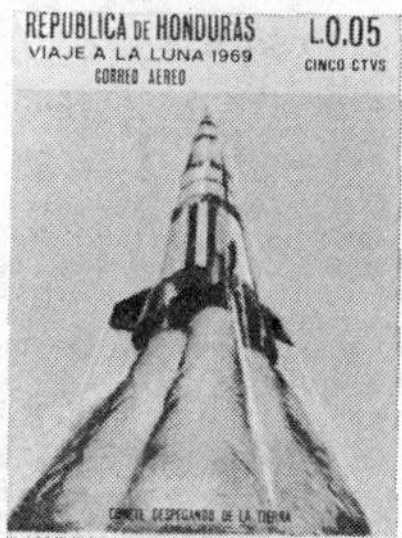

Rocket Blast-off
AP85

Designs: 10c, Close-up view of moon. 12c, Spacecraft (horiz.). 20c, Astronaut and module on moon (horiz.). 24c, Lunar landing module.

Perf. 14½x13½, 13½x14

1969, Nov. 20

C454 AP85 5c multicolored
C455 " 10c "
C456 " 12c "
C457 " 20c "
C458 " 24c "

Man's first landing on the moon, U. S. Apollo 11 mission, July 20, 1969. A 30c showing re-entry of capsule, a 1 l in design of 20c and a 1.50 l in design of 24c exist. Two souvenir sheets exist, one containing Nos. C454–C455 and 1.50 l, and the other No. C456, 30c and 1 l.

For the safe return of Apollo 13, overprints were applied in 1970 to Nos. C454–C458, the three unlisted denominations and the two souvenir sheets.

Nos. C224, C393, C395, C422, C424, CE2 and C178
Surcharged with New Value

1970 Engraved; Lithographed

C472 AP67 4c on 3c black & rose lilac 10 10
C473 AP81 5c on 7c multi. 12 12
C474 " 10c on 9c " 15 15
C475 AP82 10c on 11c multi. 15 15
C476 " 12c on 14c " 20 20
C477 APSD1 12c on 20c black & red 20 20
C478 AP61 12c on 1 l red brown 20 20
Nos. C472–C478 (7) 1.12 1.12

No. CE3 Overprinted "HABILITADO"

1970 Lithographed *Perf. 14x14½*

C479 AP81 20c bister brown, brn. & gold 40 30

Julio Adolfo Sanhueza AP86

Emblems, Map and Flag of Honduras AP87

Designs: 8c, Rigoberto Ordoñez Rodriguez. 12c, Forest Fire Brigade emblem (with map of Honduras) and emblems of fire fighters, FAO and Alliance for Progress (horiz.). 1 l, Flags of Honduras, U.N. and U.S., Arms of Honduras and emblems as on 12c.

Perf. 14½x14, 14x14½

1970, Aug. 15 Lithographed

C480 AP86 5c gold, emerald & indigo 10 10
C481 " 8c gold, org. brown & indigo 16 15
C482 AP87 12c blue & multi. 24 20
C483 " 20c yel. & multi. 40 35
C484 " 1 l gray & multi. 1.00 90
a. Souvenir sheet of 5 2.50 2.50
Nos. C480–C484 (5) 1.90 1.70

Issued to publicize the campaign against forest fires and in memory of the men who lost their lives fighting forest fires. No. C484a contains 5 imperf. stamps with simulated perforations and without gum similar to Nos. C480–C484. Black marginal inscription. Size: 120x129½mm. Sold for 1.45 l.

Hotel Honduras Maya
AP88

1970 Lithographed *Perf. 14*

C485 AP88 12c sky blue & blk. 30 30

Issued to commemorate the opening of the Hotel Honduras Maya in Tegucigalpa.

Stamps of 1952–1968 Surcharged

1971 Lithographed; Engraved

C486 AP79 4c on 1c multi. (# C387) 8
C487 AP78 5c on 1c multi. (# C369) 10
C488 " 8c on 2c multi. (# C370) 15
C489 AP65 10c on 2c multi. (# C199) 20
C490 AP67 10c on 3c multi. (# C224) 20
a. Inverted surcharge
C491 AP68 10c on 3c multi. (# C252) 20
C492 " 10c on 3c multi. (# CO71) 20
C493 AP69 10c on 2c multi. (# C251) 20
C494 AP73 10c on 2c multi. (# CO99) 20
C495 " 10c on 3c multi. (# CO100) 20
C496 AP80 10c on 3c multi. (# C389) 20
C497 AP87 15c on 12c multi. (# C482) 35
C498 " 30c on 12c multi. (# C482) 60
C499 AP83 40c on 50c multi. (# C434) 75
C500 AP85 40c on 24c multi. (# C458) 75
Nos. C486–C500 (15) 4.38

Red "OFICIAL" overprint was not obliterated on Nos. C492, C494–C495.

Nos. C454, C456–C458 Overprinted and Surcharged

Aniversario Gran Logia de Honduras 1922-1972

L 1.00

Perf. 14½x13½, 13½x14½

1972, May 15 Lithographed

C501 AP85 5c multi. 40 40
C502 " 12c " 60 60
C503 " 1 l on 20c " 1.25 1.00
C504 " 2 l on 24c " 2.50 2.00

50th anniversary of the Masonic Grand Lodge of Honduras. Overprint varies to fit stamp shape.

Soldier's Bay, Guanaja
AP89

Designs: 5c, 7c, 9c, 10c, 21, vertical.

1972, May 19 *Perf. 13*

Gold and Multicolored

C505 AP89 4c *shown* 10 10
C506 " 5c *Taps* 10 10
C507 " 6c *Yojoa Lake* 10 10
C508 " 7c *Banana Carrier, by Roberto Aguilar* 10 10
C509 " 8c *Military parade* 12 12
C510 " 9c *Orchid, national flower* 12 12
C511 " 10c *(same)* 15 15
C512 " 12c *Soldier with machine gun* 18 15
C513 " 15c *Sunset over beach* 20 15
C514 " 20c *Litter bearers* 20 15
C515 " 30c *Landscape, by Antonio Velasquez* 35 35
C516 " 40c *Ruins of Copan* 40 40
a. Souvenir sheet of 4 (Nos. C508, C513, C515–C516) 1.00 1.00
C517 AP89 50c *Girl from Huacal, by Pablo Zelaya Sierra* 50 50
a. Souvenir sheet of 4 (Nos. C506–C507, C514, C517) 90 90
C518 AP89 1 l *Trujillo Bay* 1.00 1.00
a. Souvenir sheet of 4 (Nos. C505, C509, C512, C518) 1.35 1.35
C519 AP89 2 l *Orchid, national flower* 2.00 2.00
a. Souvenir sheet of 3 (Nos. C510–C511, C519) 2.50 2.50
Nos. C505–C519, CE4 (16) 5.87 5.74

Sesquicentennial of independence (stamps inscribed 1970). Souvenir sheets have ornamental borders, control numbers and black inscriptions. Border of No. C516a is brown, No. C517a brown orange, No. C518a lilac, No. C519a emerald. Size of sheets: 114x103mm.

Sister Maria Rosa and Child
AP90

Designs: 15c, SOS Children's Village emblem (horiz.). 30c, Father José Trinidad Reyes. 40c, Kennedy Center, first SOS village in Central America (horiz.). 1 l, Boy.

1972 Photo. *Perf. 13½x13, 13x13½*

C520 AP90 10c grn., gold, brn. 10 8
C521 " 15c " " " 15 10
C522 " 30c " " " 30 15
C523 " 40c " " " 40 20
C524 " 1 l " " " 1.00 75
Nos. C520–C524 (5) 1.95 1.28

Children's Villages in Honduras (International SOS movement to save homeless children).

Map of Honduras and Society Emblem
AP91

Design: 12c, Map of Honduras, emblems of National Geographic Institute and Interamerican Geodesic Service.

1973, Mar. 27 Lithographed *Perf. 13*

C525 AP91 10c multicolored 30 20
C526 " 12c " 40 30

25th anniversaries of National Cartographic Service (10c) and of joint cartographic work (12c).

Juan Ramón Molina
AP92

Designs: 8c, Illustration from Molina's book "Habitante de la Osa." 1 l, Illustration from "Tierras Mares y Cielos." 2 l, "UNESCO."

1973, Apr. 17 Litho. *Perf. 13½*

C527 AP92 8c brn. org., blk. & red brown 12 10
C528 " 20c brt. bl. & multi. 50 40
C529 " 1 l green & multi. 1.25 1.00
C530 " 2 l org. & multi. 2.50 2.25
a. Sheet of 4 5.00 5.00

In honor of Juan Ramón Molina (1875–1908), poet, and for the 25th anniversary (in 1971) of the United Nations Educational, Scientific and Cultural Organization (UNESCO). No. C530a contains 4 stamps similar to Nos. C527–C530. Orange brown margin with red brown ornaments and inscription. Black control number. Size: 140x130mm. Exists perf. and imperf.

Nos. C520–C523, C525–C526
Overprinted in Red or Black:
"Censos de Población y Vivienda, marzo 1974. 1974, Año Mundial de Población."

Perf. 13½x13, 13x13½, 13

1973, Dec. 28 Lithographed

C531 AP90 10c multi. (R) 10 6
C532 AP91 10c " (B) 10 6
C533 " 12c " (B) 12 8
C534 AP90 15c " (R) 15 10
C535 " 30c " (R) 30 20
C536 " 40c " (R) 40 25
Nos. C531–C536 (6) 1.17 75

1974 population and housing census and for World Population Year. The overprint is in 7 lines on vertical stamps, in 5 lines on horizontal.

Issues of 1947–59 Surcharged in Red or Black.

Perf. 13x12½, 13½, 11x12½, 12

1974, June 28 Engraved

C537 AP68 2c on 1c (#C250) (R) 8
C538 " 2c on 1c (#CO69) (B) 8
C539 AP72 2c on 1c (#C289) (B) 8
C540 " 2c on 1c (#CO98) (B) 8
C541 " 3c on 1c (#C289) (B) 8
C542 AP68 3c on 1c (#C250) (R) 8
C543 AP74 1 l on 50c (#C308) (B) 1.50
C544 AP60 1 l on 2 l (#C168) (B) 1.50
C545 AP62 1 l on 2 l (#C179) (R) 1.50
Nos. C537–C545 (9) 4.98

Red "OFICIAL" overprint was not obliterated on Nos. C538 and C540.

Nos. C520–C523 Overprinted in Bright Green: "1949–1974 SOS Kinderdorfer International Honduras—Austria"

1974 Photo. *Perf. 13½x13, 13x13½*

C546 AP90 10c grn., gold & brown 15
C547 " 15c grn., gold & brown 20
C548 " 30c grn., gold & brown 30
C549 " 40c grn., gold & brown 40

25th anniversary of Children's Villages in Honduras. Overprint in 6 lines on 10c and 30c, in 4 lines on 15c and 40c.

Stamps of 1956–1973 Surcharged

1975 Lithographed; Engraved

Multicolored

C550 AP68 16c on 1c (#C250) 16
C551 AP70 16c on 1c (#C269) 16
C552 AP72 16c on 1c (#C289) 16
C553 " 16c on 1c (#CO98) 16
C554 AP78 16c on 1c (#C369) 16
C555 AP85 18c on 12c (#C456) *1.25*
C556 AP90 18c on 10c (#C520) 18
C557 AP91 18c on 10c (#C525) 18
C558 " 18c on 12c (#C526) 18
C559 AP92 18c on 8c (#C527) 18
C560 AP90 50c on 30c (#C522) 50
C561 " 1 l on 30c (#C522) 1.00
Nos. C550–C561, CE5 (13) *5.02*

Denominations not obliterated on Nos. C551, C553–C558, C560–C561; "OFICIAL" overprint not obliterated on No. C553.

Flags of Germany and Austria AP93

Designs (Flags): 2c, Belgium and Denmark. 3c, Spain and France. 4c, Hungary and Russia. 5c, Great Britain and Italy. 10c, Norway and Sweden. 12c, Honduras. 15c, United States and Switzerland. 20c, Greece and Portugal. 30c, Romania and Serbia. 1 l, Egypt and Netherlands. 2 l, Luxembourg and Turkey.

1975, June Litho. *Perf. 13*

Gold and Multicolored; Colors Listed are for Shields

C562 AP93 1c lilac 5
C563 " 2c gold 5
C564 " 3c rose gray 5
C565 " 4c light blue 7
C566 " 5c yellow 10
C567 " 10c gray 20
C568 " 12c lilac rose 25
C569 " 15c bluish green 30
C570 " 20c bright blue 40
C571 " 30c pink 60
C572 AP93 1 l salmon 2.00
C573 " 2 l yellow green 4.00
Nos. C562–C573 (12) 8.07

Souvenir Sheet

C574 AP93 Sheet of 12 *12.50*

Centenary of Universal Postal Union (in 1974). No. C574 contains 12 stamps similar to Nos. C562–C573 with shields in different colors. Black marginal inscription, 2 bars and control number; silver and dark blue ornaments. Size: 122x150mm.

Humuya Youth Center and Mrs. Arellano—AP94

Designs (Portrait of First Lady, Gloria de Lopez Arellano, IWY Emblem and): 16c, Jalteva Youth Center. 18c, Mrs. Arellano (diff. portrait) and IWY emblem. 30c, El Carmen de San Pedro Sula Youth Center. 55c, Flag of National Social Welfare Organization (vert.). 1 l, La Isla sports and recreational facilities. 2 l, Women's Social Center.

1976, Feb. Litho. *Perf. 13½*

C575 AP94 8c sal. & multi. 8
C576 " 16c yel. & multi. 16
C577 " 18c pink & multi. 18
C578 " 30c orange & multi. 30
C579 " 55c multicolored 55
C580 " 1 l " 1.00
C581 " 2 l " 2.00
Nos. C575–C581 (7) 4.27

International Women's Year 1975.

"CARE" and Globe AP95

Designs: 1c, 16c, 30c, 55c, 1 l, Care package and globe (vert.). Others like 5c.

1976, May 24 Litho. *Perf. 13½*

C582 AP95 1c blk. & lt. bl. 3
C583 " 5c rose brown & black 5
C584 " 16c black & org. 16
C585 " 18c lemon & blk. 18
C586 " 30c black & blue 30
C587 " 50c yellow green & black 50
C588 " 55c black & buff 55
C589 " 70c bright rose & black 70
C590 " 1 l black & light green 1.00
C591 " 2 l ocher & blk. 2.00
Nos. C582–C591 (10) 5.47

20th anniversary of CARE in Honduras.

Fawn in Burnt-out Forest AP96

"Sons of Liberty" AP97

Designs: 16c, COHDEFOR emblem (Corporacion Hondureña de Desarollo Forestal). 18c, Forest (horiz.). 30c, 2 l, Live and burning trees. 50c, like 10c. 70c, Emblem. 1 l, Young forest (horiz.).

1976, May 28 Litho. *Perf. 13½*

C592 AP96 10c multicolored 10
C593 " 16c multicolored 16
C594 " 18c " 18
C595 " 30c grn. & multi. 30
C596 " 50c multicolored 50
C597 " 70c brn. & multi. 70
C598 " 1 l yel. & multi. 1.00
C599 " 2 l vio. & multi. 2.00
Nos. C592–C599, CE6 (9) 5.54

Forest protection.

1977, Aug. Litho. *Perf. 12*

Designs: 2c, Raising flag of "Liberty and Union." 3c, Bunker Hill flag. 4c, Washington's Cruisers' flag. 5c, First Navy Jack. 6c, Flag of Honduras over Presidential Palace, Tegucigalpa. 18c, U.S. flag over Capitol. 55c, Grand Union flag. 2 l, Bennington flag. 3 l, Betsy Ross and her flag.

C601 AP97 1c multicolored
C602 " 2c "
C603 " 3c "
C604 " 4c "
C605 " 5c "
C606 " 6c "
C607 " 18c "
C608 " 55c "
a. Souvenir sheet of 4 *1.50*
C609 AP97 2 l multicolored
a. Souvenir sheet of 3 *3.50*
C610 AP97 3 l multicolored
a. Souvenir sheet of 3 *4.75*
Nos. C601–C610 (10) *7.50*

American Bicentennial. No. C608a contains Nos. C603, C606–C608; No. C609a contains Nos. C601, C604, C609; No. C610a contains Nos. C602, C605, C610. Black marginal inscriptions. Size: 110x85mm.

Queen Sophia of Spain AP98

Designs: 18c, King Juan Carlos. 30c, Queen Sophia and King Juan Carlos. 2 l, Arms of Guatemala and Spain (horiz.).

1977 Lithographed *Perf. 14*

C611 AP98 16c multicolored 16
C612 " 18c " 18
C613 " 30c " 30
C614 " 2 l " 2.00

Visit of King and Queen of Spain to Honduras.

Mayan Steles, Exhibition Emblems AP99

Designs: 18c, Giant head. 30c, Statue. 55c, Sun god. 1.50 l, Mayan pelota court.

1978 Litho. *Perf. 12*

C615 AP99 15c multicolored 15
C616 " 18c " 18
C617 " 30c " 30
C618 " 55c " 55

Imperf.

C619 AP99 1.50 l multi. 1.70

Honduras '78 Philatelic Exhibition. Size of No. C619: 158x109mm.

Valle's Birthplace AP100

Designs: 14c, La Merced Church, Choluteca, where del Valle was baptized. 15c, Baptismal font (vert.). 20c, Del Valle reading independence acts. 25c, Portrait, documents, map of Central America. 40c, Portrait (vert.). 1 l, Monument, Central Park, Choluteca (vert.). 3 l, Bust (vert.).

1978 Lithographed *Perf. 14*

C620 AP100 8c multicolored 8
C621 " 14c " 14
C622 " 15c " 15
C623 " 20c " 20
C624 " 25c " 25
C625 " 40c " 40
C626 " 1 l " 1.00
C627 " 3 l " 3.00
Nos. C620–C627 (8) 5.22

Bicentenary of the birth of José Cecilio del Valle (1780–1834), Central American patriot and statesman.

Rural Health Center AP101

Designs: 6c, Child at water pump. 10c, Los Laureles Dam, Tegucigalpa. 20c, Rural aqueduct. 40c, Teaching hospital, Tegucigalpa. 2 l, Parents and child. 3 l, National vaccination campaign. 5 l, Panamerican Health Organization Building, Washington, D.C.

1978, Apr. Litho. *Perf. 14*

C628 AP101 5c multicolored 5
C629 " 6c " 6
C630 " 10c " 10
C631 " 20c " 20
C632 " 40c " 40
C633 " 2 l " 2.00
C634 " 3 l " 3.00
C635 " 5 l " 5.00
Nos. 628–C635 (8) 10.81

75th anniversary of Panamerican Health Organization (in 1977).

Luis Landa and his "Botanica" AP102

Designs (Luis Landa and): 16c, Map of Honduras showing St. Ignacio. 18c, Medals received by Landa. 30c, Landa's birthplace in St. Ignacio. 2 l, Brassavola (orchid), national flower. 3 l, Women's Normal School.

1978 Photo. *Perf. 13x13½*

C636 AP102 14c multicolored 14
C637 " 16c " 16
C638 " 18c " 18
C639 " 30c " 30
C640 " 2 l " 2.00
C641 " 3 l " 3.00
Nos. C636–C641 (6) 5.78

Prof. Luis Landa (1875–1975), botanist.

Nos. C615–C618 Overprinted in Red with Argentina '78 Soccer Cup Emblem and: "Argentina Campeón / Holanda Sub-Campeón / XI Campeonato Mundial / de Football"

1978, Sept. Litho. *Perf. 12*

C642 AP99 15c multicolored 15
C643 " 18c " 18
C644 " 30c " 30
C645 " 55c " 55

Argentina's victory in World Cup Soccer Championship. Same overprint was applied to No. C619.

Central University and Coat of Arms
AP103

Designs show for each denomination a 19th century print and a contemporary photograph of same area (except 1.50 l, 5 l): No. C647, University City. 8c, Manuel Bonilla Theater. No. C650, Court House (vert.). No. C651, North Boulevard highway intersection (vert.). No. C652, National Palace. No. C653, Presidential Palace. 20c, Hospital. 40c, Cathedral. 50c, View of Tegucigalpa. 1.50 l, Aerial view of Tegucigalpa. No. C660, Arms of San Miguel de Tegucigalpa, 18th century (vert.). No. C661, Pres. Marco Aurelio Soto (1846–1908) (painting; vert.).

1978, Sept. 29

C646	AP103	6c blk. & brn.	6
C647	"	6c multicolored	6
C648	"	8c blk. & brn.	8
C649	"	8c multicolored	8
C650	"	10c blk. & brn.	10
C651	"	10c multicolored	10
C652	"	16c blk. & brn.	16
C653	"	16c multicolored	16
C654	"	20c blk. & brn.	20
C655	"	20c multicolored	20
C656	"	40c blk. & brn.	40
C657	"	40c multicolored	40
C658	"	50c blk. & brn.	50
C659	"	50c multicolored	50
C660	"	5 l blk. & brn.	5.00
C661	"	5 l multi.	5.00
	Nos. C646–C661 (16)		13.00

Souvenir Sheet

C662 AP103 1.50 l multi. 1.65

400th anniversary of founding of Tegucigalpa. Souvenir sheet shows aerial view of modern Tegucigalpa, stamp center of city. Size: 160x110mm.

In the listing the first number is for the 19th century design, the second for the 20th century design.

Goalkeeper—AP104

Designs: Various soccer scenes. 15c, 55c, vert.

1978, Nov. 20 Litho. *Perf. 12*

C663	AP104	15c multicolored	15
C664	"	30c "	30
C665	"	55c "	55
C666	"	1 l "	1.00
C667	"	2 l "	2.00
	Nos. C663–C667 (5)		4.00

7th Youth Soccer Championship, Nov. 26.

AIR POST SEMI-POSTAL STAMPS

No. C13C Surcharged with Plus Sign and Surtax in Black.

Engraved.

1929, June 5 *Perf. 12* Unwmkd.

CB1	AP1	50c+5c carmine	60	60
CB2	"	50c+10c "	75	75
CB3	"	50c+15c "	1.00	1.00
CB4	"	50c+20c "	1.25	1.25

AIR POST SPECIAL DELIVERY STAMPS

No. C052 Surcharged in Red

ENTREGA
INMEDIATA 1953
L 0.20

Perf. 13½x14.

1953, Dec. 8 Engraved Unwmkd.

CE1 AP65 20c on 1c rose lilac & olive 1.50 1.50

Transport Plane
APSD1

1956, Oct. 3 *Perf. 13x12½*

CE2 APSD1 20c black & red 75 75

Surcharges on No. CE2 (see Nos. C421, C477) eliminate its special delivery character.

Stamp Centenary Type of Air Post Issue

Design: 20c, Mailman on motorcycle.

1966, May 31 Litho. *Perf. 14x14½*

CE3 AP81 20c bister brown, brn. & gold 75 75

Centenary (in 1965) of the first Honduran postage stamp.

The "HABILITADO" overprint on No. CE3 (see No. C479) eliminates its special delivery character.

Independence Type of Air Post Issue

1972, May 19 Litho. *Perf. 13*

Gold and Multicolored

CE4 AP89 20c *Corsair plane* 25 25

Same Surcharged

1975

CE5 AP89 60c on 20c 75 75

Forest Protection Type of Air Post Issue

Design: Stag in forest.

1976, May 28 Litho. *Perf. 13½*

CE6 AP96 60c org. & multi. 60

AIR POST OFFICIAL STAMPS.

Official Stamps Nos. O78 to O81 Overprinted in Red, Green or Black

Servicio aéreo
Habilitado
VI—1930

1930 *Perf. 11, 11½.*

CO1 A24 10c deep blue (R) 1.75 1.75
CO2 " 20c yellow brown (G) 1.75 1.75
a. Vertical pair, imperf. between 15.00
b. Inverted overprint 7.00
CO3 " 50c vermilion (Bk) 1.75 1.75
CO4 " 1p emerald (R) 1.75 1.75

OA1

Green Surcharge.

CO5 OA1 5c on 6c red violet 1.50 1.50
a. "1910" for "1930" 4.00 4.00
b. "1920" for "1930" 4.00 4.00

The overprint exists in other colors and on other denominations but the status of these is questioned.

Official Stamps of 1931 Overprinted

Servicio Aéreo
Exterior.
Habilitado X.
1931.

1931 *Perf. 12.* **Unwmkd.**

CO6 O2 1c ultramarine 50 50
CO7 " 2c black brown 1.25 1.25
CO8 " 5c olive gray 1.50 1.50
CO9 " 6c orange red 1.50 1.50
a. Inverted ovpt. 35.00 35.00
CO10 " 10c dark green 1.75 1.75
CO11 " 15c olive brown 3.00 3.00
a. Inverted ovpt. 15.00 15.00
CO12 " 20c red brown 3.00 3.00
CO13 " 50c gray violet 2.00 2.00
CO14 " 1p deep orange 3.00 3.00
Nos. CO6-CO14 (9) 17.50 17.50

In the setting of the overprint there are numerous errors in the spelling and punctuation, letters omitted and similar varieties.
This set is known with blue overprint. A similar overprint is known in larger type, but its status has not been fully determined.

Postage Stamps of 1918-30 Surcharged in Various Colors

Aéreo Oficial
Vale L. 0.70
1933
a

Aéreo oficial
Vale L. 0.90
1933
b

1933 **Wmk. 209, Unwmkd.**

CO15 A39 (a) 20c on 2c orange (G) (#295) 4.75 4.75
CO16 " (") 20c on 2c ultra. (G) (#296) 4.75 4.75
CO17 " (") 20c on 2c red (G) (#297) 4.75 4.75
CO17A " (") 40c on 2c org. (Bk) (#295) 3.00 3.00
CO18 " (") 40c on 2c red (G) (#297) 10.00 10.00
CO18A " (") 40 on 2c red (Bk) (#297) 6.00 6.00
CO19 A28 (") 40c on 5c dull violet (Bk) (#246) 6.00 6.00
CO19A A28 (a) 40c on 5c blue gray (Bk) (#247) 10.00 10.00
CO20 " (") 40c on 5c dull violet (Bk) (#266) 6.00 6.00
CO20A " (") 40c on 5c blue gray (Bk) (#267) 13.00 13.00
CO20B " (") 40c on 5c blue gray (R) (#267) 20.00 20.00
CO21 A20 (") 70c on 5c bright blue (Bk) (#183) 4.25 4.25
CO22 A24 (b) 70c on 10c blue (R) (#214) 4.75 4.75
CO23 A22 (") 1l on 20c brown (Bl) (#191) 4.75 4.75
CO24 A24 (") 1l on 50c verm. (Bl) (#216) 20.00 20.00
CO25 A22 (") 1.20l on 1p yellow green (Bl) (#193) 1.50 1.50
Nos. CO15-CO25 (16) 123.50 123.50

Same Surcharges On Official Stamps of 1915-29.

CO26 O1 (a) 40c on 5c purple (Bk) (#O84) 1.25 1.25
CO27 " (") 40c on 5c purple (R) (#O84) 32.50 32.50
CO28 A24 (b) 60c on 6c red violet (Bk)(#O77) 90 90
CO29 " (") 60c on 6c red violet (G)(#O77) 32.50 32.50
CO30 A20 (a) 70c on 5c bright blue (Bk) (#O60) 7.00 7.00
CO31 A19 (") 70c on 10c dull blue (R)(#O62) 12.00 12.00
CO32 " (") 70c on 10c dull blue (Bk)(#O62) 9.00 9.00
CO33 A22 (b) 70c on 10c dull blue (R) (#O70) 6.00 6.00
CO34 A24 (") 70c on 10c deep blue (O) (#O78) 4.75 4.75
CO35 " (") 70c on 10c deep blue (C) (#O78) 6.00 6.00
CO36 A22 (") 70c on 15c lt. bl. (R) (#O71) 120.00 120.00
CO37 " (") 90c on 10c dull blue (R) (#O70) 7.00 7.00
CO38 " (") 90c on 15c light blue (R) (#O71) 4.25 4.25
CO38A A24 (") 1l on 2c deep rose (Bl) (#O76) 1.75 1.75
CO39 A23 (") 1l on 20c brn. (Bl) (#O72) 3.00 3.00
CO39A A24 (") 1l on 20c yellow brown (Bl) (#O79) 4.25 4.25
CO40 A22 (") 1l on 50c light brown (Bl) (#O73) 2.50 2.50
CO41 A24 (") 1l on 50c verm. (Bl) (#O80) 5.50 5.50
CO42 A20 (a) 1.20l on 1p yellow green (Bl) (#O65) 12.00 12.00
CO43 A24 (b) 1.20l on 1p emerald (Bl) (#O81) 2.00 2.00
Nos. CO26-CO43 (20) 274.15 274.15

Varieties of foregoing surcharges exist.

Merchant Flag and Seal of Honduras
OA2

1939, Feb. 27 *Perf. 12½* **Unwmkd.**

CO44 OA2 2c deep blue & green 15 15
CO45 " 5c dp. bl. & orange 15 15
CO46 OA2 8c dp. blue & brown 20 20
CO47 " 15c dp. blue & car. 50 45
CO48 " 46c deep blue & olive green 65 65
CO49 " 50c deep blue & vio. 85 85
CO50 " 1l deep blue & red brown 3.00 3.00
CO51 " 2l deep blue & red orange 5.50 5.50
Nos. CO44-CO51 (8) 11.00 10.95

Types of Air Post Stamps of 1952 Overprinted in Red

OFICIAL

Perf. 13½x14, 14x13½.

1952 **Engraved.** **Unwmkd.**

CO52 AP65 1c rose lilac & olive 10 10
CO53 " 2c brown & violet 15 15
CO54 " 8c deep carmine & black 20 20
CO55 AP66 16c purple & dark green 35 35
CO56 AP65 30c dark blue & black 45 45
CO57 " 1l dark green & dark brown 1.25 1.25
CO58 " 2l blue & red brown 2.50 2.50
CO59 AP66 5l red orange & black 6.50 6.50
Nos. CO52-CO59 (8) 11.50 11.50

Issued to commemorate the 500th anniversary of the birth of Queen Isabella I of Spain.

No. C222 and Types of Air Post Stamps of 1953 Overprinted in Red

OFICIAL

Engraved; Center of 1c Litho.

1953, Dec. 18 *Perf. 12½.*

Frames in Black.

CO60 AP67 1c ultramarine & violet blue 10 10
CO61 " 2c deep blue green 15 15
CO62 " 3c orange 25 25
CO63 " 5c deep carmine 30 30
CO64 " 15c dark brown 40 40
CO65 " 30c purple 75 75
CO66 " 1l olive gray 7.00 4.50
CO67 " 2l lilac rose 8.50 6.00
CO68 " 5l ultramarine 20.00 18.50
Nos. CO60-CO68 (9) 37.45 30.95

Issued to honor the United Nations.

Types of Air Post Stamps Overprinted in Red

OFICIAL

Engraved; 8c Lithographed

1956, Oct. 3 *Perf. 13x12½*

CO69 AP68 1c blk. & brn. car. 10 10
CO70 AP69 2c black & magenta 10 10
CO71 AP68 3c black & rose violet 12 12
CO72 AP69 4c black & orange 12 12
CO73 " 5c black & blue green 15 15
CO74 AP68 8c vio. & multi. 18 18
CO75 " 10c black & red brown 18 18
CO76 " 12c black & carmine rose 20 20
CO77 " 15c car. & blk. 20 20
CO78 " 20c black & olive brown 25 25
CO79 AP69 24c black & blue 30 30
CO80 AP68 25c black & rose violet 30 30
CO81 " 30c black & green 35 35
CO82 " 40c black & red orange 45 45
CO83 AP69 50c black & brown red 55 55
CO84 AP68 60c black & rose violet 65 65
CO85 " 1l blk. & brn. 2.00 1.85
CO86 AP69 2l blk. & dk. bl. 3.50 3.25
CO87 " 5l black & violet blue 8.50 8.00
Nos. CO69-CO87 (19) 18.20 17.30

Nos. C269-C278 Overprinted Vertically in Red (Horizontally on Nos. CO89 and CO91)

OFICIAL

1957, Oct. 21 **Litho.** *Perf. 13*

Frames in Black.

CO88 AP70 1c buff & ultra. 10 10
CO89 " 2c orange, purple & emerald 10 10
CO90 " 5c pink & ultra. 12 12
a. Inverted ovpt.
CO91 " 8c orange, violet & olive 15 15
CO92 " 10c violet & brn. 20 20
CO93 " 12c light green & ultramarine 20 18
CO94 " 15c green & brn. 25 20
CO95 " 30c pink & slate 50 50
CO96 " 1l blue & brn. 2.00 2.00
CO97 " 2l light green & slate 4.00 4.00
Nos. CO88-CO97 (10) 7.62 7.55

Types of Lincoln Air Post Stamps 1959 Overprinted in Red

OFICIAL

1959 **Engraved.** *Perf. 13½*

Flags in National Colors

CO98 AP72 1c ochre 12 12
CO99 AP73 2c gray olive 12 12
a. Inverted ovpt.
CO100 " 3c red brown 12 12
CO101 " 5c ultramarine 15 15
CO102 " 10c dull purple 18 18
a. Overprint omitted
CO103 " 12c red orange 20 20
CO104 AP72 15c dark brown 25 25
CO105 AP73 25c black 40 40
CO106 " 50c dk. carmine 65 65
CO107 " 1l purple 1.50 1.50
CO108 " 2l dark blue 3.00 3.00
a. Miniature sheet of 6 5.00 5.00
CO109 " 5l green 9.00 9.00
Nos. CO98-CO109 (12) 15.69 15.69

No. CO108a contains one each of the 2c, 5c, 12c, 15c, 50c and 2 l, imperf. No marginal inscription. Size: 178½x140½ mm.

No. CO55 Overprinted:
"IN MEMORIAM / Sir Winston / Churchill / 1874–1965"

1965, Dec. 20 *Perf. 14x13½*

CO110 AP66 16c purple & dk. green 2.00 2.00

See note after No. C379.

Nos. C336-C344 Overprinted in Red:

OFICIAL

1965 **Photogravure** *Perf. 14*

Black Design and Inscription

CO111 AP76 1c yellow green 10 10
CO112 " 2c pale rose lilac 10 10
CO113 " 5c lt. ultra. 18 18
CO114 " 8c bluish green 20 20
CO115 " 10c buff 35 35
CO116 " 12c lemon 45 45
CO117 " 1 l light ocher 4.50 4.50
CO118 " 2 l pale olive green 10.00 10.00
CO119 " 3 l rose 12.00 12.00
Nos. CO111-CO119 (9) 27.88 27.88

OFFICIAL STAMPS.

Type of Regular Issue of 1890 Overprinted OFICIAL in Red.

1890 *Perf. 12.* **Unwmkd.**

O1 A5 1c pale yellow 15
O2 " 2c " 15
O3 " 5c " 15
O4 " 10c " 15
O5 " 20c " 15
O6 " 25c " 15
O7 " 30c " 15
O8 " 40c " 15
O9 " 50c " 15
O10 " 75c " 15
O11 " 1p " 15
Nos. O1-O11 (11) 1.65

Type of Regular Issue of 1891 Overprinted in Red.

1891

O12 A6 1c yellow 15
O13 " 2c " 15
O14 " 5c " 15
O15 " 10c " 15
O16 " 20c " 15
O17 " 25c " 15
O18 " 30c " 15
O19 " 40c " 15
O20 " 50c " 15
O21 " 75c " 15
O22 " 1p 15
Nos. O12–O22 (11) 1.65

Nos. O1 to O22 were never placed in use. Cancellations were applied to remainders. They exist with overprint inverted, double, triple and omitted; also, imperf. and part perf.

Regular Issue of 1898 Overprinted **OFICIAL**

1898-99 ***Perf. 11½.***

O23 A12 5c dull ultramarine 25
O24 " 10c dark blue 25
O25 " 20c dull orange 35
O26 " 50c orange red 40
O27 " 1p blue green 75
Nos. O23–O27 (5) 2.00

Counterfeits of basic stamps and of overprint exist.

Regular Issue of 1911 Overprinted **OFICIAL**

1911-15 ***Perf. 12, 14.***

Carmine Overprint.

O28 A15 1c violet 1.00 35
a. Inverted overprint 2.00
b. Double overprint 2.00
O29 " 6c ultramarine 2.00 1.50
a. Inverted overprint 2.50
O30 " 10c blue 1.00 75
a. "OFICAIL" 2.50
b. Double overprint 3.50
O31 " 20c yellow 5.00 5.00
O32 " 50c brown 5.00 4.00
O33 " 1p olive green 10.00 7.50
Nos. O28–O33 (6) 24.00 19.10

Black Overprint.

O34 A15 2c green 50 50
a. "CFICIAL" 4.00
O35 " 5c carmine 1.00 1.00
O36 " 6c ultramarine 3.00 2.50
O37 " 10c blue 2.50 2.50
O38 " 20c yellow 2.00 2.00
O39 " 50c brown 4.00 3.00
Nos. O34–O39 (6) 13.00 11.50

Counterfeits of overprint of Nos. O28–O39 exist.

With Additional Surcharge **10 cts.**

1913-14

O40 A15 1c on 5c carmine 1.50 1.50
O41 " 2c on 5c carmine 1.50 1.50
O42 " 10c on 1c violet 3.00 3.00
a. "OFICIAL" inverted 7.50
O43 " 20c on 1c violet 2.00 2.00

On No. O40 the surcharge reads "1 cent."

Nos. O40–O43 exist with double surcharge.

No. O43 Surcharged Vertically in Black or Yellow **OFICIAL 10 cts.**

1914

O44 A15 10c on 20c on 1c violet (Bk) 5.00 5.00
a. Maroon surch. 20.00 20.00
O45 " 10c on 20c on 1c violet (Y) 25.00 25.00

No. O35 Surcharged **10 c**

1915

O46 A15 10c on 5c carmine 10.00 10.00

No. O39 Surcharged **OFICIAL $ 0.20**

O47 A15 20c on 50c brown 4.00 4.00

Regular Issues of 1913-14 Overprinted in Red or Black **OFICIAL**

1915 ***Perf. 11½.***

O48 A17 1c brown (R) 25 25
a. "OFICAIL" 3.00
O49 " 2c carmine (Bk) 25 25
a. "OFICAIL" 3.50
b. Double overprint 4.00
O50 A18 5c ultramarine (Bk) 25 25
a. "OFIC" 4.00
O51 " 5c ultramarine (R) 70 70
a. "OFIC"
b. "OFICAIL"
O52 " 6c purple (Bk) 1.00 1.00
a. 6c red lilac (Bk)
O53 A17 10c brown (Bk) 75 75
O54 " 20c brown (Bk) 2.00 2.00
O55 " 20c brown (R) 2.00 2.00
a. Double overprint (R + Bk) 10.00
b. "OFICAIL"
O56 A18 50c rose (Bk) 4.00 4.00
Nos. O48–O56 (9) 11.20 11.20

The 10c blue, formerly listed, had the overprint "OFICIAL" in different type from the other stamps of the series. It is stated that forty copies were overprinted for the Postmaster General but the stamp was never put in use or on sale at the post office.

No. 152 Surcharged **OFICIAL. $ 0,01**

O57 A17 1c on 2c carmine 2.00 2.00
a. "0.10" for "0.01" 6.00 6.00
b. "0.20" for "0.01" 6.00 6.00
c. Double surcharge 12.00 12.00
d. As "a," double surcharge 110.00
e. As "b," double surch. 110.00

Regular Issue of 1915-16 Overprinted **OFICIAL** in Black or Red.

1915–16

O58 A19 1c chocolate (Bk) 15 15
O59 " 2c carmine (Bk) 15 15
a. Tête bêche pair 1.25 1.25
b. Double overprint 2.00
c. Double overprint, one inverted 2.00
d. "b" and "c" in tête bêche pair
O60 A20 5c bright blue (R) 25 25
a. Invtd. ovpt. 3.00
O61 " 6c deep purple (R) 35 35
a. Black overprint 3.00
b. Invtd. overprint 2.00 2.00
O62 A19 10c dull blue (R) 30 30
O63 " 20c red brown (Bk) 50 50
a. Tête bêche pair 2.50
O64 A20 50c red (Bk) 1.50 1.50
O65 " 1p yel. green (C) 3.50 3.50
Nos. O58–O65 (8) 6.70 6.70

The 6c, 10c and 1p exist imperf.

Regular Issue of 1919 Overprinted **OFICIAL**

1921

O66 A22 1c brown 1.00 1.00
a. Invtd. ovpt. 2.00 2.00
O67 " 2c carmine 4.00 4.00
a. Invtd. ovpt. 2.00 2.00
O68 " 5c lilac rose 4.00 4.00
a. Invtd. ovpt. 2.00
O69 " 6c bright violet 40 40
a. Invtd. overprint
O70 " 10c dull blue 50 50
a. Double overprint
O71 " 15c light blue 60 60
a. Invtd. ovpt. 2.00
b. Double overprint, one inverted 4.00
O72 " 20c brown 85 85
O73 A22 50c light brown 1.25 1.25
O74 " 1p yellow green 2.50 2.50
Nos. O66–O74 (9) 15.10 15.10

Regular Issue of 1924 Overprinted **OFICIAL**

1924 ***Perf. 11, 11½.***

O75 A24 1c olive brown 10 10
O76 " 2c deep rose 15 15
O77 " 6c red violet 25 25
O78 " 10c deep blue 40 40
O79 " 20c yellow brown 60 60
O80 " 50c vermilion 1.50 1.50
O81 " 1p emerald 1.75 1.75
Nos. O75–O81 (7) 4.75 4.75

J. C. del Valle
O1

Designs: 2c, J. R. Molina. 5c, Coffee tree. 10c, J. T. Reyes. 20c, Tegucigalpa Cathedral. 50c, San Lorenzo Creek. 1p, Radio station.

Wmkd. Multiple Ovals. (209)

1929 Lithographed. ***Perf. 11½.***

O82 O1 1c blue 15 15
O83 " 2c carmine 25 25
a. 2c rose 25 25
O84 " 5c purple 30 30
O85 " 10c emerald 40 40
O86 " 20c dark blue 50 50
O87 " 50c org., grn. & blue 1.00 1.00
O88 " 1p buff 2.00 2.00
Nos. O82–O88 (7) 4.60 4.60

Nos. O82–O88 exist imperf.

REPUBLICA DE HONDURAS 1931 CORREO OFICIAL 1934 1 UN CENTAVO 1

View of Tegucigalpa
O2

Engraved.

1931 ***Perf. 12*** **Unwmkd.**

O89 O2 1c ultramarine 25 25
O90 " 2c black brown 25 25
O91 " 5c olive gray 30 30
O92 " 6c orange red 40 40
O93 " 10c dark green 45 45
O94 " 15c olive brown 50 50
O95 " 20c red brown 60 60
O96 " 50c gray violet 75 75
O97 " 1p deep orange 1.50 1.50
Nos. O89–O97 (9) 5.00 5.00

Official Stamps of 1931 Overprinted in Black

HABILITADO 1935-1938

1936–37

O98 O2 1c ultramarine 25 25
O99 " 2c black brown 25 25
O100 " 5c olive gray 30 30
O101 " 6c red orange 40 40
O102 " 10c dark green 45 45
O103 " 15c olive brown 50 50
a. Inverted ovpt. 5.00
O104 " 20c red brown 60 60
a. "1938-1935"
O105 " 50c gray violet 75 75
Nos. O98–O105 (8) 3.50 3.50

Double overprints exist on 1c and 2c. No. O97 with this overprint is fraudulent.

POSTAL TAX STAMPS.

Red Cross Francisco Morazán
PT1 PT2

Engraved; Cross Lithographed

1941 ***Perf. 12.*** **Unwmkd.**

RA1 PT1 1c blue & carmine 12 5

Obligatory on all domestic or foreign mail, the tax to be used by the Honduran Red Cross.

1941 **Engraved**

RA2 PT2 1c copper brown 12 8

Issued in commemoration of the 100th anniversary of the death of Francisco Morazán.

Mother and Child Henri Dunant
PT3 PT4

Engraved; Cross Lithographed

1945

RA3 PT3 1c olive brown, carmine & bl. 12 5

The tax was for the Honduran Red Cross.

Similar to Type of 1945.

1950 Design: 1c, Large Red Cross.

RA4 PT3 1c olive brn. & red 12 5

The tax was for the Honduran Red Cross.

1959 ***Perf. 13x13½***

RA5 PT4 1c blue & red 8 5

The tax was for the Red Cross.

Henri Dunant
PT5

Design: No. RA7, as PT5, but redrawn; country name panel at bottom, value at right, "El poder . . ." at top.

1964, Dec. 15 **Litho.** ***Perf. 11***

RA6 PT5 1c brt. grn. & red 10 8
RA7 " 1c brown & red 10 8

The tax was for the Red Cross.

Nurse and Patient
PT6

1969, June **Litho.** ***Perf. 13½***

RA8 PT6 1c light blue & red 8 8

The tax was for the Red Cross.

HORTA

(ôr'tä)

LOCATION — An administrative district of the Azores, consisting of the islands of Pico, Fayal, Flores and Corvo.

GOVT.—A district of the Republic of Portugal.

AREA—305 sq. mi.

POP.—49,000 (approx.).

CAPITAL—Horta.

1000 Reis = 1 Milreis

King Carlos

A1 A2

Chalk-surfaced Paper.

Perf. 11½, 12½, 13½.

1892-93 Typographed Unwmkd.

No.	Type	Description	Unused	Used
1	A1	5r yellow	2.00	1.00
		a. Perf. 11½	18.00	13.50
2	"	10r reddish violet	2.50	1.50
3	"	15r chocolate	2.75	1.75
4	"	20r lavender	3.50	2.25
5	"	25r deep green, perf. 11½	2.00	75
		a. Perf. 13½	2.25	1.00
6	"	50r blue	3.50	2.25
		a. Perf. 13½	6.00	2.25
7	"	75r carmine	6.00	4.00
8	"	80r yellow green	7.50	6.00
9	"	100r brown, *yellow* ('93)	6.00	4.00
		a. Perf. 12½	75.00	35.00
10	"	150r carmine, *rose* ('93)	30.00	22.50
11	"	200r dark blue, *blue* ('93)	30.00	20.00
12	"	300r dark blue, *salmon* ('93)	35.00	27.50
		Nos. 1-12 (12)	130.75	93.50

Bisects of No. 1 were used in Aug. 1894.

The reprints have shiny white gum and clean-cut perforation 13½. The white paper is thinner than that of the originals. Price, $3 each.

1897-1905 ***Perf. 11½***

Name and Value in Black Except 500r.

No.	Type	Description	Unused	Used
13	A2	2½r gray	60	35
14	"	5r orange	60	35
15	"	10r light green	60	35
16	"	15r brown	4.50	3.00
17	"	15r gray green ('99)	1.25	75
18	"	20r gray violet	1.25	75
19	"	25r sea green	2.50	30
20	"	25r carmine rose ('99)	90	65
21	"	50r blue	1.75	80
22	"	50r ultra. ('05)	7.50	4.00
23	"	65r slate blue ('98)	80	70
24	"	75r rose	1.75	1.25
25	"	75r brown, *yellow* ('05)	9.00	6.00
26	"	80r violet	1.40	1.00
27	"	100r dark blue, *blue*	1.40	1.00
28	"	115r orange brown, *pink* ('98)	1.25	90
29	"	130r gray brown, *buff* ('98)	1.25	90
30	"	150r lt. brown, *buff*	1.25	90
31	"	180r slate, *pinkish* ('98)	1.40	1.20
32	"	200r red violet, *pale lilac*	3.50	2.75
33	"	300r dark blue, *rose*	5.00	3.50
34	"	500r black & red, *blue*	7.50	5.50
		Nos. 13-34 (22)	56.95	36.90

Stamps of Portugal replaced those of Horta.

HUNGARY

(hŭng'gȧ-rĭ)

LOCATION—In Central Europe

GOVT.—Republic.

AREA—35,902 sq. mi.

POP.—10,650,000 (est. 1977).

CAPITAL—Budapest.

Prior to World War I Hungary together with Austria, comprised the Austro-Hungarian Empire.

100 Krajczár (Kreuzer) = 1 Forint
100 Fillér = 1 Korona (1900)
100 Fillér = 1 Pengö (1926)
100 Fillér = 1 Forint (1946)

> Perforations of Nos. 1-12 usually cut into the designs. Well centered stamps sell at much higher prices.

Issues of the Monarchy.

Franz Josef I

A1

Lithographed

1871 ***Perf. 9½*** **Unwmkd.**

No.	Type	Description	Unused	Used
1	A1	2k orange	250.00	100.00
		a. 2k yellow	750.00	275.00
2	"	3k light green	650.00	475.00
3	"	5k rose	275.00	17.50
		a. 5k brick red	500.00	40.00
4	"	10k blue	650.00	100.00
		a. 10k pale blue	700.00	150.00
5	"	15k yellow brown	800.00	160.00
6	"	25k violet	600.00	200.00
		a. 25k brt. violet	750.00	300.00

The first printing of No. 1, in dark yellow, was not issued because of spots on the King's face. A few copies were used at Pest.

1871-72 Engraved

No.	Type	Description	Unused	Used
7	A1	2k orange	35.00	8.50
		a. 2k yellow	175.00	17.50
		b. Bisect on cover		350.00
8	"	3k green	42.50	20.00
		a. 3k blue green	50.00	20.00
9	"	5k rose	35.00	1.50
		a. 5k brick red	120.00	9.00
10	"	10k deep blue	185.00	10.00
11	"	15k brown	165.00	20.00
		a. 15k copper brn.	1200.00	750.00
		b. 15k black brown	375.00	75.00
12	"	25k lilac	120.00	45.00

Reprints are perf. 11½ and watermarked "kr" in oval. Set price $350.

Crown of St. Stephen

A2 A3

1874-76 ***Perf. 12½ to 13½***

No.	Type	Description	Unused	Used
13	A2	2k rose lilac	25.00	1.00
14	"	3k yellow green	27.50	1.25
		a. 3k blue green	27.50	1.25
15	"	5k rose	6.00	30
		a. 5k dull red	17.50	1.00
16	"	10k blue	37.50	1.00
17	"	20k slate	350.00	5.00

Perf. 11½ and Compound

No.	Type	Description	Unused	Used
13a	A2	2k rose lilac	35.00	3.00
14b	"	3k yellow green	30.00	5.00
		c. 3k blue green	30.00	5.00
		d. Perf. 9½	650.00	300.00
5b	"	5k rose	30.00	40
		c. 5k dull red	30.00	40
		d. Perf. 9½		150.00
16a	"	10k blue	80.00	3.00
17a	"	20k slate	500.00	40.00

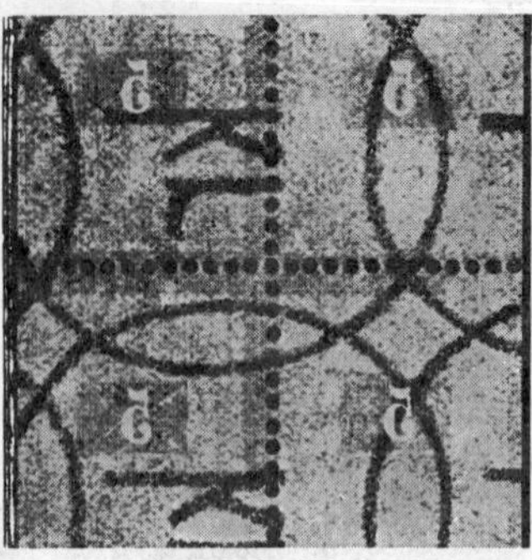

Wmk. 132

Wmkd. "kr" in Oval. (132)

1881 ***Perf. 11½, 12x11½***

No.	Type	Description	Unused	Used
18	A2	2k violet	1.00	25
		a. 2k rose lilac	1.00	25
		b. 2k slate	6.00	40
19	"	3k blue green	1.00	30
20	"	5k rose	5.50	20
21	"	10k blue	5.00	30
22	"	20k slate	7.00	60

Perf. 12½ to 13½ and Compound

No.	Type	Description	Unused	Used
18c	A2	2k violet	70.00	3.50
19a	"	3k blue green	50.00	1.50
20a	"	5k rose	40.00	90
21a	"	10k blue	50.00	2.00
22b	"	20k slate	375.00	8.00

1888-98 Typographed.

Perf. 11½, 12x11½.

Numerals in Black.

No.	Type	Description	Unused	Used
22A	A3	1k black, one plate	75	25
		c. "1" printed separately	6.50	80
23	"	2k red violet	90	30
		a. Perf. 11½	30.00	3.00
24	"	3k green	1.10	30
		a. Perf. 11½	13.50	1.50
25	"	5k rose	1.20	15
		a. Perf. 11½	15.00	85
26	"	8k orange	4.00	25
		a. "8" double	45.00	
27	"	10k blue	2.50	45
		a. Perf. 11½	50.00	37.50
28	"	12k brown & green	6.50	30
29	"	15k claret & blue	4.50	15
30	"	20k gray	9.00	2.00
		a. Perf. 11½	120.00	100.00
31	"	24k brn.violet & red	12.00	40
32	"	30k olive grn. & brn.	12.50	25
33	"	50k red & orange	25.00	80

Numerals in Red

No.	Type	Description	Unused	Used
34	A3	1fo gray blue & silver	120.00	1.25
		a. Perf. 11½	130.00	1.50
35	"	3fo lilac brn. & gold	22.50	9.00

Most of Nos. 22A to 103 exist imperforate, but were never so issued.

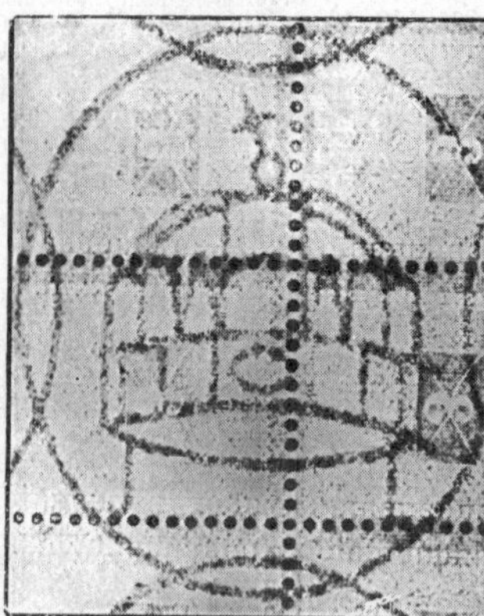

Wmk. 135

Wmkd. Crown in Oval or Circle, Sideways. (135)

1898-99 ***Perf. 12x11½, 11½***

Numerals in Black.

No.	Type	Description	Unused	Used
35A	A3	1k black	65	20
36	"	2k violet	2.25	20
37	"	3k green	2.00	15
38	"	5k rose	1.50	10
39	"	8k orange	9.00	2.00
40	"	10k blue	1.60	30
41	"	12k red brn. & grn.	30.00	2.50
		a. Perf. 11½	110.00	12.50
42	"	15k rose & blue	2.00	20
43	"	20k gray	3.50	1.25
		a. Perf. 11½	100.00	10.00
44	"	24k vio. brn. & red	3.25	1.35
		a. Perf. 11½	135.00	25.00
45	"	30k olive grn. & brn.	4.00	90
		a. Perf. 11½	25.00	7.50
46	"	50k dull red & orange	7.00	2.75
		a. Perf. 11½	175.00	30.00
		Nos. 35A-46 (12)	66.75	11.90

Nos. 35A to 46 also are found on paper with a variation of Wmk. 135, showing the crown in a circle, instead of an oval. In the watermark with circles, a four-pointed star and "VI" appear four times in the sheet in the large spaces between the intersecting circles. The paper with the circular watermark is often yellowish and thinner than that with the oval watermark

See note after No. 35.

New Currency

100 Filler = 1 Korona

"Turul" and Crown of St. Stephen

A4

Franz Josef I Wearing Hungarian Crown

A5

1900-04 Wmk. 135

Numerals in Black.

No.	Type	Description	Unused	Used
47	A4	1f gray	25	25
		a. 1f dull lilac	40	25
48	"	2f olive yellow	50	12
49	"	3f orange	25	15
50	"	4f violet	50	12
		a. Booklet pane of 6	20.00	
51	"	5f emerald	3.00	6
		a. Booklet pane of 6	25.00	
52	"	6f claret	40	20
		a. 6f violet brown	30	20
53	"	6f bistre ('01)	8.00	50
54	"	6f olive green ('04)	3.00	50
55	"	10f carmine	2.00	6
		a. Booklet pane of 6	20.00	
56	"	12f violet ('04)	2.00	40
57	"	20f brown ('01)	1.60	20
58	"	25f blue	1.40	20
		a. Booklet pane of 6	15.00	
59	"	30f orange brown	22.50	20
60	"	35f red violet ('01)	10.00	20
		a. Booklet pane of 6	45.00	
61	"	50f lake	7.50	60
62	"	60f green	35.00	40
		a. Perf. 11½	200.00	12.00
63	A5	1k brown red	35.00	60
		a. Perf. 11½	30.00	2.50
64	"	2k gray blue ('01)	175.00	5.00
		a. Perf. 11½	200.00	40.00
65	"	3k sea green	22.50	1.40
66	"	5k violet brn. ('01)	22.50	12.00
		a. Perf. 11½	275.00	125.00
		Nos. 47-66 (20)	352.90	23.16

The watermark on Nos. 47 to 66 is always the circular form of Wmk. 135 described in the note following No. 46.

Pairs imperforate between were favor prints made for an influential Budapest collector.

See note after No. 35.

Wmk. 136 Wmk. 136a

Wmkd. Crown. (136)

1908-13 *Perf. 15*

67	A4	1f slate	30	15
68	"	2f olive yellow	15	5
69	"	3f orange	30	6
70	"	5f emerald	15	4
		c. Booklet pane of 6		
71	"	6f olive green	30	6
72	"	10f carmine	12	4
		c. Booklet pane of 6		
73	"	12f violet	45	12
74	"	16f gray green ('13)	30	25
75	"	20f dark brown	3.00	10
76	"	25f blue	2.00	8
77	"	30f orange brown	2.75	8
78	"	35f red violet	4.50	10
79	"	50f lake	55	20
80	"	60f green	3.00	10
81	A5	1k brown red	4.50	15
82	"	2k gray blue	40.00	45
83	"	5k violet brown	55.00	3.50
		Nos. 67-83 (17)	117.37	5.53

See note after No. 35.

Perf. 12x11½.

1904-05 **Wmk. 136a**

67a	A4	1f slate	1.00	80
68a	"	2f olive yellow	3.50	12
69a	"	3f orange	60	30
70a	"	5f emerald	1.75	12
71a	"	6f olive green	1.10	15
72a	"	10f carmine	3.50	10
73a	"	12f violet	1.25	90
75a	"	20f dark brown	7.50	50
76a	"	25f blue	15.00	40
77a	"	30f orange brown	3.00	20
78a	"	35f red violet	12.50	25
79a	"	50f lake	10.00	1.50
		c. 50f magenta	30	50
80a	"	60f green	160.00	40
81a	A5	1k brown red	80.00	80
82a	"	2k gray blue	300.00	22.50
		c. Perf. 11½	300.00	27.50
83a	"	5k violet brown	85.00	35.00

1906 *Perf. 15.*

67b	A4	1f slate	1.25	30
68b	"	2f olive yellow	35	10
69b	"	3f orange	1.00	12
70b	"	5f emerald	35	6
71b	"	6f olive green	1.20	10
72b	"	10f carmine	80	5
73b	"	12f violet	1.50	20
75b	"	20f dark brown	3.75	25
76b	"	25f blue	3.25	20
77b	"	30f orange brown	3.25	15
78b	"	35f red violet	15.00	15
79b	"	50f lake	1.20	40
80b	"	60f green	25.00	20
81b	A5	1k brown red	22.50	30
82b	"	2k gray blue	75.00	3.00

Wmk. 137

A5a

Wmkd. Double Cross (137) Vert.

1913-16 *Perf. 15*

84	A4	1f slate	20	10
85	"	2f olive yellow	8	4
86	"	3f orange	8	5
87	"	5f emerald	30	3
88	"	6f olive green	8	5
89	"	10f carmine	6	3
90	"	12f violet, *yellow*	10	5
91	"	16f gray green	25	25
92	"	20f dark brown	15	5
93	"	25f ultramarine	15	5
94	A4	30f orange brown	15	5
95	"	35f red violet	20	5
96	"	50f lake, *blue*	25	15
		a. Cliché of 35f in plate of 50f	200.00	200.00
97	"	60f green	3.00	1.50
98	"	60f green, *salmon*	35	8
99	"	70f red brown, *green* ('16)	20	5
100	"	80f dull violet ('16)	20	5
101	A5	1k dull red	60	6
102	"	2k dull blue	1.75	25
103	"	5k violet brown	5.00	1.75
		Nos. 84-103 (20)	13.15	4.69

See note after No. 35.

Wmk. 137 Horiz.

84a	A4	1f slate	1.25	1.00
85a	"	2f olive yellow	2.50	75
87a	"	5f emerald	40	25
88a	"	6f olive green	60	25
89b	"	10f carmine	1.10	20
90a	"	12f violet, *yellow*	2.50	25
92a	"	20f dark brown	6.00	25
94a	"	30f orange brown	35.00	20
95a	"	35f red violet	100.00	50
96b	"	50f lake, *blue*	10.00	7.50
97a	"	60f green	2.50	1.75
98a	"	60f green, *salmon*	1.75	20
101a	A5	1k dull red	17.50	25
102a	"	2k dull blue	85.00	1.00

1916, July 1 *Perf. 15*

103A	A5a	10f violet brown	20	20

Although issued as a postal savings stamp, No. 103A was also valid for postage.

Queen Zita
A6

King Charles IV
A7

1916, Dec. 30

104	A6	10f violet	35	30
105	A7	15f red	35	30

Issued to commemorate the coronation of King Charles IV and Queen Zita on Dec. 30, 1916.

Harvesting (White Numerals)
A8

1916

106	A8	10f rose	15	6
107	"	15f violet	20	6

Harvesting Wheat
A9

Parliament Building at Budapest
A10

1916-18 *Perf. 15*

108	A9	2f brown orange	4	4
109	"	3f red lilac	4	4
110	"	4f slate gray ('18)	5	6
111	"	5f green	6	4
112	"	6f greenish blue	10	8
113	"	10f rose red	20	4
114	"	15f violet	3	3
115	"	20f gray brown	4	3
116	"	25f dull blue	10	6
117	"	35f brown	12	10
118	"	40f olive green	3	3

Perf. 14

119	A10	50f red violet & lilac	3	3
120	"	75f bright blue & pale blue	8	5
121	"	80f green & pale grn.	10	5
122	"	1k red brown & claret	3	3
123	"	2k olive brown & bistre	4	3
124	A10	3k dk. violet & indigo	25	10
125	"	5k dark brown & light brown	30	12
126	"	10k violet brown & violet	50	20
		Nos. 108-126 (19)	2.14	1.16

See also Nos. 335-377, 388-396.

During 1921-24 various stamps then current were punched with three holes ∴ forming a triangle. These were sold at post offices and collectors and dealers who wanted them unpunched would have to purchase them through the philatelic agency at a 10 per cent advance over face value.

King Charles IV
A11

Queen Zita
A12

1918 *Perf. 15*

127	A11	10f scarlet	5	5
128	"	15f deep violet	20	20
129	"	20f dark brown	4	4
130	"	25f bright blue	6	6
131	A12	40f olive green	5	5
132	"	50f lilac	15	15
		Nos. 127-132 (6)	55	55

Issues of the Republic.

Hungarian Stamps of 1916-18 Overprinted in Black

KÖZTÁRSASÁG

1918-19 *Perf. 15, 14* **Wmk. 137**

On Stamps of 1916-18.

153	A9	2f brown orange	5	4
154	"	3f red lilac	5	4
155	"	4f slate gray	5	4
156	"	5f green	5	4
157	"	6f greenish blue	5	4
158	"	10f rose red	5	4
159	"	20f gray brown	20	20
162	"	40f olive green	5	5
163	A10	1k red brown & claret	5	5
164	"	2k olive brn. & bistre	5	5
165	"	3k dark violet & indigo	15	15
166	"	5k dk. brn. & lt. brn.	40	40
167	"	10k violet brown & violet	45	45

On Stamps of 1918.

168	A11	10f scarlet	5	5
169	"	15f deep violet	5	5
170	"	20f dark brown	5	5
171	"	25f bright blue	12	12
172	A12	40f olive green	12	12
173	"	50f lilac	12	12
		Nos. 153-173 (19)	2.16	2.10

Nos. 153-162 and 168-173 exist with overprint inverted.

A13

A14

1919-20 *Perf. 15*

174	A13	2f brown orange	4	4
176	"	4f slate gray	5	5
177	"	5f yellow green	4	3
178	"	6f greenish blue	4	3
179	"	10f red	4	3
180	"	15f violet	6	6
181	"	20f dark brown	4	3
182	"	20f green ('20)	3	3
183	"	25f dull blue	4	3
184	"	40f olive green	4	3
185	"	40f rose red ('20)	4	4
186	"	45f orange	6	6

Perf. 14.

187	A14	50f brown violet & pale violet	6	4
188	"	60f brown & blue ('20)	4	3
189	"	95f dark blue & blue	6	6
190	"	1k red brown	6	5
191	"	1k dark blue & dull blue ('20)	4	3
192	"	1.20k dark green & green	6	5
193	"	1.40k yellow green	8	6
194	"	2k olive brown & bistre	10	8
195	"	3k dark violet & indigo	10	10
196	"	5k dk. brown & brn.	10	10
197	"	10k violet brown & red violet	40	25
		Nos. 174-197 (23)	1.62	1.31

The 3f red lilac, type A13, was never regularly issued without overprint (Nos. 204 and 312). In 1923 a small quantity was sold by the Government at public auction. Price $2.25.

Issues of the Soviet Republic.

Karl Marx
A15

Sándor Petőfi
A16

Ignác Martinovics
A17

György Dózsa
A18

Friedrich Engels
A19

Wmkd. Double Cross Horiz. (137)

1919, June 14 Litho. *Perf. 12½x12*

198	A15	20f rose & brown	75	75
		a. Wmk. vertical	4.00	3.00
199	A16	45f brown orange & dark green	75	75
		a. Wmk. vertical	7.50	7.50
200	A17	60f blue gray & brown	1.50	1.50
		a. Wmk. vertical	4.00	3.00
201	A18	75f claret & violet brown	1.75	1.75
		a. Wmk. vertical	4.00	3.00
202	A19	80f olive drab & black brown	1.50	1.50
		a. Wmk. vertical	40.00	40.00
		Nos. 198-202 (5)	6.25	6.25
		Nos. 198a-202a (5)	59.50	56.50

Stamps of 1919 Overprinted in Red

MAGYAR
TANÁCS-
KÖZTÁRSASÁG.

1919, July 21 **Typo.** *Perf. 15*

203	A13	2f brown orange	6	6
204	"	3f red lilac	6	6
205	"	4f slate gray	6	6
206	"	5f yellow green	6	6

207 A13 6f greenish blue 6 6
208 " 10f red 4 4
209 " 15f violet 6 6
210 " 20f dark brown 6 6
211 " 25f dull blue 6 6
212 " 40f olive green 6 6
213 " 45f orange 6 6

Overprinted in Red

MAGYAR TANÁCSKÖZTÁRSASÁG

Perf. 14.

214 A14 50f brown violet & pale violet 8 8
215 " 95f dark blue & blue 10 10
216 " 1k red brown 10 10
217 " 1.20k dark green & green 12 12
218 " 1.40k yellow green 12 12
219 " 2k olive brown & bistre 50 50
220 " 3k dark violet & indigo 50 50
221 " 5k dark brown & brown 50 50
222 " 10k violet brown & red violet 75 75
Nos. 203-222 (20) 3.41 3.41

"Magyar Tanacsköztarsasag" on Nos. 198 to 222 means "Hungarian Soviet Republic."

Issues of the Kingdom

Stamps of 1919 Overprinted in Black

A nemzeti hadsereg bevonulása. 1919. XI/16.

1919, Nov. 16

306 A13 5f green 60 60
307 " 10f rose red 60 60
308 " 15f violet 60 60
309 " 20f gray brown 60 60
310 " 25f dull blue 60 60
Nos. 306-310 (5) 3.00 3.00

Issued to commemorate the Romanian evacuation. The overprint reads: "Entry of the National Army—November 16, 1919".

Nos. 203 to 213 Overprinted in Black

1920, Jan. 26 *Perf. 15.*

311 A13 2f brown orange 45 45
312 " 3f red lilac 20 20
313 " 4f slate gray 45 45
314 " 5f yellow green 5 5
315 " 6f blue green 10 10
316 " 10f red 5 5
317 " 15f violet 5 5
318 " 20f dark brown 5 5
319 " 25f dull blue 10 10
320 " 40f olive green 60 60
321 " 45f orange 60 60

Nos. 214 to 222 Overprinted in Black

Perf. 14.

322 A14 50f brown violet & pale violet 60 60
323 " 95f dark blue & blue 60 60
324 " 1k red brown 60 60
325 " 1.20k dark green & green 1.00 1.00
326 " 1.40k yellow green 1.00 1.00
327 " 2k olive brown & bistre 2.25 2.25
328 " 3k dark violet & indigo 2.25 2.25
329 " 5k dark brown & brown 30 30
330 " 10k violet brown & red violet 4.00 4.00
Nos. 311-330 (20) 15.30 15.30

Types of 1916-18 Issue.
Denomination Tablets Without Inner Frame on Nos. 350 to 363.

1920-24 *Perf. 15.* **Wmk. 137**

335 A9 5f brown orange 6 5
336 " 10f red violet 6 5
337 " 40f rose red 8 6
338 " 50f yellow green 5 4
339 " 50f blue violet ('22) 6 4
340 " 60f black 6 6
341 " 1k green ('22) 6 4
342 " 1½k brown violet ('22) 8 5
343 " 2k greenish blue ('22) 6 4
344 " 2½k deep green ('22) 6 4
345 " 3k brown orange ('22) 6 5
346 " 4k light red ('22) 6 5
347 " 4½k dull violet ('22) 20 10
348 " 5k deep brown ('22) 6 4
349 " 6k dark blue ('22) 20 10
350 " 10k brown ('23) 6 5
351 " 15k slate ('23) 8 5
352 " 20k red violet ('23) 8 5
353 " 25k orange ('23) 8 4
354 " 40k gray green ('23) 8 5
355 " 50k dark blue ('23) 8 4
356 " 100k claret ('23) 8 4
357 " 150k dark green ('23) 10 5
358 " 200k green ('23) 10 4
359 " 300k rose red ('24) 12 6
360 " 350k violet ('23) 20 10
361 " 500k dark gray ('24) 25 8
362 " 600k olive bistre ('24) 30 12
363 " 800k orange yel. ('24) 35 15

Perf. 14.

364 A10 2.50k blue & gray blue 5 4
365 " 3.50k gray 8 6
366 " 10k brown ('22) 5 4
367 " 15k dark gray ('22) 5 4
368 " 20k red violet ('22) 5 4
369 " 25k orange ('22) 6 4
370 " 30k claret ('22) 6 4
371 " 40k gray green ('22) 6 4
372 " 50k deep blue ('22) 6 5
373 " 100k yellow brown ('22) 6 4
374 " 400k turquoise blue ('23) 40 20
375 " 500k bright violet ('23) 35 5
376 " 1000k lilac ('24) 25 4
377 " 2000k carmine ('24) 80 10
Nos. 335-377 (43) 5.55 2.55

Nos. 372 to 377 have colored numerals.

Madonna and Child
A23

1921, Feb. 27 **Typo.** *Perf. 12*

378 A23 50k dk. brown & blue 45 20
379 " 100k olive bistre & yellow brown 65 30

Wmk. 133

Type of 1921 Issue.
Wmkd. Four Double Crosses. (133)

1923-25 *Perf. 12*

380 A23 200k dark blue & ultramarine 30 15
381 A23 500k violet brown & violet 30 15
382 " 1000k violet & red violet 35 20
383 " 2000k greenish blue & violet 40 40
384 " 2500k olive brown & buff ('25) 45 25
385 " 3000k brown red & violet 60 30
386 " 5000k dark green & yellow green 60 30
a. Center inverted 2250.00 1800.00
387 A23 10,000k gray violet & pale blue ('25) 2.25 85
Nos. 380-387 (8) 5.25 2.60

Types of 1916–18.
Denomination Tablets Without Inner Frame on Nos. 388–394.

1924 *Perf. 15.* **Wmk. 133**

388 A9 100k claret 20 10
389 " 200k yellow green 10 6
390 " 300k rose red 10 6
391 " 400k deep blue 10 6
392 " 500k dark gray 12 8
393 " 600k olive bistre 12 10
a. "800" in upper right corner 100.00 100.00
394 " 800k orange yellow 30 20

Perf. 14½x14.

395 A10 1000k lilac 30 4
396 " 2000k carmine 50 4
Nos. 388-396 (9) 1.84 74

Nos. 395 and 396 have colored numerals.

Maurus Jókai
A24

1925, Feb. 1 *Perf. 12* **Unwmkd.**

400 A24 1000k deep green & black brown 2.50 2.00
401 " 2000k light brown & black brown 1.00 80
402 " 2500k dark blue & black brown 2.50 2.00

Birth centenary of Maurus Jokai (1825–1904), novelist.

Crown of St. Stephen
A25

Matthias Cathedral
A26

Palace at Budapest
A27

Lithographed

1926–27 *Perf. 14, 15* **Wmk. 133**

403 A25 1f dark gray 15 10
404 " 2f light blue 15 5
405 " 3f orange 20 6
406 " 4f violet 20 3
407 " 6f light green 30 8
408 " 8f lilac rose 35 3

Typographed.

409 A26 10f deep blue 35 4
410 " 16f dark violet 35 3
411 " 20f carmine 35 10
412 " 25f light brown 35 12

Perf. 14½x14.

413 A27 32f deep violet & bright violet 1.00 12
414 " 40f dk. blue & blue 1.20 12
Nos. 403-414 (12) 4.95 88

See also Nos. 428–436.

Madonna and Child
A28

1926–27 **Engraved.** *Perf. 14.*

415 A28 1p violet 12.00 20
416 " 2p red 7.50 60
417 " 5p blue ('27) 17.50 3.00

Palace at Budapest
A29

St. Stephen
A30

1926–27 **Typographed**

418 A29 30f blue green ('27) 50 10
419 " 46f ultra. ('27) 90 10
420 " 50f brn. black ('27) 80 6
421 " 70f scarlet 1.10 6

1928-29 **Engraved** *Perf. 15*

422 A30 8f yellow green 60 25
423 " 8f rose lake ('29) 45 20
424 " 16f orange red 60 25
425 " 16f violet ('29) 45 25
426 " 32f ultramarine 1.65 1.50
427 " 32f bistre ('29) 1.50 1.35
Nos. 422-427 (6) 5.25 3.80

890th death anniversary of St. Stephen, the first king of Hungary.

Wmk. 210

Types of 1926-27 Issue.
Wmkd.
Double Cross on Pyramid. (210)

1928-30 **Typographed** *Perf. 14, 15*

428 A25 1f black 20 8
429 " 2f blue 15 5
430 " 3f orange 15 8
431 " 4f violet 15 3
432 " 6f blue green 15 8
433 " 8f lilac rose 30 3
434 A26 10f deep blue ('30) 1.50 3
435 " 16f violet 50 3
436 " 20f dull red 40 6
Nos. 428-436 (9) 3.50 47

On Nos. 428 to 433 the numerals have thicker strokes than on the same values of the 1926–27 issue.

Palace at Budapest
A31

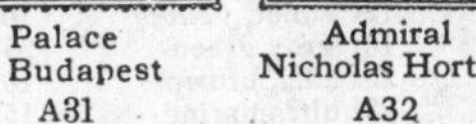

Admiral Nicholas Horthy
A32

Type A31 resembles A27 but the steamer is nearer the right of the design.

1928-31 ***Perf. 14***

437	A31	30f emerald ('31)	85	10
438	"	32f red violet	85	25
439	"	40f deep blue	80	6
440	"	46f apple green	1.00	15
441	"	50f ochre ('31)	1.10	5
		Nos. 437-441 (5)	4.60	61

1930, Mar. 1 **Litho.** ***Perf. 15***

445	A32	8f myrtle green	1.25	20
446	"	16f purple	1.25	30
447	"	20f carmine	5.00	1.20
448	"	32f olive brown	4.00	3.50
449	"	40f dark blue	6.00	1.20
		Nos. 445-449 (5)	17.50	6.40

Issued in commemoration of the tenth anniversary of the election of Admiral Nicholas Horthy as Regent, March 1, 1920.

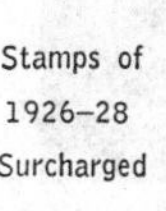

Stamps of 1926-28 Surcharged

1931, Jan. 1 ***Perf. 14, 15***

450	A25	2f on 3f orange	40	35
451	"	6f on 8f magenta	50	15
		a. Perf. 14	17.50	15.00
452	A26	10f on 16f violet	35	10

Wmk. 133

453	A25	2f on 3f orange	3.75	3.50
454	"	6f on 8f magenta	3.00	2.75
		a. Perf. 14	100.00	100.00
455	A26	10f on 16f dk. violet	2.00	1.50
456	"	20f on 25f lt. brown	1.50	75
		a. Perf. 14	1.25	75
		Nos. 450-456 (7)	11.50	9.10

St. Elizabeth

A33

Ministering to Children

A34

Photogravure.

1932, Apr. 21 ***Perf. 15*** **Wmk. 210**

458	A33	10f ultramarine	75	40
459	"	20f scarlet	75	40

Perf. 14

460	A34	32f deep violet	2.50	2.25
461	"	40f deep blue	2.25	1.50

Issued in commemoration of the 700th anniversary of the death of St. Elizabeth of Hungary.

Madonna, Patroness of Hungary

A35

1932, June 1 ***Perf. 12***

462	A35	1p yellow green	15.00	50
463	"	2p carmine	16.00	1.00
464	"	5p deep blue	60.00	5.00
465	"	10p olive bistre	150.00	40.00

Nos. 451 and 454 Surcharged **2**

1932, June 14 ***Perf. 15*** **Wmk. 210**

466	A25	2(f) on 6f on 8f magenta	50	20

Wmk. 133

467	A25	2(f) on 6f on 8f magenta	40.00	35.00

Imre Madách A36

Designs: 2f, Janos Arany. 4f, Dr. Ignaz Semmelweis. 6f, Baron Roland Eotvos. 10f, Count Stephen Szechenyi. 16f, Ferenc Deak. 20f, Franz Liszt. 30f, Louis Kossuth. 32f, Stephen Tisza. 40f, Mihaly Munkacsy. 50f, Alexander Csoma. 70f, Farkas Bolyai.

1932 ***Perf. 15.*** **Wmk. 210**

468	A36	1f slate violet	12	8
469	"	2f orange	10	4
470	"	4f ultramarine	10	4
471	"	6f yellow green	10	5
472	"	10f Prussian green	15	4
473	"	16f dull violet	35	10
474	"	20f deep rose	20	4
475	"	30f brown	50	10
476	"	32f brown violet	55	30
477	"	40f dull blue	75	7
478	"	50f deep green	1.00	6
479	"	70f cerise	1.75	10
		Nos. 468-479 (12)	5.67	1.02

Issued in honor of famous Hungarians.
See also Nos. 509-510.

No. 421 Surcharged ≡ **10** ≡

1933, Apr. 15 ***Perf. 14*** **Wmk. 133**

480	A29	10(f) on 70f scarlet	40	12

Leaping Stag and Double Cross

A47

Perf. 15

1933, July 10 **Photo.** **Wmk. 210**

481	A47	10(f) dark green	1.20	80
482	"	16(f) violet brown	4.00	2.00
483	"	20(f) carmine lake	2.00	1.00
484	"	32(f) yellow	7.50	5.00
485	"	40(f) deep blue	6.50	4.25
		Nos. 481-485 (5)	21.20	13.05

Issued to commemorate the Boy Scout Jamboree at Gödöllö, Hungary, July 20 to August 20, 1933.

Souvenir Sheet.

Franz Liszt—A48

1934, May 6 ***Perf. 15***

486	A48	20f lake	70.00	55.00

Second Hungarian Philatelic Exhibition, Budapest, and Jubilee of the First Hungarian Philatelic Society. Sold for 90f, including entrance fee. Size: 64x76mm.

Francis II Rákóczy

A49

1935, Apr. 8 ***Perf. 12***

487	A49	10f yellow green	1.40	75
488	"	16f bright violet	6.00	4.00
489	"	20f dark carmine	1.40	75
490	"	32f brown lake	12.50	6.00
491	"	40f blue	10.00	5.50
		Nos. 487-491 (5)	31.30	17.00

Bicentenary of the death of Francis II Rákóczy (1676-1735), prince of Transylvania.

Cardinal Pázmány

A50

Signing the Charter

A51

1935, Sept. 25

492	A50	6f dull green	2.25	1.50
493	A51	10f dark green	75	50
494	A50	16f slate violet	2.50	1.75
495	"	20f magenta	75	50
496	A51	32f deep claret	5.00	2.25
497	"	40f dark blue	5.00	2.75
		Nos. 492-497 (6)	16.25	9.25

Tercentenary of the founding of the University of Budapest by Peter Cardinal Pázmány.

Ancient City and Fortress of Buda

A52

Guardian Angel over Buda

A53

Shield of Buda, Cannon and Massed Flags

A54

First Hungarian Soldier to Enter Buda

A55

1936, Sept. 2 ***Perf. 11½x12½***

498	A52	10f dark green	60	35
499	A53	16f deep violet	4.50	3.00
500	A54	20f carmine lake	60	35
501	A55	32f dark brown	5.00	3.00
502	A52	40f deep blue	5.00	3.00
		Nos. 498-502 (5)	15.70	9.70

Issued in commemoration of the 250th anniversary of the recapture of Budapest from the Turks.

A56

1937, Feb. 22 ***Perf. 12***

503	A56	2f deep orange	20	20
504	"	6f yellow green	25	20
505	"	10f myrtle green	20	10
506	"	20f deep cerise	30	10
507	"	32f dark violet	85	60
508	"	40f ultramarine	1.00	50
		Nos. 503-508 (6)	2.80	1.70

Budapest International Fair.

Portrait Type of 1932.

Designs:
5f, Ferenc Kolcsey. 25f, Mihaly Vorosmarty.

1937, May 5 ***Perf. 15***

509	A36	5f brown orange	12	8
510	"	25f olive green	35	12

Pope Sylvester II, Archbishop Astrik

A59

Admiral Horthy

A67

Designs: 2f, 16f, Stephen the Church builder. 4f, 20f, St. Stephen enthroned. 5f, 25f, Sts. Gerhardt, Emerich, Stephen. 6f, 30f, St. Stephen offering holy crown to Virgin Mary. 10f, same as 1f. 32f, 50f, Portrait of St. Stephen. 40f, Madonna and Child. 70f, Crown of St. Stephen.

1938, Jan. 1 ***Perf. 12***

511	A59	1f deep violet	20	10
512	"	2f olive brown	15	6
513	"	4f bright blue	30	5
514	"	5f magenta	30	20
515	"	6f deep yel. green	30	12
516	"	10f red orange	40	5
517	"	16f gray violet	50	40
518	"	20f carmine lake	50	6
519	"	25f dark green	60	50
520	"	30f olive bistre	1.00	10
521	"	32f dp. claret, *buff*	1.75	1.25
522	"	40f Prus. green	1.25	15
523	"	50f rose violet, *greenish*	2.00	40
524	"	70f olive green, *bluish*	3.50	60
		Nos. 511-524 (14)	12.75	4.04

Issued in commemoration of the 900th anniversary of the death of St. Stephen.

1938, Jan. 1 *Perf. 12½x12*

525 A67 1p peacock green 75 15
526 " 2p brown 1.50 35
527 " 5p sapphire blue 5.00 2.00

Philatelic Exhibition Issue.
Souvenir Sheet.

St. Stephen
A68

1938, May 22 *Perf. 12* **Wmk. 210**

528 A68 20f carmine lake 12.00 10.00

Issued for the third Hungarian Philatelic Exhibition, Budapest. Green marginal inscription. Size: 146x106mm. Sheet sold only at exhibition with ticket (1p) for 1.20p.

College of Debrecen
A69

Three Students A71 George Maróthy A73

Designs: 10f, 18th century view of College. 20f, 19th century view of College. 40f, Stephen Hatvani.

Inscribed:
"Debreceni Collegium 1538-1938"
Perf. 12x12½, 12½x12

1938, Sept. 24 **Wmk. 210**

529 A69 6f deep green 20 10
530 " 10f brown 15 8
531 A71 16f brown carmine 30 25
532 A69 20f crimson 25 8
533 A73 32f slate green 85 40
534 " 40f bright blue 1.00 30
Nos. 529-534 (6) 2.75 1.21

Issued in commemoration of the 400th anniversary of the founding of Debrecen College.

Types of 1938
Overprinted in Blue or Carmine:

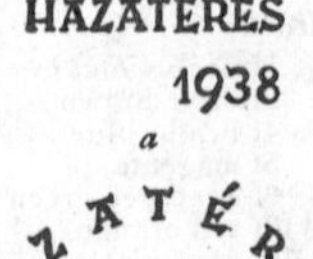

a

b

1938 *Perf. 12*

535 A59 (*a*) 20f salmon pink (Bl) 1.00 30
536 A59 (*b*) 70f brown, *greenish* (C) 1.00 35

Restoration of the territory ceded by Czechoslovakia.

The 70f exists without overprint. Price, unused, $1,650; used, $1,400.

Crown of St. Stephen A75 St. Stephen A76

Madonna, Patroness of Hungary
A77

Coronation Church, Budapest A78 Reformed Church, Debrecen A79

Cathedral, Esztergom A80 Deak Square Evangelical Church, Budapest A81

Cathedral of Kassa—A82

Perf. 15

1939, June 1 **Photo.** **Wmk. 210**

537 A75 1f brown carmine 4 3
538 " 2f Prussian green 3 3
539 " 4f ochre 5 3
540 " 5f brown violet 6 3
541 " 6f yellow green 5 3
542 " 10f bistre brown 6 3
543 " 16f rose violet 5 4
544 A76 20f rose red 7 3
545 A77 25f blue gray 8 6

Perf. 12

546 A78 30f red violet 40 5
547 A79 32f brown 20 8
548 A80 40f greenish blue 30 5
549 A81 50f olive 30 5
550 A82 70f henna brown 40 5
Nos. 537-550 (14) 2.09 59

See also Nos. 578-596.

Girl Scout Sign and Olive Branch
A83

Designs: 6f, Scout lily, Hungary's shield, Crown of St. Stephen. 10f, Girls in Scout hat and national headdress. 20f, Dove and Scout emblems.

1939, July 20 **Photo.** *Perf. 12*

Inscribed: "I. Pax-Ting."

551 A83 2f brown orange 40 30
552 " 6f green 60 40
553 " 10f brown 70 40
554 " 20f lilac rose 1.00 75

Girl Scout Jamboree at Gödöllö.

Admiral Horthy at Szeged, 1919
A87

Admiral Nicholas Horthy
A88

Cathedral of Kassa and Angel Ringing "Bell of Liberty"
A89

1940, Mar. 1

555 A87 6f green 30 20
556 A88 10f olive black & olive bistre 25 15
557 A89 20f bright rose brown 50 30

Issued in commemoration of the 20th anniversary of the election of Admiral Horthy as Regent of Hungary.

Crown of St. Stephen
A90

1940, Sept. 5

558 A90 10f dark green & yellow 20 10

Issued in commemoration of the recovery of northeastern Transylvania from Romania.

Nos. 542, 544
Overprinted
in Red or Black

DÉL·VISSZATÉR

1941, Apr. 21 *Perf. 15*

559 A75 10f bistre brown (R) 15 8
560 A76 20f rose red (Bk) 20 10

Return of the Bacska territory from Jugoslavia.

Admiral Nicholas Horthy
A92

Photogravure.

1941, June 18 *Perf. 12* **Wmk. 210**

570 A92 1p dark green & buff 35 15
571 " 2p dark brown & buff 75 40
572 " 5p dark rose violet & buff 2.00 1.40

See also Nos. 597-599.

Count Stephen Széchenyi
A93

Count Széchenyi and Royal Academy of Science
A94

Representation of the Narrows of Kazán
A95

Chain Bridge, Budapest
A96

Mercury, Train and Boat
A97

1941, Sept. 21

573 A93 10f dark olive green 10 8
574 A94 16f olive brown 20 20
575 A95 20f carmine lake 20 6
576 A96 32f red orange 35 30
577 A97 40f royal blue 35 25
Nos. 573-577 (5) 1.20 89

Issued in commemoration of the 150th anniversary of the birth of Count Stephen Széchenyi (1791-1860).

Wmk. 266

Types of 1939.

Wmkd. Double Barred Cross, Wreath and Crown. (266)

Perf. 12x12½, 12½x12, 15.

1941-43

578 A75 1f rose lake ('42) 3 3
579 " 3f dark brown 3 3
580 " 5f violet gray ('42) 4 3
581 " 6f light green ('42) 4 3
582 " 8f slate green 3 3
583 " 10f olive brown ('42) 3 3
584 " 12f red orange 3 3
585 A76 20f rose red ('42) 4 3
586 " 24f brown violet 10 8
587 A78 30f lilac ('42) 6 4
588 A82 30f rose red ('43) 5 3
589 A80 40f blue green ('42) 10 4
590 A79 40f gray black ('43) 8 4
591 A81 50f olive green ('42) 10 6
592 A80 50f bright blue ('43) 8 4
593 A82 70f copper red ('42) 10 6
594 A81 70f gray green ('43) 10 4
595 A77 80f brown bistre 12 5
596 A78 80f bistre brown ('43) 12 5
Nos. 578-596 (19) 1.28 77

Horthy Type of 1941.

Perf. 12x12½

1941, Dec. 18 Wmk. 266

597 A92 1p dark green & buff 50 5
598 " 2p dark brown & buff 20 20
599 " 5p dk. rose vio. & buff 30 30

Stephen Horthy
A98

1942, Oct. 15 *Perf. 12*

600 A98 20f black 25 25

To commemorate the death of Stephen Horthy (1904-42), son of Regent Nicholas Horthy, who died in a plane crash.

Arpád
A99

Crown of St. Stephen
A109

Portraits: 2f, King Ladislaus I. 3f, Miklós Toldi. 4f, János Hunyadi. 5f, Paul Kinizsi. 6f, Count Miklós Zrinyi. 8f, Francis II Rákóczy. 10f, Count Andrew Hadik. 12f, Arthur Görgei. 18f, 24f, Virgin Mary, Patroness of Hungary.

1943-45 *Perf.15.*

601 A99 1f greenish black 4 4
602 " 2f red orange 3 3
603 " 3f ultramarine 3 3
604 " 4f brown 3 3
605 " 5f vermilion 5 5
606 " 6f slate blue 4 4
607 " 8f dark olive green 3 3
608 " 10f brown 3 3
609 " 12f deep blue green 3 3
610 " 18f dark gray 5 5
611 A109 20f chestnut brown 3 3
612 A99 24f rose violet 20 8
613 A109 30f bright carmine 5 4
614 " 50f blue 5 4
615 " 80f yellow brown 8 5
616 " 1p green 8 5
616A " 2p brown ('45) 25 20
616B " 5p dark red violet ('45) 30 25
Nos. 601-616B (18) 1.40 1.10

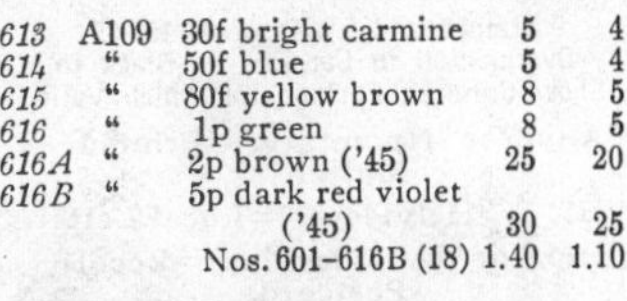

Message to the Shepherds
A110

St. Margaret
A113

Designs: 20f, Nativity. 30f, Adoration of the Magi.

1943, Dec. 1 *Perf. 12x12½*

617 A110 4f dark green 30 20
618 " 20f dull blue 30 20
619 " 30f brown orange 30 20

1944, Jan. 19 *Perf. 15*

620 A113 30f deep carmine 10 5

Canonization of St. Margaret of Hungary.

Kossuth with Family
A114

Lajos Kossuth
A117

Honvéd Drummer
A115

Design: 30f, Kossuth orating.

Perf. 12½x12, 12x12½

1944, Mar. 20

621 A114 4f yellow brown 10 8
622 A115 20f dark olive green 10 6
623 " 30f henna brown 12 8
624 A117 50f slate blue 15 12

To commemorate the 50th anniversary of the death of Louis (Lajos) Kossuth (1802-94).

St. Elizabeth
A118

Portraits: 24f, St. Margaret. 30f, Elizabeth Szilágyi. 50f, Dorothy Kanizsai. 70f, Susanna Lórántffy. 80f, Ilona Zrinyi.

1944, Aug. 1 *Perf. 15*

625 A118 20f olive 5 5
626 " 24f rose violet 8 8
627 " 30f copper red 5 5
628 " 50f dark blue 8 8
629 " 70f orange red 6 6
630 " 80f brown carmine 12 12
Nos. 625-630 (6) 44 44

Issues of the Republic

Types of Hungary, 1943 Surcharged in Carmine

1945, May 1 Wmk. 266

Blue Surface-tinted Paper.

631 A99 10f on 1f greenish black 1.60 1.60
632 " 20f on 3f ultra. 1.60 1.60
633 " 30f on 4f brown 1.60 1.60
634 " 40f on 6f slate bl. 1.60 1.60
635 " 50f on 8f dark olive green 1.60 1.60
636 " 1p on 10f brown 1.60 1.60
637 " 150f on 12f deep blue green 1.60 1.60
638 " 2p on 18f dk. gray 1.60 1.60
639 A109 3p on 20f chestnut brown 1.60 1.60
640 A99 5p on 24f rose vio. 1.60 1.60
641 A109 6p on 50f blue 1.60 1.60
642 " 10p on 80f yellow brown 1.60 1.60
643 " 20p on 1p green 1.60 1.60

Yellow Surface-tinted Paper.

644 A99 10f on 1f greenish black 1.60 1.60
645 " 20f on 3f ultra. 1.60 1.60
646 " 30f on 4f brown 1.60 1.60
647 " 40f on 6f slate bl. 1.60 1.60
648 " 50f on 8f dark olive green 1.60 1.60
649 " 1p on 10f brown 1.60 1.60
650 " 150f on 12f deep blue green 1.60 1.60
651 " 2p on 18f dark gray 1.60 1.60
652 A109 3p on 20f chestnut brown 1.60 1.60
653 A99 5p on 24f rose violet 1.60 1.60
654 A109 6p on 50f blue 1.60 1.60
655 " 10p on 80f yellow brown 1.60 1.60
656 " 20p on 1p green 1.60 1.60
Nos. 631-656 (26) 41.60 41.60

Issued to commemorate Hungary's liberation.

Types of Hungary, 1943-45, Surcharged in Carmine or Black

1945
10
fillér
a

1945

Blue Surface-tinted Paper

657 A99 10f on 4f brown (C) 4 4
658 " 10f on 10f brown (C) 40 40
659 A118 20f on 20f olive (C) 4 4
660 A99 28f on 5f vermilion 4 4
661 A109 30f on 30f brt. car. 4 4
662 A113 30f on 30f dp. car. 4 4
663 A118 30f on 30f copper red 4 4
664 A99 40f on 10f brown 4 4
665 A118 1p on 70f orange red 20 20
666 A109 1p on 80f yellow brown (C) 4 4
667 A99 2p on 4f brown 4 4
668 A109 2p on 2p brown (C) 7 7
669 " 4p on 30f brt. car. 4 4
670 A118 8p on 20f olive 4 4
671 A99 10p on 2f red org. 5.50 5.50
672 A109 10p on 80f yel. brn. 4 4
673 A118 20p on 30f copper red 4 4

Same Surcharge with Thinner Unshaded Numerals of Value.

673A A113 300p on 30f deep carmine 6 6

Surcharged Type "a."

Yellow Surface-tinted Paper.

674 A99 10f on 12f deep blue green (C) 4 4
675 " 20f on 1f greenish black (C) 4 4
676 A99 20f on 18f dark gray (C) 4 4
a. Double surcharge
677 " 40f on 24f rose violet (C) 6 6
678 A118 40f on 24f rose violet (C) 6 6
679 A109 42f on 20f chestnut brown (C) 5 5
680 " 50f on 50f blue (C) 4 4
681 A118 50f on 50f dark blue (C) 4 4
682 A99 60f on 8f dark olive green (C) 4 4
683 A118 80f on 24f rose violet 10 10
684 " 80f on 80f brown carmine (C) 4 4
685 A109 1p on 20f chestnut brown 6 6
686 " 1p on 1p green (C) 4 4
687 A99 1.50p on 6f slate blue (C) 1.00 1.00
688 " 1.60p on 12f deep blue green 5 5
689 " 3p on 3f ultramarine (C) 20 20
690 A118 3p on 50f dark blue 5 5
691 A99 5p on 8f dark olive green 5 5
692 A109 5p on 5p dark red violet (C) 25 25
693 " 6p on 50f blue 8 8
694 " 7p on 1p green 5 5
695 A99 9p on 1f greenish black 5 5

Same Surcharge with Thinner, Unshaded Numerals of Value.

696 A99 40p on 8f dark olive green 4 4
697 " 60p on 18f dark gray 4 4
698 " 100p on 12f deep blue green 4 4
Nos. 657-698 (43) 9.30 9.30

Various shades and errors of overprint exist on Nos. 657-698.

These surface-tinted stamps exist without surcharge, but were not so issued.

Construction
A124

Designs: 1.60p, Manufacturing. 2p, Railroading. 3p, Building. 5p, Agriculture. 8p, Communications. 10p, Architecture. 20p, Writing.

Perf. 12

1945, Sept. 11 Photo. Wmk. 266

700 A124 40f gray black 5.00 5.00
701 " 1.60p olive bistre 5.00 5.00
702 " 2p slate green 5.00 5.00
703 " 3p dark purple 5.00 5.00
704 " 5p dark red 5.00 5.00
705 " 8p brown 5.00 5.00
706 " 10p deep claret 5.00 5.00
707 " 20p slate blue 5.00 5.00
Nos. 700-707 (8) 40.00 40.00

Issued to commemorate the World Trade Union Conference, Paris, September 25 to October 10, 1945.

"Reconstruction"
A132

1945-46

708 A132 12p brown olive 18 20
709 " 20p bright green 3 3
710 " 24p orange brown 20 25
711 " 30p gray black 3 3
712 " 40p olive green 3 3
713 " 60p red orange 5 5
714 " 100p orange yellow 4 4

715 A132 120p bright ultra. 3 3
716 " 140p bright red 25 30
717 " 200p olive brown 5 5
718 " 240p bright blue 6 5
719 " 300p dark carmine 6 5
720 " 500p dull green 8 8
721 " 1000p red violet 8 6
722 " 3000p bright red ('46) 15 20
Nos. 708-722 (15) 1.32 1.45

Nos. 708 to 721 exist tête bêche. Price: 2½ times the price of a single.

"Liberation" A133 — Postrider A134

1946, Feb. 12

723 A133 3000p dark red 8 10
724 " 15,000p ultramarine 10 15

Photogravure; Values Typographed

1946 ***Perf. 15.***

725 A134 4000p brown orange 6 8
726 " 10,000p bright red 6 8
727 " 15,000p ultramarine 6 8
728 " 20,000p dark brown 6 8
729 " 30,000p red violet 6 8
730 " 50,000p gray black 6 8
731 " 80,000p bright ultra. 6 8
732 " 100,000p rose carmine 6 8
733 " 160,000p gray green 6 8
734 " 200,000p yellow green 8 10
735 " 500,000p red 12 15
736 " 640,000p olive bistre 12 15
737 " 800,000p rose violet 5 6
Nos. 725-737 (13) 91 1.18

Abbreviations:
Ez (Ezer) = Thousand
Mil (Milpengo) = Million
Mlrd (Milliard) = Billion
Bil (Billio-pengo) = Trillion

Arms of Hungary
A135

Photogravure; Values Typographed.

1946 **Wmk. 210**

738 A135 1mil p vermilion 20 25
739 " 2mil p ultramarine 20 25
740 " 3mil p brown 4 5
741 " 4mil p slate gray 15 16
742 " 5mil p rose violet 4 8
743 " 10mil p green 4 8
744 " 20mil p carmine 4 8
745 " 50mil p olive 4 8

Arms and Post Horn
A136 A137

746 A136 100mil p henna brown 4 5
747 " 200mil p " 4 5
748 " 500mil p " 10 12
749 " 1000mil p " 4 5
750 " 2000mil p " 4 5
751 " 3000mil p " 4 5
752 " 5000mil p " 4 6
753 " 10,000mil p " 4 10
754 " 20,000mil p " 15 18
755 " 30,000mil p " 15 18
756 " 50,000mil p " 20 25

Denomination in Carmine.

757 A137 100mlrd p olive 5 8
758 " 200mlrd p " 5 8
759 " 500mlrd p " 5 8

Dove and Letter
A138

Denomination in Carmine

760 A138 1bil p greenish blk. 12 20
761 " 2bil p " 12 20
763 " 5bil p " 6 10
764 " 10bil p " 6 10
765 " 20bil p " 6 10
766 " 50bil p " 6 10
767 " 100bil p " 6 10
768 " 200bil p " 8 10
769 " 500bil p " 8 10
770 " 1000bil p " 8 10
771 " 10,000bil p " 12 30
772 " 50,000bil p " 15 30
773 " 100,000bil p " 20 20
774 " 500,000bil p " 20 40

Denomination in Black.

775 A137 5ez ap green 6 8
776 " 10ez ap " 6 8
777 " 20ez ap " 6 8
778 " 50ez ap " 6 8
779 " 80ez ap " 6 8
780 " 100ez ap " 6 8
781 " 200ez ap " 6 8
782 " 500ez ap " 6 8
783 " 1mil ap vermilion 6 12
784 " 5mil ap " 6 12
Nos. 738-784 (46) 3.83 5.69

Denominations are expressed in "ado" or "tax" pengos.

Early Steam Locomotive
A139

Designs: 20,000ap, Recent steam locomotive. 30,000ap, Electric locomotive. 40,000ap, Diesel locomotive.

1946, July 15 ***Perf. 12*** **Wmk. 266**

785 A139 10,000ap violet brn. 2.50 2.50
786 " 20,000ap dark blue 2.50 2.50
787 " 30,000ap deep yellow green 2.50 2.50
788 " 40,000ap rose car. 2.50 2.50

Centenary of Hungarian railways.

Industry A143 — Agriculture A144

Photogravure.

1946 ***Perf. 15.*** **Wmk. 210**

788A A143 8f henna brown 25 5
789 " 10f " 25 5
790 " 12f " 25 6
791 " 20f " 25 4
792 " 30f " 20 4
793 " 40f " 20 4
794 " 60f " 30 4
795 A144 1fo dp. yel. grn. 60 4
796 " 1.40fo " 80 4
797 " 2fo " 80 4
798 " 3fo " 1.25 15
799 " 5fo " 2.50 30
800 " 10fo " 6.00 80
Nos. 788A-800 (13) 13.65 1.69

No. 796 was surcharged for Parcel Post. See Nos. Q9-Q11.

Stamps and Types of 1943-45 Overprinted in Carmine or Black to Show Class of Postage for which Valid.

"Any." or "Nyomtatv."=Printed Matter.
"Hl" or "Helyi levél"=Local Letter.
"Hlp." or "Helyi lev.-lap"=Local Postcard.
"Tl." or "Távolsági levél"=Domestic Letter.
"Tlp." or "Távolsági lev.-lap"=Domestic Postcard.

Any. I.
a

Nyomtatv
20 gr.
b

1946 **Wmk. 266**

801 A99 (a) "Any. 1. on 1f greenish black (No. 601) (C) 5 6
802 " (") "Any. 2." on 1f greenish black (No. 601) (C) 4 6
803 " (b) "Nyomtatv. 20gr" on 60f on 8f dark olive green, *yellow* (No. 682) (Bk+C) 5 7
804 A118 (a) "H l. 1" on 50f dark blue (No. 628) (C) 5 5
805 A99 (") "H l. 2" on 40f on 10f brown, *blue* (No. 664) (C+Bk) 4 6
806 " (b) "Helyi levél" on 10f brown, *blue* (Bk) 4 5
807 A118 (a) "Hlp. 1." on 8p on 20f olive, *blue* (No. 670) (C+Bk) 8 5
808 " (") "Hlp. 2." on 8p on 20f olive, *blue* (No. 670) (C+Bk) 10 12
809 " (b) "Helyi lev.-lap" on 20f olive, *blue* (C) 4 5
810 A99 (a) "Tl. 1." on 10f brown (No. 608) (Bk) 4 5
811 " (") "Tl. 2." on 10f on 4f brown, *blue* (No. 657) (Bk+C) 8 10
812 " (b) "Távolsági levél" on 18f dark gray (No. 610) (C) 6 8
813 " (a) "Tlp. 1." on 4f brown (No. 604) (Bk) 10 12
814 " (") "Tlp. 2." on 4f brown (No. 604) (Bk) 8 10
815 " (b) "Távolsági lev.-lap" on 4f brown (No. 604) (Bk) 4 5
Nos. 801-815 (15) 89 1.07

Nos. 806 and 809 were not issued without overprint.

György Dózsa
A145

Designs: 10f, Antal Budai-Nagy. 12f, Tamas Esze. 20f, Ignac Martinovics. 30f, Janos Batsanyi. 40f, Lajos Kossuth. 60f, Mihaly Tancsics. 1fo, Alexander Petőfi. 2fo, Andreas Ady. 4fo, Jozsef Attila.

1947, Mar. 15 **Photo.** **Wmk. 210**

816 A145 8f rose brown 10 5
817 " 10f deep ultramarine 10 4
818 A145 12f deep brown 10 4
819 " 20f dark yellow green 10 3
820 " 30f dark olive bistre 12 3
821 " 40f brown carmine 20 3
822 " 60f cerise 30 3
823 " 1fo dp. greenish blue 45 5
824 " 2fo dark violet 1.20 25
825 " 4fo greenish black 2.00 55
Nos. 816-825 (10) 4.67 1.10

Peace and Agriculture A155 — Postal Savings Emblem A156

1947, Sept. 22 ***Perf. 12***

826 A155 60f bright red 40 20

Peace treaty.

1947, Oct. 31

Design: 60f, Postal Savings Bank, Budapest.

827 A156 40f rose brown 20 6
828 " 60f brt. rose carm. 30 6

Issued to publicize Savings Day, October 31, 1947.

Hungarian Flag
A157

1848 Printing Press
A158

Barred Window and Dove
A159

1848 Shako, Sword and Trumpet
A160

"On your feet Hungarian, the Homeland is Calling!"
A161

Arms of Hungary
A162

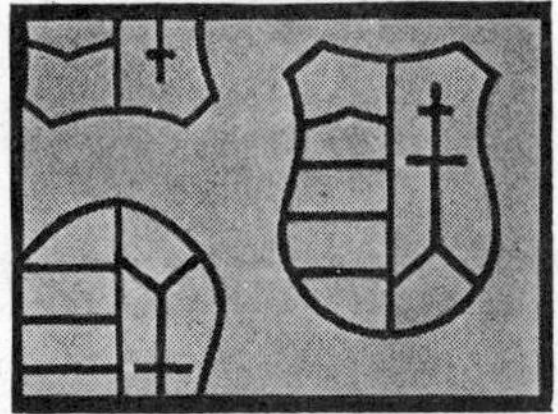
Wmk. 283

Wmkd. Double Barred Cross on Shield, Multiple. (283)

Photogravure.

1948 ***Perf. 12½x12, 12x12½.***

829	A157	8f dark rose red	25	4
830	A158	10f ultramarine	25	4
831	A159	12f copper brown	30	6
832	A160	20f deep green	1.00	4
833	A161	30f olive brown	25	5
834	A157	40f dk. vio. brown	40	5
835	A161	60f carmine lake	80	4
836	A162	1fo bright ultra.	80	6
837	"	2fo red brown	1.25	20
838	"	3fo green	2.00	50
839	"	4fo scarlet	3.50	75
		Nos. 829-839 (11)	10.80	1.83

Issued to commemorate the centenary of the beginning of Hungary's war for independence.

No. 834 is inscribed "Kossuth," No. 835 "Petofi".

Baron Roland Eötvös
A163

1948, July 27

840	A163	60f deep red	35	20

Issued to commemorate the centenary of the birth of Roland Eötvös, physicist.

Hungarian Workers
A164

1948, Oct. 17 ***Perf. 12*** **Wmk. 283**

841	A164	30f dark carmine rose	50	25
		a. Sheet of four	12.00	12.00

The 17th Trade Union Congress, Budapest, October 1948. No 841a was sold for 2 forint.

Marx Stamp of 1919 and Crowd Carrying Flags
A165

Petöfi Stamp of 1919 and Flags
A166

1949, Mar. 19

Flags in Carmine.

842	A165	40f brown	45	30
843	A166	60f olive gray	45	35

Issued to commemorate the 30th anniversary of the first Hungarian Soviet Republic.

Workers of the Five Continents and Flag
A167

1949, June 29 ***Perf. 12x12½***

Flag in Red.

844	A167	30f yellow brown	1.65	1.65
845	"	40f brown violet	1.65	1.65
846	"	60f lilac rose	1.65	1.65
847	"	1fo violet blue	1.65	1.65

Issued to publicize the 2nd Congress of the World Federation of Trade Unions, Milan, 1949.

Sándor Petöfi
A168

Perf. 12½x12

1949, July 31 **Engr.** **Unwmkd.**

848	A168	40f claret	20	15
849	"	60f dark red	25	10
850	"	1fo deep blue	50	20

Issued to commemorate the centenary of the death of Sándor Petöfi, poet.

See also Nos. 867-869.

Youth of Three Races
A169

Designs: 30f, Three fists. 40f, Soldier breaking chain. 60f, Soviet youths carrying flags. 1fo, Young workers displaying books.

Perf. 12½x12

1949, Aug. 14 **Photo.** **Wmk. 283**

Inscribed: "Budapest 1949 VIII 14-28."

851	A169	20f dark violet brown	75	75
		a. 20f blue green	2.00	2.00
852	"	30f blue green	75	75
		a. 30f violet brown	2.00	2.00
853	"	40f olive bistre	90	90
		a. 40f ultramarine	2.00	2.00
854	"	60f rose pink	75	75
855	"	1fo ultramarine	1.50	1.50
		a. 1fo olive bistre	2.00	2.00
		b. Souvenir sheet	25.00	25.00
		Nos. 851-855 (5)	4.65	4.65

Issued to publicize the World Festival of Youth and Students, Budapest, August 14–28, 1949.

No. 855b contains one each of Nos. 851a, 852a, 853a, 854 and 855a. Sheets measure 100x130mm., inscribed "V.I.T. Budapest 1949" in rose pink.

Arms of Hungarian People's Republic
A170

Arms in Bistre, Carmine Blue and Green.

1949 **Wmk. 283**

856	A170	20f green	60	60
857	"	60f carmine	25	25
858	"	1fo blue	40	40

Issued to commemorate the adoption of the Hungarian People's Republic constitution. Nos. 856-858 also exist unwatermarked; same price as watermarked.

Imperforates

Nearly all Hungarian stamps from No. 859 on were issued imperforate as well as with perforations. In most cases the imperforate quantities were smaller than the perforated ones. The imperforates were sold at five times face value, and all issued before Feb. 22, 1958, were invalid. Late in 1958, Philatelica Hungarica started selling the imperforates at four to six times face value.

Symbols of the U.P.U.
A171

1949, Nov. 1 ***Perf. 12x12½***

859	A171	60f rose red	35	35
		a. Booklet pane of 6	3.50	
860	"	1fo blue	60	60
		a. Booklet pane of 6	5.50	

Issued to commemorate the 75th anniversary of the formation of the Universal Postal Union.

Nos. 859 and 860 exist imperforate and stamps from 859a and 860a in horizontal pairs, imperforate between.

See Nos. C63, C81.

Chain Bridge—A172

1949, Nov. 20 **Wmk. 283**

861	A172	40f blue green	25	20
862	"	60f red brown	30	25
863	"	1fo blue	40	30
		Nos. 861-863, C64-C65 (5)	2.30	1.95

Issued to commemorate the centenary of the opening of the Chain Bridge at Budapest to traffic. For souvenir sheet see No. C66.

Joseph V. Stalin
A173

Perf. 12½x12

1949, Dec. 21 **Engr.** **Unwmkd.**

864	A173	60f dark red	30	12
865	"	1fo deep blue	40	15
866	"	2fo brown	80	50

Issued to commemorate the 70th anniversary of the birth of Joseph V. Stalin.

See also Nos. 1034-1035.

Petöfi Type of 1949.

1950, Feb. 5 ***Perf. 12½x12***

867	A168	40f brown	15	10
868	"	60f dark carmine	25	15
869	"	1fo dark green	60	25

Philatelic Museum, Budapest
A174

Perf. 12x12½

1950, Mar. 12 **Photo.** **Wmk. 283**

870	A174	60f gray & brown	1.50	1.25

Issued to commemorate the 20th anniversary of the establishment of the Hungarian Post Office Philatelic Museum. See also No. C68.

Coal Mining
A175

Designs: 10f, Heavy industry. 12f, Power production. 20f, Textile industry. 30f, "Cultured workers." 40f, Mechanized agriculture. 60f, Village cooperative. 1fo, Train. 1.70fo, "Holiday." 2fo, Defense. 3fo, Shipping. 4fo, Livestock. 5fo, Engineering. 10fo, Sports.

1950 **Wmk. 283**

871	A175	8f gray	45	30
872	"	10f claret	45	20
873	"	12f orange vermilion	80	60
874	"	20f blue green	40	10
875	"	30f rose violet	50	10
876	"	40f sepia	50	10
877	"	60f red	60	10
878	"	1fo gray brown, yellow & lilac	2.50	40
879	"	1.70fo dk. grn. & yel.	6.00	65
880	"	2fo violet brown & cream	3.50	35
881	"	3fo slate & cream	5.00	25
882	"	4fo black brown & salmon	30.00	5.50
883	"	5fo rose violet & yellow	20.00	2.00
884	"	10fo dk. brn. & yel.	60.00	10.00
		Nos. 871-884 (14)	130.70	20.65

Issued to publicize Hungary's Five Year Plan. See also Nos. 945-958.

Citizens Welcoming Liberators
A176

1950, Apr. 4 ***Perf. 12*** **Unwmkd.**

885	A176	40f gray black	25	15
886	"	60f rose brown	20	10
887	"	1fo deep blue	25	15
888	"	2fo brown	60	60

Issued to commemorate the fifth anniversary of Hungary's liberation.

Chess Players
A177

Wmk. 106

Design: 1fo, Iron Workers Union building and chess emblem.

Wmkd. Multiple Star. (106)

1950, Apr. 9

889	A177	60f deep magenta	75	30
890	"	1fo deep blue	1.25	40

Issued to publicize the World Chess Championship Matches, Budapest. See also No. C69.

Workers Symbolizing International Proletariat
A178

Design: 60f, Blast furnace, tractor, workers holding May pole.

1950, May 1

891	A178	40f orange brown	25	20
892	"	60f rose carmine	15	5
893	"	1fo deep blue	75	15

Issued to publicize Labor Day, May 1, 1950.

Liberty, Cogwheel, Dove and Globes—A179

Inscribed: "1950. V. 10.-24."

Design: 60f, Three workers and flag.

1950, May 10 Photo. *Perf. 12x12½*

894	A179	40f olive green	25	15
895	"	60f dark carmine	40	6

Issued to publicize the meeting of the World Federation of Trade Unions, Budapest, May 1950.

Doctor Inspecting Baby's Bath
A180

Designs: 30f, Physical Culture. 40f, Education. 60f, Boys' Camp. 1.70fo, Model plane building.

1950, June 4 Wmk. 106

896	A180	20f gray & brown	75	40
897	"	30f brown & rose lake	40	10
898	"	40f indigo & dk. grn.	40	10
899	A180	60f brn. & henna brn.	40	10
900	"	1.70fo dp. grn. & gray	1.50	60
		Nos. 896-900 (5)	3.45	1.30

Issued to publicize Children's Day.

No. 899 is inscribed, "SZABAD HAZABAN BOLDOG IFJUSAG" (Happy Youth in a Free Fatherland). Essays exist with the inscription: "UTANPOTLASUNK A JOVO HARCAIHOZ" (Youth is Our Reserve for Future Battles).

Youths Marching on Globe
A181

Working Man and Woman
A182

Designs: 30f, Foundry worker. 60f, Workers on Mt. Gellert. 1.70fo, Worker, peasant and student; flags.

Inscribed: "Budapest 1950. VI. 17-18."

Perf. 12x12½, 12½x12.

1950, June 17

901	A181	20f dark green	40	40
902	"	30f dp. red orange	15	5
903	A182	40f dark brown	15	5
904	"	60f deep claret	25	5
905	"	1.70fo dark olive green	65	20
		Nos. 901-905 (5)	1.60	75

Issued to publicize the First Congress of the Working Youth, Budapest, June 17–18, 1950.

Peonies—A183

Designs: 40f, Anemones. 60f, Pheasant's-eye. 1fo, Geraniums. 1.70fo, Bluebells.

Engraved and Lithographed.

Perf. 12½x12

1950, Aug. 20 Unwmkd.

906	A183	30f rose brown, rose pink & green	60	25
907	"	40f dark green, lilac & yellow	75	30
908	"	60f red brown, yel. & green	1.50	60
909	"	1fo purple, red & green	4.00	2.50
910	"	1.70fo dark violet & green	4.50	2.00
		Nos. 906-910 (5)	11.35	5.65

Miner
A184

Designs: 60f, High speed lathe. 1fo, Prefabricated building construction.

Perf. 12x12½

1950, Oct. 7 Photo. Wmk. 106

911	A184	40f brown	16	10
912	"	60f carmine rose	20	10
913	"	1fo bright blue	75	50

Issued to publicize the 2nd National Exhibition of Inventions.

Gen. Josef Bem and Battle at Piski
A185

Perf. 12½x12

1950, Dec. 10 Engr. Unwmkd.

914	A185	40f dark brown	35	30
915	"	60f deep carmine	40	15
916	"	1fo deep blue	85	35

Gen. Josef Bem, death centenary.
See No. C80.

Signing Petition A186

Peace Demonstrator Holding Dove A187

Design: 1fo, Mother and Children with soldier.

Perf. 12

1950, Nov. 23 Photo. Wmk. 106

917	A186	40f ultramarine & red brown	6.00	6.00
918	A187	60f red orange & dark green	1.75	1.75
919	A186	1fo olive green & dark brown	7.50	7.50

Women Swimmers
A188

Designs: 20f, Vaulting. 1fo, Mountain climbing. 1.70fo, Basketball. 2fo, Motorcycling.

1950, Dec. 2 *Perf. 12x12½*

920	A188	10f blue & gray	30	15
921	"	20f salmon & dark brown	30	20
922	"	1fo olive & green	75	40
923	"	1.70fo vermilion & brn. carmine	1.25	80
924	"	2fo salmon & pur.	2.25	1.25
		Nos. 920-924, C82-C86 (10)	10.00	6.20

Canceled to Order

The government stamp agency started about 1950 to sell canceled sets of new issues. Prices in the second ("used") column are for these canceled-to-order stamps. Postally used copies are worth more.

Worker, Peasant, Soldier and Party Flag
A189 A190

Designs: 60f, Matthias Rakosi and allegory. 1fo, House of Parliament, columns of workers and banner.

Inscribed:

"Budapest · 1951 · Februar 24."

Perf. 12½x12, 12x12½

1951, Feb. 24

925	A189	10f yellow green	8	5
926	A190	30f brown	12	8
927	"	60f carmine rose	15	12
928	A189	1fo blue	50	20

Issued to publicize the 2nd Congress of the Hungarian Workers' Party.

Mare and Foal
A191

Designs: 30f, Sow and shoats. 40f, Ram and ewe. 60f, Cow and calf.

1951, Apr. 5 *Perf. 12x12½*

929	A191	10f olive bistre & rose brown	30	15
930	"	30f rose brown & olive bistre	50	30
931	"	40f dk. grn. & brn.	75	50
932	"	60f brown orange & brown	1.00	60
		Nos. 929-932, C87-C90 (8)	7.65	5.60

Issued to encourage increased livestock production.

Flags of Russia and Hungary
A192

Russian Technician Teaching Hungarians
A193

Perf. 12½x12, 12x12½

1951, Apr. 4

933	A192	60f brownish carmine	20	4
934	A193	1fo dull violet	35	10

Issued to publicize the "Month of Friendship" between Hungary and Russia, 1951.

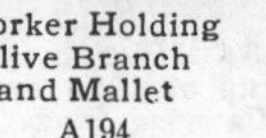

Worker Holding Olive Branch and Mallet
A194

Workers Carrying Flags
A195

Design: 1fo, Workers approaching Place of Heroes.

Perf. 12x12½, 12½x12.

1951, May 1 Photo. Wmk. 106

Inscribed: "1951 Majus 1."

935	A194	40f brown	15	4
936	A195	60f scarlet	25	5
937	A194	1fo blue	30	10

Issued to publicize Labor Day, May 1, 1951.

Leo Frankel

A196

Children of Various Races

A198

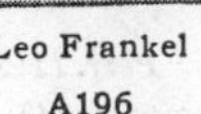

Paris Street Fighting, 1871

A197

1951, May 20

938	A196	60f dark brown	20	5
939	A197	1fo blue & red	30	12

Issued to commemorate the 80th anniversary of the Commune of Paris.

1951, June 3 *Perf. 12½x12*

Designs: 40f, Boy and girl at play. 50f, Street car and Girl Pioneer. 60f, Chemistry students. 1.70fo, Pioneer bugler.

Inscribed:

"Nemzetkozi Gyermeknap 1951."

940	A198	30f dark brown	15	10
941	"	40f green	20	10
942	"	50f brown red	25	10
943	"	60f plum	45	15
944	"	1.70fo blue	85	40
		Nos. 940-944 (5)	1.90	85

Issued to publicize the International Day of Children, June 3, 1951.

5-Year-Plan Type of 1950.

Designs as Before.

1951-52 *Perf. 12x12½.* **Wmk. 106**

945	A175	8f gray	40	10
946	"	10f claret	30	5
947	"	12f orange vermilion	30	10
948	"	20f blue green	30	5
949	"	30f rose violet	30	5
950	"	40f sepia	30	5
951	"	60f red	40	5
952	"	1fo gray brown, yellow & lilac	50	5
953	"	1.70fo dk. grn. & yel.	1.25	18
954	"	2fo violet brown & cream	1.50	12
955	"	3fo slate & cream	2.00	15
956	"	4fo black brown & salmon	2.50	35
957	"	5fo rose violet & yellow ('52)	3.00	60
958	"	10fo dark brown & yellow ('52)	6.00	2.00
		Nos. 945-958 (14)	19.05	3.90

Maxim Gorky

A199

Perf. 12½x12

1951, June 17 Engr. Unwmkd.

959	A199	60f copper red	20	10
960	A199	1fo deep blue	45	20
961	"	2fo rose violet	1.00	55

15th anniversary of the death of Gorky.

Budapest Buildings.

Railroad Workshop

A200

Building in Lehel Street

A201

Suburban Bus Terminal

A202

Rakosi House of Culture

A203

George Kilian Street School

A204

Central Construction Headquarters

A205

Photogravure.

1951 *Perf. 15* **Wmk. 106**

962	A200	20f green	30	3
963	A201	30f red orange	20	3
964	A202	40f brown	40	3
965	A203	60f red	50	3
966	A204	1fo blue	75	3
967	A205	3fo deep plum	2.00	5
		Nos. 962-967 (6)	4.15	20

The original size of Nos. 962-967, 22x18mm., was changed to 21x17mm. starting in 1958. Prices are the same. See also Nos. 1004-11, 1048-56.

Tractor Manufacture—A206

Designs: 30f, Fluoroscope examination. 40f, Checking lathework. 60f, Woman tractor operator.

1951, Aug. 20 *Perf. 12x12½*

968	A206	20f black brown	10	4
969	"	30f deep blue	10	4
970	"	40f crimson rose	15	4
971	"	60f brown	30	10
		Nos. 968-971, C91-C93 (7)	2.55	1.07

Issued to publicize the successful conclusion of the first year under Hungary's 5-year plan.

Soldiers of the People's Army

A207

1951, Sept. 29

972	A207	1fo brown	35	15

Issued to publicize Army Day, Sept. 29, 1951. See also No. C94.

A little time given to study of the arrangement of the Scott Catalogue can make it easier to use effectively.

Stamp of 1871, Portrait Replaced by Postmark

A208

Cornflower

A209

Perf. 12½x12

1951, Sept. 12 Engr. Unwmkd.

973	A208	60f olive green	1.50	1.20

Issued to commemorate the 80th anniversary of Hungary's first postage stamp. See Nos. B207-B208, C95, CB13-CB14.

1951, Nov. 4 Engr. & Litho.

Flowers: 40f, Lily of the Valley. 60f, Tulip. 1fo, Poppy. 1.70fo, Cowslip.

Foliage in Yellow Green.

974	A209	30f red violet & blue	40	10
975	"	40f dark green	75	75
976	"	60f vio. brn. & pink	60	15
977	"	1fo indigo & salmon	90	40
978	"	1.70fo red brn. & yel.	1.80	60
		Nos. 974-978 (5)	4.45	2.00

Storming of the Winter Palace

A210

Designs: 60f, Lenin speaking to soldiers. 1fo, Lenin and Stalin.

Perf. 12x12½

1951, Nov. 7 Photo. Wmk. 106

979	A210	40f gray green	25	10
980	"	60f deep blue	20	8
981	"	1fo rose lake	35	20

Issued to commemorate the 34th anniversary of the Russian Revolution.

Marchers Passing Stalin Monument

A211

1951, Dec. 16 Wmk. 106

982	A211	60f henna brown	15	10
983	"	1fo deep blue	35	20

Joseph V. Stalin, 72nd birthday.

Grand Theater, Moscow

A212

Views of Moscow: 1fo, Lenin Mausoleum. 1.60fo, Kremlin.

1952, Feb. 20 *Perf. 12*

984	A212	60f olive green & rose brown	30	15
985	"	1fo lilac rose & olive brown	60	30
986	"	1.60fo red brn. & olive	80	50

Hungarian-Soviet Friendship Month.

Rakosi and Farmers—A213

Matyas Rakosi

A214

Design: 2fo, Rakosi and Workers.

Perf. 12x12½, 12½x12.

1952, Mar. 9 Engr. Unwmkd.

987	A213	60f deep plum	20	5
988	A214	1fo dark red brown	20	8
989	A213	2fo deep violet blue	80	30

Issued to commemorate the 60th anniversary of the birth of Matyas Rakosi, communist leader.

Lajos Kossuth and Speech at Debrecen

A215

Designs: 30f, Sándor Petőfi. 50f, Gen. Josef Bem. 60f, Michael Tancsics. 1fo, Gen. János Damjanich. 1.50fo, Gen. Alexander Nagy.

1952, Mar. 15 *Perf. 12*

990	A215	20f green	20	15
991	"	30f rose violet	20	15
992	"	50f greenish black	40	30
993	"	60f brown carmine	30	15
994	"	1fo blue	50	30
995	"	1.50fo reddish brown	90	55
		Nos. 990-995 (6)	2.50	1.60

Heroes of the 1848 revolution.

No. B204 Surcharged in Black with Bars Obliterating Inscription and Surtax.

Perf. 12½x12

1952, Apr. 27 Photo. Wmk. 283

996	SP121	60f magenta	35.00	35.00

Budapest Philatelic Exhibition. Counterfeits exist.

Girl Drummer Leading Parade

A216

Designs: 60f, Workers and soldier. 1fo, Worker, flag-encircled globe and dove.

Perf. 12x12½

1952, May 1 Photo. Wmk. 106

997	A216	40f dark green & dull red	15	15
998	"	60f dark red brown & dull red	20	10
999	"	1fo sepia & dull red	45	20

Issued to publicize Labor Day, May 1, 1952.

Runner
A217

Designs: 40f, Swimmer. 50f, Fencer. 1fo, Woman gymnast.

1952, May 26 ***Perf. 11***

1000	A217	30f dark red brown	30	10
1001	"	40f deep green	35	10
1002	"	60f deep lilac rose	40	15
1003	"	1fo deep blue	70	30
		Nos. 1000-1003, C107-C108 (6)	3.65	2.15

Issued to publicize Hungary's participation in the Olympic Games, Helsinki, 1952.

Building Types of 1951.

Buildings: 8f, School, Stalinvarost. 10f, Szekesfehervar Station. 12f, Building, Ujpest. 50f, Metal works, Inotai. 70f, Grain elevator, Hajdunanas. 80f, Tiszalok dam. 4fo, Miners' union headquarters. 5fo, Workers' apartments, Ujpest.

1952 ***Perf. 15*** **Wmk. 106**

1004	A202	8f green	30	5
1005	A200	10f purple	30	3
1006	A202	12f carmine	30	5
1007	"	50f gray blue	35	6
1008	"	70f yellow brown	35	5
1009	A200	80f maroon	45	5
1010	A202	4fo olive green	2.25	10
1011	"	5fo gray black	3.25	25
		Nos. 1004-1011 (8)	7.55	64

The original size of Nos. 1004-1011 was 22x18mm. Starting in 1958, this was changed to 21x17mm. Prices are the same.

Approaching Train
A218

Design: 1fo, Railroad Construction.

1952, Aug. 10 ***Perf. 12x12½***

1012	A218	60f red brown	40	10
1013	"	1fo dp. olive grn.	60	20

Issued to publicize Railroad Day, Aug. 10, 1952.

Coal Excavator
A219

Design: 1fo, Coal breaker.

1952, Sept. 7

1014	A219	60f brown	20	10
1015	"	1fo dark green	30	20

Issued to publicize Miners' Day, Sept. 7, 1952.

Demand as well as supply determine a stamp's market value. The first is as important as the other.

Lajos Kossuth A220 — Janos Hunyadi A221

Design: 60f, Kossuth statue.

1952, Sept. 19 ***Perf. 12½x12***

1016	A220	40f olive brown, *pink*	30	10
1017	"	60f black brown, *blue*	25	10
1018	"	1fo purple, *citron*	45	20

Issued to commemorate the 150th anniversary of the birth of Lajos Kossuth.

1952, Sept. 28 Engr. Unwmkd.

Portraits: 30f, Gyorgy Dozsa. 40f, Miklos Zrinyi. 60f, Ilona Zrinyi. 1fo, Bottyan Vak. 1.50fo, Aurel Stromfeld.

1019	A221	20f purple	20	5
1020	"	30f dark green	20	5
1021	"	40f indigo	20	5
1022	"	60f dk. violet brn.	20	10
1023	"	1fo dark blue green	45	15
1024	"	1.50fo dark brown	75	45
		Nos. 1019-1024 (6)	2.00	85

Issued to publicize Army Day, Sept. 28, 1952.

Lenin and Conference at Smolny Palace
A222

Designs: 60f, Stalin and Cavalry Attack. 1fo, Marx, Engels, Lenin and Stalin.

1952, Nov. 7 **Wmk. 106**

Portraits in Olive Gray.

1025	A222	40f deep claret	10	10
1026	"	60f gray	15	5
1027	"	1fo rose red	40	10

Russian Revolution, 35th anniversary.

Peasant Woman Holding Wheat
A223

Peace Meeting—A224

Perf. 12½x12, 12x12½

1952, Nov. 22

1028	A223	60f brn. red, *citron*	20	10
1029	A224	1fo brown, *blue*	35	20

Third Hungarian Peace Congress, 1952.

Subway Construction
A225

Design: 1fo, Station and map.

1953, Jan. 19 Photo. ***Perf. 12x12½***

1030	A225	60f dark slate green	20	10
1031	"	1fo brown red	40	15

Issued to commemorate the completion of the Budapest subway extension.

Tank and Flag
A226

Design: 60f, Map of Central Europe and Soldier.

1953, Feb. 18

1032	A226	40f dk. carmine rose	20	6
1033	"	60f chocolate	30	6

Battle of Stalingrad, 10th anniversary.

Joseph V. Stalin
A227

Perf. 12x11½

1953 Engraved Wmk. 106

1034	A227	60f purple black	25	15

Souvenir Sheet.

1035	A227	2fo purple black	9.00	9.00

Death of Joseph Stalin (1879-1953). No. 1035 has red border and inscriptions; size 50x70mm.

Issue dates: 1034, Mar. 27, 1035, Mar. 9.

Workers' Rest Home, Galyateto
A228

Designs: 40f, Home at Mecsek. 50f, Parad Mineral Baths. 60f, Home at Kekes. 70f, Balatonfured Mineral Baths.

1953, April Photo. ***Perf. 12x12½***

1036	A228	30f fawn	20	5
1037	"	40f deep blue	20	5
1038	"	50f dk. olive bistre	20	8
1039	"	60f deep yel. grn.	30	8
1040	"	70f scarlet	40	12
		Nos. 1036-1040 (5)	1.30	38

Young Workers with Red Flags
A229

1953, May 1 ***Perf. 12½x12***

1041	A229	60f brown & red, *yellow*	15	6

Issued to publicize Labor Day, May 1, 1953.

Karl Marx
A230

1953, May 1 Engr. ***Perf. 11½x12***

1042	A230	1fo black, *pink*	40	5

Issued to commemorate the 70th anniversary of the death of Karl Marx. See also No. 1898.

Insurgents in the Forest
A231

Designs: 30f, Drummer and fighters. 40f, Battle scene. 60f, Cavalry attack. 1fo, Francis Rákóczy II.

1953, June 14 Photo. ***Perf. 11***

1043	A231	20f dark olive green & org. red, *greenish*	50	30
1044	"	30f violet brown & red orange	70	35
1045	"	40f gray blue & red orange, *pink*	85	50
1046	"	60f dk. olive brown & orange, *yellow*	1.25	1.00
1047	"	1fo dk. red brown & org. red, *yellow*	2.25	1.25
		Nos. 1043-1047 (5)	5.55	3.40

Issued to commemorate the 250th anniversary of the insurrection of 1703.

Building Types of 1951.

Buildings: 8f, Day Nursery, Ozd. 10f, Medical research institute, Szombathely. 12f, Apartments, Komlo. 20f, Department store, Ujpest. 30f, Brick factory, Maly. 40f, Metropolitan hospital. 50f, Sports building, Stalinvaros. 60f, Post office, Csepel. 70f, Blast furnace, Diosgyor. 1.20fo, Agricultural school, Ajkacsinger Valley. 1.70fo, Iron Works School, Csepel. 2fo, Optical works house of culture.

1953 ***Perf. 15.*** **Wmk. 106**

1048	A204	8f olive green	30	6
1049	"	10f purple	40	3
1050	A205	12f rose carmine	25	8
1051	A204	20f dark green	25	3
1052	"	30f orange	25	3
1053	"	40f dark brown	30	3
1054	A205	50f blue violet	50	10
1055	"	60f rose red	60	3
1056	A204	70f yellow brown	70	3
1056A	A205	1.20fo red	75	4
1056B	A204	1.70fo blue	1.25	10
1056C	"	2fo green	1.50	4
		Nos. 1048-1056C (12)	7.05	60

The original size of Nos. 1048-1056C was 22x18mm. Starting in 1958, this was changed to 21x17mm. Prices are the same.

Cycling
A232

Sports: 30f, Swimming. 40f, Calisthenics. 50f, Discus. 60f, Wrestling.

1953, Aug. 20 *Perf. 11*

Center in Brown

1057	A232	20f orange	35	20
1058	"	30f deep green	25	12
1059	"	40f gray blue	25	12
1060	"	50f olive green	40	20
1061	"	60f olive bistre	50	25
		Nos. 1057-1061 (5)	1.75	89

Opening of the People's Stadium, Budapest. See Nos. C123-C127.

Kazar Costume
A233

Provincial Costumes: 30f, Ersekcsanad. 40f, Kalocsa. 60f, Sioagard. 1fo, Sarkoz. 1.70fo, Boldog. 2fo, Orhalom. 2.50fo, Hosszuheteny.

1953, Sept. 12 **Engraved** *Perf. 12*

1062	A233	20f blue green	60	30
1063	"	30f chocolate	70	30
1064	"	40f ultramarine	1.00	35
1065	"	60f red	1.00	85
1066	"	1fo greenish blue	1.75	1.50
1067	"	1.70fo bright green	3.75	2.50
1068	"	2fo carmine rose	5.50	3.75
1069	"	2.50fo purple	10.00	6.50
		Nos. 1062-1069 (8)	24.30	16.05

See No. 1189.

Lenin
A234

1954, Jan. 21 *Perf. 12* **Wmk. 106**

Designs: 60f, Lenin and Stalin at meeting. 1fo, Lenin, facing left.

1073	A234	40f dark blue green	35	20
1074	"	60f black brown	30	10
1075	"	1fo dk. carmine rose	60	25

30th anniversary, death of Lenin.

Worker Reading
A235

Revolutionary and Red Flag
A236

Design: 1fo, Soldier.

Perf. 12x12½, 12½x12

1954, Mar. 21 **Photogravure**

1076	A235	40f gray bl. & red	1.20	80
1077	A236	60f brown & red	2.00	1.50
1078	A235	1fo gray & red	3.50	2.00

Issued to commemorate the 35th anniversary of the "First Hungarian Communist Republic."

Blood Test
A237

Maypole
A238

Designs: 40f, Mother receiving newborn baby. 60f, Medical examination of baby.

1954, Mar. 8 *Perf. 12*

1079	A237	30f bright blue	12	4
1080	"	40f brown bistre	15	4
1081	"	60f purple	25	5
		Nos. 1079-1081, C146-C148 (6)	2.27	93

1954, May 1 *Perf. 12½x12*

Design: 60f, Flag bearer.

1082	A238	40f olive	24	10
1083	"	60f orange red	30	12

Issued to publicize Labor Day, May 1, 1954.

Farm Woman with Fruit
A239

1954, May 24 *Perf. 12*

1084	A239	60f red orange	30	15

Issued to publicize the 3rd Congress of the Hungarian Workers Party, Budapest, May 24, 1954.

National Museum, Budapest
A240

Peppers
A241

Designs: 60f, Arms of People's Republic. 1fo, Dome of Parliament Building.

1954, Aug. 20 *Perf. 12½x12*

1085	A240	40f bright blue	25	20
1086	A240	60f reddish brown	20	6
1087	"	1fo dark brown	25	15

Fifth anniversary of the People's Republic Constitution.

Engraved, Fruit Lithographed.

1954, Sept. 11

Fruit: 50f, Tomatoes. 60f, Grapes. 80f, Apricots. 1fo, Apples. 1.20fo, Plums. 1.50fo, Cherries. 2fo, Peaches.

Fruit in Natural Colors

1088	A241	40f gray blue	20	10
1089	"	50f plum	20	10
1090	"	60f gray blue	30	15
1091	"	80f chocolate	40	20
1092	"	1fo rose violet	55	30
1093	"	1.20fo dull blue	1.00	60
1094	"	1.50fo plum	1.75	1.25
1095	"	2fo gray blue	2.00	1.25
		Nos. 1088-1095 (8)	6.40	3.95

National agricultural fair.

Maurus Jokai
A242

Janos Apacai Csere
A243

1954, Oct. 17 **Engraved**

1096	A242	60f dark brown olive	45	30
1097	"	1fo deep claret	1.00	75

Issued to commemorate the 50th anniversary of the death of Maurus Jokai, writer.

No. 1097 in violet blue is from the souvenir sheet, No. C157.

1954, Dec. 5 **Photo.** *Perf. 12x12½*

Scientists: 10f, Csoma Sandor Korosi. 12f, Anyos Jedlik. 20f, Ignaz Semmelweis. 30f, Janos Irinyi. 40f, Frigyes Koranyi. 50f, Armin Vambery. 60f, Karoly Than. 1fo, Otto Herman. 1.70fo, Tivadar Puskas. 2fo, Endre Hogyes.

1098	A243	8f dk. violet brown, *yellow*	10	4
1099	"	10f brn. car., *pink*	10	4
1100	"	12f gray, *blue*	15	4
1101	"	20f brown, *yellow*	15	4
1102	"	30f violet blue, *pink*	15	5
1103	"	40f dark green, *yellow*	15	5
1104	"	50f red brown, *pale green*	15	10
1105	"	60f blue, *pink*	20	10
1106	"	1fo olive	50	10
1107	"	1.70fo rose brown, *yellow*	80	35
1108	"	2fo blue green	1.00	50
		Nos. 1098-1108 (11)	3.45	1.41

Readers in Industrial Library
A244

Industry
A245

Designs: 1fo, Agriculture. 2fo, Liberation monument.

1955, Apr. 4 *Perf. 12½x12, 12x12½*

1109	A244	40f dark carmine & olive brown	10	5
1110	A245	60f dark green & red	15	5
1111	"	1fo chocolate & grn.	35	20
1112	A244	2fo bl. grn. & brown	75	40

10th anniversary of Hungary's liberation.

Date, Flags and Farm
A246

1955, May 1 *Perf. 12x12½*

1113	A246	1fo rose carmine	30	8

Labor Day, May 1, 1955.

Government Printing Plant
A247

1955, May 28 **Wmk. 106**

1114	A247	60f gray green & henna brown	25	8

Issued to commemorate the centenary of the establishment of the government printing plant.

Young Citizens and Hungarian Flag
A248

1955, June 15 *Perf. 12*

1115	A248	1fo red brown	35	6

Issued to publicize the second national congress of the Hungarian Youth Organization.

Truck Farmer
A249

Designs: 10f, Fisherman. 12f, Bricklayer. 20f, Radio assembler. 30f, Woman potter. 40f, Railwayman and train. 50f, Clerk and scales. 60f, Postman emptying mail box. 70f, Cattle and herdsman. 80f, Textile worker. 1fo, Riveter. 1.20fo, Carpenter. 1.40fo, Streetcar conductor. 1.70fo, Herdsman and pigs. 2fo, Welder. 2.60fo, Woman tractor driver. 3fo, Herdsman in national costume and horse. 4fo, Bus driver. 5fo, Lineman. 10fo, Coal miner.

1955 *Perf. 12x12½* **Wmk. 106**

1116	A249	8f chestnut	15	3
1117	"	10f Prussian green	15	3
1118	"	12f red orange	20	5
1119	"	20f olive green	20	3
1120	"	30f dark red	30	3
1121	"	40f brown	20	3
1122	"	50f violet blue	20	3
1123	"	60f brown red	20	3
1124	"	70f olive	25	3
1125	"	80f purple	30	8
1126	"	1fo blue	25	3
1127	"	1.20fo olive bistre	30	6
1128	"	1.40fo deep green	60	6
1129	"	1.70fo purple	70	4
1130	"	2fo rose brown	75	5
1131	"	2.60fo vermilion	85	10
1132	"	3fo green	1.20	10
1133	"	4fo peacock blue	1.80	25
1134	"	5fo orange brown	2.50	35
1135	"	10fo violet	4.00	75
		Nos. 1116-1135 (20)	15.10	2.16

Postrider Blowing Horn
A250

1955, June 25 ***Perf. 12½x12***

1136 A250 1fo rose violet 25 20

Hungarian Postal Museum, 25th anniversary.

Mihaly Csokonai Vitez
A251

Portraits: 1fo, Mihaly Vorosmarty. 2fo, Attila József.

1955, July 28 ***Perf. 12***

1137 A251 60f olive black 40 15
1138 " 1fo dark blue 60 25
1139 " 2fo rose brown 1.20 50

Issued to honor three Hungarian poets.

Bela Bartok
A252

1955, Oct. 9

1140 A252 60f light brown 50 35

Issued to commemorate the 10th anniversary of the death of Bela Bartok, composer. See also Nos. C168-C169.

Diesel Train
A253

Designs: 60f, Bus. 80f, Motorcycle. 1fo, Truck. 1.20fo, Steam locomotive. 1.50fo, Dump truck. 2fo, Freighter.

1955, Dec. 20 ***Perf. 14½***

1141 A253 40f green & violet brown 15 6
1142 " 60f deep green & olive 20 10
1143 " 80f olive green & brown 35 12
1144 " 1fo ochre & green 45 15
1145 " 1.20fo salmon & black 80 30
1146 " 1.50fo greenish black & red brown 90 60
1147 " 2fo aqua. & brn. 1.25 80
Nos. 1141-1147 (7) 4.10 2.13

Puli (Sheepdog)
A254

Puli and Steer
A255

Hungarian Pointer
A256

Hungarian Dogs: 60f, Pumi (sheepdog). 1fo, Retriever with fowl. 1.20fo, Kuvasz (sheepdog). 1.50fo, Komondor (sheepdog) and cottage. 2fo, Komondor (head).

Perf. 11x13 (A254), 12

1956, Mar. 17 **Engr. & Litho.**

1148 A254 40f yellow, black & red 25 6
1149 A255 50f blue, bistre & black 20 6
1150 A254 60f yellow green, black & red 25 6
1151 A256 80f bluish green, ochre & black 35 10
1152 " 1fo turquoise, ochre & black 45 15
1153 A254 1.20fo salmon, black & chestnut 75 25
1154 A255 1.50fo ultramarine, black & buff 90 75
1155 A254 2fo cerise, black & chestnut 1.25 1.00
Nos. 1148-1155 (8) 4.40 2.43

Pioneer Emblem
A257

Perf. 12x12½

1956, June 2 **Photo.** **Wmk. 106**

1156 A257 1fo red 25 10
1157 " 1fo gray 25 10

Pioneer movement, 10th anniversary.

Janos Hunyadi Statue
A258

Miner
A259

1956, Aug. 12 ***Perf. 12***

1158 A258 1fo brown, *yellowish* 45 15

Issued to commemorate the 500th anniversary of the defeat of the Turks at the battle of Pecs under Janos Hunyadi.

Printed in sheets of 50 with alternate vertical rows inverted and center row of perforation omitted, providing 25 tête bêche pairs, of which 5 are imperf. between.

1956, Sept. 2

1159 A259 1fo dark blue 35 15

Issued in honor of Miners' Day 1956.

Kayak Racer
A260

Sports: 30f, Horse jumping hurdle. 40f, Fencing. 60f, Women hurdlers. 1fo, Soccer. 1.50fo, Weight lifting. 2fo, Gymnastics. 3fo, Basketball.

1956, Sept. 25 ***Perf. 11*** **Wmk. 106**

Figures in brown olive.

1160 A260 20f light blue 10 6
1161 " 30f light olive green 10 6
1162 " 40f deep orange 10 6
1163 " 60f bluish green 16 10
1164 " 1fo vermilion 24 12
1165 " 1.50fo blue violet 45 24
1166 " 2fo emerald 65 40
1167 " 3fo rose lilac 1.00 60
Nos. 1160-1167 (8) 2.80 1.64

16th Olympic Games at Melbourne, Nov. 22-Dec. 8, 1956.

Franz Liszt
A261

Portrait: 1fo, Frederic Chopin facing left.

1956, Oct. 7 **Photo.** ***Perf. 12x12½***

1168 A261 1fo violet blue 1.25 1.00
1169 " 1fo magenta 1.25 1.00

Nos. 1168 and 1169 alternate in the sheet, forming horizontal se-tenant pairs.

Issued for the 29th Day of the Stamp and sold only at the Philatelic Exhibition together with entrance ticket for 4fo.

Janos Arany
A262

Arms of Hungary
A263

1957, Sept. 15 ***Perf. 12*** **Wmk. 106**

1170 A262 2ft bright blue 60 15

Issued in honor of the 75th anniversary of the death of Janos Arany, poet.

1957, Oct. 1

1171 A263 60f bright red 20 5
1172 " 1fo dp. yellow green 30 8

Trade Union Congress Emblem
A264

1957, Oct. 4

1173 A264 1fo dark carmine 30 5

Issued to publicize the fourth International Trade Union Congress, Leipzig, Oct. 4-15.

Dove and Colors
of Communist Countries—A265

Design: 1fo, Lenin.

1957, Nov. 7 **Litho.** ***Perf. 12***

1174 A265 60f gray, black & multicolor 20 3
1175 " 1fo olive bistre & indigo 30 5

Russian Revolution, 40th anniversary.

Komarom Tumbler Pigeons
A266

Pigeons: 40f, Two short-beaked Budapest pigeons. 60f, Giant domestic pigeon. 1fo, Three Szeged pigeons. 2fo, Two Hungarian fantails.

Perf. 12x12½

1957-58 **Photogravure** **Wmk. 106**

1176 A266 30f yellow green, claret & ochre 15 5
1177 " 40f ochre & black 15 5
1178 " 60f blue & gray 15 6
1179 " 1fo gray & red brn. 50 18
1180 " 2fo bright pink & gray 1.20 40
Nos. 1176-1180, C175 (6) 3.00 1.34

Issued to publicize the International Pigeon Exhibition, Budapest, Dec. 14-16.

Issue dates: 1176, Jan. 12, 1958, others, Dec. 14, 1957.

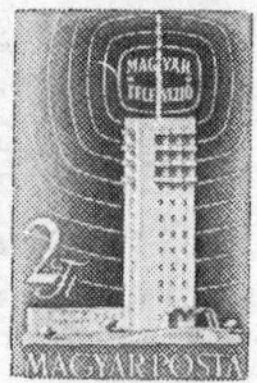

Television Station
A267

1958, Feb. 22 **Engraved** ***Perf. 12***

1181 A267 2fo rose violet 1.20 50

Souvenir Sheet.

1182 A267 2fo green 20.00 20.00

Issued to publicize the television industry.

No. 1182 measures 50½x69½mm. with gold margin inscribed: "To commemorate the Founders of Hungarian Television." Sold for 25fo.

Mother and Child
A268

Designs: 20f, Old man feeding pigeons. 40f, School boys. 60f, "Working ants and fiddling grasshopper." 1fo, Honeycomb and bee. 2fo, Handing over money.

1958, Mar. 9 Photo. *Perf. 12*

1183 A268 20f yellow green & olive gray 10 6
1184 " 30f light olive & maroon 10 6
1185 " 40f yellow bistre & brown 20 15
1186 " 60f rose carmine & greenish black 30 20
1187 " 1fo olive gray & dark brown 50 30
1188 " 2fo orange & olive gray 1.20 50
Nos. 1183-1188 (6) 2.40 1.27

Issued to publicize the value of savings and insurance.

Souvenir Sheet

Kazar Costume Type of 1953.

1958, Apr. 17 Engr. *Perf. 12*

1189 A233 10fo magenta 25.00 25.00

Issued for the Universal and International Exposition at Brussels.

No. 1189 measures 72x98mm. Marginal inscription, arms of Hungary, Belgium and exposition emblem in magenta.

Arms of Hungary
A269

1958, May 23 Litho. Wmk. 106

Arms in Original Colors

1190 A269 60f light red brown & red 10 6
1191 " 1fo gray grn. & grn. 20 8
1192 " 2fo gray & dk. brn. 50 20

Issued to commemorate the first anniversary of the law amending the constitution.

Youth Holding Book
A270

Post Horn and Town Hall, Prague
A271

1958, June 14 Photo. *Perf. 12½x12*

1193 A270 1fo brown carmine 50 15

Issued to publicize the 5th Hungarian Youth Festival at Keszthely.

Printed with alternating label, inscribed: V. IFJUSAGI TALALKOZO KESZTHELY 1958.

1958, June 30

1194 A271 60f green 20 10
a. Se-tenant with No. C184 55

Issued to commemorate the conference of Postal Ministers of Communist Countries at Prague, June 30–July 8.

Nos. 1194 and C184 printed alternating in sheets of 50.

Dolomite Flax—A272

Hungarian Thistles—A273

Flowers: 30f, Kitaibelia vitifolia. 60f, Crocuses. 1fo, Hellebore. 2fo, Lilies. 2.50fo, Pinks. 3fo, Dog roses.

Perf. 11x13, 12½x12 (A273)

1958, Aug. 12 Photo. Wmk. 106

1195 A272 20f red violet & yellow 30 6
1196 " 30f bl., yel. & grn. 20 6
1197 A273 40f brown & bistre 30 6
1198 " 60f blue green & pink 40 10
1199 " 1fo rose carmine & yellow green 50 20
1200 " 2fo grn. & yel. 1.25 25
1201 A272 2.50fo violet blue & pink 1.75 50
1202 " 3fo green & pink 2.25 90
a. Souvenir sheet of 4, perf. 12 25.00 25.00
Nos. 1195-1202 (8) 6.95 2.13

No. 1202a and a similar imperf. sheet were issued for the International Philatelic Congress at Brussels, Sept. 15–17, 1958. They contain the triangular 20f, 30f, 2.50fo and 3fo stamps printed in different colors. Sheets measure 111x111 mm. and are printed on unwatermarked, linen-finish paper. Background of stamps, marginal inscriptions and ornaments in green. No. 1202a also exists perf. 11; same price.

Paddle, Ball and Olive Branch
A274

Designs: 30f, Table tennis player (vert.). 40f, Wrestlers (vert.). 60f, Wrestlers (horiz.). 1fo, Water polo player (vert.). 2.50fo, High dive (vert.). 3fo, Swimmer (horiz.).

1958, Aug. 30 *Perf. 12* Wmk. 106

1203 A274 20f rose red, *pinkish* 15 5
1204 " 30f olive, *greenish* 15 5
1205 " 40f magenta, *yellow* 15 12
1206 " 60f brown, *bluish* 20 12
1207 " 1fo ultramarine, *bluish* 60 20
1208 " 2.50fo dk. red, *yellow* 1.25 55
1209 " 3fo greenish blue, *greenish* 1.50 85
Nos. 1203-1209 (7) 4.00 1.94

The International Wrestling and European Swimming and Table Tennis Championships, held at Budapest.

Red Flag
A275

Design: 2fo, Hand holding newspaper.

1958, Nov. 21 *Perf. 12½x12*

1210 A275 1fo brown & red 20 5
1211 " 2fo dark gray blue & red 40 10

Issued to commemorate the 40th anniversary of the founding of the Hungarian Communist Party and newspaper.

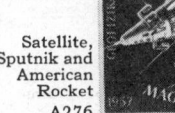

Satellite, Sputnik and American Rocket
A276

Designs: 10f, Eötvös Torsion Balance and Globe. 20f, Deep sea exploration. 30f, Icebergs, penguins and polar light. 40f, Soviet Antarctic camp and map of Pole. 60f, "Rocket" approaching moon. 1fo, Sun and observatory.

1959, Mar. 14 *Perf. 12x12½*

Size: 32x21 mm.

1212 A276 10f carmine rose & sepia 15 6
1213 " 20f bright blue & gray 15 6
1214 " 30f dark slate green & bistre 10 6

Perf. 12

Size: 35x26 mm.

1215 A276 40f slate blue & light blue 25 10

Perf. 15

Size: 58x21 mm.

1216 A276 60f Prussian blue & lemon 40 25

Perf. 12

Size: 35x26 mm.

1217 A276 1fo scarlet & yellow 75 40
1218 " 5fo brown & red brown 2.75 1.00
Nos. 1212-1218 (7) 4.55 1.93

International Geophysical Year.
See No. 1262.

"Revolution"
A277

1959, Mar. 21 *Perf. 12½x12*

1219 A277 20f vio. brn. & red 10 3
1220 " 60f blue & red 20 6
1221 " 1fo brown & red 40 10

Issued to commemorate the 40th anniversary of the proclamation of the Hungarian Soviet Republic.

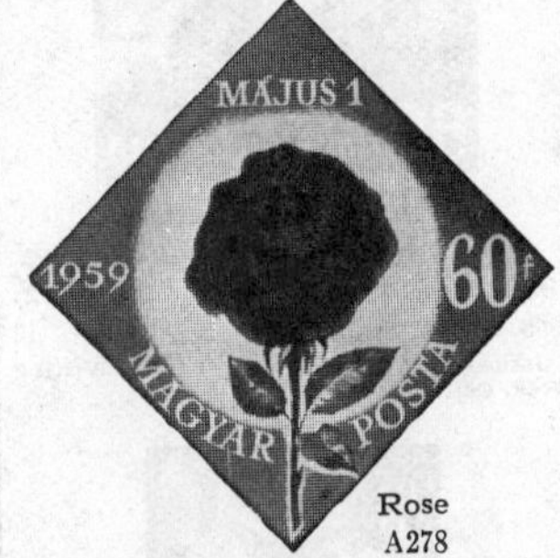

Rose
A278

1959, May 1 Photo. *Perf. 11*

1222 A278 60f lilac, dp. carmine & green 30 10
1223 " 1fo light brown, dull red & grn. 55 20

Issued for Labor Day, May 1, 1959.

Early Locomotive
A279

Designs: 30f, Diesel coach. 40f, Early semaphore (vert.). 60f, Csonka automobile. 1fo, Icarus bus. 2fo, First Lake Balaton steamboat. 2.50fo, Stagecoach.

Lithographed

1959, May 26 *Perf. 14½x15*

1224 A279 20f multicolored 20 5
1225 " 30f " 15 5
1226 " 40f " 20 6
1227 " 60f " 25 8
1228 " 1fo " 25 10
1229 " 2fo " 60 30
1230 " 2.50fo " 75 75
Nos. 1224-1230, C201 (8) 3.15 1.79

Transport Museum, Budapest.

Perf. 10½x11½

1959, May 29 Wmk. 106

1231 A279 2.50fo multi. 2.50 2.75

Designer's name on No. 1231. Printed in sheets of four with four labels to commemorate the congress of the International Federation for Philately in Hamburg.

Post Horn and World Map
A280

1959, June 1 Photo. *Perf. 12*

1232 A280 1fo cerise 40 20

Postal Ministers Conference, Berlin.

Printed in sheets of 25 stamps with 25 alternating gray labels showing East Berlin Opera House.

Great Cormorant
A281

Warrior, 10th Century
A282

Birds 20f, Little egret and nest. 30f, Purple heron and nest. 40f, Great egret. 60f, White spoonbill. 1fo, Gray heron. 2fo, Squacco heron and nest. 3fo, Glossy ibis.

1959, June 14

1233 A281 10f green & indigo 4 5
1234 " 20f gray blue & olive green 6 10
1235 " 30f orange, greenish black & violet 15 10
1236 " 40f dark green & gray 20 12
1237 " 60f deep claret & pale rose 30 15
1238 " 1fo deep blue green & black 40 15
1239 " 2fo deep orange & gray 1.00 30
1240 " 3fo bistre & brown lake 1.65 1.00
Nos. 1233-1240 (8) 3.80 1.97

1959, July 11

Designs: 20f, Warrior, 15th century. 30f, Soldier, 18th century. 40f, Soldier, 19th century. 60f, Cavalry man, 19th century. 1fo, Fencer, assault. 1.40fo, Fencer on guard. 3fo, Swordsman saluting.

1241 A282 10f gray & blue 10 4
1242 " 20f gray & dull yellow 25 4
1243 " 30f gray & gray violet 15 5
1244 " 40f gray & vermilion 15 6
1245 " 60f gray & rose lilac 15 10
1246 " 1fo indigo & light blue green 40 20
1247 " 1.40fo orange & black 75 30
1248 " 3fo black & olive green 1.50 80
Nos. 1241-1248 (8) 3.45 1.59

24th World Fencing Championships, Budapest.

Sailboat, Lake Balaton
A283

Designs: 40f, Vintager and lake (horiz.). 60f, Bathers. 1.20fo, Fishermen. 2fo, Summer guests and ship.

1959, July 11 Photo. Wmk. 106

1249 A283 30f blue, *yellow* 5 3
1250 " 40f carmine rose 8 5
1251 " 60f deep red brown 20 12
1252 " 1.20fo violet 60 20
1253 " 2fo red orange, *yellow* 85 50
Nos. 1249-1253, C202-C205 (9) 3.23 1.90

Issued to publicize Lake Balaton and the opening of the Summer University.

Haydn's Monogram
A284

Esterhazy Palace
A285

Design: 1fo, Joseph Haydn and score.

1959, Sept. 20 *Perf. 12* Wmk. 106

1254 A284 40f deep claret & yellow 20 6
1255 A285 60f Prussian blue, gray & yel. 40 20
1256 A284 1fo dark violet, light brown & orange 75 35

Designs: 40f, Schiller's monogram. 60f, Pegasus rearing from flames. 1fo, Friedrich von Schiller.

1257 A284 40f olive green, & orange 20 6
1258 A285 60f violet blue & lilac 40 20
1259 A284 1fo deep claret & orange brown 75 35
Nos. 1254-1259 (6) 2.70 1.22

Souvenir Sheet

Haydn and Schiller Monograms
A286

Imperf.

1260 A286 Sheet of two 8.50 8.50
a. 3fo magenta 3.00 3.00
b. 3fo green 3.00 3.00

Nos. 1254-56 issued to commemorate the 150th anniversary of the death of Joseph Haydn, Austrian composer; Nos. 1257-59 commemorate the 200th anniversary of the birth of Friedrich von Schiller, German poet and dramatist; No. 1260 honors both Haydn and Schiller.

No. 1260 measures 95 x 75 mm. with gray background and ochre inscriptions and frame around stamps.

Shepherd—A287

1959, Sept. 25 Engr. *Perf. 12*

1261 A287 2fo deep claret 1.80 1.80
a. With ticket 2.25 2.25

Issued to publicize the Day of the Stamp and the National Stamp Exhibition. Issued in sheets of 8 with alternating ticket. The 4fo sale price marked on the ticket was the admission fee to the National Stamp Exhibition.

Type of 1959 Overprinted in Red

1959, Sept. 24 Photo. *Perf. 15.*

1262 A276 60f dull blue & lemon 55 25

Landing of Lunik 2 on moon, Sept. 14.

60f MAGYAR POSTA

Handing over Letter
A288

1959, Oct. 4 Litho. *Perf. 12.*

1263 A288 60f multicolored 25 10

Issued for International Letter Writing Week, Oct. 4-10.

Szamuely and Lenin—A289

Designs: 40pf, Aleksander Pushkin. 60pf, Vladimir V. Mayakovsky. 1fo, Hands holding peace flag.

1959, Nov. 14 Photo. Wmk. 106

1264 A289 20f dark red & bistre 15 10
1265 " 40f brown & rose lilac, *bluish* 15 10
1266 " 60f dk. blue & bistre 20 15
1267 " 1fo blue, carmine, buff, red & grn. 40 25

Soviet Stamp Exhibition, Budapest.

European Swallowtail
A290

Worker with Banner
A291

Butterflies: 30f, Arctia hebe (horiz.). 40f, Lysandra hylas (horiz.). 60f, Apatura ilia.

Perf. 11½x12, 12x11½

1959, Nov. 20

Butterflies in Natural Colors.

1268 A290 20f black & yel. grn. 25 5
1269 " 30f lt. blue & black 40 10
1270 " 40f dark gray & orange brown 45 20
1271 " 60f dark gray & dull yellow 60 25
Nos. 1268-1271, C206-C208 (7) 6.00 2.50

1959, Nov. 30 *Perf. 14½*

Design: 1fo, Congress flag.

1272 A291 60f brn., grn. & red 15 4
1273 " 1fo brown red, red & green 20 6

Issued to commemorate the 7th Congress of the Hungarian Socialist Workers' Party.

Teacher Reading Fairy Tales
A292

Sumeg Castle
A293

Fairy Tales: 30f, Sleeping Beauty. 40f, Matt, the Goose Boy. 60f, The Cricket and the Ant. 1fo, Mashenka and the Three Bears. 2fo, Hansel and Gretel. 2.50fo, Pied Piper. 3fo, Little Red Riding Hood.

1959, Dec. 15 Litho. *Perf. 11½*

Designs in Black

1274 A292 20f gray & multi. 5 5
1275 " 30f bright pink 10 5
1276 " 40f light blue green 20 10
1277 " 60f light blue 20 10
1278 " 1fo yellow 25 12
1279 " 2fo brt. yel. green 65 25
1280 " 2.50fo orange 85 45
1281 " 3fo crimson 1.50 75
Nos. 1274-1281 (8) 3.80 1.87

Perf. 14½

1960, Feb. 1 Photo. Wmk. 106

Castles: 20fr, Tata. 30f, Diosgyor. 60f, Saros-Patak. 70f, Nagyvazsony. 1.40fo, Siklos. 1.70fo, Somlo. 3fo, Csesznek (vert.). 5fo, Koszeg (vert.). 10fo, Sarvar (vert.).

Size: 21x17½mm.

1282 A293 8f purple 3 3
1283 " 20f dark yellow green 4 3
1284 A293 30f orange brown 5 3
1285 " 60f rose red 10 3
1286 " 70f emerald 20 3

Perf. 12x11½, 11½x12

Size: 28x21 mm., 21x28 mm.

1287 A293 1.40fo ultramarine 30 5
1288 " 1.70fo dull violet ("Somló") 30 6
b. 1.70fo dull vio. ("Somlyó") 60 10
1289 " 3fo red brown 50 10
1290 " 5fo yel. green 1.10 25
1291 " 10fo carmine rose 2.25 45
Nos. 1282-1291 (10) 4.87 1.06

Tinted Paper

Perf. 14½

Size: 21x17½mm.

1282a A293 8f purple, *bluish* 10
1283a " 20f dark yellow green, *greenish* 15 5
1284a " 30f orange brown, *yellow* 15 5
1285a " 60f rose red, *pinkish* 20 5
1286a " 70f emerald, *bluish* 25 6

Perf. 12x11½

Size: 28x21mm.

1287a A293 1.40fo ultramarine, *bluish* 30 15
1288a " 1.70fo dull violet, *bluish* 50 20
Nos. 1282a-1288a (7) 1.65 61

See also Nos. 1356-1365, 1644-1646.

Halas Lace
A294

Cross-country Skier
A295

Designs: Various Halas lace patterns.

Perf. 11½

1960, Feb. 15 Litho. Wmk. 106

Sizes: 20f, 60f, 1fo, 3fo: 27x37mm.
30f, 40f, 1.50fo, 2fo: 37½x43½mm.

Inscriptions in Orange.

1292 A294 20f brown black 15 5
1293 " 30f violet 15 5
1294 " 40f Prussian blue 40 6
1295 " 60f dark brown 15 10
1296 " 1fo dark green 25 12
1297 " 1.50fo green 60 18
1298 " 2fo dark blue 1.20 30
1299 " 3fo dark carmine 1.60 75
Nos. 1292-1299 (8) 4.50 1.61

See also Nos. 1570-1577.

Souvenir Sheet

Design as on No. 1299.

1960, Sept. 3

Inscriptions in Orange

1300 Sheet of four + 4 labels 6.50 6.50
a. 3fo brn. olive 1.25 1.25
b. 3fo brt. violet 1.25 1.25
c. 3fo emerald 1.25 1.25
d. 3fo brt. blue 1.25 1.25

Issued to commemorate the Fédération Internationale de Philatélie Congress, Warsaw, Sept. 3-11. No. 1300 contains 4 stamps and 4 alternating labels, printed in colors of adjoining stamps. Bright blue marginal inscriptions. Size: 160x122mm.

Photogravure

1960, Feb. 29 *Perf. 11½x12*

Sports: 40f, Ice hockey player. 60f, Ski jumper. 80f, Woman speed skater. 1fo, Downhill skier. 1.20fo, Woman figure skater.

Inscriptions and Figures in Bister

1301 A295 30f deep blue 10 3
1302 " 40f bright green 15 3
1303 " 60f scarlet 15 3

1304 A295 80f purple 20 6
1305 " 1fo brt. greenish bl. 50 20
1306 " 1.20fo brown red 90 60
Nos. 1301-1306, B217 (7) 3.50 1.65

Issued to commemorate the 8th Olympic Winter Games, Squaw Valley, Calif., Feb. 18-29, 1960.

Clara Zetkin
A296

Portraits: No. 1308, Kato Haman. No. 1309, Lajos Tüköry. No. 1310, Giuseppe Garibaldi. No. 1311, István Türr. No. 1312, Ottó Herman. No. 1313, Ludwig van Beethoven. No. 1314, Ferenc Mora. No. 1315, Istvan Toth Bucsoki. No. 1316, Donat Banki. No. 1317, Abraham G. Pattantyus. No. 1318, Ignaz Semmelweis. No. 1319, Frédéric Joliot-Curie. No. 1320, Ferenc Erkel. No. 1321, Janos Bolyai. No. 1322, Lenin.

1960 Photogravure *Perf. 10½*

1307 A296 60f light red brown 15 3

Engraved.

1308 A296 60f pale purple 15 3
1309 " 60f rose red 15 3
1310 " 60f violet 15 3
1311 " 60f blue green 15 3
1312 " 60f blue 15 3
1313 " 60f gray brown 15 3
1314 " 60f salmon pink 15 3
1315 " 60f gray 15 3
1316 " 60f rose lilac 25 10
1317 " 60f green 15 3
1318 " 60f violet blue 15 3
1319 " 60f brown 20 5
1320 " 60f rose brown 15 3
1321 " 60f greenish blue 15 4
1322 " 60f dull red 25 20
Nos. 1307-1322 (16) 2.65 75

Nos. 1307-1308 commemorate International Women's Day, March 8.

Flower and Quill—A297
Photogravure

1960, Apr. 2 *Perf. 12* Wmk. 106

1323 A297 2fo brown, yellow & green 1.50 1.50
a. With ticket 1.75 1.75

Issued for the stamp show of the National Federation of Hungarian Philatelists. The olive green 4fo ticket pictures the Federation's headquarters and served as entrance ticket to the show. Printed in sheets of 35 stamps and 35 tickets.

Soviet Captain Ostapenko Statue
A298

Designs: 60f, Youth holding flag (horiz.).

Perf. 12½x11½, 11½x12½

1960, Apr. 4

1324 A298 40f deep carmine & brown 10 6
1325 " 60f red brown, red & green 12 6

Issued to commemorate the 15th anniversary of Hungary's liberation from the Nazis.

Boxers
A299

Sports: 10f, Rowers. 30f, Archer. 40f, Discus thrower. 50f, Girls playing ball. 60f, Javelin thrower. 1fo, Rider. 1.40fo, Wrestlers. 1.70fo, Swordsmen. 3fo, Hungarian Olympic emblem.

1960, Aug. 21 *Perf. 11½x12*

Designs in Ochre and Black

1326 A299 10f blue 4 3
1327 " 20f salmon 5 3
1328 " 30f light violet 6 3
1329 " 40f yellow 8 3
1330 " 50f deep pink 15 8
1331 " 60f gray 18 10
1332 " 1fo pale brown violet 50 15
1333 " 1.40fo lt. vio. blue 60 25
1334 " 1.70fo ochre 80 30
1335 " 3fo multicolored 2.50 75
Nos. 1326-1335, B218 (11) 6.31 2.35

Issued to commemorate the 17th Olympic Games, Rome, Aug. 25-Sept. 11.

Souvenir Sheet

Romulus and Remus Statue and Olympic Flame—A300

1336 A300 10fo multi. 20.00 20.00

Issued to commemorate the Winter and Summer Olympic Games, 1960. Size: 66½x94mm.

Woman of Mezokovesd Writing Letter
A301

Perf. 11½x12

1960, Oct. 15 Photo. Wmk. 106

1337 A301 2fo multicolored 1.75 1.75
a. With ticket 2.00 2.00

Issued to publicize the Day of the Stamp and the National Stamp Exhibition. Issued in sheets of 8 with alternating ticket. The 4fo sale price marked on the ticket was the admission fee to the National Stamp Exhibition.

The Turnip, Russian Fairy Tale
A302

Kangaroo
A303

Fairy Tales: 30f, Snow White and the Seven Dwarfs. 40f, The Miller, His Son and the Donkey. 60f, Puss in Boots. 80f, The Fox and the Raven. 1fo, The Maple-Wood Pipe. 1.70fo, The Fox and the Stork. 2fo, Momotaro (Japanese).

1960, Dec. 1 *Perf. 11½x12*

1338 A302 20f multicolored 5 3
1339 " 30f " 6 3
1340 " 40f " 15 3
1341 " 60f " 20 4
1342 " 80f " 25 7
1343 " 1fo " 60 15
1344 " 1.70fo " 1.00 40
1345 " 2fo " 1.30 75
Nos. 1338-1345 (8) 3.61 1.50

1961, Feb. 24 *Perf. 11½x12*

Animals: 30f, Bison. 40f, Brown bear. 60f, Elephants. 80fr, Tiger with cubs. 1fo, Ibex. 1.40fo, Polar bear. 2fo, Zebra and young. 2.60fo, Bison cow with calf. 3fo, Main entrance to Budapest Zoological Gardens. 30f, 60f, 80f, 1.40fo, 2fo, 2.60fo are horizontal.

1346 A303 20f org. & black 5 3
1347 " 30f yel. green & blk. brown 6 3
1348 " 40f orange brown & brown 9 3
1349 " 60f lilac rose & gray 10 5
1350 " 80f gray & yel. 15 8
1351 " 1fo blue green & brown 25 10
1352 " 1.40fo greenish blue, gray & blk. 30 15
1353 " 2fo pink & black 60 35
1354 " 2.60fo bright violet & brown 1.00 50
1355 " 3fo multi. 1.50 75
Nos. 1346-1355 (10) 4.10 2.07

Issued for the Budapest Zoo.

Castle Type of 1960

Castles: 10f, Kisvárda. 12f, Szigliget. 40f, Simon Tornya. 50f, Füzér. 80f, Egervár. 1fo, Vitány. 1.20fo, Sirok. 2fo, Boldogkő. 2.60fo, Hollókő. 4fo, Eger.

1961, Mar. 3 Photo. *Perf. 14½*

Size: 21x17½mm.

1356 A293 10f orange brown 5 3
1357 " 12f violet blue 5 3
1358 " 40f bright green 8 3
1359 " 50f brown 10 3
1360 " 80f dull claret 12 5

Perf. 12x11½

Size: 28x21mm.

1361 A293 1fo bright blue 20 3
1362 " 1.20fo rose violet 25 3
1363 " 2fo olive bistre 50 6
1364 " 2.60fo dull blue 65 10
1365 " 4fo brt. violet 1.00 25
Nos. 1356-1365 (10) 3.00 64

Child Chasing Butterfly
A304

Ferenc Rozsa, Journalist
A305

Designs: 40f, Man on operating table. 60f, Ambulance and stretcher. 1fo, Traffic light and scooter. 1.70fo, Syringe. 4fo, Emblem of Health Information Service (torch and serpent).

1961, March 17 Litho. *Perf. 10½*

Cross in Red

Size: 18x18mm.

1366 A304 30f orange brown & black 10 5
1367 " 40f blue green, blue & sepia 10 5

Size: 25x30mm.

1368 A304 60f bright violet, yel. & gray 15 5
1369 " 1fo multicolored 25 10
1370 " 1.70fo dark gray, dark blue & yellow 75 25
1371 " 4fo gray & yel. green 1.40 75
Nos. 1366-1371 (6) 2.75 1.25

Health Information Service.

Wmk. 106, Unwmkd.

1961 Photogravure *Perf. 12*

Portraits: No. 1373, Gyorgy Kilian. No. 1374, Jozsef Rippl-Ronai. No. 1375, Sandor Latinka. No. 1376, Maté Zalka. No. 1377, Jozsef Katona.

1372 A305 1fo red brown 24 5
1373 " 1fo greenish blue 24 5
1374 " 1fo rose brown 24 15
1375 " 1fo olive bistre 24 5
1376 " 1fo olive green 24 5
1377 " 1fo maroon 24 5
Nos. 1372-1377 (6) 1.44 40

Issued to commemorate variously: Press Day (No. 1372); the inauguration of the Gyorgy Kilian Sports Movement (No. 1373); the birth centenary of Jozsef Rippl-Ronai, painter (No. 1374); the 75th anniversary of the death of Sandor Latinka, revolutionary leader (No. 1375); Maté Zalka, author and revolutionist (No. 1376); Jozsef Katona, dramatist (No. 1377).

Nos. 1374, 1375 and 1377 are unwatermarked. Others in this set have Wmk. 106.

Yuri A. Gagarin and Vostok 1
A306

Roses
A307

Design: 1fo, Launching Vostok 1.

Perf. 11½x12

1961, Apr. 25 Wmk. 106

1381 A306 1fo dark blue & bistre brown 50 50
1382 " 2fo deep ultra. & bistre brown 5.00 5.00

Issued to commemorate the first man in space, Yuri A. Gagarin, Apr. 12, 1961.

1961, Apr. 29 *Perf. 12½x11½*

Design: 2fo, As 1fo, design reversed.

1383 A307 1fo green & deep carmine 25 15
1384 " 2fo green & deep carmine 35 20

Issued for May Day, 1961. Nos. 1383-1384 are printed se-tenant in sheet.

"Venus" and Moon
A308

Designs: Various Stages of Rocket.

1961, May 24 *Perf. 14½* Wmk. 106

1385	A308	40f greenish blue, bis. & black	*60*	*30*
1386	"	60f brt. blue, bistre & black	*80*	*30*
1387	"	80f ultra. & black	*1.50*	*90*
1388	"	2fo violet & yel.	*3.00*	*3.00*

Issued to commemorate the Soviet launching of the Venus space probe, Feb. 12, 1961. No. 1388 was also printed in sheets of four, perf. and imperf. Size: 130x76mm.

Warsaw Mermaid, Letter and Sea, Air and Land Transport—A309

Mermaid and: 60f, Television screen and antenna. 1fo, Radio.

1961, June 19 Photo. *Perf. 13½*

1389	A309	40f red orange & black	15	5
1390	"	60f lilac & black	25	5
1391	"	1fo bright blue & black	45	10

Issued to commemorate the conference of Postal Ministers of Communist Countries held at Warsaw.

Flag and Parliament—A310

Designs: 1.70fo, Orchid. 2.60fo, Small tortoise-shell butterfly. 3fo, Goldfinch.

1961, June 23 *Perf. 11*

Background in Silver

1392	A310	1fo green, red & black	50	50
1393	"	1.70fo red & multi.	65	65
1394	"	2.60fo purple & multi.	1.00	1.00
1395	"	3fo bl. & multi.	1.25	1.25

1961, Aug. 19

Background in Gold

1396	A310	1fo green & blk.	50	50
1397	"	1.70fo red & multi.	65	65
1398	"	2.60fo pur. & multi.	1.00	1.00
1399	"	3fo bl. & multi.	1.25	1.25
		Nos. 1392-1399 (8)	6.80	6.80

Issued to publicize the International Stamp Exhibition, Budapest, Sept. 23–Oct. 3, 1961.

Each denomination of Nos. 1392–1399 printed in sheets of four.

In gold background issue the top left inscription is changed on 1fo and 3fo.

George Stephenson

A311

Winged Wheel, Steering Wheel and Road

A312

Design: 2fo, Jenö Landler.

Perf. 12½x11½

1961, July 4 Photo. Wmk. 106

1400	A311	60f yellow olive	10	5
1401	A312	1fo blue & bistre	25	10
1402	A311	2fo yellow brown	45	20

Issued to commemorate the conference of Transport Ministers of Communist Countries held at Budapest.

Soccer

A313

Sports: 60f, Wrestlers. 1fo, Gymnast.

1961, July 8 *Perf. 14½* Unwmkd.

Emblem and Inscription in Gold, Red & Ultramarine.

1403	A313	40f ochre & black	10	5
1404	"	60f olive green & black	15	8
1405	"	1fo bistre & blk.	40	15

Issued to commemorate the 50th anniversary of the Steel Workers Sport Club (VASAS). See also No. B219.

Galloping Horses

A314

Designs: 40f, Hurdle Jump. 60f, Two trotters. 1fo, Three trotters. 1.70fo, Mares and foals. 2fo, Race horse "Baka." 3fo, Race horse "Kincsem."

1961, July 22

1406	A314	30f multicolored	10	5
1407	"	40f "	15	5
1408	"	60f "	15	5
1409	"	1fo "	50	10
1410	"	1.70fo "	75	15
1411	"	2fo "	1.00	40
1412	"	3fo "	1.50	75
		Nos. 1406-1412 (7)	4.15	1.55

Keyboard, Music and Liszt Silhouette—A315

Liszt Monument, Budapest

A316

Designs: 2fo, Academy of Music, Budapest, and bar of music. 10fo, Franz Liszt.

1961, Oct. 2 *Perf. 12* Unwmkd.

1413	A315	60f gold & black	10	10
1414	A316	1fo dark gray	35	15
1415	A315	2fo dk. blue & gray green	75	40

Souvenir Sheet

1416	A316	10fo multi.	6.00	6.00

Nos. 1413–1416 issued to commemorate the 150th anniversary of the birth, and the 75th anniversary of the death of Franz Liszt, composer. No. 1416 contains one stamp: pale green margin with gold inscription. Size: 70x98mm.

Lenin

A317

Monk's Hood

A318

1961, Oct. 22 *Perf. 11½*

1417	A317	1fo deep brown	20	5

Issued to commemorate the 22nd Congress of the Communist Party of the USSR, Oct. 17–31.

Photogravure

1961, Nov. 4 *Perf. 12* Wmk. 106

Designs: 30f, Centaury. 40f, Blue iris. 60f, Thorn apple. 1fo, Purple hollyhock. 1.70fo, Hop. 2fo, Poppy. 3fo, Mullein.

Flowers in Natural Colors

1418	A318	20f salmon & black	5	4
1419	"	30f pale green & black	8	5
1420	"	40f bright yel. & black	12	8
1421	"	60f pink & black	12	8
1422	"	1fo yellow & blk.	20	10
1423	"	1.70fo lt. bl. & blk.	50	20
1424	"	2fo light yellow & black	1.00	35
1425	"	3fo pale lilac & black	1.25	75
		Nos. 1418-1425 (8)	3.32	1.65

Nightingale

A319

Birds: 40f, Great titmouse. 60f, Chaffinch (horiz.). 1fo, Eurasian jay. 1.20fo, Golden oriole (horiz.). 1.50fo, European blackbird (horiz.). 2fo, Yellowhammer. 3fo, Lapwing (horiz.).

1961, Dec. 18 *Perf. 12* Unwmkd.

1426	A319	30f multicolored	5	3
1427	"	40f "	8	5
1428	"	60f "	12	8
1429	"	1fo "	20	12
1430	"	1.20fo "	30	18
1431	"	1.50fo "	60	20
1432	"	2fo "	85	30
1433	"	3fo "	1.25	65
		Nos. 1426-1433 (8)	3.45	1.61

Mihaly Karolyi

A320

1962, March 18

1434	A320	1fo black	20	5

Issued in memory of Mihaly Karolyi, (1875–1955), Prime Minister of Hungarian Republic (1918–19).

1962, March 29

Portrait: No. 1435, Ferenc Berkes.

1435	A320	1fo red brown	15	5

Issued to commemorate the Fifth Congress of the Hungarian Cooperative Movement, and to honor Ferenc Berkes, revolutionary. See also Nos. 1457, 1459.

Map of Europe, Train Signals and Emblem

A321

1962, May 2 Photogravure

1436	A321	1fo blue green	20	8

Issued to commemorate the 14th International Esperanto Congress of Railway Men.

Xiphophorus Helleri

A322

Tropical Fish: 30f, Macropodus opercularis. 40f, Lebistes reticulatus. 60f, Betta splendens. 80c, Puntius tetrazona. 1fo, Pterophyllum scalare. 1.20fo, Mesogonistius chaetodon. 1.50fo, Aphyosemion australe. 2fo, Hyphessobrycon innesi. 3fo, Symphysodon aequifasciata haraldi.

1962, May 5 *Perf. 11½x12*

Fish in Natural Colors, Black Inscriptions.

1437	A322	20f blue	5	3
1438	"	30f citron	6	3
1439	"	40f light blue	9	3
1440	"	60f lt. yel. green	15	3
1441	"	80f blue green	40	3
1442	"	1fo br. blue grn.	25	5
1443	"	1.20fo blue green	35	10
1444	"	1.50fo greenish blue	50	15
1445	"	2fo green	85	35
1446	"	3fo gray green & yellow	1.30	80
		Nos. 1437-1446 (10)	4.00	1.60

Globe, Soccer Ball and Flags of Colombia and Uruguay

A323

Goalkeeper—A324

Flags of: 40f, U.S.S.R. and Jugoslavia. 60f, Switzerland and Chile. 1fo, Germany and Italy. 1.70fo, Argentina and Bulgaria. 3fo, Brazil and Mexico.

Photogravure

1962, May 21 *Perf. 11* Unwmkd.

Flags in National Colors

1447	A323	30f rose & bistre	15	10
1448	"	40f pale green & bistre	20	10
1449	"	60f pale lilac & bistre	25	10
1450	"	1fo blue & bistre	50	30
1451	"	1.70fo ochre & bistre	60	50
1452	"	3fo pink & blue bistre	90	75
		Nos. 1447-1452, B224, C209A (8)	4.90	2.75

Souvenir Sheet

Perf. 12

1453	A324	10fo multicolored	7.50	7.50

Issued to commemorate the World Cup Soccer Championship, Chile, May 30–June 17. No. 1453 measures 72x92mm.

Type of 1961 and

Johann Gutenberg

A325

Portraits: No. 1456, Miklós Misztótfalusi Kis, Hungarian printer (1650–1702). No. 1457, Jozsef Pech. No. 1458, András Cházár. No. 1459, Dr. Ferenc Hutyra. No. 1460, Gábor Egressy and National Theater.

Photogravure

1962 *Perf. 12* Unwmkd.

1455	A325	1fo blue black	12	4
1456	"	1fo red brown	12	4
1457	A320	1fo blue	15	4
1458	A325	1fo violet	12	4
1459	A320	1fo deep blue	12	4
1460	A325	1fo rose red	13	5
		Nos. 1455-1460 (6)	76	25

Issued to commemorate variously: Centenary of Printers' and Papermakers' Union (Nos. 1455–1456). 75th anniversary of founding, by Joszef Pech, of Hungarian Hydroelectric Service (No. 1457). András Cházár, founder of Hungarian deaf-mute education (No. 1458). Dr. Ferenc Hutÿra, founder of Hungarian veterinary medicine (No. 1459). 125th anniversary of National Theater (No. 1460).

Malaria Eradication Emblem—A327

1962, June 25 *Perf. 15*

1461	A327	2.50fo lemon & blk.	80	40
		a. 2.50fo grn. & blk., sheet of 4	6.00	6.00

Issued for the World Health Organization drive to eradicate malaria. No. 1461a measures 112x75mm., perf. 11. Imperf. sheets with control numbers exist.

Sword-into-Plowshare Statue, United Nations, N.Y.

A328

1962, July 7 *Perf. 12*

1462	A328	1fo brown	20	5

Issued to commemorate the World Congress for Peace and Disarmament, Moscow, July 9–14.

Floribunda Rose

A329

Festival Emblem

A330

Various Roses in Natural Colors

1962 *Perf. 12½x11½*

1465	A329	20f org. brown	5	3
1466	"	40f slate green	8	3
1467	"	60f violet	12	4
1468	"	80f rose red	18	5
1469	"	1fo dark green	22	10
1470	"	1.20fo orange	40	15
1471	"	2fo dk. blue grn.	70	65
1472	A330	3fo multi.	1.50	60
		Nos. 1465-1472 (8)	3.25	1.65

No. 1472 was issued to commemorate the 8th World Youth Festival, Helsinki, July 28–Aug. 6.

Weight Lifter

A331

Oil Derrick and Primitive Oil Well

A332

1962, Sept. 16 *Perf. 12*

1473	A331	1fo copper red	30	10

Issued to commemorate the European Weight Lifting Championships.

Perf. 12x11½

1962, Oct. 8 Photo. Unwmkd.

1474	A332	1fo green	20	8

Issued to commemorate the 25th anniversary of the Hungarian oil industry.

Racing Motorcyclist—A333

Designs: 30f, Stunt racing. 40f, Uphill race. 60f, Cyclist in curve. 1fo, Start. 1.20fo, Speed racing. 1.70fo, Motorcyclist with sidecar. 2fo, Motor scooter. 3fo, Racing car.

1962, Dec. 28 *Perf. 11*

1475	A333	20f multicolored	4	3
1476	"	30f "	5	3
1477	"	40f "	6	3
1478	"	60f "	10	3
1479	A333	1fo multicolored	20	8
1480	"	1.20fo "	25	15
1481	"	1.70fo "	50	25
1482	"	2fo "	70	40
1483	"	3fo "	1.25	65
		Nos. 1475-1483 (9)	3.15	1.65

Ice Skater

A334

Designs: 20f–3fo, Various figure skating and ice dancing positions. (20f, 3fo horiz.). 10fo, Figure skater and flags of participating nations.

Perf. 12x11½, 11½x12

1963, Feb. 5 Photo. Unwmkd.

1484	A334	20f multicolored	5	3
1485	"	40f "	8	3
1486	"	60f "	12	3
1487	"	1fo "	20	6
1488	"	1.40fo "	50	20
1489	"	2fo "	75	30
1490	"	3fo "	1.25	75
		Nos. 1484-1490 (7)	2.95	1.40

Souvenir Sheet

Perf. 11½x12

1491	A334	10fo multicolored	*4.25*	*4.25*

Issued to commemorate the European Figure Skating and Ice Dancing Championships, Budapest, Feb. 5–10. No. 1491 contains one stamp, buff margin with blue inscription. Size: 66x93mm.

János Batsányi—A335

Designs: No. 1493, Helicon Monument. No. 1494, Actors before Szeged Cathedral. No. 1495, Leo Weiner, composer. No. 1496, Ferenc Entz, horticulturist. No. 1497, Ivan Markovits, inventor of Hungarian shorthand. No. 1498, Dr. Frigyes Koranyi. No. 1499, Ferenc Erkel (1810–1893), composer. No. 1500, Geza Gardonyi (1863–1922), novelist. No. 1501, Pierre de Coubertin, Frenchman, reviver of Olympic Games. No. 1502, Jozsef Eötvös, author, philosopher, educator. No. 1503, Budapest Industrial Fair emblem. No. 1504, Stagecoach and Arc de Triomphe, Paris. No. 1505, Hungary map and power lines. No. 1506, Roses.

1963 *Perf. 11* Unwmkd.

1492	A335	40f dk. carmine rose	10	3
1493	"	40f blue	10	3
1494	"	40f violet blue	10	3
1495	"	40f olive	10	3
1496	"	40f emerald	10	3
1497	"	40f dark blue	10	3
1498	"	60f dull violet	12	4
1499	"	60f bister brown	12	4
1500	"	60f gray green	12	4
1501	"	60f red brown	25	15
1502	"	60f lilac	10	4
1503	"	1fo purple	25	8
1504	"	1fo rose red	25	8
1505	A335	1fo gray	25	10
1506	"	2fo bister, rose red & light green	60	15
		Nos. 1492-1506 (15)	2.66	90

Issued to commemorate: No. 1492, Bicentenary of birth of János Batsányi (1763–1845), writer. No. 1493, 10th Youth Festival, Keszthely. No. 1494, Outdoor plays, Szeged. No. 1495, Budapest Music Competition. No. 1496, Centenary of professional horticultural training. No. 1497, Centenary of Hungarian shorthand. No. 1498, 50th anniversary of the death of Prof. Frigyes Koranyi, pioneer in fight against tuberculosis. No. 1499, Erkel Memorial Festival, Gyula. No. 1500, Birth centenary of Geza Gardonyi, writer of Hungarian historical novels for youth. No. 1501, 10th anniversary of the People's Stadium, Budapest. No. 1502, 150th anniversary of birth of Jozsef Eötvös, organizer of modern public education in Hungary. No. 1503, Budapest Industrial Fair, May 17–27. No. 1504, Paris Postal Conference, 1863. No. 1505, Rural electrification. No. 1506, 5th National Rose Show.

Ship and Chain Bridge, Budapest

A336

Bus and Parliament

A337

Designs: 20f, Trolley. 30f, Sightseeing bus and National Museum. 40f, Bus and trailer. 50f, Railroad tank car. 60f, Trolley bus. 70f, Railroad mail car. 80f, Motorcycle messenger. No. 1516, Mail plane (vert.). No. 1517, Television transmitter, Miskolc (vert.). 1.40fo, Mobile post office. 1.70fo, Diesel locomotive. 2fo, Mobile radio transmitter and stadium. 2.50fo, Tourist bus. 2.60fo, Passenger train. 3fo, P.O. parcel conveyor. 4fo, Television transmitters, Pecs (vert.). 5fo, Hydraulic lift truck and mail car. 6fo, Woman teletypist. 8fo, Map of Budapest and automatic dial phone. 10fo, Girl pioneer and woman letter carrier.

1963-64 Photogravure *Perf. 11*

1507	A336	10f bright blue	4	3
1508	"	20f dp. yel. grn.	4	3
1509	"	30f violet	4	3
1510	"	40f orange	8	3
1511	"	50f brown	10	3
1512	"	60f crimson	12	3
1513	"	70f olive gray	20	3
1514	"	80f red brn. ('64)	50	20

Perf. 12x11½, 11½x12

1515	A337	1fo rose claret	15	3
1516	"	1.20fo orge. brown	1.50	60
1517	"	1.20fo dp. vio. ('64)	20	10
1518	"	1.40fo dp. yel. grn.	30	5
1519	"	1.70fo maroon	40	5
1520	"	2fo greenish blue	45	4
1521	"	2.50fo lilac	50	8
1522	"	2 60fo olive	50	8
1523	"	3fo dk. blue ('64)	40	4
1524	"	4fo blue ('64)	60	8
1525	"	5fo olive brn. ('64)	85	10
1526	"	6fo dark olive bister ('64)	1.00	12
1527	"	8fo red lilac ('64)	1.50	35
1528	"	10fo emerald ('64)	1.80	50
		Nos. 1507-1528 (22)	11.27	2.63

Size of Nos. 1508, 1512: 20½–21x16¾–17mm.

Minute inscription in lower margin includes year date, number of stamp in set and designer's name (Bokros F. or Legrady S.).

See also Nos. 1983–1983B, 2196–2204.

Coil Stamps

1965-67 *Perf. 14*

Size: 21½x16½mm.

1508a	A336	20f deep yellow green	12	10
1512a	"	60f crimson ('67)	30	10

Black control number on back of every fifth stamp.

Motorboat—A338

Girl, Steamer and Castle—A339

Design: 60f, Sailboat.

1963, July 13 *Perf. 11*

No.	Type	Description	Unused	Used
1529	A338	20f slate green, red & black	30	12
1530	A339	40f multicolor	30	18
1531	A338	60f blue, black, brn. & orge.	50	24

Centenary of the summer resort Siofok.

Child with Towel and Toothbrush A340 — Karancsság Woman A341

Designs: 40f, Child with medicines. 60f, Girls of 3 races. 1fo, Girl and heart. 1.40fo, Boys of 3 races. 2fo, Medical examination of child. 3fo, Hands shielding plants.

1963, July 27 *Perf. 12x11½*

No.	Type	Description	Unused	Used
1532	A340	30f multicolored	8	8
1533	"	40f "	10	8
1534	"	60f "	15	10
1535	"	1fo "	20	12
1536	"	1.40fo "	40	20
1537	"	2fo "	50	40
1538	"	3fo "	1.00	75
		Nos. 1532-1538 (7)	2.43	1.73

Centenary of the International Red Cross.

1963, Aug. 18 Engraved *Perf. 11½*

Provincial Costumes: 30f, Kapuvár man. 40f, Debrecen woman. 60f, Hortobágy man. 1fo, Csököly woman. 1.70fo, Dunántul man. 2fo, Buják woman. 2.50fo, Alföld man. 3fo, Mezökövesd bride.

No.	Type	Description	Unused	Used
1539	A341	20f claret	6	5
1540	"	30f green	6	5
1541	"	40f brown	8	6
1542	"	60f bright blue	12	8
1543	"	1fo brown red	20	10
1544	"	1.70fo purple	40	20
1545	"	2fo dk. bl. green	60	30
1546	"	2.50fo dk. carmine	75	50
1547	"	3fo violet blue	1.50	80
		Nos. 1539-1547 (9)	3.77	2.14

Issued in connection with the Popular Art Exhibition in Budapest.

Slalom and 1964 Olympic Emblem A342

Sports: 60f, Downhill skiing. 70f, Ski jump. 80f, Rifle shooting on skis. 1fo, Figure skating pair. 2fo, Ice hockey. 2.60fo, Speed ice skating. 10fo, Skier and mountains (vert.).

1963-64 Photo. *Perf. 12*

1964 Olympic Emblem in Black and Red

No.	Type	Description	Unused	Used
1548	A342	40f yellow green & bister	10	5
1549	"	60f vio. & bister	10	5
1550	"	70f ultra. & bister	15	5
1551	"	80f emerald & bister	15	8
1552	"	1fo brn. orge. & bister	20	10
1553	"	2fo bright blue & bister	70	40
1554	"	2.60fo rose lake & bister	1.00	60
		Nos. 1548-1554, B234 (8)	4.00	1.83

Souvenir Sheet

Perf. 11½x12

No.	Type	Description	Unused	Used
1555	A342	10fo greenish bl., red & brn. ('64)	6.50	6.50

Issued to publicize the 9th Winter Olympic Games, Innsbruck, Austria, Jan. 29-Feb. 9, 1964. No. 1555 contains one stamp with design continuing into margin. Size of stamp: 33x42½mm. Size of sheet: 66x60mm.

Four-Leaf Clover A343 — Moon Rocket A344

Good Luck Symbols: 20f, Calendar and mistletoe (horiz.). 30f, Chimneysweep and clover. 60f, Top hat, pig and clover. 1fo, Clown with balloon and clover (horiz.). 2fo, Lanterns, mask and clover.

Perf. 12x11½, 11½x12

1963, Dec. 12 Photo. Unwmkd.

Sizes: 28x22mm. (20f, 1fo); 22x28 mm. (40f); 28x39mm. (30f, 60f, 2fo).

No.	Type	Description	Unused	Used
1556	A343	20f multicolored	5	4
1557	"	30f "	5	4
1558	"	40f "	10	5
1559	"	60f "	15	6
1560	"	1fo "	25	20
1561	"	2fo "	65	40
		Nos. 1556-1561, B235-B236 (8)	3.25	1.79

New Year 1964. The 20f and 40f issued in booklet panes of 10, perf. and imperf.; sold for 2 times and 1½ times face respectively.

Perf. 11½x12, 12x11½

1964, Jan. 8

American and Russian Spacecraft: 40f, Venus space probe. 60f, Vostok I (horiz.). 1fo, Friendship 7. 1.70fo, Vostok III & IV. 2fo, Telstar 1 & 2 (horiz.). 2.60fo, Mars I. 3fo, Radar, rockets and satellites (horiz.).

No.	Type	Description	Unused	Used
1562	A344	30f grn., yellow & bronze	5	3
1563	"	40f purple, blue & silver	10	3
1564	"	60f bl., blk., yel., silver & red	12	3
1565	"	1fo dark brown, red & silver	25	8
1566	"	1.70fo vio. bl., blk., tan & red	40	10
1567	"	2fo slate green, yel. & silver	60	25
1568	"	2.60fo dp. blue, yel. & bronze	80	30
1569	A344	3fo dp. violet, lt. bl. & silver	1.25	70
		Nos. 1562-1569 (8)	3.57	1.52

Issued to honor the achievements of space research.

Lace Type of 1960

Various Halas Lace Designs

Sizes: 20f, 2.60fo: 38x28mm. 30f, 40f, 60f, 1fo, 1.40fo, 2fo: 38x45mm.

Engraved and Lithographed

1964, Feb. 28 *Perf. 11½*

No.	Type	Description	Unused	Used
1570	A294	20f emerald & blk.	8	5
1571	"	30f dull yellow & black	10	5
1572	"	40f dp. rose & blk.	20	5
1573	"	60f olive & blk.	20	6
1574	"	1fo red org. & blk.	35	8
1575	"	1.40fo blue & black	50	20
1576	"	2fo bluish green & black	90	40
1577	"	2.60fo lt. vio. & blk.	1.40	85
		Nos. 1570-1577 (8)	3.73	1.74

Special Anniversaries-Events Issue

Inscribed: "ÉVFORDULÓK-ESEMÉNYEK"

Imre Madach A345 — Shakespeare A346

Karl Marx and Membership Card of International Working Men's Association—A347

Michelangelo A348

Lajos Kossuth and György Dózsa A349

Budapest Fair Buildings—A350

Designs: No. 1579, Ervin Szabo. No. 1580, Andras Fay. No. 1581, Aggtelek Cave scene. No. 1582, Excavating bauxite. No. 1584, Equestrian statue, Szekesfehervar. No. 1585, Bowler. No. 1586, Waterfall and forest. No. 1587, Miklos Ybl and Budapest Opera. No. 1590, Armor, saber, sword and foil. No. 1592, Galileo Galilei. No. 1593, Women basketball players. No. 1595, Two runners breaking tape.

Perf. 11½x12, 12x11½, 11

1964 Photogravure Unwmkd.

No.	Type	Description	Unused	Used
1578	A345	60f bright purple	10	5
1579	"	60f olive	10	5
1580	"	60f olive green	10	5
1581	A346	60f bluish green	10	5
1582	"	60f Prussian blue	10	5
1583	A347	60f rose red	10	5
1584	A348	60f slate blue	10	5
1585	A345	1fo carmine rose	25	8
1586	A346	1fo dull blue green	20	8
1587	A348	1fo orange brown	15	8
1588	A349	1fo ultramarine	15	8
1589	A350	1fo bright green	15	8
1590	A345	2fo yellow brown	40	10
1591	A346	2fo magenta	40	10
1592	"	2fo red brown	40	8
1593	"	2fo bright blue	50	8
1594	A348	2fo gray brown	40	8
1595	"	2fo brown red	40	8
		Nos. 1578-1595 (18)	4.10	1.27

Issued to commemorate: No. 1578, Dramatist Imre Madach (1823-1864), death centenary. No. 1579, Municipal libraries, 60th anniversary, and librarian Ervin Szabo (1877-1918). No. 1580, Writer Andras Fay (1786-1864), death centenary. No. 1582, Bauxite mining in Hungary, 30th year. No. 1583, Centenary of first Socialist International. No. 1584, King Alba Day in Székesfehérvár. No. 1585, First European Bowling Championship, Budapest. No. 1586, Congress of National Forestry Federation. No. 1587, Architect Miklos Ybl (1814-1891), 150th birth anniversary. No. 1588, City of Cegléd, 600th anniversary. No. 1589, Opening of 1964 Budapest International Fair. No. 1590, Hungarian Youth Fencing Association, 50th anniversary. Nos. 1591-1592, Shakespeare and Galileo, 400th birth anniversaries. No. 1593, 9th European Women's Basketball Championship. No. 1594, Michelangelo's 400th death anniversary. No. 1595, 50th anniversary of first Hungarian-Swedish athletic meet.

Eleanor Roosevelt A351

Design (horiz.): Nos. 1597a, 1597d, Portrait at right. Nos. 1597b, 1597c, Portrait at left.

1964, Apr. 27 *Perf. 12½*

No.	Type	Description	Unused	Used
1596	A351	2fo gray, black & buff	40	30

Miniature Sheet

Perf. 11

No.	Type	Description	Unused	Used
1597	A351	Sheet of four	5.00	5.00
		a. 2fo dp. claret, brown & black	1.00	1.00
		b. 2fo dark blue, brown & black	1.00	1.00
		c. 2fo green, brown & black	1.00	1.00
		d. 2fo olive, brown & black	1.00	1.00

Issued to honor Mrs. Eleanor Roosevelt. Sheet of four measures: 112½x76½mm.

Fencing—A352

Sport: 40f, Women's gymnastics. 60f, Soccer. 80f, Equestrian. 1fo, Running. 1.40fo, Weight lifting. 1.70fo, Gymnast on rings. 2fo, Hammer throw and javelin. 2.50fo, Boxing.

1964, June 12 Photo. *Perf. 11*

Multicolored Design and Inscription

1598	A352	30f lt. vermilion	10	3
1599	"	40f blue	10	3
1600	"	60f emerald	12	3
1601	"	80f tan	17	4
1602	"	1fo yellow	20	7
1603	"	1.40fo bister brown	30	10
1604	"	1.70fo bluish gray	50	15
1605	"	2fo gray green	75	35
1606	"	2.50fo violet gray	1.00	75
		Nos. 1598-1606, B237 (10)	4.44	2.05

Issued to publicize the 18th Olympic Games, Tokyo, Oct. 10–25.

Elberta Peaches

A353

Peaches: 40h, Blossoms (J. H. Hale). 60h, Magyar Kajszi. 1fo, Mandula Kajszi. 1.50fo, Borsi Rozsa. 1.70fo, Blossoms (Alexander). 2fo, Champion. 3fo, May-flower.

1964, July 24 *Perf. 11½*

Gray Inscriptions

1607	A353	40f multicolored	8	5
1608	"	60f "	12	5
1609	"	1fo "	20	8
1610	"	1.50fo "	30	20
1611	"	1.70fo "	35	14
1612	"	2fo "	50	24
1613	"	2.60fo "	60	45
1614	"	3fo "	75	60
		Nos. 1607-1614 (8)	2.90	1.81

Issued to publicize the National Peach Exhibition, Szeged.

Crossing Street in Safety Zone

A354

Designs: 60f, "Watch out for Children" (child and ball). 1fo, "Look before Crossing" (mother and child).

1964, Sept. 27 *Perf. 11*

1615	A354	20f multicolored	20	12
1616	"	60f "	30	12
1617	"	1fo lilac & multi.	40	20

Issued to publicize traffic safety.

Souvenir Sheet

Voskhod 1 and Globe—A355

1964, Nov. 6 *Perf. 12x11½*

1618	A355	10fo multicolored	6.00	6.00

Issued to commemorate the Russian three-manned space flight of Vladimir M. Komarov, Boris B. Yegorov and Konstantine Feoktistov. No. 1618 has gray and gold marginal inscriptions and designs. Size of stamp: 38x28mm.; size of sheet: 87x74 mm.

Arpad Bridge—A356

Danube Bridges, Budapest: 30f, Margaret Bridge. 60f, Chain Bridge. 1f, Elizabeth Bridge. 1.50f, Freedom Bridge. 2fo, Petőfi Bridge. 2.50fo, Railroad Bridge.

1964, Nov. 21 Photo. *Perf. 11x11½*

1619	A356	20f multicolored	8	3
1620	"	30f "	10	3
1621	"	60f "	15	3
1622	"	1fo "	30	6
1623	"	1.50fo "	45	20
1624	"	2fo "	70	40
1625	"	2.50fo "	1.20	75
		Nos. 1619-1625 (7)	2.98	1.50

Issued to commemorate the opening of the reconstructed Elizabeth Bridge. See also No. C250.

Ring-necked Pheasant and Hunting Rifle—A357

Designs: 30f, Wild boar. 40f, Gray partridges. 60f, Varying hare. 80f, Fallow deer. 1fo, Mouflon. 1.70fo, Red deer. 2fo, Great bustard. 2.50fo, Roebuck and roe deer. 3fo, Emblem of National Federation of Hungarian Hunters (antlers).

1964, Dec. 30 Photo. *Perf. 12x11½*

1626	A357	20f multicolored	10	5
1627	"	30f "	10	5
1628	"	40f "	15	8
1629	"	60f "	15	10
1630	"	80f "	20	10
1631	"	1fo "	20	12
1632	"	1.70fo "	40	15
1633	"	2fo "	50	20
1634	"	2.50fo "	85	50
1635	"	3fo "	1.25	85
		Nos. 1626-1635 (10)	3.90	2.20

Castle Type of 1960

Castles: 3fo, Czesznek (vert.). 4fo, Eger. 5fo, Koszeg (vert.).

1964 *Perf. 11½x12, 12x11½*

Size: 21x28mm., 28x21mm.

1644	A293	3fo red brown	40	6
1645	"	4fo bright violet	60	8
1646	"	5fo yellow green	80	10

Equestrian, Gold and Bronze Medals

A358

Designs: 30f, Women's gymnastics, silver and bronze medals. 50f, Small-bore rifle, gold and bronze medals. 60f, Water polo, gold medal. 70f, Shot put, bronze medal. 80f, Soccer, gold medal. 1fo, Weight lifting, 1 bronze and 2 silver medals. 1.20fo, Canoeing, silver medal. 1.40fo, Hammer throw, silver medal. 1.50fo, Wrestling, 2 gold medals. 1.70fo, Javelin, 2 silver medals. 3fo, Fencing, 4 gold medals.

1965, Feb. 20 *Perf. 12*

Medals in Gold, Silver or Bronze.

1647	A358	20f lt. olive grn. & dark brn.	8	3
1648	"	30f vio. & dk. brn.	10	3
1649	"	50f olive & dark brown	20	3
1650	"	60f light blue & red brown	15	6
1651	"	70f light gray & red brown	20	8
1652	"	80f yellow green & dark brn.	15	10
1653	"	1fo lilac, violet & red brown	20	10
1654	"	1.20fo lt. bl., ultra. & red brn.	30	15
1655	"	1.40fo gray & red brown	40	15
1656	"	1.50fo tan, lt. brn. & red brn.	45	30
1657	"	1.70fo pink & red brown	65	40
1658	"	3fo greenish blue & brown	1.00	75
		Nos. 1647-1658 (12)	3.88	2.18

Issued to commemorate the victories won by the Hungarian team in the 1964 Olympic Games, Tokyo, Oct. 10–25.

Arctic Exploration A359 — Chrysanthemums A360

Designs: 30f, Radar tracking rocket, ionosphere research. 60f, Rocket and earth with reflecting layer diagrams, atmospheric research. 80f, Telescope and map of Milky Way, radio astronomy. 1.50fo, Earth, compass rose and needle, earth magnetism. 1.70fo, Weather balloon and lightning, meteorology. 2fo, Aurora borealis and penguins, arctic research. 2.50fo, Satellite, earth and planets, space research. 3fo, IQSY emblem and world map. 10fo, Sun with flares and corona, snow crystals and rain.

Perf. 11½x12

1965, Mar. 25 Photo. Unwmkd.

1659	A359	20f bl., orge. & blk.	4	3
1660	"	30f gray, black & emerald	5	3
1661	"	60f lilac, black & yellow	12	3
1662	"	80f light green, yel. & blk.	15	3
1663	"	1.50fo lemon, blue & black	30	8
1664	"	1.70fo blue, pink & black	35	10
1665	"	2fo ultra., salmon & black	45	20
1666	A359	2.50fo orge. brn., yel. & blk.	70	35
1667	"	3fo light blue, citron & black	1.00	65
		Nos. 1659-1667 (9)	3.16	1.50

Souvenir Sheet

1668	A359	10fo ultra., orge. & black	4.00	4.00

Issued to publicize the International Quiet Sun Year, 1964–65. No. 1668 contains one stamp. Twelve phases of the earth shown in margin and orange inscription. Size: 62x85mm.

1965, Apr. 4

Designs: 30f, Peonies. 50f, Carnations. 60f, Roses. 1.40fo, Lilies. 1.70fo, Anemones. 2fo, Gladioli. 2.50fo, Tulips. 3fo, Mixed flower bouquet.

Flowers in Natural Colors.

1669	A360	20f gold & gray	6	3
1670	"	30f " "	8	3
1671	"	50f " "	9	3
1672	"	60f " "	12	3
1673	"	1.40fo " "	25	5
1674	"	1.70fo " "	35	6
1675	"	2fo " "	40	12
1676	"	2.50fo " "	60	30
1677	"	3fo " "	1.00	75
		Nos. 1669-1677 (9)	2.95	1.40

Issued to commemorate the 20th anniversary of liberation from the Nazis.

"Head of a Combatant" by Leonardo da Vinci

A361

Perf. 11½x12

1965, May 4 Photo. Unwmkd.

1678	A361	60f bister & orange brown	30	10

Issued to publicize the First International Renaissance Conference, Budapest.

Nikolayev, Tereshkova and View of Budapest—A362

1965, May 10 *Perf. 11*

1679	A362	1fo dull bl. & brn.	30	8

Issued to commemorate the visit of the Russian astronauts Andrian G. Nikolayev and Valentina Tereshkova (Mr. & Mrs. Nikolayev) to Budapest.

ITU Emblem, Old and New Communication Equipment

A363

1965, May 17

1680	A363	60f violet blue	20	6

Issued to commemorate the centenary of the International Telecommunication Union.

Souvenir Sheet

Austrian WIPA Stamp of 1933
A363a

1965, June 4 Photo. *Perf. 11*

1681	A363a	Sheet of 2	3.50	3.50
		a. 2fo gray & dp. ultra.	1.50	1.50

Issued to commemorate the 1965 Vienna International Philatelic Exhibition WIPA, June 4–13. No. 1681 contains two 2fo stamps and two labels in gold, dp. ultra. & red. Size: 102x74mm.

Marx and Lenin, Crowds with Flags
A364

ICY Emblem and Pulley
A365

1965, June 15 *Perf. 11½x12*

1682	A364	60f red, black & yellow	15	3

Issued to commemorate the 6th Conference of Ministers of Post of Socialist Countries, Peking, June 21–July 15.

1965, June 25

1683	A365	2fo dark red	24	12
		a. Min. sheet of 4	3.50	3.50

Issued for the International Cooperation Year, 1965. No. 1683a contains four 2fo stamps, perf. 11, each in a different color (rose red, olive, Prussian green, violet). Size of stamp: 21x38mm.; sheet: 74x97 mm.

Musical Clown
A366

Dr. Semmelweis
A367

Circus Acts: 20f, Equestrians. 40f, Elephant. 50f, Seal balancing ball. 60f, Lions. 1fo, Wildcat jumping through burning hoops. 1.50fo, Black leopards. 2.50 fo, Juggler. 3fo, Leopard and dogs. 4fo, Bear on bicycle.

1965, July 26 Photo. *Perf. 11½x12*

1684	A366	20f multicolored	5	3
1685	"	30f "	8	5
1686	"	40f "	10	8
1687	"	50f "	14	10
1688	"	60f "	18	10
1689	"	1fo "	20	10
1690	"	1.50fo "	30	15
1691	"	2.50fo "	50	15
1692	"	3fo "	70	50
1693	"	4fo "	1.10	75
		Nos. 1684-1693 (10)	3.35	2.01

1965, Aug. 20 Photo. Unwmkd.

1694	A367	60f red brown	15	5

Issued to commemorate the centenary of the death of Dr. Ignaz Philipp Semmelweis (1818–1865), who discovered the cause of puerperal fever and introduced antisepsis into obstetrics.

Runner—A368

Sport: 30f, Swimmer at start. 50f, Woman diver. 60f, Modern dancing. 80f, Tennis. 1.70fo, Fencing. 2fo, Volleyball. 2.50fo, Basketball. 4fo, Water polo. 10fo, People's Stadium, Budapest (horiz.).

1965, Aug. 20 *Perf. 11*

Size: 38x38mm.

1695	A368	20f multicolored	5	3
1696	"	30f bl. & red brn.	10	3
1697	"	50f bl. grn., blk. & red brown	15	5
1698	"	60f vio., blk. & red brown	15	8
1699	"	80f tan, olive & red brown	20	12
1700	"	1.70fo multicolored	45	20
1701	"	2fo "	50	25
1702	"	2.50fo gray, blk. & red brown	80	45
1703	"	4fo bl., red brn. & black	1.50	80
		Nos. 1695-1703 (9)	3.90	2.01

Souvenir Sheet

Perf. 12x11½

1704	A368	10fo bister, red brn. & gray	4.00	4.00

Issued to commemorate the International College Championships, "Universiade," Budapest. No. 1704 contains one stamp with gray and red brown marginal inscription. Size of stamp: 38x28mm.; sheet: 105x75mm.

Hemispheres and Warsaw Mermaid
A369

1965, Oct. 8 Photo. *Perf. 12x11½*

1705	A369	60f bright blue	20	6

Issued to commemorate the Sixth Congress of the World Federation of Trade Unions, Warsaw.

Phyllocactus Hybridus
A370

Flowers from Botanical Gardens: 30f, Cattleya Warszewiczii (orchid). 60f, Rebutia calliantha. 70f, Paphiopedilum hybridium. 80f, Opuntia cactus. 1fo, Laelia elegans (orchid). 1.50fo, Christmas cactus. 2fo, Bird-of-paradise flower. 2.50fo, Lithops Weberi. 3fo, Victoria water lily.

1965, Oct. 11 *Perf. 11½x12*

1706	A370	20f gray & multi.	3	3
1707	"	30f " "	5	3
1708	"	60f " "	12	5
1709	"	70f " "	15	5
1710	"	80f " "	20	8
1711	"	1fo " "	25	12
1712	"	1.50fo " "	35	15
1713	"	2fo " "	40	30
1714	"	2.50fo " "	70	35
1715	"	3fo " "	90	60
		Nos. 1706-1715 (10)	3.15	1.76

"The Black Stallion"
A371

Tales from the Arabian Nights: 30f, Shahriar and Scheherazade. 50f, Sinbad's Fifth Voyage (ship). 60f, Aladdin, or The Wonderful Lamp. 80f, Harun al-Rashid. 1fo, The Flying Carpet. 1.70fo, The Fisherman and the Genie. 2fo, Ali Baba and the Forty Thieves. 3fo, Sinbad's Second Voyage (flying bird).

1965, Dec. 15 Litho. *Perf. 11½*

1716	A371	20f multicolored	10	5
1717	"	30f "	10	5
1718	"	50f "	15	8
1719	"	60f "	15	8
1720	"	80f "	25	8
1721	"	1fo "	35	10
1722	"	1.70fo "	50	15
1723	"	2fo "	60	30
1724	"	3fo "	1.40	75
		Nos. 1716-1724 (9)	3.60	1.64

Congress Emblem
A372

Callimorpha Dominula
A373

1965, Dec. 9 Photo. *Perf. 11½x12*

1725	A372	2fo dark blue	30	15

Issued to commemorate the Fifth Congress of the International Federation of Resistance Fighters (FIR), Budapest.

1966, Feb. 1 Photo. *Perf. 11½x12*

Various Butterflies in Natural Colors; Black Inscription

1726	A373	20f lt. aquamarine	8	5
1727	"	60f pale violet	10	5
1728	"	70f tan	15	8
1729	"	80f light ultra.	20	8
1730	"	1fo gray	20	10
1731	"	1.50fo emerald	30	14
1732	"	2fo dull rose	40	20
1733	"	2.50fo bister	70	30
1734	"	3fo blue	1.20	85
		Nos. 1726-1734 (9)	3.33	1.85

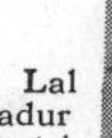

Lal Bahadur Shastri
A374

Designs: 60f, Bela Kun. 2fo, Istvan Széchenyi and Chain Bridge.

Litho.; Photo. (*1736)

1966 *Perf. 11½x12, 12x11½*

1735	A374	60f red & black	7	3
1736	"	1fo bright violet	25	5
1737	"	2fo dull yel., buff & sepia	40	10

No. 1735 commemorates the 80th anniversary of the birth of Bela Kun (1886–1939), communist labor leader; No. 1736 issued in memory of Lal Bahadur Shastri (1904–66), Indian Prime Minister; No. 1737 commemorates the 175th anniversary of the birth of Count Istvan Széchenyi (1791–1860), statesman.

See also Nos. 1764-1765, 1769-1770.

Luna 9
A375

Crocus
A376

Design: 3fo, Luna 9 sending signals from moon to earth (horiz.).

1966, Mar. 12 Photo. *Perf. 12*

1738	A375	2fo vio., blk. & yel.	65	20
1739	"	3fo lt. ultra., black & yellow	1.10	75

Issued to commemorate the first soft landing on the moon by the Russian satellite Luna 9, Feb. 3, 1966.

1966, March 12 *Perf. 11*

Flowers: 30f, Cyclamen. 60f, Ligularia sibirica. 1.40fo, Lilium bulbiferum. 1.50fo, Snake's head. 3fo, Snapdragon and emblem of Hungarian Nature Preservation Society.

Flowers in Natural Colors

1740	A376	20f brown	10	8
1741	"	30f aquamarine	15	10
1742	"	60f rose claret	20	15
1743	"	1.40fo gray	35	25
1744	"	1.50fo ultramarine	50	30
1745	"	3fo magenta & sepia	1.40	75
		Nos. 1740-1745 (6)	2.70	1.63

1966, Apr. 16

Designs: 20f, Barn swallows. 30f, Long-tailed tits. 60f, Red crossbill and pine cone. 1.40fo, Middle spotted woodpecker. 1.50fo, Hoopoe feeding young. 3fo, Forest preserve, lapwing and emblem of National Forest Preservation Society.

Birds in Natural Colors

1746	A376	20f bright green	20	15
1747	"	30f vermilion	15	10
1748	"	60f bright green	20	10
1749	"	1.40fo violet blue	35	20
1750	"	1.50fo blue	60	30

No.	Type	Description	Unused	Used
1751	A376	3fo brn., magenta & green	90	75
		Nos. 1746-1751 (6)	2.40	1.60

Nos. 1740-1751 issued to promote protection of wild flowers and birds.

Locomotive, 1947; Monoplane, 1912; Autobus, 1911; Steamer, 1853, and Budapest Railroad Station, 1846—A377

Designs: 2fo, Transportation, 1966: electric locomotive V.43; turboprop airliner IL-18; Ikarusz autobus; Diesel passenger ship, and Budapest South Railroad Station.

1966, Apr. 2 Photo. *Perf. 12*

No.	Type	Description	Unused	Used
1752	A377	1fo yellow, brown & green	20	10
1753	"	2fo pale grn., blue & brown	40	20

Issued to commemorate the re-opening of the Transport Museum, Budapest.

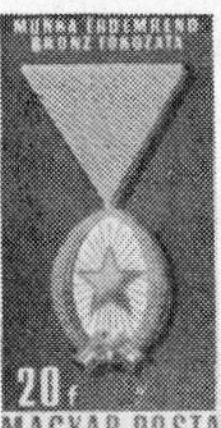

Bronze Order of Labor A378

Decorations: 30f, Silver Order of Labor. 50f, Banner Order, third class. 60f, Gold Order of Labor. 70f, Banner Order, second class. 1fo, Red Banner Order of Labor. 1.20fo, Banner Order, first class. 2fo, Order of Merit. 2.50fo, Hero of Socialist Labor. Sizes: 20f, 30f, 60f, 1fo, 2fo, 2.50fo: 19½x38mm. 50f: 21x29 mm. 70f, 25x31mm. 1.20fo: 28x38mm.

1966, Apr. 2 *Perf. 11* Unwmkd.

Decorations in Original Colors

No.	Type	Description	Unused	Used
1754	A378	20f dp. ultra.	3	3
1755	"	30f light brown	6	3
1756	"	50f blue green	10	5
1757	"	60f violet	10	5
1758	"	70f carmine	10	5
1759	"	1fo violet blue	18	10
1760	"	1.20fo bright blue	25	20
1761	"	2fo olive	50	25
1762	"	2.50fo dull blue	65	35
		Nos. 1754-1762 (9)	1.97	1.11

Portrait Type of 1966 and

Dubna Nuclear Research Institute A379

WHO Headquarters, Geneva A380

Designs: No. 1764, Pioneer girl. No. 1765, Tamás Esze. No. 1767, Old view of Buda and UNESCO emblem. No. 1768, Horse-drawn fire pump and emblem of Sopron Fire Brigade. No. 1769, Miklos Zrinyi. No. 1770, Sandor Koranyi.

1966 Litho. *Perf. 11½x12*

No.	Type	Description	Unused	Used
1763	A379	60f bl. grn. & blk.	10	3
1764	A374	60f multicolored	10	3
1765	"	60f brt. bl. & blk.	10	3
1766	A380	2fo lt. ultra. & blk.	30	6
1767	"	2fo light bl. & pur.	35	10
1768	"	2fo orange & black	40	8
1769	A374	2fo ol. bis. & brn.	35	10
1770	"	2fo multicolored	35	10
		Nos. 1763-1770 (8)	2.05	53

Issued to commemorate: No. 1763, Tenth anniversary of the United Institute for Nuclear Research, Dubna, U.S.S.R.; No. 1764, 20th anniversary of Pioneer Movement; No. 1765, 300th anniversary of the birth of Tamás Esze (1666–1708), military hero; No. 1766, Inauguration of the World Health Organization Headquarters, Geneva; No. 1767, 20th anniversary of UNESCO and 72nd session of Executive Council, Budapest, May 30–31; No. 1768, Centenary of Volunteer Fire Brigade; No. 1769, 400th anniversary of death of Miklos Zrinyi (1508–1566), hero of Turkish Wars; No. 1770, Centenary of birth of Sandor Koranyi (1866–1944), physician and scientist.

Hungarian Soccer Player and Soccer Field—A381

Jules Rimet, Cup and Soccer Ball A382

Designs (Views of Soccer play): 30f, Montevideo 1930 (Uruguay 4, Argentina 2). 60f, Rome 1934 (Italy 2, Czechoslovakia 1). 1fo, Paris 1938 (Italy 4, Hungary 2). 1.40fo, Rio de Janeiro 1950 (Uruguay 2, Brazil 1). 1.70fo, Bern 1954 (Germany 3, Hungary 2). 2fo, Stockholm 1958 (Brazil 5, Sweden 2). 2.50fo, Santiago 1962 ((Brazil 3, Czechoslovakia 1).

Souvenir Sheet

1966, May 16 Photo. *Perf. 11½x12*

No.	Type	Description	Unused	Used
1771	A381	10fo multi.	3.50	3.50

1966, June 6 *Perf. 12x11½*

No.	Type	Description	Unused	Used
1772	A382	20f blue & multi.	15	3
1773	"	30f org. & multi.	10	3
1774	"	60f multicolored	10	6
1775	"	1fo "	12	12
1776	"	1.40fo "	25	16
1777	"	1.70fo "	30	20
1778	"	2fo "	35	25
1779	A382	2.50fo multicolored	85	65
		Nos. 1772-1779, B258 (9)	2.97	2.00

Issued to publicize the World Cup Soccer Championship, Wembley, England, July 11–30. No. 1771 contains one stamp. Emerald margin with championship emblem, soccer field and names of participating countries. Size: 75x108mm.

European Red Fox A383

Hunting Trophies: 60f, Wild boar. 70f, Wildcat. 80f, Roebuck. 1.50fo, Red deer. 2.50fo, Fallow deer. 3fo, Mouflon.

1966, July 4 Photo. *Perf. 11½x12*

Animals in Natural Colors

No.	Type	Description	Unused	Used
1780	A383	20f gray & lt. brn.	20	5
1781	"	60f buff & gray	15	5
1782	"	70f lt. bl. & gray	15	5
1783	"	80f pale green & yellow bister	20	12
1784	"	1.50fo pale lemon & brown	30	20
1785	"	2.50fo gray & brown	45	30
1786	"	3fo pale pink & gray	1.00	65
		Nos. 1780-1786 (7)	2.45	1.42

The 80f and 1.50fo were issued with and without alternating labels, which show date and place when trophy was taken; the 2.50fo was issued only with labels, 20f, 60f, 70f and 3fo without labels only.

Discus Thrower and Matthias Cathedral A384

Designs: 30f, High jump and Agriculture Museum. 40f, Javelin (women's) and Parliament. 50f, Hammer throw, Mt. Gellert and Liberty Bridge. 60f, Broad jump and view of Buda. 1fo, Shot put and Chain Bridge. 2fo, Pole vault and Stadium. 3fo, Long distance runners and Millenium Monument.

1966, Aug. 30 Photo. *Perf. 12x11½*

No.	Type	Description	Unused	Used
1787	A384	20f grn., brn. & org.	10	3
1788	"	30f multicolored	20	5
1789	"	40f "	15	5
1790	"	50f "	15	10
1791	"	60f "	20	10
1792	"	1fo "	50	15
1793	"	2fo "	85	30
1794	"	3fo "	1.20	75
		Nos. 1787-1794 (8)	3.35	1.53

8th European Athletic Championships, Budapest, Aug. 30–Sept. 4. See No. C261.

Girl in the Forest by Miklos Barabas—A385

Paintings: 1fo, Mrs. Istvan Bitto by Miklos Barabas (1810–98). 1.50fo, Hunyadi's Farewell by Gyula Benczur (1844–1920). 1.70fo, Reading Woman by Gyula Benczur (horiz.). 2fo, Woman with Fagots by Mihaly Munkacsi (1844–1900). 2.50fo, Yawning Boy by Mihaly Munkacsi. 3fo, Lady in Violet by Pal Szinyei Merse (1845–1920). 10fo, Picnic in May by Pal Szinyei Merse (horiz.).

1966, Dec. 9 *Perf. 12½*

Gold Frame

No.	Type	Description	Unused	Used
1795	A385	60f multicolored	20	8
1796	"	1fo "	30	10
1797	"	1.50fo "	60	10
1798	"	1.70fo "	70	12
1799	"	2fo "	80	25
1800	"	2.50fo "	1.10	40
1801	"	3fo "	2.65	1.35
		Nos. 1795-1801 (7)	6.35	2.40

Souvenir Sheet

No.	Type	Description	Unused	Used
1802	A385	10fo multicolored	12.00	12.00

Issued to honor Hungarian painters. No. 1802 contains one stamp. Ocher margin with white inscription. Size of stamp: 56x51mm. Size of sheet: 97x89mm.

Vostoks 3 and 4—A386

Space Craft: 60f, Gemini 6 and 7. 80f, Vostoks 5 and 6. 1fo, Gemini 9 and target rocket. 1.50fo, Alexei Leonov walking ing in space. 2fo, Edward White walking in space. 2.50fo, Voskhod. 3fo, Gemini 11 docking Agena target.

1966, Dec. 29 *Perf. 11*

No.	Type	Description	Unused	Used
1803	A386	20f lt. ultra., red & black	10	5
1804	"	60f brt. blue, red & black	20	10
1805	"	80f greenish bl., red & blk.	25	12
1806	"	1fo greenish bl., red & blk.,	25	12
1807	"	1.50fo lt. grn., red & black	30	15
1808	"	2fo aquamarine, sal. & blk.	60	20
1809	"	2.50fo ultra., red & black	75	40
1810	"	3fo sky blue, red & black	1.00	60
		Nos. 1803-1810 (8)	3.45	1.74

American and Russian twin space flights.

Pal Kitaibel and Kitaibelia Vitifolia—A387

Flowers of the Carpathian Basin: 60f, Dentaria glandulosa. 1fo, Edraianthus tenuifolius. 1.50fo, Althaea pallida. 2fo, Centaurea mollis. 2.50fo, Sternbergia colchiciflora. 3fo, Iris Hungarica.

1967, Feb. 7 Photo. *Perf. 11½x12*

Flowers in Natural Colors

No.	Type	Description	Unused	Used
1811	A387	20f rose, black & gold	6	3
1812	"	60f green	10	5
1813	"	1fo violet gray	20	10
1814	"	1.50fo blue	30	15
1815	"	2fo light olive	50	30
1816	"	2.50fo gray green	80	40
1817	"	3fo yel. green	1.00	65
		Nos. 1811-1817 (7)	2.96	1.68

Issued to commemorate the 150th anniversary of the death of Pal Kitaibel (1757–1817), botanist, chemist and physician.

Militiaman
A388

1967, Feb. 18 Photo. *Perf. 11½x12*

1818 A388 2fo blue gray 30 8

Workers' Militia, 10th anniversary.

Mme. Du Barry and Louis XV, by Gyula Benczur (1844–1920)
A390

Souvenir Sheet

Painting: 10fo, Milton dictating "Paradise Lost" to his daughters, by Soma Orlai Petrics.

1967, May 6 Photo. *Perf. 12½*

1819 A390 10fo multicolored 5.50 5.50

1967, June 22

Paintings: 60f, Franz Liszt by Mihaly Munkacsi (1844–1900). 1fo, Samuel Lanyi, self-portrait, 1840. 1.50fo, Lady in Fur-lined Jacket by Jozsef Borsos (1821–1883). 1.70fo, The Lovers, by Pal Szinyei Merse (1845–1920; horiz.). 2fo, Portrait of Szidonia Deak, 1861, by Alajos Gyorgyi (1821–1863). 2.50fo, National Guardsman, 1848, by Jozsef Borsos.

Gold Frame

1820 A390 60f multicolored 10 3
1821 " 1fo " 20 4
1822 " 1.50fo " 30 6
1823 " 1.70fo " 40 12
1824 " 2fo " 50 15
1825 " 2.50fo " 65 30
1826 " 3fo " 1.50 1.20
Nos. 1820–1826 (7) 3.65 1.90

Issued to honor Hungarian painters. No. 1819 commemorates AMPHILEX 67 and the F.I.P. Congress, Amsterdam, May 11–21. No. 1819 contains one stamp; gray margin with white inscription. Size of stamp: 56x50mm.; size of sheet: 81x91mm.

See also Nos. 1863–1870, 1900–1907, 1940–1947.

Map of Hungary, Tourist Year Emblem, Plane, Train, Car and Ship—A391

1967, May 6 *Perf. 12x11½*

1827 A391 1fo brt. bl. & black 15 5

International Tourist Year, 1967.

S.S. Ferencz Deak, Schönbüchel Castle, Austrian Flag—A392

Designs: 60f, Diesel hydrobus, Bratislava Castle and Czechoslovak flag. 1fo, Diesel ship Hunyadi, Buda Castle and Hungarian flag. 1.50fo, Diesel tug Szekszard, Golubac Fortress and Yugoslav flag. 1.70fo, Towboat Miskolc, Vidin Fortress and Bulgarian flag. 2fo, Cargo ship Tihany, Galati shipyard and Romanian flag. 2.50fo, Hydrofoil Siraly I, Izmail Harbor and Russian flag.

1967, June 1 *Perf. 11½x12*

Flags in National Colors

1828 A392 30f lt. blue green 10 3
1829 " 60f orange brown 15 8
1830 " 1fo greenish blue 15 10
1831 " 1.50fo light green 30 15
1832 " 1.70fo blue 35 25
1833 " 2fo rose lilac 60 30
1834 " 2.50fo lt. olive green 1.20 70
Nos. 1828–1834 (7) 2.85 1.61

25th session of the Danube Commission.

Poodle
A393

Collie
A394

Dogs: 1fo, Hungarian pointer. 1.40fo, Fox terriers. 2fo, Pumi, Hungarian sheep dog. 3fo, German shepherd. 4fo, Puli, Hungarian sheep dog.

1967, July 7 Litho. *Perf. 12*

1835 A393 30f multicolored 10 5
1836 A394 60f " 15 10
1837 A393 1fo " 25 15
1838 A394 1.40fo " 40 20
1839 A393 2fo " 60 25
1840 A394 3fo " 1.00 50
1841 A393 4fo " 1.25 75
Nos. 1835–1841 (7) 3.75 2.00

Sterlets
A395

Fish: 60f, Pike perch. 1fo, Carp. 1.70fo, European catfish. 2fo, Pike. 2.50fo, Rapfin.

1967, Aug. 22 Photo. *Perf. 12x11½*

1842 A395 20f multicolored 20 6
1843 " 60f bister & multi. 10 6
1844 " 1fo multicolored 15 8
1845 " 1.70fo " 25 10
1846 " 2fo green & multi. 35 25
1847 A395 2.50fo gray & multi. 80 60
Nos. 1842–1847, B263 (7) 2.45 1.65

Issued to commemorate the 14th Congress of the International Federation of Anglers (C.I.P.S.), Dunaujvaros, Aug 20–28.

Prince Igor, by Aleksandr Borodin—A396

Opera Scenes: 30f, Freischütz, by Karl Maria von Weber. 40f, The Magic Flute, by Mozart. 60f, Prince Bluebeard's Castle, by Bela Bartok. 80f, Carmen, by Bizet (vert.). 1fo, Don Carlos, by Verdi (vert.). 1.70fo, Tannhäuser, by Wagner (vert.). 3fo, Laszlo Hunyadi, by Ferenc Erkel (vert.).

1967, Sept. 26 Photo. *Perf. 12*

1848 A396 20f multicolored 20 10
1849 " 30f " 20 10
1850 " 40f " 20 10
1851 " 60f " 20 10
1852 " 80f " 20 10
1853 " 1fo " 20 15
1854 " 1.70fo " 45 25
1855 " 3fo " 1.10 75
Nos. 1848–1855 (8) 2.75 1.65

Teacher, Students and Stone from Pecs University, 14th Century
A397

1967, Oct. 9 Photo. *Perf. 11½x12*

1856 A397 2fo gold & dp. grn. 50 10

Issued to commemorate the 600th anniversary of higher education in Hungary; University of Pecs was founded in 1367.

Eötvös University, and Symbols of Law and Justice—A398

1967, Oct. 12 *Perf. 12x11½*

1857 A398 2fo slate 45 10

Issued to commemorate the 300th anniversary of the School of Political Science and Law at the Lorand Eötvös University, Budapest.

Lenin as Teacher, by Sandor Legrady
A399

Paintings by Sandor Legrady: 1fo, Lenin. 3fo, Lenin on board the cruiser Aurora.

1967, Oct. 31 *Perf. 12½*

1858 A399 60f gold & multi. 10 4
1859 " 1fo " " 25 10
1860 " 3fo " " 75 30

Issued to commemorate the 50th anniversary of the Russian October Revolution.

Venus 4 Landing on Venus—A400

1967, Nov. 6 *Perf. 12*

1861 A400 5fo gold & multi. 1.25 65

Issued to commemorate the landing of the Russian automatic space station Venus 4 on the planet Venus.

Souvenir Sheet

19th Century Mail Coach and Post Horn—A401

Photogravure; Gold Impressed

1967, Nov. 21 *Perf. 12½*

1862 A401 10fo multicolored 3.75 3.75

Issued to commemorate the centenary of the Hungarian Postal Administration. No. 1862 has gray margin with symbols of telecommunication. Size: 84x95mm.

Painting Type of 1967

Paintings: 60f, Brother and Sister by Adolf Fenyes (1867–1945). 1fo, Wrestling Boys by Oszkar Glatz (1872–1958). 1.50fo, "October" by Karoly Ferenczy (1862–1917). 1.70fo, Women at the River Bank by Istvan Szönyi (1894–1960) (horiz.). 2fo, Godfather's Breakfast by Istvan Csok (1865–1961). 2.50fo, "Eviction Notice" by Gyula Derkovits (1894–1934). 3fo, Self-portrait by M. T. Czontvary Kosztka (1853–1919). 10fo, The Apple Pickers by Bela Uitz (1887–).

1967, Dec. 21 Photo. *Perf. 12½*

Gold Frame

1863 A390 60f multicolored 10 6
1864 " 1fo " 15 10
1865 " 1.50fo " 30 15
1866 " 1.70fo " 40 25
1867 " 2fo " 50 30
1868 " 2.50fo " 60 35
1869 " 3fo " 85 70
Nos. 1863–1869 (7) 2.90 1.91

Miniature Sheet

1870 A390 10fo multicolored 3.75 3.75

Issued to honor Hungarian painters. No. 1870 contains one stamp with ocher and brown margin suggesting a picture frame. Size: 78x100mm.

Biathlon
A402

Sport (Olympic Rings and): 60f, Figure skating, pair. 1fo, Bobsledding. 1.40fo, Slalom. 1.70fo, Women's figure skating. 2fo, Speed skating. 3fo, Ski jump. 10fo, Ice hockey.

1967, Dec. 30 Photo. ***Perf. 12½***

Souvenir Sheet

1871	A402	10fo lilac & multi.	3.50	3.50

1968, Jan. 29 ***Perf. 11***

1872	A402	30f multicolored	20	5
1873	"	60f "	15	5
1874	"	1fo "	15	6
1875	"	1.40fo rose & multi.	20	10
1876	"	1.70fo multicolored	20	15
1877	"	2fo "	40	20
1878	"	3fo olive & multi.	1.00	50
		Nos. 1872-1878, B264 (8)	2.90	1.61

Issued to publicize the 10th Winter Olympic Games, Grenoble, France, Feb. 6-18. No. 1871 contains one stamp (size: 43x43mm.); gray margin with Olympic, French and Hungarian flags and gold inscription. Size: 116x98mm.

Kando Statue, Miskolc, Kando Locomotive and Map of Hungary—A403

1968, Mar. 30 Photo. ***Perf. 11½x12***

1879	A403	2fo dark blue	40	10

Issued in memory of Kalman Kando (1869-1931), engineer, inventor of Kando locomotive.

Domestic Cat
A404

1968, Mar. 30 ***Perf. 11***

Multicolored

1880	A404	20f *shown*	5	5
1881	"	60f *Cream Persian*	10	5
1882	"	1fo *Smoky Persian*	20	8
1883	"	1.20fo *Domestic kitten*	30	12
1884	"	1.50fo *White Persian*	30	20
1885	"	2fo *Brown-striped Persian*	50	35
1886	"	2.50fo *Siamese*	60	40
1887	"	5fo *Blue Persian*	1.25	85
		Nos. 1880-1887 (8)	3.30	2.10

Zoltan Kodaly, by Sandor Légrády
A405

1968, Apr. 17 Photo. ***Perf. 12½***

1888	A405	5fo gold & multi.	1.20	80

Issued in memory of Zoltan Kodaly (1882-1967), composer and musicologist.

White Storks
A406

Birds: 50f, Golden orioles. 60f, Imperial eagle. 1fo, Red-footed falcons. 1.20fo, Scops owl. 1.50fo, Great bustard. 2fo, European bee-eaters. 2.50fo, Graylag goose.

1968, Apr. 25

Birds in Natural Colors

1889	A406	20f vermilion & lt. ultra.	20	15
1890	"	50f vermilion & gray	15	10
1891	"	60f vermilion & light blue	20	10
1892	"	1fo vermilion & yel. green	25	10
1893	"	1.20fo vermilion & brt. green	35	15
1894	"	1.50fo vermilion & lt. violet	40	20
1895	"	2fo vermilion & pale lilac	60	30
1896	"	2.50fo vermilion & blue green	1.20	90
		Nos. 1889-1896 (8)	3.35	2.00

International Bird Preservation Congress.

City Hall, Kecskemét
A407

Student and Agricultural College
A408

1968, Apr. 25 ***Perf. 12x11½***

1897	A407	2fo brown orange	30	15

600th anniversary of Kecskemét.

Marx Type of 1953.

1968, May 5 Engraved ***Perf. 12***

1898	A230	1fo claret	12	6

Issued to commemorate the 150th anniversary of the birth of Karl Marx (1818-1883).

1968, May 24 Photo. ***Perf. 12x11½***

1899	A408	2fo dk. olive green	35	15

Issued to commemorate the 150th anniversary of the founding of the Agricultural College at Mosonmagyaróvár.

Painting Type of 1967

Paintings: 40f, Girl with Pitcher, by Goya (1746-1828). 60f, Head of an Apostle, by El Greco (c.1541-1614). 1fo, Boy with Apple Basket and Dogs, by Pedro Nunez (1639-1700) (horiz.). 1.50fo, Mary Magdalene, by El Greco. 2.50fo, The Breakfast, by Velazquez (1599-1660) (horiz.). 4fo, The Virgin from The Holy Family, by El Greco. 5fo, The Knife Grinder, by Goya. 10fo, Portrait of a Girl, by Palma Vecchio (1480-1528).

1968, May 30 ***Perf. 12½***

Gold Frame

1900	A390	40f multicolored	6	4
1901	"	60f "	10	8
1902	"	1fo "	20	12
1903	"	1.50fo "	30	18
1904	"	2.50fo "	60	30
1905	"	4fo "	1.00	45
1906	"	5fo "	1.50	80
		Nos. 1900-1906 (7)	3.76	1.97

Souvenir Sheet

1907	A390	10fo multicolored	3.75	3.75

Issued to publicize art treasures in the Budapest Museum of Fine Arts and to publicize an art exhibition. No. 1907 contains one stamp; decorative border and marginal inscription. Size: 86½x94mm.

Lake Balaton at Badacsony
A409

Views on Lake Balaton: 40f like 20f. 60f, Tihanyi Peninsula. 1fo, Sailboats at Almadi. 2fo, Szigliget Bay.

1968-69 Litho. ***Perf. 12***

1908	A409	20f multicolored	6	5
1908A	"	40f multi. ('69)	6	3
		b. Bklt. pane of 6 (2 #1908A, 1 each #1909-1911)	75	
		c. Bklt. pane of 6 (3 #1908A, 1 each #1909-1911)	75	
		d. Bklt. pane of 6 (3 #1908A, 2 #1909, 1 #1911)	65	
1909	"	60f multicolored	10	5
1910	"	1fo "	20	10
1911	"	2fo "	40	30
		Nos. 1908-1911 (5)	82	53

Locomotive, Type 424
A410

1968, July 14 Photo. ***Perf. 12x11½***

1912	A410	2fo gold, lt. blue & slate	50	15

Centenary of the Hungarian State Railroad.

Horses Grazing—A411

Designs: 40f, Horses in storm. 60f, Horse race on the steppe. 80f, Horse-drawn sleigh. 1fo, Four-in-hand and rainbow. 1.40fo, Farm wagon drawn by 7 horses. 2fo, One rider driving five horses. 2.50fo, Campfire on the range. 4fo, Coach with 5 horses.

1968, July 25 ***Perf. 11***

1913	A411	30f multicolored	5	3
1914	"	40f "	10	5
1915	"	60f "	15	8
1916	"	80f "	20	10
1917	"	1fo "	25	12
1918	"	1.40fo "	40	20
1919	"	2fo "	35	25
1920	"	2.50fo "	60	40
1921	"	4fo "	1.20	75
		Nos. 1913-1921 (9)	3.30	1.98

Horse breeding on the Hungarian steppe (Puszta).

Mihály Tompa
A412

1968, July 30 Photo. ***Perf. 12x11½***

1922	A412	60f blue black	20	5

Issued to commemorate the centenary of the death of Mihály Tompa (1817-1868), poet.

Festival Emblem, Bulgarian and Hungarian National Costumes
A413

1968, Aug. 3 Litho. ***Perf. 12***

1923	A413	60f multicolored	20	5

Issued to publicize the 9th Youth Festival for Peace and Friendship, Sofia, Bulgaria.

Souvenir Sheet

Runners and Aztec Calendar Stone
A414

1968, Aug. 21 Photo. ***Perf. 12½***

1924	A414	10fo multicolored	4.25	4.25

Issued to publicize the 19th Olympic Games, Mexico City, Oct. 12-27. No. 1924 has gold marginal inscription and Olympic Rings in multicolor. Size: 80x101mm.

Scientific Society Emblem A415 — Hesperis A416

Photogravure

1968, Dec. 10 *Perf. 12½x11½*

1925 A415 2fo brt. bl. & blk. 40 15

Issued to publicize the work of the Society for the Popularization of Scientific Knowledge.

1968 Oct. 29 *Perf. 11½x12*

Garden Flowers: 60f, Pansy. 80f, Zinnias. 1fo, Morning-glory. 1.40fo, Petunia. 1.50fo, Portulaca. 2fo, Michaelmas daisies. 2.50fo, Dahlia.

Flowers in Natural Colors

1926 A416 20f gray 5 5
1927 " 60f light green 10 5
1928 " 80f bluish lilac 10 6
1929 " 1fo buff 15 10
1930 " 1.40fo light greenish blue 30 20
1931 " 1.50fo light blue 40 25
1932 " 2fo pale pink 50 35
1933 " 2.50fo light blue 1.00 60
Nos. 1926-1933 (8) 2.60 1.66

Pioneers Saluting Communist Party—A417

Children's Paintings: 60f, Four pioneers holding banner saluting Communist Party. 1fo, Pioneer camp.

1968, Nov. 16 Photo. *Perf. 12x11½*

1934 A417 40f buff & multi. 12 8
1935 " 60f " " 25 10
1936 " 1fo " " 50 20

Issued to commemorate the 50th anniversary of the Communist Party of Hungary. The designs are from a competition among elementary school children.

Workers, Monument by Z. Olcsai-Kiss—A418

Design: 1fo, "Workers of the World Unite!" poster by N. Por (vert.).

Perf. 11½x12, 12x11½

1968, Nov. 24 Photogravure

1937 A418 1fo gold, red, & blk. 12 5
1938 " 2fo gold & multi. 24 10

Issued to commemorate the 50th anniversary of the Communist Party of Hungary.

Human Rights Flame A419

1968, Dec. 10 *Perf. 12½x11½*

1939 A419 1fo dark red brown 15 3

International Human Rights Year.

Painting Type of 1967

Italian Paintings: 40f, Esterhazy Madonna, by Raphael. 60f, The Annunciation, by Bernardo Strozzi. 1fo, Portrait of a Young Man, by Raphael. 1.50fo, The Three Graces, by Battista Naldini. 2.50fo, Portrait of a Man, by Sebastiano del Piombo. 4fo, The Doge Marcantonio Trevisani, by Titian. 5fo, Venus, Cupid and Jealousy, by Angelo Bronzino. 10fo, Bathsheba Bathing, by Sebastiano Ricci (horiz.).

1968, Dec. 10 Photo. *Perf. 12½*

Gold Frame

1940 A390 40f multicolored 5 3
1941 " 60f " 10 6
1942 " 1fo " 15 10
1943 " 1.50fo " 30 15
1944 " 2.50fo " 60 30
1945 " 4fo " 1.00 50
1946 " 5fo " 1.50 90
Nos. 1940-1946 (7) 3.70 2.04

Miniature Sheet

Perf. 11

1947 A390 10fo multicolored 3.75 3.75

Issued to publicize art treasures in the Budapest Museum of Fine Arts. No. 1947 contains one stamp and gray margin showing Museum. Size of stamp: 62x45mm.; size of sheet: 115x72mm.

1869 and 1969 Emblems of Athenaeum Press A420 — Endre Ady A421

1969, Jan. 27 *Perf. 12½x11½*

1948 A420 2fo gold, gray, light blue & black 40 8

Centenary of Athenaeum Press, Budapest.

1969, Jan. 27 *Perf. 11½x12*

1949 A421 1fo multicolored 25 5

Issued to commemorate the 50th anniversary of the death of Endre Ady (1877-1919), lyric poet.

Olympic Medal and Women's Javelin A422

Olympic Medal and: 60f, Canadian singles (canoeing). 1fo, Soccer. 1.20fo, Hammer throw. 2fo, Fencing. 3fo, Greco-Roman Wrestling. 4fo, Kayak single. 5fo, Equestrian. 10fo, Head of Mercury by Praxiteles and Olympic torch.

1969, Mar. 7 Photo. *Perf. 12*

1950 A422 40f gold, green, brn. & gray 10 5
1951 " 60f gold, dk. blue, brn. & gray 15 5
1952 " 1fo gold, red, brn. & gray 15 10
1953 " 1.20fo gold, green, brn. & gray 20 10
1954 " 2fo gold, rose magenta, brn. & gray 25 20
1955 " 3fo gold, ultra., brn. & gray 50 20
1956 " 4fo gold, Prus. bl., brn. & gray 75 30
1957 " 5fo gold, brt. pur., brn. & gray 1.20 90
Nos. 1950-1957 (8) 3.30 1.90

Souvenir Sheet

Litho. *Perf. 11½*

1958 A422 10fo multicolored 3.75 3.75

Issued to commemorate the victories won by the Hungarian team in the 1968 Olympic Games, Mexico City, Oct. 12-27, 1968. No. 1958 contains one stamp (size: 45x38mm.) gray margin inscribed "Mexico 68" and "München 72". Size: 110x 84mm.

1919 Revolutionary Poster A423

Revolutionary Posters: 60f, Lenin. 1fo, Man breaking chains. 2fo, Industrial worker looking at family and farm. 3fo, Militia recruiter. 10fo, Shouting revolutionist with red banner (horiz.).

1969, Mar. 21 Photo. *Perf. 11½x12*

Gold Frame

1960 A423 40f red & black 5 3
1961 " 60f " " 8 3
1962 " 1fo red & black 12 5
1963 " 2fo blk., gray & red 30 10
1964 " 3fo multicolored 45 20
Nos. 1060-1064 (5) 1.00 41

Souvenir Sheet

Perf. 12½

1965 A423 10fo red, gray & black 2.00 2.00

Issued to commemorate the 50th anniversary of the proclamation of the Hungarian Soviet Republic.

The 60f red lilac with 4-line black printing on back was given away by the Hungarian Post Office.

No. 1965 contains one stamp (size: 51x 38½mm.); slate margin with white commemorative inscription. Size: 96x70mm.

Jersey Tiger—A424

Designs: Various Butterflies and Moths.

1969, Apr. 15 Litho. *Perf. 12*

Multicolored

1966 A424 40f *shown* 15 6
1967 " 60f *Eyed hawk moth* 15 6
1968 " 80f *Painted lady* 15 10
1969 " 1fo *Tiger moth* 20 12
1970 " 1.20fo *Small fire moth* 25 15
1971 " 2fo *Large blue* 60 25
1972 " 3fo *Belted oak egger* 80 40
1973 " 4fo *Peacock* 1.20 80
Nos. 1966-1973 (8) 3.50 1.94

ILO Emblem A426

Photogravure

1969, May 22 *Perf. 12x11½*

1974 A426 1fo carmine lake & lake 25 5

Issued to commemorate the 50th anniversary of the International Labor Organization.

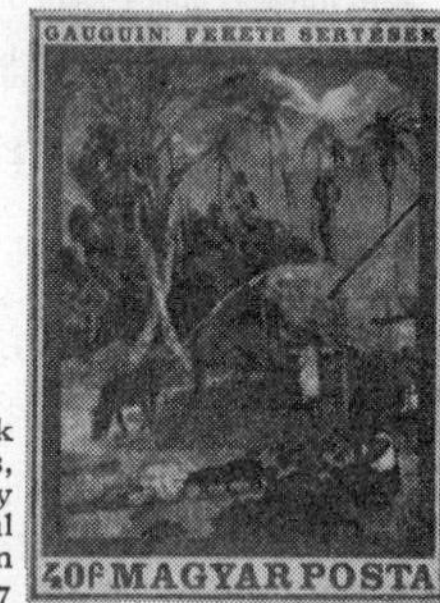

Black Pigs, by Paul Gauguin A427

French Paintings: 60f, These Women, by Toulouse-Lautrec (horiz.). 1fo, Venus in the Clouds, by Simon Vouet. 2fo, Lady with Fan, by Edouard Manet (horiz.). 3fo, La Petra Camara (dancer), by Théodore Chassériau. 4fo, The Cowherd, by Constant Troyon (horiz.). 5fo, The Wrestlers, by Gustave Courbet. 10fo, Pomona, by Nicolas Fouché.

1969, May 28 Photo. *Perf. 12½*

Gold Frame

1975 A427 40f multicolored 10 5
1976 " 60f " 15 6
1977 " 1fo " 15 12
1978 " 2fo " 35 20
1979 " 3fo " 60 35
1980 " 4fo " 80 45
1981 " 5fo " 1.25 80
Nos. 1975-1981 (7) 3.40 2.03

Miniature Sheet

1982 A427 10fo multicolored 3.75 3.75

Issued to publicize art treasures in the Budapest Museum of Fine Arts. No. 1982 contains one stamp with buff and gold margin. Size of stamp: 40x62mm.; size of sheet: 75x96½mm.

Hotel Budapest A428 — Budapest Post Office 100 A429

1969, May Photogravure *Perf. 11*

1983 A428 1fo brown 20 5

Coil Stamps

1970, Aug. 3 *Perf. 14*

1983B A429 40f gray 10 5
1983a A428 1fo brown 25 8

Yellow control number on back of every 5th stamp.

Arms and Buildings of Vac A430

Towns of the Danube Bend: 1fo, Szentendre. 1.20fo, Visegrad. 3fo, Esztergom.

1969, June 9 Litho. *Perf. 12*

1984 A430 40f multicolored 5 3
 a. Bklt. pane of 6 (4 #1984, 1 each #1985, 1987) 90
 b. Bklt. pane of 6 (3 #1984, 2 each #1985, 1986) 90
1985 A430 1fo multicolored 15 5
1986 " 1.20fo " 20 10
1987 " 3fo " 45 20

Stamps in booklet panes Nos. 1984a–1984b come in two arrangements.

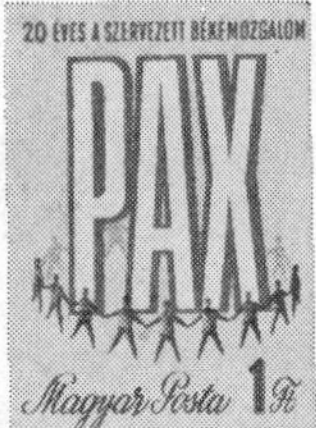

"PAX" and Men Holding Hands
A431

1969, June 17 Photo. *Perf. 11½x12*

1988 A431 1fo lt. blue, dark blue & gold 20 5

20th anniversary of Peace Movement.

The Scholar, by Rembrandt
A432

1969, Sept. 15 *Perf. 11½x12*

1989 A432 1fo sepia 20 8

Issued to publicize the 22nd International Congress of Art Historians, Budapest.

Fossilized Zelkova Leaves
A433

1969, Sept. 21 Photogravure

Designs: 60f, Greenockit calcite sphalerite crystals. 1fo, Fossilized fish, clupea hungarica. 1.20fo, Quartz crystals. 2fo, Ammonite. 3fo, Copper. 4fo, Fossilized turtle, placochelys placodonta. 5fo, Cuprite crystals.

1990 A433 40f red, gray & sepia 8 6
1991 " 60f vio., yellow & black 10 6
1992 " 1fo blue, tan & brown 15 6
1993 " 1.20fo emerald, gray & lilac 20 9
1994 " 2fo olive, tan & brown 24 15
1995 " 3fo org., brt. & dk. green 45 30
1996 " 4fo dull black grn., brn. & black 75 40
1997 " 5fo multi. 1.20 65
 Nos. 1990-1997 (8) 3.17 1.77

Issued to commemorate the centenary of the Hungarian State Institute of Geology.

Steeplechase
A434

Designs: 60f, Fencing. 1fo, Pistol shooting. 2fo, Swimmers at start. 3fo, Relay race. 5fo, Pentathlon.

Perf. 12x11½

1969, Sept. 15 Photogravure

1998 A434 40f blue & multi. 20 5
1999 " 60f multicolored 20 6
2000 " 1fo " 20 10
2001 " 2fo violet & multi. 40 15
2002 " 3fo lemon & multi. 65 30
2003 " 5fo bluish grn., gold & dark red 1.25 75
 Nos. 1998-2003 (6) 2.90 1.41

Hungarian Pentathlon Championships.

First Hungarian Postal Card
A435

1969, Oct. 1

2004 A435 60f verm. & ocher 15 4

Issued to commemorate the centenary of the postal card. Hungary and Austria both issued cards in 1869.

Mahatma Gandhi
A436

1969, Oct. 1 *Perf. 11½x12*

2005 A436 5fo green & multi. 1.50 60

Issued to commemorate the centenary of the birth of Mohandas K. Gandhi (1869–1948), leader in India's fight for independence.

World Trade Union Emblem
A437

1969, Oct. 17 Photo. *Perf. 12x11½*

2006 A437 2fo fawn & dk. blue 30 10

Issued to publicize the 7th Congress of the World Federation of Trade Unions.

Janos Balogh Nagy, Self-portrait
A438

1969, Oct. 17 *Perf. 11½x12*

2007 A438 5fo gold & multi. 1.25 50

Issued to commemorate the 50th anniversary of the death of Janos Balogh Nagy (1874–1919), painter.

St. John the Evangelist, by Anthony Van Dyck
A439

Dutch Paintings: 60f, Three Fruit Pickers (by Pieter de Molyn?). 1fo, Boy Lighting Pipe, by Hendrick Terbrugghen. 2fo, The Feast, by Jan Steen. 3fo, Woman Reading Letter, by Pieter de Hooch. 4fo, The Fiddler, by Dirk Hals. 5fo, Portrait of Jan Asselyn, by Frans Hals. 10fo, Mucius Scaevola before Porsena, by Rubens and Van Dyck.

1969–70 Photogravure *Perf. 12½*

Black and Gold Frame

2008 A439 40f multicolored 8 4
2009 " 60f " 9 5
2010 " 1fo " 15 7
2011 " 2fo " 30 15
2012 " 3fo " 50 25
2013 " 4fo " 60 30
2014 " 5fo " 1.20 70
 Nos. 2008-2014 (7) 2.92 1.56

Miniature Sheet

2015 A439 10fo multicolored 3.75 3.75

Issued to publicize treasures in the Museum of Fine Arts, Budapest and the Museum in Eger. No. 2015 contains one stamp with brown and gold frame. Size: 73x96mm.

Issue Dates: Nos. 2008–2014, Dec. 2, 1969; No. 2015, Jan. 1970.

Kiskunfelegyhaza Circling Pigeon
A440

1969, Dec. 12 Photo. *Perf. 11½x12*

2016 A440 1fo multicolored 20 8

Issued to publicize the International Pigeon Show, Budapest, Dec. 1969.

Subway
A441

1970, Apr. 3 Photo. *Perf. 12*

2017 A441 1fo black, light green & ultra. 25 8

Opening of new Budapest subway.

Souvenir Sheet

Panoramic View of Budapest 1945 and 1970, and Soviet Cenotaph—A442

1970, Apr. 3 *Perf. 12x11½*

2018 A442 Sheet of 2 3.75 3.75
 a. 5fo "1945" 1.50 1.50
 b. 5fo "1970" 1.50 1.50

Issued to commemorate the 25th anniversary of the liberation of Budapest. Size of stamps: 128x22mm. Size of sheet: 156x82mm.

Cloud Formation, Satellite, Earth and Receiving Station
A443

Lenin Statue, Budapest
A444

1970, Apr. 8 Litho. *Perf. 12*

2019 A443 1fo dk. blue, yellow & black 25 5

Issued to commemorate the centenary of the Hungarian Meteorological Service.

1970, Apr. 22 Photo. *Perf. 11*

Design: 2fo, Lenin portrait.

2020 A444 1fo gold & multi. 12 3
2021 " 2fo " " 24 4

Issued to commemorate the centenary of the birth of Lenin (1870–1924), Russian communist leader.

Franz Lehar and "Giuditta" Music
A445

1970, Apr. 30 Photo. *Perf. 12*

2022 A445 2fo multicolored 60 20

Issued to commemorate the centenary of the birth of Franz Lehar (1870–1948), composer.

Samson and Delilah, by Michele Rocca
A446

Paintings: 60f, Joseph Telling Dream, by Giovanni Battista Langetti. 1fo, Clio, by Pierre Mignard. 1.50fo, Venus and Satyr, by Sebastiano Ricci (horiz.). 2.50fo, Andromeda, by Francesco Furini. 4fo, Venus, Adonis and Cupid, by Luca Giordano. 5fo, Allegorical Feast, by Corrado Giaquinto. 10fo, Diana and Callisto, by Abraham Janssens (horiz.).

1970, June 2 Photo. ***Perf. 12½***

2023	A446	40f gold & multi.	20	6
2024	"	60f " "	15	10
2025	"	1fo " "	25	12
2026	"	1.50fo " "	30	18
2027	"	2.50fo " "	60	30
2028	"	4fo " "	1.00	50
2029	"	5fo " "	1.25	80
		Nos. 2023-2029 (7)	3.75	2.06

Miniature Sheet

Perf. 11

2030 A446 10fo gold & multi. 3.75 3.75

No. 2030 contains one horizontal stamp (size: 63x46mm.), gold marginal inscription. Size: 100x85mm.

Beethoven Statue, by Janos Pasztor, at Martonvasar

A447

1970, June 27 Litho. ***Perf. 12***

2031 A447 1fo plum, gray grn. & org. yellow 50 10

Issued to commemorate the bicentenary of the birth of Ludwig van Beethoven (1770–1827), composer. The music in the design is from Sonata 37.

Foundryman A448 — King Stephen I A449

1970, July 28 Litho. ***Perf. 12***

2032 A448 1fo multicolored 20 6

Issued to commemorate the 200th anniversary of the first Hungarian steel foundry at Diosgyor, now the Lenin Metallurgical Works.

1970, Aug. 19 Photo. ***Perf. 11½x12***

2033 A449 3fo multicolored 1.00 40

Issued to commemorate the millenary of the birth of Saint Stephen, first King of Hungary.

Women's Four on Lake Tata and Tata Castle

A450

1970, Aug. 19 Litho. ***Perf. 12***

2034 A450 1fo multicolored 20 8

Issued to commemorate the 17th European Women's Rowing Championships, Lake Tata.

Mother Giving Bread to her Children, FAO Emblem—A451

1970, Sept. 21 Litho. ***Perf. 12***

2035 A451 1fo lt. bl. & multi. 20 5

Issued to publicize the 7th European Regional Congress of the United Nations' Food and Agricultural Organization, Budapest, Sept. 21–25.

Boxing and Olympic Rings

A452

Designs (Olympic Rings and): 60f, Canoeing. 1fo, Fencing. 1.50fo, Water polo. 2fo, Woman gymnast. 2.50fo, Hammer throwing. 3fo, Wrestling. 5fo, Swimming, butterfly stroke.

1970, Sept. 26 Photo. ***Perf. 11***

2036	A452	40f lt. vio. & multi.	8	5
2037	"	60f sky bl. & multi.	10	5
2038	"	1fo org. & multi.	15	10
2039	"	1.50fo multicolored	25	15
2040	"	2fo "	40	20
2041	"	2.50fo "	50	25
2042	"	3fo "	75	45
2043	"	5fo "	1.20	60
		Nos. 2036-2043 (8)	3.43	1.85

Issued to commemorate the 75th anniversary of the Hungarian Olympic Committee. The 5fo also publicizes the 1972 Olympic Games in Munich.

Flame and Family

A453

1970, Sept. 28 Litho. ***Perf. 12***

2044 A453 1fo ultra., orange & emerald 20 5

5th Education Congress, Budapest.

Chalice, by Benedek Suky, 1440

A454

Hungarian Goldsmiths' Art: 60f, Altar burette, 1500. 1fo, Nadasdy goblet, 16th century. 1.50fo, Coconut goblet, 1600. 2fo, Silver tankard, by Mihaly Toldalaghy, 1623. 2.50fo, Communion cup of Gyorgy Rakoczy I, 1670. 3fo, Tankard, 1690. 4fo, Bell-flower cup, 1710.

1970, Oct. Photo. ***Perf. 12***

2045	A454	40f gold & multi.	20	5
2046	"	60f " "	20	6
2047	"	1fo " "	20	10
2048	"	1.50fo " "	25	15
2049	"	2fo " "	35	20
2050	"	2.50fo " "	40	25
2051	"	3fo " "	70	45
2052	"	4fo " "	1.10	75
		Nos. 2045-2052 (8)	3.40	2.01

Virgin and Child, by Giampietrino

A455

Paintings from Christian Museum, Esztergom: 60f, "Love" (woman with 3 children), by Gregorio Lazzarini. 1fo, Legend of St. Catherine, by Master of Bat. 1.50fo, Adoration of the Shepherds, by Francesco Fontebasso (horiz.). 2.50fo, Adoration of the Kings, by Master of Aranyosmarot. 4fo, Temptation of St. Anthony the Hermit, by Jan de Cock. 5fo, St. Sebastian, by Marco Palmezzano. 10fo, Lady with the Unicorn, by Painter of Lombardy.

1970, Dec. 7 Photo. ***Perf. 12½***

2053	A455	40f silver & multi.	15	5
2054	"	60f " "	20	10
2055	"	1fo " "	20	15
2056	"	1.50fo " "	30	20
2057	"	2.50fo " "	50	30
2058	"	4fo " "	75	40
2059	"	5fo " "	1.20	75
		Nos. 2053-2059 (7)	3.30	1.95

Souvenir Sheet

2060 A455 10fo silver & multi. 4.00 4.00

No 2060 contains one stamp (size: 50½x56mm.); silver margin with red inscription. Size: 70½x84½mm.

Monument to Hungarian Martyrs, by A. Makrisz

A456

1970, Dec. 30 Photo. ***Perf. 12x11½***

2061 A456 1fo ultra. & sepia 20 5

The 25th anniversary of the liberation of the concentration camps at Auschwitz, Mauthausen and Dachau.

"Marseillaise," by François Rude A457 — Béla Bartók A458

1971, March 18 Litho. ***Perf. 12***

2062 A457 3fo bister & green 60 30

Centenary of the Paris Commune.

1971

Design: No. 2064, András L. Achim.

2063 A458 1fo gray & dk. car. 40 10

2064 " 1fo gray & green 25 5

90th anniversary of the birth of Béla Bartók (1881–1945), composer, and centenary of the birth of András L. Achim (1871–1911), peasant leader. Dates of issue: No. 2063, March 25; No. 2064, Apr. 17.

Györ Castle, 1594

A459

1971, March 27

2065 A459 2fo lt. bl. & multi. 40 12

700th anniversary of Györ.

Bison Hunt—A460

Designs: 60f, Wild boar hunt. 80f, Deer hunt. 1fo, Falconry. 1.20fo, Felled stag and dogs. 2fo, Bustards. 3fo, Net fishing. 4fo, Angling.

1971, May Photogravure ***Perf. 12***

2066	A460	40f verm. & multi.	6	4
2067	"	60f plum & multi.	8	6
2068	"	80f multicolored	10	8
2069	"	1fo lilac & multi.	20	12
2070	"	1.20fo multicolored	25	25
2071	"	2fo "	50	30
2072	"	3fo "	75	40
2073	"	4fo grn. & multi.	1.20	75
		Nos. 2066-2073 (8)	3.14	2.00

World Hunting Exhibition, Budapest, Aug. 27–30. See also No. C313.

Souvenir Sheet

Portrait of a Man, by Dürer—A461

1971, May 21 ***Perf. 12½***

2074 A461 10fo gold & multi. 3.75 3.75

500th anniversary of the birth of Albrecht Dürer (1471–1528), German painter and etcher. Sheet margin design of bister brown "frame" is after a Dürer woodcut. Size: 80x111mm.

Carnation and Pioneers' Emblem
A462

1971, June 2 Photogravure *Perf. 12*

2075	A462	1fo dk. red & multi.	20	4

25th anniversary of the Hungarian Pioneers' Organization.

FIR Emblem, Resistance Fighters
A463

1971, July 3

2076	A463	1fo brown & multi.	25	5

International Federation of Resistance Fighters (FIR), 20th anniversary.

Walking in Garden, Tokyo School
A464

Japanese Prints from Museum of East Asian Art, Budapest: 60f, Geisha in Boat, by Yeishi (1756–1829). 1fo, Woman with Scroll, by Yeishi. 1.50fo, Courtesans, by Kiyonaga (1752–1815). 2fo, Awabi Fisher Women, by Utamaro (1753–1806). 2.50fo, Seated Courtesan, by Harunobu (1725–1770). 3fo, Peasant Woman Carrying Fagots, by Hokusai (1760–1849). 4fo, Women and Girls Walking, by Yeishi.

1971, July 9 ***Perf. 12½***

2077	A464	40f gold & multi.	10	3
2078	"	60f " "	15	8
2079	"	1fo " "	20	12
2080	"	1.50fo " "	25	15
2081	"	2fo " "	35	20
2082	"	2.50fo " "	40	30
2083	"	3fo " "	60	35
2084	"	4fo " "	1.20	55
		Nos. 2077-2084 (8)	3.25	1.78

Locomotive, Map of Rail System and Danube
A465

1971, July 15 Litho. *Perf. 12*

2086	A465	1fo multicolored	40	10

125th anniversary of first Hungarian railroad between Pest and Vac.

Griffin Holding Ink Balls
A466

1971, Sept. 11 Photo. *Perf. 12x11½*

2087	A466	1fo multicolored	60	50

Centenary of stamp printing in Hungary. Printed se-tenant with 2 labels showing printing presses of 1871 and 1971 and Hungary Nos. P1 and 1171.

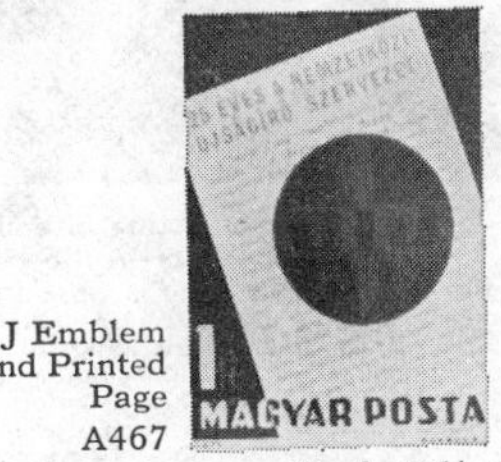

OIJ Emblem and Printed Page
A467

1971, Sept. 21 ***Perf. 11½x12***

2088	A467	1fo dk. blue, blue & gold	30	10

25th anniversary of the International Organization of Journalists (OIJ).

Josef Jacob Winterl and Barren Strawberry—A468

Plants: 60f, Bromeliaceae. 80f, Titanopsis calcarea. 1fo, Periwinkle. 1.20fo, Gymnocalycium. 2fo, White water lily. 3fo, Iris arenaria. 5fo, Peony.

1971, Oct. 29 Litho. *Perf. 12*

2089	A468	40f lt. vio. & multi.	4	5
2090	"	60f gray & multi.	10	10
2091	"	80f multicolored	15	10
2092	"	1fo "	15	12
2093	"	1.20fo lilac & multi.	25	15
2094	"	2fo gray & multi.	40	20
2095	"	3fo multicolored	75	45
2096	"	5fo "	1.20	75
		Nos. 2089-2096 (8)	3.04	1.92

Bicentenary of Budapest Botanical Gardens.

Galloping—A469

Equestrian Sports: 60f, Trotting. 80f, Horses fording river. 1fo, Jumping. 1.20fo, Start. 2fo, Polo. 3fo, Steeplechase. 5fo, Dressage.

1971, Nov. 22 Photo. *Perf. 12*

2097	A469	40f blue & multi.	4	3
2098	"	60f ocher & multi.	10	8
2099	"	80f olive & multi.	12	10
2100	"	1fo red & multi.	15	12
2101	"	1.20fo multicolored	25	15
2102	"	2fo "	40	20
2103	"	3fo violet & multi.	75	45
2104	"	5fo blue & multi.	1.20	65
		Nos. 2097-2104 (8)	3.01	1.78

Beheading of Heathen Chief Koppany
A470

Designs: 60f, Samuel Aba pursuing King Peter. 1fo, Basarad's victory over King Charles Robert. 1.50fo, Strife between King Salomon and Prince Geza. 2.50fo, Founding of Obuda Church by King Stephen I and Queen Gisela. 4fo, Reconciliation of King Koloman and his brother Almos. 5fo, Oradea Church built by King Ladislas I. 10fo, Funeral of Prince Emeric and blinding of Vazul.

1971, Dec. 10 Lithographed

2105	A470	40f buff & multi.	4	3
2106	"	60f " "	6	5
2107	"	1fo " "	15	10
2108	"	1.50fo " "	25	15
2109	"	2.50fo " "	45	25
2110	"	4fo " "	70	40
2111	"	5fo " "	1.30	70
		Nos. 2105-2111 (7)	2.95	1.68

Miniature Sheet

Perf. 11½

2112	A470	10fo buff & multi.	3.75	3.75

History of Hungary, from miniatures from Illuminated Chronicle of King Louis the Great, c. 1370. No. 2112 contains one stamp (size 44½x52mm.). Salmon and gold margin. Size of sheet: 84x93mm.

Equality Year Emblem
A471

1971, Dec. 30 Litho. *Perf. 12*

2113	A471	1fo bister & multi.	20	5

International Year Against Racial Discrimination.

Ice Hockey and Sapporo '72 Emblem—A472

Sport and Sapporo '72 Emblem: 60f, Men's slalom. 80f, Women's figure skating. 1fo, Ski jump. 1.20fo, Long-distance skiing. 2fo, Men's figure skating. 3fo, Bobsledding. 4fo, Biathlon. 10fo, Buddha.

1971, Dec. 30 ***Perf. 12***

2114	A472	40f blk. & multi.	4	3
2115	"	60f " "	8	5
2116	"	80f " "	12	10
2117	"	1fo " "	15	12
2118	"	1.20fo " "	30	15
2119	"	2fo " "	50	30
2120	"	3fo " "	75	40
2121	"	4fo " "	1.20	75
		Nos. 2114-2121 (8)	3.14	1.90

Souvenir Sheet

Perf. 11½

2122	A472	10fo gold & multi.	4.00	4.00

11th Winter Olympic Games, Sapporo, Japan, Feb. 3–13, 1972. No. 2122 contains one stamp (size 86x48mm.) Hungarian and Japanese marginal inscription and figure skating pair. Size: 132½x87½ mm.

Hungarian Locomotive—A473

Locomotives: 60f, Germany. 80f, Italy. 1fo, Soviet Union. 1.20fo, Japan. 2fo, Great Britain. 4fo, Austria. 5fo, France.

1972, Feb. 23 Photo. *Perf. 12x11½*

2123	A473	40f multicolored	4	3
2124	"	60f ocher & multi.	8	5
2125	"	80f multicolored	12	10
2126	"	1fo olive & multi.	15	12
2127	"	1.20fo ultra. & multi.	25	15
2128	"	2fo verm. & multi.	35	25
2129	"	4fo multicolored	75	45
2130	"	5fo "	1.25	75
		Nos. 2123-2130 (8)	2.99	1.90

Janus Pannonius, by Andrea Mantegna
A474

1972, Mar. 27 Litho. *Perf. 12*

2131	A474	1fo gold & multi.	25	10

500th anniversary of the death of Janus Pannonius (Johannes Czezmiczei, 1434–1472), humanist and poet.

Mariner 9—A475

Design: No. 2133, Mars 2 and 3 spacecraft.

1972, Mar. 30 Photo. *Perf. 11½x12*

2132	A475	2fo dk. bl. & multi.	40	40
2133	"	2fo multicolored	40	40
	a.	Strip #2132-2133 + label	1.20	1.20

Exploration of Mars by Mariner 9 (U.S.), and Mars 2 and 3 (U.S.S.R.). Issued in sheets containing 4 each of Nos. 2132–2133 and 4 labels inscribed in Hungarian, Russian and English.

13th Century Church Portal
A476

1972, Apr. 11

2134	A476	3fo greenish black	60	15

Centenary of the Society for the Protection of Historic Monuments.

Hungarian Greyhound—A477

Hounds: 60f, Afghan hound (head). 80f, Irish wolfhound. 1.20fo, Borzoi. 2fo, Running greyhound. 4fo, Whippet. 6fo, Afghan hound.

1972, Apr. 14 Litho. *Perf. 12*

2135	A477	40f multicolored	4	3
2136	"	60f brn. & multi.	6	5
2137	"	80f multicolored	15	8
2138	"	1.20fo "	20	12
2139	"	2fo "	40	20
2140	"	4fo "	85	40
2141	"	6fo "	1.20	75
		Nos. 2135-2141 (7)	2.90	1.63

József Imre, Emil Grósz, László Blaskovics (Ophthalmologists) A478

Design: 2fo, Allvar Gullstrand, V. P. Filatov, Jules Gonin, ophthalmologists.

1972, Apr. 17

2142	A478	1fo red, brn. & blk.	25	10
2143	"	2fo bl., brn. & black	60	30

First European Ophthalmologists' Congress, Budapest.

Girl Reading and UNESCO Emblem A479

1972, May 27 Photo. *Perf. 11½x12*

2144	A479	1fo multicolored	20	10

International Book Year 1971.

Roses A480

1972, June 1

2145	A480	1fo multicolored	20	10

15th Rose Exhibition, Budapest.

George Dimitrov A481

1972, June 18 Litho. *Perf. 12*

2146	A481	3fo black & multi.	45	15

90th anniversary, birth of George Dimitrov (1882-1949), communist leader.

Souvenir Sheet

St. Martin and the Beggar, Stained-glass Window A482

1972, June 20 *Perf. 10½*

2147	A482	10fo multicolored	3.75	3.75

Belgica 72, International Philatelic Exhibition, Brussels, June 24-July 9. No. 2147 contains one stamp and has ocher and gold decorative margin. Size: 68½x94 mm.

Gyorgy Dozsa A483

1972, June 25 Photo. *Perf. 11½x12*

2148	A483	1fo red & multi.	20	5

Gyorgy Dozsa (1474-1514), peasant leader.

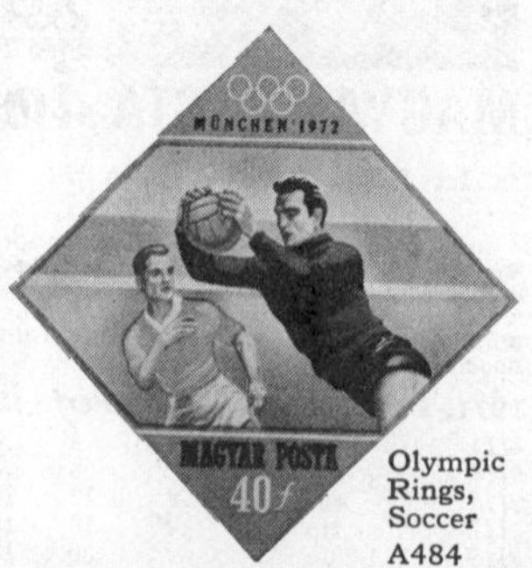

Olympic Rings, Soccer A484

Designs (Olympic Rings and): 60f, Water polo. 80f, Javelin, women's. 1fo, Kayak, women's. 1.20fo, Boxing. 2fo, Gymnastics, women's. 5fo, Fencing.

1972, July 15 *Perf. 11*

2149	A484	40f multicolored	5	3
2150	"	60f "	10	3
2151	"	80f "	12	6
2152	"	1fo lilac & multi.	20	10
2153	"	1.20fo blue & multi.	30	12
2154	"	2fo multicolored	60	25
2155	"	5fo green & multi.	1.00	75
		Nos. 2149-2155, B299 (8)	2.97	1.74

20th Olympic Games, Munich, Aug. 26-Sept. 11. See also No. C325.

Prince Geza Selecting Site of Székesfehérvár—A485

Designs: 60f, St. Stephen, first King of Hungary. 80f, Knights (country's defense). 1.20fo, King Stephen dictating to scribe (legal organization). 2fo, Sculptor at work (education). 4fo, Merchants before king (foreign relations). 6fo, View of castle and town of Székesfehérvár, 10th century. 10fo, King Andreas II presenting Golden Bull to noblemen.

1972, Aug. 20 Photo. *Perf. 12*

2156	A485	40f slate & multi.	10	5
2157	"	60f multicolored	20	8
2158	"	80f lilac & multi.	15	10
2159	"	1.20fo multicolored	25	15
2160	"	2fo bister & multi.	65	25
2161	"	4fo blue & multi.	90	45
2162	"	6fo pur. & multi.	1.20	75
		Nos. 2156-2162 (7)	3.45	1.83

Souvenir Sheet

Perf. 12½

2163	A485	10fo blk. & multi.	3.75	3.75

Millenium of the town of Székesfehérvár and 750th anniversary of the Golden Bull granting rights to lesser nobility. No. 2163 contains one stamp (94x45mm.). Reproduction of Golden Bull in gray, bister and gold margin. Size: 135x90mm.

Parliament, Budapest A486

Design: 6fo, Session room of Parliament.

1972, Aug. 20 Lithographed

2164	A486	5fo dk. bl. & multi.	85	30
2165	"	6fo multicolored	1.20	40

Constitution of 1949.

Eger, 17th Century View, and Bottle of Bull's Blood—A487

Design: 2fo, Contemporary view of Tokay and bottle of Tokay Aszu.

1972, Aug. 21 Litho. *Perf. 12*

2166	A487	1fo buff & multi.	30	10
2167	"	2fo green & multi.	75	30

1st World Wine Exhibition, Budapest, Aug. 1972.

Georgikon Emblems, Grain, Potato Flower A488

1972, Sept. 3

2168	A488	1fo multicolored	20	5

175th anniversary of the founding of the Georgikon at Keszthely, the first scientific agricultural academy.

Covered Candy Dish A489

Herend Porcelain: 40f, Vase with bird. 80f, Vase with flowers and butterflies. 1fo, Plate with Mexican landscape. 1.20fo, Covered dish. 2fo, Teapot, cup and saucer. 4fo, Plate with flowers. 5fo, Baroque vase showing Herend factory.

1972, Sept. 15

Sizes: 23x46mm. (40f, 80f, 2fo, 5fo); 33x36mm., others

2169	A489	40f gray & multi.	5	3
2170	"	60f ocher & multi.	8	5
2171	"	80f multicolored	15	10
2172	"	1fo "	20	12
2173	"	1.20fo grn. & multi.	25	15
2174	"	2fo multicolored	40	25
2175	"	4fo red & multi.	75	45
2176	"	5fo multicolored	1.00	75
		Nos. 2169-2176 (8)	2.88	1.90

Herend china factory, founded 1839.

UIC Emblem and M-62 Diesel Locomotive—A490

1972, Sept. 19 Photo. *Perf. 11½x12*

2177	A490	1fo dark red	20	5

50th anniversary of International Railroad Union Congress, Budapest, Sept. 19.

"25" and Graph A491

1972, Sept. *Perf. 11½x12*

2178	A491	1fo yellow & brown	20	5

Planned national economy, 25th anniversary.

View of Obuda, 1872 A492

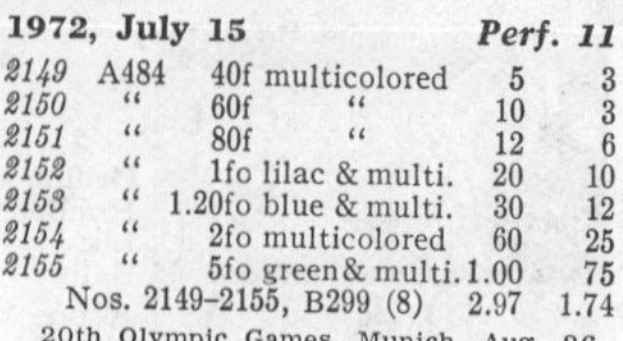

Designs: No. 2180, Budapest, 1972. No. 2181, Buda, 1872. No. 2182, Budapest, 1972. No. 2183, Pest, 1872. No. 2184, Budapest, 1972.

1972, Sept. 26 *Perf. 12x11½*

2179	A492	1fo Prussian blue & rose carmine	20	10
2180	"	1fo rose carmine & Prussian blue	20	10
2181	"	2fo ocher & olive	40	15
2182	"	2fo olive & ocher	40	15
2183	"	3fo grn. & lt. brown	60	20
2184	"	3fo lt. brn. & green	60	20
		Nos. 2179-2184 (6)	2.40	90

Centenary of unification of Obuda, Buda and Pest into Budapest. Stamps of same denomination printed se-tenant.

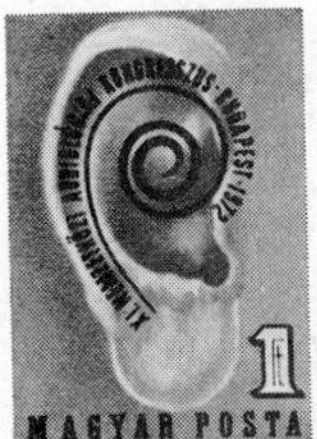

Ear and Congress Emblem
A493

1972, Oct. 3 *Perf. 11½x12*

2185 A493 1fo brn., yel. & blk. 20 5

11th International Audiology Congress, Budapest.

Flora Martos
A494

Portrait: No. 2187, Miklós Radnóti.

1972 Photogravure *Perf. 11½x12*

2186	A494	1fo grn. & multi.	15	5
2187	"	1fo brn. & multi.	15	5

75th anniversary of the birth of Flora Martos (1897–1938), Hungarian Labor Party leader, and to honor Miklós Radnóti (1909–1944), poet (No. 1287).

Issue dates: No. 2186, Nov. 5; No. 2187, Nov. 11.

Muses, by Jozsef Rippl-Ronai
A495

Stained-glass Windows, 19th–20th Centuries: 60f, 16th century scribe, by Ferenc Sebesteny. 1fo, Flight into Egypt, by Karoly Lotz and Bertalan Székely. 1.50fo, Prince Arpad's Messenger, by Jenö Percz. 2.50fo, Nativity, by Lili Sztehlo. 4fo, Prince Arpad and Leaders, by Karoly Kernstock. 5fo, King Matthias and Jester, by Jenö Haranghy.

1972, Nov. 15 *Perf. 12*

2188	A495	40f multicolored		5	3
2189	"	60f	"	10	8
2190	"	1fo	"	15	12
2191	"	1.50fo	"	30	15
2192	"	2.50fo	"	50	25
2193	"	4fo	"	80	40
2194	"	5fo	"	1.00	75
		Nos. 2188-2194 (7)		2.90	1.78

Weaver, Cloth and Cog-wheel
A496

1972, Nov. 27 Litho. *Perf. 12*

2195 A496 1fo silver & multi. 20 8

Opening of Museum of Textile Techniques, Budapest.

Main Square, Szarvas
A497

Designs: 1fo, Modern buildings, Salgotarjan. 3fo, Tokay and vineyard. 4fo, Esztergom Cathedral. 7fo, Town Hall, Kaposvar. 20fo, Veszprem.

1972–73 Lithographed *Perf. 11*

Size: 20x17mm.

2196	A497	40f brown & orange	8	3
2197	"	1fo dk. & lt. blue	20	4

Perf. 12x11½

Size: 28x21mm.

2198	A497	3fo dk. & lt. green ('73)	60	5
2199	"	4fo red brn. & org. ('73)	80	8
2200	"	7fo blue violet & lilac ('73)	1.40	15
2200A	"	20fo multi. ('73)	4.00	60
		Nos. 2196-2200A (6)	7.08	95

Coil Stamps
Types of 1963–64

Designs: 2fo, Mobile radio transmitter and stadium. 3fo, P.O. parcel conveyor. 4fo, Television transmitter (vert.). 6fo, Woman teletypist.

1972, Nov. Photo. *Perf. 14*

Size: 21½x17½mm., 17½x21½mm.

2201	A337	2fo blue green	40	15
2202	"	3fo dark blue	60	20
2203	"	4fo blue	80	25
2204	"	6fo bister	1.20	50

Black control number on back of every 5th stamp.

Minute inscription centered in lower margin: "Legrady Sandor".

Arms of Soviet Union
A498

1972, Dec. 30 Photo. *Perf. 11½x12*

2205 A498 1fo multicolored 15 8

50th anniversary of Soviet Union.

Petöfi Speaking at Pilvax Cafe
A499

Designs: 2fo, Portrait. 3fo, Petöfi on horseback, 1848–49.

1972, Dec. 30 Engr. *Perf. 12*

2206	A499	1fo rose carmine	20	10
2207	"	2fo violet	40	20
2208	"	3fo Prussian green	60	35

Sesquicentennial of the birth of Sandor Petöfi (1823–49), poet and revolutionary.

Postal Zone Map of Hungary and Letter-carrying Crow—A500

1973, Jan. 1 Litho. *Perf. 12*

2209 A500 1fo red & black 20 8

Introduction of postal code system.

Imre Madách
A501

1973, Jan. 20 Photo. *Perf. 11½x12*

2210 A501 1fo multicolored 20 8

Sesquicentennial of the birth of Imre Madách (1823–1864), poet and dramatist.

Busho Mask
A502

Designs: Various Busho masks.

1973, Feb. 17 Litho. *Perf. 12*

2211	A502	40f tan & multi.	8	5
2212	"	60f dull grn. & multi.	10	8
2213	"	80f lilac & multi.	15	10
2214	"	1.20fo multicolored	20	15
2215	"	2fo tan & multi.	35	25
2216	"	4fo multicolored	80	60
2217	"	6fo lilac & multi.	1.20	75
		Nos. 2211-2217 (7)	2.88	1.98

Busho Walk at Mohacs, ancient ceremony to drive out winter.

Nicolaus Copernicus
A503

1973, Feb. 19 Engraved *Perf. 12*

2218 A503 3fo brt. ultra. 60 20

500th anniversary of the birth of Nicolaus Copernicus (1473–1543), Polish astronomer. Printed with alternating label showing heliocentric system and view of Torun.

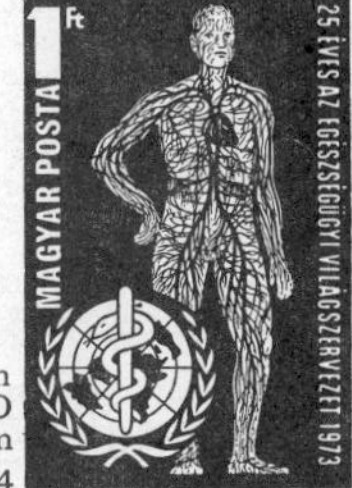

Vascular System and WHO Emblem
A504

1973, Apr. 16 Photo. *Perf. 12*

2219 A504 1fo slate green & brown red 25 10

25th anniversary of the World Health Organization.

Tank, Rocket, Radar, Plane, Ship and Soldier
A505

1973, May 9 Litho. *Perf. 12*

2220 A505 3fo blue & multi. 45 15

Philatelic Exhibition of Military Stamp Collectors of Warsaw Treaty Member States. No. 2220 was printed with alternating label showing flags of Warsaw Treaty members.

Hungary No. 1396 and IBRA '73 Emblem—A506

1973, May 11 Litho. *Perf. 12*

Multicolored

2221	A506	40f *shown*	7	5
2222	"	60f *No. 1397, POLSKA '73*	10	8
2223	"	80f *No. 1398, IBRA '73*	15	10
2224	"	1fo *No. 1399, POLSKA '73*	18	12
2225	"	1.20fo *No. B293a, IBRA '73*	25	15
2226	"	2fo *No. B293b, POLSKA '73*	40	25
2227	"	4fo *No. B293c, IBRA '73*	80	45
2228	"	5fo *No. B293d, POLSKA*	1.00	60
		Nos. 2221-2228 (8)	2.95	1.80

Publicity for IBRA '73 International Philatelic Exhibition, Munich, May 11–20; and POLSKA '73, Poznan, Aug. 15–Sept. 2. See No. C345.

Typesetting, from "Orbis Pictus," by Comenius
A507

Design: 3fo, Printer and wooden screw press, woodcut from Hungarian translation of Gospels.

1973, June 5 Photo. *Perf. 11½x12*

2229	A507	1fo black & gold	15	8
2230	"	3fo " "	45	15

500th anniversary of book printing in Hungary.

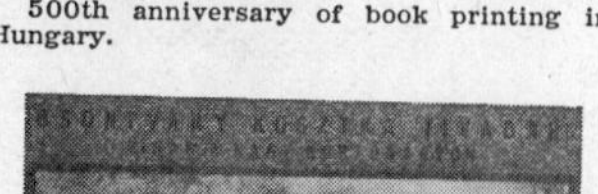

Storm over Hortobagy Puszta, by Csontvary—A508

Paintings: 60f, Mary's Well, Nazareth. 1fo, Carriage Ride by Moonlight in Athens (vert.). 1.50fo, Pilgrimage to Cedars of Lebanon (vert.). 2.50fo, The Lonely Cedar. 4fo, Waterfall at Jajce. 5fo, Ruins of Greek Theater at Taormina. 10fo, Horseback Riders on Shore.

1973, June 18 *Perf. 12½*

2231	A508	40f gold & multi.	6	4
2232	"	60f " "	8	6
2233	"	1fo " "	15	10
2234	"	1.50fo " "	25	15
2235	"	2.50fo " "	45	25
2236	"	4fo " "	70	40
2237	"	5fo " "	1.00	70
		Nos. 2231–2237 (7)	2.69	1.70

Souvenir Sheet

2238	A508	10fo gold & multi.	3.50	3.50

Paintings by Tividar Kosztka Csontvary (1853–1919). No. 2238 contains one stamp (size: 90x43mm.). Gray and gold margin with artist's signature in gold, black control number. Size: 114x75mm.

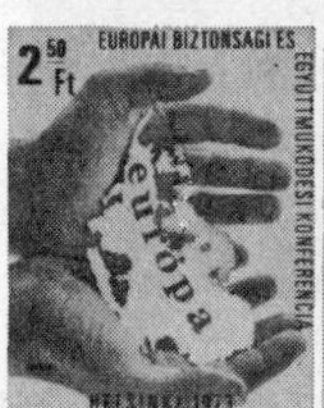

Hands Holding Map of Europe
A509

Cyclamen
A510

1973, July 3 Photo. *Perf. 11½x12*

2239	A509	2.50fo black & golden brn.	1.00	1.00
	a.	Souvenir sheet of 4+2 labels	6.00	6.00

Conference for European Security and Cooperation, Helsinki, July 1973. No. 2239 was printed in souvenir sheet of 4 stamps and 2 blue labels showing conference sites. Black marginal inscription. Size: 122x109mm.

1973, Aug. 4

Designs: Flowers.

Multicolored

2240	A510	40f *Provence roses*	6	4
2241	"	60f *shown*	8	6
2242	"	80f *Lungwort*	12	10
2243	"	1.20fo *English daisies*	20	15
2244	"	2fo *Buttercups*	40	25
2245	"	4fo *Violets*	80	50
2246	"	6fo *Poppies*	1.20	70
		Nos. 2240–2246 (7)	2.86	1.80

"Let's be Friends in Traffic"
A511

Designs: 60f, "Not even one drink." 1fo, "Light your bicycle."

1973, Aug. 18 Photo. *Perf. 12x11½*

2247	A511	40f green & orange	8	5
2248	"	60f purple & org.	10	6
2249	"	1fo indigo & org.	20	10

To publicize traffic rules.

Adoration of the Kings
A512

Paintings: 60f, Angels playing violin and lute. 1fo, Adoration of the Kings. 1.50fo, Annunciation. 2.50fo, Angels playing organ and harp. 4fo, Visitation of Mary. 5fo, Legend of St. Catherine of Alexandria. 10fo, Nativity.

1973, Nov. 3 Photo. *Perf. 12½*

2250	A512	40f gold & multi.	6	4
2251	"	60f " "	8	6
2252	"	1fo " "	15	12
2253	"	1.50fo " "	25	18
2254	"	2.50fo " "	50	30
2255	"	4fo " "	80	50
2256	"	5fo " "	1.10	75
		Nos. 2250–2256 (7)	2.94	1.95

Souvenir Sheet

Perf. 11

2257	A512	10fo gold & multi.	3.75	3.75

Paintings by Hungarian anonymous early masters from the Christian Museum at Esztergom. No. 2257 contains one stamp (49x74mm.); gold margin with white inscription and black control number. Size: 73x100mm.

Mihaly Csokonai Vitez
A513

José Marti and Cuban Flag
A514

1973, Nov. 17 Photo. *Perf. 11½x12*

2258	A513	2fo bister & multi.	40	10

Bicentenary of the birth of Mihaly Csokonai Vitez (1773–1805), poet.

1973, Nov. 30

2259	A514	1fo dark brown, red & blue	15	5

José Marti (1853–1895), Cuban national hero and poet.

Barnabas Pesti
A515

1973, Nov. 30

2260	A515	1fo bl., brn. & buff	15	5

Barnabas Pesti (1920–1944), member of Hungarian underground Communist Party.

Women's Double Kayak—A516

Designs: 60f, Water polo. 80f, Men's single kayak. 1.20fo, Butterfly stroke. 2fo, Men's fours kayak. 4fo, Men's single canoe. 6fo, Men's double canoe.

1973, Dec. 29 Litho. *Perf. 12x11*

2261	A516	40f red & multi.	6	4
2262	"	60f blue & multi.	8	6
2263	"	80f multicolored	12	10
2264	"	1.20fo grn. & multi.	18	15
2265	"	2fo car. & multi.	35	25
2266	"	4fo vio. & multi.	70	45
2267	"	6fo multicolored	1.20	80
		Nos. 2261–2267 (7)	2.69	1.85

Hungarian victories in water sports at Tampere and Belgrade.

Souvenir Sheet

Map of Europe
A517

1974, Jan. 15 Photo. *Perf. 12x11½*

Multicolored

2268	A517	Sheet of two	6.00	6.00
	a.	5fo multicolored	2.50	2.50

European Peace Conference (Arab-Israeli War), Geneva, Jan. 1974. No. 2268 contains two stamps and label showing view of Geneva. Black marginal inscription. Size: 141½x70mm.

Lenin—A518

1974, Jan. 21 Photo. *Perf. 11½x12*

2269	A518	2fo gold, dull blue & brown	30	6

50th anniversary of the death of Lenin (1870–1924).

Jozsef Boczor, Imre Békés, Tamás Elek—A519

1974, Feb. 21 *Perf. 12½*

2270	A519	3fo brn. & multi.	45	8

30th anniversary of the death in France of Hungarian resistance fighters.

Comecon Building, Moscow and Flags
A520

1974, Feb. 26 Photo. *Perf. 12x11½*

2271	A520	1fo multicolored	20	4

25th anniversary of the Council of Mutual Economic Assistance.

Bank Emblem, Coins and Banknote
A521

1974, Mar. 1 *Perf. 11½x12*

2272	A521	1fo lt. grn. & multi.	20	10

25th anniversary of the State Savings Bank.

Spacecraft on Way to Mars—A522

Designs: 60f, Mars 2 over Mars. 80f, Mariner 4. 1fo, Mars and Mt. Palomar Observatory. 1.20fo, Soft landing of Mars 3. 5fo, Mariner 9 with Mars satellites Phobos and Deimos.

1974, Mar. 11 Photo. *Perf. 12½*

2273	A522	40f gold & multi.	8	4
2274	"	60f silver & multi.	10	6
2275	"	80f gold & multi.	15	8
2276	"	1fo silver & multi.	18	10
2277	"	1.20fo gold & multi.	30	12
2278	"	5fo silver & multi.	1.00	60
		Nos. 2273–2278, C347 (7)	3.01	1.80

Exploration of Mars. See No. C348.

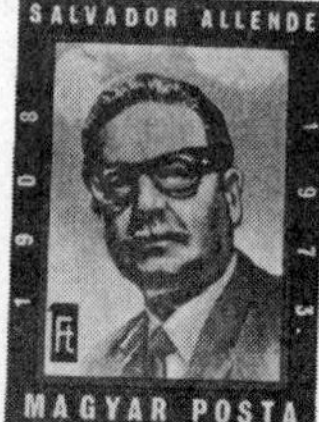

Salvador Allende
A523

1974, Mar. 27 Photo. *Perf. 11½x12*

2279	A523	1fo black & multi.	15	5

Salvador Allende (1908–1973), President of Chile.

Mona Lisa, by Leonardo da Vinci
A524

1974, Apr. 19 *Perf. 12½*

2280 A524 4fo gold & multi. 4.00 4.00

Exhibition of the Mona Lisa in Asia. Printed in sheets of 6 stamps and 6 labels with commemorative inscription.

Souvenir Sheet

Issue of 1874 and Flowers—A525

1974, May 11 Litho. *Perf. 11½*

2281	A525	Sheet of 4	3.25	3.25
	a.	2.50fo *No. 13 and mallow*	60	60
	b.	2.50fo *No. 14 and aster*	60	60
	c.	2.50fo *No. 15 and daisy*	60	60
	d.	2.50fo *No. 16 and columbine*	60	60

Centenary of the first issue inscribed "Magyar Posta" (Hungarian Post). No. 2281 has black marginal inscription. Size: 102x86mm.

Carrier Pigeon, World Map, UPU Emblem—A526

1974, May 22 Litho. *Perf. 12*

Multicolored

2282	A526	40f *shown*	10	8
2283	"	60f *Mail coach*	12	10
2284	"	80f *Old mail automobile*	15	12
2285	"	1.20fo *Balloon post*	30	20
2286	"	2fo *Mail train*	50	30
2287	"	4fo *Mail bus*	1.00	60
		Nos. 2282-2287, C349 (7)	3.67	2.20

Centenary of the Universal Postal Union.

Dove of Basel, Switzerland No. 3L1, 1845
A527

1974, June 7 Photo. *Perf. 11½x12*

2288 A527 3fo gold & multi. 1.20 1.20

INTERNABA 1974 Philatelic Exhibition, Basel, June 7-16. No. 2288 issued in sheets of 3 stamps and 3 labels showing Internaba 1974 emblem. Size: 104x125mm.

Chess Players, from 13th Century Manuscript
A528

Designs: 60f, Chess players, 15th century English woodcut. 80f, Royal chess party, 15th century Italian chess book. 1.20fo, Chess players, 17th century copper engraving by Selenus. 2fo, Farkas Kempelen's chess playing machine, 1769. 4fo, Hungarian Grand Master Geza Maroczy (1870-1951). 6fo, View of Nice and emblem of 1974 Chess Olympiad.

1974, June 6 Litho. *Perf. 12*

2289	A528	40f	multicolored	8	6
2290	"	60f	"	10	8
2291	"	80f	"	15	12
2292	"	1.20fo	"	25	15
2293	"	2fo	"	40	25
2294	"	4fo	"	80	40
2295	"	6fo	"	1.20	80
		Nos. 2289-2295 (7)		2.98	1.86

50th anniversary of International Chess Federation and 21st Chess Olympiad, Nice, June 6-30.

Souvenir Sheet

Cogwheel Railroad—A529

1974, June 25 Litho. *Perf. 12*

Multicolored

2296	A529	Sheet of 4	4.00	4.00
	a.	2.50fo *Passenger train, 1874*	75	75
	b.	2.50fo *Freight train, 1874*	75	75
	c.	2.50fo *Electric train, 1929-73*	75	75
	d.	2.50fo *Twin motor train, 1973*	75	75

Centenary of Budapest's cogwheel railroad. No. 2296 has Prussian blue margin with white inscription and multicolored Budapest coat of arms. Size: 130x95mm.

Congress Emblem (Globe and Parliament)
A530

1974, Aug. 18 Photo. *Perf. 12*

2297 A530 2fo silver, dark & light blue 40 10

4th World Congress of Economists, Budapest, Aug. 19-24.

Bathing Woman, by Károly Lotz
A531

Paintings of Nudes: 60f, Awakening, by Károly Brocky. 1fo, Venus and Cupid, by Brocky (horiz.). 1.50fo, After the Bath, by Lotz. 2.50fo, Resting Woman, by Istvan Csok (horiz.). 4fo, After the Bath, by Bertalan Szekely. 5fo, "Devotion," by Erzsebet Korb. 10fo, Lark, by Pál Szinyei Merse.

1974, Aug. *Perf. 12½*

2298	A531	40f	gold & multi.	8	5
2299	"	60f	" "	10	8
2300	"	1fo	" "	18	12
2301	"	1.50fo	" "	25	18
2302	"	2.50fo	" "	60	30
2303	"	4fo	" "	85	40
2304	"	5fo	" "	1.20	80
		Nos. 2298-2304 (7)		3.26	1.93

Souvenir Sheet

Perf. 11

2305 A531 10fo gold & multi. 3.75 3.75

No. 2305 contains one stamp (45x70mm.), gray and silver margin with black control number. Size: 74x100mm.

Mimi, by Béla Czóbel
A532

1974, Sept. 4

2306 A532 1fo multicolored 25 12

91st birthday of Béla Czóbel, Hungarian painter.

Intersputnik Tracking Station
A533

High Voltage Line "Peace" and Pipe Line "Friendship"
A534

Perf. 11½x12, 12x11½

1974, Sept. 5 Lithographed

2307	A533	1fo blue & violet	15	6
2308	A534	3fo multicolored	45	18

Technical assistance and cooperation between Hungary and USSR, 25th anniversary.

Pablo Neruda
A535

Sweden No. 1 and Lion from Royal Palace, Stockholm
A536

1974, Sept. 11 Photo. *Perf. 11½x12*

2309 A535 1fo multicolored 15 8

70th anniversary of the birth of Pablo Neruda (Neftali Ricar do Reyes, 1904-1973), Chilean poet.

1974, Sept. 21 *Perf. 12x11½*

2310 A536 3fo ultra., yel. grn. & gold 1.10 1.10

Stockholmia 74 International Philatelic Exhibition, Stockholm, Sept. 21-29. No. 2310 issued in sheets of 3 stamps and 3 labels showing Stockholmia emblem. White margin inscribed "UPU" multiple in white. Size: 126x104mm.

Tank Battle and Soldier with Anti-tank Grenade—A537

1974, Sept. 28 Litho. *Perf. 12*

2311 A537 1fo gold, org. & blk. 15 8

Army Day. See Nos. C351-C352.

Segner and Segner Crater on Moon
A538

1974, Oct. 5

2312 A538 3fo multicolored 65 18

270th anniversary of the birth of Janos Andras Segner, naturalist. No. 2312 printed se-tenant with label arranged checkerwise in sheet. Label shows Segner wheel.

Rhyparia Purpurata
A539

Lepidoptera: 60f, Melanargia galathea. 80f, Parnassius Apollo. 1fo, Celerio euphorbia. 1.20fo, Catocala fraxini. 5fo, Apatura iris. 6fo, Palaeochrysophanus hyppothoe.

1974, Nov. 11 Photo. *Perf. 12½*

2313	A539	40f multicolored	6	4
2314	"	60f violet & multi.	8	5
2315	"	80f multicolored	12	10
2316	"	1fo brn. & multi.	20	12
2317	"	1.20fo blue & multi.	25	15
2318	"	5fo pur. & multi.	1.00	45
2319	"	6fo multicolored	1.20	80
		Nos. 2313-2319 (7)	2.91	1.71

Motherhood A540 Robert Kreutz A541

1974, Dec. 24 Lithographed *Perf. 12*

2320	A540	1fo lt. blue, black & yellow	20	5

1974, Dec. 24

Multicolored

2321	A541	1fo *shown*	15	5
2322	"	1fo *István Pataki*	15	5

30th death anniversary of anti-fascist martyrs Robert Kreutz (1923–1944) and István Pataki (1914–1944).

Puppy A542

Young Animals: 60f, Siamese kittens (horiz.). 80f, Rabbit. 1.20fo, Foal (horiz.). 2fo, Lamb. 4fo, Calf (horiz.). 6fo, Piglet.

1974, Dec. 30

2323	A542	40f lt. bl. & multi.	6	4
2324	"	60f multicolored	8	5
2325	"	80f olive & multi.	12	10
2326	"	1.20fo grn. & multi.	25	12
2327	"	2fo brn. & multi.	40	15
2328	"	4fo org. & multi.	80	45
2329	"	6fo vio. & multi.	1.20	80
		Nos. 2323-2329 (7)	2.91	1.71

See Nos. 2403–2409.

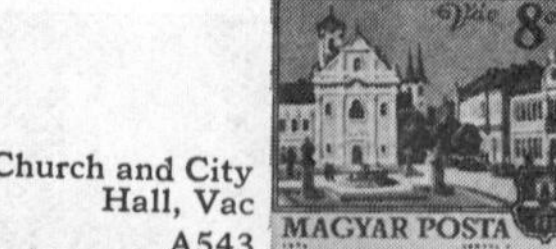

Church and City Hall, Vac A543

Designs: 5fo, View of Szolnok across Tisza River. 6fo, Skyscraper, Dunaújváros. 10fo, City Hall, Kiskunfélegyháza. 50fo, Church (Turkish Mosque), Hunyadi Statue and TV Tower, Pecs.

1974–75 Litho. *Perf. 12x11½*

2331	A543	5fo dk. bl. & ultra. ('75)	75	8
2332	"	6fo dk. brn. & org. ('75)	90	18
2333	A543	8fo dk. & brt. grn.	1.20	10
2335	"	10fo brn. & yellow	1.50	15
2338	"	50fo multicolored	7.50	2.00
		Nos. 2331-2338 (5)	11.85	2.51

Hospital, Lambarene—A544

Designs: 60f, Dr. Schweitzer, patient and microscope. 80f, Patient arriving by boat. 1.20fo, Hospital supplies arriving by ship. 2fo, Globe, Red Cross, carrier pigeons. 4fo, Nobel Peace Prize medal. 6fo, Portrait and signature of Dr. Schweitzer, organ pipes and "J. S. Bach."

1975, Jan. 14 Photogravure *Perf. 12*

2340	A544	40f gold & multi.	6	4
2341	"	60f " "	8	10
2342	"	80f " "	12	12
2343	"	1.20fo " "	20	15
2344	"	2fo " "	40	20
2345	"	4fo vio. & multi.	80	45
2346	"	6fo lilac & multi.	1.20	75
		Nos. 2340-2346 (7)	2.86	1.81

Dr. Albert Schweitzer (1875–1965), medical missionary and musician, birth centenary.

Farkas Bolyai A545 Mihály Károlyi A546

1975, Feb. 7 Litho. *Perf. 11½x12*

2347	A545	1fo gray & red brn.	15	5

Bicentenary of the birth of Farkas Bolyai (1775–1856), mathematician.

1975, Mar. 4 Lithographed *Perf. 12*

2348	A546	1fo lt. bl. & brn.	15	5

Birth centenary of Count Mihály Károlyi (1875–1955), prime minister, 1918–1919.

Woman, IWY Emblem A547

1975, Mar. 8 *Perf. 12x11½*

2349	A547	1fo aqua. & blk.	15	5

International Women's Year 1975.

"Let us Build up the Railroads" A548

Posters: 60f, "Bread starts here." 2fo, "Hungarian Communist Party—a Party of Action." 4fo, "Heavy Industry—secure base of Three-year Plan." 5fo, "Our common interest—a developed socialist society."

1975, Mar. 17 Photo. *Perf. 11*

2350	A548	40f red & multi.	6	5
2351	"	60f " "	8	5
2352	"	2fo " "	30	12
2353	"	4fo " "	65	30
2354	"	5fo " "	85	50
		Nos. 2350-2354 (5)	1.94	1.02

Hungary's liberation from Fascism, 30th anniversary.

Arrow, 1915, Pagoda and Mt. Fuji A549

Antique Cars: 60f, Swift, 1911, Big Ben and Tower of London. 80f, Model T Ford, 1908, Capitol and Statue of Liberty. 1fo, Mercedes, 1901, Towers of Stuttgart. 1.20fo, Panhard Levassor, 1912, Arc de Triomphe and Eiffel Tower. 5fo, Csonka, 1906, Fishermen's Bastion and Chain Bridge. 6fo, Emblems of Hungarian Automobile Club, Alliance Internationale de Tourisme and Federation Internationale de l'Automobile.

1975, Mar. 27 Litho. *Perf. 12*

2355	A549	40f lt. bl. & multi.	6	4
2356	"	60f lt. grn. & multi.	8	4
2357	"	80f pink & multi.	12	8
2358	"	1fo lilac & multi.	20	10
2359	"	1.20fo org. & multi.	30	15
2360	"	5fo ultra. & multi.	90	50
2361	"	6fo lilac rose & multi.	1.25	85
		Nos. 2355-2361 (7)	2.91	1.76

Hungarian Automobile Club, 75th anniversary.

The Creation of Adam, by Michelangelo—A550

1975, Apr. 23 Photo. *Perf. 12½*

2362	A550	10fo gold & multi.	3.75	3.75

500th birth anniversary of Michelangelo Buonarroti (1475–1564), Italian painter, sculptor and architect. Size of No. 2362: 126x90mm.

Academy of Science A551 Count Istvan Szechenyi A552

Design: 2fo, Dates "1975 1825."

1975, May 5 Litho. *Perf. 12*

2363	A551	1fo green & multi.	20	8
2364	"	2fo " "	40	15
2365	A552	3fo " "	60	25

Sesquicentennial of Academy of Science, Budapest, founded by Count Istvan Szechenyi.

Emblem of 1980 Olympics and Proposed Moscow Stadium—A553

1975, May 8 Photo. *Perf. 11½x12*

2366	A553	5fo lt. bl. & multi.	1.00	1.00

Socfilex 75 International Philatelic Exhibition, Moscow, May 8–18. No. 2366 issued in sheets of 3 stamps and 3 labels showing Socfilex 75 emblem (War Memorial, Berlin-Treptow). Size: 104x125 mm.

France No. 1100 and Venus of Milo—A554

1975, June 3 Photo. *Perf. 11½x12*

2367	A554	5fo lilac & multi.	1.00	1.00

ARPHILA 75 International Philatelic Exhibition, Paris, June 6–16. No. 2367 issued in sheets of 3 stamps and 3 labels showing ARPHILA 75 emblem. Size: 104x125mm.

Early Transformer, Kando Locomotive, 1902, Pylon—A555

1975, June 10 Litho. *Perf. 12*

2368	A555	1fo multicolored	20	10

Hungarian Electrotechnical Association, 75th anniversary.

Saber, Rapier, Epée and Globe A556

1975, July 11

2369	A556	1fo multicolored	20	10

32nd World Fencing Championships, Budapest, July 11–20.

Souvenir Sheet

Whale Pavilion, Oceanexpo 75
A557

1975, July 21 Photo. *Perf. 12½*

2370 A557 10fo gold & multi. 3.75 3.75

Oceanexpo 75, International Exhibition, Okinawa, July 20, 1975–Jan. 1976. No. 2370 has gold, blue and multicolored margin with Oceanexpo 75 emblem. Size: 115x94mm.

Agoston Zimmermann
A558

1975, Sept. 4 Litho. *Perf. 12*

2371 A558 1fo brown & blue 20 5

Dr. Agoston Zimmermann (1875–1963), veterinarian, birth centenary.

Symbolic of 14 Cognate Languages
A559

1975, Sept. 9

2372 A559 1fo gold & multi. 15 5

International Finno-Ugrian Congress.

Voters
A560

Design: No. 2374, Map of Hungary with electoral districts.

1975, Oct. 1

2373 A560 1fo multicolored 15 5
2374 " 1fo " 15 5

Hungarian Council System, 25th anniversary.

Fish and Waves
(Ocean Pollution)
A561

Designs: 60f, Skeleton hand reaching for rose in water glass. 80f, Fish gasping for raindrop. 1fo, Carnation wilting in polluted soil. 1.20fo, Bird dying in polluted air. 5fo, Sick human lung and smokestack. 6fo, "Stop Pollution" (raised hand protecting globe from skeleton hand).

1975, Oct. 16 Litho. *Perf. 11½*

2375 A561 40f multicolored 6 4
2376 " 60f " 8 5
2377 " 80f " 12 8
2378 " 1fo " 20 12
2379 " 1.20fo " 30 15
2380 " 5fo " 1.00 50
2381 " 6fo " 1.20 75
Nos. 2375–2381 (7) 2.96 1.69

Environmental protection.

Mariska Gárdos
(1885–1973)
A562

Portraits: No. 2383, Imre Mezö (1905–1956). No. 2384, Imre Tarr (1900–1937).

1975, Nov. 4 Litho. *Perf. 12*

2382 A562 1fo black & red orange 15 6
2383 " 1fo black & red orange 15 6
2384 " 1fo black & red orange 15 6

Famous Hungarians, birth anniversaries.

Treble Clef, Organ and Orchestra—A563

1975, Nov. 14

2385 A563 1fo multicolored 25 6

Franz Liszt Musical Academy, centenary.

Szigetcsep Icon
A564

Virgin and Child, 18th Century Icons: 60f, Graboc. 1fo, Esztergom. 1.50fo, Vatoped. 2.50fo, Tottos. 4fo, Gyor. 5fo, Kazan.

1975, Nov. 25 Photo. *Perf. 12½*

2386 A564 40f gold & multi. 6 4
2387 " 60f " " 10 5
2388 " 1fo " " 20 10
2389 " 1.50fo " " 30 12
2390 " 2.50fo " " 45 18
2391 " 4fo " " 90 45
2392 " 5fo " " 1.20 75
Nos. 2386–2392 (7) 3.21 1.69

Members' Flags, Radar, Mother and Child—A565

1975, Dec. 15 Litho. *Perf. 12*

2393 A565 1fo multicolored 20 5

20th anniversary of the signing of the Warsaw Treaty (Bulgaria, Czechoslovakia, German Democratic Rep., Hungary, Poland, Romania, USSR).

Ice Hockey, Winter Olympics' Emblem—A566

Designs (Emblem and): 60f, Slalom. 80f, Ski race. 1.20fo, Ski jump. 2fo, Speed skating. 4fo, Cross-country skiing. 6fo, Bobsled. 10fo, Figure skating, pair.

1975, Dec. 29 Photo. *Perf. 12x11½*

2394 A566 40f silv. & multi. 10 6
2395 " 60f " " 12 8
2396 " 80f " " 15 10
2397 " 1.20fo " " 25 15
2398 " 2fo " " 40 20
2399 " 4fo " " 80 40
2400 " 6fo " " 1.20 75
Nos. 2394–2400 (7) 3.02 1.74

Souvenir Sheet

Perf. 12½

2401 A566 10fo silv. & multi. 3.75 3.75

12th Winter Olympic Games, Innsbruck, Austria, Feb. 4–15, 1976. No. 2401 contains one stamp (59x36mm.); multicolored margin with Olympic rings, snowflake design and black control number. Size: 130x80mm.

"P", 5-pengö and 500-pengö Notes—A567

1976, Jan. 16 Litho. *Perf. 12*

2402 A567 1fo multicolored 25 5

Hungarian Bank Note Co., 50th anniversary.

Animal Type of 1974

Young Animals: 40f, Wild boars (horiz.). 60f, Squirrels. 80f, Lynx (horiz.). 1.20fo, Wolves. 2fo, Foxes (horiz.). 4fo, Bears. 6fo, Lions (horiz.).

1976, Jan. 26

2403 A542 40f multicolored 6 4
2404 " 60f blue & multi. 8 5
2405 " 80f multicolored 15 8
2406 " 1.20fo " 25 15
2407 " 2fo vio. & multi. 45 25
2408 " 4fo yel. & multi. 90 45
2409 " 6fo multi. 1.20 70
Nos. 2403–2409 (7) 3.09 1.72

A.G. Bell, Telephone, Molniya I and Radar—A568

1976, Mar. 10 Litho. *Perf. 11½x12*

2410 A568 3fo multicolored 1.00 1.00

Centenary of first telephone call by Alexander Graham Bell, Mar. 10, 1876. Issued in sheets of 4.

Battle of Kuruc-Labantz—A569

Paintings: 60f, Meeting of Rakoczi and Tamas Esze, by Endre Veszprem. 1fo, Diet of Onod, by Mor Than. 2fo, Camp of the Kurucs. 3fo, Ilona Zrinyi (Rakoczi's mother; vert.). 4fo, Kuruc officers (vert.). 5fo, Prince Francis II Rakoczy, by Adam Manyoki (vert.). Painters of 40f, 2fo, 3fo, 4fo, are unknown.

1976, Mar. 27 Photo. *Perf. 12½*

2411 A569 40f gold & multi. 15 4
2412 " 60f " " 20 5
2413 " 1fo " " 40 10
2414 " 2fo " " 80 20
2415 " 3fo " " 1.20 30
2416 " 4fo " " 1.60 40
2417 " 5fo " " 2.50 65
Nos. 2411–2417 (7) 6.85 1.74

Francis II Rakoczy (1676–1735), leader of Hungarian Protestant insurrection, 300th birth anniversary.

Standard Meter, Hungarian Meter Act
A570

Designs: 2fo, Istvan Krusper, his vacuum balance, standard kilogram. 3fo, Interferometer and rocket.

1976, Apr. 5 ***Perf. 11½x12***

2418 A570 1fo multicolored 20 10
2419 " 2fo " 40 20
2420 " 3fo " 60 30

Centenary of introduction of metric system in Hungary.

U.S. No. 1353 and Independence Hall, Philadelphia—A571

Photogravure and Foil Embossed

1976, May 29 ***Perf. 11½x12***

2421 A571 5fo blue & multi. 1.20 1.20

Interphil 76 International Philatelic Exhibition, Philadelphia, Pa., May 29–June 6. No. 2421 issued in sheets of 3 stamps and 3 labels showing bells. Size: 115x125mm.

"30" and Various Pioneer Activities
A572

1976, June 5 Litho. ***Perf. 12***

2422 A572 1fo multicolored 20 10

Hungarian Pioneers, 30th anniversary.

Trucks, Safety Devices, Trade Union Emblem—A573

1976, June ***Perf. 12½***

2423 A573 1fo multicolored 20 10

Labor safety.

Intelstat 4, Montreal Olympic Emblem, Canadian Flag
A574

Designs: 60f, Equestrian. 1fo, Butterfly stroke. 2fo, One-man kayak. 3fo, Fencing. 4fo, Javelin. 5fo, Athlete on vaulting horse.

1976, June 29 Photo. ***Perf. 11½x12***

2424 A574 40f dk. bl. & multi. 6 4
2425 " 60f slate green & multicolored 8 5
2426 " 1fo blue & multi. 15 10
2427 " 2fo green & multi. 30 20
2428 " 3fo brn. & multi. 60 30
2429 " 4fo bister & multi. 80 40
2430 " 5fo maroon & multi. 1.00 65
Nos. 2424-2430 (7) 2.99 1.74

21st Olympic Games, Montreal, Canada, July 17–Aug. 1. See No. C365.

Denmark No. 2 and Mermaid, Copenhagen—A575

1976, Aug. 19 Photo. ***Perf. 11½x12***

2431 A575 3fo multicolored 1.10 1.10

HAFNIA 76 International Philatelic Exhibition, Copenhagen, Aug. 20–29. No. 2431 issued in sheets of 3 stamps and 3 labels showing HAFNIA emblem. Size: 106x127mm.

Souvenir Sheet

Discovery of Body of Lajos II, by Bertalan Székely—A576

1976, Aug. 27 Photo. ***Perf. 12½***

2432 A576 20fo multicolored 4.25 4.25

450th anniversary of the Battle of Mohacs against the Turks. No. 2432 has gray margin with brown inscription and black control number. Size: 81x81mm.

Flora, by Titian
A577

1976, Aug. 27

2433 A577 4fo gold & multi. 80 40

Titian (1477–1576), Venetian painter, 400th death anniversary.

Hussar, Herend China
A578

1976, Sept. 28 Litho. ***Perf. 12***

2434 A578 4fo multicolored 80 20

Herend China manufacture, sesquicentennial.

Daniel Berzsenyi
A579

1976, Sept. 28

2435 A579 2fo black, gold & yellow 30 10

Daniel Berzsenyi (1776–1836), poet, 200th birth anniversary.

Pal Gyulai
A580

1976, Sept. 28

2436 A580 2fo org. & black 30 10

Pal Gyulai (1826–1909), poet and historian, birth sesquicentennial.

Tuscany No. 1 and Emblem—A581

1976, Oct. 13 Photo. ***Perf. 11½x12***

2437 A581 5fo org. & multi. 2.50 2.50

ITALIA 76 International Philatelic Exhibition, Milan, Oct. 14–24. No. 2437 issued in sheets of 3 stamps and 3 labels showing Italia 76 emblem. Size: 106x127 mm.

Jozsef Madzsar, M.D.
A582

Portraits: No. 2439, Ignac Bogar (1876–1933), secretary of printers' union. No. 2440, Rudolf Golub (1901–1944), miner.

1976, Nov. 4 Litho. ***Perf. 12***

2438 A582 1fo dp. brn. & red 20 5
2439 " 1fo " " 20 5
2440 " 1fo " " 20 5

Labor leaders.

Science and Culture House, Georgian Dancer, Hungarian and USSR Flags—A583

1976, Nov. 4 ***Perf. 12½x12***

2441 A583 1fo multicolored 20 5

House of Soviet Science and Culture, Budapest, 2nd anniversary.

Koranyi Sanitarium and Statue
A584

1976, Nov. 11 ***Perf. 12***

2442 A584 2fo multicolored 40 15

Koranyi TB Sanitarium, founded by Dr. Frigyes Koranyi, 75th anniversary.

Locomotive, 1875, Enese Station
A585

Designs: 60f, Steam engine No. 17, 1885, Rabatamasi Station. 1fo, Railbus, 1925, Fertoszentmiklos Station. 2fo, Express steam engine, Kapuvar Station. 3fo, Engine and trailer, 1926, Gyor Station. 4fo, Eight-wheel express engine, 1934, and Fertoboz Station. 5fo, Raba-Balaton engine, Sopron Station.

1976, Nov. 26 Litho. *Perf. 12*

2443	A585	40f multicolored	8	4
2444	"	60f "	12	5
2445	"	1fo "	20	8
2446	"	2fo "	40	20
2447	"	3fo "	60	30
2448	"	4fo "	80	40
2449	"	5fo "	1.00	65
		Nos. 2443-2449 (7)	3.20	1.72

Gyor-Sopron Railroad, centenary.

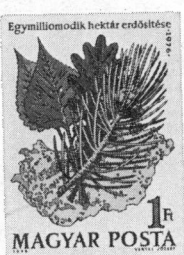

Poplar, Oak, Pine and Map of Hungary A586

1976, Dec. 14

2450	A586	1fo multicolored	20	5

Millionth hectar of reforestation.

Weight Lifting and Wrestling, Silver Medals—A587

Designs: 60f, Kayak, men's single and women's double. 1fo, Horse vaulting. 4fo, Women's fencing. 6fo, Javelin. 20fo, Water polo.

1976, Dec. 14 Photo. *Perf. 11½x12*

2451	A587	40f multicolored	8	4
2452	"	60f "	12	5
2453	"	1fo "	20	10
2454	"	4fo "	80	40
2455	"	6fo "	1.20	60
		Nos. 2451-2455 (5)	2.40	1.19

Souvenir Sheet

Perf. 12½x11½

2456	A587	20fo multicolored	*4.25*	*4.25*

Hungarian medalists in 21st Olympic Games. No. 2456 has multicolored margin with Montreal '76 and Moscow '80 emblems, Canadian flag, Olympic flame and satellite; black control number. Size: 80x96mm.

Spoonbills A588

Birds: 60f, White storks. 1fo, Purple herons. 2fo, Great bustard. 3fo, Common cranes. 4fo, White wagtails. 5fo, Garganey teals.

1977, Jan. 3 Litho. *Perf. 12*

2457	A588	40f multicolored	8	4
2458	"	60f "	12	5
2459	"	1fo "	20	10
2460	"	2fo "	40	20
2461	"	3fo "	60	30
2462	"	4fo "	80	40
2463	"	5fo "	1.00	65
		Nos. 2457-2463 (7)	3.20	1.74

Birds from Hortobagy National Park.

1976 World Champion Imre Abonyi Driving Four-in-hand—A589

Designs: 60f, Omnibus on Boulevard, 1870. 1fo, One-horse cab at Budapest Railroad Station, 1890. 2fo, Mail coach, Buda to Vienna route. 3fo, Covered wagon of Hajduszoboszlo. 4fo, Hungarian coach, by Jeremias Schemel, 1563. 5fo, Post chaise, from a Lübeck wood panel, 1430.

1977, Jan. 31 Litho. *Perf. 12x11½*

2464	A589	40f multicolored	8	4
2465	"	60f "	12	5
2466	"	1fo "	20	12
2467	"	2fo "	40	25
2468	"	3fo "	60	30
2469	"	4fo "	80	50
2470	"	5fo "	1.20	60
		Nos. 2464-2470 (7)	3.40	1.86

History of the coach.

Peacock A590

Birds: 60f, Green peacock. 1fo, Congo peacock. 3fo, Argus pheasant. 4fo, Impeyan pheasant. 6fo, Peacock pheasant.

1977, Feb. 22 Litho. *Perf. 12*

2471	A590	40f multicolored	8	4
2472	"	60f "	12	5
2473	"	1fo "	20	12
2474	"	3fo "	60	30
2475	"	4fo "	80	40
2476	"	6fo "	1.20	60
		Nos. 2471-2476 (6)	3.00	1.51

Newspaper Front Page, Factories A591

1977, Mar. 3 Litho. *Perf. 12*

2477	A591	1fo gold, black & vermilion	20	12

Nepszava newspaper, centenary.

Flowers, by Mihaly Munkacsy A592

Flowers, by Hungarian Painters: 60f, Jakab Bogdany. 1fo, Istvan Csok (horiz.). 2fo, Janos Halapy. 3fo, Jozsef Rippl-Ronai (horiz.). 4fo, Janos Tornyai. 5fo, Jozsef Koszta.

1977, Mar. 18 Photo. *Perf. 12½*

2478	A592	40f gold & multi.	8	4
2479	"	60f " "	12	5
2480	"	1fo " "	20	12
2481	"	2fo " "	40	25
2482	"	3fo " "	60	30
2483	"	4fo " "	80	50
2484	"	5fo " "	1.00	60
		Nos. 2478-2484 (7)	3.20	1.86

Newton and Double Convex Lens A593

1977, Mar. 31 Litho. *Perf. 12*

2485	A593	3fo tan & multi.	85	85

Isaac Newton (1643–1727), natural philosopher and mathematician, 250th death anniversary. No. 2485 issued in sheets of 4 stamps and 4 blue and black labels showing illustration from Newton's "Principia Mathematica," and Soviet space rocket.

Janos Vajda A594

1977, May 2 Litho. *Perf. 12*

2486	A594	1fo green, cream & black	20	12

Janos Vajda (1827–1897), poet, 150th birth anniversary.

Netherlands No. 1 and Tulips—A595

1977, May 23 Photo. *Perf. 11½x12*

2487	A595	3fo multicolored	1.00	1.00

AMPHILEX '77, International Stamp Exhibition, Amsterdam, May 26–June 5. Issued in sheets of 3 stamps and 3 yellow, brown and ocher labels showing Amphilex poster.

Scene from "Wedding at Nagyrede" A596

1977, June 14 Litho. *Perf. 12*

2488	A596	3fo multicolored	60	30

State Folk Ensemble, 25th anniversary.

Souvenir Sheet

Bath of Bathsheba, by Rubens—A597

1977, June 14 Photo. *Perf. 11*

2489	A597	20fo multicolored	4.25	4.25

Peter Paul Rubens (1577–1640), Flemish painter, 400th birth anniversary. No. 2489 has deep rose lilac margin with silver inscription and black control number. Size: 70x94mm.

Medieval View of Sopron, Fidelity Tower, Arms A598

1977, June 25 Litho. *Perf. 12x11½*

2490	A598	1fo multicolored	50	40

700th anniversary of Sopron. Printed se-tenant with label showing European Architectural Heritage medal awarded Sopron in 1975.

Race Horse Kincsem A599

1977, July 16 Litho. *Perf. 12*

2491	A599	1fo multicolored	20	10

Sesquicentennial of horse racing in Hungary. Printed se-tenant with label showing portrait of Count Istvan Szechenyi and vignette from his 1827 book "Rules of Horse Racing in Hungary."

German Democratic Republic No. 370 A600

1977, Aug. 18 Photo. *Perf. 12x11½*

2492	A600	3fo multicolored	75	75

SOZPHILEX 77 Philatelic Exhibition, Berlin, Aug. 19–28. No. 2492 issued in sheets of 3 stamps and 3 labels showing SOZPHILEX emblem.

Scythian Iron Bell, 6th Century B.C.
A601

Panel, Crown of Emperor Constantin Monomakhos
A602

Designs: No. 2494, Bronze candlestick in shape of winged woman, 12th–13th centuries. No. 2495, Centaur carrying child, copper aquamanile, 12th century. No. 2496, Gold figure of Christ, from 11th century Crucifix. Designs show art treasures from Hungarian National Museum, founded 1802.

1977, Sept. 3 Litho. *Perf. 12*

2493	A601	2fo multicolored	50	40
2494	"	2fo "	50	40
2495	"	2fo "	50	40
2496	"	2fo "	50	40
		a. Horizontal strip of 4	2.25	

Souvenir Sheet

2497	A602	10fo multicolored	3.50	3.50

50th Stamp Day. Nos. 2493–2496 printed se-tenant. No. 2497 has ornamental margin showing Museum; black inscription and control number. Size: 74x83mm.

Sputnik
A603

Spacecraft: 60f, Skylab. 1fo, Soyuz-Salyut 5. 3fo, Luna 24. 4fo, Mars 3. 6fo, Viking.

1977, Sept. 20

2498	A603	40f multicolored	8	4
2499	"	60f "	12	5
2500	"	1fo "	20	12
2501	"	3fo "	60	35
2502	"	4fo "	90	50
2503	"	6fo "	1.40	70
		Nos. 2498–2503 (6)	3.30	1.76

Space explorations, from Sputnik to Viking. See No. C375.

Janos Szanto Kovacs
A604

Ervin Szabo
A605

1977, Nov. 4 Litho. *Perf. 12*

2504	A604	1fo red & black	20	8
2505	A605	1fo " "	20	8

Janos Szanto Kovacs (1852–1908), pioneer of agrarian movement; Ervin Szabo (1877–1918), pioneer of revolutionary workers' movement.

Monument to Hungarian October Revolutionists, Omsk—A606

1977, Nov. 4

2506	A606	1fo black & red	20	10

60th anniversary of Russian October Revolution.

Hands and Feet Bathed in Thermal Spring
A607

1977, Nov. 1

2507	A607	1fo multicolored	20	10

World Rheumatism Year.

Endre Ady
A608

1977, Nov. 22 Engr. *Perf. 12*

2508	A608	1fo violet blue	40	40

Endre Ady (1877–1919), lyric poet. Issued in sheets of 4.

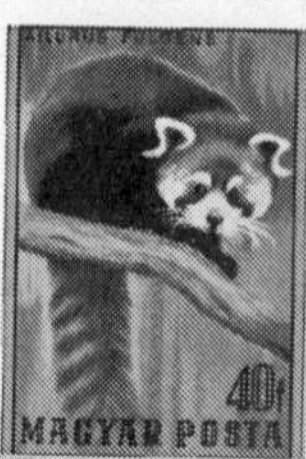

Lesser Panda
A609

Designs: 60f, Giant panda. 1fo, Asiatic black bear. 4fo, Polar bear. 6fo, Brown bear.

1977, Dec. 16 Litho. *Perf. 11½x12*

2509	A609	40f yellow & multi.	8	4
2510	"	60f " "	12	5
2511	"	1fo " "	20	12
2512	"	4fo " "	1.00	50
2513	"	6fo " "	1.40	80
		Nos. 2509–2513 (5)	2.80	1.51

Souvenir Sheet

Flags and Ships along Intercontinental Waterway—A610

1977, Dec. 28 Litho. *Perf. 12*

2514	A610	Sheet of 11, multicolored	5.00	5.00
		a. 2fo *Austria*	40	
		b. 2fo *Bulgaria*	40	
		c. 2fo *Czechoslovakia*	40	
		d. 2fo *France*	40	
		e. 2fo *Luxembourg*	40	
		f. 2fo *Jugoslavia*	40	
		g. 2fo *Hungary*	40	
		h. 2fo *Fed. Rep. of Germany*	40	
		i. 2fo *Romania*	40	
		j. 2fo *Switzerland*	40	
		k. 2fo *USSR*	40	

European Intercontinental Waterway: Danube, Main and Rhine. Center label shows map of rivers and canal; Danube fountain, Budapest, and brown control number. Size: 130x93mm.

Lancer, 17th Century
A611

Hussars: 60f, Kuruts, 1710. 1fo, Baranya, 1762. 2fo, Palatine officer, 1809. 4fo, Sandor, 1848. 6fo, Trumpeter, 5th Honved Regiment, 1900.

1978, Jan. Litho. *Perf. 11½x12*

2515	A611	40f lilac & multi.	8	4
2516	"	60f yel. green & multicolored	12	5
2517	"	1fo red & multi.	20	12
2518	"	2fo dull blue & multicolored	40	25
2519	"	4fo olive bister & multi.	1.00	50
2520	"	6fo gray & multi.	1.50	70
		Nos. 2515–2520 (6)	3.30	1.66

School of Arts and Crafts
A612

1978, Mar. 31 Litho. *Perf. 12*

2521	A612	1fo multicolored	20	10

School of Arts and Crafts, 200th anniversary.

Soccer Players, Flags of West Germany and Poland—A613

Designs (Various Soccer Scenes and Flags): No. 2523, Hungary and Argentina. No. 2524, France and Italy. No. 2525, Tunisia and Mexico. No. 2526, Sweden and Brazil. No. 2527, Spain and Austria. No. 2528, Peru and Scotland. No. 2529, Iran and Netherlands. Flags represent first round of contestants.

1978, May 25 Litho. *Perf. 12*

2522	A613	2fo multicolored	40	25
2523	"	2fo "	40	25
2524	"	2fo "	40	25
2525	"	2fo "	40	25
2526	"	2fo "	40	25
2527	"	2fo "	40	25
2528	"	2fo "	40	25
2529	"	2fo "	40	25
		Nos. 2522–2529 (8)	3.20	2.00

Souvenir Sheet

Design: 20fo, Argentina '78 emblem.

Perf. 11½

2530	A613	20fo multicolored	4.50	4.50

Argentina '78 11th World Cup Soccer Championships, Argentina, June 2–25. No. 2530 contains one stamp; multicolored margin shows flags of participants, world map and satellite. Black control number. Size: 98x76mm.

Vase, Star and Glass Blower's Tube
A614

1978, May 20 Litho. *Perf. 12*

2531	A614	1fo multicolored	20	10

Ajka Glass Works, centenary.

Canada No. 1 and Trillium—A615

1978, June 2

2532	A615	3fo multicolored	60	60

CAPEX '78, Canadian International Philatelic Exhibition, Toronto, Ont., June 9–18. Issued in sheets of 3 stamps and 3 labels showing CAPEX '78 emblem.

Souvenir Sheets

Leif Ericson and his Ship—A616

Designs: Explorers and their ships.

1978, June 10 Litho. ***Perf. 12x11½***

Multicolored

2533 Sheet of 4 2.00 2.00
a. A616 2fo *shown* 40
b. " 2fo *Columbus* 40
c. " 2fo *Vasco da Gama* 40
d. " 2fo *Ferdinand Magellan* 40

2534 Sheet of 4 2.00 2.00
a. A616 2fo *Sir Francis Drake* 40
b. " 2fo *Henry Hudson* 40
c. " 2fo *James Cook* 40
d. " 2fo *Robert Peary* 40

Nos. 2533–2534 have nautical emblems and black control numbers in margin. Size: 130x100mm.

Diesel Train, Pioneer's Kerchief
A617

Congress Emblem as Flower
A618

1978, June 10 ***Perf. 12***

2535 A617 1fo multicolored 20 10

30th anniversary of Pioneer Railroad.

1978, June

Design: No. 2537, Congress emblem, "Cuba" and map of Cuba.

2536 A618 1fo multicolored 20 10
2537 " 1fo " 20 10

11th World Youth Festival, Havana. Nos. 2536–2537 printed se-tenant.

WHO Emblem, Stylized Body and Heart
A619

Clenched Fist, Dove and Olive Branch
A620

1978, Aug. 21 Litho. ***Perf. 12***

2538 A619 1fo multicolored 20 10

Drive against hypertension.

1978, Sept. 1 Litho. ***Perf. 12***

2539 A620 1fo gray, red & black 20 10

Publication of review "Peace and Socialism," 20th anniversary.

Train, Telephone, Space Communication—A621

1978, Sept. 8 Litho. ***Perf. 12***

2540 A621 1fo multicolored 20 10

20th anniversary of Organization for Communication Cooperation of Socialist Countries.

"Toshiba" Automatic Letter Sorting Machine—A622

1978, Sept. 15 Litho. ***Perf. 11½x12***

2541 A622 1fo multicolored 20 10

Introduction of automatic letter sorting. No. 2541 printed with se-tenant label showing bird holding letter.

Eros Offering Grapes, Villa Hercules
A623

Roman Mosaics Found in Hungary: No. 2543, Tiger (Villa Hercules, Budapest). No. 2544, Bird eating berries (Balacapuszta). No. 2545, Dolphin (Aquincum). 10fo, Hercules aiming at Centaur fleeing with Deianeira (Villa Hercules).

Photogravure and Engraved

1978, Sept. 16 ***Perf. 11½***

2542 A623 2fo multicolored 40 25
2543 " 2fo " 40 25
2544 " 2fo " 40 25
2545 " 2fo " 40 25

Souvenir Sheet

2546 A623 10fo multicolored 3.50 3.50

Stamp Day. No. 2546 contains one stamp (52x35mm.); light brown and black decorative margin. Black control number. Size: 89x63mm.

Count Imre Thököly
A624

1978, Oct. 1 Photo. ***Perf. 12½***

2547 A624 1fo blk. & yellow 20 10

300th anniversary of Hungary's independence movement, led by Imre Thököly (1657–1705).

Souvenir Sheet

Hungarian Crown Jewels—A625

1978, Oct. 10

2548 A625 20fo gold & multi. 4.75 4.75

Return of Crown Jewels from United States, Jan. 6, 1978. Olive gray margin with gold inscription and black control number. Size: 76x96mm.

"The Red Coach"
A626

1978, Oct. 21 Litho. ***Perf. 12***

2549 A626 3fo red & black 60 20

Gyula Krúdy, 1878–1933, novelist.

St. Ladislas I Reliquary, Györ Cathedral
A627

1978, Nov. 15 ***Perf. 11½x12½***

2550 A627 1fo multicolored 20 10

Ladislas I (1040–1095), 900th anniversary of accession to throne of Hungary.

Miklos Jurisics Statue, Köszeg—A628

1978, Nov. 15 ***Perf. 12***

2551 A628 1fo multicolored 20 10

650th anniversary of founding of Köszeg.

Samu Czaban and Gizella Berzeviczy—A629

Photogravure and Engraved

1978, Nov. 24 ***Perf. 11½x12***

2552 A629 1fo brown, buff & red 20 10

Samu Czaban (1878–1942) and Gizella Berzeviczy (1878–1954), Communist teachers during Soviet Republic (1918–1919).

Communist Party Emblem
A630

1978, Nov. 24 Litho. ***Perf. 12***

2553 A630 1fo gray, red & black 20 5

Hungarian Communist Party, 60th anniversary.

Woman Cutting Bread
A631

Ceramics by Margit Kovacs (1902–1976): 2fo, Woman with pitcher. 3fo, Potter.

1978, Nov. 30 Litho. ***Perf. 11½x12***

2554 A631 1fo multicolored 20 20
2555 " 2fo " 40 40
2556 " 3fo " 60 60

Virgin and Child, by Dürer
A632

Dürer Paintings: 60f, Adoration of the Kings (horiz.). 1fo, Self-portrait, 1500. 2fo, St. George. 3fo, Nativity (horiz.). 4fo, St. Eustatius. 5fo, The Four Apostles. 20fo, Dancing Peasant Couple, 1514 (etching).

1979, Jan. 8 Photo. ***Perf. 12½***

2557 A632 40f gold & multi. 8 4
2558 " 60f " " 12 6
2559 " 1fo " " 20 12
2560 " 2fo " " 40 25
2561 " 3fo " " 60 30
2562 " 4fo " " 1.00 50
2563 " 5fo " " 1.20 60
Nos. 2557–2563 (7) 3.60 1.87

Souvenir Sheet

Lithographed

2564 A632 20fo buff & brn. 4.25 4.25

Albrecht Dürer (1471–1528), German painter and engraver. No. 2564 has gold and carmine margin, brown control number. Size: 78x99mm.

Human Rights Flame
A633

1979, Feb. 8 Litho. ***Perf. 11½x12***

2565 A633 1fo dk. & lt. blue 20 12

Universal Declaration of Human Rights, 30th anniversary. No. 2565 issued in sheets of 12 stamps (3x4) and 4 labels. Alternating horizontal rows inverted.

Child at Play
A634

Designs (IYC Emblem and): No. 2567, Family. No. 2568, 3 children (international friendship).

1979, Feb. *Perf. 12*

2566	A634	1fo multicolored	20	12
2567	"	1fo "	20	12
2568	"	1fo "	20	12

International Year of the Child.

SEMI-POSTAL STAMPS.

Issues of the Monarchy.

"Turul" and St. Stephen's Crown
SP1

Franz Josef I Wearing Hungarian Crown
SP2

Wmkd. Double Cross. (137)

1913, Nov. 20 Typo. *Perf. 14.*

B1	SP1	1f slate	50	50
B2	"	2f olive yellow	25	25
B3	"	3f orange	25	25
B4	"	5f emerald	20	20
B5	"	6f olive green	50	40
B6	"	10f carmine	20	15
B7	"	12f violet, *yellow*	75	75
B8	"	16f gray green	40	30
B9	"	20f dark brown	1.75	1.10
B10	"	25f ultramarine	40	30
B11	"	30f orange brown	80	40
B12	"	35f red violet	35	25
B13	"	50f lake, *blue*	4.00	1.20
B14	"	60f green, *salmon*	5.00	75
B15	SP2	1k dull red	18.00	7.50
B16	"	2k dull blue	50.00	30.00
B17	"	5k violet brown	14.00	12.00
		Nos. B1–B17 (17)	97.35	56.30

Nos. B1–B17 were sold at an advance of 2f over face value, as indicated by the label at bottom. The surtax was to aid flood victims.

Semi-Postal Stamps of 1913 Surcharged in Red, Green or Brown:

Hadi segély

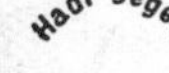

Özvegyeknek és árváknak két (2) fillér
a

Özvegyeknek és árváknak két (2) fillér
b

1914

B18	SP1 (*a*)	1f slate	30	20
B19	" (")	2f olive yellow	35	30
B20	" (")	3f orange	35	30
B21	" (")	5f emerald	20	10
B22	" (")	6f olive green	50	30
B23	" (")	10f carmine (G)	20	10
B24	" (")	12f violet, *yellow*	30	25
B25	" (")	16f gray green	20	20
B26	" (")	20f dark brown	40	25
B27	" (")	25f ultramarine	85	30
B28	" (")	30f orange brown	75	30
B29	" (")	35f red violet	2.75	1.50
B30	" (")	50f lake, *blue*	1.50	75
B31	" (")	60f grn., *salmon*	5.00	1.25
B32	SP2 (*b*)	1k dull red (Br)	50.00	30.00
B33	" (")	2k dull blue	22.50	16.50
B34	" (")	5k violet brown	16.50	12.00
		Nos. B18–B34 (17)	102.65	64.60

Regular Issue of 1913 Surcharged in Red or Green:

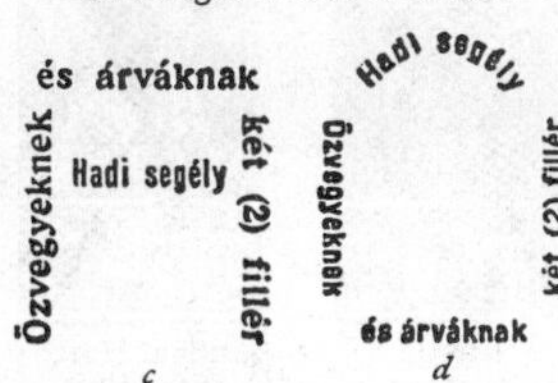

1915, Jan. 1

B35	A4 (*c*)	1f slate	12	10
B36	" (")	2f olive yellow	12	6
B37	" (")	3f orange	12	8
B38	" (")	5f emerald	8	6
B39	" (")	6f olive green	12	8
B40	" (")	10f carmine (G)	8	6
B41	" (")	12f violet, *yellow*	15	12
B42	" (")	16f gray green	35	15
B43	" (")	20f dark brown	40	30
B44	" (")	25f ultramarine	25	12
B45	" (")	30f orange brown	15	12
B46	" (")	35f red violet	20	12
B47	" (")	50f lake, *blue*	30	20
B48	" (")	60f green, *salmon*	40	20
B49	A5 (*d*)	1k dull red	75	40
B50	" (")	2k dull blue	2.00	1.20
B51	" (")	5k violet brown	5.50	4.50

Surcharged as Type "c" but in Smaller Letters

B52	A4	60f grn., *salmon*	1.00	75
		Nos. B35–B52 (18)	12.09	8.62

Nos. B18–B52 were sold at an advance of 2f over face value. The surtax to aid war widows and orphans.

Soldiers Fighting
SP3 SP4

Eagle with Sword
SP5

Harvesting
SP6

1916–17 ***Perf. 15***

B53	SP3	10f+2f rose red	15	15
B54	SP4	15f+2f dull violet	15	15
B55	SP5	40f+2f brn. car. ('17)	20	20

1917, Sept. 15

Surcharge in Red

B56	SP6	10f+1k rose	30	30
B57	"	15f+1k violet	30	30

Nos. B56 and B57 were issued in connection with the War Exhibition of Archduke Josef.

Issues of the Republic.

Semi-Postal Stamps of 1916-17 Overprinted in Black

1918

B58	SP3	10f+2f rose red	10	10
B59	SP4	15f+2f dull violet	10	10
B60	SP5	40f+2f brown carmine	10	10

Nos. B58-B60 exist with inverted overprint.

Issues of the Kingdom.

Released Prisoner Walking Home
SP7

Homecoming of Soldier
SP9

Prisoners of War—SP8

Wmk. 137 Vert. or Horiz.

1920, Mar. 11 ***Perf. 12***

B69	SP7	40f+1k dull red	50	50
B70	SP8	60f+2k gray brown	45	45
B71	SP9	1k+5k dark blue	45	45

The surtax was used to help prisoners of war return home from Siberia.

Statue of Petöfi
SP10

Griffin
SP11

Sándor Petöfi
SP12

Petöfi Addressing People
SP14

Petöfi Dying—SP13

Perf. 14 (10k, 40k), 12

1923, Jan. 23

B72	SP10	10k slate green	30	30
B73	SP11	15k dull blue	1.00	1.00
B74	SP12	25k gray brown	30	30
B75	SP13	40k brown violet	1.25	1.25
B76	SP14	50k violet brown	1.50	1.50
		Nos. B72–B76 (5)	4.35	4.35

Birth centenary of the Hungarian poet Sándor Petöfi. The stamps were on sale at double face value, for a limited time and in restricted quantities, after which the remainders were given to a charitable organization.

Child with Symbols of Peace
SP15

Mother and Infant
SP16

Instruction in Archery
SP17

Engraved.

1924, Apr. 8 ***Perf. 12.*** **Wmk. 133**

B77	SP15	300k dark blue	1.65	1.65
		a. Perf. 11½	10.00	10.00
B78	SP16	500k black brown	1.65	1.65
B79	SP17	1000k black green	1.65	1.65

Each stamp has on the back an inscription stating that it was sold at a premium of 100 per cent over the face value.

Parade of Athletes
SP18

Skiing
SP19

Skating
SP20

Diving
SP21

Fencing
SP22

Scouts Camping
SP23

Soccer
SP24

Hurdling
SP25

Perf. 12, 12½ and Compound

1925 Typographed Unwmkd.

B80	SP18	100k blue green & brown	2.00	1.50
B81	SP19	200k light brown & myrtle green	3.00	1.65
B82	SP20	300k dark blue	4.00	2.00
B83	SP21	400k deep blue & deep green	5.00	3.00
B84	SP22	500k purple brown	6.00	4.00
B85	SP23	1000k red brown	8.50	5.00

B86 SP24 2000k brown violet 6.50 6.50
B87 SP25 2500k olive brown 6.50 6.50
Nos. B80-B87 (8) 41.50 30.15

These stamps were sold at double face value, plus a premium of 10 per cent on orders sent by mail. They did not serve any postal need and were issued solely to raise funds to aid athletic associations. An inscription regarding the 100 per cent premium is printed on the back of each stamp.

Nos. B80-B87 exist imperforate. Price $60.

St. Emerich
SP26

Sts. Stephen and Gisela
SP27

St. Ladislaus
SP28

Sts. Gerhardt and Emerich
SP29

1930, May 15 ***Perf. 14*** **Wmk. 210**

B88	SP26	8f+2f deep green	75	75
B89	SP27	16f+4f brt. violet	1.00	1.00
B90	SP28	20f+4f deep rose	3.00	3.00
B91	SP29	32f+8f ultramarine	4.00	4.00

Issued in commemoration of the 900th anniversary of the death of St. Emerich, son of Stephen I, king, saint and martyr.

St. Ladislaus
SP30

Holy Sacrament
SP31

1938, May 16 **Photo.** ***Perf. 12***

B92	SP30	16(f)+16f dull slate blue	3.00	3.00
B93	SP31	20(f)+20f dark carmine	3.00	3.00

Souvenir Sheet.

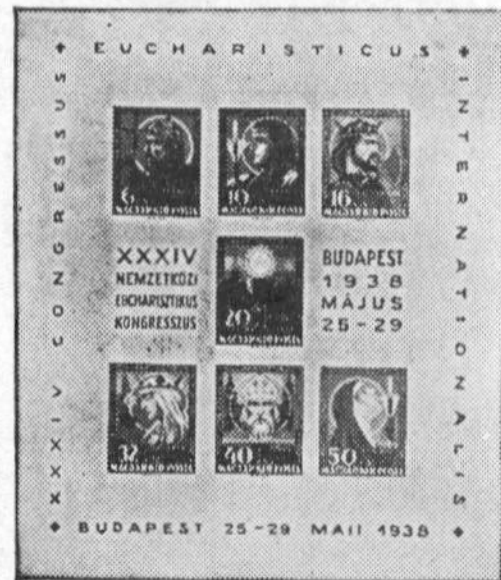

SP32

B94	SP32	Sheet of seven	18.50	18.50
	a.	6f+6f deep grren (*St. Stephen*)	2.00	2.00
	b.	10f+10f deep orange (*St. Emerich*)	2.00	2.00
	c.	16f+16f slate blue (*St. Ladislaus*) (B92)	2.00	2.00
	d.	20f+20f dark carmine (*Holy Sacrament*) (B93)	2.00	2.00
	e.	32f+32f deep claret (*St. Elizabeth*)	2.00	2.00
	f.	40f+40f slate green (*St. Maurice*)	2.00	2.00
	g.	50f+50f rose violet (*St. Margaret*)	2.00	2.00

Printed in sheets measuring 136½x155 mm. Nos. B94c and B94d are slightly smaller than B92 and B93.

Issued in commemoration of the Eucharistic Congress in Budapest, May, 1938.

St. Stephen, Victorious Warrior
SP33

St. Stephen, Offering Crown
SP34

SP35

1938, Aug. 12 ***Perf. 12***

B95	SP33	10(f)+10f violet brown	3.00	3.00
B96	SP34	20(f)+20f red org.	3.00	3.00

Souvenir Sheet.

B97	SP35	Sheet of seven	18.50	18.50
	a.	6(f)+6f dark blue green (*St. Stephen the Missionary*)	2.00	2.00
	b.	10(f)+10f violet brown (*Victorious Warrior*) (B95)	2.00	2.00
	c.	16(f)+16f bistre brown (*Seated Upon Throne*)	2.00	2.00
	d.	20(f)+20f red orange (*Offering Crown*) (B96)	2.00	2.00
	e.	32(f)+32f slate blue (*Receives Bishops and Monks*)	2.00	2.00
	f.	40(f)+40f dull blue (*St. Gisela, St. Stephen and St. Emerich*)	2.00	2.00
	g.	50(f)+50f dark violet (*St. Stephen on Bier*)	2.00	2.00

Death of St. Stephen, 900th anniversary. Size of No. B97: 153x112½mm.

Statue Symbolizing Recovered Territories
SP36

Castle of Munkács
SP37

Admiral Horthy Entering Komárom
SP38

Cathedral of Kassa
SP39

Girl Offering Flowers to Soldier
SP40

1939, Jan. 16

B98	SP36	6f+3f myrtle green	70	70
B99	SP37	10f+5f olive green	40	30
B100	SP38	20f+10f dark red	50	40
B101	SP39	30f+15f greenish blue	1.20	90
B102	SP40	40f+20f dark blue gray	1.20	90
		Nos. B98-B102 (5)	4.00	3.20

The surtax was for the aid of "Hungary for Hungarians" patriotic movement.

Memorial Tablets
SP41

Gáspár Károlyi, Translator of the Bible into Hungarian
SP42

Albert Molnár de Szenci, Translator of the Psalms—SP43

Prince Gabriel Bethlen
SP44

Susanna Lórántffy
SP45

SP46

Perf. 12x12½, 12½x12.

1939 **Photogravure** **Wmk. 210**

B103	SP41	6f+3f green	60	40
B104	SP42	10f+5f claret	60	40
B105	SP43	20f+10f copper red	80	50
B106	SP44	32f+16f bistre	1.20	1.20
B107	SP45	40f+20f chalky bl.	1.20	1.20
		Nos. B103-B107 (5)	4.40	3.70

Souvenir Sheets.

Perf. 12

B108	SP46	32f olive & violet brown	16.50	16.50

Imperf.

B109	SP46	32f blue green, copper red & gold	16.50	16.50

Issued to commemorate National Protestant Day. The surtax was used to erect an International Protestant Institute.

The souvenir sheets sold for 1.32p each. Size: 77x110mm.

Issue dates: Nos. B103-B107, Oct. 2. Nos. B108-B109, Oct. 27.

Boy Scout Flying Kite
SP47

Allegory of Flight
SP48

Archangel Gabriel from Millennium Monument, Budapest, and Planes
SP49

1940, Jan. 1 ***Perf. 12½x12***

B110	SP47	6f+6f yellow green	40	35
B111	SP48	10f+10f chocolate	80	65
B112	SP49	20f+20f copper red	1.00	1.00

The surtax was used for the Horthy National Aviation Fund.

SP50

Soldier Protecting Family from Floods
SP51

Souvenir Sheet
Perf. 12

1940, May 6 Photo. Wmk. 210

B113 SP50 20f+1p dark blue green 2.25 2.25

1940, May

B114 SP51 10f+ 2f gray brown 20 20
B115 " 20f+ 4f orange red 30 30
B116 " 20f+50f red brown 85 85

The surtax on Nos. B113–B116 was used to aid flood victims. No. B113 has sheet marginal decorations and inscriptions in terra cotta. Size: 79½x111mm.

Hunyadi Coat of Arms
SP52

Hunyadi Castle
SP53

King Matthias
SP54

Corvin Codex
SP56

Equestrian Statue of King Matthias
SP55

Equestrian Statue of King Matthias
SP57

1940 *Perf. 12½x12, 12x12½.*

B117 SP52 6f+3f blue green 40 40
B118 SP53 10f+5f golden brown 40 35
B119 SP54 16f+8f dark olive bistre 50 45
B120 SP55 20f+10f brick red 65 50
B121 SP56 32f+16f dark gray 90 80
Nos. B117–B121 (5) 2.85 2.50

Souvenir Sheet.

B122 SP57 20f+1p dark blue green & pale green 2.25 2.25

Issued in commemoration of the 500th anniversary of the birth of King Matthias (1440–1490) at Kolozsvar, Transylvania. The surtax was used for war relief.
No. B122 measures 79½x112mm.
Issue dates: July 1, Nos. B117–B121. Nov. 7, No. B122.

Hungarian Soldier
SP58

Virgin Mary and Szekler, Symbolizing the Return of Transylvania
SP59

Szekler Mother Offering Infant Son to the Fatherland
SP60

1940, Dec. 2 Photo. *Perf. 12½x12*

B123 SP58 10f+50f dark blue green 60 50
B124 SP59 20f+50f brown carmine 90 85
B125 SP60 32f+50f yellow brown 1.20 1.00

Issued in commemoration of the occupation of Transylvania. The surtax was for the Pro-Transylvania movement.

Symbol for Drama
SP61

Symbol for Sculpture
SP62

Symbol for Art
SP63

Symbol for Literature
SP64

SP65

Perf. 12x12½, 12½x12

1940, Dec. 15

B126 SP61 6f+ 6f dk. green 1.00 90
B127 SP62 10f+10f olive bis. 1.00 90
B128 SP63 16f+16f dk. violet 1.00 90
B129 SP64 20f+20f terra cotta 1.00 90

Souvenir Sheet.

1941, Jan. 5 ***Imperf.***

B130 SP65 Sheet of four 3.00 3.00
a. 6f+6f olive brown 60 60
b. 10f+10f henna brown 60 60
c. 16f+16f dark blue green 60 60
d. 20f+20f rose violet 60 60

The surtax on Nos. B126–B130 was used for the Pension and Assistance Institution for Artists.
No. B130 measures 123x84mm.

Winged Head of Pilot
SP66

Boy Scout with Model Plane
SP67

Glider in Flight
SP68

Our Lady of Loreto, Patroness of Hungarian Pilots
SP69

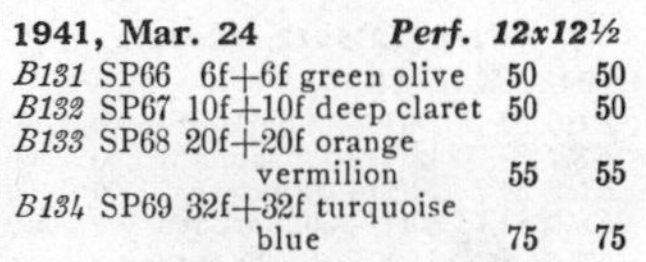
1941, Mar. 24 ***Perf. 12x12½***

B131 SP66 6f+6f green olive 50 50
B132 SP67 10f+10f deep claret 50 50
B133 SP68 20f+20f orange vermilion 55 55
B134 SP69 32f+32f turquoise blue 75 75

The surtax was used to finance civilian and army pilot training through the Horthy National Aviation Fund.

Infantry
SP70

Designs: 12(f)+18f, Heavy artillery. 20(f)+30f, Plane and tanks. 40(f)+60f, Cavalryman and cyclist.

1941, Dec. 1 Photo. Wmk. 266

Inscribed: "Honvedeink Karacsonyara 1941."

B135 SP70 8(f)+12f dark green 25 25
B136 " 12(f)+18f olive green 25 25
B137 " 20(f)+30f slate 30 30
B138 " 40(f)+60f red brn. 50 50

The surtax was for the benefit of the Army.

Soldier and Emblem
SP74

1941, Dec. 1

B139 SP74 20(f)+40(f) dark red 1.75 1.50

The surtax was for the soldiers' Christmas.

Aviator and Plane
SP75

Aviators and Plane
SP78

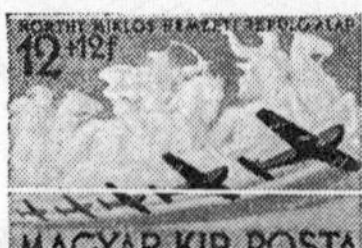

Planes and Ghostly Band of Old Chiefs
SP76

Plane and Archer
SP77

Perf. 12½x12, 12x12½

1942, Mar. 15

B140	SP75	8(f)+8f dark green	60	60
B141	SP76	12(f)+12f sapphire	60	60
B142	SP77	20(f)+20f brown	60	60
B143	SP78	30(f)+30f dark red	60	60

The surtax aided the Horthy National Aviation Fund.

Blood Transfusion
SP79

Bandaging Wounded Soldier
SP80

Radio and Carrier Pigeons
SP81

Widows and Orphans
SP82

1942, Sept. 1 *Perf. 12½x12*

B144	SP79	3(f)+18f dark olive & red	1.20	1.20
B145	SP80	8(f)+32f deep brn. & red	1.20	1.20
B146	SP81	12(f)+50f deep claret & red	1.20	1.20
B147	SP82	20f+1p slate blue & red	1.20	1.20

The surtax aided the Hungarian Red Cross. Sheets of 10.

Widow of Stephen Horthy
SP83

Magdalene Horthy Mother of Stephen Horthy
SP85

Red Cross Nurse Aiding Soldier
SP84

1942, Dec. 1 *Perf. 13, Imperf.*

B148	SP83	6f+1p violet blue & red	3.00	3.00
		a. Sheet of four	16.00	16.00
B149	SP84	8f+1p dark olive green & red	3.00	3.00
		a. Sheet of four	16.00	16.00
B150	SP85	20f+1p dark red brown & red	3.00	3.00
		a. Sheet of four	16.00	16.00

The surtax aided the Hungarian Red Cross.

King Ladislaus I
SP86 SP87

King Béla IV
SP88 SP89

King Lajos the Great
SP90 SP91

1942, Dec. 21 *Perf. 12* **Wmk. 266**

B151	SP86	6(f)+6f olive gray	50	50
B152	SP87	8(f)+8f green	50	50
B153	SP88	12(f)+12f dull violet	50	50
B154	SP89	20(f)+20f Prussian green	50	50
B155	SP90	24(f)+24f brown	50	50
B156	SP91	30(f)+30f rose car.	50	50
		Nos. B151-B156 (6)	3.00	3.00

To commemorate the 900th anniversary of the birth of St. Ladislaus (1040–95), the 700th anniversary of the beginning of the country's reconstruction by King Béla IV (1206–70) and the 600th anniversary of the accession of King Lajos the Great (1326–82).

The surtax aided war invalids and their families.

Archer on Horseback
SP92

Warrior with Shield and Battle Ax
SP93 SP94

Knight with Sword and Shield
SP95

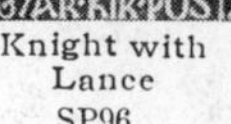
Knight with Lance
SP96

Musketeer
SP97

Hussar
SP98

Artilleryman
SP99

Old Magyar Arms
SP100

1943

B157	SP92	1(f)+1f dark gray	10	5
B158	SP93	3(f)+1f dull violet	45	45
B159	SP94	4(f)+1f lake	10	8
B160	SP95	8(f)+2f green	10	8
B161	SP96	12(f)+2f bistre brn.	10	10
B162	SP97	20(f)+2f deep claret	12	10
B163	SP98	40(f)+4f gray violet	15	10
B164	SP99	50(f)+6f org. brn.	25	15
B165	SP100	70(f)+8f slate blue	30	25
		Nos. B157-B165 (9)	1.67	1.36

The surtax aided war invalids.

Model Glider
SP101

Gliders
SP102

White-tailed Sea Eagle and Planes
SP103

ME-109E Fighter and Gliders
SP104

1943, July 17

B166	SP101	8(f)+8f green	65	65
B167	SP102	12(f)+12f royal blue	65	65
B168	SP103	20(f)+20f chestnut	65	65
B169	SP104	30(f)+30f rose carmine	65	65

The surtax aided the Horthy National Aviation Fund.

Stephen Horthy
SP105

1943, Aug. 16

B170	SP105	30(f)+20f deep rose violet	40	40

The surtax aided the Horthy National Aviation Fund.

Nurse and Soldier
SP106

Designs: 30(f)+30f, Soldier, nurse, mother and child. 50(f)+50f, Nurse keeping lamp alight. 70(f)+70f, Wounded soldier and tree shoot.

1944, Mar. 1

Cross in Red.

B171	SP106	20(f)+20f brown	20	25
B172	"	30(f)+30f henna	20	25
B173	"	50(f)+50f brn. vio.	20	25
B174	"	70(f)+70f Prussian blue	20	25

The surtax aided the Hungarian Red Cross.

Issues of the Republic

Types of 1944
Surcharged in Red or Black:

BÉKE
3P
A NÉPFŐISKOLÁKERT
+9P
a

BÉKE 4 P
A NÉP-
FŐISKOLÁKÉRT
+12P
b

1945, July 23 *Perf. 12* **Wmk. 266**

B175	A115 (*a*)	3p+9p on 20f dark olive green, *yellow*	30	30
B176	A114 (*b*)	4p+12p on 4f yellow brown, *blue* (Bk)	30	30
B177	A117 (")	8p+24p on 50f slate blue, *yellow*	30	30
B178	A115 (*a*)	10p+30p on 30f henna brown, *blue* (Bk)	30	30

The surtax was for the Peoples Universities. "Béke" means "peace".

Imre Sallai and Sandor Fürst
SP110

Designs: 3p+3p, L. Kabok and Iles Monus. 4p+4p, Ferenc Rozsa and Zoltan Schonerz. 6p+6p, Anna Koltai and Mrs. Paul Knurr. 10p+10p, George Sarkozi and Imre Nagy. 15p+15p, Vilmos Tartsay and Jeno Nagy. 20p+20p, Janos Kiss and Andreas Bajcsy-Zsilinszky. 40p+40p, Endre Sagvari and Otto Hoffmann.

1945, Oct. 6 Photogravure

B179 SP110 2p+2p yel. brown 1.00 1.00
B180 " 3p+3p deep red 1.00 1.00
B181 " 4p+4p dk. purple 1.00 1.00
B182 " 6p+6p dark yellow green 1.00 1.00
B183 " 10p+10p deep car. 1.00 1.00
B184 " 15p+15p dark slate green 1.00 1.00
B185 " 20p+20p dk. brown 1.00 1.00
B186 " 40p+40p dp. blue 1.00 1.00
Nos. B179-B186 (8) 8.00 8.00

The surtax was for child welfare.

Andreas Bajcsy-Zsilinszky and Eagle
SP111

1945, May 27

B187 SP111 1p+1p dark brown violet 25 25

Issued to commemorate the 1st anniversary of the death of Andreas Bajcsy-Zsilinszky, hanged by the Nazis for anti-fascist activities.

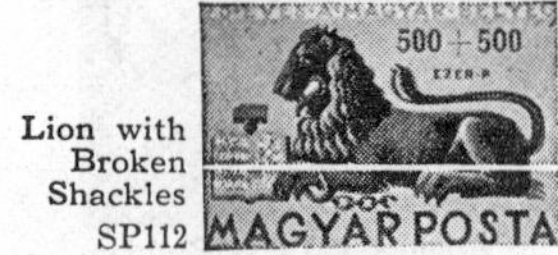

Lion with Broken Shackles
SP112

1946, May 1

B188 SP112 500,000p+500,000p dark green 1.00 1.00
B189 " 1,000,000p+1,000,000p brown 1.00 1.00
B190 " 1,500,000p+1,500,000p red 1.00 1.00
B191 " 2,000,000p+2,000,000p slate blue 1.00 1.00

Issued to commemorate the 75th anniversary of Hungary's first postage stamp. The surtax was for the benefit of postal employees.

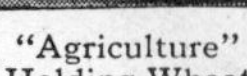

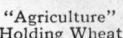

"Agriculture" Holding Wheat
SP113

Physician with Syringe
SP114

1946, Sept. 7 Photogravure

B192 SP113 30f+60f deep yellow green 4.00 4.00
B193 " 60f+1.20fo rose brown 4.00 4.00
B194 " 1fo+2fo deep blue 4.00 4.00

1st Agricultural Congress and Exhibition.

Perf. 12½x12

1947, May 16 **Wmk. 210**

Designs: 12f+50f, Physician examining X-ray picture. 20f+50f, Nurse and child. 60f+50f, Prisoner of war starting home.

B195 SP114 8(f)+50f ultra. 3.00 3.00
B196 " 12(f)+50f choc. 3.00 3.00
B197 " 20(f)+50f dark green 3.00 3.00
B198 " 60(f)+50f dark red 80 80

The surtax was for charitable purposes.

Franklin D. Roosevelt and Freedom of Speech Allegory
SP115

Designs (Pres. F. D. Roosevelt and Allegory): 12f+12f, Freedom of Religion. 20f+20f, Freedom from Want. 30f+30f, Freedom from Fear.

1947, June 11 Photo. ***Perf. 12x12½***

Portrait in Sepia

B198A SP115 8f+8f dk. red 3.00 3.00
B198B " 12f+12f deep green 3.00 3.00
B198C " 20f+20f brown 3.00 3.00
B198D " 30f+30f blue 3.00 3.00
Nos. B198A-B198D, CB1-CB1C (8) 24.00 24.00

Honoring Franklin D. Roosevelt (1882-1945), U.S. president.

Nos. B198A-B198D and CB1-CB1C were also printed in sheets of 4 of each denomination (size: 117x96mm.). Price, set of 8, $90.

A souvenir sheet contains one each of Nos. B198A-B198D with border inscriptions and decorations in brown. Size: 161x122mm. Price $40.

Lenin
SP118

XVI Century Mail Coach
SP119

Designs: 60f+60f, Soviet Cenotaph, Budapest. 1fo+1fo, Joseph V. Stalin.

1947, Oct. 29 Photo. **Wmk. 283**

B199 SP118 40f+40f olive green & org. brown 6.00 6.00
B200 " 60f+60f red & slate blue 1.50 1.50
B201 " 1fo+1fo violet & brown black 6.00 6.00

The surtax was for the Hungarian-Soviet Cultural Association.

1947, Dec. 21 ***Perf. 12x12½***

B202 SP119 30f (+50f) henna brown 12.00 12.00
a. Sheet of 4 60.00 60.00

Issued in sheets of four stamps to commemorate Stamp Day, December 21, 1947. The surtax paid admission to a philatelic exhibition in any one of eight Hungarian towns, where the stamps were sold.

Globe and Carrier Pigeon
SP120

Woman Worker
SP121

1948, Oct. 17 ***Perf. 12½x12***

B203 SP120 30f(+1fo) greenish blue 4.50 4.50
a. Sheet of 4 30.00 30.00

Issued in sheets of four stamps at the 5th National Hungarian Stamp Exhibition, Budapest. Each stamp sold for 1.30 forint, which included admission to the exhibition.

1949, Mar. 8

B204 SP121 60f+60f magenta 80 80

Issued to publicize International Woman's Day, March 8, 1949. The surtax was for the Democratic Alliance of Hungarian Women.

Aleksander S. Pushkin
SP122

Aleksander S. Pushkin
SP123

1949, June 6 Photogravure

B205 SP122 1fo+1fo carmine lake 5.00 5.00

Souvenir Sheet.

Perf. 12½x12, Imperf.

B206 SP123 1fo+1fo red violet & car. lake 15.00 15.00

150th anniversary of the birth of Aleksander S. Pushkin. The surtax was for the Hungarian-Russian Culture Society.

Size of No. B206: 51½x60½mm.

Type of Regular Issue of 1951.

Perf. 12½x12

1951, Oct. 6 **Engr.** **Unwmkd.**

B207 A208 1fo+1fo red 10.00 10.00
B208 " 2fo+2fo blue 15.00 15.00

Issued to commemorate the 80th anniversary of Hungary's first postage stamp.

Postwoman Delivering Mail
SP124

1953, Nov. 1 ***Perf. 12*** **Wmk. 106**

B209 SP124 1fo+1fo blue green 2.00 2.00
B210 " 2fo+2fo rose violet 2.00 2.00

Issued to publicize Stamp Day, November 1, 1953.

Stamps of 1955 Surcharged in Red or Lake

Photogravure

1957, Jan. 31 ***Perf. 12x12½***

B211 A249 20f+20f olive green (R) 20 10
B212 " 30f+30f dk. red (L) 20 15
B213 " 40f+40f brown (R) 30 20
B214 " 60f+60f brown red (L) 40 35
B215 " 1fo+1fo blue (R) 60 50
B216 A249 2fo+2fo rose brown (R) 1.25 1.25
Nos. B211-B216 (6) 2.95 2.55

The surtax was for the Hungarian Red Cross.

Winter Olympic Type of 1960.

Design: Olympic Games emblem.

Perf. 11½x12

1960, Feb. 29 **Wmk. 106**

B217 A295 2fo+1fo multi. 1.50 70

Issued to commemorate the 8th Olympic Winter Games, Squaw Valley, Calif., Feb. 18-29, 1960.

Olympic Type of 1960.

Design: 2fo+1fo, Romulus and Remus.

Perf. 11½x12

1960, Aug. 21 **Photo.** **Wmk. 106**

B218 A299 2fo+1fo multi. 1.35 60

Issued to commemorate the 17th Olympic Games, Rome, Aug. 25-Sept. 11.

Sport Club Type of 1961.

Sport: 2fo+1fo, Sailboats.

1961, July 8 ***Perf. 14½*** **Unwmkd.**

B219 A313 2fo+1fo multi. 1.00 60

Issued to commemorate the 50th anniversary of the Steel Workers Sport Club (VASAS).

St. Margaret's Island and Danube
SP125

Views of Budapest: No. B221, Fishermen's Bastion. No. B222, Coronation Church and Chain Bridge. No. B223, Mount Gellert.

Photogravure

1961, Sept. 24 ***Perf. 12*** **Unwmkd.**

B220 SP125 2fo+1fo red brown, olive bistre & blue 90 90
B221 " 2fo+1fo red brown, olive bistre & blue 90 90
B222 " 2fo+1fo red brown, olive bistre & blue 90 90
B223 " 2fo+1fo red brown, olive bistre & blue 90 90
a. Horiz. strip of 4 4.00 4.00

Issued for Stamp Day, 1961, and to publicize the Budapest International Stamp Exhibition.

Nos. B220-B223 are printed se-tenant in sheet and show a continuous air view of Budapest. No. B223a contains one each of Nos. B220-B223.

Miniature presentation sheets, perf. and imperf., contain one each of Nos. B220-B223; size: 204x66½mm.

Soccer Type of Regular Issue, 1962.

Design: Flags of Spain and Czechoslovakia.

1962, May 21 ***Perf. 11***

Flags in Original Colors

B224 A323 4fo+1fo light green & bistre 1.50 50

Issued to commemorate the World Cup Soccer Championship, Chile, May 30-June 17.

Austrian Stamp of 1850 with Pesth Postmark
SP126

Designs: No. B226, Dozsa stamp of 1919 (No. 201). No. B227, Ski stamp of 1955 (No. C164). No. B228, Butterfly stamp of 1959 (No. C208).

Lithographed and Engraved

1962, Sept. 22 ***Perf. 11*** **Unwmkd.**

Design and Inscription in Dark Brown

B225 SP126 2fo+1fo yellow 75 75
B226 " 2fo+1fo pale pink 75 75
B227 " 2fo+1fo pale bl. 75 75
B228 " 2fo+1fo pale yellow green 75 75
a. Horiz. strip of four 3.25 3.25
b. Souv. sheet of 4 5.00 5.00

Issued to commemorate the 35th Stamp Day and the 10th anniversary of Mabeosz, the Hungarian Philatelic Federation. Nos. B225–B228 are printed se-tenant in sheet. No. B228a contains one each of Nos. B225–B228. No. B228b contains one each of Nos. B225–B228. Size: 90x111mm.

Emblem, Cup and Soccer Ball
SP127

Photogravure

1962, Nov. 18 ***Perf. 11½x12***

B229 SP127 2fo+1fo multi. 75 50

Issued to commemorate the winning of the "Coupe de l'Europe Centrale" by the Steel Workers Sport Club (VASAS) in the Central European Soccer Championships.

Hyacinth
SP128

1963, Oct. 24 ***Perf. 11½x12***

Size: 32x43mm.

Multicolored

B230 SP128 2fo+1fo *Hyacinth* 75 75
B231 " 2fo+1fo *Narcissus* 75 75
B232 " 2fo+1fo *Chrysanthemum* 75 75
B233 " 2fo+1fo *Tiger lily* 75 75
a. Horiz. strip of 4 3.25 3.25
b. Miniature sheet of 4 4.50 4.50

Issued for Stamp Day, 1963. Nos. B230–B233 printed se-tenant. No. B233a contains one each of Nos. B230–B233. No. B233b contains four stamps similar to Nos. B230–B233 with perf. 11 and stamp size: 25x32mm. Size of sheet: 76x90mm.

Winter Olympic Type of 1963.

Design: 4fo+1fo, Bobsledding.

1963, Nov. 11 ***Perf. 12***

B234 A342 4fo+1fo greenish bl. & bister 1.60 50

Issued to commemorate the 9th Olympic Winter Games, Innsbruck, Austria, Jan. 29–Feb. 9, 1964.

New Year Type of Regular Issue

Good Luck Symbols: 2.50fo+1.20fo, Horseshoe, mistletoe and clover. 3fo+1.50fo, Pigs, clover and balloon (horiz.).

Perf. 12x11½, 11½x12

1963, Dec. 12 **Photo.** **Unwmkd.**

Sizes: 28x39mm. (※B235); 28x22mm. (※B206)

B235 A343 2.50fo+1.20fo multicolored 1.00 40
B236 " 3fo+1.50fo multicolored 1.00 60

Issued for New Year 1964. The surtax was for the modernization of the Hungarian Postal and Philatelic Museum.

Olympic Type of Regular Issue

Design: 3fo+1fo, Water polo.

1964, June 12 ***Perf. 11***

B237 A352 3fo+1fo multi. 1.20 50

18th Olympic Games, Tokyo, Oct. 10–25.

Exhibition Hall—SP129

1964, July 23 **Photogravure**

B238 SP129 3fo+1.50fo black, red orge. & gray 60 20

Issued to publicize the Tennis Exhibition, Budapest Sports Museum.

Twirling Woman Gymnast
SP130

1964, Sept. 4 ***Perf. 11½x12***

Size: 27x38mm.

Multicolored

B239 SP130 2fo+1fo *Lilac* 70 70
B240 " 2fo+1fo *Mallards* 70 70
B241 " 2fo+1fo *Gymnast* 70 70
B242 " 2fo+1fo *Rocket & globe* 70 70
a. Horiz. strip of 4 3.00 3.00
b. Souv. sheet of 4 4.00 4.00

Issued to commemorate the 37th Stamp Day and to publicize the International Topical Stamp Exhibition, IMEX. No. B242a contains one each of Nos. B239–B242. No. B242b contains 4 stamps similar to Nos. B239–B242 but perf. 11 and stamp size: 20x28mm. Size of sheet: 84x100mm. Sheet has buff margin and silver and red inscription.

13th Century Tennis
SP131

History of Tennis: 40f+10f, Indoor tennis, 16th century. 60f+10f, Tennis, 18th century. 70f+30f, Tennis court and castle. 80f+40f, Tennis court, Fontainebleau (buildings). 1fo+50f, Tennis, 17th century. 1.50fo+50f, W. C. Wingfield, Wimbledon champion 1877, and Wimbledon Cup. 1.70fo+50f, Davis Cup, 1900. 2fo+1fo, Bela Kehrling (1891–1937), Hungarian champion.

Lithographed and Engraved

1965, June 15 ***Perf. 12*** **Unwmkd.**

B243 SP131 30f+10f maroon, *dull orange* 8 4
B244 " 40f+10f black, *pale lilac* 15 4
B245 " 60f+10f green, *olive* 20 8
B246 " 70f+30f lilac, *bright green* 25 10
B247 " 80f+40f dark blue, *lt. violet* 30 12
B248 " 1fo+50f green, *yellow* 40 20
B249 " 1.50fo+50f sepia, *lt. olive green* 45 25
B250 " 1.70fo+50f indigo, *light blue* 60 35
B251 " 2fo+1fo dark red, *lt. green* 1.00 65
Nos. B243–B251 (9) 3.43 1.83

Flood Scene
SP132

Design: 10fo+5fo, Relief commemorating 1838 flood.

1965, Aug. 14 **Photo.** ***Perf. 12x11½***

B252 SP132 1fo+50f orange brown & blue 40 40

Souvenir Sheet

B253 SP132 10fo+5fo golden brn. & buff 3.50 3.50

The surtax was for aid to 1965 flood victims. No. B253 contains one stamp; gray margin with map of Danube showing high-water marks. Size: 113x77mm.

Geranium Stamp of 1950 (No. 909)
SP133

Designs: No. B255, Red deer stamp of 1953 (No. C120). No. B256, Ice skater stamp of 1963 (No. 1489). No. B257, Gagarin stamp of 1961 (No. 1382).

Perf. 12x11½

1965, Oct. 30 **Photo.** **Unwmkd.**

Stamps in Original Colors

B254 SP133 2fo+1fo gray & dark blue 85 85
B255 " 2fo+1fo gray & red 85 85
B256 " 2fo+1fo gray & ocher 85 85
B257 " 2fo+1fo gray & violet 85 85
a. Horiz. strip of 4 3.75 3.75
b. Souv. sheet of 4 4.25 4.25

Issued for Stamp Day, 1965. Nos. B254–B257 printed se-tenant. No. B257a contains one each of Nos. B254–B257. No. B254b contains 4 stamps similar to Nos. B254–B257 but perf. 11 and stamp size: 32x23mm. Size of sheet: 101x85mm. Gray margin and ocher inscription.

Soccer Type of Regular Issue

Design: 3fo+1fo, Championship emblem and map of Great Britain showing cities where matches were held.

1966, June 6 **Photo.** ***Perf. 12x11½***

B258 A382 3fo+1fo multi. 75 50

Issued to publicize the World Cup Soccer Championship, Wembley, England, July 11–30.

Woman Archer and Danube at Visegrad
SP134

Designs: No. B260, Gloria Hungariae grapes and Lake Balaton. No. B261, Red poppies and ruins of Diosgyor Castle. No. B262, Russian space dogs Ugolek and Veterok.

1966, Sept. 16 **Photo.** ***Perf. 12x11½***

B259 SP134 2fo+50f multi. 80 80
B260 " 2fo+50f " 80 80
B261 " 2fo+50f " 80 80
B262 " 2fo+50f " 80 80
a. Horiz. strip of 4 3.50 3.50
b. Souv. sheet of 4 4.25 4.25

Issued for Stamp Day, 1966. No. B262a contains one each of Nos. B259–B262. No. B262b contains 4 stamps similar to Nos. B259–B262 but perf. 11 and stamp size: 29x21mm. Size of sheet: 98x84½mm. Margin inscribed in pale green "MABEOSZ" and circle in very small letters, forming continuous rows.

Anglers, C.I.P.S. Emblem and View of Danube
SP135

1967, Aug. 22 **Photo.** ***Perf. 12x11½***

B263 SP135 3fo+1fo lt. ultra. & multi. 60 50

See note after No. 1847

Olympic Type of Regular Issue

Design: 4fo+1fo, Indoor stadium and Winter Olympics emblem.

1968, Jan. 29 **Photo.** ***Perf. 11***

B264 A402 4fo+1fo multi. 60 50

Issued to commemorate the 10th Winter Olympic Games, Grenoble, France, Feb. 6–18.

Jug, Western Hungary, 1618
SP136

Hungarian Earthenware: No. B266, Tiszafüred vase, 1847. No. B267, Toby jug, 1848. No. B268, Decorative Baja plate, 1870. No. B269a, Jug, Northern Hungary, 1672. No. B269b, Decorative Mezőcsat plate, 1843. No. B269c, Decorative Moragy plate, 1860. No. B269d, Pitcher, Debrecen, 1793.

1968, Oct. 5 **Litho.** ***Perf. 12***

B265 SP136 1fo+50f ultra. & multicolored 50 40
B266 " 1fo+50f sky blue & multicolored 50 40
B267 " 1fo+50f sepia & multicolored 50 40
B268 " 1fo+50f yel. brn. & multi. 50 40

Miniature Sheet

B269 SP136 Sheet of 4 3.50 3.50
a. 2fo+50f ultra. & multicolored 75 75
b. 2fo+50f yellow brown & multi. 75 75
c. 2fo+50f olive & multicolored 75 75
d. 2fo+50f bright rose & multi. 75 75

Issued for 41st Stamp Day. No. B269 contains 4 stamps (size: 25x36mm.). Size of sheet: 74x96mm. See Nos. B271–B275.

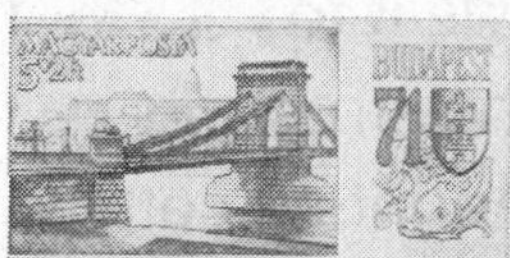

Suspension Bridge, Buda Castle and Arms of Budapest
SP137

Lithographed and Engraved

1969, May 22 ***Perf. 12***

B270 SP137 5fo+2fo sepia, pale yellow & gray 1.20 1.20

Budapest 71 Philatelic Exposition.

Folk Art Type of 1968

Hungarian Wood Carvings: No. B271, Stirrup cup from Okorag, 1880. No. B272, Jar with flower decorations from Felsőtiszavidek, 1898. No. B273, Round jug, Somogyharsagy, 1935. No. B274, Two-legged jug, Alföld, 1740. No. B275a, Carved panel (farm couple), Csorna, 1879. No. B275b, Tankard, Okany, 1914. No. B275c, Round jar with soldiers, Sellye, 1899. No. B275d, Square box with 2 women, Lengyeltoti, 1880.

1969, Sept. 13 Litho. ***Perf. 12***

B271 SP136 1fo+50f rose claret & multi. 50 40
B272 " 1fo+50f dp. bister & multicolored 50 40
B273 " 1fo+50f blue & multicolored 50 40
B274 " 1fo+50f lt. blue green & multi. 50 40

Miniature Sheet

B275 SP136 Sheet of 4 3.50 3.50
a. 2fo+50f ultra. & multicolored 70 70
b. 2fo+50f brown orange & multi. 70 70
c. 2fo+50f lt. brown & multicolored 70 70
d. 2fo+50f blue green & multi. 70 70

Issued for the 42nd Stamp Day. No. B275 contains 4 stamps (size: 25x36mm.). Size of sheet: 74x96mm.

Fishermen's Bastion, Coronation Church and Chain Bridge
SP138

King Matthias I Corvinus
SP139

Designs: No. B277, Parliament and Elizabeth Bridge. No. B278, Castle and Margaret Bridge.

1970, Mar. 7 Litho. ***Perf. 12***

B276 SP138 2fo+1fo golden brn. & multi. 70 60
B277 " 2fo+1fo blue & multicolored 70 60
B278 SP138 2fo+1fo light violet & multi. 70 60

Budapest 71 Philatelic Exhibition, commemorating the centenary of Hungarian postage stamps.

1970, Aug. 22 Photo. ***Perf. 11½x12***

Initials and Paintings from Bibliotheca Corvina: No. B280, Letter "A." No. B281, Letter "N." No. B282, Letter "O." No. B283a, Ransanus Speaking before King Matthias. No. B283b, Scholar and letter "Q." No. B283c, Portrait of Appianus and letter "C." No. B283d, King David and letter "A."

B279 SP139 1fo+50f multi. 50 40
B280 " 1fo+50f " 50 40
B281 " 1fo+50f " 50 40
B282 " 1fo+50f " 50 40

Miniature Sheet

B283 SP139 Sheet of 4 3.50 3.50
a. 2fo+50f multicolored 75 75
b. 2fo+50f " 75 75
c. 2fo+50f " 75 75
d. 2fo+50f " 75 75

Issued for the 43rd Stamp Day. No. B283 contains 4 stamps (size: 22½x32mm.). Size of sheet: 66½x84mm.

View of Buda, 1470—SP140

Designs: No. B285, Buda, 1600. B286, Buda and Pest, about 1638. No. B287, Buda and Pest, 1770. No. B288a, Buda, 1777. No. B288b, Buda, 1850. No. B288c, Buda, 1895. No. B288d, Budapest, 1970.

1971, Feb. 26 Litho. ***Perf. 12***

B284 SP140 2fo+1fo black & yellow 80 80
B285 " 2fo+1fo black & pink 80 80
B286 " 2fo+1fo black & pale green 80 80
B287 " 2fo+1fo black & pale salmon 80 80

Souvenir Sheet

Perf. 10½

B288 SP140 Souv. sheet 3.50 3.50
a. 2fo+1fo black & pale salmon 75 75
b. 2fo+1fo black & pale green 75 75
c. 2fo+1fo black & lilac 75 75
d. 2fo+1fo black & pink 75 75

"Budapest 71" International Stamp Exhibition for the centenary of Hungarian postage stamps, Budapest, Sept. 4–12. No. B288 contains 4 stamps (size: 39½x18 mm.). Black marginal inscription. Size: 114½x73½mm.

Iris and No. P1
SP141

Designs: No. B290, Daisy and No. 199. No. B291, Poppy and No. 391. No. B292, Rose and No. B128. No. B293a, Carnations and No. 200. No. B292b, Dahlia and No. 1069. No. B293c, Tulips and No. C196. No. B293d, Anenomes and No. C251.

1971, Sept. 4 Photo. ***Perf. 12x11½***

B289 SP141 2fo+1fo silver & multicolored 90 80
B290 " 2fo+1fo silver & multicolored 90 80
B291 " 2fo+1fo silver & multicolored 90 80
B292 " 2fo+1fo silver & multicolored 90 80

Souvenir Sheet

Perf. 11½

B293 SP141 Souv. sheet of 4 3.50 3.50
a. 2fo+1fo silver & multicolored 75 35
b. 2fo+1fo " " 75 75
c. 2fo+1fo " " 75 75
d. 2fo+1fo " " 75 75

Centenary of first Hungarian postage stamps and in connection with Budapest 71 International Stamp Exhibition, Sept. 4–12. No. B293 has light yellow margin with commemorative inscription. Size: 115x98mm.

Miskólcz Postmark, 1818–43
SP142

Postmarks: No. B295, Szegedin, 1827–48. No. B296, Esztergom, 1848–51. No. B297, Budapest 1971 Exhibition. No. B298a, Paar family signet, 1593. No. B298b, Courier letter, 1708. No. B298c, First well-known Hungarian postmark "V. TOKAI," 1752. No. B298d, Letter, 1705.

1972, May ***Perf. 12x11½***

B294 SP142 2fo+1fo bl. & blk. 85 85
B295 " 2fo+1fo yellow & black 85 85
B296 " 2fo+1fo yel. grn. & black 85 85
B297 " 2fo+1fo verm. & multicolored 85 85

Souvenir Sheet

B298 SP142 Souvenir sheet 3.50 3.50
a. 2fo+1fo yel. grn. & multi. 80 80
b. 2fo+1fo brown & multi. 80 80
c. 2fo+1fo ultra. & multi. 80 80
d. 2fo+1fo red & multi. 80 80

9th Congress of National Federation of Hungarian Philatelists (Mabeosz). No. B298 contains 4 stamps (size: 32x23mm.). Parchment-like margin with black inscription. Size: 105x90mm.

Olympic Type of Regular Issue

Design: 3fo+1fo, Wrestling and Olympic rings.

1972, July 15 Photo. ***Perf. 11***

B299 A484 3fo+1fo multi. 60 40

20th Olympic Games, Munich, Aug. 26–Sept. 11.

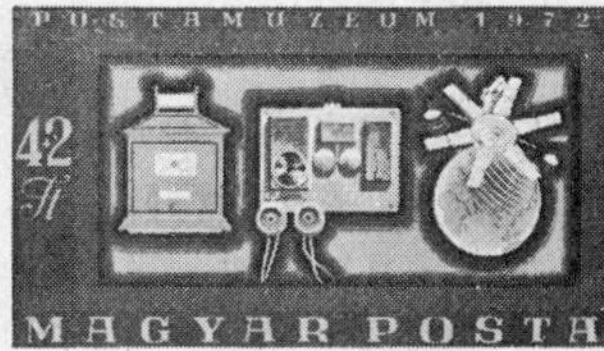

Historic Mail Box, Telephone and Molnya Satellite—SP143

Design: No. B301, Post horn, Tokai postmark, and Nos. 183, 1802, 1809.

1972, Oct. 27 Litho. ***Perf. 12***

B300 SP143 4fo+2fo green & multi. 1.25 1.25
B301 " 4fo+2fo blue & multi. 1.25 1.25

Reopening of the Post and Philatelic Museums, Budapest.

Bird on Silver Disk, 10th Century
SP144

Treasures from Hungarian National Museum. No. B303, Ring with serpent's head, 11th century. No. B304, Lovers, belt buckle, 12th century. No. B305, Flower, belt buckle, 15th century. No. B306a, Opal pendant, 16th century. No. B306b, Jeweled belt buckle, 18th century. No. B306c, Flower pin, 17th century. No. B306d, Rosette pendant, 17th century.

1973, Sept. 22 Litho. ***Perf. 12***

B302 SP144 2fo+50f brown & multicolored 85 85
B303 " 2fo+50f brt. rose lilac & multi. 85 85
B304 " 2fo+50f dk. blue & multicolored 85 85
B305 " 2fo+50f brt. grn. & multi. 85 85

Souvenir Sheet

B306 SP144 Souv. sheet of 4 3.50 3.50
a. 2fo+50f brown & multi. 75 75
b. 2fo+50f carmine & multi. 75 75
c. 2fo+50f olive green & multi. 75 75
d. 2fo+50f bright blue & multi. 75 75

46th Stamp Day. No. B306 contains 4 stamps (size: 25x35mm.). Buff margin with brown inscription and black control number. Size: 75x100mm.

Gothic Wall Fountain
SP145

Visegrad Castle and Bas-reliefs
SP146

Designs: No. B308, Wellhead, Anjou period. No. B309, Twin lion-head wall fountain. B310, Fountain with Hercules riding dolphin. No. B311a, Raven panel. No. B311b, Visegrad Madonna. B311c, Lion panel. No. B311d, Visegrad Castle. Designs show artworks from Visegrad Palace of King Matthias Corvinus I, 15th century.

1975, Sept. 13 Litho. ***Perf. 12***

B307 SP145 2fo+1fo green & multicolored 1.00 1.00
B308 " 2fo+1fo verm. & multicolored 1.00 1.00
B309 " 2fo+1fo blue & multicolored 1.00 1.00
B310 " 2fo+1fo lilac & multicolored 1.00 1.00
a. Horizontal strip of 4 4.25 4.25

Souvenir Sheet

Multicolored

B311 SP146 Sheet of 4 4.50 4.50
a. 2fo+1fo, 21x32mm. 1.00 1.00
b. 2fo+1fo, 47x32mm. 1.00 1.00
c. 2fo+1fo, 21x32mm. 1.00 1.00
d. 2fo+1fo, 99x32mm. 1.00 1.00

European Architectural Heritage Year 1975 and 48th Stamp Day. Nos. B307–B310 printed se-tenant. No. B311 has buff margin with lilac inscription and black control number. Size: 128x99mm.

Condition is the all-important factor of price. Prices quoted are for stamps in fine condition.

Knight
SP147

Gothic Sculptures,
Buda Castle—SP148

Designs: Gothic sculptures from Buda Castle.

1976 Photogravure *Perf. 12*

Multicolored

B312	SP147	2.50+1fo *shown*	1.00	1.00
B313	"	2.50+1fo *Armor-bearer*	1.00	1.00
B314	"	2.50+1fo *Apostle*	1.00	1.00
B315	"	2.50+1fo *Bishop*	1.00	1.00
		a. Horizontal strip of 4	4.25	4.25

Souvenir Sheet

B316	SP148	Sheet of 4	4.25	4.25
		a. 2.50+1fo Man with hat	90	90
		b. 2.50+1fo Woman with wimple	90	90
		c. 2.50+1fo Man with cloth cap	90	90
		d. 2.50+1fo Man with fur hat	90	90

49th Stamp Day. Nos. B312–B315 printed se-tenant.

No. B316 issued in connection with 10th Congress of National Federation of Hungarian Philatelists (Mabeosz). Buff margin with sepia inscription and emblem, black control number. Size: 106x100mm.

Issue dates: No. B316, May 22. Nos. B312–B315, Sept. 4.

Young Runners
SP149

1977, Apr. 2 Litho. *Perf. 12*

B317	SP149	3fo+1.50fo multi.	90	75

Sports promotion among young people.

Young Man and Woman, Profiles
SP150

1978, Apr. 1 Litho. *Perf. 12*

B318	SP150	3fo+1.50fo multicolored	90	55

Hungarian Communist Youth Movement, 60th anniversary.

"Generations," by Gyula Derkovits
SP151

1978, May 6 Litho. *Perf. 12*

B319	SP151	3fo+1.50fo multi.	90	75

Szocfilex '78, Szombathely. No. B319 printed in sheets of 3 stamps and 3 labels showing Szocfilex emblem.

AIR POST STAMPS

Issues of the Monarchy.

AP1

Typographed.

1918, July 4 *Perf. 14.* **Wmk. 137**

No.	Type	Description	Unused	Used
C1	AP1	1k 50f on 75f bright blue & pale blue (R)	8.00	8.00
		a. Inverted surch.	100.00	100.00
C2	"	4k 50f on 2k olive brown & bistre (Bl)	5.00	5.00

Counterfeits exist.

AP2

1920, Nov. 7

No.	Type	Description	Unused	Used
C3	AP2	3k on 10k violet brown & violet (G)	1.60	1.60
C4	"	8k on 10k violet brown & violet (R)	1.60	1.60
		a. Double surch.	450.00	
C5	"	12k on 10k violet brown & violet (Bl)	1.60	1.60

Icarus
AP3

1924, Apr. 11 *Perf. 14.*

No.	Type	Description	Unused	Used
C6	AP3	100k red brown & red	75	65
C7	"	500k blue green & yellow green	75	65
C8	"	1000k bistre brown & brown	80	70
C9	"	2000k dark blue & light blue	80	70

1925, Apr. 20 **Wmk. 133**

No.	Type	Description	Unused	Used
C10	AP3	5000k dull violet & brt. violet	1.75	1.75
C11	"	10000k red & dull vio.	1.75	1.75

Mythical "Turul"
AP4

"Turul" Carrying Messenger
AP5 AP6

1927-30 Engraved. *Perf. 14.*

No.	Type	Description	Unused	Used
C12	AP4	4f orange ('30)	40	30
C13	"	12f deep green	50	30
C14	"	16f red brown	60	40
C15	"	20f carmine	60	40
C16	"	32f brown violet	2.50	1.75
C17	"	40f dp. ultramarine	2.00	40
C18	AP5	50f claret	2.00	1.25
C19	"	72f olive green	2.00	80
C20	"	80f deep violet	2.00	80
C21	"	1p emerald ('30)	3.50	85
C22	AP5	2p red ('30)	7.50	4.50
C23	"	5p dark blue ('30)	17.50	17.50
		Nos. C12-C23 (12)	41.10	29.25

1931, Mar. 27

Overprint in Second Color.

No.	Type	Description	Unused	Used
C24	AP6	1p orange & black	40.00	27.50
C25	"	2p dull violet & green	40.00	27.50

Monoplane over Danube Valley
AP7

Worker Welcoming Plane, Double Cross and Sun Rays
AP8

Spirit of Flight on Plane Wing
AP9

"Flight" Holding Propeller
AP10

Photogravure.

1933, June 20 *Perf. 15.* **Wmk. 210**

No.	Type	Description	Unused	Used
C26	AP7	10f blue green	1.50	25
C27	"	16f purple	1.75	40

Perf. 12½x12.

No.	Type	Description	Unused	Used
C28	AP8	20f carmine	3.50	25
C29	"	40f blue	3.50	50
C30	AP9	48f gray black	5.00	1.50
C31	"	72f bistre brown	7.50	3.00
C32	AP10	1p yellow green	12.00	2.50
C33	"	2p violet brown	25.00	12.00
C34	"	5p dark gray	125.00	75.00
		Nos. C26-C34 (9)	184.75	95.40

Fokker F VII over Mail Coach
AP11

Plane over Parliament
AP12

Airplane
AP13

1936, May 8 *Perf. 12x12½.*

No.	Type	Description	Unused	Used
C35	AP11	10f bright green	25	15
C36	"	20f crimson	30	15
C37	"	36f brown	60	40
C38	AP12	40f bright blue	60	40
C39	"	52f red orange	1.50	1.50
C40	AP12	60f bright violet	14.00	1.00
C41	"	80f dk. slate green	1.50	1.50
C42	AP13	1p dk. yel. green	1.50	50
C43	"	2p brown carmine	4.50	1.50
C44	"	5p dark blue	17.50	14.00
		Nos. C35-C44 (10)	42.25	21.10

Issues of the Republic.

Loyalty Tower, Sopron
AP14

Cathedral of Esztergom
AP15

Liberty Bridge, Budapest
AP16

Palace Hotel, Lillafüred
AP17

Vajdahunyad Castle, Budapest
AP18

Visegrád Fortress on the Danube
AP19

Lake Balaton
AP20

Parliament Building, Budapest
AP21

Perf. 12½x12.

1947, Mar. 5 Photo. **Wmk. 210**

No.	Type	Description	Unused	Used
C45	AP14	10f rose lake	50	20
C46	AP15	20f gray green	50	10
C47	AP16	50f copper brown	50	10
C48	AP17	70f olive green	50	12
C49	AP18	1fo gray blue	75	20
C50	AP19	1.40fo brown	1.00	40
C51	AP20	3fo green	2.50	15
C52	AP21	5fo rose violet	5.50	1.50
		Nos. C45-C52 (8)	11.75	2.77

Johannes Gutenberg and Printing Press
AP22

Designs: 2f, Columbus. 4f, Robert Fulton. 5f, George Stephenson. 6f, David Schwarz and Ferdinand von Zeppelin. 8f, Thomas A. Edison. 10f, Louis Bleriot. 12f, Roald Amundsen. 30f, Kalman Kando. 40f, Alexander S. Popov.

Perf. 12x12½.

1948, May 15 **Wmk. 283**

No.	Type	Description	Unused	Used
C53	AP22	1f orange red	15	15
C54	"	2f deep magenta	15	15
C55	"	4f blue	15	15
C56	"	5f orange brown	20	20
C57	"	6f green	20	20
C58	"	8f deep red violet	20	20
C59	"	10f brown	35	35
C60	"	12f blue green	40	40
C61	"	30f brown rose	85	85
C62	"	40f blue violet	1.00	1.00
		Nos. C53-C62 (10)	3.65	3.65

Explorers and inventors.
See also Nos. CB3-CB12.

Plane and Symbols of the U. P. U.
AP23

1949, Nov. 1

No.	Type	Description	Unused	Used
C63	AP23	2fo orange brown	1.20	1.20
		a. Bklt. pane of 6	10.00	

Issued to commemorate the 75th anniversary of the formation of the Universal Postal Union.
See also No. C81.

Chain Bridge
AP24

Symbols of Labor—AP25

1949, Nov. 20

No.	Type	Description	Unused	Used
C64	AP24	1.60fo scarlet	60	60
C65	"	2fo olive	75	60

Souvenir Sheet

Perf. 12½x12

No.	Type	Description	Unused	Used
C66	AP25	50fo car. lake	180.00	180.00

Issued in sheets measuring 137½x99 mm., with sheet design in gray and cream.
Nos. C64-C66 commemorate the centenary of the opening of the Chain Bridge, Budapest.

Postman and Mail Carrying Vehicles
AP26

1949, Dec. 11 *Perf. 12.*

No.	Type	Description	Unused	Used
C67	AP26	50f lilac gray	3.50	3.50
		Sheet of 4	20.00	20.00

Stamp Day, 1949. Issued in sheets of 4.

Plane, Globe, Stamps and Stagecoach
AP27

1950, Mar. 12 ***Perf. 12x12½.***

C68 AP27 2fo red brown & yellow 3.25 3.25

Issued to commemorate the 20th anniversary of the establishment of the Hungarian Post Office Philatelic Museum.

Chess Emblem, Globe and Plane
AP28

1950, Apr. 9 ***Perf. 12.*** **Wmk. 106**

C69 AP28 1.60fo brown 2.00 1.00

Issued to publicize the World Chess Championship Matches, Budapest.

Globes, Parliament Building and Chain Bridge—AP29

1950, May 16 ***Perf. 12x12½***

C70 AP29 1fo red brown 60 20

Issued to publicize the meeting of the World Federation of Trade Unions, Budapest, May 1950.

Statue of Liberty and View of Budapest
AP30

Designs: 30f, Crane and apartment house. 70f, Steel mill. 1fo, Stalinyec tractor. 1.60fo, Steamship. 2fo, Reaping-threshing machine. 3fo, Passenger train. 5fo, Matyas Rakosi Steel Mill, Csepel. 10fo, Budaörs Airport.

Perf. 12½x12.

1950, Oct. 29 Engraved. Unwmkd.

C71 AP30 20f claret 10 5
C72 " 30f blue violet 40 10
C73 " 70f violet brown 25 10
C74 " 1fo yellow brown 25 15
C75 " 1.60fo ultramarine 50 20
C76 " 2fo red orange 70 25
C77 " 3fo olive black 1.20 40
C78 " 5fo gray blue 1.50 75
C79 " 10fo chestnut 6.00 1.25
Nos. C71-C79 (9) 10.90 3.25

See also Nos. C167 and C172.

Souvenir Sheet.

Gen. Josef Bem and Battle at Piski—AP31

1950, Dec. 10 Engr. ***Imperf.***

C80 AP31 2fo deep plum 15.00 15.00

Issued in sheets measuring 98x78mm., to commemorate Stamp Day and the Budapest Stamp Exhibition.

U.P.U. Type of 1949.
Perf. 12x12½, Imperf.

1950, July 2 Photo. Wmk. 106

C81 AP23 3fo dark carmine & dk. brown 35.00 35.00
Sheet of 4 250.00 250.00

No. C81 was printed in numbered sheets of four. Marginal inscription at top: "75e Anniversaire de l'Union Postale Universelle."

Volleyball—AP32

Designs: 40f, Javelin-throwing. 60f, Sports badge. 70f, Soccer. 3fo, Glider meet.

1950, Dec. 2

C82 AP32 30f lilac & magenta 30 20
C83 " 40f olive & indigo 35 20
C84 " 60f olive, dark brown & orange red 75 40
C85 " 70f gray & dark brown 1.00 60
C86 " 3fo buff & dark brown 2.75 2.00
Nos. C82-C86 (5) 5.15 3.40

Mare and Foal—AP33

Designs: 70f, Sow and shoats. 1fo, Ram and ewe. 1.60fo, Cow and calf.

Photogravure

1951, Apr. 5 ***Perf. 12x12½***

C87 AP33 20f olive green & rose brown 35 30
C88 " 70f red brown & olive bistre 75 50
C89 " 1fo turq. & brown 1.50 1.00
C90 " 1.60fo brown & red brown 2.50 2.25

Issued to encourage increased livestock production.

Telegraph Linemen
AP34

Designs: 1fo, Workers on vacation. 2fo, Air view of Stalin Bridge.

1951, Aug. 20

C91 AP34 70f henna brown 30 20
C92 " 1fo blue green 60 20
C93 " 2fo deep plum 1.00 45

Issued to publicize the successful conclusion of the first year under Hungary's 5-year plan.

Tank Column
AP35

1951, Sept. 29 ***Perf. 12½x12***

C94 AP35 60f deep blue 40 20

Issued to publicize Army Day, Sept. 29, 1951.

Souvenir Sheet.

AP36

1951, Oct. 6 Engraved Unwmkd.

C95 AP36 60f olive green 30.00 30.00

Issued in sheets measuring 77x97½mm., on the occasion of a stamp exhibition to commemorate the 80th anniversary of Hungary's first postage stamp.

Twelve hundred copies in rose lilac, perforated and imperforate, were presented to exhibitors and members of the arranging committee of the exhibition. Price, both rose lilac sheets, $375.

See also Nos. CB13-CB14.

Avocet—AP37

Hungarian Birds: 30f, White stork. 40f, Golden oriole. 50f, Kentish plover. 60f, Black-winged stilt. 70f, Lesser gray shrike. 80f, Great bustard. 1fo, Red-footed falcon. 1.40fo, European bee-eater. 1.60fo, Glossy ibis. 2.50fo, Great white egret.

Perf. 13x11.

1952, Mar. 16 Photo. Wmk. 106

Birds in Natural Colors.

C96 AP37 20f emerald, *greenish* 20 10
C97 " 30f sage green, *grayish* 20 10
C98 " 40f brown, *cream* 20 10
C99 " 50f orange, *cream* 20 10
C100 " 60f deep carmine 25 10
C101 " 70f red org., *cream* 25 20
C102 " 80f olive, *cream* 35 20
C103 " 1fo deep blue, *bluish* 60 25
C104 AP37 1.40fo gray, *grayish* 1.25 75
C105 " 1.60fo orange brown, *cream* 1.75 90
C106 " 2.50fo rose violet, *cream* 2.25 1.20
Nos. C96-C106 (11) 7.50 4.00

Hammer Thrower—AP38

Design: 2fo, Stadium, Budapest.

1952, May 26 ***Perf. 11***

C107 AP38 1.70fo dp. red org. 90 75
C108 " 2fo olive brn. 1.00 75

Issued to publicize Hungary's participation in the Olympic Games, Helsinki, 1952.

Leonardo da Vinci
AP39

Design: 2fo, Victor Hugo.

1952, June 15 ***Perf. 12½x12.***

C109 AP39 1.60fo dark Prussian green 85 35
C110 " 2fo deep plum 85 35

Commemorating anniversaries of the birth of Leonardo da Vinci (500th) and Victor Hugo (150th).

Red Squirrel
AP40

Hedgehog
AP41

Designs: 40f, Hare. 50f, Beech marten. 60f, Otter. 70f, Red fox. 80f, Fallow deer. 1fo, Roe deer. 1.50fo, Boar. 2fo, Red deer.

1953, Mar. 4 ***Perf. 12x12½.***

C111 AP40 20f yellow green & copper brown 30 10
C112 AP41 30f orange brown & brown 35 10
C113 " 40f green & brown black 50 10
C114 AP40 50f light brown & brown 30 20
C115 AP41 60f green & brown 30 20
C116 " 70f olive green & red brown 35 25
C117 AP40 80f gray green & brown 90 30
C118 AP41 1fo yellow green & brown 1.10 60
C119 " 1.50fo olive bistre & black 2.00 1.50
C120 AP40 2fo brown orange & dk. brown 3.00 2.00
Nos. C111-C120 (10) 9.10 5.35

Children at Balaton Lake
AP42

Design: 1.50fo, Workers' Home at Lillafured.

1953, Apr. 19 ***Perf. 12.***

C121 AP42 1fo bright greenish blue 25 20
C122 " 1.50fo deep red lilac 60 40

Water Polo
AP43

Sports: 1fo, Boxing. 2fo, Soccer. 3fo, Track. 5fo, Stadium.

1953, Aug. 20 ***Perf. 11.***

Center in Brown or Olive Brown (No. C127)

C123 AP43 80f aquamarine 75 20
C124 " 1fo rose lilac 75 25
C125 " 2fo green 1.50 60
C126 " 3fo brown rose 2.25 1.25
C127 " 5fo greenish blue 3.00 1.50
Nos. C123–C127 (5) 8.25 3.80

Opening of People's Stadium, Budapest.

No. C125 Overprinted in Black

LONDON-WEMBLEY 1953. XI. 25.

6:3

1953, Dec. 3

C128 AP43 2fo grn. & brn. 15.00 15.00

Issued to publicize Hungary's success in the soccer matches at Wembley, England, Nov. 25, 1953. Counterfeits exist.

Janos Bihari and Scene from Verbunkos—AP44

Portraits: 40f, Ferenc Erkel. 60f, Franz Liszt. 70f, Mihaly Mosonyi. 80f, Karl Goldmark. 1fo, Bela Bartok. 2fo, Zoltan Kodaly.

1953, Dec. 5 Photo. ***Perf. 12***

Frames and Portraits in Brown

C129 AP44 30f blue gray 10 8
C130 " 40f orange 10 10
C131 AP44 60f green 15 10
C132 " 70f red 20 10
C133 " 80f gray blue 30 20
C134 " 1fo olive bistre 65 35
C135 " 2fo violet 1.25 80
Nos. C129–C135 (7) 2.75 1.73

Hungarian composers.

Carrot Beetle
AP45

May (or June) Beetle
AP46

Designs: Various beetles. 60f, Bee.

Perf. 12½x12, 12x12½.

1954, Feb. 6 **Wmk. 106**

C136 AP45 30f deep orange & dark brn. 20 10
C137 AP46 40f green & dark brown 20 15
C138 " 50f rose brown & black 40 20
C139 " 60f violet, dark brn. & yel. 30 20
C140 AP45 80f greenish gray, purple & rose 40 30
C141 " 1fo ochre & blk. 1.50 40
C142 AP46 1.20fo dull green & dark brown 1.50 60
C143 " 1.50fo olive brown & dk. brown 1.50 1.00
C144 " 2fo henna brn. & dk. brown 2.25 1.75
C145 AP45 3fo blue green & dk. brown 3.00 2.75
Nos. C136–C145 (10) 11.25 7.45

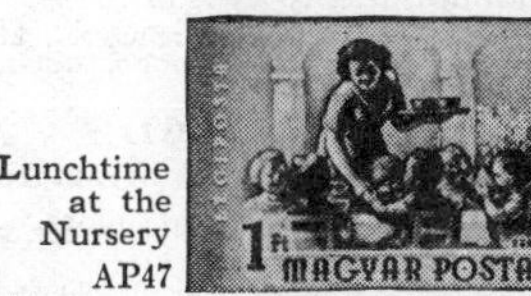

Lunchtime at the Nursery
AP47

Designs: 1.50fo, Mother taking child from doctor. 2fo, Nurse and children.

1954, Mar. 8 ***Perf. 12.***

C146 AP47 1fo olive green 25 10
C147 " 1.50fo red brown 50 30
C148 " 2fo blue green 1.00 40

Model Glider Construction—AP48

Boy Flying Model Glider
AP49

Designs: 60f, Gliders. 80f, Pilot leaving plane. 1fo, Parachutists. 1.20fo, Biplane. 1.50fo, Plane over Danube. 2fo, Jet planes.

1954, June 25 ***Perf. 11***

C149 AP48 40f brown olive & dark blue gray 10 8
C150 AP49 50f gray & red brown 15 10
C151 AP48 60f red brown & dark blue gray 20 10
C152 AP49 80f vio. & sepia 25 12
C153 AP48 1fo brown & dark blue gray 35 15
C154 AP49 1.20fo olive & sepia 50 20
C155 AP48 1.50fo claret & dark blue gray 85 70
C156 AP49 2fo bl. & dk. brown 1.50 85
Nos. C149–C156 (8) 3.90 2.30

Souvenir Sheet

Maurus Jokai
AP50

1954, Oct. 17 **Engr.** ***Perf. 12½x12***

C157 AP50 1fo violet blue 12.00 12.00

Stamp Day. Size: 51x71mm.
Exists imperforate.

Children on Sled
AP51

Skaters
AP52

Designs: 50f, Ski racer. 60f, Ice yacht. 80f, Ice hockey. 1fo, Ski jumper. 1.50fo, Downhill ski racer. 2fo, Man and woman exhibition-skating.

1955 **Photogravure** ***Perf. 12***

C158 AP51 40f greenish blue, dark brown & red brown 20 10
C159 AP52 50f olive green, dark brown & salmon 30 10
C160 AP51 60f light blue, salmon & dark brown 40 15
C161 AP52 80f green, bistre & brown black 50 25
C162 AP51 1fo blue, dark brown & salmon 80 40
C163 AP52 1.20fo olive green, brown black & salmon 1.50 60
C164 AP51 1.50fo gray green, salmon & dark brown 2.00 1.25
C165 AP52 2fo gray, brown & cerise 2.50 1.50
Nos. C158–C165 (8) 8.20 4.35

The 1.20fo and 2fo were issued Jan. 27; others Feb. 26.

Souvenir Sheet

Government Printing Plant
AP53

1955, May 28 ***Perf. 12x12½***

C166 AP53 5fo henna brown & gray green 9.00 9.00

Issued in sheets measuring 97x76½mm. to commemorate the centenary of the establishment of the government printing plant.

No. C78 Printed on Aluminum Foil

Perf. 12½x12

1955, Oct. 5 **Engraved.** **Unwmkd.**

C167 AP30 5fo gray blue 10.00 10.00

Issued to publicize the International Congress of the Light Metal Industry and to commemorate 20 years of aluminum production in Hungary. Imperfs. exist.

Bela Bartok
AP54

Photogravure.

1955, Oct. 9 ***Perf. 12*** **Wmk. 106**

C168 AP54 1fo gray green 40 40
C169 " 1fo violet brown 90 90
a. With ticket 12.50 12.50

Issued to commemorate the tenth anniversary of the death of Bela Bartok, composer. No. C169a was issued for the Day of the Stamp, Oct. 16, 1955. The 5fo sales price, marked on the attached ticket, was the admission fee to any one of 14 simultaneous stamp shows.

"Esperanto"—AP55

Lazarus Ludwig Zamenhof
AP56

1957, June 8

C170 AP55 60f red brown 25 10
C171 AP56 1fo dark green 40 20

Issued to commemorate the 10th anniversary of the death of L. L. Zamenhof, inventor of Esperanto.

Type of 1950.
Design: 20fo, Budaörs Airport.

Perf. 12½x12

1957, July 18 Engraved. Unwmkd.

C172 AP30 20fo dark slate green 8.00 6.50
Punched 3 holes 7.00 6.00

A few days after issuance, stocks of No. C172 were punched with three holes and used on domestic surface mail.

Courier and Fort Buda
AP57

Design: No. C174, Plane over Budapest.

Photogravure.

1957, Oct. 13 *Perf. 12* Wmk. 106

C173 AP57 1fo olive bistre & brn., *buff* 1.00 1.00
C174 " 1fo olive bistre & deep claret, *buff* 1.00 1.00
a. Strip, Nos. C173 and C174+label 3.00 3.00

Printed in sheets containing 10 each of Nos. C173–C174, flanking a center label. The triptych sold for 6fo. Issued for Stamp Day, Oct. 20th.

Type of Regular Pigeon Issue.
Design: 3fo, Two carrier pigeons.

1957, Dec. 14 *Perf. 12x12½*

C175 A266 3fo red, green, gray & black 85 60

Issued to publicize the International Pigeon Exhibition at Budapest, Dec. 14–16.

Hungarian Pavilion, Brussels
AP58

Designs: 40f, Map, lake and local products. 60f, Parliament. 1fo, Chain Bridge, Budapest. 1.40fo, Arms of Hungary and Belgium. 2fo, Fountain, Brussels (vert.). 3fo, City Hall, Brussels (vert.). 5fo, Exposition emblem.

Perf. 14½x15

1958, Apr. 17 Litho. Wmk. 106

C176 AP58 20f red orange & red brown 40 10
C177 " 40f light blue & brown 40 20
C178 " 60f crimson & sepia 15 10
C179 " 1fo bistre & red brown 30 15
C180 " 1.40fo dull violet & multicolor 50 25
C181 " 2fo golden brown & dark brown 70 30
C182 " 3fo blue green & sepia 1.75 60
C183 " 5fo gray olive, black, red, blue & yellow 3.50 1.10
Nos. C176–C183 (8) 7.70 2.80

Issued for the Universal and International Exposition at Brussels.

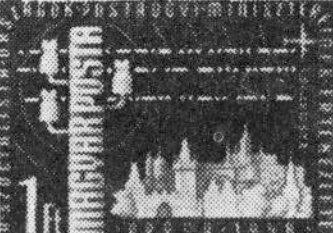

View of Prague and Morse Code
AP59

1958, June 30 Photo. *Perf. 12x12½*

C184 AP59 1fo rose brown 30 20

See No. 1194a for se-tenant pair.
Issued to commemorate the conference of Postal Ministers of Communist Countries at Prague, June 30–July 8.

Post Horn, Pigeon and Pen
AP60

Design: No. C185, Stamp under magnifying glass.

1958, Oct. 25 *Perf. 12* Wmk. 106

C185 AP60 1fo dp. car. & bis. 75 65
C186 " 1fo yellow green & bistre 75 65
a. Strip, Nos. C185 and C186+label 2.00 2.00

Issued for the National Stamp Exhibition, Budapest, Oct. 25–Nov. 2.
Printed in sheets containing 10 each of Nos. C185–C186, flanking a center label.
No. C185 inscribed: "XXXI Belyegnap 1958."

1958, Oct. 26

Designs: 60f, as No. C186. 1fo, Ship, plane, locomotive and pen surrounding letter.

C187 AP60 60f deep plum & grayish buff 30 10
C188 " 1fo blue & grayish buff 50 20

Issued for Letter Writing Week.

Plane over Heroes' Square Budapest
AP61

Design: 5fo, Plane over Tower of Sopron.

Perf. 12½x12

1958, Nov. 3 Engraved. Wmk. 106

C189 AP61 3fo gray, rose vio. & red 1.20 50
C190 " 5fo gray, dark blue & red 1.75 90

Issued to commemorate the 40th anniversary of Hungarian air post stamps.

Same
Without Commemorative Inscription

Plane over: 20f, Szeged. 30f, Sarospatak. 70f, Gyor. 1fo, Budapest, Opera House. 1.60fo, Veszprém. 2fo, Budapest, Chain Bridge. 3fo, Sopron. 5fo, Heroes' Square, Budapest. 10fo, Budapest, Academy of Science and Parliament. 20fo, Budapest.

1958, Dec. 31 Engraved Wmk. 106

Yellow Paper
and Vermilion Inscriptions.

C191 AP61 20f green 15 10
C192 " 30f violet 10 10
C193 " 70f brown violet 15 10
C194 " 1fo blue 30 10
C195 " 1.60fo purple 40 12
C196 " 2fo Prussian green 40 20
C197 " 3fo brown 70 20
C198 " 5fo olive green 1.00 30
C199 " 10fo dark blue 2.00 50
C200 " 20fo brown 4.00 1.25
Nos. C191–C200 (10) 9.20 2.97

Transport Type of Regular Issue.
Design: 3fo, Early plane.

1959, May Litho. *Perf. 14½x15*

C201 A279 3fo dull lilac, black, yel. & brown 75 40

Transport Museum, Budapest.

Tihany
AP62

Designs: 70f, Ship. 1fo, Heviz and water lily. 1.70fo, Sailboat and fisherman statue.

1959, July 15 Photo. *Perf. 11½x12*

C202 AP62 20f bright green 15 15
C203 " 70f bright blue 20 15
C204 " 1fo ultramarine & carmine rose 40 25
C205 " 1.70fo red brown, *yellow* 70 45

Issued to publicize Lake Balaton and the opening of the Summer University.

Moth-Butterfly Type of 1959

Butterflies: 1fo, Lycaena virgaureae. 2fo, Acherontia atropos (horiz.). 3fo, Red admiral.

Perf. 11½x12, 12x11½

1959, Nov. 20 Wmk. 106

Butterflies in Natural Colors.

C206 A290 1fo black & light blue green 60 30
C207 " 2fo black & lilac 1.30 60
C208 " 3fo dark gray & emerald 2.40 1.00

Souvenir Sheet

Rockets in Orbit, Gagarin, Titov & Glenn—AP63

Perf. 11, Imperf.

1962, March 29 Unwmkd.

C209 AP63 10fo multi. 17.50 17.50

Issued to honor astronants Yuri A. Gagarin and Gherman Titov of Russia and John H. Glenn, Jr., USA. No. C209 contains one stamp with black margin. Sheet size: 110x70mm.

Soccer Type of 1962.
Flags of Hungary and Great Britain.

1962, May 21 Photo. *Perf. 11*

Flags in National Colors

C209A A323 2fo greenish & bister 80 40

Issued to commemorate the World Cup Soccer Championship, Chile, May 30–June 17.

Glider and Lilienthal's 1898 Design
AP64

Designs: 30f, Icarus and Aero Club emblem. 60f, Light monoplane and 1912 aerobatic plane. 80f, Airship GZ-1 and Montgolfier balloon. 1fo, IL-18 Malev and Wright 1903 plane. 1.40fo, Stunt plane and Nyesterov's 1913 plane. 2fo, Helicopter and Asboth's 1929 helicopter. 3fo, Supersonic bomber and Zhukovski's turbomotor. 4fo, Space rocket and Tsiolkovsky's rocket.

1962, July 19 *Perf. 15* Unwmkd.

C210 AP64 30f bl. & dull yel. 5 5
C211 " 40f yellow green & ultra. 6 5
C212 " 60f ultra. & verm. 9 6
C213 " 80f greenish blue & silver 10 8
C214 " 1fo lilac, silver, & blue 20 12
C215 " 1.40fo blue & orange 30 18
C216 " 2fo bluish green & brown 40 30
C217 " 3fo vio., silver & blue 80 40
C218 " 4fo grn., silver & black 1.20 75
Nos. C210–C218 (9) 3.20 1.99

Issued to show flight development: "From Icarus to the Space Rocket."

Earth, TV Screens and Rockets
AP65

Design: 2fo, Andrian G. Nikolayev, Pavel R. Popovich and rockets.

1962, Sept. 4 *Perf. 12*

C219 AP65 1fo dark blue & org. brown 80 50
C220 " 2fo dark blue & org. brown 90 80

First group space flight of Vostoks 3 and 4, Aug. 11–15, 1962. Printed in alternating horizontal rows.

John H. Glenn, Jr.
AP66

Astronauts: 40f, Yuri A. Gagarin. 60f, Gherman Titov. 1.40fo, Scott Carpenter. 1.70fo, Andrian G. Nikolayev. 2.60fo, Pavel R. Popovich. 3fo, Walter Schirra.

1962, Oct. 27 *Perf. 12x11½*

Portraits in Bister

C221 AP66 40f purple 20 8
C222 " 60f dark green 20 10
C223 " 1fo dk. bl. grn. 25 15
C224 " 1.40fo dark brown 25 20
C225 " 1.70fo deep blue 35 25
C226 " 2.60fo violet 75 40
C227 " 3fo red brown 1.00 70
Nos. C221–C227 (7) 3.00 1.88

Issued to honor the first seven astronauts and in connection with the Astronautical Congress in Paris.

Eagle Owl
AP67

Birds: 40f, Osprey. 60f, Marsh harrier. 80f, Booted eagle. 1fo, African fish eagle. 2fo, Lammergeier. 3fo, Golden eagle. 4fo, Kestrel.

1962, Nov. 18 Litho. ***Perf. 11½***

Birds in Natural Colors

C228	AP67	30f yel. grn. & blk.	10	4
C229	"	40f org. yel. & blk.	10	5
C230	"	60f bistre & blk.	15	6
C231	"	80f lt. grn. & blk.	20	10
C232	"	1fo olive bistre & black	25	15
C233	"	2fo bluish green & black	35	20
C234	"	3fo lt. vio. & blk.	75	35
C235	"	4fo dp. org. & blk.	1.20	80
		Nos. C228–C235 (8)	3.10	1.75

Radio Mast and Albania No. 623
AP68

Designs (Communication symbols and rocket stamps of various countries): 30f, Bulgaria No. C77 (vert.). 40f, Czechoslovakia No. 1108. 50f, Communist China No. 380. 60f, North Korea. 80f, Poland No. 875. 1fo, Hungary No. 1386. 1.20fo, Mongolia No. 189 (vert.). 1.40fo, German Democratic Rep. No. 580. 1.70fo, Romania No. 1200. 2fo, Russia No. 2456 (vert.). 2.60fo, North Viet Nam.

Perf. 12x11½, 11½x12

1963, May 9 Photo. **Unwmkd.**

Stamp Reproductions in Original Colors

C236	AP68	20f olive green	10	5
C237	"	30f rose lake	10	5
C238	"	40f violet	10	5
C239	"	50f bright blue	13	5
C240	"	60f orange brn.	20	6
C241	"	80f ultramarine	20	8
C242	"	1fo dull red brn.	25	10
C243	"	1.20fo aquamarine	30	12
C244	"	1.40fo olive	40	20
C245	"	1.70fo brown olive	45	25
C246	"	2fo rose lilac	60	35
C247	"	2.60fo bluish grn.	1.00	60
		Nos. C236–C247 (12)	3.83	1.96

Issued to commemorate the 5th Conference of Postal Ministers of Communist Countries, Budapest.

Souvenir Sheet

Globe and Spaceships—AP69

Perf. 11½x12, Imperf.

1963, July 13 **Unwmkd.**

C248	AP69	10fo dark & light blue	11.00	11.00

Issued to commemorate the space flights of Valeri Bykovski, June 14–19, and Valentina Tereshkova, first woman cosmonaut, June 16–19, 1963. No. C248 contains one stamp. Margin in dark and light blue, gold, ocher and gray showing portraits of Bykovski and Tereshkova and stars. Sheet size: 63x93mm.

Souvenir Sheet

Mt. Fuji and Stadium—AP70

1964, Sept. 22 Photo. ***Perf. 11½x12***

C249	AP70	10fo multicolored	4.50	4.50

Issued to commemorate the 18th Olympic Games, Tokyo, Oct. 10–24. No. C249 contains one stamp; violet margin. Size: 56x83mm. Exists imperf.

Souvenir Sheet

Bridge Type of 1964

Design: 10fo, Elizabeth Bridge.

1964, Nov. 21 Photo. ***Perf. 11***

C250	A356	10fo silver & dp. green	4.00	4.00

Issued to commemorate the opening of the reconstructed Elizabeth Bridge. No. C250 contains one stamp; silver and green margin. Size of stamp: 59x20mm. Size of sheet: 95x51mm.

Lt. Col. Alexei Leonov in Space
AP71

Design: 2fo, Col. Pavel Belyayev, Lt. Col. Alexei Leonov and Voskhod 2.

1965, Apr. 17 Photo. ***Perf. 11½x12***

C251	AP71	1fo vio. & gray	50	20
C252	"	2fo rose claret & ocher	1.20	90

Issued to commemorate the space flight of Voskhod 2 and of Lt. Col. Alexei Leonov, the first man floating in space.

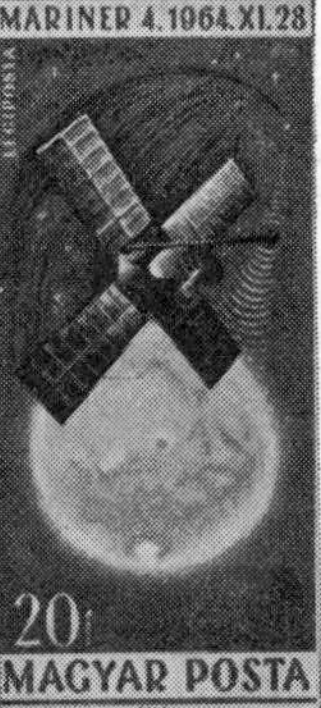

Mariner IV (USA)
AP72

Plane over Helsinki
AP73

Designs: 30f, San Marco satellite (Italy). 40f, Molniya satellite (USSR). 60f, Moon rocket, 1965, (USSR). 1fo, Shapir rocket (France). 2.50fo, Zond III satellite (USSR). 3fo, Syncom III satellite (USA). 10fo, Rocket sending off satellites (horiz.).

1965, Dec. 31 Photo. ***Perf. 11***

C253	AP72	20f ultra., black & org. yel.	15	4
C254	"	30f brn., vio. & yel.	25	5
C255	"	40f violet, brown & pink	25	7
C256	"	60f lt. pur., blk. & org. yel.	30	10
C257	"	1fo red lilac, black & buff	35	20
C258	"	2.50fo rose claret, black & gray	80	50
C259	"	3fo blue green, blk. & bister	1.20	85
		Nos. C253–C259 (7)	3.30	1.81

Souvenir Sheet

1965, Dec. 20

C260	AP72	10fo brt. bl., yel. & dk. olive	5.00	5.00

Issued to honor new achievements in space research. No. C260 contains one stamp; bright blue margin showing Vostok 2 and Gemini 4 capsules. Size: 105x84mm.

Sport Type of Regular Issue

Souvenir Sheet

Design: 10fo, Women hurdlers and Ferihegy airport.

1966, Sept. 4 Photo. ***Perf. 12x11½***

C261	A384	10fo brt. blue, brn. & red	4.50	4.50

Issued to commemorate the 8th European Athletic Championships, Budapest, Aug. 30–Sept. 4. No. C261 contains one stamp; light gray margin with brown and red inscription. Size: 105x75mm.

1966–67 Photo. ***Perf. 12x11½***

Plane over Cities Served by Hungarian Airlines: 50f, Athens. 1fo, Beirut. 1.10fo, Frankfort on the Main. 1.20fo, Cairo. 1.50fo, Copenhagen. 2fo, London. 2.50fo, Moscow. 3fo, Paris. 4fo, Prague. 5fo, Rome. 10fo, Damascus. 20fo, Budapest.

C262	AP73	20f brn. orange	10	10
C263	"	50f brown	10	10
C264	"	1fo blue	15	8
C265	"	1.10fo black	17	10
C266	"	1.20fo orange	18	10
C267	"	1.50fo blue green	22	10
C268	"	2fo bright blue	30	12
C269	"	2.50fo bright red	35	15
C270	"	3fo yellow green	45	20
C271	"	4fo brown red	90	60
C272	"	5fo brt. purple	75	35
C273	"	10fo violet blue ('67)	1.50	50
C274	"	20fo gray olive ('67)	3.00	90
		Nos. C262–C274 (13)	8.17	3.40

See also No. C276.

Souvenir Sheet

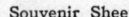

Icarus Falling—AP73a

1968, May 11 Photo. ***Perf. 11***

C275	AP73a	10fo blk., ultra., pink & gold	4.50	4.50

Issued in memory of the astronauts Edward H. White (USA), Vladimir M. Komarov and Yuri A. Gagarin (USSR). No. C275 shows portraits of the astronauts in margin against ultramarine background. Gold inscription. Size: 94½x76½mm.

Type of 1966–67 without "Legiposta" Inscription

Design: 2.60fo, Malev Airlines jet over St. Stephen's Cathedral, Vienna.

1968, July 4 Photo. ***Perf. 12x11½***

C276	AP73	2.60fo violet	40	15

Issued to commemorate the 50th anniversary of regular airmail service between Budapest and Vienna.

Women Swimmers and Aztec Calendar Stone
AP74

Aztec Calendar Stone, Olympic Rings and: 60f, Soccer. 80f, Wrestling. 1fo, Canoeing. 1.40fo, Gymnast on rings. 3fo, Fencing. 4fo, Javelin.

1968, Aug. 21 Photo. ***Perf. 12***

C277	AP74	20f bright blue & multi.	15	10
C278	"	60fr green & multi.	10	5
C279	"	80f car. rose & multi.	15	10
C280	"	1fo greenish bl. & multi.	20	12
C281	"	1.40fo violet & multi.	40	15
C282	"	3fo bright lilac & multi.	1.00	40
C283	"	4fo green & multi.	1.20	75
		Nos. C277–C283, CB31 (8)	3.60	2.02

Issued to publicize the 19th Olympic Games, Mexico City, Oct. 12–27.

Souvenir Sheet

Apollo 8 Trip Around the Moon
AP75

1969, Feb. Photogravure *Perf. 12½*

C284	AP75	10fo multi.	5.50	5.50

Issued to commemorate man's first flight around the moon, Dec. 21–27, 1968. No. C284 has multicolored margin inscribed with the names of the American astronauts Col. Frank Borman, Capt. James Lovell and Maj. William Anders. Size: 110x81mm.

Soyuz 4 and 5, and Men in Space
AP76

Design: No. C286, Soyuz 4 and 5.

1969, Mar. 21 Photo. *Perf. 12x11½*

C285	AP76	2fo multicolored	60	60
C286	"	2fo dk. blue, lt. blue & red	60	60
	a.	Strip, #C285–C286 + label	1.40	

First team flights of Russian spacecraft Soyuz 4 and 5, Jan. 16, 1969.

Nos. C285–C286 are printed with connecting label showing radar screen and astronaut; sheets of 8 contain 4 horizontal strips of Nos. C285–C286 and label.

Journey to the Moon, by Jules Verne—AP77

Designs: 60f, Tsiolkovski's space station. 1fo, Luna 1. 1.50fo, Ranger 7. 2fo, Luna 9 landing on moon. 2.50fo, Apollo 8 in orbit around moon. 3fo, Soyuz 4 and 5 docking in space. 4fo, Lunar landing module landing on moon. 10fo, Apollo 11 astronauts on moon and lunar landing module.

1969 Photo. *Perf. 12x11½*

C287	AP77	40f multicolored	15	10
C288	"	60f "	20	10
C289	"	1fo "	20	10
C290	"	1.50fo "	25	15
C291	"	2fo "	30	20
C292	"	2.50fo "	40	30
C293	"	3fo "	90	40
C294	"	4fo "	1.40	75
		Nos. C287–C294 (8)	3.80	2.10

Souvenir Sheet

Perf. 11

C295	AP77	10fo multi.	12.00	12.00

Moon landing issue. See note after Algeria No. 427.

No. C295 has multicolored margin with commemorative inscription. Size of stamp: 74x49mm. Size of sheet: 132x88mm. Issue dates: Nos. C287–C294, Nov. 1, No. C295, Aug. 15.

Daimler, 1886—AP78

Automobiles: 60f, Peugeot, 1894. 1fo, Benz, 1901. 1.50fo, Cudell mail truck, 1902. 2fo, Rolls Royce, 1908. 2.50fo, Model T Ford, 1908. 3fo, Vermorel, 1912. 4fo, Csonka mail car, 1912.

1970, March Photo. *Perf. 12*

C296	AP78	40f ocher & multi.	5	3
C297	"	60f multicolored	10	4
C298	"	1fo red & multi.	15	8
C299	AP78	1.50fo blue & multi.	20	15
C300	"	2fo multicolored	30	20
C301	"	2.50fo vio. & multi.	40	25
C302	"	3fo multicolored	90	30
C303	"	4fo "	1.20	75
		Nos. C296–C303 (8)	3.30	1.80

American Astronauts on Moon
AP79

Design: No. C305, Soyuz 6, 7 and 8 in space.

1970, Mar. 20 Photo. *Perf. 11*

C304	AP79	3fo blue & multi.	90	90
C305	"	3fo carmine rose & multi.	90	90

Landing of Apollo 12 on moon, Nov. 14, 1969, and group flight of Russian spacecraft Soyuz 6, 7 and 8, Oct. 11–13, 1969.

Nos. C304–C305 issued also in sheets of 4. Size: 112½x78mm.

"Rain at Foot of Fujiyama," by Hokusai, and Pavilion
AP80

Design: 3fo, Sun Tower, Peace Bell and globe.

1970, Apr. 30 Photo. *Perf. 12½*

C306	AP80	2fo multicolored	80	70
C307	"	3fo "	1.00	90

Issued to publicize EXPO '70 International Exhibition, Osaka, Japan, Mar. 15–Sept. 13.

Miniature Sheets

Phases of Apollo 13 Moon Flight
AP81

Designs of Vignettes of No. C308: Apollo 13 over moon; return to earth; capsule with parachutes; capsule floating, aircraft carrier and helicopter.

Designs of Vignettes of No. C309: Soyuz 9 on way to launching pad; launching of Soyuz 9 capsule in orbit; astronauts Andrian Nikolayev and Vitaly Sevastyanov.

Designs of Vignettes of No. C310: Luna 16 approaching moon; module on moon; landing; nose cone on ground.

Designs of Vignettes of No. C311: Lunokhod 1 on moon; trajectories of Luna 17 around earth and moon.

1970–71 Lithographed *Perf. 11½*

Multicolored

C308	AP81	Sheet of 4	4.00	4.00

Photogravure

C309	AP81	Sheet of 4	4.00	4.00
C310	AP81	Sheet of 4 ('71)	4.00	4.00
C311	"	Sheet of 4 ('71)	4.00	4.00

Nos. C308–C311 were valid for postage only as full sheets. Each contains four 2.50fo vignettes which were not valid singly.

No. C308 was issued to commemorate the aborted moon flight and safe return of Apollo 13, American spaceship, Apr. 11–17, 1970. Size: 111x90mm. Issued June 10.

No. C309 was issued to commemorate the 424-hour flight of Soyuz 9, Russian spaceship, June 1–9. Size: 106½x86½ mm. Issued Sept. 4.

No. C310 was issued to commemorate Luna 16, the unmanned, automated Russian moon mission, Sept. 12–24, 1970. Size: 107½x85½mm. Issued Jan. 15, 1971.

No. C311 was issued to commemorate Luna 17, unmanned, automated Russian moon mission, Nov. 10–17, 1970. Size: 107½x85½mm. Issued Mar. 8, 1971.

Souvenir Sheet

American Astronauts on Moon
AP82

1971, March 31 *Perf. 12½*

C312	AP82	10fo multicolored	4.00	4.00

Apollo 14 moon landing, Jan. 31–Feb. 9, 1971. Size of C312: 118x67½mm.

See also Nos. C315, C326–C328.

Hunting Type of Regular Issue

Souvenir Sheet

Design: 10fo, Red deer group.

1971, Aug. 27 Photo. *Perf. 11*

C313	A460	10fo multicolored	4.00	4.00

World Hunting Exhibition, Budapest, Aug. 27–30. No. C313 contains one stamp (size: 70x45mm.). Gray green and gold margin with commemorative inscription in Hungarian, French, German, English and Russian. Size: 145x98mm.

Astronauts Volkov, Dobrovolsky and Patsayev—AP83

Souvenir Sheet

1971, Oct. 4 Photo. *Perf. 12½*

C314	AP83	10fo multicolored	3.00	3.00

In memory of the Russian astronauts Vladislav N. Volkov, Lt. Col. Georgi T. Dobrovolsky and Victor I. Patsayev, who died during the Soyuz 11 space mission, June 6–30, 1971. Silver and black margin. Size: 133x90mm.

Apollo 14 Type of 1971

Souvenir Sheet

Design: 10fo, American Lunar Rover on moon.

1972, Jan. 20 Photo. *Perf. 12½*

C315	AP82	10fo multi.	4.00	4.00

Apollo 15 moon mission, July 26–Aug. 7, 1971. Multicolored margin with Apollo 15 badge showing explorations of Lunar Rover, and names of American astronauts David Scott, Alfred Worden and James Irwin. Size: 120x75mm.

Soccer and Hungarian Flag—AP84

Various Scenes from Soccer and National Flags of: 60f, Romania. 80f, German Federal Republic. 1fo, Great Britain. 1.20fo, Jugoslavia. 2fo, Soviet Union. 4fo, Italy. 5fo, Belgium.

1972, Apr. 29

C316	AP84	40f gold & multi.	5	4
C317	"	60f " "	7	6
C318	"	80f " "	10	8
C319	"	1fo " "	15	12
C320	"	1.20fo " "	20	15
C321	"	2fo " "	40	25
C322	"	4fo " "	1.20	60
C323	"	5fo " "	1.50	90
	a.	Sheet of 8	4.00	3.00
		Nos. C316–C323 (8)	3.67	2.20

European Soccer Championships for the Henri Delaunay Cup. Nos. C316–C323 printed se-tenant in sheets of 8 (2x4). Margin inscribed in black with names of event and participating countries Size: 147x197mm.

Nos. C316–C321 were later issued individually in sheets of 20 and in partly changed colors.

Souvenir Sheet

Olympic Rings and Globe—AP85

1972, June 10 Photo. *Perf. 12½*

C324	AP85	10fo multi.	10.00	10.00

20th Olympic Games, Munich, Aug. 26–Sept. 11. No. C324 contains one stamp. Blue and multicolored margin. Size: 117x 68mm.

Olympic Type of Regular Issue

Souvenir Sheet

Design: 10fo, Equestrian and Olympic Rings.

1972, July 15 Photo. *Perf. 12½*

C325	A484	10fo multicolored	4.00	4.00

20th Olympic Games, Munich, Aug. 26–Sept. 11. No. C325 contains one stamp (43x43mm.). Pale green, gold and lilac rose decorative margin. Size: 115x90mm.

Souvenir Sheets

Apollo 14 Type of 1971

Design: 10fo, Astronaut in space, Apollo 16 capsule and badge.

1972, Oct. 10 Photo. *Perf. 12½*

C326	AP82	10fo bl. & multi.	4.00	4.00

Apollo 16 U.S. moon mission, Apr. 15–27, 1972. Multicolored margin showing moon surface. White marginal inscription with date of mission and names of astronauts: J. W. Young, T. K. Mattingly, C. M. Duke. Size: 119x75mm.

1973, Jan. 15

Design: 10fo, Astronaut exploring moon (vert.).

C327	AP82	10fo bl. & multi.	4.00	4.00

Apollo 17 U.S. moon mission, Dec. 7–19, 1972. No. C327 contains one vertical stamp. Moon surface and landing module shown in multicolored margin; gold inscription with names of astronauts: Eugene Cernan, Ronald Evans, Harrison Schmitt. Size: 69½x110mm.

1973, Mar. 12 Photo. *Perf. 12½*

Design: 10fo, Venus 8.

C328	AP82	10fo multicolored	3.25	3.25

Venus 8 USSR space mission, Mar. 27–July 22, 1972. No. C328 contains one stamp. Pictures of constellations in margin. Size: 109x92½mm.

Equestrian (Pentathlon), Olympic Rings and Medal
AP86

Designs (Olympic Rings and Medals): 60f, Weight lifting. 1fo, Canoeing. 1.20fo, Swimming, women's. 1.80fo, Boxing. 4fo, Wrestling. 6fo, Fencing. 10fo, Allegorical figure lighting flame (vert.)

1973, Mar. 31

C329	AP86	40f multicolored	6	4
C330	"	60f "	10	8
C331	"	1fo bl. & multi.	15	12
C332	"	1.20fo multicolored	30	15
C333	"	1.80fo "	40	20
C334	"	4fo "	1.00	45
C335	"	6fo "	1.35	90
		Nos. C329-C335 (7)	3.36	1.94

Souvenir Sheet
Perf. 11

C336	AP86	10fo bl. & multi.	4.75	4.75

Hungarian medalists at 20th Olympic Games. No. C336 contains one stamp (size: 44x71mm.). Brown and multicolored margin with Mercator map, Olympic medals, emblem of Montreal 76, and Intelsat 4. Size: 132x88mm.

Wrens
AP87

1973, Apr. 16 Litho. *Perf. 12*

Multicolored

C337	AP87	40f *shown*	6	4
C338	"	60f *Rock thrush*	9	6
C339	"	80f *Robins*	12	8
C340	"	1fo *Firecrests*	15	12
C341	"	1.20fo *Linnets*	25	15
C342	"	2fo *Blue titmice*	40	25
C343	"	4fo *White-spotted blue throat*	80	45
C344	"	5fo *Gray wagtails*	1.60	1.00
		Nos. C337-C344 (8)	3.47	2.15

Souvenir Sheet
Exhibition Type of Regular Issue

Design: 10fo, Bavaria No. 1 with mill wheel cancellation; Munich City Hall, TV Tower and Olympic tent.

1973, May 11 Litho. *Perf. 11*

C345	A506	10fo multicolored	4.00	4.00

IBRA '73 Philatelic Exhibition, Munich, May 11–20. No. C345 contains one stamp (size: 83x45mm.). Light olive margin with multicolored IBRA emblem and Budapest '61 and '71 exhibition emblems. Size: 130x81mm.

Souvenir Sheet

Skylab over Earth—AP88

1973, Oct. 16 Photo. *Perf. 12½*

C346	AP88	10fo dk. blue, lt. bl. & yel.	4.00	4.00

First U.S. manned space station. No. C346 contains one stamp with blue margin showing interior of Skylab. Size: 115x76mm.

Space Type of Regular Issue

Designs: 6fo, Mars "canals" and Giovanni V. Schiaparelli. 10fo, Mars 7 spacecraft.

1974, Mar. 11 Photo. *Perf. 12½*

C347	A522	6fo gold & multi.	1.20	80

Souvenir Sheet

C348	A522	10fo gold & multi.	4.00	4.00

Mars exploration. No. C348 contains one stamp; dark blue and multicolored margin showing planets and stars. Gold marginal inscription. Size: 95x90mm.

UPU Type of 1974

1974, May 22 Litho. *Perf. 12*

Multicolored

C349	A526	6fo *UPU emblem and TU-154 jet*	1.50	80

Souvenir Sheet

C350	A526	Sheet of 4	4.00	4.00
	a.	2.50fo *Mail coach*	75	75
	b.	2.50fo *Old mail automobile*	75	75
	c.	2.50fo *Jet*	75	75
	d.	2.50fo *Apollo 15*	75	75

Centenary of Universal Postal Union. No. C350 has bister UPU emblem in center where 4 stamps meet, and silver margin with blue inscription. Size: 130x105mm.

Army Day Type of 1974

Designs: 2fo, Ground-to-air missiles (vert.). 3fo, Parachutist, helicopter, supersonic jets.

1974, Sept. 28 Litho. *Perf. 12*

C351	A537	2fo gold, emerald & black	30	15
C352	"	3fo gold, bl. & blk.	70	30

Carrier Pigeon, Elizabeth Bridge, Mt. Gellert
AP89

1975, Feb. 7 Litho. *Perf. 12*

C353	AP89	3fo multicolored	1.50	1.50

Carrier Pigeons' Olympics, Budapest, Feb. 7–9. No. C353 printed checkerwise with black and violet coupon showing Pigeon Olympics emblem.

Sputnik 2, Apollo-Soyuz Emblem
AP90

Spacecraft and Apollo-Soyuz Emblem: 60f, Mercury-Atlas 5. 80f, Lunokhod I on moon. 1.20fo, Lunar rover, Apollo 15 mission. 2fo, Soyuz take-off, Baikonur. 4fo, Apollo take-off, Cape Kennedy. 6fo, Apollo-Soyuz link-up. 10fo, Apollo, Soyuz, American and Russian flags over earth (horiz.).

1975, July 7 Photo. *Perf. 12x11½*

C354	AP90	40f silv. & multi.	8	6
C355	"	60f silv. & multi.	10	6
C356	"	80f silv. & multi.	20	10
C357	"	1.20fo silv. & multi.	25	15
C358	"	2fo silv. & multi.	40	20
C359	"	4fo silv. & multi.	80	40
C360	"	6fo silv. & multi.	1.40	75
		Nos. C354-C360 (7)	3.23	1.72

Souvenir Sheet
Perf. 12½

C361	AP90	10fo bl. & multi.	4.00	4.00

Apollo Soyuz space test project (Russo-American cooperation), launching July 15; link-up July 17. No. C361 contains one stamp (size: 59x38mm.); deep carmine margin with various space mission emblems, white inscription and black control number. Size: 128x99mm.

Souvenir Sheet

Map of Europe and Cogwheels
AP91

1975, July 30 Litho. *Perf. 12½*

C362	AP91	10fo multi.	4.50	4.50

European Security and Cooperation Conference, Helsinki, July 30–Aug. 1. No. C362 has gray and multicolored margin showing flags of participating nations. Size: 156x82mm.

Souvenir Sheet

Hungary Nos. 1585, 1382, 2239, 2280, C81—AP92

1975, Sept. 9 Photo. *Perf. 12½*

C363	AP92	10fo multi.	4.00	4.00

30 years of stamps. No. C363 has purple margin with white inscription and border, black control number. Size: 149x95mm.

A similar souvenir sheet with blue margin, no denomination and no postal validity was released for the 25th anniversary of Filatelica Hungarica.

Souvenir Sheet

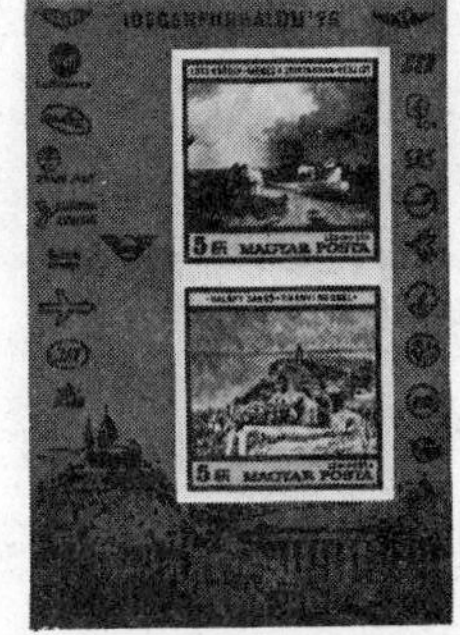

Paintings by Károly Lotz and János Halápi—AP93

1976, Mar. 19 Photo. *Perf. 12½*

C364	AP93	Sheet of 2, multi.	4.00	4.00
	a.	5fo *Horses in Storm*	1.50	1.50
	b.	5fo *Morning at Tihany*	1.50	1.50

Tourist publicity. Dark violet blue margin with view of Pest and airline emblems in gold foil. Nos. C364a and C364b se-tenant, imperf. between. Size of sheet: 95x135mm.

Souvenir Sheet

Montreal Olympic Stadium—AP94

1976, June 29 Litho. *Perf. 12½*

C365	AP94	20fo red, gray & black	4.50	4.50

21st Olympic Games, Montreal, Canada, July 17–Aug. 1. No. C365 has green, red and gray margin showing transfer of Olympic Flame by laser beam from Athens to Montreal. Size: 129x84mm.

U.S. Mars Mission
AP95

Designs: 60f, Viking in space. 1fo, Viking on moon. 2fo, Venus, rocket take-off. 3fo, Venyera 9 in space. 4fo, Venyera 10, separation in space. 5fo, Venyera on moon. 20fo, Viking 1 landing on Mars (vert.).

1976, Nov. 11 Photo. *Perf. 11*

C366	AP95	40f silver & multi.	8	4
C367	"	60f " "	12	5
C368	"	1fo " "	20	12
C369	"	2fo " "	40	25
C370	"	3fo " "	60	30
C371	"	4fo " "	80	40
C372	"	5fo " "	1.25	60
		Nos. C366-C372 (7)	3.45	1.76

Souvenir Sheet
Perf. 12½

C373	AP95	20fo black & multi.	4.75	4.75

US–USSR space missions. No. C373 contains one stamp (size: 41x64mm.); yellow and multicolored margin shows emblems of various missions. Size: 95x81mm.

Hungary No. CB33—AP96

1977, Apr. Litho. ***Perf. 11½x12***

C374	AP96	3fo multicolored	80	80

European stamp exhibitions. Issued in sheets of 3 stamps and 3 labels. Labels show exhibition emblems respectively: 125th anniversary of Brunswick stamps, Brunswick, May 5–8; Regiofil XII, Lugano, June 17–19; centenary of San Marino Stamps, Riccione, Aug. 27–29.

Souvenir Sheet

Space Type 1977

Design: 20fo, Viking on Mars.

1977, Sept. 20 Litho. ***Perf. 11½***

C375	A603	20fo multicolored	4.50	4.50

Space explorations. No. C375 has multicolored margin showing signs of the Zodiac; silver control number. Size: 98x78mm.

Souvenir Sheet

"EUROPA," Map and Dove—AP97

1977, Oct. 3 ***Perf. 12½***

C376	AP97	20fo multi.	5.00	5.00

European Security Conference, Belgrade, Oct.–Nov. No. C376 shows flags of participating nations, arms of Belgrade and control number. Size: 125x76mm.

TU-154, Malev over Europe AP98

Planes, Airlines, Maps: 1.20fo, DC-8, Swissair, Southeast Asia. 2fo, IL-62, CSA, North Africa. 2.40fo, A 300B Airbus, Lufthansa, Northwest Europe. 4fo, Boeing 747, Pan Am, North America. 5fo, TU-144, Aeroflot, Northern Europe. 10fo, Concorde, Air France, South America. 20fo, IL-86, Aeroflot, Northeast Asia.

1977, Oct. 26 Litho. ***Perf. 11½x12***

Size: 32x21mm.

C377	AP98	60f org. & blk.	12	6
C378	"	1.20fo vio. & blk.	25	15
C379	"	2fo yel. & blk.	40	25
C380	"	2.40fo bl. green & black	50	30
C381	"	4fo ultra. & black	80	50
C382	"	5fo dp. rose & black	1.00	65
C383	"	10fo bl. & blk.	2.00	1.30

Perf. 12x11½

Size: 37½x29mm.

C384	AP98	20fo grn. & black	4.00	2.60
		Nos. C377–C384 (8)	9.07	5.81

Methods and style of listing are detailed in "Special Notices" at the front of this volume.

Montgolfier Brothers and Balloon, 1783—AP99

Designs: 60f, David Schwarz and airship, 1850. 1fo, Alberto Santos-Dumont and airship flying around Eiffel Tower, 1873. 2fo, Konstantin E. Tsiolkovsky, airship and Kremlin, 1857. 3fo, Roald Amundsen, airship Norge, Polar bears and map, 1872. 4fo, Hugo Eckener, Graf Zeppelin over Mt. Fuji, 1930. 5fo, Count Ferdinand von Zeppelin, Graf Zeppelin over Chicago, 1932. 20fo, Graf Zeppelin over Budapest, 1931.

1977, Nov. 1 Photo. ***Perf. 12x11½***

C385	AP99	40f gold & multi.	8	4
C386	"	60f " "	12	6
C387	"	1fo " "	20	12
C388	"	2fo " "	40	25
C389	"	3fo " "	60	38
C390	"	4fo " "	80	50
C391	"	5fo " "	1.00	65
		Nos. C385–C391 (7)	3.20	2.00

Souvenir Sheet

Perf. 12½

C392	AP99	20fo silver & multi.	4.50	4.50

History of airships. No. C392 contains one stamp (60x36mm.); multicolored margin shows air routes on world map, 1931 commemorative cancellation and black control number. Size: 97x78mm.

Moon Station AP100

Science Fiction Paintings by Pal Varga: 60f, Moon settlement. 1fo, Spaceship near Phobos. 2fo, Exploration of asteroids. 3fo, Spaceship in gravitational field of Mars. 4fo, Spaceship and rings of Saturn. 5fo, Spaceship landing on 3rd Jupiter moon.

1978, Mar. 10 Litho. ***Perf. 11***

C393	AP100	40f multicolored	8	4
C394	"	60f "	12	6
C395	"	1fo "	20	12
C396	"	2fo "	40	25
C397	"	3fo "	60	38
C398	"	4fo "	80	50
C399	"	5fo "	1.00	65
		Nos. C393–C399 (7)	3.20	2.00

Louis Bleriot and La Manche—AP101

Designs: 60f, J. Alcock and R. W. Brown, Vickers Vimy, 1919. 1fo, A. C. Read and Navy Curtiss NC-4, 1919. 2fo, H. Köhl, G. Hünefeld, J. Fitzmaurice, Junkers W33, 1928. 3fo, A. Johnson, J. Mollison, Gipsy Moth, 1930. 4fo, G. Endresz, S. Magyar, Lockheed Sirius, 1931. 5fo, W. Gronau, Dornier WAL, 1932. 20fo, Wilbur and Orville Wright and their plane.

1978, May 10 Litho. ***Perf. 12***

C400	AP101	40f multicolored	8	4
C401	"	60f "	12	6
C402	"	1fo "	20	12
C403	"	2fo "	40	25
C404	"	3fo "	60	38
C405	"	4fo "	80	50
C406	"	5fo "	1.00	65
		Nos. C400–C406 (7)	3.20	2.00

Souvenir Sheet

C407	AP101	20fo multi.	4.50	4.50

75th anniversary of first powered flight by Wright brothers. No. C407 contains one stamp (75x25mm.); orange, yellow and black margin showing Concorde and Daedalus; dark blue control number. Size: 95x79mm.

Souvenir Sheet

Jules Verne and "Voyage from Earth to Moon"—AP102

Lithographed

1978, Aug. 21 ***Perf. 12½x11½***

C408	AP102	20fo multi.	4.50	4.50

Jules Verne (1828–1905), French science fiction writer, birth sesquicentennial. No. C408 has multicolored margin showing rockets and space stations. Size: 97x78mm.

Vladimir Remek Postmarking Mail on Board Salyut 6—AP103

1978, Sept. 1 Photo. ***Perf. 11½x12***

C409	AP103	3fo multicolored	60	60

PRAGA '78 International Philatelic Exhibition, Prague, Sept. 8–17. Issued in sheets of 3 stamps and 3 labels, showing PRAGA '78 emblem and Golden Tower, Prague. FISA emblems in margin.

AIR POST SEMI-POSTAL STAMPS.

Roosevelt Type of Semipostal Stamps, 1947

Designs (F. D. Roosevelt, Plane and Place): 10f+10f, Casablanca. 20f+20f, Tehran. 50f+50f, Yalta (map). 70f+70f, Hyde Park.

Perf. 12x12½

1947, June 11 Photo. Wmk. 210

Portrait in Sepia

CB1	SP115	10f+10f red vio.	3.00	3.00
CB1A	"	20f+20f brown olive	3.00	3.00
CB1B	"	50f+50f violet	3.00	3.00
CB1C	"	70f+70f black	3.00	3.00

Honoring Franklin D. Roosevelt (1882–1945), U.S. President.

A souvenir sheet contains one each of Nos. CB1–CB1C with border inscriptions and decorations in brown. Size: 161x122mm. Price $60.

See note below Nos. B198A–B198D.

Souvenir Sheets.

Chain Bridge, Budapest—SPAP1

Perf. 12x12½

1948, May 15 Photo. Wmk. 283

CB1D	SPAP1	2fo+18fo brn. car., sheet	85.00	85.00

Gray margin design. Size: 74½x65mm.

Chain Bridge—SPAP2

1948, Oct. 16

CB2	SPAP2	3fo+18fo deep greenish blue, sheet	75.00	75.00

Olive bister margin design. Size: 75x65mm.

Type of Air Post Stamps of 1948. Portraits at Right.

Writers: 1f, William Shakespeare. 2f, Francois Voltaire. 4f, Johann Wolfgang von Goethe. 5f, Lord Byron. 6f, Victor Hugo. 8f, Edgar Allen Poe. 10f, Sandor Petöfi. 12f, Mark Twain. 30f, Count Leo Tolstoy. 40f, Maxim Gorky.

1948, Oct. 16 Photogravure

CB3	AP22	1f deep ultra	20	20
CB4	"	2f rose carmine	20	20
CB5	"	4f deep yellow grn.	20	20
CB6	"	5f deep rose lilac	20	20
CB7	"	6f deep blue	20	20
CB8	"	8f olive brown	25	25
CB9	"	10f red	35	35
CB10	"	12f deep violet	35	35
CB11	"	30f orange brown	70	70
CB12	"	40f sepia	90	90
		Nos. CB3–CB12 (10)	3.55	3.55

Sold at a 50 per cent increase over face, half of which aided reconstruction of the Chain Bridge and the other half the hospital for postal employees.

Souvenir Sheets. Type of Air Post Souvenir Sheet of 1951.

Perf. 12½x12

1951, Sept. 12 Engr. Unwmkd.

CB13	AP36	1fo+1fo red	30.00	30.00
CB14	"	2fo+2fo blue	30.00	30.00

Issued in sheets measuring 77 x 97½ mm., on the occasion of a stamp exhibition to commemorate the 80th anniversary of Hungary's first postage stamp.

Children Inspecting Stamp Album
SPAP3

Design: 2fo+2fo, Children at stamp exhibition.

Perf. 12x12½

1952, Oct. 12 Photo. Wmk. 106

CB15	SPAP3	1fo+1fo blue	2.00	2.00
CB16	"	2fo+2fo brown red	2.75	2.75

Issued to publicize stamp week, Oct. 11–19, 1952.

Globe and Mailbox
SPAP4

Designs: 1fo+50f, Mobile post office. 2fo+1fo, Telegraph pole. 3fo+1.50fo, Radio. 5fo+2.50fo, Telephone. 10fo+5fo, Post horn.

1957, June 20 *Perf. 12x12½, 12*

Cross in Red.

Size: 32x21mm.

CB17	SPAP4	60f+30f bis. brn.	40	30
CB18	"	1fo+50f lilac	60	40
CB19	"	2fo+1fo orange vermilion	1.20	50
CB20	"	3fo+1.50fo blue	1.50	70
CB21	"	5fo+2.50fo gray	2.25	1.50

Size: 46x31mm.

CB22	SPAP4	10fo+5fo pale green	5.00	3.50
		Nos. CB17–CB22 (6)	10.95	6.90

The surtax was for the benefit of hospitals for postal and telegraph employees.

Parachute of Fausztusz Verancsics, 1617
SPAP5

History of Hungarian Aviation: No. CB24, Balloon of David Schwarz, 1897. No. CB25, Monoplane of Ernö Horvath, 1911. No. CB26, PKZ-2 helicopter, 1918.

Engraved and Lithographed

1967, May 6 *Perf. 10½*

CB23	SPAP5	2fo+1fo sepia & yellow	90	90
CB24	"	2fo+1fo sepia & lt. blue	90	90
CB25	"	2fo+1fo sepia & lt. green	90	90
CB26	"	2fo+1fo sepia & pink	90	90
		a. Horiz. strip of 4	4.00	4.00
		b. Souv. sheet of 4	4.25	4.25

Issued to publicize "AEROFILA 67" International Airmail Exhibition, Budapest, Sept. 3–10. Nos. CB26a–CB26b each contain one each of Nos. CB23–CB26. No. CB26b has tan margin with brown inscription. Size: 116x91mm.

1967, Sept. 3

Aviation, 1967: No. CB27, Parachutist. No. CB28, Helicopter Mi-1. No. CB29, TU-154 jet. No. CB30, Space station Luna 12.

CB27	SPAP5	2fo+1fo slate & light green	75	75
CB28	"	2fo+1fo slate & buff	75	75
CB29	"	2fo+1fo slate & yellow	75	75
CB30	"	2fo+1fo slate & pink	75	75
		a. Horiz. strip of 4	3.25	3.25
		b. Souv. sheet of 4	3.50	3.50

Issued to commemorate (in connection with AEROFILA 67) the 7th Congress of FISA (Fédération Internationale des Sociétés Aérophilatéliques) and the 40th Stamp Day. Nos. CB30a–CB30b each contain one each of Nos. CB27–CB30. No. CB30b has light blue margin with black inscription. Size: 115x90mm.

Olympic Games Airmail Type

Design: 2fo+1fo, Equestrian.

1968, Aug. 21 Photo. *Perf. 12*

CB31	AP74	2fo+1fo multi.	40	35

Issued for the 19th Olympic Games, Mexico City, Oct. 12–27.

1st Hungarian Airmail Letter, 1918, Plane—SPAP6

Designs: No. CB33, Letter, 1931, and Zeppelin. No. CB34, Balloon post letter, 1967, and balloon. No. CB35, Letter, 1969, and helicopter.

1974, Oct. 19 Lithographed *Perf. 12*

CB32	SPAP6	2fo+1fo multi.	1.40	1.20
CB33	"	2fo+1fo "	1.40	1.20
CB34	"	2fo+1fo "	1.40	1.20
CB35	"	2fo+1fo "	1.40	1.20

Souvenir Sheet

Multicolored

CB36	SPAP6	Sheet of 4	3.75	3.75
		a. 2fo+1fo *No. C1*	80	80
		b. 2fo+1fo *No. C7*	80	80
		c. 2fo+1fo *No. C305*	80	80
		d. 2fo+1fo *No. C312*	80	80

AEROPHILA, International Airmail Exhibition, Budapest, Oct. 19–27.

Nos. CB32–CB33 and CB34–CB35 printed se-tenant. No. CB36 contains 4 stamps (size: 35x25mm.). Light and Prussian blue border and inscription. Black control number. Size: 106x90mm.

SPECIAL DELIVERY STAMPS.

Issue of the Monarchy.

Crown of St. Stephen
SD1

Wmkd. Double Cross. (137)

1916 Typographed. *Perf. 15.*

E1	SD1	2f gray green & red	10	10

Issue of the Republic.

Special Delivery Stamp of 1916 Overprinted

KÖZTÁRSASÁG

1919

E2	SD1	2f gray green & red	10	10

General Issue.

SD2

1919

E3	SD2	2f gray green & red	6	6

REGISTRATION STAMPS.

Nos. 625, 609 and 626 Overprinted in Carmine

Ajl. 1.
a

Ajánlás
b

"Ajl." or "Ajánlás" = Registered Letter.

1946 *Perf. 15.* **Wmk. 266**

F1	A118 (*a*)	"Ajl. 1." on 20f olive	5	5
F2	A99 (")	"Ajl. 2." on 12f deep blue green	5	5
F3	A118 (*b*)	"Ajánlás" on 24f rose violet	5	5

POSTAGE DUE STAMPS.

Issues of the Monarchy.

D1

Perf. 11½, 11½x12.

1903 Typographed Wmk. 135

J1	D1	1f green & black	25	25
J2	"	2f " "	2.00	1.50
J3	"	5f " "	9.00	4.50
J4	"	6f " "	7.50	4.50
J5	"	10f " "	65.00	2.75
J6	"	12f " "	1.50	1.50
		a. Perf. 11½	100.00	80.00
J7	"	20f green & black	12.00	1.75
		a. Perf. 11½	120.00	27.50
J8	"	50f green & black	10.00	10.00
		a. Perf. 11½	160.00	140.00
J9	"	100f green & black	75	75
		Nos. J1–J9 (9)	108.00	27.50

1908–09 *Perf. 15* **Wmk. 136**

J10	D1	1f green & black	35	35
J11	"	2f " "	30	30
J12	"	5f " "	1.80	1.20
J13	"	6f " "	40	40
J14	"	10f " "	1.50	40
J15	"	12f " "	40	40
J16	"	20f green & black	7.50	40
		c. Center inverted		*1750.00*
J17	"	50f green & black	80	80
		Nos. J10–J17 (8)	13.05	4.25

1905 *Perf. 11½x12* **Wmk. 136a**

J12a	D1	5f green & black	120.00	120.00
J13a	"	6f " "	7.00	7.00
J14a	"	10f " "	120.00	7.50
J15a	"	12f " "	15.00	12.00
J17a	"	50f " "	3.50	3.50
J18	D1	100f green & black	3.00	3.00

1906 *Perf. 15.*

J11b	D1	2f green & black	2.50	2.50
J12b	"	5f " "	1.50	1.50
J13b	"	6f " "	1.50	1.50
J14b	"	10f " "	10.00	60
J15b	"	12f " "	40	50
J16b	"	20f green & black	14.00	50
		d. Center inverted	1200.00	
J17b	"	50f green & black	60	60

1914 *Perf. 15* **Wmk. 137 Horiz.**

J19	D1	1f green & black	25	25
J20	"	2f " "	25	25
J21	"	5f " "	30	30
J22	"	6f " "	35	35
J23	"	10f " "	70	60
J24	"	12f " "	30	30

J25 D1 20f green & black 35 35
J26 " 50f " " 40 40
Nos. J19–J26 (8) 2.90 2.80

1914 Wmk. 137 Vert.

J20a D1 2f green & black 50.00 50.00
J21a " 5f " " 5.00 5.00
J22a " 6f " " 14.00 14.00
J25a " 20f " " 1200.00 750.00
J26a " 50f " " 5.00 4.00

No. J9 Surcharged in Red **20**

1915 Wmk. 135

J27 D1 20f on 100f green & black 1.00 1.00
a. On No. J18, Wmk. 136a 25.00 25.00

1915-22 Wmk. 137

J28 D1 1f green & red 10 8
J29 " 2f " " 10 8
J30 " 5f " " 20 15
J31 " 6f " " 10 8
J32 " 10f " " 5 5
J33 " 12f " " 15 10
J34 " 15f " " 20 15
J35 " 20f " " 5 5
J36 " 30f " " 15 15
J37 " 40f " " ('20) 10 8
J38 " 50f green & red ('20) 10 6
a. Center inverted 30.00
J39 " 120f green & red ('20) 15 10
J40 " 200f " " ('20) 8 8
J41 " 2k " " ('22) 30 25
J42 " 5k " " ('22) 10 10
J43 " 50k " " ('22) 10 10
Nos. J28–J43 (16) 2.03 1.66

Issues of the Republic.

Postage Due Stamps of 1914-18 Overprinted in Black KÖZTÁRSASÁG

1918–19

On Issue of 1914.

J44 D1 50f green & black 60 60

On Stamps and Type of 1915-18.

J45 D1 2f green & red 10 10
J46 " 3f " " 6 6
a. "KOZTARSASAG" omitted 65.00
J47 " 10f green & red 6 6
J48 " 20f " " 6 6
J49 " 40f " " 6 6
a. Inverted overprint 5.00 5.00
J50 " 50f green & red 6 6
a. Center and overprint inverted 6.00 6.00
Nos. J44–J50 (7) 1.00 1.00

Issues of the Kingdom

D3

1919–20 Typographed

J65 D3 2f green & black 8 8
a. Inverted center 200.00
J66 " 3f green & black 8 8
J67 " 20f " " 8 8
J68 " 40f " " 8 8
J69 " 50f " " 8 8
Nos. J65–J69 (5) 40 40

Postage Due Stamps of this type have been overprinted "Magyar Tanácsköztarsasag" but have not been reported as having been issued without the additional overprint heads of wheat.

New Overprint in Black over "Magyar Tanacskoztarsasag" 1919

1920

J70 D3 2f green & black 50 50
J71 " 3f " " 50 50
J72 " 10f " " 1.75 1.75
J73 D3 20f green & black 50 50
J74 " 40f " " 50 50
J75 " 50f " " 50 50
Nos. J70–J75 (6) 4.25 4.25

D5 D6

1921–25 Red Surcharge.

J76 D5 100f on 15f violet 10 6
J77 " 500f on 15f violet 10 6
J78 " 2½k on 10f red violet 10 6
J79 " 3k on 15f violet 10 6
J80 " 6k on 1½k violet('22) 10 6
J81 " 9k on 40f olive green 10 6
J82 " 10k on 2½k green ('23) 10 6
J83 " 12k on 60f blk. brown 10 6
J84 " 15k on 1½k violet ('22) 10 6
J85 " 20k on 2½k green ('23) 15 6
J86 " 25k on 1½k violet ('22) 10 6
J87 " 30k on 1½k violet ('22) 10 6
J88 " 40k on 2½k green ('23) 15 6
J89 " 50k on 1½k violet ('22) 10 6
J90 " 100k on 4½k dull violet ('23) 15 8
J91 " 200k on 4½k dull violet ('23) 15 8
J92 " 300k on 4½k dull violet ('23) 20 8
J93 " 500k on 2k greenish blue ('23) 25 10
J94 " 500k on 3k orange brown ('25) 45 25
J95 " 1000k on 2k greenish blue ('23) 40 20
J96 " 1000k on 3k orange brown ('25) 50 25
J97 " 2000k on 2k greenish blue ('23) 50 15
J98 " 2000k on 3k orange brown ('25) 75 30
J99 " 5000k on 5k brown ('24) 90 45
Nos. J76–J99 (24) 5.75 2.78

Lithographed.

1926 *Perf. 14, 15.* Wmk. 133

J100 D6 1f rose red 10 10
J101 " 2f " 15 10
J102 " 3f " 30 15
J103 " 4f " 15 5
J104 " 5f " 50 25
a. Perf. 15 1.25 50
J105 " 8f rose red 15 5
J106 " 10f " 15 8
J107 " 16f " 25 5
J108 " 32f " 60 20
J109 " 40f " 75 10
J110 " 50f " 60 15
J111 " 80f " 1.20 35
Nos. J100–J111 (12) 4.90 1.63

See also Nos. J117–J123.

Air Post Stamps of 1924 Surcharged in Red or Green PORTÓ 2 FILLÉR

1926 *Perf. 14* Wmk. 137

J112 AP3 1f on 500k blue green & yel. grn. (R) 30 25
J113 " 2f on 1000k bistre brown & brown (G) 30 25
J114 " 3f on 2000k dark blue & lt. blue (R) 30 25

Wmk. 133

J115 AP3 5f on 5000k dull violet & brt. vio. (G) 65 60
J116 " 10f on 10000k red & dull violet (G) 45 35
Nos. J112–J116(5) 2.00 1.70

Type of 1926 Issue.

1928-32 *Perf. 14, 15.* Wmk. 210

J117 D6 2f rose red 15 10
J118 " 4f " ('32) 15 5
J119 " 8f " 15 5
J120 " 10f " 20 5
J121 " 16f " 30 20
J122 " 20f " 40 5
J123 " 40f " 85 15
Nos. J117–J123 (7) 2.20 65

Postage Due Stamps of 1926 Surcharged in Black 20 20

1931–33 Wmk. 133

J124 D6 4(f) on 5f rose red 30 15
J125 " 10(f) on 16f rose red 80 80
J126 " 10(f) on 80f rose red ('33) 60 25
J127 " 12(f) on 50f rose red ('33) 60 25
J128 " 20(f) on 32f rose red 60 35
Nos. J124–J128 (5) 2.90 1.80

Surcharged on No. J121

1931 *Perf. 15.* Wmk. 210

J129 D6 10(f) on 16f rose red 85 60

Figure of Value
D7

Coat of Arms and Post Horn
D8

1934 Photogravure. Wmk. 210

J130 D7 2f ultramarine 10 5
J131 " 4f " 10 5
J132 " 6f " 10 5
J133 " 8f " 10 5
J134 " 10f " 15 5
J135 " 12f " 25 8
J136 " 16f " 25 8
J137 " 20f " 25 12
J138 " 40f " 50 15
J139 " 80f " 60 35
Nos. J130–J139 (10) 2.60 1.03

1941

J140 D8 2f brown red 10 6
J142 " 4f " 10 6
J143 " 6f " 10 6
J144 " 8f " 10 6
J145 " 10f " 10 6
J146 " 12f " 10 6
J147 " 16f " 25 15
J148 " 20f " 25 15
J150 " 40f " 30 20
Nos. J140–J150(9) 1.40 86

1941-44 Wmk. 266

J151 D8 2f brown red 8 4
J152 " 3f " 8 4
J153 " 4f " 8 4
J154 " 6f " 10 8
J155 " 8f " 10 4
J156 " 10f " 12 4
J157 " 12f " 12 4
J158 " 16f " 15 4
J159 " 18f " ('44) 15 10
J160 " 20f " 10 4
J161 " 24f " 15 8
J162 " 30f " ('44) 12 8
J163 " 36f " ('44) 12 10
J164 " 40f " 12 10
J165 " 50f " 15 8
J166 " 60f " ('44) 20 8
Nos. J151–J166(16) 1.94 1.02

Issues of the Republic.

Types of Hungary Postage Due Stamps, 1941-44, Surcharged in Carmine 1945 10 fillér

Photogravure.

1945 *Perf. 15* Wmk. 266

Blue Surface-tinted Paper.

J167 D8 10f on 2f brown red 6 4
J168 " 10f on 3f " 6 4
J169 " 20f on 4f " 6 4
J170 " 20f on 6f " 6.50 6.50
J171 " 20f on 8f " 6 4
J172 " 40f on 12f " 10 6
J173 " 40f on 16f " 10 6
J174 " 40f on 18f " 10 6
J175 " 60f on 24f " 6 4
J176 " 80f on 30f " 8 6
J177 " 90f on 36f " 6 4
J178 " 1p on 10f " 6 4
J179 " 1p on 40f " 8 6
J180 " 2p on 20f " 8 8
J181 " 2p on 50f " 8 8
J182 " 2p on 60f " 8 8

Surcharged in Black, Thicker Type.

J183 D8 10p on 3f brown red 8 8
J184 " 12p on 8f " 10 10
J185 " 20p on 24f " 12 12
Nos. J167–J185 (19) 7.92 7.62

D9

1946–50 *Perf. 15* Wmk. 210

Numerals in Deep Magenta

J186 D9 4f magenta 60 10
J187 " 10f " 1.25 10
J188 " 20f " 60 10
J189 " 30f " 60 10
J190 " 40f " 1.00 10
J191 " 50f " ('50) 2.00 30
J192 " 60f " 1.75 20
J193 " 1.20fo " 3.00 20
J194 " 2fo " 4.50 30
Nos. J186–J194 (9) 15.30 1.50

1951 Wmk. 106

Numerals in Deep Magenta

J194A D9 4f magenta 8 4
J194B " 10f " 8 4
J194C " 20f " 8 4
j. "fiellr" 5.00
J194D " 30f magenta 20 4
J194E " 40f " 25 5
J194F " 50f " 1.00 8
J194G " 60f " 40 5
J194H " 1.20fo " 1.00 10
J194I " 2fo " 1.50 20
Nos. J194A–J194I (9) 4.59 64

Nos. J194A–J194I are found in both large format (about 18x22mm.) and small (about 17x21mm.).

D10 D11

Typographed.

1951 *Perf. 14½x15* Unwmkd.

Paper with Vertical Lines in Green.

Blue Surcharge.

J195 D10 8f dark brown 8 8
J196 " 10f " 12 10
J197 " 12f " 25 25

Photogravure.

1951 *Perf. 14½.* **Wmk. 106**

No.	Design	Denomination	Unused	Used
J198	D11	4f brown	4	3
J199	"	6f "	5	3
J200	"	8f "	5	3
J201	"	10f "	6	3
J202	"	14f "	8	3
J203	"	20f "	10	3
J204	"	30f "	12	3
J205	"	40f "	15	4
J206	"	50f "	30	5
J207	"	60f "	35	10
J208	"	1.20fo "	35	15
J209	"	2fo "	60	25
		Nos. J198–J209 (12)	2.25	80

D12

D13

Photo., Numeral Typo. in Black

1953

Numerals 4½mm. High

No.	Design	Denomination	Unused	Used
J210	D12	4f dull green	4	3
J211	"	6f "	5	3
J212	"	8f "	5	3
J213	"	10f "	4	3
J214	"	12f "	4	3
J215	"	14f "	5	6
J216	"	16f "	6	6
J217	"	20f "	6	3
J218	"	24f "	12	6
J219	"	30f "	10	4
J220	"	36f "	15	6
J221	"	40f "	12	5
J222	"	50f "	20	5
J223	"	60f "	25	5
J224	"	70f "	25	6
J225	"	80f "	35	10
J226	"	1.20fo "	50	12
J227	"	2fo "	80	15
		a. Small "2" (3mm. high)	1.00	60
		Nos. J210–J227 (18)	3.23	1.04

Issued to commemorate the 50th anniversary of the first Hungarian postage due stamp.

Photo., Numeral Typo. in Black on Nos. J228–J243.

1958 *Perf. 14½* **Wmk. 106**

Size: 21x16½mm.

No.	Design	Denomination	Unused	Used
J228	D13	4f red	5	3
J229	"	6f "	5	3
J230	"	8f "	5	3
J231	"	10f "	5	3
J232	"	12f "	5	3
J233	"	14f "	5	3
J234	"	16f "	5	3
J235	"	20f "	5	3
J236	"	24f "	5	3
J237	"	30f "	5	3
J238	"	36f "	6	3
J239	"	40f "	10	4
J240	"	50f "	15	5
J241	"	60f "	20	6
J242	"	70f "	25	8
J243	"	80f "	35	10

Perf. 12

Size: 31x21mm.

No.	Design	Denomination	Unused	Used
J244	D13	1.20fo dk. red brn.	50	15
J245	"	2fo "	80	20
		Nos. J228–J245 (18)	2.91	1.01

Photo., Numeral Typo. in Black on Nos. J246–J261.

1965–69 *Perf. 11½* **Unwmkd.**

Size: 21x16½mm.

No.	Design	Denomination	Unused	Used
J246	D13	4f red	6	3
J247	"	6f "	6	3
J248	"	8f "	5	3
J249	"	10f "	5	3
J250	"	12f "	5	3
J251	"	14f "	5	3
J252	"	16f "	5	3
J253	"	20f "	5	3
J254	"	24f "	6	3
J255	"	30f "	8	3
J256	"	36f "	8	3
J257	"	40f "	10	3
J258	"	50f "	15	4
J259	"	60f "	20	5
J260	D13	70f red	25	8
J261	"	80f "	30	10

Perf. 11½x12

Size: 31x21mm.

No.	Design	Denomination	Unused	Used
J262	D13	1fo dk. red brn. ('69)	20	8
J263	"	1.20fo " " "	40	15
J264	"	2fo " " "	50	20
J265	"	4fo " " " ('69)	1.00	15
		Nos. J246–J265 (20)	3.74	1.21

Mail Plane and Truck
D14

Designs: 20f, Money order cancelling machine. 40f, Scales in self-service P.O. 80f, Automat for registering parcels. 1fo, Keypunch operator. 1.20fo, Mail plane and truck. 2fo, Diesel mail train. 3fo, Mailman on motorcycle with sidecar. 4fo, Rural mail delivery.

1973, Dec. Photogravure *Perf. 11*

Size: 21x18mm.

No.	Design	Denomination	Unused	Used
J266	D14	20f brown & verm.	5	3
J267	"	40f dull bl. & verm.	10	3
J268	"	80f violet & verm.	30	3
J269	"	1fo olive green & vermilion	25	6

Perf. 12x11½

Size: 28x22mm.

No.	Design	Denomination	Unused	Used
J270	D14	1.20fo grn. & verm.	40	10
J271	"	2fo lilac & verm.	50	15
J272	"	3fo bright blue & vermilion	75	30
J273	"	4fo org. brown & vermilion	1.00	40
		Nos. J266–J273 (8)	3.35	1.10

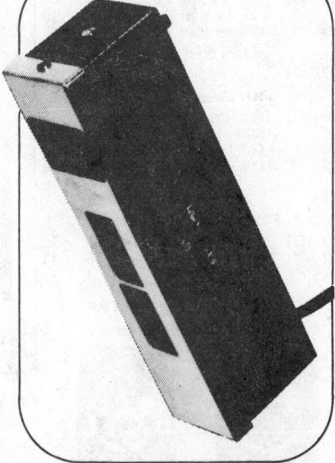

OFFICIAL STAMPS.

O1

Typographed.

1921-23 *Perf. 15.* **Wmk. 137**

O1 O1 10f brn. violet & black 10 6
O2 " 20f olive brown & blk. 10 6
a. Inverted center 120.00 100.00
O3 " 60f blk. brown & black 10 6
O4 " 100f dull rose & black 10 5
O5 " 250f blue & black 10 6
O6 " 350f gray & black 20 15
O7 " 500f lt. brown & black 10 6
O8 " 1000f lilac brown & blk. 10 6
O9 " 5k brown ('23) 10 5
O10 " 10k chocolate ('23) 10 5
O11 " 15k gray black ('23) 10 8
O12 " 25k orange ('23) 10 8
O13 " 50k brown & red ('22) 10 5
O14 " 100k bistre & red ('22) 10 5
O15 " 150k green & red ('23) 15 10
O16 " 300k dull red & red ('23) 15 10
O17 " 350k violet & red ('23) 25 12
O18 " 500k orange & red ('22) 25 15
O19 " 600k olive bistre & red ('23) 30 20
O20 " 1000k blue & red ('22) 40 15
Nos. O1-O20 (20) 3.00 1.74

Stamps of 1921 Surcharged in Red **15 KORONA 15**

1922

O21 O1 15k on 20f olive brown & black 15 10
O22 " 25k on 60f black brown & black 15 10

Stamps of 1921 Overprinted in Red **KORONA**

1923

O23 O1 350k gray & black 15 10

With Additional Surcharge of New Value in Red.

O24 O1 150k on 100f dull rose & black 20 10
O25 " 2000k on 250f blue & black 45 35

1923-24

Paper with Gray Moiré on Face.

O26 O1 500k org. & red ('23) 30 15
O27 " 1000k blue & red ('23) 40 15
O28 " 3000k violet & red ('24) 50 40
O29 " 5000k blue & red ('24) 60 50

1924

Wmkd. Four Double Crosses. (133)

O30 O1 500k orange & red 75 40
O31 " 1000k blue & red 75 45

NEWSPAPER STAMPS.

Issues of the Monarchy.

St. Stephen's Crown and Post Horn
N1 N2

Typographed.

1871-72 *Imperf.* **Unwmkd.**

P1 N1 (1k) vermilion red 42.50 25.00
P2 N2 (1k) rose red ('72) 10.00 1.75
a. (1k) vermilion 10.00 1.75
b. Printed on both sides

Reprints of No. P2 are on watermarked paper. Price $250.

Letter with Crown and Post Horn
N3

1874

P3 N3 1k orange 4.50 50

1881 Wmkd. "kr" in Oval. (132)

P4 N3 1k orange 1.00 20
a. 1k lemon yellow 7.50 4.00
b. Printed on both sides

Wmkd. Crown in Oval or Circle.

1898 **(135)**

P5 N3 1k orange 1.00 25

See watermark note after No. 46.

N5

1900 Wmkd. Crown in Circle. (135)

P6 N5 (2f) red orange 50 12

1905 Wmkd. Crown. (136a)

P7 N5 (2f) red orange 60 12
a. Wmk. 136 ('08) 60 12

Wmkd. Double Cross. (137)

1914-22

P8 N5 (2f) orange 10 6
a. Wmk. horiz. 1.20 1.00
P9 N5 (10f) deep blue ('20) 6 6
P10 " (20f) lilac ('22) 8 8

NEWSPAPER TAX STAMPS.

Issues of the Monarchy.

NT1 NT2

NT3 Wmk. 91

Wmkd. "ZEITUNGS-MARKEN" in Double-lined Capitals across the Sheet. (91); Unwmkd. from 1871.

1868 **Typographed.** *Imperf.*

PR1 NT1 1k blue 7.50 1.50
a. Pair, one sideways
PR2 NT2 2k brown 20.00 22.50
a. 2k red brown 200.00 60.00

1868

PR2B NT3 1k blue *4000.00 3250.00*

No. PR2B was issued for the Military Border District only. All used copies are precancelled (overprinted with newspaper text). A similar 2k was not issued.

1889-90 Wmkd. "kr" in Oval. (132)

PR3 NT1 1k blue 1.40 80
PR4 NT2 2k brown 5.50 4.50

1898 Wmkd. Crown in Oval. (135)

PR5 NT1 1k blue 7.50 6.00

These stamps did not pay postage, but represented a fiscal tax collected by the postal authorities on newspapers.

Nos. PR3 and PR5 have a tall "k" in "kr".

PARCEL POST STAMPS.

Stamps and Types of 1943-45 Overprinted in Black or Carmine

Cs. 5-l. *a* **Csomag 5 kg.** *b*

"Cs." or "Csomag"=Parcel.

1946 *Perf. 15.* **Wmk. 266**

Q1 A118 (*a*) "Cs. 5-l." on 70f orange red (No. 629) 10 8
Q2 A109 (") "Cs. 5-l." on 30f bright carmine (No. 613) 5.00 5.00
Q3 A99 (") "Cs. 5-2." on 24f rose violet (No. 612) 10 10
Q4 A118 (") "Cs. 10-l." on 70f orange red (No. 629) 10 10
Q5 " (") "Cs. 10-l." on 80f yel. brn. (No. 615) 5.00 5.00
Q6 " (") "Cs. 10-2." on 80f brown carmine (No. 630) 10 10
Q7 A99 (*b*) "Csomag 5kg." on 2p on 4f brown, *blue* (No. 667) (C+Bk) 20 20
Q8 A118 (") "Csomag 10kg." on 30f copper red, *blue* 15 15
Nos. Q1-Q8 (8) 10.75 10.73

No. Q8 was not issued without overprint.

No. 796 Surcharged with New Value in Red or Black.

1954 **Wmk. 210**

Q9 A144 1.70fo on 1.40fo deep yellow green 60 20
Q10 " 2fo on 1.40fo deep yel. grn. (Bk) 70 30
Q11 " 3fo on 1.40fo deep yellow green 85 50

OCCUPATION STAMPS.

Issued under French Occupation.

Forged overprints exist.

ARAD ISSUE.

Stamps of Hungary Overprinted in Red or Blue **Occupation française**

On Issue of 1916-18.

Wmkd. Double Cross. (137)

1919 *Perf. 15, 14.*

1N1 A9 2f brown orange 6 6
1N2 " 3f red lilac 5 5
1N3 " 5f green 25 25
1N4 " 6f greenish blue 6 6
a. Inverted overprint 50
1N5 " 10f rose red (Bl) 6 6
1N6 " 15f violet 6 6
a. Double overprint 2.00
1N7 " 20f gray brown 4.00 4.00
1N8 " 35f brown 4.00 4.00
1N9 " 40f olive green 5.00 5.00
1N10 A10 50f red violet & lilac (Bl) 12 12
1N11 " 75f bright blue & pale blue (Bl) 8 8
1N12 " 80f green & pale green (Bl) 8 8
1N13 A10 1k red brown & claret (Bl) 60 60
1N14 " 2k olive brown & bistre (Bl) 50 50
a. Inverted overprint 75
1N15 " 3k dark violet & indigo (Bl) 80 80
1N16 " 5k dark brown & lt. brown (Bl) 1.00 1.00
1N17 " 10k violet brown & violet (Bl) 5.50 5.50
Nos. 1N1-1N17 (17) 22.22 22.22

With Additional Surcharge:

45 *a* **45** *b* **50** *c* **50** *d*

1N18 A9 (*a*) 45f on 2f brown orange 20 20
1N19 " (*b*) 45f on 2f brown orange 40 40
1N20 " (*c*) 50f on 3f red lilac 40 40
1N21 " (*d*) 50f on 3f red lilac 20 20

On Issue of 1918.

1N22 A11 10f scarlet (Bl) 4.00 4.00
1N23 " 20f dark brown 8 8
1N24 " 25f bright blue 8 8
a. Inverted overprint 1.00
1N25 A12 40f olive green 8 8

On Issue of 1918-19, Overprinted "Köztarsasag".

1N26 A9 2f brown orange 5 5
a. Inverted overprint 1.00
1N27 " 4f slate gray 5 5
1N28 " 5f green 5 5
1N29 " 6f greenish blue 10 10
a. Inverted overprint 1.00
1N30 " 10f rose red (Bl) 5.00 5.00
1N31 " 20f gray brown 50 50
1N32 A11 25f bright blue 10 10
a. Inverted overprint 1.00
1N33 A9 40f olive green 10 10
1N34 A12 40f olive green 9.00 9.00
a. Inverted overprint 3.00
1N35 " 50f lilac 25 25
1N36 A10 1k red brown & claret (Bl) 15 15
1N37 " 3k dark violet & indigo (Bl) 1.00 1.00
Nos. 1N26-1N37 (12) 16.35 16.35

With Additional Surcharge:

10 *e* **10** *f*

1N38 A10 (*e*) 10k on 1k red brown & claret (Bl) 3.00 3.00
1N39 " (*f*) 10k on 1k red brown & claret (Bl) 4.00 4.00

On Issue of 1919.

Inscribed "MAGYAR POSTA".

1N40 A13 10f red (Bl) 10 10

SEMI-POSTAL STAMPS.

Hungarian Semi-Postal Stamps of 1916-17 Overprinted "Occupation francaise" in Blue or Red.

Wmkd. Double Cross. (137)

1919 *Perf. 15.*

1NB1 SP3 10f+2f rose red 5.00 5.00
1NB2 SP4 15f+2f dull violet (R) 25 25
1NB3 SP5 40f+2f brn. car. 25 25

SPECIAL DELIVERY STAMP.

Hungarian Special Delivery Stamp of 1916 Overprinted "Occupation francaise"

Wmkd. Double Cross. (137)

1919 *Perf. 15.*

1NE1 SD1 2f gray green & red 10 10

POSTAGE DUE STAMPS.

Hungarian Postage Due Stamps of 1915 Overprinted "Occupation francaise".

Wmkd. Double Cross. (137)

1919 *Perf. 15.*

1NJ1 D1 2f green & red 40 40
1NJ2 " 10f " " 40 40
1NJ3 " 12f " " 60 60
1NJ4 " 15f " " 80 80
1NJ5 " 20f " " 1.00 1.00

Hungarian Newspaper Stamp of 1914 Surcharged — Occupation française 12 Porto 12

Imperf.

1NJ6 N5 12f on 2f orange 30 30
1NJ7 " 15f on 2f " 30 30
1NJ8 " 30f on 2f orange 40 40
a. Double surcharge 2.50
1NJ9 " 50f on 2f orange 40 40
1NJ10 " 100f on 2f " 40 1.00
Nos. 1NJ1-1NJ10 (10) 5.00 5.00

NEWSPAPER STAMP.

Hungarian Newspaper Stamp of 1914 Overprinted "Occupation francaise".

1919 *Imperf.* **Wmk. 137**

1NP1 N5 (2f) orange 6 6

Issued under Romanian Occupation.

FIRST DEBRECEN ISSUE.

The first Debrecen overprint was applied to numerous other stamps, also in other colors than are listed. These varieties were not sold to the public but to a favored few.

Excellent forgeries of this overprint are plentiful.

Hungarian Stamps of 1913-19 Overprinted [ZONA DE OCUPATIE P F T 1919 ROMANA] in Blue, Red or Black

Wmkd. Double Cross. (137)

1919 *Perf. 15, 14½x14.*

On Stamps of 1913

2N1 A4 2f olive yel. (Bl) 10.00 10.00
2N2 " 3f orange (Bl) 15.00 15.00
2N3 " 6f olive grn. (R) 1.75 1.75

On Stamps of 1916

2N4 A8 10f rose (Bl) 6.00 6.00
2N5 " 15f violet (Bk) 4.50 4.50

On Stamps of 1916-18.

2N6 A9 2f brown orange (Bl) 5 5
2N7 " 3f red lilac (Bl) 5 5
2N8 " 5f green (Bl) 8 8
2N9 " 6f greenish blue(R) 5 5
2N10 " 15f violet (Bk) 5 5
2N11 " 20f gray brn. (Bl) 10.00 10.00
2N12 " 25f dull blue (Bk) 25 25
2N13 " 35f brown (Bl) 2.00 2.00
2N14 " 40f olive green (Bl) 25 25
2N15 A10 50f red violet & lilac (Bl) 30 30
2N16 " 75f bright blue & pale blue(Bk) 12 12
2N17 " 80f green & pale green (R) 20 20
2N18 " 1k red brown & claret (Bl) 25 25
2N19 " 2k olive brown & bistre (Bk) 12 12
2N20 " 3k dark violet & indigo (R) 1.25 1.25
a. Blue overprint 3.75 3.75
b. Black overprint 45.00 45.00
2N21 A10 5k dark brown & lt. brown(Bk) 1.25 1.25
2N22 " 10k violet brown & violet (Bl) 8.00 8.00

With New Value Added.

2N23 A9 35f on 3f red lilac(Bl) 10 10
2N24 " 45f on 2f brown orange (Bl) 10 10
2N25 A10 3k on 75f bright blue & pale blue (Bk) 50 50
2N26 A10 5k on 75f bright blue & pale blue (Bk) 25 25
2N27 " 10k on 80f green & pale green (R) 60 60

On Stamps of 1918.

2N28 A11 10f scarlet (Bl) 1.75 1.75
2N29 " 20f dark brown(R) 30 30
a. Black overprint 50 50
b. Blue overprint 4.00 4.00
2N30 A11 25f bright blue(R) 25 25
a. Black overprint 1.25 1.25
2N31 A12 40f olive green (Bl) 15 15
2N32 " 50f lilac (Bl) 90 90

On Stamps of 1918-19, Overprinted "Köztarsasag".

2N33 A9 2f brown orange(Bl) 10 10
2N34 " 3f red lilac (Bl) 1.75 1.75
2N35 " 4f slate gray (R) 5 5
2N36 " 5f green (Bl) 5 5
2N37 " 6f greenish blue (R) 70 70
2N38 " 10f rose red (Bl) 50 50
2N39 A11 10f scarlet (Bl) 85 85
2N40 " 15f dp. violet (Bk) 1.50 1.50
2N41 A9 20f gray brown (Bl) 15 15
2N42 A11 20f dk. brn. (Bk) 1.25 1.25
b. Red overprint 1.25 1.25
2N43 A9 40f olive green (Bl) 10 10
2N44 A10 1k red brown & claret (Bl) 10 10
2N45 " 2k olive brown & bister (Bk) 1.25 1.25
2N46 " 3k dark violet & indigo (R) 40 40
a. Blue overprint 2.75 2.75
b Black overprint 30.00 30.00
2N47 A10 5k dark & light brown (Bk) 30.00 30.00
2N48 " 10k vio. brown & violet (Bl) 40.00 40.00
2N49 A11 25f bright blue(R) 15 15
a. Black overprint 50 50
2N50 A12 40f olive grn. (Bl) 8.00 8.00
2N51 " 50f lilac (Bl) 10 10

On Stamps of 1919.

2N52 A13 5f green (Bl) 5 5
2N53 " 6f greenish bl. (Bk) 30 30
2N54 " 10f red (Bl) 5 5
2N55 " 20f dark brown (Bl) 5 5
2N56 " 25f dull blue (Bk) 6 6
2N57 " 45f orange (Bl) 50 50
2N58 A14 5k dark brown & brn. (Bl)

No. 2N58 is handstamped. Counterfeits exist.

Same Overprint on No. 103A

2N59 A5a 10f vio. brn. (R) 1.75 1.75
Nos. 2N1-2N57, 2N59 (58) 156.18 156.18

SEMI-POSTAL STAMPS.

Overprinted like Regular Issues in Blue or Black

Wmkd. Double Cross. (137)

1919 *Perf. 15.*

2NB1 SP3 10f+2f rose red (Bl) 12 12
2NB2 SP4 15f+2f dull violet (Bk) 25 25
2NB3 SP5 40f+2f brown carmine (Bl) 20 20

Same Overprint on Hungary Nos. B58-B60 (with "Köztarsasag")

1919

2NB4 SP3 10f+2f rose red (Bl) 40 40
2NB5 SP4 15f+2f dull violet (Bk) 8.00 8.00
2NB6 SP5 40f+2f brown carmine (Bl) 50 50

SPECIAL DELIVERY STAMP.

Hungarian Special Delivery Stamp of 1916 Overprinted like Regular Issues.

Wmkd. Double Cross. (137)

1919 *Perf. 15.*

2NE1 SD1 2f gray green & red(Bl) 10 10

POSTAGE DUE STAMPS.

Hungarian Postage Due Stamps of 1914-19 Overprinted in Black like Regular Issues.

Wmkd. Double Cross. (137)

1919 *Perf. 15*

On Stamp of 1914

2NJ1 D1 50f green & blk. 25.00 25.00

On Stamps of 1915

2NJ2 D1 1f green & red 2.50 2.50
2NJ3 " 2f " " 5 5
2NJ4 " 5f " " 30.00 30.00
2NJ5 " 6f " " 2.50 2.50
2NJ6 " 10f " " 5 5
2NJ7 " 12f " " 10.00 10.00
2NJ8 " 15f " " 50 50
2NJ9 " 20f " " 50 50
2NJ10 " 30f " " 50 50

On Stamps of 1918-19, Overprinted "Köztarsasag".

2NJ11 D1 2f green & red 50 50
2NJ12 " 3f " " 50 50
2NJ13 " 10f " " 50 50
2NJ14 " 20f " " 50 50
2NJ15 " 40f " " 50 50
2NJ16 " 50f " " 50 50
Nos. 2NJ1-JNJ16 (16) 74.60 74.60

NEWSPAPER STAMP.

Hungarian Newspaper Stamp of 1914 Overprinted like Regular Issues.

1919 *Imperf.* **Wmk. 137**

2NP1 N5 (2f) orange (Bl) 5 5
a. Inverted overprint
b. Double overprint

SECOND DEBRECEN ISSUE.

Counterfeits exist.

Mythical "Turul" OS5

Throwing Lariat—OS6

Hungarian Peasant—OS7

Typographed

1920 *Perf. 11½* **Unwmkd.**

3N1 OS5 2f light brown 15 15
3N2 " 3f red brown 15 15
3N3 " 4f gray 20 20
3N4 " 5f light green 15 15
3N5 " 6f slate 20 20
3N6 " 10f scarlet 15 15
3N7 " 15f dark violet 25 25
3N8 " 20f dark brown 15 15
3N9 OS6 25f ultramarine 20 20
3N10 " 30f buff 20 20
3N11 " 35f claret 20 20
3N12 " 40f olive green 20 20
3N13 " 45f salmon 20 20
3N14 " 50f pale violet 20 20
3N15 " 60f yellow green 20 20
3N16 " 75f Prussian blue 20 20
3N17 OS7 80f gray green 20 20
3N18 " 1k brown red 25 25
3N19 " 2k chocolate 50 50
3N20 " 3k brown violet 80 80
3N21 OS7 5k bistre brown 80 80
3N22 " 10k dull violet 1.00 1.00
Nos. 3N1-3N22 (22) 6.55 6.55

Thick, Glazed Paper.

3N23 OS5 2f light brown 30 30
3N24 " 3f red brown 30 30
3N25 " 4f gray 30 30
3N26 " 5f light green 20 20
3N27 " 6f slate 50 50
3N28 " 10f scarlet 20 20
3N29 " 15f dark violet 50 50
3N30 " 20f dark brown 20 20
3N31 OS7 80f gray green 45 45
3N32 " 1k brown red 45 45
3N33 " 1.20k orange 5.00 5.00
3N34 " 2k chocolate 1.00 1.00
Nos. 3N23-3N34 (12) 9.40 9.40

SEMI-POSTAL STAMPS.

Carrying Wounded—SP1

Typographed.

1920 *Perf. 11½.* **Unwmkd.**

3NB1 SP1 20f green 20 20
3NB2 " 50f gray brown 20 20
3NB3 " 1k blue green 35 35
3NB4 " 2k dark green 50 50

Colored Paper

3NB5 SP1 20f green, *blue* 40 40
3NB6 " 50f brown, *rose* 30 30
3NB7 " 1k dark green, *green* 40 40
Nos. 3NB1-3NB7 (7) 2.35 2.35

POSTAGE DUE STAMPS.

D1

Wmkd. Double Cross. (137)

1920 Typographed *Perf. 15*

3NJ1 D1 5f blue green 15 15
3NJ2 " 10f " 15 15
3NJ3 " 20f " 15 15
3NJ4 " 30f " 15 15
3NJ5 " 40f " 15 15
Nos. 3NJ1-3NJ5 (5) 75 75

Issued under Romanian Occupation.

TEMESVAR ISSUE.

OS1

OS2

OS3

OS4

Wmkd. Double Cross. (137)

1919 *Perf. 15*

4N1 OS1 30f on 2f brown orange (Bl) 10 10
a. Red surcharge 20 20
b. Inverted surcharge (R)

4N2 OS2 1k on 4f slate gray (R) 10 10
4N3 OS3 150f on 3f red lilac (Bk) 15 15
4N4 " 150f on 5f green (Bk) 20 20
4N5 OS4 3k on 2f gray green & red (Bk) 20 20
a. Blue surcharge 20 20
Nos. 4N1-4N5 (5) 75 75

POSTAGE DUE STAMPS.

D1

D2

1919 *Perf. 15* Wmk. 137
4NJ1 D1 40f on 15f+2f violet (Bk) 5 5
a. Red surcharge 20 20
4NJ2 D2 60f on 2f green & red (Bk) 20 20
a. Red surcharge 75 75
4NJ3 D2 60f on 10f green & red (Bk) 20 20
a. Red surcharge 75 75

Issued under Romanian Occupation.

FIRST TRANSYLVANIA ISSUE.

Both the first and second Transylvania overprints were applied to numerous other stamps and in colors other than listed. These varieties were not sold to the public but to a favored few.
Counterfeits are plentiful.

Issued in Kolozsvar (Cluj)

Hungarian Stamps of 1916-18 Overprinted

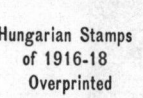

BANI

Wmkd. Double Cross. (137)
1919 *Perf. 15, 14.*

On Stamp of 1916, White Numerals
5N1 A8 15b violet 1.00 1.00

On Stamps of 1916-18.
5N2 A9 2b brown orange 5 5
5N3 " 3b red lilac 5 5
5N4 " 5b green 5 5
5N5 " 6b greenish blue 6 6
5N6 " 15b violet 5 5
5N7 " 25b dull blue 5 5
5N8 " 35b brown 5 5
5N9 " 40b olive green 6 6
5N10 A10 50b red violet & lilac 6 6
5N11 " 75b bright blue & pale blue 5 5
5N12 " 80b green & pale green 5 5
5N13 " 1 l red brown & claret 6 6
5N14 " 2 l olive brown & bistre 10 10
5N15 " 3 l dark violet & indigo 1.00 1.00
5N16 " 5 l dark brown & light brown 50 50
5N17 " 10 l vio. brn. & vio. 1.25 1.25

On Stamps of 1918.
5N18 A11 10b scarlet 15.00 15.00
5N19 " 15b deep violet 2.00 2.00
5N20 " 20b dark brown 5 5
a. Gold overprint *12.50 12.50*
b. Silver overprint *12.50 12.50*
5N21 " 25b bright blue 15 15
5N22 A12 40b olive green 6 6

On No. 103A
5N23 A5a 10b violet brown 10 10
Nos. 5N1-5N23 (23) 21.84 21.84

SEMI-POSTAL STAMPS.

Hungarian Semi-Postal Stamps of 1913-17 Overprinted like Regular Issues.

On Issue of 1913.
Wmkd. Double Cross. (137)
1919 *Perf. 14.*
5NB1 SP1 1 l on 1f slate 9.00 9.00
5NB2 " 1 l on 2f olive yellow 30.00 30.00
5NB3 " 1 l on 3f orange 9.00 9.00
5NB4 " 1 l on 5f emerald 1.00 1.00
5NB5 " 1 l on 10f carmine 1.00 1.00
5NB6 " 1 l on 12f violet, *yellow* 2.00 2.00
5NB7 " 1 l on 16f gray green 1.50 1.50
5NB8 " 1 l on 25f ultra. 27.50 27.50
5NB9 " 1 l on 35f red violet 1.50 1.50
5NB10 SP2 1 l on 1k dull red 27.50 27.50

On Issue of 1916-17.
Perf. 15.
5NB11 SP3 10b+2b rose red 6 6
5NB12 SP4 15b+2b dull vio. 6 6
5NB13 SP5 40b+2b brown carmine 6 6
Nos. 5NB1-5NB13 (13) 110.18 110.18

SPECIAL DELIVERY STAMP.

Hungarian Special Delivery Stamp of 1916 Overprinted like Regular Issues.
Wmkd. Double Cross. (137)
1919 *Perf. 15.*
5NE1 SD1 2b gray green & red 5 5

POSTAGE DUE STAMPS.

Hungarian Postage Due Stamps of 1914-18 Overprinted like Regular Issues.

On Stamp of 1914.
Wmkd. Double Cross. (137)
1919 *Perf. 15.*
5NJ1 D1 50b green & black 3.00 3.00

On Stamps of 1915
5NJ2 D1 1b green & red 80.00 80.00
5NJ3 " 2b " " 20 20
5NJ4 " 5b " " 15.00 15.00
5NJ5 " 10b " " 20 20
5NJ6 " 15b " " 1.75 1.75
5NJ7 " 20b " " 20 20
5NJ8 " 30b " " 7.50 7.50
Nos. 5NJ1-5NJ8 (8) 107.85 107.85

NEWSPAPER STAMP.

Hungarian Newspaper Stamp of 1914 Overprinted like Regular Issues.
1919 *Imperf.* Wmk. 137
5NP1 N5 2b orange 35 35

SECOND TRANSYLVANIA ISSUE.

Counterfeits are plentiful.

Issued in Nagyvarad (Oradea)

Bani

Hungarian Stamps of 1916-19 Overprinted

Wmkd. Double Cross. (137)
1919 *Perf. 15, 14.*

On Stamps of 1913-16.
6N1 A4 2b olive yellow 1.25 1.25
6N2 " 3b orange 3.50 3.50
6N3 " 6b olive green 20 20
6N4 " 16b gray green 10.00 10.00
6N5 " 50b lake, *blue* 30 30
6N6 " 70b red brown & green 10.00 10.00

On Stamps of 1916-18.
6N7 A9 2b brown orange 5 5
6N8 " 3b red lilac 5 5
6N9 " 5b green 6 6
6N10 " 6b greenish blue 12 12
6N11 " 10b rose red 15 15
6N12 " 15b violet 5 5
6N13 " 20b gray brown 4.00 4.00
6N14 " 25b dull blue 6 6
6N15 " 35b brown 6 6
6N16 " 40b olive green 6 6
6N17 A10 50b red violet & lilac 6 6
6N18 " 75b bright blue & pale blue 5 5
6N19 " 80b green & pale green 6 6
6N20 " 1 l red brown & claret 10 10
6N21 " 2 l olive brown & bistre 6 6
6N22 " 3 l dark violet & indigo 1.00 1.00
6N23 " 5 l dark brown & light brown 50 50
6N24 " 10 l violet brown & violet 80 80

On Stamps of 1918.
6N25 A11 10b scarlet 50 50
6N26 " 20b dark brown 5 5
6N27 " 25b bright blue 8 8
6N28 A12 40b olive green 10 10

On Stamps of 1918-19, Overprinted "Köztarsasag".
6N29 A9 2b brown orange 60 60
6N30 " 3b red lilac 5 5
6N31 " 4b slate gray 5 5
6N32 " 5b green 6 6
6N33 " 6b greenish blue 25 25
6N34 " 10b rose red 5.00 5.00
6N35 " 20b gray brown 20 20
6N36 " 40b olive green 6 6
6N37 A10 1 l red brown & claret 5 5
6N38 " 3 l dark violet & indigo 10 10
6N39 " 5 l dark brown & light brown 1.25 1.25
6N40 A11 10b scarlet 40.00 40.00
6N41 " 20b dark brown 50 50
6N42 " 25b bright blue 15 15
6N43 A12 50b lilac 5 5

On Stamps of 1919.
Inscribed "MAGYAR POSTA".
6N44 A13 5b yellow green 5 5
6N45 " 10b red 5 5
6N46 " 20b dark brown 6 6
6N47 " 25b dull blue 20 20
6N48 " 40b olive green 8 8
6N49 A14 5 l dark brown & brown 1.75 1.75

On No. 103A
6N50 A5a 10b violet brown 10 10
Nos. 6N1-6N50 (50) 83.93 83.93

SEMI-POSTAL STAMPS.

Hungarian Semi-Postal Stamps of 1913-17 Overprinted like Regular Issues.

On Stamps of 1913.
Wmkd. Double Cross. (137)
1919 *Perf. 14*
6NB1 SP1 1 l on 1f slate 50 50
6NB2 " 1 l on 2f olive yellow 1.25 1.25
6NB3 " 1 l on 3f orange 50 50
6NB4 " 1 l on 5f emer ald 10 10
6NB5 " 1 l on 6f olive green 30 30
6NB6 " 1 l on 10f carmine 10 10
6NB7 " 1 l on 12f violet, *yellow* 22.50 22.50
6NB8 " 1 l on 16f gray green 60 60
6NB9 " 1 l on 20f dark brown 4.00 4.00
6NB10 " 1 l on 25f ultra. 1.25 1.25
6NB11 " 1 l on 35f red violet 1.25 1.25

On Stamp of 1915
Wmkd. Crown in Circle. (135)
Perf. 11½.
6NB12 A4 5b emerald 2.00 2.00

On Stamps of 1916-17.
Wmkd. Double Cross. (137)
Perf. 15.
6NB13 SP3 10b+2b rose red 20 20
6NB14 SP4 15b+2b dull violet 5 5
6NB15 SP5 40b+2b brn. car. 5 5
Nos. 6NB1-6NB15 (15) 34.65 34.65

SPECIAL DELIVERY STAMP.

Hungarian Special Delivery Stamp of 1916 Overprinted like Regular Issues.
Wmkd. Double Cross. (137)
1919 *Perf. 15.*
6NE1 SD1 2b gray green & red 5 5

POSTAGE DUE STAMPS.

Hungarian Postage Due Stamps of 1915 Overprinted like Regular Issues.
Wmkd. Double Cross. (137)
1919 *Perf. 15.*
6NJ1 D1 1b green & red *8.00 8.00*
6NJ2 " 2b " " 5 5
6NJ3 " 5b " " 1.50 1.50
6NJ4 " 6b " " 1.00 1.00
6NJ5 " 10b " " 5 5
6NJ6 " 12b " " 35 35
6NJ7 " 15b " " 35 35
6NJ8 " 20b " " 5 5
6NJ9 " 30b " " 40 40
Nos. 6NJ1-6NJ9 (9) *11.75 11.75*

NEWSPAPER STAMP.

Hungarian Newspaper Stamp of 1914 Overprinted like Regular Issues.
1919 *Imperf.* Wmk. 137
6NP1 N5 2b orange 5 5

Issued under Serbian Occupation.

Forged overprints abound.

FIRST BARANYA ISSUE.

Hungarian Stamps of 1913-18 Overprinted in Black or Red:

1919 1919

Baranya *a* Baranya *b*

Wmkd. Double Cross. (137)
1919 *Perf. 15.*

On Issue of 1913-16.
7N1 A4 (*a*) 6f olive green (R) 30 40
7N2 " (") 50f lake, *blue* 10 20
7N3 " (") 60f green, *salmon* 20 35
7N4 " (") 70f red brown & green (R) 85 1.20
7N5 " (") 70f red brown & green (Bk) 10 20
7N6 " (") 80f dull vio. (R) 2.50 3.25

On Issue of 1916-18.
7N7 A9 (*a*) 2f brown orange (Bk) 2.75 3.25
7N8 " (") 2f brn. org. (R) 5 5
7N9 " (") 3f red lilac (Bk) 5 5
7N10 " (") 3f red lilac (R) 25 30
7N11 " (") 5f green (Bk) 25 30
7N12 " (") 5f green (R) 5 5
7N13 " (") 6f greenish blue (Bk) 75 75
7N14 " (") 6f greenish blue (R) 80 80
7N15 " (") 15f violet 5 5
7N16 " (") 20f gray brown 27.50 27.50
7N17 " (") 25f dull blue 2.25 2.75
7N18 " (") 35f brown 3.50 4.00
7N19 " (") 40f olive green 25.00 27.50

7N20 A10 (*b*) 50f red violet & lilac 85 1.10
7N21 " (") 75f bright blue & pale blue 6 10
7N22 " (") 80f green & pale green 15 25
7N23 " (") 1k red brown & claret 10 15
7N24 " (") 2k olive brown & bistre 15 25
7N25 " (") 3k dark violet & indigo 20 30
7N26 " (") 5k dark brown & light brown 60 80
7N27 " (") 10k violet brown & violet 2.75 3.50

OS8

7N28 OS8 45f on 2f brn. orange 10 15
7N29 " 45f on 5f green 5 5
7N30 " 45f on 15f violet 5 5

On Issue of 1918.

7N31 A11(*a*) 10f scarlet (Bk) 5 5
7N32 " (") 20f dk. brn. (Bk) 5 5
7N33 " (") 20f dk. brn. (R) *30.00*
7N34 " (") 25f dp. blue (Bk) 65 75
7N35 " (") 25f deep blue (R) 45 45
7N36 A12(") 40f olive green (Bk) 4.00 4.25
7N37 " (") 40f olive green (R) 16.00

On Issue of 1918-19 (Köztarsasag).

7N38 A9 (*a*) 2f brown orange (Bk) 2.75 3.25
7N39 A12(") 40f olive green (Bk) *125.00* *125.00*
7N40 " (") 40f olive green (R) 25.00 30.00

With New Value Added.

7N41 OS8 45f on 2f brown orange (Bk) 85 1.10
7N42 " 45f on 2f brown orange (R) 10 15

Overprints "a" and "b" were set in groups of 25. In each group two stamps have the figures "1" of "1919" with serifs.
No. 7N33 is considered a proof by some specialists.

SEMI-POSTAL STAMPS.

Hungarian Semi-Postal Stamps Overprinted like Regular Issues.

On Stamp of 1915

Wmkd. Double Cross. (137)

1919 *Perf. 15.*

7NB1 A4 (*a*) 50f+2f lake, *blue* 12.00

On Stamps of 1916.

7NB2 SP3 (*a*) 10f+2f rose red 10 20
7NB3 SP4 (") 15f+2f dull violet 15 30

SPECIAL DELIVERY STAMP.

SD1

Wmkd. Double Cross. (137)

1919 *Perf. 15*

7NE1 SD1 105f on 2f gray green & red 45 60

POSTAGE DUE STAMPS.

D1

Wmkd. Double Cross. (137)

1919 *Perf. 15.*

7NJ1 D1 2f green & red 3.00 4.00
7NJ2 " 10f " " 50 60
7NJ3 " 20f " " 80 95

With New Value Added.

7NJ4 D1 40f on 2f green & red 75 95

SECOND BARANYA ISSUE.

Forged overprints exist.

1919

Hungarian Stamps of 1916-19 Surcharged in Black and Red

BARANYA 100

On Stamps of 1916-18.

8N1 A9 20f on 2f brn. org. 3.75 4.25
8N2 " 50f on 5f green 85 1.00
8N3 " 150f on 15f violet 80 1.00
8N4 A10 200f on 75f bright blue & pale blue 25 35

On Stamp of 1918-19, Overprinted "Köztarsasag"

8N5 A11 150f on 15f dp. violet 15 15

On Stamps of 1919.

8N6 A13 20f on 2f brn. org. 10 10
8N7 " 30f on 6f greenish blue 20 20
8N8 " 50f on 5f yel. grn. 8 8
8N9 " 100f on 25f dull blue 8 8
8N10 " 100f on 40f olive green 8 8
8N11 " 100f on 45f orange 35 35
8N12 " 150f on 20f dk. brown 40 40

On No. 103A

8N13 A5a 10f on 10f vio. brn. 20 30
Nos. 8N1-8N13 (13) 7.29 8.34

SPECIAL DELIVERY STAMP.

Hungarian Special Delivery Stamp of 1916 Surcharged like Regular Issues.

Wmkd. Double Cross. (137)

1919 *Perf. 15.*

8NE1 SD1 10f on 2f gray green & red 15 15

NEWSPAPER STAMP.

Hungarian Newspaper Stamp of 1914 Surcharged like Regular Issues.

Wmkd. Double Cross. (137)

1919 *Imperf.*

8NP1 N5 10f on 2f orange 10 10

Issued under Serbian Occupation.

TEMESVAR ISSUE.

Hungarian Stamps of 1916-18 Surcharged in Black, Blue or Brown:

10 filler
a *b*

1919

9N1 A9 (*a*) 10f on 2f brown orange (Bl) 5 5
a. Black surcharge 5.00 7.00
9N2 A9 (*b*) 30f on 2f brown orange (Bk) 8 8
a. Inverted surcharge
9N3 A11 (*b*) 50f on 20f dark brown (Bl) 6 6
a. Inverted surcharge
9N4 A9 (") 1k 50f on 15f violet (Bk) 60 75
a. Brown surcharge 1.75 2.00
b. Double surcharge (Bk)

SEMI-POSTAL STAMP.

Hungarian Semi-Postal Stamp of 1916 Surcharged in Blue

45 fillér

Wmkd. Double Cross. (137)

1919 *Perf. 15.*

9NB1 SP3 45f on 10f+2f rose red 10 20

POSTAGE DUE STAMPS.

Hungarian Postage Due Stamps of 1915 Surcharged

60 FILLÉR

Wmkd. Double Cross. (137)

1919 *Perf. 15.*

9NJ1 D1 40f on 2f grn. & red 85 95
9NJ2 " 60f on 2f " " 85 95
9NJ3 " 100f on 2f " " 85 95

Issued under Serbian Occupation

Forged overprints exist.

BANAT, BACSKA, ISSUE

Postal authorities at Temesvar applied these overprints. The stamps were available for postage, but were chiefly used to pay postal employees' salaries.

Hungarian Stamps of 1913-19 Overprinted in Black or Red:

Bánát Bácska 1919.
a
Bánát, Bácska 1919.
b

1919

Type "a" on Stamp of 1913

10N1 A4 50f lake, *blue* 4.00 4.00

Type "a" on Stamps of 1916-18

10N2 A9 2f brown orange 8 8
10N3 " 3f red lilac 8 8
10N4 " 5f green 8 8
10N5 " 6f greenish blue 10 10
10N6 " 15f violet 10 10
10N7 " 35f brown 5.00 5.00

Type "b"

10N8 A10 50f red violet & lilac (R) 3.00 3.00
10N9 " 75f bright blue & pale blue 10 10
10N10 " 80f grn. & pale grn. 10 10
10N11 " 1k red brown & claret 10 10
10N12 " 2k olive brown & bistre 10 10
a. Red overprint 3.00 3.00
10N14 A10 3k dark violet & indigo 4.00 4.00
10N15 " 5k dark brown & light brown 25 25
10N16 " 10k violet brown & violet 60 60

Type "a" on Stamps of 1918

10N17 A11 10f scarlet 8 8
10N18 " 20f dark brown 8 8
10N19 " 25f bright blue 8 8
10N20 A12 40f olive green 8 8
10N21 " 50f lilac 10 10

Type "a" on Stamps of 1919 Inscribed "Magyar Posta"

10N22 A13 10f red 60 60
10N23 " 20f dark brown 60 60
10N24 " 25f dull blue 75 75

Type "a" on Stamps of 1918-19 Overprinted "Köztarsasag"

10N25 A9 4f slate gray 8 8
10N26 " 4f slate gray (R) 4.00 4.00
10N27 A9 5f green 8 8
10N28 " 6f greenish blue 8 8
10N29 " 10f rose red 1.40 1.40
10N30 A11 15f deep violet 1.00 1.00
10N31 A9 20f gray brown 2.50 2.50
10N32 A11 25f bright blue 1.25 1.25
10N33 A9 40f olive green 8 8
10N34 " 40f olive grn. (R) 3.50 3.50

Type "b"

10N35 A10 1k red brown & claret 10 10
10N36 " 2k olive brown & bistre 2.00 2.00
10N37 " 3k dark violet & indigo 2.25 2.25
10N38 " 5k dark brown & light brown 2.25 2.25
10N39 " 10k violet brown & violet 4.00 4.00

Type "a" on Temesvár Issue

10N40 A9 10f on 2f brown orange (Bl & Bk) 9 9
10N41 " 1k 50f on 15f violet 10 10

OS9

10N42 OS9 50f on 10f violet brown 50 50
Nos. 10N1-10N42 (41) 45.32 45.32

SEMI-POSTAL STAMPS

Semi-Postal Stamps of 1916-17 Overprinted Type "a" in Black

1919

10NB1 SP3 10f+2f rose red 15 15
10NB2 SP4 15f+2f dull violet 15 15
10NB3 SP5 40f+2f brn. car. 15 15

Same Overprint on Temesvar Issue.

10NB4 SP3 45f on 10f+2f rose red (Bl & Bk) 40 40

SPECIAL DELIVERY STAMP

SD1

Black Surcharge.

1919

10NE1 SD1 30f on 2f gray grn. & red 40 40

POSTAGE DUE STAMPS

Postage Due Stamps of 1914-15 Overprinted Type "a" in Black

1919

10NJ1 D1 2f green & red 10 10
10NJ2 " 10f " " 10 10
10NJ3 " 15f " " 3.00 3.00
10NJ4 " 20f " " 10 10
10NJ5 " 30f " " 1.50 1.50
10NJ6 " 50f green & black 3.00 3.00
Nos. 10NJ1-10NJ6 (6) 7.80 7.80

NEWSPAPER STAMP

Stamp of 1914 Overprinted Type "a" in Black

1919

10NP1 N5 (2f) orange 12 12

SZEGED ISSUE

The "Hungarian National Government, Szeged, 1919", as the overprint reads, was an anti-Bolshevist government which opposed the Soviet Republic then in control at Budapest.

Excellent counterfeits of the overprint exist.

Hungary Stamps of 1916–19 Overprinted in Various Colors — MAGYAR NEMZETI KORMÁNY Szeged, 1919.

On Stamps of 1916-18.

1919 *Perf. 15, 14*

1 A9 2f brown orange (G) 15 15
2 " 3f red lilac (G) 10 10
3 " 5f green (R) 15 15
4 " 6f greenish blue (R) 7.50 7.50
5 " 15f violet (R) 15 15
6 A10 50f red violet & lilac (R) 2.50 2.50
7 " 75f bright blue & pale blue (R) 15 15
8 " 80f green & pale green (R) 50 50
9 " 1k red brown & claret (G) 20 20
10 " 2k olive brown & bistre (R) 20 20
11 " 3k dark violet & indigo (R) 40 40
12 " 5k dark brown & light brown (R) 25.00 25.00
13 " 10k violet brown & violet (R) 25.00 25.00

With New Value Added.

14 A9 45f on 3f red lilac (R & G) 15 15
15 A10 10k on 1k red brown & claret (Bl & G) 1.25 1.25

On Stamps of 1918.

16 A11 10f scarlet (G) 15 15
17 " 20f dark brown (R) 15 15
18 " 25f bright blue (R) 6.00 6.00
19 A12 40f olive green (R) 25 25

On Stamps of 1918-19, Overprinted "Köztarsasag".

20 A9 3f red lilac (G) 6.00 6.00
21 " 4f slate gray (R) 20 20
22 " 5f green (R) 4.00 4.00
23 " 6f greenish blue (R) 50 50
24 " 10f rose red (G) 1.50 1.50
25 A11 10f scarlet (G) 75 75
26 " 15f deep violet (R) 20 20
27 A9 20f gray brown (R) 25.00 25.00
28 A11 20f dark brown (R) 25.00 25.00
29 " 25f bright blue (R) 3.50 3.50
30 A9 40f olive green (R) 20 20
31 A12 50f light (R) 20 20
32 A10 3k dark biolet & indigo (R) 25.00 25.00

With New Value Added.

33 A9 20f on 2f brn. org. (R&G) 20 20

On Stamps of 1919. Inscribed "Magyar Posta".

34 A13 20f dark brown (R) 20.00 20.00
35 " 25f dull blue (R) 15 15
Nos. 1-35 (35) 182.35 182.35

SEMI-POSTAL STAMPS

Szeged Overprint on Semi-Postal Stamps of 1916–17 in Green or Red

1919

B1 SP3 10f+2f rose red (G) 10 10
B2 SP4 15f+2f dull violet (R) 15 15
B3 SP5 40f+2f brown carmine (G) 60 60

With Additional Overprint "Köztarsasag."

B4 SP5 40f+2f brown carmine (Bk & G) 2.50 2.50

SPECIAL DELIVERY STAMP

Szeged Overprint on Special Delivery Stamp of 1916 in Red

1919

E1 SD1 2f gray green & red 25 25

POSTAGE DUE STAMPS

Szeged Overprint on Stamps of 1915–18 in Red

1919

J1 D1 2f green & red 30 30
J2 " 6f " " 1.50 1.50
J3 " 10f " " 30 30
J4 " 12f " " 30 30
J5 " 20f " " 30 30
J6 " 30f " " 50 50

D1

Red Surcharge.

J7 D1 50f on 2f gray green & red 25 25
J8 " 100f on 2f gray green & red 25 25
Nos. J1-J8 (8) 3.70 3.70

NEWSPAPER STAMP

Szeged Overprint on Stamp of 1914 in Green

Wmkd. Double Cross. (137)

1919 *Imperf.*

P1 N5 (2f) orange 20 20

ICELAND

(īs′lȧnd)

LOCATION — An island in the North Atlantic Ocean, east of Greenland.

GOVT.—Republic.

AREA—39,758 sq. mi.

POP.—220,000 (est. 1976).

CAPITAL—Reykjavík.

Iceland became a republic on June 17, 1944. Formerly this country was united with Denmark under the government of King Christian X who, as the ruling sovereign of both countries, was assigned the dual title of King of each. Although the two countries were temporarily united in certain affairs beyond the King's person, both were acknowledged as sovereign States.

96 Skillings = 1 Rigsdaler
100 Aurar (singular "Eyrir") = 1 Krona (1876)

> Prices of early Icelandic stamps vary according to condition. Quotations for Nos. 1–7 are for fine copies. Very fine to superb specimens sell at much higher prices, and inferior or poor copies sell at reduced prices, depending on the condition of the individual specimen.

Numeral of Value
A1

Wmk. 112

Wmkd. Crown. (112)

1873 Typographed *Perf. 14x13½*

1 A1 2s ultramarine 500.00 750.00
  a. Imperf. 500.00
2 " 4s dark carmine 95.00 375.00
  a. Imperf. 550.00
3 " 8s brown 140.00 375.00
  a. Imperf. 160.00
4 " 16s yellow 700.00 850.00
  a. Imperf. 275.00

Perf. 12½.

5 A1 3s gray 175.00 600.00
  a. Imperf. 500.00
6 " 4s carmine 600.00 800.00
7 " 16s yellow 65.00 250.00

False and favor cancellations are often found on Nos. 1–7. The imperforate varieties lack gum.

Small numeral — Large "3"

A2 A3 A3a

1876

8 A2 5a blue 130.00 170.00

Perf. 14x13½.

9 A2 5a blue 170.00 225.00
10 " 6a gray 57.50 11.00
11 " 10a carmine 100.00 3.25
  a. Imperf. 300.00 350.00
12 " 16a brown 55.00 22.50
13 " 20a dark violet 17.50 47.50
14 " 40a green 52.50 57.50

1882–98

15 A3 3a orange 27.50 9.00
16 A2 5a green 25.00 5.00
17 " 20a blue 110.00 16.00
  a. 20a ultramarine 250.00 70.00
18 " 40a red violet 18.00 22.50
  a. Perf. 13 ('98) 3000.00
19 " 50a bl. & car. ('92) 40.00 30.00
20 " 100a brn. & vio. ('92) 52.50 45.00
See note after No. 68.

1896–1901 *Perf. 13*

21 A3 3a orange ('97) 35.00 4.75
22 A3a 3a yellow ('01) 3.50 11.00
23 A2 4a rose & gray ('99) 10.00 10.00
24 " 5a green 3.00 1.25
25 " 6a gray ('97) 6.00 9.00
26 " 10a carmine ('97) 4.00 1.25
27 " 16a brown 35.00 35.00
28 " 20a dull blue ('98) 12.50 10.00
  a. 20a dull ultra. 160.00 10.00
29 " 25a yellow brown & blue ('00) 11.00 8.50
30 " 50a bl. & car. ('98) 225.00 375.00
See note after No. 68.

Black and Red Surcharge.

Surcharged þrír 3

1897 *Perf. 13*

31 A2 3a on 5a green 375.00 275.00
  a. Perf. 14x13½ 1600.00
  b. Invtd. surch. 1000.00 650.00

Surcharged þrír 3

32 A2 3a on 5a green 325.00 225.00
  a. Inverted surcharge 1000.00 650.00
  b. Perf. 14x13½ 900.00

Black Surcharge.

Surcharged þrír

33 A2 3a on 5a green 375.00 300.00

Surcharged þrír

33A A2 3a on 5a green 325.00 275.00
Excellent counterfeits are known.

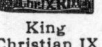

King Christian IX
A4

Wmk. 113

Wmkd. Crown. (113)

1902–04 *Perf. 13*

34 A4 3a orange 3.75 1.30
35 " 4a gray & rose 2.00 45
36 " 5a yellow green 8.00 20
37 " 6a gray brown 9.00 3.50
38 " 10a carmine rose 4.50 20
39 " 16a chocolate 3.00 3.00
40 " 20a deep blue 1.50 1.60
  a. Inscribed "PJONUSTA" 50.00 55.00
41 " 25a brown & green 1.50 1.60
42 " 40a violet 2.00 1.30
43 " 50a gray & blue black 2.75 10.00
44 " 1k slate blue & yellow brown 4.50 3.75
44A " 2k olive brown & bright blue ('04) 14.00 30.00
44B " 5k orange brown & slate blue ('04) 75.00 70.00
Nos. 34-44B (13) 131.50 126.90

Stamps of 1882-1901 Overprinted — í GILDI '02—'03

Wmkd. Crown. (112)

1902–03 *Perf. 13*

Red Overprint

45 A2 5a green 65 3.50
  a. Invtd. overprint 15.00
  b. "I" before Gildi omitted 27.50
  c. '03-'03 60.00
  d. 02'-'03 60.00
  e. Pair, one without overprint 30.00
46 " 6a gray 65 3.50
  a. Double overprint 37.50
  b. Invtd. overprint 30.00
  c. '03-'03 110.00
  d. 02'-'03 110.00
  e. Pair, one with inverted overprint 40.00
  f. Pair, one without overprint 45.00
  g. Same as "f", invtd. 75.00
47 " 20a dull blue 65 3.50
  a. Inverted ovpt. 20.00 20.00
  b. "I" before Gildi omitted 55.00
  c. 02'-'03 150.00
48 " 25a yel. brn. & blue 65 5.50
  a. Inverted ovpt. 20.00 20.00
  b. '03-'03 60.00
  c. 02'-'03 60.00
  d. Dbl. ovpt. 110.00

Black Overprint.

49 A3 3a orange 85.00 200.00
  b. Inverted ovpt. 110.00
  c. "I" before Gildi omitted 100.00
  d. '03-'03 100.00
  e. 02'-'03 100.00 200.00
50 A3a 3a yellow 65 1.00
  a. Double overprint 65.00
  b. Invtd. overprint 11.00
  c. "I" before Gildi omitted 90.00
  d. 02'-'03 90.00
51 A2 4a rose & gray 13.00 22.50
  a. Double overprint 65.00
  b. Invtd. ovpt. 27.50 40.00
  c. Double overprint, one inverted 110.00
  d. "I" before Gildi omitted 27.50
  e. '03-'03 77.50
  f. 02'-'03 77.50 80.00
  g. Pair, one with inverted ovpt. 77.50
52 " 5a green 170.00 190.00
  a. Inverted ovpt. 180.00 200.00
  b. Pair, one without overprint 190.00
  c. Same as "b", inverted 190.00

53 A2 6a gray 225.00 250.00
- *a.* Inverted ovpt. 275.00 300.00
- *b.* Pair, one without overprint 275.00

54 " 10a carmine 65 *5.50*
- *a.* Invtd. overprint 11.00 16.00
- *b.* Pair, one without overprint 42.50

55 " 16a brown 8.50 20.00
- *a.* Inverted ovpt. 40.00
- *b.* "I" before Gildi omitted 77.50
- *c.* '03-'03 120.00
- *d.* 02'-'03 120.00

56 " 20a dull blue *3750.00*
- *a.* Inverted ovpt. *4750.00*

57 " 25a yel. brn. & bl. *3000.00*
- *a.* Inverted ovpt. *4000.00*

58 " 40a red violet 65 *27.50*
- *a.* Inverted ovpt. 15.00 35.00

59 " 50a blue & carmine 2.50 *35.00*
- *a.* Double overprint 60.00 65.00
- *b.* 02'-'03 60.00
- *c.* '03-'03 60.00

Perf. 14x13½.

Red Overprint.

60 A2 5a green 550.00 750.00
- *a.* '03-'03 575.00
- *b.* 02'-'03 575.00

61 " 6a gray 550.00 750.00
- *a.* 02'-'03 575.00

62 " 20a blue *2250.00 3750.00*

Black Overprint.

63 A3 3a orange 525.00 600.00
- *a.* Inverted ovpt. 575.00
- *b.* 02'-'03 575.00
- *c.* '03-'03 575.00

64 A2 10a carmine *3000.00 3250.00*

65 " 16a brown 475.00 625.00
- *a.* Inverted ovpt. 525.00
- *b.* 02'-'03 525.00
- *d.* '03-'03 525.00

65C " 20a dull blue *3250.00 4000.00*

66 " 40a red violet 11.00 *50.00*
- *a.* Inverted ovpt. 27.50
- *b.* '03-'03 72.50
- *c.* 02'-'03 72.50

67 " 50a blue & carmine 12.50 *60.00*
- *a.* Inverted overprint 65.00 77.50
- *b.* '03-'03 72.50
- *c.* 02'-'03 72.50
- *d.* As "c." invtd. 190.00

68 " 100a brown & violet 27.50 32.50
- *a.* Inverted ovpt. 40.00 50.00
- *b.* 02'-'03 120.00
- *c.* '03-'03 120.00

"I GILDI" means "valid."

In 1904 Nos. 20, 22–30, 45–59 (except 49, 52, 53, 56 and 57) and No. 68 were reprinted for the Postal Union. The reprints are perforated 13 and have the watermark of the 1902 issue (type 113). Price $40 each. A few copies have been found without the overprint. Price $80 each.

Kings Christian IX and Frederik VIII
A5

Typo., Center Engr.
Wmkd. Crown. (113)

1907–08 ***Perf. 13***

71 A5 1e yellow grn. & red 1.00 40
72 " 3a yellow brown & ochre 2.00 25
73 " 4a gray & red 1.00 40
74 " 5a green 30.00 20
75 " 6a gray & gray brn. 16.00 1.20
76 " 10a scarlet 50.00 20
77 " 15a red & green 3.50 20
78 " 16a brown 4.00 16.00
79 " 20a blue 4.50 1.00
80 " 25a bis. brn. & green 2.50 4.00
81 " 40a claret & violet 3.00 6.00
82 " 50a gray & violet 3.00 5.00
83 " 1k blue & brown 15.00 25.00
84 " 2k dark brown & dark green 15.00 27.50
85 " 5k brown & slate 80.00 110.00
Nos. 71–85 (15) 230.50 197.35

See also Nos. 99–107.

Jon Sigurdsson
A6

King Frederik VIII
A7

1911 **Typo. and Embossed**

86 A6 1e olive green 1.25 30
87 " 3a light brown 1.50 3.25
88 " 4a ultramarine 75 75
89 " 6a gray 4.00 6.75
90 " 15a violet 12.00 70
91 " 25a orange 15.00 14.00
Nos. 86–91 (6) 34.50 25.75

Issued to commemorate the centenary of the birth of Jon Sigurdsson (1811–1879), statesman and author.

1912, Feb. 17

92 A7 5a green 16.00 5.50
93 " 10a red 16.00 5.50
94 " 20a pale blue 27.50 7.50
95 " 50a claret 9.00 14.00
96 " 1k yellow 16.00 25.00
97 " 2k rose 16.00 22.50
98 " 5k brown 90.00 95.00
Nos. 92–98 (7) 190.50 175.00

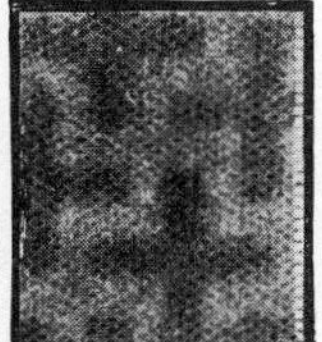

Wmk. 114

King Christian X
A8

Typo., Center Engr.
Wmkd. Multiple Crosses. (114)

1915–18 ***Perf. 14x14½***

99 A5 1e yellow green & red 3.75 4.75
100 " 3a bistre brown 1.75 70
101 " 4a gray & red 1.75 3.50
102 " 5a green 32.50 25
103 " 6a gray & gray brn. 7.50 32.50
104 " 10a scarlet 1.75 25
107 " 20a blue 75.00 3.00
Nos. 99–107 (7) 124.00 44.95

1920–22 **Typographed**

108 A8 1e yellow green & red 50 50
109 " 3a bistre brown 2.50 5.00
110 " 4a gray & red 1.75 1.00
111 " 5a green 1.25 75
112 " 5a olive green ('22) 1.75 25
113 " 6a dark gray 7.50 4.00
114 " 8a dark brown 3.25 85
115 " 10a red 75 3.25
116 " 10a green ('21) 1.50 50
117 " 15a violet 17.50 20
118 " 20a deep blue 1.00 7.00
119 " 20a chocolate ('22) 35.00 45
120 " 25a brown & green 7.50 50
121 " 25a red ('21) 5.00 10.00
122 " 30a red & green 22.50 1.20
123 " 40a claret 22.50 75
124 " 40a dark blue ('21) 45.00 5.50
125 " 50a dk. gray & claret 80.00 5.00
126 " 1k dp. bl. & dk. brn. 55.00 25
127 " 2k olive brown & myrtle green 85.00 7.00
Revenue cancellation 1.00
128 " 5k brown & indigo 40.00 7.50
Revenue cancellation 85
Nos. 108–128 (21) 436.75 61.45

Revenue cancellations consisting of "TOLLUR" boxed in frame are found on stamps used to pay the tax on parcel post packages entering Iceland.

See also Nos. 176–187, 202.

A9

A10

A11

1921–25 ***Perf. 13*** **Wmk. 113**

130 A9 5a on 16a brown 1.40 16.00
131 A11 5a on 16a brown 85 3.25
132 A10 20a on 25a brn. & grn. 3.00 2.00
133 A11 20a on 25a bistre brown & green 1.75 2.25
134 A9 20a on 40a violet 3.00 8.00
135 A11 20a on 40a claret & violet 5.00 8.00
137 A9 30a on 50a gray & blue black ('25) 8.50 12.00
Revenue cancel 4.00
138 " 50a on 5k orange brn. & slate bl. ('25) 35.00 12.00
Revenue cancel 4.00
Nos. 130–138 (8) 58.50 63.50

No. 111 Surcharged **10 aur.**

1922 ***Perf. 14x14½*** **Wmk. 114**

139 A8 10a on 5a green 2.00 1.00

Stamps of 1902-12 Surcharged **Kr. 10**

Wmkd. Crown. (113)

1924–30 ***Perf. 13***

140 A7 10k on 50a claret ('25) 120.00 120.00
Revenue cancellation 11.00
141 " 10k on 1k yellow 190.00 210.00
Revenue cancellation 32.50
142 A4 10k on 2k olive brown & blue ('29) 35.00 11.00
Revenue cancellation 2.25
143 A5 10k on 5k brown & slate ('30) 190.00 210.00
Revenue cancellation 3.50

"Tollur" is a revenue cancellation.

Landing the Mail
A12

Designs: 7a, 50a, Landing the mail. 10a, 35a, View of Reykjavik. 20a, Museum building.

Wmkd. Multiple Crosses. (114)

1925, Sept. 12 **Typo.** ***Perf. 14x15***

144 A12 7a yellow green 37.50 3.75
145 " 10a deep blue & brown 37.50 25
146 " 20a vermilion 37.50 15
147 " 35a deep blue 50.00 4.50
148 " 50a yellow green & brown 50.00 50
Nos. 144–148 (5) 212.50 9.15

No. 91 Surcharged **2 krónur**

1925 ***Perf. 13*** **Wmk. 113**

149 A6 2k on 25a orange 45.00 45.00
Revenue cancellation 3.75

No. 124 Surcharged in Red **EIN KRÓNA**

1926

150 A8 1k on 40a dark blue 42.50 10.00
Revenue cancellation 6.00

Parliament Building
A15

Designs: 5a, Viking ship in storm. 7a, Parliament meeting place, 1690. 10a, Viking funeral. 15a, Vikings naming land. 20a, The dash for Thing. 25a, Gathering wood. 30a, Thingvalla Lake. 35a, Iceland woman in national costume. 40a, Iceland flag. 50a, First Althing, 930 A.D. 1k, Map of Iceland. 2k, Winter-bound home. 5k, Woman spinning. 10k, Viking Sacrifice to Thor.

Perf. 12½x12

1930, Jan. 1 **Litho.** **Unwmkd.**

152 A15 3a dull violet & gray violet 2.50 5.00
153 " 5a dark blue & slate green 2.50 5.00
154 " 7a grn. & gray green 2.50 5.00
155 " 10a dark violet & lilac 6.00 6.00
156 " 15a deep ultramarine & blue gray 2.50 5.00
157 " 20a rose red & salmon 27.50 30.00
- *a.* Dbl. impression 150.00

158 " 25a dark brown & light brown 4.50 6.00
159 " 30a dark green & slate green 4.50 6.00
160 " 35a ultramarine & blue gray 4.50 6.00
161 " 40a dk. ultra., red & slate green 4.50 6.00
162 " 50a red brown & cinnamon 50.00 65.00
163 " 1k olive green & gray green 50.00 65.00
164 " 2k turquoise blue & gray green 50.00 65.00
165 " 5k orange & yellow 32.50 50.00
166 " 10k magenta & dull rose 32.00 50.00
- *a.* Imperf. (pair) 75.00

Nos. 152–166 (15) 276.50 375.00

Issued in commemoration of the millenary of the founding of the "Althing", the Icelandic Parliament, which is the oldest in the world.

Gullfoss (Golden Falls)
A30

Engraved.

1931-32 ***Perf. 14.*** **Unwmkd.**

170 A30 5a gray 11.00 30
171 " 20a red 7.00 15
172 " 35a ultramarine 20.00 6.00
173 " 60a red lilac ('32) 9.00 40
174 " 65a red brown ('32) 1.50 30
175 " 75a greenish blue ('32) 62.50 10.00
Revenue cancellation 65
Nos. 170–175 (6) 111.00 17.15

Type of 1920 Christian X Issue.
Redrawn.
Wmkd. Multiple Crosses. (114)

1931–33 **Typo.** ***Perf. 14x14½***

176 A8 1e yellow green & red 30 35
177 " 3a bistre brown 3.00 3.50
178 " 4a gray & red 1.00 50
179 " 6a dark gray 1.00 1.50
180 " 7a yellow green ('33) 20 40
181 " 10a chocolate 37.50 25
182 " 25a brown & green 9.00 80
183 " 30a red & green 10.00 2.00
184 " 40a claret 60.00 6.00
185 " 1k dark blue & light brown 32.50 3.50
Revenue cancellation 70
186 " 2k choc. & dk. grn. 85.00 20.00
Revenue cancellation 1.25
187 " 10k yellow green & black 130.00 40.00
Revenue cancellation 2.50
Nos. 176–187 (12) 369.50 78.80

On the redrawn stamps the horizontal lines of the portrait and the oval are closer together than on the 1920 stamps and are crossed by many fine vertical lines.

See also No. 202.

Condition is the all-important factor of price. Prices quoted are for stamps in fine condition.

Dynjandi Falls
A31

Mount Hekla
A32

Perf. 12½

1935, June 28 Engr. **Unwmkd.**

193	A31	10a blue	10.00	15
194	A32	1k greenish gray	27.50	20

Matthias Jochumsson
A33

King Christian X
A34

1935, Nov. 11

195	A33	3a gray green	25	1.65
196	"	5a gray	8.50	25
197	"	7a yellow green	15.00	60
198	"	35a blue	30	40

Issued to commemorate the centenary of the birth of Matthias Jochumsson, poet.

1937, May 14 ***Perf. 13x12½***

199	A34	10a green	2.00	*9.00*
200	"	30a brown	2.00	*4.50*
201	"	40a claret	2.00	*4.50*

Issued to commemorate the 25th anniversary of the accession to the throne of King Christian X.

Christian X Type of 1931–33.
Typographed.

1937 ***Perf. 11½*** **Unwmkd.**

202	A8	1e yellow green & red	30	40

Geyser
A35 A36

1938–47 Engraved ***Perf. 14***

203	A35	15a deep rose violet	2.50	2.75
		a. Imperf., pair	*1100.00*	
204	"	20a rose red	14.00	15
205	"	35a ultramarine	60	30
206	A36	40a dk. brown ('39)	7.50	5.50
207	"	45a brt. ultra. ('40)	50	40
208	"	50a dk. slate green	14.00	25
208A	"	60a brt. ultra. ('43)	3.75	40
		c. Perf. 11½ ('47)	1.25	1.50
208B	"	1k indigo ('45)	1.00	20
		d. Perf. 11½ ('47)	1.25	1.50
		Nos. 203–208B (8)	43.85	9.95

University of Iceland
A37

1938, Dec. 1 ***Perf. 13½***

209	A37	25a dark green	7.00	7.50
210	"	30a brown	7.00	7.50
211	"	40a brt. red violet	7.00	7.50

20th anniversary of independence.

No. 198 Surcharged with New Value.

1939, Mar. 17 ***Perf. 12½***

212	A33	5a on 35a blue	65	65
		a. Double surcharge	*120.00*	

New York World's Fair Issue.

Trylon and Perisphere
A38

Leif Ericsson's Ship and Route to America
A39

Statue of Thorfinn Karlsefni
A40

1939 Engraved. ***Perf. 14.***

213	A38	20a crimson	2.75	3.75
214	A39	35a brt. ultramarine	3.00	4.50
215	A40	45a bright green	3.00	4.50
216	"	2k dark gray	45.00	72.50

Codfish
A41

Herring
A42

Flag of Iceland
A43

Perf. 14, 14x13½

1939–45 Engraved

217	A41	1e Prussian blue	15	1.25
		a. Perf. 14x13½	1.10	1.50
218	A42	3a dark violet	15	15
		a. Perf. 14x13½	1.40	1.10
219	A41	5a dark brown	15	15
		a. Bklt. pane of 5	1.50	
		c. Perf. 14x13½	1.65	45
220	A42	7a dark green	2.50	3.00
221	"	10a green ('40)	18.00	20
		a. Bklt. pane of 5	100.00	
		b. Perf. 14	22.50	20
222	"	10a slate gray ('45)	20	15
		a. Booklet pane of 5	1.50	
223	"	12a dark green ('43)	20	20
224	A41	25a brt. red ('40)	6.00	15
		a. Bklt. pane of 5	32.50	
		b. Perf. 14x13½	25.00	25
225	"	25a henna brown ('45)	25	15
		a. Bklt. pane of 5	2.25	
226	A42	35a carmine ('43)	40	15
227	A41	50a dark blue green ('43)	40	15
		Typographed.		
228	A43	10a car. & ultra.	1.40	30
		Nos. 217–228 (12)	29.80	6.00

Statue of Thorfinn Karlsefni
A44

1939–47 Engraved ***Perf. 14***

229	A44	2k dark gray	1.50	15
		a. Perf. 11½ ('47)	5.50	60
230	"	5k dark brown ('43)	12.50	25
		a. Perf. 11½ ('47)	20.00	80
231	"	10k brown yel. ('45)	14.00	1.40
		a. Perf. 11½ ('47)	15.00	16.00

New York World's Fair Issue of 1939
Overprinted "1940" in Black.

1940, May 11 ***Perf. 14***

232	A38	20a crimson	12.50	20.00
233	A39	35a bright ultra.	12.50	20.00
234	A40	45a bright green	12.50	20.00
235	"	2k dark gray	85.00	140.00

No. 195 Surcharged in Red

1941, Mar. 6 ***Perf. 12½***

236	A33	25a on 3a gray green	60	50

Statue of Snorri Sturluson
A45

Jon Sigurdsson
A46

1941, Nov. 17 **Engr.** ***Perf. 14***

237	A45	25a rose red	1.00	1.00
238	"	50a deep ultra.	2.50	2.50
239	"	1k dk. olive green	2.50	2.50

Issued to commemorate the 700th anniversary of the death of Snorri Sturluson, writer and historian.

Republic

1944, June 17 ***Perf. 14x13½***

240	A46	10a gray black	35	35
		a. Booklet pane of 5	2.50	
241	"	25a dark red brown	55	40
242	"	50a slate green	55	40
243	"	1k blue black	90	40
244	"	5k henna	7.50	10.00
245	"	10k golden brown	35.00	52.50
		Nos. 240–245 (6)	44.85	62.05

Founding of Republic of Iceland, June 17, 1944.

Eruption of Hekla Volcano
A47

A48

Designs: 35a, 60a, Close view of Hekla.

Engraved.

1948, Dec. 3 ***Perf. 14*** **Unwmkd.**

246	A47	12a dk. violet brown	15	15
247	A48	25a green	2.00	15
248	A47	35a carmine rose	40	15
249	"	50a brown	2.25	15
250	"	60a bright ultra.	7.75	70
251	A48	1k orange brown	18.50	15
252	"	10k violet black	62.50	50
		Nos. 246–252 (7)	93.55	1.95

Pack Train and U.P.U. Monument, Bern
A49

Designs: 35a, Reykjavik. 60a, Map. 2k, Thingvellir Road.

1949, Oct. 9

253	A49	25a dark green	20	20
254	"	35a deep carmine	20	20
255	"	60a blue	40	65
256	"	2k orange red	1.00	65

Issued to commemorate the 75th anniversary of the formation of the Universal Postal Union.

Trawler
A50

Jon Arason
A51

Designs: 20a, 75a, 1k, Tractor plowing. 60a, 5k, Flock of sheep. 5a, 90a, 2k, Vestmannaeyjar harbor. 25a, 1.25k, 1.50k, Same as 10a.

1950–54 ***Perf. 13.***

257	A50	5a dark brown ('54)	8	15
258	"	10a gray	15	25
259	"	20a brown	15	15
260	"	25a carmine ('54)	15	15
261	"	60a green	6.50	13.00
262	"	75a red orange ('52)	35	8
263	"	90a carmine	25	15
264	"	1k chocolate	2.50	12
265	"	1.25k red violet ('52)	6.00	15
266	"	1.50k deep ultra.	5.50	25
267	"	2k purple	10.00	15
268	"	5k dark green	17.50	45
		Nos. 257–268 (12)	49.13	15.05

1950, Nov. 7 ***Perf. 14***

269	A51	1.80k carmine	1.60	1.40
270	"	3.30k green	45	1.20

Issued to commemorate the 400th anniversary of the death of Bishop Jon Arason.

Mail Delivery, 1776
A52

Design: 3k, Airmail, 1951.

1951, May 13

271	A52	2k dp. ultramarine	1.25	50
272	"	3k dark purple	1.50	90

Issued to commemorate the 175th anniversary of Iceland's postal service.

Parliament Building
A53

1952, Apr. 1 *Perf. 13x12½*

273 A53 25k gray black 150.00 8.50

Sveinn Björnsson A54 — Reykjabok A55

1952, Sept. 1 *Perf. 13½*

274 A54 1.25k deep blue 1.35 20
275 " 2.20k deep green 40 *2.25*
276 " 5k indigo 3.00 60
277 " 10k brown red 14.00 9.00

Issued to honor Sveinn Björnsson, first President of Iceland.

1953, Oct. 1 *Perf. 13½x13*

Designs: 70a, Lettering manuscript. 1k, Corner of 15th century manuscript, "Stjorn." 1.75k, Reykjabok. 10k, Corner from law manuscript.

278 A55 10a black 10 10
279 " 70a green 25 25
280 " 1k carmine 30 15
281 " 1.75k blue 10.00 50
282 " 10k orange brown 7.00 35
Nos. 278-282 (5) 17.65 1.35

No. 248 Surcharged With New Value and Bars in Black.

1954, Mar. 31 *Perf. 14*

283 A47 5a on 35a car. rose 10 10
a. Bars omitted 50.00
b. Inverted surcharge 120.00

Hannes Hafstein A56 — Icelandic Wrestling A57

Portraits: 2.45k, in oval. 5k, fullface.

1954, June 1 Engraved *Perf. 13*

284 A56 1.25k deep blue 2.25 20
285 " 2.45k dark green 10.00 12.00
286 " 5k carmine 6.00 60

Issued to commemorate the 50th anniversary of the appointment of the first native minister to Denmark.

1955, Aug. 9 *Perf. 14* **Unwmkd.**

Design: 1.25k, Diving.

287 A57 75a brown 30 20
288 " 1.25k dark blue 35 20

See also Nos. 300-301.

Skoga Falls A58

Ellidaar Power Plant A59

Waterfalls: 60a, Goda. 2kr, Detti. 5kr, Gull. Electric Power Plants: 1.50kr, Sogs. 2.45kr, Andakilsar. 3kr, Laxar.

Perf. 11½, 13½x14 **(A59)**

1956, Apr. 4 **Unwmkd.**

289 A58 15a violet blue 12 12
290 A59 50a dull green 20 12
291 " 60a brown 1.40 1.10
292 " 1.50k violet 5.00 15
293 " 2k sepia 1.00 15
294 " 2.45k gray black 3.75 3.50
295 " 3k dark blue 2.50 35
296 A58 5k dark green 5.00 85
Nos. 289-296 (8) 18.97 6.34

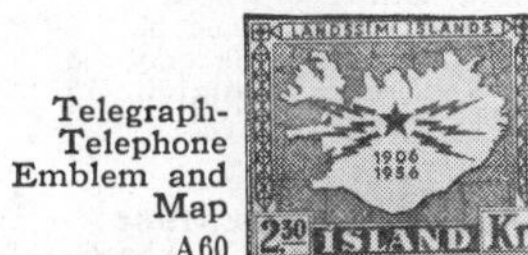

Telegraph-Telephone Emblem and Map A60

1956, Sept. 29 Engr. *Perf. 13*

297 A60 2.30k ultramarine 18 *50*

Issued to commemorate the 50th anniversary of Telegraph and Telephone service in Iceland.

Northern Countries Issue.

Whooper Swans A60a

1956, Oct. 30 *Perf. 12½*

298 A60a 1.50k rose red 75 75
299 " 1.75k ultramarine 5.00 5.00

To emphasize the bonds among Denmark, Finland, Iceland, Norway and Sweden.

Sports Type of 1955.

Designs: 1.50k, Icelandic wrestling. 1.75k, Diving.

1957, Apr. 1 Engraved *Perf. 14*

300 A57 1.50k carmine 65 20
301 " 1.75k ultramarine 30 20

Type of 1952 Air Post Stamps; Plane Omitted.

Glaciers: 2k, Snaefellsjokull. 3k, Eiriksjokull. 10k, Oraefajokull.

1957, May 8 *Perf. 13½x14*

302 AP16 2k green 1.50 18
303 " 3k dark blue 1.50 20
304 " 10k reddish brown 2.50 35

Bessastadir, President's Residence A61

1957, Aug. 1 Engraved **Unwmkd.**

305 A61 25k gray black 10.00 2.00

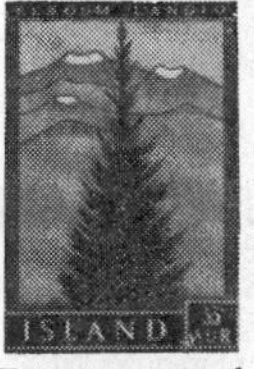

Evergreen and Volcanoes A62 — Jonas Hallgrimsson A63

Design: 70a, Birch.

1957, Sept. 4 *Perf. 13½x13*

306 A62 35a green 7 7
307 " 70a blue green 8 8

Issued to publicize a reforestation program.

1957, Nov 16

308 A63 5k green & black 1.50 55

Issued to commemorate the 150th anniversary of the birth of Jonas Hallgrimsson, poet.

Willow Herb A64 — Icelandic Pony A65

Design: 2.50k, Wild pansy.

1958, July 8 Litho. **Unwmkd.**

309 A64 1k green, blue & rose red 20 20
310 " 2.50k multicolored 45 45

1958, Sept. 27 Engraved

311 A65 10a gray black 6 6
312 " 2.25k brown 45 12

See also No. 324.

Flag A66 — Old Icelandic Government Building A67

Perf. 13½x14

1958, Dec. 1 Litho. **Unwmkd.**

Size: 17½x21mm.

313 A66 3.50k brt. ultra. & red 1.20 55

Size: 23x26½mm.

314 A66 50k bright ultramarine & red 5.00 3.75

40th anniversary of Icelandic flag.

1958, Dec. 9 Photo. *Perf. 11½*

315 A67 2k deep green 50 15
316 " 4k deep brown 60 25

See also Nos. 333-334.

Jon Thorkelsson Teaching—A68

1959, May 5 Engraved *Perf. 13½*

317 A68 2k green 60 50
318 " 3k dull purple 60 55

Issued to commemorate the bicentenary of the death of Jon Thorkelsson, headmaster of Skaholt.

Sockeye Salmon A69

Eider Ducks A70

Design: 25k, Gyrfalcon.

1959-60 Engraved. *Perf. 14*

319 A69 25a dark blue 10 10
320 A70 90a chestnut & black 12 10
321 " 2k olive green & black 30 15
322 A69 5k gray green 2.50 50

Lithographed. *Perf. 11½*

323 A70 25k dull purple, gray & yellow ('60) 6.00 6.00
Nos. 319-323 (5) 9.02 6.85

Pony Type of 1958.

1960, Apr. 7 Engr. *Perf. 13½x13*

324 A65 1k dark carmine 25 12

"The Outlaw" by Einar Jonsson A71 — Wild Geranium A72

1960, Apr. 7 *Perf. 14*

325 A71 2.50k reddish brown 25 15
326 " 4.50k ultramarine 50 50

Issued to publicize World Refugee Year, July 1, 1959–June 30, 1960.

Europa Issue, 1960.

Common Design Type

1960, Sept. 18 Photo. *Perf 11½*

Size: 32½x22mm.

327 CD3 3k green & light green 1.25 65
328 " 5.50k dark blue & light blue 1.00 1.40

1960-62 Photogravure *Perf. 11½*

Flowers: 50a, Bellflower. 2.50k, Dandelion. 3.50k, Buttercup.

329 A72 50a gray green, green & violet ('62) 8 6
330 " 1.20k sepia, violet & green 15 8
331 " 2.50k brown, yellow & green 25 12
332 " 3.50k dull blue, yel. & green ('62) 50 20

See also Nos. 363-366, 393-394.

Building Type of 1958

1961, Apr. 11 *Perf. 11½* **Unwmkd.**

333 A67 1.50k deep blue 35 10
334 " 3k dark carmine 35 10

Jon Sigurdsson A73 — Reykjavik A74

Typographed and Embossed

1961, June 17 *Perf. 12½x14*

335 A73 50a crimson 10 10
336 " 3k dark blue 40 20
337 " 5k deep plum 75 50

Issued to commemorate the 150th anniversary of the birth of Jon Sigurdsson (1811-1879), statesman and scholar.

Common Design Types pictured in section at front of book.

1961, Aug. 18 Photo. ***Perf. 11½***

338 A74 2.50k blue & green 30 20
339 " 4.50k lilac & violet blue 75 40

Municipal charter of Reykjavik, 175th anniversary.

Europa Issue, 1961
Common Design Type

1961, Sept. 18
Size: 32x22½mm.

340 CD4 5.50k multicolored 75 75
341 " 6k " 75 75

Benedikt Sveinsson A75 — University of Iceland A76

Design: 1.40k, Björn M. Olsen.

1961, Oct. 6 Photo. ***Perf. 11½***

342 A75 1k red brown 15 12
343 " 1.40k ultramarine 15 12
344 A76 10k green 1.40 60
a. Souvenir sheet of 3 60 60

Issued to commemorate the 50th anniversary of the founding of the University of Iceland and to honor Benedikt Sveinsson (1827–1899), statesman, and Björn M. Olsen (1850–1919), first rector.

No. 344a contains one each of Nos. 342–344, imperf. Green marginal inscription. Size: 99x50mm.

Production Institute
A77

New Buildings: 4k, Fishing Research Institute. 6k, Farm Bureau.

1962, July 6 ***Perf. 11½*** **Unwmkd.**

345 A77 2.50k ultramarine 25 15
346 " 4k dull green 50 20
347 " 6k brown 60 30

Europa Issue, 1962
Common Design Type

1962, Sept. 17 ***Perf. 11½***
Size: 32½x22½mm.

348 CD5 5.50k yel., lt. green & brown 25 20
349 " 6.50k lt. grn., green & brown 40 40

Map Showing Submarine Telephone Cable
A78

1962, Nov. 20 **Granite Paper**

350 A78 5k multicolored 75 50
351 " 7k grn., lt. blue & red 50 30

Issued to commemorate the inauguration of the submarine telephone cable from Newfoundland, via Greenland and Iceland to Scotland.

Sigurdur Gudmundsson, Self-portrait A79 — Herring Boat A80

Design: 5.50k, Knight slaying dragon, Romanesque door from Valthjofsstad Church, ca. 1200A.D.

1963, Feb. 20 Photo. ***Perf. 11½***

352 A79 4k bister brown & choc. 45 25
353 " 5.50k gray olive & brown 25 25

Issued to commemorate the centenary of the founding of the National Museum of Iceland, and to honor the first curator, Sigurdur Gudmundsson.

1963, Mar. 21

354 A80 5k multicolored 85 30
355 " 7.50k " 25 25

Issued for the "Freedom from Hunger" campaign of the U.N. Food and Agriculture Organization.

View of Akureyri
A81

1963, July 2 ***Perf. 11½*** **Unwmkd.**

356 A81 3k gray green 20 15

Europa Issue, 1963
Common Design Type

1963, Sept. 16
Size: 32½x23mm.

357 CD6 6k orge. brn. & yel. 40 30
358 " 7k blue & yellow 40 30

M.S. Gullfoss
A82

1964, Jan. 17 Photo. ***Perf. 11½***

359 A82 10k ultra., black & gray 1.25 90
a. Accent on 2nd "E" omitted 14.00 12.00

Issued to commemorate the 50th anniversary of the Iceland Steamship Company.

Scout Emblem and "Be Prepared" A83 — Icelandic Coat of Arms A84

1964, Apr. 24

360 A83 3.50k multicolored 50 20
361 " 4.50k " 50 30

Issued to honor the Boy Scouts.

1964, June 17 ***Perf. 11½***

362 A84 25k multicolored 2.50 1.50

20th anniversary, Republic of Iceland.

Flower Type of 1960–62.

Flowers: 50a, Eight-petal dryas. 1k, Crowfoot (Ranunculus glacialis). 1.50k, Buck bean. 2k, Clover (trifolium repens).

1964, July 15
Flowers in Natural Colors

363 A72 50a violet blue & light violet bl. 8 5
364 " 1k gray & dk. gray 8 5
365 " 1.50k brn. & pale brn. 15 6
366 " 2k olive & pale olive 20 8

Europa Issue, 1964
Common Design Type

1964, Sept. 14 Photo. ***Perf. 11½***
Granite Paper
Size: 22½x33mm.

367 CD7 4.50k golden brown, yellow & Prus. green 50 25
368 " 9k blue, yellow & dk. brn. 50 25

Runner
A85

1964, Oct. 20 ***Perf. 11½*** **Unwmkd.**

369 A85 10k lt. grn. & black 1.10 60

18th Olympic Games, Tokyo, Oct. 10–25.

ITU Emblem
A86

1965, May 17 Photo. ***Perf. 11½***

370 A86 4.50k green 75 25
371 " 7.50k bright ultra. 25 25

Issued to commemorate the centenary of the International Telecommunication Union.

Surtsey Island, April 1964
A87

Designs: 1.50k, Underwater volcanic eruption, November, 1963 (vert.). 3.50k, Surtsey, September, 1964.

1965, June 23 ***Perf. 11½*** **Unwmkd.**

372 A87 1.50k bl., bister & blk. 55 35
373 " 2k multicolored 60 60
374 " 3.50k blue, black & red 80 55

Issued to commemorate the emergence of a new volcanic island off the southern coast of Iceland.

Europa Issue, 1965
Common Design Type

1965, Sept. 27 Photo. ***Perf. 11½***
Size: 33x22½mm.

375 CD8 5k tan, brown & bright green 60 35
376 " 8k bright green, brn. & yellow green 60 40

Einar Benediktsson
A88

Engraved and Lithographed

1965, Nov. 16 ***Perf. 14*** **Unwmkd.**

377 A88 10k bright blue & brown 1.75 1.35

Issued to honor the poet Einar Benediktsson (1864–1940).

White-tailed Sea Eagle A89 — National Costume A90

1965–66 Photo. ***Perf. 11½***

378 A89 50k multi. ('66) 4.50 4.00
379 A90 100k multicolored 5.50 5.00

Issue dates: No. 378, Apr. 26, 1966; No. 379, Dec. 3, 1965.

West Iceland
A91

Designs: 4k, North Iceland. 5k, East Iceland. 6.50k, South Iceland.

1966, Aug. 4 Photo. ***Perf. 11½***

380 A91 2.50k multicolored 30 15
381 " 4k " 40 18
382 " 5k " 45 20
383 " 6.50k " 50 20

Europa Issue, 1966
Common Design Type

1966, Sept. 26 Photo. ***Perf. 11½***
Size: 22½x33mm.

384 CD9 7k greenish blue, lt. blue & red 35 25
385 " 8k brn., buff & red 35 30

Literary Society Emblem
A92

1966, Nov. 18 Engraved ***Perf. 11½***

386 A92 4k ultramarine 35 20
387 " 10k vermilion 60 50

Issued to commemorate the 150th anniversary of the Icelandic Literary Society.

Common Loon
A93

1967, March 16 Photo. ***Perf. 11½***

388 A93 20k multicolored 2.50 1.75

Europa Issue, 1967

Common Design Type

1967, May 2 Photo. *Perf. 11½*

Size: 22½x33mm.

389 CD10 7k yellow, brown & dk. blue 35 35
390 " 8k emerald, gray & dk. blue 40 35

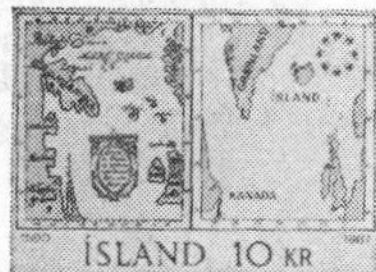

Old and New Maps of Iceland and North America
A94

1967, June 8 Photo. *Perf. 11½*

391 A94 10k blk., tan & lt. bl. 50 40

Issued to commemorate EXPO '67 International Exhibition, Montreal, Apr. 28–Oct. 27, 1967. The old map, drawn about 1590 by Sigurdur Stefansson, is at the Royal Library, Copenhagen.

Symbols of Trade, Fishing, Husbandry and Industry
A95

1967, Sept. 14 Photo. *Perf. 11½*

392 A95 5k dk. blue, yellow & emerald 40 30

Issued to commemorate the 50th anniversary of the Icelandic Chamber of Commerce.

Flower Type of 1960–62

Flowers: 50a, Saxifraga oppositifolia. 2.50k, Orchis maculata.

1968, Jan. 17 Photo. *Perf. 11½*

Flowers in Natural Colors

393 A72 50a grn. & dk. brn. 10 10
394 " 2.50k dk. brown, yel. & green 25 15

Europa Issue, 1968

Common Design Type

1968, Apr. 29 Photo. *Perf. 11½*

Size: 33½x23mm.

395 CD11 9.50k dull yel., car. rose & blk. 35 30
396 " 10k brt. yel. green, blk. & org. 35 30

Right-hand Driving
A96

1968, May 21 Photo. *Perf. 11½*

397 A96 4k yellow & brown 20 12
398 " 5k lt. reddish brown 25 15

Issued to publicize the introduction of right-hand driving in Iceland, May 26, 1968.

Fridrik Fridriksson, by Sigurjón Olafsson
A97

1968, Sept. 5 Photo. *Perf. 11½*

399 A97 10k sky blue & dark gray 45 35

Issued to commemorate the centenary of the birth of the Rev. Fridrik Fridriksson (1868–1961), founder of the YMCA in Reykjavik and writer.

Reading Room, National Library
A98

Prime Minister Jon Magnusson (1859–1926)
A99

1968, Oct. 30 Photo. *Perf. 11½*

Granite Paper

400 A98 5k yellow & brown 30 15
401 " 20k lt. bl. & dp. ultra. 1.00 75

Issued to commemorate the sesquicentennial of the National Library, Reykjavik.

1968, Dec. 12 Granite Paper

402 A99 4k carmine lake 25 15
403 " 50k dark brown 3.50 2.50

Issued to commemorate the 50th anniversary of independence.

Nordic Cooperation Issue

Five Ancient Ships
A99a

1969, Feb. 28 Engraved *Perf. 12½*

404 A99a 6.50k vermilion 30 20
405 " 10k bright blue 30 30

See footnote after Norway No. 524.

Europa Issue, 1969

Common Design Type

1969, Apr. 28 Photo. *Perf. 11½*

Size: 32½x23mm.

406 CD12 13k pink & multi. 50 35
407 " 14.50k yel. & multi. 50 40

Flag of Iceland and Rising Sun
A100

1969, June 17 Photo. *Perf. 11½*

408 A100 25k gray, gold, vio. blue & red 1.00 60
409 " 100k lt. bl., gold, vio. blue & red 4.00 3.50

25th anniversary, Republic of Iceland.

Boeing 727
A101

Design: 12k, Rolls Royce 400.

1969, Sept. 3 Photo. *Perf. 11½*

410 A101 9.50k dark blue & sky blue 30 30
411 " 12k dark blue & ultra. 45 30

50th anniversary of Icelandic aviation.

Snaefellsjökull Mountain
A102

Views: 4k, Laxfoss. 5k, Hattver (vert.). 20k, Fjardargil (vert.).

1970, Jan. 6 Photo. *Perf. 11½*

412 A102 1k multicolored 15 10
413 " 4k " 20 15
414 " 5k " 20 15
415 " 20k " 90 40

First Meeting of Icelandic Supreme Court
A103

1970, Feb. 16 Photo. *Perf. 11½*

416 A103 6.50k multicolored 25 20

Issued to commemorate the 50th anniversary of the Icelandic Supreme Court.

Column from "Skarosbók," 1363 (Law Book)
A104

Icelandic Manuscripts: 15k, Preface to "Flateyjarbók" (History of Norwegian Kings), 1387–1394. 30k, Initial from "Flateyjarbók" showing Harald Fairhair cutting fetters of Dofri.

1970, Mar. 20 Photo. *Perf. 11½*

417 A104 5k multicolored 20 20
418 " 15k " 60 50
419 " 30k " 1.40 1.00

Europa Issue, 1970

Common Design Type

1970, May 4 Photo. *Perf. 11½*

Size: 32x22mm.

420 CD13 9k brown & yellow 40 20
421 " 25k brt. grn. & bister 80 60

Nurse
A105

Grimur Thomsen
A106

The Rest, by Thorarinn B. Thorlaksson
A107

1970, June 19 Photo. *Perf. 11½*

422 A105 7k ultra. & lt. blue 30 20
423 A106 10k indigo & light greenish blue 45 35
424 A107 50k gold & multi. 2.00 1.50

No. 422 commemorates the 50th anniversary (in 1969) of the Icelandic Nursing Association; No. 423 the 150th anniversary of the birth of Grimur Thomsen (1820–1896), poet; No. 424 publicizes the International Arts Festival, Reykjavik, June 1970.

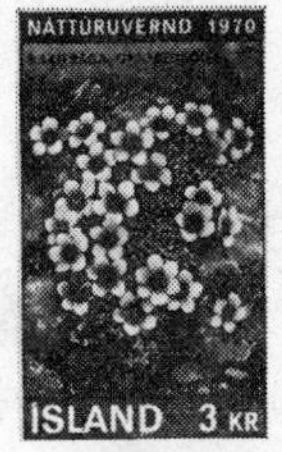

Saxifraga Oppositifolia
A108

Lakagigar
A109

1970, Aug. 25 Photo. *Perf. 11½*

425 A108 3k multicolored 12 12
426 A109 15k " 45 35

European Nature Conservation Year.

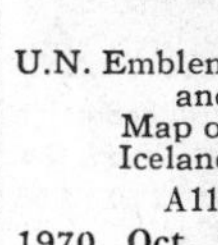

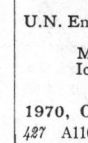

U.N. Emblem and Map of Iceland
A110

1970, Oct. 23 Photo. *Perf. 11½*

427 A110 12k multicolored 50 50

25th anniversary of United Nations.

"Flight," by Asgrimur Jonsson
A111

1971, March 26 Photo. *Perf. 11½*

428 A111 10k multicolored 40 25

Joint northern campaign for the benefit of refugees.

Europa Issue, 1971

Common Design Type

1971, May 3 Photo. *Perf. 11½*

Size: 33x22mm.

429 CD14 7k rose claret, yel. & black 25 20
430 " 15k ultra., yellow & black 40 30

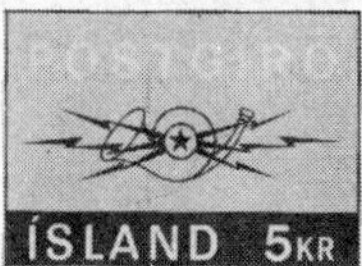

Postal Checking Service Emblem—A112

1971, June 22 Photo. *Perf. 11½*

431 A112 5k vio. blue & lt. bl. 12 12
432 " 7k dk. green & yellow green 20 20

Introduction of Postal Checking Service, Apr. 30, 1971.

Tryggvi Gunnarsson
A113

Haddock Freezing Plant
A114

Design: 30k, Patriotic Society emblem.

1971, Aug. 19 Photo. *Perf. 11½*

433 A113 30k lt. bl. & vio. blk. 1.25 90
434 " 100k gray & vio. blk. 4.50 3.25

Centenary of the Icelandic Patriotic Society and to honor Tryggvi Gunnarsson (1835–1917), founder and president.

1971, Nov. 18

Designs: 7k, Cod fishing. 20k, Lobster canning plant.

435 A114 5k multicolored 15 15
436 " 7k " 20 20
437 " 20k green & multi. 60 50

Fish industry.

Herdubreid Mountain
A115

Engraved and Lithographed

1972, Mar. 9 *Perf. 14*

438 A115 250k blue & multi. 2.50 2.50

Europa Issue 1972
Common Design Type

1972, May 2 Photo. *Perf. 11½*

Size: 22x32mm.

439 CD15 9k lt. violet & multi. 25 25
440 " 13k yel. grn. & multi. 50 35

"United Municipalities"
A116

1972, June 14 Photo. *Perf. 11½*

441 A116 16k multicolored 45 40

Centenary of legislation for local government.

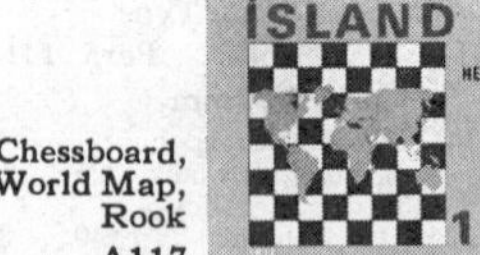

Chessboard, World Map, Rook
A117

1972, July 2 Litho. *Perf. 13*

442 A117 15k lt. olive & multi. 55 50

World Chess Championship, Reykjavik, July–Sept. 1972.

Hothouse Tomatoes
A118

Designs: 12k, Steam valve and natural steam. 40k, Hothouse roses.

1972, Aug. 23 Photo. *Perf. 11½*

443 A118 8k Prus. bl. & multi. 25 25
444 A118 12k green & multi. 25 25
445 " 40k dk. pur. & multi. 1.10 1.00

Hothouse gardening in Iceland, using natural steam and hot springs.

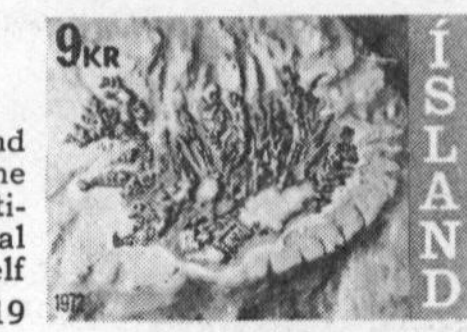

Iceland and the Continental Shelf
A119

1972, Sept. 27 Litho. *Perf. 13*

446 A119 9k blue & multi. 25 25

To publicize Iceland's offshore fishing rights.

Europa Issue 1973
Common Design Type

1973, Apr. 30 Photo. *Perf. 11½*

Size: 32½x22mm.

447 CD16 13k violet & multi. 60 50
448 " 25k olive & multi. 50 50

Iceland No. 1 and Messenger
A120

Designs (First Issue of Iceland and): 15k, No. 5 and pony train. 20k, No. 2 and mailboat "Esja." 40k, No. 3 and mail truck. 80k, No. 4 and Beech-18 mail plane.

1973, May 23 *Perf. 13x13½*

Lithographed and Engraved

449 A120 10k dull blue, black & ultra. 25 25
450 " 15k grn., blk. & gray 25 25
451 " 20k maroon, black & carmine 40 40
452 " 40k vio., blk. & brn. 65 65
453 " 80k olive, black & yellow 2.00 2.00
Nos. 449-453 (5) 3.55 3.55

Centenary of Iceland's first postage stamps.

Nordic Cooperation Issue

Nordic House, Reykjavik
A120a

1973, June 26 Engr. *Perf. 12½*

454 A120a 9k multicolored 20 20
455 " 10k " 50 25

A century of postal cooperation among Denmark, Finland, Iceland, Norway and Sweden, and in connection with the Nordic Postal Conference, Reykjavik.

Ásgeir Ásgeirsson
A121

1973, Aug. 1 Engr. *Perf. 13x13½*

456 A121 13k carmine 50 30
457 " 15k blue 40 35

Ásgeir Ásgeirsson (1894–1972), President of Iceland 1952–1968.

Islandia 73 Emblem
A122

Design: 20k, Islandia 73 emblem; different arrangement.

1973, Aug. 31 Photo. *Perf. 11½*

458 A122 17k gray & multi. 60 40
459 " 20k brown, ocher & yellow 35 35

Islandia 73 Philatelic Exhibition, Reykjavik, Aug. 31–Sept. 9.

Man and WMO Emblem
A123

The Settlement, Tapestry by Vigdis Kristjansdottir
A124

1973, Nov. 14 Photo. *Perf. 12½*

460 A123 50k silv. & multi. 1.00 1.00

Centenary of international meteorological cooperation.

1974 Photogravure *Perf. 11½*

Designs: 13k, Establishment of Althing, painting by Johannes Johannesson (horiz.). 15k, Gudbrandur Thorlakkson, Bishop of Holar 1571–1627. 17k, Age of Sturlungar (Fighting Vikings), drawing by Thorvaldur Skulason. 20k, Stained glass window honoring Hallgrimur Petursson (1614–74), hymn writer. 25k, Illumination from Book of Flatey, 14th century. 30k, Conversion to Christianity (altarpiece, Skalholt), mosaic by Nina Tryggvadottir. 40k, Wood carving (family and plants), 18th century. 60k, Curing the Catch, cement bas-relief. 70k, Age of Writing (Saemundur Riding Seal), sculpture by Asmundur Sveinsson. 100k, Virgin and Child with Angels, embroidered antependium, Stafafell Church, 14th century.

461 A124 10k multicolored 20 20
462 " 13k " 30 30
463 " 15k " 35 35
464 " 17k " 40 35
465 " 20k " 50 50
466 " 25k " 50 50
467 " 30k " 60 60
468 " 40k " 1.00 1.00
469 " 60k " 1.50 1.25
470 " 70k " 1.60 1.50
471 " 100k " 2.50 2.00
Nos. 461-471 (11) 9.45 8.55

1100th anniversary of settlement of Iceland.

Issue dates: 10k, 13k, 30k, 70k, Mar. 12; 17k, 25k, 100k, June 11; 15k, 20k, 40k, 60k, July 16.

Europa Issue 1974

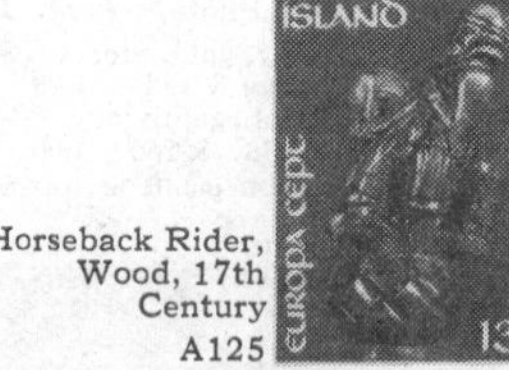

Horseback Rider, Wood, 17th Century
A125

Design: 20k, "Through the Sound Barrier," contemporary bronze by Asmundur Sveinsson.

1974, Apr. 29 Photo. *Perf. 11½*

472 A125 13k brn. red & multi. 20 20
473 " 20k gray & multi. 50 50

Clerk selling Stamps, UPU Emblem
A126

Design: 20k, Mailman delivering mail.

1974, Oct. 9 Photo. *Perf. 11½*

474 A126 17k ocher & multi. 30 30
475 " 20k olive & multi. 30 30

Centenary of Universal Postal Union.

Volcanic Eruption, Heimaey, 1973
A127

Design: 25k, Volcanic eruption, night view.

1975, Jan. 23 Photo. *Perf. 11½*

476 A127 20k multicolored 40 40
477 " 25k " 35 35

Volcanic eruption, Jan. 23, 1973.

Europa Issue 1975

Bird, by Thorvaldur Skulason
A128

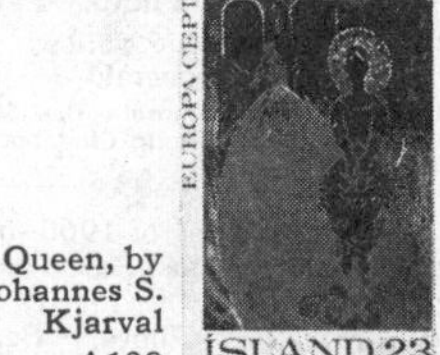

Sun Queen, by Johannes S. Kjarval
A129

1975, May 12 Photo. *Perf. 11½*

478 A128 18k multicolored 25 25
479 A129 23k gold & multi. 30 30

Stephan G. Stephansson
A130

1975, Aug. 1 Engr. *Perf. 13*

480 A130 27k green & brown 70 50

Stephan G. Stephansson (1853–1927), Icelandic poet and settler in North America; centenary of Icelandic emigration to North America.

Petursson, by Hjalti Thorsteinsson
A131

Einar Jonsson, Self-portrait
A132

Portraits: 23k, Arni Magnusson, by Hjalti Thorsteinsson. 30k, Jon Eiriksson, sculpture by Olafur Olafsson.

1975, Sept. 18 **Engr.** ***Perf. 13***

481 A131 18k slate green & indigo 25 25
482 " 23k Prussian blue 30 30
483 " 30k deep magenta 35 35
484 A132 50k indigo 60 60

Famous Icelanders: Hallgrimur Petursson (1614–1674), minister and religious poet; Arni Magnusson (1663–1730), historian, registrar and manuscript collector; Jon Eiriksson (1728–1787), professor of law and cabinet member; Einar Jonsson (1874–1954), sculptor, painter and writer.

Red Cross
A133

1975, Oct. 15 Photo. ***Perf. 11½x12***

485 A133 23k multicolored 30 30

Icelandic Red Cross, 50th anniversary.

Abstract Painting, by Nina Tryggvadottir
A134

1975, Oct. 15 ***Perf. 12x12½***

486 A134 100k multicolored 1.75 1.50

International Women's Year 1975.

Thorvaldsen Statue, by Thorvaldsen
A135

Saplings Growing in Bare Landscape
A136

1975, Nov. 19 **Photo.** ***Perf. 11½***

487 A135 27k lt. vio. & multi. 70 45

Centenary of Thorvaldsen Society, a charity honoring Bertel Thorvaldsen (1768–1844), sculptor.

1975, Nov. 19 ***Perf. 12x11½***

488 A136 35k multicolored 50 40

Reforestation.

Langjökull Glacier, by Asgrimur Jonsson
A137

1976, Mar. 18 **Photo.** ***Perf. 11½***

489 A137 150k gold & multi. 2.50 2.00

Asgrimur Jonsson (1876–1958), painter, birth centenary.

Europa Issue 1976

Wooden Bowl
A138

Design: 45k, Spinning wheel (vert.).

1976, May 3 **Photo.** ***Perf. 11½***

490 A138 35k verm. & multi. 50 50
491 " 45k blue & multi. 80 60

No. 9 with First Day Cancel
A139

1976, Sept. 22 **Photo.** ***Perf. 11½***

Granite Paper

492 A139 30k bister, black & gray blue 40 30

Centenary of aurar stamps.

Decree Establishing Postal Service
A140

1976, Sept. 22 **Engr.** ***Perf. 13***

Design: 45k, Conclusion of Decree with signatures.

493 A140 35k dark brown 55 40
494 " 45k dark blue 50 40

Iceland's Postal Service, bicentenary.

Federation Emblem, People
A141

1976, Dec. 2 **Photo.** ***Perf. 12½***

Granite Paper

495 A141 100k multicolored 1.35 1.00

Icelandic Federation of Labor, 60th anniversary.

Five Water Lilies
A142

Ofaerufoss, Eldgja
A143

Photogravure and Engraved

1977, Feb. 2 ***Perf. 12½***

496 A142 35k brt. green & multicolored 50 50
497 " 45k ultra. & multi. 60 60

Nordic countries cooperation for protection of the environment and 25th Session of Nordic Council, Helsinki, Feb. 19.

Europa Issue 1977

Design: 85k, Kirkjufell Mountain, seen from Grundarfjord.

1977, May 2 **Photo.** ***Perf. 12***

498 A143 45k multicolored 60 60
499 " 85k " 90 90

Harlequin Duck
A144

1977, June 14 **Photo.** ***Perf. 11½***

500 A144 40k multicolored 45 40

Wetlands conservation, European campaign.

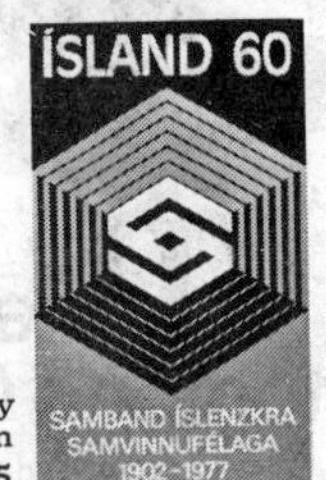

Society Emblem
A145

1977, June 14

501 A145 60k vio. bl. & ultra. 70 70

Federation of Icelandic Cooperative Societies, 75th anniversary.

Hot Springs, Therapeutic Bath, Emblem
A146

1977, Nov. 16 **Photo.** ***Perf. 11½***

502 A146 90k multicolored 1.00 80

World Rheumatism Year.

Stone Marker
A147

1977, Dec. 12 **Engr.** ***Perf. 11½***

503 A147 45k dark blue 70 45

Touring Club of Iceland, 50th anniversary.

Thorvaldur Thoroddsen
A148

Design: 60k, Briet Bjarnhedinsdottir.

1977, Dec. 12 **Engr.** ***Perf. 11½***

504 A148 50k brown & slate green 50 50
505 " 60k green & violet brown 60 60

Thorvaldur Thoroddsen (1855–1921), geologist, scientist and writer; Briet Bjarnhedinsdottir (1856–1940), Founder of Icelandic Women's Association and Reykjavik city councillor.

Europa Issue 1978

Bailiff's Residence, Videy Island, 1752
A149

Design: 120k, Husavik Church, 1906 (vert.).

1978, May 2 **Photo.** ***Perf. 11½***

506 A149 80k multicolored 80 80
507 " 120k " 1.20 1.20

Alexander Johannesson, Junkers Planes
A150

Design: 100k, Fokker Friendship plane over mountains.

1978, June 21 **Photo.** ***Perf. 12½***

508 A150 60k multicolored 48 45
509 " 100k " 80 80

50th anniversary of domestic flights in Iceland.

Skeioara River Bridge
A151

1978, Aug. 17 **Photo.** ***Perf. 11½***

510 A151 70k multicolored 55 55

Lava near Mt. Hekla, by Jon Stefansson—A152

1978, Nov. 16 **Photo.** ***Perf. 12***

511 A152 1000k multi. 8.00 8.00

Jon Stefansson (1881–1962), Icelandic painter.

Ship to Shore Rescue
A153

1978, Dec. 1 **Engr.** ***Perf. 13***

512 A153 60k black 48 45

National Life Saving Association, 50th anniversary.

Halldor Hermannsson
A154

Lighthouse
A155

1978, Dec. 1

513 A154 150k indigo 1.20 1.20

Halldor Hermannsson (1878–1958), historian and librarian.

1978, Dec. 1 Photo. *Perf. 11½*

514 A155 90k multicolored 70 70

Centenary of Icelandic lighthouses.

SEMI-POSTAL STAMPS.

Shipwreck and Rescue by Breeches Buoy
SP1

Children Gathering Rock Plants
SP2

Old Fisherman at Shore—SP3

Engraved.

1933, Apr. 28 ***Perf. 14*** **Unwmkd.**

B1	SP1	10a+10a red brown	1.25	2.50
B2	SP2	20a+20a orange red	1.25	2.50
B3	SP1	35a+25a ultra.	1.25	2.50
B4	SP3	50a+25a blue green	1.25	2.50

Receipts from the surtax were devoted to a special fund for use in various charitable works especially those indicated on the stamps: "Slysavarnir" (Rescue work), "Barnahaeli" (Asylum for scrofulous children), "Elliheimili" (Asylum for the Aged).

Souvenir Sheets.

King Christian X—SP4

1937, May 15 **Typographed**

B5	SP4	Sheet of three	37.50	*125.00*
		a. 15a violet	8.00	*22.50*
		b. 25a red	8.00	*22.50*
		c. 50a blue	8.00	*22.50*

25th anniversary of the accession to the throne of King Christian X. Sheet sold for 2kr. Size: 132x115mm.

SP5

Designs: 30a, 40a, Ericsson statue, Reykjavik. 60a, Iceland's position on globe.

1938, Oct. 9 **Photo.** ***Perf. 12***

B6	SP5	Sheet of three	4.00	*20.00*
		a. 30a scarlet	90	*3.50*
		b. 40a purple	90	*3.50*
		c. 60a deep green	90	*3.50*

Leif Ericsson Day Oct. 9, 1938. Size: 144½x100mm.

Ill Child
SP6

Red Cross Nurse and Patient
SP7

Nurse Covering Patient
SP8

Elderly Couple
SP9

Rescue at Sea
SP10

Engraved.

1949, June 8 ***Perf. 14*** **Unwmkd.**

B7	SP6	10a+10a olive green	40	55
B8	SP7	35a+15a carmine	40	55
B9	SP8	50a+25a chocolate	45	55
B10	SP9	60a+25a brt. ultra.	45	55
B11	SP10	75a+25a slate gray	60	60
		Nos. B7-B11 (5)	2.30	2.80

The surtax was for charitable purposes.

Nos. 262 and 265 Surcharged in Black — Hollandshjálp 1953 +25

1953, Feb. 12 ***Perf 13*** **Unwmkd.**

B12	A50	75a+25(a) red orange	35	1.35
B13	"	1.25k+25(a) red violet	75	1.35

The surtax was for flood relief in the Netherlands.

St. Thorlacus
SP11

Cathedral at Skalholt
SP12

Portrait: 1.75(k)+1.25(k), Bishop Jon Thorkelsson Vidalin.

1956, Jan. 23 ***Perf. 11½***

B14	SP11	75a+25a carmine	25	40
B15	SP12	1.25k+75a dark brown	25	40
B16	SP11	1.75k+1.25k black	60	80

Issued to commemorate the 900th anniversary of the Bishopric of Skalholt.

The surtax was for the rebuilding of Skalholt, former cultural center of Iceland.

Ambulance
SP13

1963, Nov. 15 **Photo.** **Unwmkd.**

B17	SP13	3k+50a multi.	15	15
B18	"	3.50k+50a "	30	20

Centenary of International Red Cross.

Rock Ptarmigan in Summer
SP14

Design: 4.50k+50a, Rock ptarmigan in winter.

1965, Jan. 27 **Photo.** ***Perf. 12½***

Granite Paper

B19	SP14	3.50k+50a multi.	40	40
B20	"	4.50k+50a blk., lt. blue & gray	60	60

Ringed Plover's Nest
SP15

Arctic Terns
SP16

Design: 5k+50a, Rock ptarmigan's nest.

1967, Nov. 22 **Photo.** ***Perf. 11½***

B21	SP15	4k+50a multi.	40	40
B22	"	5k+50a "	40	40

1972, Nov. 22 **Litho.** ***Perf. 13***

B23	SP16	7k+1k bl. & multi.	25	25
B24	"	9k+1k multi.	30	30

AIR POST STAMPS.

No. 115 Overprinted

Wmkd. Multiple Crosses. (114)

1928, May 31 ***Perf. 14x14½***

C1	A8	10a red	90	3.00

Same Overprint on No. 82.

1929, June 29 ***Perf. 13*** **Wmk. 113**

C2	A5	50a gray & violet	25.00	30.00

Gyrfalcon
AP1

Perf. 12½x12

1930, Jan. 1 **Litho.** **Unwmkd.**

C3	AP1	10a deep ultramarine & gray blue	12.00	32.50
		a. Imperf., pair		

Parliament Millenary Issue.

Snaefellsjokull, Extinct Volcano
AP2

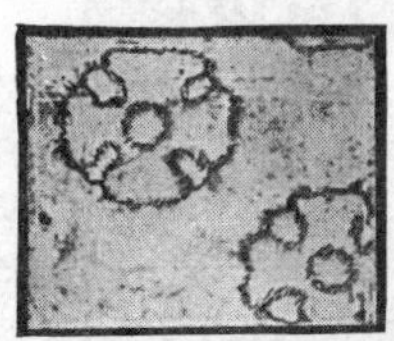
Wmk. 47

Designs: 20a, Fishing boat. 35a, Iceland pony. 50a, Gullfoss (Golden Falls). 1k, Ingolfour Arnarson Statue.

Wmkd. Multiple Rosette. (47)

1930, June 1 **Typo.** ***Perf. 14***

C4	AP2	15a orange brown & dull blue	12.00	25.00
C5	"	20a bistre brown & slate blue	12.00	25.00
C6	"	35a olive green & brown	27.50	40.00
C7	"	50a deep green & deep blue	27.50	40.00
C8	"	1k olive green & dark red	27.50	40.00
		Nos. C4-C8 (5)	106.50	170.00

Regular Issue of 1920 Overprinted — Zeppelin 1931

Perf. 14x14½

1931, May 25 **Wmk. 114**

C9	A8	30a red & green	30.00	55.00
C10	"	1k deep blue & dark brown	13.00	55.00
C11	"	2k olive brown & myrtle green	35.00	55.00

Nos. 185, 128 and 187 Overprinted in Red

1933, June 16

C12	A8	1k dark blue & lt. brown	150.00	250.00
C13	"	5k brn. & indigo	375.00	600.00
C14	"	10k yellow green & black	675.00	1300.00

Excellent counterfeit overprints exist.

Issued in commemoration of the visit of the Italian Flying Armada en route from Rome to Chicago; also for the payment of the charges on postal matter sent from Iceland to the United States via the Italian seaplanes.

Plane over Thingvalla Lake
AP7

Designs: 10a, 20a, Plane over Thingvalla Lake. 25a, 50a, Plane and Aurora Borealis. 1k, 2k, Map of Iceland.

Perf. 12½x14

1934, Sept. 1 Engr. Unwmkd.

C15 AP7 10a blue 75 1.00
C16 " 20a emerald 1.75 1.75
a. Perf. 14 6.50 3.00
C17 " 25a dark violet 6.00 6.00
a. Perf. 14 8.50 6.00
C18 " 50a red violet, perf. 14 3.00 1.50
C19 " 1k dark brown 13.00 14.00
C20 " 2k red orange 5.50 3.75
Nos. C15-C20 (6) 30.00 28.00

Thingvellir, Old Site of the Parliament
AP10

Isafjörthur
AP11

Eyjafjörthur
AP12

Mt. Strandatindur AP13 Mt. Thyrill AP14

Aerial View of Reykjavik
AP15

1947, Aug. 18 Perf. 14

C21 AP10 15a red orange 20 45
C22 AP11 30a gray black 20 50
C23 AP12 75a brown red 30 35
C24 AP13 1k indigo 35 35
C25 AP14 2k chocolate 1.00 1.00
C26 AP15 3k dark green 1.00 80
Nos. C21-C26 (6) 3.05 3.45

Snaefellsjokull
AP16

Views: 2.50k, Eiriksjokull. 3.30k, Oraefajokull.

Perf. 13½x14

1952, May 2 Unwmkd.

C27 AP16 1.80k slate blue 5.00 4.25
C28 " 2.50k green 10.00 85
C29 " 3.30k deep ultra. 5.00 1.50

Vickers Viscount and Plane of 1919
AP17

Design: 4.05k, Skymaster and plane of 1919.

1959, Sept. 3 Engraved. *Perf. 13½*

C30 AP17 3.50k steel blue 55 45
C31 " 4.05k green 25 20

Issued to commemorate the 40th anniversary of air transportation in Iceland.

AIR POST OFFICIAL STAMPS.

No. C3 Overprinted In Red

Þjónustumerki

Perf. 12½x12

1930, Jan. 1 Unwmkd.

CO1 AP1 10a deep ultra. & gray bl. 27.50 *90.00*
a. Imperf.

OFFICIAL STAMPS.

O1 O2 O3

Wmkd. Crown. (112)

1873 Typographed *Perf. 14x13½*

O1 O1 4s green *3250.00 3250.00*
a. Imperf. 90.00
O2 " 8s red lilac 275.00 250.00
a. Imperf. 275.00

Perf. 12½

O3 O1 4s green 50.00 *150.00*

The imperforate varieties lack gum.

1876-95 *Perf. 14x13½*

O4 O2 3a yellow 14.00 25.00
O5 " 5a brown 4.25 7.50
a. Imperf. 185.00
O6 " 10a blue 25.00 6.25
a. 10a ultramarine 200.00 20.00
O7 " 16a carmine 7.50 15.00
O8 " 20a yellow green 6.25 12.50
O9 " 50a rose lilac ('95) 35.00 35.00

1898-1902 *Perf. 13*

O10 O2 3a yellow 5.00 11.00
O11 " 4a gray ('01) 15.00 15.00
O12 " 10a ultra. ('02) 15.00 37.50

A 5a brown, perf. 13, Wmk. 112, exists. It was not regularly issued.
See note after No. O30.

Wmkd. Crown. (113)

1902 *Perf. 13*

O13 O3 3a buff & black 1.50 75
O14 " 4a dp. green & black 2.50 75
O15 " 5a orange brown & black 80 1.40
O16 " 10a ultra. & black 1.00 1.40
O17 " 16a carmine & black 1.10 6.00
O18 " 20a green & black 6.00 2.50
O19 " 50a violet & black 2.75 5.00
Nos. O13-O19 (7) 15.65 17.80

Stamps of 1876-1901 Overprinted in Black **Í GILDI '02—'03**

Wmkd. Crown. (112)

1902-03 *Perf. 13*

O20 O2 3a yellow 70 1.00
a. "I" before Gildi omitted 12.00
b. Inverted overprint 6.00 7.25
c. Same as "a" invtd. 100.00
d. Pair, one with inverted overprint 40.00
e. '03-'03 65.00
f. 02'-'03 65.00
O21 " 4a gray 70 1.00
a. "I" before Gildi omitted 32.50
b. Inverted overprint 14.00 16.00
e. '03-'03 95.00 100.00
f. 02'-'03 95.00
g. Pair, one without ovpt. 32.50
h. Pair, one with invtd. ovpt. 35.00 40.00
i. "L" only of "I GILDI" invtd. 170.00
O22 " 5a brown 50 1.00
O23 " 10a ultramarine 55 1.00
a. "I" before Gild omitted 18.00
b. Inverted overprint 9.00 9.00
c. '03-'03 60.00
d. 02'-'03 60.00
e. "L" only of "I GILDI" 21.00
f. Same as "e" invtd. 30.00
g. "IL" only of "I GILDI" 24.00
O24 " 20a yellow green 50 *12.50*
Nos. O20-O24 (5) 2.95 16.50

Perf. 14x13½.

O25 O2 3a yellow 150.00 300.00
a. "02'-'03" 240.00
O26 " 5a brown 5.00 *55.00*
a. Inverted overprint 10.00 *62.50*
b. '03-'03 65.00
c. 02'-'03 65.00
d. "L" only of "I GILDI" invtd. 165.00
O27 " 10a blue 200.00 *350.00*
a. "I" before Gildi omitted 225.00
b. Inverted overprint 225.00 *400.00*
c. '03-'03 240.00
d. 02'-'03 240.00
O28 " 16a carmine 5.00 *30.00*
a. "I" before Gildi omitted 120.00
b. Double overprint 27.50 55.00
c. Double overprint, one inverted 60.00
d. Inverted overprint 30.00 50.00
e. '03-'03 120.00
O29 " 20a yellow green 4.50 *30.00*
a. Inverted overprint 47.50 47.50
b. '03-'03 100.00
c. 02'-'03 100.00
d. "I" before Gildi omitted 85.00
O30 " 50a red lilac 3.75 *27.50*
a. "I" before Gildi omitted 17.50
b. Invtd. overprint 65.00
Nos. O25-O30 (6) 368.25 *792.50*

Nos. O10-O12, O20-O24, O28 and O30 were reprinted in 1904. They have the watermark of 1902 (type 113) and are perforated 13. Price $40 each.

A few copies have been found without overprint. Price $80 each.

King Christian IX and King Frederick VIII
O4

King Christian X
O5

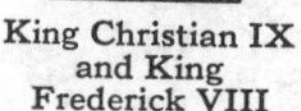

Engraved Center.
Wmkd. Crown. (113)

1907-08 *Perf. 13*

O31 O4 3a yellow & gray 2.50 2.75
O32 " 4a green & gray 1.50 2.25
O33 " 5a brown orange & gray 4.50 2.00
O34 " 10a deep blue & gray 1.00 1.75
O35 " 15a light blue & gray 1.75 2.75
O36 O4 16a carmine & gray 1.75 7.50
O37 " 20a yel. grn. & gray 5.50 1.00
O38 " 50a violet & gray 2.75 2.25
Nos. O31-O38 (8) 21.25 22.25

Wmkd. Multiple Crosses. (114)

1918 *Perf. 14x14½*

O39 O4 15a light blue & gray 4.50 12.50

1920-30 Typographed.

O40 O5 3a yellow & gray 1.75 1.75
O41 " 4a deep green & gray 65 1.75
O42 " 5a orange & gray 60 15
O43 " 10a dark blue & gray 1.00 15
O44 " 15a light blue & gray 30 15
O45 " 20a yellow green & gray 17.50 1.75
O46 " 50a violet & gray 16.00 60
O47 " 1k carmine & gray 16.00 1.00
O48 " 2k blue & black ('30) 4.50 4.00
O49 " 5k brown & blk. ('30) 20.00 13.00
Nos. O40-O49 (10) 78.30 24.30

Nos. 97 and 98 Overprinted **Þjónusta.**

1922, May *Perf. 13* Wmk. 113

O50 A7 2k rose 55.00 35.00
a. Larger letters, without period 18.00 22.50
O51 " 5k brown 120.00 90.00

No. 115 Surcharged **20 aur. Þjónusta**

1923 *Perf. 14x14½* Wmk. 114

O52 A8 20a on 10a red 7.50 1.00

Parliament Millenary Issue.
Nos. 152 to 166 Overprinted in Red or Blue

Þjónustumerki

Perf. 12½x12

1930, Jan. 1 Unwmkd.

O53 A15 3a dull violet & gray violet 9.50 20.00
O54 " 5a dark blue & slate green 9.50 20.00
O55 " 7a green & gray green 9.50 20.00
O56 " 10a dark violet & lilac (Bl) 9.50 20.00
O57 " 15a deep ultra. & blue gray 9.50 20.00
O58 " 20a rose red & salmon (Bl) 9.50 20.00
O59 " 25a dark brown & light brn. (Bl) 9.50 20.00
O60 " 30a dark green & slate green 9.50 20.00
O61 " 35a ultramarine & blue gray 9.50 20.00
O62 " 40a dark ultra., red & slate green (Bl) 9.50 20.00
O63 " 50a red brown & cinnamon (Bl) 100.00 120.00
O64 " 1k olive green & gray green 100.00 120.00
O65 " 2k turquoise blue & gray grn. 100.00 120.00
O66 " 5k org. & yel. (Bl) 100.00 120.00
O67 " 10k magenta & dull rose (Bl) 100.00 120.00
Nos. O53-O67 (15) 595.00 800.00

Type of 1920 Issue Redrawn
Typographed.

1931 Wmkd. Multiple Crosses. (114)

O68 O5 20a yel. grn. & gray 15.00 55

For differences in redrawing see note after No. 187.

No. 82 Overprinted in Black **Þjónusta**

Overprint 15 mm. long.

1936, Dec. 7 *Perf. 13* Wmk. 113

O69 A5 50a gray & violet 12.00 10.00

Same Overprint on Nos. 180 and 115.

Wmkd. Multiple Crosses. (114)

Perf. 14x14½.

O70	A8	7a yellow green	1.75	*11.00*
O71	"	10a red	1.75	65

IFNI

(if'ni)

LOCATION—An enclave in southern Morocco on the Atlantic coast.

GOVT.—Former Spanish possession.

AREA—580 sq. mi.

POP.—51,517 (est. 1964).

CAPITAL—Sidi Ifni.

Ifni was ceded to Spain by Morocco in 1860, but the Spanish did not occupy it until 1934. Sidi Ifni was also the administrative capital for Spanish West Africa. Spain turned Ifni back to Morocco June 30, 1969.

100 Centimos = 1 Peseta

Stamps of Spain, 1936-40, Overprinted in Red or Blue — TERRITORIO DE IFNI

Perf. 10 to 11, Imperf.

1941-42 **Unwmkd.**

1	A159	1c green (imperf.)	7.00	6.00
2	A160	2c org. brown (Bl)	7.00	6.00
3	A161	5c gray brown	1.50	50
5	"	10c dk. carmine (Bl)	4.50	1.85
		a. Red overprint	6.75	4.00
6	"	15c light green	1.20	55
7	A166	20c bright violet	1.20	55
8	"	25c deep claret	1.20	55
9	"	30c blue	1.20	75
10	"	40c Prussian green	2.00	45
11	"	50c indigo	6.00	1.50
12	"	70c blue	6.00	3.75
13	"	1p gray black	6.00	38
14	"	2p dull brown	60.00	10.00
15	"	4p dull rose (Bl)	225.00	45.00
16	"	10p light brown	400.00	100.00
		Nos. 1-16 (15)	729.80	177.83

Nomads
A1

Marksman
A2

Alcazaba Fortress
A3

1943 Lithographed ***Perf. 12½***

17	A1	1c brown & lilac rose	8	8
18	A2	2c yellow green & slate blue	8	8
19	A3	5c magenta & violet	8	8
20	A1	15c slate green & green	30	30
21	A2	20c violet & red brown	30	30
22	A1	40c rose violet & violet	38	38
23	A2	45c brown violet & red	45	45
24	A3	75c indigo & blue	45	45
25	A1	1p red & brown	2.65	2.25
26	A2	3p blue violet & slate green	3.00	2.75
27	A3	10p black brown & black	22.50	17.50
		Nos. 17-27 (11)	30.27	24.62

Nos. 17-27 exist imperforate.

1947, Feb. ***Perf. 10***

28	A1	50c vio. brn. & gray black (*Nomad Family*)	9.00	90

Stamps of Spain, 1939-48, Overprinted in Carmine — Territorio de Ifni

Perf. 9½x10½, 11, 13.

1948, Aug. 2

29	A161	5c gray brown	3.50	90
30	A194	15c gray green	3.50	90
31	A167	90c dark green	12.00	3.00
32	A166	1p gray black	50	38

Spain Nos. 769 and 770 Overprinted in Violet Blue or Carmine — Territorio de Ifni

1949, Oct. 9 ***Perf. 12½x13***

33	A202	50c red brn. (VB)	2.75	1.50
34	"	75c vio. blue (C)	2.75	1.50

75th anniversary of the Universal Postal Union. See No. C40.

Stamps of Spain, 1938-48, Overprinted in Blue or Carmine — Territorio de Ifni

Perf. 13, 13½, 12½x13, 9½x10½.

1949 **Unwmkd.**

35	A160	2c org. brown (Bl)	22	15
37	A161	10c dk. carmine (Bl)	22	15
38	"	15c dark green (II)	22	15
39	A166	25c brown violet	30	22
40	"	30c blue	30	30
41	A195	40c red brown	30	30
42	"	45c carmine rose (Bl)	50	45
43	A166	50c indigo	45	30
44	A195	75c dark violet blue	70	38
47	A167	1.35p purple	4.00	3.00
48	A166	2p dull brown	3.00	1.75
49	"	4p dull rose (Bl)	11.00	4.50
50	"	10p light brown	21.00	12.50
		Nos. 35-50 (13)	42.21	24.15

Gen. Francisco Franco and Desert Scene—A4

Perf. 12½x13

1951, July 18 Photo. **Unwmkd.**

51	A4	50c deep orange	75	15
52	"	1p chocolate	6.00	1.25
53	"	5p blue green	42.50	9.50

Visit of Gen. Francisco Franco, 1950.

View of Granada and Globe
A5

1952, Dec. 10 ***Perf. 13x12½***

54	A5	5c red orange	8	6
55	"	35c dark olive green	8	6
56	"	60c brown	30	8

400th anniversary of the death of Leo Africanus (c. 1485-c. 1554), Arab traveler and scholar, author of "Descrittione dell' Africa."

Musician
A6

Design: 60c, Two musicians.

1953, June 1 ***Perf. 12½x13***

57	A6	15c olive gray	10	6
58	"	60c brown	10	6

Issued to promote child welfare.

Fish and Jellyfish—A7

Design: 60c, Fish and seaweed.

1953, Nov. 23

59	A7	15c dark green	12	12
60	"	60c brown	45	12

Colonial Stamp Day, Nov. 23, 1953.

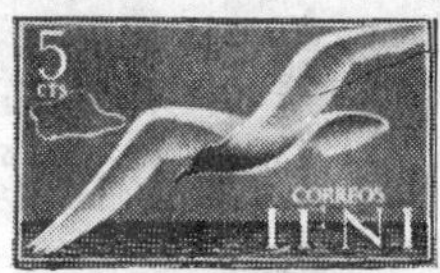

Sea Gull—A8

Cactus
A9

Design: 25c, 60c, 2p, 5p, Salsola vermiculata.

Perf. 12½x13, 13x12½

1954, Apr. 22

61	A8	5c red orange	8	5
62	A9	10c olive	8	5
63	"	25c brown carmine	8	5
64	A8	35c olive gray	8	5
65	A9	40c rose lilac	8	5
66	"	60c dark brown	8	5
67	A8	1p brown	11.50	38
68	A9	1.25p carmine rose	8	8
69	"	2p deep blue	8	8
70	"	4.50p olive green	45	22
71	"	5p olive black	50.00	5.00
		Nos. 61-71 (11)	62.59	6.06

Mother and Child
A10 A11

1954, June 1 ***Perf. 13x12½***

72	A10	15c dark gray green	12	6
73	A11	60c dark brown	12	6

Lobster—A12

Design: 60c, Hammerhead shark.

1954, Nov. 23 ***Perf. 12½x13***

74	A12	15c olive green	8	6
75	"	60c rose brown	22	10

Issued to publicize Colonial Stamp Day.

Farmer Plowing and Statue of "Justice"
A13

1955, June 1 Photo. **Unwmkd.**

76	A13	50c gray olive	8	6

Squirrel—A14

1955, Nov. 23

77	A14	70c yellow green	22	8

Issued to publicize Colonial Stamp Day.

Senecio Antheuphorbium—A15

Design: 50c, Limoniastrum Ifniensis.

1956, June 1 ***Perf. 13x12½***

78	A15	20c bluish green	8	8
79	"	50c brown	22	8

Arms of Sidi Ifni and Shepherd
A16

1956, Nov. 23 ***Perf. 12½x13***

80	A16	70c light green	15	8

Issued for Colonial Stamp Day.

Rock Doves
A17

1957, June 1 Photo. ***Perf. 13x12½***

81	A17	70c yel. grn. & brown	30	15

Jackal
A18

Design: 70c, Jackal's head (vertical).

Perf. 12½x13, 13x12½

1957, Nov. 23

82 A18 20c emerald & light brown 8 6
83 " 70c green & brown 22 10

Issued for the Day of the Stamp, 1957.

Basketball Players A19 — Red-legged Partridges A20

Design: 70c, Cyclists.

1958, June 1 *Perf. 13x12½*

84 A19 20c bluish green 8 6
85 " 70c olive green 22 10

Types of 1957 inscribed "Pro-Infancia 1959."

Designs: 20c, Goat. 70c, Ewe and lamb.

Perf. 13x12½, 12½x13

1959, June 1

86 A17 20c dull green 8 4
87 A18 70c yellow green 15 10

Issued to promote child welfare.

1960, June 10 *Perf. 13x12½*

Design: 80c, Camels.

88 A20 35c slate green 8 5
89 " 80c Prussian green 15 7

White Stork—A21

Birds: 50c, 1.50p, 5p, European goldfinches. 75c, 2p, 10p, Skylarks (vert.).

1960 *Perf. 12½x13* **Unwmkd.**

90 A21 25c violet 5 5
91 " 50c olive black 6 5
92 " 75c dull purple 8 5
93 " 1p orange vermilion 8 5
94 " 1.50p brt. greenish bl. 22 6
95 " 2p red lilac 22 8
96 " 3p dark blue 75 22
97 " 5p red brown 1.50 38
98 " 10p olive 5.25 1.15
Nos. 90-98 (9) 8.21 2.09

Map of Ifni A22

General Franco—A23

Design: 70c, Government palace.

Perf. 13x12½, 12½x13

1961, Oct. 1 **Photogravure**

99 A22 25c gray violet 6 5
100 A23 50c olive brown 6 5
101 " 70c bright green 6 5
102 " 1p red orange 15 6

Issued to commemorate the 25th anniversary of the nomination of Gen. Francisco Franco as Head of State.

Admiral Jofre Tenoria A24 — Mailman A25

Design: 50c, Cesareo Fernandez-Duro (1830–1908), writer.

1962, July 10 *Perf. 13x12½*

103 A24 25c dull violet 6 5
104 " 50c deep blue green 6 5
105 " 1p orange brown 15 6

1962, Nov. 23 **Unwmkd.**

Design: 35c, Hands, letter and winged wheel.

106 A25 15c dark blue 6 5
107 " 35c lilac rose 6 5
108 " 1p rose brown 15 6

Issued for Stamp Day.

Golden Tower, Seville A26 — Butterflies A27

1963, Jan. 29 **Photogravure**

109 A26 50c green 6 5
110 " 1p brown orange 6 6

Issued for flood relief in Seville.

1963, July 6 *Perf. 13x12½*

Design: 50c, Butterfly and flower.

111 A27 25c deep blue 6 5
112 " 50c light green 6 5
113 " 1p carmine rose 15 6

Issued for child welfare.

Child with Flowers and Arms A28

1963, July 12 *Perf. 12½x13*

114 A28 50c gray olive 6 6
115 " 1p reddish brown 6 6

Issued for Barcelona flood relief.

Beetle (Steraspis Speciosa) A29 — Mountain Gazelle A30

Design: 50c, Grasshopper.

1964, Mar. 6 *Perf. 13x12½*

116 A29 25c violet blue 6 6
117 " 50c olive green 6 6
118 " 1p red brown 15 6

Issued for Stamp Day 1963.

1964, June 1 **Photogravure**

Design: 50c, Head of roebuck.

119 A30 25c bright violet 6 6
120 " 50c slate black 6 6
121 " 1p orange red 15 6

Issued for child welfare.

Bicycle Race A31

1964, Nov. 23 *Perf. 12½x13*

Design: 1p, Motorcycle race.

122 A31 50c brown 6 6
123 " 1p orge. vermilion 6 6
124 " 1.50p Prussian green 15 6

Issued for Stamp Day, 1964.

Man A32 — Two Boys in School A33

Cable Cars, Sidi Ifni A34

Perf. 13x12½, 12½x13

1965, Mar. 1 **Photo.** **Unwmkd.**

125 A32 50c dark green 6 6
126 A33 1p orange verm. 6 6
127 A34 1.50p dark blue 15 6

Issued to commemorate 25 years of peace after the Spanish Civil War.

Eugaster Fernandezi A35

Insect: 1p, Halter halteratus.

1965, June 1 **Photo.** **Unwmkd.**

128 A35 50c purple 6 6
129 " 1p rose red 6 6
130 " 1.50p violet blue 15 6

Issued for child welfare.

Eagle A36

Arms of Sidi Ifni A37

Perf. 13x12½, 12½x13

1965, Nov. 23 **Photo.**

131 A36 50c dk. red brown 6 6
132 A37 1p orange verm. 6 6
133 A36 1.50p greenish blue 15 6

Issued for Stamp Day 1965.

Jetliner over Sidi Ifni A38 — Syntomis Alicia A39

Design: 2.50p, Two 1934 biplanes (horiz.).

Perf. 13x12½, 12½x13

1966, June 1 **Photo.** **Unwmkd.**

134 A38 1p orange brown 8 6
135 " 1.50p bright blue 15 8
136 " 2.50p dull violet 2.10 1.20

Issued for child welfare.

1966, Nov. 23 **Photo.** *Perf. 13*

Designs: 40c, 4p, Danais chrysippus (butterfly).

137 A39 10c green & red 5 5
138 " 40c dk. brown & golden brn. 6 6
139 " 1.50p violet & yellow 8 8
140 " 4p dk. purple & brt. blue 30 15

Issued for Stamp Day, 1966.

Coconut Palms A40

Designs: 40c, 4p, Cactus.

1967, June 1 **Photo.** *Perf. 13*

141 A40 10c dp. green & brn. 5 5
142 " 40c Prus. green & ocher 6 6
143 " 1.50p bl. grn. & sepia 8 8
144 " 4p sepia & ocher 30 15

Issued for child welfare.

Sidi Ifni Harbor
A41

1967, Sept. 28 Photo. *Perf. 12½x13*

145 A41 1.50p grn. & red brn. 22 8

Modernization of harbor installations.

Needlefish (Skipper)
A42

Fish: 1.50p, John Dory (vert.). 3.50p, Gurnard (Trigla lucerna).

1967, Nov. 23 Photo. *Perf. 13*

146 A42 1p blue & green 8 8
147 " 1.50p vio. blk. & yel. 8 8
148 " 3.50p brt. bl. & scarlet 30 15

Issued for Stamp Day 1967.

Zodiac Issue

Pisces—A43

Signs of the Zodiac: 1.50p, Capricorn. 2.50p, Sagittarius.

1968, Apr. 25 Photo. *Perf. 13*

149 A43 1p brt. magenta, *light yellow* 6 6
150 " 1.50p brown, *pink* 8 8
151 " 2.50p dk. vio., *yellow* 30 15

Issued for child welfare.

Mailing a Letter
A44

Designs: 1.50p, Carrier pigeon carrying letter. 2.50p, Stamp under magnifying glass.

1968, Nov. 23 Photo. *Perf. 12½x13*

152 A44 1p orange yellow & slate green 8 8
153 " 1.50p bright blue & violet black 8 8
154 " 2.50p emerald & violet black 22 15

Issued for Stamp Day.

SEMI-POSTAL STAMPS

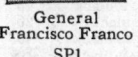

General Francisco Franco
SP1

Fennec
SP2

Perf. 13x12½

1950, Oct. 19 Unwmkd.

B1 SP1 50c+10c sepia 75 60
B2 " 1p+25c blue 22.50 7.25
B3 " 6.50p+1.65p dull green 7.50 3.50

The surtax was for child welfare.

1951, Nov. 30

B4 SP2 5c+5c brown 8 8
B5 " 10c+5c red orange 8 8
B6 " 60c+15c olive brown 38 12

Colonial Stamp Day, Nov. 23, 1951.

Mother and Child
SP3

Common Shag
SP4

1952, June 1

B7 SP3 5c+5c brown 8 8
B8 " 50c+10c brown black 8 8
B9 " 2p+30c deep blue 2.25 75

The surtax was for child welfare.

1952, Nov. 23

B10 SP4 5c+5c brown 15 13
B11 " 10c+5c brn. carmine 15 13
B12 " 60c+15c dark green 38 13

Colonial Stamp Day, Nov. 23, 1952.

Musician Type of Regular Issue

1953, June 1 *Perf. 12½x13*

B13 A6 5c+5c rose brown 10 6
B14 " 10c+5c rose violet (*As No. 58*) 10 6

The surtax was for child welfare.

Fish Type of Regular Issue

1953, Nov. 23

B15 A7 5c+5c dark blue 12 12
B16 " 10c+5c bright red violet (*As No. 60*) 12 12

Colonial Stamp Day, Nov. 23, 1953.

Type of Regular Issue.

1954, June 1 *Perf. 13x12½*

B17 A10 5c+5c orange 12 6
B18 A11 10c+5c rose violet 12 6

The surtax was for child welfare.

Type of Regular Issue.

Design: 10c+5c, Hammerhead shark.

1954, Nov. 23 *Perf. 12½x13*

B19 A12 5c+5c brown orange 8 6
B20 " 10c+5c violet 8 6

Issued to publicize Colonial Stamp Day.

"Dama de Elche" Protecting Caravan
SP5

1955, June 1 Photo. Unwmkd.

B21 A13 10c+5c rose lilac 6 6
B22 SP5 25c+10c violet 6 6

The surtax was to help Ifni people.

Squirrel Type of Regular Issue

1955, Nov. 23

Design: 15c+5c, Squirrel holding nut.

B23 A14 5c+5c red brown 6 6
B24 " 15c+5c olive bistre 6 6

Issued to publicize Colonial Stamp Day.

Type of Regular Issue.

Flower: 15c+5c, Limoniastrum Ifniensis.

1956, June 1 *Perf. 13x12½*

B25 A15 5c+5c greenish gray 8 6
B26 " 15c+5c bistre 8 6

The tax was for child welfare.

Dorcas Gazelles and Arms of Spain
SP6

Design: 15c+5c, Arms of Sidi Ifni, boat and woman with drum.

1956, Nov. 23

B27 SP6 5c+5c dark brown 8 6
B28 " 15c+5c golden brown 8 6

Issued for Colonial Stamp Day.

Dove Type of Regular Issue

Designs: 5c+5c, Rock doves. 15c+5c, Stock doves.

1957, June 1 Photo. *Perf. 13x12½*

B29 A17 5c+5c orange brown & olive green 8 6
B30 " 15c+5c bistre & violet brown 8 6

The surtax was for child welfare.

Type of Regular Issue.

Designs: 10c+5c, Jackal (horizontal). 15c+5c, Head of jackal (vertical).

Perf. 12½x13, 13x12½

1957, Nov. 23 Photo. Unwmkd.

B31 A18 10c+5c red lilac & brown 8 6
B32 " 15c+5c dark bistre & greenish black 8 6

Issued for the Day of the Stamp, 1957.

Swallows and Arms of Valencia and Sidi Ifni—SP7

1958, Mar. 6 *Perf. 12½x13*

B33 SP7 10c+5c orange brown 8 6
B34 " 15c+10c bistre 8 6
B35 " 50c+10c brown olive 15 8

The surtax was to aid the victims of the Valencia flood, Oct. 1957.

Sport Type of Regular Issue, 1958

Designs: 10c+5c, Basketball players. 15c+5c, Cyclists.

1958, June 1 Photo. *Perf. 13x12½*

B36 A19 10c+5c orange brown 8 6
B37 " 15c+5c bistre brown 8 6

The surtax was for child welfare.

Guitarfish
SP8

Sailboats
SP9

Design: 10c+5c, Spotted dogfish.

Perf. 13x12½, 12½x13

1958, Nov. 23

B38 SP9 10c+5c brown red 12 6
B39 SP8 25c+10c dull violet 12 6
B40 SP9 50c+10c olive 15 8

Issued for the Day of the Stamp, 1958.

Donkey and Man
SP10

Soccer
SP11

Type of Regular Issue, 1957, and SP10.

Design: 10c+5c, Ewe and lamb.

1959, June 1 Photo. Unwmkd.

Perf. 12½x13, 13x12½

B41 A18 10c+5c light red brown 8 6
B42 SP10 15c+5c golden brown 8 6

The surtax was for child welfare.

1959, Nov. 23 *Perf. 13x12½*

Designs: 20c+5c, Soccer players. 50c+20c, Javelin thrower.

B43 SP11 10c + 5c fawn 6 6
B44 " 20c + 5c slate green 6 6
B45 " 50c + 20c olive gray 30 10

Issued for the Day of the Stamp, 1959.

Type of Regular Issue, 1960

Designs: 10c+5c, Camels. 15c+5c, Wild boars.

1960, June 10 *Perf. 13x12½*

B46 A20 10c+5c maroon 6 6
B47 " 15c+5c bistre brn. 6 6

The surtax was for child welfare.

Santa Maria del Mar
SP12

Design: 20c+5c, 50c+20c, New school building (horiz.).

Perf. 13x12½, 12½x13

1960, Dec. 29 Photogravure

B48 SP12 10c+5c orange brn. 6 5
B49 " 20c+5c dark slate green 6 5
B50 " 30c+10c red brown 6 5
B51 " 50c+20c sepia 15 5

Issued for Stamp Day, 1960.

Type of 1959 inscribed: "Pro-Infancia 1961"

Designs: 10c+5c, 80c+20c, Pole vaulting (horiz.). 25c+10c, Soccer player.

Perf. 12½x13, 13x12½

1961, June 21 Unwmkd.

B52 SP11 10c+5c rose brown 10 7

B53 SP11 25c+10c gray violet 10 7
B54 " 80c+20c dark green 12 10

The surtax was for child welfare.

Camel Rider and Truck
SP13

Design: 25c+10c, 1p+10c, Ship in Sidi Ifni harbor.

1961, Nov. 23 ***Perf. 12½x13***

B55 SP13 10c+5c rose brown 6 6
B56 " 25c+10c dk. purple 6 6
B57 " 30c+10c dark red brown 6 6
B58 " 1p+10c red orange 15 8

Issued for Stamp Day 1961.

AIR POST STAMPS.

Stamps formerly listed as Nos. C1–C29 were privately overprinted. These include 1936 stamps of Spain overprinted "VIA AEREA" and plane, and 1939 stamps of Spain, type AP30, overprinted "IFNI" or "Territorio de Ifni."

Oasis
AP1

The Sanctuary
AP2

Lithographed

1943 ***Perf. 12½*** **Unwmkd.**

C30 AP2 5c cerise & violet brown 38 38
C31 AP1 25c yellow green & olive green 38 38
C32 AP2 50c indigo & turquoise green 55 55
C33 AP1 1p purple & greenish blue 55 55
C34 AP2 1.40p gray green & blue 55 55
C35 AP1 2p magenta & org. brown 2.00 1.50
C36 AP2 5p brn. & purple 2.75 2.25
C37 AP1 6p bright blue & gray green 25.00 21.00
Nos. C30-C37 (8) 32.16 27.16

Nos. C30-C37 exist imperforate.

Type of Spain, 1939-47, Overprinted in Carmine **IFNI**

1947, Nov. 29

C38 AP30 5c dull yellow 3.00 90
C39 " 10c dk. blue green 3.00 90

Spain No. C126 Overprinted in Carmine **Territorio de Ifni**

1949, Oct. 9 ***Perf. 12½x13***

C40 A202 4p dark olive green 2.75 1.50

Issued to commemorate the 75th anniversary of the formation of the Universal Postal Union.

Spain, Nos. C110 and C112 to C116, Overprinted in Blue or Carmine **Territorio de Ifni**

1949 ***Perf. 10***

C41 AP30 25c reddish brown (Bl) 75 22
C42 " 50c brown 90 38
C43 " 1p chalky blue 90 38
C44 " 2p light gray green 3.25 1.00
C45 " 4p gray blue 10.00 4.50
C46 " 10p bright purple 12.50 9.00
Nos. C41-C46 (6) 28.30 15.48

Lope Sancho de Valenzuela and Sheik
AP3

Woman Holding Dove
AP4

1950, Nov. 23 Photo. ***Perf. 13x12½***

C47 AP3 5p brown black 3.75 75

Issued to publicize Stamp Day, November 23, 1950.

1951, Apr. 22 Engraved ***Perf. 10***

C48 AP4 5p red 21.00 5.25

Issued to commemorate the 500th anniversary of the birth of Queen Isabella I of Spain.

Ferdinand the Catholic
AP5

Perf. 13x12½

1952, July 18 Photo. Unwmkd.

C49 AP5 5p brown 28.50 5.25

Issued to commemorate the 500th anniversary of the birth of Ferdinand the Catholic of Spain.

Plane and Mountain Gazelle
AP6

1953, Apr. 1

C50 AP6 60c light green 8 6
C51 " 1.20p brown carmine 38 6
C52 " 1.60p light brown 45 7
C53 " 2p deep blue 2.25 30
C54 " 4p greenish black 1.50 30
C55 " 10p brt. red violet 6.50 1.50
Nos. C50-C55 (6) 11.16 2.29

SPECIAL DELIVERY STAMPS.

Type A3 inscribed "URGENTE"

1943 ***Perf. 12½.***

E1 A3 25c slate green & carmine 1.85 1.60

Spain, No. E20, Overprinted in Blue **Territorio de Ifni**

1949 ***Perf. 10.*** **Unwmkd.**

E2 SD10 25c carmine 45 30

INDO-CHINA

(ĭn'dō-chī'nȧ)

LOCATION—It comprised the French possessions on the Cambodian Peninsula in southeastern Asia, bordering on the South China Sea and the Gulf of Siam.

GOVT.—Former French Colony and Protectorate.

AREA—280,849 sq. mi.

POP.—27,030,000 (estimated 1949).

CAPITAL—Hanoi.

In 1949, Indo-China was divided into Cambodia, Laos and Viet Nam each issuing its own stamps.

100 Centimes = 1 Franc
100 Cents = 1 Piastre (1918)

Stamps of French Colonies Surcharged in Black or Red:

INDO-CHINE 89
5
R D
a

INDO-CHINE 1889
5
R—D
b

1889 ***Perf. 14x13½*** **Unwmkd.**

1 A9 (*a*) 5c on 35c deep violet, *orange* (Bk) 3.00 2.50
 a. Without date 90.00 70.00
 b. Inverted surcharge 200.00 200.00
2 " (*b*) 5c on 35c deep violet, *orange* (R) 35.00 30.00
 a. Date in smaller type 70.00 60.00
 b. Inverted surcharge, #2 375.00 375.00
 c. As "a," invtd. surcharge 500.00 500.00

Navigation and Commerce
A3

France
A4

Name of Colony in Blue or Carmine

1892–1900 Typographed

3 A3 1c *lilac blue* 20 15
4 " 2c brown, *buff* 40 20
5 " 4c claret, *lavender* 40 20
6 " 5c green, *greenish* 40 15
7 " 5c yellow green ('00) 20 10
8 " 10c *lavender* 1.65 30
9 " 10c red ('00) 60 30
10 " 15c bl., quadrille paper 9.00 20
11 " 15c gray ('00) 2.25 10
12 " 20c red, *green* 2.50 1.25
13 " 25c *rose* 4.00 80
 a. "INDO-CHINE" omitted 1750.00 1150.00
14 " 25c blue ('00) 6.00 60
15 " 30c brown, *bistre* 6.50 2.00
16 " 40c red, *straw* 6.00 2.00
17 " 50c carmine, *rose* 16.50 6.00
18 " 50c brown, *azure* ('00) 7.00 2.75
19 " 75c deep violet, *orange* 10.00 6.00
 a. "INDO-CHINE" inverted 1850.00 1500.00
20 " 1fr bronze green, *straw* 16.50 10.00
 a. "INDO-CHINE" double 185.00 150.00
21 " 5fr red lilac, *lavender* ('96) 42.50 35.00
Nos. 3-21 (19) 132.60 68.10

Nos. 11 and 14 Surcharged in Black **5**

1903

22 A3 5c on 15c gray 30 25
23 " 15c on 25c blue 45 25

1904-06

24 A4 1c olive green 15 10
25 " 2c violet brown, *buff* 20 10
26 " 4c claret, *bluish* 10 10
27 " 5c deep green 15 10
28 " 10c carmine 50 10
29 " 15c orange brown, *blue* 30 10
30 " 20c red, *green* 80 25
31 " 25c deep blue 5.00 40
32 " 30c pale brown 1.50 85
33 " 35c *yellow* ('06) 6.00 40
34 " 40c *bluish* 1.50 40
35 " 50c bistre brown 2.00 75
36 " 75c red, *orange* 17.50 10.00
37 " 1fr pale green 8.00 1.50
38 " 2fr brown, *orange* 17.50 15.00
39 " 5fr deep violet, *lilac* 90.00 70.00
40 " 10fr orange brown, *green* 70.00 60.00
Nos. 24-40 (17) 221.20 160.15

Annamite Girl
A5

Cambodian Girl
A6

Cambodian Woman
A7

Annamite Women
A8

Muong Woman
A9

Laotian Woman
A10

Cambodian Woman
A11

1907 ***Perf. 14x13½***

41 A5 1c olive brown & black 7 7
42 " 2c yellow brown & black 8 8
43 " 4c blue & black 20 20
44 " 5c green & black 15 10
45 " 10c red & black 20 10
46 " 15c violet & black 40 25
47 A6 20c violet & black 80 45

48 A6 25c blue & black 1.50 20
49 " 30c brown & black 3.00 2.00
50 " 35c olive green & black 40 20
51 " 40c yellow brown & black 1.00 55
52 " 45c orange & black 3.25 2.00
53 " 50c carmine & black 4.00 2.00

Perf. 13½x14

54 A7 75c vermilion & black 3.00 3.00
55 A8 1fr car. & black 16.00 5.00
56 A9 2fr green & black 5.00 4.00
57 A10 5fr blue & black 16.00 10.00
58 A11 10fr purple & black 35.00 30.00
Nos. 41-58 (18) 90.05 60.20

Stamps of 1904-06 Surcharged in Black or Carmine **05** *a* **10** *b*

1912 *Perf. 14x13½*

59 A4 (*a*) 5c on 4c claret, *bluish* 2.00 1.75
60 " (") 5c on 15c orange brn., *blue* (C) 10 10
61 " (") 5c on 30c pale brn. 15 15
62 " (*b*) 10c on 40c *bluish* (C) 25 25
63 " (") 10c on 50c bistre brown (C) 20 20
64 " (") 10c on 75c red, *orange* 1.85 1.65
Nos. 59-64 (6) 4.55 4.10

Two spacings between the surcharged numerals are found on Nos. 59 to 64.

Stamps of 1907 Surcharged with New Values in Cents or Piastres in Black, Red or Blue **4 CENTS**

1919

65 A5 2/5c on 1c olive brown & black 10 10
66 " 4/5c on 2c yellow brown & black 30 20
67 " 1 3/5c on 4c bl. & blk. (R) 40 20
68 " 2c on 5c grn. & black 20 10
a. Inverted surch. 25.00
69 " 4c on 10c red & black (Bl) 20 10
a. Closed "4" 1.50 10
b. Double surch. 25.00
70 " 6c on 15c vio. & blk. 60 20
a. Inverted surch. 25.00
71 A6 8c on 20c vio. & blk. 80 60
72 " 10c on 25c blue & blk. 60 10
73 " 12c on 30c brown & black 1.85 20
74 " 14c on 35c olive green & black 20 15
a. Closed "4" 2.50 1.25
75 " 16c on 40c yellow brown & black 1.65 50
76 " 18c on 45c orange & black 2.00 1.00
77 " 20c on 50c carmine & black (Bl) 2.65 20
78 A7 30c on 75c vermilion & black (Bl) 2.65 60
79 A8 40c on 1fr carmine & black (Bl) 5.00 1.00
80 A9 80c on 2fr green & black (R) 6.00 2.00
a. Double surcharge 75.00 65.00
81 A10 2pi on 5fr blue & black (R) 35.00 30.00
82 A11 4pi on 10fr purple & black (R) 50.00 47.50
Nos. 65-82 (18) 110.20 84.75

Types of 1907 Issue Surcharged with New Values in Black or Red

2 CENTS *c* **12 CENTS** *d*

1922

88 A5 (*c*) 1c on 5c ochre & black 20
89 A5 (*c*) 2c on 10c gray green & black 50
90 A6 (") 6c on 30c light red & black 60
91 " (") 10c on 50c light blue & black 70
92 " (") 11c on 55c violet & black, *bluish* 60
93 " (*d*) 12c on 60c light blue & black, *pinkish* (R) 75
Nos. 88-93 (6) 3.35

Nos. 88 to 93 were sold officially in Paris but were never placed in use in the colony.

Nos. 88-93 exist without surcharge but were not regularly issued in that condition. Price, Nos. 88-91 each $50; Nos. 92-93 each $25.

A12

A13

"CENTS" below Numerals.

1922-23 *Perf. 14x13½*

94 A12 1/10c black & salmon 5 5
a. Double impression of frame
95 " 1/5c blue & black 6 5
96 " 2/5c olive brn. & black 6 6
a. Head and value double 90.00 85.00
97 " 4/5c rose & black, *lavender* 6 6
98 " 1c yel. brn. & black 6 6
99 " 2c gray green & black 8 6
100 " 3c violet & black 6 6
101 " 4c orange & black 6 6
a. Head and value double 35.00 35.00
102 " 5c carmine & black 6 6
a. Head and value double 110.00 100.00
103 A13 6c dull red & black 7 6
104 " 7c olive grn. & black 10 10
105 " 8c black, *lavender* 25 20
106 " 9c ochre & black, *greenish* 30 20
107 " 10c blue & black 10 8
108 " 11c violet & black 10 10
109 " 12c brown & black 10 10
a. Head and value dbl. (11c+12c) 125.00 125.00
110 " 15c orange & black 20 12
111 " 20c blue & black, *straw* 30 17
112 " 40c vermilion & black, *bluish* 60 30
113 " 1pi blue green & black, *greenish* 1.40 1.25
114 " 2pi vio. brn. & black, *pinkish* 2.50 1.75
Nos. 94-114 (21) 6.57 4.95

Plowing near Tower of Confucius
A14

Bay of Along
A15

Angkor Wat, Cambodia—A16

Carving Wood—A17

That Luang Temple, Laos
A18

Founding of Saigon
A19

1927

115 A14 1/10c light olive green 6 6
116 " 1/5c yellow 6 6
117 " 2/5c light blue 8 8
118 " 4/5c deep brown 10 10
119 " 1c orange 15 6
120 " 2c blue green 20 10
121 " 3c indigo 15 10
122 " 4c lilac rose 30 27
123 " 5c deep violet 20 8
a. Booklet pane of 10 10.00
124 A15 6c deep red 60 10
a. Booklet pane of 10 10.00
125 " 7c light brown 15 10
126 " 8c gray green 35 35
127 " 9c red violet 40 40
128 " 10c light blue 50 20
129 " 11c orange 50 40
130 " 12c myrtle green 20 20
131 A16 15c dull rose & olive brown 2.50 2.50
132 " 20c violet & slate 1.00 40
133 A17 25c orange brown & lilac rose 3.00 2.00
134 " 30c deep blue & olive gray 1.50 75
135 A18 40c vermilion & light blue 2.00 70
136 " 50c light green & slate 3.00 1.00
137 A19 1pi dark blue, black & yellow 5.00 3.00
a. Yel. omitted 45.00
138 " 2pi red, deep blue & orange 6.00 4.00
Nos. 115-138 (24) 28.00 17.01

Colonial Exposition Issue.

Common Design Types

Engraved.

Name of Country in Black.

Surcharged with New Values.

1931 *Perf. 12½*

140 CD71 4c on 50c violet 85 45
141 CD72 6c on 90c red org. 1.00 1.00
142 CD73 10c on 1.50fr dull blue 1.25 65

Junk
A20

Tower at Ruins of Angkor Thom
A21

Planting Rice
A22

Apsaras, Celestial Dancer
A23

1931-41 Photo. *Perf. 13, 13½*

143 A20 1/10c Prussian blue 4 4
144 " 1/5c lake 4 4
145 " 2/5c orange red 6 6
146 " 1/2c red brown 6 6
147 " 4/5c dark violet 6 6
148 " 1c black brown 6 6
149 " 2c dark green 6 6
150 A21 3c deep brown 6 6
151 " 3c dk. green ('34) 1.50 15
152 " 4c dark blue 12 8
153 " 4c dark green ('38) 17 17
153A " 4c yel. org. ('41) 6 6
154 " 5c deep violet 8 6
154A " 5c deep green ('41) 8 8
155 " 6c orange red 6 6
a. Bklt. pane 5 + 1 label
156 " 7c black ('38) 6 6
157 " 8c rose lake ('38) 6 6
157A " 9c black, *yellow* ('41) 6 6
158 A22 10c dark blue 27 10
158A " 10c ultramarine, *pink* ('41) 5 5
159 " 15c dark brown 1.85 10
160 " 15c dark blue ('33) 5 5
161 " 18c blue ('38) 8 6
162 " 20c rose 6 6
163 " 21c olive green 8 6
164 " 22c dark green ('38) 6 6
165 " 25c deep violet 1.00 40
165A " 25c dark blue ('41) 6 6
166 " 30c org. brn. ('32) 7 6
167 A23 50c dark brown 6 6
168 " 60c dull violet ('32) 6 5
168A " 70c light blue ('41) 6 6
169 " 1pi yellow green 20 6
170 " 2pi red 30 6
Nos. 143-170 (34) 7.00 2.63

Nos. 166, 167, 169 and 170 were issued without the letters "RF" in 1943, by the Vichy Government, but were not placed on sale in the colony.

Emperor Bao-Dai
A24

King Sisowath Monivong
A25

For Use in Annam.

1936 Engraved. *Perf. 13.*

171 A24 1c brown 20 20
172 " 2c green 20 20
173 " 4c violet 40 20
174 " 5c red brown 30 20
175 " 10c lilac rose 60 60
176 " 15c ultramarine 60 60
177 " 20c scarlet 85 60
178 " 30c plum 1.00 85
179 " 50c slate green 1.25 1.25
180 " 1pi rose violet 1.75 1.00
181 " 2pi black 2.00 1.40
Nos. 171-181 (11) 9.15 7.10

For Use in Cambodia.

182 A25 1c brown 20 20
183 " 2c green 20 20
184 " 4c violet 40 40
185 " 5c red brown 40 40
186 " 10c lilac rose 1.00 85
187 " 15c ultramarine 1.25 1.00
188 " 20c scarlet 80 60
189 " 30c plum 80 80
190 " 50c slate green 80 80
191 " 1pi rose violet 1.00 80
192 " 2pi black 1.25 1.00
Nos. 182-192 (11) 8.10 7.05

Common Design Types
pictured in section at front of book.

Paris International Exposition Issue.

Common Design Types

1937

193	CD74	2c deep violet	30	20
194	CD75	3c dark green	30	20
195	CD76	4c carmine rose	20	20
196	CD77	6c dark brown	20	20
197	CD78	9c red	20	20
198	CD79	15c ultramarine	20	20
		Nos. 193–198 (6)	1.40	1.20

Colonial Arts Exhibition Issue.

Souvenir Sheet.

Common Design Type

1937 *Imperf.*

199	CD79	30c dull violet	1.50	1.35

Issued in sheets measuring 118x99mm. containing one stamp.

Governor-General Paul Doumer

A26

1938 Photo. *Perf. 13½x13*

200	A26	5c rose carmine	30	20
201	"	6c brown	30	20
202	"	18c bright blue	25	15

Issued in commemoration of the 35th anniversary of the Trans-Indo-Chinese Railway.

New York World's Fair Issue.

Common Design Type

1939 Engraved. *Perf. 12½x12.*

203	CD82	13c carmine lake	10	10
204	"	23c ultramarine	15	15

Mot Cot Pagoda, Hanoi

A27

1939 *Perf. 13*

205	A27	6c black brown	30	25
206	"	9c vermilion	20	20
207	"	23c ultramarine	20	20
208	"	39c rose violet	30	25

Golden Gate International Exposition.

Angkor Wat and Marshal Pétain

A27a

1941 Engraved *Perf. 12½x12*

209	A27a	10c dark carmine	10	
209A	"	25c blue	10	

Nos. 209–209A were issued by the Vichy government and were not placed on sale in the colony.

King Norodom Sihanouk of Cambodia
A28

Harnessed Elephant on Parade
A29

Lithographed.

1941 *Pin-perf. 12½.* Unwmkd.

Without Gum.

210	A28	1c red orange	20	20
211	"	6c violet	40	40
212	"	25c deep ultramarine	8.00	6.00

Coronation of Norodom Sihanouk, King of Cambodia, October, 1941.

Gum

Nos. 210–261 were issued without gum.

1942

213	A29	3c reddish brown	35	30
214	"	6c crimson	35	30

Fête of Nam-Giao in Annam.

No. 165 Surcharged in Black

10
cents

1942 *Perf. 13*

214A	A22	10c on 25c deep violet	10	8

View of Saigon Fair

A30

1942 *Perf. 13½*

215	A30	6c carmine rose	7	7

Saigon Fair of 1942.

Nam-Phuong, Empress of Annam
A31

Marshal Pétain
A32

1942 *Pin-perf. 11½*

216	A31	6c carmine rose	20	15

1943–44 *Perf. 12, 13½*

217	A32	1c black brown	5	5
218	"	3c olive brown	5	5
219	"	6c rose red	5	5
220	"	10c dull green ('44)	8	8
221	"	40c dark blue	6	5
222	"	40c slate blue	40	40
		Nos. 217–222 (6)	69	68

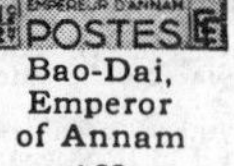

Bao-Dai, Emperor of Annam
A33

Norodom Sihanouk, King of Cambodia
A34

Perf. 13½.

223	A33	½c brown	5	5
224	"	6c carmine rose	25	15

1943 *Perf. 11½*

225	A34	1c brown	15	12
226	"	6c red	5	5

Sisavang-Vong, King of Laos
A35

Family, Country and Labor
A36

227	A35	1c bistre brown	5	5
228	"	6c carmine rose	5	5

1943 *Perf. 12*

229	A36	6c carmine rose	7	7

National revolution, 3rd anniversary.

Admiral Rigault de Genouilly

A37

François Chasseloup-Laubat

A38

Admiral André A. P. Courbet

A39

1943 *Perf. 11½, 12, 12x11½*

230	A37	6c carmine rose	12	10
231	A38	6c "	8	8
232	A39	6c "	25	8

A 5c dull brown, type A37, was not regularly issued without the Viet Nam overprint. A 3c light brown, type A39, was prepared but not issued.

Pigneau de Behaine, Bishop of Adran
A40

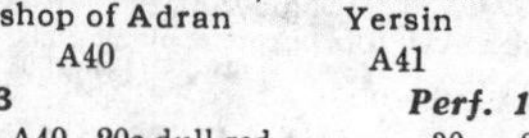

Alexandre Yersin
A41

1943 *Perf. 12*

233	A40	20c dull red	30	20

1943-45 *Perf. 12x11½.*

234	A41	6c carmine rose	30	25
235	"	15c violet brown ('45)	6	6
236	"	1pi yellow green ('45)	8	8

Issued to honor Dr. Alexandre Yersin (1863-1943), the Swiss bacteriologist who introduced rubber culture into Indo-China.

Lt. M. J. François Garnier

A42

1943 *Perf. 12*

237	A42	1c dull olive bistre	15	15

A 15c brown violet was prepared but not issued.

Alexandre de Rhodes

A43

1943–44 *Pin-perf., Perf. 12*

238	A43	15c dark violet brown	6	6
239	"	30c orange brown	6	6
		a. 30c yel. brown, perf. 13½	8	8

Nos. 239 and 239a carry the monogram "EF".

Athlete Giving Olympic Salute

A44

1944 *Perf. 12*

241	A44	10c dark violet brown & yellow	70	70
242	"	50c dull red	70	70

Adm. Pierre de La Grandière

A45

243	A45	1c dull brown	6	6
244	"	5c dark brown	6	6

The upper left corner of No. 244 contains the denomination "5c" instead of "EF" monogram.

Auguste Pavie
A46

1944 *Perf. 12*
245 A46 4c orange yellow 5 5
246 " 10c dull green 5 5

A 20c dark red, type A46, was not regularly issued without the Viet Nam overprint.

Governor-General Pierre Pasquier
A47

Governor-General Paul Doumer
A50

247 A47 5c brown violet 10 10
248 " 10c dull green 6 6

Joost Van Vollenhoven
A48

249 A48 1c olive brown 6 6
250 " 10c green 10 5

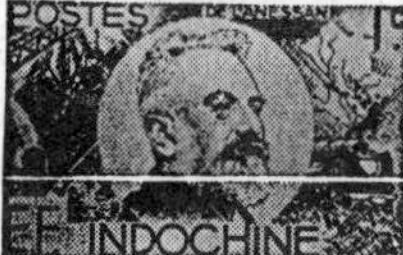

Governor-General J. M. A. de Lanessan
A49

251 A49 1c dull gray brown 5 5
252 " 15c dull rose violet 10 10

1944
253 A50 2c red violet 5 5
254 " 4c light brown 6 6
255 " 10c yellow green 8 8

Admiral Charner
A51

Doudart de Lagrée
A52

256 A51 10c green 5 5
257 " 20c brown red 7 7
258 " 1pi pale yellow green 15 15

1944
259 A52 1c dull gray brown 5 5
260 " 15c dull rose violet 10 10
261 " 40c bright blue 7 7

Nos. 209–209A Overprinted in Black

RF

1946 *Perf. 12½x12.* **Unwmkd.**
262 A27a 10c dark carmine 10 10
263 " 25c blue 30 30

SEMI-POSTAL STAMPS.

+

No. 45 Surcharged

5 c

1914 *Perf. 14x13½.* **Unwmkd.**
B1 A5 10c+5c red & black 20 15

Nos. 44–46 Surcharged

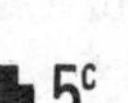

1915–17
B2 A5 5c+5c green & black 15 15
a. Double surcharge 40.00 40.00
B3 " 10c+5c red & black 60 40
B4 " 15c+5c violet & black 60 40
a. Triple surcharge 45.00 40.00
b. Quadruple surcharge 40.00 35.00

Nos. B2–B4 Surcharged with New Values in Blue or Black.

1918
B5 A5 4c on 5c+5c green & black (Bl) 1.25 85
a. Closed "4" 65.00 60.00
B6 " 6c on 10c+5c red & black 1.00 85
B7 " 8c on 15c+5c violet & black 4.00 3.00
a. Double surcharge 50.00 45.00

France Nos. B5–B10 Surcharged

INDOCHINE
10 CENTS

1918
B8 SP5 10c on 15c+10c gray green 10 10
a. Double surcharge 12.00
B9 " 16c on 25c+15c deep blue 1.00 1.00
B10 SP6 24c on 35c+25c slate & violet 1.50 1.50
a. Double surch. 75.00
B11 SP7 40c on 50c+50c pale brown & dark brown 1.50 1.50
B12 SP8 80c on 1fr+1fr claret & maroon 4.00 4.00
B13 " 4pi on 5fr+5fr deep blue & black 52.50 52.50
Nos. B8–B13 (6) 60.60 60.60

Curie Issue

Common Design Type with Inscription and Date in Upper Margin.

1938 **Engraved.** *Perf. 13.*
B14 CD80 18c+5c brt. ultra. 3.25 3.25

French Revolution Issue

Common Design Type

Name and Value Typo. in Black.

1939 Photogravure.
B15 CD83 6c+2c green 2.50 2.50
B16 " 7c+3c brown 2.50 2.50
B17 " 9c+4c red orange 2.50 2.50
B18 " 13c+10c rose pink 2.50 2.50
B19 " 23c+20c blue 2.50 2.50
Nos. B15–B19 (5) 12.50 12.50

Common Design Type and

Tonkinese Sharpshooter
SP1

Legionary
SP2

1941 Photogravure *Perf. 13½*
B19A SP1 10c+10c red 25
B19B CD86 15c+30c maroon 25
B19C SP2 25c+10c blue 25

Nos. B19A–B19C were issued by the Vichy government, and were not placed on sale in the colony.

Nos. 209–209A were surcharged "OEUVRES COLONIALES" and surtax (including change of denomination of the 25c to 5c). These were issued in 1944 by the Vichy government and not placed on sale in the colony.

Portal and Flags, City University, Hanoi
SP3

Coat of Arms and Sword
SP4

Lithographed.

1942–44 *Perf. 11½.* **Unwmkd.**
B20 SP3 6c+2c carmine rose 15 15
B21 " 15c+5c brown violet 20 20

10c +2c

No. B20 Surcharged in Black

a

B22 SP3 (a) 10c+2c on 6c+2c car. rose ('44) 5 5

1942–44 *Perf. 12*
B23 SP4 6c+2c red & blue 15 15
B24 " 15c+5c violet black, red & blue 20 20

No. B23 Surcharged in Black.

B25 SP4 (a) 10c+2c on 6c+2c red & blue ('44) 5 5

Aviator Do-Huu-Vi
SP5

1944
B26 SP5 6c+2c carmine rose 12 12

No. B26 Surcharged in Black.

B27 SP5 (a) 10c+2c on 6c+2c carmine rose 5 5

Surcharge arranged to fit size of stamp.

Aviator Roland Garros
SP6

B28 SP6 6c+2c rose carmine 8 8

No. B28 Surcharged in Black.

B29 SP6 (a) 10c+2c on 6c+2c rose carmine 5 5

Cathedral of Orléans
SP7

B30 SP7 15c+60c brown violet 30 25
B31 " 40c+1.10pi blue 35 30

Type of France, 1945, Surcharged in Black

INDOCHINE
2 P + 2 P

Engraved.

1945 *Perf. 13.* **Unwmkd.**
B32 A152 50c+50c on 2fr green 10 10
B33 " 1pi+1pi on 2fr henna brown 10 10
B34 " 2pi+2pi on 2fr Prussian green 25 25

AIR POST STAMPS.

Airplane—AP1

Photogravure.

1933–41 *Perf. 13½* **Unwmkd.**
C1 AP1 1c olive brown 6 6
C2 " 2c dark green 6 6
C3 " 5c yellow green 8 8
C4 " 10c red brown 20 20
C5 " 11c rose carmine ('38) 12 10
C6 " 15c deep blue 18 18
C6A " 16c bright pink ('41) 10 7
C7 " 20c greenish gray 25 20
C8 " 30c orange brown 15 10
C9 " 36c carmine rose 65 8
C10 " 37c olive green ('38) 15 10
C10A " 39c dark olive green ('41) 15 6
C11 " 60c dark violet 20 12
C12 " 66c olive green 20 12
C13 " 67c bright blue ('38) 25 18
C13A " 69c brt. ultra. ('41) 25 25
C14 " 1pi black 15 10
C15 " 2pi yellow orange 40 15
C16 " 5pi purple 55 10
C17 " 10pi deep red 1.00 20
Nos. C1–C17 (20) 5.15 2.51

See also Nos. C27–C28.

Stamps of type AP1 without "RF" monogram were issued in 1942 and 1943 by the Vichy Government, but were not placed on sale in the colony. On the Vichy stamps, the figure of value has been moved to the lower left corner of the vignette.

Governor-General Paul Doumer
AP2

1938

C18 AP2 37c red orange 6 6

Issued in commemoration of the 35th anniversary of the Trans-Indo-Chinese Railway.

Victory Issue
Common Design Type
Engraved.

1946 *Perf. 12½.* Unwmkd.

C19 CD92 80c red orange 20 15

Chad to Rhine Issue
Common Design Types

1946

C20 CD93 50c yellow green 12 12
C21 CD94 1pi violet 12 12
C22 CD95 1.50pi carmine 12 12
C23 CD96 2pi violet brown 15 15
C24 CD97 2.50pi deep blue 20 20
C25 CD98 5pi orange red 30 30
Nos. C20–C25 (6) 1.01 1.01

UPU Issue
Common Design Type

1949 *Perf. 13.*

C26 CD99 3pi deep blue, dark violet, green & red 90 85

Plane Type of 1933.

1949 Photogravure. *Perf. 13½*

C27 AP1 20pi dk. bl. green 4.00 1.50
C28 " 30pi brown 4.00 1.50

AIR POST SEMI-POSTAL STAMP.

French Revolution Issue
Common Design Type
Photogravure.

1939 *Perf. 13* Unwmkd.

Name and Value Typo. in Orange.

CB1 CD83 39c+40c brown black 8.00 8.00

V4

V5

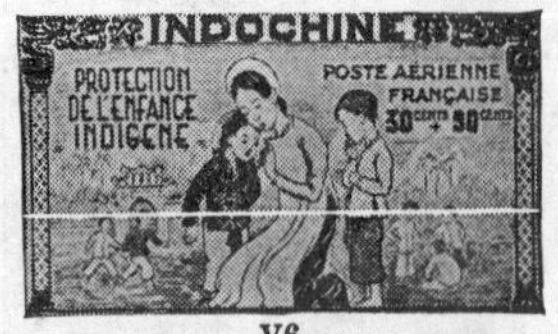

V6

Stamps of the above designs, and of Cameroun type V10 inscribed "Indochine", were issued in 1942 by the Vichy Government, but were not placed on sale in the colony.

POSTAGE DUE STAMPS.

French Colonies No. J21 Surcharged **5**

1904 *Imperf.* Unwmkd.

J1 D1 5c on 60c brown, *buff* 3.50 2.50

French Colonies Nos. J10–J11 Surcharged in Carmine

1905

J2 D1 5c on 40c black 10.00 3.25
J3 " 10c on 60c black 10.00 5.50
J4 " 30c on 60c black 10.00 5.50

Dragon from Steps of Angkor Wat
D1 D2

1908 Typographed. *Perf. 14x13½.*

J5 D1 2c black 20 20
J6 " 4c deep blue 20 20
J7 " 5c blue green 20 20
J8 " 10c carmine 80 20
J9 " 15c violet 1.00 75
J10 " 20c chocolate 20 20
J11 " 30c olive green 25 20
J12 " 40c claret 3.00 2.50
J13 " 50c greenish blue 1.20 20
J14 " 60c orange 4.00 3.50
J15 " 1fr gray 8.00 5.50
J16 " 2fr yellow brown 6.00 4.50
J17 " 5fr red 10.00 7.00
Nos. J5–J17 (13) 35.05 25.15

Surcharged with New Values in Cents or Piasters

1919

J18 D1 4/5c on 2c black 40 20
J19 " 1 3/5c on 4c deep blue 40 30
J20 " 2c on 5c blue green 80 40
J21 " 4c on 10c carmine 40 30
J22 " 6c on 15c violet 1.35 1.00
J23 " 8c on 20c chocolate 1.75 40
J24 " 12c on 30c olive grn. 1.75 40
J25 " 16c on 40c claret 1.75 40
J26 " 20c on 50c greenish blue 3.00 1.65
J27 " 24c on 60c orange 75 60
 a. Closed "4" 7.00 4.00
J28 " 40c on 1fr gray 75 20
 a. Closed "4" 7.00 4.00
J29 " 80c on 2fr yel. brn. 10.00 6.50
J30 " 2pi on 5fr red 12.00 7.50
 a. Double surcharge 50.00 40.00
 b. Triple surch. 50.00 35.00
Nos. J18–J30 (13) 35.10 19.85

"CENTS" below Numerals.

1922

J31 D2 2/5c black 6 6
J32 " 4/5c red 10 7
J33 " 1c buff 10 5
J34 " 2c gray green 20 5
J35 " 3c violet 20 6
J36 " 4c orange 15 5
 a. "4 CENTS" omitted 250.00
 b. "4 CENTS" double 20.00 20.00
J37 D2 6c olive green 27 15
J38 " 8c black, *lavender* 20 6
J39 " 10c deep blue 40 8
J40 " 12c ochre, *greenish* 40 25
J41 " 20c deep blue, *straw* 40 10
J42 " 40c red, *bluish* 33 13
J43 " 1p brown violet, *pinkish* 1.25 90
Nos. J31–J43 (13) 4.06 2.01

Pagoda of Mot Cot, Hanoi
D3

Dragon of Annam
D4

1927 *Perf. 14x13½, 13½x14.*

J44 D3 2/5c violet brown & orange 10 8
J45 " 4/5c violet & black 10 7
J46 " 1c brown red & slate 40 30
J47 " 2c green & brown olive 40 35
J48 " 3c red brown & blue 40 30
J49 " 4c indigo & brown 40 35
J50 " 6c deep red & verm. 40 40
J51 " 8c olive brn. & vio. 40 40
J52 D4 10c deep blue 45 20
J53 " 12c olive 1.50 1.25
J54 " 20c rose 1.00 20
J55 " 40c blue green 1.00 90
J56 " 1pi red orange 6.00 4.75
Nos. J44–J56 (13) 12.55 9.55

D5

Value Surcharged in Black.

1931-41 *Perf. 13.*

J57 D5 1/5c red, *orange* ('38) 4 4
J58 " 2/5c " " 4 4
J59 " 4/5c " " 5 5
J60 " 1c " " 6 6
J61 " 2c " " 5 5
J62 " 2½c ("2,5") " ('40) 5 5
J63 " 3c " " ('38) 5 5
J64 " 4c " " 5 5
J65 " 5c " " ('38) 8 8
J66 " 6c " " 6 6
J67 " 10c " " 6 5
J68 " 12c " " 8 8
J69 " 14c " " ('38) 12 12
J70 " 18c " " ('41) 15 15
J71 " 20c " " 12 12
J72 " 50c " " 12 12
J72A " 1pi " " 3.00 2.25

Value Surcharged in Blue.

J73 D5 1pi red, *orange* 65 65
Nos. J57–J73 (18) 4.83 4.07

Numeral of Value
D6 D7

Perf. 12, 13½ and Compound

1944 Lithographed Unwmkd.

J74 D6 1c red, *orange* 3 3
J75 " 2c " " 6 6
J76 " 3c " " 5 5
J77 " 4c " " 5 5
J78 " 6c " " 5 5
J79 " 10c " " 8 8
J80 D7 12c blue, *pinkish* 8 8
J81 " 20c " " 7 7
J82 " 30c " " 6 6
Nos. J74–J82 (9) 53 53

OFFICIAL STAMPS.

Regular Issues of 1931–32 Overprinted in Blue or Red.

Overprinted SERVICE (vertical)

1933 *Perf. 13, 13½.* Unwmkd.

O1 A20 1c black brown (Bl) 20 10
O2 " 2c dark green (Bl) 20 15

Overprinted **SERVICE**

O3 A21 3c deep brown (Bl) 40 30
 a. Inverted ovpt. 30.00
O4 " 4c dark blue (R) 40 30
 a. Inverted ovpt. 30.00
O5 " 5c deep violet (Bl) 60 10
O6 " 6c orange red (Bl) 60 10

Overprinted **SERVICE** (arched)

O7 A22 10c dark blue (R) 20 15
O8 " 15c dark brown (Bl) 1.00 60
O9 " 20c rose (Bl) 85 10
O10 " 21c olive green (Bl) 85 60
O11 " 25c deep violet (Bl) 20 10
O12 " 30c orange brown (Bl) 85 30

Overprinted **S E R V I C E**

O13 A23 50c dark brown (Bl) 4.50 1.50
O14 " 60c dull violet (Bl) 60 60
O15 " 1pi yel. green (Bl) 10.00 4.00
O16 " 2pi red (Bl) 3.75 3.25
Nos. O1–O16 (16) 25.20 12.25

Type of Regular Issue, 1922-23

Overprinted diagonally in Black or Red "SERVICE"

1934 *Perf. 14x13.*

O17 A13 1c olive green 20 15
O18 " 2c brown orange 20 20
O19 " 3c yellow green 20 15
O20 " 4c cerise 40 30
O21 " 5c yellow 10 10
O22 " 6c orange red 1.65 1.00
O23 " 10c gray green (R) 1.00 85
O24 " 15c ultramarine 60 40
O25 " 20c gray black (R) 40 20
O26 " 21c light violet 3.00 2.50
O27 " 25c rose lake 3.75 1.85
O28 " 30c lilac gray 50 40
O29 " 50c brt. violet 3.00 2.50
O30 " 60c gray 4.00 2.50
O31 " 1pi blue (R) 9.00 6.00
O32 " 2pi deep red 12.00 10.00
Nos. O17–O32 (16) 40.00 29.10

The value tablet has colorless numeral and letters on solid background.

PARCEL POST STAMPS.

French Colonies No. 50 Overprinted **INDO-CHINE TIMBRE COLIS POSTAUX**

1891 *Perf. 14x13½.* Unwmkd.

Q1 A9 10c *lavender* 4.00 1.00

The overprint on No. Q1 was also handstamped in shiny ink.

Indo-China No. 8 Overprinted **Colis Postaux**

1898

Q2 A3 10c *lavender* 6.00 5.00

Nos. 8 and 9 Overprinted **TIMBRE COLIS POSTAUX**

1902

Q3 A3 10c *lavender* 15.00 8.50
 a. Inverted ovpt. 22.50 12.00
Q4 " 10c red 14.00 5.50
 a. Inverted ovpt. 17.50 10.00
 b. Double ovpt. 17.50 10.00

INDONESIA

(ĭn'dô-nē'zhȧ)

LOCATION—In the East Indies.
GOVT.—Republic.
AREA—575,450 sq. mi.
POP.—143,280,000 (est. 1977).
CAPITAL—Djakarta.

Formerly Netherlands Indies, Indonesia achieved independence late in 1949 and the Republic of Indonesia was proclaimed Aug. 15, 1950. See "Netherlands Indies" for earlier issues.

100 Sen = 1 Rupiah

United States of Indonesia.

Mountain, Palms and Flag of Republic
A49

Perf. 12½x12

1950, Jan. 17 Photo. Unwmkd.
Size: 20½x26mm.
333 A49 15s red 30 12

1950, June *Perf. 11½*
Size: 18x23mm.
334 A49 15s red 4.00 30

Netherlands Indies Nos. 307-315 Overprinted in Black

1950-51 *Perf. 12½*
335 A42 1s gray 20 9
336 " 2s claret 20 9
337 " 2½s olive brown 30 20
338 " 3s rose pink 20 9
339 " 4s green 25 15
340 " 5s blue 20 8
341 " 7½s dark green 20 12
342 " 10s violet 20 5
343 " 12½s bright red 20 8

Netherlands Indies Nos. 317-330 Overprinted in Black

Perf. 11½, 12½x12.
345 A43 20s gray black 4.00 3.50
346 " 25s ultramarine 20 10
347 A44 30s bright red 2.50 2.50
348 " 40s gray green 40 20
349 " 45s claret 60 30
350 A45 50s orange brown 40 12
351 " 60s brown 3.25 2.75
352 " 80s scarlet 2.00 25

Overprint 12 mm. High.
Perf. 12½x12.
353 A46 1r purple 30 10
354 " 2r olive green 165.00 115.00
355 " 3r red violet 110.00 50.00
356 " 5r dark brown 40.00 12.50
357 " 10r gray 70.00 16.00
358 " 25r orange brown 20.00 7.00
Nos. 335-358 (23) 420.60 211.27

Republic of Indonesia.

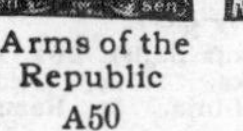

Arms of the Republic
A50

Doves in Flight
A51

Perf. 12½x12

1950, Aug. 17 Photo. Unwmkd.
359 A50 15s red 45 8
360 " 25s dull green 1.10 40
361 " 1r sepia 4.25 60

Issued to commemorate the 5th anniversary of Indonesia's proclamation of independence.

1951, Oct. 24 Engraved *Perf. 12*
362 A51 7½s blue green 1.75 25
363 " 10s violet 50 30
364 " 20s red 1.65 75
365 " 30s carmine rose 1.75 1.00
366 " 35s ultramarine 1.75 1.00
367 " 1r sepia 14.00 2.00
Nos. 362-367 (6) 21.40 5.40

Issued to commemorate the sixth anniversary of the formation of the United Nations Organization and the first anniversary of its acceptance of the Republic of Indonesia as a member.

A52

Post Office
A53

Mythological Hero
A54

Pres. Sukarno
A55

1951-53 Photogravure. *Perf. 12½*
368 A52 1s gray 4 4
369 " 2s plum 4 4
370 " 2½s brown 2.50 20
371 " 5s carmine rose 4 4
372 " 7½s green 4 4
373 " 10s blue 18 4
374 " 15s purple 15 4
375 " 20s rose red 18 4
376 " 25s deep green 20 4
377 A53 30s red orange 10 4
378 " 35s purple 14 4
379 " 40s dull green 16 4
380 " 45s deep claret 20 4
381 " 50s brown 4.00 4
382 A54 60s dark brown 4 3
383 " 70s gray 6 3
384 " 75s ultramarine 8 8
385 " 80s claret 10 10
386 " 90s gray green 12 10
Nos. 368-386 (19) 8.37 1.06

Perf. 12½x12
387 A55 1r purple 5 4
388 " 1.25r deep orange 5 4
389 " 1.50r brown 5 4
390 " 2r green 5 4
391 " 2.50r rose brown 5 4
392 " 3r blue 5 4
392A " 4r apple green 5 4
393 " 5r brown 5 4
394 " 6r rose lilac 5 4
395 " 10r slate 5 4
396 " 15r yellow 5 4
397 " 20r sepia 5 4
398 " 25r scarlet 5 4
399 " 40r yellow green 10 4
400 " 50r violet 20 8
Nos. 387-400 (15) 95 64

Nos. 368-376, 387, 390, 392, 393, 395, 398 were issued in 1951; Nos. 377-386, 388-389, 391, 392A, 394, 396-397, 399-400 in 1953.

Prices are for the later Djakarta printings which have thicker numerals and a darker over-all impression. Earlier printings by Joh. Enschede and Sons, Haarlem, Netherlands, sell for more.

Melati Flowers
A56

Crowd Releasing Doves
A57

1953, Dec. 22 *Perf. 12½*
401 A56 50s blue green 3.50 30

Issued to commemorate the 25th anniversary of the formation of the Indonesian Women's Congress.

1955, Apr. 18 *Perf. 13x12½*
402 A57 15s gray 35 20
403 " 35s brown 50 25
404 " 50s deep magenta 1.20 30
405 " 75s blue green 70 30

Asian-African Conference, Bandung, April 18-24.

Proclamation of Independence
A58

Voters
A59

1955, Aug. 17 Photo. *Perf. 12½*
406 A58 15s green 40 20
407 " 35s ultramarine 40 35
408 " 50s brown 1.00 15
409 " 75s magenta 75 40

Ten years of independence.

1955, Sept. 29 *Perf. 12*
Without gum.
410 A59 15s rose violet 30 15
411 " 35s green 60 35
412 " 50s carmine rose 1.20 25
413 " 75s light ultramarine 60 25

First free elections in Indonesia.

Mas Soeharto Postmaster General
A60

Helmet, Wreath and Monument
A61

1955, Sept. 27 *Perf. 12½*
414 A60 15s brown 65 15
415 " 35s dark carmine 1.10 30
416 " 50s ultramarine 4.00 30
417 " 75s dull green 2.25 20

Issued to mark 10 years of Indonesia's Postal, Telegraph and Telephone system.

1955, Nov. 10
418 A61 25s bluish green 65 10
419 " 50s ultramarine 2.00 20
420 " 1r dark car. rose 4.00 25

Issued in honor of the soldiers killed in the war of liberation from the Netherlands.

Torch, Book and Map
A62

Lesser Malay Chevrotain
A63

1956, May 26 Photogravure
421 A62 25s ultramarine 1.25 6
422 A62 50s carmine rose 3.75 25
423 " 1r dark green 2.50 30

Issued to publicize the Asia-Africa Student Conference, Bandung, May, 1956.

1956 *Perf. 12½x13½* Unwmkd.

Animals: 5s, 10s, Lesser Malay chevrotain. 20s, 25s, Otter. 35s, Malayan pangolin. 50s, Banteng. 75s, Asiatic two-horned rhinoceros.

424 A63 5s deep ultramarine 3 3
425 " 10s yellow brown 3 3
426 " 15s rose violet 3 3
427 " 20s dull green 3 3
428 " 25s deep claret 3 3
429 " 35s bright violet blue 3 3
430 " 50s brown 3 3
431 " 75s dark brown 4 4
Nos. 424-431 (8) 25 25

See Nos. 450-456.

Dancing Girl and Gate
A64

Telegraph Key
A65

1956, Oct. 7 *Perf. 12½x12*
432 A64 15s slate green 38 12
433 " 35s brown violet 75 18
434 " 50s blue black 1.35 20
435 " 75s deep claret 1.85 15

Issued to commemorate the 200th anniversary of the founding of the city of Jogjakarta.

1957, May 10 Unwmkd.
436 A65 10s light crimson 85 8
437 " 15s bright blue 18 8
438 " 25s gray 30 8
439 " 50s brown red 40 12
440 " 75s light blue green 60 10
Nos. 436-440 (5) 2.33 46

Indonesian telegraph system centenary.

Thrift Symbolism
A66

Douglas DC-3
A67

Design: 15s, 1r, People and hands holding wreath of rice and cotton.

1957, July 12 Photo. *Perf. 12½*
441 A66 10s blue 20 15
442 " 15s rose carmine 30 20
443 " 50s green 40 12
444 " 1r bright violet 1.00 10

Issued to publicize Cooperation Day, July 12.

1958, Apr. 9 *Perf. 12½x12*

Aircraft: 15s, Helicopter. 30s, Miles Magister. 50s, Two-motor plane of Indonesian Airways. 75s, De Havilland Vampire.

445 A67 10s reddish brown 5 4
446 " 15s blue 8 4
447 " 35s orange 12 6
448 " 50s bright green 15 8
449 " 75s gray 50 13
Nos. 445-449 (5) 90 35

Issued for National Aviation Day, April 9.

Animal Type of 1956.

Animals: 30s, Otter. 40s, 45s, Malayan pangolin. 60s, 70s, Banteng 80s, 90s, Asiatic two-horned rhinoceros.

1958 Photogravure *Perf. 12½x13½*
450 A63 30s orange 3 3
451 " 40s brt. yel. green 3 3
452 " 45s rose lilac 3 3
453 " 60s dark blue 3 3

454 A63 70s orange vermilion 3 3
455 " 80s red 5 5
456 " 90s yellow green 5 5
Nos. 450-456 (7) 25 25

Thomas Cup
A68

1958, Aug. 15 ***Perf. 13½x13***

457 A68 25s rose carmine 4 4
458 " 50s orange 10 5
459 " 1r brown 15 5

Issued to commemorate Indonesia's victory in the 1958 Thomas Cup World Badminton Championship.

Satellite Circling Globe
A69

1958, Oct. 15 Litho. ***Perf. 12½x12***

460 A69 10s dark green, pink & light blue 30 5
461 " 15s violet, gray & pale bluish green 8 8
462 " 35s brown, blue & pink 10 10
463 " 50s blue, reddish brown & gray 20 12
464 " 75s black, violet & buff 20 15
Nos. 460-464 (5) 88 50

International Geophysical Year, 1957-58.

Bicyclist and Map
A70

1958, Nov. 15 Photo. ***Perf. 13½x13***

465 A70 25s bright blue 5 5
466 " 50s brown carmine 10 8
467 " 1r gray 25 18

Bicycle Tour of Java, Aug. 15-30.

Man Looking into Light
A71

Wild Boar (Babirusa)
A72

Designs: 15s, Hands and flame. 35s, Woman holding candle. 50s, Family hailing torch. 75s, Torch and "10."

1958, Dec. 10 ***Perf. 12½x12***

468 A71 10s gray brown 3 3
469 " 15s dull red brown 6 3
470 " 35s ultramarine 8 6
471 " 50s pale brown 12 8
472 " 75s light blue green 18 10
Nos. 468-472 (5) 47 30

Issued to commemorate the tenth anniversary of the signing of the Universal Declaration of Human Rights.

1959, June 1 Photo. ***Perf. 12***

Animals: 15s, Anoa (smallest buffalo). 20s, Orangutan. 50s, Javan rhinoceros. 75s, Komodo dragon (lizard). 1r, Malayan tapir.

473 A72 10s olive bistre & sepia 5 3
474 " 15s orange brown & sepia 5 3
475 " 20s light olive green & sepia 5 3
476 A72 50s bistre brown & sepia 6 3
477 " 75s deep rose & sepia 8 3
478 " 1r blue green & blk. 10 3
Nos. 473-478 (6) 39 18

Issued to publicize wildlife preservation.

A73

Factories
A74

1959, Aug. 17 Litho. ***Perf. 12***

479 A73 20s blue & red 4 3
480 " 50s rose red & black 4 3
481 " 75s brown & red 6 3
482 " 1.50r light green & black 15 3

Issued to commemorate the introduction of the constitution of 1945 embodying "guided democracy."

1959, Oct. 26 Photo. ***Perf. 12***

Designs: 20s, 75s, Cogwheel and train. 1.15r, Means of transportation.

483 A74 15s bright green & black 3 3
484 " 20s dull orange & black 3 3
485 " 50s red & black 8 3
486 " 75s bright greenish blue & black 10 5
487 " 1.15r magenta & black 15 6
Nos. 483-487 (5) 39 20

11th Colombo Plan Conference, Jakarta.

Mother and Child, WRY Emblem
A75

Tea Plantation
A76

Designs: 15s, 75s, Destroyed town and fleeing family. 20s, 1.15r, World Refugee Year emblem.

Perf. 12½x12

1960, Apr. 7 **Unwmkd.**

488 A75 10s claret & black 3 3
489 " 15s bistre & black 3 3
490 " 20s orange brown & black 5 3
491 " 50s green & black 8 3
492 " 75s dk. blue & blk. 10 6
493 " 1.15r scarlet & black 12 10
Nos. 488-493 (6) 41 28

Issued to publicize World Refugee Year, July 1, 1959-June 30, 1960.

1960 ***Perf. 12x12½***

Designs: 5s, Oil palms. 10s, Sugar cane and railroad. 15s, Coffee. 20s, Tobacco. 50s, Coconut palms. 75s, Rubber plantation. 1.15r, Rice.

494 A76 5s gray 3 3
495 " 10s red brown 3 3
496 " 15s plum 3 3
497 " 20s ochre 3 3
498 " 25s brt. blue grn. 3 3
499 " 50s deep blue 6 3
500 " 75s scarlet 8 3
501 " 1.15r plum 12 3
Nos. 494-501 (8) 41 24

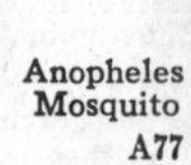

Anopheles Mosquito
A77

1960, Nov. 12 Photo. ***Perf. 12x12½***

502 A77 25s carmine rose 5 3
503 " 50s orange brown 5 3
504 " 75s bright green 8 3
505 " 3r orange 20 5

Issued to commemorate World Health Day, Nov. 12, 1960, and to promote malaria control.

Pres. Sukarno with Hoe—A78

1961, Feb. 15 ***Perf. 12½x12***

506 A78 75s gray 10 8

Planned National Development.

Dayak Dancer of Borneo—A79

Designs: 10s, Ambonese boat. 15s, Tangkubanperahu crater. 20s, Bull races. 50s, Toradja houses. 75s, Balinese temple. 1r, Lake Toba. 1.50r, Balinese dancer and musicians. 2r, Buffalo hole, view. 3r, Borobudur Temple, Java.

1961 ***Perf. 13½x13***

507 A79 10s rose lilac 5 5
508 " 15s gray 5 5
509 " 20s orange 5 5
510 " 25s orange vermilion 5 5
511 " 50s carmine rose 5 5
512 " 75s red brown 6 6
513 " 1r bright green 15 6
514 " 1.50r bistre brown 30 7
515 " 2r greenish blue 45 10
516 " 3r gray 60 12
Set of 4 souvenir sheets 3.50 2.50
Nos. 507-516 (10) 1.81 66

Issued for tourist publicity.

The four souvenir sheets among them contain one each of Nos. 507-516 imperf., with two or three stamps to a sheet and English marginal inscriptions: "Visit Indonesia" and "Visit the Orient Year." Size: 139x105 or 105x139.

Sports Hall and Thomas Cup
A80

Photogravure

1961, June 1 ***Perf. 13½x12½***

517 A80 75s pale vio. & blue 6 5
518 " 1r citron & dark green 10 10
519 " 3r salmon pink & dark blue 25 20

Issued to commemorate the 1961 Thomas Cup World Badminton Championship.

New Buildings and Workers
A81

1961, July 6 **Unwmkd.**

520 A81 75s violet & greenish bl. 6 6
521 " 1.50r emerald & buff 10 8
522 " 3r dark red & salmon 18 12

16th anniversary of independence.

Sultan Hasanuddin
A82

Portraits: 20s, Abdul Muis. 30s, Surjopranoto. 40s, Tengku Tjhik Di Tiro. 50s, Teuku Umar. 60s, K. H. Samanhudi. 75s, Captain Pattimura. 1r, Raden Adjeng Kartini. 1.25r, K. H. Achmad Dahlan. 1.50r, Tuanku Imam Bondjol. 2r, Si Singamangaradja XII. 2.50r, Mohammad Husni Thamrin. 3r, Ki Hadjar Dewantoro. 4r, Djenderal Sudirman. 4.50r, Dr. G. S. S. J. Ratulangie. 5r, Pangeran Diponegoro. 6r, Dr. Setyabudi. 7.50r, H. O. S. Tjokroaminoto. 10r, K. H. Agus Salim. 15r, Dr. Soetomo.

Photogravure

1961-62 ***Perf. 13½x12½*** **Unwmkd.**

Black Inscriptions; Portraits in Sepia

523 A82 20s olive 3 3
524 " 25s gray olive 3 3
525 " 30s bright lilac 3 3
526 " 40s brown orange 3 3
527 " 50s bluish green 6 3
528 " 60s green ('62) 3 3
529 " 75s lt. red brown 6 3
530 " 1r light blue 8 3
531 " 1.25r lt. olive grn. ('62) 4 3
532 " 1.50r emerald 20 4
533 " 2r orange red ('62) 6 4
534 " 2.50r rose claret 20 5
535 " 3r gray blue 24 5
536 " 4r olive green 30 5
537 " 4.50r red lilac ('62) 8 5
538 " 5r brick red 32 5
539 " 6r bister ('62) 10 5
540 " 7.50r violet blue ('62) 15 8
541 " 10r green ('62) 18 12
542 " 15r dp. orange ('62) 30 15
Nos. 523-542 (20) 2.52 1.00

Issued to honor national heroes. The 25s, 75s, 1.50r and 5r on Aug. 17, Independence Day; 40s, 50s and 4r on Oct. 5, Army Day; 20s, 30s, 1r, 2.50r and 3r on Nov. 10, Republic Day; 60s, 2r, 7.50r and 15r on Oct. 5, 1962; 1.25r, 4.50r, 6r and 10r on Nov. 10, 1962.

Symbols of Census—A83

1961, Sept. 15 ***Perf. 13½x12½***

543 A83 75s rose violet 20 6

First census in Indonesia.

Djataju—A84

Scenes from Ramayana Ballet: 40s, Hanuman. 1r, Dasamuka. 1.50r, Kidang Kentjana. 3r, Dewi Sinta. 5r, Rama.

Perf. 12x12½

1962, Jan. 15 **Unwmkd.**

544 A84 30s ochre & red brn. 3 3
545 " 40s rose lilac & vio. 3 3
546 " 1r green & claret 3 3
547 " 1.50r salmon pink & dark green 6 3
548 " 3r pale green & deep blue 12 6
549 " 5r brown orange & dk. brown 20 8
Nos. 544-549 (6) 47 26

Asian Games Emblem
A85

Main Stadium
A86

Designs: 10s, Basketball. 15s, Main Stadium, Jakarta. 20s, Weight lifter. 25s, Hotel Indonesia. 30s, Cloverleaf intersection. 40s, Discus thrower. 50s, Woman diver. 60s, Soccer. 70s, Press House. 75s, Boxers. 1r, Volleyball. 1.25r, 2r, 3r, 5r, Asian Games emblem. 1.50r, Badminton. 1.75r, Wrestlers. 2.50r, Woman rifle shooter. 4.50r, Hockey. 6r, Water polo. 7.50r, Tennis. 10r, Table tennis. 15r, Bicyclist. 20r, Welcome Monument.

1962 Photogravure *Perf. 12½*

550 A85 10s green & yellow 4 3
551 A86 15s greenish black & bister 4 3
552 A85 20s red lilac & light green 4 3
553 A86 25s car. & lt. green 4 3
554 " 30s blue grn. & yel. 6 3
555 A85 40s ultra. & pale bl. 6 3
556 " 50s chocolate & gray 6 3
557 " 60s lilac rose & violet gray 6 3
558 " 70s dark brn. & rose 6 3
559 " 75s choc. & orange 6 3
560 " 1r purple & lt. blue 8 6
561 " 1.25r dark blue & rose carmine 8 6
562 " 1.50r red org. & lilac 8 6
563 " 1.75r dark car. & rose 10 8
564 " 2r brn. & yel. green 10 8
565 " 2.50r dp. blue & lt. grn. 12 8
566 " 3r black & dk. red 15 10
567 " 4.50r dk. green & red 20 10
568 " 5r gray green & lemon 25 15
569 " 6r brown red & deep yellow 25 15
570 " 7.50r red brn. & sal. 30 20
571 " 10r dark blue & blue 35 20
572 " 15r dull violet & pale violet 50 25
573 " 20r dark green & olive bister 60 40
Nos. 550-573 (24) 3.68 2.27

4th Asian Games, Jakarta.

Helpful notes abound in the "Information for Collectors" section at the front of this volume.

Malaria Eradication Emblem A87 — Atom Diagram A88

1962, Apr. 7 *Perf. 12½x12*

574 A87 40s dull blue & violet blue 3 3
575 " 1.50r yellow orange & brown 5 5
576 " 3r green & indigo 15 8
577 " 6r lilac & black 25 20

Issued for the World Health Organization drive to eradicate malaria. The 1.50r and 6r have Indonesian inscription on top.

Photogravure

1962, Sept. 24 *Perf. 12x12½*

578 A88 1.50r dk. blue & yel. 12 8
579 " 4.50r brick red & yel. 20 18
580 " 6r green & yellow 30 20

Development through science.

Pacific Travel Association Emblem A89 — Mechanized Plow A90

Designs: 1.50r, Prambanan Temple and Mount Merapi. 6r, Balinese Meru (Buildings), Pura Taman Ajun.

1963, Mar. 14 **Unwmkd.**

581 A89 1r green & indigo 6 3
582 " 1.50r olive & indigo 6 3
583 " 3r ocher & indigo 6 6
584 " 6r deep orange & indigo 12 12

Issued to publicize the 12th conference of the Pacific Area Travel Association, Bandung.

Perf. 12½x12, 12x12½

1963, Mar. 21 Photogravure

Design: 1r, 3r, Hand holding rice stalks (vert.).

585 A90 1r blue & yellow 5 3
586 " 1.50r brt. grn. & indigo 5 5
587 " 3r rose car. & orge. 8 6
588 " 6r orange & black 12 12

Issued for the "Freedom from Hunger" campaign of the U.N. Food and Agriculture Organization. English inscription on 3r and 6r.

Long-Armed Lobster—A91

Fish: 1.50r, Little tuna. 3r, River roman. 6r, Chinese pompano.

1963, Apr. 6 *Perf. 12½x12*

589 A91 1r vermilion, black & yel. 8 3
590 " 1.50r ultramarine, black & yel. 8 3
591 " 3r Prussian blue, bister & car. 8 5
592 " 6r olive green, blk. & ocher 16 8

Pen and Conference Emblem
A92

Designs: 1.50r, Pen, Emblem and map of Africa and Southeast Asia. 3r, Globe, pen and broken chain (vert.). 6r, Globe, hand holding pen and broken chain (vert.).

Perf. 12½x12, 12x12½

1963, Apr. 24 Photo. **Unwmkd.**

593 A92 1r lt. bl. & dp. orge. 5 3
594 " 1.50r pale violet & maroon 5 3
595 " 3r olive, bl. & blk. 6 4
596 " 6r brick red & black 12 8

Asian-African Journalists' Conference.

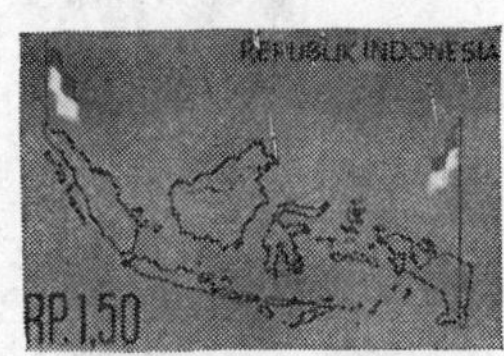

"Indonesia's Flag from Sabang to Merauke"—A93

Designs: 4.50r, Parachutist landing in New Guinea. 6r, Bird of paradise and map of New Guinea.

1963, May 1 *Perf. 12½x12*

597 A93 1.50r orange brown, black & red 3 3
598 " 4 50r multicolored 6 6
599 " 6r " 12 12

Issued to mark the acquisition of Netherlands New Guinea (West Irian).

Centenary Emblem
A94

Design: 1.50r, 6r, Red Cross.

1963, May 8 *Perf. 12*

600 A94 1r bright grn. & red 5 3
601 " 1.50r light blue & red 5 3
602 " 3r gray & red 8 6
603 " 6r yel. bister & red 15 8

Centenary of the International Red Cross.

Bank of Indonesia, Djalan A95 — Daneswara, God of Prosperity A96

1963, July 5 Photo. *Perf. 12*

604 A95 1.75r lt. bl. & purple 3 3
605 A96 4r citron & slate green 5 3
606 A95 6r lt. grn. & brn. 10 6
607 A96 12r orange & dark red brown 20 10

Issued for National Banking Day.

Standard Bearers—A97

Designs: 1.75r, "Pendet" dance. 4r, GANEFO building, Senajan, Jakarta. 6r, Archery. 10r, Badminton. 12r, Javelin. 25r, Sailing. 50r, Torch.

1963, Nov. 10 *Perf. 12½* **Unwmkd.**

608 A97 1.25r gray violet & dark brown 6 3
609 " 1.75r orange & olive green 6 3
610 " 4r emerald & dark brown 6 3
611 " 6r rose brown & black 6 3
612 " 10r lt. olive green & dark brown 6 3
613 " 12r rose carmine & greenish black 10 8
614 " 25r blue & dk. blue 12 10
615 " 50r red & black 15 10
Nos. 608-615 (8) 67 43

Issued to commemorate the 1st Games of the New Emerging Forces, GANEFO, Jakarta, Nov. 10-22.

Pres. Sukarno A98 — Trailer Truck A99

1964 Photo. *Perf. 12½x12*

616 A98 6r brn. & dk. blue 3 3
617 " 12r bister & plum 3 3
618 " 20r blue & orange 3 3
619 " 30r red orange & bl. 3 3
620 " 40r green & brown 3 3
621 " 50r red & dp. grn. 5 5
622 " 75r vio. & red orge. 5 5
623 " 100r silver & red brown 8 8
624 " 250r dk. bl. & silver 8 8
625 " 500r red & gold 10 10
Nos. 616-625 (10) 51 51

1964 *Perf. 12x12½, 12½x12*

Designs: 1r, Oxcart. 1.75r, Freighter. 2r, Lockheed Electra plane. 2.50r, Buginese sailboat (vert.). 4r, Mailman with bicycle. 5r, Dakota plane. 7.50r, Teletype operator. 10r, Diesel train. 15r, Passenger ship. 25r, Convair Coronado Plane. 35r, Telephone switchboard operator.

626 A99 1r dull claret 3 3
627 " 1.25r red brown 3 3
628 " 1.75r Prussian blue 3 3
629 " 2r red orange 3 3
630 " 2.50r bright blue 3 3
631 " 4r bluish green 3 3
632 " 5r olive bister 5 3
633 " 7.50r bright green 5 3
634 " 10r orange 6 3
635 " 15r dark blue 8 3
636 " 25r violet blue 8 3
637 " 35r red brown 10 3
Nos. 626-637 (12) 60 36

Ramses II
A100

Design: 6r, 18r, Kiosk of Trajan, Philae.

1964, March 8 *Perf. 12½x12*

638 A100 4r olive bister & olive green 5 3
639 " 6r greenish blue & olive green 8 3
640 " 12r rose & olive grn. 10 8
641 " 18r emerald & olive green 15 10

Issued to publicize the UNESCO world campaign to save historic monuments in Nubia.

Stamps of Netherlands Indies and Indonesia—A101

1964, Apr. 1 *Perf. 12½*

642 A101 10r gold, dark blue & red orange 10 6

Centenary of postage stamps in Indonesia.

Indonesian Pavilion—A102

1964, May 16 *Perf. 12½x12*

643 A102 25r silver, black, red & dark blue 10 6
644 " 50r gold, Prussian bl., red & green 15 12

New York World's Fair, 1964–65.

Thomas Cup
A103

1964, Aug. 15 *Perf. 12½x13½*

645 A103 25r bright green, gold & red 10 5
646 " 50r ultramarine, gold & red 15 5
647 " 75r pur., gold & red 25 15

Thomas Cup Badminton World Championship, 1964.

Cruisers and Map of West Irian
A104

Designs: 30r, Submarine. 40r, Torpedo boat.

Perf. 12½x12

1964, Oct. 5 Photo. **Unwmkd.**

648 A104 20r yellow & brn. 8 8
649 " 30r rose & black 12 12
650 " 40r brt. grn. & ultra. 16 16

Issued to honor the Indonesian Navy.

Map of Africa and Asia and Mosque
A105

Design: 15r, 50r, Mosque and clasped hands.

1965, Mar. 6. Photo. *Perf. 12½*

651 A105 10r lt. bl. & purple 5 3
652 " 15r orge. & red brn. 5 3
653 " 25r brt. grn. & brn. 8 4
654 " 50r brn. red & blk. 15 5

Issued to publicize the Afro-Asian Islamic Conference, Bandung, March, 1965.

Hand Holding Scroll
A106

Design: 25r, 75r, Conference emblem (globe, cotton and grain).

1965, Apr. 18 *Perf. 12½* **Unwmkd.**

655 A106 15r silver & dp. car. 6 3
656 " 25r aqua., gold & red 6 3
657 " 50r gold & dp. ultra. 8 4
658 " 75r pale violet, gold & red 10 5

Issued to commemorate the 10th anniversary of the First Afro-Asian Conference.

Nos. 618–623 and Nos. 634–636 Surcharged in Revalued Currency in Orange or Black

Sen

1965, Dec. *Perf. 12x12½, 12½x12*

659 A99 10s on 10r orange 4 4
660 " 15s on 15r dk. blue (O) 6 4
661 A98 20s on 20r bl. & org. (O) 8 6
662 A99 25s on 25r vio. bl. 10 6
663 A98 30s on 30r red org. & blue (O) 10 6
664 " 40s on 40r green & brown (O) 12 8
665 " 50s on 50r red & dp. green (O) 15 10
666 " 75s on 75r violet & red orange (O) 20 12
667 " 100s on 100r silver & red brown (O) 25 14
Nos. 659–667 (9) 1.10 70

The surcharge on Nos. 659–660 and No. 662 is in two lines and larger.

Pres. Sukarno
A107

1966–67 Photo. *Perf. 12½x12*

668 A107 1s sepia & Prus. grn. 3 3
669 " 3s sepia & lt. olive green 3 3
670 " 5s sepia & dp. car. 3 3
671 " 8s sepia & Prus. grn. 3 3
672 " 10s sepia & vio. blue 3 3
673 " 15s sepia & black 3 3
674 " 20s sepia & dp. green 3 3
675 " 25s sepia & dk. red brown 3 3
676 " 30s sepia & dp. blue 3 3
677 " 40s sepia & red brn. 3 3
678 " 50s sepia & brt. vio. 3 3
679 " 80s sepia & orange 6 3
680 " 1r sepia & emerald 6 3
681 " 1.25r sepia & dk. gray olive 8 4
682 " 1.50r sepia & emerald 8 4
683 " 2r sepia & magenta 8 5
684 " 2.50r sepia & gray 8 5
685 " 5r sepia & ocher 12 5
686 " 10r sepia & olive green 15 5
686A " 12r grn. & org. ('67) 28 6
686B " 25r green & bright purple ('67) 30 7
Nos. 668–686B (21) 1.62 80

The 12r is inscribed "1967" instead of "1966."

Dockyard Workers
A108

Gen. Ahmad Yani
A109

Designs: 40s, Lighthouse. 50s, Fishermen. 1r, Maritime emblem (wheel and eagle). 1.50r, Sailboat. 2r, Loading dock. 2.50r, Diver emerging from water. 3r, Liner at pier.

1966 Photo. *Perf. 12x12½*

687 A108 20s lt. ultra. & grn. 3 3
688 " 40s pink & dk. bl. 3 3
689 " 50s green & brown 4 3
690 " 1r sal., blue & yel. 5 5
691 " 1.50r dull lilac & dull green 8 5
692 " 2r gray & dp. org. 10 5
693 " 2.50r rose lilac & dark red 12 5
694 " 3r brt. grn. & blk. 15 6
a. Souv. sheet 2.50 2.00
Nos. 687–694 (8) 60 35

Issued for Maritime Day. Nos. 687–690 issued Sept. 23; Nos. 691–694, Oct. 23.

No. 694a contains one imperf. stamp similar to No. 694. Ocher margin with black and white inscription. Size: 59x77½mm.

1966, Nov. 10

Heroes of the Revolution: No. 696, Lt. Gen. R. Suprapto. No. 697, Lt. General Harjono. No. 698, Lt. Gen. S. Parman. No. 699, Maj. Gen. D. I. Pandjaitan. No. 700, Maj. Gen. Sutojo Siswomihardjo. No. 701, Brig. General Katamso. No. 702, Colonel Soegijono. No. 703, Capt. Pierre Andreas Tendean. No. 704, Adj. Insp. Karel Satsuit Tubun.

Deep Blue Frame

695 A109 5r orange brown 15 10
696 " 5r bright green 15 10
697 " 5r gray brown 15 10
698 " 5r olive 15 10
699 " 5r gray 15 10
700 " 5r bright purple 15 10
701 " 5r red lilac 15 10
702 " 5r slate green 15 10
703 A109 5r dull rose lilac 15 10
704 " 5r orange 15 10
Nos. 695–704 (10) 1.50 1.00

Issued to honor military men killed during the Communist uprising, October, 1965.

Tjlempung, Java
A110

Aviator and MiG-21
A111

Musical Instruments and Maps: 1r, Sasando, Timor. 1.25r, Foi doa, Flores. 1.50r, Kultjapi, Sumatra. 2r, Arababu, Sangihe and Talaud Islands. 2.50r, Drums, West New Guinea. 3r, Katjapi, Celebes. 4r, Hape, Borneo. 5r, Gangsa, Bali. 6r, Serunai, Sumatra. 8r, Rebab, Java. 10r, Trompet, West New Guinea. 12r, Totobuang, Moluccas. 15r, Drums, Nias. 20r, Kulintang, Celebes. 25r, Keledi, Borneo.

Photogravure

1967 *Perf. 12½x12* **Unwmkd.**

705 A110 50s red & gray 3 3
706 " 1r brn. & dp. org. 3 3
707 " 1.25r maroon & ultra. 3 3
708 " 1.50r grn. & lt. violet 3 3
709 " 2r violet blue & yellow bister 4 4
710 " 2.50r olive green & dull red 5 4
711 " 3r brt. green & dull claret 6 4
712 " 4r vio. bl. & orange 8 5
713 " 5r dull red & blue 10 6
714 " 6r blk. & brt. pink 15 6
715 " 8r red brown & bright green 20 8
716 " 10r lilac & red 30 8
717 " 12r olive green & lilac 35 12
718 " 15r violet & lt. olive green 40 15
719 " 20r gray & sepia 50 20
720 " 25r black & green 65 25
Nos. 705–720 (16) 3.00 1.29

Issue Dates: 1.25r, 10r, 12r, 15r, 20r, 25r—March 1; others Feb. 1.

1967, Apr. 9 *Perf. 12½*

Designs: 4r, Traffic control tower and 990A Convair jetliner. 5r, Hercules transport plane.

721 A111 2.50r multicolored 8 5
722 " 4r " 12 8
723 " 5r " 20 12

Issued for Aviation Day.

Thomas Cup with Victory Dates
A112

Design: 12r, Thomas Cup and globe.

1967, May 31 *Perf. 12x12½*

724 A112 5r multicolored 12 8
725 " 12r " 30 15

Issued to commemorate the Thomas Cup Badminton World Championship of 1967.

Balinese Girl in Front of Temple Gate
A113

1967, July 1 Photo. *Perf. 12½*
726 A113 12r multicolored 30 20
a. Souv. sheet 70 70

Issued for International Tourist Year, 1967. See also No. 739.
No. 726a contains one imperf. stamp similar to No. 726. Yellow ITY emblem and blue inscription in margin. Size: 84½x78mm.

Heroes of the Revolution Monument, Lubang Buaja
A114

Designs: 5r, Full view of monument (horiz.). 7.50r, Shrine at monument.

Perf. 12x12½, 12½x12

1967, Aug. 17 Photogravure
727 A114 2.50r pale green & dark brown 8 5
728 " 5r brt. rose lilac & pale brn. 12 8
729 " 7.50r pink & Prus. green 20 12

Issued to publicize the "Heroes of the Revolution" Monument in Lubang Buaja.

Forest Fire, by Raden Saleh—A115

Design: 50r, Fight to Death, by Raden Saleh.

1967, Oct. 30 Photo. *Perf. 12½*
730 A115 25r org. & gray grn. 45 40
a. Souv. sheet 1.25 1.25
731 " 50r vio. brn. & org. 1.00 90

Issued to honor the Indonesian painter Raden Saleh (1813–1880). No. 730a contains one No. 730. Marginal inscription in dark blue and orange and Raden Saleh's portrait in orange in margin. Size: 95x63 mm.

Human Rights Flame
A116

1968, Jan. 1 Photo. *Perf. 12½*
732 A116 5r green, lt. violet blue & red 15 3
733 " 12r green, olive bister & red 25 8

International Human Rights Year 1968.

Armed Forces College Emblem
A117

1968, Jan. 29 Litho. *Perf. 12½*
734 A117 10r lt. blue, yellow & brown 25 8

Integration of the Armed Forces College.

WHO Emblem and "20"
A118

Design: 20r, World Health Organization emblem.

1968, Apr. 7 Photo. *Perf. 12½*
735 A118 2r dp. yellow, pale yel. & dk. brn. 10 3
736 " 20r emerald & black 40 10

Issued to commemorate the 20th anniversary of the World Health Organization.

Trains of 1867 and 1967 and Railroad's Emblem—A119

1968, May 15 Photo. *Perf. 12½x12*
737 A119 20r multicolored 40 15
738 " 30r " 60 25

Indonesian railroad centenary (in 1967).

Tourist Type of 1967

Design: 30r, Butterfly dancer from West Java.

1968, July 1 *Perf. 12½*
739 A113 30r gray & multi. 50 25
a. Souv. sheet 1.50 1.50

Issued for tourist publicity. No. 739a contains one No. 739 and a multicolored perforated label with commemorative inscriptions in English and Indonesian. Size: 85x88½mm.

Bosscha Observatory and Andromeda Nebula—A120

Design: 30r, Observatory, globe and sky (vert.).

1968, Sept. 20 Photo. *Perf. 12½x12*
740 A120 15r ultra. & yellow 25 10
741 " 30r violet & orange 50 15

Bosscha Observatory, 40th anniversary.

Weight Lifting
A121

Designs: 7.50r+7.50r, Sailing (horiz.). 12r, Basketball. 30r, Dove, Olympic flame and emblem (horiz.).

1968, Oct. 12 *Perf. 12½*
742 A121 5r ocher, black & green 10 5
743 " 7.50r+7.50r rose red & multi. 25 15
a. Left half 12 7
b. Right half 12 7
c. Souv. sheet 1.00 80
744 " 12r blue & multi. 20 12
745 " 30r bl. green & multi. 50 20

Issued to commemorate the 19th Olympic Games, Mexico City, Oct. 12–27. No. 743 is perforated vertically in the center, dividing it into two separate stamps, each inscribed "Republic Indonesia" and "7.50r." There is no gutter along the center perforation; and the design is continous over the two stamps.
No. 743c contains one No. 743 with track design surrounding the stamps. Margin inscribed "Mexico 68" Olympic rings and emblem. Size: 95x63mm.

Eugenia Aquea Burm. f.—A122

Fruits: 15r, Papaya. 30r, Durian (vert.).

1968, Dec. 20 Photographed
Perf. 12½x12, 12x12½
746 A122 7.50r multicolored 10 5
747 " 15r " 20 15
a. Souvenir sheet of 1 40 40
748 A122 30r multicolored 40 20
a. Souvenir sheet of 1 1.50 1.50

Issued for the 11th Social Day.
No. 747a has pink margin with blue inscription, size 95x62mm; No. 748a, blue margin, orange inscription, size 63x95mm.

Globe, ILO and UN Emblems
A123

Designs: 7.50r, 25r, ILO and UN emblems.

1969, Feb. 1 Photo. *Perf. 12½*
749 A123 5r yellow green
" 7. & scarlet 10 5
750 " 50r org. & dk. green 15 5
751 " 15r lilac & orange 25 10
752 25r blue green & dull red 35 15

Issued to commemorate the 50th anniversary of the International Labor Organization.

R. Dewi Sartika
A124

Portraits: No. 754, Tjoet Nja Din. No. 755, Tjoet Nja Meuthia. No. 756, General Gatot Subroto. No. 757, Sutan Sjahrir. No. 758, Dr. F. L. Tobing. Nos. 753–755 show portraits of women.

1969, Mar. 1 Photo. *Perf. 12½x12*
753 A124 15r green & purple 25 8
754 " 15r red lilac & green 25 8
755 " 15r dk. blue & verm. 25 8
756 " 15r lilac & dk. blue 25 8
757 " 15r lemon & red 25 8
758 " 15r pale brn. & blue 25 8
Nos. 753-758 (6) 1.50 48

Heroes of Indonesian independence.

Red Crosses
A125

Design: 20r, Red Cross surrounded by arms.

1969, May 5 Photo. *Perf. 12*
759 A125 15r green & dp. red 20 12
760 " 20r org. yel. & red 30 24

Issued to commemorate the 50th anniversary of the League of Red Cross Societies.

"Family Planning Leads to National Development and Prosperity"
A126

Design: 10r, Family, birds and factories.

1969, June 2 Photo. *Perf. 12½*
761 A126 10r bl. grn. & orange 15 10
762 " 20r gray & magenta 25 20

Issued to publicize the Planned Parenthood Conference of Southeast Asia and Oceania, Bandung, June 1–7.

Map of Bali and Mask
A127

Designs: 15r, Map of Bali and woman carrying basket with offerings on head. 30r, Map of Bali and cremation ceremony.

1969, July 1 Litho. *Perf. 12½x12*

No.	Type	Description	Unused	Used
763	A127	12r gray & multi.	18	7
764	"	15r lilac & multi.	22	8
765	"	30r multicolored	40	10
		a. Souv. sheet	1.20	80

Issued for tourist publicity.

No. 765a contains one No. 765; multicolored border and inscription. Size: 96½x62½mm.

Agriculture A128 — Radar, Djatiluhur Station A129

Designs: 5r, Religious coexistence (roofs of mosques and churches). 10r, Social welfare (house and family). 12r, Import-export (cargo and ship). 15r, Clothing industry (cloth and spindles). 20r, Education (school children). 25r, Research (laboratory). 30r, Health care (people and syringe). 40r, Fishing (fish and net). 50r, Statistics (charts).

1969 Photogravure *Perf. 12x12½*

No.	Type	Description	Unused	Used
766	A128	5r yel. green & blue	6	3
767	"	7.50r rose brn. & yel.	8	4
768	"	10r slate & red	14	4
769	"	12r blue & dp. org.	16	7
770	"	15r slate grn. & org.	18	6
771	"	20r purple & yellow	25	8
772	"	25r orange & black	35	10
773	"	30r car. rose & gray	40	10
774	"	40r green & orange	55	20
775	"	50r sepia & orange	60	20
		Nos. 766-775 (10)	2.77	92

Five-year Development Plan.
See No. 968a.

1969, Sept. 29 *Perf. 12½*

Design: 30r, Communications satellite and earth.

No.	Type	Description	Unused	Used
776	A129	15r multicolored	20	15
777	"	30r "	40	30

Vickers Vimy and Borobudur Temple—A130

Design: 100r, Vickers Vimy and map of Indonesia.

1969, Nov. 1 Photo. *Perf. 13½x12½*

No.	Type	Description	Unused	Used
778	A130	75r deep orange & dull purple	60	20
779	"	100r yellow & green	1.00	30

Issued to commemorate the 50th anniversary of the first flight from England to Australia (via Java).

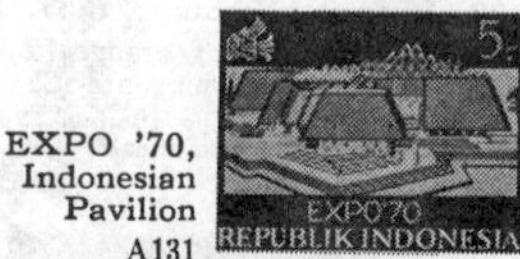

EXPO '70, Indonesian Pavilion A131

Designs: 15r, Garuda, symbol of Indonesian EXPO '70 committee. 30r, like 5r.

1970, Feb. 15 Photo. *Perf. 12x12½*

No.	Type	Description	Unused	Used
780	A131	5r brn., yel. & green	6	3
781	"	15r dark blue, yellow green & red	15	8
782	"	30r red, yel. & dk. bl.	30	10

Issued to publicize EXPO '70 International Exposition, Osaka, Japan, Mar. 15–Sept. 13.

Upraised Hands, Bars and Scales of Justice A132

1970, Mar. 15 Photo. *Perf. 12½*

No.	Type	Description	Unused	Used
783	A132	10r red org. & purple	15	5
784	"	15r brt. grn. & pur.	20	5

Rule of law and justice in Indonesia.

U.P.U. Monument, Bern A133

Design: 30r, U.P.U. Headquarters, Bern.

1970, May 20 Photo. *Perf. 12x12½*

No.	Type	Description	Unused	Used
785	A133	15r emerald & copper red	40	10
786	"	30r ocher & blue	75	15

Issued to commemorate the inauguration of the new Universal Postal Union Headquarters in Bern, Switzerland.

Timor Dancers A134

Design: 45r, Bali dancers.

1970, July 1 Photo. *Perf. 12*

No.	Type	Description	Unused	Used
787	A134	20r pink & multi.	30	12
788	"	45r lt. blue & multi.	70	28
		a. Souvenir sheet	1.00	1.00

Issued for tourist publicity. No. 788a contains one No. 788; yellow, blue and orange decorative margin. Size: 62½x96mm. Sold for 60r.

Asian Productivity Year A135 — Independence Proclamation Monument A136

1970, Aug. 1 Photo. *Perf. 12*

No.	Type	Description	Unused	Used
789	A135	5r emerald, org. & red	20	3
790	"	30r vio., org. & red	60	15

1970, Aug. 17

No.	Type	Description	Unused	Used
791	A136	40r lt. ultramarine & magenta	5.00	25

The 25th anniversary of independence.

Post and Telecommunications Emblems A137 — Postal Worker and Telephone Dial A138

Perf. 12x12½, 12½x12

1970, Sept. 27 Photogravure

No.	Type	Description	Unused	Used
792	A137	10r grn., ocher & yel.	3.00	6
793	A138	25r pink, blk. & yel.	4.50	15

25th anniversary of the postal service.

U.N. Emblem A139 — Education Year and UNESCO Emblems A140

1970, Oct. 10 Photo. *Perf. 12½*

No.	Type	Description	Unused	Used
794	A139	40r purple, red & yellow green	7.50	20

25th anniversary of the United Nations.

1970, Nov. 16 Photo. *Perf. 12½*

Design: 50r, similar to 25r, but without oval background.

No.	Type	Description	Unused	Used
795	A140	25r yellow, dark red & brown	3.50	20
796	"	50r lt. blue, black & dark red	7.00	30

International Education Year.

Batik Worker—A141

Designs: 50r, Woman with bamboo musical instrument (angklung; vert.). 75r, Menangkabau house and family in traditional costumes.

1971, May 26 Litho. *Perf. 12½*

No.	Type	Description	Unused	Used
797	A141	20r multicolored	45	8
798	"	50r "	1.10	20
		a. Souvenir sheet	1.75	1.75
799	A141	75r multicolored	1.65	30

"Visit Asian lands." No. 798a contains one stamp; multicolored margin. Size: 64x97mm. Sold for 70r.

Fatahillah Park, Djakarta—A142

Designs: 30f, City Hall. 65r, Lenong Theater performance. 80r, Ismail Marzuki Cultural Center.

1971, June 19 Photo. *Perf. 12½*

No.	Type	Description	Unused	Used
800	A142	15r yellow green, brown & blue	60	6
801	"	65r org. brn., dk. brn. & lt. green	1.85	20
802	"	80r olive, blue & magenta	2.50	25

Souvenir Sheet

No.	Type	Description	Unused	Used
803	A142	30r blue, yellow & lilac rose	2.00	1.50

444th anniversary of Djakarta. No. 803 contains one stamp; maps of Djakarta, 1619, and present in margin. Size: 120x103mm. Sold for 60r.

Rama and Sita A143

Design: 100r, Rama with bow.

1971, Aug. 31

No.	Type	Description	Unused	Used
804	A143	30r yel., grn. & blk.	45	15
805	"	100r bl., red & blk.	1.85	50

International Ramayana Festival.

Carrier Pigeon and Conference Emblem A144

1971, Sept. 20

No.	Type	Description	Unused	Used
806	A144	50r ocher & dp. brn.	50	18

5th Asian Regional Postal Conference.

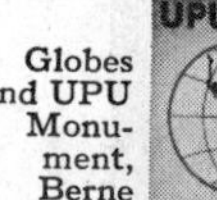

Globes and UPU Monument, Berne A145

1971, Oct. 4 Photo. *Perf. 13½x13*

No.	Type	Description	Unused	Used
807	A145	40r bl. & dull violet	40	18

Universal Postal Union Day.

Boy Writing, UNICEF Emblem A146

Design: 40r, Boy with sheaf of rice and UNICEF emblem.

1971, Dec. 11 *Perf. 12½*

No.	Type	Description	Unused	Used
808	A146	20r orange & multi.	20	10
809	"	40r blue & multi.	40	20

25th anniversary of United Nations International Children's Fund (UNICEF).

Lined Tang A147

Fish: 30r, Moorish goddess. 40r, Imperial angelfish.

1971, Dec. 27 Litho. *Perf. 12½*

No.	Type	Description	Unused	Used
810	A147	15r lilac & multi.	65	6
811	"	30r dull green & multi.	1.35	14
812	"	40r blue & multi.	1.65	30

See Nos. 834-836, 859-861, 926-928, 959-961.

U.N. Emblem A148 — Radio Tower A149

Design: 100r, Road and dam.

1972, Mar. 28 Photo. *Perf. 12½*

813 A148 40r lt. greenish blue & blue 60 20
814 A149 75r dk. car., yel. & greenish blue 90 30
815 A148 100r grn., yel. & blk. 1.20 40

United Nations Economic Commission for Asia and the Far East (ECAFE), 25th anniversary.

"Your Heart is your Health" A150 — Woman Weaver, Factories A151

1972, Apr. 7

816 A150 50r multicolored 45 18

World Health Day.

1972, Apr. 22

817 A151 35r orange, yel. & purple 30 10

50th anniversary of the Textile Technology Institute.

Book Readers A152

1972, May 15 *Perf. 13½x12½*

818 A152 75r blue & multi. 60 30

International Book Year 1972.

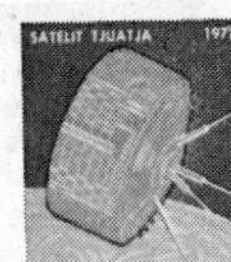

Weather Satellite A153

1972, July 20 Photo. *Perf. 12½*

Multicolored

819 A153 35r *shown* 45 10
820 " 50r *Astronaut on moon* 60 18
821 " 60r *Indonesian rocket Kartika 1* 75 20

Space achievements.

Hotel Indonesia—A154

1972, Aug. 5

822 A154 50r grn., lt. bl. & car. 40 18

Hotel Indonesia, 10th anniversary.

Silat (Self Defense) A155 — Family, Houses of Worship A156

Designs (Olympic Emblems and): 35r, Running. 50r, Diving. 75r, Badminton. 100r, Olympic Stadium.

1972, Aug. 26 Photogravure

823 A155 20r lt. blue & multi. 40 10
824 " 35r multicolored 60 15
825 " 50r yel. grn. & multi. 80 25
826 " 75r multicolored 1.20 30
827 " 100r " 1.60 40
Nos. 823-827 (5) 4.60 1.20

20th Olympic Games, Munich, Aug. 26–Sept. 11.

1972, Sept. 27 *Perf. 12½x13½*

Designs: 75r, Healthy family. 80r, Working family (national prosperity).

828 A156 30r lemon & multi. 50 12
829 " 75r lilac & multi. 1.25 28
830 " 80r multicolored 1.35 30

Family planning.

Moluccas Dancer A157 — Thomas Cup, Shuttlecock A158

Designs: 60r, Man, woman and Toradja house, Celebes. 100fr, West Irian house (horiz.).

1972, Oct. 28 Photo. *Perf. 12½x13½*

831 A157 30r olive pink & brn. 38 12
832 " 60r multicolored 75 28
833 " 100r lt. bl., brn. & dull yellow 1.20 40

Fish Type of 1971

Fish: 30r, Butterflyfish. 50r, Regal angelfish. 100r, Spotted triggerfish.

1972, Dec. 4 Litho. *Perf. 12½*

834 A147 30r blue & multi. 38 12
835 " 50r " " 60 20
836 " 100r " " 1.20 40

1973, Jan. 2 Litho. *Perf. 12½*

Designs (Thomas Cup, Shuttlecock and): 75r, National monument and Istora Sports Hall. 80r, Indonesian flag and badminton player.

837 A158 30r emerald & bright blue 20 12
838 " 75r dull green & dark carmine 80 30
839 " 80r gold & red 80 30

Thomas Cup Badminton World Championship 1973.

WMO Emblem, Anemometer, Wayang Figure A159

1973, Feb. 15 Litho. *Perf. 13½x12½*

840 A159 80r bl., grn. & claret 60 30

Centenary of international meteorological cooperation.

"Health Begins at Home" A160

1973, Apr. 7 Photo. *Perf. 12½*

841 A160 80r dk. green, orange & ultra. 60 30

25th anniversary of the World Health Organization.

Ceremonial Mask, Java A161 — Hand Putting Coin into Bank A162

1973, June 1 Photo. *Perf. 12½*

Multicolored

842 A161 30r *shown* 30 12
843 " 60r *Mask, Kalimantan* 60 25
844 " 100r *Mask, Bali* 90 40

Tourist publicity.

1973, July 2 Photo. *Perf. 12½*

Design: 30r, Symbolic coin bank and hand (horiz.).

845 A162 25r yellow, lt. brown & black 25 12
846 " 30r grn., yel. & gold 30 15

National savings movement.

Chess A163 — INTERPOL Emblem and Policemen A164

Designs: 60r, Karate. 75r, Hurdling (horiz.).

1973, Aug. 4 Photo. *Perf. 12½*

847 A163 30r red, yel. & black 30 12
848 " 60r black, ocher & light green 60 25
849 " 75r blk., lt. bl. & rose 75 40

8th National Sports Week.

1973, Sept. 3

Design: 50r, INTERPOL emblem and guard statue from Sewu Prambanan Temple (vert.).

850 A164 30r yel., grn. & blk. 30 12
851 " 50r yel., brn. & blk. 40 20

50th anniversary of International Police Organization.

Batik Worker and Parang Rusak Pattern—A165

Batik designs: 80r, Man and Pagi Sore pattern. 100r, Man and Merak Ngigel pattern.

1973, Oct. 9 Photo. *Perf. 12½*

852 A165 60r multicolored 60 20
853 " 80r " 80 30
854 " 100r " 1.00 40

Farmer, Grain, UN and FAO Emblems A166

1973, Oct. 24 Photo. *Perf. 12½*

855 A166 30r lilac & multi. 24 12

World Food Program, 10th anniversary.

Houses of Worship A167

Designs: 30r, Classroom. 60r, Family and home.

1973, Nov. 10

856 A167 20r dk. blue, lt. blue & vermilion 20 8
857 " 30r ocher, blk. & yel. 30 12
858 " 60r lt. green, yellow & black 60 24

Family planning.

Fish Type of 1971

Fish: 40r, Acanthurus leucosternon. 65r, Chaetodon trifasciatus. 100r, Pomacanthus annularis.

1973, Dec. 10 Litho. *Perf. 12½*

859 A147 40r multicolored 40 18
860 " 65r " 70 28
861 " 100r " 95 45

Adm. Sudarso and Battle of Arafuru—A168

1974, Jan. 15

862 A168 40r brt. bl. & multi. 35 16

12th Navy Day.

Bengkulu Costume A169

Designs: Regional Costumes.

1974, Mar. 28 Litho. *Perf. 12½*

Multicolored

863 A169 5r *shown*
864 " 7.50r *Kalimantan, Timor*
865 " 10r *Kalimantan, Tengah*
866 " 15r *Jambi*
867 " 20r *Sulawesi, Tenggara*
868 " 25r *Nusatenggara, Timor*
869 " 27.50r *Maluku*
870 " 30r *Lampung*
871 " 35r *Sumatra, Barat*
872 " 40r *Aceh*
873 " 45r *Nusatenggara, Barat*
874 " 50r *Riouw*
875 " 55r *Kalimantan, Barat*
876 " 60r *Sulawesi, Utara*
877 " 65r *Sulawesi, Tengah*
878 " 70r *Sumatra, Selatan*
879 " 75r *Java, Barat*
880 " 80r *Sumatra, Utara*
881 " 90r *Yogyakarta*
882 " 95r *Kalimantan, Selatan*
883 " 100r *Java, Timor*
884 " 120r *Irian, Java*
885 " 130r *Java, Tengah*
886 " 135r *Sulawesi, Selatan*
887 " 150r *Bali*
888 " 160r *Djakarta*
Nos. 863-888 (26) *22.50*

Tourist publicity.

Baladewa
A170

Designs (Figures from Shadow Plays): 80r, Kresna. 100r, Bima.

1974, June 1 Photo. *Perf. 12½*

889 A170 40r lt. vio. & multi. 38 12
890 " 80r salmon & multi. 75 20
891 " 100r rose & multi. 90 25

Pres. Suharto
A171

Family and WPY Emblem
A172

1974–76 Photo. *Perf. 12½*

Portrait in Dark Brown

901 A171 40r lt. grn. & black 30 12
903 " 50r ultra. & black 40 15
906 " 65r brt. pink & blk. 50 20
908 " 75r yellow & blk. 60 25
912 " 100r buff & black 80 32
913 " 150r citron & black 1.20 50
914 " 200r green & blue 1.50 65
915 " 300r brown orange & carmine 2.25 95
916 " 400r green & yel. 3.00 1.25
917 A171 500r lilac & car. 3.75 1.60
Nos. 901-917 (10) 14.30 5.99

Nos. 914–917 have wavy lines in background.

Issue dates: Nos. 901–913, Aug. 17, 1974. Nos. 914–917, Aug. 17, 1976.

1974, Aug. 19

918 A172 65r ultra., gray & ocher 40 20

World Population Year 1974.

"Welfare"
A173

"Development"
A174

"Religion"
A175

1974, Sept. 9

919 A173 25r green & multi. 20 6
920 A174 40r yel. grn. & multi. 35 12
921 A175 65r dk. vio. brown & multi. 50 20

Family planning.

Mailmen with Bicycles, UPU Emblem—A176

Designs (UPU Emblem and): 40r, Horse-drawn mail cart. 65r, Mailman on horseback. 100r, Sailing ship, 18th century.

1974, Oct. 9

922 A176 20r dk. grn. & multi. 15 6
923 " 40r dull bl. & multi. 30 12
924 " 65r blk. brn. & yel. 50 20
925 " 100r maroon & multi. 75 32

Centenary of Universal Postal Union.

Fish Type of 1971

Fish: 40fr, Zebrasoma veliferum. 80r, Euxiphipops navarchus. 100r, Synchiropus splendidus.

1974, Oct. 30 Photo. *Perf. 12½*

926 A147 40r blue & multi. 30 12
927 " 80r " " 60 24
928 " 100r " " 75 32

Drill Team Searching for Oil—A177

Designs (Pertamina Emblem and): 75r, Oil refinery. 95r, Pertamina telecommunications and computer center. 100r, Gasoline truck and station. 120r, Plane over storage tanks. 130r, Pipes and tanker. 150r, Petro-chemical storage tanks. 200r, Off-shore drilling platform. 95r, 100r, 120r, 130r, vertical.

1974, Dec. 10 *Perf. 13½*

929 A177 40r black & multi. 35 12
930 " 75r " " 60 20
931 " 95r " " 80 28
932 " 100r " " 85 30
933 " 120r " " 1.00 35
934 " 130r " " 1.10 38
935 " 150r " " 1.25 45
936 " 200r " " 1.75 60
Nos. 929-936 (8) 7.70 2.68

Pertamina State Oil Enterprise, 17th anniversary.

Spittoon, Sumatra
A178

Artistic Metalware: 75r, Condiment dish, Sumatra. 100r, Condiment dish, Kalimantan.

1975, Feb. 24 Photo. *Perf. 12½*

937 A178 50r red & black 35 15
938 " 75r green & black 55 24
939 " 100r brt. bl. & multi. 75 30

Blood Donors' Emblem
A179

Globe, Standard Meter and Kilogram
A180

1975, Apr. 7

940 A179 40r yel., red & green 30 12

"Give blood, save lives."

1975, May 20

941 A180 65r blue, red & yel. 50 20

Centenary of International Meter Convention, Paris, 1875.

Farmer, Teacher, Mother, Policewoman and Nurse—A181

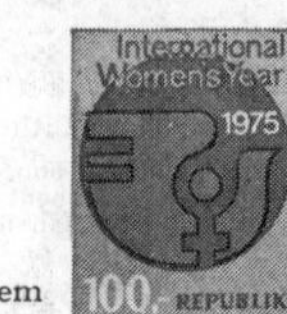

IWY Emblem
A182

1975, June 26 Photo. *Perf. 12½*

942 A181 40r multicolored 30 12
943 A182 100r " 75 30

International Women's Year 1975.

Dendrobium Pakarena
A183

Orchids: 70r, Aeridachnis bogor. 85r, Vanda genta.

1975, July 21

944 A183 40r multicolored 30 12
945 " 70r " 50 22
946 " 85r " 75 32

See Nos. 1010–1012, 1036–1038.

Stupas and Damaged Temple
A184

Designs (UNESCO Emblem and): 40r, Buddha statues, stupas and damaged wall. 65r, Stupas and damaged wall (horiz.). 100r, Buddha statue and stupas (horiz.).

1975, Aug. 10 *Perf. 12½*

947 A184 25r yel., brn. & org. 20 8
948 " 40r blk., grn. & yel. 30 12
949 " 65r lemon, claret & green 60 25
950 " 100r bister, brown & slate blue 75 30

UNESCO campaign to save Borobudur Temple, Java.

Banjarmasin Battle—A185

Battle Scenes: 40r, Batua, Sept. 8, 1946. 75r, Margarana, Nov. 20, 1946. 100r, Palembang, Jan. 1, 1947.

1975, Aug. 17

951 A185 25r yellow & black 20 8
952 " 40r org. verm. & red 30 12
953 " 75r verm. & black 55 22
954 " 100r orange & black 75 30

Indonesian independence, 30th anniversary.

"Education"
A186

Heroes' Monument, Surabaya
A187

Designs: 25r, "Religion." 40r, "Prosperity."

1975, Oct. 20 Photo. *Perf. 12½*

955 A186 20r blue, salmon & black 20 6

956 A186 25r emerald, salmon & black 24 8
957 " 40r dp. orange, blue & black 36 12

Family planning.

1975, Nov. 10

958 A187 100r maroon & grn. 80 32

War of independence, 30th anniversary.

Fish Type of 1971

Fish: 40r, Coris angulata. 75r, Chaetodon ephippium. 150r, Platax pinnatus (vert.).

1975, Dec. 15 Litho. *Perf. 12½*

959 A147 40r multicolored 30 12
960 " 75r " 55 22
961 " 150r " 1.10 45

Thomas Cup A188

Designs: 40r, Uber Cup. 100r, Thomas and Uber Cups.

1976, Jan. 31 Photo. *Perf. 12½*

962 A188 20r blue & multi. 15 6
963 " 40r multicolored 30 12
964 " 100r green & multi. 75 32

Indonesia, Badminton World Champions.

Refugees on Truck and New Village—A189

Designs: 50r, Neglected and restored village streets. 100r, Derelict and rebuilt houses.

1976, Feb. 28 Photo. *Perf. 12½*

965 A189 30r yel. & multi. 24 9
966 " 50r blue & multi. 36 16
967 " 100r ocher & multi. 72 32

World Human Settlements Day.

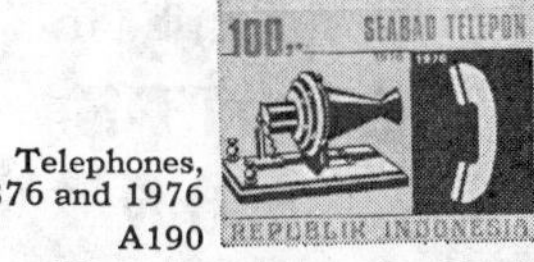

Telephones, 1876 and 1976 A190

1976, Mar. 10 Photo. *Perf. 12½*

968 A190 100r yellow, orange & brown 72 32
a. Bklt. pane of 8 (4 #968, 4 #775, 2 labels) ('78) 5.25

Centenary of first telephone call by Alexander Graham Bell, Mar. 10, 1876.

Eye and WHO Emblem A191

Design: 40r, Blind man, eye and World Health Organization emblem.

1976, Apr. 7 Photo. *Perf. 12½*

969 A191 20r yellow, lt. green & black 15 6
970 " 40r yel., bl. & blk. 30 12

Foresight prevents blindness.

Montreal Stadium—A192

1976, May 17

971 A192 100r ultramarine 72 22

21st Olympic Games, Montreal, Canada, July 17–Aug. 1.

Lake Tondano, Celebes A193

Designs: 40r, Lake Kelimutu, Flores. 75r, Lake Maninjau, Sumatra.

1976, June 1

972 A193 35r lt. grn. & blk. 25 10
973 " 40r gray, rose & light green 30 12
974 " 75r bl. & slate grn. 55 22
a. Bklt. pane of 8 (7 #974, #998, 2 labels) ('78) 4.50

Tourist publicity.

Radar Station A194

Designs: 50r, Master control radar station. 100r, Apalata satellite.

1976, July 8 Photo. *Perf. 12½*

975 A194 20r multicolored 15 6
976 " 50r green & black 40 16
977 " 100r multicolored 75 32
a. Bklt. pane of 9 (4 #977, 5 #987, label) ('78) 4.50

Inauguration of domestic satellite system.

Arachnis Flos-aeris—A195

Orchids: 40r, Vanda putri serang. 100r, Coelogyne pandurata.

1976, Sept. 7

978 A195 25r multicolored 20 8
979 " 40r " 30 12
980 " 100r " 75 32

Tree and Mountain A196

1976, Oct. 4

981 A196 20r grn., bl. & brn. 15 6

16th National Reforestation Week.

Dagger and Sheath from Timor—A197

Historic Daggers and Sheaths: 40r, from Borneo. 100r, from Aceh.

1976, Nov. 1 *Perf. 12½*

982 A197 25r multicolored 20 8
983 " 40r " 30 15
a. Souvenir sheet 4.50 4.50
984 A197 100r grn. & multi. 75 32

No. 983a contains one No. 983; multicolored decorative margin. Size: 94x63 mm. Exists imperf.

Open Book A198

Children Reading A199

1976, Dec. 8 Photo. *Perf. 12½*

985 A198 20r multicolored 15 6
986 A199 40r " 30 12

Better books for children.

UNICEF Emblem A200

Ballot Box A201

1976, Dec. 11

987 A200 40r multicolored 30 12

United Nations Children Fund, 30th anniversary.

1977, Jan. 5 Photo. *Perf. 12½*

Designs: 75r, Ballot box, grain and factory. 100r, Coat of arms.

988 A201 40r multicolored 30 12
989 " 75r " 55 24
990 " 100r " 75 32

1977 elections.

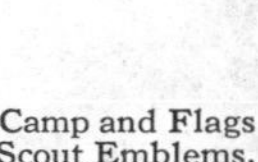

Camp and Flags Scout Emblems, A202

1977, Feb. 28

Designs: 30r, Tent, emblems and trees. 40r, Boy and Girl Scout flags and emblems.

991 A202 25r multicolored 20 8
992 " 30r " 24 10
993 " 40r " 30 12

11th National Scout Jamboree.

Letter with "AOPU" A203

Anniversary Emblem, Djakarta Arms A204

Design: 100r, Stylized bird and letter.

1977, Apr. 1 Photo. *Perf. 12½*

994 A203 65r multicolored 40 20
995 " 100r " 60 32

Asian-Oceanic Postal Union, 15th convention.

1977, May 23 Photo. *Perf. 12½*

Designs: Anniversary emblem and arms of Djakarta in different arrangements.

996 A204 20r orange & blue 12 6
997 " 40r emerald & blue 24 12
998 " 100r slate & blue 60 32
a. Souvenir sheet 75

450th anniversary of Djakarta. No. 998a contains one stamp; ocher and blue margin shows modern building. Size: 73x 95mm. No. 998a also issued imperf.

Rose A205

Various Sports Emblems A206

Design: No. 1000, Envelope.

1977, May 26 Photo. *Perf. 12½*

999 A205 100r green, black & red 60 32
a. Souvenir sheet 75
1000 A205 100r green, black & red 60 32
a. Souvenir sheet of 4 2.75

Amphilex 77 Philatelic Exhibition, Amsterdam, May 26–June 5. Nos. 999–1000 printed se-tenant. No. 999a contains one stamp similar to No. 999 with blue background; multicolored decorative margin. Size: 73x64mm. No. 1000a contains 2 each of Nos. 999–1000; green margin with black inscription. Size: 72x96mm.

Nos. 999a, 1000a exist imperf.

1977, June 22

Designs: 50r, 100r, Different sports emblems,

1001 A206 40r silver & multi. 24 12
1002 " 50r " " 30 16
1003 " 100r gold & multi. 60 32

9th National Sports Week.

Contest Trophy A207

Emblem A208

1977, July 20

1004 A207 40r grn. & multi. 24 12
1005 A208 100r yel. & multi. 60 32

10th National Koran Reading Contest, July 20–27.

Map of ASEAN Countries, Satellite A209

Designs: 35r, Map of ASEAN countries. 50r, Flags of founding members: Indonesia, Malaysia, Philippines, Singapore and Thailand; ship, plane and train.

1977, Aug. 8

1006 A209 25r multicolored 15 8
1007 " 35r " 22 12
1008 " 50r " 30 16

Association of South East Asian Nations (ASEAN), 10th anniversary.

Uniform, Jakarta Regiment
A210

1977, Aug. 19

1009 A210 25r green, gold & brown 15 8

Indonesia-Pakistan Economic and Cultural Organization, 1968–1977.

Orchid Type of 1975

Orchids: 25r, Taeniophyllum. 40r, Phalaenopsis violacea. 100r, Dendrobium spectabile.

1977, Oct. 28 Photo. ***Perf. 12½***

1010 A183 25r org. & multi. 15 8
1011 " 40r blue & multi. 24 12
1012 " 100r yellow green & multi. 60 32
a. Souvenir sheet 65

No. 1012a contains one stamp similar to No. 1012 with blue background. Yellow margin with blue inscription. Size: 87x71mm. No. 1012a exists imperf.

Child and Mosquito
A211

1977, Nov. 7 ***Perf. 12½***

1013 A211 40r brt. green, red & black 24 12

National Health campaign to eradicate malaria.

Proboscis Monkey—A212

Designs: 40r, Indian elephant. 100r, Tiger.

1977, Dec. 22

1014 A212 20r multicolored 12 6
1015 " 40r " 24 12
1016 " 100r " 60 32
a. Souvenir sheet 65

Wildlife protection. No. 1016a contains one No. 1016; multicolored decorative margin. Size: 94x63mm. Exists imperf.

Conference Emblem
A213

Mother and Child
A214

1978, Mar. 27 Photo. ***Perf. 12½***

1017 A213 100r light blue & ultramarine 60 32

United Nations Conference on Technical Cooperation among Developing Countries.

1978, Apr. 7 Photo. ***Perf. 12½***

Design: 75r, Mother and child, symbolic design.

1018 A214 40r lt. grn. & blue 24 12
1019 " 75r org. red & brn. 45 24

Promotion of breast feeding.

Dome of The Rock, Jerusalem—A215

1978, May 15 Photo. ***Perf. 12½***

1020 A215 100r multicolored 60 32

Palestinian fighters and their families.

Argentina '78 Emblem
A216

Head and "Blood Circulation"
A217

1978, June 1

1021 A216 40r multicolored 24 12
1022 " 100r " 60 32

11th World Cup Soccer Championships, Argentina, June 1–25.

1978, June 17 Photo. ***Perf. 12½***

1023 A217 100r blk., bl. & red 60 32

World Health Day and drive against hypertension.

Leather Puppets—A218

Art from Wayang Museum, Djakarta: 75r, Wooden puppets. 100r, Actors with puppet masks.

1978, July 22 Litho. ***Perf. 12½***

1024 A218 40r multicolored 24 12
1025 " 75r " 45 24
1026 " 100r " 60 32

Congress Emblem
A219

IAAY Emblem
A220

1978, Aug. 1

1027 A219 100r slate 60 32

27th Congress of World Confederation of Organizations of Teachers (WCOTP), Djakarta, June 26–Aug. 2.

1978, Aug. 16 Photo. ***Perf. 12½***

1028 A220 100r org. & dk. bl. 60 32

International Anti-Apartheid Year.

Congress Emblem
A221

Youth Pledge Emblem
A222

Design: 100r, People and trees.

1978, Oct. 16 Photo. ***Perf. 12½***

1029 A221 40r emerald & blue 24 12
1030 " 100r emerald & black 60 32

8th World Forestry Congress, Djakarta.

1978, Oct. 28

1031 A222 40r dark brown & red 24 12
1032 " 100r sal., brown & red 60 32

50th anniversary of the Youth Pledge.

Porcupine Anteater—A223

Designs: 75r, Deer. 100r, Clouded tiger.

1978, Nov. 1

1033 A223 40r multicolored 24 12
1034 " 75r " 45 24
1035 " 100r " 60 32

Wildlife protection.

Orchid Type of 1975

Orchids: 40r, Phalaenopsis sri rejeki. 75r, Dendrobium macrophilium. 100r, Cymbidium fynlaysonianum.

1978, Dec. 22 Photo. ***Perf. 12½***

1036 A183 40r multicolored 12 5
1037 " 75r " 25 10
1038 " 100r " 35 15

Douglas DC-3, 1949, over Volcano—A224

Designs: 75r, Douglas DC-9 over village. 100r, Douglas DC-10 over temple.

1979, Jan. 26 Photo. ***Perf. 12½***

1039 A224 40r multicolored 12 5
1040 " 75r " 25 10
1041 " 100r " 35 15

Garuda Indonesian Airways, 30th anniversary.

Badminton

A225 A226

Design: 40r, Thomas Cup and badminton player.

1979, Feb. 24 Photo. ***Perf. 12½***

1042 A225 40r car. & blue 12 5
1043 " 100r car. & ocher 35 15
1044 A226 100r " " 35 15

11th Thomas Cup, Djakarta, May 24–June 2. Nos. 1043–1044 printed se-tenant in sheets of 100.

Paphiopedilum Lowii
A227

Orchids: 100r, Vanda limbata. 125r, Phalaenopsis gigantea.

1979, Mar. 22 Photo. ***Perf. 12½***

1045 A227 60r multicolored 35 18
1046 " 100r " 60 32
1047 " 125r " 75 38

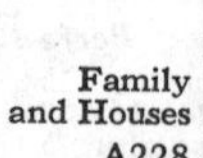

Family and Houses
A228

Third Five-year Plan: 60r, Pylon and fields. 100r, School and clinic. 125r, Factories and trucks. 150r, Motorized mail delivery.

1979, Apr. 1

1048 A228 35r grn. & olive 22 10
1049 " 60r blue & olive 35 18
1050 " 100r bl. & dk. brn. 60 32
1051 " 125r red brn. & ol. 75 40
1052 " 150r car. & yellow 90 48
Nos. 1048–1052 (5) 2.82 1.48

SEMI-POSTAL STAMPS.

Symbols of Olympic Games SP43 — Wings and Flame SP44

Perf. 12½x12

1951, Jan. 2 Photo. Unwmkd.

B58	SP43	5s+3s gray green	5	5
B59	"	10s+5s dark violet blue	6	6
B60	"	20s+5s orange red	7	7
B61	"	30s+10s dark brown	20	20
B62	"	35s+10s ultramarine	1.00	1.00
		Nos. B58-B62 (5)	1.38	1.38

Issued to publicize the Asiatic Olympic Games of 1951 at New Delhi, India.

1951, Oct. 15

B63	SP44	5s+3s olive green	5	5
B64	"	10s+5s dull blue	5	5
B65	"	20s+5s red	8	8
B66	"	30s+10s brown	12	12
B67	"	35s+10s ultramarine	15	15
		Nos. B63-B67 (5)	45	45

Issued to publicize the second National Games, Djakarta, October 21-28, 1951.

No. 378 Surcharged in Black

19 53
BENTJANA ALAM
+10s

1953, May 8 *Perf. 12½*

B68	A53	35s+10s purple	18	14

The surcharge reads "Natural Disaster." Surtax was for emergency relief following volcanic eruption and floods.

Merapi Erupting SP45 — Young Musicians SP46

1954, Apr. 15 Litho. *Perf. 12½x12*

B69	SP45	15s+10s blue green	8	6
B70	"	35s+15s purple	15	12
B71	"	50s+25s red	20	16
B72	"	75s+25s violet blue	25	20
B73	"	1r+25s carmine	35	28
B74	"	2r+50s blk. brn.	2.00	64
B75	"	3r+1r gray green	6.25	2.50
B76	"	5r+2.50r org. brn.	9.00	3.50
		Nos. B69-B76 (8)	18.28	7.46

The surtax was for victims of the Merapi volcano eruption.

1954, Dec. 22 Photo. *Perf. 12½*

Designs: 15s+10s, Parasol dance. 35s+15s, Girls playing dakon. 50s+15s, Boy on stilts. 75s+25s, Bamboo flute players. 1r+25s, Javanese dancer.

B77	SP46	10s+10s dark purple	3	3
B78	"	15s+10s dark green	3	3
B79	"	35s+15s carminerose	3	3
B80	"	50s+15s rose brown	5	5
B81	"	75s+25s ultramarine	10	10
B82	"	1r+25s red orange	18	18
		Nos. B77-B82 (6)	42	42

The surtax was for child welfare.

Scout Emblem SP47

Scout Signaling SP48

Designs: 50s+25s, Campfire. 75s+25s, Scout feeding fawn. 1r+50s, Scout saluting.

1955, June 27 *Perf. 12½* **Unwmkd.**

B83	SP47	15s+10s blue green	8	6
B84	SP48	35s+15s ultramarine	8	6
B85	"	50s+25s scarlet	10	8
B86	"	75s+25s brown	12	10
B87	"	1r+50s violet	20	15
		Nos. B83-B87 (5)	58	45

Issued to commemorate the First National Boy Scout Jamboree.

Blind Weaver SP49 — Red Cross and Heart SP50

Designs: 35s+15s, Basket weaver. 50s+25s, Boy studying map. 75s+50s, Woman reading Braille.

1956, Jan. 4

B88	SP49	15s+10s deep green	4	4
B89	"	35s+15s yellow brown	8	8
B90	"	50s+25s rose carmine	60	40
B91	"	75s+50s ultramarine	30	28

The surtax was for the benefit of the blind.

1956, July 26 Lithographed

Designs: 35s+15s, 50s+15s, Transfusion bottle. 75s+25s, 1r+25s, Outstretched hands.

Cross in Red

B92	SP50	10s+10s ultramarine	4	4
B93	"	15s+10s carmine	8	8
B94	"	35s+15s light brown	10	10
B95	"	50s+15s blue green	10	10
B96	"	75s+25s orange	15	10
B97	"	1r+25s bright purple	18	12
		Nos. B92-B97 (6)	65	54

The surtax was for the Indonesian Red Cross.

Invalids Doing Batik Work SP51

Designs: 15s+10s, Amputee painting. 35s+15s, Lathe operator. 50s+15s, Crippled child learning to walk. 75s+25s, Treating amputee. 1r+25s, Painting with artificial hand.

1957, Mar. 26 Photo. *Perf. 12½*

B98	SP51	10s+10s deep blue	5	5
B99	"	15s+10s brown	6	6
B100	"	35s+15s red	8	8
B101	"	50s+15s deep violet	15	10
B102	"	75s+25s green	20	12
B103	"	1r+25s dark carmine rose	25	18
		Nos. B98-B103 (6)	79	59

The surtax was for rehabilitation of invalids.

Kembodja Flower SP52

Designs: 15s+10s, Michelia. 35s+15s, Sunflower. 50s+15s, Jasmine. 75s+50s, Orchid.

1957, Dec. 23 *Perf. 13½x12½*

Flowers in Natural Colors.

B104	SP52	10s+10s blue	50	30
B105	"	15s+10s deep yellow green	45	30
B106	"	35s+15s dark red brown	15	10
B107	"	50s+15s olive & dark brown	15	10
B108	"	75s+50s rose brown	20	15
		Nos. B104-B108 (5)	1.45	95

Children SP53 — Indonesian Scout Emblem SP54

Design: 15+10s, 50+25s, 1r+50s, Girl and boy.

1958, July 1 Photo. *Perf. 12½x12*

B109	SP53	10s+10s blue	3	3
B110	"	15s+10s rose brown	5	5
B111	"	35s+15s gray green	5	8
B112	"	50s+25s gray olive	8	8
B113	"	75s+50s brn. car.	10	10
B114	"	1r+50s brown	14	14
		Nos. B109-B114 (6)	45	45

The surtax was for orphans.

1959, July 17 Photo. Unwmkd.

Design: 15s + 10s, 50s + 25s, 1r + 50s, Scout emblem and compass.

Emblem in Red.

B115	SP54	10s+5s bistre	3	3
B116	"	15s+10s bluish green	4	4
B117	"	20s+10s lilac gray	4	4
B118	"	50s+25s olive	8	8
B119	"	75s+35s yel. brn.	12	12
B120	"	1r+50s dark gray	20	20
		Nos. B115-B120 (6)	51	51

Issued for the 10th World Scout Jamboree, Makiling National Park near Manila, July 17-26.

Palm-leaf Ribs, Gong and 5 Rings SP55

Young Couple Holding Sharpened Bamboo Weapon SP56

Design: 20s+10s, 75s+35s, Bamboo musical instrument and 5-ring emblem.

1960, Feb. 14 *Perf. 12½x12*

B121	SP55	15s+5s bistre & dark brown	3	3
B122	"	20s+10s green & black	3	3
B123	"	50s+25s blue & purple	5	5
B124	"	75s+35s olive & dark green	10	8
B125	SP56	1.15r+50s carmine & black	15	12
		Nos. B121-B125 (5)	36	31

Issued to commemorate the All-Indonesian Youth Congress, Bandung, Feb. 14-21, 1960.

Social Emblem SP57 — Pineapple SP58

Designs: 15s+15s, Rice, lotus and cotton. 20s+20s, Lotus blossom and tree. 50s+25s, Girl and boy. 75s+25s, Watering of plant in man's hand. 3r+50s, Woman nursing infant.

Inscribed: "Hari Sosial Ke III."

Perf. 12½x12

1960, Dec. 20 Photo. Unwmkd.

B126	SP57	10s+10s ochre & black	3	3
B127	"	15s+15s deep claret & black	3	3
B128	"	20s+20s blue & black	5	5
B129	"	50s+25s bistre brown & black	6	6
B130	"	75s+25s emerald & black	18	8
B131	"	3r+50s red & black	30	12
		Nos. B126-B131 (6)	65	37

3rd Social Day, Dec. 20.

Type of 1960 Overprinted: "BENTJANA ALAM 1961"

Designs: 15s+10s, Coffee. 20s+15s, Tobacco. 75s+25s, Rubber plantation.

1961, Feb. 17 *Perf. 12x12½*

B132	A76	15s+10s plum	5	3
B133	"	20s+15s ochre	5	3
B134	"	75s+25s scarlet	10	5

The surtax was for flood relief.

1961, Dec. 20 *Perf. 12½x13½*

Designs: 75s+25s, Mangosteen. 3r+1r, Rambutan.

B135	SP58	20s+10s blue, yellow & red	10	8
B136	"	75s+25s gray, green & deep claret	16	10
B137	"	3r+1r green, yellow & red	45	20

Issued for the 4th Social Day.

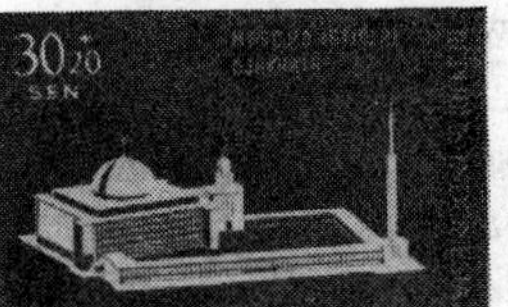

Istiqlal Mosque, Djakarta SP59

Designs: 40s+20s, 3r+1r, Different view of mosque.

1962, Feb. 22 *Perf. 12½x12*

B138	SP59	30s+20s Prussian green & yellow	8	4
B139	"	40s+20s dark red & yellow	8	8
B140	"	1.50r+50s brown & yellow	20	10
B141	"	3r+1r grn. & yel.	35	18

Issued for the benefit of the new Istiqlal Mosque.

National Monument, Djakarta
SP60

Design: 1.50r+50s, 6r+1.50r, Aerial view of monument.

1962, May 20 Photo. *Perf. 12x12½*

B142 SP60 1r+50s orange brn. & blk. 5 5
B143 " 1.50r+50s olive grn. & ultra. 6 6
B144 " 3r+1r lilac rose & dk. green 12 12
B145 " 6r+1.50r violet blue & red 18 18

Vanda Tricolor
SP61

Orchids: 1.50r+50s, Phalaenopsis amabilis (vert.). 3fr+1fr, Dendrobium phalaenopsis (vert.). 6fr+1.50fr, Paphiopedilum praestans.

Perf. 13½x12½, 12½x13½

1962, Dec. 20 Unwmkd.

Orchids in Natural Colors

B146 SP61 1r+50s ultra. & yellow 6 4
B147 " 1.50r+50s greenish blue & verm. 6 4
B148 " 3r+1r deep blue & ochre 6 4
B149 " 6r+1.50r orange & dull violet 12 12

Issued for the 5th Social Day.

West Irian Monument, Djakarta
SP62

1963, Feb. 15 *Perf. 12½x13½*

B150 SP62 1r+50s rose red & black 5 3
B151 " 1.50r+50s magenta & dark brown 5 3
B152 " 3r+1r blue & dark brown 10 6
B153 " 6r+1.50r green & brown 20 12

The surtax was for the construction of the West Irian Monument in Djakarta.

Erupting Volcano—SP63

1963, June 29 Photo. *Perf. 13½x13*

B154 SP63 4r+2r rose red 8 6
B155 " 6r+3r greenish bl. 12 10

The surtax was for victims of national natural disasters.

Papilio Blumei, Celebes
SP64

Malaysian Fantails
SP65

Butterflies: 4r+1r, Charaxes Dehaani, Java. 6r+1.50r, Graphium, West Irian. 12r+3r, Troides Amphrysus, Sumatra.

1963, Dec. 20 *Perf. 12x12½*

B156 SP64 1.75r+50s bl., grn. & dk. brn. 8 5
B157 " 4r+1r orge. yel., blk. & dark brown 8 5
B158 " 6r+1.50r yel. grn., red lilac & black 8 5
B159 " 12r+3r dp. orge., dark brown & green 15 12

Issued for the 6th Social Day.

Perf. 12½x13½

1965, Jan. 25 Photo. Unwmkd.

Birds: 6r+1.50r, Zebra doves. 12r+3r, Black drongos. 20r+5r, Black-naped orioles. 30r+7.50r, Javanese sparrows.

B160 SP65 4r+1r dull yellow, lilac & black 6 3
B161 " 6r+1.50r green, black & pink 6 6
B162 " 12r+3r olive & blk. 8 8
B163 " 20r+5r gray, yellow & red 15 8
B164 " 30r+7.50r carmine rose, slate blue & black 25 12
Nos. B160-B164 (5) 60 37

Issued for the 7th Social Day.

Type of Regular Issue, 1964, Inscribed Vertically "Conefo"

1965 *Perf. 12½x12*

B165 A98 1r+1r orange red & brown 3 3
B166 " 1.25r+1.25r orange red & brown 3 3
B167 " 1.75r+1.75r orge. red & brn. blk. 3 3
B168 " 2r+2r orge. red & slate green 3 3
B169 " 2.50r+2.50r orge. red & red brn. 3 3
B170 " 4r+3.50r orange red & dp. blue 3 3
B171 " 6r+4r orange red & emerald 3 3
B172 " 10r+5r orge. red & yel. brown 3 3
B173 " 12r+5.50r orge. red & orange 5 3
B174 " 15r+7.50r orge. red & bl. grn. 5 3
B175 " 20r+10r orge. red & dk. gray 5 3
B176 " 25r+10r orange red & purple 6 3
B177 " 40r+15r verm. & plum 8 3
B178 " 50r+15r orge. red & dp. violet 3 3
B179 " 100r+25r orge. red & dark olive gray 6 3
Nos. B165-B179 (15) 62 45

Conference of New Emerging Forces.

Makara Mask and Magic Rays
SP66

Family and Produce
SP67

1965, July 17 *Perf. 12*

B180 SP66 20r+10r red & dk. bl. 6 6
B181 " 30r+15r bl. & dk. red 10 10

Issued to publicize the fight against cancer.

1965, Aug. 17 Photo. *Perf. 12½*

State Principles: 20r+10r, Humanitarianism; clasped hands, globe, flags and chain. 25r+10r, Nationalism; map of Indonesia and tree. 40r+15r, Democracy; conference and bull's head. 50r+15r, Belief in God; houses of worship and star.

B182 SP67 10r+5r terra cotta, yel. & black 5 3
B183 " 20r+10r dp. yel., red & black 5 3
B184 " 25r+10r rose red, red, grn. & blk. 5 4
B185 " 40r+15r blue, red & black 5 5
B186 " 50r+15r lilac, yel. & black 5 5
Nos. B182-B186 (5) 25 20

Samudra Beach Hotel and Pres. Sukarno—SP68

Designs: 25r+10r, 80r+20r, Ambarrukmo Palace Hotel and Pres. Sukarno.

1965, Dec. 1 Photo. *Perf. 12½*

B187 SP68 10r+5r dk. blue & lt. blue green 3 3
B188 " 25r+10r vio. black & yellow green 5 5
B189 " 40r+15r dk. brown & violet blue 8 8
B190 " 80r+20r dk. purple & orange 10 10

Issued for tourist publicity.

Gloriosa
SP69

Flowers: 40r+15r, Magaguabush. 80r+20r, Balsam. 100r+25r, Crape myrtle.

1965, Dec. 20 Photo. *Perf. 12*

Flowers in Natural Colors

B191 SP69 30r+10r dp. blue 5 3
B192 " 40r+15r " 8 5
B193 " 80r+20r " 10 6
B194 " 100r+25r " 15 12

Dated "1966"

Flowers: 10s+5s, Senna. 20s+5s, Crested barleria. 30s+10s, Scarlet ixora. 40s+10s, Rose of China (hibiscus).

1966, Feb. 10

Flowers in Natural Colors

B195 SP69 10s+5s Prus. blue 3 3
B196 " 20s+5s green 5 5
B197 " 30s+10s " 6 6
B198 " 40s+10s Prus. blue 12 12

Nos. B191-B198 issued for the 8th Social Day, Dec. 20, 1965. An imperf. souvenir sheet contains one No. B198. Green margin with yellow and white inscription. Size: 58x78mm.

Type of 1965 Inscribed:
"BENTJANA ALAM / NASIONAL 1966"

Flowers: 15s+5s, Gloriosa. 25s+5s, Magaguabush. 30s+10s, Balsam. 80s+20s, Crape myrtle.

1966, May 2

Flowers in Natural Colors

B199 SP69 15s+5s blue 5 3
B200 " 25s+5s dark blue 8 5
B201 " 30s+10s " 12 6
B202 " 80s+20s light blue 35 20

The surtax was for victims of national natural disasters.

Reticulated Python—SP70

Reptiles: 3r+50s, Bloodsucker. 4r+75s, Salt-water crocodile. 6r+1r, Hawksbill turtle (incorrectly inscribed *chelonia mydas*, "green turtle").

1966, Dec. 20 Photo. *Perf. 12½x12*

B203 SP70 2r+25s multi. 5 5
B204 " 3r+50s " 8 8
B205 " 4r+75s " 12 12
B206 " 6r+1r " 16 16

Flooded Village
SP71

Buddha and Stupa, Borobudur Temple
SP72

Designs: 2.50r+25s, Landslide. 4r+40s, Fire destroying village. 5r+50s, Erupting volcano.

1967, Dec. 20 Photo. *Perf. 12½*

B207 SP71 1.25r+10s dull vio. blue & yellow 6 6
B208 " 2.50r+25s dull vio. blue & yellow 12 12
B209 " 4r+40s dp. orange & black 18 18
B210 " 5r+50s dp. org. & black 24 24
a. Souv. sheet of 2 12.50 10.00

The surtax was for victims of national natural disasters.

No. B210a contains one each of Nos. B209–B210. Black and deep orange marginal inscription. Size: 95½x89½mm.

1968, Mar. 1 Photo. *Perf. 12½*

Designs: No. B211, Musicians. No. B212, Sudhana and Princess Manohara. No. B213, Procession with elephant and horses.

B211 SP72 2.50r+25s brt. grn. & gray olive 10 10
B212 " 2.50r+25s brt. grn. & gray olive 10 10
B213 " 2.50r+25s brt. grn. & gray olive 10 10
Strip of 3, #B211–B213 30 30
a. Souvenir sheet of 3 12.50 10.00
B214 " 7.50r+75s org. & gray olive 25 25

The surtax was to help save Borobudur Temple in Central Java, c. 800 A.D.

Nos. B211–B213 were printed se-tenant in same sheet. Continuous design shows a frieze from Borobudur.

No. B213a contains one each of Nos. B211–B213 with marginal decoration and inscription in bright green and orange. Size: 95x64½mm.

Scout with Pickax
SP73

Designs: 10r+1r, Bugler. 30r+3r, Scouts singing around campfire (horiz.).

1968, June 1 Photo. *Perf. 12½*

Size: 28½x44½ mm.

B215 SP73 5r+50s dp. orange & brown 20 10
B216 " 10r+1r brown & gray olive 30 22

Size: 68x28½mm.

B217 SP73 30r+3r olive gray & green 70 65

Surtax for Wirakarya Scout Camp.

Woman with Flower
SP74

1969, Apr. 21 Photo. *Perf. 13½x12½*

B218 SP74 20r+2r emerald, red & yellow 40 20

Emancipation of Indonesian women.

Noble Voluta
SP75

Sea shells: 7.50r+50s, Common hairy triton. 10r+1r, Spider conch. 15r+1.50r, Murex ternispina.

1969, Dec. 20 Photo. *Perf. 12½*

B219 SP75 5r+50s multi. 8 6
B220 " 7.50r+50s " 12 10
B221 " 10r+1r " 16 12
B222 " 15r+1.50r " 24 20

Issued for the 12th Social Day, Dec. 20.

Chrysocoris Javanus
SP76

Insects: 15r+1.50r, Dragonfly. 20r+2r, Carpenter bee.

1970, Dec. 21 Photo. *Perf. 12½*

B223 SP76 7.50r+50c multi. *1.80* 4
B224 " 15r+1.50r " *5.50* 8
B225 " 20r+2r " *6.00* 12

The 13th Social Day, Dec. 20.

SPECIAL DELIVERY STAMPS

Garuda
SD1
Photogravure

1967 *Perf. 13½x12½* **Unwmkd.**

E1 SD1 10r light ultra. & dull purple 25 10
E2 " 15r org. & dull purple 50 30

1968 Inscribed "1968"

E3 SD1 10r lt. ultra. & dull purple ('68) 16 10
E4 " 15r orange & dull purple ('68) 24 18
E5 " 20r yel. & dull purple 28 25
E6 " 30r bright green & dull purple 40 40
E7 " 40r lilac & dull purple 55 50
Nos. E3–E7 (5) 1.63 1.43

1969 Same Inscribed "1969"

E8 SD1 20r yel. & dull purple 38 20
E9 " 30r bright green & dull purple 50 30
E10 " 40r lilac & dull purple 65 40

POSTAGE DUE STAMPS

Netherlands Indies Nos. J57 to J59 Surcharged in Black

BAJAR
2½
sen
PORTO

1950 *Perf. 14½x14* **Wmk. 228**

J60 D7 2½s on 50c yellow 40 30
J61 " 5s on 100c apple grn. 1.20 70
J62 " 10s on 75c aquamarine 1.60 90

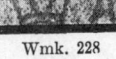

D8

Wmk. 228

Wmkd. Small Crown and C of A Multiple. (228)

Lithographed.

1951-52 *Perf. 12½* **Wmk. 228**

J63 D8 2½s vermilion 10 6
J64 " 5s " 10 5
J65 " 10s " 10 8
J66 " 20s blue ('52) 20 12
J67 " 25s olive bistre ('52) 50 35
J68 " 50s vermilion 4.00 3.00
J69 " 1r citron 4.00 2.00
Nos. J63–J69 (7) 9.00 5.66

1953-55 **Unwmkd.**

J70 D8 15s lt. magenta ('55) 20 10
J71 " 30s red brown 20 16
J72 " 40s green 20 18

1958-61 *Perf. 13½x12½*

J73 D8 10s orange 5 3
J74 " 15s " ('59) 5 3
J74A " 20s " ('61) 12 5
J75 " 25s " 20 8
J76 " 30s " ('60) 20 8
J77 " 50s " 2.00 55
J78 " 100s " ('60) 1.00 20
Nos. J73–J78 (7) 3.62 1.02

1962-65 *Perf. 13½x12½*

J79 D8 50s lt. bluish green 3 3
J80 " 100s bister 3 3
J81 " 250s blue 3 3
J82 " 500s dull yellow 6 6
J83 " 750s pale lilac 10 10
J84 " 1000s salmon 15 15
J85 " 50r red ('65) 5 5
J86 " 100r maroon ('65) 10 10
Nos. J79–J86 (8) 55 55

"1966"
D9
Photogravure

1966 *Perf. 13½x12½* **Unwmkd.**

J91 D9 5s dull green & dull yellow 5 3
J92 " 10s red & lt. blue 5 3
J93 " 20s dk. blue & pink 6 3
J94 " 30s brown & rose 8 4
J95 " 40s plum & bister 8 4
J96 " 50s olive green & pale lilac 8 4
J97 " 100s dk. red & yellow green 12 4
J98 " 200s bright green & pink ('67) 15 10
J99 " 500s yellow & light blue ('67) 20 16
J100 " 1000s rose lilac & yellow ('67) 35 20
Nos. J91–J100 (10) 1.22 71

Type of 1966 Dated "1967"

1967 Photo. *Perf. 13½x12½*

J101 D9 50s olive green & pale lilac 5 4
J102 " 100s dark red & yellow green 10 4
J103 " 200s brt. grn. & pink 12 8
J104 " 500s yellow & lt. blue 22 17
J105 " 1000s rose lilac & yel. 40 20
J106 " 15r orange & gray 30 25
J107 " 25r lilac & citron 50 40
Nos. J101–J107 (7) 1.69 1.18

Similar stamps inscribed "Bajar/1968/Sumbangan Ongkos Tjetak" are for revenue purposes.

Type of 1966 Dated "1973"
Inscribed "BAYAR PORTO"

1973 Photogravure *Perf. 13½x12½*

J114 D9 25r lilac & citron

Denominations of 65r and 125r exist, dated "1974".

Type of 1966 Dated "1975"
Inscribed "BAYAR PORTO"

1975 Photo. *Perf. 13½x12½*

J115 D9 25r lilac & citron 15 15

Nos. 706, 709, 712–713, 716, 718 Surcharged in Red

BAYAR PORTO

1978 Photo. *Perf. 12½x12*

J118 A110 25r on 1r 15
J119 " 50r on 2r 30
J120 " 100r on 4r 60
J121 " 200r on 5r 1.20
J122 " 300r on 10r 1.80
J123 " 400r on 15r 2.40
Nos. J118–J123 (6) 6.45

Surcharged in Black

J124 A110 25r on 1r 15
J125 " 50r on 2r 30
J126 " 100r on 4r 60
J127 " 200r on 5r 1.20
J128 " 300r on 10r 1.80
J129 " 400r on 15r 2.40
Nos. J124–J129 (6) 6.45

Issue dates: Nos. J118–J123, June 3. Nos. J124–J129, Sept. 1.

Riouw Archipelago

100 Sen = 1 Rupiah

(1 rupiah = 1 Malayan dollar)

Indonesia Nos. 371-386 Overprinted in Black

RIAU

a *b*

Overprint "a"

1954 ***Perf. 12½.*** **Unwmkd.**

No.	Type	Description		
1	A52	5s carmine rose		
2	"	7½s green		
3	"	10s blue		
4	"	15s purple		
5	"	20s rose red		
6	"	25s deep green		

Overprint "b"

No.	Type	Description		
7	A53	30s red orange		
8	"	35s purple		
9	"	40s dull green		
10	"	45s deep claret		
11	"	50s brown		
12	A54	60s dark brown		
13	"	70s gray		
14	"	75s ultramarine		
15	"	80s claret		
16	"	90s gray green		

Netherlands Indies Nos. 325-330 Overprinted Type "a" in Black

Perf. 12½x12.

No.	Type	Description		
17	A46	1r purple		
18	"	2r olive green		
19	"	3r red violet		
20	"	5r dark brown		
21	"	10r gray		
22	"	25r orange brown		
		Nos. 1-22 (22)	*200.00*	*200.00*

Indonesia Nos. 424-428, 450 and 430 Overprinted Type "b" or

RIAU

c

1957-64 Photo. ***Perf. 12½x13½***

No.	Type	Overprint	Description
23	A63	(*b*)	5s deep ultramarine
24	"	(*c*)	10s yellow brown
25	"	(*b*)	10s yellow brown
25A	"	(")	15s rose violet ('64)
26	"	(")	20s dull green ('60)
28	"	(")	25s deep claret
29	"	(")	30s orange
30	"	(*c*)	50s brown
31	"	(*b*)	50s brown

The "b" overprint measures 12mm. in this set. Type "c" overprints were issued in 1957. No. 428 also exists with "c" overprint.

Sukarno Type of Indonesia Overprinted Type "a"

1960 ***Perf. 12½x12***

No.	Type	Description	Unused	Used
32	A55	1.25r deep orange	8	8
33	"	1.50r brown	15	15
34	"	2.50r rose brown	25	25
35	"	4r apple green	28	28
36	"	6r rose lilac	40	40
37	"	15r yellow	90	90
38	"	20r sepia	1.25	1.25
39	"	40r yellow green	1.75	1.75
40	"	50r violet	2.25	2.25
		Nos. 32-40 (9)	7.31	7.31

INGERMANLAND

(See North Ingermanland.)

INHAMBANE

(ĭn'yăm·bä'nĕ)

LOCATION—East Africa.

GOVT.—A district of Mozambique, former Portuguese colony.

AREA——21,000 sq. mi. (approx.).

POP.—248,000 (approx.).

CAPITAL—Inhambane.

Stamps of Inhambane were replaced by those of Mozambique. See Mozambique.

1000 Reis = 1 Milreis

100 Centavos = 1 Escudo (1914)

Stamps of Mozambique Overprinted

CENTENARIO

DE

S. ANTONIO

—

Inhambane

MDCCCXCV

On 1886 Issue.

1895, July 1 *Perf. 12½* **Unwmkd.**

Without Gum

No.	Type	Description	Unused	Used
1	A2	5r black	25.00	22.50
2	"	10r green	22.50	18.50
		a. Perf. 13½	65.00	55.00
3	"	20r rose	40.00	35.00
4	"	25r lilac		
5	"	40r chocolate	42.50	35.00
6	"	50r blue	42.50	35.00
		a. Perf. 13½	37.50	37.50
7	"	100r yellow brown		
8	"	200r gray violet	60.00	55.00
9	"	300r orange	60.00	55.00

On 1894 Issue

Perf. 11½

No.	Type	Description	Unused	Used
10	A3	50r light blue	37.50	30.00
		a. Perf. 12½	45.00	37.50
11	"	75r rose	40.00	32.50
12	"	80r yellow green	40.00	32.50
13	"	100r brown, *buff*	72.50	52.50
14	"	150r carmine, *rose*	50.00	40.00

700th anniversary of the birth of St. Anthony of Padua.

The status of Nos. 4 and 7 is questionable. No. 3 is always discolored.

King Carlos

A1

1903, Jan. 1 Typo. *Perf. 11½*

Name and Value in Black except 500r.

No.	Type	Description	Unused	Used
15	A1	2½r gray	50	35
16	"	5r orange	50	35
17	"	10r light green	75	35
18	"	15r gray green	1.00	75
19	"	20r gray violet	1.25	75
20	"	25r carmine	1.00	75
21	"	50r brown	2.50	1.75
22	"	65r dull blue	10.00	7.50
23	"	75r lilac	2.50	2.00
		a. Imperf.		
24	"	100r dark blue, *blue*	2.50	1.75
25	"	115r orange brown, *pink*	4.50	4.25
26	"	130r brown, *straw*	4.50	4.25
27	"	200r red violet, *pink*	4.50	4.25
28	"	400r dull blue, *straw*	7.50	6.75
29	"	500r black & red, *blue*	10.00	7.75
30	"	700r gray black, *straw*	13.50	12.00
		Nos. 15-30 (16)	67.00	55.55

No. 22 Surcharged in Black

50

RÉIS

1905

No.	Type	Description	Unused	Used
31	A1	50r on 65r dull blue	3.00	2.50

Nos. 15-21, 23-30 Overprinted in Carmine or Green

REPUBLICA

1911

No.	Type	Description	Unused	Used
32	A1	2½r gray	30	30
33	"	5r orange	30	30
34	"	10r light green	30	30
35	"	15r gray green	35	35
36	"	20r gray violet	35	35
37	"	25r carmine (G)	70	50
38	"	50r brown	35	25
39	"	75r lilac	55	35
40	"	100r dark blue, *blue*	55	35
41	"	115r orange brown, *pink*	70	50
42	"	130r brown, *straw*	70	50
43	"	200r red violet, *pink*	85	75
44	"	400r dull blue, *straw*	1.50	1.25
45	"	500r black & red, *blue*	1.50	1.25
46	"	700r gray blk., *straw*	2.10	1.75
		Nos. 32-46 (15)	11.10	9.05

No. 31 Overprinted in Red

1914

No.	Type	Description	Unused	Used
47	A1	50r on 65r dull blue	1.75	1.25
		a. "Republica" inverted		

Vasco da Gama Issue of Various Portuguese Colonies.

Common Design Types CD20-CD27 Surcharged

REPUBLICA

INHAMBANE

¼ C.

1913

On Stamps of Macao.

No.	Type	Description	Unused	Used
48	CD20	¼c on ½a bl. green	1.50	1.35
49	CD21	½c on 1a red	1.50	1.35
50	CD22	1c on 2a red violet	1.50	1.35
		a. Inverted surch.	6.50	6.50
51	CD23	2½c on 4a yel. grn.	1.50	1.35
52	CD24	5c on 8a dark blue	1.50	1.35
53	CD25	7½c on 12a violet brown	2.75	2.25
54	CD26	10c on 16a bistre brown	2.00	1.35
55	CD27	15c on 24a bistre	2.00	1.35
		Nos. 48-55 (8)	14.25	11.70

On Stamps of Portuguese Africa.

No.	Type	Description	Unused	Used
56	CD20	¼c on 2½r bl. green	1.20	1.00
57	CD21	½c on 5r red	1.20	1.00
58	CD22	1c on 10r red violet	1.20	1.00
59	CD23	2½c on 25r yel. grn.	1.20	1.00
60	CD24	5c on 50r dk. blue	1.20	1.00
61	CD25	7½c on 75r violet brown	2.50	2.25
62	CD26	10c on 100r bis. brn.	1.50	1.40
63	CD27	15c on 150r bistre	1.50	1.40
		Nos. 56-63 (8)	11.50	10.05

On Stamps of Timor

No.	Type	Description	Unused	Used
64	CD20	¼c on ½a bl. green	1.50	1.25
		a. Inverted surch.	13.50	13.50
65	CD21	½c on 1a red	1.50	1.25
66	CD22	1c on 2a red violet	1.50	1.25
67	CD23	2½c on 4a yel. grn.	1.50	1.25
68	CD24	5c on 8a dark blue	1.50	1.25
69	CD25	7½c on 12a violet brown	2.75	2.25
70	CD26	10c on 16a bis. brn.	2.00	1.35
71	CD27	15c on 24a bistre	2.00	1.35
		Nos. 64-71 (8)	14.25	11.20

Ceres

A2

1914 Typographed *Perf. 15x14*

Name and Value in Black.

No.	Type	Description	Unused	Used
72	A2	¼c olive brown	70	60
73	"	½c black	70	60
		a. Imperf.		
74	"	1c blue green	70	65
75	"	1½c lilac brown	70	65
76	"	2c carmine	70	65
77	"	2½c light violet	35	30
78	"	5c deep blue	85	65
79	"	7½c yellow brown	1.25	85
80	"	8c slate	1.25	85
81	"	10c orange brown	1.25	85
82	"	15c plum	1.50	1.25
83	"	20c yellow green	1.50	1.25
84	"	30c brown, *green*	2.00	2.00
85	"	40c brown, *pink*	2.00	2.00
86	"	50c orange, *salmon*	3.25	2.50
87	"	1e green, *blue*	3.25	2.50
		Nos. 72-87 (16)	21.95	18.15

No. 31 Overprinted in Carmine

1915 *Perf. 11½*

No.	Type	Description	Unused	Used
88	A1	50c on 65r dull blue	4.50	4.50

Nos. 15-21, 23-30 Overprinted Locally

REPUBLICA

1917

No.	Type	Description	Unused	Used
89	A1	2½r gray	10.00	7.50
90	"	5r orange	10.00	7.50
91	"	15r gray green	2.25	1.75
92	"	20r gray violet	1.60	1.40
93	"	50r brown	1.90	1.50
94	"	75r lilac	1.90	1.50
95	"	100r blue, *blue*	1.90	1.50
96	"	115r orange brown, *pink*	1.90	1.50
97	"	130r brown, *straw*	1.90	1.50
98	"	200r red violet, *pink*	1.90	1.50
99	"	400r dull blue, *straw*	2.50	2.00
100	"	500r black & red, *blue*	3.00	2.25
101	"	700r gray black, *straw*	7.00	6.00
		Nos. 89-101 (13)	47.75	37.40

The stamps of Inhambane have been superseded by those of Mozambique.

Common Design Types pictured in section at front of book.

ININI

(ē·nē·nē')

LOCATION—In northeastern South America, adjoining French Guiana.

GOVT.—Former territory of French Guiana.

AREA—30,301 sq. mi.

POP.—5,024 (1946).

CAPITAL—St. Elie.

Inini was separated from French Guiana in 1930 and reunited with it in 1946 when the colony became an overseas department of France.

100 Centimes = 1 Franc

Stamps of French Guiana, 1929-40, Overprinted in Black

TERRITOIRE

DE L'ININI

1932-40 *Perf. 13½x14.* **Unwmkd.**

No.	Type	Description	Unused	Used
1	A16	1c gray lilac & greenish blue	5	5
2	"	2c dark red & blue green	5	5
3	"	3c gray lilac & greenish blue ('40)	6	6
4	"	4c olive brown & red violet ('38)	6	6
5	"	5c Prussian blue & red orange	6	6
6	"	10c magenta & brown	6	6
7	"	15c yellow brown & red orange	6	6
8	"	20c dark blue & olive green	6	6
9	"	25c dark red & dark brown	12	12

Overprinted in Black, Red or Blue:

Territoire de l'ININI

Perf. 14x13½.

No.	Type	Description	Unused	Used
10	A17	30c dull green & light green	15	15
11	"	30c green & brown ('40)	6	6
12	"	35c Prussian green & olive ('38)	10	10
13	"	40c red brown & olive gray	8	8
14	"	45c olive green & light green ('40)	12	12
15	"	50c dark blue & olive gray	6	6
16	"	55c violet blue & carmine ('38)	50	50
17	"	60c salmon & green ('40)	6	6
18	"	65c salmon & green ('38)	15	15
19	"	70c indigo & slate blue ('40)	15	15
20	"	75c indigo & slate blue (Bl)	55	55
21	"	80c black & violet blue (R) ('38)	12	12
22	"	90c dark red & vermilion	15	15
23	"	90c red violet & brown ('39)	15	15
24	"	1fr light violet & brown	4.00	3.50
25	"	1fr carmine & light red ('38)	12	12
26	"	1fr black & violet blue ('40)	8	8

Overprinted in Black or Red

Territoire de l'ININI

No.	Type	Description	Unused	Used
27	A18	1.25fr black brown & blue green ('33)	12	12
28	"	1.25fr rose & light red ('39)	15	15
29	"	1.40fr olive brown & red violet ('40)	15	15
30	"	1.50fr dark blue & light blue	12	12
31	"	1.60fr olive brown & blue green ('40)	20	20

32 A18 1.75fr brn. red & black brown ('33) 5.50 4.00
33 " 1.75fr violet blue ('38) 20 20
34 " 2fr dark green & rose red 8 8
35 " 2.25fr violet blue ('39) 15 15
36 " 2.50fr copper red & brown ('40) 20 20
37 " 3fr brown red & red violet 10 10
38 " 5fr dull violet & yellow green 12 12
39 " 10fr olive gray & deep ultra. (R) 10 10
40 " 20fr indigo & vermilion 15 15
Nos. 1-40 (40) 14.52 12.52

Colonial Arts Exhibition Issue.
Souvenir Sheet.
Common Design Type

1937 ***Imperf.***
41 CD75 3fr red brown 3.00 3.00

Issued in sheets measuring 118x99mm. containing one stamp.

New York World's Fair Issue.
Common Design Type

1939 Engraved. ***Perf. 12½x12.***
42 CD82 1.25fr carmine lake 1.25 1.25
43 " 2.25fr ultramarine 1.25 1.25

French Guiana Nos. 170A-170B Overprinted "ININI" in Green or Red.

1941 **Engraved** ***Perf. 12½x12***
44 A21a 1fr deep lilac (G) 15
45 " 2.50fr blue (R) 15

Nos. 44-45 were issued by the Vichy government, and were not placed on sale in the territory. This is also true of four stamps of French Guiana types A16-A18 without "RF" and overprinted "TERRITOIRE DE L'ININI," released in 1944.

SEMI-POSTAL STAMPS
Common Design Type
Photo.; Name & Value Typo. in Black

1939 ***Perf. 13.*** **Unwmkd.**
B1 CD83 45(c)+25(c) green 3.75 3.75
B2 " 70(c)+30(c) brown 3.75 3.75
B3 " 90(c)+35(c) red orange 3.75 3.75
B4 " 1.25fr+1fr rose pink 3.75 3.75
B5 " 2.25fr+2fr blue 3.75 3.75
Nos. B1-B5 (5) 18.75 18.75

Common Design Type and French Guiana Nos. B9 and B11 Overprinted "ININI" in Blue or Red

1941 **Photogravure** ***Perf. 13½***
B6 SP1 1fr+1fr red (B) 50
B7 CD86 1.50fr+3fr maroon 45
B8 SP2 2.50fr+1fr blue (R) 45

Nos. B6-B8 were issued by the Vichy government, and were not placed on sale in Inini.

Nos. 44-45 were surcharged "OEUVRES COLONIALES" and surtax (including change of denomination of the 2.50fr to 50c). These were issued in 1944 by the Vichy government and not placed on sale in Inini.

AIR POST SEMI-POSTAL STAMPS.

Stamps of French Guiana type V6 and Cameroun type V10 inscribed "Inini" were issued in 1942 by the Vichy Government, but were not placed on sale in the territory.

POSTAGE DUE STAMPS.
Postage Due Stamps of French Guiana, 1929,

Overprinted in Black **TERRITOIRE DE L'ININI**

1932 ***Perf. 13½x14*** **Unwmkd.**
J1 D3 5c indigo & Prussian blue 6 6
J2 D3 10c bistre brown & Prussian green 5 5
J3 " 20c green & rose red 6 6
J4 " 30c olive brown & rose red 8 8
J5 " 50c violet & olive brown 15 15
J6 " 60c brown red & olive brown 15 15

Overprinted in Black or Red **TERRITOIRE DE L'ININI**

1932-41
J7 D4 1fr deep blue & orange brown 20 20
J8 " 2fr brown red & bluish green 30 30
J9 " 3fr violet & black (R) 1.40 1.40
J10 " 3fr violet & blk. ('41) 35 35
Nos. J1-J10 (10) 2.80 2.80

IONIAN ISLANDS
(ī-ō′nĭ-ăn ī′lăndz)

LOCATION—A group of seven Islands, of which six—Corfu, Paxos, Lefkas (Santa Maura), Cephalonia, Ithaca and Zante—are in the Ionian Sea west of Greece, and a seventh—Cerigo (Kithyra)—is in the Mediterranean south of Greece.

GOVT.—Integral part of Kingdom of Greece.

AREA—752 sq. miles

POP.—231,510 (1938).

These islands were occupied by Italian forces in 1941. The Italians withdrew in 1943 and German forces continued the occupation, using current Greek stamps without overprinting, except for Zante.

For stamps of the Italian occupation of Corfu, see Corfu.

Issued under Italian Occupation.

Issue for Cephalonia and Ithaca.

Prices of stamps overprinted by letterpress in pairs are for unsevered pairs. Single stamps, unused, sell for one third the price of a pair; used, one half the price of a pair.

Handstamped overprints were also applied to pairs, with "isola" instead of "isole".

Stamps of Greece, 1937-38, Overprinted in Pairs Vertically, Reading Down, or Horizontally (H) in Black

ITALIA
Occupazione Militare
Italiana isole
Cefalonia e Itaca

Perf. 12½x12, 13½x12, 12x13½.
1941 **Wmk. 252, Unwmkd.**
N1 A69 5l brown red & blue 1.00 1.00
a. Overprint reading up 2.00 2.00
N2 A70 10l blue & red brown (on No. 413) (H) 1.00 1.00
N3 A71 20l black & green (H) 1.00 1.00
a. Overprint inverted 60.00
N4 A72 40l green & black 1.00 1.00
a. Overprint reading up 1.25 1.25
N5 A73 50l brown & black 1.00 1.00
a. Overprint reading up 1.00 1.00
N6 A74 80l indigo & yellow brown (H) 1.25 1.25
a. Overprint inverted 75.00 65.00
N7 A67 1d green (H) 10.00 7.00
N8 A84 1.50d green (H) 13.50 8.00
a. Overprint inverted 35.00 35.00
N9 A75 2d ultramarine 1.00 1.00
a. Overprint reading up 1.25 1.25
N10 A76 5d red 2.50 2.00
N11 A77 6d olive brown 3.00 2.25
a. Overprint reading up 6.00 5.00
N12 A78 7d dark brown 3.00 2.50
a. Overprint reading up 3.50 3.00
N13 A67 8d dp. blue (H) 22.50 15.00
N14 A79 10d red brown 7.50 5.00
a. Overprint reading up 10.00 7.00
N15 A80 15d green 15.00 8.00
a. Overprint reading up 20.00 12.00
N16 A81 25d dk. blue (H) 30.00 25.00
a. Overprint inverted 100.00 90.00
N17 A84 30d orange brown (H) 52.50 30.00
a. Overprint inverted 70.00 65.00

A variety with wrong font "C" in "Cephalonia" is found in several positions in each sheet of all denominations except those overprinted on single stamps. It sells for about five times the price of a normal pair.

Several other minor spelling errors in the overprint occur on several denominations in one of the printings.

Forgeries exist of many of the higher priced stamps and minor varieties of Nos. N1-N17, NC1-NC11 and NRA1-NRA5.

General Issue.

Stamps of Italy, 1929, Overprinted in Red or Black **ISOLE JONIE**

1941 ***Perf. 14.*** **Wmk. 140**
N18 A90 5c olive brn. (R) 15 15
N19 A92 10c dark brown (R) 15 15
N20 A91 20c rose red 15 15
N21 A94 25c deep green 15 15
N22 A95 30c olive brown (R) 15 15
a. "SOLE" for "ISOLE" 5.50
N23 " 50c purple (R) 15 15
N24 A94 75c rose red 15 15
N25 " 1.25l deep blue (R) 15 15
Nos. N18-N25 (8) 1.20 1.20

The stamps overprinted "Isole Jonie" were issued for all the Ionian Islands except Cerigo which used regular postage stamps of Greece.

Issued under German Occupation.
ZANTE ISSUE.

Nos. N21 and N23 with Additional Handstamped Overprint in Black

1943 ***Perf. 14*** **Wmk. 140**
N26 A94 25c deep green 10.00 25.00
a. Carmine overprint 10.00 25.00
N27 A95 50c purple 10.00 25.00
a. Carmine overprint 10.00 25.00

No. N19 with this overprint is a proof. Price, black $17.50; carmine $45.

Nos. N26-N27 were in use 8 days, then were succeeded by stamps of Greece.

Forgeries of Nos. N26-N27, NC13 and their cancellations are plentiful.

Greek stamps with Italian overprints for the islands of Cerigo (Kithyra), Paxos and Lefkas (Santa Maura) are fraudulent.

OCCUPATION AIR POST STAMPS.

Issued under Italian Occupation.

Issue for Cephalonia and Ithaca.

Stamps of Greece Overprinted in Pairs Vertically, Reading Down, or Horizontally (H) in Black

ITALIA
Occupazione Militare
Italiana isole
Cefalonia e Itaca

Perf. 13x12½, 12½x13.
1941 **Unwmkd.**

On Greece Nos. C22, C23, C25 and C27 to C30.

Grayish Paper

NC1 AP16 1d deep red 12.00 12.00
NC1A AP17 2d dull blue 42.50
NC2 AP19 7d blue violet (H) 72.50 90.00
NC3 AP21 25d rose (H) 45.00 35.00
a. Overprint inverted 150.00 150.00
NC4 AP22 30d dk. green 45.00 25.00
a. Overprint reading up 35.00 30.00
b. Horizontal overprint on single stamp 65.00 40.00
NC5 AP23 50d vio. (H) 325.00 175.00
NC6 AP24 100d brown 200.00 100.00
a. Overprint reading up 200.00 110.00

No. NC1A is known only with overprint reading up.

On Greece Nos. C31 to C34.

Reengraved; White Paper

NC7 AP16 1d red 5.00 4.50
NC8 AP17 2d gray blue 1.50 1.50
a. Overprint reading up 3.00 3.00
b. Horiz. ovpt. on pair
c. Horizontal overprint on single stamp 15.00 12.00
NC9 AP18 5d violet (H) 2.50 2.00
a. Overprint inverted 10.00
b. Vert. ovpt. on single stamp, up or down 40.00 30.00
NC10 AP19 7d deep ultramarine (H) 4.00 3.25
a. Overprint inverted 35.00 30.00

Overprinted Horizontally on No. C36.

Rouletted 13½.
NC11 D3 50l violet brown 35.00 25.00
a. Pair, one without overprint 75.00
b. On No. C36a 165.00 65.00

See footnote following No. N17.

General Issue.

Italy No. C13 Overprinted in Red **ISOLE JONIE**

1941 ***Perf. 14.*** **Wmk. 140**
NC12 AP3 50c olive brown 15 15
a. "SOLE" for "ISOLE" 7.00

Issued for use in all the Ionian Islands except Cerigo which used air post stamps of Greece.

No. NC12 with additional overprint "BOLLO" is a revenue stamp.

Issued under German Occupation.
ZANTE ISSUE.

No. NC12 with Additional Hand-stamped Overprint in Black

1943 *Perf. 14.* **Wmk. 140**

NC13 AP3 50c olive brown 10.00 *25.00*
 a. "SOLE" for "ISOLE" *400.00*
 b. Carmine overprint 110.00 165.00

See note after No. N27.

OCCUPATION POSTAGE DUE STAMPS.
General Issue.

Postage Due Stamps of Italy, 1934, Overprinted in Black **ISOLE JONIE**

1941 *Perf. 14.* **Wmk. 140**

NJ1	D6	10c blue	15	22
NJ2	"	20c rose red	15	22
NJ3	"	30c red orange	22	30
NJ4	D7	1 l red orange	22	30

See footnote after No. N25.

OCCUPATION POSTAL TAX STAMPS.
Issued under Italian Occupation.
Issue for Cephalonia and Ithaca.

Greece No. RA56 with Additional Overprint on Horizontal Pair in Black

ITALIA

Occupazione Militare Italiana isole Cefalonia e Itaca

Serrate Roulette 13½.

1941 **Unwmkd.**

NRA1 D3 10 l carmine (Bl+Bk) 4.50 4.00
 a. Blue overprint double 25.00 15.00
 b. Inverted ovpt. 40.00 35.00

Same Overprint Reading Down on Vertical Pairs of Nos. RA61-63.

Perf. 13½x12.

NRA2 PT7 10 l bright rose, *pale rose* 4.00 3.00
 a. Overprint on horiz. pair 20.00 15.00
 b. Horizontal overprint on single stamp *150.00 150.00*
 c. Overprint reading up 4.00 3.00
NRA3 " 50 l gray green, *pale green* 1.00 1.00
 a. Overprint reading up 6.00 6.00
 b. Overprint on horizontal pr. 10.00 10.00
 c. Horizontal overprint on single stamp 12.00 12.00
NRA4 " 1d dull blue, *light blue* 7.50 6.00
 a. Overprint reading up 7.50 6.00

Same Overprint Reading Down on Vertical Pair of No. RA65.

NRA5 PT7 50 l gray green, *pale green* 75.00 50.00
 a. Overprint reading up 85.00

Nos. NRA5 and NRA5a were not placed in use on any compulsory day.

See footnote following No. N17.

IRAN

(ē'rän'; ī-rän')

(Persia)

(pûr'shȧ; -zhȧ)

LOCATION—In western Asia, bordering on the Persian Gulf and the Gulf of Oman.
GOVT.—Kingdom.
AREA—628,060 sq. mi.
POP.—33,590,000 (est. 1976).
CAPITAL—Tehran.

20 Shahis (or Chahis) = 1 Kran
10 Krans = 1 Toman
100 Centimes = 1 Franc = 1 Kran (1881)
100 Dinars = 1 Rial (1933)
100 Rials = 1 Pahlavi

> Prices of early stamps vary according to condition. Quotations for Nos. 1–20, 33–40 are for fine copies. Very fine to superb specimens sell at much higher prices, and inferior or poor copies sell at reduced prices, depending on the condition of the individual specimen.

Many issues have handstamped surcharges. As usual with such surcharges there are numerous inverted, double and similar varieties.

Value Numeral below Lion

Coat of Arms
A1 A2

Typographed.

1870 *Imperf.* **Unwmkd.**

1 A1 1s dull violet 32.50
 a. Printed on both sides 275.00
2 " 2s green 32.50
 a. Printed on both sides 275.00
 b. Tête bêche pair
3 " 4s greenish blue 32.50
 a. Printed on both sides 450.00
4 " 8s red 32.50
 a. Printed on both sides 275.00

Prices for used copies of Nos. 1–4 are omitted as postmarked copies are not known. Used copies with pen cancellation exist. Many shades exist.

Thick Wove Paper

1875 *Imperf.*

6 A2 1s black 110.00 55.00
7 " 2s blue 110.00 55.00
8 " 4s vermilion 110.00 55.00
9 " 8s yellow green 50.00 20.00

No. 6 has spacing of 3–5mm.; No. 15, 2mm. or less. Nos. 6–14 were printed in horizontal strips of four.

Rouletted.

11 A2 1s black 57.50 27.50
12 " 2s blue 50.00 22.50
 a. Tête bêche pair
13 " 4s vermilion 57.50 27.50
14 " 8s yellow green 65.00 22.50
 a. Tête bêche pair *4000.00 2500.00*

Four varieties of each.

Nos. 11 to 14 also exist pin-perforated and percé en scie.

Medium to Thin White or Grayish Paper

1876 *Imperf.*

15 A2 1s gray black 5.00 10.00
 a. Printed on both sides 550.00 550.00
 b. Laid paper 325.00
16 " 2s gray blue 165.00 55.00
 a. Printed on both sides 375.00
17 A2 2s black 225.00
 a. Tête bêche pair *4500.00*
18 " 4s vermilion 57.50 20.00
 a. Printed on both sides 200.00 100.00
19 " 1k rose 165.00 14.00
 a. Printed on both sides 325.00
 b. Laid paper 500.00 50.00
 c. 1k yellow (error)
 d. Tête bêche pair *6000.00*
20 " 4k yellow 250.00 17.50
 a. Printed on both sides 325.00
 b. Laid paper 450.00 75.00
 c. Tête bêche pair

Nos. 16, 18–20 were printed in blocks of 4. No. 15 in a block of 4 and vertical strip of 4. No. 17 in a vertical strip of 4.

The 2s black and the vertical-strip printing on the 1s are on medium to thick grayish wove paper. Both printings of the 1s are found in black as well as gray black.

No. 19c was not regularly issued.

Reprints:

1875 and 1876 issues.

The reprints of the 1sh and 1kr stamps are readily told; the pearls of the circle are heavier, the borders of the circles containing the Persian numeral of value are wider and the figure "1" below the lion is always Roman.

The reprints of the 2 shahi have the outer line of the frame at the left and at the bottom broken and on some specimens entirely missing.

The only distinguishing mark by which to tell the 4 shahi and 4 kran stamps is the frame, the outer line of which is of the same thickness as the inner line, while on the originals the inner line is very thin and the outer line thick; another feature of some of the reprints is a break in the ornament in the lower part of the circle below the figure "4".

In the reprints of the 8 shahi stamps the small scroll nearest to the circles with Persian numerals at the bottom of the stamp touches the frame below it; the inner and outer lines of the frame are of equal thickness, while in the originals the outer line is much heavier than the inner one.

All reprints are found cancelled to order.

Shah Nasr-ed-Din—A3

Perf. 10½, 12, 13, 11x10½, 12x10½, 13x10½.

1876 **Typographed**

27 A3 1s lilac & black 6.00 1.50
28 " 2s green & black 10.00 1.25
29 " 5s rose & black 3.00 30
30 " 10s blue & black 15.00 3.00

Bisects of the 5s (surcharged "2½") and the 10s (surcharged "5 Shahi" or "5 Shahy") exist. Experts variously attribute them to local shortages, a postmaster's inventiveness or fraudulence.

1878 **Typographed** ***Imperf.***

33 A2 1k carmine rose 57.50 15.00
34 " 1k red, *yellow* 550.00 27.50
 a. Tête bêche pair *1100.00*
35 " 4k ultramarine 85.00 32.50
36 " 5k gold 400.00 100.00
37 " 5k violet 110.00 65.00
38 " 5k red bronze *1100.00* 225.00
39 " 5k violet bronze *1100.00* 200.00
40 " 1t bronze, *blue* *3250.00 1500.00*

Four varieties of each.

Nos. 33 and 34 are printed from redrawn clichés. They have wide colorless circles around the corner numerals.

The reprints of the 1 kran and 1 toman are printed from the same die as the reprints of the 1 shahi and 1 kran of the 1876 issue; on these and on the reprints of the 5 krans the outer frame is of irregular thickness. The impression of the reprints of this issue is better than that of the originals.

Nasr-ed-Din A6 Sun A7

Typographed

1879 ***Perf. 12, 13, 10½x12, 12x13.***

41 A6 1k brown & black 27.50 1.50
 a. Imperf., pair 100.00
 b. Inverted center *600.00*
42 " 5k blue & black 7.50 75
 a. Imperf., pair 150.00 100.00
 b. Inverted center 160.00

1880

43 A6 1s red & black 7.50 2.00
 a. Imperf., pair 200.00
44 " 2s yellow & black 12.00 2.00
 a. Imperf., pair 175.00
45 " 5s green & black 12.00 40
46 " 10s violet & black 37.50 4.00
 a. Imperf., pair 175.00

The 2, 5 and 10sh of this issue and the 1 and 5kr of the 1879 issue have been reprinted from a new die which resembles the 5 shahi envelope. The aigrette is shorter than on the original stamps and touches the circle above it.

Lithographed.

1881 ***Perf. 12, 13, 12x13***

47 A7 5c dull violet 7.50 1.00
48 " 10c rose 7.50 1.00
49 " 25c green 250.00 20.00

1882 **Engraved, Border Litho.**

50 A7 5c bl. vio. & violet 8.00 1.00
51 " 10c dp. pink & rose 8.00 50
52 " 25c dp. grn. & grn. 47.50 50

A8

Shah Nasr-ed-Din
A9 A10

A11

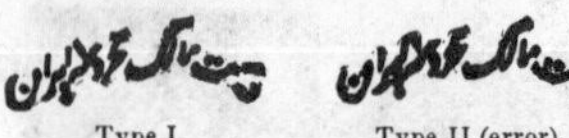

Type I. Type II (error).

Type I. Three dots at right end of scroll.
Type II. Two dots at right end of scroll.

1882–84 Engr. *Perf. 11½ to 13.*

No.	Type	Description	Unused	Used
53	A8	5s green, type I	3.75	15
		a. 5s green, type II	7.50	75
54	A9	10s buff, orange & black	9.00	75
55	A10	50c buff, orange & black	40.00	4.00
56	"	50c gray & black ('84)	15.00	4.00
57	"	1fr blue & black	15.00	1.50
58	"	5fr rose red & blk.	15.00	1.50
59	A11	10fr buff, red & blk.	15.00	6.00

Halves of the 10s, 50c and 1fr surcharged with Arabic characters in red or black are frauds. The 50c and 1fr surcharged with a large "5" surrounded by rays are also frauds.

A12

A13

1885–86 Typo. *Perf. 12, 12½, 13*

No.	Type	Description	Unused	Used
60	A12	1c green	6.00	75
61	"	2c rose	6.00	75
62	"	5c dull blue	7.50	15
		a. 5c violet blue	75.00	3.75
63	A13	10c brown	4.50	15
64	"	1k slate	6.00	30
65	"	5k dull vio. ('86)	37.50	1.50

Nos. 53, 54, 56 and 58 Surcharged in Black:

OFFICIEL 6 — *a*
OFFICIEL 12 — *b*
OFFICIEL 18 — *c*
OFFICIEL 1T — *d*
OFFICIEL 3 — *e*
OFFICIEL 8 — *f*

1885

No.	Type	Description	Unused	Used
66	(*a*)	6c on 5s green, type I	30.00	1.50
		a. 6s on 5s green, type II	60.00	15.00
67	(*b*)	12c on 50c gray & black	60.00	6.00
68	(*c*)	18c on 10s buff, orange & blk.	60.00	12.50
69	(*d*)	1t on 5fr rose red & black	52.50	6.00

1887

No.	Type	Description	Unused	Used
70	(*e*)	3c on 5s grn., type I	15.00	7.50
		a. 3c on 5s green, type II	30.00	15.00
71	(*a*)	6c on 10s buff, org. & black	15.00	7.50
72	(*f*)	8c on 50c gray & black	45.00	13.50

The word "OFFICIEL" indicated that the surcharged stamps were officially authorized.

Surcharges on the same basic stamps of values other than those listed are believed to be bogus.

Counterfeits of Nos. 66–72 abound.

A14

A15

Perf. 11, 13½, 11x13½.

1889 Typographed

No.	Type	Description	Unused	Used
73	A14	1c pale rose	30	15
74	"	2c pale blue	22	5
75	"	5c lilac	30	3
76	"	7c brown	1.25	45
77	A15	10c black	45	15
78	"	1k red orange	45	15
79	"	2k rose	1.50	75
80	"	5k green	3.75	1.50
		Nos. 73–80 (8)	8.22	3.23

All values exist imperforate.

A16

A17

1891 *Perf. 10½, 11½*

No.	Type	Description	Unused	Used
81	A16	1c black	30	15
82	"	2c brown	60	15
83	"	5c deep blue	15	6
84	"	7c gray	32.50	2.25
85	"	10c rose	60	15
86	"	14c orange	60	15
87	A17	1k green	9.00	15
88	"	2k orange	52.50	2.25
89	"	5k ochre yellow	75	60
		Nos. 81–89 (9)	97.00	5.91

A18

Shah Nasr-ed-Din
A19

1894 *Perf. 12½.*

No.	Type	Description	Unused	Used
90	A18	1c lilac	38	3
91	"	2c blue green	38	3
92	"	5c ultramarine	38	3
93	"	8c brown	38	6
		Perf. 11½x11.		
94	A19	10c orange	75	30
95	"	16c rose	3.75	75
96	"	1k red & yellow	2.25	30
97	"	2k brown orange & pale blue	2.25	30
98	"	5k violet & silver	3.00	45
99	"	10k red & gold	10.00	2.25
100	"	50k green & gold	7.50	3.00
		Nos. 90–100 (11)	31.02	7.50

Reprints exist. Price, set $5.
See also Nos. 104–112, 136–144.

A20

A21

Violet or Magenta Surcharge

1897 *Perf. 12½, 11½x11*

No.	Type	Description	Unused	Used
101	A20	5c on 8c brown (V)	75	5
102	A21	1k on 5k violet & silver (V)	1.50	1.50
103	"	2k on 5k violet & silver (M)	2.25	1.50

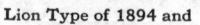

Lion Type of 1894 and

Shah Muzaffar-ed-Din
A22

1898 Typographed *Perf. 12½*

No.	Type	Description	Unused	Used
104	A18	1c gray	45	4
105	"	2c pale brown	45	8
106	"	3c dull violet	45	8
107	"	4c vermilion	45	8
108	"	5c yellow	45	4
109	"	8c orange	1.50	30
110	"	10c light blue	75	4
111	"	12c rose	75	8
112	"	16c green	2.25	15
113	A22	1k ultramarine	3.00	15
114	"	2k pink	1.50	15
115	"	3k yellow	1.50	30
116	"	4k gray	1.50	1.00
117	"	5k emerald	1.50	1.25
118	"	10k orange	4.50	1.50
119	"	50k bright violet	9.00	4.50
		Nos. 104–119 (16)	30.00	9.74

Unauthorized reprints of Nos. 104–119 were made from original clichés. Price for set, $3.

See also Nos. 145–151.

Stamps of 1898 Handstamped in Violet:

a *b* *c* *d* *e*

f *g* *h*

1899

No.	Type	Description	Unused	Used
120	(*a*)	1c gray	1.50	8
121	(*b*)	2c pale brown	1.50	8
122	(")	3c dull violet	1.50	8
123	(*c*)	4c vermilion	1.50	8
124	(")	5c yellow	1.50	8
125	(*d*)	8c orange	2.25	45
126	(")	10c light blue	1.50	15
127	(")	12c rose	1.50	22
128	(")	16c green	2.25	45
129	(*e*)	1k ultramarine	2.25	45
130	(*f*)	2k pink	4.50	30
131	(")	3k yellow	12.00	4.50
132	(*g*)	4k gray	12.00	4.50
133	(")	5k emerald	6.00	3.00
134	(*h*)	10k orange	21.00	5.25
135	(")	50k bright violet	15.00	7.50

The handstamped control marks on Nos. 120–135 exist sideways, inverted and double. Counterfeits are plentiful.

Types of 1894–98.

1899 Typographed. *Perf. 12½*

No.	Type	Description	Unused	Used
136	A18	1c gray, *green*	75	4
137	"	2c brown, *green*	75	4
138	"	3c violet, *green*	75	4
139	"	4c red, *green*	75	8
140	"	5c yellow, *green*	75	4
141	"	8c orange, *green*	2.25	45
142	"	10c pale blue, *green*	75	8
143	"	12c lake, *green*	1.50	15
144	"	16c green, *green*	3.75	45
145	A22	1k red	3.75	45
146	"	2k deep green	6.75	90
147	"	3k lilac brown	7.50	2.25
148	"	4k orange red	7.50	2.25
149	"	5k gray brown	12.00	2.25
150	"	10k deep blue	30.00	3.75
151	A22	50k brown	12.00	3.75
		Nos. 136–151 (16)	91.50	16.97

Unauthorized reprints of Nos. 136–151 were made from original clichés. Price for set, $5.

Nos. 104–111 Handstamped in Violet

(Struck once on every two stamps.)

1900

No.	Type	Description	Unused	Used
152	A18	1c gray	15.00	75
153	"	2c pale brown	15.00	75
154	"	3c dull violet	22.50	15
155	"	4c vermilion	30.00	1.50
156	"	5c yellow	7.50	15
158	"	10c light blue	52.50	22.50
159	"	12c rose	22.50	75

Pairs of Nos. 152–159 sell for three times the price of singles.

This control mark, in genuine state, was not applied to the 8c orange (Nos. 109, 125).

Same Overprint Handstamped on Nos. 120–127 in Violet.
(Struck once on each block of four.)

No.	Type	Description	Unused	Used
160	A18	1c gray	30.00	75
161	"	2c pale brown		
162	"	3c dull violet		
163	"	4c vermilion	30.00	75
164	"	5c yellow	15.00	15
166	"	10c light blue	15.00	45
167	"	12c rose	15.00	75

Blocks of four of Nos. 160–167 sell for six times the price of singles.

Counterfeits exist of Nos. 152–167.

No. 93 Surcharged in Violet

1900

No.	Type	Description	Unused	Used
168	A18	5c on 8c brown	3.00	8

No. 145 Surcharged in Violet

12CH

1901

No.	Type	Description	Unused	Used
169	A22	12c on 1k red	7.50	2.25
		a. Blue surcharge	7.50	2.25

Some specialists state that No. 169 with black surcharge was made for collectors.

A23

1902 Violet Surcharge.

No.	Type	Description	Unused	Used
171	A23	5k on 50k brown	30.00	7.50
		a. Blue surcharge	37.50	15.00

Nos. 136–151 Overprinted in Black

This "Tabriz" overprint exists in five types.

1902

No.	Type	Description	Unused	Used
173	A18	1c gray, *green*	60	22
174	"	2c brown, *green*	60	22

175 A18 3c violet, *green* 60 22
176 " 4c red, *green* 60 30
177 " 5c yellow, *green* 60 22
178 " 8c orange, *green* 90 60
179 " 10c pale blue, *green* 90 30
180 " 12c lake, *green* 90 40
181 " 16c green, *green* 90 75
182 A22 1k red 1.75 60
183 " 2k deep green
184 " 3k lilac brown
185 " 4k orange red
186 " 5k gray brown
187 " 10k deep blue
188 " 50k brown

Counterfeits of the overprint of Nos. 173–188 are plentiful. Practically all examples with overprint sideways, inverted, double and double with one inverted are frauds.

Same Overprint on Stamps of 1899–1902. Violet and Black Overprints.
Overprinted on Nos. 122–123, 125

189 A18 3c dull violet 50
190 " 4c vermilion 50
191 " 8c orange 50

Overprinted on Nos. 152 to 157.

194 A18 1c gray 40
195 " 2c pale brown 40
196 " 3c dull violet 40
197 " 4c vermilion 40
198 " 5c yellow 50
199 " 8c orange 50

Overprinted on Nos. 160 to 165.

200 A18 1c gray 35
201 " 2c pale brown 35
202 " 3c dull violet 40
203 " 4c vermilion 40
204 " 5c yellow 40
205 " 8c orange 40

Some specialists believe that Nos. 189–191, 194–205 were not regularly issued.

Overprinted on No. 168.

206 A18 5c on 8c brown 1.50 10

Overprinted on Nos. 171 and 171a.

207 A23 5k on 50k brown 7.50 3.00
a. On #171a 7.50 3.00

Overprinted on Nos. 169 and 169a.

209 A22 12c on 1k red 1.50 30
a. On #169a 1.50 30

Nos. 142 and 145 Surcharged in Violet

1902

211 A18 5c on 10c pale blue, *green* 90 45
a. Blue surcharge 90 45
b. Black surcharge 90 45
c. Rose surcharge 90 45
d. Magenta surcharge 5.00
215 A22 5c on 1k red 1.50 75
a. Blue surcharge 1.50 75
b. Black surcharge 1.50 75
c. Rose surcharge 1.50 75

Initials of Victor Castaigne, Postmaster of Meshed
A24

1902 Typographed. *Imperf.*

222 A24 1c black 225.00 57.50
b. Invtd. center 1100.00 850.00
223 A24 2c black 165.00 57.50
b. "2" in right upper corner 2250.00 1750.00
c. Printed on both sides 600.00
224 " 3c black 150.00 85.00
225 " 5c violet 150.00 42.50
a. "5" in right upper corner 400.00 275.00
b. Printed on both sides 1650.00 1000.00
c. Invtd. center 2250.00 1100.00
226 " 5c black 150.00 45.00
a. Persian "5" in lower left corner 450.00
b. Invtd. center 2250.00 1650.00
227 " 12c dull blue 400.00 250.00
228 " 1k rose 3000.00 500.00

The design of No. 228 differs slightly from the illustration.

Pin-perforated

234 A24 12c dull blue 1350.00 135.00

The post office at Meshed having exhausted its stock of stamps, the postmaster issued the above series provisionally. The center of the design is the seal of the postmaster who also wrote his initials upon the upper part, using black ink for the 1 kran and red ink for the other values.

Unauthorized reprints and forgeries exist. The unauthorized reprints include pin-perforated examples of Nos. 222–226.

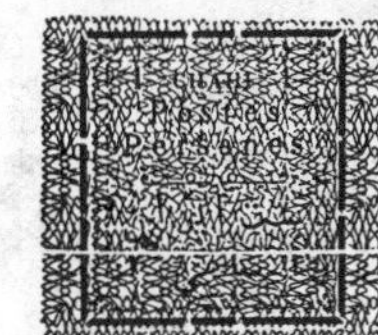

A25

TWO TYPES:

Type I. "CHAHI" or "KRANS" are in capital letters.

Type II. Only "C" of "Chahi" or "K" of "Krans" is a capital.

The 3c and 5c sometimes have a tall narrow figure in the upper left corner. The 5c is also found with the cross at the upper left broken or missing. These varieties are known with many of the overprints that were applied to type A25.

Handstamp Overprinted in Black

1902 Typeset *Imperf.*

TYPE I.

235 A25 1c gray & buff 15.00 5.00
236 " 2c brown & buff 15.00 5.00
237 " 3c green & buff 15.00 5.00
238 " 5c red & buff 15.00 5.00
239 " 12c ultra. & buff 15.00 5.00
Nos. 235–239 (5) 75.00 25.00

Counterfeits abound.

The 3c with violet overprint is believed not to have been regularly issued.

Handstamp Overprinted in Rose

1902

TYPE I.

247 A25 1c gray & buff 1.50 30
a. With Persian numerals "2" 3.50
248 " 2c brown & buff 4.50 15
249 " 3c dp. green & buff 7.50 15
250 " 5c red & buff 1.50 8
251 " 10c olive yel. & buff 4.50 30
252 " 12c ultra. & buff 7.50 75
253 " 1k violet & blue 22.50 1.50
254 A25 2k olive grn. & blue 30.00 4.50
256 " 10k dk. blue & blue 75.00 15.00
257 " 50k red & blue 150.00 45.00

A 5k exists with both types of overprint. Status doubtful.

Nos. 247–257 and the 12c on brown paper and on blue paper with blue quadrille lines are known without overprint but are not believed to have been regularly issued in this condition.

The 1c to 10k, A25 type I, with violet overprint are believed not to have been regularly issued. Five denominations also exist with overprint in blue, black or green.

TYPE II.

280 A25 1c gray & yellow 7.50 15
a. Tête bêche pair
281 " 2c brown & yellow 7.50 30
282 " 3c dark green & yellow 7.50 45
a. "Persans" 17.50 5.00
283 " 5c red & yellow 7.50 8
a. Tête bêche, pair
284 " 10c olive yellow & yellow 15.00 75
285 " 12c blue & yellow 15.00 75
286 " 1k violet & blue
287 " 2k yellow green & blue
289 " 10k dark blue & blue
290 " 50k orange red & blue

The same overprint in violet was applied to nine denominations of the Type II stamps, but these are believed not to have been regularly issued. The overprint also exists in blue, black and green.

Counterfeits of the overprint on Nos. 247–257, 280–290 are plentiful.

Five stamps of type A25, type II, in high denominations (10, 20, 25, 50 and 100 tomans), with "Postes 1319" lion overprint in blue, were used only on money orders, not for postage. They are usually numbered on the back in red, blue or black.

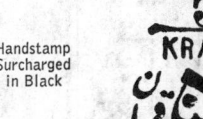

Handstamp Surcharged in Black

1902

TYPE I.

308 A25 5k on 5k ochre & blue 15.00 3.00

Counterfeits of No. 308 abound.

This surcharge in rose, violet, blue or green is considered bogus.

This surcharge on 50k orange red and blue, and on 5k ocher and blue, type II, is considered bogus.

Handstamp Overprinted Diagonally in Black

P.L.
TEHERAN

1902

TYPE I.

315 A25 2c brown & buff 10.00 2.50
a. Rose ovpt. 10.00 2.50

TYPE II.

316 A25 2c brown & yellow 10.00 2.50
a. Rose ovpt. 10.00 2.50

"P. L." stands for "Poste Locale."

Counterfeits of Nos. 315–316 exist.

Some specialists believe that Type II stamps were not used officially for this overprint.

Handstamp Overprinted in Black or Rose

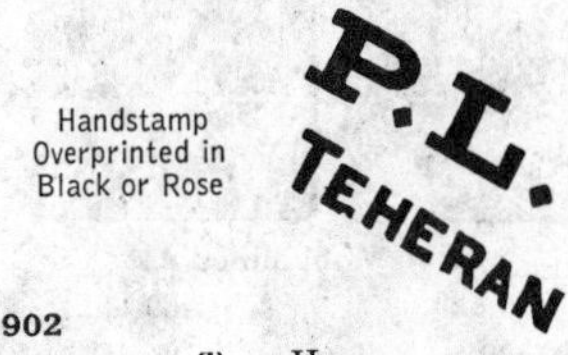

1902

TYPE II

317 A25 2c brown & yellow 10.00 2.50
318 " 2c brn. & yellow (R) 10.00 2.50

Overprinted in Blue

1903

TYPE I.

321 A25 1k violet & blue 12.00

TYPE II.

336 A25 1c gray & yellow 3.00
337 " 2c brown & yellow 3.00
338 " 5c red & yellow 3.00
339 " 10c olive yel. & yel. 3.00
340 " 12c blue & yellow 7.50
Nos. 321–340 (6) 31.50

The overprint also exists in violet and black, but it is doubtful whether such items were regularly issued.

Forgeries of Nos. 321, 336–340 abound. Genuine unused examples are seldom found.

Arms of Persia
A26

Shah Muzaffar-ed-Din
A27

1903–04 Typo. *Perf. 12½*

351 A26 1c violet 8 3
352 " 2c gray 15 3
353 " 3c green 15 3
354 " 5c rose 38 3
355 " 10c yellow brown 38 3
356 " 12c blue 38 3

Engraved

Perf. 11½x11.

357 A27 1k violet 60 3
358 " 2k ultramarine 45 3
359 " 5k orange brown 90 18
360 " 10k rose red 1.20 38
361 " 20k orange ('04) 1.80 1.50
362 " 30k green ('04) 2.65 2.25
363 " 50k green 20.00 10.00
Nos. 351–363 (13) 29.12 14.55

No. 355 exists with blue diagonal surcharge "1 CHAHI"; its status is questioned.

No. 353 Surcharged in Violet or Blue

1 CHAHI

1903

364 A26 1c on 3c green (V) 3.00 30
365 " 2c on 3c green (Bl) 7.50 4.50

A 2c surcharge on No. 354 exists, but its status is dubious.

No. 360 Surcharged in Blue

12CH

366 A27 12c on 10k rose red 4.00 1.00
a. Black surcharge 4.00 1.00
b. Violet surcharge 4.00 1.00

No. 363 Surcharged in Blue or Black

2 TOMANS

1903

368 A27 2t on 50k green (Bl) 30.00 10.00
a. Rose surcharge 30.00 10.00
b. Black surcharge 30.00 15.00
370 A27 3t on 50k green (Bk) 30.00 15.00
a. Violet surcharge 30.00 22.50
b. Rose surcharge 30.00 22.50

No. 363 Surcharged in Blue or Black

3TOMANS

1904

372 A27 2t on 50k green (Bl) 30.00 15.00
375 " 3t on 50k green (Bk) 30.00 15.00

The 2t on 50k also exists with surcharge in rose, violet, black and magenta; the 3t on 50k in rose, violet and blue. Prices about the same unused; about 50 percent higher used.

Nos. 98 and 99 Surcharged in Various Colors

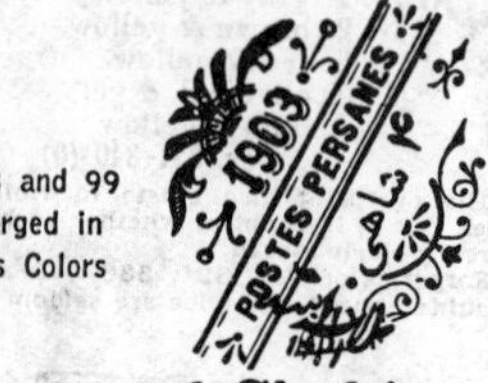

4 Chahis

1903 *Perf. 11½x11*

383 A19 4c on 5k (R & Bk) 3.00 2.25
384 " 8c on 5k (G & Car) 3.00 2.25
  a. Grn. & blk. surch. 4.50
386 " 16c on 5k (O & G) 3.00 2.25
387 " 3k on 5k (Bl & Car) 3.00 2.25
388 " 4k on 5k (RBrn & G) 3.00 2.25
389 " 2t on 5k (Car & O) 3.75 2.25
390 " 2t on 10k (Bl & Bk) 3.75 2.25
391 " 3t on 5k (Bk & Car) 3.75 2.25
392 " 3t on 10k (G & DkBl) 4.50 2.25

The surcharge is found in many color varieties and combinations on Nos. 383–392.

No. 352 Overprinted in Violet

1904 *Perf. 12½.*

393 A26 2c gray 15.00 3.00
  a. Black overprint 15.00 3.75
  b. Rose overprint 15.00 3.75

This overprint also exists in blue, violet blue, maroon and gray, but these were not regularly issued.

The 2c overprinted "Controle" in various types is said to be a revenue stamp.

Stamps of 1903 Surcharged in Black:

a

b

c

1904

400 A26 (a) 3c on 5c rose 3.75 8
401 " (b) 6c on 10c brown 7.50 8
402 A27 (c) 9c on 1k violet 7.50 8

Stamps of 1903 Surcharged in Black, Magenta or Violet:

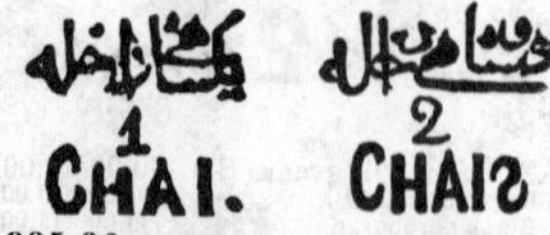

1905–06

404 A26 1c on 3c green ('06) 3.75 15
405 A27 1c on 1k violet 7.50 3.00
406 A27 2c on 5k org. brown 7.50 3.00
407 A26 1c on 3c green (M) ('06) 50 3
408 A27 1c on 1k violet (M) 2.50 1.00
409 " 2c on 5k orange brown (V) 2.50 1.00
  Nos. 404–409 (6) 24.25 8.18

Nos. 145, 146, 182 and 183 Surcharged Diagonally in Black

1 CHAHI
SERVICE INTERIEUR

On Regular Issue of 1899.

1906

414 A22 1c on 1k red 7.50 3.75
415 " 1c on 2k dp. grn. 7.50 3.75

On Overprinted Issue of 1902.

416 A22 1c on 1k red 7.50 3.75
417 " 1c on 2k dp. grn. 7.50 3.75

Blue or violet examples of this surcharge on the same stamps are believed to have been privately produced.

Nos. 355 and 358 Surcharged in Violet **1 CHAI**

419 A26 1c on 10c brown 50.00 50.00
420 A27 2c on 2k ultra. 60.00 60.00

Forgeries of Nos. 419–420 exist.

A28

Typeset; "Provisoire"
Overprint Handstamped in Black

1906 *Imperf.*

422 A28 1c violet 75 6
  a. Irregular pin perf. or perf. 10½ 7.50 30
423 A28 2c gray 75 6
424 " 3c green 75 8
425 " 6c red 75 8
426 " 10c brown 7.50 75
427 " 13c blue 15 15
  Nos. 422–427 (6) 10.65 1.18

Stamps of type A28 have a faint background pattern of tiny squares within squares, an ornamental frame and open rectangles for the value corners.

The 3c and 6c also exist perforated.

Nos. 422–427 are known without overprint but were probably not issued in that condition. Nearly all values are known with overprint inverted and double.

Forgeries exist.

Lion Type of 1903 and

Shah Mohammed Ali

A29 A30

1907–09 Typo. *Perf. 12½*

428 A26 1c violet, *blue* 8 3
429 " 2c gray, *blue* 8 3
430 A26 3c green, *blue* 8 3
431 " 6c rose, *blue* 8 3
432 " 9c orange, *blue* 8 3
433 " 10c brown, *blue* 15 5

Engraved *Perf. 11, 11½*

434 A29 13c dark blue 60 8
435 " 1k red 60 4
436 " 26c red brown 60 4
437 " 2k deep green 60 4
438 " 3k pale blue 75 15
439 " 4k bright yellow 20.00 50
440 " 4k bistre 1.50 30
441 " 5k dark brown 1.50 45
442 " 10k pink 2.25 45
443 " 20k gray black 2.25 45
444 " 30k dark violet 3.75 75
445 A30 50k gold, vermilion & black ('09) 4.00 2.25
  Nos. 428–445 (18) 38.95 5.70

Frame of No. 445 lithographed. Nos. 434–444 were issued in 1908.

Forgeries of Nos. 428–445 exist.

Nos. 428–429 Overprinted in Black

1909 *Perf. 12½.*

446 A26 1c violet, *blue* 37.50 15.00
447 " 2c gray, *blue* 37.50 15.00

Counterfeits of Nos. 446–447 exist.

Coat of Arms

A31

1909 Typographed. *Perf. 12½x12.*

448 A31 1c orange & maroon 20 3
449 " 2c violet & maroon 20 3
450 " 3c yel. grn. & maroon 30 3
451 " 6c red & maroon 30 3
452 " 9c gray & maroon 30 3
453 " 10c red violet & maroon 30 3
454 " 13c dark blue & maroon 40 3
455 " 1k silver, violet & bistre brown 3.00 8
456 " 26c dk. grn. & maroon 20 10
457 " 2k silver, dark green & bistre brown 5.00 8
458 " 3k silver, gray & bistre brown 10.00 15
459 " 4k silver, blue & bistre brown 12.50 45
460 " 5k gold, brown & bistre brown 20.00 50
461 " 10k gold, orange & bistre brown 30.00 1.25
462 " 20k gold, olive green & bistre brown 30.00 1.85
463 " 30k gold, carmine & bistre brown 35.00 2.25
  Nos. 448–463 (16) 147.70 6.92

The unauthorized "reprints" of Nos. 448–463 abound. Originals have clean, bright colors and centers stand out clearly. Nos. 460–463 originals have gleaming gold margins; reprint margins appear as blackish yellow. Price for reprints, Nos. 448–463, $5.

Types of 1907-08 Surcharged in Red or Black:

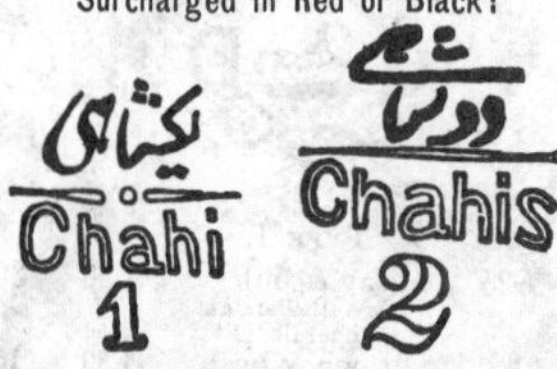

1910 Blue Paper *Imperf.*

464 A26 1c on 1c violet 13.50 11.50
465 " 1c on 2c gray 13.50 11.50
466 " 1c on 3c green 13.50 11.50
467 " 1c on 6c rose (Bk) 13.50 11.50
468 A26 1c on 9c orange 22.50 22.50
469 " 1c on 10c brown 22.50 22.50

White Paper.

470 A29 2c on 13c dp. blue 32.50 22.50
471 " 2c on 26c red brown (Bk) 32.50 22.50
472 " 2c on 1k red (Bk) 32.50 22.50
473 " 2c on 2k dp. green 32.50 22.50
474 " 2c on 3k pale blue 32.50 22.50
475 " 2c on 4k brt. yel. 32.50 22.50
476 " 2c on 4k bistre 32.50 22.50
477 " 2c on 5k dk. brown 32.50 22.50
478 " 2c on 10k pink (Bk) 45.00 22.50
479 " 2c on 20k gray blk. 45.00 22.50
480 " 2c on 30k dk. vio. 45.00 22.50
  Nos. 464–480 (17) 494.00 338.50

Nos. 464–480 were prepared for use on newspapers, but nearly the entire printing was sold to stamp dealers. The issue is generally considered speculative.

Shah Ahmed

A32

Engr. (center), Typo. (frame)
Perf. 11½, 11½x11, 11½x12

1911–13

481 A32 1c green & orange *10* 3
482 " 2c red & sepia *10* 3
483 " 3c gray brown & green *10* 3
  a. 3c bistre brown & green *10*
484 " 5c brn. & car. ('13) *10* 3
485 " 6c gray & carmine *10* 3
486 " 6c green & red brown ('13) *10* 3
487 " 9c yel. brown & violet *20* 3
488 " 10c red & orange brown *20* 3
489 " 12c green & ultra. ('13) *20* 3
490 " 13c vio. & ultramarine *5.00* 3
491 " 1k ultra. & carmine *1.00* 5
492 " 24c vio. & green ('13) *1.25* 3
493 " 26c ultra. & green *5.00* 30
494 " 2k green & red violet *1.50* 5
495 " 3k violet & black *5.00* 5
496 " 4k ultra. & gray ('13) *25.00* 1.25
497 " 5k red & ultramarine *20.00* 22
498 " 10k olive bistre & claret *25.00* 50
499 " 20k vio. brn. & bistre *30.00* 50
500 " 30k red & green *30.00* 50
  Nos. 481–500 (20) *149.95* 3.75

Unauthorized "reprints" of Nos. 481–500 are ubiquitous. Perf. 11½x12. Price, set of reprints, $5.

The reprints include inverted centers for some denominations.

Stamps of 1911 Overprinted in Black

1912

501 A32 1c green & orange 10 8
502 " 2c red & sepia 20 8
503 " 3c gray brown & green 30 5
504 " 6c gray & carmine 50 5
505 " 9c yel. brown & violet 50 8
506 " 10c red & orange brown 50 8
507 " 13c violet & ultra. 3.00 75
508 " 1k ultra. & carmine 10.00 40
509 " 26c ultra. & green 15.00 1.50
510 " 2k grn. & red violet 10.00 30
511 " 3k violet & black 10.00 45
512 " 5k red & ultra. 15.00 45
513 " 10k olive bistre & claret 25.00 1.85
514 " 20k vio. brn. & bis. 25.00 2.25
515 " 30k red & green 35.00 3.75
  Nos. 501-515 (15) 150.10 12.12

The "Officiel" overprint does not signify that the stamps were intended for use on official correspondence but that they were issued by authority. It was applied to the stocks in Persian post offices after a large quantity of stamps had been stolen during the Russian occupation of Tabriz.

The "Officiel" overprint has been counterfeited.

In 1912 this overprint, reading "Sultan Mohammed Ali Shah Kajar," was handstamped on outgoing mail in the Persian Kurdistan region occupied by the forces of the former Shah Mohammed Ali. It was applied after the stamps were on cover and is found on 8 of the Shah Ahmed stamps of 1911 (1c, 2c, 3c, 6c, 9c, 13c, 1k and 26c). Some specialists add the 10c. Forgeries exist.

Nos. 490 and 493 Surcharged:

1 CH 1914 — *a*

3 CH 1914 — *b*

1914

535 A32 (*a*) 1c on 13c violet & ultramarine 3.00 8

536 " (*b*) 3c on 26c ultra. & green 3.00 8

In 1914 a set of 19 stamps was prepared as a coronation issue. The 10 lower values each carry a different portrait; the 9 higher values show buildings and scenes. The same set printed with black centers was overprinted in red "SERVICE." The stamps were never placed in use, but were sold to stamp dealers in 1923.

Nos. 484 and 489 Surcharged in Black or Violet:

c

d

1915

537 A32 (*c*) 1c on 5c brown & carmine 3.00 8

538 " (") 2c on 5c brown & carmine (V) 3.00 8

539 " (") 2c on 5c brown & carmine 30.00 3.00

540 " (*d*) 6c on 12c green & ultramarine 4.50 8

Nos. 455, 454 Surcharged:

e

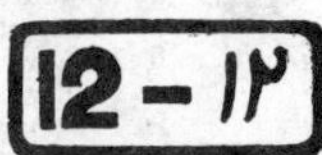

f

1915 ***Perf. 12½x12.***

541 A31 (*e*) 5c on 1k silver, vio. & brown 4.50 8

542 " (*f*) 12c on 13c dark blue & maroon 6.00 15

Nos. 448–453, 455 Overprinted ۱۳۳۳

1915

543 A31 1c orange & maroon 30 15

544 " 2c violet & maroon 45 8

545 " 3c green & maroon 75 8

546 " 6c red & maroon 75 8

547 " 9c gray & maroon 75 8

548 " 10c red vio. & maroon 4.50 30

549 A31 1k silver, violet & bistre brown 4.50 15

Nos. 543–549 (7) 12.00 92

This overprint ("1333") also exists on the 2k, 10k, 20k and 30k, but they were not issued.

Imperial Crown
A33

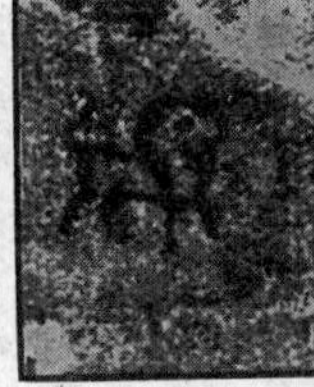

Wmk. 161

King Darius, Ahura-Mazda overhead
A34

Ruins of Persepolis
A35

Engraved, Typographed

1915 **Wmkd. Lion. (161)**

Perf. 11, 11½ or Compound.

560 A33 1c carmine & indigo 8 4

561 " 2c blue & carmine 8 4

562 " 3c dark green 8 4

a. Inverted center

564 A33 5c red 8 4

565 " 6c olive green & car. 15 8

a. Inverted center

566 A33 9c yel. brown & violet 15 8

567 " 10c blue green & yellow brown 30 8

568 " 12c ultramarine 30 15

569 A34 1k silver, yellow brown & gray 75 30

570 A33 24c yellow brown & dark brown 30 15

571 A34 2k silver, blue & rose 75 30

572 " 3k silver, violet & brown 75 30

573 " 5k silver, brown & green 75 30

574 A35 1t gold, purple & black 75 45

575 " 2t gold, green & brown 75 45

576 " 3t gold, claret & red brown 75 45

577 " 5t gold, blue & indigo 75 60

Nos. 560–577 (17) 7.52 3.85

Coronation of Shah Ahmed.

Nos. 560–568, 570 are engraved. Nos. 569, 571–573 are engraved except for silver margins. Nos. 574–577 have centers engraved, frames typographed.

The 3c and 6c with inverted centers are considered genuine errors. Unauthorized reprints exist of these varieties and of other denominations with inverted centers.

Nos. 455, 461–463 Overprinted ۱۳۳۴

Typographed.

1915 ***Perf. 12½x12.*** **Unwmkd.**

582 A31 1k silver, violet & bistre brn. 5.00 75

583 " 10k gold, orange & bistre brown 10.00 2.25

584 " 20k gold, olive green & bistre brn. 100.00 30.00

585 " 30k gold, carmine & bistre brn. 35.00 4.50

Counterfeits exist of the overprints on Nos. 582–585 and 588, and of the surcharges on Nos. 586–587.

No. 491 Surcharged 24 Chahis

1917 ***Perf. 11½***

586 A32 12c on 1k ultramarine & carmine *200.00 80.00*

587 " 24c on 1k ultramarine & carmine *50.00 35.00*

No. 448 Overprinted "1335" in Persian Numerals.

1917 ***Perf. 12½x12***

588 A31 1c orange & maroon 35.00 4.50

Overprint on No. 588 is similar to date in "k" and "l" surcharges.

Stamps of 1909 Surcharged:

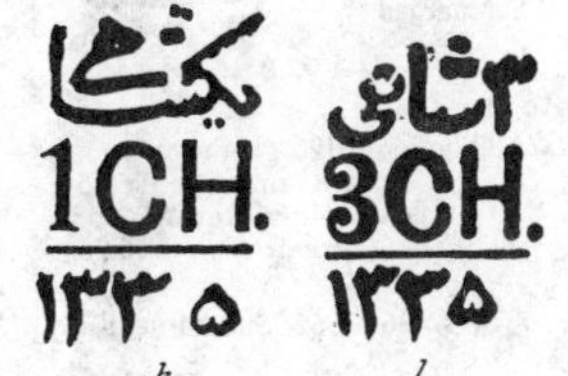

k *l*

1917

589 A31 (*k*) 1c on 2c violet & maroon 3.75 8

590 " (") 1c on 9c gray & maroon 3.75 8

591 " (") 1c on 10c violet & maroon 3.75 8

592 " (*l*) 3c on 9c gray & maroon 3.75 8

593 " (") 3c on 10c violet & maroon 3.75 8

594 " (") 3c on 26c green & maroon 5.25 15

Same Surcharge on No. 488.

595 A32 (*k*) 1c on 10c red & orange brown 3.75 8

596 " (*l*) 3c on 10c red & orange brown 3.75 8

Nos. 454 and 491 Surcharged Type "e."

597 A31 5c on 13c dark blue & maroon 2.00 5

598 A32 5c on 1k ultra. & car. 2.00 5

Nos. 488–489 Surcharged

599 A32 6c on 10c red & orange brown 4.00 75

600 " 6c on 12c green & ultramarine 5.25 8

Status of No. 599 is questioned.

No. 457 Overprinted ۱۳۳۶

1918

601 A31 2k silver, dark green & bistre brown 7.50 75

Nos. 459–460 Surcharged:

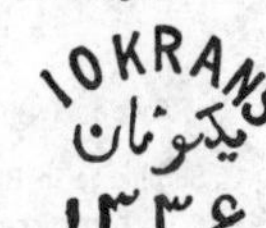

1918

602 A31 24c on 4k silver, blue & bistre brown 7.50 75

603 " 10k on 5k gold, brown & bistre brown 15.00 75

The surcharges of Nos. 602–603 have been counterfeited.

Nos. 457–463 Overprinted ۱۳۳۷

1918

603A A31 2k silver, dark green & bistre brown 5.00 75

604 " 3k silver, gray & bistre brown 15.00 75

604A " 4k silver, blue & bistre brown 15.00 1.50

604B " 5k gold, brown & bistre brown 15.00 75

605 " 10k gold, orange & bistre brown 25.00 2.25

605A " 20k gold, olive green & bistre brn. 100.00 15.00

606 " 30k gold, carmine & bistre brown 50.00 3.00

Nos. 603A-606 (7) 225.00 24.00

Nos. 489, 488 and 491 Surcharged:

m

6 CHAHIS ۱۳۳۷ — *n*

607 A32 (*m*) 3c on 12c green & ultramarine 5.25 8

608 " (*n*) 6c on 10c red & orange brown 3.75 8

609 " (*m*) 6c on 1k ultra. & carmine 3.75 8

Nos. 571–577 Overprinted in Black or Red

Novembre ۱۳۳۷–1918

1918 **Wmkd. Lion. (161)**

610 A34 2k silver, blue & rose 3.00 2.50

611 " 3k silver, violet & brown (R) 3.00 2.50

612 " 5k silver, brown & green (R) 5.00 2.50

613 A35 1t gold, purple & black (R) 4.00 2.50

614 " 2t gold, grn. & brown 5.00 3.00

615 " 3t gold, claret & red brown 5.00 3.00

616 " 5t gold, blue & indigo (R) 5.00 4.00

Nos. 610–616 (7) 30.00 20.00

The overprint commemorates the end of World War I. Counterfeits of this overprint are plentiful.

A36

Typographed

1919 ***Perf. 11½*** **Unwmkd.**

617 A36 1c yellow & black 30 4

618 " 3c green & black 45 6

619 " 5c rose & black 75 15

620 " 6c violet & black 1.50 8

621 " 12c blue & black 3.00 30

Nos. 617-621 (5) 6.00 63

Nos. 617–621 exist imperf., in colors other than the originals, with centers inverted and double impressions. Some specialists call them fraudulent, others call them reprints.

Nos. 75, 85–86 Surcharged in Various Colors

دو قران 1919 2 Kr.

1919 ***Perf. 10½, 11, 11½, 13½***

622 A14 2k on 5c lilac (Bk) 6.00 75

623 " 3k on 5c lilac (Br) 1.50 75

624 " 4k on 5c lilac (G) 1.50 75

625 " 5k on 5c lilac (V) 1.50 75

626 A16 10k on 10c rose (Bl) 1.50 75
627 " 20k on 10c rose (G) 1.50 75
628 " 30k on 10c rose (Br) 1.50 1.50
629 " 50k on 14c org. (V) 1.50 75
Nos. 622-629 (8) 16.50 6.75

Nos. 622-629 exist with inverted and double surcharge. Some specialists consider these fraudulent.

Nos. 486, 489 Handstamp Surcharged

1 KRAN BENADERS

1921 *Perf. 11½, 11½x11*

630 A32 10c on 6c green & red brown 15.00 3.00
631 " 1k on 12c green & ultramarine 15.00 3.00

Counterfeits exist.

No. 489 Surcharged

6 CHAHIS

632 A32 6c on 12c green & ultramarine 4.50 15

Nos. 486, 489 Surcharged in Violet:

10 Ch. (o) 1 Kr. (p)

1921

633 A32 (o) 10c on 6c green & red brown 22.50 3.00
634 " (p) 1k on 12c green & ultramarine 22.50 6.00

Counterfeits exist.

Coronation Issue of 1915 Overprinted

1921 *Perf. 11, 11½* **Wmk. 161**

635 A33 3c dark green 3.00 1.50
a. Center and overprint inverted 20.00
636 " 5c red 3.00 2.25
637 " 6c olive green & carmine 3.00 2.25
638 " 10c blue green & yellow brown 3.00 2.25
639 " 12c ultramarine 4.50 3.00
640 A34 1k silver, yellow brown & gray 3.75 2.25
641 " 2k silver, blue & rose 4.50 3.75
642 " 5k silver, brown & green 7.50 5.00
643 A35 2t gold, green & brown 7.50 5.00
644 " 3t gold, claret & red brown 7.50 5.00
645 " 5t gold, blue & indigo 7.50 5.00
Nos. 635-645 (11) 54.75 37.25

Counterfeits of this Feb. 21, 1921, overprint are plentiful. Inverted overprints exist on all values; some specialists consider them fraudulent.

Stamps of 1911-13 Overprinted

CONTROLE 1922

Perf. 11½, 11½x11.

1922 **Unwmkd.**

646 A32 1c green & orange 20 3
a. Invtd. overprint 15.00
647 " 2c red & sepia 20 3
648 " 3c brown & green 20 3
649 " 5c brn. & carmine 10.00 5.00
650 " 6c green & red brown 20 3
651 " 9c yel. brn. & vio. 50 3
652 " 10c red & org. brn. 50 3
653 A32 12c green & ultra. 50 3
654 " 1k ultra. & car. 3.00 3
655 " 24c violet & green 1.50 3
656 " 2k grn. & red vio. 5.00 3
657 " 3k violet & black 5.00 3
658 " 4k ultra. & gray 35.00 5.00
659 " 5k red & ultra. 12.50 8
660 " 10k olive bistre & claret 25.00 8
661 " 20k violet brown & bistre 25.00 15
662 " 30k red & green 25.00 15
Nos. 646-662 (17) 149.30 10.70

The status of inverted overprints on 5c and 12c is dubious. Unlisted inverts on other denominations are generally considered fraudulent. Counterfeits of this overprint exist.

Nos. 653, 655 Surcharged

3CH.

1922

663 A32 3c on 12c green & ultramarine 75 5
664 " 6c on 24c violet & green 5.25 5

Nos. 661-662 Surcharged:

10 chahis 1 Kran

1923

665 A32 10c on 20k violet brn. & bistre 3.75 1.50
666 " 1k on 30k red & green 5.25 2.25

Shah Ahmed
A37 A38

Engraved

1924-25 *Perf. 11½, 11x11½*

667 A37 1c orange 3 3
668 " 2c magenta 3 3
669 " 3c orange brown 3 3
670 " 6c black brown 8 3
671 " 9c dark green 8 3
672 " 10c dark violet 15 8
673 " 12c red 8 4
674 " 1k dark blue 15 8
675 " 2k indigo & red 45 15
a. Center inverted 700.00
676 " 3k dark violet & red brown 1.50 15
677 " 5k red & brown 5.25 45
678 " 10k choc. & lilac 4.50 75
679 " 20k dk. grn. & brn. 7.50 1.25
680 " 30k orange & black brown 9.00 1.85
Nos. 667-680 (14) 28.83 4.95

SIX CHAHIS.

Type I. P.re.

Type II. P.re.

Surcharge in Black, "1924" etc.

1924 **Typographed.** *Perf. 11.*

681 A38 1c yellow brown 15 3
682 " 2c gray 15 3
683 " 3c deep rose 15 3
684 " 6c orange (I) 75 3
a. 6c orange (II) 75 3

The 1c was surcharged "Chahis" by error. Later the "s" was blocked out in black.

Similar Surcharge, Dated 1925

1925

686 A38 2c yellow green 15 3
687 " 3c red 15 3
689 " 6c chalky blue 60 3
690 " 9c light brown 1.25 8
691 " 10c gray 3.75 15
694 " 1k emerald 3.75 15
695 " 2k lilac 10.00 30
Nos. 686-695 (7) 19.65 77

A39

Gold Overprint on Treasury Department Stamps.

1925

697 A39 1c red 1.00 45
698 " 2c yellow 1.00 45
699 " 3c yellow green 1.00 45
700 " 5c dark gray 3.00 2.25
701 " 10c deep orange 1.00 45
702 " 1k ultramarine 1.00 45
Nos. 697-702 (6) 8.00 4.50

Nos. 697 to 702 all have in the center the Persian lion in a sunburst but with a different frame for each denomination.

The overprint reads: "Post—Provisional Government—of Pahlavi—9th Abanmah—1304—1925".

Issued in commemoration of the deposition of Shah Ahmed and the establishing of the provisiona. government of Riza Khan Pahlavi.

Nos. 667-670 Overprinted

1926 *Perf. 11½, 11x11½*

703 A37 1c orange 8 5
704 " 2c magenta 30 5
705 " 3c orange brown 30 8
706 " 6c black brown 7.50 5.25

Overprinted to commemorate the Pahlavi government of 1925. Counterfeits of No. 706 exist.

Stamps of 1909 Overprinted

Règne de Pahlavi 1926

1926 *Perf. 11½, 12½x12*

707 A31 1c orange & maroon 25 4
708 " 2c violet & maroon 25 4
709 " 3c yellow green & maroon 20 4
a. Invtd. overprint 20.00
710 " 6c red & maroon 30 4
711 " 9c gray & maroon 50 4
712 " 10c red violet & maroon 50 4
713 " 13c dk. bl. & maroon 2.00 4
714 " 1k silver, violet & bistre brown 2.00 4
715 " 26c dark green & maroon 3.00 4
716 " 2k silver, dark green & bistre brown 3.00 4
717 " 3k silver, gray & bistre brown 3.00 8
718 " 4k silver, blue & bistre brown 40.00 15
719 " 5k gold, brown & bistre brown 25.00 15
720 " 10k gold, orange & bistre brown 60.00 15
721 A31 20k gold, olive grn. & bis. brown 80.00 30
722 " 30k gold, carmine & bistre brown 80.00 40
Nos. 707-722 (16) 300.00 1.63

Overprinted to commemorate the Pahlavi government in 1926.

Nos. 707-722, perf. 11½, are on thick paper. Nos. 707-718, perf. 12½x12 are on thin paper and generally sell at higher prices.

Riza Shah Pahlavi
A40 A41

1926-29 **Typographed** *Perf. 11*

723 A40 1c yellow green 30 5
724 " 2c gray violet 60 5
725 " 3c emerald 1.00 5
727 " 6c magenta 2.00 5
728 " 9c rose 8.00 5
729 " 10c bistre brown 10.00 13
730 " 12c deep orange 8.00 10
731 " 15c pale ultra. 10.00 10
733 A41 1k dull blue ('27) 10.00 1.00
734 " 2k brt. violet ('29) 20.00 8.50
Nos. 723-734 (10) 69.90 10.08

Redrawn

1928

740 A40 1c yellow green 40 4
741 " 2c gray violet 40 4
742 " 3c emerald 45 4
743 " 6c rose 1.10 4

On the redrawn stamps much of the shading of the face, throat, collar, etc., has been removed. The letters of "Postes Persanes" and those in the circle at upper right are smaller. The redrawn stamps measure 20¼x25¾mm. instead of 19¾x25¼mm.

Riza Shah Pahlavi
A42 A43

Perf. 12x12½, 11½x12½

1929 **Photogravure**

744 A42 1c yellow green & cerise 15 4
745 " 2c scarlet & brt. blue 15 4
746 " 3c magenta & myrtle green 15 4
747 " 6c yellow brown & olive green 15 4
748 " 9c Prussian blue & vermilion 45 4
749 " 10c blue grn. & choc. 75 4
750 " 12c gray blk. & pur. 1.25 4
751 " 15c citron & ultra. 1.50 4
752 " 1k dull bl. & black 5.25 4
753 " 24c olive green & red brown 3.00 4

Engraved.

Perf. 11½.

754 A42 2k brown orange & dark violet 5.25 10
755 " 3k dark green & deep rose 7.50 30
756 " 5k red brown & deep green 7.50 40
757 " 1t ultramarine & deep rose 9.00 60
758 " 2t car. & black 22.50 3.00

Engraved and Typographed.

No.	Type	Description	Unused	Used
759	A43	3t gold & dp. vio.	17.50	2.75
		Nos. 744-759 (16)	82.05	7.55

Riza Shah Pahlavi
A44

1931-32 Lithographed. *Perf. 11.*

No.	Type	Description	Unused	Used
760	A44	1c olive brown & ultramarine	30	3
761	“	2c red brown & black	45	3
762	“	3c lilac rose & olive	30	3
763	“	6c red org. & violet	60	3
764	“	9c ultra. & red org.	3.00	4
765	“	10c vermilion & gray	9.00	8
766	“	11c blue & dull red	11.00	90
767	“	12c turquoise blue & lilac rose	9.00	6
768	“	16c black & red	6.00	10
769	“	1k carmine & turquoise blue	7.50	15
770	“	27c dark gray & dull blue	6.00	10
		Nos. 760-770 (11)	53.15	1.55

Riza Shah Pahlavi
A45 A46

1933-34

No.	Type	Description	Unused	Used
771	A45	5d olive brown	15	3
772	“	10d blue	15	3
773	“	15d gray	30	3
774	“	30d emerald	30	3
775	“	45d turquoise blue	60	3
776	“	50d magenta	75	3
777	“	60d green	1.50	3
778	“	75d brown	1.50	5
779	“	90d red	1.50	10
780	A46	1r dk. rose & blk.	1.50	3
781	“	1.20r gray black & rose	7.50	10
782	“	1.50r citron & blue	7.50	22
783	“	2r light blue & chocolate	5.25	10
784	“	3r magenta & grn.	9.00	15
785	“	5r dark brown & red orange	22.50	3.00
		Nos. 771-785 (15)	60.00	3.96

"Justice"
A47

"Education"
A49

Ruins of Persepolis—A48

Tehran Airport—A50

Sanatorium at Sakhtessar—A51

Cement Factory, Chah-Abdul-Azim—A52

Gunboat "Palang"—A53

Railway Bridge over Karun River—A54

Post Office and Customs Building, Tehran—A55

1935, Feb. 21 Photo. *Perf. 12½*

No.	Type	Description	Unused	Used
786	A47	5d red brn. & grn.	15	3
787	A48	10d red orange & gray black	15	3
788	A49	15d magenta & Prussian blue	22	6
789	A50	30d black & green	40	10
790	A51	45d olive green & red brown	60	10
791	A52	75d grn. & dk. brn.	3.00	20
792	A53	90d blue & carmine rose	2.25	30
793	A54	1r red brown & purple	6.75	1.50
794	A55	1½r violet & ultra.	4.50	2.25
		Nos. 786-794 (9)	18.02	4.57

Issued in commemoration of the 10th anniversary of the reign of Riza Shah Pahlavi.

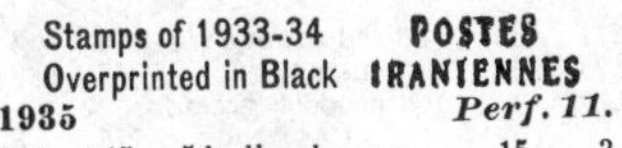

Stamps of 1933-34 Overprinted in Black POSTES IRANIENNES

1935 *Perf. 11.*

No.	Type	Description	Unused	Used
795	A45	5d olive brown	15	3
796	“	10d blue	30	3
797	“	15d gray	30	3
798	“	30d emerald	1.50	3
799	“	45d turquoise blue	75	30
800	“	50d magenta	75	4
801	“	60d green	75	3
802	“	75d brown	3.75	50
803	“	90d red	3.75	3.00
804	A46	1r dk. rose & blk.	6.75	5.50
805	“	1.20r gray black & rose	4.50	15
806	“	1.50r citron & blue	3.75	15
807	“	2r lt. blue & choc.	4.50	15
808	“	3r magenta & green	6.00	30
809	“	5r dark brown & red orange	45.00	30.00
		Nos. 795-809 (15)	82.50	40.24

Same Overprint on Stamps of 1929.

1935 *Perf. 12, 12x12½*

No.	Type	Description	Unused	Used
810	A42	1c yellow green & cerise	*125.00*	*35.00*
811	“	2c scarlet & bright blue	30.00	15.00
812	“	3c magenta & myrtle green	15.00	7.50
813	“	6c yellow brown & olive green	15.00	7.50
814	“	9c Prussian blue & vermilion	9.00	7.50

Perf. 11½.

No.	Type	Description	Unused	Used
815	A42	1t ultramarine & deep rose	9.00	45
816	“	2t carmine & black	12.50	75
817	A43	3t gold & deep violet	15.00	2.25
		Nos. 810-817 (8)	*230.50*	*75.95*

No. 817 is overprinted vertically.

Same Overprint on Stamps of 1931-32.

1935 *Perf. 11*

No.	Type	Description	Unused	Used
818	A44	1c olive brown & ultramarine	100.00	*40.00*
819	“	2c red brown & black	7.50	6.00
820	“	3c lilac rose & olive	4.50	4.00
821	“	6c red orange & violet	22.50	12.50
822	“	9c ultramarine & red orange	22.50	12.50
823	“	11c blue & dull red	75	5
824	“	12c turquoise blue & lilac rose	75.00	*35.00*
825	“	16c black & red	75	22
826	“	27c dark gray & dull blue	75	8
		Nos. 818-826 (9)	234.25	*110.35*

Riza Shah Pahlavi
A56

Photogravure.

1935 Size: 19x27mm. *Perf. 11*

No.	Type	Description	Unused	Used
827	A56	5d violet	15	3
828	“	10d lilac rose	15	3
829	“	15d turquoise blue	15	3
830	“	30d emerald	45	3
831	“	45d orange	75	3
832	“	50d dull light brown	75	3
833	“	60d ultramarine	6.00	3
834	“	75d red orange	1.85	3
835	“	90d rose	1.85	3

Size: 21½x31 mm.

No.	Type	Description	Unused	Used
836	A56	1r dull lilac	3.75	3
837	“	1.50r blue	10.00	40
838	“	2r dk. olive green	9.00	8
839	“	3r dark brown	9.00	15
840	“	5r slate black	9.00	1.90
		Nos. 827-840 (14)	52.85	2.83

Riza Shah Pahlavi
A57 A58

1936-37 Lithographed. *Perf. 11*

Size: 20x27 mm.

No.	Type	Description	Unused	Used
841	A57	5d bright violet	15	3
842	“	10d magenta	15	3
843	“	15d brt. ultramarine	15	3
844	“	30d yellow green	15	3
845	“	45d vermilion	15	3
846	“	50d black brown ('37)	45	3
847	“	60d brown orange	60	3
848	“	75d rose lake	75	3
849	“	90d rose red	90	3

Size: 23x31 mm.

No.	Type	Description	Unused	Used
850	A57	1r turquoise green	1.25	3
851	“	1.50r deep blue	3.00	3
852	“	2r bright blue	3.75	3
853	“	3r violet brown	3.75	8
854	“	5r slate green	18.50	50
855	“	10r dark brown & ultra. ('37)	27.50	3.75
		Nos. 841-855 (15)	61.20	4.69

1938-39 *Perf. 11*

Size: 20x27 mm.

No.	Type	Description	Unused	Used
856	A58	5d light violet	15	3
857	“	10d magenta	15	3
858	“	15d violet blue	15	3
859	“	30d bright green	15	3
860	“	45d vermilion	15	3
861	“	50d black brown	45	3
862	“	60d brown orange	60	3
863	“	75d rose lake	60	3
864	“	90d rose red ('39)	60	3

Size: 22½x30 mm

No.	Type	Description	Unused	Used
865	A58	1r turquoise green	1.50	3
866	“	1.50r deep blue	5.25	3
867	“	2r light blue ('39)	6.00	8
868	“	3r violet brown	7.50	8
869	“	5r gray green ('39)	9.00	30
870	“	10r dark brown & ultra. ('39)	25.00	1.25
		Nos. 856-870 (15)	57.25	2.04

A set of 10 denominations in this Riza Shah Pahlavi design was prepared in 1939, but is considered not to have been issued by the government for regular postal purposes. The set exists perf. 13 and imperf., with each denomination also printed in miniature sheets of 4, both perf. and imperf.

Crown Prince and Princess Fawziya
A59

Perf. 11½

1939, Apr. 25 Photo. Unwmkd.

No.	Type	Description	Unused	Used
871	A59	5d red brown	25	5
872	“	10d bright violet	25	5
873	“	30d emerald	75	27
874	“	90d red	3.75	27
875	“	1.50r bright blue	5.00	85
		Nos. 871-875 (5)	10.00	1.49

Issued to commemorate the wedding of Crown Prince Mohammed Riza Pahlavi to Princess Fawziya of Egypt, March 15, 1939.

Bridge over Karun River
A60

Veresk Bridge, North Iran
A61

Granary, Ahwaz
A62

Train and Bridge
A63

Museum, Side View
A64 A67

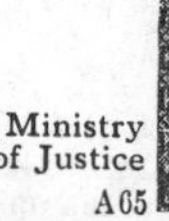

Ministry of Justice
A65

School Building
A66

Mohammed Riza Pahlavi
A68 A69

Lithographed.

1942–46 *Perf. 11* **Unwmkd.**

876	A60	5d violet	8	3
877	A60	5d red orange ('44)	15	3
878	A61	10d magenta	15	3
879	"	10d peacock green ('44)	15	3
880	A62	20d light red violet	30	3
881	"	20d magenta ('44)	15	3
882	A63	25d rose carmine	75	3
883	"	25d violet ('44)	15	3
884	A64	35d emerald	15	3
885	A65	50d ultramarine	75	3
886	"	50d emerald ('44)	75	3
887	A66	70d dull violet brn.	15	3
888	A67	75d rose lake	3.00	3
889	"	75d rose car. ('46)	3.75	3
890	A68	1r carmine	3.00	3
891	"	1r maroon ('45)	6.00	3
892	"	1.50r red	2.25	3
893	"	2r light blue	3.00	3
894	"	2r sage green ('44)	6.00	3
895	"	2.50r dark blue	1.50	3
896	"	3r peacock green	30.00	12
897	"	3r brt. violet ('44)	12.50	3
898	"	5r sage green	60.00	30
899	"	5r light blue ('44)	3.75	3
900	A69	10r brown orange & black	30.00	1.85
901	"	10r dk. org. brn. & black ('44)	10.00	12
902	"	20r choc. & vio.	350.00	11.50
903	"	20r orange & black ('44)	10.00	22
904	"	30r gray black & emerald	*1500.00*	6.75
905	"	30r emerald & black ('44)	8.00	22
906	"	50r dull blue & brown red	35.00	13.00
907	"	50r bright violet & black ('45)	8.00	60
908	"	100r rose red & black ('45)	350.00	9.00
909	"	200r blue & black ('45)	200.00	5.75
		Nos. 876-909 (34)	*2639.43*	50.09

Sixteen denominations of this issue were handstamped at Tabriz in 1945–46 in Persian characters: "Azerbaijan National Government, Dec. 12, 1945." A rebel group did this overprinting while the Russian army held that area.

Flag of Persia—A70

Designs: 50d, Docks at Bandar Shapur. 1.50r, Motor convoy. 2.50r, Gorge and railway viaduct. 5r, Map and Mohammed Riza Pahlavi.

Inscribed:
"En souvenir des efforts de l'Iran pour la Victoire."

Engraved and Lithographed.

1949, Apr. 28 *Perf. 12½* **Unwmkd.**

910	A70	25d multicolored	25	25

Engraved.

911	A70	50d purple	45	25
912	"	1.50r carmine rose	1.50	25
913	"	2.50r deep blue	6.50	50
914	"	5r green	6.75	1.25
		Nos. 910-914 (5)	15.45	2.50

Iran's contribution toward the victory of the Allied Nations in World War II.

Bridge over Zaindeh River
A71

National Bank—A72

Former Ministry of P.T.T.
A73

Mohammed Riza Pahlavi
A74

Designs: 5d–20r, Various views and buildings.

Lithographed.

1949-50 *Perf. 10½.* **Unwmkd.**

915	A71	5d rose & dark green	4	3
916	"	10d ultra. & brown	4	3
917	"	20d violet & ultra.	8	3
918	"	25d black brown & deep blue	15	3
919	"	50d green & ultra.	15	3
920	"	75d dk. brown & red	32	3
921	A72	1r violet & green	45	3
922	"	1.50r dark green & vermilion	32	3
923	"	2r deep carmine & black brown	32	3
924	"	2.50r chalky blue & blue	32	3
925	"	3r violet blue & red orange	75	3
926	"	5r dp. car. & violet	75	8
927	A73	10r carmine & blue green ('50)	10.00	13
928	"	20r brown black & red ('50)	150.00	12.00
929	A74	30r chocolate & dp. blue ('50)	22.50	3.00
930	"	50r red & deep blue ('50)	35.00	3.75
		Nos. 915-930 (16)	221.19	19.29

Globes and Pigeons—A75

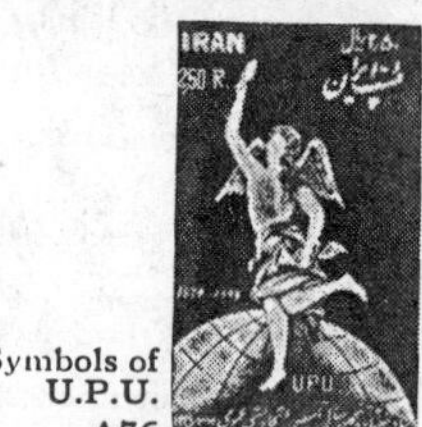
Symbols of U.P.U.
A76

1950, Mar. 16 **Photogravure**

931	A75	50d brown carmine	22.50	15.00
932	A76	2.50r deep blue	37.50	22.50

Issued to commemorate the 75th anniversary (in 1949) of the formation of the Universal Postal Union.

Riza Shah Pahlavi and his Tomb
A77

1950, May 7

933	A77	50d brown	6.25	2.00
934	"	2r sepia	13.50	3.00

Issued to commemorate the re-burial of Riza Shah Pahlavi, May 12, 1950.

Mohammed Riza Pahlavi
A78

Various Portraits.

1950, Oct. 26 Engraved ***Perf. 12½***

Center in Black.

935	A78	25d carmine	33	40
936	"	50d orange	75	40
937	"	75d brown	9.00	2.00
938	"	1r green	10.00	1.35
939	"	2.50r deep blue	15.00	1.20
940	"	5r brown lake	25.00	1.65
		Nos. 935-940 (6)	60.08	7.00

31st birthday of Shah Mohammed Riza Pahlavi.

Shah and Queen Soraya
A79

A80

1951, Feb. 12 Litho. ***Perf. 10½***

941	A79	5d rose violet	1.40	30
942	"	25d orange red	1.40	45
943	"	50d emerald	4.00	75
944	A80	1r brown	4.00	60
945	"	1.50r carmine	4.00	75
946	"	2.50r blue	7.00	90
		Nos. 941-946 (6)	21.80	3.75

Issued to commemorate the wedding of Mohammed Riza Pahlavi to Soraya Esfandiari.

Farabi
A81

1951, Feb. 20

947 A81 50d red 1.65 75
948 " 2.50r blue 8.50 1.25

Issued to commemorate the millenary of the death of Farabi, Persian philosopher.

Mohammed Riza Pahlavi
A82 A83

Photogravure.

1951–52 *Perf. 10½* **Unwmkd.**

950 A82 5d brown orange 6 3
951 " 10d violet 6 3
952 " 20d chocolate ('52) 8 3
953 " 25d blue ('52) 8 3
954 " 50d green 45 3
955 " 75d rose 30 3
956 A83 1r gray green 1.50 3
957 " 1.50r cerise 60 3
958 " 2r chocolate 1.20 3
959 " 2.50r deep blue 1.20 3
960 " 3r red orange 1.50 3
961 " 5r dark green 6.00 15
962 " 10r olive ('52) 13.50 30
963 " 20r org. brn. ('52) 9.00 45
964 " 30r violet blue('52) 9.00 60
965 " 50r blk. brn. ('52) 15.00 1.20
Nos. 950–965 (16) 59.53 3.03

See also Nos. 975–977.

Oil Well and Mosque—A84

Oil Well, Mosque and Monument—A85

1953, Feb. 20 Lithographed

966 A84 50d green & yellow 60 10
967 A85 1r lilac rose & yellow 90 30
968 A84 2.50r blue & yellow 2.50 80
969 A85 5r blk. brn. & yel. 3.75 1.25

Discovery of oil at Qum.

Abadan Oil Refinery—A86

Oil Wells—A87

Designs: 1r, Storage tanks. 5r, Pipe lines. 10r, Abadan refinery and wells.

1953, Mar. 20 Photogravure

970 A86 50d blue green 30 20
971 " 1r rose 60 20
972 A87 2.50r bright ultra. 1.20 60
973 A86 5r red orange 1.85 80
974 " 10r dark violet 3.75 1.25
Nos. 970–974 (5) 7.70 3.05

Nationalization of oil industry, 2nd anniversary.

Shah Types of 1951–52

1953–54 Photogravure. *Perf. 10½.*

975 A82 50d dark gray green 7.00 4
976 A83 1r dark blue green 30 4
977 " 1.50r cerise ('54) 30 3

The background has been highlighted on the 1r and 1.50r.

Gymnast
A88

Archery—A89

Designs: 3r, Climbing Mt. Demavend. 5r, Ancient polo. 10r, Lion hunting.

1953, Oct. 26

978 A88 1r deep green 1.50 65
979 A89 2.50r bright greenish blue 2.00 2.50
980 " 3r gray 21.00 3.25
981 A88 5r bistre 17.50 6.25
982 " 10r rose lilac 23.00 6.50
Nos. 978–982 (5) 65.00 19.15

Mother with Children and UN Emblem
A90

1953, Oct. 24

983 A90 1r blue green & dark green 60 30
984 " 2.50r light blue & indigo 90 60

United Nations Day, Oct. 24.

Herring—A91

Refrigeration Compressor
A92

Processing Equipment, National Fisheries
A93

Designs: 2.50r, Sardines. 10r, Sturgeon.

1954, Jan. 31

985 A91 1r multicolored 1.35 60
986 " 2.50r " 22.50 3.00
987 A92 3r vermilion 11.00 2.50
988 A93 5r deep blue green 11.00 4.50
989 A91 10r multicolored 23.50 9.00
Nos. 985–989 (5) 69.35 19.60

Nationalization of fishing industry.

Broken Shackles
A94

Mother Feeding Baby
A95

Designs: 3r, Torch and flag. 5r, Citizen holding flag of Iran.

1954, Aug. 19 Lithographed

990 A94 2r multicolored 1.25 50
991 " 3r " 6.25 1.00
992 " 5r " 9.00 1.50

Issued to commemorate the first anniversary of the return of the royalist government.

1954, Oct. 24 Photogravure

Center in Orange

993 A95 2r red lilac 2.25 1.00
994 " 3r violet blue 2.25 1.65

Issued to honor the United Nations.

Woodsman Felling Tree—A96

Designs: 2.50r, Laborer carrying firewood. 5fr, Worker operating saw. 10r, Wooden galley.

1954, Dec. 11

995 A96 1r brown & greenish blk. 15.00 6.50
996 " 2.50r greenish black & blue 30.00 13.50
997 " 5r lilac & dark brown 90.00 25.00
998 " 10r blue & claret 60.00 32.50

Issued to publicize the fourth World Forestry Congress, Dehra Dun, India, 1954.

Mohammed Riza Pahlavi
A97 A98

1954–55 **Unwmkd.**

999 A97 5d yellow brown 3 3
1000 " 10d violet 3 3
1001 " 25d scarlet 3 3
1002 " 50d black brown 13 3
1003 A98 1r blue green 20 3
1004 " 1.50r cerise 40 4
1005 " 2r ochre 60 4
1006 " 2.50r blue 80 4
1007 " 3r olive 80 4
1008 " 5r dk. slate grn. 1.20 7
1009 " 10r lilac rose 7.00 30
1010 " 20r indigo 9.00 2.00
1011 " 30r dp. yel. brn. 100.00 8.00
1012 " 50r deep orange 10.00 2.00
1013 " 100r light violet 400.00 40.00
1014 " 200r yellow 70.00 8.00
Nos. 999–1014 (16) 600.22 60.68

See also Nos. 1023–1036.

Regional Costume
A99

Wmk. 306

Regional Costumes: 1r, 2r, Men's costumes. 2.50r, 3r, 5r, Women's costumes.

Wmkd. Arms of Iran (306)

1955, June 26 Photo. *Perf. 11*

1015 A99 1r bluish gray & black 1.35 50
1016 " 2r dull rose & blk. 3.25 1.50
1017 " 2.50r buff & black 10.00 3.75
1018 " 3r rose lilac & blk. 5.00 1.75
1019 " 5r gray brown & black 6.50 2.50
Nos. 1015–1019 (5) 26.10 10.00

Parliament Gate—A100

Designs: 3r, Statue of Liberty (vertical). 5r, Old Gate of Parliament.

1955, Aug. 6 *Perf. 11*

1020 A100 2r red vio. & grn. 1.10 35
1021 " 3r dark blue & aquamarine 4.50 85
1022 " 5r Prussian green & red orange 4.75 1.35

50th anniversary of constitution.

Shah Types of 1954–55

1955–56 *Perf. 11* **Wmk. 306**

1023 A97 5d violet ('56) 12 3
1024 " 10d carmine ('56) 5 3
1025 " 25d brown 7 3
1026 " 50d dark carmine 12 3
1027 A98 1r dark blue green 22 3

1028 A98 1.50r red brn. ('56) 6.75 3
1029 " 2r olive green ('56) 70 3
1030 " 2.50r blue ('56) 45 3
1031 " 3r bistre 85 10
1032 " 5r red lilac 1.15 15
1033 " 10r bright greenish blue 5.75 45
1034 " 20r slate green 18.50 90
1035 " 30r red org. ('56) 45.00 9.50
1036 " 50r red brn. ('56) 67.50 7.50
Nos. 1023–1036 (14) 147.23 18.34

U.N. Emblem and Globes—A101

1955, Oct. 24 ***Perf. 11x12½***

1039 A101 1r deep carmine & orange 80 40
1040 " 2.50r dark blue & greenish blue 1.20 80

Issued to commemorate the tenth anniversary of the United Nations, Oct. 24, 1955.

Wrestlers
A102

1955, Oct. 26 ***Perf. 11*** **Wmk. 306**

1041 A102 2.50r multicolored 2.00 1.20

Issued to commemorate victory in international wrestling competitions.

Garden, Nemazi Hospital
A103

Soldier
A105

Nemazi Hospital, Shiraz
A104

Designs: 5r, Gate of the Koran. 10r, Hafiz of Shiraz.

1956, Mar. 21 ***Perf. 11x12½***

1042 A103 50d multicolored 1.25 50
1043 A104 1r " 2.50 75
1044 A105 2.50r " 3.75 1.75
1045 A104 5r " 5.00 3.25
1046 A105 10r " 7.50 3.75
Nos. 1042–1046 (5) 20.00 10.00

Opening of Nemazi Hospital, Shiraz.

Arms of Iran and Olympic Rings
A106

Tomb at Maragheh
A107

1956, May 15 **Wmk. 306**

1047 A106 5r rose lilac 10.00 5.00

Issued to commemorate the 10th anniversary of the National Olympic Committee.

Photogravure

1956, May 26 ***Perf. 11x12½***

Designs: 2.50r, Astrolabe. 5r, Nasr-ud-Din of Tus.

1048 A107 1r orange 1.00 40
1049 " 2.50r deep ultra. 2.00 45
1050 " 5r sepia & purple 4.00 1.00

Issued to commemorate the 700th anniversary of the death of Nasr-ud-Din of Tus, mathematician.

World Health Organization Emblem
A108

Perf. 11x12½

1956, Sept. 19 **Wmk. 306**

1051 A108 6r cerise 1.65 90

Issued to commemorate the 6th Regional Congress of the World Health Organization.

Scout Bugler and Camp
A109

Design: 5r, Scout badge and Shah in scout uniform.

1956, Aug. 5 ***Perf. 12½x11***

1052 A109 2.50r ultra. & blue 4.00 2.50
1053 " 5r lilac & red lilac 8.00 3.50

National Boy Scout Jamboree.

Former Telegraph Office, Tehran
A110

Design: 6r, Telegraph lines and ancient monument.

1956, Oct. 26

1054 A110 2.50r bright blue & grn., *bluish* 3.00 1.25
1055 " 6r rose carmine & lilac 4.50 2.25

Centenary of Persian telegraph system.

U. N. Emblem and People of the World
A111

Design: 2.50r, U. N. Emblem and scales.

1956, Oct. 24

1056 A111 1r bluish green 60 30
1057 " 2.50r blue & green 1.00 60

Issued in honor of United Nations Day, Oct. 24.

Shah and Pres. Iskander Mirza of Pakistan—A112

1956, Oct. 31

1058 A112 1r multicolored 45 25

Issued to commemorate the visit of Pres. General Iskander Mirza of Pakistan to Tehran, Oct. 31–Nov. 10.

Mohammed Riza Pahlavi
A113 A114

Photogravure.

1956-57 ***Perf. 13½x11*** **Wmk. 306**

1058A A113 5d bright carmine & red ('57) 5 3
1058B " 10d violet blue & dull violet('57) 5 3
1059 " 25d dark brown & brown ('57) 5 3
1059A " 50d brown & olive brown ('57) 12 3
1060 " 1r brown & bright green ('57) 12 3
1061 " 1.50r bright lilac & brown 22 3
1062 " 2r red violet & red 33 3
1063 " 2.50r ultramarine & blue ('57) 33 3
1064 " 3r brown & dark olive bistre 60 3
1065 " 5r vermilion & maroon 65 3
1066 A114 6r dark violet & bright lilac 90 3
1067 " 10r light blue & green ('57) 1.10 20
1068 " 20r green & blue ('57) 2.25 60
1069 " 30r rose red & org. ('57) 11.00 5.00
1070 " 50r dark green & olive green ('57) 4.50 1.65
1071 " 100r lilac & cerise ('57) 135.00 40.00
1072 " 200r deep plum & violet blue ('57) 45.00 13.50
Nos. 1058A–1072 (17) 202.27 61.28

See also Nos. 1082–1098.

Lord Baden-Powell
A115

Railroad Tracks
A116

Train and Map—A117

1957, Feb. 22 ***Perf. 12½***

1073 A115 10r dark green & brown 4.00 2.00

Centenary of the birth of Robert Baden-Powell, founder of the Boy Scout movement.

Perf. 11x12½, 12½x11

1957, May 2

Design: 10r, Train and mosque.

1074 A116 2.50r greenish black, bl. & ochre 2.50 60
1075 A117 5r multicolored 6.25 1.75
1076 A116 10r black, yellow & blue 7.50 3.75

Opening of the Tehran Meshed-Railway.

Pres. Giovanni Gronchi of Italy and Shah—A118

Wmk. 316

Wmkd. Persian Inscription. (316)

Design: 6r, Ruins of Persepolis and Colosseum in Rome and flags.

1957, Sept. 7 **Photo.** ***Perf. 11***

1077 A118 2r slate blue, green & red 75 30
1078 " 6r slate blue, green & red 2.25 1.25

Issued to commemorate the visit of Pres. Giovanni Gronchi of Italy to Iran, Sept. 7.

Queen Soraya and Hospital
A119

1957, Sept. 29 ***Perf. 11*** **Wmk. 316**
1079 A119 2r lt. blue & green 60 20
Sixth Medical Congress, Ramsar.

Globes Showing Location of Iran
A120
Lithographed.

1957, Oct. 22 ***Perf. 12½x11***
1080 A120 10r black, light blue, yellow & red 3.75 80
Issued to commemorate the International Cartographic Conference, Tehran.

Mohammed Riza Pahlavi and King Faisal II—A121

1957, Oct. 18 **Photogravure**
1081 A121 2r slate blue, green & red 45 15
Visit of King Faisal of Iraq, Oct. 19.

Shah Types of 1956–57.

1957-58 ***Perf. 11*** **Wmk. 316**
1082 A114 5d vio. & pur. ('58) 3 3
1083 " 10d claret & rose carmine ('58) 3 3
1084 " 25d rose carmine & brick red ('58) 3 3
1085 " 50d green & olive green ('58) 3 3
1086 " 1r dark green ('58) 3 3
1087 " 1.50r claret & red lilac 12 3
1088 " 2r blue & greenish blue 50 3
1089 " 2.50r dk. blue & blue ('58) 25 3
1090 " 3r rose carmine & vermilion 50 3
1091 " 5r violet blue ('58) 35 3
1092 A113 6r bright blue('58) 50 3
1093 " 10r dp. green ('58) 1.25 13
1094 " 20r green & olive green ('58) 1.50 35
1095 " 30r violet blue & dk. brn. ('58) 5.00 1.25
1096 " 50r dark brown & light brown ('58) 7.50 1.25
1097 " 100r rose lilac & carmine rose ('58) 100.00 7.50
1098 " 200r violet & yellow brown ('58) 62.50 9.00
Nos. 1082-1098 (17) 180.12 19.81

Weight Lifter
A122

Modern and Old Houses, Radio Transmitter
A123

1957, Nov. 8 ***Perf. 11x14½***
1099 A122 10r bl., green & red 1.85 40
Iran's victories in weight lifting.

1958, Feb. 22 **Lithographed**
1100 A123 10r brown, ochre & blue 1.85 90
30th anniversary of radio in Iran.

Oil Derrick and Symbolic Flame
A124

Train on Viaduct
A125

Photogravure.

1958, Mar. 10 ***Perf. 11*** **Wmk. 316**
1101 A124 2r gray & multi. 1.00 25
1102 " 10r multicolored 2.00 50
Issued to commemorate the 50th anniversary of the drilling of Persia's first oil well.

1958, Apr. 24 ***Perf. 11*** **Wmk. 316**
Design: 8r, Train and map.
1103 A125 6r dull purple 3.00 80
1104 " 8r green 3.00 1.25
Opening of Tehran-Tabriz railway line.

Exposition Emblem
A126

1958, Apr. 17 ***Perf. 12½x11***
1105 A126 2.50r blue & lt. blue 45 10
1106 " 6r carmine & salmon 75 20
World's Fair, Brussels, Apr. 17–Oct.19.

Mohammed Riza Pahlavi
A127

U.N. Emblem and Map of Iran
A128

Photogravure.

1958-59 ***Perf. 11*** **Wmk. 316**
1107 A127 5d blue violet 5 3
1108 " 10d light vermilion 5 3
1109 " 25d crimson 5 3
1110 " 50d bright blue 18 3
1111 " 1r dark green 27 3
1113 " 2r dark brown 4.00 3
1115 " 3r dk. red brown 4.75 4
1117 " 6r bright blue 55 3
1118 " 8r magenta 1.65 3
1120 " 14r blue violet 6.75 3
1121 " 20r green 2.25 20
a. Wmd. 306 9.00
1122 " 30r brt. car. rose 4.75 38
1123 " 50r rose violet 12.00 75
1124 " 100r red orange 5.50 1.50
1125 " 200r slate green 12.00 2.75
Nos. 1107-1125 (15) 54.80 5.89
See also Nos. 1138–1151, 1173–1179.

1958, Oct. 24
1126 A128 6r bright blue 75 45
1127 " 10r dark violet & green 1.10 75
Issued for United Nations Day, Oct. 24.

Globe and Hands
A129

1958, Dec. 10
1128 A129 6r dark red brown & brown 60 40
1129 " 8r dark green & gray green 1.00 60
Issued to commemorate the tenth anniversary of the signing of the Universal Declaration of Human Rights.

Rudagi
A130
Design: 5r, Rudagi, different pose.

1958, Dec. 24 **Photo.** **Wmk. 306**
1130 A130 2.50r bluish black 1.35 20
1131 " 5r violet 4.00 80
1132 " 10r dark brown 6.75 1.00
Issued to commemorate the 1100th anniversary of the birth of Rudagi, blind Persian poet.

Flag—A130a
Perf. 14½x11

1959, May 8 **Wmk. 316**
1132A A130a 1r multicolored 45 40
1132B " 6r " 1.10 40
Centenary of the Red Cross.

Wrestlers, Flag and Globe
A131

1959, Oct. 7 **Litho.** ***Perf. 11x12½***
1133 A131 6r multicolored 3.00 80
World Wrestling Championships, Tehran.

Globe, U. N. Building and Hand Holding Torch of Freedom
A132

1959, Oct. 24 **Photo.** ***Perf. 11***
1134 A132 6r gray brown, red & bistre 60 50
Issued for United Nations Day, Oct. 24.

Mohammed Riza Pahlavi and Pres. Ayub Khan of Pakistan
A133

1959, Nov. 9 **Litho.** ***Perf. 11x16***
1135 A133 6r multicolored 75 40
Issued to commemorate the visit of Pres. Ayub Khan of Pakistan to Iran.

ILO Emblem
A134

1959, Nov. 12 ***Perf. 16***
1136 A134 1r blue 45 30
1137 " 5r brown 75 45
Issued to commemorate the 40th anniversary of the International Labor Organization.

Shah Type of 1958–59.

Photogravure.

1959-63 ***Perf. 11*** **Wmk. 316**
1138 A127 5d red brown ('60) 3 3
1139 " 10d Prus. grn. ('60) 3 3
a. 10d Prussian blue ('63) 1.00 1.00
1140 " 25d orange 3 3
1141 " 50d scarlet 10 3
1142 " 1r deep violet 10 3
1143 " 3r olive 75 3
1144 " 8r brown olive 50 3
1145 " 10r olive black ('60) 50 3
1146 " 14r yellow green 65 3
1147 " 20r slate green ('60) 1.00 18
1148 " 30r chocolate ('60) 1.35 18
1149 " 50r deep blue ('60) 3.75 45
1150 " 100r green ('60) 47.50 1.80
1151 " 200r cerise ('60) 110.00 2.75
Nos. 1138-1151 (14) 166.29 5.63

Pahlavi Foundation Bridge, Karun River—A135
Design: 5r, Bridge, different view.

1960, Feb. 29 **Litho.** ***Perf. 16x11***
1152 A135 1r dark brown & bright blue 40 10
1153 " 5r blue & emerald 1.00 30
Issued to commemorate the opening of Pahlavi Foundation Bridge at Khorramshahr on the Karun River.

Uprooted Oak Emblem
A136

Design: 6r, Arched frame.

1960, Apr. 7 *Perf. 11*

1154 A136 1r bright ultra. 15 8
1155 " 6r gray olive 22 18

Issued to publicize World Refugee Year, July 1, 1959–June 30, 1960.

Mosquito A137 — Man with Spray Gun A138

Design: 3r, Mosquito on water.

1960, Apr. 7 **Wmk. 316**

1156 A137 1r blk. & red, *yel.* 38 20
1157 A138 2r light blue, ultra. & black 75 30
1158 A137 3r black & red, *yellow green* 1.10 50

Issued to publicize malaria control.

Polo Player
A139

Design: 6r, Persian archer.

1960, June 9 **Litho.** **Wmk. 316**

1159 A139 1r deep claret 60 30
1160 " 6r dark blue & light blue 1.00 70

Issued to commemorate the 17th Olympic Games, Rome, Aug. 25–Sept. 11.

Shah Riza Pahlavi and King Hussein of Jordan
A140

1960, July 6 *Perf. 11*

1161 A140 6r multicolored 1.00 30

Visit of King Hussein of Jordan to Tehran.

Iranian Scout Emblem in Flower A141 — Tents and Pillars of Persepolis A142

1960, July 18

1162 A141 1r green 30 15
1163 A142 6r brown bright blue & buff 45 30

3rd National Boy Scout Jamboree.

Shah and Queen Farah—A143

1960, Sept. 9 **Litho.** *Perf. 11*

1164 A143 1r green 1.00 40
1165 " 5r blue 3.00 80

Issued to commemorate the marriage of Shah Mohammed Riza Pahlavi and Farah Diba.

U. N. Emblem and Globe
A144

1960, Oct. 24 **Wmk. 316**

1166 A144 6r blue, black & light brown 50 20

15th anniversary of the United Nations.

Shah Riza Pahlavi and Queen Elizabeth II—A145

1961, Mar. 2 **Litho.** *Perf. 11*

1167 A145 1r light red brown 30 10
1168 " 6r bright ultra. 75 30

Issued to commemorate the visit of Queen Elizabeth II to Tehran, Feb. 1961.

Girl Playing Arganoon A146 — Safiaddin Amavi A147

1961, Apr. 10 *Perf. 11* **Wmk. 316**

1169 A146 1r dark brn. & buff 40 10
1170 A147 6r greenish gray 60 20

International Congress of Music, Tehran.

Shah Type of 1958–59 Redrawn

1961–62 **Litho.** *Perf. 11*

1173	A127	25d orange	25	3
1174	"	50d scarlet	25	3
1175	"	1r deep violet	90	3
1176	"	2r chocolate	1.75	3
1177	"	3r olive brown	2.25	3
1178	"	6r brt. blue ('62)	9.00	3
1179	"	8r brn. olive ('62)	3.75	3
		Nos. 1173-1179 (7)	18.15	21

On Nos. 1173–1179 (lithographed), a single white line separates the lower panel from the shah's portrait. On Nos. 1107–1125, 1138–1151 (photogravure), two lines, one in color and one in white, separate panel from portrait. Other minor differences exist.

Shah and Queen Farah Holding Crown Prince—A148

1961, June 2 **Lithographed**

1186 A148 1r bright pink 1.00 40
1187 " 6r light blue 4.00 1.65

Issued to commemorate the birth of the Crown Prince Riza Cyrus Ali, Oct. 31, 1960.

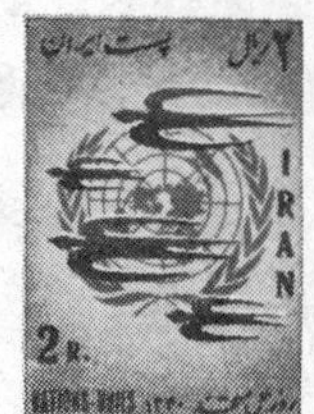

Swallows and U.N. Emblem A149 — Planting Tree A150

1961, Oct. 24 *Perf. 11*

1188 A149 2r blue & carmine rose 40 12
1189 " 6r blue & violet 55 25

Issued for United Nations Day, Oct. 24.

1962, Jan. 11

1190 A150 2r olive green, citron & dark blue 40 12
1191 " 6r ultra., green & pale blue 50 25

Tree Planting Day.

Worker and Symbols of Labor and Agriculture A151 — Map, Family and Cogwheel A152

1962, March 15 **Lithographed**

1192 A151 2r blue green, brown & black 30 12
1193 " 6r light ultra., brown & black 45 25

Issued for Workers' Day.

1962, Mar. 20 *Perf. 11*

1194 A152 2r black, yellow & lilac 22 6
1195 " 6r black, blue & ultramarine 40 18

Social Insurance Week.

Sugar Refinery, Khuzistan
A153

1962, Apr. 14 **Wmk. 316**

1196 A153 2r dk. & lt. blue & green 30 12
1197 " 6r ultramarine, buff & blue 50 25

Opening of sugar refinery in Khuzistan.

Karaj Dam—A154

1962, May 15

1198 A154 2r dark brown & gray green 40 12
1199 " 6r violet blue & light blue 80 30

Inauguration of Karaj Dam, renamed Amir Kabir Dam.

Sefid Rud Dam—A155

1962, May 19 **Lithographed**

1200 A155 2r dark green, lt. blue & buff 35 12
1201 " 6r red brown, slate green & light blue 85 40

Inauguration of Sefid Rud Dam.

"UNESCO" and U.N. Emblem A156 — Malaria Eradication Emblem and Sprayer A157

1962, June 2 *Perf. 11* **Wmk. 316**

1202 A156 2r black, emerald & red 22 12
1203 " 6r blue, emerald & red 45 30

Issued to commemorate the 15th anniversary of UNESCO (U.N. Educational, Scientific and Cultural Organization).

1962, June 20

Designs: 2r, Emblem and arrow piercing mosquito (horiz.). 10r, Emblem and globe (horiz.). Size: 2r and 10r, 40x25 mm.; 6r, 29½x34½mm.

1204 A157 2r black & bluish green 25 15
1205 " 6r pink & violet blue 45 15
1206 " 10r light blue & ultramarine 60 30

Issued for the World Health Organization drive to eradicate malaria.

Oil Field and U.N. Emblem
A158

1962, Sept. 1 Photogravure

1207 A158 6r greenish blue & brown 60 25
1208 " 14r gray & sepia 90 50

Issued to commemorate the 2nd Petroleum Symposium of ECAFE (U.N. Economic Commission for Asia and the Far East).

Mohammed Riza Pahlavi
A159

Palace of Darius, Persepolis
A160

Perf. 11, 10½x11

1962 Photogravure **Wmk. 316**

1209 A159 5d green 3 3
1210 " 10d chestnut 3 3
1211 " 25d dark blue 3 3
1212 " 50d Prussian green 30 3
1213 " 1r orange 30 3
1214 " 2r violet blue 15 3
1215 " 5r dark brown 45 4
1216 A160 6r blue 90 4
1217 " 8r yellow green 45 4
1218 " 10r greenish blue 45 4
1219 " 11r slate green 45 12
1220 " 14r purple 60 15
1221 " 20r red brown 1.20 18
1222 " 50r vermilion 2.50 60
Nos. 1209-1222 (14) 7.84 1.39

See also Nos. 1331–1344.

Hippocrates and Avicenna
A161

1962, Oct. 7 Lithographed

1226 A161 2r brown, buff & ultramarine 80 25
1227 " 6r green, pale grn. & ultra. 1.20 45

Near and Middle East Medical Congress.

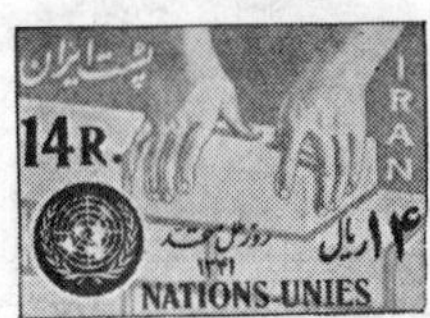

Hands Laying Bricks
A162

Design: 6r, Houses and U.N. emblem (vert.).

1962, Oct. 24

1228 A162 6r dk. bl. & ultra. 60 18
1229 " 14r dark blue & emerald 1.00 45

Issued for United Nations Day, Oct. 24.

Crown Prince Receiving Flowers
A163

1962, Oct. 31

1230 A163 6r blue gray 2.00 90
1231 " 14r dull green 5.00 2.10

Issued for Children's Day, Oct. 31, the second birthday of Crown Prince Riza Cyrus Ali.

Map of Iran and Persian Gulf
A164

1962, Dec. 12 *Perf. 11* **Wmk. 316**

1232 A164 6r dk. & lt. blue, violet blue & rose 55 15
1233 " 14r dk. & lt. blue, pink & rose 1.00 35

The Persian Gulf Seminar.

Hilton Hotel, Tehran
A165

1963, Jan. 21 Photogravure

1234 A165 6r deep blue 2.00 40
1235 " 14r dk. red brown 3.00 80

Opening of the Royal Tehran Hilton Hotel.

Mohammed Riza Shah Dam
A166

1963, Mar. 14 Lithographed

Center Multicolored

1236 A166 6r violet blue 2.00 45
1237 " 14r dark brown 4.00 90

Issued to commemorate the inauguration of the Mohammed Riza Shah Dam.

Worker with Pickax
A167

1963, Mar. 15

1238 A167 2r cream & black 60 12
1239 " 6r light bl. & blk. 90 25

Issued for Labor Day.

Stylized Bird over Globe
A168

Designs: 6r, Stylized globe and "FAO." 14r, Globe in space and wheat emblem.

1963, Mar. 21 *Perf. 11*

1240 A168 2r ultramarine, lt. bl. & bister 45 15
1241 " 6r light ultra., ocher & black 80 25
1242 " 14r slate blue & ocher 2.50 45

Issued for the "Freedom from Hunger" campaign of the U.N. Food and Agriculture Organization.

Shah and List of Bills—A169

1963, Mar. 21 **Wmk. 316**

1243 A169 6r grn. & lt. blue 1.50 40
1244 " 14r grn. & dull yel. 3.00 80

Issued to commemorate the first anniversary of the signing of six socioeconomic bills by Shah Mohammed Riza Pahlavi.

Shah and King of Denmark—A170

1963, May 3 Litho. *Perf. 11*

1245 A170 6r indigo & dark ultramarine 2.00 40
1246 " 14r dark brown & red brown 4.00 80

Visit of King Frederik IX of Denmark.

Flags, Shah Mosque, Isfahan, and Taj Mahal, Agra—A171

1963, May 19

1247 A171 6r blue, yellow green & red 2.00 40
1248 " 14r multicolored 4.00 80

Issued to commemorate the visit of Dr. Sarvepalli Radhakrishnan, president of India.

Chahnaz Dam
A172

1963, June 8 *Perf. 11* **Wmk. 316**

1249 A172 6r ultra., blue & green 1.00 45
1250 " 14r dark green, blue & buff 2.00 75

Inauguration of Chahnaz Dam.

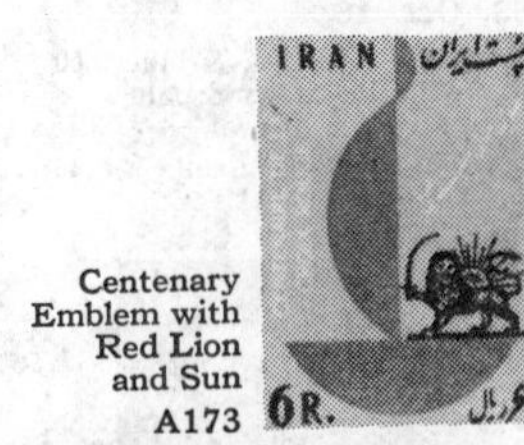

Centenary Emblem with Red Lion and Sun
A173

1963, June 10

1251 A173 6r blue, gray & red 2.50 50
1252 " 14r buff, gray & red 3.75 1.00

Centenary of International Red Cross.

Shah and Queen Juliana
A174

Wmk. 349

Wmkd. Persian Inscription and Crown in Circle (349)

Circles are 95mm. apart.

1963, Oct. 3 ***Perf. 11x10½***

1253 A174 6r ultra. & blue 3.00 50
1254 " 14r slate green & dull green 4.00 1.00

Visit of Queen Juliana of the Netherlands.

Literacy Corps Emblem and Soldier Teaching Village Class
A175

1963, Oct. 15 **Litho.** ***Perf. 10½***

1255 A175 6r multicolored 2.00 40
1256 " 14r " 3.00 80

Issued to publicize the Literacy Corps.

Gen. Charles de Gaulle and View of Tehran—A176

1963, Oct. 16

1257 A176 6r ultra. & blue 2.50 50
1258 " 14r brown & pale brown 3.75 1.00

Visit of General de Gaulle of France.

Fertilizer Plant, Oil Company Emblem and Map
A177

Design: 14r, Factory and Iranian Oil Company emblem (horiz.).

Perf. 10½x11, 11x10½

1963, Oct. 18 **Wmk. 316**

1259 A177 6r blk., yel. & red 3.00 50
1260 " 14r blk., bl. & yel. 5.00 1.00

Opening of Shiraz Chemical Factory.

Pres. Lübke of Germany and Mosque in Tehran
A178

1963, Oct. 23 ***Perf. 10½*** **Wmk. 349**

1261 A178 6r ultra. & dk. bl. 2.50 45
1262 " 14r gray & brown 3.75 75

Issued to commemorate the visit of President Heinrich Lübke of Germany.

U.N. Emblem and Iranian Flag
A179

1963, Oct. 24

1263 A179 8r brn., emerald, ultra. & red 1.00 25

Issued for United Nations Day.

U.N. Emblem and Jets
A180

1963, Oct. 24

1264 A180 6r multicolored 1.00 30

Issued to honor Iranian jet fighters with U.N. Force in the Congo.

Crown Prince Riza
A181

Pres. Brezhnev of U.S.S.R.
A182

1963, Oct. 31

1265 A181 2r brown 85 20
1266 " 6r blue 1.65 40

Issued for Children's Day on Crown Prince Riza's 3rd birthday.

1963, Nov. 16 ***Perf. 10½*** **Wmk. 349**

1267 A182 6r dark brown, yellow & blue 3.75 45
1268 A182 11r dark brown, yellow & red 2.50 1.00

Issued to commemorate the visit of Leonid I. Brezhnev, President of the Presidium of the Supreme Soviet of the USSR.

Atatürk's Mausoleum, Ankara
A183

Design: 5r, Kemal Atatürk.

1963, Nov. 28 **Lithographed**

1269 A183 4r gray, red brown & dark green 2.00 10
1270 " 5r red, yel. & blk. 2.00 25

Issued to commemorate the 25th anniversary of the death of Kemal Atatürk, president of Turkey.

Scales and Globe
A184

1963, Dec. 10

1271 A184 6r bright yellow green, black & ultra. 1.40 30
1272 " 14r orange brown, black & buff 1.65 50

Issued to commemorate the 15th anniversary of the Universal Declaration of Human Rights.

Mother and Child
A185

Map of Iran, Chamber of Industry and Mines Emblem
A186

1963, Dec. 16

1273 A185 2r multicolored 1.00 25
1274 " 4r " 2.00 50

Issued for Mother's Day.

1963, Dec. 17 **Lithographed**

1275 A186 8r blue green, buff & dark blue 2.00 30

Issued to honor the Chamber of Industry and Mines.

Factories and Hand Holding Bill
A187

Designs: 4r, Factories and bills on scale. 6r, Man on globe carrying torch of education. 8r, Tractor, map and yardstick. 10r, Forest. 12r, Gate of Parliament and heads of man and woman.

1964, Jan. 26 ***Perf. 10½*** **Wmk. 349**

1276 A187 2r dark gray, lilac & brn. 75 15
1277 " 4r brown & gray 75 15
1278 " 6r multicolored 1.25 30
1279 " 8r " 1.00 35
1280 " 10r slate grn., gray green & red 2.00 45
1281 " 12r red org. & brn. 2.50 60
Nos. 1276-1281 (6) 8.25 2.00

Issued to commemorate the second anniversary of six socioeconomic bills: 2r, Shareholding for factory workers. 4r, Sale of shares in government factories. 6r, Creation of Army of Education. 8r, Land reforms. 10r, Nationalization of forests. 12r, Reforms in parliamentary elections.

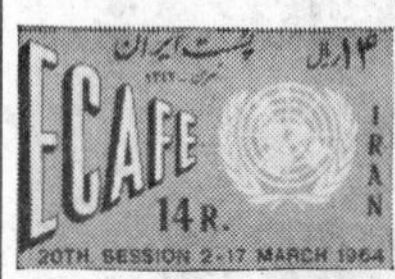

"ECAFE" and UN Emblem
A188

Flowering Branch
A189

1964, March 2 **Wmk. 349**

1282 A188 14r brt. grn. & blk. 2.00 55

Issued to commemorate the 20th session of ECAFE (Economic Commission for Asia and the Far East), March 2–17.

1964, March 5 ***Perf. 10½***

1283 A189 50d emerald, black & orange 10 3
1284 " 1r brt. blue, black & orange 10 6

Novrooz, Iranian New Year, Mar. 21.

Anemometer
A190

Mosque and Arches, Isfahan
A191

1964, March 23 **Lithographed**

1285 A190 6r brt. bl. & vio. bl. 75 25

Issued to commemorate the United Nations Fourth World Meteorological Day, March 23.

1964, Apr. 7 ***Perf. 10½***

Design: 11r, Griffon and winged bull, Persepolis.

1286 A191 6r lilac, grn. & blk. 1.40 45
1287 " 11r org., brn. & blk. 1.65 75

Issued for tourist publicity.

Rudagi and Musical Instrument
A192

1964, May 16 **Photo.** **Wmk. 349**

1288 A192 6r blue 1.40 30
1289 " 8r red brown 1.65 50

The inscription translates: "Wisdom is better than eye and sight." Issued to commemorate the opening of an institute for the blind.

Sculpture, Persepolis

A193

Designs: 4r, Achaemenian horse-drawn mail cart, map of Iran (horiz.). 6r, Vessel with sculptured animals. 10r, Head of King Shapur, sculpture.

Lithographed

1964, June 5 *Perf. 10½* Wmk. 349

1290 A193 2r gray & blue 1.00 20
1291 " 4r violet blue, light blue & blue 3.00 30
1292 " 6r brn. & yellow 2.00 50
1293 " 10r yel. & olive grn. 2.00 1.00

Issued to commemorate the opening of the "7000 Years of Persian Art" exhibition in Washington, D.C.

Shah and Emperor Haile Selassie I

A194

1964, Sept. 14 *Perf. 10½* Wmk. 349

1294 A194 6r ultra. & lt. blue 75 20

Issued to commemorate the visit of Emperor Haile Selassie I of Ethiopia.

Tooth and Dentists' Association Emblem A195

"2 I.D.A." A196

1964, Sept. 14 Lithographed

1295 A195 2r bl., red & dk. bl. 50 12
1296 A196 4r ultra., blue & pale brown 50 25

Iranian Dentists' Association, 2nd congress.

Research Institute, Microscope, Wheat and Locust

A197

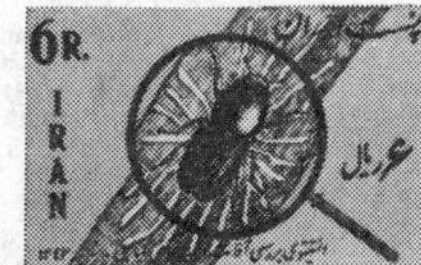

Beetle under Magnifying Glass

A198

1964, Sept. 23 *Perf. 10½* Wmk. 349

1297 A197 2r red, org. & brn. 1.00 20
1298 A198 6r bl., brn. & ind. 2.00 40

Issued to publicize the fight against plant diseases and damages.

Mithras (Mehr) on Ancient Seal A199

Eleanor Roosevelt A200

1964, Oct. 8 Lithographed

Size: 26x34mm.

1299 A199 8r orange & brn. orange 1.20 25

Mehragan celebration. See also No. 1406.

1964, Oct. 11

1300 A200 10r violet blue & rose violet 1.25 40

Issued to honor Eleanor Roosevelt (1884–1962).

Clasped Hands and U.N. Emblem A201

Symbolic Airplane and U.N. Emblem A202

1964, Oct. 24 *Perf. 10½* Wmk. 349

1301 A201 6r ultra., yellow, red & black 1.00 20
1302 A202 14r org., ultra. & red 1.40 40

Issued for United Nations Day.

Persian Gymnast A203

Polo Player A204

1964, Oct. 26

1303 A203 4r tan, sepia & Prussian blue 75 20
1304 A204 6r red & black 1.35 40

18th Olympic Games, Tokyo, Oct. 10–25.

Crown Prince Riza

A205

1964, Oct. 31 Lithographed

1305 A205 1r dull grn. & brn. 60 15
1306 " 2r deep rose & ultramarine 1.40 30
1307 " 6r ultra. & red 2.00 45

Issued for Children's Day on Crown Prince Riza's 4th birthday.

U.N. Emblem, Flame and Smokestack

A206

1964, Nov. 16 *Perf. 10½* Wmk. 349

1308 A206 6r blk., lt. bl. & car. 60 25
1309 " 8r black, emerald & carmine 1.00 30

Issued to commemorate the Petro-Chemical Conference and Gas Seminar, Nov.–Dec. 1964.

Shah and King Baudouin

A207

1964, Nov. 17

1310 A207 6r blk., org. & yel. 50 20
1311 " 8r black, orange & emerald 70 25

Visit of King Baudouin of Belgium.

Rhazes—A208

1964, Dec. 27 *Perf. 10½* Wmk. 349

1312 A208 2r multicolored 60 20
1313 " 6r " 1.00 40

Issued to commemorate the 1100th anniversary of the birth of Rhazes (abu-Bakr Muhammad ibn-Zakariya al-Razi), Persian-born Mohammedan physician.

Shah and King Olav V

A209

1965, Jan. 7 Lithographed

1314 A209 2r dk. brown & lilac 50 12
1315 " 4r brown & green 70 20

Visit of King Olav V of Norway.

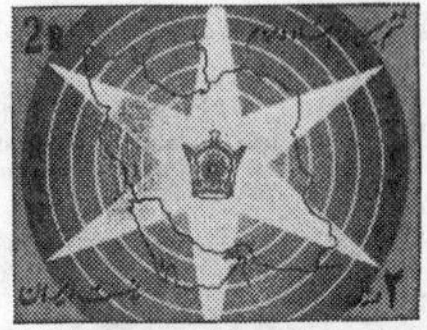

Map of Iran and Six-pointed Star

A210

1965, Jan. 26 *Perf. 10½* Wmk. 349

1316 A210 2r black, bright blue & orange 40 12

Issued to commemorate the third anniversary of the Shah's six socioeconomic bills.

Woman and U.N. Emblem A211

Green Wheat and Tulip A212

1965, Mar. 1 *Perf. 10½* Wmk. 349

1317 A211 6r black & blue 50 18
1318 " 8r ultra. & red 70 25

Issued to commemorate the 18th session of the United Nations commission on the status of women.

1965, Mar. 6

1319 A212 50d multicolored 10 3
1320 " 1r " 10 6

Novrooz, Iranian New Year, Mar. 21.

Pres. Habib Bourguiba and Minarets of Tunis Mosque

A213

1965, Mar. 14 Litho. *Perf. 10½*

1321 A213 4r multicolored 80 15

Visit of Pres. Habib Bourguiba of Tunisia.

Map of Iran and Trade Mark of Iranian Oil Co.—A214

1965, Mar. 20 **Lithographed**

1322	A214	6r multicolored	80	25
1323	"	14r "	1.65	60

Issued to commemorate the 14th anniversary of the nationalization of the oil industry.

ITU Emblem, Old and New Communication Equipment
A215

1965, May 17 ***Perf. 10½*** **Wmk. 349**

1324	A215	14r deep carmine rose & gray	60	35

Issued to commemorate the centenary of the International Telecommunication Union.

ICY Emblem
A216

1965, June 22 **Litho.** ***Perf. 10½***

1325	A216	10r slate green & gray blue	50	25

International Cooperation Year, 1965.

Iran Airways Emblem
A217

1965, July 17 ***Perf. 10½*** **Wmk. 349**

1326	A217	14r multicolored	60	45

Tenth anniversary of Iran Airways.

Hands Holding Book
A218

Map and Flags of Turkey, Iran and Pakistan—A219

1965, July 21 **Lithographed**

1327	A218	2r dk. brown, org. brown & buff	30	12
1328	A219	4r multicolored	50	20

Issued to commemorate the first anniversary of the signing of the Regional Cooperation for Development Pact by Turkey, Iran and Pakistan.

Iranian Scout Emblem and Ornament—A220

1965, July 23

1329	A220	2r multicolored	25	12
		a. Pair, imperf., horiz.	25.00	

Issued to commemorate the Middle East Rover Moot (senior Boy Scout assembly).

Majlis Gate
A221

1965, Aug. 5 ***Perf. 10½*** **Wmk. 349**

1330	A221	2r lilac rose & brn.	20	5

60th anniversary of Iranian constitution.

Types of Regular Issue, 1962
Wmk. 349

1964-65 **Photo.** ***Perf. 10½***

1331	A159	5d dk. slate grn. ('65)	3	3
		a. Wmk. 353	3	3
		b. Perf. 11x10½	50	20
1332	A159	10d chestnut	3	3
		a. Perf. 11x10½	3	3
1333	A159	25d dk. blue ('65)	15	7
		a. Perf. 11x10½	25	7
1334	A159	50d Prussian green	3	3
		a. Perf. 11x10½	50	20
1335	A159	1r orange	7	3
		a. Perf. 11x10½	50	20
1336	A159	2r violet blue	12	4
1337	"	5r dark brown	33	6
		a. Perf. 11x10½	33	6
1338	A160	6r blue ('65)	45	10
1339	"	8r yel. grn. ('65)	45	10
1340	"	10r greenish bl. ('65)	65	10
1341	"	11r slate grn. ('65)	80	12
1342	"	14r purple ('65)	95	18
1343	"	20r red brn. ('65)	1.35	18
1344	"	50r org. verm. ('65)	2.65	60
		Nos. 1331-1344 (14)	8.06	1.67

Dental Congress Emblem
A222

1965, Sept. 7 **Litho.** ***Perf. 10½***

1345	A222	6r gray, ultra., & carmine	40	18

Iranian Dentists' Association, 3rd congress.

Classroom and Literacy Corps Emblem
A223

Alphabets on Globe
A224

Designs: 6r, UNESCO emblem and open book (diamond shape). 8r, UNESCO emblem and inscription (horiz.). 14r, Shah Riza Pahlavi and inscription in six languages.

1965, Sept. 8

		Size: 31x35mm.		
1346	A223	2r multicolored	15	10
		Size: 25x30mm.		
1347	A224	5r multicolored	20	18
		Size: 30x30mm.		
1348	A223	6r multicolored	25	20
		Size: 35x23mm.		
1349	A223	8r dk. blue, carm., emerald & buff	20	25
		Size: 34x46mm.		
1350	A223	14r citron, dark bl. & brown	45	40
		Nos. 1346-1350 (5)	1.35	1.13

Issued to publicize the World Congress Against Illiteracy, Tehran, Sept. 8-19.

Mohammed Riza Pahlavi—A225

1965, Sept. 16 **Litho.** ***Perf. 10½***

1351	A225	1r crimson, rose red & gray	15	6
1352	"	2r dark red, rose red & yellow	15	8

25th anniversary of the reign of Shah Mohammed Riza Pahlavi.

Emblem of Persian Medical Society
A226

1965, Sept. 21 **Wmk. 349**

1353	A226	5r ultra., dp. ultra. & gold	22	18

14th Medical Congress, Ramsar.

Pres. Jonas of Austria—A227

1965, Sept. 30

1354	A227	6r blue, bright blue & gray	30	18

Visit of President Franz Jonas of Austria.

Mithras (Mehr) on Ancient Seal
A228

Wmk. 353

Wmkd. Persian Inscription and Coat of Arms in Circle (353)

1965, Oct. 8 **Lithographed**

1355	A228	4r brt. green, gold, brown & black	25	18

Issued to commemorate the Mehragan celebration during month of Mehr, Sept. 23-Oct. 22. Persian inscription of watermark vertical on No. 1355.

U.N. Emblem
A229

1965, Oct. 24 ***Perf. 10½*** **Wmk. 353**

1356	A229	5r blue, green & rose carmine	22	18

20th anniversary of the United Nations.

Symbolic Arches
A230

1965, Oct. 26

1357	A230	3r violet blue, blk., yellow & red	18	12

Exhibition of Iranian Commodities.

Crown Prince Riza
A231

1965, Oct. 31

1358	A231	2r brown & yellow	35	12

Issued for Children's Day on Crown Prince Riza's 5th birthday.

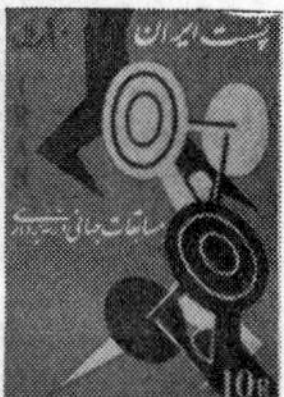

Weight Lifters
A232

1965, Nov. 1

1359 A232 10r brt. blue, violet & bright pink 35 20

World Weight Lifting Championships, Tehran.

Open Book
A233

1965, Dec. 1 ***Perf. 10½*** **Wmk. 353**

1360 A233 8r blue, brt. pink & black 30 20

Issued for Book Week.

Shah and King Faisal
A234

1965, Dec. 8 **Lithographed**

1361 A234 4r olive bister & brown 20 12

Visit of King Faisal of Saudi Arabia.

Scales and Olive Branch
A235

1965, Dec. 12

1362 A235 14r multicolored 50 25

Human Rights Day (Dec. 10).

Tractor, "Land Reform"
A236

Symbols of Reform Bills: 2r, Trees, nationalization of forests. 3r, Factory and gear wheel, sale of shares in government factories. 4r, Wheels, shareholding for factory workers. 5r, Parliament gate, women's suffrage. 6r, Children before blackboard, Army of Education. 7r, Caduceus, Army of Hygiene. 8r, Scales, creation of rural courts. 9r, Two girders, creation of Army of Progress.

1966, Jan. 26 ***Perf. 10½*** **Wmk. 353**

1363	A236	1r org. & brown	3	3
1364	"	2r dull grn. & grn.	6	5
1365	"	3r silver & gray	10	8
1366	"	4r lt. & dk. violet	12	10
1367	"	5r rose & brown	15	12
1368	"	6r olive & brown	18	15
1369	"	7r blue & vio. blue	22	20
1370	"	8r ultra. & dp.ultra.	25	20
1371	"	9r brn. orange & dark brown	28	25
		Nos. 1363-1371 (9)	1.39	1.18

Issued to commemorate parliamentary approval of the Shah's reform plan.

Mohammed Riza Pahlavi
A237

Ruins of Persepolis
A238

Photogravure

1966-71 ***Perf. 10½*** **Wmk. 353**

1372	A237	5d green	3	3
1373	"	10d chestnut	3	3
1374	"	25d dark blue	3	3
1375	"	50d Prussian green	3	3
1376	"	1r orange	5	3
1377	"	2r violet	8	3
1377A	"	4r claret brn. ('68)	12	6
1378	"	5r dark brown	18	6
1379	A238	6r deep blue	20	6
1380	"	8r yellow green	27	6
		a. 8r dull green ('71)	24	6
1381	A238	10r Prussian blue	35	6
1382	"	11r slate green	42	12
1383	"	14r purple	48	15
1384	"	20r brown	75	15
1385	"	50r copper red	1.75	60
1386	"	100r bright blue	4.75	1.25
1387	"	200r chestnut brn.	8.00	2.50
		Nos. 1372-1387 (17)	17.52	5.25

Set, except 4r, issued Feb. 22, 1966.

Student Nurse Taking Oath
A239

Narcissus
A240

1966, Feb. 24 **Lithographed**

1388 A239 5r bright pink & magenta 30 15

1389 " 5r lt. bl. & brt. bl. 30 15

Issued for Nurses' Day. Nos. 1388-1389 were printed in sheets of 50 arranged checkerwise.

1966, March 7

1390 A240 50d ultra., yellow & emerald 9 5

1391 " 1r lilac, yellow & emerald 9 8

Novrooz, Iranian New Year, Mar. 21.

Oil Derricks in Persian Gulf
A241

1966, March 20 ***Perf. 10½***

1392 A241 14r black, brt. blue & brt. rose lilac 50 40

Formation of six offshore oil companies.

Radio Tower
A242

Designs: 2r, Radar (horiz.). 6r, Emblem and waves. 8r, Compass rose and waves. 10r, Tower and waves.

1966, Apr. 27 **Litho.** **Wmk. 349**

1393	A242	2r dark green	10	6
1394	"	4r ultra. & dp. org.	15	12
1395	"	6r gray olive & plum	22	18
1396	A242	8r bright blue & dark blue	27	22
1397	"	10r brown & bister	35	30
		Nos. 1393-1397 (5)	1.09	88

Issued to commemorate the inauguration of the radio telecommunication system of the Central Treaty Organization of the Middle East (CENTO).

WHO Headquarters, Geneva
A243

1966, May 3 **Wmk. 353**

1398 A243 10r brt. blue, yel. & black 35 25

Issued to commemorate the inauguration of the opening of the World Health Organization Headquarters, Geneva.

World Map—A244

1966, May 14 **Lithographed**

1399 A244 6r blue & multi. 25 20

1400 " 8r multicolored 30 25

Issued to commemorate the 18th Conference of the International Council of Women, Tehran, May, 1966.

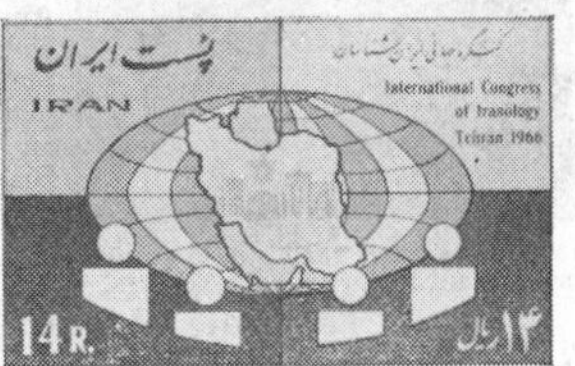

Globe, Map of Iran and Ruins of Persepolis—A245

1966, Sept. 5 ***Perf. 10½*** **Wmk. 353**

1401 A245 14r multicolored 55 30

International Iranology Congress, Tehran.

Emblem of Iranian Medical Society
A246

1966, Sept. 21

1402 A246 4r ultra., greenish blue & bister 18 10

15th Medical Congress, held at Ramsar.

Gate of Parliament, Mt. Demavend and Congress Emblem
A247

Design: 8r, Senate building, Mt. Demavend and emblem.

1966, Oct. 2 ***Perf. 10½*** **Wmk. 353**

1403 A247 6r brick red, ultra. & dark green 25 18

1404 " 8r lt. lilac, ultra. & dark green 30 25

Issued to commemorate the 55th Inter-parliamentary Union Conference, Tehran.

President Cemal Gürsel of Turkey
A248

1966, Oct. 2 **Lithographed**

1405 A248 6r vio. & dk. brn. 25 18

Visit of Pres. Cemal Gürsel of Turkey.

Mithras Type of 1964

1966, Oct. 8

Size: 30x40mm.

1406 A199 6r olive bister & brown 25 15

Mehragan celebration.

Farmers
A249

1966, Oct. 13

1407 A249 5r olive bister & brown 50 45

Establishment of rural courts of justice.

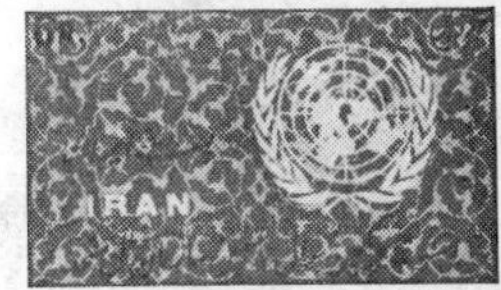

U.N. Emblem—A250

1966, Oct. 24 ***Perf. 10½*** **Wmk. 353**

1408 A250 6r brn. org. & black 25 18

21st anniversary of United Nations.

Crown Prince Riza
A251

Symbolic Woman's Face
A252

1966, Oct. 31 **Lithographed**

1409 A251 1r ultramarine 10 6

1410 " 2r violet 20 10

Issued for Children's Day on Crown Prince Riza's 6th birthday. Nos. 1409-1410 are printed se-tenant.

1966, Nov. 6

1411 A252 5r gold, black & ultra. 22 18

Issued to commemorate the founding of the Iranian Women's Organization.

Film Strip and Song Bird
A253

1966, Nov. 6

1412 A253 4r black, red lilac & violet 18 10

First Iranian children's film festival.

"Census Count" A254 Book Cover A255

1966, Nov. 11

1413 A254 6r dk. brn. & gray 25 18

National census.

1966, Nov. 15

1414 A255 8r tan, brown & ultra. 30 25

Issued to publicize Book Week.

Riza Shah Pahlavi
A256

Design: 2r, Riza Shah Pahlavi without kepi.

1966, Nov. 16 **Lithographed**

1415 A256 1r slate blue 30 6
1416 " 1r brown 30 6
1417 " 2r gray green 30 10
1418 " 2r violet blue 30 10

Issued to commemorate Riza Shah Pahlavi (1877–1944), founder of modern Iran. The two stamps of each denomination are printed se-tenant.

EROPA Emblem and Map of Persia
A257

1966, Dec. 4 ***Perf. 10½*** **Wmk. 353**

1419 A257 8r dark brown & emerald 30 25

Issued to publicize the 4th General Assembly of the Organization of Public Administrators, EROPA.

Shah Giving Land Reform Papers to Farmers
A258

1967, Jan. 9 ***Perf. 10½*** **Wmk. 353**

1420 A258 6r olive bister, yel. & brown 25 18

Issued to commemorate the 5th anniversary of the approval of the land reform laws.

Shah and 9-Star Crescent
A259

Design: 2r, Torch and 9-star crescent.

Lithographed

1967, Jan. 26 ***Perf. 10½*** **Wmk. 353**

1421 A259 2r multicolored 10 6
1422 " 6r " 30 18

Issued to commemorate the 5th anniversary of the Shah's reforms, the "White Revolution."

Ancient Sculpture of Bull
A260

Designs: 5r, Sculptured mythical animals. 8r, Pillar from Persepolis.

Perf. 10½

1967, Feb. 25 **Litho.** **Wmk. 353**

1423 A260 3r dk. brn. & ocher 15 6
1424 " 5r Prus. grn., brn. & ocher 18 12
1425 " 8r violet, black & silver 30 18

Issued to publicize Museum Week.

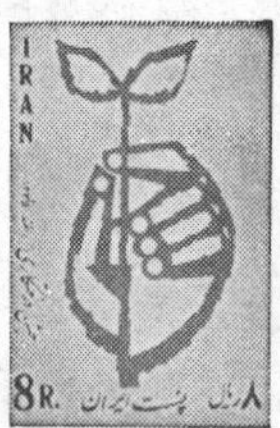

Planting Tree A261 Goldfish A262

1967, March 6

1426 A261 8r brn. org. & grn. 30 18

Issued to commemorate Tree Planting Day.

1967, March 11

Design: 8r, Swallows.

Size: 26x20mm.

1427 A262 1r lt. blue, brown & vermilion 6 3

Size: 35x27mm.

1428 A262 8r blue, vio. blue & red 40 18

Issued for Novrooz, Iranian New Year.

Microscope, Animals and Emblem
A263

1967, March 11 ***Perf. 10½***

1429 A263 5r black, gray & magenta 22 12

Second Iranian Veterinary Congress.

Pres. Arif of Iraq, Mosque—A264

1967, March 14 **Litho.** **Wmk. 353**

1430 A264 6r brt. bl. & green 25 18

Visit of President Abdul Salam Mohammed Arif of Iraq.

Fireworks
A265

1967, March 17

1431 A265 5r vio. bl. & multi. 22 15

Issued for United Nations Stamp Day.

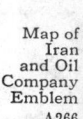

Map of Iran and Oil Company Emblem
A266

1967, March 20

1432 A266 6r multicolored 25 18

Nationalization of Iranian Oil Industry.

Fencers
A267

1967, March 23

1433 A267 5r violet & bister 22 15

International Youth Fencing Championships, Tehran.

Shah and King of Siam
A268

1967, Apr. 23 ***Perf. 10½*** **Wmk. 353**

1434 A268 6r brn. orange & dark brown 25 18

Visit of King Phumiphon Aduldet of Siam.

Old and Young Couples—A269

1967, Apr. 24 **Lithographed**

1435 A269 5r olive bister & violet blue 22 15

15th anniversary of Social Insurance.

Skier and Iranian Olympic Emblem
A270

Designs: 6r, Assyrian soldiers, Olympic rings and tablet inscribed "I.O.C." 8r, Wrestlers and Iranian Olympic emblem.

1967, May 5

1436 A270 3r brown & black 12 6
1437 " 6r multicolored 18 15
1438 " 8r ultra. & brown 30 25

Issued to commemorate the 65th International Olympic Congress, Tehran, May 2–11.

Lions International
A271

Design: 7r, Lions International emblem (vert.).

1967, May 11

Size: 41½x30½mm.

1439 A271 3r multicolored 15 6

Size: 36x42mm.

1440 A271 7r multicolored 30 15

50th anniversary of Lions International.

President Stoica of Romania
A272

1967, May 13

1441 A272 6r org. & dk. blue 25 12

Visit of Pres. Chivu Stoica of Romania.

International Tourist Year Emblem
A273

1967, June 6 ***Perf. 10½*** **Wmk. 353**

1442 A273 3r brick red & ultra. 15 7

International Tourist Year, 1967.

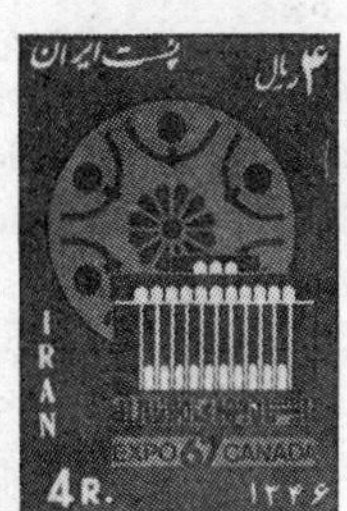

Iranian Pavilion and Ornament
A274

1967, June 7 Lithographed

1443 A274 4r dark brown, red & gold 18 10
1444 " 10r red, dark brown & gold 35 25

Issued to commemorate EXPO '67 International Exhibition, Montreal, Apr. 28–Oct. 27.

Stamp of 1870, No. 1
A275

1967, July 23 ***Perf. 10½*** **Wmk. 353**

1445 A275 6r ultra., lt. blue & rose claret 25 18
1446 " 8r dk. grn., lt. grn. & rose claret 30 22

Centenary of first Persian postage stamp.

World Map and School Children
A276

Globe and Oriental Musician
A277

1967, Sept. 8 Litho. Wmk. 353

1447 A276 3r ultra. & brt. bl. 12 7
1448 " 5r brown & yellow 22 15

World campaign against illiteracy.

1967, Sept. 10 ***Perf. 10½***

1449 A277 14r brown orange & dark brown 48 25

Issued to publicize the International Conference on Music Education in Oriental Countries, Sept. 1967.

Child's Hand Holding Adult's
A278

Winged Wild Goat
A279

Perf. 10½

1967, Sept. 14 Litho. Wmk. 353

1450 A278 8r dk. brn. & yel. 48 35

Issued to commemorate the introduction of Children's Villages in Iran. (Modelled after Austrian SOS Villages for homeless children).

1967, Sept. 19

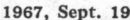

1451 A279 8r dk. brn. & lemon 35 25

Festival of Arts, Persepolis.

U.N. Emblem
A280

1967, Oct. 17

1452 A280 6r olive bister & violet blue 25 18

Issued for United Nations Day.

Shah and Empress Farah
A281

1967, Oct. 26 ***Perf. 10½*** **Wmk. 353**

Various Frames

1453 A281 2r silver, bl. & brn. 20 8
1454 " 10r silver, bl. & vio. 40 25
1455 " 14r lt. bl., bl., gold & violet 45 30

Issued to commemorate the coronation of Shah Mohammed Riza Pahlavi and Empress Farah, Oct. 26, 1967.

Nos. 1453–1455 also exist part perforate and ungummed. Price per pair, $8.

Crown Prince Riza
A282

Pres. Traikov of Bulgaria
A283

1967, Oct. 31 Lithographed

1456 A282 2r silver & violet 15 12
1457 " 8r silver & red brn. 35 25

Issued for Children's Day on Crown Prince Riza's 7th birthday.

1967, Nov. 20

1458 A283 10r lilac & dark brown 35 30

Visit of Pres. Georgi Traikov of Bulgaria.

Persian Boy Scout Emblem
A284

1967, Dec. 3 ***Perf. 10½*** **Wmk. 353**

1459 A284 8r olive & red brn. 30 25

Issued to publicize Cooperation Week of the Iranian Boy Scouts, Dec. 5–12.

Hands Holding Chain Link
A285

1967, Dec. 6 Lithographed

1460 A285 6r multicolored 25 15

Issued to publicize Cooperation Year.

Sheik Sabah of Kuwait
A286

1968, Jan. 10 ***Perf. 10½*** **Wmk. 353**

1461 A286 10r lt. blue & slate green 35 30

Visit of Sheik Sabah of Kuwait.

List of Shah's 12 Reform Laws
A287

1968, Jan. 27 Litho. Wmk. 353

1462 A287 2r slate grn., brn. & salmon 20 5
1463 " 8r violet, dk. grn. & lt. green 40 25
1464 " 14r brn., pink & light lilac 60 40

"White Revolution of King and People."

Almond Blossoms
A288

Haji Firooz (New Year Singer)
A289

Design: 2r, Tulips.

1968, Mar. 12 ***Perf. 10½*** **Wmk. 353**

1465 A288 1r multicolored 6 3
1466 " 2r bluish gray & multicolored 9 4
1467 " 2r brt. rose lilac & multicolored 9 4
1468 A289 6r multicolored 30 18

Issued for Novrooz, Iranian New Year.

Oil Worker and Derrick
A290

1968, Mar. 19 Lithographed

1469 A290 14r green, black & orange yellow 48 30

Issued to commemorate the 17th anniversary of the nationalization of the oil industry.

WHO Emblem
A291

1968, Apr. 7 ***Perf. 10½*** **Wmk. 353**

1470 A291 14r brn., bl. & org. 48 30

Issued to commemorate the 20th anniversary of the World Health Organization.

Marlik Chariot, Ancient Sculpture
A292

1968, Apr. 13

1471 A292 8r bl., brn. & buff 30 15

Fifth World Congress of Persian Archaeology and Art, Tehran.

Shah and King Hassan II
A293

1968, Apr. 16

1472 A293 6r brt. vio. & buff 25 15

Visit of King Hassan II of Morocco.

Human Rights Flame
A294

Soccer Player
A295

Design: 14r, Frameline inscription reads, "International Conference on Human Rights Tehran 1968"; "Iran" at left.

1968, May 5 ***Perf. 10½*** **Wmk. 353**

1473 A294 8r red & dk. green 35 22
1474 " 14r vio. blue & blue 48 40

Issued for International Human Rights Year. The 8r commemorates the Iranian Human Rights Committee; the 14r, the International Conference on Human Rights, Tehran, 1968.

1968, May 10 Lithographed

1475 A295 8r multicolored 35 22
1476 " 10r " 45 30

Asian Soccer Cup Finals, Tehran.

Tehran Oil Refinery
A296

1968, May 21 *Perf. 10½* **Wmk. 353**

1477 A296 14r brt. bl. & multi. 55 30

Opening of the Tehran Oil Refinery.

Queen Farah as Girl Guide
A297

1968, June 24 Litho. *Perf. 10½*

1478 A297 4r brt. rose lilac & blue green 30 10
1479 " 6r car. & brown 60 15

Great Camp of Iranian Girl Guides.

Anopheles Mosquito, Congress Emblem
A298

Winged Figure with Banner, and Globe
A299

1968, Sept. 7 *Perf. 10½* **Wmk. 353**

1480 A298 6r bright purple & black 27 15
1481 " 14r dark green & magenta 50 40

Issued to publicize the 8th International Congress on Tropical Medicine and Malaria, Tehran, Sept. 7–15.

1968, Sept. 8 Lithographed

1482 A299 6r light violet, bister & blue 27 15
1483 " 14r dull yellow, slate green & brown 50 40

World campaign against illiteracy.

Ornamental Horse and Flower
A300

1968, Sept. 11

1484 A300 14r slate green, org. & yel. green 55 40

2nd Festival of Arts, Shiraz—Persepolis.

INTERPOL Emblem and Globe
A301

1968, Oct. 6 *Perf. 10½* **Wmk. 353**

1485 A301 10r dk. brown & bl. 42 25

Issued to commemorate the 37th General Assembly of the International Police Organization (INTERPOL) in Tehran.

Police Emblem on Iran Map in Flag Colors
A302

1968, Oct. 7 Lithographed

1486 A302 14r multicolored 55 40

Issued for Police Day.

Peace Dove and U.N. Emblem
A303

1968, Oct. 24

1487 A303 14r blue & vio. bl. 55 40

Issued for United Nations Day.

Empress Farah—A304

Designs: 8r, Shah Mohammed Riza Pahlavi. 10fr, Shah, Empress and Crown Prince.

1968, Oct. 26

1488 A304 6r multicolored 1.50 60
1489 " 8r " 1.50 60
1490 " 10r " 1.50 60

Issued to commemorate the first anniversary of the coronation of Shah Riza Pahlavi and Empress Farah.

Shah's Crown and Bull's Head Capital
A305

1968, Oct. 30

1491 A305 14r ultra., gold, silver & red 55 40

Festival of Arts and Culture.

UNICEF Emblem and Child's Drawing
A306

Children's Drawings and UNICEF Emblem: 3r, Boat on lake, house and trees (horiz.). 5r, Flowers (horiz.).

1968, Oct. 31 Lithographed

1492 A306 2r dk. brown & multi. 9 4
1493 " 3r dk. grn. & multi. 15 6
1494 " 5r multicolored 20 15

Issued for Children's Day.

Labor Union Emblem
A307

Factory and Insurance Company Emblem
A308

Designs: 8r, Members of Army of Hygiene, and Insurance Company emblem. 10r, Map of Persia, Insurance Company emblem, car, train, ship and plane.

1968, Nov. 6 *Perf. 10½* **Wmk. 353**

1495 A307 4r silver & vio. blue 18 10
1496 A308 5r multicolored 20 12
1497 " 8r ultra., gray & yellow 30 22
1498 " 10r multicolored 35 30

Issued to publicize Insurance Day.

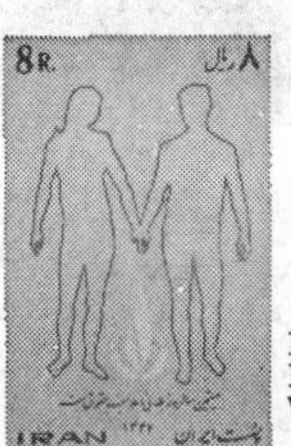

Human Rights Flame, Man and Woman
A309

1968, Dec. 10 Litho. *Perf. 10½*

1499 A309 8r lt. blue, violet blue & carmine 35 22

International Human Rights Year.

Symbols of Shah's Reform Plan
A310

Design: Each stamp shows symbols of 3 of the Shah's reforms. Nos. 1500–1503 are printed se-tenant in blocks of 4. The block shows the 12 symbols in a circle with a medallion in the center picturing 3 heads and a torch.

969, Jan. 26 *Perf. 10½* **Wmk. 353**

1500 A310 2r ocher, green & lilac 30 7
1501 " 4r lilac, ocher & green 30 15
1502 " 6r lilac, ocher & green 40 20
1503 " 8r lilac, ocher & green 60 30

Declaration of the Shah's Reform Plan.

Shah Mohammed Riza Pahlavi and Crowd—A311

1969, Feb. 1 Lithographed

1504 A311 6r red, blue & brn. 30 15

Issued to commemorate the 10,000th day of the reign of Shah Mohammed Riza Pahlavi.

European Goldfinch
A312

Designs: 2r, Ring-necked pheasant. 8r, Roses.

1969, Mar. 6 *Perf. 10½* **Wmk. 353**

1505 A312 1r multicolored 6 3
1506 " 2r " 15 5
1507 " 8r " 30 22

Issued for Novrooz, Iranian New Year.

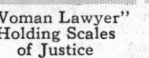

"Woman Lawyer" Holding Scales of Justice
A313

Workers, ILO and U.N. Emblems
A314

1969, Apr. 8 Litho. *Perf. 10½*

1508 A313 6r black & brt. blue 25 12

Issued to publicize the 15th General Assembly of Women Lawyers, Tehran, Apr. 8–14.

1969, Apr. 30 *Perf. 10½* **Wmk. 353**

1509 A314 10r blue & vio. blue 42 25

Issued to commemorate the 50th anniversary of the International Labor Organization.

Freestyle Wrestlers and Ariamehr Cup—A315

1969, May 6 **Lithographed**

1510 A315 10r lilac & multi. 35 25

Issued to commemorate the third round of the International Freestyle Wrestling Championships.

Birds and Flower
A316

1969, June 10 *Perf. 10½* **Wmk. 353**

1511 A316 10r vio. bl. & multi. 35 25

Issued to publicize Handicrafts Day.

Boy Scout Symbols
A317

1969, July 9 *Perf. 10½* **Wmk. 353**

1512 A317 6r lt. blue & multi. 35 15

Issued to publicize Philia 1969, an outdoor training course for Boy Scout patrol leaders.

Lady Serving Wine, Safavi Miniature, Iran
A318

Designs: No. 1514, Lady on Balcony, Mogul miniature, Pakistan. No. 1515, Sultan Suleiman Receiving Sheik Abdul Latif, 16th century miniature, Turkey.

1969, July 21 **Lithographed**

1513 A318 25r multicolored 90 65
1514 " 25r " 90 65
1515 " 25r " 90 65

Issued to commemorate the 5th anniversary of the signing of the Regional Cooperation for Development Pact by Turkey, Iran and Pakistan.

Neil A. Armstrong and Col. Edwin E. Aldrin on Moon—A319

1969, July 26

1516 A319 24r bister, blue & brown 1.35 1.35

See note after Algeria No. 427.

Quotation from Shah's Declaration on Education and Art
A320

1969, Aug. 6 *Perf. 10½* **Wmk. 353**

1517 A320 10r car., cream & emerald 35 25

Issued to commemorate the anniversary of educational and art reforms.

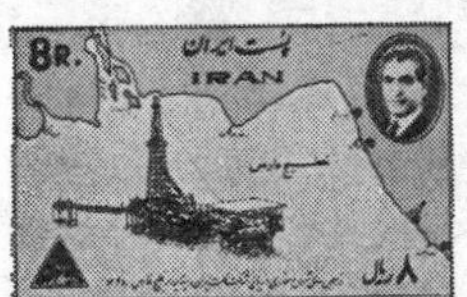

Offshore Oil Rig in Persian Gulf
A321

1969, Sept. 1 **Lithographed**

1518 A321 8r multicolored 30 22

Issued to commemorate the 10th anniversary of marine drillings by the Iran-Italia Oil Co.

Dancers Forming Flower
A322

Crossed-out Fingerprint, Moon and Rocket
A323

1969, Sept. 6 *Perf. 10½* **Wmk. 353**

1519 A322 6r multicolored 30 15
1520 " 8r " 35 22

3rd Festival of Arts, Shiraz and Persepolis, Aug. 30–Sept. 9.

1969, Sept. 8 **Lithographed**

1521 A323 4r multicolored 25 10

World campaign against illiteracy.

Persepolis, Simulated Stamp with UPU Emblem, and Shah—A324

1969, Sept. 28

1522 A324 10r lt. blue & multi. 60 25
1523 " 14r multicolored 60 40

Issued to publicize the 16th Congress of the Universal Postal Union, Tokyo.

Fair Emblem
A325

Justice
A326

Designs: 14r, like 8r, inscribed "ASIA 69." 20r, Fair emblem, world map and "ASIA 69" (horiz.).

1969, Oct. 5 *Perf. 10½* **Wmk. 353**

1524 A325 8r rose & multi. 35 22
1525 " 14r blue & multi. 48 35
1526 " 20r tan & multi. 65 50

2nd Asian Trade Fair, Tehran.

1969, Oct. 13 **Lithographed**

1527 A326 8r blue green & dark brown 30 22

Rural Courts of Justice Day.

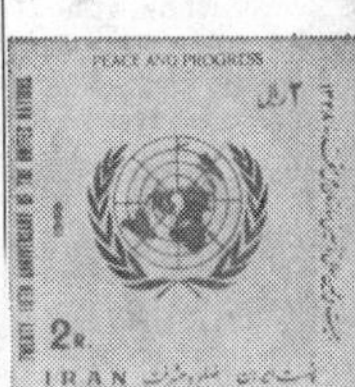

U.N. Emblem
A327

Emblem and Column Capital, Persepolis
A328

1969, Oct. 24

1528 A327 2r lt. bl. & dp. blue 12 6

25th anniversary of the United Nations.

1969, Oct. 28

1529 A328 2r dp. blue & multi. 12 6

2nd Festival of Arts and Culture. See also No. 1577, 1681, 1735.

Child's Drawing and UNICEF Emblem
A329

Children's Drawings and UNICEF Emblem: 1r, Boy and birds (vert.). 5r, Dinner.

1969, Oct. 31 *Perf. 10½* **Wmk. 353**

Size: 28x40mm., 40x28mm.

1530 A329 1r lt. blue & multi. 10 6
1531 " 2r lt. green & multi. 12 6
1532 " 5r lt. lilac & multi. 25 14

Children's Week. See Nos. 1578–1580.

Globe Emblem
A330

1969, Nov. 6

1533 A330 8r dk. brn. & blue 30 22

Issued to publicize the meeting of the National Society of Parents and Educators, Tehran.

Satellite Communications Station
A331

1969, Nov. 19 **Lithographed**

1534 A331 6r blk. brn. & bister 24 15

Issued to publicize the first Iranian Satellite Communications Earth Station, Hamadan.

Mahatma Gandhi
A332

1969, Dec. 29 *Perf. 10½* **Wmk. 353**

1535 A332 14r gray & dark rose brown 70 30

Issued to commemorate the centenary of the birth of Mohandas K. Gandhi (1869–1948), leader in India's fight for independence.

Globe, Flags and Emblems
A333

Design: 6r, Globe and Red Cross, Red Lion and Sun, and Red Crescent Emblems.

1969, Dec. 31

1536 A333 2r red & multi. 18 6
1537 " 6r " " 28 16

50th anniversary of the League of Red Cross Societies.

Symbols of Reform Laws and Shah
A334

1970, Jan. 26 **Litho.** **Wmk. 353**

1538 A334 1r bister & multi. 20 6
1539 " 2r multicolored 20 6

Declaration of the Shah's Reform Plan.

Pansies
A335

New Year's Table
A336

1970, Mar. 6 *Perf. 10½* Wmk. 353

1540 A335 1r multicolored 8 3
1541 A336 8r " 55 25

Issued for the Iranian New Year.

Chemical Plant, Kharg Island, and Iranian Oil Company Emblem
A337

Designs (Iranian Oil Company Emblem and): 2r, Shah's portrait and quotation. 4r, Laying of gas pipe line and tractor. 8r, Tankers at pier of Kharg Island (vert.). 10r, Tehran refinery.

1970, Mar. 20 *Perf. 10½* Wmk. 353

1542 A337 2r gray & multi. 40 6
1543 " 4r multicolored 50 10
1544 " 6r lt. blue & multi. 50 15
1545 " 8r multicolored 70 22
1546 " 10r " 90 28
Nos. 1542-1546 (5) 3.00 81

Issued to commemorate the 20th anniversary of the nationalization of the oil industry in Iran.

EXPO '70 Emblem
A338

Radar, Satellite and Congress Emblem—A339

1970, Mar. 27 Lithographed

1547 A338 4r bright rose lilac & violet blue 30 10
1548 " 10r lt. blue & purple 55 28

Issued to publicize EXPO '70 International Exposition, Osaka, Japan, Mar. 15-Sept. 13.

1970, Apr. 20 *Perf. 10½* Wmk. 353

1549 A339 14r multicolored 1.00 35

Issued to publicize the Asia-Australia Telecommunications Congress, Tehran.

U.P.U. Headquarters, Bern
A340

1970, May 10

1550 A340 2r gray, brown & lilac rose 22 6
1551 A340 4r lilac, brown & lilac rose 30 10

Issued to commemorate the inauguration of the new Universal Postal Union Headquarters, Bern.

Productivity Year Emblem
A341

1970, May 19 *Perf. 10½* Wmk. 353

1552 A341 8r gray & multi. 50 22

Asian Productivity Year, 1970.

Bird Bringing Baby
A342

1970, June 15 Lithographed

1553 A342 8r brn. & dk. blue 70 30

Issued to commemorate the 50th anniversary of Iranian School for Midwives.

Tomb of Cyrus the Great, Meshed-Morghab in Fars—A343

Designs: 8r, Pillars of Apadana Palace, Persepolis (vert.). 10r, Bas-relief from a Mede tomb, Iraq. 14r, Achaemenian officers, bas-relief, Persepolis.

1970, June 21 Photo. *Perf. 13*

1554 A343 6r gray, red & vio. 60 25
1555 " 8r pale rose, blk. & blue green 60 35
1556 " 10r yel., red & brn. 90 45
1557 " 14r blue, black & red brown 1.00 55

2500th anniversary of the founding of the Persian Empire by Cyrus the Great.
See also Nos. 1561-1571, 1589-1596, 1605-1612.

Seeyo-Se-Pol Bridge, Isfahan—A344

Designs: No. 1559, Saiful Malook Lake, Pakistan (vert.). No. 1560, View of Fethiye, Turkey (vert.).

Perf. 10½

1970, July 21 Litho. Wmk. 353

1558 A344 2r multicolored 30 20
1559 A344 2r multicolored 30 20
1560 " 2r " 40 20

Issued to commemorate the 6th anniversary of the signing of the Regional Cooperation for Development Pact by Iran, Turkey and Pakistan.

Queen Buran, Dirhem Coin
A345

Wine Goblet with Lion's Head
A346

Designs: No. 1562, Achaemenian eagle amulet. No. 1563, Mithridates I, dirhem coin. No. 1564, Sassanidae art (arch, coin, jugs). No. 1566, Shapur I, dirhem coin. No. 1567, Achaemenian courier. No. 1568, Winged deer. No. 1569, Ardashir I, dirhem coin. No. 1570, Seal of Darius I (chariot, palms, lion). 14r, Achaemenian tapestry.

Photogravure

1970 *Perf. 13* Wmk. 353

1561 A345 1r gold & multi. 65 15
1562 A346 2r " " 65 20
1563 A345 2r " " 65 20
1564 A346 2r lilac & multi. 50 20
1565 " 6r " " 65 30
1566 A345 6r " " 95 30
1567 " 6r " " 95 30
1568 A346 8r " " 95 60
1569 A345 8r " " 95 60
1570 " 8r " " 95 60
1571 " 14r lt. blue & multi. 1.10 1.25
Nos. 1561-1571 (11) 8.95 4.70

2500th anniversary of the founding of the Persian Empire by Cyrus the Great.
Issue dates: 1r, Nos. 1563, 1566, 1569, Aug. 22; Nos. 1562, 1565, 1568, 14r, Aug. 6; others, Sept. 22.

Candle and Globe
A347

Persian Decoration
A348

1970, Sept. 8 Litho. *Perf. 10½*

1572 A347 1r lt. blue & multi. 12 5
1573 " 2r pale sal. & multi. 20 6

Issued to publicize World Literacy Day.

1970, Sept. 14

1574 A348 6r multicolored 30 15

Issued to publicize the Isfahan International Congress of Architects, Sept. 1970.

Emblem
A349

U.N. Emblem, Dove and Scales—A350

1970, Sept. 28 *Perf. 10½*

1575 A349 2r lt. bl. & purple 15 6

Issued to publicize the Congress of Election Committees of Persian States and Tehran.

1970, Oct. 24 Litho. Wmk. 353

1576 A350 2r lt. bl., magenta & dark blue 15 6

Issued for United Nations Day.

Festival Type of 1969

1970, Oct. 28 *Perf. 10½*

1577 A328 2r orange & multi. 18 5

3rd Festival of Arts and Culture.

UNICEF Type of 1969

Children's Drawings and UNICEF Emblem: 50d, Herdsman and goats. 1r, Family picnic. 2r, Mosque.

1970, Oct. 31 Size: 43½x31mm.

1578 A329 50d black & multi. 9 3
1579 " 1r " " 12 5
1580 " 2r " " 25 6

Issued for Children's Week.

Shah Mohammed Riza Pahlavi
A351

1971, Jan. 26 *Perf. 10½* Wmk. 353

1581 A351 2r lt. blue & multi. 25 10

Publicizing the "White Revolution of King and People" and the 12 reform laws.

Sheldrake—A352

Designs: 2r, Ruddy shelduck. 8r, Flamingo (vert.).

1971, Jan. 30 Lithographed

1582 A352 1r multicolored 17 5
1583 " 2r " 25 6
1584 " 8r " 60 22

International Wetland and Waterfowl Conference, Ramsar.

Riza Shah Pahlavi
A353

1971, Feb. 22 *Perf. 10½* Wmk. 353

1585	A353	6r multicolored	60	15

50th anniversary of the Pahlavi dynasty's accession to power.

Rooster
A354

Designs: 2r, Barn swallow and nest. 6r, Hoopoe.

1971, Mar. 6 Photo. *Perf. 13½x13*

1586	A354	1r multicolored	22	5
1587	"	2r "	40	6
1588	"	6r "	60	16

Novrooz, Iranian New Year.

Shapur II Hunting—A355

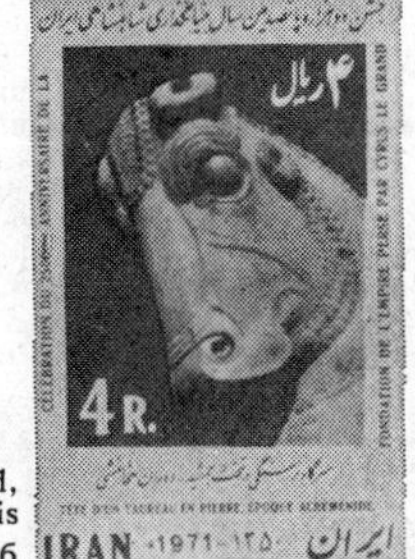

Bull's Head, Persepolis
A356

Designs: 1r, Harpist, mosaic. No. 1591, Investiture of Ardashir I, bas-relief. 5r Winged lion ornament. 6r, Persian archer, bas-relief. 8r, Royal audience, bas-relief. 10r, Bronze head of Parthian prince.

1971 Lithographed *Perf. 10½*

1589	A356	1r multicolored	60	18
1590	A355	2r black & brn. org.	75	18
1591	"	2r lilac, golden brn. & black	75	18
1592	A356	4r purple & multi.	60	18
1593	"	5r multicolored	75	38
1594	"	6r multicolored	75	45
1595	"	8r lt. blue & multi.	1.00	65
1596	"	10r dp. bister, black & slate	1.00	85
		Nos. 1589-1596 (8)	6.20	3.05

2500th anniversary of the founding of the Persian Empire by Cyrus the Great.

Issue dates: 4r, 5r, 6r, 8r, May 15; others, June 15.

Prisoners Leaving Jail
A357

1971, May 20 Litho. Wmk. 353

1597	A357	6r multicolored	50	15
1598	"	8r "	70	22

Rehabilitation of Prisoners Week.

Religious School, Chaharbagh, Ispahan
A358

Designs: No. 1600, Mosque of Selim, Edirne, Turkey. No. 1601, Badshahi Mosque, Lahore, Pakistan (horiz.).

Perf. 10½

1971, July 21 Litho. Wmk. 353

1599	A358	2r multicolored	20	6
1600	"	2r "	20	6
1601	"	2r "	20	6

7th anniversary of Regional Cooperation among Iran, Pakistan and Turkey.

"Fifth Festival of Arts"
A359

1971, Aug. 26 Litho. and Typo.

1602	A359	2r lt. & dk. green, red & gold	18	6

5th Festival of Arts, Shiraz-Persepolis.

"Fight Against Illiteracy"
A360

1971, Sept. 8 Lithographed

1603	A360	2r green & multi.	18	6

International Literacy Day, Sept. 8.

Kings Abdullah and Hussein II of Jordan
A361

1971, Sept. 11

1604	A361	2r yellow green, black & red	20	5

50th anniversary of the Hashemite Kingdom of Jordan.

Shahyad Aryamehr Monument
A362

Designs: 1r, Aryamehr steel mill, near Isfahan. 3r, Senate Building, Tehran. 11r, Shah Abbas Kabir Dam, Zayandeh River.

1971, Sept. 22

1605	A362	1r blue & multi.	40	25
1606	"	2r multicolored	65	25
1607	"	3r brt. pink & multi.	65	38
1608	"	11r orange & multi.	1.25	65

2500th anniversary of the founding of the Persian empire by Cyrus the Great.

Shah Mohammed Riza Pahlavi
A363

Designs: 2r, Riza Shah Pahlavi. 5r, Stone tablet with proclamation of Cyrus the Great (horiz.). 10r, Crown of present empire (erroneously inscribed *Le Couronne*).

1971, Oct. 12

1609	A363	1r gold & multi.	65	15
1610	"	2r " "	55	22
1611	"	5r " "	65	38
1612	"	10r " "	1.20	75

2500th anniversary of the founding of the Persian empire by Cyrus the Great.

Ghatour Railroad Bridge—A364

1971, Oct. 7

1613	A364	2r multicolored	30	6

Iran-Turkey railroad.

Racial Equality Emblem
A365

Mohammed Riza Pahlavi
A366

1971, Oct. 24

1614	A365	2r lt. blue & multi.	18	6

International Year Against Racial Discrimination.

Perf. 13½x13

1971, Oct. 26 Photo. Wmk. 353

Size: 20½x28mm.

1615	A366	5d lilac	3	3
1616	"	10d henna brown	3	3
1617	"	50d brt. blue green	6	3
1618	"	1r dp. yellow green	10	3
1619	"	2r brown	10	3

Size: 27x36½mm.

1620	A366	6r slate green	20	3
1621	"	8r violet blue	40	3
1622	"	10r red lilac	50	3
1623	"	11r blue green	80	20
1624	"	14r bright blue	80	7
1625	"	20r carmine rose	1.00	8
1626	"	50r yellow bister	2.00	25
		Nos. 1615-1626 (12)	6.02	84

See also Nos. 1650-1661B, 1768-1772.

Child's Drawing and Emblem
A367

Designs: No. 1631, Ruins of Persepolis (vert.). No. 1632, Warrior, mosaic (vert.).

1971, Oct. 31 Litho. *Perf. 10½*

1630	A367	2r multicolored	20	6
1631	"	2r "	20	6
1632	"	2r "	20	6

Children's Week.

UNESCO Emblem and "25"
A368

1971, Nov. 4

1633	A368	6r ultramarine & rose claret	30	12

25th anniversary of United Nations Educational, Scientific and Cultural Organization (UNESCO).

Domestic Animals and Emblem
A369

1971, Nov. 22

1634	A369	2r gray, blk. & car.	18	6

4th Iranian Veterinarians' Congress.

ILO Emblem, Cog Wheels and Globe
A370

1971, Dec. 4

1635	A370	2r blk., org. & blue	18	6

7th International Labor Organization Conference for the Asian Region.

UNICEF Emblem, Bird Feeding Young
A371

1971, Dec. 16 ***Perf. 13x13½***

1636 A371 2r lt. bl., magenta & black 20 8

25th anniversary of United Nations International Children's Fund (UNICEF).

Mohammed Riza Pahlavi
A372

Perf. 10½

1972, Jan. 26 **Wmk. 353**

1637 A372 2r lt. grn. & multi. 20 6
a. 20r Souvenir sheet 2.00 2.00

"White Revolution of King and People" and the 12 reform laws. No. 1637a contains one stamp with simulated perforations. Gold and black typographed margin has medallions showing 12 reform laws. Size: 81x94mm.

Pin-tailed Sand-grouse
A373

Designs: No. 1639, Rock ptarmigan. 2r, Yellow-billed waxbill and red-cheeked cordon-bleu.

1972, Mar. 5 Litho. ***Perf. 13x13½***

1638 A373 1r lt. grn. & multi. 10 4
1639 " 1r lt. blue & multi. 10 4
1640 " 2r yellow & multi. 30 8

Iranian New Year.

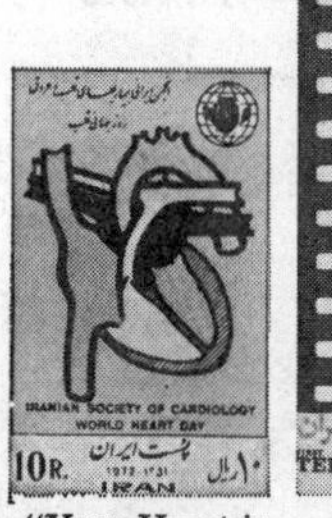

"Your Heart is your Health"
A374

Film Strip and Winged Antelope
A375

1972, Apr. 4 ***Perf. 10½***

1641 A374 10r lemon & multi. 1.00 25

World Health Day and for the Iranian Society of Cardiology.

1972, Apr. 16 **Litho. & Engr.**

Design: 8r, Film strips and winged antelope.

1642 A375 6r ultra. & gold 60 25
1643 " 8r yellow & multi. 85 25

Tehran International Film Festival.

Rose and Bud
A376

Designs: 2r, Yellow roses. 5r, Red rose.

1972, May 5 **Lithographed**

1644 A376 1r lt. blue & multi. 17 5
1645 " 2r multicolored 25 10
1646 " 5r blue & multi. 60 20

See also Nos. 1711–1713.

Persian Woman, by Behzad
A377

Paintings: No. 1648, Fisherman, by Cevat Dereli (Turkey). No. 1649, Young Man, by Abdur Rehman Chughtai (Pakistan).

1972, July 21 **Wmk. 353**

1647 A377 5r gray & multi. 85 20
1648 " 5r " " 85 20
1649 " 5r " " 85 20

Regional Cooperation for Development Pact among Iran, Turkey and Pakistan, 8th anniversary.

Shah Type of 1971

1972–73 **Photo.** ***Perf. 13½x13***

Bister Frame & Crown

Size: 20½x28mm.

1650 A366 5d lilac 3 3
1651 " 10d henna brown 3 3
1652 " 50d brt. blue green 6 3
1653 " 1r dp. yellow green 10 3
a. Brown frame & crown ('73) 10 3
1654 A366 2r brown 10 3

Size: 27x36½mm.

1655 A366 6r slate green 30 3
1656 " 8r violet blue 50 3
1657 " 10r red lilac 60 3
1658 " 11r blue green 80 20
1659 " 14r dull blue 80 5
1660 " 20r carmine rose 1.25 10
1661 " 50r greenish blue 2.50 25
1661A " 100r violet ('73) 2.50 50
1661B " 200r slate ('73) 5.00 90
Nos. 1650–1661B (14) 14.57 2.24

Festival Emblem
A378

1972, Aug. 31 **Litho.** ***Perf. 10½***

1662 A378 6r emerald, red & black 40 15
1663 " 8r brt. magenta, black & green 85 20

6th Festival of Arts, Shiraz-Persepolis, Aug. 31–Sept. 8.

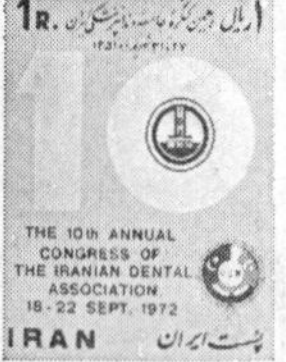

Pens and Emblem
A379

"10" and Emblems
A380

1972, Sept. 8

1664 A379 1r lt. blue & multi. 10 3
1665 " 2r yellow & multi. 20 6

World Literacy Day, Sept. 8.

1972, Sept. 18

1666 A380 1r lilac & multi. 10 3
1667 " 2r dull yel. & multi. 20 6

10th Congress of Iranian Dentists' Association, Sept. 18–22.

Asian Broadcasting Union Emblem
A381

Persia No. 450 on Cover
A382

1972, Oct. 1

1668 A381 6r lt. grn. & multi. 40 15
1669 " 8r gray & multi. 85 20

9th General Assembly of Asian Broadcasting Union, Tehran, Oct. 1972.

1972, Oct. 9

1670 A382 10r lt. bl. & multi. 1.00 30

International Stamp Day.

Chess and Olympic Rings—A383

Designs (Olympic Rings and): 2r, Hunter. 3r, Archer. 5r, Equestrians. 6r, Polo. 8r, Wrestling.

1972, Oct. 17

1671 A383 1r brown & multi. 20 5
1672 " 2r blue & multi. 12 6
1673 " 3r lilac & multi. 30 9
1674 " 5r bl. grn. & multi. 40 15
1675 " 6r red & multi. 50 18
1676 " 8r yel. grn. & multi. 50 22
a. Souv. sheet of 6 2.00 1.50
Nos. 1671–1676 (6) 2.02 75

20th Olympic Games, Munich, Aug. 26–Sept. 11. No. 1676a contains 6 imperf. stamps similar to Nos. 1671–1676. Gold border and multicolored marginal emblems. Size: 176x105mm.

Communications Symbol, U.N. Emblem
A384

Children and Flowers
A385

1972, Oct. 24

1677 A384 10r multicolored 90 20

United Nations Day.

1972, Oct. 31 **Litho.** **Wmk. 353**

Children's Drawings and Emblem: No. 1679, Puppet show. 6r, Boys cutting wood (horiz.).

1678 A385 2r gray & multi. 20 6
1679 " 2r bister & multi. 20 6
1680 " 6r pink & multi. 60 20

Children's Week.

Festival Type of 1969

Design: 10r, Crown, emblems and column capital, Persepolis.

1972, Nov. 11

1681 A328 10r dp. bl. & multi. 1.00 20

10th anniversary of White Revolution and Festival of Culture and Art.

Family Planning Emblem
A386

1972, Dec. 5

1682 A386 1r blue & multi. 10 3
1683 " 2r brt. pink & multi. 20 6

To promote family planning.

Scout Emblem
A387

1972, Dec. 9

1684 A387 2r multicolored 20 8

Iranian Scout Organization, 20th anniversary.

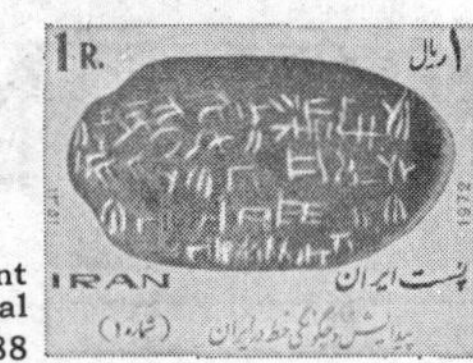

Ancient Seal
A388

Designs: Various ancient seals.

1973, Jan. 5 ***Perf. 10½***

1685 A388 1r bl., red & brn. 25 7
1686 " 1r yellow & multi. 25 7
1687 " 1r pink & multi. 25 7
1688 " 2r light brick red & multicolored 25 10
1689 " 2r dull orange & multicolored 25 10
1690 " 2r olive & multi. 25 10
Nos. 1685–1690 (6) 1.50 51

Development of writing.

Books and Book Year Emblem
A389

"12 Improvements by the King"
A390

Design: 6r, Illuminated page, 10th century, from Shahnameh, by Firdousi.

1973, Jan. 10

1691 A389 2r black & multi. 20 6
1692 " 6r yellow & multi. 40 12

International Book Year 1972.

1973, Jan. 26 **Lithographed**

Designs: 2r, 10r, 12 circles symbolizing 12 improvements. 6r, like 1r.

Size: 29x43mm.

1693 A390 1r gold, ultramarine, red & yellow 8 3
1694 " 2r silver, plum, olive & yellow 12 6

Size: 65x84mm.

1695 A390 6r gold, ultramarine, red & yellow 60 60

Souvenir Sheet

Imperf.

1696 A390 10r silver, plum, olive & yellow 60 60

10th anniversary of the introduction of the King's socioeconomic reforms. No. 1696 contains one stamp; silver and black marginal inscription. Size: 71x90½mm.

Blue Surgeon-fish
A391

Fish: No. 1698, Gilthead. No. 1699, Banded sergeant major. No. 1700, Pork-fish. No. 1701, Black-spot snapper.

1973, Mar. 6 ***Perf. 10½*** **Wmk. 353**

1697 A391 1r multicolored 12 5
1698 " 1r " 12 5
1699 " 2r " 25 10
1700 " 2r " 25 10
1701 " 2r " 25 10
Nos. 1697-1701 (5) 99 40

Iranian New Year.

WHO Emblem
A392

1973, Apr. 7 **Litho.** **Wmk. 353**

1702 A392 10r brn., grn. & red 90 20

25th anniversary of the World Health Organization.

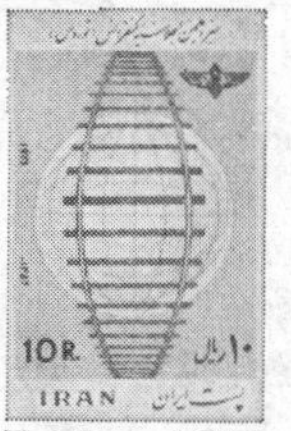

Soccer
A393

Tracks and Globe
A394

1973, Apr. 13

1703 A393 14r org. & multi. 90 28

15th Asian Youth Football (soccer) Tournament.

1973, May 10 ***Perf. 10½*** **Wmk. 353**

1704 A394 10r dk. grn., lilac & vio. blue 90 20

13th International Railroad Conference.

Clay Tablet with Aryan Script
A395

Designs: Clay tablets with various scripts.

1973, June 5 ***Perf. 10½***

Multicolored

1705 A395 1r *shown* 25 7
1706 " 1r *Kharoshthi* 25 7
1707 " 1r *Achaemenian* 25 7
1708 " 2r *Parthian(Mianeh)* 38 10
1709 " 2r *Parthian (Arsacide)* 38 10
1710 " 2r *Gachtak (Dabireh)* 50 10
Nos. 1705-1710 (6) 2.01 51

Development of writing.

Flower Type of 1972

Flowers: 1r, Orchid. 2r, Hyacinth. 6r, Columbine.

1973, June 20

1711 A376 1r green & multi. 20 4
1712 " 2r magenta & multi. 20 6
1713 " 6r dull bl. & multi. 40 15

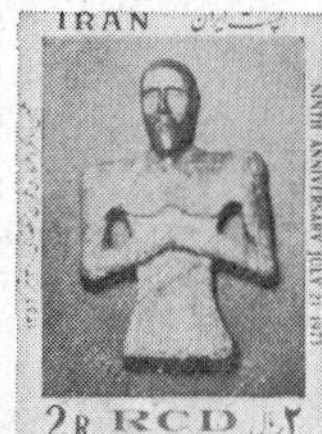

Statue, Shahdad Kerman, Persia, 4000 B.C.
A396

Designs: No. 1714, Head from mausoleum of King Antiochus I (69-34 B.C.), Turkey. No. 1716, Street, Mohenjo-Daro, Pakistan.

1973, July 21

1714 A396 2r brown & multi. 20 6
1715 " 2r green & multi. 20 6
1716 " 2r blue & multi. 20 6

Regional Cooperation for Development Pact among Iran, Turkey and Pakistan, 9th anniversary. Nos. 1714-1716 printed se-tenant.

Shah, Oil Pump, Refinery and Tanker
A397

1973, Aug. 4

1717 A397 5r blue & black 30 10

Nationalization of oil industry.

Soldiers and Rising Sun
A398

Gymnasts and Globe
A399

Perf. 10½

1973, Aug. 19 **Litho.** **Wmk. 353**

1718 A398 2r ultra. & multi. 15 6

20th anniversary of return of monarchy.

1973, Aug. 23

1719 A399 2r olive & multi. 12 6
1720 A399 2r vio. blue & multi. 12 6

7th International Congress of Physical Education and Sports for Girls and Women, Tehran, Aug. 19-25.

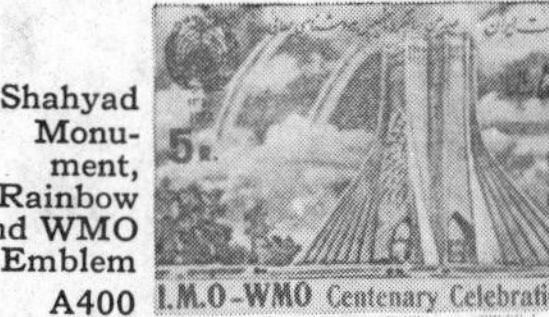

Shahyad Monument, Rainbow and WMO Emblem
A400

1973, Sept. 4

1721 A400 5r multicolored 40 10

Centenary of international meteorological cooperation.

Festival Emblem
A401

1973, Aug. 31

1722 A401 1r silver & multi. 20 4
1723 " 5r gold & multi. 30 12

7th Festival of Arts, Shiraz-Persepolis.

Wrestlers
A402

"Literacy as Light"
A403

1973, Sept. 6 **Litho.** **Wmk. 353**

1724 A402 6r lt. grn. & multi. 30 15

World Wrestling Championships, Tehran, Sept. 6-14.

1973, Sept. 8

1725 A403 2r multicolored 12 6

World Literacy Day, Sept. 8.

Audio-Visual Equipment
A404

1973, Sept. 11

1726 A404 10r yellow & multi. 70 20

Tehran International Audio-Visual Exhibition, Sept. 11-24.

Warrior Taming Winged Bull
A405

1973, Sept. 16

1727 A405 8r bl. gray & multi. 40 15

International Council of Military Sports, 25th anniversary.

abu-al-Rayhan al-Biruni
A406

1973, Sept. 16

1728 A406 10r brown & black 75 35

Millennium of the birth of abu-al-Rayhan al-Biruni (973-1048), philosopher and mathematician.

Soccer Cup
A407

INTERPOL Emblem
A408

Perf. 10½

1973, Oct. 2 **Litho.** **Wmk. 353**

1729 A407 2r lilac, blk. & buff 12 6

Soccer Games for the Crown Prince's Cup.

1973, Oct. 7

1730 A408 2r multicolored 12 6

50th anniversary of International Criminal Police Organization.

Symbolic Arches and Globe
A409

1973, Oct. 8

1731 A409 10r orange & multi. 60 20

25th anniversary of World Federation for Mental Health.

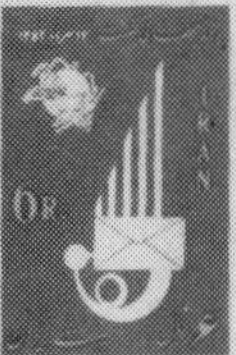

UPU Emblem, Letter and Post Horn
A410

Honeycomb
A411

1973, Oct. 9

1732 A410 6r blue & orange 30 12

World Post Day, Oct. 9.

1973, Oct. 24

1733	A411	2r lt. brn. & multi.	12	6
1734	"	2r gray olive & multicolored	12	6

5th anniversary of the United Nations Volunteer Program.

Festival Type of 1969

Design: 2r, Crown and column capital, Persepolis.

1973, Oct. 26

1735	A328	2r yellow & multi.	12	6

Festival of Culture and Art.

Turkish Bosporus Bridge, Flag
A412

Design: 8r, Kemal Ataturk and Riza Shah Pahlavi.

1973, Oct. 29 Litho. *Perf. 10½*

1736	A412	2r multicolored	20	6
1737	"	8r "	40	15

50th anniversary of the Turkish Republic.

Mother and Child, Emblem
A413

Children's Drawings and Emblem: No. 1739, Wagon (horiz.). No. 1740, House and garden with birds.

1973, Oct. 31

1738	A413	2r multicolored	15	6
1739	"	2r "	15	6
1740	"	2r "	15	6

Children's Week.

Cow, Wheat and FAO Emblem
A414

1973, Nov. 4

1741	A414	10r multicolored	75	20

10th anniversary of World Food Program.

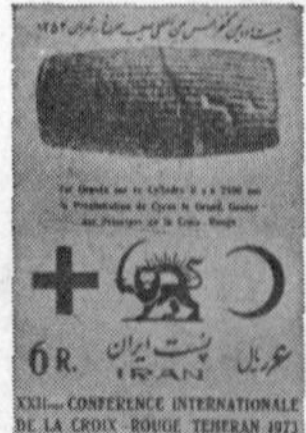

Proclamation of Cyrus the Great; Red Cross, Lion and Crescent Emblems
A415

1973, Nov. 8

1742	A415	6r lt. bl. & multi.	50	15

22nd International Red Cross Conference, Tehran 1972.

"Film Festival"
A416

Globe and Travelers
A417

Perf. 10½

1973, Nov. 26 Litho. Wmk. 353

1743	A416	2r black & multi.	12	6

2nd International Tehran Film Festival.

1973, Nov. 26

1744	A417	10r orange & multi.	50	20

12th annual Congress of International Association of Tour Managers.

Human Rights Flame
A418

Score and Emblem
A419

1973, Dec. 10

1745	A418	8r lt. blue & multi.	30	15

25th anniversary of Universal Declaration of Human Rights.

1973, Dec. 21

Design: No. 1747, Score and emblem (diff.).

1746	A419	10r yellow green, red & black	60	20
1747	"	10r lt. blue, ultra. & red	60	20

Dedicated to the art of music.

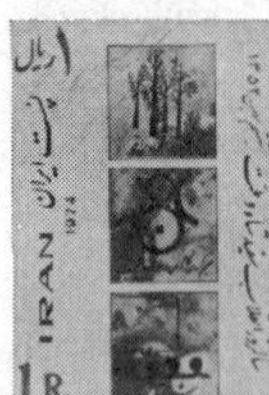

Forestry, Printing, Education
A420

Designs (Symbols of Reforms): No. 1749, Land reform, sales of shares, women's suffrage. No. 1750, Army of progress, irrigation, women's education. No. 1751, Hygiene, rural courts, housing.

1974, Jan. 26 Litho. *Perf. 10½*

1748	A420	1r lt. blue & multi.	4	3
1749	"	1r " " "	4	3
1750	"	2r " " "	10	6
1751	"	2r " " "	10	6

Souvenir Sheet

1752	A420	20r multicolored	80	80

"White Revolution of King and People" and 12 reform laws. No. 1752 combines symbolic designs of Nos. 1748–1751 within multicolored frame. Size: 76½x102mm.

Pir Amooz Ketabaty Script
A421

Various Scripts: No. 1754, Mo Eghely Ketabaty. No. 1755, Din Dabireh, Avesta script. No. 1756, Pir Amooz, Naskh style. No. 1757, Pir Amooz, decorative style. No. 1758, Decorative and architectural style.

Lithographed

1974, Feb. 14 *Perf. 10½* Wmk. 353

1753	A421	1r silver, ocher & multicolored	12	5
1754	"	1r gold, gray & multicolored	12	5
1755	"	1r silver, yellow & multicolored	12	5
1756	"	2r gold, gray & multicolored	22	10
1757	"	2r gold, slate & multicolored	22	10
1758	"	2r gold, claret & multicolored	22	10
		Nos. 1753–1758 (6)	1.02	45

Development of writing.

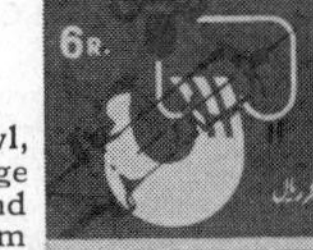

Fowl, Syringe and Emblem
A422

1974, Feb. 23

1759	A422	6r red brn. & multi.	28	15

5th Iranian Veterinary Congress.

Monarch Butterfly
A423

Designs: Various butterflies.

Perf. 10½

1974, Mar. 6 Litho. Wmk. 353

1760	A423	1r rose lilac & multi.	12	6
1761	"	1r brt. rose & multi.	12	6
1762	"	2r lt. blue & multi.	25	10
1763	"	2r green & multi.	25	10
1764	"	2r bister & multi.	25	10
		Nos. 1760–1764 (5)	99	42

Novrooz, Iranian New Year.

Mevlana
A424

1974, Mar. 12 *Perf. 13*

1765	A424	2r pale vio. & multi.	20	6

700th anniversary of the death of Jalaludin Mevlana (1207–1273), poet.

Shah Type of 1971

1974 Photogravure *Perf. 13½x13*

Size: 20½x28mm.

1768	A366	50d orange & blue	3	3
1769	"	1r emerald & blue	6	3
1770	"	2r red & blue	10	3

Size: 27x36½mm.

1771	A366	10r lt. green & blue	35	3
1772	"	20r lilac & blue	70	12
		Nos. 1768–1772 (5)	1.24	24

Palace of the Forty Columns
A425

Lithographed

1974, Apr. 11 *Perf. 10½* Wmk. 353

1773	A425	10r multicolored	60	10

9th Medical Congress of the Near and Middle East, Isfahan.

Onager
A426

Athlete and Games Emblem
A427

1974, Apr. 13

Gold & Multicolored

1774	A426	1r *shown*	10	5
1775	"	2r *Great bustard*	20	6
1776	"	6r *Fawn and deer*	30	12
1777	"	8r *Caucasian black grouse*	40	15

International Council for Game and Wildlife Preservation. Nos. 1774–1777 printed se-tenant.

1974, Apr. 30 Multicolored

1778	A427	1r *shown*	20	3
1779	"	1r *Table tennis*	20	3
1780	"	2r *Wrestling*	40	6
1781	"	2r *Hurdles*	40	6
1782	"	6r *Weight lifting*	60	15
1783	"	8r *Basketball*	60	20
		Nos. 1778–1783 (6)	2.40	53

7th Asian Games, Tehran; first issue.

Lion of Venice—A428

Design: 8r, Audience with the Doge of Venice (painting).

1974, May 5

1784	A428	6r multicolored	30	12
1785	"	8r "	40	15

Safeguarding Venice.

Links and Grain
A429

1974, May 13 Litho. *Perf. 10½*

1786 A429 2r multicolored 10 4

Cooperation Day.

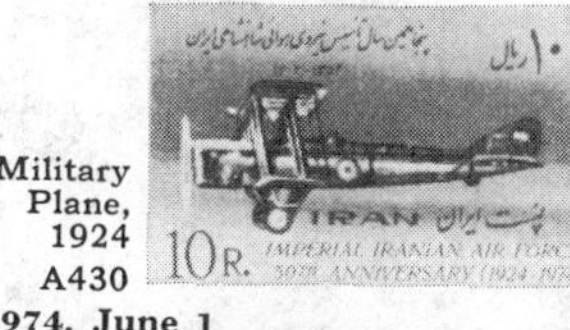

Military Plane, 1924
A430

1974, June 1

Multicolored

1787 A430 10r *shown* 60 10
1788 " 10r *Jet, 1974* 60 10

50th anniversary of Iranian Air Force.

Swimmer and Games Emblem A431

Bicyclists and Games Emblem A432

Perf. 10½

1974, July 1 Litho. **Wmk. 353**

Gold and Multicolored

1789 A431 1r *shown* 8 5
1790 " 1r *Tennis, men's doubles* 8 5
1791 " 2r *Wrestling* 8 7
1792 " 2r *Hockey* 12 7
1793 " 4r *Netball* 20 10
1794 " 10r *Tennis, women's singles* 40 10
Nos. 1789–1794 (6) 96 44

7th Asian Games, Tehran; second issue.

1974, Aug. 1

Multicolored

1795 A432 2r *shown* 17 4
1796 " 2r *Soccer* 17 4
1797 " 2r *Fencing* 17 4
1798 " 2r *Small-bore rifle shooting* 17 4

7th Asian Games, Tehran; third issue.

Ghaskai Costume A433

Gold Winged Lion Cup A434

Regional Costumes: No. 1800, Kurdistan, Kermanshah District. No. 1801, Kurdistan, Sanandaj District. No. 1802, Mazandaran. No. 1803, Bakhtiari. No. 1804, Torkaman.

1974, July 6

1799 A433 2r lt. ultra. & multi. 20 7
1800 " 2r buff & multi. 20 7
1801 " 2r green & multi. 20 7
1802 " 2r lt. blue & multi. 20 7
1803 " 2r gray & multi. 20 7
1804 " 2r dull grn. & multi. 20 7
Nos. 1799–1804 (6) 1.20 42

Nos. 1799–1804 printed se-tenant.

1974, July 13

1805 A434 2r dull grn. & multi. 12 5

Iranian Soccer Cup.

Tabriz Rug, Late 16th Century A435

King Carrying Vases, Bas-relief A436

1974, July 21

Designs: No. 1807, Anatolian rug, 15th century. No. 1808, Kashan rug, Lahore.

1806 A435 2r brown & multi. 17 4
1807 " 2r blue & multi. 17 4
1808 " 2r red & multi. 17 4

10th anniversary of the Regional Cooperation for Development Pact among Iran, Turkey and Pakistan. Nos. 1806–1808 printed se-tenant.

Perf. 10½

1974, Aug. 15 Litho. **Wmk. 353**

1809 A436 2r black & multi. 12 5

8th Iranian Arts Festival, Shiraz-Persepolis.

Aryamehr Stadium, Tehran—A437

Designs: No. 1811, Games' emblem and inscription. No. 1812, Aerial view of games' site.

1974

1810 A437 6r multicolored 30 12

Souvenir Sheets

1811 A437 10r multicolored 50 50
1812 " 10r " 50 50

7th Asian Games, Tehran; fourth and fifth issues. Nos. 1811–1812 contain one stamp each (51x38mm.), gold and multicolored margins with sports emblems. Size: 73x94mm.

Issue dates: Nos. 1811–1812, Sept. 1; No. 1810, Sept. 16.

"Welfare" A438

"Education" A439

1974, Sept. 11

1813 A438 2r org. & multi. 10 4
1814 A439 2r blue & multi. 10 4

Welfare and free education.

Map of Hasanlu, 1000–800 B.C.
A440

1974, Sept. 24

1815 A440 8r multicolored 32 16

2nd International Congress of Architecture, Shiraz-Persepolis, Sept. 1974.

Achaemenian Mail Cart and UPU Emblem—A441

Design: 14r, UPU emblem and letters.

Perf. 10½

1974, Oct. 9 Litho. **Wmk. 353**

1816 A441 6r org., grn. & blk. 30 12
1817 " 14r multicolored 50 28

Centenary of Universal Postal Union.

Road Through Farahabad Park
A442

Design: 2r, Recreation Building.

1974, Oct. 16

1818 A442 1r multicolored 8 3
1819 " 2r " 12 4

Inauguration of Farahabad Park, Tehran.

Farahnaz Dam and Mohammed Riza Pahlavi
A443

Designs: 5d, Khark Island petro-chemical plant. 10d, Ghatour Railroad Bridge. 1r, Tehran oil refinery. 2r, Satellite communication station, Hamadan, and Mt. Alvand. 6r, Aryamehr steel mill, Isfahan. 8r, University of Tabriz. 10r, Shah Abbas Kabir Dam. 14r, Rudagi Music Hall. 20r, Shayad Monument. 50r, Aryamehr Stadium.

1974–75 Photo. *Perf. 13x13½*

Size: 28x21mm.

Frame & Shah in Brown

1820 A443 5d slate green 3 3
1821 " 10d orange 3 3
1822 " 50d blue green 3 3
1823 " 1r ultramarine 4 3
1824 " 2r deep lilac 8 3

Size: 36x26½mm.

Frame & Shah in Dark Blue

1825 A443 6r brown 24 3
1826 " 8r greenish blue 32 3
1827 " 10r deep lilac 40 7
a. Value in Persian omitted 1.00 1.00
1828 A443 14r deep green 50 5
1829 " 20r magenta 80 5
1830 " 50r violet 2.00 12
Nos. 1820–1830 (11) 4.47 50

Issued dates: 50d, 1r, 2r, Oct. 16, 1974; 14r, Nov. 1974; others Mar. 6, 1975.

1975–77 **Size: 28x21mm.**

Frame & Shah in Green

1831 A443 5d orange ('77) 3 3
1832 " 10d rose mag. ('77) 3 3
1833 " 50d lilac 3 3
1834 " 1r dark blue 4 3
1835 " 2r brown 8 3

Size: 36x26½mm.

Frame & Shah in Brown

1836 A443 6r violet blue ('76) 24 8
1837 " 8r dp. orange ('77) 32 16
1838 " 10r dp. yel. grn. ('76) 40 12
1839 " 14r lilac 50 13
1840 " 20r brt. green ('76) 80 24
1841 " 50r dp. blue ('76) 2.00 60
Nos. 1831–1841 (11) 4.47 1.48

Festival Emblem, Crown and Column Capital, Persepolis
A444

1974, Oct. 26 Litho. *Perf. 10½*

1842 A444 2r multicolored 12 6

Festival of Culture and Art.

Destroyer "Palang" and Flag
A445

1974, Nov. 5

1843 A445 10r multicolored 40 10

Navy Day.

Girl at Spinning Wheel
A446

Designs: Children's drawings.

1974, Nov. 7 *Perf. 10½*

Multicolored

1844 A446 2r *shown* 10 6
1845 " 2r *Scarecrow* (vert.) 10 6
1846 " 2r *Picnic* 10 6

Children's Week.

Winged Ibex
A447

1974, Nov. 25 Litho. **Wmk. 353**

1847 A447 2r vio., org. & black 12 6

Third Tehran International Film Festival.

WPY Emblem
A448

1974, Dec. 1

1848 A448 8r orange & multi. 32 16

World Population Year.

Gold Bee
A449

Design: 8r, Gold crown, gift of French people to Empress Farah. Bee pin was gift of the Italian people.

1974, Dec. 20

1849 A449 6r multicolored 24 12
1850 " 8r " 32 16

14th wedding anniversary of Shah Riza Pahlavi and Empress Farah.

Angel with Banner
A450

1975, Jan. 7 Lithographed *Perf. 10½*

1851 A450 2r org. & vio. blue 10 4

International Women's Year 1975.

Symbols of Agriculture, Industry and the Arts
A451

Tourism Year 75 Emblem
A452

Perf. 10½

1975, Jan. 26 Litho. Wmk. 353

1852 A451 2r multicolored 10 4

"White Revolution of King and People."

1975, Feb. 17

1853 A452 6r multicolored 24 12

South Asia Tourism Year 1975.

"Farabi" in Shape of Musical Instrument or Alembic
A453

Ornament, Rug Pattern
A454

1975, Mar. 1

1854 A453 2r brn. red & multi. 10 4

Abu-Nasr al-Farabi (870 ?–950), physician, musician and philosopher, 1100th birth anniversary.

1975, Mar. 6

Multicolored

1855 A454 1r *shown* 6 3
1856 " 1r *Blossoms and cypress trees* 6 3
1857 " 1r *Shah Abbasi flower* 6 3

Novrooz, Iranian New Year. Nos. 1855–1857 printed se-tenant in sheets of 45 stamps and 15 labels.

Nasser Khosrov
A455

Formula
A456

1975, Mar. 11

1858 A455 2r blk., gold & red 10 4

Nasser Khosrov, poet, 1000th birth anniversary.

Perf. 10½

1975, May 5 Litho. Wmk. 353

1859 A456 2r buff & multi. 10 4

5th Biennial Symposium of Iranian Biochemical Society.

Charioteer, Bas-relief, Persepolis
A457

Design: 2r, Heads of Persian warriors, bas-relief from Persepolis (vert.).

1975, May 5

1860 A457 2r lt. brn. & multi. 8 4
1861 " 10r blue & multi. 40 20

Rotary International, 70th anniversary.

Signal Fire, Persian Castle
A458

Design: 8r, Communications satellite.

1975, May 17

1862 A458 6r multicolored 24 12
1863 " 8r lilac & multi. 32 16

7th World Telecommunications Day.

Cooperation, Men and Women Linking Hands
A459

1975, May 13

1864 A459 2r multicolored 10 4

Cooperation Day.

Jet, Shayad Monument, Statue of Liberty—A460

Perf. 10½

1975, May 29 Litho. Wmk. 353

1865 A460 10r org. & multi. 40 20

Iran Air's first flight to New York, May 1975.

Emblem
A461

1975, June 5

1866 A461 6r blue & multi. 24 12

World Environment Day.

Dam
A462

1975, June 10

1867 A462 10r multicolored 40 20

9th International Congress on Irrigation and Drainage.

Resurgence Party Emblem
A463

Girl Scout Symbols
A464

Perf. 10½

1975, July 1 Litho. Wmk. 353

1868 A463 2r multicolored 10 4

Organization of Resurgence Party.

1975, July 16

1869 A464 2r multicolored 12 4

2nd National Girl Scout Camp, Tehran, July 1976.

Festival of Tus
A465

1975, July 17

1870 A465 2r gray, lilac & violet 10 4

Festival of Tus in honor of Firdausi (940–1020), Persian poet born near Tus in Khorasan.

Ceramic Plate, Iran
A466

Designs: No. 1872, Camel leather vase, Pakistan (vert.). No. 1873, Porcelain vase, Turkey (vert.).

1975, July 21

1871 A466 2r bister & multi. 8 4
1872 " 2r " " 8 4
1873 " 2r " " 8 4

Regional Cooperation for Development Pact among Iran, Pakistan and Turkey.

Majlis Gate
A467

Perf. 10½

1975, Aug. 5 Litho. Wmk. 353

1874 A467 10r multicolored 40 20

Iranian Constitution, 70th anniversary.

Column with Stylized Branches
A468

Flags over Globe
A469

Perf. 10½

1975, Aug. 21 Litho. Wmk. 353

1875 A468 8r red & multi. 32 16

9th Iranian Arts Festival, Shiraz-Persepolis.

1975, Sept. 8

1876 A469 2r vio. bl. & multi. 10 4

International Literacy Symposium, Persepolis.

Stylized Globe
A470

1975, Sept. 13

1877 A470 2r violet & multi. 10 4

3rd Tehran International Trade Fair.

World Map and Envelope
A471

Perf. 10½

1975, Oct. 9 Litho. Wmk. 353

1878 A471 14r ultra. & multi. 56 28

World Post Day, Oct. 9.

Crown, Column Capital, Persepolis
A472

Perf. 10½

1975, Oct. 26 Litho. Wmk. 353

1879 A472 2r ultra. & multi. 10 4

Festival of Culture and Art. See No. 1954.

Face and Film
A473

1975, Nov. 2

1880 A473 6r multicolored 24 12

Tehran International Festival of Children's Films.

"Mother's Face" A474 | Girl A475

Design: No. 1882, 2r, "Our House" (horiz.). All designs after children's drawings.

1975, Nov. 5

1881 A474 2r multicolored 8 4
1882 A475 2r " 8 4
1883 " 2r " 8 4

Children's Week.

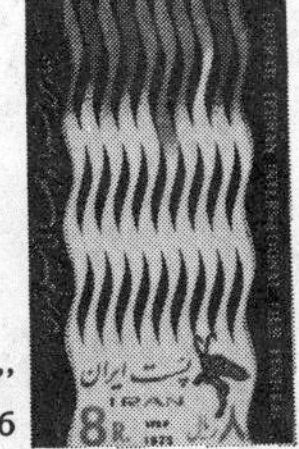

"Film"
A476

Perf. 10½

1975, Dec. 4 Litho. Wmk. 353

1884 A476 8r multicolored 32 16

4th Tehran International Film Festival.

Symbols of Reforms A477 | People A478

Design: No. 1887, Five reform symbols.

Perf. 10½

1976, Jan. 26 Litho. Wmk. 353

1885 A477 2r green & multi. 8 4
1886 A478 2r greenish blue & multicolored 8 4
1887 A477 2r lilac & multi. 8 4

"White Revolution of King and People."

Motorcycle Policeman
A479

Police Helicopter
A480

1976, Feb. 16

1888 A479 2r multicolored 8 4
1889 A480 6r " 24 12

Highway Police Day.

Soccer Cup A481 | Candlestick A482

Perf. 10½

1976, Feb. 24 Litho. Wmk. 353

1890 A481 2r orange & multi. 8 4

3rd International Youth Soccer Cup, Shiraz and Ahvaz.

1976, Mar. 6

Designs: No. 1892, Incense burner. No. 1893, Rose water container.

1891 A482 1r olive & multi. 4 3
1892 " 1r claret & multi. 4 3
1893 " 1r Prus. blue & multicolored 4 3

Novrooz, Iranian New Year. Nos. 1891–1893 printed se-tenant.

Telephones, 1876 and 1976 A483 | Eye Within Square A484

1976, Mar. 10

1894 A483 10r multicolored 40 20

Centenary of first telephone call by Alexander Graham Bell, Mar. 10, 1876.

Perf. 10½

1976, Apr. 29 Litho. Wmk. 353

1895 A484 6r black & multi. 24 12
a. Perf. 12½ 50

World Health Day: "Foresight prevents blindness."

Nurse with Infant
A485

Young Man Holding Old Man's Hand
A486

Design: No. 1897, Engineering apprentices.

1976, May 10

1896 A485 2r lt. bl. & multi. 8 4
1897 " 2r " " 8 4
1898 A486 2r org. & multi. 8 4

Royal Organization of Social Services, 30th anniversary.

Map of Iran, Men Linking Hands A487 | Waves and Ear Phones A488

1976, May 13 Wmk. 353

1899 A487 2r yellow & multi. 8 4

Iranian Cooperatives, 10th anniversary.

1976, May 17

1900 A488 14r gray & multi. 56 28

World Telecommunications Day.

Emblem, Woman with Flag, Man with Gun
A489

1976, June 6

1901 A489 2r bister & multi. 8 4

To publicize the power of stability.

Map of Iran, Columns of Persepolis, Nasser Khosrov A490 | Riza Shah Pahlavi A491

1976, July 6 Litho. *Perf. 10½*

1902 A490 6r yellow & multi. 24 12

Tourist publicity.

1976, July 21 Litho. Wmk. 353

Designs: 6r, Mohammed Ali Jinnah. 8r, Kemal Ataturk.

1903 A491 2r gray & multi. 8 4
1904 " 6r " " 24 12
1905 " 8r " " 32 16

Regional Cooperation for Development Pact among Iran, Turkey and Pakistan, 12th anniversary.

Torch, Montreal and Iranian Olympic Emblems
A492

1976, Aug. 1

1906 A492 14r multicolored 56 28

21st Olympic Games, Montreal, Canada, July 17–Aug. 1.

Riza Shah Pahlavi in Coronation Robe A493 | Festival Emblem A494

Designs: 2r, Shahs Riza and Mohammed Riza Pahlavi (horiz.). 14r, 20r, Shah Mohammed Riza Pahlavi in coronation robe and crown.

1976 *Perf. 10½* Wmk. 353

1907 A493 2r lilac & multi. 8 4
1908 " 6r blue & multi. 24 12
1909 " 14r grn. & multi. 56 28

Souvenir Sheet
Imperf.

1910 A493 20r multicolored 90

50th anniversary of Pahlavi dynasty and 35th anniversary of reign of Shah Mohammed Riza Pahlavi. No. 1910 contains one stamp, size: 43x62mm.; decorative yellow margin. Size: 75x100mm.

1976, Aug. 29 Litho. *Perf. 10½*

1911 A494 10r multicolored 40 20

10th Iranian Arts Festival, Shiraz-Persepolis.

Iranian Scout Emblem
A495

Cancer Radiation Treatment
A496

1976, Oct. 2 Litho. *Perf. 10½*

1912 A495 2r lt. blue & multi. 8 4

10th Asia Pacific Conference, Tehran 1976.

1976, Oct. 6

1913 A496 2r black & multi. 8 4

Fight against cancer.

Target, Police Woman Receiving Decoration
A497

1976, Oct. 7

1914 A497 2r lt. blue & multi. 8 4

Police Day.

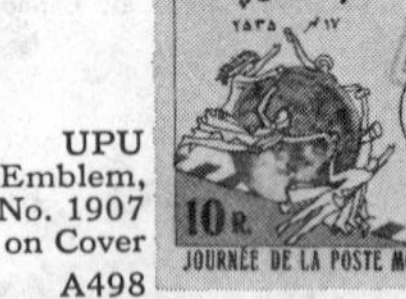

UPU Emblem, No. 1907 on Cover
A498

1976, Oct. 9

1915 A498 10r multicolored 40 20

International Post Day.

Crown Prince Riza with Cup
A499

1976, Oct. 10

1916 A499 6r multicolored 24 12

National Society of Village Culture Houses, anniversary.

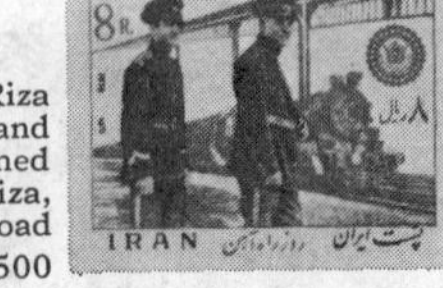

Shahs Riza and Mohammed Riza, Railroad
A500

1976, Oct. 15

1917 A500 8r black & multi. 32 16

Railroad Day.

Emblem and Column Capital, Persepolis
A501

Census Emblem
A502

1976, Oct. 26

1918 A501 14r blue & multi. 56 28

Festival of Culture and Art, Persepolis.

1976, Oct. 30

1919 A502 2r gray & multi. 8 4

National Census of Population and Housing, 1976.

Flowers and Birds
A503

Mohammed Ali Jinnah
A504

Designs: No. 1921, Flowers and bird. No. 1922, Flowers and butterfly. Designs are from covers of children's books.

1976, Oct. 31 *Perf. 10½*

1920 A503 2r multicolored 8 4
1921 " 2r " 8 4
1922 " 2r " 8 4

Children's Week.

1976, Dec. 25 Litho. **Wmk. 353**

1923 A504 10r multicolored 40 20

Mohammed Ali Jinnah (1876–1948), first Governor General of Pakistan, birth centenary.

Development and Agriculture Corps—A505

17-Point Reform Law: 5d, Land reform. 10d, Nationalization of forests. 50d, Sale of shares of state-owned industries. 1r, Profit sharing for factory workers. 2r, Woman suffrage. 3r, Education Corps formation. 5r, Health Corps. 8r, Establishment of village courts. 10r, Nationalization of water resources. 12r, Reconstruction program, urban and rural. 14r, Administrative and educational reorganization. 20r, Sale of factory shares. 30r, Commodity pricing. 50r, Free education. 100r, Child care. 200r, Care of the aged (social security).

1977, Jan. 26 Photo. *Perf. 13x13½*

Frame and Shah's Head in Gold

Size: 28x21mm.

1924 A505 5d rose & green 3 3
1925 " 10d light green & brown 3 3
1926 " 50d yel. & vio. bl. 3 3
1927 " 1r lilac & vio. bl. 4 3
1928 " 2r org. & green 8 4
1929 " 3r lt. blue & red 12 6
1930 " 5r blue green & magenta 20 10

Size: 37x27mm.

1931 A505 6r brn., maroon & black 24 12
1932 " 8r ultra., maroon & black 32 16
1933 " 10r lt. green, blue & black 40 20
1934 " 12r vio., maroon & black 48 24
1935 " 14r orange, red & black 56 28
1936 " 20r gray, ocher & black 80 40
1937 " 30r blue, green & black 1.20 60
1938 " 50r yel., brown & black 2.00 1.00
1939 " 100r multicolored 4.00 2.00
1940 " 200r " 8.00 4.00
Nos. 1924-1940 (17) 18.53 9.32

"White Revolution of King and People" reform laws.

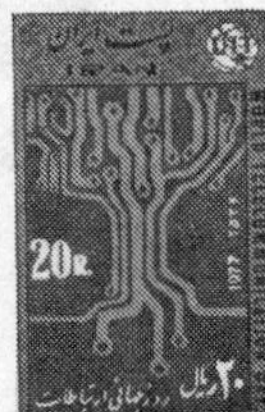

Man in Guilan Costume
A506

Electronic Tree
A507

Design: 2r, Woman in Guilan costume (Northern Iran).

1977, Mar. 6 *Perf. 13* **Wmk. 353**

1941 A506 1r multicolored 4 3
1942 " 2r " 8 4

Novrooz, Iranian New Year.

1977, May 17 Photo. *Perf. 13*

1943 A507 20r multicolored 80 40

World Telecommunications Day.

Riza Shah Dam
A508

1977, May 31 *Perf. 13x13½*

1944 A508 5r multicolored 20 10

Inauguration of Riza Shah Dam.

Olympic Rings
A509

1977, June 23 Litho. *Perf. 10½*

1945 A509 14r multicolored 56 28

Olympic Day.

Terra-cotta Jug, Iran
A510

Designs: No. 1947, Terra-cotta bullock cart, Pakistan. No. 1948, Terra-cotta pot with human face, Turkey.

Wmk. 353

1977, July 21 Photo. *Perf. 13x13½*

1946 A510 5r vio. & multi. 20 10
1947 " 5r emerald & multi. 20 10
1948 " 5r green & multi. 20 10

Regional Cooperation for Development Pact among Iran, Turkey and Pakistan, 13th anniversary.

Flowers with Scout Emblems, Map of Asia
A511

1977, Aug. 5 Litho. *Perf. 13*

1949 A511 10r multicolored 40 20

2nd Asia-Pacific Jamboree, Nishapur.

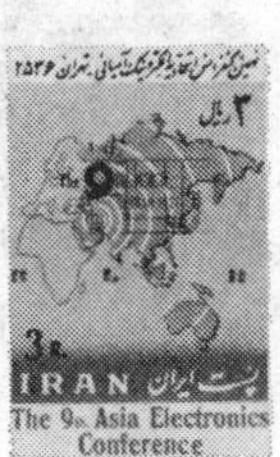

Map of Eastern Hemisphere with Iran
A512

Tree of Learning, Symbolic Letters
A513

1977, Sept. 20 Photo. **Wmk. 353**

1950 A512 3r multicolored 12 6

9th Asian Electronics Conference, Tehran.

1977, Oct. 8 *Perf. 13* **Wmk. 353**

1951 A513 10r multicolored 40 20

Honoring the teachers.

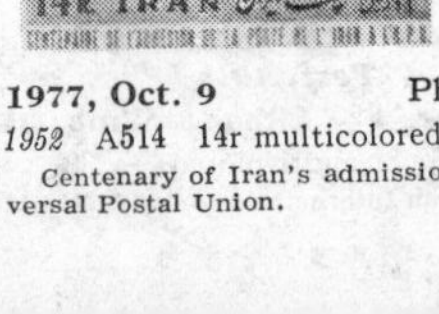

Globe, Envelope, UPU Emblem
A514

1977, Oct. 9 Photogravure

1952 A514 14r multicolored 56 28

Centenary of Iran's admission to the Universal Postal Union.

Folk Art
A515

1977, Oct. 16

1953 A515 5r multicolored 20 10

Festival of Folk Art.

Festival Type of 1975

Design: 20r, similar to 1975 issue, but with small crown within star.

1977, Oct. 26 ***Perf. 10½***

1954 A472 20r bis., grn., car. & black 80 40

Festival of Culture and Art.

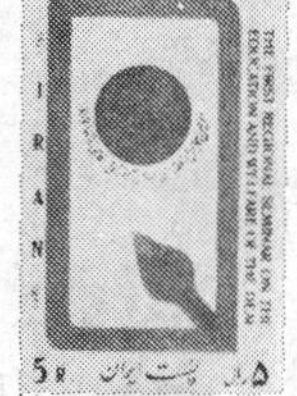

Joust A516 · Emblem A517

Designs: No. 1956, Rapunzel. No. 1957, Little princess with attendants.

1977, Oct. 31 **Photogravure**

1955 A516 3r multicolored 12 6
1956 " 3r " 12 6
1957 " 3r " 12 6

Children's Week. Nos. 1955–1957 printed se-tenant.

1977, Nov. 7 ***Perf. 13*** **Wmk. 353**

1958 A517 5r multicolored 20 10

First Regional Seminar on the Education and Welfare of the Deaf.

Mohammad Iqbal A518 · African Sculpture A519

1977, Nov. 9 **Litho.** ***Perf. 10½***

1959 A518 5r multicolored 20 10

Mohammad Allama Iqbal (1877–1938), poet and philosopher.

1977, Dec. 14

1960 A519 20r multicolored 80 40

African art.

Shah Mosque, Isfahan
A520

Designs: 1r, Ruins, Persepolis. 2r, Khajou Bridge, Isfahan. 5r, Imam Riza Shrine, Meshed. 9r, Warrior frieze, Persepolis. 10r, Djameh Mosque, Isfahan. 20r, King on throne, bas-relief. 25r, Sheik Lotfollah Mosque. 30r, Ruins, Persepolis (diff. view). 50r, Ali Ghapou Palace, Isfahan. 100r, Bas-relief, Tagh Bastan. 200r, Horseman and prisoners, bas-relief, Naqsh Rostam.

Wmk. 353

1978 **Photo.** ***Perf. 13x13½***

"Iran" and Head in Gold

Size: 28x21mm.

1961 A520 1r deep brown 3 3
1962 " 2r emerald 6 3
1963 " 3r magenta 12 3
1964 " 5r Prussian blue 20 4

Size: 36x27mm.

1965 A520 9r sepia 28
1966 " 10r bright blue 30
1967 " 20r rose 60
1968 " 25r ultramarine 75
1969 " 30r magenta 90
1970 " 50r dp. yel. grn. 1.50
1971 " 100r dark blue 3.00
1972 " 200r violet blue 6.00
Nos. 1961–1972 (12) 13.74

Persian Rug
A521

Designs: Persian rugs.

Wmk. 353

1978, Feb. 11 **Litho.** ***Perf. 10½***

1973 A521 3r silver & multi. 10 6
1974 " 5r " " 15 10
1975 " 10r " " 30 20

Opening of Carpet Museum.

Iranian Man A522 · Mohammed Riza Pahlavi A523

Design: 5r, Iranian woman.

1978, Mar. 6 ***Perf. 13***

1976 A522 3r yel. & multi. 10 6
1977 " 5r lt. bl. & multi. 15 10

Novrooz, Iranian New Year.

1978, Mar. 15

1978 A523 20r multicolored 60 40

Father's Day.

Riza Shah Pahlavi and Crown Prince Inspecting Girls' School—A524

Designs (Riza Shah Pahlavi and Crown Prince Mohammed Riza Pahlavi): 5r, Inauguration of Trans-Iranian railroad. 10r, At stairs of Palace, Persepolis. 14r, Shah handing Crown Prince (later Shah) officer's diploma at Tehran Officers' Academy.

1978, Mar. 15

1979 A524 3r multicolored 10 6
1980 " 5r " 15 10
1981 " 10r " 30 20
1982 " 14r " 42 28

Riza Shah Pahlavi (1877–1944), founder of Pahlavi dynasty.

Communications Satellite over Map of Iran—A525

1978, Apr. 18 **Litho.** ***Perf. 10½***

1983 A525 20r multicolored 60 15

International Telecommunications Union, 7th meeting, Tehran, and 10th anniversary of Iran's membership.

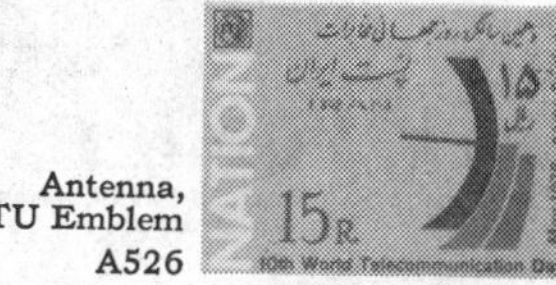

Antenna, ITU Emblem
A526

1978, May 17 **Litho.** ***Perf. 10½***

1984 A526 15r multicolored 45 12

10th World Telecommunications Day.

Welfare Legion Emblem A527 · Pink Roses, Iran A528

Photogravure

1978, June 13 ***Perf. 13x13½***

1985 A527 10r multicolored 30 8

Universal Welfare Legion, 10th anniversary.

Wmk. 353

1978, July 21 **Photo.** ***Perf. 13½x13***

Designs: 10r, Yellow rose, Turkey. 15r, Red roses, Pakistan.

1986 A528 5r multicolored 15 4
1987 " 10r " 30 8
1988 " 15r " 45 12

Regional Cooperation for Development Pact among Iran, Turkey and Pakistan, 14th anniversary.

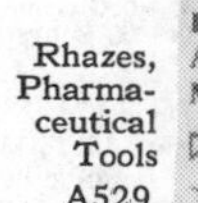

Rhazes, Pharmaceutical Tools
A529

1978, Aug. 26 ***Perf. 13*** **Wmk. 353**

1989 A529 5r multicolored 15 4

Pharmacists' Day. Rhazes (850–923), chief physician of Great Hospital in Baghdad.

Girl Scouts, Aryamehr Arch
A530

1978, Sept. 2 ***Perf. 10½***

1990 A530 5r multicolored 15 4

23rd World Girl Scouts Conference, Tehran, Sept. 1978.

Shah Riza Pahlavi
A531

Design: 5r, Mohammed Riza Shah Pahlavi.

1978, Sept. 11 **Litho.** ***Perf. 10½***

1991 A531 3r multicolored 10 3
1992 " 5r " 15 4

Bank Melli Iran, 50th anniversary.

Girl and Bird
A532

1978, Oct. 31 **Photo.** ***Perf. 13***

1993 A532 3r multicolored 10 3

Children's Week.

Envelope, Map of Iran, UPU Emblem
A533

1978, Nov. 22 ***Perf. 13x13½***

1994 A533 14r gold & multi. 42 28

World Post Day, Oct. 22.

Communications Symbols and Classroom—A534

1978, Nov. 22 ***Perf. 10½***

1995 A534 10r multicolored 30 8

Faculty of Communications, 50th anniversary.

Human Rights Flame
A535

1978, Dec. 17 **Photo.** ***Perf. 13***

1996 A535 20r bl., blk. & gold 60 15

Universal Declaration of Human Rights, 30th anniversary.

SEMI-POSTAL STAMPS.

Lion and Bull, Persepolis
SP1

Persian Soldier, Persepolis
SP2

Palace of Darius the Great
SP3

Tomb of Cyrus the Great, Pasargadae
SP4

King Darius on his Throne
SP5

Perf. 13x13½, 13½x13

1948, Jan. 30 Engr. Unwmkd.

B1	SP1	50d+25d emerald	60	60
B2	SP2	1r+50d red	60	60
B3	SP3	2½r+1¼r blue	60	60
B4	SP4	5r+2½r purple	1.25	1.25
B5	SP5	10r+5r vio. brown	1.50	1.50
		Nos. B1-B5 (5)	4.55	4.55

The surtax was for reconstruction of the tomb of Avicenna (980–1037), Arab physician and philosopher, at Hamadan.

Ardashir II
SP6

Shapur I and Valerian
SP7

Designs: 1r+50d, King Narses, Naqsh-i-Rustam. 5r+2½r, Taq-i-Kisra, Ctesiphon. 10r+5r, Ardashir I and Ahura Mazda.

1949, June 11

B6	SP6	50d+25d green	15	15
B7	"	1r+50d vermilion	30	30
B8	SP7	2½r+1¼r blue	30	30
B9	"	5r+2½r magenta	1.10	1.10
B10	"	10r+5r greenish gray	1.25	1.25
		Nos. B6-B10 (5)	3.10	3.10

The surtax was for reconstruction of Avicenna's tomb at Hamadan.

Gunbad-i-Ali
SP8

Alaviyan, Hamadan
SP9

Seldjukide Coin
SP10

Designs: 1r+½r, Masjid-i-Jami, Isfahan. 5r+2½r, Masjid-i-Jami, Ardistan.

1949, Dec. 22

B11	SP8	50d+25d blue green	15	15
B12	"	1r+½r dark brown	30	30
B13	SP9	2½r+1¼r blue	30	30
B14	"	5r+2½r red	1.10	1.10
B15	SP10	10r+5r olive gray	1.25	1.25
		Nos. B11-B15 (5)	3.10	3.10

The surtax was for reconstruction of Avicenna's tomb at Hamadan.

Book, Crescent and Flag
SP11

1950, Oct. 2 Litho. *Perf. 11*

B16	SP11	1.50r+1r multi.	7.00	5.00

Issued to publicize the Economic Conference of the Islamic States.

Tomb of Baba Afzal at Kashan
SP12

Gorgan Vase
SP13

Designs: 2½r+1¼r, Tower of Ghazan. 5r+2½r, Masjid-i Gawhar. 10r+5r, Mihrab of the Mosque at Rezaieh.

1950, Aug. 23 Engr. *Perf. 13x13½*

B17	SP12	50d+25d dk. green	15	15
B18	SP13	1r+½r blue	30	30
B19	"	2½r+1¼r chocolate	30	30
B20	SP12	5r+2½r red	1.10	1.10
B21	"	10r+5r gray	1.25	1.25
		Nos. B17-B21 (5)	3.10	3.10

The surtax was for reconstruction of Avicenna's tomb at Hamadan.

Mohammed Riza Pahlavi and Map
SP14

Monument to Fallen Liberators of Azerbaijan—SP15

Designs: 1r+50d, Marching troops. 1.50r+75d, Running advance with flag. 2.50r+1.25r, Mohammed Riza Pahlavi. 3r+1.50r, Parade of victors.

1950, Dec. 12 Lithographed

B22	SP14	10d+5d black brown	7.00	1.75
B23	SP15	50d+25d black brown	8.50	1.75
B24	"	1r+50d brown lake	12.00	2.50
B25	SP14	1.50r+75d orange vermilion	17.50	4.25
B26	"	2.50r+1.25r blue	21.00	4.75
B27	SP15	3r+1.50r ultra.	21.00	6.00
		Nos. B22-B27 (6)	87.00	21.00

Issued to commemorate the 4th anniversary of the liberation of Azerbaijan Province from communists.

The surtax was for families of Persian soldiers who died in the struggle.

Koran Gate at Shiraz
SP16

Saadi
SP17

Design: 50d+50d, Tomb of Saadi, Shiraz.

Perf. 11x10½, 10½x11.

1952, Apr. 30 Photo. Unwmkd.

B28	SP16	25d+25d dull blue green	65	38
B29	"	50d+50d brown olive	1.65	85
B30	SP17	1.50r+50d vio. bl.	2.75	1.25

770th birthday of Saadi, Persian poet. The surtax was to help complete Saadi's tomb at Shiraz.

Three stamps of same denominations and colors, with values enclosed in tablets, were prepared but not officially issued.

View of Hamadan
SP18

Avicenna
SP19

Designs: 2½r+1¼r, Gonbad Qabus (tower of tomb). 5r+2½r, Old tomb of Avicenna. 10r+5r, New tomb.

Perf. 13x13½, 13½x13.

1954, Apr. 21 Engr. Unwmkd.

B31	SP18	50d+25d dp. green	45	45
B32	SP19	1r+½r vio. brown	30	30
B33	"	2½r+1¼r blue	30	30
B34	SP18	5r+2½r verm.	75	75
B35	"	10r+5r olive gray	1.25	1.25
		Nos. B31-B35 (5)	3.05	3.05

The surtax was for reconstruction of Avicenna's tomb at Hamadan.

Mother with Children and Ruins
SP20

Lithographed

1963, Feb. 4 *Perf. 10½* Wmk. 316

B36	SP20	14r+6r dk. bl., grn. & lt. brown	1.00	50

The surtax was for the benefit of survivors of the Kazvin earthquake.

AIR POST STAMPS.

Type of 1909 Overprinted

مخصوص پست هوائی

POSTE AÉRIENNE

Typographed

1927 *Perf. 11½.* Unwmkd.

C1	A31	1c orange & maroon	30	8
C2	"	2c violet & maroon	30	15
C3	"	3c green & maroon	45	8
C4	"	6c red & maroon	60	8
C5	"	9c gray & maroon	60	8
C6	"	10c red violet & maroon	75	8
C7	"	13c dark blue & maroon	75	22
C8	"	1k silver, violet & bistre brown	2.25	45
C9	"	26c dark green & maroon	2.25	30
C10	"	2k silver, dark green & bistre brown	3.00	2.25
C11	"	3k silver, gray & bistre brown	4.50	2.25
C12	"	4k silver, blue & bistre brown	7.50	3.75
C13	"	5k gold, brown & bistre brown	7.50	5.25
C14	"	10k gold, orange & bistre brown	110.00	90.00
C15	"	20k gold, olive grn. & bis. brn.	100.00	85.00
C16	"	30k gold, carmine & bistre brown	100.00	100.00
		Nos. C1-C16 (16)	340.75	290.02

Counterfeit overprints are plentiful. They are found on Nos. 448-463, perf. 12½x12 instead of 11½.

Nos. C1-C16 exist without overprint. Price, set $500.

AP1

AP2

AP3

AP4

AP5

Airplane, Value and "Poste aérien Surcharged on Revenue Stamps

1928 *Perf. 11.*

No.	Type	Description	Unused	Used
C17	AP1	3k yellow brown	45.00	30.00
C18	AP2	5k dark brown	5.25	2.25
C19	AP3	1t gray violet	7.50	6.00
C20	AP4	2t olive bistre	8.00	6.75
C21	AP5	3t deep green	9.00	7.50
		Nos. C17-C21 (5)	74.75	52.50

AP6

AP7

"Poste aerienne".

1928-29

No.	Type	Description	Unused	Used
C22	AP6	1c emerald	20	5
		a. 1c yellow green	10	5
		b. Double overprint	20.00	
C23	"	2c light blue	20	5
C24	"	3c bright rose	8	5
C25	"	5c olive brown	8	5
		a. "5" omitted	150.00	75.00
		b. Horizontal pair, imperf. between	*150.00*	
C26	"	10c dark green	15	6
		a. "10" omitted	5.00	
		b. "1" inverted	5.00	
C27	AP7	1k dull violet	20	10
		a. "1" inverted	5.00	
C28	"	2k orange	40	20
		Nos. C22-C28 (7)	1.31	56

Revenue Stamps

Similar to Nos. C17 to C21, Overprinted like Nos. C22 to C28: "Poste aerienne".

1929

No.	Type	Description	Unused	Used
C29	AP1	3k yellow brown	22.50	7.50
C30	AP2	5k dark brown	4.50	1.50
C31	AP3	10k violet	7.50	5.50
C32	AP4	20k olive green	9.00	4.00
C33	AP5	30k deep green	9.00	4.00
		Nos. C29-C33 (5)	52.50	22.50

Riza Shah Pahlavi and Eagle AP8

1930, July 6 Photo. ***Perf. 12½x11½***

No.	Type	Description	Unused	Used
C34	AP8	1c olive bistre & bright blue	10	10
C35	"	2c blue & gray black	10	10
C36	"	3c olive green & dark violet	10	10
C37	"	4c dark violet & peacock blue	10	10
C38	"	5c light green & magenta	10	10
C39	"	6c magenta & blue green	10	10
C40	"	8c dark gray & deep violet	10	10
C41	"	10c deep ultramarine & vermilion	10	10
C42	"	12c slate & orange	20	10
C43	"	15c orange brown & olive green	40	20
C44	"	1k Prussian blue & scarlet	80	40

Engraved

No.	Type	Description	Unused	Used
C45	AP8	2k black & ultra.	60	60
C46	"	3k dark brown & gray green	80	80
C47	"	5k deep red & gray black	1.35	1.00
C48	"	1t orange & violet	4.00	3.00
C49	"	2t dark green & red brown	3.00	3.00
C50	"	3t brown violet & slate blue	27.50	20.00
		Nos. C34-C50 (17)	39.45	29.90

Same Overprinted in Black

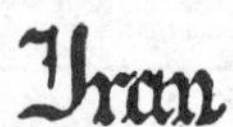

1935 Photogravure

No.	Type	Description	Unused	Used
C51	AP8	1c olive bistre & bright blue	10	10
C52	"	2c blue & gray black	20	10
C53	"	3c olive green & dark violet	10	10
C54	"	4c dark violet & peacock blue	10	10
C55	"	5c light green & magenta	10	10
C56	"	6c magenta & blue green	10	10
C57	"	8c dark gray & deep violet	20	10
C58	"	10c deep ultramarine & vermilion	30	10
C59	"	12c slate & orange	30	10
C60	"	15c orange brown & olive green	50	10
C61	"	1k Prussian blue & scarlet	7.50	1.25

Engraved

No.	Type	Description	Unused	Used
C62	AP8	2k black & ultra.	1.00	85
C63	"	3k dark brown & gray green	3.00	2.50
C64	"	5k deep red & gray black	2.00	1.00
C65	"	1t orange & violet	30.00	20.00
C66	"	2t dark green & red brown	5.00	2.00
C67	"	3t brown violet & slate blue	5.00	2.50
		Nos. C51-C67 (17)	55.50	31.10

Plane Over Mt. Demavend AP9

Plane above Mosque—AP10

Photogravure.

1953, Jan. 21 ***Perf. 11*** **Unwmkd.**

No.	Type	Description	Unused	Used
C68	AP9	50d blue green	8	3
C69	AP10	1r carmine rose	15	3
C70	"	2r dark blue	15	6
C71	"	3r dark brown	15	6
C72	"	5r purple	25	6
C73	"	10r orange vermilion	75	10
C74	"	20r violet blue	1.25	17
C75	"	30r olive	2.50	25
C76	"	50r brown	4.00	40
C77	"	100r black brown	18.50	3.00
C78	"	200r dark blue green	12.00	3.00
		Nos. C68-C78 (11)	39.78	7.16

AP11

Golden Dome Mosque and Oil Well AP12

1953, May 4 Litho. ***Perf. 10½***

Mosque in Deep Yellow.

No.	Type	Description	Unused	Used
C79	AP11	3r violet	3.75	2.25
C80	AP12	5r chocolate	11.50	3.75
C81	AP11	10r blue green	15.00	7.50
C82	AP12	20r red violet	75.00	20.00

Discovery of oil at Qum.

Globe and U.N. Emblem—AP13

Perf. 10½x12½

1957, Oct. 24 Photo. Wmk. 316

No.	Type	Description	Unused	Used
C83	AP13	10r bright red lilac & rose	2.00	1.00
C84	"	20r dull violet & rose violet	3.00	1.65

United Nations Day, Oct. 24, 1957.

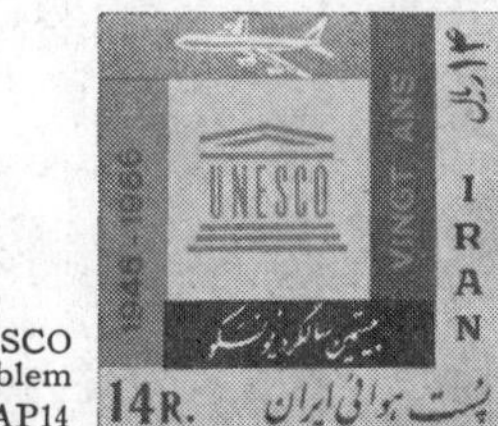

UNESCO Emblem AP14

Lithographed

1966, June 20 ***Perf. 10½*** **Wmk. 353**

No.	Type	Description	Unused	Used
C85	AP14	14r multicolored	55	15

20th anniversary of UNESCO.

No. B36 Surcharged in Maroon, Brown or Red

1969, Dec. 4 ***Perf. 10½*** **Wmk. 316**

No.	Type	Description	Unused	Used
C86	SP20	4r on 14r+6r multi. (M)	40	12
C87	"	10r on 14r+6r " (B)	70	15
C88	"	14r on 14r+6r " (R)	90	15

Issued to commemorate the 50th anniversary of the first England-Australia flight, made by Capt. Ross Smith and Lt. Keith Smith.

IATA Emblem and Persepolis AP15

Wmk. 353

1970, Oct. 27 Photo. ***Perf. 13x13½***

No.	Type	Description	Unused	Used
C89	AP15	14r multicolored	3.00	25

Issued to commemorate the 26th meeting of the International Air Transport Association (IATA), Tehran.

"UIT" AP16

1972, May 17 Litho. ***Perf. 10½***

No.	Type	Description	Unused	Used
C90	AP16	14r multicolored	1.60	25

4th World Telecommunications Day.

Shah and Jet AP17

Photogravure

1974, June 1 ***Perf. 13*** **Wmk. 353**

No.	Type	Description	Unused	Used
C91	AP17	4r orange & black	14	8
C92	"	10r blue & black	40	10
C93	"	12r dull yel. & black	50	14
C94	"	14r lt. grn. & black	55	18
C95	"	20r red lilac & black	80	20
C96	"	50r dull bl. & black	2.00	50
		Nos. C91-C96 (6)	4.39	1.20

Crown Prince at Controls of Light Aircraft—AP18

1974, Oct. 31 Litho. *Perf. 10½*

C97 AP18 14r gold & multi. 55 18

Crown Prince Riza's 14th birthday.

OFFICIAL STAMPS.

Four bicolored stamps of this design (1s, 2s, 5s, 10s), with centers embossed, exist, but were never issued or used in Iran. They are known imperforate and in many trial colors.

Shah Muzaffar-ed-Din
O1

No. 145 Surcharged in Black

1902 *Perf. 12½.*

O5 O1 5c on 1k red 1.50 75
O6 " 10c on 1k red 1.50 75
O7 " 12c on 1k red 3.00 1.50

Nos. 351–363 Overprinted in Black **Service**

1903–06

O8 A26 1c violet 3 3
O9 " 2c gray 5 3
O10 " 3c green 5 3
O11 " 5c rose 5 3
O12 " 10c yellow brown 22 3
O13 " 12c blue 45 3

Perf. 11½x11.

O14 A27 1k violet 60 3
O15 " 2k ultramarine 75 8
a. Violet overprint 4.50 3.00
O16 A27 5k orange brown 1.50 30
O17 " 10k rose red 1.50 60
a. Violet overprint 12.00
O18 A27 20k orange ('06) 2.25 1.25
O19 " 30k green ('06) 3.75 1.50
O20 " 50k green 25.00 11.00
Nos. O8–O20 (13) 36.20 14.94

Overprinted on Nos. 368, 370a

O21 A27 2t on 50k grn.(Bl) 30.00 22.50
O22 " 3t on 50k green(V) 30.00 22.50

Overprinted on Nos. 372, 375, New Value Surcharged in Blue or Black

1905

O23 A27 2t on 50k grn.(Bl) 30.00 22.50
O28 " 3t on 50k grn.(Bk) 30.00 22.50

The 2t on 50k also exists with surcharge in black and magenta; the 3t on 50k in violet and magenta. Prices about the same.

Regular Issue of 1909 Overprinted **Service**

There is a space between the word "Service" and the Turkish characters.

1911 *Perf. 12½x12.*

O31 A31 1c orange & maroon 1.50 8
O32 " 2c violet & maroon 1.50 8
O33 " 3c yellow green & maroon 1.50 8
O34 " 6c red & maroon 1.50 8
O35 " 9c gray & maroon 1.50 8
O36 A31 10c multicolored 1.50 15
O38 " 1k " 6.00 22
O40 " 2k " 15.00 3.75
Nos. O31–O40 (8) 30.00 4.52

The 13c, 26c and 3k to 30k denominations were not regularly issued with this overprint.

Counterfeits exist.

Regular Issue of 1915 Overprinted **SERVICE**

Wmkd. Lion. (161)

1915 *Perf. 11, 11½.*

O41 A33 1c carmine & indigo 6 3
O42 " 2c blue & carmine 6 3
O43 " 3c dark green 6 3
O44 " 5c red 6 3
O45 " 6c olive grn. & car. 6 3
O46 " 9c yel. brown & violet 6 3
O47 " 10c multicolored 8 3
O48 " 12c ultramarine 8 8
O49 A34 1k multicolored 8 8
O50 A33 24c " 8 8
O51 A34 2k silver, blue & rose 30 22
O52 " 3k silver, vio. & brown 30 22
O53 " 5k multicolored 30 22
O54 A35 1t gold, purple & black 30 30
O55 " 2t gold, grn. & brn. 60 50
O56 " 3t multicolored 90 45
O57 " 5t gold, bl. & indigo 1.25 85
Nos. O41–O57 (17) 4.63 3.21

Coronation of Shah Ahmed.

Coat of Arms
O2 O3

Lithographed.

1941 *Perf. 11* Unwmkd.

For Internal Postage.

O58 O2 5d violet 8 3
O59 " 10d magenta 15 3
O60 " 25d carmine 15 3
O61 " 50d brown black 15 3
O62 " 75d claret 30 3

Size: 22½x30mm.

O63 O2 1r peacock green 75 3
O64 " 1½r deep blue 3.00 3
O65 " 2r light blue 4.50 3
O66 " 3r violet brown 6.00 3
O67 " 5r gray green 15.00 6
O68 " 10r dk. brn. & blue 57.50 20
O69 " 20r chalky blue & bright pink 110.00 1.00
O70 " 30r vio. & brt.grn. 165.00 1.75
O71 " 50r turquoise green & dk. brown 200.00 12.00
Nos. O58–O71 (14) 562.58 15.38

Perf. 13½x13

1974, Feb. 25 Photo. Wmk. 353

Size: 20x28mm.

O72 O3 5d violet & lilac 3 3
O73 " 10d magenta & greenish blue 3 3
O74 " 50d org. & lt. green 3 3
O75 " 1r green & gold 4 3
O76 " 2r emerald & orange 7 3

Perf. 13

Size: 23x37mm.

O77 O3 6r slate grn. & org. 20 5
O78 " 8r ultra. & yellow 28 5
O79 " 10r dark blue & lilac 35 6
O80 " 11r purple & lt. blue 40 7
O81 " 14r red & lt. ultra. 45 13
O82 " 20r vio. blue & orange 70 20
O83 " 50r dark brown & bright green 1.25 50
Nos. O72–O83 (12) 3.83 1.21

Perf. 13½x13

1977–78 Photo. Wmk. 353

Size: 20x28mm

O87 O3 1r blk. & lt. green 4 3
O88 " 2r brown & gray 8 4
O89 " 3r ultra. & orange 10 6
O90 " 5r green & rose 15 5

Perf. 13

Size: 23x37mm.

O91 O3 6r dark blue & lt. blue ('78) 20 12
O92 " 8r red & blue green ('78) 25 15
O93 " 10r dark green & yellow green 30 6
O94 " 15r bl. & rose lilac ('78) 45 8
O95 " 20r purple & yellow 60 10
O96 " 30r brn. & ocher ('78) 90 20
O97 " 50r black & gold ('78) 1.50 75
Nos. O87–O97 (11) 5.37 1.64

NEWSPAPER STAMP.

No. 429 Overprinted *Imprimés*

1909 *Perf. 12½* Unwmkd.

P1 A26 2c gray, *blue* 60 15

PARCEL POST STAMPS.

Colis Postaux

Colis Postaux

Regular issues of 1907–08 (types A26, A29) with the handstamps above in blue, black or green are of questionable status as issued stamps.

Regular Issue of 1915 Overprinted in Black **COLIS POSTAUX**

Wmkd. Lion. (161)

1915 *Perf. 11, 11½.*

Q19 A33 1c carmine & indigo 4 3
Q20 " 2c blue & carmine 4 3
Q21 " 3c dark green 4 3
Q22 " 5c red 4 3
Q23 " 6c olive green & carmine 4 3
Q24 " 9c yel. brn. & violet 4 3
Q25 " 10c blue green & yellow brown 5 3
Q26 " 12c ultramarine 5 3
Q27 A34 1k multicolored 20 15
Q28 A33 24c " 6 15
Q29 A34 2k " 20 15
Q30 " 3k " 20 15
Q31 " 5k " 20 15
Q32 A35 1t " 30 20
Q33 " 2t gold, grn. & brn. 40 20
Q34 " 3t multicolored 60 20
Q35 " 5t " 80 40
Nos. Q19–Q35 (17) 3.30 1.99

Coronation of Shah Ahmed.

Post Horn
PP1

Black frame and "IRAN" (reversed) are printed on back of Nos. Q36–Q65, to show through when stamp is attached to parcel.

Typographed.

1958 *Perf. 12½* Wmk. 306

Q36 PP1 50d olive bistre 3 3
Q37 " 1r carmine 4 3
Q38 " 2r blue 10 4
a. Imperf., pair 15.00
Q39 " 3r green 10 3
Q40 " 5r purple 40 3
Q41 " 10r orange brown 75 4
Q42 " 20r deep orange 1.00 4
Q43 " 30r lilac 1.65 25
Q44 " 50r dark carmine 2.00 30
Q45 " 100r yellow 4.00 40
Q46 " 200r light green 6.00 80
Nos. Q36–Q46 (11) 16.07 1.99

1961–66 Wmk. 316

Q51 PP1 5r purple ('66) 25 10
Q52 " 10r org. brown('62) 60 20
Q53 " 20r orange 1.10 40
Q54 " 30r red lilac ('63) 1.65 60
Q55 " 50r dk. car. ('63) 2.00 1.00
Q56 " 100r yellow ('64) 7.00 2.00
Q57 " 200r emerald ('64) 8.00 4.00
Nos. Q51–Q57 (7) 20.60 8.30

1967–74 Wmk. 353

Q58 PP1 2r blue ('74) 8 4
Q59 " 5r dk. pur. ('69) 20 10
Q60 " 10r orange brown 40 20
Q61 " 20r orange ('69) 60 40
Q62 " 30r red lilac 80 20
Q63 " 50r red brown ('68) 1.25 1.00
Q64 " 100r yellow 2.50 1.25
Q65 " 200r emerald ('69) 6.00 4.00
Nos. Q58–Q65 (8) 11.83 7.19

POSTAL TAX STAMPS

Red Lion and Sun Emblem
PT1

Lithographed.

1950 *Perf. 11* Unwmkd.

RA1 PT1 50d grn. & car. rose 1.20 10
RA2 " 2r violet & lilac rose 50 10

1955 Wmk. 306

RA3 PT1 50d emerald & car. rose 2.40 20

1957–58 Wmk. 316

RA4 PT1 50d emerald & rose lilac 20 30
RA5 " 2r violet & carmine rose ('58) 60 30

1965 *Perf. 10½* Wmk. 349

RA6 PT1 50d emerald & car. rose ('65) 40 4
RA7 " 2r violet & lilac rose ('65) 50 10

1965–66 Wmk. 353

RA8 PT1 50d emerald & carmine rose 4 4
RA9 " 2r violet & carmine rose ('66) 20 5

No. RA8 was printed in two types: I. Without diagonal line before Persian "50." II. With line.

1976, Sept. Photo. *Perf. 13x13½*

RA10 PT1 50d emerald & red 4 4

No. RA10 is redrawn and has vertical watermark.

Nos. RA1–RA10 were obligatory on all mail. The tax was for hospitals.

The 2.25r and 2.50r of type PT1 were used only on telegrams.

BUSHIRE

Stamps issued under British occupation are listed under "Bushire" in Volume I.

ISRAEL

(ĭz′râ-ĕl ; -rī-ĕl)

LOCATION—In western Asia bordering on the Mediterranean Sea.

GOVT.—Republic.

AREA—7,993 sq. mi.

POP.—3,610,000 (est. 1977).

CAPITAL—Jerusalem.

When the British mandate of Palestine ended in May, 1948, the Jewish state of Israel was proclaimed by the Jewish National Council in Palestine.

1000 Mils = 1 Pound
1000 Prutot = 1 Pound (1949)
100 Agorot = 1 Pound (1960)

Tabs

Stamps of Israel are printed in sheets with tabs (labels) usually attached below the bottom row, sometimes at the sides. Stamps with tab attached are priced by issue or separately through No. 86. From No. 87 onward, stamps with tab attached sell for 10 to 100 per cent higher prices than those quoted, except where noted otherwise.

Tabs of the following numbers are in two parts, perforated between: 9, 15, 23–37, 44, 46–47, 50, 55, 62–65, 70–72, 74–77, 86–91, 94–99, 104–118, 123–126, 133–136B, 138–141, 143–151, 160–161, 165–167, 178–179, 182, 187–189, 203, 211–213, 222–223, 228–237, 243–244, 246–250, 256–258, 269–270, 272–273, 275, 294–295, 312, 337–339, 341–344, 346–347, 353–354, C1–C13, C22–C30.

Ancient Judean Coins
A1 A2

Designs: Nos. 1–6, Various coins.

Perf. 10, 11 and Compound.

1948, May 16 Typo. Unwmkd.

1 A1 3m orange 60 25
a. Rouletted 1.00 30
2 " 5m yellow green 60 10
a. Booklet pane of 6 15.00
b. Rouletted 3.00 50
3 " 10m red violet 1.10 12
a. Booklet pane of 6 20.00
b. Rouletted 7.00 1.50
4 " 15m red 1.75 15
a. Booklet pane of 6 22.50
5 " 20m bright ultra. 4.00 18
a. Booklet pane of 6 25.00
6 " 50m orange brown 8.25 30
Nos. 1–6 (6) 16.30 1.10
Nos. 1–6, with tabs 325.00
Nos. 1a, 2b, 3b with tabs 425.00

Size: 34½x22mm.

7 A2 250m dark slate green 70.00 30.00
8 " 500m red brown, *cream* 275.00 125.00

Size: 36½x24mm.

9 A2 1000m black blue, *pale blue* 300.00 200.00
Nos. 7–9 (3) 645.00 355.00
Nos. 7–9, with tabs *7000.00*
Nos. 1–9 exist imperf

Flying Scroll
A3

1948, Sept. 26 Litho. *Perf. 11½*

10 A3 3m brn. red & ultra. 75 30
11 " 5m dull grn. & ultra. 1.25 40
12 " 10m dp. car. & ultra. 1.50 65
13 " 20m dp. ultra. & ultra. 3.00 1.15
14 " 65m brown & red 18.50 6.00
Nos. 10–14 (5) 25.00 8.50
With tabs 300.00

Jewish New Year, 5709.

Flag of Israel
A4

1949, Mar. 31

15 A4 20(m) bright blue 1.75 50
With tab 85.00

Issued to commemorate the appointment of the government by the Knesset.

Souvenir Sheet.

A5

1949, May 1 *Imperf.*

16 A5 Sheet of four 165.00 45.00
a. 10(m) dark carmine rose 22.50 6.00

Issued in sheets measuring 75½ x 95 mm., to commemorate the first anniversary of the inauguration of Israeli postage stamps.

The sheet was sold at "TABUL," First National Stamp Exhibition, in Tel Aviv, May 1-6, 1949. Tickets, costing 100 mils, covered the entrance fee and one sheet.

Bronze Half-Shekel of 67 A.D.
A6

Hebrew University, Jerusalem
A7

Approach to Jerusalem
A8

"The Negev" by Reuven Rubin
A9

1949–50 *Perf. 11½, 14* Unwmkd.

17 A6 3(p) gray black 30 20
18 " 5(p) purple 15 5
a. Booklet pane of 6
19 " 10(p) green 18 5
a. Booklet pane of 6
20 " 15(p) deep rose 25 5
a. Booklet pane of 6
21 " 30(p) dark blue 35 5
a. Booklet pane of 6
22 " 50(p) brown 1.25 30
23 A7 100(p) Pruss. grn. ('50) 60 20
With tab 35.00
24 A8 250(p) orange brown & gray 1.75 1.25
With tab 60.00
25 A9 500(p) deep orange & brown ('50) 11.00 9.00
With tab 300.00
Nos. 17–25 (9) 15.83 11.15
Nos. 17–22 with tabs (6) 125.00
Tête bêche pairs, Nos. 18–21 60.00 60.00

Each of Nos. 17–22 portrays a different coin. For other stamps of coin design, see Nos. 38–43, 56–61, 80–83.

No. 23 was issued to commemorate the 25th anniversary of the Hebrew University in Jerusalem.

Well at Petah Tikva
A10

1949, Aug. 10 *Perf. 11*

27 A10 40(p) dark green & brown 11.00 85
With tab 100.00

Issued to commemorate the 70th anniversary of the founding of Petah Tikva.

Arms and Service Insignia: Air Force
A11

1949, Sept. 20 *Perf. 11½*

28 A11 5(p) dark blue 85 25
29 " 10(p) dull green (*Navy*) 1.65 40
30 " 35(p) dull reddish brown (*Army*) 8.50 2.50
With tabs 725.00

Jewish New Year, 5710.

Running Stag
A12

1950, Mar. 26

31 A12 40(p) purple 1.25 75
a. Booklet pane of 4 5.25
32 " 80(p) rose red 1.25 1.00
a. Booklet pane of 4 10.50
b. Nos. 31 and 32 tête bêche 35.00 27.50
With tabs 160.00

Issued to commemorate the 75th anniversary (in 1949) of the formation of the Universal Postal Union.

Struggle for Free Immigration
A13

Arrival of Immigrants
A14

1950, Apr. 23

33 A13 20(p) dull brown 5.00 2.50
34 A14 40(p) dull green 8.00 6.00
With tabs 625.00

Issued to publicize Independence Day, April 22, 1950.

Fruit and Star of David
A15

1950, Aug. 31 Litho. *Perf. 14*

35 A15 5p violet blue & orange 35 20
36 " 15p red brn. & green 1.10 75
With tabs 80.00

Jewish New Year, 5711.

Runner and Track
A16

1950, Oct. 1

37 A16 80p olive & slate black 3.50 2.25
With tab 90.00

3rd Maccabiah, Ramat Gan, Sept. 27, 1950.

Coin Type of 1949 Redrawn

Designs: Various coins.

1950

38 A6 3p gray black 8 8
39 " 5p purple 5 5
a. Tête bêche pair 1.50 1.50
b. Booklet pane of 6 35
40 " 10p green 5 5
a. Tête bêche pair 60 50
b. Booklet pane of 6 60
41 " 15p deep rose 5 5
a. Tête bêche pair 1.00 90
42 " 30p dark blue 5 5
a. Tête bêche pair 2.00 2.00
b. Booklet pane of 6 1.25
43 " 50p brown 10 10
Nos. 38–43 (6) 38 38
With tabs 4.25

Inscription at left measures 11 mm. on Nos. 38–43; 9mm. on Nos. 17–22.

Detail from Tablet, "Founding of Tel Aviv"—A17

1951, Mar. 22

44 A17 40p dark brown 75 50
With tab 40.00

40th anniversary of Tel Aviv.

Young Man Holding Outline Map of Israel
A18

1951, Apr. 30 **Lithographed**

45 A18 80p red brown 25 28
With tab 7.50

Issued to promote the sale of Independence Bonds.

Metsudat Yesha
A19

Hakastel
A20

1951, May 9 **Unwmkd.**

46 A19 15p red brown 30 15
47 A20 40p deep blue 1.25 65
With tabs 85.00

3rd anniversary of proclamation of State of Israel.

Tractor and Wheat A21 — Tree A22

Plower and National Fund Stamp of 1902
A23

1951, June 24 *Perf. 14*

48 A21 15p red brown 18 15
49 A22 25p Prussian green 20 15
50 A23 80p dull blue 1.75 1.50
With tabs 150.00

Jewish National Fund, 50th anniversary.

Theodor Zeev Herzl A24 — Carrier Pigeons A25

1951, Aug. 14

51 A24 80p gray green 35 35
With tab 8.25

23rd Zionist Congress, Jerusalem.

1951, Sept. 16

Designs: 15(p), Girl holding dove and fruit. 40(p), Scrolls of the law.

52 A25 5(p) blue 10 8
53 " 15(p) cerise 10 8
54 " 40(p) rose violet 20 18
With tabs 6.50

Jewish New Year, 5712.

Menorah and Emblems of Twelve Tribes
A26

1952, Feb. 27

55 A26 1000p dark blue & gray 17.50 8.00
With tab 300.00

Redrawn Coin Type of 1950.

1952, Mar. 30 **Various Coins**

56 A6 20p orange 10 3
a. Tête bêche pair 1.25 1.25
57 " 35p olive green 10 10
58 " 40p orange brown 10 3
59 " 45p red violet 12 6
a. Tête bêche pair 2.75 2.75
60 " 60p carmine 10 3
61 " 85p aquamarine 40 12
Nos. 56-61 (6) 92 37
With tabs 15.00

Thistle and Yad Mordecai Battlefield
A27

Battlefields: 60p, Cornflower and Deganya. 110p, Anemone and Safed.

1952, Apr. 29

62 A27 30p lilac rose & violet brown 15 10
63 " 60p ultra. & gray blk. 25 20
64 " 110p crimson & gray 75 50
With tabs 40.00

Issued for the 4th anniversary of the proclamation of the State of Israel.

Manhattan Skyline and American Zionists' House—A28

1952, May 13

65 A28 220p dark blue & gray 1.25 90
With tab 25.00

Opening of American Zionists' House, Tel Aviv.

Figs
A29

Designs: 40p, Lily. 110p, Dove. 220p, Nut cluster.

Perf. 14

1952, Sept. 3 **Litho.** **Unwmkd.**

66 A29 15p dark green & yellow 12 10
67 " 40p purple, blue & yellow 20 20
68 " 110p carmine & gray 55 60
69 " 220p orange yellow, dark brown & green 1.00 80
Nos. 66-69 (4) 1.87 1.70
With tabs 40.00

Jewish New Year, 5713.

Chaim Weizmann and Presidential Standard—A30

1952, Dec. 9

70 A30 30p slate 12 10
71 " 110p black 60 40
With tabs 20.00

Dr. Chaim Weizmann (1874–1952), president of Israel, 1948–1952.

Numeral Incorporating Agricultural Scenes—A31

1952, Dec. 31

72 A31 110p brown, buff & emerald 40 30
With tab 21.00

70th anniversary of B.I.L.U. (Bet Yaakov Lechu Venelcha) immigration.

Five Anemones and State Emblem
A32

1953, Apr. 19

73 A32 110p greenish blue, blue black & red 40 30
With tab 7.00

5th anniversary of State of Israel.

Rabbi Moshe ben Maimon (Maimonides) A33 — Holy Ark, Jerusalem A34

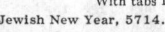

Wmk. 301

Watermarked ISRAEL in Hebrew Characters. (301)

1953, Aug. 3 *Perf. 14x13*

74 A33 110p brown 25 20
With tab 2.50

7th International Congress of History of Science, Jerusalem, Aug. 4–11.

1953, Aug. 11

Holy Arks: 45p, Petah Tikva. 200p, Safed.

75 A34 20p sapphire 6 4
76 " 45p brown red 8 6
77 " 200p purple 20 20
With tabs 10.00

Jewish New Year, 5714.

Combined Ball-Globe A35 — Desert Rose A36

Perf. 14

1953, Sept. 20 **Litho.** **Unwmkd.**

78 A35 110p blue & dark brown 30 25
With tab 7.00

4th Maccabiah, Sept. 20–29, 1953.

1953, Sept. 22

79 A36 200p multicolored 30 25
With tab 8.00

Conquest of the Desert Exhibition, Sept. 22–Oct. 14.

Redrawn Type of 1950.

1954, Jan. 5 Various Coins

80 A6 80p olive bistre 8 6
81 " 95p blue green 8 6
82 " 100p fawn 8 5
83 " 125p violet blue 18 12
Nos. 80-83 (4) 42 29
With tabs 3.50

Marigold and Ruins at Yehiam
A37

Design: 350p, Narcissus and bridge at Gesher.

1954, May 5 Lithographed

84 A37 60p dark blue, magenta & olive gray 10 10
85 " 350p dark brown, green & yellow 40 35
With tabs 3.50

Memorial Day and 6th anniversary of proclamation of State of Israel.

Theodor Zeev Herzl
A38

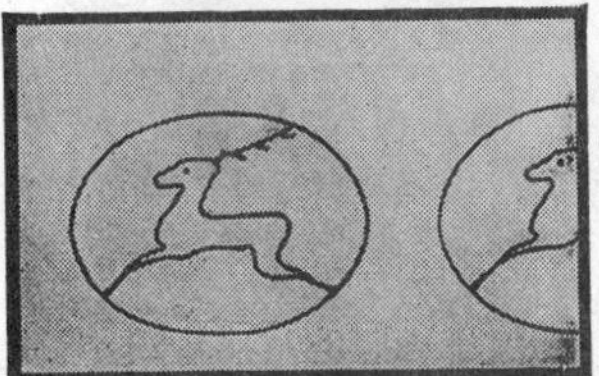

Wmk. 302

Wmkd. Multiple Stag. (302)

1954, July 21

86 A38 160p dark blue, dark brown & cream 18 12
With tab 1.35

Theodor Zeev Herzl (1860–1904), founder of Zionist movement.

Bearers with Grape Cluster—A39

1954, Sept. 8 *Perf. 13x14*

87 A39 25p dark brown 8 8

Jewish New Year, 5715.

19th Century Mail Coach and Jerusalem Post Office—A40

Design: 200p, Mail truck and present G.P.O., Jerusalem.

1954, Oct. 13 *Perf. 14*

88 A40 60p blue, blk. & yel. 12 12
89 " 200p dark green, black & red 25 20
With tabs 6.00

TABIM, National Stamp Exhibition, Jerusalem, Oct. 13–18.

Baron Edmond de Rothschild and Grape Cluster—A41

1954, Nov. 23 *Perf. 13x14*

90 A41 300p dark blue green 25 20
With tab 1.10

Baron Edmond de Rothschild (1845–1934).

Lighted Oil Lamp—A42

1955, Jan. 13 *Perf. 13x14*

91 A42 250p dark blue 22 15
With tab 1.10

Teachers' Association, 50th anniversary.

Parachutist and Barbed Wire
A43

Lighted Menorah
A44

1955, Mar. 31 Litho. *Perf. 14*

92 A43 120p dark Prus. green 18 18
With tab 60

Jewish volunteers from Palestine who served in British army in World War II.

1955, Apr. 26

93 A44 150p dark green, black & orange 18 18
With tab 65

7th anniversary of proclamation of State of Israel.

Immigration by Ship
A45

Designs: 10p, Immigration by plane. 25p, Agricultural training. 30p, Gardening. 60p, Vocational training. 750p, Scientific education.

1955, May 10 *Perf. 14* Unwmkd.

94 A45 5p bright blue & black 3 3
95 " 10p red & black 3 3
96 " 25p deep green & black 3 3
97 " 30p orange & black 4 4
98 " 60p lilac rose & black 6 6
99 A45 750p olive bistre & blk. 50 40
With tab 2.75
Nos. 94-99 (6) 69 59

20th anniversary of Israel's Youth Immigration Institution.

Musicians with Tambourine and Cymbals
A46

Musician with: 60p, Ram's Horn. 120p, Loud Trumpet. 250p, Harp.

1955, Aug. 25 Photo. **Wmk. 302**

100 A46 25p dark green & orange 6 4

Unwmkd.

101 A46 60p dark gray & orange 8 8
102 " 120p dark blue & yellow 10 10
103 " 250p red brown & orange 12 12

Jewish New Year, 5716.
See Nos. 121–122.

Ambulance—A47

1955, Nov. 1 *Perf. 14* **Wmk. 301**

104 A47 160p green, red & black 15 10

25th anniversary of Magen David Adom (Israeli Red Cross).

Twelve Tribes Issue.

Mandrake, Reuben
A48

Designs: 20p, Gates of Sechem, Simeon. 30p, Ephod, Levi. 40p, Lion, Judah. 50p, Scales, Dan. 60p, Stag, Naphtali. 80p, Tents, Gad. 100p, Tree, Asher. 120p, Sun and stars, Issachar. 180p, Ship, Zebulon. 200p, Sheaf of wheat, Joseph. 250p, Wolf, Benjamin.

1955-57 *Perf. 13x14.* **Wmk. 302**

105 A48 10p bright green 3 3
106 " 20p red lilac ('56) 3 3
107 " 30p bright ultramarine 5 3
108 " 40p brown ('56) 4 3
109 " 50p greenish blue ('56) 5 3
110 " 60p lemon 6 3
111 " 80p deep violet ('56) 8 3
a. Bklt. pane of 6 75
112 " 100p vermilion 8 4
a. Bklt. pane 6 ('57) 1.20
113 " 120p olive ('56) 10 4
114 " 180p lilac rose ('56) 12 5
115 " 200p green ('56) 12 7
116 " 250p gray ('56) 15 9
Nos. 105-116 (12) 91 50
With tabs 2.50

See also Nos. 133–136B.

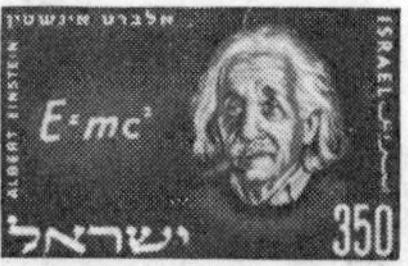

Albert Einstein and Equation of his Relativity Theory—A49

1956, Jan. 3 *Perf. 13x14*

117 A49 350p brown 40 35
With tab 1.00

Albert Einstein (1879–1955), German-born American theoretical physicist.

Technion, Haifa—A50

1956, Jan. 3 **Wmk. 302**

118 A50 350p light olive green & black 25 20

Israel Institute of Technology, 30th anniversary.

"Eight Years of Israel"
A51

Jaffa Oranges
A52

1956, Apr. 12 Litho. *Perf. 14*

119 A51 150p multicolored 10 10

8th anniversary of proclamation of State of Israel.

1956, May 20 *Perf. 14* **Wmk. 302**

120 A52 300p blue green & orange 20 15

4th International Congress of Mediterranean Citrus Growers.

New Year Type of 1955 and

Musician with Double Oboe—A53

Musician with: 30p, Lyre. 50p, Cymbals.

1956, Aug. 14 Photo. *Perf. 14x13*

121 A46 30p brn. & brt. blue 5 5

Perf. 14

122 A46 50p purple & orange 5 5
123 A53 150p dark blue green & orange 10 8
With tabs 50

Jewish New Year, 5717.

Haganah Insignia
A54

Bezalel Museum and Antique Lamp
A55

Defense Issue.

1957, Jan. 1 *Perf. 13x14*

124 A54 20p+80p bright green 10 5
125 " 50p+150p carmine rose 12 6
126 " 50p+350p ultramarine 25 10

Divided denomination used to show increased postal rate.

1957, Apr. 29 Litho. *Perf. 14*

127 A55 400p multicolored 20 8

Bezalel National Museum, Jerusalem, 50th anniversary.

Jet Plane and "9" A56

Horse and Seal A57

1957, Apr. 29

128 A56 250p deep blue & black 15 3

9th anniversary of proclamation of State of Israel.

1957, Sept. 4 *Perf. 14* Wmk. 302

Ancient Seals: 160p, Lion. 300p, Gazelle.

129 A57 50p ochre & black, *light blue* 5 3

***Perf. 14x13* Photo. Unwmkd.**

130 A57 160p green & black, *bistre brown* 8 3
131 " 300p deep carmine & black, *pink* 15 6

Jewish New Year, 5718.

TABIL Souvenir Sheet

Bet Alpha Synagogue Mosaic A58

1957, Sept. 17 Litho. *Roulette 13*

132 A58 Sheet of four 75 50
a. 100p multicolored 15 10
b. 200p " 15 10
c. 300p " 15 10
d. 400p " 15 10

Issued to publicize the First Israel International Stamp exhibition, Tel Aviv, Sept. 17–23. Sheet measures 103x105mm.

Tribes Type of 1955–57.

Photogravure.

1957–59 *Perf. 13x14* Unwmkd.

133 A48 10p bright green ('58) 10 5
133A " 20p red lilac 10 10
133C " 40p brown ('59) 2.75 1.35
134 " 50p greenish blue 15 12
a. Booklet pane of 6 1.50 ('58)
135 " 60p lemon 15 12
136 " 100p vermilion 25 15
a. Booklet pane of 6 2.50 ('58)
136B " 120p olive ('58) 60 25
Nos. 133-136B (7) 4.10 2.14
With tabs 55.00

Hammer Thrower A59

1958, Jan. 20 *Perf. 14x13*

137 A59 500p bistre & carmine 30 25

Maccabiah Games, 25th anniversary.

Ancient Ship—A60

Ships: 20p, Three-master used for "illegal immigration." 30p, Cargo ship "Shomron." 1000p, Passenger ship "Zion."

Lithographed.

1958, Jan. 27 *Perf. 14* Wmk. 302

Size: 36½x22½mm.

138 A60 10p ochre, red & black 4 4

Photogravure.

Perf. 13x14.

139 A60 20p bright green, black & brown 4 4
140 " 30p red, black & greenish blue 4 4

Size: 56½x22½mm.

141 A60 1000p bright blue, black & green 65 65

Issued to honor Israel's merchant fleet.

Menorah and Olive Branch A61

Lithographed.

1958, Apr. 21 *Perf. 14* Unwmkd.

142 A61 400p gold, blk. & green 22 20

Memorial Day and 10th anniversary of proclamation of State of Israel.

Dancing Youths Forming "10" A62

1958, July 2

143 A62 200p dark orange & dark green 20 10

First World Conference of Jewish Youth, Jerusalem, July 28–Aug. 1.

Convention Center, Jerusalem A63

1958, July 2

144 A63 400p violet & orange, *yellow* 22 20

10th Anniversary of Independence Exhibition, Jerusalem, June 5–Aug. 21.

Wheat—A64

Designs: 60p, Barley. 160p, Grapes. 300p, Figs.

1958, Aug. 27 Photo. *Perf. 14x13*

145 A64 50p bistre & brown 5 3
146 " 60p citron & black 5 4
147 " 160p violet & red lilac 8 5
148 " 300p yellow green & dark green 12 10

Jewish New Year, 5719.

"Love Thy Neighbor . . ." A65

1958, Dec. 10 Litho. *Perf. 14*

149 A65 750p yellow, gray & green 40 35
With tab 2.50

Universal Declaration of Human Rights, 10th anniversary.

Designing and Printing Stamps A66

Radio and Telephone A67

Designs: 120p, Mobile post office. 500p, Teletype.

1959, Feb. 25 *Perf. 14* Wmk. 302

150 A66 60p olive, black & red 5 5
151 " 120p " " " 8 5
152 A67 250p " " " 15 12
153 " 500p " " " 30 20

Decade of postal activities in Israel.

Shalom Aleichem A68

Cyclamen A69

Portraits: No. 155, Chaim Nachman Bialik. No. 156, Eliezer Ben-Yehuda.

Photogravure.

1959 *Perf. 14x13* Unwmkd.

154 A68 250p yellow green & red brown 20 15
155 " 250p ochre & olive gray 22 20

Lithographed

Perf. 14

156 A68 250p blue & violet blue 25 22
With tab 60

No. 154 commemorates the centenary of the birth of Shalom Aleichem (Solomon Rabinowitz), Yiddish writer; No. 155, the 25th anniversary of the death of Chaim N. Bialik, Hebrew poet; No. 156, the centenary of the birth of Eliezer Ben-Yehuda, father of modern Hebrew.

1959, May 11 *Perf. 14* Wmk. 302

Flowers: 60p, Anemone. 300p, Narcissus.

Flowers in Natural Colors

157 A69 60p deep green 5 5
158 " 120p deep plum 10 5
159 " 300p blue 30 30

Memorial Day and 11th anniversary of proclamation of State of Israel.

Buildings, Tel Aviv A70

1959, May 4

160 A70 120p multicolored 15 10

50th anniversary of Tel Aviv.

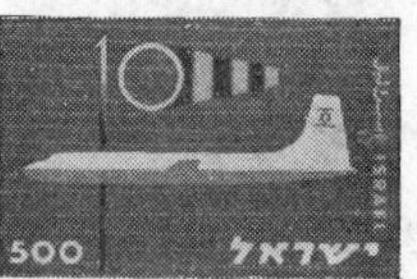

Bristol Britannia and Windsock A71

1959, July 22

161 A71 500p multicolored 35 32

Civil Aviation in Israel, 10th anniversary.

Pomegranates A72

Designs: 200p, Olives. 350p, Dates.

Perf. 14x13

1959, Sept. 9 Photo. Unwmkd.

162 A72 60p pale lilac gray, black brown & crimson 5 5
163 " 200p gray olive & olive green 8 5
164 " 350p brown & dp. org. 35 30
With tabs 1.00

Jewish New Year, 5720.

Merhavya — A73
Judean Coin (66-70 A.D.) — A74

Settlements: 120p, Yesud Ha-Maala. 180p, Deganya.

1959, Nov. 25 Photo. *Perf. 13x14*

165 A73 60p citron & dark green 6 4
166 " 120p red brown & ochre 15 6
167 " 180p blue & dark green 25 25
With tabs 3.00

50th anniversary of the settlements of Merhavya and Deganya and 75th anniversary of Yesud Ha-Maala.

Perf. 13x14

1960, Jan. 6–July 6 Unwmkd.

Denominations in Black

168 A74 1a brown, *pinkish* 3 3
a. On surface colored paper 6 5
As "a", with tab 40
b. Pair, one without black ovpt.
169 " 3a bright red, *pinkish* 3 3
170 " 5a gray, *pinkish* 3 3
171 " 6a bright green, *light blue* 3 3
171A " 7a gray, *bluish* 5 4
172 " 8a magenta, *lt. blue* 5 4
173 " 12a greenish blue, *light blue* 5 4
a. Black ovpt. omitted
174 " 18a orange 8 8
175 " 25a blue 10 8
176 " 30a carmine 18 12
177 " 50a bright lilac 35 12
Nos. 168-177 (11) 98 64
With tabs 2.25

Operation "Magic Carpet"
A75

Design: 50a, Resettled family in front of house, grapes and figs.

1960, Apr. 7 *Perf. 13x14* Unwmkd.

178 A75 25a red brown 18 18
179 " 50a green 30 30

World Refugee Year, July 1, 1959–June 30, 1960.

Sand Lily
A76

Design: 32a, Evening primrose.

1960, Apr. 27 Litho. *Perf. 14*

180 A76 12a multicolored 8 5
181 " 32a brown, yellow & green 25 20
With tabs 75

Memorial Day and 12th anniversary of proclamation of State of Israel. See Nos. 204–206, 238–240.

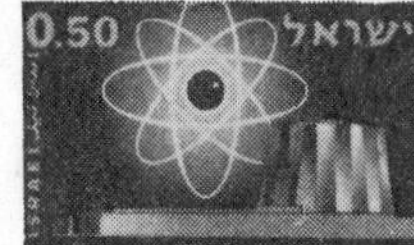

Atom Diagram and Atomic Reactor—A77

1960, July 6 *Perf. 14* Wmk. 302

182 A77 50a blue, red & black 50 50
With tab 1.00

Installation of Israel's first atomic reactor.

Theodor Herzl and Rhine at Basel — A78
King Saul — A79

1960, Aug. 31 Litho. *Perf. 14*

183 A78 25a gray brown 25 25
With tab 60

Theodor Zeev Herzl (1860–1904), founder of Zionist Movement.

1960, Aug. 31 Wmk. 302

Designs: 25a, King David. 40a, King Solomon.

Kings in Multicolor

184 A79 7a emerald 5 4

Unwmkd.

185 A79 25a brown 5 5
186 " 40a blue 55 50
Nos. 184-186 with tabs 2.00

Jewish New Year, 5721. See Nos. 208–210.

Jewish Postal Courier, Prague, 18th Century—A80

Perf. 13x14

1960, Oct. 9 Photo. Unwmkd.

187 A80 25a olive black, *gray* 50 45
With tab 4.25
a. Souvenir sheet 25.00 12.50

Issued on the occasion of the National Stamp Exhibition "TAVIV," Tel Aviv, Oct. 9–19.

No. 187a contains one stamp in lower left corner. The entire sheet shows part of a 1741 engraving of a parade. Size: 192x135mm. Sold only at Exhibition for 50a.

Henrietta Szold and Hadassah Medical Center—A81

1960, Dec. 14 *Perf. 13x14*

188 A81 25a turquoise blue & violet gray 25 20
With tab 60

Issued to commemorate the centenary of the birth of Henrietta Szold, founder of Hadassah, American Jewish women's organization.

Shields of Jerusalem and First Zionist Congress—A82

1960, Dec. 14 *Perf. 14* Unwmkd.

189 A82 50a violet blue & turquoise blue 40 35
With tab 1.10

25th Zionist Congress, Jerusalem, 1960.

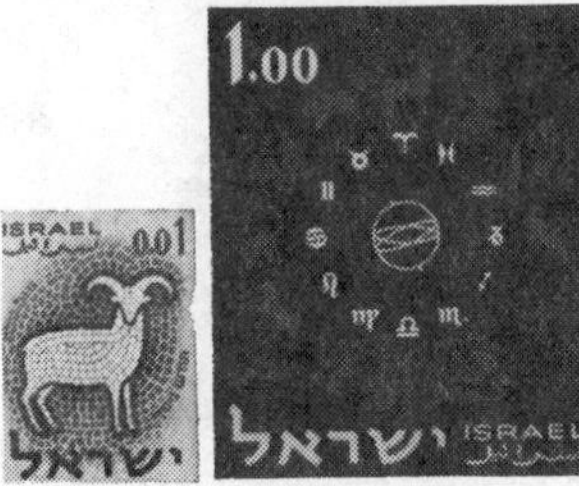

Ram — A83
Signs of Zodiac — A84

Signs of the Zodiac: 2a, Bull. 6a, Twins. 7a, Crab. 8a, Lion. 10a, Virgin. 12a, Scales. 18a, Scorpion. 20a, Archer. 25a, Goat. 32a, Water bearer. 50a, Fishes.

1961, Feb. 27 Photo. *Perf. 13x14*

190 A83 1a emerald 3 3
191 " 2a red 3 3
192 " 6a ultramarine 3 3
193 " 7a brown 5 3
194 " 8a green 5 3
a. Bklt. pane of 6 ('65) 50
195 " 10a orange 5 3
196 " 12a violet 5 5
a. Bklt. pane of 6 ('65) 50
197 " 18a lilac rose 8 8
198 " 20a olive 10 5
199 " 25a red lilac 12 5
200 " 32a gray 25 15
201 " 50a greenish blue 75 10

Lithographed

Perf. 14

202 A84 £1 dark blue, gold & light blue 1.25 50
Nos. 190-202 (13) 2.84 1.16
With tabs 6.50

Booklet pane sheets (Nos. 194a, 196a) of 36 (9x4) contain 6 panes of 6, with gutters dividing the sheet in four sections. Each sheet yields 4 tete beche pairs and 4 tete beche gutter pairs, or strips. See also Nos. 215–217.

Vertical strips of 6 of the 1a, 10a and No. 216 (5a) are from larger sheets from which coils were produced. Regular sheets of 50 are arranged 10x5.

Javelin Thrower and "7"
A85

1961, Apr. 18 Litho. *Perf. 14*

203 A85 25a multicolored 50 40
With tab 1.00

Issued to commemorate the 7th International Congress of the Hapoël Sports Organization, Ramat Gan, May 1961.

Flower Type of 1960

Flowers: 7a, Myrtle. 12a, Sea onion. 32a, Oleander.

1961, Apr. 18 Unwmkd.

Flowers in Natural Colors

204 A76 7a green 10 8
205 " 12a rose carmine 25 25
206 " 32a brt. greenish bl. 45 30

Issued for Memorial Day and the 13th anniversary of the proclamation of the State of Israel.

Scaffold Around "10" and Sapling
A86

1961, June 14 Photo. *Perf. 14*

207 A86 50a Prussian blue 55 55

Issued to commemorate a decade of achievements through Israel bonds.

Type of 1960.

Designs: 7a, Samson. 25a, Judas Maccabaeus. 40a, Bar Cocheba.

1961, Aug. 21 Litho. *Perf. 14*

Multicolored Designs

208 A79 7a red orange 5 5
209 " 25a gray 25 15
210 " 40a lilac 55 45
With tabs 1.85

Jewish New Year, 5722.

Bet Hamidrash Synagogue, Medzibozh—A87

1961, Aug. 21 Photo. *Perf. 13x14*

211 A87 25a dk. brn. & yel. 30 25
With tab 75

Bicentenary of death of Rabbi Israel Baal-Shem-Tov, founder of Hasidism.

Pine Cone—A88

Design: 30a, Symbolic trees.

1961, Dec. 26 *Perf. 13x14* Unwmkd.

212 A88 25a grn., yel. & blk. 30 25
213 " 30a orange, green & indigo 30 25
With tabs 4.50

Issued to commemorate the achievements of Israel's afforestation program.

Cello, Harp, French Horn and Kettle Drum
A89

1961, Dec. 26 Litho. *Perf. 14*

214 A89 50a multicolored 60 55
With tab 4.50

Israel Philharmonic Orchestra, 25th anniversary.

Zodiac Type of 1961 Surcharged with New Value

1962, Mar. 18 Photo. *Perf. 13x14*

215 A83 3a on 1a light lilac 3 3
a. Without overprint 100.00
216 A83 5a on 7a gray 5 4
217 " 30a on 32a emerald 25 15
a. Without overprint 35.00

See note after No. 202.

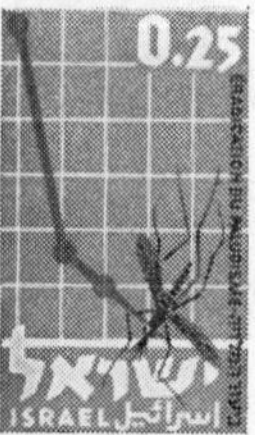

Anopheles Maculipennis and Chart Showing Decline of Malaria in Israel
A90

View of Rosh Pinna
A91

1962, Apr. 30 *Perf. 14x13*

218	A90	25a ochre, red & black	45	30

Issued for the World Health Organization drive to eradicate malaria.

1962, Apr. 30 **Unwmkd.**

219	A91	20a yellow, green & brown	30	25

Issued to commemorate the 80th anniversary of Rosh Pinna, agricultural settlement in Eastern Upper Galilee.

Flame ("Hear, O Israel . . .")
A92

Yellow Star of David and Six Candles
A93

1962, Apr. 30 **Photogravure**

220	A92	12a black, orange & red	25	20

Perf. 14

221	A93	55a multicolored	75	70
		Nos. 220-221 with tabs 2.25		

Issued for Heroes and Martyrs Day in memory of the 6,000,000 Jewish victims of Nazi persecution.

Vautour Fighter-Bomber—A94

Design: 30a, Fighter-Bombers in formation.

1962, Apr. 30 *Perf. 13x14*

222	A94	12a blue	20	25
223	"	30a olive green	45	45
		With tabs 2.25		

Issued for Memorial Day and the 14th anniversary of the proclamation of the state of Israel.

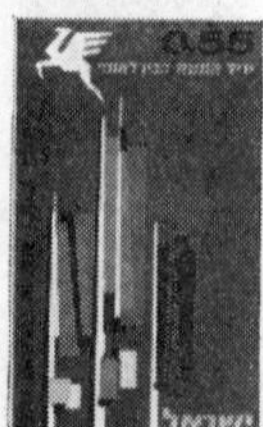

Symbolic Flags
A95

1962, June 5 *Perf. 14*

224	A95	55a multicolored	60	50
		With tab 1.00		

Issued to publicize the Near East International Fair, Tel Aviv, June 5–July 5.

Wolf and Lamb, Isaiah 11:6
A96

Designs: 28a, Leopard and kid, Isaiah 11:6. 43a, Child and asp, Isaiah 11:8.

1962, Sept. 5

225	A96	8a buff, red & blk.	10	7
226	"	28a buff, lilac & blk.	35	30
227	"	43a buff, org. & blk.	75	65
		With tabs 4.50		

Jewish New Year, 5723.

Boeing 707—A97

1962, Nov. 7 *Perf. 13x14*

228	A97	55a blue, dark blue & rose lilac	70	60
		With tab 1.60		
		a. Souvenir sheet	4.50	2.00

Issued in sheets of 15 to publicize the El Al Airline and in connection with the El Al Philatelic Exhibition, Tel Aviv, Nov. 7–14.

No. 228a contains one stamp in greenish blue, dark blue & rose lilac with greenish blue color continuing into margin design (No. 228 has white perforations). Sheet design shows globe and compass rose. Size: 193x136mm. Sold for £1 for one day at philatelic counters in Jerusalem, Haifa and Tel Aviv and for one week at the El Al Exhibition.

Cogwheel Symbols of UJA Activities—A98

1962, Dec. 26 *Perf. 13x14* **Unwmkd.**

229	A98	20a orange red, silver & blue	45	40

Issued to commemorate the 25th anniversary of the United Jewish Appeal (United States) and its support of immigration, settlement, agriculture and care of the aged and sick.

Janusz Korczak—A99

1962, Dec. 26 **Photogravure**

230	A99	30a olive grn. & blk.	45	40

Issued to commemorate Dr. Janusz Korczak (Henryk Goldszmit, 1879–1942), physician, pedagogue and writer, killed in Treblinka concentration camp.

Pennant Coral Fish—A100

Red Sea fish: 6a, Orange butterflyfish. 8a, Lionfish. 12a, Zebra-striped angelfish.

1962, Dec. 26 **Litho.** *Perf. 14*

Fish in Natural Colors

231	A100	3a green	8	8
232	"	6a purple	12	10
233	"	8a brown	15	12
234	"	12a dark blue	18	15
		Nos. 231-234 (4)	53	45
		With tabs 1.25		

See also Nos. 246-249.

Stockade at Dawn—A101

Design: 30a, Completed stockade at night.

1963, Mar. 21 *Perf. 14* **Unwmkd.**

235	A101	12a yellow brn., blk. & yellow	20	20
236	"	30a dp. plum, black & light blue	35	35
		With tab 1.75		

Issued to commemorate the 25th anniversary of the "Stockade and Tower" villages.

Hand Offering Food to Bird
A102

1963, Mar. 21 **Photo.** *Perf. 13x14*

237	A102	55a gray & black	60	75
		With tab 1.75		
		a. Bklt. pane of 4	27.50	

Issued for the "Freedom from Hunger" campaign of the U.N. Food and Agriculture Organization.

Issued in sheets of 15 (5x3) with 5 tabs. The booklet pane sheet of 16 (4x4) is divided into 2 panes of 8 (4x2) by horizontal gutter. The 4 stamps at left in each pane are inverted in relation to the 4 at right, making 4 horizontal tete beche pairs down the center of the sheet.

Flower Type of 1960

Flowers: 8a, White lily. 30a, Hollyhock. 37a, Tulips.

1963, Apr. 25 **Litho.** *Perf. 14*

Flowers in Natural Colors

238	A76	8a slate	20	15
239	"	30a yellow green	60	50
240	"	37a sepia	80	30
		With tabs 7.25		

Issued for Memorial Day and the 15th anniversary of the proclamation of the State of Israel.

Typesetter, 19th Century
A103

1963, June 19 **Photo.** *Perf. 14x13*

241	A103	12a tan & vio. brn.	45	30
		With tab 3.25		
		a. Sheet of 16	65.00	50.00

Issued to commemorate the centenary of the Hebrew press in Palestine. Printed in sheets of 16; the background of the sheet shows page of first issue of "Halbanon" newspaper, giving each stamp different background.

"The Sun Beat upon the Head of Jonah"
A104

Hoe Clearing Thistles
A105

Designs: 30a, "There was a mighty tempest in the sea." 55a, "Jonah was in the belly of the fish" (30a, 55a, horiz.).

Perf. 14x13, 13x14

1963, Aug. 21 **Unwmkd.**

242	A104	8a orange, lilac & black	10	5
243	"	30a multicolored	30	20
244	"	55a "	50	50
		With tabs 4.50		

Jewish New Year, 5724.

1963, Aug. 21 *Perf. 14*

245	A105	37a multicolored	30	25
		With tab 1.00		

Issued to commemorate 80 years of agricultural settlements in Israel and to publicize the "Year of the Pioneers."

Fish Type of 1962

Red Sea Fish: 2a, Undulate triggerfish. 6a, Radiate turkeyfish. 8a, Bigeye. 12a, Imperial angelfish.

1963, Dec. 16 **Litho.** *Perf. 14*

Fish in Natural Colors

246	A100	2a violet blue	6	5
247	"	6a green	10	8
248	"	8a orange	12	12
249	"	12a olive green	18	15
		Nos. 246-249 (4)	46	40
		With tabs 1.50		

S.S. Shalom, Sailing Vessel and Ancient Map of Coast Line
A106

Photogravure

1963, Dec. 16 *Perf. 13x14* **Unwmkd.**

250	A106	£1 ultra., bright green & lilac	2.50	2.00
		With tab	17.50	

Maiden voyage of S.S. Shalom.

"Old Age and Survivors Insurance"
A107

Izhak Ben-Zvi
A108

Designs (Insurance): 25a, Maternity. 37a, Large family. 50a, Workers' compensation.

1964, Feb. 24 Litho. *Perf. 14*

251 A107 12a multicolored 10 8
252 " 25a " 20 20
253 " 37a " 50 30
254 " 50a " 75 50
Nos. 251-254 (4) 1.55 1.08
With tabs 11.00

Issued to commemorate the 10th anniversary of the National Insurance Institute.

1964, Apr. 13 Photo. *Perf. 14x13*

255 A108 12a dark brown 20 12

Issued in memory of Izhak Ben-Zvi, president of Israel 1952-63.

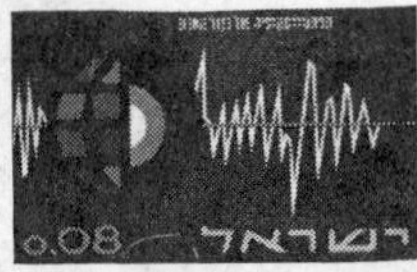

Terrestrial Spectroscopy
A109

Designs: 35a, Macromolecules of the living cell. 70a, Electronic computer.

1964, Apr. 13 *Perf. 14*

256 A109 8a multicolored 12 10
257 " 35a " 40 30
258 " 70a " 85 75
With tabs 5.50

Issued to commemorate the 16th anniversary of the proclamation of the State of Israel and to publicize Israel's contribution to science.

Basketball Players
A110

Serpent of Aesculapius and Menorah
A111

Designs: 8a, Runner. 12a, Discus thrower. 50a, Soccer.

1964, June 24 *Perf. 14x13*

259 A110 8a bright brick red & dark brown 10 10
260 " 12a rose lilac & dark brown 15 15
261 " 30a blue, carmine & dark brown 35 35
262 " 50a yellow grn., org. red & dk. brn. 50 45

Issued to commemorate Israel's participation in the 18th Olympic Games, Tokyo, Oct. 10-25.

1964, Aug. 5 Unwmkd.

263 A111 £1 olive bister & slate green 90 80

Issued to commemorate the 6th World Congress of the Israel Medical Association, Haifa, Aug. 3-13.

Ancient Glass Vase—A112

Designs: Different glass vessels, 1st to 3rd centuries.

1964, Aug. 5 Lithographed

264 A112 8a vio., brn. & orge. 12 10
265 " 35a olive, green & blue green 40 35
266 " 70a bright car. rose, blue & violet bl. 65 55
With tabs 2.50

Jewish New Year, 5725.

Steamer Bringing Immigrants
A113

Eleanor Roosevelt
A114

1964, Nov. 2 Litho. *Perf. 14*

267 A113 25a slate bl., blue grn. & black 25 22
With tab 55

Issued to commemorate the 30th anniversary of the blockade runners bringing immigrants to Israel.

1964, Nov. 2 Photo. *Perf. 14x13*

268 A114 70a dull purple 80 60

Issued to honor Eleanor Roosevelt (1884-1962).

Chess Board, Knight and Emblem of Chess Olympics—A115

Design: 70a, Chess board, rook and emblem of Chess Olympics.

1964, Nov. 2 *Perf. 13x14*

269 A115 12a sepia 30 20
270 " 70a green 1.10 80
With tabs 2.50

16th Chess Olympics, Tel Aviv, Nov. 1964.

"Africa-Israel Friendship"
A116

Perf. 14x13

1964, Nov. 30 Photo. Unwmkd.

271 A116 57a olive, blk., gold & red brown 1.00 75
With tab 5.00
a. Souv. sheet 3.75 3.00

Issued to commemorate TABAI, National Stamp Exhibition, dedicated to African-Israel friendship, Haifa, Nov. 30-Dec. 6. No. 271a contains one imperf. stamp, red brown margin and control number, black and gold inscription. Size: 124x78mm. Sold for £1.

View of Masada from West
A117

Designs: 36a, Northern Palace, lower terrace. £1, View of Northern Palace (vert.).

1965, Feb. 3 Photo. *Perf. 13x14*

272 A117 25a dull green 35 30
273 " 36a bright blue 60 50
274 " £1 dk. red brown 1.10 90
With tabs 4.00

Issued to publicize the ruins of Masada, the last stronghold in the war against the Romans, 66-73 A D.

Book Fair Emblem
A118

Arms of Ashdod
A119

1965, Mar. 24 Photo. *Perf. 13x14*

275 A118 70a gray olive, brt. bl. & blk. 75 65

Issued to publicize the Second International Book Fair, Jerusalem, April 1965.

1965-66 *Perf. 13x14*

Town Emblems: 1a, Lydda (Lod). 2a, Qiryat Shemona. 5a, Petah Tikva. 6a, Nazareth. 8a, Beersheba. 10a, Bet Shean. 12a, Tiberias. 20a, Elat. 25a, Acre (Akko). 35a, Dimona. 37a, Zefat. 50a, Rishon Leziyyon. 70a, Jerusalem. £1, Tel Aviv-Jaffa. £3, Haifa.

Size: 17x22½mm.

276 A119 1a brown 3 3
277 " 2a lilac rose 3 3
278 " 5a gray 4 3
279 " 6a violet 5 3
280 " 8a orange 7 4
a. Bklt. pane of 6 45
281 " 10a emerald 8 4
282 " 12a dark purple 10 5
a. Bklt. pane of 6 60
283 " 15a green 10 5
284 " 20a rose red 15 10
285 " 25a ultramarine 20 10
286 " 35a magenta 30 15
287 " 37a olive 30 25
288 " 50a greenish blue 30 20

Perf. 14x13

Size: 22x27mm.

289 A119 70a dark brown 40 30
290 " £1 dark green 65 50
291 " £3 dk. car. rose 2.00 55
Nos. 276-291 (16) 4.80 2.45
With tabs 11.00

Dates of issue: Nos. 283-286, Mar. 24, 1965. No. 290, Nov. 24, 1965. No. 291, Mar. 14, 1966. Others, Feb. 2, 1966.

The uncut booklet pane sheets of 36 are divided into 4 panes (2 of 6 stamps, 2 of 12) by horizontal and vertical gutters. Half of the stamps in the 2 panes of 12 are inverted, causing 4 horizontal tête bêche pairs and 4 horizontal tête bêche gutter pairs.

Vertical strips of 6 of the 1a, 5a and 10a are from larger sheets, released Jan. 10, 1967, from which coils were produced. Regular sheets of 50 are arranged 10x5.

No. 290 also comes tagged (1975).

See also Nos. 334-336, 386-393.

Hands Reaching for Hope, and Star of David
A120

"Irrigation of the Desert"
A121

1965, Apr. 27 *Perf. 14x13* Unwmkd.

292 A120 25a gray, blk. & yel. 35 35
With tab 85

Issued to commemorate the 20th anniversary of the liberation of Nazi concentration camps.

1965, Apr. 27 Photogravure

293 A121 37a olive bister & bl. 50 35

Issued for Memorial Day and the 17th anniversary of the proclamation of the state of Israel.

Telegraph Pole and Syncom Satellite
A122

1965, July 21 *Perf. 13x14* Unwmkd.

294 A122 70a violet, black & greenish blue 60 60

Issued to commemorate the centenary of the International Telecommunication Union.

Symbol of Cooperation and U.N. Emblem
A123

1965, July 21 Litho. *Perf. 14*

295 A123 36a gray, dp. claret, bl., red & bister 60 50

International Cooperation Year, 1965.

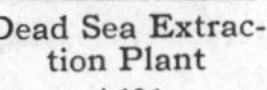

Dead Sea Extraction Plant
A124

"Let There be Light . ."
A125

Design: 12a, Industrial crane, Dead Sea and chemicals.

1965, July 21

296 A124 12a multicolored 10 10
297 " 50a " 50 50

Dead Sea chemical industry.

1965, Sept. 7 Photo. *Perf. 13x14*

Genesis 1, The Creation: 8a, Firmament and waters. 12a, Dry land and vegetation. 25a, Heavenly lights. 35a, Fish and fowl. 70a, Man.

298 A125 6a dark purple, lilac & gold 10 8
299 " 8a brt. green, dark blue & gold 10 8
300 " 12a red brown, black & gold 12 8
301 " 25a dark purple, pink & gold 25 20
302 " 35a lt. & dark blue & gold 40 30
303 " 70a deep claret, carm. & gold 1.10 80
Nos. 298-303 (6) 2.07 1.54

Jewish New Year, 5726. Sheets of 20 (10x2).

Charaxes Jasius
A126

Flags over Rooftops
A127

Butterflies: 6a, Papilio Alexanor Maccabaeus. 8a, Daphnis Nerii. 12a, Zegris Eupheme Uarda.

1965, Dec. 15 Litho. *Perf. 14*

Butterflies in Natural Colors

304 A126 2a lt. olive green 3 3
305 " 6a lilac 5 4
306 " 8a ocher 8 6
307 " 12a blue 15 15

1966, Apr. 20 Litho. *Perf. 14*

Designs: 30a, Fireworks over Tel Aviv. 80a, Warships and Super Mirage jets, Haifa.

308 A127 12a multicolored 8 8
309 " 30a " 20 20
310 " 80a " 55 55

Issued for the 18th anniversary of the proclamation of the state of Israel.

Memorial, Upper Galilee
A128

1966, Apr. 20 Photo. *Perf. 14x13*

311 A128 40a olive gray 50 50

Issued for Memorial Day.

Knesset Building, Jerusalem—A129

Perf. 13x14

1966, June 22 Photo. Unwmkd.

312 A129 £1 deep blue 1.00 1.00
With tab 2.00

Issued to commemorate the inauguration of the Knesset Building (Parliament). Sheets of 12.

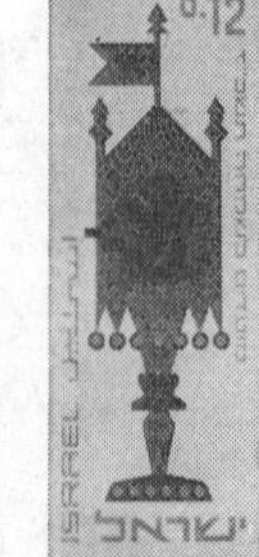
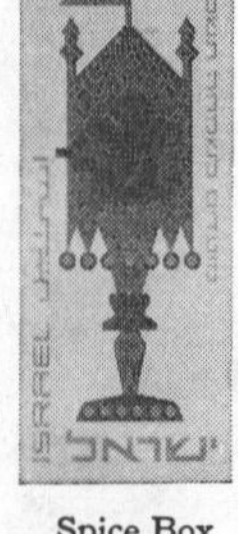
Road Sign and Motorcyclist
A130

Spice Box
A131

Designs (Road Signs and): 5a, Bicyclist. 10a, Pedestrian. 12a, Child playing ball. 15a, Automobile.

1966, June 22 *Perf. 14*

313 A130 2a slate, red brown & lilac rose 3 3
314 " 5a olive bister, slate & lilac rose 5 3
315 " 10a violet, light blue & lilac rose 10 10
316 " 12a blue, green & lilac rose 12 12
317 " 15a green, red & lilac rose 15 15
Nos. 313-317 (5) 45 43

Issued to publicize traffic safety.

Perf. 13x14

1966, Aug. 24 Photo. Unwmkd.

Ritual Art Objects: 15a, Candlesticks. 35a, Kiddush cup. 40a, Torah pointer. 80a, Hanging lamp.

318 A131 12a silver, gold, black & blue 8 8
319 " 15a silver, gold, black & lilac 10 10
320 " 35a silver, gold, blk. & emerald 20 20
321 " 40a silver, gold, blk. & violet blue 25 25
322 " 80a silver, gold, blk. & red 60 60
Nos. 318-322 (5) 1.23 1.23

Jewish New Year, 5727.

Bronze Panther, Avdat, 1st Century, B.C.—A132

Designs: 30a, Stone menorah, Tiberias, 2nd Century. 40a, Phoenician ivory sphinx, 9th century, B.C. 55a, Gold earring (calf's head), Ashdod, 6th–4th centuries B.C. 80a, Miniature gold capital, Persia, 5th century, B.C. £1.15, Gold drinking horn (ram's head), Persia, 5th century, B.C. (vert.).

1966, Oct. 26 Litho. *Perf. 14*

323 A132 15a dp. blue & yel. brown 12 10
324 " 30a vio. brown & bister 25 15
325 " 40a sepia & yellow bister 30 25
326 " 55a Prus. green, dp. yel. & brown 45 35
327 " 80a lake, dp. yellow & brown 60 50

Perf. 13x14

328 A132 £1.15 violet, gold & brown 1.50 1.25
Nos. 323-328 (6) 3.22 2.60
With tabs 10.00

Israel Museum, Jerusalem. Sheets of 12.

Coach and Mailman of Austrian Levant
A133

Microscope and Cells
A134

Designs: 15a, Turkish mailman and caravan. 40a, Palestinian mailman and locomotive. £1, Israeli mailman and jet liner.

1966, Dec. 14 Photo. *Perf. 14*

329 A133 12a ocher & green 8 8
330 " 15a lt. grn., brown & dp. carmine 12 10
331 " 40a bright rose & dark blue 25 20
332 " £1 greenish blue & brown 55 50

Issued for Stamp Day.

1966, Dec. 14 *Perf. 14x13*

333 A134 15a red & dark slate green 15 12
With tab 30

Campaign against cancer.

Arms Type of 1965–66

Town Emblems: 40a, Mizpe Ramon. 55a, Ashkelon. 80a, Rosh Pinna.

1967, Feb. 8 *Perf. 13x14* Unwmkd.

334 A119 40a dark olive 25 15
335 " 55a dk. carmine rose 30 25
336 " 80a red brown 60 40
With tabs 3.75

Port of Acre—A135

Ancient Ports: 40a, Caesarea. 80a, Jaffa.

1967, March 22 Photo. *Perf. 13x14*

337 A135 15a dark brown 10 10
338 " 40a dark blue green 30 25
339 " 80a deep blue 60 55

Page of Shulhan Aruk and Crowns
A136

1967, March 22 *Perf. 13½x13*

340 A136 40a dk. & lt. blue, gray & gold 45 45
With tab 80

Issued to commemorate the 400th anniversary of the publication (in 1565) of the Shulhan Aruk, a compendium of Jewish religious and civil law, by Joseph Karo (1488–1575).

War of Independence Memorial
A137

1967, May 10 *Perf. 13x14* Unwmkd.

341 A137 55a lt. blue, indigo & silver 50 40
With tab 90

Issued for Memorial Day, 1967.

Auster Plane over Convoy on Jerusalem Road
A138

Military Aircraft: 30a, Mystère IV jet fighter over Dead Sea area. 80a, Mirage jet fighters over Masada.

1967, May 10 Photogravure

342 A138 15a lt. olive green & dk. bl. green 15 8
343 " 30a ocher & dk. brn. 25 18
344 " 80a greenish blue & violet blue 55 50

Issued for Independence Day, 1967.

Israeli Ships in Straits of Tiran
A139

Torah, Scroll of the Law
A140

Designs: 15a, Star of David, sword and olive branch (vert.). 80a, Wailing (Western) Wall, Jerusalem.

Perf. 14x13, 13x14

1967, Aug. 16 Photo. Unwmkd.

345 A139 15a dark red, black & yellow 10 10
346 " 40a Prussian green 15 15
347 " 80a deep violet 45 45

Victory of the Israeli forces, June, 1967.

1967, Sept. 13 *Perf. 13x14*

Designs: Various ancient, decorated Scrolls of the Law.

348 A140 12a gold & multi. 10 8
349 " 15a silver & multi. 12 10
350 " 35a gold & multi. 15 15
351 " 40a silver & multi. 20 20
352 " 80a gold & multi. 50 50
Nos. 348-352 (5) 1.07 1.03

Jewish New Year, 5728. Sheets of 20 (10x2).

Chaim Weizmann
A141

Design: 40a, Lord Balfour.

1967, Nov. 2 Photo. *Perf. 13x14*

353 A141 15a dark green 20 20
354 " 40a brown 40 40

Issued to commemorate the 50th anniversary of the Balfour Declaration, which established the right to a Jewish national home in Palestine. Issued in sheets of 15.

Emblem and Doll
A142

Nubian Ibex
A143

Designs: 30a, Hebrew inscription. 40a, French inscription.

1967, Nov. 2 Litho. *Perf. 14*

355 A142 30a yel. & multi. 25 20
356 " 40a brt. bl. & multi. 30 25
357 " 80a brt. grn. & multi. 70 60

Issued for International Tourist Year, 1967. Issued in sheets of 15.

1967, Dec. 27 Litho. *Perf. 13*

Designs: 18a, Caracal lynx. 60a, Dorcas gazelles.

Animal in Ocher & Brown

358 A143 12a dull purple 8 8
359 " 18a bright green 12 12
360 " 60a bright blue 40 35

Flags Forming Soccer Ball
A144

1968, Mar. 11 Photo. *Perf. 13*

361 A144 80a ocher & multi. 50 50

Pre-Olympic soccer tournament.

Welcoming Immigrants
A145

Resistance Fighter
A146

Design: 80a, Happy farm family.

Lithographed

1968, Apr. 24 *Perf. 14* Unwmkd.

362 A145 15a lt. grn. & multi. 12 10
363 " 80a cream & multi. 45 40

Issued for Independence Day, 1968.

1968, Apr. 24 Photo. *Perf. 14x13*

364 A146 60a brown olive 32 30

Issued to commemorate the 25th anniversary of the Warsaw Ghetto Uprising. Design from Warsaw Ghetto Memorial.

Sword and Laurel
A147

Rifles and Helmet
A148

1968, Apr. 24 Litho. *Perf. 14*

365 A147 40a gold & multi. 25 20
366 A148 55a black & multi. 30 25

No. 365 issued to honor the Zahal defense army on Independence Day; No. 366 issued for Memorial Day, 1968.

Candle and Prison Window
A149

Moshe Sharett
A150

1968, June 5 Photo. *Perf. 14x13*

367 A149 80a black, gray & sepia 40 40

Issued to honor those who died for freedom.

1968, June 5 Unwmkd.

368 A150 £1 deep brown 50 50

Issued to publicize the 27th Zionist Congress, and in memory of Prime Minister Moshe Sharett (1894–1965).

Knot Forming Star of David
A151

Dome of the Rock and Absalom's Tomb
A152

1968, Aug. 21 Litho. *Perf. 13*

369 A151 30a multicolored 20 20

50 years of Jewish Scouting. Sheets of 15 (5x3).

1968, Aug. 21 Photo. *Perf. 14x13*

Views of Jerusalem: 15a, Church of the Resurrection. 35a, Tower of David and City Wall. 40a, Yemin Moshe District and Mount of Olives. 60a, Israel Museum and "Shrine of the Book."

370 A152 12a gold & multi. 5 5
371 " 15a " " 8 5
372 " 35a " " 12 12
373 " 40a " " 25 20
374 " 60a " " 35 35
Nos. 370-374 (5) 85 77

Jewish New Year, 5729. Sheets of 15 (5x3).

Detail from Lions' Gate, Jerusalem (St. Stephen's Gate)
A153

1968, Oct. 8 *Perf. 13x14* Unwmkd.

375 A153 £1 brown orange 60 55
a. Souv. sheet 80 80

Issued to publicize TABIRA. National Philatelic Exhibition. No. 375a contains one imperf. stamp. Olive green margin shows wall of Old City with Lions' Gate. Brown marginal inscription. Size: 121x75mm. Sold only at exhibition for £1.50. Issued in sheets of 15 (5x3).

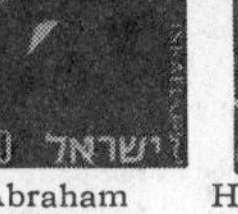

Abraham Mapu
A154

Handicapped Boys Playing Basketball
A155

1968, Oct. 8 Photo. *Perf. 14x13*

376 A154 30a dark olive green 20 18

Issued to commemorate the 160th anniversary of the birth of Abraham Mapu (1808–1867), novelist and historian.

1968, Nov. 6 Photo. *Perf. 14x13*

377 A155 40a green & yel. grn. 30 25

Issued to publicize the 17th Stoke-Mandeville Games for the Paralyzed, Nov. 4–13. Sheets of 15 (5x3).

Port of Elat—A156

Ports of Israel: 60a, Ashdod. £1, Haifa.

1969, Feb. 19 *Perf. 13x14* Unwmkd.

378 A156 30a deep magenta 15 15
379 " 60a brown 35 35
380 " £1 dull green 50 50

Gun Carrier
A157

Design: 80a, Destroyer.

1969, Apr. 16 Photo. *Perf. 13x14*

381 A157 15a olive & multi. 12 10
382 " 80a lt. blue, violet & green 40 40

Issued for Independence Day 1969.

Israel's Flag at Half-mast
A158

Worker and ILO Emblem
A159

1969, Apr. 16

383 A158 55a vio., gold & blue 35 30

Issued for Memorial Day.

1969, Apr. 16

384 A159 80a dark blue green 50 40

Issued to commemorate the 50th anniversary of the International Labor Organization.

Hand Holding Torch
A160

Arms of Hadera
A161

1969, July 9 Photo. *Perf. 14x13*

385 A160 60a gold & multi. 35 35
With tab 1.20

Issued to publicize the 8th Maccabiah.

1969–73 *Perf. 13x14*

Town Emblems: 3a, Hertseliya. 5a, Holon. 15a, Bat Yam. 18a, Ramla. 20a, Kefar Sava. 25a, Giv'atayim. 30a, Rehovot. 40a, Netanya. 50a, Bene Beraq. 60a, Nahariyya. 80a, Ramat Gan.

386 A161 2a green 3 3
387 " 3a deep magenta 3 3
388 " 5a orange 3 3
389 " 15a bright rose 18 12
c. Bklt. pane of 6 (2#389+4#389A) ('71) 90
389A A161 18a ultra. ('70) 22 12
d. Bklt. pane of 6 ('71) 1.00
e. Bklt. pane of 6 (1#281+5#389A) ('73) 90
389B A161 20a brown ('70) 35 15
f. Bklt. pane of 5 + label ('73) 1.25
390 A161 25a dark blue 40 15
390A " 30a brt. pink ('70) 45 12
391 " 40a purple 60 25
392 " 50a greenish blue 75 20
392A " 60a olive ('70) 90 25
393 " 80a dark green 1.10 25
Nos. 386-393 (12) 5.04 1.70
With tabs 6.50

Nos. 389c, 389d and 389e were also sold in uncut sheets of 36. See note after No. 291 about similar sheets of Nos. 280a and 282a.

Noah Building the Ark
A162

The Story of the Flood: 15a, Animals boarding the Ark. 35a, The Ark during the flood. 40a, Noah sending out the dove. 60a, Noah and the rainbow.

1969, Aug. 13 *Perf. 14* Unwmkd.

394 A162 12a multicolored 12 10
395 " 15a " 12 10
396 " 35a " 15 12
397 " 40a " 20 18
398 " 60a " 45 35
Nos. 394-398 (5) 1.04 85

Jewish New Year, 5730. Sheets of 15 (5x3).

King David by Marc Chagall
A163

Atom Diagram and Test Tube
A164

1969, Sept. 24 Photo. ***Perf. 14***
399 A163 £3 multicolored 2.50 1.50
With tab 4.00

1969, Nov. 3 ***Perf. 14x13***
400 A164 £1.15 violet blue & multi. 1.25 75
With tab 4.25

Issued to commemorate the 25th anniversary of the Weizmann Institute of Science.

Joseph Trumpeldor A165 — Dum Palms, Emeq Ha-Arava A166

1970, Jan. 21 Photo. ***Perf. 14x13***
401 A165 £1 dark purple 60 60

Issued to commemorate the 50th anniversary of the defense of Tel Hay under the leadership of Joseph Trumpeldor.

1970, Jan. 21

Views: 3a, Tahana Waterfall. 5a, Nahal Baraq Canyon, Negev. 6a, Cedars in Judean Hills. 30a, Soreq Cave, Judean Hills.

402 A166 2a olive 3 3
403 " 3a deep blue 3 3
404 " 5a orange red 3 3
405 " 6a slate green 5 3
406 " 30a bright purple 18 18
Nos. 402-406 (5) 32 30

Issued to publicize nature reserves.

Magic Carpet Shaped as Airplane A167 — Levi Eshkol A168

1970, Jan. 21 Litho. ***Perf. 13***
407 A167 30a multicolored 20 20
With tab 40

Issued to commemorate the 20th anniversary of "Operation Magic Carpet" which airlifted the Yemeni Jews to Israel.

1970, Mar. 11 Litho. ***Perf. 14***
408 A168 15a blue & multi. 15 10

Issued in memory of Levi Eshkol (1895-1969), Prime Minister of Israel.

Mania Shochat A169 — Camel and Train A170

Portrait: 80a, Ze'ev Jabotinsky (1880-1940), writer and Zionist leader.

1970, Mar. 11 Photo. ***Perf. 14x13***
409 A169 40a dp. plum & buff 25 20
410 " 80a green & cream 40 40
With tabs 1.75

No. 409 commemorates the 60th anniversary of Ha-Shomer (Watchmen defense organization); No. 410 the 50th anniversary of the defense of Jerusalem.

1970, Mar. 11 Litho. ***Perf. 13***
411 A170 80a orange & multi. 85 45
With tab 1.50

Opening of Dimona-Oron Railroad.

Scene from "The Dibbuk"—A171

1970, Mar. 11 Photo. ***Perf. 14x13***
412 A171 £1 multicolored 75 60
With tab 1.50

Habimah National Theater, 50th anniversary.

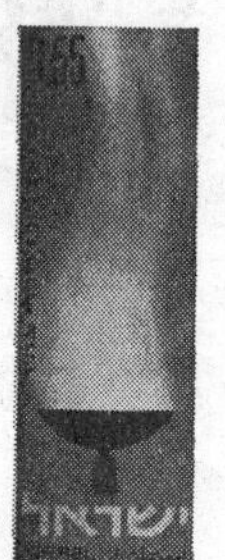

Memorial Flame A172 — Orchis Laxiflorus A173

1970, May 6 Photo. ***Perf. 13x14***
413 A172 55a vio., pink & blk. 50 30

Issued for Memorial Day, 1970.

1970, May 6 Litho. ***Perf. 14***

Flowers: 15a, Iris mariae. 80a, Lupinus pilosus.

414 A173 12a pale gray, plum & green 12 7
415 " 15a multicolored 15 12
416 " 80a pale bl. & multi. 55 50
With tabs 1.75

Issued for Independence Day, 1970.

Charles Netter A174 — 420 Class Yachts A175

Design: 80a, Agricultural College (Mikwe Israel) and garden.

1970, May 6 Photo. ***Perf. 14x13***
417 A174 40a lt. green, dark brown & gold 30 20
418 " 80a gold & multi. 50 50
With tabs 1.75

Centenary of first agricultural college in Israel; its founder, Charles Netter.

1970, July 8 Photo. ***Perf. 14x13***

Designs: Various 420 Class yachts.

419 A175 15a greenish blue, black & silver 10 10
420 A175 30a olive, red, black & silver 20 18
421 " 80a ultra., black & silver 50 50
With tabs 1.75

World "420" Class Sailing Championships.

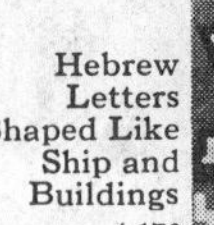

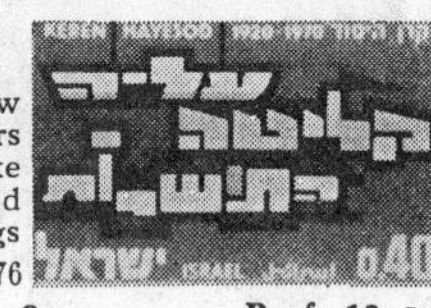

Hebrew Letters Shaped Like Ship and Buildings A176

1970, July 8 ***Perf. 13x14***
422 A176 40a gold & multi. 32 25

Issued to commemorate the 50th anniversary of the Keren Hayesod, a Zionist Fund to maintain schools and hospitals in Palestine.

Arava Plane A177

1970, July 8
423 A177 £1 brt. blue, black & silver 85 50

First Israeli designed and built aircraft.

Bird (Exiles) and Sun (Israel) A178

1970, Sept. 7 Litho. ***Perf. 14***
424 A178 80a yellow & multi. 65 60

Issued to commemorate "Operation Ezra and Nehemiah," the exodus of Iraqi Jews.

Old Synagogue, Cracow A179

Historic Synagogues: 15a, Great Synagogue, Tunis. 35a, Portuguese Synagogue, Amsterdam. 40a, Great Synagogue, Moscow. 60a, Shearith Israel Synagogue, New York.

Perf. 14, 13 (15a)
1970, Sept. 7 Photogravure
425 A179 12a gold & multi. 6 5
426 " 15a " " 10 8
427 " 35a " " 18 15
428 " 40a " " 20 20
429 " 60a " " 40 40
Nos. 425-429 (5) 94 88

Jewish New Year, 5731.

Tel Aviv Post Office, 1920 A180

1970, Oct. 18 Photo. ***Perf. 14***
430 A180 £1 multicolored 65 60
a. Souvenir sheet 2.25 1.25

Issued to publicize the National Stamp Exhibition "TABIT" Tel Aviv, Oct. 18-29. No. 430a contains an imperf. stamp similar to No. 430; brown margin with orange yellow and black inscription and dark red picture of modern post office. Size: 122x74½mm. Sold for £1.50.

Mother and Child A181

1970, Oct. 18 ***Perf. 13x14***
431 A181 80a dp. grn., yellow & gray 45 45
With tab 1.25

Issued to commemorate the 50th anniversary of WIZO, Women's International Zionist Organization.

Paris Quai, by Camille Pissarro—A182

Paintings from Tel Aviv Museum: 85a, The Jewish Wedding, by Josef Israels. £2, Flowers in a Vase, by Fernand Leger.

1970, Dec. 22 Litho. ***Perf. 14***
432 A182 85a black & multi. 45 45
433 " £1 " " 55 55
434 " £2 " " 1.50 1.20

Hammer and Menorah Emblem A183 — Persian Fallow Deer A184

1970, Dec. 22
435 A183 35a gold & multi. 25 25

General Federation of Labor in Israel (Histadrut), 50th anniversary.

1971, Feb. 16 Litho. ***Perf. 13***

Animals of the Bible: 3a, Asiatic wild ass. 5a, White oryx. 78a, Cheetah.

436 A184 2a multicolored 3 3
437 " 3a " 3 3
438 " 5a " 3 3
439 " 78a " 55 45

"Samson and Dalila," Israel National Opera—A185

Designs: No. 441, Inn of the Ghosts, Cameri Theater. No. 442, A Psalm of David, Inbal Dance Theater.

1971, Feb. 16 ***Perf. 14x13***
440 A185 50a bister & multi. 35 30
441 " 50a lt. grn. & multi. 35 30
442 " 50a blue & multi. 35 30

Theater art in Israel.

Basketball
A186

Defense Forces
Emblem—A187

Designs: No. 444, Runner. No. 445, Athlete on rings.

1971, Apr. 13 Litho. *Perf. 14*

443	A186	50a green & multi.	30	35
444	"	50a ocher & multi.	30	35
445	"	50a lt. vio. & multi.	30	35

9th Hapoel Games.

1971, Apr. 13 Photo. *Perf. 14x13*

446	A187	78a multicolored	45	40

Memorial Day, 1971, and to honor the war dead.

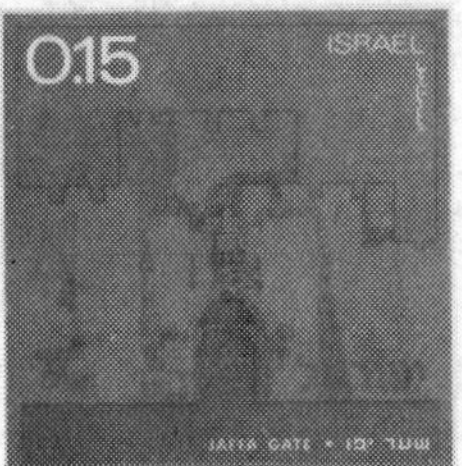

Jaffa Gate, Jerusalem
A188

Gates of Jerusalem: 18c, New Gate. 35c, Damascus Gate. 85c, Herod's Gate.

1971, Apr. 13 *Perf. 14*

Size: 41x41mm.

447	A188	15a gold & multi.	20	12
448	"	18a " "	25	15
449	"	35a " "	45	27
450	"	85a " "	1.10	65
		a. Souvenir sheet of 4	6.00	4.00

Independence Day, 1971. No. 450a contains 4 stamps similar to Nos. 447-450, but smaller (27x27mm.). Gold marginal inscription. Size: 93x93mm. It was sold at the Jerusalem Exhibition for £2.

See also Nos. 488-491.

"He Wrote . . . Words of the Covenant"—A189

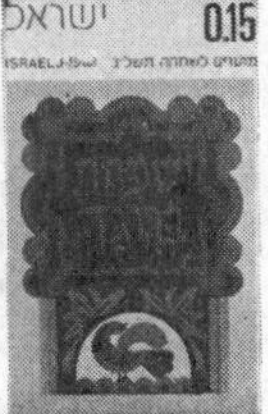

"You shall rejoice in your feast"
A190

Designs: 85a, "First Fruits . . ." Exodus 23:19. £1.50, ". . . Feast of Weeks" Exodus 34:22. The quotation on 50a is from Exodus 34:28. The quotations are in English on the tabs.

1971, May 25 Photo. *Perf. 14x13*

451	A189	50a yellow & multi.	40	30
452	"	85a " "	75	55
453	"	£1.50 " "	1.10	85
		With tabs 4.00		

For the Feast of Weeks (Shabuoth).

1971, Aug. 24 Photo. *Perf. 14x13*

Designs: 18a, "You shall dwell in booths for seven days. . ." Leviticus 23:42. 20a, "That I made the people of Israel dwell in booths. . ." Lev. 23:43. 40a, ". . . when you have gathered in the produce of the land" Lev. 23:39. 65a, ". . . then I will give you your rains in their season" Lev. 26:4. The quotation on 15a is from Deuteronomy 16:14. The quotations are in English on tabs.

454	A190	15a yellow & multi.	5	5
455	"	18a " "	6	6
456	"	20a " "	10	10
457	"	40a " "	15	15
458	"	65a " "	30	30
		Nos. 454-458 (5)	66	66
		With tabs 1.80		

For the Feast of Tabernacles (Sukkoth).

Sun Shining on Fields
A191

1971, Aug. 24 *Perf. 14*

459	A191	40a gold & multi.	25	22

50th anniversary of the first cooperative settlement in Israel, at Emeq (Valley of Israel).

Retort and Grain
A192

Negev
A193

1971, Oct. 25 Litho. *Perf. 14*

460	A192	£1 green & multi.	65	50

50th anniversary of Volcani Institute of Agricultural Research.

Tagging

Starting in 1975, vertical luminescent bands were overprinted on various regular and commemorative stamps.

In the 1971–75 regular series, values issued both untagged and tagged are: 20a, 25a, 30a, 35a, 45a, 50a, 65a, £1.10, £1.30, £2 and £3. Also No. 290 was re-issued with tagging in 1975.

Regular issues from 1975 onward, including the £1.70, are tagged unless otherwise noted.

Tagged commemoratives include Nos. 562–563 and all from Nos. 567–569 onward unless otherwise noted.

1971–75 Photo. *Perf. 13x14*

Landscapes: 3a, Judean desert. 5a, Gan Ha-Shelosha. 18a, Kinneret. 20a, Tel Dan. 22a, Fishermen, Yafo. 25a, Arava. 30a, En Avedat. 35a, Brekhat Ram, Golan Heights. 45a, Grazing sheep, Mt. Hermon. 50a, Rosh Pinna. 55a, Beach and park, Netanya. 65a, Plain of Zebulun. 70a, Shore, Engedi. 80a, Beach at Elat. 88a, Boats in Akko harbor. 95a, Hamifratz Hane'elam (lake). £1.10, Aqueduct near Acco. £1.30, Zefat. £1.70, Upper Nazareth. £2, Coral Island. £3, Haifa.

461	A193	3a deep blue ('72)	30	22
462	"	5a green ('72)	3	3
463	"	15a deep orange	20	15
464	"	18a bright magenta	80	35
464A	"	20a dk. green ('73)	12	6
465	"	22a brt. blue ('72)	1.75	70
465A	"	25a org. red ('74)	3	3
466	"	30a brt. rose ('72)	3	3
466A	"	35a plum ('73)	3	3
467	"	45a dull vio. bl. ('73)	18	15
468	"	50a green	18	15
469	"	55a olive ('72)	20	18
469A	"	65a black ('73)	20	18
470	"	70a dp. car. ('72)	30	22
470A	"	80a dp. ultra. ('74)	18	15
471	"	88a greenish blue	1.50	80
472	"	95a org. verm. ('73)	1.35	75

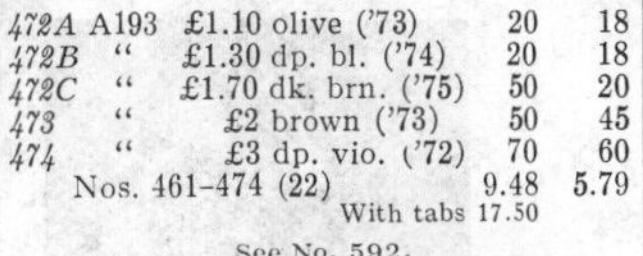

472A	A193	£1.10 olive ('73)	20	18
472B	"	£1.30 dp. bl. ('74)	20	18
472C	"	£1.70 dk. brn. ('75)	50	20
473	"	£2 brown ('73)	50	45
474	"	£3 dp. vio. ('72)	70	60
		Nos. 461-474 (22)	9.48	5.79
		With tabs 17.50		

See No. 592.

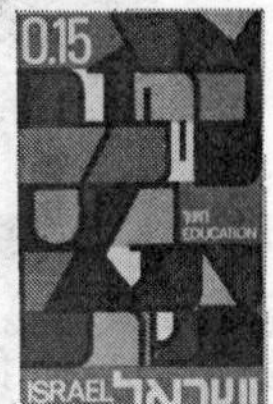

"Get Wisdom" Proverbs 4:7
A194

Abstract Designs: 18a, Mathematical and scientific formula. 20a, Tools and engineering symbols. 40a, Abbreviations of various college degrees.

1972, Jan. 4 Lithographed *Perf. 14*

475	A194	15a brt. grn. & multi.	10	5
476	"	18a multicolored	15	6
477	"	20a "	18	12
478	"	40a red, blk. & gold	30	25

The Scribe, Sculpture by Boris Schatz—A195

Works by Israeli Artists: 55a, Young Girl (Sarah), by Abel Pann. 70a, Zefat (landscape), by Menahem Shemi (horiz.). 85a, Old Jerusalem, by Jacob Steinhardt. £1, Resurrection (abstract), by Aharon Kahana.

Perf. 13x14* (40a, 85a), *14

1972, Mar. 7

479	A195	40a black & tan	25	10
480	"	55a red brn. & multi.	30	25
481	"	70a lt. grn. & multi.	40	30
482	"	85a black & yellow	75	40
483	"	£1 black & multi.	1.00	60
		Nos. 479-483 (5)	2.70	1.65

Exodus
A196

"Let My People Go"
A197

Passover 1972: 45a, Baking unleavened bread. 95a, Seder.

1972, Mar. 7 Litho. *Perf. 13*

484	A196	18a buff & multi.	10	5
485	"	45a " "	35	25
486	"	95a " "	60	50
		With tabs 2.25		

1972, Mar. 7 *Perf. 14*

487	A197	55a black, blue & yellow green	70	30
		With tab 7.50		

No. 487 inscribed in Hebrew, Arabic, Russian and English.

Gate Type of 1971

Gates of Jerusalem: 15a, Lions' Gate. 18a, Golden Gate. 45a, Dung Gate. 55a, Zion Gate.

1972, Apr. 17 Photo. *Perf. 14*

Size: 40x40mm.

488	A188	15a gold & multi.	15	5
489	"	18a " "	18	10
490	"	45a " "	45	25
491	"	55a " "	55	45
		a. Souvenir sheet of 4	3.25	2.25

Independence Day 1972. No. 491a contains 4 stamps similar to Nos. 488-491, but 27x27mm. Gold marginal inscription. Size: 93x93mm. Sold for £2.

Jethro's Tomb
A198

1972, Apr. 17 Litho. *Perf. 13*

492	A198	55a multicolored	60	25

Flowers
A199

1972, Apr. 17 *Perf. 14*

493	A199	55a multicolored	35	25

Memorial Day 1972.

Hebrew Words Emerging from Opened Ghetto
A200

Printed Page
A201

1972, June 6 *Perf. 13*

494	A200	70a blue & multi.	55	35
		With tab 3.50		

400th anniversary of the death of Rabbi Isaac ben Solomon Ashkenazi Luria ("Ari") (1534–1572), Palestinian cabalist.

1972, June 6 *Perf. 14x13*

495	A201	95a blk., red & blue	55	35

International Book Year 1972.

Satellite Earth Station, Satellite and Rainbow
A202

1972, June 6 *Perf. 13*

496	A202	£1 tan & multi.	75	35

Opening of satellite earth station in Israel.

17th Century Ark, Ancona
A203

Candelabrum and "25"
A204

Holy Arks from: 45a, Padua, 1729. 70a, Parma, 17th century. 95a, Reggio Emilia, 1756. Arks moved to Israel from Italian synagogues.

1972, Aug. 8 Photo. *Perf. 14x13*

497	A203	15a dp. brn. & yel.	20	5
498	"	45a dp. green, yel. green & gold	30	15
499	"	70a brn. red, yellow & blue	55	25
500	"	95a magenta & gold	75	40
		Nos. 497-500 (4)	1.80	85
		With tabs	6.00	

Jewish New Year, 5733.

1972, Aug. 8

501	A204	£1 silver, blue & magenta	65	25

25th anniversary of the State of Israel.

Brass Menorah, Morocco, 18th–19th Century
A205

Menorahs: 25a, Brass, Poland, 18th century. 70a, Silver, Germany, 17th century.

1972, Nov. 7 Litho. *Perf. 14x13*

502	A205	12a emerald, blk. & blue green	10	6
503	"	25a lilac rose, black & orange	17	12
504	"	70a bl., blk. & vio.	50	33

Hanukkah (Festival of Lights), 1972.

Child's Drawing
A206

Pendant
A207

Designs: Children's drawings.

1973, Jan. 16 Litho. *Perf. 14*

Sizes: 22½x37mm. (2a, 55a); 17x48mm. (3a).

505	A206	2a black & multi.	3	3
506	"	3a multicolored	3	3
507	"	55a "	30	18
		With tabs	70	

Youth Wing of Israel Museum, Jerusalem (2a, 3a) and Youth Workshops, Tel Aviv Museum (55a).

1973, Jan. 16 Photo. *Perf. 14x13*

508	A207	18a silver & multi.	22	10
		With tab	50	

Immigration of North African Jews.

Levi, by Marc Chagall
A208

Tribes of Israel: No. 510, Simeon. No. 511, Reuben. No. 512, Issachar. No. 513, Zebulun. No. 514, Judah. No. 515, Dan. No. 516, Gad. No. 517, Asher. No. 518, Naphtali. No. 519, Joseph. No. 520, Benjamin.

1973 Lithographed *Perf. 14*

509	A208	£1 multicolored	50	30
510	"	£1 gray grn. & multi.	50	30
511	"	£1 olive & multi.	50	30
512	"	£1 gray bl. & multi.	50	30
513	"	£1 lemon & multi.	50	30
514	"	£1 gray & multi.	50	30
515	"	£1 bl. grn. & multi.	50	30
516	"	£1 gray & multi.	50	30
517	"	£1 yel. grn. & multi.	50	30
518	"	£1 sepia & multi.	50	30
519	"	£1 olive & multi.	50	30
520	"	£1 tan & multi.	50	30
		Nos. 509-520 (12)	6.00	3.60

Designs from stained glass windows by Marc Chagall, Hadassah-Hebrew University Medical Center Synagogue, Jerusalem.

Issue dates: Nos. 509–514, Mar. 27; Nos. 515–520, Aug. 21.

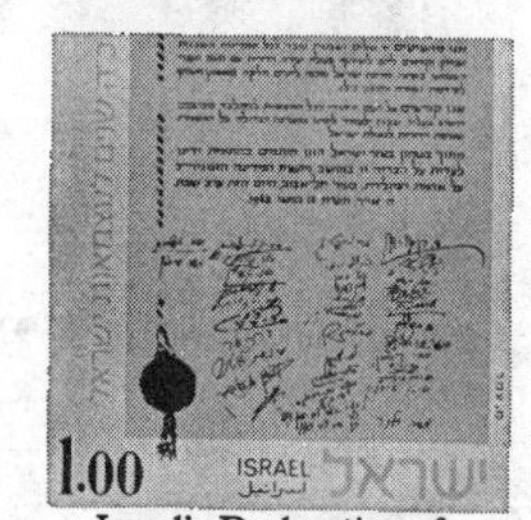

Israel's Declaration of Independence—A209

1973, May 4 Photo. *Perf. 14*

521	A209	£1 ocher & multi.	75	22
		a. Souvenir sheet	3.00	2.25

25 years of independence. No. 521a contains one stamp. Text of Declaration and 25th anniversary symbol in margin which has simulated perforations and silver frame. Size: 65x146mm. Sold for £1.50.

Star of David and Runners
A210

1973, May 4 Lithographed

522	A210	£1.10 multicolored	65	25

9th Maccabiah.

Prison-cloth Hand
A211

1973, May 4 Photogravure

523	A211	55a blue black	30	20

To honor the heroes and martyrs of the Holocaust, 1933–1945.

Flame
A212

Prophet Isaiah
A213

1973, May 4 Lithographed

524	A212	65a multicolored	50	18

Memorial Day 1973.

1973, Aug. 21 Photo. *Perf. 13x14*

Prophets: 65a, Jeremiah. £1.10, Ezekiel.

525	A213	18a multicolored	9	3
526	"	65a "	33	20
527	"	£1.10 ultra. & multi.	55	30

Jewish New Year, 5734.

Torch of Learning, Cogwheel
A214

Rescue Boat and Danish Flag
A215

1973, Oct. 24 *Perf. 14x13*

528	A214	£1.25 slate & multi.	50	25

50th anniversary of the Technion, Israel Institute of Technology.

1973, Oct. 24 *Perf. 13x14*

529	A215	£5 bis., red & black	2.50	1.25

30th anniversary of the rescue by the Danes of the Jews in Denmark.

Spectators at Stamp Show
A216

Design: £1, Spectators, different design.

1973, Dec. 19 Litho. *Perf. 13*

530	A216	20a brown & multi.	10	3
531	"	£1 " "	50	18

JERUSALEM '73 Philatelic Exhibition, Mar.25–Apr. 2, 1974.

Souvenir Sheets

Israel No. 7—A217

Designs (First Issue): £2, No. 8. £3, No. 9.

1974, Feb. 19 Photo. *Perf. 14x13*

532	A217	£1 silver & dark slate green	60	50
533	"	£2 silver & red brn.	1.20	1.10
534	"	£3 silver & blk. bl.	2.40	2.25

Jerusalem '73 Philatelic Exhibition, Mar. 25–Apr. 2, 1974 (postponed from Dec. 1973), commemorating 25th anniversary of State of Israel. Sheets have silver margin with embossed replica of Hebrew silver shekel shown on stamps. Marginal inscriptions in stamp colors. Size: 121x75mm. Each sheet was sold with a 50 per cent surcharge.

Soldier with Prayer Shawl
A218

Quill and Inkwell with Hebrew Letters
A219

1974, Apr. 23 *Perf. 13x14*

535	A218	£1 black & lt. blue	50	20

Memorial Day 1974.

1974, Apr. 23 *Perf. 14x13*

536	A219	£2 gold & black	80	25

50th anniversary of Hebrew Writers Assn.

Lady in Blue, by Moshe Kisling
A220

Designs: £2, Mother and Child, Sculpture by Chana Orloff. £3, Girl in Blue, by Chaim Soutine.

1974, June 11 Litho. *Perf. 14*

537	A220	£1.25 multicolored	50	20
538	"	£2 "	75	30
539	"	£3 "	1.25	50

Art works from Tel Aviv, En Harod and Jerusalem Museums.

Wrench
A221

1974, June 11

540	A221	25a multicolored	15	15

50th anniversary of the Working Youth Movement.

Istanbuli Synagogue, Jerusalem
A222

Designs: Interiors of restored synagogues in Jerusalem's Old City.

1974, Aug. 6 Photo. ***Perf. 13x14***

Multicolored

541 A222 25a *shown* 15 12
542 " 70a *Emtzai Synagogue* 25 20
543 " £1 *Rabbi Yohanan Synagogue* 35 30

Jewish New Year, 5735.

Lady Davis Technical Center "AMAL," Tel Aviv—A223

Designs: 60a, Elias Sourasky Library, Tel Aviv University. £1.45, Mivtahim Rest Home, Zikhron Yaaqov.

1974, Aug. 6 ***Perf. 13½x14***

544 A223 25a violet black 15 12
545 " 60a dark blue 25 20
546 " £1.45 maroon 50 45

Modern Israeli architecture.

David Ben-Gurion
A224

1974, Nov. 5 ***Perf. 14***

547 A224 25a brown 12 10
548 " £1.30 slate green 65 60

David Ben-Gurion (1886–1973), first Prime Minister and Minister of Defense of Israel.

Arrows on Globe
A225

Dove Delivering Letter
A226

1974, Nov. 5 Litho. ***Perf. 14***

549 A225 25a blk. & multi. 12 10

Photogravure

550 A226 £1.30 gold & multi. 65 60

Centenary of Universal Postal Union.

Hebrew University, Mount Scopus, Jerusalem—A227

1975, Jan. 14 Lithographed ***Perf. 13***

551 A227 £2.50 multicolored 80 60

50th anniversary of the Hebrew University in Jerusalem.

Girl Carrying Plant
A228

Welder
A229

Designs: 35a, Bird singing in tree. £2, Boy carrying potted plant.

1975, Jan. 14 ***Perf. 14***

552 A228 1a multicolored 3 3
553 " 35a " 12 10
554 " £2 " 68 60

Arbor Day.

1975, Jan. 14 Photo. ***Perf. 14x13***

Designs: 80a, Tractor driver. £1.20, Electrical lineman.

555 A229 30a multicolored 12 10
556 " 80a " 28 22
557 " £1.20 ultra. & multi. 40 35

Occupational safety and publicity for the Institute for Safety and Hygiene.

Hebrew University Synagogue, Jerusalem—A230

Modern Israeli architecture: £1.30, Yad Mordecai Museum. £1.70, Bat Yam City Hall.

Perf. 14, 13½x14 (#559)

1975, Mar. 5 Photogravure

558 A230 80a brown 28 25
559 " £1.30 slate green 42 35
560 " £1.70 brown olive 56 50

Harry S. Truman
A231

1975, Mar. 5 Engraved ***Perf. 14***

561 A231 £5 dark brown 1.75 1.50

Harry S. Truman (1884–1972), 33rd President of the United States.

Eternal Flame over Soldier's Grave
A232

Memorial Tablet
A233

1975, Apr. 10 Photo. ***Perf. 14x13***

562 A232 £1.45 blk. & multi. 50 35

Memorial Day 1975.

1975, Apr. 10

563 A233 £1.45 black, red & gray 50 35

In memory of soldiers missing in action.

Obstacle Race
A234

Designs: £1.70, Bicycling. £3, Netball.

1975, Apr. 10 ***Perf. 13x14***

564 A234 25a purple & org. 8 5
565 " £1.70 red, green & dark blue 56 45
566 " £3 dark blue & emerald 1.00 80

10th Hapoel Games in connection with the 50th anniversary of the Hapoel Organization.

Hanukkah, by Mortiz D. Oppenheim
A235

Paintings: £1.40, The Purim Players, by Jankel Adler (horiz.). £4, Yom Kippur, by Maurycy Gottlieb.

1975, June 17 Litho. ***Perf. 14***

567 A235 £1 multicolored 30 25
568 " £1.40 " 42 35
569 " £4 " 1.20 1.00

Paintings of religious holidays.

Old Couple
A236

1975, June 17 Photo. ***Perf. 13x14***

570 A236 £1.85 multicolored 65 50
With tab 1.25

International Gerontological Association, 10th triennial conference, Jerusalem.

Zalman Shazar
A237

Pioneer Women's Emblem
A238

1975, Aug. 6 Photo. ***Perf. 14x13***

571 A237 35a silver & black 12 5
With tab 30

Zalman Shazar (1889–1974), poet, journalist, third president of Israel.

1975, Aug. 6 ***Perf. 14½***

572 A238 £5 multicolored 1.25 1.10

Pioneer Women, 50th anniversary.

Gideon
A239

Judges of Israel: £1, Deborah. £1.40, Jephthah.

1975, Aug. 6 ***Perf. 13x14***

573 A239 35a violet & multi. 10 5
574 " £1 green & multi. 30 25
575 " £1.40 brown & multi. 42 35

Jewish New Year, 5736.

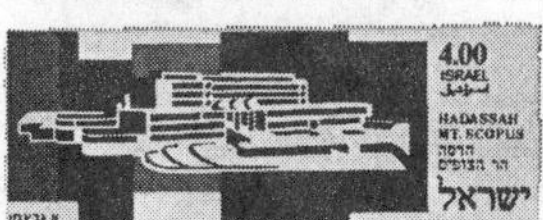

Hebrew University, Mt. Scopus
A240

1975, Oct. 14 Photo. ***Perf. 14x13***

576 A240 £4 multicolored 1.20 90

Return of Hadassah to Mt. Scopus, Jerusalem.

Collared Pratincoles
A241

Birds: £1.70, Spur-winged plover. £2, Black-winged stilts.

1975, Oct. 14 Litho. ***Perf. 13***

577 A241 £1.10 pink & multi. 33 25
578 " £1.70 lemon & multi. 50 35
579 " £2 multicolored 60 45

Protected birds.

Butterfly and Factory (Air Pollution)
A242

Designs: 80a, Fish and tanker (water pollution). £1.70, Ear and jet (noise pollution).

1975, Dec. 9 Photo. *Perf. 14*

580	A242	50a car. & multi.	15	10
581	"	80a grn. & multi.	24	18
582	"	£1.70 org. & multi.	50	35

Environmental protection.

Star of David
A243

1975–78 *Perf. 13x14*

584	A243	75a violet blue & car. ('77)	10	5
588	"	£1.85 violet blue & lt. brown	55	35
590	"	£2.45 violet blue & brt. green ('76)	70	30
591	"	£5.40 violet blue & olive ('78)	65	30

Landscape Type of 1971–75

Design: £10, View of Elat and harbor.

1976, Aug. 17 Photo. *Perf. 14x14½*

592	A193	£10 Prussian blue	2.50	2.00

No. 592 is not tagged.

"In the days of Ahasuerus. ."
A247

Designs (from Book of Esther): 80a, "He set the royal crown on her head." £1.60, "Thus shall it be done to the man whom the king delights to honor."

1976, Feb. 17 Photo. *Perf. 14*

593	A247	40a multicolored	12	10
594	"	80a "	24	20
595	"	£1.60 "	45	40
	a.	Souvenir sheet of 3	1.50	1.50

Purim Festival. No. 595a contains 3 stamps similar to Nos. 593–595, perf. 13x 14; multicolored decorative margin inscribed "Purim 1976." Size: 125½x85 mm. Sold for £4.

Border Settlement, Barbed Wire—A248

1976, Feb. 17

596	A248	£1.50 olive & multi.	42	35

Border settlements, part of Jewish colonization of Holy Land.

Symbolic Key
A249

1976, Feb. 17

597	A249	£1.85 multicolored	52	45

Bezalel Academy of Arts and Design, Jerusalem. 70th anniversary.

"200" U.S. Flag
A250

1976, Apr. 25 Photo. *Perf. 13x14*

598	A250	£4 gold & multi.	1.12	1.00

American Bicentennial.

Dancers of Meron, by Reuven Rubin
A251

1976, Apr. 25 Litho. *Perf. 14*

599	A251	£1.30 multicolored	40	35

Lag Ba-Omer festival.

8th Brigade Monument, Ben-Gurion Airport
A252

1976, Apr. 25 Photo. *Perf. 14x13*

600	A252	£1.85 multicolored	52	50

Memorial Day 1976.

Souvenir Sheet

Tourism, Sport and Industry—A253

1976, Apr. 25

601	A253	Sheet of 3	2.80	2.80
	a.	£1 multicolored	28	
	b.	£2 "	56	
	c.	£4 "	1.12	

No. 601 has buff margin with blue inscription. Size: 112x75mm. Sold for £10.

High Jump
A254

Designs: £2.40, Diving. £4.40, Gymnastics.

1976, June 23 *Perf. 13x14*

602	A254	£1.60 black & red	45	30
603	"	£2.40 blk. & vio. bl.	65	45
604	"	£4.40 black & red lilac	1.25	1.00

21st Olympic Games, Montreal, Canada, July 17–Aug. 1.

Tents and Suns
A255

1976, June 23 *Perf. 14*

605	A255	£1.50 grn. & multi.	42	40

Israel Camping Union.

"Truth"
A256

Pawn
A257

Design: £1.50, "Judgment" (scales). £1.90, "Peace" (dove and olive branch).

1976, Aug. 17 Photo. *Perf. 14x13*

Tagged

606	A256	45a gold & multi.	12	10
607	"	£1.50 " "	42	35
608	"	£1.90 " "	52	45

Festivals 5737.

1976, Oct. 19 Litho. *Perf. 14*

Design: £1.60, Rook.

609	A257	£1.30 multicolored	32	25
610	"	£1.60 "	40	35

22nd Men's and 7th Women's Chess Olympiad, Haifa, Oct. 24–Nov. 11.

Byzantine Building, 6th Century
A258

Designs: 70a, City wall, 7th century B.C. £2.40, Robinson's Arch. £2.80, Steps to Gate of Hulda. Both from area leading to 2nd Temple, 1st century B.C. £5, Wall, Omayyad Palace, 8th century A.D.

1976 Lithographed *Perf. 14*

611	A258	70a multicolored	18	15
612	"	£1.30 "	32	25
613	"	£2.40 "	60	50
614	"	£2.80 "	70	60
615	"	£5 "	1.20	1.00
		Nos. 611–615 (5)	3.00	2.50

Excavations in Old Jerusalem.

Issue dates, Nos. 612–614, Oct. 19. Nos. 611, 615, Dec. 14.

Clearing the Land, 1890
A259

Designs: 10a, Building harbor wall. 60a, Road building (vert.). £1.40, Plower and horse-drawn plow. £1.80, Planting trees.

1976, Dec. 14 Photo. *Perf. 13*

616	A259	5a brown & gold	3	3
617	"	10a purple & gold	3	3
618	"	60a gold & car.	16	15
619	"	£1.40 gold & blue	36	35
620	"	£1.80 green & gold	52	50
		Nos. 616–620 (5)	1.10	1.06

Work of the pioneers.

"Let's Pull up Grandfather's Carrot"—A260

1977, Feb. 15 Litho. *Perf. 14*

621	A260	£2.60 multicolored	75	70

Voluntary service.

Doves, Jew and Arab Shaking Hands
A261

Designs: £1.40, Arab and Jew holding hands, and flowers. £2.70, Peace dove, Arab and Jew dancing. Illustrations for the book "My Shalom–My Peace."

1977, Feb. 15

622	A261	50a multicolored	12	10
623	"	£1.40 "	36	35
624	"	£2.70 "	62	60

Children's drawings for peace.

"By the Rivers of Babylon . . ."—A262

Drawings by Efraim Moshe Lilien: £1.80, Abraham (vert.). £2.10, "May our eyes behold thee when thou returnest to Zion in compassion."

Perf. 14x13, 13x14

1977, Feb. 15 Photogravure

625	A262	£1.70 gray, brown & black	40	30
626	"	£1.80 yellow, black & brown	42	30
627	"	£2.10 lt. green & dark green	48	35

Souvenirs for 5th Zionist Congress, 1902.

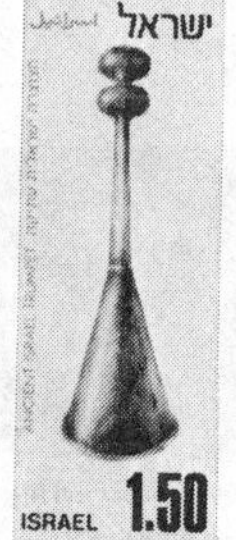

Trumpet
A263

Embroidered Sabbath Cloth
A264

Designs: £2, Lyre. £5, Cymbals.

1977, Apr. 17 Litho. *Perf. 14*

628 A263 £1.50 multicolored 36 35
629 " £2 " 48 45
630 " £5 " 1.20 1.10

Ancient musical instruments, Haifa Music Museum and Amli Library.

1977, Apr. 17 *Perf. 13x14*

631 A264 £3 buff & multi. 72 70

Importance of Sabbath observation in Jewish life.

Parachutists' Memorial, Bilu-Gedera, Tel Aviv
A265

1977, Apr. 17 *Perf. 13x14*

632 A265 £3.30 gray, black & green 80 75

Memorial Day 1977.

Fencing A266

ZOA Convention Emblem A267

Designs: £2.50, Shot put. £3.50, Judo.

1977, June 23 Photo. *Perf. 14x13*

633 A266 £1 gray, bl. & blk. 25 25
634 " £2.50 gray, red & blk. 60 60
635 " £3.50 gray, emerald & black 85 85

10th Maccabiah.

1977, June 23 *Perf. 14*

636 A267 £4 silver & multi. 1.00 90

Convention of Zionist Organization of America (ZOA), Jerusalem, June 1977.

Petah Tikva—A268

1977, June 23 *Perf. 14x13*

637 A268 £1.50 multicolored 36 35

Centenary of Petah Tikva.

Sarah
A269

Matriarchs of the Bible: £1.50, Rebekah. £2, Rachel. £3, Leah.

1977, Aug. 16 Photo. *Perf. 14*

638 A269 70a multicolored 15 14
639 " £1.50 " 30 28
640 " £2 " 40 36
641 " £3 " 60 55

Jewish New Year 5738.

Police A270

Illuminated Page A271

Designs: No. 643, Frontier Guards. No. 644, Civil Guard.

1977, Aug. 16 Litho. *Perf. 14*

642 A270 £1 multicolored 18 18
643 " £1 " 18 18
644 " £1 " 18 18

Israel Police Force, established Mar. 26, 1948.

1977, July 21 Photo. *Perf. 14x13*

645 A271 £4 multicolored 75 72

Fourth centenary of Hebrew printing at Safad.

Farm Growing from Steel Helmet A272

Koffler Accelerator A273

1977, Oct. 18 Litho. *Perf. 14*

646 A272 £3.50 multicolored 60 60

Fighting Pioneer Youth (NAHAL), established 1949.

1977, Oct. 18 Photo. *Perf. 14x13*

647 A273 £8 black & blue 1.50 1.40

Inauguration of Koffler accelerator at Weizmann Institute of Science, Rehovot. Untagged.

Caesarea
A274

Scenes: £1, Arava on the Dead Sea. £20, Rosh Pinna.

1977–78 *Perf. 13½x14*

Size: 27x22mm.

649 A274 10a violet blue 3 3
664 " £1 olive bister 18 18

Perf. 14½x14

Size: 27½x26½

672 A274 £20 orange & dk. green ('78) 2.25 2.10

The 10a and £20 are untagged.

Scott's editorial staff cannot undertake to identify, authenticate or appraise stamps and postal markings.

Listings of stamps issued since this Catalogue went to press will be found in Scott's Monthly Stamp Journal.

First Holy Land Locomotive
A276

Locomotives: £1.50, Jezreel Valley train. £2, British Mandate period. £2.50, Israel Railways.

1977, Dec. 13 Photo. *Perf. 13x14*

674 A276 65a multicolored 10 10
675 " £1.50 " 25 25
676 " £2 " 35 35
677 " £2.50 " 40 40
a. Souvenir sheet of 4 1.50 1.50

Railways in the Holy Land. No. 677a contains one each of Nos. 674–677; blue border and black marginal inscription. Size: 111x74mm. Sold for £10.

Cypraea Isabella
A277

Designs: Red Sea shells.

1977, Dec. 13 Litho. *Perf. 14*

Multicolored

678 A277 £2 *shown* 30 30
679 " £2 *Lioconcha castrensis* 30 30
680 " £2 *Glorípallium pallium* 30 30
681 " £2 *Malea pomum* 30 30

Street in Jerusalem, by Haim Glicksberg (1904–1970)
A278

Paintings: £3.80, Thistles, by Leopold Krakauer (1890–1954). £4.40, An Alley in Zefat, by Mordekhai Levanon (1901–1968).

1978, Feb. 14

682 A278 £3 multicolored 40 40
683 " £3.80 " 55 55
684 " £4.40 " 65 65

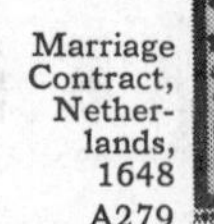

Marriage Contract, Netherlands, 1648
A279

Marriage Contracts (Ketubah): £3.90, Morocco, 1897. £6, Jerusalem, 1846.

1978, Feb. 14

685 A279 75a multicolored 8 8
686 " £3.90 " 60 60
687 " £6 " 90 90

Eliyahu Golomb
A280

Designs: Portraits.

1978, Apr. 23 Photo. *Perf. 14x13*

Multicolored

688 A280 £2 *shown* 25 25
689 " £2 *Dr. Moshe Sneh* 25 25
690 " £2 *David Raziel* 25 25
691 " £2 *Yitzhak Sadeh* 25 25
692 " £2 *Abraham Stern* 25 25
Nos. 688-692 (5) 1.25 1.25

Heroes of underground movement. Nos. 688–692 issued in sheets of 15.

Souvenir Sheet

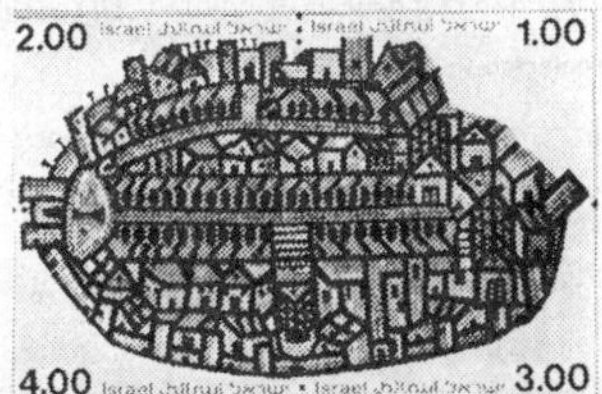

Jerusalem, Mosaic, from Madaba Map—A281

1978, Apr. 23 Litho. *Perf. 14*

693 A281 Sheet of 4 2.00 2.00
a. £1 multicolored 18
b. £2 " 38
c. £3 " 55
d. £4 " 75

Tabir '78 National Stamp Exhibition, Jerusalem, Apr. 23. Size of No. 693: 111x76½mm. Sold for £15.

Flowers
A282

Design: Flowers, after children's paintings on Memorial Wall in Yad-Lebanim Museum, Petah Tikva. Each stamp shows different flowers.

1978, Apr. 23 *Perf. 14*

694 Sheet of 15, multi. 3.00
a. A282 £1.50 single stamp 20 20

Memorial Day.

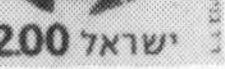

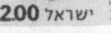

Theodor Herzl A283

Chaim Weizmann A284

1978, July 5 Photo. *Perf. 14x13*

695 A283 £2 gray & gray olive 25 25
696 A284 £2 buff & vio. blue 25 25

Theodor Herzl (1860–1904), writer, founder of Zionism, and Chaim Weizmann (1874–1952), chemist, first president of Israel.

Hatiqwa, 1st Verse
A285

YMCA Building, Jerusalem
A286

1978, July 4 *Perf. 13x14*

697 A285 £8.40 multicolored 75 75

Centenary of Israeli National Anthem, Hatiqwa, by poet Naftali Herz Imber.

1978, July 4 Litho. *Perf. 13*

698 A286 £5.40 multicolored 60 60

Centenary of Young Men's Christian Association in Jerusalem.

Rabbi Kook (1865–1935)
A287

Abraham and Isaac
A288

Design: No. 700, Rabbi Ouziel (1880–1963).

1978, Aug. 22 Photo. *Perf. 14x13*

699 A287 £2 pale gray & slate green 25 25
700 " £2 pale gray & dark purple 25 25

1978, Aug. 22 *Perf. 14*

Patriarchs: £5.20, Isaac. £6.60, Jacob.

701 A288 £1.10 multicolored 14 10
702 " £5.20 " 65 40
703 " £6.60 " 85 45

Festivals 5739.

Families and Houses
A289

1978, Aug. 22 *Perf. 13x14*

704 A289 £5.10 multicolored 65 40

Social welfare.

David Ben-Gurion
A290

Star of David and Growing Tree
A291

Design: No. 706, Ze'ev Jabotinsky.

1978, Oct. 31 Photo. *Perf. 14x13*

705 A290 £2 buff & vio. brn. 25 18
706 " £2 gray & indigo 25 18

30 years of independence. David Ben-Gurion (1886–1973), first Prime Minister, and Ze'ev Vladimir Jabotinsky (1880–1940), leader of World Union of Zionist Revisionists.

1978, Oct. 31 Litho. *Perf. 14*

707 A291 £8.40 multicolored 1.00 65

United Jewish Appeal, established 1939 in U.S. to help Israel.

Old and New Hospital Buildings
A292

1978, Oct. 31

708 A292 £5.40 multicolored 65 45

Opening of new Shaare Zedek Medical Center, Jerusalem.

Silver and Enamel Vase, India
A293

Designs: £3, Elephant with howdah, Persia, 13th century. £4, Mosque lamp, glass and enamel, Syria, 14th century.

1978, Oct. 31

709 A293 £2.40 multicolored 30 20
710 " £3 " 36 26
711 " £4 " 50 35

Leo Arie Mayer Memorial Museum for Islamic Art, Jerusalem.

Menachem Ussishkin (1863–1941)
A294

Iris Lortetii
A295

Portraits: No. 713, Berl Katzenelson (1878–1944). No. 714, Max Nordau (1849–1923).

1978, Dec. 26 Photo. *Perf. 14x13*

712 A294 £2 citron & slate green 25 18
713 " £2 gray & vio. bl. 25 18
714 " £2 buff & black 25 18

30th anniversary of independence.

1978, Dec. 26 Litho. *Perf. 14*

Protected Wild Flowers: £5.40, Iris haynei. £8.40, Iris nazarena.

715 A295 £1.10 multicolored 14 10
716 " £5.40 " 65 45
717 " £8.40 " 1.05 70

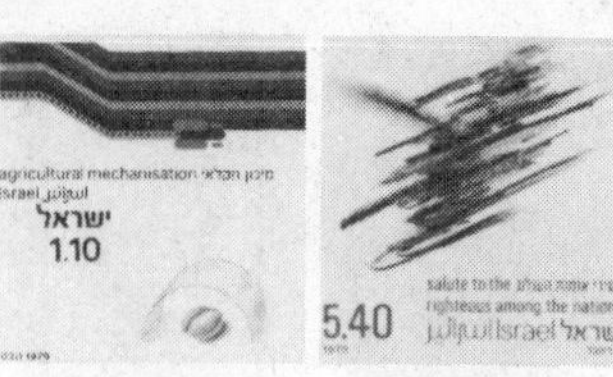

Agricultural Mechanization
A296

"Hope from Darkness"
A297

Symbolic Designs: £2.40, Seawater desalination. £4.30, Electronics. £5, Chemical fertilizers.

1979, Feb. 13 Litho. *Perf. 13*

718 A296 £1.10 multicolored 14 10
719 " £2.40 " 30 20
720 " £4.30 " 55 40
721 " £5 " 62 45

Technological Achievements.

1979, Feb. 13

722 A297 £5.40 multicolored 65 45

Salute to "the Righteous among Nations," an award to those who helped during Nazi period.

Jewish Brigade Flag
A298

1979, Feb. 13 Photo. *Perf. 14*

723 A298 £5.10 bl., yel. & blk. 62 45

Jewish Brigade served with British Armed Forces during WWII.

Paper (Prayer for Peace) in Crevice of Western Wall
A299

Weightlifting
A300

1979, Mar. 26 Photo. *Perf. 14x13*

724 A299 £10 multicolored 1.25 90
a. Souvenir sheet 1.50

Signing of peace treaty between Israel and Egypt, Mar. 26. No. 724a contains one imperf. stamp; brown margin shows Western (Wailing) Wall. Size: 117x77mm.

1979, Apr. 23 Litho. *Perf. 13*

Designs: £6, Tennis. £11, Gymnastics.

725 A300 £1.50 multicolored 18 12
726 " £6 " 75 52
727 " £11 " 1.38 95

11th Hapoel Games.

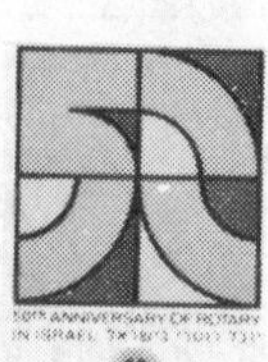

"50" and Rotary Emblem
A301

1979, Apr. 23 Photogravure

728 A301 £7 multicolored 88 65

Rotary International in Israel, 50th anniversary.

Navy Memorial, Ashdod
A302

1979, Apr. 23

729 A302 £5.10 multicolored 62 45

Memorial Day.

AIR POST STAMPS.

Doves Pecking at Grapes
AP1

Marisa Eagle
AP2

Designs: 30p, Beth Shearim eagle. 40p, Mosaic bird. 50p, Stylized dove. 250p, Mosaic dove and olive branch.

Lithographed.

1950, June 25 *Perf. 11½* Unwmkd.

No.	Type	Description	Unused	Used
C1	AP1	5p bright greenish blue	1.00	60
C2	"	30p gray	35	35
C3	"	40p dark green	90	60
C4	"	50p henna brown	1.35	60
C5	AP2	100p rose carmine	16.00	10.00
C6	"	250p dark gray blue	4.50	2.00
		Nos. C1-C6 (6)	24.10	14.15
		With tabs 300.00		

Haifa Bay and City Seal
AP3

Design: 120p, Haifa, Mt. Carmel and city seal.

1952, Apr. 13 *Perf. 14*

Seal in Gray

No.	Type	Description	Unused	Used
C7	AP3	100p ultramarine	50	50
C8	"	120p purple	60	60
		With tabs 27.50		

Stamps were available only on purchase of a ticket to the National Stamp Exhibition, Haifa. Price, including ticket, 340 pruta.

Olive Tree
AP4

Tanur Cascade
AP5

Coast at Tel Aviv-Jaffa
AP6

Designs: 70p, En Gev, Sea of Galilee. 100p, Road to Jerusalem. 150p, Lion Rock. 350p, Bay of Elat, Red Sea. 750p, Lake Hule. 3000p, Tomb of Rabbi Meir Baal Haness, Tiberias.

1953-56 Lithographed.

No.	Type	Description	Unused	Used
C9	AP4	10p olive green	8	5
C10	"	70p violet	12	15
C11	"	100p green	15	10
C12	"	150p orange brown	20	15
C13	"	350p carmine rose	45	25
C14	AP5	500p dull & dk. blue	75	40
C15	AP6	750p brown	80	35
C16	"	1000p dp. bl. grn.	4.75	4.00
		With tab 135.00		
C17	AP6	3000p claret	3.00	1.50
		Nos. C9-C17 (9)	10.30	6.95
		Nos. C9-C15, C17 with tab 8.50		

Dates of issue: 1000p, Mar. 16, 1953; 10p, 100p, 500p, Mar. 2, 1954; 70p, 150p, 350p, Apr. 6, 1954; 750p, Aug. 21, 1956; 3000p, Nov. 13, 1956.

Old Town, Zefat
AP7

Designs: 20a, Ashkelon, Afridar Center. 25a, Acre, tower and boats. 30a, Haifa, view from Mt. Carmel. 35a, Capernaum, ancient synagogue (horiz.). 40a, Jethro's tomb (horiz.). 50a, Jerusalem (horiz.). 65a, Tiberias, tower and lake (horiz.). £1, Jaffa (horiz.).

Perf. 13x14, 14x13

1960-61 Photo. Unwmkd.

No.	Type	Description	Unused	Used
C18	AP7	15a light lilac & black	15	5
C19	"	20a bright yellow green & black	18	8
C20	"	25a orange & black ('61)	25	15
C21	"	30a greenish blue & black ('61)	60	45
C22	"	35a yellow green & black ('61)	75	60
C23	"	40a light violet & black ('61)	80	70
C24	"	50a olive & black ('61)	60	35
C25	"	65a lt. ultra. & black	75	60
C26	"	£1 pink & black ('61)	1.50	1.50
		Nos. C18-C26 (9)	5.58	4.48
		With tabs 17.50		

Dates of issue: Nos. C18, C19, C25, Feb. 24, 1960. Nos. C20-C22, June 14, 1961. Nos. C23, C24, C26, Oct. 26, 1961.

Port of Elat ('Aqaba)—AP8

Lithographed

1962, Feb. 21 *Perf. 14* Wmk. 302

No.	Type	Description	Unused	Used
C27	AP8	£3 multicolored	5.50	3.50
		With tab	16.50	

Houbara Bustard
AP9

Birds: 5a, Sinai rose finch (horiz.). 20a, White-breasted kingfisher (horiz.). 28a, Mourning wheatear (horiz.). 30a, Blue-cheeked bee eater. 40a, Graceful prinia. 45a, Palestine sunbird. 70a, Scops owl. £1, Purple heron. £3, White-tailed Sea eagle.

Photogravure

1963 *Perf. 13x14, 14x13* Unwmkd.

No.	Type	Description	Unused	Used
C28	AP9	5a dp. vio. & multi.	10	5
C29	"	20a red & multi.	22	15
C30	"	28a emerald & multi.	30	20
C31	"	30a orange & multi.	30	20
C32	AP9	40a multicolored	35	30
C33	"	45a yel. & multi.	40	35
C34	"	55a multicolored	45	35
C35	"	70a blk. & multi.	50	40
C36	"	£1 multicolored	75	50
C37	"	£3 ultra. & multi.	2.50	1.75
		Nos. C28-C37 (10)	5.87	4.25
		With tabs 11.50		

Dates of issue: Nos. C28-C30, Apr. 15. Nos. C31-C33, June 19. Nos. C34-C36, Feb. 13. No. C37, Oct. 23.

Diamond and Boeing 707
AP10

Designs (Boeing 707 and): 10a, Textiles. 30a, Symbolic stamps. 40a, Vase and jewelry. 50a, Chick and egg. 55a, Melon, avocado and strawberries. 60a, Gladioli. 80a, Electronic equipment and chart. £1, Heavy oxygen isotopes (chemical apparatus). £1.50, Women's fashions.

1968 Photogravure *Perf. 13x14*

No.	Type	Description	Unused	Used
C38	AP10	10a ultra. & multi.	6	5
C39	"	30a gray & multi.	18	16
C40	"	40a multicolored	24	20
C41	"	50a "	30	25
C42	"	55a "	33	28
C43	"	60a slate green, lt. green & red	36	30
C44	"	80a yellow, brown & lt. blue	48	40
C45	"	£1 dk. blue & org.	60	50
C46	"	£1.50 multicolored	90	75
C47	"	£3 pur. & lt. blue	1.75	1.50
		Nos. C38-C47 (10)	5.20	4.39

Issued to publicize Israeli exports. Sheets of 15 (5x3).

Dates of issue: Nos. C38-C41, Mar. 11; No. C47, Feb. 7; Nos. C42-C43, C45, Nov. 6; Nos. C44, C46, Dec. 23.

POSTAGE DUE STAMPS.

Types of Regular Issue Overprinted in Black דמי דאר

Designs: Various coins, as on postage denominations.

Typographed.

1948, May 28 *Perf. 11* Unwmkd.

Yellow Paper.

No.	Type	Description	Unused	Used
J1	A1	3m orange	3.50	3.00
J2	"	5m yellow green	5.00	4.50
J3	"	10m red violet	15.00	7.50
J4	"	20m ultramarine	37.50	30.00
J5	"	50m orange brown	100.00	100.00
		Nos. J1-J5 (5)	161.00	145.00
		With tabs (blank) *2750.00*		

The 3m, 20m and 50m are known with overprint omitted.

Nos. J1-J5 exist imperf.

D1

Running Stag
D2

Perf. 11½

1949, Dec. 18 Litho. Unwmkd.

No.	Type	Description	Unused	Used
J6	D1	2(p) orange	10	10
J7	"	5(p) purple	15	15
J8	"	10(p) yellow green	20	20
J9	"	20(p) vermilion	60	50
J10	"	30(p) violet blue	90	65
J11	"	50(p) orange brown	1.40	1.00
		Nos. J6-J11 (6)	3.35	2.60
		With tabs (blank) 125.00		

1952, Nov. 30 *Perf. 14* Unwmkd.

No.	Type	Description	Unused	Used
J12	D2	5p orange brown	3	3
J13	"	10p Prussian blue	3	3
J14	"	20p magenta	4	4
J15	"	30p gray black	6	6
J16	"	40p green	7	7
J17	"	50p brown	10	10
J18	"	60p purple	12	12
J19	D2	100p red	20	20
J20	"	250p blue	50	50
		Nos. J12-J20 (9)	1.15	1.15
		With tabs (blank) 9.00		

OFFICIAL STAMPS.

Redrawn Type of 1950 Overprinted in Black בול שרות

1951, Feb. 1 *Perf. 14* Unwmkd.

No.	Type	Description	Unused	Used
O1	A6	5p bright red violet	8	8
O2	"	15p vermilion	12	10
O3	"	30p ultramarine	25	20
O4	"	40p orange brown	35	25
		Nos. O1-O4 (4)	80	63
		With tabs 25.00		

ITALIAN COLONIES

General Issues for all Colonies.

100 Centesimi=1 Lira

Types of Italy, Dante Alighieri Society Issue, in New Colors and Overprinted in Red or Black

COLONIE ITALIANE

Wmkd. Crowns. (140)

1932, July 11 ***Perf. 14***

No.	Type	Description	Unused	Used
1	A126	10c gray black	25	25
2	"	15c olive brown	25	25
3	"	20c slate green	25	25
4	"	25c dark green	25	25
5	"	30c red brown (Bk)	25	25
6	"	50c blue black	25	25
7	"	75c car. rose (Bk)	40	40
8	"	1.25 l dark blue	40	25
9	"	1.75 l violet	1.10	1.35
10	"	2.75 l orange (Bk)	1.10	1.35
11	"	5 l+2 l olive green	1.10	1.35
12	"	10 l+2.50 l dp. blue	1.10	1.35
		Nos. 1-12 (12)	6.70	7.55

Types of Italy, Garibaldi Issue, in New Colors and Inscribed:

"POSTE COLONIALI ITALIANE".

1932, July 1 **Photogravure**

No.	Type	Description	Unused	Used
13	A138	10c green	75	90
14	"	20c carmine rose	75	90
15	"	25c green	75	90
16	"	30c green	75	90
17	"	50c carmine rose	75	90
18	A141	75c carmine rose	75	90
19	"	1.25 l deep blue	75	90
20	"	1.75 l+25c dp. blue	3.25	4.50
21	A144	2.55 l+50c olive brown	3.25	4.50
22	A145	5 l+1 l deep blue	3.25	4.50
		Nos. 13-22 (10)	15.00	19.80

Plowing with Oxen

A1

Pack Camel

A2

Lioness

A3

Wmk. 140

1933, Mar. 27 **Wmk. 140**

No.	Type	Description	Unused	Used
23	A1	10c olive brown	1.50	1.85
24	A2	20c dull violet	1.50	1.85
25	A3	25c green	1.50	1.85
26	A1	50c purple	1.50	1.85
27	A2	75c carmine	1.50	1.85
28	A3	1.25 l blue	1.50	1.85
29	A1	2.75 l red orange	3.75	5.00
30	A2	5 l+2 l gray grn.	12.00	20.00
31	A3	10 l+2.50 l orange brown	12.00	20.00
		Nos. 23-31 (9)	36.75	56.10

Annexation of Eritrea by Italy, 50th anniversary.

Agricultural Implements

A4

Arab and Camel

A5

"Eager with New Life"

A7

Steam Roller

A6

1933 **Photo.** ***Perf. 14***

No.	Type	Description	Unused	Used
32	A4	5c orange	1.25	1.50
33	A5	25c green	1.25	1.50
34	A6	50c purple	1.25	1.50
35	A4	75c carmine	1.25	1.50
36	A5	1.25 l deep blue	1.25	1.50
37	A6	1.75 l rose red	1.25	1.50
38	A4	2.75 l dark blue	1.25	1.50
39	A5	5 l brownish black	5.00	7.50
40	A6	10 l bluish black	5.00	7.50
41	A7	25 l gray black	12.50	20.00
		Nos. 32-41 (10)	31.25	45.50

10th anniversary of Fascism. Each denomination bears a different inscription.

Issue dates: 25 l, Dec. 26. Others, Oct. 5.

Mercury and Fasces

A8

1934, Apr. 18

No.	Type	Description	Unused	Used
42	A8	20c red orange	45	65
43	"	30c slate green	45	65
44	"	50c indigo	45	65
45	"	1.25 l blue	45	65

15th annual Trade Fair, Milan.

Scoring a Goal

A9

Soccer Kickoff

A10

1934, June 5

No.	Type	Description	Unused	Used
46	A9	10c olive green	2.75	3.75
47	"	50c purple	3.75	4.75
48	"	1.25 l blue	7.50	10.00
49	A10	5 l brown	15.00	21.50
50	"	10 l gray blue	20.00	30.00
		Nos. 46-50 (5)	49.00	70.00

2nd World Soccer Championship.

SEMI-POSTAL STAMPS

Many issues of Italy and Italian Colonies include one or more semi-postal denominations. To avoid splitting sets, these issues are generally listed as regular postage, airmail, etc., unless all values carry a surtax.

AIR POST STAMPS.

Dante Alighieri Society Issue.

Italian Air Post Stamps of 1932 in New Colors and Overprinted in Red or Black

COLONIE ITALIANE

Wmkd. Crowns. (140)

1932, July 11 ***Perf. 14***

No.	Type	Description	Unused	Used
C1	AP10	50c gray black (R)	65	35
C2	AP11	1 l indigo (R)	65	35
C3	"	3 l gray (R)	90	1.25
C4	"	5 l olive brn. (R)	90	1.25
C5	AP10	7.70 l+2 l carmine rose	90	1.25
C6	AP11	10 l+2.50 l orange	90	1.25
		Nos. C1-C6 (6)	4.90	5.70

Leonardo da Vinci

AP1

1932, Sept. 7 **Photo.** ***Perf. 14½***

No.	Type	Description	Unused	Used
C7	AP1	100 l deep green & brown	8.00	13.50

Garibaldi Issue

Types of Italian Air Post Stamps of 1932 in New Colors and Inscribed:

"POSTE AEREA COLONIALE ITALIANA"

1932, July 1

No.	Type	Description	Unused	Used
C8	AP13	50c carmine rose	65	1.00
C9	AP14	80c green	65	1.00
C10	AP13	1 l+25c olive brn.	2.25	3.25
C11	"	2 l+50c olive brn.	2.25	3.25
C12	AP14	5 l+1 l olive brn.	2.25	3.25
		Nos. C8-C12 (5)	8.05	11.75

Eagle—AP2

Savoia Marchetti 55

AP3

Savoia Marchetti 55 over Map of Eritrea—AP4

1933 ***Perf. 14.***

No.	Type	Description	Unused	Used
C13	AP2	50c orange brn.	1.50	2.00
C14	"	1 l black violet	1.50	2.00
C15	AP3	3 l carmine	1.50	2.65
C16	"	5 l olive brown	1.50	2.65
C17	AP2	7.70 l + 2 l slate	8.50	14.00
C18	AP3	10 l + 2.50 l dp. blue	8.50	14.00
C19	AP4	50 l dark violet	8.50	14.00
		Nos. C13-C19 (7)	31.50	51.30

50th anniversary of Italian Government of Eritrea.

Issue dates: 50 l, June 1. Others, Mar. 27.

Macchi-Castoldi Seaplane

AP5

Savoia S73

AP6

Winding Propeller

AP7

"More Efficient Machinery"

AP8

1933–34

No.	Type	Description	Unused	Used
C20	AP5	50c orange brown	1.75	2.40
C21	AP6	75c red violet	1.75	2.40
C22	AP5	1 l bistre brown	1.75	2.40
C23	AP6	3 l olive gray	1.75	2.40
C24	AP5	10 l deep violet	1.75	2.40
C25	AP6	12 l blue green	1.75	2.40
C26	AP7	20 l gray black	6.00	8.50
C27	AP8	50 l blue ('34)	13.50	20.00
		Nos. C20-C27 (8)	30.00	42.90

Tenth anniversary of Fascism.

Issue dates: 50 l, Dec. 26. Others, Oct. 5.

Natives Hailing Dornier Wal

AP9

1934, Apr. 24

C28	AP9	25 l brown olive	8.00	13.50

Issued in honor of Luigi Amadeo, Duke of the Abruzzi (1873–1933).

Airplane over Stadium AP10

Goalkeeper Leaping AP11

Seaplane and Soccer Ball—AP12

1934, June

C29	AP10	50c yellow brown	1.75	3.25
C30	"	75c deep violet	1.75	3.25
C31	AP11	5 l brown black	8.50	13.50
C32	"	10 l red orange	8.50	13.50
C33	AP10	15 l car. rose	8.50	13.50
C34	AP11	25 l green	12.00	20.00
C35	AP12	50 l blue green	13.50	20.00
		Nos. C29-C35 (7)	54.50	87.00

World Soccer Championship Games, Rome. Issue dates: 50 l, June 21. Others, June 5.

AIR POST SPECIAL DELIVERY STAMPS.

Garibaldi Type of Italy

Wmkd. Crowns. (140)

1932, Oct. 6 Photo. ***Perf. 14***

CE1	APSD1	2.25 l+1 l dark violet & slate	2.50	3.25
CE2	"	4.50 l+1.50 l dark brown & green	2.50	3.25

ITALIAN EAST AFRICA

LOCATION — In eastern Africa, bordering on the Red Sea and Indian Ocean.

GOVT.—Former Italian Colony.

AREA—665,977 sq. mi. (estimated)

POP.—12,100,000 (estimated).

CAPITAL—Asmara.

This colony was formed in 1936 and included Ethiopia and the former colonies of Eritrea and Italian Somaliland. For previous issues see listings under these headings.

100 Centesimi = 1 Lira

Grant's Gazelle A1

Eagle and Lion A2

King Victor Emmanuel III A3

Fascist Legionary A5

Statue of the Nile A4

Desert Road—A6

Wmk. 140

Wmkd. Crowns. (140)

1938, Feb. 7 Photo. ***Perf. 14***

1	A1	2c red orange	15	15
2	A2	5c brown	15	12
3	A3	7½c dark violet	22	22
4	A4	10c olive brown	15	12
5	A5	15c slate green	15	15
6	A3	20c crimson	15	12
7	A6	25c green	15	12
8	A1	30c olive brown	15	15
9	A2	35c sapphire	22	22
10	A3	50c purple	15	12
		Engraved		
11	A5	75c carmine lake	27	20
12	A6	1 l olive green	27	12
13	A3	1.25 l deep blue	27	22
14	A4	1.75 l orange	2.65	12
15	A2	2 l cerise	27	22
16	A6	2.55 l dark brown	1.00	1.00
17	A1	3.70 l purple	9.00	4.75
18	A5	5 l blue	1.00	27
19	A2	10 l henna brown	2.65	1.00
20	A4	20 l dull green	2.65	1.35
		Nos. 1-20 (20)	21.67	10.74

Augustus Caesar (Octavianus) A7

Goddess Abundantia A8

1938, Apr. 25 Photo. ***Perf. 14***

21	A7	5c bistre brown	27	35
22	A8	10c copper red	27	35
23	A7	25c deep green	35	40
24	A8	50c purple	35	40
25	A7	75c crimson	35	40
26	A8	1.25 l deep blue	35	40
		Nos. 21-26, C12-C13 (8)	2.77	3.40

Bimillenary of the birth of Augustus Caesar (Octavianus), first Roman emperor.

Native Boat A9

Native Soldier A10

Statue Suggesting Italy's Conquest of Ethiopia A11

1940, May 11 **Wmk. 140**

27	A9	5c olive brown	15	20
28	A10	10c red orange	15	20
29	A11	25c green	60	75
30	A9	50c purple	60	75
31	A10	75c rose red	60	75
32	A11	1.25 l dark blue	60	75
33	A10	2 l+75c rose carmine	65	85
		Nos. 27-33, C14-C17 (11)	5.35	7.05

Issued in connection with the first Triennial Overseas Exposition held at Naples.

Hitler and Mussolini ("Two Peoples, One War") A12

1941, June 19

34	A12	5c ochre	15
35	"	10c chestnut	15
36	"	20c black	40
37	"	25c turquoise green	40
38	"	50c rose lilac	40
39	"	75c rose carmine	40
40	"	1.25 l bright ultramarine	45
		Nos. 34-40 (7)	2.35

Issued in commemoration of the Rome-Berlin Axis.

Four stamps of type AP8, without "Posta Aerea", were prepared in 1941, but not issued. Price, each $8.50.

SEMI-POSTAL STAMPS

Many issues of Italy and Italian Colonies include one or more semi-postal denominations. To avoid splitting sets, these issues are generally listed as regular postage, air-mail, etc., unless all values carry a surtax.

AIR POST STAMPS.

Plane Flying over Mountains AP1

Mussolini Carved in Stone Cliff AP2

Airplane over Lake Tsana—AP3

Bataleur Eagle AP4

Eagle Attacking Serpent AP5

Wmkd. Crowns. (140)

1938, Feb. 7 Photo. ***Perf. 14***

C1	AP1	25c slate green	40	40
C2	AP2	50c olive brown	9.00	12
C3	AP3	60c red orange	20	40
C4	AP1	75c orange brown	1.10	35
C5	AP4	1 l slate blue	12	12
		Engraved.		
C6	AP2	1.50 l violet	20	20
C7	AP3	2 l slate blue	20	27
C8	AP1	3 l carmine lake	27	45
C9	AP4	5 l red brown	1.20	55
C10	AP2	10 l violet brown	2.40	1.00
C11	AP1	25 l slate blue	3.75	2.25
		Nos. C1-C11 (11)	18.84	6.11

1938, Apr. 25 **Photogravure**

C12	AP5	50c bistre brown	33	40
C13	"	1 l purple	50	70

Bimillenary of the birth of Augustus Caesar (Octavianus), first Roman emperor.

Tractor AP6

Plane over City
AP7

1940, May 11

C14 AP6 50c olive gray 40 55
C15 AP7 1 l purple 40 55
C16 AP6 2 l+75c gray blue 60 85
C17 AP7 5 l+2.50 l red brown 60 85

Issued in connection with the first Triennial Overseas Exposition held at Naples.

Hitler and Mussolini ("Two Peoples, One War")—AP8

AP9

1941, Apr. 24

C18 AP8 1 l slate blue 8.00
C19 AP9 1 l slate blue 65

Issued in commemoration of the Rome-Berlin Axis.

AIR POST SPECIAL DELIVERY STAMPS.

Plow and Airplane
APSD1

Wmkd. Crowns. (140)

1938, Feb. 7 Engr. ***Perf. 14***

CE1 APSD1 2 l slate blue 20 27
CE2 " 2.50 l dark brown 27 40

SPECIAL DELIVERY STAMPS

King Victor Emmanuel III—SD1

Wmkd. Crowns. (140)

1938, Apr. 16 Engraved ***Perf. 14***

E1 SD1 1.25 l dark green 20 20
E2 " 2.50 l dark carmine 32 50

POSTAGE DUE STAMPS.

Italy, Nos. J28 to J40, Overprinted in Black **A.O.I.**

1941 ***Perf. 14.*** **Wmk. 140**

J1 D6 5c brown 30
J2 " 10c blue 30
J3 D6 20c rose red 45
J4 " 25c green 45
J5 " 30c red orange 60
J6 " 40c black brown 75
J7 " 50c violet 90
J8 " 60c slate black 1.00
J9 D7 1 l red orange 12.50
J10 " 2 l green 12.50
J11 " 5 l violet 12.50
J12 " 10 l blue 12.50
J13 " 20 l carmine rose 12.50
Nos. J1-J13 (13) 67.25

In 1943 a set of 11 "Segnatasse" stamps, picturing a horse and rider and inscribed "A. O. I.," was prepared but not issued. Price, $4.

ITALIAN SOMALILAND

(See Somalia in Vol. IV.)

ITALIAN STATES

MODENA

(mô'dȧ-nä)

LOCATION—In northern Italy.
GOVT.—Former Duchy.
AREA—1,003 sq. mi.
POP.—448,000 (approx.).
CAPITAL—Modena.

In 1852, when the first postage stamps were issued, Modena was under the rule of Duke Francis V of the House of Este-Lorraine. In June, 1859, he was overthrown and the Duchy was annexed to the Kingdom of Sardinia which on March 17, 1861, became the Kingdom of Italy.

100 Centesimi = 1 Lira

Prices of Modena stamps vary according to condition. Quotations are for fine copies, the unused with original gum. Very fine to superb specimens sell at much higher prices, and inferior to poor copies sell at reduced prices, depending on the condition of the individual specimens.

Coat of Arms
A1

Typographed

1852 ***Imperf.*** **Unwmkd.**

Without Period After Figures of Value.

1 A1 5c *green* 175.00 32.50
 a. Pair, one with period 350.00 650.00
2 " 10c *rose* 150.00 45.00
 a. "EENT. 10" 2250.00 850.00
 b. "1 " of "10" inverted 2250.00 850.00
 c. "CNET" 300.00 600.00
 d. No period after "CENT" 450.00 250.00
 e. Pair, one with period after "10" 350.00 900.00
3 " 15c *yellow* 17.50 15.00
 a. "CETN 15." 2750.00 300.00
 b. No period after "CENT" 90.00 150.00
4 " 25c *buff* 20.00 15.00
 a. No period after "CENT" 100.00 200.00
 b. "ENT. 25" omitted 300.00
5 " 40c *blue* 135.00 75.00
 a. 40c pale blue 3000.00 275.00
 b. No period after "CENT" 400.00 350.00
 c. As "a," no period after "CENT"
 d. Pair, one with period after "40" 275.00 1000.00

Unused examples of No. 5a lack gum.

With Period After Figures of Value.

6 A1 5c *green* 13.50 22.50
 a. 5c olive green 100.00 40.00
 As "a," without gum 12.00
 b. "ENT" 2400.00 1200.00
 c. "CNET" 1800.00 1100.00
 d. As "a," "CNET" 900.00 600.00
 e. "C[illegible]NT" 1750.00 1000.00
 f. As "a," "CEN1" 900.00 600.00
 g. As "a," no period after "5" 300.00 600.00
 h. Double impression 425.00
 i. As "a," double impression 400.00
7 " 10c *rose* 70.00 120.00
 a. "CENE" 300.00 600.00
 b. "CNET" 300.00 550.00
 c. "CE6T" 250.00 650.00
 d. "CEZT" 2000.00 1500.00
 e. Double impression 300.00
8 " 40c *blue* 17.50 90.00
 a. "CNET" 125.00 400.00
 b. "CENE" 200.00 600.00
 c. "CE6T" 200.00 600.00
 d. "49" 125.00 350.00
 e. "4C" 250.00 750.00
 f. "CEN.T"

Wmk. 157

Wmkd. Large Letter A. (157)

9 A1 1 l black 12.00 1000.00
 a. With period after "LIRA" 100.00 1350.00

Provisional Government.

Coat of Arms
A2

1859 **Unwmkd.**

10 A2 5c green 140.00 325.00
 a. 5c emerald 185.00 375.00
 b. 5c dark green 160.00 325.00
11 " 15c brown 185.00 1500.00
 a. 15c gray brown 60.00
 b. 15c black brown 350.00 1000.00
 c. No period after "15" 350.00
 d. Period before "CENT" 450.00
 e. Double impression 275.00
12 " 20c lilac 20.00 325.00
 a. 20c violet 140.00 65.00
 b. 20c blue violet 160.00 80.00
 c. No period after "20" 30.00 450.00
 d. "ECNT" 140.00 1500.00
 e. "N" inverted 90.00 650.00
 f. Double impression 1000.00
13 " 40c carmine 40.00 600.00
 a. 40c brown rose 40.00 600.00
 b. No period after "40" 110.00 1100.00
 c. Period before "CENT" 150.00 1250.00
 d. Inverted "5" before the "C"
14 " 80c buff 45.00 7500.00
 a. 80c brown orange 50.00 7500.00
 b. "CENT 8" 100.00
 c. "CENT 0" 100.00
 d. No period after "80" 100.00
 e. "N" inverted 150.00

The reprints of the 1859 issue have the word "CENT" and the figures of value in different type from the originals. There is no frame line at the bottom of the small square in the lower right corner.

NEWSPAPER TAX STAMPS.

NT1

NT2

Typographed.

1853 ***Imperf.*** **Unwmkd.**

B. G. CEN. 9 — Type I.
B. G. CEN. 9. — Type II.

PR1 NT1 9c *violet*, (I) 4250.00 1350.00
PR2 " 9c *violet*, (II) 110.00 60.00
 a. No period after "9" 300.00 120.00

All known unused examples of No. PR1 lack gum.

1855-57

PR3 A1 9c *violet* 75
 a. No period after "9" 1.50
PR4 " 10c *gray vio.* ('57) 20.00 125.00
 a. "CEN1" 140.00 550.00

No. PR3 was never placed in use.

1859

PR5 NT2 10c black 185.00 800.00

These stamps did not pay postage, but were a fiscal tax collected by the postal authorities on newspapers arriving from foreign countries.

The stamps of Modena were superseded by those of Sardinia in February, 1860.

PARMA

(pär'mȧ)

LOCATION—Comprising the present provinces of Parma and Piacenza in northern Italy.
GOVT.—A former independent Duchy.
AREA—2,750 sq. mi. (1860).
POP.—500,000 (1860).
CAPITAL—Parma.

Parma was annexed to Sardinia in 1860.

100 Centesimi = 1 Lira

Prices of Parma stamps vary according to condition. Quotations are for fine copies. Very fine to superb specimens sell at much higher prices, and inferior or poor copies sell at reduced prices, depending on the condition of the individual specimen.

Prices for unused are for copies with gum except No. 8 which is known only without gum. Copies of other stamps without gum sell for about a third less.

Crown and Fleur-de-lis
A1 A2

Typographed.

1852 ***Imperf.*** **Unwmkd.**

1 A1 5c *yellow* 25.00 45.00
2 " 10c *white* 25.00 45.00
3 " 15c *pink* 600.00 25.00
 a. Tête bêche pair 22,500.00
 b. Dbl. impression 1350.00
4 " 25c *violet* 2250.00 70.00
5 " 40c *blue* 550.00 135.00
 a. 40c *pale blue* 1250.00 150.00

1854-55

6 A1 5c orange yellow 1200.00 300.00
 a. 5c lemon yel. 2000.00 350.00
 b. Dbl. impression

7 A1 15c red 1600.00 72.50
8 " 25c red brn. ('55) 5000.00 100.00
a. Dbl. impression

No. 8 unused is without gum.

1857-59

9 A2 15c red ('59) 50.00 *200.00*
10 " 25c red brown 110.00 50.00
11 " 40c blue, wide "O" ('58) 20.00 *185.00*
a. Narrow "O" in "40" 27.50 *225.00*

Provisional Government.

A3

1859

12 A3 5c yellow green 100.00 *5500.00*
a. 5c blue green 200.00 *1650.00*
13 " 10c brown 75.00 *275.00*
a. 10c deep brown 75.00 *275.00*
b. "1" of "10" inverted 250.00 *2000.00*
c. Thick "O" in "10" 125.00 *400.00*
14 " 20c pale blue 135.00 100.00
a. 20c deep blue 135.00 110.00
b. Thick "O" in "20" 175.00 120.00
15 " 40c red 100.00 *2500.00*
a. 40c brown red *2750.00 2500.00*
b. Thick "O" in "40" 125.00 *2500.00*
16 " 80c orange yellow *1600.00 6500.00*
a. 80c olive yellow *1600.00 6500.00*
d. Thick "O" in "80" *2000.00*

Nos. 12–16 exist in two other varieties: with spelling "CFNTESIMI" and with small "A" in "STATI." These are priced about 50 per cent more than normal stamps.

NEWSPAPER TAX STAMPS.

NT1

Typographed.

1853-57 *Imperf.* **Unwmkd.**

PR1 NT1 6c *rose* ('57) 20.00
a. 6c *deep rose* 125.00 125.00
PR2 " 9c *blue* 12.50 *10,000.00*

These stamps belong to the same class as the Newspaper Tax Stamps of Modena, Austria, etc. No. PR1 was not regularly issued.

Note following No. 16 also applies to Nos. PR1–PR2.

The stamps of Parma were superseded by those of Sardinia in 1860.

ROMAGNA

(rô-män'yä)

LOCATION — Comprised the present Italian provinces of Forlì, Ravenna, Ferrara and Bologna.

GOVT.—Formerly one of the Roman States.

AREA—5,626 sq. mi.

POP.—1,341,091 (1853).

CAPITAL—Ravenna.

Postage stamps were issued when a provisional government was formed pending the unification of Italy. In 1860 Romagna was annexed to Sardinia and since 1862 the postage stamps of Italy have been used.

100 Bajocchi = 1 Scudo

> Prices of Romagna stamps vary according to condition. Quotations are for fine copies. Very fine to superb specimens sell at much higher prices, and inferior or poor copies sell at reduced prices, depending on the condition of the individual specimen.

A1

Typographed.

1859 *Imperf.* **Unwmkd.**

1 A1 ½b *straw* 12.50 *200.00*
2 " 1b *drab* 12.50 *90.00*
3 " 2b *buff* 15.00 *90.00*
4 " 3b *dark green* 20.00 *225.00*
5 " 4b *fawn* 150.00 100.00
6 " 5b *gray violet* 20.00 *300.00*
7 " 6b *yellow green* 125.00 *4500.00*
8 " 8b *rose* 80.00 *950.00*
9 " 20b *gray green* 80.00 *1750.00*

These stamps have been reprinted several times. The reprints usually resemble the originals in the color of the paper but there are impressions on incorrect colors and also in colors on white paper. They often show broken letters and other injuries. The Y shaped ornaments between the small circles in the corners are broken and blurred and the dots outside the circles are often missing or joined to the circles.

Forged cancellations are plentiful.

The stamps of Romagna were superseded by those of Sardinia in February, 1860.

ROMAN STATES

(rō'măn stāts)

LOCATION — Comprised most of the central Italian Peninsula, bounded by the former Kingdom of Lombardy-Venetia and Modena on the north, Tuscany on the west, and the Kingdom of Naples on the southeast.

GOVT. — Formerly under the direct government of the See of Rome.

AREA—16,000 sq. mi.

POP.—3,124,758 (1853).

CAPITAL—Rome.

Upon the formation of the Kingdom of Italy, the area of the Roman States was greatly reduced and in 1870 they disappeared from the political map of Europe. Postage stamps of Italy have been used since that time.

100 Bajocchi = 1 Scudo

100 Centesimi = 1 Lira (1867)

> Prices of Roman States stamps vary according to condition. Quotations are for fine copies. Very fine to superb specimens sell at much higher prices, and inferior or poor copies sell at reduced prices depending on the condition of the individual specimen.
> Prices for unused are for copies with original gum.

Papal Arms

A1 A2

A3 A4

A5

A6

A7

A8

A9

A10

A11

Typographed.

1852 *Imperf.* **Unwmkd.**

1 A1 ½b *dull violet* 30.00 *90.00*
a. ½b *gray blue* 175.00 45.00
b. ½b *gray lilac* 120.00 80.00
c. ½b *gray* 150.00 45.00
d. ½b *reddish violet* 600.00 250.00
e. ½b *dark violet* 140.00 150.00
f. Tête bêche pair *5000.00*
i. Double impression *2000.00*
j. Impression on both sides *3000.00*
2 A2 1b *blue green* 40.00 8.50
a. 1b *gray green* 55.00 5.00
c. Printed with grayish greasy ink 200.00 10.00
d. Double impression *2000.00*
e. Impression on both sides *3000.00*
3 A3 2b *greenish white* 3.00 *17.50*
a. 2b *yellow green* 65.00 3.25
d. Printed with grayish greasy ink 275.00 10.00
e. No period after "BAJ" (*greenish white*) 150.00 10.00
f. As "a," no period after "BAJ" 100.00 15.00
g. Double impression *1350.00*
4 A4 3b *brown* 65.00 11.00
a. 3b *light brown* 70.00 12.00
b. 3b *yellow brown* 100.00 30.00
c. 3b *yellow buff* 7.00 *50.00*
g. Printed with grayish greasy ink 900.00 40.00
h. Impression on both sides *2750.00*
i. Double impression *2000.00*
5 A5 4b *lemon* 60.00 27.50
a. 4b *yellow* 60.00 27.50
b. 4b *rose brown* 600.00 27.50
c. 4b *gray brown* 700.00 27.50
f. Impression on both sides *3000.00*
g. Ribbed paper 70.00 30.00
h. Printed with grayish greasy ink *1000.00* 40.00
6 A6 5b *rose* 50.00 4.00
a. 5b *pale rose* 100.00 5.00
c. Impression on both sides *3000.00*
d. Double impression *2400.00*
e. Printed with grayish greasy ink 275.00 13.50
7 A7 6b *grayish green* 100.00 13.50
a. 6b *gray* 140.00 16.50
b. 6b *grayish lilac* 150.00 50.00
c. Printed with grayish greasy ink 400.00 45.00
d. Double impression *2000.00*
8 A8 7b *blue* 150.00 30.00
b. Double impression *1000.00*
c. Printed with grayish greasy ink 400.00 50.00

9 A9 8b black 50.00 15.00
c. Double impression
d. Printed with grayish greasy ink 450.00 55.00
10 A10 50b dull blue 2250.00 900.00
a. 50b deep blue (worn impression) 2500.00 900.00
11 A11 1sc rose 1000.00 *2000.00*

Counterfeits exist of Nos. 10–11. Fraudulent cancellations are found on No. 11.

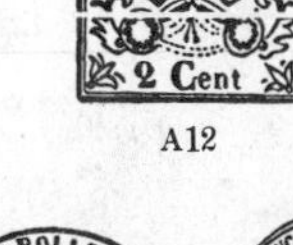

A12

A13 A14

A15 A16

A17 A18

1867 Glazed Paper. *Imperf.*

12 A12 2c *green* 45.00 *85.00*
a. No period after "Cent" 55.00 *100.00*
13 A13 3c *gray* 225.00 *3000.00*
a. 3c *lilac gray* 500.00 *900.00*
14 A14 5c *light blue* 55.00 *110.00*
a. No period after "5" 150.00 *275.00*
15 A15 10c *vermilion* 225.00 17.50
a. Double impression *1500.00*
16 A16 20c *copper red* (unglazed) 40.00 20.00
a. No period after "20" 175.00 65.00
b. No period after "CENT" 175.00 65.00
17 A17 40c *yellow* 50.00 *165.00*
a. No period after "40" 50.00 *165.00*
18 A18 80c *lilac rose* 50.00 *250.00*
a. No period after "80" 120.00 *450.00*

Imperforate stamps on unglazed paper, or in colors other than listed, are unfinished remainders of the 1868 issue.

Fraudulent cancellations are found on Nos. 13, 14, 17, 18.

1868 Glazed Paper. *Perf. 13.*

19 A12 2c *green* 2.00 *17.50*
a. No period after "Cent" 2.25 *120.00*
20 A13 3c *gray* 17.50 *1250.00*
a. 3c *lilac gray* *1000.00 5000.00*
21 A14 5c *light blue* 4.00 *15.00*
a. No period after "5" 6.00 *20.00*
b. No period after "Cent" 25.00 *80.00*
c. 5c *light blue* (unglazed, imperf., without gum) 10.00
22 A15 10c *orange vermilion* 85 *3.50*
a. 10c *vermilion* 120.00 4.00
b. 10c *vermilion* (unglazed) 1.00 1.10
c. 10c *vermilion* (unglazed, imperf., without gum)

23 A16 20c *deep crimson* 1.00 *6.00*
a. 20c *magenta* 1.35 *6.00*
b. 20c *magenta* (unglazed) 1.35 *6.00*
c. 20c *magenta* (imperf., without gum) 75
d. 20c *copper red* (unglazed) 275.00 6.50
e. 20c *deep crimson* (imperf., without gum) 75
f. No period after "20" (*copper red*) *500.00* 25.00
g. No period after "20" (*magenta*) 4.50 13.50
h. No period after "20" (*deep crimson*) 2.25 *6.00*
i. No period after "CENT" (*copper red*) *500.00* 25.00
j. No period after "CENT" (*magenta*) 4.50 15.00
k. No period after "CENT" (*deep crimson*) 4.50 15.00
24 A17 40c *greenish yellow* 2.00 *45.00*
a. 40c *yellow* 2.00 *45.00*
b. 40c *orange yellow* 2.75 *45.00*
c. No period after "40" 2.50 *45.00*
25 A18 80c *rose lilac* 7.00 *135.00*
a. 80c *bright rose* *850.00* *6000.00*
b. 80c *rose* (unglazed) 7.00
c. No period after "80" (*rose lilac*) 25.00

All values except the 3c are known imperforate vertically or horizontally.

Double impressions are known of the 5c. 10c, 20c (all three colors), 40c and 80c.

Fraudulent cancellations are found on Nos. 20, 24 and 25.

The stamps of the 1867 and 1868 issues have been privately reprinted; many of these reprints are well executed and it is difficult to distinguish them from the originals. Most reprints show more or less pronounced defects of the design. On the originals the horizontal lines between stamps are unbroken, while on most of the reprints these lines are broken. Most of the perforated reprints gauge 11½.

Roman States stamps were replaced by those of Italy in 1870.

SARDINIA

(sär·dĭn'ĭ·ȧ)

LOCATION—An island in the Mediterranean Sea off the west coast of Italy and a large area in northwestern Italy, including the cities of Genoa, Turin and Nice.

GOVT.—A former Kingdom.

As a result of war and revolution, most of the former independent Italian States were joined to the Kingdom of Sardinia in 1859 and 1860. On March 17, 1861, the name was changed to the Kingdom of Italy.

100 Centesimi = 1 Lira

Prices of Sardinia stamps vary according to condition. Quotations for Nos. 1–9 are for fine copies. Very fine to superb specimens sell at much higher prices, and inferior or poor copies sell at reduced prices, depending on the condition of the individual specimen.

Prices for unused are for copies with original gum.

King Victor Emmanuel II

A1 A2

A3 A4

Lithographed.

1851 ***Imperf.*** **Unwmkd.**

1 A1 5c gray black 800.00 750.00
a. 5c black 800.00 750.00
2 " 20c blue 850.00 80.00
a. 20c deep blue 900.00 90.00
3 " 40c rose 900.00 1350.00
a. 40c violet rose 1250.00 1650.00

1853 **Embossed**

4 A2 5c *blue green* 900.00 400.00
a. Double embossing *1800.00*
5 " 20c *dull blue* 1150.00 80.00
a. Double embossing 500.00
6 " 40c *pale rose* 900.00 375.00
a. Double embossing *1500.00*

1854 **Litho. & Embossed.**

7 A3 5c yellow green *6500.00* 250.00
a. Double embossing 700.00
b. 5c green 50.00
8 " 20c blue *2250.00* 70.00
a. Double embossing *300.00*
b. 20c indigo 30.00
9 " 40c rose *16,000.00* 1100.00
a. Double embossing *3000.00*
b. 40c brown rose 25.00

Nos. 7b, 8b and 9b, differing in shade from the original stamps, were prepared but not issued.

Typographed Frame in Color.

Colorless Embossed Center.

1855-63 ***Imperf.*** **Unwmkd.**

Stamps of this issue vary greatly in color, paper and sharpness of embossing as between the early (1855-59) printings and the later (1860-63) ones. Year dates after each color name indicate whether the stamp falls into the Early or Late printing group.

As a rule, early printings are on smooth thick paper with sharp embossing, while later printings are usually on paper varying from thick to thin and of inferior quality with embossing less distinct and printing blurred. The outer frame shows a distinct design on the early printings, while this design is more or less blurred or even a solid line on the later printings.

10 A4 5c green ('62-63) 1.50 *6.00*
a. 5c yellow green ('62-63) 1.50 *6.00*
b. 5c olive green ('60-61) 50.00 15.00
c. 5c yellow green ('55-59) *250.00* 25.00
d. 5c myrtle green ('57) *1350.00* 100.00
e. 5c emerald ('55-57) *900.00* 100.00
f. Head inverted *1200.00*
g. Double head, one inverted *1750.00*
11 " 10c bistre ('63) 1.00 *3.00*
a. 10c ochre ('62) 200.00 6.00
b. 10c olive bistre ('62) 12.00 4.00
c. 10c olive brown ('61) 25.00 7.00
d. 10c reddish brown ('61) 40.00 10.00
e. 10c gray brown ('61) 30.00 6.00
f. 10c olive gray ('60-61) 30.00 25.00
g. 10c gray ('60) 60.00 20.00
h. 10c brown ('59) 30.00 20.00
i. 10c violet brown ('59) 125.00 55.00
j. 10c dark brown ('58) *300.00* 90.00
k. Head inverted *1000.00*
l. Double head, one inverted *1250.00*
12 " 20c indigo ('62) 10.00 3.75
a. 20c blue ('61) 15.00 3.50
b. 20c light blue ('60-61) 25.00 3.50
c. 20c Prussian blue ('59-60) 50.00 10.00
d. 20c indigo('57-58) 100.00 6.00
e. 20c sky blue ('55-56) *800.00* 35.00
f. 20c cobalt ('55) *800.00* 45.00
g. Head inverted *500.00*
h. Double head, one inverted *800.00*

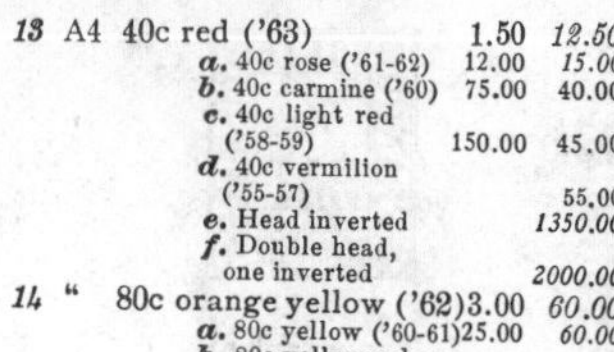

13 A4 40c red ('63) 1.50 *12.50*
a. 40c rose ('61-62) 12.00 *15.00*
b. 40c carmine ('60) 75.00 40.00
c. 40c light red ('58-59) 150.00 45.00
d. 40c vermilion ('55-57) 55.00
e. Head inverted *1350.00*
f. Double head, one inverted *2000.00*
14 " 80c orange yellow ('62) 3.00 *60.00*
a. 80c yellow ('60-61) 25.00 *60.00*
b. 80c yellow ochre ('59) *200.00* 100.00
c. 80c ochre ('58) 50.00 100.00
d. 80c brown orange ('58) 75.00 100.00
e. Head inverted *5000.00*
15 " 3l bronze ('61) 90.00 *1200.00*

Forgeries of the inverted and double head varieties have been made by applying a faked head embossing to printer's waste without head. These forgeries are plentiful.

Fraudulent cancellations are found on Nos. 13–15.

The 5c, 20c and 40c have been reprinted; the embossing of the reprints is not as sharp as that of the originals, the colors are dull and blurred.

NEWSPAPER STAMPS.

N1

Typographed and Embossed.

1861 ***Imperf.*** **Unwmkd.**

P1 N1 1c black 50 85
a. Numeral "2" 75.00 *500.00*
b. Figure of value inverted *400.00* *7000.00*
c. Double impression *1100.00*
P2 " 2c black 12.00 15.00
a. Numeral "1" *2500.00* *7000.00*
b. Figure of value inverted *400.00* *7000.00*

Forgeries of the varieties of the embossed numerals have been made from printer's waste without numerals.

The stamps of Sardinia were superseded in 1862 by those of Italy, which were identical with the 1855 issue of Sardinia, but perforated. Until 1863, imperforate and perforated stamps were issued simultaneously.

TUSCANY

(tŭs'kȧ·nĭ)

LOCATION — In the north central part of the Apennine Peninsula.

GOVT. — A former Grand Duchy, now a department of Italy.

AREA—8,890 sq. mi.

POP.—2,892,000 (approx.).

CAPITAL—Florence.

Tuscany was annexed to Sardinia in 1860.

60 Quattrini = 20 Soldi = 12 Crazie = 1 Lira

100 Centesimi = 1 Lira (1860)

Prices of Tuscany stamps vary according to condition. They were narrowly spaced. Quotations are for fine copies. Very fine to superb copies with margins all around sell at much higher prices. Inferior specimens with designs partly cut away sell at greatly reduced prices, depending on the individual specimen.

Prices for unused stamps are for copies with original gum. Copies without gum sell for about 40 per cent less.

Lion of Tuscany

A1

Wmk. 185

(Reduced Illustration)

The watermark consists of twelve crowns, arranged in four rows of three, with horizontal and vertical lines between them. Only parts of the watermark appear on each stamp.

Wmkd. Crowns in the Sheet. (185)

1851-52 **Typographed.** ***Imperf.***

Blue, Grayish Blue or Gray Paper.

1 A1 1q black ('52) 1100.00 375.00
2 " 1s ochre 2000.00 600.00
a. 1s orange 2000.00 600.00
b. 1s yellow 2000.00 600.00
3 " 2s scarlet *7000.00* 1750.00
4 " 1cr carmine 1000.00 30.00
a. 1cr brown carmine 1100.00 30.00
5 " 2cr blue 725.00 22.50
a. 2cr greenish blue 725.00 35.00
6 " 4cr green 1000.00 30.00
a. 4cr bluish green 1000.00 40.00
7 " 6cr blue 1000.00 30.00
a. 6cr slate blue 1000.00 30.00
b. 6cr indigo 1000.00 30.00
8 " 9cr gray lilac 2750.00 65.00
a. 9cr deep violet 2750.00 65.00
9 " 60cr red ('52) *15,000.00* *5500.00*

The first paper was blue, later paper more and more grayish. Stamps on distinctly blue paper sell about 20 percent higher, except Nos. 3 and 9 which were issued on blue paper only. Examples without watermark are proofs.

Reprints of Nos. 3 and 9 have re-engraved value labels, color is too brown and impressions blurred and heavy. Paper same as originals.

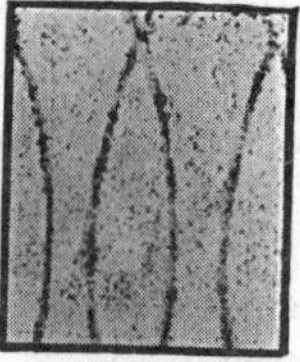

Wmk. 184

Wmkd.

Interlaced Wavy Lines. (184)

Wmk. 184 has double lined letters diagonally across the sheet readiing: "II R R POSTE TOSCANE".

1857–59 **White Paper.**

10 A1 1q black 210.00 275.00
11 " 1s yellow *5750.00* 950.00
12 " 1cr carmine 1350.00 125.00
13 " 2cr blue 400.00 25.00
14 " 4cr blue green 1250.00 65.00
15 " 6cr deep blue *1650.00* 50.00
16 " 9cr gray lilac ('59) *4500.00* *1500.00*

Provisional Government.

Coat of Arms—A2

1860

17 A2 1c brown lilac 300.00 165.00
a. 1c red lilac 300.00 165.00
b. 1c gray lilac 300.00 165.00
18 " 5c green 1350.00 60.00
a. 5c olive grn. 1350.00 60.00
b. 5c yel. grn. 1350.00 60.00
19 " 10c gray brown 165.00 13.50
a. 10c dp. brown 165.00 13.50
b. 10c purple brown 165.00 13.50
20 " 20c blue 725.00 35.00
a. 20c deep blue 725.00 35.00
b. 20c gray blue 725.00 35.00
21 " 40c rose 950.00 65.00
a. 40c carmine 950.00 65.00
22 " 80c pale red brown *2500.00* 210.00
a. 80c brown orange *2500.00* 210.00
23 " 3l ochre *30,000.00 14,000.00*

Dangerous counterfeits exist of Nos. 1–PR1c.

NEWSPAPER TAX STAMP.

NT1

Typographed.

1854 *Imperf.* Unwmkd.

Yellowish Pelure Paper.

PR1 NT1 2s black 3.25
a. Tête bêche pair 125.00
b. Tête bêche pair, one stamp on back 125.00
c. Dbl. impression 100.00

This stamp represented a fiscal tax on newspapers coming from foreign countries. It was not cancelled when used.

The stamps of Tuscany were superseded by those of Sardinia in 1861.

TWO SICILIES

(tōō sĭs'ĭ-lĭz)

LOCATION — Formerly comprised the island of Sicily and the lower half of the Apennine Peninsula.

GOVT. — A former independent Kingdom.

CAPITAL—Naples.

The Kingdom was annexed to Sardinia in 1860.

200 Tornesi = 100 Grana = 1 Ducat

Prices of Two Sicilies stamps vary according to condition. Quotations for Nos. 1–18 are for fine copies. Very fine to superb specimens sell at much higher prices, and inferior or poor copies sell at reduced prices, depending on the condition of the individual specimen.

Prices for unused are for copies with original gum.

Naples

Coat of Arms
A1 A2

A3

A4

A5

A6

A7

Wmk. 186

Wmkd.

Fleurs-de-Lis in Sheet. (186)

1858 Engraved. *Imperf.*

1 A1 ½g pale lake 300.00 90.00
a. ½g rose lake 325.00 100.00
b. ½g lake 350.00 165.00
c. ½g carmine lake 400.00 140.00
2 A2 1g pale lake 110.00 15.00
a. 1g rose lake 140.00 17.50
b. 1g brown lake 120.00 17.50
c. 1g carmine lake 120.00 22.50
d. Printed on both sides *500.00*
e. Double impression 75.00
3 A3 2g pale lake 50.00 3.50
a. 2g rose lake 55.00 3.50
b. 2g lake 125.00 13.50
c. 2g carmine lake 150.00 15.00
d. Impression of 1g on reverse *850.00*
e. Double impression *125.00* 30.00
f. Printed on both sides *750.00*
4 A4 5g rose lake 325.00 25.00
a. 5g brown lake 350.00 35.00
b. 5g carmine lake 650.00 45.00
c. Double impression 475.00 50.00
d. Printed on both sides *2500.00*
5 A5 10g rose lake 600.00 55.00
a. 10g lake 625.00 65.00
b. 10g car. lake 700.00 65.00
c. Printed on both sides *4000.00*
d. Double impression 125.00
6 A6 20g rose lake 750.00 165.00
a. 20g lake 800.00 175.00
b. Double impression *225.00*
7 A7 50g rose lake *2100.00* 1350.00
a. 50g lake *2250.00* 1500.00
b. Double impression *4000.00*

As a secret mark, the engraver, G. Masini, placed a minute letter of his name just above the lower outer line of each stamp. There were three plates of the 2g, one plate of the 50g, and two plates of each of the other values.

Nos. 1 to 7, except No. 3, have been reprinted in bright rose and Nos. 1 and 7 in dull brown. The reprints are on thick unwatermarked paper. Price $8 each.

Provisional Government.

A8

A9

1860

8 A8 ½t deep blue *47,500.00 5000.00*
9 A9 ½t blue *7250.00* 1750.00
a. ½t deep blue *7250.00* 1750.00

100 varieties of each.

No. 8 was made from the plate of No. 1, which was altered by changing the "G" to "T".

No. 9 was made from the same plate after a second alteration erasing the coat of arms and inserting the Cross of Savoy. Dangerous counterfeits exist of Nos. 8–9.

Sicily

Ferdinand II
A10

Engraved.

1859 *Imperf.* Unwmkd.

10 A10 ½g orange 160.00 *600.00*
a. ½g yellow *1500.00* 800.00
b. ½g olive yellow *5000.00*
c. Printed on both sides *7000.00*
11 " 1g dark brown *6500.00* 500.00
a. 1g olive brown (I) *6750.00* 525.00
12 " 1g olive green 55.00 90.00
a. 1g grayish olive green (II) 125.00 55.00
b. 1g olive brn. (II) 400.00 50.00
c. Double impression *1800.00 2000.00*
13 " 2g blue 60.00 40.00
a. 2g deep blue *500.00* 100.00
b. Printed on both sides *5000.00*
14 " 5g carmine 325.00 275.00
a. 5g deep rose 450.00 300.00
b. 5g brick red 650.00 300.00
15 " 5g vermilion 110.00 *800.00*
a. 5g orange vermilion 110.00 *800.00*
16 " 10g dark blue 200.00 140.00
a. 10g indigo 225.00 150.00
17 " 20g dk. gray violet 225.00 250.00
18 " 50g dk. brown red 165.00 *2500.00*

There were three plates each for the 1g and 2g, two each for the ½g and 5g and one plate each for the other values.

Nos. 10a, 10b, 11, 11a, 14, 14a, 14b and 15 are printed from Plate I on which the stamps are 2 to 2½mm. apart. On almost all stamps from Plate I, the S and T of POSTA touch.

Nos. 12a, and 15a are from Plate II and No. 12 is from Plate III. On both Plates II and III stamps are spaced 1½mm. apart. Most stamps from Plate II have a white line about 1mm. long below the beard.

The ½g blue is stated to be a proof of which two copies are known used on cover.

Fraudulent cancellations are known on Nos. 10, 15, 15a and 18.

Neapolitan Provinces.

King Victor Emmanuel II
A11

Lithographed.

Center Embossed.

1861 *Imperf.* Unwmkd.

19 A11 ½t green 3.50 *35.00*
a. ½t yellow green 4.00 *35.00*
b. ½t emerald 275.00 100.00
c. ½t blk. (error) *3000.00 6000.00*
d. Head inverted (green) 60.00
e. Head inverted (yellow green) *3000.00*
f. Printed on both sides *5000.00*
20 A11 ½g bistre brown 25.00 *85.00*
a. ½g brown 27.50 *85.00*
b. ½g gray brown 450.00 85.00
c. Head invtd. *850.00*
21 " 1g black 40.00 8.00
a. Head inverted *750.00*
22 " 2g blue 13.50 4.00
a. 2g deep blue 13.50 3.75
b. Head inverted *125.00 200.00*
c. 2g black (error) *9000.00*
23 " 5g carmine rose 25.00 25.00
a. 5g vermilion 30.00 37.50
b. 5g lilac rose 45.00 45.00
c. Head invtd. *400.00 1500.00*
e. Printed on both sides *3000.00*
25 " 10g orange 15.00 *45.00*
a. 10g ochre *450.00* 125.00
b. 10g bistre 30.00 *60.00*
26 " 20g yellow 90.00 *300.00*
a. Head inverted *3250.00*
27 " 50g gray 5.00 *2500.00*
a. 50g slate 8.50 *2500.00*
b. 50g slate blue 12.50 *2750.00*

Counterfeits of the inverted head varieties of this issue are plentiful. See note on forgeries after Sardinia No. 15.

Fraudulent cancellations are found on Nos. 19–20, 23–27.

Stamps similar to those of Sardinia 1855–61, type A4 but with inscriptions in larger, clearer lettering, were prepared in 1861 for the Neapolitan Provinces. They were not officially issued although a few are known postally used. Denominations: 5c, 10c, 20c, 40c and 80c.

Stamps of Two Sicilies were replaced by those of Italy in 1862.

ITALY

(ĭt'ȧ-lĭ)

LOCATION—Southern Europe.

GOVT.—Republic.

AREA—119,764 sq. mi.

POP.—56,450,000 (est. 1977).

CAPITAL—Rome.

Formerly a Kingdom, Italy became a republic in June, 1946.

100 Centesimi = 1 Lira

See Sardinia for stamps formerly listed as Italy Nos. 1–16 and black 1c and 2c newspaper stamps, type N1.

Prices

of Italy Nos. 17–91, J1–J27, O1–O8 and Q1–Q6 are for specimens in fine condition with original gum. Very fine to superb specimens sell at higher prices. Copies without gum or with perforations cutting into the design sell at much lower prices.

King Victor Emmanuel II
A4 A5

Typographed; Head Embossed.

1862 *Perf. 11½x12.* Unwmkd.

17 A4 10c bistre *3750.00* 125.00
a. 10c yel. brown *3750.00* 125.00
b. 10c brown *8500.00* 165.00
19 " 20c dark blue 8.00 15.00
20 " 40c red 150.00 80.00
21 " 80c orange 25.00 *850.00*

The outer frame shows a distinct design on the early printings, while this design is more or less blurred, or even a solid line, on the later printings.

The 20c and 40c exist perf. 11½. These are remainders of Sardinia with forged perforations.

Counterfeit cancellations are often found on No. 21.

Lithographed; Head Embossed.

1863 *Imperf.*

22 A4 15c blue 60.00 20.00
a. Head inverted 9000.00
b. Double head 75.00 35.00

Two types of No. 23:
Type I. First "C" in bottom line nearly closed.
Type II. "C" open. Line broken below "Q."

1863 **Lithographed**

23 A5 15c blue (type II) 85 1.40
a. Type I 325.00 3.75

No. 23a unused without gum, price $7.

A6

A7

King Victor Emmanuel II
A8 A13

Wmk. 140

Wmkd. Crown. (140)

1863-77 **Typographed** *Perf. 14*

24 A6 1c gray green 1.50 30
a. Imperf., pair 4250.00
25 A7 2c orange brown ('65) 6.50 25
a. Imperf., pair 135.00 200.00
26 A8 5c slate green 225.00 30
27 " 10c buff 325.00 30
a. 10c orange brown 350.00 30
28 " 10c blue ('77) 850.00 70
29 " 15c blue 325.00 35
a. Imperf., pair 2250.00
30 " 30c brown 10.00 70
a. Imperf., pair 3500.00
31 " 40c carmine 700.00 60
a. 40c rose 700.00 60
32 " 60c lilac 12.00 7.00
33 A13 2 l vermilion 15.00 30.00

Nos. 26 to 32 have the head of type A8 but with different corner designs for each value.

Early printings of Nos. 24-27, 29-33 were made in London, later printings in Turin. Prices are for Turin printings. London printings of 1c, 2c, 30c, 60c and 2 l sell for more.

No. 29 Surcharged in Brown

1865

Type I. Dots flanking stars in oval, and dot in eight check-mark ornaments in corners.
Type II. Dots in oval, none in corners.
Type III. No dots.

34 A8 20c on 15c blue (I) 210.00 30
a. Type II 1750.00 4.00
b. Type III 650.00 50
c. Invtd. surch. (I) 11,000.00
d. Dbl. surch. (I)
e. Double surch. (III) 4500.00

A15

1867-77 **Typographed.**

35 A15 20c blue 175.00 15
36 " 20c orange ('77) 700.00 20

Official Stamps Surcharged in Blue

1877

37 O1 2c on 2c lake 30.00 5.50
a. Inverted surcharge 250.00
38 " 2c on 5c lake 30.00 6.50
a. Inverted surcharge 200.00
39 " 2c on 20c lake 250.00 1.50
a. Inverted surcharge 175.00
40 " 2c on 30c lake 60.00 2.00
a. Inverted surcharge 175.00
41 " 2c on 1 l lake 120.00 2.00
a. Inverted surcharge 175.00
42 " 2c on 2 l lake 150.00 2.50
a. Inverted surcharge 200.00
43 " 2c on 5 l lake 190.00 5.00
a. Inverted surcharge 200.00
44 " 2c on 10 l lake 95.00 6.00
a. Inverted surcharge 175.00

King Humbert I
A17

1879 **Typographed** *Perf. 14*

45 A17 5c blue green 10.00 22
46 " 10c claret 90.00 22
47 " 20c orange 80.00 20
48 " 25c blue 120.00 30
49 " 30c brown 55.00 1000.00
50 " 50c violet 7.50 2.25
51 " 2 l vermilion 30.00 75.00

Nos. 45 to 51 have the head of type A17 with different corner designs for each value.

Arms of Savoy
A24

King Humbert I
A25

A26

A27

A28

A29

1889

52 A24 5c dark green 150.00 65
53 A25 40c brown 4.50 75
54 A26 45c gray green 600.00 1.00
55 A27 60c violet 4.50 3.00
56 A28 1 l brown & yellow 7.50 1.10
a. 1 l brown & orange 7.50 1.10
57 A29 5 l green & claret 5.00 165.00

Forged cancellations exist on Nos. 49, 51 and 57.

Parcel Post Stamps of 1884-86 Surcharged in Black

Valevole
per le stampe
Cmi = 2

1890

58 PP1 2c on 10c olive gray 1.40 1.50
a. Inverted surch. 40.00 100.00
59 " 2c on 20c blue 1.75 2.00
60 " 2c on 50c claret 17.50 8.00
a. Inverted surcharge 4250.00
61 " 2c on 75c bl. green 1.75 1.50
62 " 2c on 1.25 l orange 17.50 7.00
a. Invtd. surch. 6000.00 4250.00
63 " 2c on 1.75 l brown 7.50 20.00

Stamps of 1879 Surcharged

Cmi 2

1890-91

64 A17 2c on 5c blue green. ('91) 15.00 22.50
a. "2" with thin tail 25.00 40.00
65 A17 20c on 30c brown 100.00 2.00
66 " 20c on 50c violet 110.00 12.00

On Nos. 65-66 the period is omitted in the surcharge.

Arms of Savoy
A33

King Humbert I
A34

A35 A36

A37 A38

1891-96 **Typographed.**

67 A33 5c green 160.00 50
68 A34 10c claret ('96) 5.00 20
69 A35 20c orange ('95) 5.00 20
70 A36 25c blue 5.00 25
71 A37 45c olive green ('95) 4.25 50
72 A38 5 l blue & rose 27.50 37.50

Arms of Savoy
A39

A40 A41

1896-97

73 A39 1c brown 3.00 65
74 A40 2c orange brown 3.00 20
75 A41 5c green ('97) 7.50 15

A42

A43

A44

Coat of Arms

A45

A46

King Victor Emmanuel III

1901-26

76 A42 1c brown 10 10
a. Imperf., pair 300.00 300.00
77 A43 2c orange brown 10 5
a. Double impression 17.50 17.50
b. Imperf., pair 67.50 67.50
78 A44 5c blue green 25.00 5
a. Imperf., pair
79 A45 10c claret 30.00 10
a. Imperf., pair 3750.00
80 " 20c orange 3.75 5
81 " 25c deep blue 27.50 12
a. 25c ultramarine 27.50 12
82 A46 25c green & pale green ('26) 25 6
83 A45 40c brown 135.00 1.50
84 " 45c olive green 2.75 10
a. Imperf., pair 115.00 135.00
85 " 50c violet 140.00 4.00
86 A46 75c dark red & rose ('26) 1.60 15
87 " 1 l brown & green 1.50 5
a. Imperf., pair 45.00 45.00
88 " 1.25 l blue & ultra. ('26) 1.75 10
89 " 2 l dark green & orange ('23) 7.50 50
90 " 2.50 l dark green & orange ('26) 25.00 1.00
91 " 5 l blue & rose 7.50 50
Nos. 76-91 (16) 409.30 8.43

The borders of Nos. 79 to 81, 83 to 85, 87, 89 and 91 differ slightly for each denomination.

On Nos. 82, 86, 88 and 90, the value is expressed as "Cent. 25," etc.

No. 80 Surcharged in Black

C. 15

1905

92 A45 15c on 20c orange 35.00 20
a. Double surcharge 850.00

King Victor Emmanuel III
A47

No. 93

No. 111

No. 123

Engraved.

1906 *Perf. 12* **Unwmkd.**

93 A47 15c slate 27.50 20
a. Imperf. horiz. or vert., pair 150.00 60.00
b. Booklet pane of 6 200.00

King Victor Emmanuel III

A48 A49

Typographed.

1906-19 *Perf. 14.* **Wmk. 140**

No.	Type	Description	Unused	Used
94	A48	5c green	8	5
		a. Imperf., pair	20.00	20.00
		b. Printed on both sides	50.00	
95	"	10c claret	10	5
		a. Imperf., pair	20.00	20.00
96	"	15c slate ('19)	75	6
		a. Imperf., pair	60.00	60.00

The frame of No. 95 differs in several details.

1908–27

No.	Type	Description	Unused	Used
97	A49	20c brn. orange ('25)	50	5
98	"	20c green ('25)	50	5
99	"	20c lilac brown ('26)	55	6
100	"	25c blue	40	6
		a. Imperf., pair	30.00	30.00
		b. Printed on both sides	55.00	55.00
101	"	25c light green ('27)	4.50	1.50
102	"	30c org. brown ('22)	75	10
103	"	30c gray ('25)	1.10	10
104	"	40c brown	70	6
		a. Imperf., pair	60.00	60.00
105	"	50c violet	40	6
		a. Imperf., pair	40.00	40.00
106	"	55c dull violet ('20)	4.50	2.50
107	"	60c carmine ('17)	80	6
108	"	60c blue ('23)	10.00	12.50
109	"	60c brn. org. ('26)	3.75	10
110	"	85c red brown ('20)	3.50	60
		Nos. 97-110 (14)	31.95	17.80

The upper panels of Nos. 104 and 105 are in solid color with white letters. A body of water has been added to the background.

A50 A51

Redrawn.

Perf. 13x13½, 13½x14.

1909-17 Typographed. **Unwmkd.**

No.	Type	Description	Unused	Used
111	A50	15c slate black	135.00	30
112	"	20c brn. org. ('16)	17.50	60

No. 111 is similar to No. 93, but the design has been redrawn and the stamp is 23mm. high instead of 25mm. There is a star at each side of the coat collar, but one is not distinct. See illustrations next to A47.

Wmkd. Crown. (140)

Perf. 14.

No.	Type	Description	Unused	Used
113	A50	20c brn. orange ('17)	1.60	6
		a. Imperf., pair	5.00	5.00

Stamps overprinted "Prestito Nazionale, 1917", or later dates, are Thrift or Postal Savings Stamps.

1910, Nov. 1

No.	Type	Description	Unused	Used
114	A51	10 l gray grn. & red	40.00	3.25

Giuseppe Garibaldi

A52 A53

Perf. 14x13½

1910, Apr. 15 **Unwmkd.**

No.	Type	Description	Unused	Used
115	A52	5c green	7.50	6.50
116	"	15c claret	17.50	16.50

50th anniversary of freedom of Sicily.

1910, Dec. 1

No.	Type	Description	Unused	Used
117	A53	5c claret	60.00	25.00
118	"	15c green	90.00	35.00

50th anniversary of the plebiscite of the southern Italian provinces in 1860.

Symbols of Rome and Turin

A54

Symbol of Valor

A55

Genius of Italy

A56

Glory of Rome

A57

1911, May 1 Engraved *Perf. 14x13½*

No.	Type	Description	Unused	Used
119	A54	2c brown	1.20	1.00
120	A55	5c deep green	4.00	5.00
121	A56	10c carmine	4.00	5.00
122	A57	15c slate	3.50	5.00

Issued to commemorate the 50th anniversary of the union of Italian States to form the Kingdom of Italy.

Nos. 115 to 122 were sold at a premium over their face value.

King Victor Emmanuel III

A58

Campanile, Venice

A59

1911, Oct. Re-engraved *Perf. 13½*

No.	Type	Description	Unused	Used
123	A58	15c slate	10.00	7
		a. Imperf., pair	50.00	50.00
		b. Printed on both sides	150.00	150.00
		c. Bklt. pane of 6	65.00	

The re-engraved stamp is 24 mm. high. The stars at each side of the coat collar show plainly and the "C" of "Cent" is nearer the frame than in No. 93. See illustrations next to A47.

1912, Apr. 25 *Perf. 14x13½*

No.	Type	Description	Unused	Used
124	A59	5c indigo	2.50	3.75
125	"	15c dark brown	7.50	7.50

Issued to commemorate the re-erection of the Campanile at Venice.

Nos. 120-121 Surcharged in Black 2 2

1913, Mar. 1

No.	Type	Description	Unused	Used
126	A55	2c on 5c deep green	90	90
127	A56	2c on 10c carmine	1.20	1.20

No. 122 Surcharged in Violet 2 2

No.	Type	Description	Unused	Used
128	A57	2c on 15c slate	90	90

No. 123 Surcharged ≡ CENT 20 ≡

1916

No.	Type	Description	Unused	Used
129	A58	20c on 15c slate	6.00	7
		a. Bklt. pane of 6	40.00	
		b. Invtd. surch.	100.00	67.50
		c. Dbl. surch.	52.50	40.00

Old Seal of Republic of Trieste

A60

Allegory of Dante's Divine Comedy

A61

Italy Holding Laurels for Dante

A62

Dante Alighieri

A63

Perf. 14

1921, June 5 Litho. **Wmk. 140**

No.	Type	Description	Unused	Used
130	A60	15c black & rose	1.10	4.00
131	"	25c blue & rose	1.10	4.00
132	"	40c brown & rose	1.10	4.00

Issued to commemorate the reunion of Venezia Giulia with Italy.

1921, Sept. 28 Typographed

No.	Type	Description	Unused	Used
133	A61	15c violet brown	1.50	1.75
		a. Imperf., pair	15.00	15.00
134	A62	25c gray green	1.50	1.75
		a. Imperf., pair	15.00	15.00
135	A63	40c brown	1.50	1.75
		a. Imperf., pair	15.00	15.00

600th anniversary of the death of Dante.

The 15c gray, type A61, was not issued. Price $40.

Nos. 133–135 exist in part perforate pairs.

"Victory"

A64

Engraved

1921, Nov. 1 *Perf. 14, 14x13½*

No.	Type	Description	Unused	Used
136	A64	5c olive green	45	65
137	"	10c red	90	1.50
138	"	15c slate green	1.75	2.50
139	"	25c ultramarine	90	1.50

Third anniversary of the victory on the Piave.

Nos. 136–137, 139 exist imperf.

Flame of Patriotism Tempering Sword of Justice

A65

Giuseppe Mazzini

A66

Mazzini's Tomb

A67

1922, Sept. 20 Typo. *Perf. 14*

No.	Type	Description	Unused	Used
140	A65	25c maroon	2.75	4.50
141	A66	40c violet brown	4.00	4.50
142	A67	80c dark blue	2.75	4.50

Issued to commemorate the 50th anniversary of the death of Giuseppe Mazzini (1805–1872), patriot and writer.

Nos. 95, 96, 100 and 104 Overprinted in Black

IX CONGRESSO FILATELICO ITALIANO TRIESTE 1922

1922, June 4 *Perf. 14* **Wmk. 140**

No.	Type	Description	Unused	Used
142A	A48	10c claret	175.00	100.00
142B	"	15c slate	150.00	75.00
142C	A49	25c blue	150.00	75.00
142D	"	40c brown	175.00	100.00

9th Italian Philatelic Congress, Trieste. Counterfeits exist.

Christ Preaching The Gospel

A68

Portrait at upper right and badge at lower right differ on each value. Portrait at upper left is of Pope Gregory XV. Others: 20c, St. Theresa. 30c, St. Dominic. 50c, St. Francis of Assisi. 1 l, St. Francis Xavier.

1923, June 11

No.	Type	Description	Unused	Used
143	A68	20c olive green & brown orange	2.50	9.00
144	"	30c claret & brown orange	2.50	9.00
145	"	50c violet & brown orange	2.00	8.00
146	"	1 l blue & brown orange	2.00	8.00

Issued to commemorate the 300th anniversary of the Propagation of the Faith. Practically the entire issue was delivered to speculators.

Nos. 143–146 exist imperf. and part perf.

Stamps of Previous Issues, Surcharged:

Cent. 7½
a

10
CENTESIMI
b

DIECI
c

Lire 1,75
e

Cent. 25
d

1923–25

No.	Type		Description	Unused	Used
147	A49	(a)	7½c on 85c choc. ('24)	25	35
			a. Double surcharge	225.00	325.00
148	A42	(b)	10c on 1c brown	25	6
			a. Inverted surcharge	5.00	5.00
149	A43	(")	10c on 2c orange brown	25	6
			a. Inverted surcharge	15.00	15.00
150	A48	(c)	10c on 15c slate ('25)	28	6
151	A49	(a)	20c on 25c blue ('25)	30	7
152	A45	(d)	25c on 45c olive green ('24)	40	55
153	A49	(a)	25c on 60c blue ('24)	2.25	40
154	"	(")	30c on 50c violet ('25)	25	7
155	"	(")	30c on 55c dull violet ('25)	45	30
156	"	(")	50c on 40c brn.	35	6
			a. Inverted surcharge	90.00	90.00
			b. Double surcharge	75.00	75.00
157	"	(")	50c on 55c dull violet	27.50	3.00
			a. Inverted surcharge	500.00	800.00
158	A51	(e)	1.75 l on 10 l gray green & red ('25)	7.50	6.00
			Nos. 147-158 (12)	40.03	10.98

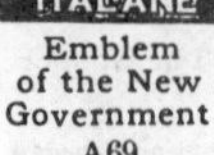

Emblem of the New Government
A69

Wreath of Victory, Eagle and Fasces
A70

Symbolical of Fascism and Italy
A71

Perf. 14

1923, Oct. 24 Engraved Unwmkd.

No.	Type	Description	Unused	Used
159	A69	10c dark green	1.20	1.75
		a. Imperf., pair	125.00	125.00
160	"	30c dark violet	1.20	1.75
161	"	50c brown carmine	1.65	2.25

Typographed.
Wmkd. Crowns. (140)

No.	Type	Description	Unused	Used
162	A70	1 l blue	1.65	1.50
163	"	2 l brown	2.50	2.00
164	A71	5 l black & blue	6.50	7.50
		a. Imperf., pair	165.00	165.00
		Nos. 159-164 (6)	14.70	16.75

Issued in commemoration of the anniversary of the March of the Fascisti on Rome.

Fishing Scene
A72

Designs: 15c, Mt. Resegone. 30c, Fugitives bidding farewell to native mountains. 50c, Part of Lake Como. 1l, Manzoni's home, Milan. 5l, Alessandro Manzoni. The first four designs show scenes from Manzoni's work "I Promessi Sposi".

1923, Dec. 29 ***Perf. 14***

No.	Type	Description	Unused	Used
165	A72	10c brn. red & black	1.00	2.00
166	"	15c bl. green & blk.	1.00	2.00
167	"	30c black & slate	1.00	2.00
		a. Imperf., pair	1000.00	
168	"	50c org. brn. & blk.	1.00	2.00
169	"	1 l blue & black	20.00	30.00
		a. Imperf., pair	275.00	300.00
170	"	5 l vio. & black	250.00	450.00
		a. Imperf., pair	650.00	
		Nos. 165-170 (6)	274.00	488.00

Issued to commemorate the 50th anniversary of the death of Alessandro Manzoni.

Nos. 136-139 Surcharged

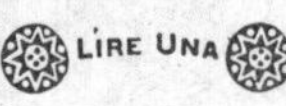

1924, Feb.

No.	Type	Description	Unused	Used
171	A64	1 l on 5c olive green	15.00	22.50
		a. Perf. 14x13½	21.00	40.00
172	"	1 l on 10c red	10.00	15.00
		a. Perf. 14x13½	15.00	25.00
173	"	1 l on 15c slate green	11.50	18.50
		a. Perf. 14x13½	18.50	30.00
174	"	1 l on 25c ultra.	10.00	15.00
		h. Perf. 14x13½	15.00	25.00

Surcharge forgeries exist.

Nos. 95, 102, 105, 108, 110, 87 and 89 Overprinted in Black or Red

CROCIERA
ITALIANA
1924

1924, Feb. 16

No.	Type	Description	Unused	Used
174A	A48	10c claret	1.20	3.25
174B	A49	30c orange brown	1.20	3.25
174C	"	50c violet	1.20	3.25
174D	"	60c blue (R)	15.00	15.00
174E	"	85c chocolate (R)	6.00	8.50
174F	A46	1 l brn. & green	42.50	65.00
174G	"	2 l dark green & orange	37.50	65.00
		Nos. 174A-174G (7)	104.60	163.25

These stamps were sold on an Italian warship which made a cruise to South American ports in 1924.

Overprint forgeries exist of Nos. 174D–174G.

Stamps of 1901–22 with Advertising Labels Attached.
Perf. 14 all around, Imperf. between.

1924–25

No.	Type	Description	Unused	Used
96b	A48	15c+Bitter Campari	90	1.20
96c	"	15c+Cordial Campari	90	1.20
96d	"	15c+Columbia	7.25	9.00
100c	A49	25c+Abrador	22.50	7.50
100d	"	25c+Coen	47.50	6.00
100e	"	25c+Piperno	300.00	67.50
100f	"	25c+Reinach	22.50	7.50
100g	"	25c+Tagliacozzo	135.00	55.00
102a	"	30c+Columbia	7.25	7.50
105b	"	50c+Coen	300.00	6.00
105c	"	50c+Columbia	4.00	60
105d	"	50c+De Montel	60	90
105e	"	50c+Piperno	275.00	17.50
105f	"	50c+Reinach	42.50	6.00
105g	"	50c+Siero Casali	6.00	4.75
105h	"	50c+Singer	40	40
105i	"	50c+Tagliacozzo	600.00	37.50
105j	A49	50c+Tantal	60.00	7.50
87b	A46	1 l+Columbia	160.00	40.00
		Nos. 96b-87b (19)	1992.30	283.55

No. 113 with Columbia label and No. E3 with Cioccolato Perugina label were prepared but not issued. Prices $12.50 and $2.50.

King Victor Emmanuel III
A78

Perf. 11, 13½ (No. 177)

1925-26 Engraved. Unwmkd.

No.	Type	Description	Unused	Used
175	A78	60c brown carmine	25	10
		a. Perf. 13½	6.00	35
		b. Imperf., pair	75.00	75.00
176	"	1 l dark blue	25	10
		a. Perf. 13½	1.50	20
		b. Imperf., pair	75.00	75.00
177	"	1.25 l dark blue ('26)	4.00	85
		a. Perf. 11	80.00	12.00
		b. Imperf., pair	225.00	

Issued to commemorate the twenty-fifth year of the reign of King Victor Emmanuel III.

Nos. 175 to 177 exist with sideways watermark of fragments of letters or a crown, which are normally on the sheet margin.

St. Francis and His Vision
A79

Monastery of St. Damien
A80

Assisi Monastery—A81

St. Francis' Death—A82

St. Francis—A83

1926, Jan. 30 ***Perf. 14*** **Wmk. 140**

No.	Type	Description	Unused	Used
178	A79	20c gray green	20	20
179	A80	40c dark violet	20	20
180	A81	60c red brown	20	20
		a. Imperf., pair	210.00	210.00

Perf. 11
Unwmkd.

No.	Type	Description	Unused	Used
181	A83	30c slate black	20	15
		a. Perf. 13½	12.00	1.25
182	A82	1.25 l dark blue	30	25
		a. Perf. 13½	350.00	5.50

Perf. 13½

No.	Type	Description	Unused	Used
183	A83	5 l+2.50 l dk. brown	8.00	15.00
		Nos. 178-183 (6)	9.10	16.00

Issued to commemorate the 700th anniversary of the death of St. Francis of Assisi.

Alessandro Volta
A84

Typographed.

1927 ***Perf. 14.*** **Wmk. 140**

No.	Type	Description	Unused	Used
188	A84	20c dark carmine	25	25
189	"	50c greenish black	2.25	20
190	"	60c chocolate	1.50	75
191	"	1.25 l ultramarine	2.00	1.00

Issued to commemorate the centenary of the death of Alessandro Volta.

The 20c in purple is Cyrenaica No. 25 with overprint omitted.

King Victor Emmanuel III
A85 A86

1927-29 Size: 17½x22mm. ***Perf. 14***

No.	Type	Description	Unused	Used
192	A85	50c brown & slate	85	5
		a. Imperf., pair	100.00	100.00

Perf. 11 **Engraved Unwmkd.**

Size: 19x23mm.

No.	Type	Description	Unused	Used
193	A85	1.75 l deep brown	4.50	6
		a. Perf. 13½ ('29)	3250.00	200.00
		b. Perf. 11x13½ ('29)	3250.00	450.00
		c. Perf. 13½x11 ('29)	3250.00	450.00
194	"	1.85 l black	90	30
195	"	2.55 l brown carmine	5.75	1.75
196	"	2.65 l deep violet	7.00	8.00
		Nos. 192-196 (5)	19.00	10.16

Typographed.

1928-29 ***Perf. 14.*** **Wmk. 140**

No.	Type	Description	Unused	Used
197	A86	7½c light brown	75	75
198	"	15c brn. orange ('29)	1.00	12
199	"	35c gray black ('29)	2.00	2.00
200	"	50c dull violet	2.00	7

Emmanuel Philibert, Duke of Savoy
A87

Statue of Philibert, Turin
A88

Philibert and Italian Soldier of 1918
A89

1928 ***Perf. 11, 14.***

No.	Type	Description	Unused	Used
201	A87	20c red brn. & ultra.	50	50
		a. Perf. 13½	14.00	10.00
202	"	25c deep red & blue green	50	50
		a. Perf. 13½	12.50	7.50
203	"	30c blue green & red brown	1.10	65
		a. Center invtd.	5000.00	1100.00
		b. Perf. 13½	4.00	2.50
204	A89	50c org. brn. & blue	35	15
205	"	75c deep red	1.00	35
206	A88	1.25 l blue & black	1.25	50
207	A89	1.75 l blue green	2.50	1.50
208	A87	5 l violet & blue green	7.50	7.50
209	A89	10 l black & pink	12.00	14.00
210	A88	20 l violet & black	17.50	20.00
		Nos. 201-210 (10)	44.20	45.65

Issued to commemorate the 400th anniversary of the birth of Emmanuel Philibert, Duke of Savoy; 10th anniversary of the victory of 1918; Turin Exhibition.

She-wolf Suckling Romulus and Remus
A90 A95a

Julius Caesar A91 · Augustus Caesar A92 · "Italia" A93

King Victor Emmanuel III
A94 A95

Photogravure.

1929-42 ***Perf. 14*** **Wmk. 140**

No.	Type	Description	Unused	Used
213	A90	5c olive brown	3	3
214	A91	7½c deep violet	5	3
215	A92	10c dark brown	3	3
216	A93	15c slate green	3	3
217	A91	20c rose red	3	3
218	A94	25c deep green	3	3
219	A95	30c olive brown	3	3
		a. Imperf., pair	175.00	
220	A93	35c deep blue	3	3
221	A95	50c purple	3	3
		a. Imperf., pair	85.00	85.00
222	A94	75c rose red	3	3
222A	A91	1 l dark purple ('42)	5	3
223	A94	1.25 l deep blue	3	3
224	A92	1.75 l red orange	3	3
225	A93	2 l carmine lake	3	3
226	A95a	2.55 l slate green	10	3
226A	"	3.70 l purple ('30)	10	10
227	"	5 l rose red	5	3
228	A93	10 l purple	22	7
229	A91	20 l light green	1.60	90
230	A92	25 l bluish slate	3.25	3.50
231	A94	50 l deep violet	3.75	4.00
		Nos. 213-231 (21)	9.53	9.05

See Nos. 427-438, 441-459.

Stamps of the 1929-42 issue overprinted "G.N.R." are 1943 local issues of the Guardia Nazionale Repubblicana.

Courtyard of Monte Cassino
A96

Monks Laying Cornerstone
A98

St. Benedict of Nursia
A100

Designs: 25c, Fresco, "Death of St. Benedict." 75c+15c, 5 l+1 l, Monte Cassino Abbey.

1929, Aug. 1 **Photo.** **Wmk. 140**

No.	Type	Description	Unused	Used
232	A96	20c red orange	30	25
233	"	25c dark green	30	25
234	A98	50c+10c olive brn.	1.50	2.25
235	"	75c+15c crimson	1.50	2.25
236	A96	1.25 l+25c sapphire	1.50	2.25
237	A98	5 l+1 l dark violet	3.00	4.75

Engraved.

Unwmkd.

No.	Type	Description	Unused	Used
238	A100	10 l+2 l slate green	4.00	6.00
		Nos. 232-238 (7)	12.10	18.00

Issued in commemoration of the 14th centenary of the founding of the Abbey of Monte Cassino by St. Benedict in 529 A.D. The premium on some of the stamps was given to the committee for the celebration of the centenary.

Prince Humbert and Princess Marie José
A101

1930, Jan. 8 **Photo.** **Wmk. 140**

No.	Type	Description	Unused	Used
239	A101	20c orange red	25	30
240	"	50c+10c olive brn.	1.00	1.25
241	"	1.25 l+25c deep blue	2.25	3.00

Issued in commemoration of the marriage of Prince Humbert of Savoy with Princess Marie José of Belgium.

The surtax on Nos. 240 and 241 was for the benefit of the Italian Red Cross Society.

The 20c in green is Cyrenaica No. 35 with overprint omitted.

Ferrucci Leading His Army
A102

Fabrizio Maramaldo Killing Ferrucci
A103

Francesco Ferrucci—A104

1930, July 10

No.	Type	Description	Unused	Used
242	A102	20c rose red	30	25
243	A103	25c deep green	40	30
244	"	50c purple	20	12
245	"	1.25 l deep blue	1.10	1.20
246	A104	5 l+2 l orange red	6.00	10.00
		Nos. 242-246 (5)	8.00	11.87

Issued in commemoration of the fourth centenary of the death of Francesco Ferrucci, Tuscan warrior.

Helenus and Aeneas
A106

Designs: 20c, Anchises and Aeneas watch passing of Roman Legions. 25c, Aeneas feasting in shade of Albunea. 30c, Ceres and her children with fruits of Earth. 50c, Harvesters at work. 75c, Woman at loom, children and calf. 1.25 l, Anchises and his sailors in sight of Italy. 5 l+1.50 l, Shepherd piping by fireside. 10 l+2.50 l, Aeneas leading his army.

1930, Oct. 21 **Photo.** ***Perf. 14***

No.	Type	Description	Unused	Used
248	A106	15c olive brown	40	25
249	"	20c orange	40	25
250	"	25c green	60	20
251	"	30c dull violet	75	25
252	"	50c violet	50	12
253	"	75c rose red	90	90
254	"	1.25 l blue	1.25	65

Engraved

Unwmkd.

No.	Type	Description	Unused	Used
255	A106	5 l+1.50 l red brn.	17.50	30.00
256	"	10 l+2.50 l gray grn.	17.50	30.00
		Nos. 248-256 (9)	39.80	62.62

Bimillenary of the birth of Virgil. Surtax on Nos. 255-256 was for the National Institute Figli del Littorio.

See Nos. C23-C26.

Arms of Italy (Fascist Emblems Support House of Savoy Arms)
A115

1930, Dec. 16 **Photo.** **Wmk. 140**

No.	Type	Description	Unused	Used
257	A115	2c deep orange	10	10

St. Anthony being Installed as a Franciscan
A116

Olivares Hermitage, Portugal
A118

St. Anthony Freeing Prisoners
A120

St. Anthony's Death—A121

St. Anthony Succoring the Poor
A122

Designs: 25c, St. Anthony preaching to the fishes. 50c, Basilica of St. Anthony, Padua.

Perf. 14

1931, Mar. 9 **Photo.** **Wmk. 140**

No.	Type	Description	Unused	Used
258	A116	20c dull violet	60	20
259	"	25c gray green	75	20
260	A118	30c brown	1.00	30
261	"	50c violet	65	10
262	A120	1.25 l blue	4.00	75

Engraved

Unwmkd.

No.	Type	Description	Unused	Used
263	A121	75c brown red	5.00	1.50
		a. Perf. 12	90.00	45.00
264	A122	5 l+2.50 l olive green	18.50	22.50
		Nos. 258-264 (7)	30.50	25.55

Issued to commemorate the seventh centenary of the death of Saint Anthony of Padua.

Tower of Meloria—A123

Training Ship "Amerigo Vespucci"
A124

Cruiser "Trento"—A125

1931, Nov. 29 Photo. Wmk. 140

265 A123 20c rose red 40 20
266 A124 50c purple 60 10
267 A125 1.25 l dark blue 2.50 75

Issued in commemoration of the 50th anniversary of the inauguration of the Royal Naval Academy at Leghorn (Livorno) in 1881.

Giovanni Boccaccio A126

Designs: 15c, Niccolo Machiavelli. 20c, Paolo Sarpi. 25c, Count Vittorio Alfieri. 30c, Ugo Foscolo. 50c, Count Giacomo Leopardi. 75c, Giosue Carducci. 1.25 l, Carlo Giuseppe Botta. 1.75 l, Torquato Tasso. 2.75 l, Francesco Petrarca. 5 l+2 l, Ludovico Ariosto. 10 l+2.50 l, Dante Alighieri.

1932, Mar. 14 ***Perf. 14***

268 A126 10c olive brown 33 20
269 " 15c slate green 40 20
270 " 20c rose red 40 20
271 " 25c deep green 50 25
272 " 30c olive brown 70 25
273 " 50c violet 25 10
274 " 75c carmine rose 1.40 60
275 " 1.25 l deep blue 1.10 50
276 " 1.75 l orange 1.40 40
277 " 2.75 l gray 4.75 7.50
278 " 5 l+2 l carmine rose 8.00 14.00
279 " 10 l+2.50 l olive green 9.00 16.00
Nos. 268-279 (12) 28.23 40.20

Issued to commemorate the Dante Alighieri Society, a national literary association founded to promote development of the Italian language and culture. The surtax was added to the Society funds to help in its work.

See also Nos. C28–C34.

View of Caprera—A138

Garibaldi Carrying His Dying Wife A141

Garibaldi Memorial A144

Giuseppe Garibaldi A145

Designs: 20c, 30c, Garibaldi meeting Victor Emmanuel II. 25c, 50c, Garibaldi at Battle of Calatafimi. 1.25 l, Garibaldi's tomb. 1.75 l+25c, Rock of Quarto.

1932, Apr. 6

280 A138 10c gray black 50 20
281 " 20c olive brown 50 20
282 " 25c dull green 1.20 25
283 " 30c orange 1.20 30
284 " 50c violet 65 10
285 A141 75c rose red 3.25 1.75
286 " 1.25 l deep blue 2.40 75
287 " 1.75 l+25c blue gray 8.00 12.00
288 A144 2.55 l+50c red brown 9.00 14.00
289 A145 5 l+1 l copper red 9.50 16.00
Nos. 280-289 (10) 36.20 45.55

Issued to commemorate the 50th anniversary of the death of Giuseppe Garibaldi, patriot.

See also Nos. C35–C39.

Plowing with Oxen and Tractor A146

Designs: 10c, Soldier guarding mountain pass. 15c, Marine, battleship and seaplane. 20c, Head of Facist youth. 25c, Hands of workers and tools. 30c, Flags, Bible and altar. 35c, "New roads for the new Legions." 50c, Mussolini statue, Bologna. 60c, Hands with spades. 75c, Excavating ruins. 1 l, Steamers and galleons. 1.25 l, Italian flag, map and points of compass. 1.75 l, Flag, athlete and stadium. 2.55 l, Mother and child. 2.75 l, Emblems of drama, music, art and sport. 5 l+2.50 l, Roman emperor.

1932, Oct. 27 Photogravure

290 A146 5c dark brown 20 20
291 " 10c dark brown 25 20
292 " 15c dark gray green 25 25
293 " 20c carmine rose 25 15
294 " 25c deep green 25 20
295 " 30c dark brown 40 25
296 " 35c dark blue 2.00 2.50
297 " 50c purple 17 10
298 " 60c orange brown 2.00 2.00
299 " 75c carmine rose 1.00 60
300 " 1 l black violet 1.25 90
301 " 1.25 l deep blue 50 30
302 " 1.75 l orange 1.10 30
303 " 2.55 l dark gray 9.50 16.50
304 " 2.75 l slate green 11.00 18.50
305 " 5 l+2.50 l carmine rose 17.50 28.50
Nos. 290-305 (16) 47.62 71.45

Commemorating the 10th anniversary of the Fascist government and the March on Rome.

See also Nos. C40–C41, E16–E17.

Statue of Athlete A162

Cross in Halo, St. Peter's Dome A163

1933, Aug. 16 ***Perf. 14***

306 A162 10c dark brown 40 25
307 " 20c rose red 50 30
308 " 50c purple 60 20
309 " 1.25 l blue 2.25 1.75

Issued in connection with the International University Games at Turin, September, 1933.

1933, Oct. 23

Designs: 25c, 50c, Angel with cross. 1.25 l, as 20c. 2.55 l, + 2.50 l, Cross with doves.

310 A163 20c rose red 40 15
311 " 25c green 90 25
312 " 50c purple 50 9
313 " 1.25 l deep blue 1.50 1.00
314 " 2.55 l+2.50 l black 3.25 6.00
Nos. 310-314 (5) 6.55 7.49

Issued at the solicitation of the Order of the Holy Sepulchre of Jerusalem to mark the Holy Year.

See also Nos. CB1–CB2.

Anchor of the "Emanuele Filiberto" A166

Antonio Pacinotti A172

Designs: 20c, Anchor. 50c, Gabriele d'Annunzio. 1.25 l, St. Vito's Tower. 1.75 l, Symbolizing Fiume's annexation. 2.55 l+2 l, Victor Emmanuel III arriving aboard "Brindisi." 2.75 l+2.50 l, Galley, gondola and battleship.

1934, Mar. 12

315 A166 10c dark brown 1.60 35
316 " 20c rose red 40 25
317 " 50c purple 40 15
318 " 1.25 l blue 80 1.00
319 " 1.75 l+1 l indigo 1.25 2.75
320 " 2.55 l+2 l dull violet 1.25 2.75
321 " 2.75 l+2.50 l olive green 1.25 2.75
Nos. 315-321 (7) 6.95 10.00

10th anniversary of annexation of Fiume. See Nos. C56–C61, CE5–CE7.

1934, May 23

322 A172 50c purple 1.50 20
323 " 1.25 l sapphire 1.50 1.00

75th anniversary of invention of the dynamo by Antonio Pacinotti (1841–1912), scientist.

Guarding the Goal A173

Players A175

Soccer Players—A174

1934, May 23

324 A173 20c red orange 2.50 2.00
325 A174 25c green 2.50 75
326 " 50c purple 1.60 30
327 " 1.25 l blue 5.50 5.00
328 A175 5 l+2.50 l brown 20.00 27.50
Nos. 324-328 (5) 32.10 35.55

2nd World Soccer Championship. See Nos. C62–C65.

Luigi Galvani A176

1934, Aug. 16

329 A176 30c brown, *buff* 2.75 40
330 " 75c carmine, *rose* 2.75 1.60

International Congress of Electro-Radio-Biology.

Carabinieri Emblem A177

Cutting Barbed Wire A178

Designs: 20c, Sardinian Grenadier and soldier throwing grenade. 25c, Alpine Infantry. 30c, Military courage. 75c, Artillery. 1.25 l, Acclaiming the Service. 1.75 l+1 l, Cavalry. 2.55 l+2 l, Sapping Detail. 2.75 l+2 l, First aid.

1934, Sept. 6 Photo. Wmk. 140

331 A177 10c dark brown 80 40
332 A178 15c olive green 80 45
333 " 20c rose red 80 40
334 A177 25c green 1.20 45
335 A178 30c dark brown 1.60 60
336 " 50c purple 1.20 20
337 " 75c carmine rose 4.00 1.75
338 " 1.25 l dark blue 4.00 1.50
339 A177 1.75 l+1 l red orange 8.00 13.00
340 A178 2.55 l+2 l dp. claret 9.00 16.00
341 " 2.75 l+2 l violet 9.00 16.00
Nos. 331-341 (11) 40.40 50.75

Centenary of Military Medal of Valor. See Nos. C66–C72.

Man Holding Fasces A187

Standard Bearer, Bayonet Attack A188

Design: 30c, Eagle and soldier.

1935, Apr. 23 ***Perf. 14***

342 A187 20c rose red 32 35
343 " 30c dark brown 2.25 2.00
344 A188 50c purple 28 15

Issued in honor of the University Contests.

Fascist Flight Symbolism A190

Leonardo da Vinci A191

1935, Oct. 1

345 A190 20c rose red 2.75 45
346 " 30c brown 15.00 85

347	A191	50c purple	19.00	25
348	"	1.25 l dark blue	5.00	1.50

International Aeronautical Salon, Milan.

Vincenzo Bellini A192 — Bellini's Villa A194

Bellini's Piano A193

1935, Oct. 15

349	A192	20c rose red	1.20	40
350	"	30c brown	1.60	60
351	"	50c violet	1.20	30
352	"	1.25 l dark blue	4.00	1.75
353	A193	1.75 l+1 l red org.	12.50	21.00
354	A194	2.75 l+2 l olive black	12.50	21.00
		Nos. 349-354 (6)	33.00	45.05

Issued to commemorate the centenary of the death of Vincenzo Bellini (1801-1835), operatic composer.

See also Nos. C79-C83.

Map of Italian Industries A195

Designs: 20c, 1.25 l, Map of Italian Industries. 30c, 50c, Cogwheel and plow.

1936, Mar. 23

355	A195	20c red	20	20
356	"	30c brown	28	25
357	"	50c purple	20	20
358	"	1.25 l blue	1.35	55

The 17th Milan Trade Fair.

Flock of Sheep A197

Ajax Defying the Lightning A199 — Bust of Horace A200

Designs: 20c, 1.25 l+1 l, Countryside in Spring. 75c, Capitol. 1.75 l+1 l, Pan piping. 2.55 l+1 l, Dying warrior.

Wmkd. Crowns. (140)

1936, July 1 Photo. *Perf. 14*

Inscribed: "Bimillenario Oraziano."

359	A197	10c deep green	1.50	25
360	"	20c rose red	75	30
361	A199	30c olive brown	1.50	40
362	A200	50c purple	1.10	15
363	A197	75c rose red	1.85	85
364	"	1.25 l+1 l dark blue	9.00	16.00
365	A199	1.75 l+1 l car. rose	9.00	16.00
366	A197	2.55 l+1 l slate blk.	9.00	16.00
		Nos. 359-366 (8)	33.70	49.95

Issued to commemorate the 2000th anniversary of the birth of Quintus Horatius Flaccus (Horace), Roman poet. See Nos. C84-C88.

Child Holding Wheat A204 — Child Giving Salute A205

Child and Fasces A206 — "Il Bambino" by della Robbia A207

1937, June 28

367	A204	10c yellow brown	55	30
368	A205	20c carmine rose	55	30
369	A204	25c green	75	35
370	A206	30c dark brown	1.10	60
371	A205	50c purple	75	20
372	A207	75c rose red	3.25	1.00
373	A205	1.25 l dark blue	4.25	1.25
374	A206	1.75 l+75c orange	12.00	20.00
375	A207	2.75 l+1.25 l dark blue green	9.00	18.00
376	A205	5 l+3 l blue gray	9.00	18.00
		Nos. 367-376 (10)	41.20	60.00

Issued to commemorate the Summer Exhibition for Child Welfare. The surtax on Nos. 374 to 376 was used to support summer camps for children.

See also Nos. C89-C94.

Rostral Column A208

Designs: 15c, Army Trophies. 20c, Augustus Caesar (Octavianus) offering sacrifice. 25c, Cross and Roman Standards. 30c, Julius Caesar and Julian Star. 50c, Augustus receiving acclaim. 75c, Augustus Caesar. 1.25 l, Symbolizing maritime glory of Rome. 1.75 l+1 l, Sacrificial Altar. 2.55 l+2 l, Capitol.

Inscribed: "Bimillenario Augusteo."

1937, Sept. 23

377	A208	10c myrtle green	75	20
378	"	15c olive brown	75	25
379	"	20c red	75	20
380	"	25c green	75	20
381	"	30c olive bistre	1.10	25
382	"	50c purple	75	15
383	"	75c scarlet	1.50	55
384	"	1.25 l dark blue	1.85	70
385	"	1.75 l+1 l plum	15.00	25.00
386	A208	2.55 l+2 l slate blk.	15.00	25.00
		Nos. 377-386 (10)	38.20	52.00

Issued to commemorate the bimillenary of the birth of Emperor Augustus Caesar (Octavianus) on the occasion of the exhibition opened in Rome by Mussolini, Sept. 22, 1937.

See also Nos. C95-C99.

Gasparo Luigi Pacifico Spontini A218 — Antonius Stradivarius A219

Count Giacomo Leopardi A220 — Giovanni Battista Pergolesi A221

Giotto di Bondone A222

1937, Oct. 25

387	A218	10c dark brown	40	28
388	A219	20c rose red	40	28
389	A220	25c dark green	40	28
390	A221	30c dark brown	40	40
391	A220	50c purple	40	22
392	A221	75c crimson	1.40	1.50
393	A222	1.25 l deep blue	1.65	1.65
394	A218	1.75 l deep orange	1.65	1.00
395	A219	2.55 l+2 l gray green	13.50	17.50
396	A222	2.75 l+2 l red brown	13.50	17.50
		Nos. 387-396 (10)	33.70	40.61

Issued to commemorate the centennials of Spontini, Stradivarius, Leopardi, Pergolesi and Giotto.

Guglielmo Marconi A223 — Romulus Plowing A224

1938, Jan. 24

397	A223	20c rose pink	90	40
398	"	50c purple	32	20
399	"	1.25 l blue	80	1.25

Guglielmo Marconi (1874-1937), electrical engineer, inventor of wireless telegraphy.

1938, Oct. 28

Designs: 20c, Augustus Caesar (Octavianus). 25c, Dante. 30c, Columbus. 50c, Leonardo da Vinci. 75c, Victor Emmanuel II and Garibaldi. 1.25 l, Tomb of Unknown Soldier, Rome. 1.75 l, Blackshirts' March on Rome, 1922. 2.75 l, Map of Italian East Africa and Iron Crown of Monza. 5 l, Victor Emmanuel III.

400	A224	10c brown	25	15
401	"	20c carmine rose	25	15
402	"	25c dark green	25	15
403	"	30c olive brown	25	25
404	"	50c light violet	25	10
405	"	75c rose red	50	45
406	"	1.25 l deep blue	75	40
407	"	1.75 l violet black	90	35
408	"	2.75 l slate green	4.00	6.00
409	"	5 l light red brown	6.00	8.50
		Nos. 400-409 (10)	13.40	16.50

Issued to commemorate the proclamation of the Empire. See also Nos. C100-C105.

Wood-burning Engine and Streamlined Electric Engine A234

Wmkd. Crowns. (140)

1939, Dec. 15 Photo. *Perf. 14*

410	A234	20c rose red	35	25
411	"	50c bright violet	30	10
412	"	1.25 l deep blue	1.40	90

Centenary of Italian railroads.

Adolf Hitler and Benito Mussolini A235

Hitler and Mussolini—A236

1941

413	A235	10c deep brown	15	18
414	"	20c red orange	20	30
415	"	25c deep green	20	25
416	A236	50c violet	25	12
417	"	75c rose red	30	42
418	"	1.25 l deep blue	40	55
		Nos. 413-418 (6)	1.50	1.82

Rome-Berlin Axis.

Stamps of type A236 in the denominations and colors of Nos. 413 to 415 were prepared but not issued. They were sold for charitable purposes in 1948. Price $6.50 each.

Galileo Teaching Mathematics at Padua—A237

Designs: 25c, Galileo presenting telescope to Doge of Venice. 50c, Galileo Galilei. 1.25 l, Galileo studying at Arcetri.

1942, Sept. 28

419	A237	10c dark orange & lake	25	28
420	"	25c gray green & green	30	28
421	"	50c brn. vio. & violet	35	22
		a. Frame missing	600.00	
422	A237	1.25 l Prussian blue & ultramarine	60	65

Issued to commemorate the 300th anniversary of the death of Galileo Galilei (1564-1642).

Statue of Rossini A241 — Gioacchino Rossini A242

1942, Nov. 23 Photogravure

423	A241	25c deep green	15	17
424	"	30c brown	20	22
425	A242	50c violet	20	17
426	"	1 l blue	25	33

Issued to commemorate the 150th anniversary of the birth of Gioacchino Antonio Rossini (1792-1868), operatic composer.

"Victory for the Axis"
A243

"Discipline is the Weapon of Victory"
A244

"Everything and Everyone for Victory"
A245

"Arms and Hearts Must Be Stretched Out Towards the Goal"
A246

Perf. 14 all around, Imperf. between.

1942 Photogravure **Wmk. 140**

427	A243	25c deep green	10	12
428	A244	25c "	10	12
429	A245	25c "	10	12
430	A246	25c "	10	12
431	A243	30c olive brown	15	22
432	A244	30c olive brown	15	22
433	A245	30c "	15	22
434	A246	30c "	15	22
435	A243	50c purple	7	8
436	A244	50c "	7	8
437	A245	50c "	7	8
438	A246	50c "	7	8
		Nos. 427-438 (12)	1.28	1.68

Issued in honor of the Italian Army.
The left halves of Nos. 431-438 are type A95.

She-Wolf Suckling Romulus and Remus
A247 — Wmk. 87

Wmkd. Honeycomb. (87)
Perf. 10½x11½, 11x11½, 11½, 14.

1944, Jan. Litho. **Without Gum**

439	A247	50c rose violet & bistre rose	40	40

Unwmkd.

440	A247	50c rose violet & pale rose	10	10

Nos. 439-440 exist imperf., part perf.

Types of 1929.

1945, May ***Perf. 14*** **Unwmkd.**

With Gum.

441	A93	15c slate green	12	12
442	"	35c deep blue	12	12
443	A91	1 l deep violet	18	18

Types of 1929 Redrawn.
(Fasces removed.)

King Victor Emmanuel III A248 — Julius Caesar A249

Photogravure.

1944-45 ***Perf. 14*** **Wmk. 140**

444	A248	30c dark brown	12	18
445	"	50c purple	60	35
446	"	60c slate green ('45)	18	18
447	A249	1 l deep violet ('45)	55	18

Augustus Caesar A250 — "Italia" A251

1945 ***Perf. 14*** **Unwmkd.**

448	A250	10c dark brown	15	20
448A	A249	20c rose red	20	10
449	A251	50c dark violet	12	10
450	A248	60c slate green	20	10
451	A251	60c red orange	15	20
452	A249	1 l deep violet	20	10
452A	"	1 l deep violet, redrawn	10	10
452B	A251	2 l deep carmine	30	20
452C	"	10 l purple	3.50	1.75
		Nos. 448-452C (9)	4.92	2.85

She-Wolf Suckling Romulus and Remus
A252

Wmk. 277

1945 Wmkd. Winged Wheel. (277)

453	A249	20c rose red	22	5
454	A248	60c slate green	22	22
455	A249	1 l deep violet	22	5
456	A251	1.20 l dark brown	22	22
457	"	2 l dark red	22	5
458	A252	5 l dark red	22	5
459	A251	10 l purple	3.00	1.85
		Nos. 453-459 (7)	4.32	2.49

Nos. 452A and 457 are redrawings of types A249 and A251. In the redrawn 1L, the "L" of "LIRE" extends under the "IRE" and the letters of "POSTE ITALIANE" are larger. In the original the "L" extends only under the "I."

In the redrawn 2L, the "2" is smaller and thinner, and the design is less distinct.

No. 224 Surcharged in Black — L. 2,50

1945, Mar. **Wmk. 140**

460	A92	2.50 l on 1.75 l red orange	10	10
		a. Six bars at left	50	50

Loggia dei Mercanti, Bologna A253 — Basilica of San Lorenzo, Rome A254

Stamps of Italian Social Republic Surcharged in Black.

1945, May 2 Photo. ***Perf. 14***

461	A253	1.20 l on 20c crimson	8	8
462	A254	2 l on 25c green	8	8
		a. 2½ mm. between "2" and "LIRE"	90	90

Breaking Chain A255 — United Family and Scales A256

Planting Tree A257 — Tying Tree A258 — Torch A259

"Italia" and Sprouting Oak Stump
A260

Photogravure.

1945-47 ***Perf. 14.*** **Wmk. 277**

463	A255	10c rose brown	4	3
464	A256	20c dark brown	4	3
464A	A259	25c bright blue green ('46)	6	3
465	A257	40c slate	6	3
465A	A255	50c deep violet ('46)	6	3
466	A258	60c dark green	6	3
467	A255	80c carmine rose	10	3
468	A257	1 l dark green	6	3
469	A259	1.20 l chestnut	10	10
470	A258	2 l dark claret brown	8	3
471	A259	3 l red	10	3
471A	"	4 l red org. ('46)	40	3
472	A256	5 l deep blue	30	3
472A	A257	6 l dp. vio. ('47)	2.50	3
473	A255	10 l slate	1.00	10
473A	A257	15 l dp. blue ('46)	4.50	3
474	A259	20 l dk. red vio.	2.00	4
475	A260	25 l dark green	10.00	10
476	"	50 l dk. vio. brn.	7.00	4
		Nos. 463-476 (19)	28.46	80

See also Nos. 486-488.

United Family and Scales
A261

1946 **Engraved.** ***Perf. 14***

477	A261	100 l car. lake	125.00	40
		a. Perf. 14x13¼	175.00	60

Cathedral of St. Andrea, Amalfi A262 — Church of St. Michael, Lucca A263

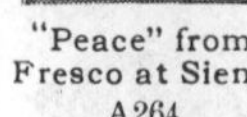

"Peace" from Fresco at Siena A264 — Signoria Palace, Florence A265

View of Cathedral Domes, Pisa
A266

Republic of Genoa—A267

"Venice Crowned by Glory," by Paolo Veronese—A268

Oath of Pontida—A269

1946, Oct. 30

478	A262	1 l brown	4	4
479	A263	2 l dark blue	5	4
480	A264	3 l dark blue green	5	4
481	A265	4 l deep orange	5	4
482	A266	5 l deep violet	4	4
483	A267	10 l carmine rose	15	6
484	A268	15 l deep ultramarine	30	30
485	A269	20 l red brown	15	6
		Nos. 478-485 (8)	83	62

Proclamation of the Republic.

Types of 1945.
Photogravure.

1947-48 *Perf. 14.* **Wmk. 277**

486	A255	8 l dark green ('48)	1.50	3
487	A256	10 l red orange	17.50	3
488	A259	30 l dk. blue ('48)	80.00	10

St. Catherine Giving Mantle to Beggar
A270

Designs: 5 l, St. Catherine carrying cross. 10 l, St. Catherine, arms outstretched. 30 l, St. Catherine and scribe.

1948, Mar. 1 Photogravure

489	A270	3 l yellow green & gray green	12	12
490	"	5 l violet & blue	18	18
491	"	10 l red brown & vio.	30	30
492	"	30 l bis. & gray brn.	3.00	3.00
		Nos. 489-492, C127-C128 (6)	42.60	32.60

Issued to commemorate the 600th anniversary of the birth of St. Catherine of Siena, Patroness of Italy.

"Constitutional Government"
A271

1948, Apr. 12

493	A271	10 l rose violet	50	50
494	"	30 l blue	1.50	75

Issued to commemorate the proclamation of the constitution of January 1, 1948.

Uprising at Palermo, Jan. 12, 1848
A272

Designs (Revolutionary scenes): 4 l, Rebellion at Padua. 5 l, Proclamation of statute, Turin. 6 l, "Five Days of Milan." 8 l, Daniele Manin proclaming the Republic of Venice. 10 l, Defense of Vicenza. 12 l, Battle of Curtatone. 15 l, Battle of Gioto. 20 l, Insurrection at Bologna. 30 l, "Ten Days of Brescia." 50 l, Garibaldi in Rome fighting. 100 l, Death of Goffredo Mameli.

1948, May 3

495	A272	3 l dark brown	7	10
496	"	4 l red violet	13	10
497	"	5 l deep blue	38	10
498	"	6 l deep yellow green	30	60
499	"	8 l brown	22	60
500	"	10 l orange red	38	20
501	"	12 l dark gray green	50	75
502	"	15 l gray black	2.75	65
503	"	20 l carmine rose	10.00	1.75
504	"	30 l bright ultra.	2.75	30
505	"	50 l violet	42.50	85
506	"	100 l blue black	67.50	9.00
		Nos. 495-506 (12)	127.48	15.00

Centenary of the Risorgimento, uprisings of 1848-49 which led to Italian unification.

Alpine Soldier and Bassano Bridge
A273

1948, Oct. 1 *Perf. 14* **Wmk. 277**

507	A273	15 l dark green	1.10	70

Issued to commemorate the reopening of the Bridge of Bassano, October 3, 1948.

Gaetano Donizetti
A274

1948, Oct. 23 Photogravure

508	A274	15 l dark brown	1.10	80

Issued to commemorate the centenary of the death of Gaetano Donizetti, composer.

Fair Buildings—A275

1949, Apr. 12

509	A275	20 l dark brown	5.00	1.10

27th Milan Trade Fair, April 1949.

Standard of Doges of Venice
A276

Designs: 15 l, Clock strikers, Lion Tower and Campanile of St. Mark's. 20 l, Lion standard and Venetian galley. 50 l, Lion tower and gulls.

1949, Apr. 12 **Buff Background**

510	A276	5 l red brown	15	12
511	"	15 l dark green	1.75	60
512	A276	20 l deep red brown	2.00	12
513	"	50 l dark blue	13.00	75

Issued to commemorate 50th anniversary of the Biennial Art Exhibition of Venice.

"Transportation" and Globes
A277

1949, May 2 *Perf. 14* **Wmk. 277**

514	A277	50 l bright ultra.	15.00	3.50

Issued to commemorate the 75th anniversary of the formation of the Universal Postal Union.

Workman and Ship
A278

1949, May 30 Photogravure

515	A278	5 l dark green	6.50	4.25
516	"	15 l violet	15.00	6.50
517	"	20 l brown	60.00	11.00

European Recovery Program.

The Vascello, Rome
A279

1949, May 18

518	A279	100 l brown	150.00	50.00

Centenary of Roman Republic.

Giuseppe Mazzini
A280

Vittorio Alfieri
A281

1949, June 1

519	A280	20 l gray	6.00	90

Issued to commemorate the erection of a monument to Giuseppe Mazzini (1805-1872), Italian patriot and revolutionary.

1949, June 4 Photogravure

520	A281	20 l brown	7.00	90

Issued to commemorate the 200th anniversary of the birth of Vittorio Alfieri, tragic dramatist.

Basilica of St. Just, Trieste
A282

1949, June 8

521	A282	20 l brown red	9.00	8.00

Trieste election, June 12, 1949.

Staff of Aesculapius, Globe
A283

1949, June 13 *Perf. 14* **Wmk. 277**

522	A283	20 l violet	8.50	7.25

Issued to commemorate the second World Health Congress, Rome, 1949.

Lorenzo de Medici
A284

Andrea Palladio
A285

1949, Aug. 4

523	A284	20 l violet blue	5.00	90

Issued to commemorate the 500th anniversary of the birth of Lorenzo de Medici.

1949, Aug. 4

524	A285	20 l violet	4.75	3.75

Issued to honor Andrea Palladio (1518-1580), architect.

Tartan and Fair Buildings
A286

1949, Aug. 16

525	A286	20 l red	2.00	90

Issued to publicize the 133th Levant Fair, Bari, September, 1949.

Voltaic Pile
A287

Alessandro Volta
A288

1949, Sept. 14 Engraved *Perf. 14*

526	A287	20 l rose carmine	3.00	60
		a. Perf. 13x14	17.50	3.50
527	A288	50 l deep blue	32.50	9.00
		a. Perf. 13x14	175.00	42.50

Issued to commemorate the 150th anniversary of the invention of the Voltaic Pile.

Holy Trinity Bridge
A289

1949, Sept. 19 **Photogravure**

528 A289 20 l deep green 4.50 75

Issued to publicize plans to reconstruct Holy Trinity Bridge, Florence.

Gaius Valerius Catullus
A290

Domenico Cimarosa
A291

1949, Sept. 19 ***Perf. 14*** **Wmk. 277**

529 A290 20 l bright blue 7.00 75

Issued to commemorate the 2000th anniversary of the death of Gaius Valerius Catullus, lyric poet.

1949, Dec. 28

530 A291 20 l violet black 3.75 75

Issued to commemorate the bicentenary of the birth of Domenico Cimarosa, composer.

Milan Fair Scene—A292

1950, Apr. 12 **Photogravure**

531 A292 20 l brown 2.75 75

The 28th Milan Trade Fair.

Flags and Italian Automobile
A293

1950, Apr. 29

532 A293 20 l violet gray 3.50 75

Issued to publicize the 32nd International Auto Show, Turin, May 4–14, 1950.

Pitti Palace, Florence
A294

"Perseus" by Cellini
A295

Composite of Italian Cathedrals and Churches
A296

1950, May 22

533 A294 20 l olive green 4.00 30
534 A295 55 l blue 20.00 2.75

Issued to commemorate the 5th General Conference of the United Nations Educational, Scientific and Cultural Organization.

1950, May 29

535 A296 20 l violet 3.00 45
536 " 55 l blue 15.00 90

Holy Year, 1950.

Gaudenzio Ferrari
A297

Radio Mast and Tower of Florence
A298

1950, July 1 ***Perf. 14*** **Wmk. 277**

537 A297 20 l gray green 6.00 1.00

Issued to honor Gaudenzio Ferrari.

1950, July 15 **Photogravure**

538 A298 20 l purple 8.00 3.00
539 " 55 l blue 80.00 42.50

Issued to commemorate the International Shortwave Radio Conference, Florence, 1950.

Ludovico A. Muratori
A299

Guido d'Arezzo
A300

1950, July 22

540 A299 20 l brown 4.00 80

Issued to commemorate the 200th anniversary of the death of Ludovico A. Muratori, writer.

1950, July 29

541 A300 20 l dark green 6.50 85

Issued to commemorate the 900th anniversary of the death of Guido d'Arezzo, music teacher and composer

Tartan and Fair Buildings
A301

1950, Aug. 21

542 A301 20 l chestnut brown 5.00 85

Levant Fair, Bari, September, 1950.

G. Marzotto and A. Rossi
A302

Tobacco Plant
A303

1950, Sept. 11

543 A302 20 l indigo 60 50

Issued to honor the pioneers of the Italian wool industry.

1950, Sept. 11

Designs: 20 l, Mature plant, different background. 55 l, Girl holding tobacco plant.

544 A303 5 l deep claret & green 1.25 1.25
545 " 20 l brown & green 8.00 60
546 " 55 l dp. ultra. & brn. 42.50 8.50

Issued to publicize the European Tobacco Conference, Rome, 1950.

Arms of the Academy of Fine Arts
A304

Augusto Righi
A305

1950, Sept. 16

547 A304 20 l olive brown & red brown 3.00 80

Issued to commemorate the 200th anniversary of the founding of the Academy of Fine Arts, Venice.

1950, Sept. 16

548 A305 20 l cream & gray black 3.00 80

Issued to commemorate the centenary of the birth of Augusto Righi, physicist.

Blacksmith, Aosta Valley
A306

1851 Stamp of Tuscany
A307

Designs: 1 l, Auto mechanic. 2 l, Mason. 5 l, Potter. 6 l, Lace-making. 10 l, Weaving. 12 l, Sailor steering boat. 15 l, Shipbuilding. 20 l, Fisherman. 25 l, Sorting oranges. 30 l, Woman carrying grapes. 35 l, Olive picking. 40 l, Wine cart. 50 l, Shepherd and flock. 55 l, Plowing. 60 l, Grain cart. 65 l, Girl worker in hemp field. 100 l, Husking corn. 200 l, Woodcutter.

1950, Oct. 20 ***Perf. 14*** **Wmk. 277**

549 A306 50c violet blue 5 5
550 " 1 l dark blue violet 5 3
551 " 2 l sepia 5 3
552 " 5 l dark gray 33 3
553 " 6 l chocolate 5 3
554 " 10 l deep green 2.00 3
555 " 12 l deep bl. green 60 4
556 " 15 l dark gray blue 60 4
557 " 20 l blue violet 4.75 3
558 " 25 l brown orange 2.40 3
559 " 30 l magenta 45 3
560 " 35 l crimson 2.40 5
561 " 40 l brown 15 4
562 " 50 l violet 3.25 4
563 " 55 l deep blue 15 7
564 " 60 l red 5.75 18
565 " 65 l dark green 20 8

Engraved.

Perf. 13x14, 14x13

566 A306 100 l brn. orange 30.00 12
a. Perf. 13 30.00 25
b. Perf. 14 35.00 25
567 " 200 l olive brown 4.25 25
a. Perf. 14 4.25 25
Nos. 549-567 (19) 57.48 1.20

See also Nos. 668–673A.

1951, Mar. 27 **Photo.** ***Perf. 14***

Design: 55 l, Tuscany 6 cr.

568 A307 20 l red vio. & red 2.75 1.20
569 " 55 l ultramarine & blue 11.00 13.00

Centenary of Tuscany's first stamps.

Italian Automobile
A308

1951, Apr. 2

570 A308 20 l dark green 3.50 1.00

Issued to publicize the 33rd International Automobile Exhibition, Turin, April 4-15, 1951.

Altar of Peace, Medea
A309

1951, Apr. 11

571 A309 20 l blue violet 4.25 1.00

Issued to publicize the consecration of the Altar of Peace at Redipuglia Cemetery, Medea.

Helicopter over Leonardo da Vinci Heliport
A310

P. T. T. Building, Milan Fair
A311

1951, Apr. 12 **Photogravure**

572 A310 20 l brown 3.50 1.10
573 A311 55 l deep blue 27.50 21.00

29th Milan Trade Fair.

Symbols of the International Gymnastic Festival
A312

Statue of Diana, Spindle and Turin Tower
A313

Photogravure.

1951, May 18 ***Perf. 14*** **Wmk. 277**

Fleur-de-lis in Red

574 A312 5 l dark brown 13.50 *75.00*
575 " 10 l Prussian green 13.50 *75.00*
576 " 15 l violet blue 13.50 *75.00*

International Gymnastic Festival and Meet, Florence, 1951.

Fake cancellations exist on Nos. 574–576.

1951, Apr. 26

577 A313 20 l purple 7.25 1.35

Tenth International Exhibition of Textile Art and Fashion, Turin, May 2–16.

Landing of Columbus
A314

1951, May 5

578 A314 20 l Prussian green 3.75 1.35

500th anniversary of birth of Columbus.

Reconstructed Abbey of Montecassino
A315

Design: 55 l, Montecassino Ruins.

1951, June 18

579 A315 20 l violet 3.00 60
580 " 55 l bright blue 27.50 9.00

Issued to commemorate the reconstruction of the Abbey of Montecassino.

Pietro Vannucci (Il Perugino)
A316

Stylized Vase
A317

Cartouche of Amenhotep III and Pitcher—A318

1951, July 23

581 A316 20 l brn. & red brn. 3.75 2.00

Issued to commemorate the 500th anniversary (in 1950) of the birth of Pietro Vannucci, painter.

1951, July 23

582 A317 20 l greenish gray & black 2.50 1.25
583 A318 55 l violet blue & pale salmon 14.00 15.00

Triennial Art Exhibition, Milan, 1951.

Cyclist
A319

1951, Aug. 23

584 A319 25 l gray black 3.25 1.65

Issued to publicize the World Bicycle Championship Races, Milan, Aug.-Sept. 1951.

Tartan and Globes—A320

1951, Sept. 8 **Photogravure**

585 A320 25 l deep blue 3.50 1.00

15th Levant Fair, Bari, September 1951.

"La Figlia di Jorio" by Michetti
A321

1951, Sept. 15 ***Perf. 14*** **Wmk. 277**

586 A321 25 l dark brown 4.75 1.00

Issued to commemorate the centenary of the birth of Francesco Paolo Michetti, painter.

Sardinia Stamp of 1851
A322

1951, Oct. 5

587 A322 10 l dk. brown & gray 1.25 1.25
588 " 25 l rose red & blue green 1.85 1.25
589 " 60 l violet blue & red orange 6.25 6.25

No. 588 shows a 20c Sardinia stamp, No. 589 a 40c. Issued to commemorate the centenary of Sardinia's first postage stamp.

Mercury—A323

Roman Census—A324

1951, Oct. 31

590 A323 10 l green 1.50 85
591 A324 25 l violet gray 2.50 1.00

Issued to publicize the 3rd Industrial and the 9th General Italian Census.

Winter Scene
A325

Trees—A326

1951, Nov. 21

592 A325 10 l olive & dull grn. 1.50 1.25
593 A326 25 l dull green 3.00 90

Issued to publicize the Festival of Trees.

Giuseppe Verdi—A327

Designs: Portraits of Verdi, various backgrounds.

1951, Nov. 19 **Engraved**

594 A327 10 l violet brown & dark green 1.20 1.85
595 " 25 l red brown & dark brown 4.50 1.20
596 " 60 l deep green & indigo 12.00 4.25

Issued to commemorate the 50th anniversary of the death of Giuseppe Verdi, composer.

Vincenzo Bellini
A328

Photogravure.

1952, Jan. 28 ***Perf. 14*** **Wmk. 277**

597 A328 25 l gray & gray blk. 2.50 50

Issued to commemorate the 150th anniversary of the birth of Vincenzo Bellini, composer.

Palace of Caserta and Statuary—A329

1952, Feb. 1

598 A329 25 l dull green & olive bistre 2.50 50

Issued to honor Luigi Vanvitelli, architect.

Statues of Athlete and River God Tiber—A330

1952, Mar. 22

599 A330 25 l brown & slate black 1.10 50

Issued on the occasion of the first International Exhibition of Sports Stamps.

Milan Fair Buildings—A331

1952, Apr. 12 **Engraved**

600 A331 60 l ultramarine 12.00 5.50

30th Milan Trade Fair.

Leonardo da Vinci
A332

Virgin of the Rocks
A332a

Photogravure

1952 ***Perf. 14*** **Wmk. 277**

601 A332 25 l deep orange 60 12

Engraved.

Perf. 13

Unwmkd.

601A A332a 60 l ultramarine 3.50 3.75

Wmk. 277

601B A332 80 l brn. carmine 11.00 18
c. Perf. 14x13 10.00 50

Issued to commemorate the 500th anniversary of the birth of Leonardo da Vinci.

First Stamps and Cathedral Bell Towers of Modena and Parma—A333

1952, May 29 ***Perf. 14***

602 A333 25 l black & red brown 1.75 30
603 " 60 l black & ultra. 6.00 5.75

Issued to commemorate the centenary of the first postage stamps of Modena and Parma.

Globe and Torch
A334

Lion of St. Mark
A335

1952, June 7

604 A334 25 l bright blue 3.00 50

Issued to honor the Overseas Fair at Naples and Italian labor throughout the world.

1952, June 14

605 A335 25 l black & yellow 2.00 45

26th Biennial Art Exhibition, Venice.

"P" and Basilica of St. Anthony
A336

Flag and Basilica of St. Just
A337

1952, June 19

606 A336 25 l blue gray, red & dark blue 3.50 50

30th International Sample Fair of Padua.

1952, June 28

607 A337 25 l deep green, dark brown & red 2.10 50

4th International Sample Fair of Trieste.

Fair Entrance and Tartan
A338

1952, Sept. 6 ***Perf. 14*** **Wmk. 277**

608 A338 25 l dark green 1.35 50

16th Levant Fair, Bari, Sept. 1952.

Girolamo Savonarola
A339

Mountain Peak and Climbing Equipment
A340

1952, Sept. 20

609 A339 25 l purple 1.75 50

Issued to commemorate the 500th anniversary of the birth of Girolamo Savonarola.

1952, Oct. 4

610 A340 25 l gray 1.00 35

Issued to publicize the National Exhibition of the Alpine troops, Oct. 4, 1952.

Colosseum and Plane—A341

1952, Sept. 29

611 A341 60 l violet blue & dark blue 8.00 8.00

Issued to publicize the first International Civil Aviation Conference, Rome, Sept. 1952.

Guglielmo Cardinal Massaia and Map—A342

1952, Nov. 21 **Engraved** ***Perf. 13***

612 A342 25 l brn. & dk. brn. 1.75 50

Issued to commemorate the centenary of the establishment of the first Catholic mission in Ethiopia.

Symbols of Army, Navy and Air Force
A343

Sailor, Soldier and Aviator
A344

Design: 60 l, Boat, plane and tank.

1952, Nov. 3 **Photo.** ***Perf. 14***

613 A343 10 l dark green 12 5
614 A344 25 l black & dark brown 75 5
615 " 60 l black & blue 3.75 1.35

Issued to publicize Armed Forces Day, Nov. 4, 1952.

Antonio Mancini
A345

Vincenzo Gemito
A346

1952, Dec. 6

616 A345 25 l dark green 1.20 40
617 A346 25 l brown 1.20 40

Issued to commemorate the birth centenaries of Antonio Mancini, painter, and Vincenzo Gemito, sculptor.

Martyrs, Jailer and Artist Boldini
A347

1952, Dec. 31

618 A347 25 l gray black & dark blue 1.75 50

Issued to commemorate the centenary of the deaths of the five Martyrs of Belfiore.

Antonello da Messina
A349

1953, Feb. 21 **Photo.** ***Perf. 14***

621 A349 25 l carmine lake 2.75 50

Issued to commemorate the Messina Exhibition of the paintings of Antonello and his 15th century contemporaries.

Racing Cars—A350

1953, Apr. 24

622 A350 25 l violet 85 50

20th 1,000-mile auto race.

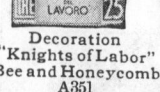

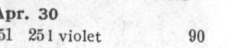

Decoration "Knights of Labor" Bee and Honeycomb
A351

Arcangelo Corelli
A352

1953, Apr. 30

623 A351 25 l violet 90 50

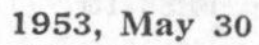

1953, May 30

624 A352 25 l dark brown 1.00 40

Issued to commemorate the 300th anniversary of the birth of Arcangelo Corelli, composer.

St. Clare of Assisi and Convent of St. Damien
A353

"Italia" after Syracusean Coin
A354

1953, June 27

625 A353 25 l brn. & dull red 85 18

Issued to commemorate the 700th anniversary of the death of St. Clare of Assisi.

1953–54 ***Perf. 14*** **Wmk. 277**

Size: 17x21mm.

626 A354 5 l gray 8 4
627 " 10 l orange vermilion 15 4
628 " 12 l dull green 12 4
628A " 13 l brt. lilac rose ('54) 8 5
629 " 20 l brown 80 5
630 " 25 l purple 2.65 4
631 " 35 l rose carmine 40 8
632 " 60 l blue 3.00 12
633 " 80 l orange brown 37.50 12
Nos. 626-633 (9) 44.78 58

See Nos. 661-662, 673B-689, 785-788, 998A-998W, 1288-1295.

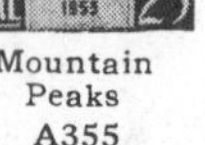

Mountain Peaks
A355

Tyche, Goddess of Fortune
A356

1953, July 11

634 A355 25 l blue green 2.00 18

Festival of the Mountain.

1953, July 16

635 A356 25 l dark brown 1.25 12
636 " 60 l deep blue 3.75 70

Issued to publicize the International Exposition of Agriculture, Rome, 1953.

Continents Joined by Rainbow
A357

1953, Aug. 6

637 A375 25 l org. & Pruss. bl. 3.00 12
638 " 60 l lilac rose & dk. vio. blue 18.00 1.75

Issued to commemorate the 4th anniversary of the signing of the North Atlantic Treaty.

Luca Signorelli
A358

Agostino Bassi
A359

1953, Aug. 13

639 A358 25 l dark brown & dull green 1.00 18

Issued to publicize the opening of an exhibition of the works of Luca Signorelli, painter.

1953, Sept. 5

640 A359 25 l dk. gray & brn. 85 18

6th International Microbiology Congress, Rome, Sept. 6-12, 1953.

Siena—A360

Rapallo—A361

Views: 20 l, Seaside at Gardone. 25 l, Mountain, Cortina d'Ampezzo. 35 l, Roman ruins, Taormina. 60 l, Rocks and sea, Capri.

1953, Dec. 31 ***Perf. 14***

641 A360 10 l dark brown & red brown 12 3
642 A361 12 l light blue & gray 25 12
643 " 20 l brown orange & dark brown 30 4
644 A360 25 l dark green & pale blue 60 4
645 A361 35 l cream & brn. 1.20 12
646 " 60 l bl. grn. & indigo 3.00 30
Nos. 641-646 (6) 5.47 65

Lateran Palace, Rome
A362

Television Screen and Aerial
A363

1954, Feb. 11

647 A362 25 l dk. brn. & choc. 1.00 12
648 " 60 l blue & ultra. 3.00 70

Issued to commemorate the 25th anniversary of the signing of the Lateran Pacts.

1954, Feb. 25

649 A363 25 l purple 1.10 12
650 " 60 l dp. blue green 4.50 1.00

Issued to commemorate the introduction of regular national television service.

"Italia" and Quotation from Constitution—A364

1954, Mar. 20

651 A364 25 l purple 1.25 5

Issued as propaganda for the payment of taxes.

Vertical Flight Trophy A365 — Eagle Perched on Ruins A366

1954, Apr. 24

652 A365 25 l gray black 70 45

Issued to publicize the experimental transportation of mail by helicopter, April 1954.

1954, June 1

653 A366 25 l gray, orange brn. & black 50 12

Issued to commemorate the 10th anniversary of Italy's resistance movement.

Alfredo Catalani A367

1954, June 19 *Perf. 14*

654 A367 25 l dark greenish gray 70 12

Issued to commemorate the centenary of the birth of Alfredo Catalani, composer.

Marco Polo, Lion of St. Mark and Dragon A368

Perf. 14, 13 (60 l)

1954, July 8 Engraved

655 A368 25 l red brown 75 12
656 " 60 l gray green 2.75 1.00
a. Perf. 13x12 4.00 2.25

Issued to commemorate the 700th anniversary of the birth of Marco Polo.

Automobile and Cyclist A369

1954, Sept. 6 Photo. *Perf. 14*

657 A369 25 l deep grn. & red 60 12

Issued to commemorate the 60th anniversary of the founding of the Italian Touring Club.

St. Michael Overpowering the Devil A370 — Pinocchio and Group of Children A371

1954, Oct. 9

658 A370 25 l rose red 1.00 12
659 " 60 l blue 2.25 1.00

Issued to publicize the 23rd general assembly of the International Criminal Police, Rome 1954.

1954, Oct. 26

660 A371 25 l rose red 65 18

Issued to honor Carlo Lorenzini, creator of Pinocchio.

Italia Type of 1953–54

1954, Dec. 28 Engraved *Perf. 13*

Size; 22½x27½mm.

661 A354 100 l brown 32.50 12
662 " 200 l deep blue 4.00 25

Madonna, Perugino A372 — Amerigo Vespucci and Map A373

Design: 60 l, Madonna of the Pieta, Michelangelo.

1954, Dec. 31 Photo. *Perf. 14*

663 A372 25 l brown & bistre 42 12
664 " 60 l black & cream 1.40 1.10

Issued to mark the end of the Marian Year.

1954, Dec. 31 Engraved *Perf. 13*

665 A373 25 l deep plum 50 12
a. Perf. 13x14 5.00 1.20
666 " 60 l blue black 1.65 1.10
a. Perf. 13x14 2.50 1.20

Issued to commemorate the 500th anniversary of the birth of Amerigo Vespucci, explorer, 1454 (1451?)–1512.

Silvio Pellico A374

Perf. 14

1955, Jan. 24 Photo. **Wmk. 277**

667 A374 25 l brt. blue & vio. 75 12

Centenary of death of Silvio Pellico (1789–1854), dramatist.

Wmk. 303

St. George, by Donatello A374a

Types of 1950 ("Italy at Work").

Wmk. Multiple Stars. (303)

1955-57 Photogravure. *Perf. 14*

668 A306 50c violet blue 8 10
669 " 1 l dark blue violet 8 5
670 " 2 l sepia 8 5
671 " 15 l dark gray blue 80 5
672 " 30 l magenta 32.50 30
673 " 50 l violet 16.00 5
673A " 65 l dk. grn. ('57) 16.00 20.00
Nos. 668-673A (7) 65.54 20.60

Italia Type of 1953–54
Photogravure

1955–58 *Perf. 14* **Wmk. 303**

Size: 17x21mm.

673B A354 1 l gray ('58) 3 3
674 " 5 l slate 6 3
675 " 6 l ochre ('57) 6 3
676 " 10 l orange vermilion 12 3
677 " 12 l dull green 18 3
678 " 13 l bright lilac rose 30 3
679 " 15 l gray violet ('56) 18 3
680 " 20 l brown 25 3
681 " 25 l purple 75 3
682 " 35 l rose carmine 30 3
683 " 50 l olive ('58) 1.50 3
685 " 60 l blue 25 3
686 " 80 l brown orange 38 3
687 " 90 l lt. red brn. ('58) 1.85 3

See Nos. 998A–998T for small-size set.

Engraved.

Perf. 13½

Size: 22½x28 mm.

688 A354 100 l brown ('56) 24.00 5
a. Perf. 13½x12 24.00 38
b. Perf. 13½x14 375.00 13.50
689 " 200 l gray blue ('57) 4.75 12
690 A374a 500 l green ('57) 2.25 12
690A " 1000 l rose car. ('57) 2.25 25
Nos. 673B-690A (18) 39.46 96

Nos. 690–690A were printed on ordinary and fluorescent paper.
See also Nos. 785–788.

"Italia" A375 — Oil Derrick and Old Roman Aqueduct A376

1955, Mar. 15 Photo. *Perf. 14*

691 A375 25 l rose violet 5.25 12

Issued as propaganda for the payment of taxes.

1955, June 6

Design: 60 l, Marble columns and oil field on globe.

692 A376 25 l olive green 1.40 12
693 " 60 l henna brown 3.00 1.00

Issued to publicize the fourth World Petroleum Congress, Rome, June 6-15, 1955.

Antonio Rosmini A377

1955, July 1 *Perf. 14* **Wmk. 303**

694 A377 25 l sepia 2.50 12

Issued to commemorate the centenary of the death of the philosopher, Antonio Rosmini.

Girolamo Fracastoro and Stadium at Verona A378

1955, Sept. 1

695 A378 25 l gray blk. & brown 85 12

International Medical Congress, Verona, Sept. 1–4.

Basilica of St. Francis, Assisi A379

1955, Oct. 4

696 A379 25 l black & cream 80 12

Issued in honor of St. Francis and to commemorate the 7th centenary (in 1953) of the Basilica in Assisi.

Young Man at Drawing Board A380

1955, Oct. 15

697 A380 25 l Prussian green 85 12

Centenary of technical education in Italy.

Harvester A381

F.A.O. Headquarters, Rome—A382

1955, Nov. 3

698 A381 25 l rose red & brown 70 12
699 A382 60 l black & bright purple 1.75 55

Issued to commemorate the 50th anniversary of the International Institute of Agriculture and the 10th anniversary of the Food and Agriculture Organization, successor to the Institute.

Giacomo Matteotti A383 Battista Grassi A384

1955, Nov. 10

700 A383 25 l rose brown 90 12

Issued to honor the 70th anniversary of the birth of Giacomo Matteotti, Italian socialist leader.

1955, Nov. 19

701 A384 25 l dark green 90 12

Issued to commemorate the 30th anniversary of the death of Battista Grassi, zoologist.

"St. Stephen Giving Alms" A385

"St. Lorenzo Giving Alms" A386

1955, Nov. 26

702	A385	10 l black & cream	22	18
703	A386	25 l ultra. & cream	75	12

Issued to commemorate the 500th anniversary of the death of Fra Angelico, painter.

Giovanni Pascoli A387

1955, Dec. 31

704 A387 25 l gray black 80 12

Issued to commemorate the centenary of the birth of Giovanni Pascoli, poet.

Ski Jump "Italia"—A388

Stadiums at Cortina: 12 l, Skiing. 25 l, Ice skating. 60 l, Ice racing, Lake Misurina.

1956, Jan. 26 Photogravure

705	A388	10 l blue grn. & org.	12	12
706	"	12 l yellow & black	18	12
707	"	25 l violet black & orange brown	45	8
708	A388	60 l sapphire & orange	1.40	90

Issued to commemorate the VII Winter Olympic Games at Cortina d'Ampezzo, Jan. 26-Feb. 5, 1956.

Mail Coach and Tunnel Exit A389

1956, May 19 ***Perf. 14*** **Wmk. 303**

709 A389 25 l dark blue green 50 12

Issued to commemorate the 50th anniversary of the Simplon Tunnel.

Arms of Republic and Symbols of Industry A390

1956, June 2

710	A390	10 l gray & slate blue	12	12
711	"	25 l pink & rose red	28	6
712	"	60 l light blue & bright blue	2.75	85
713	"	80 l org. & brown	9.50	12

Tenth anniversary of the Republic.

Amedeo Avogadro—A391

1956, Sept. 8

714 A391 25 l black violet 40 12

Issued to commemorate the centenary of the death of Amedeo Avogadro, physicist.

Europa Issue.

"Rebuilding Europe" A302

1956, Sept. 15

715	A392	25 l dark green	2.25	10
716	"	60 l blue	12.50	30

Issued to symbolize the cooperation among the six countries comprising the Coal and Steel Community.

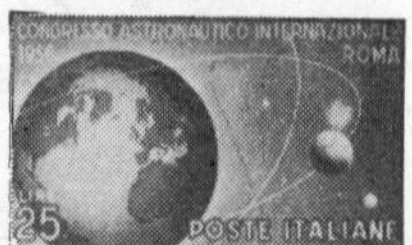

Globe and Satellites—A393

1956, Sept. 22

717 A393 25 l intense blue 1.00 12

Issued to commemorate the 7th International Astronautical Congress, Rome, Sept. 17–22.

Globe A394

1956, Dec. 29 Litho. Unwmkd.

718	A394	25 l red & blue green, *pink*	17	5
719	"	60 l blue green & red, *pale blue green*	45	25

Italy's admission to the United Nations. The design, viewed through red and green glasses, becomes three-dimensional.

Postal Savings Bank and Notes A395

1956, Dec. 31 Photo. Wmk. 303

720 A395 25 l slate blue & deep ultramarine 30 12

80th anniversary of Postal Savings.

Ovid A396 Antonio Canova A397

Paulina Borghese as Venus A398

1957, June 10 ***Perf. 14***

721 A396 25 l olive green & black 25 12

Issued to commemorate the 2000th anniversary of the birth of the poet Ovid (Publius Ovidius Naso).

1957, July 15 **Engraved**

Design: 60 l, Sculpture: Hercules and Lichas.

722	A397	25 l brown	18	12
723	"	60 l gray	55	50
724	A398	80 l violet blue	85	13

Issued to commemorate the bicentenary of the birth of Antonio Canova, sculptor.

Traffic Light A399 "United Europe" A400

Photogravure.

1957, Aug. 7 ***Perf. 14*** **Wmk. 303**

725 A399 25 l green, black & red 25 6

Issued to publicize a campaign for careful driving.

1957, Sept. 16 Litho. ***Perf. 14***

Flags in Original Colors

726 A400 25 l light blue 25 6

Perf. 13

727 A400 60 l violet blue 1.25 25

Issued to publicize a united Europe for peace and prosperity.

Giosue Carducci A401 Filippino Lippi A402

1957, Oct. 14 Engraved ***Perf. 14***

728 A401 25 l brown 18 12

Issued to commemorate the 50th anniversary of the death of the poet Giosue Carducci.

1957, Nov. 25 ***Perf. 14*** **Wmk. 303**

729 A402 25 l reddish brown 18 12

Issued to commemorate the 500th anniversary of the birth of Filippino Lippi, painter.

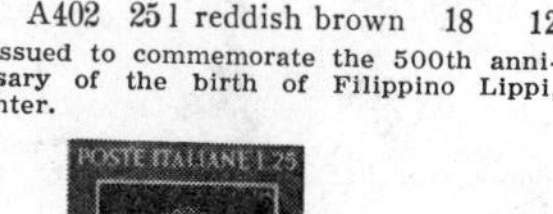

Cicero A403

1957, Nov. 30 **Photogravure**

730 A403 25 l brown red 18 10

Issued to commemorate the 2000th anniversary of the death of Marcus Tullius Cicero, Roman statesman and writer.

St. Domenico Savio and Students of Various Races A404

1957, Dec. 14

731 A404 15 l brt. lilac & blk. 18 12

Issued to commemorate the centenary of the death of St. Domenico Savio.

St. Francis of Paola A405 Giuseppe Garibaldi A406

1957, Dec. 21 **Engraved**

732 A405 25 l black 25 7

Issued to commemorate the 450th anniversary of the death of St. Francis of Paola, patron saint of seafaring men.

1957, Dec. 14 ***Perf. 14x13, 13x14***

Design: 110 l, Garibaldi monument (horizontal).

733 A406 15 l slate green 10 12
734 " 110 l dull purple 90 12

Issued to commemorate the 150th anniversary of the birth of Giuseppe Garibaldi.

Peasant, Dams and Map of Sardinia—A407

1958, Feb. 1 Engraved ***Perf. 14***

738 A407 25 l bluish green 12 7

Issued to commemorate the completion of the Flumendosa-Mulargia irrigation system.

Immaculate Conception Statue, Rome, and Lourdes Basilica
A408

1958, Apr. 16 ***Perf. 14*** **Wmk. 303**

739 A408 15 l rose claret 8 5
740 " 60 l blue 18 18

Issued to commemorate the centenary of the apparition of the Virgin Mary at Lourdes.

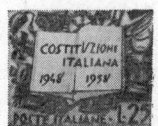

Book and Symbols of Labor Industry and Agriculture
A409

Designs: 60 l, "Tree of Freedom" (vert.). 110 l, Montecitorio Palace.

1958, May 9 Photo. ***Perf. 14***

741 A409 25 l blue green & ochre 18 5
742 " 60 l black brown & blue 25 18
743 " 110 l olive bistre & black brown 80 5

10th anniversary of the constitution.

Brussels Fair Emblem
A410

Prologue from Pagliacci
A411

1958, June 12

744 A410 60 l blue & yellow 18 18

Issued for the International and Universal Exposition at Brussels.

1958, July 10

745 A411 25 l dark blue & dark red 12 7

Issued to commemorate the centenary of the birth of Ruggiero Leoncavallo, composer.

Scene from La Bohème
A412

1958, July 10 Engraved **Unwmkd.**

746 A412 25 l dark blue 12 7

Issued to commemorate the centenary of the birth of Giacomo Puccini, composer.

Giovanni Fattori, Self-portrait
A413

"Ave Maria on the Lake" by Giovanni Segantini
A414

1958, Aug. 7 ***Perf. 13x14*** **Wmk. 303**

747 A413 110 l reddish brown 55 18

Issued to commemorate the 50th anniversary of the death of Giovanni Fattori, painter.

1958, Aug. 7 ***Perf. 14***

748 A414 110 l slate, *buff* 55 18

Issued to commemorate the centenary of the birth of Giovanni Segantini, painter.

Map of Brazil, Plane and Arch of Titus
A415

1958, Aug. 23 Photo. ***Perf. 14***

749 A415 175 l Prussian grn. 1.60 1.50

Issued to honor Italo-Brazilian friendship on the occasion of Pres. Giovanni Gronchi's visit to Brazil.

Europa Issue, 1958.
Common Design Type

1958, Sept. 13

Size: 20½x35½mm.

750 CD1 25 l red & blue 7 7
751 " 60 l blue & red 18 18

Issued to show the European Postal Union at the service of European integration.

½g Stamp of Naples
A416

Evangelista Torricelli
A417

Design: 60 l, 1g Stamp of Naples.

Perf. 14x13½, 13½

1958, Oct. 4 Engraved **Unwmkd.**

752 A416 25 l brown red 12 6
753 " 60 l black & red brown 18 18

Centenary of the stamps of Naples.

1958, Oct. 20 ***Perf. 14*** **Wmk. 303**

754 A417 25 l rose claret 38 22

Issued to commemorate the 350th anniversary of the birth of Evangelista Torricelli, mathematician and physicist.

"The Triumph of Caesar," Montegna
A418

Persian Style Bas-relief, Sorrento
A419

Designs: 25 l, Coats of Arms of Trieste, Rome and Trento (horiz.). 60 l, War memorial bell of Rovereto.

1958, Nov. 3 Engr. ***Perf. 14x13½***

755 A418 15 l green 6 6
756 " 25 l gray 12 7
757 " 60 l rose claret 12 25

Issued to commemorate the 40th anniversary of Italy's victory in World War I.

1958, Nov. 27 Photogravure

758 A419 25 l sepia, *bluish* 13 6
759 " 60 l violet blue, *bluish* 35 35

Visit of the Shah of Iran to Italy.

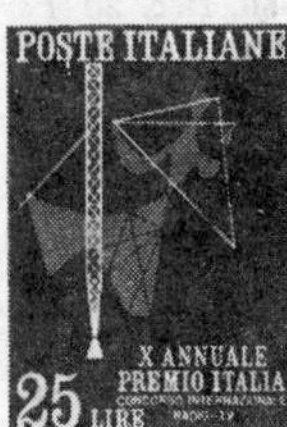

Eleonora Duse
A420

Dancers and Antenna
A421

Engraved.

1958, Dec. 11 ***Perf. 14*** **Unwmkd.**

760 A420 25 l bright ultramarine 18 7

Issued to commemorate the centenary of the birth of Eleonora Duse, actress.

1958, Dec. 29 Photo. **Wmk. 303**

Design: 60 l, Piano, dove and antenna.

761 A421 25 l red, blue & black 6 6
762 " 60 l ultramarine & black 15 15

Issued to commemorate the 10th anniversary of the Prix Italia (International Radio and Television Competitions).

Stamp of Sicily
A422

Design: 60 l, Stamp of Sicily, 5g.

Perf. 14x13½

1959, Jan. 2 Engraved **Unwmkd.**

763 A422 25 l Prussian green 6 6
764 " 60 l deep orange 15 15

Centenary of the stamps of Sicily.

Common Design Types pictured in section at front of book.

Dome of St. Peter's and Tower of Lateran Palace
A423

Perf. 14

1959, Feb. 11 Photo. **Wmk. 303**

765 A423 25 l ultramarine 15 7

Issued to commemorate the 30th anniversary of the Lateran Pacts.

Map of North Atlantic and NATO Emblem—A424

1959, Apr. 4

766 A424 25 l dk. blue & ochre 6 6
767 " 60 l dk. blue & grn. 15 15

Issued to commemorate the tenth anniversary of the North Atlantic Treaty Organization.

Arms of Paris and Rome
A425

1959, Apr. 9

768 A425 15 l blue & red 7 7
769 " 25 l blue & red 12 7

Issued to publicize the cultural ties between Rome and Paris.

"A Gentle Peace Has Come"
A426

Statue of Lord Byron
A427

1959, Apr. 13 Engraved **Unwmkd.**

770 A426 25 l olive green 12 7

International War Veterans Association convention, Rome.

1959, Apr. 21

771 A427 15 l black 12 7

Issued to commemorate the unveiling in Rome of a statue of Lord Byron by Bertel Thorvaldson, Danish sculptor.

Camillo Prampolini
A428

1959, Apr. 27 ***Perf. 14*** **Unwmkd.**

772 A428 15 l carmine rose 38 12

Camillo Prampolini, socialist leader and reformer, birth centenary.

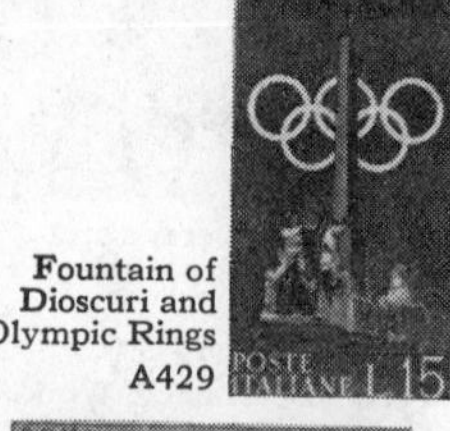

Fountain of Dioscuri and Olympic Rings
A429

Baths of Carcalla—A430

1959, June 23 Photo. Wmk. 303

Designs: 25 l, Capitoline tower. 60 l, Arch of Constantine. 110 l, Ruins of Basilica of Massentius.

Designs in Dark Sepia

No.	Type	Denomination & color	Unused	Used
773	A429	15 l red orange	7	7
774	"	25 l blue	7	7
775	A430	35 l bistre	12	12
776	"	60 l rose lilac	18	18
777	"	110 l yellow	30	12
		Nos. 773-777 (5)	74	56

1960 Olympic Games in Rome.

Victor Emanuel II, Garibaldi, Cavour, Mazzini
A431

Battle of San Fermo
A432

Designs: 25 l, "After the Battle of Magenta" by Fattori and Red Cross (vert.). 60 l, Battle of Palestro. 110 l, "Battle of Magenta" by Induno (vert.).

1959, June 27 Engraved Unwmkd.

No.	Type	Denomination & color	Unused	Used
778	A431	15 l gray	8	7
779	"	25 l brown & red	8	7
780	A432	35 l dark violet	12	12
781	"	60 l ultramarine	18	18
782	"	110 l magenta	30	12
		Nos. 778-782 (5)	76	56

Issued to commemorate the centenary of the war of independence. No. 779 commemorates the centenary of the Red Cross idea. Cross photogravure on No. 779.

Labor Monument, Geneva
A433

Stamp of Romagna
A434

1959, July 20 *Perf. 14x13, 14*

No.	Type	Denomination & color	Unused	Used
783	A433	25 l violet	6	6
784	"	60 l brown	18	12

Issued to commemorate the 40th anniversary of the International Labor Organization.

Italia Type of 1953-54
Photo.; Engr. (100 l, 200 l)

1959-66 *Perf. 14* Wmk. 303

Size: 17x21mm.

No.	Type	Denomination & color	Unused	Used
785	A354	30 l bistre brn. ('60)	30	4
786	"	40 l lilac rose ('60)	1.50	5
786A	"	70 l Prussian green ('60)	50	5
787	"	100 l brown	1.00	3
787A	A354	130 l gray & dull red ('66)	40	6
788	"	200 l deep blue	1.00	3
		Nos. 785-788 (6)	4.70	26

1959, Sept. 1 Photogravure

Design: 60 l, Stamp of Romagna, 20b.

No.	Type	Denomination & color	Unused	Used
789	A434	25 l pale brown & black	12	5
790	"	60 l gray green & black	15	15

Centenary of the stamps of Romagna.

Europa Issue, 1959.
Common Design Type

1959, Sept. 19

Size: 22 x 27½ mm.

No.	Type	Denomination & color	Unused	Used
791	CD2	25 l olive green	12	6
792	"	60 l blue	12	12

Stamp of 1953 with Facsimile Cancellation
A435

Aeneas Fleeing with Father and Son, by Raphael
A436

1959, Dec. 20 *Perf. 14* Wmk. 303

No.	Type	Denomination & color	Unused	Used
793	A435	15 l gray, rose carmine & black	8	8

Italy's first Stamp Day, Dec. 20, 1959.

1960, Apr. 7 Engraved Unwmkd.

No.	Type	Denomination & color	Unused	Used
794	A436	25 l lake	8	8
795	"	60 l gray violet	15	15

Issued to publicize World Refugee Year, July 1, 1959-June 30, 1960. Design is detail from "The Fire in the Borgo."

Garibaldi's Proclamation to the Sicilians—A437

King Victor Emmanuel and Garibaldi Meeting at Teano
A438

Design: 60 l, Volunteers embarking, Quarto, Genoa.

Photogravure

1960, May 5 *Perf. 14* Wmk. 303

No.	Type	Denomination & color	Unused	Used
796	A437	15 l brown	6	6

Perf. 13x14, 14x13

Engraved Unwmkd.

No.	Type	Denomination & color	Unused	Used
797	A438	25 l rose claret	12	6
798	A437	60 l ultramarine	18	18

Centenary of the liberation of Southern Italy (Kingdom of the Two Sicilies) by Garibaldi.

Emblem of 17th Olympic Games
A439

Olympic Stadium—A440

Statues: 15 l, Roman Consul on way to the games. 35 l, Myron's Discobolus. 110 l, Seated boxer. 200 l, Apoxyomenos by Lysippus.

Stadia: 25 l, Velodrome. 60 l, Sports palace. 150 l, Small sports palace.

Photogravure, Engraved.
Wmk. 303, Unwmkd.

1960 *Perf. 14x13½, 13½x14*

No.	Type	Denomination & color	Unused	Used
799	A439	5 l yellow brown	5	6
800	A440	10 l deep orange & dark blue	5	6
801	A439	15 l ultramarine	7	6
802	A440	25 l light violet & brown	7	6
803	A439	35 l rose claret	12	12
804	A440	60 l bluish green & brown	18	12
805	A439	110 l plum	30	5
806	A440	150 l blue & brn.	95	65
807	A439	200 l green	1.00	6
		Nos. 799-807 (9)	2.79	1.24

Issued to commemorate the 17th Olympic Games, Rome, Aug. 25-Sept. 11.

The photogravure denominations (5, 10, 25, 60, 150 lire) are watermarked; the engraved (15, 35, 110 and 200 lire) are unwatermarked.

Bottego Statue, Parma
A441

Michelangelo da Caravaggio
A442

Engraved

1960 *Perf. 14* Unwmkd.

No.	Type	Denomination & color	Unused	Used
808	A441	30 l brown	12	6

Issued to commemorate the centenary of the birth of Vittorio Bottego, explorer.

Europa Issue, 1960.
Common Design Type

1960 Photogravure Wmk. 303

Size: 37x27mm.

No.	Type	Denomination & color	Unused	Used
809	CD3	30 l dark green & bistre brown	6	6
810	"	70 l dark blue & salmon	15	15

Engraved

1960 *Perf. 13x13½* Unwmkd.

No.	Type	Denomination & color	Unused	Used
811	A442	25 l orange brown	12	7

Issued to commemorate the 350th anniversary of the death of Michelangelo da Caravaggio (Merisi), painter.

Mail Coach and Post Horn
A443

Photogravure

1960 *Perf. 14* Wmk. 303

No.	Type	Denomination & color	Unused	Used
812	A443	15 l black brown & orange brown	12	7

Issued for Stamp Day, Dec. 20.

Slave, by Michelangelo
A444

Designs from Sistine Chapel by Michelangelo: 5 l, 10 l, 115 l, 150 l, Heads of various "slaves." 15 l, Joel. 20 l, Libyan Sybil. 25 l, Isaiah. 30 l, Eritrean Sybil. 40 l, Daniel. 50 l, Delphic Sybil. 55 l, Cumaean Sybil. 70 l, Zachariah. 85 l, Jonah. 90 l, Jeremiah. 100 l, Ezekiel. 200 l, Self-portrait. 500 l, Adam. 1000 l, Eve.

Photogravure

1961, March 6 *Perf. 14* Wmk. 303

Size: 17x21mm.

No.	Type	Denomination & color	Unused	Used
813	A444	1 l gray	3	3
814	"	5 l brown orange	9	3
815	"	10 l red orange	12	4
816	"	15 l bright lilac	12	4
817	"	20 l Prussian green	18	4
818	"	25 l brown	55	4
819	"	30 l purple	25	4
820	"	40 l rose red	18	4
821	"	50 l olive	1.25	4
822	"	55 l red brown	18	8
823	"	70 l blue	25	4
824	"	85 l slate green	25	4
825	"	90 l lilac rose	60	4
826	"	100 l violet gray	2.50	4
827	"	115 l ultramarine	38	3

Engraved

No.	Type	Denomination & color	Unused	Used
828	A444	150 l chocolate	3.00	7
829	"	200 l dark blue	6.00	7
		a. Perf. 13½	6.00	7

Perf. 13½

Size: 22x27mm.

No.	Type	Denomination & color	Unused	Used
830	A444	500 l blue green	3.75	12
831	"	1000 l brown red	3.75	90
		Nos. 813-831 (19)	23.43	1.77

Map Showing Flight from Italy to Argentina
A445

Designs: 185 l, Italy to Uruguay. 205 l, Italy to Peru.

1961, Apr. Photo. *Perf. 14*

No.	Type	Denomination & color	Unused	Used
832	A445	170 l ultramarine	5.50	6.50
833	"	185 l dull green	5.50	6.50
834	"	205 l violet black	12.00	13.50
		a. 205 l rose lilac	325.00	

Issued to commemorate the visit of President Gronchi to South America, April 1961.

Nos. 832-833 and 834a were issued Apr. 4, to become valid on Apr. 6. The map of Peru on No. 834a was drawn incorrectly and the stamp was therefore withdrawn on Apr. 4. A corrected design in new color (No. 834) was issued Apr. 6.

Statue of Pliny, Como Cathedral
A446

Ippolito Nievo
A447

1961, May 27

835 A446 30 l brown 22 22

Issued to commemorate the 1900th anniversary of the birth of Pliny the Younger, Roman consul and writer.

1961, June 8 *Perf. 14* Wmk. 303

836 A447 30 l multicolored 22 22

Issued to commemorate the centenary of the death of Ippolito Nievo (1831–1861), writer.

St. Paul Aboard Ship
A448

1961, June 28

837 A448 30 l multicolored 18 18
838 " 70 l " 60 60

Issued to commemorate the 1,900th anniversary of St. Paul's arrival in Rome. The design is after a miniature from the Bible of Borso D'Este.

Cavalli Gun and Gaeta Fortress
A449

Designs: 30 l, Carignano palace, Turin. 40 l, Montecitorio palace, Rome. 70 l, Palazzo Vecchio, Florence. 115 l, Villa Madama, Rome. 300 l, Steel construction, Italia '61 Exhibition, Turin.

1961, Aug. 12 Photogravure

839 A449 15 l dark blue & reddish brn. 12 5
840 " 30 l dark blue & red brown 18 5
841 " 40 l blue & brown 60 38
842 " 70 l brn. & pink 90 12
843 " 115 l orange brown & dk. blue 3.50 6
844 " 300 l bright green & red 9.00 9.00
Nos. 839-844 (6) 14.30 9.66

Centenary of Italian unity.

Europa Issue, 1961
Common Design Type

1961, Sept. 18 *Perf. 14* Wmk. 303
Size: 36½x21mm.

845 CD4 30 l carmine 6 6
846 " 70 l yellow green 15 15

Giandomenico Romagnosi
A450

Engraved

1961, Nov. 28 *Perf. 13½* Unwmkd.

847 A450 30 l green 12 6

Issued to commemorate the bicentenary of the birth of Giandomenico Romagnosi, jurist and philosopher.

Design from 1820 Sardinia Letter Sheet
A451

Photogravure

1961, Dec. 3 *Perf. 14* Wmk. 303

848 A451 15 l lilac rose & black 7 7

Issued for Stamp Day 1961.

Family Scene
"I am the Lamp that Glows so Gently . . ."
A452

1962, Apr. 6 *Perf. 14* Wmk. 303

849 A452 30 l red 30 12
850 " 70 l blue 65 55

Issued to commemorate the 50th anniversary of the death of Giovanni Pascoli, poet.

Pacinotti's Dynamo
A453

1962, June 12

851 A453 30 l rose & black 30 12
852 " 70 l ultra. & black 60 60

Issued to commemorate the 50th anniversary of the death of Antonio Pacinotti (1841–1912), physicist and inventor of the ring winding dynamo.

St. Catherine of Siena, by Andrea Vanni
A454

Lion of St. Mark
A455

Design: 70 l, St. Catherine, 15th century woodcut.

1962, June 26 Photogravure

853 A454 30 l black 30 7

Engraved and Photogravure

854 A454 70 l red & black 60 60

Issued to commemorate the 500th anniversary of the canonization of St. Catherine of Siena, Patroness of Italy.

1962, Aug. 25 Photogravure

Design: 30 l, Stylized camera eye.

855 A455 30 l blue & black 60 12
856 " 70 l red org. & blk. 85 70

Issued to mark the 30th anniversary of the International Film Festival in Venice.

Motorcyclist and Bicyclist
A456

Designs: 70 l, Group of cyclists. 300 l, Bicyclist.

1962, Aug. 30

857 A456 30 l green & black 60 6
858 " 70 l blue & black 30 25
859 " 300 l dp. org. & blk. 5.00 5.00

World Bicycle Championship Races.

Europa Issue, 1962
Common Design Type

1962, Sept. 17
Size: 37x21mm.

860 CD5 30 l carmine 42 7
861 " 70 l blue 80 55

Swiss and Italian Flags, Eugenio and Angela Lina Balzan Medal
A457

1962, Oct. 25 *Perf. 14* Wmk. 303

862 A457 70 l rose red, green & brown 18 18

Issued to commemorate the first distribution of the Balzan Prize by the International Balzan Foundation for Italian-Swiss Cooperation.

Malaria Eradication Emblem
A458

Stamps of 1862 and 1961
A459

1962, Oct. 31 Photogravure

863 A458 30 l light violet 30 12
864 " 70 l light blue 60 60

Issued for the World Health Organization drive to eradicate malaria.

1962, Dec. 2

865 A459 15 l purple, buff & bistre 12 6

Issued for Stamp Day and to commemorate the centenary of Italian postage stamps.

Holy Spirit Descending on Apostles
A460

1962, Dec. 8

866 A460 30 l orange & dark bl. grn., *buff* 25 6
867 " 70 l dk. blue green & org., *buff* 50 55

Issued to commemorate the 21st Ecumenical Council of the Roman Catholic Church, Vatican II. The design is an illumination from the Codex Syriacus.

Statue of Count Camillo Bensi di Cavour
A461

1962, Dec. 10 Engraved Unwmkd.

868 A461 30 l dark green 22 6

Centenary of Court of Accounts.

Count Giovanni Pico della Mirandola
A462

Gabriele D'Annunzio
A463

Photogravure

1963, Feb. 25 *Perf. 14* Wmk. 303

869 A462 30 l gray black 12 6

Issued to commemorate the 500th anniversary of the birth of Pico della Mirandola (1463–1494), Renaissance scholar.

1963, Mar. 12 Engraved Unwmkd.

870 A463 30 l dark green 12 6

Issued to commemorate the centenary of the birth of Gabriele d'Annunzio, author and soldier.

Sower
A464

Design: 70 l, Harvester tying sheaf, sculpture from Maggiore Fountain, Perugia.

1963, Mar. 21 Photo. Wmk. 303

871 A464 30 l rose car. & brn. 12 6
872 " 70 l blue & brown 42 25

Issued for the "Freedom from Hunger" campaign of the U.N. Food and Agriculture Organization.

Mt. Viso, Alpine Club Emblem, Ax and Rope
A465

Map of Italy and "INA" Initials
A466

1963, Mar. 30 *Perf. 14* Wmk. 303

873 A465 115 l dark brown & bright blue 45 12

Issued to commemorate the centenary of the founding of the Italian Alpine Club.

1963, Apr. 4

874 A466 30 l green & black 12 6

Issued to commemorate the 50th anniversary of the National Insurance Institute.

Globe and Stamp
A467

1963, May 7 Photo. *Perf. 14*

875 A467 70 l blue & green 18 18

Issued to commemorate the centenary of the first International Postal Conference, Paris, 1863.

Crosses and Centenary Emblem on Globe
A468

1963, June 8 *Perf. 14* Wmk. 303

876 A468 30 l dark gray & red 25 12
877 " 70 l dull bl. & red 50 50

Issued to commemorate the centenary of the founding of the International Red Cross.

Roman Column, Globe and Highways
A469

1963, Aug. 21 *Perf. 14* Wmk. 303

878 A469 15 l gray olive & dark blue 12 7
879 " 70 l dull bl. & brn. 38 25

Issued to commemorate the United Nations Tourist Conference, Rome, Aug. 21–Sept. 5.

Europa Issue, 1963
Common Design Type

1963, Sept. 16
Size: 27½x23mm.

880 CD6 30 l rose & brown 12 6
881 " 70 l brown & green 18 18

Bay of Naples, Vesuvius and Sailboats
A470

Athlete on Greek Vase
A471

1963, Sept. 21 *Perf. 14* Wmk. 303

882 A470 15 l blue & orange 12 6
883 A471 70 l dark green & orange brown 15 15

Issued to commemorate the 4th Mediterranean Games, Naples, Sept. 21–29.

Giuseppe Gioachino Belli
A472

Stamps Forming Flower
A473

1963, Nov. 14 *Perf. 14* Wmk. 303

884 A472 30 l red brown 12 6

Issued to commemorate the centenary of the death of Giuseppe Gioachino Belli (1791–1863), poet.

1963, Dec. 1

885 A473 15 l blue & carmine 12 6

Issued for Stamp Day.

Pietro Mascagni and Old Costanzi Theater, Rome
A474

Design: No. 886, Giuseppe Verdi and La Scala, Milan.

1963 Photogravure

886 A474 30 l gray green & yellow brown 12 6
887 " 30 l yellow brown & gray green 12 6

Issued to commemorate the 150th anniversary of the birth of Giuseppe Verdi (1813–1901), composer (No. 886), and the centenary of the birth of Pietro Mascagni (1863–1945), composer (No. 887). Dates of issue: No. 886, Oct. 10; No. 887, Dec. 7.

Galileo Galilei
A475

Nicodemus by Michelangelo
A476

1964, Feb. 15 *Perf. 14* Wmk. 303

888 A475 30 l orange brown 12 6
889 " 70 l black 15 15

Issued to commemorate the 400th anniversary of the birth of Galileo Galilei (1564–1642), astronomer and physicist.

1964, Feb. 18 Photogravure

890 A476 30 l brown 6 6

Issued to commemorate the 400th anniversary of the death of Michelangelo Buonarroti (1475–1564), artist. Head of Nicodemus (self-portrait ?) from the Pieta, Florence Cathedral. See also No. C137.

Carabinieri—A477

Design: 70 l, Charge of Pastrengo, 1848, by De Albertis.

1964, June 5 *Perf. 14* Wmk. 303

891 A477 30 l violet blue & red 12 6
892 " 70 l brown 15 15

Issued to commemorate the 150th anniversary of the Carabinieri (police corps).

Giambattista Bodoni
A478

Unwmkd.

1964, July 30 Engr. *Perf. 14x13*

893 A478 30 l carmine 12 6
a. Perf. 13 18 18

Issued to commemorate the 150th anniversary of the death of Giambattista Bodoni (1740–1813), printer and type designer (Bodoni type).

Europa Issue, 1964
Common Design Type
Photogravure

1964, Sept. 14 *Perf. 14* Wmk. 303
Size: 21x37mm.

894 CD7 30 l brt. rose lilac 12 6
895 " 70 l blue green 12 12

Walled City
A479

Left Arch of Victor Emanuel Monument, Rome
A480

1964, Oct. 15 Photo. *Perf. 14*

896 A479 30 l emerald & dk. brown 12 12
897 " 70 l bl. & dk. brn. 12 12

Engraved
Unwmkd.

898 A479 500 l red 90 90

Issued to commemorate the 7th Congress of European Towns. The buildings in design are: Big Ben, London; Campodoglio, Rome; Town Hall, Bruges; Römer, Frankfurt; Town Hall, Paris; Belfry, Zurich; Gate, Kampen (Holland).

1964, Nov. 4 Photo. Wmk. 303

899 A480 30 l dk. red brown 12 12
900 " 70 l blue 12 12

Issued to commemorate the pilgrimage to Rome of veterans living abroad.

Giovanni da Verrazano and Verrazano-Narrows Bridge, New York Bay—A481

1964, Nov. 21 *Perf. 14* Wmk. 303

901 A481 30 l blk. & brown 12 12

Issued to commemorate the opening of the Verrazano-Narrows Bridge connecting Staten Island and Brooklyn, New York, and to honor Giovanni da Verrazano (1485–1528), discoverer of New York Bay. See also No. C138.

Italian Sports Stamps, 1934–63
A482

1964, Dec. 6 Photo. *Perf. 14*

902 A482 15 l golden brown & dark brown 12 12

Issued for Stamp Day.

Italian Soldiers in Concentration Camp
A483

Victims Trapped by Swastika
A484

Designs: 15 l, Italian soldier, sailor and airman fighting for the Allies. 70 l, Guerrilla fighters in the mountains. 115 l, Marchers with Italian flag. 130 l, Ruins of city and torn Italian flag.

1965, Apr. 24 Photo. Wmk. 303

903 A483 10 l black 5 5
904 " 15 l grn. & rose car. 5 5
905 A484 30 l plum 6 6
906 A483 70 l deep blue 12 18
907 A484 115 l rose carmine 18 12
908 " 130 l green, sepia & red 25 12
Nos. 903-908 (6) 71 58

Issued to commemorate the 20th anniversary of the Italian resistance movement during World War II.

Antonio Meucci, Guglielmo Marconi and ITU Emblem—A485

1965, May 17 *Perf. 14*

909 A485 70 l red & dark grn. 12 12

Issued to commemorate the centenary of the International Telecommunication Union.

Sailboats of Flying Dutchman Class—A486

Designs: 70 l, Sailboats of 5.5-meter class (vert.). 500 l, Sailboats, Lightning class.

1965, May 31 Photo. Wmk. 303

No.	Type	Description	Unused	Used
910	A486	30 l blk. & dull rose	12	12
911	"	70 l blk. & ultra.	12	12
912	"	500 l blk. & gray bl.	75	75

Issued to publicize the World Yachting Championships, Naples and Alassio.

Mont Blanc and Tunnel
A487

1965, June 16 *Perf. 14* Wmk. 303

No.	Type	Description	Unused	Used
913	A487	30 l black	6	6

Issued to commemorate the opening of the Mont Blanc Tunnel connecting Entrayes, Italy, and Le Polerins, France.

Alessandro Tassoni and Scene from "Seccia Rapita"
A488

Photogravure

1965, Sept. 20 *Perf. 14* Unwmkd.

No.	Type	Description	Unused	Used
914	A488	40 l black & multi.	12	6

Issued to commemorate the 400th anniversary of the birth of Alessandro Tassoni (1565–1635), poet. Design is from 1744 engraving by Bartolomeo Soliani.

Europa Issue, 1965
Common Design Type

1965, Sept. 27 Wmk. 303
Size: 36½x27mm.

No.	Type	Description	Unused	Used
915	CD8	40 l ocher & olive green	12	6
916	"	90 l ultra. & olive green	15	15

Dante, 15th Century Bust
A489

House under Construction
A490

Designs (from old Manuscripts): 40 l, Dante in Hell. 90 l, Dante in Purgatory led by Angel of Chastity. 130 l, Dante in Paradise interrogated by St. Peter on faith (horiz.).

Perf. 13½x14, 14x13½

1965, Oct. 21 Photo. Unwmkd.

No.	Type	Description	Unused	Used
917	A489	40 l multicolored	12	4
918	"	90 l "	15	12
919	"	130 l "	25	6

***Perf. 14* Wmk. 303**

No.	Type	Description	Unused	Used
920	A489	500 l slate green	75	75

Issued to commemorate the 700th anniversary of the birth of Dante Alighieri (1265–1321), poet.

1965, Oct. 31 *Perf. 14* Wmk. 303

No.	Type	Description	Unused	Used
921	A490	40 l buff, black & orange brown	12	6

Issued for Savings Day.

Jet Plane, Moon and Airletter Border
A491

Design: 40 l, Control tower and plane.

1965, Nov. 3

No.	Type	Description	Unused	Used
922	A491	40 l dk. Prus. blue & red	12	6

Unwmkd.

No.	Type	Description	Unused	Used
923	A491	90 l red, green, deep blue & buff	15	15

Night air postal network.

Map of Italy with Milan-Rome Highway
A492

Two-Man Bobsled
A493

1965, Dec. 5 Photo. *Perf. 13x14*

No.	Type	Description	Unused	Used
924	A492	20 l blue, black, ocher & gray	6	6

Issued for Stamp Day.

1966, Jan. 24 *Perf. 14* Wmk. 303

Design: 90 l, Four-man bobsled.

No.	Type	Description	Unused	Used
925	A493	40 l dull blue, gray & red	12	12
926	"	90 l violet & blue	15	15

Issued to commemorate the International Bobsled Championships, Cortina d'Ampezzo.

Woman Skater
A494

Benedetto Croce
A495

Designs: 40 l, Skier holding torch (horiz.). 500 l, Ice hockey.

1966, Feb. 5 Photogravure

No.	Type	Description	Unused	Used
927	A494	40 l black & red	12	6
928	"	90 l violet & red	15	13
929	"	500 l brown & red	80	80

Winter University Games.

1966, Feb. 25 *Perf. 14* Wmk. 303

No.	Type	Description	Unused	Used
930	A495	40 l brown	12	6

Issued to commemorate the centenary of the birth of Benedetto Croce (1866–1952), philosopher, statesman and historian.

Arms of Venice and Other Cities in Venezia—A496

1966, Mar. 22 Photo. Unwmkd.

No.	Type	Description	Unused	Used
932	A496	40 l gray & multi.	12	6

Centenary of Venezia's union with Italy.

Battle of Bezzecca
A497

1966, July 21 *Perf. 14* Wmk. 303

No.	Type	Description	Unused	Used
933	A497	90 l olive green	18	13

Issued to commemorate the centenary of the unification of Italy and of the Battle of Bezzecca.

Umbrella Pine
A498

Carnations
A499

Designs: 25 l, Apples. 50 l, Florentine iris. 55 l, Cypresses. 90 l, Daisies. 170 l, Olive tree. 180 l, Juniper.

1966–68 *Perf. 13½x14* Unwmkd.

No.	Type	Description		Unused	Used
934	A498	20 l multi.		8	7
934A	"	25 l "	('67)	15	6
935	A499	40 l "		15	7
935A	A498	50 l "	('67)	12	6
935B	"	55 l "	('68)	12	12
936	A499	90 l "		22	6
937	A498	170 l "		45	6
937A	"	180 l "	('68)	60	5
		Nos. 934–937A (8)		1.89	55

Tourist Attractions
A500

"I" in Flag Colors
A501

1966, May 28 *Perf. 14* Wmk. 303

No.	Type	Description	Unused	Used
938	A500	20 l yel., org. & blk.	6	6

Issued for tourist publicity and in connection with the National Conference on Tourism, Rome.

Perf. 13½x14

1966, June 2 Photo. Unwmkd.

No.	Type	Description	Unused	Used
939	A501	40 l multicolored	12	6
940	"	90 l "	15	15

20th anniversary of the Republic of Italy.

Singing Angels, by Donatello
A502

Madonna, by Giotto
A503

Perf. 13½x14

1966, Sept. 24 Photo. Unwmkd.

No.	Type	Description	Unused	Used
941	A502	40 l multicolored	12	6

Issued to commemorate the centenary of the death of Donatello (1386–1466), sculptor.

Europa Issue. 1966
Common Design Type

1966, Sept. 26 *Perf. 14* Wmk. 303
Size: 22x38mm.

No.	Type	Description	Unused	Used
942	CD9	40 l bright purple	12	6
943	"	90 l bright blue	15	12

Perf. 13½x14

1966, Oct. 20 Photo. Unwmkd.

No.	Type	Description	Unused	Used
944	A503	40 l multicolored	12	6

Issued to commemorate the 700th anniversary of the birth of Giotto di Bondone (1266?–1337), Florentine painter.

Italian Patriots
A504

1966, Nov. 3 *Perf. 14* Wmk. 303

No.	Type	Description	Unused	Used
945	A504	40 l gray & dull grn.	12	6

Issued to commemorate the 50th anniversary of the execution by Austrians of four Italian patriots: Fabio Filzi, Cesare Battisti, Damiano Chiesa and Nazario Sauro.

Postrider
A505

Perf. 14x13½

1966, Dec. 4 Photo. Unwmkd.

No.	Type	Description	Unused	Used
946	A505	20 l multicolored	6	6

Issued for Stamp Day.

Globe and Compass Rose
A506

1967, March 20 Photo. Wmk. 303

No.	Type	Description	Unused	Used
947	A506	40 l dull blue	12	6

Centenary of Italian Geographical Society.

Arturo Toscanini
A507

1967, March 25 *Perf. 14*

948 A507 40 l dp. vio. & cream 12 5

Birth centenary of Arturo Toscanini (1867–1957), conductor.

Seat of Parliament on Capitoline Hill, Rome
A508

1967, March 25 *Perf. 14*

949 A508 40 l sepia 12 6
950 " 90 l rose lilac & blk. 25 12

Issued to commemorate the 10th anniversary of the Treaty of Rome, establishing the European Common Market.

Europa Issue, 1967
Common Design Type

1967, Apr. 10 *Perf. 14* Wmk. 303
Size: 22x28mm.

951 CD10 40 l plum & pink 12 7
952 " 90 l ultramarine & pale gray 25 12

Alpine Ibex, Grand Paradiso Park
A509

National Parks: 40 l, Brown bear, Abruzzi Apennines (horiz.). 90 l, Red deer, Stelvio Pass, Ortler Mountains (horiz.). 170 l, Oak and deer, Circeo.

Perf. 13½x14, 14x13½

1967, Apr. 22 **Photogravure**

953 A509 20 l multicolored 8 5
954 " 40 l " 12 4
955 " 90 l " 22 6
956 " 170 l " 55 18

Claudio Monteverdi and Characters from "Orfeo"
A510

1967, May 15 ***Perf. 14***

957 A510 40 l bister brown & brown 15 6

Issued to commemorate the 4th centenary of the birth of Claudio Monteverdi (1567–1643), composer.

Bicyclists and Mountains
A511

Designs: 90 l. Three bicyclists on the road. 500 l, Group of bicyclists.

Perf. 14x13½

1967, May 15 Photo. Unwmkd.

958 A511 40 l multicolored 12 4
959 " 90 l brt. bl. & multi. 25 6
960 " 500 l yel. grn. & multi. 1.35 75

50th Bicycle Tour of Italy.

Luigi Pirandello and Stage
A512

1967, June 28 ***Perf. 14x13***

961 A512 40 l black & multi. 12 6

Issued to commemorate the centenary of the birth of Luigi Pirandello (1867–1936), novelist and dramatist.

Stylized Mask
A513

1967, June 30 *Perf. 14* Wmk. 303

962 A513 20 l green & black 10 6
963 " 40 l car. rose & blk. 12 6

10th "Festival of Two Worlds," Spoleto.

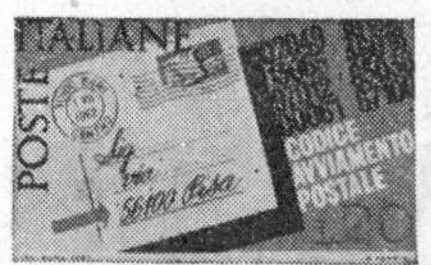

Postal Card with Postal Zone Number
A514

Design: 40 l, 50 l, Letter addressed with postal zone number.

1967–68

Unwmkd.; Wmk. 303 (25 l, 50 l)

964 A514 20 l multicolored 10 6
965 " 25 l " ('68) 10 5
966 " 40 l " 15 6
967 " 50 l " ('68) 15 5

Issued to publicize the introduction of postal zone numbers, July 1, 1967.

Pomilio PC-1 Biplane and 1917 Airmail Postmark
A515

1967, July 18 Photo. **Wmk. 303**

968 A515 40 l black & lt. blue 12 6

Issued to commemorate the 50th anniversary of the first airmail stamp, Italy No. C1.

St. Ivo Church, Rome
A516

1967, Aug. 2 ***Perf. 14*** **Unwmkd.**

969 A516 90 l multicolored 25 12

Issued to commemorate the 300th anniversary of the death of Francesco Borromini (1599–1667), architect.

Umberto Giordano and "Improvisation" from Opera Andrea Chenier
A517

1967, Aug. 28 **Wmk. 303**

970 A517 20 l blk. & org. brn. 8 6

Issued to commemorate the centenary of the birth of Umberto Giordano (1867–1948), composer.

Oath of Pontida, by Adolfo Cao
A518

ITY Emblem
A519

1967, Sept. 2

971 A518 20 l dark brown 8 6

Issued to commemorate the 800th anniversary of the Oath of Pontida, which united the Lombard League against Emperor Frederick I.

Perf. 13½x14

1967, Oct. 23 Photo. **Unwmkd.**

972 A519 20 l black, citron & bright blue 8 6
973 " 50 l black, orange & bright blue 12 6

Issued for International Tourist Year, 1967.

Lions Emblem
A520

Soldier at the Piave
A521

1967, Oct. 30 ***Perf. 14x13½***

974 A520 50 l multicolored 15 5

50th anniversary of Lions International.

1967, Nov. 9 ***Perf. 13x14***

975 A521 50 l multicolored 15 5

50th anniversary of Battle of the Piave.

Enrico Fermi at Los Alamos and Model of 1st Atomic Reactor
A522

"Day and Night" and Pigeon Carrying Italy No. 924
A523

Wmk. 303

1967, Dec. 2 Photo. ***Perf. 14***

976 A522 50 l org. brn. & blk. 15 6

Issued to commemorate the 25th anniversary of the first atomic chain reaction under Enrico Fermi (1901–1954), Chicago, Ill.

Perf. 13½x14

1967, Dec. 3 **Unwmkd.**

977 A523 25 l multicolored 12 6

Issued for Stamp Day, 1967.

Scouts at Campfire
A524

St. Aloysius Gonzaga, by Pierre Legros
A525

1968, Apr. 23 ***Perf. 13x14***

978 A524 50 l multicolored 15 6

Issued to honor the Boy Scouts.

Europa Issue, 1968
Common Design Type

1968, Apr. 29 *Perf. 14x13* Wmk. 303
Size: 36½x26mm.

979 CD11 50 l black, rose & slate green 12 7
980 " 90 l black, blue & brown 30 12

Perf. 13½x14

1968, May 28 Photo. **Wmk. 303**

981 A525 25 l red brown & dull violet 10 6

Issued to commemorate the 400th anniversary of the birth of Aloysius Gonzaga (1568–1591), Jesuit priest who ministered to victims of the plague.

Arrigo Boito and Mephistopheles
A526

1968, June 10 ***Perf. 14*** **Unwmkd.**

982 A526 50 l multicolored 15 5

Issued to commemorate the 50th anniversary of the death of Arrigo Boito (1842–1918), composer and librettist.

Francesco Baracca and "Planes," by Giacomo Balla—A527

1968, June 19

983 A527 25 l multicolored 10 6

Issued to commemorate the 50th anniversary of the death of Major Francesco Baracca (1888–1918), World War I aviator.

Giambattista Vico
A528

Bicycle Wheel and Velodrome, Rome
A529

Designs: No. 985, Tommaso Campanella. No. 986, Gioacchino Rossini.

Perf. 14x13½

1968 Engraved Wmk. 303

984 A528 50 l ultramarine 18 6
985 " 50 l black 18 5
a. Perf. 13½ 75 12
986 A528 50 l carmine rose 18 5

No. 984 commemorates the 300th birth anniversary of Giambattista Vico (1668–1744), philosopher; No. 985, the 400th birth anniversary of Tommaso Campanella (1568–1639), Dominican monk, philosopher, poet and teacher; No. 986, death centenary of Gioacchino Rossini (1792–1868), composer.

Issue dates: No. 984, June 24; No. 985, Sept. 5; No. 986, Oct. 25.

Perf. 13x14

1968, Aug. 26 Photo. Unwmkd.

Design: 90 l, Bicycle and Sforza Castle, Imola.

987 A529 25 l slate, rose & brown 12 6
988 " 90 l slate, blue & vermilion 38 12

Issued to publicize the Bicycling World Championships. The 25 l commemorates the track championships at the Velodrome in Rome, the 90 l, the road championships at Imola.

"The Small St. Mark's Place," by Canaletto—A531

1968, Sept. 30 *Perf. 14* Unwmkd.

989 A531 50 l pink & multi. 18 6

Issued to commemorate the 200th anniversary of the death of Canaletto (Antonio Canale, 1697–1768), Venetian painter.

"Mobilization" A533

Symbolic Designs: 25 l, Trench war. 40 l, The Navy. 50 l, The Air Force. 90 l, The Battle of Vittorio Veneto. 180 l, The Unknown Soldier.

1968, Nov. 2 Photo. Unwmkd.

990 A533 20 l brown & multi. 15 5
991 " 25 l blue & multi. 15 6
992 " 40 l multicolored 22 12
993 " 50 l " 22 5
994 " 90 l green & multi. 30 12
995 " 180 l blue & multi. 45 18
Nos. 990-995 (6) 1.49 58

Issued to commemorate the 50th anniversary of the Allies' Victory in World War I.

Emblem A534

1968, Nov. 20 *Perf. 14x13½*

996 A534 50 l black, blue, green & red 18 5

Issued to commemorate the 50th anniversary of the Postal Checking Service.

Parabolic Antenna, Fucino A535

1968, Nov. 25 Photo. *Perf. 14*

997 A535 50 l multicolored 18 5

Issued to publicize the expansion of the space communications center at Fucino.

Development of Postal Service A536

1968, Dec. 1 Wmk. 303

998 A536 25 l car. & yellow 12 6

Issued for the 10th Stamp Day.

Fluorescent Paper

was introduced in 1968 for regular and special delivery issues. These stamps are about 1 mm. smaller each way than the non-fluorescent ones they replaced, except Nos. 690-690A which remained the same size.

Commemorative or nonregular stamps issued only on fluorescent paper are Nos. 935B, 937A, 965, 967 and from 981 onward unless otherwise noted.

Italia Type of 1953-54

Small Size: 16x19½-20mm.

Photo.; Engr. (100 l, 150 l, 200 l, 300 l, 400 l)

Fluorescent

1968-76 *Perf. 14* Wmk. 303

998A A354 1 l dark gray 3 4
998B " 5 l slate 3 4
998C " 6 l ocher 3 4
998D " 10 l org. vermilion 4 4
998E " 15 l gray violet 5 4
998F " 20 l brown 7 4
998G " 25 l purple 8 4
998H " 30 l bister brown 10 4
998I " 40 l lilac rose 13 4
998J " 50 l olive 16 4
998K " 55 l violet ('69) 17 4
998L " 60 l blue 18 4
998M " 70 l Prus. green 24 4
998N " 80 l brown orange 25 4
998O " 90 l lt. red brown 30 4
998P " 100 l reddish brown 32 4
998Q " 125 l ocher & lilac ('74) 40 4
998R " 130 l gray & dull red 42 4
998S " 150 l violet ('76) 45 4
998T " 180 l gray & violet brown ('71) 60 4
998U " 200 l slate blue 64 4
998V " 300 l Prus. green ('72) 1.10 10
998W " 400 l dull red ('76) 1.20 15
Nos. 998A-998W (23) 6.99 1.09

Memorial Medal A537

Perf. 14

1969, Apr. 22 Photo. Unwmkd.

999 A537 50 l pink & black 18 6

Centenary of the State Audit Bureau.

Europa Issue, 1969

Common Design Type

1969, Apr. 28 *Perf. 14x13*

Size: 35½x25½mm.

1000 CD12 50 l magenta & multi. 22 7
1001 " 90 l blue & multi. 38 12

Niccolo Machiavelli A538

ILO Emblem A539

1969, May 3 *Perf. 14x13½*

1002 A538 50 l blue & multi. 18 5

Issued to commemorate the 500th anniversary of the birth of Niccolo Machiavelli (1469-1527), statesman and political philosopher.

Photogravure

1969, June 7 *Perf. 14* Wmk. 303

1003 A539 50 l green & black 32 7
1004 " 90 l car. & black 40 12

Issued to commemorate the 50th anniversary of the International Labor Organization.

Federation Emblem, Tower of Superga Basilica and Matterhorn A540

1969, June 26 *Perf. 14* Unwmkd.

1005 A540 50 l gold, bl. & car. 18 5

Issued to commemorate the 50th anniversary of the Federation of Italian Philatelic Societies.

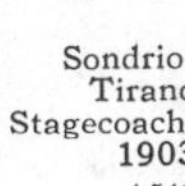

Sondrio-Tirano Stagecoach, 1903 A541

1969, Dec. 7 Engraved Wmk. 303

1006 A541 25 l violet blue 12 6

Issued for the 11th Stamp Day.

Downhill Skier A542

Design: 90 l, Sassolungo and Sella Group, Dolomite Alps.

Photogravure

1970, Feb. 6 *Perf. 13x14* Unwmkd.

1007 A542 50 l blue & multi. 22 7
1008 " 90 l " " 30 12

Issued to publicize the World Alpine Ski Championships, Val Gardena, Bolzano Province, Feb. 6-15.

Galatea, by Raphael A543

Painting: 50 l, Madonna with the Goldfinch (detail), by Raphael.

1970, Apr. 6 Photo. *Perf. 14x13*

1009 A543 20 l multicolored 12 5
1010 " 50 l " 15 6

Issued to commemorate the 450th anniversary of the death of Raphael (1483-1520).

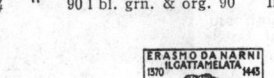

Symbol of Flight, Colors of Italy and Japan A544

1970, May 2 *Perf. 14* Unwmkd.

1011 A544 50 l multicolored 25 6
1012 " 90 l " 32 12

Issued to commemorate the 50th anniversary of Arturo Ferrarin's flight from Rome to Tokyo, Feb. 14-May 31, 1920.

Europa Issue, 1970

Common Design Type

1970, May 4 Wmk. 303

Size: 36x20mm.

1013 CD13 50 l red & orange 45 7
1014 " 90 l bl. grn. & org. 90 12

Gattamelata, Bust by Donatello A545

1970, May 30 Engr. *Perf. 14x13*

1015 A545 50 l slate green 18 5

Issued to commemorate the 6th centenary of the birth of Erasmo de' Narni, called Il Gattamelata (1370-1443), condottiere.

Runner A546

Design: 180 l, Swimmer.

Photogravure

1970, Aug. 26 *Perf. 14* Unwmkd.

1016 A546 20 l multicolored 10 5
1017 " 180 l " 45 12

Issued to publicize the 1970 World University Games, Turin, Aug. 26-Sept. 6.

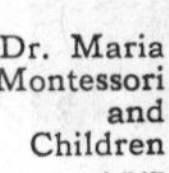

Dr. Maria Montessori and Children A547

1970, Aug. 31 *Perf. 14x13*

1018 A547 50 l multicolored 18 6

Issued to commemorate the centenary of the birth of Maria Montessori (1870-1952), educator and physician.

Map of Italy and Quotation of Count Camillo Cavour—A548

1970, Sept. 19 *Perf. 14* **Unwmkd.**

1019 A548 50 l multicolored 18 6

Issued to commemorate the centenary of the union of the Roman States with Italy.

Loggia of St. Mark's Campanile, Venice
A549

Perf. 14x13½

1970, Sept. 26 Engraved **Wmk. 303**

1020 A549 50 l red brown 18 6

Issued to commemorate the 400th anniversary of the death of Iacopo Tatti "Il Sansovino" (1486–1570), architect.

Garibaldi at Battle of Dijon
A550

1970, Oct. 15 Photo. *Perf. 14*

1021 A550 20 l gray & dk. bl. 12 6

1022 " 50 l brt. rose lilac & dk. blue 15 6

Centenary of Garibaldi's participation in the Franco-Prussian War during Battle of Dijon.

Tree and U.N. Emblem
A551

1970, Oct. 24 *Perf. 13x14* **Unwmkd.**

1023 A551 25 l blk., sepia & grn. 45 5

1024 " 90 l blk., brt. bl. & yellow green 75 12

25th anniversary of the United Nations.

Rotary Emblem
A552

1970, Nov. 12 *Perf. 14* **Wmk. 303**

1025 A552 25 l bluish violet & orange 90 5

1026 " 90 l bluish violet & orange 2.40 12

Rotary International, 65th anniversary.

Telephone Dial and Trunk Lines
A553

1970, Nov. 24

1027 A553 25 l yellow green & dark red 52 5

1028 " 90 l ultra. & dark red 1.15 12

Issued to publicize the completion of the automatic trunk telephone dialing system.

"Man Damaging Nature"
A554

Virgin and Child, by Fra Filippo Lippi—A556

Mail Train
A555

1970, Nov. 28 *Perf. 14* **Wmk. 303**

1029 A554 20 l carmine lake & green 12 6

1030 " 25 l dark blue & emerald 15 6

For European Nature Conservation Year.

1970, Dec. 6 Engraved

1031 A555 25 l black 12 5

For the 12th Stamp Day.

1970, Dec. 12 Photo. **Unwmkd.**

1032 A556 25 l multicolored 8 5

Christmas 1970. See No. C139.

Saverio Mercadante
A557

1970, Dec. 17 **Wmk. 303**

1033 A557 25 l violet & gray 12 5

Death centenary of Saverio Mercadante (1795–1870), composer.

Mercury, by Benvenuto Cellini
A558

Bramante's Temple, St. Peter in Montorio—A559

1971, Mar. 20 Photo. *Perf. 14*

1034 A558 50 l Prussian blue 18 6

400th anniversary of the death of Benvenuto Cellini (1500–1571), sculptor.

Photogravure and Engraved

1971, Apr. 8 *Perf. 13x14*

1035 A559 50 l ocher & black 18 6

Honoring Bramante (Donato di Angelo di Antonio, 1444–1514), architect.

Adenauer, Schuman, De Gasperi
A560

Perf. 14x13½

1971, Apr. 28 Photo. **Wmk. 303**

1036 A560 50 l black & light greenish blue 22 6

1037 " 90 l blk. & lilac rose 38 12

20th anniversary of the European Coal and Steel Community.

Europa Issue, 1971

Common Design Type

1971, May 3 *Perf. 14*

1038 CD14 50 l verm. & dk. red 25 6

1039 " 90 l brt. rose lilac & dk. lilac 42 12

Giuseppe Mazzini, Italian Flag
A561

Perf. 14x13½

1971, June 12 Unwmkd.

1040 A561 50 l multicolored 22 4

1041 " 90 l " 38 12

25th anniversary of the Italian Republic.

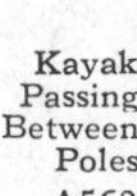

Kayak Passing Between Poles
A562

Design: 90 l, Kayak in free descent.

1971, June 16 Photo. *Perf. 14*

1042 A562 25 l multicolored 15 5

1043 " 90 l " 30 12

Canoe Slalom World Championships, Merano.

Skiing, Basketball, Volleyball
A563

Design: 50 l, Gymnastics, cycling, track and swimming.

Perf. 13½x14

1971, June 26 Photo. **Unwmkd.**

1044 A563 20 l emerald, ocher & black 12 4

1045 " 50 l dull blue, org. & black 15 4

Youth Games.

Plane Circling Globe and "A"
A564

Designs: 50 l, Ornamental "A." 150 l, Tail of B747 in shape of "A."

1971, Sept. 16 *Perf. 14x13½*

1046 A564 50 l slate green, black & red 27 6

1047 " 90 l multicolored 40 12

1048 " 150 l " 55 25

25th anniversary of the founding of ALITALIA, Italian airlines.

Grazia Deledda
A565

Child in Barrel Made of Banknote
A566

Photogravure and Engraved

Perf. 13½x14

1971, Sept. 28 **Wmk. 303**

1049 A565 50 l blk. & salmon 18 5

Centenary of the birth of Grazia Deledda (1871–1936), novelist.

Perf. 13x14

1971, Oct. 27 Photo. **Unwmkd.**

1050 A566 25 l black & multi. 12 5

1051 " 50 l multicolored 15 5

Publicity for postal savings bank.

UNICEF Emblem and Children
A567

Design: 90 l, Children hailing UNICEF emblem.

1971, Nov. 26 *Perf. 14x13*

1052 A567 25 l pink & multi. 27 5

1053 " 90 l multicolored 55 12

25th anniversary of the United Nations International Children's Fund (UNICEF).

Packet Tirrenia and Postal Ensign
A568

1971, Dec. 5 *Perf. 14* **Wmk. 303**

1054 A568 25 l slate green 12 5

Stamp Day.

Nativity
A569

Design: 90 l, Adoration of the Kings. Both designs are from miniatures in Evangelistary of Matilda in Nonantola Abbey, 12th–13th centuries.

Perf. 14x13

1971, Dec. 10 Photo. **Unwmkd.**

1055 A569 25 l gray & multi. 15 5

1056 " 90 l " " 30 12

Christmas 1971.

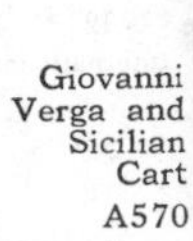

Giovanni Verga and Sicilian Cart A570

1972, Jan. 27

1057 A570 25 l org. & multi. 10 5
1058 " 50 l multicolored 15 5

Giovanni Verga (1840–1922), writer and playwright.

Giuseppe Mazzini A571

Engraved

1972, Mar. 10 *Perf. 13* **Wmk. 303**

1059 A571 25 l black & Prus. green 12 5
1060 " 90 l black 22 12
1061 " 150 l blk. & rose red 55 18

Centenary of the death of Giuseppe Mazzini (1805–1872), patriot and writer.

Flags, Milan Fair A572

Designs: 50 l, 90 l, Different abstract views.

Perf. 14x13½

1972, Apr. 14 Photo. **Unwmkd.**

1062 A572 25 l emerald & blk. 12 5
1063 " 50 l dp. org. & blk. 18 5
1064 " 90 l blue & black 25 12

50th anniversary of the Milan Sample Fair.

Europa Issue 1972

Common Design Type

1972, May 2 *Perf. 13x14*

Size: 26x36mm.

1065 CD15 50 l multicolored 22 5
1066 " 90 l " 38 12

Alpine Soldier and Pack Mule A573

Designs: 50 l, Mountains, Alpinist's hat, pick and laurel. 90 l, Alpine soldier and mountains.

1972, May 10 *Perf. 14x13*

1067 A573 25 l olive & multi. 15 5
1068 " 50 l blue & multi. 22 5
1069 " 90 l green & multi. 38 12

Centenary of the Alpine Corps.

Brenta Mountains, Society Emblem A574

Designs (Emblem and): 50 l, Mountain climber and Brenta Mountains. 180 l, Sunset over Mt. Crozzon.

Perf. 14x13

1972, Sept. 2 Photo. **Unwmkd.**

1070 A574 25 l multicolored 12 5
1071 " 50 l " 25 5
1072 " 180 l " 50 12

Tridentine Alpinist Society centenary.

Conference Emblem, Seating Diagram A575

1972, Sept. 21

1073 A575 50 l multicolored 18 5
1074 " 90 l " 25 12

60th Conference of the Inter-Parliamentary Union, Montecitorio Hall, Rome.

St. Peter Damian, by Giovanni di Paoli, c. 1445 A576

1972, Sept. 21 Photogravure

1075 A576 50 l multicolored 18 5

900th anniversary of the death of St. Peter Damian (1007–1072), church reformer, cardinal, papal legate.

The Three Graces, by Canova A577

1972, Oct. 13 Engr. **Wmk. 303**

1076 A577 50 l black 18 5

Sesquicentennial of the death of Antonio Canova (1757–1822), sculptor.

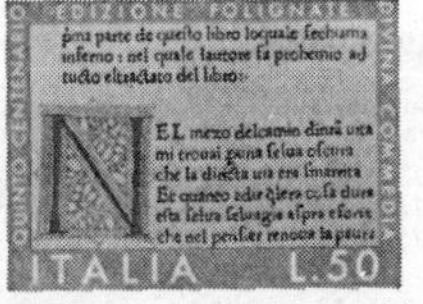

Page from Divine Comedy, Foligno Edition A578

Designs (Illuminated First Pages): 90 l, Mantua edition (vert.). 180 l, Jesina edition.

Perf. 14x13½, 13½x14

1972, Nov. 23 Photo. **Unwmkd.**

1077 A578 50 l ocher & multi. 25 5
1078 " 90 l multicolored 30 12
1079 " 180 l " 55 12

500th anniversary of three illuminated editions of Dante's Divine Comedy.

Angel A579

Designs: 25 l, Christ Child in cradle (horiz.). 150 l, Angel. All designs from 18th century Neapolitan crèche.

Perf. 13x14, 14x13

1972, Dec. 6 Photogravure

1080 A579 20 l multicolored 15 6
1081 " 25 l " 15 5
1082 " 150 l " 50 18

Christmas 1972.

Passenger and Mail Autobus A580

1972, Dec. 16 Engr. **Wmk. 303**

1083 A580 25 l magenta 12 5

Stamp Day.

Leòn Battista Alberti A581

Lorenzo Perosi A582

1972, Dec. 16 *Perf. 14*

1084 A581 50 l ultra. & ocher 18 5

Leòn Battista Alberti (1404–1472), architect, painter, organist and writer.

1972, Dec. 20 Photo. **Unwmkd.**

1085 A582 50 l dk. vio. brown & orange 22 5
1086 " 90 l blk. & yel. grn. 38 12

Centenary of the birth of Lorenzo Perosi (1872–1956), priest and composer.

Luigi Orione and Boys A583

Ship Exploring Ocean Floor A584

1972, Dec. 30

1087 A583 50 l lt. bl. & dk. bl. 22 6
1088 " 90 l ocher & slate green 38 12

Centenary of the birth of Luigi Orione (1872–1940), founder of CARITAS; Catholic Welfare Organization.

1973, Feb. 15 Photo. *Perf. 13x14*

1089 A584 50 l multicolored 15 6

Centenary of the Naval Hydrographic Institute.

Palace Staircase, Caserta A585

1973, Mar. 1 Engr. *Perf. 14x13½*

1090 A585 25 l gray olive 10 5

Bicentenary of the death of Luigi Vanvitelli (1700–1773), architect.

Schiavoni Shore—A586

The Tetrarchs, 4th Century Sculpture A587

Designs: 50 l, "Triumph of Venice," by Vittore Carpaccio. 90 l, Bronze horses from St. Mark's. 300 l, St. Mark's Square covered by flood.

1973 Photogravure *Perf. 14*

1091 A586 20 l ultra & multi. 6 6
1092 A587 25 l " " 6 5
1093 A586 50 l " " 15 5
1094 A587 90 l " " 22 12
1095 A586 300 l " " 80 80
Nos. 1091-1095 (5) 1.29 1.08

Save Venice campaign. Issue dates: No. 1091, Mar. 5; others Apr. 10.

Verona Fair Emblem A588

Title Page for Book about Rosa A589

1973, Mar. 10 *Perf. 13x14*

1096 A588 50 l multicolored 15 5

75th International Fair, Verona.

1973, Mar. 15 *Perf. 14*

1097 A589 25 l orange & black 10 5

300th anniversary of death of Salvator Rosa (1615–1673), painter and poet.

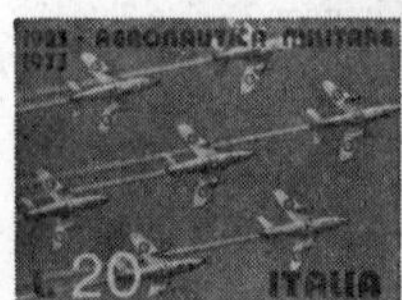

G-91 Jet Fighters A590

Designs: 25 l, Formation of S-55 seaplanes. 50 l, G-91Y fighters. 90 l, Fiat CR-32's flying figure 8. 180 l, Campini-Caproni jet, 1940.

1973, Mar. 28 *Perf. 14x13½*

1098 A590 20 l multicolored 7 6
1099 " 25 l " 7 5
1100 " 50 l lilac & multi. 15 5
1101 " 90 l multicolored 22 12
1102 " 180 l " 50 12
Nos. 1098-1102, C140 (6) 1.39 58

50th anniversary of military aviation.

Soccer Field and Ball

A591

Design: 90 l, Soccer players and goal.

1973, May 19 Photo. *Perf. 14x13½*

1103 A591 25 l olive, blk. & light green 12 5
1104 " 90 l green & multi. 22 12

75th anniversary of Italian Soccer Federation.

Alessandro Manzoni, by Francisco Hayez
A592

Villa Rotunda, by Palladio
A593

1973, May 22 Engraved

1105 A592 25 l black & brown 12 5

Centenary of the death of Alessandro Manzoni (1785–1873), novelist and poet.

1973, May 30 Photo. Unwmkd.
Perf. 13x14

1106 A593 90 l black, yellow & lemon 25 12

Andrea Palladio (1508–1580), architect.

Spiral and Cogwheels

A594

1973, June 20 *Perf. 14x13*

1107 A594 50 l gold & multi. 12 5

50th anniversary of the State Supply Office.

Europa Issue 1973

Common Design Type

1973, June 30 Litho. *Perf. 14*

Size: 36x20mm.

1108 CD16 50 l lilac, gold & yellow 18 5
1109 " 90 l lt. blue green, gold & yellow 25 12

Catcher and Diamond

A595

Design: 90 l, Diamond and batter.

1973, July 21 Photo. *Perf. 14x13½*

1110 A595 25 l multicolored 10 5
1111 " 90 l " 25 12

International Baseball Cup.

Viareggio by Night

A596

1973, Aug. 10 Photo. *Perf. 13x14*

1112 A596 25 l black & multi. 12 5

Viareggio Carnival.

Assassination of Minzoni

A597

1973, Aug. 23 *Perf. 14x13*

1113 A597 50 l multicolored 12 6

50th anniversary of the death of Giovanni Minzoni (1885–1923), priest and social worker.

Gaetano Salvemini

A598

1973, Sept. 8 *Perf. 14x13½*

1114 A598 50 l pink & multi. 15 6

Centenary of the birth of Gaetano Salvemini (1873–1957), historian, anti-Fascist.

Palazzo Farnese, Caprarola, by Vignola

A599

1973, Sept. 21 Engr. *Perf. 14x13½*

1115 A599 90 l choc. & yellow 30 12

400th anniversary of the death of Giacomo da Vignola (real name, Giacomo Barocchio), 1507–1573, architect.

St. John the Baptist, by Caravaggio

A600

Lithographed & Engraved

1973, Sept. 28 *Perf. 14*

1116 A600 25 l blk. & dull yel. 12 6

400th anniversary of the birth of Michelangelo da Caravaggio (1573–1610?), painter.

Tower of Pisa

A601

1973, Oct. 8 Photogravure

1117 A601 50 l multicolored 12 5

8th century of Leaning Tower of Pisa.

Sandro Botticelli
A602

Trevi Fountain, Rome
A603

1973–74 Photo. *Perf. 14x13½*

Multicolored

1118 A602 50 l *shown* 15 6
1119 " 50 l *Giambattista Piranesi* 15 6
1120 " 50 l *Paolo Veronese* 15 6
1121 " 50 l *Andrea del Verrocchio* 15 6
1122 " 50 l *Giovanni Battista Tiepolo* 15 6
1123 " 50 l *Francesco Borromini* 15 6
1124 " 50 l *Rosalba Carriera* 15 6
1125 " 50 l *Giovanni Bellini* 15 6
1126 " 50 l *Andrea Mantegna* 15 6
1127 " 50 l *Raphael* 15 6
Nos. 1118–1127(10) 1.50 60

Famous artists.

Issue dates: Nos. 1118–1122, Nov. 5, 1973. Nos. 1123–1127, May 25, 1974.

Photogravure and Engraved

1973, Nov. 10 *Perf. 13½x14*

Designs: No. 1129, Immacolatella Fountain, Naples. No. 1130, Pretoria Fountain, Palermo.

1128 A603 25 l black & multi. 10 5
1129 " 25 l " " 10 5
1130 " 25 l " " 10 5

See Nos. 1166–1168, 1201–1203, 1277–1279, 1341–1343.

Angels, by Agostino di Duccio
A604

Map of Italy, Rotary Emblems
A605

Sculptures by Agostino di Duccio: 25 l, Virgin and Child. 150 l, Angels with flute and trumpet.

1973, Nov. 26

1131 A604 20 l yel. grn. & blk. 12 5
1132 " 25 l lt. bl. & black 12 5
1133 " 150 l yellow & black 38 15

Christmas 1973.

1973, Nov. 28 Photogravure

1134 A605 50 l red, green & dark blue 12 5

50th anniversary of Rotary International of Italy.

Caravelle

A606

Engraved

1973, Dec. 2 *Perf. 14* Wmk. 303

1135 A606 25 l Prussian blue 12 5

15th Stamp Day.

Medal of Valor
A607

Enrico Caruso
A608

Perf. 13½x14

1973, Dec. 10 Photo. Unwmkd.

1136 A607 50 l gold & multi. 15 5

Gold Medal of Valor, 50th anniversary.

1973, Dec. 15 Engraved

Design: 50 l, Caruso as Duke in Rigoletto.

1137 A608 50 l magenta 15 5

Centenary of the birth of Enrico Caruso (1873–1921), operatic tenor.

Christ Crowning King Roger
A609

Luigi Einaudi
A610

Design: 50 l, King William II offering model of church to the Virgin, mosaic from Monreale Cathedral. The design of 20 l, is from a mosaic in Martorana Church, Palermo.

Lithographed and Engraved

Perf. 13½x14

1974, Mar. 4 Unwmkd.

1138 A609 20 l indigo & buff 15 6
1139 " 50 l red & lt. green 15 6

Norman art in Sicily.

1974, Mar. 23 Engr. *Perf. 14x13½*

1140 A610 50 l green 12 6

Luigi Einaudi (1874–1961), President of Italy.

Guglielmo Marconi

A611

Design: 90 l, Marconi and world map.

1974, Apr. 24 Photo. *Perf. 14x13½*

1141 A611 50 l bl. grn. & gray 15 5
1142 " 90 l violet & multi. 22 12

Centenary of the birth of Guglielmo Marconi (1874–1937), Italian inventor and physicist.

Europa Issue 1974

David, by Giovanni L. Bernini
A612

Design: 90 l, David, by Michelangelo.

1974, Apr. 29 Photo. *Perf. 13½x14*

1143 A612 50 l salmon, ultra. & gray 15 5
1144 " 90 l green, ultra. & buff 30 12

Customs Frontier Guards, 1774, 1795, 1817
A613

Uniforms of Customs Service: 50 l, Lombardy Venetia, 1848, Sardinia, 1815, Tebro Battalion, 1849. 90 l, Customs Guards, 1866, 1880 and Naval Marshal, 1892. 180 l, Helicopter pilot, Naval and Alpine Guards, 1974. All bordered with Italian flag colors.

1974, June 21 Photo. *Perf. 14*

1145 A613 40 l multicolored 12 5
1146 " 50 l " 12 5
1147 " 90 l " 30 12
1148 " 180 l " 45 12

Customs Frontier Guards bicentenary.

Sprinter
A614

Design: 50 l, Pole vault.

1974, June 28 Photo. *Perf. 14x13*

1149 A614 40 l multicolored 15 5
1150 " 50 l " 15 5

European Athletic Championships, Rome.

Sharpshooter
A615

Design: 50 l, Bersaglieri emblem.

1974, June 27

1151 A615 40 l multicolored 15 5
1152 " 50 l green & multi. 15 5

50th anniversary of the Bersaglieri Veterans Association.

View of Portofino
A616

1974, July 10 *Perf. 14*

1153 A616 40 l *shown* 15 5
1154 " 40 l *View of Gradara* 15 5

Tourist publicity.

Petrarch
A617

Design: 50 l, Petrarch at his desk (from medieval manuscript).

Lithographed and Engraved

1974, July 19 *Perf. 13½x14*

1155 A617 40 l ocher & multi. 15 5
1156 " 50 l ocher, yel. & bl. 15 5

600th anniversary of the death of Petrarch (1304–1374), poet.

Tommaseo Statue, by Ettore Ximenes, Shibenik
A618

Giacomo Puccini
A619

1974, July 19

1157 A618 50 l green & pink 15 5

Death centenary of Niccolo Tommaseo (1802–1874), writer, Venetian education minister.

1974, Aug. 16 Photogravure

1158 A619 40 l multicolored 15 5

50th death anniversary of Giacomo Puccini (1858–1924), composer.

King Roland, Woodcut
A620

1974, Sept. 9 Engr. *Perf. 14x13½*

1159 A620 50 l car. & vio. bl. 15 5

500th anniversary of the birth of Lodovico Ariosto (1474–1533), poet. The design is from a contemporary illustration of Ariosto's poem "Orlando Furioso."

Quotation from Menippean Satire by Varro
A621

1974, Sept. 21

1160 A621 50 l ocher & dk. red 15 5

Marcus Terentius Varro (116–27 B.C.), Roman scholar and writer.

"October," 15th Century Mural
A622

1974, Sept. 28 Photo. *Perf. 14*

1161 A622 50 l multicolored 15 5

14th International Wine Congress, Trento.

"UPU" and Emblem
A623

Design: 90 l, Letters, "UPU" and emblem.

1974, Oct. 19 Photo. *Perf. 14*

1162 A623 50 l multicolored 15 5
1163 " 90 l " 22 6

Centenary of Universal Postal Union.

St. Thomas Aquinas, by Francesco Traini
A624

Bas-relief from Ara Pacis
A625

1974, Oct. 25 *Perf. 13x14*

1164 A624 50 l multicolored 15 5

St. Thomas Aquinas (1225–1274), scholastic philosopher, 700th death anniversary.

1974, Oct. 26

1165 A625 50 l multicolored 15 5

Centenary of the Ordini Forensi (Bar Association).

Fountain Type of 1973

Designs: No. 1166, Oceanus Fountain, Florence. No. 1167, Neptune Fountain, Bologna. No. 1168, Fontana Maggiore, Perugia.

Photogravure and Engraved

1974, Nov. 9 *Perf. 13x14*

1166 A603 40 l black & multi. 13 5
1167 " 40 l " " 13 5
1168 " 40 l " " 13 5

St. Francis Adoring Christ Child, by Presepe di Greccio—A626

Photogravure and Engraved

1974, Nov. 26 *Perf. 14x13½*

1169 A626 40 l multicolored 15 5

Christmas 1974.

Masked Dancers
A627

1974, Dec. 1 Photo. *Perf. 13½x14*

Multicolored

1170 A627 40 l *Pulcinella* 12 5
1171 " 50 l *shown* 22 5
1172 " 90 l *Pantaloon* 22 6

16th Stamp Day 1974.

God Admonishing Adam, by Jacopo della Quercia
A628

Courtyard, Uffizi Gallery, Florence, by Giorgio Vasari
A629

1974, Dec. 20 Engraved *Perf. 14*

1173 A628 90 l dk. violet blue 27 12

Lithographed and Engraved

1174 A629 90 l multicolored 27 12

Italian artists: Jacopo della Quercia (1374–c.1438), sculptor, and Giorgio Vasari (1511–1574), architect, painter and writer.

Angel with Tablet
A630

Angels' Bridge, Rome—A631

Angel with Cross
A632

Designs: 50 l, Angel holding column. 150 l, Angel holding Crown of Thorns. The angels are statues by Giovanni Bernini on the Angels' Bridge (San Angelo).

1975, Mar. 25 Photo. *Perf. 14*

1175 A630 40 l multicolored 12 6
1176 " 50 l blue & multi. 12 6
1177 A631 90 l " " 18 6
1178 A630 150 l vio. & multi. 38 12
1179 A632 180 l multicolored 45 12
Nos. 1175-1179 (5) 1.25 42

Holy Year 1975.

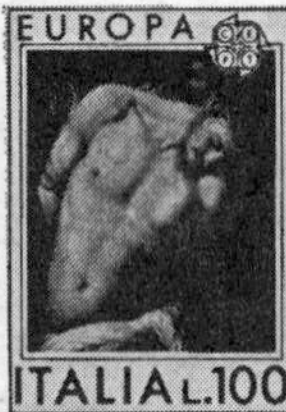

Pitti Madonna, by Michelangelo
A633

Flagellation of Jesus, by Caravaggio
A634

Designs (Works of Michelangelo): 50 l, Niche in Vatican Palace. 90 l, The Flood, detail from Sistine Chapel.

1975, Apr. 18 Engr. *Perf. 13½x14*

1180 A633 40 l dull green 12 6
1181 " 50 l sepia 12 6
1182 " 90 l red brown 25 12

500th birth anniversary of Michelangelo Buonarroti (1475-1564), sculptor, painter and architect.

Europa Issue 1975

Design: 150 l, Apparition of Angel to Hagar and Ishmael, by Tiepolo (detail).

1975, Apr. 29 Photo. *Perf. 13x14*

1183 A634 100 l multicolored 25 10
1184 " 150 l " 38 12

Four Days of Naples, by Marino Mazzacurati
A635

Resistance Fighters of Cuneo, by Umberto Mastroianni
A636

Design: 100 l, Martyrs of Ardeatine Caves, by Francesco Coccia.

1975, Apr. 23

1185 A635 70 l multicolored 12 7
1186 A636 100 l olive & multi. 25 7
1187 " 150 l multicolored 38 7

30th anniversary of victory of the resistance movement.

Globe and IWY Emblems
A637

1975, May *Perf. 14x13½*

1188 A637 70 l multicolored 18 5

International Women's Year 1975.

Satellite, San Rita Launching Platform
A638

1975, May 28 *Perf. 13½x14*

1189 A638 70 l multicolored 18 5

San Marco satellite project.

View of Isola Bella—A639

Paintings: No. 1191, Baths of Montecatini. No. 1192, View of Cefalù.

1975, June 16 Photo. *Perf. 14*

1190 A639 150 l grn. & multi. 42 6
1191 " 150 l blue green & multi. 42 6
1192 " 150 l red brown & multi. 42 6

Tourist publicity.
See Nos. 1221-1223, 1263-1265, 1314-1316.

Artist and Model, Armando Spadini
A640

Painting: No. 1194, Flora, by Guido Reni.

1975, June 20 Engr. *Perf. 14*

1193 A640 90 l blk. & multi. 30 12
1194 " 90 l multicolored 30 12

50th death anniversary of Armando Spadini and 400th birth anniversary of Guido Reni.

Palestrina
A641

1975, June 27 Engr. *Perf. 13½x14*

1195 A641 100 l magenta & tan 25 6

Giovanni Pierluigi da Palestrina (1525-1594), composer of sacred music, 450th birth anniversary.

Emmigrants and Ship
A642

1975, June 30 Photo. *Perf. 14x13½*

1196 A642 70 l multicolored 18 6

Italian emigration centenary.

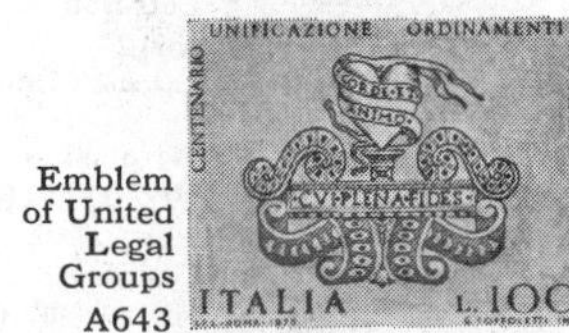

Emblem of United Legal Groups
A643

Photogravure and Engraved

1975, July 25 *Perf. 14x13½*

1197 A643 100 l yellow, green & red 25 6

Centenary of unification of Italian legal organizations.

Locomotive Wheels
A644

1975, Sept. 15 Photo. *Perf. 14x13½*

1198 A644 70 l multicolored 25 5

International Railroad Union, 21st congress, Bologna.

Salvo D'Acquisto, by Vittorio Pisano
A645

1975, Sept. 23

1199 A645 100 l multicolored 25 5

Salvo D'Acquisto died in 1943 saving 22 people.

Stylized Syracusean Italia
A646

1975, Sept. 26 Photo. *Perf. 13½x14*

1200 A646 100 l org. & multi. 25 5

Centenary of unification of the State Archives.

Fountain Type of 1973

Designs: No. 1201, Rosello Fountain, Sassari. No. 1202, Fountain of the 99 Faucets, Aquila. No. 1203, Piazza Fontana, Milan.

Photogravure and Engraved

1975, Oct. 20 *Perf. 13x14*

1201 A603 70 l blk. & multi. 25 5
1202 " 70 l " " 25 5
1203 " 70 l " " 25 5

Antonio Vivaldi
A647

1975, Nov. 14 Photo. *Perf. 14x13½*

Multicolored

1204 A647 100 l *Alessandro Scarlati* 25 5
1205 " 100 l *shown* 25 5
1206 " 100 l *Gaspare Spontini* 25 5
1207 " 100 l *F. B. Busoni* 25 5
1208 " 100 l *Francesco Cilea* 25 5
1209 " 100 l *Franco Alfano* 25 5
Nos. 1204-1209 (6) 1.50 30

Famous musicians.
See Nos. 1243-1247, 1266-1270.

Annunciation to the Shepherds
A648

"The Magic Orchard"
A649

Designs: 100 l, Nativity. 150 l, Annunciation to the Kings. Designs from painted wood panels, portal of Alatri Cathedral, 14th century.

Lithographed and Engraved

1975, Nov. 25 *Perf. 13½x14*

1210 A648 70 l grn. & multi. 18 5
1211 " 100 l ultra. & multi. 25 5
1212 " 150 l brown & multi. 30 6

Christmas 1975.

Perf. 14x13½, 13½x14

1975, Dec. 7 Photogravure

Designs (Children's Drawings): 70 l, Children on Horseback (horiz.). 150 l, Village and procession (horiz.).

1213 A649 70 l multicolored 18 5
1214 " 100 l " 25 5
1215 " 150 l " 30 6

17th Stamp Day.

Boccaccio, by Andrea del Castagno
A650

State Advocate's Office, Rome
A651

Design: 150 l, Frontispiece for "Fiammetta", 15th century woodcut.

Engraved and Lithographed

1975, Dec. 22 *Perf. 13½x14*

1216 A650 100 l yel. green & black 30 5
1217 " 150 l buff & multi. 38 6

Giovanni Boccaccio (1313–1375), writer, 600th death anniversary.

1976, Jan. 30 Photo. *Perf. 13½x14*

1218 A651 150 l multicolored 30 6

State Advocate's Office, centenary.

ITALIA 76 Emblem
A652

Majolica Plate, Deruta
A653

Design: 180 l, Milan Fair pavilion.

1976, Mar. 27 Photo. *Perf. 13½x14*

1219 A652 150 l black, red & green 35 5
1220 " 180 l blk., red grn. & blue 40 12

ITALIA 76 International Philatelic Exhibition, Milan, Oct. 14–24.

Tourist Type of 1975

Paintings: No. 1221, Fenis Castle. No. 1222, View of Ischia. No. 1223, Itria Valley.

1976, May 21 Photo. *Perf. 14*

1221 A639 150 l grn. & multi. 35 5
1222 " 150 l plum & multi. 35 5
1223 " 150 l yel. & multi. 35 5

Tourist publicity.

Europa Issue 1976

1976, May 22 *Perf. 13½x14*

Design: 180 l, Ceramic vase in shape of woman's head, Caltagirone.

1224 A653 150 l multicolored 35 10
1225 " 180 l brn. & multi. 42 12

Italian Flags
A654

Italian Presidents
A655

1976, June 1

1226 A654 100 l multicolored 25 5
1227 A655 150 l " 30 6

30th anniversary of Italian Republic.

Fortitude, by Giacomo Serpotta, 1656–1732
A656

Paintings: No. 1229, Woman at Table, by Umberto Boccioni, 1882–1916. No. 1230, The Gunner's Letter, by F. T. Marinetti, 1876–1944.

1976, July 26 Engr. *Perf. 14*

1228 A656 150 l blue 38 12

Lithographed and Engraved

1229 A656 150 l multicolored 38 12
1230 " 150 l black & red 38 12

Italian art.

St. George, by Vittore Carpaccio
A657

Design: No. 1231, Dragon, by Vittore Carpaccio, after painting in Church of St. George Schiavoni, Venice.

Perf. 14x13½

1976, July 30 Engraved

1231 A657 150 l rose lake 35 6
1232 " 150 l " " 35 6

Vittore Carpaccio (1460–1526), Venetian painter, 350th death anniversary. Nos. 1231–1232 printed se-tenant in sheets of 20 stamps and 10 labels with commemorative inscription.

Flora, by Titian
A658

1976, Sept. 15 Engr. *Perf. 14*

1233 A658 150 l carmine 35 6

Titian (1477–1576), Venetian painter, 400th death anniversary.

St. Francis, 13th Century Fresco
A659

1976, Oct. 2 Engr. *Perf. 14*

1234 A659 150 l brown 35 6

St. Francis of Assisi, 750th death anniversary.

Cart, from Trajan's Column
A660

Designs: 100 l, Emblem of Kingdom of Sardinia. 150 l, Marble mask, 19th century mail box. 200 l, Hand canceler, 19th century. 400 l, Automatic letter sorting machine.

1976, Oct. 14 Photo. *Perf. 14x13½*

1235 A660 70 l multicolored 18 5
1236 " 100 l " 25 5
1237 " 150 l " 38 6
1238 A660 200 l multicolored 45 6
1239 " 400 l " 90 12
Nos. 1235–1239 (5) 2.16 34

ITALIA 76 International Philatelic Exhibition, Milan, Oct. 14–24.

Girl and Animals
A661

Designs (Children's Drawings): 100 l, Trees, rabbit and flowers. 150 l, Boy healing tree.

1976, Oct. 17 *Perf. 13½x14*

1240 A661 40 l multicolored 12 5
1241 " 100 l " 25 5
1242 " 150 l " 35 6

18th Stamp Day and nature protection.

Vivaldi Type of 1975

1976, Nov. 22 Photo. *Perf. 14x13½*

Multicolored

1243 A647 170 l *Lorenzo Ghiberti* 45 6
1244 " 170 l *Domenico Ghirlandaio* 45 6
1245 " 170 l *Sassoferrato* 45 6
1246 " 170 l *Carlo Dolci* 45 6
1247 " 170 l *Giovanni Piazzetta* 45 6
Nos. 1243–1247 (5) 2.25 30

Famous painters.

The Visit, by Silvestro Lega
A662

1976, Dec. 7 Photo. *Perf. 14x13½*

1248 A662 170 l multicolored 40 6

Silvestro Lega (1826–1895), painter, sesquicentennial of birth.

Adoration of the Kings, by Bartolo di Fredi
A663

Design: 120 l, Nativity, by Taddeo Gaddi.

1976, Dec. 11 *Perf. 13½x14*

1249 A663 70 l multicolored 25 5
1250 " 120 l " 42 6

Christmas 1976.

Fountain Type of 1973

Designs: No. 1251, Antique Fountain, Gallipoli. No. 1252, Madonna Fountain, Verona. No. 1253, Silvio Cosini Fountain, Palazzo Doria, Genoa.

Lithographed and Engraved

1976, Dec. 21 *Perf. 13½x14*

1251 A603 170 l blk. & multi. 42 6
1252 " 170 l " " 42 6
1253 " 170 l " " 42 6

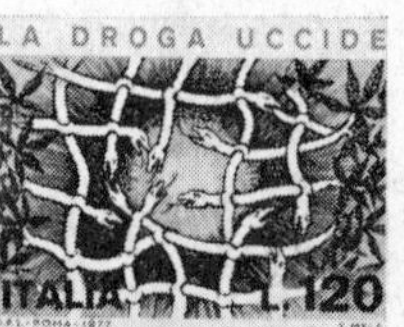

Snakes Forming Net
A664

Design: 170 l, Drug addict and poppy.

1977, Feb. 28 Photo. *Perf. 14x13½*

1254 A664 120 l multicolored 30 6
1255 " 170 l " 38 6

Fight against drug abuse.

Micca Setting Fire
A665

1977, Mar. 5

1256 A665 170 l multicolored 38 6

Pietro Micca (1677–1706), patriot who set fire to the powder magazine of Turin Citadel, 300th birth anniversary.

Globe with Cross in Center
A666

Design: 120 l, People of the World united as brothers by St. John Bosco.

1977, Mar. 29 Photo. *Perf. 13x13½*

1257 A666 70 l multicolored 15 5
1258 " 120 l " 30 6

Honoring the Salesian missionaries.

Italian Constitution, Article 53
A667

1977, Apr. 14 Photo. *Perf. 14*

1259 A667 120 l bister, brown & black 30 6
1260 " 170 l lt. grn., grn. & black 38 6

"Pay your taxes."

Europa Issue 1977

Taormina
A668

Design: 200 l, Castle del Monte.

1977, May 2

1261 A668 170 l multicolored 38 6
1262 " 200 l " 45 6

Tourist Type of 1975

Paintings: No. 1263, Canossa Castle. No. 1264, Fermo. No. 1265, Castellana Caves.

1977, May 30 Photo. *Perf. 14*

1263 A639 170 l brn. & multi. 38 6

1264 A639 170 l violet & multi. 38 6
1265 " 170 l gray & multi. 38 6

Tourist publicity.

Vivaldi Type of 1975

1977, June 27 *Perf. 14x13½*

Multicolored

1266 A647 70 l *Filippo Brunelleschi* 15 5
1267 " 70 l *Pietro Aretino* 15 5
1268 " 70 l *Carlo Goldoni* 15 5
1269 " 70 l *Luigi Cherubini* 15 5
1270 " 70 l *Eduardo Bassini* 15 5
Nos. 1266-1270 (5) 75 25

Famous artists, writers and scientists.

Justice, by Andrea Delitio
A669

Painting: No. 1272, Winter, by Giuseppe Arcimboldi, 1527-c.1593.

1977, Sept. 5 Engr. & Litho. *Perf. 14*

1271 A669 170 l multicolored 38 10
1272 " 170 l " 38 10

Corvette Caracciolo—A670

Italian Ships: No. 1274, Hydrofoil gunboat Sparviero. No. 1275, Paddle steamer Ferdinando Primo. No. 1276, Passenger liner Saturnia.

Photogravure and Engraved

1977, Sept. 23 *Perf. 14x13½*

1273 A670 170 l multicolored 38 10
1274 " 170 l " 38 10
1275 " 170 l " 38 10
1276 " 170 l " 38 10

Printed se-tenant in sheets of 40 stamps and 20 labels showing alternately arms of Italian Navy and Merchant Marine.

See Nos. 1323-1326.

Fountain Type of 1973

Designs: No. 1277, Pacassi Fountain, Gorizia. No. 1278, Fraterna Fountain, Isernia. No. 1279, Palm Fountain, Palmi.

Lithographed and Engraved

1977, Oct. 18 *Perf. 13x14*

1277 A603 120 l blk. & multi. 30 6
1278 " 120 l " " 30 6
1279 " 120 l " " 30 6

Volleyball
A671

Designs (Children's Drawings): No. 1281, Butterflies and net. No. 1282, Flying kites.

1977, Oct. 23 Photo. *Perf. 13x14*

1280 A671 120 l multicolored 30 6
1281 A671 120 l multicolored 30 6
1282 " 120 l " 30 6

19th Stamp Day. Nos. 1280-1282 printed in sheets of 24 stamps and 8 labels with Stamp Day emblem.

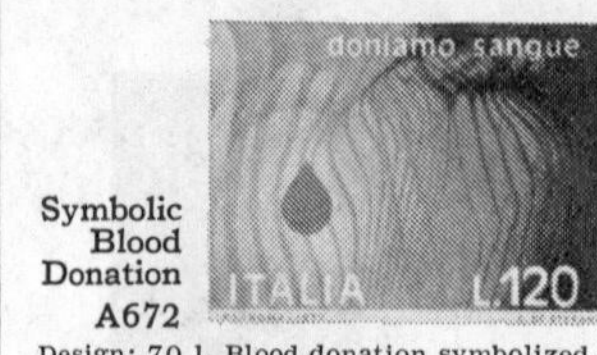

Symbolic Blood Donation
A672

Design: 70 l, Blood donation symbolized.

1977, Oct. 26 *Perf. 14x13½*

1283 A672 70 l multicolored 15 6
1284 " 120 l " 30 6

Blood donors.

Quintino Sella and Italy No. 24
A673

1977, Oct. 23 *Perf. 13½x14*

1285 A673 170 l olive & black brown 38 10

Quintino Sella (1827-1884), statesman, engineer, mineralogist, birth sesquicentenary.

Italia Type of 1953-54 and A674

Italia
A674

1977-79 *Perf. 14* Wmk. 303

Size: 16x20mm.

Photogravure

1288 A354 120 l dark blue & emerald 30 4

Photogravure and Engraved

1292 A354 170 l grn. & ocher 38 4

Lithographed and Engraved

1295 A354 350 l red, ocher & purple 75 12

Engr. *Perf. 14x13½* Unwmkd.

1306 A674 3000 l multi. ('79) 6.00
1307 " 4000 l multi. ('79) 8.00
1308 " 5000 l multi. ('78) 10.00

Dina Galli
A675

Perf. 13½x14

1977, Dec. 2 Photo. Unwmkd.

1309 A675 170 l multicolored 38 10

Dina Galli (1877-1951), actress, birth centenary.

Adoration of the Shepherds, by Pietro Testa—A676

Design: 120 l, Adoration of the Shepherds, by Gian Jacopo Caraglio.

Lithographed and Engraved

1977, Dec. 13 *Perf. 14*

1310 A676 70 l black & olive 15 6
1311 " 120 l black & blue green 30 6

Christmas 1977.

La Scala
A677

Design: 200 l, La Scala, auditorium.

1978, Mar. 15 Litho. *Perf. 13½x14*

1312 A677 170 l multicolored 38 15
1313 " 200 l " 45 15

La Scala Opera House, Milan, bicentenary.

Tourist Type of 1975

Paintings: 70 l, Gubbio. 200 l, Udine. 600 l, Paestum.

1978, Mar. 30 Photo. *Perf. 14*

1314 A639 70 l multicolored 15 3
1315 " 200 l " 45 15
1316 " 600 l " 1.20 15

Tourist publicity.

Giant Grouper
A678

Designs (outline of "Amerigo Vespucci" in background): No. 1318, Leatherback turtle. No. 1319, Mediterranean monk seal. No. 1320, Audouin's gull.

1978, Apr. 3 *Perf. 14x13*

1317 A678 170 l multicolored 38 15
1318 " 170 l " 38 15
1319 " 170 l " 38 15
1320 " 170 l " 38 15

Endangered species in Mediterranean. Nos. 1317-1320 printed se-tenant with blue and black label in sheets of 10.

Europa Issue

Castel Nuovo, Angevin Fortifications, Naples
A679

Design: 200 l, Pantheon, Rome.

1978, Apr. 29 Litho. *Perf. 14x13½*

1321 A679 170 l multicolored 38 15
1322 " 200 l " 45 15

Ship Type of 1977

Designs: No. 1323, Cruiser Benedetto Brin. No. 1324, Frigate Lupo. No. 1325, Ligurian brigantine Fortuna. No. 1326, Container ship Africa.

1978, May 8 Lithographed & Engr.

1323 A670 170 l multicolored 38 15
1324 " 170 l " 38 15
1325 " 170 l " 38 15
1326 " 170 l " 38 15

Printed se-tenant in sheets of 40 stamps and 20 labels showing alternately nautical astrolabe and sextant.

Matilde Serao
A680

Constitution
A681

Designs: Portraits of famous Italians.

1978, May 10 Engr. *Perf. 14x13½*

Multicolored

1327 A680 170 l *shown* 38 15
1328 " 170 l *Vittorino da Feltre* 38 15
1329 " 170 l *Victor Emmanuel II* 38 15
1330 " 170 l *Pope Pius IX* 38 15
1331 " 170 l *Marcello Malpighi* 38 15
1332 " 170 l *Antonio Meucci* 38 15
Nos. 1327-1332 (6) 2.28 90

Nos. 1327-1332 printed se-tenant (2x3) in sheets of 36.

1978, June 2 Litho. *Perf. 13½x14*

1333 A681 170 l multicolored 38 15

30th anniversary of Constitution.

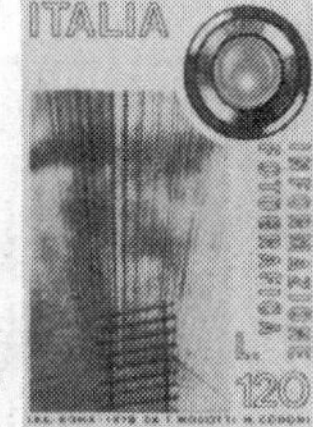

Telegraph Wires and Lens
A682

1978, June 30 Photogravure

1334 A682 120 l lt. bl. & gray 30 10

Photographic information.

The Lovers, by Tranquillo Cremona (1837–1878)
A683

Design: 520 l, The Cook (woman with goose), by Bernardo Strozzi (1581–1644).

Engraved and Lithographed

1978, July 12 **Perf. 14**

1335	A683	170 l multicolored		38	15
1336	"	520 l	"	1.10	22

Holy Shroud of Turin, by Giovanni Testa, 1578—A684

1978, Sept. 8 **Photo.** **Perf. 14**

1337	A684	220 l yel., red & black	55	15

400th anniversary of the transfer of the Holy Shroud from Savoy to Turin.

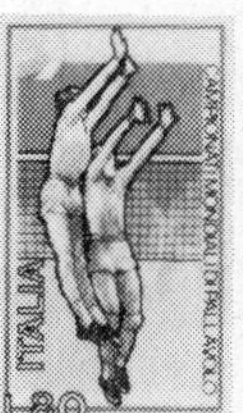

Volleyball A685 — Mother and Child, by Masaccio A686

Design: 120 l, Volleyball (diff.).

1978, Sept. 20

1338	A685	80 l multicolored		20	5
1339	"	120 l	"	30	10

Men's Volleyball World Championship.

1978, Oct. 18 **Engr.** **Perf. 13½x14**

1340	A686	170 l indigo	38	15

Masaccio (real name Tommaso Guidi; 1401–1428), painter, 550th death anniversary.

Fountain Type of 1973

Designs: No 1341, Neptune Fountain, Trent. No. 1342, Fortuna Fountain, Fano. No. 1343, Cavallina Fountain, Genzano di Lucania.

1978, Oct. 25 **Litho. & Engr.**

1341	A603	120 l blk. & multi.		30	10
1342	"	120 l	" "	30	10
1343	"	120 l	" "	30	10

Virgin and Child, by Giorgione
A687

Adoration of the Kings, by Giorgione—A688

1978, Nov. 8 **Engr.** **Perf. 13x14**

1344	A687	80 l dark red	20	6

Photogravure **Perf. 14x13½**

1345	A688	120 l multicolored	30	10

Christmas 1978.

Flags as Flowers
A689

1978, Nov. 26 **Photo.** **Perf. 13x14**

Designs: No. 1347, European flags. No. 1348, "People hailing Europe."

1346	A689	120 l multicolored		30	10
1347	"	120 l	"	30	10
1348	"	120 l	"	30	10

20th Stamp Day on theme "United Europe."

State Printing Office, Stamps
A690

Design: 220 l, Printing press and stamps.

1979, Jan. 6 **Photo.** **Perf. 14x13½**

1349	A690	170 l multicolored		45	15
1350	"	220 l	"	55	20

50th anniversary of first stamps printed by State Printing Office.

St. Francis Washing Lepers, 13th Century Painting—A691

1979, Jan. 22

1351	A691	80 l multicolored	20	10

Leprosy relief.

Bicyclist Carrying Bike
A692

1979, Jan. 27 **Perf. 13½x14**

1352	A692	170 l multicolored		45	15
1353	"	220 l	"	55	20

World Crosscountry Bicycle Championships.

Virgin Mary, by Antonello da Messina
A693

Painting: 520 l, Haystack, by Ardengo Soffici (1879–1964).

1979, Feb. 15 **Engr.** **Perf. 14**

1354	A693	170 l multicolored		35	15
1355	"	520 l	"	1.05	60

Albert Einstein and his Equation
A694

Lithographed and Engraved

1979, Mar. 14 **Perf. 13x14**

1356	A694	120 l multicolored	35	10

Albert Einstein (1879–1955), theoretical physicist.

Tourist Type of 1975

Paintings: 70 l, Asiago. 90 l, Castelsardo. 170 l, Orvieto. 220 l, Scilla.

1979, Mar. 30 **Photo.** **Perf. 14**

1357	A639	70 l grn. & multi.	18	8
1358	"	90 l car. & multi.	22	10
1359	"	170 l ultramarine & multi.	35	15
1360	"	220 l gray & multi.	65	30

SEMI-POSTAL STAMPS.

Many issues of Italy and Italian Colonies include one or more semi-postal denominations. To avoid splitting sets, these issues are generally listed as regular postage, airmail, etc., unless all values carry a surtax.

Italian Flag
SP1

Italian Eagle Bearing Arms of Savoy
SP2

Wmkd. Crown. (140)

1915-16 Typographed. ***Perf. 14.***

B1 SP1 10c+5c rose 1.75 2.50
B2 SP2 15c+5c slate 1.75 2.50
B3 " 20c+5c orange 7.25 9.00

No. B2 Surcharged **20**

1916

B4 SP2 20c on 15c+5c slate 5.50 11.00
a. Double ovpt. 250.00
b. Inverted ovpt. 250.00 250.00

Regular Issues of 1906–16 Overprinted in Blue or Red **B.L.P.**

1921

B5 A48 10c claret (Bl) 275.00 75.00
B6 A50 20c brown orange (Bl) 275.00 37.50
B7 A49 25c blue (R) 55.00 9.00
B8 " 40c brown (Bl) 16.50 1.50
a. Inverted ovpt. 22.50 22.50

Regular Issues of 1901–22 Overprinted in Black, Blue, Brown or Red

1922-23

B9 A48 10c claret ('23) (Bk) 32.50 7.50
a. Blue overprint 40.00 12.50
b. Brown ovpt. 40.00 12.50
B10 " 15c slate (Bl) 65.00 30.00
a. Red overprint 85.00 37.50
B11 A50 20c brn. org. (Bk) 65.00 30.00
a. Blue ovpt. 185.00 45.00
B12 A49 25c blue ('23) (Bk or Bl) 32.50 9.00
b. Red overprint 80.00 37.50
B12A " 30c orange brown (Bk) 40.00 12.50
B13 " 40c brown (Bl) 55.00 15.00
a. Black ovpt. 55.00 15.00
b. As "a," invtd. ovpt. 45.00
B14 " 50c violet ('23) (Bk) 185.00 52.50
a. Blue ovpt.
B15 " 60c car. (Bk) 600.00 350.00
B15A " 85c choc. (Bk) 80.00 37.50
B16 A46 1 l brown & green ('23) (Bk) *1650.00* 575.00
a. Invtd. ovpt. *850.00*

The stamps overprinted "B. L. P." were sold by the Government below face value to the National Federation for Assisting War Invalids. Most of them were affixed to special envelopes (Buste Lettere Postali) which bore advertisements. The Federation was permitted to sell these envelopes at a reduction of 5c from the face value of each stamp. The profits for the war invalids were derived from the advertisements.

Prices of Nos. B5–B16 unused are for stamps with original gum. Most copies without gum or with part gum sell for about a quarter of prices quoted. Uncanceled stamps affixed to the special envelopes usually sell for about half price.

The overprint on Nos. B9–B16 is wider (13½mm.) than that on Nos. B5–B8 (11mm.). The 1922–23 overprint exists both typographed and lithographed on 10c, 15c, 20c and 25c; only lithographed on 40c, 50c, 60c and 1 l; and only typographed on 30c and 85c.

Counterfeits of the B.L.P. overprints exist.

Administering Fascist Oath
SP3

1923, Oct. 29 ***Perf. 14x14½***

B17 SP3 30c+30c brown 12.00 *30.00*
B18 " 50c+50c violet 12.00 *30.00*
B19 " 1 l+1 l gray 12.00 *30.00*

The surtax was given to the Benevolent Fund of the Black Shirts (the Italian National Militia).

Anniversary of the March of the Fascisti on Rome.

St. Maria Maggiore
SP4

Pope Opening Holy Door
SP8

Designs: 30c+15c, St. John Lateran. 50c+25c, St. Paul's Church. 60c+30c, St. Peter's Basilica. 5l+2.50 l, Pope closing Holy Door.

1924, Dec. 24 ***Perf. 12***

B20 SP4 20c+10c dark green & brown 90 1.75
B21 " 30c+15c dark brown & brown 90 1.75
B22 " 50c+25c vio. & brn. 1.10 2.00
B23 " 60c+30c deep rose & brown 1.10 2.00
B24 SP8 1 l+50c deep blue & violet 1.50 3.00
B25 " 5 l+2.50 l orange brown & violet 3.00 7.50
Nos. B20–B25 (6) 8.50 18.00

The surtax was contributed toward the Holy Year expenses.

Castle of St. Angelo
SP10

Victor Emmanuel II
SP14

Designs: 50c+20c, 60c+30c, Aqueduct of Claudius. 1.25 l+50c, 1.25 l+60c, Capitol, Roman Forum. 5 l+2 l, 5 l+2.50 l, People's Gate.

Engraved.

1926, Oct. 26 ***Perf. 11*** **Unwmkd.**

B26 SP10 40c+20c dark brown & black 1.75 2.50
B27 " 60c+30c brown red & olive brown 1.75 2.50
B28 " 1.25 l+60c blue green & black 1.75 2.50
B29 " 5 l+2.50 l dark blue & black 3.50 8.50

1928, Mar. 1

B30 SP10 30c+10c dull violet & black 1.75 3.50
B31 " 50c+20c olive green & slate 1.75 3.50
B32 SP10 1.25 l+50c deep blue & black 3.50 7.00
B33 " 5 l+2 l brown red & black 8.00 16.50

The tax on Nos. B26 to B33 was devoted to the charitable work of the Voluntary Militia for National Defense.

1929, Jan. 4 Photo. ***Perf. 14***

B34 SP14 50c+10c olive green 2.00 2.00

Commemorative of the 50th anniversary of the death of King Victor Emmanuel II. The surtax was for veterans.

Type of 1926 Issue.
Designs in same order.

1930, July 1 **Engraved**

B35 SP10 30c+10c dark grn. & violet 1 00 1.50
B36 " 50c+10c dk. green & blue green 1.00 1.50
B37 " 1.25 l+30c indigo & green 1.25 2.00
B38 " 5 l+1.50 l black brown & olive brown 6.50 12.00

The surtax was for the charitable work of the Voluntary Militia for National Defense.

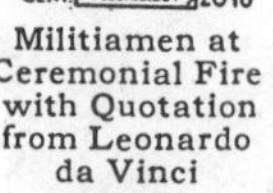

Militiamen at Ceremonial Fire with Quotation from Leonardo da Vinci
SP15

Symbolical of Pride for Militia
SP16

Symbolical of Militia Guarding Immortality of Italy
SP17

Militia Passing Through Arch of Constantine
SP18

1935, July 1 Photo. **Wmk. 140**

B39 SP15 20c+10c rose red 4.75 6.50
B40 SP16 25c+15c green 4.75 6.50
B41 SP17 50c+30c purple 4.75 6.50
B42 SP18 1.25 l+75c blue 4.75 6.50
Nos. B39-B42, CB3 (5) 25.75 35.00

The surtax was for the Militia.

Roman Battle
SP19

Roman Warriors
SP20

1941, Dec. 13

B43 SP19 20c+10c rose red 60 75
B44 " 30c+15c brown 60 75
B45 SP20 50c+25c violet 60 75
B46 " 1.25 l+1 l blue 75 1.10

Issued to commemorate the 2,000th anniversary of the birth of Livy (59 B. C.-17 A. D.), Roman historian.

AIR POST STAMPS.

Special Delivery Stamp No. E1 Overprinted

ESPERIMENTO POSTA AEREA
MAGGIO 1917
TORINO-ROMA • ROMA-TORINO

1917, May ***Perf. 14*** **Wmk. 140**

C1 SD1 25c rose red 8.25 7.25

Type of SD3 Surcharged in Black

IDROVOLANTE
NAPOLI - PALERMO - NAPOLI
25 CENT. 25

1917, June 27

C2 SD3 25c on 40c violet 13.50 11.50

Type SD3 was not issued without surcharge.

AP2

1926–28 **Typographed**

C3 AP2 50c rose red ('28) 1.80 3.00
C4 " 60c gray 1.20 2.00
C5 " 80c brown violet & brown ('28) 4.25 9.00
C6 " 1 l blue 90 1.50
C7 " 1.20 l brown ('27) 7.25 14.00
C8 " 1.50 l buff 4.00 7.50
C9 " 5 l gray green 11.00 20.00
Nos. C3-C9 (7) 30.40 57.00

Nos. C4 and C6 Surcharged

Cent. 50

1927, Sept. 16

C10 AP2 50c on 60c gray 2.40 4.00
a. Pair, one without surcharge 400.00
C11 " 80c on 1 l blue 4.75 10.00

Pegasus
AP3

Wings
AP4

Spirit of Flight
AP5

Arrows
AP6

1930–32 Photogravure **Wmk. 140**

C12 AP4 25c dark green ('32) 4 4
C13 AP3 50c olive brown 4 4
C14 AP5 75c orange brn. ('32) 4 4
C15 AP4 80c orange red 15 15
C16 AP5 1 l purple 4 4
C17 AP6 2 l deep blue 6 6
C18 AP3 5 l dark green 6 6
C19 " 10 l deep carmine 65 50
Nos. C12–C19 (8) 1.08 93

The 50c, 1 l and 2 l were reprinted in 1942 with labels similar to those of Nos. 427–438, but were not issued. Price, set of 3, $100.

Statue of Ferrucci
AP7

1930, July 10

C20 AP7 50c purple 90 2.00
C21 " 1 l orange brown 90 2.00
C22 " 5 l+2 l brown violet 3.00 6.00

Issued to commemorate the 400th anniversary of the death of Francesco Ferrucci, Tuscan warrior.

Jupiter Sending Forth his Eagle
AP8

1930, Oct. 21 Photo. Wmk. 140

C23 AP8 50c light brown 60 1.75
C24 " 1 l orange 1.25 3.25

Engraved
Unwmkd.

C25 AP8 7.70 l+1.30 l violet brown 9.50 20.00
C26 " 9 l+2 l indigo 9.50 20.00

Issued to commemorate the bimillenary of the birth of Virgil.
The surtax on Nos. C25 and C26 was for the National Institute Figli del Littorio.

Trans-Atlantic Squadron
AP9

1930, Dec. 15 Photo. Wmk. 140

C27 AP9 7.70 l Pruss. blue & gray 275.00 325.00
a. Seven stars instead of six 700.00 *1500.00*

Issued in connection with the flight by Italian aviators from Rome to Rio de Janeiro, Dec., 1930–Jan. 12, 1931.

Leonardo da Vinci's Flying Machine
AP10

Leonardo da Vinci
AP11

Leonardo da Vinci
AP12

1932

C28 AP10 50c olive brown 90 2.00
C29 AP11 1 l violet 90 2.00
C30 " 3 l brown red 1.85 4.00
C31 " 5 l deep green 2.10 4.50
C32 AP10 7.70 l+2 l dark blue 4.00 6.50
C33 AP11 10 l+2.50 l black brown 4.50 6.50
Nos. C28-C33 (6) 14.25 25.00

Engraved
Unwmkd.

C34 AP12 100 l bright blue & greenish black 35.00 50.00
a. Thin paper 65.00 100.00

Issued to commemorate the Dante Alighieri Society and especially Leonardo da Vinci, the great painter and architect, to whom the invention of a flying machine has been attributed. The surtax was for the benefit of the Society.

Inscription on No. C34: "Man with his large wings by beating against the air will be able to dominate it and lift himself above it".

Issue dates: Nos. C28–C33, Mar. 14; No. C34, Aug. 6.

Garibaldi's Home at Caprera
AP13

Farmhouse where Anita Garibaldi Died
AP14

Designs: 50c, 1 l+25c, Garibaldi's home, Caprera. 2 l + 50c, Anita Garibaldi. 5 l + 1 l, Giuseppe Garibaldi.

1932, Apr. 6 Photo. Wmk. 140

C35 AP13 50c copper red 60 1.25
C36 AP14 80c deep green 90 1.75
C37 AP13 1 l+25c red brn. 1.85 3.50
C38 " 2 l+50c deep blue 3.00 6.00
C39 AP14 5 l+1 l deep green 3.50 7.00
Nos. C35-C39 (5) 9.85 19.50

Issued to commemorate the 50th anniversary of the death of Giuseppe Garibaldi, patriot. The surtax was for the benefit of the Garibaldi Volunteers.

Eagle Sculpture and Airplane
AP17

Design: 75c, Italian buildings from the air.

1932, Oct. 27 ***Perf. 14***

C40 AP17 50c dark brown 1.50 3.00
C41 " 75c orange brown 3.00 5.50

Issued to commemorate the 10th anniversary of the Fascist government and the March on Rome.

Graf Zeppelin Issue.

Zeppelin over Pyramid of Caius Cestius—AP19

Designs: 5 l, Tomb of Cecilia Metlella. 10 l, Stadium of Mussolini. 12 l, St. Angelo Castle and Bridge. 15 l, Roman Forum. 20 l, Imperial Avenue.

1933, Apr. 24

C42 AP19 3 l black & green 11.00 *20.00*
C43 " 5 l green & brown 6.25 *20.00*
C44 AP19 10 l carmine & dull blue 6.25 *25.00*
C45 " 12 l dark blue & red orange 6.25 *30.00*
C46 " 15 l drk. brn. & gray 6.25 *35.00*
C47 AP19 20 l orange brown & blue 6.25 *40.00*
a. Vertical pair, imperf. btwn. *1000.00*
Nos. C42-C47 (6) 43.75 *170.00*

Balbo's Trans-Atlantic Flight Issue.

Italian Flag | King Victor Emmanuel III | Allegory "Flight"
AP25

Italian Flag | King Victor Emmanuel III | Colosseum at Rome; Towers of Chicago
AP26

1933, May 20

C48 AP25 5.25 l + 19.75 l red, green & ultramarine 45.00 *300.00*
a. Stamp at left without overprint *10,000.00*
C49 AP26 5.25 l + 44.75 l green, red & ultramarine 45.00 *300.00*

Issued in connection with the flight from Rome to Chicago of a squadron of twenty-four seaplanes under the command of General Italo Balbo. Twenty of these machines were designated to transport mail. The stamps were divided into three sections as illustrated. The first section displays the Italian flag in the national colors and is overprinted with first four letters of the name of one of the twenty pilots. This section had no franking value but it formed an essential part of the stamp, since, without it, a letter would not have been transported. The second section bears the ordinary postage, registration and special delivery fees and the third section represents the air post fee.

No. C49 was overprinted "VOLO DI RITORNO NEW YORK–ROMA" for the return flight, New York to Rome. As the flight was canceled, the stamp was not issued. Price $8,500.

Type of Air Post Stamp of 1930 Surcharged in Black

5

1934, Jan. 18

C52 AP6 2 l on 2 l yellow 7.50 *30.00*
C53 " 3 l on 2 l yellow green 3.75 *35.00*
C54 " 5 l on 2 l rose 3.75 *40.00*
C55 " 10 l on 2 l violet 3.75 *45.00*

For use on mail carried on a special flight from Rome to Buenos Aires.

View of Fiume Harbor
AP28

Designs: 50c, 1 l+50c, Monument to the Dead. 2 l+1.50 l, Venetian Lions. 3 l+2 l, Julian wall.

1934, Mar. 12

C56 AP28 25c green 30 50
C57 " 50c brown 30 50
C58 " 75c orange brown 30 50
C59 " 1 l+50c dull violet 35 75
C60 " 2 l+1.50 l dull blue 35 75
C61 " 3 l+2 l black brown 35 75
Nos. C56-C61 (6) 1.95 3.75

Annexation of Fiume, 10th anniversary.

Airplane and View of Stadium
AP32

Soccer Player and Plane
AP33

Airplane and Stadium Entrance
AP35

Airplane over Stadium
AP34

1934, May 24

C62 AP32 50c carmine rose 1.85 3.50
C63 AP33 75c gray blue 2.50 4.50
C64 AP34 5 l+2.50 l olive green 9.00 17.50
C65 AP35 10 l+5 l brown black 11.00 20.00

2nd World Soccer Championships.

Zeppelin under Fire
AP36

Air Force Memorial
AP40

Designs: 25c, 80c, Zeppelin under fire. 50c, 75c, Motorboat patrol. 1l+50c, Desert infantry. 2l+1l, Plane attacking troops.

1934, Apr. 24

C66	AP36	25c dark green	60	1.00
C67	"	50c gray	60	1.00
C68	"	75c dark brown	60	1.00
C69	"	80c slate blue	1.00	1.50
C70	"	1l+50c red brown	2.75	4.00
C71	"	2l+1l bright blue	3.25	5.00
C72	AP40	3l+2l brown black	4.00	6.00
		Nos. C66–C72 (7)	12.80	19.50

Issued in commemoration of the centenary of the institution of the Military Medal of Valor.

King Victor Emmanuel III
AP41

1934, Nov. 5

C73	AP41	1l purple	50	*10.00*
C74	"	2l bright blue	50	*10.00*
C75	"	4l red brown	1.00	*20.00*
C76	"	5l dull green	1.00	*20.00*
C77	"	8l rose red	16.50	*60.00*
C78	"	10l brown	16.50	*60.00*
		Nos. C73–C78 (6)	36.00	*180.00*

65th birthday of King Victor Emmanuel III and the nonstop flight from Rome to Mogadiscio.

Muse Playing Harp—AP42

Angelic Dirge for Bellini
AP43

Scene from Bellini Opera, La Sonnambula—AP44

1935, Sept. 24

C79	AP42	25c dull yellow	80	75
C80	"	50c brown	80	75
C81	"	60c rose carmine	1.60	1.00
C82	AP43	1l + 1l purple	7.25	13.50
C83	AP44	5l + 2l green	9.50	18.50
		Nos. C79–C83 (5)	19.95	34.50

Issued in commemoration of the centenary of the death of Vincenzo Bellini, (1801–1835), operatic composer.

Seaplane in Flight
AP45

Designs: 50c, 1l+1l, Monoplane over valley. 60c, Oak and eagle. 5l+2l, Ruins of ancient Rome.

1936, July 1

C84	AP45	25c deep green	1.00	1.50
C85	"	50c dark brown	1.35	2.00
C86	"	60c scarlet	1.60	2.50
C87	"	1l+1l violet	6.75	12.00
C88	"	5l+2l slate blue	9.50	17.50
		Nos. C84–C88 (5)	20.20	35.50

Issued to commemorate the 2000th anniversary of the birth of Quintus Horatius Flaccus (Horace).

Child of the Balilla AP49 — Heads of Children AP50

1937, June 28

C89	AP49	25c dk. blue green	1.60	2.00
C90	AP50	50c brown	2.25	2.00
C91	AP49	1l purple	1.60	2.00
C92	AP50	2l+1l dark blue	7.25	14.00
C93	AP49	3l+2l orange	9.50	16.00
C94	AP50	5l+3l rose lake	9.50	16.00
		Nos. C89–C94 (6)	31.70	52.00

Issued to commemorate the Summer Exhibition for Child Welfare. The surtax on Nos. C92-C94 was used to support summer camps for poor children.

Prosperous Italy—AP51

Designs: 50c, Prolific Italy. 80c, Apollo's steeds. 1 l+1 l, Map and Roman Standard. 5 l+1 l, Augustus Caesar.

1937, Sept. 23

C95	AP51	25c red violet	1.60	2.50
C96	"	50c olive brown	1.60	2.50
C97	"	80c orange brown	3.25	5.00
C98	"	1l+1l dark blue	8.50	15.00
C99	"	5l+1l dull vio.	12.50	20.00
		Nos. C95–C99 (5)	27.45	45.00

Issued in commemoration of the bimillenary of the birth of Augustus Caesar (Octavianus) on the occasion of the exhibition opened in Rome by Mussolini on September 22nd, 1937.

King Victor Emmanuel III
AP56

Designs: 25c, 3l, King Victor Emmanuel III. 50c, 1l, Dante Alighieri. 2l, 5l, Leonardo da Vinci.

1938, Oct. 28

C100	AP56	25c dull green	25	50
C101	"	50c dark yellow brown	25	50
C102	"	1l violet	45	85
C103	"	2l royal blue	65	1.25
C104	AP56	3l brn. carmine	1.25	2.25
C105	"	5l deep green	2.25	3.75
		Nos. C100–C105 (6)	5.10	9.10

Proclamation of the Empire.

Plane and Clasped Hands
AP59

Swallows in Flight—AP60

Photogravure.

1945–46 *Perf. 14* **Wmk. 277**

C106	AP59	1l slate blue	5	5
C107	AP60	2l dark blue	5	5
C108	AP59	3.20l red orange	9	20
C109	AP60	5l dark green	35	5
C110	AP59	10l car. rose	5	5
C111	AP60	25l dk. bl. ('46)	10.00	3.25
C112	AP59	50l dark green ('46)	13.50	7.50
		Nos. C106–C112 (7)	24.09	11.15

1947, Apr. 21

C113	AP60	25l brown	15	5
C114	AP59	50l violet	25	5

See also No. C130–C131.

No. C108 Surcharged in Black

1947, July 1

C115	AP59	6l on 3.20l red orange	25	25
		a. Pair, one without surch.	*1000.00*	
		b. Inverted surcharge		*2500.00*

Radio on Land AP61 — Plane over Capitol Bell Tower AP65

Designs: 6l, 25l, Radio on land. 10l, 35l, Radio at sea. 20l, 50l, Radio in the skies.

1947, Sept. 1 Photo. *Perf. 14*

C116	AP61	6l deep violet	4	12
C117	"	10l dark car. rose	10	12
C118	"	20l deep orange	50	25
C119	"	25l aquamarine	15	30
C120	"	35l bright blue	20	42
C121	"	50l lilac rose	40	60
		Nos. C116–C121 (6)	1.39	1.81

Issued to commemorate the 50th anniversary of radio.

1948

C123	AP65	100l green	2.50	4
C124	"	300l lilac rose	1.75	25
C125	"	500l ultramarine	1.75	40

Engraved.

C126	AP65	1000l dark brown	2.50	90
		a. Vertical pair, imperf. between	250.00	
		b. Perf. 14x13	3.00	1.00

See also No. C132–135.

St. Catherine Carrying Cross
AP66

Design: 200 l, St. Catherine with outstretched arms.

1948, Mar. 1 **Photogravure.**

C127	AP66	100l blue violet & brn. orange	30.00	20.00
C128	"	200l dp. bl. & bis.	9.00	9.00

600th anniversary of the birth of St. Catherine of Siena, patroness of Italy.

Giuseppe Mazzini
AP67

1955, Dec. 31 *Perf. 14* **Wmk. 303**

C129	AP67	100l Prussian green	3.00	1.25

Giuseppe Mazzini (1805–1872), patriot.

Types of 1945-46, 1948

1955–62 *Perf. 14* **Wmk. 303**

C130	AP60	5l green ('62)	5	5
C131	AP59	50l violet ('57)	40	25
C132	AP65	100l green	1.50	5
C133	"	300l lilac rose	90	50
C134	"	500l ultra. ('56)	1.10	1.10

Engraved.
Perf. 13½

C135	AP65	1000 l maroon ('59)	2.50	2.00
		Nos. C130–C135 (6)	6.45	3.95

Fluorescent Paper

See note below No. 998.

No. C132 was issued on both ordinary and fluorescent paper.

Airmail stamps issued only on fluorescent paper are Nos. C139–C140.

Type of 1945–46
Surcharged in Ultramarine

1956

Visita
del Presidente
della Repubblica
negli U.S.A.
e nel Canada

L 120

1956, Feb. 24

C136	AP59	120l on 50l magenta	2.25	1.65

Issued to commemorate the visit of President Giovanni Gronchi to the United States and Canada.

Madonna of Bruges, by Michelangelo
AP68

Photogravure

1964, Feb. 18 *Perf. 14* **Wmk. 303**

C137	AP68	185 l black	50	60

400th anniversary of the death of Michelangelo Buonarroti (1475–1564), artist.

Verrazano Type of Regular Issue, 1964.

1964, Nov. 21 *Perf. 14* **Wmk. 303**

C138	A481	130 l black & dull green	18	18

See note after No. 901.

Adoration of the Kings, by Gentile da Fabriano
AP69

1970, Dec. 12 Photo. Unwmkd.

C139 AP69 150 l multicolored 42 18

Christmas 1970.

Aviation Type of Regular Issue

Design: 150 l, F-140S Starfighter over Aeronautical Academy, Pozzuoli.

1973, Mar. 28 Photo. ***Perf. 14x13½***

C140 A590 150 l multicolored 38 1

50th anniversary of military aviation.

AIR POST SEMI-POSTAL STAMPS

Holy Year Issue.

Dome of St. Peter's, Dove with Olive Branch, Church of the Holy Sepulcher
SPAP1

Photogravure.

1933, Oct. 23 *Perf. 14* Wmk. 140

CB1 SPAP1 50c+25c orange brown 1.00 1.50
CB2 " 75c+50c brown violet 1.40 2.50

Symbolical of Military Air Force
SPAP2

1935, July 1

CB3 SPAP2 50c+50c brown 6.75 9.00

The surtax was for the Militia.

AIR POST SPECIAL DELIVERY STAMPS.

Garibaldi, Anita Garibaldi, Plane
APSD1

Photogravure.

1932, June 2 *Perf. 14* Wmk. 140

CE1 APSD1 2.25 l+1 l deep red & gray violet 3.25 6.50
CE2 " 4.50 l+1.50 l deep green & olive brown 4.75 9.00

Issued in commemoration of the fiftieth anniversary of the death of Giuseppe Garibaldi.

Airplane and Sunburst
APSD2

1933–34

CE3 APSD2 2 l gray black ('34) 10 10
CE4 " 2.25 l gray black 4.75 6.00

Flag Raising before Fascist Headquarters
APSD3

1934, Mar. 12

CE5 APSD3 2 l+1.25 l deep blue 1.90 3.00
CE6 " 2.25 l+1.25 l olive green 35 1.00
CE7 " 4.50 l+2 l carmine rose 35 1.00

Issued in commemoration of the tenth anniversary of the annexation of Fiume.

Triumphal Arch in Rome
APSD4

1934, Aug. 31

CE8 APSD4 2 l+1.25 l brn. 3.25 5.00
CE9 " 4.50 l+2 l copper red 4.00 6.00

Issued in commemoration of the centenary of the institution of the Military Medal of Valor.

AIR POST OFFICIAL STAMPS

Type of Air Post Stamp of 1933 (Balbo Flight Issue)

Overprinted ***SERVIZIO DI STATO***

1933 *Perf. 14* Wmk. 140

CO1 AP26 5.25 l+44.75 l red, green & red vio. 1500.00 *4500.00*

Type of Air Post Stamp of 1934
Overprinted in Gold Crown and
"SERVIZIO DI STATO"

1934

CO2 AP41 10 l bl. black 550.00 *2000.00*

65th birthday of King Victor Emmanuel III and the non-stop flight from Rome to Mogadiscio.

PNEUMATIC POST STAMPS.

PN1

Typographed.

1913–28 *Perf. 14* **Wmk. 140**

D1 PN1 10c brown 1.50 3.00
D2 " 15c brn. violet ('28) 1.50 3.00
a. 15c dull violet ('21) 1.85 4.00
D3 " 15c rose red ('28) 1.50 3.00
D4 " 15c claret ('28) 1.50 3.00
D5 " 20c brn. violet ('25) 4.50 9.00
D6 " 30c blue ('23) 2.65 6.00
D7 " 35c rose red ('27) 7.50 15.00
D8 " 40c deep red ('26) 9.00 18.00
Nos. D1–D8 (8) 29.65 60.00

Stamps of 1913-26 Surcharged

Cent. 15

1924-27

D9 PN1 15c on 10c brown 1.50 3.00
D10 " 15c on 20c brown violet ('27) 3.00 6.00
D11 " 20c on 10c brown ('25) 3.00 6.00
D12 " 20c on 15c dull violet ('25) 1.85 4.00
D13 " 35c on 40c deep red ('27) 6.00 12.00
D14 " 40c on 30c blue ('25) 2.65 5.50
Nos. D9–D14 (6) 18.00 36.50

Dante Alighieri
PN2

Galileo Galilei—PN3

1933, Mar. 29 **Photogravure**

D15 PN2 15c dark violet 12 18
D16 PN3 35c rose red 12 18

Dante Alighieri
PN4

Galileo Galilei
PN5

1945, Oct. 22 **Wmk. 277**

D17 PN4 60c dull brown 12 18
D18 PN5 1.40 l dull blue 12 18

Minerva
PN6

1947, Nov. 15

D19 PN6 3 l rose lilac 7.00 8.00
D20 " 5 l aquamarine 8 12

1958–66 **Wmk. 303**

D21 PN6 10 l rose red 8 8
D22 " 20 l sapphire ('66) 8 8

SPECIAL DELIVERY STAMPS.

Victor Emmanuel III
SD1

Wmkd. Crowns. (140)

1903-26 Typographed. *Perf. 14.*

E1 SD1 25c rose red 12.00 18
a. Imperf., pair 110.00 110.00
E2 " 50c dull red ('20) 1.35 18
E3 " 60c dull red ('22) 1.35 30
E4 " 70c dull red ('25) 30 7
E5 " 1.25 l deep blue ('26) 38 4
Nos. E1–E5 (5) 15.38 77

Victor Emmanuel III
SD2

1908–26

E6 SD2 30c blue & rose 70 50
E7 " 2 l blue & red ('25) 1.50 2.10
E8 " 2.50 l blue & red ('26) 1.50 90

The 1.20 lire blue and red (see No. E12) was prepared in 1922, but not issued. Price $60.

SD3

1917, Nov.

E9 SD3 25c on 40c violet 12.00 9.00

Type SD3 not issued without surcharge.

No. E6 Surcharged

1921, Oct.

E10 SD2 1.20 l on 30c blue & rose 1.50 2.10
a. Comma in value omitted 3.75 6.00
b. Double surch. 50.00

No. E2 Surcharged **Cent. 60**

1922, Jan. 9

E11 SD1 60c on 50c dull red 12.00 30
a. Inverted surch. 50.00 50.00
b. Double surch. 140.00
c. Imperf., pair 150.00 150.00

Type of 1908 Surcharged

Lire 1,60

1924, May

E12 SD2 1.60 l on 1.20 l blue & red 1.50 2.75
a. Double surch., one inverted 47.50 47.50

No. E3 Surcharged like No. E11.

1925, Apr. 11

E13 SD1 70c on 60c dull red 30 30
a. Inverted surch. 42.50 42.50

Victor Emmanuel III
SD4

1932-33 **Photogravure.**

E14 SD4 1.25 l green 6 5
E15 " 2.50 l dp. org. ('33) 8 8

Ancient Pillars and Entrenchments
SD5

Design: 2.50 l, Head of Mussolini, trophies of flags, etc.

1932, Oct. 27

E16 SD5 1.25 l deep green 1.10 60
E17 " 2.50 l deep orange 3.25 8.50

"Italia"—SD7

1945, Aug. *Perf. 14* **Wmk. 277**

E18 SD7 5 l rose carmine 8 8

Winged Foot
SD8

Rearing Horse and Torch-Bearer
SD9

1945-51

E19 SD8 5 l henna brown 6 6
E20 SD9 10 l deep blue 12 6
E21 " 15 l dark carmine rose ('47) 2.25 12
E22 SD8 25 l bright red org. ('47) 17.50 18
E23 " 30 l dp. violet('46) 2.25 18
E24 " 50 l lilac rose('51) 32.50 6
E25 SD9 60 l car. rose ('48) 13.50 25
Nos. E19–E25 (7) 68.18 91

Type of Regular Issue of 1948.
Inscribed: "Espresso."

1948, Sept. 18 Photo. *Perf. 14*

E26 A272 35 l vio. (*Naples*) 12.00 6.00

Centenary of the Risorgimento, uprisings of 1848–49 which led to Italian unification.

Type of 1945-51

1955, July 7 *Perf. 14* **Wmk. 303**

E32 SD8 50 l lilac rose 1.85 6

Etruscan Winged Horses
SD10

1958–76 **Photogravure**

Size: 36½x20¼ mm.

E33 SD10 75 l magenta 30 6
E34 " 150 l dull bl. grn. ('66) 3.75 6
a. Size: 36x20mm. ('68) 30

Size: 36x20mm.

E35 SD10 250 l blue ('74) 60 5
E36 " 300 l brown ('76) 60 5

Nos. E34a, E35–E36 are fluorescent.

AUTHORIZED DELIVERY STAMPS.

For the payment of a special tax for the authorized delivery of correspondence privately instead of through the post office.

Coat of Arms
AD1 AD2

Typographed.

1928 *Perf. 14.* **Wmk. 140**

EY1 AD1 10c dull blue 1.00 12
a. Perf. 11 4.50 38

1930 **Photogravure.** *Perf. 14.*

EY2 AD2 10c dark brown 6 3

No. EY2 Surcharged in Black

1945

EY3 AD2 40(c) on 10c dark brown 18 18

Coat of Arms "Italia"
AD3 AD4

1945–46 **Photogravure** **Wmk. 277**

EY4 AD3 40c dark brown 12 12
EY5 " 1 l dk. brown('46) 25 25

1947-52 **Size: 27½x22½ mm.**

EY6 AD4 1 l brt. greenish blue 60 12
EY7 " 8 l brt. red ('48) 8.00 18

Size: 20½x16½ mm.

EY8 AD4 15 l violet ('49) 27.50 6
EY9 " 20 l rose vio. ('52) 1.10 7

1955–77 *Perf. 14* **Wmk. 303**

Size: 20½x16½ mm.

EY11 AD4 20 l rose violet 25 5
EY12 " 30 l Prus. green ('65) 12 5
EY13 " 35 l ocher ('74) 18 5
EY14 " 110 l lt. ultra. ('77) 25 6

POSTAGE DUE STAMPS.

Unused prices for Postage Due stamps are for examples with full original gum. Stamps without gum, with part gum or privately gummed sell for much less.

D1

Lithographed.

1863 *Imperf.* **Unwmkd.**

No.	Type	Description	Unused	Used
J1	D1	10c yellow	500.00	65.00
		a. 10c yel. orange	550.00	65.00

Price for Nos. J1 and J1a without original gum, each $35.

D2 D3

Typographed.

1869 *Perf. 14* **Wmk. 140**

No.	Type	Description	Unused	Used
J2	D2	10c buff	500.00	9.00

1870-1925

No.	Type	Description	Unused	Used
J3	D3	1c buff & magenta	1.00	1.00
		a. Numeral inverted	450.00	325.00
J4	"	2c buff & magenta	4.50	6.00
		a. Numeral invtd.	2750.00	550.00
J5	"	5c buff & magenta	18	8
		a. Numeral inverted	50	50
J6	"	10c buff & magenta ('71)	18	8
		a. Numerals inverted	75	75
		b. Imperf., pair		
J7	"	20c orange & magenta ('94)	40	8
		a. Imperf., pair	35.00	35.00
		b. Numerals inverted	4.00	4.00
J8	"	30c buff & magenta	50	8
		a. Numerals inverted	1.25	1.25
		b. Imperf., pair		
J9	"	40c buff & magenta	60	8
		a. Numerals inverted	40.00	40.00
J10	"	50c buff & magenta	75	8
		a. Numerals inverted	3.75	3.75
		b. Imperf., pair		325.00
J11	"	60c buff & magenta	27.50	8
		a. Numerals inverted	45.00	45.00
J12	"	60c buff & brown ('25)	9.50	75
J13	"	1 l light blue & brown	800.00	3.00
		a. Numeral inverted		6000.00
J14	"	1 l blue & magenta ('94)	50	15
		a. Imperf., pair	35.00	35.00
		b. Numeral invtd.	1500.00	1250.00
J15	"	2 l light blue & brown	725.00	3.75
		a. Numeral inverted	1000.00	275.00
J16	"	2 l blue & magenta ('03)	8.50	8
		a. Numeral inverted	900.00	1100.00
J17	"	5 l blue & brown ('74)	50.00	1.85
		a. Numeral inverted		60.00
J18	"	5 l blue & magenta ('03)	30.00	18
		a. Numeral inverted		
J19	"	10 l blue & brown ('74)	1500.00	6.00
		a. Numerals inverted		37.50
J20	"	10 l blue & magenta ('94)	42.50	15

D4

1884–1903

No.	Type	Description	Unused	Used
J21	D4	50 l green	6.75	4.00
J22	"	50 l yellow ('03)	12.00	4.00
J23	"	100 l claret	8.50	3.50
J24	"	100 l blue ('03)	9.00	2.50

Nos. J3 & J4 Surcharged in Black

1890-91

No.	Type	Description	Unused	Used
J25	D3	10c on 2c buff & magenta	40.00	5.00
J26	"	20c on 1c buff & magenta	80.00	3.00
		a. Inverted surcharge		850.00
J27	"	30c on 2c buff & magenta	275.00	2.00
		a. Inverted surcharge		300.00

Coat of Arms

D6 D7

1934 Photogravure.

No.	Type	Description	Unused	Used
J28	D6	5c brown	7	3
J29	"	10c blue	4	3
J30	"	20c rose red	4	3
J31	"	25c green	4	3
J32	"	30c red orange	4	3
J33	"	40c black brown	4	3
J34	"	50c violet	4	3
J35	"	60c slate black	15	3
J36	D7	1 l red orange	5	3
J37	"	2 l green	20	3
J38	"	5 l violet	80	4
J39	"	10 l blue	1.60	4
J40	"	20 l carmine rose	2.10	4
		Nos. J28-J40 (13)	5.21	42

Coat of Arms

D8 D9

1945-46 *Perf. 14.* **Unwmkd.**

No.	Type	Description	Unused	Used
J41	D8	5c brown ('46)	5	25
J42	"	10c blue	5	5
J43	"	20c rose red ('46)	5	5
J44	"	25c dark green	5	5
J45	"	30c red orange	5	5
J46	"	40c black brown	5	5
J47	"	50c violet	5	5
J48	"	60c black	10	10
J49	D9	1 l red orange	1.75	5
J50	"	2 l green	25	5
J51	"	5 l violet	25	5
J52	"	10 l blue	25	12
J53	"	20 l carmine rose	30	12
		Nos. J41-J53 (13)	3.25	1.04

Nos. J41 and J43 are printed on grayish paper and have yellow gum.

Wmk. 277

No.	Type	Description	Unused	Used
J54	D8	10c dark blue	12	18
J55	"	25c dark green	60	75
J56	"	30c red orange	60	75
J57	"	40c black brown	12	12
J58	"	50c violet ('46)	2.25	50
J59	"	60c blue black ('46)	2.25	60
J60	D9	1 l red orange	12	6
J61	"	2 l dark green	25	12
J62	"	5 l violet	8.50	8
J63	"	10 l dark blue	11.50	8
J64	"	20 l carmine rose	13.50	8
		Nos. J54-J64 (11)	39.81	3.32

D10

1947–54 Photo. *Perf. 14*

No.	Type	Description	Unused	Used
J65	D10	1 l red orange	5	3
J66	"	2 l dark green	10	3
J67	"	3 l carmine	65	50
J68	"	4 l brown	40	30
J69	"	5 l violet	2.00	3
J70	"	6 l violet blue	2.00	12
J71	"	8 l rose violet	3.00	1.00
J72	"	10 l deep blue	1.50	3
J73	D10	12 l golden brown	2.00	42
J74	"	20 l lilac rose	47.50	3
J75	"	25 l dark red ('54)	47.50	80
J76	"	50 l aquamarine	32.50	3
J77	"	100 l org. yel. ('52)	2.25	7

Engraved

Perf. 13½x14

No.	Type	Description	Unused	Used
J78	D10	500 l deep blue & dk. carmine ('52)	5.00	30
		a. Perf. 11x13	4.50	35
		b. Perf. 13	3.50	35
		Nos. J65-J78 (14)	146.45	3.69

Photogravure

1955–66 *Perf. 14* **Wmk. 303**

No.	Type	Description	Unused	Used
J83	D10	5 l violet	5	5
J85	"	8 l rose violet	72.50	72.50
J86	"	10 l deep blue	4	5
J87	"	20 l lilac rose	6	5
J88	"	25 l dark red	6	5
J89	"	30 l gray brown ('61)	12	5
J90	"	40 l dull brown ('66)	12	5
J91	"	50 l aquamarine	15	5
J92	"	100 l org. yellow ('58)	20	5

Engraved

Perf. 14x14½

No.	Type	Description	Unused	Used
J93	D10	500 l dp. bl. & dk. car. ('61)	1.75	25
		Nos. J83-J93 (10)	75.05	73.15

MILITARY STAMPS.

Regular Stamps, 1929-42, Overprinted in Black

P.M.

1943 *Perf. 14.* **Wmk. 140**

No.	Type	Description	Unused	Used
M1	A90	5c olive brown	12	18
M2	A92	10c dark brown	12	18
M3	A93	15c slate green	12	18
M4	A91	20c rose red	12	18
M5	A94	25c deep green	12	18
M6	A95	30c olive brown	12	18
M7	"	50c purple	12	12
M8	A91	1 l dark purple	30	30
M9	A94	1.25 l deep blue	18	25
M10	A92	1.75 l red orange	18	25
M11	A93	2 l carmine lake	25	30
M12	A95a	5 l rose red	25	30
M13	A93	10 l purple	35	42
		Nos. M1-M13 (13)	2.35	3.02

Due to a shortage of regular postage stamps during 1944-45, this issue was used for ordinary mail. "P. M." stands for "Posta Militare."

MILITARY AIR POST STAMPS.

Air Post Stamps, 1930 Overprinted in Black

P.M.

1943 *Perf. 14* **Wmk. 140**

No.	Type	Description	Unused	Used
MC1	AP3	50c olive brown	12	18
MC2	AP5	1 l purple	12	18
MC3	AP6	2 l deep blue	18	35
MC4	AP3	5 l dark green	25	42
MC5	"	10 l deep carmine	35	60
		Nos. MC1-MC5 (5)	1.02	1.73

MILITARY AIR POST SPECIAL DELIVERY STAMP.

No. CE3 Overprinted in Black

P.M.

1943 *Perf. 14.* **Wmk. 140**

No.	Type	Description	Unused	Used
MCE1	APSD2	2 l gray black	25	42

MILITARY SPECIAL DELIVERY STAMP.

No. E14 Overprinted in Black

P.M.

1943 *Perf. 14* **Wmk. 140**

No.	Type	Description	Unused	Used
ME1	SD4	1.25 l green	18	25

OFFICIAL STAMPS.

O1

Typographed.

1875 *Perf. 14.* **Wmk. 140**

No.	Type	Description	Unused	Used
O1	O1	2c lake	60	50
O2	"	5c "	60	65
O3	"	20c "	15	20
O4	"	30c "	15	25
O5	"	1 l "	1.50	3.00
O6	"	2 l "	9.50	9.00
O7	"	5 l "	40.00	65.00
O8	"	10 l "	70.00	35.00

Nos. O1–O8 surcharged "2 C" are listed as Nos. 37–44.

Stamps inscribed "Servizio Commissioni" were used in connection with the postal service but not for the payment of postage.

NEWSPAPER STAMP.

N1

Typo., Numeral Embossed

1862 *Imperf.* **Unwmkd.**

No.	Type	Description	Unused	Used
P1	N1	2c buff	22.50	35.00
		a. Numeral double	75.00	450.00

Black 1c and 2c stamps of similar type are listed under Sardinia.

PARCEL POST STAMPS.

King Humbert I

PP1

Typographed.

1884-86 *Perf. 14.* **Wmk. 140**

Various Frames.

No.	Type	Description	Unused	Used
Q1	PP1	10c olive gray	35.00	5.00
Q2	"	20c blue	60.00	8.50
Q3	"	50c claret	6.00	1.50
Q4	"	75c blue green	6.00	1.50
Q5	"	1.25 l orange	12.00	3.50
Q6	"	1.75 l brown	12.00	15.00

Nos. Q1–Q6 overprinted "Valevole per le stampe" and surcharged "Cml. 2" are listed as Nos. 58–63.

Parcel Post stamps from No. Q7 onward were used by affixing them to the waybill so that one half remained on it following the parcel, the other half staying on the receipt given the sender. Most used halves are right halves. Complete stamps were and are obtainable canceled, probably to order.

Both unused and used prices are for complete stamps.

PP2

1914–22 *Perf. 13* **Wmk. 140**

No.	Type	Description	Unused	Used
Q7	PP2	5c brown	20	25
Q8	"	10c deep blue	20	25
Q9	"	20c black ('17)	25	25
Q10	"	25c red	25	25
Q11	"	50c orange	30	35
Q12	"	1 l violet	40	18
Q13	"	2 l green	1.00	25
Q14	"	3 l bistre	1.75	50
Q15	"	4 l slate	2.00	50
Q16	"	10 l rose lilac ('22)	12.00	1.20
Q17	"	12 l red brn. ('22)	47.50	47.50
Q18	"	15 l olive grn. ('22)	55.00	55.00
Q19	"	20 l brn. violet ('22)	55.00	60.00
		Nos. Q7–Q19 (13)	175.85	166.48

Halves Used

Q7	3	Q14	4
Q8	3	Q15	4
Q9	3	Q16	18
Q10	3	Q17	75
Q11	3	Q18	75
Q12	3	Q19	75
Q13	3		

Imperfs exist. Price per pair: 20c, 25c, 50c, 2 l, 4 l, 10 l, $50 each; 3 l, $60; 12 l, 15 l, 20 l, $200 each.

No. Q7 Surcharged

60 CENT. 60

Q20	PP2	30c on 5c brown	25	50
		Half stamp		4
Q21	PP2	60c on 5c brown	38	75
		Half stamp		4
Q22	PP2	1.50 l on 5c brown	2.50	4.25
		Half stamp		25
		a. Double surch.	25.00	

No. Q16 Surcharged

LIRE 3 LIRE 3

Q23	PP2	3 l on 10 l rose lilac	2.50	4.25
		Half stamp		20

PP3

1927-39 Wmkd. Crowns. (140)

Q24	PP3	5c brown ('38)	5	8
Q25	"	10c deep blue ('39)	5	8
Q26	"	25c red ('32)	5	8
Q27	"	30c ultramarine	5	8
Q28	"	50c orange ('32)	5	8
Q29	"	60c red	5	8
Q30	"	1 l lilac ('31)	5	8
Q31	"	1 l brown violet ('36)	7.50	9.00
Q32	"	2 l green ('32)	5	8
Q33	"	3 l bistre	5	8
		a. Printed on both sides	30.00	
Q34	"	4 l gray	8	8
Q35	"	10 l rose lilac ('34)	30	30
Q36	"	20 l lilac brown ('33)	60	65
		Nos. Q24-Q36 (13)	8.93	10.75

Price of used halves, Nos. Q24-Q36, each 3 cents.

Nos. Q24-Q30, Q32-Q36 Overprinted Between Halves in Black

1945 Perf. 13 Wmk. 140

Q37	PP3	5c brown	12	18
Q38	"	10c deep blue	12	18
Q39	"	25c red	12	18
Q40	"	30c ultramarine	3.00	3.75
Q41	"	50c orange	12	18
Q42	"	60c red	12	18
Q43	"	1 l lilac	12	18
Q44	"	2 l green	12	18
Q45	"	3 l bistre	18	30
Q46	"	4 l gray	25	38
Q47	"	10 l rose lilac	1.25	1.75
Q48	"	20 l lilac brown	2.25	3.00
		Nos. Q37-Q48 (12)	7.77	10.44

Halves Used

Q37	3	Q43	3
Q38	3	Q44	3
Q39	3	Q45	3
Q40	18	Q46	3
Q41	3	Q47	4
Q42	3	Q48	13

Type of 1927.
With Fasces Removed.

1946 Typographed.

Q55	PP3	1 l lilac	60	18
Q56	"	2 l green	30	18
Q57	"	3 l yellow orange	1.00	50
Q58	"	4 l gray	1.35	30
Q59	"	10 l rose lilac	12.00	3.00
Q60	"	20 l lilac brown	20.00	9.50
		Nos. Q55-Q60 (6)	35.25	13.66

Halves Used

Q55	6	Q58	6
Q56	6	Q59	25
Q57	6	Q60	30

PP4

PP5

Perf. 13, 13x14, 12½x13

1946-54 Photogravure Wmk. 277

Q61	PP4	25c dull violet blue ('48)	6	12
Q62	"	50c brown ('47)	6	12
Q63	"	1 l golden brown ('47)	6	12
Q64	"	2 l lt. bl. green ('47)	20	17
Q65	"	3 l red orange ('47)	15	17
Q66	"	4 l gray black ('47)	1.75	1.25
Q67	"	5 l lilac rose ('47)	6	12
		a. Perf. 13	15	12
Q68	PP4	10 l violet	1.50	25
		a. Perf. 13	1.50	12
Q69	PP4	20 l lilac brown	85	18
		a. Perf. 13	15.00	18
Q70	PP4	30 l plum ('52)	60	70
		a. Perf. 13	1.75	70
Q71	PP4	50 l rose red	8.00	1.20
		a. Perf. 13	15.00	1.50
Q72	PP4	100 l sapphire	12.00	8.00
		a. Perf. 13	80.00	9.00
Q73	PP4	200 l green ('48)	25.00	12.00
		a. Perf. 13	30.00	12.00
Q74	PP4	300 l brn. car. ('48)	275.00	110.00
		a. Perf. 13	275.00	110.00
Q75	PP4	500 l brown ('48)	60.00	18.50

Engraved *Perf. 13*

Q76	PP5	1000 l ultra. ('54)	1100.00	525.00
		Nos. Q61-Q76 (16)	1485.29	677.10

Halves Used

Q61	3	Q70	3
Q62	3	Q70a	6
Q63	3	Q71	3
Q64	3	Q71a	6
Q65	3	Q72	3
Q66	3	Q72a	12
Q67	3	Q73	18
Q67a	3	Q73a	25
Q68	3	Q74	30
Q68a	3	Q74a	40
Q69	3	Q75	18
Q69a	6	Q76	1.25

Types of 1946-54
Photogravure.

1955-59 *Perf. 12½x13* Wmk. 303

Without Imprint

Q77	PP4	25c violet blue	60	60
Q77A	"	50c brown ('56)	5.50	6.00
Q78	"	5 l lilac rose ('59)	8	3
Q79	"	10 l violet	6	3
Q80	"	20 l lilac brown	12	6
Q81	"	30 l plum ('56)	17	12
Q82	"	40 l dull violet ('57)	12	13
Q83	"	50 l rose red	13	12
Q84	"	100 l sapphire	25	18
Q85	"	150 l org. brn. ('57)	60	42
Q86	"	200 l green ('56)	42	25
Q87	"	300 l brn. car. ('58)	55	50
Q88	"	400 l gray black ('57)	70	60
Q89	"	500 l brown ('57)	95	85

Engraved *Perf. 13*

Q90	PP5	1000 l ultra. ('57)	1.65	90
Q91	"	2000 l red brown & carmine ('57)	4.25	2.50
		Nos. Q77-Q91 (16)	16.15	13.29

Price of used halves, Nos. Q77-Q89, each 3 cents. Nos. Q90-Q91, each 40 cents.

1960-66 Photo. *Perf. 12½x13*

Q92	PP4	60 l bright lilac	12	12
Q93	"	140 l dull red	42	30
Q94	"	280 l yellow	70	60
Q95	"	600 l olive bistre	1.10	85
Q96	"	700 l blue ('66)	1.25	1.00
Q97	"	800 l dp. org. ('66)	1.65	1.10
		Nos. Q92-Q97 (6)	5.24	3.97

Halves Used

Q92	4	Q95	40
Q93	5	Q96	25
Q94	18	Q97	25

Imprint: "I.P.S.-Off. Carte Valori-Roma"

1973, Mar. Photo. Wmk. 303

Q98	PP4	20 l lilac brown	8	5
Q99	"	30 l plum	10	8

PARCEL POST AUTHORIZED DELIVERY STAMPS.

For the payment of a special tax for the authorized delivery of parcels privately instead of through the post office.

Both unused and used prices are for complete stamps.

PAD1

Photogravure

1953 *Perf. 13* Wmk. 277

QY1	PAD1	40 l orange red	1.10	1.10
QY2	"	50 l ultra.	70.00	70.00
QY3	"	75 l brown	55.00	55.00
QY4	"	110 l lilac rose	50.00	50.00

Halves Used

QY1	25	QY3	2.40
QY2	35	QY4	3.00

1956-58 *Perf. 12½x13* Wmk. 303

QY5	PAD1	40 l orange red	2.50	2.50
QY6	"	50 l ultramarine	4.00	4.00
QY7	"	60 l bright vio. bl. ('58)	10.00	10.00
QY8	"	75 l brown	175.00	175.00
QY9	"	90 l lilac ('58)	25	25
QY10	"	110 l lilac rose	135.00	135.00
QY11	"	120 l greenish blue ('58)	25	25
		Nos. QY5-QY11 (7)	327.00	327.00

Halves Used

QY5	15	QY9	5
QY6	15	QY10	2.75
QY7	15	QY11	5
QY8	2.25		

1960-76

QY12	PAD1	70 l grn. ('66)	35.00	35.00
QY13	"	80 l brown	17	17
QY14	"	110 l orange yel.	25	25
QY15	"	140 l black	30	30
QY16	"	150 l carmine rose ('68)	30	30
QY17	"	180 l red ('66)	70	70
QY18	"	240 l dk. bl. ('66)	50	50

Perf. 13½

QY19	PAD1	500 l ocher ('76)	1.10	1.10
		Nos. QY12-QY19 (8)	38.32	38.32

Halves Used

QY12	2.25	QY16	5
QY13	5	QY17	8
QY14	5	QY18	8
QY15	5	QY19	12

OCCUPATION STAMPS.

Issued under Austrian Occupation.

Emperor Karl of Austria
OS1 OS2

1918 *Perf. 12½.* Unwmkd.

N1	OS1	2c on 1h greenish blue	7	7
N2	"	3c on 2h red orange	4	4
N3	"	4c on 3h olive gray	6	6
N4	"	6c on 5h olive green	12	12
N5	"	7c on 6h violet	12	12
		a. Perf. 12½x11½	5.50	5.50
N6	"	11c on 10h org. brown	8	8
N7	"	13c on 12h blue	8	8
N8	OS1	16c on 15h bright rose	8	8
N9	"	22c on 20h red brown	6	6
		a. Perf. 11½	3.50	3.50
N10	"	27c on 25h ultra.	35	35
N11	"	32c on 30h slate	18	18
N12	"	43c on 40h olive bistre	8	8
		a. Perf. 11½	3.50	3.50
N13	"	53c on 50h deep green	8	8
N14	"	64c on 60h rose	12	12
N15	"	85c on 80h dull blue	6	6
N16	"	95c on 90h dark violet	12	12
N17	OS2	2 l 11c on 2k rose, *straw*	30	30
N18	"	3 l 16c on 3k green, *blue*	95	95
N19	"	4 l 22c on 4k rose, *green*	1.20	1.20
		Nos. N1-N19 (19)	4.15	4.15

Emperor Karl
OS3

1918

N20	OS3	2c on 1h greenish bl.	2.00
N21	"	3c on 2h orange	2.00
N22	"	4c on 3h olive gray	2.00
N23	"	6c on 5h yel. green	2.00
N24	"	11c on 10h dark brown	2.00
N25	"	22c on 20h red	2.00
N26	"	27c on 25h blue	2.00
N27	"	32c on 30h bistre	2.00
N28	"	48c on 45h dark slate	2.00
N29	"	53c on 50h deep green	2.00
N30	"	64c on 60h violet	2.00
N31	"	85c on 80h rose	2.00
N32	"	95c on 90h brown violet	2.00
N33	OS2	1 l 16c on 1k olive bistre, *blue*	2.00
		Nos. N20-N33 (14)	28.00

Nos. N20 to N33 inclusive were never placed in use in the occupied territory. They were, however, on sale at the Post Office in Vienna for a few days before the Armistice.

OCCUPATION SPECIAL DELIVERY STAMPS

Special Handling Stamps of Bosnia Surcharged **3 Centesimi**

1918 *Perf. 12½.* Unwmkd.

NE1	SH1	3c on 2h vermilion	4.75	4.75
NE2	"	6c on 5h deep green	4.75	4.75

Nos. NE1-NE2 are on yellowish paper. Reprints on white paper sell for about 70 cents a set.

OCCUPATION POSTAGE DUE STAMPS.

Postage Due Stamps of Bosnia Surcharged **6 Centesimi**

1918 *Perf. 12½.* Unwmkd.

NJ1	D2	6c on 5h red	2.10	2.10
		a. Perf. 11½	3.75	4.00
NJ2	"	11c on 10h red	2.10	2.10
		a. Perf. 11½	3.75	4.00
NJ3	"	16c on 15h red	70	60
NJ4	"	27c on 25h "	70	60
NJ5	"	32c on 30h "	70	60
NJ6	"	43c on 40h "	70	60
NJ7	"	53c on 50h "	70	60
		Nos. NJ1-NJ7 (7)	7.70	7.20

OCCUPATION NEWSPAPER STAMPS.

Austrian Military Newspaper Stamps Surcharged **3 Centesimi**

1918 *Perf. 12½.* Unwmkd.

NP1	MN1	3c on 2h blue	18	18
		a. Perf. 11½	1.20	1.20
NP2	"	7c on 6h orange	35	35
NP3	"	11c on 10h carmine	42	42
NP4	"	22c on 20h brown	25	25
		a. Perf. 11½	1.80	1.80

Issued jointly by the Allied Military Government of the United States and Great Britain, for civilian use in areas under Allied occupation.

OS4

Offset Printing.

"Italy Centesimi" (or "Lira") in Black

1943		*Perf. 11.*	Unwmkd.	
1N1	OS4	15c pale orange	5	12
1N2	"	25c pale citron	5	12
1N3	"	30c light gray	5	12
1N4	"	50c light violet	5	12
1N5	"	60c orange yellow	5	12
1N6	"	1 l light yellow green	5	12
1N7	"	2 l deep rose	5	12
1N8	"	5 l light blue	25	30
1N9	"	10 l buff	50	65
		Nos. 1N1–1N9 (9)	1.10	1.79

Italy Nos. 217, 220 and 221 Overprinted in Blue, Vermilion, Carmine or Orange

GOVERNO MILITARE ALLEATO

1943, Dec. 10		*Perf. 14*	Wmk. 140	
1N10	A91	20c rose red (Bl)	30	35
1N11	A93	35c deep blue (C)	2.10	2.75
		a. 35c deep blue (V)	3.00	4.00
1N12	A95	50c purple (C)	12	18
		a. 50c purple (O)	25	30

Nos. 1N1–1N9 were for use in Sicily, Nos. 1N10–1N13 for use in Naples.

Venezia Giulia.

Stamps of Italy, 1929 to 1945 Overprinted in Black:

A.M.G. V.G. *a* A.M.G. V.G. *b*

On Stamps of 1929.

1945-47		*Perf. 14.*	Wmk. 140	
1LN1	A92 (*a*)	10c dark brown	4	4
1LN1A	A91 (")	20c rose red ('47)	6	6

On Stamps of 1945.

1945		*Perf. 14.*	Wmk. 277	
1LN2	A249 (*a*)	20c rose red	4	4
1LN3	A248 (")	60c slate green	6	6
1LN4	A249 (")	1 l deep violet	4	4
1LN5	A251 (")	2 l dark red	5	5
1LN6	A252 (*b*)	5 l "	6	6
1LN7	A251 (*a*)	10 l purple	10	10
		Nos. 1LN2–1LN7 (6)	35	35

On Stamps of 1945.

1945-46			Unwmkd.	
1LN7A	A250 (*a*)	10c dark brown ('46)	5	5
1LN7B	A249 (")	20c rose red ('46)	5	5
1LN8	A251 (")	60c red orange	8	8

On Air Post Stamp of 1930.

1945		*Perf. 14.*	Wmk. 140	
1LN9	AP3 (*a*)	50c olive brown	5	5

On Stamp of 1929.

1946				
1LN10	A91	(*a*) 20 l light green	12	18

On Stamps of 1945.
Wmk. 277.

1LN11	A260 (*a*)	25 l dark green	12	18
1LN12	" (")	50 l dark violet brown	25	30

Italy No. 477 Overprinted in Black

A.M.G. V.G. *c*

1LN13	A261 (*c*)	100 l carmine lake	75	90

Stamps of Italy, 1945–47 Overprinted Type "a" in Black

1947				
1LN14	A259	25c brt. bl. green	3	3
1LN15	A258	2 l dk. claret brn.	3	3
1LN16	A259	3 l red	4	4
1LN17	"	4 l red orange	5	5
1LN18	A257	6 l deep violet	5	5
1LN19	A259	20 l dk. red violet	30	30
		Nos. 1LN14–1LN19 (6)	50	50

Some denominations of the Venezia Giulia A.M.G. issues exist with inverted overprint; several values exist in horizontal and vertical pairs, one stamp without overprint.

OCCUPATION AIR POST STAMPS.

Italy Nos. C106-C107 and C109-C113 Overprinted in Black

A.M.G. V.G. *c*

1946-47		*Perf. 14*	Wmk. 277	
1LNC1	AP59	1 l slate bl. ('47)	5	5
1LNC2	AP60	2 l dk. bl. ('47)	5	5
1LNC3	"	5 l dk. grn. ('47)	5	5
1LNC4	AP59	10 l carmine rose ('47)	5	8
1LNC5	AP60	25 l dark blue	12	18
1LNC6	"	25 l brown ('47)	70	80
1LNC7	AP59	50 l dark green	18	25
		Nos. 1LNC1–1LNC7 (7)	1.20	1.46

Nos. 1LNC5 and 1LNC7 exist with inverted overprint; No. 1LNC5 with double overprint, one inverted.

OCCUPATION SPECIAL DELIVERY STAMPS.

Italy Nos. E20 and E23 Overprinted Type "c" in Black.

1946		*Perf. 14*	Wmk. 277	
1LNE1	SD9	10 l deep blue	12	18
1LNE2	SD8	30 l deep violet	18	25

Issues of ITALIAN SOCIAL REPUBLIC.

On Sept. 15, 1943, Mussolini proclaimed the establishment of a Republican fascist party and a new fascist government. This government's authority covered only the Northern Italy area occupied by the Germans.

Italy Nos. 218, 219, 221 to 223 and 231 Overprinted in Black or Red:

a *b* *c*

1944			*Perf. 14.*	Wmk. 140	
1	A94	(*a*)	25c deep green	6	8
2	A95	(*b*)	30c olive brown (R)	6	8
3	"	(*c*)	50c purple (R)	6	8
4	A94	(*a*)	75c rose red	6	8
5	"	(*b*)	1.25 l dp. blue (R)	6	8
5A	"	(")	50 l dp. violet (R)	225.00	*600.00*

Nos. 1 to 5 exist with overprint inverted. Counterfeits of No. 5A exist.

Italy Nos. 427 to 438 Overprinted Same in Black or Red.

6	A243 (*a*)	25c deep green	18	25
7	A244 (")	25c "	18	25
8	A245 (")	25c "	18	25
9	A246 (")	25c "	18	25
10	A243 (*b*)	30c olive brown (R)	25	30
11	A244 (")	30c " "	25	30
12	A245 (")	30c " "	25	30
13	A246 (")	30c " "	25	30
14	A243 (*c*)	50c purple (R)	12	18
15	A244 (")	50c " "	12	18
16	A245 (")	50c " "	12	18
17	A246 (")	50c " "	12	18
		Nos. 6–17 (12)	2.20	2.92

Loggia dei Mercanti, Bologna A1 — Basilica of San Lorenzo, Rome A2 — Drummer Boy A3

1944		Photogravure	*Perf. 14*	
18	A1	20c crimson	3	5
19	A2	25c green	3	5
20	A3	30c brown	3	5
21	"	75c dark red	3	5

Church of St. Ciriaco, Ancona A4 — Monte Cassino Abbey A5 — Loggia dei Mercanti, Bologna A6

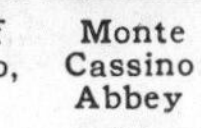
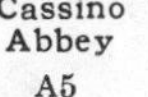

Basilica of San Lorenzo, Rome A7 — Statue of "Rome" A8 — Basilica of St. Maria delle Grazie Milan A9

1944			Unwmkd.	
22	A4	5c brown	5	12
23	A5	10c brown	5	6
24	A6	20c rose red	5	6
25	A7	25c deep green	5	6
26	A3	30c brown	5	12
27	A8	50c purple	5	6
28	A3	75c dark red	12	18
29	A5	1 l purple	5	12
30	A9	1.25 l blue	5	25
31	"	3 l deep green	6	*50*
		Nos. 22–31 (10)	58	*1.53*

Bandiera Brothers A10

1944, Dec. 6				
32	A10	25c deep green	6	*30*
33	A10	1 l purple	6	*42*
34	"	2.50 l rose red	5	*1.75*

To commemorate the centenary of the execution of Attilio Bandiera (1811-44) and Emilio Bandiera (1819-44), revolutionary patriots who were shot at Cosenza, July 23, 1844, by Neapolitan authorities after an unsuccessful raid.

This set was overprinted in 1945 by the committee of the National Philatelic Convention to publicize that gathering at Venice.

SPECIAL DELIVERY STAMPS.

Italy Nos. E14 and E15 Overprinted in Red or Black

REPUBBLICA SOCIALE ITALIANA

1944		*Perf. 14.*	Wmk. 140	
E1	SD4	1.25 l green (R)	6	6
E2	"	2.50 l deep orange	6	25

Cathedral, Palermo SD1

1944			Photogravure	
E3	SD1	1.25 l green	6	12

AUTHORIZED DELIVERY STAMP.

Italy No. EY2 Overprinted

1944		*Perf. 14*	Wmk. 140	
EY1	AD2	10c dark brown	12	12

POSTAGE DUE STAMPS.

Italy Nos. J28 to J40 Overprinted in Black

1944		*Perf. 14*	Wmk. 140	
J1	D6	5c brown	5	10
J2	"	10c blue	5	10
J3	"	20c rose red	5	10
J4	"	25c green	5	10
J5	"	30c red orange	5	10
J6	"	40c black brown	5	10
J7	"	50c violet	5	10
J8	"	60c slate black	50	75
J9	D7	1 l red orange	5	10
J10	"	2 l green	1.10	1.25
J11	"	5 l violet	14.00	18.50
J12	"	10 l blue	22.50	26.50
J13	"	20 l carmine rose	22.50	26.50
		Nos. J1–J13 (13)	61.00	74.30

PARCEL POST STAMPS.

Both unused and used prices are for complete stamps.

Italian Parcel Post Stamps and Types of 1927-39 Overprinted in Black

REP. SOC. ITALIANA

1944		*Perf. 13*	Wmk. 140	
Q1	PP3	5c brown	65	1.50
Q2	"	10c deep blue	65	1.50
Q3	"	25c carmine	65	1.50
Q4	"	30c ultramarine	65	1.50
Q5	"	50c orange	65	1.50
Q6	"	60c red	65	1.50
Q7	"	1 l lilac	65	1.50
Q8	"	2 l green	37.50	65.00
Q9	"	3 l yellow orange	1.65	4.00
Q10	"	4 l gray	1.65	4.00
Q11	"	10 l rose lilac	27.50	50.00

Q12 PP3 20 l lilac brown 80.00 135.00
Nos. Q1-Q12 (12) 152.85 268.50

No parcel post service existed in 1944. Nos. Q1–Q12 were used undivided, for regular postage.

ITALIAN OFFICES ABROAD.

Stamps listed under this heading were issued for use in the Italian Post Offices which, for various reasons, were maintained from time to time in foreign countries.

GENERAL ISSUE.

100 Centesimi=1 Lira

> Prices of early Italian Offices Abroad vary according to condition. Quotations for Nos. 1–11 are for fine copies. Very fine to superb specimens sell at much higher prices, and inferior or poor copies sell at reduced prices, depending on the condition of the individual specimen.

Italian Stamps with Corner Designs Slightly Altered and Overprinted ESTERO

Wmkd. Crown. (140)

1874-78 *Perf. 14.*

1 A6 1c gray green 30 3.75
a. Inverted overprint 5000.00
c. 2 dots in lower right corner 7.50 37.50
d. Three dots in upper right corner 110.00 175.00
e. Without ovpt. 200.00
2 A7 2c orange brown 42 4.25
a. Without ovpt. 150.00
3 A8 5c slate green 42.50 3.00
a. Lower right corner not altered 2000.00 400.00
4 " 10c buff 150.00 9.00
a. Upper left corner not altered 2000.00 250.00
b. None of the corners altered 10,000.00 10,000.00
c. Lower corners not altered 3500.00 550.00
5 " 10c blue ('78) 35.00 1.85
6 A15 20c blue 135.00 4.25
7 " 20c orange ('78) 425.00 1.85
8 A8 30c brown 70 1.20
a. None of the corners altered 5000.00
b. Right lower corner not altered
c. Double ovpt. 550.00
9 " 40c rose 55 1.85
10 " 60c lilac 90 16.00
11 A13 2 l vermilion 16.50 85.00

1881

12 A17 5c green 1.50 1.85
13 " 10c claret 65 75
14 " 20c orange 65 75
a. Double overprint 250.00
15 " 25c blue 65 90
16 " 50c violet 90 11.00
17 " 2 l vermilion 3.50

The "Estero" stamps were used in various parts of the world, South America, Africa, Turkey, etc.

Forged cancellations exist on Nos. 1–2, 9–11, 16.

OFFICES IN CHINA

PEKING.

(pē-king')

100 Cents=1 Dollar

Italian Stamps of 1901-16 Handstamped PECHINO 2 CENTS.

Wmkd. Crown (140), Unwmkd.

1917 *Perf. 12, 13½, 14.*

1 A48 2c on 5c green 17.50 7.50
c. 4c on 5c green 750.00
3 A48 4c on 10c claret (No. 95) 42.50 20.00
c. 4c on 10c claret (No. 79)
5 A58 6c on 15c slate 90.00 40.00
b. 8c on 15c slate 425.00 185.00
7 " 8c on 20c on 15c slate 450.00 175.00
8 A50 8c on 20c brown orange (No. 112) 750.00 275.00
9 A49 20c on 50c violet 3500.00 1100.00
b. 40c on 50c violet 575.00 250.00
11 A46 40c on 1 l brown & green 17,500.00 3000.00

Inverted surcharges are found on Nos. 1, 3, 3c, 5, 7–9; prices same. Double surcharge one inverted exist on Nos. 1, 3; price about double.

Excellent forgeries exist of the higher priced stamps of Offices in China.

Italian Stamps of 1901-16 Overprinted Pechino

1917-18

12 A42 1c brown 90 1.25
13 A43 2c orange brown 90 1.25
a. Double ovpt. 37.50
14 A48 5c green 25 30
a. Double ovpt. 25.00
15 A48 10c claret 25 30
16 A50 20c brown orange (No. 112) 1.60 1.85
17 A49 25c blue 30 35
18 " 50c violet 40 45
19 A46 1 l brown & green 75 90
20 " 5 l blue & rose 90 1.10
21 A51 10 l gray green & red 8.50 11.00
Nos. 12-21 (10) 14.75 18.75

Italy No. 113, the watermarked 20c brown orange, was also overprinted "Pechino," but not issued. Price $1.85.

Italian Stamps of 1901-16 Surcharged:

1 CENT Pechino *a* — 2 dollari Pechino *b*

TWO DOLLARS.
Type I. Surcharged "2 dollari" as illustrated "*b*".
Type II. Surcharged "2 DOLLARI".
Type III. Surcharged "2 dollari". "Pechino" measures 11½ mm. wide, instead of 13 mm.

1918-19 *Perf. 14.*

22 A42 (*a*) ½c on 1c brown 6.25 7.00
a. Surcharged "1 cents" 32.50 32.50
23 A43 (") 1c on 2c orange brown 30 35
a. Surcharged "1 cents" 18.50 18.50
24 A48 (") 2c on 5c green 30 35
25 " (") 4c on 10c claret 30 35
26 A50 (") 8c on 20c brown orange (No. 112) 75 90
27 A49 (") 10c on 25c blue 75 90
28 " (") 20c on 50c violet 75 90
29 A46 (") 40c on 1 l brown & green 10.00 12.00
30 " (*b*) $2 on 5 l blue & rose (type I) 60.00 67.50
a. Type II 12,000.00 7500.00
b. Type III 1500.00 900.00

Italy No. 100 Surcharged 10 CENTS Pechino

1919

32 A49 10c on 25c blue 30 50

SPECIAL DELIVERY STAMPS.

Italian Special Delivery Stamp 1908 Overprinted Pechino

1917 *Perf. 14.* **Wmk. 140**

E1 SD2 30c blue & rose 85 1.10

No. E1 Surcharged 12 CENTS

1918

E2 SD2 12c on 30c blue & rose 8.00 9.50

POSTAGE DUE STAMPS.

Italian Postage Due Stamps Overprinted Pechino

1917 *Perf. 14.* **Wmk. 140**

J1 D3 10c buff & magenta 35 45
J2 " 20c " " 35 45
J3 " 30c " " 35 45
J4 " 40c " " 65 90

Nos. J1-J4 Surcharged 8 CENTS

1918

J5 D3 4c on 10c buff & magenta 9000.00 7500.00
J6 " 8c on 20c buff & magenta 20 30
J7 " 12c on 30c buff & magenta 8.00 10.00
J8 " 16c on 40c buff & magenta 22.50 25.00

In 1919, the same new values were surcharged on Italy Nos. J6–J9 in a different style: four lines to cancel the old denomination, and "-PECHINO- 4 CENTS". These were not issued. Price 90 cents each.

TIENTSIN.

(tin'tsin')

Italian Stamps of 1906 Handstamped TIENTSIN 2 CENTS

Wmkd. Crown (140), Unwmkd.

1917 *Perf. 12, 13½, 14.*

1 A48 2c on 5c green 42.50 20.00
c. 4c on 5c green 2100.00
2 " 4c on 10c claret 80.00 55.00
4 A58 6c on 15c slate 165.00 80.00
b. 4c on 15c slate 400.00 250.00

Italian Stamps of 1901-16 Overprinted Tientsin

1917-18

5 A42 1c brown 1.00 1.35
a. Invtd. ovpt. 22.50 22.50
6 A43 2c orange brown 1.00 1.35
7 A48 5c green 30 38
8 " 10c claret 30 38
9 A50 20c brown orange (No. 112) 1.65 2.00
10 A49 25c blue 35 40
11 " 50c violet 40 45
12 A46 1 l brown & green 80 90
13 " 5 l blue & rose 1.00 1.20
14 A51 10 l gray green & red 9.00 11.00
Nos. 5-14 (10) 15.80 19.41

Italy No. 113, the watermarked 20c brown orange, was also overprinted "Tientsin," but not issued. Price $1.75.

Italian Stamps of 1901-16 Surcharged:

1 CENT Tientsin *a* — 2 Dollari Tientsin *b*

TWO DOLLARS.
Type I. Surcharged "2 Dollari" as illustrated "*b*".
Type II. Surcharged "2 dollari".
Type III. Surcharged "2 Dollari". "Tientsin" measures 10 mm. wide instead of 13 mm.

1918-21 *Perf. 14.*

15 A42 (*a*) ½c on 1c brown 4.75 5.50
a. Inverted surcharge 22.50 22.50
b. Surcharged "1 cents" 37.50 37.50
16 A43 (*a*) 1c on 2c orange brown 35 40
a. Surcharged "1 cents" 22.50 22.50
b. Invtd. surch. 22.50 22.50
17 A48 (") 2c on 5c green 35 40
18 " (") 4c on 10c claret 35 40
19 A50 (") 8c on 20c brn. org. (No. 112) 55 70
20 A49 (") 10c on 25c blue 55 70
21 " (") 20c on 50c violet 80 90
22 A46 (") 40c on 1 l brown & green 7.25 9.00
23 " (*b*) $2 on 5 l blue & rose (I) 55.00 60.00
a. Type II 1750.00 1100.00
b. Type III ('21) 1650.00 950.00
Nos. 15-23 (9) 69.95 78.00

SPECIAL DELIVERY STAMPS.

Italian Special Delivery Stamp of 1908 Overprinted Tientsin

1917 *Perf. 14.* **Wmk. 140**

E1 SD2 30c blue & rose 90 1.15

No. E1 Surcharged 12 CENTS

1918

E2 SD2 12c on 30c blue & rose 8.00 10.00

POSTAGE DUE STAMPS.

Italian Postage Due Stamps Overprinted Tientsin

1917 *Perf. 14.* **Wmk. 140**

J1 D3 10c buff & magenta 35 40
a. Double ovpt. 15.00
J2 " 20c buff & magenta 35 40
J3 " 30c " " 35 40
a. Double ovpt. 15.00
J4 " 40c buff & magenta 60 80

Nos. J1-J4 Surcharged 8 CENTS

1918

J5 D3 4c on 10c buff & magenta 550.00 600.00
J6 " 8c on 20c buff & magenta 20 30
J7 " 12c on 30c buff & magenta 8.00 9.50
J8 " 16c on 40c buff & magenta 21.50 24.00

In 1919, the same new values were surcharged on Italy Nos. J6–J9 in a different style: four lines to cancel the old denomination, and "-TIENTSIN- 4 CENTS". These were not issued. Price 90 cents each.

OFFICES IN CRETE

40 Paras=1 Piastre
100 Centesimi=1 Lira (1906)

Italy Nos. 70 and 81 Surcharged in Red or Black

1 PIASTRA 1 *a* — LA CANEA 1 PIASTRA 1 *b*

1900-01 *Perf. 14.* **Wmk. 140**

1 A36 (*a*) 1pi on 25c blue 80 55
2 A45 (*b*) 1pi on 25c deep blue (Bk) ('01) 80 55

Italian Stamps Overprinted LA CANEA

1906

On Stamps of 1901–16

3 A42 1c brown 15 15
a. Pair, one without ovpt. 60.00
4 A43 2c orange brown 15 10
a. Imperf., pair 150.00
b. Double ovpt. 37.50

5 A44 5c blue green 30 20
6 A45 10c claret 55.00 27.50
7 " 15c on 20c orange 35 30
8 " 25c blue 1.10 1.00
9 " 40c brown 80 80
10 " 45c olive green 70 80
11 " 50c violet 90 95
12 A46 1 l brown & green 2.65 2.65
13 " 5 l blue & rose 32.50 40.00
Nos. 3-13 (11) 94.60 74.45

1907-10

On Stamps of 1906-08.

14 A48 5c green 15 20
a. Inverted overprint 60.00
15 " 10c claret 20 27
16 A49 25c blue 35 40
17 " 40c brown 3.25 3.50
18 " 50c violet 45 55
Nos. 14-18 (5) 4.40 4.92

On Stamp of 1909.
Violet Overprint.

1912 *Perf. 13x13½.* **Unwmkd.**

19 A50 15c slate black 20 30

SPECIAL DELIVERY STAMP.

Special Delivery Stamp of Italy Overprinted LA CANEA

1906 *Perf. 14.* **Wmk. 140**

E1 SD1 25c rose red 65 75

OFFICES IN AFRICA

40 Paras—1 Piastre
100 Centesimi=1 Lira (1910)

BENGASI

Italy No. 81 Surcharged in Black BENGASI 1 PIASTRA 1

1901 **Wmkd. Crown. (140)** *Perf. 14.*

1 A45 1pi on 25c deep blue 10.00 4.25

Same Surcharge on Italy No. 100.

1911

2 A49 1pi on 25c blue 7.00 5.50

TRIPOLI

Italian Stamps of 1901–09 Overprinted in Black or Violet Tripoli di Barberia

1909 **Wmk. 140**

2 A42 1c brown 20 30
a. Inverted overprint 22.50
3 A43 2c orange brown 30 35
4 A48 5c green 8.00 1.75
a. Double ovpt. 60.00
5 " 10c claret 30 35
a. Double ovpt. 30.00 30.00
6 A49 25c blue 45 40
7 " 40c brown 55 45
8 " 50c violet 60 55

Perf. 13½x14 **Unwmkd.**

9 A50 15c slate black (V) 35 35
Nos. 2-9 (8) 10.75 4.50

Italian Stamps of 1901 Overprinted TRIPOLI DI BARBERIA

1909 *Perf. 14.* **Wmk. 140**

10 A46 1 l brown & green 45.00 15.00
11 " 5 l blue & rose 20.00 22.50

Same Overprint on Italy Nos. 76-77.

1915

12 A42 1c brown 40
13 A43 2c orange brown 30

Nos. 12-13 were prepared but not issued.

SPECIAL DELIVERY STAMPS.

Italy Nos. E1, E6 Overprinted TRIPOLI DI BARBERIA

1909 *Perf. 14.* **Wmk. 140**

E1 SD1 25c rose red 50 60
E2 SD2 30c blue & rose 1.50 1.75

Tripoli was ceded by Turkey to Italy in October, 1912, and became known as the Colony of Libia. Later issues will be found under Libya.

OFFICES IN THE TURKISH EMPIRE

40 Paras=1 Piastre

Various powers maintained post offices in the Turkish Empire before World War I by authority of treaties which ended with the signing of the Treaty of Lausanne in 1923. The foreign post offices were closed Oct. 27, 1923.

GENERAL ISSUES.

Italian Stamps of 1906-08

Surcharged 10 Parà 10

Printed at Turin.
Wmkd. Crown (140) or Unwmkd., as in Italy.

1908 *Perf. as in Italy*

1 A48 10pa on 5c green 20 20
2 " 20pa on 10c claret 30 20
3 A49 40pa on 25c blue 35 20
4 " 80pa on 50c violet 45 30

See also Janina Nos. 1-4.

Surcharged in Violet 30 Parà 30

5 A47 30pa on 15c slate 20 20
Nos. 1-5 (5) 1.50 1.10

Nos. 1, 2, 3 and 5 were first issued in Janina, Albania, and subsequently for general use. They can only be distinguished by the cancellations.

Italian Stamps of 1901-08 Surcharged:

10 PARA (a)

1 PIASTRA (b) 2 PIASTRE (c)

Printed at Constantinople.

1908 **First Printing.**

6 A48 (a) 10pa on 5c grn. 42.50 27.50
7 " (") 20pa on 10c claret 42.50 27.50
8 A47 (") 30pa on 15c slate 165.00 120.00
9 A49 (b) 1pi on 25c blue 165.00 120.00
a. "PIASTRE" 200.00 150.00
10 " (c) 2pi on 50c violet 350.00 225.00
11 A46 (") 4pi on 1 l brown &green *1500.00* *900.00*
12 " (") 20pi on 5 l blue & rose *4750.00* *3000.00*

On Nos. 8, 9 and 10 the surcharge is at the top of the stamp. No. 11 has the "4" closed at the top. No. 12 has the "20" wide, as in type "c".

Second Printing.
Surcharged:

10 PARA (d)

1 PIASTRA (e) 2 PIASTRE (f)

13 A48 (d) 10pa on 5c green 40 40
14 " (") 20pa on 10c claret 40 40
15 A47 (") 30pa on 15c slate 3.25 2.25
a. Double surch. 15.00 15.00
16 A49 (e) 1pi on 25c blue 90 75
a. "PIPSTRA" 11.50 11.50
b. "1" omitted 11.50 11.50
17 A49 (f) 2pi on 50c violet 11.00 11.00
a. Surcharged "20 PIASTRE" 90.00 75.00
b. "20" with "0" scratched out 37.50 37.50
c. "2" 5 mm. from "PIASTRE" 30.00 30.00
18 A46 (") 4pi on 1 l brown & green 235.00 150.00
19 " (") 20pi on 5 l blue & rose 800.00 475.00
Nos. 13-19 (7) 1050.95 639.80

On No. 18 the "4" is open at the top.

Third Printing.

Surcharged in Red 30 PARA

20 A47 30pa on 15c slate 40 30
a. Dbl. surcharge 15.00 15.00

Fourth Printing.
Surcharged:

4 PIASTRE (h) 4 20 PIASTRE (i) 20

20B A46 (h) 4pi on 1 l brown & green 10.00 4.00
c. Inverted "S" 24.00 12.00
20D A46 (i) 20pi on 5 l blue & rose 37.50 20.00
i. Inverted "S" 115.00 60.00

Fifth Printing.
Surcharged:

4 PIASTRE (k) 4 20 PIASTRE (l) 20

20E A46 (k) 4pi on 1 l brown & green 6.75 3.75
f. Surch. "20 PIASTRE" 235.00
20G " (l) 20pi on 5 l blue & rose 6.75 3.75
h. Dbl. surch. 225.00 200.00

Italian Stamps of 1906-19

Surcharged 2 PIASTRE

1921

21 A48 1pi on 5c green 47.50 55.00
22 " 2pi on 15c slate 20 20
23 A50 4pi on 20c brn. org. (No. 113) 1.75 2.50
24 A49 5pi on 25c blue 1.75 2.50
a. Dbl. surch. 45.00
25 A49 10pi on 60c carmine 20 20
Nos. 21-25 (5) 51.40 60.40

On No. 25 the "10" is placed above "PIASTRE".

Italian Stamps of 1901-19 Surcharged

PARA 30 (n) PIASTRE 1 PARA 20 (o)

1922

26 A42 (n) 10pa on 1c brown 25 35
27 A43 (") 20pa on 2c orange brown 25 35
28 A48 (") 30pa on 5c green 35 40
29 " (o) 1pi 20pa on 15c slate 50 35
30 A50 (n) 3pi on 20c brown orange (No. 113) 2.75 1.15
31 A49 (o) 3pi 30pa on 25c blue 55 55
32 (") 7pi 20pa on 60c carmine 70 40
33 A46 (n) 15pi on 1 l brown & green 1.65 2.35
Nos. 26-33 (8) 7.00 5.90

Italy No. 100 Surcharged Piastre 3,75

34 A49 3.75pi on 25c blue 30 35

Italian Stamps of 1901-20
Surcharged:

30 PARÀ (q) PIASTRE 3,75 (r)

1922

35 A48 (q) 30pa on 5c grn. 1.50 2.00
36 A49 (r) 1.50pi on 25c blue 40 55
37 " (") 3.75pi on 40c brown 25 25
38 " (") 4.50pi on 50c violet 40 40
39 " (") 7.50pi on 60c car. 45 50
40 " (") 15pi on 85c red brown 1.50 2.00
41 A46 (") 18.75pi on 1 l brown & green 1.25 1.35

On No. 40 the numerals of the surcharge are above "PIASTRE".

Surcharged 45 PIASTRE

42 A46 45pi on 5 l blue & rose 50.00 55.00
43 A51 90pi on 10 l gray green & red 65.00 75.00

Italian Stamps of 1901–17 Surcharged 1,50 PIASTRE (t)

44 A43 (q) 30pa on 2c orange brown 15 20
45 A50 (t) 1.50pi on 20c brown orange (No. 113) 30 35
Nos. 35-45 (11) 121.20 137.60

Italian Stamps of 1901-20 Surcharged in Black or Red 1½ PIASTRE

46 A48 30pa on 5c green 15 20
47 " 1½pi on 10c claret 20 25
48 A49 3pi on 25c blue 35 35
49 " 3¾pi on 40c brown 35 25
50 " 4½pi on 50c violet 5.50 5.50
51 " 7½pi on 85c red brn. 1.00 1.10
a. "PIASIRE" 4.50 4.50
52 A46 7½pi on 1 l brown & green (R) 1.35 1.50
a. Double surch. 22.50 22.50
b. "PIASIRE" 6.75 6.75
53 " 15pi on 1 l brown & green 20.00 21.50
54 " 45pi on 5 l blue & rose 9.50 11.00
55 A51 90pi on 10 l gray green & red 9.50 11.00
Nos. 46-55 (10) 47.90 52.65

Italian Stamps of 1901-20
Surcharged:

4 PIASTRE 20 PARA (v) 15 PIASTRE (w)

45 PIASTRE (x)

1923

56 A49 (o) 1pi 20pa on 25c blue 2.00
57 " (") 3pi 30pa on 40c brown 2.00
58 " (v) 4pi 20pa on 50c violet 2.00
58A " (o) 7pi20pa on 60c carmine 12.00
59 " (w) 15pi on 85c red brown 2.00
60 A46 (o) 18pi 30pa on 1 l brn. & green 2.75
61 " (x) 45pi on 5 l blue & rose 2.00
62 A51 (") 90pi on 10 l gray green & red 2.00
Nos. 56-62 (8) 26.75

Nos. 56-62 were not issued.

SPECIAL DELIVERY STAMPS.

Italian Special Delivery Stamps Surcharged.

1908 *Perf. 14.* **Wmk. 140**

Surcharged LEVANTE 1 PIASTRA 1

E1 SD1 1pi on 25c rose red 30 30

Surcharged LEVANTE 60 Parà 60

1910

E2 SD2 60pa on 30c blue & rose 40 40

Surcharged 15 PIASTRE

1922

E3 SD2 15pi on 1.20 l on 30c blue & rose 3.25 4.00

On No. E3, lines obliterate the first two denominations.

Surcharged 15 PIASTRE

E4 SD2 15pi on 30c blue & rose 55.00 60.00

Surcharged 15 PIASTRE

1924

E5 SD2 15pi on 1.20 l blue & red 1.65

No. E5 was not regularly issued.

ALBANIA.

Stamps of Italy Surcharged in Black ALBANIA 10 Parà 10

1902 *Perf. 14.* **Wmk. 140**

1 A44 10pa on 5c green 40 35
2 A45 35pa on 20c orange 1.60 1.35
3 " 40pa on 25c blue 1.35 1.00

1907

4 A48 10pa on 5c green 8.00 9.00
5 " 20pa on 10c claret 2.00 1.35
6 A45 80pa on 50c violet 2.65 2.65

CONSTANTINOPLE.

(kŏn'stăn·tĭ·nō'p'l)

Stamps of Italy Surcharged in Black or Violet Costantinopoli 10 Parà 10

Wmk. 140, Unwmkd. (*3)

1909–11 *Perf. 14, 12*

1 A48 10pa on 5c green 20 20
2 " 20pa on 10c claret 20 20
3 A47 30pa on 15c slate (V) 20 20
4 A49 1pi on 25c blue 20 20
a. Dbl. surch. 15.00 15.00
5 " 2pi on 50c violet 27 27

Surcharged COSTANTINOPOLI 4 PIASTRE 4

6 A46 4pi on 1 l brown & green 38 27
7 " 20pi on 5 l blue & rose 1.50 1.65
8 A51 40pi on 10 l gray green & red 1.15 1.65
Nos. 1-8 (8) 4.10 4.64

Italian Stamps of 1901-19 Surcharged:

COSTANTINOPOLI PIASTRE 1 PARA 20 *a* — COSTANTINOPOLI PIASTRE 3 *b*

1922

9 A48 (*b*) 20pa on 5c green 2.00 2.35
10 " (*a*) 1pi 20pa on 15c slate 13 20
11 A49 (*b*) 3pi on 30c orange brown 20 27
12 " (*a*) 3pi 30pa on 40c brown 20 27
13 A46 (") 7pi 20pa on 1 l brown & green 20 27
Nos. 9-13 (5) 2.73 3.36

Italian Stamps of 1901-20 Surcharged COSTANTINOPOLI PIASTRE 1 PARÀ 20

1923

14 A48 30pa on 5c green 33 40
15 A49 1pi 20pa on 25c blue 33 40
16 " 3pi 30pa on 40c brown 33 40
17 " 4pi 20pa on 50c violet 33 40
18 " 7pi 20pa on 60c car. 33 40
19 " 15pi on 85c red brown 33 40
20 A46 18pi 30pa on 1 l brown & green 50 55
21 " 45pi on 5 l blue & rose 60 70
22 A51 90pi on 10 l gray green & red 95 1.10
Nos. 14-22 (9) 4.03 4.75

SPECIAL DELIVERY STAMP.

King Victor Emmanuel III
SD1

Type of Italian Special Delivery Stamp of 1909 Surcharged in Black.

Wmkd. Crowns. (140)

1923 *Perf. 14.*

E1 SD1 15pi on 1.20 l blue & red 80 1.10

POSTAGE DUE STAMPS.

Italian Postage Due Stamps of 1870-1903 Overprinted Costantinopoli

Wmkd. Crown. (140)

1922 *Perf. 14.*

J1 D3 10c buff & magenta 65 65
J2 " 30c buff & magenta 65 65
J3 " 60c buff & magenta 65 65
J4 " 1 l blue & magenta 65 65
J5 " 2 l bl. & magenta *400.00* *375.00*
J6 " 5 l blue & magenta 67.50 60.00
Nos. J1-J6 (6) *470.10* *437.60*

A circular control mark, having the appearance of a cancellation, was applied to each block of four of these stamps.

DURAZZO.

(dŏŏ·rät'sō)

Stamps of Italy Surcharged in Black or Violet Durazzo 10 Parà 10

Wmk. 140, Unwmkd. (*3)

1909–11 *Perf. 14, 12*

1 A48 10pa on 5c green 20 40
2 " 20pa on 10c claret 20 27
3 A47 30pa on 15c slate (V) 3.00 1.35
4 A49 1pi on 25c blue 20 27
5 " 2pi on 50c violet 20 27

Surcharged DURAZZO 4 PIASTRE 4

6 A46 4pi on 1 l brown & green 35 40
7 " 20pi on 5 l blue & rose 17.50 17.50
8 A51 40pi on 10 l gray green & red 5.50 11.00
Nos. 1-8 (8) 27.15 31.46

No. 3 Surcharged ≡ CENT 20 ≡

1916 *Perf. 12* **Unwmkd.**

9 A47 20c on 30pa on 15c slate 70 1.35

JANINA.

(yä'nē·nä)

Stamps of Italy Surcharged 10 Parà 10

Wmkd. Crown. (140)

1902-07 *Perf. 14.*

1 A44 10pa on 5c green 40 40
2 A45 35pa on 20c orange 60 85
3 " 40pa on 25c blue 6.00 2.00
4 " 80pa on 50c violet ('07) 6.00 4.50

Surcharged in Black or Violet Janina 10 Parà 10

1909–11 *Perf. 14, 12*

Wmk. 140, Unwmkd. (*7)

5 A48 10pa on 5c green 20 27
6 " 20pa on 10c claret 20 27
7 A47 30pa on 15c slate (V) 20 27
8 A49 1pi on 25c blue 20 27
9 " 2pi on 50c violet 38 40

Surcharged JANINA 4 PIASTRE 4

10 A46 4pi on 1 l brown & green 50 60
11 " 20pi on 5 l blue & rose 27.50 27.50
12 A51 40pi on 10 l gray green & red 5.50 11.50
Nos. 5-12 (8) 34.68 41.08

JERUSALEM.

(jē·rōō'sȧ·lĕm)

Stamps of Italy Surcharged in Black or Violet Gerusalemme 10 Parà 10

Wmk. 140, Unwmkd. (*3)

1909–11 *Perf. 14, 12*

1 A48 10pa on 5c green 40 *2.00*
2 " 20pa on 10c claret 40 *2.00*
3 A47 30pa on 15c slate (V) 40 *2.00*
4 A49 1pi on 25c blue 40 *2.00*
5 " 2pi on 50c violet 70 *5.00*

Surcharged GERUSALEMME 4 PIASTRE 4

6 A46 4pi on 1 l brown & green 1.10 *11.00*
7 " 20pi on 5 l blue & rose 80.00 *150.00*
8 A51 40pi on 10 l gray green & red 10.00 *65.00*
Nos. 1-8 (8) 93.40 *239.00*

Forged cancellations exist on Nos. 1–8.

SALONIKA.

(sä'lō·nē'kȧ)

Stamps of Italy Surcharged in Black or Violet Salonicco 10 Parà 10

Wmk. 140, Unwmkd. (*3)

1909–11 *Perf. 14, 12*

1 A48 10pa on 5c green 20 27
2 " 20pa on 10c claret 20 27
3 A47 30pa on 15c slate (V) 20 27
4 A49 1pi on 25c blue 20 27
5 " 2pi on 50c violet 38 40

Surcharged SALONICCO 4 PIASTRE 4

6 A46 4pi on 1 l brown & green 50 70
7 A46 20pi on 5 l blue & rose 55.00 57.50
8 A51 40pi on 10 l gray green & red 5.50 11.00
Nos. 1-8 (8) 62.18 70.68

SCUTARI.

(skōō'ta·rē)

Stamps of Italy Surcharged in Black or Violet Scutari di Albania 10 Parà 10

Wmk. 140, Unwmkd. (*3)

1909–11 *Perf. 14, 12*

1 A48 10pa on 5c green 20 27
2 " 20pa on 10c claret 20 27
3 A47 30pa on 15c slate(V) 3.00 1.35
4 A49 1pi on 25c blue 20 27
5 " 2pi on 50c violet 35 40

Surcharged SCUTARI DI ALBANIA 4 PIASTRE 4

6 A46 4pi on 1 l brown & green 40 50
7 " 20pi on 5 l blue & rose 1.10 1.35
8 A51 40pi on 10 l gray green & red 15.00 20.00
Nos. 1-8 (8) 20.45 24.41

Surcharged like Nos. 1–5

1915

9 A43 4pa on 2c orange brown 20 27

No. 3 Surcharged ≡ CENT 20 ≡

1916 *Perf. 12* **Unwmkd.**

10 A47 20c on 30pa on 15c slate 70 1.35

SMYRNA.

(smûr'nȧ)

Stamps of Italy Surcharged in Black or Violet Smirne 10 Parà 10

Wmk. 140, Unwmkd. (*3)

1909–11 *Perf. 14, 12*

1 A48 10pa on 5c green 20 13
2 " 20pa on 10c claret 20 13
3 A47 30pa on 15c slate (V) 20 13
4 A49 1pi on 25c blue 20 13
5 " 2pi on 50c violet 35 35

Surcharged SMIRNE 4 PIASTRE 4

6 A46 4pi on 1 l brown & green 50 50
7 " 20pi on 5 l blue & rose 1.75 2.00
8 A51 40pi on 10 l gray green & red 5.50 8.00
Nos. 1-8 (8) 8.90 11.37

Italian Stamps of 1901-22 Surcharged:

SMIRNE PIASTRE 1 PARÀ 20 *a* — SMIRNE PIASTRE 3 *b*

1922

9 A48 (*b*) 20pa on 5c green 1.50
10 " (*a*) 1pi 20pa on 15c slate 13
11 A49 (*b*) 3pi on 30c org. brn. 13
12 " (*a*) 3pi 30pa on 40c brown 13
13 A46 (") 7pi 20pa on 1 l brown & green 13
Nos. 9-13 (5) 2.02

Nos. 9–13 were not issued.

VALONA.

(vȧ·lō′nä)

Stamps of Italy Surcharged in Black or Violet **Valona 10 Parà 10**

Wmk. 140, Unwmkd. (#3)

1909–11 *Perf. 14, 12*

1 A48 10pa on 5c green 20 27
2 " 20pa on 10c claret 20 27
3 A47 30pa on 15c slate (V) 3.00 1.35
4 A49 1pi on 25c blue 20 27
5 " 2pi on 50c violet 27 35

Surcharged **VALONA 4 PIASTRE 4**

6 A46 4pi on 1 l brown & green 35 40
7 " 20pi on 5 l blue & rose 1.20 1.50
8 A51 40pi on 10 l gray green & red 16.00 22.50
Nos. 1-8 (8) 21.42 26.91

Italy No. 123 Surcharged in Violet or Red Violet **VALONA 30 PARA 30**

1916

9 A58 30pa on 15c slate(V) 40 70
a. Red violet surcharge 70 1.35

No. 9 Surcharged **CENT 20**

10 A58 20c on 30pa on 15c slate 20 40

AEGEAN ISLANDS

(ē·jē′ȧn ī′lȧndz)

(Dodecanese.)

A group of islands in the Aegean Sea off the coast of Turkey. They were occupied by Italy during the Tripoli War and were ceded to Italy by Turkey in 1924 by the Treaty of Lausanne. Stamps of Italy overprinted with the name of the island were in use at the post offices maintained in the various islands.

Rhodes, on the island of the same name, was capital of the entire group.

100 Centesimi = 1 Lira

GENERAL ISSUE.

Italian Stamps of 1907–08 Overprinted **EGEO**

1912 *Perf. 14* **Wmkd. Crown. (140)**

1 A49 25c blue 2.25 2.00
a. Inverted ovpt. 37.50 30.00
2 " 50c violet 2.25 2.00
a. Inverted ovpt. 37.50 30.00

Virgil Issue.

Types of Italian Stamps of 1930 Overprinted in Red or Blue

ISOLE ITALIANE DELL'EGEO

Wmkd. Crowns. (140)

1930 Photogravure *Perf. 14*

3 A106 15c violet black 40 55
4 " 20c orange brown 40 55
5 " 25c dark green 40 55
6 " 30c light brown 40 55
7 " 50c dull violet 40 55
8 " 75c rose red 40 55
9 " 1.25 l gray blue 40 55

Engraved.

Unwmkd.

10 A106 5 l+1.50 l dk. vio. 2.00 3.50
11 " 10 l+2.50 l olive brown 2.00 3.50
Nos. 3-11, C4-C7 (13) 12.05 17.60

St. Anthony of Padua Issue.

Types of Italian Stamps of 1931 Overprinted in Blue or Red **ISOLE ITALIANE DELL'EGEO**

Wmkd. Crowns. (140)

1932 Photogravure. *Perf. 14.*

12 A116 20c black brown 4.00 4.00
13 " 25c dull green 4.00 4.00
14 A118 30c brown orange 4.00 4.00
15 " 50c dull violet 4.00 4.00
16 A120 1.25 l gray blue 4.00 4.00

Engraved

Unwmkd.

17 A121 75c light red 4.00 4.00
18 A122 5 l+2.50 l dp. org. 4.00 4.00
Nos. 12-18 (7) 28.00 28.00

Dante Alighieri Society Issue.

Types of Italian Stamps of 1932 Overprinted

ISOLE DELL' ITALIANE EGEO

1932 Photogravure **Wmk. 140**

19 A126 10c greenish gray 20 25
20 " 15c black violet 20 25
21 " 20c brown orange 20 25
22 " 25c deep green 20 25
23 " 30c deep orange 20 25
24 " 50c dull violet 20 25
25 " 75c rose red 40 50
26 " 1.25 l blue 50 60
27 " 1.75 l olive brown 60 75
28 " 2.75 l carmine rose 70 90
29 " 5 l+2 l dp. violet 80 1.00
30 " 10 l+2.50 l dark brown 95 1.15
Nos. 19-30 (12) 5.15 6.40

See Nos. C8–C14.

Soccer Issue.

Types of Italy, "Soccer" Issue, Overprinted in Black or Red

ISOLE ITALIANE DELL'EGEO

1934

31 A173 20c brown rose (Bk) 3.00 3.25
32 A174 25c green (R) 3.00 3.25
33 " 50c violet (R) 25.00 2.00
34 " 1.25 l gray blue (R) 4.00 6.50
35 A175 5 l+2.50 l blue (R) 5.00 8.50
Nos. 31-35 (5) 40.00 23.50

See Nos. C28–C31.

Types of Medal of Valor Issue of Italy, Overprinted in Red or Black

ISOLE ITALIANE DELL'EGEO

1935

36 A177 10c slate gray (R) 12.00 13.50
37 A178 15c brown (Bk) 12.00 13.50
38 " 20c red orange (Bk) 12.00 13.50
39 A177 25c dp grn. (R) 12.00 13.50
40 A178 30c lake (Bk) 12.00 13.50
41 " 50c olive green (Bk) 12.00 13.50
42 " 75c rose red (Bk) 12.00 13.50
43 " 1.25 l deep blue (R) 12.00 13.50
44 A177 1.75 l+1 l pur. (R) 5.00 13.50
45 A178 2.55 l+2 l dark carmine (Bk) 5.00 13.50
46 " 2.75 l+2 l orange brown (Bk) 5.00 13.50
Nos. 36-46 (11) 111.00 148.50

See Nos. C32–C38, CE3–CE4.

Types of Italy, 1937, Overprinted in Blue or Red **ISOLE ITALIANE DELL'EGEO**

1938 *Perf. 14.* **Wmk. 140**

47 A208 10c dark brown (Bl) 25 33
48 " 15c purple (R) 25 33
49 " 20c yellow bistre (Bl) 25 33
50 " 25c myrtle green (R) 25 33
51 " 30c deep claret (Bl) 25 33
52 A208 50c slate green (R) 25 33
53 " 75c rose red (Bl) 50 65
54 " 1.25 l dark blue (R) 50 65
55 " 1.75 l+1 l deep orange (Bl) 2.75 3.25
56 " 2.55 l+2 l olive brown (R) 2.75 3.25
Nos. 47-56 (10) 8.00 9.78

Bimillenary of birth of Augustus Caesar (Octavianus), first Roman emperor. See Nos. C39–C43.

Type of Italy, 1937, Overprinted in Red **ISOLE ITALIANE DELL'EGEO**

1938

57 A222 1.25 l deep blue 80 55
58 " 2.75 l+2 l brown 80 1.10

Issued to commemorate the 600th anniversary of the death of Giotto di Bondone, Italian painter.

Statue of Roman Wolf
A1

Arms of Rhodes
A2

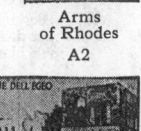

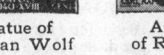

Dante's House, Rhodes
A3

1940 Photogravure

59 A1 5c light brown 12 12
60 A2 10c pale orange 12 12
61 A3 25c blue green 50 50
62 A1 50c rose violet 50 50
63 A2 75c dull vermilion 50 50
64 A3 1.25 l dull blue 50 50
65 A2 2 l + 75c rose 50 50
Nos. 59-65, C44-C47 (11) 6.84 6.84

Triennial Overseas Exposition, Naples.

AIR POST STAMPS.

Ferrucci Issue.

Types of Italian Air Post Stamps of 1930 Overprinted in Blue or Red **ISOLE ITALIANE DELL'EGEO**

1930 *Perf. 14* **Wmk. 140**

C1 AP7 50c brown violet (Bl) 50 1.00
C2 " 1 l dark blue (R) 50 1.00
C3 " 5 l+2 l deep carmine (Bl) 4.00 5.75

Nos. C1 to C3 were sold at Rhodes only.

Virgil Issue.

Types of Italian Air Post Stamps of 1930 Overprinted in Red or Blue

ISOLE ITALIANE DELL'EGEO

Photogravure.

C4 AP8 50c deep green (R) 1.10 65
C5 " 1 l rose red (Bl) 85 1.10

Engraved

Unwmkd.

C6 AP8 7.70 l+1.30 l dark brown (R) 1.65 2.50
C7 " 9 l+2 l gray (R) 1.65 2.50

Dante Alighieri Society Issue.

Types of Italian Air Post Stamps of 1932 Overprinted

ISOLE DELL' ITALIANE EGEO

1932 **Wmkd. Crowns. (140)**

C8 AP10 50c carmine rose 60 80
C9 AP11 1 l deep green 30 40
C10 AP11 3 l dull violet 30 40
C11 " 5 l deep orange 30 40
C12 AP10 7.70 l+2 l olive brown 75 1.00
C13 AP11 10 l+2.50 l dark blue 75 1.00
Nos. C8-C13 (6) 3.00 4.00

Leonardo da Vinci
AP12

1932 Photogravure. *Perf. 14½*

C14 AP12 100 l deep blue & greenish gray 11.00 12.00

Types of Italian Air Post Stamps of 1932 (Garibaldi Commemorative Issue) Overprinted in Red or Blue **ISOLE ITALIANE DELL'EGEO**

1932

C15 AP13 50c deep green 6.00 7.50
C16 AP14 80c copper red 6.00 7.50
C17 AP13 1 l+25c dull blue 6.00 7.50
C18 " 2 l+50c red brown 6.00 7.50
C19 AP14 5 l+1 l bluish slate 6.00 7.50
Nos. C15-C19 (5) 30.00 37.50

See Nos. CE1–CE2.

Graf Zeppelin over Rhodes
AP17

1933 *Perf. 14.*

C20 AP17 3 l olive brown 40.00 30.00
C21 " 5 l deep violet 12.00 *30.00*
C22 " 10 l dark green 12.00 *30.00*
C23 " 12 l dark blue 12.00 *30.00*
C24 " 15 l carmine rose 12.00 *30.00*
C25 " 20 l gray black 12.00 *30.00*
Nos. C20-C25 (6) 100.00 *180.00*

Balbo Flight Issue.

Types of Italian Air Post Stamps of 1933 Overprinted

ISOLE ITALIANE DELL EGEO

1933 *Perf. 14.* **Wmk. 140**

C26 AP25 5.25 l+19.75 l green, red & blue gray 37.50 *50.00*
C27 AP26 5.25 l+44.75 l red, grn. & blue gray 37.50 *50.00*

Soccer Issue.

Types of Italian Air Post Stamps of 1934 Overprinted in Black or Red

ISOLE ITALIANE DELL'EGEO

1934

C28 AP32 50c brown (R) 1.20 2.50
C29 AP33 75c rose red (Bk) 1.20 2.50
C30 AP34 5 l+2.50 l red orange (Bk) 4.75 6.50
C31 AP35 10 l+5 l grn. (R) 4.75 6.50

Types of Medal of Valor Issue of Italy Overprinted in Red or Black

ISOLE ITALIANE DELL'EGEO

1935

C32 AP36 25c deep green (Bk) 20.00 16.50

C33 AP36 50c black brown (R) 20.00 16.50
C34 " 75c rose (Bk) 20.00 16.50
C35 " 80c dark brown (Bk) 20.00 16.50
C36 " 1 l + 50c olive green (Bk) 10.00 16.50
C37 " 2 l + 1 l deep blue (R) 10.00 16.50
C38 AP40 3 l + 2 l violet (R) 10.00 16.50
Nos. C32-C38 (7) 110.00 115.50

Types of Italy Air Post Stamps, 1937, Overprinted in Blue or Red ISOLE ITALIANE DELL'EGEO

1938 ***Perf. 14.*** **Wmk. 140**

C39 AP51 25c dull gray violet (R) 55 55
C40 " 50c green (R) 70 70
C41 " 80c bright blue (R) 80 80
C42 " 1 l + 1 l rose lake (Bl) 4.00 4.00
C43 " 5 l + 1 l rose red (Bl) 5.50 5.50
Nos. C39-C43 (5) 11.55 11.55

Bimillenary of the birth of Augustus Caesar (Octavianus).

Statues of Stag and Roman Wolf AP18

Plane over Government Palace, Rhodes—AP19

1940 Photogravure.

C44 AP18 50c olive black 90 90
C45 AP19 1 l dark violet 90 90
C46 AP18 2 l + 75c dark blue 1.15 1.15
C47 AP19 5 l + 2.50 l copper brown 1.15 1.15

Triennial Overseas Exposition, Naples.

AIR POST SPECIAL DELIVERY STAMPS.

Type of Italian Garibaldi Air Post Special Delivery Stamps Overprinted in Blue or Ochre ISOLE ITALIANE DELL'EGEO

1932 ***Perf. 14*** **Wmkd. Crowns. (140)**

CE1 APSD1 2.25 l + 1 l blue & rose (Bl) 6.00 7.50
CE2 " 4.50 l + 1.50 l ochre & gray (O) 6.00 7.50

Types of Medal of Valor Issue of Italy, Overprinted in Black ISOLE ITALIANE DELL'EGEO

1935

CE3 APSD4 2 l + 1.25 l deep blue 10.00 16.50
CE4 " 4.50 l + 2 l green 10.00 16.50

ISSUES FOR THE INDIVIDUAL ISLANDS.

Italian Stamps of 1901-20 Overprinted with Names of Various Islands as Caso *a* CASO *b*

The 1912-22 issues of each island have type "a" overprint in black on all values except 15c (type A58) and 20c on 15c, which have type "b" overprint in violet.

CALCHI.

(käl'kē)

Overprinted "Karki" in Black or Violet

1912-22 ***Perf. 13½, 14*** **Wmk. 140**

1 A43 2c orange brown 1.15 55
a. Double overprint 45.00
2 A48 5c green 13 20
a. Double overprint 45.00
3 A48 10c claret 13 20
4 " 15c slate ('22) 1.65 2.00
a. Double overprint 50.00
5 A50 20c brn. org. ('21) 90 1.65
6 A49 25c blue 20 27
7 " 40c brown 20 27
8 " 50c violet 20 27

Unwmkd.

9 A58 15c slate (V) 4.75 2.35
10 A50 20c brn. org. ('17) 16.00 17.50
Nos. 1-10 (10) 25.31 25.26

No. 9 Surcharged CENT 20

1916 ***Perf. 13½***

11 A58 20c on 15c slate 20 35

Ferrucci Issue.

Types of Italian Stamps of 1930 Overprinted in Red or Blue CALCHI

1930 ***Perf. 14.*** **Wmk. 140**

12 A102 20c violet (R) 18 22
13 A103 25c dark green (R) 18 22
14 " 50c black (R) 18 22
15 " 1.25 l deep blue (R) 18 22
16 A104 5 l + 2 l deep carmine (Bl) 1.10 1.25
Nos. 12-16 (5) 1.82 2.13

Garibaldi Issue.

Types of Italian Stamps of 1932 Overprinted in Red or Blue CARCHI

1932

17 A138 10c brown 1.00 1.00
18 " 20c red brown (Bl) 1.00 1.00
19 " 25c deep green 1.00 1.00
20 " 30c bluish slate 1.00 1.00
21 " 50c red violet (Bl) 1.00 1.00
22 A141 75c copper red (Bl) 1.00 1.00
23 " 1.25 l dull blue 1.00 1.00
24 " 1.75 l + 25c brown 1.00 1.00
25 A144 2.55 l + 50c org. (Bl) 1.00 1.00
26 A145 5 l + 1 l dull violet 1.00 1.00
Nos. 17-26 (10) 10.00 10.00

CALINO.

(kä-lē'nō)

Overprinted "Calimno" in Black or Violet

1912-21 ***Perf. 13½, 14*** **Wmk. 140**

1 A43 2c orange brown 1.15 55
2 A48 5c green 27 20
3 " 10c claret 13 20
4 " 15c slate ('21) 1.00 1.65
5 A50 20c brn. org. ('21) 1.00 1.65
6 A49 25c blue 85 27
7 " 40c brown 20 27
8 " 50c violet 20 27

Unwmkd.

9 A58 15c slate (V) 4.75 2.35
10 A50 20c brn. org. ('17) 9.00 10.00
Nos. 1-10 (10) 18.55 17.41

No. 9 Surcharged CENT 20

1916 ***Perf. 13½***

11 A58 20c on 15c slate 2.35 2.75

Ferrucci Issue.

Types of Italian Stamps of 1930 Overprinted in Red or Blue CALINO

1930 ***Perf. 14.*** **Wmk. 140**

12 A102 20c violet (R) 18 22
13 A103 25c dark green (R) 18 22
14 A102 50c black (R) 18 22
15 " 1.25 l deep blue (R) 18 22
16 A104 5 l + 2 l deep carmine (Bl) 1.10 1.25
Nos. 12-16 (5) 1.82 2.13

Garibaldi Issue.

Types of Italian Stamps of 1932 Overprinted in Red or Blue CALINO

1932

17 A138 10c brown 1.00 1.00
18 " 20c red brn. (Bl) 1.00 1.00
19 " 25c deep green 1.00 1.00
20 " 30c bluish slate 1.00 1.00
21 " 50c red violet (Bl) 1.00 1.00
22 A141 75c copper red (Bl) 1.00 1.00
23 " 1.25 l dull blue 1.00 1.00
24 " 1.75 l + 25c brown 1.00 1.00
25 A144 2.55 l + 50c orange (Bl) 1.00 1.00
26 A145 5 l + 1 l dull vio. 1.00 1.00
Nos. 17-26 (10) 10.00 10.00

CASO.

(kä'sō)

Overprinted "Caso" in Black or Violet

1912-21 ***Perf. 13½, 14*** **Wmk. 140**

1 A43 2c orange brown 1.15 55
2 A48 5c green 13 20
3 " 10c claret 13 20
4 " 15c slate ('21) 90 1.65
5 A50 20c brn. org. ('20) 55 1.65
6 A49 25c blue 20 27
7 " 40c brown 20 27
8 " 50c violet 20 27

Unwmkd.

9 A58 15c slate (V) 4.75 2.35
10 A50 20c brn. org. ('17) 9.00 10.00
Nos. 1-10 (10) 17.21 17.41

No. 9 Surcharged CENT 20

1916 ***Perf. 13½***

11 A58 20c on 15c slate 20 35

Ferrucci Issue.

Types of Italian Stamps of 1930 Overprinted in Red or Blue CASO

1930 ***Perf. 14.*** **Wmk. 140**

12 A102 20c violet (R) 18 22
13 A103 25c dark green (R) 18 22
14 " 50c black (R) 18 22
15 " 1.25 l deep blue (R) 18 22
16 A104 5 l + 2 l deep carmine (Bl) 1.10 1.25
Nos. 12-16 (5) 1.82 2.13

Garibaldi Issue.

Types of Italian Stamps of 1932 Overprinted in Red or Blue CASO

1932

17 A138 10c brown 1.00 1.00
18 " 20c red brown (Bl) 1.00 1.00
19 " 25c deep green 1.00 1.00
20 " 30c bluish slate 1.00 1.00
21 " 50c red violet (Bl) 1.00 1.00
22 A141 75c copper red (Bl) 1.00 1.00
23 " 1.25 l dull blue 1.00 1.00
24 " 1.75 l + 25c brown 1.00 1.00
25 A144 2.55 l + 50c orange (Bl) 1.00 1.00
26 A145 5 l + 1 l dull vio. 1.00 1.00
Nos. 17-26 (10) 10.00 10.00

COO.

(kō'ō)

(Cos, Kos)

Overprinted "Cos" in Black or Violet

1912-22 ***Perf. 13½, 14*** **Wmk. 140**

1 A43 2c orange brown 1.15 55
2 A48 5c green 5.75 2.25
3 " 10c claret 13 20
4 " 15c slate ('22) 90 1.65
5 A50 20c brn. org. ('21) 55 1.65
6 A49 25c blue 4.00 1.65
7 " 40c brown 20 27
8 " 50c violet 20 27

Unwmkd.

9 A58 15c slate (V) 4.75 2.35
10 A50 20c brown orange ('17) 5.50 6.00
Nos. 1-10 (10) 23.13 16.84

No. 9 Surcharged CENT 20

1916 ***Perf. 13½***

11 A58 20c on 15c slate 2.35 2.75

Ferrucci Issue.

Types of Italian Stamps of 1930 Overprinted in Red or Blue COO

1930 ***Perf. 14*** **Wmk. 140**

12 A102 20c violet (R) 18 22
13 A103 25c dark green (R) 18 22
14 " 50c black (R) 18 22
15 " 1.25 l deep blue (R) 18 22
16 A104 5 l + 2 l deep carmine (Bl) 1.10 1.25
Nos. 12-16 (5) 1.82 2.13

Garibaldi Issue.

Types of Italian Stamps of 1932 Overprinted in Red or Blue COO

1932

17 A138 10c brown 1.00 1.00
18 " 20c red brown (Bl) 1.00 1.00
19 " 25c deep green 1.00 1.00
20 " 30c bluish slate 1.00 1.00
21 " 50c red violet (Bl) 1.00 1.00
22 A141 75c copper red (Bl) 1.00 1.00
23 " 1.25 l dull blue 1.00 1.00
24 " 1.75 l + 25c brown 1.00 1.00
25 A144 2.55 l + 50c org. (Bl) 1.00 1.00
26 A145 5 l + 1 l dull vio. 1.00 1.00
Nos. 17-26 (10) 10.00 10.00

LERO.

(lĕ'rō)

Overprinted "Leros" in Black or Violet

1912-22 ***Perf. 13½, 14.*** **Wmk. 140**

1 A43 2c orange brown 1.15 55
2 A48 5c green 13 20
3 " 10c claret 13 20
4 " 15c slate ('22) 90 1.65
5 A50 20c brn. org. ('21) 20.00 21.50
6 A49 25c blue 5.00 2.25
7 " 40c brown 20 27
8 " 50c violet 20 27

Unwmkd.

9 A58 15c slate (V) 4.75 2.35
10 A50 20c brn. org. ('17) 5.50 6.00
Nos. 1-10 (10) 37.96 35.24

No. 9 Surcharged CENT 20

1916 ***Perf. 13½***

11 A58 20c on 15c slate 2.00 2.35

Ferrucci Issue.

Types of Italian Stamps of 1932 Overprinted in Red or Blue LERO

1930 ***Perf. 14***

12 A102 20c violet (R) 18 22
13 A103 25c dark green (R) 18 22
14 " 50c black (R) 18 22
15 " 1.25 l deep blue (R) 18 22
16 A104 5 l + 2 l deep carmine (Bl) 1.10 1.25
Nos. 12-16 (5) 1.82 2.13

Garibaldi Issue.

Types of Italian Stamps of 1932 Overprinted in Red or Blue LERO

1932

17 A138 10c brown 1.00 1.00
18 " 20c red brn. (Bl) 1.00 1.00
19 " 25c deep green 1.00 1.00

20	A138	30c bluish slate	1.00	1.00
21	"	50c red violet (Bl)	1.00	1.00
22	A141	75c copper red (Bl)	1.00	1.00
23	"	1.25 l dull blue	1.00	1.00
24	"	1.75 l+25c brown	1.00	1.00
25	A144	2.55 l+50c org. (Bl)	1.00	1.00
26	A145	5 l+1 l dull violet	1.00	1.00
		Nos. 17-26 (10)	10.00	10.00

LISSO.

(lis'sō)

Overprinted "Lipso" in Black or Violet

1912-22 *Perf. 13½, 14.* **Wmk. 140**

1	A43	2c orange brown	1.15	55
2	A48	5c green	13	20
3	"	10c claret	13	20
4	"	15c slate ('22)	1.00	1.65
5	A50	20c brn. org. ('21)	1.00	1.65
6	A49	25c blue	20	27
7	"	40c brown	20	27
8	"	50c violet	20	27

Unwmkd.

9	A58	15c slate (V)	4.75	2.35
10	A50	20c brn. org. ('17)	5.50	6.00
		Nos. 1-10 (10)	14.26	13.41

No. 9 Surcharged CENT 20

1916 *Perf. 13½*

11	A58	20c on 15c slate	20	35

Ferrucci Issue.

Types of Italian Stamps of 1930 Overprinted in Red or Blue LISSO

1930 *Perf. 14.* **Wmk. 140**

12	A102	20c violet (R)	18	22
13	A103	25c dark green (R)	18	22
14	"	50c black (R)	18	22
15	"	1.25 l deep blue (R)	18	22
16	A104	5 l+2 l deep carmine (Bl)	1.10	1.25
		Nos. 12-16 (5)	1.82	2.13

Garibaldi Issue.

Types of Italian Stamps of 1932 Overprinted in Red or Blue LIPSO

1932

17	A138	10c brown	1.00	1.00
18	"	20c red brn. (Bl)	1.00	1.00
19	"	25c deep green	1.00	1.00
20	"	30c bluish slate	1.00	1.00
21	"	50c red violet (Bl)	1.00	1.00
22	A141	75c copper red (Bl)	1.00	1.00
23	"	1.25 l dull blue	1.00	1.00
24	"	1.75 l+25c brown	1.00	1.00
25	A144	2.55 l+50c org. (Bl)	1.00	1.00
26	A145	5 l+1 l dull vio.	1.00	1.00
		Nos. 17-26 (10)	10.00	10.00

NISIRO.

(nē'sē-rō)

Overprinted "Nisiros" in Black or Violet

Wmkd. Crown. (140)

1912-22 *Perf. 13½, 14.*

1	A43	2c orange brown	1.15	55
2	A48	5c green	13	20
3	"	10c claret	13	20
4	"	15c slate ('22)	2.35	2.75
5	A50	20c brn. org. ('21)	11.50	13.00
6	A49	25c blue	20	27
7	"	40c brown	20	27
8	"	50c violet	20	27

Unwmkd.

9	A58	15c slate (V)	4.75	2.35
10	A50	20c brown orange ('17)	11.00	12.00
		Nos. 1-10 (10)	31.61	31.86

No. 9 Surcharged CENT 20

1916 *Perf. 13½*

11	A58	20c on 15c slate	20	35

Ferrucci Issue.

Types of Italian Stamps of 1930 Overprinted in Red or Blue NISIRO

1930 *Perf. 14* **Wmk. 140**

12	A102	20c violet (R)	18	22
13	A103	25c deep green (R)	18	22
14	"	50c black (R)	18	22
15	"	1.25 l deep blue (R)	18	22
16	A104	5 l+2 l deep carmine (Bl)	1.10	1.25
		Nos. 12-16 (5)	1.82	2.13

Garibaldi Issue

Types of Italian Stamps of 1932 Overprinted in Red or Blue NISIRO

1932

17	A138	10c brown	1.00	1.00
18	"	20c red brn. (Bl)	1.00	1.00
19	"	25c deep green	1.00	1.00
20	"	30c bluish slate	1.00	1.00
21	"	50c red violet (Bl)	1.00	1.00
22	A141	75c copper red (Bl)	1.00	1.00
23	"	1.25 l dull blue	1.00	1.00
24	"	1.75 l+25c brown	1.00	1.00
25	A144	2.55 l+50c org. (Bl)	1.00	1.00
26	A145	5 l+1 l dull violet	1.00	1.00
		Nos. 17-26 (10)	10.00	10.00

PATMO.

(pät'mō)

Overprinted "Patmos" in Black or Violet

Wmkd. Crown. (140)

1912-22 *Perf. 13½, 14.*

1	A43	2c orange brown	1.15	55
2	A48	5c green	13	20
3	"	10c claret	13	20
4	"	15c slate ('22)	90	1.65
5	A50	20c brn. org. ('21)	20.00	21.50
6	A49	25c blue	20	27
7	"	40c brown	20	27
8	"	50c violet	20	27

Unwmkd.

9	A58	15c slate (V)	4.75	2.35
10	A50	20c brn. org. ('17)	5.50	6.00
		Nos. 1-10 (10)	33.16	33.26

No. 9 Surcharged CENT 20

1916 *Perf. 13½*

11	A58	20c on 15c slate	1.65	2.00

Ferrucci Issue.

Types of Italian Stamps of 1930 Overprinted in Red or Blue PATMO

1930 *Perf. 14.* **Wmk. 140**

12	A102	20c violet (R)	18	22
13	A103	25c dark green (R)	18	22
14	"	50c black (R)	18	22
15	"	1.25 l deep blue (R)	18	22
16	A104	5 l+2 l deep carmine (Bl)	1.10	1.25
		Nos. 12-16 (5)	1.82	2.13

Garibaldi Issue.

Types of Italian Stamps of 1932 Overprinted in Red or Blue PATMO

1932

17	A138	10c brown	1.00	1.00
18	"	20c red brn. (Bl)	1.00	1.00
19	"	25c deep green	1.00	1.00
20	"	30c bluish slate	1.00	1.00
21	"	50c red violet (Bl)	1.00	1.00
22	A141	75c copper red (Bl)	1.00	1.00
23	"	1.25 l dull blue	1.00	1.00
24	"	1.75 l+25c brown	1.00	1.00
25	A144	2.55 l+50c org. (Bl)	1.00	1.00
26	A145	5 l+1 l dull vio.	1.00	1.00
		Nos. 17-26 (10)	10.00	10.00

PISCOPI.

(pēs'kō-pē)

Overprinted "Piscopi" in Black or Violet

Wmkd. Crowns. (140)

1912-21 *Perf. 13½, 14*

1	A43	2c orange brown	1.15	55
2	A48	5c green	13	20
3	"	10c claret	13	20
4	"	15c slate ('21)	1.65	2.00
5	A50	20c brn. org. ('21)	6.75	7.50
6	A49	25c blue	20	27
7	"	40c brown	20	27
8	"	50c violet	20	27

Unwmkd.

9	A58	15c slate (V)	4.75	2.35
10	A50	20c brn. org. ('17)	5.50	6.00
		Nos. 1-10 (10)	20.66	19.61

No. 9 Surcharged CENT 20

1916 *Perf. 13½*

11	A58	20c on 15c slate	20	35

Ferrucci Issue.

Types of Italian Stamps of 1930 Overprinted in Red or Blue PISCOPI

1930 *Perf. 14* **Wmk. 140**

12	A102	20c violet (R)	18	22
13	A103	25c dark green (R)	18	22
14	"	50c black (R)	18	22
15	"	1.25 l deep blue (R)	18	22
16	A104	5 l+2 l deep carmine (Bl)	1.10	1.25
		Nos. 12-16 (5)	1.82	2.13

Garibaldi Issue.

Types of Italian Stamps of 1932 Overprinted in Red or Blue PISCOPI

1932

17	A138	10c brown	1.00	1.00
18	"	20c red brown (Bl)	1.00	1.00
19	"	25c deep green	1.00	1.00
20	"	30c bluish slate	1.00	1.00
21	"	50c red violet (Bl)	1.00	1.00
22	A141	75c copper red (Bl)	1.00	1.00
23	"	1.25 l dull blue	1.00	1.00
24	"	1.75 l+25c brown	1.00	1.00
25	A144	2.55 l+50c org. (Bl)	1.00	1.00
26	A145	5 l+1 l dull violet	1.00	1.00
		Nos. 17-26 (10)	10.00	10.00

RHODES.

(rōdz)

(Rodi)

Overprinted "Rodi" in Black or Violet

Wmkd. Crown. (140)

1912-24 *Perf. 13½, 14.*

1	A43	2c orange brown	13	20
2	A48	5c green	13	20
		a. Double overprint	45.00	
3	A48	10c claret	13	20
4	"	15c slate ('21)	10.00	10.00
5	A45	20c orange ('16)	13	20
6	A50	20c brn. orange ('19)	35	40
		a. Double overprint	15.00	
7	A49	25c blue	20	20
8	"	40c brown	20	20
9	"	50c violet	20	20
10	"	85c red brown ('22)	2.10	2.75
11	A46	1 l brn. & grn. ('24)	20	

No. 11 was not regularly issued.

Unwmkd.

12	A58	15c slate (V)	5.75	2.25
13	A50	20c brown orange ('17)	25.00	27.50
		Nos. 1-10, 12-13 (12)	44.32	44.30

No. 12 Surcharged CENT 20

1916 *Perf. 13½*

14	A58	20c on 15c slate	25.00	27.50

Windmill, Rhodes
A1

Medieval Galley
A2

Christian Knight
A3

Crusader's Tomb
A5

Crusader Kneeling in Prayer
A4

No Imprint

Lithographed

1929 *Perf. 11.* **Unwmkd.**

15	A1	5c magenta	75	12
16	A2	10c olive brown	75	12
17	A3	20c rose red	75	12
18	"	25c green	75	12
19	A4	30c dark blue	1.00	18
20	A5	50c dark brown	1.25	6
21	"	1.25 l dark blue	1.50	25
22	A4	5 l magenta	12.00	4.25
23	"	10 l olive brown	20.00	14.00
		Nos. 15-23 (9)	38.75	19.22

Issued in commemoration of the visit of the King and Queen of Italy to the Aegean Islands. The stamps are inscribed "Rodi" but were available for use in all the Aegean Islands.

Nos. 15-23 and C1-C4 were used in eastern Crete in 1941-42 with Greek postmarks.

See also Nos. 55-63.

Ferrucci Issue.

Types of Italian Stamps of 1930 Overprinted in Red or Blue RODI

1930 *Perf. 14* **Wmk. 140**

24	A102	20c violet (R)	18	22
25	A103	25c dark green (R)	18	22
26	"	50c black (R)	18	22
27	"	1.25 l deep blue (R)	18	22
28	A104	5 l+2 l deep carmine (Bl)	1.10	1.25
		Nos. 24-28 (5)	1.82	2.13

Hydrological Congress Issue.

Rhodes Issue of 1929 Overprinted XXI Congresso Idrologico

1930 *Perf. 11.* **Unwmkd.**

29	A1	5c magenta	50	75
30	A2	10c olive brown	50	75
31	A3	20c rose red	75	1.00
32	"	25c green	1.00	1.35
33	A4	30c dark blue	50	70
34	A5	50c dark brown	175.00	25.00
35	"	1.25 l dark blue	135.00	25.00
36	A4	5 l magenta	20.00	30.00
37	"	10 l olive green	20.00	30.00
		Nos. 29-37 (9)	353.25	114.55

Rhodes Issue of 1929 Overprinted in Blue or Red 1931 CONGRESSO EUCARISTICO ITALIANO

1931

38	A1	5c magenta (Bl)	30	35
39	A2	10c olive brown (R)	30	35
40	A3	20c rose red (Bl)	30	35
41	"	25c green (R)	42	50

42 A4 30c dark blue (R) 50 60
43 A5 50c dk. brown (R) 19.00 10.00
44 " 1.25 l dark blue (R) 17.50 12.50
Nos. 38-44 (7) 38.32 24.65

Italian Eucharistic Congress, 1931.

Garibaldi Issue.

Types of Italian Stamps of 1932
Overprinted in Red or Blue **RODI**

1932 *Perf. 14* **Wmk. 140**

45 A138 10c brown 1.00 1.00
46 " 20c red brn. (Bl) 1.00 1.00
47 " 25c deep green 1.00 1.00
48 " 30c bluish slate 1.00 1.00
49 " 50c red violet (Bl) 1.00 1.00
50 A141 75c copper red (Bl) 1.00 1.00
51 " 1.25 l dull blue 1.00 1.00
52 " 1.75 l+25c brown 1.00 1.00
53 A144 2.55 l+50c org. (Bl) 1.00 1.00
54 A145 5 l+1 l dull violet 1.00 1.00
Nos. 45-54 (10) 10.00 10.00

Types of Rhodes Issue of 1929.
Imprint:
"Officina Carte-Valori Roma".

1932

55 A1 5c rose lake 6 6
56 A2 10c dark brown 6 6
57 A3 20c red 6 6
58 " 25c dull green 6 6
59 A4 30c dull blue 6 6
60 A5 50c black brown 6 6
61 " 1.25 l deep blue 6 6
62 A4 5 l rose lake 18 12
63 " 10 l olive brown 30 18
Nos. 55-63 (9) 90 72

Aerial View of Rhodes
A6

Map of Rhodes
A7

Deer and Palm
A8

Lithographed.

1932 *Perf. 11* **Wmk. 140**

Shield in Red.

64 A6 5c black & green 60 75
65 " 10c black & violet blue 60 75
66 " 20c black & dull yellow 60 75
67 " 25c lilac & black 60 75
68 " 30c black & pink 60 75

Shield and Map Dots in Red.

69 A7 50c black & gray 60 75
70 " 1.25 l red brown & gray 60 75
71 " 5 l dark blue & gray 5.50 6.00
72 " 10 l dark green & gray 15.00 16.50
73 " 25 l choc. & gray 375.00 400.00
Nos. 64-73 (10) 399.70 427.75

Issued to commemorate the 20th anniversary of the Italian occupation and the 10th anniversary of Fascist rule.

1935, Apr. Photo. **Wmk. 140**

74 A8 5c orange 1.20 1.50
75 " 10c brown 1.20 1.50
76 " 20c carmine rose 1.20 1.50
77 " 25c green 1.20 1.50
78 " 30c purple 1.20 1.50
79 " 50c red brown 1.20 1.50
80 " 1.25 l blue 1.20 1.50
81 " 5 l yellow 85.00 100.00
Nos. 74-81 (8) 93.40 110.50

Holy Year.

WEIHNACHTEN WEIHNACHTEN
1944 1944

The above overprints on No. 55 are stated to have been prepared locally for use on German military correspondence, but banned by postal authorities in Berlin.

SEMI-POSTAL STAMPS.

Rhodes
Nos. 55 to 62
Surcharged in Black
or Red

CENT. 5
PRO
ASSISTENZA
EGEO

1943 *Perf. 14.* **Wmk. 140**

B1 A1 5c+5c rose lake 18 18
B2 A2 10c+10c dk. brown 18 18
B3 A3 20c+20c red 18 18
B4 " 25c+25c dull green 18 18
B5 A4 30c+30c dull blue (R) 25 25
B6 A5 50c+50c blk. brown 38 38
B7 " 1.25 l+1.25 l deep blue (R) 50 50
B8 A4 5 l+5 l rose lake 42.50 17.50
Nos. B1-B8 (8) 44.35 19.35

The surtax was for general relief.

Rhodes Nos. 55
to 58, 60 and 61
Surcharged in Black
or Red

£. 3
PRO SINISTRATI
DI GUERRA

1944

B9 A1 5c+3 l rose lake 12 12
B10 A2 10c+3 l dk. brn. (R) 12 12
B11 A3 20c+3 l red 12 12
B12 " 25c+3 l dull green (R) 12 12
B13 A5 50c+3 l black brown (R) 18 18
B14 " 1.25 l+5 l deep blue (R) 5.50 5.50
Nos. B9-B14 (6) 6.16 6.16

The surtax was for war victims.

Rhodes Nos. 62
and 63
Surcharged in Red

\+ 10
FEBBRAIO
1945

1945

B17 A4 5 l+10 l rose lake 3.00 3.00
B18 " 10 l+10 l olive brown 3.00 3.00

The surtax was for the Red Cross.

AIR POST STAMPS.

Symbolical of Flight
AP18

Wmkd. Crown. (140)

1934 Typographed. *Perf. 14.*

C1 AP18 50c black & yellow 6 6
C2 " 80c black & magenta 30 30
C3 " 1 l black & green 18 6
C4 " 5 l black & red violet 60 80

The only foreign revenue stamps listed in this Catalogue are those authorized for prepayment of postage.

AIR POST SEMI-POSTAL STAMPS.

Rhodes
Nos. C1 to C4
Surcharged
in Silver

PRO
SINISTRATI
DI
GVERRA
£. 2

1944 *Perf. 14.* **Wmk. 140**

CB1 AP18 50c+2 l black & yellow 50 50
CB2 " 80c+2 l black & magenta 1.25 1.25
CB3 " 1 l+2 l black & green 1.25 1.25
CB4 " 5 l+2 l black & red violet 17.50 17.50

The surtax was for war victims.

SPECIAL DELIVERY STAMPS.

Stag—SD1

Wmkd. Crowns. (140)

1936 Photogravure. *Perf. 14.*

E1 SD1 1.25 l green 18 12
E2 " 2.50 l vermilion 55 38

Nos. 58 and 57
Surcharged
in Black

LIRE 1,25
ESPRESSO

1943

E3 A3 1.25 l on 25c dull green 12 18
E4 " 2.50 l on 20c red 12 18

SEMI-POSTAL SPECIAL DELIVERY STAMPS.

Rhodes Nos. E1
and E2 Surcharged
in Red or Black

L.RE 1,25 PRO
ASSISTENZA EGEO

1943 *Perf. 14* **Wmk. 140**

EB1 SD1 1.25 l+1.25 l green (R) 4.25 3.75
EB2 " 2.50 l+2.50 l vermilion 8.00 5.00

The surtax was for general relief.

POSTAGE DUE STAMPS.

Maltese Cross
PD1

Immortelle
PD2

Wmkd. Crown. (140)

1934 Photogravure. *Perf. 13.*

J1 PD1 5c vermilion 8 5
J2 " 10c carmine 8 5
J3 " 20c dark green 8 5
J4 " 30c purple 8 5
J5 " 40c dark blue 8 5
J6 PD2 50c vermilion 8 5
J7 " 60c carmine 8 5
J8 " 1 l dark green 12 5
J9 " 2 l purple 12 5
Nos. J1-J9 (9) 80 45

PARCEL POST STAMPS.

Both unused and used prices are for complete stamps.

PP1

PP2

Wmkd. Crowns. (140)

1934 Photogravure. *Perf. 13.*

Q1 PP1 5c vermilion 15 7
Q2 " 10c carmine 15 7
Q3 " 20c dark green 15 7
Q4 " 25c purple 22 7
Q5 " 50c dark blue 22 7
Q6 " 60c black 22 7
Q7 PP2 1 l vermilion 22 7
Q8 " 2 l carmine 22 7
Q9 " 3 l dark green 22 7
Q10 " 4 l purple 38 7
Q11 " 10 l dark blue 45 7
Nos. Q1-Q11 (11) 2.60 77

Price of used halves, Nos. Q1-Q11, each 3 cents.

See note preceding No. Q7 of Italy.

SCARPANTO.

(skär'pän-tō)

Overprinted "Scarpanto"
in Black or Violet

1912-22 *Perf. 13½, 14.* **Wmk. 140**

1 A43 2c orange brown 1.15 55
2 A48 5c green 13 20
3 " 10c claret 13 20
4 " 15c slate ('22) 2.00 2.35
5 A50 20c brn. org. ('21) 4.75 5.50
6 A49 25c blue 90 40
7 " 40c brown 20 27
8 " 50c violet 20 27

Unwmkd.

9 A58 15c slate (V) 4.75 2.35
10 A50 20c brn. orange ('17) 16.00 17.50
Nos. 1-10 (10) 30.21 29.59

No 9
Surcharged

CENT 20

1916 *Perf. 13½*

11 A58 20c on 15c slate 20 35

Ferrucci Issue.

Types of Italian Stamps of 1930
Overprinted in Red or Blue **SCARPANTO**

1930 *Perf. 14.* **Wmk. 140**

12 A102 20c violet (R) 18 22
13 A103 25c dk. green (R) 18 22
14 " 50c black (R) 18 22
15 " 1.25 l deep blue (R) 18 22
16 A104 5 l+2 l deep car. (Bl) 1.10 1.25
Nos. 12-16 (5) 1.82 2.13

Garibaldi Issue.

Types of Italian Stamps of 1932
Overprinted in Red or Blue **SCARPANTO**

1932

17 A138 10c brown 1.00 1.00
18 " 20c red brn. (Bl) 1.00 1.00
19 " 25c deep green 1.00 1.00
20 " 30c bluish slate 1.00 1.00
21 " 50c red violet (Bl) 1.00 1.00
22 A141 75c copper red (Bl) 1.00 1.00
23 " 1.25 l dull blue 1.00 1.00
24 " 1.75 l+25c brown 1.00 1.00
25 A144 2.55 l+50c org. (Bl) 1.00 1.00
26 A145 5 l+1 l dull violet 1.00 1.00
Nos. 17-26 (10) 10.00 10.00

SIMI.

(sē'mē)

Overprinted "Simi"
in Black or Violet

1912-21 *Perf. 13½, 14* **Wmk. 140**

1 A43 2c orange brown 1.15 55
2 A48 5c green 1.85 70
3 " 10c claret 13 20

4 A48 15c slate ('21) 27.50 30.00
5 A50 20c brn. org. ('21) 5.50 6.00
6 A49 25c blue 50 40
7 A49 40c brown 20 27
8 " 50c violet 20 27

Unwmkd.

9 A58 15c slate (V) 4.75 2.35
10 A50 20c brn. org. ('17) 9.00 10.00
Nos. 1-10 (10) 50.78 50.74

No. 9 Surcharged CENT 20

1916 *Perf. 13½*

11 A58 20c on 15c slate 1.65 2.00

Ferrucci Issue.

Types of Italian Stamps of 1930 Overprinted in Red or Blue SIMI

1930 *Perf. 14.* **Wmk. 140**

12 A102 20c violet (R) 18 22
13 A103 25c dk. green (R) 18 22
14 " 50c black (R) 18 22
15 " 1.25 l deep blue (R) 18 22
16 A104 5 l+2 l deep car. (Bl) 1.10 1.25
Nos. 12-16 (5) 1.82 2.13

Garibaldi Issue.

Types of Italian Stamps of 1932 Overprinted in Red or Blue SIMI

1932

17 A138 10c brown 1.00 1.00
18 " 20c red brn. (Bl) 1.00 1.00
19 " 25c deep green 1.00 1.00
20 " 30c bluish slate 1.00 1.00
21 " 50c red violet (Bl) 1.00 1.00
22 A141 75c copper red (Bl) 1.00 1.00
23 " 1.25 l dull blue 1.00 1.00
24 " 1.75 l+25c brown 1.00 1.00
25 A144 2.55 l+50c org. (Bl) 1.00 1.00
26 A145 5 l+1 l dull vio. 1.00 1.00
Nos. 17-26 (10) 10.00 10.00

STAMPALIA.

(stäm'pȧ-lē'ä)

Overprinted "Stampalia" in Black or Violet

1912-21 *Perf. 13½, 14* **Wmk. 140**

1 A43 2c orange brown 1.15 55
2 A48 5c green 13 20
3 " 10c claret 13 20
4 " 15c slate ('21) 1.65 2.35
5 A50 20c brn. org. ('21) 3.75 4.50
6 A49 25c blue 20 27
7 " 40c brown 20 27
8 " 50c violet 20 27

Unwmkd.

9 A58 15c slate (V) 4.75 2.35
10 A50 20c brn. org. ('17) 16.00 17.50
Nos. 1-10 (10) 28.16 28.46

No. 9 Surcharged CENT 20

1916 *Perf. 13½*

11 A58 20c on 15c slate 20 35

Ferrucci Issue.

Types of Italian Stamps of 1930 Overprinted in Red or Blue STAMPALIA

1930 *Perf. 14.* **Wmk. 140**

12 A102 20c violet (R) 18 22
13 A103 25c dark green (R) 18 22
14 " 50c black (R) 18 22
15 " 1.25 l deep blue (R) 18 22
16 A104 5 l+2 l deep car. (Bl) 1.10 1.25
Nos. 12-16 (5) 1.82 2.13

Garibaldi Issue.

Types of Italian Stamps of 1932 Overprinted in Red or Blue STAMPALIA

1932

17 A138 10c brown 1.00 1.00
18 " 20c red brn. (Bl) 1.00 1.00
19 " 25c deep green 1.00 1.00
20 " 30c bluish slate 1.00 1.00
21 " 50c red violet (Bl) 1.00 1.00
22 A141 75c copper red (Bl) 1.00 1.00
23 A141 1.25 l dull blue 1.00 1.00
24 " 1.75 l+25c brown 1.00 1.00
25 A144 2.55 l+50c org. (Bl) 1.00 1.00
26 A145 5 l+1 l dull vio. 1.00 1.00
Nos. 17-26 (10) 10.00 10.00

IVORY COAST

(ī'vō-rī kōst)

LOCATION—West coast of Africa, bordering on Gulf of Guinea.

GOVT.—Republic.

AREA—127,520 sq. mi.

POP.—5,150,000 (est. 1977).

CAPITAL—Abidjan.

The former French colony of Ivory Coast became part of French West Africa and used its stamps, starting in 1945. On Dec. 4, 1958, Ivory Coast became a republic, with full independence on Aug. 7, 1960.

100 Centimes = 1 Franc

Navigation and Commerce A1

Perf. 14x13½.

1892-1900 Typographed. Unwmkd.

Name of Colony in Blue or Carmine.

1 A1 1c *lilac blue* 60 60
2 " 2c brown, *buff* 80 80
3 " 4c claret, *lavender* 1.20 1.00
4 " 5c green, *greenish* 4.50 2.75
5 " 10c *lavender* 5.00 3.00
6 " 10c red ('00) 40.00 35.00
7 " 15c bl., quadrille paper 6.00 4.00
8 " 15c gray ('00) 3.00 1.00
9 " 20c red, *green* 5.00 4.00
10 " 25c *rose* 6.00 75
11 " 25c blue ('00) 10.00 8.00
12 " 30c brown, *bistre* 9.00 9.00
13 " 40c red, *straw* 6.00 6.00
14 " 50c carmine, *rose* 25.00 18.50
15 " 50c brown, *azure* ('00) 7.00 3.00
16 " 75c deep violet, *orange* 10.00 9.00
17 " 1fr bronze green *straw* 12.00 10.00
Nos. 1-17 (17) 151.10 116.40

Nos. 12, 16-17 Surcharged in Black 0,05

1904

18 A1 0,05c on 30c brown, *bistre* 22.50 22.50
19 " 0,10c on 75c violet, *orange* 3.50 3.50
20 " 0,15c on 1fr bronze green, *straw* 5.50 5.50

Gen. Louis Faidherbe A2

Oil Palm A3 — Dr. N. Eugène Ballay A4

1906-07

Name of Colony in Red or Blue.

21 A2 1c slate 40 40
22 " 2c chocolate 40 40
23 " 4c choc., *gray blue* 60 60
a. Name double 50.00 45.00
24 " 5c green 60 60
25 " 10c carmine (B) 2.00 1.60
26 A3 20c *azure* 3.00 2.40
27 " 25c blue, *pinkish* 2.00 1.60
28 " 30c choc., *pinkish* 3.00 2.40
30 " 35c *yellow* 3.00 1.40
31 " 45c choc., *greenish* 4.00 3.75
32 " 50c deep violet 4.50 4.00
33 " 75c blue, *orange* 4.50 4.00
34 A4 1fr *azure* 13.50 12.00
35 " 2fr blue, *pink* 13.50 13.50
36 " 5fr car., *straw* (B) 25.00 25.00
Nos. 21-36 (15) 80.00 73.65

Stamps of 1892-1900 Surcharged in Carmine or Black 05 *a* 10 *b*

1912

37 A1 (*a*) 5c on 15c gray (C) 10 10
38 " (") 5c on 30c brown, *bistre* (C) 30 30
39 " (*b*) 10c on 40c red, *straw* 20 20
a. Pair, one without surcharge 60.00
40 " (") 10c on 50c brown, *azure* (C) 40 40
41 " (") 10c on 75c deep vio., *org.* 2.00 2.00
Nos. 37-41 (5) 3.00 3.00

Two spacings between the surcharged numerals are found on Nos. 37 to 41.

River Scene—A5

1913-35

42 A5 1c vio. brn. & violet 6 6
43 " 2c brown & black 6 6
44 " 4c vio. & vio. brown 6 6
45 " 5c yellow green & blue green 10 10
a. Booklet pane of 4 2.00
46 " 5c chocolate & olive brown ('22) 7 7
47 " 10c red orange & rose 20 20
a. Booklet pane of 4 3.50
48 " 10c yellow green & blue green ('22) 5 5
49 " 10c carmine rose, *bluish* ('26) 5 5
50 " 15c orange & rose ('17) 10 10
51 " 20c black & gray 8 7
52 " 25c ultra. & blue 1.60 1.10
53 " 25c black & violet ('22) 10 10
54 " 30c choc. & brown 30 20
55 " 30c red orange & rose ('22) 30 30
56 " 30c light blue & rose red ('26) 8 8
57 " 30c dull green & green ('27) 10 10
58 " 35c violet & orange 10 10
59 " 40c gray & blue green 30 20
60 " 45c red orange & choc. 12 8
61 " 45c deep rose & maroon ('34) 1.35 1.25
62 " 50c black & violet 90 75
63 " 50c ultramarine & blue ('22) 10 10
64 " 50c olive green & blue ('25) 5 5
65 " 60c violet, *pinkish* ('25) 8 8
66 " 65c carmine rose & olive green ('26) 35 35
67 " 75c brown & rose 12 12
68 " 75c indigo & ultra. ('34) 90 85
69 " 85c red violet & black ('26) 25 25
70 A5 90c brown red & rose ('30) 3.50 3.50
71 " 1fr orange & black 30 25
72 " 1.10fr dull green & dark brown ('28) 1.75 1.75
73 " 1.50fr light blue & dp. blue ('30) 2.00 1.50
74 " 1.75fr light ultramarine & magenta ('35) 3.25 1.50
75 " 2fr brown & blue 1.00 50
76 " 3fr red violet ('30) 2.00 1.25
77 " 5fr dark blue & chocolate 1.85 1.25
Nos. 42-77 (36) 23.58 18.38

Nos. 45, 47, 50 and 58 exist on both ordinary and chalky paper.

Stamps and Type of 1913-34 Surcharged 60

1922-34

78 A5 50c on 45c deep rose & maroon ('34) 60 50
79 " 50c on 75c indigo & ultra. ('34) 50 50
80 " 50c on 90c brown red & rose ('34) 50 50
81 " 60c on 75c violet, *pinkish* ('22) 10 10
82 " 65c on 15c orange & rose ('25) 20 20
83 " 85c on 75c brown & rose ('25) 20 20
Nos. 78-83 (6) 2.10 2.00

Stamps and Type of 1913 Surcharged with New Value and Bars

1924-27

84 A5 25c on 2fr brown & blue (R) ('24) 20 20
85 " 25c on 5fr dark blue & chocolate ('24) 20 20
86 " 90c on 75c brown red & cerise ('27) 20 20
87 " 1.25fr on 1fr dark blue & ultramarine (R) ('26) 10 10
88 " 1.50fr on 1fr light blue & dark blue ('27) 30 30
89 " 3fr on 5fr brown red & blue green ('27) 85 85
90 " 10fr on 5fr dull red & rose lilac ('27) 4.50 4.50
91 " 20fr on 5fr blue green & verm. ('27) 5.75 5.75
Nos. 84-91 (8) 12.10 12.10

Colonial Exposition Issue.

Common Design Types

Name of Country in Black.

1931 Engraved. *Perf. 12½.*

92 CD70 40c deep green 60 60
93 CD71 50c violet 1.75 1.75
94 CD72 90c red orange 40 40
95 CD73 1.50fr dull blue 1.75 1.75

Stamps of Upper Volta 1928, Overprinted Côte d'Ivoire

1933 *Perf. 13½x14.*

96 A5 2c brown & lilac 5 5
97 " 4c black & yellow 6 5
98 " 5c indigo & gray blue 12 10
99 " 10c indigo & pink 15 12
100 " 15c brown & blue 17 15
101 " 20c brown & green 20 20
102 A6 25c brown & yellow 60 50
103 " 30c dp. green & green 60 50
104 " 45c brown & blue 2.00 1.85

105 A6 65c indigo & blue 1.00 85
106 " 75c black & lilac 1.10 90
107 " 90c brown red & lilac 80 60

Overprinted

Côte d'Ivoire

108 A7 1fr brown & green 80 65
109 " 1.50fr ultramarine & grayish 80 65

Surcharged Côte d'Ivoire 1F.25

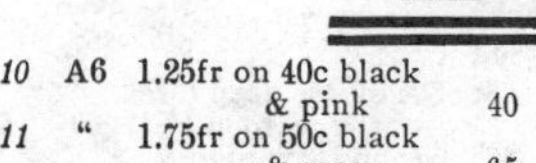

110 A6 1.25fr on 40c black & pink 40 35
111 " 1.75fr on 50c black & green 65 55
Nos. 96–111 (16) 9.50 8.07

Baoulé Woman
A6

Rapids on Comoe River
A9

Mosque at Bobo-Dioulasso
A7

Coastal Scene—A8

1936–44 *Perf. 13*

112 A6 1c carmine rose 6 6
113 " 2c ultramarine 6 6
114 " 3c deep green ('40) 6 6
115 " 4c chocolate 6 6
116 " 5c violet 6 6
117 " 10c Prussian blue 8 5
118 " 15c copper red 6 6
119 A7 20c ultramarine 8 8
120 " 25c copper red 10 10
121 " 30c blue green 10 10
122 " 30c brown ('40) 8 8
123 A6 35c deep green ('38) 8 8
124 A7 40c carmine rose 6 6
125 " 45c brown 15 13
126 " 45c blue green ('40) 10 10
127 " 50c plum 8 7
128 " 55c dark violet ('38) 10 10
129 A8 60c car. rose ('40) 10 10
130 " 65c red brown 8 6
131 " 70c red brown ('40) 10 10
132 " 75c dark violet 12 10
133 " 80c black brown ('38) 12 10
134 " 90c carmine rose 1.85 1.10
135 " 90c dark green ('39) 15 15
136 " 1fr dark green 90 30
137 " 1fr car. rose ('38) 10 6
138 A8 1fr dark violet ('40) 7 7
139 " 1.25fr copper red 10 10
140 " 1.40fr ultramarine ('40) 8 8
141 " 1.50fr ultramarine 6 6
141A " 1.50fr greenish black ('44) 10 10
142 " 1.60fr blk. brown ('40) 15 15
143 A9 1.75fr carmine rose 10 10
144 " 1.75fr dull blue ('38) 10 10
145 " 2fr ultramarine 10 8
146 " 2.25fr dark blue ('39) 8 8
147 " 2.50fr rose red ('40) 10 10
148 " 3fr green 15 12
149 " 5fr chocolate 17 12
150 " 10fr violet 22 18
151 " 20fr copper red 50 35
Nos. 112–151 (41) 6.97 5.17

Stamps of types A7–A9 without "RF" were issued in 1944, but were not placed on sale in the colony.

Paris International Exposition Issue.

Common Design Types

1937 *Perf. 13.*

152 CD74 20c deep violet 30 30
153 CD75 30c dark green 30 30
154 CD76 40c carmine rose 40 40
155 CD77 50c dk. brn. & bl. 30 30
156 CD78 90c red 30 30
157 CD79 1.50fr ultramarine 40 40
Nos. 152–157 (6) 2.00 2.00

Colonial Arts Exhibition Issue.

Souvenir Sheet.
Common Design Type

1937 *Imperf.*

158 CD76 3fr sepia 1.50 1.50
Size: 118x99mm.

Louis Gustave Binger
A10

1937 *Perf. 13.*

159 A10 65c red brown 6 5

Issued in commemoration of the death of Governor General Louis Gustave Binger and the 50th anniversary of his exploration of the Niger.

Caillie Issue

Common Design Type

1939 Engraved *Perf. 12½x12.*

160 CD81 90c orange brown & orange 20 20
161 " 2fr bright violet 30 30
162 " 2.25fr ultramarine & dark blue 20 20

New York World's Fair Issue.

Common Design Type

1939

163 CD82 1.25fr carmine lake 25 25
164 " 2.25fr ultramarine 25 25

Ebrié Lagoon and Marshal Pétain—A11

1941

165 A11 1fr green 15
166 " 2.50fr deep blue 15

It is doubtful whether Nos. 165–166 were placed in use.

Common Design Types pictured in section at front of book.

Republic

Elephant
A12

President Felix Houphouet-Boigny
A13

Engraved.

1959, Oct. 1 *Perf. 13* Unwmkd.

167 A12 10fr black & emerald 20 10
168 " 25fr violet brown & olive 40 25
169 " 30fr olive black & greenish blue 45 30

Imperforates

Most Ivory Coast stamps from 1959 onward exist imperforate in issued and trial colors, and also in small presentation sheets in issued colors.

1959, Dec. 4

170 A13 25fr violet brown 45 25

Issued to commemorate the first anniversary of the proclamation of the Republic.

Bété Mask
A14

Designs: Masks of 5 tribes: Bété, Gueré, Baoulé, Senufo and Guro. Nos. 174–176 are horizontal.

1960 *Perf. 13*

171 A14 50c pale brown & violet brown 6 5
172 " 1fr violet & magenta 6 4
173 " 2fr ultramarine & blue green 6 4
174 " 4fr dk. green & org. 10 8
175 " 5fr vermilion & brn. 12 10
176 " 6fr dk. brn. & violet 15 12
177 " 45fr dark green & brown violet 85 35
178 " 50fr dark brown & greenish blue 1.00 40
179 " 85fr carmine & slate green 1.65 85
Nos. 171–179 (9) 4.05 2.03

C.C.T.A. Issue

Common Design Type

1960, May 16 Engraved *Perf. 13*

180 CD106 25fr greenish blue & violet 60 55

Emblem of the Entente
A14a

1960, May 29 Photo. *Perf. 13x13½*

181 A14a 25fr multicolored 65 65

Issued to commemorate the first anniversary of the Entente (Dahomey, Ivory Coast, Niger and Upper Volta).

Young Couple with Olive Branch and Globe—A15

1961, Aug. 7 Engraved *Perf. 13*

182 A15 25fr emerald, bistre & black 45 30

First anniversary of Independence.

Blood Lilies
A16

Designs: Various Local Plants and Orchids.

1961–62

183 A16 5fr dk. green, red & orange ('62) 15 12
184 " 10fr ultra., claret & yellow 20 10
185 " 15fr orge., rose lilac & green ('62) 30 15
186 " 20fr brown, dk. red & yellow 40 25
187 " 25fr green, red brown & yel. 55 30
188 " 30fr black, carmine & green 60 40
189 " 70fr green, verm. & yellow 1.40 60
190 " 85fr brown, lilac, yellow & grn. 1.75 1.10
Nos. 183–190 (8) 5.35 3.02

Early Letter Carrier and Modern Mailman
A17

1961, Oct. 14 *Perf. 13* Unwmkd.

191 A17 25fr choc., emerald & blue 50 40

Issued for Stamp Day, 1961.

Ayamé Dam—A18

1961, Nov. 18 Engraved

192 A18 25fr greenish blue, black & green 40 25

Swimming Race—A19

Sports: 20fr, Basketball. 25fr, Soccer.

1961, Dec. 23 Perf. 13 Unwmkd.

193 A19 5fr multicolored 10 8
194 " 20fr green, gray & red brown 35 30
195 " 25fr blue, olive green & red brown 45 30

Abidjan Games, Dec. 24–31. See No. C17.

Palms—A20

1962, Feb. 5 Photo. Perf. 12x12½

196 A20 25fr brown, blue & orange 40 25

Issued to commemorate the 17th session of the Commission for Technical Co-operation in Africa South of the Sahara, Abidjan, Feb. 5–16.

Fort Assinie and Assinie River

A21

1962, May 26 Engraved Perf. 13

197 A21 85fr Prussian green, green & dull red brown 1.35 75

Centenary of the Ivory Coast post.

African and Malagasy Union Issue

Common Design Type

1962, Sept. 8 Photo. Perf. 12½x12

198 CD110 30fr multicolored 1.00 75

First anniversary of African and Malagasy Union.

Fair Emblem, Cotton and Spindles

A22

1963, Jan. 26 Engr. Perf. 13

199 A22 50fr green, brown org. & sepia 70 40

Bouake Fair, Jan. 26–Feb. 4.

Stylized Map of Africa

A23

1963, May 25 Photo. Perf. 12½x12

200 A23 30fr ultramarine & emerald 60 60

Issued to commemorate the conference of African heads of state for African unity, Addis Ababa.

Hartebeest

A24

UNESCO Emblem, Scales and Globe

A25

Designs: 1fr, Yellow-backed duiker (horiz). 2fr, Potto. 4fr, Beecroft's hyrax (horiz.). 5fr, Water chevrotain. 15fr, Forest hog (horiz.). 20fr, Wart hog (horiz.). 25fr, Bongo (antelope). 45fr, Cape hunting dogs, or hyenas (horiz.). 50fr, Black-and-white colobus (monkey).

1963–64 Engraved Perf. 13

201 A24 1fr chocolate, green & yellow ('64) 10 5
202 " 2fr blk., dk. bl., gray olive & brn. ('64) 10 5
203 " 4fr red brn., dk. bl., brn. & blk. ('64) 15 5
204 " 5fr slate green, brn. & citron ('64) 15 5
205 " 10fr olive, green & ocher 25 13
206 " 15fr red brown, grn. & blk. ('64) 40 20
207 " 20fr red orange, green & black 60 25
208 " 25fr red brn. & green 65 25
209 " 45fr chocolate, blue grn. & yel. grn. 1.10 65
210 " 50fr red brown, green & black 1.20 60
a. Miniature sheet of 4 3.25 3.25
Nos. 201–210 (10) 4.70 2.28

No. 210a contains one each of Nos. 205, 207 and Nos. 209–210. Size: 170x100mm. See also Nos. 218–220.

1963, Dec. 10 Unwmkd.

211 A25 85fr dk. bl., blk. & org. 1.25 75

Issued to commemorate the 15th anniversary of the Universal Declaration of Human Rights.

Sun Radiating from Ivory Coast over Africa

A26

Weather Station and Balloon

A27

1964, Mar. 17 Photo. Perf. 12x12½

212 A26 30fr green, dull violet & red 50 30

Issued to commemorate the Inter-African Conference of National Education Ministers.

1964, March 23 Perf. 13x12½

213 A27 25fr multicolored 45 35

World Meteorological Day, Mar. 23.

Physician Vaccinating Child

A28

1964, May 8 Engraved Perf. 13

214 A28 50fr dk. brn., bl. & red 75 50

Issued to honor the National Red Cross.

Wrestlers, Globe and Torch—A29

Design: 35fr, Globe, torch and several athletes (vert.).

1964, June 27 Perf. 13 Unwmkd.

215 A29 35fr green, violet & dark red brown 70 50
216 " 65fr dark blue, ocher & red brown 1.25 1.00

18th Olympic Games, Tokyo, Oct. 10–25.

Europafrica Issue, 1964

Common Design Type

Design: 30fr, White man and black man beneath tree of industrial symbols.

1964, July 20 Photo. Perf. 12x13

217 CD116 30fr multicolored 45 30

Animal Type of 1963–64.

Designs: 5fr, Manatee (horiz.). 10fr, Pigmy hippopotamus (horiz.). 15fr, Royal antelope.

1964, Oct. 17 Engraved Perf. 13

218 A24 5fr yel. grn., slate green & brown 20 8
219 " 10fr sepia, Prus. grn. & deep claret 30 15
220 " 15fr lilac rose, green & orange brn. 50 20

Co-operation Issue

Common Design Type

1964, Nov. 7 Perf. 13 Unwmkd.

221 CD119 25fr green, dark brown & red 45 35

Korhogo Mail Carriers with Guard, 1914

A30

1964 Nov. 28 Engraved

222 A30 85fr blk. brn., bl. & brown red 1.25 90

Issued for Stamp Day 1964.

Potter—A31

Artisans: 10fr, Wood carvers. 20fr, Ivory carver. 25fr, Weaver.

1965, Mar. 27 Engraved Perf. 13

223 A31 5fr magenta, green & black 7 5
224 " 10fr red lilac, green & black 20 10
225 " 20fr bister, deep blue & dark brown 30 15
226 " 25fr brn., olive & car. 40 25

Unloading Mail, 1900

A32

1965, Apr. 24 Perf. 13 Unwmkd.

227 A32 30fr multicolored 50 35

Issued for Stamp Day, 1965.

ITU Emblem, Old and New Telecommunication Equipment

A32a

1965, May 17

228 A32a 85fr maroon, bright green & dk. bl. 1.35 90

Issued to commemorate the centenary of the International Telecommunication Union.

Abidjan Railroad Station

A33

1965, June 12 Engraved Perf. 13

229 A33 30fr magenta, blue & brown olive 50 35

Pres. Felix Houphouet-Boigny and Map of Ivory Coast

A34

1965, Aug. 7 Photo. Perf. 12½x13

230 A34 30fr multicolored 50 35

Fifth anniversary of Independence.

Hammerhead Stork
A35

Birds: 1fr, Bruce's green pigeon (horiz.). 2fr, Spur-winged goose (horiz.). 5fr, Stone partridge. 15fr, White-breasted guinea fowl. 30fr, Namaqua dove (horiz.). 50fr, Lizard buzzard (horiz.). 75fr, Yellow-billed stork. 90fr, Forest (or Latham's) francolin.

1965–66 Engraved *Perf. 13*

231 A35 1fr yellow green, purple & yellow ('66) 15 15
232 " 2fr slate green, blk. & red ('66) 15 15
233 " 5fr dark olive, dark brown & brown red ('66) 20 20
234 " 10fr red lilac, black & red brown 20 12
235 " 15fr slate green, gray & vermilion 30 18
236 " 30fr slate green, maroon & red brown 60 30
237 " 50fr brown, black & chalky blue 90 50
238 " 75fr orange, maroon & slate green 1.25 60
239 " 90fr emerald, black & brown ('66) 1.85 1.00
Nos. 231-239 (9) 5.60 3.20

Mail Train, 1906
A36

1966, March 26 Engraved *Perf. 13*

240 A36 30fr green, black & maroon 55 35

Issued for Stamp Day.

Baoulé Mother and Child, Carved in Wood
A37

Designs: 10fr, Ointment jar with Wanigougo mask lid. 20fr, Atié carved drums. 30fr, Bété female ancestral figure.

1966, Apr. 9 Unwmkd.

241 A37 5fr blk. & emerald 15 12
242 " 10fr purple & black 25 18
243 " 20fr orange & black 50 35
244 " 30fr red & black 70 40

Issued to commemorate the International Negro Arts Festival, Dakar, Senegal, Apr. 1–24.

Hotel Ivoire
A38

1966, Apr. 30 Engraved *Perf. 13*

245 A38 15fr bl., green, red & olive 30 20

Farm Tractor
A39

1966, Aug. 7 Photo. *Perf. 12½x12*

246 A39 30fr multicolored 45 35

The 6th anniversary of independence.

Uniformed Teacher and Villagers
A40

1966, Sept. 1 Engraved *Perf. 13*

247 A40 30fr dk. red, indigo & dark brown 45 35

National School of Administration.

Veterinarian Treating Cattle
A41

1966, Oct. 22 Engraved *Perf. 13*

248 A41 30fr olive, blue & dp. brown 50 40

Campaign against cattle plague.

Man and Waves Radiating from UNESCO Emblem
A42

Delivery of Gift Parcels
A43

1966, Nov. 14 Engraved *Perf. 13*

249 A42 30fr deep blue & violet brown 50 40

Issued to commemorate the 20th anniversary of UNESCO (United Nations Educational, Scientific and Cultural Organization).

1966, Dec. 11 Engraved *Perf. 13*

250 A43 30fr dk. blue, brown & black 50 40

Issued to commemorate the 20th anniversary of UNICEF (United Nations International Children's Emergency Fund).

Bouaké Hospital and Red Cross
A44

1966, Dec. 20

251 A44 30fr red brown, red & lilac 50 40

Sikorsky S-43 Seaplane and Boats
A45

1967, March 25 Engraved *Perf. 13*

252 A45 30fr indigo, blue green & brn. 60 40

Issued for Stamp Day and to commemorate the 30th anniversary of the Sikorsky S-43 flying boat route.

Pineapple Harvest
A46

Designs: 30fr, Cabbage tree. 100fr, Bananas.

1967 Engraved *Perf. 13*

253 A46 20fr emerald, choc. & lt. brown 30 15
254 " 30fr multicolored 45 20
255 " 100fr brt. bl., lt. olive & brown 1.65 90

Issue Dates: 20fr, 100fr, March 25; 30fr, June 24.

Genie, Protector of Assamlangangan
A47

1967, July 31 Engr. *Perf. 13*

256 A47 30fr green, black & maroon 45 20

Issued to commemorate the 25th Congress of the International PEN Club (writers' organization), Abidjan, July 31–Aug. 5.

Old and New Houses
A48

1967, Aug. 7 Photo. *Perf. 12½x12*

257 A48 30fr multicolored 45 25

The 7th anniversary of independence.

Lions Emblem and Elephant's Head
A49

1967, Sept. 2 Photo. *Perf. 12½x13*

258 A49 30fr lt. blue & multi. 60 45

50th anniversary of Lions International.

Monetary Union Issue

Common Design Type

1967, Nov. 4 Engraved *Perf. 13*

259 CD125 30fr carmine, slate green & black 40 30

Issued to commemorate the 5th anniversary of the West African Monetary Union.

Allegory of French Recognition of Ivory Coast
A50

Tabou Radio Station
A51

1967, Nov. 17 Photo. *Perf. 13x12½*

260 A50 90fr multicolored 1.25 75

20th anniversary of the Days of Recognition. See No. 298.

1968, Mar. 9 Engraved *Perf. 13*

261 A51 30fr dk. green, brown & brt. green 50 30

Issued for Stamp Day.

Cotton Mill
A52

Designs: 5fr, Palm oil extraction plant. 15fr, Abidjan oil refinery. 20fr, Unloading raw cotton and spinning machine (vert.). 30fr, Flour mill. 50fr, Cacao butter extractor. 70fr, Instant coffee factory (vert.). 90fr, Saw mill and timber.

1968 Engraved *Perf. 13*

262 A52 5fr vermilion, slate green & black 8 6
263 " 10fr dk. green, gray & olive bister 12 8
264 " 15fr vermilion, lt. ultra. & blk. 30 15
265 " 20fr Prus. bl. & choc. 30 15
266 " 30fr dk. grn., brt. blue & brn. 50 25
267 " 50fr red, bright green & blk. 70 35
268 " 70fr dark brown, blue & brn. 1.00 60
269 " 90fr dp. blue, black & brown 1.35 65
Nos. 262-269 (8) 4.35 2.29

Issue dates: 5fr, 15fr, June 8. 10fr, 20fr, 90fr, Mar. 23. Others, Oct. 5.

Canoe Race
A53

Design: 100fr, Runners.

1968, Apr. 6 Engraved *Perf. 13*

270 A53 30fr slate blue, lt. green & brown 50 30
271 " 100fr vio. bl., brt. rose lilac & slate blue 1.50 90

Issued to publicize the 19th Olympic Games, Mexico City, Oct. 12–27.

Queen Pokou Sacrificing her Son
A54

1968, Aug. 7 Photo. ***Perf. 12½x12***

272 A54 30fr multicolored 45 25

The 8th anniversary of independence.

Vaccination, WHO Emblem and Elephant's Head
A55

1968, Sept. 28 Engr. ***Perf. 13***

273 A55 30fr chocolate, brt. blue & maroon 50 30

Issued to commemorate the 20th anniversary of the World Health Organization.

Antelope in Forest
A56

1968, Oct. 26 Engraved ***Perf. 13***

274 A56 30fr ultra., brown & olive 60 30

Protection of fauna and flora.

Abidjan Museum and Carved Screen—A57

1968, Nov. 2

275 A57 30fr vio. blue, olive & rose magenta 45 25

Anthropological Museum, Abidjan.

Human Rights Flame and Statues of "Justitia"—A58

1968, Nov. 9 Engraved ***Perf. 13***

276 A58 30fr slate, orange & dark brown 50 30

International Human Rights Year.

"Ville de Maranhao" at Grand Bassam—A59

1969, Mar. 8 Engraved ***Perf. 13***

277 A59 30fr brown, bright blue & green 55 30

Issued for Stamp Day.

Hotel Ivoire, Abidjan—A60

1969, Mar. 29

278 A60 30fr verm., blue & grn. 45 25

Opening of Hotel Ivoire.

Carved Figure A61

Mountains and Hertzian Telecommunications Tower, Man A62

1969, July 5 Engraved ***Perf. 13***

279 A61 30fr red lilac, black & red orange 45 25

Issued to publicize the Ivory Coast art exhibition at the Fine Arts Museum, Vevey, Switzerland, July 12–Sept. 22.

1969, Aug. 7 Engraved ***Perf. 13***

280 A62 30fr dull brown, slate & green 50 30

The 9th anniversary of independence.

Development Bank Issue
Common Design Type

Design: Development Bank emblem and Ivory Coast coat of arms.

1969, Sept. 6

281 CD130 30fr ocher, green & maroon 45 25

Issued to commemorate the 5th anniversary of the African Development Bank.

Arms of Bouake A63

Sport Fishing and SKAL Emblem A64

Coats of Arms: 15fr, Abidjan. 30fr, Ivory Coast.

1969 Photogravure ***Perf. 13***

282	A63	10fr	multicolored	13	5
283	"	15fr	"	22	8
284	"	30fr	"	35	12

Issue Dates: 10fr, Oct. 25; 15fr, Dec. 27; 30fr, Dec. 20.
See Nos. 335–336.

1969, Nov. 22 Engraved ***Perf. 13***

Design: 100fr, Vacation village and SKAL emblem.

285 A64 30fr brown, dk. blue & violet blue 50 30

286 " 100fr green, brown & violet blue 1.50 75

Issued to commemorate the First International Congress in Africa of the SKAL Tourist Association, Abidjan, Nov. 23–28.

ASECNA Issue
Common Design Type

1969, Dec. 13 Engraved ***Perf. 13***

287 CD132 30fr vermilion 45 25

University Center, Abidjan—A65

1970, Feb. 26 Engraved ***Perf. 13***

288 A65 30fr indigo & yel. grn. 40 20

Issued to commemorate the 10th anniversary of higher education in Ivory Coast.

Gabriel Dadié and Telegraph Operator
A66

1970, Mar. 7 Engraved ***Perf. 13***

289 A66 30fr dark red, slate green & black 40 20

Issued for Stamp Day. Gabriel Dadié (1891–1953) was the first native-born postal administrator.

University of Abidjan—A67

1970, Mar. 21 Photogravure

290 A67 30fr Prus. bl., dk. pur. & dk. yel. grn. 40 20

Issued to commemorate the 3rd General Assembly of the Association of French-language Universities (A.U.P.E.L.F.).

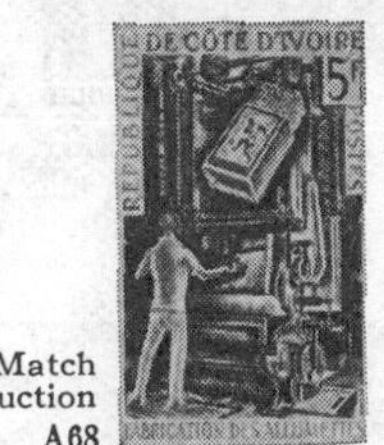

Safety Match Production
A68

Designs: 20fr, Textile industry. 50fr, Shipbuilding.

1970, May 9 Engraved ***Perf. 13***

291 A68 5fr blue, dark brown & ocher 7 3

292 " 20fr rose red, slate & green 25 10

293 " 50fr dark green, brown & bright blue 60 30

Radar, Classroom with Television
A69

1970, May 17

294 A69 40fr red, green & gray olive 60 50

Issued for World Telecommunications Day.

U.P.U. Headquarters Issue
Common Design Type

1970, May 20

295 CD133 30fr lilac, bright green & olive 50 25

U.N. Emblem, Lion, Antelopes and Plane
A70

1970, June 27 Engraved ***Perf. 13***

296 A70 30fr dark red brown, ultramarine & dark green 55 40

25th anniversary of the United Nations.

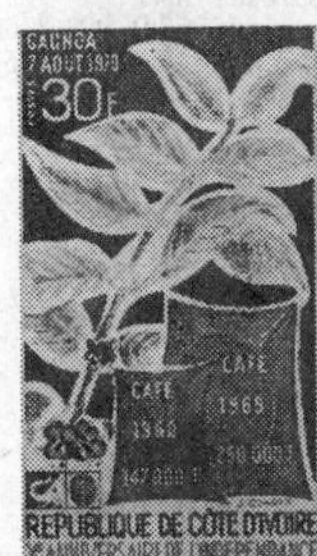

Coffee Branch and Bags Showing Increased Production
A71

1970, Aug. 7 Engraved ***Perf. 13***

297 A71 30fr orange, bluish green & gray 40 20

Tenth anniversary of independence.

Type of 1967.

1970, Oct. 29 Photo. ***Perf. 12x12½***

298 A50 40fr multicolored 55 30

The 5th Congress of the Ivory Coast Democratic Party.

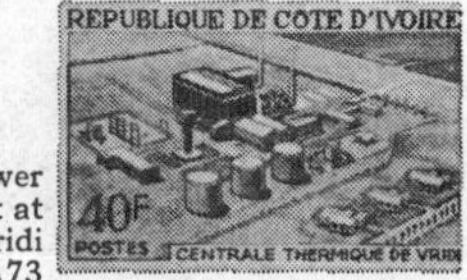

Power Plant at Uridi
A73

1970, Nov. 21 Engraved ***Perf. 13***

299 A73 40fr multicolored 55 25

Certain unlisted issues of Ivory Coast, starting in 1970, are mentioned and briefly described in "For the Record" at the back of this volume.

Postal Service Autobus, 1925
A74

1971, Mar. 6 Engraved ***Perf. 13***

300 A74 40fr dp. grn., dk. brn. & golden brn. 50 25

Stamp Day, 1971.

Marginella Desjardini
A75

Marine Life: 1fr, Aporrhais pes gallinae (shell). 5fr, Crab. 10fr, Marine annelid worms (vert.). No. 305, Natica fanel, marine snail (vert.). No. 306, Starfish (vert.). No. 307, Xenorhora digitata. 25fr, Prometheus cone. 35fr, Crayfish (vert.). No. 310, Conus genuanus (shell). No. 311, Scallop. 45fr, Strombus bubonius. 50fr, Lobster (vert.). 65fr, Rat cowrie.

1971–72 Engraved *Perf. 13*

301 A75 1fr olive & multi. 8 6
302 " 5fr red & multi. 10 8
303 " 10fr emerald & multi. 17 10
304 " 15fr brt. blue & multi. 25 12
305 " 15fr dp. carmine & multi. ('72) 25 10
306 " 20fr ocher & carmine 30 20
307 " 20fr vermilion & multi. ('72) 35 15
308 " 25fr dk. car., rose brn. & black ('72) 35 20
309 " 35fr yellow & multi. 45 25
310 " 40fr emerald & multi. 70 40
311 " 40fr brown & multi. 55 30
312 " 45fr multi. ('72) 60 40
313 " 50fr green & multi. 90 55
314 " 65fr blue, rose brn. & slate grn. ('72) 90 60
Nos. 301-314 (14) 5.95 3.51

Issue dates: Nos. 304, 306, 310, Apr. 24, 1971; 5fr, 35fr, 50fr, June 5, 1971; 1fr, 10fr, No. 311, Oct. 23, 1971; 25fr, 65fr, Jan. 29, 1972; Nos. 305, 307, 45fr, June 3, 1972.

Sub-marine Cable Station, 1891
A76

1971, May 17

315 A76 100fr blue, ocher & olive 1.10 70

3rd World Telecommunications Day.

Apprentice and Lathe
A77

1971, June 19 Engr. *Perf. 13*

316 A77 35fr green, slate & orange brown 45 25

Technical instruction and professional training.

Map of Africa and Telecommunications System
A78

1971, June 26 *Perf. 13x12½*

317 A78 45fr magenta & multi. 55 30

Pan-African Telecommunications system.

Bondoukou Market—A79

1971, Aug. 7 Engraved *Perf. 13*
Size: 48x27mm.

318 A79 35fr ultra., brown & slate 45 25

11th anniversary of independence. See No. C46.

White, Black and Yellow Girls
A80

Design: 45fr, Boys of all races encircling globe.

1971, Oct. 10 Photo. *Perf. 13*

319 A80 40fr blue & multi. 50 25
320 " 45fr emerald & multi. 55 30

International Year Against Racial Discrimination.

Gaming Table and Lottery Tickets
A81

1971, Nov. 13 *Perf. 12½*

321 A81 35fr green & multi. 40 25

National lottery.

Electric Power Installations
A82

1971, Dec. 18 *Perf. 13*

322 A82 35fr red brn. & multi. 50 25

Cogwheel and Workers
A83

1972, Mar. 18 Engr. *Perf. 13*

323 A83 35fr orange, blue & dark brown 40 20

Technical Cooperation Week.

"Your Heart is your Health"
A84

Girls Reading, Book Year Emblem
A85

1972, Apr. 7 Photo. *Perf. 12½x13*

324 A84 40fr blue, olive & red 50 30

World Health Day.

Perf. 12½x13, 13x12½

1972, Apr. 22 Engraved

Design: 35fr, Boys reading (horiz.).

325 A85 35fr slate green, brn. & orange 40 20
326 A85 40fr black, orange & bright green 50 30

International Book Year 1972.

Postal Sorting Center, Abidjan
A86

1972, May 13 *Perf. 13*

327 A86 40fr dk. green, rose lilac & bister 50 25

Stamp Day 1972.

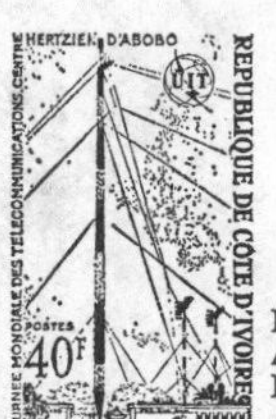

Hertzian Center, Abobo, and ITU Emblem
A87

1972, May 17 Engraved *Perf. 13*

328 A87 40fr blue, red & green 50 25

4th World Telecommunications Day.

Computer Operator, Punch Card
A88

1972, June 24

329 A88 40fr brt. green, blue & red 50 30

Development of computerized information.

View of Odienné—A89

1972, Aug. 7 Engraved *Perf. 13*

330 A89 35fr bl., grn. & brown 40 25

12th anniversary of independence.

West African Monetary Union Issue
Common Design Type

1972, Nov. 2 Engraved *Perf. 13*

331 CD136 40fr brown, gray & red lilac 45 20

10th anniversary of West African Monetary Union.

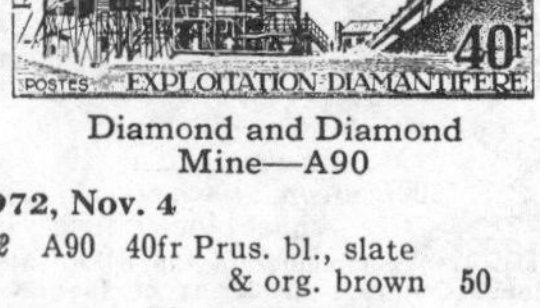

Diamond and Diamond Mine—A90

1972, Nov. 4

332 A90 40fr Prus. bl., slate & org. brown 50 25

Diamond industry.

Pasteur Institute, Louis Pasteur
A91

1972, Nov. 21

333 A91 35fr violet blue, green & brown 45 30

Sesquicentennial of the birth of Louis Pasteur (1822–1895), chemist and bacteriologist.

Children at Village Pump
A92

1972, Dec. 9 Engraved *Perf. 13*

334 A92 35fr dark red, green & black 40 20

Water campaign. See No. 360.

Arms Type of 1969

Coats of Arms: 5fr, Daloa. 10fr, Gagnoa.

1973 Photogravure *Perf. 12*

335 A63 5fr multicolored 7 3
336 " 10fr " 10 5

Nos. 335–336 are 16½-17x22mm. and have "DELRIEU" below design at right. Nos. 282–284 are 17x23mm. and have no name at lower right.

Dr. Armauer G. Hansen
A93

1973, Feb. 3 Engraved *Perf. 13*

342 A93 35fr lilac, dp. blue & brown 45 25

Centenary of the discovery of the Hansen bacillus, the cause of leprosy.

Lake Village Bletankoro—A94

1973, Mar. 10 Engraved *Perf. 13*

343 A94 200fr chocolate, blue & green 2.25 1.25

Gray Triggerfish
A95

Fish: 20fr, Goatfish. 25fr, Cephalopholis taeniops. 35fr, Priacanthus arenatus. 50fr, Razorfish.

1973–74 Engraved *Perf. 13*

344 A95 15fr indigo & slate green 18 12
345 " 20fr lilac & multi. 27 18
346 " 25fr slate green & rose ('74) 20 8
347 " 35fr rose red & slate green 45 25

348 A95 50fr black, ultra. & rose red 65 45
Nos. 344-348 (5) 1.75 1.08

Issue dates: 1973—50fr, Mar. 24; 15fr, 20fr, July 7; 35fr, Dec. 1. 1974—25fr, Mar. 2.

Children A96

1973, Apr. 7 Engr. *Perf. 13*
354 A96 40fr green, black & dull red 50 25

Establishment of first children's village in Africa (SOS villages for homeless children).

Parliament, Abidjan—A97

1973, Apr. 24 Photo. *Perf. 13x12½*
355 A97 100fr multicolored 1.10 60

112th session of the Inter-parliamentary Council.

Teacher and PAC Store A98

1973, May 12 Photo. *Perf. 13x12½*
356 A98 40fr multicolored 40 20

Commercial Action Program (PAC).

Mother, Typist, Dress Form and Pot A99

1973, May 26
357 A99 35fr multicolored 35 20

Technical instruction for women.

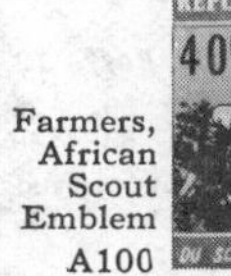

Farmers, African Scout Emblem A100

1973, July 16 Photo. *Perf. 13x12½*
358 A100 40fr multicolored 40 25

24th Boy Scout World Conference, Nairobi, Kenya, July 16-21.

Party Headquarters, Yamoussokro—A101

1973, Aug. 7 Photo. *Perf. 13*
359 A101 35fr multicolored 35 20

Children at Dry Pump A102

1973, Aug. 16 Engraved
360 A102 40fr multicolored 40 20

African solidarity in drought emergency.

African Postal Union Issue
Common Design Type

1973, Sept. 12 Engraved *Perf. 13*
361 CD137 100fr purple, black & red 1.00 60

Decorated Arrow Heads A103

1973, Sept. 15 Photo. *Perf. 12½x13*
362 A103 5fr black, brown red & brown 7 7

Abidjan Museum.

Ivory Coast No. 1—A104

1973, Oct. 9 Engraved *Perf. 13*
363 A104 40fr emerald, black & orange 45 30

Stamp Day.

Highway Intersection A105

1973, Oct. 13
364 A105 35fr blue, blk. & grn. 35 20

Indenie-Abidjan intersection.

Map of Africa, Federation Emblem A106

Elephant Emblem A107

1973, Oct. 26 Photo. *Perf. 13*
365 A106 40fr ultra., red brn. & vio. blue 35 20

18th General Assembly of the International Social Security Federation, Abidjan, Oct. 26-Nov. 3.

1973, Nov. 19
366 A107 40fr black & bister 35 20

7th World Congress of the Universal Federation of World Travel Agents' Associations, Abidjan.

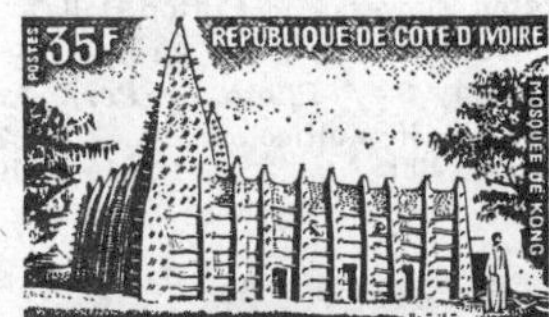

Kong Mosque—A108

1974, Mar. 9
367 A108 35fr bl., grn. & brn. 28 12

People and Sun A109

1974, Apr. 20 Photo. *Perf. 13*
368 A109 35fr multicolored 30 20

Permanent Mission to U.N.

Grand Lahou Post Office—A110

1974, May 17 Engraved *Perf. 13*
369 A110 35fr multicolored 30 20

Stamp Day 1974.

Map and Flags of Members A110a

1974, May 29 Photo. *Perf. 13x12½*
370 A110a 40fr blue & multi. 35 15

15th anniversary of the Council of Accord.

Pres. Houphouet-Boigny
A111 A112

1974-76 Engraved *Perf. 13*
371 A111 25fr grn., org. & brn. 20 8
a. Booklet pane of 10 2.50
b. Booklet pane of 20 5.00
373 A112 35fr org., grn. & brn. 28 10
a. Booklet pane of 10 3.50
b. Booklet pane of 20 7.00
374 A112 40fr grn., org. & brn. 33 12
a. Booklet pane of 10 4.00
b. Booklet pane of 20 8.00
375 A112 60fr blue, carmine & brn. ('76) 50 10
376 " 65fr carmine, blue & brn. ('76) 50 15
Nos. 371-376 (5) 1.81 55

Arms of Ivory Coast A113

WPY Emblem A114

1974-77 Photo. *Perf. 12*
377 A113 30fr emerald, brown & gold 30 12
378 " 35fr brown, emerald & gold 28 10
a. Booklet pane of 10 3.50
b. Booklet pane of 20 7.00
379 A113 40fr vio. bl., emerald & gold 32 12
a. Booklet pane of 10 4.00
b. Booklet pane of 20 8.00

Inscribed: "COTE D'IVOIRE"

380 A113 60fr carmine, gold & emerald 45 25
381 " 65fr green, gold & emerald 50 30
382 " 70fr blue, gold & emerald 55 35
Nos. 377-382 (6) 2.40 1.24

Issue dates: Nos. 378-379, June 29, 1974. Nos. 380-382, Jan. 1976, No. 377, 1977.

1974, Aug. 19 Engraved *Perf. 13*
383 A114 40fr emerald & blue 35 20

World Population Year, 1974.

Cotton Harvest A115

1974, Sept. 21 Litho. *Perf. 12½x13*
384 A115 50fr multicolored 40 20

UPU Emblem A116

1974, Oct. 9 Engraved *Perf. 13*
385 A116 40fr multicolored 35 20

Centenary of Universal Postal Union. See Nos. C59-C60.

Plowing Farmer, Service Emblem A117

1974, Dec. 7 Photogravure *Perf. 13*
386 A117 35fr multicolored 30 15

14th anniversary of independence.

National Library—A118

1975, Jan. 9 Photo. ***Perf. 13***

387 A118 40fr multicolored 35 15

National Library, first anniversary.

Follereau and Blind Students A119

1975, Jan. 26 Engr. ***Perf. 13***

388 A119 35fr multicolored 30 15

Raoul Follereau, pioneer educator of the blind and lepers.

Congress Emblem A120

Flowering Coffee Branch A121

1975, Mar. 4 Photo. ***Perf. 12½x13***

389 A120 40fr blk. & emerald 35 20

52nd Congress of the International Association of Seed Crushers, Abidjan, Mar. 2–7.

1975, Mar. 15 ***Perf. 13½x13***

Design: 10fr, Branch with beans.

390 A121 5fr blk., org. & grn. 5 3
391 " 10fr brn. & multi. 8 6

Coffee cultivation.

Sassandra Wharf—A122

1975, Apr. 19 Engr. ***Perf. 13***

392 A122 100fr multi. 75 50

Letter Sorting A123

1975, Apr. 26 Photo. ***Perf. 13***

393 A123 40fr multicolored 35 25

Stamp Day.

Cotton Flower A124

Cotton Bolls A125

1975, May 3 Photo. ***Perf. 13***

394 A124 5fr multicolored 7 7
395 A125 10fr " 15 10

Cotton cultivation.

Marie Kore, Women's Year Emblem—A126

1975, May 19 Engraved ***Perf. 13***

396 A126 45fr lt. blue, yellow grn. & brown 40 30

International Women's Year.

Fort Dabou—A127

1975, June 7 Engr. ***Perf. 13***

397 A127 50fr multicolored 40 30

Abidjan Harbor—A128

Designs: 40fr, Grand Bassam wharf, 1906 (vert.). 100fr, Planned harbor expansion on Locodjro.

1975, July 1 Photo. ***Perf. 13***

398 A128 35fr multicolored 30 20

Miniature Sheet

399 A128 Sheet of 3 1.60 1.60
 a. 40fr multicolored 30 30
 b. 100fr " 75 75

25th anniversary of Abidjan Harbor. No. 399 also contains a 35fr (No. 398). Nos. 399a–399b were issued in miniature sheet only. Size of sheet: 155x100mm.

Cacao Pods on Tree A129

1975, Aug. 2

400 A129 35fr multicolored 28 15

Farm Workers A130

1975, Oct. 4 Photo. ***Perf. 13x12½***

401 A130 50fr multicolored 40 25

National Organization for Rural Development.

Railroad Bridge, N'zi River—A131

1975, Dec. 7 Photo. ***Perf. 13***

402 A131 60fr multicolored 50 30

15th anniversary of independence.

Baoulé Mother and Child, Carved in Wood A132

1976, Jan. 24 Litho. ***Perf. 13***

403 A132 65fr black & multi. 55 35

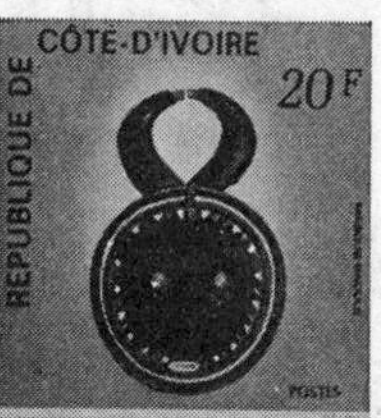

Baoulé Mask A133

Design: 150fr, Chief Abron's chair.

1976, Feb. 7 Photo. ***Perf. 12½***

404 A133 20fr blue & multi. 15 10
405 " 150fr buff, black & brown 1.20 75

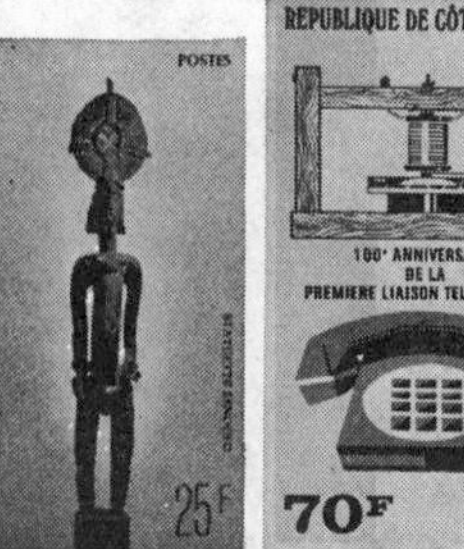

Senufo Statuette A134

Telephones 1876 and 1976 A135

1976, Feb. 21 ***Perf. 13x13½***

406 A134 25fr ocher & multi. 20 15

1976, Mar. 10 Litho. ***Perf. 12***

407 A135 70fr multicolored 55 40

Centenary of first telephone call by Alexander Graham Bell, Mar. 10, 1876.

Ivory Coast Map, Pigeon, Carving A136

1976, Apr. 10 Photo. ***Perf. 12½***

408 A136 65fr multicolored 50 40

20th Stamp Day.

Smiling Trees and Cat A137

Children with Books A138

1976, June 5 Litho. ***Perf. 12½***

409 A137 65fr multicolored 50 30

Nature protection.

1976, July 3 Photo. ***Perf. 12½x13***

410 A138 65fr multicolored 50 35

Books for children.

Runner, Maple Leaf, Olympic Rings—A139

Design: 60fr, Javelin, maple leaf, Olympic rings (vert.).

1976, July 17 Litho. ***Perf. 12***

411 A139 60fr multicolored 50 35
412 " 65fr " 50 40

21st Olympic Games, Montreal, Canada, July 17–Aug. 1.

Cashew A140

1976, Sept. 18 ***Perf. 12½***

413 A140 65fr blue & multi. 50 30

Highway and Conference Emblem—A141

1976, Oct. 25 Litho. *Perf. 12½x12*

414 A141 60fr multicolored 50 35

3rd African Highway Conference, Abidjan, July 25–30.

Pres. Houphouet-Boigny A142

1976–77 Photo. *Perf. 13½x12½*

415	A142	35fr brn., red lilac & blk. ('77)	25	5
416	"	40fr brt. grn., ocher & brn. blk.	30	6
		a. Bklt. pane of 12 (8 #416, 4 #417)	4.00	
417	A142	45fr ocher, brt. grn. & brn. blk.	35	8
418	"	60fr brn., magenta & brn. blk.	50	10
419	"	65fr grn., org. & brn. black	50	15
		Nos. 415-419 (5)	1.90	44

The 40fr issued in booklet only; 45fr in booklet and coil; 35fr, 60fr and 65fr in coil only.

Stamps from booklets are imperf. on one side or two adjoining sides. Coils have control number on back of every 10th stamp.

John Paul Jones, American Marine and Ship

A143

Designs: 125fr, Count de Rochambeau and grenadier of Touraine Regiment. 150fr, Admiral Count Jean Baptiste d'Estaing and French marine. 175fr, Marquis de Lafayette and grenadier of Soissons Regiment. 200fr, Thomas Jefferson, American soldier, Declaration of Independence. 500fr, George Washington, U.S. flag, Continental officer.

1976, Nov. 27 Litho. *Perf. 11*

421	A143	100fr multicolored	75	35
422	"	125fr "	1.00	40
423	"	150fr "	1.15	50
424	"	175fr "	1.25	55
425	"	200fr "	1.50	60
		Nos. 421-425 (5)	5.65	2.40

Souvenir Sheet

426 A143 500fr multicolored 4.00 2.00

American Bicentennial.

No. 426 has multicolored margin showing four American soldiers; black inscriptions. Size: 101x76mm.

Certain countries cancel stamps in full sheets and sell them (usually with gum) for less than face value. Dealers generally sell "CTO" (canceled to order) stamps for much less than postally used copies.

"Development and Solidarity" A144

1976, Dec. 7 Photo. *Perf. 13*

427 A144 60fr multicolored 50 30

16th anniversary of independence.

Benin Head, Ivory Coast Arms A145

1977, Jan. 15 Photo. *Perf. 13*

428 A145 65fr gold, dk. brn. & green 50 30

2nd World Black and African Festival, Lagos, Nigeria, Jan. 15–Feb. 12.

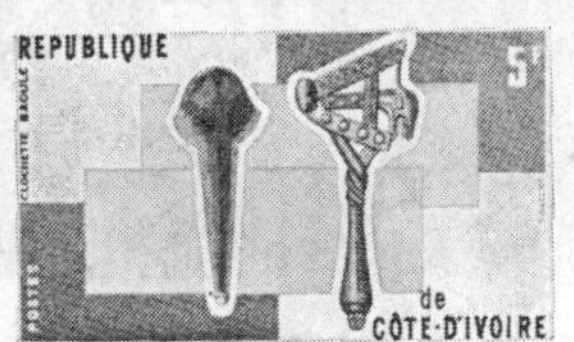

Baoule Bells—A146

Musical Instruments: 10fr, Senufo balafon. 20fr, Dida drum.

1977, Mar. 5 Engr. *Perf. 13*

429	A146	5fr multicolored	8	8
430	"	10fr black & red	10	8
431	"	20fr green, violet & black	17	10

Air Afrique Plane Unloading Mail A147

1977, Apr. 9 Litho. *Perf. 13*

432 A147 60fr multicolored 50 35

Stamp Day 1977.

Sassenage Castle, Grenoble—A148

1977, May 21 Litho. *Perf. 12½*

433 A148 100fr multicolored 75 50

10th anniversary of International French Language Council.

Orville and Wilbur Wright, "Wright Flyer," 1903

A149

Designs: 75fr, Louis Bleriot crossing English Channel, 1909. 100fr, Ross Smith and Vickers-Vimy (flew England-Australia, 1919). 200fr, Charles A. Lindbergh and "Spirit of St. Louis" (flew New York-Paris, 1927). 300fr, Supersonic jet Concorde, 1976. 500fr, Lindbergh in flying suit and "Spirit of St. Louis."

1977, June 27 Litho. *Perf. 14*

434	A149	60fr multicolored	50	25
435	"	75fr "	60	30
436	"	100fr "	75	30
437	"	200fr "	1.50	60
438	"	300fr "	2.25	90
		Nos. 434-438	5.60	2.35

Souvenir Sheet

439 A149 500fr multicolored 4.00 1.75

History of aviation.

No. 439 has multicolored margin with map of Lindbergh's transatlantic flight. Size: 117x91mm.

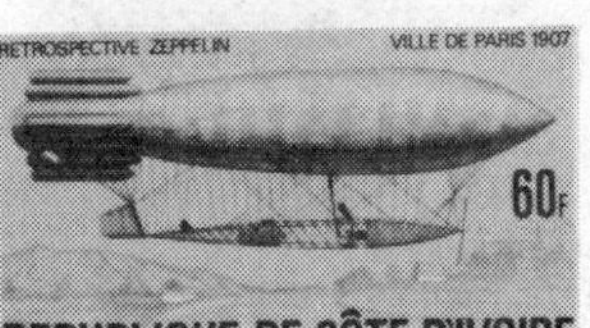

Santos Dumont's "Ville de Paris," 1907

A150

Designs: 65fr, LZ 1 at takeoff. 150fr, "Schwaben" LZ 10 over Germany. 200fr, "Bodensee" LZ 120, 1919. 300fr, LZ 127 over Sphinx and pyramids.

1977, Sept. 3 Litho. *Perf. 11*

440	A150	60fr multicolored	45	20
441	"	65fr "	45	20
442	"	150fr "	1.10	45
443	"	200fr "	1.50	60
444	"	300fr "	2.25	90
		Nos. 440-444 (5)	5.75	2.35

History of the Zeppelin. Exist imperf.

See No. C63.

Congress Emblem

A151

1977, Sept. 12 Photo. *Perf. 12½*

445 A151 60fr lt. & dk. green 50 35

17th International Congress of Administrative Sciences in Africa, Abidjan, Sept. 12–16.

Yamoussoukro A152

1977, Nov. 12 Photo. *Perf. 13½x14*

446 A152 65fr multicolored 50 35

Yamoussoukro, first Ivory Coast container ship.

Hand Holding Produce, Generators, Factories A153

1977, Dec. 7 Photo. *Perf. 13½*

447 A153 60fr multicolored 50 35

17th anniversary of independence.

Presidents Giscard d'Estaing and Houphouet-Boigny—A154

1978, Jan. 11 *Perf. 13*

448	A154	60fr multicolored	50	35
449	"	65fr "	50	35
450	"	100fr "	75	55
		a. Souvenir sheet, 500fr	4.00	4.00

Visit of Pres. Valery Giscard d'Estaing. No. 450a contains one stamp; multicolored margin with arms of Ivory Coast and French and Ivory Coast flags. Size: 160x120mm.

St. George and the Dragon, by Rubens

A155

Rubens Paintings: 150fr, Child's head. 250fr, Annunciation. 300fr, The Birth of Louis XIII. 500fr, Virgin and Child.

1978, Mar. 4 Litho. *Perf. 13½*

451	A155	65fr gold & multi.	50	25
452	"	150fr " "	1.10	45
453	"	250fr " "	1.90	70
454	"	300fr " "	2.25	85

Souvenir Sheet

455 A155 500fr gold & multi. 4.00 1.75

Peter Paul Rubens (1577–1640), 400th birth anniversary. No. 455 has multicolored margin showing cherubs surrounding Virgin. Size: 96x115mm.

Royal Guards—A156

Design: 65fr, Cosmological figures.

1978, Apr. 1 **Litho.** ***Perf. 12½***

456 A156 60fr multicolored 45 25
457 " 65fr " 50 30

Rural Postal Center—A157

1978, Apr. 8

458 A157 60fr multicolored 45 25

Stamp Day.

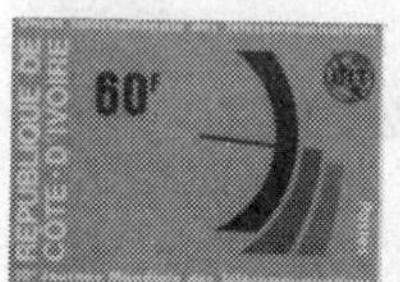

Antenna, ITU Emblem A158

1978, May 17 ***Perf. 13***

459 A158 60fr multicolored 45 25

10th World Telecommunications Day.

Svante August Arrhenius, Electrolytic Apparatus—A159

Designs: 75fr, Jules Bordet, child, mountains, eagle and Petri dish. 100fr, André Gide, and St. Peter's, Rome. 200fr, John Steinbeck and horse farm. 300fr, Children with flowers and UNICEF emblem. 500fr, Max Planck, rockets and earth.

1978, May 27 **Litho.** ***Perf. 13½***

460 A159 60fr multicolored 45 25
461 " 75fr " 55 35
462 " 100fr " 75 45
463 " 200fr " 1.50 90
464 " 300fr " 2.25 1.35
Nos. 460-464 (5) 5.50 3.30

Souvenir Sheet

465 A159 500fr multicolored 4.00 1.85

Nobel Prize winners. No. 465 has multicolored margin showing outer space and head of Alfred Nobel. Size: 120x82mm.

Soccer Ball, Player and Argentina '78 Emblem—A160

Designs (Soccer Ball, Argentina '78 Emblem and): 65fr, Player (vert.). 100fr, Player. 150fr, Goalkeeper. 300fr, Ball as sun, and player (vert.). 500fr, Ball as globe with Argentina on map of South America.

1978, June 17

466 A160 60fr multicolored 45 25
467 " 65fr " 50 30
468 " 100fr " 75 45
469 " 150fr " 1.10 65
470 " 300fr " 2.25 1.35
Nos. 466-470 (5) 5.05 3.00

Souvenir Sheet

471 A160 500fr multicolored 4.00 2.00

11th World Cup Soccer Championship, Argentina, June 1-25. No. 471 has multicolored margin showing stadium, Ivory Coast and World Cup flags. Size: 103x78 mm.

Miniodes Discolor A161

Butterflies: 65fr, Charaxes lactetinctus. 100fr, Papilio zalmoxis. 200fr, Papilio antimachus.

1978, July 8 **Photo.** ***Perf. 14x13***

472 A161 60fr multicolored 45 25
473 " 65fr " 50 30
474 " 100fr " 75 45
475 " 200fr " 1.50 90

Cricket A162

Insects: 20fr, 60fr, Various hemiptera. 65fr, Goliath beetle.

1978, Aug. 26 **Litho.** ***Perf. 12½***

476 A162 10fr multicolored 7 5
477 " 20fr " 15 10
478 " 60fr " 45 25
479 " 65fr " 50 50

Stylized Figures Emerging from TV Screen—A163

Design: 65fr, Passengers on train made up of TV sets.

1978, Sept. 18 ***Perf. 13***

480 A163 60fr multicolored 45 25
481 " 65fr " 50 35

Educational television programs.

Map of Ivory Coast, Mobile Drill Platform Ship A164

Designs (Map of Ivory Coast, Ram at Discovery Site and): 65fr, Gold goblets. 500fr, Pres. Houphouet-Boigny holding gold goblets.

1978, Oct. 18 **Litho.** ***Perf. 12½x12***

482 A164 60fr multicolored 45 25
483 " 65fr " 50 35

Souvenir Sheet

484 A164 500fr multicolored 4.00 2.00

First anniversary of announcement of oil discovery off the coast of Ivory Coast. No. 484 has multicolored margin showing mobile drill platform ship. Size: 90x109mm.

National Assembly, Paris, UPU Emblem A165

1978, Dec. 2 **Litho.** ***Perf. 13½***

485 A165 200fr multicolored 1.50 90

Congress of Paris, centenary.

Drummer A166 **Poster A167**

1978, Dec. 7 **Photo.** ***Perf. 12½x13***

486 A166 60fr multicolored 45 25

18th anniversary of independence.

1978, Dec. 12

Design: 65fr, Arrows made of flags, and television screen.

487 A167 60fr multicolored 45 25
488 " 65fr " 50 35

Technical cooperation among developing countries with the help of educational television.

Plowing—A168

1979, Jan. 27 **Photo.** ***Perf. 13***

489 A168 100fr multicolored 75 45

The first price column gives the catalogue value of an unused stamp, the second that of a used stamp.

Canceled-to-order stamps are often from remainders. Most collectors of canceled stamps prefer postally used specimens.

King Hassan II, Pres. Houphouet-Boigny, Flags and Map of Morocco and Ivory Coast—A169

1979, Jan. 27 **Photo.** ***Perf. 13***

490 A169 60fr multicolored 45 30
491 " 65fr " 50 35
492 " 500fr " 3.75 2.25

Visit of King Hassan of Morocco to Ivory Coast.

Horus A170

Design: 500fr, Vulture with Ankh and cartouches.

1979, Feb. 17 **Litho.** ***Perf. 12½***

493 A170 200fr multicolored 1.50 90
494 " 500fr " 3.75 2.25

UNESCO drive to save Temples of Philae.

Locranthus A171

Flowers: 60fr, Vanda Joséphine. 65fr, Renanthera storiei.

1979, Feb. 24

495 A171 30fr multicolored 22 15
496 " 60fr " 45 30
497 " 65fr " 50 35

Hippopotamus A172

1979, Mar. 24 **Photo.** ***Perf. 13x13½***

498 A172 50fr multicolored 50 40

Wildlife protection.

SEMI-POSTAL STAMPS.

No. 47
Surcharged in Red

1915 *Perf. 14x13½* Unwmkd.

B1 A5 10c+5c red orange & rose 25 25
a. Double surcharge 17.50 17.50

Issued on ordinary and chalky paper.

Curie Issue
Common Design Type

1938 *Perf. 13.*

B2 CD80 1.75fr+50c bright ultramarine 3.75 3.00

French Revolution Issue
Common Design Type

1939 Photogravure

Name and Value Typo. in Black.

B3 CD83 45(c)+25(c) green 2.00 2.00
B4 " 70(c)+30(c) brown 2.00 2.00
B5 " 90(c)+35(c) red orange 2.00 2.00
B6 " 1.25fr+1fr rose pink 2.00 2.00
B7 " 2.25fr+2fr blue 2.00 2.00
Nos. B3-B7 (5) 10.00 10.00

1941

Stamps of 1936-38 Surcharged in Red or Black

SECOURS
+ 1 fr.
NATIONAL

B8 A7 50c+1fr plum (Bk) 30 30
B9 A8 80c+2fr black brown (R) 4.50 4.50
B10 " 1.50fr+2fr ultra. (R) 4.50 4.50
B11 A9 2fr+3fr ultra-marine (Bk) 4.50 4.50

Common Design Type and

Native Engineer—SP1

Senegalese Light Artillery SP2

1941 Photogravure *Perf. 13½*

B12 SP1 1fr + 1fr red 25
B13 CD86 1.50fr + 3fr claret 25
B14 SP2 2.50fr + 1fr blue 25

It is doubtful whether Nos. B12–B14 were placed in use. They were issued by the Vichy government.

Nos. 165–166 were surcharged "OEUVRES COLONIALES" and surtax (including change of denomination of the 2.50fr to 50c). These were issued in 1944 by the Vichy government and not placed on sale in the colony.

Republic
Anti-Malaria Issue
Common Design Type
Perf. 12½x12

1962, Apr. 7 Engraved Unwmkd.

B15 CD108 25fr+5fr olive green 60 60

Issued for the World Health Organization drive to eradicate malaria.

Freedom from Hunger Issue
Common Design Type

1963, Mar. 21 *Perf. 13*

B16 CD112 25fr+5fr red lilac, dk. vio. & brn. 70 70

AIR POST STAMPS.

Common Design Type
Engraved.

1940 *Perf. 12½x12.* Unwmkd.

C1 CD85 1.90fr ultramarine 8 8
C2 " 2.90fr dark red 8 8
C3 " 4.50fr dk. gray green 12 12
C4 " 4.90fr yellow bistre 12 12
C5 " 6.90fr deep orange 40 40
Nos. C1-C5 (5) 80 80

Common Design Types

1942

C6 CD88 50c carmine & blue 7
C7 " 1fr brown & black 10
C8 " 2fr dark green & red brown 18
C9 " 3fr dark blue & scarlet 25
C10 " 5fr violet & dark red 30

Frame Engraved,
Center Typographed.

C11 CD89 10fr multicolored 35
C12 " 20fr " 45
C13 " 50fr " 50 60
Nos. C6-C13 (8) 2.20

There is doubt whether Nos. C6–C12 were officially placed in use.

Republic

Lapalud Place and Post Office, Abidjan—AP1

Designs: 200fr, Houphouet-Boigny Bridge. 500fr, Ayamé dam.

Engraved.

1959, Oct. 1 *Perf. 13* Unwmkd.

C14 AP1 100fr multicolored 1.75 60
C15 " 200fr " 3.25 1.50
C16 " 500fr " 8.00 3.25

Sports Type of 1961.
Sport: 100fr, High Jump.

1961, Dec. 23

C17 A19 100fr rose lilac, black & bl. 1.75 1.25

Abidjan Games, Dec. 24–31.

Air Afrique Issue
Common Design Type

1962, Feb. 17 *Perf. 13* Unwmkd.

C18 CD107 50fr Prussian blue, chocolate & org. brown 1.00 75

Founding of Air Afrique (African Airlines).

Village in Man Region—AP2

Design: 200fr, Street in Odienné (vert.).

1962, June 23 Engraved *Perf. 13*

C19 AP2 200fr gray, green, & dk. brown 3.25 1.35
C20 " 500fr slate green & dull red brn. 7.00 3.00

U.N. Headquarters, New York AP3

1962, Sept. 20 *Perf. 13*

C21 AP3 100fr multicolored 1.65 1.10

Issued to commemorate the second anniversary of admission to the United Nations.

Sassandra Bay—AP4

Design: 50fr, Moossou bridge. 200fr, Comoe river.

1963 *Perf. 13* Unwmkd.

C22 AP4 50fr brn., blue & slate green 75 40
C23 " 100fr red brown, slate grn. & blue 1.65 1.00
C24 " 200fr brown, slate green & yel. green 3.25 1.50

African Postal Union Issue
Common Design Type

1963, Sept. 8 Photo. *Perf. 12½*

C25 CD114 85fr org. brown, ocher & red 1.40 1.10

1963 Air Afrique Issue
Common Design Type

1963, Nov. 19 *Perf. 13x12* Unwmkd.

C26 CD115 25fr crimson, gray, black & green 50 40

Ramses II and Queen Nefertari AP5

1964, Mar. 7 Engraved *Perf. 13*

C27 AP5 60fr carmine, black & red brown 1.20 1.00

Issued to publicize the UNESCO campaign to save historic monuments in Nubia.

Arms of Republic—AP6

1964, June 13 Photogravure

C28 AP6 200fr ultra., yellow green & gold 3.00 1.25

President John F. Kennedy AP7

1964, Nov. 14 *Perf. 12½* Unwmkd.

C29 AP7 100fr gray, claret brn. & blk. 1.75 1.25
a. Souv. sheet of 4 7.25 7.25

Issued in memory of Pres. John F. Kennedy (1917–63). No. C29a contains four No. C29; black marginal inscription. Size: 90x128½mm.

Liana Bridge, Lieupleu—AP8

1965, Dec. 4 Engraved *Perf. 13*

C30 AP8 100fr olive grn., dk. green & dk. red brown 1.50 1.00

Street in Kong—AP9

1966, March 5 Engraved *Perf. 13*

C31 AP9 300fr brt. bl., bister brown & vio. brown 4.75 2.50

Air Afrique Issue, 1966
Common Design Type

1966, Aug. 20 Photo. *Perf. 13*

C32 CD123 30fr dark green, blk. & gray 50 30

Issued to commemorate the introduction of DC-8F planes by Air Afrique.

Air Afrique Headquarters AP10

1967, Feb. 4 Engraved *Perf. 13*

C33 AP10 500fr emerald, indigo & ocher 7.50 3.25

Issued to commemorate the opening of Air Afrique headquarters in Abidjan.

African Postal Union Issue, 1967

Common Design Type

1967, Sept. 9 Engraved *Perf. 13*

C34 CD124 100fr black, vio. & car. lake 1.65 1.00

See note after Cameroun No. C90.

Senufo Village—AP11

Design: 500fr, Tiegba village.

1968 Engraved *Perf. 13*

C35 AP11 100fr olive bis., grn. & ocher 1.65 1.00

C36 " 500fr Prus. blue, olive green & brown 7.00 3.00

Issue dates: 100fr, Feb. 17; 500fr, Apr. 27.

PHILEXAFRIQUE Issue

Street in Grand Bassam, by Achalme AP12

1969, Jan. 11 Photo. *Perf. 12x12½*

C37 AP12 100fr grn. & multi. 1.65 1.65

Issued to publicize PHILEXAFRIQUE Philatelic Exhibition in Abidjan, Feb. 14–23. Printed with alternating green label.

2nd PHILEXAFRIQUE Issue

Common Design Type

Designs: 50fr, Ivory Coast No. 130 and view of San Pedro. 100fr, Ivory Coast No. 149 and man wearing chief's garments (vert.). 200fr, Ivory Coast No. 77 and Exhibition Hall, Abidjan.

1969, Feb. 14 Engraved *Perf. 13*

C38 CD128 50fr green, brn. red & deep blue 90 90

C39 " 100fr brown, orange & dp. blue 1.75 1.75

C40 " 200fr brown, gray & deep blue 3.25 3.25

a. Min. sheet of 3 6.00 6.00

Issued to commemorate the opening of PHILEXAFRIQUE, Abidjan, Feb. 14. No. C40a contains one each of Nos. C38–C40. Size: 158x99mm.

Man Waterfall—AP13

Mount Niangbo—AP14

1970 Engraved *Perf. 13*

C41 AP13 100fr ocher, slate green & violet blue 1.40 80

C42 AP14 200fr henna brown, green & light olive 3.00 1.25

Issue dates: 100fr, Jan. 6; 200fr, July 18.

San Pedro Harbor—AP15

1971, March 21 Engraved *Perf. 13*

C43 AP15 100fr slate green, red brown & bright blue 1.25 70

Treichville Swimming Pool—AP16

1971, May 29 Photo. *Perf. 12½*

C44 AP16 100fr multicolored 1.25 75

Aerial View of Coast Line—AP17

1971, July 3 Engr. *Perf. 13*

C45 AP17 500fr multicolored 6.50 3.00

Tourist publicity for the African Riviera.

Bondoukou Market Type of Regular Issue

Design: 200fr, Similar to No. 318, but without people at left and in center.

Embossed on Gold Paper

1971, Aug. 7 *Perf. 12½*

Size: 36x26mm.

C46 A79 200fr gold, ultra. & black 2.75 2.25

11th anniversary of independence.

African Postal Union Issue, 1971

Common Design Type

Design: 100fr, Ivory Coast coat of arms and UAMPT building, Brazzaville, Congo.

1971, Nov. 13 Photo. *Perf. 13x13½*

C47 CD135 100fr bl. & multi. 1.25 70

Lion of St. Mark—AP18

Design: 200fr, Waves and St. Mark's Basilica, Venice.

1972, Feb. 5 Photo. *Perf. 12½*

C48 AP18 100fr yel. & multi. 1.50 1.00

C49 " 200fr bl. & multi. 3.50 2.25

UNESCO campaign to save Venice.

Kawara Mosque—AP19

1972, Apr. 29 Engr. *Perf. 13*

C50 AP19 500fr blue, brown & ocher 6.00 2.75

View of Gouessesso—AP20

Designs: 200fr, Jacqueville Lake. 500fr, Kossou Dam.

1972 Engraved *Perf. 13*

C51 AP20 100fr bl., slate grn. & ocher 1.25 70

C52 " 200fr brn., blue & slate grn. 3.00 1.25

C53 " 500fr Prus. bl., grn. & brown 6.00 3.00

Issue dates: 100fr, June 10; 200fr, Oct. 28; 500fr, Nov. 17.

Akakro Radar Earth Station—AP21

1972, Nov. 27 Engraved *Perf. 13*

C54 AP21 200fr bright blue, slate grn. & chocolate 3.00 1.50

The Judgment of Solomon, by Nandjui Legue—AP22

1973, Aug. 26 Photo. *Perf. 13*

C55 AP22 500fr multicolored 5.50 3.00

6th World Peace Conference for Justice.

Sassandra River Bridge—AP23

1974, May 4 Engraved *Perf. 13*

C56 AP23 100fr black & yel. green 75 45

C57 " 500fr slate green & brown 4.00 2.25

Vridi Soap Factory, Abidjan—AP24

1974, July 6 Photogravure *Perf. 13*

C58 AP24 200fr multicolored 1.65 1.00

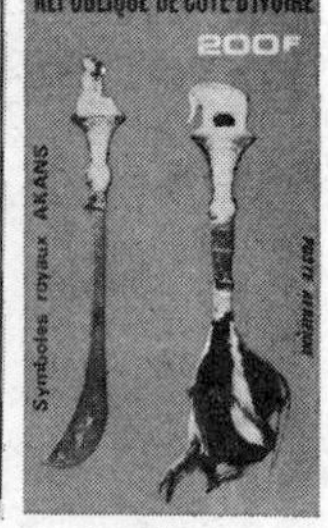

UPU Emblem, Ivory Coast Flag, Post Runner and Jet AP25

Fly Whisk and Panga Knife, Symbols of Akans Royal Family AP26

1974, Oct. 9 Photo. *Perf. 13*

C59 AP25 200fr multicolored 2.00 1.50

C60 " 300fr " 3.00 2.25

Centenary of Universal Postal Union.

1976, Apr. 3 Photo. *Perf. 12½x13*

C61 AP26 200fr brt. blue & multi. 1.65 1.00

Tingrela Mosque AP27

1977, May 7 Engr. *Perf. 13*

C62 AP27 500fr multicolored 4.00 2.25

Zeppelin Type of 1977

Souvenir Sheet

Design: "Graf Zeppelin" LZ 127 over New York.

1977, Sept. 3 Litho. *Perf. 11*

C63 A150 500fr multicolored 4.00 1.75

History of the Zeppelin. Exists imperf. No. C63 has multicolored margin showing zeppelin; black inscription. Size: 92x105mm.

Philexafrique II—Essen Issue

Common Design Types

Designs: No. C64, Elephant and Ivory Coast No. 239. No. C65, Pheasant and Bavaria No. 1.

1978, Nov. 1 Litho. *Perf. 13x12½*

C64 CD138 100fr multi. 75 45

C65 CD139 100fr " 75 45

Nos. C64–C65 printed se-tenant.

AIR POST SEMI-POSTAL STAMPS.

Stamps of Dahomey types V1, V2, V3 and V4 inscribed "Côte d'Ivoire" were issued in 1942 by the Vichy Government, but were not placed on sale in the colony.

POSTAGE DUE STAMPS.

Natives
D1

Numeral of Value
D2

Typographed.

1906-07 *Perf. 14x13½.* Unwmkd.

J1	D1	5c green, *greenish*	85	85
J2	"	10c red brown	70	70
J3	"	15c dark blue	1.25	1.25
J4	"	20c *yellow*	2.35	2.35
J5	"	30c red, *straw*	2.75	2.75
J6	"	50c violet	2.00	2.00
J7	"	60c *buff*	10.00	10.00
J8	"	1fr *pinkish*	10.00	10.00
		Nos. J1-J8 (8)	29.90	29.90

1914

J9	D2	5c green	5	5
J10	"	10c rose	5	5
J11	"	15c gray	5	5
J12	"	20c brown	5	5
J13	"	30c blue	8	8
J14	"	50c black	15	15
J15	"	60c orange	20	20
J16	"	1fr violet	25	25
		Nos. J9-J16 (8)	88	88

Type of 1914 Issue Surcharged **2F.**

1927

J17	D2	2fr on 1fr lilac rose	30	30
J18	"	3fr on 1fr org. brown	30	30

Republic

Guéré Mask
D3

Mask
D4

1960 Engraved. *Perf. 14x13*

Denomination Typographed in Black

J19	D3	1fr purple	5	5
J20	"	2fr bright green	6	6
J21	"	5fr orange yellow	10	10
J22	"	10fr ultramarine	20	20
J23	"	20fr lilac rose	40	40
		Nos. J19-J23 (5)	81	81

1962, Nov. 3 Typo. *Perf. 13½x14*

Designs: Various masks and heads, Bingerville school of art.

J24	D4	1fr org. & brt. blue	4	4
J25	"	2fr black & red	6	6
J26	"	5fr red & dk. green	10	10
J27	"	10fr green & lilac	25	25
J28	"	20fr dk. purple & blk.	40	40
		Nos. J24-J28 (5)	85	85

Baoulé Weight
D5

Gold Weight
D6

Designs: Various Baoulé weights.

1968, May 18 Photo. *Perf. 13*

J29	D5	5fr citron, brown & blue green	8	8
J30	"	10fr lt. blue, brown & blue green	12	12
J31	"	15fr salmon, brown & blue green	35	35
J32	"	20fr gray, carmine & blue green	40	40
J33	"	30fr bister, brown & blue green	55	55
		Nos. J29-J33 (5)	1.50	1.50

1972, May 27 Engraved

Designs: Various gold weights.

J34	D6	20fr vio. bl. & org. red	35	35
J35	"	40fr verm. & ocher	55	55
J36	"	50fr orange & choc.	70	70
J37	"	100fr slate green & ocher	1.40	1.40

MILITARY STAMP

Coat of Arms
M1

Typographed

1967, Jan. 1 *Perf. 13x14* Unwmkd.

M1	M1	multicolored	70	70

OFFICIAL STAMPS

Ivory Coast Coat of Arms—O1

1974, Jan. 1 Photo. *Perf. 12*

O1	O1	(35fr) green & multi.	35	20
O2	"	(75fr) orange & multi.	65	40
O3	"	(100fr) lilac rose & multi.	85	60
O4	"	(250fr) vio. & multi.	2.25	1.35

PARCEL POST STAMPS.

Postage Due Stamps of French Colonies Overprinted.

Overprinted in Black

Côte - d'Ivoire
COLIS
Postaux

1903 *Imperf.* Unwmkd.

Q1	D1	50c lilac	10.00	9.00
Q2	"	1fr rose, *buff*	10.00	9.00

Overprinted in Black

Colis
Postaux

Q3	D1	50c lilac	1000.00	1000.00
Q4	"	1fr rose, *buff*	1000.00	1000.00

Overprinted

Côte d'Ivoire
Colis Postaux

Red Overprint.

Q5	D1	50c lilac	35.00	35.00
		a. Inverted overprint	70.00	70.00

Blue Black Overprint

Q6	D1	1fr rose, *buff*	20.00	20.00
		a. Inverted overprint	60.00	60.00

Surcharged in Black

Cote d Ivoire

Colis Postaux

1903

Q7	D1	50c on 15c pale green	3.75	3.75
		a. Inverted surcharge	40.00	40.00
Q8	"	50c on 60c brown, *buff*	10.00	9.00
		a. Inverted surcharge	40.00	40.00

Surcharged in Black:

Cote d'Ivoire / ✕✕ 1FR / Colis Postaux — *a*

Cote d'Ivoire / 1FR / Colis Postaux — *b*

Cote d'Ivoire / fr 1 fr / Colis Postaux — *c*

Cote d'Ivoire / fr 1 fr / Colis Postaux — *d*

Cote d'Ivoire / fr 1 fr / Colis Postaux — *e*

Cote d'Ivoire / fr 1 fr / Colis Postaux — *f*

Côte d'Ivoire / UN FR / Colis Postaux — *g*

Côte d'Ivoire / UN FR / Colis Postaux — *h*

1903

Q9	(*a*)	1fr on 5c blue	1100.00	900.00
Q10	(*b*)	1fr on 5c blue	1000.00	800.00
Q11	(*c*)	1fr on 5c blue	4.00	3.75
		a. Inverted surcharge	80.00	80.00
Q12	(*d*)	1fr on 5c blue	6.00	5.00
Q13	(*e*)	1fr on 5c blue	1200.00	1200.00
Q14	(*f*)	1fr on 5c blue	1850.00	1650.00
Q15	(*g*)	1fr on 5c blue	27.50	27.50
Q16	(*h*)	1fr on 5c blue	900.00	900.00
Q17	(*c*)	1fr on 10c gray brown	6.00	6.00
		a. Inverted surcharge	60.00	60.00
Q18	(*d*)	1fr on 10c gray brn.	7.00	6.00
		a. Inverted surcharge	60.00	60.00
Q19	(*g*)	1fr on 10c gray brown	1350.00	1350.00
Q20	(*h*)	1fr on 10c gray brown	15,000.00	

Some authorities regard Nos. Q9 and Q10 as essays. A sub-type of type "a" has smaller, bold "XX" without serifs.

Surcharged in Black:

Côte d'Ivoire / fr 4 fr / Colis Postaux — *i*

Cote d Ivoire / fr 4 fr / Colis Postaux — *k*

Côte d'Ivoire / fr 4 fr / Colis Postaux — *l*

Q21	(*i*)	4fr on 60c brn., *buff*	40.00	30.00
		a. Double surcharge	50.00	
Q22	(*k*)	4fr on 60c brown, *buff*	70.00	60.00
Q23	(*l*)	4fr on 60c brown, *buff*	250.00	185.00

Surcharged in Black

Colis Postaux

Côte d'Ivoire

Q24	D1	4fr on 15c green	40.00	30.00
		a. One large star	55.00	55.00
		b. Two large stars	50.00	40.00
Q25	"	4fr on 30c rose	40.00	30.00
		a. One large star	55.00	55.00
		b. Two large stars	50.00	40.00

Overprinted in Black

C. P.
Cote d'Ivoire

1904

Q26	D1	50c lilac	8.00	8.00
		a. Inverted overprint		
Q27	"	1fr rose, *buff*	8.00	8.00
		a. Inverted overprint		

Overprinted in Black

Cote d'Ivoire
C. P.

Q28	D1	50c lilac	9.00	9.00
		a. Inverted overprint	40.00	40.00
Q29	"	1fr rose, *buff*	12.00	12.00
		a. Inverted overprint	45.00	45.00

Surcharged in Black

Colis Postaux

Cote d'Ivoire

Q30	D1	4fr on 5c blue	85.00	85.00
Q31	"	8fr on 15c green	85.00	85.00

Overprinted in Black

Cote d'Ivoire
C.
P.

1905

Q32	D1	50c lilac	10.00	10.00
Q33	"	1fr rose, *buff*	10.00	10.00

Surcharged in Black

Cote d'Ivoire
2 Francs
C. P.

Q34	D1	2fr on 1fr rose, *buff*	50.00	50.00
Q35	"	4fr on 1fr rose, *buff*	80.00	80.00
		a. Italic "4"	375.00	375.00
Q36	"	8fr on 1fr rose, *buff*	250.00	250.00

Nearly all the Parcel Post stamps are to be found without the circumflex accent on the "o" of "Cote".

JAPAN

(jȧ·păn')

LOCATION — In the north Pacific Ocean east of China.
GOVT.—Constitutional Monarchy.
AREA—142,726 sq. mi.
POP.—113,860,000 (est. 1977).
CAPITAL—Tokyo.

1000 Mon = 10 Sen
100 Sen = 1 Yen (or En)
10 Rin = 1 Sen

Counterfeits of Nos. 1–71 are plentiful. Some are excellent and deceive many collectors.

Nos. 1–54A were printed from hand engraved plates of 40. Each stamp in the sheet is slightly different.

Pair of Dragons Facing Characters of Value
A1

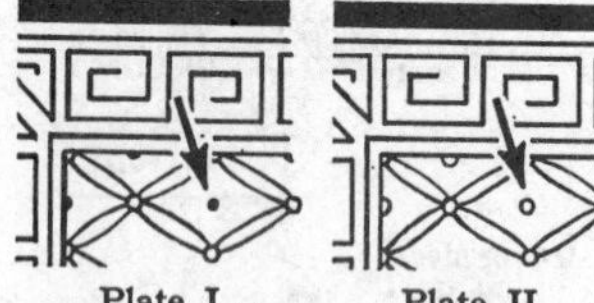

Plate I   Plate II

48 mon.
Plate I. Solid dots in inner border.
Plate II. Tiny circles replace dots.

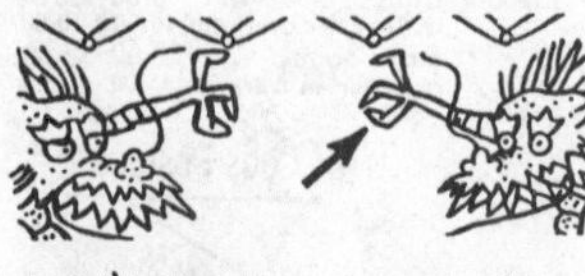

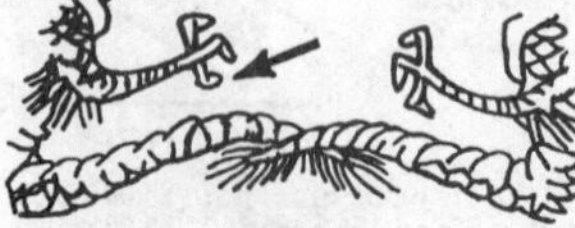

Plate I

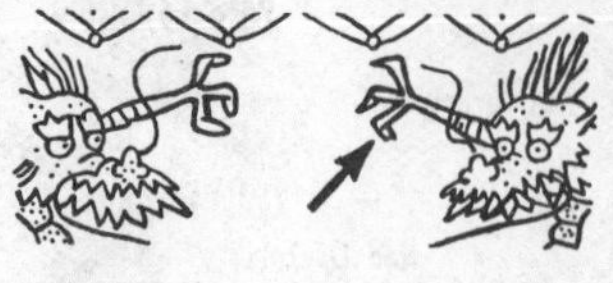

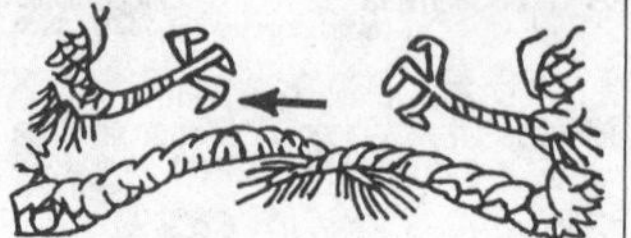

Plate II

100 mon.
Plate I. Lowest dragon claw at upper right and at lower left point upward.
Plate II. Same two claws point downward.

Plate I   Plate II

200 mon.
Plate I. Dot in upper left corner.
Plate II. No dot. (Some Plate I copies show dot faintly; these can be mistaken for Plate II.)

Plate I   Plate II

500 mon.
Plate I. Lower right corner of Greek-type border incomplete
Plate II. Short horizontal line completes corner border pattern.

Engraved
Native Laid Paper Without Gum
1871, Apr. 20 *Imperf.* Unwmkd.
Denomination in Black.

1	A1	48m brown (I)	140.00	150.00
		a. 48m red brn. (I)	140.00	150.00
		b. Wove paper (I)	150.00	165.00
		c. 48m brn. (II)	140.00	150.00
		d. Wove paper (II)	225.00	250.00
2	"	100m blue (I)	120.00	135.00
		a. Wove paper (I)	200.00	225.00
		b. Plate II	450.00	400.00
		c. Wove paper (II)	600.00	600.00
3	"	200m vermilion (I)	165.00	150.00
		a. Wove paper (I)	300.00	325.00
		b. Plate II	1500.00	1000.00
		c. Wove paper (II)		
4	"	500m blue green (I)	200.00	225.00
		a. 500m greenish blue (I)	200.00	225.00
		b. 500m grn. (I)	650.00	700.00
		c. 500m yellow green (I)	800.00	750.00
		d. Wove paper (I)	275.00	275.00
		e. 500m blue green (II)	500.00	750.00
		f. 500m greenish blue (II)	500.00	*900.00*
		g. Wove paper (II)	1500.00	1750.00
		h. Denomination inverted (I)		*75,000.00*

Dragons and Denomination
A1a

½ sen.
Plate I. Same as 48m Plate II. Measures not less than 19.8x19.8 mm. Some subjects on this plate measure 20.3x20.2mm.
Plate II. Same as 48m Plate II. Measures not more than 19.7x19.3 mm. Some subjects measure 19.3x18.7mm.

Plates I & II

Plate III

1 sen.
Plate I. Same as 100m Plate I. Narrow space between frameline and Greek-type border.
Plate II. Same as 100m Plate II. Same narrow space between frameline and border.
Plate III. Space between frameline and border is much wider. Frameline thinner. Shading on dragon heads heavier than on Plates I and II.

Native Laid Paper.
With or Without Gum.
1872 *Perf. 9–12 & compound*
Denomination in Black.

5	A1a	½s brown (II)	100.00	120.00
		a. ½s red brn. (II)	100.00	120.00
		b. ½s gray brown (II)	100.00	120.00
		c. Wove paper (II)	900.00	800.00
		d. ½s brn. (I)	100.00	120.00
		e. ½s red brn. (I)	100.00	120.00
		f. ½s gray brn. (I)	100.00	120.00
		g. Wove paper (I)	150.00	165.00
6	"	1s blue (II)	110.00	110.00
		a. Wove paper (II)	500.00	550.00
		b. Plate I	1000.00	1850.00
		c. Wove paper (I)		
		d. Plate III	*5000.00*	1200.00
		e. Wove paper (III)		
7	"	2s vermilion	300.00	275.00
		a. Wove paper	350.00	275.00
8	"	5s blue green	500.00	500.00
		a. 5s yel. green	500.00	500.00
		b. Wove paper	900.00	900.00

In 1896 the government made imperforate imitations of Nos. 6–7 to include in a presentation collection.

Imperial Crest and Branches of Kiri Tree
A2

Dragons and Chrysanthemum Crest
A3

Imperial Chrysanthemum Crest
A4

Imperial Crest and Branches of Kiri Tree
A5

1872–73
Perf. 9 to 13 and Compound.
Native Wove or Laid Paper of Varying Thickness.

9	A2	½s brown, *wove* 半	18.00	18.00
		a. Upper character in left label has 2 diagonal top strokes missing	1000.00	850.00
		b. Laid paper	80.00	
		c. As "a," laid paper	1150.00	
10	"	1s blue, *wove*	45.00	32.50
		a. Laid paper	40.00	25.00
11	"	2s vermilion, *wove*	90.00	35.00
12	"	2s dull rose, *laid*	70.00	30.00
		a. Wove paper	110.00	40.00
13	"	2s yellow, *laid* ('73)	75.00	17.50
		a. Wove paper ('73)	200.00	27.50
14	"	4s rose, *laid* ('73)	55.00	18.00
		a. Wove paper ('73)	250.00	40.00
15	A3	10s bl. green, *wove*	165.00	100.00
16	A3	10s yellow green, *laid*	500.00	300.00
		a. Wove paper ('73)	650.00	550.00
17	A4	20s lilac, *wove*	325.00	225.00
		a. 20s violet, *wove*	325.00	225.00
		b. 20s red violet, *laid*		
18	A5	30s gray, *wove*	375.00	325.00

Nos. 9b and 9c were never put in use.

1874 Foreign Wove Paper

24	A2	4s rose	500.00	150.00
25	A5	30s gray		*5000.00*

A6

Chrysanthemum Crest
A7   A8

Type A6 differs from A2 by the addition of a syllabic character in a box covering crossed kiri branches above SEN. Stamps of type A6 differ for each value in border and spandrel designs.

In type A7, the syllabic character appears just below the buckle. In type A8, it appears in an oval frame at bottom center below SE of SEN.

With Syllabic Characters.

イ	ロ	ハ	ニ	ホ	ヘ	ト	チ
i	ro	ha	ni	ho	he	to	chi
1	2	3	4	5	6	7	8

リ	ヌ	ル	チ	ワ	カ	ヨ	タ
ri	nu	ru	wo	wa	ka	yo	ta
9	10	11	12	13	14	15	16

レ	ソ	ツ	子	ナ	ラ	ム
re	so	tsu	ne	na	ra	mu
17	18	19	20	21	22	23

1874
Perf. 9½ to 12½ and Compound
Native Laid or Wove Paper.

28	A6	2s yellow	225.00	300.00

Syll.	Un.	Used	Syll.	Un.	Used
1		300.00	16	225.00	

29	A7	6s violet brown (Syll. 2)	1100.00	400.00

Syll.	Un.	Used	Syll.	Un.	Used
2	1350.00	475.00	7		550.00
3		850.00	8		500.00
4		550.00	9		600.00
5		550.00	10		2500.00
6		700.00	11		2250.00
			12		1100.00

30	A4	20s red violet (Syll. 3)	*6500.00*	

Syll.	Un.	Used	Syll.	Un.	Used
1	*20,000.00*		2	*7000.00*	

No. 30, syllabic 1, is known only with specimen (mihon) dot.

31	A5	30s gray. (Syll. 1)	1850.00	2000.00
		a. Very thin laid paper	2000.00	2250.00

Perf. 11 to 12½ and Compound.

1874 Foreign Wove Paper

32	A6	½s brown (Syll. 1)	16.50	13.50

Syll.	Un.	Used	Syll.	Un.	Used
			2	32.50	27.50

33	A6	1s blue	110.00	16.00

Syll.	Un.	Used	Syll.	Un.	Used
1	150.00	18.00	7	175.00	17.50
2	150.00	17.50	8	125.00	17.50
3	135.00	17.50	9	110.00	17.50
4	110.00	16.00	10	150.00	30.00
5	275.00	62.50	11	135.00	17.50
6	110.00	17.50	12	175.00	30.00

34 A6 2s yellow 120.00 13.50

Syll.	Un.	Used	Syll.	Un.	Used
1	275.00	15.00	13	*1650.00*	15.00
2	125.00	15.00	14	*2100.00*	16.50
3	135.00	15.00	15	125.00	15.00
4	125.00	13.50	16	*1650.00*	15.00
5	285.00	15.00	17	125.00	15.00
6	1350.00	20.00	18	125.00	13.50
7	1500.00	15.00	19	125.00	13.50
8	120.00	15.00	20	120.00	13.50
9	120.00	15.00	21	190.00	13.50
10	*2000.00*	30.00	22	*2100.00*	15.00
11	135.00	15.00	23	200.00	15.00
12	*2000.00*	15.00			

35 A6 4s rose (Syll. 1) 950.00 250.00

36 A7 6s violet brown 110.00 32.50

10	400.00	165.00	15		*1850.00*
11	325.00		16	110.00	32.50
13		*4000.00*	17	110.00	32.50
14	200.00	100.00	18	140.00	45.00

37 A3 10s yel. grn. (Syll. 2) 65.00 40.00

1	250.00	85.00	3	650.00	275.00

38 A4 20s violet 165.00 50.00

4	185.00	50.00	5	165.00	55.00

39 A5 30s gray (Syll. 1) 165.00 50.00

1875

Perf. 9 to 13 and Compound.

40 A6 ½s gray (Syll. 2,3) 12.50 10.00

4	20.00				

41 A6 1s brown 32.50 9.00

5	375.00	45.00	14	35.00	10.00
7		165.00	15	32.50	9.00
8		165.00	16	32.50	9.00
12	400.00	70.00	17	32.50	9.00
13	37.50	11.50			

42 A6 4s grn. (Syll. 1) 100.00 15.00

2	135.00	16.50	3	120.00	15.00

43 A7 6s orange 80.00 11.50

10	165.00	45.00	15		
11	150.00	32.50	16	80.00	11.50
13	120.00	22.50	17	80.00	11.50
14	165.00	27.50			

44 A8 6s orange 80.00 11.50

19	90.00	11.50	21	100.00	12.50
20	80.00	11.50	22	*2500.00*	*1000.00*

Dragons
A9

Wild Goose
A10

Wagtail
A11

Imperial Crest
A11a

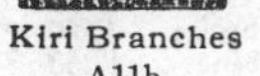

Kiri Branches
A11b

Goshawk
A12

45 A9 10s ultra. (Syll. 4) 90.00 12.50

5	*2000.00*	350.00			

46 A10 12s rose (Syll. 1) 165.00 90.00

2	185.00	120.00	3	*2250.00*	500.00

47 A11 15s lilac 175.00 110.00

1	175.00	110.00	3	265.00	150.00
2	185.00	110.00			

48 A11a 20s rose (Syll. 8) 60.00 11.50
49 A11b 30s violet 100.00 45.00

2	100.00	45.00	4	110.00	45.00
3	100.00	50.00			

50 A12 45s lake 250.00 120.00

1	250.00	120.00	3	1150.00	425.00
2	1200.00	450.00			

Issue dates: No. 46, syll. 2, 1882. No. 46, syll. 3, 1883. Others, 1875.

The 1s brown on laid paper, type A6, formerly listed as No. 50A, is one of several stamps of the preceding issue which exist on a laid type paper. They are difficult to identify and mainly of interest to specialists.

Without Syllabic Characters.

1875

51 A2 1s brown *3750.00* 500.00
52 " 4s green 200.00 60.00

Branches of Kiri Tree Tied with Ribbon
A13

Imperial Crest and Kiri Branches
A14

1875–76

53 A13 1s brown 45.00 11.50
54 " 2s yellow 70.00 10.00
54A A14 5s green ('76) 160.00 75.00

Chrysanthemum Crest
A15 A16

Imperial Crest, Star and Kiri Branches
A17

Sun, Kikumon and Kiri Branches
A18

Imperial Crest and Kiri Branches
A19

Kikumon
A20

1876–77 Typographed.

Perf. 8 to 14 and Compound.

55 A15 5r slate 17.50 8.00
56 A16 1s black 22.50 3.00
  a. Horiz. pair, imperf. btwn.
57 A16 2s brown olive 30.00 2.50
58 " 4s blue green 30.00 3.00
  a. 4s green 30.00 3.00
59 A17 5s brown 55.00 21.50
60 " 6s orange ('77) 110.00 35.00
61 " 8s violet brown ('77) 60.00 5.00
62 " 10s blue ('77) 40.00 3.00
63 " 12s rose ('77) 200.00 120.00
64 A18 15s yellow green ('77) 135.00 3.00
65 " 20s dark blue ('77) 160.00 13.50
66 " 30s violet ('77) 200.00 90.00
  a. 30s red violet 200.00 90.00
67 A18 45s carmine ('77) 500.00 425.00

1879

68 A16 1s maroon 12.00 1.25
69 " 2s dark violet 18.00 2.00
70 " 3s orange 40.00 17.50
71 A18 50s carmine 150.00 15.00

1883

72 A16 1s green 6.00 40
73 " 2s carmine rose 6.00 20
74 A17 5s ultramarine 15.00 35

1888-92

75 A15 5r gray black ('89) 5.00 30
76 A16 3s lilac rose ('92) 14.00 30
77 " 4s olive bistre 12.50 30
78 A17 8s blue lilac 17.50 50
79 " 10s brown orange 17.50 20
80 A18 15s purple 60.00 25
81 " 20s orange 70.00 80
  a. 20s yellow 70.00 80
82 A19 25s blue green 120.00 60
83 A18 50s brown 100.00 4.00
84 A20 1y carmine 160.00 4.00

Stamps of types A16–A18 differ for each value, in backgrounds and ornaments.

Most of Nos. 55–84 are found with telegraph or telegraph office cancellations. These sell at considerably lower prices than postally used copies.

Cranes and Imperial Crest
A21

1894, Mar. 9

Perf. 11½ to 13 and Compound.

85 A21 2s carmine 8.50 1.40
86 " 5s ultramarine 22.50 7.00

Issued to commemorate the 25th wedding anniversary of Emperor Meiji (Mutsuhito) and Empress Haru.

Gen. Yoshihisa Kitashirakawa
A22 A23

Field Marshal Akihito Arisugawa
A24 A25

1896, Aug. 1 Engraved

87 A22 2s rose 10.00 1.25
88 A23 5s dp. ultramarine 42.50 2.00
89 A24 2s rose 10.00 1.25
90 A25 5s dp. ultramarine 42.50 2.00

Victory in Chinese-Japanese War (1894–95).

Chrysanthemum Crest
A26 A27

A28 A29

1899–1907 Typographed

Perf. 11½ to 14 and Compound.

91 A26 5r gray 5.50 20
92 " ½s gray ('01) 2.00 12
93 " 1s light red brown 2.50 12
94 " 1½s ultra. ('00) 13.00 70
95 " 1½s violet ('06) 6.00 12
  a. Bklt. pane of 6 250.00
96 " 2s light green 4.50 10
  a. Bklt. pane of 6 30.00
97 " 3s violet brown 5.50 10
  a. Double impression
98 " 3s rose ('06) 4.50 10
  a. Bklt. pane of 6 100.00
99 " 4s rose 4.50 40
  a. 4s pink ('06) 4.50 50
  b. Booklet pane of 6 (4s pink) 25.00
  c. Booklet pane of 6 (4s rose) 75.00
100 " 5s orange yellow 15.00 12
101 A27 6s maroon ('07) 20.00 85
  a. Bklt. pane of 6 225.00
102 " 8s olive green 35.00 1.10
103 " 10s deep blue 8.00 10
  a. Booklet pane of 6 30.00
104 " 15s purple 25.00 40
105 " 20s red orange 35.00 10
106 A28 25s blue green 70.00 40
107 " 50s red brown 65.00 45
108 A29 1y carmine 75.00 50
  Nos. 91–108 (18) 396.00 5.98

Boxes for Rice Cakes and Marriage Certificates
A30

Symbols of Korea and Japan
A31

1900, Apr. 28

Perf. 11½ to 12½ and Compound

109 A30 3s carmine 11.50 70

Issued in commemoration of the wedding of the Crown Prince Yoshihito and Princess Sadako.

1905, July 1

110 A31 3s rose red 60.00 8.50

Issued to commemorate the amalgamation of the postal services of Japan and Korea. Korean stamps were withdrawn from sale June 30, 1905, but remained valid until Aug. 31. No. 110 was used in the Korea and China Offices of Japan, as well as in Japan proper.

Field-piece and Japanese Flag
A32

Empress Jingo
A33

1906, Apr. 29

111 A32 1½s blue 17.50 1.65
112 " 3s carmine rose 32.50 5.00

Issued to commemorate the triumphal military review following the Russo-Japanese War.

1908 Engraved.

113 A33 5y green 600.00 5.00
114 " 10y dark violet 750.00 12.50

The frame of No. 114 differs slightly from the illustration.

Chrysanthemum Crest
A34 A35

A36

Perf. 12, 12x13, 13x13½.

1913 Typographed. Unwmkd.

No.	Type	Description	Unused	Used
115	A34	⅛s brown	5.50	30
116	"	1s orange	6.00	30
117	"	1⅛s light blue	9.00	40
		a. Bklt. pane of 6	100.00	
118	"	2s green	10.00	25
		a. Bklt. pane of 6	100.00	
119	"	3s rose	15.00	20
		a. Bklt. pane of 6	100.00	
120	A35	4s red	25.00	7.50
		a. Bklt. pane of 6	150.00	
121	"	5s violet	27.50	25
122	"	10s deep blue	70.00	15
		a. Bklt. pane of 6	400.00	
123	"	20s claret	130.00	80
124	"	25s olive green	130.00	1.10
125	A36	1y yellow green & maroon	675.00	7.50
		Nos. 115-125 (11)	1103.00	18.75

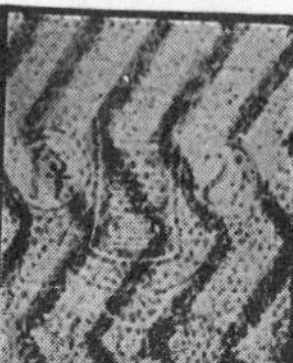

Wmk. 141

Granite Paper.

1914-25 Wmkd. Zigzag Lines. (141)

Size: 19x22½mm. ("Old Die").

No.	Type	Description	Unused	Used
127	A34	⅛s brown	1.75	8
128	"	1s orange	2.00	8
129	"	1⅛s blue	2.25	8
		a. Bklt. pane of 6	75.00	
		d. As "a," imperf.		
130	"	2s green	2.50	8
		a. Bklt. pane of 6	65.00	
131	"	3s rose	1.50	8
		a. Bklt. pane of 6	85.00	
132	A35	4s red	17.50	80
		a. Bklt. pane of 6	90.00	
133	"	5s violet	10.00	15
134	"	6s brown ('19)	17.50	1.50
136	"	8s gray ('19)	18.00	7.00
137	"	10s deep blue	5.50	8
		a. Bklt. pane of 6	85.00	
138	"	13s olive brn. ('25)	20.00	1.35
139	"	20s claret	60.00	40
140	"	25s olive green	14.00	50
141	A36	30s org. brn. ('19)	18.00	30
143	"	50s dk. brown ('19)	25.00	40
145	"	1y yellow green & maroon	120.00	50
		b. Imperf., pair		
146	A33	5y green	375.00	4.00
147	"	10y violet	600.00	6.00
		Nos. 127-147, Old Die (18)	1310.50	23.38

1924-33

"New Die" Size: 18½x22mm. (Flat Plate), or 18½x22½mm. (Rotary).

No.	Type	Description	Unused	Used
127a	A34	⅛s brown	1.65	20
128a	"	1s orange	1.65	20
129b	"	1⅛s blue	1.50	10
		c. Bklt. pane of 6 ('30)	15.00	
131b	"	3s rose	1.35	10
		c. Bklt. pane of 6 ('28)	17.00	
133a	A35	5s violet	16.00	10
135	A35	7s red orange ('30)	9.00	15
138a	A35	13s bister brown ('25)	6.00	12
140a	"	25s olive green	72.50	12
142	A36	30s orge. & grn. ('29)	25.00	20
144	"	50s yellow brown & dark blue ('29)	14.00	22
145a	A36	1y yellow green & maroon	110.00	50
		Nos. 127a-145a, New Die (11)	258.65	2.01

See also Nos. 212-213, 239-241, 243, 245, 249-252, 255.

Enthronement Issue.

Ceremonial Cap
A37

Imperial Throne
A38

Enthronement Hall, Kyoto
A39

Perf. 12½

1915, Nov. 10 Typo. Unwmkd.

No.	Type	Description	Unused	Used
148	A37	1⅛s red & black	1.35	35
149	A38	3s orange & violet	1.50	45

Engraved

Perf. 12x12½

No.	Type	Description	Unused	Used
150	A39	4s carmine rose	8.50	2.00
151	"	10s ultramarine	15.00	4.50

Enthronement of Emperor Yoshihito.

Mandarin Duck
A40

Ceremonial Cap
A41

1916, Nov. 3 Typo. *Perf. 12½*

No.	Type	Description	Unused	Used
152	A40	1⅛s grn., red & yel.	1.85	50
153	"	3s red & yellow	3.00	60
154	A41	10s ultramarine & dark blue	300.00	125.00

Issued in commemoration of the nomination of the Prince Heir Apparent, later Emperor Hirohito.

Dove and Olive Branch
A42 A43

Perf. 12, 12½, 13½x13

1919, July 1 Engraved

No.	Type	Description	Unused	Used
155	A42	1⅛s dark brown	1.25	35
156	A43	3s gray green	1.25	35
157	A42	4s rose	4.00	1.35
158	A43	10s dark blue	11.00	3.00

Restoration of peace after World War I.

Census Officer, A.D. 652
A44

Meiji Shrine, Tokyo
A45

Perf. 12½

1920, Sept. 25 Typo. Unwmkd.

No.	Type	Description	Unused	Used
159	A44	1⅛s red violet	3.50	1.50
160	"	3s vermilion	3.50	1.65

Issued to commemorate the taking of the first modern census in Japan. Not available for foreign postage except to China.

1920, Nov. 1 Engraved

No.	Type	Description	Unused	Used
161	A45	1⅛s dull violet	1.75	80
162	"	3s rose	1.75	80

Issued to commemorate the dedication of the Meiji Shrine. Not available for foreign postage except to China.

National and Postal Flags
A46

Ministry of Communications Building, Tokyo—A47

Typo. (A46), Engr. (A47)

1921, Apr. 20 *Perf. 12½, 13x13½*

No.	Type	Description	Unused	Used
163	A46	1⅛s gray grn. & red	1.25	75
164	A47	3s violet brown	2.00	85
165	A46	4s rose & red	45.00	17.50
166	A47	10s dark blue	135.00	55.00

Issued to commemorate the 50th anniversary of the establishment of postal service and this issuance of the first Japanese postage stamps.

Battleships "Katori" and "Kashima"
A48

1921, Sept. 3 Litho. *Perf. 12½*

No.	Type	Description	Unused	Used
167	A48	1⅛s violet	1.85	75
168	"	3s olive green	2.00	75
169	"	4s rose red	20.00	6.50
170	"	10s deep blue	27.50	9.00

Issued to commemorate the return of Crown Prince Hirohito from his European visit.

Mount Fuji
A49

Mt. Niitaka, Taiwan
A50

Granite Paper.

Perf. 13x13½.

1930-37 Typographed Wmk. 141

Size: 18½x22mm. ("New Die").

No.	Type	Description	Unused	Used
171	A49	4s green ('37)	4.75	15
172	"	4s orange	6.50	10
174	"	8s olive green	13.50	10
175a	A49	20s blue ('37)	25.00	25.00
176	A49	20s brown violet	50.00	12
		Nos. 171-176 (5)	99.75	25.47

1922-29

Size: 19x22½mm. ("Old Die").

No.	Type	Description	Unused	Used
171a	A49	4s green	7.00	70
172a	"	4s orange ('29)	65.00	2.75
173	A49	8s rose	15.00	4.00
174a	A49	8s olive green ('29)	225.00	57.50
175	A49	20s deep blue	16.50	30
176a	A49	20s brown violet ('29)	75.00	1.20
		Nos. 171a-176a (6)	403.50	66.45

See also Nos. 242, 246, 248.

Engraved.

1923, Apr. 16 *Perf. 12½* Unwmkd.

No.	Type	Description	Unused	Used
177	A50	1⅛s orange	6.00	3.00
178	"	3s dark violet	10.00	2.75

Issued to commemorate the first visit of Crown Prince Hirohito to Taiwan. The stamps were sold only in Taiwan, but were valid throughout the empire.

Cherry Blossoms
A51

Sun and Dragonflies
A52

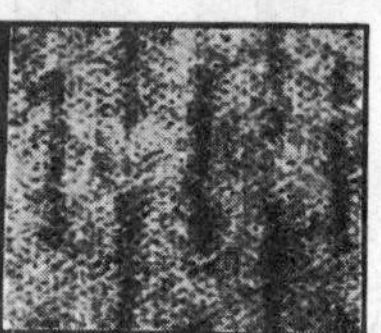

Wmk. 142

Lithographed.

Granite Paper.

Wmkd. Parallel Lines. (142)

1923 Without Gum. *Imperf.*

No.	Type	Description	Unused	Used
179	A51	⅛s gray	2.00	1.50
180	"	1⅛s light blue	2.25	65
181	"	2s red brown	2.25	65
182	"	3s bright rose	1.75	50
183	"	4s gray green	12.50	7.50
184	"	5s dull violet	6.50	60
185	"	8s red orange	20.00	15.00
186	A52	10s deep brown	12.50	60
187	"	20s deep blue	17.50	65
		Nos. 179-187 (9)	77.25	27.65

Nos. 179 to 187 exist rouletted and with various perforations. These were made privately.

Empress Jingo—A53

Granite Paper.

Perf. 12, 13x13½.

1924 Engraved **Wmk. 141**

188 A53 5y gray green 225.00 2.00
189 " 10y dull violet 400.00 1.50

See also Nos. 253–254.

Cranes
A54

Phoenix
A55

Perf. 10½ to 13½ and Compound.

1925, May 10 Litho. **Unwmkd.**

190 A54 1½s gray violet 1.25 50
191 A55 3s silver & brown orange 2.75 1.25
a. Vert. pair, imperf. btwn. 500.00
192 A54 8s light red 12.00 3.50
193 A55 20s silver & gray green 45.00 10.50

Issued to commemorate the 25th wedding anniversary of the Emperor Yoshihito (Taisho) and Empress Sadako.

Mt. Fuji
A56

Yomei Gate, Nikko
A57

Nagoya Castle
A58

Granite Paper.

Perf. 13½x13

1926–37 Typographed **Wmk. 141**

194 A56 2s green 1.75 8
195 A57 6s carmine 10.00 12
196 A58 10s dark blue 8.50 8
197 " 10s carmine ('37) 12.50 6.00

See also Nos. 244, 247.

Baron Hisoka Maejima
A59

Map of World on Mollweide's Projection
A60

Perf. 12½, 13x13½

1927, June 20 **Unwmkd.**

198 A59 1½s lilac 2.50 65
199 " 3s olive green 2.50 75
200 A60 6s carmine rose 40.00 15.00
201 " 10s blue 50.00 15.00

Issued to commemorate the 50th anniversary of Japan's joining the Universal Postal Union. Baron Maejima (1835–1919) organized Japan's modern postal system and was postmaster general.

Phoenix
A61

Enthronement Hall, Kyoto
A62

1928, Nov. 10 Engr. *Perf. 12½*

Yellow Paper.

202 A61 1½s deep green 1.00 15
203 A62 3s red violet 1.00 20
204 A61 6s carmine rose 3.00 75
205 A62 10s deep blue 4.00 1.00

Enthronement of Emperor Hirohito.

Great Shrines of Ise
A63

Map of Japanese Empire
A64

1929, Oct. 2 *Perf. 12½*

206 A63 1½s gray violet 1.75 60
207 " 3s carmine 2.00 60

58th rebuilding of the Ise Shrines.

1930, Sept. 25 **Unwmkd.**

208 A64 1½s deep violet 2.00 65
209 " 3s deep red 3.00 85

Issued in connection with the taking of the second census in the Japanese Empire.

Meiji Shrine
A65

1930, Nov. 1 Lithographed

210 A65 1½s green 2.00 65
211 " 3s brown orange 2.50 75

10th anniversary of dedication of Meiji Shrine.

Coil Stamps.

Wmkd. Zigzag Lines. (141)

1933 Typo. *Perf. 13 Horiz.*

212 A34 1½s light blue 12.00 12.00
213 " 3s rose 10.00 10.00

Japanese Red Cross Badge
A66

Red Cross Building, Tokyo
A67

Perf. 12½

1934, Oct. 1 Engraved **Unwmkd.**

214 A66 1½s green & red 2.00 65
215 A67 3s dull vio. & red 2.50 75
216 A66 6s dark carmine & red 12.50 2.50
217 A67 10s blue & red 15.00 3.00

15th International Red Cross Congress. Sheets of 20 with commemorative marginal inscription.

White Tower of Liaoyang and Warship "Hiei"
A68

Akasaka Detached Palace, Tokyo
A69

1935, Apr. 2

218 A68 1½s olive green 1.65 60
219 A69 3s red brown 2.00 75
220 A68 6s carmine 10.00 2.00
221 A69 10s blue 13.50 2.50

Visit of Emperor Kang Teh of Manchukuo (Henry Pu-yi) to Tokyo, April 6, 1935. Sheets of 20 with commemorative marginal inscription.

Mt. Fuji
A70

Granite Paper.

1935 Typo. *Perf. 13x13½*

222 A70 1½s rose carmine 7.50 12
a. Min. sheet of 20 200.00 225.00

Issued to pay postage on New Year's cards from Dec. 1 to 31, 1935. After Jan. 1, 1936, used for ordinary letter postage. No. 222 was issued in sheets of 100.

Fuji-Hakone National Park Issue.

Mt. Fuji—A71

Fuji from Lake Ashi-no-ko—A72

Fuji from Lake Kawaguchi—A73

Fuji from Mishima—A74

Granite Paper.

1936, July 10 Photo. **Wmk. 141**

223 A71 1½s red brown 3.50 1.10
224 A72 3s dark green 6.00 1.75
225 A73 6s carmine rose 15.00 5.00
226 A74 10s dark blue 17.50 7.50

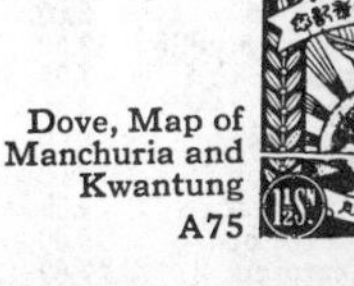

Dove, Map of Manchuria and Kwantung
A75

Shinto Shrine, Port Arthur
A76

Headquarters of Kwantung Government
A77

Granite Paper.

1936, Sept. 1 Litho. *Perf. 12½*

227 A75 1½s gray violet 6.00 6.00
228 A76 3s red brown 9.00 7.50
229 A77 10s dull green 140.00 140.00

Issued to commemorate the 30th anniversary of Japanese administration of Kwantung Leased Territory and the South Manchuria Railway Zone. Sold only in Kwantung Territory and South Manchuria Railway Zone, but valid throughout Japan.

Imperial Diet Building—A78

Grand Staircase—A79

1936, Nov. 7 Engraved *Perf. 13*

230 A78 1½s green 2.50 65
231 A79 3s brown violet 3.00 80
232 " 6s carmine 7.00 2.25
233 A78 10s blue 10.00 4.00

Issued in commemoration of the opening of the new Diet Building, Tokyo.

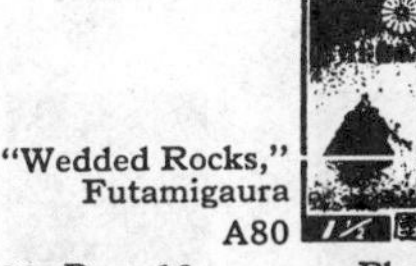

"Wedded Rocks," Futamigaura
A80

1936, Dec. 10 Photogravure

234 A80 1½s rose carmine 4.00 15

Issued to pay postage on New Year's greeting cards.

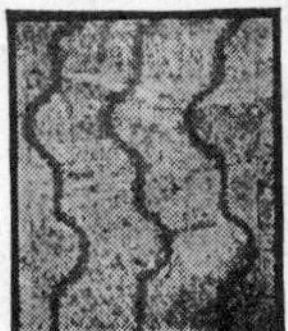

Wmk 257

After 1945, Wmk. 257 exists also in a narrow spacing on a small number of issues.

Types of 1913-26.
Typographed
Wmkd. Curved Wavy Lines. (257)

1937 ***Perf. 13½x13, 13x13½.***

No.	Type	Description	Unused	Used
239	A34	½s brown	2.00	40
240	"	1s orange yellow	2.50	40
241	"	3s rose	1.25	8
242	A49	4s green	4.50	12
243	A35	5s violet	6.00	8
244	A57	6s crimson	9.00	1.10
245	A35	7s red orange	9.00	8
246	A49	8s olive bistre	10.00	40
247	A58	10s carmine	7.00	8
248	A49	20s blue	15.00	30
249	A35	25s olive green	40.00	65
250	A36	30s orange & green	25.00	20
251	"	50s brown orange & dark blue	100.00	70
252	"	1y yellow green & maroon	60.00	40
		Nos. 239-252 (14)	291.25	4.99

Engraved.

No.	Type	Description	Unused	Used
253	A53	5y gray green	375.00	5.50
254	"	10y dull violet	400.00	4.50

Coil Stamp

1938 Typo. ***Perf. 13 Horiz.***

No.	Type	Description	Unused	Used
255	A34	3s rose	4.00	4.00

New Year's Decoration
A81

1937, Dec. 15 Photo. ***Perf. 13***

No.	Type	Description	Unused	Used
256	A81	2s scarlet	4.00	15

Issued to pay postage on New Year's cards, later for ordinary use.

Trading Ship
A82

Rice Harvest
A83

Gen. Maresuke Nogi
A84

Power Plant
A85

Admiral Heihachiro Togo
A86

Mount Hodaka
A87

Garambi Lighthouse, Taiwan
A88

Diamond Mountains, Korea
A89

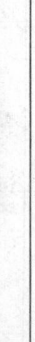

Meiji Shrine, Tokyo
A90

Yomei Gate, Nikko
A91

Plane and Map of Japan
A92

Kasuga Shrine, Nara
A93

Mount Fuji and Cherry Blossoms
A94

Horyu Temple, Nara
A95

Miyajima Torii, Itsukushima Shrine
A96

Golden Pavilion, Kyoto
A97

Great Budda, Kamakura
A98

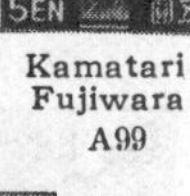

Kamatari Fujiwara
A99

Plum Blossoms
A100

Typographed or Engraved.

1937-45 ***Perf. 13*** **Wmk. 257**

No.	Type	Description	Unused	Used
257	A82	½s purple	20	15
258	A83	1s fawn	35	10
259	A84	2s crimson	20	8
		a. Bklt. pane of 20	50.00	
		b. 2s pink, perf. 12 ('45)	30	12
		c. 2s vermilion ('44)	1.75	1.50
260	A85	3s green ('39)	20	8
261	A86	4s dark green	22	8
		a. Bklt. pane of 20	3.00	
262	A87	5s dark ultramarine ('39)	70	8
263	A88	6s orange ('39)	1.25	50
264	A89	7s deep green ('39)	15	8
265	A90	8s dark purple & pale violet ('39)	20	10
266	A91	10s lake ('38)	2.25	8
267	A92	12s indigo ('39)	20	10
268	A93	14s rose lake & pale rose ('38)	30	10
269	A94	20s ultramarine ('40)	30	8
270	A95	25s dark brown & pale brown ('38)	25	10
271	A96	30s peacock blue ('39)	45	8
		a. Imperf., pair	375.00	
272	A97	50s olive & pale olive ('39)	35	8
		a. 50s olive (forest omitted)		
273	A98	1y brown & pale brown ('39)	1.60	12
274	A99	5y deep gray green ('39)	30.00	60
275	A100	10y dark brown violet ('39)	15.00	40
		Nos. 257-275 (19)	54.17	2.99

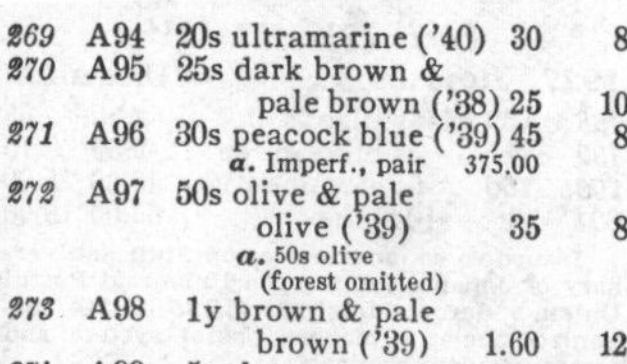

Nos. 257 to 261, 265, 268, 270, 272 and 273 are typographed; the others are engraved.

Coil Stamps.
Perf. 13 Horizontally.

1938-39 Typographed.

No.	Type	Description	Unused	Used
276	A82	½s purple ('39)	3.00	3.00
277	A84	2s crimson	3.50	3.50
278	A86	4s dark green	3.50	3.50
279	A93	14s rose lake & pale rose	55.00	55.00

For other stamps of types A84 and A86, see Nos. 329, 331, 333 and 351. For others of types A88, A99 and A100, see Nos. 341, 360 and 361.

Nikko National Park Issue

Mount Nantai
A101

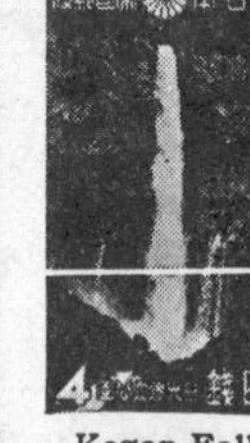

Kegon Falls
A102

Sacred Bridge, Nikko
A103

Mount Hiuchi
A104

Photogravure.

1938, Dec. 25 ***Perf. 13*** **Unwmkd.**

No.	Type	Description	Unused	Used
280	A101	2s brown orange	90	35
281	A102	4s olive green	90	35
282	A103	10s deep rose	4.00	1.50
283	A104	20s dark blue	4.00	1.50
		a. Souvenir sheet	35.00	37.50

No. 283a measures 128x181mm., containing one each of Nos. 280 to 283. Sold for 50s.

Daisen and Inland Sea National Parks Issue

Mount Daisen
A106

Yashima Plateau, Inland Sea
A107

Abuto Kwannon Temple
A108

Tomo Bay, Inland Sea—A109

1939, Apr. 20

No.	Type	Description	Unused	Used
285	A106	2s light brown	75	35
286	A107	4s yellow green	90	60
287	A108	10s dull rose	6.00	2.00
288	A109	20s blue	6.00	2.00
		a. Souvenir sheet	16.00	17.00

No. 288a measures 127x181mm., containing one each of Nos. 285 to 288. Sold for 50s.

Aso National Park Issue

View from Kuju Village, Kyushu
A111

Mount Naka—A112

Crater of Mount Naka
A113

Volcanic Cones of Mt. Aso
A114

1939, Aug. 15

No.	Type	Description	Unused	Used
290	A111	2s olive brown	85	40
291	A112	4s yellow green	3.00	1.25
292	A113	10s carmine	17.50	4.50
293	A114	20s sapphire	25.00	7.50
		a. Souvenir sheet	65.00	75.00

No. 293a measures 126x181 mm., containing one each of Nos. 290 to 293. Sold for 50s.

Globe
A116

Tsunetami Sano
A117

1939, Nov. 15 *Perf. 12½*

Cross in Carmine.

295	A116	2s brown	1.50	65
296	A117	4s yellow green	1.50	65
297	A116	10s crimson	8.50	2.25
298	A117	20s sapphire	8.50	2.25

Issued to commemorate the 75th anniversary of the founding of the International Red Cross Society.

Sacred Golden Kite
A118

Mount Takachiho
A119

Five Ayu Fish and Saké Jar
A120

Kashiwara Shrine
A121

1940 Engraved *Perf. 12*

299	A118	2s brown orange	90	40
300	A119	4s dark green	60	25
301	A120	10s dark carmine	4.00	1.65
302	A121	20s dark ultramarine	85	65

Issued to commemorate the 2,600th anniversary of the legendary date of the founding of Japan.

Daisetsuzan Natl. Park Issue

Mt. Hokuchin, Hokkaido—A122

Mt. Asahi, Hokkaido—A123

Sounkyo Gorge—A124

Tokachi Mountain Range—A125

1940, Apr. 20 Photo. *Perf. 13*

303	A122	2s brown	75	35
304	A123	4s yellow green	2.00	65
305	A124	10s carmine	7.00	1.65
306	A125	20s sapphire	8.00	1.65
		a. Souvenir sheet	190.00	200.00

No. 306a measures 126½x180 mm., containing one each of Nos. 303 to 306. Sold for 50s.

Kirishima National Park Issue.

Mt. Karakuni, Kyushu—A127

Mt. Takachiho—A128

Torii of Kirishima Shrine—A129

Lake of the Six Kwannon—A130

1940, Aug. 21

308	A127	2s brown	75	40
309	A128	4s green	90	50
310	A129	10s carmine	6.00	1.60
311	A130	20s deep ultramarine	7.50	1.75
		a. Souvenir sheet	120.00	140.00

No. 311a measures 127x181mm., containing one each of Nos. 308 to 311. Sold for 50s.

Education Minister with Rescript on Education
A132

Characters Signifying Loyalty and Filial Piety
A133

1940, Oct. 25 Engr. *Perf. 12½*

313	A132	2s purple	75	35
314	A133	4s green	85	35

Issued to commemorate the 50th anniversary of the imperial rescript on education, given by Emperor Meiji to clarify Japan's educational policy.

Daiton and Niitaka-Arisan National Parks Issue.

Mt. Daiton, Taiwan—A134

Central Peak of Mt. Niitaka
A135

Buddhist Temple on Mt. Kwannon
A136

View from Mt. Niitaka—A137

1941, Mar. 10 Photo. *Perf. 13*

315	A134	2s brown	70	50
316	A135	4s bright green	85	60
317	A136	10s rose red	2.25	1.00
318	A137	20s brilliant ultra.	2.50	1.00
		a. Souvenir sheet	40.00	45.00

No. 318a measures 127x181mm., containing one each of Nos. 315 to 318. Sold with No. 323a in same folder for 90s.

Tsugitaka-Taroko National Park Issue.

Seisui Precipice, East Taiwan Coast
A139

Taroko Gorge
A141

Mt. Tsugitaka—A140

Upper River Takkiri District
A142

1941, Mar. 10

320	A139	2s brown	75	35
321	A140	4s bright green	90	50
322	A141	10s rose red	2.25	1.00
323	A142	20s brilliant ultra.	2.50	1.00
		a. Souvenir sheet	40.00	45.00

No. 323a measures 128x182 mm., containing one each of Nos. 320 to 323. Sold with No. 318a in same folder for 90s.

War Factory Girl
A144

Building of Wooden Ship
A145

Hyuga Monument and Mt. Fuji
A146

War Worker and Planes
A147

Palms and Map of "Greater East Asia"
A148

"Enemy Country Surrender"
A149

Aviator Saluting and Japanese Flag
A150

Torii of Yasukuni Shrine
A151

Mt. Fuji and Cherry Blossoms
A152

Torii of Miyajima
A153

Garambi Lighthouse, Taiwan—A154

Typographed; Engraved.

1942-45 *Perf. 13.* **Wmk. 257**

325	A144	1s org. brown ('43)	8	3
328	A145	2s green	10	3
329	A84	3s brown ('44)	12	3
330	A146	4s emerald	8	3
331	A86	5s brown lake	10	3
332	A147	6s light ultra. ('44)	15	3
		a. Imperf., pair		
333	A86	7s org. verm. ('44)	8	3
334	A148	10s crim. & dull rose	12	3
		a. Dull rose (map) omitted	350.00	350.00
335	A149	10s light gray ('45)	1.75	1.75

No.	Type	Description	Unused	Used
336	A150	15s dull blue	45	5
337	A151	17s gray violet ('43)	12	3
338	A152	20s blue ('44)	12	3
339	A151	27s rose brown ('45)	15	6
340	A153	30s bluish green ('44)	60	5
341	A88	40s dull violet	35	3
342	A154	40s dk. violet ('44)	1.00	25
		Nos. 325, 328-342 (16)	5.37	2.49

Nos. 325 to 335, 337 to 340 and 342 are typographed. Nos. 336 and 341 are engraved. Nos. 329, 331, 333, 334 and 342 were issued with and without gum. No. 335 was issued only without gum.

Nos. 328 and 342 exist with watermark sideways. No. 328 exists printed on gummed side.

Most stamps of the above series exist in numerous shades.

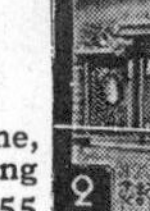

Kenkoku Shrine, Hsinking
A155

Boys of Japan and Manchukuo
A156

Orchid Crest of Manchukuo
A157

Engraved

1942 *Perf. 12* **Unwmkd.**

No.	Type	Description	Unused	Used
343	A155	2s brown	40	20
344	A156	5s olive	60	20
345	A155	10s red	1.25	75
346	A157	20s dark blue	2.00	1.00

The 2s and 5s were issued Mar. 1 for the 10th anniversary of the creation of Manchukuo; 10s and 20s on Sept. 15 for the 10th anniversary of Japanese diplomatic recognition of Manchukuo.

C-59 Locomotive
A158

Yasukuni Shrine, Tokyo
A159

1942, Oct. 14 **Photogravure**

No.	Type	Description	Unused	Used
347	A158	5s Prussian green	2.25	90

Issued to commemorate the 70th anniversary of Japan's first railway.

1944, June 29 *Perf. 13*

No.	Type	Description	Unused	Used
348	A159	7s Prussian green	60	30

75th anniversary of Yasukuni Shrine.

Kwantung Shrine and Map of Kwantung Peninsula
A160

1944, Oct. 1

No.	Type	Description	Unused	Used
349	A160	3s red brown	1.65	1.40
350	"	7s gray violet	1.90	1.65

Issued to commemorate the dedication of Kwantung Shrine, Port Arthur.

Sun and Cherry Blossoms
A161

Sunrise at Sea and Plane
A162

Coal Miners
A163

Yasukuni Shrine
A164

Lithographed, Typographed.
Without Gum.

1945-47 *Imperf.* **Wmk. 257**

No.	Type	Description	Unused	Used
351	A84	2s rose red	15	3
352	A161	3s rose carmine	15	3
353	A162	5s green	15	3
		a. 5s blue	4.00	4.00
354	A149	10s light gray	4.00	4.00
354A	"	10s blue	16.50	
355	A152	10s red orange	15	3
		a. Double impression	15.00	15.00
356	"	20s ultra. ('46)	15	3
357	A153	30s brt. blue ('46)	30	6
		a. Double impression	20.00	
358	A163	50s dk. brn. ('46)	20	3
		a. Souvenir sheet of 5 ('47)	7.50	7.50
359	A164	1y deep olive green ('46)	75	35
360	A99	5y dp. gray grn.	2.00	18
361	A100	10y dark brown violet	25.00	40
		Nos. 351-354, 355-361 (11)	33.00	5.17

Nos. 351 and 354 are typographed. The other stamps in this set are printed by offset lithography.

No. 358a was issued with marginal inscriptions to commemorate the Sapporo (Hokkaido) Philatelic Exhibition, November, 1947.

Nos. 351 to 361 are on grayish paper, and Nos. 355 to 361 also exist on white paper. See also No. 404.

Most stamps of the above series exist in numerous shades and with private perforation or roulette.

Baron Hisoka Maejima
A165

Horyu Temple Pagoda
A166

"Thunderstorm below Fuji," by Hokusai
A167

"First Geese," Print by Hokusai
A168

Kintai Bridge, Iwakuni
A169

Kiyomizu Temple, Kyoto
A170

Goldfish
A171

Noh Mask
A172

Plum Blossoms
A173

Characters Read Right to Left
Lithographed.
Without Gum.

1946-47 *Imperf.* **Wmk. 257**

No.	Type	Description	Unused	Used
362	A165	15s dark green	25	4
363	A166	30s dull lilac	25	4
364	A167	1y deep ultramarine	30	5
		a. 1y ultramarine	50	5
		b. 1y light blue	45	5
365	A168	1.30y olive bistre	90	15
366	A169	1.50y dark gray	90	15
367	A170	2y vermilion	1.10	6
		a. Souvenir sheet of 5 ('47)	6.50	6.50
368	A171	5y lilac rose	2.50	8
		Nos. 362-368 (7)	6.20	57

Nos. 363 and 368 exist both with and without gum.

No. 367a was issued in sheets measuring 113x71mm., with marginal inscriptions and ornaments, to commemorate the "Know Your Stamps" exhibition, Kyoto, August 19 to 24, 1947.

Nos. 362 and 369 exist with watermark horizontal.

See also Nos. 384-387, 512A.

Engraved.

No.	Type	Description	Unused	Used
369	A172	50y bistre brown	35.00	40
370	A173	100y brn. car. ('47)	27.50	40

Perf. 13.

No.	Type	Description	Unused	Used
371	A172	50y bistre brown, with gum ('47)	27.50	30
372	A173	100y brown carmine, with gum ('47)	27.50	30

Lithographed

Perf. 13x13½, 12, 12x12½

No.	Type	Description	Unused	Used
373	A166	30s dull lilac	60	60

Typographed.
Unwmkd.
Rouletted in Colored Lines.
With Gum.

No.	Type	Description	Unused	Used
374	A166	30s deep lilac	40	50

Medieval Postman's Bell
A175

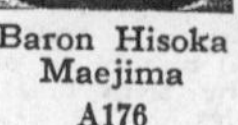

Baron Hisoka Maejima
A176

Design of First Japanese Stamp
A177

Communication Symbols
A178

Perf. 12½, 13½x13

1946, Dec. 12 **Engr.** **Unwmkd.**

With Gum.

No.	Type	Description	Unused	Used
375	A175	15s orange	1.75	65
376	A176	30s deep green	4.00	1.85
377	A177	50s carmine	1.25	65
378	A178	1y deep blue	1.25	65
		a. Souvenir sheet (imperf.)	100.00	100.00

Issued to commemorate the 75th anniversary of government postal service in Japan.

No. 378a measures 183x125mm., is ungummed and contains one each of Nos. 375-378, with marginal inscriptions in orange. There were two printings: I. (2,000 sheets.) The four colors were printed simultaneously. Arched top inscription in high relief. II. (49,000 sheets.) Stamps were printed in one step, sheet inscriptions in another. Top inscription flat, almost level with paper's surface. First printing price $300.

Mother and Child, Diet Building
A180

Bouquet of Japanese May Flowers
A181

Perf. 12½

1947, May 3 **Litho.** **Wmk. 257**

No.	Type	Description	Unused	Used
380	A180	50s rose brown	40	15
381	A181	1y bright ultramarine	50	15
		a. Souvenir sheet (imperf.)	5.00	5.00
		b. As "a," 50s omitted	1000.00	
		c. As "a," 1y omitted	1000.00	

Issued to commemorate the inauguration of the constitution of May 3, 1947.

No. 381a measures 128x180mm, and contains one each of Nos. 380-381, with inscriptions and text in brown orange.

A182

1947, Aug. 15 **Photo.** *Perf. 12½*

No.	Type	Description	Unused	Used
382	A182	1.20y brown	1.75	50
383	"	4y bright ultra.	3.50	50

Issued to commemorate the reopening of foreign trade on a private basis.

The ornaments on No. 383 differ from those shown in the illustration.

Types of 1946 Redrawn.
Characters Read Left to Right
Typographed.

1947-48 *Perf. 13.* **Wmk. 257**

No.	Type	Description	Unused	Used
384	A166	30s deep lilac	60	7
385	"	1.20y light olive green	75	4
		a. Souvenir sheet of 15	85.00	85.00
386	A170	2y vermilion ('48)	1.75	4
387	A168	4y light ultra.	2.00	4

No. 385a was issued with marginal inscriptions to commemorate the "Know Your Stamps" Exhibition, Tokyo, May, 1947.

On No. 386, the chrysanthemum crest has been eliminated and the top inscription centered.

Plum Blossoms
A183

1947 Typographed *Imperf.*

388 A183 10y dark brn. violet 20.00 30

This stamp is similar to type A100 but with new inscription "Nippon Yubin" (Japan Post), reading from left to right. The characters for the denomination are likewise transposed.

Numeral
A184

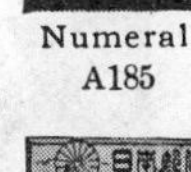

Numeral
A185

Baron
Hisoka Maejima
A186

Whaling
A187

National Art,
Imperial Treasure
House, Nara
A188

1947 Typo. *Perf. 13x13½*

389 A184 35s green 30 4

Lithographed.

390 A185 45s lilac rose 35 6
 a. Imperf., pair 300.00
 b. Perf. 11x13½ 1.50

391 A186 1y dull brown 85 4

Typographed.

392 A187 5y blue 1.85 6
 a. Imperf., pair 225.00
 b. Perf. 11x13½ 22.50

Engraved.

Perf. 13½x13.

393 A188 10y lilac 11.50 6
 a. Imperf., pair
 Nos. 389-393 (5) 14.85 26

No. 389 was produced on both rotary and flat press. Sheets of the rotary press printing have a border. Those of the flat press printing have none.

Lily of the Valley
A188a

1947, Sept. 13 *Perf. 12½* **Unwmkd.**

394 A188a 2y dk. Prus. green 1.75 50

Issued to commemorate Relief of Ex-convicts Day, Sept. 13, 1947.

Souvenir Sheets.

A189

Lithographed

1947 *Imperf.* **Wmk. 257**

Without Gum.

395 A189 Sheet of 5, ultra. 2.00 2.25

Issued in connection with Stamp Hobby Week, November 1–7, 1947. Sheet size: 113½x71½mm., on white or grayish paper.

"Benkei," 1880 Locomotive
A190

Engraved

1947, Oct. 14 **Unwmkd.**

396 A190 4y deep ultra. 15.00 16.50

75th anniversary of railway service in Japan. Size: 114½x71½mm.

Hurdling
A191

Diving
A192

Discus Throwing
A193

Volleyball
A194

1947, Oct. 25 Photo. *Perf. 12½*

With Gum.

397 A191 1.20y red violet 4.50 1.50
398 A192 1.20y " 4.50 1.50
399 A193 1.20y " 4.50 1.50
400 A194 1.20y " 4.50 1.50

Issued to commemorate the 2nd National Athletic Meet, held in Kanazawa, Oct. 30–Nov. 3. Sheets of 80 (10x8) comprising 20 blocks containing each of the 4 designs.

Souvenir Sheets.

A195

Lithographed.

1948 *Imperf.* **Wmk. 257**

Without Gum.

401 A195 Sheet of two 6.50 6.50

Same, Inscribed with Three instead of Two Japanese Characters at Bottom Center.

402 A195 Sheet of two 8.00 8.00

Philatelic exhibitions at Osaka (No. 401) and Nagoya (No. 402). Nos. 401 and 402 contain 2 No. 368. Size: 113½x70½mm.

Stylized Tree
A196

National Art
Treasure, Nara
A197

Photogravure.

1948, Apr. 1 *Perf. 12½* **Unwmkd.**

403 A196 1.20y dp. yel. grn. 60 18

Forestation movement. Sheets of 30, marginal inscription.

Coal Miners Type of 1946, and Type A197.

Lithographed.

With Gum.

1948 *Perf. 13.* **Wmk. 257**

404 A163 50s dark brown 50 5

Typographed.

405 A197 10y rose violet 9.00 5

See also No. 515A.

School Children
A198

Photogravure.

1948, May 3 *Perf. 12½* **Unwmkd.**

406 A198 1.20y dark carmine 50 15

Reorganization of Japan's educational system. Sheets of 30, marginal inscription.

Souvenir Sheets.

No. 402 Overprinted at Top, Bottom and Sides with Japanese Characters and Flowers in Green.

1948, Apr. 3 *Imperf.* **Wmk. 257**

407 A195 Sheet of 2 35.00 35.00
 a. Ovpt. inverted
 b. Ovptd. on No. 401 600.00

Mishima Philatelic Exhibition, Apr. 3–9. Experts question the status of No. 407a.

No. 395 Overprinted at Top and Bottom With Japanese Characters in Plum

1948, Apr. 18

408 A189 Sheet of 5, ultra. 10.00 11.50

Issued to commemorate the centenary of the death of Katsushika Hokusai, painter.

Sampans on Inland Sea,
Near Suma—A199

Engraved and Lithographed.

1948, Apr. 22 *Imperf.* **Unwmkd.**

Without Gum.

409 A199 Sheet of two 6.00 4.75

Issued to commemorate the Communications Exhibition, Tokyo, Apr. 27–May 3, 1948. Sheet contains two 2y deep carmine stamps with border and inscriptions in green. Size: 113x71mm.

Sheet exists with green border omitted.

1948, May 20

410 A199 Sheet of two, ultramarine border 10.00 10.00

Aomori Newspaper and Stamp Exhibition. Border design of apples and apple blossoms. Size: 115x69mm.

Type A199

With Altered Border and Inscriptions

1948, May 23

411 A199 Sheet of two, blue border 10.00 10.00

Fukushima Stamp Exhibition. Border design of cherries and crossed lines. Size: 112x70mm.

Horse Race
A200

1948, June 6 Photo. *Perf. 12½*

With Gum.

412 A200 5y brown 1.50 50

Issued to commemorate the 25th anniversary of the enforcement of Japan's horse racing laws. Each sheet contains 30 stamps and two labels, with marginal inscription.

Numerals

A201 A202

Lithographed.

1948, Sept. 10 *Perf. 13* **Wmk. 257**

413 A201 1.50y blue 1.10 10
414 A202 3.80y light brown 2.75 1.50

Souvenir Sheet.

Types A201 and A202.

1948, Sept. 20 *Imperf.*

415 Sheet of four 22.50 22.50

Kumamoto Stamp Exhibition, Sept. 20. Sheet contains two each of 1.50y deep blue (A201) and 3.80y brown (A202), with inscriptions at left. Size: 114x70mm.

Rectifying
Tower
A203

Perf. 12½

1948, Sept. 14 Photo. **Unwmkd.**

416 A203 5y dk. olive bistre 2.00 60

Government alcohol monopoly.

Swimmer
A204

Runner
A205

Designs: No. 419, High jumper. No. 420, Baseball players. No. 421, Bicycle racers.

1948

417 A204 5y blue 2.25 65
418 A205 5y green 4.50 1.40
419 " 5y green 4.50 1.40
420 " 5y green 4.50 1.40

421 A205 5y green 4.50 1.40
Nos. 417-421 (5) 20.25 6.25

Issued to commemorate the 3rd National Athletic Meet. The swimming matches were held at Yawata, Sept. 16-19, and the field events in Fukuoka, Oct. 29-Nov. 3. Nos. 418-421 were printed in sheets of 80 comprising 20 blocks containing each of the 4 designs.

"Beauty Looking Back," Print by Moronobu
A206

1948, Nov. 29 ***Perf. 13***

422 A206 5y brown 30.00 15.00
a. Sheet of five 160.00 140.00

Philatelic Week, Nov. 29-Dec. 5. Sheets of 5 with marginal inscriptions.

Souvenir Sheet.

1948, Dec. 3 ***Imperf.***

Without Gum

423 A206 5y brown, sheet of 1 22.50 20.00

Kanazawa and Takaoka stamp exhibitions. Marginal inscriptions and maple leaf ornaments. Size: 71x115mm.

Child Playing Hane-tsuki
A207

1948, Dec. 13 **Litho.** ***Perf. 13***

424 A207 2y scarlet 2.50 75

Issued to pay postage on New Year's cards, later for ordinary use.

Farm Woman
A208

Whaling
A209

Miner
A210

Tea Picking
A211

Girl Printer
A212

Factory Girl with Cotton Bobbin
A213

Mt. Hodaka
A214

Planting
A215

Postman
A216

Blast Furnace
A217

Locomotive Assembly
A218

Typographed, Engraved.

1948-49 ***Perf. 13x13½*** **Wmk. 257**

425 A208 2y green 60 6
a. Overprinted with 4 characters in frame 50 40
b. As "a," ovpt. inverted
426 A209 3y light greenish blue ('49) 1.00 7
427 A210 5y olive bistre 8.00 7
a. Booklet pane of 20 37.50
428 A211 5y bl. green ('49) 12.50 1.50
429 A212 6y red orange ('49) 2.00 6
430 A210 8y brown orange ('49) 3.25 7
a. Booklet pane of 20 25.00
431 A213 15y blue 1.00 7
432 A214 16y ultra. ('49) 2.75 1.60
433 A215 20y dark green ('49) 9.00 8
434 A216 30y vio. blue ('49) 10.00 8
435 A217 100y carmine lake ('49) 175.00 30
436 A218 500y dp. blue ('49) 110.00 40
Nos. 425-436 (12) 335.10 4.36

No. 425a has a red control overprint of four characters ("Senkyo Jimu", or "Election Business") arranged vertically in a rectangular frame. Each candidate received 1,000 copies.

Nos. 432, 435-436 are engraved.

See also Nos. 511-512, 514-515, 518, 520, 521A-521B.

Souvenir Sheets.

Typographed and Lithographed.

1948, Oct. 16 ***Imperf.***

437 A213 15y blue, sheet of 1 27.50 28.50

Issued in sheets measuring 114x71 mm., containing a single stamp at upper left, to honor the Nagano Stamp Exhibition, October 16th. Ornamental design and Japanese inscriptions in brown orange.

1948, Nov. 2 ***Imperf.***

438 A210 5y olive bister, sheet of 2 28.50 28.50

Issued in sheets measuring 115x72mm., containing two stamps at upper right, to honor the Shikoku Traveling Stamp Exhibition, November, 1948. Map and Japanese inscriptions in light ultramarine.

Sampans on Inland Sea—A219

Engraved.

1949 ***Perf. 13x13½*** **Wmk. 257**

439 A219 10y rose lake 15.00 5.00
440 " 10y carmine rose 9.00 3.50
441 " 10y orange verm. 8.00 3.00
442 A214 16y bright blue 5.00 1.50

Nos. 439-441 were issued in sheets of 20 stamps with marginal inscription publicizing expositions at Takamatsu (No. 439), Okayama (No. 440) and Matsuyama (No. 441).

No. 442 was issued in sheets of 20 stamps with marginal inscription publicizing the Nagano Peace Exposition, April 1 to May 31, 1949.

Ice Skater
A221

Ski Jumper
A222

Photogravure.

1949 ***Perf. 12*** **Unwmkd.**

444 A221 5y violet 1.75 65
445 A222 5y ultramarine 1.90 65

Issued for the winter events of the 4th National Athletic Meet—skating at Suwa Jan. 27-30 and skiing at Sapporo Mar. 3-6. Issue dates: No. 444, Jan. 27; No. 445, Mar. 3.

Steamer in Beppu Bay
A223

1949, Mar. 10 **Engr.** ***Perf. 13x13½***

Center in Ultramarine.

446 A223 2y carmine 50 22
447 " 5y green 3.00 50

Scene at Fair
A224

Stylized Trees
A225

1949, Mar. 15 **Photo.** ***Perf. 13***

448 A224 5y bright rose 1.65 50
a. Imperf. 1.25 60
b. Sheet of 20, imperf. 45.00 45.00

Issued to publicize the Japan Foreign Trade Fair, Yokohama, 1949.

No. 448 was printed in sheets of 50 (10x5); No. 448a in sheets of 20 (4x5) with marginal inscriptions (No. 448b).

1949, Apr. 1 ***Perf. 12*** **Unwmkd.**

449 A225 5y bright green 1.75 50

Issued to publicize the forestation movement.

Yoshino-Kumano National Park Issue.

Lion Rock—A226

Daiho-zan (Mt. Ohmine)—A227

Doro-kyo—A228

Bridge Pier Rocks—A229

1949, Apr. 10 **Photo.** ***Perf. 13***

450 A226 2y brown 60 18
451 A227 5y yellow green 1.25 40
452 A228 10y scarlet 7.00 1.65
453 A229 16y blue 2.25 50
a. Souvenir sheet 12.50 14.00
b. As "a," 10y omitted

No. 453a measures 127x181mm., containing one each of Nos. 450 to 453 with Japanese and English inscriptions in brown. No gum. Sold for 40y.

Boy
A230

Radio Tower and Star
A231

1949, May 5 ***Perf. 12***

455 A230 5y rose brown & orange 3.50 70
a. Orange omitted 400.00

Children's Day, May 5, 1949.

Souvenir Sheets.

1949, May 5 ***Imperf.***

456 A230 5y rose brown & orange, sheet of 10 185.00 185.00

Children's Exhibition at Inuyama, Apr. 1-May 31. Marginal inscriptions, top and bottom in rose brown. Size: 142½x90 mm.

1949, May 11 ***Perf. 13***

457 A231 20y dp. blue, sheet of one 45.00 45.00

Electrical Communication Week, May 11-18. Outer frame, ornaments and inscriptions in brown and light brown. Size: 71x107½mm.

Symbols of Communication
A232

Central Meteorological Observatory, Tokyo
A233

Engraved.

1949, June 1 *Perf. 12* **Wmk. 257**

458 A232 8y brt. ultramarine 1.75 50

Issued to commemorate the establishment of the Post Ministry and the Ministry of Electricity and Communication.

1949, June 1 *Perf. 12½* **Unwmkd.**

459 A233 8y deep green 1.75 50

Issued to commemorate the 57th anniversary of the establishment of the Central Meteorological Observatory.

Fuji-Hakone National Park Issue.

Mt. Fuji in Autumn—A234

Lake Kawaguchi—A235

Fuji from Mt. Shichimen—A236

Shinobuno Village and Mt. Fuji
A237

1949, July 15 Photo. *Perf. 13*

460 A234 2y yellow brown 1.15 25
461 A235 8y yellow green 1.75 50
462 A236 14y carmine lake 1.00 22
463 A237 24y blue 1.50 25
a. Souvenir sheet 15.00 16.50

No. 463a measures 127x180mm., containing one each of Nos. 460 to 463 with Japanese and English inscriptions in yellow brown. Sold for 55y.

Allegory of Peace—A238

Doves over Nagasaki
A239

Perf. 13x13½, 13½x13

1949 Photogravure. **Unwmkd.**

465 A238 8y yellow brown 3.50 90
466 A239 8y green 2.00 65

Issued to publicize the establishment of Hiroshima as the City of Eternal Peace and of Nagasaki as the International City of Culture. Issue dates: No. 465, Aug. 6; No. 466, Aug. 9.

Boy Scout
A240

Pen Nib of Newspaper Stereotype Matrix
A241

1949, Sept. 22 *Perf. 13x13½*

467 A240 8y brown 4.00 1.00

Issued to publicize the National Boy Scout Jamboree.

1949, Oct. 1 *Perf. 13½x13*

468 A241 8y deep blue 3.50 75

Issued to publicize National Newspaper Week.

Racing Swimmer Poised for Dive
A242

Javelin Thrower
A243

1949 *Perf. 13½*

469 A242 8y dull blue 1.85 75

Perf. 12.

470 A243 8y black brown 2.50 90
471 " 8y black brown (*Yacht Racing*) 2.50 90
472 " 8y black brown (*Relay Race*) 2.50 90
473 " 8y black brown (*Tennis*) 2.50 90
Nos. 469-473 (5) 11.85 4.35

Nos. 469 to 473 were issued to commemorate the 4th National Athletic Meet. The swimming matches were held at Yokohama, Sept. 15–18 and the fall events at Tokyo, Oct. 30.

Nos. 470–473 were printed in sheets of 80 with the four designs se-tenant in each sheet. Issue dates: No. 469, Sept. 15; Nos. 470–473, Oct. 30.

Map and Envelopes Forming "75"
A244

Symbols of U.P.U.
A245

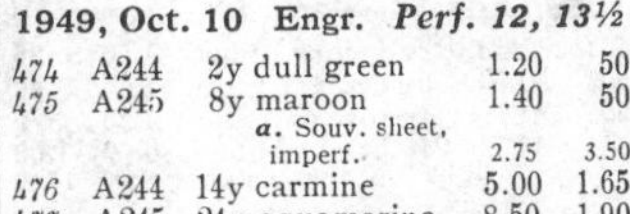

1949, Oct. 10 **Engr.** *Perf. 12, 13½*

474 A244 2y dull green 1.20 50
475 A245 8y maroon 1.40 50
a. Souv. sheet, imperf. 2.75 3.50
476 A244 14y carmine 5.00 1.65
477 A245 24y aquamarine 8.50 1.90
a. Imperf., pair

Issued to commemorate the 75th anniversary of the formation of the Universal Postal Union.

No. 475a contains one each of Nos. 474 and 475.

Floating Zenith Telescope
A246

"Moon and Geese," Print by Hiroshige
A247

1949, Oct. 30 Photo. *Perf. 12*

478 A246 8y dark blue green 2.00 55

Issued to commemorate the 50th anniversary of the Mizusawa Latitudinal Observatory.

1949, Nov. 1 *Perf. 13x13½*

479 A247 8y purple 40.00 22.50
a. Sheet of five 225.00 175.00

Postal Week, Nov. 1–7. Sheets of 5, inscribed in top margin.

Dr. Hideyo Noguchi
A248

Yukichi Fukuzawa
A249

Soseki Natsume
A250

Shoyo Tsubouchi
A251

Danjuro Ichikawa
A252

Joseph Hardy Niijima
A253

Hogai Kano
A254

Kanzo Uchimura
A255

Ichiyo Higuchi
A256

Ogai Mori
A257

Shiki Masaoka
A258

Shunso Hishida
A259

Amane Nishi
A260

Kenjiro Ume
A261

Hisashi Kimura
A262

Inazo Nitobe
A263

Torahiko Terada
A264

Tenshin Okakura
A265

Engraved.

1949-52 *Perf. 12½.* **Unwmkd.**

480 A248 8y green 5.00 40
481 A249 8y deep olive ('50) 1.65 40
a. Imperf., pair
482 A250 8y dark Prussian green ('50) 1.65 40
483 A251 8y Prus. grn. ('50) 1.65 40
484 A252 8y dark vio. ('50) 4.50 85
485 A253 8y violet brn. ('50) 1.65 40
486 A254 8y dark green ('51) 2.75 50
487 A255 8y deep purple ('51) 2.75 50
488 A256 8y carmine ('51) 6.50 70
489 A257 8y violet brn. ('51) 8.00 70
490 A258 8y chocolate ('51) 5.00 70
491 A259 8y dark blue ('51) 4.50 70

492	A260	10y dark green ('52)	32.50	1.65
493	A261	10y brown vio. ('52)	4.50	60
494	A262	10y carmine ('52)	1.85	60
495	A263	10y dark green ('52)	2.25	60
496	A264	10y chocolate ('52)	2.10	60
497	A265	10y dark blue ('52)	2.50	60
		Nos. 480-497 (18)	91.30	11.30

Tiger

A266

Microphones of 1925 and 1950

A267

1950, Feb. 1 Photo. *Perf. 12*

498	A266	2y dark red	3.75	50

Sheets reproducing five of these stamps in the form of a cross, against a gray green background, were awarded as sixth prize in the national lottery. Price $90.

1950, Mar. 21 *Perf. 13*

499	A267	8y ultramarine	1.85	50

25th anniversary of broadcasting in Japan. Sheets of 20 with marginal inscription.

Dove and Olive Twig on Letter Box

A268

1950, Apr. 20 *Perf. 12*

500	A268	8y dp. yellow green	1.65	50

Day of Posts, Apr. 20.

Akan National Park Issue.

Lake Akan and Mt. Akan—A269

Lake Kutcharo, Hokkaido—A270

Mt. Akan-Fuji—A271

Lake Mashu—A272

1950, July 15 *Perf. 13* **Unwmkd.**

501	A269	2y yellow brown	1.50	25
502	A270	8y dp. yel. green	1.65	40
503	A271	14y rose carmine	4.25	70
504	A272	24y bright blue	6.00	1.00
		a. Souvenir sheet	15.00	16.50

No. 504a measures 127x180½mm., and contains one each of Nos. 501 and 504 with inscriptions in yellow brown in top and bottom margins. Sold for 55y.

Gymnast on Rings

A273

Designs: No. 506, Pole vault. No. 507, Soccer. No. 508, Equestrian.

1950, Oct. 28 *Perf. 13½x13*

505	A273	8y rose brown	16.50	4.00
506	"	8y "	16.50	4.00
507	"	8y "	16.50	4.00
508	"	8y "	16.50	4.00

Issued to commemorate the 5th National Athletic Meet. Sheets of 20 stamps in which each horizontal row contains all four designs.

Types of 1947-49 and

Ishiyama-dera Pagoda

A274

Hisoka Maejima

A275

Long-tailed Cock of Tosa

A276

Goddess Kannon

A277

Himeji Castle

A278

Nyoirin Kannon of Chuguji Temple

A280

Phoenix Hall, Byodoin Temple

A279

Perf. 13x13½, 13½x13 (14y)

1950-52 Typographed **Unwmkd.**

509	A274	80s carmine ('51)	60	50
		a. Sheet of 1	5.00	6.00
		Photogravure		
510	A275	1y dk. brown ('51)	75	10
		a. Souv. sheet of 4	8.50	8.50
		Typographed		
511	A208	2y green ('51)	90	6
512	A209	3y light greenish blue ('51)	20.00	35
512A	A168	4y lt. ultra. ('52)	18.50	30
513	A276	5y dp. grn. & orge. brown ('51)	2.75	8
		a. Orange brown omitted	125.00	
514	A212	6y red orge. ('51)	2.00	6
515	A210	8y dark orange brown ('51)	22.50	30
515A	A197	10y rose vio. ('52)	25.00	1.20
516	A277	10y red brown & lilac ('51)	2.50	4
		Engraved		
517	A278	14y brn. car. ('51)	10.00	8.00
		a. Sheet of 1	18.50	20.00
		Typographed		
518	A215	20y dk. green ('51)	22.50	25
		Engraved		
519	A279	24y dp. ultra.	16.50	5.00
		a. Sheet of 1	16.50	16.50
		Typographed		
520	A216	30y vio. blue ('52)	50.00	50
		Photogravure		
521	A280	50y dk. brn. ('51)	60.00	12
		c. Sheet of 1	100.00	110.00
		Engraved		
521A	A217	100y car. lake ('52)	115.00	25
521B	A218	500y dp. blue ('52)	80.00	25
		Nos. 509-521B (17)	449.50	17.36

Nos. 509a, 517a, 519a and 521c are inscribed in lower margin. Size: 75-76x51-52mm.

No. 510a was issued to commemorate the 80th anniversary of Japan's postal service. Sheet contains four of No. 510, with inscriptions in right margin. Size: 87x64mm.

On No. 512A, characters read from left to right.

See also Nos. 557-559, 580, 623, 636-636A, 672, 879A, 885, 916, 1244, 1256.

Girl and Rabbit

A281

1951, Jan. 1 Photo. *Perf. 12*

522	A281	2y rose pink	2.40	30

Sheets measuring 102x90mm., reproducing five of these stamps, were awarded as ninth prize in the national lottery. Price $20.

Scenic Spots Issue

Mt. Zao

Skiers on Mt. Zao

A282 A283

1951 *Perf. 13*

523	A282	8y olive	8.50	1.10
524	A283	24y blue	8.50	1.20

Nihon-daira Plateau

Tea Picking

A284

Mt. Fuji Seen from Nihon-daira

A285

525	A284	8y olive green	7.50	75
526	A285	24y bright blue	27.50	4.00

Hakone Hot Springs

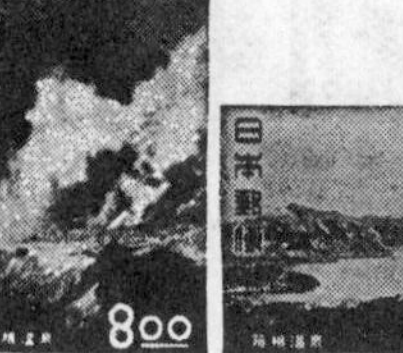

Hot Springs, Hakone

A286

Lake Ashi, Hakone

A287

527	A286	8y chestnut brn.	5.00	70
528	A287	24y deep blue	4.00	85

Akame 48 Waterfalls

Senju-no-taki Waterfall

A288

Ninai-no-taki Waterfall

A289

529	A288	8y deep green	5.00	70
530	A289	24y deep blue	4.00	85

Wakanoura & Tomogashima

Pavilion, Wakanoura Bay

A290

Wakanoura Bay

A291

531	A290	8y brown	3.75	70
532	A291	24y bright blue	3.00	80

Uji River

Uji River

A292

View from Uji Bridge

A293

Engraved.

Perf. 13x13½, 13½x13

533	A292	8y brown	3.50	70
534	A293	24y deep blue	3.00	80

Nagasaki

Oura Catholic Church, Nagasaki

A294

Sofuku Temple Gate
A295

Photogravure.
Perf. 13½

535	A294	8y carmine rose	5.50	70
536	A295	24y dull blue	3.50	80

Marunuma & Sugenuma Lakes

Marunuma
A296

Sugenuma
A297

537	A296	8y rose violet	5.50	70
538	A297	24y dull blue grn.	3.50	80

Shosenkyo Gorge

Kakuenpo (peak)
A298

Nagatoro Bridge
A299

539	A298	8y brown red	6.00	70
540	A299	24y deep Prussian green	5.00	80
		Nos. 523-540 (18)	112.25	17.65

Boy's Head and Seedling
A300

1951, May 5 *Perf. 13½*

541	A300	8y orange brown	12.50	1.60

Issued to publicize Children's Day, May 5, 1951.

Towada National Park Issue.

Oirase River
A301

Lake Towada
A302

View from Kankodai
A303

Mt. Hakkoda from Mt. Yokodake
A304

Photogravure.

1951, July 20 *Perf. 13x13½*

542	A301	2y brown	1.40	25
543	A302	8y green	4.00	45
544	A303	14y dark red	3.00	60
545	A304	24y blue	4.00	75
		a. Souvenir sheet	16.50	17.50

No. 545a contains one each of Nos. 542–545, with brown inscriptions in top and bottom margins. Size: 126x180mm. Sold for 55y.

Chrysanthemum
A305

National Flag
A306

1951, Sept. 9 *Perf. 13½*

546	A305	2y orange brown	1.50	40
547	A306	8y slate bl. & red	3.50	80
548	A305	24y blue green	6.00	80

Signing of the peace treaty of 1951.

Putting the Shot
A307

Hockey
A308

1951, Oct. 27

549	A307	2y orange brown	1.75	60
550	A308	2y gray blue	1.75	60

6th National Athletic Meet, Hiroshima, Oct. 27–31. Nos. 549–550 printed se-tenant.

Okina Mask
A309

1952, Jan. 16 Photo. *Perf. 13½x13*

551	A309	5y crimson rose	5.00	30

Sheets reproducing four of these stamps with Japanese inscriptions and floral ornament at left were awarded as sixth prize in the national lottery. Price $22.50.

Southern Cross from Ship
A310

Earth and Big Dipper
A311

1952, Feb. 19

552	A310	5y purple	3.50	60
553	A311	10y dark green	7.00	90

Issued to commemorate the 75th anniversary of Japan's admission to the Universal Postal Union.

Red Cross and Lilies
A312

Red Cross Nurse
A313

1952, May 1

554	A312	5y rose red & dark red	3.00	50
555	A313	10y dk. grn. & red	6.00	75
		a. Red Cross omitted		

Issued to commemorate the 75th anniversary of the formation of the Japanese Red Cross Society.

Goldfish
A314

Japanese Serow
A315

1952 *Perf. 13x13½*

556	A314	35y red orange	1.00	4

Types of 1951.
Redrawn; Zeros Omitted.

1952 **Unwmkd.**

557	A275	1y dark brown	15	3
558	A280	50y dark brown	2.75	4

Typographed.

559	A274	4y deep claret & pale rose	60	3
		a. Background (pale rose) omitted		

Ornamental frame and background added, denomination at upper left, Japanese characters at upper right.

Photogravure.

560	A315	8y brown	20	3

Japan Alps (Chubu-Sangaku) National Park Issue.

Mt. Yarigatake
A316

Kurobe Valley
A317

Mt. Shiroumadake
A318

Norikuradake Range
A319

Perf. 13½x13, 13x13½

1952, July 5

561	A316	5y brown	2.00	28
562	A317	10y blue green	7.50	75
563	A318	14y bright red	2.50	70
564	A319	24y bright blue	5.00	75
		a. Souvenir sheet (imperf.)	27.50	30.00

No. 564a measures 127x181mm., and contains one each of Nos. 561-564 with inscriptions in brown in top and bottom margins. Sold for 60y.

Yasuda Hall, Tokyo University
A320

Yomei Gate, Nikko
A321

1952, Oct. 1 **Engr.** *Perf. 13*

565	A320	10y dull green	6.50	1.10

Issued to commemorate the 75th anniversary of the founding of Tokyo University.

1952, Oct. 15 Photo. *Perf. 13x13½*

566	A321	45y blue	1.60	4

Mountain Climber
A322

Design: No. 568, Wrestlers.

1952, Oct. 18 **Dated "1952."**

567	A322	5y ultramarine	4.00	70
568	"	5y brown	4.00	70

7th National Athletic Meet, Fukushima, Oct. 18–22. Nos. 567–568 printed se-tenant.

Bandai - Asahi National Park Issue.

Mt. Azuma—A323

Mt. Asahi—A324

Mt. Bandai—A325

Mt. Gatsun—A326

Photogravure.

1952, Oct. 18 *Perf. 13* **Unwmkd.**

569 A323 5y brown 1.75 20
570 A324 10y olive green 7.00 60
571 A325 14y rose red 2.50 60
572 A326 24y blue 4.50 75
a. Souvenir sheet (imperf.) 27.50 30.00

No. 572a measures 127x181mm., and contains one each of Nos. 569 to 572 with inscriptions in brown in top and bottom margins. Sold for 60y.

Kirin
A327

Flag of Crown Prince
A328

Engraved and Photogravure

1952, Nov. 10 *Perf. 13½*

573 A327 5y red orange & purple 1.20 30
574 " 10y red orange & dark green 1.40 40
575 A328 24y deep blue 6.00 80
a. Souvenir sheet (imperf.) 55.00 60.00

Issued to commemorate the nomination of Crown Prince Akihito as Heir Apparent.

No. 575a measures 130x129mm., and contains one each of Nos. 573-575 with background design of phoenix and clouds in violet brown and blue. Sold for 50y.

Sambaso Doll
A329

First Electric Lamp in Japan
A330

Perf. 13½x13

1953, Jan, 1 Photo. **Unwmkd.**

576 A329 5y carmine 4.75 30

Issued to pay postage on New Year's cards, later for ordinary use.

Sheets measuring 102x89mm., reproducing four of these stamps, were awarded as sixth pri-e in the national lottery. Price $25.

1953, Mar. 25

577 A330 10y brown 4.50 80

Issued to commemorate the 75th anniversary of electric lighting in Japan.

"Kintai Bridge," Print by Hiroshige
A331

Kintai Bridge as Rebuilt in 1953
A332

1953, May 3 *Perf. 13*

578 A331 10y chestnut 4.00 60
579 A332 24y blue 3.75 80

Kannon Type of 1951.

Redrawn; Zeros Omitted.

1953-54 Typographed.

580 A277 10y red brn. & lilac 1.25 3
a. Booklet pane 10 + 2 labels (souvenir) ('54) 80.00 80.00
b. Bklt. pane 10 + 2 labels ('54) 20.00

No. 580a was issued in honor of Philatelic Week 1954. The inscriptions on the two labels are arranged in two rows of boldface characters.

On No. 580b, the label inscriptions are arranged in three rows of mixed heavy and thin characters.

See also Nos. 611a and 672.

Shikotsu-Toya National Park Issue.

Lake Shikotsu, Hokkaido
A333

Mt. Yotei—A334

1953, July 25 Photo. *Perf. 13*

581 A333 5y ultramarine 1.45 25
582 A334 10y green 4.00 50
a. Souvenir sheet 15.00 16.00

No. 582a measures 148x105mm. and contains one each of Nos. 581 and 582, imperforate, with inscriptions in ultramarine in top and bottom margins. No gum. Sold for 20 yen.

Akita Dog
A335

Cormorant Fishing
A336

1953 **Unwmkd.**

583 A335 2y gray 12 3

Engraved.

584 A336 100y dark red 8.50 6
a. Imperf., pr. 400.00

Ise-Shima National Park Issue.

Futamigaura Beach
A337

Namikiri Coast—A338

1953, Oct. 2 Photogravure

585 A337 5y red 1.50 30
586 A338 10y blue 3.50 50
a. Souvenir sheet 10.00 11.00

No. 586a measures 147x105mm. and contains one each of Nos. 585 and 586, imperforate, with inscriptions in blue in top and bottom margins. No gum.

Phoenix—A339

Design: 10y, Japanese crane in flight.

1953, Oct. 12 Engr. *Perf. 12½*

587 A339 5y brown carmine 1.50 45

Photogravure.

588 A339 10y dark blue 3.50 75

Nos. 587-588 were issued on the occasion of the return of Crown Prince Akihito from his visit to Europe and America. Issued in sheets of 20 with marginal inscription.

Rugby Match
A340

Judo
A341

1953, Oct. 22 *Perf. 13½*

589 A340 5y black 4.00 1.00
590 A341 5y blue green 4.00 1.00

8th National Athletic Meet, Matsuyama, Oct. 22-26. Nos. 589-590 printed se-tenant.

Sky and Top of Observatory—A342

1953, Oct. 29

591 A342 10y dark gray blue 6.50 80

Issued to commemorate the 75th anniversary of the Tokyo Astronomical Observatory.

Unzen National Park Issue.

Mt. Unzen from Golf Course
A343

Mt. Unzen from Chijiwa Beach
A344

1953, Nov. 20 *Perf. 13*

592 A343 5y red 1.30 40
593 A344 10y blue 3.50 60
a. Souvenir sheet 10.00 11.00

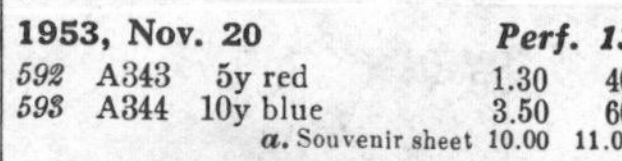

No. 593a measures 148x105mm. and contains one each of Nos. 592 and 593, imperforate. No gum.

Toy Horse
A345

Racing Skaters
A346

1953, Dec. 25 *Perf. 13½x13*

594 A345 5y rose 3.25 25

Issued to pay postage on New Year's cards, later for ordinary use. A sheet reproducing four of these stamps was awarded as sixth prize in the national lottery. Price $20.

1954, Jan. 16

595 A346 10y blue 2.25 60

Issued to publicize the World Speed Skating Matches for Men, Sapporo City, Jan. 16-17, 1954.

Golden Hall, Chusonji Temple
A347

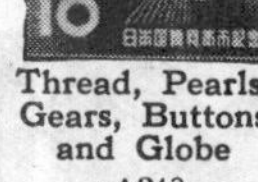
Thread, Pearls, Gears, Buttons and Globe
A348

1954, Jan. 20

596 A347 20y olive green 65 5

1954, Apr. 10

597 A348 10y dark red 2.00 70

Issued to publicize the International Trade Fair, Osaka, Apr. 10-23, 1954.

Little Cuckoo
A349

Wrestlers
A350

1954, May 10 *Perf. 13x13½*

598 A349 3y blue green 15 5
a. Imperf., pair 350.00

1954, May 22 **Engraved**

599 A350 10y deep green 1.75 70

Issued to publicize the World Free Style Wrestling Championship Matches, Tokyo, 1954.

Jo-Shin-etsu National Park Issue

Mt. Asama—A351

Mt. Tanikawa—A352

1954, June 25 *Perf. 13*

600	A351	5y dark gray brn.	1.50	25
601	A352	10y dark blue green	3.00	50
		a. Souvenir sheet	10.00	11.00

No. 601a measures 147x105mm. and contains one each of Nos. 600 and 601, imperforate and ungummed, with inscriptions in ultramarine in top and bottom margins.

Table Tennis
A353

Archery
A354

1954, Aug. 22 Engr. *Perf. 12*

602	A353	5y dull brown	3.00	50
603	A354	5y gray green	3.00	50

9th National Athletic Meet, Sapporo, Aug. 22–26. Nos. 602–603 printed se-tenant in sheets of 20.

Morse Telegraph Instrument
A355

I. T. U. Monument
A356

Perf. 13x13½, 13½x13

1954, Oct. 13

604	A355	5y dk. purple brown	1.50	30
605	A356	10y deep blue	3.00	70

Issued to commemorate the 75th anniversary of Japanese membership in the International Telecommunication Union.

Daruma Doll—A357

1954, Dec. 20 Photo. *Perf. 13½x13*

606	A357	5y black & red	2.75	25

Sheets reproducing four of these stamps with Japanese inscriptions and ornaments were awarded as fifth prize in the national lottery. Price $20.

Chichibu-Tama National Park Issue

Mountain Stream, Tama Gorge
A358

Chichibu Mountains—A359

1955, Mar. 1 Engraved *Perf. 13*

607	A358	5y blue	1.50	25
608	A359	10y red brown	2.00	40
		a. Souvenir sheet	10.00	11.00

No. 608a measures 148x106 mm. and contains one each of Nos. 607 and 608, imperforate and ungummed, with inscriptions in gray in top and bottom margins.

Bridge and Iris
A360

1955, Mar. 15 *Perf. 13x13½*

609	A360	500y deep plum	12.00	10

Paper Carp as Flown on Boys' Day
A361

Mandarin Ducks
A362

Photogravure.

1955, May 16 *Perf. 13* **Unwmkd.**

610	A361	10y multicolored	3.00	70

Issued to publicize the 15th congress of the International Chamber of Commerce, Tokyo, May 16-21, 1955.

1955-64

611	A362	5y light blue & red brown	15	5
		a. Bklt. pane of 12 (4 No. 611 + 8 No. 580) ('59)	10.00	
		b. Bklt. pane of 12 (4 No. 611 + 8 No. 725) ('63)	11.00	
		c. Bklt. pane of 4 ('64)	3.00	
		d. Imperf., pair	375.00	

See also Nos. 738, 881d, 914b.

Rikuchu-Kaigan National Park Issue

Bentenzaki Cape
A363

Jodogahama Beach—A364

1955, Sept. 30

612	A363	5y deep green	1.35	25
613	A364	10y rose lake	2.00	40
		a. Souvenir sheet	10.00	11.00

No. 613a measures 148x104 mm. and contains one each of Nos. 612 and 613, imperforate and ungummed, with inscriptions in ultramarine in top and bottom margins. Sold for 20y.

Girl Athletes
A365

Runners
A366

1955, Oct. 30 Engraved

614	A365	5y brown lake	1.35	40
615	A366	5y bluish black	1.35	40

10th National Athletic Meet, Kanagawa Prefecture. Nos. 614–615 printed se-tenant in sheets of 20.

See also Nos. 639–640, 657.

"A Girl Blowing Glass Toy," by Utamaro—A367

1955, Nov. 1 Photogravure

616	A367	10y multicolored	10.00	4.00

Issued in honor of the 150th anniversary of the death of Utamaro, woodcut artist, and to publicize Philatelic Week, November, 1955. Issued in sheets of 10.

Kokeshi Dolls
A368

Table Tennis
A369

1955, Dec. 30 *Perf. 13* **Unwmkd.**

617	A368	5y olive green & red	1.65	12

Sheets reproducing four of these stamps, were awarded as fifth prize in the New Year's lottery. Price $12.50.

1956, Apr. 2 *Perf. 13x13½*

618	A369	10y red brown	1.00	30

International Table Tennis Championship, Tokyo, Apr. 2–11.

Judo
A370

1956, May 2 *Perf. 13*

619	A370	10y green & lilac	1.40	30

Issued to publicize the first World Judo Championship Meet, Tokyo, May 3, 1956.

Boy and Girl with Paper Carp
A371

1956, May 5

620	A371	5y light blue & black	90	30

Issued to commemorate the establishment of World Children's Day, May 5, 1956.

Water Plants, Lake Akan
A372

Big Purple Butterfly
A373

1956 *Perf. 13* **Unwmkd.**

621	A372	55y light blue, green & black	4.50	8
622	A373	75y multicolored	4.00	12

See also Nos. 887A, 917.

Castle Type of 1951.
Redrawn; Zeros Omitted.

1956 Engraved *Perf. 13½x13*

623	A278	14y gray olive	2.75	50

Saikai National Park Issue.

Osezaki Promontory
A374

Kujukushima—A375

1956, Oct. 1 Photogravure

624	A374	5y red brown	75	20

Engraved and Photogravure

625	A375	10y light blue & indigo	1.00	25
		a. Souvenir sheet	10.00	11.00

No. 625a measures 147x104mm, and contains one each of Nos. 624 and 625, imperforate and ungummed, with marginal inscription in olive. Sold for 20y.

Palace Moat and Modern Tokyo
A376

1956, Oct. 1 Engraved

626	A376	10y dull purple	2.00	40

Issued to commemorate the 500th anniversary of the founding of Tokyo.

Sakuma Dam
A377

1956, Oct. 15 *Perf. 13* **Unwmkd.**

627	A377	10y dark blue	1.25	30

Completion of Sakuma Dam.

Long Jump A378 — Basketball A379

1956, Oct. 28 ***Perf. 13½x13***

628 A378 5y brown violet 90 25
629 A379 5y steel blue 90 25

11th National Athletic Meet, Hyogo Prefecture. Nos. 628–629 printed se-tenant in sheets of 20.
See also No. 658.

Kabuki Actor Ebizo Ichikawa by Sharaku—A380

1956, Nov. 1 Photo. ***Perf. 13***

630 A380 10y multicolored 8.50 3.50

Stamp Week. Sheets of 10.

Mount Manaslu—A381

1956, Nov. 3

631 A381 10y multicolored 3.50 1.00

Issued in honor of the Japanese expedition which climbed Mount Manaslu in the Himalayas on May 9 and 11, 1956.

Electric Locomotive and Hiroshige's "Yui Stage" A382

1956, Nov. 19 ***Perf. 13*** **Unwmkd.**

632 A382 10y dark olive bistre, black & green 4.00 80

Electrification of Tokaido Line.

Cogwheel, Vacuum Tube and Ship—A383

1956, Dec. 18 **Engraved**

633 A383 10y ultramarine 60 25

Japanese Machinery Floating Fair.

Toy Whale A384 — United Nations Emblem A385

1956, Dec. 20 **Photogravure**

634 A384 5y multicolored 1.25 12
a. Imperf., pair

Sheets reproducing four of these stamps, with inscriptions and ornaments, were awarded as sixth prize in the national lottery. Price $10.

Photogravure and Engraved
Perf. 13½x13

1957, Mar. 8 **Unwmkd.**

635 A385 10y light blue & dk. carmine 65 25

Issued to commemorate Japan's admission to the United Nations, Dec. 18, 1956.

Temple Type of 1950
Redrawn; Zeros Omitted.

1957–59 **Engraved** ***Perf. 13x13½***

636 A279 24y violet 3.75 35
636A " 30y rose lilac ('59) 7.50 15
b. Imperf., pair

I. G. Y. Emblem, Penguin and "Soya" A386 — Atomic Reactor A387

1957, July 1 **Photogravure** ***Perf. 13***

637 A386 10y blue, yellow & black 60 35

International Geophysical Year.

1957, Sept. 18 **Engraved** ***Perf. 13***

638 A387 10y dark purple 32 12

Issued to commemorate the completion of Japan's atomic reactor at Tokai-Mura, Ibaraki Prefecture.

Sports Type of 1955.

Designs: No. 639, Girl on parallel bars. No. 640, Boxers.

1957, Oct. 26 ***Perf. 13*** **Unwmkd.**

639 A366 5y ultramarine 25 8
640 " 5y dark red 25 8

12th National Athletic Meet, Shizuoka Prefecture. Nos. 639–640 printed se-tenant in sheets of 20.

"Girl Bouncing Ball," by Suzuki Harunobu A388

1957, Nov. 1 **Photogravure**

641 A388 10y multicolored 3.00 1.00

Issued to publicize the 1957 Stamp Week. Issued in sheets of 10. See also Nos. 646, 671, 728, 757.

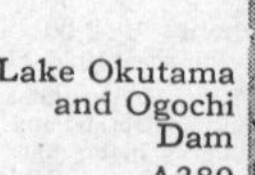

Lake Okutama and Ogochi Dam A389

1957, Nov. 26 **Engr.** ***Perf. 13½***

642 A389 10y ultramarine 35 8

Issued to commemorate the completion of Ogochi Dam, part of the Tokyo water supply system.

Modern and First Japanese Blast Furnaces A390 — Toy Dog (Inu-hariko) A391

1957, Dec. 1 **Photo.** **Unwmkd.**

643 A390 10y orange & dark purple 35 8

Centenary of Japan's iron industry.

1957, Dec. 20 ***Perf. 13½x13***

644 A391 5y multicolored 35 8

Issued for New Year 1958. Sheets reproducing four of No. 644, with inscriptions and ornaments, were awarded as fifth prize in the New Year lottery. Price $4.25.

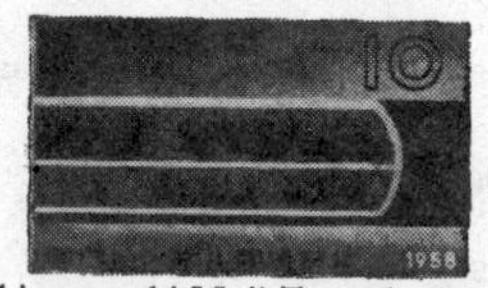

Shimonoseki-Moji Tunnel—A392

1958, Mar. 9 ***Perf. 13x13½***

645 A392 10y multicolored 30 8

Issued to commemorate the completion of the Kan-Mon Underwater Highway connecting Honshu and Kyushu Islands.

Stamp Week Type of 1957.

Design: 10y, Woman with Umbrella, woodcut by Kiyonaga.

1958, Apr. 20 ***Perf. 13*** **Unwmkd.**

646 A388 10y multicolored 1.10 20

Stamp Week, 1958. Sheets of 10.

Statue of Ii Naosuke and Harbor A393

Engraved.

1958, May 10 ***Perf. 13*** **Unwmkd.**

647 A393 10y gray blue & carmine 25 8

Issued to commemorate the centenary of the opening of the ports of Yokohama, Nagasaki and Hakodate to foreign powers.

National Stadium A394

Designs: 10y, Torch and emblem. 14y, Runner. 24y, Woman diver.

1958, May 24 **Photogravure**

648 A394 5y bl. green, bistre & pink 20 8
649 " 10y multicolored 30 8
650 " 14y " 65 12
651 " 24y " 75 15

3rd Asian Games, Tokyo.

Kasato Maru, Map and Brazilian Flag—A395

1958, June 18

652 A395 10y multicolored 25 8

Issued to commemorate 50 years of Japanese emigration to Brazil.

Sado-Yahiko Quasi-National Park Issue

Sado Island and Local Dancer A396

Mt. Yahiko and Echigo Plain A397

1958, Aug. 20 ***Perf. 13*** **Unwmkd.**

653 A396 10y multicolored 65 8
654 A397 10y " 65 8

Stethoscope—A398

1958, Sept. 7 **Photo.** ***Perf. 13***

655 A398 10y Prussian green 30 10

Issued to commemorate the 5th International Congress on Diseases of the Chest and the 7th International Congress of Bronchoesophagology.

"Kyoto" (Sanjo Bridge), Print by Hiroshige A399

1958, Oct. 5

656 A399 24y multicolored 3.50 50

Issued for International Letter Writing Week, Oct. 5–11. See also No. 679.

Sports Types of 1955–56.

Designs: No. 657, Weight lifter. No. 658, Girl badminton player.

1958, Oct. 19 **Engraved**

657	A365	5y gray blue	30	10
658	A379	5y claret	30	10

13th National Athletic Meet, Toyama Prefecture. Nos. 657–658 printed se-tenant in sheets of 20.

Keio University and Yukichi Fukuzawa
A400

1958, Nov. 8 **Engraved** ***Perf. 13½***

659	A400	10y magenta	25	10

Centenary of Keio University.

Globe and Playing Children
A401

1958, Nov. 23 **Photo.** ***Perf. 13***

660	A401	10y deep green	30	8

Issued to publicize the 9th International Conference of Social Work and the 2nd International Study Conference on Child Welfare.

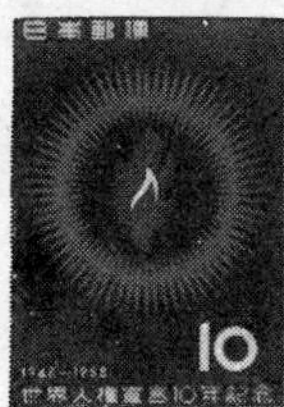

Flame: Symbol of Human Rights
A402

1958, Dec. 10 ***Perf. 13*** **Unwmkd.**

661	A402	10y multicolored	35	8

Issued to commemorate the tenth anniversary of the signing of the Universal Declaration of Human Rights.

Toy of Takamatsu (Tai-Ebisu)
A403

Tractor and Map of Kojima Bay
A404

1958, Dec. 20 ***Perf. 13½***

662	A403	5y multicolored	40	8

Issued for New Year 1959. Sheets reproducing four of No. 662, with inscriptions and ornaments, were awarded as prizes in the New Year lottery. Size: 103x89mm. Price $4.

1959, Feb. 1 ***Perf. 12½***

663	A404	10y claret & bistre brown	30	8

Issued to commemorate the completion of the embankment closing Kojima Bay for reclamation.

Akiyoshidai Quasi-National Park Issue

Karst Plateau
A405

Akiyoshi Cave
A406

1959, Mar. 16 **Photo.** ***Perf. 13½***

664	A405	10y green, blue & ochre	85	12
665	A406	10y multicolored	1.10	12

Map of Southeast Asia
A407

1959, Mar. 27

666	A407	10y deep carmine	28	8

Issued to publicize the Asian Cultural Congress, marking the 2,500th anniversary of the death of Buddha, Tokyo, March 27–31.

Ceremonial Fan
A408

Prince Akihito and Princess Michiko
A409

Photogravure; Portraits Engraved

1959, Apr. 10

667	A408	5y magenta & vio.	20	8
668	A409	10y red brown & dull purple	70	12
		a. Souvenir sheet (imperf.)	3.50	3.75
669	A408	20y orange brown & brown	90	12
670	A409	30y yellow green & dark green	1.20	16

Issued to commemorate the wedding of Crown Prince Akihito and Princess Michiko, Apr. 10, 1959. No. 668a contains one each of Nos. 667–668 and measures 128½ x 88mm.; red brown marginal inscriptions.

Type of 1957.

Design: 10y, Women Reading Poetry Print by Eishi Fujiwara.

1959, May 20 **Photo.** ***Perf. 13***

671	A388	10y multicolored	2.75	1.00

Issued to publicize Stamp Week, 1959. Issued in sheets of 10.

Redrawn Kannon Type of 1953.

Coil Stamp

Perf. 13 Horizontally

1959, Jan. 20 **Typo.** **Unwmkd.**

672	A277	10y red brn. & lilac	7.50	7.50

Measuring Glass, Tape Measure and Scales
A410

Nurses Carrying Stretcher
A411

1959, June 5 **Photo.** ***Perf. 13***

673	A410	10y lt. blue & black	28	8

Adoption of the metric system.

1959, June 24

674	A411	10y olive grn. & red	28	8

Centenary of the Red Cross idea.

Mt. Fuji and Lake Motosu
A412

1959, July 21 **Engraved** ***Perf. 13***

675	A412	10y green, blue & sepia	50	10

Issued to commemorate the establishment of Natural Park Day and the first Natural Park Convention, Yumoto, Nikko, July 21, 1959.

Yaba-Hita-Hiko Quasi-National Park Issue

Ao Cave Area of Yabakei—A413

Hita, Mt. Hiko and Great Cormorant—A414

1959, Sept. 25 **Photo.** ***Perf. 13***

676	A413	10y multicolored	1.10	12
677	A414	10y "	1.10	12

Golden Dolphin, Nagoya Castle
A415

Japanese Crane, IATA Emblem
A416

1959, Oct. 1

678	A415	10y bright blue, gold & black	55	12

350th anniversary of Nagoya.

Hiroshige Type of 1958.

Design: 30y, "Kuwana," the 7-ri Crossing Point, print by Hiroshige.

1959, Oct. 4 **Unwmkd.**

679	A399	30y multicolored	5.00	70

Issued for International Letter Writing Week, Oct. 4-10.

1959, Oct. 12 **Engraved**

680	A416	10y bright greenish blue	35	8

Issued to publicize the 15th General Meeting of the International Air Transport Association.

Shoin Yoshida and PTA Symbol
A417

Throwing the Hammer
A418

1959, Oct. 27 **Photo.** ***Perf. 13***

681	A417	10y brown	35	8

Issued to commemorate the centenary of the death of Shoin Yoshida, educator, and in connection with the Parent-Teachers Association convention.

1959, Oct. 25 **Engraved**

Design: No. 683, Woman Fencer.

682	A418	5y gray blue	45	8
683	"	5y olive bistre	45	8

14th National Athletic Meet, Tokyo. Nos. 682–683 printed se-tenant in sheets of 20.

Globes
A419

1959, Nov. 2 **Photogravure**

684	A419	10y brown red	38	8

Issued to commemorate the 15th session of GATT (General Agreement on Tariffs and Trade), Tokyo, Oct. 12–Nov. 21.

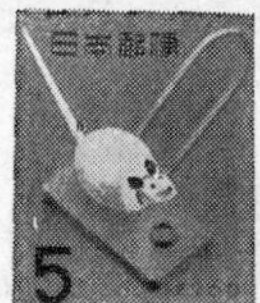

Toy Mouse of Kanazawa
A420

1959, Dec. 19 ***Perf. 13½*** **Unwmkd.**

685	A420	5y gold, red, green & black	60	12

Issued for New Year 1960. Sheets reproducing four of No. 685, with marginal inscription and ornaments, were awarded as prizes in national lottery. Price $3.

Yukio Ozaki and Clock Tower, Ozaki Memorial Hall
A421

Nara Period Artwork, Shosoin Treasure House
A422

1960, Feb. 25 **Photo.** ***Perf. 13½***

686	A421	10y red brown & dark brown	28	8

Issued to commemorate the completion of Ozaki Memorial Hall, erected in memory of Yukio Ozaki (1858–1954), statesman.

1960, Mar. 10

687	A422	10y olive gray	30	8

Issued to mark the 1250th anniversary of the transfer of the capital to Nara.

Scenic Trio Issue

Bay of Matsushima—A423

Ama-no-hashidate (Heavenly Bridge)—A424

Miyajima from the Sea—A425

1960 **Engraved**

688 A423 10y maroon & blue green 1.10 30
689 A424 10y green & light blue 1.25 30
690 A425 10y violet black & blue green 1.25 30

Issue dates: No. 688, Mar. 15. No. 689, July 15. No. 690, Nov. 15.

Mil awa Bay Quasi-National Park Issue

Takeshima, off Gamagori
A426

1960, Mar. 20 Photo. *Perf. 13½*

691 A426 10y multicolored 65 12

Poetess Isé, 13th Century Painting
A427

1960, Apr. 20 *Perf. 13* **Unwmkd.**

692 A427 10y multicolored 3.00 1.25

Stamp Week, 1960.

Kanrin Maru
A428

Design: 30y, Pres. Buchanan receiving first Japanese diplomatic mission.

1960, May 17 **Engraved**

693 A428 10y blue green & brown 70 15
694 " 30y car. & indigo 85 12

Issued to commemorate the centenary of the Japan-United States Treaty of Amity and Commerce. Nos. 694 and 693 form pages of an open book when placed next to each other. Souvenir sheet is No. 703.

Crested Ibis (Toki)
A429

Radio Waves Encircling Globe
A430

1960, May 24 Photo. *Perf. 13½*

695 A429 10y gray, pink & red 60 12

Issued to commemorate the 12th International Congress for Bird Preservation.

1960, June 1 **Engraved**

696 A430 10y carmine rose 25 12

Issued to commemorate the 25th anniversary of the International Radio Program by the Japanese Broadcasting Corporation.

Abashiri Quasi-National Park Issue

Flower Garden (Gensei Kaen)
A431

1960, June 15 **Photogravure**

697 A431 10y multicolored 1.10 15

Ashizuri Quasi-National Park Issue

Cape Ashizuri
A432

1960, Aug. 1 **Unwmkd.**

698 A432 10y multicolored 1.10 18

Rainbow Spanning Pacific, Cherry Blossoms and Pineapples
A433

Henri Farman's Biplane and Jet
A434

1960, Aug. 20 *Perf. 13½*

699 A433 10y multicolored 90 25

Issued to commemorate the 75th anniversary of Japanese contract emigration to Hawaii.

1960, Sept. 20 *Perf. 13*

700 A434 10y brown & chalky blue 45 12

50th anniversary of Japanese aviation.

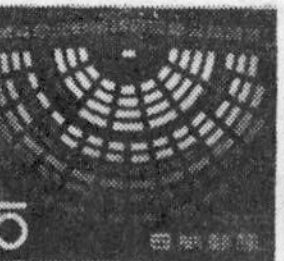

Seat Plan of Diet
A435

"Red Fuji" by Hokusai and Diet Building
A436

1960, Sept. 27

701 A435 5y indigo & orange 25 12
702 A436 10y blue & red brown 40 12

49th Inter-Parliamentary Conference.

Souvenir Sheet
Type A428

1960, Sept. 27 **Engraved**

703 Sheet of two 8.50 9.00

Issued to commemorate the visit of Prince Akihito and Princess Michiko to the United States.

The sheet contains one each of Nos. 693–694. Dull rose inscription, 1860–1960 date and U.S. and Japanese flags. Size: 120x76mm.

"Night Snow at Kambara," by Hiroshige—A437

1960, Oct. 9 **Photogravure**

704 A437 30y multicolored 10.00 1.75

Issued for International Letter Writing Week, Oct. 9–15. See also Nos. 735, 769.

Japanese Fencing (Kendo)
A438

Okayama Astrophysical Observatory
A439

Design: No. 706, Girl gymnast and vaulting horse.

1960, Oct. 23 Engr. *Perf. 13½*

705 A438 5y dull blue 35 15
706 " 5y rose violet 35 15

15th National Athletic Meet, Kumamoto. Nos. 705–706 printed se-tenant in sheets of 20.

1960, Oct. 19

707 A439 10y bright violet 50 12

Issued to commemorate the opening of the Okayama Astrophysical Observatory.

Lt. Naoshi Shirase and Map of Antarctica
A440

Little Red Calf of Aizu, Gold Calf of Iwate
A441

1960, Nov. 29 **Photogravure**

708 A440 10y fawn & black 60 15

Issued to commemorate the 50th anniversary of the first Japanese Antarctic expedition.

1960, Dec. 20 *Perf. 13½* **Unwmkd.**

709 A441 5y multicolored 55 10

Issued for New Year 1961. Sheets reproducing four of No. 709, with ornamental side panels, one inscribed, were awarded as prizes in the New Year lottery. Size: 102x89mm. Price $3.50.

Diet Building at Night
A442

Opening of First Session
A443

Photogravure; Engraved (10y).

1960, Dec. 24

710 A442 5y gray & dk. blue 25 12
711 A443 10y carmine 25 12

70th anniversary of the Japanese Diet.

Narcissus
A444

Nojima Cape Lighthouse and Fisherwomen
A445

Designs: No. 713, Plum blossoms. No. 714, Camellia japonica. No. 715, Cherry blossoms. No. 716, Peony. No. 717, Iris. No. 718, Lily. No. 719, Morning-glory. No. 720, Bellflower. No. 721, Gentian. No. 722, Chrysanthemum. No. 723, Camellia sasanqua.

1961 Photogravure *Perf. 13½*

712 A444 10y lilac, yellow & green 2.25 60
713 " 10y brn., grn. & yel. 1.65 60
714 " 10y lemon, green, pink & yel. 1.35 50
715 " 10y gray, brn., pink, yel. & black 1.35 50
716 " 10y black, green, pink & yel. 1.35 50
717 " 10y gray, purple, green & yel. 85 28
718 " 10y gray green, yel. & brown 75 25
719 " 10y light blue, green & lilac 75 25
720 " 10y light yellow green, violet & green 75 25
721 " 10y orange, violet blue & green 75 25
722 " 10y blue, yellow & green 75 25
723 " 10y slate, pink, yellow & grn. 75 25
Nos. 712–723 (12) 13.30 4.48

South Boso Quasi-National Park Issue

1961, March 15

724 A445 10y multicolored 75 10

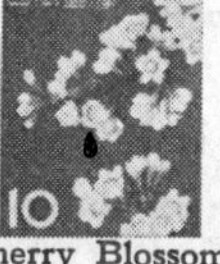

Cherry Blossoms
A446

Hisoka Maejima
A447

Photogravure

1961, Apr. 1 *Perf. 13* **Unwmkd.**

725 A446 10y lilac rose & gray 18 7
a. Lilac rose omitted 350.00
b. Imperf., pair 250.00
c. Bklt. pane of 4 2.25
d. Gray omitted 300.00

See No. 611b.

Coil Stamp

1961, Apr. 25 *Perf. 13 Horiz.*

726 A446 10y lilac rose & gray 1.65 1.65

1961, Apr. 20 *Perf. 13*

727 A447 10y olive & black 65 8

Issued to commemorate the 90th anniversary of Japan's modern postal service from Tokyo to Osaka, inaugurated by Deputy Postmaster General Hisoka Maejima.

Type of 1957

Design: "Dancing Girl" from a "Screen of Dancers."

1961, Apr. 20 *Perf. 13½*

728 A388 10y multicolored 1.50 65

Stamp Week, 1961. Sheets of 10 (5x2).

Lake Biwa Quasi-National Park Issue

Lake Biwa
A448

1961, Apr. 25

729 A448 10y black, dark blue & yellow grn. 60 15

Rotary Emblem and People of Various Races—A449

1961, May 29 **Engraved** *Perf. 13*

730 A449 10y gray & orange 28 8

Issued to commemorate the 52nd convention of Rotary International, Tokyo, May 29–June 1, 1961.

Faucet, Wheat, Insulator & Cogwheel
A450

Sun, Earth and Meridian
A451

1961, July 7 Photo. *Perf. 13½*

731 A450 10y violet & aqua. 30 12

Aichi irrigation system, Kiso river.

1961, July 12

732 A451 10y yellow, red & black 32 12

Issued to commemorate the 75th anniversary of Japanese standard time.

San'in Kaigan Quasi-National Park Issue

Parasol Dance on Dunes of Tottori
A452

1961, Aug. 15

733 A452 10y multicolored 60 12

Onuma Lake and Komagatake Volcano
A453

Gymnast on Horizontal Bar
A454

Onuma Quasi-National Park Issue

1961, Sept. 15

734 A453 10y green, red brown & blue 60 12

Hiroshige Type of 1960

1961, Oct. 8 *Perf. 13*

Design: 30y, "Hakone," print by Hiroshige from the 53 Stages of the Tokaido.

735 A437 30y multicolored 6.00 2.00

Issued for International Letter Writing Week, Oct. 8–14.

1961, Oct. 8 **Engraved** *Perf. 13½*

Design: No. 737, Women rowing.

736 A454 5y blue green 35 8
737 " 5y ultramarine 35 8

16th National Athletic Meet, Akita. Nos. 736–737 printed se-tenant in sheets of 20.

See also Nos. 770–771, 816–817, 852–853.

Coil Stamp
Duck Type of 1955.

1961, Oct. 2 Photo. *Perf. 13 Horiz.*

738 A362 5y light blue & red brown 1.20 1.35

National Diet Library and Book
A455

Papier Maché Tiger
A456

1961, Nov. 1 *Perf. 13½*

739 A455 10y dp. ultra. & gold 30 8

Issued to commemorate the opening of the new National Diet Library, Tokyo.

1961, Dec. 15 *Perf. 13½*

740 A456 5y multicolored 40 12

Issued for New Year 1962. Sheets reproducing four of No. 740, with marginal decorations and inscriptions, were awarded as fifth prize in the New Year lottery. Size: 102x90mm. Price $3.50.

Fuji-Hakone-Izu National Park Issue

Mt. Fuji from Lake Ashi
A457

Minokake-Iwa at Irozaki
A458

Mt. Fuji from Mitsu Pass
A459

Mt. Fuji from Cape of Ose
A460

Photogravure

1962, Jan. 16 *Perf. 13½* **Unwmkd.**

741 A457 5y deep green 45 15
742 A458 5y dark blue 45 15
743 A459 10y red brown 80 25
744 A460 10y black 80 25

Kitanagato-Kaigan Quasi-National Park Issue

Omishima
A461

1962, Feb. 15 *Perf. 13½*

745 A461 10y ultramarine, red & yellow 55 12

Perotrochus Hirasei
A462

Sacred Bamboo
A463

Shari-den of Engakuji
A464

Yomei Gate, Nikko
A465

Noh Mask
A466

Copper Pheasant
A466a

Wind God, Fujin, by Sotatsu
A467

Japanese Crane
A468

Mythical Winged Woman, Chusonji
A469

1962–65 *Perf. 13* **Unwmkd.**

746 A462 4y dk. brown & red ('63) 12 7
747 A463 6y gray grn. & car. 12 7
748 A464 30y violet black 1.00 8
749 A465 40y rose red 1.10 8
750 A466 70y yellow brn. & black ('65) 1.00 8
751 A466a 80y crim. & brown ('65) 1.10 8
752 A467 90y brt. blue green 5.50 12
753 A468 100y pink & blk. ('63) 4.25 8
754 A469 120y purple 4.00 12
Nos. 746–754 (9) 18.19 78

See also Nos. 888, 888A, 890.

Coil Stamp.
Perf. 13 Horiz.

755 A464 30y dull vio. ('63) 2.50 2.75

Hinamatsuri, Doll Festival
A470

1962, March 3 *Perf. 13½*

756 A470 10y brown, black, blue & car. 1.15 25

The Doll Festival is celebrated March 3 in honor of young girls.

Type of 1957

Design: Dancer from "Flower Viewing Party" by Naganobu Kano.

1962, Apr. 20 Photo. *Perf. 13½*

757 A388 10y multicolored 2.00 1.00

Stamp Week, 1962. Sheets of 10.

Kinkowan Quasi-National Park Issue

Sakurajima Volcano and Kagoshima Bay—A471

1962, Apr. 30

758 A471 10y multicolored 50 12

Kongo-Ikoma Quasi-National Park Issue

Mount Kongo—A472

1962, May 15 *Perf. 13½*

759 A472 10y gray blue, dk. green & sal. 50 12

Suigo Quasi-National Park Issue

Suigo Park Scene and Iris
A473

1962, June 1 *Perf. 13½*

760 A473 10y multicolored 50 12

Train Emerging from Hokuriku Tunnel
A474

1962, June 10 Photogravure

761 A474 10y olive gray 55 12

Issued to commemorate the opening of Hokuriku Tunnel between Tsuruga and Imajo, Fukui Prefecture.

Star Festival (Tanabata Matsuri)
A475

Boy Scout Hat on Map of Southeast Asia
A476

1962, July 7 ***Perf. 13½*** **Unwmkd.**

762 A475 10y multicolored 50 12

The Tanabata festival is celebrated on the evening of July 7.

1962, Aug. 3

763 A476 10y red org., black & bistre 25 12

Issued to commemorate the Asian Boy Scout Jamboree, Mt. Fuji, Aug. 3–7.

Nikko National Park Issue

Ozegahara Swampland and Mt. Shibutsu—A477

Fumes on Mt. Chausu, Nasu
A478

Lake Chuzenji and Mt. Nantai
A479

Senryu-kyo Narrows, Shiobara
A480

1962, Sept. 1

764 A477 5y greenish blue 25 8
765 A478 5y maroon 25 8
766 A479 10y purple 38 8
767 A480 10y olive 38 8

Wakato Suspension Bridge
A481

Perf. 13½x13

1962, Sept. 26 **Engr.** **Unwmkd.**

768 A481 10y rose red 85 25

Issued to commemorate the opening of Wakato Bridge over Dokai Bay in North Kyushu.

Hiroshige Type of 1960

Design: 40y, "Nihonbashi," print by Hiroshige from the 53 Stages of the Tokaido.

1962, Oct. 7 Photogravure ***Perf. 13***

769 A437 40y multicolored 5.50 1.40

Issued for International Letter Writing Week, Oct. 7–13.

Sports Type of 1961

Design: No. 770, Woman softball pitcher. No. 771, Rifle shooting.

1962, Oct. 21 Engraved ***Perf. 13½***

770 A454 5y bluish black 25 8
771 " 5y brown violet 25 8

17th National Athletic Meeting, Okayama. Nos. 770–771 printed se-tenant in sheets of 20.

Shichi-go-san Festival
A482

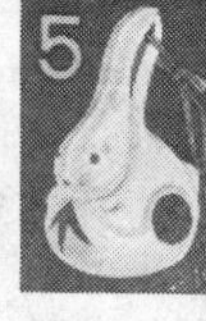

Rabbit Bell
A483

1962, Nov. 15 Photo. ***Perf. 13½***

772 A482 10y multicolored 60 12

This festival for 7 and 3-year-old girls and 5-year-old boys is celebrated on Nov. 15.

1962, Dec. 15

773 A483 5y multicolored 25 12

Issued for New Year 1963. Sheets reproducing four of No. 773 with marginal decorations and inscriptions were awarded as prizes in the New Year lottery. Price $3.

Ishizuchi Quasi-National Park Issue

Mt. Ishizuchi—A484

1963, Jan. 11 ***Perf. 13½*** **Unwmkd.**

774 A484 10y multicolored 28 12

Setsubun, Spring Festival, Bean Scattering Ceremony
A485

Map of City, Birds, Ship and Factory
A486

1963, Feb. 3 Photogravure

775 A485 10y multicolored 40 12

1963, Feb. 10

776 A486 10y chocolate 18 8

Issued to commemorate the consolidation of the communities of Moji, Kokura, Wakamatsu, Yawata and Tobata into Kita-Kyushu City.

Unzen-Amakusa National Park Issue

"Frost Flowers" on Mt. Fugen
A487

Amakusa Island and Mt. Unzen
A488

1963, Feb. 15

777 A487 5y gray blue 25 8
778 A488 10y carmine rose 25 8

Hakusan National Park Issue

Green Pond, Midorigaike
A489

Hakusan Range
A490

Photogravure

1963, Mar. 1 ***Perf. 13½*** **Unwmkd.**

779 A489 5y violet brown 25 8
780 A490 10y dark green 25 8

Genkai Quasi-National Park Issue

Keya-no-Oto Rock
A491

1963, Mar. 15

781 A491 10y multicolored 25 8

Wheat Emblem and Globe
A492

1963, Mar. 21

782 A492 10y dark green 18 8

Issued for the "Freedom from Hunger" campaign of the U.N. Food and Agriculture Organization.

"Portrait of Heihachiro Honda," Yedo Screen—A493

1963, Apr. 20 ***Perf. 13½***

783 A493 10y multicolored 1.00 1.00

Issued to publicize Stamp Week, 1963.

World Map and Centenary Emblem
A494

1963, May 8

784 A494 10y multicolored 18 8

Centenary of the International Red Cross.

Globe and Leaf with Symbolic River System
A495

1963, May 15 Photogravure

785 A495 10y blue 18 8

Issued to commemorate the 5th Congress of the International Commission on Irrigation and Drainage.

Bandai-Asahi National Park Issue

Ito-dake, Asahi Range
A496

Lake Hibara and Mt. Bandai
A497

1963, May 25 ***Perf. 13½*** **Unwmkd.**

786 A496 5y green 25 8
787 A497 10y red brown 25 8

Lidth's Jay
A498

Designs: No. 789, Rock ptarmigan. No. 790, Eastern turtle dove. No. 791, Japanese white stork. No. 792, Bush warbler. No. 792A, Meadow bunting.

1963–64 *Perf. 13½*

Design and Inscription

788	A498	10y light green	1.00	65
789	"	10y blue	28	8
790	"	10y pale yellow	28	8
791	"	10y greenish bl. ('64)	28	8
792	"	10y green ('64)	28	8
792A	"	10y light rose brown ('64)	25	8
		Nos. 788–792A (6)	2.37	1.05

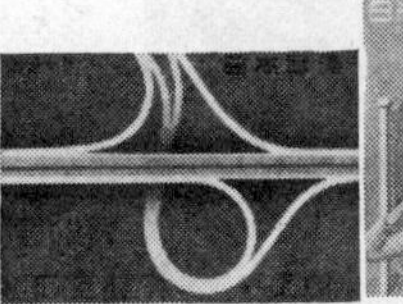

Intersection at Ritto, Shiga
A499

Girl Scout and Flag
A500

1963, July 15 *Perf. 13½* **Unwmkd.**

793 A499 10y blue green, black & orge. 18 8

Issued to commemorate the opening of the Nagoya-Kobe expressway, linking Nagoya with Kyoto, Osaka and Kobe.

1963, Aug. 1 **Photogravure**

794 A500 10y multicolored 18 8

Issued to commemorate the Asian Girl Scout and Girl Guides Camp, Togakushi Heights, Nagano, Aug. 1–7.

Inland Sea National Park Issue

View of Nashu
A501

Whirlpool at Naruto
A502

1963, Aug. 20

795 A501 5y olive bister 20 8
796 A502 10y dark green 20 8

Daisetsuzan National Park Issue

Lake Shikaribetsu, Hokkaido
A503

Mt. Kurodake from Sounkyo Valley
A504

1963, Sept. 1 *Perf. 13½* **Unwmkd.**

797 A503 5y dp. Prussian blue 20 8
798 A504 10y rose violet 20 8

Parabolic Antenna for Space Communications—A505

1963, Sept. 9 **Photogravure**

799 A505 10y multicolored 18 8

Issued to publicize the 14th General Assembly of the International Scientific Radio Union, Tokyo.

"Great Wave off Kanagawa," by Hokusai—A506

1963, Oct. 10 *Perf. 13*

800 A506 40y gray, dark blue & yellow 3.00 60

Issued for International Letter Writing Week, Oct. 6–12. Design from Hokusai's "36 Views of Fuji." Printed in sheets of 10 (5x2).

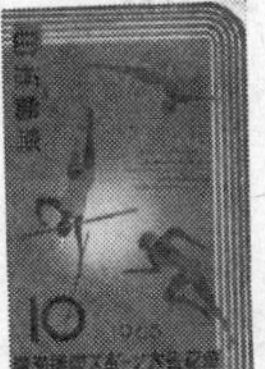

Diver, Pole Vaulter and Relay Runner
A507

Woman Gymnast
A508

1963, Oct. 11 *Perf. 13½*

801 A507 10y blue, ocher, black & red 15 6

Issued to commemorate the Tokyo International (Pre-Olympic) Sports Meet, Tokyo, Oct. 11–16.

Engraved

1963, Oct. 27 *Perf. 13½* **Unwmkd.**

Design: No. 803, Japanese wrestling (sumo).

802 A508 5y slate green 15 5
803 " 5y brown 15 5

18th National Athletic Meet, Yamaguchi. Nos. 802–803 printed se-tenant in sheets of 20.

Phoenix Tree and Hachijo Island
A509

Toy Dragons of Tottori and Yamanashi
A510

Izu Islands Quasi-National Park Issue

1963, Dec. 10 **Photogravure**

804 A509 10y multicolored 18 6

1963, Dec. 16

805 A510 5y gold, pink, aqua., indigo & red 12 5

a. Aquamarine omitted

Issued for New Year 1964. Sheets containing four of No. 805 were awarded as fifth prize in the New Year lottery. Price $2.50.

Wakasa Bay Quasi-National Park Issue

Wakasa-Fuji from Takahama
A511

1964, Jan 25 *Perf. 13½*

806 A511 10y multicolored 18 6

Nichinan-Kaigan Quasi-National Park Issue

Agave and View from Horikiri Pass
A512

1964, Feb. 20 **Unwmkd.**

807 A512 10y multicolored 18 6

Ise-Shima National Park Issue

Uji Bridge—A513

View of Toba—A514

1964, Mar. 15 **Photogravure**

808 A513 5y sepia 15 4
809 A514 10y red lilac 15 4

Regional Festival Issue

Takayama Festival Float and Mt. Norikura—A515

Design: No. 811, Yamaboko floats and Gion Shrine, Kyoto.

1964 **Photogravure** *Perf. 13½*

810 A515 10y lt. grn. & multi. 20 3
811 " 10y greenish blue & multi. 20 3

No. 810 issued to publicize the annual Takayama spring and autumn festivals, Takayama City, Gifu Prefecture. No. 811 to publicize the annual Gion festival of Kyoto, July 10–30.

Issue dates: No. 810, Apr. 15. No. 811, July 15.

Yadorigi Scene from Genji Monogatari Scroll
A516

1964, Apr. 20

814 A516 10y multicolored 25 15

Stamp Week, 1964. Sheets of 10 (2x5).

Himeji Castle
A517

1964, June 1 *Perf. 13½*

815 A517 10y dark brown 15 10

Restoration of Himeji Castle.

Sports Type of 1961

Designs: No. 816, Handball. No. 817, Woman athlete on beam.

1964, June 6 *Perf. 13½*

816 A454 5y slate green 12 10
817 " 5y rose red 12 10

19th National Athletic Meeting, Niigata. Nos. 816–817 printed se-tenant in sheets of 20.

Cable Cross Section, Map of Pacific Ocean
A518

Tokyo Expressway Crossing Nihonbashi
A519

1964, June 19

818 A518 10y gray green, deep magenta & yel. 15 10

Opening of the transpacific cable.

1964, Aug. 1 **Photogravure**

819 A519 10y grn., silver & blk. 15 10

Opening of the Tokyo Expressway.

Coin-like Emblems
A520

1964, Sept. 7 *Perf. 13½* **Unwmkd.**

820 A520 10y scarlet, gold & black 15 10

Issued to commemorate the annual general meeting of the International Monetary Fund, International Bank for Reconstruction and Development, International Financial Corporation and the International Development Association, Tokyo, Sept. 7–11.

Athletes, Olympic Flame and Rings
A521

National Stadium, Tokyo
A522

Designs: 30y, Nippon Bodokan (fencing hall). 40y, National Gymnasium. 50y, Komazawa Gymnasium.

1964

821 A521 5y dk. bl., verm., black & gold 12 3
822 A522 10y dk. brn., gold, orange & blk. 15 3
823 " 30y ultra., black, gold & red 40 4
824 " 40y gold, black, red & ultra. 40 15
825 " 50y brick red, gold, black & ultra. 50 18
a. Souv. sheet of 5 3.00 3.50
Nos. 821-825 (5) 1.57 43

Issued to commemorate the 18th Olympic Games, Tokyo, Oct. 10–25. No. 825a contains one each of Nos. 821–825. Black inscription and emblem of Tokyo Olympic Games in margin. Size: 92½x143mm.

Issue dates: 5y, Sept. 9. Others, Oct. 10.

Hand with Grain, Cow and Fruit
A523

Express Train
A524

1964, Sept. 15 ***Perf. 13½***

826 A523 10y vio. brn. & gold 15 3

Draining of Hachirogata Lagoon, providing new farmland for the future.

1964, Oct. 1

827 A524 10y blue & black 20 10

Opening of the new Tokaido railroad line.

Mt. Fuji Seen from Tokaido, by Hokusai—A525

1964, Oct. 4 ***Perf. 13***

828 A525 40y multicolored 1.40 35

Issued for International Letter Writing Week, Oct. 4–10. Issued in sheets of 10 (5x2). See Nos. 850, 896, 932, 971, 1016.

"Straw Snake" Mascot
A526

1964, Dec. 15 Photo. ***Perf. 13½***

829 A526 5y crimson, black & yellow 10 8

Issued for New Year 1965. Sheets containing four of No. 829 were awarded as prizes in the New Year lottery (issued Jan. 20, 1965). Price $1.75.

Daisen-Oki National Park Issue

Mt. Daisen—A527

Paradise Cove, Oki Islands
A528

1965, Jan. 20 ***Perf. 13½*** **Unwmkd.**

830 A527 5y dark blue 15 4
831 A528 10y brown orange 15 6

Niseko-Shakotan-Otarukaigan Quasi-National Park Issue

Niseko-Annupuri
A529

1965, Feb. 15 Photogravure

832 A529 10y multicolored 20 6

Meteorological Radar Station on Mt. Fuji—A530

1965, Mar. 10 Photo. ***Perf. 13½***

833 A530 10y multicolored 15 10

Issued to commemorate the completion of the Meteorological Radar Station on Kengamine Heights of Mt. Fuji.

Jo-Shin-etsu Kogen National Park Issue

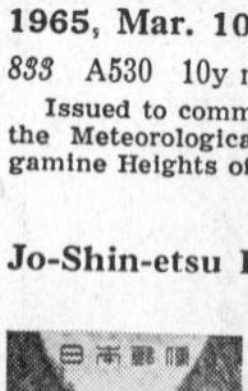

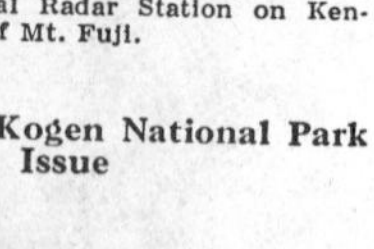

Kiyotsu Gorge
A531

Lake Nojiri and Mt. Myoko
A532

1965, Mar. 15

834 A531 5y brown 15 4
835 A532 10y magenta 15 6

Communications Museum, Tokyo
A533

1965, Mar. 25 ***Perf. 13½*** **Unwmkd.**

836 A533 10y green 15 3

Issued to commemorate the Philatelic Exhibition celebrating the completion of the Communications Museum.

"The Prelude" by Shoen Uemura
A534

1965, Apr. 20 Photogravure

837 A534 10y gray & multi. 45 15

Issued for Stamp Week, 1965.

Playing Children, Cows and Swan
A535

Stylized Tree and Sun
A536

1965, May 5 ***Perf. 13½*** **Unwmkd.**

838 A535 10y pink & multi. 15 3

Opening of the National Garden for Children, Tokyo-Yokohama.

1965, May 9

839 A536 10y multicolored 15 3

Issued to publicize the forestation movement and the forestation ceremony, Tottori Prefecture.

Globe, Old and New Communication Equipment—A537

1965, May 17

840 A537 10y bright blue, yellow & black 15 3

Issued to commemorate the centenary of the International Telecommunication Union.

Aso National Park Issue

Crater of Mt. Naka, Kyushu
A538

Five Central Peaks of Aso and Mountain Road
A539

1965, June 15 Photo. ***Perf. 13½***

841 A538 5y carmine rose 15 4
842 A539 10y deep green 15 6

ICY Emblem and Doves—A540

1965, June 26 **Unwmkd.**

843 A540 40y multicolored 50 12

Issued for the International Cooperation Year, 1965, and to commemorate the 20th anniversary of the United Nations.

Horse Chase, Soma
A541

Chichibu Festival Scene
A542

1965 Photo. ***Perf. 13x13½***

844 A541 10y multicolored 30 10
845 A542 10y multicolored 35 10

No. 844 issued to publicize the ancient Soma Nomaoi Festival, Fukushima Prefecture; No. 845, to publicize the festival dedicated to the Chichibu Myoken Shrine (built 1584).

Issue dates: No. 844, July 16. No. 845, Dec. 3.

Meiji Maru, Black-tailed Gulls
A543

1965, July 20 ***Perf. 13½***

846 A543 10y green, gray, black & yellow 15 3

25th Maritime Day, July 20.

Drop of Blood, Girl's Face and Bloodmobile
A544

1965, Sept. 1 ***Perf. 13½***

847 A544 10y yellow green, black & red 15 3

Issued to publicize the national campaign for blood donations, Sept. 1–30.

Tokai Atomic Power Station and Structure of Alpha Uranium
A545

1965, Sept. 21 Photogravure
848 A545 10y multicolored 15 3

Issued to publicize the Ninth General Conference of the International Atomic Energy Agency, IAEA, Tokyo, Sept. 21–30.

People and Flag
A546

1965, Oct. 1
849 A546 10y multicolored 15 3

Tenth national census.

Hokusai Type of 1964

Design: No. 850, "Waters at Misaka" by Hokusai (Mt. Fuji seen across Lake Kawaguchi).

1965, Oct. 6 ***Perf. 13*** **Unwmkd.**
850 A525 40y multicolored 90 30

Issued for International Letter Writing Week, Oct. 6–12. Issued in sheets of 10 (5x2).

Emblems and Diagram of Seats in National Diet—A547

1965, Oct. 15 ***Perf. 13½***
851 A547 10y multicolored 15 3

Issued to commemorate the 75th anniversary of national suffrage, the 40th anniversary of universal suffrage and the 20th anniversary of women's suffrage.

Sports Type of 1961

Designs: No. 852, Gymnast on vaulting horse. No. 853, Walking race.

1965, Oct. 24 Engraved ***Perf. 13½***
852 A454 5y red brown 10 3
853 " 5y yellow green 10 3

20th National Athletic Meeting, Gifu. Nos. 852–853 printed se-tenant in sheets of 20.

Profile and Infant
A548

1965, Oct. 30 Photogravure ***Perf. 13***
854 A548 30y car. lake, yel. & light blue 38 8

Issued to commemorate the Eighth International Conference of Otorhinolaryngology and the 11th International Conference of Pediatrics.

Shiretoko National Park Issue

Mt. Iwo from Shari Coast, Hokkaido
A549

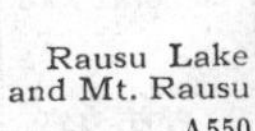

Rausu Lake and Mt. Rausu
A550

1965, Nov. 15 ***Perf. 13½***
855 A549 5y Prussian green 15 4
856 A550 10y bright blue 15 6

Aurora Australis, Map of Antarctica and "Fuji"—A551

1965, Nov. 20
857 A551 10y bl., yel. & dk. bl. 15 3

Issued to publicize the Antarctic expedition, which left on the observation ship "Fuji," Nov. 20, 1965.

"Secret Horse" Straw Toy, Iwate Prefecture
A552

Telephone Dial and 1890 Switchboard
A553

1965, Dec. 10
858 A552 5y lt. blue & multi. 12 10

Issued for New Year 1966. Sheets containing four of No. 858 were awarded as prizes in the New Year lottery (issued Jan. 20, 1966). Price $1.50.

1965, Dec. 16
859 A553 10y multicolored 15 8

Issued to commemorate the 75th anniversary of telephone service in Japan.

Japanese Spiny Lobster
A554

Carp
A555

1966–67 Photogravure ***Perf. 13***

Multicolored; Background in Colors Indicated

860 A554 10y green & ultra. 20 3
861 A555 10y blue green 20 3
862 " 10y dk. blue (*Bream*) 20 3
863 " 10y dk. ultra. (*Skipjack tuna*) 20 3
864 " 10y bister & dk. grn. (*3 Ayu*) 20 3
865 " 15y greenish blue & yellow (*Eel*) 30 3
866 " 15y bright green (*Jack mackerel*) 30 3
867 " 15y brt. grn. & blue (*Chum salmon*) 30 3
868 " 15y light blue green (*Yellowtail*) ('67) 35 3
869 A555 15y bright green (*Tiger puffer*) ('67) 38 3
870 A554 15y ultra. & green (*Squid*) ('67) 50 8
871 " 15y chalky blue (*Turbo cornutus*) ('67) 50 8
Nos. 860-871 (12) 3.63 46

Famous Gardens Issue

Kobuntei Pavilion and Plum Blossoms, Kairakuen Garden, Ibaragi
A556

Japanese Cranes and Okayama Castle, Korakuen Garden, Okayama
A557

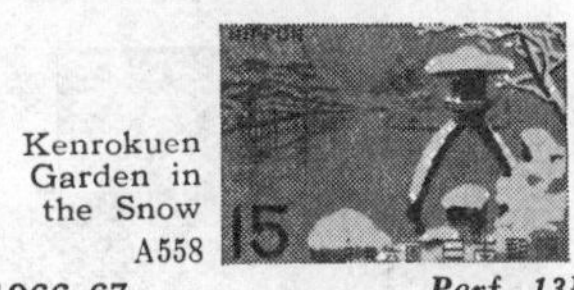

Kenrokuen Garden in the Snow
A558

1966–67 ***Perf. 13½***
872 A556 10y gold, black & green 30 8
873 A557 15y blue, black & magenta 35 8
874 A558 15y silver, green & dk. brown ('67) 35 8

Dates of issue: 10y, Feb. 25; No. 873, Nov. 3; No. 874, Jan. 25, 1967.

Zao Quasi-National Park Issue

Crater Lake, Zao
A559

1966, March 15
875 A559 10y multicolored 20 6

Muroto-Anan Coast Quasi-National Park Issue

Muroto Cape
A560

Senba Cliffs, Anan Coast
A561

1966, March 22 ***Perf. 13½***
876 A560 10y multicolored 20 3
877 A561 10y " 20 3

AIPPI Emblem
A562

1966, Apr. 11 ***Perf. 13***
878 A562 40y multicolored 50 8

Issued to commemorate the 26th General Assembly of the International Association for the Protection of Industrial Properties, Tokyo, April 11–16.

"Butterflies" by Takeji Fujishima
A563

Photogravure and Engraved

1966, Apr. 20 ***Perf. 13½***
879 A563 10y gray & multi. 35 8

Stamp Week, 1966. Sheets of 10 (2x5).

Inscribed "NIPPON." Types of 1951–63 and

Goldfish
A564

Chrysanthemums
A565

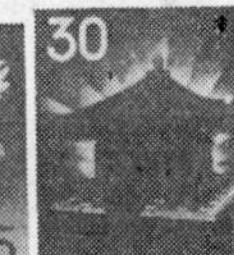

Golden Hall, Chusonji
A565a

Yomei Gate, Nikko
A565b

Ancient Clay Horse (Haniwa)
A567

Katsura Palace Garden
A568

Central Hall, Enryakuji Temple
A566

Bodhisattva Playing Flute (from Todaiji Lantern)
A570

Designs: 1y, Hisoka Maejima. 20y, Wistaria. 25y, Hydrangea. 35y, Luminescent squid. 45y, Lysichiton camtschatsense (white flowers). 50y, Nyoirin Kannon. 75y, Big purple butterfly. 90y, Wind god (Fujin). 120y, Mythical winged woman. 500y, Deva King statue, South Gate, Todaiji.

1966–69 Photogravure ***Perf. 13***
879A A275 1y olive bister ('68) 12 8
880 A564 7y olive & deep orange 40 7

881 A565 15y blue & yellow (blue "15") 45 3
b. Bklt. pane of 2 + label ('67) 3.25
c. Bklt. pane of 4 ('67) 2.25
d. Bklt. pane of 4 (2 # 881 + 2 # 611) ('67) 4.50
e. Imperf., pair 300.00
881A " 20y violet & multi. ('67) 65 3
882 " 25y grn. & lt. ultra. 45 3
882A A565a 30y dp. ultra. & gold ('68) 55 3
883 A564 35y bl., gray & blk. 50 3
883A A565b 40y blue green & brown ('68) 55 3
884 A565 45y blue & multi. ('67) 55 3
885 A280 50y dk. car. rose 3.00 3

Engraved

886 A566 60y slate green 1.00 3

Photogravure

887 A567 65y orange brown 4.00 4
887A A373 75y rose, black, yel. & pur. 1.00 4
888 A467 90y gold & brown 1.85 4
888A A468 100y verm. & black ('68) 1.20 3

Engraved

889 A568 110y brown 1.65 3
890 A469 120y red 2.00 3
891 A570 200y Prus. green (22x33 mm) 2.65 3
891A " 500y dull pur. ('69) 6.50 5
Nos. 879A-891A (19) 29.07 71

Nos. 880-881 were also issued with fluorescent frame on July 18, 1966.

See also Nos. 913-915, 918, 926, 1072, 1081.

UNESCO Emblem
A571

Map of Pacific Ocean
A572

1966, July 2 Photogravure *Perf. 13*

892 A571 15y multicolored 20 3

Issued to commemorate the 20th anniversary of the founding of the United Nations Educational, Cultural and Scientific Organization (UNESCO).

1966, Aug. 22 *Perf. 13*

893 A572 15y bister brown, dull bl. & rose 20 3

11th Pacific Science Congress, Tokyo, Aug. 22-Sept. 10.

Amakusa Bridges, Kyushu
A573

Emblem of Post Office Life Insurance and Family
A574

1966, Sept. 24 Photo. *Perf. 13*

894 A573 15y multicolored 20 3

Issued to commemorate the completion of five bridges linking Misumi Harbor, Kyushu, with Amakusa islands.

1966, Oct. 1

895 A574 15y yel. grn. & multi. 20 3

Issued to commemorate the 50th anniversary of post office life insurance service.

Hokusai Type of 1964

Design: 50y, "Sekiya on the Sumida" (horseback riders and Mt. Fuji) from Hokusai's "36 Views of Fuji."

1966, Oct. 6

896 A525 50y multicolored 1.50 40

Issued for International Letter Writing Week, Oct. 6-12. Printed in sheets of 10 (5x2).

Sharpshooter
A575

Design: No. 898, Hop, skip and jump.

1966, Oct. 23 Engraved *Perf. 13½*

897 A575 7y ultramarine 15 3
898 " 7y carmine rose 15 3

21st National Athletic Meet, Oita, Oct. 23-28. Nos. 897-898 printed se-tenant in sheets of 20.

National Theater
A576

Kabuki Scene
A577

Bunraku Puppet Show
A578

1966, Nov. 1 *Perf. 13, 13½*

899 A576 15y multicolored 20 4
900 A577 25y " 90 30
901 A578 50y " 90 38

Inauguration of first National Theater in Japan. Nos. 900-901 issued in sheets of 10.

Rice Year Emblem
A579

Ittobori Carved Sheep, Nara Prefecture
A580

1966, Nov. 21 *Perf. 13½*

902 A579 15y red, blk. & ocher 20 3

Issued to publicize the International Rice Year under sponsorship of the U.N. Food and Agricultural Organization.

1966, Dec. 10 Photo. *Perf. 13½*

903 A580 7y blue, gold, black & pink 12 3

Issued for New Year 1967. Sheets containing four of No. 903 were awarded as prizes in the New Year lottery. Price $1.40.

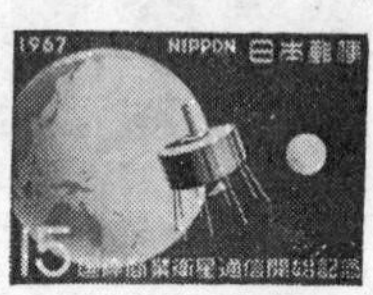

International Communications Satellite, Lani Bird 2
A581

1967, Jan. 27 *Perf. 13½*

904 A581 15y dark Prussian blue & sepia 20 3

Inauguration in Japan of International commercial communications service via satellite.

Around the World Air Route and Jet Plane—A582

1967, March 6 Photo. *Perf. 13½*

905 A582 15y multicolored 20 3

Issued to publicize the inauguration of Japan Air Lines Tokyo-London service via New York, which completes the around the world air route.

Library of Modern Japanese Literature—A583

1967, Apr. 11

906 A583 15y greenish blue, lt. & dk. brn. 20 3

Issued to commemorate the opening of the Library of Modern Japanese Literature, Komaba Park, Meguro-ku, Tokyo.

Painting Type of 1966

Design: 15y, Lakeside (seated woman), by Seiki (Kiyoteru) Kuroda.

1967, Apr. 20

907 A563 15y multicolored 1.00 30

Stamp Week, 1967. Sheets of 10 (2x5).

Kobe Harbor
A584

1967, May 8 Photo. *Perf. 13x13½*

908 A584 50y multicolored 60 18

Issued to commemorate the 5th Congress of the International Association of Ports and Harbors, Tokyo, May 8-13.

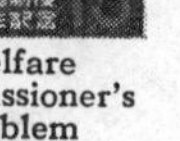

Welfare Commissioner's Emblem
A585

Traffic Light, Automobile and Children
A586

1967, May 12 *Perf. 13½*

909 A585 15y dk. brn. & gold 20 3

Issued to commemorate the 50th anniversary of the Welfare Commissioner System.

1967, May 22 *Perf. 13x13½*

910 A586 15y emerald, red, blk. & yellow 20

Issued to publicize traffic safety.

South Japan Alps National Park Issue

Kita and Kai-Koma Mountains
A587

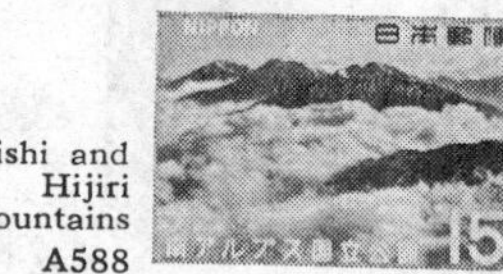

Akaishi and Hijiri Mountains
A588

1967, July 10

911 A587 7y Prussian blue 15 3
912 A588 15y rose lilac 20 3

Types of 1956-67

Inscribed "NIPPON" and Redrawn

Original 20y
No. 881A

Redrawn 20y
No. 915

1967-69 Photogravure *Perf. 13*

913 A564 7y brt. yel. green & dp. orange 22 3
914 A565 15y blue & yellow (white "15") 28 3
a. Pane of 10 (5x2) ('68) 3.00
b. Bklt. panes of 4 with gutter (6 #914 + 2 #611) ('68) 2.75
c. Imperf., pair 225.00
d. Blue shading omitted
e. Bklt. panes of 2 & 4 with gutter ('68) 17.50
915 A565 20y violet & multi. ('69) 65 3
916 A280 50y bright carmine 70 3
917 A372 55y lt. blue, green & black ('69) 65 3
918 A567 65y deep orange 1.20 3
Nos. 913-918 (6) 3.70 18

Issued for use in facer-canceling machines. Issue dates: 7y, Aug. 1; 15y, 50y, July 1; 65y, July 20, 1967; 20y, Apr. 1, 1969; 55y, Sept. 1, 1969.

On No. 913 the background has been lightened and a frame line of shading added at top and right side.

No. 914a is imperf. on four sides.

The two panes of Nos. 914b and 914e are connected by a vertical creased gutter 21 mm. wide. The left pane of No. 914b consists of 2 No. 914 and 2 No. 611; the right pane, 4 of No. 914. The left pane of 2 of No. 914e includes a 4-line inscription.

On No. 915 the wistaria leaves do not touch frame at left and top. On No. 881A they do.

Coil Stamp

1968, Jan. 9 ***Perf. 13 Horiz.***

926 A565 15y blue & yellow (white "15") 65 45

Mitochondria and Protein Model
A589

1967, Aug. 19 **Photo.** ***Perf. 13***

927 A589 15y gray & multi. 20 3

Issued to commemorate the 7th International Biochemistry Congress, Tokyo, Aug. 19–25.

Gymnast on Horizontal Bar
A590

Universiade Emblem
A591

1967, Aug. 26

928 A590 15y red & multi. 15 4
929 A591 50y yellow & multi. 65 30

Issued to commemorate the World University Games, Universiade 1967, Tokyo, Aug. 26–Sept. 4.

Paper Lantern, ITY Emblem
A592

"Sacred Mt. Fuji" by Taikan Yokoyama
A593

1967, Oct. 2 **Photo.** ***Perf. 13***

930 A592 15y ultra. & multi. 20 4
931 A593 50y multicolored 2.50 1.65

International Tourist Year, 1967. No. 931 issued in sheets of 10.

Hokusai Type of 1964

Design: 50y, "Kajikazawa, Koshu" (fisherman and waves) from Hokusai's "36 Views of Fuji."

1967, Oct. 6

932 A525 50y multicolored 2.25 50

Issued for International Letter Writing Week, Oct. 6–12. Sheets of 10 (5x2).

Athlete, Wild Primrose and Chichibu Mountains
A594

1967, Oct. 22 **Photo.** ***Perf. 13***

933 A594 15y gold & multi. 30 12

22nd National Athletic Meet, Saitama, Oct. 22–27.

Miroku Bosatsu, Koryuji Temple, Kyoto
A595

Kudara Kannon, Horyuji Temple, Nara
A596

Golden Hall and Pagoda, Horyuji Temple, Nara
A597

1967, Nov. 1 **Photogravure**

934 A595 15y multicolored 40 30

Engraved

935 A596 15y pale green, black & red 40 30

Photogravure and Engraved

936 A597 50y multicolored 2.50 85

National treasures of Asuka Period (6th–7th centuries). No. 936 issued in sheets of 10.

Highway and Congress Emblem
A598

1967, Nov. 5 **Photo.** ***Perf. 13***

937 A598 50y multicolored 65 15

Issued to publicize the 13th World Road Congress, Tokyo, Nov. 5–11.

Chichibu-Tama National Park Issue

Mt. Kumotori
599

Lake Chichibu
A600

1967, Nov. 27

938 A599 7y olive 15 3
939 A600 15y red lilac 20 3

Climbing Monkey Toy (Noborizaru), Miyazaki Prefecture
A601

1967, Dec. 11 **Photo.** ***Perf. 13***

940 A601 7y multicolored 12 8

Issued for New Year 1968. Sheets containing four of No. 940 were awarded as prizes in the New Year lottery. Price $1.25.

Sobo Katamuki Quasi-National Park Issue

Mt. Sobo
A602

Takachiho Gorge
A603

1967, Dec. 20

941 A602 15y multicolored 25 10
942 A603 15y " 25 10

Girl, Boy and Sakura Maru
A604

1968, Jan. 19 **Photo.** ***Perf. 13***

943 A604 15y ultra., ocher & black 20 3

Issued to commemorate the centenary of the Meiji Era, and to publicize the first Japanese Youth Good Will Cruise in celebration of the centenary.

Ashura, Kofukuji Temple, Nara
A605

Gakko Bosatsu, Todaiji Temple, Nara
A606

Kichijo Ten, Yakushiji Temple, Nara
A607

1968, Feb. 1 **Engraved** ***Perf. 13***

944 A605 15y sepia & carmine 35 30

Engraved and Photogravure

945 A606 15y dk. brn., pale grn. & orange 60 35

Photogravure

946 A607 50y multicolored 1.85 70

Issued to show National Treasures of the Nara Period (710–784).

Yatsugatake-Chushin-Kogen Quasi-National Park Issue

Grazing Cows and Mt. Yatsugatake
A608

Mt. Tateshina
A609

1968, Mar. 21 **Photo.** ***Perf. 13***

947 A608 15y multicolored 25 12
948 A609 15y " 25 12

Young Dancer (Maiko) in Tenjuan Garden, by Bakusen Tsuchida
A610

1968, Apr. 20 **Photo.** ***Perf. 13***

949 A610 15y multicolored 55 20

Stamp Week, 1968. Sheets of 10 (5x2).

Rishiri-Rebun Quasi-National Park Issue

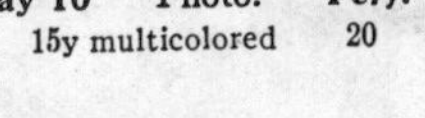

Rishiri Isl. Seen from Rebun Isl.
A611

1968, May 10 **Photo.** ***Perf. 13***

950 A611 15y multicolored 20 3

Gold Lacquer and Mother-of-Pearl Box
A612

"The Origin of Shigisan" Painting from Chogo-sonshiji, Nara
A613

Bodhisattva Samantabhadra
A614

1968, June 1 Engr. and Photo.

951 A612 15y lt. bl. & multi. 50 30

Photogravure

952 A613 15y tan & multi. 50 50
953 A614 50y sepia & multi. 3.50 1.40

Issued to show national treasures of the Heian Period (8–12th centuries).

Memorial Tower and Badge of Hokkaido
A615

1968, June 14

954 A615 15y grn., vio. blue, bister & red 20 3

Centenary of development of Hokkaido.

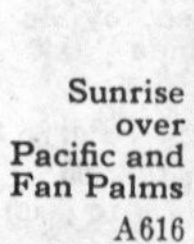

Sunrise over Pacific and Fan Palms
A616

1968, June 26 Photo. *Perf. 13*

955 A616 15y black, orange & red orange 20 10

Return of Bonin Islands to Japan by U.S.

Map of Japan Showing Postal Codes
A617

Two types of inscription:

Type I (enlarged)

あなたの住所にも郵便番号を

"Postal code also on your address"

Type II (enlarged)

あて名に郵便番号を

"Don't omit postal code on the address"

1968, July 1

956 A617 7y yel. grn. & red (I) 2.00 35
957 " 7y yellow green & red (II) 2.00 35
958 " 15y sky blue & carmine (I) 1.35 15
a. Bklt. panes of 4 with gutter (3 #958+3 #959+2 #611) 11.50
959 A617 15y sky blue & carmine (II) 1.35 15

Issued to publicize the introduction of the postal code system. The two types of the same denomination are printed se-tenant in sheets of 100 (10x10).

The double booklet pane, No. 958a, comes in two forms, the positions of the Postal Code types being transposed.

Coil Stamps

Perf. 13 Horiz.

959A A617 15y sky blue & car. (I) 55 55
959B " 15y sky blue & car. (II) 55 55

Nos. 959A–959B alternate in coil.

Hida-Kisogawa Quasi-National Park Issue

Kiso River
A618

Inuyama Castle
A619

1968, July 20 *Perf. 13½*

960 A618 15y multicolored 20 3
961 A619 15y " 20 3

Youth Hostel Emblem, Trees and Sun
A620

1968, Aug. 6 Photo. *Perf. 13*

962 A620 15y citron & multi. 20 3

Issued to publicize the 27th International Youth Hostel Congress, Tokyo, Aug. 6–20.

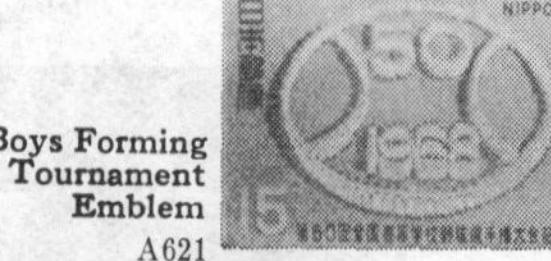

Boys Forming Tournament Emblem
A621

Pitcher and Tournament Flag
A622

1968, Aug. 9

963 A621 15y yel. green, yel., black & red 25 12
964 A622 15y red, yellow & black 25 12

Issued to commemorate the 50th All-Japan High School Baseball Championship Tournament, Koshi-en Baseball Grounds, Aug. 9. Nos. 963–964 printed checkerwise in sheets of 20 (5x4).

Minamoto Yoritomo, Jingoji, Kyoto
A623

Heiji Monogatari Scroll Painting—A624

Red-threaded Armor, Kasuga Shrine, Nara
A625

1968, Sept. 16 Photo. *Perf. 13*

965 A623 15y black & multi. 45 30
966 A624 15y tan & multi. 50 35

Photogravure and Engraved

967 A625 50y multicolored 1.60 1.35

National treasures of Kamakura period (1180–1192 to 1333).

Towada-Hachimantai National Park

Mt. Iwate, seen from Hachimantai
A626

Lake Towada, seen from Mt. Ohanabe
A627

1968, Sept. 16 Photogravure

968 A626 7y red brown 15 3
969 A627 15y green 20 3

Gymnast, Tojimbo Cliff and Narcissus
A628

1968, Oct. 1 Photo. *Perf. 13*

970 A628 15y multicolored 20 4

23rd National Athletic Meet, Fukui Prefecture, Oct. 1–6.

Hokusai Type of 1964

Design: 50y, "Fujimihara in Owari Province" (cooper working on a barrel) from Hokusai's "36 Views of Fuji."

1968, Oct. 7

971 A525 50y multicolored 1.50 45

Issued for International Letter Writing Week, Oct. 7–13. Sheets of 10 (5x2).

Centenary Emblem, Sun and First Western Style Warship
A629

Imperial Carriage Arriving in Tokyo (1868), by Tomone Kobori—A630

1968, Oct. 23

972 A629 15y vio. blue, red, gold & gray 30 3
973 A630 15y multicolored 35 3

Meiji Centenary Festival.

Old and New Lighthouses
A631

1968, Nov. 1 Photo. *Perf. 13*

974 A631 15y multicolored 20 3

Issued to commemorate the centenary of the first western style lighthouse in Japan.

Ryo'o Court Dance and State Hall, Imperial Palace
A632

1968, Nov. 14

975 A632 15y multicolored 35 10

Completion of the new Imperial Palace.

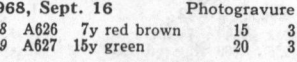

Kirishima-Yaku National Park Issue

Mt. Takachiho
A633

Mt. Motobu, Yaku Island
A634

1968, Nov. 20

976 A633 7y purple 15 3
977 A634 15y orange 20 3

Carved Toy Cock of Yonezawa, Yamagata Prefecture
A635

Human Rights Flame, Dancing Children and Globe
A636

1968, Dec. 5 Photo. ***Perf. 13***

978 A635 7y lt. blue & multi. 12 8

Issued for New Year 1969. Sheets containing 4 of No. 978 were awarded as prizes in the New Year lottery. Price $1.25.

1968, Dec. 10

979 A636 50y orange & multi. 50 15

International Human Rights Year.

Striped Squirrel
A637

Kochomon Cave and Road—A638

1968, Dec. 14

980 A637 15y emerald & black 20 3

Issued to promote saving.

Echizen-Kaga-Kaigan Quasi-National Park Issue

1969, Jan 27 Photogravure

981 A638 15y multicolored 20 3

Silver Pavilion, Jishoji Temple, Kyoto
A639

Pagoda, Anrakuji Temple, Nagano
A640

Winter Landscape by Sesshu
A641

1969, Feb. 10 Photo. ***Perf. 13***

982 A639 15y multicolored 35 15

Photogravure and Engraved

983 A640 15y lt. grn. & multi. 35 15

Photogravure

984 A641 50y tan, black & vermilion 1.85 1.20

Issued to show national treasures of the Muromachi Period (1333–1572).

Chokai Quasi-National Park Issue

Mt. Chokai, seen from Tobishima Island
A642

1969, Feb. 25 Photogravure

985 A642 15y brt. blue & multi. 20 3

Koya-Ryujin Quasi-National Park Issue

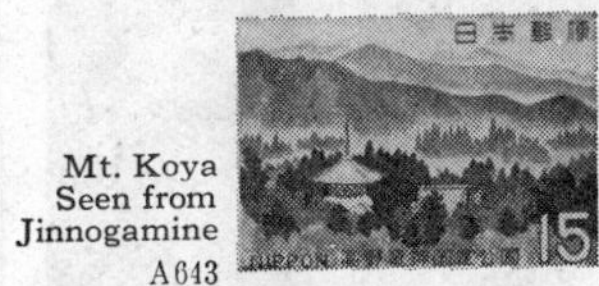

Mt. Koya Seen from Jinnogamine
A643

Mt. Gomadan and Rhododendron
A644

1969, Mar. 25 Photogravure ***Perf. 13***

986 A643 15y multicolored 20 3
987 A644 15y " 20 3

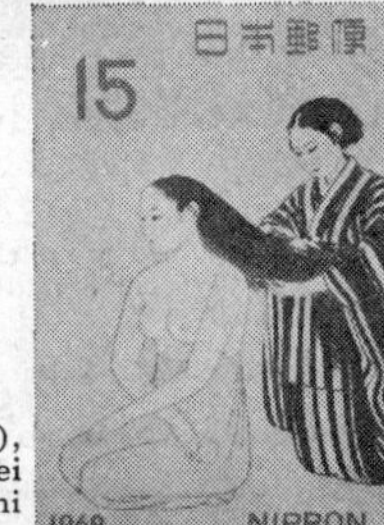

Hair (Kami), by Kokei Kobayashi
A645

1969, Apr. 20 Photo. ***Perf. 13***

988 A645 15y multicolored 45 22

Issued for Philatelic Week.

Mother and Son Crossing Street
A646

Tokyo-Nagoya Expressway and Sakawagawa Bridge
A647

1969, May 10 Photo. ***Perf. 13***

989 A646 15y lt. bl., red & grn. 20 3

National traffic safety campaign.

1969, May 26

990 A647 15y multicolored 30 3

Completion of Tokyo-Nagoya Expressway.

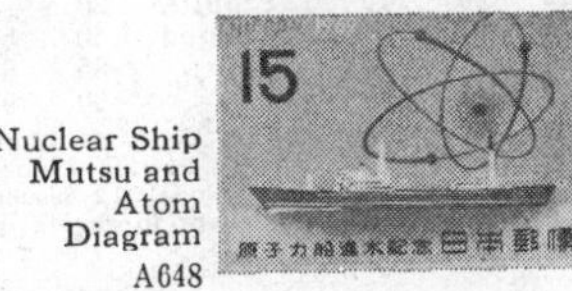

Nuclear Ship Mutsu and Atom Diagram
A648

1969, June 12

991 A648 15y gray, black, pink & blue 20 3

Issued to publicize the launching of the first Japanese nuclear ship, Mutsu.

Museum of Modern Art and Palette
A649

1969, June 11 Photo. ***Perf. 13½***

992 A649 15y lt. blue, brown, yellow & black 20 3

Issued to commemorate the opening of the new National Museum of Modern Art, Tokyo.

Cable Ship KKD Maru and Map of Japan Sea
A650

1969, June 25

993 A650 15y lt. blue, black & ocher 20 3

Issued to commemorate the completion of the Japan sea cable between Naoetsu, Japan, and Nakhodka, Russia.

Postcards and Postal Code Symbol
A651

Mailbox and Postal Code Symbol
A652

1969, July 1 Photo. ***Perf. 13***

997 A651 7y yellow green & carmine 30 12
998 A652 15y sky blue & car. 35 12

Issued to commemorate the first anniversary of the postal code system and to promote its use.

Lions Emblem and Rose
A653

1969, July 2

999 A653 15y blue, black, rose & gold 20 3

Issued to publicize the 52nd Convention of Lions International, Tokyo, July 2–5.

Shimokita Hanto Quasi-National Park Issue

Hotoke-ga-ura on Shimokita Peninsula, Northern Honshu
A654

1969, July 15

1000 A654 15y multicolored 20 3

Himeji Castle, Hyogo Prefecture
A655

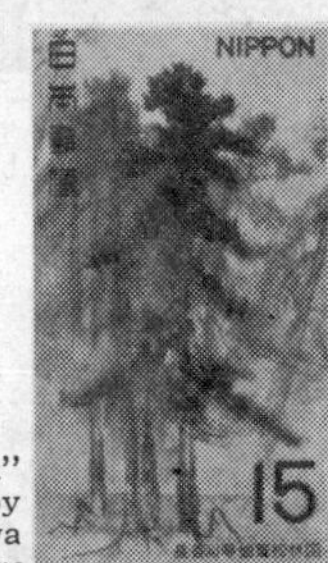

"Pine Forest" (Detail), by Tohaku Hasegawa
A656

"Cypress," Attributed to Eitoku Kano
A657

1969, July 21 Photo. and Engr.

1001 A655 15y lt. bl. & multi. 35 25

Photogravure

1002 A656 15y pale brn. & blk. 35 25
1003 A657 50y gold & multi. 1.50 1.00

Issued to show national treasures of the Momoyama period (1573–1614). The 50y is in sheets of 10 (2x5); Nos. 1001–1002 in sheets of 20 (5x4).

Hyobosen-Ushiroyama-Nagisan Quasi-National Park Issue

Harano-fudo Waterfall A658 — Mt. Nagisan A659

1969, Aug. 20

1004 A658 15y multicolored 20 3
1005 A659 15y " 20 3

Akan National Park Issue

Mt. O-akan, Hokkaido A660 — Mt. Iwo A661

1969, Aug. 25 Photo. *Perf. 13*

1006 A660 7y bright blue 15 3
1007 A661 15y sepia 20 3

Angling, by Taiga Ikeno A662 — The Red Plum, by Korin Ogata A663

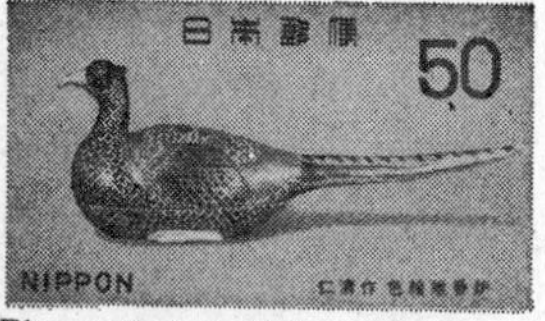

Pheasant-shaped Incense Burner A664

Design: No. 1010, The White Plum, by Korin Ogata.

Perf. 13x13½

1969, Sept. 25 Photogravure

1008 A662 15y multicolored 30 8

Perf. 13

1009 A663 15y gold & multi. 35 8
1010 " 15y " " 35 8

Photogravure and Engraved

1011 A664 50y multicolored 1.00 35

Issued to show national treasures of the Edo Period (1615–1867). Nos. 1009–1010 printed se-tenant.

Birds Circling Globe and UPU Congress Emblem A665

Woman Reading Letter, by Utamaro A666

Designs (UPU Congress Emblem and): 50y, Two Women Reading a Letter, by Harunobu. 60y, Man Reading a Letter (Miyako Dennai), by Sharaku.

1969, Oct. 1 Photo. *Perf. 13*

1012 A665 15y red & multi. 20 3
1013 A666 30y multicolored 50 50
1014 " 50y " 65 65
1015 " 60y " 90 90

Issued to commemorate the 16th Congress of the Universal Postal Union, Tokyo, Oct. 1–Nov. 16. No. 1012 issued in sheets of 20 (5x4), others in sheets of 10 (5x2.

Hokusai Type of 1964

Design: 50y, "Passing through Koshu down to Mishima" from Hokusai's 36 Views of Fuji.

1969, Oct. 7 Photo. *Perf. 13*

1016 A525 50y multicolored 1.25 55

Issued for International Letter Writing Week Oct. 7–13. Sheets of 10 (5x2).

Rugby Player, Camellia and Oura Catholic Church A667

1969, Oct. 26

1017 A667 15y lt. ultramarine & multi. 20 3

24th National Athletic Meet, Nagasaki, Oct. 26–31.

Rikuchu Coast National Park Issue

Cape Kitayama A668

Goishi Coast A669

1969, Nov. 20 Photo. *Perf. 13*

1018 A668 7y gray & dk. blue 12 3
1019 A669 15y salmon & dark red 20 3

Worker in Hard Hat A670 — Dog Amulet, Hokkeji, Nara A671

1969, Nov. 26

1020 A670 15y ultra., black yel. & brown 20 3

Issued to commemorate the 50th anniversary of the International Labor Organization.

1969, Dec. 10

1021 A671 7y orange & multi. 12 10

Issued for New Year 1970. Sheets containing 4 of No. 1021 were awarded as prizes in the New Year lottery. Price $1.25.

Iki-Tsushima Quasi-National Park Issue

Aso Bay and Tsutsu Women with Horse A672

1970, Feb. 25 Photo. *Perf. 13*

1022 A672 15y multicolored 20 3

First EXPO '70 Issue

Fireworks over EXPO '70 A673 — Cherry Blossoms Around Globe A674

Irises, by Korin Ogata (1658–1716) A675

1970, Mar. 14 Photo. *Perf. 13*

1023 A673 7y red & multi. 10 3
1024 A674 15y gold & multi. 20 3
1025 A675 50y " " 70 15
a. Souvenir sheet of 3 1.25 1.25
b. Bklt. panes of 4 & 3 with gutter 2.50

Issued to publicize EXPO '70 International Exposition, Senri, Osaka, Mar. 15–Sept. 13. No. 1025a contains one each of Nos. 1023–1025 se-tenant. Black marginal inscription and gold EXPO '70 emblem. Size: 143x93mm.

No. 1025b contains a pane of 4 of No. 1023 and a pane of 3 embracing one each of Nos. 1023–1025. A 35mm. gutter separates the panes.

Woman with Hand Drum, by Saburosuke Okada A676

1970, Apr. 20 Photo. *Perf. 13*

1026 A676 15y multicolored 40 15

Issued for Stamp Week, Apr. 20–26.

Yoshino-Kumano National Park Issue

Mt. Yoshino A677 — Nachi Waterfall A678

1970, Apr. 30 Photo. *Perf. 13*

1027 A677 7y gray & pink 12 3
1028 A678 15y pale bl. & green 20 3

Second EXPO '70 Issue

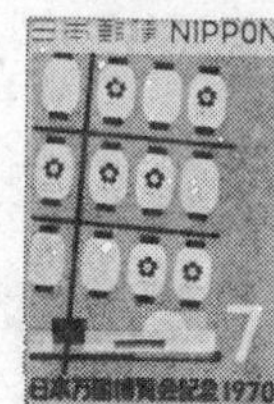

Pole Lanterns at EXPO A679 — View of EXPO Within Globe A680

Grass in Autumn Wind, by Hoitsu Sakai (1761–1828) A681

1970, June 15 Photo. *Perf. 13*

1029 A679 7y red & multi. 10 3
1030 A680 15y blue & multi. 20 3
1031 A681 50y silver & multi. 70 10
a. Souvenir sheet of 3 1.25
b. Booklet panes of 4 & 3 with gutter 2.50

Issued to publicize EXPO '70. No. 1031a contains one each of Nos. 1029–1031 se-tenant. Black marginal inscription and silver EXPO '70 emblem. Size: 143x93mm.

No. 1031b contains a pane of 4 of No. 1029 and a pane of 3 embracing one each of Nos. 1029–1031. A 35mm. gutter separates the panes.

Buildings and Postal Code Symbol
A682

1970, July 1 Photo. ***Perf. 13***

1032 A682 7y emerald & violet 25 10

1033 " 15y brt. bl. & choc. 35 10

Postal code system.

"Maiden at Dojo Temple"
A683

Scene from "Sukeroku"
A684

"The Subscription List" (Kanjincho)—A685

1970, July 10

1034 A683 15y multicolored 25 15

1035 A684 15y " 25 20

1036 A685 50y " 65 50

Issued to publicize the Kabuki Theater.

Girl Scout
A686

1970, July 26

1037 A686 15y multicolored 20 3

50th anniversary of Japanese Girl Scouts.

Noto Hanto Quasi-National Park Issue

Kinoura Coast and Festival Drum
A687

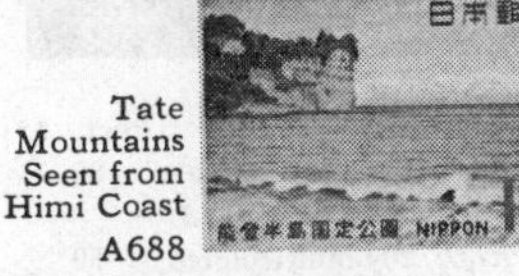

Tate Mountains Seen from Himi Coast
A688

1970, Aug. 1

1038 A687 15y multicolored 20 3

1039 A688 15y " 20 3

Sunflower and U.N. Emblem
A689

1970, Aug. 17

1040 A689 15y lt. blue & multi. 20 3

Issued to publicize the 4th United Nations Congress on the Prevention of Crime and the Treatment of Offenders, Kyoto, Aug. 17–26.

Myogi-Arafune-Sakukogen Quasi-National Park Issue

Mt. Myogi
A690

Mt. Arafune
A691

1970, Sept. 11 Photo. ***Perf. 13***

1041 A690 15y multicolored 20 3

1042 A691 15y " 20 3

G.P.O., Tokyo, by Hiroshige III
A692

Equestrian, Mt. Iwate and Paulownia
A693

1970, Oct. 6

1043 A692 50y multicolored 85 30

Issued for International Letter Writing Week, Oct. 6–12. Sheets of 10 (5x2). Design from wood block series, "Noted Places in Tokyo."

1970, Oct. 10 Photo. ***Perf. 13***

1044 A693 15y silver & multi. 30 8

25th National Athletic Meet, Morioka, Oct. 10–16.

Hodogaya Stage, by Hiroshige III
A694

Tree and U.N. Emblem
A695

1970, Oct. 20

1045 A694 15y multicolored 30 8

Centenary of telegraph service in Japan.

1970, Oct. 24

Design: 50y, U.N. emblem and Headquarters with flags.

1046 A695 15y olive, apple green & gold 20 3

1047 " 50y multicolored 65 15

25th anniversary of United Nations.

Vocational Training Competition Emblem
A696

Diet Building and Doves
A697

1970, Nov. 10 Photo. ***Perf. 13***

1048 A696 15y multicolored 20 3

The 19th International Vocational Training Competition, Chiba City, Nov. 10–19.

1970, Nov. 29

1049 A697 15y multicolored 20 3

80th anniversary of Japanese Diet.

Wild Boar, Folk Art, Arai City, Niigata Prefecture
A698

1970, Dec. 10

1050 A698 7y multicolored 15 10

New Year 1971. Sheets containing 4 of No. 1050 were awarded as prizes in the New Year lottery. Price $1.25.

Gen-jo-raku
A699

Ko-cho
A700

Tai-hei-raku—A701

1971, Apr. 1 Photo. ***Perf. 13***

1051 A699 15y multicolored 20 3

1052 A700 15y " 20 3

1053 A701 50y " 65 15

Gagaku, classical Japanese court entertainment.

Woman Voter and Parliament
A702

Pines and Maple Leaves
A703

1971, Apr. 10 Photo. ***Perf. 13***

1054 A702 15y org. & multi. 20 3

25th anniversary of woman suffrage.

1971, Apr. 18

1055 A703 7y emerald & vio. 12 3

National forestation campaign.

Woman of Tokyo, by Kiyokata Kaburagi
A704

1971, Apr. 19

1056 A704 15y gray & multi. 30 4

Philatelic Week, Apr. 19–25.

Mailman
A705

Mailbox
A706

Railroad Post Office
A707

1971, Apr. 20

1057 A705 15y blk. & org. brn. 20 3

1058 A706 15y multicolored 20 3

1059 A707 15y " 20 3

Centenary of Japanese postage stamps.

Titmouse
A708

Penguins
A709

1971, May 10 Photo. ***Perf. 13***

1060 A708 15y emerald, black & bister 20 3

25th Bird Week.

1971, June 23 Photo. ***Perf. 13***

1061 A709 15y dk. blue, yellow & green 20 3

Tenth anniversary of the Antarctic Treaty pledging peaceful uses of and scientific co-operation in Antarctica.

Saikai National Park Issue

Goto Wakamatsu Seto Region
A710

Kujukushima ("99 Islands"), Kyushu
A711

1971, June 26 Photo. ***Perf. 13***

1062 A710 7y dark green 10 3
1063 A711 15y deep brown 15 3

Arabic Numerals and Postal Code Symbol
A712

1971, July 1

1064 A712 7y emerald & red 25 12
1065 " 15y blue & carmine 35 10

Promotion for postal code system.

Inscribed "NIPPON"
Types of 1951–69 and

Little Cuckoo A713 | Mute Swan A714 | Sika Deer A715

Beetle A716 | Pine A717 | Golden Eagle A717a

Bronze Phoenix, Uji A718 | Burial Statue of Warrior, Ota A718a | Buddha, Sculpture, 685 A718b

Tentoki Sculpture, 11th Century A718c | Bazara-Taisho, c. 710–794 A718d

Goddess Kissho
A718e

Designs: 25y, Hydrangea. 70y, Noh mask. 80y, Pheasant. No. 1076, Wind God Fujin. 120y, Mythical winged woman. 1081, Bodhisattva.

1971–75 Photogravure ***Perf. 13***

1067 A713 3y emerald 12 3
a. Bklt. pane of 20 ('72) 2.75
1068 A714 5y bright blue 12 3
1069 A715 10y yel. green & sepia ('72) 17 3
a. Bklt. pane of 6 (2 #1069, 4 #1071 with gutter btwn.) ('72) 1.25
1070 A716 12y deep brown 17 3
1071 A717 20y green & sepia ('72) 22 3
a. Pane of 10 (5x2) ('72) 2.25
1072 A565 25y emerald & lt. ultra. ('72) 28 3
1074 A466 70y dp. org. & blk. 85 4
1075 A466a 80y crim. & brown 85 4
1076 A467 90y org. & dk. brn. 1.10 4
1077 A717a 90y orange & brown ('73) 95 4
1079 A469 120y dk. brn. & lt. green ('72) 1.10 4
1080 A718 150y lt. & dk. grn. 1.50 4
1081 A570 200y dp. carmine (18x22mm.; '72) 2.10 5
1082 A718a 200y red brown ('74) 2.25 10
1083 A718b 300y dk. bl. ('74) 2.75 10
1084 A718c 400y car. rose ('74) 3.50 15
1085 A718d 500y green ('74) 4.25 25
1087 A718e 1000y multi. ('75) 9.00 1.00
a. Miniature sheet 9.50
Nos. 1067–1087 (18) 31.28 2.07

No. 1071a is imperf. on four sides.
No. 1087a contains one stamp; black marginal inscription. Size: 51x102mm.
See Nos. 1249–1250.

Coil Stamp
Perf. 13 Horiz.

1088 A717 20y green & sepia ('72) 35 30

Boy Scout Bugler
A719

1971, Aug. 2

1090 A719 15y lt. bl. & multi. 15 3

13th World Boy Scout Jamboree, Asagiri Plain, Aug. 2–10.

Rose and Rings
A720

1971, Oct. 1

1091 A720 15y ultra. & multi. 15 3

50th anniversary of Japanese Conciliation System.

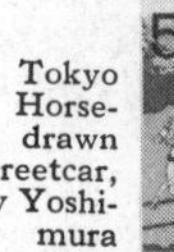

Tokyo Horse-drawn Streetcar, by Yoshimura
A721

1971, Oct. 6

1092 A721 50y multicolored 75 30

International Letter Writing Week. Sheets of 10 (5x2).

Emperor's Flag, Chrysanthemums and Phoenix
A722

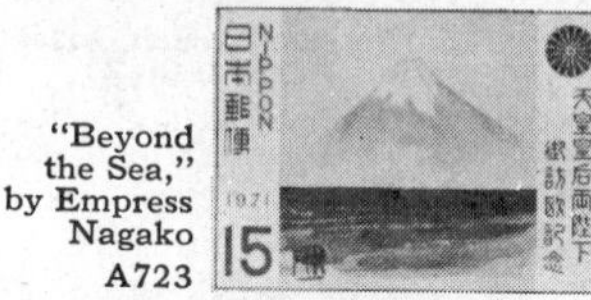

"Beyond the Sea," by Empress Nagako
A723

1971, Oct. 14

1093 A722 15y gold, violet, red & blue 30 3
1094 A723 15y gold, violet, red & blue 30 3
a. Souvenir sheet of 2 85 85

European trip of Emperor Hirohito and Empress Nagako, Sept. 28–Oct. 15. Nos. 1093–1094 printed se-tenant in sheets of 20 (5x4). No. 1094a contains 2 imperf. stamps similar to Nos. 1093–1094. Violet map of Asia, Africa and Europe in background. Size: 140x110mm.

Tennis, Cape Shiono-misaki, Plum Blossoms
A724

Child's Face and "100"
A725

1971, Oct. 24 Photo. ***Perf. 13***

1095 A724 15y org. & multi. 15 3

26th National Athletic Meet, Wakayama Prefecture, Oct. 24–29.

1971, Oct. 27

1096 A725 15y pink, carmine & black 15 3

Centenary of Japanese Family Registration System.

Tiger, by Gaho Hashimoto
A726

Design: No. 1098, Dragon, from "Dragon and Tiger," by Gaho Hashimoto.

1971, Nov. 1 Engraved ***Perf. 13***

1097 A726 15y olive & multi. 28 3
1098 " 15y " " 28 3

Centenary of Government Printing Works. Nos. 1097–1098 printed checkerwise in sheets of 20 (5x4).

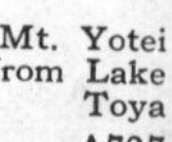

Mt. Yotei from Lake Toya
A727

Mt. Showa-Shinzan
A728

Treasure Ship
A729

Shikotsu-Toya National Park Issue

1971, Dec. 6

1099 A727 7y slate grn. & yel. 12 8
1100 A728 15y pink & vio. bl. 15 8

1971–72

1101 A729 7y emerald, gold & orange 15 10
1102 " 10y lt. blue, orange & gold ('72) 15 10

New Year 1972. Sheets containing 3 of No. 1102 were awarded as prizes in the New Year lottery. Price $1.75.

Issue dates: 7y, Dec. 10, 1971; 10y, Jan. 11, 1972.

Downhill Skiing
A730

Designs (Olympic Rings and): No. 1104, Bobsledding. 50y, Figure skating, pairs.

1972, Feb. 3 Photogravure ***Perf. 13***

Size: 24x34mm.

1103 A730 20y ultra. & multi. 20 6
1104 " 20y " " 20 6

Size: 49x34mm.

1105 A730 50y ultra. & multi. 60 22
a. Souvenir sheet of 3 1.25 1.25

11th Winter Olympic Games, Sapporo, Feb. 3–13. No. 1105a contains Nos. 1103–1105, printed se-tenant with design extending into margin, which includes Sapporo '72 emblem and commemorative inscription. Size: 144x93mm.

Bunraku, Ningyo Jyoruri Puppet Theater
A731 A732

A733

1972, Mar. 1 Photo. ***Perf. 13½***

1106 A731 20y gray & multi. 30 4

Perf. 12½x13

1107 A732 20y multicolored 30 4

Litho. & Engr. *Perf. 13½x13*

1108 A733 50y multicolored 60 18

Japanese classical entertainment.

Express Train on New Sanyo Line
A734

Taishaku-kyo Valley
A735

Hiba Mountains Seen from Mt. Dogo
A736

1972, Mar. 15 Photo. *Perf. 13*

1109 A734 20y multicolored 25 4

Centenary of first Japanese railroad.

Hiba-Dogo-Taishaku Quasi-National Park Issue

1972, Mar. 24

1110 A735 20y gray & multi. 20 4
1111 A736 20y green & multi. 20 4

Heart and U.N. Emblem
A737

1972, Apr. 15

1112 A737 20y gray, red & black 20 12

"Your heart is your health," World Health Day.

"A Balloon Rising," by Gakuryo Nakamura
A738

1972, Apr. 20

1113 A738 20y vio. bl. & multi. 30 15

Philatelic Week, Apr. 20-26.

Shurei Gate, Okinawa
A739

Camellia
A740

1972, May 15

1114 A739 20y ultra. & multi. 20 12

Ratification of the Reversion Agreement with U.S. under which the Ryukyu Islands were returned to Japan.

1972, May 20

1115 A740 20y brt. grn., vio. blue & yel. 20 12

National forestation campaign and 23rd Arbor Day, May 21.

Kurikoma Quasi-National Park Issue

Mt. Kurikoma and Kijiyama Kokeshi Doll
A741

Naruko-kyo Gorge and Naruko Kokeshi Doll
A742

1972, June 20 Photo. *Perf. 13*

1116 A741 20y blue & multi. 20 12
1117 A742 20y red & multi. 20 12

Envelope and Postal Code Symbol—A743

Mailbox and Postal Code Symbol—A744

1972, July 1

1118 A743 10y bl., blk. & gray 15 10
1119 A744 20y emerald & org. 25 10

Publicity for the postal code system.

Chubu Sangaku National Park Issue

Mt. Hodaka
A745

Mt. Tate
A746

1972, Aug. 10 Photo. *Perf. 13*

1120 A745 10y rose & violet 15 10
1121 A746 20y blue & buff 25 10

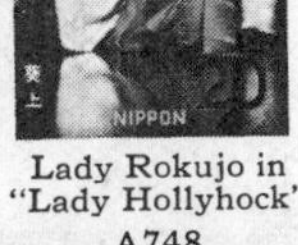

Ghost in "Tamura"
A747

Lady Rokujo in "Lady Hollyhock"
A748

"Hagoromo" (Feather Robe)—A749

1972, Sept. 20 Engraved

1122 A747 20y multicolored 30 8

Photogravure

1123 A748 20y multicolored 30 8

Perf. 13½x13

1124 A749 50y multicolored 65 15

Noh, classical public entertainment.

School Children
A750

Eitai Bridge, Tokyo, by Hiroshige III
A751

1972, Oct. 5 Photo. *Perf. 13*

1125 A750 20y lt. ultra., vio. blue & car. 20 4

Centenary of modern education system.

1972, Oct. 9

1126 A751 50y multicolored 65 15

International Letter Writing Week, Oct. 9-15.

Inauguration of Railway Service, by Hiroshige III
A752

Locomotive, Class C62
A753

1972, Oct. 14

1127 A752 20y multicolored 20 4
1128 A753 20y " 20 4

Centenary of Japanese railroad system.

Kendo (Fencing) and Sakurajima Volcano
A754

1972, Oct. 22

1129 A754 10y yellow & multi. 12 4

27th National Athletic Meet, Kagoshima Prefecture, Oct. 22-27.

Boy Scout Shaking Hand of Cub Scout
A755

1972, Nov. 4

1130 A755 20y yellow & multi. 20 4

50th anniversary of the Boy Scouts of Japan.

U.S. Ship, Yokohama Harbor
A756

"Clay Plate with Plum Blossoms"
A757

1972, Nov. 28 Photo. *Perf. 13*

1131 A756 20y multicolored 20 4

Centenary of Japanese customs. Wood block by Hiroshige III (d. 1896).

1972, Dec. 11

1132 A757 10y blue & multi. 12 4

New Year 1973. Art work by Kenzan Ogata (1663-1743). Sheets containing 3 of No. 1132 were awarded as prizes in the New Year lottery. Price $1.75.

Mt. Tsurugi Quasi-National Park Issue

Mt. Tsurugi
A758

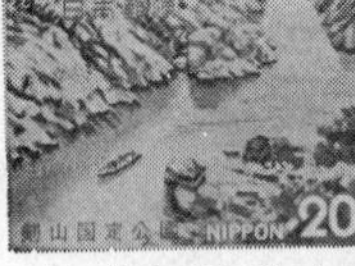

Oboke Valley
A759

1973, Feb. 20 Photogravure *Perf. 13*

1133 A758 20y multicolored 20 4
1134 A759 20y " 20 4

Meiji Forests Quasi-National Park Issue

Mt. Takao
A760

Minoo Falls
A761

1973, Mar. 12 Photo. *Perf. 13*

1135 A760 20y multicolored 20 4
1136 A761 20y " 20 4

Phoenix Tree
A762

Sumiyoshi Shrine Visitor
A763

1973, Apr. 7 Photogravure *Perf. 13*

1137 A762 20y brt. grn., yel. & dark blue 17 4

National forestation campaign.

1973, Apr. 20

1138 A763 20y multicolored 17 4

Philatelic Week, Apr. 20–26. Design from painting by Ryusei Kishida (1891–1929) of his daughter, "A Portrait of Reiko Visiting Sumiyoshi Shrine."

Suzuka Quasi-National Park Issue

Mt. Kamagatake
A764

Mt. Haguro
A765

1973, May 25 Photo. *Perf. 13*

1139 A764 20y multicolored 20 10
1140 A765 20y " 20 10

Ogasawara National Park Issue

Chichijima Beach
A766

Coral Reef on Minami Island
A767

1973, June 26

1141 A766 10y greenish bl. & Prus. blue 9 4
1142 A767 20y lilac & dk. pur. 17 4

5th anniversary of the return of the Bonin (Ogasawara Islands) to Japan.

Tree and Postal Code Symbol
A768

Mailman and Postal Code Symbol
A769

1973, July 1 Photogravure *Perf. 13*

1143 A768 10y brt. grn. & gold 12 10
1144 A769 20y bl., pur. & car. 22 10

Postal code system, 5th anniversary.

Nishi-Chugoku-Sanchi Quasi-National Park Issue

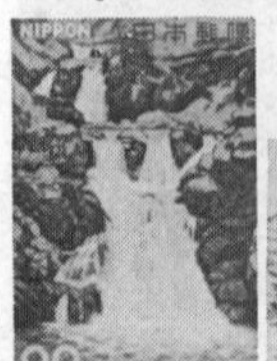

Sandan Gorge
A770

Mt. Shinnyu
A771

1973, Aug. 28 Photo. *Perf. 13*

1145 A770 20y multicolored 17 4
1146 A771 20y " 17 4

Tenryu-Okumikawa Quasi-National Park Issue

Tenryu Valley—A772

Mt. Horaiji—A773

1973, Sept. 18 Photo. *Perf. 13*

1147 A772 20y lilac & multi. 17 4
1148 A773 20y violet blue, lt. blue & silver 17 4

Cock, by Jakuchu Ito (1716–1800)
A774

Woman Runner at Start
A775

1973, Oct. 6

1149 A774 50y gold & multi. 40 25

International Letter Writing Week, Oct. 7–13. Sheets of 10.

1973, Oct. 14

1150 A775 10y silver & multi. 9 4

28th National Athletic Meet, Chiba Prefecture, Oct. 14–19.

Kan Mon Bridge
A776

1973, Nov. 14 Engr. *Perf. 13*

1151 A776 20y blk., rose & yel. 17 4

Opening of Kan Mon Bridge connecting Honshu and Kyushu.

Old Man and Dog
A777

Designs: No. 1153, Old man and wife pounding rice mortar, which yields gold. No. 1154, Old man sitting in tree and landlord admiring tree.

1973, Nov. 20 Photogravure

1152 A777 20y multicolored 17 4
1153 " 20y " 17 4
1154 " 20y " 17 4

Folk tale "Hanasaka-jijii" (The Old Man Who Made Trees Bloom).

Bronze Lantern, Muromachi Period
A778

1973, Dec. 10

1155 A778 10y emerald, black & orange 15 10

New Year 1974. Sheets containing 3 of No. 1155 were awarded as prizes in the New Year lottery. Price $1.50.

Nijubashi, Tokyo
A779

Imperial Palace, Tokyo
A780

1974, Jan. 26 Photo. *Perf. 13*

1156 A779 20y gold & multi. 17 4
1157 A780 20y " " 17 4
a. Souvenir sheet of 2 40 40

50th anniversary of the wedding of Emperor Hirohito and Empress Nagako. No. 1157a contains one each of Nos. 1156–1157, gold border and black inscription. Size: 145x94mm.

Young Wife
A781

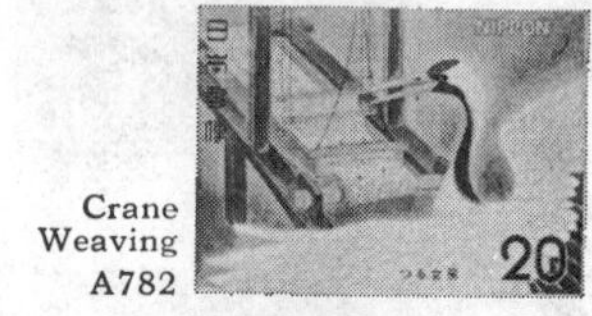

Crane Weaving
A782

Cranes in Flight
A783

1974, Feb. 20 Photo. *Perf. 13*

1158 A781 20y multicolored 17 4
1159 A782 20y " 17 4
1160 A783 20y " 17 4

Folk tale "Tsuru-nyobo" (Crane becomes wife of peasant).

Iriomote National Park Issue

Marudu Falls
A784

Marine Scene
A785

1974, Mar. 15

1161 A784 20y multicolored 17 4
1162 A785 20y " 17 4

"Finger," by Ito Shinsui
A786

Nambu Red Pine Sapling and Mt. Iwate
A787

1974, Apr. 20 Photo. *Perf. 13*

1163 A786 20y multicolored 22 12

Philatelic Week, Apr. 20–27.

1974, May 18

1164 A787 20y multicolored 17 4

National forestation campaign.

Supreme Court Building
A788

1974, May 23 Engraved

1165 A788 20y reddish brown 17 4

Completion of Supreme Court Building, Tokyo.

Midget Using Bowl as Boat
A789

Designs: No. 1167, Midget fighting demon. No. 1168, Princess and midget changed into prince with magic hammer.

1974, June 10 Photo. *Perf. 13*

1166 A789 20y yel. & multi. 20 4
1167 " 20y bister & multi. 20 4
1168 " 20y " " 20 4

Folk tale "Issun Hoschi" (The Story of the Mini-mini Boy).

"Police," by Kunimasa Baido
A790

1974, June 17 *Perf. 13*

1169 A790 20y multicolored 20 4

Centenary of the Tokyo Metropolitan Police Department.

Iriomote Wildcat
A791

Japanese Otter
A792

Ogasawara Flying Fox
A793

Design: No. 1172, Black hare.

1974 Litho. & Engr.; Photo. & Engr.

1170	A791	20y multicolored	20	10
1171	A792	20y sepia & multi.	20	10
1172	"	20y verm. & multi.	20	10
1173	A793	20y multicolored	20	10

Nature conservation.

Issue dates: No. 1170, Mar. 25; No. 1171, June 25; No. 1172, Aug. 30; No. 1173, Nov. 15.

Transfusion Bottle, Globe, Doves
A794

1974, July 1 Photogravure

1174	A794	20y brt. blue & multicolored	20	4

International Red Cross Blood Donations Year.

Discovery of Kaguya Hime in Shining Bamboo
A795

Kaguya Hime as Grown-up Beauty
A796

Kaguya Hime and Escorts Returning to Moon
A797

1974, July 29 Photo. *Perf. 13*

1175	A795	20y multicolored	20	4
1176	A796	20y "	20	4
1177	A797	20y "	20	4

Folk tale "Kaguya Hime" or "Tale of the Bamboo Cutter."

Rich and Poor Men with Wens
A798

Designs: No. 1179, Poor man dancing with spirits. No. 1180, Rich man with two wens, poor man without wen, spirits.

1974, Sept. 9 Photogravure *Perf. 13*

1178	A798	20y multicolored	20	4
1179	"	20y "	20	4
1180	"	20y "	20	4

Folk tale "Kobutori Jiisan," or "The Old Man who had his Wen Taken by Spirits."

Goode's Projection and Diet
A799

"Aizen" by Ryushi Kawabata—A800

1974, Oct. 1 Photo. *Perf. 13*

1181	A799	20y multicolored	30	12
1182	A800	50y "	40	12

Interparliamentary Union, 61st Meeting, Tokyo, Nov. 2–11.

Pine and Hawk, by Sesson
A801

UPU Emblem
A802

Tending Cow, Fan by Sotatsu Tawaraya—A803

1974, Oct. 7

1183	A801	50y sepia, black & dark brown	35	6

International Letter Writing Week, Oct. 6–12.

1974, Oct. 9

1184	A802	20y multicolored	14	4
1185	A803	50y "	35	6

Centenary of Universal Postal Union.

Soccer Players and Sailboat
A804

1974, Oct. 20 Photogravure

1186	A804	10y multicolored	7	3

29th National Athletic Meet, Ibaraki Prefecture, Oct. 20–25.

Various Mushrooms
A805

1974, Nov. 2

1187	A805	20y multicolored	14	4

9th International Congress on the Cultivation of Edible Fungi, Japan, Nov. 4–13.

Steam Locomotive Class D51
A806

Class C57
A807

Class 8620
A808

Class C11
A809

Designs: Steam locomotives.

1974, Nov. 26 Photo. *Perf. 13*

Multicolored

1188	A806	20y *shown*	20	4
1189	A807	20y "	20	4

1975, Feb. 25

1190	A806	20y *Class D52*	20	4
1191	A807	20y *Class C58*	20	4

1975, Apr. 3

1192	A808	20y *shown*	20	4
1193	A809	20y "	20	4

1975, May 15 Photo. *Perf. 13*

1194	A806	20y *Class 9600*	20	4
1195	A807	20y *Class C51*	20	4

1975, June 10 Photo. & Engr.

1196	A806	20y *Class 7100*	20	4
1197	"	20y *Class 150*	20	4
		Nos. 1188–1197 (10)	2.00	40

Japanese National Railways. Nos. 1188–1189, 1190–1191, 1192–1193, 1194–1195, 1196–1197 printed se-tenant in sheets of 20 (5x4).

Ornamental Nail Cover, Katsura Palace
A810

1974, Dec. 10

1198	A810	10y blue & multi.	7	3

New Year 1975. Sheets containing 3 of No. 1198 were awarded as prizes in the New Year Lottery. Price $1.50.

Short-tailed Albatrosses
A811

Bonin Island Honey-eater
A812

Temminck's Robin
A813

Ryukyu-Yamagame Tortoise
A814

Design: No. 1200, Japanese cranes.

1975–76 Photo. & Engr. *Perf. 13*

1199	A811	20y multicolored	14	4
1200	"	20y "	14	4
1201	A812	20y "	14	4
1202	A813	50y "	35	10
1203	A814	50y "	35	10
		Nos. 1199–1203 (5)	1.12	32

Nature conservation.

Issue dates: No. 1199, Jan. 16; No. 1200, Feb. 13; No. 1201, Aug. 8; No. 1202, Feb. 27, 1976; No. 1203, Mar. 25, 1976.

Taro Urashima Releasing Turtle
A815

Palace of the Sea God and Fish
A816

Smoke from Casket Making Taro an Old Man
A817

1975, Jan. 28 Photo. *Perf. 13*

1204	A815	20y multicolored	14	4
1205	A816	20y "	14	4
1206	A817	20y "	14	4

Folk tale "Legend of Taro Urashima."

Kan-mon-sho (Seeing and Hearing), by Shiko Munakata
A818

1975, Mar. 20 Photo. *Perf. 13*

1207 A818 20y brn. & multi. 14 4

Japan Broadcasting Corporation, 50th anniversary.

Old Man Feeding Mouse
A819

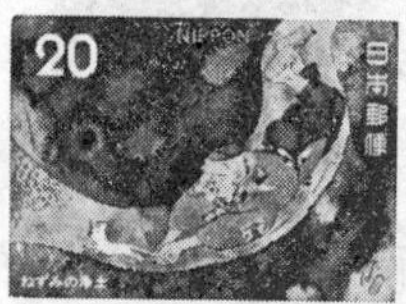

Man Following Mouse Underground
A820

Mice Entertaining and Bringing Gifts
A821

1975, Apr. 15 Photo. *Perf. 13*

1208	A819	20y multicolored	14	4
1209	A820	20y "	14	4
1210	A821	20y "	14	4

Folk tale "Paradise for the Mice."

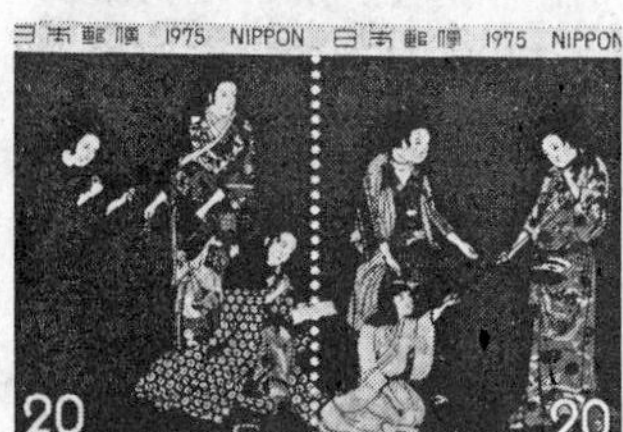

Matsuura Screen (detail), 16th Century
A822 A823

1975, Apr. 21

1211	A822	20y gold & multi.	14	4
1212	A823	20y " "	14	4

Philatelic Week, Apr. 21–27. Nos. 1211–1212 printed se-tenant in sheets of 10 (2x5).

Oil Derricks, Congress Emblem
A824

1975, May 10 Photo. *Perf. 13*

1213 A824 20y multicolored 14 4

9th World Petroleum Congress, Tokyo, May 11–16.

Trees and River
A825

IWY Emblem, Sun and Woman
A826

1975, May 24

1214 A825 20y green & multi. 14 4

National forestation campaign.

1975, June 23

1215 A826 20y orange & multi. 14 4

International Women's Year 1975.

Okinawan Dancer, EXPO 75 Emblem
A827

Birds in Flight (Bingata)
A828

Aquapolice and Globe—A829

1975, July 19 Photo. *Perf. 13*

1216	A827	20y ultra. & multi.	14	4
1217	A828	30y bl. grn. & multi.	20	5
1218	A829	50y ultra. & multi.	35	15
	a.	Souvenir sheet of 3	1.00	

Oceanexpo 75, First International Ocean Exposition, Okinawa, July 20, 1975–Jan. 18, 1976. No. 1218a contains one each of Nos. 1216–1218; black marginal inscription and silver EXPO 75 emblem. Size: 144x94mm.

Historic Ship Issue

Kentoshi-sen 7th–9th Centuries
A830

Ships: No. 1220, Kenmin-sen, 7th–9th centuries. No. 1221, Goshuin-sen, merchant ship, 16th–17th centuries. No. 1222, Tenchi-maru, state barge, built 1630. No. 1223, Sengoku-bune (cargo ship) and fishing vessel. No. 1224, Shoheimaru, 1852, European-type sailing ship. No. 1225, Taisei-maru, four-mast bark training ship, 1903. No. 1226, Tenyomaru, first Japanese passenger liner, 1907. No. 1227, Asama-maru, passenger liner. No. 1228, Kinai-maru, transpacific freighter and Statue of Liberty. No. 1229, Container ship. No. 1230, Tanker.

1975–76 Engraved *Perf. 13*

1219	A830	20y rose red	14	4
1220	"	20y sepia	14	4
1221	"	20y light olive	14	4
1222	"	20y dark blue	14	4
1223	"	50y violet blue	35	10
1224	"	50y lilac	35	10
1225	A830	50y gray	35	10
1226	"	50y dark brown	35	10
1227	"	50y olive green	35	10
1228	"	50y olive brown	35	10
1229	"	50y ultramarine	35	10
1230	"	50y violet blue	35	10
		Nos. 1219–1230 (12)	3.36	96

Nos. 1219–1220, 1221–1222, 1223–1224, 1225–1226, 1227–1228 printed se-tenant checkerwise in sheets of 20 (5x4).

Issue dates: Nos. 1219–1220, Aug. 30; Nos. 1221–1222, Sept. 25, 1975; Nos. 1223–1224, Mar. 11; Nos. 1225–1226, Apr. 12; Nos. 1227–1228, June 1, 1976; Nos. 1229–1230, Aug. 18, 1976.

Apple and Apple Tree
A831

Peacock, by Korin Ogata
A832

1975, Sept. 17 Photo. *Perf. 13*

1231 A831 20y gray, blk. & red 14 4

Centenary of apple cultivation in Japan.

1975, Oct. 6 Photo. *Perf. 13*

1232 A832 50y gold & multi. 35 6

International Letter Writing Week, Oct. 6–12.

American Flag and Cherry Blossoms
A833

Japanese Flag and Dogwood
A834

1975, Oct. 14

1233	A833	20y ultra. & multi.	14	4
1234	A834	20y green & multi.	14	4
	a.	Souvenir sheet of 2	45	45

Visit of Emperor Hirohito and Empress Nagako to the United States, Oct. 1–14. No. 1234a contains one each of Nos. 1233–1234; black, green and ultramarine marginal decoration and inscription. Size: 143½x93mm.

Savings Box and Coins
A835

1975, Oct. 24

1235 A835 20y multicolored 14 4

Japan's Postal Savings System, centenary.

Weight Lifter
A836

1975, Oct. 25

1236 A836 10y multicolored 7 3

30th National Athletic Meet, Mie Prefecture, Oct. 26–31.

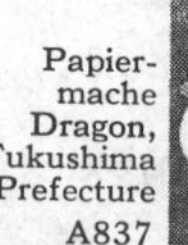

Papier-mache Dragon, Fukushima Prefecture
A837

1975, Dec. 13 Photo. *Perf. 13*

1237 A837 10y multicolored 7 3

New Year 1976. Sheets containing 3 of No. 1237 were awarded as prizes in the New Year Lottery. Price $1.50.

Inscribed "NIPPON"
Types of 1951–1974 and

Japanese Narcissus
A841

Noh Mask, Old Man
A843

Guardian Dog, Katori Shrine
A845

Sho-Kannon, Yakushiji Temple
A846

Designs: 50y, Nyoirin Kannon, Chuguji Temple. 150y, Bronze phoenix, Uji. 200y, Clay burial figure of warrior, Ota.

1976 Photogravure *Perf. 13*

1244	A280	50y emerald	55	4
	a.	Booklet panes of 2 & 4 with gutter	3.50	
1245	A841	60y multicolored	65	4
1248	A843	140y lilac rose & lilac	1.40	4
1249	A718	150y red orange & brown	1.40	4
1250	A718a	200y red orange	1.75	10
1251	A845	250y blue	2.25	10
1253	A846	350y dk. vio. brn.	3.00	12
		Nos. 1244–1253 (7)	11.00	48

Coil Stamp
Perf. 13 Horiz.

1256 A280 50y emerald 85 4

No. 1244a contains a pane of 2 No. 1244 and inscription; and a pane of 4 No. 1244. A 42mm. gutter separates the panes.

Hikone Folding Screen (detail), 17th Century
A850 A851

1976, Apr. 20 Photo. *Perf. 13*

1258	A850	50y gold & multi.	35	10
1259	A851	50y " "	35	10

Philatelic Week, Apr. 20–26. Nos. 1258–1259 printed se-tenant in sheets of 10 (2x5).

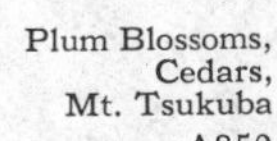

Plum Blossoms, Cedars, Mt. Tsukuba
A852

1976, May 22

1260 A852 50y multicolored 50 10

National forestation campaign.

Green Tree Frog
A853

Bitterlings
A854

Sticklebacks
A855

Photogravure and Engraved

1976 ***Perf. 13***

1261 A853 50y multicolored 35 10
1262 A854 50y " 35 10
1263 A855 50y " 35 10

Nature conservation.
Issue dates: No. 1261, July 20; No. 1262, Aug. 26; No. 1263, Sept. 16.

Kite and Crows, by Yosa Buson
A856

Gymnasts and Stadium
A857

1976, Oct. 6 Photo. ***Perf. 13***

1264 A856 100y gray, black & buff 70 20

International Letter Writing Week, Oct. 6–12.

1976, Oct. 23 Photo. ***Perf. 13***

1265 A857 20y multicolored 14 4

31st National Athletic Meet, Saga Prefecture, Oct. 24–29.

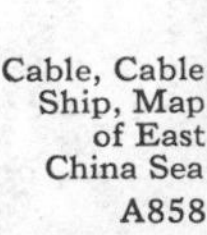

Cable, Cable Ship, Map of East China Sea
A858

1976, Oct. 25

1266 A858 50y bl., blk. & silver 35 10

Opening of Sino-Japanese cable between Shanghai and Reihoku-cho, Kumamoto Prefecture.

Classical Court Dance
A859

Imperial Coach
A860

1976, Nov. 10 Photo. ***Perf. 13***

1267 A859 50y multicolored 35 10
1268 A860 50y " 35 10
a. Souvenir sheet of 2 1.00 1.00

Emperor Hirohito's accession to the throne, 50th anniversary. No. 1268a contains one each of Nos. 1267–1268; gold and black decorative margin and inscription. Size: 144x94mm.

Kindergarten Class
A861

1976, Nov. 16

1269 A861 50y multicolored 35 10

Centenary of first Kindergarten in Japan.

Healthy Family
A862

Bamboo Toy Snake
A863

1976, Nov. 24

1270 A862 50y multicolored 35 10

National Health Insurance, 50th anniversary.

1976, Dec. 1 Photo. ***Perf. 13***

1271 A863 20y multicolored 14 4

New Year 1977. Sheets containing two of No. 1271 were awarded as prizes in the New Year lottery. Price $1.50.

National Treasures

East Pagoda, Yakushiji Temple, c. 730
A864

Deva King in Armor Holding Spear, Nara Period
A865

1976, Dec. 9 Photo. ***Perf. 13***

1272 A864 50y multicolored 35 10

Engraved

1273 A865 100y grn. & multi. 70 20

Golden Pavilion, Toshodai-ji Temple, 8th Century—A866

Praying Women, from Heike Nokyo Sutra, 12th Century
A867

Photogravure and Engraved

1977, Jan. 20 ***Perf. 13***

1274 A866 50y multicolored 35 10

Photogravure

1275 A867 100y multicolored 70 20

Comic Picture Scroll, by Toba Sojo Kakuyu (1053–1140)—A868

Saint on Cloud, 11th Century Wood Carving, Byodoin Temple
A869

1977, March 25 Photo. ***Perf. 13***

1276 A868 50y multicolored 35 10

Engraved

1277 A869 100y multicolored 70 20

Noblemen on Way to Court, from Picture Scroll, Heian Period
A870

Statue of Seitaka-doji, Messenger, Kamakura Period
A871

1977, June 27 Photo. ***Perf. 13***

1278 A870 50y multicolored 35 10

Engraved

1279 A871 100y multicolored 70 20

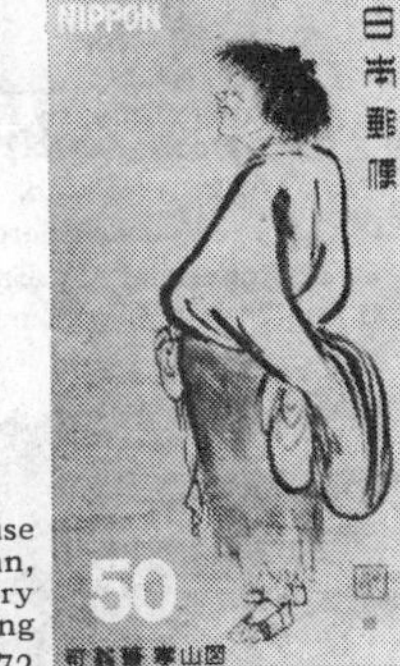

The Recluse Han Shan, 14th Century Painting
A872

Tower, Matsumoto Castle, 16th Century—A873

1977, Aug. 25 Photo. ***Perf. 13***

1280 A872 50y multicolored 35 10

Photogravure and Engraved

1281 A873 100y blk. & multi. 70 20

Pine and Flowers, Chishakuin Temple, Kyoto, 1591—A874

Main Hall, Kiyomizu Temple, 1633
A875

1977, Nov. 16 Photo. *Perf. 13*

1282	A874	50y multicolored	35	10

Engraved

1283	A875	100y multicolored	70	20

Scene from Tale of Genji, by Sotatsu Tawaraya—A876

Inkstone Case, by Koetsu Honami—A877

1978, Jan. 26 Photo. *Perf. 13*

1284	A876	50y multicolored	40	12

Photogravure and Engraved

1285	A877	100y blk. & multi.	80	25

Family Enjoying Cool Evening, by Morikage Kusumi—A878

Yomeimon, Toshogu Shrine, 1636—A879

1978, Mar. 3 Photo. *Perf. 13*

1286	A878	50y gray & multi.	40	12

Photogravure and Engraved

1287	A879	100y multicolored	80	25

Horseshoe Crabs
A884

Graphium Doson Albidum
A885

Cicada
A887

Firefly
A886

Dragonfly
A888

1977 Photogravure *Perf. 13*

1292	A884	50y multicolored	35	10

Photogravure and Engraved

1293	A885	50y multicolored	35	10
1294	A886	50y "	35	10
1295	A887	50y "	35	10

Photogravure

1296	A888	50y multicolored	35	10
		Nos. 1292–1296 (5)	1.75	50

Issue dates: No. 1292, Feb. 18; No. 1293, May 18; No. 1294, July 22; No. 1295, Aug. 15; No. 1296, Sept. 14.

Figure Skating
A889

Figure Skating Pair
A890

1977, Mar. 1

1297	A889	50y silver & multi.	35	10
1298	A890	50y " "	35	10

World Figure Skating Championships, National Yoyogi Stadium, March 1–6.

Sun Shining on Forest
A891

1977, Apr. 16 Photo. *Perf. 13*

1299	A891	50y grn. & multi.	35	10

National forestation campaign.

Women Weavers (Detail from Folding Screen)
A892 A893

1977, Apr. 20

1300	A892	50y gold & multi.	35	10
1301	A893	50y " "	35	10

Philatelic Week, Apr. 20–26. Nos. 1300–1301 printed se-tenant in sheets of 10 (5x2).

Nurses
A894

1977, May 30 Photo. *Perf. 13*

1302	A894	50y multicolored	35	10

16th Quadrennial Congress of the International Council of Nurses, Tokyo, May 30–June 3.

Fast Breeder Reactor, Central Part
A895

1977, June 6

1303	A895	50y multicolored	35	10

Experimental fast breeder reactor "Joyo," which began operating Apr. 24, 1977.

Workers and Safety Emblems
A896

Work on High-rise Buildings
A897

Cargo Unloading
A898

Machinery Work
A899

1977, July 1

1304	A896	50y multicolored	35	10
1305	A897	50y "	35	10
1306	A898	50y "	35	10
1307	A899	50y "	35	10
		Strip of 4 (#1304–1307)	1.40	

National Safety Week, July 1–July 7. Nos. 1304–1307 printed se-tenant in sheet of 100.

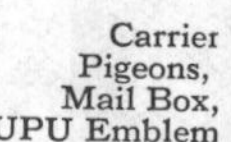

Carrier Pigeons, Mail Box, UPU Emblem
A900

Design: 100y, UPU emblem, Postal Service flag of Meiji era, world map.

1977, June 20 Photo. *Perf. 13*

1308	A900	50y multicolored	35	10
1309	"	100y "	70	20
		a. Souvenir sheet of 2	1.20	

Centenary of Japan's admission to Universal Postal Union. No. 1309a contains one each of Nos. 1308–1309; multicolored margin. Size: 144x93mm.

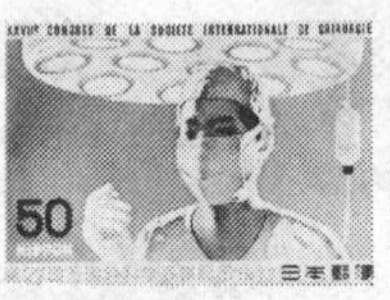

Surgeon in Operating Room
A901

1977, Sept. 3 Photo. *Perf. 13*

1310	A901	50y multicolored	35	10

27th Congress of the International Surgeon's Society on the 75th anniversary of its founding, Kyoto, Sept. 3–8.

Child Using Telephone, Map of New Cable Route—A902

1977, Aug. 26

1311	A902	50y multicolored	35	10

Inauguration of underwater telephone cable linking Okinawa, Luzon and Hong Kong.

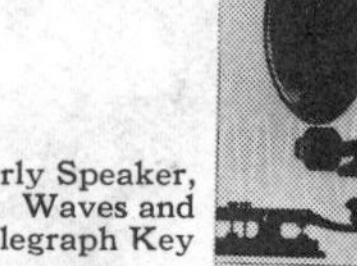

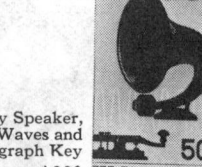

Early Speaker, Waves and Telegraph Key
A903

1977, Sept. 24 Photo. *Perf. 13*

1312	A903	50y multicolored	35	10

50th anniversary of amateur radio in Japan.

Bicyclist, Mt. Iwaki and Iwaki River
A904

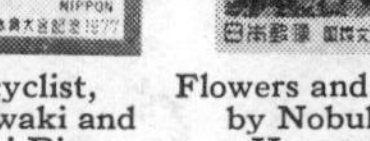

Flowers and Ducks, by Nobuharu Hasegawa
A905

1977, Oct. 1

1313	A904	20y multicolored	14	4

32nd National Athletic Meet, Aomori Prefecture, Oct. 2–7.

1977, Oct. 6

1314	A905	100y multicolored	70	20

International Letter Writing Week, Oct. 6–12.

Dinosaur, Stars, Museum
A906

1977, Nov. 2 Photo. ***Perf. 13***
1315 A906 50y multicolored 35 10

Centenary of National Science Museum.

Decorated Horse, Fushimi Toy
A907

Tokyo Subway, 1927
A908

1977, Dec. 1 Photo. ***Perf. 13***
1316 A907 20y multicolored 14 4

New Year 1978. Sheets containing two of No. 1316 were awarded as prizes in the New Year lottery. Price $1.50.

1977, Dec. 6

Design: No. 1318, Subway, 1977.

1317 A908 50y multicolored 35 10
1318 " 50y " 35 10

Tokyo Subway, 50th anniversary. Nos. 1317–1318 printed se-tenant in sheets of 20.

Primrose
A909

Pinguicula Ramosa
A910

Dicentra
A911

Photogravure and Engraved

1978 ***Perf. 13***
1319 A909 50y multicolored 40 12
1320 A910 50y " 40 12
1321 A911 50y " 40 12

Nature protection.
Issue dates: No. 1319, Apr. 12. No. 1320, June 8. No. 1321, July 25.

Kanbun Bijinzu Folding Screen, Edo Era
A912 A913

1978, Apr. 20 Photo. ***Perf. 13***
1322 A912 50y multicolored 40 12
1323 A913 50y " 40 12

Philatelic Week, Apr. 16–22. Nos. 1322–1323 printed se-tenant in sheets of 10 (5x2).

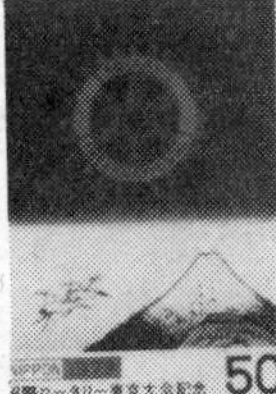

Rotary Emblem, Mt. Fuji
A914

Congress Emblem, by Taro Okamoto
A915

1978, May 13 Photo. ***Perf. 13***
1324 A914 50y multicolored 40 12

69th Rotary International Convention, Tokyo, May 14–18.

1978, May 15
1325 A915 50y multicolored 40 12

23rd International Ophthalmological Congress, Kyoto, May 14–20.

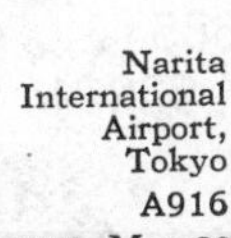

Narita International Airport, Tokyo
A916

1978, May 20
1326 A916 50y multicolored 40 12

Opening of Tokyo International Airport.

Rainbow, Japanese Cedars, Cape Ashizuri
A917

Lion, by Sotatsu Tawaraya, Lions Emblem
A918

1978, May 20
1327 A917 50y multicolored 40 12

National forestation campaign.

1978, June 21 Photo. ***Perf. 13***
1328 A918 50y multicolored 40 12

61st Lions International Convention, Tokyo, June 21–24.

Sumo Print Issues

Grand Champion Hidenoyama with Sword Bearer and Herald, by Kunisada I (Toyokuni III)
A919 A920

Ekoin Drum Tower, Ryogoku, by Hiroshige
A921

Photogravure and Engraved

1978, July 1 ***Perf. 13***
1329 A919 50y multicolored 40 12
1330 A920 50y " 40 12

Photogravure

1331 A921 50y multicolored 40 12

Nos. 1329–1330 printed se-tenant in sheets of 20 (4x5).

Champions Tanikaze and Onogawa in Ring-entry Ceremony, 1782, by Shunsho
A922 A923

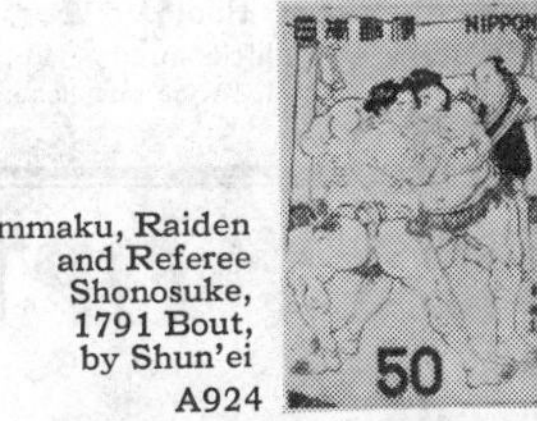

Jimmaku, Raiden and Referee Shonosuke, 1791 Bout, by Shun'ei
A924

Photogravure and Engraved

1978, Sept. 9 ***Perf. 13***
1332 A922 50y multicolored 40 12
1333 A923 50y " 40 12
1334 A924 50y " 40 12

Nos. 1332–1333 printed se-tenant in sheets of 20 (4x5).

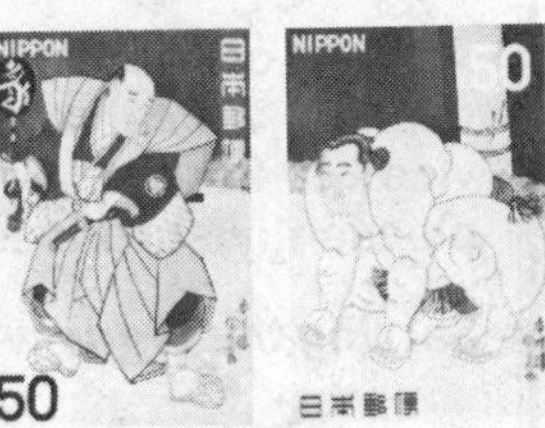

Referee Shonosuke and Champion Onomatsu, by Kunisada I
A925 A926

Children's Sumo Play, by Utamaro
A927

1978, Nov. 11 ***Perf. 13***
1335 A925 50y multicolored 40 12
1336 A926 50y " 40 12
1337 A927 50y " 40 12

Nos. 1335–1336 printed se-tenant in sheets of 20 (4x5).

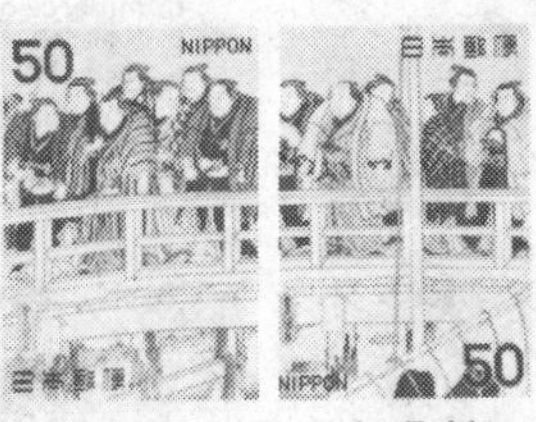

Wrestlers on Ryogoku Bridge, by Kunisada I
A928 A929

Bow-receiving Ceremony at Tournament, by Kunisada II
A930

1979, Jan. 13 ***Perf. 13***
1338 A928 50y multicolored 40 12
1339 A929 50y " 40 12
1340 A930 50y " 40 12

Nos. 1338–1339 printed se-tenant in sheets of 20 (4x5).

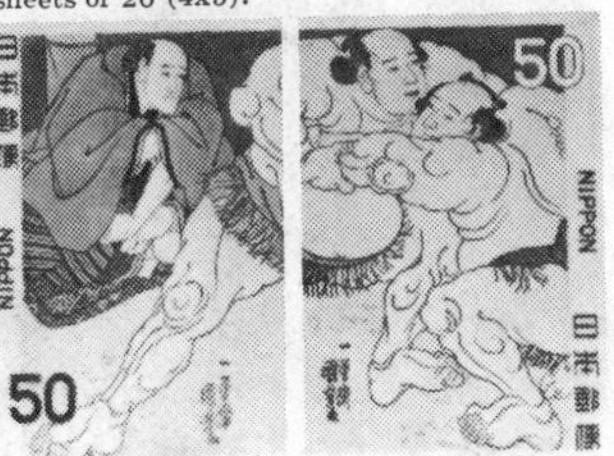

Takekuma and Iwamigata (Hidenoyama) Wrestling, by Kuniyoshi
A931 A932

Daidozan (Great Child Mountain) in Ring-entry Ceremony, by Sharaku
A933

1979, Mar. 10 ***Perf. 13***
1341 A931 50y multicolored 40 12
1342 A932 50y " 40 12
1343 A933 50y " 40 12

Nos. 1341–1342 printed se-tenant in sheets of 20 (4x5).

Radio Gymnastics Emblem
A934

1978, Aug. 1 Photo. ***Perf. 13***
1344 A934 50y multicolored 40 12

Radio gymnastics program exercises, 50th anniversary.

Chamber of Commerce and Industry
A935

1978, Aug. 28 Photo. ***Perf. 13***

1345 A935 50y multicolored 40 12

Tokyo Chamber of Commerce, centenary.

Symbolic Sculptures, Tokyo Stock Exchange
A936

Copper Pheasant, from Door, Tenkyuin Temple
A937

1978, Sept. 14 Engr. ***Perf. 13***

1346 A936 50y lilac, green & brown 40 12

Centenary of the Tokyo and Osaka Stock Exchanges.

1978, Oct. 6 Photo. ***Perf. 13***

1347 A937 100y multicolored 80 25

International Letter Writing Week, Oct. 6–12.

Softball and Mt. Yarigatake
A938

Artificial Hip, Orthopedists' Emblem
A939

1978, Oct. 14

1348 A938 20y multicolored 15 5

33rd National Athletic Meet, Nagano Prefecture, Oct. 15–20.

1978, Oct. 16

1349 A939 50y multicolored 40 12

14th World Congress of International Society of Orthopedic Surgeons (50th anniversary), Kyoto, Oct. 15–20.

Telescope and Stars
A940

Sheep Bell, Nakayama Toy
A941

1978, Dec. 1 Photogravure

1350 A940 50y multicolored 40 12

Tokyo Astronomical Observatory, centenary.

1978, Dec. 4

1351 A941 20y multicolored 16 5

New Year 1978. Sheets containing two of No. 1351 were awarded as prizes in the New Year Lottery. Price $1.75.

Family and Human Rights Emblem
A942

Hands Shielding Children
A943

1978, Dec. 4

1352 A942 50y multicolored 40 12

Human Rights Week, Dec. 4–10.

1979, Feb. 16 Photo. ***Perf. 13***

1353 A943 50y multicolored 40 12

Education of the handicapped, centenary.

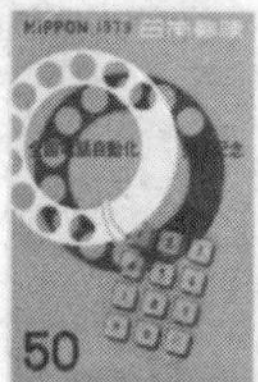

Telephone Dials
A944

1979, Mar. 14 Photo. ***Perf. 13***

1354 A944 50y multicolored 40 12

Completion of nation-wide telephone automatization.

SEMI-POSTAL STAMPS

Douglas Plane over Japan Alps
SP1

Wmkd. Zigzag Lines. (141)

1937, June 1 Photo. ***Perf. 13***

B1	SP1	2s+2s rose carmine	2.00	60
B2	"	3s+2s purple	2.00	60
B3	"	4s+2s green	4.00	60

The surtax was for the Patriotic Aviation Fund to build civil airports.

Nos. 259 and 261 Surcharged in Blue or Red

1942, Feb. 16 ***Perf. 13*** **Wmk. 257**

B4	A84	2s+1s crimson (Bl)	60	50
B5	A86	4s+2s dark green (R)	60	50

Issued to commemorate the fall of Singapore to Japanese forces.

Tank Corps Attack, Bataan
SP2

Pearl Harbor under Japanese Attack
SP3

Photogravure.

1942, Dec. 8 ***Perf. 12*** **Unwmkd.**

B6	SP2	2s+1s rose brown	1.75	1.10
B7	SP3	5s+2s sapphire	2.25	1.10

Issued to commemorate the first anniversary of the "Greater East Asia War."
The surtax was for national defense.

SP4

1947, Nov. 25 ***Perf. 12½*** **Wmk. 257**

B8	SP4	1.20(y)+80(s) dark rose red	75	50

Issued to publicize Japan's first Community Chest drive. The surtax was for charitable purposes.

Nurse
SP5

Bird Feeding Young
SP6

1948, Oct. 1 ***Perf. 12½*** **Unwmkd.**

B9	SP5	5y+2.50y bright red	6.00	1.20
B10	SP6	5y+2.50y emerald	6.00	1.20

Souvenir Sheet.

SP7

Imperf.

Wmk. 257

B11	SP7	Sheet of 2	32.50	35.00

The surtax on Nos. B9–B11 was divided between the Red Cross and Community Chest organizations.
No. B11 contains 1 each of Nos. B9–B10, imperf. Size: 128x90mm.

Javelin Thrower
SP8

Designs: No. B13, Wrestlers. No. B14, Diver. No. B15, Water polo. No. B16, Woman gymnast. No. B17, Judo. No. B18, Fencing. No. B19, Basketball. No. B20, Rowing. No. B21, Sailing. No. B22, Boxing. No. B23, Volleyball. No. B24, Bicyclist. No. B25, Equestrian. No. B26, Field hockey. No. B27, Pistol shooting. No. B28, Modern pentathlon. No. B29, Weight lifter. No. B30, Women's kayak doubles. No. B31, Soccer.

Engraved

1961, Oct. 11 ***Perf. 13½*** **Unwmkd.**

B12	SP8	5y+5y bistre	95	65
B13	"	5y+5y dark green	95	65
B14	"	5y+5y carmine	95	65
		a. Souv. sheet of 3 ('64)	3.00	3.25

1962, June 23

B15	SP8	5y+5y green	65	32
B16	"	5y+5y dark purple	65	32
B17	"	5y+5y dk. carmine	65	32
		a. Souv. sheet of 3 ('64)	2.25	2.50

1962, Oct. 10

B18	SP8	5y+5y brick red	40	35
B19	"	5y+5y slate green	40	35
B20	"	5y+5y violet	40	35
		a. Souv. sheet of 3 ('64)	1.85	2.00

1963, June 23

B21	SP8	5y+5y blue	42	35
B22	"	5y+5y dark brown	42	35
B23	"	5y+5y brown	42	35
		a. Souv. sheet of 3 ('64)	2.75	3.00

1963, Nov. 11

B24	SP8	5y+5y dark blue	16	12
B25	"	5y+5y olive	16	12
B26	"	5y+5y black	16	12
B27	"	5y+5y claret	16	12
		a. Souv. sheet of 4 ('64)	2.75	3.00

1964, June 23

B28	SP8	5y+5y bluish violet	22	12
B29	"	5y+5y deep olive	22	12
B30	"	5y+5y greenish blue	22	12
B31	SP8	5y+5y rose claret	22	12
		a. Souv. sheet of 4 ('64)	2.75	3.00
		Nos. B12-B31 (20)	8.78	5.97

Nos. B12–B31 were issued to raise funds for the 1964 Olympic Games in Tokyo.
The six souvenir sheets were issued Aug. 20, 1964. Each contains one each of the stamps in the set it follows. Size: 134x60mm. Nos. B14a, B20a, B23a and B27a, exist imperf.

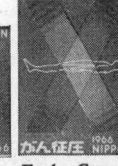

Cobalt Treatment Unit
SP9

Early Cancer Detection with X-rays
SP10

1966, Oct. 21 Photo. ***Perf. 13***

B32	SP9	7y+3y yel. orange & black	17	14
B33	SP10	15y+5y multicolored	35	20

Issued to commemorate the 9th International Anticancer Congress, Tokyo, Oct. 23–29. The surtax was for the fight against cancer and for research.

EXPO '70 Emblem and Globe
SP11

Cherry Blossoms, Mural, Chishakuin Temple—SP12

1969, Mar. 15 Photo. ***Perf. 13***

B34	SP11	15y+5y blue, ocher & vermilion	1.10	1.10
B35	SP12	50y+10y gold, brown & green	2.00	2.00

Issued to publicize EXPO '70, International Exhibition, Osaka, 1970.

Ice Hockey, Sapporo Olympic Emblem
SP13

Design: No. B37, Ski jump and Sapporo Olympic Games emblem (vert.).

1971, Feb. 6 Photo. ***Perf. 13***

B36	SP13	15y+5y multi.	40	18
B37	"	15y+5y "	40	18

To promote the 11th Winter Olympic Games, Sapporo, Japan, 1972.

Blue Dragon, East Wall—SP14

Murals from ancient tomb mound: No. B39, Two men, east wall (vert.). 50y+10y, Four women, west wall (vert.).

1973, Mar. 26 Photo. ***Perf. 13***

Size: 48x27mm., 27x48mm.

B38	SP14	20y+5y multi.	45	18
B39	"	20y+5y "	45	18

Photogravure and Engraved

Size: 33x48mm.

B40	SP14	50y+10y multi.	85	35

Surtax was for restoration work on the murals of the Takamatsu-zuka tomb mound, discovered in March, 1972, and excavated in Nara Prefecture.

Reefs, by Hyakusui Hirafuku—SP15

1974, Mar. 2 Photo. ***Perf. 13***

B41	SP15	20y+5y multi.	30	15

The surtax was for the International Ocean Exposition, Okinawa, 1975.

AIR POST STAMPS.

Regular Issue of 1914 Overprinted in Red or Blue

Granite Paper.

Wmkd. Zigzag Lines. (141)

1919, Oct. 3 *Perf. 13x13½*

C1 A34 1½s blue (R) 165.00 65.00
C2 " 3s rose (Bl) 275.00 140.00

Excellent counterfeits of Nos. C1 and C2 exist.

Passenger Plane over Lake Ashi
AP1

Granite Paper.

1929-34 Engraved *Perf. 13½x13*

C3 AP1 8½s orange brown 20.00 15.00
C4 " 9½s rose ('34) 8.50 3.00
C5 " 16½s yellow green 9.00 4.50
C6 " 18s ultramarine 12.00 3.50
C7 " 33s gray 22.50 2.50
Nos. C3-C7 (5) 72.00 28.50

Issue dates: 9½s, Mar. 1, 1934; others, Oct. 6, 1929.

Souvenir Sheet.

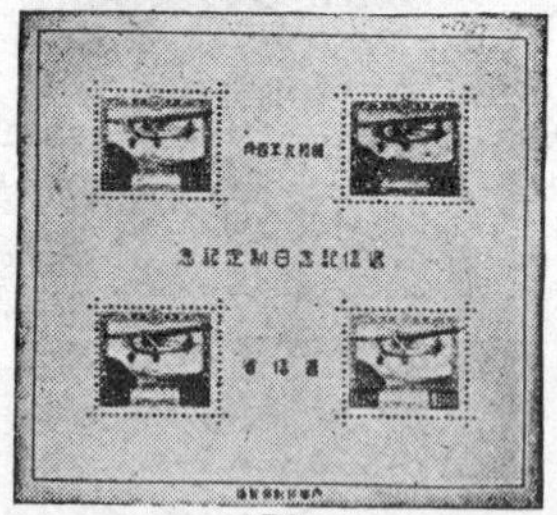

AP2

1934, Apr. 20 **Granite Paper**

C8 AP2 Sheet of 4 750.00 750.00

Communications Commemoration Day (first observance of establishment of the postal service and issuance of Nos. 1–4). Contains one each of Nos. C4–C7. Issued at Philatelic Exhibition, Tokyo, Apr. 20–27. Sold only at exhibition post office. Size: 110x100mm.

Southern Green Pheasant
AP3

Perf. 13x13½

1950, Jan. 10 Engr. Unwmkd.

C9 AP3 16y gray 10.00 4.00
C10 " 34y brown violet 25.00 4.00
C11 " 59y carmine 35.00 8.00
C12 " 103y orange yellow 18.50 6.50
C13 " 144y olive 21.50 6.50
Nos. C9-C13 (5) 110.00 29.00

Pagoda and Plane
AP4

1951 Photogravure.

C14 AP4 15y purple 1.50 85
C15 " 20y blue 12.00 60
C16 " 25y yellow green 7.50 15
C17 " 30y brown red 7.00 15
C18 " 40y gray black 3.50 15
Nos. C14-C18 (5) 31.50 1.90

Issue dates: 25y, 30y, Dec. 20. Others, Sept. 1.

Plane and Mt. Tsurugi-dake
AP5

1952, Feb. 11

C19 AP5 55y bright blue 85.00 20.00
C20 " 75y brownish red 55.00 8.00
C21 " 80y magenta 8.50 2.65
C22 " 85y black 6.00 2.65
C23 " 125y olive bistre 6.00 2.50
C24 " 160y Prus. green 12.00 2.65
Nos. C19-C24 (6) 172.50 38.45

Redrawn; Underlined Zeros Omitted

1952-62

C25 AP4 15y purple ('62) 70 15
C26 " 20y blue 15.00 30
C27 " 25y yel. green ('53) 60 4
C28 " 30y brown red 4.75 4
C29 " 40y gray blk. ('53) 2.00 8
C30 AP5 55y bright blue 25.00 2.25
C32 " 75y brownish red 60.00 5.50
C33 " 80y magenta 30.00 1.40
C34 " 85y black 2.00 1.40
C36 " 125y olive bistre 3.00 1.40
C38 " 160y Prus. green 10.00 1.40
Nos. C25-C38 (11) 153.05 13.96

See also No. C43.

Great Buddha of Kamakura
AP6

1952, Aug. 15 *Perf. 13½*

C39 AP6 70y red brown 1.75 8
C40 " 80y blue 2.50 8
C41 " 115y olive green 2.00 30
C42 " 145y Prussian green 4.00 45

Coil Stamp

Redrawn Type of 1952-62.

1961, Oct. 2 *Perf. 13 Horiz.*

C43 AP4 30y brown red 15.00 12.50

MILITARY STAMPS.

Stamps of Regular Issues Overprinted 軍事

Perf. 11½ to 13½.

1910 On No. 98 Unwmkd.

M1 A26 3s rose 140.00 35.00

1913 On No. 119.

M2 A34 3s rose 190.00 100.00

1914 On No. 131. Wmk. 141

M3 A34 3s rose 32.50 17.50

Nos. M1–M3 overprint type I has 3.85 mm. between characters; type II, 4 to 4.5 mm. (movable type).

On No. 37, Offices in China.

1921

M4 A34 3s rose *5000.00 4000.00*

No. M4 is a provisional military stamp issued at the Japanese Post Office, Tsingtao, China. The overprint differs from the illustration, being 12mm. high with thicker characters. Counterfeits are plentiful.

1924 On Japan No. 131

M5 A34 3s rose 62.50 35.00
a. 3s rose (#131b) 75.00 50.00

On Nos. M5 and M5a the overprint measures 16mm. high.

Excellent forgeries exist of Nos. M1–M5.

JAPANESE OFFICES ABROAD

Offices in China

Regular Issues of Japan Overprinted in Red or Black. 那支

Perf. 11½, 12, 12½, 13½, 13x13½.

1900-06 Unwmkd.

1 A26 5r gray (R) 4.00 4.00
2 " ½s gray (R) ('01) 2.00 85
3 " 1s lt. red brn. (R) 2.00 85
4 " 1½s ultramarine 6.50 2.50
5 " 1½s violet ('06) 3.50 1.15
a. Bklt. pane of 6
6 " 2s light green (R) 3.50 85
a. Bklt. pane of 6
7 " 3s violet brown 4.00 85
8 " 3s rose ('06) 2.50 60
a. Booklet pane of 6
9 " 4s rose 4.00 1.50
a. Bklt. pane of 6
10 " 5s org. yellow (R) 11.00 1.50
11 A27 6s maroon ('06) 15.00 13.50
12 " 8s olive green (R) 6.50 6.00
13 " 10s deep blue 6.00 60
a. Bklt. pane of 6
14 " 15s purple 15.00 1.50
15 " 20s red orange 14.00 60
16 A28 25s blue green (R) 30.00 3.00
17 " 50s red brown 32.50 2.25
18 A29 1y carmine 65.00 2.25
Nos. 1-18 (18) 227.00 44.35

No. 6 with black overprint is bogus.

1900

19 A30 3s carmine 35.00 25.00

No. 19 was issued in commemoration of the wedding of Crown Prince Yoshihito and Princess Sadako.

1908

20 A33 5y green 400.00 40.00
21 " 10y dark violet 700.00 100.00

On Nos. 20–21 the space between characters of the overprint is 6½mm. instead of 1½mm.

1913 *Perf. 12, 12x13, 13x13½*

22 A34 ½s brown 8.00 6.00
23 " 1s orange 8.75 6.00
24 " 1½s light blue 27.50 10.00
a. Bklt. pane of 6
25 " 2s green 30.00 15.00
a. Bklt. pane of 6
26 " 3s rose 15.00 4.50
a. Bklt. pane o f6
27 A35 4s red 42.50 35.00
a. Bklt. pane of 6
28 " 5s violet 42.50 27.50
29 " 10s deep blue 42.50 7.50
a. Bklt. pane of 6
30 " 20s claret 175.00 60.00
31 " 25s olive green 65.00 10.00
32 A36 1y yellow green & maroon 600.00 400.00
Nos. 22-32 (11) 1056.75 581.50

Wmkd. Zigzag Lines. (141)

1914-21 Granite Paper.

33 A34 ½s brown 1.50 85
34 " 1s orange 1.50 85
35 " 1½s blue 1.85 85
a. Bklt. pane of 6
36 " 2s green 1.85 90
a. Bklt. pane of 6
37 " 3s rose 1.45 85
a. Bklt. pane of 6
38 A35 4s red 5.50 3.00
a. Bklt. pane of 6
39 " 5s violet 11.00 1.85
40 " 6s brown ('20) 20.00 15.00
41 " 8s gray ('20) 22.50 18.50
42 " 10s deep blue 10.00 1.40
a. Bklt. pane of 6
43 " 20s claret 30.00 2.75
44 " 25s olive green 35.00 3.75
45 A36 30s org. brn. ('20) 57.50 18.50
46 " 50s dk. brn. ('20) 62.50 30.00
47 " 1y yel. green & maroon ('18) 80.00 5.50
48 A33 5y green 1000.00 400.00
49 " 10y violet('21) 1500.00 725.00
Nos. 33-49 (17) 2842.15 1229.55

On Nos. 48–49 the space between characters of overprint is 4½mm., instead of 6½mm. on Nos. 20–21 and 1½mm. on all lower values.

Counterfeit overprints exist of Nos. 1–49.

Offices in Korea

Regular Issue of Japan Overprinted in Red or Black 鮮朝

Perf. 11½, 12, 12½.

1900 Unwmkd.

1 A26 5r gray (R) 15.00 8.00
2 " 1s lt. red brn. (R) 16.50 5.00
3 " 1½s ultramarine 200.00 150.00
4 " 2s light green (R) 17.50 11.00
5 " 3s violet brown 13.50 4.75
6 " 4s rose 57.50 30.00
7 " 5s orange yel. (R) 60.00 30.00
8 A27 8s olive grn. (R) 185.00 160.00
9 " 10s deep blue 30.00 5.00
10 " 15s purple 67.50 6.00
11 " 20s red orange 65.00 5.00
12 A28 25s bl. green (R) 175.00 60.00
13 " 50s red brown 150.00 20.00
14 A29 1y carmine 425.00 15.00
Nos. 1-14 (14) 1477.50 509.75

1900

15 A30 3s carmine 65.00 22.50

No. 15 was issued to commemorate the wedding of Crown Prince Yoshihito.

Counterfeit overprints exist of Nos. 1–15.

Taiwan (Formosa)

Numeral of Value and Imperial Crest
A1

Lithographed.

1945 *Imperf.* **Unwmkd.**

1 A1 3s carmine 13.50 15.00
2 " 5s blue green 8.00 8.00
3 " 10s pale blue 18.50 20.00

Additional values, prepared, but not issued, were: 30s, 40s, 50s, 1y, 5y and 10y. The entire set of nine was overprinted by Chinese authorities after World War II and issued for use in Taiwan.

JUBALAND

See Oltre Giuba in Vol. III.

JUGOSLAVIA

(Yugoslavia)

(yōō'gō-slä'vĭ-ȧ)

LOCATION — In southern Europe, bordering on the Adriatic Sea.

GOVT.—Republic.

AREA—98,766 sq. mi.

POP.—21,720,000 (est. 1977).

CAPITAL—Belgrade.

On Dec. 1, 1918, Bosnia and Herzegovina, Croatia, Dalmatia, Montenegro, Serbia and Slovenia united to form a kingdom which was later called Jugoslavia. Other listings may be found under all except Slovenia. A republic was proclaimed Nov. 29, 1945.

100 Heller = 1 Krone
(Bosnia & Herzegovina)
100 Filler = 1 Krone
(Croatia-Slavonia)
100 Paras = 1 Dinar (General Issues)

Counterfeits exist of most of the 1918–19 overprints for Bosnia and Herzegovina, Croatia-Slavonia and Slovenia.

Issues for BOSNIA AND HERZEGOVINA

Stamps of Bosnia and Herzegovina, 1910, Overprinted or Surcharged in Black or Red:

DRŽAVA S.H.S.

1918 1918

Bosna i Hercegovina

a

ДРЖАВА С.Х.С.

1918 1918

Босна и Херцеговина

b

DRŽAVA
S. H. S.

1918 1918

Bosna i Hercegovina

c

1918 *Perf. 12½* **Unwmkd.**

No.	Type		Description	Unused	Used
1L1	A4	(*a*)	3h olive green	40	40
1L2	"	(*b*)	5h dark green(R)	5	5
1L3	"	(*a*)	10h carmine	5	5
1L4	"	(")	20h dark brown (R)	5	5
1L5	"	(")	25h deep blue (R)	5	5
1L6	A4	(*b*)	30h green	5	5
1L7	"	(")	40h orange	5	5
1L8	"	(")	45h brown red	5	5
1L9	"	(")	50h dull violet	20	20
1L10	"	(*a*)	60h on 50h dull violet	12	12
1L11	"	(*b*)	80h on 6h org. brn.	10	30
1L12	"	(*a*)	90h on 35h myrtle green	10	10
1L13	A17	(*c*)	2k gray green	20	30
1L14	A4	(*b*)	3k on 3h olive grn.	40	50
1L15	A17	(*c*)	4k on 1k maroon	1.50	1.50
1L16	A4	(*b*)	10k on 2h violet	2.75	3.50
			Nos. 1L1–1L16 (16)	6.12	7.27

Nos. 1L1–1L16 exist with overprint or surcharge inverted, double or double inverted; in v ɔng color, etc. Price $4 to $12.

Bosnian Girl
A1

1918 Typographed. *Perf. 11½.*

No.	Type	Description	Unused	Used
1L17	A1	2(h) ultramarine	15	20
1L18	"	6(h) violet	60	1.50
1L19	"	10(h) rose	30	30
1L20	"	20(h) green	30	30

Imperforate stamps of this type (A1) are newspaper stamps of Bosnia.

Nos. 1L17 and 1L18 Surcharged ■ 3 ■

1918 *Imperf.*

No.	Type	Description	Unused	Used
1L21	A1	3(h) on 2(h) ultra.	15	15
		a. Double surcharge	*12.00*	
1L22	"	5(h) on 6(h) violet	15	15
		a. Double surcharge	*12.00*	

Stamps of Bosnia and Herzegovina, 1906-17, Overprinted or Surcharged in Black or Red:

КРАЉЕВСТВО

С. Х. С.

d

KRALJEVSTVO

S. H. S.

e

KRALJEVSTVO

S. H. S.

1919 *Perf. 12½*

No.	Type		Description	Unused	Used
1L25	A23	(*d*)	3h claret	10	20
1L26	"	(*e*)	5h green	10	10
1L27	"	(")	10h on 6h dark gray	7	7
1L28	A24	(*d*)	20h on 35h myrtle green	10	10
1L29	A23	(*e*)	25h ultramarine	10	10
1L30	"	(*d*)	30h orange red	20	20
1L31	A24	(*d*)	45h olive brown	20	20
1L32	A27	(")	45h on 80h orange brown	10	10
			a. Perf. 11½	2.50	3.00
1L33	A24	(*e*)	50h slate blue	20.00	20.00
1L34	"	(")	50h on 72h dark blue (R)	10	10
1L35	"	(*d*)	60h brown violet	10	10
1L36	A27	(*e*)	80h org. brown	10	10
			a. Perf. 11½	*10.00*	*11.00*
1L37	"	(*d*)	90h dark violet	10	10
			a. Perf. 11½	2.50	3.00
1L38	A17	(*f*)	2k gray green	20	30
			a. Imperf.		
			b. Perf. 9½	3.00	3.00
1L39	A26	(*d*)	3k car., *green*	40	50
1L40	A28	(*e*)	4k carmine, *green*	1.50	1.75
1L41	A26	(*d*)	5k dark violet, *gray*	1.50	1.75
1L42	A28	(*e*)	10k dark violet, *gray*	3.00	4.00
			Nos. 1L25–1L42 (18)	27.97	29.77

Nos. 1L32, 1L36, 1L37, 1L40 and 1L42 have no bars in the overprint.

Nos. 1L25 to 1L42 exist with inverted overprint or surcharge.

Stamps of 1918 Surcharged 

1920 *Imperf.*

No.	Type	Description	Unused	Used
1L43	A1	2(h) on 6(h) violet	125.00	150.00
1L44	"	2(h) on 10(h) rose	52.50	65.00
1L45	"	2(h) on 20(h) green	2.00	4.00

SEMI-POSTAL STAMPS.

Issues for BOSNIA AND HERZEGOVINA

Leading Blind Soldier
SP1

Wounded Soldier
SP2

Semi-Postal Stamps of Bosnia and Herzegovina, 1918 Overprinted in Black.

1918 *Perf. 12½, 13* **Unwmkd.**

No.	Type	Description	Unused	Used
1LB1	SP1	10h greenish blue	70	1.25
		a. Overprinted as No. 1LB2	15.00	20.00
1LB2	SP2	15h red brown	1.50	2.00
		a. Overprinted as No. 1LB1	15.00	20.00

Bosnian Semi-Postal Stamps of 1916 Overprinted like No. 1LB2.

No.	Type	Description	Unused	Used
1LB3	SP1	5h green	120.00	120.00
		a. Overprinted as No. 1LB1	*225.00*	*225.00*
1LB4	SP2	10h magenta	65.00	65.00

Inverted and double overprints exist on Nos. 1LB1–1LB4.

Mail Wagon
SP3

Bridge at Mostar
SP4

Scene near Sarajevo—SP5

Regular Issue of Bosnia, 1906 Surcharged in Black.

1919

No.	Type	Description	Unused	Used
1LB5	SP3	10h+10h on 40h orange red	1.25	1.50
1LB6	SP4	20h+10h on 20h dark brown	75	1.00
1LB7	SP5	45h+15h on 1k maroon	4.00	4.00

Nos. 1LB5–1LB7 exist with surcharge inverted. Price each $7.50.

SPECIAL DELIVERY STAMPS.

Issues for BOSNIA AND HERZEGOVINA

Lightning
SD1 SD2

Bosnian Special Delivery Stamps Overprinted in Black.

1918 *Perf. 12½, 13.* **Unwmkd.**

No.	Type	Description	Unused	Used
1LE1	SD1	2h vermilion	4.00	4.00
		a. Inverted overprint	20.00	
		b. Overprinted as No. 1LE2	30.00	32.50
1LE2	SD2	5h deep green	1.50	1.50
		a. Inverted overprint	12.50	
		b. Overprinted as No. 1LE1	30.00	32.50

POSTAGE DUE STAMPS.

Issues for BOSNIA AND HERZEGOVINA

Postage Due Stamps of Bosnia and Herzegovina, 1916, Overprinted in Black or Red:

ДРЖАВА С.Х.С.
БОСНА И
ХЕРЦЕГОВИНА

хелера

a

DRŽAVA S.H.S.
BOSNA I
HERCEGOVINA

HELERA

b

1918 *Perf. 12½, 13.* **Unwmkd.**

No.	Type		Description	Unused	Used
1LJ1	D2	(*a*)	2h red	5	8
1LJ2	"	(*b*)	4h "	30	60
1LJ3	"	(*a*)	5h "	5	8
1LJ4	"	(*b*)	6h "	30	45
1LJ5	"	(*a*)	10h "	5	5
1LJ6	"	(*b*)	15h "	5.50	5.50
1LJ7	"	(*a*)	20h "	5	5
1LJ8	"	(*b*)	25h "	30	60
1LJ9	"	(*a*)	30h "	30	60
1LJ10	"	(*b*)	40h "	5	8
1LJ11	"	(*a*)	50h "	80	1.00

DRŽAVA S.H.S.
BOSNA I
HERCEGOVINA

KRUNA

c

ДРЖАВА С.Х.С.
Босна и
ХЕРЦЕГОВИНА

круна

d

1LJ12 D2 (*c*) 1k dark blue(R) 40 40
1LJ13 " (*d*) 3k dark blue(R) 30 30
Nos. 1LJ1-1LJ13 (13) 8.45 9.79

Nos. 1LJ1-1LJ13 exist with overprint double or inverted. Price $3 to $7.
Nos. 1LJ1-1LJ11 exist with type "b" overprint instead of type "a," and vice versa. Price, each $10.

Stamps of Bosnia and Herzegovina, 1900-04, Surcharged

ПОРТО **PORTO**

5 x **20h**

e *f*

1919

1LJ14 A2 (*e*) 2h on 35h blue 30 60
1LJ15 " (") 5h on 45h greenish blue 50 65
1LJ16 " (*f*) 10h on 10h red 5 10
1LJ17 " (*e*) 15h on 40h org. 25 40
1LJ18 " (*f*) 20h on 5h green 6 10
1LJ19 " (*e*) 25h on 20h pink 20 30
1LJ20 " (*f*) 30h on 30h bistre brown 20 30
1LJ21 " (*e*) 1k on 50h red lilac 10 15
1LJ22 " (") 3k on 25h blue 25 25

Postage Due Stamps of Bosnia and Herzegovina, 1904 Surcharged:

КРАЉЕВСТВО СРБА, ХРВАТА И СЈОВЕНАЦА **40** — KRALJEVSTVO SRBA, HRVATA I SLOVENACA **50**

40 хелера 40 — **50 helera 50**

g *h*

1LJ23 D1 (*g*) 40h on 6h black, red & yellow 5 10
1LJ24 " (*h*) 50h on 8h black, red & yellow 6 10
1LJ25 " (") 200h black, red & green 4.00 5.00
1LJ26 " (") 4k on 7h black, red & yellow 20 30
Nos. 1LJ14-1LJ26 (13) 6.22 8.35

Nos. 1LJ14-1LJ26 exist with overprint double or inverted. Price, $3 to $6.

Methods and style of listing are detailed in "Special Notices" at the front of this volume.

Issues for
CROATIA-SLAVONIA.
(krô-ā'shĭ-*ȧ*-slā-vō'nĭ-*ȧ*)

Stamps of Hungary Overprinted in Blue.

A1

Wmkd. Double Cross. (137)

1918 *Perf. 15.*

On Stamps of 1913.

2L1 A1 6f olive green 1.35 1.85
2L2 " 50f lake, *blue* 1.25 1.75

A2

A3

On Stamps of 1916.

2L3 A2 10f violet 35.00 45.00
a. Inverted overprint *75.00*
2L4 A3 15f red 35.00 45.00

A4

On Hungary Nos. 106-107.
White Numerals.

2L4A A4 10f rose *300.00 325.00*
2L5 " 15f violet 12.50 15.00
a. Inverted overprint

On Stamps of 1916-18.
Colored Numerals.

2L6 A4 2f brown orange 3 5
2L7 " 3f red lilac 3 5
2L8 " 5f green 3 5
2L9 " 6f greenish blue 5 20
2L10 " 10f rose red 2.00 2.75
a. Overprinted on back
2L11 " 15f violet 3 5
2L12 " 20f gray brown 6 10
a. Overprinted like No. 2LB1
2L13 " 25f dull blue 3 5
2L14 " 35f brown 6 10
2L15 " 40f olive green 15 20

Nos. 2L6-2L15 exist with overprint double or inverted. Price $3 to $7.
Nos. 2L6-2L9 exist in pairs, one without overprint.

A5

A6

2L16 A5 50f red violet & lilac 3 5
2L17 " 75f bright blue & pale blue 5 10
2L18 " 80f green & pale green 5 10
2L19 A6 1k red brown & claret 3 5
a. Double overprint
2L20 " 2k olive brown & bis. 10 15
a. Inverted overprint
2L21 A6 3k dark violet & indigo 25 50
a. Inverted overprint
2L22 " 5k dark brown & light brown 1.50 2.50
2L23 " 10k violet brown & violet 12.00 20.00

Stamps of Hungary Overprinted in Blue, Black or Red.

A7

A8

2L24 A7 10f scarlet (Bl) 3 5
a. Black overprint
b. Overprinted like No. 2L6
2L25 " 20f dark brown (Bk) 3 5
a. Double overprint
b. Blue overprint, inverted
c. Overprinted like No. 2L6
2L26 " 25f deep blue (R) 60 1.25
a. Inverted overprint
2L27 A8 40f olive green (Bl) 10 15
a. Inverted overprint
b. Overprinted like No. 2L6
Nos. 2L6-2L27 (22) 17.24 28.55

Many other stamps of the 1913-18 issues of Hungary, the Semi-Postal Stamps of 1915-16 and Postage Due Stamps were surreptitiously overprinted but were never sold through the post office.

Freedom of Croatia-Slavonia
A9

Lithographed.

1918 *Perf. 11½.* Unwmkd.

2L28 A9 10(f) rose 2.00 2.00
2L29 " 20(f) violet 2.50 2.50
2L30 " 25(f) blue 4.50 4.50
2L31 " 45(f) greenish blk. 40.00 40.00

Commemorating the attaining of independence by Croatia, Slavonia and Dalmatia.
Nos. 2L28 to 2L31 exist imperforate, but were not officially issued in this condition.
Excellent counterfeits of Nos. 2L28 to 2L31 exist.

Allegory of Freedom
A10

Youth with Standard
A11

Falcon, Symbol of Liberty
A12

1919 *Perf. 11½*

2L32 A10 2(f) brown orange 8 8
a. Perf. 12½ 1.50 1.25
2L33 " 3(f) violet 8 8
a. Perf. 12½ 1.25 1.00
2L34 " 5(f) green 8 8
a. Perf. 12½ *45.00 45.00*
2L35 A11 10(f) red 8 8
a. Perf. 12½ 50 50
2L36 " 20(f) black brown 8 8
a. Perf. 12½ 40 30
2L37 " 25(f) deep blue 8 8
2L38 A11 45(f) dk. olive grn. 15 15
2L39 A12 1k carmine rose 18 18
2L40 " 3k dark violet 60 60
2L41 " 5k deep brown 1.50 1.25
Nos. 2L32-2L41 (10) 2.91 2.66

Nos. 2L32-2L41 exist imperf. Price, set $25.

SEMI-POSTAL STAMPS.
Issues for
CROATIA-SLAVONIA.

SP1

SP2

SP3

Wmkd. Double Cross. (137)

1918 *Perf. 15.*

2LB1 SP1 10f+2f rose red 70 *3.50*
a. Double overprint
b. Overprinted like No. 2L6
2LB2 SP2 15f+2f dull violet 15 *60*
a. Double overprint
b. Inverted overprint
2LB3 SP3 40f+2f brown carmine 35 *1.20*
a. Inverted overprint
b. Overprinted like No. 2LB1

SPECIAL DELIVERY STAMP.
Issue for
CROATIA-SLAVONIA.

SD1

Hungary No. E1 Overprinted in Black.

Wmkd. Double Cross. (137)

1918 *Perf. 15.*

2LE1 SD1 2f gray grn. & red 15 15
a. Overprinted like No. 2L6

POSTAGE DUE STAMPS.
Issues for
CROATIA-SLAVONIA.

D1

Postage Due Stamps of Hungary Overprinted in Blue.

1918 Wmkd. Crown. (136) *Perf. 15.*

2LJ1 D1 50f green & black 200.00 200.00

Wmkd. Double Cross. (137)

2LJ2 D1 1f green & red 7.50 7.50
a. Invtd. overprint 20.00 20.00
2LJ3 " 2f green & red 85 85
2LJ4 " 10f " " 60 60
2LJ5 " 12f green & red 42.50 42.50
a. Invtd. ovpt.
b. Double overprint
2LJ6 " 15f green & red 50 50
a. Double overprint
2LJ7 " 20f green & red 50 50

2LJ8	D1	30f green & red	1.25	1.25
2LJ9	"	50f green & black	12.50	12.50
		Nos. 2LJ2-2LJ9 (8)	66.20	66.20

NEWSPAPER STAMPS.

Issues for CROATIA-SLAVONIA.

N1 N2

Hungary No. P8 Overprinted in Black.

1918 *Imperf.* **Wmk. 137**

2LP1	N1	(2f) orange	10	20

1919 Lithographed. **Unwmkd.**

2LP2	N2	2(f) yellow	10	20

Issues for SLOVENIA

(slō·vē'nĭ·ȧ)

Chain Breaker

A1 A2

Lithographed at Ljubljana.

Fine Impression.

3, 5, 10, 15f: The chain on the right wrist is short, extending only about half way to the frame.
10f: Numerals are 8½mm. high.
20, 25, 30, 40f: The distant mountains show faintly between the legs of the male figure.
40f: Numerals 7mm. high. The upright strokes of the "4" extend to the same height; the "0" is 3mm. wide.

1919 *Perf. 11½.* **Unwmkd.**

3L1	A1	3(f) violet	12	5
3L2	"	5(f) green	15	5
3L3	"	10(f) carmine rose	25	5
3L4	"	15(f) blue	12	5
3L5	A2	20 (f) brown	35	10
3L6	"	25(f) blue	20	5
3L7	"	30(f) lilac rose	20	5
3L8	"	40(f) bistre	25	7
		Nos. 3L1-3L8 (8)	1.64	47

Various stamps of this series exist imperforate and part perforate. Many shades exist.

Allegories of Freedom

A3 A4

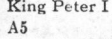

King Peter I

A5

1919-20 ***Perf. 11½***

Typographed at Ljubljana and Vienna.

Coarse Impression.

3, 5, 15f: The chain on the right wrist touches the bottom tablet.
10f: Numerals are 7½mm. high.
15f: The curled end of the loin cloth appears above the letter "H" in the bottom tablet.
20, 25, 30, 40f: The outlines of the mountains have been redrawn and they are more distinct than on the lithographed stamps.
40f: Numerals 8mm. high. The left slanting stroke of the "4" extends much higher than the main vertical stroke. The "0" is 2¼mm. wide and encloses a much narrower space than on the lithographed stamp.

3L9	A1	3(f) violet	12	3
3L10	"	5(f) green	20	3
3L11	"	10(f) red	30	3
3L12	"	15(f) blue	1.00	15
3L13	A2	20(f) brown	35	10
3L14	"	25(f) blue	30	5
3L15	"	30(f) carmine rose	35	5
3L16	"	30(f) deep red	90	20
3L17	"	40(f) orange	35	8
3L18	A3	50(f) green	35	10
		a. 50(f) dark green	35	10
		b. 50(f) olive grn.	6.00	1.85
3L19	"	60(f) dark blue	50	10
		a. 60 (f) vio. blue	1.25	30
3L20	A4	1k vermilion	35	10
		a. 1k red orange	65	20
3L21	"	2k blue	35	10
		a. 2k dull ultra.	1.50	25
3L22	A5	5k brown lake	45	10
		a. 5k lake	20.00	2.75
		b. 5k dull red	90	15
3L23	"	10k deep ultra.	2.00	55
		Nos. 3L9-3L23 (15)	7.87	1.77

Nos. 3L9-3L23 exist imperf. Price, set $90.

Many of the series exist part perforate.

Many shades exist of lower values.

Serrate Roulette 13½.

3L24	A1	5(f) light green	6	4
		a. Roul. x perf. 11½	85.00	85.00
3L25	A1	10(f) carmine	10	4
		a. Roul. x perf. 11½	45.00	45.00
3L26	A1	15(f) slate blue	20	10
		a. Roul. x perf. 11½	75.00	80.00
3L27	A2	20(f) dark brown	45	8
		a. Serrate x straight roul.	75	15
3L28	A2	30(f) carmine rose	30	12
		a. Serrate x straight roul.	75	12
		b. Roul. x perf. 11½	25.00	25.00
3L29	A3	50(f) green	30	5
		a. Roul. x perf. 11½	2.00	2.00
3L30	A3	60(f) dark blue	60	10
		a. 60(f) violet blue	60	12
		b. Roul. x perf. 11½	30.00	30.00
3L31	A4	1k vermilion	90	15
		a. 1k rose red	90	15
		b. Roul. x perf. 11½	25.00	27.50
3L32	A4	2k blue	15.00	2.25
		Nos. 3L24-3L32 (9)	17.91	2.93

Thick Wove Paper.

1920 Lithographed. ***Perf. 11½.***

3L40	A5	15k gray green	6.00	7.50
3L41	"	20k dull violet	2.00	2.50

On Nos. 3L40-3L41 the horizonal lines have been removed from the value tablets. They are printed over a background of pale brown wavy lines.

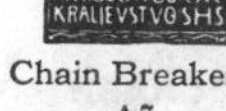

Chain Breaker Freedom

A7 A8

King Peter I

A9

Dinar Values.

Type I. Size 21x30½mm.

Type II. Size 22x32½mm.

Thin to Thick Wove Paper.

1920 ***Serrate Roulette 13½***

3L42	A7	5p olive green	5	3
3L43	"	10p green	5	3
3L44	"	15p brown	5	3
3L45	"	20p carmine	60	1.00
3L46	"	25p chocolate	30	30
3L47	A8	40p dark violet	5	10
3L48	"	45p yellow	5	15
3L49	"	50p dark blue	5	3
3L50	"	60p red brown	5	3
3L51	A9	1d dark brown (I)	5	3
		Perf. 11½.		
3L52	A9	2d gray violet (II)	5	3
3L53	"	4d greenish black (I)	30	30
3L54	"	6d olive brown (II)	15	25
3L55	"	10d brown red (II)	30	30
		Nos. 3L42-3L55 (14)	2.10	2.61

The 2d and 6d have a background of pale red wavy lines, the 10d of gray lines.

Counterfeits exist of No. 3L45.

POSTAGE DUE STAMPS

Issues for SLOVENIA

D1

Lithographed.

1919 ***Perf. 11½.*** **Unwmkd.**

Ljubljana Print.

Numerals 9½ mm. high.

3LJ1	D1	5(f) carmine	10	5
3LJ2	"	10(f) "	10	10
3LJ3	"	20(f) "	10	10
3LJ4	"	50(f) "	20	10

Nos. 3LJ1-3LJ4 were also printed in scarlet and dark red.

Numerals 8mm. high.

3LJ5	D1	1k dark blue	35	30
3LJ6	"	5k "	65	30
3LJ7	"	10k "	1.25	80
		Nos. 3LJ1-3LJ7 (7)	2.75	1.75

1920 Vienna Print

Numerals 11 to 12 mm. high.

3LJ8	D1	5(f) red	25	7
3LJ9	"	10(f) "	25	8
3LJ10	"	20(f) "	35	12
3LJ11	"	50(f) "	1.00	30

Numerals 7mm. high

3LJ12	D1	1k Prussian blue	75	50
		a. 1k dark blue	8.00	7.50
3LJ13	"	5k Prussian blue	2.00	50
		a. 5k dark blue	13.00	12.00
3LJ14	"	10k Prussian blue	4.50	3.00
		a. 10k dark blue	22.50	22.50
		Nos. 3LJ8-3LJ14 (7)	9.10	4.57

Nos. 3LJ8-3LJ14 exist imperf. Price, set $40.

No. 3L4 Surcharged in Red

1920 ***Perf. 11½.***

On Lithographed Stamps.

3LJ15	A1	5p on 15(f) blue	5	5
3LJ16	"	10p on 15(f) blue	75	75
3LJ17	"	20p on 15(f) blue	8	5
3LJ18	"	50p on 15(f) blue	8	5

Nos. 3L7, 3L12, 3L26, 3L28, 3L28a Surcharged in Dark Blue

3LJ19	A2	1d on 30(f) lilac rose	20	20
3LJ20	"	3d on 30(f) "	35	25
3LJ21	"	8d on 30(f) "	1.75	85
		Nos. 3LJ15-3LJ21 (7)	3.26	2.20

On Typographed Stamps.

Perf. 11½.

3LJ22	A1	5p on 15(f) pale blue	11.50	2.50
3LJ23	"	10p on 15(f) pale blue	40.00	17.50
3LJ24	"	20p on 15(f) pale blue	13.50	5.50
3LJ25	"	50p on 15(f) pale blue	8.50	5.50

Serrate Roulette 13½.

3LJ26	A1	5p on 15(f) slate blue	2.25	60
3LJ27	"	10p on 15(f) slate blue	9.00	4.50
3LJ28	"	20p on 15(f) slate blue	2.25	60
3LJ29	"	50p on 15(f) slate blue	2.25	60
3LJ30	A2	1d on 30(f) deep rose	2.75	1.00
		a. Serrate x straight roulette	7.50	3.00
3LJ31	A2	3d on 30(f) deep rose	3.25	1.25
		a. Serrate x straight roulette	4.75	2.75
3LJ32	A2	8d on 30(f) deep rose	75.00	9.00
		a. Serrate x straight roulette	72.50	8.50
		Nos. 3LJ26-3LJ32 (7)	96.75	17.55

The para surcharges were printed in sheets of 100, ten horizontal rows of ten. There were: 5p three rows, 10p one row, 20p three rows, 50p three rows. The dinar surcharges were in a setting of 50, arranged in vertical rows of five. There were: 1d five rows, 3d three rows, 8d two rows.

NEWSPAPER STAMPS.

Issues for SLOVENIA

Eros

N1

Lithographed.

1919 *Imperf.* **Unwmkd.**

Ljubljana Print.

2 4 6 10

3LP1	N1	2(f) gray	5	15
3LP2	"	4(f) "	15	25
3LP3	"	6(f) "	4.25	6.00
3LP4	"	10(f) "	10	15
3LP5	"	30(f) "	15	25
		Nos. 3LP1-3LP5 (5)	4.70	6.80

1920 Vienna Print.

2 4 6 10

3LP6	N1	2(f) gray	15	25
3LP7	"	4(f) "	5.50	6.50
3LP8	"	6(f) "	2.50	3.00
3LP9	"	10(f) "	9.00	11.00
3LP10	"	2(f) blue	25	35
3LP11	"	4(f) "	10	15
3LP12	"	6(f) "	*85.00*	*90.00*
3LP13	"	10(f) "	10	15
		Nos. 3LP6-3LP13 (8)	*102.60*	*111.40*

Nos. 3LP1, 3LP10 Surcharged:

On Ljubljana Print.

3LP14	N1 (a)	2p on 2f gray	40	60
3LP15	" (")	4p on 2f "	40	60
3LP16	" (")	6p on 2f "	65	95
3LP17	" (b)	10p on 2f "	1.00	1.20
3LP18	" (")	30p on 2f "	1.00	1.35

On Vienna Print.

3LP19	N1 (a)	2p on 2f blue	8	20
3LP20	" (")	4p on 2f "	8	20
3LP21	" (")	6p on 2f "	8	20
3LP22	" (b)	10p on 2f "	16	30
3LP23	" (")	30p on 2f "	20	40
		Nos. 3LP14–3LP23 (10)	4.05	6.00

The five surcharges were arranged in a setting of 100, in horizontal rows of ten. There were: 2p three rows, 4p three rows, 6p two rows, 10p one row and 30p one row. The sheets were perforated 11½ horizontally between the groups of the different values.

SEMI-POSTAL STAMPS

Issue for CARINTHIA PLEBISCITE.

SP1

Nos. 3LP2, 3LP1 Surcharged With Various Designs in Dark Red.

1920

4LB1	SP1	5p on 4f gray	10	10
4LB2	"	15p on 4f "	12	12
4LB3	"	25p on 4f "	15	20
4LB4	"	45p on 2f "	25	30
4LB5	"	50p on 2f "	15	20
4LB6	"	2d on 2f "	1.75	2.50
		Nos. 4LB1–4LB6 (6)	2.52	3.42

Nos. 4LB1 to 4LB6 have a different surcharge on each stamp but each includes the letters "K.G.C.A." which signify Carinthian Governmental Commission, Zone A.

Sold at three times face value for the benefit of the Plebiscite Propaganda Fund.

GENERAL ISSUES.

For Use throughout the Kingdom.

King Alexander A1 — King Peter I A2

Engraved.

1921, Jan. 16 *Perf. 12.* **Unwmkd.**

1	A1	2(p) olive brown	5	3
2	"	5(p) deep green	5	3
3	"	10(p) carmine	5	3
4	"	15(p) violet	5	3
5	"	20(p) black	5	3
6	"	25(p) dark blue	5	3
7	"	50(p) olive green	5	5
8	"	60(p) vermilion	12	5
9	"	75(p) purple	6	5
10	A2	1d orange	15	5
11	"	2d olive bistre	30	5
12	"	4d dark green	50	5
13	"	5d carmine rose	3.00	10
14	"	10d red brown	6.00	50
		Nos. 1–14 (14)	10.49	1.08

Exist imperf. Price, set $22.50.

Nos. B1–B3 Surcharged:

дин. 1 din.

дин. 8 din.

in Black, Brown, Green or Blue

1922-24

15	SP1 (a)	1d on 10(p) carmine (Bk)	10	3
16	SP2 (b)	1d on 15(p) violet brown (Bk) ('24)	15	3
17	SP3 (a)	1d on 25(p) light blue (Br)	10	3
18	SP2 (b)	3d on 15(p) violet brown (G)	1.25	10
		a. Blue surch.	2.50	20
19	" (")	8d on 15(p) violet brown (G)	3.75	20
		a. Dbl. surch.	37.50	32.50
		b. 9d on 15(p) violet brown (error)	*85.00*	
20	" (")	20d on 15(p) violet brown (Bk)	9.25	50
21	" (")	30d on 15(p) violet brown (Bl)	24.00	1.25
		Nos. 15–21 (7)	38.60	2.14

A3

1923, Jan. 23 Engraved

22	A3	1d red brown	1.00	10
23	"	5d carmine	7.50	15
24	"	8d violet	11.00	30
25	"	20d green	27.50	40
26	"	30d red orange	80.00	1.25
		Nos. 22–26 (5)	127.00	2.20

Nos. 8 and 24 Surcharged in Black or Blue **пара 20 para**

1924, Feb. 18

27	A1	20p on 60(p) vermilion	60	5
28	A3	5d on 8d violet (Bl)	7.50	45

The color of the surcharge on No. 28 varies, including blue, blue black, greenish black and black.

A4 — A5

1924, July 1 *Perf. 14.*

29	A4	20(p) black	60	6
30	"	50(p) dark brown	75	6
31	"	1d carmine	75	6
32	"	2d myrtle green	1.50	6
33	"	3d ultramarine	1.25	8
34	"	5d orange brown	4.25	8
35	A5	10d dark violet	17.50	30
36	"	15d olive green	11.50	35
37	"	20d vermilion	10.50	25
38	"	30d dark green	9.50	60
		Nos. 29–38 (10)	58.10	1.90

No. 33 Surcharged **п 50 р**

1925, June 5

39	A4	25p on 3d ultramarine	10	8
40	"	50p on 3d ultramarine	12	8

King Alexander

A6 — A7

1926-27 Typographed *Perf. 13*

41	A6	25(p) deep green	10	4
42	"	50(p) olive brown	25	3
43	"	1d scarlet	40	3
44	"	2d slate black	50	3
45	"	3d slate blue	85	3
46	"	4d red orange	4.75	3
47	"	5d violet	3.50	3
48	"	8d black brown	7.50	10
49	"	10d olive brown	7.00	3
50	"	15d brown ('27)	12.00	20
51	"	20d dk. violet ('27)	17.50	30
52	"	30d orange ('27)	45.00	70
		Nos. 41–52 (12)	99.35	1.55

Semi-Postal Stamps of 1926 Overprinted **XXXX** over the Red Surcharge.

1928, July

53	A6	1d scarlet	1.00	10
		a. Surcharge "0.50" inverted		
54	"	2d black	2.50	10
55	"	3d deep blue	2.75	25
56	"	4d red orange	9.25	1.25
57	"	5d bright violet	3.00	20
58	"	8d black brown	4.50	75
59	"	10d olive brown	7.00	50
60	"	15d brown	55.00	5.50
61	"	20d violet	25.00	2.85
62	"	30d orange	65.00	5.75
		Nos. 53–62 (10)	175.00	17.25

With Imprint at Foot

1931-34 *Perf. 12½.*

63	A7	25p black	1.50	6
64	"	50p green	1.25	3
65	"	75p slate green	20	3
66	"	1d red	1.50	3
67	"	1.50d pink	40	3
68	"	1.75d deep rose ('34)	60	35
69	"	3d slate blue	3.00	4
70	"	3.50d ultramarine ('34)	85	28
71	"	4d deep orange	2.50	3
72	"	5d purple	2.50	3
73	"	10d dark olive	8.00	3
74	"	15d deep brown	7.00	15
75	"	20d dark violet	20.00	15
76	"	30d rose	8.00	45
		Nos. 63–76 (14)	57.30	1.69

Type of 1931 Issue. Without Imprint at Foot.

1932-33

77	A7	25p black	25	12
78	"	50p green	45	6
79	"	1d red	90	6
80	"	3d slate blue ('33)	2.75	6
81	"	4d dp. org. ('33)	6.25	6
82	"	5d purple ('33)	7.50	6
83	"	10d dk. olive ('33)	18.50	10
84	"	15d dp. brown ('33)	25.00	20
85	"	20d dk. violet ('33)	47.50	20
86	"	30d rose ('33)	55.00	55
		Nos. 77–86 (10)	164.10	1.47

See also Nos. 102–115.

Nos. 41 to 52 Overprinted

ЈУГОСЛАВИЈА

JUGOSLAVIJA

1933, Sept. 5 *Perf. 13.*

87	A6	25(p) deep green	10	3
88	"	50(p) olive brown	10	3
89	"	1d scarlet	30	3
90	A6	2d slate black	1.75	20
91	"	3d slate blue	2.00	6
92	"	4d red orange	1.00	5
93	"	5d violet	2.50	3
94	"	8d black brown	5.00	18
95	"	10d olive brown	10.00	10
96	"	15d brown	12.50	1.40
97	"	20d dark violet	25.00	70
98	"	30d orange	27.50	1.00
		Nos. 87–98 (12)	87.75	3.81

Semi-Postal Stamps of 1926 Overprinted like Nos. 87 to 98 and Four Bars over the Red Surcharge of 1926.

1933, Sept. 5

99	A6	25p green	50	20
100	"	50p olive brown	50	10
101	"	1d scarlet	1.75	40

Nos. 99–101 exist with double impression of bars. Price, each $5.50 unused, $4.50 used.

King Alexander Memorial Issue.

Type of 1931-34 Issues Borders in Black.

1934, Oct. 17

102	A7	25p black	10	5
103	"	50p green	10	5
104	"	75p slate green	20	15
105	"	1d red	15	5
106	"	1.50d pink	20	5
107	"	1.75d deep rose	25	25
108	"	3d slate blue	35	5
109	"	3.50d ultramarine	45	10
110	"	4d deep orange	60	10
111	"	5d purple	80	10
112	"	10d dark olive	2.75	10
113	"	15d deep brown	4.00	15
114	"	20d dark violet	6.00	15
115	"	30d rose	4.75	30
		Nos. 102–115 (14)	20.70	1.65

King Peter II A10

1935-36 *Perf. 13x12½.*

116	A10	25(p) brown black	3	3
117	"	50(p) yellow orange	3	3
118	"	75(p) turquoise green	10	3
119	"	1d brown red	10	3
120	"	1.50d scarlet	8	3
121	"	1.75d cerise	25	15
122	"	2d magenta ('36)	17	5
123	"	3d brown orange	15	5
124	"	3.50d ultramarine	25	5
125	"	4d yellow green	1.10	15
126	"	4d slate blue ('36)	15	5
127	"	10d bright violet	45	10
128	"	15d brown	85	25
129	"	20d bright blue	4.00	20
130	"	30d rose pink	2.10	35
		Nos. 116–130 (15)	9.81	1.55

The abbreviation "Din." is in Cyrillic characters on Nos. 116, 118, 120, 123, 125, 126, 128 and 130.

King Alexander A11 — Nikola Tesla A12

Perf. 12½x11½, 11½

1935, Oct. 9

131	A11	75(p) turquoise green	20	20
132	"	1.50d scarlet	20	20
133	"	1.75d dark brown	1.25	1.25
134	"	3.50d ultramarine	1.25	1.25
135	"	7.50d rose carmine	1.25	1.25
		Nos. 131–135 (5)	4.15	4.15

Issued in commemoration of the first anniversary of the death of King Alexander.

Perf. 12½x11½

1936, May 28 Lithographed

136 A12 75p yellow green & dark brown 35 20
137 " 1.75d dull blue & indigo 50 30

Issued to honor the 80th birthday of Nikola Tesla (1856–1943), electrical inventor.

Lettering at side in Roman, at bottom in Serbian on No. 136. This arrangement is reversed on No. 137.

Memorial Church, Oplenac A13 — Coats of Arms of Jugoslavia, Greece, Romania and Turkey A14

1937, July 1

138 A13 3d Prussian green 50 15
a. Perf. 12½ 4.00 2.00
139 " 4d dark blue 55 20

"Little Entente," 16th anniversary. "Jugoslavia" in Cyrillic characters on No. 138.

Perf. 11, 11½, 12½

1937, Oct. 29 Photogravure

140 A14 3d peacock green 55 12
141 " 4d ultramarine 85 18

Balkan Entente. "Jugoslavia" in Latin characters on No. 141.

King Peter II A16

1939–40 Typographed *Perf. 12½*

142 A16 25p black ('40) 5 5
143 " 50p orange ('40) 5 3
144 " 1d yellow green 8 3
145 " 1.50d red 8 3
146 " 2d deep magenta ('40) 15 10
147 " 3d dull red brown 15 5
148 " 4d ultramarine 15 5
148A " 5d dark blue ('40) 20 20
148B " 5.50d dark violet brown ('40) 20 10
149 " 6d slate blue 45 8
150 " 8d sepia 45 10
151 " 12d bright violet 85 15
152 " 16d dull violet 1.20 35
153 " 20d blue ('40) 1.20 30
154 " 30d brt. pink ('40) 2.25 50
Nos. 142–154 (15) 7.51 2.12

Arms of Jugoslavia, Greece, Romania and Turkey
A17 A18

1940, June 1

155 A17 3d ultramarine 50 15
156 A18 3d ultramarine 50 15
157 A17 4d dark blue 50 20
158 A18 4d dark blue 50 20

Balkan Entente.

Cyrillic and Roman inscriptions alternate in each sheet of 3d and of 4d. Price, se-tenant pairs of the two values, unused or used, $4.

Bridge at Obod A19

1940, Sept. 29 Lithographed

159 A19 5.50d slate green & dull green 2.75 2.25

Issued to commemorate the Zagreb Philatelic Exhibition and the 500th anniversary of Johann Gutenberg's invention of printing. The first press in the Jugoslav area was located at Obod in 1493.

Issues for Federal Republic.

Types of Serbia, 1942–43, Surcharged in Green or Vermilion

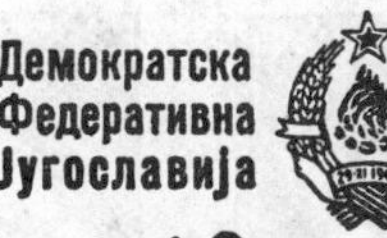

1944, Dec. *Perf. 11½.* **Unwmkd.**

Overprinted with Pale Green Network.

159A OS4 5d (3d+2d) rose pink (G) 20 55
159B " 10d (7d+3d) dark slate green (V) 20 55

Similar Surcharge on Serbia 2N37 to 2N39 Without Network

1945, Jan. 24

159C OS4 5d (3d+2d) rose pink (G) 15 45
159D " 10d (7d+3d) dark slate green (V) 15 55
159E " 25d (4d+21d) ultramarine (Bk) 25 60

Marshal Tito (Josip Broz) A20 — Prohor Pcinski Monastery A21

1945 Photogravure. *Perf. 12½.*

160 A20 25p bright blue green 50 15
161 " 50p deep green 30 8
162 " 1d crimson rose 2.50 25
163 " 2d dk. car. rose 50 6
164 " 4d deep blue 1.00 8
165 " 5d deep green 8 60
166 " 6d dark purple 50 8
167 " 9d orange brown 1.25 30
168 " 10d deep rose 8 60
169 " 20d orange 3.50 40
170 " 25d dark purple 17 95
171 " 30d deep blue 30 1.10
Nos. 160–171 (12) 10.68 4.65

1945, Aug. 2 Typo. *Perf. 11½*

172 A21 2d red 1.25 20

Issued to commemorate the first anniversary of the formation of the Popular Antifascist Chamber of Deputies of Macedonia, August 2, 1944.

Partisans
A22 A23

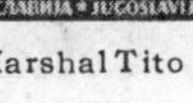

Marshal Tito A24 — Partisan Girl and Flag A26

City of Jaice A25

1945, Oct. 10 Litho. *Perf. 12½*

173 A22 50p olive gray 6 6
174 " 1d blue green 10 6
175 A23 1.50d orange brown 15 6
176 A24 2d scarlet 10 6
177 A25 3d red brown 1.00 6
178 A24 4d dark blue 20 6
179 A25 5d dk. yel. green 75 10
180 A26 6d black 40 8
181 " 9d deep plum 50 20
182 A23 12d ultramarine 60 15
183 A22 16d blue 70 12
184 A23 20d orange verm. 1.25 50
Nos. 173–184 (12) 5.81 1.51

See also Nos. 211 to 214.

"Labor" and "Agriculture"
A27 A28

1945, Nov. 29 Photo. *Perf. 12*

185 A27 2d brown carmine 2.75 2.50
186 A28 2d brown carmine 2.75 2.50
187 A27 4d deep blue 2.75 2.00
188 A28 4d deep blue 2.75 2.00
189 A27 6d dark slate green 2.75 2.00
190 A28 6d dark slate green 2.75 2.00
191 A27 9d red orange 2.75 2.00
192 A28 9d red orange 2.75 2.00
193 A27 16d bright ultra. 2.75 2.00
194 A28 16d bright ultra. 2.75 2.00
195 A27 20d dark brown 2.75 2.00
a. Souvenir sheet (perf. 11½) 12.50 17.50
196 A28 20d dark brown 2.75 2.00
a. Souvenir sheet (perf. 11½) 12.50 17.50
Nos. 185–196 (12) 33.00 25.00
Se-tenant pairs, Nos. 185–196 45.00 45.00

Issued to commemorate the inauguration of the constitution for the Democratic Federation of Jugoslavia, November 29, 1945.

No. 195a measures 148x110mm. and contains one each of Nos. 191 and 195, with gold marginal inscriptions in Latin alphabet.

No. 196a is similar to No. 195a, except left inscriptions are in Cyrillic characters and stamps are Nos. 192 and 196.

Parade of Armed Forces A31 — Svetozar Markovic A32

Lithographed.

1946, May 9 *Perf. 12½.* **Unwmkd.**

199 A31 1.50d org. yel. & red 1.00 50
200 A31 2.50d cerise & red 1.25 80
201 " 5d blue & red 3.00 2.25

Issued to commemorate the first anniversary of victory over fascism.

Type of 1945 Surcharged with New Values in Black.

1946, Apr. 1

202 A26 2.50(d) on 6d bright red 1.50 5
203 " 8(d) on 9d org. 1.50 10

1946, Sept. 22

204 A32 1.50d blue green 1.75 1.25
205 " 2.50d deep red lilac 2.25 1.50

Issued to commemorate the centenary of the birth of Svetozar Markovic, Serbian socialist.

Latin and Cyrillic spellings of Jugoslavia are transposed on No. 205.

People's Theater, Sofia A33

Sigismund Monument, Warsaw A35

Designs: 1d, Prague. 2½d, Victory Monument, Belgrade. 5d, Spassky Tower, Kremlin.

Lithographed.

1946, Dec. 8 *Perf. 11½.* **Unwmkd.**

206 A33 ½d dark brown & yellow brown 15 15
207 " 1d greenish black & emerald 15 15
208 A35 1½d dark carmine rose & rose 25 20
209 " 2½d henna brown & brown orange 35 30
210 " 5d dark blue & blue 65 35
Nos. 206–210 (5) 1.55 1.15

Issued to commemorate the Pan-Slavic Congress held at Belgrade, December 1946.

Types of 1945.

1947, Jan. 15 Litho. *Perf. 12½.*

211 A26 2.50d red orange 50 10
212 A25 3d dull red 85 10
213 " 5d dark blue 2.00 15
214 A26 8d orange 1.35 8

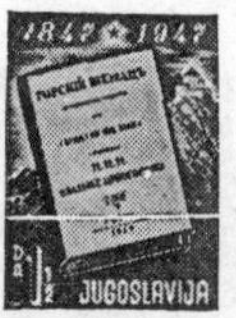

Gorski Vijenac A38 — Peter P. Nyegosh A39

1947, June 8 Typographed

215 A38 1.50d Prussian green & black 30 30
216 A39 2.50d olive bistre & dark carmine 45 35
217 A38 5d blue & black 70 45

Issued to commemorate the centenary of the Montenegrin national epic "Gorski Vijenac" (Wreath of Mountains) by Peter Petrovich Nyegosh.

Girls' Physical Training Classes
A40

Girl Runner
A41

Physical Culture Parade—A42

1947, June 15 Litho. *Perf. 11.*

218	A40	1.50d brown	30	30
219	A41	2.50d red	45	45
220	A42	4d violet blue	75	65

Issued to commemorate the national sports meet held at Belgrade, June 15–22, 1947.

Map and Star
A43

1947, Sept. 16 Typographed

231	A43	2.50d deep carmine & dark blue	25	15
232	"	5d orange brown & dark green	30	15

Annexation of Julian Province.

Music and One-string Gusle
A44

Vuk Karadzić
A45

Perf. 11½x12, 12½

1947, Sept. 27

233	A44	1.50d green	35	20
234	A45	2.50d orange red	45	30
235	A44	5d violet blue	65	45

Centenary of Serbian literature.

Symbols of Industry and Agriculture, Map and Flag
A46

Danube River Scene
A47

1948, Apr. 8 Litho. *Perf. 12½*

236	A46	1.50(d) green, blue & salmon	12	5
237	"	2.50(d) red brown, blue & salmon	15	10
238	"	5(d) dark blue, blue & salmon	30	25

International Fair, Zagreb, May 8–17.

1948, July 30 **Unwmkd.**

239	A47	2d green	40	40
240	"	3d carmine	50	50
241	"	5d blue	60	60
242	"	10d brown orange	1.00	1.00

Danube Conference, Belgrade.

Marchers with Party Flag
A48

Laurent Kosir
A49

1948, July 21 *Perf. 11½, 12½*

243	A48	2d dark green	30	25
244	"	3d dark red	45	30
245	"	10d dark blue violet	90	50

Issued to commemorate the 5th Congress of the Communist Party in Jugoslavia, July 21, 1948.

Commemorative inscription in Latin characters on No. 245.

1948, Aug. 21 *Perf. 12½*

246	A49	3d claret	20	15
247	"	5d blue	30	30
248	"	10d red orange	30	20
249	"	12d dull green	75	50

Issued to commemorate the 80th anniversary of the death of Laurent Kosir, recognized by Jugoslavia as inventor of the postage stamp.

Arms of Bosnia and Herzegovina
A50

Arms of Jugoslavia
A51

1948, Nov. 29 *Perf. 12½, 12x11½.*

Arms of Jugoslav Peoples Republics.

250	A50	3d green	1.00	1.00
251	"	3d rose lilac (*Macedonia*)	1.00	1.00
252	"	3d gray blue (*Serbia*)	1.00	1.00
253	"	3d gray (*Montenegro*)	1.00	1.00
254	"	3d rose (*Croatia*)	1.00	1.00
255	"	3d orange (*Slovenia*)	1.00	1.00
256	A51	10d deep carmine	2.50	2.50
		Nos. 250–256 (7)	8.50	8.50

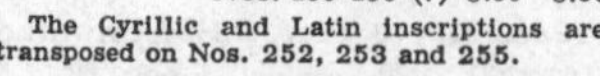

The Cyrillic and Latin inscriptions are transposed on Nos. 252, 253 and 255.

Franc Presern—A52

1949, Feb. 8 Photo. *Perf. 11½*

257	A52	3d dark blue	40	30
258	"	5d brown orange	50	35
259	"	10d olive black	65	60

Issued to commemorate the centenary of the death of Franc Presern, poet.

Ski Jump, Planica
A53

Ski Jumper
A54

Lithographed.

1949, Mar. 20 *Perf. 12½x11½*

260	A53	10d magenta	1.50	1.25
261	A54	12d slate gray	1.50	1.25

Issued to commemorate the International Ski Championship Meet, Planica, March 13–20, 1949.

Soldiers
A55

Farmers
A56

Arms and Flags of Macedonia and Jugoslavia
A57

1949, Aug. 2 *Perf. 12½*

262	A55	3d carmine rose	55	60
263	A56	5d dull blue	55	60
264	A57	12d red brown	5.50	7.50

Issued to commemorate the fifth anniversary of the liberation of Macedonia.

It is reported that No. 264 was not sold to the public at post offices.

Postal Communications
A58

Early Steam Locomotive
A60

Design: 5d, Plane, locomotive and stage coach (horiz.).

1949, Sept. 8 **Unwmkd**

265	A58	3d red	3.25	3.7
266	"	5d blue	60	6
267	"	12d brown	60	6

Issued to commemorate the 75th anniversary of the formation of the Universal Postal Union.

1949, Dec. 15 **Photogravure**

Designs: Locomotives.

269	A60	2d blue green	1.00	4
270	"	3d carmine rose (*Modern, Steam*)	1.00	4
271	"	5d blue (*Diesel*)	2.50	6
272	"	10d deep orange (*Electric*)	17.50	12.5

Centenary of Jugoslav railroads.

Official Stamps Nos. 07 and 08 Surcharged:

3 = 3 =

1949 **Typographed**

272A	O1	3d on 8d chocolate	20	
272B	"	3d on 12d violet	30	1

Stamps of 1945 and 1947 Overprinted or Surcharged in Black:

F
N
R
JUGOSLAVIJA FNR JUGOSLAVIJA

ФНР

ФНР ЈУГОСЛАВИЈА

≡ D3

FNR JUGOSLAVIJA F N R

Lithographed

273	A22 (*a*)	50p olive gray	5	3
274	" (")	1d blue green	5	3
275	A24 (*b*)	2d scarlet	8	3
276	A26 (*c*)	3d on 8d orange	25	10
277	A25 (*d*)	3d dull red	8	5
278	" (")	5d dark blue	20	15
279	A23 (*a*)	10d on 20d orange vermilion	35	10
280	" (")	12d ultramarine	20	10
281	A22 (")	16d blue	35	15
282	A23 (")	20d orange verm.	80	25
		Nos. 273–282 (10)	2.41	99

On No. 279 the surcharge includes a rule below "JUGOSLAVIJA" and "D 10" with two bars over "20D".

See also Nos. 286–289.

Surveying for Highway
A61

Bridge, Map and Automobile
A62

Highway Completion Symbolized—A63

Photogravure.

1950, Jan. 16 *Perf. 12½.* **Unwmkd.**

No.	Type	Description	Unused	Used
283	A61	2d blue green	50	40
284	A62	3d rose brown	40	20
285	A63	5d violet blue	1.00	1.00

Issued to commemorate the completion of the Belgrade-Zagreb highway, December, 1949.

Types of 1945 Overprinted in Black.

1950 *Perf. 12½* **Unwmkd.**

No.	Type	Description	Unused	Used
286	A22 (*a*)	1d brownish orange	10	3
287	A24 (*b*)	2d blue green	15	3
288	A25 (*d*)	3d rose pink	20	3
289	" (")	5d blue	30	6

Marshal Tito A64

Child Eating A65

1950, Apr. 30 **Engraved**

No.	Type	Description	Unused	Used
290	A64	3d red	1.00	50
291	"	5d dull blue	1.00	50
292	"	10d brown	14.00	7.75
293	"	12d olive black	2.00	2.00

Issued to mark Labor Day, May 1, 1950.

1950, June 1 **Photogravure.**

No.	Type	Description	Unused	Used
294	A65	3d brown red	60	15

Issued to publicize Children's Day, June 1.

Boy and Model Plane A66

Map and Chess Symbols A67

Designs: 3d, Glider aloft. 5d, Parachutists. 10d, Aviatrix. 20d, Glider on field.

1950, July 2 **Engraved**

No.	Type	Description	Unused	Used
295	A66	2d dark green	60	40
296	"	3d brown red	60	40
297	"	5d violet	60	40
298	"	10d chocolate	1.50	1.00
299	"	20d ultramarine	15.00	9.50
		Nos. 295-299 (5)	18.30	11.70

Third Aviation Meet, July 2–11.

1950, Aug. 20 **Photo.** *Perf. 11½.*

Designs: 3d, Rook and ribbon. 5d, Globe and chess board. 10d, Allegory of international chess. 20d, View of Dubrovnik, knight and ribbon.

No.	Type	Description	Unused	Used
300	A67	2d red brown & rose brown	1.00	40
301	"	3d black brown, gray brown & dull yellow	50	35
302	"	5d dark green, blue & buff	1.00	60
303	"	10d claret, blue & orange yellow	2.00	1.25
304	"	20d dark blue, blue & orange yellow	16.00	9.50
		Nos. 300-304 (5)	20.50	12.10

Issued to publicize the International Chess Matches, Dubrovnik, August 1950.

Electrification A68

Coal and Logs for Export A69

Designs: 50p, Metallurgy. 2d, Agriculture. 3d, Construction. 5d, Fishing. 7d, Mining. 10d, Fruit-growing. 12d, Lumbering. 16d, Gathering sunflowers. 20d, Livestock raising. 30d, Book manufacture. 50d, Loading ship.

Engraved

1950-51 *Perf. 12½.* **Unwmkd.**

No.	Type	Description	Unused	Used
305	A68	50p dark brown ('51)	5	10
306	"	1d blue green	20	3
307	"	2d orange	25	3
308	"	3d rose red	25	3
309	"	5d ultramarine	45	3
310	"	7d gray	45	6
311	"	10d chocolate	85	6
312	"	12d vio. brown ('51)	3.00	15
313	"	16d violet blue ('51)	4.00	45
314	"	20d olive grn. ('51)	3.50	25
314A	"	30d red brown ('51)	7.50	1.60
315	"	50d violet ('51)	22.00	16.50
		Nos. 305-315 (12)	42.50	19.29

See also Nos. 343-354, 378-384A.

1950, Sept. 23 **Photogravure**

No.	Type	Description	Unused	Used
316	A69	3d red brown	50	15

Zagreb International Fair, 1950.

Early Sailing Vessel "Dubrovnik" A70

Partisans with Flag A71

Designs: 3d, Partisans in boat. 5d, Loading freighter. 10d, Transatlantic ship "Zagreb." 12d, Sailboats. 20d, Naval gun and ship.

1950, Nov. 29

No.	Type	Description	Unused	Used
317	A70	2d brown violet	35	30
318	"	3d orange brown	35	20
319	"	5d dull green	35	20
320	"	10d chalky blue	70	45
321	"	12d dark blue	1.75	90
322	"	20d red brown	7.00	3.50
		Nos. 317-322 (6)	10.50	5.55

Issued to honor the Jugoslav navy. Inscriptions on Nos. 318, 320 and 322 are in Cyrillic characters.

1951, Mar. 27 **Engraved**

No.	Type	Description	Unused	Used
323	A71	3d red & red brown	8.25	5.00

Issued to commemorate the 10th anniversary of Jugoslavia's resistance to Nazi Germany.

Stane Rozman A72

Design: 5d, Post-boy during Slovene insurrection.

1951, Apr. 27 **Photogravure**

No.	Type	Description	Unused	Used
324	A72	3d brown red	70	55
325	"	5d dark blue	1.00	95

Issued to commemorate the 10th anniversary of the Slovene insurrection.

Children Painting A73

1951, June 3

No.	Type	Description	Unused	Used
326	A73	3d red	1.75	30

Issued to publicize Children's Day, June 3.

Zika Jovanovich A74

Serbian Revolutionists A75

1951, July 7

No.	Type	Description	Unused	Used
327	A74	3d brown red	75	55
328	A75	5d deep blue	1.25	95

Issued to commemorate the 10th anniversary of the Serbian insurrection.

Sava Kovacevich A76

Kovacevich Leading Revolutionists A77

1951, July 13

No.	Type	Description	Unused	Used
329	A76	3d rose pink	1.00	55
330	A77	5d light blue	1.75	95

Issued to commemorate the 10th anniversary of the Montenegrin insurrection.

Monument to Marko Oreskovich A78

Design: 5d, Monument to wounded.

1951, July 27

No.	Type	Description	Unused	Used
331	A78	3d brown lake	90	55
332	"	5d greenish black	1.35	95

Issued to commemorate the 10th anniversary of the Croatian insurrection.

Sium Bolaj A79

Revolutionists of Bosnia and Herzegovina A80

1951, July 27

No.	Type	Description	Unused	Used
333	A79	3d rose brown	75	30
334	A80	5d blue	1.25	70

Issued to commemorate the 10th anniversary of the revolution in Bosnia and Herzegovina.

Primoz Trubar A81

National Handicrafts A82

Portraits: 12d, Marko Marulic. 20d, Tsar Stefan Duschan.

1951, Sept. 9 **Engraved**

No.	Type	Description	Unused	Used
335	A81	10d slate gray	1.10	65
336	"	12d brown orange	1.10	65
337	"	20d violet	9.00	6.00

Issued to publicize Jugoslav cultural anniversaries. No. 337 is inscribed in Cyrillic.

1951, Sept. 15 **Litho.** *Perf. 11½*

No.	Type	Description	Unused	Used
338	A82	3d multicolored	4.00	50

Zagreb International Fair, 1951.

Mirce Acev A83

Monument at Skoplje A84

1951, Oct. 11

No.	Type	Description	Unused	Used
339	A83	3d deep plum	1.00	55
340	A84	5d indigo	1.75	95

Issued to commemorate the 10th anniversary of the Macedonian insurrection.

Soldier and Emblem A85

Peter P. Nyegosh A86

1951, Dec. 22 **Photo.** *Perf. 12½*

No.	Type	Description	Unused	Used
341	A85	15d deep carmine	85	10

Issued to publicize Army Day, Dec. 22, 1951. See also No. C54.

1951, Nov. 29 **Engraved.**

No.	Type	Description	Unused	Used
342	A86	15d deep claret	3.25	1.00

Issued to commemorate the centenary of the death of Peter Nyegosh. See note after No. 217.

Types of 1950-51.

1951-52 **Engraved.**

Designs: 15d, Gathering sunflowers. 25d, Agriculture. 35d, Construction. 75d, Lumbering. 100d, Metallurgy.

No.	Type	Description	Unused	Used
343	A68	1d gray ('52)	15	3
344	"	2d rose car. ('52)	40	3
345	"	5d orange ('52)	1.50	3
346	"	10d emerald ('52)	4.00	15
347	"	15d rose car. ('52)	8.25	1.25
348	"	20d purple	3.50	5
349	"	25d yel. brown ('52)	4.25	5
350	"	30d blue	2.00	3
351	"	35d red brown ('52)	2.75	10
352	"	50d greenish blue	1.50	5
353	"	75d purple ('52)	2.75	10
354	"	100d sepia ('52)	3.25	30
		Nos. 343-354 (12)	34.30	2.17

Marshal Tito
A87 A88

Design: 50d, Figure facing left.

Perf. 11½

1952, May 25 Photo. Unwmkd.

355 A87 15(d) dark brown 1.00 75
356 A88 28(d) red brown 2.50 2.25
357 A87 50(d) dark gray green 13.00 13.50

60th birthday of Marshal Tito.

Child with Ball—A89

1952, June 1 Litho. *Perf. 12½*

358 A89 15(d) bright rose 7.50 1.00

Issued to publicize Children's Day, June 1.

Girl Gymnast A90 — Split, Dalmatia A91

Designs: 10(d), Runner. 15(d), Swimmer. 28(d), Boxer. 50(d), Basketball. 100(d), Soccer.

1952, July 10 *Perf. 12½*

359 A90 5(d) dark brown & buff, *cream* 1.00 50
360 " 10(d) dark brown & buff, *yellow* 1.00 50
361 " 15(d) indigo & lilac, *pink* 1.25 50
362 " 28(d) dark brown & salmon, *cream* 4.00 2.00
363 " 50(d) dark green & green 8.25 2.50
364 " 100(d) dark brown & blue, *lilac* 20.00 11.50
Nos. 359-364 (6) 35.50 17.50

15th Olympic Games, Helsinki, 1952.
Nos. 360, 362 and 364 are inscribed in Cyrillic characters.
Nos. 359-364 exist imperf. Price $250.

1952, Sept. 10 Lithographed

Designs: 28(d), Naval scene. 50(d), St. Stefan.

365 A91 15(d) deep claret 2.00 50
366 " 28(d) dark brown 3.00 80
367 " 50(d) gray 11.00 8.00

Issued to commemorate the 10th anniversary of the formation of the Jugoslav navy.

Belgrade, 16th Century—A92

1952, Sept. 14 Engr. *Perf. 11½*

368 A92 15d violet brown 18.50 16.00

Issued on the occasion of the first Jugoslav Philatelic Exhibition, Sept. 14-20, 1952. Sold only at the exhibition.

Marching Workers and Congress Flag—A93

1952, Nov. 2 *Perf. 11½*

369 A93 15d red brown 3.25 2.50
370 " 15d dark violet blue 3.25 2.50
371 " 15d dark brown 3.25 2.50
372 " 15d blue green 3.25 2.50

Issued to publicize the 6th Jugoslav Communist Party Congress, Zagreb, 1952.

Nikola Tesla A94 — Woman Pouring Water A95

1953, Jan. 7 Unwmkd.

373 A94 15d brown carmine 90 20
374 " 30d chalky blue 4.00 75

Issued to commemorate the 10th anniversary of the death of Nikola Tesla.

1953, Mar. 24 Litho. *Perf. 11½*

Designs: 30d, Hands holding two birds. 50d, Woman holding Urn.

375 A95 15(d) dk. olive green 1.50 25
376 " 30(d) chalky blue 2.50 50
377 " 50(d) henna brown 14.00 3.50

Issued to honor the United Nations.
See also Nos. RA19 and RAJ16.

Types of 1950-52.

1953-55 Lithographed. *Perf. 12½.*

Designs: 8d, Mining. 17d, Livestock raising.

378 A68 1d dull gray 1.75 10
379 " 2d carmine 5.50 10
380 " 5d orange 8.50 10
381 " 8d blue 4.50 20
382 " 10d yellow green 11.00 10
383 " 12d lt. violet brown 60.00 30
384 " 15d rose red 23.50 12
384A " 17d violet brn. ('55) 6.00 10
Nos. 378-384A (8) 120.75 1.12

Automobile Climbing Mt. Lovcen—A96

Designs: 30d, Motorcycle and auto at Opatija. 50d, Racers leaving Belgrade. 70d, Auto near Mt. Triglav.

1953, May 10 Photo. *Perf. 12½*

385 A96 15d salmon & deep plum 45 10
386 " 30d blue & dark blue 50 15
387 " 50d ochre & choc. 75 25
388 " 70d light blue green & olive green 4.50 1.00

Issued to publicize the International Automobile and Motorcycle Races, 1953.

President Tito A97 — Star and Flag-encircled Globe A98

1953, June 28 Engr. Unwmkd.

389 A97 50d deep purple 8.00 1.50

Issued to commemorate Marshal Tito's election to the presidency, January 14, 1953.

Engraved; Star Typographed

1953, July 25

390 A98 15d gray & green 3.50 3.25

Issued to publicize the 38th Esperanto Congress, Zagreb, July 25-Aug. 1, 1953.

Macedonian Revolutionary A99 — Nicolas Karev A100

1953, Aug. 2 Lithographed

391 A99 15d dk. red brown 1.75 75
392 A100 30d dull green 5.00 3.25

Issued to commemorate the 50th anniversary of the Macedonian insurrection of 1903.

Family A101 — Branko Radicevic A102

1953, Sept. 6 Photogravure

393 A101 15 (d) deep green *42.50* *3.00*

Issued to commemorate the 10th anniversary of the liberation of Istria and the Slovene coast.

1953, Oct. 1 Engraved

394 A102 15 (d) lilac 8.25 4.75

Issued to commemorate the 10th anniversary of the death of Branko Radicevic, poet.

View of Jajce A103

Designs: 30(d), First meeting place. 50(d), Marshal Tito addressing Assembly.

1953, Nov. 29 *Perf. 12½x12*

395 A103 15(d) dark green 1.75 85
396 " 30(d) rose carmine 2.75 2.00
397 " 50(d) dark brown 18.00 18.00

Issued to commemorate the 10th anniversary of the 2nd Assembly of the National Republic of Jugoslavia.

Ground Squirrel A104 — Lammergeier A105

Designs: 5d, Lynx. 10d, Red deer. 15d, Brown bear. 17d, Chamois. 25d, White pelican. 35d, Black beetle. 50d, Bush cricket. 65d, Adriatic lizard. 70d, Salamander. 100d, Trout.

1954, June 30 Photo. *Perf. 11½*

398 A104 2d green, slate & cream 35 10
399 " 5d gray green & dark yellow brown 35 10
400 " 10d gray & dark orange brown 35 10
401 " 15d gray blue & dark orange brown 50 20
402 " 17d brown violet, dark brown & cream 50 20
403 " 25d purple, gray blue & org. yellow 1.00 30
404 A105 30d violet blue & dark brown 1.00 35
405 " 35d brown & blue black 1.00 40
406 " 50d olive green & violet brown 7.50 3.75
407 " 65d lake & gray black 15.00 6.25
408 " 70d blue green & orange brown 13.50 6.25
409 " 100d ultramarine & black brown 25.00 22.50
Nos. 398-409 (12) 66.05 40.50

See also Nos. 497-505.

Ljubljana, 17th Century A106

1954, July 29 Engraved

410 A106 15d violet black, dark green & dark brown 18.50 18.50

Issued on the occasion of the second Jugoslav Philatelic Exhibition, July 29 - Aug. 8, 1954. Sold for 50d, which included admission to the exhibition.

Revolutionary Flag A107

Designs: 30d, Cannon. 50d, Revolutionary seal. 70d, Karageorge.

Engraved and Typographed

1954, Oct. 3 *Perf. 12½*

411 A107 15d red, ochre & dark blue 1.50 30
412 " 30d dark green, salmon buff & chocolate 3.50 60
413 " 50d dark blue, bistre & brown red 5.00 80
414 " 70d chocolate, gray green & dark green 32.50 8.00

Issued to commemorate the 150th anniversary of the first Serbian insurrection.

Vatroslav Lisinski
A108

Portraits: 30d, Andrea Kacic-Miosic. 50d, Jure Vega. 70d, Jovan Jovanovic-Zmai. 100d, Philip Visnic.

1955, Dec. 25 Engraved

415 A108 15d dark green 4.00 1.50
416 " 30d chocolate 4.75 2.75
417 " 50d deep claret 5.50 4.25
418 " 70d indigo 11.00 9.50
419 " 100d purple 37.50 40.00
Nos. 415-419 (5) 62.75 58.00

Scene from "Robinja"
A109

"A Midsummer Night's Dream"
A110

Photogravure.
Glazed Paper

1955 *Perf. 12x11½, 12½* **Unwmkd.**

420 A109 15(d) brown lake 1.50 1.00
421 A110 30(d) dark blue 7.00 5.00

Issued to commemorate the Festival at Dubrovnik.

Dragon Emblem of Ljubljana
A111

1955 Engraved *Perf. 12½*

422 A111 15(d) dark green & brown 6.00 1.25

Issued to publicize the first International Exhibition of Graphic Arts in Ljubljana, July 3–Sept. 3, 1955.

Symbol of Sign Language
A112

Hops
A113

1955, Aug. 23

423 A112 15(d) rose lake 3.00 45

Issued to publicize the 2nd World Congress of Deaf Mutes in Zagreb, Aug. 23–27.

1955, Sept. 24 Photo. *Perf. 11½*

Medicinal Flowers: 10(d), Tobacco. 15(d), Poppy. 17(d), Linden. 25(d), Chamomile. 30(d), Salvia. 50(d), Dog Rose. 70(d), Gentian. 100(d), Adonis.

Flowers in Natural Colors.

424 A113 5(d) peacock green & chestnut 10 6
425 " 10(d) yellow orange, green & red brown 10 6
426 " 15(d) brown & plum 10 6
427 " 17(d) red brown & dark red brown 20 8
428 " 25(d) light & dark ultramarine 20 12
429 " 30(d) gray black & violet 30 18
430 " 50(d) chocolate & dark green 4.50 1.50
431 " 70(d) light & dark violet brown 4.50 1.50
432 " 100(d) light & dark gray 11.50 5.00
Nos. 424-432 (9) 21.50 8.56

"Peace" Statue, New York
A114

Woman and Dove
A115

1955, Oct. 24 Litho. *Perf. 12½*

433 A114 30(d) light blue & black 4.00 2.00

United Nations, 10th anniversary.

1955, Nov. 29 Engraved

434 A115 15(d) dull violet 75 20

Issued to commemorate the tenth anniversary of the "New Jugoslavia."

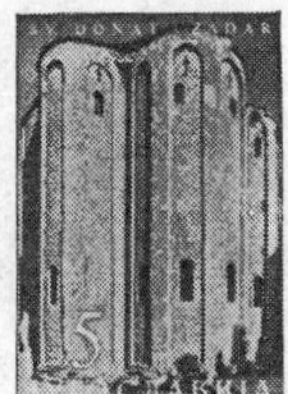

St. Donat, Zadar
A116

Cornice, Cathedral at Sibenik
A117

Jugoslav Art: 10d, Relief of a King, Split. 15d, Griffin, Studenica Monastery. 20d, Figures, Trogir Cathedral. 25d, Fresco, Sopocani Monastery. 30d, Tombstone, Radimlje. 40d, Ciborium, Kotor Cathedral. 50d, St. Martin from Tryptich, Dubrovnik. 70d, Figure, Belec Church. 100d, Rihard Jakopic, self-portrait. 200d, "Peace" Statue, New York.

1956, Mar. 24 Photo. *Perf. 11½*

435 A116 5d blue violet 25 12
436 " 10d slate green 25 12
437 " 15d olive brown 25 12
438 A116 20d brown carmine 50 25
439 " 25d black brown 50 25
440 " 30d deep claret 50 25
441 A117 35d olive green 1.00 40
442 " 40d red brown 1.25 40
443 A116 50d olive brown 1.50 75
444 " 70d dark green 8.50 4.25
445 " 100d dark purple 22.50 17.50
446 " 200d deep blue 47.50 40.00
Nos. 435-446 (12) 84.50 64.41

13th Century Tower, Zagreb
A118

Chalky Paper.

1956, Apr. 20 Engr. *Perf. 11½*

447 A118 15d violet brown, bistre brown & gray 70 20
a. Miniature sheet 6.25 3.50

Issued to publicize the Third Jugoslavia Philatelic Exhibition (JUFIZ III), Zagreb, May 20-27, 1956.

No. 447a contains four copies of No. 447 and measures 111x75mm. It was sold at the exhibition, tipped into a folder, for 75 dinars.

See also No. C56.

Induction Motor
A119

Designs: 15d, Transformer. 30d, Electronic controls. 50d, Nikola Tesla.

Perf. 11½x12½

1956, July 10 Photo. **Unwmkd.**

448 A119 10d olive green 30 10
449 " 15d brown red 40 25
450 " 30d blue 85 45
451 " 50d dull purple 3.25 1.35

Issued to commemorate the centenary of the birth of Nikola Tesla, inventor.

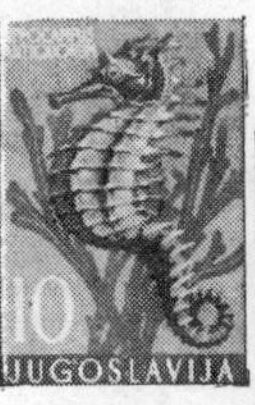

Sea Horse
A120

Paper Nautilus
A121

Designs: 20d, European rock lobster. 25d, "Sea Prince." 30d, Sea perch. 35d, Red mullet. 50d, Scorpion fish. 70d, Wrasse. 100d, Dory.

Granite Paper

1956, Sept. 10 *Perf. 11½*

Animals in natural colors,

452 A120 10d bright green 15 7
453 A121 15d ultra. & black 15 7
454 " 20d deep blue 20 7
455 " 25d violet blue 50 9
456 " 30d bright greenish blue 55 9
457 " 35d dk. blue green 85 12
458 " 50d indigo 2.75 1.10
459 " 70d slate green 2.75 1.10
460 " 100d dark blue 16.00 6.00
Nos. 452-460 (9) 23.90 8.71

Nos. 453, 455, 457 and 459 are inscribed in Cyrillic characters.

Runner
A122

Centaury
A123

Designs: 15d, Paddling kayak. 20d, Skiing. 30d, Swimming. 35d, Soccer. 50d, Water polo. 70d, Table tennis. 100d, Sharpshooting.

1956, Oct. 24 Litho. *Perf. 12½*

Design and Inscription in Bistre.

461 A122 10d dark carmine 15 3
462 " 15d dark blue 15 3
463 " 20d ultramarine 35 7
464 " 30d olive green 35 7
465 " 35d dark brown 50 7
466 " 50d green 50 15
467 " 70d brown violet 5.00 2.75
468 " 100d dark red 7.00 4.75
Nos. 461-468 (8) 14.00 7.92

Issued to commemorate the 16th Olympic Games at Melbourne, Nov. 22-Dec. 8, 1956.

Nos. 462, 464, 466 and 468 have Latin characters at the top and Cyrillic characters at the bottom.

Granite Paper.

1957, May 25 Photo. *Perf. 11½*

Medicinal Plants: 15d, Belladonna. 20d, Autumn crocus. 25d, Marsh mallow. 30d, Valerian. 35d, Woolly Foxglove. 50d, Aspidium. 70d, Green Winged Orchid. 100d, Pyrethrum.

Flowers in Natural Colors.

469 A123 10d dk. blue & green 15 4
470 " 15d violet 15 4
471 " 20d light olive green & brown 15 4
472 " 25d deep claret & dark blue 25 6
473 " 30d lilac rose & claret 25 8
474 " 35d dark gray & dull purple 30 10
475 " 50d deep green & chocolate 2.00 55
476 " 70d pale brown & green 2.25 55
477 " 100d gray & brown 8.50 4.00
Nos. 469-477 (9) 14.00 5.46

See also Nos. 538-546, 597-605, 689-694, 772-777.

Hand Holding Factory
A124

1957, June 25 Engr. *Perf. 12½*

478 A124 15d dk. carmine rose 30 8
479 " 30d violet blue 1.50 30

Issued to publicize the Congress of Workers' Councils, Belgrade, June 25.

No. 479 inscribed in Cyrillic characters.

Gymnasts
A125

Various Gymnastic Poses.

1957, July 1 Photogravure

480 A125 10d olive green & black 20 5
481 " 15d brn. red & blk. 20 5

482 A125 30d Prussian blue & black 50 15
483 " 50d brown & black 4.00 1.35

Issued to publicize the Second Gymnastic Meet, Zagreb, July 10-14.

Montenegro
A126

National Costumes: 15d, Macedonia. 30d, Croatia. 50d, Serbia. 70d, Bosnia and Herzegovina. 100d, Slovenia. (50d, 70d and 100d arranged vertically.)

Background in Bistre Brown.

1957, Sept. 24 Typo. *Perf. 12½*

484 A126 10d dark brown, ultramarine & red 10 3
485 " 15d dark brown, black & red 10 3
486 " 30d dark brown, green & red 10 3
487 " 50d dk. brn. & green 40 25
488 " 70d dk. brn. & blk. 1.00 45
489 " 100d dark brown, green & red 8.00 4.25
Nos. 484-489 (6) 9.70 5.04

Revolutionists
A127

Simon Gregorcic
A128

Engraved and Lithographed.

1957, Nov. 7 *Perf. 11½x12½*

490 A127 15d ochre & red 75 10

Issued to commemorate the 40th anniversary of the Russian Revolution.

1957, Dec. 3 Engr. *Perf. 12½*

Portraits: 30d, Anton Linhart, dramatist and historian. 50d, Oton Kucera, physicist. 70d, Stevan Mokranjac, composer. 100d, Jovan Sterija Popovic, writer.

491 A128 15d sepia 25 5
492 " 30d indigo 35 12
493 " 50d reddish brown 60 12
494 " 70d dull violet 7.00 2.75
495 " 100d olive green 25.00 18.00
Nos. 491-495 (5) 33.20 21.04

Issued to honor famous men of Jugoslavia.

"Young Man on Fire"
A129

Stylized Bird
A130

1958, Apr. 22 Photogravure

496 A129 15d deep plum 60 10

Issued to commemorate the seventh congress of the Union of Jugoslav Communists, Ljubljana, Apr. 22.

Types of 1954.

Game Birds: 10d, Mallard. 15d, Capercaillie. 20d, Ring-necked pheasant. 25d, Coot. 30d, Water rail. 35d, Great bustard. 50d, Rock partridge. 70d, Woodcock. 100d, Eurasian crane.

Granite Paper.

1958, May 25 *Perf. 11½*

Birds in Natural Colors

497 A104 10d brown 15 4
498 A104 15d dark car. rose 15 4
499 " 20d black violet 15 4
500 A105 25d yellow green 30 10
501 A104 30d blue green 35 10
502 A105 35d dark olive bistre 40 15
503 " 50d lilac 1.25 50
504 A104 70d bright blue 2.25 50
505 A105 100d chestnut brn. 8.75 5.00
Nos. 497-505 (9) 13.75 6.47

1958, June 14 Engr. *Perf. 12½*

506 A130 15d bluish black 85 15

Issued to commemorate the opening of the Postal Museum in Belgrade.

Flag and Laurel
A131

1958, July 1 Unwmkd.

507 A131 15d brown carmine 60 10

Issued to commemorate the 15th anniversary of the victory over the Germans at Sutjeska, Bosnia.

Onufrio Well, Dubrovnik—A132

1958, Aug. 10 Litho. *Perf. 12½*

508 A132 15d black & brown 85 15

Issued to commemorate the 450th anniversary of the birth of Marin Drzic, dramatist.

Sisak Steel Works
A133

Titograd Hotel and Open-Air Theater
A134

Industrial Progress Designs: 2d, Crude oil production. 5d, Shipbuilding. 10d, Sisak steel works. 15d, Jablanica hydroelectric works. 17d, Lumber industry. 25d, Overpass, Zagreb-Ljubljana highway. 30d, Litostroy turbine factory. 35d, Lukavac coke plant. 50d, Bridge at Skoplje. 70d, Railroad station, Sarajevo. 100d, Triple bridge, Ljubljana. 200d, Mestrovic station, Zagreb. 500d, Parliament, Belgrade.

Coil stamps

1958 Typo. *Perf. 12½ Horiz.*

509 A133 10d green 7.50 3.00
510 " 15d orange verm. 6.00 3.00

Engraved.

Perf. 12½

511 A133 2d olive 3 3
512 " 5d brown red 3 3
513 " 10d green 10 4
514 " 15d orange verm. 20 4
515 " 17d deep claret 10 3
516 " 25d slate 20 3
517 " 30d blue black 15 3
518 " 35d rose red 15 3
519 A134 40d carmine rose 30 3
520 " 50d bright blue 40 3
521 " 70d orange verm. 70 3
522 " 100d green 80 4
523 " 200d red brown 1.75 8
524 " 500d intense blue 4.00 25
Nos. 509-524 (16) 22.41 6.72

See also Nos. 555-562, 627-645, 786-789, 830-840.

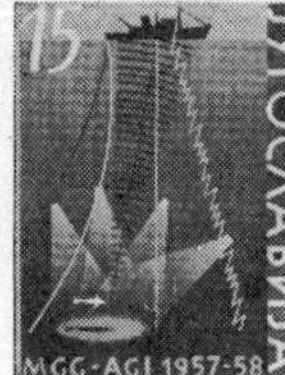

Ocean Exploration
A135

1958, Oct. 24 Unwmkd.

525 A135 15d brown violet 85 35

Issued for the International Geophysical Year, 1957-58. See also No. C58.

White and Black Hands Holding Scales
A136

1958, Dec. 10 *Perf. 12½*

526 A136 30d steel blue 1.60 1.35

Issued to commemorate the tenth anniversary of the signing of the Universal Declaration of Human Rights.

Dubrovnik
A137

Designs: No. 528, Bled. No. 529, Postojna grotto. No. 530, Ohrid. No. 531, Opatija. No. 532, Plitvice National Park. No. 533, Split. No. 534, Sveti Stefan. No. 535, Exhibition Hall, Belgrade.

1959, Feb. 16 Litho. *Perf. 12½*

527 A137 10d crimson rose & citron 7 3
528 " 10d light green & light violet blue 7 3
529 " 15d greenish blue & purple 8 3
530 " 15d grn. & brt. blue 8 3
531 " 20d light green & greenish blue 15 3
532 " 20d olive bistre & bright green 15 3
533 " 30d yellow orange & purple 30 5
534 " 30d light violet blue & gray olive 30 5
535 " 70d gray & greenish blue 3.25 1.60
Nos. 527-535 (9) 4.45 1.88

Issued to publicize Jugoslavian tourist attractions. Nos. 527, 530, 532 and 534 are inscribed in Cyrillic characters. See also Nos. 650-658, 695-700.

Red Flags
A138

1959, Apr. 20 *Perf. 12½* Unwmkd.

536 A138 20d multicolored 25 5

Issued to commemorate the 40th anniversary of the Jugoslav Communist Party.

Dubrovnik, 15th Century
A139

1959, May 24 Engr. *Perf. 11½*

537 A139 20d yel. grn., dk. grn. & blue 1.85 1.65

Issued to commemorate the Fourth Jugoslavia Philatelic Exhibition (JUFIZ IV), Dubrovnik.

Type of 1957.

Medicinal Plants: 10d, Lavender. 15d, Black Alder. 20d, Scopolia. 25d, Monkshood. 30d, Bilberry. 35d, Juniper. 50d, Primrose. 70d, Pomegranate. 100d, Jimson weed.

Granite Paper.

1959, May 25 Photogravure

Flowers in Natural Colors.

538 A123 10d light blue & dark blue 8 4
539 " 15d bright yellow & carmine 8 4
540 " 20d dark olive bistre & maroon 8 4
541 " 25d apple green & dark purple 15 8
542 " 30d pink & dark blue 20 8
543 " 35d bistre brown & violet blue 25 15
544 " 50d brown & green 1.25 35
545 " 70d yellow & ochre 1.75 60
546 " 100d light brown & brown 5.50 3.25
Nos. 538-546 (9) 9.34 4.63

Tug of War
A140

Sports: 15d, High jump and runners. 20d, Ring and parallel bar exercises. 35d, Women gymnasts. 40d, Sailors doing gymnastics. 55d, Field ball and basketball. 80d, Swimming. 100d, Festival emblem (vert.).

1959, June 26 Litho. *Perf. 12½*

547 A140 10d dark slate green & ochre 4 3
548 " 15d violet blue & sepia 4 3
549 " 20d olive bistre & dull lilac 4 3
550 " 35d deep claret & gray 15 5
551 " 40d violet & gray 15 10
552 " 55d slate green & olive bistre 20 10
553 " 80d indigo & olive 1.35 60
554 " 100d purple & bistre 4.50 2.25
Nos. 547-554 (8) 6.47 3.19

Issued to publicize the Physical Culture Festival.

Types of 1958; Designs as before.

Designs: 8d, Lumber industry. 15d, Overpass, Zagreb-Ljubljana highway. 20d, Jablanica hydroelectric works. 40d, Titograd Hotel. 55d, Bridge at Skoplje. 80d, Railroad Station, Sarajevo.

1959 Typographed.

Coil Stamps

Perf. 12½ Horizontally

555 A133 15d green 2.25 65
556 " 20d org. vermilion 2.25 65

Engraved.

Perf. 12½

557 A133 8d deep claret 20 3
558 " 15d green 30 3
559 " 20d org. vermilion 50 3
560 A134 40d bright blue 1.10 3
561 " 55d carmine rose 2.00 3
562 " 80d org. vermilion 3.25 3
Nos. 555-562 (8) 11.85 1.48

JAPAN...

a fine album of historical interest and oriental beauty

For the convenience of collectors, the White Ace Japan Album is available in sections. This way you can buy the part for which you have the most stamps, then purchase the other section later. Since White Ace Albums are looseleaf style, they have this added flexibility feature. And to keep your album always current, supplements are issued annually. The binder, gold-stamped in gold leaf, is jumbo size with 1¼" rings for added capacity. Sheet lifters, standard equipment in all White Ace Binders, prevent damage to pages.

Wondering why we suggest Japan, why we have created a White Ace Album for this far-off country? Because her stamps are interesting and beautiful, because there is enough variety to make collecting challenging, but not too much, to make it frustrating . . . and it costs so little to make a collection of them. In the past decade many collectors have discovered Japan as a new collecting field. As a matter of fact, you can say that this album has been produced by popular demand.

So, . . . open up new philatelic vistas. Try your hand at Japan . . . with White Ace, philately's premium album.

Part One Pages (1871-1939)	$4.50
Part Two Pages (1940-1954)	8.75
Part Three Pages (1955-1969)	8.25
Part Four Pages (1970-1978).........	10.50
Matching Border Blanks (Pack of 10)................................	1.60
Deluxe Gold-Stamped Binder	7.50

White Ace

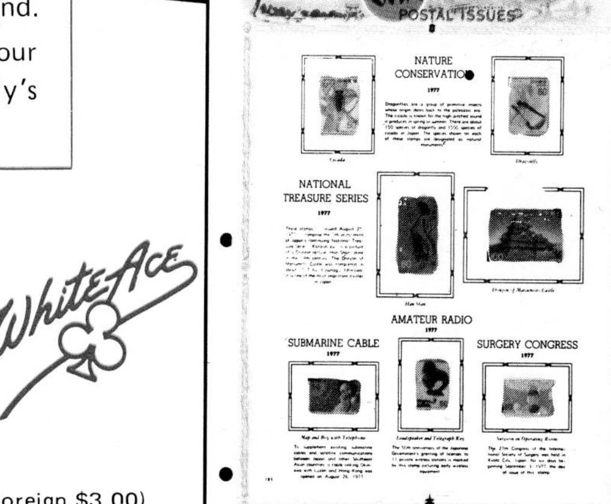

On Mail Orders, Please add $1.25 for Packing (Canada & Foreign $3.00)

A PRODUCT OF

THE WASHINGTON PRESS

MAPLEWOOD, NEW JERSEY 07040

Fair Emblem A141 — Athletics A142

1959, Sept. 5 Litho. Unwmkd.

563 A141 20d light violet bl. & black 1.10 25

50th International Fair at Zagreb.

1960, Apr. 25 *Perf. 12½*

Sports: 20d, Swimming. 30d, Skiing. 35d, Wrestling. 40d, Bicycling. 55d, Yachting. 80d, Horseback riding. 100d, Fencing.

564 A142 15d orange, gray & yellow 6 3
565 " 20d light violet, blue & brown 8 3
566 " 30d gray brown & ultramarine 11 3
567 " 35d light brown, lilac & gray 25 15
568 " 40d light green, olive green & gray 28 18
569 " 55d gray, green & blue gray 45 22
570 " 80d gray, carmine & ochre 1.20 45
571 " 100d gray, violet & ochre 1.45 75
Nos. 564-571 (8) 3.88 1.84

17th Olympic Games.

Hedgehog—A143

Animals: 20d, Red squirrel. 25d, Pine marten. 30d, Hare. 35d, Red fox. 40d, Badger. 55d, Wolf. 80d, Roe deer. 100d, Wild bear.

1960, May 25 Photo. *Perf. 12x11½*

Animals in Natural Colors

572 A143 15d bluish black 10 3
573 " 20d olive 10 3
574 " 25d Prus. green 10 4
575 " 30d slate green 15 10
576 " 35d sepia 20 12
577 " 40d maroon 35 12
578 " 55d ultramarine 50 35
579 " 80d violet blue 60 40
580 " 100d henna brown 2.40 1.30
Nos. 572-580 (9) 4.50 2.49

"Jugoslavia" in Latin letters on Nos. 573, 575, 577, 579.

See also Nos. 663-671.

Lenin A144 — Atomic Accelerator A145

1960, June 22 Engr. *Perf. 12½*

581 A144 20d dark green & slate green 15 10

90th anniversary of the birth of Lenin.

1960, Aug. 23 Unwmkd.

Designs: 20d, Generator. 40d, Nuclear reactor.

582 A145 15d green 10 3
583 " 20d maroon 15 3
584 " 40d violet blue 40 15

Nuclear energy exposition, Belgrade.

Serbian National Theater, Novi Sad A146 — Ivan Cankar, Writer A147

Designs: 20d, Woman from Croatian play. 40d, Edward Rusijan and early plane. 55d, Symbolic hand holding fruit. 80d, Atom and U.N. emblem.

1960, Oct. 24 *Perf. 12½*

585 A146 15d gray black 4 3
586 " 20d brown 6 3
587 " 40d dark gray blue 12 3
588 " 55d dull claret 30 10
589 " 80d dark green 50 13
Nos. 585-589 (5) 1.02 32

Issued to commemorate the following: Centenary of the Serbian National Theater, Novi Sad (No. 585). Centenary of the Croatian National Theater, Zagreb (No. 586). 50th anniversary of the first flight in Jugoslavia (No. 587). 15th anniversary of the Jugoslav Republic (No. 588). 15th anniversary of the United Nations (No. 589).

1960, Dec. 24 Engr. *Perf. 12½*

Portraits: 20d, Silvije Strahimir Kranjcevic, poet. 40d, Paja Jovanovic, painter. 55d, Dura Jaksic, writer and painter. 80d, Mihajlo Pupin, electro-technician. 100d, Ruder Boskovic, mathematician.

590 A147 15d dark green 5 3
591 " 20d henna brown 8 3
592 " 40d olive bistre 12 5
593 " 55d magenta 18 5
594 " 80d dark blue 55 12
595 " 100d Prussian blue 1.00 50
Nos. 590-595 (6) 1.98 78

Issued to honor famous Jugoslavs.

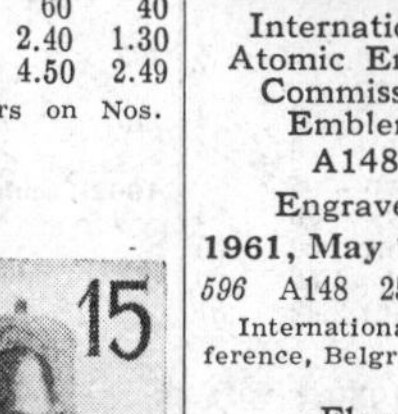

International Atomic Energy Commission Emblem A148 — Victims' Monument, Kragujevac A149

Engraved and Lithographed

1961, May 15 *Perf. 12½*

596 A148 25d multicolored 20 4

International Nuclear Electronic Conference, Belgrade.

Flower Type of 1957.

Medicinal plants: 10d, Yellow foxglove. 15d, Marjoram. 20d, Hyssop. 25d, Scarlet haw. 40d, Rose mallow. 50d, Soapwort. 60d, Clary. 80d, Blackthorn. 100d, Marigold.

Granite Paper

1961, May 25 Photo. *Perf. 11½*

Flowers in Natural Colors.

597 A123 10d light blue & greenish blue 4 3
598 " 15d gray & chestnut 5 3
599 " 20d buff & green 6 4
600 A123 25d lt. vio. & violet 9 5
601 " 40d lt. ultramarine & ultramarine 13 6
602 " 50d lt. blue & blue 22 8
603 " 60d beige & dark carmine rose 35 15
604 " 80d lt. green & grn. 65 25
605 " 100d reddish brown & chocolate 1.25 70
Nos. 597-605 (9) 2.84 1.39

1961, July 3 *Perf. 12x12½*

Granite Paper

Monuments: 15d, Stevan Filipovic, Valjevo. 20d, Relief from Insurrection, Bozansko Grahovo. 60d, Victory, Nova Gradiska. 100d, Marshall Tito, Titovo Uzice.

Gold Frames and Inscriptions

606 A149 15d crimson & brown 6 5
607 " 20d brown & olive bistre 8 5
608 " 25d blue green & gray olive 12 5
609 " 60d violet 32 15
610 " 100d indigo & black 65 40
Nos. 606-610 (5) 1.23 70

Souvenir Sheet

Imperf.

611 A149 500d indigo & black 40.00 35.00

Issued to commemorate the 20th anniversary of the National Insurrection. No. 611 contains one stamp with gray margin, indigo inscription and gold ornaments. Size: 64x82mm.

Men of Five Races—A150

National Assembly Building, Belgrade—A151

Lithographed

1961, Sept. 1 *Perf. 11½* Unwmkd.

613 A150 25d brown 15 5

Engraved

614 A151 50d blue green 30 6

Miniature Sheet

Imperf.

615 A150 1000d claret 10.00 7.50

Issued to commemorate the conference of Non-aligned Nations, Belgrade, Sept. 1961. See also Nos. C59-C60.

No. 615 has gold border and measures 72x65mm.

St. Clement, 14th Century Wood Sculpture—A152

1961, Sept. 10 Engr. *Perf. 12½*

616 A152 25d sepia & olive 20 4

Issued to publicize the 12th International Congress for Byzantine Studies.

Serbian Women—A153

Regional Costumes: 25d, Montenegro. 30d, Bosnia and Herzegovina. 50d, Macedonia. 65d, Croatia. 100d, Slovenia.

1961, Nov. 28 Lithographed

617 A153 15d beige, brown & red 8 6
618 " 25d beige, red brown & black 10 6
619 " 30d beige, brown & dk. red 12 6
620 " 50d multicolored 20 10
621 " 65d brown, red & yellow 25 16
622 " 100d multicolored 1.40 75
Nos. 617-622 (6) 2.15 1.19

Luka Vukalovic A154 — Hands with Flower and Rifle A155

1961, Dec. 15 Engraved

623 A154 25d slate blue 20 3

Centenary of Herzegovina insurrection.

1961, Dec. 22

624 A155 25d red & vio. blue 15 3

20th anniversary of Jugoslav army.

Miladinov Brothers—A156

1961, Dec. 25 Lithographed

625 A156 25d buff & claret 20 4

Issued to commemorate the centenary of the Macedonian folksong "Koder," and to honor Dimitri and Konstantin Miladinov, brothers who collected and published folksongs. Monument is at Struga.

Types of 1958;

Designs as Before.

Designs: 5d, Shipbuilding. 8d, Lumber industry. 10d, Sisak steel works. 15d, Overpass. 20d, Jablanica hydroelectric works. 25d, Cable factory, Svetozarevo. 30d, Litostroy turbine factory. 40d, Lukavac coke plant. 50d, Zenica steel works. 65d, Sevojno copper works. 100d, Crude oil production. 150d, Titograd hotel. 200d, Bridge, Skoplje. 300d, Railroad station, Sarajevo. 500d, Triple bridge, Ljubljana. 1000d, Mestrovic station, Zagreb. 2000d, Parliament, Belgrade.

Coil Stamps

Typographed

Perf. 12½ Horizontally

1961-62 Unwmkd.

627 A133 10d dk. red brn. 2.75 75
628 " 15d emerald 3.75 65

Engraved

Perf. 12½

629 A133 5d dull orange 3 3
630 " 8d gray 3 3
631 " 10d dk. red brown 3 3
632 " 15d emerald 4 3

No.	Type	Description	Unused	Used
633	A133	20d violet blue	5	3
634	"	25d vermilion	6	3
635	"	30d red brown	10	3
636	"	40d dp. claret ('62)	12	3
637	"	50d gray blue	20	3
638	"	65d green	20	3
639	"	100d yellow olive	2.50	3
640	A134	150d carmine ('62)	70	15
641	"	200d slate green ('62)	60	3
642	"	300d olive ('62)	1.00	5
643	"	500d dull violet	1.50	4
644	"	1000d bistre brown	3.50	30
645	"	2000d claret	6.00	50
		Nos. 627-645 (19)	23.16	2.80

Isis of Kalabsha

A157

Joy of Motherhood by Frano Krsinic

A158

Design: 50d, Ramses II, Abu Simbel.

1962, Apr. 7 Engraved *Perf. 12½*

No.	Type	Description	Unused	Used
646	A157	25d greenish black, *cream*	25	7
647	"	50d brown, *buff*	40	10

Issued to commemorate the 15th anniversary (in 1961) of UNESCO (United Nations Educational and Scientific Organization.)

1962, Apr. 7

No.	Type	Description	Unused	Used
648	A158	50d black, *cream*	40	10

Issued to commemorate the 15th anniversary (in 1961) of UNICEF (United Nations International Childrens Emergency Fund).

Anopheles Mosquito

A159

1962, Apr. 7

No.	Type	Description	Unused	Used
649	A159	50d black, *gray*	35	10

Issued for the World Health Organization drive to eradicate malaria.

Scenic Type of 1959

Designs: No. 650, Portoroz. No. 651, Jajce. No. 652, Zadar. No. 653, Popova Sapka. No. 654, Hvar. No. 655, Bay of Kotor. No. 656, Danube, Iron Gate. No. 657, Rab. No. 658, Zagreb.

1962, Apr. 24 Lithographed

No.	Type	Description	Unused	Used
650	A137	15d olive & chalky blue	15	3
651	"	15d blue green & bistre	15	3
652	"	25d blue & red brown	15	3
653	"	25d dk. blue & pale blue	15	3
654	"	30d blue & brown orange	30	5
655	"	30d gray & chalky blue	30	5
656	"	50d olive & greenish blue	60	5
657	"	50d blue & olive	60	5
658	"	100d dark green & gray blue	5.50	75
		Nos. 650-658 (9)	7.90	1.07

Issued to publicize Jugoslavian tourist attractions. Nos. 651, 653, 655 and 656 are inscribed in Cyrillic characters.

Marshal Tito, by Augustincic

A160

Pole Vault

A161

Design: 50d, 200d, Sideview of bust by Antun Augustincic.

Engraved

1962, May 25 *Perf. 12½* Unwmkd.

No.	Type	Description	Unused	Used
659	A160	25d dark green	10	3
660	"	50d dark brown	25	5
661	"	100d dark blue	70	30
662	"	200d greenish blk.	1.70	95
		a. Souvenir sheet of 4	5.00	5.00

70th birthday of Pres. Tito (Josip Broz).

No. 662a contains one each of Nos. 659-662, imperf., with dark green marginal inscription. Size: 76x104mm.

Animal Type of 1960

Designs: 15d, Crested newt. 20d, Fire salamander. 25d, Yellow-bellied toad. 30d, Pond frog. 50d, Pond turtle. 65d, Lizard. 100d, Emerald lizard. 150d, Leopard snake. 200, European viper (adder).

1962, June 8 Photo. *Perf. 12x11½*

Animals in Natural Colors

No.	Type	Description	Unused	Used
663	A143	15d green	10	3
664	"	20d purple	10	3
665	"	25d chocolate	10	3
666	"	30d violet blue	20	5
667	"	50d dark red	20	10
668	"	65d bright green	20	10
669	"	100d black	40	30
670	"	150d brown	1.30	75
671	"	200d carmine rose	3.00	1.95
		Nos. 663-671 (9)	5.60	3.34

Latin inscription on Nos. 666-669.

1962, July 10 Litho. *Perf. 12½*

Sports: 25d, Woman discus thrower (horiz.). 30d, Long distance runners. 50d, Javelin thrower (horiz.). 65d, Shot put. 100d, Women runners (horiz.). 150d, Hop, step and jump. 200d, High jump (horiz.).

Athletes in Black.

No.	Type	Description	Unused	Used
672	A161	15d blue	5	3
673	"	25d magenta	5	3
674	"	30d emerald	5	3
675	"	50d red	15	5
676	"	65d violet blue	15	5
677	"	100d green	35	20
678	"	150d orange	60	30
679	"	200d orange brown	1.40	70
		Nos. 672-679 (8)	2.80	1.39

Issued to publicize the 7th European Athletic Championships, Belgrade, Sept. 12-16. See also No. C61.

Child at Play

A162

Lithographed and Engraved

1962, Oct. 1 *Perf. 12½* Unwmkd.

No.	Type	Description	Unused	Used
680	A162	25d red & black	25	3

Issued for Children's Week.

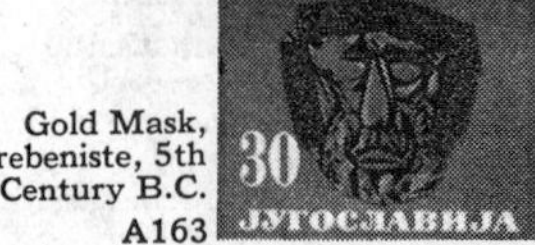

Gold Mask, Trebeniste, 5th Century B.C.

A163

Bathing the Infant Christ, Fresco, Decani Monastery

A164

Jugoslav Art Treasures: 25d, Horseman and bird, bronze vase (5th cent. B.C.). 50d, God Kairos, marble relief. 65d, "The Pigeons of Nerezi," fresco (12th cent.). 150d, Archangel Gabriel, icon (14th cent.).

1962, Nov. 28 Photogravure

No.	Type	Description	Unused	Used
681	A163	25d Prussian blue, black & gold	10	6
682	"	30d gold, sapphire & black	12	6
683	A164	50d dark green, brown & gold	20	6
684	"	65d multicolored	45	20
685	"	100d "	55	25
686	A163	150d "	2.25	2.15
		Nos. 681-686 (6)	3.67	2.78

Latin letters on Nos. 681, 683-684, 686.

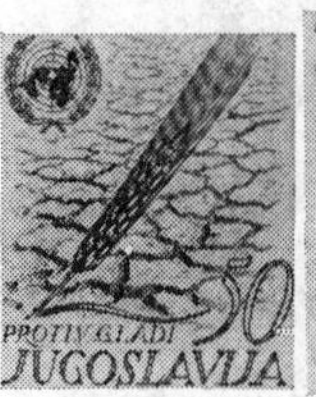

Parched Earth and Wheat

A165

Dr. Andrija Mohorovicic and U.N. Emblem

A166

1963, Mar. 21 Engr. *Perf. 12½*

No.	Type	Description	Unused	Used
687	A165	50d dark brown, *tan*	30	8

Issued for the "Freedom from Hunger" campaign of the U.N. Food and Agriculture Organization.

1963, March 23 Unwmkd.

No.	Type	Description	Unused	Used
688	A166	50d dark blue, *gray*	30	8

Issued to commemorate the United Nations Third World Meteorological Day, March 23. Dr. Andrija Mohorovicic (1857-1936) was director of the Zagreb meteorological observatory.

Flower Type of 1957

Medicinal Plants: 15d, Lily of the valley. 25d, Iris. 30d, Bistort. 50d, Henbane. 65d, St. John's wort. 100d, Caraway.

1963, May 25 Photo. *Perf. 11½*

Flowers in Natural Colors; Granite Paper

No.	Type	Description	Unused	Used
689	A123	15d gray grn. & grn.	8	4
690	"	25d lt. blue, ultra. & purple	8	4
691	"	30d gray & black	8	4
692	"	50d reddish brown & red brown	18	4
693	"	65d pale brn. & brn.	50	15
694	"	100d slate & black	1.50	50
		Nos. 689-694 (6)	2.42	81

Scenic Type of 1959

Designs: 15d, Pula. 25d, Vrnjacka Banja. 30d, Crikvenica. 50d, Korcula. 65d, Durmitor mountain. 100d, Ljubljana.

1963, June 6 Litho. *Perf. 12½*

No.	Type	Description	Unused	Used
695	A137	15d multicolored	5	3
696	"	25d "	5	3
697	"	30d "	5	3
698	"	50d "	20	10
699	"	65d "	30	10
700	"	100d "	80	35
		Nos. 695-700 (6)	1.45	64

Issued to publicize Jugoslavian tourist attractions. Nos. 696 and 699 are inscribed in Cyrillic characters.

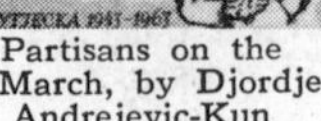

Partisans on the March, by Djordje Andrejevic-Kun

A167

Sutjeska (Gorge)

A168

Design: No. 702A, As 15d, but inscribed "Vis 1944-1964." 50d, Partisans in battle.

Engraved and Lithographed; Lithographed (No. 702)

1963-64 *Perf. 12½, 11½*

No.	Type	Description	Unused	Used
701	A167	15d gray & dark slate green	5	3
702	A168	25d dk. slate green	5	3
702A	A167	25d gray & dark car. rose ('64)	15	3
703	"	50d tan & purple	25	6

Issued to commemorate (Nos. 701, 702-703) the 20th anniversary of the Partisan Battle of Sutjeska; (No. 702A) the 20th anniversary of the arrival of the Jugoslav General Staff on the island of Vis.

Gymnast on Vaulting Horse

A169

Mother, by Ivan Meštrović

A170

Gymnasts: 50d, Parallel bars. 100d, Rings.

1963, July 6 Litho. *Perf. 12½*

No.	Type	Description	Unused	Used
704	A169	25d olive grn. & blk.	10	5
705	"	50d brt. bl. & black	20	15
706	"	100d olive bister & black	75	60

5th Gymnastics Europa Prize.

1963, Sept. 28 Engraved

Sculptures by Meštrović: 50d, "Reminiscences" (woman). 65d, Head of Kraljević Marko. 100d, Indian on Horseback.

No.	Type	Description	Unused	Used
707	A170	25d brown, *buff*	25	12
708	"	50d slate green, *greenish*	30	15
709	"	65d greenish black, *grayish*	85	50
710	"	100d black, *grayish*	1.50	1.00

Issued to honor Ivan Meštrović (1883-1962), sculptor.

Children with Toys

A171

1963, Oct. 5 Lithographed

No.	Type	Description	Unused	Used
711	A171	25d multicolored	25	8

Issued for Children's Week.

Soldier with Gun and Flag
A172

Lithographed and Engraved

1963, Oct. 20 *Perf. 12½* **Unwmkd.**

712	A172	25d verm., tan & gold	15	6

Issued to commemorate the 20th anniversary of the founding of the Jugoslavian Democratic Federation.

Relief from Tombstone, Herzegovina
A173

Dositej Obradović
A174

Art through the centuries: 30d, Horseback trio, Split Cathedral (horiz.). 50d, King and queen on horseback, Beram Church, Istria (horiz.). 65d, Archangel Michael, Dominican monastery, Dubrovnik. 100d, Man pouring water, fountain, Ljubljana. 150d, Archbishop Eufrasie, mosaic, Porec Basilica, Istria.

1963, Nov. 29 **Photogravure**

713	A173	25d olive, gold, black & gray	10	4
714	"	30d gold, black, carmine & vio.	10	4
715	"	50d pale green, gold, black, red & blue	15	4
716	"	65d green, gold, black & red	35	10
717	"	100d dark blue, gold & black	55	25
718	"	150d gold, black, vio., brn. & tan	1.60	1.40
		Nos. 713-718 (6)	2.85	1.87

Issued for the Day of the Republic.

1963, Dec. 10 **Engraved**

Portraits: 30d, Vuk Stefanović Karadžić, reformer of Serbian language. 50d, Franc Miklošič, Slovenian philologist. 65d, Ljudevit Gaj, reformer of Croatian language. 100d, Peter Petrovich Nyegosh, Montenegrin prince, bishop and poet.

Variously Toned Paper

719	A174	25d black	12	8
720	"	30d "	12	8
721	"	50d "	12	8
722	"	65d "	60	45
723	"	100d "	80	55
		Nos. 719-723 (5)	1.76	1.24

Issued to honor famous Jugoslavian men.

Vanessa Io
A175

Fireman Rescuing Child
A176

Designs (Butterflies and Moths): 30d, Vanessa antiopa. 40d, Daphnis nerii. 50d, Parnassius apollo. 150d, Saturnia pyri. 200d, Papilio machaon.

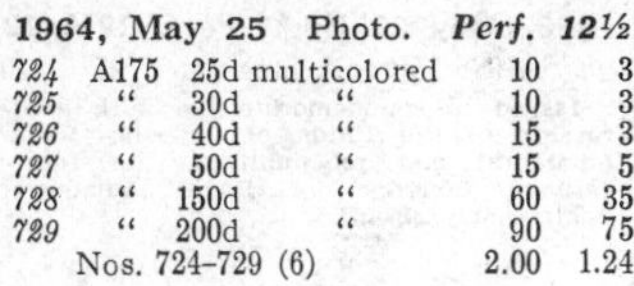

1964, May 25 Photo. *Perf. 12½*

724	A175	25d multicolored	10	3
725	"	30d "	10	3
726	"	40d "	15	3
727	"	50d "	15	5
728	"	150d "	60	35
729	"	200d "	90	75
		Nos. 724-729 (6)	2.00	1.24

1964, June 14 **Lithographed**

730	A176	25d red & black	25	3

Centenary of voluntary firemen.

Runner
A177

Designs: 30d, Boxing. 40d, Rowing. 50d, Basketball. 150d, Soccer. 200d, Water polo.

1964, July 1 *Perf. 12½* **Unwmkd.**

Gray Background

731	A177	25d black & yellow	5	3
732	"	30d black & violet	5	3
733	"	40d black & emerald	10	3
734	"	50d black & verm.	15	3
735	"	150d black & yellow	65	30
736	"	200d black & blue	90	70
		Nos. 731-736 (6)	1.90	1.12

18th Olympic Games, Tokyo, Oct. 10–25.

U.N. Flag over Scaffolding
A178

Design: 25d, Upheaval of the earth and scaffolding.

1964, July 26 **Engraved**

737	A178	25d red brown	10	6
738	"	50d blue	25	8

Issued to commemorate the first anniversary of the earthquake at Skoplje and the international assistance.

Serbian Women
A179

Friedrich Engels
A180

Regional Costumes: 30d, Slovenia. 40d, Bosnia and Herzegovina. 50d, Croatia. 150d, Macedonia. 200d, Montenegro.

1964, Aug. 5 **Lithographed**

Costumes Multicolored

740	A179	25d violet & brown	10	3
741	"	30d slate & green	10	3
742	"	40d reddish brown & black	15	3
743	"	50d blue & black	20	3
744	"	150d dull grn. & sepia	55	30
745	"	200d tan, red & brn.	70	65
		Nos. 740-745 (6)	1.80	1.07

Lithographed and Engraved

1964, Sept. 27 *Perf. 11½* **Unwmkd.**

Design: 50d, Karl Marx.

746	A180	25d black, *buff*	10	3
747	"	50d black, *pinkish*	25	5

Issued to commemorate the centenary of the First Socialist International, founded in London, Sept. 28, 1864.

Children at Play
A181

1964, Oct. 4 Lithographed *Perf. 12½*

748	A181	25d verm., pink & gray grn.	25	3

Issued for Children's Week.

The Victor by Ivan Meštrović
A182

1964, Oct. 20 **Engraved** *Perf. 11½*

749	A182	25d gold & black, *pinkish*	20	3

Issued to commemorate the 20th anniversary of the Liberation of Belgrade.

Initial from Evangel of Hilandar
A183

Hand, "Liberty and Equality"
A184

Art through the centuries: 30d, Initial from Evangel of Miroslav (musician). 40d, Detail from Cetigne octavo, 1494 (saint with scroll). 50d, Miniature from Evangel of Trogir, 13th century (female saint). 150d, Miniature from Hrovoe Missal, 15th century (knight on horseback). 200d, Miniature from 14th century manuscript (symbolic fight), (horiz.).

Perf. 11½x12, 12x11½

1964, Nov. 29 Photo. **Unwmkd.**

750	A183	25d multicolored	10	3
751	"	30d "	10	3
752	"	40d "	10	3
753	"	50d "	20	4
754	"	150d "	40	30
755	"	200d "	90	60
		Nos. 750-755 (6)	1.80	1.03

Issued for Day of the Republic.

1964, Dec. 7 *Perf. 12*

Designs: 50d, Dove over factory, "Peace and Socialism." 100d, Smokestacks, "Building Socialism."

756	A184	25d dull violet, gold, yellow & red	10	3
757	"	50d dk. bl., gold, yel. & red	15	3
758	"	100d dk. bl., gold, yel. & red	55	30

Jugoslav Communist League, 8th congress.

Table Tennis Player
A185

Titograd
A186

Design: 150d, Table tennis player from back.

1965, Apr. 15 Litho. *Perf. 12½*

759	A185	50d multicolored	20	10
760	"	150d "	70	55

Issued to commemorate the 28th Table Tennis Championships, Ljubljana, Apr. 15–25.

1965, May 8 **Engraved**

Views: 30d, Skoplje. 40d, Sarajevo. 50d, Ljubljana. 150d, Zagreb. 200d, Belgrade.

761	A186	25d claret	10	5
762	"	30d chocolate	10	5
763	"	40d violet black	10	5
764	"	50d slate green	30	10
765	"	150d dark purple	40	30
766	"	200d dark blue	80	60
		Nos. 761-766 (6)	1.80	1.15

Issued to commemorate the 20th anniversary of the liberation of Jugoslavia from the Nazis.

Young Pioneer
A187

ITU Emblem and Television Tower
A188

1965, May 10 **Litho. & Engr.**

767	A187	25d black & tan, *buff*	20	3

Issued to commemorate the Young Pioneer Games "20 Years of Freedom."

1965, May 17 **Engraved**

768	A188	50d dark blue	25	10

Issued to commemorate the centenary of the International Telecommunication Union.

Iron Gate, Danube—A189

Arms of Jugoslavia and Romania and Djerdap Dam—A190

Design: 50d (55b), Iron Gate hydroelectric plant and dam.

1965, May 20 Litho. *Perf. 12½x12*

769 A189 25d (30b) lt. blue & green 5 3
770 " 50d (55b) light blue & dark red 18 3

Miniature Sheet

Perf. 13½x13

771 A190 Sheet of 4 2.00 1.25
a. 100d multi. 25 12
b. 150d " 35 18

Nos. 769–771 were issued simultaneously by Jugoslavia and Romania to commemorate the start of the construction of the Iron Gate hydroelectric plant. Nos. 769–770 were valid for postage in both countries.

No. 771 contains one each of Nos. 771a, 771b and Romania Nos. 1747a and 1747b. Only Nos. 771a and 771b were valid in Jugoslavia. Size: 104x80mm. Sold for 500d.

See also Romania Nos. 1745–1747.

Flower Type of 1957

Medicinal Plants: 25d, Milfoil. 30d, Rosemary. 40d, Inula. 50d, Belladonna. 150d, Mint. 200d, Foxglove.

1965, May 25 Photo. *Perf. 11½*

Granite Paper

Flowers in Natural Colors

772 A123 25d deep carmine 15 3
773 " 30d olive bister 15 3
774 " 40d red brown 15 3
775 " 50d dark blue 20 3
776 " 150d violet blue 60 25
777 " 200d purple 1.25 90
Nos. 772-777 (6) 2.50 1.27

ICY Emblem
A191

1965, June 26 Litho. *Perf. 12½*

778 A191 50d dark blue & dull blue 20 4

International Cooperation Year, 1965.

Sibenik A192 — Cat A193

Scenic Views: 25d, Rogaska Slatina. 40d, Prespa Lake. 50d, Prizren. 150d, Scutari. 200d, Sarajevo.

1965, July 6 *Perf. 12½* Unwmkd.

779 A192 25d multicolored 12 3
780 " 30d " 12 3
781 " 40d " 12 3
782 " 50d " 12 3
783 " 150d " 55 20
784 " 200d " 1.00 75
Nos. 779-784 (6) 2.03 1.07

1965, Oct. 3 Litho. *Perf. 12½*

785 A193 30d maroon & bright yellow 30 5

Issued for Children's Week.

Nos. 630 and 634 Surcharged in Maroon and Type of 1958

1965 Engraved *Perf. 12½*

786 A133 5d on 8d gray 20 3
787 " 20d emerald 30 3
788 " 30d red orange 45 3
789 " 50d on 25d verm. 45 10

Branislav Nusic A194 — Marshal Tito A195

Portraits: 50d, Antun Gustav Matos, poet. 60d, Ivan Mazuranic, writer. 85d, Fran Levstik, writer. 200d, Josif Pancic, physician and botanist. 500d, Dimitrije Tucovic, political writer.

1965, Nov. 28 Engraved

Variously Toned Paper

790 A194 30d dull red 8 3
791 " 50d indigo 12 3
792 " 60d brown 15 5
793 " 85d dark blue 18 5
794 " 200d dk. olive green 85 60
795 " 500d deep claret 1.25 80
Nos. 790-795 (6) 2.63 1.56

Issued to honor famous Jugoslavian men.

1966, Feb. 4 Litho. *Perf. 12½*

796 A195 20p bluish green 30 5
797 " 30p rose pink 35 5

Rowing
A196

Designs: 30p, Long jump. 50p, Ice hockey. 3d, Hockey sticks and puck. 5d, Oars and scull.

1966, March 1 Engraved

798 A196 30p dk. carm. rose 6 3
799 " 50p dark purple 10 3
800 " 1d gray green 16 3
801 " 3d dark red brown 85 65
802 " 5d dark blue 1.15 75
Nos. 798-802 (5) 2.32 1.49

Issued to publicize: 25th Balkan Games (30p); World ice hockey championship (50p, 3d); Second rowing championships (1d, 5d).

"T" from 15th Century Psalter A197 — Radio Amateurs' Emblem A198

Art through the Centuries (Initials from Medieval Manuscripts): 50p, Cyrillic "V," Divosh Evangel, 14th century. 60p, "R," Gregorius I, Libri moralium, 12th century. 85p, Cyrillic "P," Miroslav Evangel, 12th century. 2d, Cyrillic "B," Radomir Evangel, 13th century. 5d, "F," Passional, 11th century.

1966, Apr. 25 Photo. *Perf. 12*

803 A197 30p multicolored 6 3
804 " 50p " 10 3
805 " 60p " 12 3
806 " 85p " 15 4
807 " 2d " 85 65
808 " 5d " 1.15 75
Nos. 803-808 (6) 2.43 1.53

1966, May 23 Engr. *Perf. 12½x12*

809 A198 85p dark blue 25 10

Issued to commemorate the 20th anniversary of the Union of Jugoslav Radio Amateurs, and to publicize the International Congress of Radio Amateurs, Opatija, May 23–28.

Stag Beetle A199 — Serbia No. 2, 1866 A200

Beetles: 50p, Floral beetle. 60p, Oil beetle. 85p, Ladybird. 2d, Rosalia alpina. 5d, Aquatic beetle.

1966, May 25 Photo. *Perf. 12x12½*

810 A199 30p gray, black & bister 6 3
811 " 50p gray, emerald & black 10 3
812 " 60p bluish blk., slate green & gray 15 3
813 " 85p dull orange, dp. orange & black 30 8
814 " 2d gray, ultra. & black 85 65
815 " 5d tan, brn. & blk. 1.15 85
Nos. 810-815 (6) 2.61 1.67

Lithographed and Engraved

1966, June 25 *Perf. 12½* Unwmkd.

Stamps of Serbia: 50p, No. 3. 60p, No. 4. 85p, No. 5. 2d, No. 6. 10d, No. 1.

816 A200 30p bister brown & olive green 6 3
817 " 50p ocher & brown 10 3
818 " 60p light olive green & orange 15 10
819 " 85p ultra. & dk. car. 50 20
820 " 2d gray grn. & bl. 1.25 80
Nos. 816-820 (5) 2.06 1.16

Souvenir Sheet

Imperf.

821 A200 10d dark blue & dark green 2.50 2.50

Issued to commemorate the centenary of Serbia's first postage stamps. No. 821 contains one stamp. Gray and gold margin with black commemorative inscription. Size: 62x72½mm.

Leather Shield with Farmer, Soldier and Woman A201 — Bishop Strossmayer and Franjo Racki A202

1966, July 2 *Perf. 12½*

822 A201 20p pale green, gold & red brown 4 3
823 " 30p buff, gold & deep magenta 5 4
824 " 85p lt. gray, gold & Prus. blue 16 10
825 " 2d light blue, gold & violet 60 50

25th anniversary of National Revolution.

1966, July 15

826 A202 30p dull olive, black & buff 20 5

Issued to commemorate the centenary of the Academy of Arts and Sciences, founded by Bishop Josip Juraj Strossmayer with Franjo Rački as first president.

Mostar Bridge, Neretva River
A203

1966, Sept. 24 Engraved *Perf. 12½*

827 A203 30p rose claret 2.50 25

400th anniversary of Mostar Bridge.

Medieval View of Sibenik
A204

1966, Sept. 24

828 A204 30p deep plum 50 6

900th anniversary of Sibenik.

Girl A205 — Shipbuilding A206

1966, Oct. 2 Lithographed

829 A205 30p ultra., org., red & black 1.25 10

Issued for Children's Week.

1966 Engraved *Perf. 12½*

Designs: 10p, Sisak steel works. 15p, Overpass. 20p, Jablonica hydroelectric works. 30p, Litostroy turbine factory. 40p, Lukavac coke factory. 50p, Zenica steel works. 60p, Cable factory, Svetozarevo. 65p, Sevojno copper works. 85p, Lumber industry. 1d, Crude oil production.

830 A206 5p dull orange 3 3
831 " 10p brown 3 3
832 " 15p violet blue 4 3
833 " 20p emerald 10 3
834 " 30p vermilion 25 3
835 " 40p deep claret 15 3
836 " 50p gray blue 18 3
837 " 60p red brown 20 3
838 " 65p green 25 3
839 " 85p dull purple 35 3
840 " 1d yellow olive 45 3
Nos. 830-840 (11) 2.03 33

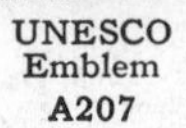

UNESCO Emblem
A207

Santa Claus
A208

1966, Nov. 4 **Lithographed**

841 A207 85p violet blue 25 12

20th anniversary of UNESCO.

1966, Nov. 25 **Litho.** ***Perf. 12½***

Designs: 15p, Stylized winter landscape. 30p, Stylized Christmas tree.

842 A208 15p org. & dk. blue 6 3
843 " 20p org. & purple 8 3
844 " 30p org. & slate grn. 15 3

1966, Dec. 23 **Photo.** ***Perf. 12½***

845 A208 15p gold & dk. blue 50 30
846 " 20p gold & red 50 30
847 " 30p gold & green 50 30
Nos. 842-847 (6) 1.79 99

Nos. 842–847 were issued for New Year, 1967.

Wolf's Head Coin of Durad I, 1373
A209

Medieval Coins: 50p, ½d of King Stefan, c. 1461 (arms of Bosnia). 60d, Dinar of Serbia (portrait of Durad Brankovic). 85p, Dinar of Ljubljana, c. 1250 (heraldic eagle). 2d, Dinar of Split, c. 1403–1413 (shield with arms of Duke Hrvoje Vukcic). 5d, Dinar of Emperor Stefan Dusan, c. 1346–1355 (Emperor on horseback).

1966, Nov. 28 **Photogravure**

Coins in Silver, Gray and Black

848 A209 30p verm. & black 10 3
849 " 50p ultra. & black 10 3
850 " 60p magenta & blk. 10 3
851 " 85p violet & black 15 4
852 " 2d dk. olive bister & black 35 15
853 " 5d brt. grn. & blk. 1.10 75
Nos. 848-853 (6) 1.90 1.03

Arnica
A210

Marshal Tito
A211

Medicinal Plants: 50p, Flax. 85p, Oleander. 1.20d, Gentian. 3d, Laurel. 5d, African rue.

1967, May 25 **Photo.** ***Perf. 11½***

Granite Paper

Flowers in Natural Colors

854 A210 30p scarlet 5 3
855 " 50p yellow brown 7 3
856 " 85p violet 12 4
857 " 1.20d magenta 25 6
858 " 3d dark blue 45 15
859 " 5d deep green 1.30 85
Nos. 854-859 (6) 2.24 1.16

Issued to commemorate Youth Day, May 25.

1967, May 25 **Engraved** ***Perf. 12½***

Size: 20x27½mm.

860 A211 5p orange 10 8
861 " 10p dark red brown 10 8
862 " 15p dark violet blue 10 8
863 " 20p green 10 8
864 " 30p vermilion 10 8
865 " 40p black 10 8
866 " 50p Prussian green 10 8
867 " 60p lilac 12 10
868 " 85p deep blue 20 18
869 " 1d plum 25 22
Nos. 860-869 (10) 1.27 1.06

Issued to commemorate the 75th birthday of President Tito. Printed in sheets of 15.

Nos. 860–869 were reissued in 1967 with slight differences including thinner paper and slightly darker shades.

See also Nos. 924–939.

Coil Stamps

1968-69 **Photo.** ***Perf. 12½ Horiz.***

869A A211 20p green 10 3
869B " 30p vermilion 15 3
869C " 50p vermilion ('69) 15 3

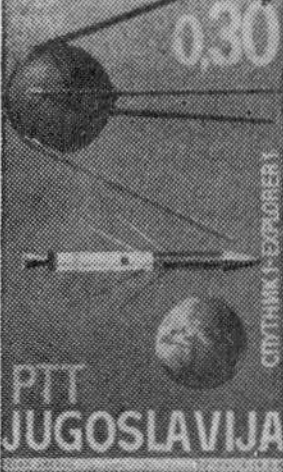

EXPO Emblem, Sputnik 1 and Explorer 1
A212

ITY Emblem, St. Tripun's Church, Kotor
A213

Space Craft: 50p, Tiros, Telstar and Molniya. 85p, Luna 9 and lunar satellite. 1.20d, Mariner 4, and Venus 3. 3d, Vostok, Gemini and Agena Rocket. 5d, Astronaut walking in space.

1967, June 26 **Photo.** ***Perf. 11½***

870 A212 30p ultra. & multi. 4 3
871 " 50p yellow & multi. 8 3
872 " 85p slate & multi. 12 3
873 " 1.20d multicolored 35 6
874 " 3d violet & multi. 45 15
875 " 5d blue & multi. 1.50 1.25
Nos. 870-875 (6) 2.54 1.55

Issued to commemorate EXPO '67, International Exhibition, Montreal, Apr. 28–Oct. 27, 1967, and the 18th Congress of the International Astronautical Federation, Belgrade.

1967, July 17 **Engraved**

Designs (ITY Emblem and): 50p, Municipal Building, Maribor. 85p, Cathedral, Trogir. 1.20d, Fortress gate, Niš. 3d, Drina Bridge, Višegrad. 5d, Daut-pasha's Bath, Skoplje.

876 A213 30p slate blue & light olive 8 6
877 " 50p brown & dull violet 10 6
878 " 85p dark blue & deep claret 16 6
879 " 1.20d deep claret & brown 25 10
880 " 3d brn. & slate grn. 50 15
881 " 5d slate grn. & brn. 1.25 1.00
Nos. 876-881 (6) 2.34 1.43

Issued for International Tourist Year, 1967.

Partridge
A214

Designs: 50p, Pike. 1.20d, Red deer. 5d, Peregrine falcon.

1967, Sept. 22 **Photo.** ***Perf. 14***

882 A214 30p bister & multi. 4 3
883 " 50p multicolored 5 3
884 " 1.20d vio. bl. & multi. 15 12
885 " 5d multicolored 1.25 1.00

Issued to commemorate the opening of the International Fishing and Hunting Exposition and Fair at Novi Sad.

Congress Emblem with Sputnik 1
A215

Lithographed and Engraved

1967, Sept. 25 ***Perf. 12½***

886 A215 85p dk. blue, light blue & gold 25 4

Issued to publicize the 18th Congress of the International Astronautical Federation, Belgrade, Sept. 25–30.

Old Theater and Castle, Ljubljana
A216

Child's Drawing: Winter Scene
A217

1967, Sept. 29 **Engraved** ***Perf. 12½***

887 A216 30p sepia & dk. grn. 20 3

Centenary of Slovene National Theater.

1967, Oct. 2 **Lithographed**

888 A217 30p multicolored 60 3

International Children's Week, Oct. 2–8.

Lenin by Mestrovic
A218

4-Leaf Clover
A219

1967, Nov. 7 **Engraved** ***Perf. 12½***

889 A218 30p dark purple 10 3
890 " 85p olive gray 25 5

Souvenir Sheet

Imperf.

891 A218 10d magenta 2.50 2.25

Issued to commemorate the 50th anniversary of the Russian October Revolution. No. 891 contains one stamp, buff margin with gold decoration and inscription. Size: 60x77mm.

1967, Nov. 15 **Photo.** ***Perf. 14***

Designs: 30p, Chimney sweep. 50p, Horseshoe and flower.

Dated "1968"

892 A219 20p gold, emerald & ultramarine 4 3
893 " 30p gold, yel. & vio. 4 3
894 " 50p gold, lilac & crimson 25 6

Issued for New Year 1968. See also Nos. 957–959.

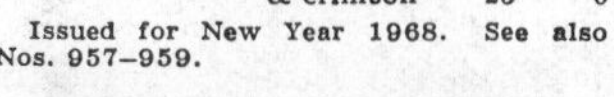

The Young Sultana, by Vlaho Bucovac—A220

Paintings: 85p, The Watchtower, by Dura Jaksic (vert.). 2d, Visit to the Family, by Josip Petkovsek. 3d, The Cock Fight, by Paja Jovanovic. 5d, "Spring" (woman and children), by Ivana Kobilca (vert.).

Perf. 11½x12, 12x11½

1967, Nov. 28 **Engr. and Litho.**

895 A220 85p multicolored 20 10
896 " 1d " 30 15
897 " 2d " 40 30
898 " 3d " 50 50
899 " 5d " 1.75 1.75
Nos. 895-899 (5) 3.15 2.80

Issued for the Day of the Republic, Nov. 29. See also Nos. 942–946, 995–1000.

Ski Jump
A221

Annunciation
A222

Sport: 1d, Figure skating pair. 2d, Downhill skiing. 5d, Ice hockey.

1968, Feb. 5 **Engr.** ***Perf. 12½***

900 A221 50p dk. blue & dark purple 10 6
901 " 1d brn. & slate grn. 20 12
902 " 2d slate grn. & lake 40 20
903 " 5d slate green & dark blue 1.00 80

Issued to commemorate the 10th Winter Olympic Games, Grenoble, France, Feb. 6–18.

1968, Apr. 20 **Photo.** ***Perf. 13½***

Medieval Icons: 50p, Madonna, St. George's Church, Prizren. 1.50d, St. Sava and St. Simeon. 2d, Christ's descent into hell, Ohrid. 3d, Crucifixion, St. Clement's Church, Ohrid. 5d, Madonna, Church of Our Lady of the Bell Tower, Split.

906 A222 50p gold & multi. 10 3
907 " 1d " " 12 3
908 " 1.50d " " 25 4
909 " 2d " " 40 10
910 " 3d " " 60 15
911 " 5d " " 1.75 1.75
Nos. 906-911 (6) 3.22 2.10

European Bullfinch
A223

800-meter Race for Women
A224

Finches: 1d, Goldfinch. 1.50d, Chaffinch. 2d, European greenfinch. 3d, Red crossbill. 5d, Hawfinch.

1968, May 25 **Photo.** ***Perf. 11½***

Birds in Natural Colors

912 A223 50p bister 10 3
913 " 1d rose lake 16 3
914 " 1.50d gray blue 20 3
915 " 2d deep orange 35 15
916 " 3d olive green 48 15
917 " 5d pale violet 1.10 1.05
Nos. 912-917 (6) 2.39 1.44

Issued for Youth Day.

Lithographed and Engraved

1968, June 28 ***Perf. 12½***

Sports: 1d, Basketball. 1.50d, Gymnast on vaulting horse. 2d, Rowing. 3d, Water polo. 5d, Wrestling.

918 A224 50p dk. brown & dk. red brown 5 3
919 " 1d Prus. bl. & blk. 12 3
920 " 1.50d slate & dk. brn. 20 3

921 A224 2d bister & slate green 32 15
922 " 3d black brown & indigo 55 25
923 " 5d dk. green & violet black 1.15 1.05
Nos. 918-923 (6) 2.39 1.54

Issued to publicize the 19th Olympic Games, Mexico City, Oct. 12–27.

Tito Type of 1967

1968–72 Engraved *Perf. 12½*

Size: 20x27½mm.

924 A211 20p dark blue 7 3
925 " 25p lake 10 3
926 " 30p green 10 3
927 " 50p vermilion 15 3
928 " 70p black 20 3
929 " 75p slate green 20 3
930 " 80p olive 20 3
930A " 80p red org. ('72) 25 3
931 " 90p olive 15 3
932 " 1.20d dark blue 80 3
932A " 1.20d slate green ('72) 30 3
933 " 1.25d deep blue 30 3
934 " 1.50d slate green 30 3

Size: 20x30½mm.

935 A211 2d sepia 30 6
936 " 2.50d Prus. green 85 16
937 " 5d deep plum 1.00 10
938 " 10d violet black 1.75 20
939 " 20d bluish black 3.50 55
Nos. 924-939 (18) 10.52 1.46

The shading of the background of Nos. 924–939 has been changed from the 1967 issue to intensify the contrast around the portrait.

Cannon and Laurel Wreath
A225

Mother Nursing Twins, Fresco by Jan of Kastav
A226

1968, Aug. 2 Photo. *Perf. 12½*

940 A225 50p org. brn. & gold 20 3

65th anniversary of the Ilinden uprising.

1968, Sept. 9 Lithographed

941 A226 50p black & multi. 20 3

Issued to commemorate the 25th anniversary of the annexation of Istria and the Slovene Coast to Jugoslavia.

Painting Type of 1967

Paintings: 1d, Lake Klansko, by Marko Pernhart. 1.50d, Bavarian Landscape, by Milan Popovic. 2d, Porta Terraferma, Zadar, by Ferdo Quiquerez. 3d, Mt. Triglav seen from Bohinj, by Anton Karinger. 5d, Studenica Monastery, by Djordje Krstic.

Engraved and Lithographed

1968, Oct. 3 *Perf. 14x13½*

942 A220 1d gold & multi. 12 3
943 " 1.50d " " 20 3
944 " 2d " " 25 6
945 " 3d " " 50 30
946 " 5d " " 2.00 1.50
Nos. 942-946 (5) 3.07 1.92

Aleksa Santic—A227

1968, Oct. 5 Engraved *Perf. 12½*

947 A227 50p dark blue 15 3

Issued to commemorate the centenary of the birth of Aleksa Santič (1868–1924), poet.

"Going for a Walk" (child's drawing)
A228

1968, Oct. 6 Lithographed

948 A228 50p multicolored 25 3

Issued for Children's Week.

Karl Marx, by N. Mitric
A229

Old Theater and Belgrade Castle
A230

1968, Oct. 11 Engraved

949 A229 50d dark car. rose 15 3

Issued to commemorate the 150th anniversary of the birth of Karl Marx (1818–1883).

1968, Nov. 22 Engraved *Perf. 12½*

950 A230 50p olive brown & slate green 15 3

Issued to commemorate the centenary of the Serbian National Theater, Belgrade.

Hasan Brkić
A231

The Family, by J. Soldatovic
A232

Portraits: 75p, Ivan Milutinovič. 1.25d, Rade Končar. 2d, Kuzman Josifovski. 2.50d, Tone Tomšič. 5d, Moša Pijade.

1968, Nov. 28 Engr. *Perf. 12½*

951 A231 50p violet black 15 3
952 " 75p black 25 20
953 " 1.25d red brown 35 30
a. Souv. sheet of 6 17.50 17.50
954 " 2d bluish black 45 30
955 " 2.50d slate green 60 30
956 " 5d claret 2.75 2.75
a. Souv. sheet of 6 17.50 17.50
Nos. 951-956 (6) 4.55 3.88

Issued to commemorate the 25th anniversary of the 2nd Assembly of the National Republic of Jugoslavia. No. 953a contains 2 each of Nos. 951–953; No. 956a contains 2 each of Nos. 954–956. Sheets have gold border and label with commemorative inscription. Size: 154x107mm.

Type of New Year's Issue, 1967

Dated "1969"

Designs: 20p, 4-leaf clover. 30p, Chimney sweep. 50p, Horseshoe and flower.

1968, Nov. 25 Photo. *Perf. 14*

957 A219 20p gold, bluish lilac & deep blue 6 3
958 A219 30p gold, green & dk. violet blue 6 3
959 " 50p gold, yel. & car. 15 10

Issued for New Year 1969.

1968, Dec. 10 Engraved *Perf. 12½*

960 A232 1.25d dark blue 30 10

International Human Rights Year.

ILO Emblem
A233

Dove, Hammer and Sickle Emblem
A234

Lithographed and Engraved

1969, Jan. 27 *Perf. 12½*

961 A233 1.25d red & black 30 10

Issued to commemorate the 50th anniversary of the International Labor Organization.

Inscribed: "SKJ 1919–1969"

Engraved and Photogravure

1969, Mar. 11 *Perf. 12½*

Designs: 75p, Graffiti "TITO" and five-pointed star. 1.25d, Five-pointed crystal.

962 A234 50p black & red 10 3
963 " 75p olive bister & black 15 3
964 " 1.25d red & black 35 10
a. Souv. sheet of 9 5.00 5.00

Issued to commemorate the 50th anniversary of the Communist Federation of Jugoslavia and to publicize the 9th party congress.

No. 964a contains 9 stamps (3x3): 4 No. 962, 2 each of Nos. 963–964 and one 10d brown, engraved stamp showing Marshal Tito in 1943. Gold marginal inscription. Size: 115x135mm.

Nos. 962–964 issued in sheets of 50; the 10d Tito stamp was issued in the souvenir sheet only.

St. Nikita, from Manasija Monastery
A235

1969, Apr. 7 Photo. *Perf. 13½*

Frescoes from Monasteries: 75p, Apostles, Zakopani. 1.25d, Crucifixion, Studenica. 2d, Wedding at Cana, Kalenic. 3d, Angel at the Grave, Milseva. 5d, Pietá, Nerezi.

965 A235 50p gold & multi. 12 3
966 " 75p " " 15 3
967 " 1.25d " " 20 3
968 " 2d " " 45 10
969 " 3d " " 75 15
970 " 5d " " 1.75 1.50
Nos. 965-970 (6) 3.42 1.84

Roman Memorial and View of Ptuj
A236

1969, Apr. 23 Engraved *Perf. 11½*

971 A236 50p violet brown 25 3

Issued to commemorate the 1900th anniversary of Ptuj, the Roman Petovio. Issued in sheets of 9 (3x3) with marginal inscription.

Vasil Glavinov
A237

Thin-leafed Peony
A238

1969, May 8 *Perf. 12x12½*

972 A237 50p ocher & rose lilac 25 3

Issued to commemorate the centenary of the birth of Vasil Glavinov, Macedonian socialist. Issued in sheets of 9 (3x3) with marginal inscription.

1969, May 25 Photo. *Perf. 11½*

Medicinal Plants: 75p, Coltsfoot. 1.25d, Primrose. 2d, Hellebore. 2.50d, Violets. 5d, Anemones.

Flowers in Natural Colors

973 A238 50p yellow brown 12 3
974 " 75p dull purple 20 3
975 " 1.25d blue 25 3
976 " 2d brown 40 3
977 " 2.50d plum 60 12
978 " 5d green 1.50 1.50
Nos. 973-978 (6) 3.07 1.76

See Nos. 1056–1061, 1140–1145.

Eber, by Vasa Ivankovic
A239

Paintings of Sailing Ships: 1.25d, Tare, by Franasovic. 1.50d, Brig Sela, by Vasa Ivankovic. 2.50d, Dubrovnik galleon, 16th century. 3.25d, Madre Mimbelli, by Antoine Roux. 5d, The Virgin Saving Seamen from Disaster, 16th century ikon.

1969, July 10 Photo. *Perf. 11½*

979 A239 50p gold & multi. 12 3
980 " 1.25d " " 20 3
981 " 1.50d " " 25 3
982 " 2.50d " " 40 5
983 " 3.25d " " 60 25
984 " 5d " " 3.00 2.50
Nos. 979-984 (6) 4.57 2.89

Issued to commemorate the 20th anniversary of the Dubrovnik Summer Festival.

Emblem of Games for Deaf
A240

1969, Aug. 9 Engraved *Perf. 12½*

985 A240 1.25d deep claret & dull violet 40 15

Issued to publicize the 11th World Games for the Deaf, Belgrade, Aug. 9–16.

Lipice Horse
A241

Horses: 75p, Bosnian mountain horse. 3.25d, Ljutomer trotter. 5d, Half-breed.

1969, Sept. 26 Photo. *Perf. 11½*

986	A241	75p multicolored	10	3
987	"	1.25d olive & multi.	20	3
988	"	3.25d brown & multi.	40	3
989	"	5d multicolored	1.25	1.00

Issued to commemorate the 50th anniversary of the Zagreb Veterinary College.

Children and Birds, by Tanja Vucanik, 13 years
A242

1969, Oct. 5 Litho. *Perf. 12½*

990	A242	50p org., blk. & gray	15	8

Issued for Children's Week.

Arms of Belgrade
A243

Josip Smodlaka
A244

Coats of Arms: No. 992, Skoplje (bridge and mountain). No. 993, Titograd (bridge and fortifications).

1969 Lithographed *Perf. 12½*

991	A243	50p gold & multi.	18	3
992	"	50p " "	18	3
993	"	50p " "	18	3

The 25th anniversary of the liberation of the capitals of the Federated Republics. See Nos. 1017-1020.

1969, Nov. 9 Engraved

994	A244	50p dark blue	15	3

Issued to commemorate the centenary of the birth of Josip Smodlaka (1869-1956), leader in Jugoslavia's fight for independence.

Painting Type of 1967

Paintings of Nudes: 50p, The Little Gypsy with the Rose, by Nikola Martinoski (vert.). 1.25d, Girl on a Red Chair, by Sava Sumanovic (vert.). 1.50d, Woman Combing her Hair, by Marin Tartaglia (vert.). 2.50d, Olympia, by Miroslav Kraljevic. 3.25d, The Bather, by Jovan Bijelic (vert.). 5d, Woman on a Couch, by Matej Sternen.

Photogravure and Engraved

1969, Nov. 29 *Perf. 13½*

995	A220	50p multicolored	18	6
996	"	1.25d "	25	6
997	"	1.50d "	30	8
998	"	2.50d "	60	10
999	"	3.25d "	1.00	20
1000	"	5d "	5.00	5.00
		Nos. 995-1000 (6)	7.33	5.50

University of Ljubljana
A245

1969, Dec. 9 Engraved *Perf. 11½*

1001	A245	50p slate green	12	3

University of Ljubljana, 50th anniversary.

Seal of Zagreb University
A246

Jovan Cvijic, Geographer
A247

Photogravure and Engraved

1969, Dec. 17 *Perf. 12½*

1002	A246	50p gold, bl. & brn.	12	3

Issued to commemorate the 300th anniversary of the University of Zagreb.

Europa Issue, 1969

Common Design Type

1969, Dec. 20 Photo. *Perf. 11½*

1003	CD12	1.25d greenish gray, buff & brown	1.25	75
1004	"	3.25d rose lilac, gray & dk. blue	10.00	9.00

Issued to commemorate Jugoslavia's admission to the Conference of European Postal and Telecommunications Administrations.

1970, Feb. 16 Engraved *Perf. 12½*

Portraits: 1.25d, Dr. Andrija Stampar, hygienist. 1.50d, Joakim Krcovski, author. 2.50d, Marko Miljanov, Montenegrin patriot-hero. 3.25d, Vaca Pelagic, socialist. 5d, Oton Zupancic, Slovenian poet.

1005	A247	50p reddish brn.	7	3
1006	"	1.25d brownish blk.	18	3
1007	"	1.50d lilac	24	10
1008	"	2.50d slate green	35	18
1009	"	3.25d reddish brn.	50	20
1010	"	5d blue violet	1.40	1.00
		Nos. 1005-1010 (6)	2.74	1.54

Issued to honor famous Jugoslavs.

Punishment of Dirce, Pulj
A248

Mosaics from the 1st-4th Centuries: 1.25d, Cerberus, Bitola (horiz.). 1.50d, Angel of the Annunciation, Porec. 2.50d, Hunters, Gamzigard. 3.25d, Bull and cherry tree (horiz.). 5d, Virgin and Child enthroned, Porec.

1970, Mar. 16 Photo. *Perf. 13½*

1011	A248	50p gold & multi.	12	3
1012	"	1.25d " "	18	3
1013	"	1.50d " "	25	4
1014	"	2.50d " "	40	15
1015	"	3.25d " "	60	30
1016	"	5d " "	1.80	1.40
		Nos. 1011-1016 (6)	3.35	1.95

Common Design Types

pictured in section at front of book.

Arms Type of 1969

Coats of Arms: No. 1017, Sarajevo (arcade). No. 1018, Zagreb (castle). No. 1019, Ljubljana (dragon and tower). No. 1020a, Jugoslavia (embossed coat of arms.)

1970 Lithographed *Perf. 12½*

1017	A243	50p gold & multi.	15	3
1018	"	50p " "	15	3
1019	"	50p " "	15	3

Souvenir Sheet

1020	A243	Sheet of 7	5.00	5.00
		a. 12d gold & black	2.00	2.00

Issued to commemorate the 25th anniversary of the liberation of Jugoslavia. No. 1020 contains one each of Nos. 991-993, 1017-1019, one No. 1020a and 2 labels with commemorative inscriptions. Black control number in margin. Size: 88x106mm. Issue dates: No. 1017, Apr. 6, No. 1018, May 8, No. 1019, May 9, No. 1020, May 15.

Lenin, by S. Stojanovic
A249

Design: 1.25d, Lenin sculpture facing left.

1970, Apr. 22 Engraved

1021	A249	50p rose lilac	8	3
1022	"	1.25d blue gray	30	6

Issued to commemorate the centenary of the birth of Lenin (1870-1924), Russian communist leader.

Basketball
A250

1970, Apr. 25

1023	A250	1.25d plum	30	10

Issued to commemorate the 6th World Basketball Championships, Ljubljana, May 10-23.

Europa Issue, 1970

Common Design Type

1970, May 4 Photo. *Perf. 11½*

Size: 32½x23mm.

1024	CD13	1.25d lt. blue, dark blue & light greenish bl.	30	20
1025	"	3.25d rose lilac, plum & gray	75	50

Istrian Short-haired Hound
A251

Jugoslav Breeds of Dogs: 1.25d, Jugoslav tricolor hound. 1.50d, Istrian hard-haired hound. 2.50d, Balkan hound. 3.25d, Dalmatian. 5d, Shara mountain dog.

1970, May 25 Photo. *Perf. 11½*

Granite Paper

1026	A251	50p tan & multi.	10	3
1027	"	1.25d olive & multi.	18	3
1028	"	1.50d vio. & multi.	25	10
1029	"	2.50d slate & multi.	35	15
1030	"	3.25d multicolored	50	15
1031	"	5d "	1.25	1.10
		Nos. 1026-1031 (6)	2.63	1.56

Telegraph Circuit
A252

Championship Emblem (Athlete)
A254

Bird (Child's Drawing)
A253

1970, June 20 Litho. *Perf. 12½*

1032	A252	50p henna brown, gold & black	12	3

Issued to commemorate the centenary of telegraph service in Montenegro.

1970, Oct. 5

1033	A253	50p multicolored	20	10

Issued for Children's Week, Oct. 5-11.

1970, Oct. 22 Engraved

1034	A254	1.25d car. & slate	25	3

Issued to publicize the 17th World Gymnastics Championships, Ljubljana, Oct. 22-27.

U.N. Emblem and Hand Holding Dove, by Makoto
A255

Lithographed and Engraved

1970, Oct. 24 *Perf. 11½*

1035	A255	1.25d dk. brown, blk. & gold	30	8

25th anniversary of the United Nations.

Ascension, by Teodor D. Kracun
A256

Baroque Paintings: 75p, Abraham's Sacrifice, by Federiko Benkovic. 1.25d, Holy Family, by Francisek Jelovsek. 2.50d, Jacob's Ladder, by Hristofor Zefarovic. 3.25d, Baptism of Christ, by unknown Serbian painter. 5.75d, The Coronation of Mary, by Tripo Kokolja.

Engraved and Photogravure

1970, Nov. 28 *Perf. 13½x14*

1036	A256	50p gold & multi.	8	3
1037	"	75p " "	15	3

1038 A256 1.25d gold & multi. 25 4
1039 " 2.50d " " 40 5
1040 " 3.25d " " 50 5
1041 " 5.75d " " 1.75 1.75
Nos. 1036–1041 (6) 3.13 1.95

Alpine Rhododendron
A257

Design: 3.25d, Bearded vulture and European Nature Protection Year emblem.

1970, Dec. 14 Photo. *Perf. 11½*
1042 A257 1.25d multicolored 2.25 1.50
1043 " 3.25d " 10.00 9.00

European Nature Protection Year. Sheets of 9.

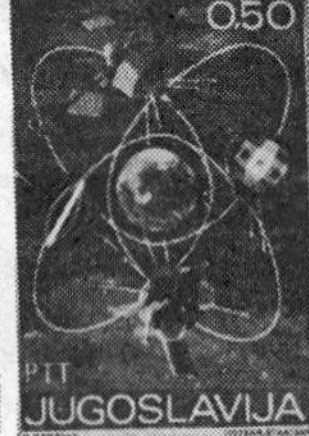

Frano Supilo
A258

British, French, Canadian, Italian Satellites—A259

Lithographed and Engraved

1971, Jan. 25 *Perf. 12½*
1044 A258 50p black & buff 15 3

Centenary of the birth of Frano Supilo (1870–1917), Croat leader for independence from Austria-Hungary. Sheets of 9.

1971, Feb. 8 Photo. *Perf. 13½*

Designs: 75p, Satellite. 1.25d, Automated moon exploration. 2.50d, Various spacecraft (horiz.). 3.25d, First experimental space station (horiz.). 5.75d, Astronauts on moon (horiz.).

1045 A259 50p blue & multi. 10 3
1046 " 75p multicolored 15 3
1047 " 1.25d " 35 6
1048 " 2.50d brown & multi. 75 40
1049 " 3.25d multicolored 1.25 75
1050 " 5.75d " 2.50 2.50
Nos. 1045–1050 (6) 5.10 3.77

"Space in the service of science." Sheets of 9.

Proclamation of the Commune, Town Hall, Paris
A260

Lithographed and Engraved

1971, March 18 *Perf. 11½*
1051 A260 1.25d bister brn. & gray brown 30 15

Centenary of the Paris Commune.

Europa Issue, 1971
Common Design Type

1971, May 4 Photo. *Perf. 11½*
Size: 33x23 mm.
1052 CD14 1.50d Prus. bl., pale green & dark blue 30 10
1053 CD14 4d magenta, pink & dark magenta 1.10 80

Circles
A261

Prince Lazar, Fresco, Lazarica Church
A262

Design: 1.25d, 20 circles.

1971, May 5 *Perf. 13½*
1054 A261 50p gold, red & blk. 55 25
1055 " 1.25d " " " 1.65 1.00

2nd Congress of Managers of Autonomous States.

Flower Type of 1969

Medicinal Plants: 50p, Common mallow. 1.50d, Common buckthorn. 2d, Water lily. 2.50d, Poppy. 4d, Wild chicory. 6d, Physalis.

1971, May 25 Photo. *Perf. 11½*
Flowers in Natural Colors.
1056 A238 50p lt. ultramarine 10 3
1057 " 1.50d olive bister 25 3
1058 " 2d dull blue 35 4
1059 " 2.50d dark carmine 40 20
1060 " 4d deep bister 75 20
1061 " 6d orange brown 1.35 1.25
Nos. 1056–1061 (6) 3.20 1.75

1971, June 28 Photo. *Perf. 13½*
1062 A262 50p gray & multi. 15 3

600th anniversary of founding of Krusevac by Prince Lazar Hrebeljanovic (1329–1389).

View of Krk
A263

Views: 5p, Krusevac. 10p, Castle and church, Gradacac. 20p, Church and bridge, Bohinj. 35p, Shore and mountains, Omis. 40p, Peje. 50p, Memorial column, Krusevac. 60p, Logar Valley. 75p, Bridge and church, Bohinj. 80p, Church, Piran. 1d, Street, Bitolj. 1.20d, Minaret, Pocitelj. 1.25d, 1.50d, Gate tower, Ercegnovi. 2d, Cathedral and City Hall Square, Novi Sad. 2.50d, Crna River.

1971–73 Engraved *Perf. 13*
1063 A263 5p orange ('73) 3 3
1064 " 10p brown ('72) 3 3
1065 " 20p vio. blk. ('73) 4 3
1066 " 30p green 50 3
a. 30p olive gray ('72) 5 3
1067 A263 35p brn. car. ('73) 9 3
1068 " 40p black ('72) 7 3
1069 " 50p vermilion 60 3
1070 " 50p green ('72) 13 3
1071 " 60p purple ('72) 13 3
1072 " 75p slate green 40 3
1073 " 80p rose red ('72) 24 3
1073A " 1d vio. brown 24 3
1073B " 1.20d slate grn. ('72) 60 3
1073C " 1.25d deep blue 30 3
1073D " 1.50d bluish black ('73) 30 3
1073E " 2d blue ('72) 60 5
1073F " 2.50d dull pur. ('73) 50 5
Nos. 1063–1073F (17) 4.80 55

Issued with and without fluorescent bars. See type A323.

Emperor Constantine, 4th Century
A264

UNICEF Emblem, Children in Balloon
A265

Tourist Issue

1971, Sept. 20 Photo. *Perf. 13½*

Antique Bronzes: 1.50d, Boy with fish. 2d, Hercules, replica after Lysippus. 2.50d, Satyr. 4d, Head of Aphrodite. 6d, Citizen of Emona, 1st century tomb.

1074 A264 50p rose & multi. 8 3
1075 " 1.50d multicolored 18 3
1076 " 2d " 25 3
1077 " 2.50d lemon & multi. 35 15
1078 " 4d ocher & multi. 50 30
1079 " 6d multicolored 2.00 2.00
Nos. 1074–1079 (6) 3.36 2.54

Antique bronzes excavated in Jugoslavia. Sheets of 9.

1971, Oct. 4 Litho. *Perf. 13x13½*
1080 A265 50p multicolored 15 3

Children's Week, Oct. 3–10.

Woman in Serbian Costume, by Katarina Ivanovic
A266

Portraits, 19th Century: 1.50d, The Merchant Ivanisevic, by Anastasije Bocaric. 2d, Ana Kresic, by Vjekoslav Karas. 2.50d, Pavle Jagodic, by Konstantin Danil. 4r, Luiza Pesjakova, by Mihael Stroj. 6d, Old Man and view of Ljubljana, by Matevz Langus.

Engraved and Photogravure

1971, Nov. 29 *Perf. 13½x14*
1081 A266 50p gold & multi. 12 3
1082 " 1.50d " " 25 5
1083 " 2d " " 35 8
1084 " 2.50d " " 50 10
1085 " 4d " " 60 30
1086 " 6d " " 2.50 2.50
Nos. 1081–1086 (6) 4.32 3.06

See Nos. 1120–1125.

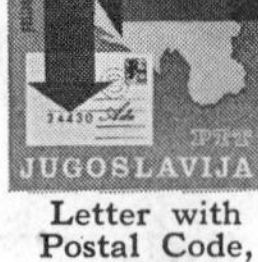

Letter with Postal Code, Map of Jugoslavia
A267

Damjan Gruev
A268

Photogravure

1971, Dec. 15 *Perf. 13½x14*
1087 A267 50p ultra. & multi. 12 3

Introduction of postal code system.

1971, Dec. 22 Engr. *Perf. 12½*
1088 A268 50p dark blue 12 3

Centenary of the birth of Damjan (Dame) Gruev (1871–1906), Macedonian revolutionist.

Sapporo '72 Emblem, Speed Skating
A269

Engraved and Typographed

1972, Feb. 3 *Perf. 11½*
Gold and Multicolor
1089 A269 1.25d *shown* 45 20
1090 " 6d *Slalom* 3.50 3.00

11th Winter Olympic Games, Sapporo, Japan, Feb. 3–13. Sheets of 9.

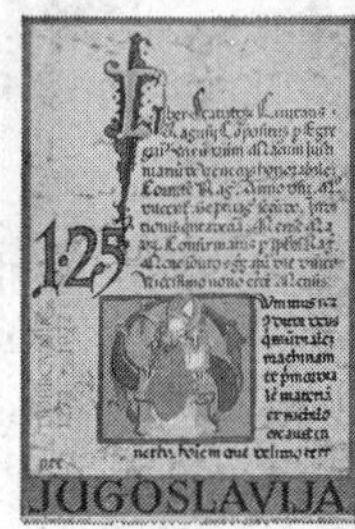

First Page of Statute of Dubrovnik
A270

Lithographed & Engraved

1972, Mar. 15 *Perf. 13½*
1091 A270 1.25d gold & multi. 30 4

700th anniversary of the Statute of Dubrovnik, a legal code given by Prince Marko Justiniani.

Ski Jump Track, Planica
A271

Water Polo and Olympic Rings
A272

1972, Mar. 21 *Perf. 11½*
1092 A271 1.25d black light blue & grn. 30 4

World Ski Jump Championships, Planica, Mar. 22–26.

1972, Apr. 17 Litho. *Perf. 12½x12*
Multicolored
1093 A272 50p *shown* 7 3
1094 " 1.25d *Basketball* 18 3
1095 " 2.50d *Butterfly stroke* 35 25
1096 " 3.25d *Boxing* 45 25
1097 " 5d *Running, women's* 80 50
1098 " 6.50d *Yachting* 2.25 3.25
Nos. 1093–1098 (6) 4.10 3.31

20th Olympic Games, Munich, Aug. 26–Sept. 10. Sheets of 9.

Europa Issue 1972

Common Design Type

1972, May 4 Photo. *Perf. 11½*

1100 CD15 1.50d bl., grn. & yel. 27 10
1101 " 5d bright rose, magenta & orange 1.75 1.10

Wall Creeper A275

Marshal Tito, by Bozidar Jakac A276

Birds: 1.25d, Little bustard. 2.50d, Red-billed chough. 3.25d, Spoonbill. 5d, Eagle owl. 6.50d, Rock ptarmigan.

1972, May 8

Birds in Natural Colors

1102 A275 50p gray violet 9 3
1103 " 1.25d ocher 20 3
1104 " 2.50d gray olive 40 5
1105 " 3.25d light plum 50 35
1106 " 5d red brown 75 50
1107 " 6.50d violet 1.50 1.35
Nos. 1102-1107 (6) 3.44 2.31

Nature protection.

1972, May 25 Litho. *Perf. 12½*

1108 A276 50p cream & dark brown 15 5
1109 " 1.25d gray & indigo 65 55

Souvenir Sheet

Imperf.

1110 A276 10d gray & black brown 3.00 3.00

80th birthday of Pres. Tito. Sheets of 9. No. 1110 contains one stamp. Gold margin with brown border and inscription. Size: 60x75mm. Printed in blocks of 4.

First Locomotive Built in Serbia, 1882
A277

Design: 5d, Modern Jugoslavian electric locomotive.

1972, June 12 Photo. *Perf. 11½*

1111 A277 1.50d multicolored 27 10
1112 " 5d " 1.35 80

International Railroad Union, 50th anniversary.

Glider
A278

1972, July 8 Photo. *Perf. 12½*

1113 A278 2d blue gray, gold & black 40 15

13th World Gliding Championships, Vrsac Airport, July 9-23. Sheets of 9.

Pawn on Chessboard
A279

Design: 6d, Chessboard, emblems of King and Queen.

1972, Sept. 18 *Perf. 11½*

1114 A279 1.50d multicolored 35 3
1115 " 6d " 1.25 1.00

20th Men's and 5th Women's Chess Olympiad, Skoplje, Sept.-Oct. Sheets of 9.

Boy on Rocking Horse A280

Goce Delchev A281

1972, Oct. 2 Litho. *Perf. 12½*

1116 A280 80p org. & multi. 15 3

Children's Week, Oct. 2-8.

1972, Oct. 16 *Perf. 13*

1117 A281 80p yellow green & black 15 3

Centenary of the birth of Goce Delchev (1872-1903), Macedonian freedom fighter.

Grga Martic, by Ivan Mestrovic
A282

1972, Nov. 3 *Perf. 12½*

1118 A282 80p red, yel. green & black 15 3

Sesquicentennial of the birth of Brother Grga Martic (1822-1905), Franciscan administrator, educator and poet.

Serbian National Library, Belgrade
A283

1972, Nov. 25 Engr. *Perf. 11½x12*

1119 A283 50p chocolate 12 3

140th anniversary of the Serbian National Library and opening of new building.

Painting Type of 1971

Still-Life Paintings: 50p, by Milos Tenkovic (horiz.). 1.25d, by Jozef Pekovsek. 2.50d, by Katarina Jovanovic (horiz.). 3.25d, by Konstantin Danil (horiz.). 5d, by Nikola Masic. 6.50d, by Celestin Medovic (horiz.).

Perf. 14x13½, 13½x14

1972, Nov. 28 Engr. & Photo.

1120 A266 50p gold & multi. 9 3
1121 " 1.25d " " 23 3
1122 " 2.50d " " 40 15
1123 A266 3.25d gold & multi. 58 30
1124 " 5d " " 80 50
1125 " 6.50d " " 1.50 1.10
Nos. 1120-1125 (6) 3.60 2.11

Battle of Stubica, by Krsto Hegedusic—A284

Design: 6d, Battle of Krsko, by Gojmir Anton Kos.

1973, Jan. 29 Photo. *Perf. 11½*

1126 A284 2d gold & multi. 40 8
1127 " 6d " " 1.60 1.20

400th anniversary of the Croatian-Slovenian Rebellion (2d) and 500th anniversary of the beginning of the peasant rebellions in Slovenia (6d). Sheets of 9.

Radoje Domanovic
A285

1973, Feb. 3 Litho. *Perf. 12½*

1128 A285 80p tan & brown 30 10

Centenary of the birth of Radoje Domanovic (1873-1908), Serbian writer. Sheets of 9.

Skofja Loka
A286

1973, Feb. 15 *Perf. 11½*

1129 A286 80p brown & buff 30 10

Millennium of the founding of Skofja Loka. Sheets of 9.

Novi Sad, by Peter Demetrovic
A287

Old Engravings: 1.25d, Zagreb, by Josef Szeman. 2.50d, Kotor, by Pierre Mortier. 3.25d, Belgrade, by Mancini. 5d, Split, by Louis-Francois Cassas. 6.50d, Kranj, by Matthaus Merian.

Engraved and Photogravure

1973, Mar. 15 *Perf. 13½*

1130 A287 50p gold, buff & black 9 3
1131 " 1.25d gold, gray & black 23 3
1132 " 2.50d gold & black 40 25
1133 " 3.25d " " 58 30
1134 " 5d gold, buff & black 80 50
1135 " 6.50d gold & black 1.10 1.00
Nos. 1130-1135 (6) 3.20 2.11

Championship Poster
A288

1973, Apr. 5 Litho. *Perf. 13½x13*

1136 A288 2d multicolored 35 15

32nd International Table Tennis Championships, Sarajevo, Apr. 5-15. Sheets of 9.

Europa Issue, 1973

Common Design Type

1973, Apr. 30 Photo. *Perf. 11½*

Size: 32½x23mm.

1138 CD16 2d dk. blue, lilac & light green 35 20
1139 " 5.50d pur., citron & salmon pink 2.00 1.35

Sheets of 9.

Flower Type of 1969

Medicinal Plants: 80p, Birthwort. 2d, Globe thistles. 3d, Olive branch. 4d, Corydalis. 5d, Mistletoe. 6d, Comfrey.

1973, May 25 Photo. *Perf. 11½*

Flowers in Natural Colors

1140 A238 80p orange & grn. 12 3
1141 " 2d dull blue & bl. 35 10
1142 " 3d olive & black 50 25
1143 " 4d yel. grn. & grn. 70 40
1144 " 5d orange & sepia 85 55
1145 " 6d lilac & green 2.00 1.50
Nos. 1140-1145 (6) 4.52 2.83

Anton Jansa and Bee
A291

1973, Aug. 25 Engraved *Perf. 12½*

1147 A291 80p black 18 6

200th anniversary of the death of Anton Jansa (1734-1773), teacher, wrote book on apiculture. Sheets of 9.

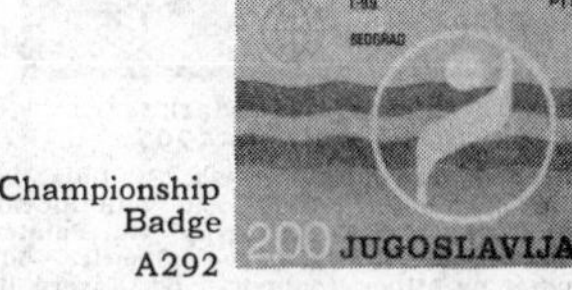

Championship Badge
A292

1973, Sept. 1 Litho. *Perf. 13½x13*

1148 A292 2d multicolored 35 22

World water sport championships (swimming, water polo, water jumps, figure swimming), Belgrade, Sept. 1-9. Sheets of 9.

"Greeting the Sun," by Ivan Vucovic
A293

Post Horn
A294

1973, Oct. 1 *Perf. 12½*

1149 A293 80p multicolored 18 6

Children's Week, Oct. 1-7. Sheets of 9.

Coil Stamps

1973–77 Photo. ***Perf. 14½x14***

1150	A294	30p brown	5	3
1151	"	50p gray blue	8	3
1152	"	80p rose red ('74)	12	3
1153	"	1d yel. grn. ('77)	12	3
1154	"	1.20d pink ('74)	18	3
1155	"	1.50d rose ('77)	18	3
		Nos. 1150–1155 (6)	73	18

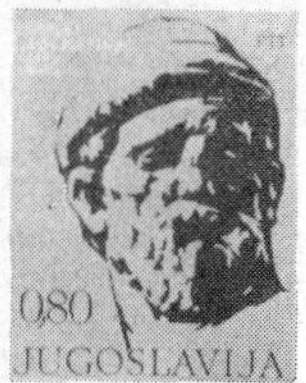

Juraj Dalmatinac
A295

1973, Oct. 8 Litho. ***Perf. 12½***

1158	A295	80p greenish gray & olive black	15	6

500th anniversary of the death of Juraj Dalmatinac, sculptor and architect. Sheets of 9.

Nadezda Petrovic, Self-Portrait
A296

Lithographed & Engraved

1973, Oct. 12 ***Perf. 11½***

1159	A296	2d gold & multi.	35	22

Centenary of the birth of Nadezda Petrovic (1873–1915), painter. Sheets of 9.

Interior, by Marko Celebonovic—A297

Paintings of Interiors: 2d, St. Duja, by Emanuel Vidovic. 3d, Room with Slovak Woman, by Marino Tartaglia. 4d, Painter with Easel, by Miljenko Stancic. 5d, Studio, by Milan Konjovic. 6d, Tavern in Stara Loka, by France Slana.

1973, Oct. 20 Photo. ***Perf. 13½***

1160	A297	80p gold & multi.	12	6
1161	"	2d " "	35	22
1162	"	3d " "	50	35
1163	"	4d " "	65	45
1164	"	5d " "	80	55
1165	"	6d " "	1.25	1.00
		Nos. 1160–1165 (6)	3.67	2.63

Paintings by Jugoslav artists. Sheets of 9.

Dragojlo Dudic
A298

Lithographed and Engraved

1973, Nov. 29 ***Perf. 12½***

Gray and Indigo

1166	A298	80p *shown*	12	6
1167	"	80p *Strahil Pindzur*	12	6
1168	"	80p *Boris Kidric*	12	6
1169	"	80p *Radoje Dakic*	12	6

Gray and Plum

1170	A298	2d *Josip Mazar-Sosa*	35	22
1171	"	2d *Zarko Zrenjanin*	35	22
1172	"	2d *Emin Duraku*	35	22
1173	"	2d *Ivan-Lola Ribar*	35	22
		Nos. 1166–1173 (8)	1.88	1.12

Republic Day, Nov. 29, honoring national heroes who perished during World War II. Nos. 1166–1173 printed se-tenant in sheets of 8 (4x2).

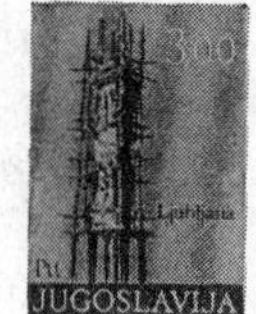

Memorial, by O. Boljka, Ljubljana
A299

Winged Globe, by D. Dzamonja, at Podgaric
A300

Sculptures: 4.50d, Tower by D. Dzamonja, at Kozara. 5d, Memorial, by B. Grabulovski, at Belcista. 10d, Abstract, by M. Zivkovic, at Sutjeska. 50d, Stone "V," by Zivkovic, at Kragujevac.

1974 Engraved ***Perf. 12½***

1174	A299	3d slate green	50	33
1175	"	4.50d brown lake	75	40
1176	"	5d dark violet	90	50
1177	A300	10d slate green	1.75	80
1178	"	20d dull purple	3.50	1.50
1179	"	50d indigo	8.70	4.00
		Nos. 1174–1179 (6)	16.10	7.53

Issue dates: 3d, 4.50d, 5d, Jan. 1; 10d, 20d, 50d, May 15.

Metric Measure
A301

1974, Jan. 10 Litho. ***Perf. 13***

1180	A301	80p plum & multi.	15	6

Centenary of introduction of metric system.

Ice Skating
A302

1974, Jan. 29

1181	A302	2d multicolored	35	22

European Ice Skating Championships, Zagreb, Jan. 29–Feb. 2.

Diligence, 1874
A303

Designs: 2d, New UPU Headquarters, Bern. 8d, Jet plane.

Lithographed and Engraved

1974, Feb. 25 ***Perf. 11½***

1182	A303	80p bister & black	12	6
1183	"	2d rose car. & blk.	35	22
1184	"	8d ultra. & black	1.40	95

Centenary of the Universal Postal Union.

Montenegro No. 1
A304

Lithographed and Engraved

1974, Mar. 11 ***Perf. 13***

Multicolored

1185	A304	80p *shown*	12	6
1186	"	6d *Montenegro No. 7*	1.05	65

Centenary of first Montenegrin postage stamps.

Marshal Tito
A305

Lenin, by Nandor Glid
A306

1974 Lithographed ***Perf. 13***

1193	A305	50p green	10	3
1196	"	80p vermilion	15	3
1198	"	1.20d slate green	25	3
1201	"	2d gray blue	50	5

Issued with and without fluorescence.

1974, Apr. 20 Litho. ***Perf. 13***

1204	A306	2d black & silver	35	22

50th anniversary of the death of Lenin (1870–1924).

Europa Issue 1974

Lepenski Vir Statue, c. 4950 B.C.
A307

Design: 6d, Widow and Child, by Ivan Mestrovic.

1974, Apr. 29 Photo. ***Perf. 11½***

1205	A307	2d multicolored	75	40
1206	"	6d "	2.25	1.50

Great Tit
A308

1974, May 25 Photo. ***Perf. 11½***

Multicolored

1207	A308	80p *shown*	12	3
1208	"	2d *Rose*	35	22
1209	"	6d *Cabbage butterfly*	2.00	90

Youth Day. Issued in sheets of 9.

Congress Poster
A309

1974, May 27 Litho. ***Perf. 11½***

1210	A309	80p gold & multi.	12	3
1211	"	2d silver & multi.	35	22
1212	"	6d ocher & multi.	1.00	85

10th Congress of Jugoslav League of Communists, Belgrade, May 27–30.

Radar Ground Station, Ivanjica
A311

Games Emblem and Soccer Cup
A312

Design: 6d, Intelsat IV circling earth.

1974, June 7 Engraved ***Perf. 13***

1214	A311	80p gray	15	8
1215	"	6d violet gray	1.50	85

Opening of first satellite ground station in Jugoslavia at Ivanjica. Sheets of 9.

1974, June 13 Litho. ***Perf. 13***

1216	A312	4.50d violet blue & multi.	1.00	50

World Cup Soccer Championship, Munich, June 13–July 7. Sheets of 9.

Klek Mountain, Edelweiss, Mountaineers' Emblem
A313

1974, June 15

1217	A313	2d green & multi.	35	20

Centenary of mountaineering in Jugoslavia. Sheets of 9.

Children's Dance, by Jano Knjazovic—A314

Paintings: 2d, "Crucified Rooster," by Ivan Generalic (vert.). 5d, Laundresses, by Ivan Lackovic (vert.). 8d, Dance, by Janko Brasic.

1974, Sept. 9 Photo. ***Perf. 11½***

1218	A314	80p multicolored	12	6
1219	"	2d "	35	20
1220	"	5d "	85	50
1221	"	8d "	1.40	80

Jugoslav primitive art.

Cock and Flower, by Kaca Milinojsin
A315

Designs (Children's Paintings): 3.20d, Girl and Boy, by Ewa Medrzecka (vert.). 5d, Cat and Kitten, by Jelena Anastasijevic.

1974, Oct. 7 Litho. ***Perf. 13***

1222 A315 1.20d multicolored 18 9
1223 " 3.20d " 55 35
1224 " 5d " 85 50

Children's Week, Oct. 1-7, and Joy of Europe meeting in Belgrade. Sheets of 9.

Library and Primoz Trubar Statue
A316

1974, Oct. 21 Engr. ***Perf. 13***

1225 A316 1.20d black 18 9

200th anniversary of the National University Library, Ljubljana.

White Peonies, by Petar Dobrovic
A317

Paintings of Flowers: 2d, Carnations, by Vilko Gecan. 3d, Flowers, still-life, by Milan Konjovic. 4d, White Vase, by Sava Sumanovic. 5d, Larkspur, by Stane Kregar. 8d, Roses, by Petar Lubarda.

1974, Nov. 28 Photo. ***Perf. 11½***

1226 A317 80p gold & multi. 12 10
1227 " 2d " " 35 20
1228 " 3d " " 50 30
1229 " 4d " " 70 40
1230 " 5d " " 85 53
1231 " 8d " " 1.40 1.25
Nos. 1226-1231 (6) 3.92 2.78

Paintings by Jugoslav artists. Sheets of 9.

Title Page and View of Belgrade
A318

1975, Jan. 8 Litho. ***Perf. 13***

1232 A318 1.20d citron 18 9

Sesquicentennial of the first publication of Matica Srpska, literary journal.

Map of Europe and Dove
A319

1975, Jan. 30 ***Perf. 12x11½***

1233 A319 3.20d bl. & multi. 75 50
1234 " 8d multicolored 2.50 1.25

Interparliamentary Union for European Cooperation and Security, 2nd Conference, Belgrade, Jan. 31-Feb. 6.

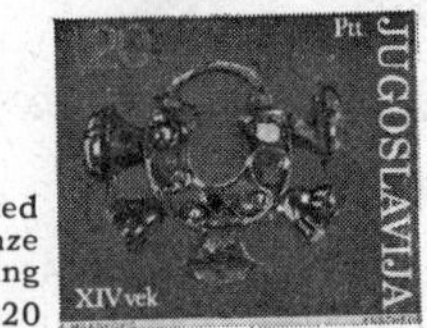

Gold-plated Bronze Earring
A320

Designs: 2.10d, Silver bracelet, 18th century. 3.20d, Silver gilt belt buckle, 18th century. 5d, Silver ring with Nike cameo, 14th century. 6d, Silver necklace, 17th century. 8d, Bronze gilt bracelet, 14th century.

1975, Feb. 25 Photo. ***Perf. 14x13***

1235 A320 1.20d multicolored 18 9
1236 " 2.10d " 36 20
1237 " 3.20d " 55 35
1238 " 5d " 85 50
1239 " 6d " 1.00 60
1240 " 8d " 1.40 80
Nos. 1235-1240 (6) 4.34 2.54

Antique jewelry in Jugoslav museums.

Svetozar Markovic, by Stevan Bodnarov
A321

1975, Feb. 26 Engraved ***Perf. 13***

1241 A321 1.20d blue black 18 9

Svetozar Markovic (1846-1875), writer and poet, death centenary.

Fettered Woman, by Frano Krsinic
A322

1975, Mar. 8 Photo. ***Perf. 14½x14***

1242 A322 3.20d gold & sepia 55 35

International Women's Year 1975.

Street, Ohrid—A323

Views: 25p, Budva. 75p, City Hall, Rijeka (Fiume). Nos. 1245, 1246, Street, Ohrid. 1.50d, Church, Bihac. 2.10d, Street and fountain, Hvar. 3.20d, Skofja Loka. 3.40d, Main Square, Vranje. 4.90d, Mosque, Perast.

1975-77 Lithographed ***Perf. 13***

1243 A323 25p carmine ('76) 3 3
1244 " 75p purple ('76) 9 3
1245 " 1d dull purple 12 3
1246 " 1d dull grn. ('76) 12 3
1247 " 1.50d rose red ('76) 18 4
1248 " 2.10d gray green 25 5
1249 " 3.20d dull blue 38 6
1250 " 3.40d gray green ('77) 40 8
1251 " 4.90d dull bl. ('76) 60 20
Nos. 1243-1251 (9) 2.17 55

Europa Issue 1975

Still Life with Eggs, by Mosa Pijade
A325

Painting: 8d, Three Graces, by Ivan Radovic.

1975, Apr. 28

1252 A325 3.20d gold & multi. 75 50
1253 " 8d " " 2.00 1.60

Srem Front Fighters' Monument, by Dusan Dzamonja
A326

1975, May 9 Litho. ***Perf. 13½***

1254 A326 3.20d red & multi. 50 35

30th anniversary of victory over Fascism in World War II and the liberation of Jugoslavia.

Garland Flower
A327

1975, May 24 Photo. ***Perf. 14x14½***
Multicolored

1255 A327 1.20d *shown* 18 9
1256 " 2.10d *Garden balsam* 36 20
1257 " 3.20d *Rose mallow* 55 35
1258 " 5d *Geranium* 86 50
1259 " 6d *Crocus* 1.00 60
1260 " 8d *Oleander* 1.40 80
Nos. 1255-1260 (6) 4.35 2.54

Youth Day.

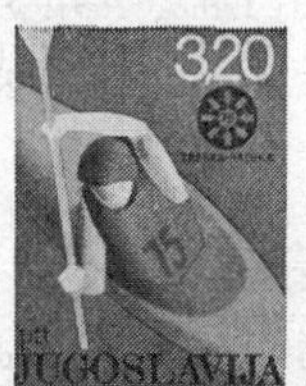

Kayak
A328

1975, June 20 Litho. ***Perf. 13½***

1261 A328 3.20d greenish bl. & multi. 55 35

9th World Championship of Wild Water Racing, Radika River, June 24-25, and 14th World Championship of Canoe-Slalom, Treska River, June 28-29.

Ambush, Herzegovinian Insurgents, by Ferdo Quiquerez—A329

1975, July 9 Photo. ***Perf. 13½x14½***

1262 A329 1.20d gold & multi. 18 9

Bosnian and Herzegovinian Uprising, centenary.

Stjepan Mitrov Ljubisa (1824-1878)
A330

Portraits: 2.10d, Ivan Prijatelj (1875-1937). 3.20d, Jakov Ignjatovic (1824-1889). 5d, Dragojla Jarnevic (1824-1889). 6d, Svetozar Corovic (1875-1919). 8d, Ivana Brlic-Mazuranic (1874-1938).

1975, Sept. 16 Litho. ***Perf. 13***

1263 A330 1.20d brick red & black 18 9
1264 " 2.10d dull green & black 36 20
1265 " 3.20d olive bister & black 55 35
1266 " 5d brown org. & black 86 50
1267 " 6d yellow grn. & black 1.00 60
1268 " 8d Prus. blue & black 1.40 80
Nos. 1263-1268 (6) 4.35 2.54

Jugoslav writers.

Young Lion
A331

Design: 6d, Baby carriage. Both designs from children's drawings.

1975, Oct. 1 Litho. ***Perf. 13½***

1269 A331 3.20d multi. 55 35
1270 " 6d " 1.50 90

"Joy of Europe" Children's Meeting, Belgrade, Oct. 2-7.

Peace Dove
A332

1975, Oct. 10

1271 A332 3.20d multi. 55 35
1272 " 8d " 1.75 80

European Security and Cooperation Conference, Helsinki, July 30-Aug. 1.

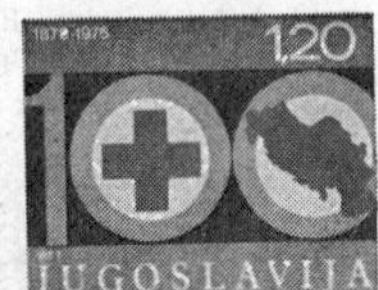

Red Cross, "100", Map of Jugoslavia
A333

Design: 8d, Red Cross and people seeking help.

1975, Nov. 1 Litho. ***Perf. 13½x13***

1273 A333 1.20d red & multi. 18 9
1274 " 8d " " 1.40 85

Centenary of Red Cross in Jugoslavia.

Soup Kitchen, by Dorde Andrejevic-Kun
A334

Paintings: 2.10d, People at the Door, by Vinko Grdan. 3.20d, Drunks in Coach, by Marijan Detoni (horiz.). 5d, Workers' Lunch, by Tone Kralj (horiz.). 6d, Water Wheel, by Lazar Licenoski. 8d, The Hanging, by Krsto Hegedusic.

Perf. 14½x13½, 13½x14½

1975, Nov. 28 Photogravure

1275 A334 1.20d gold & multi. 18 9
1276 " 2.10d " " 36 20
1277 " 3.20d " " 55 35
1278 " 5d " " 86 50
1279 " 6d " " 1.00 60
1280 " 8d " " 1.40 80
Nos. 1275-1280 (6) 4.35 2.54

Social paintings by 20th century Jugoslav artists. Sheets of 9.

Diocletian's Palace, 304 A.D.
A335

Designs: 3.20d, House of Ohrid, 19th century (vert.). 8d, Gracanica Monastery, Kosovo, 1321.

1975, Dec. 10 Engr. ***Perf. 13½***

1281 A335 1.20d dark brown 18 9
1282 " 3.20d bluish black 55 35
1283 " 8d dk. vio. brn. 1.40 80

European Architectural Heritage Year 1975. Sheets of 9.

Ski Jump, Games Emblem
A336

Design: 8d, Figure skating, pair.

1976, Feb. 4 Engr. ***Perf. 13½***

1284 A336 3.20d dark blue 55 35
1285 " 8d rose claret 1.40 80

12th Winter Olympic Games, Innsbruck, Austria, Feb. 4-15.

Red Flag
A337

1976, Feb. 14 Lithographed

1286 A337 1.20d red & multi. 18 9

"Red Flag" workers demonstration, Kragujevac, Feb. 15, 1876.

Svetozar Miletic
A338

1976, Feb. 23 ***Perf. 13½x13***

1287 A338 1.20d greenish gray & dull grn. 18 9

Svetozar Miletic (1826-1901), lawyer, founder of United Serbian Youth.

Bora Stankovic
A339

1976, Mar. 31 Litho. ***Perf. 13½x13***

1288 A339 1.20d lemon, olive & maroon 18 9

Borislav ("Bora") Stankovic (1876-1927), writer. Sheets of 9.

Europa Issue 1976

King Matthias, by Jakob Pogorelec, 1931
A340

Design: 8d, Bowl, 14th century.

1976, Apr. 26 Photo. ***Perf. 11½***

1289 A340 3.20d multicolored 55 35
1290 " 8d " 1.40 80

Ivan Cankar
A341

1976, May 8 Litho. ***Perf. 13½x13***

1291 A341 1.20d org. & plum 18 9

Ivan Cankar (1876-1918), Slovenian writer.

Train on Viaduct in Bosnia
A342

Design: 8d, Train on viaduct in Montenegro.

1976, May 15 Engr. ***Perf. 13½***

1292 A342 3.20d dp. magenta 55 35
1293 " 8d deep blue 1.40 80

Inauguration of the Belgrade-Bar railroad.

Hawker Dragonfly
A343

Fresh-water Fauna: 2.10d, Winkle. 3.20d, Rudd. 5d, Green frog. 6d, Ferruginous duck. 8d, Muskrat.

1976, May 25 Lithographed

1294 A343 1.20d yel. & multi. 18 9
1295 " 2.10d blue & multi. 36 20
1296 " 3.20d vio. & multi. 55 35
1297 " 5d multicolored 86 50
1298 A343 6d multi. 1.00 60
1299 " 8d " 1.40 80
Nos. 1294-1299 (6) 4.35 2.54

Youth Day.

Vladimir Nazor
A344

1976, May 29 ***Perf. 13***

1300 A344 1.20d pale lilac & dull blue 18 9

Vladimir Nazor, Croatian writer, birth centenary.

Battle of Vucji Dol, 1876—A345

1976, June 16 Litho. ***Perf. 13***

1301 A345 1.20d gold, brown & buff 18 9

Liberation of Montenegro from Turkey, centenary.

Serbian Pitcher
A346

Water Pitchers: 2.10d, Slovenia. 3.20d, Bosnia-Herzegovina. 5d, Vojvodina 6d, Macedonia. 8d, Kosovo.

1976, June 22 Photo. ***Perf. 14x13***

1302 A346 1.20d dk. carmine & multi. 18 9
1303 " 2.10d olive & multi. 36 20
1304 " 3.20d red & multi. 55 35
1305 " 5d brn. & multi. 86 50
1306 " 6d dk. green & multi. 1.00 60
1307 " 8d dk. blue & multi. 1.40 80
Nos. 1302-1307 (6) 4.35 2.54

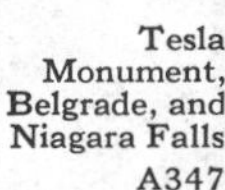

Tesla Monument, Belgrade, and Niagara Falls
A347

1976, July 10 Engr. ***Perf. 13***

1308 A347 5d slate green & indigo 86 50

Nikola Tesla (1856-1943), electrical engineer and inventor, 120th birth anniversary. Sheets of 9.

Long Jump
A348

Designs (Olympic Rings and): 3.20d, Soccer. 5d, Target shooting. 8d, Rowing, single scull.

1976, July 17

1309 A348 1.20d brn. carmine 18 9
1310 " 3.20d slate green 55 35
1311 " 5d brown 86 50
1312 " 8d bluish blk. 1.40 80

21st Olympic Games, Montreal, Canada, July 17-Aug. 1. Sheets of 9.

World Map and Peace Dove
A349

1976, Aug. 16 Litho. ***Perf. 13***

1313 A349 4.90d multicolored 85 50

5th Summit Conference of Non-Aligned Countries, Colombo, Sri Lanka, Aug. 9-19. Sheets of 9.

Children's Train
A350

Design: 4.90d, Navy Day (submarine). Both designs from children's drawings.

1976, Oct. 2 Litho. ***Perf. 13***

1314 A350 4.90d multicolored 85 50
1315 " 8d " 1.40 80

"Joy of Europe" Children's Meeting, Belgrade, Oct. 2-7.

Herzegovinian Fugitives, by Uros Predic—A351

Paintings: 1.20d, Battle of the Montenegrins, by Djura Jaksic (vert.). 2.10d, Nikola S. Zrinjski at Siget, by Oton Ivekovic (vert.). 5d, Uprising at Razlovci, by Borko Lazeski. 6d, Enthroning of Slovenian Duke at Gospovetsko Field, by Anton Gojmir Kos. 8d, Break-through at Solun Front, by Veljko Stanojevic.

Perf. 13½x12½, 12½x13½

1976, Nov. 29 Photogravure

1316 A351 1.20d gold & multi. 18 9
1317 " 2.10d " " 36 20
1318 " 3.20d " " 55 35
1319 " 5d " " 86 50
1320 " 6d " " 1.00 60
1321 " 8d " " 1.40 80
Nos. 1316-1321 (6) 4.35 2.54

Historical paintings by 19th-20th centuries Jugoslav painters. Sheets of 9.

No. 839 Surcharged with New Value and 3 Bars in Rose

1976, Dec. 8 Engr. ***Perf. 12½***

1322 A206 1d on 85p dull pur. 18 8

Mateja Nenadovic
A352

Rajko Zinzifov
A353

1977, Feb. 4 Photo. ***Perf. 13½x14***

1323 A352 4.90d multicolored 58 36

Prota Mateja Nenadovic (1777–1854), Serbian Duke, archbishop and writer, 200th birth anniversary.

1977, Feb. 10 Litho. ***Perf. 13x13½***

1324 A353 1.50d brn. & sepia 18 9

Rajko Zinzifov (1839–1877), writer, death centenary.

Phlox
A354

Flowers: 3.40d, Lily. 4.90d, Bleeding heart. 6d, Zinnia. 8d, Spreading marigold. 10d, Horseshoe geranium.

1977, Mar. 8 ***Perf. 13½x13***

1325 A354 1.50d multicolored 18 12
1326 " 3.40d " 40 22
1327 " 4.90d " 58 36
1328 " 6d " 72 40
1329 " 8d " 96 58
1330 " 10d " 1.20 70
Nos. 1325–1330 (6) 4.04 2.38

Croatian Music Institute
A355

1977, Apr. 4 Engr. ***Perf. 13***

1331 A355 4.90d blue & sepia 58 36

Croatian Music Institute, Zagreb, 150th anniversary.

Alojz Kraigher
A356

1977, Apr. 11 Litho. ***Perf. 13½***

1332 A356 1.50d lemon & brn. 18 12

Alojz Kraigher (1877–1959), Slovenian writer, birth centenary.

Europa Issue 1977

Boka Kotorska, by Milo Milunovic
A357

Design: 10d, Zagorje in November, by Ljubo Babic.

1977, May 4 Photo. ***Perf. 11½***

1333 A357 4.90d gold & multi. 58 36
1334 " 10d " " 1.20 95

Issued in sheets of 9.

Marshal Tito, by Omer Mujadzic
A358

Mountain Range and Gentian
A359

1977, May 25 ***Perf. 11½x12***

1335 A358 1.50d gold & multi. 25 12
1336 " 4.90d " " 58 36
1337 " 8d " " 95 70

85th birthday of Pres. Tito. Sheets of 9.

1977, June 6 Litho. ***Perf. 13x13½***

Design: 10d, Plitvice Lakes Falls, trees, robin and environmental protection emblem.

1338 A359 4.90d multicolored 58 36
1339 " 10d " 1.20 85

World Environment Day.

Petar Kočić
A360

1977, June 15 ***Perf. 13½***

1340 A360 1.50d pale green & brown 25 12

Petar Kočić (1877–1916), writer.

Map of Europe and Peace Dove
A361

1977, June 15 Litho. ***Perf. 13½***

1341 A361 4.90d multicolored 58 36
1342 " 10d " 1.20 70

Security and Cooperation Conference, Belgrade, June 15.

Child on Float
A362

Design: 10d, Fruit picking. Both designs from children's drawings.

1977, Oct. 3 Litho. ***Perf. 13½***

1343 A362 4.90d multicolored 58 36
1344 " 10d " 1.20 70

"Joy of Europe" Children's Meeting.

Sava Congress Center, Belgrade
A363

1977, Oct. 4 Litho. ***Perf. 13½***

1345 A363 4.90d blue & multi. 58 36
1346 " 10d carmine & multi. 1.20 70

European Security and Cooperation Conference, Belgrade.

Exhibition Emblem
A364

1977, Oct. 20 Litho. ***Perf. 13½***

1347 A364 4.90d gold & multi. 58 36

Balkanfila 1977, 6th International Philatelic Exhibiton of Balkan Countries, Belgrade, Oct. 24–30.

Double Flute and Shepherd
A365

Designs (Landscape and Musician): 3.40d, 4.90d, 6d, Various string instruments. 8d, Bagpipes. 10d, Panpipes.

1977, Oct. 25 Engr. ***Perf. 13½***

1348 A365 1.50d ocher & red brown 18 12
1349 " 3.40d grn. & brn. 40 25
1350 " 4.90d dk. brn. & yellow 60 36
1351 " 6d blue & red brown 72 42
1352 " 8d brick red & sepia 95 48
1353 " 10d slate green & bister 1.20 70
Nos. 1348–1353 (6) 4.05 2.33

Musical instruments from Belgrade Ethnographical Museum.

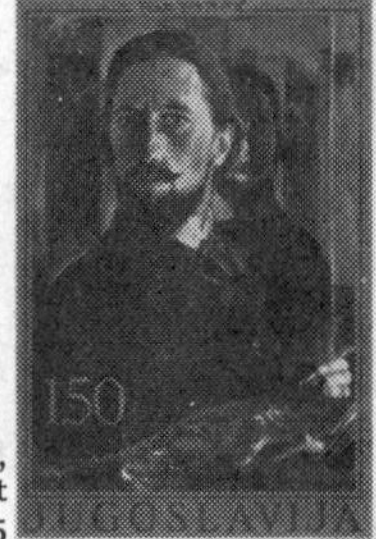

Ivan Vavpotic, Self-portrait
A366

Self-portraits: 3.40d, Mihailo Vukotic. 4.90d, Kosta Hakman. 6d, Miroslav Kraljevic. 8d, Nikola Martinovski. 10d, Milena Pavlovic-Barili.

Perf. 13½x12½

1977, Nov. 26 Photogravure

1354 A366 1.50d gold & multi. 18 12
1355 " 3.40d " " 40 25
1356 " 4.90d " " 60 36
1357 " 6d " " 72 42
1358 " 8d " " 95 48
1359 " 10d " " 1.20 70
Nos. 1354–1359 (6) 4.05 2.33

Jugoslav art.

Festival of Testaccio, by Klovic
A367

Julija Klovic, by El Greco
A368

1978, Jan. 14 Photo. ***Perf. 13½***

1360 A367 4.90d multicolored 60 36
1361 A368 10d " 1.20 70

Julija Klovic (1498–1578), Croat miniaturist, 400th death anniversary.

Stampless Cover, Banaviste to Kubin, 1869
A369

Designs: 3.40d, Mailbox. 4.90d, Ericsson telephone, 1900. 10d, Morse telegraph, 1844.

1978, Jan. 28 ***Perf. 13x14***

1362 A369 1.50d multicolored 18 12
1363 " 3.40d " 40 25
1364 " 4.90d " 60 36
1365 " 10d " 1.20 70

Post Office Museum, Belgrade.

Battle of Pirot, by Andreja Milenkovic
A370

1978, Feb. 20 Litho. ***Perf. 13½***

1366 A370 1.50d gold, black & slate green 18 12

Centenary of Serbo-Turkish War.

S-49A, 1949
A371

Planes: 3.40d, Galeb, 1961. 4.90d, Utva-75, 1976. 10d, Orao, 1974.

1978, Apr. 24 Litho. ***Perf. 13½***

1367 A371 1.50d multicolored 18 12
1368 " 3.40d " 40 25
1369 " 4.90d " 60 36
1370 " 10d " 1.20 70

Aeronautical Day.

Europa Issue 1978

View of Golubac
A372

Design: 10d, St. Naum Monastery, Ohrid.

1978, May 3 Photo. ***Perf. 11½***

1371 A372 4.90d multicolored 60 36
1372 " 10d " 1.20 70

Boxing Glove A373 — Honeybee A374

1978, May 5 Litho. *Perf. 13½*

1373 A373 4.90d multicolored 60 36

Amateur Boxing Championships.

1978, May 25 Photo. *Perf. 11½*

Bees of Jugoslavia: 3.40d, Halictus scabiosae. 4.90d, Blue carpenter bee. 10d, Large earth bumblebee.

1374 A374 1.50d multicolored 18 12
1375 " 3.40d " 40 25
1376 " 4.90d " 60 36
1377 " 10d " 1.20 70

Filipovic and Radovic A375

1978, June 19 Litho. *Perf. 13½*

1378 A375 1.50d dk. purple & dull olive 18 12

Filip Filipovic (1878–1938) and Radovan Radovic (1878–1906), revolutionaries.

Marshal Tito A376 — Congress Emblem A377

1978, June 20

1379 A376 2d red & multi. 25 15
1380 A377 4.90d " " 60 36

Souvenir Sheet

Imperf.

1381 A376 15d red & multi. 2.00

11th Congress of Yugoslav League of Communists, Belgrade, June 20–23. No. 1381 has dark olive green margin with gold inscription. Size: 70x93mm.

Nos. 1246, 1248 Surcharged with New Value and Two Bars in Brown

1978 Litho. *Perf. 13*

1382 A323 2d on 1d 25 15
1383 " 3.40d on 2.10d 40 25

Issue dates: No. 1382, July 17; No. 1383, Aug. 1.

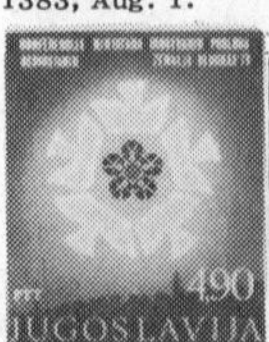

Conference Emblem over Belgrade A378 — Championship Emblem A379

1978, July 25 Photo. *Perf. 13½*

1384 A378 4.90d bl. & lt. bl. 60 36

Conference of Foreign Ministers of Non-aligned Countries, Belgrade, July 25–29.

1978, Aug. 10 Litho. *Perf. 13½x13*

1385 A379 4.90d multicolored 60 36

14th Kayak and Canoe Still-water Championships, Lake Sava, Aug. 10–14.

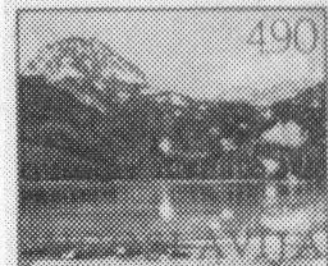

Mt. Triglav, North Rock A380 — Black Lake, Mt. Durmitor A381

1978, Aug. 26 Photo. *Perf. 14*

1386 A380 2d multicolored 25 15

Bicentenary of first ascent of Mt. Triglav by Slovenian climbers.

1978, Sept. 20

Design: 10d, Tara River.

1387 A381 4.90d multicolored 60 36
1388 " 10d " 1.25 75

Protection of the environment.

Night Sky A382

1978, Sept. 30 Litho. *Perf. 13x12½*

1389 A382 4.90d blue black, black & gold 60 36

29th Congress of International Astronautical Federation, Dubrovnik, Oct. 1–8.

People in Forest A383

Design: 10d, Family around pond. Both designs from children's drawings.

1978, Oct. 2 *Perf. 13½x13*

1390 A383 4.90d multicolored 60 36
1391 " 10d " 1.25 75

"Joy of Europe" Children's Meeting.

Seal on Insurrection Declaration A384

1978, Oct. 5 *Perf. 13½*

1392 A384 2d gold, brown & black 25 15

Centenary of Kresna uprising.

Teachers' College A385

1978, Oct. 16

1393 A385 2d multicolored 25 15

Teachers' Training Institute, Sombor, bicentenary.

Red Cross A386

1978, Oct. 21

1394 A386 2d lt. blue, black & red 25 15

Croatian Red Cross, centenary.

Metallic Sculpture XXII, by Dusan Dzamonja A387

Modern Sculptures: 3.40d, Circulation in Space I, by Vojin Bakic (vert.). 4.90d, Tectonic Octopode, by Olga Jevric (vert.). 10d, Tree of Life, by Drago Trsar.

Perf. 13½x13, 13x13½

1978, Nov. 4 Lithographed

1395 A387 2d multicolored 25 15
1396 " 3.40d " 40 25
1397 " 4.90d " 60 36
1398 " 10d " 1.20 70

Crossing of Neretva Pass, by Ismet Mujezinovic A388

1978, Nov. 10 Litho. *Perf. 13*

1399 A388 2d multicolored 25 15

35th anniversary of Battle of Neretva.

Workers Leaving Factory, by Marijan Detoni A389 — Pine Cone A390

Engravings: 3.40d, Workers, by Maksim Sedej. 4.90d, Lumberjacks, by Daniel Ozmo. 6d, Meal Break, by Pivo Karamatijevic. 10d, Hanged Man and Raped Woman, by Djordje Andrejevic Kun.

1978, Nov. 28 Photo. *Perf. 14x13½*

1400 A389 2d gold, black & buff 25 15
1401 " 3.40d gold & black 40 25
1402 " 4.90d gold, yellow & black 60 36
1403 " 6d gold, buff & black 75 45
1404 A389 10d gold, cream & black 1.20 70
Nos. 1400–1404 (5) 3.20 1.91

Republic Day.

1978, Dec. 11 Photo. *Perf. 13x12½*

Multicolored

1405 A390 1.50d *shown* 18 12
1406 " 1.50d *Squirrel* 18 12
1407 " 2d *Maple leaves* 25 15
1408 " 2d *Stag* 25 15
a. Bklt. pane of 8 2.00
1409 A390 3.40d *Leaves* 40 25
1410 " 3.40d *Partridge* 40 25
1411 " 4.90d *Oak leaves* 60 36
1412 " 4.90d *Grouse* 60 36
a. Bklt. pane of 8 4.00
Nos. 1405–1412 (8) 2.86 1.76

New Year 1979. Nos. 1405–1412 printed se-tenant in sheets of 25.

No. 1408a contains 4 each of Nos. 1407–1408; No. 1412a 2 each of Nos. 1409–1412.

Nos. 1064, 868, 1198 Surcharged with New Value and Bars

1978 Engr.; Litho. *Perf. 12½, 13½*

1413 A263 35p on 10p brown 4 3
1414 A211 60p on 85p dp. bl. 8 3
1415 A305 80p on 1.20d slate green 10 5

First Masthead of Politika A391

1979, Jan. 25 Litho. *Perf. 13½*

1416 A391 2d gold & black 25 15

75th anniversary of publication of Politika daily newspaper.

Red Flags and Emblem A392 — Child and IYC Emblem A393

1979, Feb. 15

1417 A392 2d red & gold 25 15

11th Meeting of Self-managers, Kragujevac, Feb. 15–16.

1979, Mar. 1 Photo. *Perf. 11½x12*

1418 A393 4.90d gold & violet blue 60 36

International Year of the Child.

SEMI-POSTAL STAMPS.

Giving Succor to Wounded
SP1

Wounded Soldier
SP2

Symbolical of National Unity—SP3

Engraved

1921, Jan. 30 ***Perf. 12*** **Unwmkd.**

B1	SP1	10(p) carmine	10	12
B2	SP2	15(p) violet brown	10	12
B3	SP3	25(p) light blue	17	20

Nos. B1 to B3 were sold at double face value, the excess being for the benefit of invalid soldiers.

У.Р.И. U.R.I.

This overprint was applied to 500,000 copies of No. B1 in 1923 and they were given to the Society for Wounded Invalids (Uprava Ratnih Invalida) which sold them for 2d apiece. These overprinted stamps had no franking power, but some were used through ignorance.

Regular Issue of 1926–27
Surcharged in Dark Red **+0·25**

1926, Nov. 1 ***Perf. 13***

B5	A6	25p+25p green	10	3
B6	"	50p+50p olive brown	10	3
B7	"	1d+50p scarlet	20	3
B8	"	2d+50p black	40	14
B9	"	3d+50p slate blue	25	10
B10	"	4d+50p red orange	90	30
B11	"	5d+50p bright violet	70	20
B12	"	8d+50p black brown	2.75	55
B13	"	10d+1d olive brown	3.00	30
B14	"	15d+1d brown	8.50	85
B15	"	20d+1d dark violet	7.00	70
B16	"	30d+1d orange	25.00	2.75
		a. Double surcharge	55.00	40.00
		Nos. B5-B16 (12)	48.90	5.98

The surtax on these stamps was intended for a fund for relief of sufferers from floods.

Cathedral at Duvno
SP4

King Tomislav
SP6

Kings Tomislav and Alexander
SP5

Perf. 12½, 11½x12

1929, Nov. 1 **Typographed**

B17	SP4	50p(+50p) olive grn.	55	60
B18	SP5	1d(+50p) red	55	60
B19	SP6	3d(+1d) blue	2.50	2.25

Issued to commemorate the millenary of the Croatian kingdom. The surtax was used to create a War Memorial Cemetery in France and to erect a monument to Serbian soldiers who died there.

View of Dobropolje
SP7

View of Kajmaktchalan
SP9

War Memorial
SP8

1931, Apr. 1 ***Perf. 12½, 11½***

B20	SP7	50p+50p blue green	8	10
B21	SP8	1d+1d scarlet	12	15
B22	SP9	3d+3d deep blue	18	20

The surtax was added to a fund for a War Memorial to Serbian soldiers who died in France during World War I.

SP10

SP12

SP11

Black Overprint.

1931, Nov. 1 ***Perf. 12½, 11½x12***

B23	SP10	50p(+50p) olive green	8	*45*
B24	SP11	1d(+50p) red	10	*50*
B25	SP12	3d(+1d) blue	30	*60*

Surtax for War Memorial fund.

Rower on Danube at Smederevo
SP13

Bled Lake—SP14

Danube near Belgrade
SP15

View of Split Harbor
SP16

Zagreb Cathedral
SP17

Prince Peter
SP18

1932, Sept. 2 **Litho.** ***Perf. 11½***

B26	SP13	75p+50p dull green & light blue	75	1.45
B27	SP14	1d+½d scarlet & light blue	85	1.55
B28	SP15	1½d+½d rose & green	95	1.65
B29	SP16	3d+1d blue & light blue	1.25	2.00
B30	SP17	4d+1d red orange & light blue	6.50	6.50
B31	SP18	5d+1d dull violet & lilac	5.50	6.00
		Nos. B26-B31 (6)	15.80	19.15

Issued in connection with the European Rowing Championship Races held at Belgrade.

+0·25
XI int. kongres
Pen-Klubova
u Dubrovniku 1933.

King Alexander
SP19

Prince Peter
SP20

1933, May 25 **Typo.** ***Perf. 12½***

B32	SP19	50p+25p black	4.50	4.75
B33	"	75p+25p yel. grn.	4.50	4.75
B34	"	1.50d+50p rose	4.50	4.75
B35	"	3d+1d bl. violet	4.50	4.75
B36	"	4p+1d dk. green	4.50	4.75
B37	"	5d+1d orange	4.50	4.75
		Nos. B32-B37 (6)	27.00	28.50

Issued in connection with the Eleventh International Congress of P. E. N. (Poets, Editors and Novelists) Clubs at Dubrovnik, May 25-27, 1933.

The labels at the foot of the stamps are printed in either Cyrillic or Latin letters and each bears the amount of a premium for the benefit of the local P. E. N. Club at Dubrovnik.

1933, June 28

B38	SP20	75p+25p slate grn.	25	40
B39	"	1½d+½d deep red	25	40

Issued in connection with the sixtieth anniversary meeting of the National Sokols (Sports Associations) at Ljubljana, July 1st, 1933.

Eagle Soaring over City
SP22

Athlete and Eagle
SP23

1934, June 1 ***Perf. 12½***

B40	SP22	75p+25p green	4.50	1.50
B41	"	1.50d+50p carmine	6.75	2.00
B42	"	1.75d+25p brown	11.50	2.75

20th anniversary of Sokols of Sarajevo.

1934, June 1

B43	SP23	75p+25p Prussian green	3.25	1.10
B44	"	1.50d+50p carmine	5.75	1.75
B45	"	1.75d+25p choc.	9.50	2.50

60th anniversary of Sokols of Zagreb.

Mother and Children
SP24 SP25

Perf. 12½x11½

1935, Dec. 25 **Photogravure**

B46	SP24	1.50d+1d dk. brn. & brown	2.10	1.30
		a. Perf. 11½	15.00	15.00
B47	SP25	3.50d+1.50d bright ultramarine & blue	2.50	1.50

The surtax was for "Winter Help."

Queen Mother Marie
SP26

Prince Regent Paul
SP27

1936, May 3 **Lithographed**

B48	SP26	75(p)+25(p) greenish bl.	1.00	90
B49	"	1.50(d)+50(p) rose pink	1.15	1.00
B50	"	1.75(d)+75(p) brn.	1.40	1.10
B51	"	3.50(d)+1(d) brt. blue	1.30	1.05

Nos. B48 and B50 are printed in Slavic. Nos. B49 and B51 are printed in Roman letters.

1936, Sept. 20 **Typographed**

B52	SP27	75p+50p turquoise green & red	45	*2.10*
B53	"	1.50d+50p cerise & red	40	*1.85*

The surtax was for the benefit of the Red Cross.

Princes Tomislav and Andrej
SP28 SP29

Perf. 11½x12½, 12½x11½

1937, May 1

B54 SP28 25p+25p red brown 30 40
B55 " 75p+75p emerald 40 50
B56 SP29 1.50d+1d org. red 45 55
B57 " 2d+1d magenta 50 60

Souvenir Sheet.

National Costumes SP30

1937, Sept. 12 ***Perf. 14***

B57A SP30 Sheet of four 1.85 2.75
b. 1d blue green 30 40
c. 1.50d bright violet 30 40
d. 2d rose red 30 40
e. 4d dark blue 30 40

Issued in sheets measuring 109x150mm. containing one each of the four stamps with inscriptions in margins. Issued for the First Jugoslavian Philatelic Exhibition at Belgrade and sold only at the exhibition post office at 15d each.

SP31  SP32

Perf. 11½x12½, 12½x11½.

1938, May 1 **Photogravure**

B58 SP31 50p+50(p) dk. brn. 55 60
B59 SP32 1d+1(d) dk. grn. 65 70
B60 SP31 1.50d+1.50(d) scarlet 85 90
B61 SP32 2d+2(d) magenta 90 95

The surtax was for the benefit of Child Welfare.

Bridge and Anti-aircraft Lights SP33

1938, May 28 ***Perf. 11½x12½***

B62 SP33 1d+50(p) dark green 90 90
B63 " 1.50d+1(d) scarlet 1.25 1.20
a. Perf. 11½ 15.00 15.00
B64 " 2d+1(d) rose vio. 1.50 1.40
a. Perf. 11½ 13.50 13.50
B65 " 3d+1.50(d) dp. bl. 1.75 1.60

International Aeronautical Exhibition, Belgrade.

Cliff at Demir-Kapiya SP34

Modern Hospital—SP35

Runner Carrying Torch SP36 **Alexander I SP37**

Perf. 11½x12½, 12½x11½

1938, Aug. 1

B66 SP34 1(d)+1d slate green & deep green 1.10 1.20
B67 SP35 1.50(d)+1.50d scarlet 1.50 1.60
B68 SP36 2(d)+2d claret & deep rose 1.75 1.85
B69 SP37 3(d)+3d dp. bl. 1.75 1.85

The surtax was to raise funds to build a hospital for railway employees.

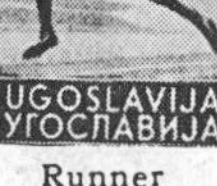

Runner SP38 **Shot-Putter SP41**

Hurdlers—SP39

Pole Vaulter—SP40

1938, Sept. 11

B70 SP38 50(p)+50p orange brown 1.50 1.50
B71 SP39 1(d)+1d slate green & deep green 2.25 2.25
B72 SP40 1.50(d)+1.50d rose & dk. magenta 2.00 2.00
B73 SP41 2(d)+2d dk. blue 3.00 3.00

Ninth Balkan Games.

Stamps of 1938 Overprinted in Black

SALVATE PARVULOS *a* SALVATE PARVULOS *b*

1938, Oct. 1

B75 SP31 (*a*) 50p+50(p) dark brown 85 85
B76 SP32 (*b*) 1d+1d dk. grn. 90 95
B77 SP31 (*a*) 1.50d+1.50(d) scarlet 95 1.00
B78 SP32 (*b*) 2d+2d magenta 1.25 1.30

The surtax was for the benefit of Child Welfare.

Postriders—SP43

Designs: 1+1d, Rural mail delivery. 1.50+1.50d, Mail train. 2+2d, Mail bus. 4+4d, Mail plane.

1939, Mar. 15 **Photo.** ***Perf. 11½***

B79 SP43 50(p)+50p buff, bistre & brown 75 70
B80 " 1(d)+1d slate green & deep green 85 80
B81 " 1.50(d)+1.50d red, copper red & brown carmine 1.10 1.00
B82 " 2(d)+2d deep plum & rose lilac 1.50 1.40
B83 " 4(d)+4d indigo & slate blue 2.50 2.75
Nos. B79-B83 (5) 6.70 6.65

Issued in commemoration of the centenary of the present postal system in Jugoslavia. The surtax was used for the Railway Benevolent Association.

The Cyrillic and Latin inscriptions are transposed on Nos. B82 and B83.

Child Eating—SP48

Children at Seashore SP49 **Children in Crib SP51**

Boy Planing Board—SP50

1939, May 1 ***Perf. 12½***

B84 SP48 1(d)+1d black & dp. bl. grn. 1.35 1.35
B85 SP49 1.50(d)+1.50d orange brown & salmon 1.75 1.75
a. Perf. 11½ 30.00 25.00
B86 SP50 2(d)+2d maroon & vio. rose 2.00 2.00
B87 SP51 4(d)+4d indigo & royal bl. 2.50 2.75

The surtax was for the benefit of Child Welfare.

Czar Lazar of Serbia SP52 **Milosh Obilich SP53**

1939, June 28 ***Perf. 11½***

B88 SP52 1d+1d slate green & blue green 1.50 1.25
B89 SP53 1.50d+1.50d maroon & brt. carmine 1.50 1.25

Battle of Kossovo, 550th anniversary.

Training Ship "Jadran" SP54

Designs: 1d+50p, Steamship "King Alexander." 1.50+1d, Freighter "Triglan." 2+1.50d, Cruiser "Dubrovnik."

1939, Sept. 6 **Engraved**

B90 SP54 50p+50p brn. org. 1.30 1.40
B91 " 1d+50p dull grn. 1.60 1.75
B92 " 1.50d+1d deep rose 1.50 1.65
B93 " 2d+1.50d dk. bl. 1.75 2.00

Issued to honor the Jugoslav Navy and Merchant Marine. The surtax aided a Marine Museum.

Motorcycle and Sidecar SP58 **Motorcycle SP60**

Racing Car—SP59

Racing Car—SP61

1939, Sept. 3 **Photogravure**

B94 SP58 50p+50p brown, red org. & yellow 1.50 1.30
B95 SP59 1d+1d black, blue green & peacock green 1.75 1.45

B96 SP60 1.50d+1.50d chocolate & copper red 2.00 1.60
B97 SP61 2d+2d indigo, dark blue & ultramarine 3.00 2.75

Issued to commemorate the Automobile and Motorcycle Races held at Belgrade. The surtax was for the Race Organization and the State Treasury.

Unknown Soldier Memorial
SP62

1939, Oct. 9 ***Perf. 12½***

B98 SP62 1d+50p slate green & green 1.60 1.70
B99 " 1.50d+1d red & rose red 1.70 1.80
B100 " 2d+1.50d deep claret & violet rose 1.90 2.10
B101 " 3d+2d deep blue & blue 1.90 2.10

Issued in commemoration of the 5th anniversary of the assassination of King Alexander.
The surtax was used to aid World War I invalids.
The Cyrillic and Latin inscriptions are transposed on Nos. B99 and B101.

Postman Delivering Mail
SP64

Postman Emptying Mail Box
SP65

Parcel Post Delivery Wagon
SP66

Parcel Post—SP67

Repairing Telephone Wires
SP68

1940, Jan. 1

B102 SP64 50p+50p brown & deep orange 1.25 1.10
B103 SP65 1d+1d slate green & blue green 1.50 1.30
B104 SP66 1.50d+1.50d red brn. & scarlet 1.85 1.60
B105 SP67 2d+2d dull violet & red lilac 2.10 1.80
B106 SP68 4d+4d slate blue & blue 2.50 2.75
Nos. B102-B106 (5) 9.20 8.55

The surtax was used for the employees of the Postal System in Belgrade.

Croats' Arrival at Adriatic in 640
SP69

King Tomislav
SP70

Death of Matija Gubec
SP71

Anton and Stjepan Radic
SP72

Map of Jugoslavia
SP73

1940, Mar. 1 Typo. ***Perf. 11½***

B107 SP69 50p+50p brown orange 80 80
B108 SP70 1d+1d green 90 90
B109 SP71 1.50d+1.50d bright red 1.00 1.00
B110 SP72 2d+2d dark cerise 1.20 1.20
B111 SP73 4d+2d dark blue 1.40 1.50
Nos. B107-B111 (5) 5.30 5.40

The surtax was used for the benefit of postal employees in Zagreb.

Children Playing in Snow
SP74

Children at Seashore
SP75

Photogravure.

1940, May 1 ***Perf. 11½, 12½***

B112 SP74 50p+50p brown orange & orange yellow 75 65
B113 SP75 1d+1d slate green & dark green 85 70
B114 SP74 1.50d+1.50d brown red & scarlet 70 60
B115 SP75 2d+2d maroon & violet rose 1.00 95

The surtax was for Child Welfare.

Air Post Stamps of 1937 Surcharged in Carmine

0·50
+0·50

Perf. 11½x12½, 12½x11½.

1940, Dec. 23

B116 AP6 50(p)+50(p) on 5d brown violet 60 75
B117 AP7 1(d)+1(d) on 10d brown lake 65 80
B118 AP8 1.50(d)+1.50(d) on 20d dark green 70 85
B119 AP9 2(d)+2(d) on 30d ultramarine 80 1.00

The surtax was used to fight tuberculosis.

St. Peter's Cemetery at Ljubljana—SP76

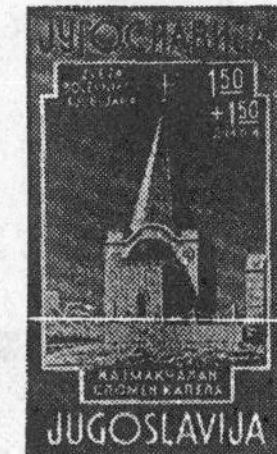

Croatian, Serbian and Slovenian
SP77

Chapel at Kajmaktchalan
SP78

Memorial at Brezje
SP79

1941, Jan. 1 ***Perf. 12½***

B120 SP76 50p+50p gray green & yellow green 80 95
B121 SP77 1d+1d brown carmine & dull rose 85 1.00
B122 SP78 1.50d+1.50d myrtle green & blue green 90 1.05
B123 SP79 2d+2d gray blue & pale lilac 95 1.10

The surtax was for the Ljubljana War Veterans Association.

Kamenita Gate, Zagreb
SP80

13th Century Cathedral, Zagreb
SP81

1941, Mar. 16 Engr. ***Perf. 11½***

B124 SP80 1.50d+1.50d choc. 1.00 1.10
B125 SP81 4d+3d blue blk. 1.00 1.10

2nd Philatelic Exhibition of Croatia, at Zagreb, Mar. 16–27.
Nos. B124–B125 exist perf. 9½ on right side. Price, each $25.

1941, April

B126 SP80 1.50+1.50d bl. blk. 20.00 35.00
B127 SP81 4d+3d choc. 20.00 35.00

Issued for a regional philatelic exhibition at Slavonski Brod. Nos. B126–B127 with gold overprint, "Nezavisna Drzava Hrvatska," are Croatia Nos. B1–B2.
Nos. B126–B127 exist perf. 9½ on right side. Price, each $55 unused, $70 used.

Issues for Federal Republic.

Carrying Wounded Soldier
SP82

Child
SP83

Perf. 11½

1945, Sept. 15 Typo. **Unwmkd.**

B131 SP82 1d+4d dp. ultra. 1.85 1.85
B132 SP83 2d+6d scarlet 1.85 1.85

The surtax was for the Red Cross.

Russia, Jugoslavia Flags—SP84

1945, Oct. 20 Photogravure

B133 SP84 2d+5d multi. 1.50 1.75

Issued to commemorate the 1st anniversary of the liberation of Belgrade.

Communications Symbols
SP85

Flag and Young Laborers
SP86

1946, May 10 ***Perf. 12½***

B134 SP85 1.50d+1d emerald 5.25 4.75
B135 " 2.50d+1.50d carmine rose 5.25 4.75

B136 SP85 5d+2d gray bl. 5.25 4.75
B137 " 8d+3.50d dull brown 5.25 4.75

Issued to commemorate the first PTT Congress since liberation, May 10, 1946.
Inscription in lower panel on Nos. B135 and B136 is in Latin characters.

1946, Aug. 1 Lithographed

Flag in Red or Carmine and Deep or Dark Blue.

B138 SP86 50p+50p brown & buff 4.75 2.50
B139 " 1.50d+1d dk. green & lt. green 4.75 2.00
B140 " 2.50d+2d rose vio. & rose lilac 4.75 2.00
B141 " 5d+3d gray blue & blue 4.75 2.50

Inscription at top differs on each denomination and the Cyrillic and Latin spellings of Jugoslavia are transposed on Nos. B139 and B141.
The surtax aided railroad reconstruction carried out by Jugoslav youths.

Handstand on Horizontal Bar
SP87

1947, Sept. 5 *Perf. 11½*

B142 SP87 1.50d+50p dark green 50 50
B143 " 2.50d+50p carmine 55 55
B144 " 4d+50p brt. bl. 60 60

Issued to commemorate the 1947 Balkan Games, September 5th to 7th at Ljubljana.

Young Railway Laborers
SP88

1947, Sept. 25 Typo. *Perf. 11½x12*

B145 SP88 1d+50p orange 40 30
B146 " 1.50d+ 1d yel. grn. 40 30
B147 " 2.50d+1.50d carmine lake 40 30
B148 " 5d+2d deep blue 40 30

The surtax was for youth brigades employed in the construction of the Samac-Sarajevo railway.

Symbolizing Protection of "B.C.G." Vaccine
SP89

Dying Serpent
SP91

"Illness" and "Recovery"
SP90

1948, Apr. 1 Litho. *Perf. 12½*

B149 SP89 1.50(d)+1(d) slate black & red 55 45
B150 SP90 2.50(d)+2(d) greenish gray, olive black & red 55 45
B151 SP91 5(d)+3(d) dark blue & car. 55 45

Issued to publicize the fight against tuberculosis. The surtax was for the Jugoslav Red Cross.

Juro Danicic
SP92

Shot Put
SP93

Portraits: 2.50d+1d, Franjo Racki. 4d+2d, Josip J. Strossmayer.

1948, July 28 *Perf. 11*

B152 SP92 1.50(d)+50(p) black green 55 45
B153 " 2.50d+1d dk. red 55 45
B154 " 4(d)+2(d) dark blue 55 45

Issued on the occasion of the 80th anniversary of the Jugoslav Academy of Arts and Sciences, Zagreb. The surtax was for the Academy.
"JUGOSLAVIJA" (Latin characters) on No. B153.

1948, Sept. 10 *Perf. 12½*

Designs: 3d+1d, Hurdles. 5d+2d, Pole vault.

B155 SP93 2d+1d dull green 75 65
B156 " 3d+1d rose 75 65
B157 " 5d+2d dull blue 75 65

Balkan and Central Europe Games, 1948. Latin and Cyrillic spellings of "Jugoslavia" transposed on No. B156. On sale 4 days.

AIR POST STAMPS.

Dubrovnik
AP1

Lake Bled
AP2

Falls of Jaice
AP3

Church at Oplenac
AP4

Bridge at Mostar
AP5

Perf. 12½

1934, June 15 Typo. Unwmkd.

C1 AP1 50p violet brown 30 15
C2 AP2 1d green 30 15
C3 AP3 2d rose red 1.00 40
C4 AP4 3d ultramarine 1.00 40
C5 AP5 10d vermilion 2.75 2.00
Nos. C1-C5 (5) 5.35 3.10

King Alexander Memorial Issue.

Border in Black

1935, Jan. 1

C6 AP4 3d ultramarine 3.75 2.25

St. Naum Convent
AP6

Port of Rab
AP7

Sarajevo
AP8

Ljubljana—AP9

Perf. 12½, 11½x12½, 12½x11½.

1937, Sept. 12 Photogravure

C7 AP6 50p brown 12 5
C8 AP7 1d yellow green 12 5
C9 AP8 2d blue gray 15 7
C10 AP9 2.50d rose red 18 7
C11 AP6 5d brown violet 20 15
C12 AP7 10d brown lake 30 20
C13 AP8 20d dark green 50 35
C14 AP9 30d ultramarine 85 60
Nos. C7-C14 (8) 2.42 1.54

Cathedral of Zagreb
AP10

Bridge at Belgrade
AP11

1940, Aug. 15 Litho. *Perf. 12½*

C15 AP10 40d Prussian green & pale green 3.00 3.75
C16 AP11 50d slate blue & gray blue 3.00 3.75

Issues for Federal Republic.

Plane over Terrace of Kalimegdan, Belgrade
AP12

Plane over Dubrovnik
AP13

Typographed.

1947, Apr. 21 *Perf. 11½* **Unwmkd.**

Cyrillic Inscription at Top

C17 AP12 50p olive gray & brown violet 15 3
C18 AP13 1d magenta & olive gray 35 6
C19 AP12 2d blue & black 40 8
C20 AP13 5d green & gray 55 15
C21 AP12 10d olive bistre & chocolate 70 25
C22 AP13 20d ultra. & olive 1.35 40

Roman Inscription at Top

C23 AP12 50p olive gray & brown violet 15 3
C24 AP13 1d magenta & olive gray 35 6
C25 AP12 2d blue & black 40 8
C26 AP13 5d green & gray 55 15
C27 AP12 10d olive bistre & chocolate 70 25
C28 AP13 20d ultra. & olive 1.35 40
Nos. C17-C28 (12) 7.00 1.94

Sheets of each denomination contain alternately stamps with Cyrillic or Roman inscription at top. Price, 6 se-tenant pairs, $75.

Laurent Kosir and Birthplace
AP14

1948, Aug. 27 **Engraved.**

C29 AP14 15d red violet 1.85 1.25

Issued in sheets of 25 stamps and 25 labels to commemorate the 80th anniversary of the death of Laurent Kosir, recognized by Jugoslavia as inventor of the postage stamp.

Nos. 262 to 264 Overprinted in Blue or Carmine

AVIONSKA POSTA

1949, Aug. 25 *Perf. 12½* **Unwmkd.**

C30 A55 3d carmine rose 3.00 5.25
C31 A56 5d dull blue (C) 3.00 5.25
C32 A57 12d red brown 3.00 5.25

Issued to commemorate the fifth anniversary of the liberation of Macedonia.
It is reported that No. C32 was not sold to the public at the post office.

Souvenir Sheet.

Electric Train
AP15

Perf. 11½x12½

1949, Dec. 15 Photogravure

C33 AP15 10d lilac rose 82.50 50.00
a. Imperf. 82.50 50.00

Centenary of Jugoslav railroads. Size: 47x69mm.

Iron Gate, Derdap—AP16

Belgrade—AP17

Designs: 2d, Cascades, Plitvice. 3d, Carolina. 6d, Roman bridge, Mostar. 10d, Ohrid. 20d, Gulf of Kotor. 30d, Dubrovnik. 50d, Bled.

Engraved.

1951, June 16 *Perf. 12½* **Unwmkd.**

C34	AP16	1d deep orange	15	3
C35	"	2d dark green	15	3
C36	"	3d dark red	35	5
C37	"	6d ultramarine	6.00	6.75
C38	"	10d dark brown	60	8
C39	"	20d greenish black	70	8
C40	"	30d deep claret	1.10	8
C41	"	50d dark purple	1.25	25
C42	AP17	100d dk. gray bl.	35.00	6.50
		Nos. C34-C42 (9)	45.30	13.85

Souvenir Sheet.

1951, June 16 *Imperf.*

C43	AP17	100d red brown	150.00	140.00

Mostar Bridge Type of 1951 Overprinted "ZEFIZ 1951" in Carmine.

Perf. 12½.

C44	AP16	6d dark green	2.25	2.25

Nos. C43-C44 were issued for Zagreb Philatelic Exhibition, June 16-26.

No. C43 has red brown frame and marginal inscription, "ZEFIZ 1951". Size: 69x71mm.

See also Nos. C50-C53.

View on Mt. Kapaonik AP18 — Plane and Parachutists AP19

Designs: 5d, Mt. Triglav. 20d, Mt. Kalnik.

Photogravure.

1951, July *Perf. 12½* **Unwmkd.**

Inscribed "UIAA-1951."

C45	AP18	3d lilac rose	3.00	2.00
C46	"	5d blue	3.00	2.00
C47	"	20d blue green	75.00	55.00

Issued to publicize the 12th assembly of the International Union of Mountaineers, Bled, July 13-18, 1951.

1951, Aug. 16 **Engraved.**

C48	AP19	6d carmine	5.00	2.50

Type of 1951 Overprinted in Carmine — I SVETSKO TAKMIČENJE PADOBRANACA 1951

C49	AP16	50d blue	65.00	55.00

First World Parachute Championship, Bled, Aug. 16-20, 1951.

Types of 1951

1951-52

Designs: 5d, Cascades, Plitvice. 100d, Carniola. 200d, Roman bridge, Mostar.

C50	AP16	5d yel. brn. ('52)	10	5
C51	AP16	100d green	1.25	8
C52	"	200d dp. car. ('52)	1.50	30
C53	AP17	500d blue vio. ('52)	4.00	90

Marshal Tito, Tank, Factory and Planes AP20

1951, Dec. 22

C54	AP20	150d deep blue	8.00	6.50

Issued to publicize Army Day, Dec. 22, 1951 and to commemorate the 10th anniversary of the formation of the first military unit of "New" Jugoslavia.

Star and Flag-encircled Globe AP21

1953, July 30 **Engraved.**

C55	AP21	300d bl. & green	250.00	250.00

Issued to publicize the 38th Esperanto Congress, Zagreb, July 25-Aug. 1, 1953.

13th Century Tower, Zagreb AP22

Chalky Paper.

1956, May 20 *Perf. 11½* **Unwmkd.**

C56	AP22	30d gray, violet blue & org. red	3.25	2.00

Jugoslav International Philatelic Exhibition, JUFIZ III, Zagreb, May 20-27.

Workers and Cogwheel AP23 — Moon and Earth with Satellites AP24

1956, June 15 **Photogravure**

Glossy Paper.

C57	AP23	30d carmine rose & black	3.25	2.25

10th anniversary of technical education.

1958, Oct. 24 **Engraved** *Perf. 12½*

C58	AP24	300d dark blue	8.00	3.25

Issued for the International Geophysical Year, 1957-58.

Types of Regular Issue, 1961.

1961, Sept. 1 *Perf. 11½*

C59	A150	250d dark purple	1.50	1.35
C60	A151	500d violet blue	3.50	2.50

See note after No. 615.

Type of Athletic Regular Issue, 1962

Souvenir Sheet

Design: Army Stadium, Belgrade.

Lithographed

1962, Sept. 12 *Imperf.* **Unwmkd.**

C61	A161	600d vio. & black	3.50	3.25

Issued to commemorate the Seventh European Athletic Championships, Belgrade, Sept. 12-16. No. C61 has gray margin and black inscription. Size: 56½x71mm.

POSTAGE DUE STAMPS.

King Alexander D1

1921 *Perf. 11½* **Unwmkd.**

Red or Black Surcharge.

J1	D1	10p on 5p green (R)	30	15
J2	"	30p on 5p green (Bk)	25	15

D2

D3

1921-22 Typo. *Perf. 11½*

J3	D2	10p rose	20	5
J4	"	30p yellow green	30	20
J5	"	50p violet	30	5
J6	"	1d brown	40	5
J7	"	2d blue	45	5
J8	D3	5d orange	8.50	60
J9	"	10d violet brown	12.50	70
		a. Cliché of 10p in sheet of 10d	60.00	125.00
J10	"	25d pink	45.00	2.25
J11	"	50d green	37.50	1.65
		Nos. J3-J11 (9)	105.15	5.60

1924 *Perf. 9, 10½, 11½*

J12	D3	10p rose red	20	10
J13	"	30p yellow green	50	30
J14	"	50p violet	25	10
J15	"	1d brown	40	10
J16	"	2d deep blue	70	5
J17	"	5d orange	12.50	10
J18	"	10d violet brown	40.00	20
J19	"	25d pink	85.00	85
J20	"	50d green	115.00	75
		Nos. J12-J20 (9)	254.55	2.55

Nos. J19-J20 Surcharged — 10

1928

J21	D3	10(d) on 25d pink	5.75	50
J22	"	10(d) on 50d green	5.75	50
		a. Invtd. surch.	40.00	25.00

A second type of "1" in surcharge has flag projecting horizontally. Price, each $15 unused, $3 used.

Coat of Arms D4

Numeral of Value D5

1931 Typographed *Perf. 12½*

With Imprint at Foot.

J23	D4	50p violet	2.00	30
J24	"	1d deep magenta	3.50	15
J25	"	2d deep blue	8.75	15
J26	"	5d orange	3.75	30
J27	"	10d chocolate	10.00	1.10
		Nos. J23-J27 (5)	28.00	2.00

1932 Without Imprint at Foot

J28	D4	50p violet	5	3
J29	"	1d deep magenta	5	3
J30	"	2d deep blue	10	3
J31	"	5d orange	15	10
J32	"	10d chocolate	35	20
		Nos. J28-J32 (5)	70	39

1933 *Perf. 9, 10½, 11½.*

Overprint in Green, Blue or Maroon

J33	D5	50p violet (G)	20	10
J34	"	1d brown (Bl)	30	10
		a. Perf. 10½	5.00	1.25
J35	"	2d blue (M)	60	15
		a. Perf. 10½	2.50	80
J36	"	5d orange (Bl)	2.00	25
J37	"	10d violet brown (Bl)	9.00	1.50
		Nos. J33-J37 (5)	12.10	2.10

Issues for Federal Republic.

Redrawn Type OD5, German Occupation of Serbia, Overprinted in Black

1945 *Perf. 12½* **Unwmkd.**

J37A	OD5	10d red	60	60
J37B	"	20d ultramarine	60	60

In the redrawn design the eagle is replaced by a colorless tablet.

Coat of Arms D6

Torches and Star D7

1945 Lithographed *Perf. 12½*

Numerals in Black.

J38	D6	2d brown violet	8	1.25
J39	"	3d violet	8	1.25
J40	"	5d green	8	1.25
J41	"	7d orange brown	8	1.25
J42	"	10d rose lilac	8	1.25
J43	"	20d blue	8	1.25
J44	"	30d light blue green	35	2.00
J45	"	40d rose red	35	2.00

Numerals in Color of Stamp.

J46	D6	1d blue green	20	3
J47	"	1.50d blue	40	3
J48	"	2d vermilion	40	3
J49	"	3d violet brown	40	3
J50	"	4d rose violet	40	3
		Nos. J38-J50 (13)	2.98	11.65

1946-47 Typographed **Unwmkd.**

J51	D7	50p deep orange ('47)	10	3
J52	"	1d orange	10	3
J53	"	2d dark blue	10	3
J54	"	3d yellow green	35	3
J55	"	5d bright purple	35	3
J56	"	7d crimson	70	5
J57	"	10d bright pink ('47)	1.25	15
J58	"	20d rose lake ('47)	1.75	40
		Nos. J51-J58 (8)	4.70	75

Latin inscription at top, Cyrillic at bottom on 50p, 2d, 5d and 10d.

Nos. J47, J49 and J50 Overprinted in Black — ФНРЈУГОСЛАВИЈА / FNR JUGOSLAVIJA

1950 Lithographed

J64	D6	1.50d blue	7	5
J65	"	3d violet brown	8	6
J66	"	4d rose violet	25	15

Type of 1946-47

1951-52 Typo. *Perf. 12½*

J67	D7	1d brown ('52)	20	3
J68	"	2d emerald	20	3
J69	"	5d blue	40	3
J70	"	10d scarlet	65	3
J71	"	20d purple	95	10
J72	"	30d orange yel. ('52)	1.50	10
J73	"	50d ultramarine	3.00	30
J74	"	100d dp. plum ('52)	6.25	50
		Nos. J67-J74 (8)	13.15	1.12

Latin inscription at top, Cyrillic at bottom on 2d, 5d and 10d.

1962 Lithographed *Perf. 12½*

J75	D7	10d red orange	1.25	10
J76	"	20d purple	1.25	10
J77	"	30d orange	1.75	12
J78	"	50d ultramarine	6.00	60
J79	"	100d rose lake	5.25	60
		Nos. J75-J79 (5)	15.50	1.52

Latin inscription at top, Cyrillic at bottom on 10d.

OFFICIAL STAMPS.

Issues for the Federal Republic

Arms of the Federated People's Republic
O1

Typographed.

1946, Nov. 1 *Perf. 12½.* **Unwmkd.**

O1	O1	50p orange	25	3
O2	"	1d blue green	25	3
O3	"	1.50d olive green	40	3
O4	"	2.50d red	40	3
O5	"	4d yellow brown	60	5
O6	"	5d deep blue	90	5
O7	"	8d chocolate	1.50	18
O8	"	12d violet	1.75	35
		Nos. O1-O8 (8)	6.05	75

The Cyrillic and Latin inscriptions are transposed on Nos. O2, O4, O6 and O8.

POSTAL TAX STAMPS.

The surtax was for the Red Cross unless otherwise noted.

Red Cross Emblem
PT1

Dr. Vladen Djordjevic
PT2

Lithographed.

1933, Sept. 17 *Perf. 13* **Unwmkd.**

RA1 PT1 50p dk. blue & red 20 10

During "Red Cross Week," September 17th to 23rd inclusive, each inland letter had to bear a copy of No. RA1 in addition to the regular postage.

1936, Sept. 20 Typo. *Perf. 12.*

RA2 PT2 50p brn. black & red 30 10

During "Red Cross Week," September 20th to 26th inclusive, each inland letter had to bear a copy of No. RA2 in addition to the regular postage.

Aiding the Wounded
PT3

1938, Sept. 18 Litho. *Perf. 12½.*

RA3 PT3 50p dark blue, red, yellow & green 50 10

1940, Sept. 15 Redrawn

RA4 PT3 50p slate bl. & red 1.25 20

The inscription at the upper right of this stamp and the numerals of value are in smaller characters.

Obligatory on all letters during the second week of September. The funds were used to aid the Red Cross.

Issues for Federal Republic.

Ruined Dwellings
PT4

Red Cross Nurse
PT5

Lithographed.

1947, Jan. 1 *Perf. 12½.* **Unwmkd.**

RA5 PT4 50p brown & scarlet 10 5

1948, Oct. 1

RA6 PT5 50p dark violet blue & red 15 5

Nurse and Child
PT6

Nurse Holding Book
PT7

1949, Nov. 5

RA7 PT6 50p red & brown 15 5

1950, Oct. 1

RA8 PT7 50p dk. green & red 15 5

Obligatory Oct. 1-8, 1950.

Hands Raising Red Cross Flag
PT8

Nurse
PT9

1951, Oct. 7

RA9 PT8 50p vio. blue & red 15 5

Obligatory Oct. 7-14, 1951.

1952, Oct. 5 Photo. *Perf. 12½*

RA10 PT9 50p gray & car. 15 8

Child Receiving Blood Transfusion
PT10

Youths Carrying Flags
PT11

1953, Oct. 25 Lithographed

RA11 PT10 2(d) red vio. & red 15 5

1954, Nov. 1

RA12 PT11 2(d) gray green & red 10 5

Infant
PT11a

1954, Oct. 4

RA12A PT11a 2(d) brown & salmon 60 1.25

The tax was for Children's Week.

Girl
PT12

Nurse Opening Window
PT13

1955, Oct. 2 *Perf. 12½* **Unwmkd.**

RA13 PT12 2(d) dull red 10 5

The tax was for child welfare.

1955, Oct. 31

RA14 PT13 2(d) violet black & red 10 5

Ruins in the Snow
PT14

Children and Goose
PT15

1956, May 6 *Perf. 12½*

RA15 PT14 2d sepia & red 8 3

1956, Sept. 30

RA16 PT15 2d gray green 8 3

The tax was for child welfare.

Plane over Temporary Shelter
PT16

1957, May 5 Lithographed.

RA17 PT16 2d light blue, black & carmine 8 3

Girl and Boy Pioneers
PT17

1957, Sept. 30 *Perf. 12½* **Unwmkd.**

RA18 PT17 2d rose & gray 6 3

Issued for Children's Week. Obligatory Oct. 2-6.

Redrawn Type of Regular Issue, 1953

1958, May 4 *Perf. 12½x12*

RA19 A95 2d multicolor 10 5

On No. RA19 the U. N. Emblem has been left out, Cyrillic inscriptions at left added, country name in Latin letters.

Playing Children
PT18

Helping Hand and Family
PT19

1958, Oct. 5 Litho. *Perf. 12½*

RA20 PT18 2d bright yellow & black 6 3

Issued for Children's Week, Oct. 5-11.

1959, May 3

RA21 PT19 2d blue violet & red 8 3

Issued for the centenary of the Red Cross. Obligatory May 3-9, 1959.

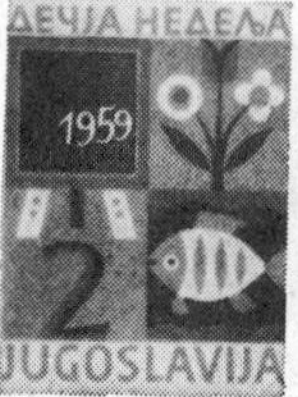

Blackboard, Flower and Fish
PT20

"Reconstruction"
PT21

1959, Oct. 5 **Unwmkd.**

RA22 PT20 2d ochre & Prussian green 8 3

Issued for Children's Week. Obligatory on domestic mail, Oct. 5-11.

1960, May 8 *Perf. 12½*

RA23 PT21 2d slate & red 10 5

Obligatory May 8-14.

Girl and Toys
PT22

Blood Donor Symbolism
PT23

1960, Oct. 2 Litho. *Perf. 12½*

RA24 PT22 2d red 6 3

Issued for Children's Week. Obligatory on domestic mail Oct. 2-8.

1961, May 7

RA25 PT23 2d multicolored 6 5

Obligatory May 7-13. Exists imperf. Price $12.50.

Bird Holding Flower
PT24

1961, Oct. 1

RA26 PT24 2d orange & violet 6 3

Issued for Children's Week. Obligatory on domestic mail, Oct. 1–7.

Bandages and Symbols of Home, Industry, Weather, Transportation, Fire and Flood
PT25

1962, Apr. 30 ***Perf. 12½***

RA27 PT25 5d red brown, gray & red 6 3

Obligatory on domestic mail May 6–12.

Centenary Emblem
PT26

Parachute Drop of Supplies, Jugoslav Flag
PT27

1963, May 5 ***Perf. 12½*** **Unwmkd.**

RA28 PT26 5d dull yellow, red & gray 12 3

Issued to commemorate the centenary of the founding of the International Red Cross. Obligatory on all domestic mail during Red Cross Week, May 5–11.

1964, Apr. 27 **Lithographed**

RA29 PT27 5d blue, rose & dark blue 5 3

Obligatory on domestic mail, May 3–9.

Children in Circle
PT28

1965, May 2 **Litho.** ***Perf. 12½***

RA30 PT28 5d tan & red 5 3

The tax was for the Red Cross. Obligatory on domestic mail, May 2–8, 1965.

Arrows
PT29

1966, Apr. 28 **Litho.** ***Perf. 12½***

RA31 PT29 5p gray & multi. 5 3

The tax was for the Red Cross. Obligatory on domestic mail, May 1–7, 1966.

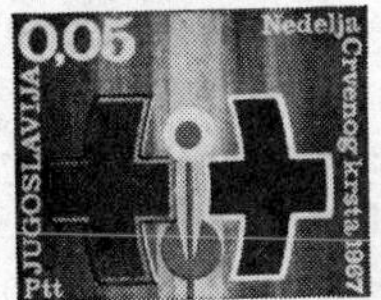

Crosses and Flower
PT30

1967, Apr. 28 **Litho.** ***Perf. 12½***

RA32 PT30 5p violet, red & yellow green 5 3

Honeycomb and Red Cross
PT31

Aztec Calendar Stone and Olympic Rings
PT32

1968, Apr. 30 **Litho.** ***Perf. 12***

RA33 PT31 5p multicolored 5 3

The tax was for the Red Cross. Obligatory on all domestic mail May 5–11, 1968.

1968, Oct. 12 ***Perf. 12½***

RA34 PT32 10p black & multi. 5 3

The tax was for the Jugoslav Olympic Committee.

Red Cross, Hands and Globe
PT33

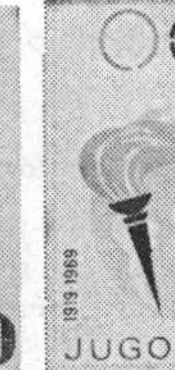

Globe, Olympic Torch and Rings
PT34

1969, May 18 **Litho.** ***Perf. 12***

RA35 PT33 20p red org., dull red & black 5 3

1969, Nov. 24 **Litho.** ***Perf. 11***

RA36 PT34 10p gold & multi. 5 3

The surtax was for the Jugoslav Olympic Committee in connection with its 50th anniversary.

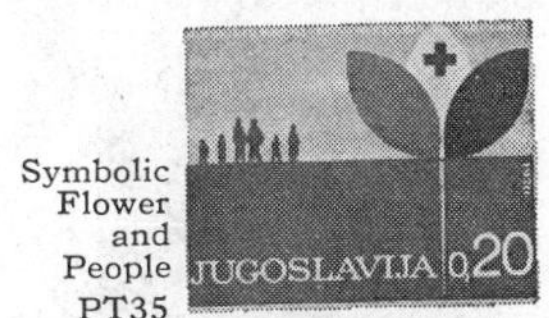

Symbolic Flower and People
PT35

1970, Apr. 27 **Litho.** ***Perf. 13***

RA37 PT35 20p violet blue, org. & red 5 3

Olympic Flag
PT36

1970, June 10 **Litho.** ***Perf. 13x13½***

RA38 PT36 10p multicolored 5 3

Issued for Olympic Week.

Red Cross Encircling Globe
PT37

1971, Apr. 26 **Litho.** ***Perf. 12½***

RA39 PT37 20p bl., yel. & red 5 3

Olympic Rings and Disk
PT38

1971, June 15 **Litho.** ***Perf. 12½***

RA40 PT38 10p blue & black 5 3

Olympic Week.

Red Cross and Hemispheres
PT39

1972, Apr. 27 ***Perf. 13½x13***

RA41 PT39 20p red & multi. 5 3

Olympic Rings, TV Tower, Munich and Sapporo Emblems
PT40

Red Cross, Crescent and Lion Emblems
PT41

1972, May ***Perf. 13x13½***

RA42 PT40 10p ultra. & multi. 5 3

Tax was for the Jugoslav Olympic Committee.

1973, Apr. 24 **Litho.** ***Perf. 13x13½***

RA43 PT41 20p blue & multi. 5 3

Globe and Olympic Rings
PT42

1973, June 1 **Litho.** ***Perf. 13x13½***

RA44 PT42 10p multicolored 8 3

Olympic Week.

Drop of Blood, Red Cross Emblems
PT43

1974, Apr. 25 **Litho.** ***Perf. 13***

RA45 PT43 20p red & multi. 4 3

Olympic Rings
PT44

1974, June 1 **Litho.** ***Perf. 13***

RA46 PT44 10p blue & multi. 10 10

Olympic Week.

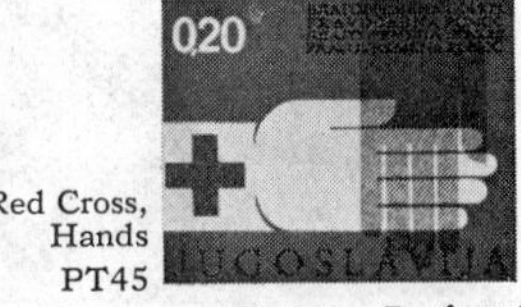

Red Cross, Hands
PT45

1975, Apr. 23 **Photo.** ***Perf. 11½***

RA47 PT45 20p bl., car. & blk. 5 3

Olympic Rings
PT46

1975, June 2 **Litho.** ***Perf. 13½***

RA48 PT46 10p multicolored 3 3

Olympic Week, June 2–9. Tax for Olympic fund.

Ruin and Clock
PT47

1975, July 26 **Litho.** ***Perf. 13x13½***

RA49 PT47 30p gray, dk. blue & black 5 3

Solidarity Week, July 26–Aug. 1.

POSTAL TAX DUE STAMPS.

The tax of Nos. RAJ1–RAJ9, RAJ11–RAJ12, RAJ14 and RAJ18 was for the Red Cross.

Red Cross Emblem PTD1 — Cross and Map of Jugoslavia PTD2

Lithographed.

1933 *Perf. 13.* **Unwmkd.**

RAJ1 PTD1 50p dull green & red 30 10

Type of Postal Tax Stamp of 1947 Inscribed: "PORTO."

1947 *Perf. 12½*

RAJ2 PT4 50p blue green & scarlet 40 15

Type of Postal Tax Stamp of 1948, Inscribed: "PORTO."

1948

RAJ3 PT5 50p dark green & red 35 15

Type of Postal Tax Stamp of 1949 Inscribed: "PORTO."

1949

RAJ4 PT6 50p red & violet 35 15

1950 *Perf. 12½.* **Unwmkd.**

RAJ5 PTD2 50p red brown & red 35 15

Type of Postal Tax Stamp of 1951. Inscribed: "PORTO."

1951

RAJ6 PT8 50p emerald & red 35 15

Red Cross PTD3

Photogravure.

1952 *Perf. 12½.* **Unwmkd.**

RAJ7 PTD3 50p gray & car. 35 15

Type of Postal Tax Stamp of 1953 Inscribed: "PORTO."

1953 Lithographed.

RAJ8 PT10 2(d) yellow brown & red 35 15

Type of Postal Tax Stamp of 1954 Inscribed: "PORTO."

1954

RAJ9 PT11 2(d) lilac & red 20 10

Type of Postal Tax Stamp of 1955. Inscribed: "PORTO."

1955

RAJ10 PT12 2(d) yel. green 25 10

The tax was for child welfare.

Type of Postal Tax Stamp of 1955. Inscribed: "PORTO."

1955

RAJ11 PT13 2(d) dark violet brown & red 30 15

Type of Postal Tax Stamp of 1956. Inscribed: "PORTO."

1956

RAJ12 PT14 2d blue green & red 15 6

Type of Postal Tax Stamp of 1956 Inscribed: "PORTO."

1956

RAJ13 PT15 2d violet brown 15 6

Type of Postal Tax Stamp of 1957 Inscribed: "PORTO."

1957

RAJ14 PT16 2d gray, black & carmine 20 6

Type of Postal Tax Stamp, 1957 Inscribed: "PORTO."

1957

RAJ15 PT17 2d light blue, bistre & green 15 6

Redrawn Type of Regular Issue, 1953, inscribed "PORTO."

1958 *Perf 12½x12*

RAJ16 A95 2d multicolor 25 15

See note after No. RA19.

Child With Toy PTD4

1958 Lithographed. *Perf. 12½*

RAJ17 PTD4 2d light ultramarine & black 15 6

Issued for Children's Week, Oct. 5–11.

Type of Postal Tax Stamp, 1959, Inscribed "PORTO."

1959

RAJ18 PT19 2d yellow orange & red 18 10

Type of Postal Tax Stamp, 1959, Inscribed "PORTO."

Design: Tree, cock and wheat.

1959

RAJ19 PT20 2d ochre & maroon 12 6

Type of Postal Tax Stamp, 1960, Inscribed: "porto."

1960

RAJ20 PT21 2d violet brown & red 22 15

Type of Postal Tax Stamp, 1960, Inscribed: "PORTO."

Design: Boy, tools and ball.

1960

RAJ21 PT22 2d Prussian blue 12 5

Type of Postal Tax Stamp, 1961, Inscribed "PORTO"

1961, May 7

RAJ22 PT23 2d multicolored 20 10

Exists imperf. Price $12.50.

Type of Postal Tax Stamp, 1961. Inscribed "PORTO"

1961, Oct. 1

RAJ23 PT24 2d apple green & brown 12 5

Type of Postal Tax Stamp, 1962, Inscribed: "PORTO."

1962, Apr. 30

RAJ24 PT25 5d brown red, blue & red 12 5

Type of Postal Tax Stamp, 1963, Inscribed: "PORTO."

1963, May 5

RAJ25 PT26 5d red orange, red & gray 20 8

OFFICES ABROAD

King Peter II A1

Typographed.

1943 *Perf. 12½* **Unwmkd.**

1K1	A1	2d dark blue	30	*6.00*
1K2	"	3d slate	35	*6.00*
1K3	"	5d carmine	40	*6.25*
1K4	"	10d black	45	*6.25*

V. Vodnik A2 — Peter Nyegosh A3

Designs: 3d, Ljudovit Gaj. 4d, Vuk Stefanović Karadžić. 5d, Bishop Joseph Strossmayer. 10d, Karageorge.

1943, Dec. 1 Engr. *Perf. 12½x13*

1K5	A2	1d red orange & black	50	*10.00*
1K6	A3	2d yel. grn. & blk.	55	*10.50*
1K7	A2	3d dp. ultra. & black	60	*11.00*
1K8	A3	4d dark purple & brown black	65	*11.50*
1K9	A2	5d brown violet & brown black	70	*12.00*
1K10	A3	10d brown & brown black	75	*12.50*
		Nos. 1K5–1K10 (6)	3.75	*67.50*

25th anniversary of the Union of Liberated Jugoslavia. Valid on ships of the Jugoslav Navy and Mercantile Marine.

Nos. 1K5–1K10 overprinted diagonally "1945" in London were not issued. In 1950, they were sold by the Jugoslav Government without postal validity. Later they appeared with the additional overprint of the outline of a plane at upper left in carmine or black.

Souvenir Sheet.

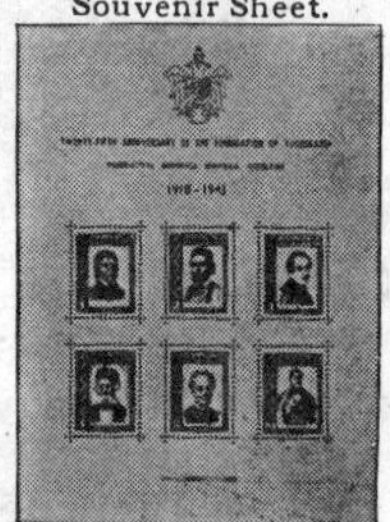

A8

Perf. 13½.

Center in Black.

1K11 A8 Sheet of 6 15.00

No. 1K11 contains one each of Nos. 1K5–1K10. Size: 126x164mm.

SEMI-POSTAL STAMPS.

Nos. 1K1–1K4 Surcharged in Orange or Black — **CRVENI KRST + 12.50**

1943 *Perf. 12½.* **Unwmkd.**

1KB1	A1	2d+12.50(d) dark blue (O)	1.50	*12.50*
1KB2	"	3d+12.50(d) slate (O)	1.50	*12.50*
1KB3	A1	5d+12.50(d) carmine (Bk)	1.50	*12.50*
1KB4	"	10d+12.50(d) black (O)	1.50	*12.50*

The surtax was for the Red Cross.

LJUBLJANA
(Lubiana, Laibach)
Italian Occupation.

Under Italian occupation in 1941, the western half of Slovenia was known as the Province of Ljubljana (Lubiana to the Italians, Laibach to the Germans) and a quisling administration was set up under the profascist General Rupnik.

100 Centesimi = 1 Lira

Jugoslavia Nos. 127, 128 and 142 to 154 Overprinted in Black — **Co. Ci.**

Perf. 12½, 13x12½.

1941 **Unwmkd.**

N1	A16	25p black	15	20
N2	"	50p orange	15	20
N3	"	1d yellow green	15	20
N4	"	1.50d red	15	20
N5	"	2d deep magenta	15	20
N6	"	3d dull red brown	15	20
N7	"	4d ultramarine	15	20
N8	"	5d dark blue	20	20
N9	"	5.50d dk. violet brn.	20	20
N10	"	6d slate blue	35	35
N11	"	8d sepia	55	55
N12	A10	10d bright violet	65	65
N13	A16	12d bright violet	80	80
N14	A10	15d brown	100.00	110.00
N15	A16	16d dull violet	80	80
N16	"	20d blue	1.50	1.75
N17	"	30d bright pink	17.50	17.50
		Nos. N1–N17 (17)	123.60	134.20

Jugoslavia Nos. 127 and 142 to 154 Overprinted in Black — **R.Commissariato Civile Territori Sloveni occupati LUBIANA**

N18	A16	25p black	15	20
N19	"	50p orange	15	20
N20	"	1d yellow green	15	20
N21	"	1.50d red	15	20
N22	"	2d deep magenta	15	20
N23	"	3d dull red brown	25	25
N24	"	4d ultramarine	20	25
N25	"	5d dark blue	65	65
N26	"	5.50d dk. violet brn.	30	30
N27	"	6d slate blue	30	30
N28	"	8d sepia	45	45
N29	A10	10d bright violet	1.10	1.10
N30	A16	12d bright violet	45	45
N31	"	16d dull violet	1.00	1.00
N32	"	20d blue	4.25	4.25
N33	"	30d bright pink	40.00	40.00

Jugoslavia Nos. 145 and 148 Surcharged in Black — **R.Commissariato Civile Territori Sloveni occupati LUBIANA Din**

N34	A16	50p on 1.50d red	30	30
N35	"	1d on 4d ultramarine	30	30
		Nos. N18–N35 (18)	50.30	50.60

German Occupation.

Stamps of Italy, 1929-42, Overprinted or Surcharged in Blue, Carmine, Black or Green

a

b

c

1944 *Perf. 14.* Wmk. 140

N36 A90 (*a*) 5c olive brown (Bl) 20 25
N37 A92 (*b*) 10c dark brown (Bl) 20 25
N38 A93 (*a*) 15c slate green (C) 25 30
N39 A91 (*b*) 20c rose red (Bl) 15 20
N40 A94 (*a*) 25c deep green (C) 15 20
N41 A95 (*b*) 30c olive brown (Bl) 20 25
N42 A93 (*a*) 35c dp. blue (C) 20 25
N43 A95 (*b*) 50c purple (C) 20 25
N44 A94 (*a*) 75c rose red (Bl) 25 30
N45 A91 (*b*) 1 l dp. vio. (Bl) 30 40
N46 A94 (*a*) 1.25 l dp. blue (C) 25 30
N47 A92 (*b*) 1.75 l red orange (Bl) 90 1.25
N48 A93 (*a*) 2 l carmine lake (Bl) 30 35
N49 A90 (*c*) 2.55 l on 5c olive brown (Bk) 30 40
N50 A94 (*a*) 5 l on 25c deep green (Bl) 35 45
N51 A93 (*b*) 10 l purple (Bl) 3.25 3.50
N52 A91 (*a*) 20 l on 20c rose red (G) 1.75 2.25
N53 A93 (*b*) 25 l on 2 l car. lake (G) 2.75 3.75
N54 A92 (*a*) 50 l on 1.75 l red orange (C) 4.00 6.00
Nos. N36-N54 (19) 15.95 20.90

Krizna Jama
A1

Cerknica Lake
A2

Designs: 20c, Railroad Bridge, Borovnica. 25c, Landscape near Ljubljana. 50c, Church, Ribnica. 75c, View, Ljubljana. 1 l, Old Castle, Ljubljana. 1.25 l, Kocevje (Gottschee). 1.50 l, Borovnica Falls. 2 l, Castle, Konstanjevnica. 2.50 l, Castle, Turjak. 3 l, Castle, Zuzemperk. 5 l, View of Krk. 10 l, View of Otolac. 20 l, Farm, Carniola. 30 l, Castle and church, Tabor.

Perf. 10½x11½, 11½x10½.

1945 Photogravure. Unwmkd.

N55 A1 5c black 15 20
N56 A2 10c red orange 15 20
N57 " 20c brown carmine 15 20
N58 " 25c dark slate green 15 20
N59 A1 50c deep violet 15 20
N60 A2 75c vermilion 15 20
N61 " 1 l dark olive green 15 25
N62 A1 1.25 l dark blue 15 25
N63 " 1.50 l olive black 20 30
N64 A2 2 l ultramarine 25 35
N65 " 2.50 l brown 30 45
N66 A1 3 l bright red violet 50 70
N67 A2 5 l dark red brown 50 90
N68 " 10 l slate green 1.00 2.00
N69 A2 20 l sapphire 5.50 7.50
N70 A1 30 l rose pink 60.00 67.50
Nos. N55-N70 (16) 69.45 81.40

SEMI-POSTAL STAMPS.

Italian Occupation.

Jugoslavia Nos. B116 to B119 with Additional Overprint in Black

R.Commissariato Civile Territori Sloveni occupati LUBIANA

Perf. 11½x12½, 12½x11½.

1941 Unwmkd.

NB1 AP6 50p+50p on 5d brown violet 12.00 14.50
NB2 AP7 1d+1d on 10d brown lake 12.00 14.50
NB3 AP8 1.50d+1.50d on 20d dark green 12.00 14.50
NB4 AP9 2d+2d on 30d ultramarine 12.00 14.50

German Occupation.

Italy Nos. E14 and E15 Surcharged in Red:

1944 Wmk. 140

NB5 SD4 1.25 l+50 l green 20.00 25.00
NB6 " 2.50 l+50 l deep orange 20.00 25.00

The surtax aided the Red Cross.

Same, Surcharged in Blue or Green:

NB7 SD4 1.25 l+50 l green 20.00 25.00
NB8 " 2.50 l+50 l deep orange (G) 20.00 25.00

The surtax aided the Homeless Relief Fund.

The German and Slovenian inscriptions in the surcharges are transposed on Nos. NB6 and NB8.

Italy Nos. C12-C14, C16-C18 Surcharged "DEN WAISEN," "SIROTAM," Heraldic Eagle and Surtax in Blue or Red.

1944 Wmk. 140

NB9 AP4 25c+10 l dk. grn 7.00 8.50
NB10 AP3 50c+10 l olive brown 7.00 8.50
NB11 AP5 75c+20 l orange brown 7.00 8.50
NB12 " 1 l+20 l purple 7.00 8.50
NB13 AP6 2 l+20 l deep blue (R) 7.00 8.50
NB14 AP3 5 l+20 l dk. grn. 7.00 8.50
Nos. NB9-NB14 (6) 42.00 51.00

The surcharge aided orphans

Same, Surcharged "WINTERHILFE," "ZIMSKA POMOC," Heraldic Eagle and Surtax in Blue or Red.

NB15 AP4 25c+10 l dk. grn. 7.00 8.50
NB16 AP3 50c+10 l olive brown 7.00 8.50
NB17 AP5 75c+20 l orange brown 7.00 8.50
NB18 " 1 l+20 l purple 7.00 8.50
NB19 AP6 2 l+20 l deep blue (R) 7.00 8.50
NB20 AP3 5 l+20 l dark green 7.00 8.50
Nos. NB15-NB20 (6) 42.00 51.00

The surcharge was for winter relief.

AIR POST STAMPS.

Italian Occupation.

Jugoslavia Nos. C7 to C16 Overprinted in Black

R.Commissariato Civile Territori Sloveni occupati LUBIANA

Perf. 12½, 12½x11½, 11½x12½.

1941 Unwmkd.

NC1 AP6 50p brown 55 55
NC2 AP7 1d yellow green 55 55
NC3 AP8 2d blue gray 85 85
NC4 AP9 2.50d rose red 85 85
NC5 AP6 5d brown violet 1.40 1.40
NC6 AP7 10d brown lake 1.40 1.40
NC7 AP8 20d dark green 10.00 10.00
NC8 AP9 30d ultramarine 40.00 40.00
NC9 AP10 40d Prus. grn. & pale grn. 125.00 135.00
NC10 AP11 50d slate bl. & gray blue 70.00 70.00
a. Invtd. ovpt. 300.00
Nos. NC1-NC10 (10) 250.60 260.60

German Occupation.

Italy Nos. C12 to C14 and C16 to C19 Overprinted in Carmine, Green or Blue

a

b

1944 *Perf. 14.* Wmk. 140

NC11 AP4 (*a*) 25c dark green (C) 1.50 2.00
NC12 AP3 (*b*) 50c olive brown (C) 4.75 6.00
NC13 AP5 (*a*) 75c orange brown (G) 2.50 3.25
NC14 " (*b*) 1 l purple (C) 6.00 8.00
NC15 AP6 (*a*) 2 l deep blue (Bl) 2.75 4.00
NC16 AP3 (*b*) 5 l dark green (C) 3.50 4.75
NC17 " (*a*) 10 l deep carm. (G) 2.75 4.00
Nos. NC11-NC17 (7) 23.75 32.00

AIR POST SPECIAL DELIVERY STAMP.

German Occupation.

Italy No. CE3 Overprinted in Blue

1944 *Perf. 14* Wmk. 140

NCE1 APSD2 2 l gray black 6.00 6.00

SPECIAL DELIVERY STAMP

German Occupation.

Italy No. E14 Overprinted in Green

1944 *Perf. 14.* Wmk. 140

NE1 SD4 1.25 l green 1.25 1.50

POSTAGE DUE STAMPS.

Italian Occupation.

Jugoslavia Nos. J28 to J32 Overprinted in Black **Co. Ci.**

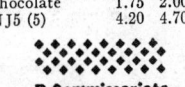

1941 *Perf. 12½* Unwmkd.

NJ1 D4 50p violet 20 20
NJ2 " 1d rose 20 20
NJ3 " 2d deep blue 30 30
NJ4 " 5d orange 1.75 2.00
NJ5 " 10d chocolate 1.75 2.00
Nos. NJ1-NJ5 (5) 4.20 4.70

Same Overprinted in Black

R.Commissariato Civile Territori Sloveni occupati LUBIANA

NJ6 D4 50p violet 10 15
NJ7 " 1d rose 10 15
NJ8 " 2d deep blue 35 35
NJ9 " 5d orange 18.50 18.50
NJ10 " 10d chocolate 5.00 5.00
Nos NJ6-NJ10 (5) 24.05 24.15

Same Overprinted in Black

R. Commissariato Civile Territori Sloveni occupati LUBIANA

NJ11 D4 50p violet 40 40
NJ12 " 1d rose 70 80
NJ13 " 2d deep blue 15.00 17.50

German Occupation.

Postage Due Stamps of Italy, 1934, Overprinted or Surcharged in Various Colors

a

b

c

d

1944 *Perf. 14.* Wmk. 140

NJ14 D6 (*a*) 5c brown (Br) 1.40 1.60
NJ15 " (*b*) 10c blue (Bl) 1.40 1.60
NJ16 " (*a*) 20c rose red (R) 20 25
NJ17 " (*b*) 25c green (G) 20 25
NJ18 " (*c*) 30c on 50c violet (Bk) 20 25
NJ19 " (*d*) 40c on 5c brown (Bl) 20 25
NJ20 " (*a*) 50c violet (V) 20 25
NJ21 D7 (*b*) 1 l red org. (R) 30 30
NJ22 " (*a*) 2 l green (Bl) 40 50
Nos. NJ14-NJ22 (9) 4.50 5.25

Fiume-Kupa Zone.

Italian Occupation.

ZONA OCCUPATA FIUMANO KUPA

O.N.M.I.

Four issues of 1941-42 consist of overprints on Jugoslav stamps of 1939-41: (a.) 14 stamps overprinted "ZONA OCCUPATO FIUMANO KUPA" and "ZOFK ZOFK ZOFK." (b.) 3 stamps overprinted as illustrated. (c.) 1 stamp surcharged "MEMENTO AVDERE SEMPER." "L1," etc. (d) 3 stamps overprinted in arch: "Pro Maternite e Infanzia."

Issues for Istria and the Slovene Coast. (Zone B).

Grapes A1

Olive Branch A2

Sailboat, Pola A3

Designs: 50c, Donkey. Nos. 25–26, Ruined home. 2 l, Duino Castle. 5 l, Birthplace of Vladimir Gortan. 10 l, Plowing. Nos. 33–34, Tuna. 30 l, Viaduct at Solkan, Soca River.

Perf. 11½, 12, 10½x11½.

1945-46 Photogravure.

No.	Type	Description	Unused	Used
23	A1	25c dark green	12	10
24	"	50c red brown	4	4
25	"	1(l) green	4	4
26	"	1(l) red	4	4
27	A2	1.50(l) olive brown	8	4
28	"	2(l) dk. Pruss. green	4	4
29	A3	4(l) red	4	4
30	"	4(l) bright blue	6	4
31	"	5(l) gray black	6	6
32	"	10(l) brown	30	20
33	"	20(l) blue	1.90	65
34	"	20(l) dark violet	3.75	1.35
35	"	30(l) magenta	2.50	80
		Nos. 23–35 (13)	8.97	3.44

The first (Ljubljana) printing is perf. 10½x11½ and consists of Nos. 23–24, 26–28, 30–32, 34–35. The second (Zagreb) printing is perf. 12 and consists of Nos. 23–25, 27–29, 31–33, 35. The third (Belgrade) printing is perf. 11½ and consists of Nos. 25, 28, 40–41.

Nos. 33 and 35 Surcharged with New Values and Bars in Black.

1946 ***Perf. 11½.*** **Unwmkd.**

No.	Type	Description	Unused	Used
36	A3	1(l) on 20(l) blue	55	35
37	"	2(l) on 30(l) magenta	55	35

Types of 1945.

Design: 3 l, Duino Castle.

No.	Type	Description	Unused	Used
40	A2	3(l) crimson	13	5
41	A3	6(l) ultramarine	13	5

Types of Jugoslavia and of Official Stamps of 1946 Surcharged in Black

VOJNA UPRAVA
JUGOSLAVENSKE
ARMIJE

a

VOJNA UPRAVA
JUGOSLAVENSKE
ARMIJE
≡ L 1.50 ≡
b

1947 ***Perf. 12½*** **Unwmkd.**

No.	Type	Description	Unused	Used
42	A26 (a)	1 l on 9d lilac rose	3	3
43	O1 (b)	1.50 l on 50p blue	3	3
44	A26 (a)	2 l on 9d lilac rose	3	3
45	O1 (b)	3 l on 50p blue	3	3
46	A26 (a)	5 l on 9d lilac rose	4	3
47	O1 (b)	6 l on 50p blue	4	3
48	A26 (a)	10 l on 9d lilac rose	6	3
49	O1 (b)	15 l on 50p blue	9	3
50	A26 (a)	35 l on 9d lilac rose	12	5
51	O1 (b)	50 l on 50p blue	20	7
		Nos. 42–51 (10)	67	36

POSTAGE DUE STAMPS.

Nos. 23, 24
34 and 35
Surcharged
in Black

PORTO
1.-
▬ Lit.

1945 ***Perf. 10½x11½.*** **Unwmkd.**

No.	Type	Description	Unused	Used
J1	A3	50c on 20(l) dark violet	40	30
J2	A1	1 l on 25c dark green	2.50	80
J3	A3	2 l on 30(l) magenta	40	20
J4	A1	4 l on 50c red brown	45	30
J5	"	8 l on 50c "	45	30
J6	"	10 l on 50c "	2.50	1.35
J7	"	20 l on 50c "	3.00	1.50
		Nos. J1–J7 (7)	9.70	4.75

Nos. 25 and 35
Surcharged
in Black

Lira
1.-
PORTO

1945 ***Perf. 12***

No.	Type	Description	Unused	Used
J8	A1	1 l on 1 l green	20	12
J9	"	2 l on 1 l "	20	15
J10	"	4 l on 1 l "	45	20
J11	A3	10 l on 30(l) magenta	65	45
J12	"	20 l on 30(l) "	3.25	1.50
J13	"	30 l on 30(l) "	3.25	1.35
		Nos. J8–J13 (6)	8.00	3.77

The surcharges are arranged to fit the designs of the stamps.

No. 23
Surcharged
in Black

PORTO
1.-
▬ Lira

1946

No.	Type	Description	Unused	Used
J14	A1	1 l on 25c dark green	20	8
J15	"	2 l on 25c "	20	10
J16	"	4 l on 25c "	30	10

No. 33 Surcharged in Black

PORTO
Lira
10.-

No.	Type	Description	Unused	Used
J17	A3	10 l on 20(l) blue	75	25
J18	"	20 l on 20(l) "	3.50	1.35
J19	"	30 l on 20(l) "	3.50	1.35
		Nos. J14–J19 (6)	8.45	3.23

Type of Jugoslavia
Postage Due Stamps,
1946,
Surcharged in Black

Vojna Uprava
Jugoslavenske
Armije
≡ L 1 ≡

1947

No.	Type	Description	Unused	Used
J20	D7	1 l on 1d bright blue green	10	12
J21	"	2 l on 1d bright blue green	8	12
J22	"	6 l on 1d bright blue green	15	20
J23	"	10 l on 1d bright blue green	20	25
J24	"	30 l on 1d bright blue green	50	60
		Nos. J20–J24 (5)	1.03	1.29

TRIESTE, ZONE B

See listing under that heading, Vol. IV.

KARELIA

(kȧ-rē'lĭ-ȧ)

LOCATION—In northwestern Soviet Russia.

GOVT.—An autonomous republic of the Soviet Union.

AREA—55,198 sq. mi. (approx.).

POP.—270,000 (approx.).

CAPITAL—Petrozavodsk (Kalininsk).

In 1921 the Karelians rebelled and for a short period a form of sovereignty independent of Russia was maintained.

100 Pennia = 1 Markka

Bear A1

Lithographed.

1922 ***Perf. 11½, 12.*** **Unwmkd.**

No.	Type	Description	Unused	Used
1	A1	5(p) dark gray	8.00	*25.00*
2	"	10(p) light blue	8.00	*25.00*
3	"	20(p) rose red	8.00	*25.00*
4	"	25(p) yellow brown	8.00	*25.00*
5	"	40(p) magenta	8.00	*25.00*
6	"	50(p) gray green	8.00	*25.00*
7	"	75(p) orange yellow	8.00	*25.00*
8	"	1m pink & gray	8.00	*25.00*
9	"	2m yellow green & gray	16.00	*35.00*
10	"	3m light blue & gray	16.00	*35.00*
11	"	5m red lilac & gray	20.00	*65.00*
12	"	10m light brown & gray	20.00	*65.00*
13	"	15m grn. & carmine	20.00	*65.00*
14	"	20m rose & green	20.00	*65.00*
15	"	25m yellow & blue	20.00	*65.00*
		Nos. 1–15 (15)	196.00	

Nos. 1–15 were valid Jan. 31–Feb. 16, 1922. Counterfeits abound.

OCCUPATION STAMPS.

Issued under Finnish Occupation.

Issued in the Russian territory of Eastern Karelia under Finnish military administration.

Types of Finland Stamps, 1930 Overprinted in Black:

ITÄ-
KARJALA
Sot.hallinto
On A26

ITÄ-KARJALA
Sot.hallinto
On A27–A28

1941 ***Perf. 14*** **Unwmkd.**

No.	Type	Description	Unused	Used
N1	A26	50p bright yellow green	30	40
N2	"	1.75m dark gray	35	50
N3	"	2m deep orange	85	1.25
N4	"	2.75m yellow orange	40	50
N5	"	3½m light ultra.	1.00	1.25
N6	A27	5m rose violet	2.50	3.50
N7	A28	10m pale brown	2.75	4.00
		Nos. N1–N7 (7)	8.15	11.40

Types of Finland Stamps, 1930 Overprinted in Green:

ITÄ-
KARJALA
Sot. hallinto
On A26

ITÄ-KARJALA
Sot. hallinto
On A27–A29

No.	Type	Description	Unused	Used
N8	A26	50p bright yellow green	30	45
N9	"	1.75m dark gray	35	50
N10	"	2m deep orange	50	1.00
N11	"	2.75m yellow orange	35	50
N12	"	3½m light ultra.	75	1.00
N13	A27	5m rose violet	1.75	1.75
N14	A28	10m pale brown	2.75	4.00
N15	A29	25m green	3.00	4.25
		Nos. N8–N15 (8)	9.75	13.45

Mannerheim Type of Finland Overprinted

ITÄ-KARJALA
Sot.hallinto

1942

No.	Type	Description	Unused	Used
N16	A48	50p dk. yel. green	35	60
N17	"	1.75m slate blue	35	60
N18	"	2m red orange	35	60
N19	"	2.75m brown orange	30	60
N20	"	3.50m bright ultra.	25	60
N21	"	5m brown violet	25	60
		Nos. N16–N21 (6)	1.85	3.60

Same Overprint on Ryti Type of Finland.

No.	Type	Description	Unused	Used
N22	A49	50p dk. yel. green	25	60
N23	"	1.75m slate blue	25	60
N24	"	2m red orange	25	60
N25	"	2.75m brown orange	35	60
N26	"	3.50m bright ultra.	35	60
N27	"	5m brown violet	35	60
		Nos. N22–N27 (6)	1.80	3.60

The overprint translates, "East Karelia Military Administration."

OCCUPATION SEMI-POSTAL STAMP.

Arms of East Karelia SP1

Engraved.

1943 ***Perf. 14*** **Unwmkd.**

No.	Type	Description	Unused	Used
NB1	SP1	3.50m+1.50m dark olive	55	1.50

This surtax aided war victims in East Karelia.

KATANGA

Katanga province seceded from the Congo (ex-Belgian) Republic in July, 1960, but established nations did not recognize it as an independent state. The United Nations declared the secession ended in September, 1961.

During the secession, Congo stamps were overprinted "KATANGA" at Elisabethville, and a few were surcharged. Also a set of Katanga stamps in new designs was released. These stamps were tolerated in the international mails, but the government authorizing them was not recognized.

KHMER

See Cambodia in Vol. II.

KIAUCHAU

(jyou'jō')

(Kiautschou)

LOCATION—A district of China on the south side of the Shantung peninsula.

GOVT.— A former German colony.

AREA—200 sq. mi.

POP.—192,000 (approx. 1914).

The area was seized by Germany in 1897 and through negotiations that followed was leased to Germany by China.

100 Pfennig = 1 Mark
100 Cents = 1 Dollar (1905)

Tsingtau Issue.

1900

Stamps of Germany, Offices in China 1898, with Additional Surcharge:

5 Pfg. (a) 5 Pfg. (b) 5 Pfg. (c)

"China" Overprint at 56° Angle.

No.	Type	Description	Unused	Used
1	A10 (a)	5pfg on 10pf carmine	47.50	42.50
		c. Double surcharge, one inverted	450.00	

2 A10 (*b*) 5pfg on 10pf carmine 47.50 42.50
c. Double surcharge, one inverted 450.00
3 " (*c*) 5pfg on 10pf carmine 47.50 42.50
c. Double surcharge, one inverted 450.00

"China" Overprint at 48° Angle.

1a A10 (a) 5pf on 10pf carmine 150.00 150.00
b. Dbl. surch. 600.00 725.00
2a " (b) 5pf on 10pf carmine 150.00 150.00
b. Dbl. surch. 600.00 725.00
3a " (c) 5pf on 10pf carmine 150.00 150.00
b. Dbl. surch. 600.00 725.00

Surcharged:

5 Pf. *a* **5 Pf.** *e* **5 Pf.** *J*

"China" Overprint at 48° Angle on Nos. 4–9.

4 A10 (*d*) 5pf on 10pf carmine *3000.00 3500.00*
a. Double surcharge *4250.00 4750.00*
5 " (*e*) 5pf on 10pf carmine *3000.00 3500.00*
a. Double surcharge *4250.00 4750.00*
6 " (*f*) 5pf on 10pf carmine *3000.00 3500.00*
a. Double surcharge *4250.00 4750.00*
b. "5fP" instead of "5Pf"
c. Same as "b", double surcharge

With Additional Handstamp **5**

7 A10 (*d*) 5pf on 10pf carmine *30,000.00 35,000.00*
8 " (*f*) 5pf on 10pf carmine *30,000.00 35,000.00*
a. "5fP" instead of "5Pf"

With Additional Handstamp **5 Pf.**

9 A10 (*f*) 5pf on 10pf carmine *6000.00 8000.00*
a. Double surcharge *9500.00 11,000.00*
b. Double surcharge of type "f"
c. "5fP" instead of "5Pf"
d. Same as "c" double surcharge

On Nos. 1–9, a blue or violet line is drawn through "PF. 10 PF." All exist without this line. All copies of Nos. 1b, 2b and 3b lack the colored line.

Kaiser's Yacht "Hohenzollern"
A1 A2

Typographed.

1900 ***Perf. 14*** **Unwmkd.**

10 A1 3pf brown 2.50 2.25
11 " 5pf green 1.90 1.10
12 " 10pf carmine 3.25 2.25
13 " 20pf ultramarine 10.00 11.00
14 " 25pf orange & black, *yellow* 20.00 22.50
15 " 30pf orange & black, *salmon* 20.00 22.50
16 " 40pf lake & black 22.50 27.50
17 " 50pf purple & black, *salmon* 22.50 30.00
18 " 80pf lake & black, *rose* 40.00 65.00

Engraved.

Perf. 14½x14

19 A2 1m carmine 67.50 75.00
20 " 2m blue 100.00 110.00
21 " 3m black violet 100.00 *225.00*
22 " 5m slate & carmine 325.00 *725.00*
Nos. 10–22 (13) 735.15 *1319.10*

A3

A4

1905 Typographed.

23 A3 1c brown 1.90 1.90
24 " 2c green 2.75 1.65
25 " 4c carmine 5.00 1.35
26 " 10c ultramarine 13.50 6.50
27 " 20c lake & black 37.50 27.50
28 " 40c lake & black, *rose* 95.00 110.00

Engraved.

29 A4 $½ carmine 80.00 80.00
30 " $1 blue 165.00 110.00
31 " $1½ black violet 1100.00 1350.00
32 " $2½ slate & car. 1900.00 *3250.00*

1905–09 **Wmkd. Lozenges. (125)**

Typographed.

33 A3 1c brown ('06) 70 1.35
34 " 2c green ('09) 70 1.10
35 " 4c carmine ('09) 1.10 1.10
36 " 10c ultra. ('09) 1.35 *2.50*
37 " 20c lake & blk. ('08) 2.25 *22.50*
38 " 40c lake & blk., *rose* 3.25 *55.00*

Engraved.

39 A4 $½ carmine ('07) 5.50 *67.50*
40 " $1 blue ('06) 8.00 *50.00*
41 " $1½ black violet 10.00 *190.00*
42 " $2½ slate & car. 27.50 *600.00*
Nos. 33–42 (10) 60.35

KIONGA

(kyōng'gȧ)

LOCATION—Southeast Africa and northeast Mozambique, on Indian Ocean south of Rovuma River.

GOVT. — Formerly part of German East Africa.

AREA—400 sq. mi.

This territory, occupied by Portuguese troops during World War I was allotted to Portugal by the Treaty of Versailles. Later it became part of Mozambique.

100 Centavos = 1 Escudo

King Carlos
A1

Lourenco Marques No. 149 Surcharged in Red.

Perf. 11½

1916, May 29 **Unwmkd.**

1 A1 ½c on 100r blue, *blue* 12.50 12.50
2 " 1c on 100r blue, *blue* 12.50 12.50
3 " 2½c on 100r blue, *blue* 12.50 12.50
4 " 5c on 100r blue, *blue* 12.50 12.50

Most of the stock of Lourenço Marques No. 149 used for these surcharges lacked gum.

KOREA

(kô·rē'ȧ)

(Corea)

(Chosen, Tyosen, Tai Han)

LOCATION—A peninsula extending from Manchuria between the Yellow Sea and the Sea of Japan.

GOVT —Republic.

AREA—85,246 sq. mi. (South Korea, 38,452 sq. mi.)

POP.—South Korea, 36,440,000 (est. 1977).

CAPITAL—Seoul.

Korea or Corea, for centuries under Chinese influence, declared itself an independent monarchy in 1895. Administrative control was assumed by Japan in 1904 and annexation followed in 1910.

Postage stamps of Japan were used in Korea from 1905 to 1945.

At the end of World War II, American forces occupied South Korea and Russian forces occupied North Korea, with the 38th parallel of latitude as the dividing line. A republic was established in 1948 following an election in South Korea. North Korea has issued its own stamps. See note following air post listings.

100 Mon = 1 Tempo
5 Poon = 1 Cheun
100 Sen = 1 Yen
1000 Re = 100 Cheun = Weun
100 Weun = 1 Hwan (1953)
100 Chun = 1 Won (1962)

Stylized Yin Yang
A1 A2

Perf. 8½ to 11½

1884 Typographed **Unwmkd.**

1 A1 5m rose 8.00
2 A2 10m blue 4.00

Reprints of Nos. 1–2 exist.

A3

A4 A5

1885

3 A3 25m orange 2.50
4 A4 50m green 2.50
5 A5 100m blue & pink 2.50

Nos. 3 to 5 were never placed in use.

Yin Yang
A6

Two types of 50p:
I. No period after "50."
II. Period after "50."

Perf. 11½, 12, 12½, 13 and Compound

1895 Lithographed.

6 A6 5p green 5.00 2.00
a. 5p pale yel. green 10.00 5.00
b. Imperf. horiz., pair 15.00
c. Imperf. vert., pair 20.00 20.00
d. Vertical pair, imperf. between 25.00 25.00
e. Horizontal pair, imperf. between 25.00 25.00
7 " 10p deep blue 6.75 3.00
a. Horizontal pair, imperf. between 20.00 20.00
b. Imperf. horiz., pair
8 " 25p maroon 5.50 3.00
a. Horizontal pair, imperf. between 25.00 25.00
b. Imperf. horiz., pair 20.00 20.00
9 " 50p purple (II) 2.50 1.50
a. Horizontal pair, imperf. between 35.00 35.00
b. Imperf. horiz., pair 20.00 20.00
c. Imperf. vert., pair 20.00 20.00
d. Type I 5.00 3.75

Overprinted "Tai Han" in Korean and Chinese Characters

한뎌

1897 Red Overprint.

10 A6 5p green 8.50 4.50
a. 5p pale yel. green 25.00 20.00
b. Inverted overprint 20.00 20.00
c. Without overprint at bottom 15.00 15.00
d. Without overprint at top 15.00 15.00
f. Double overprint at top 20.00 20.00
g. Overprint at bottom in black 22.50 22.50
h. Pair, one without overprint 50.00 50.00
i. Double overprint at top, inverted at bottom
11 " 10p deep blue 10.00 6.50
a. Without overprint at bottom 20.00 20.00
b. Without overprint at top 20.00 20.00
c. Double overprint at top 25.00 25.00
d. Bottom overprint inverted 20.00 20.00
e. Top overprint double, one in black 35.00 35.00
f. Top overprint omitted, bottom overprint inverted
12 " 25p maroon 11.00 7.50
a. Overprint at bottom inverted 25.00 25.00
b. Overprint at bottom in black 30.00 30.00
c. Bottom overprint omitted 17.50 17.50
e. Top overprint double, one in black 35.00 35.00
f. Top and bottom overprints double, one of each in black 50.00 50.00
g. Pair, one without overprint 50.00 50.00
13 " 50p purple 12.50 7.50
a. Without overprint at bottom 30.00 30.00
b. Without overprint at top 30.00 30.00
c. Bottom overprint double 25.00 25.00
e. Pair, one without overprint 75.00 75.00

1900 Black Overprint.

13F A6 5p green 60.00 45.00
13G " 10p deep blue 60.00 45.00
h. Without overprint at bottom
14 " 25p maroon 75.00 50.00
a. Without overprint at bottom 85.00 75.00
b. Without overprint at top 85.00 75.00
c. Double overprint at bottom 85.00 75.00
15 " 50p purple 65.00 50.00
a. Without overprint at bottom 85.00 75.00

These stamps with black overprint, also No. 16A, are said not to have been officially authorized.

Nos. 6a and 8 Surcharged in Red or Black

1900

15B A6 1ch on 5p yellow green (R) *250.00 200.00*
16 " 1ch on 25p maroon 37.50 37.50

Same Surcharge in Red or Black on Nos. 10, 12, 12c and 14.

16A A6 1ch on 5p green (R) 50.00 50.00
b. 1ch on 5p pale yellow green 50.00 50.00
17 " 1ch on 25p maroon 12.50 10.00
a. Figure "1" omitted 35.00
b. Overprint at bottom omitted (No. 12c) 25.00
17C " 1ch on 25p maroon (on No. 14) *100.00 90.00*

Counterfeit overprints and surcharges of Nos. 10–17C exist.

A8

A9

A10

A11

A12

A13

A14

A15

A16 A17

1900 Typo. *Perf. 11*

18 A8 2re gray 2.00 1.25
a. Perf. 10 3.00 1.25
19 A9 1ch yellow green 2.00 1.25
a. Perf. 10 2.00 1.25
20 A10 2ch blue, perf. 10 10.00 7.50
a. Horizontal pair, imperf. between 60.00
21 A11 3ch orange red 2.50 1.50
a. Imperf. horiz. 30.00 30.00
b. Perf. 10 2.50 1.75
22 A12 4ch carmine 4.00 2.50
a. Perf. 10 12.00 9.00
23 A13 5ch pink 3.00 2.00
a. Perf. 10 4.00 3.00
24 A14 6ch deep blue 4.00 2.50
a. Perf. 10 5.00 4.00
25 A15 10ch purple 5.50 3.00
26 A16 15ch gray violet 5.50 3.50
a. Perf. 10 60.00 50.00
27 A17 20ch red brown 7.00 4.00
a. Perf. 10 110.00 100.00
Nos. 18-27 (10) 45.50 29.00

Reprints of No. 24 were made in light blue, perf. 12x13, in 1905 for a souvenir booklet. Price $10.

A18

A19

A20

A21

1901 *Perf. 11*

30 A18 2ch pale blue 4.00 3.50
a. Perf. 10 15.00 15.00
31 A19 50ch olive green & pink 25.00 22.50
32 A20 1wn rose, black & blue 50.00 40.00
33 A21 2wn purple & yellow green 60.00 50.00

See also Nos. 52–54.

Emperor's Crown
A22

1902 *Perf. 11½*

34 A22 3ch orange 10.00 8.50
a. Imperf., pair 70.00

Issued in commemoration of the fortieth year of the reign of Emperor Kwang My.

Nos. 8 and 9 Surcharged in Black

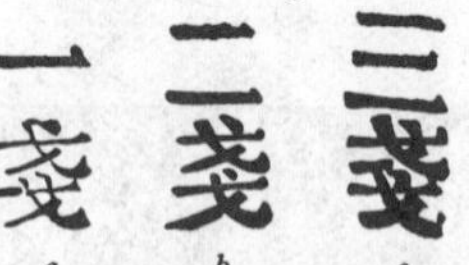
a *b* *c*

Perf. 11½, 12, 12½, 13 and Compound

1902

35 A6 (*a*) 1ch on 25p maroon 3.00 2.25
a. Inverted surcharge 50.00
b. Horizontal pair, imperf. between 35.00
c. Imperf. 15.00
d. Imperf. horizontally 15.00
e. On No. 12 37.50 30.00
36 A6 (*b*) 2ch on 25p maroon 5.00 2.50
a. Inverted surcharge 50.00 45.00
b. Imperf. 15.00
c. Double surcharge 50.00 50.00
d. On No. 12 40.00 32.50
e. 2ch on 50p purple 85.00 75.00
f. As "e," character "cheun" unabbreviated (in two rows instead of one) 125.00 100.00
37 " (*c*) 3ch on 50p purple 5.00 3.00
a. Inverted surcharge 30.00 30.00
b. With character "cheun" unabbreviated (in two rows instead of one) 60.00 50.00
c. Same as b, inverted 85.00 70.00
d. Horizontal pair, imperf. between 25.00
e. Vertical pair, imperf. between 25.00
f. Double surcharge 30.00
g. On No. 13 20.00 20.00
38 " (") 3ch on 25p maroon 27.50 17.50

There are several sizes of these surcharges. Counterfeit surcharges exist.

Falcon
A23

1903 ***Perf. 13½x14.***

39 A23 2re slate 1.25 1.00
40 " 1ch violet brown 2.00 1.25
41 " 2ch green 2.00 1.25
42 " 3ch orange 2.25 1.25
43 " 4ch rose 2.75 2.50
44 " 5ch yellow brown 3.75 2.75
45 " 6ch lilac 4.50 3.00
46 " 10ch blue 5.00 3.50
47 " 15ch red, *straw* 8.00 5.00
48 " 20ch violet brown, *straw* 8.00 5.00
49 " 50ch red, *green* 14.00 10.00
50 " 1wn vio., *lavender* 22.50 17.50
51 " 2wn violet, *orange* 50.00 40.00
Nos. 39-51 (13) 126.00 94.00

Types of 1901.
Thin, Semi-Transparent Paper.

1903 *Perf. 12½*

52 A19 50ch pale olive green & pale pink *65.00 65.00*
53 A20 1wn rose, black & blue *100.00 90.00*
54 A21 2wn light violet & light green *100.00 90.00*

Most examples of Nos. 52–54 unused are from souvenir booklets made up in 1905 when the Japanese withdrew all Korean stamps from circulation.

Issued under U. S. Military Rule.

Stamps of Japan Nos. 331, 268, 342, 332, 339 and 337 Surcharged in Black

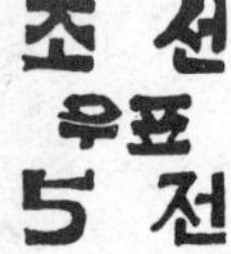

1946, Feb. 1 *Perf. 13* **Wmk. 257**

55 A86 5ch on 5s brown lake 5.00 7.00
56 A93 5ch on 14s rose lake & pale rose 50 75
a. 5ch on 40s dark violet (error) 200.00
57 A154 10ch on 40s dark violet 35 50
58 A147 20ch on 6s lt. ultra. 35 50
a. 20ch on 27s rose brown (error) 225.00
59 A151 30ch on 27s rose brown 35 50
a. 30ch on 6s light ultramarine (error) 50.00
b. Double surch. 35.00
60 A151 5wn on 17s gray violet 2.50 5.00
Nos. 55-60 (6) 9.05 14.25

Five essays for this provisional issue exist both with and without additional overprint of two Chinese characters ("specimen") in vermilion. The essays are: 20ch on Japan No. 269; 50ch on No. 272; 1wn on No. 336; 1wn on No. 273; 10wn on No. 265.

Korean Family and Flag
A24

Arms of Korea
A25

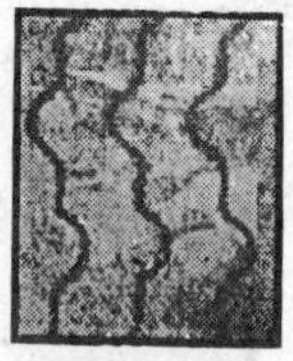
Wmk. 257

Wmkd. Curved Wavy Lines. (257)

1946, May 1 Litho. *Perf. 10½*

61 A24 3ch orange yellow 25 25
62 " 5ch green 30 15
63 " 10ch carmine 30 15
64 " 20ch dark blue 35 20
65 A25 50ch brown violet 60 40
66 " 1wn light brown 90 60
Nos. 61-66 (6) 2.70 1.75

Liberation from Japan.

Imperfs., Part Perfs.

Imperforate and part-perforate examples of a great many Korean stamps from No. 61 onward exist.

The imperfs. include Nos. 61–74, 77, 80–90, 93–97, 116–117, 119–126, 132–173, 182–186, 195, 197–199, 202A, 203, 204–205, 217, 428, etc.

The part-perfs. include Nos. 62–65, 69, 72–73, 109, 111–113, 132, etc.

As the field is so extensive, the editors, while reluctant to delete such varieties already listed, believe that they belong more properly in a specialized catalogue.

Dove
A26

1946, Aug. 15 **Unwmkd.**

67 A26 50ch deep violet 2.25 1.75

First anniversary of liberation.

Flags of United States and Korea—A27

1946, Sept. 9 ***Perf. 11***

68 A27 10wn carmine 2.75 2.50

Issued to commemorate the resumption of postal communication with the United States.

Astronomical Observatory, Kyungju—A28

Hibiscus with Rice
A29

Map of Korea
A30

Gold Crown of Silla Dynasty
A31

Admiral Li Sun-sin
A32

1946 *Rouletted 12*

69	A28	50ch dark blue	35	25
70	A29	1wn buff	30	30
		a. Perf. 11	1.25	1.00
71	A30	2wn indigo	75	30
		a. Perf. 11	35.00	12.50
72	A31	5wn magenta	3.00	2.25
		a. Perf. 11	9.00	6.00
73	A32	10wn emerald	4.00	2.50
		Nos. 69-73 (5)	8.40	5.60

Korean Phonetic Alphabet
A33

1946, Oct. 9 *Perf. 11*

74	A33	50ch deep blue	1.25	1.00

Issued to commemorate the 500th anniversary of the introduction of the Korean phonetic alphabet (Hangul).

Li Jun
A34

Admiral Li Sun-sin
A35

Perf. 11½x11, 11½.

1947, Aug. 1 **Litho.** **Wmk. 257**

75	A34	5wn light blue green	3.50	2.50
76	A35	10wn light blue	3.50	2.50

Presentation Sheets

Starting in 1947 with No. 75, nearly 100 Korean stamps were printed in miniature or souvenir sheets and given to government officials and others. These sheets were released in quantities of 300 to 4,000. In 1957 the Ministry of Communications began to sell the souvenir sheets at post offices at face value to be used for postage. They are listed from No. 244a onward.

Letter-encircled Globe
A36

1947, Aug. 1 *Perf. 11½x11*

77	A36	10wn light blue	3.50	2.50

Issued to commemorate the resumption of international mail service between Korea and all countries of the world.

Granite Paper

Starting with No. 77, most Korean stamps, except those on Laid Paper, are on Granite Paper. Granite Paper is noted above listings if the issue was printed on both ordinary and Granite Paper, such as Nos. 360a–374A.

Arch of Independence, Seoul
A37

Tortoise Ship, First Ironclad War Vessel
A38

1948, Apr.

78	A37	20wn rose	3.50	2.50
79	A38	50wn dull red brown	9.00	5.00

Republic

Flag and Ballot
A39

Woman and Man Casting Ballots
A40

Perf. 11x11½

1948, May 10 **Litho.** **Wmk. 257**

80	A39	2wn orange	1.25	50
81	"	5wn lilac rose	2.50	1.50
82	"	10wn light violet	5.00	3.00
83	A40	20wn carmine	7.50	6.00
84	"	50wn blue	10.00	9.00
		Nos. 80-84 (5)	26.25	20.00

South Korea election of May 10, 1948.

Korean Flag and Olive Branches
A41

Olympic Torchbearer and Map of Korea
A42

Perf. 11x11½, 11½x11

1948, June 1

85	A41	5wn green	32.50	32.50
86	A42	10wn purple	7.50	6.50

Issued to commemorate Korea's participation in the 1948 Olympic Games.

National Assembly—A43

1948, July 1 *Perf. 11½* **Wmk. 257**

87	A43	4wn orange brown	6.00	5.00

Opening of the Assembly July 1, 1948.

Korean Family and Capitol
A44

Pres. Syngman Rhee
A46

Flag of Korea—A45

1948, Aug. 1 **Lithographed**

88	A44	4wn emerald	7.50	4.50
89	A45	10wn orange brown	5.00	4.50

Issued to commemorate the signing of the new constitution, July 17, 1948.

1948, Aug. 5

90	A46	5wn deep blue	7.50	4.00

Inauguration of Korea's first president, Syngman Rhee.

Dove
A47

Hibiscus
A48

Two types of 5wn:

I. "1948" 3mm. wide; top inscription 9mm. wide; periods in "8.15." barely visible.

II. "1948" 4mm. wide; top inscription 9½mm; periods in "8.15." bold and strong.

1948 *Perf. 11, 11x11½*

91	A47	4wn blue	13.00	12.00
92	A48	5wn rose lilac (II)	11.50	10.50
		a. Type I	40.00	40.00

Issued to commemorate the establishment of Korea's republican government.

Li Jun
A49

Observatory, Kyungju
A50

1948, Oct. 1 *Perf. 11½x11*

93	A49	4wn rose carmine	25	15
94	A50	14wn deep blue	50	25
		a. 14wn light blue	20.00	12.50

Doves over U. N. Emblem
A51

Korean Citizen and Census Date
A52

1949, Feb. 12 *Perf. 11* **Wmk. 257**

95	A51	10wn blue	13.50	10.00

Issued to commemorate the arrival of the United Nations Commission on Korea, Feb. 12, 1949.

1949, Apr. 25

96	A52	15wn purple	10.00	7.50

Census of May 1, 1949.

Korean Boy and Girl
A53

1949, May 5

97	A53	15wn purple	9.00	6.00

Issued to commemorate the 20th anniversary of Children's Day, May 5, 1949.

Postman
A54

Worker and Factory
A55

Rice Harvesting
A56

Japanese Cranes
A57

Diamond Mountains
A58

Ginseng Plant
A59

South Gate, Seoul
A60

Tabo Pagoda, Kyungju
A61

1949 Lithographed. *Perf. 11.*

98	A54	1wn rose	1.50	1.00
99	A55	2wn dark blue gray	40	20
100	A56	5wn yellow green	1.00	1.00
101	A57	10wn blue green	35	25
102	A58	20wn orange brown	30	20
103	A59	30wn blue green	65	30
		a. Vert. pair, imperf. between	12.50	
104	A60	50wn violet blue	50	30
105	A61	100wn dull yel. green	50	30
		Nos. 98-105 (8)	5.20	3.55

Phoenix and Yin Yang
A62

1949, Aug. 25

106	A62	15wn deep blue	6.50	5.00

Issued to commemorate the first anniversary of Korea's independence.

Express Train "Sam Chun Li"
A63

1949, Sept. 18 *Perf. 11½x12*

107	A63	15wn violet blue	12.50	10.00

50th anniversary of Korean railroads.

Korean Flag
A64

Perf. 11½x11

1949, Oct. 15 **Wmk. 257**

108	A64	15wn red orange, yellow & dark blue	7.50	6.50

Issued to commemorate the 75th anniversary of the formation of the Universal Postal Union.

No. 108 exists unwatermarked. Some specialists say the unwatermarked copies are counterfeit.

Hibiscus
A65

Magpies and Map of Korea
A66

Stylized Bird and Globe
A67

Diamond Mountains
A68

Admiral Li Sun-sin
A69

Lithographed.

1949 *Perf. 11* **Wmk. 257**

109	A65	15wn vermilion	30	20
110	A66	65wn deep blue	30	20
111	A67	200wn green	35	20
112	A68	400wn brown	35	25
113	A69	500wn deep blue	35	20
		Nos. 109-113 (5)	1.65	1.05

Canceled to Order

More than 100 Korean stamps and souvenir sheets were canceled to order, the cancellation incorporating the date "67.9. 20." These include 81 stamps between Nos. 111 and 327, 18 airmail stamps between Nos. C6 and C26, and 5 souvenir sheets between Nos. 313 and 332.

Ancient Postal Medal (Ma-Pae)
A70

Revolutionists
A71

1950, Jan. 1

114	A70	15wn yellow green	6.00	4.00
115	"	65wn red brown	5.00	3.00

Issued to commemorate the 50th anniversary of Korea's entrance into the Universal Postal Union.

1950, Mar. 10 *Perf. 11½*

116	A71	15wn olive	7.00	3.00
117	"	65wn light violet	3.50	3.00

Issued to mark the 41st anniversary of Korea's declaration of Independence.

Korean Emblem and National Assembly
A72

1950, May 30

118	A72	30wn blue, red, brown & green	5.00	4.00

Issued to commemorate the second national election of the Korean Republic.

Syngman Rhee
A73

Korean Flag and White Mountains
A74

Flags of United Nations and Korea, Map of Korea—A75

1950, Nov. 20 *Perf. 11* **Wmk. 257**

119	A73	100wn blue	1.00	85
120	A74	100wn green	1.50	1.00
121	A75	200wn dark green	1.50	1.00

Crane
A76

Tiger Mural
A77

Dove and Flag
A78

Postal Medal
A79

Mural from Ancient Tomb
A80

Ordinary Paper

1951 *Perf. 11* **Unwmkd.**

122	A76	5wn orange brown	75	50
123	A77	20wn purple	50	50
124	A78	50wn green	75	75
125	A79	100wn deep blue	2.00	1.25
126	A80	1000wn green	7.50	1.50
		Nos. 122-126 (5)	11.50	4.50

Roulette 12

122a	A76	5wn orange brown	75	50
123a	A77	20wn purple	1.00	1.00
124a	A78	50wn green	1.25	50
125a	A79	100wn blue	1.50	1.25

No. 126 also exists perforated 12½. See also Nos. 187-189.

No. 93 Surcharged with New Value and Wavy Lines in Blue.

1951 *Perf. 11½x11* **Wmk. 257**

127	A49	100wn on 4wn rose carmine	60	40
		a. Invtd. surch.	30.00	

Nos. 109, 101, 102 and 104 Surcharged in Blue or Brown

Perf. 11

128	A65	200wn on 15wn vermilion	1.00	50
		a. Inverted surch.	6.50	6.50
129	A57	300wn on 10wn blue green (Br)	2.25	1.25
		a. Invtd. surch.	12.50	
130	A58	300wn on 20wn orange brown	1.25	1.00
		a. Invtd. surch.	12.50	
131	A60	300wn on 50wn violet blue (Br)	2.50	1.75
		Nos. 127-131 (5)	7.60	4.90

Size of surcharge varies. Numeral upright on Nos. 129 and 131; numeral slanted on Nos. 175 and 179. See also Nos. 174-181.

On No. 130, the zeros in "300" are octagonal; on No. 177B they are oval.

Flags of U.S.A. and Korea and Statue of Liberty—A81

Design (blue stamps): Flags, U. N. emblem and doves.

1951-52 *Perf. 11* **Wmk. 257**

Flags in Natural Colors, Participating Country at Left.

132	A81	500wn green	3.00	3.00
133	"	500wn blue	3.00	3.00
134	"	500wn green (*Australia*)	2.50	2.50
135	"	500wn blue (*Australia*)	2.50	2.50
136	"	500wn green (*Belgium*)	2.50	2.50
137	"	500wn blue (*Belgium*)	2.50	2.50
138	"	500wn green (*Britain*)	2.50	2.50
139	"	500wn blue (*Britain*)	2.50	2.50
140	"	500wn green (*Canada*)	2.50	2.50
141	"	500wn blue (*Canada*)	2.50	2.50
142	"	500wn green (*Colombia*)	2.50	2.50
143	"	500wn blue (*Colombia*)	2.50	2.50
144	"	500wn green (*Denmark*)	4.50	4.50
145	"	500wn blue (*Denmark*)	4.50	4.50
146	"	500wn green (*Ethiopia*)	2.50	2.50
147	"	500wn blue (*Ethiopia*)	2.50	2.50
148	"	500wn green (*France*)	2.50	2.50
149	"	500wn blue (*France*)	2.50	2.50
150	"	500wn green (*Greece*)	2.50	2.50
151	"	500wn blue (*Greece*)	2.50	2.50
152	"	500wn green (*India*)	4.00	4.00
153	"	500wn blue (*India*)	4.00	4.00
154	"	500wn green (*Italy*)	4.00	4.00
		a. Flag without crown ('52)	7.50	
155	"	500wn blue (*Italy*)	4.00	4.00
		a. Flag without crown ('52)	7.50	
156	"	500wn green (*Luxembourg*)	4.00	4.00
157	"	500wn blue (*Luxembourg*)	4.00	4.00
158	"	500wn green (*Netherlands*)	2.50	2.50

159 A81 500wn blue (*Netherlands*) 2.50 2.50
160 " 500wn green (*New Zealand*) 2.50 2.50
161 " 500wn blue (*New Zealand*) 2.50 2.50
162 " 500wn green (*Norway*) 4.00 4.00
163 " 500wn blue (*Norway*) 4.00 4.00
164 " 500wn green (*Philippines*) 2.50 2.50
165 " 500wn blue (*Philippines*) 2.50 2.50
166 " 500wn green (*Sweden*) 2.50 2.50
167 " 500wn blue (*Sweden*) 2.50 2.50
168 " 500wn green (*Thailand*) 2.50 2.50
169 " 500wn blue " 2.50 2.50
170 " 500wn green (*Turkey*) 2.50 2.50
171 " 500wn blue " 2.50 2.50
172 " 500wn green (*Union of South Africa*) 2.50 2.50
173 " 500wn blue " 2.50 2.50
Nos. 132-173 (42) 122.00 122.00

Twenty-two imperf. souvenir sheets of two, containing the green and the blue stamps for each participating country (including both types of Italy) were issued. Size: 140x90mm. Price, set $200.

Stamps of 1948-49
Surcharged Type "d" in Blue or Brown

1951 ***Perf. 11½x11, 11.*** **Wmk. 257**

174 A49 300wn on 4wn rose carmine 75 60
a. Invtd. surch. 40.00 40.00
175 A57 300wn on 10wn blue green (Br) 60 50
a. Invtd. surch. 35.00 30.00
176 A50 300wn on 14wn deep blue (Br) 1.00 85
a. 300wn on 14wn light blue 100.00 75.00
b. Invtd. surch. 35.00 35.00
177 A65 300wn on 15wn vermilion 75 50
a. Invtd. surch. 22.50 22.50
177B A58 300wn on 20wn org. brown 1.50 1.25
178 A59 300wn on 30wn blue green (Br) 75 50
a. Invtd. surch. 35.00 35.00
179 A60 300wn on 50wn violet blue (Br) 75 50
180 A66 300wn on 65wn deep blue (Br) 60 50
a. Invtd. monad 15.00 15.00
181 A61 300wn on 100wn dull yellow green 1.00 75
a. Invtd. surch. 35.00 30.00
Nos. 174-181 (9) 7.70 5.95

"300" slanted on Nos. 175, 177B and 179; "300" upright on Nos. 129 and 131. The surcharge exists double on several of these stamps.

No. 177B differs from No. 130 in detail noted after No. 131.

Syngman Rhee and "Good Luck"
A82

1952, Sept. 10 **Litho.** ***Perf. 12½.***

182 A82 1000wn dark green 1.25 1.00

Issued to publicize the second inauguration of President Syngman Rhee, Aug. 15, 1952.

Sok Kul Am, Near Kyungju
A83

Bool Gook Temple, Kyungju
A84

Tombstone of Mu Yal Wang
A85

Choong Yul Sa Shrine, Tongyung
A86

Typographed.

1952 ***Perf. 12½*** **Wmk. 257**

183 A83 200wn henna brown 50 10
184 A84 300wn green 50 12
185 A85 500wn carmine 65 60
186 A86 2000wn deep blue 80 10

Lithographed.

Rough Perf. 10-11, 11½x11 and Compound

186A A83 200wn henna brn. 80 30
186B A84 300wn green 1.20 40
Nos. 183-186B (6) 4.45 1.62

Types of 1951.
(Designs Slightly Smaller)

1952-53 ***Rough Perf. 10-11***

187 A77 20wn purple 2.00 75
187A A78 50wn green 2.00 25
187B A79 100wn deep blue 1.25 30
187C A80 1000wn green 35.00 2.50

(Designs Slightly Larger)

Perf. 12½

187D A78 50wn green 75 40
188 A79 100wn deep blue 75 40
189 A80 1000wn green ('53) 2.50 60

1953 Type of 1952.

189A A85 500wn deep blue 9.00 *75.00*

All copies of No. 189A were affixed to postal cards before sale.

See also Nos. 191-192, 203B, 248.

Types of 1952 and

Planting Trees
A87

Lithographed.

1953, Apr. 5 ***Perf. 12½*** **Wmk. 257**

190 A87 1h aquamarine 25 20
191 A85 2h aquamarine 25 25
192 " 5h bright green 50 25
193 A87 10h bright green 75 15
194 A86 20h brown 1.50 50
Nos. 190-194 (5) 3.25 1.35

See also Nos. 203A, 247.

Map and YMCA Emblem
A88

1953, Oct. 25 ***Perf. 13½***

195 A88 10h dk. slate blue & red 1.25 1.00

Issued to commemorate the 50th anniversary of the establishment of the Korean Young Men's Christian Association.

Tombstone of Mu Yal Wang—A88a

Sika Deer
A89 A90

1954, Apr. ***Perf. 12½***

196 A88a 5h dark green 15 10
197 A89 100h brown carmine 1.75 35
198 A90 500h brown orange 3.50 90
199 " 1000h bistre brown 7.00 1.25

See also Nos. 203C, 203D, 238-239, 248A, 250-251, 259, 261-262, 269-270, 279, 281-282.

Dok Do (Dok Island)
A91

Design: 10h, Dok Do, lateral view.

1954, Sept. 15

200 A91 2h claret 15 10
201 " 5h blue 25 15
202 " 10h blue green 50 20

Moth and Flag
A92

Pagoda Park, Seoul
A92a

1954, Apr. 16 ***Perf. 12½*** **Wmk. 257**

202A A92 10h brown 75 35
203 A92a 30h dark blue 85 25

See also Nos. 203E, 260, 280.

Types of 1952-54.

1955-56 ***Perf. 12½*** **Unwmkd.**

Laid Paper.

203A A87 1h aqua. ('56) 25 20
203B A85 2h aqua. ('56) 25 20
203C A88a 5h brt. green ('56) 25 20
203D A89 100h brn. carmine 2.25 50
203E A92a 200h violet 2.25 75
Nos. 203A-203E (5) 5.25 1.85

On No. 203C the right hand character is redrawn as in illustration above No. 212D.

Nos. 203A and 203C are found on horizontally and vertically laid paper.

Erosion Control on Mountainside
A93

1954, Dec. 12 **Wmk. 257**

204 A93 10h dark green & yellow green 40 20
205 " 19h dark green & yellow green 60 35

Issued to publicize the 1954 forestation campaign.

Presidents Syngman Rhee and Dwight Eisenhower Shaking Hands
A94

1954, Dec. 25 ***Perf. 13½***

206 A94 10h violet blue 40 25
207 " 19h brown 60 40
208 " 71h dull green 1.50 75

Issued to publicize the adoption of the United States-Korea mutual defense treaty.

"Reconstruction"
A95

Lithographed.

1955, Feb. 10 ***Perf. 12½*** **Wmk. 257**

209 A95 10h brown 75 35
210 " 15h violet 50 50
211 " 20h blue 110.00 4.00
212 " 50h plum 2.00 25

Issued to publicize Korea's industrial reconstruction.

1955, Oct. 19 ***Perf. 12½*** **Unwmkd.**

Laid Paper.

212A A95 15h violet 60 25
212B " 20h blue 90 35
212C " 50h plum 1.25 25

No. 212B is found on horizontally and vertically laid paper.

Same with Right Character at Top Redrawn.

Original

Redrawn

1956, June 5 ***Perf. 12½*** **Unwmkd.**

Laid Paper.

212D A95 10h brown 1.25 30
212E " 15h violet 90 30
212F " 20h blue 75 25
g. Bklt. pane of 6 12.50

Nos. 212D-212F are found on horizontally and vertically laid paper. See also Nos. 248B, 256, 272, 276.

Rotary Emblem
A96

Syngman Rhee
A98

1955, Feb. 23 ***Perf. 13½*** **Wmk. 257**

213 A96 20h violet 50 30
214 " 25h dull green 60 40
215 " 71h magenta 90 75

Rotary International, 50th anniversary.

1955, Mar. 26

217 A98 20h deep blue 2.75 1.25

Issued to commemorate the 80th birthday of Pres. Syngman Rhee, Apr. 26.

Flag and Arch of Independence
A99

1955, Aug. 15 Litho. *Perf. 13½*

218 A99 40h Prussian green 60 40
219 " 100h lake 90 60

Tenth anniversary of independence.

United Nations Emblem in Circle of Clasped Hands
A100

Olympic Torch and Runners
A101

1955, Oct. 24

221 A100 20h bluish green 90 50
222 " 55h aquamarine 1.50 75

United Nations, 10th anniversary.

1955, Oct. 23

223 A101 20h claret 1.00 50
224 " 55h dark green 1.50 75

36th National Athletic Meet.

Adm. Li Sun-sin, Navy Flag and Tortoise Ship—A102

Perf. 13x13½

1955, Nov. 11 **Unwmkd.**

Laid Paper.

225 A102 20h violet blue 1.75 1.25

Korean Navy, 10th anniversary.

Rhee Monument near Seoul
A103

Syngman Rhee
A104

1956 *Perf. 13½x13*

226 A103 20h dull green 1.50 90

81st birthday of Pres. Syngman Rhee.
No. 226 is found on horizontally and vertically laid paper.

Perf. 13x13½

1956, Aug. 15 **Unwmkd.**

227 A104 20h brown 1.00 75
228 " 55h violet blue 2.00 1.00

Third inauguration of Pres. Syngman Rhee.

Olympic Rings and Torch
A105

1956, Nov. 1 Litho. *Perf. 12½*

Laid Paper

229 A105 20h red orange 1.25 75
230 " 55h bright green 2.25 1.25

Issued to commemorate the 16th Olympic Games in Melbourne, Nov. 22–Dec. 8, 1956.

Central Post Office, Seoul
A107

Stamp of 1884
A108

Mail Delivered by Donkey—A109

1956, Dec. 4 Laid Paper Unwmkd.

232 A107 20h lt. blue green 60 50
233 A108 50h light carmine 90 60
234 A109 55h green 1.20 90

Issued to commemorate Postal Day.

Types of 1954 Redrawn and

Hibiscus
A110

King Sejong
A111

Kyungju Observatory
A112

No Hwan Symbol;
Redrawn Character

1956, Dec. 4 ***Perf. 12½*** **Unwmkd.**

Laid Paper.

235 A110 10h lilac rose 40 15
236 A111 20h lilac 75 15
237 A112 50h violet 90 15
238 A89 100h brown carmine 1.00 30
239 A90 500h brown orange 5.00 50
Nos. 235–239 (5) 8.05 1.25

On Nos. 238–239, the character after numeral has been omitted and the last character of the inscription has been redrawn as illustrated above No. 212D.
Nos. 235–236 are found on horizontally and vertically laid paper.
See also Nos. 240–242, 253, 255, 258, 273, 275, 278, 291d, 291f, B3–B4.

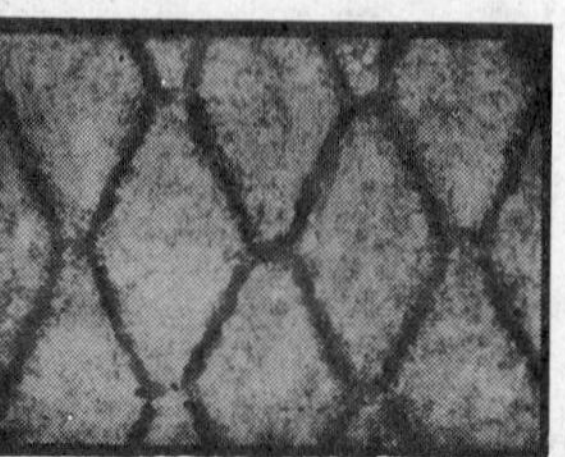

Wmk. 312

Types of 1956.
Wmkd. Zigzag Lines (312)

1957, Jan. 21 ***Perf. 12½***

240 A110 10h lilac rose 45 25
241 A111 20h red lilac 60 50
242 A112 50h violet 1.25 25

Telecommunication Symbols
A117

1957, Jan. 31 ***Perf. 13½***

243 A117 40h light ultramarine 60 35
244 " 55h bright green 90 60
a. Souvenir sheet of 2 225.00

Issued to commemorate the 5th anniversary of Korea's joining the International Telecommunication Union.
No. 244a contains one each of Nos. 243–244, imperf., with blue gray marginal inscriptions. Size: 110x83mm.

Boy Scout and Emblem
A118

1957, Feb. 27 **Wmk. 312**

245 A118 40h pale purple 65 50
246 " 55h light magenta 1.20 75
a. Souvenir sheet of 2 300.00

50th anniversary of Boy Scout movement.
No. 246a contains one each of Nos. 245–246, imperf., with marginal inscriptions.

Types of 1953–56.
**Top Right Character Redrawn;
Hwan Symbol Retained.**

1957 ***Perf. 12½*** **Wmk. 312**

247 A87 1h aquamarine 40 15
248 A85 2h aquamarine 25 20
248A A88a 5h bright green 75 20
248B A95 15h violet 1.50 25

Redrawn Types of 1954, 1956 and

Planting Trees
A119

South Gate, Seoul
A120

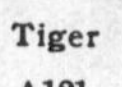

Tiger
A121

Diamond Mountains
A122

Lithographed.
**No Hwan Symbol;
Redrawn Character.**

1957 ***Perf. 12½*** **Wmk. 312**

249 A119 2h aquamarine 10 10
a. Min. sheet 8.00
250 A88a 4h aquamarine 10 10
a. Min. sheet 8.00
251 " 5h emerald 15 10
252 A120 10h green 15 10
a. Min. sheet 8.00
253 A110 20h lilac rose 30 10
a. Min. sheet 8.00
254 A121 30h pale lilac 30 10
a. Min. sheet 9.00
255 A111 40h red lilac 35 10
a. Booklet pane of 6 20.00
b. Min. sheet 8.00
256 A95 50h lake 50 12
257 A122 55h violet brown 1.25 75
a. Min. sheet 9.00
258 A112 100h violet 1.00 18
a. Min. sheet 30.00
259 A89 200h brn. carmine 2.50 18
a. Min. sheet 8.00
260 A92a 400h bright violet 4.00 50
a. Min. sheet 10.00
261 A90 500h ochre 6.00 1.50
262 " 1000h dk. olive bis. 12.00 4.00
Nos. 249–262 (14) 28.70 7.93

The "redrawn character" is illustrated above No. 212D.
The miniature sheets, Nos. 249a–250a, 252a–254a, 255b and 257a–260a contain one stamp and are imperf. Each sheet has a fancy border in the color of the stamp, and black inscriptions. Size: 110x83mm.
See also Nos. 268, 271, 274, 277, 291c, 291e.

Mercury and Flags of Korea and U.S.A.
A123

1957, Nov. 7 ***Perf. 13½*** **Wmk. 312**

263 A123 40h deep orange 50 30
264 " 205h emerald 1.50 75
a. Souvenir sheet of 2 110.00

Issued to publicize the treaty of friendship, commerce and navigation between Korea and the United States.
No. 264a contains one each of Nos. 263–264, imperf., with black marginal inscription and emerald border. Size: 112x 88½mm.

Star of Bethlehem and Pine Cone
A124

Designs: 25h, Christmas tree and tassel. 30h, Christmas tree, window and dog.

Lithographed

1957, Dec. 11 ***Perf. 12½***

265 A124 15h orange, brown & green 75 50
a. Souv. sheet 165.00
266 " 25h light green, yellow & red 1.00 75
a. Souv. sheet 165.00
267 " 30h blue, light green & yellow 1.50 1.00
a. Souv. sheet 165.00

Issued for Christmas and the New Year.
The imperf. souvenir sheets each contain a single impression of No. 265, 266 or 267, with marginal inscriptions in black and borders in color. Size: 90x61mm.

Redrawn Types of 1954–57.

Wmk. 317

Wmkd. Communications Department Emblem (317)

1957–59 Lithographed *Perf. 12½*

268 A119 2h aquamarine 10 10
269 A88a 4h aquamarine 10 10
270 " 5h emerald ('58) 15 15
271 A120 10h green 20 15
272 A95 15h violet ('58) 15 15
273 A110 20h lilac rose 20 15
274 A121 30h pale lilac ('58) 25 15
275 A111 40h red lilac 45 15
276 A95 50h lake ('58) 75 15
277 A122 55h violet brown ('59) 90 1.25
278 A112 100h violet 1.25 40
279 A89 200h brown carmine ('59) 2.00 50
280 A92a 400h brt. vio. ('59) 4.00 3.50
281 A90 500h ochre ('58) 6.00 1.75
282 " 1000h dark olive bistre ('58) 12.00 2.25
Nos. 268–282 (15) 28.50 10.90

Nos. 268–282 have no hwan symbol, and final character of inscription is the redrawn one illustrated above No. 212D.
See also No. 291B.

Winged Envelope
A125

1958, May 20 Wmk. 317

283 A125 40h dark blue & red 1.00 60
a. Souvenir sheet 110.00

Issued for the Second Postal Week.
No. 283a contains one of No. 283, imperf., with dark blue border and black marginal inscriptions. Size: 90x60mm.

Children Looking at Industrial Growth
A126

Design: 40h, Hibiscus forming "10".

1958, Aug. 15 *Perf. 13½*

284 A126 20h gray 50 20
285 " 40h dark carmine 75 30
a. Souvenir sheet of 2 27.50

10th anniversary of Republic of Korea.
No. 285a contains one each of Nos. 284–285, imperf., with gray border and black marginal inscriptions. Size: 109½x83 mm.

UNESCO Building, Paris
A127

1958, Nov. 3 Wmk. 317

286 A127 40h orange & green 60 50
a. Souv. sheet 25.00

Issued to commemorate the opening of UNESCO (U. N. Educational, Scientific and Cultural Organization). Headquarters in Paris, Nov. 3.
No. 286a contains one No. 286, imperf., with orange border and black marginal inscriptions. Size: 90x60mm.

Children Flying Kites
A128

Christmas Tree and Fortune Screen
A129

Children in Costume
A130

1958, Dec. 11 Litho. *Perf. 12½*

287 A128 15h yellow green 60 50
a. Souv. sheet 16.00
288 A129 25h blue, red & yellow 60 50
a. Souv. sheet 16.00
289 A130 30h yellow, ultramarine & red 1.00 75
a. Souv. sheet 16.00

Issued for Christmas and the New Year.
The three souvenir sheets are imperf. and measure 90x61mm. Each contains a single impression of No. 287, 288 or 289 with marginal inscriptions and colored borders.

Flag and Pagoda Park
A131

1959, Mar. 1 *Perf. 13½*

290 A131 40h rose lilac & brn. 75 35
a. Souvenir sheet 10.00

Issued to commemorate the 40th anniversary of Independence Movement Day.
No. 290a is imperf. and contains one copy of No. 290. Sheet measures 90x61 mm. and has rose lilac border and black inscriptions.

Korean Marines Landing
A132

1959, Apr. 15

291 A132 40h olive green 75 40
a. Souvenir sheet 5.00

Korean Marine Corps, 10th anniversary.
No. 291a contains one of No. 291, imperf., with marginal inscriptions in black. Size: 88x60mm.

Souvenir Sheet.
Types of 1956–57.
Wmk. 317

1959, May 20 Litho. *Imperf.*

291B Sheet of 4 1.35 1.75
c. A120 10h green 30 35
d. A111 20h lilac rose 30 35
e. A121 30h pale lilac 30 35
f. A111 40h red lilac 30 35

Issued to commemorate the Third Postal Week, May 20–26. Marginal inscriptions in pale lilac. Size: 70x105mm.

WHO Emblem and Family
A133

1959, Aug. 17 *Perf. 13½* Wmk. 317

292 A133 40h pink & rose violet 60 30
a. Souvenir sheet 6.00

Issued to commemorate the 10th anniversary of Korea's joining the World Health Organization.
No. 292a contains one No. 292, imperf., with marginal inscription in rose violet. Size: 89½x61mm.

Diesel Train—A134

1959, Sept. 18 Lithographed.

293 A134 40h brown & bistre 65 35
a. Souvenir sheet 6.00

60th anniversary of Korean railroads.
No. 293a contains one No. 293, imperf., with brown marginal inscriptions. Size: 90x60mm.

Relay Race and Emblem
A135

1959, Oct. 3

294 A135 40h light blue & red brown 65 40
a. Souvenir sheet 5.00

40th National Athletic Meet.
No. 294a contains one No. 294, imperf., with marginal inscriptions in red brown. Size: 90x60mm.

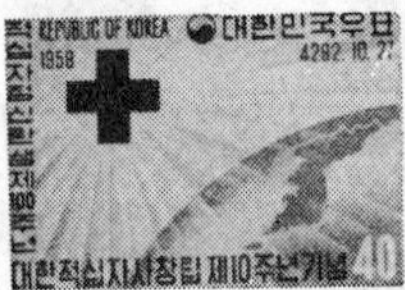

Red Cross and Korea Map
A136

Design: 55h, Red Cross superimposed on globe.

1959, Oct. 27 *Perf. 13½*

295 A136 40h red & blue green 40 20
296 " 55h pale lilac & red 60 30
a. Souv. sheet 12.00

Centenary of the Red Cross idea.
No. 296a contains one each of Nos. 295–296, imperf., with blue green marginal inscriptions. Size: 110x60mm.

Old Postal Flag and New Communications Flag
A137

1959, Dec. 4

297 A137 40h blue & red 65 35
a. Souvenir sheet 5.00

Issued to commemorate the 75th anniversary of the Korean postal system.
No. 297a contains one No. 297, imperf., with blue marginal inscriptions. Size: 90x60mm.

Mice and Chinese Happy New Year Character
A138

Designs: 25h, Children singing Christmas hymns. 30h, Red-crested crane.

1959, Dec. 15 *Perf. 12½*

298 A138 15h gray, violet blue & pink 40 30
a. Souvenir sheet 6.00
299 " 25h blue, red & emerald 50 30
a. Souvenir sheet 6.00
300 " 30h light lilac, black & red 60 30
a. Souvenir sheet 6.00

Issued for Christmas and the New Year.
The three souvenir sheets are imperf. and measure 90x60mm. Each contains a single impression of No. 298, 299 or 300 with marginal inscriptions in violet blue, blue and black respectively.

UPU Monument and Means of Transportation
A139

Lithographed.

1960, Jan. 1 *Perf. 13½* Wmk. 317

301 A139 40h greenish blue & brown 60 30
a. Souvenir sheet 5.00

Issued to commemorate the 60th anniversary of Korean membership in the Universal Postal Union.
No. 301a contains one No. 301, imperf., with brown marginal inscriptions. Size: 90x60mm.

Bee, Honeycomb and Clover
A140

Snail and Money Bag
A141

1960, Apr. 1 *Perf. 12½* Wmk. 317

302 A140 10h emerald, brown & orange 15 10
303 A141 20h pink, bl. & brn. 35 20

Issued to encourage systematic saving by children. See No. 313, souvenir sheet.
See also Nos. 377–380.

Uprooted Oak Emblem and Yin Yang
A142

Dwight D. Eisenhower
A143

1960, Apr. 7 *Perf. 13½* Wmk. 312

304 A142 40h emerald, car. & ultra. 50 25
a. Souv. sheet 15.00

Issued to publicize World Refugee Year, July 1, 1959–June 30, 1960.
No. 304a contains one No. 304, imperf., with emerald marginal inscriptions. Size: 89x61mm.

1960, June 19 Litho. Wmk. 317

305 A143 40h blue, red & bluish green 70 40
a. Souvenir sheet 8.00

Issued to commemorate President Eisenhower's visit to Korea, June 19.
No. 305a contains one No. 305, imperf., with blue marginal inscriptions and red border at bottom. Size: 89x60mm.

Children in School and Ancient Home Teaching
A144

1960, Aug. 3 *Perf. 13½* Wmk. 317

306 A144 40h citron, claret & orange brn. 60 35
a. Souvenir sheet 2.25

Issued to commemorate the 75th anniversary of the modern educational system.
No. 306a contains one No. 306, imperf., with marginal inscriptions in claret. Size: 90x60mm.

Hibiscus and House of Councilors
A145

1960, Aug. 8

307 A145 40h blue 60 30
a. Souvenir sheet 3.00

Inaugural session, House of Councilors.
No. 307a contains one No. 307, imperf., with marginal inscriptions in blue. Size: 90x60mm.

Woman Holding Torch and Man with Flag
A146

1960, Aug. 15

308 A146 40h bistre, light blue & brown 55 25
a. Souvenir sheet 2.00

15th anniversary of liberation.
No. 308a contains one No. 308, imperf., with marginal inscription in brown. Size: 90x60mm.

Weight Lifter
A147

Design: 40h, South Gate, Seoul, and Olympic emblem.

1960, Aug. 25 Lithographed

309 A147 20h brown, light blue & salmon 30 15
310 " 40h brown, lt. blue & dark blue 60 25
a. Souvenir sheet of 2 5.00

Issued to commemorate the 17th Olympic Games, Rome, Aug. 25–Sept. 11.
No. 310a contains one each of Nos. 309–310, imperf., with marginal inscriptions in dark blue. Size: 89x60mm.

Swallow and Telegraph Pole
A148

1960, Sept. 28 *Perf. 13½*

311 A148 40h light blue, lilac & gray 50 25
a. Souvenir sheet 1.50

Issued to commemorate the 75th anniversary of the establishment of telegraph service.
No. 310a contains one each of Nos. 309–with marginal inscriptions in lilac. Size: 90x60mm.

Students and Sprout
A149

1960, Oct. 1 Wmk. 317

312 A149 40h blue, salmon pink & emerald 50 25
a. Souvenir sheet 1.50

Rebirth of the Republic.
No. 312a contains one No. 312, imperf., with blue marginal inscriptions. Size: 90x60mm.

Souvenir Sheet

Savings Types of 1960.

1960, Oct. 7 *Imperf.*

313 Sheet of two 1.25 1.25
a. A140 10h emerald, brn. & org. 60 60
b. A141 20h pink, blue & brn. 60 60

Issued to commemorate the Fourth Postal Week, Oct. 7–13, and International Letter Writing Week, Oct. 3–9. Blue marginal inscriptions. Size: 90x60mm.

Torch
A150

1960, Oct. 15 *Perf. 13½*

314 A150 40h dark blue, light blue & yellow 50 25
a. Souvenir sheet 1.50

Cultural Month (October).
No. 314a contains one No. 314, imperf., with dark blue marginal inscriptions. Size: 90x60mm.

U.N. Flag, Globe and Laurel
A151

U.N. Emblem and Grave Markers
A152

1960, Oct. 24 Lithographed

315 A151 40h rose lilac, blue & green 50 25
a. Souvenir sheet 2.75

15th anniversary of United Nations.
No. 315a contains one No. 315, imperf., with marginal inscriptions in blue and green. Size: 90x60mm.

1960, Nov. 1 Wmk. 317

316 A152 40h salmon & brown 50 25
a. Souvenir sheet 2.50

Issued to commemorate the establishment of the U.N. Memorial Cemetery, Tanggok, Pusan, Korea.
No. 316a contains one No. 316, imperf., with black marginal inscriptions and border. Size: 90x60mm.

"Housing, Agriculture, Population"
A153

1960, Nov. 15 *Perf. 13½*

317 A153 40h greenish blue rose carmine & pale brown 50 25
a. Souvenir sheet 1.25

Issued to publicize the 1960 census.
No. 317a contains one No. 317, imperf., with greenish blue marginal inscriptions. Size: 90x60mm.

Boy and Head of Ox
A154

Star of Bethlehem and Korean Sock
A155

Girl Giving New Year's Greeting
A156

1960, Dec. 15 Litho. *Perf. 12½*

318 A154 15h gray, brown & orange yellow 40 25
a. Souvenir sheet 4.00
319 A155 25h violet blue, red & green 50 25
a. Souvenir sheet 4.00
320 A156 30h red, violet blue & yellow 60 30
a. Souvenir sheet 4.00

Issued for Christmas and the New Year.
The three souvenir sheets each contain a single impression of No. 318, 319 or 320, imperf., with marginal inscriptions and borders in three colors. Size: 90x60 mm.

U.N. Emblem, Windsock and Ancient Rain Gauge—A157

1961, March 23 *Perf. 13½*

321 A157 40h light blue & ultramarine 60 30
a. Souv. sheet 1.25

Issued to commemorate the First World Meteorological Day. No. 321a contains No. 321, imperf., with marginal inscription in ultramarine. Size: 90x60mm.

Children, Globe and U.N. Emblem
A158

1961, Apr. 7 Wmk. 317

322 A158 40h salmon & brown 60 30
a. Souvenir sheet 1.25

Issued to commemorate the Tenth World Health Day. No. 322a contains No. 322, imperf., with marginal inscription in brown. Size: 90x60mm.

Students Demonstrating
A159

1961, Apr. 19 Lithographed

323 A159 40h red. green & ultramarine 60 40
a. Souvenir sheet 1.50

Issued to commemorate the first anniversary of the Korean April revolution.
No. 323a contains No. 323 imperf. with marginal inscription in green. Size: 90x60mm.

Workers
A160

1961, May 6

324 A160 40h bright green 60 30
a. Souvenir sheet 1.50

Issued to commemorate the International Conference on Community Development, Seoul. No. 324a contains No. 324, imperf. with marginal inscription in bright green. Size: 90x60mm.

Girl Scout
A161

1961, May 10

325 A161 40h bright green 65 40
a. Souvenir sheet 6.00

15th anniversary of Korea's Girl Scouts. No. 325a contains No. 325, imperf., with bright green marginal inscription. Size: 90x60mm.

Soldier's Grave
A162

Soldier with Torch
A163

Lithographed

1961, June 6 ***Perf. 13½*** **Wmk. 317**

326 A162 40h black & olive gray 50 30
a. Souvenir sheet 1.00

Issued for the 6th National Mourning Day. No. 326a contains No. 326, imperf., with marginal inscription in olive gray. Size: 90x60mm.

1961, June 16

327 A163 40h brown & yellow 65 35
a. Souvenir sheet 1.00

Issued to commemorate the Military Revolution of May 16, 1961. No. 327a contains No. 327, imperf. with marginal inscription in brown. Size: 90x60mm.

Map of Korea, Torch and Broken Chain
A164

1961, Aug. 15 ***Perf. 13½*** **Wmk. 317**

328 A164 40h dark blue, vermilion & aquamarine 65 40
a. Souvenir sheet 1.00

Issued to commemorate the 16th anniversary of liberation. No. 328a contains No. 328 imperf. with dark blue marginal inscription. Size: 90x60mm.

Flag and Servicemen
A165

1961, Oct. 1 **Lithographed**

329 A165 40h violet blue, red & brown 65 40
a. Souv. sheet 1.20

Issued for Armed Forces Day. No. 329a contains No. 329 imperf. with violet blue marginal inscription. Size: 90x60mm.

Kyongbok Palace Art Museum
A166

1961, Nov. 1 ***Perf. 13½*** **Wmk. 317**

330 A166 40h beige & dark brown 50 30
a. Souvenir sheet 1.00

Issued to commemorate the 10th National Exhibition of Fine Arts. No. 330a contains one No. 330, imperf., with marginal inscription in dark brown. Size: 90x60mm.

"UNESCO," Candle and Laurel
A167

1961, Nov. 4

331 A167 40h light green & dark blue 50 30
a. Souvenir sheet 1.00

Issued to commemorate the 15th anniversary of UNESCO.

No. 331a contains one No. 331 imperf. with marginal inscription in dark blue. Size: 96x60mm.

Mobile X-Ray Unit
A168

1961, Nov. 16

332 A168 40h rose beige & red brown 50 30
a. Souvenir sheet 1.00

Issued to publicize Tuberculosis Prevention Week.

No. 332a contains one No. 332, imperf., with marginal inscription in red brown. Size: 90x60mm.

Ginseng
A169

King Sejong and Hangul Alphabet
A170

Tristram's Woodpecker
A171

Rice Farmer
A172

Ancient Drums
A173

Lithographed

1961–62 ***Perf. 12½*** **Unwmkd.**

338	A169	20h rose brown ('62)	75	20
339	A170	30h pale purple	1.00	20
340	A171	40h dk. blue &red	1.00	20
341	A172	40h dark green ('62)	1.25	20
342	A173	100h red brown	1.25	50
		Nos. 338-342 (5)	5.25	1.30

See Nos. 363-366, 368, 388-392, 517-519, B5-B7.

Globe with Map of Korea and ITU Emblem
A175

1962, Jan. 31 ***Perf. 13½*** **Unwmkd.**

348 A175 40h vermilion & dark blue 60 30
a. Souv. sheet 1.25

Issued to commemorate the 10th anniversary of Korea's joining the International Telecommunication Union. No. 348a contains No. 348 imperf. with dark blue marginal inscription. Size: 90x60mm.

Atomic Reactor and Atom Symbol
A176

1962, Mar. 30 Litho. ***Perf. 13½***

349 A176 40h lt. blue, slate green & olive gray 50 35

Issued to commemorate the inauguration of the Triga Mark II atomic reactor.

Malaria Eradication Emblem and Mosquito
A177

1962, Apr. 7 **Unwmkd.**

350 A177 40h green & red orange 60 40
a. Souvenir sheet 1.25

Issued for the World Health Organization drive to eradicate malaria. No. 350a contains No. 350 imperf. with dark green marginal inscription. Size: 90x60mm.

YWCA Emblem and Girl
A178

1962, Apr. 20 ***Perf. 13½***

351 A178 40h pink & dk. blue 60 35

Issued to commemorate the 40th anniversary of the Korean Young Women's Christian Association.

South Gate and FPA Emblem
A179

1962, May 12 **Wmk. 317**

352 A179 40h light blue, dk. violet & red 45 30

Issued to publicize the meeting of the Federation of Motion Picture Producers in Asia, May 12-16.

Men Pushing Cogwheel
A180

Soldiers on Hang Kang Bridge
A181

Yin Yang and Factory
A182

Lithographed

1962, May 16 *Perf. 13½* Wmk. 317

353	A180	30h brown & pale olive	75	50
		a. Souv. sheet, Korean text	3.00	
		b. Souv. sheet, English text	3.00	
354	A181	40h brown, lt. blue & citron	75	50
		a. Souv. sheet, Korean text	3.00	
		b. Souv. sheet, English text	3.00	
355	A182	200h ultra., yellow & red	2.00	75
		a. Souv. sheet, Korean text	3.00	
		b. Souv. sheet, English text	3.50	

Issued to commemorate the first anniversary of the May 16th Revolution.

The souvenir sheets contain one stamp each imperf. and the text of the revolutionary pledges in Korean or English respectively. Size: 90x140mm. The sheets with English text also exist with "E" in "POSTAGE" omitted. The English-text sheets are not watermarked except those with "E" omitted. Price, each $9.

Tortoise Warship, 16th Century
A183

Design: 4w, Tortoise ship, heading right.

1962, Aug. 14 *Perf. 13½* Unwmkd.

356	A183	2w dk. blue & pale blue	75	50
357	"	4w black, bluish green & lilac	1.25	1.00

Issued to commemorate the 370th anniversary of Korea's victory in the naval battle with the Japanese off Hansan Island.

Flag, Scout Emblem and Tents
A184

Lithographed

1962, Oct. 5 *Perf. 13½* Wmk. 312

358	A184	4w brn., blue & red	60	35
		a. Souvenir sheet	90	

Wmk. 317

359	A184	4w grn., blue & red	60	35
		a. Souvenir sheet	90	

Issued to commemorate the 40th anniversary of Korean Boy Scouts. Nos. 358a and 359a contain one stamp each, imperf. and unwmkd. Marginal inscription in brown on No. 358a, in green on No. 359a. Size: 90x60mm.

Types of 1961-62 and

Hanabusaya Asiatica
A185

Miruk Bosal
A186

Long-horned Beetle
A186a

Symbols of Thrift and Development
A186b

Meesun Blossoms and Fruit
A186c

Library of Early Buddhist Scriptures
A186d

Sika Deer
A186e

King Songdok Bell, 8th Century
A186f

Bodhisattva in Cavern Temple, Silla Dynasty
A187

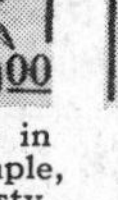

Tile of Silla Dynasty
A187a

Designs: 20ch, Jin-Do dog. 1w, Folk dancers. 1.50w, Miruk Bosal. 2w, Ginseng. 3w, King Sejong. 4w, Rice farmer. 5w, Dragon waterpot. 10w, Ancient drums. 500w, Blue dragon fresco, Koguryo dynasty.

Ordinary Paper
Lithographed

1962-66 *Perf. 12½* Unwmkd.

Size: 22x25mm., 25x22mm.

360	A186	20ch golden brown	75	50
361	A185	40ch blue	75	50
362	A186	50ch claret brown	75	50
363	A169	1w bright bl. ('63)	1.00	50
364	"	2w red brown	1.00	50
365	A170	3w violet brown	1.25	50
366	A172	4w green	1.50	50
367	A186	5w greenish blue	1.50	75
368	A173	10w red brown	7.50	1.00
369	A186c	20w lilac rose ('63)	3.00	2.00
370	A186d	40w dull pur. ('63)	7.50	4.00
		Nos. 360-370 (11)	26.50	11.25

1964-66 Granite Paper

360a	A186	20ch orange brown	50	25
361a	A185	40ch blue	50	25
362a	A186	50ch claret brown	50	25
362B	A186a	60ch black ('66)	50	25
363a	A169	1w bright blue	50	25
363B	A186	1.50w dk. slate grn. ('66)	50	25
364a	A169	2w red brown	50	25
365a	A170	3w violet brown	50	25
366a	A172	4w green	50	25
367a	A186	5w greenish blue	50	25
367B	A186b	7w lilac rose ('66)	1.00	50
368a	A173	10w red brown	1.25	50
369a	A186c	20w lilac rose	1.25	50
370a	A186d	40w violet brown	4.00	1.00
371	A186e	50w red brown	3.00	1.00
372	A186f	100w slate green	7.50	1.00
373	A187	200w dk. & light grn. ('65)	5.00	1.50
374	A187a	300w slate grn. & buff ('65)	8.50	2.50
374A	"	500w dk. & light blue ('65)	10.00	4.00
		Nos. 360a-374A (Granite Paper set) (19)	46.50	15.00

The paper of Nos. 360a to 374A contains a few colored fibers; the paper of Nos. 385-396 contains many fibers.

See also Nos. 385-396, 516, 521-522, 582-584, 1076-1079, B8.

Map, Mackerel and Trawler
A188

1962, Oct. 10 *Perf. 13½*

375	A188	4w dark blue & greenish blue	50	35

Issued to commemorate the 10th anniversary of the Pacific Fishery Council.

ICAO Emblem and Plane
A189

1962, Dec. 11 *Perf. 13½*

376	A189	4w blue & brown	60	35
		a. Souv. sheet	1.75	

Issued to commemorate the 10th anniversary of Korea's joining the International Civil Aviation Organization. No. 376a contains one imperf. stamp, brown marginal inscription. Size: 90x60mm.

Savings Types of 1960

1962-64 *Perf. 12½* Unwmkd.

377	A140	1w emerald, brown & orange ('63)	60	40
		a. Granite paper	1.00	50
378	A141	2w pink, bl. & brn.	90	60
		a. Granite paper	1.25	75

Wmk. 317

379	A140	1w emerald, brown & org. ('64)	5.00	3.00
380	A141	2w pink, bl. & brn. ('64)	2.50	1.00

Wheat Emblem
A190

Lithographed

1963, Mar. 21 *Perf. 13½* Wmk. 317

381	A190	4w emerald, dark blue & ocher	45	24
		a. Souvenir sheet	1.20	

Issued for the "Freedom from Hunger" campaign of the U.N. Food and Agriculture Organization.

No. 381a contains one No. 381 imperf., with dark blue marginal inscriptions. Size: 89x60mm.

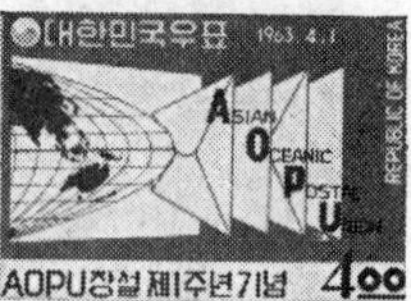

Globe and Letters—A191

1963, Apr. 1

382	A191	4w rose lilac, olive & dark blue	45	24
		a. Souvenir sheet	1.20	

Issued to commemorate the first anniversary of the formation of the Asian-Oceanic Postal Union, AOPU. No. 382a contains one imperf. stamp, rose lilac marginal inscription. Size: 90x60mm.

Centenary Emblem and World Map
A192

1963, May 8 Lithographed

383	A192	4w orge., red & gray	60	25
384	"	4w lt. bl., red & gray	60	25
		a. Souv. sheet of 2	1.25	

Issued to commemorate the centenary of the International Red Cross. No. 384a contains 2 imperf. stamps similar to Nos. 383-384, portrait of Henri Dunant in margin, red and light blue inscription. Size: 139x90mm.

Types of 1961-63

Designs: 20ch, Jin-Do dog. 40ch, Hanabusaya. 50ch, Miruk Bosal. 1w, Folk dancers. 2w, Ginseng. 3w, King Sejong. 4w, Rice farmer. 10w, Ancient drums. 20w, Meesun blossoms and fruit. 40w, Library of early Buddhist scriptures. 50w, Deer. 100w, King Songdok bell, 8th century.

1963-64 *Perf. 12½* Wmk. 317

Granite Paper

Size: 22x25mm., 25x22mm.

385	A186	20ch golden brn. ('64)	25	15
386	A185	40ch blue	25	15
387	A186	50ch claret brn. ('64)	25	15
388	A169	1w bright blue	30	25
389	"	2w red brown	25	25
390	A170	3w violet brown	50	25
391	A172	4w green	50	40
392	A173	10w red brown	1.25	40
393	A186c	20w lilac rose ('64)	1.50	1.25
394	A186d	40w dull purple	5.00	1.00
395	A186e	50w brown	5.00	1.50
396	A186f	100w slate green	10.00	3.00
		Nos. 385-396 (12)	25.05	8.75

Hibiscus and "15"
A193

1963, Aug. 15 *Perf. 13½* Wmk. 317

398	A193	4w violet blue, pale blue & red	60	30

15th anniversary of the Republic.

Army Nurse and Corps Emblem
A194

1963, Aug. 26 **Lithographed**

399 A194 4w citron, grn. & blk. 50 30

Army Nurses Corps, 15th anniversary.

First Five-Year Plan Issue

Transformer and Power Transmission Tower
A195

Irrigated Rice Fields
A196

Designs: No. 402, Cement factory. No. 403, Coal Miner. No. 404, Oil refinery. No. 405, Fishing industry (ships). No. 406, Cargo ship and cargo. No. 407, Fertilizer plant and grain. No. 408, Radar and telephone. No. 409, Transportation (plane, train, ship and map).

1962-66 ***Perf. 12½*** **Unwmkd.**

400 A195 4w org. & dk. vio. 85 50
401 A196 4w lt. bl. & vio. bl. 85 50

Wmk. 317

402 A195 4w dk. bl. & gray ('63) 75 40
403 A196 4w buff & brn. ('63) 75 40
404 A195 4w yel. & ultra. ('64) 65 40
405 A196 4w lt. bl. & blk. ('64) 65 40

Unwmkd.

406 A195 4w pale pink & vio. blue ('65) 50 30
407 A196 4w bister brown & black ('65) 50 30
408 A195 7w yellow bister & black ('66) 50 35
409 A196 7w vio. bl. & lt. bl. ('66) 50 35
Nos. 400-409 (10) 6.50 3.90

Issued to publicize the Economic Development Five-Year Plan.
Issue dates: Nos. 400-401, Dec. 28, 1962. Nos. 402-403, Sept. 1, 1963. Nos. 404-405, June 15, 1964. Nos. 406-407, June 1, 1965. Nos. 408-409, June 1, 1966.

Ramses Temple, Abu Simbel
A197 A198

Lithographed

1963, Oct. 1 ***Perf. 13½*** **Wmk. 317**

410 A197 3w gray & olive gray 60 35
411 A198 4w gray & olive gray 75 50
a. Souv. sheet of 2 2.50

Issued to publicize the UNESCO world campaign to save historic monuments in Nubia. Nos. 410-411 printed se-tenant. No. 411a contains two imperf. stamps similar to Nos. 410-411. Olive gray marginal inscription. Sze: 90x60mm.

Rugby and Torch Bearer
A199

1963, Oct. 4 ***Perf. 13½*** **Wmk. 317**

412 A199 4w pale blue, red brn. & dk. grn. 65 35

44th National Athletic Games.

Nurse and Mobile X-Ray Unit
A200

Eleanor Roosevelt
A201

1963, Nov. 6 ***Perf. 13½***

413 A200 4w orge. & bluish blk. 50 30

Issued to commemorate the tenth anniversary of the Korean National Tuberculosis Association.

1963, Dec. 10 **Litho.** **Wmk. 317**

Design: 4w, Hands holding torch and globe.

414 A201 3w light red brown & dark blue 40 20
415 " 4w dull orange, olive & dk. blue 60 35
a. Souv. sheet of 2 1.20

Issued to honor Eleanor Roosevelt on the 15th anniversary of the Universal Declaration of Human Rights. No. 415a contains two imperf. stamps similar to Nos. 414-415. Dark blue and light red brown marginal inscription. Size: 88x59mm.

Korean Flag and U.N. Headquarters
A202

Tang-piri (Recorder)
A203

1963, Dec. 12 ***Perf. 13½*** **Wmk. 317**

416 A202 4w greenish blue, olive & black 50 30
a. Souv. sheet 1.00

Issued to commemorate the 15th anniversary of Korea's recognition by the United Nations. No. 416a contains one imperf. stamp Black marginal inscription. Size: 90x60mm.

1963, Dec. 17 **Unwmkd.**

Musical Instruments: No. 418, Pyenkyeng (chimes). No. 419, Chang-ko (drums). No. 420, Tai-keum (large flute). No. 421, Taipyeng-so (Chinese oboe). No. 422, Na-bal (brass trumpet). No. 423, Hyang-pipa (Chinese short lute). No. 424, Wul-keum (banjo). No. 425, Kaya-ko (zither, horiz.). No. 426, Wa-kong-hu (harp, horiz.).

417 A203 4w pink, blk. & carm. 50 25
418 " 4w bl., bl. grn. & blk. 50 25
419 " 4w rose, violet blue & brown 50 25
420 A203 4w tan, dark green & brown 50 25
421 " 4w yellow, violet blue & brown 50 25
422 " 4w gray, brn. & vio. 50 25
423 " 4w pink, vio. blue & red brown 50 25
424 " 4w greenish blue, black & blue 50 25
425 " 4w rose, red brown & black 50 25
426 " 4w lilac, blk. & blue 50 25
Nos. 417-426 (10) 5.00 2.50

Pres. Chung Hee Park and Capitol
A204

1963, Dec. 17 **Wmk. 317**

427 A204 4w blk. & brt. grn. 1.75 85

Inauguration of Pres. Chung Hee Park.

Symbols of Metric System
A205

1964, Jan. 1 **Lithographed**

428 A205 4w multicolored 50 25

Introduction of the metric system.

UNESCO Emblem and Yin Yang
A206

1964, Jan. 30 ***Perf. 13½*** **Wmk. 317**

429 A206 4w red, lt. bl. & ultra. 50 25

Issued to commemorate the 10th anniversary of the Korean National Commission for UNESCO.

Industrial Census—A207

1964, Mar. 23 ***Perf. 13½*** **Wmk. 317**

430 A207 4w gray, black & red brown 50 25

National Mining and Industrial Census.

YMCA Emblem and Head
A208

1964, Apr. 12 **Lithographed**

431 A208 4w apple green, dk. blue & red 50 25

Issued to commemorate the 50th anniversary of the Korean Young Men's Christian Association.

Unisphere, Ginseng and Cargo Ship—A209

Design: 100w, Korean pavilion and globe.

1964, Apr. 22 ***Perf. 13½*** **Wmk. 317**

432 A209 40w buff, red brown & green 1.50 50
433 " 100w blue, red brn. & ultra. 2.50 1.50
a. Souv. sheet 5.00

Issued for the New York World's Fair, 1964-65. No. 433a contains two imperf. stamps similar to Nos. 432-433. Red brown marginal inscription. Size: 90x60mm.

Secret Garden, Changdok Palace, Seoul—A210

Views: 2w, Whahong Gate, Suwon. 3w, Uisang Pavilion, Yangyang-gun. 4w, Maitreya Buddha, Bopju Temple at Mt. Songni. 5w, Paekma River and Rock of Falling Flowers. 6w, Anab Pond, Kyongju. 7w, Choksok Pavilion, Chinju. 8w, Kwanghan Pavilion. 9w, Whaom Temple, Mt. Chiri. 10w, Chonjeyon Falls, Soguipo.

1964, May 25 ***Perf. 13½*** **Wmk. 317**

Light Blue Background

434 A210 1w green 15 10
435 " 2w gray 15 10
436 " 3w dark green 25 15
437 " 4w emerald 25 15
438 " 5w violet 35 15
439 " 6w violet blue 50 20
a. Souv. sheet of 2 (5w, 6w) 1.00
440 " 7w dark brown 50 20
a. Souv. sheet of 2 (4w, 7w) 1.00
441 " 8w brown 50 25
a. Souv. sheet of 2 (3w, 8w) 1.00
442 " 9w light violet 1.00 40
a. Souv. sheet of 2 (2w, 9w) 1.00
443 " 10w slate green 1.00 50
a. Souv. sheet of 2 (1w, 10w) 1.00
Nos. 434-443 (10) 4.65 2.20
Nos. 439a-443a (5) 5.00

The five souvenir sheets contain 2 imperf. stamps each, and have marginal inscriptions; size: 90x60mm.

Globe and Wheel—A211

1964, July 1 **Litho.** ***Perf. 13½***

444 A211 4w light olive green, dull brn. & ocher 50 25
a. Souvenir sheet 1.10

Issued to honor the Colombo Plan for co-operative economic development of south and southeast Asia. No. 444a contains one imperf. stamp similar to No. 444 with dull brown inscriptions and light olive green bar. Size: 90x60mm.

Hands and World Health Organization Emblem
A212

1964, Aug. 17 *Perf. 13½* Wmk. 317

445 A212 4w brt. yellow green, yel. grn. & blk. 50 25
a. Souvenir sheet 1.00

Issued to commemorate the 15th anniversary of Korea's joining the United Nations. No. 445a contains one imperf. stamp similar to No. 445 with black marginal inscription and yellow green bar. Size: 90x60 mm.

Runner—A213

1964, Sept. 3

446 A213 4w red lilac, green & pink 60 30

Issued to commemorate the 45th National Athletic Meet, Inchon, Sept. 3-8.

UPU Monument, Bern
A214

1964, Sept. 15

447 A214 4w pink, red brown & blue 50 35
a. Souvenir sheet 1.00

Issued to commemorate the 90th anniversary of the first International Congress for establishing the UPU. No. 447a contains one imperf. stamp similar to No. 447 with red brown inscription and blue bar. Size: 90x60mm.

Crane Hook and Emblem
A215

1964, Sept. 29 *Perf. 13½* Wmk. 317

448 A215 4w red brown & dull green 50 35

Issued to commemorate the 5th Convention of the International Federation of Asian and Western Pacific Contractors' Association (IFAWPCA), Seoul, Sept. 29–Oct. 7.

Methods and style of listing are detailed in "Special Notices" at the front of this volume.

Marathon Runners
A216

Designs: No. 450, Equestrian. No. 451, Gymnast. No. 452, Rowing. No. 453, "V", Olympic rings, laurel and track (vert.).

1964, Oct. 10 Lithographed

449 A216 4w violet blue, lilac rose & green 35 20
a. Souv. sheet 50
450 " 4w brown, red brn. & dark blue 35 20
a. Souv. sheet 50
451 " 4w dark blue, red brn. & lilac rose 35 20
a. Souv. sheet 50
452 " 4w greenish blue, vio. bl. & brn. 35 20
a. Souv. sheet 50
453 " 4w brt. grn., dk. grn. & red brown 35 20
a. Souv. sheet 50
Nos. 449-453 (5) 1.75 1.00
Nos. 449a-453a (5) 2.50

Issued to commemorate the 18th Olympic Games, Tokyo, Oct. 10–25. The souvenir sheets are unwatermarked and contain one imperf. stamp each, marginal inscription and Olympic rings. Size: 90x60mm.

Stamp of 1885 A217 — Yong Sik Hong A218

1964, Dec. 4 *Perf. 13½* Unwmkd.

454 A217 3w lilac, violet & & dull bl. grn. 50 25
455 A218 4w gray, violet blue & black 70 35

Issued to commemorate the 80th anniversary of the Korean postal system. Yong Sik Hong (1855–1884) was Korea's first general postmaster.

Pine Branch and Cones
A219

Designs: No. 457, Plum Blossoms. No. 458, Forsythia. No. 459, Azalea. No. 460, Lilac. No. 461, Sweetbrier. No. 462, Garden balsam. No. 463, Hibiscus. No. 464, Crape myrtle. No. 465, Chrysanthemum lucidum. No. 466, Paulownia coreana. No. 467, Bamboo.

1965 Lithographed *Perf. 13½*

456 A219 4w pale green, dp. green & brown 30 20
a. Souv. sheet 60
457 " 4w gray, black, rose & yellow 30 20
a. Souv. sheet 60
458 " 4w lt. bl., yel. & brn. 30 20
a. Souv. sheet 60
459 " 4w brt. grn., lilac rose & salmon 40 20
a. Souv. sheet 60
460 A219 4w red lilac & bright green 35 20
a. Souv. sheet 60
461 " 4w yel. grn., grn., carm. & brown 25 20
a. Souv. sheet 60
462 " 4w blue, grn. & red 30 20
a. Souv. sheet 60
463 " 4w bluish gray, rose red & green 30 20
a. Souv. sheet 60
464 " 4w multicolored 35 20
a. Souv. sheet 60
465 " 4w pale green, dark brown, green & carmine rose 40 20
a. Souv. sheet 60
466 " 4w buff, olive green & brown 40 20
a. Souv. sheet 60
467 " 4w ultra. & emerald 35 20
a. Souv. sheet 60
Nos. 456-467 (12) 4.00 2.40
Nos. 456a-467a (12) 7.20

Souvenir sheets, Nos. 456a-467a, each contain one imperf. stamp, with marginal inscription in one color and bars in another. Size: 90x60mm.

Dancing Women, PATA Emblem and Tabo Tower—A220

1965, Mar. 26

468 A220 4w lt. bl. grn., dk. brn. & dk. vio. blue 50 30
a. Souv. sheet 1.00

Issued to commemorate the 14th conference of the Pacific Travel Association, Seoul, March 26–April 2. No. 468a contains one imperf. stamp similar to No. 468 with dark violet blue and dark brown inscriptions and light blue green bar. Size: 90x60mm.

Map of Viet Nam and Flag of Korean Assistance Group
A221

1965, Apr. 20 *Perf. 13½*

469 A221 4w blk., lt. yel. grn. & greenish bl. 50 30
a. Souv. sheet 1.00

Issued to honor the Korean military assistance group in Viet Nam. No. 469a contains one imperf. stamp similar to No. 469 with greenish blue and black marginal inscription and bar. Size: 90x60mm.

Symbols of 7-Year Plan
A222

1965, May 1 Lithographed

470 A222 4w emerald, dark grn. & dk. brn. 40 25

Issued to publicize the 7-year plan for increased food production.

Scales with Families and Homes
A223

1965, May 8

471 A223 4w light & dark green & gray 45 25
a. Souv. sheet 1.00

Issued to publicize May as Month of Family Planning. No. 471a contains one imperf. stamp similar to No. 471 with dark green marginal inscription and gray bar. Size: 89x60mm.

ITU Emblem, Old and New Communication Equipment
A224

1965, May 17

472 A224 4w lt. bl., car. & blk. 45 25
a. Souv. sheet 1.00

Issued to commemorate the centenary of the International Telecommunication Union. No. 472a contains one imperf. stamp similar to No. 472 with black and red marginal inscription and black bar. Size: 89x60mm.

U.N. Emblem and Flags of Australia, Belgium, Great Britain, Canada and Colombia—A225

Gen. Douglas MacArthur and Flags of Korea, U.N. and U.S.A.
A226

U.N. Emblem and Flags: No. 474, Denmark, Ethiopia, France, Greece and India. No. 475, Italy, Luxembourg, Netherlands, New Zealand and Norway. No. 476, Philippines, Sweden, Thailand, Turkey and South Africa.

1965, June 25

Flags in Original Colors

473 A225 4w gray & vio. blue 35 15
a. Souv. sheet 40
474 " 4w greenish blue & violet blue 35 15
a. Souv. sheet 40
475 " 4w greenish blue & violet blue 35 15
a. Souv. sheet 40
476 " 4w greenish blue & violet blue 35 15
a. Souv. sheet 40
477 A226 10w lt. bl., blk., vio. blue & red 75 45
a. Souv. sheet 80
Nos. 473-477 (5) 2.15 1.05
Nos. 473a-477a (5) 2.40

Issued to commemorate the 15th anniversary of the participation of U.N. Forces in the Korean war. The souvenir sheets contain one imperf. stamp each and have marginal inscriptions and bars in stamp colors. Size: 90x60mm.

Flag, Factories and "20"
A227

South Gate, Seoul, Fireworks and Yin Yang
A228

1965, Aug. 15 **Lithographed**

478 A227 4w lt. bl., violet blue & red 30 15
479 A228 10w violet blue, lt. blue & red 75 35

Issued to commemorate the 20th anniversary of liberation from the Japanese.

Factory, Leaf and Ants
A229

1965, Sept. 20 ***Perf. 13½***

480 A229 4w brt. yel. green, brn. & bister 45 20

Issued to publicize the importance of saving.

Parabolic Antenna, Telephone Dial and Punched Tape—A230

Telegraph Operator, 1885
A231

1965, Sept. 28

481 A230 3w light blue, black & olive 25 15
482 A231 10w citron, Prussian blue & black 60 35

Issued to commemorate the 80th anniversary of telegraph service between Seoul and Inchon.

Korean Flag and Capitol, Seoul
A232

1965, Sept 28

483 A232 3w orange, slate grn. & blue green 45 25

15th anniversary of recapture of Seoul.

Pole Vault
A233

1965, Oct. 5

484 A233 3w blk., lilac & sal. 45 25

Issued to publicize the 46th National Athletic Meet, Kwangju, Oct. 5–10.

ICY Emblem
A234

U.N. Flag and Headquarters, N.Y.
A235

1965, Oct. 24 **Lithographed**

485 A234 3w lt. & dk. green & orge. brown 35 20
a. Souv. sheet 60
486 A235 10w lt. blue, violet blue & green 60 35
a. Souv. sheet 70

Issued for the International Cooperation Year, 1965, and to commemorate the 20th anniversary of the United Nations. Nos. 485a–486a contain one imperf. stamp each with marginal inscriptions in stamp colors. Size: 90x60mm.

Child Posting Letter
A236

Design: 10w, Air mail envelope and telephone.

1965, Dec. 4 ***Perf. 13½***

487 A236 3w bl. green, black, green & red 40 20
488 " 10w olive, dk. blue & red 65 35

Tenth Communications Day

Children with Sled
A237

Children and South Gate
A238

1965, Dec. 11 **Litho.** ***Perf. 12½***

489 A237 3w pale green, vio. blue & red 40 30
490 A238 4w lt. blue green, vio. blue & red 90 60
a. Souv. sheet of 2 1.25

Issued for Christmas and the New Year. No. 490a contains two imperf. stamps similar to Nos. 489–490; marginal inscription in red, pale green and violet blue. Size: 90x60mm.

Freedom House
A239

1966, Feb. 15 ***Perf. 12½*** **Unwmkd.**

491 A239 7w brt. green, black & citron 35 25
492 " 39w lilac, black & pale green 1.00 60
a. Souv. sheet 2.00

Issued to commemorate the opening of "Freedom House" at Panmunjom. No. 492a contains two imperf. stamps similar to Nos. 491–492. Lilac and black marginal inscription. Size: 90x60mm.

Wildlife Issue

Mandarin Ducks
A240

Birds: 5w, Japanese cranes. 7w, Ring-necked pheasants.

1966 **Litho.** ***Perf. 12½***

493 A240 3w multicolored 30 20
a. Souv. sheet 35
494 " 5w multicolored 40 25
a. Souv. sheet 45
495 " 7w multicolored 50 30
a. Souv. sheet 60

Issued Mar. 15, 1966.

Alaska Pollack
A241

Fish: 5w, Manchurian trout. 7w, Yellow corvina.

496 A241 3w blue, dark brown & yellow 30 20
a. Souv. sheet 35
497 " 5w greenish blue, blk. & magenta 40 25
a. Souv. sheet 45
498 " 7w brt. greenish bl., black & yellow 50 30
a. Souv. sheet 60

Issued June 15, 1966.

Firefly
A242

Insects: 5w, Grasshopper. 7w, Silk butterfly (sericinus telamon).

499 A242 3w multicolored 30 20
a. Souvenir sheet 35
500 " 5w dp. yel. & multi. 40 25
a. Souvenir sheet 45
501 " 7w lt. bl. & multi. 50 30
a. Souvenir sheet 60

Issued Sept. 15, 1966.

Badger
A243

Animals: 5w, Asiatic black bear. 7w, Tiger.

502 A243 3w multicolored 30 20
a. Souvenir sheet 35
503 " 5w multicolored 40 25
a. Souvenir sheet 45
504 " 7w multicolored 50 30
a. Souvenir sheet 60
Nos. 493–504 (12) 4.80 3.00
Nos. 493a–504a (12) 5.60

Issued Dec. 15, 1966.

Souvenir sheets Nos. 493a–504a each contain one imperf. stamp with multicolored marginal inscriptions and bars. Size: 90x60mm.

Hwansung-gun and Kwangnung Forests
A244

Symbolic Newspaper Printing and Pen
A245

1966, Apr. 5 ***Perf. 12½*** **Unwmkd.**

505 A244 7w green & brown 40 25

Forestation Movement.

1966, Apr. 7 **Lithographed**

506 A245 7w lt. blue, violet brown & yel. 40 25

Tenth Newspaper Day.

Children and Bell
A246

1966, May 1 ***Perf. 12½*** **Unwmkd.**

507 A246 7w org., grn. & blue 45 25

Proper guidance of young people.

WHO Headquarters, Geneva
A247

1966, May 3 **Lithographed**

508 A247 7w lt. bl., blk. & yel. 25 15
a. Souv. sheet 65
509 " 39w bluish gray, yel. & red 70 40

Issued to commemorate the inauguration of the World Health Organization Headquarters, Geneva. No. 508a contains one imperf. stamp similar to No. 508. Black and light blue marginal inscription, blue bar. Size: 89x60mm.

Girl Scout and Flag
A248

1966, May 10

510 A248 7w yel., emerald & dark blue 75 45

Girl Scouts of Korea, 20th anniversary.

Pres. Park and Flags of Korea, Malaysia, Thailand and China
A249

1966, May 10

511 A249 7w multicolored 85 50

Issued to commemorate the state visit of President Chung Hee Park to Malaysia, Thailand and China.

Women's Ewha University, Seoul, and Student
A250

1966, May 31

512 A250 7w light blue, violet blue & dp. org. 75 30

Issued to commemorate the 80th anniversary of modern education for women.

Types of 1961–66 Inscribed "Republic of Korea," and

Porcelain Incense Burner, 11th–12th Centuries
A253

Celadon Vessel, 12th Century
A254

Unjin Miruk Buddha, Kwanchok Temple
A255

Designs: 60ch, Long-horned beetle. 1w, Folk dancers. 2w, Ginseng. 3w, King Sejong. 5w, Dragon waterpot. 7w, Symbols of thrift and development.

Lithographed

1966, Aug. 20 *Perf. 12½* Unwmkd.

Size: 22x19mm., 19x22mm.

Granite Paper

516	A186a	60ch gray green	10	8
517	A169	1w green	15	8
518	"	2w blue green	15	8
519	A170	3w dull red brown	15	8
521	A186	5w gray green	18	8
522	A186b	7w greenish blue	30	8

Size: 22x25mm.

523	A253	13w violet blue	40	10
524	A254	60w green	1.25	30
525	A255	80w slate green	1.75	40
		Nos. 516-525 (9)	4.43	1.28

Souvenir Sheet

Carrier Pigeons—A258

1966, July 13 *Imperf.* Wmk. 317

Red Brown Surcharge

534 A258 7w on 40h emerald & dark green 80 50

Issued for the 6th International Letter Writing Week, June 13–19. No. 534 was not issued without surcharge. Size: 90x 60mm.

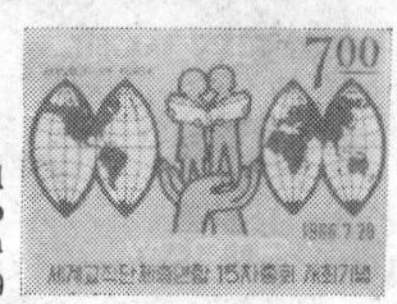

Children and World Map Projection
A259

1966, July 28 *Perf. 12½* Unwmkd.

535 A259 7w light & dark. vio. blue & gray 45 25
a. Souv. sheet 65

Issued to commemorate the 15th annual assembly of WCOTP (World Conference of Teaching Profession), Seoul, July 28–Aug. 9. No. 535a contains one imperf. stamp with marginal inscription and bar. Size: 90x60mm.

Factory, Money Bag and Honeycomb
A260

1966, Sept. 1 *Perf. 12½* Unwmkd.

536 A260 7w multicolored 45 25

Issued to publicize systematic saving.

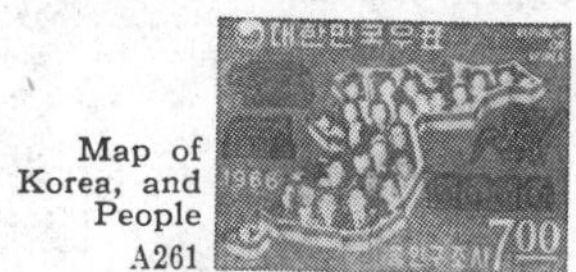

Map of Korea, and People
A261

1966, Sept. 1 Lithographed

537 A261 7w multicolored 45 25

Ninth national census.

CISM Emblem and Round-Table Conference
A262

1966, Sept. 29 *Perf. 12½* Unwmkd.

538 A262 7w multicolored 45 25
a. Souvenir sheet 85

Issued to publicize the 21st General Assembly of the International Military Sports Council (CISM), Seoul, Sept. 29–Oct. 9. No. 538a contains one imperf. stamp, marginal inscription and bar. Size: 90x60mm.

Flags of Korea and Viet Nam and Korean Soldiers
A263

1966, Oct. 1

539 A263 7w multicolored 65 40

Issued to commemorate the first anniversary of Korean combat troops in Viet Nam.

Wrestlers
A264

1966, Oct. 10

540 A264 7w red brown, buff & black 60 35

Issued to publicize the 47th National Athletic Meet, Seoul, Oct. 10–15.

Lions Emblem and Map of Southeast Asia
A265

1966, Oct. 15

541 A265 7w multicolored 40 25
a. Souvenir sheet 1.00

Issued to publicize the 5th East and Southeast Asia Lions Convention, Seoul, Oct. 15–17. No. 541a contains one imperf. stamp and marginal inscription. Size: 90x60mm.

Seoul University Emblem
A266

1966, Oct. 15 Lithographed

542 A266 7w multicolored 40 25

20th anniversary of Seoul University.

Anticommunist League Emblem
A267

1966, Oct. 31 *Perf. 12½* Unwmkd.

543 A267 7w multicolored 35 25
a. Souv. sheet 80

Issued to publicize the 12th Conference of the Asian Anticommunist League, Seoul, Oct. 31–Nov. 7. No. 543a contains one imperf. stamp similar to No. 543 with multicolored marginal inscription and tan bar. Size: 89x60mm.

Presidents Park and Johnson, Flags of U.S. and Korea
A268

1966, Oct. 31 Litho. *Perf. 12½*

544 A268 7w multicolored 75 25
545 " 83w " 1.75 1.00
a. Souv. sheet 3.50

Issued to commemorate the visit of President Lyndon B. Johnson to Korea. No. 545a contains 2 imperf. stamps similar to Nos. 544–545 with multicolored marginal inscription. Size 90x60mm.

UNESCO Emblem and Symbols of Learning
A269

1966, Nov. 4

546 A269 7w multicolored 40 30
a. Souv. sheet 85

Issued to commemorate the 20th anniversary of UNESCO (United Nations Educational, Cultural and Scientific Organization). No. 546a contains one imperf. stamp with marginal inscription in black & red brown and gray bar. Size: 89x60mm.

Good Luck Bag and "Joy"
A270

Ram and "Completion"
A271

Perf. 12½x13, 13x12½

1966, Dec. 10

547 A270 5w multicolored 30 20
a. Souvenir sheet 75
548 A271 7w multicolored 40 30
a. Souvenir sheet 1.00

Issued for Christmas and the New Year. Souvenir sheets Nos. 547a–548a each contain one imperf. stamp with multicolored marginal inscriptions and bars. Size 90x60 mm.

Syncom Satellite over Globe
A272

1967, Jan. 31 Litho. *Perf. 12½*

549 A272 7w dk. bl. & multi. 45 25
a. Souvenir sheet 1.25

Issued to commemorate the 15th anniversary of Korea's membership in the International Telecommunication Union. No. 549a contains one imperf. stamp with multicolored marginal inscription and bar. Size: 90x60mm.

Presidents Park and Lübke
A273

Perf. 12½

1967, March 2 Litho. Unwmkd.

550 A273 7w multicolored 65 40
a. Souvenir sheet 1.50

Issued to commemorate the visit of Pres. Heinrich Lübke of Germany, March 2–6. No. 550a contains one imperf. stamp with multicolored marginal inscription and bars. Size: 90x60mm.

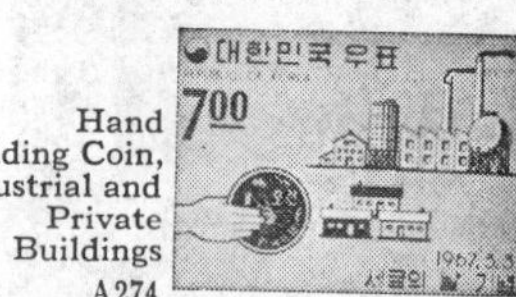

Hand Holding Coin, Industrial and Private Buildings
A274

1967, March 3

551 A274 7w light green & black brown 45 25

Issued to commemorate the first anniversary of the National Taxation Office.

Folklore Series

Okwangdae Clown
A275

Perfect Peace Dance
A276

Girls on Seesaw A277 — Korean Shuttlecock A278

Designs: 5w, Sandi mask and dance (horiz.). 7w, Hafoe mask.

1967, Mar. 15 Litho. *Perf. 12½*

552 A275 4w gray, blk. & yel. 25 15
a. Souvenir sheet 30
553 " 5w multicolored 35 20
a. Souvenir sheet 40
554 " 7w multicolored 45 30
a. Souvenir sheet 65

1967, June 15

Designs: 4w, Sword dance (horiz.). 7w, Buddhist Monk dance.

555 A276 4w multicolored 25 15
a. Souv. sheet 30
556 " 5w multicolored 35 20
a. Souv. sheet 40
557 " 7w multicolored 45 30
a. Souv. sheet 65

1967, Sept. 15

Designs: 4w, Girls on swing (horiz.). 7w, Girls dancing in the moonlight.

558 A277 4w multicolored 25 15
a. Souv. sheet 30
559 " 5w multicolored 35 20
a. Souv. sheet 40
560 " 7w multicolored 45 30
a. Souv. sheet 65

1967, Dec. 15

Designs: 5w, Girls celebrating full moon (horiz.). 7w, Archery.

561 A278 4w multicolored 25 15
a. Souv. sheet 30
562 " 5w multicolored 35 20
a. Souv. sheet 40
563 " 7w multicolored 45 30
a. Souv. sheet 65
Nos. 552-563 (12) 4.20 2.60
Nos. 552a-563a (12) 5.40

Souvenir sheets Nos. 552a-563a each contain one imperf. stamp with multicolored marginal inscriptions and bars. Size: 90x60mm.

JCI Emblem and Kyung-hoe Pavilion
A279

1967, Apr. 13 Litho. *Perf. 12½*

564 A279 7w dk. brown, brt. grn., bl. & red 45 30
a. Souvenir sheet 85

Issued to publicize the International Junior Chamber of Commerce Conference, Seoul, Apr. 13-16. No. 654a contains one imperf. stamp with multicolored marginal inscription and bars. Size: 90x60mm.

Emblem, Map of Far East
A280

1967, Apr. 24 *Perf. 12½* Unwmkd.

565 A280 7w vio. blue & multi. 45 25
a. Souvenir sheet 85

Issued to publicize the 5th Asian Pacific Dental Congress, Seoul, Apr. 24-28. No. 565a contains one imperf. stamp similar to No. 565 with multicolored marginal inscription and bar. Size: 90x60mm.

EXPO '67 Korean Pavilion
A281

1967, Apr. 28

566 A281 7w yel., blk. & red 50 35
567 " 83w lt. bl., blk. & red 1.75 90
a. Souv. sheet 1.75

Issued to commemorate EXPO '67, International Exhibition, Montreal, Apr. 28-Oct. 27, 1967. No. 567a contains 2 imperf. stamps similar to Nos. 566-567 with black and red marginal inscription. Size: 90x60mm.

Worker, Soldier, Emblem and Buildings
A282

1967, May 1

568 A282 7w multicolored 45 25

Veterans' Day, May 1.

Seond Five-Year Plan Issue

Nut and Arrows
A283

Designs: No. 570, Iron wheel and rail. No. 571, Express highway. No. 572, Cloverleaf intersection. No. 573, Rising income for fishermen and farmers (oysters, silk worm, mushrooms and bull's head). No. 574, Machine industry (cogwheels, automobile, wrench and motor). No. 575, Harbor. No. 576, Housing projects plans. No. 577, Atomic power plant. No. 578, Four Great River Valley development.

1967-71 Litho. *Perf. 12½*

569 A283 7w blk., red brn. & dull orange 60 35
570 " 7w dull orange, yel. & black 60 35
571 " 7w green, blue & olive ('68) 50 25
572 " 7w dark brown, yel. & green ('68) 50 25

Perf. 13x12½

573 A283 7w brn., grn., yellow & orange ('69) 35 15
574 " 7w dark blue, lilac rose & buff ('69) 35 15
575 " 10w dk. bl., blue, yel. & green ('70) 30 15
576 " 10w lt. bl., blue, grn. & red ('70) 30 15

Photogravure

Perf. 13

577 A283 10w blk., carmine & blue ('71) 30 15
578 " 10w black, green & brown ('71) 30 15
Nos. 569-578 (10) 4.10 2.10

Issued to publicize the Second Economic Development Five-Year Plan.

Issue dates: Nos. 569-570, June 1, 1967. Nos. 571-572, Dec. 5, 1968. Nos. 573-574, Dec. 5, 1969. Nos. 575-576, Dec. 5, 1970. Nos 577-578, Dec. 5, 1971.

President Park and Phoenix
A284

1967, July 1 *Perf. 12½* Unwmkd.

579 A284 7w multicolored 1.50 85
a. Souv. sheet 2.00

Issued to commemorate the inauguration of President Chung Hee Park for a second term, July 1, 1967. No. 579a contains one imperf. stamp similar to No. 579. Violet blue, red and green marginal inscription. Size: 90x60mm.

Korean Boy Scout, Emblem and Tents
A285

Design: 20w, Korean Boy Scout emblem, bridge and tents.

1967, Aug. 10 Litho. *Perf. 12½*

580 A285 7w multicolored 40 25
a. Souv. sheet 60
581 " 20w multicolored 80 50
a. Souv. sheet 1.20

Issued to commemorate the 3rd Korean Boy Scout Jamboree, Hwarangdae, Seoul, Aug. 10-15. Souvenir sheets Nos. 580a-581a each contain one imperf. stamp with multicolored marginal inscriptions and bars. Size: 90x60mm.

Types of 1962-66 Redrawn
(Inscribed "Republic of Korea")

Designs: 20w, Meesun blossoms and fruit. 40w, Library of early Buddhist scriptures. 50w, Deer.

1967, Aug. 25 Granite Paper

582 A186c 20w green & light blue green 1.00 20
583 A186d 40w dark green & light olive 2.00 30
584 A186e 50w dark brown & bister 3.00 50

The printing of redrawn designs of the regular issue of 1962-66 became necessary upon discovery of large quantities of counterfeits, made to defraud the post. The position of the denominations was changed and elaborate fine background tracings were added.

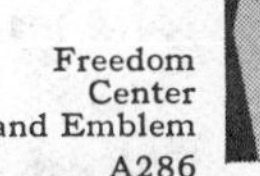

Freedom Center and Emblem
A286

Hand Breaking Chain A287 — Boxing A288

1967, Sept. 25 Litho. *Perf. 12½*

586 A286 5w multicolored 30 15
a. Souv. sheet 35
587 A287 7w multicolored 50 25
a. Souv. sheet 1.00

Issued to commemorate the first Conference of the World Anti-Communist League, WACL, Taipei, China, Sept. 25-29. Souvenir sheets Nos. 586a-587a each contain one imperf. stamp with multicolored marginal inscriptions. Size: 89x60mm.

1967, Oct. 5

Design: 7w, Women's basketball.

588 A288 5w tan & multi. 50 30
589 " 7w pale rose & multi. 75 50

Issued to publicize the 48th National Athletic Meet, Seoul, Oct. 5-10.

Students' Memorial, Kwangjoo A289 — Symbolic Water Cycle A290

1967, Nov. 3 Litho. *Perf. 12½*

590 A289 7w lt. grn. & multi. 45 25

Issued for Student Day commemorating 1929 students' uprising against Japan.

1967, Nov. 20

591 A290 7w multicolored 45 25

Hydrological Decade (UNESCO), 1965-74.

Children Spinning Top A291 — Monkey and Oriental Zodiac A292

1967, Dec. 10

592 A291 5w salmon, orange & violet blue 30 20
a. Souv. sheet 60
593 A292 7w yel. bister, brn. & violet blue 40 35
a. Souv. sheet 1.25

Issued for Christmas and New Year. Souvenir sheets Nos. 592a-593a each contain one imperf. stamp with multicolored marginal inscription and bars. Size: 90x60mm.

Parabolic Antenna and Electric Waves
A293

1967, Dec. 21

594 A293 7w lt. blue, black & yellow 45 25
a. Souv. sheet 1.00

Issued to commemorate the opening of the national microwave communications network, Dec. 21. No. 594a contains one imperf. stamp; black marginal inscription, blue border and marginal design. Size: 90x60mm.

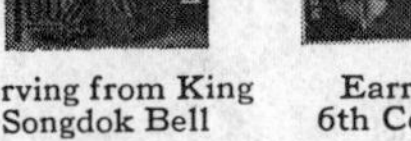

Carving from King Songdok Bell A294 — Earrings, 6th Century A295

Flag
A296

Perf. 13x12½

1968, Feb. 1 Litho. Unwmkd.

Granite Paper

595 A294 1w yellow & brown 25 15
596 A295 5w dk. grn. & yellow 35 15
597 A296 7w dark blue & red 60 20

WHO Emblem A297 **EATA Emblem and Korean Buildings** A298

1968, Apr. 7 *Perf. 12½* Unwmkd.

598 A297 7w multicolored 45 25
a. Souv. sheet 1.00

Issued to commemorate the 20th anniversary of the World Health Organization. No. 598a contains one imperf. stamp; multicolored marginal inscription and border. Size: 90x60mm.

1968, Apr. 9 Lithographed

599 A298 7w multicolored 45 25
a. Souv. sheet 95

Issued to publicize the 2nd General Meeting of the East Asia Travel Association (EATA), Seoul, Apr. 9–13. No. 599a contains one imperf. stamp; yellow decorrative margin with pink border and dark blue inscription. Size: 90x60mm.

Door Knocker, Factories and Emblem
A299

1968, May 6 *Perf. 12½* Unwmkd.

600 A299 7w multicolored 50 30
a. Souv. sheet 95

Issued to commemorate the 2nd Conference of the Confederation of Asian Chambers of Commerce and Industry, Seoul. No. 600a contains one imperf. stamp; multicolored marginal inscription and design. Size: 90x60mm.

Pres. Park and Emperor Haile Selassie
A300

1968, May 18 Lithographed

601 A300 7w multicolored 85 45
a. Souv. sheet 2.75

Issued to commemorate the visit of Emperor Haile Selassie I, May 18–20. No. 601a contains one imperf. stamp; multicolored border. Size 90x60mm.

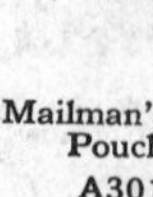

Mailman's Pouch
A301

Mailman
A302

1968, May 31 *Perf. 12½* Unwmkd.

602 A301 5w multicolored 30 15
603 A302 7w " 40 25

First Postman's Day, May 31, 1968.

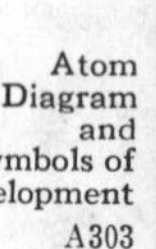

Atom Diagram and Symbols of Development
A303

1968, June 1 Lithographed

604 A303 7w dk. blue, citron & vermilion 45 25

Issued to promote science and technology.

Kyung Hee University and Conference Emblem
A304

1968, June 18 Unwmkd.

605 A304 7w bl., pink & blk. 50 30
a. Souv. sheet 3.50

Issued to publicize the 2nd Conference of the International Association of University Presidents. No. 605a contains one imperf. stamp. Light blue margin with black and blue inscription and pink emblem. Size: 90x60mm.

Liberated People
A305

1968, July 1 Litho. *Perf. 12½*

606 A305 7w multicolored 45 25

Issued to publicize the movement to liberate people under communist rule.

Peacock and Industrial Plant
A306

1968, Aug. 15 *Perf. 12½* Unwmkd.

607 A306 7w multicolored 50 30

Republic of Korea, 20th anniversary.

Fair Entrance
A307

1968, Sept. 9 *Perf. 12½* Unwmkd.

608 A307 7w lilac & multi. 50 25

Issued to publicize the first Korean Trade Fair, Seoul, Sept. 9–Oct. 18.

Assembly Emblem and Pills A308 **Soldier, Insigne and Battle Scene** A309

1968, Sept. 16 Lithographed

609 A308 7w multicolored 45 25

Issued to commemorate the 3rd General Assembly of the Federation of Asian Pharmaceutical Associations, Seoul, Sept. 16–21.

1968, Oct. 1

Designs: No. 611, Sailor, insigne and ship's guns. No. 612, Servicemen and flags. No. 613, Aviator, insigne and planes. No. 614, Marine, insigne and landing group.

610 A309 7w green & orange 50 30
611 " 7w light & dk. blue 50 30
612 " 7w dk. bl. & orange 50 30
613 " 7w dk. bl. & lt. blue 50 30
614 " 7w orange & green 50 30
Nos. 610–614 (5) 2.50 1.50

Issued to commemorate the 20th anniversary of the Korean armed forces. Nos. 610–614 are printed in vertical se-tenant strips in sheets of 50.

Colombo Plan Emblem and Globe
A310

1968, Oct. 8 Litho. *Perf. 12½*

615 A310 7w dk. brown, pale salmon & green 45 25

Issued to commemorate the 19th meeting of the Consultative Committee of the Colombo Plan, Seoul, Oct. 8–28.

Bicycling (Type I) A311

제19회 올림픽대회기념
대한민국우표
Type II
(2nd line flush left)

Designs (Olympic Rings and): No. 617, Bicycling, Type II. Nos. 618–619, Wrestling. Nos. 620–621, Boxing. Nos. 622–623, Olympic flame, "68" and symbols of various sports events.

1968, Oct. 12 *Perf. 12½* Unwmkd.

616 A311 7w pink & multi. (I) 50 25
617 " 7w " " (II) 50 25
a. Souv. sheet of 2 1.20
618 " 7w olive & multi. (I) 50 25
619 " 7w " " (II) 50 25
a. Souv. sheet of 2 1.20
620 " 7w org. & multi. (I) 50 25
621 " 7w " " (II) 50 25
a. Souv. sheet of 2 1.20
622 " 7w bluish green & multi. (I) 50 25
623 A311 7w bluish green & multi. (II) 50 25
a. Souv. sheet of 2 1.20
Nos. 616–623 (8) 4.00 2.00

Issued to commemorate the 19th Olympic Games, Mexico City, Oct. 12–27.

Types I and II of each design of Nos. 616–623 are printed se-tenant in sheets of 50. The position of the "7" is reversed on Nos. 619, 621 and 623 as are the designs of Nos. 619 and 621.

The souvenir sheets Nos. 617a, 619a, 621a and 623a each contain the 2 imperf. stamps of the 2 types under which they are listed. Black inscriptions and Olympic emblem in color of stamp background in margins. Size: 90x60mm.

"Search for Knowledge" and School Girls
A312

1968, Oct. 15

624 A312 7w multicolored 35 25

Issued to commemorate the 60th anniversary of public secondary education for women.

Coin and Statistics
A313

1968, Nov. 1

625 A313 7w multicolored 35 25

National Wealth Survey.

Memorial to Students' Uprising
A314

1968, Nov. 23

626 A314 7w gray & multi. 35 25

Issued to commemorate the anti-communist students' uprising, Nov. 23, 1945.

Men With Banners Declaring Human Rights—A315

1968, Dec. 10

627 A315 7w multicolored 45 30

Issued for the 20th anniversary of the Declaration of Human Rights.

Christmas Decorations A316 **Cock and Good Luck Characters** A317

1968, Dec. 11

628 A316 5w salmon & multicolored 1.00 60
a. Souv. sheet 1.25
629 A317 7w multicolored 1.00 60
a. Souv. sheet 1.25

Issued for Christmas and the New Year. Souvenir sheets Nos. 628a–629a each contain one imperf. stamp with multicolored marginal inscriptions and bars. Size: 90x60mm.

UN Emblems and Korean House
A318

1968, Dec. 12

630 A318 7w lt. blue & multi. 45 25

Issued to commemorate the 20th anniversary of the recognition of the Republic of Korea by the United Nations.

Boy Scout Emblem
A319

Torch, Map and Students Demonstrating against Japan, 1919
A320

1968, Sept. 30 Litho. *Perf. 12½*

631 A319 7w black & multi. 45 25

Regional Boy Scout conference.

1969, Mar. 1 *Perf. 12½* **Unwmkd.**

632 A320 7w multicolored 45 25

50th anniversary of Sam-il movement.

Hyun Choong Sa Shrine and Tortoise Ships
A321

1969, Apr. 28 *Perf. 12½* **Unwmkd.**

633 A321 7w deep blue, green & brown 60 40

Issued to commemorate the completion of the Hyun Choong Sa Shrine at Onyang, dedicated to the memory of Adm. Li Sunsin.

Pres. Park and Tuanku Nasiruddin of Malaysia
A322

1969, Apr. 29 Lithographed

634 A322 7w yellow & multi. 65 40
a. Souv. sheet 2.50

Issued to commemorate the visit of Tuanku Ismail Nasiruddin, ruler of Malaysia, Apr. 29, 1969. No. 634a contains one imperf. stamp with multicolored marginal inscription. Size: 90x60mm.

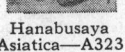

Hanabusaya Asiatica—A323

Flag of Korea—A324

Ancient Drums
A325

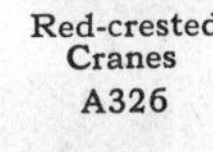

Red-crested Cranes
A326

Highway and Farm
A327

Pitcher (12–13th Centuries)
A328

Ceramic Duck (Water Jar)
A329

Library of Early Buddhist Scriptures
A330

Miruk Bosal
A333

Designs: 1w, Old man's mask. No. 637, Stone lamp, 8th century. No. 638, Chipmunk. No. 644, Tiger lily. No. 649, Bee. No. 651, Vase, Yi dynasty, 17th–18th centuries. No. 653, Gold crown, Silla Dynasty.

Zeros Omitted except 7w No. 639.
Perf. 13x12, 12x13 (Litho.);
13½x12½, 12½x13½ (Photo.).
Litho. (40ch, Nos. 641, 650); others Photo.
Granite Paper (Litho.); Ordinary Paper (Photo.)

1969–74 **Unwmkd.**

No.	Type	Description	Unused	Used
635	A323	40ch green	5	3
636	A326	1w dark rose brown ('74)	5	3
637	A328	5w bright plum	10	5
638	A326	5w maroon ('74)	10	5
639	A324	7w blue ("7⁰⁰")	15	8
640	"	7w blue ("7")	15	8
641	A325	10w ultramarine	25	12
642	A324	10w ultra. ("10") ('70)	20	12
643	A326	10w blue & dark blue ('73)	15	5
		a. Bklt. pane of 6 ('74)	75	
644	A323	10w green & multi. ('73)	15	5
645	A327	10w green, red & gray ('73)	15	5
647	A328	20w green	50	15
648	A329	30w dull green ('70)	60	18
649	A326	30w yellow & dark brown ('74)	50	12
650	A330	40w vio. bl. & pink	75	25
651	A328	40w ultra. & lilac	75	20
652	A333	100w deep claret & yellow	2.00	90
653	A333	100w brn. & yel. ('74)	1.00	60
		Nos. 635-653 (18)	7.60	3.11

Red Cross, Faces and Doves
A336

1969, May 5 Litho. *Perf. 12½*

654 A336 7w multicolored 40 25
a. Souv. sheet 1.25

Issued to commemorate the 50th anniversary of the League of Red Cross Societies. No. 654a contains one imperf. stamp with dark blue green marginal inscription and yellow green border. Size: 89x59mm.

Savings Bank, Factories and Highway
A337

1969, May 20 *Perf. 12½* **Unwmkd.**

655 A337 7w yel. grn. & multi. 40 20

Second Economy Drive.

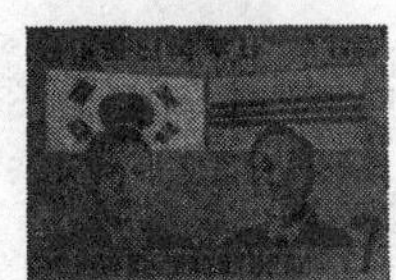

Pres. Park, Pres. Thieu and Flags of Korea and Viet Nam
A338

1969, May 27 **Lithographed**

656 A338 7w pink & multi. 60 40
a. Souv. sheet 2.00

Issued to commemorate the visit of Pres. Nguyen Van Thieu of Viet Nam, May 27. No. 656a contains one imperf. stamp with multicolored marginal inscription and ornament. Size: 90x60mm.

"Reforestation and Parched Fields"
A339

Growing and Withering Plants
A340

1969, June 10

657 A339 7w multicolored 40 20
658 A340 7w " 40 20

Issued to publicize the need for prevention of damages from floods and droughts.

Apollo 11, Separation of Second Stage—A341

Designs: No. 660, Apollo 11, separation of 3rd Stage. No. 661, Orbits of command and landing modules around moon. No. 662, Astronauts gathering rock samples on moon. 40w, Spacecraft splashdown.

1969, Aug. 15 *Perf. 12½* **Unwmkd.**

Granite Paper

659 A341 10w indigo, bl. & red 20 15
660 " 10w " " " 20 15
661 " 20w indigo, bl., red & lemon 40 25
662 " 20w indigo, bl., red & lemon 40 25
663 " 40w indigo, bl. & red 75 50
a. Souv. sheet of 5 2.25
Nos. 659-663 (5) 1.95 1.30

Issued to commemorate man's first landing on the moon, July 20, 1969. U. S. astronauts Neil A. Armstrong and Col. Edwin E. Aldrin, Jr., with Lieut. Col. Michael Collins piloting Apollo 11. Nos. 659–663 printed se-tenant in sheets of 50 (5x10).

No. 663a contains 5 imperf. stamps with simulated perforations similar to Nos. 659–663. Light blue margin with white commemorative inscriptions. Size: 159x109mm.

Fable Issue

Girl and Stepmother
A342

Kongji and Patji (Cinderella): 7w, Sparrows help Kongji separate rice. 10w, Ox helps Kongji to weed a field. 20w, Kongji in a sedan chair on the way to the palace.

1969–70 Litho. *Perf. 12½*

664 A342 5w apple green & multi. 15 10
a. Souv. sheet 20
665 " 7w yellow & multi. 20 10
a. Souv. sheet 25
666 " 10w lt. vio. & multi. 30 20
a. Souv. sheet 35
667 " 20w lt. grn. & multi. 50 35
a. Souv. sheet 75

Issued Sept. 1, 1969.

The Sick Princess
A343

"The Hare's Liver": 7w, Hare riding to the palace on back of turtle. 10w, Hare telling a lie to the King to save his life. 20w, Hare mocking the turtle.

Perf. 13x12½

668 A343 5w yellow & multi. 15 10
a. Souv. sheet 20
669 " 7w lt. vio. & multi. 20 10
a. Souv. sheet 25
670 " 10w lt. greenish blue & multicolored 30 20
a. Souv. sheet 35
671 " 20w lt. yellow green & multicolored 50 35
a. Souv. sheet 75

Issued Nov. 1, 1969.

Mother Meeting Tiger
A344

"The Sun and the Moon": 7w, Tiger disguised as mother at children's house. 10w, Tiger, and children on tree. 20w, Children safe on cloud, and tiger falling to his death.

672 A344 5w orange & multi. 15 10
a. Souvenir sheet 20
673 A344 7w gray grn. & multi. 20 10
a. Souvenir sheet 25
674 A344 10w lt. grn. & multi. 30 20
a. Souvenir sheet 35
675 A344 20w gray & multi. 50 35
a. Souvenir sheet 75

Issued Jan. 5, 1970.

Woodcutter Stealing Fairy's Clothes
A345

Designs: No. 677, Woodcutter with wife and children. No. 678, Wife taking children to heaven. No. 679, Husband joining family in heaven.

676 A345 10w dull blue green & multi. 30 16
a. Souvenir sheet 40
677 A345 10w buff & multi. 30 16
a. Souvenir sheet 40
678 A345 10w lt. greenish blue & multi. 30 16
a. Souvenir sheet 40
679 A345 10w pink & multi. 30 16
a. Souvenir sheet 40

Issued Mar. 5, 1970.

Heungbu and Wife Release Healed Swallow
A346

Designs: No. 681, Heungbu and wife finding gold treasure in gourd. No. 682, Nolbu and wife with large gourd. No. 683, Demon emerging from gourd punishing evil Nolbu and wife.

Perf. 12½

680 A346 10w lt. greenish blue & multi. 30 16
a. Souvenir sheet 40
681 A346 10w orange & multi. 30 16
a. Souvenir sheet 40
682 A346 10w apple green & multi. 30 16
a. Souvenir sheet 40
683 A346 10w tan & multi. 30 16
a. Souvenir sheet 40
Nos. 664-683 (20) 5.85 3.53
Nos. 664a-683a (20) 7.85

Issued May 5, 1970.
Souvenir sheets Nos. 664a–683a each contain one imperf. stamp with black marginal inscriptions and ornamental border in background color of stamps. Size: 90x60mm.

1869 Locomotive and Diesel Train
A347

Design: No. 685, Early locomotive.

Perf. 12½

1969, Sept. 18 Litho. Unwmkd.

684 A347 7w yellow & multi. 35 12
685 " 7w green & multi. 35 12

70th anniversary of Korean Railroads.

Formation of F-5A Planes
A348

Design: No. 687, F-4D Phantom.

1969, Oct. 1 Photo. *Perf. 13½x13*

686 A348 10w blue, blk. & car. 45 25

Lithographed *Perf. 13x12½*

687 A348 10w multicolored 45 25

20th anniversary of Korean Air Force.

Cha-jun Game
A349

1969, Oct. 3

688 A349 7w apple green, dk. blue & black 35 25

Issued to commemorate the 10th National Festival of Traditional Skills.

Institute of Science and Technology
A350

1969, Oct. 23

689 A350 7w bister, green & chocolate 35 25

Issued to commemorate the completion of the Korean Institute of Science and Technology, Hongnung, Seoul.

Pres. Park and Diori Hamani
A351

1969, Oct. 27

690 A351 7w yel. grn. & multi. 50 25
a. Souv. sheet 1.75

Issued to commemorate the visit of Diori Hamani, President of Nigeria, Oct. 27. No. 690a contains one imperf. stamp with multicolored marginal inscription. Size: 90x60mm.

Korean Wrestling
A352

Sports: No. 692, Fencing. No. 693, Korean karate (tackwondo). No. 694, Volleyball (vert.). No. 695, Soccer (vert.).

1969, Oct. 28 *Perf. 13x12½, 12½x13*

691 A352 10w yel. grn. & multi. 30 20
692 " 10w blue & multi. 30 20
693 " 10w green & multi. 30 20
694 " 10w olive & multi. 30 20
695 " 10w ultra. & multi. 30 20
Nos. 691-695 (5) 1.50 1.00

Issued to commemorate the 50th National Athletic Meet, Seoul, Oct. 28–Nov. 2.

Allegory of National Education Charter
A353

1969, Dec. 5 Litho. *Perf. 12½x13*

696 A353 7w dull yel. & multi. 40 25

Issued to commemorate the first anniversary of the proclamation of the National Education Charter.

Toy Dogs and Lattice Pattern
A354

Candle, Lattice Door and Fence
A355

1969, Dec. 11 Photo. *Perf. 13½*

697 A354 5w green & multi. 30 15
698 A355 7w blue & multi. 40 25

Issued for New Year 1970.

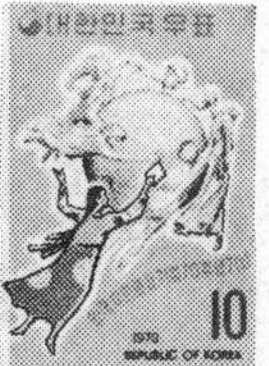

UPU Monument, Bern, and Korean Woman
A356

Education Year Emblem and Book
A357

1970, Jan. 1 Photo. *Perf. 13x13½*

699 A356 10w multicolored 35 25

Issued to commemorate the 70th anniversary of Korea's admission to the Universal Postal Union.

1970, Mar. 10 Litho. *Perf. 12½x13*

700 A357 10w pink & multi. 45 25

International Education Year 1970.

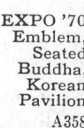

EXPO '70 Emblem, Seated Buddha, Korean Pavilion
A358

1970, March 15 *Perf. 13x12½*

701 A358 10w multicolored 40 25

Issued to publicize EXPO '70 International Exhibition, Osaka, Japan, March 15–Sept. 13.

Korean Youths and 4-H Club Emblem
A359

1970, Mar. 28 *Perf. 12½x13*

702 A359 10w yellow & multi. 35 25

Issued to publicize the 15th Korean 4-H Club Central Contest, Suwon, March 28.

Money and Bank Emblem
A360

1970, Apr. 9 Litho. *Perf. 13x12½*

703 A360 10w yellow & multi. 35 25

Issued to commemorate the 3rd annual Board of Governors' meeting of the Asian Development Bank, Seoul, Apr. 9–11.

Royal Palanquin
A361

1899 Streetcar
A362

Historic Means of Transportation: No. 706, Emperor Sunjong's Cadillac, 1903. No. 707, Nieuport biplane, 1922.

Perf. 13x13½, 13½x13

1970, May 20 Photogravure

704 A361 10w citron & multi. 30 15
705 A362 10w yellow & multi. 30 15
706 " 10w ocher & multi. 30 15
707 " 10w aqua. & multi. 30 15

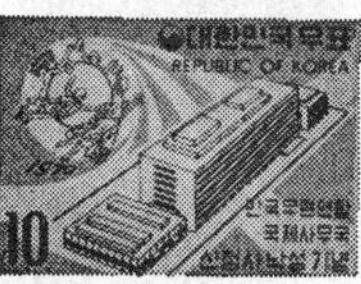

U.P.U. Headquarters
A363

1970, May 30 *Perf. 13½x13*

708 A363 10w multicolored 35 25

Issued to commemorate the inauguration of the new Universal Postal Union Headquarters in Bern, Switzerland.

Map, Radar and Satellite—A364

1970, June 2 *Perf. 13x13½*

709 A364 10w sky blue, violet blue & black 35 25

Issued to commemorate the completion of the Kum San Earth Station of the International Satellite Consortium (INTELSAT).

"PEN" and Manuscript Paper
A365

1970, June 28 Photo. *Perf. 13x13½*

710 A365 10w blue green, blue & carmine 35 25

Issued to publicize the 37th International P.E.N. Congress (Poets, Playwrights, Editors, Essayists and Novelists), Seoul, June 28–July 4.

Seoul-Pusan Expressway—A366

1970, June 30

711 A366 10w multicolored 40 30

Opening of Seoul-Pusan Expressway.

Postal Code Symbol and Number
A367

Mail Sorting Machine
A368

1970, July 1

712 A367 10w multicolored 35 20

Issued to publicize the introduction of postal zone numbers, July 1, 1970.

1970, July 2

713 A368 10w lt. vio. & multi. 35 20
  a. Souv. sheet of 4 14.00

Mechanization of Korean postal system.
No. 713a contains 2 each of Nos. 712–713. Size: 130x90mm.

Boy and Children's Hall
A369

1970, July 25

714 A369 10w pink & multi. 35 25

Opening of Children's Hall, July 25.

Paintings Issue

Jongyangsa Temple and Mt. Kumgang, by Chong Son (1676–1759)
A370

The Fierce Tiger, by Shim Sa-yung (1707–1769)
A371

Paintings: No. 716, Mountains and Rivers, by Yi In-moon (1745–1821). No. 717, Mountains and Rivers in Moonlight, by Kim Doo-ryang (1696–1763).

Perf. 13x13½, 13½x13

1970, Aug. 31 Photogravure

715 A370 10w blue & multi. 35 20
  a. Souvenir sheet of 2 55
716 A370 10w buff & multi. 35 20
  a. Souvenir sheet of 2 55
717 A371 10w multicolored 35 20
  a. Souvenir sheet of 2 55

Nos. 715a–717a have simulated perforations and white marginal inscriptions. No. 715a has blue margin, No. 716a–717a have yellow margins. Background color of stamps on No. 717a is yellow instead of greenish gray as on No. 717. Size: 129x90mm.

1970, Oct. 30

Paintings: No. 719, Cats and Sparrows, by Pyun Sang-byuk (18th century). No. 720, Dog with puppies, by Yi Am (1499–?).

718 A371 30w multicolored 60 40
  a. Souvenir sheet of 2 1.25
719 A371 30w multicolored 60 40
  a. Souvenir sheet of 2 1.25
720 A371 30w multicolored 60 40
  a. Souvenir sheet of 2 1.25

Nos. 718a–720a have been ocher margins with white inscriptions. Size: 129x89mm. Nos. 718–720, 718a–720a exist imperf. (same prices).

1970, Dec. 30

Paintings: No. 721, Cliff and Boat, by Kim Hong-do (1745–?). No. 722, Cock, Hens and Chick, by Pyun Sang-byuk (early 18th century). No. 723, Woman Playing Flute, by Shin Yun-bok (late 18th century).

721 A371 10w yellow brown, black & red 35 20
  a. Souvenir sheet of 2 60
722 A371 10w pale rose, black & green 35 20
  a. Souvenir sheet of 2 60
723 A371 10w multicolored 35 20
  a. Souvenir sheet of 2 60
  Nos. 715-723 (9) 3.90 2.40
  Nos. 715a-723a (9) 7.20

Nos. 721a–723a have ocher margins with white inscriptions. Size: 129x89mm. Nos. 721a–723a exist imperf.

P.T.T.I. Emblem and Map of Far East
A372

1970, Sept. 6 Litho. *Perf. 13x12½*

724 A372 10w lt. yellow green, bl. & dk. blue 35 25

Issued to publicize the opening of the Councillors' Meeting of the Asian Chapter of the Postal, Telegraph and Telephone International Organization, Sept. 6–12.

Korean WAC and Emblem
A373

1970, Sept. 6 Photo. *Perf. 13x13½*

725 A373 10w blue & multi. 35 25

Issued to commemorate the 20th anniversary of the founding of the Korean Women's Army Corps.

Pres. Park, Korean Flag and Means of Transportation
A374

Pres. Park, Highways, Factories
A375

1970 *Perf. 13x13½, 13½x13*

726 A374 10w violet blue, blk. & car. 60 30
727 A375 10w dk. bl., greenish blue & black 50 25

Presidents Park and Hernandez, Flags of Korea, Salvador—A376

1970, Sept. 28 Litho. *Perf. 13x12½*

728 A376 10w dark blue, red & black 35 25
  a. Souvenir sheet 3.00

Visit of Gen. Fidel Sanchez Hernandez, President of El Salvador. No. 728a contains one imperf. stamp. Marginal inscription in black, red and dark blue. Size: 90x60mm.

People and Houses
A377

1970, Oct. 1 Litho. *Perf. 13x12½*

729 A377 10w lilac & multi. 35 20

Issued to publicize the national census of population and housing, Oct. 1.

Diver—A378

Designs: No. 731, Field hockey. No. 732, Baseball.

1970, Oct. 6 Photo. *Perf. 12½x13½*

730 A378 10w lilac, lt. brown & black 24 18
  a. Souvenir sheet of 2 60
731 A378 10w lt. green, yellow & brown 24 18
  a. Souvenir sheet of 2 60
732 A378 10w grn., blue & car. 24 18
  a. Souvenir sheet of 2 60

Issued to publicize the 51st National Athletic Games, Seoul, Oct. 6–11. Nos. 730a–732a each contain 2 imperf. stamps with marginal inscriptions and decorations in colors of stamps. Size: 90x85mm.

Police Emblem and Activities
A379

1970, Oct. 21 Litho. *Perf. 12½*

733 A379 10w ultra. & multi. 35 25

The 25th Policemen's Day.

Freedom Bell, U.N. Emblem over Globe
A380

1970, Oct. 24 Photo. *Perf. 13x13½*

734 A380 10w blue & multi. 35 25

25th anniversary of United Nations.

Kite and Holly
A380a

Boar
A381

1970, Dec. 1 Litho. *Perf. 13*

735 A380a 10w lt. blue & multi. 25 18
  a. Souvenir sheet of 3 60
736 A381 10w green & multi. 25 18
  a. Souvenir sheet of 3 60

New Year 1971. Nos. 735a and 736a contain 3 stamps each. No. 735a has black and pink marginal inscription; No. 736a has black, green and violet inscription. Size: 90x60mm.

Pres. Park Quotation, Globe and Telecommunications Emblems
A382

1970, Dec. 4 Photogravure

737 A382 10w multicolored 35 25

For the 15th Communications Day.

Power Dam—A383

Coal Mining
A384

Highway Intersection
A385

Designs: No. 739, Crate wrapped in world map, and ships. No. 740, Irrigation project and farm (vert.). No. 742, Cement factory (vert.). No. 743, Fertilizer factory. No. 744, Increased national income (scales). No. 745, Increased savings (factories, bee and coins).

1971 ***Perf. 13x13½, 13½x13***

738 A383 10w blue & multi. 20 12
a. Souvenir sheet 40
739 A383 10w pale lilac & multicolored 20 12
a. Souvenir sheet 40
740 A383 10w green & multi. 20 12
a. Souvenir sheet 40
741 A384 10w blue green, lt. blue & black 20 12
a. Souvenir sheet of 2 50
742 A384 10w lt. blue, violet & brt. magenta 20 12
a. Souvenir sheet of 2 50
743 A384 10w violet, green & bister 20 12
a. Souvenir sheet of 2 50
744 A384 10w pink & multi. 20 12
a. Souvenir sheet of 2 50
745 A384 10w lt. blue green & multicolored 20 12
a. Souvenir sheet of 2 50
746 A385 10w violet & multi. 20 12
a. Souvenir sheet of 2 50
Nos. 738-746 (9) 1.80 1.08
Nos. 738a-746a (9) 4.20

Economic Development. Nos. 738a-740a each contain one imperf. stamp; Nos. 741a-746a, each two imperf. stamps. All have marginal inscriptions in stamp colors. Size: 90x60mm.

Torch, Globe and Spider
A386

1971, Mar. 1 Litho. ***Perf. 12½x13***

747 A386 10w gray & multi. 35 25

March, the month for anti-espionage and victory over communism.

Reservist, Reserve Forces Emblem
A387

1971, Apr. 3 Photo. ***Perf. 13½x13***

748 A387 10w lt. ultra. & multi. 35 25

Home Reserve Forces Day, Apr. 3.

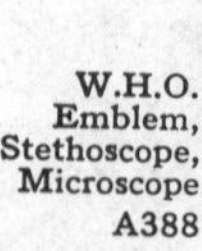

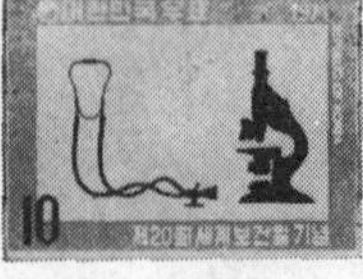

W.H.O. Emblem, Stethoscope, Microscope
A388

1971, Apr. 7

749 A388 10w lt. bl., pur. & yel. 35 25

20th World Health Day, Apr. 7.

Subway Tunnel and Train
A389

Soccer Player
A390

1971, Apr. 12 Litho. ***Perf. 12½x13***
Granite Paper

750 A389 10w multicolored 35 25

Seoul subway construction start.

1971, May 2

751 A390 10w green, dk. brown & black 40 30

First Asian Soccer Games, Seoul, May 2-13.

Veterans Flag and Veterans
A391

Girl Scouts and Emblem
A392

1971, May 8 Photo. ***Perf. 13x13½***

752 A391 10w ultra. & multi. 35 25

20th Korean Veterans Day.

1971, May 10

753 A392 10w lilac & multi. 40 30

25th anniversary of the Korean Federation of Girl Scouts.

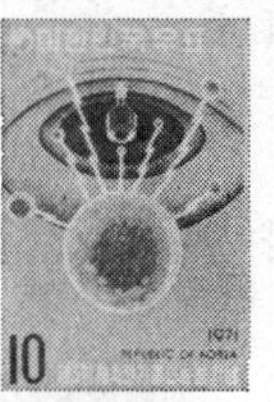

Torch and Development
A393

"Telecommunication"
A394

1971, May 16

754 A393 10w lt. blue & multi. 35 25

10th anniversary of May 16th revolution.

1971, May 17

755 A394 10w blue & multi. 35 25

3rd World Telecommunications Day.

Security Council
A395

Korean Flag
A396

United Nations Organizations: No. 756, Intl. Labor Org. (ILO). No. 757, Food and Agriculture Org. (FAO). No. 758, General Assembly (U.N. Headquarters). No. 759, U.N. Educational, Cultural and Scientific Org. (UNESCO). No. 760, World Health Org. (WHO). No. 761, World Bank. No. 762, Intl. Development Association (IDA). No. 763, Security Council. No. 764, Intl. Finance Corp. (IFC). No. 765, Intl. Monetary Fund. No. 766, Intl. Civil Aviation Org. (ICAO). No. 767, Economic and Social Council. No. 768, Korean Flag. No. 769, Trusteeship Council. No. 770, Universal Postal Union. No. 771, Intl. Telecommunications Union (ITU). No. 772, World Meteorological Org. (WMO). No. 773, Intl. Court of Justice. No. 774, Intl. Maritime Consultative Org. No. 775, U.N. Children's Fund (UNICEF). No. 776, Intl. Atomic Energy Agency. No. 777, U.N. Industrial Development Org. No. 778, U.N. Commission for the Unification and Rehabilitation of Korea. No. 779, U.N. Development Program. No. 780, U.N. Conference on Trade and Development.

1971, May 30 ***Perf. 13½x13***

756 A395 10w grn., blk. & pink 25 20
757 " 10w pink, blk. & blue 25 20
758 " 10w blue, black, green & pink 25 20
759 " 10w pink, blk. & blue 25 20
760 " 10w grn., blk. & pink 25 20
761 " 10w pink, blk. & blue 25 20
762 " 10w blue, blk. & pink 25 20
763 " 10w grn., blk. & pink 25 20
764 " 10w blue, blk. & pink 25 20
765 " 10w pink, blk. & blue 25 20
766 " 10w blue, blk. & pink 25 20
767 " 10w grn., blk. & pink 25 20
768 A396 10w blue, blk. & pink 25 20
769 A395 10w grn., blk. & pink 25 20
770 " 10w blue, blk. & pink 25 20
771 " 10w pink, blk. & blue 25 20
772 " 10w blue, blk. & pink 25 20
773 " 10w grn., blk. & pink 25 20
774 " 10w blue, blk. & pink 25 20
775 " 10w pink, blk. & blue 25 20
776 " 10w grn., blk. & pink 25 20
777 " 10w pink, blk. & blue 25 20
778 " 10w blue, blk. & pink 25 20
779 " 10w pink, blk. & blue 25 20
780 " 10w grn., blk. & pink 25 20
Nos. 756-780 (25) 6.25 5.00

To honor the United Nations and its various organizations and agencies. Sheet of 50 incorporates two each of Nos. 756-780.

Boat Ride, by Shin Yun-bok—A397

Man and Boy under Pine Tree
A398

Paintings by Shin Yun-bok: No. 782, Greeting travelers. No. 783, Tea ceremony. No. 784, Lady traveling with servants. No. 785, Man and woman on the road.

Perf. 13x13½, 13½x13

1971, June 20 Photogravure

781 A397 10w multicolored 30 15
a. Souvenir sheet of 2 60
782 A397 10w multicolored 30 15
a. Souvenir sheet of 2 60
783 A397 10w multicolored 30 15
a. Souvenir sheet of 2 60
784 A397 10w multicolored 30 15
a. Souvenir sheet of 2 60
785 A397 10w multicolored 30 15
a. Souvenir sheet of 2 60
786 A398 10w multicolored 30 15
a. Souvenir sheet of 2 60
Nos. 781-786 (6) 1.80 90
Nos. 781a-786a (6) 3.60

Nos. 781-785 printed se-tenant in vertical rows. Nos. 781a-786a have yellow margins with black inscriptions. Size: 123x90mm.

Types A397-A398 with Inscription at Left

1971, July 20

Paintings: No. 787, Farmyard scene, by Kim Deuk-shin. No. 788, Family living in valley, by Lee Chae-kwan. No. 789, Man reading book under pine tree, by Lee Chae-kwan.

787 A397 10w pale grn. & multi. 30 20
a. Souvenir sheet of 2 60
788 A398 10w pale grn. & multi. 30 20
a. Souvenir sheet of 2 60
789 A398 10w lt. yellow green & multi. 30 20
a. Souvenir sheet of 2 60

Nos. 787a-789a have yellow margins with black inscriptions. Size: 123½x90mm.

Teacher and Students, by Kim Hong-do
A399

Paintings by Kim Hong-do (Yi Dynasty): No. 791, Wrestlers. No. 792, Dancer and musicians. No. 793, Weavers. No. 794, At the Well.

1971, Aug. 20 ***Perf. 13½x13***

790 A399 10w black, lt. green & rose 35 20
a. Souvenir sheet of 2 1.00
791 A399 10w black, lt. green & rose 35 20
a. Souvenir sheet of 2 1.00
792 A399 10w black, lt. green & rose 35 20
a. Souvenir sheet of 2 1.00
793 A399 10w black, lt. green & rose 35 20
a. Souvenir sheet of 2 1.00
794 A399 10w black, lt. green & rose 35 20
a. Souvenir sheet of 2 1.00
Nos. 790-794 (5) 1.75 1.00
Nos. 790a-794a (5) 5.00

Nos. 790-794 printed se-tenant in horizontal rows in sheets of 25 (5x5). Nos. 790a-794a have yellow margins with black inscriptions. Size: 123½x90mm.

Pres. Park, Highway and Phoenix
A400

1971, July 1 ***Perf. 13½x13***

795 A400 10w grn., blk. & org. 75 40
a. Souvenir sheet of 2 1.75

Inauguration of President Chung Hee Park for a third term, July 1.

No. 795a contains 2 stamps with black and green marginal inscription. Size: 89x60mm.

Campfire and Tents
A401

1971, Aug. 2 Photo. *Perf. 13x13½*

796 A401 10w bl. grn. & multi. 40 25

13th Boy Scout World Jamboree, Asagiri Plain, Japan, Aug. 2–10.

Symbol of Conference
A402

1971, Sept. 27 *Perf. 13*

797 A402 10w multicolored 40 25
a. Souvenir sheet of 2 1.75

Asian Labor Ministers' Conference, Seoul, Sept. 27–30. No. 797a has multicolored marginal inscription. Size: 90x60mm.

Archers—A403

Design: No. 799, Judo.

1971, Oct. 8 Photo. *Perf. 13x13½*

798 A403 10w salmon & multi. 30 18
a. Souvenir sheet of 3 75
799 A403 10w brt. bl. & multi. 30 18
a. Souvenir sheet of 3 75

52nd National Athletic Meet. Nos. 798a and 799a have black marginal inscriptions with blue and tan decoration. Size: 89x85mm.

Taeguk on Palette
A404

1971, Oct. 11 *Perf. 13½x13*

800 A404 10w yellow & multi. 35 25

20th National Fine Arts Exhibition.

Physician, Globe and Emblem
A405

1971, Oct. 13

801 A405 10w multicolored 35 25

7th Congress of the Confederation of Medical Associations in Asia and Oceania.

Symbols of Contest Events
A406

1971, Oct. 20 Photo. *Perf. 13x13½*

802 A406 10w multicolored 35 25
a. Souvenir sheet of 2 1.25

2nd National Skill Contest for High School Students. No. 802a has black and blue marginal inscription. Size: 90x60 mm.

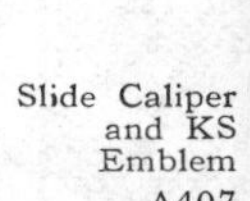

Slide Caliper and KS Emblem
A407

1971, Nov. 11 *Perf. 13x13½*

803 A407 10w multicolored 35 25

10th anniversary of industrial standardization in Korea.

Rats
A408

Japanese Crane
A409

1971, Dec. 1

804 A408 10w multicolored 20 18
a. Souvenir sheet of 3 50
805 A409 10w multicolored 20 18
a. Souvenir sheet of 3 50

New Year 1972. No. 804a has black, carmine and blue marginal inscription; No. 805a has black, carmine and slate green inscription. Size: 90x60mm.

Emblem of Hangul Hakhoe and Hangul Letters
A410

1971, Dec. 3 Photogravure

806 A410 10w dk. bl. & multi. 25 20

50th anniversary of Korean Language Research Society (Hangul Hakhoe).

Red Cross Headquarters and Map of Korea
A411

1971, Dec. 31 *Perf. 13½x13*

807 A411 10w multicolored 35 20
a. Souvenir sheet of 2 50

First South and North Korean Red Cross Conference, Panmunjom, Aug. 20, 1971. No. 807a has blue marginal inscription. Size: 123x89mm.

Globe and Book
A412

1972, Jan. 5 *Perf. 13x13½*

808 A412 10w multicolored 35 30
a. Souvenir sheet of 2 1.00

International Book Year 1972. No. 808a has black and lilac marginal inscription and light green border. Size: 90x60mm.

Intelsat 4 Sending Signals to Korea
A413

1972, Jan. 31 *Perf. 13½x13*

809 A413 10w dk. bl. & multi. 30 25

Korea's entry into International Telecommunications Union, 20th anniversary.

Figure Skating, Sapporo '72 Emblem
A414

Map of Korea with Forest Sites
A415

Design: No. 811, Speed skating.

1972, Feb. 3 *Perf. 13x13½*

810 A414 10w lt. & dk. blue & carmine 30 15
811 " 10w lt. & dk. blue & carmine 30 15
a. Souvenir sheet of 2 3.00

11th Winter Olympic Games, Sapporo, Japan, Feb. 3–13. No. 811a contains one each of Nos. 810–811. Dark and light blue marginal inscription. Size: 90x60 mm.

1972, Mar. 10 Photo. *Perf. 13x13*

812 A415 10w buff, blue green & red 25 20

Publicity for forests planted to mark hope for re-unification of Korea.

Junior Chamber of Commerce Emblem and Beetles
A416

1972, Mar. 19 *Perf. 13½x13*

813 A416 10w pink & multi. 25 20

Junior Chamber of Commerce, 20th anniversary.

U.N. Emblem, Agriculture and Industry
A417

1972, Mar. 28 *Perf. 13x13½*

814 A417 10w vio., grn. & car. 25 20

Economic Commission for Asia and the Far East (ECAFE), 25th anniversary.

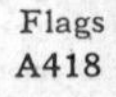

Flags
A418

1972, Apr. 1 *Perf. 13½x13*

815 A418 10w blue & multi. 25 20

Asian-Oceanic Postal Union, 10th anniversary.

Korean Flag
A419

YWCA Emblem, Butterflies
A420

1972, Apr. 1 Photo. *Perf. 13x13½*

816 A419 10w yellow & multi. 25 25

Homeland Reserve Forces Day, Apr. 1.

1972, Apr. 20

817 A420 10w violet & multi. 25 20

50th anniversary of the Young Women's Christian Association of Korea.

Community Projects
A421

Korean Flag and Inscription
A422

1972, May 1 *Perf. 13x13½*

818 A421 10w pink & multi. 25 20

Rural rehabilitation and construction movement.

1972, May 1

819 A422 10w green & multi. 25 20

Anti-espionage and victory over communism month.

Children with Balloons
A423

1972, May 5 *Perf. 13½x13*

820 A423 10w yellow & multi. 25 20

Children's Day, May 5.

King Munyong's Gold Earrings
A424

Design: No. 822, Gold ornament from King's crown (vert.).

Perf. 13½x13, 13x13½

1972, May 10

821 A424 10w green & multi. 25 20
822 " 10w " " 25 20

National treasures from tomb of King Munyong of Paekche, who reigned 501–523.

Kojo Island
A425

Design: No. 823, Crater Lake.

1972, May 30 ***Perf. 13½x13***

823	A425	10w bl. grn. & multi.	30	20
824	"	10w grn. & multi.	30	20

National parks.

Daisy, Environment Emblem
A426

1972, May 30 Litho. ***Perf. 13x13½***

825	A426	10w green & multi.	25	20
	a.	Souvenir sheet of 2	1.50	

U.N. Conference on Human Environment, Stockholm, June 5–16. No. 825a has blue and green marginal inscription. Size: 90x60mm.

Gwanghwa Gate, Flags of Participants
A427

1972, June 14

826	A427	10w yellow & multi.	25	20

7th Meeting of Asian-Pacific Council (ASPAC).

Farm and Fish Hatchery
A428

Weight Lifting
A429

Third Five-Year Plan Issue

1972, July 1 Photo. ***Perf. 13½x13***

Multicolored

827	A428	10w *shown*	20	12
828	"	10w *Steel industry and products*	20	12
829	"	10w *Globe and cargo*	20	12

3rd Economic Development Five-Year Plan.

1972, Aug. 26 Photo. ***Perf. 13x13½***

Multicolored

830	A429	20w *shown*	25	15
831	"	20w *Judo*	25	15
	a.	Souv. sheet of 2	75	
832	A429	20w *Boxing*	25	15
833	"	20w *Wrestling*	25	15
	a.	Souv. sheet of 2	75	

20th Olympic Games, Munich, Aug. 26–Sept. 11. Nos. 830–831, 832–833 each printed checkerwise in sheets of 20 (4x5). No. 831a contains one each of Nos. 830–831; No. 833a one each of Nos. 832–833; violet marginal inscriptions. Size: 90x60mm.

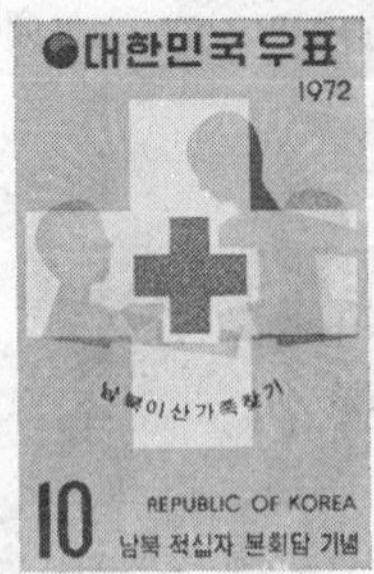

Families Reunited by Red Cross
A430

1972, Aug. 30 Photo. ***Perf. 13½x13***

834	A430	10w lt. bl. & multi.	25	20
	a.	Souv. sheet of 2	1.00	

Plenary meeting of the South-North Red Cross Conference, Pyongyang, Aug. 30, 1972. No. 834a has blue marginal inscription. Size: 123x90mm.

Bulkuk-sa Temple, Kyongju Park
A431

Bopju-sa Temple, Mt. Sokri Park
A432

1972, Sept. 20 Photo. ***Perf. 13½x13***

835	A431	10w brown & multi.	25	20
836	A432	10w blue & multi.	25	20

National parks.

"5" and Conference Emblem
A433

1972, Sept. 25 ***Perf. 13x13½***

837	A433	10w vio. blue & multi.	25	15

Fifth Asian Judicial Conference, Seoul, Sept. 25–29.

Lions Emblem, Taeguk Fan
A434

1972, Sept. 28 ***Perf. 13½x13***

838	A434	10w multicolored	25	15

11th Orient and Southeast Asian Lions Convention, Seoul, Sept. 28–30.

Scout Taking Oath, Korean Flag and Scout Emblem
A435

1972, Oct. 5

839	A435	10w yellow & multi.	25	15

Boy Scouts of Korea, 50th anniversary.

Children and Ox
A436

Children in Balloon
A437

1972, Dec. 1 Photo. ***Perf. 13x13½***

840	A436	10w green & multi.	20	12
	a.	Souvenir sheet of 2	30	
841	A437	10w blue & multi.	20	12
	a.	Souvenir sheet of 2	30	

New Year 1973. Nos. 840a–841a have blue, red and green marginal inscriptions. Size: 90x60mm.

Mt. Naejang Park and Temple
A438

Mt. Sorang and Madeung-ryong Pass
A439

1972, Dec. 10 ***Perf. 13x13½, 13½x13***

842	A438	10w multicolored	25	20
843	A439	10w "	25	20

National parks.

Pres. Park, Korean Flag and Modern Landscape—A440

1972, Dec. 27 ***Perf. 13x13½***

844	A440	10w multicolored	40	20
	a.	Souvenir sheet of 2	60	

Inauguration of Chung Hee Park for a 4th term as president of Korea.

No. 844a has black and green marginal inscription. Size: 129½x90mm.

Tourism Issue

Kyongbok Palace (National Museum)
A441

Mt. Sorak and Kejo-am Temple
A442

1973 Photo. ***Perf. 13½x13***

845	A441	10w multicolored	20	15
846	A442	10w "	20	15

Palmi Island and Beach
A443

Sain-am Rock, Mt. Dokjol
A444

Perf. 13x13½

847	A443	10w multicolored	20	15
848	A444	10w "	20	15

Shrine for Adm. Li Sun-sin
A445

Limestone Cavern, Kusan-ni
A446

849	A445	10w multicolored	20	15
850	A446	10w "	20	15

Namhae Bridge
A447

Hongdo Island
A448

Perf. 13½x13

851	A447	10w multicolored	20	15
852	A448	10w "	20	15

Mt. Mai
A449

Tangerine Orchard, Cheju Island
A450

853	A449	10w multicolored	20	15
854	A450	10w "	20	15

Issue dates: Nos. 845–846, Feb. 20. Nos. 847–848, Apr. 20. Nos. 849–850, June 20. Nos. 851–852, Aug. 20. Nos. 853–854, Oct. 20.

Praying Family
A451

1973, Mar. 1 *Perf. 13x13½*

855 A451 10w yellow & multi. 20 15

Prayer for national unification.

Flags of Korea and South Viet Nam, Victory Sign
A452

1973, Mar. 1

856 A452 10w violet & multi. 20 15

Return of Korean Expeditionary Force from South Viet Nam.

Workers, Factory, Cogwheel
A453

Satellite, WMO Emblem
A454

1973, Mar. 10 **Unwmkd.**

857 A453 10w blue & multi. 20 15

10th Labor Day.

1973, Mar. 23

858 A454 10w blue & multi. 20 15
a. Souvenir sheet of 2 35

Centenary of International Meteorological Cooperation. No. 858a has blue marginal inscription. Size: 90x60mm.

King's Ceremonial Robe
A455

Traditional Korean Costumes (Yi dynasty): No. 860, Queen's ceremonial dress. No. 861, King's robe. No. 862, Queen's robe. No. 863, Crown Prince. No. 864, Princess. No. 865, Courtier. No. 866, Royal bridal gown. No. 867, Official's wife. No. 868, Military official.

1973 **Photo.** *Perf. 13½x13*

859 A455 10w ocher & multi. 25 12
a. Souvenir sheet of 2 (#1) 40

860 A455 10w salmon & multi. 25 12
a. Souvenir sheet of 2 (#2) 40

861 A455 10w rose lilac & multi. 25 12
a. Souvenir sheet of 2 (#3) 40

862 A455 10w apple grn. & multicolored 25 12
a. Souvenir sheet of 2 (#4) 40

863 A455 10w lt. bl. & multi. 25 12
a. Souvenir sheet of 2 (#5) 40

864 A455 10w lilac rose & multicolored 25 12
a. Souvenir sheet of 2 (#6) 40

865 A455 10w yellow & multi. 25 12
a. Souvenir sheet of 2 (#7) 40

866 A455 10w lt. blue & multi. 25 12
a. Souvenir sheet of 2 (#8) 40

867 A455 10w ocher & multi. 25 12
a. Souvenir sheet of 2 (#9) 40

868 A455 10w lilac rose & multicolored 25 12
a. Souvenir sheet of 2 (#10) 40

Nos. 859-868 (10) 2.50 1.20
Nos. 859a-868a (10) 4.00

Nos. 859a-868a have black and blue marginal inscriptions. Size: 124x90mm.

Parenthetical numbers after souvenir sheet listings appear in top marginal inscriptions.

Issue dates: Nos. 859-860, Mar. 30. Nos. 861-862, May 30. Nos. 863-864, July 30. Nos. 865-866, Sept. 30. Nos. 867-868, Nov. 30.

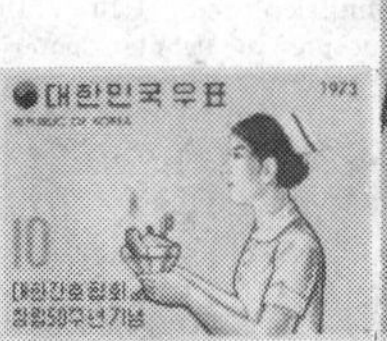

Nurse Holding Lamp
A456

Homeland Reservists and Flag
A457

1973, Apr. 1 *Perf. 13½x13*

869 A456 10w rose & multi. 25 12

50th anniversary of Korean Nurses Association.

1973, Apr. 7 *Perf. 13x13½*

870 A457 10w yellow & multi. 25 12

Homeland Reserve Forces Day on 5th anniversary of their establishment.

Table Tennis Player, and Globe
A458

1973, May 23 *Perf. 13x13½*

871 A458 10w pink & multi. 25 12

Victory of Korean women's table tennis team, 32nd International Table Tennis Championships, Sarajevo, Jugoslavia, Apr. 5-15.

World Vision Children's Choir
A459

1973, June 25 *Perf. 13x13½*

872 A459 10w multicolored 25 12

20th anniversary of World Vision International, a Christian service organization.

Converter, Pohang Steel Works
A460

1973, July 3 *Perf. 13x13½*

873 A460 10w blue & multi. 20 12

Inauguration of Pohang iron and steel plant.

INTERPOL Emblem
A461

1973, Sept. 3 *Perf. 13½x13*

874 A461 10w lt. vio. & multi. 20 12

50th anniversary of the International Criminal Police Organization (INTERPOL).

Children with Stamp Albums
A462

1973, Oct. 12 *Perf. 13½x13*

875 A462 10w dp. grn. & multi. 25 12
a. Souvenir sheet of 2 40

Philatelic Week, Oct. 12-18. No. 875a contains 2 No. 875. Blue and red marginal inscription. Size: 90x60mm.

Woman Hurdler—A463

1973, Oct. 12 *Perf. 12½x13½*

Multicolored

876 A463 10w *shown* 20 12
877 " 10w *Tennis player* 20 12

54th National Athletic Meet, Pusan, Oct. 12-17.

Soyang River Dam, Map Showing Location
A464

1973, Oct. 15 *Perf. 13½x13*

878 A464 10w blue & multi. 20 12

Inauguration of Soyang River Dam and hydroelectric plant.

Fire from Match and Cigarette
A465

1973, Nov. 1 *Perf. 13x13½*

879 A465 10w multicolored 20 12

10th Fire Prevention Day.

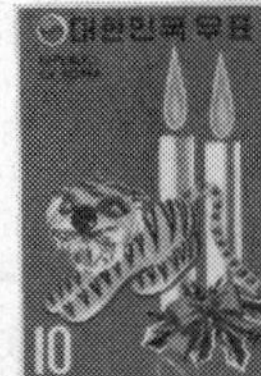

Tiger and Candles
A466

Toys
A467

1973, Dec. 1 **Photo.** *Perf. 13x13½*

880 A466 10w emerald & multicolored 20 12
a. Souvenir sheet of 2 30

881 A467 10w blue & multi. 20 12
a. Souvenir sheet of 2 30

New Year 1974. Nos. 880a-881a have multicolored marginal inscriptions. Size: 90x60mm.

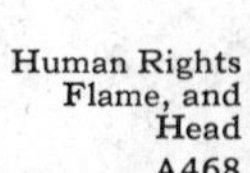

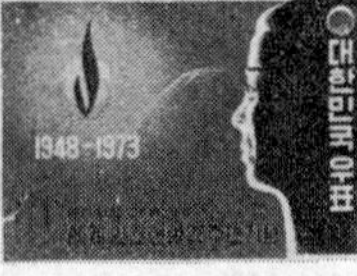

Human Rights Flame, and Head
A468

1973, Dec. 10 *Perf. 13½x13*

882 A468 10w orange & multi. 20 12

25th anniversary of Universal Declaration of Human Rights.

Musical Instruments Issue

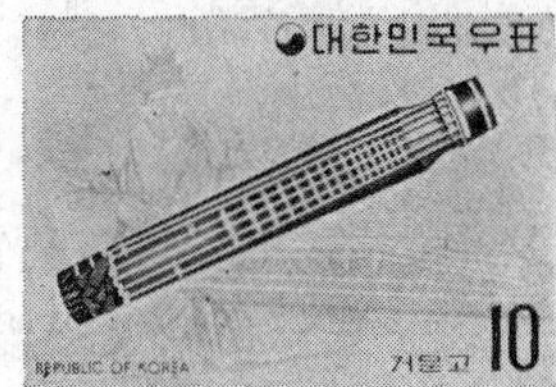

Komunko, Six-stringed Zither—A469

Design: 30w, Nagak, shell trumpet.

1974, Feb. 20 **Photo.** *Perf. 13x13½*

883 A469 10w lt. bl., blk. & brn. 20 10
a. Souvenir sheet of 2 (#1) 20

884 A469 30w org. & multi. 30 20
a. Souvenir sheet of 2 (#2) 55

1974, Apr. 20

Designs: 10w, Tchouk; wooden hammer in slanted box, used to start orchestra. 30w, Eu; crouching tiger, used to stop orchestra.

885 A469 10w brt. bl. & multi. 15 10
a. Souvenir sheet of 2 (#3) 20

886 A469 30w lt. grn. & multi. 30 20
a. Souvenir sheet of 2 (#4) 55

1974, June 20

Designs: 10w, A-chaing, 7-stringed instrument. 30w, Kyobang-ko, drum.

887 A469 10w dull yel. & multi. 15 10
a. Souvenir sheet of 2 (#5) 20

888 A469 30w salmon pink & multi. 30 20
a. Souvenir sheet of 2 (#6) 55

1974, Aug. 20

Designs: 10w, So, 16-pipe ritual instrument. 30w, Kaikeum, 2-stringed fiddle.

889 A469 10w lt. blue & multi. 15 10
a. Souvenir sheet of 2 (#7) 20

890 A469 30w bright pink & multi. 30 20
a. Souvenir sheet of 2 (#8) 55

1974, Oct. 20

Designs: 10w, Pak (clappers). 30w, Pyenchong (bell chimes).

891 A469 10w lt. lilac & multi. 15 10
a. Souvenir sheet of 2 (#9) 20

892 A469 30w lemon & multi. 30 20
a. Souvenir sheet of 2 (#10) 55

Nos. 883-892 (10) 2.30 1.50
Nos. 883a-892a (10) 3.75

Marginal inscription in black on Nos. 883a-885a, 887a-892a, and in blue green on No. 886a. Size: 124x90mm.

Fruit Issue

Apricots
A470

1974, Mar. 30 Photo. *Perf. 13x13½*

Multicolored

893	A470	10w *shown*	15	10
	a.	Souvenir sheet of 2 (#1)	20	
894	A470	30w *Strawberries*	30	20
	a.	Souvenir sheet of 2 (#2)	55	

1974, May 30

895	A470	10w *Peaches*	15	10
	a.	Souvenir sheet of 2 (#3)	20	
896	A470	30w *Grapes*	30	20
	a.	Souvenir sheet of 2 (#4)	55	

1974, July 30

897	A470	10w *Pears*	15	10
	a.	Souvenir sheet of 2 (#5)	20	
898	A470	30w *Apples*	30	20
	a.	Souvenir sheet of 2 (#6)	55	

1974, Sept. 30

899	A470	10w *Cherries*	15	10
	a.	Souvenir sheet of 2 (#7)	20	
900	A470	30w *Persimmons*	30	20
	a.	Souvenir sheet of 2 (#8)	55	

1974, Nov. 30

901	A470	10w *Tangerines*	15	10
	a.	Souvenir sheet of 2 (#9)	20	
902	A470	30w *Chestnuts*	30	20
	a.	Souvenir sheet of 2 (#10)	55	
		Nos. 893-902 (10)	2.25	1.50
		Nos. 893a-902a (10)	3.75	

Nos. 893a–902a have black and light blue marginal inscriptions. Size: 90x60mm.

Reservist and Factory
A471

1974, Apr. 6 Photo. *Perf. 13½x13*

903 A471 10w yel. & multi. 20 15

Homeland Reserve Forces Day.

WPY Emblem and Scales
A472

1974, Apr. 10 *Perf. 13x13½*

904	A472	10w salmon & multi.	20	15
	a.	Souvenir sheet of 2	40	

World Population Year 1974. No. 904a contains 2 No. 904. Blue and red marginal inscription. Size: 90x60mm.

Train and Communications Emblem
A473

1974, Apr. 22 *Perf. 13½x13*

905 A473 10w multicolored 20 15

19th Communications Day.

Emblem and Stylized Globe
A474

1974, May 6 Photo. *Perf. 13*

906 A474 10w red lilac & multi. 20 15

22nd Session of International Chamber of Commerce (Eastern Division), Seoul, May 6–8.

New Dock at Inchon
A475

1974, May 10

907 A475 10w yellow & multi. 20 15

Dedication of dock, Inchon.

UNESCO Emblem, "20" and Yin Yang
A476

1974, June 14 Photo. *Perf. 13*

908 A476 10w org. yel. & multi. 20 15

20th anniversary of the Korean National Commission for UNESCO.

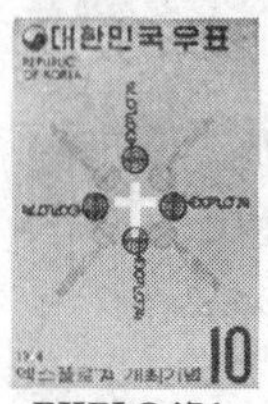

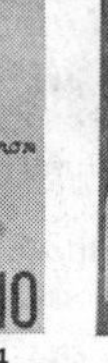

EXPLO '74 Emblems
A477

Subway, Bus and Plane
A478

Design: No. 910, EXPLO emblem rising from map of Korea.

1974, Aug. 13 Photo. *Perf. 13*

909	A477	10w org. & multi.	15	10
910	"	10w blue & multi.	15	10

EXPLO '74, International Christian Congress, Yoido Islet, Seoul, Aug. 13–18.

1974, Aug. 15

911 A478 10w green & multi. 15 10

Inauguration of Seoul subway (first in Korea), Aug. 15, 1974.

Target Shooting—A479

Design: 30w, Rowing.

1974, Oct. 8 Photo. *Perf. 13x13½*

912	A479	10w multicolored	15	10
913	"	30w "	30	15

55th National Athletic Meet.

UPU Emblem
A480

1974, Oct. 9 *Perf. 13*

914	A480	10w yellow & multi.	15	10
	a.	Souvenir sheet of 2	35	

Centenary of Universal Postal Union. No. 914a contains 2 No. 914, yellow margin with blue and red inscription. Size: 90x60mm. See No. C43.

International Landmarks
A481

1974, Oct. 11

915 A481 10w multicolored 15 10

International People to People Conference, Seoul, Oct. 11–14.

Korea Nos. 1–2
A482

1974, Oct. 17

916	A482	10w lilac & multi.	15	10
	a.	Souvenir sheet of 2	35	

Philatelic Week, Oct. 17–23, and 90th anniversary of first Korean postage stamps. No. 916a contains 2 No. 916, black and lilac marginal inscription. Size: 90x60mm.

Taekwondo and Kukkiwon Center
A483

1974, Oct. 18

917 A483 10w yel. grn. & multi. 15 10

First Asian Taekwondo (self-defense) Games, Seoul, Oct. 18–20.

Presidents Park and Ford, Flags and Globe—A484

1974, Nov. 22 Photo. *Perf. 13*

918	A484	10y multicolored	40	20
	a.	Souvenir sheet of 2	50	

Visit of Pres. Gerald R. Ford to South Korea. No. 918a contains 2 No. 918, multicolored margin. Size: 90x60mm.

Yook Young Soo
A485

1974, Nov. 29

919	A485	10w green	20	10
920	"	10w orange	20	10
921	"	10w lilac	20	10
922	"	10w blue	20	10
	a.	Souvenir sheet of 4	80	

Yook Young Soo (1925–1974), wife of Pres. Park. Nos. 919–922 printed se-tenant in sheets of 40. No. 922a contains one each of Nos. 919–922, blue marginal inscription. Size: 90x123mm.

Rabbits
A486

Good-luck Purse
A487

1974, Dec. 1 Litho. *Perf. 12½x13*

923	A486	10w multicolored	15	12
	a.	Souvenir sheet of 2	40	
924	A487	10w multicolored	15	12
	a.	Souvenir sheet of 2	40	

New Year 1975. Nos. 923a–924a have multicolored marginal inscriptions. Size: 90x60mm.

Good-luck Key and Pigeon
A488

1975, Jan. 1 Photo. *Perf. 13*

925 A488 10w lt. blue & multi. 15 12

Introduction of National Welfare Insurance System.

UPU Emblem and "75"
A489

UPU Emblem and Paper Plane
A490

1975, Jan. 1

926	A489	10w yellow & multi.	15	10
927	A490	10w lt. blue & multi.	15	10

75th anniversary of Korea's membership in Universal Postal Union.

Dr. Schweitzer, Map of Africa, Hypodermic Needle
A491

1975, Jan. 14

928	A491	10w olive	10	8
929	"	10w bright rose	10	8
930	"	10w orange	10	8
931	"	10w bright green	10	8

Dr. Albert Schweitzer (1875–1965), medical missionary, birth centenary. Nos. 928–931 printed se-tenant in sheets of 40 (4x10).

Folk Dance Issue

Dancer
A492

Designs: No. 933, Dancer with fan. No. 934, Woman with butterfly sleeves. No. 935, Group of women. No. 936, Pongsan mask dance. No. 937, Pusan mask dance. No. 938, Buddhist drum dance. No. 939, Bara (cymbals) dance. No. 940, Sogo dance. No. 941, Bupo Nori.

1975, Feb. 20 Photo. *Perf. 13*

932 A492 10w emerald & multi. 15 10
a. Souvenir sheet of 2 (#1) 20
933 A492 10w brt. bl. & multi. 15 10
a. Souvenir sheet of 2 (#2) 20

1975, Apr. 20

934 A492 10w yel. grn. & multi. 15 10
a. Souvenir sheet of 2 (#3) 20
935 A492 10w yellow & multi. 15 10
a. Souvenir sheet of 2 (#4) 20

1975, June 20

936 A492 10w pink & multi. 15 10
a. Souvenir sheet of 2 (#5) 20
937 A492 10w blue & multi. 15 10
a. Souvenir sheet of 2 (#6) 20

1975, Aug. 20

938 A492 20w yellow & multi. 20 10
a. Souvenir sheet of 2 (#7) 30
939 A492 20w sal. & multi. 20 10
a. Souvenir sheet of 2 (#8) 30

1975, Oct. 20

940 A492 20w blue & multi. 20 10
a. Souvenir sheet of 2 (#9) 30
941 A492 20w yellow & multi. 20 10
a. Souvenir sheet of 2 (#10) 30
Nos. 932-941 (10) 1.70 1.00
Nos. 932a-941a (10) 2.40

Nos. 932a-941a have black marginal inscriptions. Size: 90x60mm.

Globe and Rotary Emblem
A493

1975, Feb. 23

942 A493 10w multicolored 15 5

Rotary International, 70th anniversary.

Women and IWY Emblem
A494

1975, Mar. 8

943 A494 10w multicolored 15 10

International Women's Year 1975.

Flower Issue

Violets
A495

Anemones
A496

Designs: No. 946, Rhododendron. No. 947, Clematis patens. No. 948, Thistle. No. 949, Iris. No. 950, Broad-bell flowers. No. 951, Bush clover. No. 952, Camellia. No. 953, Gentian.

1975, Mar. 15

944 A495 10w orange & multi. 15 10
945 A496 10w yellow & multi. 15 10

1975, May 15

946 A495 10w dk. grn. & multi. 15 10
947 A496 10w yel. grn. & multi. 15 10

1975, July 15

948 A495 10w emerald & multicolored 15 10
949 " 10w blue & multi. 15 10

1975, Sept. 15

950 A495 20w yel. & multi. 15 10
951 " 20w blue green & multicolored 15 10

1975, Nov. 15

952 A495 20w yel. & multi. 15 10
953 A496 20w sal. & multi. 15 10
Nos. 944-953 (10) 1.50 1.00

Forest and Water Resources—A497

1975, Mar. 20

954 A497 Strip of 4, multi. 40 30
a. 10w *Saemaeul forest* 9 7
b. 10w *Dam and reservoir* 9 7
c. 10w *Green forest* 9 7
d. 10w *Timber industry* 9 7

National Tree Planting Month, Mar. 21–Apr. 20. No. 954 printed in sheets of 20 (4x5).

Map of Korea, HRF Emblem
A498

1975, Apr. 12 Photo. *Perf. 13*

955 A498 10w blue & multi. 40 20

Homeland Reserve Forces Day.

Lily
A499

Ceramic Jar
A500

Ceramic Vase
A501

Adm. Li Sun-sin
A502

1975, Oct. 10 Photo. *Perf. 13½x13*

957 A499 6w grn. & blue green 20 10
964 A500 50w gray green & brown 45 30
965 A501 60w brn. & yellow 54 52
969 A502 100w carmine 60 40

Metric System Symbols
A507

1975, May 20 *Perf. 13*

975 A507 10w salmon & multi. 15 10

Centenary of International Meter Convention, Paris, 1875.

Praying Soldier, Incense Burner
A508

1975, June 6 Photo. *Perf. 13*

976 A508 10w multicolored 15 10

20th Memorial Day.

Flags of Korea, U.N. and U.S.
A509

Designs (Flags of): No. 978, Ethiopia, France, Greece, Canada, South Africa. No. 979, Luxembourg, Australia, Great Britain, Colombia, Turkey. No. 980, Netherlands, Belgium, Philippines, New Zealand, Thailand.

1975, June 25 Photo. *Perf. 13*

977 A509 10w dk. bl. & multi. 10 6
978 " 10w " " 10 6
979 " 10w " " 10 6
980 " 10w " " 10 6

25th anniversary of beginning of Korean War. No. 977-980 printed se-tenant in sheets of 20 (4x5).

Presidents Park and Bongo, Flags of Korea and Gabon
A510

1975, July 5

981 A510 10w blue & multi. 15 10
a. Souvenir sheet of 2 35

Visit of Pres. Albert Bongo of Gabon, July 5–8.

No. 981a contains 2 No. 981, black and red marginal inscription. Size: 96x60mm.

Scout Emblem, Tents and Neckerchief
A511

1975, July 29 Photo. *Perf. 13*

Multicolored

982 A511 10w *shown* 8 6
983 " 10w *Pick and oath* 8 6
984 " 10w *Tents* 8 6
985 " 10w *Ax, rope and tree* 8 6
986 " 10w *Campfire* 8 6
Nos. 982-986 (5) 40 30

Nordjamb 75, 14th Boy Scout Jamboree, Lillehammer, Norway, July 29–Aug. 7. Nos. 982-986 printed se-tenant in sheets of 50 (10x5).

Flame and Broken Chain
A512

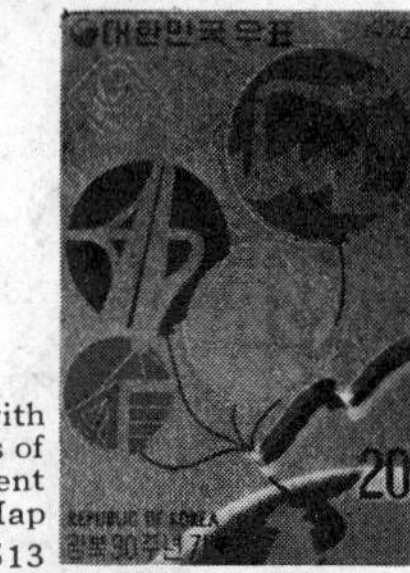

Balloons with Symbols of Development over Map
A513

1975, Aug. 15 *Perf. 13½x13*

987 A512 20w gold & multi. 15 10
988 A513 20w silver & multi. 15 10

30th anniversary of liberation.

Taekwondo
A514

1975, Aug. 26 *Perf. 13*

989 A514 20w multicolored 15 10

2nd World Taekwondo Championships, Seoul, Aug. 25–Sept. 1.

National Assembly and Emblem
A515

1975, Sept. 1 Photo. *Perf. 13½x13*

990 A515 20w multicolored 15 10

Completion of National Assembly Building.

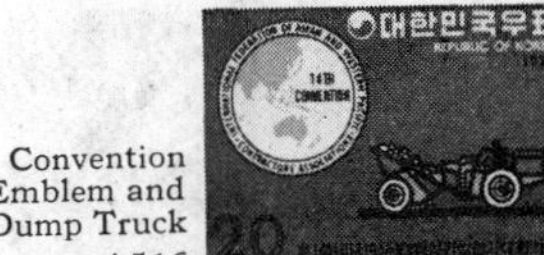

Convention Emblem and Dump Truck
A516

1975, Sept. 7 Photo. *Perf. 13½x13*

991 A516 20w ultra. & multi. 15 10

14th Convention of the International Federation of Asian and Western Pacific Contractors

Cassegrainian Telescope and Morse Key
A517

1975, Sept. 28

992 A517 20w red lilac, orange & black 15 10

90th anniversary of Korean telecommunications system.

Stalactite Cave, Yeongweol
A518

View of Mt. Sorak
A519

1975, Sept. 28

993 A518 20w multicolored 15 10
994 A519 20w " 15 10

International Tourism Day.

Armed Forces Flag and Missiles
A519a

1975, Oct. 1 Photo. ***Perf. 13***

994A A519a 20w multicolored 15 10

Armed Forces Day.

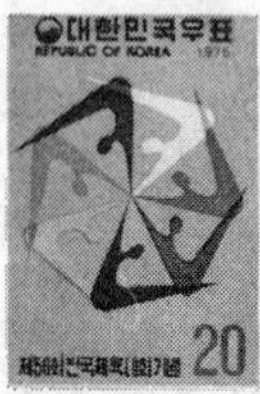

Gymnastics
A520

Handball
A521

1975, Oct. 7 Photo. ***Perf. 13***

995 A520 20w yel. & multi. 15 10
996 A521 20w multicolored 15 10

56th National Athletic Meet, Taegu, Oct. 7–12.

Stamp Collecting Kangaroo
A522

Hands and UN Emblem
A523

1975, Oct. 8

997 A522 20w multicolored 15 10

Philatelic Week, Oct. 8–14.

1975, Oct. 24

998 A523 20w multicolored 15 10

United Nations, 30th anniversary.

Red Cross and Activities
A524

Emblem and Dove
A525

1975, Oct. 30

999 A524 20w org., red & grn. 15 10

Korean Red Cross, 70th anniversary.

1975, Nov. 30 Photo. ***Perf. 13***

1000 A525 20w multicolored 15 10

Asian Parliamentary Union, 10th anniversary.

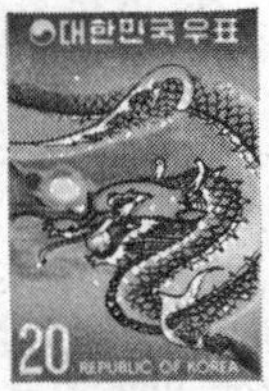

Children Playing
A526

Dragon
A527

1975, Dec. 1

1001 A526 20w multicolored 15 10
a. Souvenir sheet of 2 30
1002 A527 20w multicolored 15 10
a. Souvenir sheet of 2 30

New Year 1976. Nos. 1001a–1002a have black marginal inscriptions. Size: 90x60mm.

Inchong-Bukpyong Railroad
A528

1975, Dec. 5 Photo. ***Perf. 13***

1003 A528 20w multicolored 15 10

Opening of electric cross-country railroad.

Butterfly Issue

Dilipa Fenestra
A529

Butterflies: No. 1005, Luehdorfia puziloi. No. 1006, Papilio xuthus linne. No. 1007, Parnassius bremeri. No. 1008, Colias erate esper. No. 1009, Byasa alcinous klug. No. 1010, Hestina assimilis. No. 1011, Graphium sarpedon. No. 1012, Fabriciana nerippe. No. 1013, Nymphalis xanthomelas.

1976, Jan. 20 Photo. ***Perf. 13***

1004 A529 20w deep rose & multicolored 15 10
1005 " 20w deep blue & multicolored 15 10

1976, Mar. 20

1006 A529 20w yel. & multi. 15 10
1007 " 20w yellow green & multi. 15 10

1976, June 20

1008 A529 20w light violet & multicolored 15 10
1009 " 20w citron & multicolored 15 10

1976, Aug. 20

1010 A529 20w yel. & multi. 15 10
1011 " 20w light gray & multicolored 15 10

1976, Oct. 20

1012 A529 20w light green & multicolored 15 10
1013 " 20w lilac & multi. 15 10
Nos. 1004–1013 (10) 1.50 1.00

Emblems of Science, Industry and KIST
A530

1976, Feb. 10 Photo. ***Perf. 13***

1014 A530 20w multicolored 15 10

Korean Institute of Science and Technology (KIST), 10th anniversary.

Siberian Bustard
A531

White-naped Crane
A532

1976, Feb. 20 Photo. ***Perf. 13x13½***

1015 A531 20w *shown* 15 10
1016 A532 20w *shown* 15 10

1976, May 20

1017 A531 20w *Blue-winged pitta* 15 10
1018 A532 20w *Tristram's woodpecker* 15 10

1976, July 20

1019 A531 20w *Wood pigeon* 15 10
1020 A532 20w *Oyster catcher* 15 10

1976, Sept. 20

1021 A531 20w *Black-faced spoonbill* 15 10
1022 A532 20w *Black stork* 15 10

1976, Nov. 20

1023 A531 20w *Whooper swan* 15 10
1024 A532 20w *Black vulture* 15 10
Nos. 1015–1024 (10) 1.50 1.00

1876 and 1976 Telephones, Globe
A533

1976, Mar. 10

1025 A533 20w multicolored 15 10

Centenary of first telephone call by Alexander Graham Bell, Mar. 10, 1876.

Homeland Reserves
A534

1976, Apr. 3 Photo. ***Perf. 13½x13***

1026 A534 20w multicolored 15 10

8th Homeland Reserve Forces Day.

"People and Eye"
A535

1976, Apr. 7 ***Perf. 13x13½***

1027 A535 20w multicolored 15 10

World Health Day; "Foresight prevents blindness."

Pres. Park, Village Movement Flag
A536

Intellectual Pursuits
A537

1976, Apr. 22

Blue and Multicolored

1028 A536 20w *shown* 15 10
1029 A537 20w *shown* 15 10
1030 " 20w *Village improvement* 15 10
1031 " 20w *Agriculture* 15 10
1032 " 20w *Income from production* 15 10
Strip of 5, #1028–1032 80

6th anniversary of Pres. Park's New Village Movement for National Prosperity. Nos. 1028–1032 printed se-tenant in sheets of 50 (10x5).

Mohenjo-Daro
A538

1976, May 1 ***Perf. 13½x13***

1033 A538 20w multicolored 15 10

UNESCO campaign to save the Mohenjo-Daro excavations in Pakistan.

13-Star and 50-Star Flags
A539

Girl Scouts, Campfire and Emblem
A540

Designs (Bicentennial Emblem and): No. 1035, Statue of Liberty. No. 1036, Map of U.S. and Mt. Rushmore monument. No. 1037, Liberty Bell. No. 1038, First astronaut on moon.

1976, May 8 ***Perf. 13x13½***

1034 A539 100w black, deep blue & red 60 30
a. Souvenir sheet 75
1035 A539 100w black, deep blue & red 60 30
1036 " 100w black, deep blue & red 60 30
1037 " 100w black, deep blue & red 60 30

1038 A539 100w black, deep blue & red 60 30

Nos. 1034–1038 (5) 3.00 1.50

American Bicentennial. No. 1034a contains one No. 1034, black marginal inscription. Size: 90x60mm.

1976, May 10

1039 A540 20w org. & multi. 15 10

Korean Federation of Girl Scouts, 30th anniversary.

Stupas, Buddha of Borobudur
A541

"Life Insurance"
A542

1976, June 10

1040 A541 20w multicolored 15 10

UNESCO campaign to save the Borobudur Temple, Java.

1976, July 1 Photo. ***Perf. 13x13½***

1041 A542 20w multicolored 15 10

National Life Insurance policies: "Over 100 billion-won," Apr. 30, 1976.

Volleyball
A543

Design: No. 1043, Boxing.

1976, July 17

1042 A543 20w multicolored 15 10
1043 " 20w " 15 10

21st Olympic Games, Montreal, Canada, July 17–Aug. 1.

Children and Books
A544

1976, Aug. 10 ***Perf. 13½x13***

1044 A544 20w brn. & multi. 15 10

Books for children.

Civil Defense Corps, Flag and Members
A545

1976, Sept. 15 ***Perf. 13x13½***

1045 A545 20w multicolored 15 10

Civil Defense Corps, first anniversary.

Chamsungdan, Mani Mountain
A546

Front Gate, Tongdosa Temple
A547

1976, Sept. 28 ***Perf. 13½x13***

1046 A546 20w multicolored 15 10
1047 A547 20w " 15 10

International Tourism Day.

Cadets and Academy
A548

1976, Oct. 1

1048 A548 20w multicolored 15 10

Korean Military Academy, 30th anniversary.

Leaves and Stones, by Cheong Ju
A549

1976, Oct. 5 ***Perf. 13x13½***

1049 A549 20w black, gray & red 15 10
a. Souvenir sheet of 2 35

Philatelic Week, Oct. 5–11. No. 1049a has black and gray marginal inscription. Size: 90x60mm.

Snake-headed Figure, Bas-relief
A550

Door-pull and Cranes
A551

1976, Dec. 1 Photo. ***Perf. 13x13½***

1050 A550 20w multicolored 15 10
a. Souvenir sheet of 2 30
1051 A551 20w multicolored 15 10
a. Souvenir sheet of 2 30

New Year 1977. No. 1050a has black, No. 1051a ultramarine marginal inscription. Size: 90x60mm.

Arrows, Cogwheels, Worker at Lathe
A552

Design: No. 1053, Arrows, cogwheels, ship in dock.

1977, Jan. 20 Photo. ***Perf. 13½x13***

1052 A552 20w multicolored 15 10
1053 " 20w " 15 10

4th Economic Development Five-Year Plan.

Satellite Antenna and Microwaves
A553

1977, Jan. 31 ***Perf. 13x13½***

1054 A553 20w multicolored 15 10

Membership in International Telecommunications Union, 25th anniversary.

Korean Broadcasting Center
A554

1977, Feb. 16 ***Perf. 13½x13***

1055 A554 20w multicolored 15 10

50th anniversary of broadcasting in Korea.

Parents and Two Children
A555

1977, Apr. 1 Photo. ***Perf. 13½x13***

1056 A555 20w bright green & orange 15 10

Family planning.

Reservist on Duty
A556

Head with Symbols
A557

1977, Apr. 2 ***Perf. 13x13½***

1057 A556 20w multicolored 15 10

9th Homeland Reserve Forces Day.

1977, Apr. 21 Photo. ***Perf. 13x13½***

1058 A557 20w deep lilac & multicolored 15 10

10th anniversary of Science Day.

Book, Map, Syringe
A558

1977, Apr. 25

1059 A558 20w blue & multi. 15 10

35th International Meeting on Military Medicine.

Boy with Flowers and Dog
A559

1977, May 5

1060 A559 20w multicolored 15 10

Proclamation of Children's Charter, 20th anniversary.

Veteran's Emblem and Flag
A560

1977, May 8

1061 A560 20w multicolored 15 10

25th anniversary of Korean Veterans' Day.

Buddha, 8th Century, Sokkulam Grotto
A561

1977, May 25 Photo. ***Perf. 13x13½***

1062 A561 20w sepia & olive 15 10
a. Souvenir sheet of 2 30

"2600th" anniversary of birth of Buddha. No. 1062a has dark green marginal inscription. Size: 90x60mm.

Ceramic Issues

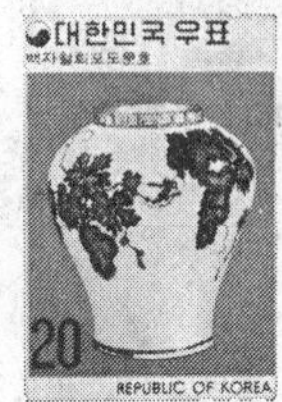

Jar with Grape Design, 17th Century
A562

Celadon Vase, Bamboo Design, 12th Century
A563

1977, Mar. 15 Photo. ***Perf. 13x13½***

1063 A562 20w violet brown & multi. 15 10
1064 A563 20w gray, green & bister 15 10

Ceramic, national treasures.

Celadon Jar with Peonies
A564

Vase with Willow Reed Peony Pattern
A565

Perf. 13x13½, 13½x13

1977, June 15 Photogravure

1065 A564 20w multicolored 12 10
1066 A565 20w " 12 10

Celadon Man-shaped Wine Jug
A566

Celadon Melon-shaped Vase
A567

1977, July 15

1067 A566 20w multicolored 12 10
1068 A567 20w " 12 10

1977, Aug. 15

Designs: No. 1069, White porcelain bowl with inlaid lotus vine design. No. 1070, Black Koryo ware vase with plum blossom vine.

1069 A564 20w multicolored 12 10
1070 A565 20w " 12 10

Punch'ong Jar—A568

Celadon Cylindrical Vase—A569

1977, Nov. 15

1071 A568 20w multicolored 12 10
1072 A569 20w " 12 10

Types of 1962–66
Designs as Before

1976–77 Litho. ***Perf. 12½***

Granite Paper

1076 A187 200w brown & lt. green 1.00 80
1077 A187a 300w slate grn. & sal. ('76) 1.50 1.20
1078 " 300w brn. & sal. 1.50 1.20
1079 " 500w purple & lt. green 2.50 2.00

Magpie
A570

Nature Protection
A571

"Family Planning"
A572

Ceramic Horseman
A573

Muryangsu Hall, Busok Temple
A575

Pagoda, Pobjusa Temple
A576

Gold Crown, from Chonmachong Mound
A577

Monster Mask Tile, 6th or 7th Century
A578

Flying Angels from Bronze Bell from Sangwon-sa, 725 A.D.
A579

1977–78 Photo. ***Perf. 12½x13½***

1088 A570 3w lt. bl. & black 3 3
1091 A571 20w multicolored 12 10
1092 A572 20w emerald & black ('78) 12 10
1097 A573 80w light brown & sepia 48 40
1099 A575 200w salmon & brown 1.00 80
1100 A576 300w brn. purple 1.50 1.20
1101 A577 500w multi. 2.50 2.00

Perf. 13½x13, 13 (1000w)

1102 A578 500w brn. & pur. 2.50 2.00
1103 A579 1000w slate grn. ('78) 5.00 4.00
Nos. 1088–1103 (9) 13.25 10.63

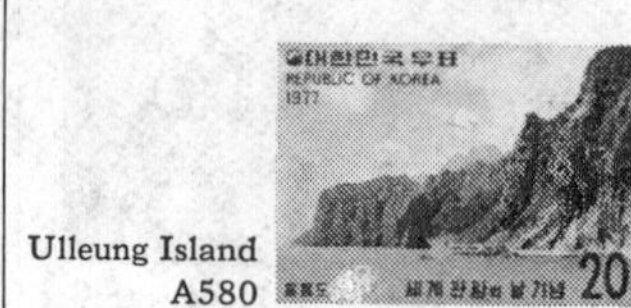

Ulleung Island
A580

Design: No. 1105, Haeundae Beach.

1977, Sept. 28 Photo. ***Perf. 13***

1104 A580 20w multicolored 12 10
1105 " 20w " 12 10

World Tourism Day.

Armed Forces
A581

1977, Oct. 1 Photo. ***Perf. 13***

1106 A581 20w grn. & multi. 12 10

Armed Forces Day.

Mt. Inwang after the Rain, by Chung Seon (1676–1759)
A582 A583

1977, Oct. 4

1107 A582 20w multicolored 12 10
1108 A583 20w " 12 10
a. Souvenir sheet of 2 30

Philatelic Week, Oct. 4–10. No. 1108a has black marginal inscription. Size: 90x60mm.

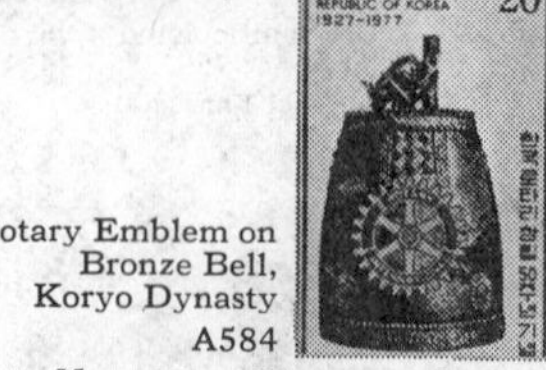

Rotary Emblem on Bronze Bell, Koryo Dynasty
A584

1977, Nov. 10 Photo. ***Perf. 13***

1109 A584 20w multicolored 12 10

Korean Rotary Club, 50th anniversary.

Korean Flag on Mt. Everest
A585

1977, Nov. 11

1110 A585 20w multicolored 12 10

Korean Mt. Everest Expedition, reached peak, Sept. 15, 1977.

Children and Kites
A586

Horse-headed Figure, Bas-relief
A587

1977, Dec. 1 Photo. ***Perf. 13***

1111 A586 20w multicolored 12 10
a. Souvenir sheet of 2 30
1112 A587 20w multicolored 12 10
a. Souvenir sheet of 2 30

New Year 1978. Nos. 1111a and 1112a have black marginal inscriptions. Size: 90x60mm.

Clay Pigeon Shooting
A588

Designs: No. 1114, Air pistol shooting. No. 1115, Air rifle shooting and target.

1977, Dec. 3

1113 A588 20w multicolored 12 10
a. Souvenir sheet of 2 30
1114 A588 20w multicolored 12 10
a. Souvenir sheet of 2 30
1115 A588 20w multicolored 12 10
a. Souvenir sheet of 2 30

42nd World Shooting Championships, Seoul, 1978.

Nos. 1113a–1115a have black marginal inscriptions. Size: 90x60mm. Issued in 1978.

Boeing 727 over Globe, ICAO Emblem
A589

1977, Dec. 11

1116 A589 20w multicolored 12 10

25th anniversary of Korea's membership in the International Civil Aviation Organization.

Plane, Cargo, Freighter and Globe
A590

1977, Dec. 22 Photogravure ***Perf. 13***

1117 A590 20w multi. 12 10

Korean exports.

Ships and World Map
A591

1978, Mar. 13 Photo. ***Perf. 13***

1118 A591 20w multicolored 12 10

Maritime Day.

Stone Pagoda Issue

Four Lions Pagoda, Hwaom-sa
A592

Kyongch'on sa Temple
A594

Punhwang-sa Temple
A593

Design: No. 1120, Seven-storied pagoda, T'appyongri.

1978, Mar. 20 Photo. ***Perf. 13***

1119 A592 20w light green & multicolored 12 10
1120 " 20w ocher & multi. 12 10

1978, May 20

Design: No. 1122, Miruk-sa Temple.

1121 A593 20w lt. grn. & blk. 12 10
1122 " 20w grn., brn. & yellow 12 10

1978, June 20

Designs: No. 1123, Tabo Pagoda, Pulguk-sa. No. 1124, Three-storied pagoda, Pulguk-sa.

1123 A592 20w gray, lt. green & black 12 10
1124 " 20w lilac & black 12 10

1978, July 20 ***Perf. 13½x12½***

Design: No. 1126, Octagonal Pagoda, Wolchong-sa Temple.

1125 A594 20w gray & brown 12 10
1126 " 20w lt. grn. & blk. 12 10

1978, Nov. 20 ***Perf. 13x13½***

Designs: No. 1127, 13-storied pagoda, Jeonghye-sa. No. 1128, Three-storied pagoda, Jinjeon-sa.

1127 A592 20w pale green & multicolored 12 10
1128 " 20w lilac & multi. 12 10
Nos. 1119-1128 (10) 1.20 1.00

Ants and Coins
A595

Reservist with Flag
A596

1978, Apr. 1

1129 A595 20w multicolored 12 10

Importance of saving.

1978, Apr. 1

1130 A596 20w multicolored 12 10

10th Homeland Reserve Forces Day.

Seoul Cultural Center
A597

1978, Apr. 1

1131 A597 20w multicolored 12 10

Opening of Seoul Cultural Center.

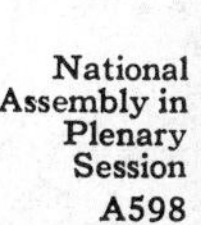

National Assembly in Plenary Session
A598

1978, May 31

1132 A598 20w multicolored 12 10

30th anniversary of National Assembly.

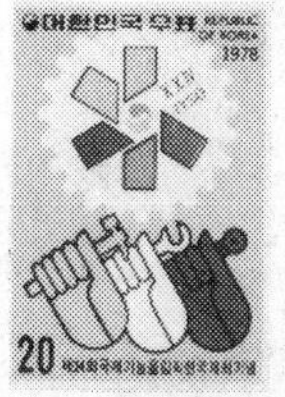

Hands Holding Tools, Competition Emblem
A599

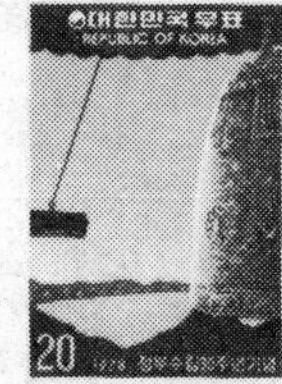

Bell of Joy and Crater Lake, Mt. Baegdu
A600

1978, Aug. 5 **Photo.** ***Perf. 13***

1133 A599 20w multicolored 12 10
a. Souvenir sheet of 2 30

24th World Youth Skill Olympics, Busan, Aug. 30–Sept. 15. No. 1133a has black and red marginal inscription. Size: 90x60mm.

1978, Aug. 15

1134 A600 20w multicolored 12 10

Founding of republic, 30th anniversary.

Helpful notes abound in the "Information for Collectors" section at the front of this volume.

Nurse, Badge and Flowers
A601

Sobaeksan Observatory
A602

1978, Aug. 26

1135 A601 20w multicolored 12 10

Army Nurse Corps, 30th anniversary.

1978, Sept. 13 **Photo.** ***Perf. 13***

1136 A602 20w multicolored 12 10

Opening of Sobaeksan National Observatory.

Kyunghoeru Pavilion, Kyongbok Palace, Seoul
A603

Design: No. 1138, Baeg Do (island).

1978, Sept. 28

1137 A603 20w multicolored 12 10
1138 " 20w " 12 10

Tourist publicity.

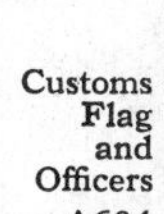

Customs Flag and Officers
A604

1978, Sept. 28

1139 A604 20w multicolored 12 10

Centenary of first Korean Custom House, Busan.

Armed Forces
A605

1978, Oct. 1 **Photo.** ***Perf. 13***

1140 A605 20w multicolored 12 10

Armed Forces, 30th anniversary.

Clay Figurines, Silla Dynasty
A606

Portrait of a Lady, by Shin Yoon-bok
A607

1978, Oct. 1

1141 A606 20w lt. grn. & blk. 12 10

Culture Month, October 1978.

1978, Oct. 24

1142 A607 20w multicolored 12 10
a. Souvenir sheet of 2 30

Philatelic Week, Oct. 24–29. No. 1142a has black marginal inscription. Size: 90x60mm.

Young Men, YMCA Emblem
A608

1978, Oct. 28

1143 A608 20w multicolored 12 10

75th anniversary of founding of Korean Young Men's Christian Association.

Hand Protecting Against Fire
A609

1978, Nov. 1 **Photo.** ***Perf. 13***

1144 A609 20w multicolored 12 10

Fire Prevention Day, Nov. 1.

Winter Landscape
A610

Ram-headed Figure, Bas-relief
A611

1978, Dec. 1 **Photo.** ***Perf. 13x13½***

1145 A610 20w multicolored 12 10
a. Souvenir sheet of 2 30
1146 A611 20w multicolored 12 10
a. Souvenir sheet of 2 30

New Year 1979. Nos. 1145a–1146a have black marginal inscriptions. Size: 90x60mm.

Hibiscus, Students, Globe
A612

President Chung Hee Park
A613

1978, Dec. 5

1147 A612 20w multicolored 12 10

Proclamation of National Education Charter, 10th anniversary.

1978, Dec. 27

1148 A613 20w multicolored 12 10
a. Souvenir sheet of 2 30

Inauguration of Chung Hee Park for fifth term as president. No. 1148a has black and ultramarine marginal inscription. Size: 90x60mm.

The only foreign revenue stamps listed in this Catalogue are those authorized for prepayment of postage.

Attractive slip cases are available for most Scott Albums.

Golden Mandarinfish
A614

Lace-bark Pines
A615

1979, Feb. 20 **Photo.** ***Perf. 13x13½***

1149 A614 20w multicolored 12 10
1150 A615 20w " 12 10

Nature conservation.

Samil Monument
A624

1979, Mar. 1 **Photo.** ***Perf. 13x13½***

1159 A624 20w multicolored 12 10

60th anniversary of Samil independence movement.

Worker and Bulldozer
A625

1979, Mar. 10 ***Perf. 13½x13***

1160 A625 20w multicolored 12 10

Labor Day.

SEMI-POSTAL STAMPS.

Field Hospital
SP1

Nurses Supporting Patient
SP2

Perf. 13½x14, 14x13½.

1953, Aug. 1 Litho. Wmk. 257
Crosses in Red.

B1 SP1 10h+5h blue green 1.50 1.00
B2 SP2 10h+5h blue 1.50 1.00

The surtax was for the Red Cross. Nos. B1–2 exist imperf.

Type of Regular Issue, 1956, with Added Inscription at Upper Left.
1957, Sept. 1 *Perf. 12½* Wmk. 312
Granite Paper

B3 A111 40h+10h light blue green 75 45

Wmk. 317

B4 A111 40h+10 light blue green 75 40

The surtax was for flood relief.

Rice Farmer Type of Regular Issue, 1961–62
1963, July 10 *Perf. 12½* Wmk. 317

B5 A172 4w+1w dark blue 50 35

The surtax was for flood victims in southern Korea.

1965, Oct. 1 *Perf. 12½* Unwmkd.

B6 A172 4w+2w indigo 50 35

The surtax was for flood relief.

1965, Oct. 11

B7 A172 4w+2w magenta 50 30

The surtax was for a scholarship fund.

Type of Regular Issue 1964–66.
1966, Nov. 10 Litho. *Perf. 12½*
Granite Paper

B8 A186b 7w+2w car. rose 60 30

The surtax was to help the needy.

Soldier with Wife and Child
SP3

Reservist
SP4

1967, June 20 *Perf. 12½x13*

B9 SP3 7w+3w rose lilac & black 50 30

The surtax was for veterans of the war in Viet Nam and their families.

1968, Aug. 1 Litho. *Perf. 13x12½*

B10 SP4 7w+3w grn. & black 1.75 1.25

Issued for the fund-raising drive to arm reservists.

Flag
SP5

"Pin of Love"
SP6

1968, Nov. 1 Litho. Unwmkd.

B11 SP5 7w+3w dark blue & red 4.00 1.50

The surtax was for disaster relief.

1969, Feb. 15

B12 SP5 7w+3w light green, dk. blue & red 1.25 75

Surtax for military helicopter fund.

Flag Type of 1968 Redrawn
Zeros Omitted
1969, Nov. 1 Litho. *Perf. 13x12½*

B13 SP5 7w+3w dk. bl. & red 1.25 75

The surtax was for the searchlight fund.

1972, Aug. 1 Photo. *Perf. 13½x12½*

B14 SP6 10w+5w bl. & car. 50 25

Disaster relief.

"Pin of Love"
SP7

Paddle and Ball
SP8

Perf. 12½x13½

1973, July 1 Photogravure

B15 SP7 10w+5w multi. 50 25

Disaster relief.

Perf. 13½x12½

1973, Aug. 1 Photogravure

B16 SP8 10w+5w multi. 50 25

Surtax was for gymnasium to be built to commemorate the victory of the Korean women's table tennis team at the 32nd World Table Tennis Championships.

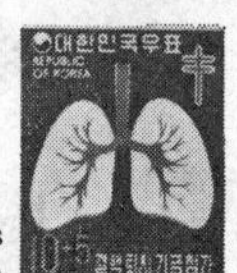

Lungs
SP9

1974, Nov. 1 *Perf. 13½x12½*

B17 SP9 10w+5w grn. & red 50 25

Surtax was for tuberculosis control.

No. 647 Surcharged 수해구제 +10

Perf. 13½x12½

1977, July 25 Photogravure

B18 A328 20w+10w green 25 20

Surtax was for flood relief.

Prices of premium quality never hinged stamps will be in excess of catalogue price.

AIR POST STAMPS

Four-motor Plane and Globe
AP1

Perf. 11½x11.

1947, Oct. 1 Litho. Wmk. 257

C1 AP1 50wn carmine rose 1.75 1.25
a. Horizontal pair, imperf. between 40.00

Type of 1947.
1949–50 Redrawn *Perf. 11*

C2 AP1 150wn blue 75 75
a. "KORFA" 11.00 9.00
C3 " 150wn green ('50) 2.50 *5.00*

Lines of shading more widely spaced, and many other minor differences.

Plane and Korea Map
AP2

Douglas C-47 and Ship
AP3

1950, Jan. 1

C4 AP2 60wn light blue 3.50 3.00

No. C2 Surcharged with New Value and Wavy Lines in Black.
1951, Oct. 10

C5 AP1 500wn on 150wn blue 1.00 75
a. "KORFA" 11.00 9.00
b. Surcharge inverted 75.00

Perf. 13x12½.

1952, Oct. 15 Litho. Wmk. 257

C6 AP3 1200wn red brown 10 8
C7 " 1800wn light blue 20 12
C8 " 4200wn purple 30 20

Nos. C6–C8 exist imperf.

1953, Apr. 5

C9 AP3 12h deep blue 25 25
C10 " 18h purple 40 25
C11 " 42h Prussian green 75 30

Douglas DC-7 over East Gate, Seoul
AP4

1954, June 15 *Perf. 12½*

C12 AP4 25h brown 20 10
C13 " 35h deep pink 30 15
C14 " 38h dark green 40 15
C15 " 58h ultramarine 50 20
C16 " 71h deep blue 50 30
Nos. C12–C16 (5) 1.90 90

Nos. C12–C16 exist imperf.

Type of 1954 Redrawn.
1956, July 20 Unwmkd.
Laid Paper.

C17 AP4 70h brt. bluish grn. 1.00 50
C18 " 110h brown 1.25 60
C19 " 205h magenta 1.50 75

Nos. C18–C19 are found on horizontally and vertically laid paper.

1957, July *Perf. 12½* Wmk. 312
Granite Paper.

C20 AP4 70h brt. bluish grn. 50 30
C21 " 110h brown 75 40
C22 " 205h magenta 1.25 60

On the redrawn stamps, Nos. C17–C22, the lines of the entire design are lighter, and the colorless character at right end of bottom row has been redrawn as in illustration above No. 212D.

Girl on Palace Balcony
AP5

Designs: 100h, Suwon Castle. 200h, Songnyu Gate, Tuksu Palace. 400h, Kyunghoeru Pavilion.

Lithographed
1961, Dec. 1 *Perf. 12½* Unwmkd.

C23 AP5 50h lt. blue & vio. 35 20
C24 " 100h pale green & sepia 75 25
C25 " 200h pale green & brown 1.25 40
C26 " 400h green & pale blue 1.75 75

Values in Won; Same Designs; Underlined Zeros Added
1962–63

C27 AP5 5w lt. bl. & vio. ('63) 50 12
C28 " 10w pale green & sepia 75 24
C29 " 20w pale green & brown ('63) 1.25 45
C30 " 40w green & pale blue ('63) 2.00 80

1964, May 10 *Perf. 12½* Wmk. 317
Granite Paper

C32 AP5 10w pale grn. & sepia 75 25
C33 " 20w pale grn. & brn. 1.25 40
C34 " 40w pale blue & grn. 2.00 1.00

1964, Oct. *Perf. 12½* Unwmkd.

Designs: 39w, Girl on palace balcony. 64w, Suwon Castle. 78w, Songnyu Gate, Tuksu Palace. 112w, Kyunghoeru Pavilion.

Granite Paper

C35 AP5 39w violet blue & gray olive 75 25
C36 " 64w blue & greenish gray 1.00 35
C37 " 78w greenish blue & ultra. 1.25 45
C38 " 112w blue & green 2.00 65

World Map and Plane
AP6

Designs: 135w, Plane over eastern hemisphere. 145w, Plane over world map. 180w, Plane over world map.

1973, Dec. 30 Photo. *Perf. 13x12½*

C39 AP6 110w pink & multi. 65 50
C40 " 135w yellow green & red 80 60
C41 " 145w lt. bl. & rose 90 65
C42 " 180w lilac & yellow 1.10 75

UPU Type of 1974
1974, Oct. 9 Photogravure *Perf. 13*

C43 A480 110w bl. & multi. 75 50
a. Souvenir sheet of 2 1.50

Centenary of Universal Postal Union. No. C43a contains 2 No. C43, blue margin with dark blue and red inscription. Size: 90x60mm.

North Korea

Stamps issued by the Korean People's Republic have not been listed because the U. S. Treasury Department (Foreign Assets Control Section) has prohibited their purchase abroad and importation.

LA AGUERA

(See Aguera.)

LAOS

(lä'ōz; louz)

LOCATION—In northwestern Indo-China.

GOVT.—Republic.

AREA—89,320 sq. mi.

POP.—3,460,000 (est. 1977).

CAPITAL—Vientiane.

Before 1949, Laos was part of the French colony of Indo-China and used its stamps until 1951. The kingdom was replaced by the Lao Peoples Democratic Republic Dec. 2, 1975.

100 Cents = 1 Piaster
100 Cents = 1 Kip (1955)

Boat on Mekong River
A1

King Sisavang-Vong
A2

Laotian Woman
A3

Designs: 50c, 60c, 70c, Luang Prabang. 1pi, 2pi, 3pi, 5pi, 10pi, Temple at Vientiane.

Engraved.

1951-52 Perf. 13 Unwmkd.

1	A1	10c dark green & emerald	4	4
2	"	20c dk. car. & car.	10	10
3	"	30c indigo & deep ultramarine	75	55
4	A3	30c indigo & purple ('52)	25	15
5	A1	50c dark brown	25	20
6	"	60c red & red orange	20	20
7	"	70c ultramarine & blue green	20	20
8	A3	80c bright green & dark blue green ('52)	25	20
9	A1	1pi dk. pur. & pur.	35	35
10	A3	1.10pi dark plum & carmine ('52)	45	20
11	A2	1.50pi black brown & violet brown	55	35
12	A3	1.90pi indigo & deep blue ('52)	85	65
13	A1	2pi dark green & gray green	12.00	1.80
14	"	3pi dk. car. & red	60	45
15	A3	3pi chocolate & black brown ('52)	1.00	60
16	A1	5pi indigo & deep ultramarine	80	60
17	"	10pi black brown & violet brown	2.00	90
		Nos. 1-17 (17)	20.64	7.54

A booklet containing 26 souvenir sheets was issued in 1952 on the anniversary of the first issue of Laos stamps. Each sheet contains a single stamp in the center (Nos. 1-17, C2-C4, J1-J6), measures 130x89 mm., and is inscribed "Royaume du Laos" in Laotian and in French. Price $100.

U. P. U. Monument and King Sisavang-Vong
A4

1952, Dec. 1

18	A4	80c indigo, blue & purple	40	35
19	"	1pi dark carmine, carmine & orange brown	40	35
20	"	1.20pi dark purple, purple & ultramarine	40	35
21	"	1.50pi dark green, blue green & dark brown	40	35
22	"	1.90pi black brown, violet brown & dark Prussian green	40	35
		Nos. 18-22, C5-C6 (7)	7.00	5.75

Issued to publicize Laos' admission to the Universal Postal Union, May 13, 1952.

Musicians
A5

1953, July 14

23	A5	4.50pi indigo & blue green	65	60
24	"	6pi gray & dk. brn.	90	60

Composite of Laotian Temples—A6

1954, Mar. 4

25	A6	2pi indigo & purple	25.00	15.00
26	"	3pi black brown & dark red	25.00	20.00

Issued to commemorate the 50th anniversary of the accession of King Sisavang-Vong. See No. C13.

Buddha Statue and Monks—A7

1956, May 24 Engr. Perf. 13

27	A7	2k reddish brown	2.25	1.65
28	"	3k black	2.25	1.65
29	"	5k chocolate	2.75	2.25
		Nos. 27-29, C20-C21 (5)	44.25	35.55

2500th anniversary of birth of Buddha.

U.N. Emblem
A8

1956, Dec. 14 Perf. 13½x13

30	A8	1k black	50	40
31	"	2k blue	60	60
32	"	4k bright red	75	70
33	"	6k purple	1.00	90
		Nos. 30-33, C22-C23 (6)	9.85	9.60

Issued to commemorate the first anniversary of the admission of Laos to the United Nations.

Khouy Player—A9

Khene Player
A10

Musical Instrument: 8k, Ranat.

1957, Mar. 25 Perf. 13 Unwmkd.

34	A9	2k multicolored	1.10	90
35	A10	4k "	1.10	1.00
36	A9	8k orange, blue & red brown	1.10	1.00
		Nos. 34-36, C24-C26 (6)	8.30	6.40

Harvesting Rice—A11

Drying Rice—A12

Designs: 16k, Winnowing rice. 26k, Polishing rice.

1957, July 22 Engraved Perf. 13

37	A11	3k multicolored	75	50
38	A12	5k grn, sepia & red	1.00	60
39	"	16k blue, olive & pur.	1.75	1.25
40	A11	26k red brown, green & sepia	3.00	1.85

Elephants—A13

Various Elephants: 10c, 20c, 2k, horizontal. 30c, 5k, 10k, 13k, vertical.

1958, Mar. 17

41	A13	10c multicolored	20	10
42	"	20c "	20	10
43	"	30c "	20	10
44	"	2k "	20	15
45	"	5k "	85	85
46	"	10k "	1.00	1.00
47	"	13k "	1.50	1.35
		Nos. 41-47 (7)	4.15	3.65

Globe and Goddess—A14

UNESCO Building and Mother with Children
A15

Designs: 70c, UNESCO building, globe and mother with children. 1k, UNESCO building and Eiffel tower.

1958, Nov. 3 Engraved Perf. 13

48	A14	50c multicolored	15	10
49	A15	60c emerald, violet & maroon	15	10
50	"	70c ultramarine, rose red & brn.	15	12
51	A14	1k olive bistre, claret & greenish blue	15	12

Issued to commemorate the opening of UNESCO (U.N. Educational, Scientific and Cultural Organization) Headquarters in Paris, Nov. 3.

King Sisavang-Vong
A16

1959, Sept. **Unwmkd.**

52	A16	4k rose claret	20	20
53	"	6.50k orange red	20	20
54	"	9k bright pink	20	20
55	"	13k green	30	30

Dancers
A17

Student and Torch of Learning
A18

Portal of Wat Phou, Pakse
A19

Designs: 3k, Globe, key of knowledge and girl student. 5k, Dancers and temple.

1959, Oct. 1 **Engraved** ***Perf. 13***

56	A17	1k violet black, olive & blue	12	10
57	A18	2k maroon & black	12	10
58	A17	3k slate green & violet	20	20
59	A18	5k rose violet, yellow & bright green	30	30

1959, Nov. 2 ***Perf. 13*** **Unwmkd.**

Historic Monuments: 1.50k, That Inghang, Savannakhet (horiz.). 2.50k, Phou Temple, Pakse (horiz.). 7k, That Luang, Vientiane. 11k, That Luang, Vientiane (horiz.). 12.50k, Phousi, Luang Prabang.

60	A19	50c sepia, grn. & org.	4	4
61	"	1.50k multicolored	6	6
62	"	2.50k purple, violet blue & olive	10	10
63	"	7k violet, olive & claret	12	12
64	"	11k brown, carmine & green	20	20
65	"	12.50k blue, violet & bistre	25	25
		Nos. 60-65 (6)	77	77

Funeral Urn and Monks
A20

King Sisavang-Vong
A21

Designs: 6.50k, Urn under canopy. 9k, Catafalque on 7-headed dragon carriage.

1961, Apr. 29 **Engr.** ***Perf. 13***

66	A20	4k black, bistre & orange	30	30
67	A20	6.50k black & bistre	30	30
68	"	9k black & bistre	30	30
69	A21	25k black	75	75

Issued in memory of King Sisavang-Vong (1885-1959) and to commemorate the funeral, Apr. 23-29, 1961.

King Savang Vatthana
A22

Boy and Malaria Eradication Emblem
A23

1962, Apr. 16 ***Perf. 13***

Portrait in Brown and Carmine

70	A22	1k ultramarine	10	10
71	"	2k lilac rose	10	10
72	"	5k greenish blue	15	15
73	"	10k olive	35	35

1962, July 19 **Engraved**

Designs: 9k, Girl. 10k, Malaria eradication emblem.

74	A23	4k bluish green, black & buff	12	12
75	"	9k light blue, blk. & light brown	25	20
76	"	10k olive, bistre & rose red	45	40

Issued for the World Health Organization drive to eradicate malaria. A souvenir sheet exists.

Stamp Day—A24

Royal Messenger
A25

Designs: 50c, Modern mail service (truck, train, plane). 1k, Ancient mail service (messenger on elephant).

1962, Nov. 15 ***Perf. 13*** **Unwmkd.**

77	A24	50c multicolored	30	30
78	"	70c "	30	30
79	A25	1k deep claret, green & black	35	35
80	"	1.50k multicolored	35	35

Issued for Stamp Day.

Souvenir sheets exist. One contains the 50c and 70c; the other, the 1k and 1.50k. The sheets exist both perf. and imperf.

Fishermen with Nets—A26

Threshing Rice
A27

Designs: 5k, Plowing and planting in rice paddy. 9k, Woman with infant harvesting rice.

1963, Mar. 21 ***Perf. 13***

81	A26	1k green, bister & pur.	15	15
82	A27	4k bister, blue & grn.	15	15
83	A26	5k grn., bister & indigo	15	15
84	A27	9k grn., vio. bl. & ocher	40	40
		a. Min. sheet of 4	2.50	2.50

Issued for the "Freedom from Hunger" campaign of the U.N. Food and Agriculture Organization.

No. 84a contains one each of Nos. 81-84, imperf. Size: 219x100½mm.

Queen Khamphouy Handing out Gifts
A28

1963, Oct. 10 **Engraved**

85	A28	4k brn., dp. car. & bl.	15	15
86	"	6k grn., red, yel., & bl.	25	25
87	"	10k blue, deep carmine & dark brown	30	30
		a. Min. sheet of 3	2.00	2.00

Centenary of the International Red Cross.

No. 87a contains one each of Nos. 85-87. Size: 140x100mm.

Man Holding U.N. Emblem
A29

1963, Dec. 10 ***Perf. 13*** **Unwmkd.**

88	A29	4k dark blue, deep org. & vio. brn.	25	20

Issued to commemorate the 15th anniversary of the Universal Declaration of Human Rights.

Temple of That Luang, Map of Nubia and Ramses II—A30

1964, March 8 **Engraved**

89	A30	4k multicolored	15	15
90	"	6k "	20	20
91	"	10k "	30	30
		a. Min. sheet of 3	1.10	1.10

Issued to publicize the UNESCO world campaign to save historic monuments in Nubia. No. 91a contains one each of Nos. 89-91. Sold for 25k. Size: 184x99mm.

Ceremonial Chalice—A31

Designs: 15k, Buddha. 20k, Soldier leading people through Mekong River Valley. 40k, Royal Palace, Luang Prabang.

1964, July 30 ***Perf. 13*** **Unwmkd.**

92	A31	10k multicolored	30	20
93	"	15k "	35	30
94	"	20k "	45	40
95	"	40k "	75	70
		a. Min. sheet of 4	2.50	2.50

Issued to emphasize "Neutral and Constitutional Laos." When the stamps are arranged in a block of four with 40k and 15k in first row and 10k and 20k in second row, the map of Laos appears. No. 95a contains one each of Nos. 92-95. Size: 138x139mm.

Prince Vet and Wife Mathie
A32

Lao Women
A33

Scenes from Buddhist Legend of Phra Vet Sandone: 32k, God of the Skies sending his son to earth. 45k, Phaune's daughter with beggar husband. 55k, Beggar cornered by guard and dogs.

1964, Dec. 3 **Photo.** ***Perf. 13x12½***

96	A32	10k multicolored	35	35
97	"	32k "	45	45
98	"	45k "	60	60
99	"	55k "	80	80
		a. Min. sheet of 4	2.75	2.75

No. 99a contains 4 imperf. stamps similar to Nos. 96-99. Black control number. Size: 104x179mm.

1964, Dec. 15 **Engraved** ***Perf. 13***

100	A33	25k blk., org. brown & pale olive	35	35

See Nos. C43-C45 and miniature sheet No. C45a.

Cethosia Biblis—A34

Butterflies: 25k, Precis cebrene. 40k, Dysphania militaris.

1965, Mar. 13 ***Perf. 13*** **Unwmkd.**

Size: 36x36mm.

101 A34 10k black, brown red & lt. green 40 35
102 " 25k blk., orge. & vio. 55 50

Size: 48x27mm.

103 A34 40k multicolored 85 75

See also No. C46.

Teacher and School, American Aid
A35

Designs: 25k, Woman at Wattay Airport, French aid (horiz.). 45k, Woman bathing child and food basket, Japanese aid. 55k, Musicians broadcasting, British aid (horiz.).

1965, Mar. 30 Engraved ***Perf. 13***

104 A35 25k bl. grn., brn. & carmine rose 30 25
105 " 45k olive grn. & brn. 60 60
106 " 55k brt. bl. & bister 70 70
107 " 75k multicolored 1.00 1.00

Issued to publicize foreign aid to Laos.

Hophabang Temple
A36

1965, Apr. 23 ***Perf. 13*** **Unwmkd.**

108 A36 10k multicolored 30 25

Telewriter, Map of Laos and Globe—A37

Designs: 30k, Communication by satellite and map of Laos. 50k, Globe, map of Laos and radio.

1965, June 15 Engraved ***Perf. 13***

109 A37 5k violet blue, brown & red lilac 10 10
110 " 30k blue, orange brown & slate green 45 40
111 " 50k crimson, light blue & bister 65 60
a. Min. sheet of 3 3.00 3.00

Centenary of International Telecommunications Union. No. 111a contains one each of Nos. 109–111. Size: 148x99mm.

Nos. 52–53 Surcharged in Dark Blue with New Value and Bars.

1965 ***Perf. 13*** **Unwmkd.**

112 A16 1k on 4k rose claret 20 12
113 " 5k on 6.50k org. red 25 12

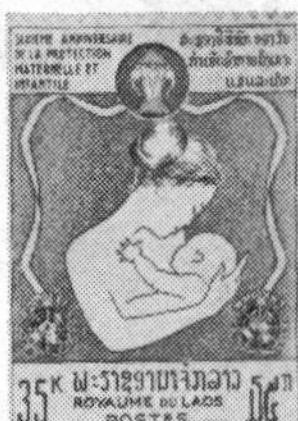

Mother and Child, UNICEF and WHO Emblems
A38

Map of Laos and U.N. Emblem
A39

1965, Sept. 15 Engraved ***Perf. 13***

114 A38 35k light ultra. & dark red 50 40
a. Min. sheet 2.50 2.50

Issued to commemorate the sixth anniversary of the Mother and Child Protection movement. No. 114a contains one No. 114. Size: 130x100mm.

1965, Nov. 3 ***Perf. 12½x13***

115 A39 5k emerald, gray & violet blue 15 15
116 " 25k lilac rose, gray & violet blue 35 30
117 " 40k blue, gray & violet blue 50 50

Issued to commemorate the 20th anniversary of the United Nations. Although first day covers were canceled "Oct. 24," the actual day of issue is reported to have been Nov. 3.

Tikhy (Hockey)
A40

Folklore: 10k, Two bulls fighting. 25k, Canoe race. 50k, Rocket festival.

1965, Dec. 23 Engraved ***Perf. 13***

118 A40 10k orge., brn. & gray 15 15
119 " 20k green, verm. & dark blue 30 30
120 " 25k brt. bl. & multi. 30 22
121 " 50k orge. & multi. 60 60

Slaty-headed Parakeet
A41

Birds: 15k, White-crested laughing thrush. 20k, Osprey. 45k, Bengal roller.

1966, Jan. 26 Engraved ***Perf. 13***

122 A41 5k car. rose, olive & brown 20 20
123 " 15k bluish green, brn. & black 25 25
124 " 20k dull blue, sepia & bister 30 30
125 " 45k violet, Prussian blue & sepia 70 70

WHO Headquarters, Geneva
A42

1966, May 3 Engraved ***Perf. 13***

126 A42 10k bl. grn. & indigo 15 12
127 " 25k car. & dk. green 30 25
128 " 50k ultra. & black 60 60
a. Min. sheet of 3 2.75 2.75

Issued to commemorate the inauguration of the World Health Organization Headquarters, Geneva. No. 128a contains one each of Nos. 126–128. Sold for 150k. Size: 149x100mm.

Ordination of Buddhist Monk
A43

Folklore: 25k, Women building ceremonial sand hills. 30k, Procession of the Wax Pagoda (vert.). 40k, Wrist-tying ceremony (3 men, 3 women) (vert.).

1966, May 20 ***Perf. 13***

129 A43 10k multicolored 15 12
130 " 25k " 30 25
131 " 30k " 40 35
132 " 40k " 50 40

UNESCO Emblem
A44

1966, July 7 Engraved ***Perf. 13***

133 A44 20k ocher & gray 20 15
134 " 30k brt. blue & gray 35 35
135 " 40k brt. grn. & gray 45 35
136 " 60k crimson & gray 65 50
a. Min. sheet 3.25 3.25

Issued to commemorate the 20th anniversary of the United Nations Educational, Scientific and Cultural Organization (UNESCO). No. 136a contains one each of Nos. 133–136. Size: 139x139mm. Sold for 250k.

Addressed Envelope, Carrier Pigeon, Globe and Hand with Quill Pen—A45

1966, Sept. 7 Engraved ***Perf. 13***

137 A45 5k red, brn. & blue 20 15
138 " 20k blue green, black & lilac 35 30
139 " 40k blue, red brown & dk. olive bister 50 45
140 " 45k brt. rose lilac, bl. grn. & blk. 60 55
a. Min. sheet 2.50 2.50

Issued for International Letter Writing Week, Oct. 6–12. No. 140a contains one each of Nos. 137–140. Size: 130x98mm. Sold for 250k.

Sculpture from Siprapouthbat Temple
A46

Sculptures: 20k, from Visoun Temple. 50k, from Xiengthong Temple. 70k, from Visoun Temple.

1967, Jan. Engraved ***Perf. 12½x13***

141 A46 5k olive grn. & grn. 10 10
142 " 20k brown olive & gray blue 25 25
143 " 50k dark brown & deep claret 50 50
144 " 70k dark brown & dk. magenta 65 65

General Post Office
A47

1967, Apr. 6 Engraved ***Perf. 13***

145 A47 25k brown, green & violet brown 30 20
146 " 50k indigo, brt. blue & green 60 50
147 " 70k dk. red, green & brown 80 60

Inauguration of the new Post and Telegraph Headquarters.

Snakehead
A48

Fish: 35k, Giant catfish. 45k, Spiny eel. 60k, Knifefish.

1967, June 8 Engr. ***Perf. 13x12½***

148 A48 20k dull blue, bister & black 25 18
149 " 35k aquamarine, bister & gray 40 30
150 " 45k pale green, bister & olive brown 60 40
151 " 60k slate green, bister & black 75 50

Drumstick Tree Flower
A49

Blossoms: 55k, Turmeric. 75k, Peacock flower. 80k, Pagoda tree.

1967, Aug. 10 Engr. ***Perf. 12½x13***

152 A49 30k red lilac, yellow & green 20 25
153 " 55k org., magenta & light green 55 45
154 " 75k bl., red & lt. grn. 65 50
155 " 80k brt. grn., magenta & yellow 80 65

Banded Krait—A50

Reptiles: 40k, Marsh crocodile. 100k, Malayan moccasin. 200k, Water monitor.

1967, Dec. 7 Engraved *Perf. 13*

156 A50 5k emerald, indigo & yellow 10 10
157 " 40k sepia, lt. green & yellow 35 30
158 " 100k lt. grn., brown & ocher 1.00 80
159 " 200k green, black & bister 2.00 2.00

Human Rights Flame—A51

1968, Feb. 8 Engraved *Perf. 13*

160 A51 20k brt. green, red & green 25 20
161 " 30k brown, red & grn. 35 30
162 " 50k brt. blue, red & green 60 50
a. Souv. sheet of 3 2.00 2.00

Issued for International Human Rights Year. No. 162a contains one each of Nos. 160–162. Green marginal inscription. Size: 189x100mm. Sold for 250k.

WHO Emblem A52

1968, July 5 Engr. *Perf. 12½x13*

163 A52 15k rose vio., verm. & ocher 18 18
164 " 30k brt. blue, brt. green & ocher 30 25
165 " 70k vermilion, plum & ocher 70 30
166 " 110k brown, brt. rose lilac & ocher 1.20 85
167 " 250k brt. green, brt. blue & ocher 2.40 1.65
a. Souv. sheet of 5 4.75 4.75
Nos. 163-167 (5) 4.78 3.23

Issued for the 20th anniversary of the World Health Organization. No. 167a contains one each of Nos. 163–167. Ocher marginal inscriptions. Size: 129x114½ mm. Sold for 500k.

Parade and Memorial Arch A53

Designs: 20k, Armored Corps with tanks. 60k, Three soldiers with Laotian flag.

1968, July 15 *Perf. 13*

168 A53 15k multicolored 15 10
169 A53 20k multicolored 20 12
170 " 60k " 65 35
Nos. 168-170, C52-C53 (5) 4.75 3.07

Issued to honor the Laotian Army. For souvenir sheet see No. C53a.

Chrysochroa Mnizechi A54

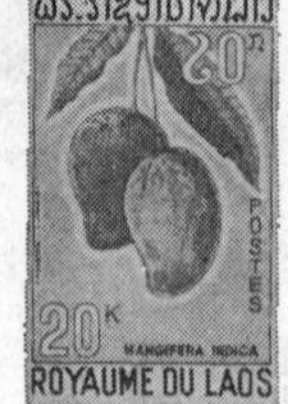

Mangoes A55

Insects: 50k, Aristobia approximator. 90k, Eutaenia corbetti.

1968, Aug. 28 Engraved *Perf. 13*

171 A54 30k vio. blue, green & yellow 30 20
172 " 50k lilac, black & ocher 50 40
173 " 90k bis., blk. & org. 75 60
Nos. 171-173, C54-C55 (5) 4.05 2.95

1968, Oct. 3 Engraved *Perf. 13*

Fruits: 50k, Tamarind. 180k, Jackfruit (horiz.). 250k, Watermelon (horiz.).

174 A55 20k indigo, lt. blue & emerald 18 12
175 " 50k lt. blue, emerald & brown 55 50
176 " 180k sepia, orange & yellow green 1.50 1.35
177 " 250k sepia, bister & emerald 2.00 1.75

Hurdling A56

Sports: 80k, Tennis. 100k, Soccer. 110k, High jump.

1968, Nov. 15 Engraved *Perf. 13*

178 A56 15k bister brown, indigo & green 12 10
179 " 80k blue green, indigo & olive 75 48
180 " 100k emerald, indigo & brown 90 60
181 " 110k salmon rose, indigo & brn. 1.00 60

Issued to commemorate the 19th Olympic Games, Mexico City, Oct. 12–27.

Wedding of Kathanam and Nang Sida A57

Design: 200k, Thao Khathanam battling the serpent Ngou Xouang and the giant bird Phanga Houng. Design from panels of the central gate of Ongtu Temple, Vientiane. Design of 150k is from east gate.

1969, Feb. 28 Photo. *Perf. 12x13*

182 A57 150k blk., gold & red 1.20 75
183 " 200k " " " 1.75 1.00

Soukhib Ordered to Attack A58

Scenes from Royal Ballet: 15k, Pharak pleading for Nang Sita. 20k, Thotsakan reviewing his troops. 30k, Nang Sita awaiting punishment. 40k, Pharam inspecting troops. 60k, Hanuman preparing to rescue Nang Sita.

1969 Photogravure *Perf. 14*

184 A58 10k multicolored 15 12
185 " 15k blue & multi. 20 18
186 " 20k lt. blue & multi. 20 18
187 " 30k salmon & multi. 25 20
188 " 40k " " 30 25
189 " 60k pink & multi. 50 40
Nos. 184-189, C56-C57 (8) 4.85 3.98

ILO Emblem and Basket Weavers at Vientiane Vocational Center—A59

1969, May 2 Engraved *Perf. 13*

190 A59 30k claret & violet 30 20
191 " 60k slate green & violet brown 60 40

Issued to commemorate the 50th anniversary of the International Labor Organization. See No. C58.

Chinese Pangolin—A60

1969, Oct. 1 Photo. *Perf. 13x12*

192 A60 15k multicolored 10 10
193 " 30k " 20 20
Nos. 192-193, C59-C61 (5) 2.00 1.90

That Luang, Luang Prabang A61

King Sisavang-Vong A62

1969, Oct. 29 Engraved *Perf. 13*

194 A61 50k dk. green, blue & bister 60 30
195 A62 70k maroon & buff 90 50

Issued to commemorate the 10th anniversary of the death of King Sisavang-Vong. Nos. 194–195 are printed se-tenant with connecting label with dark green commemorative inscription.

Carved Capital from Wat Xieng-thong A63

1970, Jan. 10 Photo. *Perf. 12x13*

196 A63 70k multicolored 70 70

See Nos. C65–C66.

Kongphene (Midday) Drum A64

Designs: 55k, Kongthong (bronze) drum.

1970, Mar. 30 Engraved *Perf. 13*

197 A64 30k blue gray, olive & orange 50 30
198 " 55k ocher, black & yellow green 90 60

See No. C67.

Lenin Explaining Electrification Plan, by L. Shmatko—A65

1970, Apr. 22 Litho. *Perf. 12½x12*

199 A65 30k blue & multi. 25 18
200 " 70k rose red & multi. 60 42

Issued to commemorate the centenary of the birth of Lenin (1870–1924), Russian communist leader.

Silk Weaver and EXPO Emblem
A66

Design: 70k, Woman winding silk thread and EXPO '70 emblem.

1970, July 7 Engraved *Perf. 13*

201 A66 30k deep rose, dark brown & black 20 18
202 " 70k blue & multi. 50 50

Issued to publicize the Laotian silk industry and to commemorate EXPO '70 International Exposition, Osaka, Japan, Mar. 15–Sept. 13. See No. C69.

Wild Boar
A67

1970, Sept. 7 Engraved *Perf. 13*

203 A67 20k grn. & dp. brown 10 10
204 " 60k deep brown & olive bister 35 35

See Nos. C70–C71.

Buddha, U.N. Headquarters and Emblem
A68

1970, Oct. 24 Size: 22x36mm.

205 A68 30k ultra., brown & rose red 25 18
206 " 70k bright green, sepia & violet 60 42

United Nations, 25th anniversary. See No. C75.

Nakhanet, Symbol of Arts and Culture—A69

Design: 58k, Rahu swallowing the moon.

1971, Feb. 5

207 A69 70k henna brown, orange & olive 65 42
208 " 85k bl., grn. & yellow 75 50

See No. C76.

Silver-smithing
A70

Designs: 30k, Pottery. 70k, Boat building.

1971, Apr. 12 Engraved *Perf. 13*

Size: 36x36mm.

209 A70 30k bl. grn. & multi. 25 18
210 " 50k multicolored 40 30

Size: 47x36 mm.

211 A70 70k red brn. & multi. 50 35

Laotian and African Children, U.N. Emblem—A71

Design: 60k, Women musicians, elephants and U.N. emblem.

1971, May 1 Engraved *Perf. 13*

212 A71 30k lt. green, brown & black 25 18
213 " 60k yellow, purple & dull red 60 40

International year against racial discrimination.

Miss Rotary, Wat Ho Phrakeo
A72

Dendrobium Aggregatum
A73

Design: 30k, Monk on roof of That Luang and Rotary emblem (horiz.).

1971, June Engraved *Perf. 13*

214 A72 30k purple & ocher 35 20
215 " 70k gray olive, dark blue & rose 65 40

Rotary International, 50th anniversary.

Perf. 12½x13, 13x12½

1971, July Photogravure

Orchids: 50k, Asocentrum ampullaceum (horiz.). 70k, Trichoglottis fasciata (horiz.).

Size: 26x36, 36x26mm.

216 A73 30k gray bl. & multi. 15 15
217 " 50k " " 25 25
218 " 70k " " 35 35

See Nos. 230–232, C79, C89.

Palm Civet
A74

Animals: 40k, like 25k. 50k, Lesser Malay chevrotain. 85k, Sika deer.

1971, Sept. 16 Engr. *Perf. 13*

219 A74 25k purple, dark blue & black 15 15
220 " 40k green, olive bister & black 20 20
221 " 50k brt. grn. & ocher 25 25
222 " 85k slate grn., grn. & brown orange 40 40
Nos. 219–222, C83 (5) 2.00 1.75

Types of 1952–57 with Ornamental Panels and Inscriptions.

Designs: 30k, Laotian woman. 40k, So player (like No. C25). 50k, Rama (like No. C19).

1971, Nov. 2

223 A3 30k brn. vio. & brown 20 18
a. Souvenir sheet of 3 2.25 2.25
224 A10 40k sepia, blk. & verm. 24 24
225 AP7 50k ultramarine, black & salmon 40 40

20th anniversary of Laotian independent postal service. All stamps inscribed: "Vingtième Anniversaire de la Philatélie Lao," "Postes" and "1971." No. 223a contains No. 223 and 60k and 85k in design of 30k. Sheet has brown commemorative inscription and control number. Size: 178½x109mm. Sold for 250k. See also No. C84.

Children Learning to Read
A75

Design: 70k, Old-style scribe writing on palm leaves.

1972, Jan. 30 Engraved *Perf. 13*

Size: 36x22mm.

226 A75 30k blue green 18 18
227 " 70k brown 42 42

International Book Year 1972. See No. C

Nam Ngum Hydroelectric Dam, Monument and ECAFE Emblem—A76

1972, Mar. 28 Engraved *Perf. 13*

228 A76 40k green, ultra. & light brown 20 20
229 " 80k grn., brn. olive & dark blue 45 45

25th anniversary of the Economic Commission for Asia and the Far East (ECAFE), which helped build the Nam Ngum Hydroelectric Dam. See No. C88.

Orchid Type of 1971

Orchids: 40k, Rynchostylis giganterum. 60k, Paphiopedilum exul. 80k, Cattleya (horiz.).

1972, May 5 Photogravure *Perf. 13*

Size: 26x36, 36x26mm.

230 A73 40k lt. blue & multi. 20 20
231 " 60k multicolored 30 30
232 " 80k lt. blue & multi. 40 40

See No. C89.

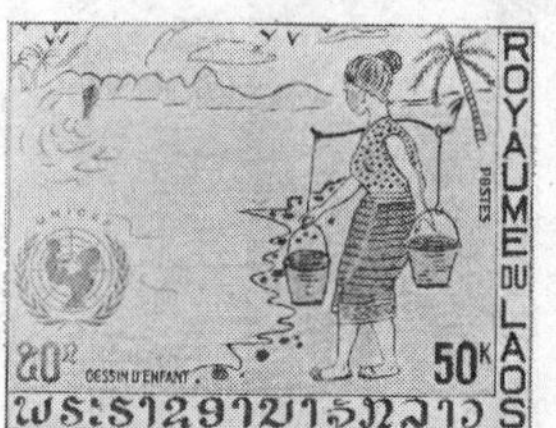

Woman Carrying Water, UNICEF Emblem—A77

Design: 80k, Child learning bamboo-weaving, UNICEF emblem. Designs are children's drawings.

1972, July 20 Engraved *Perf. 13*

233 A77 50k blue & multi. 30 30
234 " 80k brown & multi. 45 45

25th anniversary (in 1971) of the United Nations International Children's Fund (UNICEF). See No. C90.

Attopeu Costume, Religious Ceremony
A78

Lion from Wat That Luang and Lions Emblem
A79

Design: 90k, Phongsaly festival costume.

1973, Feb. Engraved *Perf. 13*

235 A78 40k maroon & multi. 12 12
236 " 90k multicolored 25 25

See Nos. C101–C102.

1973, Mar. 30 Engraved *Perf. 13*

237 A79 40k violet blue, rose claret & lilac 20 20
238 " 80k purple, orange brown & yellow 40 40

Lions International of Laos. See No. C103.

Dr. Hansen, Map of Laos, "Dok Hak" Flowers—A80

1973, June 28 Engraved *Perf. 13*

239 A80 40k multicolored 15 15
240 " 80k " 30 30

Centenary of the discovery by Dr. Armauer G. Hansen of the Hansen bacillus, the cause of leprosy.

Wat Vixun, Monk Blessing Girl Scouts
A81

1973, Sept. 1 Engraved *Perf. 13*

241 A81 70k ocher & brown 42 42

25th anniversary of Laotian Scout Movement. See Nos. C106–C107.

INTERPOL Headquarters
A82

1973, Dec. 22 Engr. *Perf. 13x12½*

242 A82 40k greenish blue 20 20
243 " 80k brown 40 40

50th anniversary of International Criminal Police Organization. See No. C110.

Boy Mailing Letter A83 — Eranthemum Nervosum A84

1974, Apr. 30 Engr. *Perf. 13*

244	A83	70k blue, light green & ocher	20	20
245	"	80k light green, blue & ocher	25	25

Centenary of Universal Postal Union. See Nos. C114-C115.

1974, May 31

Flowers: 50k, Water lilies (horiz.). 80k, Scheffler's kapokier (horiz.).

Size: 26x36, 36x26mm.

246	A84	30k lt. grn. & violet	8	8
247	"	50k vio. blue & multi.	12	12
248	"	80k brn. org. & multi.	20	30

See No. C116.

Mekong River Ferry—A85

Design: 90k, Samlo (passenger tricycle; vert.).

1974, July 31 Engraved *Perf. 13*

249	A85	25k red brn. & choc.	8	8
250	"	90k brown olive & light olive	25	25

See No. C117.

Marconi, Indigenous Transmission Methods, Transistor Radio—A86

1974, Aug. 28 Engr. *Perf. 13*

251	A86	60k multicolored	15	15
252	"	90k "	25	25

Birth centenary of Guglielmo Marconi (1874-1937), Italian electrical engineer and inventor. See No. C118.

Diastocera Wallichi Tonkinensis A87

Insects: 90k, Macrochenus isabellunus. 100k, Purpuricenus malaccensis.

1974, Oct. 23 Engr. *Perf. 13*

253	A87	50k bl. grn. & multi.	20	20
254	"	90k yel. grn. & multi.	35	35
255	"	100k brn. & multi.	40	40

See No. C119.

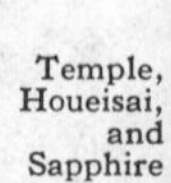

Temple, Houeisai, and Sapphire A88

Design: 110k, Gold panning at Attopeu.

1975, Feb. 1 Engr. *Perf. 13x12½*

256	A88	100k bl., brn. & grn.	30	30
257	"	110k bl., brn. & yel.	40	40

King Sisavang-Vong, Princes Souvanna Phouma and Souphanou-Vong—A89

1975, Feb. 21 Engraved *Perf. 13*

258	A89	80k olive & multi.	30	24
259	"	300k multicolored	1.00	90
260	"	420k "	1.25	1.25

First anniversary of Peace Treaty of Vientiane.

Certain unlisted issues of Laos, starting in 1975, are mentioned and briefly described in "For the Record" at the back of this volume.

Fortuneteller Working on Forecast for New Year (Size of pair: 100x27mm.)

A90 A91

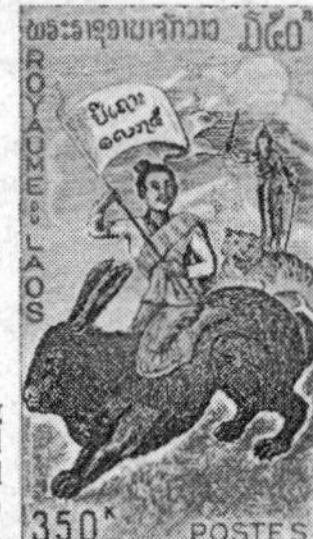

New Year Riding Rabbit, and Tiger (Old Year) A92

1975, Apr. 14 Engr. *Perf. 13*

261	A90	40k bister & red brn.	10	10
262	A91	200k bister, red brn. & slate	45	45
263	A92	350k blue & multi.	90	90

New Year 1975, Year of the Rabbit. Nos. 261-262 printed se-tenant.

U.N. Emblem, "Equality" A93

Design: 200k, IWY emblem, man and woman.

1975, June 19 Engraved

264	A93	100k dull blue & violet blue	30	30
265	"	200k multicolored	60	60
		a. Miniature sheet of 2	1.00	1.00

International Women's Year 1975. No. 265a contains one each of Nos. 264-265. Size: 133x100mm.

Scene from Vet Sandone Legend A94

Designs: Scenes from Buddhist legend of Prince Vet Sandone.

1975, July 22 Photo. *Perf. 13*

266	A94	80k multicolored	40	30
267	"	110k "	55	40
268	"	120k "	60	45
269	"	130k "	65	50

Buddha, Stupas of Borobudur A95

Design: 200k, Borobudur sculptures and UNESCO emblem.

1975, Aug. 20 Engraved *Perf. 13*

270	A95	100k indigo & multi.	25	25
271	"	200k multicolored	50	50
		a. Miniature sheet of 2	1.35	1.35

UNESCO campaign to save Borobudur Temple, Java. No. 271a contains one each of Nos. 270-271. Size: 130x100mm.

Coat of Arms of Republic A96 — Thathiang Pagoda, Vientiane A97

1976, Dec. 2 Litho. *Perf. 14*

272	A96	1k blue & multi.	3	3
273	"	2k rose & multi.	3	3
274	"	5k bright green & multicolored	3	3
275	"	10k lilac & multi.	5	5
276	"	200k org. & multi.	1.10	1.10
		a. Miniature sheet of 5	2.50	2.50
		Nos. 272-276 (5)	1.24	1.24

No. 276a contains one each of Nos. 272-276. Size: 165x71mm.

1976, Dec. 18 *Perf. 13½*

Designs: 2k, 80k, 100k, Phonsi Pagoda, Luang Prabang. 30k, 300k, like 1k.

277	A97	1k multicolored	3	3
278	"	2k "	3	3
279	"	30k "	14	14
280	"	80k "	36	36
281	A97	100k multicolored	45	45
282	"	300k "	1.35	1.35
		Nos. 277-282 (6)	2.36	2.36

Silversmith A98

Handicrafts: 2k, Weaver. 20k, Potter. 50k, Basket weaver (vert.).

Perf. 13x12½, 12½x13

1977, Apr. 1 Lithographed

283	A98	1k multicolored	5	5
284	"	2k "	5	5
285	"	20k "	15	15
286	"	50k "	30	30

Miniature sheets of 2 exist, perf. and imperf.

Cosmonauts A. A. Gubarev, G. M. Grechko A99

Government Palace, Vientiane, Kremlin, Moscow—A100

Designs: 20k, 50k, Lenin speaking on Red Square. 60k, like 5k. 250k, like 100k.

Perf. 12x12½, 12½x12

1977, Oct. 31 Lithographed

287	A99	5k multicolored	3	3
288	"	20k "	8	8
289	"	50k "	20	20
290	"	60k "	22	20
291	A100	100k "	40	40
		a. Souvenir sheet of 3	1.00	1.00
292	A100	250k multicolored	1.00	1.00
		a. Souvenir sheet of 3	1.50	1.50
		Nos. 287-292 (6)	1.93	1.91

60th anniversary of Russian October Revolution. No. 291a contains one each of Nos. 288, 290-291; No. 292a one each of Nos. 287, 289, 292. Sheets have red marginal inscriptions. Size: 140x82mm.

Soldiers with Flag A101

Designs: 40k, Fighters and burning house (horiz.). 300k, Anti-aircraft battery.

Perf. 12½x12, 12x12½

1978, Sept. Lithographed

293	A101	20k multicolored	5	5
294	"	40k "	10	10
295	"	300k "	85	85

Army Day.

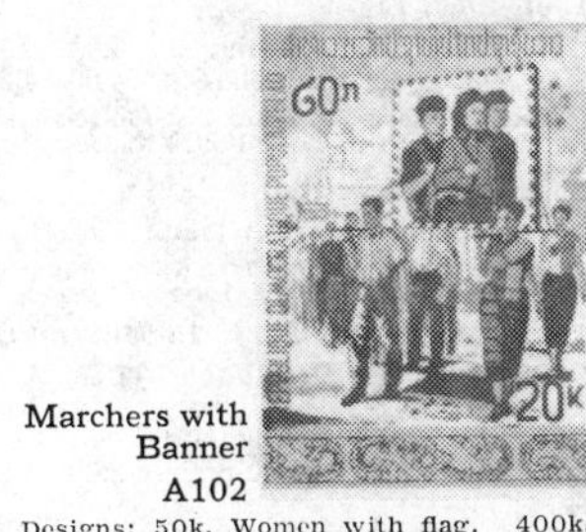

Marchers with Banner
A102

Designs: 50k, Women with flag. 400k, Dancer.

1978, Dec. Lithographed ***Perf. 11½***

296	A102	20k multicolored	5	5
297	"	50k "	15	15
298	"	400k "	1.20	1.20

National Day. A second printing in slightly different colors and with rough perforation exists.

Electronic Tree, Map of Laos, ITU Emblem
A103

Design: 250k, Electronic tree, map of Laos and broadcast tower.

1978 **Litho.** ***Perf. 12½***

299	A103	30k multicolored	12	12
300	"	250k "	1.00	1.00

World Telecommunications Day, 1978.

Woman Mailing Letter
A104

Designs: 10k, 80k, Processing mail. 100k, like 5k.

1978

301	A104	5k multicolored	3	3
302	"	10k "	4	4
303	"	80k "	32	32
304	"	100k "	40	40

Asian-Oceanic Postal Union, 15th anniversary.

Prices of premium quality never hinged stamps will be in excess of catalogue price.

A well-informed dealer has services to offer that would be helpful toward building your collection.

Use the **Yellow Pages** to fulfill your philatelic requirements.

A well-informed dealer has services to offer that would be helpful toward building your collection.

SEMI-POSTAL STAMPS

Laotian Children
SP1

Engraved.

1953 *Perf. 13.* Unwmkd.

Cross in Red.

B1 SP1 1.50pi+1pi indigo & violet brown 1.15 1.15
B2 " 3pi+1.50pi dark blue green & red 1.15 1.15
B3 " 3.90pi+2.50pi dark brown & violet brown 1.15 1.15

The surtax was for the Red Cross.

Nos. 52 and 46 Surcharged: "1k ANNEE MONDIALE DU REFUGIE 1959–1960."

1960

B4 A16 4k+1k rose claret 55 55
B5 A13 10k+1k multi. 55 55

Issued to publicize World Refugee Year, July 1, 1959–June 30, 1960. The surcharge was for aid to refugees.

Flooded Village
SP2

Designs: 40k+10k, Flooded market place and truck. 60k+15k, Flooded airport and plane.

1967, Jan. 18 Engraved *Perf. 13*

B6 SP2 20k+5k multi. 25 25
B7 " 40k+10k " 50 50
B8 " 60k+15k " 75 75
a. Miniature sheet of 3 2.75 2.75

The surtax was for victims of the Mekong Delta flood. No. B8a contains one each of Nos. B6–B8. Size: 148x99mm. Sold for 250k.

Women Working in Tobacco Field
SP3

1967, Oct. 5 Engraved *Perf. 13*

B9 SP3 20k+5k multi. 30 30
B10 " 50k+10k " 55 55
B11 " 60k+15k " 70 70
a. Souv. sheet of 3 3.00 3.00

Issued to commemorate the 10th anniversary of the Laotian Red Cross. No. B11a contains one each of Nos. B9–B11 with red marginal inscription. Size: 183x100mm. Sold for 250k+30k.

Nos. 184–189 Surcharged: "Soutien aux Victimes / de la Guerre / + 5k"

1970, May 1 Photo. *Perf. 14*

B12 A58 10k+5k multi. 20 15
B13 " 15k+5k " 20 15
B14 " 20k+5k " 25 20
B15 " 30k+5k " 30 25
B16 A58 40k+5k multi. 45 35
B17 " 60k+5k " 60 50
Nos. B12–B17, CB1–CB2 (8) 5.35 4.95

AIR POST STAMPS

Weaving—AP1

Design: 3.30pi, Wat Pra Keo.

Engraved.

1952, Apr. 13 *Perf. 13* Unwmkd.

C1 AP1 3.30pi dark purple & purple 85 40
C2 " 10pi ultramarine & blue green 1.65 1.00
C3 " 20pi deep claret & red 2.25 1.50
C4 " 30pi black brown & dark brown violet 3.25 2.50

See note following No. 17.

U. P. U. Monument and King Sisavang-Vong
AP2

1952, Dec. 1

C5 AP2 25pi violet blue & indigo 2.50 2.00
C6 " 50pi dark brown & violet brown 2.50 2.00

Issued to publicize Laos' admission to the Universal Postal Union, May 13, 1952.

AP3

AP4

Designs: Various Buddha statues.

1953, Nov. 18

C7 AP3 4pi dark green 25 15
C8 AP4 6.50pi dark blue green 32 25
C9 " 9pi blue green 50 32
C10 AP3 11.50pi red, yellow & dk. violet brown 55 35
C11 AP4 40pi purple 1.00 65
C12 " 100pi olive 3.00 2.25
Nos. C7–C12 (6) 5.62 3.97

Issued on the occasion of Great Oath of Laos ceremony.

Composite of Laotian Temples
AP5

1954, Mar. 4 Unwmkd.

C13 AP5 50pi indigo & blue green 75.00 75.00

Issued to commemorate the 50th anniversary of the accession of King Sisavang-Vong.

Ravana—AP6

Sita and Rama
AP7

Scenes from the Ramayana: 4k, Hanuman, the white monkey. 5k, Ninh Laphath, the black monkey. 20k, Lucy with a friend of Ravana. 30k, Rama.

1955, Oct. 28 Engr. *Perf. 13*

C14 AP6 2k blue green, emerald & indigo 60 55
C15 " 4k red brown, dark red brown & vermilion 80 65
C16 " 5k scarlet, sepia & olive 1.25 1.00
C17 AP7 10k black, orange & brown 2.25 1.85
C18 " 20k violet, dark green & olive 2.75 2.50
C19 " 30k ultramarine, black & salmon 3.50 3.50
Nos. C14–C19 (6) 11.15 10.05

Buddha Type of Regular Issue, 1956.

1956, May 24

C20 A7 20k carmine rose 18.50 15.00
C21 " 30k olive & olive bistre 18.50 15.00

2500th anniversary of birth of Buddha.

U. N. Emblem—AP8

1956, Dec. 14

C22 AP8 15k light blue 3.00 3.00
C23 " 30k deep claret 4.00 4.00

Issued to commemorate the first anniversary of the admission of Laos to the United Nations.

Types of Regular Issue, 1957.

Musical Instruments: 12k, Khong vong. 14k, So. 20k, Kong.

1957, March 25 *Perf. 13* Unwmkd.

C24 A9 12k multicolored 1.50 1.00
C25 A10 14k " 1.50 1.00
C26 " 20k bl. grn., yellow green & purple 2.00 1.50

Monk Receiving Alms
AP9

Monks Meditating in Boat—AP10

Designs: 18k, Smiling Buddha. 24k, Ancient temple painting (horse and mythological figures.)

1957, Nov. 5

C27 AP9 10k dark purple, pale brown & dark green 50 50
C28 AP10 15k dk. vio. brn., brown orange & yellow 50 50
C29 AP9 18k slate green & olive 80 70
C30 AP10 24k claret, orange yellow & black 1.20 1.00

No. C28 measures 48x27mm. No. C30, 48x36mm.

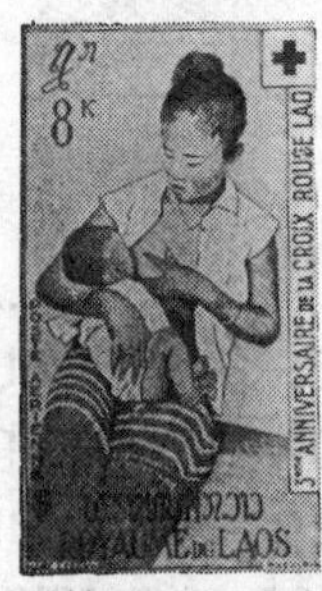

Mother Nursing Infant
AP11

1958, May 2

Cross in Red.

C31 AP11 8k lilac gray & dark gray 1.00 75
C32 " 12k red brown & brown 1.50 1.00
C33 " 15k slate green & bluish green 1.75 1.25
C34 " 20k bistre & violet 2.25 1.50

3rd anniversary of Laotian Red Cross.

Plain of Stones, Xieng Khouang
AP12

Papheng Falls, Champassak
AP13

Designs: 15k, Buffalo cart. 19k, Buddhist monk and village.

1960, July 1 Engraved *Perf. 13*

C35	AP12	9.50k blue, olive & claret	25	25
C36	AP13	12k violet blue, red brown & gray green	32	32
C37	"	15k yellow green, olive gray & claret	40	40
C38	AP12	19k multi.	50	50

Pou Gneu Nha Gneu Legend
AP14

Garuda
AP15

Hanuman, the White Monkey
AP16

Nang Teng One Legend
AP17

1962, Feb. 19 *Perf. 13* Unwmkd.

C39	AP14	11k green, carmine & ochre	30	30
C40	AP15	14k ultra. & orange	30	30
C41	AP16	20k multicolored	45	45
C42	AP17	25k "	45	45

Issued for the Magna Bousa festival.

Yao Hunter
AP18

Phayre's Flying Squirrel
AP19

People of Laos: 10k, Kha hunter. 50k, Meo woman.

1964, Dec. 15 Engraved *Perf. 13*

C43	AP18	5k yel. grn., slate, orange red & brown	12	8
C44	"	10k rose lilac, slate & red brown	15	15
C45	"	50k vio., red brown & olive bister	75	75
		a. Miniature sheet of 4	2.00	2.00

No. C45a contains one each of No. 100 and Nos. C43–C45. Size: 150x116mm. C45a exists imperf.

Butterfly Type of 1965

Design: 20k, Atlas moth.

1965, Mar. 13

Size: 48x27mm.

C46	A34	20k brown, bister & dark brown	75	60

1965, Oct. 7 Engraved *Perf. 13*

Designs: 25k, Leopard cat. 75k, Javan mongoose. 100k, Crestless porcupine. 200k, Binturong.

C47	AP19	25k dk. brown, yel. green & ocher	30	25
C48	"	55k brown & blue	60	40
C49	"	75k bright green & brown	80	50
C50	"	100k ocher, brown & black	1.00	80
C51	"	200k red & black	2.25	1.75
		Nos. C47–C51 (5)	4.95	3.70

Army Type of Regular Issue

Design: 200k, 300k, Parading service flags before National Assembly Hall.

1968, July 15 Engraved *Perf. 13*

C52	A53	200k multicolored	1.50	1.00
C53	"	300k "	2.25	1.50
		a. Souvenir sheet of 5	6.25	6.25

Issued to honor the Laotian Army. No. C53a contains one each of Nos. 168–170 and C52–C53. Blue marginal inscription. Size: 139x109mm. Sold for 600k.

Insect Type of Regular Issue

Insects: 120k, Dorysthenes walkeri (horiz.). 160k, Megaloxantha bicolor (horiz.).

1968, Aug. 28 Engraved *Perf. 13*

C54	A54	120k brown, orange & black	1.10	75
C55	"	160k rose carmine, Prus. blue & yellow	1.40	1.00

Ballet Type of Regular Issue

Designs: 110k, Sudagnu battling Thotsakan. 300k, Pharam dancing with Thotsakan.

1969 Photogravure *Perf. 14*

C56	A58	110k multicolored	75	65
		a. Souvenir sheet of 4	3.75	3.75
C57	A58	300k multicolored	2.50	2.00
		a. Souvenir sheet of 4	7.50	7.50

No. C56a contains imperf. stamps similar to Nos. 187–189 and C56. No. C57a contains imperf. stamps similar to Nos. 184–186, C57. Each has black marginal inscriptions and control number; size: 106x106mm. No. C56a sold for 480k; No. C57a for 650k.

Timber Industry, Paksane
AP20

1969, May 2 Engraved *Perf. 13*

C58	AP20	300fr olive bister & black	3.00	2.25

Issued to commemorate the 50th anniversary of the International Labor Organization.

Animal Type of Regular Issue

Animals: 70k, Asiatic black bear. 120k, White-handed gibbon (vert.). 150k, Tiger.

1969, Oct. 1 Photo. *Perf. 12x13*

C59	A60	70k multicolored	35	30
C60	"	120k "	60	55
C61	"	150k "	75	75

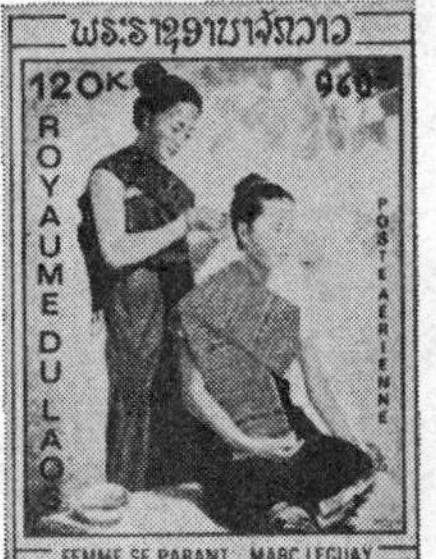

Hair-dressing, by Marc Leguay
AP21

Paintings: No. C63, Village Market, by Marc Leguay (horiz.). No. C64, Tree on the Bank of the Mekong, by Marc Leguay (horiz.).

1969–70 Photo. *Perf. 12x13, 13x12*

C62	AP21	120k multicolored	1.25	75
C63	"	150k "	1.75	1.10
C64	"	150k multi. ('70)	1.75	1.10

See Nos. C72–C74.

Wat Xiengthong, Luang Prabang
AP22

Design: 100k, Library, Wat Sisaket (vert.).

1970, Jan. 10 *Perf. 12x13, 13x12*

C65	AP22	100k multicolored	90	60
C66	"	120k "	1.10	80

Drum Type of 1970

Design: 125k, Pong wooden drum (vert.).

1970, Mar. 30 Engraved *Perf. 13*

C67	A64	125k ocher, brown & orange	2.25	1.50

Franklin D. Roosevelt
AP23

1970, Apr. 12

C68	AP23	120k olive & slate	1.10	90

Issued to commemorate the 25th anniversary of the death of Pres. Franklin D. Roosevelt (1882–1945).

EXPO '70 Type of Regular Issue

Design: 125k, Woman boiling cocoons in kettle, and spinning silk thread.

1970, July 7 Engraved *Perf. 13*

C69	A66	125k olive & multi.	85	85

See note after No. 202.

Animal Type of Regular Issue.

Designs: 210k, Leopard. 500k, Gaur.

1970, Sept. 7 Engraved *Perf. 13*

C70	A67	210k blk., olive gray & maroon	90	90
C71	"	500k ocher, greenish black & brn.	3.75	3.25

Painting Type of 1969–70

Paintings by Marc Leguay: 100k, Village Foot Path. 120k, Rice Field in Rainy Season (horiz.). 150k, Village Elder.

Perf. 11½x13, 13x11½

1970, Dec. 21 Photogravure

C72	AP21	100k multicolored	60	60
C73	"	120k "	70	70
C74	"	150k "	90	90

U.N. Type of Regular Issue

Design: 125k, Earth Goddess Nang Thorani wringing her hair; U.N. Headquarters and emblem.

1970, Oct. 24 Size: 26x36mm.

C75	A68	125k brt. blue, pink & dk. green	1.00	75

United Nations, 25th anniversary.

Hanuman and Nang Matsa—AP24

1971, Feb. 5

C76	AP24	125k multicolored	1.10	75

Orchid Type of Regular Issue

Design: 125k, Brasilian cattleya.

1971, July Photo. *Perf. 13x12½*

Size: 48x27mm.

C79	A73	125k gray bl. & multi.	70	65

Laotian and French Women, That Luang Pagoda and Arms
AP25

1971 Engraved *Perf. 13*

C80	AP25	30k brn. & dull red	30	30
C81	"	70k violet & lilac	70	70
C82	"	100k slate green & green	1.00	1.00

Kinship between the cities Keng Kok, Laos, and Saint Astier, France.

Animal Type of Regular Issue

Design: 300k, Javan rhinoceros.

1971, Sept.

C83	A74	300k brown & yellow green	1.00	75

Type of 1957 with Ornamental Panel and Inscription.

Design: 125k, Monk receiving alms (like No. C27).

1971, Nov. 2 Engraved *Perf. 13*

C84	AP9	125k dark purple, pale brown & dark green	75	75

20th anniversary of Laotian independent postal service. No. C84 inscribed: "Vingtième Anniversaire de la Philatélie Lao," "Poste Aerienne" and "1971."

Sunset Over the Mekong, by Chamnane Prisayane—AP26

Design: 150k, "Quiet Morning" (village scene), by Chamnane Prisayane.

1971, Dec. 20 Photo. *Perf. 13x12*

C85	AP26	125k blk. & multi.	40	40
C86	"	150k " "	50	50

Book Year Type of Regular Issue

Design: 125k, Father teaching children to read palm leaf book.

1972, Jan. 30 Engraved *Perf. 13*

Size: 48x27mm.

C87	A75	125k bright purple	75	75

International Book Year 1972.

Dam Type of Regular Issue

Design: 145k, Nam Ngum Hydroelectric Dam and ECAFE emblem.

1972, Mar. 28 Engraved *Perf. 13*

C88	A76	145k brn., blue & grn.	90	90

See note after No. 229.

Orchid Type of Regular Issue 1971

Design: 150k, Vanda teres (horiz.).

1972, May 5 Photo. *Perf. 13x12½*

Size: 48x27mm.

C89	A73	150k green & multi.	75	75

UNICEF Type of Regular Issue

Design: 120k, Boy riding buffalo to water hole (child's drawing).

1972, July Engraved *Perf. 13*

C90	A77	120k multicolored	70	70

See note after No. 234.

Nakharath, Daughter of the Dragon King
AP27

Wood carvings from Wat Sikhounvieng Dongmieng, Vientiane: 120k, Nang Kinnali, Goddess from Mt. Kailath. 150k, Norasing, Lion King from Himalayas.

1972, Sept. 15 Engraved *Perf. 13*

C91	AP27	100k blue green	30	30
C92	"	120k violet	35	35
C93	"	150k brown orange	45	45

Presentation of Wax Castles—AP28

Design: 125k, Procession.

1972, Nov. 18 Engr. *Perf. 13*

C94	AP28	110k orange brown	75	75
C95	"	125k dp. magenta	1.00	1.00

That Luang religious festival.

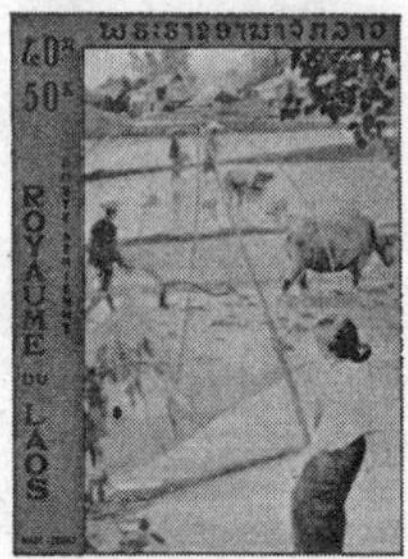

Workers in Rice Field, by Leguay
AP29

Paintings by Mark Leguay: No. C97, Women and water buffalo in rice field. 70k (Nos. C98–C99), Rainy Season in Village. 120k, Mother and Child.

1972, Dec. 23 Photo. *Perf. 13*

C96	AP29	50k multicolored	25	25
C97	"	50k "	25	25
C98	"	70k "	35	35
C99	"	70k "	35	35
C100	"	120k yellow & multi.	50	50
		Nos. C96–C100 (5)	1.70	1.70

Nos. C97, C99 have denomination and frame at right.

Costume Type of Regular Issue

Women's Costumes: 120k, Luang Prabang marriage costume. 150k, Vientiane evening costume.

1973, Feb. Engraved *Perf. 13*

C101	A78	120k multicolored	35	35
C102	"	150k brown & multi.	45	45

Lions Club Emblems, King Sayasettha-Thirath—AP30

1973, Mar. 30 Engraved *Perf. 13*

C103	AP30	150k rose & multi.	75	70

Lions Club of Vientiane.

Rahu with Rockets and Sputnik
AP31

Design: 150k, Laotian festival rocket and U.S. lunar excursion module.

1973, May 11 Engraved *Perf. 13*

C104	AP31	80k ultra. & multi.	50	25
C105	"	150k buff & ultra.	90	40

Space achievements.

Dancing Around Campfire—AP32

Design: 125k, Boy Scouts helping during Vientiane Flood, 1966.

1973, Sept. 1 Engraved *Perf. 13*

C106	AP32	110k vio. & orange	65	30
C107	"	125k Prus. green & bister	75	35

25th anniversary of Laotian Scout Movement.

Sun Chariot and WMO Emblem—AP33

Design: 90k, Nang Mékhala, the weather goddess, and WMO emblem (vert.).

1973, Oct. 24 Engraved *Perf. 13*

C108	AP33	90k violet, red & ocher	55	30
C109	"	150k ocher, red & brown olive	90	50

Centenary of international meteorological cooperation.

Woman in Poppy Field, INTERPOL Emblem—AP34

1973, Dec. 22 Engraved *Perf. 13*

C110	AP34	150k vio., yellow green & red	90	40

50th anniversary of International Criminal Police Organization.

Phra Sratsvady, Wife of Phra Phrom
AP35

Designs: 110k, Phra Indra on 3-headed elephant Erawan. 150k, Phra Phrom, the Creator, on phoenix. Designs show giant sculptures in park at Thadeua.

1974, Mar. 23 Engraved *Perf. 13*

C111	AP35	100k lilac, red & black	55	35
C112	"	110k carmine, vio. & brown	60	50
C113	"	150k ocher, violet & sepia	75	60

UPU Emblem, Women Reading Letter—AP36

1974 Engraved *Perf. 13*

C114	AP36	200k lt. brown & carmine	90	80
C115	"	500k lilac & red	2.00	1.60
	a.	Souvenir Sheet	6.50	6.50

Centenary of Universal Postal Union. No. C115a contains one No. C115; maroon decorative margin with control number. Size: 135x105mm.

Issue dates: 200k, Apr. 30; 500k, Oct. 9.

Flower Type of 1974

1974, May 31

Design: 500k, Pitcher plant.

Size: 36x36mm.

C116	A84	500k brn. orange & light green	1.40	1.25

Transportation Type of Regular Issue

Design: 250k, Sampan.

1974, July 31 Engraved *Perf. 13*

C117	A85	250k green & olive green	65	55

Marconi Type of 1974

Design: Old and new means of communications.

1974, Aug. 28 Engraved *Perf. 13*

C118	A86	200k vio. bl. & brn.	50	50

Birth centenary of Guglielmo Marconi (1874–1937), Italian electrical engineer and inventor.

Insect Type of 1974

Design: 110k, Sternocera multipunctata.

1974, Oct. 23 Engr. *Perf. 13*

C119	A87	110k grn. & multi.	45	35

AIR POST SEMI-POSTAL STAMPS

Nos. C56–C57 Surcharged: "Soutien aux Victimes / de la Guerre / + 5k"

1970, May 1 Photo. *Perf. 13*

CB1	A58	110k+5k multi.	1.10	1.10
CB2	"	300k+5k "	2.25	2.25

The surtax was for war victims.

POSTAGE DUE STAMPS.

Vat-Sisaket Monument
D1

Boat and Raft
D2

Engraved.

1952-53 *Perf. 13½x13.* Unwmkd.

J1	D1	10c dark brown	15	15
J2	"	20c purple	15	15
J3	"	50c carmine	10	10
J4	"	1pi dark green	15	15
J5	"	2pi deep ultramarine	15	15
J6	"	5pi rose violet	55	55
J7	D2	10pi indigo ('53)	70	70
		Nos. J1-J7 (7)	1.95	1.95

See note following No. 17.

Serpent
D3

1973, Oct. 31 Photo. *Perf. 13*

J8	D3	10k yellow & multi.	10	10
J9	"	15k emerald & multi.	10	10
J10	"	20k blue & multi.	10	10
J11	"	50k scarlet & multi.	15	15

LATAKIA

(lä'tä·kē'ä)

LOCATION—A division of Syria in Western Asia.

GOVT.—French Mandate.

AREA—2,500 sq. mi.

POP.—278,000 (approx. 1930).

CAPITAL—Latakia.

This territory, included in the Syrian Mandate to France under the Versailles Treaty, was formerly known as Alaouites. The name Latakia was adopted in 1930. See Alaouites and Syria.

100 Centimes = 1 Piastre

Stamps of Syria Overprinted in Black or Red

LATTAQUIE **LATTAQUIE**

or

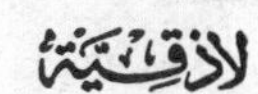

Perf. 12x12½, 13½.

1931-33 Unwmkd.

1	A6	10c red violet	20	20
2	"	10c violet brown ('33)	25	25
3	A7	20c dark blue (R)	20	20
4	"	20c brown orange ('33)	25	25
5	A8	25c gray green (R)	20	20
6	"	25c dark blue gray (R) ('33)	30	30
7	A9	50c violet	50	50
8	A15	75c orange red ('32)	50	50
9	A10	1p green (R)	50	50
10	A11	1.50p bis. brown (R)	85	85
11	"	1.50p deep green ('33)	1.25	1.25
12	A12	2p dark violet (R)	90	90
13	A13	3p yel. green (R)	1.40	1.40
14	A14	4p orange	1.40	1.40
15	A15	4.50p rose carmine	1.40	1.40
16	A16	6p greenish black (R)	1.40	1.40
17	A17	7.50p dull blue (R)	1.40	1.40
18	A18	10p deep brown (R)	2.00	2.00
19	A19	15p dp. green (R)	2.50	2.50
20	A20	25p violet brown	5.50	5.50
21	A21	50p dk. brn. (R)	4.00	4.00
22	A22	100p red orange	13.50	13.50
		Nos. 1-22 (22)	40.40	40.40

AIR POST STAMPS

Air Post Stamps of Syria, 1931, Overprinted in Black or Red

لاذقية

LATTAQUIE

1931-33 *Perf. 13½.* Unwmkd.

C1	AP2	50c ocher	30	30
		a. Inverted overprint	225.00	225.00
C2	"	50c black brown (R) ('33)	30	30
C3	"	1p chestnut brown	60	60
C4	"	2p Prus. blue (R)	1.00	1.00
C5	"	3p blue green (R)	1.20	1.20
C6	"	5p red violet	2.50	2.50
C7	"	10p slate green (R)	3.50	3.50
C8	"	15p orange red	4.50	4.50
C9	"	25p orange brown	5.00	5.00
C10	"	50p black (R)	10.00	10.00
C11	"	100p magenta	11.00	11.00
		Nos. C1-C11 (11)	39.90	39.90

POSTAGE DUE STAMPS.

Postage Due Stamps of Syria, 1931, Overprinted like Regular Issue.

1931 *Perf. 13½.* Unwmkd.

J1	D7	8p *gray blue* (R)	5.50	5.50
J2	D8	15p *dull rose* (R)	5.00	5.00

Stamps of Latakia were superseded in 1937 by those of Syria.

LATVIA

(lăt'vĭ·ȧ)

(Lettonia, Lettland)

LOCATION — In northern Europe, bordering on the Baltic Sea and the Gulf of Riga.

GOVT.—Former independent Republic.

AREA—25,395 sq. mi.

POP.—1,994,506 (estimated 1939).

CAPITAL—Riga.

Latvia was created a sovereign state following World War I and was admitted to the League of Nations in 1922. In 1940 it became a republic in the Union of Soviet Socialist Republics.

100 Kapeikas = 1 Rublis
100 Santims = 1 Lat (1923)

Arms
A1

Printed on the Backs of German Military Maps.

Lithographed.

1918, Dec. 18 *Imperf.* Unwmkd.

1	A1	5k carmine	30	30

Perf. 11½.

2	A1	5k carmine	30	30

Stamps from outer rows of the sheets sometimes have no printing on the back.

Redrawn.

Paper with Ruled Lines.

1919 *Imperf.*

3	A1	5k carmine	15	15
4	"	10k dark blue	20	20
5	"	15k green	25	20

Perf. 11½.

6	A1	5k carmine	75	75
7	"	10k dark blue	75	75
8	"	15k deep green	1.25	1.25
		Nos. 3-8 (6)	3.35	3.30

In the redrawn design the wheat heads are thicker, the ornament at lower left has five points instead of four, and there are minor changes in other parts of the design.

The sheets of this and subsequent issues were usually divided in half by a single line of perforation gauging 10. Thus stamps are found with this perforation on one side.

1919 Pelure Paper *Imperf.*

9	A1	3k lilac	3.00	3.00
10	"	5k carmine	10	10
11	"	10k deep blue	20	20
12	"	15k dark green	15	15
13	"	20k orange	15	15
13A	"	25k gray	12.50	12.50
14	"	35k dark brown	30	30
15	"	50k purple	25	25
16	"	75k emerald	3.00	3.00
		Nos. 9-16 (9)	19.65	19.65

Perf. 11½, 9½

17	A1	3k lilac	10.00	10.00
18	"	5k carmine	1.50	1.50
19	"	10k deep blue	2.00	2.00
20	"	15k dark green	2.00	2.00
21	"	20k orange	2.00	2.00
22	"	35k dark brown	3.50	3.50
23	"	50k purple	4.00	4.00
24	"	75k emerald	10.00	10.00
		Nos. 17-24 (8)	35.00	35.00

Nos. 17 to 24 are said to be unofficially perforated varieties of Nos. 9 to 16.

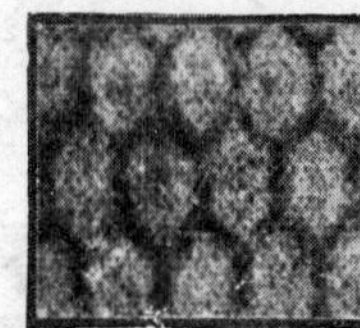

Wmk. 108

Wmkd. Honeycomb. (108)

1919 *Imperf.*

25	A1	3k lilac	6	6
26	"	5k carmine	6	6
27	"	10k deep blue	8	8
28	"	15k deep green	8	8
29	"	20k orange	20	20
30	"	25k gray	35	35
31	"	35k dark brown	25	25
32	"	50k purple	15	15
33	"	75k emerald	20	20
		Nos. 25-33 (9)	1.43	1.43

The variety "printed on both sides" exists for 3k, 10k, 15k, 20k and 35k. See also Nos. 57–58, 76–82.

Liberation of Riga
A2

Rising Sun
A4

1919 **Wmk. 108**

43	A2	5k carmine	25	18
44	"	15k deep green	25	18
45	"	35k brown	45	30

Unwmkd.

Pelure Paper

49	A2	5k carmine	12.50	10.00
50	"	15k deep green	10.00	10.00
51	"	35k brown	12.50	10.00

1919 *Imperf.*

55	A4	10k gray blue	25	25

Perf. 11½.

56	A4	10k gray blue	50	50

Type of 1918

1919 Laid Paper *Perf. 11½*

57	A1	3r slate & orange	1.25	65
58	"	5r gray brown & orange	1.15	50

Independence Issue.

Allegory of One Year of Independence
A5

Wove Paper

1919, Nov. 18 **Unwmkd.**

Size: 33x45 mm.

59	A5	10k brown & rose	75	75

Laid Paper.

60	A5	10k brown & rose	1.50	1.50

Size: 28x38 mm.

61	A5	10k brown & rose	25	25
		a. Imperf.		

62 A5 35k indigo & green 25 25
a. Vertical pair, imperf. between 25.00 25.00

There are two types of Nos. 59 and 60. In type I the trunk of the tree is not outlined. In type II it has a distinct white outline.

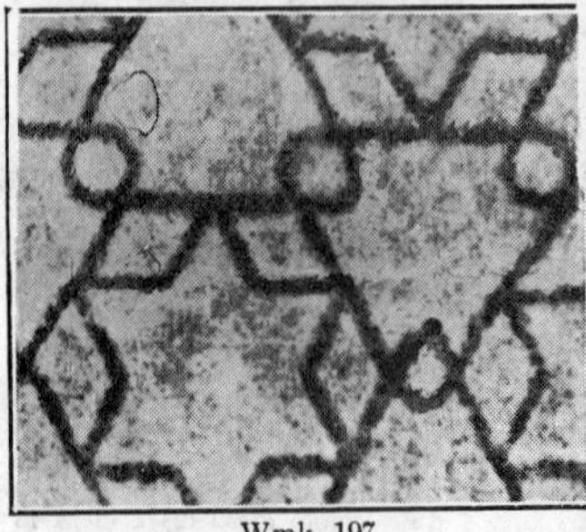

Wmk. 197

Thick Wove Paper.

Wmkd. Star and Triangles. (197)

Blue Design on Back.

63 A5 1r green & red 50 50
Nos. 59-63 (5) 3.25 3.25

No. 63 was printed on the backs of unfinished 5r bank notes of the Workers and Soldiers Council, Riga.

Warrior Slaying Dragon

A6

Wove Paper.

1919-20 ***Perf. 11½*** **Unwmkd.**

64 A6 10k brown & carmine 15 15
a. Horizontal pair, imperf. between 10.00 10.00

65 " 25k indigo & yellow green 25 25
a. Pair, imperf. between 25.00 25.00

66 " 35k black & blue ('20) 35 35
a. Horizontal pair, imperf. between 25.00 25.00

67 " 1r dark green & brown ('20) 75 75
a. Imperf. vert., pair 25.00 25.00
b. Horizontal pair, imperf. between 25.00 25.00

Issued in honor of the liberation of Kurzeme (Kurland). The paper sometimes shows impressed quadrille lines.

Latgale Relief Issue.

Latvia Welcoming Home Latgale Province

A7

1920, Mar.

Brown and Green Design on Back.

68 A7 50k dark green & rose 25 30
a. Imperf. vertically, pair 25.00

69 A7 1r slate green & brown 30 35
a. Imperf vert., pair 25.00

No. 68-69 were printed on the backs of unfinished bank notes of the government of Colonel Bermondt-Avalov and on the so-called German "Ober-Ost" money.

First National Assembly Issue.

Latvia Hears Call to Assemble

A8

1920

70 A8 50k rose 50 25
a. Imperf., pair 8.00 8.00

71 " 1r blue 50 15
a. Vertical pair, imperf. between 15.00 15.00
b. Imperf., pair 10.00 10.00

72 " 3r dark brown & green 1.00 65

73 " 5r slate & vio. brn. 1.25 75

Type of 1918 Issue.

Wove Paper.

1920-21 ***Perf. 11½.*** **Unwmkd.**

76 A1 5k carmine 12 12

78 " 20k orange 25 25

79 " 40k lilac ('21) 35 25

80 " 50k violet 35 30

81 " 75k emerald 35 20

82 " 5r gray brown & orange ('21) 1.25 40
Nos. 76-82 (6) 2.67 1.52

No. 63 Surcharged in Black, Brown or Blue

1920, Sept. 1

83 A5 10r on 1r green & red (Bk) 2.00 1.50

84 " 20r on 1r green & red (Br) 7.00 6.00

85 " 30r on 1r green & red (Bl) 9.00 7.50

Types of 1919 Surcharged

2
DIWI
RUBLI

1920-21 ***Perf. 11½*** **Wmk. 108**

86 A1 2r on 10k deep blue 2.00 1.50

87 A2 2r on 35k brown 1.00 90

No. 62 Surcharged in Red

DIWI
RUBLI
2

Unwmkd.

88 A5 2r on 35k indigo & green 1.00 90

No. 70 Surcharged in Blue

DIVI
2 RUB. 2

1921

90 A8 2r on 50k rose 75 75

A9

Red or Blue Surcharge.

1920-21

91 A9 1r on 35k black & blue (R) 75 50

92 " 2r on 10k brown & rose (Bl) 75 50

93 " 2r on 25k indigo & green (R) 1.00 75
a. Imperf.

On Nos. 92 and 93 the surcharge reads "DIVI 2 RUBLI."

No. 83 with Added Surcharge

Desmit
rubli.

1921 **Wmk. 197**

94 A5 10r on 10r on 1r green & red 2.00 2.00

Latgale Relief Issue of 1920 Surcharged in Black or Blue

1921, May 31 **Unwmkd.**

95 A7 10r on 50k grn. & rose 2.00 1.50
a. Imperf.

96 " 20r on 50k green & rose 7.50 5.00

97 " 30r on 50k green & rose 6.00 3.50

98 " 50r on 50k green & rose 10.00 7.50

99 " 100r on 50k green & rose (Bl) 20.00 17.50
Nos. 95-99 (5) 45.50 35.00

Excellent counterfeits exist.

Arms and Stars for Vidzeme, Kurzeme and Latgale

A10

Wmk. 181

Wmkd. Wavy Lines.

(Similar to 181)

Perf. 10, 11½ and Compound.

1921-22 Typographed

Type I, slanting cipher in value.
Type II, upright cipher in value.

101 A10 50k violet (II) 50 20

102 " 1r orange yellow 50 40

103 " 2r deep green 30 10

104 " 3r bright green 40 40

105 " 5r rose 1.25 10

106 " 6r deep claret 2.25 60

107 " 9r orange 1.50 50

108 " 10r blue (I) 1.50 10

109 A10 15r ultramarine 3.50 1.50
a. Printed on both sides 45.00

110 " 20r dull lilac (II) 15.00 3.00
Nos. 101-110 (10) 26.70 6.90

Nos. 101 to 131 sometimes show letters of a paper maker's watermark "PACTIEN LIGAT MILLS".

Coat of Arms

A11 A12

1922, Aug. 21 ***Perf. 11½***

111 A11 50r dark brown & pale brn. (I) 25.00 6.00

112 " 100r dark blue & pale blue (I) 27.50 5.00

1923-25 ***Perf. 10, 11, 11½.***

2 SANTIMS.

Type A, tail of "2" ends in an upstroke.
Type B, tail of "2" is nearly horizontal.

113 A12 1s violet 20 10

114 " 2s org. yellow (A) 30 12

115 " 4s dark green 75 10
a. Horizontal pair, imperf. between 25.00 22.50

116 " 5s lt. green ('25) 1.25 10

117 " 6s green, *yellow* ('25) 3.50 20

118 " 10s rose red (I) 1.00 10
a. Horizontal pair, imperf. between 25.00 22.50

119 " 12s claret 20 20

120 " 15s brown, *salmon* 3.00 10
a. Horizontal pair, imperf. between 17.50 15.00

121 " 20s deep blue (II) 1.50 5

122 " 25s ultramarine ('25) 30 10

123 " 30s pink (I) ('25) 3.50 20

124 " 40s lilac (I) 2.00 10

125 " 50s lilac gray (II) 3.50 12

126 A11 1 l dark brown & pale brown 10.00 35

127 " 2 l dk. blue & bl. 15.00 75

130 " 5 l deep green & pale green 50.00 5.00

131 " 10 l carmine rose & pale rose (I) 5.00 6.00
Nos. 113-131 (17) 101.00 13.69

Value in "Santims" (1s); "Santimi" (2s-6s) or "Santimu" (others).
See note after No. 110.

Stamps of 1920-21 Surcharged

15
SANTIMU

1927 ***Perf. 11½*** **Unwmkd.**

132 A1 15s on 40k lilac 75 50

133 " 15s on 50k violet 1.50 1.50

Stamp of 1920 Surcharged

134 A8 1 l on 3r brown & green 7.50 7.50

Wmk. 212

Types of 1923-25 Issue.

Wmkd. Multiple Swastikas. (212)

1927-33 *Perf. 10, 11½.*

No.	Type	Description	Unused	Used
135	A12	1s dull violet	30	5
136	"	2s orange yellow (A)	30	12
137	"	2s orange yellow (B) ('33)	20	5
138	"	3s orange red ('31)	30	5
139	"	4s dark green ('29)	2.50	1.50
140	"	5s light green ('31)	50	5
141	"	6s green, *yellow*	12	5
142	"	7s dark geen ('31)	50	20
143	"	10s red (I)	1.75	15
144	"	10s green, *yellow* (I) ('32)	7.50	5
145	"	15s brown, *salmon*	6.00	5
146	"	20s pink (I)	6.00	8
147	"	20s pink (II)	4.00	5
148	"	30s light blue (I)	2.50	10
149	"	35s dark blue ('31)	2.00	5
150	"	40s dull lilac (I) ('29)	2.00	8
151	"	50s gray (II)	3.00	8
152	A11	1 l dark brown & pale brown	8.00	25
153	"	2 l dark blue & blue ('31)	17.50	25
154	"	5 l green & pale green ('33)	90.00	15.00
		Nos. 135-154 (20)	154.97	18.26

The paper of Nos. 141, 144 and 145 is colored on the surface only.

See note above No. 113 for types A and B, and note above No. 101 for types I and II.

Type of 1927-33 Issue.

Paper Colored Through.

1931-33 *Perf. 10.*

No.	Type	Description	Unused	Used
155	A12	6s green, *yellow*	20	15
156	"	10s green, *yellow* (I) ('33)	17.50	5
157	"	15s brown, *salmon*	2.00	5

View of Rezekne

A13

Designs (Views of Cities): 15s, Jelgava. 20s, Cesis (Wenden). 30s, Liepaja (Libau). 50s, Riga. 1 l, Riga Theater.

Lithographed

1928, Nov. 18 *Perf. 10, 11½*

No.	Type	Description	Unused	Used
158	A13	6s dp. grn. & violet	75	25
159	"	15s dark brown & olive green	75	25
160	"	20s cerise & blue green	1.50	45
161	"	30s ultra. & vio. brn.	1.75	25
162	"	50s dark gray & plum	1.75	1.00
163	"	1 l black brown & brown	3.50	1.50
		Nos. 158-163 (6)	10.00	3.70

Issued in commemoration of the tenth anniversary of Latvian Independence.

Riga Exhibition Issue.

Stamps of 1927-33 Overprinted

Latvijas ražojumu izstāde Rīgā. 1932.g.10.–18.IX.

1932, Aug. 30 *Perf. 10, 11*

No.	Type	Description	Unused	Used
164	A12	3s orange	1.00	50
165	"	10s grn., *yellow* (I)	2.00	75
166	"	20s pink (I)	3.00	75
167	"	35s dark blue	4.00	1.25

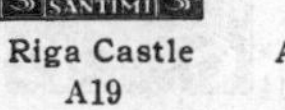

Riga Castle

A19

Arms and Shield

A20

Allegory of Latvia

A21

Ministry of Foreign Affairs

A22

1934, Dec. 15 Litho. *Perf. 10½, 10*

No.	Type	Description	Unused	Used
174	A19	3s red orange	10	10
175	A20	5s yellow green	25	12
176	"	10s gray green	2.25	10
177	A21	20s deep rose	2.25	10
178	A22	35s dark blue	30	30
179	A19	40s brown	20	20
		Nos. 174-179 (6)	5.35	92

Atis Kronvalds

A23

A. Pumpurs

A24

Juris Maters

A25

Mikus Krogzemis (Auseklis)

A26

1936, Jan. 4 *Perf. 11½* **Wmk. 212**

No.	Type	Description	Unused	Used
180	A23	3s vermilion	2.25	2.25
181	A24	10s green	2.25	2.25
182	A25	20s rose pink	2.25	2.25
183	A26	35s dark blue	2.25	2.25

President Karlis Ulmanis

A27

Lithographed

1937, Sept. 4 *Perf. 10, 11½*

No.	Type	Description	Unused	Used
184	A27	3s orange red & brown orange	25	25
185	"	5s yellow green	25	25
186	"	10s dark slate green	50	50
187	"	20s rose lake & brown lake	1.00	50
188	"	25s black violet	1.25	75
189	"	30s dark blue	1.25	75
190	"	35s indigo	1.25	75
191	"	40s light brown	1.50	1.00
192	"	50s olive black	1.75	1.25
		Nos. 184-192 (9)	9.00	6.00

60th birthday of President Ulmanis.

Independence Monument, Rauna (Ronneburg)

A28

Independence Monument, Jelgava

A30

Monument Entrance to Cemetery at Riga—A29

War Memorial, Valka

A31

Independence Monument, Iecava

A32

Independence Monument, Riga

A33

Tomb of Col. Kalpaks

A34

Lithographed.

1937, July 12 *Perf. 10* **Unwmkd.**

Thick Paper.

No.	Type	Description	Unused	Used
193	A28	3(s) vermilion	40	40
194	A29	5(s) yellow green	40	40
195	A30	10(s) deep green	40	40
196	A31	20(s) carmine	1.50	1.50
197	A32	30(s) light blue	2.00	2.00

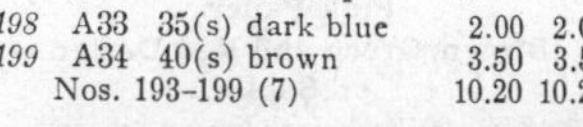

Perf. 11½ **Engraved** **Wmk. 212**

Thin Paper

No.	Type	Description	Unused	Used
198	A33	35(s) dark blue	2.00	2.00
199	A34	40(s) brown	3.50	3.50
		Nos. 193-199 (7)	10.20	10.20

View of Vidzeme

A35

View of Latgale

A36

General J. Balodis—A37

President Karlis Ulmanis

A38

Riga Waterfront

A39

View of Kurzeme

A40

View of Zemgale

A41

1938, Nov. 17 *Perf. 10, 10½x10*

No.	Type	Description	Unused	Used
200	A35	3(s) brown orange	12	5
		a. Booklet pane of 4	25.00	
201	A36	5(s) yellow green	12	10
		a. Booklet pane of 4	25.00	
202	A37	10(s) dark green	25	12
		a. Booklet pane of 2	25.00	
203	A38	20(s) red lilac	35	18
		a. Booklet pane of 2	15.00	
204	A39	30(s) deep blue	1.00	25
205	A40	35(s) indigo	1.00	25
		a. Booklet pane of 2	25.00	
206	A41	40(s) rose violet	1.00	30
		Nos. 200-206 (7)	3.84	1.25

The 20th anniversary of the Republic.

School, Riga—A42

Castle of Jelgava

A43

Riga Castle—A44

Independence Monument, Riga—A45

Symbol of Freedom

A46

Community House
Daugavpils—A47

Powder Tower and
War Museum, Riga
A48

President Karlis Ulmanis
A49

1939, May 13 Photo. *Perf. 10*

207	A42	3(s) brown orange	25	25
208	A43	5(s) deep green	25	25
209	A44	10(s) dk. slate green	1.25	1.00
210	A45	20(s) dk. car. rose	1.50	1.25
211	A46	30(s) bright ultra.	1.25	1.00
212	A47	35(s) dark blue	1.50	1.50
213	A48	40(s) brown violet	2.00	1.00
214	A49	50(s) greenish black	2.50	1.00
		Nos. 207-214 (8)	10.50	7.25

Issued in commemoration of the fifth anniversary of National Unity Day.

Harvesting Wheat A50 — Apple A51

1939, Oct. 8

215	A50	10(s) slate green	50	25
216	A51	20(s) rose lake	75	25

Issued in commemoration of the eighth Agricultural Exposition held near Riga.

Arms and Stars for
Vidzeme, Kurzeme and Latgale
A52

1940

217	A52	1(s) dk. vio. brown	25	25
218	"	2(s) ochre	25	25
219	"	3(s) red orange	5	10
220	"	5(s) dark olive brown	5	10
221	"	7(s) dark green	10	25
222	"	10(s) dk. blue green	1.00	15
224	"	20(s) rose brown	1.00	20
225	"	30(s) dp. red brown	1.25	40
226	"	35(s) bright ultra.	40	75
228	"	50(s) dk. slate green	1.35	50
229	"	1 l olive green	1.75	50
		Nos. 217-229 (11)	7.45	3.45

SEMI-POSTAL STAMPS

"Mercy" Assisting
Wounded Soldier
SP1

Typographed.

1920 *Perf. 11½.* Unwmkd.

Brown and Green Design on Back.

B1	SP1	20(30)k dark brown & red	35	50
B2	"	40(55)k dark blue & red	35	50
B3	"	50(70)k dark green & red	35	50
B4	"	1(1.30)r dark slate & red	35	50

Wmkd. Star and Triangles. (197)

Blue Design on Back.

B5	SP1	20(30)k dark brown & red	40	50
B6	"	40(55)k dark blue & red	40	50
		a. Vertical pair, imperf. between	25.00	
B7	"	50(70)k dark green & red	40	50
B8	"	1(1.30)r dark slate & red	50	60

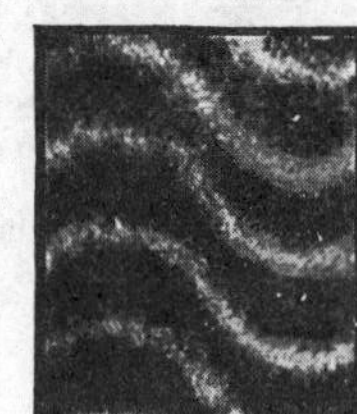

Wmk. 145

Wmkd.
Wavy Lines. (Similar to 145)
Imperf.

Pink Paper.

Brown, Green and Red Design on Back.

B9	SP1	20(30)k dark brown & red	50	75
B10	"	40(55)k dark blue & red	50	75
B11	"	50(70)k dark green & red	50	75
B12	"	1(1.30)r dark slate & red	1.00	1.25
		Nos. B1-B12 (12)	5.60	7.60

These semi-postal stamps were printed on the backs of unfinished bank notes of the Workers and Soldiers Council, Riga, and the Bermondt-Avalov Army.

Nos. B1–B8 Surcharged RUB. 2 RUB.

1921 *Perf. 11½.* Unwmkd.

Brown and Green Design on Back.

B13	SP1	20k+2r dark brown & red	1.75	2.50
B14	"	40k+2r dark blue & red	1.75	2.50
B15	"	50k+2r dark green & red	1.75	2.50
B16	"	1r+2r dark slate & red	1.75	2.50

Wmkd. Star and Triangles. (197)

Blue Design on Back.

B17	SP1	20k+2r dark brown & red	12.50	12.50
B18	"	40k+2r dark blue & red	12.50	12.50
B19	SP1	50k+2r dark green & red	12.50	12.50
B20	"	1r+2r dark slate & red	12.50	12.50
		Nos. B13-B20 (8)	57.00	60.00

Regular Issue of 1923–25 Surcharged in Blue

Wmkd. Wavy Lines. (Similar to 181)

1923 ***Perf. 10.***

B21	A12	1s+10s violet	35	50
B22	"	2s+10s yellow	35	50
B23	"	4s+10s dark green	35	50

The surtax benefited the Latvian War Invalids Society.

Lighthouse and Harbor, Liepaja
(Libau)
SP2

Church at Liepaja SP5 — Coat of Arms of Liepaja SP6

Designs: 15s (25s), City Hall, Liepaja. 25s, (35s), Public Bathing Pavilion, Liepaja.

1925, May 29 ***Perf. 11½***

B24	SP2	6s (12s) red brown & deep blue	1.00	1.50
B25	"	15s (25s) dark blue & brown	1.00	1.50
B26	"	25s (35s) violet & dark green	1.50	1.75
B27	SP5	30s (40s) dark blue & lake	5.00	6.00
B28	SP6	50s (60s) dark green & violet	6.50	8.00
		Nos. B24-B28 (5)	15.00	18.75

Tercentenary of Liepaja (Libau). The surtax benefited that city. Exist imperf.

President Janis Cakste
SP7

1928, Apr. 18 Engraved

B29	SP7	2s(12s) red orange	2.50	2.50
B30	"	6s(16s) deep green	2.50	2.50
B31	"	15s(25s) red brown	2.50	2.50
B32	"	25s(35s) deep blue	2.50	2.50
B33	"	30s(40s) claret	2.50	2.50
		Nos. B29-B33 (5)	12.50	12.50

The surtax helped erect a monument to Janis Cakste, first president of the Latvian Republic.

Venta River
SP8

Allegory, "Latvia"
SP9

View of Jelgava
SP10

National Theater, Riga
SP11

View of Cesis
(Wenden)
SP12

Riga Bridge and Trenches
SP13

Wmkd. Multiple Swastikas. (212)

Lithographed

1928, Nov. 18 ***Perf. 11½, Imperf.***

B34	SP8	6s(16s) green	3.00	3.00
B35	SP9	10s(20s) scarlet	3.00	3.00
B36	SP10	15s(25s) maroon	3.00	3.00
B37	SP11	30s(40s) ultra.	3.00	3.00
B38	SP12	50s(60s) dark gray	3.00	3.00
B39	SP13	1 l(1.10 l) choc.	3.00	3.00
		Nos. B34-B39 (6)	18.00	18.00

The surtax on Nos. B34 to B39 was given to a committee for the erection of a Liberty Memorial.

Z. A. Meierovics
SP14

1929, Aug. 22 *Perf. 11½ Imperf.*

B46	SP14	2s (4s) orange	2.50	2.50
B47	"	6s (12s) dp. green	2.50	2.50
B48	"	15s (25s) red brown	2.50	2.50
B49	"	25s (35s) deep blue	2.50	2.50
B50	"	30s (40s) ultra.	2.50	2.50
		Nos. B46-B50 (5)	12.50	12.50

The surtax was used to erect a monument to Z. A. Meierovics, Latvian statesman.

Tuberculosis Cross
SP15

Allegory of Hope for the Sick
SP16

Gustavs Zemgals
SP17

Riga Castle
SP18

Janis Cakste, First President of Latvia
SP19

Daisies and Double-barred Cross
SP20

President Alberts Kviesis
SP21

Tuberculosis Sanatorium, near Riga
SP22

Cakste, Kviesis and Zemgals
SP23

1930, Dec. 4 Typo. *Perf. 10, 11½*

B56	SP15	1s(2s) dark violet & red orange	50	50
B57	"	2s(4s) orange & red orange	50	50
		a. Cliché of 1s(2s) in plate of 2s(4s)	*300.00*	*400.00*
B58	SP16	4s(8s) dark green & red	1.00	1.00
B59	SP17	5s(10s) bright green & dk. brown	1.50	1.50
B60	SP18	6s(12s) olive green & bistre	1.25	1.25
B61	SP19	10s(20s) deep red & black	2.00	2.00
B62	SP20	15s(30s) maroon & dull green	1.75	1.75
B63	SP21	20s(40s) rose lake & indigo	2.25	2.25
B64	SP22	25s(50s) Prussian blue, dark violet & red	2.75	2.75
B65	SP23	30s(60s) ultramarine, dark violet & olive green	3.00	3.00
		Nos. B56-B65 (10)	16.50	16.50

The surtax was for the Latvian Anti-Tuberculosis Society.

J. Rainis and New Buildings, Riga—SP24

Character from Play and Rainis
SP25

Characters from Plays
SP26

Rainis and Lyre
SP27

Flames, Flag and Rainis
SP28

Perf. 11½

1930, May 23 **Wmk. 212**

B66	SP24	1s (2s) dull violet	70	70
B67	SP25	2s (4s) yellow orge.	70	70
B68	SP26	4s (8s) deep green	80	80
B69	SP27	6s (12s) yellow green & red brown	80	80
B70	SP28	10s (20s) dark red	10.00	12.50
B71	SP27	15s (30s) red brown & yel. grn.	10.00	12.50
		Nos. B66-B71 (6)	23.00	28.00

Sold at double face value, surtax going to memorial fund for J. Rainis (Jan Plieksans, 1865–1929), writer and politician.

Exist imperf. Price twice that of perf. stamps.

Nos. B56 to B65 Surcharged in Black

1931, Aug. 19 *Perf. 10, 11½*

B72	SP18	9s on 6s (12s) olive green & bistre	1.00	1.50
B73	SP15	16s on 1s (2s) dark violet & red orange	15.00	15.00
B74	"	17s on 2s (4s) org. & red orange	2.00	2.50
B75	SP16	19s on 4s (8s) dark green & red	5.00	6.00
B76	SP17	20s on 5s (10s) bright green & dark brown	3.00	4.00
B77	SP20	23s on 15s (30s) maroon & dull green	1.50	1.50
B78	SP19	25s on 10s (20s) dp. red & black	4.00	5.00
B79	SP21	35s on 20s (40s) rose lake & indigo	6.00	6.00
B80	SP22	45s on 25s (50s) Prussian blue, dk. & vio. red	17.50	20.00
B81	SP23	55s on 30s (60s) ultramarine, dark violet & olive green	17.50	20.00
		Nos. B72-B81 (10)	72.50	81.50

The surcharge replaces the original total price, including surtax.

Nos. B73 to B81 have no bars in the surcharge. The surtax aided the Latvian Anti-Tuberculosis Society.

Lacplesis, the Deliverer
SP29

Designs: 1s, Kriva telling stories under Holy Oak. 2s, Enslaved Latvians building Riga under knight's supervision. 4s, Death of Black Knight. 5s, Spirit of Lacplesis over freed Riga.

Inscribed: "AIZSARGI" (Army Reserve)

Perf. 10½, Imperf.

1932, Feb. 10

B82	SP29	1s (11s) violet brown & bluish	2.50	2.50
B83	"	2s (17s) ochre & olive green	2.50	2.50
B84	"	3s (23s) red brown & orange brown	2.50	2.50
B85	"	4s (34s) dark green & green	2.50	2.50
B86	"	5s (45s) green & emerald	2.50	2.50
		Nos. B82-B86 (5)	12.50	12.50

The surtax aided the Militia Maintenance Fund.

Marching Troops
SP30

Infantry in Action
SP31

Nurse Binding Soldier's Wound
SP32

Army Soup Kitchen
SP33

Gen. J. Balodis
SP34

1932, May *Perf. 10½, Imperf.*

B87	SP30	6s (25s) olive brn. & red violet	5.00	5.00
B88	SP31	7s (35s) dark blue green & dk. bl.	5.00	5.00
B89	SP32	10s (45s) olive grn. & black brown	5.00	5.00
B90	SP33	12s (55s) lake & olive green	5.00	5.00
B91	SP34	15s (75s) red orange & brown vio.	5.00	5.00
		Nos. B87-B91 (5)	25.00	25.00

The surtax aided the Latvian Home Guards.

Symbolical of Unified Latvia
SP35

Symbolical of the Strength of the Latvian Union
SP36

Aid to the Sick
SP37

"Charity"
SP38

Wmkd. Multiple Swastikas. (212)

1936, Dec. 28 Litho. *Perf. 11½*

B92	SP35	3s orange red	1.50	1.75
B93	SP36	10s green	1.50	1.75
B94	SP37	20s rose pink	1.50	1.75
B95	SP38	35s blue	1.50	1.75

Souvenir Sheets.

SP39

1938, May 12 Perf. 11 Wmk. 212

B96 SP39 Sheet of two 7.50 10.00
 a. 35(s) dark blue (*Justice Palace, Riga*) 2.00 2.50
 b. 40(s) chocolate (*Power Station, Kegums*) 2.00 2.50

Issued in sheets measuring 140x100 mm. Sold for 2 lats. The surtax of 1.25 l was for the National Reconstruction Fund.

Overprinted in Blue with Dates 1934 1939 and $\frac{15}{V}$

1939

B97 SP39 Sheet of two 8.50 11.00

Issued in commemoration of the fifth anniversary of National Unity Day. Sold for 2 lats. The surtax was for the National Reconstruction Fund.

AIR POST STAMPS

Blériot XI
AP1

Wmkd. Wavy Lines. (Similar to 181)
Lithographed

1921, July 30 Perf. 11½

C1 AP1 10r emerald 3.00 1.50
 a. Imperf. 10.00 10.00
C2 " 20r dark blue 3.00 1.50
 a. Imperf. 10.00 10.00

1928, May 1

C3 AP1 10s deep green 1.75 75
C4 " 15s red 1.75 75
C5 " 25s ultramarine 2.50 75
 a. Pair, imperf. between 40.00

Nos. C1 to C5 sometimes show letters of a paper maker's watermark "PACTIEN LIGAT MILLS".

Wmkd. Multiple Swastikas. (212)

1931-32 Perf. 11, 11½.

C6 AP1 10s deep green 2.00 75
C7 " 15s red 3.00 1.25
C8 " 25s deep blue ('32) 4.00 1.75

Type of 1921 Overprinted or Surcharged in Black

LATVIJA-AFRIKA
1933.

1933, May 26 Imperf. Wmk. 212

C9 AP1 10s deep green 7.50 7.50
C10 " 15s red 7.50 7.50
C11 " 25s deep blue 12.00 12.00
C12 " 50s on 15s red 90.00 90.00
C13 " 100s on 25s deep blue 90.00 90.00
 Nos. C9-C13 (5) 207.00 207.00

Issued to commemorate and finance a flight from Riga to Bathurst, Gambia. The plane crashed at Neustettin, Germany.
Counterfeits exist of Nos. C1-C13.

AIR POST SEMI-POSTAL STAMPS.

Durbes Castle, Rainis Birthplace
SPAP1

Perf. 11½

1930, May 26 Litho. Wmk. 212

CB1 SPAP1 10s (20s) red & olive green 7.50 10.00
 a. Imperf. 12.50 15.00
CB2 SPAP1 15s (30s) dark yellow green & copper red 7.50 10.00
 a. Imperf. 12.50 15.00

The surtax was for the Rainis Memorial Fund.

Nos. C6-C8 Surcharged in Magenta, Blue or Red

LATVIJAS AIZSARGI

1931, Dec. 5

CB3 AP1 10s+50s deep green (M) 9.00 10.00
 a. Imperf. 12.50 15.00
CB4 AP1 15s+1 l red (Bl) 9.00 10.00
 a. Imperf. 12.50 15.00
CB5 AP1 25s+1.50 l deep blue (R) 9.00 10.00
 a. Imperf. 12.50 15.00

The surtax was for the Latvian Home Guards.

SPAP2

1932, June 17 Perf. 10½

CB6 SPAP2 10s (20s) dark slate green & green 12.50 15.00
 a. Imperf. 15.00 17.50
CB7 " 15s (30s) bright red & buff 12.50 15.00
 a. Imperf. 15.00 17.50
CB8 " 25s (50s) deep blue & gray 12.50 15.00
 a. Imperf. 15.00 17.50

The surtax was for the Latvian Home Guards.

Icarus
SPAP3

Leonardo da Vinci
SPAP4

Wright Brothers Biplane
SPAP6

Bleriot Monoplane
SPAP7

Charles Balloon
SPAP5

1932, Dec. Perf. 10, 11½

CB9 SPAP3 5s (25s) olive bis. & green 12.50 15.00
 a. Imperf. 15.00 17.50
CB10 SPAP4 10s (50s) olive brown & gray green 12.50 15.00
 a. Imperf. 15.00 17.50
CB11 SPAP5 15s (75s) red brown & gray green 12.50 15.00
 a. Imperf. 15.00 17.50
CB12 SPAP6 20s (1 l) gray green & lilac rose 12.50 15.00
 a. Imperf. 15.00 17.50
CB13 SPAP7 25s (1.25 l) brown & blue 12.50 15.00
 a. Imperf. 15.00 17.50
 Nos. CB9-CB13 (5) 62.50 75.00
 Nos. CB9a-CB13a (5) 75.00 87.50

Issued to honor pioneers of aviation. The surtax of four times the face value was for wounded Latvian aviators.

Icarus Falling
SPAP8

Monument to Aviators
SPAP9

Proposed Tombs for Aviators
SPAP10 SPAP11

1933, Mar. 15 Perf. 11½

CB14 SPAP8 2s (52s) black & ochre 7.50 10.00
 a. Imperf. 8.50 11.00
CB15 SPAP9 3s (53s) black & red orange 7.50 10.00
 a. Imperf. 8.50 11.00
CB16 SPAP10 10s (60s) black & dark yellow green 7.50 10.00
 a. Imperf. 8.50 11.00
CB17 SPAP11 20s (70s) black & cerise 7.50 10.00
 a. Imperf. 8.50 11.00

The 50s surtax was for wounded Latvian aviators.

Monoplane Taking Off
SPAP12

Designs: 7 (57), Biplane under fire at Riga. 35 (1.35 l), Map and planes.

1933, June 15 Perf. 11½ Wmk. 212

CB18 SPAP12 3s (53s) orange & slate blue 12.50 15.00
 a. Imperf. 15.00 17.50
CB19 " 7s (57s) slate blue & dark brown 12.50 15.00
 a. Imperf. 15.00 17.50
CB20 " 35s (1.35 l) deep ultramarine & olive black 12.50 15.00
 a. Imperf. 15.00 17.50

The surtax was for wounded Latvian aviators.

American Gee-Bee
SPAP13

English Seaplane S6B
SPAP14

Graf Zeppelin over Riga
SPAP15

DO-X
SPAP16

1933, Sept. 5 Perf. 11½

CB21 SPAP13 8s (68s) brn. & gray blk. 25.00 30.00
 a. Imperf. 27.50 32.50
CB22 SPAP14 12s (1.12 l) brown carmine & olive grn. 25.00 30.00
 a. Imperf. 27.50 32.50
CB23 SPAP15 30s (1.30 l) blue & gray black 25.00 30.00
 a. Imperf. 27.50 32.50
CB24 SPAP16 40s (1.90 l) brown violet & indigo 25.00 30.00
 a. Imperf. 27.50 32.50

The surtax was for wounded Latvian aviators.

OCCUPATION STAMPS.
Issued under German Occupation.

German Stamps of 1905-18 Handstamped

LIBAU

1919 Perf. 14, 14½ Wmk. 125

Red Overprint.

1N1 A22 2½pf gray 350.00 350.00
1N2 A16 5pf green 200.00 90.00
1N3 A22 15pf dark violet 300.00 75.00
1N4 A16 20pf blue violet 110.00 35.00
1N5 " 25pf orge. & blk., *yellow* 300.00 210.00
1N6 " 50pf pur. & blk., *buff* 300.00 210.00

Blue Overprint.

1N7 A22 2½pf gray 350.00 350.00
1N8 A16 5pf green 110.00 45.00
1N9 " 10pf carmine 90.00 25.00
1N10 A22 15pf dark violet 250.00 150.00
1N11 A16 20pf blue violet 125.00 55.00
1N12 " 25pf orge. & blk., *yellow* 350.00 300.00
1N13 " 50pf purple & blk., *buff* 350.00 300.00

Inverted and double overprints exist, as well as counterfeit overprints.

Some experts believe that Nos. 1N1-1N7 were not officially issued. All used copies are cancelled to order.

LATVIJA
1941
1. VII

Russia Nos. 734, 616, 735, 617, 736 and 619A were overprinted in black or dark green with the three lines above in 1941. They were used in Latvia under the German occupation in July-September, 1941, and were replaced by German stamps in October, 1941.

Kurland

Four stamps of Germany were surcharged for use in Kurzeme in April, 1945, during World War II. Those are Germany Nos. 509, 511A and 516 (5pf, 10pf, 20pf with Hitler's head), surcharged "KURLAND" and "6", and No. MQ1 (red brown military parcel post stamp) surcharged "Kurland" and "12". After the Germans capitulated to the Russians May 8, 1945, in the territory of Latvia, these surcharged stamps were replaced by stamps of Russia.

Issued under Russian Occupation.

The following stamps were issued at Mitau during the occupation of Kurland by the West Russian Army under Colonel Bermondt-Avalov.

Stamps of Latvia Handstamped

Wmkd. Honeycomb. (108)

1919 ***Imperf.***

On Stamps of 1919.

2N1 A1 3k lilac 10.00 12.50
2N2 " 5k carmine 10.00 12.50
2N3 " 10k deep blue 70.00 75.00
2N4 " 20k orange 10.00 12.50
2N5 " 25k gray 10.00 12.50
2N6 " 35k dark brown 10.00 12.50
2N7 " 50k purple 10.00 12.50
2N8 " 75k emerald 16.50 20.00

On Riga Liberation Stamps.

2N9 A2 5k carmine 7.25 9.00
2N10 " 15k deep green 7.25 9.00
2N11 " 35k brown 8.75 9.00

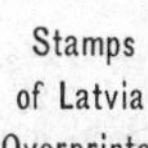
Stamps of Latvia Overprinted

On Stamps of 1919.

2N12 A1 3k lilac 4.00 5.00
2N13 " 5k carmine 4.00 5.00
2N14 " 10k deep blue 70.00 75.00
2N15 " 20k orange 8.00 9.00
2N16 " 25k gray 20.00 25.00
2N17 " 35k dark brown 12.00 13.50
2N18 " 50k purple 12.00 13.50
2N19 " 75k emerald 12.00 13.50

On Riga Liberation Stamps.

2N20 A2 5k carmine 4.00 5.00
2N21 " 15k deep green 4.00 5.00
2N22 " 35k brown 4.00 5.00
a. Inverted overprint 75.00

The letters "Z. A." are the initials of "Zapadnaya Armiya"—i.e. Western Army.

Russian Stamps of 1909-17 Surcharged Like Illustration

On Stamps of 1909-12. Unwmkd.

Perf. 14, 14½x15.

2N23 A14 10k on 2k green 1.25 1.50
a. Inverted surcharge 25.00
2N24 A15 30k on 4k carmine 2.00 2.25
2N25 A14 40k on 5k claret 1.60 1.75
2N26 A15 50k on 10k dk. blue 1.60 1.75
2N27 A9 70k on 15k red brown & blue 1.60 1.75
a. Invtd. surch. 50.00
2N28 A6 90k on 20k blue & carmine 2.50 2.75
2N29 A9 1r on 25k green & violet 2.50 2.75
2N30 " 1½r on 35k red brown & green 16.50 20.00
2N31 A6 2r on 50k violet & green 3.00 3.50
a. Invtd. surch. 40.00
2N32 A9 4r on 70k brown & orange 8.00 9.00

Perf. 13½

2N33 A7 6r on 1r pale brown, brown & orange 10.00 12.50

On Stamps of 1917.

Imperf.

2N34 A14 20k on 3k red 1.50 1.75
2N35 " 40k on 5k claret 25.00 27.50
2N36 A10 10r on 3½r maroon & lt. green 25.00 27.50
a. Inverted surch. 80.00
Nos. 2N1-2N36 (36) 425.80 487.75

Eight typographed stamps of this design were prepared in 1919, but never placed in use. They exist both perforated and imperforate.

Arms of Soviet Latvia
OS1

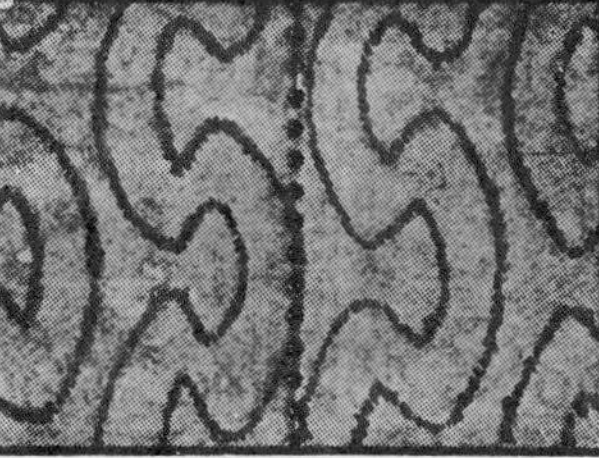

Wmk. 265

Wmkd. Multiple Waves. (265)

1940 Typographed ***Perf. 10***

2N45 OS1 1s dark violet 25 25
2N46 " 2s orange yellow 25 20
2N47 " 3s orange vermilion 5 10
2N48 " 5s dark olive green 5 5
2N49 " 7s turquoise green 10 15
2N50 " 10s slate green 75 15
2N51 " 20s brown lake 1.25 25
2N52 " 30s light blue 1.50 50
2N53 OS1 35s bright ultra. 5 10
2N54 " 40s chocolate 1.00 25
2N55 " 50s light gray 1.25 25
2N56 " 1 l light brown 2.50 50
2N57 " 5 l bright green 15.00 7.50
Nos. 2N45-2N57 (13) 24.00 10.25

LEBANON

(lĕb'ȧ-nŭn)

(Grand Liban)

LOCATION—In Asia Minor, bordering on the Mediterranean Sea.
GOVT.—Republic.
AREA—4,015 sq. mi.
POP.—3,060,000 (est. 1977).
CAPITAL—Beirut.

Formerly a part of the Syrian Province of Turkey, Lebanon was occupied by French forces after World War I. It was mandated to France after it had been declared a separate state. Limited autonomy was granted in 1927 and full independence achieved in 1941. The French issued two sets of occupation stamps (with "T.E.O." overprint) for Lebanon in late 1919. The use of these and later occupation issues (of 1920-24, with overprints "O.M.F." and "Syrie-Grand Liban") was extended to Syria, Cilicia, Alaouites and Alexandretta. By custom, these are all listed under Syria.

100 Centimes = 1 Piastre

Issued under French Mandate.

Stamps of France 1900-21 Surcharged

GRAND
LIBAN
50
CENTIEMES

1924 ***Perf. 14x13½.*** **Unwmkd.**

1 A16 10c on 2c violet brn. 40 40
a. Inverted surch. 8.00 8.00
2 A22 25c on 5c orange 40 20
3 " 50c on 10c green 30 20
4 A20 75c on 15c slate green 90 70
5 A22 1pi on 20c red brown 50 30
a. Double surch. 8.00 8.00
b. Invtd. surch. 8.00 8.00
6 " 1.25pi on 25c blue 1.20 75
7 " 1.50pi on 30c orange 70 45
8 " 1.50pi on 30c red 70 45
9 A20 2.50pi on 50c dull blue 70 40
a. Inverted surch. 9.00 9.00

Surcharged

GRAND LIBAN
2 PIASTRES

10 A18 2pi on 40c red & pale blue 1.20 1.00
a. Inverted surch. 9.00 9.00
11 " 3pi on 60c violet & ultramarine 3.00 2.75
12 " 5pi on 1fr claret & olive green 3.00 2.75
13 " 10pi on 2fr orange & pale blue 4.50 3.00
a. Inverted surch. 15.00 15.00
14 " 25pi on 5fr dark blue & buff 6.50 5.50
a. Inverted surch. 30.00 30.00
Nos. 1-14 (14) 24.00 18.85

Broken and missing letters and varieties of spacing are numerous in these surcharges.

Stamps of France, 1923, (Pasteur) Surcharged "GRAND LIBAN" and New Values.

15 A23 50c on 10c green 40 30
a. Invtd. surch. 9.00 9.00
16 " 1.50pi on 30c red 60 40
17 " 2.50pi on 50c blue 40 30
a. Invtd. surch. 9.00 9.00

Commemorative Stamps of France, 1924, (Olympic Games) Surcharged "GRAND LIBAN" and New Values.

18 A24 50c on 10c gray green & yellow green 12.00 12.00
a. Inverted surcharge 100.00
19 A25 1.25pi on 25c rose & dark rose 12.00 12.00
a. Inverted surcharge 100.00
20 A26 1.50pi on 30c brown red & black 12.00 12.00
a. Inverted surcharge 100.00
21 A27 2.50pi on 50c ultramarine & dark blue 12.00 12.00
a. Invtd. surch. 100.00

Stamps of France, 1900-24, Surcharged

G^d Liban
0, P. 25
لبنان الكبير
١/٤ القرش
c

1924-25

22 A16 0p10 on 2c vio. brn. 10 10
23 A22 0p25 on 5c orange 30 30
24 " 0p50 on 10c green 40 40
25 A20 0p75 on 15c gray green 30 30
26 A22 1pi on 20c red brn. 20 20
27 " 1p25 on 25c blue 50 50
28 " 1p50 on 30c red 40 40
29 " 1p50 on 30c org. 20.00 18.00
30 " 2pi on 35c violet ('25) 40 40
31 A20 3pi on 60c light violet ('25) 60 60
32 " 4pi on 85c verm. 60 60

Surcharged

Grand Liban
2 Piastres
لبنان الكبير
غرش ٢

33 A18 2pi on 40c red & pale blue 20 20
a. Second line of Arabic reads "2 Piastre" (singular) 70 50
34 " 2pi on 45c green & blue ('25) 6.00 6.00
35 " 3pi on 60c violet & ultramarine 60 60
36 " 5pi on 1fr claret & olive green 1.10 1.00
37 " 10pi on 2fr orange & pale blue 2.50 2.50
38 " 25pi on 5fr dark blue & buff 3.00 3.00
Nos. 22-38 (17) 37.20 35.10

Last line of surcharge on No. 33 has four characters, with a 9-like character between the third and fourth in illustration. Last line on No. 33a is as illustrated.

The surcharge may be found inverted on most of Nos. 22-38, and double on some values.

Stamps of France 1923-24 (Pasteur) Surcharged Type "c"

39 A23 0p50 on 10c green 20 10
a. Invtd. surch. 7.00 7.00
b. Double surcharge 5.00 5.00
40 " 0p75 on 15c green 50 50
41 " 1p50 on 30c red 50 45
a. Invtd. surch. 7.00 7.00
42 " 2pi on 45c red 70 60
a. Invtd. surch. 7.00 7.00
43 " 2p50 on 50c blue 25 15
a. Invtd. surch. 7.00 7.00
b. Double surch. 7.00 7.00
44 " 4pi on 75c blue 75 60
Nos. 39-44 (6) 2.90 2.40

France Nos. 198 to 201 (Olympics) Surcharged Type "c"

45 A24 0p50 on 10c gray grn. & yel. green 12.00 12.00

46 A25 1p25 on 25c rose & dark rose 12.00 12.00
47 A26 1p50 on 30c brown red & black 12.00 12.00
48 A27 2p50 on 50c ultra. & dk. blue 12.00 12.00

France No. 219 (Ronsard) Surcharged Type "c"

49 A28 4pi on 75c blue, *bluish* 60 60
a. Inverted surch. 13.50 13.50

Cedar of Lebanon
A1

Crusader Castle, Tripoli
A3

View of Beirut—A2

Designs: 50c, Crusader Castle, Tripoli. 75c, Beit-ed-Din Palace. 1p, Temple of Jupiter, Baalbek. 1.25p, Mouktara Palace. 1.50p, Harbor of Tyre. 2p, View of Zahle. 2.50p, Ruins at Baalbek. 3p, Square at Deir-el-Kamar. 5p, Castle at Sidon. 25p, Square at Beirut.

1925 Litho. *Perf. 12½, 13½*

50 A1 0p10 dark violet 8 6

Photogravure.

51 A2 0p25 olive black 15 13
52 " 0p50 yellow green 8 7
53 " 0p75 brown orange 15 12
54 " 1pi magenta 50 50
55 " 1p 25 deep green 60 50
56 " 1p 50 rose red 15 10
57 " 2pi dark brown 40 10
58 " 2p 50 peacock blue 60 40
59 " 3pi orange brown 60 40
60 " 5pi violet 70 60
61 A3 10pi violet brown 1.00 1.00
62 A2 25pi ultramarine 4.00 4.00
Nos. 50-62 (13) 9.01 7.98

Stamps of 1925 Surcharged

3P·50 ٣غ ١/٢

and Bars.

1926

63 A2 3p50 on 0p75 brn. org. 20 20
64 " 4pi on 0p25 olive blk. 60 60
65 " 6pi on 2p50 peacock blue 30 30
66 " 12pi on 1p25 dp. green 30 30
67 " 20pi on 1p25 dp. green 1.50 1.50

Stamps of 1925 Surcharged

4P·50 ٤غ ١/٢

and Bars

68 A2 4p50 on 0p75 brn. org. 60 60
69 " 7p50 on 2p50 peacock blue 60 60
70 " 15pi on 25pi ultramarine 60 60
Nos. 63-70 (8) 4.70 4.70

No. 51 Surcharged

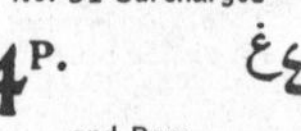

and Bars.

1927

71 A2 4pi on 0p 25 olive black 60 60

Issues of Republic under French Mandate

Stamps of 1925 Issue Overprinted in Black or Red

République Libanaise

1927

72 A1 0p10 dark violet (R) 5 5
a. Black overprint 8.00 8.00
73 A2 0p50 yellow green 6 6
74 " 1pi magenta 6 6
75 " 1p50 rose red 20 18
76 " 2pi dark brown 40 20
77 " 3pi orange brown 25 15
78 " 5pi violet 60 40
79 A3 10pi violet brown 65 35
80 A2 25pi ultramarine 3.25 2.00
Nos. 72-80 (9) 5.52 3.45

On Nos. 72 and 79 the overprint is set in two lines. On all stamps the double bar obliterates GRAND LIBAN.

Same Overprint on Provisional Issues of 1926-27.
15 PIASTRES ON 25 PIASTRES.

TYPE I. "République Libanaise" at foot of stamp.
TYPE II. "République Libanaise" near top of stamp.

81 A2 4pi on 0p25 olive black 20 8
82 " 4p50 on 0p75 brn. org. 20 18
83 " 7p50 on 2p50 peacock blue 20 15
84 " 15pi on 25pi ultramarine (Type I) 3.00 2.25
a. Type II 3.00 3.00

Most of Nos. 72–84 are known with overprint double, inverted or on back as well as face.

Stamps of 1927 Overprinted in Black or Red

الجمهورية اللبنانية

1928

86 A1 0p10 dark violet (R) 15 15
a. French overprint omitted 5.00 5.00
87 A2 0p50 yellow green (Bk) 50 50
a. Arabic overprint inverted 3.00 3.00
88 " 1pi magenta (Bk) 15 15
a. Invtd. ovpt. 6.00 6.00
89 " 1p50 rose red (Bk) 60 60
90 " 2pi dark brown (R) 1.00 1.00
90A " 2pi dark brown (Bk+R) 12.50 12.50
91 " 3pi org. brn. (Bk) 45 45
92 " 5pi violet (Bk+R) 1.20 1.20
93 " 5pi violet (R) 1.40 1.40
a. French ovpt. above Arabic 1.00 1.00
94 A3 10pi vio. brown (Bk) 1.20 1.20
a. Double overprint 5.00 5.00
b. Double overprint inverted
c. Invtd. overprint 6.00 6.00
95 A2 25pi ultra. (Bk+R) 3.25 3.25
95A " 25pi ultramarine (R) 6.00 4.75
Nos. 86-95A (12) 28.40 27.15

On all stamps the double bar with Arabic overprint obliterates Arabic inscription.

Same Overprint on Nos. 81–84

96 A2 4pi on 0p25 olive black (Bk+R) 45 45
97 " 4p50 on 0p75 brown orange (Bk) 70 70
98 " 7p50 on 2p50 peacock blue (Bk+R) 1.80 1.80
99 " 7p50 on 2p50 peacock blue (R) 1.20 1.20
100 " 15pi on 25pi ultramarine (II) (Bk+R) 3.50 3.00
a. Arabic overprint inverted
101 " 15pi on 25pi ultramarine (I) (R) 6.00 5.00
Nos. 96-101 (6) 13.65 12.15

The new values are surcharged in black. The initials in () refer to the colors of the overprints.

Stamps of 1925 Surcharged in Red or Black

Republique Libanaise
4P. ٤غ
الجمهورية اللبنانية

1928-29 *Perf. 13½.*

102 A2 0p50 on 0p75 brown orange (Bk) ('29) 30 30
103 " 2pi on 1p25 deep green 30 30
104 " 4pi on 0p25 olive black 32 32
a. Double surcharge 5.00 5.00
105 " 7p50 on 2p50 peacock blue 40 40
a. Double surcharge 5.00 5.00
b. Inverted surcharge 5.00 5.00
106 " 15pi on 25pi ultra. 3.75 3.75
Nos. 102-106 (5) 5.07 5.07

On Nos. 103, 104 and 105 the surcharged numerals are 3½mm. high, and have thick strokes.

No. 86 Surcharged in Red **05** ٠٥

1928

107 A1 (0p)05 on 0p10 dark violet 8 8

Silkworm, Cocoon and Moth
A4

1930, Feb. 11 Typo. *Perf. 11*

108 A4 4pi black brown 5.00 5.00
109 " 4½pi vermilion 4.50 4.50
110 " 7½pi dark blue 4.50 4.50
111 " 10pi dark violet 4.50 4.50
112 " 15pi dark green 4.50 4.50
113 " 25pi claret 4.50 4.50
Nos. 108-113 (6) 27.50 27.50

Sericultural Congress, Beirut.
Presentation imperfs. exist.

Pigeon Rocks, Ras Beirut
A5

View of Bickfaya—A8

Beit-ed-Din Palace
A10

Crusader Castle, Tripoli
A11

Ruins of Venus Temple, Baalbek
A12

Ancient Bridge, Dog River
A13

Belfort Castle—A14

Afka Falls—A19

Designs: 0p20, Cedars of Lebanon. 0p25, Ruins of Bacchus Temple, Baalbek. 1pi, Crusader Castle, Sidon Harbor. 5pi, Arcade of Beit-ed-Din Palace. 6pi, Tyre Harbor. 7.50pi, Ruins of Sun Temple, Baalbek. 10pi, View of Hasbeya. 25pi, Government House, Beirut. 50pi, View of Deir-el-Kamar. 0p75, 100pi, Ruins at Baalbek.

1930–35 Litho. *Perf. 12½, 13½*

114 A5 0p10 brown orange 6 6
115 " 0p20 yellow brown 7 7
116 " 0p25 deep blue 6 6

Photogravure.

117 A8 0p50 orange brown 40 30
118 A11 0p75 olive brown ('32) 15 15
119 A8 1pi deep green 30 20
120 " 1pi brn. violet ('35) 30 20
121 A10 1.50pi violet brown 50 40
122 " 1.50pi dp. green ('32) 20 20
123 A11 2pi Prussian blue 80 30
124 A12 3pi black brown 80 20
125 A13 4pi orange brown 80 10
126 A14 4p50 carmine 80 40
127 " 5pi greenish black 40 20
128 A13 6pi brown violet 60 60
129 A10 7.50pi deep blue 80 20
130 " 10pi dk. olive grn. 1.40 20
131 A19 15pi black violet 1.85 40
132 " 25pi blue green 2.75 40
133 A8 50pi apple green 10.00 3.50
134 A11 100pi black 10.00 5.00
Nos. 114-134 (21) 33.04 13.14

See also Nos. 135, 144, 152–155.

Pigeon Rocks Type of 1930–35
Redrawn.

1934 Lithographed. *Perf 12½x12.*

135 A5 0p10 dull orange 1.25 1.00

Lines in rocks and water more distinct. Printer's name "Hélio Vaugirard, Paris," in larger letters.

Cedar of Lebanon
A23

President Emile Eddé
A24

Dog River Panorama
A25

1937-40 Typo. *Perf. 14x13½*

137 A23 0p10 rose carmine 6 6
137A " 0p20 aqua. ('40) 10 10
137B " 0p25 pale rose lilac ('40) 10 10
138 " 0p50 magenta 7 7
138A " 0p75 brown ('40) 15 15

Engraved

Perf. 13

139 A24 3pi dark violet 40 25
140 " 4pi black brown 15 8
141 " 4p50 carmine 20 12
142 A25 10pi brown carmine 35 20
142A " 12½pi deep ultramarine ('40) 20 18
143 " 15pi dk. grn. ('38) 30 15
143A " 20pi chestnut ('40) 25 20
143B " 25pi crimson ('40) 35 30
143C " 50pi dk. vio. ('40) 90 80
143D " 100pi sepia ('40) 1.25 1.00
Nos. 137-143D (15) 4.83 3.76

Nos. 137A, 137B, 138A, 142A, 143A, 143B, 143C, and 143D exist imperforate.

View of Bickfaya
A26

Type A8 Redrawn.

1937 Photogravure. *Perf. 13½*

144 A26 0p50 orange brown 2.50 1.65

Arabic inscriptions more condensed.

Stamps of 1930-37 Surcharged in Black or Red

1937-42 *Perf. 13, 13½.*

145 A24 2pi on 3pi dk. violet 20 20
146 " 2½pi on 4pi black brown 20 20
146A " 2½pi on 4pi black brown (R) ('42) 50 50
147 A10 6pi on 7.50pi deep blue (R) 75 75

Stamps of 1930-35 and Type of 1937-40 Surcharged in Black or Red

7.50

Perf. 13½, 13.

148 A8 7.50pi on 50pi apple green 65 65
149 A11 7.50pi on 100pi black (R) 60 60
150 A25 12.50pi on 7.50pi dark blue (R) 1.25 1.25

Type of 1937-40 Surcharged in Red

12½

1939 Engraved *Perf. 13*

151 A25 12½pi on 7.50pi dark blue 15 15
Nos. 145-151 (8) 4.30 4.30

Type of 1930-35 Redrawn

Imprint: "Beiteddine-Imp.-Catholique-Beyrouth-Liban."

1939 Lithographed. *Perf. 11½.*

152 A10 1pi dark slate green 40 10
153 " 1.50pi brown violet 40 35
154 " 7.50pi carmine lake 40 35

Bridge Type of 1930-35

Imprint: "Degorce" instead of "Hélio Vaugirard".

1940 Engraved *Perf. 13*

155 A13 5pi greenish blue 12 8

Exists imperforate.

Independent Republic

Amir Beshir Shehab—A27

1942, Sept. 18 Litho. *Perf. 11½*

156 A27 0p50 emerald 1.20 1.20
157 " 1.50pi sepia 1.20 1.20
158 " 6pi rose pink 1.20 1.20
159 " 15pi dull blue 1.20 1.20

Issued to commemorate the first anniversary of the Proclamation of Independence, November 26, 1941.

Nos. 156 to 159 exist imperforate.

Nos. 140, 154 and 142A Surcharged in Blue, Green or Black

1943 *Perf. 13, 11½.*

160 A24 2pi on 4pi black brown (Bl) 2.25 1.85
161 A10 6pi on 7.50pi carmine lake (G) 20 15
162 A25 10pi on 12½pi deep ultramarine (Bk) 20 15

The surcharge is arranged differently on each value.

Parliament Building
A28

Government House, Beirut
A29

1943 Lithographed *Perf. 11½*

163 A28 25pi salmon rose 5.50 5.50
164 A29 50pi bluish green 5.50 5.50
165 A28 150pi light ultra. 5.50 5.50
166 A29 200pi dull vio. brn. 5.50 5.50

Second anniversary of Proclamation of Independence. Nos. 163-166 exist imperforate. See Nos. C82-C87.

Quarantine Station, Beirut—A30

1943, July 8 Photogravure

Black Overprint

167 A30 10pi cerise 2.25 2.25
168 " 20pi light blue 2.25 2.25
Nos. 167-168, C88-C90 (5) 9.50 9.50

Arab Medical Congress, Beirut.

Nos. 163 to 166 Overprinted in Blue, Violet, Red or Black

1944

169 A28 25pi salmon rose (Bl) 7.50 7.50
170 A29 50pi bluish green (V) 7.50 7.50
171 A28 150pi lt. ultra. (R) 7.50 7.50
172 A29 200pi dull violet brown (Bk) 7.50 7.50
Nos. 169-172, C91-C96 (10) 98.50 98.50

Issued to commemorate the return to office of the president and his ministers, November 22, 1943.

Type of 1930 and No. 142A Surcharged in Violet, Black or Carmine

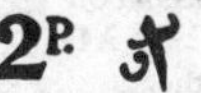

Engraved.

1945 *Perf. 13.* Unwmkd.

173 A13 2pi on 5pi dark blue green (V) 20 15
174 " 3pi on 5pi dark blue green (Bk) 20 15
175 A25 6pi on 12½pi deep ultramarine (Bk) 40 30
176 " 7½pi on 12½pi deep ultramarine (C) 45 40

The trees are at the bottom on Nos. 175 and 176.

Citadel of Jubayl (Byblos)
A31

Crusader Castle, Tripoli—A32

1945 Lithographed *Perf. 11½*

177 A31 15pi violet brown 1.60 1.25
178 " 20pi deep green 1.60 1.25
179 A32 25pi deep blue 1.60 1.25
180 " 50pi deep carmine 2.25 1.25

See also Nos. 229-233.

Soldiers and Flag of Lebanon
A33

1946 Lithographed

Stripes of Flag in Red Orange.

181 A33 7.50pi red & pale lilac 75 15
182 " 10pi lilac & pale lilac 1.00 15
183 " 12.50pi chocolate & yellow green 1.25 15
184 " 15pi sepia & pink 2.25 15
185 " 20pi ultra. & pink 2.00 20
186 " 25pi dark green & yellow grn. 3.00 50
187 " 50pi dark blue & pale blue 4.50 1.25
188 " 100pi gray black & pale blue 7.00 3.50
Nos. 181-188 (8) 21.75 6.05

Type of 1946 Overprinted in Red

V

1946, May 8

Stripes of Flag in Red.

189 A33 7.50pi chocolate & pink 75 15
190 " 10pi dk. vio. & pink 1.00 15
191 " 12.50pi brown red & pale lilac 1.25 20
192 " 15pi light green & yel. green 1.35 25
193 " 20pi slate green & yel. green 2.00 20
194 " 25pi slate blue & pale blue 3.00 50
195 " 50pi ultra. & gray 4.50 1.25
196 " 100pi black & pale blue 7.00 3.50
Nos. 189-196 (8) 20.85 6.20

See Nos. C101-C106 and note after No. C106.

Cedar of Lebanon
A34

Night Herons over Mt. Sanin
A35

1946-47 *Perf. 10½* Unwmkd.

197 A34 50c red brn. ('47) 8 5
198 " 1pi purple ('47) 12 5
199 " 2.50pi violet 20 8
200 " 5pi red 40 10
201 " 6pi gray ('47) 50 12

Perf. 11½.

202 A35 12.50pi dp. carmine 3.00 15
Nos. 197-202 (6) 4.30 55

Cedar of Lebanon
A36

Crusader Castle, Tripoli
A37

1947 Litho. *Perf. 14x13½*

203 A36 50c dark brown 40 10
204 " 2.50pi bright green 75 10
205 " 5pi carmine rose 1.00 15

Perf. 11½

206 A37 12.50pi rose pink 2.75 15
207 " 25pi ultramarine 3.25 25
208 " 50pi turq. green 10.00 55
209 " 100pi violet 17.50 3.75
Nos. 203-209 (7) 35.65 5.05

Cedar
A38

Zebaide Aqueduct
A39

1948 *Perf. 14x13½*

210 A38 50c blue 10 5
211 " 1pi yellow brown 20 6
212 " 2.50pi rose violet 40 6
213 " 3pi emerald 75 6
214 " 5pi crimson 1.00 8

Perf. 11½.

215 A39 7.50pi rose red 1.50 10
216 " 10pi dull violet 2.00 10
217 " 12.50pi blue 3.00 20
218 " 25pi blue violet 5.00 60
219 " 50pi green 10.00 3.25
Nos. 210-219 (10) 23.95 4.56

See also Nos. 227A-228A, 234-237.

Europa A40 — Avicenna A41

1948 **Lithographed**

220 A40 10pi dark red & orange red 2.00 1.75
221 " 12.50pi purple & rose 2.00 1.75
222 " 25pi olive green & pale green 2.50 1.75
223 A41 30pi orange brown & buff 3.50 2.25
224 " 40pi Prussian green & buff 5.00 2.25
Nos. 220–224 (5) 15.00 9.75

Issued to honor the United Nations Educational, Scientific and Cultural Organization.

Nos. 220 to 224 exist imperforate (see note after No. C145).

Camel Post Rider A42

1949, Aug. 16 *Perf. 11½* **Unwmkd.**

225 A42 5pi violet 80 50
226 " 7.50pi red 1.40 90
227 " 12.50pi blue 1.75 1.40
Nos. 225–227, C148–C149 (5) 13.95 7.80

Issued to commemorate the 75th anniversary of the formation of the Universal Postal Union.

See note after No. C149.

Cedar Type of 1948 Redrawn and Jubayl Type of 1945

1949 **Litho.** *Perf. 14x13½*

227A A38 50c blue 15 5
228 " 1pi red orange 35 10
228A " 2.50pi rose lilac 3.50 55

Perf. 11½

229 A31 7.50pi rose red 1.00 10
230 " 10pi violet brown 2.00 15
231 " 12.50pi deep blue 4.00 15
232 " 25pi violet 8.00 40
233 " 50pi green 14.00 2.50
Nos. 227A–233 (8) 33.00 4.00

On No. 227A in left numeral tablet, top of "P" stands higher than flag of the 1¼mm. high "5." On No. 210, tops of "P" and the 2mm. "5" are on same line.

On No. 228, "1 P." is smaller than on No. 211, and has no line below "P."

On No. 228A, the "O" does not touch tablet frame; on No. 212, it does. No. 228A exists on gray paper.

Cedar Type of 1948 Redrawn and

Ancient Bridge across Dog River A43

1950 **Lithographed** *Perf. 14x13½*

234 A38 50c rose red 20 5
235 " 1pi salmon 30 5
236 " 2.50pi violet 50 5
237 " 5pi claret 1.00 6

Cedar slightly altered and mountains eliminated.

Perf. 11½

238 A43 7.50pi rose red 1.00 10
239 " 10pi rose violet 1.50 10
240 " 12.50pi light blue 2.00 15
241 " 25pi deep blue 5.00 75
242 " 50pi emerald 10.00 3.75
Nos. 234–242 (9) 21.50 5.06

See Nos. 251–255, 310–312.

Flags and Building A44

1950, Aug. 8 *Perf. 11½*

243 A44 7.50pi gray 40 10
244 " 12.50pi lilac rose 40 15
Nos. 243–244, C150–C153 (6) 4.85 2.65

Issued to publicize the Conference of Emigrants, 1950. See note after C153.

Nos. 213 and 201 Surcharged with New Value and Bars in Carmine.

1950 *Perf. 14x13½, 10½* **Unwmkd.**

245 A38 1pi on 3pi emerald 25 5
246 A34 2.50pi on 6pi gray 25 5

Cedar of Lebanon A45

1951 **Litho.** *Perf. 14x13½*

247 A45 50c rose red 15 5
248 " 1pi light brown 25 5
249 " 2.50pi slate gray 1.40 8
250 " 5pi rose lake 1.25 10

Bridge Type of 1950, Redrawn.
Typographed *Perf. 11½*

251 A43 7.50pi red 1.40 18
252 " 10pi dull rose vio. 2.00 15
253 " 12.50pi blue 3.50 30
254 " 25pi dull blue 5.00 60
255 " 50pi green 10.00 5.50
Nos. 247–255 (9) 24.95 7.01

Nos. 238-242 are lithographed from a fine-screen halftone; "P" in the denomination has serifs. Nos. 251-255 are typographed and much coarser; "P" without serifs.

Cedar of Lebanon A46 — Ruins at Baalbek A47

Design: 50pi, 100pi, Beaufort Castle.

1952 **Lithographed** *Perf. 14x13½*

256 A46 50c emerald 40 10
257 " 1pi orange brown 40 10
258 " 2.50pi greenish blue 60 15
259 " 5pi carmine rose 80 25

Perf. 11½

260 A47 7.50pi red 1.00 40
261 " 10pi bright violet 2.00 50
262 " 12.50pi blue 2.00 50
263 " 25pi violet blue 3.25 1.00
264 " 50pi dark blue grn. 6.50 1.50
265 " 100pi chocolate 15.00 5.50
Nos. 256–265 (10) 31.95 10.00

Cedar of Lebanon A48 — Postal Administration Building A49

1953 *Perf. 14x13½*

266 A48 50c blue 40 5
267 " 1pi rose lake 40 5
268 A48 2.50pi lilac 60 15
269 " 5pi emerald 1.00 20

Perf. 11½

270 A49 7.50pi carmine rose 1.60 35
271 " 10pi dp. yel. green 2.00 50
272 " 12.50pi aquamarine 3.00 60
273 " 25pi ultramarine 4.00 85
274 " 50pi violet brown 7.00 2.00
Nos. 266–274 (9) 20.00 4.75

See also No. 306.

Cedar ot Lebanon A50 — Gallery, Beit-ed-Din Palace A51

1954 *Perf. 14x13½*

275 A50 50c blue 10 10
276 " 1pi deep orange 20 10
277 " 2.50pi purple 40 20
278 " 5pi blue green 60 20

Perf. 11½

279 A51 7.50pi deep carmine 1.25 40
280 " 10pi dull olive grn 2.00 40
281 " 12.50pi blue 3.00 60
282 " 25pi violet blue 5.00 1.00
283 " 50pi aquamarine 7.50 2.50
284 " 100pi black brown 15.00 4.50
Nos. 275–284 (10) 35.05 10.00

Arab Postal Union Issue

Globe A52

1955, Jan. 1 **Litho.** *Perf. 13½x13*

285 A52 12.50pi blue green 30 20
286 " 25pi violet 40 20

Issued to commemorate the founding of the Arab Postal Union, July 1, 1954. See No. C197.

Cedar of Lebanon A53 — Jeita Cave A54

1955 *Perf. 14x13½*

287 A53 50c violet blue 10 4
288 " 1pi vermilion 15 4
289 " 2.50pi purple 30 4
290 " 5pi emerald 50 4

Perf. 11½

291 A54 7.50pi deep orange 65 5
292 " 10pi yellow green 1.10 6
293 " 12.50pi blue 1.00 5
294 " 25pi dp. violet blue 2.75 15
295 " 50pi dark gray grn. 3.50 35
Nos. 287–295 (9) 10.05 82

See also Nos. 308–309, 315–318, 341–343A.

Cedar of Lebanon A55 — Globe and Columns A56

1955 *Perf. 13x13½* **Unwmkd.**

296 A55 50c dark blue 10 4
297 " 1pi deep orange 15 4
298 " 2.50pi deep violet 20 4
299 " 5pi green 25 5
300 A56 7.50pi yellow orange & copper red 40 6
301 " 10pi emerald & sal. 50 5
302 " 12.50pi ultramarine & blue green 60 8
303 " 25pi deep ultramarine & brt. pink 1.00 15
304 " 50pi dark green & light blue 1.40 27
305 " 100pi dk. brn. & sal. 2.40 65
Nos. 296–305 (10) 7.00 1.43

Cedar Type of 1953 Redrawn.

1956 **Litho.** *Perf. 13x13½*

306 A48 2.50pi violet 1.25 10

No. 306 measures 17x20½mm. The "2p.50" is in Roman numerals.

Cedar Type of 1955 Redrawn and Bridge Type of 1950, Second Redrawing

1957 **Lithographed** *Perf. 13x13½*

308 A53 50c lt. ultramarine 10 4
309 " 2.50pi claret 30 5

Perf. 11½

310 A43 7.50pi vermilion 60 6
311 " 10pi brn. orange 1.00 5
312 " 12.50pi blue 1.00 6
Nos. 308–312 (5) 3.00 26

On Nos. 308 and 309 numerals are slanted and clouds slightly changed.

Nos. 310–312 inscribed "Liban" instead of "Republique Libanaise," and different Arabic characters.

Runners A57

Design: 12.50pi, Soccer players.

1957, Sept. 12 **Litho.** *Perf. 13*

313 A57 2.50pi dark brown 30 20
314 " 12.50pi bluish black 50 25

Second Pan-Arab Games, Beirut. See Nos. C243–C244.

A souvenir sheet of four contains one each of Nos. 313–314, C243–C244.

Cedar Type of 1955 Redrawn and

Workers A58 — Ancient Potter A59

1957 *Perf. 13x13½* **Unwmkd.**

315 A53 50c light blue 10 4
316 " 1p light brown 10 4
317 " 2.50p bright violet 20 4
318 " 5p light green 30 5

Perf. 11½, 13½x13 (A59)

319 A58 7.50p crimson rose 40 5
320 " 10p dull red brown 60 5
321 " 12.50p bright blue 70 5
322 A59 25p dull blue 1.10 12
323 " 50p yellow green 1.50 20
324 " 100p sepia 3.00 60
Nos. 315-324 (10) 8.00 1.24

The word "piaster" is omitted on No. 315; on Nos. 316 and 318 there is a line below "P"; on No. 317 there is a period between "2" and "50."

Nos. 315-318 are 16mm. wide and have three shading lines above tip of cedar. See No. 343A and footnote.

Cedar of Lebanon
A60

Soldier and Flag
A61

1958 Lithographed. *Perf. 13*

325 A60 50c blue 15 5
326 " 1p dull orange 20 5
327 " 2.50p violet 25 4
328 " 5p yellow green 30 4
329 A61 12.50p bright blue 50 10
330 " 25p dark blue 60 10
331 " 50p orange brown 1.00 20
332 " 100p black brown 2.00 40
Nos. 325-332 (8) 5.00 98

مؤتمر المحامين العرب
من ١ الى ٥ ايلول ١٩٥٩

No. 304 Surcharged

30P. ٣٠ق

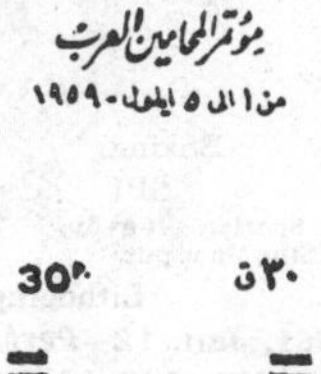

1959, Sept. 1

333 A56 30p on 50p dark green & light blue 50 40

Arab Lawyers Congress. See No. C265.

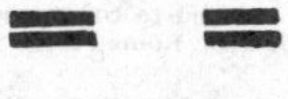

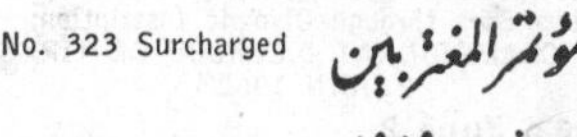

No. 323 Surcharged

مؤتمر المغتربين
صيف - ١٩٥٩

30P. ٣٠ق

1959 *Perf. 13½x13*

334 A59 30p on 50p yel. grn. 40 15
335 " 40p on 50p yel. grn. 50 20

Issued to welcome the convention of the Association of Arab Emigrants in the United States.

Nos. 329-330 and 323 Surcharged with New Value and Bars.

1959 *Perf. 13, 13½x13*

336 A61 7.50p on 12.50p bright blue 15 6
337 " 10p on 12.50p brt. bl. 20 6
338 " 15p on 25p dk. blue 25 8
339 A59 40p on 50p yel. grn. 60 27
Nos. 336-339, C271 (5) 2.70 87

Arab League Center, Cairo
A62

Lithographed.

1960 *Perf. 13x13½* **Unwmkd.**

340 A62 15p light blue green 40 30

Issued to commemorate the opening of the Arab League Center and the Arab Postal Museum in Cairo.

Cedar Type of 1955, Second Redrawing.

1960 Lithographed *Perf. 13x13½*

341 A53 50c light violet 15 5
342 " 1p rose claret 15 5
343 " 2.50p ultramarine 20 5
343A " 5p light green 30 7

Nos. 341-343A are 16½-17mm. wide and have two shading lines above cedar. In other details they resemble the redrawn A53 type of 1957 (Nos. 315-318).

President Fuad Chehab
A63 A64

1960 Photogravure *Perf. 13½*

344 A63 50c deep green 10 4
345 " 2.50p olive 10 5
346 " 5p green 10 5
347 " 7.50p rose brown 20 6
348 " 15p bright blue 30 15
349 " 50p lilac 70 18
350 " 100p brown 1.25 35
Nos. 344-350 (7) 2.75 88

Nos. 343A and 340 Overprinted in Red

1960, Nov. Litho. *Perf. 13x13½*

351 A53 5p light green 15 10
352 A62 15p light blue green 30 20

Arabian Oil Conference, Beirut.

1961, Feb. Litho. *Perf. 13½x13*

353 A64 2.50p blue & light blue 8 5
354 " 7.50p dark violet & pink 12 5
355 " 10p red brn. & yel. 20 6

Cedar
A65

Post Office, Beirut
A66

Lithographed

1961 *Perf. 13* **Unwmkd.**

356 A65 2.50p green 25 4

Redrawn

357 A65 2.50p orange 20 12
358 " 5p maroon 20 12
359 " 10p black 25 12

Nos. 357-359 have no clouds.

Perf. 11½

361 A66 2.50p rose carmine 20 12
362 " 5p bright green 25 12
363 " 15p dark blue 40 21
Nos. 356-363 (7) 1.75 85

Cedars
A67

Design: 10p, 15p, 50p, 100p, View of Zahle.

1961 Lithographed *Perf. 13*

365 A67 50c yellow green 5 6
366 " 1p brown 5 6
367 " 2.50p ultramarine 5 4
368 " 5p carmine 15 4
369 " 7.50p violet 20 4
370 " 10p dark brown 35 5
371 " 15p dark blue 45 10
372 " 50p dark green 80 20
373 " 100p black 1.40 55
Nos. 365-373 (9) 3.50 1.14

See also Nos. 381-384.

Unknown Soldier Monument
A68

Design: 15p, Soldier and flag.

1961, Dec. 30 *Perf. 12* **Unwmkd.**

374 A68 10p yel., black & red 15 8
375 " 15p multicolored 20 12

Issued to commemorate the anniversary of Lebanon's independence and the evacuation of foreign troops, Dec. 31, 1946. See also Nos. C329-C330.

Bugler
A69

Scout Carrying Flag and Scout Emblem—A70

Designs: 2.50p, First aid. 6p, Lord Baden-Powell. 10p, Scouts building campfire.

1962, Mar. 1 Lithographed *Perf. 12*

376 A69 50c yellow green, black & yel. 10 5
377 A70 1p multicolored 10 5
378 " 2.50p dark red, black & green 10 5
379 A69 6p multicolored 20 5
380 A70 10p deep blue, black & yellow 25 10
Nos. 376-380, C331-C333 (8) 1.95 90

50th anniversary of Lebanese Boy Scouts.

Type of 1961 Redrawn.

Designs as Before.

1962 *Perf. 13* **Unwmkd.**

381 A67 50c yellow green 15 5
382 " 1p brown 15 5
383 " 2.50p ultramarine 20 5
384 " 15p dark blue 2.00 15
Nos. 381-384, C341-C342 (6) 6.35 91

Temple of Nefertari, Abu Simbel
A71

Cherries
A72

1962, Aug. 1 *Perf. 13* **Unwmkd.**

390 A71 5p light ultra. 30 10
391 " 15p brown lake & maroon 40 20

Campaign to save the historic monuments in Nubia. See Nos. C351-C352.

1962 Lithographed

Designs: 50c, 2.50p, 7.50p, Cherries. 1p, 5p, Figs. 10p, 17.50p, 30p, Grapes. 50p, Oranges. 100p, Pomegranates.

Vignette Multicolored

392 A72 50c violet blue 15 4
393 " 1p gray blue 15 4
394 " 2.50p brown 20 5
395 " 5p bright blue 20 6
396 " 7.50p lilac rose 10 6
397 " 10p chocolate 15 8
398 " 17.50p slate 35 12
399 " 30p slate green 60 20
400 " 50p green 90 50
401 " 100p brown black 2.00 1.00
Nos. 392-401 (10) 4.80 2.15

Elementary Schoolboy
A73

1962, Oct. 1 Litho. *Perf. 12*

404 A73 30p multicolored 40 25

Students' Day, Oct. 1. See No. C355.

Cedar of Lebanon
A74 A75

1963-64 *Perf. 13x13½* **Unwmkd.**

405 A74 50c green 20 3
406 A75 50c gray green ('64) 3 3
407 " 2.50p ultra. ('64) 5 5
408 " 5p brt. pink ('64) 7 5
409 " 7.50p orange ('64) 9 5
410 " 17.50p rose lilac ('64) 45 14
Nos. 405-410 (6) 89 35

Bicyclist A76 — Hyacinth A77

Designs: 5p, Basketball. 10p, Track.

1964, Feb. 11 Lithographed *Perf. 13*

415 A76 2.50p rose claret & red brown 10 4
416 " 5p blue & org. brn. 15 6
417 " 10p dull lilac & brn. 20 10
Nos. 415-417, C385-C387 (6) 1.35 85

Issued to commemorate the 4th Mediterranean Games, Naples, Sept. 21–29, 1963.

1964 *Perf. 13x13½* Unwmkd.

Multicolored

Size: 26x27mm.

418 A77 50c *shown* 6 4
419 " 1p " 5 4
420 " 2.50p " 5 5
421 " 5p *Cyclamen* 8 5
422 " 7.50p " 10 6

Perf. 13

Size: 26x37mm.

423 A77 10p *Poinsettia* 15 7
424 " 17.50p *Anemone* 35 13
425 " 30p *Iris* 60 25
426 " 50p *Poppy* 1.35 40
Nos. 418-426 (9) 2.79 1.09

See also Nos. C391–C397.

Temple of the Sun, Baalbek A78

1965, Jan. 11 Litho. *Perf. 13x13½*

429 A78 2.50p black & red org. 10 8
430 " 7.50p black & blue 30 27
Nos. 429-430, C420-C423 (6) 1.50 1.25

International Festival at Baalbek.

Swimmer A79

Designs: 7.50p, Fencer. 10p, Basketball (vert.).

1965, Jan. 23 Engr. *Perf. 13*

431 A79 2.50p magenta, greenish blue & black 10 10
432 " 7.50p slate green, maroon & brn. 30 30
433 " 10p indigo, brown & green 40 40
Nos. 431-433, C424-C426 (6) 1.70 1.50

Issued to commemorate the 18th Olympic Games, Tokyo, Oct. 10–25, 1964.

Golden Oriole A80

Birds: 5p, Bullfinch. 10p, European goldfinch. 15p, Hoopoe. 17.50p, Rock partridge. 32.50p, European bee-eater.

1965 Engraved *Perf. 13*

434 A80 5p multicolored 7 4
435 " 10p dull blue, yel. & carmine 13 6
436 " 15p olive brn., dark brown & org. 18 10
437 " 17.50p chocolate, dk. blue & red 22 10
438 " 20p olive, blk. & orange 35 20
439 " 32.50p brt. green, yel. & brown 45 30
Nos. 434-439 (6) 1.40 80

Cow and Calf A81

Designs: 1p, Rabbit. 2.50p, Ewe and lamb.

1965 Photogravure *Perf. 11x12*

440 A81 50c yel., brn. & red 5 5
441 " 1p pink & black 10 5
442 " 2.50p lt. green, dark brown & yel. 10 5

Hippodrome, Beirut A82

Designs: 1p, Pigeon Rocks. 2.50p, Tabarja. 5p, Ruins, Beit-Méry. 7.50p, Statue and ruins, Anjar.

1966 *Perf. 12x11½* Unwmkd.

443 A82 50c gold & multi. 10 3
444 " 1p " " 10 3
445 " 2.50p " " 10 3
446 " 5p " " 5 5
447 " 7.50p " " 10 8
Nos. 443-447 (5) 45 22

See also Nos. C486–C492.

ITY Emblem and Cedars A83

1967 Photogravure *Perf. 11x12*

448 A83 50c lemon, black & bright blue 5 3
449 " 1p salmon, black & bright blue 5 3
450 " 2.50p gray, black & bright blue 5 5
451 " 5p lt. rose lilac, black & bright blue 5 5
452 " 7.50p yellow, black & bright blue 5 5
Nos. 448-452 (5) 25 21

Issued for International Tourist Year, but used as a regular issue.

See also Nos. C515–C522.

Goat and Kid A84

Designs: 1p, Castle. 2.50p, Sheep. 5p, Camels. 10p, Donkey. 15p, Horses.

1968, Feb. Photo. *Perf. 12x11½*

453 A84 50c multicolored 5 3
454 " 1p " 5 3
455 " 2.50p " 5 3
456 " 5p " 5 3
457 " 10p " 12 4
458 " 15p " 15 6
Nos. 453-458 (6) 47 22

See also Nos. C534–C539.

No. 439 Surcharged

25P ٢٥ق

1972, Apr. Engr. *Perf. 13*

459 A80 25p on 32.50p multi. 18 10

Nos. 447 and 452 Surcharged with New Value and Bars

Photogravure

1972, May *Perf. 12x11½, 11x12*

460 A82 5p on 7.50p multi. 5 3
461 A83 5p on 7.50p " 5 3

Cedar of Lebanon A85

1974 Lithographed *Perf. 11*

462 A85 50c orange & olive 3 3

SEMI-POSTAL STAMPS

Regular Issue of 1925 Surcharged in Red or Black

Secours aux Réfugiés

اعانات للاجئين

Aff^{t} 0^{P}.25 — الاجرة ١/٤ غ

1926 *Perf. 14x13½.* Unwmkd.

B1 A2 0p25+0p25 olive blk. 1.40 1.40
B2 " 0p50+0p25 yel. grn. 1.40 1.40
B3 " 0p75+0p25 brn. org. 1.40 1.40
B4 " 1pi+0p50 magenta 1.40 1.40
B5 " 1pi25+0p50 deep green 2.00 2.00
B6 " 1p50+0p50 rose red 2.00 2.00
a. Double surcharge 9.00
B7 " 2pi+0p75 dk. brn. 1.25 1.25
B8 " 2p50+0p75 peacock blue 2.00 2.00
B9 " 3pi+1pi org. brn. 2.00 2.00
B10 " 5pi+1pi violet 1.65 1.65
B11 A3 10pi+2pi vio. brn. 1.65 1.65
B12 A2 25pi+5pi ultra. 2.00 2.00
Nos. B1-B12 (12) 20.15 20.15

On No. B11 the surcharge is set in six lines to fit the shape of the stamp. All values of this series exist with inverted surcharge. Price, each $10.

See Nos. CB1–CB4.

Boxing SP1

Sports: 5p+5p, Wrestling. 7.50p+7.50p, Shot put.

Lithographed

1961, Jan. 12 *Perf. 13* Unwmkd.

B13 SP1 2.50p+2.50p blue & brown 10 8
B14 " 5p+5p org. & brn. 15 12
B15 " 7.50p+7.50p violet & brown 25 20
Nos. B13-B15, CB12-CB14 (6) 6.50 5.35

Issued to commemorate the 17th Olympic Games, Rome, Aug. 25–Sept. 11, 1960.

Nos. B13–B15 with Arabic and French Overprint in Black, Blue or Green and two Bars through Olympic Inscription: "CHAMPIONNAT D'EUROPE DE TIR, 2 JUIN 1962"

1962, June 2

B16 SP1 2.50p+2.50p blue & brown (Bk) 25 18
B17 " 5p+5p orange & brown (G) 40 27
B18 " 7.50p+7.50p violet & brown (Bl) 50 50
Nos. B16-B18, CB15-CB17 (6) 4.15 3.95

Issued to publicize the European Marksmanship Championships held in Lebanon.

AIR POST STAMPS.

Nos. 10 to 13 with Additional Overprint

Poste par Avion

1924 *Perf. 14x13½.* Unwmkd.

C1 A18 2pi on 40c red & pale blue 2.50 2.50
a. Double surcharge 12.50
C2 " 3pi on 60c violet & ultramarine 2.50 2.50

C3 A18 5pi on 1fr claret & olive green 2.50 2.50
a. Double surcharge and overprint 15.00
C4 " 10pi on 2fr orange & pale blue 2.50 2.50
a. Inverted surcharge and overprint 30.00 30.00

Nos. 33, 35-37 Overprinted

Avion طيارة

C5 A18 2pi on 40c red & pale blue 3.00 3.00
C6 " 3pi on 60c violet & ultramarine 3.00 3.00
C7 " 5pi on 1fr claret & olive green 3.00 3.00
a. Overprint reversed 20.00
C8 A18 10pi on 2fr orange & pale blue 3.00 3.00
a. Overprint reversed 20.00
b. Double surcharge 20.00

AVION

Nos. 57, 59-61 Overprinted in Green طيارة

1925

C9 A2 2pi dark brown 1.00 1.00
C10 " 3pi orange brown 1.00 1.00
C11 " 5pi violet 1.00 1.00
a. Inverted overprint 9.00
C12 A3 10pi violet brown 1.00 1.00

Nos. 57, 59-61 Overprinted in Red

c

1926

C13 A2 2pi dark brown 1.20 1.20
C14 " 3pi orange brown 1.20 1.20
C15 " 5pi violet 1.20 1.20
C16 A3 10pi violet brown 1.20 1.20

Nos. C13-C16 exist with inverted overprint. Price, each $10.

Issues of Republic under French Mandate

Nos. C13-C16 Overprinted

République Libanaise

d

1927

C17 A2 2pi dark brown 1.00 1.00
C18 " 3pi orange brown 1.00 1.00
C19 " 5pi violet 1.00 1.00
C20 A3 10pi violet brown 1.00 1.00

On No. C20 the overprint is set in two lines.

الجمهورية اللبنانية

Nos. C17-C20 with Additional Overprint

e

Black Overprint

1928

C21 A2 2pi dark brown 3.00 3.00
a. Double overprint 7.00
b. Inverted overprint 7.00
C22 A2 3pi orange brown 3.00 3.00
a. Double overprint 7.00
C23 A2 5pi violet 3.00 3.00
a. Double overprint 8.00
C24 A3 10pi violet brown 3.00 3.00
a. Double overprint 8.00

Red Overprint.

C25 A2 2pi dark brown 1.00 1.00
C26 " 3pi orange brown 1.00 1.00
C27 " 5pi violet 1.00 1.00
C28 A3 10pi violet brown 1.00 1.00
Nos. C21-C28 (8) 16.00 16.00

On Nos. C21 to C28 the airplane is always in red. The red overprint of a silhouetted plane and "Republique Libanaise," as on Nos. C25-C27, was also applied to Nos. C9-C12. These are believed to have been essays, and were not regularly issued.

Nos. 52, 54 and 62 Overprinted Type "e" in Red or Black.

1929

C33 A2 0p50 yellow green (R) 20 20
a. Inverted overprint 12.00 12.00
C34 A2 1pi magenta (Bk) 40 40
a. Inverted overprint 12.00 12.00
C35 A2 25pi ultramarine (R) 55.00 55.00
a. Inverted overprint

No. 62 with Surcharge Added in Red.

Two types of surcharge:
I. The "5" of "15 P." is italic. The "15" is 4mm. high. Arabic characters for "Lebanese Republic" and for "15 P." are on same line in that order.
II. The "5" is in Roman type (upright) and smaller; "15" is 3½mm. high. Arabic for "Lebanese Republic" is centered on line by itself, with Arabic for "15 P." below right end of line.

C36 A2 15pi on 25pi ultramarine (I) 85.00 85.00
a. Type II (#106) 200.00 200.00

Nos. 102 Overprinted Type "c" in Blue

C37 A2 0p50 on 0p75 brown orange 20 20
a. Airplane inverted 12.00
b. French and Arabic surcharge inverted 10.00
c. "P" omitted 5.00
d. Airplane double 10.00

AP1

1930 Red Surcharge.

C38 AP1 2pi on 1p25 dp. grn. 50 50
a. Inverted surcharge 12.00 12.00

Airplane over Racheya AP2

Designs: 1pi, Plane over Broumana. 2pi, Baalbek. 3pi, Hasroun. 5pi, Byblos. 10pi, Kadicha River. 15pi, Beirut. 25pi, Tripoli. 50pi, Kabeljas. 100pi, Zahle.

1930-31 Photogravure *Perf. 13½.*

C39 AP2 50c dk. violet ('31) 20 20
C40 " 1pi yel. grn. ('31) 20 20
C41 " 2pi dp. org. ('31) 40 40
C42 " 3pi magenta ('31) 40 40
C43 " 5pi indigo 40 40
C44 " 10pi orange red 60 60
C45 " 15pi orange brown 60 60
C46 " 25pi gray violet ('31) 85 85
C47 " 50pi deep claret 3.25 3.25
C48 " 100pi olive brown 3.25 3.25
Nos. C39-C48 (10) 10.15 10.15

Nos. C39 to C48 exist imperforate.

Tourist Publicity Issue.

Skiing in Lebanon AP12

Bay of Jounie AP13

1936, Oct. 12

C49 AP12 50c slate green 60 60
C50 AP13 1pi red orange 80 80
C51 AP12 2pi black violet 80 80
C52 AP13 3pi yellow green 1.00 1.00
C53 AP12 5pi brn. carmine 1.00 1.00
C54 AP13 10pi orange brown 1.00 1.00
C55 " 15pi dk. carmine 15.00 15.00
C56 AP12 25pi green 40.00 40.00
Nos. C49-C56 (8) 60.20 60.20

Nos. C49 to C56 exist imperforate.

Lebanese Pavilion at Exposition AP14

1937, July 1 *Perf. 13½*

C57 AP14 50c olive black 40 40
C58 " 1pi yellow green 40 40
C59 " 2pi dark red orange 40 40
C60 " 3pi dark olive green 40 40
C61 " 5pi deep green 60 60
C62 " 10pi carmine lake 3.25 3.25
C63 " 15pi rose lake 3.25 3.25
C64 " 25pi orange brown 4.50 4.50
Nos. C57-C64 (8) 13.20 13.20

Paris International Exposition.

Arcade of Beit-ed-Din Palace AP15

Ruins of Baalbek—AP16

1937-40 Engraved *Perf. 13*

C65 AP15 50c ultra. ('38) 5 5
C66 " 1pi henna brn. ('40) 8 8
C67 " 2pi sepia ('40) 10 10
C68 " 3pi rose ('40) 45 45
C69 " 5pi light green ('40) 18 18
C70 AP16 10pi dull violet 15 10
C71 " 15pi turq. bl. ('40) 60 60
C72 " 25pi violet ('40) 1.65 1.35
C73 " 50pi yel. grn. ('40) 3.00 1.50
C74 " 100pi brown ('40) 80 70
Nos. C65-C74 (10) 7.06 5.11

Nos. C65-C74 exist imperforate.

Medical College of Beirut—AP17

1938, May 9 Photo. *Perf. 13*

C75 AP17 2pi green 75 75
C76 " 3pi orange 75 75
C77 " 5pi lilac gray 75 75
C78 " 10pi lake 1.50 1.50

Medical Congress.

Maurice Noguès and View of Beirut—AP18

1938, July 15 *Perf. 11*

C79 AP18 10pi brn. car. 1.40 1.40
a. Souvenir sheet of 4, perf. 13½ 15.00 15.00
b. Perf. 13½ 3.50 3.50

10th anniversary of first Marseille-Beirut flight, by Maurice Noguès.

No. C79a has marginal inscriptions in French and Arabic. Size: 161x120mm. Exists imperf.; price $250.

Independent Republic

Plane Over Mt. Lebanon AP19

1942, Sept. 18 Litho. *Perf. 11½*

C80 AP19 10pi dark brown violet 2.25 2.25
C81 " 50pi dark gray green 2.25 2.25

First anniversary of the Proclamation of Independence, November 26, 1941.
Nos. C80 and C81 exist imperforate.

Bechamoun AP20

Rachaya Citadel AP21

Air View of Beirut AP22

1943, May 1 *Perf. 11½*

C82 AP20 25pi yel. green 2.00 1.75
C83 " 50pi orange 2.50 2.00
C84 AP21 100pi buff 2.25 2.00
C85 " 200pi blue violet 2.50 2.25
C86 AP22 300pi sage green 8.00 8.00
C87 " 500pi sepia 17.50 17.50
Nos. C82-C87 (6) 34.75 33.50

Issued to commemorate the second anniversary of the Proclamation of Independence. Nos. C82 to C87 exist imperforate.

Bhannes Sanatorium AP23

1943, July 8 Photogravure

Black Overprint.

C88 AP23 20pi orange 1.25 1.25
C89 " 50pi steel blue 1.25 1.25
C90 " 100pi rose violet 2.50 2.50

Arab Medical Congress, Beirut.

Nos. C82 to C87 Overprinted in Red, Blue or Violet

1944, Nov. 23

C91	AP20	25pi yel. grn. (R)	3.00	3.00
C92	"	50pi orange (Bl)	5.00	5.00
C93	AP21	100pi buff (V)	7.00	7.00
C94	"	200pi bl. vio. (R)	11.00	11.00
C95	AP22	300pi sage green (R)	15.00	15.00
C96	"	500pi sepia (Bl)	27.50	27.50
		Nos. C91-C96 (6)	68.50	68.50

Issued to commemorate the return to office of the President and his ministers, November 22, 1943.

Falls of Litani

AP24

The Cedars

AP25

Lithographed.

1945, July *Perf. 11½* **Unwmkd.**

C97	AP24	25pi gray brown	90	60
C98	"	50pi rose violet	1.65	75
C99	AP25	200pi violet	6.50	1.65
C100	"	300pi brn. black	12.00	3.50

Lebanese Soldiers at Bir Hacheim

AP26

1946, May 8

C101	AP26	15pi blue blk., org. & red org.	60	20
C102	"	20pi red, lilac & blue	60	30
C103	"	25pi bright blue, org. & red	60	50
C104	"	50pi gray black, blue & red	1.25	50
C105	"	100pi purple, pink & red	3.00	1.00
C106	"	150pi brown, pink & red	4.00	2.00
		Nos. C101-C106 (6)	10.05	4.50

Issued to commemorate the 1st anniversary of the victory of the Allied Nations in World War II.

Three imperf. souvenir sheets of 14 exist. They contain one each of Nos. C101-C106 and 189-196 in changed colors. Size: 142x228mm. One has sepia inscriptions, and one on thin white card has blue inscriptions. Price $27.50 each. The third, with blue inscriptions, is on thick honeycombed chamois card. Price $100.

Night Herons over Mt. Sanin

AP27

1946, Sept. 11

C107	AP27	10pi orange	2.00	90
C108	"	25pi ultramarine	3.00	40
C109	"	50pi blue green	5.00	1.25
C110	"	100pi dark violet brown	10.00	4.00

Symbols of Communications

AP28

1946, Nov. 22

C111	AP28	25pi deep blue	50	40
C112	"	50pi green	1.00	60
C113	"	75pi orange red	1.50	1.00
C114	"	150pi brown black	3.00	2.00

Arab Postal Congress, Sofar, 1946.

Stone Tablet, Dog River and Pres. Bechara el-Khoury

AP29

1947, Feb. 11

C115	AP29	25pi ultramarine	70	50
C116	"	50pi dull rose	1.25	1.00
C117	"	75pi gray black	1.50	1.50
C118	"	150pi blue green	3.00	2.50

Issued to commemorate the evacuation of foreign troops from Lebanon, Dec. 31, 1946.

Bay of Jounie—AP30

Government House, Beirut

AP31

1947, Feb. 11 **Grayish Paper**

C119	AP30	5pi dp. blue green	20	7
C120	"	10pi rose violet	40	8
C121	"	15pi vermilion	60	10
C122	"	20pi orange	80	15
		a. 20pi red orange, white paper	1.00	15
C123	"	25pi deep blue	1.00	15
C124	"	50pi henna brn.	2.00	32
C125	"	100pi chocolate	4.00	55
C126	AP31	150pi dk. violet brown	9.00	90
C127	"	200pi slate	14.00	3.75
C128	"	300pi black	17.50	9.00
		Nos. C119-C128 (10)	49.50	15.07

See also Nos. C145A-C147B.

Post Horn and Letter

AP32

Phoenician Galley

AP33

1947, June 17 **Lithographed**

C129	AP32	10pi bright ultra.	70	40
C130	"	15pi rose carmine	90	60
C131	"	25pi bright blue	1.40	1.00
C132	AP33	50pi dark slate green	3.00	1.25
C133	"	75pi purple	4.00	1.75
C134	AP33	100pi dark brown	5.00	3.00
		Nos. C129-C134 (6)	15.00	8.00

Issued to commemorate Lebanon's participation in the 12th congress of the Universal Postal Union, Paris, 1947.

Lebanese Village

AP34

1948, Sept. 1 *Perf. 11½*

C135	AP34	5pi deep orange	50	10
C136	"	10pi rose lilac	1.00	15
C137	"	15pi org. brown	2.00	20
C138	"	20pi slate	2.50	25
C139	"	25pi Prus. blue	5.00	90
C140	"	50pi gray black	9.00	1.40
		Nos. C135-C140 (6)	20.00	3.00

Apollo

AP35

Minerva

AP36

1948, Nov. 23 **Unwmkd.**

C141	AP35	7.50pi bl. & lt. blue	1.25	1.25
C142	"	15pi black & gray	1.75	1.25
C143	"	20pi rose brown & rose	3.00	1.75
C144	AP36	35pi carmine rose & rose	5.00	3.25
C145	"	75pi blue green & light green	9.00	5.00
		Nos. C141-C145 (5)	20.00	12.50

Issued to honor the United Nations Educational, Scientific and Cultural Organization.

Nos. C141 to C145 exist imperforate, and combined with Nos. 220 to 224 in an imperforate souvenir sheet on thin buff cardboard, measuring 141x195mm., with black inscriptions in top margin in Arabic and at bottom in French. Price $125.

Bay Type of 1947 Redrawn

1949 **White Paper.**

C145A	AP30	10pi rose lilac	4.00	1.00
C146	"	15pi dark green	6.00	1.25
C147	"	20pi orange	12.00	1.75
C147A	"	25pi dark blue	45.00	2.00
C147B	"	50pi brick red	120.00	20.00
		Nos. C145A-C147B (5)	187.00	26.00

In the redrawn designs, Nos. C145A, C147 and C147B have zeros with broader centers than in the 1947 issue (Nos. C120, C122 and C124).

Helicopter Mail Delivery

AP37

1949, Aug. 16 *Perf. 11½* **Unwmkd.**

C148	AP37	25pi deep blue	4.00	2.00
C149	"	50pi green	6.00	3.00
		a. Souvenir sheet of 5	12.50	12.50

Issued to commemorate the 75th anniversary of the formation of the Universal Postal Union.

No. 149a measures 135x188mm. and contains one each of Nos. 225-227, C148 and C149, with marginal inscriptions in green. Exists on thin cardboard.

Homing Birds—AP38

Pres. Bechara el-Khoury—AP39

1950, Aug. 8 **Lithographed**

C150	AP38	5pi violet blue	70	30
C151	"	15pi rose violet	1.00	60
C152	AP39	25pi chocolate	85	50
C153	"	35pi gray green	1.50	1.00
		a. Souvenir sheet of 6	25.00	25.00

Conference of Emigrants, 1950.

No. C153a measures 135x185mm. and contains one each of Nos. 243, 244 and C150 to C153, with marginal inscriptions in dark brown. The paper is chamois.

Crusader Castle, Sidon Harbor—AP40

1950, Sept. 7

C154	AP40	10pi chocolate	50	20
C155	"	15pi dark green	75	20
C156	"	20pi crimson	1.75	30
C157	"	25pi ultramarine	3.00	1.25
C158	"	50pi gray black	5.00	2.50
		Nos. C154-C158 (5)	11.00	4.45

1951, June 9 **Redrawn** **Typo.**

C159	AP40	10pi greenish blk.	40	10
C160	"	15pi black brown	75	15
C161	"	20pi vermilion	85	20
C162	"	25pi deep blue	1.35	25
C163	"	35pi lilac rose	2.25	1.75
C164	"	50pi indigo	5.00	1.50
		Nos. C159-C164 (6)	10.60	3.95

Nos. C154-C158 are lithographed from a fine-screen halftone; Nos. C159-C164 are typographed and much coarser, with larger plane and many other differences.

Khaldé International Airport, Beirut—AP41

Design: 50pi to 300pi, Amphitheater, Byblos.

1952 **Lithographed** *Perf. 11½*

C165	AP41	5pi crimson	10	10
C166	"	10pi dark gray	20	10
C167	"	15pi rose lilac	40	10
C168	"	20pi brown orange	60	25
C169	"	25pi greenish blue	70	25
C170	"	35pi violet blue	1.00	30
C171	"	50pi blue green	4.00	40
C172	"	100pi deep blue	25.00	1.75
C173	"	200pi dk. blue green	17.50	2.75
C174	"	300pi black brown	22.50	6.00
		Nos. C165-C174 (10)	72.00	12.00

Lockheed Constellation

AP42

1953, Oct. 1

No.	Type	Description	Unused	Used
C175	AP42	5pi yellow green	15	5
C176	"	10pi deep plum	35	5
C177	"	15pi scarlet	40	7
C178	"	20pi aquamarine	60	10
C179	"	25pi blue	1.35	15
C180	"	35pi org. brown	2.25	25
C181	"	50pi violet blue	4.00	35
C182	"	100pi black brown	7.00	4.00
		Nos. C175–C182 (8)	16.10	5.02

Ruins at Baalbek AP43

Irrigation Canal, Litani AP44

1954, Mar.

No.	Type	Description	Unused	Used
C183	AP43	5pi yellow green	20	5
C184	"	10pi dull purple	30	5
C185	"	15pi carmine	40	9
C186	"	20pi brown	50	12
C187	"	25pi dull blue	60	20
C188	"	35pi black brown	1.00	32
C189	AP44	50pi dark olive green	3.00	45
C190	"	100pi deep car.	6.00	60
C191	"	200pi dark brown	10.00	1.10
C192	"	300pi dk. gray bl.	18.00	2.00
		Nos. C183–C192 (10)	40.00	4.98

Khladé International Airport, Beirut AP45

1954, April 23 *Perf. 11½*

No.	Type	Description	Unused	Used
C193	AP45	10pi pink & rose red	40	40
C194	"	25pi deep blue & gray blue	75	60
C195	"	35pi dull brown & yel. brown	1.20	75
C196	"	65pi deep green & green	2.25	1.75

Opening of Beirut's International Airport. Exist imperf.

Arab Postal Union Type of Regular Issue, 1955

1955, Jan. 1 *Perf. 13½x13*

No.	Type	Description	Unused	Used
C197	A52	2.50pi yel. brown	15	15

Issued to commemorate the founding of the Arab Postal Union, July 1, 1954.

Rotary Emblem AP47

1955, Feb. 23 *Perf. 11½*

No.	Type	Description	Unused	Used
C198	AP47	35pi dull green	75	50
C199	"	65pi dull blue	1.25	75

Rotary International, 50th anniversary.

Skiing Among the Cedars AP48

1955, Feb. 24 Lithographed

No.	Type	Description	Unused	Used
C200	AP48	5pi blue green	40	30
C201	"	15pi crimson	60	20
C202	"	20pi lilac	1.00	20
C203	AP48	25pi blue	1.50	20
C204	"	35pi olive brown	2.50	40
C205	"	50pi chocolate	4.00	50
C206	"	65pi deep blue	7.00	1.25
		Nos. C200–C206 (7)	17.00	3.05

See also Nos. C233-C235.

Tourist AP49

1955, Sept. 10 *Perf. 13* **Unwmkd.**

No.	Type	Description	Unused	Used
C207	AP49	2.50pi brown violet & light blue	10	10
C208	"	12.50pi ultramarine & light blue	35	20
C209	"	25pi indigo & light blue	65	25
C210	"	35pi olive green & light blue	90	40
		a. Sheet of four	4.00	4.00

Issued to commemorate the Tourist Year. No. C210a measures 110x170mm. and is printed on cardboard. It contains one each of Nos. C207–C210, imperf., with marginal inscriptions in brown.

Oranges—AP50

Grapes AP51

Designs: 65pi, 100pi, 200pi, Apples.

1955, Oct. 15

No.	Type	Description	Unused	Used
C211	AP50	5pi yellow green & yellow	20	10
C212	"	10pi dark green & deep orange	25	10
C213	"	15pi yellow green & red orange	40	10
C214	"	20pi olive & yellow orange	45	10
C215	AP51	25pi blue & violet blue	60	15
C216	"	35pi grn. & claret	1.00	25
C217	"	50pi black brown & dull yel.	1.25	25
C218	AP50	65pi grn. & lemon	2.75	30
C219	"	100pi yellow green & dp. orange	4.00	65
C220	"	200pi green & car.	5.00	3.00
		Nos. C211–C220 (10)	15.90	5.00

United Nations Emblem AP52

1956, Jan. 23 *Perf. 11½*

No.	Type	Description	Unused	Used
C221	AP52	35pi violet blue	3.00	2.50
C222	"	65pi green	4.00	3.50

Issued to commemorate the tenth anniversary of the United Nations (in 1955).

An imperf. souvenir sheet contains one each of Nos. C221 and C222. Price $45.

Temple of the Sun Colonnade, Masks and Lion's Head—AP53

Temple of Bacchus, Baalbek AP54

Design: 35pi, 65pi, Temple of the Sun colonnade, masks and violoncello.

1956, Dec. 10 Litho. *Perf. 13*

No.	Type	Description	Unused	Used
C223	AP53	2.50pi dark brown	35	20
C224	"	10pi green	45	30
C225	AP54	12.50pi light blue	50	45
C226	"	25pi bright vio. blue	75	55
C227	AP53	35pi red lilac	1.20	70
C228	"	65pi slate blue	2.25	1.25
		Nos. C223–C228 (6)	5.50	3.45

International Festival at Baalbek.

Skiing Type of 1955 Redrawn and

Irrigation Canal, Litani AP55

1957 Lithographed *Perf. 11½*

No.	Type	Description	Unused	Used
C229	AP55	10pi bright violet	25	10
C230	"	15pi orange	30	10
C231	"	20pi yellow green	40	10
C232	"	25pi slate blue	55	10
C233	AP48	35pi gray green	1.50	20
C234	"	65pi deep claret	2.50	40
C235	"	100pi brown	3.50	1.00
		Nos. C229–C235 (7)	9.00	2.00

Different Arabic characters used for the country name; letters in "Liban" larger.

Pres. Camille Chamoun and King Saud—AP56

King Saud, Pres. Chamoun, King Hussein, Pres. Kouatly, King Faisal, Pres. Nasser—AP57

Pres. Chamoun and: No. C237, King Hussein. No. C238, Pres. Kouatly. No. C239, King Faisal. No. C240, Pres. Nasser. 25pi, Map of Lebanon.

1957, July 15 Lithographed *Perf. 13*

No.	Type	Description	Unused	Used
C236	AP56	15pi green	50	30
C237	"	15pi blue	50	30
C238	"	15pi red lilac	50	30
C239	"	15pi red orange	50	30
C240	"	15pi claret	50	30
C241	"	25pi blue	50	30
C242	AP57	100pi dull red brown	3.00	2.25
		Nos. C236–C242 (7)	6.00	4.05

Issued to commemorate the Congress of Arab Leaders, Beirut, Nov. 12-15, 1956.

Fencing AP58

Design: 50pi, Pres. Chamoun and stadium with flags.

1957, Sept. 12 *Perf. 13* **Unwmkd.**

No.	Type	Description	Unused	Used
C243	AP58	35pi claret	1.25	75
C244	"	50pi light green	1.75	1.00

Issued to commemorate the second Pan-Arab Games, Beirut. See note on souvenir sheet below No. 314.

Symbols of Communications AP59

Power Plant, Chamoun AP60

1957 *Perf. 13x13½, 11½(AP60)*

No.	Type	Description	Unused	Used
C245	AP59	5p bright green	20	10
C246	"	10p yellow orange	20	10
C247	"	15p brown	40	10
C248	"	20p maroon	40	12
C249	"	25p violet blue	40	15
C250	AP60	35p violet brown	60	15
C251	"	50p green	1.20	20
C252	"	65p sepia	1.60	28
C253	"	100p dark gray	2.00	80
		Nos. C245–C253 (9)	7.00	2.00

Plane at Airport—AP61

Cogwheel—AP62

1958–59 *Perf. 13* **Unwmkd.**

No.	Type	Description	Unused	Used
C254	AP61	5p green	15	8
C255	"	10p magenta	20	10
C256	"	15p dull violet	30	12
C257	"	20p orange verm.	45	20
C258	"	25p dk. vio. blue	60	20
C259	AP62	35p greenish gray	75	20
C260	"	50p aquamarine	90	20
C261	"	65p pale brown	1.60	30
C262	"	100p bright ultra.	2.00	60
		Nos. C254–C262 (9)	6.95	2.00

Nos. C259 and C261 Surcharged in Black or Dark Blue

Lithographed.

1959 *Perf. 13* **Unwmkd.**

C263	AP62	30p on 35p greenish gray	40	35
C264	"	40p on 65p pale brown (Bl)	60	50

Arab Engineers Congress.

No. C217 Overprinted as Illustrated and Surcharged with New Value and Bars.

1959, Sept. 1

C265	AP51	40p on 50p black brown & dull yellow	75	45

Arab Lawyers Congress.

Myron's Discobolus
AP63

Wreath and Hand Holding Torch
AP64

Design: 30p, Weight lifter.

1959, Oct. 11 **Litho.** *Perf. 11½*

C266	AP63	15p dull bluish green	30	20
C267	"	30p dk. vio. brn.	60	30
C268	AP64	40p ultramarine	90	40

3rd Mediterranean Games, Beirut.
A souvenir sheet on white cardboard contains one each of Nos. C266–C268, imperf., with black marginal inscriptions. Size: 104x129mm. Sold for 100 piastres. Price $8.

Soldiers and Flag
AP65

Hands Planting Tree
AP66

1959, Nov. 25 *Perf. 13½x13*

C269	AP65	40p sepia, brick red & slate	60	40
C270	"	60p sepia, dark grn. & brick red	90	60

Lebanon's independence, 1941–1959.

No. C234 Surcharged with New Value and Bars.

1959, Dec. 15 *Perf. 11½*

C271	AP48	40p on 65p deep claret	1.50	40

1960, Jan. 18 **Litho.** *Perf. 11½*

C272	AP66	20p rose violet & green	50	30
C273	"	40p dark brown & green	70	50

Issued to commemorate the 25th anniversary of the Friends of the Tree Society.

Postal Administration Building
AP67

1960, Feb. *Perf. 13* **Unwmkd.**

C274	AP67	20p green	40	25

President Fuad Chehab
AP68

Uprooted Oak Emblem
AP69

1960, Mar. 12 **Photo.** *Perf. 13½*

C275	AP68	5p green	5	5
C276	"	10p Prussian blue	8	5
C277	"	15p orange brown	12	8
C278	"	20p brown	20	7
C279	"	30p olive	30	15
C280	"	40p dull red	35	18
C281	"	50p blue	45	25
C282	"	70p red lilac	65	25
C283	"	100p dark green	1.00	45
		Nos. C275–C283 (9)	3.20	1.53

1960, Apr. 7 **Litho.** *Perf. 13½x13*

Size: 20½x36½mm.

C284	AP69	25p yellow brown	40	40
C285	"	40p green	75	50
		a. Souvenir sheet of 2	15.00	15.00

Size: 20x36mm.

C284b	AP69	25p yellow brown	75	75
C285b	"	40p green	1.25	1.25

Issued to publicize World Refugee Year, July 1, 1959–June 30, 1960.
No. C285a contains one each of Nos. C284–C285, imperf., with marginal inscriptions in black. Size: 89½x109mm. Sold for 150 piastres.
Nos. C284b–C285b appear fuzzy and pale when compared to the bolder, clear-cut printing of Nos. C284–C285.
Nos. C284b–C285b exist with carmine surcharges of "30P.+15P." (on C284b) and "20P.+10P." (on C285b), repeated in Arabic, with ornaments covering original denominations.

Martyrs' Monument—AP70

Design: 70p, Statues from Martyrs' monument (vert.).

Perf. 13x13½, 13½x13

1960, May 6 **Unwmkd.**

C286	AP70	20p rose lilac & green	35	20
C287	"	40p Prussian green & dark green	50	25
C288	"	70p gray olive & black	85	75

Martyrs of May 6th.

Pres. Chehab and King of Morocco—AP71

1960, June 1 *Perf. 13x13½*

C289	AP71	30p chocolate & dark brown	60	40
C290	"	70p black, dark brown & buff	1.10	80

Visit of King Mohammed V of Morocco.
A souvenir sheet on white cardboard contains one each of Nos. C289–C290, imperf., with black marginal inscriptions.

Child Learning to Walk
AP72

Bird, Ribbon of Flags and Map of Beirut
AP73

Design: 60p, Mother and child.

1960, Aug. 16 **Litho.** *Perf. 13½x13*

C291	AP72	20p dark red & buff	40	20
C292	"	60p blue & light blue	80	50

Day of Mother and Child, Mar. 21–22.
See also Nos. CB10–CB11.

Perf. 13½x13, 13x13½

1960, Sept. 20 **Unwmkd.**

Designs: 40p, Cedar and birds. 70p, Globes and cedar (horiz.).

C293	AP73	20p multicolored	25	15
C294	"	40p violet, blue & green	45	25
C295	"	70p multicolored	70	30

Issued to honor the Union of Lebanese Emigrants in the World. A souvenir sheet contains one each of Nos. C293–C295, imperf., printed on cardboard with black marginal inscriptions. Size: 110x140mm. Sold for 150p. Price $6.

Pres. Chehab and Map of Lebanon
AP74

1961, Feb. **Litho.** *Perf. 13½x13*

C296	AP74	5p blue green & yellow green	10	6
C297	"	10p brown & bistre	20	6
C298	"	70p violet & rose lilac	1.00	50

Casino, Maameltein—AP75

1961 *Perf. 13x13½*

C299	AP75	15p rose claret	20	12
C300	"	30p greenish blue	30	18
C301	"	40p brown	40	25
C302	"	200p bistre brown & dull blue	2.50	1.75
		Nos. C296–C302 (7)	4.70	2.92

On Nos. C299–C301, the denomination, inscription and trees differ from type AP75.

U.N. Headquarters, New York
AP76

Designs: 20p, U.N. Emblem and map of Lebanon. 30p, U.N. Emblem and symbolic building. 20p, 30p are vertical.

Perf. 13½x13, 13x13½

1961, May 5

C306	AP76	20p lake & lt. bl.	25	15
C307	"	30p green & beige	35	20
C308	"	50p violet blue & greenish blue	60	40
		a. Souv. sheet of 3	3.00	3.00

Issued to commemorate the 15th anniversary (in 1960) of the United Nations.
No. C308a contains one each of Nos. C306–C308, imperf., against a light blue background showing U.N. emblem. Black inscription. Sheet sold for 125p. Size: 100x140mm.

Pottery Workers—AP77

Design: 70p, Weaver.

Perf. 13x13½

1961, July 11 **Litho.** **Unwmkd.**

C309	AP77	30p deep rose	50	30
C310	"	70p ultramarine	1.50	75

Issued for Labor Day, 1961.

Fireworks—AP78

Water Skiing—AP79

Design: 70p, Tourists on boat ride through cave.

Perf. 13½x13, 13x13½

1961, Aug. 8

C311	AP78	15p lt. purple & dark blue	30	20
C312	AP79	40p blue & pink	70	60
C313	"	70p dull green & pink	1.00	75

Issued to publicize tourist month.

Highway Circle at Dora, Beirut Suburb—AP80

1961, Aug. *Perf. 11½*

C314	AP80	35p yellow green	50	20
C315	"	50p orange brn.	60	40
C316	"	100p gray	90	60

Beach at Tyre AP81 — Afka Falls AP82

1961, Sept. Litho. *Perf. 13*

C317	AP81	5p carmine rose	10	5
C318	"	10p bright violet	20	8
C319	"	15p bright blue	30	10
C320	"	20p orange	30	12
C321	"	30p bright green	40	20
C322	AP82	40p deep claret	40	25
C323	"	50p ultramarine	50	25
C324	"	70p yellow green	70	45
C325	"	100p dark brown	1.10	50
		Nos. C317-C325 (9)	4.00	2.00

See also Nos. C341-C342.

Entrance to UNESCO Building AP83

"UNESCO" and Cedar AP84

Design: 50p, UNESCO headquarters, Paris.

1961, Nov. 20 *Perf. 12* Unwmkd.

C326	AP83	20p blue, buff & black	30	15
C327	AP84	30p lt. green, blk. & magenta	40	25
C328	AP83	50p multicolored	60	35

Issued to commemorate the 15th anniversary of UNESCO (U.N. Educational, Scientific and Cultural Organization).

Emir Bechir and Fakhr-el-Din El Maani—AP85

Design: 25p, Cedar emblem.

1961, Dec. 30 Lithographed

C329	AP85	25p multicolored	30	20
C330	"	50p "	60	30

See note after No. 375.

Scout Types of Regular Issue, 1962.

Designs: 15p, Trefoil and cedar emblem. 20p, Hand making Scout sign. 25p, Lebanese Scout emblem.

1962, March 1 *Perf. 12* Unwmkd.

C331	A70	15p green, black & red	25	15
C332	A69	20p lilac, black & yellow	35	20
C333	A70	25p multicolored	55	25

Issued to commemorate the 50th anniversary of the Lebanese Boy Scouts.

Arab League Building, Cairo AP86

1962, March 22 *Perf. 13*

C334	AP86	20p ultra. & light blue	30	30
C335	"	30p red brown & pink	40	40
C336	"	50p green & greenish blue	60	50

Arab League Week, Mar. 22-28. See also Nos. C372-C375.

Blacksmith—AP87

Farm Tractor—AP88

Perf. 13½x13, 13x13½

1962, May 1 Lithographed

C337	AP87	5p green & lt. blue	15	5
C338	"	10p blue & pink	25	6
C339	AP88	25p bright violet & pink	40	18
C340	"	35p carmine rose & blue	50	27

Issued for Labor Day.

Types of 1961 Redrawn with Large Numerals Similar to Redrawn Regular Issue of 1962.

1962 *Perf. 13*

C341	AP81	5p carmine rose	10	6
C342	AP82	40p deep claret	3.75	55

Hand Reaching for Malaria Eradication Emblem AP89 — Bas-relief of Isis, Kalabsha Temple, Nubia AP90

Design: 70p, Malaria eradication emblem.

1962, July 1 Litho. *Perf. 13½x13*

C349	AP89	30p tan & brown	45	25
C350	"	70p bluish lilac & violet	70	55

Issued for the World Health Organization drive to eradicate malaria.

1962, Aug. 1 *Perf. 13* Unwmkd.

C351	AP90	30p yellow green	75	60
C352	"	50p slate	1.65	80

Campaign to save historic monuments in Nubia.

Spade, Heart, Diamond, Club AP91 — College Student AP92

1962, Sept.

C353	AP91	25p carmine rose, blk. & red	1.25	1.00
C354	"	40p multicolored	1.25	1.00

Issued to commemorate the European Bridge Championship Tournament.

1962, Oct. 1 *Perf. 12*

C355	AP92	45p multicolored	60	40

Issued for Students' Day, Oct. 1.

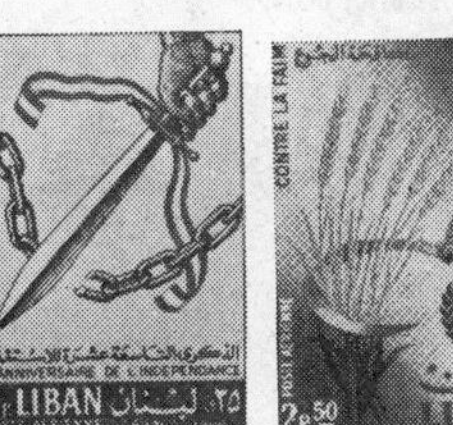

Sword Severing Chain AP93 — Harvest AP94

Lithographed

1962, Nov. 22 *Perf. 13* Unwmkd.

C356	AP93	25p violet, light blue & red	50	40
C357	"	25p blue, light blue & red	50	40
C358	"	25p green, light blue & red	50	40

19th anniversary of independence.

Fruit Type of Regular Issue, 1962

Designs: 5p, Apricots. 10p, 30p, Plums. 20p, 40p, Apples. 50p, Pears. 70p, Medlar. 100p, Lemons.

1962 Vignette Multicolored

C359	A72	5p orange brown	15	10
C360	"	10p black	20	10
C361	"	20p brown	40	20
C362	"	30p gray	50	30
C363	"	40p dark gray	60	30
C364	"	50p light brown	75	40
C365	"	70p gray olive	1.00	40
C366	"	100p blue	1.40	60
		Nos. C359-C366 (8)	5.00	2.40

1963, Mar. 21 Litho. *Perf. 13*

Design: 15p, 20p, U.N. Emblem and hand holding Wheat Emblem (horiz.).

C367	AP94	2.50p ultra. & yel.	10	6
C368	"	5p gray green & yellow	10	6
C369	"	7.50p rose lilac & yellow	20	6
C370	"	15p rose brown & pale grn.	30	18
C371	"	20p rose & pale green	40	25
		Nos. C367-C371 (5)	1.10	61

Issued for the "Freedom from Hunger" campaign of the U.N. Food and Agriculture Organization.

Redrawn Type of 1962, Dated "1963"

Design: Arab League Building, Cairo.

1963, Mar. *Perf. 12* Unwmkd.

C372	AP86	5p violet & lt. bl.	10	7
C373	"	10p grn. & lt. bl.	20	20
C374	"	15p claret & lt. bl.	30	30
C375	"	20p gray & lt. bl.	40	40

Issued for Arab League Week.

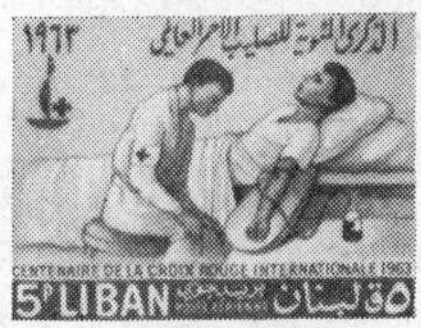

Blood Transfusion AP95

Design: 35p, 40p, Nurse and infant (vert.).

1963, Oct. 5 *Perf. 13* Unwmkd.

C376	AP95	5p green & red	6	6
C377	"	20p greenish blue & red	20	15
C378	"	35p org., red & blk.	40	30
C379	"	40p purple & red	45	35

Centenary of International Red Cross.

Lyre Player and Columns AP96

1963, Nov. 7 *Perf. 13* Unwmkd.

C380	AP96	35p light blue, orge. & blk.	60	50

International Festival at Baalbek.

Lebanon Flag, Rising Sun AP97

1964, Jan. 8 Lithographed

C381 AP97 5p bluish green, verm. & yel. 15 15
C382 " 10p yellow green, verm. & yel. 20 20
C383 " 25p ultra., verm. & yellow 45 45
C384 " 40p gray, verm. & yellow 55 55

20th anniversary of Independence.

Sports Type of Regular Issue, 1964.

Designs: 15p, Tennis. 17.50p, Swimming (horiz.). 30p, Skiing (horiz.).

1964, Feb. 11 *Perf. 13* Unwmkd.

C385 A76 15p grn. & orge. brown 20 15
C386 " 17.50p blue & orange brown 25 20
C387 " 30p blue green & orge. brn. 45 30
a. Souv. sheet of 3 3.50 3.50

Issued to commemorate the 4th Mediterranean Games, Naples, Sept. 21–29, 1963. No. C387a contains three imperf. stamps similar to Nos. C385–C387 with simulated orange brown perforations and green marginal inscription. Size: 152x112 mm. Sold for 100p.

Anemone
AP98

1964, June 9 *Perf. 13* Unwmkd.

Multicolored

C391 AP98 5p *Lily* 20 15
C392 " 10p *Ranunculus* 25 15
C393 " 20p *shown* 30 20
C394 " 40p *Tuberose* 55 35
C395 " 45p *Rhododendron* 60 35
C396 " 50p *Jasmine* 70 35
C397 " 70p *Yellow broom* 90 45
Nos. C391–C397 (7) 3.50 2.00

Girls Jumping Rope—AP99

Design: 20p, 40p, Boy on hobbyhorse (vert.).

1964, Apr. 8

C398 AP99 5p emerald, orange & red 10 10
C399 " 10p yellow brown, orange & red 15 15
C400 " 20p deep ultra., lt. bl. & orge. 25 25
C401 " 40p lilac, light blue & yellow 40 40

Issued for Children's Day.

Flame and U.N. Emblem
AP100

Design: 40p, Flame, U.N. emblem and broken chain.

1964, May 15 Litho. Unwmkd.

C402 AP100 20p salmon, orge. & brown 20 15
C403 " 40p lt. blue, gray bl. & orge. 35 30

Issued to commemorate the 15th anniversary (in 1963) of the Universal Declaration of Human Rights.

Arab League Conference—AP101

1964, Apr. 20 *Perf. 13x13½*

C404 AP101 5p blk. & pale sal. 20 20
C405 " 10p black 25 25
C406 " 15p green 55 35
C407 " 20p dk. brn. & pink 75 40

Arab League meeting.

Child in Crib
AP102

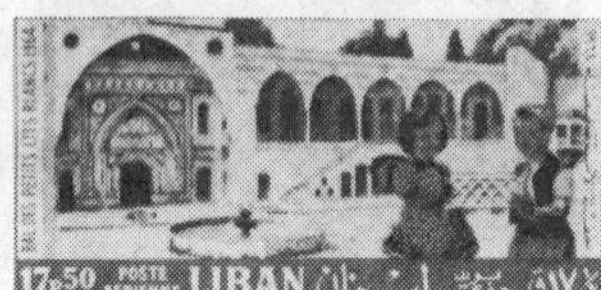

Beit-ed-Din Palace and Children
AP103

1964, July 20 *Perf. 13½x13, 13½*

C408 AP102 2.50p multi. 10 5
C409 " 5p " 10 5
C410 " 15p " 20 10
C411 AP103 17.50p " 25 15
C412 " 20p " 30 15
C413 " 40p " 45 40
Nos. C408–C413 (6) 1.40 90

Issued to publicize the Ball of the Little White Beds, Beirut, for the benefit of children's hospital beds.

Clasped Hands and Map of Lebanon
AP104

Perf. 13½x13

1964, Oct. 16 Litho. *Perf. 13½x13*

C414 AP104 20p yellow green, yel. & gray 25 20
C415 " 40p slate, yellow & gray 50 40

Issued to publicize the Congress of the International Lebanese Union.

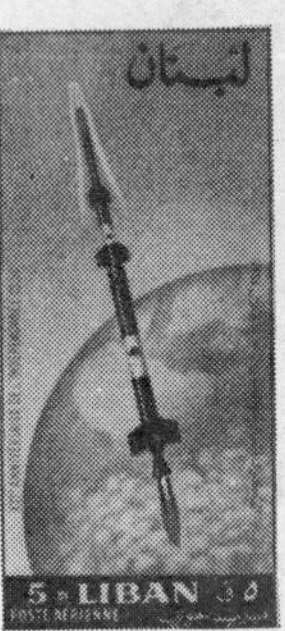

Rocket Leaving Earth
AP105

Woman in Costume
AP107

Battle Scene—AP106

1964, Nov. 24 *Perf. 13½* Unwmkd.

C416 AP105 5p multicolored 20 20
C417 " 10p " 20 20
C418 AP106 40p slate blue & black 60 60
C419 " 70p dp. claret & black 80 80

21st anniversary of independence.

1965, Jan. 11 Litho. *Perf. 13½*

Design: 10p, 15p, Man in costume.

C420 AP107 10p multicolored 10 8
C421 " 15p " 15 12
C422 " 25p grn. & multi. 30 25
C423 " 40p brn. & multi. 55 45

International Festival at Baalbek.

Equestrian
AP108

Designs: 25p, Target shooting (vert.). 40p, Gymnast on rings.

1965, Jan. 23 Engraved *Perf. 13*

C424 AP108 15p slate green & black 20 15
C425 " 25p green & pur. 25 25
C426 " 40p orange brown & indigo 45 30
a. Souv. sheet 6.00 6.00

Issued to commemorate the 18th Olympic Games, Tokyo, Oct. 10–25, 1964. No. C426a contains 3 imperf. stamps similar to Nos. C424–C426. Ocher marginal inscription. Sold for 100p. Size: 140x100mm.

Heliconius Cybria
AP109

Designs: 30p, Pericallia matronula. 40p, Red admiral. 45p, Satyrus semele. 70p, Machaon. 85p, Aurore. 100p, Morpho cypris. 200p, Erasmia sanguiflua. 300p, Papilio crassus. 500p, Charaxes ameliae.

1965 *Perf. 13* Unwmkd.

Size: 36x22mm.

C427 AP109 30p verm., yel. & dk. brn. 25 15
C428 " 35p olive bis., dk. bl. & red 30 20
C429 " 40p slate green, orge. & brn. 35 25

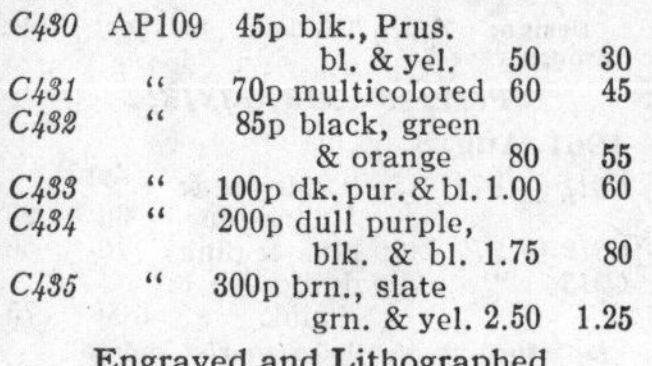

C430 AP109 45p blk., Prus. bl. & yel. 50 30
C431 " 70p multicolored 60 45
C432 " 85p black, green & orange 80 55
C433 " 100p dk. pur. & bl. 1.00 60
C434 " 200p dull purple, blk. & bl. 1.75 80
C435 " 300p brn., slate grn. & yel. 2.50 1.25

Engraved and Lithographed

Perf. 12

Size: 35x25mm.

C436 AP109 500p lt. ultra. & black 5.00 2.50
Nos. C427–C436 (10) 13.05 7.05

Pope Paul VI and Pres. Chehab
AP110

1965, June 28 Photo. *Perf. 12*

C437 AP110 45p gold & brt. violet 2.00 1.65
a. Souv. sheet 25.00 25.00

Issued to commemorate the visit of Pope Paul VI to Lebanon. No. C437a is imperf. and contains one stamp similar to No. C437. Size: 99x80mm. Sold for 50p.

Cedars of Friendship
AP111

1965, Oct. 16 Photo. *Perf. 13x12½*

C438 AP111 40p multicolored 50 15

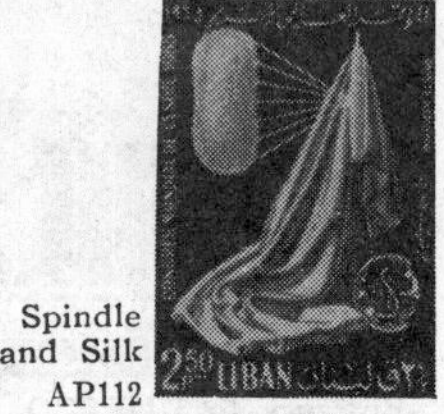

Cocoon, Spindle and Silk
AP112

Design: 15p, 30p, 40p, 50p, Silk weaver at loom.

1965, Oct. 16 *Perf. 12½x13*

Design in Buff and Bright Green

C439 AP112 2.50p brown 10 4
C440 " 5p dark olive green 10 4
C441 " 7.50p Prus. blue 5 4
C442 " 15p deep ultra. 15 8
C443 " 30p deep claret 30 20
C444 " 40p brown 50 25
C445 " 50p rose brown 60 35
Nos. C439–C445 (7) 1.80 1.00

Parliament Building
AP113

1965, Oct. 26 *Perf. 13x12½*

C446 AP113 35p red, buff & brown 35 20
C447 " 40p emerald, buff & brown 45 20

Centenary of the Lebanese parliament.

U.N. Headquarters, N.Y., U.N. Emblem and Lebanese Flags
AP114

1965, Nov. 10 Engraved *Perf. 12*

C448 AP114 2.50p dull blue 5 5
C449 " 10p magenta 10 8
C450 " 17.50p dull violet 15 12
C451 " 30p green 30 25
C452 " 40p brown 40 30
Nos. C448-C452 (5) 1.00 80

20th anniversary of the United Nations.
A souvenir sheet contains one 40p imperf. stamp in bright rose lilac, with marginal inscriptions. Size: 100x80mm. Sold for 50p. Price $8.

Playing Card King, Laurel and Cedar
AP115

1965, Nov. 15 Photo. *Perf. 12½x13*

C453 AP115 2.50p sal. pink, gold & grn. 10 4
C454 " 15p lt. rose lilac, gold & grn. 20 8
C455 " 17.50p bl., gold & green 25 12
C456 " 40p lt. vio., gold & green 40 20

International Bridge Championships.
A souvenir sheet contains two imperf. stamps similar to Nos. C454 and C456. Violet gray margin with emerald inscriptions. Size: 105x85mm. Sold for 75p. Price $8.

Dagger in Map of Palestine
AP116

1965, Dec. 13 *Perf. 12½x11*

C457 AP116 50p multicolored 50 40

Deir Yassin massacre, Apr. 9, 1948.

ITU Emblem, Old and New Communication Equipment and Syncom Satellite—AP117

1966, Apr. 13 *Perf. 13x12½*

C458 AP117 2.50p multi. 10 5
C459 " 15p " 15 10
C460 " 17.50p " 25 20
C461 " 25p " 50 25
C462 " 40p " 60 40
Nos. C458-C462 (5) 1.60 1.00

Issued to commemorate the centenary (in 1965) of the International Telecommunication Union.

Folk Dancers Before Temple of Bacchus—AP118

Designs: 7.50p, 15p, Dancers before Temple of Jupiter (vert). 30p, 40p, Orchestra before Temple of Bacchus.

1966, July 20 *Perf. 12* Unwmkd.

Gold Frame

C463 AP118 2.50p brown vio., blue & org. 10 5
C464 " 5p magenta, blue & org. 10 5
C465 " 7.50p violet blue, bl. & pink 10 7
C466 " 15p purple, blue & pink 15 10
C467 " 30p dk. green, org. & bl. 25 20
C468 " 40p violet, org. & blue 40 35
Nos. C463-C468 (6) 1.10 82

11th International Festival at Baalbek.

WHO Headquarters, Geneva
AP119

1966, Aug. 25 Engraved *Perf. 12*

C469 AP119 7.50p dp. yel. grn. 6 6
C470 " 17.50p carmine rose 15 15
C471 " 25p blue 20 20

Issued to commemorate the opening of World Health Organization Headquarters, Geneva.

Skier
AP120

Designs: 5p, Children on toboggan. 17.50p, Cedar in snow. 25p, Ski lift.

1966, Sept. 15 Photo. *Perf. 12x11½*

C472 AP120 2.50p multicolored 15 5
C473 " 5p " 15 5
C474 " 17.50p " 20 10
C475 " 25p " 40 25

International Festival of Cedars.

Sarcophagus of King Ahiram with Early Alphabet—AP121

Designs: 15p, Phoenician ship. 20p, Map of the Mediterranean Sea showing Phoenician travel routes, and ship. 30p, Phoenician with alphabet tablet.

Lithographed and Engraved

1966, Sept. 25 *Perf. 12*

C476 AP121 10p dull grn., blk. & lt. brown 10 10
C477 " 15p rose lilac, brn. & ocher 15 15
C478 AP121 20p tan, dk. brn. & blue 20 20
C479 " 30p org., dk. brn. & yellow 40 40

Invention of alphabet by Phoenicians.

Child in Bathtub and UNICEF Emblem
AP122

Designs (UNICEF Emblem and): 5p, Boy in rowboat. 7.50p, Girl skier. 12p, Girl feeding bird. 20p, Boy doing homework. 50p, Children of various races (horiz.).

1966, Oct. 10 Photo. *Perf. 11½x12*

C480 AP122 2.50p multi. 5 5
C481 " 5p " 10 5
C482 " 7.50p " 15 10
C483 " 15p " 20 15
C484 " 20p " 30 25
Nos. C480-C484 (5) 80 60

Miniature Sheet

Imperf.

C485 AP122 50p dull yellow & multi. 2.75 2.75

Issued for World Children's Day and the United Nations Children's Emergency Fund (UNICEF). No. C485 contains one horizontal stamp (43x33mm.), green cedars in margin. Size: 100x69½mm.

Scenic Type of Regular Issue, 1966

Designs: 10p, Waterfall, Djezzine. 15p, Castle of the Sea, Saida. 20p, Amphitheater, Jubayl (Byblos). 30p, Temple of the Sun, Baalbek. 50p, Beit-ed-Din Palace. 60p, Church of Christ the King, Nahr-el-Kalb. 75p, Abu Bakr Mosque, Tripoli.

1966, Oct. 12 *Perf. 12x11½*

C486 A82 10p gold & multi. 8 3
C487 " 15p " " 12 6
C488 " 20p " " 15 8
C489 " 30p " " 25 12
C490 " 50p " " 40 15
C491 " 60p " " 60 20
C492 " 75p " " 80 30
Nos. C486-C492 (7) 2.40 94

Symbolic Water Cycle
AP123

Daniel Bliss
AP124

Designs: 15p, 20p, Different wave pattern without sun.

1966, Nov. 15 Photo. *Perf. 12½*

C493 AP123 5p red, blue & vio. blue 5 5
C494 " 10p org., bl. & brn. 10 10
C495 " 15p org., emerald & dk. brown 15 15
C496 " 20p org., emerald & greenish blue 25 25

Hydrological Decade (UNESCO), 1965-74.

1966, Dec. 3

Designs: 30p, Chapel, American University, Beirut. 50p, Daniel Bliss, D.D., and American University (horiz.).

C497 AP124 20p grn., yellow & brown 25 12
C498 " 30p red brn., grn. & blue 25 18

Souvenir Sheet

Imperf.

C499 AP124 50p grn., brn. & org. brn. 1.20 1.20

Issued to commemorate the centenary of the American University, Beirut, founded by the Rev. Daniel Bliss (1823-1916). Nos. C497-C498 are printed each with alternating labels showing University emblem.
No. C499 contains one stamp (size: 59x37mm.), tan margin with brown inscription. Size: 124x85mm.

Flags of Arab League Members, Hand Signing Scroll—AP125

1967, Aug. 2 Photo. *Perf. 12x11½*

C500 AP125 5p brn. & multi. 5 5
C501 " 10p multicolored 10 10
C502 " 15p blk. & multi. 15 15
C503 " 20p multicolored 20 20

Signing of Arab League Pact in 1945.

Veteran's War Memorial Building, San Francisco—AP126

Design: 10p, 20p, 30p, Scroll, flags of Lebanon and United Nations.

1967, Sept. 1 Photo. *Perf. 12x11½*

C504 AP126 2.50p bl. & multi. 5 5
C505 " 5p multicolored 5 5
C506 " 7.50p " 7 5
C507 " 10p bl. & multi. 10 7
C508 " 20p multi. 18 10
C509 " 30p " 27 15
Nos. C504-C509 (6) 72 47

Issued to commemorate the 22nd anniversary of the San Francisco Pact, the United Nations Charter.

Ruins at Baalbek—AP127

Designs: 10p, Ruins at Anjar. 15p, Bridge over Ibrahim River and ruins. 20p, Boat on underground lake, Jaita cave. 50p, St. George's Bay, Beirut.

1967, Sept. 25 *Perf. 12½*

C510 AP127 5p multicolored 8 5
C511 " 10p " 12 7
C512 " 15p vio. & multi. 20 10
C513 " 20p brn. & multi. 25 15

Souvenir Sheet
Imperf.

C514 AP127 50p multi. 5.00 5.00

Issued for International Tourist Year, 1967. No. C514 contains one stamp; gray margin with map and flag of Lebanon. Size: 112x90mm.

View of Tabarja
AP128

Views: 15p, Pigeon Rock and shore, Beirut. 17.50p, Beit-ed-Din Palace. 20p, Ship at Sidon. 25p, Tripoli. 30p, Beach at Byblos. 35p, Ruins, Tyre. 40p, Temple of Bacchus, Baalbek.

1967, Oct. *Perf. 12x11½*

C515	AP128	10p multi.	7	3
C516	"	15p "	12	6
C517	"	17.50p "	15	10
C518	"	20p "	15	10
C519	"	25p "	20	10
C520	"	30p "	25	10
C521	"	35p "	30	10
C522	"	40p "	45	10
		Nos. C515-C522 (8)	1.69	69

Issued for International Tourist Year, 1967, but used as a regular airmail issue.

AP129

1967, Oct. 30 Engr. *Perf. 12*

C523	AP129	2.50p orange	5	5
C524	"	5p magenta	5	5
C525	"	7.50p brown	7	5
C526	"	10p blue	12	6
C527	"	15p green	24	10
		Nos. C523-C527 (5)	53	31

Issued for India Day.

Globe and Arabic Inscription
AP130

Design: 10p, 20p, 30p, U.N. emblem.

1967, Nov. 25 Engraved *Perf. 12*

C528	AP130	2.50p rose	10	10
C529	"	5p gray blue	10	10
C530	"	7.50p green	10	10
C531	"	10p brt. car.	10	10
C532	"	20p vio. blue	20	10
C533	"	30p dk. green	35	10
		Nos. C528-C533 (6)	95	60

Issued to commemorate Lebanon's admission to the United Nations. A 100p rose red souvenir sheet in the globe design exists. Size: 109x83mm. Price $4.

Basking Shark
AP131

Fish: 30p, Needlefish. 40p, Pollack. 50p, Cuckoo wrasse. 70p, Red mullet. 100p, Rainbow trout.

1968, Feb. Photo. *Perf. 12x11½*

C534	AP131	20p multicolored	20	6
C535	"	30p "	20	8
C536	"	40p "	30	15
C537	"	50p "	45	20
C538	"	70p "	70	25
C539	"	100p "	90	30
		Nos. C534-C539 (6)	2.75	1.04

Ski Jump
AP132

Designs: 5p, 7.50p, 10p, Downhill skiers (various). 25p, Congress emblem (skis and cedar).

1968 *Perf. 12½x11½*

C540	AP132	2.50p multi.	5	3
C541	"	5p "	8	5
C542	"	7.50p "	8	5
C543	"	10p "	10	5
C544	"	25p "	30	18
		Nos. C540-C544 (5)	61	36

Issued to publicize the 26th International Ski Congress, Beirut. A 50p imperf. souvenir sheet exists in design of the 25p. Size: 120x91mm. Price $4.

Emir Fakhreddine II
AP133

Designs: 2.50p, Emira Khaskiah. 10p, Citadel of Sidon (horiz.). 15p, Citadel of Chekif and grazing sheep (horiz.). 17.50p, Citadel of Beirut and harbor (horiz.).

Perf. 11½x12, 12x11½

1968, Feb. 20 Lithographed

C546	AP133	2.50p multicolored	3	3
C547	"	5p "	5	5
C548	"	10p "	6	5
C549	"	15p "	15	8
C550	"	17.50p "	20	10
		Nos. C546-C550 (5)	49	31

Issued in memory of the Emir Fakhreddine II. A 50p imperf. souvenir sheet exists showing the Battle of Anjar. Size: 118x86mm. Price $5.

Roman Bust
AP134

Ruins of Tyre: 5p, Colonnade (horiz.). 7.50p, Arch (horiz.). 10p, Banquet, bas-relief.

Lithographed and Engraved

1968, Mar. 20 *Perf. 12*

C552	AP134	2.50p pink, brn. & buff	5	5
C553	"	5p yel., brown & lt. blue	10	5
C554	"	7.50p lt. greenish blue, brn. & yellow	10	5
C555	"	10p salmon, brn. & lt. blue	15	10
		a. Souvenir sheet	5.00	5.00

Issued to publicize the excavations at Tyre. No. C555a contains one dark brown and light blue stamp, perf. 10½x11½. Yellow margin with dark brown inscription and light blue map of the Eastern Mediterranean. Size: 118x79mm. Sold for 50p. Exists imperf.

Emperor Justinian
AP135

Design: 15p, 20p, Justinian and map of the Mediterranean (horiz.).

Perf. 11½x12, 12x11½

1968, May 10 Photogravure

C556	AP135	5p blue & multi.	5	5
C557	"	10p " "	10	6
C558	"	15p red & multi.	15	10
C559	"	20p blue & multi.	20	10

Issued to honor Beirut as the site of one of the greatest law schools in antiquity, and to honor the Emperor Justinian (483–565), who compiled and preserved the Roman law.

Arab League Emblem
AP136

1968, June 6 Photo. *Perf. 12x11½*

C560	AP136	5p org. & multi.	5	3
C561	"	10p multicolored	10	7
C562	"	15p pink & multi.	15	10
C563	"	20p multicolored	20	15

Issued for Arab League Week.

Cedar and Globe Emblem—AP137

1968, July 10

C564	AP137	2.50p salmon pink, brown & green	5	3
C565	"	5p gray, brown & green	5	5
C566	"	7.50p brt. bl., brn. & green	7	5
C567	AP137	10p yel. grn., brn. & green	10	7

3rd Congress of Lebanese World Union.

Temple of Jupiter, Baalbek
AP138

Designs: 10p, Fluted pilasters, cella of Bacchus Temple. 15p, Corniche, south peristyle of Jupiter Temple (horiz.). 20p, Gate, Bacchus Temple. 25p, Ceiling detail, south peristyle of Bacchus Temple.

1968, Sept. 25 Photo. *Perf. 12½*

C568	AP138	5p gold & multi.	10	10
C569	"	10p " "	10	10
C570	"	15p " "	15	15
C571	"	20p " "	20	20
C572	"	25p " "	25	25
		Nos. C568-C572 (5)	80	80

13th Baalbek International Festival.

Broad Jump and Phoenician Statue
AP139

Designs: 10p, High jump and votive stele, Phoenician, 6th century B.C. 15p, Fencing and Olmec jade head, 500–400 B.C. 20p, Weight lifting and axe in shape of human head, Vera Cruz region. 25p, Aztec stone calendar and Phoenician ship.

1968, Oct. 19 Photo. *Perf. 12x11½*

C573	AP139	5p light ultra., yel. & gray	5	3
C574	"	10p magenta, lt. ultra. & blk.	7	7
C575	"	15p citron, ocher & brown	12	8
C576	"	20p deep orange, brown & ocher	16	13
C577	"	25p light brown	25	20
		Nos. C573-C577 (5)	65	51

Issued to commemorate the 19th Olympic Games, Mexico City, Oct. 12–27.

Human Rights Flame and Tractor
AP140

Designs (Human Rights Flame and): 15p, People. 25p, Boys of 3 races placing hands on globe.

1968, Dec. 10 Litho. *Perf. 11½*

C578	AP140	10p multicolored	8	5
C579	"	15p yel. & multi.	12	10
C580	"	25p lilac & multi.	20	15

International Human Rights Year.

Minshiya Stairs, Deir El-Kamar
AP141

Views in Deir El-Kamar: 15p, The Seraglio Kiosk. 25p, Old paved city road.

1968, Dec. 26

C581 AP141 10p multicolored 8 8
C582 " 15p " 12 8
C583 " 25p " 20 20

Centenary of the first Municipal Council in Lebanon, established in Deir El-Kamar by Daoud Pasha.

Nurse Treating Child, and U.N. Emblem—AP142

Designs: 10p, Grain, fish, grapes and jug. 15p, Mother and children. 20p, Reading girl and Phoenician alphabet. 25p, Playing children.

1969, Jan. 20 Litho. *Perf. 12*

C584 AP142 5p black, light blue & sepia 5 3
C585 " 10p black, brt. yel. & green 7 7
C586 " 15p black, red lilac & vermilion 12 8
C587 " 20p black, citron & blue 16 13
C588 " 25p black, pink & bister brown 20 15
Nos. C584-C588 (5) 60 46

Issued to commemorate the 22nd anniversary of UNICEF (United Nations Children's Fund).

Silver Coin from Byblos, 5th Century B.C.—AP143

Designs (National Museum, Beirut): 5p, Gold dagger, Byblos, 18th century B.C. 7.50p, King Dining in the Land of the Dead, sarcophagus of Ahiram, 13–12th century B.C. 30p, Breastplate with cartouche of Amenemhat III (1849–1801 B.C.). 40p, Phoenician bird vase from Khalde, 8th century B.C.

Photogravure; Gold Impressed

1969, Feb. 20 *Perf. 12*

C589 AP143 2.50p green, yellow & lt. blue 3 3
C590 " 5p violet, brown & yellow 5 5
C591 " 7.50p dull yellow, brown & pink 7 5
C592 " 30p bl. & multi. 20 17
C593 " 40p multi. 30 20
Nos. C589-C593 (5) 65 50

Issued to publicize the International Congress of Museum Councils. Issued to commemorate the 20th anniversary of the International Council of Museums (ICOM).

Water Skier
AP144

Designs: 5p, Water ballet. 7.50p, Parachutist (vert.). 30p, Yachting (vert.). 40p, Regatta.

1969, Mar. 3 Litho. *Perf. 11½*

C594 AP144 2.50p multi. 5 5
C595 " 5p " 5 5
C596 " 7.50p " 5 5
C597 " 30p " 20 20
C598 " 40p " 35 35
Nos. C594-C598 (5) 70 70

Tomb of Unknown Soldier at Military School—AP145

Designs: 2.50p, Frontier guard. 7.50p, Soldiers doing forestry work. 15p, Army engineers building road. 30p, Ambulance and helicopter. 40p, Ski patrol.

1969, Aug. 1 Litho. *Perf. 12x11½*

C599 AP145 2.50p multi. 5 5
C600 " 5p " 5 5
C601 " 7.50p " 5 5
C602 " 15p " 10 6
C603 " 30p " 20 13
C604 " 40p " 30 15
Nos. C599-C604 (6) 75 49

25th anniversary of independence.

Crosses and Circles
AP146

Design: 85p, Crosses and cedar.

1971, Jan. 6 Photo. *Perf. 11½x12*

C605 AP146 15p black & red 15 15
C606 " 85p " " 85 75

Lebanese Red Cross, 25th anniversary.

Foil Fencing
AP147

Designs: 10p, Flags of participating Arab countries. 15p, Flags of participating non-Arab countries. 40p, Sword fencing. 50p, Saber fencing.

1971, Jan. 15 Litho. *Perf. 12*

C607 AP147 10p yel. & multi. 6 6
C608 " 15p " " 10 10
C609 " 35p " " 24 24
C610 " 40p " " 27 27
C611 " 50p " " 33 33
Nos. C607-C611 (5) 1.00 1.00

Tenth World Fencing Championships, held in Lebanon.

Agricultural Workers, Arab Painting, 12th Century
AP148

1971, Feb. 1

C612 AP148 10p silver & multi. 10 6
C613 " 40p gold & multi. 30 30

International Labor Organization.

U.P.U. Building and Monument, Bern
AP149

1971, Feb. 15 Litho. *Perf. 12*

C614 AP149 15p yel., blk. & dp. orange 10 10
C615 " 35p dp. org., yel. & black 24 24

Opening of new Universal Postal Union Headquarters in Bern, Switzerland.

Ravens Burning Owls
AP150

Design: 85p, Jackal and lion. Designs of the 15p and 85p are after 13th–14th century paintings, illustrations for the "Kalila wa Dumna."

1971, March 1 Photo. *Perf. 11*
Size: 30x30mm.

C616 AP150 15p gold & multi. 15 10

Size: 38½x29mm. *Perf. 12x11½*

C617 AP150 85p gold & multi. 75 55

Children's Day.

Map and Flag of Arab League
AP151

1971, March 20 *Perf. 12x11½*

C618 AP151 30p org. & multi. 20 15
C619 " 70p yel. & multi. 50 40

25th anniversary of the founding of the Arab League.

Kahlil Gibran
AP152

Designs: No. C620, Symbolic design for Imam al Ouzai. No. C621, Bechara el Khoury. No. C622, Hassan Kamel al Sabbah.

1971, Apr. 10

C620 AP152 25p lt. green, gold & brown 20 16
C621 " 25p yellow, gold & brown 20 16
C622 AP152 25p yellow, gold & brown 20 16
C623 " 25p lt. green, gold & brown 20 16

Famous Lebanese men.

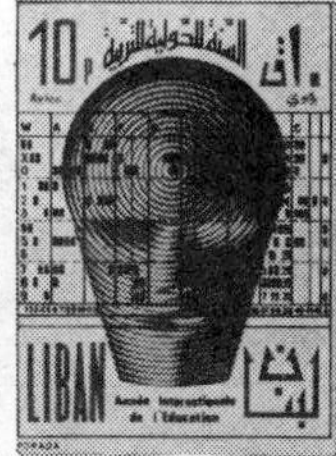

Education Year Emblem, Computer Card
AP153

1971, Apr. 30 Photo. *Perf. 11½x12*

C624 AP153 10p blk., vio. & bl. 10 6
C625 " 40p black, orange & yellow 30 24

International Education Year.

Jamhour Substation
AP154

Designs: 10p, Maameltein Bridge. 15p, Hotel Management School. 20p, Litani Dam. 25p, Television set wiring. 35p, Temple of Bziza. 40p, Jounieh Port. 45p, Airport radar. 50p, Flower. 70p, New School of Sciences. 85p, Oranges. 100p, Arbanieh earth satellite station.

1971, May Litho. *Perf. 12*

C626 AP154 5p multicolored 6 3
C627 " 10p " 8 5
C628 " 15p " 10 6
C629 " 20p " 17 10
C630 " 25p " 20 10
C631 " 35p " 30 10
C632 " 40p " 30 10
C633 " 45p " 30 15
C634 " 50p " 40 15
C635 " 70p " 60 15
C636 " 85p " 70 20
C637 " 100p " 80 30
Nos. C626-C637 (12) 4.01 1.49

Dahr-el-Bacheq Sanatorium
AP155

Design: 100p, Different view of Dahr-el-Bacheq Sanatorium.

1971, June 1

C638 AP155 50p gray & multi. 40 25
C639 " 100p multicolored 70 45

Campaign against tuberculosis.

Solar Wheel (Festival Emblem)
AP156

Design: 85p, Corinthian capital.

1971, July 1 Photo. *Perf. 11*

C640	AP156	15p ultra. & org.	15	10
C641	"	85p org. & ultra.	70	55

16th Baalbek International Festival.

155mm. Cannon AP157

Designs: 25p, Mirage fighters flying over Baalbek ruins. 40p, Army Headquarters. 70p, Naval patrol boat.

1971, Aug. 1 *Perf. 12x11½*

C642	AP157	15p gold & multi.	15	10
C643	"	25p " "	20	15
C644	"	40p " "	30	20
C645	"	70p " "	65	40

Army Day.

Wooden Console, Al Aqsa Mosque AP158

1971, Aug. 21 *Perf. 12*

C646	AP158	15p dark brown & ocher	20	15
C647	"	35p dark brown & ocher	45	30

2nd anniversary of the burning of Al Aqsa Mosque in Jerusalem.

Lenin AP159

1971, Oct. 1 *Perf. 12x11½*

C648	AP159	30p gold & multi.	30	20
C649	"	70p multicolored	70	50

Centenary of the birth of Lenin (1870–1924), Russian communist leader.

U.N. Emblem, World Map AP160

1971, Oct. 24 *Perf. 13x12½*

C650	AP160	15p multicolored	15	10
C651	"	85p "	85	50

25th anniversary of the United Nations (in 1970).

The Rape of Europa, Mosaic from Byblos AP161

1971, Nov. 20 Litho. *Perf. 12*

C652	AP161	10p silver & multi.	10	7
C653	"	40p gold & multi.	40	26

Publicity for World Lebanese Union (ULM).

Nos. C435–C436 Surcharged

Engr.; Engr. & Litho.

1972, May *Perf. 13, 12*

C654	AP109	100p on 300p multi.	1.00	60
C655	"	100p on 500p multi.	1.00	60
C656	"	200p on 300p multi.	2.00	1.20

The numerals on No. C655 are taller (5mm.) and bars spaced 1½mm. apart.

No. C554 Surcharged

(Reduced)

Lithographed and Engraved

1972, June *Perf. 12*

C657	AP134	5p on 7.50p multi.	6	4

Hibiscus AP162 Lebanese House AP163

1973 Lithographed *Perf. 12*

Multicolored

C658	AP162	2.50p *shown*	3	3
C659	"	5p *Roses*	5	4
C660	"	15p *Tulips*	15	8
C661	"	25p *Lilies*	25	6
C662	"	40p *Carnations*	30	20
C663	"	50p *Iris*	50	27
C664	"	70p *Apples*	70	8
C665	"	75p *Grapes*	70	35
C666	"	100p *Peaches*	1.00	55
C667	"	200p *Pears*	2.00	90
C668	"	300p *Cherries*	3.00	1.40
C669	"	500p *Oranges*	5.00	2.50
		Nos. C658–C669 (12)	13.68	6.46

1973 *Perf. 14*

Designs: Old Lebanese houses.

C670	AP163	35p yel. & multi.	35	10
C671	"	50p lt. bl. & multi.	40	15
C672	"	85p buff & multi.	70	20
C673	"	100p multi.	80	30

Woman with Rose AP164

Lebanese Costumes: 10p, Man. 20p, Man on horseback. 25p, Woman playing mandolin.

1973, Sept. 1 Litho. *Perf. 14*

C674	AP164	5p yel. & multi.	5	4
C675	"	10p " "	10	6
C676	"	20p " "	20	12
C677	"	25p " "	25	15

Swimming, Temple at Baalbek—AP165

Designs: 10p, Running and portal. 15p, Woman athlete and castle. 20p, Women's volleyball and columns. 25p, Basketball and aqueduct. 50p, Women's table tennis and buildings. 75p, Football and building. 100p, Soccer and cedar.

1973, Sept. 25 Photo. *Perf. 11½x12*

C678	AP165	5p multicolored	5	4
C679	"	10p "	10	6
C680	"	15p grn. & multi.	15	8
C681	"	20p multicolored	20	12
C682	"	25p ultra. & multi.	25	15
C683	"	50p org. & multi.	50	30
C684	"	75p violet & multi.	75	45
C685	"	100p multicolored	1.25	85
		a. Souvenir sheet	1.50	1.50
		Nos. C678–C685 (8)	3.25	2.05

5th Pan-Arabic Scholastic Games, Beyrouth. No. C685a contains one stamp with simulated perforations similar to No. C685; gold inscription and denomination; lilac and multicolored margin with gold inscription. Size: 119x70mm.

View of Brasilia—AP166

Designs: 20p, Old Salvador (Bahia). 25p, Lebanese sailing ship enroute from the Old World to South America. 50p, Dom Pedro I and Emir Fakhr al-Din II.

1973, Nov. 15 Litho. *Perf. 12*

C686	AP166	5p gold & multi.	5	4
C687	"	20p " "	20	12
C688	"	25p " "	25	15
C689	"	50p " "	50	35

Sesquicentennial of Brazil's independence.

Inlay Worker AP167

1973, Dec. 1

Multicolored

C690	AP167	10p *shown*	10	4
C691	"	20p *Weaver*	20	10
C692	"	35p *Glass blower*	30	15
C693	"	40p *Potter*	40	20
C694	"	50p *Metal worker*	45	25
C695	"	70p *Cutlery maker*	65	30
C696	"	85p *Lace maker*	85	40
C697	"	100p *Handicraft Museum*	1.00	55
		Nos. C690–C697 (8)	3.95	1.99

Lebanese handicrafts.

Camp Site, Log Fire and Scout Emblem—AP168

Designs: 5p, Lebanese Scout emblem and map. 7½p, Lebanese Scout emblem and map of Middle East. 10p. Lord Baden-Powell, ruins of Baalbek. 15p, Girl Guide, camp and emblem. 20p, Lebanese Girl Guide and Scout emblems. 25p, Scouts around camp fire. 30p, Symbolic globe with Lebanese flag and Scout emblem. 35p, Flags of participating nations. 50p, Old man, and Scout chopping wood.

1974, Aug. 24 Litho. *Perf. 12*

C698	AP168	2.50p multicolored	5	3
C699	"	5p "	5	3
C700	"	7.50p "	10	4
C701	"	10p "	10	6
C702	"	15p "	15	10
C703	"	20p "	20	15
C704	"	25p "	25	17
C705	"	30p "	30	20
C706	"	35p "	45	25
C707	"	50p "	55	30
		Nos. C698–C707 (10)	2.20	1.33

11th Arab Boy Scout Jamboree, Smar-Jubeil, Aug. 1974. Nos. C702–C703 are for the 5th Girl Guide Jamboree, Deir-el-Kamar. Nos. C698–C702 and C703–C707 printed vertically se-tenant.

Mail Train and Postman Loading Mail, UPU Emblem—AP169

Designs (UPU Emblem and): 20p, Postal container hoisted onto ship. 25p, Postal Union Congress Building, Lausanne, and UPU Headquarters, Bern. 50p, Fork-lift truck loading mail on plane.

1974, Nov. 4 Photo. *Perf. 11½x12*

C708	AP169	5p multicolored	5	3
C709	"	20p "	20	15
C710	"	25p "	25	17
C711	"	50p ultra. & multi.	50	40

Centenary of Universal Postal Union.

Congress Building, Sofar AP170

Designs (Arab Postal Union Emblem and): 20p, View of Sofar. 25p, APU Headquarters, Cairo. 50p, Ministry of Post, Beirut.

1974, Dec. 4 Litho. *Perf. 13x12½*

C712	AP170	5p org. & multi.	5	3
C713	"	20p yel. & multi.	20	15
C714	"	25p blue & multi.	25	17
C715	"	50p multicolored	1.00	65

Arab Postal Union, 25th anniversary.

Mountain Road, by Omar Onsi AP171

Paintings: No. C717, Clouds, by Moustapha Farroukh. No. C718, Woman, by Gebran Kahlil Gebran. No. C719, Embrace, by Cesar Gemayel. No. C720, Self-portrait, by Habib Serour. No. C721, Portrait of a Man, by Daoud Corm.

1974, Dec. 6 Litho. *Perf. 13x12½*

C716	AP171	50p lilac & multi.	50	35
C717	"	50p blue & multi.	50	35
C718	"	50p green & multi.	50	35
C719	"	50p light violet & multi.	50	35
C720	"	50p brn. & multi.	50	35
C721	"	50p gray brown & multi.	50	35
		Nos. C716-C721 (6)	3.00	2.10

Lebanese painters.

Hunter Spearing Lion AP172

1974, Dec. 13

Designs: 10p, Statue of Astarte. 25p, Dogs hunting boar, tiled panel. 35p, Greco-Roman tomb.

C722	AP172	5p blue & multi.	5	3
C723	"	10p lilac & multi.	10	6
C724	"	25p multicolored	25	15
C725	"	35p "	30	20

Excavations at Hermel.

UNESCO Emblems and Globe AP173

1974, Dec. 16 *Perf. 12½x13*

C726	AP173	5p vio. & multi.	5	3
C727	"	10p bister & multi.	10	6
C728	"	25p blue & multi.	25	15
C729	"	35p multicolored	30	20

International Book Year 1972.

Symbolic Stamp under Magnifying Glass AP174

Designs (Symbolic): 10p, Post horns. 15p, Stamp printing. 20p, Mounted stamp.

1974, Dec. 20 *Perf. 13x12½*

C730	AP174	5p blue & multi.	5	3
C731	"	10p olive & multi.	10	6
C732	"	15p brn. & multi.	15	15
C733	"	20p lilac & multi.	20	20

Stamp day.

Georgina Rizk AP175

Designs: 5p, 25p, Georgina Rizk in Lebanese costume. 50p, Like 20p.

1974, Dec. 21

C734	AP175	5p multicolored	5	3
C735	"	20p vio. & multi.	20	15
C736	"	25p yel. & multi.	25	17
C737	"	50p blue & multi.	50	40
		a. Souvenir sheet of 4	1.40	1.40

Georgina Rizk, Miss Universe 1971. No. C737a contains 4 stamps similar to Nos. C734-C737 with simulated perforations. Buff and multicolored margin with portrait of Miss Rizk. Size: 156x112mm.

UNICEF Emblem, Helicopter, Camel, Supplies AP176

Designs (UNICEF Emblem and): 25p, Child welfare clinic. 35p, Kindergarten class. 70p, Girls in chemistry laboratory.

1974, Dec. 28 Litho. *Perf. 12½x13*

C738	AP176	20p multicolored	20	15
C739	"	25p "	25	17
C740	"	35p blue & multi.	35	25
C741	"	70p " "	70	45
		a. Souvenir sheet of 4	2.25	2.25

United Nations Children's Fund (UNICEF), 25th anniversary. No. C741a contains 4 stamps similar to Nos. C738-C741 with simulated perforations; multicolored margin with UNICEF emblem and black inscription. Size: 157x112mm. Sold for 200p.

Discus and Olympic Rings AP177

1974, Dec. 30 *Perf. 13x12½*

Multicolored

C742	AP177	5p *shown*	5	3
C743	"	10p *Shot put*	10	7
C744	"	15p *Weight lifting*	20	10
C745	"	35p *Running*	40	25
C746	"	50p *Wrestling*	55	35
C747	"	85p *Javelin*	90	60
		a. Souvenir sheet of 6	2.50	2.50
		Nos. C742-C747 (6)	2.20	1.40

20th Olympic Games, Munich, Aug. 26-Sept. 11, 1972. No. C747a contains 6 stamps similar to Nos. C742-C747 with simulated perforations. Multicolored margin with black inscription. Size: 175x130mm.

Clouds and Environment Emblem AP178

1975

Multicolored

C748	AP178	5p *shown*	5	3
C749	"	25p *Landscape*	25	17
C750	"	30p *Flowers and tree*	30	20
C751	"	40p *Waves*	40	30
		a. Souvenir sheet of 4	1.65	1.65

U.N. Conference on Human Environment, Stockholm, June 5-16, 1972. No. C751a contains four stamps similar to Nos. C748-C751 with simulated perforations. Multicolored margin with black inscription. Size: 103x114mm. Sold for 150p.

Archaeology AP179

Designs (Symbols of): 25p, Science and medicine. 35p, Justice and commerce. 70p, Industry and commerce.

1975, Aug. Litho. *Perf. 12½x13*

C752	AP179	20p multicolored	20	15
C753	"	25p "	25	17
C754	"	35p bl. & multi.	35	25
C755	"	70p buff & multi.	70	45

Beirut University City.

Stamps of 1971-73 Overprinted with Various Overall Patterns Including Cedars in Blue, Red, Orange, Lilac, Brown or Green

1978 Lithographed *Perf. 12, 14*

Multicolored

C758	AP162	2.50p (#C658; B)	3	3
C759	"	5p (#C659; R)	5	4
C760	AP164	5p (#C674; B)	5	4
C761	"	10p (#C675; B)	10	6
C762	AP167	10p (#C690; O)	10	6
C763	AP162	15p (#C660; R)	15	10
C764	AP164	20p (#C676; B)	20	10
C765	AP167	20p (#C691; B)	20	10
C766	AP162	25p (#C661; L)	25	15
C767	AP164	25p (#C677; B)	25	15
C768	AP163	35p (#C670; Br)	35	15
C769	AP162	40p (#C662; L)	40	15
C770	AP167	40p (#C693; G)	40	15
C771	AP154	45p (#C633; L)	45	15
C772	AP162	50p (#C663; L)	50	15
C773	AP163	50p (#C671; L)	50	15
C774	AP167	50p (#C694; Br)	50	15
C775	AP154	70p (#C635; L)	70	15
C776	AP162	70p (#C664; L)	70	15
C777	AP167	70p (#C695; B)	70	15
C778	AP162	75p (#C665; B)	75	15
C779	AP154	85p (#C636; R)	85	18
C780	AP163	85p (#C672; B)	85	18
C781	AP167	85p (#C696; G)	85	18
C782	AP162	100p (#C666; O)	1.00	30
C783	AP163	100p (#C673; B)	1.00	30
C784	AP167	100p (#C697; L)	1.00	30
C785	AP162	200p (#C667; O)	2.00	60
C786	"	300p (#C668; O)	3.00	90
C787	"	500p (#C669; O)	5.00	1.50
		Nos. C758-C787 (30)	22.88	6.92

Heart and Arrow AP180

1978, Apr. 7 Litho. *Perf. 12*

C788	AP180	50p blue, black & red	50	30

World Health Day and drive against hypertension.

Poet Mikhail Naimy and Sannine Mountains—AP181

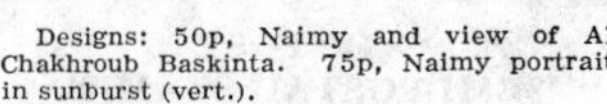

Designs: 50p, Naimy and view of Al Chakhroub Baskinta. 75p, Naimy portrait in sunburst (vert.).

1978, May 17

C789	AP181	25p gold & multi.	25	15
C790	"	50p " "	50	30
C791	"	75p " "	75	45

Mikhail Naimy Festival.

AIR POST SEMI-POSTAL STAMPS.

Nos. C13-C16 Surcharged Like Nos. B1-B12.

1926 *Perf. 13½*

CB1 A2 2pi+1pi dark brown 3.00 3.00
CB2 " 3pi+2pi org. brown 3.00 3.00
CB3 " 5pi+3pi violet 3.00 3.00
CB4 A3 10pi+5pi violet brn. 3.00 3.00

These stamps were sold for their combined values, original and surcharged. The latter represented their postal franking value and the former was a contribution to the relief of refugees from the Djebel Druze War.

Independent Republic.

Natural Bridge, Faraya
SPAP1

Bay of Jounie
SPAP2

Lithographed.

1947, June 27 *Perf. 11½* Unwmkd.

Cross in Carmine.

CB5 SPAP1 12.50pi+25pi bright blue green 6.00 6.00
CB6 " 25pi+50pi blue 6.00 6.00
CB7 SPAP2 50pi+100pi chocolate 6.00 6.00
CB8 " 75pi+150pi brt. purple 12.50 12.50
CB9 " 100pi+200pi slate 20.00 15.00
Nos. CB5-CB9 (5) 50.50 45.50

The surtax was for the Red Cross.

Type of Air Post Stamps, 1960.

1960, Aug. 16 *Perf. 13½x13*

CB10 AP72 20p+10p dark red & buff 60 30
CB11 " 60p+15p blue & light blue 1.20 60

Day of Mother and Child, Mar. 21-22.

Type of Semi-Postal Issue, 1961. (Olympic Games)

Sports: 15p+15p, Fencing. 25p+25p, Bicycling. 35p+35p, Swimming.

1961, Jan. 12 *Perf. 13* Unwmkd.

CB12 SP1 15p+15p red & red brown 2.00 1.65
CB13 " 25p+25p blue grn. & red brown 2.00 1.65
CB14 " 35p+35p vio. blue & red brown 2.00 1.65

Issued to commemorate the 17th Olympic Games, Rome, Aug. 25-Sept. 11, 1960.
An imperf. souvenir sheet exists, containing one each of Nos. CB12-CB14. Black and gray marginal inscription. Size: 136x117mm. Price $12.50.

Nos. CB12-CB14 with Arabic and French Overprint in Green, Red or Maroon and two Bars through Olympic Inscription: "CHAMPIONNAT D'EUROPE DE TIR, 2 JUIN 1962"

1962, June 2

CB15 SP1 15p+15p red & red brown (G) 50 50
CB16 " 25p+25p blue grn. & red brn. (M) 1.00 1.00
CB17 " 35p+35p vio. blue & red brn. (R) 1.50 1.50

Issued to publicize the European Marksmanship Championships held in Lebanon.

POSTAGE DUE STAMPS.

Postage Due Stamps of France, 1893-1920, Surcharged like Regular Issue.

1924 *Perf. 14x13½.* Unwmkd.

J1 D2 50c on 10c chocolate 1.65 1.25
J2 " 1pi on 20c olive green 1.65 1.25
J3 " 2pi on 30c red 1.65 1.25
J4 " 3pi on 50c vio. brown 1.65 1.25
J5 " 5pi on 1fr red brown, *straw* 1.65 1.25
Nos. J1-J5 (5) 8.25 6.25

Postage Due Stamps of France, 1893-1920, Surcharged

Gd Liban
2 Piastres
لبنان الكبير
غرش ٢

1924

J6 D2 0p50 on 10c chocolate 1.65 1.25
J7 " 1pi on 20c olive green 1.65 1.25
J8 " 2pi on 30c red 1.65 1.25
J9 " 3pi on 50c violet brown 1.65 1.25
J10 " 5pi on 1fr red brown, *straw* 1.65 1.25
Nos. J6-J10 (5) 8.25 6.25

Ancient Bridge across Dog River
D3

Designs: 1p, Village scene. 2p, Pigeon Rocks, near Beirut. 3p, Belfort Castle. 5p, Venus Temple at Baalbek.

1925 Photogravure. *Perf. 13½.*

J11 D3 0p50 brown, *yellow* 10 10
J12 " 1pi violet, *rose* 30 30
J13 " 2pi *blue* 40 40
J14 " 3pi *red orange* 1.00 1.00
J15 " 5pi *blue green* 1.25 1.25
Nos. J11-J15 (5) 3.05 3.05

Nos. J11 to J15 Overprinted

République Libanaise

1927

J16 D3 0p50 brown, *yellow* 20 20
J17 " 1pi violet, *rose* 50 50
J18 " 2pi *blue* 60 60
J19 " 3pi *red orange* 1.40 1.40
J20 " 5pi *blue green* 1.85 1.85
Nos. J16-J20 (5) 4.55 4.55

Nos. J16 to J20 with Additional Overprint

الجمهورية اللبنانية

1928

J21 D3 0p50 brown, *yellow* (Bk+R) 50 50
J22 " 1pi violet, *rose* (Bk) 60 60
J23 " 2pi *blue* (Bk+R) 1.00 1.00
J24 " 3pi *red orange* (Bk) 2.00 1.75
J25 " 5pi *blue green* (Bk+R) 2.50 1.75
Nos. J21-J25 (5) 6.60 5.60

No. J23 has not the short bars in the upper corners.

Postage Due Stamps of 1925 Overprinted in Red like Nos. J21-J25.

1928

J26 D3 0p50 brown, *yellow* (R) 20 20
J27 " 2pi *blue* (R) 1.35 1.35
J28 " 5pi *blue green* (R) 5.00 4.00

No. J28 has not the short bars in the upper corners.

D4

Bas-relief of a Ship
D5

D6

D7

D8

Bas-relief from Sarcophagus of King Ahiram—D9

D10

1930-40 Photo.; Engr. (No. J35)

J29 D4 0p50 *rose* 20 20
J30 D5 1pi *gray blue* 45 45
J31 D6 2pi *yellow* 40 40
J32 D7 3pi *blue green* 50 50
J33 D8 5pi *orange* 2.25 2.25
J34 D9 8pi *light rose* 1.25 1.25
J35 D8 10pi dk. green ('40) 2.00 2.00
J36 D10 15pi black 1.10 1.10
Nos. J29-J36 (8) 8.15 8.15

Nos. J29-J36 exist imperf.

Independent Republic

National Museum, Beirut
D11

Lithographed.

1945 *Perf. 11½* Unwmkd.

J37 D11 2pi brn. black, *yellow* 1.50 1.50
J38 " 5pi ultramarine, *rose* 1.50 1.50
J39 " 25pi blue, *blue green* 3.00 3.00
J40 " 50pi dark blue, *blue* 3.00 3.00

D12

1947

J41 D12 5pi *green* 2.00 60
J42 " 25pi *yellow* 17.50 90
J43 " 50pi *blue* 10.00 2.50

Hermel Monument
D13

1948

J44 D13 2pi *yellow* 1.00 60
J45 " 3pi *pink* 3.00 90
J46 " 10pi *blue* 8.00 2.50

D14

1950

J47 D14 1pi carmine rose 50 10
J48 " 5pi violet blue 1.50 50
J49 " 10pi gray green 3.00 90

D15

1952

J50 D15 1pi deep rose lilac 10 6
J51 " 2pi bright violet 20 10
J52 " 3pi dark blue green 30 15
J53 " 5pi blue 35 15
J54 " 10pi chocolate 55 30
J55 " 25pi black 5.50 75
Nos. J50-J55 (6) 7.00 1.51

D16

D17

1953

J56 D16 1pi carmine rose 6 5
J57 " 2pi blue green 8 5
J58 " 3pi orange 10 8
J59 " 5pi lilac rose 15 8
J60 " 10pi brown 30 15
J61 " 15pi deep blue 60 30
Nos. J56-J61 (6) 1.29 71

1955 *Perf. 13* Unwmkd.

J62 D17 1pi orange brown 5 4
J63 " 2pi yellow green 10 4
J64 " 3pi blue green 10 4
J65 " 5pi carmine lake 13 5
J66 " 10pi gray green 18 10
J67 " 15pi ultramarine 20 13
J68 " 25pi red lilac 45 30
Nos. J62-J68 (7) 1.21 70

Cedar of Lebanon
D18

Emir Fakhreddine II
D19

1966 Photogravure *Perf. 11½*

J69	D18	1p bright green	5	5
J70	"	5p rose lilac	5	5
J71	"	15p ultramarine	15	15

1968 Lithographed *Perf. 11*

J72	D19	1p dk. & lt. gray	3	3
J73	"	2p dk. & lt. blue green	3	3
J74	"	3p dp. org. & yellow	3	3
J75	"	5p bright rose lilac & pink	5	5
J76	"	10p olive & lemon	8	8
J77	"	15p vio. & pale violet	10	10
J78	"	25p brt. blue & lt. blue	25	20
		Nos. J72-J78 (7)	57	52

POSTAL TAX STAMPS.

R1

Fiscal Stamp Surcharged in Violet

طابع الجيش

٥ قروش ٥

Wmkd. A T 39 Multiple.

1945 *Perf. 13½*

RA1 R1 5pi on 30c red brn. 12.50 75

The tax was for the Lebanese Army.

No. RA1 Overprinted in Black

طابع فلسطين

1948

RA2 R1 5pi on 30c red brn. 12.50 1.25

Fiscal Stamps Surcharged in Various Colors

ضريبة فلسطين

٥ قروش ٥

RA3	R1	5pi on 15pi dk. vio. blue (R)	13.00	1.25
		a. Brown surch.	27.50	3.50
RA4	"	5pi on 25c dk. blue green (R)	13.00	1.25
RA5	"	5pi on 30c red brn. (Bl)	17.50	1.25
RA6	"	5pi on 60c light ultra. (Br)	27.50	1.25
RA7	"	5pi on 3pi salmon rose (Ult)	13.00	1.25

Fiscal Stamp Surcharged Type "b" and Overprinted طابع قضائي

RA8 R1 5pi on 10pi red *60.00* 2.50

Fiscal Stamp Surcharged Type "b" with Top Arabic characters replaced by ضريبة فلسطين

RA9 R1 5pi on 3pi rose (Bk+V) 12.50 1.25

Fiscal Stamp Surcharged in Black and Violet

ضريبة فلسطين

5 ٥

RA10 R1 5pi on 3pi salmon rose *275.00* 20.00

The tax was to aid the war in Palestine.

Family among Ruins
R2

Lithographed

1956 *Perf. 13* **Unwmkd.**

RA11 R2 2.50pi brown 1.00 12

The tax was for earthquake victims. These stamps were obligatory on all inland mail and all mail going to Arab countries.

Building a House
R3

1957 *Perf. 13½x13*

RA12 R3 2.50p brown 1.00 12

1958

RA13 R3 2.50p dark blue grn. 45 10

Type of 1957 Redrawn.

1959

RA14 R3 2.50p light brown 75 8

On No. RA14 the denomination is on top and the Arabic lines are at the bottom of design.

Building a House
R4 R5

1961 *Perf. 13½x13* **Unwmkd.**

RA15 R4 2.50p yellow brown 50 12

1962 *Perf. 13½x14*

RA16 R5 2.50p blue green 40 15

The tax was for the relief of earthquake victims.

LIBERIA

(lī·bēr'ī·ȧ)

LOCATION—On the west coast of Africa between Ivory Coast and Sierra Leone.

GOVT.—Republic.

AREA—43,000 sq. mi. (approx.).

POP.—1,800,000 (est. 1977).

CAPITAL—Monrovia.

100 Cents = 1 Dollar

"Liberia"
A1

Lithographed.

1860 *Perf. 12.* **Unwmkd.**

Thick Paper.

1	A1	6c red	55.00	70.00
		a. Imperf.	75.00	
2	"	12c deep blue	20.00	27.50
		a. Imperf.	75.00	
3	"	24c green	20.00	27.50
		a. Imperf.	75.00	

Nos. 1 to 3: Stamps set very close together. Margins small and perforation close to or touching the design. Copies of the 12c occasionally show traces of a frame line around the design.

Medium to Thin Paper.

With a single-line frame around each stamp, about 1mm. from the border.

1864 *Perf. 11, 12.*

7	A1	6c red	40.00	55.00
		a. Imperf.	70.00	
8	"	12c blue	40.00	55.00
		a. Imperf.	70.00	
9	"	24c light green	40.00	55.00
		a. Imperf.	70.00	

Nos. 7 to 9: Stamps set about 5 mm. apart. Margins large and perforation usually outside the frame line.

Without Frame Line.

1866-69

13	A1	6c light red	17.50	25.00
14	"	12c light blue	15.00	25.00
15	"	24c lt. yellow green	15.00	25.00

Nos. 13 to 15: Stamps set 2 to 2½ mm. apart with small margins. Stamps are usually without frame line but those from one transfer show broken and irregular parts of a frame.

With Frame Line.

1880 *Perf. 10½.*

16	A1	1c ultramarine	3.00	5.00
17	"	2c rose	3.00	5.00
		a. Imperf., pair	75.00	
18	"	6c violet	2.50	5.00
19	"	12c yellow	3.50	6.00
20	"	24c rose red	4.00	7.00

From Arms of Liberia
A2

1881

21 A2 3c black 3.50 3.50

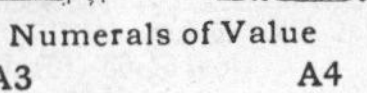
Numerals of Value
A3 A4

1882 *Perf. 11½, 12, 14*

22	A3	8c blue	15.00	7.50
23	A4	16c red	5.00	4.00

On No. 22 the openings in the figure "8" enclose a pattern of slanting lines. Compare with No. 32.

Canceled to Order

Beginning with the issue of 1885, prices in the used column are for "canceled to order" stamps. Postally used copies sell for much more.

Numerals of Value
A5 A6

From Arms of Liberia
A7

Numeral of Value
A8

1885 *Perf. 10½, 11, 12, 11½x10½, 14, 14½.*

24	A5	1c carmine	80	80
		a. 1c rose	80	80
		b. Imperf., pair	2.50	
25	"	2c green	80	80
		a. Imperf., pair	3.50	
26	"	3c violet	80	80
		a. Imperf., pair	4.00	
27	"	4c brown	90	90
		a. Imperf., pair	4.00	
28	"	6c olive gray	90	90
		a. Imperf., pair	3.50	3.50
29	A6	8c bluish gray	2.00	2.00
		a. 8c lilac	2.00	2.00
		b. Imperf., pair	10.00	
30	"	16c yellow	3.25	3.25
		a. Imperf., pair	12.50	
31	A7	32c deep blue	7.50	7.50
		a. Imperf., pair	25.00	
		Nos. 24-31 (8)	16.95	16.95

In the 1885 printing, the stamps are spaced 2mm. apart and the paper is medium. In the 1892 printing, the stamps are 4½mm. apart.

Imperf. pairs with 2mm. spacing sell for higher prices.

1889 *Perf. 12, 14*

32	A8	8c blue	4.00	3.50
		a. Imperf., pair	15.00	

The openings in the figure "8" are filled with network. See No. 22.

Numeral in Star
A9

Oil Palm
A11

Elephant—A10

Pres. Hilary R. W. Johnson
A12

Vai Woman in Full Dress
A13

Coat of Arms
A14

Liberian Star
A15

Coat of Arms
A16

Hippopotamus
A17

Liberian Star
A18

President Johnson
A19

Wmk. 143

Engraved.

1892–96 *Perf. 15* **Wmk. 143**

33 A9 1c vermilion 40 40
a. 1c blue (error) 35.00
34 " 2c blue 40 40
a. 2c vermilion (error) 35.00
35 A10 4c green & black 1.50 1.00
a. Center inverted 55.00 55.00
36 A11 6c blue green 60 60
37 A12 8c brown & black 75 1.00
a. Center inverted 150.00 150.00
38 " 10c chrome yellow & indigo ('96) 75 75
39 A13 12c rose red 75 75
40 " 15c slate ('96) 75 75
41 A14 16c lilac 2.00 2.00
42 " 20c vermilion ('96) 2.00 2.00
43 A15 24c olive green, *yellow* 1.25 1.25
44 " 25c yel. grn. ('96) 1.50 1.50
45 A16 30c steel blue ('96) 5.00 5.00
46 " 32c greenish blue 3.00 3.00
47 A17 $1 ultra. & black 5.50 5.50
a. $1 blue & black 6.50 6.50

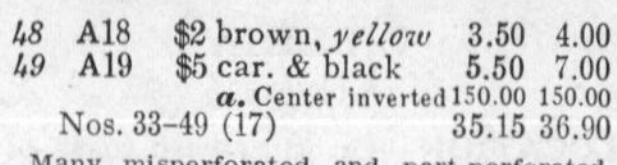

48 A18 $2 brown, *yellow* 3.50 4.00
49 A19 $5 car. & black 5.50 7.00
a. Center inverted 150.00 150.00
Nos. 33–49 (17) 35.15 36.90

Many misperforated and part-perforated varieties exist.

The 1c, 2c and 4c were issued in sheets of 60; 6c, sheet of 40; 8c, 10c, sheets of 30; 12c, 15c, 24c, 25c, sheets of 20; 16c, 20c, 30c, sheets of 15; $1, $2, $5, sheets of 10.

No. 36 Surcharged:

5 5 5 5

Five Cents
a

Five Cents
b

1893

50 A11 (*a*) 5c on 6c blue green 1.25 1.25
a. "5" with short flag 4.00 4.00
b. Both 5's with short flags 2.00 2.00
c. "i" dot omitted 15.00 15.00
d. Surcharge "b" 25.00 25.00

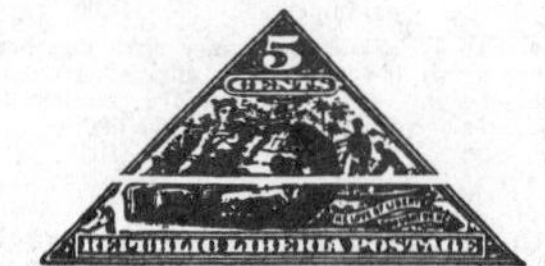

"Commerce," Globe and Krumen
A22

Engraved.

1894 ***Imperf.*** **Unwmkd.**

52 A22 5c carmine & black 3.00 3.00

Rouletted

53 A22 5c carmine & black 5.00 5.00

Oil Palm
A23

Hippopotamus
A24

Elephant
A25

Liberty
A26

Perf. 14 to 16

1897–1905 **Wmk. 143**

54 A23 1c lilac rose 60 50
a. 1c violet 75 75
55 " 1c deep green ('00) 75 70
56 " 1c light green ('05) 1.25 70
57 A24 2c bistre & black 1.50 1.25
58 " 2c orange red & black ('00) 2.00 1.25
59 " 2c rose & blk. ('05) 1.50 1.25
60 A25 5c lake & black 1.50 1.25
a. 5c lilac rose & blk. 1.50 1.25
61 " 5c gray blue & black ('00) 3.00 2.00
62 " 5c ultramarine & black ('05) 2.25 2.00
a. Center inverted 300.00
63 A26 50c red brn. & blk. 2.00 2.00
Nos. 54–63 (10) 16.35 12.90

A27

Two types:
I. 13 pearls above "Republic Liberia."
II. 10 pearls.

Lithographed

1897 ***Perf. 14*** **Unwmkd.**

64 A27 3c red & green (I) 25 25
a. Type II *1.00* 10

Official Stamps Handstamped in Black ORDINARY

1901–02 **Wmk. 143.**

On Nos. O7–O8, O10–O12.

64B A14 16c lilac *250.00 250.00*
64C A15 24c olive green, *yellow* 225.00 225.00
64D A17 $1 blue & black *900.00 900.00*
64E A18 $2 brn., *yel.* *1500.00 1500.00*
64F A19 $5 car. & blk. *3000.00 3000.00*

On Stamps with "O S" Printed.

65 A23 1c green 25.00 25.00
66 A9 2c blue 65.00 65.00
66A A24 2c bis. & black 60.00
67 " 2c orange red & black 25.00 25.00
68 A25 5c gray blue & black 20.00 20.00
69 A22 5c vio. & green (No. O26) 165.00 165.00
70 A25 5c lake & black 110.00 110.00
71 A12 10c yellow & blue black 25.00 25.00
a. "O S" omitted
72 A13 15c slate 25.00 25.00
73 A14 16c lilac 160.00 160.00
74 " 20c vermilion 30.00 30.00
75 A15 24c olive green, *yellow* 30.00 30.00
76 " 25c yellow green 30.00 30.00
a. "O S" omitted
77 A16 30c steel blue 25.00 25.00
78 A26 50c red brown & black 35.00 35.00
79 A17 $1 ultramarine & black 185.00 185.00
a. "O S" omitted
80 A18 $2 brn., *yel.* *1000.00 1000.00*
81 A19 $5 carmine & black *1750.00 1750.00*
a. "O S" omitted *2000.00 2000.00*

On Stamps with "O S" Handstamped.

82 A23 1c deep green 40.00 40.00
83 A24 2c orange red & black 40.00 40.00
84 A25 5c lake & black 70.00 70.00
85 A12 10c yellow & blue black 60.00 60.00
86 A14 20c vermilion 70.00 70.00
87 A15 24c olive green, *yellow* 70.00 70.00
88 " 25c yellow green 85.00 85.00
89 A16 30c steel blue 185.00 185.00
90 " 32c greenish blue 110.00 110.00

Varieties of Nos. 65–90 include double and inverted overprints.

Hippopotamus
A28

Liberty
A29

1902 Carmine Surcharge.

91 A28 75c on $1 ultramarine & black 8.50 8.50
a. Thin "C" and comma 12.00 12.00
b. Inverted surcharge 35.00 35.00
c. As "a" inverted

Surcharged on Official Stamp No. O10.

92 A17 75c on $1 blue & black *1500.00*
a. Thin "C" and comma *1650.00*

Surcharged on Official Stamp No. O23a.

93 A17 75c on $1 ultramarine & black *1500.00*
a. Thin "C" and comma *1650.00*

Engraved

1903 ***Perf. 14.*** **Unwmkd.**

94 A29 3c black 30 15
a. Printed on both sides 45.00
b. Perf. 12 5.00 5.00

Stamps of 1892 Surcharged in Blue

TEN Cents.
a

FIFTEEN Cents.
b

1903 **Wmk. 143**

95 A14 (*a*) 10c on 16c lilac 2.00 2.00
96 A15 (*b*) 15c on 24c olive green, *yellow* 3.00 3.00
97 A16 (") 20c on 32c greenish blue 4.00 4.00

Nos. 50, O3 and 45 Surcharged in Black or Red

A30

A31

A32

1904

98 A30 1c on 5c on 6c blue green 50 35
a. "5" with short flag 1.25 1.25
b. Both 5's with short flags 7.00 7.00
c "i" dot omitted
d. Surcharge on #50d 10.00 10.00
e. Inverted surcharge 5.50 5.50
99 A31 2c on 4c grn. & black 1.25 1.50
a. Pair, one without surcharge 27.50
b. Double surcharge
c. Double surcharge, red and black 50.00
d. Surcharged on back also 15.00
e. "Official" overprint missing 25.00
100 A32 2c on 30c steel blue (R) 6.00 6.00

African Elephant
A33

Mercury
A34

Chimpanzee
A35

Great Blue Touraco
A36

Agama
A37

Egret
A38

Head of Liberty From Coin
A39

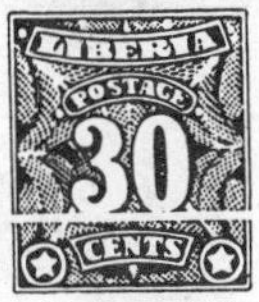

Numeral of Value
A40

Liberian Flag
A41

Pygmy Hippopotamus
A42

Liberty with Star of Liberia on Cap
A43

Mandingos
A44

Executive Mansion and Pres. Arthur Barclay
A45

Engraved

1906 *Perf. 14* **Unwmkd.**

101 A33 1c green & black 1.00 50
a. Center inverted 25.00 25.00
b. Imperf., pair 10.00
102 A34 2c carmine & black 20 10
a. Center inverted 17.50 17.50
b. Imperf., pair 4.00
103 A35 5c ultra. & black 2.00 75
a. Center inverted 90.00 90.00
104 A36 10c red brown & black 3.00 75
a. Center inverted 35.00 35.00
105 A37 15c purple & deep green 7.50 2.50
a. Center inverted 85.00 85.00
106 A38 20c orange & black 6.50 2.00
a. Imperf., pair 15.00
b. Center inverted 85.00 85.00
107 A39 25c dull blue & gray 70 25
a. Center inverted 30.00 30 00
b. Imperf., pair 40.00 40.00
108 A40 30c deep violet 75 25
109 A41 50c deep green & black 75 25
a. Imperf., pair 15.00
b. Center inverted 30.00 30.00
110 A42 75c brown & black 7.50 2.00
a. Imperf., pair 15.00
b. Center inverted 65.00 65.00
111 A43 $1 rose & gray 2.00 30
a. Center inverted 47.50 40.00
112 A44 $2 deep green & black 3.00 35
a. Center inverted 52.50 52.50
113 A45 $5 red brn. & blk. 6.00 50
a. Imperf., pair 20.00
Nos. 101-113 (13) 40.90 10.50

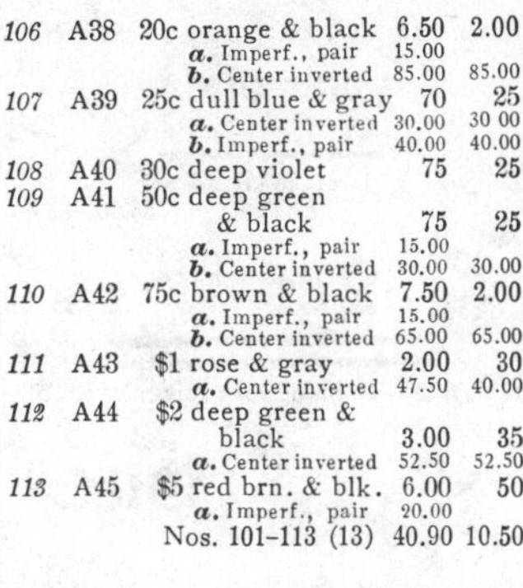

No. 104 Surcharged in Black

Inland 3 Cents

1909

114 A36 3c on 10c red brown & black 4.00 4.00

Coffee Plantation
A46

President Arthur Barclay
A47

S. S. Pres. Daniel E. Howard, former Gunboat Lark
A48

Commerce with Caduceus—A49

Vai Woman Spinning Cotton
A50

Blossom and Fruit of Pepper Plant
A51

Circular House
A52

President Barclay
A53

Men in Canoe
A54

Liberian Village
A55

1909-12 ***Perf. 14***

115 A46 1c yellow green & black 40 40
116 A47 2c lake & black 40 40
a. Center inverted 40.00 35.00
117 A48 5c ultra. & black 40 40
a. Center inverted 35.00 30.00
118 A49 10c plum & black, perf. 12½ ('12) 40 40
a. Imperf., pair 10.00
119 A50 15c indigo & black 50 40
a. Center inverted 30.00 30.00
120 A51 20c rose & green 2.50 40
a. Center inverted 40.00 35.00
b. Imperf.
121 A52 25c dk. brown & blk. 75 40
a. Imperf.
b. Center inverted 40.00 35.00
122 A53 30c dark brown 2.50 40
123 A54 50c green & black 2.00 40
a. Center inverted 60.00 50.00
124 A55 75c red brown & blk. 1.50 40
Nos. 115-124 (10) 11.35 4.00

Rouletted.

125 A49 10c plum & black 75 75

Stamps and Types of 1909-12 Surcharged in Blue or Red

3 CENTS INLAND POSTAGE

1910-12 ***Rouletted***

126 A49 3c on 10c plum & black (Bl) 40 25
a. "3" inverted
126B " 3c on 10c black & ultra. (R) 25.00 5.00

No. 126B is roulette 7. It also exists in roulette 13.

Perf. 12½, 14, 12½x14.

127 A49 3c on 10c plum & black (Bl) ('12) 40 30
a. Imperf., pair 20.00
b. Double surcharge, one inverted 20.00
c. Double vertical surcharge
127E " 3c on 10c black & ultramarine (R) ('12) 20.00 80

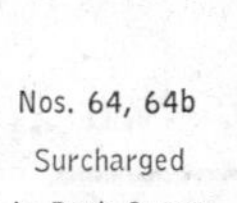
Nos. 64, 64b Surcharged in Dark Green

1913

128 A27 8c on 3c red & grn. (I) 25 20
a. Surch. on No. 64b 2.50 10
b. Double surcharge 5.00
c. Imperf., pair 16.00
d. Inverted surcharge 20.00

Stamps of Preceding Issues Surcharged

1914

2 CENTS
a

5
b

1914

On Issue of 1906.

129 A39 (*a*) 2c on 25c dull blue & gray 9.00 5.00
130 A40 (*b*) 5c on 30c deep violet 9.00 5.00

On Issue of 1909.

131 A52 (*a*) 2c on 25c brown & black 9.00 5.00
132 A53 (*b*) 5c on 30c dark brown 9.00 5.00
133 A54 (*a*) 10c on 50c green & black 9.00 5.00
Nos. 129-133 (5) 45.00 25.00

Liberian House—A57

Providence Island, Monrovia Harbor
A58

Wmk. 116

Wmkd. Crosses and Circles. (116)

1915 **Engraved** ***Perf. 14***

134 A57 2c red 20 8
135 A58 3c dull violet 20 8

Stamps of 1906-09 Surcharged with New Values in Dark Blue, Black or Red:

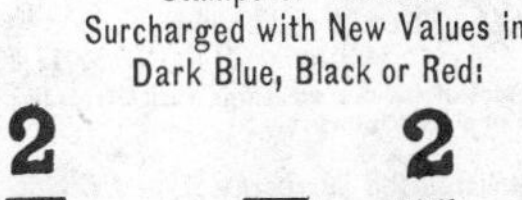

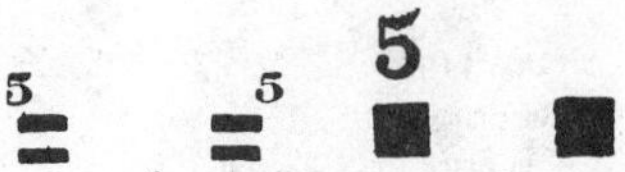

1915-16 **Unwmkd.**

136 A50 (*c*) 2c on 15c indigo & black (R) 1.00 1.00
137 A52 (*d*) 2c on 25c brown & blk. (R) 6.00 6.00
138 A51 (*e*) 5c on 20c rose & green (Bk) 1.25 1.25
139 A53 (*f*) 5c on 30c dark brown (R) 5.00 5.00
a. Double surcharge 12.00 12.00
140 " (*g*) 5c on 30c dark brown (R) 22.50 22.50

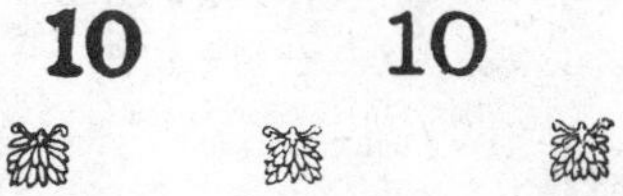

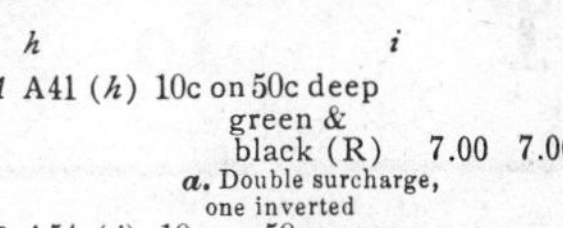

141 A41 (*h*) 10c on 50c deep green & black (R) 7.00 7.00
a. Double surcharge, one inverted
142 A54 (*i*) 10c on 50c green & black (R) 11.00 11.00
a. Double surcharge red & black 30.00 30.00
b. Blue surcharge 30.00 30.00
143 " (") 10c on 50c green & black (Bk) 8.50 8.50

20 25 cts.
xxxxx

j k

144 A55 (*j*) 20c on 75c red brown & black (Bk) 4.00 4.00

145 A43 (*k*) 25c on $1 rose & gray (Bk) 22.50 22.50

50 50
Cents Cents

l m

146 A44 (*l*) 50c on $2 deep green & black (R) 8.00 8.00
a. "Ceuts" 15.00 15.00

147 " (*m*) 50c on $2 deep green & blk. (R) 275.00 275.00

1

n

148 A45 $1 on $5 red brown & black (Bk) 17.50 17.50
a. Double surcharge 40.00 40.00

1

o

149 A45 $1 on $5 red brown & black (R) 17.50 17.50

The color of the red surcharge varies from light dull red to almost brown.

Handstamped Surcharge, Type "*i*."

150 A54 10c on 50c green & black (Dk Bl) 12.00 12.00

No. 119 Surcharged in Black 2

151 A50 2c on 15c indigo & black 150.00

No. 119 Surcharged in Red 2

152 A50 2c on 15c indigo & black 25.00 20.00
a. Double surch. 60.00

Nos. 116–117 Surcharged in Black or Red

1 1c

a1 b1

one cemt 1ct

c1 d1

one one 1c

e1 f1

1cent 1 c 1
******

g1 h1

one c one 1cts

i1 j1

Two cemts k2

l2 Two cents

2cents m2

n2 Two cts

2c o2

p2 2. 2.

two c two q2

r2 2 2

two s2

t2 2cent

153 A47 1c on 2c lake & black 2.50 2.50
Strip of 10 types 35.00

154 A48 2c on 5c ultramarine & black (R) 2.50 2.50
Strip of 10 types (R) 35.00
a. Black surch. 10.00 10.00
Strip of 10 types (Bk)

The 10 types of surcharge are repeated in illustrated sequence on 1c on 2c in each horiz. row and on 2c on 5c in each vert. row of sheets of 100 (10x10).

No. 116 and Type of 1909 Surcharged:

one ct.

155 A47 1c on 2c lake & black 55.00 55.00

2ct

156 A48 2c on 5c turquoise & black 50.00 50.00

1916

Nos. 18–20 Surcharged 5

1916

157 A1 3c on 6c violet 25.00 25.00
a. Inverted surcharge 50.00 50.00

158 " 5c on 12c yellow 2.00 2.00
a. Inverted surcharge 7.00 7.00
b. Surch. sideways 10.00

159 " 10c on 24c rose red 2.00 2.00
a. Inverted surcharge 12.00 12.00
b. Surcharge sideways

Unused prices for Nos. 157–159 are for copies without gum.

Nos. 44 and 108 Surcharged

FOUR 1917 CENTS   1917 FIVE CENTS

p r

1917 **Wmk. 143**

160 A15 (*p*) 4c on 25c yellow green 5.00 5.00
a. "OUR" 10.00 10.00
b. "FCUR" 10.00 10.00

Unwmkd.

161 A40 (*r*) 5c on 30c deep violet 40.00 40.00

No. 118 Surcharged in Red 3 CENTS

1918

162 A49 3c on 10c plum & black 2.00 2.00
a. "3" inverted 5.00 5.00

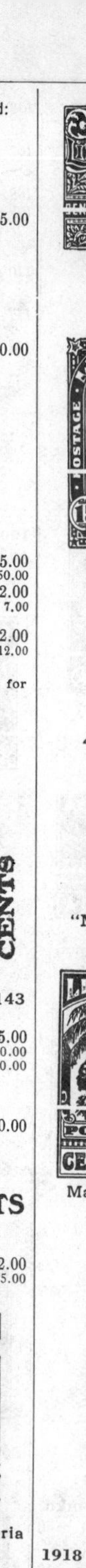

Bongo Antelope A59

Symbols of Liberia A61

Two-spot Palm Civet—A60

Value Numeral A62

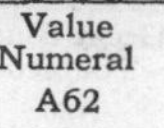

Palm-nut Vulture A66

Oil Palm A63

Mercury A64

Traveler's Tree—A65

"Mudskipper" or Bommi Fish A67

Mandingos A68

"Liberia" A71

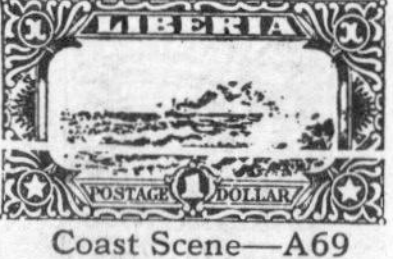

Coast Scene—A69

Liberia College—A70

1918 Engraved ***Perf. 12½, 14***

163	A59	1c deep green & black	75	20
164	A60	2c rose & black	75	20
165	A61	5c gray blue & black	15	8
166	A62	10c dark green	20	10
167	A63	15c blk. & dk. green	2.75	25
168	A64	20c claret & black	30	10
169	A65	25c dk. grn. & green	3.25	25
170	A66	30c red vio. & black	8.50	50
171	A67	50c ultra. & black	12.00	80
172	A68	75c olive bistre & black	85	12

173 A69 $1 yellow brown & blue 4.50 15
174 A70 $2 lt. vio. & black 5.50 15
175 A71 $5 dark brown 5.50 35
Nos. 163-175 (13) 45.00 3.25

Nos. 163-164, F10-F14 Surcharged

A72

A74

A73

1920

176 A72 3c on 1c green & black 1.00 1.00
a. "CEETS" 12.50 12.50
b. Double surcharge 4.00 4.00
c. Triple surcharge 5.00 5.00

177 A73 4c on 2c rose & black 1.00 1.00
a. Inverted surcharge 10.00 10.00
b. Double surcharge 4.00 4.00
c. Double surcharge, one inverted 10.00
d. Triple surcharge, one inverted 10.00 10.00
e. Quadruple surcharge 12.00 12.00
f. Typewritten surcharge
g. Same as "f" but inverted
h. Printed and typewritten surcharges, both inverted

178 A74 5c on 10c blue & black 2.50 2.50
a. Inverted surcharge 3.75 3.75
b. Double surcharge 6.00 6.00
c. Double surcharge, one inverted 6.00 6.00
d. Typewritten surcharge ("five") 50.00
e. Printed and typewritten surcharges 50.00

179 " 5c on 10c orange red & black 2.50 2.25
a. 5c on 10c orange & black 3.50 2.50
b. Inverted surcharge 6.00
c. Double surcharge 6.00
d. Double surcharge, one inverted 7.50 7.00
e. Typewritten surcharge in violet 50.00 50.00
f. Typewritten surcharge in black
g. Printed and typewritten surcharges 50.00

180 " 5c on 10c green & black 2.50 2.25
a. Double surcharge 6.00 6.00
b. Double surcharge, one inverted 9.00 9.00
c. Inverted surcharge 9.00
d. Quadruple surcharge 18.50 18.50
e. Typewritten surcharge 50.00
f. Printed and typewritten surcharges

181 " 5c on 10c vio. & blk. (Monrovia) 3.00 2.50
a. Double surcharge, one inverted 9.00 9.00

182 " 5c on 10c mag. & blk. (Robertsport) 2.00 1.75
a. Double surcharge 9.00 9.00
b. Double surcharge, one inverted 9.00 9.00
c. Double surcharge, both inverted 18.50
Nos. 176-182 (7) 14.50 13.25

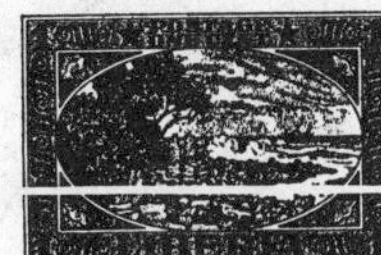
Cape Mesurado—A75

President Daniel E. Howard
A76

Arms of Liberia
A77

Crocodile—A78

Pepper Plant—A79

Leopard—A80

Village Scene—A81

Krumen in Dugout—A82

Rapids in St. Paul's River
A83

Bongo Antelope—A84

Hornbill—A85

Elephant—A86

1921 ***Perf. 14.*** **Wmk. 116**

183 A75 1c green 10 8
184 A76 5c deep blue & black 10 10
185 A77 10c red & dull blue 20 10
186 A78 15c dull vio. & green 3.75 50
187 A79 20c rose red & green 1.75 30
188 A80 25c orange & black 3.00 50
189 A81 30c green & dull violet 25 12
190 A82 50c orange & ultra. 35 15
191 A83 75c red & blk. brn. 50 15
a. Center inverted 30.00
192 A84 $1 red & black 20.00 1.25
193 A85 $2 yellow & ultra. 6.50 75
194 A86 $5 carmine rose & violet 20.00 1.00
Nos. 183-194 (12) 56.50 5.00

Stamps of 1914-21 Overprinted "1921"

195 A75 1c green 7.50 20
196 A57 2c red 7.50 20
197 A58 3c dull violet 10.00 20
198 A76 5c dp. blue & black 1.75 20
199 A77 10c red & dull blue 17.50 20
200 A78 15c dull violet & green 9.00 60
201 A79 20c rose red & grn., ovpt. invtd. 4.00 40
202 A80 25c orange & black 9.00 60
203 A81 30c grn. & dull violet 1.00 20
204 A82 50c orange & ultra. 1.75 20
205 A83 75c red & blk. brn. 2.50 20
206 A84 $1 red & black 25.00 1.00
207 A85 $2 yellow & ultra. 9.00 1.00
208 A86 $5 carmine rose & violet 22.50 1.25
Nos. 195-208 (14) 128.00 6.45

Overprint exists inverted in Nos. 195-208 and normal on No. 201.

First Settlers Landing at Cape Mesurado from U. S. S. Alligator
A87

1923 Lithographed.

209 A87 1c light blue & black 6.00 30
210 " 2c claret & olive gray 11.00 30
211 " 5c olive green & indigo 11.00 30
212 " 10c blue green & violet 50 30
213 " $1 rose & brown 1.50 30
Nos. 209-213 (5) 30.00 1.50

Centenary of founding of Liberia.

Memorial to J. J. Roberts, First President—A88

Hall of Representatives, Monrovia
A89

Liberian Star—A90

Pres. Charles Dunbar Burgess King
A91 A92

Hippopotamus—A93

Antelope—A94

West African Buffalo
A95

Grebos Making Dumboy
A96

Pineapple—A97

Carrying Ivory Tusk
A98

Rubber Planter's House—A99

Stockton Lagoon—A100

Grebo Houses—A101

1923 *Perf. 13½x14½, 14½x13½*

White Paper

214 A88 1c yellow green & deep green 3.00 8
215 A89 2c claret & brown 3.00 8
216 A90 3c lilac & black 25 8
217 A91 5c blue vio. & blk. 22.50 10
218 A92 10c slate & brown 20 10
219 A93 15c bistre & blue 14.00 40
220 A94 20c blue green & violet 2.00 40
221 A95 25c org. red & brn. 30.00 50

White, Buff or Brownish Paper

222 A96 30c dk. brown & vio. 30 10
223 A97 50c dull vio. & org. 50 25
224 A98 75c gray & blue 75 55
225 A99 $1 deep red & dark violet 3.50 85
a. White paper 20.00
226 A100 $2 orange & blue 3.00 75
a. Buff or brownish paper
227 A101 $5 deep green & brown 7.00 75
a. White paper 20.00
Nos. 214-227 (14) 90.00 4.99

Nos. 222-224 on buff or brownish paper sell for about 10% more.

No. 163 Surcharged

Two Cents

1926 *Perf. 14.* **Unwmkd.**

228 A59 2c on 1c deep green & black 3.00 3.00
a. Surcharged with ornamental design as on official stamp No. O155 15.00

No. 163 Surcharged in Red

Two Cents

1927

229 A59 2c on 1c deep green & black 6.00 6.00
a. "Ceuts" 7.50
b. "Vwo" 10.00
c. "Twc" 7.50
d. Double surcharge 17.50
e. Wavy lines omitted 15.00

Palms—A102

Map of Africa
A103

President King
A104

1928 **Engraved.** *Perf. 12.*

230 A102 1c green 20 20
231 " 2c dark violet 30 30
232 " 3c bistre brown 30 30
233 A103 5c ultramarine 75 50
234 A104 10c olive gray 1.00 50
235 A103 15c dull violet 4.00 2.00
236 " $1 red brown 30.00 15.00
Nos. 230-236 (7) 36.55 18.80

Regular Issue of 1918
Surcharged in Various Colors and Styles, "1936" and New Values.

1936 *Perf. 12½, 14.*

248 A60 1c on 2c rose & black (Bl) 35 35
249 A61 3c on 5c gray blue & black (Bl) 15 15
250 A62 4c on 10c dark green (Br) 15 15
251 A63 6c on 15c green & black (Bl) 35 35
252 A64 8c on 20c claret & black (V) 20 20
253 A66 12c on 30c red violet & black (V) 60 60
254 A67 14c on 50c ultramarine & black (Bl) 70 70
255 A68 16c on 75c olive bistre & black (Br) 40 40
256 A69 18c on $1 yellow brown & blue (Bk) 40 40
a. 22c on $1 yel. brown & blue 7.50
257 A70 22c on $2 light violet & black (V) 50 50
258 A71 24c on $5 dark brown (Bk) 60 60
Nos. 248-258 (11) 4.40 4.40

Official Stamps of 1918
Surcharged in various colors and styles with 6 pointed star, "1936" and New Values.

1936

259 A60 1c on 2c rose & black (Bl) 25 25
260 A61 3c on 5c gray blue & black (Bl) 10 10
261 A62 4c on 10c ultra. (Bl) 10 10
262 A63 6c on 15c chocolate & dk. grn. (Bl) 25 25
263 A64 8c on 20c gray lilac & black (V) 15 15
264 A66 12c on 30c bright violet & black (V) 50 50
a. "193" instead of "1936" 15.00
265 A67 14c on 50c maroon & black (Bl) 60 60
266 A68 16c on 75c car. brown & black (Bk) 30 30
267 A69 18c on $1 olive bistre & turquoise blue (Bk) 30 30
268 A70 22c on $2 olive bistre & black (Bl) 40 40
269 A71 24c on $5 yellow green (Bk) 50 50
270 A65 25c chocolate & green (Bk) 60 60
Nos. 259-270 (12) 4.05 4.05

Hornbill—A106

Designs: 2c, Bushbuck. 3c, West African dwarf buffalo. 4c, Pygmy hippopotamus. 5c, Lesser egret. 6c, Pres. E. J. Barclay.

Perf. Compound of 11½, 12, 12½, 14.

1937, Apr. 10 **Engr.** **Unwmkd.**

271 A106 1c green & black 1.00 50
272 " 2c carmine & black 1.00 40
273 " 3c violet & black 1.00 50
274 " 4c orange & black 1.50 80
275 " 5c blue & black 1.50 65
276 " 6c green & black 50 15
Nos. 271-276 (6) 6.50 3.00

Coast Line of Liberia, 1839
A107

Seal of Liberia, Map and Farming Scenes—A108

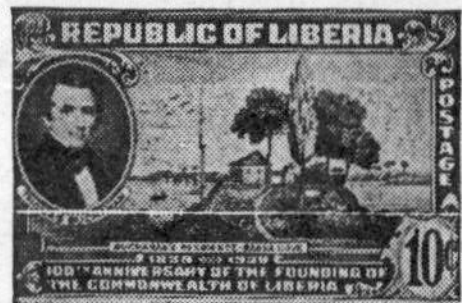
Thomas Buchanan and Residence at Bassa Cove
A109

1940, July 29 **Engr.** *Perf. 12*

277 A107 3c dark blue 10 8
278 A108 5c dull red brown 15 12
279 A109 10c dark green 20 18

Issued in commemoration of the 100th anniversary of the founding of the Commonwealth of Liberia.

Nos. 277-279 Overprinted in Red or Blue

1941, Feb. 21

280 A107 3c dark blue (R) 2.50 2.50
281 A108 5c dull red brown (Bl) 2.50 2.50
282 A109 10c dark green (R) 2.50 2.50
Nos. 280-282, C14-C16 (6) 13.50 13.50

Royal Antelope
A110

Bay-thighed Diana Monkey
A115

Designs: 2c, Water chevrotain. 3c, White-shouldered duiker. 4c, Bushbuck. 5c, Zebra antelope.

1942 **Engraved.**

283 A110 1c violet & fawn 50 25
284 " 2c bright ultra. & yellow brown 50 25
285 " 3c bright green & yellow brown 1.00 50
286 " 4c blk. & red org. 1.25 1.00
287 " 5c olive & fawn 1.50 1.00
288 A115 10c red & black 2.50 1.25
Nos. 283-288 (6) 7.25 4.25

Stamps of 1928-37 Surcharged with New Values and Bars or X's in Violet, Black, Red Brown or Blue.

Perf. 12, 12 x 12½, 14.

1944-46 **Unwmkd.**

288A A102 1c on 2c dark violet (Bk) (#231) 10.00 10.00
289 A106 1c on 4c orange & black (Bk) 60.00 50.00
289A A104 1c on 10c olive gray (RBr) (#234) 12.50 7.50
290 A106 2c on 3c violet & black (#273) 60.00 50.00
290A A103 2c on 5c ultra. (Bk) (#233) 3.00 3.00
290B " 2c on 5c ultra. (Bl) (#233) 12.50 7.50
291 A102 3c on 2c dark violet (#231) 30.00
292 A106 4c on 5c blue & black 12.50 7.50
292A A104 4c on 10c olive gray (Bk) (#234) 3.50 3.50
b. Double surch., one inverted
293 A106 5c on 1c green & black (Bk) 75.00 50.00

294 A106 6c on 2c carmine & black (Bk) (#272) 12.50 10.00
295 " 10c on 6c green & black (#276) 12.50 10.00

Surcharges on Nos. 289, 290, 293, 294 are found inverted. Prices same as normal.

Pres. Franklin D. Roosevelt Reviewing Troops—A116

1945, Nov. 26 Engraved *Perf. 12½*

Grayish Paper

296 A116 3c brt. violet & blk. 20 18
297 " 5c dark blue & black 40 35

In memory of Pres. Franklin D. Roosevelt (1882–1945).

See also No. C51.

Monrovia Harbor—A117

1947, Jan. 2

298 A117 5c deep blue 15 12

Issued to commemorate the opening of the Monrovia Harbor Project, Feb. 16, 1946. See No. C52.

1947, May 16

Without Inscription at Top

299 A117 5c violet 15 12

See also No. C53.

First United States Postage Stamps and Arms of Liberia
A118

1947, June 6

300 A118 5c carmine rose 15 15

Issued to commemorate the centenary of United States postage stamps and the 87th anniversary of Liberian postal issues.

See Nos. C54–C56, C56a.

Matilda Newport Firing Cannon
A119

Engraved and Photogravure.

1947, Dec. 1 Center in Gray Black.

301 A119 1c bright blue green 10 7
302 " 3c bright red violet 15 10
303 " 5c bright ultramarine 20 15
304 " 10c yellow 1.00 30
Nos. 301–304, C57 (5) 2.70 1.02

Issued to commemorate the 125th anniversary of Matilda Newport's defense of Monrovia, December 1, 1822.

Liberian Star
A120

Liberty
A121

Arms of Liberia
A122

Map of Liberia
A123

1947, Dec. 22 Engraved

305 A120 1c dark green 5 5
306 A121 2c bright red violet 8 8
307 A122 3c bright purple 10 10
308 A123 5c dark blue 17 12
Nos. 305–308, C58–C60 (7) 2.20 1.85

Centenary of independence.

Natives Approaching Village
A124

Rubber Tapping and Planting
A125

Landing of First Colonists
A126

Jehudi Ashmun and Defenders
A127

1949, Apr. 12 Litho. *Perf. 11½*

309 A124 1c multicolored 60 75
310 A125 2c " 60 75
311 A126 3c " 60 75
312 A127 5c " 60 75
Nos. 309–312, C63–C64 (6) 4.00 5.00

Nos. 309–312 exist perf. 12½ and sell at a much lower price. The status of the perf. 12½ set is indefinite.

Pres. Joseph J. Roberts
A128

Designs (Liberian Presidents): 2c, Stephen Benson. 3c, Daniel B. Warner. 4c, James S. Payne. 5c, Executive mansion. 6c, Edward J. Roye. 7c, A. W Gardner and A. F. Russell. 8c, Hilary R. W. Johnson. 9c, Joseph J. Cheeseman. 10c, William D. Coleman. 15c, Garretson W. Gibson. 20c, Arthur Barclay. 25c, Daniel E. Howard. 50c, Charles D. B. King. $1, Edwin J. Barclay.

Engraved.

1948–50 *Perf. 12½.* Unwmkd.

Caption and Portrait in Black.

313 A128 1c green ('48) 2.25 4.50
314 " 2c salmon pink 50 50
315 " 3c rose violet 50 50
a. "1876–1878" added 12.50 25.00
316 " 4c light olive green 50 75
317 " 5c ultramarine 60 75
318 " 6c red orange 75 1.25
319 " 7c light blue 1.00 1.75
320 " 8c carmine 1.00 2.00
321 " 9c red violet 1.50 1.50
322 " 10c yellow ('50) 1.00 45
323 " 15c yellow orange 1.15 55
324 " 20c blue gray 1.75 1.00
325 " 25c cerise 2.25 1.50
326 " 50c aquamarine 4.50 1.25
327 " $1 rose lilac 7.50 1.00
Nos. 313–327, C65 (16) 27.75 20.00

See also Nos. 371–378, C118.

Pres. Joseph J. Roberts
A129

1950

328 A129 1c green & black 25 20

Hand Holding Book
A130

1950, Feb. 14

329 A130 5c deep blue 30 12

National Literacy Campaign. See No. C66.

U.P.U. Monument—A131

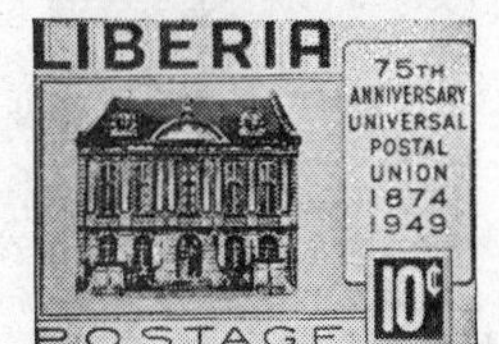

First U.P.U. Building, Bern
A132

1950, Apr. 21 Engr. Unwmkd.

330 A131 5c green & black 20 20
331 A132 10c red violet & black 40 40

Universal Postal Union, 75th anniversary (in 1949).

Nos. 330–331 exist imperf., same price.

See Nos. C67, C67a.

Jehudi Ashmun and Seal of Liberia
A133

John Marshall, Ashmun and Map of Town of Marshall—A134

Designs (Map or View and Two Portraits): 2c, Careysburg, Gov. Lott Carey (1780–1828), freed American slave, and Jehudi Ashmun (1794–1828), American missionary credited as founder of Liberia. 3c, Town of Harper, Robert Goodlow Harper (1765–1825), American statesman, and Ashmun. 5c, Upper Buchanan, Gov. Thomas Buchanan and Ashmun. 10c, Robertsport, Pres. Joseph J. Roberts and Ashmun.

1952, Apr. 10 *Perf. 10½*

332 A133 1c deep green 4 4
333 " 2c scarlet & indigo 5 5
334 " 3c purple & green 8 8
335 A134 4c brown & green 10 10
336 A133 5c ultramarine & orange red 18 10
337 A134 10c orange red & dark blue 20 18
Nos. 332–337, C68–C69 (8) 2.15 1.60

Nos. 332–337 exist imperf. Price about three times that of the perf. set.

See No. C69a.

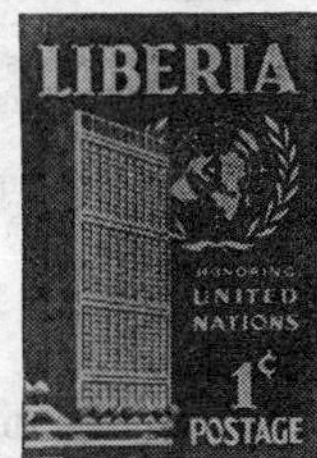

U. N. Headquarters Building—A135

Scroll and Flags—A136

Design: 10c, Liberia arms, letters "UN" and emblem.

1952, Dec. 20 *Perf. 12½* Unwmkd.

338 A135 1c ultramarine 8 8
339 A136 4c car. & ultra. 15 15
340 " 10c red brn. & yel. 30 30
a. Souvenir sheet 2.00 2.00

See also No. C70.

No. 340a measures 153x85½mm., and contains one each of Nos. 338–340 with marginal inscriptions in ultramarine.

Nos. 338–340 and 340a exist imperforate. Same prices as above.

Pepper Bird—A137

Roller—A138

Birds: 4c, Hornbill. 5c, Kingfisher. 10c, Jacana. 12c, Weaver.

1953, Nov. 18 *Perf. 10½*

341 A137 1c light blue & deep carmine 6 6
342 A138 3c brown orange & dark violet blue 8 6
343 A137 4c yel. & dk.brown 10 8
344 " 5c rose lilac & dark blue green 18 8
345 A138 10c dull green & magenta 35 15
346 " 12c red brn. & org. 50 15
Nos. 341-346 (6) 1.27 58

Exist imperf. Price, set unused $1.85.

Tennis A139 — Callichilia Stenosepala A140

Designs: 5c, Soccer. 25c, Boxing.

1955, Jan. 26 **Litho.** *Perf. 12½*

347 A139 3c red & light green 6 6
348 " 5c black & orange 10 7
349 " 25c rose vio. & yel. 40 25
Nos. 347-349, C88-C90 (6) 1.21 90

See No. C90a.

1955, Sept. 28 **Unwmkd.**

Various Native Flowers: 7c, Gomphia subcordata. 8c, Listrostachys caudata. 9c, Musaenda isertiana.

350 A140 6c yellow green, orange & yellow 8 8
351 " 7c emerald, yellow & carmine 8 8
352 " 8c yellow green, buff & blue 15 15
353 " 9c orange & green 20 20
Nos. 350-353, C91-C92 (6) 91 91

Rubber Tapping A141

1955, Dec. 5 *Perf. 12½*

354 A141 5c emerald & yellow 15 15

Issued to commemorate the 50th anniversary of Rotary International. No. 354 exists printed entirely in emerald. See also Nos. C97-C99.

Statue of Liberty
A142

Coliseum, New York City
A143

Design: 6c, Globe inscribed FIPEX.

1956, Apr. 28 *Perf. 12*

355 A142 3c bright green & dark red brown 5 5
356 A143 4c Prussian green & bistre brown 10 8
357 " 6c gray & red lilac 15 15
Nos. 355-357, C100-C102 (6) 90 73

Issued to commemorate the Fifth International Philatelic Exhibition (FIPEX), New York City, Apr. 28-May 6, 1956.

Kangaroo and Emu—A144

Discus Thrower
A145

Designs: 8c, Goddess of Victory and Olympic symbols. 10c, Classic chariot race.

1956, Nov. 15 **Litho.** **Unwmkd.**

358 A144 4c light olive green & golden brown 10 6
359 A145 6c emerald & gray 15 6
360 A144 8c light ultramarine & reddish brown 20 10
361 " 10c rose red & black 25 15
Nos. 358-361, C104-C105 (6) 1.35 77

Issued to commemorate the 16th Olympic Games at Melbourne, Nov. 22-Dec. 8, 1956.

Idlewild Airport, New York
A146

Design: 5c, Roberts Field, Liberia, plane and Pres. Tubman.

Lithographed and Engraved

1957, May 4 *Perf. 12*

362 A146 3c orange & dark blue 6 6
363 " 5c red lilac & black 12 6
Nos. 362-363, C107-C110 (6) 2.23 99

Issued to commemorate the first anniversary of direct air service between Roberts Field, Liberia, and Idlewild, New York, (Kennedy).

Orphanage Playground
A147

Designs (Orphanage and): 5c, Teacher and pupil. 6c, Singing boys and national anthem. 10c, Children and flag.

1957, Nov. 25 **Litho.** *Perf. 12*

364 A147 4c green & red 8 6
365 " 5c blue green & red brown 10 6
366 " 6c brt. vio. & bistre 15 10
367 " 10c ultramarine & rose carmine 25 15
Nos. 364-367, C111-C112 (6) 1.33 82

Issued to commemorate the founding of the Antoinette Tubman Child Welfare Foundation.

Windmill and Dutch Flag
A148

Designs: No. 369, German flag and Brandenburg Gate. No. 370, Swedish flag, palace and crowns.

Engraved and Lithographed.

1958, Jan. 10 *Perf. 10½* **Unwmkd.**

Flags in Original Colors.

368 A148 5c reddish brown 12 10
369 " 5c blue 12 10
370 " 5c lilac rose 12 10
Nos. 368-370, C114-C117 (7) 1.46 96

Issued to commemorate the European tour of Pres. Tubman in 1956.

Presidential Types of 1948-50.

Designs as before.

1958-60 **Engraved.** *Perf. 12*

Caption and Portrait in Black.

371 A129 1c salmon pink 50 35
372 A128 2c bright yellow 50 35
373 " 10c blue gray 55 55
374 " 15c bright blue & black ('59) 30 30
375 " 20c dark red 70 60
376 " 25c blue 70 60
377 " 50c red lilac & black ('59) 1.00 80
378 " $1 bis. brn. ('60) 5.00 75
Nos. 371-378, C118 (9) 10.00 4.80

Many shades of 1c.

Open Globe Projection
A149

Designs: 5c, U.N. Emblem and building. 10c, U.N. Emblem. 12c, U.N. Emblem and initials of agencies.

1958, Dec. 10 **Litho.** *Perf. 12*

379 A149 3c gray, blue & black 10 7
380 A149 5c blue & chocolate 15 8
381 " 10c black & orange 30 18
382 " 12c black & carmine 40 24

Issued to commemorate the 10th anniversary of the Universal Declaration of Human Rights. See No. C119.

People of Africa on the March A150 — Symbols of UNESCO A151

1959, Apr. 15

383 A150 20c orange & brown 40 25

African Freedom Day, Apr. 15. See also No. C120.

1959, May 11 **Unwmkd.**

384 A151 25c deep plum & emerald 50 30

Issued to commemorate the opening of UNESCO (U. N. Educational, Scientific and Cultural Organization) Headquarters in Paris, Nov. 3, 1958.

See also No. C121 and souvenir sheet, No. C121a.

Abraham Lincoln
A152

1959, Nov. 20 **Engr.** *Perf. 12*

385 A152 10c ultra. & black 30 30
386 " 15c orange & black 40 40
a. Souvenir sheet, imperf. 1.50 1.50

Issued to commemorate the 150th anniversary of the birth of Abraham Lincoln. See No. C122.

No. 386a contains one each of Nos. 385-386 and C122. Size: 140x82mm.; black marginal inscription.

Touré, Tubman and Nkrumah
A153

1960, Jan. 27 **Litho.** **Unwmkd.**

387 A153 25c crimson & black 50 40

Issued to commemorate the 1959 "Big Three" conference of Pres. Sékou Touré of Guinea, Pres. William V. S. Tubman of Liberia and Prime Minister Kwame Nkrumah of Ghana at Saniquellie, Liberia. See also No. C123.

World Refugee Year Emblem A154 — Map of Africa A155

1960, Apr. 7 *Perf. 11½*

388 A154 25c emerald & blk. 50 35

Issued to publicize World Refuge Year, July 1, 1959–June 30, 1960. See No. C124 and souvenir sheet No. C124a.

1960, May 11 **Litho.** *Perf. 11½*

389 A155 25c green & black 50 35

Issued to commemorate the 10th anniversary of the Commission for Technical Co-operation in Africa South of the Sahara (C.C.T.A.). See also No. C125.

Weight Lifter and Porter
A156

Liberian Stamps of 1860
A157

Designs: 10c, Rower and canoeists (horiz.). 15c, Walker and porter.

1960, Sept. 6 **Unwmkd.**

390 A156 5c dark brown & emerald 15 10
391 " 10c brown & red lilac 25 15
392 " 15c brown & orange 40 30

Issued to commemorate the 17th Olympic Games, Rome, Aug. 25–Sept. 11. See also Nos. C126–C127.

1960, Dec. 1 **Litho.** *Perf. 11½*

393 A157 5c multicolored 15 10
394 " 20c " 50 40

Issued to commemorate the centenary of Liberian postage stamps. See Nos. C128–C129.

Laurel Wreath
A158

1961, May 19 *Perf. 11½* **Unwmkd.**

395 A158 25c red & dark blue 50 35

Issued to commemorate Liberia's membership in the United Nations Security Council. Exists imperf. See Nos. C130–C131 and note after No. C131.

Anatomy Class—A159

1961, Sept. 8 *Perf. 11½*

396 A159 25c green & brown 50 30

Issued to commemorate the 15th anniversary of the United Nations Educational, Scientific and Cultural Organization (UNESCO). See also Nos. C132–C133.

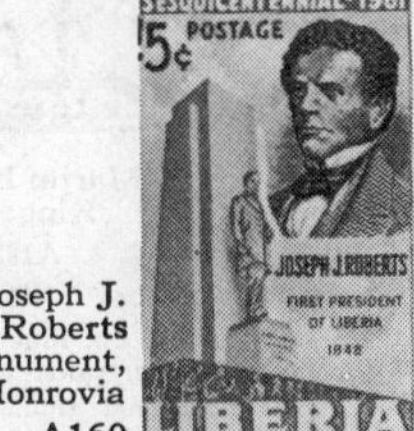

Joseph J. Roberts Monument, Monrovia
A160

Design: 10c, Pres. Roberts and old and new presidential mansions (horiz.).

1961, Oct. 25 **Lithographed**

397 A160 5c orange & sepia 10 6
398 " 10c ultra. & sepia 25 15

Issued to commemorate the 150th anniversary of the birth of Joseph J. Roberts, first president of Liberia.

See No. C134 and souvenir sheet No. C134a.

Boy Scout—A161

Design: Insignia and Scouts camping.

1961, Dec. 4 *Perf. 11½* **Unwmkd.**

399 A161 5c lilac & sepia 10 6
400 " 10c ultra. & bistre 20 15

Issued to honor the Boy Scouts of Liberia. Nos. 399–400 exist imperf. See Nos. C135–C136.

Dag Hammarskjold and U.N. Emblem—A162

1962, Feb. 1 *Perf. 12*

401 A162 20c black & ultra. 40 30

Issued in memory of Dag Hammarskjold, Secretary General of the United Nations, 1953–61. See Nos. C137–C138.

Malaria Eradication Emblem
A163

1962, Apr. 7 **Litho.** *Perf. 12½*

402 A163 25c dk. green & red 50 35

Issued for the World Health Organization drive to eradicate malaria. See Nos. C139–C140.

United Nations Emblem
A164

1962, Oct. 22 *Perf. 12x12½*

403 A164 20c grn. & yel. bis. 40 20

Issued to mark the observance of United Nations Day, Oct. 24, as a national holiday. See Nos. C144–C145.

Treasury Department Building, Monrovia—A165

Buildings: 1c, 80c, Executive Mansion, Monrovia. 10c, Information Service. 15c, Capitol.

1962–64

403A A165 1c violet blue & dp. org. ('64) 15 10
404 " 5c lt. blue & pur. 10 10
405 " 10c bistre & brown 20 15
406 " 15c salmon & dk. bl. 30 25
406A " 80c brn. & yellow ('64) 1.60 1.00
Nos. 403A-406A, C146-C148 (9) 7.00 3.90

"FAO" Emblem and Food Bowl
A166

1963, Mar. 21 *Perf. 12½*

407 A166 5c aqua. & dk. car. 15 10

Issued for the "Freedom from Hunger" campaign of the U.N. Food and Agriculture Organization. See also Nos. C149–C150.

Rocket in Space—A167

Design: 15c, Space capsule and globe.

1963, May 27 **Litho.** *Perf. 12½*

408 A167 10c deep violet blue & yellow 25 15
409 " 15c blue & red brown 35 25

Issued to honor achievements in space exploration for peaceful purposes. See also Nos. C151–C152.

Red Cross—A168

Design: 10c, Centenary emblem and torch (vert.).

1963, Aug. 26 *Perf. 11½* **Unwmkd.**

410 A168 5c blue grn. & red 12 10
411 " 10c gray & red 25 15

Issued to commemorate the centenary of the International Red Cross. See Nos. C153–C154.

Palm Tree and Scroll
A169

Ski Jump
A170

1963, Oct. 28 *Perf. 12½*

412 A169 20c brown & green 40 30

Issued to commemorate the conference of African heads of state for African Unity, Addis Ababa, May, 1963. See No. C156.

1963, Dec. 11 *Perf. 12½* **Unwmkd.**

413 A170 5c rose red & dark violet blue 10 8

Issued to publicize the 9th Winter Olympic Games, Innsbruck, Austria, Jan. 29–Feb. 9, 1964. See also Nos. C157–C159.

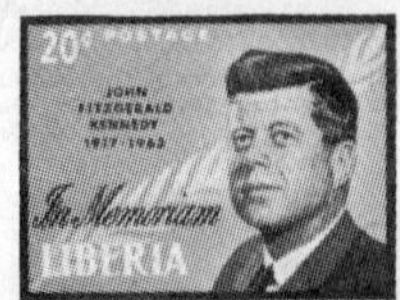

John F. Kennedy
A171

1964, Apr. 6 **Lithographed**

414 A171 20c black & bright blue 50 35

Issued in memory of John F. Kennedy (1917–63). See Nos. C160–C161.

Syncom Satellite—A172

Designs (Satellites): 15c, Relay I (vert.). 25c, Mariner II.

1964, June 22 *Perf. 12½* **Unwmkd.**

415 A172 10c orange & emerald 25 15
416 " 15c bright carmine rose & violet 30 20
417 " 25c bl., orge., & blk. 60 40

Issued to publicize progress in space communications and the peaceful uses of outer space. See No. C162.

Mt. Fuji—A173

Designs: 15c, Torii and Olympic flame. 25c, Cherry blossoms and stadium.

1964, Sept. 15 **Lithographed**

418 A173 10c orange yellow & emerald 15 10
419 " 15c lt. red & purple 30 20
420 " 25c ocher & red 50 30

Issued for the 18th Olympic Games, Tokyo, Oct. 10–25, 1964. See No. C163.

Boy Scout Emblem and Scout Sign
A174

"Emancipation" by Thomas Ball
A175

Design: 10c, Bugle and Liberian Scout emblem (horiz.).

1965, Mar. 8 **Litho.** *Perf. 12½*

421 A174 5c lt. blue & brn. 10 8
422 " 10c dk. grn. & ocher 20 15

Issued to honor the Liberian Boy Scouts. See Nos. C164–C165.

1965, May 3 ***Perf. 12½*** **Unwmkd.**

Designs: 20c, Abraham Lincoln and John F. Kennedy (horiz.). 25c, Lincoln by Augustus St. Gaudens, Lincoln Park, Chicago.

423 A175 5c dark gray & brown orange 12 8
424 " 20c emerald & light gray 40 25
425 " 25c maroon & blue 50 35

Issued to commemorate the centenary of the death of Abraham Lincoln See No. C166.

ICY Emblem—A176

1965, June 21 **Litho.** ***Perf. 12½***

426 A176 12c orange & brown 25 15
427 " 25c violet bl. & brn. 50 30
428 " 50c emerald & brn. 1.00 50

International Cooperation Year. See No. C167.

ITU Emblem, Old and New Communication Equipment
A177

1965, Sept. 21 ***Perf. 12½*** **Unwmkd.**

429 A177 25c brt. green & red brown 50 35
430 " 35c blk. & carmine rose 70 45

Issued to commemorate the centenary of the International Telecommunication Union. See No. C168.

Pres. Tubman and Liberian Flag
A178

1965, Nov. 29 **Lithographed**

431 A178 25c red, ultra. & brn. 50 35

Issued in honor of President William V. S. Tubman's 70th birthday. See No. C169 and souvenir sheet No. C169a.

Churchill in Admiral's Uniform
A179

Pres. Joseph J. Roberts
A180

Designs: 15c, Churchill giving "V" sign (vert.).

1966, Jan. 18 **Litho.** ***Perf. 12½***

432 A179 15c orange & black 30 20
433 " 20c blk. & brt. grn. 40 25

Issued in memory of Sir Winston Spencer Churchill (1874–1965), statesman and World War II leader. See Nos. C170–C171.

1966–69 **Lithographed** ***Perf. 12½***

Presidents: 2c, Stephen Benson. 3c, Daniel Bashiel Warner. 4c, James S. Payne. 5c, Edward James Roye. 10c, William D. Coleman. 25c, Daniel Edward Howard. 50c, Charles Dunbar Burgess King. 80c, Hilary R. W. Johnson. $1, Edwin J. Barclay. $2, Joseph James Cheeseman ("Cheesman" on stamp).

434 A180 1c blk. & brick red 3 3
435 " 2c black & yellow 4 4
436 " 3c black & lilac 6 4
437 " 4c apple green & black ('67) 8 8
438 " 5c blk. & dull org. 10 5
439 " 10c pale green & black ('67) 20 10
440 " 25c black & lt. blue 50 10
441 " 50c black & brt. lilac rose 1.00 90
442 " 80c dp. rose & black ('67) 1.60 1.30
443 " $1 black & ocher 2.00 20

Perf. 11½x11

443A A180 $2 black & dp. red lilac ('69) 4.00 3.50
Nos. 434–443A, C182 (12) 10.11 6.74

Soccer Players and Globe
A181

Designs: 25c, World Championships Cup, ball and shoes (vert.). 35c, Soccer player dribbling (vert.).

1966, May 3 **Litho.** ***Perf. 12½***

444 A181 10c brt. green & dark brown 20 12
445 " 25c brt. pink & brn. 50 35
446 " 35c brown & orange 70 45

Issued to publicize the World Cup Soccer Championships, Wembley, England, July 11–30. See No. C172.

Pres. Kennedy Taking Oath of Office
A182

Designs: 20c, 1964 Kennedy stamps, Nos. 414 and C160.

1966, Aug. 16 **Litho.** ***Perf. 12½***

447 A182 15c red & black 40 15
448 " 20c bright blue & red lilac 50 20

Issued to commemorate the third anniversary of President Kennedy's death (Nov. 22). See Nos. C173–C175.

Children on Seesaw and UNICEF Emblem
A183

Design: 80c, Boy playing doctor.

1966, Oct. 25 ***Perf. 12½*** **Unwmkd.**

449 A183 5c brt. blue & red 12 10
450 " 80c org. brn. & yel. green 1.60 75

Issued to commemorate the 20th anniversary of the United Nations Children's Emergency Fund (UNICEF).

Giraffe
A184

Jamboree Badge
A185

Designs: 3c, Lion. 5c, Slender-nosed crocodile (horiz.). 10c, Baby chimpanzees. 15c, Leopard (horiz.). 20c, Black rhinoceros (horiz.). 25c, Elephant.

451 A184 2c multicolored 6 5
452 " 3c " 8 6
453 " 5c " 10 8
a. Black omitted ("5¢ LIBERIA" and imprint) 15.00
454 " 10c multicolored 20 12
455 " 15c " 30 20
456 " 20c " 40 30
457 " 25c " 50 35
Nos. 451–457 (7) 1.64 1.16

1967, March 23 **Litho.** ***Perf. 12½***

Designs: 25c, Boy Scout emblem and various sports (horiz.). 40c, Scout at campfire and vision of moon landing (horiz.).

458 A185 10c brt. lilac rose & green 20 12
459 " 25c brt. red & blue 50 35
460 " 40c bright green & brn. orange 80 45

Issued to publicize the 12th Boy Scout World Jamboree, Farragut State Park, Idaho, Aug. 1–9. See No. C176.

Pre-Hispanic Sculpture of Mexico
A186

Designs: 25c, Aztec Calendar and Olympic rings. 40c, Mexican pottery, sombrero and guitar (horiz.).

1967, June 20 **Litho.** ***Perf. 12½***

461 A186 10c ocher & violet 20 12
462 " 25c lt. blue, orange & black 50 35
463 " 40c yel. grn. & car. 80 45

Issued to publicize the 19th Olympic Games, Mexico City. See No. C177.

WHO Office for Africa
A187

Design: 5c, WHO Office for Africa (horiz.).

1967, Aug. 28 **Litho.** ***Perf. 12½***

464 A187 5c blue & yellow 10 6
465 " 80c bright green & yellow 1.65 1.25

Issued to commemorate the inauguration of the World Health Organization Regional Office for Africa in Brazzaville, Congo.

Boy Playing African Rattle
A188

Africans Playing Native Instruments: 3c, Tom-tom and soko violin (horiz.). 5c, Mang harp (horiz.). 10c, Alimilim. 15c, Xylophone drums. 25c, Large tom-toms. 35c, Large harp.

1967, Oct. 16 **Litho.** ***Perf. 14***

466 A188 2c violet & multi. 4 3
467 " 3c blue & multi. 6 4
468 " 5c lilac rose & multi. 10 6
469 " 10c yel. grn. & multi. 20 15
470 " 15c violet & multi. 30 20
471 " 25c ocher & multi. 50 30
472 " 35c dp. rose & multi. 70 45
Nos. 466–472 (7) 1.90 1.23

Ice Hockey
A189

Pres. William Tubman
A190

Designs: 25c, Ski jump. 40c, Bobsledding.

1967, Nov. 20 **Litho.** ***Perf. 12½***

473 A189 10c emerald & violet blue 20 15
474 " 25c greenish blue & deep plum 50 40
475 " 40c ocher & org. brn. 80 60

Issued to publicize the 10th Winter Olympic Games, Grenoble, France, Feb. 6–18, 1968. See No. C178.

1967, Dec. 22 **Litho.** ***Perf. 12½***

476 A190 25c ultra. & brown 50 40

Souvenir Sheet

Imperf.

477 A190 50c ultra. & brown 1.00 1.00

Issued to commemorate the inauguration of President Tubman, Jan. 1, 1968. No. 477 contains one stamp with simulated perforations and picture frame. Size: 76½x76½mm.

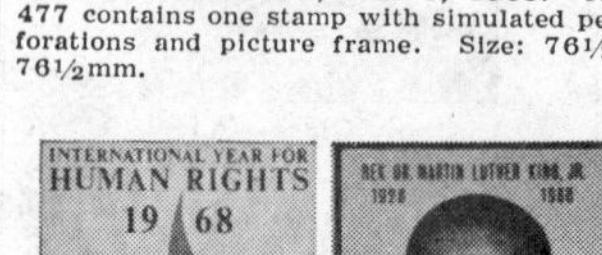

Human Rights Flame
A191

Martin Luther King, Jr.
A192

1968, Apr. 26 **Litho.** ***Perf. 12½***

478 A191 3c verm. & dp. blue 6 4
479 " 80c brn. & emerald 1.60 1.00

Issued for International Human Rights Year. See No. C179.

968, July 11 *Perf. 12½* **Unwmkd.**

Designs: 15c, Mule-drawn hearse and r. King. 35c, Dr. King and Lincoln onument by Daniel Chester French oriz.).

80 A192 15c brt. bl. & brown 30 25
81 " 25c indigo & brn. 50 40
82 " 35c olive & black 70 55

Issued in memory of the Rev. Dr. Martin uther King, Jr. (1929–1968). American ivil rights leader. See No. C180.

Javelin and Diana Statue, Mexico City
A193

Designs: 25c, Discus, pyramid and serent god Quetzalcoatl. 35c, Woman diver nd Xochicalco from ruins near Cuernavaca.

968, Aug. 22 **Litho.** *Perf. 12½*

83 A193 15c deep violet & orange brown 30 20
84 " 25c red & brt. blue 50 30
85 " 35c brn. & emerald 70 40

Issued to publicize the 19th Olympic ames, Mexico City, Oct. 12–27. See also o. C181.

Pres. Wm. V. S. Tubman
A194

Unification Monument, Voinjama-Lofa County—A195

1968, Dec. 30 *Perf. 12½* **Unwmkd.**

486 A194 25c silver, black & brown 50 40

Souvenir Sheet

Imperf.

487 A195 80c silver, ultra. & red 1.60 1.60

Issued to commemorate the 25th anniversary of President Tubman's administration. No. 487 measures 78x78mm.

"ILO" with Cogwheel and Wreath
A196

1969, Apr. 16 **Litho.** *Perf. 12½*

488 A196 25c lt. blue & gold 50 40

Issued to commemorate the 50th anniversary of the International Labor Organization. See No. C183.

Red Roofs, by Camille Pisarro
A197

Paintings: 3c, Prince Balthasar Carlos on Horseback, by Velazquez (vert.). 10c, David and Goliath, by Caravaggio. 12c, Still Life, by Jean Baptiste Chardin. 15c, The Last Supper, by Leonardo da Vinci. 20c, Regatta at Argenteuil, by Claude Monet. 25c, Judgment of Solomon, by Giorgione. 35c, Sistine Madonna, by Raphael.

1969, June 26 **Litho.** *Perf. 11*

489 A197 3c gray & multi. 6 3
490 " 5c " " 10 8
491 " 10c lt. bl. & multi. 20 15
492 " 12c gray & multi. 25 20
493 " 15c " " 30 22
494 " 20c " " 40 28
495 " 25c " " 50 35
496 " 35c " " 70 50
Nos. 489-496 (8) 2.51 1.81

See also Nos. 502–509.

African Development Bank Emblem
A198

1969, Aug. 12 **Litho.** *Perf. 12½*

497 A198 25c blue & brown 50 40
498 " 80c yel. grn. & red 1.60 1.00

Issued to commemorate the 5th anniversary of the African Development Bank.

Moon Landing and Liberia No. C174
A199

Designs: 15c, Memorial tablet left on moon, rocket, earth and moon (horiz.). 35c, Take-off from moon.

1969, Oct. 15 **Litho.** *Perf. 12½*

499 A199 15c blue & bister 30 6
500 " 25c dk. violet blue & orange 50 10
501 " 35c gray & red 70 15

Issued to commemorate man's first landing on the moon, July 20, 1969. U.S. astronauts Neil A. Armstrong and Col. Edwin E. Aldrin, Jr., with Lieut. Col. Michael Collins piloting Apollo 11. See No. C184.

Painting Type of 1969

1969, Nov. 18 **Litho.** *Perf. 11*

Paintings: 3c, The Gleaners, by Francois Millet. 5c, View of Toledo, by El Greco (vert.). 10c, Heads of Negroes, by Rubens. 12c, The Last Supper, by El Greco. 15c, Dancing Peasants, by Brueghel. 20c, Hunters in the Snow, by Brueghel. 25c, Detail from Descent from the Cross, by Rogier van der Weyden (vert.). 35c, The Ascension, by Murillo (vert., inscribed "The Conception").

502 A197 3c lt. blue & multi. 6 3
503 " 5c " " " 10 6
504 " 10c " " " 20 15
505 " 12c gray & multi. 24 18
506 " 15c " " 30 22
507 " 20c lt. blue & multi. 40 28
508 " 25c gray & multi. 50 40
509 " 35c lt. blue & multi. 70 50
Nos. 502-509 (8) 2.50 1.82

Peace Dove, U. N. Emblem and Atom
A200

1970, Apr. 16 **Litho.** *Perf. 12½*

510 A200 5c green & silver 10 8

Issued to commemorate the 25th anniversary of the United Nations. See No. C185.

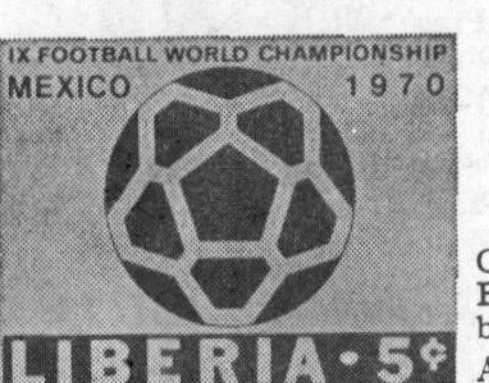

Official Emblem
A201

Designs: 10c, Statue of rain god Tlaloc (vert.). 25c, Jules Rimet cup and sculptured wall (vert.). 35c, Sombrero and soccer ball. 55c, Two soccer players.

1970, June 10 **Litho.** *Perf. 12½*

511 A201 5c pale blue & brown 10 8
512 " 10c emerald & ocher 20 15
513 " 25c deep rose lilac & gold 50 35
514 " 35c vermilion & ultra. 70 45

Souvenir Sheet

Perf. 11½

515 A201 55c brt. blue, yellow & green 1.10 1.00

Issued to commemorate the 9th World Soccer Championships for the Jules Rimet Cup, Mexico City, May 30–June 21, 1970. No. 515 contains one horizontal stamp; view of playing field of Aztec Stadium in margin and inscription. Size: 126x76½ mm.

EXPO '70 Emblem, Japanese Singer and Festival Plaza
A202

Designs (EXPO '70 Emblem and): 3c, Male Japanese singer, EXPO Hall and floating stage. 5c, Tower of the Sun and view of exhibition. 7c, Tanabata Festival. 8c, Awa Dance Festival. 25c, Sado-Okesa Dance Festival. 50c, Ricoh Pavilion with "eye," and Mt. Fuji (vert.).

1970, July **Lithographed** *Perf. 11*

516 A202 2c multicolored 5 5
517 " 3c " 6 6
518 " 5c " 10 8
519 " 7c " 15 12
520 " 8c " 20 15
521 " 25c " 50 40
Nos. 516-521 (6) 1.06 86

Souvenir Sheet

522 A202 50c multicolored 1.00 80

Issued to publicize EXPO '70 International Exhibition, Osaka, Japan, Mar. 15–Sept. 13. No. 522 contains one stamp, blue and black marginal inscription. Size: 79½x113½mm.

U.P.U. Headquarters and Monument, Bern
A203

Design: 80c, Like 25c (vert.).

1970, Aug. 25 *Perf. 12½*

523 A203 25c blue & multi. 50 30
524 " 80c multicolored 1.60 80

Issued to commemorate the inauguration of the new Universal Postal Union Headquarters in Bern.

Napoleon as Consul, by Joseph Marie Vien, Sr.
A204

Paintings of Napoleon: 5c, Visit to a School, by unknown painter. 10c, Napoleon Bonaparte, by François Pascal Gerard. 12c, The French Campaign, by Ernest Meissonier. 20c, Napoleon Signing Abdication at Fontainebleau, by François Bouchot. 25c, Napoleon Meets Pope Pius VII, by Jean-Louis Demarne. 50c, Napoleon's Coronation, by Jacques Louis David.

1970, Oct. 20 **Litho.** *Perf. 11*

525 A204 3c blue & multi. 6 4
526 " 5c " " 10 8
527 " 10c " " 20 15
528 " 12c " " 25 20
529 " 20c " " 40 30
530 " 25c " " 50 40
Nos. 525-530 (6) 1.51 1.17

Souvenir Sheet

Imperf.

531 A204 50c blue & multi. 1.00 80

Issued to commemorate the 200th anniversary of the birth of Napoleon Bonaparte (1769–1821). No. 531 contains one stamp with simulated perforations and decorative margin. Size: 76x101mm.

Pres. Tubman
A205

1970, Nov. 20 Litho. *Perf. 13½*

532 A205 25c multicolored 50 35

Souvenir Sheet

Imperf.

533 A205 50c multicolored 1.00 80

Issued in honor of President William V. S. Tubman's 75th birthday. No. 533 contains one imperf. stamp with simulated perforations. Gray and lilac margin with black inscription. Size 85½x110½mm.

Adoration of the Kings, by Rogier van der Weyden

A206

Paintings (Adoration of the Kings, by): 5c, Hans Memling. 10c, Stefan Lochner. 12c, Albrecht Altdorfer (vert.). 20c, Hugo van der Goes, Adoration of the Shepherds. 25c, Hieronymus Bosch (vert.). 50c, Andrea Mantegna (triptych).

Perf. 13½x14, 14x13½

1970, Dec. 21 Lithographed

534 A206 3c multicolored 6 4
535 " 5c " 10 8
536 " 10c " 20 15
537 " 12c " 25 20
538 " 20c " 40 30
539 " 25c " 50 40
Nos. 534-539 (6) 1.51 1.17

Souvenir Sheet

Imperf.

540 A206 50c multicolored 1.00 80

Christmas 1970.

No. 540 contains one stamp (size: 60x 40mm.). Gray margin with green and red inscription. Size: 99½x69mm.

Dogon Tribal Mask

A207

African Tribal Ceremonial Masks: 2c, Bapendé. 5c, Baoulé. 6c, Dédougou. 9c, Dan. 15c, Bamiléké. 20c, Bapendé mask and costume. 25c, Bamiléké mask and costume.

1971, Feb. 24 Litho. *Perf. 11*

541 A207 2c lt. grn. & multi. 6 3
542 " 3c pink & multi. 8 4
543 " 5c lt. blue & multi. 12 8
544 " 6c lt. green & multi. 15 10
545 " 9c lt. blue & multi. 25 20
546 " 15c pink & multi. 40 30
547 " 20c lt. green & multi. 50 40
548 " 25c pink & multi. 65 50
Nos. 541-548 (8) 2.21 1.65

Astronauts on Moon

A208

Designs: 5c, Astronaut and lunar transport vehicle. 10c, Astronaut with U.S. flag on moon. 12c, Space capsule in Pacific Ocean. 20c, Astronaut leaving capsule. 25c, Astronauts Alan B. Shepard, Stuart A. Roosa and Edgar D. Mitchell.

1971, May 20 Litho. *Perf. 13½*

549 A208 3c vio. bl. & multi. 8 6
550 " 5c " " " 12 8
551 " 10c " " " 25 18
552 " 12c " " " 35 25
553 " 20c " " " 50 35
554 " 25c " " " 65 50
Nos. 549-554 (6) 1.95 1.42

Apollo 14 moon landing, Jan. 31–Feb. 9. See No. C186.

Map, Liberian Women and Pres. Tubman

A209

Design: 3c, Pres. Tubman and women at ballot box (vert.).

1971, May 27 *Perf. 12½*

555 A209 3c ultra. & brown 10 6
556 " 80c green & brown 1.60 1.00

25th anniversary of women's suffrage.

Hall of Honor, Munich, and Olympic Flag—A210

Munich Views and Olympic Flag: 5c, General view. 10c, National Museum. 12c, Max Joseph's Square. 20c, Propylaeum on King's Square. 25c, Liesel-Karlstadt Fountain.

1971, June 28 Litho. *Perf. 11*

557 A210 3c multicolored 8 6
558 " 5c " 12 8
559 " 10c " 25 20
560 " 12c " 35 25
561 " 20c " 50 35
562 " 25c " 65 50
Nos. 557-562 (6) 1.95 1.44

Publicity for the 20th Summer Olympic Games, Munich, Germany, 1972. See No. C187.

Boy Scout, Emblem and U. S. Flag

A211

Designs (Boy Scout, National Flag and Boy Scout Emblem of): 5c, German Federal Republic. 10c, Australia. 12c, Great Britain. 20c, Japan. 25c, Liberia.

1971, Aug. 6 Litho. *Perf. 13½*

563 A211 3c multicolored 8 6
564 " 5c " 12 8
565 " 10c " 25 18
566 " 12c " 35 25
567 " 20c " 50 35
568 " 25c " 65 50
Nos. 563-568 (6) 1.95 1.42

13th Boy Scout World Jamboree, Asagiri Plain, Japan, Aug. 2–10. See No. C188.

Pres. Tubman

A212

1971, Aug. 23 *Perf. 12½*

569 A212 3c blk., ultra. & brn. 10 6
570 " 25c black, brt. rose lilac & brown 50 35

In memory of Pres. William V. S. Tubman (1895–1971).

Zebra and UNICEF Emblem—A213

Animals (UNICEF Emblem and Animals with their Young): 7c, Koala. 8c, Llama. 10c, Red fox. 20c, Monkey. 25c, Brown bear.

1971, Oct. 1 *Perf. 11*

571 A213 5c multicolored 12 8
572 " 7c " 17 12
573 " 8c " 20 15
574 " 10c " 25 20
575 " 20c " 50 40
576 " 25c " 65 50
Nos. 571-576 (6) 1.89 1.45

25th anniversary of United Nations International Children's Fund (UNICEF). See No. C189.

Sapporo 72 Emblem, Long-distance Skiing, Sika Deer—A214

Designs (Sapporo 72 Emblem and): 3c, Sledding and black woodpecker. 5c, Ski Jump and brown bear. 10c, Bobsledding and murres. 15c, Figure skating and pikas. 25c, Downhill skiing and Japanese cranes.

1971, Nov. 4 *Perf. 13x13½*

577 A214 2c multicolored 6 3
578 " 3c " 6 4
579 " 5c " 12 8
580 " 10c " 25 20
581 " 15c " 30 25
582 " 25c " 65 50
Nos. 577-582 (6) 1.44 1.10

11th Winter Olympic Games, Sapporo, Japan, Feb. 3–13, 1972. See No. C190.

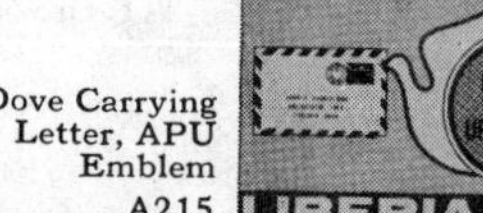

Dove Carrying Letter, APU Emblem

A215

1971, Dec. 9 *Perf. 12½*

583 A215 25c ultra. & dp. org. 50 30
584 " 80c gray & dp. brn. 1.60 1.10

10th anniversary of African Postal Union.

Pioneer Fathers' Monument, Monrovia

A216

Pres. William R. Tolbert, Jr.

A217

Designs: 3c, 25c, Sailing ship "Elizabeth," Providence Island (horiz.). 35c, as 20c.

1972, Jan. 1

585 A216 3c bl. & brt. green 8 6
586 " 20c orange & blue 40 30
587 " 25c orange & purple 50 40
588 " 35c lilac rose & bright green 70 55

Sesquicentennial of founding of Liberia. See No. C191.

1972, Jan. 1

Design: 25c, Pres. Tolbert and map of Liberia (horiz.).

589 A217 25c emerald & brn. 50 40
590 " 80c blue & brown 1.60 80

Inauguration of William R. Tolbert, Jr. as 19th president of Liberia.

Soccer and Swedish Flag—A218

Designs (Olympic Rings, "Motion" Symbol and): 5c, Swimmers at start and Italian flag. 10c, Equestrian and British flag. 12c, Bicycling and French flag. 20c, Long jump and American flag. 25c, Running and Liberian flag.

1972, May 19 Litho. *Perf. 11*

591 A218 3c lemon & multi. 8 6
592 " 5c lt. lilac & multi. 12 8
593 " 10c multicolored 25 18
594 " 12c gray & multi. 35 25
595 " 20c lt. blue & multi. 50 38
596 " 25c pink & multi. 65 50
Nos. 591-596 (6) 1.95 1.45

20th Olympic Games, Munich, Aug. 26–Sept. 10. See No. C192.

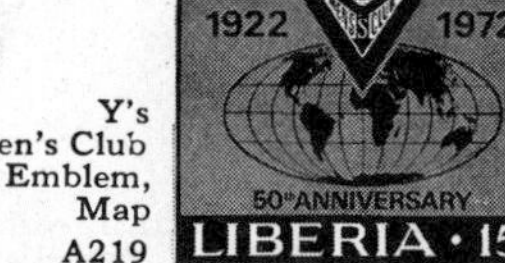

Y's Men's Club Emblem, Map

A219

Design: 90c, Y's Men's Club emblem and globe; inscribed "fifty and forward."

1972, June 12 *Perf. 13½*

597 A219 15c purple & gold 30 23
598 " 90c violet blue & emerald 1.80 1.25

International Y's Men's Club, 50th anniversary.

Astronaut and Lunar Rover—A220

Designs: 5c, Moon scene reflected in astronaut's helmet. 10c, Astronauts with cameras. 12c, Astronauts placing scientific equipment on moon. 20c, Apollo 16 badge. 25c, Astronauts riding lunar rover.

1972, June 26

599 A220 3c lt. blue & multi. 6 6
600 " 5c red org. & multi. 12 8
601 " 10c pink & multi. 25 18
602 " 12c yellow & multi. 35 25
603 " 20c lt. vio. & multi. 55 35
604 " 25c emerald & multi. 65 50
Nos. 599-604 (6) 1.98 1.42

Apollo 16 U.S. moon mission, Apr. 15–27, 1972. See No. C193.

Emperor Haile Selassie A221

1972, July 21 *Perf. 14x14½*

605 A221 20c olive grn. & yel. 40 30
606 " 25c maroon & yel. 50 40
607 " 35c brown & yellow 70 55

80th birthday of Emperor Haile Selassie of Ethiopia.

Ajax, 1809, and Figurehead—A222

1972, Sept. 6 *Perf. 11*

Multicolored

608 A222 3c *shown* 6 6
609 " 5c *Hogue, 1811* 12 10
610 " 7c *Ariadne, 1816* 18 15
611 " 15c *Royal Adelaide, 1828* 35 30
612 " 20c *Rinaldo, 1860* 50 40
613 " 25c *Nymphe, 1888* 60 50
Nos. 608-613 (6) 1.81 1.51

Famous sailing ships and their figureheads. See No. C194.

Pres. Tolbert Taking Oath, Richard A. Henries—A223

1972, Oct. 23 Litho. *Perf. 13½*

614 A223 15c green & multi. 30 23
615 " 25c vio. bl. & multi. 50 40

Pres. William R. Tolbert, Jr. sworn in as 19th President of Liberia, July 23, 1971. See No. C195.

Klaus Dibiasi, Italy, Diving A224

Designs (Flag, Olympic Emblems and): 8c, Valery Borzov, USSR, running. 10c, Hideaki Yanagida, Japan, wrestling. 12c, Mark Spitz, USA, swimming. 15c, Kipchoge Keino, Kenya, steeplechase. 25c, Richard Meade, Great Britain, equestrian. 55c, Hans Winkler, Germany, grand prix jumping.

1973, Jan. 5 Litho. *Perf. 11*

616 A224 5c lt. bl. & multi. 10 10
617 " 8c violet & multi. 17 17
618 " 10c multicolored 20 20
619 " 12c green & multi. 25 25
620 " 15c orange & multi. 30 30
621 " 25c pale sal. & multi. 50 50
Nos. 616-621 (6) 1.52 1.52

Souvenir Sheet

622 A224 55c multicolored 1.10 85

Gold medal winners in 20th Olympic Games. No. 622 contains one stamp; blue margin with gold medal design. Size: 95x70mm.

Astronaut on Moon and Apollo 17 Badge—A225

Designs (Apollo 17 Badge and): 3c, Astronauts on earth in lunar rover. 10c, Astronauts collecting yellow lunar dust. 15c, Astronauts in lunar rover exploring moon crater. 20c, Capt. Eugene A. Cernan, Dr. Harrison H. Schmitt and Comdr. Ronald E. Evans on launching pad. 25c, Astronauts on moon with scientific equipment.

1973, Mar. 28 Litho. *Perf. 11*

623 A225 2c blue & multi. 4 4
624 " 3c " " 6 6
625 " 10c " " 20 20
626 " 15c " " 30 30
627 " 20c " " 40 40
628 " 25c " " 50 50
Nos. 623-628 (6) 1.50 1.50

Apollo 17 U.S. moon mission, Dec. 7–19, 1972. See No. C196.

Locomotive, England—A226

Designs: Locomotives, 1895–1905.

1973, May 4

Multicolored

629 A226 2c *shown* 4 4
630 " 3c *Netherlands* 6 6
631 " 10c *France* 25 18
632 " 15c *United States* 35 28
633 " 20c *Japan* 50 38
634 " 25c *Germany* 65 50
Nos. 629-634 (6) 1.85 1.44

See No. C197.

OAU Emblem and Flags—A227

1973, May 24 Litho. *Perf. 13½*

635 A227 3c multicolored 6 6
636 " 5c " 10 8
637 " 10c " 20 15
638 " 15c " 30 23
639 " 25c " 50 40
640 " 50c " 1.00 75
Nos. 635-640 (6) 2.16 1.67

10th anniversary of the Organization for African Unity.

WHO Emblem, Edward Jenner and Roses—A228

Designs (WHO Emblem and): 4c, Sigmund Freud and pansies. 10c, Jonas E. Salk and chrysanthemums. 15c, Louis Pasteur and scabiosa caucasia. 20c, Emil von Behring and rhododendron. 25c, Alexander Fleming and tree mallows.

1973, June 26 Litho. *Perf. 11*

641 A228 1c gray & multi. 3 3
642 " 4c orange & multi. 7 7
643 " 10c lt. blue & multi. 25 18
644 " 15c rose & multi. 38 28
645 " 20c blue & multi. 50 38
646 " 25c yel. grn. & multi. 65 50
Nos. 641-646 (6) 1.88 1.44

25th anniversary of the World Health Organization. See No. C198.

Stanley Steamer, 1910—A229

Designs: Classic automobiles.

1973, Sept. 11 Litho. *Perf. 11*

Multicolored

647 A229 2c *shown* 4 4
648 " 3c *Cadillac, 1903* 6 6
649 " 10c *Clement-Bayard, 1904* 25 18
650 " 15c *Rolls Royce, 1907* 38 28
651 " 20c *Maxwell, 1905* 50 38
652 " 25c *Chadwick, 1907* 65 50
Nos. 647-652 (6) 1.88 1.44

See No. C199.

Copernicus, Armillary Sphere, Satellite Communication—A230

Portraits of Copernicus and: 4c, Eudoxus solar system. 10c, Aristotle, Ptolemy, Copernicus and satellites. 15c, Saturn and Apollo spacecraft. 20c, Orbiting astronomical observatory. 25c, Satellite tracking station.

1973, Dec. 14 Litho. *Perf. 13½*

653 A230 1c yellow & multi. 3 3
654 " 4c lt. vio. & multi. 8 6
655 " 10c lt. blue & multi. 25 18
656 " 15c yel. grn. & multi. 38 28
657 " 20c bister & multi. 50 38
658 " 25c pink & multi. 65 50
Nos. 653-658 (6) 1.89 1.43

500th anniversary of the birth of Nicolaus Copernicus (1473–1543), Polish astronomer. See No. C200.

Radio Tower, Map of Africa A231

Designs: 15c, 25c, Map of Liberia, Radio tower and man listening to broadcast. 17c, like 13c.

1974, Jan. 16 Litho. *Perf. 13½*

659 A231 13c multicolored 27 20
660 " 15c yellow & multi. 30 22
661 " 17c lt. gray & multi. 35 25
662 " 25c brt. grn. & multi. 50 40

20th anniversary of Radio ELWA, Monrovia.

Thomas Coutts, 1817; Aureal, 1974; UPU Emblem—A232

Designs (UPU Emblem and): 3c, Jet, satellite, Post Office, Monrovia, ship. 10c, US and USSR telecommunication satellites. 15c, Mail runner and jet. 20c, Futuristic mail train and mail truck. 25c, American Pony Express rider.

1974, Mar. 4 Litho. *Perf. 13½*

663 A232 2c ocher & multi. 4 4
664 " 3c lt. grn. & multi. 6 6
665 " 10c lt. bl. & multi. 25 20
666 " 15c pink & multi. 38 30
667 " 20c gray & multi. 50 40
668 " 25c lt. lilac & multi. 65 50
Nos. 663-668 (6) 1.88 1.50

Centenary of Universal Postal Union. See No. C201.

See "Special Notices" at the front of this volume for data on the listing methods of this Catalogue, abbreviations, condition, prices and examination.

Fox Terrier—A233

1974, Apr. 16 Litho. *Perf. 13½*

Light Ultramarine and Multicolored

No.	Type	Description	Unused	Used
669	A233	5c *shown*	10	8
670	"	10c *Boxer*	20	12
671	"	16c *Chihuahua*	33	20
672	"	19c *Beagle*	38	30
673	"	25c *Golden retriever*	50	40
674	"	50c *Collie*	1.00	65
		Nos. 669-674 (6)	2.51	1.75

See No. C202.

Soccer Game, West Germany and Chile—A234

Designs: Games between semi-finalists, and flags of competing nations.

1974, June 4 Litho. *Perf. 11*

Multicolored

No.	Type	Description	Unused	Used
675	A234	1c *shown*	3	3
676	"	2c *Australia and East Germany*	6	4
677	"	5c *Brazil and Jugoslavia*	12	8
678	"	10c *Zaire and Scotland*	25	18
679	"	12c *Netherlands and Uruguay*	32	22
680	"	15c *Sweden and Bulgaria*	40	28
681	"	20c *Italy and Haiti*	55	38
682	"	25c *Poland and Argentina*	65	50
		Nos. 675-682 (8)	2.38	1.71

World Cup Soccer Championship, Munich, June 13–July 7. See No. C203.

Chrysiridia Madagascariensis—A235

Tropical Butterflies: 2c, Catagramma sorana. 5c, Erasmia pulchella. 17c, Morpho cypris. 25c, Agrias amydon. 40c, Vanessa cardui.

1974, Sept. 11 Litho. *Perf. 13½*

No.	Type	Description	Unused	Used
683	A235	1c gray & multi.	3	3
684	"	2c " "	4	4
685	"	5c " "	10	8
686	"	17c " "	35	25
687	"	25c " "	50	40
688	"	40c " "	80	60
		Nos. 683-688 (6)	1.82	1.40

See No. C204.

Pres. Tolbert and Medal—A236

Design: $1, Pres. Tolbert, medal and Liberian flag (vert.).

1974, Dec. 10 Litho. *Perf. 13½*

No.	Type	Description	Unused	Used
689	A236	3c multicolored	6	6
690	"	$1 "	2.00	1.20

Pres. William R. Tolbert, Jr., recipient of 1974 Family of Man Award.

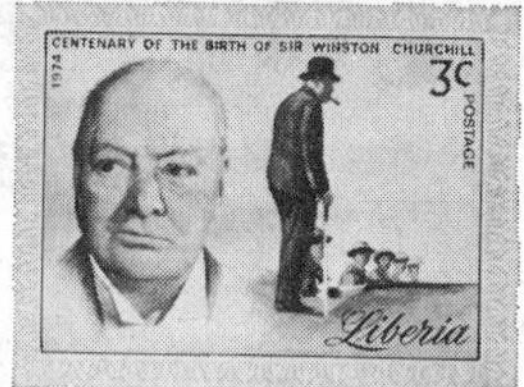

Winston Churchill, 1940—A237

Designs (Churchill and): 10c, RAF planes in dog fight. 15c, In naval launch on way to Normandy. 17c, In staff car reviewing troops in desert. 20c, Aboard landing craft crossing Rhine. 25c, In conference with Pres. Roosevelt.

1975, Jan. 17 Litho. *Perf. 13½*

No.	Type	Description	Unused	Used
691	A237	3c multicolored	6	6
692	"	10c "	20	12
693	"	15c "	30	18
694	"	17c "	34	25
695	"	20c "	40	30
696	"	25c "	50	40
		Nos. 691-696 (6)	1.80	1.31

Sir Winston Churchill (1874–1965), birth centenary. See No. C205.

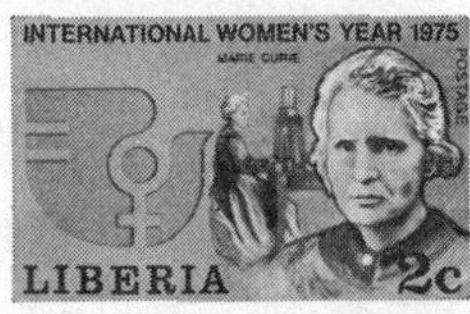

Women's Year Emblem and Marie Curie—A238

Designs (Women's Year Emblem and): 3c, Mahalia Jackson with microphone. 5c, Joan of Arc. 10c, Eleanor Roosevelt and children. 25c, Matilda Newport firing cannon. 50c, Valentina Tereshkova in space suit.

1975, Mar. 14 Litho. *Perf. 14½*

No.	Type	Description	Unused	Used
697	A238	2c citron & multi.	4	4
698	"	3c dull org. & multi.	6	6
699	"	5c lilac rose & multi.	10	8
700	"	10c yellow & multi.	20	15
701	"	25c yel. grn. & multi.	50	33
702	"	50c lilac & multi.	1.00	70
		Nos. 697-702 (6)	1.90	1.36

International Women's Year 1975. See No. C206.

Old State House, Boston, U.S. No. 627—A239

Designs: 10c, George Washington, U.S. No. 644. 15c, Town Hall and Court House, Philadelphia, U.S. No. 798. 20c, Benjamin Franklin, U.S. No. 835. 25c, Paul Revere's Ride, U.S. No. 618. 50c, Santa Maria, U.S. No. 231.

1975, Apr. 25 Litho. *Perf. 13½*

No.	Type	Description	Unused	Used
703	A239	5c multicolored	15	7
704	"	10c "	30	12
705	"	15c "	45	18
706	"	20c "	60	25
707	"	25c "	75	30
708	"	50c "	1.50	60
		Nos. 703-708 (6)	3.75	1.52

American Revolution Bicentennial. See No. C207.

Dr. Schweitzer, Hospital and Baboon Mother—A240

Designs (Dr. Schweitzer and): 3c, Elephant, and tribesmen poling boat. 5c, Water buffalo, egret, man and woman paddling canoe. 6c, Antelope and dancer. 25c, Lioness, woman cooking outdoors. 50c, Zebra and colt, doctor's examination at clinic.

1975, June 26 Litho. *Perf. 13½*

No.	Type	Description	Unused	Used
709	A240	1c multicolored	3	3
710	"	3c "	6	6
711	"	5c "	10	7
712	"	6c "	12	8
713	"	25c "	50	35
714	"	50c "	1.00	75
		Nos. 709-714 (6)	1.81	1.34

Dr. Albert Schweitzer (1875–1965), medical missionary, birth centenary. See No. C208.

American-Russian Handshake in Space—A241

Designs (Apollo-Soyuz Emblem and): 5c, Apollo. 10c, Soyuz. 20c, Flags and maps of U.S. and U.S.S.R. 25c, A. A. Leonov, and V. N. Kubasov. 50c, D. K. Slayton, V. D. Brand, T. P. Stafford.

1975, Sept. 18 Litho. *Perf. 13½*

No.	Type	Description	Unused	Used
715	A241	5c multicolored	10	6
716	"	10c "	20	8
717	"	15c "	30	10
718	"	20c "	40	25
719	"	25c "	50	30
720	"	50c "	1.00	65
		Nos. 715-720 (6)	2.50	1.44

Apollo Soyuz space test project (Russo-American cooperation), launching July 15; link-up, July 17. See No. C209.

Presidents Tolbert, Siaka Stevens; Treaty Signing; Liberia and Sierra Leone Maps—A242

1975, Oct. 3 Litho. *Perf. 13½*

No.	Type	Description	Unused	Used
721	A242	2c gray & multi.	4	4
722	"	3c " "	6	6
723	A242	5c gray & multi.	10	7
724	"	10c " "	20	12
725	"	25c " "	50	35
726	"	50c " "	1.00	70
		Nos. 721-726 (6)	1.90	1.34

Mano River Union Agreement between Liberia and Sierra Leone, signed Oct. 3, 1973.

Figure Skating—A243

Designs (Winter Olympic Games Emblem and): 4c, Ski jump. 10c, Slalom. 25c, Ice hockey. 35c, Speed skating. 50c, Two-man bobsled.

1976, Jan. 23 Litho. *Perf. 13½*

No.	Type	Description	Unused	Used
727	A243	1c lt. bl. & multi.	3	3
728	"	4c " "	8	6
729	"	10c " "	20	12
730	"	25c " "	50	30
731	"	35c " "	70	45
732	"	50c " "	1.00	65
		Nos. 727-732 (6)	2.51	1.61

12th Winter Olympic Games, Innsbruck, Austria, Feb. 4–15. See No. C210.

Pres. Tolbert Taking Oath of Office—A244

Designs: 25c, Pres. Tolbert at his desk (vert.). $1, Seal and flag of Liberia, $400 commemorative gold coin.

1976, Apr. 5 Litho. *Perf. 13½*

No.	Type	Description	Unused	Used
733	A244	3c multicolored	6	6
734	"	25c "	50	35
735	"	$1 "	2.00	1.20

Inauguration of President William R. Tolbert, Jr., Jan. 5, 1976.

Weight Lifting and Olympic Rings A245

Designs (Olympic Rings and): 3c, Pole vault. 10c, Hammer and shot put. 25c, Yachting. 35c, Women's gymnastics. 50c, Hurdles.

1976, May 4 Litho. *Perf. 13½*

No.	Type	Description	Unused	Used
736	A245	2c gray & multi.	4	4
737	"	3c orange & multi.	6	6
738	"	10c lt. vio. & multi.	20	12
739	"	25c lt. grn. & multi.	50	35
740	"	35c yel. & multi.	70	45
741	"	50c pink & multi.	1.00	60
		Nos. 736-741 (6)	2.50	1.62

21st Olympic Games, Montreal, Canada, July 17–Aug. 1. See No. C211.

A. G. Bell, Telephone and Receiver, 1876, UPU Emblem—A246

Designs (UPU Emblem and): 4c, Horse-rawn mail coach and ITU emblem. 5c, ntelsat IV satellite, radar and ITU emblem. 25c, A. G. Bell, ship laying under-vater cable, 1976 telephone. 40c, A. G. Bell, futuristic train, telegraph and telehone wires. 50c, Wright brothers' plane, Zeppelin and Concorde.

976, June 4 Litho. *Perf. 13½*

'42	A246	1c green & multi.	4	4
43	"	4c ocher & multi.	8	5
44	"	5c org. & multi.	10	8
45	"	25c green & multi.	50	35
'46	"	40c lilac & multi.	80	50
47	"	50c blue & multi.	1.00	60
		Nos. 742–747 (6)	2.52	1.62

Centenary of first telephone call by Alexander Graham Bell, Mar. 10, 1876. See No. C212.

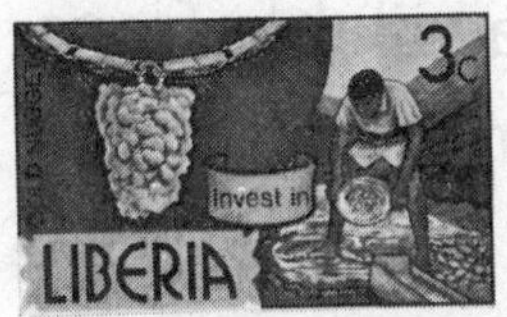

Gold Nugget on Chain, Gold Panner—A247

Designs: 1c, Mano River bridge and boat. 5c, "V" ring and hand with ring and bracelet. 10c, Tire and man tapping rubber tree. 25c, Mesurado shrimp. 55c, Barracuda, Lake Piso.

1976–77 Lithographed *Perf. 14½*

'48	A247	1c multicolored	3	3
'50	"	3c "	6	3
'52	"	5c "	10	5
'54	"	10c "	20	8
'55	"	25c "	50	15
'60	"	55c "	1.10	35
		Nos. 748–760 (6)	1.99	69

Issue dates: 3c, 5c, July 26; 10c, 25c, Nov. 26, 1976, 1c, 55c, July 19, 1977.

Rhinoceros—A249

African Animals: 3c, Zebra antelope. 5c, Chimpanzee (vert.). 15c, Pigmy hippopotamus. 25c, Leopard. $1, Gorilla (vert.).

1976, Sept. 1 Litho. *Perf. 13½*

763	A249	2c orange & multi.	4	4
764	"	3c gray & multi.	6	6
765	"	5c blue & multi.	10	8
766	"	15c brt. bl. & multi.	30	15
767	"	25c ultra. & multi.	50	35
768	"	$1 multicolored	2.00	1.20
		Nos. 763–768 (6)	3.00	1.88

See No. C213.

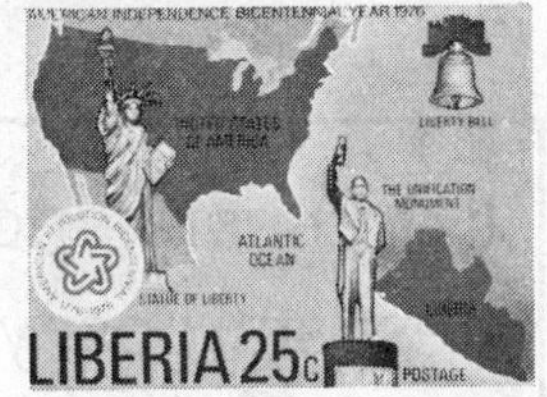

Maps of U.S. and Liberia; Statue of Liberty, Unification Monument, Voinjama and Liberty Bell

A250

Designs: $1, George Washington, Gerald R. Ford, Joseph J. Roberts (1st Pres. of Liberia), William R. Tolbert, Jr., Bicentennial emblem, U.S. and Liberian flags.

1976, Sept. 21 Litho. *Perf. 13½*

769	A250	25c multicolored	50	35
770	"	$1 "	2.00	1.00

American Bicentennial and visit of Pres. William R. Tolbert, Jr. to the United States, Sept. 21–30. See No. C214.

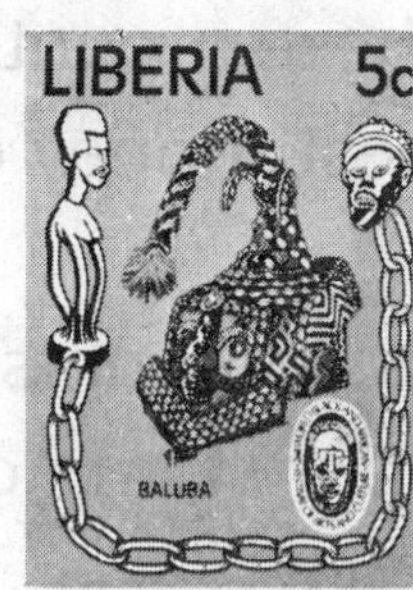

Baluba Masks and Festival Emblem

A251

Tribal Masks: 10c, Bateke. 15c, Basshilele. 20c, Igungun. 25c, Masai. 50c, Kifwebe.

1977, Jan. 20 Litho. *Perf. 13½*

771	A251	5c yellow & multi.	10	8
772	"	10c green & multi.	20	12
773	"	15c salmon & multi.	30	18
774	"	20c lt. bl. & multi.	40	25
775	"	25c violet & multi.	50	35
776	"	50c lemon & multi.	1.00	60
		Nos. 771–776 (6)	2.50	1.58

FESTAC '77, 2nd World Black and African Festival, Lagos, Nigeria, Jan. 15–Feb. 12. See No. C215.

Latham's Francolin—A252

Birds of Liberia: 10c, Narina trogon. 15c, Rufous-crowned roller. 20c, Brown-cheeked hornbill. 25c, Common bulbul. 50c, Fish eagle. 80c, Gold Coast touraco.

1977, Feb. 18 Litho. *Perf. 14*

777	A252	5c multicolored	10	8
778	"	10c "	20	12
779	"	15c "	30	18
780	"	20c "	40	25
781	"	25c "	50	30
782	"	50c "	1.00	65
		Nos. 777–782 (6)	2.50	1.58

Souvenir Sheet

783	A252	80c multicolored	1.60	1.60

No. 783 has multicolored margin showing various birds. Size: 105x77mm.

Edmund Coffin, Military Dressage, USA—A253

Designs: 15c, Alwin Schockemohle, single jump, Germany (vert.). 20c, Christine Stuckelberger, Switzerland, single dressage. 25c, Prize of the Nations (team), France.

1977, Apr. 22 Litho. *Perf. 13½*

784	A253	5c ocher & multi.	10	10
785	"	15c " "	30	15
786	"	20c " "	40	25
787	"	25c " "	50	35
		Nos. 784–787, C216 (5)	2.40	1.60

Equestrian gold medal winners in Montreal Olympic Games. See No. C217.

Elizabeth II Wearing Crown—A254

Designs: 25c, Elizabeth II Prince Philip, Pres. and Mrs. Tubman. 80c, Elizabeth II, Prince Philip, royal coat of arms.

1977, May 23 Litho. *Perf. 13½*

788	A254	15c silver & multi.	45	20
789	"	25c " "	75	30
790	"	80c " "	2.40	1.00

25th anniversary of the reign of Queen Elizabeth II. See No. C218.

Jesus Blessing Children

A255

Designs: 25c, The Good Shepherd. $1, Jesus and the Samaritan Woman. Designs after stained-glass windows, Providence Baptist Church, Monrovia.

1977, Nov. 3 Litho. *Perf. 13½*

791	A255	20c lt. bl. & multi.	40	30
792	"	25c " "	50	35
793	"	$1 " "	2.00	1.25

Christmas 1977.

Dornier DOX, 1928—A256

Progress of Aviation: 3c, Piggyback space shuttle, 1977. 5c, Eddie Rickenbacker and Douglas DC 3. 25c, Charles A. Lindbergh and Spirit of St. Louis. 35c, Louis Bleriot and Bleriot XI. 50c, Orville and Wilbur Wright and flying machine, 1903. 80c, Concorde landing at night at Dulles Airport, Washington, D.C.

1978, Jan. 6 Litho. *Perf. 13½*

794	A256	2c multicolored	4	4
795	"	3c "	6	6
796	"	5c "	10	12
797	"	25c "	50	35
798	"	35c "	70	45
799	"	50c "	1.00	65
		Nos. 794–799 (6)	2.40	1.67

Souvenir Sheet

800	A256	80c multicolored	1.60	1.60

No. 800 has multicolored margin showing space shuttle over earth. Size: 119x81mm.

Baladeuse by Santos-Dumont, 1903—A257

Airships: 3c, Baldwin's, 1908, and US flag. 5c, Tissandier brothers'. 1883. 25c, Parseval PL VII, 1912. 40c, Nulli Secundus II, 1908. 50c, R34 rigid airship, 1919.

1978, Mar. 9 Litho. *Perf. 13½*

801	A257	2c multicolored	4	4
802	"	3c "	6	6
803	"	5c "	10	8
804	"	25c "	50	35
805	"	40c "	80	50
806	"	50c "	1.00	65
		Nos. 801–806 (6)	2.50	1.68

75th anniversary of the Zeppelin. See No. C219.

Soccer, East Germany and Brazil—A258

Soccer Games: 2c, Poland and Argentina (vert.). 10c, West Germany and Netherlands. 25c, Jugoslavia and Brazil. 35c, Poland and Italy (vert.). 50c, Netherlands and Uruguay.

1978, May 16 Litho. *Perf. 13½*

807	A258	2c multicolored	4	3
808	"	3c "	6	4
809	"	10c "	20	14
810	"	25c "	50	35
811	"	35c "	70	48
812	"	50c "	1.00	70
		Nos. 807–812 (6)	2.50	1.74

11th World Cup Soccer Championships, Argentina, June 1–25. See No. C220.

Coronation Chair

A259

Designs: 25c, Imperial state crown. $1, Buckingham Palace (horiz.).

1978, June 12

813	A259	5c multicolored	10	8
814	"	25c "	50	35
815	"	$1 "	2.00	1.40

25th anniversary of coronation of Queen Elizabeth II. See No. C221.

Jinnah, Liberian and Pakistani Flags
A260

1978, June **Litho.** ***Perf. 13***

816	A260	30c multicolored	*1.50*

Mohammed Ali Jinnah (1876–1948), first Governor General of Pakistan.

Carter and Tolbert Families—A261

Designs: 25c, Pres. Tolbert, Rosalynn Carter and Pres. Carter at microphone, Robertsfield Airport. $1, Jimmy Carter and William R. Tolbert, Jr. in motorcade from airport.

1978, Oct. 26 **Litho.** ***Perf. 13½***

817	A261	5c multicolored	10	8
818	"	25c "	50	35
819	"	$1 "	2.00	1.60

Pres. Carter's visit to Liberia, Apr. 1978.

Soccer Game: Italy–France
A262

Soccer Games: 1c, Brazil–Spain (horiz.). 10c, Poland–West Germany (horiz.). 27c, Peru–Scotland. 35c, Austria–West Germany. 50c, Argentina the victor.

1978, Dec. 8 **Litho.** ***Perf. 13½***

820	A262	1c multicolored	3	3
821	"	2c "	4	3
822	"	10c "	20	15
823	"	27c "	55	35
824	"	35c "	70	48
825	"	50c "	1.00	70
		Nos. 820–825 (6)	2.52	1.74

1978 World Cup Soccer winners. See No. C222.

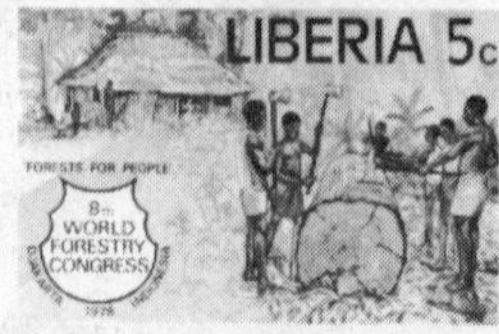

Liberian Lumbermen—A263

Designs: 10c, Hauling timber by truck (vert.). 25c, Felling trees with chain saw. 50c, Moving logs.

1978, Dec. 15 **Litho.** ***Perf. 13½x14***

826	A263	5c multicolored	10	8
827	"	10c "	20	15
828	"	25c "	50	35
829	"	50c "	1.00	70

8th World Forestry Congress, Djakarta, Indonesia.

"25" and Waves
A264

Design: $1, Radio tower and waves.

1979, Apr. 6 **Litho.** ***Perf. 14x13½***

830	A264	35c multicolored	70	48
831	"	$1 "	2.00	1.40

25th anniversary of Radio ELWA.

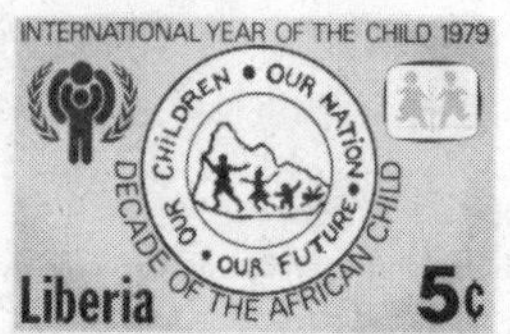

Emblems of IYC, African Child's Decade and SOS Village—A265

Designs: 25c, $1, like 5c, with UNICEF emblem replacing SOS emblem. 35c, like 5c.

1979, Apr. 6 ***Perf. 13½x14***

832	A265	5c multicolored	10	8
833	"	25c "	50	35
834	"	35c "	70	42
835	"	$1 "	2.00	1.40

International Year of the Child and Decade of the African Child.

SEMI-POSTAL STAMPS.

No. 127 Surcharged in Red **+ 2c**

1915 *Perf. 14.* Unwmkd.

B1 A49 2c+3c on 10c plum & black 50 50
a. Double red surcharge
b. Double blue surcharge
c. Both surcharges double
d. Pair, one without "2c"

Same Surcharge On Official Stamp of 1912.

B2 A49 2c+3c on 10c black & ultra. 50 50
a. Double surcharge

Regular Issue of 1918 Surcharged in Black and Red

1918 *Perf. 12½, 14.*

B3 A59 1c+2c deep green & black 50 50
B4 A60 2c+2c rose & black 50 50
a. Double surcharge, one inverted
b. Inverted surcharge, cross double
c. Inverted surcharge, cross omitted 15.00
B5 A61 5c+2c gray blue & black 20 20
a. Imperf., pair 8.00
B6 A62 10c+2c dark green 20 20
a. Inverted surcharge 5.00 5.00
B7 A63 15c+2c black & dark green 20 20
B8 A64 20c+2c claret & black 40 40
B9 A65 25c+2c dark green & green 75 75
B10 A66 30c+2c red violet & black 50 50
B11 A67 50c+2c ultra. & blk. 75 75
B12 A68 75c+2c olive bistre & black 1.50 1.50
B13 A69 $1+2c yellow brown & blue 2.50 2.50
B14 A70 $2+2c light violet & black 3.00 3.00
B15 A71 $5+2c dark brn. 10.00 10.00
Nos. B3-B15 (13) 21.00 21.00

Nos. 277-279 Surcharged in Red or Blue

RED CROSS
TWO ✠ CENTS

1941 *Perf. 12.* Unwmkd.

B16 A107 3c+2c dk. bl. (R) 1.50 1.50
B17 A108 5c+2c dull red brown (Bl) 1.50 1.50
B18 A109 10c+2c dark green (R) 1.50 1.50

Research
SP1

Lithographed and Engraved

1954 *Perf. 12½* Unwmkd.

B19 SP1 5c+5c rose lilac & black 20 10

The surtax was for the Liberian Government Hospital. No. B19 exists imperforate.

AIR POST STAMPS.

Regular Issue of 1928 Surcharged in Black "AIR MAIL" and New Values.

1936, Feb. 28 *Perf. 12* Unwmkd.

C1 A102 6c on 2c violet 110.00 70.00
C2 " 6c on 3c bis. brown 110.00 70.00

Same Surcharge on Official Stamp of 1928

C3 A102 6c on 1c green 110.00 70.00
m. Surcharged on No. 230 (error) 425.00

Many counterfeits exist.

Waco Plane—AP1

1936, Sept. 30 Engraved *Perf. 14*

C3A AP1 1c yellow green & black 15 8
C3B " 2c carmine & black 15 8
C3C " 3c purple & black 30 8
C3D " 4c orange & black 30 8
C3E " 5c blue & black 30 8
C3F " 6c green & black 30 10
Nos. C3A-C3F (6) 1.50 50

Issued in September, 1936 in commemoration of Liberia's first air mail service of February 28, 1936.

Nos. C3A-C3F exist in pairs imperf. between (price, $50 each) and in pairs imperf. (price $15 each).

Eagle in Flight
AP1a

Sikorsky Amphibian
AP5

Tri-motor Plane
AP2

Albatross
AP3

Egrets—AP4

1938, Sept. 12 Photo. *Perf. 12½*

C4 AP1a 1c green 10 10
C5 AP2 2c red orange 15 10
C6 AP3 3c olive green 15 10
C7 AP4 4c orange 20 10
C8 " 5c bright blue green 30 10
C9 AP2 10c violet 30 15
C10 AP5 20c magenta 40 15
C11 AP3 30c gray black 60 15
C12 AP1a 50c brown 80 15
C13 AP5 $1 blue 1.50 25
Nos. C4-C13 (10) 4.50 1.35

Nos. 280-282 Overprinted in Red or Dark Blue

AIR MAIL

1941, Feb. 25 *Perf. 12.*

C14 A107 3c dark blue (R) 2.00 2.00
C15 A108 5c dull red brown (Dk. Bl) 2.00 2.00
C16 A109 10c dark green (R) 2.00 2.00

Nos. C4-C13 Surcharged in Black

First Flight
LIBERIA · U.S.
1941
—— 50c

1941 *Perf. 12½.*

C17 AP1a 50c on 1c green 2500.00 225.00
C18 AP2 50c on 2c red orange 150.00 85.00
C19 AP3 50c on 3c olive green 150.00 85.00
C20 AP4 50c on 4c orange 60.00 35.00
C21 " 50c on 5c bright blue green 60.00 35.00
C22 AP2 50c on 10c violet 60.00 35.00
C23 AP5 50c on 20c magenta 2000.00 60.00
C24 AP3 50c on 30c gray black 55.00 30.00
C25 AP1a 50c brown 55.00 30.00
C26 AP5 $1 blue 60.00 30.00

Nos. C17 to C26 with Additional Overprint of Two Bars, Obliterating "1941".

1942

C27 AP1a 50c on 1c green 8.00 8.00
C28 AP2 50c on 2c red org. 8.00 7.00
C29 AP3 50c on 3c olive green 7.50 7.00
C30 AP4 50c on 4c orange 6.00 7.50
C31 " 50c on 5c bright blue green 3.50 3.50
C32 AP2 50c on 10c violet 5.00 5.00
C33 AP5 50c on 20c magenta 5.00 5.00
C34 AP3 50c on 30c gray black 6.00 6.00
C35 AP1a 50c brown 6.00 6.00
C36 AP5 $1 blue 5.00 5.00
Nos. C27-C36 (10) 60.00 60.00

Plane and Air Route from United States to South America and Africa
AP6

Plane over House
AP7

1942-44 Engraved. *Perf. 12.*

C37 AP6 10c rose 15 15
C38 AP7 12c brt. ultra. ('44) 20 15
C39 " 24c turq. green ('44) 20 15
C40 AP6 30c bright green 20 15
C41 AP6 35c red lilac ('44) 15 8
C42 " 50c violet 20 15
C43 " 70c olive gray ('44) 40 12
C44 " $1.40 scarlet ('44) 1.00 45
Nos. C37-C44 (8) 2.50 1.40

Air Post Stamps of 1938 Surcharged with New Values and Large Dot, Bar or Diagonal Line in Violet, Blue, Black or Violet and Black.

1944-45 *Perf. 12½.*

C45 AP2 10c on 2c red orange (V+Bk) 35.00 25.00
C46 AP4 10c on 5c bright blue green (V+Bk) ('45) 15.00 15.00
C46A AP1 30c on 1c yel. grn. & blk. (Bk) 100.00 55.00
C47 AP3 30c on 3c olive green (V) 120.00 55.00
C48 AP4 30c on 4c orange (V+Bk) 15.00 15.00
C48A AP1 50c on 3c purple & black (Bk) 27.50 27.50
C48B " 70c on 2c carmine & black (Bk) 55.00 55.00
C49 AP3 $1 on 3c olive green (Bl) 25.00 25.00
C50 AP1a $1 on 50c brown (V) 35.00 25.00
Nos. C45-C50 (9) 427.50 297.50

These surcharges were handstamped with the possible exception of the large "10 CTS." of No. C46 and the "30 CTS." of No. C48. On No. C47, the new value was created by handstamping a small, violet, broken "0" beside the large "3" of the basic stamp.

Surcharges on Nos. C46A, C48A, C48B are found inverted. Prices same as normal.

Franklin D. Roosevelt Reviewing Troops
AP8

1945, Nov. 26 Engraved

C51 AP8 70c brown & black, *grayish* 1.50 1.50

In memory of Pres. Franklin D. Roosevelt (1882–1945).

Copies on thick white paper appeared later on the stamp market at reduced prices.

Opening Monrovia Harbor Project
AP9

1947, Jan. 2

C52 AP9 24c bright bluish green 1.50 1.50

Issued to commemorate the opening of the Monrovia Harbor Project, February 16, 1946.

1947, May 16

Without Inscription at Top.

C53 AP9 25c dark carmine 40 30

First United States Postage Stamps and Arms of Liberia—AP10

1947, June 6

C54	AP10	12c green	15	15
C55	"	25c brt. red violet	20	20
C56	"	50c bright blue	25	25
		a. Souvenir sheet of 4	75.00	

Centenary of United States postage stamps and 87th anniversary of Liberian stamps.

No. C56a contains one each of Nos. 300 and C54–C56. Size: 88x162mm. Exists imperf., same price.

Matilda Newport Firing Cannon
AP11

1947, Dec. 1 **Engr. & Photo.**

C57	AP11	25c scarlet & gray black	1.25	40

See note after No. 304.

Monument to Joseph J. Roberts
AP12

Flag of Liberia
AP13

Centenary Monument
AP14

1947, Dec. 22 **Engraved**

C58	AP12	12c brick red	30	20
C59	AP13	25c carmine	50	30
C60	AP14	50c red brown	1.00	1.00

Centenary of independence.

L. I. A. Plane in Flight
AP15

1948, Aug. 17 ***Perf. 11½.***

C61	AP15	25c red	2.00	1.00
C62	"	50c deep blue	1.00	1.00

Issued to commemorate the first flight of Liberian International Airways, August 17, 1948.

Map and Citizens—AP16

Farm Couple, Arms and Agricultural Products
AP17

1949, Apr. 12 **Litho.** ***Perf. 11½***

C63	AP16	25c multicolored	80	1.00
C64	AP17	50c "	80	1.00

Nos. C63–C64 exist perf. 12½. Definite information concerning the perf. 12½ set has not reached the editors. The set also exists imperf.

Type of Regular Issue of 1948-50.
Design: William V. S. Tubman.

1949, July 21 **Engr.** ***Perf. 12½***

C65	A128	25c blue & black	1.00	75

See also No. C118.

Sun and Open Book
AP18

U. P. U. Monument
AP19

1950, Feb. 14 **Engr.** ***Perf. 12½***

C66	AP18	25c rose carmine	1.00	1.00
		a. Souvenir sheet of 2	1.50	1.50

Campaign for National Literacy.

No. C66a contains two imperf. stamps similar to Nos. 329 and C66, with marginal inscriptions in blue. Size: 139½x82½ mm.

1950, Apr. 21

C67	AP19	25c orange & violet	3.75	3.75
		a. Souvenir sheet of 3	10.00	10.00

Universal Postal Union, 75th anniversary (in 1949).

No. C67a contains one each of Nos. 330–331 and C67, imperf. Marginal inscription in gray. Size: 215x251mm.

No. C67 exists imperf.

Map of Monrovia, James Monroe and Ashmun
AP20

Design: 50c, Jehudi Ashmun, President Tubman and map.

1952, Apr. 1 ***Perf. 10½***

C68	AP20	25c lilac rose & black	50	45
C69	"	50c dk. bl. & car.	1.00	60
		a. Souvenir sheet of 8	20.00	20.00

Nos. C68–C69 exist imperf. Price about three times that of the perf. set.

Nos. C68–C69 exist with center inverted. Price $75 each.

No. C69a contains one each of Nos. 332 and C68, and types of Nos. 333–337 and C69 with centers in black; imperf. Margins show arms and ornaments in black. Size: 215x252mm.

The 25c exists in colors of the 50c and vice versa. Price, each $5.

Flags of Five Nations
AP21

1952, Dec. 10 ***Perf. 12½***

C70	AP21	25c ultra. & car.	75	60
		a. Souvenir sheet	3.00	3.00

No. C70a measures 153x85½mm., and contains marginal inscriptions in ultramarine.

Nos. C70 and C70a exist imperforate.

Road Building
AP22

Designs: 25c, Ships in Monrovia harbor. 35c, Diesel locomotive. 50c, Free port, Monrovia. 70c, Roberts Field. $1, Wm. V. S. Tubman bridge.

1953, Aug. 3 **Lithographed**

C71	AP22	12c orange brown	15	15
C72	"	25c lilac rose	35	25
C73	"	35c purple	50	30
C74	"	50c orange	70	35
C75	"	70c dull green	1.10	50
C76	"	$1 blue	1.50	70
		Nos. C71–C76 (6)	4.30	2.25

Flags, Emblem and Children
AP23

1954, Sept. 27

Size: 51x39mm.

C77	AP23	$5 blue, red, violet blue & black	30.00	27.50

A reproduction of No. C77, size 63x49 mm., was prepared for presentation purposes. Price $25.

Half the proceeds from the sale of No. C77 was given to the United Nations International Children's Emergency Fund.

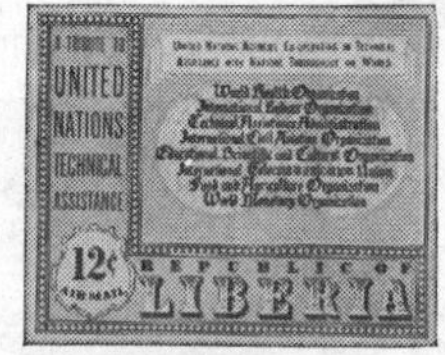

UN Technical Assistance Agencies
AP24

Designs: 15c, Printing instruction. 20c, Sawmill maintenance. 25c, Geography class.

1954, Oct. 25

C78	AP24	12c black & blue	22	12
C79	"	15c dk. brn. & yel.	30	15
C80	"	20c blk. & yel. grn.	40	22
C81	"	25c vio. blue & red	50	32

Issued to publicize the United Nations Technical Assistance program.

Type of 1953 Inscribed:
"Commemorating Presidential Visit U. S. A.—1954."
Designs as before.

1954, Nov. 19

C82	AP22	12c vermilion	25	10
C83	AP22	25c blue	50	20
C84	"	35c carmine rose	70	25
C85	"	50c rose violet	1.00	35
C87	"	70c orange brown	1.40	60
C87	"	$1 dull green	2.00	75
		Nos. C82–C87 (6)	5.85	2.25

Issued to publicize the visit of Pres. William V. S. Tubman to the United States. Exist imperforate.

Baseball—AP25

Designs: 12c, Swimming. 25c, Running.

1955, Jan. 26 **Litho.** ***Perf. 12½***

C88	AP25	10c ultra. & pink	15	12
C89	"	12c chocolate & blue	20	15
C90	"	25c cerise & lt. grn.	30	25
		a. Souvenir sheet	12.50	12.50

No. C90a contains one each of Nos. 349 and C90 with colors transposed. Rose violet inscriptions. Size: 89½x139mm. Exists imperf.; same price.

Costus—AP26

Design: 25c, Barteria nigritiana.

1955, Sept. 28 ***Perf. 12½*** **Unwmkd.**

C91	AP26	20c vio., grn. & yel.	15	15
C92	"	25c grn., red & yel.	25	25

U.N. Emblem
AP27

U.N. Charter
AP28

Designs: 15c, General Assembly. 25c, Gabriel L. Dennis signing U. N. Charter for Liberia.

1955, Oct. 24 ***Perf. 12*** **Unwmkd.**

C93	AP27	10c ultra. & red	20	10
C94	"	15c violet & black	30	15
C95	"	25c green & red brown	50	20
C96	AP28	50c brick red & green	1.00	40

Issued to commemorate the tenth anniversary of the United Nations, Oct. 24, 1955.

Rotary International Headquarters, Evanston, Ill.
AP29

Design: 15c, View of Monrovia.

1955, Dec. 5 **Litho.** ***Perf. 12½***

C97	AP29	10c dp. ultra. & red	20	15
C98	"	15c reddish brown, red & bistre	30	20

Souvenir Sheet.

C99 AP29 50c deep ultramarine & red 2.00 2.00

No. C99 measures 127x76 mm. Design as C97, but redrawn and with leaves omitted. Marginal inscription in deep ultramarine: "50th anniversary of Rotary International," 1905-1955 and "Service Above Self."

No. C97-C99 were issued to commemorate the 50th anniversary of Rotary International.

Nos. C97-C99 exist without Rotary emblem; No. C97 printed entirely in deep ultramarine; No. C98 with bistre impression omitted.

New York Coliseum—AP30

Statue of Liberty
AP31

Design: 12c, Globe inscribed FIPEX.

1956, Apr. 28 ***Perf. 12*** **Unwmkd.**

C100 AP30 10c rose red & ultramarine 15 10
C101 " 12c orange & purple 20 15
C102 AP31 15c aquamarine & red lilac 25 20

Souvenir Sheet.

C103 AP31 50c light green & brown 2.00 2.00

Issued to commemorate the Fifth International Philatelic Exhibition (FIPEX), New York City, Apr. 28–May 6, 1956.

No. C103 measures 76x127mm. Marginal inscription in brown: Fifth International Philatelic Exhibition, 1956.

Olympic Park, Melbourne—AP32

Designs: 20c, 40c, Map of Australia and Olympic torch.

1956, Nov. 15 ***Perf. 12*** **Unwmkd.**

C104 AP32 12c emerald & violet 25 15
C105 " 20c multicolored 40 25

Souvenir Sheet.

C106 AP32 40c multicolored 3.00 3.00

Issued to commemorate the 16th Olympic Games, Melbourne, Nov. 22-Dec. 8.

No. C106 measures 127x76mm. Marginal inscription in black: "1956 Melbourne Australia."

Type of Regular Issue, 1957.

Designs: 12c, 25c, Idlewild airport, New York. 15c, 50c, Roberts Field, Liberia, plane and Pres. Tubman.

Lithographed and Engraved

1957, May 4 ***Perf. 12***

C107 A146 12c bright green & dark blue 25 12
C108 " 15c red brown & black 30 20
C109 " 25c carmine & dark blue 50 25
C110 A146 50c light ultra. & black 1.00 30

Issued to commemorate the first anniversary of direct air service between Roberts Field, Liberia, and Idlewild, New York, (Kennedy).

Type of Regular Issue, 1957

Designs (Orphanage and): 15c, Nurse inoculating boy. 35c, The Kamara triplets. 70c, Children and flag.

1957, Nov. 25 **Litho.** ***Perf. 12***

C111 A147 15c light blue & brown 25 15
C112 " 35c maroon & light gray 50 30

Souvenir Sheet.

C113 A147 70c ultramarine & rose carmine 1.40 1.25

Issued to commemorate the founding of the Antoinette Tubman Child Welfare Foundation.

No. C113 measures 127x77mm. and contains one stamp. Brown marginal inscription: Republic of Liberia; Antoinette Tubman Child Welfare Foundation and pictures of Kamara triplets.

Type of Regular Issue, 1958.

Designs: 10c, Italian flag and Colosseum. No. C115, French flag and Arc de Triomphe. No. C116, Swiss flag and chalet. No. C117, Vatican flag and St. Peter's.

Engraved and Lithographed.

1958, Jan. 10 ***Perf. 10½***

Flags in Original Colors.

C114 A148 10c dark gray 20 12
C115 " 15c dp. yel. green 30 18
C116 " 15c ultramarine 30 18
C117 " 15c purple 30 18

Issued to commemorate the European tour of Pres. Tubman in 1956.

Type of Regular Issue, 1948-50.

Design: William V. S. Tubman.

1958 **Engraved** ***Perf. 12***

C118 A128 25c light green & black 75 50

Souvenir Sheet.

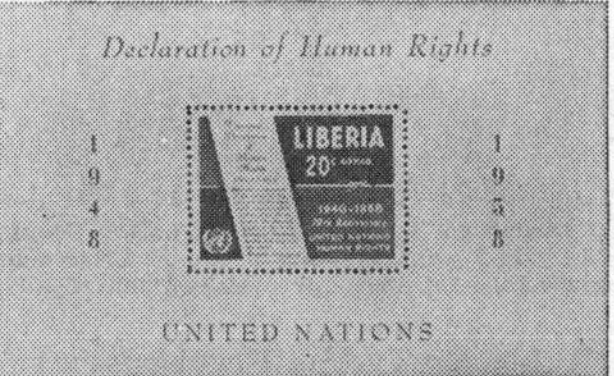

Preamble to Declaration of Human Rights—AP33

1958, Dec. 10 **Litho.** ***Perf. 12***

C119 AP33 20c blue & red 2.75 2.75

Issued to commemorate the tenth anniversary of the signing of the Universal Declaration of Human Rights. No. C119 measures 127x76½mm.

Liberians Reading Proclamation
AP34

UNESCO Building, Paris
AP35

1959, Apr. 15 **Unwmkd.**

C120 AP34 25c blue & brown 50 25

African Freedom Day, Apr. 15.

1959, May 1

C121 AP35 25c ultra. & red 50 35
a. Souvenir sheet 2.25 2.25

Issued to commemorate the opening of UNESCO (U. N. Educational, Scientific and Cultural Organization) Headquarters in Paris, Nov. 3, 1958.

No. C121a measures 76½ x 127½ mm. and contains one each of Nos. 384 and C121. Marginal inscription in red and U. N. emblem in ultramarine.

Lincoln Type of Regular Issue

1959, Nov. 20 **Engraved.** ***Perf. 12***

C122 A152 25c emerald & black 75 60

Issued to commemorate the 150th anniversary of the birth of Abraham Lincoln.

For souvenir sheet see No. 386a.

Touré, Tubman and Nkrumah
AP36

1960, Jan. 27 **Litho.** **Unwmkd.**

C123 AP36 25c beige, violet blue & black 50 35

See note after No. 387.

WRY Type of Regular Issue, 1960.

1960, Apr. 7 ***Perf. 11½***

C124 A154 25c ultra. & blk. 75 40
a. Souv. sheet 3.50 3.50

Issued to publicize World Refugee Year, July 1, 1959–June 30, 1960.

No. C124a contains one each of Nos. 388 and C124, imperf. Black marginal inscription. Size: 133½x83mm.

Map of Africa
AP37

1960, May 11 ***Perf. 11½***

C125 AP37 25c ultra. & brn. 60 50

See note after No. 389.

Olympic Games Issue.

Type of Regular Issue, 1960.

Designs: 25c, Javelin thrower and hunter (horiz.). 50c, Runner and stadium (horiz.).

1960, Sept. 6 ***Perf. 11½***

C126 A156 25c brown & bright ultra. 80 50

Souvenir Sheet

Imperf.

C127 A156 50c lilac & brown 3.50 3.50

Nos. C126–C127 issued to commemorate the 17th Olympic Games, Rome, Aug. 25–Sept. 11.

Black marginal inscription on No. C127. Size: 127x76mm.

Stamp Centenary Type of 1960

1960, Dec. 1 **Litho.** ***Perf. 11½***

C128 A157 25c multicolored 60 50

Souvenir Sheet

C129 A157 50c multicolored 1.75 1.75

Issued to commemorate the centenary of Liberian postage stamps.

No. C129 measures 130x79mm. Brown engraved marginal inscription and portraits of Presidents Benson (1860) and Tubman (1960).

Globe, Dove and U.N. Emblem
AP38

Design: 50c, Globe and dove.

1961, May 19 ***Perf. 11½*** **Unwmkd.**

C130 AP38 25c indigo & red 50 35

Souvenir Sheet

C131 AP38 50c red brown & emerald 2.00 2.00

Issued to commemorate Liberia's membership in the United Nations Security Council. No. C131 measures 127x76mm. with black marginal inscription.

A second souvenir sheet contains one each of Nos. 395, C130 and the 50c from No. C131, imperf. Size: 133x83mm. Marginal inscriptions in dark blue, ornaments in light blue.

No. C130 exists imperf.

Science Class—AP39

Design: 50c, Science class, different design.

1961, Sept. 8 **Lithographed**

C132 AP39 25c purple & brn. 50 35

Souvenir Sheet

C133 AP39 50c blue & brn. 1.50 1.50

Issued to commemorate the 15th anniversary of the United Nations Educational, Scientific and Cultural Organization, UNESCO. No. C133 has black marginal inscription. Size: 125x75mm.

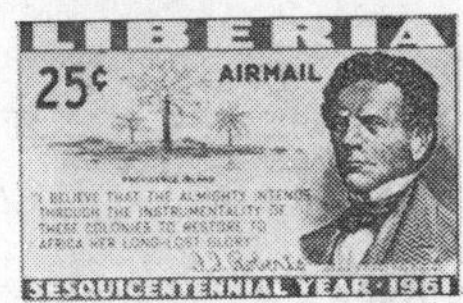

Joseph J. Roberts and Providence Island
AP40

1961, Oct. 25 **Litho.** ***Perf. 11½***

C134 AP40 25c emerald & sepia 50 35
a. Souvenir sheet of three 1.50 1.50

Issued to commemorate the 150th anniversary of the birth of Joseph J. Roberts, first president of Liberia.

No. C134a contains three imperf. stamps similar to Nos. 397–398 and C134, but printed in different colors; 5c, emerald & sepia. 10c, orange & sepia. 25c, ultramarine & sepia. Gold marginal inscription. Size: 140x84mm.

Boy Scout
AP41

1961, Dec. 4 ***Perf. 11½*** **Unwmkd.**

C135 AP41 25c emerald & sepia 50 35

Souvenir Sheet

Scout Type of Regular Issue.

Design: Like No. 399.

C136 A161 35c dull blue & sepia 1.50 1.50

Nos. C135–C136 issued to honor the Boy Scouts of Liberia. No. C136 contains one stamp and has gold marginal inscription. Size: 126x76mm. Nos. C135–C136 exist imperf.

Type of Regular Issue, 1962

Dag Hammarskjold

1962, Feb. 1 ***Perf. 12*** **Unwmkd.**

C137 A162 25c black & red lilac 50 30

Souvenir Sheet

Imperf.

C138 A162 50c blk. & ultra. 1.50 1.50

Nos. C137–C138 issued in memory of Dag Hammarskjold, Secretary General of the United Nations, 1953–61. No. C138 contains one stamp. Black and ultramarine marginal inscription. Size: 127x 76mm.

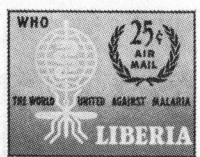

Malaria Eradication Emblem

AP42

1962, Apr. 7 ***Perf. 12½***

C139 AP42 25c purple & org. 50 30

Souvenir Sheet

Imperf.

C140 AP42 50c dark red & ultra. 1.25 1.25

Issued for the World Health Organization drive to eradicate malaria. No. C140 contains one stamp, ultramarine and gold marginal inscription. Size: 126x76mm.

Pres. Tubman, Statue of Liberty, New York Skyline and Flags of U.S. and Liberia—AP43

1962, Sept. 17 Litho. ***Perf. 11½x12***

C141 AP43 12c multicolored 25 15
C142 " 25c " 50 40
C143 " 50c " 1.00 75

Issued to commemorate President Tubman's visit to the United States in 1961.

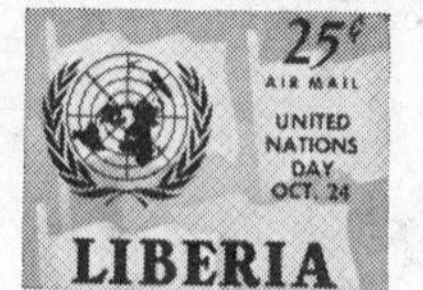

United Nations Emblem and Flags

AP44

Design: 50c, U.N. emblem.

1962, Oct. 22 ***Perf. 12x12½***

C144 AP44 25c lt. ultra. & dk. blue 50 35

Souvenir Sheet

Imperf.

C145 AP44 50c br. greenish blue & blk. 1.00 1.00

Issued to mark the observance of United Nations Day, Oct. 24, as a national holiday. No. C145 contains one stamp. Gold marginal inscription. Size: 126½x76mm.

Building Type of Regular Issue

Buildings: 12c, 70c, Capitol. 50c, Information Service. $1, Treasury Department Building, Monrovia.

1962–63 ***Perf. 12x12½, 12 (70c)***

C146 A165 12c br. yel. grn. & maroon 25 15
C147 " 50c org. & ultra. 1.00 90
C147A " 70c brt. pink & dk. bl. ('63) 1.40 1.00
C148 " $1 sal. & black ('63) 2.00 25

"FAO" Emblem and Globe

AP45

Design: 50c, "FAO" and U.N. Emblems.

1963, Mar. 21 ***Perf. 12½*** **Unwmkd.**

C149 AP45 25c dark green & yellow 50 25

Souvenir Sheet

Perf. 12

C150 AP45 50c emerald & ultra. 1.50 1.50

Issued for the "Freedom from Hunger" campaign of the U.N. Food and Agriculture Organization. No. C150 contains one stamp. Gold inscription, ultramarine U.N. emblem and emerald FAO emblem in margin. Size: 127x76mm.

Type of Regular Issue, 1963

Designs: 25c, Telstar satellite (vert.). 50c, Telstar and rocket (vert.).

1963, May 27 Litho. ***Perf. 12½***

C151 A167 25c Prussian blue & orange 50 30

Souvenir Sheet

Perf. 12

C152 A167 50c dp. vio. & yel. 1.00 80

Issued to honor achievements in space exploration for peaceful purposes. No. C152 contains one stamp. Deep violet marginal inscription. Size: 126½x76mm.

Red Cross Type of Regular Issue

Design: 25c, Red Cross and globe. 50c, Centenary emblem and globe.

1963, Aug. 26 ***Perf. 12*** **Unwmkd.**

C153 A168 25c purple & red 50 30
C154 " 50c deep ultra. & red 1.00 60

Centenary of the International Red Cross.

Map of Africa

AP46

1963, Oct. 28 ***Perf. 12½***

C156 AP46 25c red org. & grn. 50 30

See note after No. 412.

Olympic Type of Regular Issue

Designs: 10c, Torch and mountains. 25c, Mountains (horiz.). 50c, Torch, background like No. 413.

1963, Dec. 11 Litho. ***Perf. 12½***

C157 A170 10c vio. blue & red 20 12
C158 " 25c green & orange 50 30

Souvenir Sheet

Perf. 12

C159 A170 50c gray & red 1.00 1.00

Issued to publicize the 9th Winter Olympic Games, Innsbruck, Austria, Jan 29–Feb. 9, 1964. No. C159 contains one stamp. Gray and red marginal inscription. Size: 128x77mm.

Kennedy Type of Regular Issue, 1964

Designs: 25c, John F. Kennedy (vert.). 50c, John F. Kennedy (like No. 414).

1964, Apr. 6 ***Perf. 12½*** **Unwmkd.**

C160 A171 25c blk. & red lilac 50 30

Souvenir Sheet

Perf. 12

C161 A171 50c black & red lilac 1.50 1.50

Issued in memory of John F. Kennedy (1917–63). No. C161 contains one stamp, black and red lilac marginal inscription. Size: 127x77mm.

An imperf. miniature sheet containing one of No. C160 exists. No marginal inscription.

Satellite Type of Regular Issue

Souvenir Sheet

Design: Launching rocket separating from booster in space (vert.).

1964, June 22 Lithographed

C162 A172 50c vio. blue & red 1.25 1.25

Issued to publicize progress in space communications and the peaceful uses of outer space. Size: 127x77mm.

Olympic Type of Regular Issue

Souvenir Sheet

Design: 50c, Runner and Olympic rings.

1964, Sept. 15 ***Perf. 12*** **Unwmkd.**

C163 A173 50c greenish blue & red 1.00 75

Issued for the 18th Olympic Games, Tokyo, Oct. 10–25, 1964. No. C163 contains one stamp, greenish blue and red marginal inscriptions. Size: 128x77mm.

Scout Type of Regular Issue, 1965

Designs: 25c, Liberian flag and fleur-de-lis. 50c, Globe and Scout emblem.

1965, Mar. 8 Litho. ***Perf. 12½***

C164 A174 25c crimson & ultra. 50 30

Souvenir Sheet

Perf. 12

C165 A174 50c yellow & lilac 1.35 1.35

Issued to honor the Liberian Boy Scouts. No. C165 contains one stamp. Lilac marginal inscription. Size: 128x77mm.

Lincoln Type of Regular Issue

Souvenir Sheet

Design: 50c, Lincoln and John F. Kennedy (horiz.).

1965, May 3 ***Perf. 12*** **Unwmkd.**

C166 A175 50c deep plum & light gray 1.35 1.35

Issued to commemorate the centenary of the death of Abraham Lincoln. No. C166 contains one stamp. Gray marginal inscription. Size: 127x77mm.

ICY Type of Regular Issue, 1965

Souvenir Sheet

1965, June 21 Lithographed

C167 A176 50c carmine rose & brown 1.25 1.25

Issued to commemorate the United Nations International Cooperation Year. No. C167 contains one stamp; margin inscribed in brown: "U.N. Twentieth Anniversary" and "1945 1965" in carmine rose. Size: 127x77mm.

ITU Type of Regular Issue, 1965

1965, Sept. 21 ***Perf. 12½*** **Unwmkd.**

C168 A177 50c red orange & violet blue 1.00 50

Issued to commemorate the centenary of the International Telecommunication Union.

Tubman Type of Regular Issue

Design: 25c, Pres. Tubman and coat of arms.

1965, Nov. 29 Litho. ***Perf. 12½***

C169 A178 25c ultramarine, red & brown 50 30
a. Souv. sheet 1.30 1.30

Issued in honor of President Tubman's 70th birthday. No. C169a contains two imperf. stamps similar to Nos. 431 and C169. Score of National Anthem in background and inscription in margin. Size: 127x76mm.

Churchill Type of Regular Issue

Designs: 25c, "Angry Lion" portrait by Karsh and Parliament, London. 50c, "Williamsburg Award Dinner" portrait by Karsh and map of Europe.

1966, Jan. 18 Litho. ***Perf. 12½***

C170 A179 25c blk. & vio. bl. 50 40

Souvenir Sheet

Perf. 12

C171 A179 50c black & red lilac 1.25 1.25

Issued in memory of Sir Winston Spencer Churchill (1874–1965), statesman and World War II leader. No. C171 contains one stamp. Black and red lilac marginal inscription. Size: 127x77mm.

Soccer Type of Regular Issue

Souvenir Sheet

Design: 50c, Soccer match in stadium.

1966, May 3 Litho. ***Perf. 11½***

C172 A181 50c ultramarine & red brown 1.35 1.35

Issued to publicize the World Cup Soccer Championships, Wembley, England, July 11–30. No. C172 contains one stamp; ultramarine marginal inscription. Size: 127x 76mm.

Kennedy Type of Regular Issue

Designs: 25c, U.N. General Assembly and Pres. Kennedy. 35c, Pres. Kennedy and rocket on launching pad, Cape Kennedy. 40c, Flame on grave at Arlington.

1966, Aug. 16 Litho. ***Perf. 12½***

C173 A182 25c ultra., black & ocher 60 30
C174 " 35c dark violet blue & pink 80 45

Souvenir Sheet

Perf. 11½

C175 A182 40c dark violet bl. & multi. 1.25 1.25

Issued to commemorate the third anniversary of President Kennedy's death. No. C175 contains one stamp. Picture of White House at night in margin and quotation: ". . . We shall pay any price, bear any burden, meet any hardship. . . ."

Size: 76½x127mm.

Boy Scout Type of Regular Issue

Souvenir Sheet

Design: 50c, Scout at campfire and vision of moon landing.

1967, March 23 Litho. ***Perf. 12½***

C176 A185 50c brt. red lilac & scarlet 1.00 1.00

See note after No. 460.

No. C176 contains one stamp. Scarlet marginal inscription and bright red lilac fleur-de-lis emblems. Size: 127x77mm.

Olympic Type of Regular Issue

Souvenir Sheet

Design: 50c, Pre-Hispanic sculpture, serape and Olympic rings (horiz.).

1967, June 20 Litho. ***Perf. 12½***

C177 A186 50c violet & car. 1.35 1.00

Issued to publicize the 19th Olympic Games, Mexico City. No. C177 contains one stamp. Marginal inscription and Olympic torch design in carmine and violet. Size: 127x76½mm.

Winter Olympic Games Type of Regular Issue
Souvenir Sheet

Design: 50c, Woman skater.

1967, Nov. 20 Litho. ***Perf. 11½***

C178 A189 50c verm. & black 1.00 80

Issued to publicize the 10th Winter Olympic Games, Grenoble, Feb. 6–18, 1968. No. C178 contains one stamp; vermilion and black marginal design and inscription. Size: 127x76½mm.

Human Rights Type of Regular Issue
Souvenir Sheet

1968, Apr. 26 Litho. ***Perf. 11½***

C179 A191 80c blue & red 2.00 1.20

Issued for International Human Rights Year. No. C179 contains one stamp. Blue marginal inscription and U.N. emblem. Size: 127x77mm.

M. L. King Type of Regular Issue
Souvenir Sheet

Design: 55c, Pres. Kennedy congratulating Dr. King.

1968, July 11 Litho. ***Perf. 11½***

C180 A192 55c brn. & black 1.10 80

Issued in memory of Rev. Dr. Martin Luther King, Jr. (1929–1968), American civil rights leader. No. C180 contains one stamp. Brown and black inscription and Noble Prize medal in margin. Size: 127x76mm.

Olympic Type of Regular Issue
Souvenir Sheet

Design: 50c, Steeplechase and ancient sculpture.

1968, Aug. 22 Litho. ***Perf. 11½***

C181 A193 50c bright blue & org. brown 1.00 1.00

Issued to publicize the 19th Olympic Games, Mexico City, Oct. 12–27. No. C181 contains one stamp. Orange brown and bright blue marginal inscriptions and Olympic rings. Size: 127x76½mm.

President Type of Regular Issue 1966–69

Design: 25c, Pres. William V. S. Tubman.

1969, Feb. 18 Litho. ***Perf. 11½x11***

C182 A180 25c blk. & emerald 50 40

ILO Type of Regular Issue

Design: 80c, "ILO" surrounded by cogwheel and wreath (vert.).

1969, Apr. 16 Litho. ***Perf. 12½***

C183 A196 80c emerald & gold 1.60 1.20

See note after No. 488.

Apollo 11 Type of Regular Issue
Souvenir Sheet

Design: 65c, Astronauts Neil A. Armstrong, Col. Edwin E. Aldrin, Jr., and Lieut. Col. Michael Collins (horiz.).

1969, Oct. 15 Litho. ***Perf. 11½***

C184 A199 65c dk. violet blue & brt. red 1.25 1.25

See note after No. 501. No. C184 contains one stamp; commemorative inscription, Apollo 11 on launching pad and lunar landing module on moon in margin. Size: 126x76mm.

U.N. Type of 1970

Design: $1, U.N. emblem, olive branch and plane as symbols of peace and progress (vert.).

1970, Apr. 16 Litho. ***Perf. 12½***

C185 A200 $1 ultra. & silver 1.75 1.25

Issued to commemorate the 25th anniversary of the United Nations.

Apollo 14 Type of Regular Issue
Souvenir Sheet

Design: 50c, Moon, earth and star.

1971, May 20 Litho. ***Imperf.***

C186 A208 50c multicolored 1.00 1.00

Apollo 14 moon landing. No. C186 contains one stamp. Bright pink inscription in margin and picture of landing craft over moon. Size: 127x85mm.

Souvenir Sheet

Olympic Yachting Village, Kiel, and Yachting—AP47

1971, June 28 Litho. ***Perf. 14½x14***

C187 AP47 Souvenir Sheet of 2 1.20 1.20
- *a.* 25c multicolored 50 50
- *b.* 30c multicolored 60 60

Publicity for the 20th Summer Olympic Games, and the yachting races in Kiel, Germany, 1972. Size of No. C187: 114x 84mm.

Boy Scout Type of Regular Issue
Souvenir Sheet

Design: 50c, Boy Scouts of various nations cooking (horiz.).

1971, Aug. 6 Litho. ***Perf. 15***

C188 A211 50c multicolored 1.00 1.00

13th Boy Scout World Jamboree, Asagiri Plain, Japan, Aug. 2–10. No. C188 contains one stamp; blue margin with black inscription and pictures of 2 Girl Scouts. Size: 101x76mm.

UNICEF Type of Regular Issue
Souvenir Sheet

Design: 50c, UNICEF emblem and Bengal tigress with cubs.

1971, Oct. 1 ***Imperf.***

C189 A213 50c multicolored 1.00 1.00

25th anniversary of United Nations International Children's Fund (UNICEF). No. C189 contains one stamp with simulated perforations. Black inscriptions and light yellow green leaves in margin. Size: 102x76mm.

Souvenir Sheet

Japanese Royal Family—AP48

1971, Nov. 4 ***Perf. 15***

C190 AP48 50c multicolored 1.25 1.00

11th Winter Olympic Games, Sapporo, Japan, Feb. 3–13, 1972. Size of No. C190: 101x75mm.

Sesquicentennial Type of Regular Issue
Souvenir Sheet

Design: 50c, Sailing ship "Elizabeth" between maps of America and Africa (horiz.).

1972, Jan. 1 Litho. ***Imperf.***

C191 A216 50c car. & vio. bl. 1.25 1.25

Sesquicentennial of founding of Liberia. No. C191 contains one stamp. Decorative margin with inscription in carmine and violet blue. Size: 126x77mm.

Olympic Type of Regular Issue
Souvenir Sheet

Design: 55c, View of Olympic Stadium and symbol of "Motion."

1971, May 19 Litho. ***Perf. 15***

C192 A218 55c multicolored 1.10 1.10

20th Olympic Games, Munich, Aug. 26–Sept. 10. No. C192 has yellow green margin with black inscription, multicolored Olympic rings and "Motion" symbol. Size: 101x69mm.

Apollo 16 Type of Regular Issue
Souvenir Sheet

Design: 55c, Lt. Comdr. Thomas K. Mattingly, 2nd, Capt. John W. Young and Lt. Col. Charles M. Duke, Jr.

1972, June 26 Litho. ***Perf. 15***

C193 A220 55c pink & multi. 1.10 1.10

Apollo 16 U.S. moon mission, Apr. 15–27, 1972. No. C193 has multicolored margin with Apollo 16 badge. Size: 96x71 mm.

Ship Type of 1972
Souvenir Sheet

Design: Lord Nelson's flagship Victory, and her figurehead (1765).

1972, Sept. 6 Litho. ***Perf. 15***

C194 A222 50c multicolored 1.00 1.00

No. C194 has multicolored margin with signal flags, rigging and sea gulls. Size: 101½x75½mm.

Pres. Tolbert Type of 1972.
Souvenir Sheet

1972, Oct. 23 Litho. ***Perf. 15***

C195 A223 55c multicolored 1.10 1.10

Pres. William R. Tolbert, Jr. sworn in as 19th President of Liberia, July 23, 1971. No. C195 contains one stamp with Liberian flag and coat of arms in margin; brown commemorative inscription. Size: 96x71mm.

Apollo 17 Type of Regular Issue
Souvenir Sheet

Design: 55c, Apollo 17 badge, moon and earth.

1973, Mar. 28 Litho. ***Perf. 11***

C196 A225 55c blue & multi. 1.10 1.10

Apollo 17 moon mission, Dec. 7–19. 1972. No. C196 has multicolored margin with eagle flying over moon. Size: 101x 76mm.

Locomotive Type of Regular Issue
Souvenir Sheet

Design: 55c, Swiss locomotive.

1973, May 4 Litho. ***Perf. 11***

C197 A226 55c multicolored 1.10 1.10

No. C197 has multicolored margin showing old train. Size: 101x76mm.

WHO Type of Regular Issue 1973
Souvenir Sheet

Design: 55c, WHO emblem, Paul Ehrlich and poppy anemones.

1973, June 26 Litho. ***Perf. 11***

C198 A228 55c light violet & multi. 1.10 1.10

25th anniversary of the World Health Organization. No. C198 has multicolored margin with WHO emblems. Size: 102x 76mm.

Automobile Type of Regular Issue
Souvenir Sheet

Design: Franklin 10 HP cross-engined 1904–1905 models.

1973, Sept. 11 Litho. ***Perf. 11***

C199 A229 55c multicolored 1.10 1.10

No. C199 contains one stamp. Multicolored margin shows various classic cars. Size: 101½x76mm.

Copernicus Type of Regular Issue
Souvenir Sheet

Design: 55c, Copernicus and concept of orbiting station around Mars.

1973, Dec. 14 Litho. ***Perf. 13½***

C200 A230 55c gray & multi. 1.10 1.10

500th anniversary of birth of Nicolaus Copernicus (1473–1543), Polish astronomer. No. C200 contains one stamp; multicolored margin shows US rocket in space. Size: 114x76mm.

UPU Type of Regular Issue
Souvenir Sheet

Design: 55c, UPU emblem and English coach, 1784.

1974, Mar. 4 Litho. ***Perf. 13½***

C201 A232 55c multicolored 2.00 1.10

Centenary of Universal Postal Union. No. C201 contains one stamp and multicolored margin showing satellites in space. Size: 115x76mm.

Dog Type of Regular Issue
Souvenir Sheet

Design: Hungarian sheepdog (kuvasz).

1974, Apr. 16 Litho. ***Perf. 13½***

C202 A233 75c multicolored 1.50 1.50

No. C202 contains one stamp; multicolored margin showing various dogs. Size: 114x76mm.

Soccer Type of Regular Issue
Souvenir Sheet

Design: 60c, World Soccer Championship Cup and Munich Stadium.

1974, June 4 Litho. ***Perf. 11***

C203 A234 60c multicolored 1.20 1.20

World Cup Soccer Championship, Munich, June 13–July 7. No. C203 contains one stamp; light blue margin with flags of competing nations and black inscription. Size: 101x76mm.

Butterfly Type of Regular Issue
Souvenir Sheet

Design: 60c, Pierella nereis.

1974, Sept. 11 Litho. ***Perf. 13½***

C204 A235 60c gray & multi. 1.20 1.20

Tropical butterflies. No. C204 contains one stamp. Multicolored margin with butterfly design. Size: 113x76mm.

Churchill Type of 1974
Souvenir Sheet

Design: 60c, Churchill at easel painting landscape.

1975, Jan. 17 Litho. ***Perf. 13½***

C205 A237 60c multicolored 1.20 1.20

Sir Winston Churchill (1874–1965), birth centenary. No. C205 contains one stamp with multicolored margin showing St. Paul's and bombed houses. Size: 113x76 mm.

Women's Year Type of 1975
Souvenir Sheet

Design: 75c, Vijaya Lakshmi Pandit, Women's Year emblem and dais of U.N. General Assembly.

1975, Mar. 14 Litho. ***Perf. 13***

C206 A238 75c gray & multi. 1.50 1.50

International Women's Year 1975. No. C206 contains one stamp; multicolored margin, Women's Year emblems and view of U.N. Headquarters, New York. Size: 105x 80mm.

American Bicentennial Type
Souvenir Sheet

Design: 75c, Mayflower and U.S. No. 548.

1975, Apr. 25 Litho. *Perf. 13½*

C207 A239 75c multicolored 3.00 1.50

American Revolution Bicentennial. No. C207 contains one stamp. Multicolored margin shows Plymouth Plantation Village, Colonial Period. Size: 78x100mm.

Dr. Schweitzer Type, 1975
Souvenir Sheet

Design: 60c, Dr. Schweitzer as surgeon in Lambarene Hospital.

1975, June 26 Litho. *Perf. 13½*

C208 A240 60c multicolored 1.20 1.20

Dr. Albert Schweitzer (1875–1965), medical missionary, birth centenary. No. C208 contains one stamp. Multicolored margin shows Dr. Schweitzer and deer. Size: 75x97mm.

Apollo-Soyuz Type, 1975
Souvenir Sheet

Design: 75c, Apollo-Soyuz link-up and emblem.

1975, Sept. 18 Litho. *Perf. 13½*

C209 A241 75c multicolored 1.50 1.50

Apollo Soyuz space test project (Russo-American cooperation), launching July 15; link-up, July 17. No. C209 contains one stamp, multicolored margin shows earth in space. Size: 115x78mm.

Winter Olympic Games Type, 1976
Souvenir Sheet

Design: 75c, Downhill skiing and Olympic Games emblem.

1976, Jan. 23 Litho. *Perf. 13½*

C210 A243 75c multicolored 1.50 1.50

12th Winter Olympic Games, Innsbruck, Austria, Feb. 4–15. No. C210 contains one stamp, multicolored margin shows ski jump and mountains. Size: 115x77mm.

Olympic Games Type, 1976
Souvenir Sheet

Design: 75c, Dressage and jumping.

1976, May 4 Litho. *Perf. 13½*

C211 A245 75c multicolored 1.50 1.50

21st Olympic Games, Montreal, Canada, July 17–Aug. 1. No. C211 contains one stamp, multicolored margin shows various sports. Size: 115x77mm.

Bell Type
Souvenir Sheet

Design: 75c, A. G. Bell making telephone call, UPU and ITU emblems.

1976, June 4 Litho. *Perf. 13½*

C212 A246 75c ocher & multi. 1.50 1.50

Centenary of first telephone call by Alexander Graham Bell, Mar. 10, 1876. No. C212 contains one stamp, multicolored margin showing satellites and rocket. Size: 115x77mm.

Animal Type of 1976
Souvenir Sheet

Design: 50c, Elephant (vert.).

1976, Sept. 1 Litho. *Perf. 13½*

C213 A249 50c org. & multi. 1.00 1.00

No. C213 contains one stamp, multicolored margin showing birds. Size: 103x78mm.

Bicentennial Type of 1976
Souvenir Sheet

Design: 75c, Like No. 770.

1976, Sept. 21 Litho. *Perf. 13½*

C214 A250 75c multicolored 1.50 1.50

American Bicentennial and visit of Pres. William R. Tolbert, Jr. to the United States, Sept. 21–30. No. C214 contains one stamp, yellow margin showing U.S. and Liberian flags and seals. Size: 77x103mm.

Mask Type of 1977
Souvenir Sheet

Design: 75c, Ibo mask and Festival emblem.

1977, Jan. 20 Litho. *Perf. 13½*

C215 A251 75c lilac & multi. 1.50 1.50

FESTAC '77, 2nd World Black and African Festival, Lagos, Nigeria, Jan. 15–Feb. 12. No. C215 contains one stamp; multicolored margin shows map of Liberia, elephant and palm. Size: 102x77mm.

Equestrian Type of 1977

Designs: 55c, Military dressage (team), USA. 80c, Winners receiving medals (vert.).

1977, Apr. 22 Litho. *Perf. 13½*

C216 A253 55c ocher & multi. 1.10 75

Souvenir Sheet

C217 A253 80c ocher & multi. 1.60 1.60

Equestrian gold medal winners in Montreal Olympic Games. No. C217 has multicolored margin showing equestrian scenes. Size: 77x103mm.

Elizabeth II Type of 1977
Souvenir Sheet

Design: 75c, Elizabeth II, laurel and crowns.

1977, May 23 Litho. *Perf. 13½*

C218 A254 75c silver & multi. 3.00 1.00

25th anniversary of the reign of Queen Elizabeth II. No. C218 has light blue and multicolored margin showing crown and laurel emblem. Size: 116x79mm.

Zeppelin Type of 1978
Souvenir Sheet

Design: 75c, Futuristic Goodyear aerospace airship.

1978, Mar. 9 Litho. *Perf. 13½*

C219 A257 75c multicolored 1.50 1.50

75th anniversary of the Zeppelin. No. C219 has multicolored margin showing New York Harbor. Size: 108x81mm.

Soccer Type of 1978
Souvenir Sheet

Design: 75c, Soccer game Netherlands and Uruguay (vert.).

1978, May 16 Litho. *Perf. 13½*

C220 A258 75c multicolored 1.50

11th World Soccer Championships, Argentina, June 1–25. No. C220 has multicolored margin showing goalkeeper catching ball and Argentina '78 emblem. Size: 103x78mm.

Coronation Type of 1978
Souvenir Sheet

Design: 75c, Coronation coach (horiz.).

1978, June 12

C221 A259 75c multicolored 1.50

Coronation of Queen Elizabeth II. No. C221 has multicolored margin showing Windsor Castle. Size: 104x83mm.

Soccer Winners' Type of 1978
Souvenir Sheet

Design: 75c, Argentine team (horiz.).

1978, Dec. 8 Litho. *Perf. 13½*

C222 A261 75c multicolored 1.50

1978 Soccer Cup Winner. No. C222 has multicolored margin showing various teams, emblems and soccer balls. Size: 128x103mm.

Prices of premium quality never hinged stamps will be in excess of catalogue price.

AIR POST SEMI-POSTAL STAMPS.

No. 277-279

Surcharged in Red or Blue and Dark Blue

941 *Perf. 12.* **Unwmkd.**

B1 A107 3c+2c dark blue (R) 2.00 2.00
B2 A108 5c+2c dull red brown (Bl & Dk Bl) 2.00 2.00
B3 A109 10c+2c dark green (R) 2.00 2.00

Nurses Taking Oath

SPAP1

Designs: 20c+5c, Liberian Government Hospital. 5c+5c, Medical examination.

954, June 21 **Litho. & Engr.**

Size: 39½x28½mm.

B4 SPAP1 10c+5c carmine & black 20 15
B5 " 20c+5c emerald & black 35 15

Size: 45x34mm.

B6 SPAP1 25c+5c ultramarine, carmine & black 40 25

The surtax was for the Liberian Government Hospital. Nos. CB4-CB6 exist imperforate. No. B6 exists with carmine impression omitted.

AIR POST SPECIAL DELIVERY STAMP.

No. 278 Surcharged in Dark Blue

SPECIAL DELIVERY
AIR MAIL
10 CENTS 10

941 *Perf. 12.* **Unwmkd.**

E1 A108 10c on 5c dull red brown 2.00 2.00

AIR POST REGISTRATION STAMP.

No. 278 Surcharged in Dark Blue

941 *Perf. 12.* **Unwmkd.**

F1 A108 10c on 5c dull red brown 2.00 2.00

SPECIAL DELIVERY STAMP.

No. 278 Surcharged in Dark Blue

SPECIAL DELIVERY
10 CENTS 10

1941 *Perf. 12.* **Unwmkd.**

E1 A108 10c on 5c dull red brown 2.00 2.00

REGISTRATION STAMPS.

R1

Lithographed.

1893 *Perf. 14, 15* **Unwmkd.**

Without Value Surcharged.

F1 R1 (10c) black (Buchanan) 150.00 150.00
F2 " (10c) black ("Grenville") 1100.00 1100.00
F3 " (10c) black (Harper) 1100.00 1100.00
F4 " (10c) black (Monrovia) 25.00 25.00
F5 " (10c) black (Robertsport) 300.00 300.00

Types of 1893 Surcharged in Black

10 CENTS 10

10 CENTS 10

1894 *Perf. 14*

F6 R1 10c blue, *pink* (Buchanan) 3.50 3.50
F7 " 10c green, *buff* (Harper) 3.50 3.50
F8 " 10c red, *yellow* (Monrovia) 3.50 3.50
F9 " 10c rose, *blue* (Robertsport) 3.50 3.50

Nos. F6-F9 exist imperf. or with one "10" omitted. Price, $5 each.

President Garretson W. Gibson

R6

1903 **Engraved** *Perf. 14*

F10 R6 10c blue & black (Buchanan) 1.50 25
a. Center inverted 75.00
F11 " 10c orange red & black ("Grenville") 1.50
a. Center inverted 75.00
b. 10c orange & blk. 2.50 25
F12 " 10c green & black (Harper) 1.50 25
a. Center inverted 75.00
F13 " 10c violet & black (Monrovia) 1.50 25
a. Center inverted 75.00
b. 10c lilac & black 2.50
F14 " 10c magenta & black (Robertsport) 1.50 25
a. Center inverted 75.00
Nos. F10-F14 (5) 7.50
Nos. F10, F11b, F12-F14 (5) 1.25

S.S. Quail on Patrol—R7

Serrate Roulette 12.

1919 **Lithographed.**

F15 R7 10c black & blue (Buchanan) 60 1.20

Serrate Roulette 12, Perf. 14

F16 R7 10c ochre & black ("Grenville") 60 1.20
F17 " 10c green & black (Harper) 60 1.20
F18 " 10c violet & blue (Monrovia) 60 1.20
F19 " 10c rose & black (Robertsport) 60 1.20
Nos. F15-F19 (5) 3.00 6.00

Gabon Viper

R8

Wmkd. Crosses and Circles. (116)

1921 **Engraved.** *Perf. 13x14.*

F20 R8 10c claret & black (Buchanan) 35.00 3.00
F21 " 10c red & black (Greenville) 20.00 3.00
F22 " 10c ultramarine & blk. (Harper) 27.50 3.00
F23 " 10c orange & black (Monrovia) 20.00 3.00
a. Imperf., pair 175.00
F24 " 10c green & black (Robertsport) 20.00 3.00
a. Imperf., pair 175.00
Nos. F20-F24 (5) 122.50 15.00

Preceding Issue Overprinted "1921".

F25 R8 10c claret & black (Buchanan) 22.50 6.00
F26 " 10c red & black (Greenville) 25.00 6.00
F27 " 10c ultramarine & blk. (Harper) 22.50 6.00
F28 " 10c orange & black (Monrovia) 20.00 6.00
F29 " 10c green & black (Robertsport) 22.50 6.00
Nos. F25-F29 (5) 112.50 30.00

Nos. F25-F29 exist with "1921" inverted. Price same as normal.

Passengers Going Ashore from Ship

R9

Designs: No. F31, Transporting merchandise, shore to ship (Greenville). No. F32, Sailing ship (Harper). No. F33, Ocean liner (Monrovia). No. F34, Canoe in surf (Robertsport).

1924 **Lithographed.** *Perf. 14*

F30 R9 10c gray & carmine 6.00 45
F31 " 10c gray & bl. grn. 6.00 45
F32 " 10c gray & orange 6.00 45
F33 " 10c gray & blue 6.00 45
F34 " 10c gray & violet 6.00 45
Nos. F30-F34 (5) 30.00 2.25

No. 278 Surcharged in Dark Blue

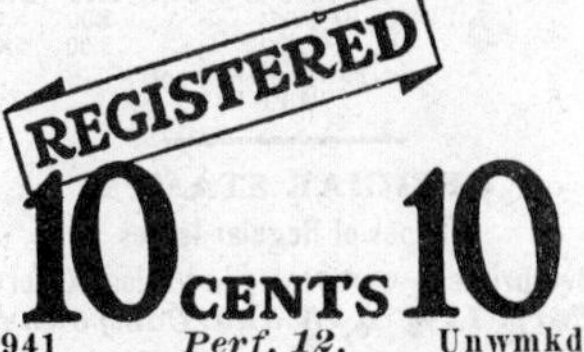

1941 *Perf. 12.* **Unwmkd.**

F35 A108 10c on 5c dull red brown 2.00 2.00

POSTAGE DUE STAMPS.

D1

D2

1892 *Perf. 11* **Unwmkd.**

J1 D1 3c on 3c violet 75 75
a. Imperf., pair 5.00
b. Inverted surcharge 20.00 20.00
c. As "a," inverted surcharge 50.00

Perf. 12.

J2 D1 6c on 6c olive gray 4.00 4.00
a. Imperf., pair 12.00
b. Inverted surcharge 30.00 30.00

Engraved.

Figures of Value Typo. in Black.

1893 *Perf. 14, 15.* **Wmk. 143.**

J3 D2 2c orange, *yellow* 1.00 65
J4 " 4c rose, *rose* 1.00 65
J5 " 6c brown, *buff* 1.00 90
J6 " 8c blue, *blue* 1.00 90
J7 " 10c green, *lilac rose* 1.35 1.10
J8 " 20c violet, *gray* 1.35 1.10
a. Center inverted 60.00 60.00
J9 " 40c olive brown, *greenish* 2.35 2.00
Nos. J3-J9 (7) 9.05 7.30

All values of the above set exist imperforate.

MILITARY STAMPS

"LFF" are the initials of "Liberian Frontier Force." Nos. M1-M7 were issued for the use of troops sent to guard the frontier.

Issues of 1905, 1906 and 1909 Surcharged

L F F
1c

1916 **Wmk. 143**

M1 A23 1c on 1c lt. green 85.00 85.00
a. "L F Ⅎ" 135.00 135.00
b. "F L F" 135.00 135.00
c. Inverted surch. 100.00 100.00

Unwmkd.

M2 A33 1c on 1c grn. & blk. 350.00 350.00
a. "L F Ⅎ" 375.00 375.00
b. "F L F" 375.00 375.00
M3 A46 1c on 1c yellow green & black 2.50 2.50
a. "L F Ⅎ" 5.00 5.00
b. "F L F" 5.00 5.00
M4 A47 1c on 2c lake & blk. 2.50 2.50
a. "L F Ⅎ" 5.00 5.00
b. "F L F" 5.00 5.00

Surcharge exists sideways on Nos. M2, M5; double on Nos. M1-M4; inverted on Nos. M2-M4.

Nos. 046, 059-060 Surcharged

L F F
1c

M5 A33 1c on 1c green & black 350.00 350.00
a. "L F Ⅎ" 375.00 375.00
b. "F L F" 375.00 375.00
M6 A46 1c on 1c emerald & black 2.50 2.50
a. "L F Ⅎ" 5.00 5.00
b. "F L F" 5.00 5.00
c. "LFF 1c" inverted 6.50 6.50
d. "L F Ⅎ 1c" inverted 9.00
e. "F L F 1c" inverted 9.00

M7 A47 1c on 2c carmine rose & brown 2.50 2.50
- *a.* "LF d" 5.00 5.00
- *b.* "FLF" 5.00 5.00
- *c.* Pair, one without "LFF 1c"

OFFICIAL STAMPS.

Types of Regular Issues

Overprinted OFFICIAL in Various Colors.

Perf. 12½ to 15 and Compound.

1892 **Wmk. 143.**

O1 A9 1c vermilion 40 40
O2 " 2c blue 40 40
O3 A10 4c green & black 40 40
O4 A11 6c blue green 40 40
O5 A12 8c brown & black 40 40
O6 A13 12c rose red 1.00 1.00
O7 A14 16c red lilac 1.00 1.00
- *a.* "OFFICSL"

O8 A15 24c olive green, *yel.* 1.00 1.00
O9 A16 32c greenish blue 1.00 1.00
- *a.* "OFFICSL"

O10 A17 $1 blue & black 13.50 5.00
O11 A18 $2 brown, *yellow* 8.00 4.00
O12 A19 $5 carmine & blk. 11.00 4.50
Nos. O1–O12 (12) 38.50 19.50

1893

O13 A11 (*a*) 5c on 6c bl. grn. (No. 50) 75 75
- *a.* "5" with short flag 4.00 4.00
- *b.* Both 5's with short flags 4.00 4.00
- *c.* "i" dot omitted 15.00 15.00
- *d.* Ovpt. on #50d 35.00 35.00

1894

Overprinted "O S" in Various Colors.

O15 A9 1c vermilion 40 40
O16 " 2c blue 60 50
- *a.* Imperf.

O17 A10 4c green & black 75 65
O18 A12 8c brown & black 75 65
O19 A13 12c rose red 1.00 75
O20 A14 16c red lilac 1.00 75
O21 A15 24c olive green, *yel.* 1.00 85
O22 A16 32c greenish blue 1.50 1.00
O23 A17 $1 blue & black 6.50 6.50
- *a.* $1 ultramarine & black 6.50 6.50

O24 A18 $2 brown, *yellow* 6.50 5.50
O25 A19 $5 carmine & blk. 30.00 20.00
Nos. O15–O25 (11) 50.00 37.55

Unwmkd.

Imperf.

O26 A22 5c violet & green 2.50 2.50

Rouletted.

O27 A22 5c violet & green 2.50 2.50

Regular Issue of 1896-1905

Overprinted "O S" in Black or Red.

1898-1905 ***Perf. 14, 15*** **Wmk. 143**

O28 A23 1c lilac rose 50 50
O29 " 1c deep green ('00) 50 50
O30 " 1c lt. grn. (R) ('05) 50 50
O31 A24 2c bistre & black 1.00 35
- *a.* Pair, one without overprint 25.00

O32 " 2c orange red & black ('00) 1.50 75
O33 " 2c rose & blk. ('05) 2.00 1.25
O34 A25 5c lake & black 1.50 75
O35 " 5c gray blue & black ('00) 2.00 75
O36 " 5c ultramarine & blk. (R) ('05) 2.00 90
O37 A12 10c chrome yellow & indigo 1.00 1.00
O38 A13 15c slate 1.00 1.00
O39 A14 20c vermilion 1.50 1.25
O40 A15 25c yellow green 1.00 1.00
O41 A16 30c steel blue 2.00 1.50
O42 A26 50c red brn. & blk. 2.00 1.50
Nos. O28–O42 (15) 20.00 13.50

Liberty
O1

Red Overprint.

1903 ***Perf. 14*** **Unwmkd.**

O43 O1 3c green 25 15
- *a.* Overprint omitted 7.50
- *b.* Inverted overprint

Two overprint types: I. Thin, sharp, dark red. II. Thick, heavier, orange red. Same price.

Palm
O2

Coat of Arms
O3

1904 Black Surcharge. **Wmk. 143.**

O44 O2 1c on 5c on 6c blue green 1.50 1.50
- *a.* "5" with short flag 2.00
- *b.* Both "5s" with straight flag 7.50 7.50

Red Surcharge.

O45 O3 2c on 30c steel blue 5.00 5.00
- *a.* Double surcharge, red and black
- *b.* Surcharge on back also

Types of Regular Issue Overprinted in Various Colors

a

1906 **Unwmkd.**

O46 A33 1c green & black (R) 60 40
O47 A34 2c car. & black (Bl) 15 15
- *a.* Center and overprint inverted 10.00 7.50
- *b.* Invtd. overprint 6.00

O48 A35 5c ultra. & blk. (Bk) 60 40
- *a.* Invtd. ovpt. 6.00 6.00
- *b.* Center and overprint invtd. 30.00

O49 A36 10c dull violet & black (R) 75 60
- *a.* Inverted overprint
- *b.* Center and overprint invtd. 40.00

O50 A37 15c brn. & blk. (Bk) 3.25 60
- *a.* Inverted ovpt. 6.00
- *b.* Overprint omitted
- *c.* Center and overprint invtd. 40.00

O51 A38 20c deep green & black (R) 75 60
- *a.* Overprint omitted

O52 A39 25c plum & gray (Bl) 45 15
- *a.* With second overprint in blue, inverted

O53 A40 30c dark brown (Bk) 50 20
O54 A41 50c orange brown & deep green (G) 75 20
- *a.* Invtd. overprint 4.00

O55 A42 75c ultramarine & black (Bk) 1.40 1.00
- *a.* Invtd. overprint 12.50 7.50
- *b.* Ovpt. omitted 30.00

O56 A43 $1 deep green & gray (R) 80 20
- *a.* Inverted overprint

O57 A44 $2 plum & black (Bl) 2.00 20
- *a.* Ovpt. omitted 30.00

O58 A45 $5 org. & blk. (Bk) 4.00 25
- *a.* Ovpt. omitted 15.00
- *b.* Inverted overprint 8.50 5.00

Nos. O46–O58 (13) 16.00 4.95

Nos. O52, O54, O55, O56 and O58 are known with center inverted.

1909-12

O59 A46 1c emerald & black (R) 30 30
O60 A47 2c carmine rose & brown (Bl) 30 30
- *a.* Ovpt. omitted

O61 A48 5c turquoise & black (Bk) 40 30
- *a.* Double overprint, one inverted 10.00

O62 A49 10c black & ultra. (R) ('12) 50 30
O63 A50 15c claret & black (Bl) 50 40
O64 A51 20c bistre & green (Bk) 1.00 50
O65 A52 25c ultramarine & green (Bk) 1.00 30
- *a.* Double overprint 6.50 6.50

O66 A53 30c dark blue (R) 75 30
O67 A54 50c brown & green (Bk) 1.25 35
- *a.* Center inverted 30.00
- *b.* Inverted overprint 5.00 4.00

O68 A55 75c purple & black (R) 1.50 30
Nos. O59–O68 (10) 7.50 3.35

Nos. O63, O64, O67 and O68 are known without overprint and with center inverted.

Rouletted.

O69 A49 10c blk. & ultra. (R) 1.00 1.00

Nos. 126B and 127E Overprinted type "a" ("OS") in Red.

1910-12 ***Rouletted***

O70 A49 3c on 10c black & ultramarine 1.00 50

Perf. 12½, 14, 12½x14.

O71 A49 3c on 10c black & ultra. ('12) 1.00 50
- *a.* Pair, one without surcharge, the other with double surcharge of which one is inverted
- *b.* Double surcharge, one inverted 7.50

Stamps of Preceding Issues Surcharged with New Values like Regular Issue and

CENTS 20 OFFICIAL

c

1914

On Nos. O52 and 110.

O72 A39 (*a*) 2c on 25c plum & gray 17.50 7.50
O73 A42 (*c*) 20c on 75c brown & black 7.50 5.00

On Nos. O66 and O68.

O74 A53 (*b*) 5c on 30c dark blue 7.50 5.00
O75 A55 (*c*) 20c on 75c purple & black (R) 10.00 5.00

Official Stamps of 1906-09 Surcharged Like Regular Issues of Same Date.

1915-16

O76 A50 (*c*) 2c on 15c claret & blk. (Bk) 1.00 75
O77 A52 (*d*) 2c on 25c ultra. & green (Bk) 6.00 6.00
O78 A51 (*e*) 5c on 20c bistre & grn. (Bk) 1.00 75
O79 A53 (*g*) 5c on 30c dark blue (R) 6.00 6.00
O80 A54 (*i*) 10c on 50c brown & green (Bk) 5.00 3.00
O81 A55 (*j*) 20c on 75c purple & black (R) 3.00 3.00
O82 A43 (*k*) 25c on $1 deep green & gray (R) 13.50 13.50
- *a.* "25" double 15.00
- *b.* "OS" inverted 15.00

O83 A44 (*l*) 50c on $2 plum & black (Bk) 30.00 30.00
- *a.* "Ceuts" 45.00 45.00

O84 " (*m*) 50c on $2 plum & black (Br) 16.50 16.50
O85 A45 (*n*) $1 on $5 orange & black (Bk) 16.50 16.50

Handstamped Surcharge.

O86 A54 (*i*) 10c on 50c brown & green (Bk) 10.00 10.00

Nos. O60–O61 Surcharged like Nos. 153–154 in Black or Red

O87 A47 1c on 2c carmine rose & brown 2.50 2.50
Strip of 10 types 35.00

O88 A48 2c on 5c turquoise & black (R) 2.50 2.5
Strip of 10 types (R) 35.00
- *a.* Black surch. 10.00 10.0

Strip of 10 types (Bk) 110.00

See note following Nos. 153–154.

Official Stamps of 1909

Surcharged like Nos. 155–156.

O90 A47 1c on 2c carmine rose & brown 40.00 40.0
O91 A48 2c on 5c turquoise & black 32.50 32.5

No. O42 Surcharged 10 10

O92 A26 10c on 50c red brown & black (Bk) 10.00 10.0

No. O53 Surcharged like No. 161.

1917

O96 A40 5c on 30c dk. brown 15.00 15.0
- *a.* "FIV" 22.50 22.5

The editors consider the 1915–17 issue unnecessary and speculative.

No. O62 Surcharged in Red like No. 162

1918

O97 A49 3c on 10c blk. & ultra. 1.50 1.5

Types of Regular Issue of 1918

Overprinted Type "a" ("OS")

in Black, Blue or Red

1918 ***Perf. 12½, 14.*** **Unwmkd**

O98 A59 1c deep green & red brown (Bk) 50 2
O99 A60 2c red & black (Bl) 50 2
O100 A61 5c ultramarine & black (R) 1.00 1(
O101 A62 10c ultramarine (R) 50 1(
O102 A63 15c chocolate & dk. green (Bl) 2.50 4
O103 A64 20c gray lilac & black (R) 75 1
O104 A65 25c chocolate & green (Bk) 4.00 5(
O105 A66 30c bright violet & black (R) 5.00 5(
O106 A67 50c maroon & black (Bl) 6.00 5(
- *a.* Ovpt. omitted 15.00

O107 A68 75c carmine brown & black (Bl) 2.50 2(
O108 A69 $1 olive bistre & turquoise blue (Bk) 4.50 2(
O109 A70 $2 olive bistre & black (R) 7.50 2(
O110 A71 $5 yel. grn. (Bk) 10.00 25
Nos. O98–O110 (13) 45.25 3.50

Official Stamps of 1918

Surcharged like Regular Issue.

1920

O111 A59 3c on 1c green & red brown 1.50 1.00
- *a.* "CEETS" 12.50
- *b.* Double surcharge 5.00 5.00
- *c.* Double surcharge, one inverted 10.00 10.00
- *d.* Triple surcharge 5.00 5.00

O112 A60 4c on 2c red & blk. 1.00 1.00
- *a.* Inverted surcharge 4.00 4.00
- *b.* Double surcharge 5.00 5.00
- *c.* Double surcharge, one inverted 10.00 10.00
- *d.* Triple surch. 10.00 10.00

Types of Regular Issues of 1915–21

Overprinted **OFFICIAL**

Wmkd. Crosses and Circles. (116)

1921 ***Perf. 14***

O113 A57 2c rose red 3.00 10
O114 A58 3c brown 1.00 10
O115 A79 20c brown & ultra. 1.50 40

Same, Overprinted "O S"

116 A75 1c deep green 1.00 10
117 A76 5c deep blue & brn. 1.00 10
118 A77 10c red violet & black 50 10
119 A78 15c black & green 3.00 50
a. Double overprint
120 A80 25c orange & green 4.00 50
121 A81 30c brown & red 1.00 11
122 A82 50c green & black 1.00 12
a. Overprinted "S" only
123 A83 75c blue & violet 2.00 12
124 A84 $1 blue & black 13.00 75
125 A85 $2 grn. & orange 10.00 1.25
126 A86 $5 green & blue 11.00 2.00
Nos. O113-O126 (14) 53.00 6.25

Preceding Issues Overprinted "1921"

921

127 A75 1c deep green 1.25 10
128 A57 2c rose red 1.25 10
129 A58 3c brown 1.25 15
130 A76 5c dp. blue & brown 50 15
131 A77 10c red vio. & blk. 2.00 15
132 A78 15c black & green 3.00 15
133 A79 20c brown & ultra. 3.00 50
134 A80 25c orange & green 5.00 1.00
135 A81 30c brown & red 2.00 15
136 A82 50c green & black 3.75 15
137 A83 75c blue & violet 1.50 15
138 A84 $1 blue & black 10.00 2.00
139 A85 $2 orange & grn. 12.50 2.50
140 A86 $5 green & blue 10.00 4.00
Nos. O127-O140 (14) 57.00 11.25

Types of Regular Issue of 1923
Overprinted "O S"
Perf. 13½x14½, 14½x13½.

923

White Paper

141 A88 1c blue green & black 5.00 10
142 A89 2c dull red & yellow brown 5.00 15
143 A90 3c gray bl. & blk. 5.00 15
144 A91 5c orange & dark green 5.00 15
145 A92 10c olive bistre & dark violet 5.00 15
146 A93 15c yellow green & blue 1.00 30
147 A94 20c violet & indigo 1.00 30
148 A95 25c brn. & red brn. 10.00 30

White, Buff or Brownish Paper

149 A96 30c deep ultramarine & brown 1.00 20
a. Overprint omitted
150 A97 50c dull bistre & red brown 1.00 30
151 A98 75c gray & green 1.00 20
152 A99 $1 red org. & green 2.00 75
a. Overprint omitted 7.50
153 A100 $2 red lilac & vermilion 3.00 1.10
154 A101 $5 blue & brown violet 5.00 85
Nos. O141-O154 (14) 50.00 5.00

No. 098 Surcharged in Red Brown — **Two Cents**

926 ***Perf. 14.*** **Unwmkd.**

155 A59 2c on 1c deep green & red brown 4.00 4.00
a. "Gents" 12.50
b. Surcharged in black 10.00
c. Same as "b", "Gents" 16.50

No. 098 Surcharged in Black — **Two Cents**

926

156 A59 2c on 1c dp. grn. & red brown 1.50 1.50
a. Inverted surcharge
b. "Gents" 10.00

No. 098 Surcharged in Red — **Two Cents**

1927

O157 A59 2c on 1c dp. grn. & red brown 15.00 15.00
a. "Ceuts" 20.00 20.00
b. "Vwo" 20.00 20.00
c. "Twc" 20.00 20.00

Regular Issue of 1928
Overprinted in Red or Black **OFFICIAL SERVICE**

1928 ***Perf. 12.***

O158 A102 1c green (R) 20 10
O159 " 2c gray vio. (R) 1.50 50
O160 " 3c bis. brn. (Bk) 1.50 15
O161 A103 5c ultramarine (R) 50 25
O162 A104 10c olive gray (R) 2.50 1.00
O163 A103 15c dull violet (R) 1.50 50
O164 " $1 red brn. (Bk) 25.00 10.00
Nos. O158-O164 (7) 32.70 12.50

No. O162 Surcharged with New Value and Bar in Black.

1945 ***Perf. 12.*** **Unwmkd.**

O165 A104 4c on 10c olive gray (Bk) 10.00 10.00

LIBYA

(lē'byä ; lĭb'ĭ-ȧ)

(Libia)

LOCATION—North Africa, bordering on Mediterranean Sea.

GOVT.—Republic.

AREA—679,358 sq. mi.

POP.—2,630,000 (est. 1977).

CAPITALS—Tripoli and Bengazi.

In 1939, the four northern provinces of Libya, a former Italian colony, were incorporated in the Italian national territory. Included in the territory is the former Turkish Vilayet of Tripoli, annexed in 1912. Libya became a kingdom on Dec. 24, 1951. The Libyan Arab Republic was established Sept. 1, 1969. "People's Socialist . . ." was added to its name in 1977. See Cyrenaica and Tripolitania.

100 Centesimi = 1 Lira
Military Authority Lira (1951)
Franc (1951)
1,000 Milliemes = 1 Pound (1952)
1,000 Dirhams = 1 Dinar (1972)

Stamps of Italy Overprinted
Libia in Black.
Wmkd. Crown. (140)

1912-22 ***Perf. 14***

1 A42 1c brown ('15) 12 18
a. Double ovpt. 50.00 50.00
2 A43 2c orange brown 8 12
3 A48 5c green 8 5
a. Double ovpt. 10.00 10.00
b. Imperf., pair 30.00
c. Inverted ovpt. *1250.00*
d. Pair, one without overprint 25.00 25.00
4 " 10c claret 8 5
a. Pair, one without overprint 25.00 25.00
b. Double ovpt. 15.00 15.00
5 " 15c slate ('22) 30 30
6 A45 20c orange ('15) 18 18
a. Double ovpt. 35.00 35.00
b. Pair, one without overprint 65.00
7 A50 20c brn. org. ('18) 18 18
8 A49 25c blue 18 12
9 " 40c brown 42 25
10 A45 45c olive green ('17) 55 65
a. Inverted ovpt. 60.00
11 A49 50c violet 90 30
12 " 60c brn. car. ('18) 65 75
13 A46 1 l brown & green ('15) 16.50 65
14 A46 5 l bl. & rose ('15) 35.00 42.50
15 A51 10 l gray green & red ('15) 4.75 6.00
Nos. 1-15 (15) 59.97 52.28

Overprinted **LIBIA** in Violet.

1912 **Unwmkd.**

16 A58 15c slate 7.50 30
a. Bl. black ovpt. *2000.00* 3.50

No. 16 Surcharged — **CENT 20**

1916, Mar. **Unwmkd.**

19 A58 20c on 15c slate 7.50 1.20

Roman Legionary
A1

Diana of Ephesus
A2

Ancient Galley Leaving Tripoli
A3

"Victory"
A4

Wmk. 140

Wmkd. Crown. (140)

1921 **Engraved** ***Perf. 14***

20 A1 1c black & gray brown 25 30
21 " 2c black & red brown 25 30
22 " 5c black & green 25 18
a. 5c black & red brown (error) 700.00
b. Center inverted 20.00 20.00
c. Imperf., pair 75.00 75.00
23 A2 10c black & rose 25 18
a. Center inverted 20.00 20.00
24 " 15c black brown & brown orange 1.75 30
a. Center inverted 32.50 32.50
25 " 25c dark blue & blue 25 12
a. Center inverted 5.00 5.00
b. Imperf., pair 125.00 125.00
26 A3 30c black & black brn. 1.20 25
a. Center inverted 400.00 275.00
27 " 50c blk. & olive green 1.20 6
a. 50c black & brown (error) 150.00
b. Center inverted *1000.00* 550.00
28 " 55c black & violet 60 60
29 A4 1 l dk. brn. & brown 90 12
30 " 5 l black & dark blue 1.80 1.00
31 " 10 l dark blue & olive green 6.75 6.75
Nos. 20-31 (12) 15.45 10.16

Nos. 20-31 also exist perf. 14x13, with prices somewhat higher.

See also Nos. 47-61.

Italy Nos. 136-139 Overprinted **LIBIA**

1921, April

33 A64 5c olive green 38 50
a. Double ovpt. 50.00 50.00
34 " 10c red 38 50
a. Double overprint 50.00 50.00
b. Inverted ovpt. 65.00 65.00
35 " 15c slate green 50 70
36 " 25c ultramarine 60 80

Issued to commemorate the third anniversary of the victory of the Piave.

Nos. 11, 8 Surcharged — **C. 40**

1922, June 1

37 A49 40c on 50c violet 55 25
38 " 80c on 25c blue 65 75

Libian Sibyl
A6

Perf. 14½x14

1924-31 **Unwmkd.**

39 A6 20c deep green 18 5
a. Perf. 11 ('26) 25.00 12
40 " 40c brown 60 30
a. Perf. 11 ('26) 5.00 60
41 " 60c deep blue 30 6
a. Perf. 11 ('26) 1.20 12
42 " 1.75 l orange ('31) 18 12
43 " 2 l carmine 75 38
a. Perf. 11 ('29) 3.75 1.00
44 " 2.55 l violet ('31) 1.20 1.50
Nos. 39-44 (6) 3.21 2.41

Type of 1921
Perf. 13½ to 14

1924-40 **Unwmkd.**

47 A1 1c blk. & gray brn. 30 38
a. Perf. 11 32.50
48 " 2c blk. & red brn. 38 45
a. Perf. 11 32.50
49 " 5c black & green 50 18
a. Perf. 11 7.00 1.50
50 " 7½c black & brown ('31) 25 30
51 A2 10c black & dull red 6 5
a. Perf. 11 4.75 38
b. Center invt. 35.00
52 " 15c black brown & orange 60 18
a. Perf. 11 25.00 1.65
b. Center invtd., perf. 11 425.00
53 " 25c dark blue & bl. 3.00 5
a. Center invtd. 35.00 30.00
54 A3 30c blk. & blk. brn. 7 12
a. Perf. 11 18.50 38
55 " 50c black & olive green 6 5
a. Perf. 11 275.00 10
b. Center invtd. 450.00 450.00
56 " 55c blk. & violet 100.00 110.00
57 A4 75c violet & red ('31) 12 6
58 " 1 l dk. brn. & brn. 3.75 12
a. Perf. 11 3.75 12
59 A3 1.25 l indigo & ultramarine ('31) 12 6
60 A4 5 l black & dark blue ('40) 9.00 9.00
a. Perf. 11 ('37) *900.00* 47.50

Perf. 11

61 A4 10 l dk. bl. & olive green ('37) 125.00 47.50
Nos. 47-61 (15) 243.21 168.50

Italy Nos. 197 and 88
Overprinted **Libia**

1929 ***Perf. 14.*** **Wmk. 140**

62 A86 7½c light brown 3.00 3.75
63 A46 1.25 l blue & ultra. 6.00 2.10

Italy No. 193 Overprinted **LIBIA**

1929 ***Perf. 11.*** **Unwmkd.**

64 A85 1.75 l deep brown 2.40 30

Water Carriers—A7

Man of Tripoli
A8

Designs: 25c, Minaret. 30c, 1.25 l, Tomb of Holy Man near Tagiura. 50c, Statue of Emperor Claudius at Leptis. 75c, Ruins of gardens.

Inscribed:
"VIII Fiera Campionaria."

1934, Feb. 17 Photo. *Perf. 14*

64A	A7	10c brown	1.85	2.75
64B	A8	20c carmine rose	1.85	2.75
64C	"	25c green	1.85	2.75
64D	A7	30c dark brown	1.85	2.75
64E	A8	50c purple	1.85	2.75
64F	A7	75c rose	1.85	2.75
64G	"	1.25 l blue	35.00	47.50
		Nos. 64A-64G (7)	46.10	64.00

8th Sample Fair, Tripoli. See Nos. C14-C18.

Bedouin Woman
A15

Highway Memorial Arch
A16

1936, May 11 *Perf. 14* Wmk. 140

65	A15	50c purple	50	50
66	"	1.25 l deep blue	1.00	1.25

10th Sample Fair, Tripoli.

1937, Mar. 15

67	A16	50c copper red	90	1.00
68	"	1.25 l sapphire	90	1.50

Issued to commemorate the opening of a coastal road to the Egyptian frontier. See Nos. C28-C29.

Nos. 67-68 Overprinted in Black

XI FIERA
DI TRIPOLI

1937, Apr. 24

69	A16	50c copper red	3.00	4.25
70	"	1.25 l sapphire	3.00	4.25

11th Sample Fair, Tripoli. See Nos. C30-C31.

Roman Wolf and Lion of St. Mark
A17

View of Fair Buildings
A18

1938, Mar. 12

71	A17	5c brown	17	17
72	A18	10c olive brown	25	25
73	A17	25c green	25	25
74	A18	50c purple	40	17
75	A17	75c rose red	50	60
76	A18	1.25 l dark blue	65	1.00
		Nos. 71-76, C32-C33 (8)	3.72	4.29

12th Sample Fair, Tripoli.

Augustus Caesar (Octavianus)
A19

Goddess Abundantia
A20

1938, Apr. 25

77	A19	5c olive brown	27	27
78	A20	10c brown red	27	27
79	A19	25c dk. yellow green	33	33
80	A20	50c dark violet	33	33
81	A19	75c orange red	45	45
82	A20	1.25 l dull blue	45	45
		Nos. 77-82, C34-C35 (8)	3.20	3.22

Issued to commemorate the bimillenary of the birth of Augustus Caesar (Octavianus), first Roman emperor.

Desert City—A21

View of Ghadames—A22

1939, Apr. 12 Photogravure

83	A21	5c olive brown	20	27
84	A22	20c red brown	27	33
85	A21	50c rose violet	33	40
86	A22	75c scarlet	40	45
87	A21	1.25 l gray blue	45	55
		Nos. 83-87, C36-C38 (8)	2.53	3.26

13th Sample Fair, Tripoli.

Modern City—A23

Oxen and Plow—A24

Mosque—A25

1940, June 3 *Perf. 14* Wmk. 140

88	A23	5c brown	13	20
89	A24	10c red orange	13	20
90	A25	25c dull green	33	40
91	A23	50c dark violet	33	40
92	A24	75c crimson	33	40
93	A25	1.25 l ultramarine	33	40
94	A24	2 l+75c rose lake	50	65
		Nos. 88-94, C39-C42 (11)	3.94	5.15

Triennial Overseas Exposition, Naples.

"Two Peoples, One War," Hitler and Mussolini—A26

1941, May 16

95	A26	5c orange	7	*70*
96	"	10c brown	7	*70*
97	"	20c dull violet	13	*70*
98	"	25c green	13	*70*
99	"	50c purple	20	*70*
100	"	75c scarlet	20	*3.00*
101	"	1.25 l sapphire	30	*3.00*
		Nos. 95-101, C43 (8)	1.40	*14.50*

Issued to commemorate the Rome-Berlin Axis.

United Kingdom of Libya

Stamps of Cyrenaica 1950 Surcharged in Black

— ليبيا —

2 MAL.
LIBYA

For Use in Tripolitania.

1951, Dec. 24 *Perf. 12½* Unwmkd.

102	A2	1 mal on 2m rose carmine	18	12
103	"	2 mal on 4m dk. grn.	18	12
104	"	4 mal on 8m red org.	25	12
105	"	5 mal on 10m purple	60	18
106	"	6 mal on 12m red	70	25
		a. Inverted surch.	50.00	50.00
107	"	10 mal on 20m deep blue	1.20	80
		a. Arabic '20' for '10'	27.50	35.00
108	A3	24 mal on 50m choc. & ultramarine	1.75	1.50
109	"	48 mal on 100m blue blk. & car. rose	11.00	9.00
110	"	96 mal on 200m violet & purple	20.00	18.50
111	"	240 mal on 500m dark green & orange	55.00	55.00
		Nos. 102-111 (10)	90.86	85.59

The surcharge is larger on Nos. 108 to 111.

Same Surcharge in Francs.

For Use in Fezzan.

112	A2	2fr on 2m rose car.	25	25
113	"	4fr on 4m dark green	25	25
114	"	8fr on 8m red orange	30	30
115	"	10fr on 10m purple	30	42
116	"	12fr on 12m red	1.75	1.75
117	"	20fr on 20m dp. blue	3.00	3.00
118	A3	48fr on 50m choc. & ultramarine	24.00	24.00
119	"	96fr on 100m bl. blk. & car. rose	37.50	37.50
120	"	192fr on 200m violet & purple	47.50	47.50
121	A3	480fr on 500m dk. grn. & orange	65.00	65.
		Nos. 112-121 (10)	179.85	179.

The surcharge is larger on Nos. 118-12
A second printing of Nos. 118-121 h an elongated first character in second l of Arabic surcharge.

Cyrenaica Nos. 65-77 Overprinted in Black

LIBYA

For Use in Cyrenaica.

122	A2	1m dark brown	25	
123	"	2m rose carmine	25	
124	"	3m orange	50	
125	"	4m dark green	15.00	12.
126	"	5m gray	85	
127	"	8m red orange	85	
128	"	10m purple	1.35	1.
129	"	12m red	1.35	1.
130	"	20m deep blue	1.35	1.
131	A3	50m choc. & ultra.	9.00	9.
132	"	100m blue black & carmine rose	18.00	12
133	"	200m violet & purple	42.50	40.
134	"	500m dark green & orange	150.00	150.
		Nos. 122-134 (13)	241.25	230.

Wider spacing between the two lines Nos. 131-134.

King Idris

A27 A28

Perf. 11½

1952, Apr. 15 Engr. Unwmk

135	A27	2m yellow brown	5	
136	"	4m gray	5	
137	"	5m blue green	14.00	
138	"	8m vermilion	25	
139	"	10m purple	14.00	
140	"	12m lilac rose	25	
141	"	20m deep blue	14.00	
142	"	25m chocolate	15.00	
143	A28	50m brown & blue	1.20	
144	"	100m gray black & carmine rose	1.75	
145	"	200m dk. bl. & pur.	3.50	3.
146	"	500m dark green & brn. orange	17.50	11.
		Nos. 135-146 (12)	81.55	16.

Globe
A29

Wmk. 195

Wmkd.
Iultiple Crown and Arabic F (195)

955, Jan. 1 Photo. ***Perf. 13½x13***

47 A29 5m yellow brown 90 70
48 " 10m green 1.50 1.25
49 " 30m violet 4.25 2.40

rab Postal Union founding, July 1, 1954.

Nos. 147-149 Overprinted

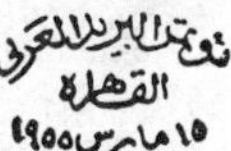

955, Aug. 1

50 A29 5m yellow brown 40 30
51 " 10m green 60 50
52 " 30m violet 1.80 80

Arab Postal Congress, Cairo, Mar. 15.

Emblems of Tripolitania, Cyrenaica and Fezzan with Royal Crown
A30

Wmk. 310

Wmkd. Multiple Crescent and Star (310)

955 Engraved ***Perf. 11½***

53 A30 2m lemon 1.00 25
54 " 3m slate blue 5 5
55 " 4m gray green 1.00 25
56 " 5m light blue green 42 5
57 " 10m violet 75 5
58 " 18m crimson 18 12
59 " 20m orange 35 12
60 " 30m blue 85 6
61 " 35m brown 50 12
62 " 40m rose carmine 85 18
63 " 50m olive 80 22

Size: 27½x32½mm.

64 A30 100m dk. grn. & pur. 1.25 38
65 " 200m ultramarine & rose carmine 10.00 60
66 " 500m grn. & orange 12.00 7.50

Size: 26½x32mm.

67 A30 £1 ocher, brown & grn., *yellow* 18.00 11.00
Nos. 153-167 (15) 48.00 20.95

See also Nos. 177-179, 192-206A.

No. 136 Surcharged ▮ 5 0 ▮

955, Aug. 25 **Unwmkd.**

68 A27 5m on 4m gray 1.20 1.00

Tomb of El Senussi, Jagbub
A31

Perf. 13x13½

1956, Sept. 14 Photo. **Wmk. 195**

169 A31 5m green 18 12
170 " 10m bright violet 25 18
171 " 15m rose carmine 38 38
172 " 30m sapphire 1.15 75

Issued to commemorate the centenary of the death of the Imam Seyyid Mohammed Aly El Senussi (in 1859).

Map, Flags and U.N. Headquarters
A32

Globe and Postal Emblems
A33

1956, Dec. 14 Litho. ***Perf. 13½x13***

173 A32 15m blue, ochre & olive bistre 38 18
174 " 35m blue, ochre & violet brown 60 42

Issued to commemorate the first anniversary of Libya's admission to the United Nations.

1957 ***Perf. 13½x13*** **Wmk. 195**

175 A33 15m blue 1.80 60
176 " 500m yellow brown 9.00 6.50

Issued to commemorate the Arab Postal Congress, Tripoli, Feb. 9, 1957.

Emblems Type of 1955.
Engraved.

1957 ***Perf. 11½*** **Wmk. 310**

177 A30 1m *yellow* 25 12
178 " 2m bistre brown 25 12
179 " 4m brown carmine 25 12

U. N. Emblem and Broken Chain
A34

Photogravure.

1958, Dec. 10 ***Perf. 14*** **Unwmkd.**

180 A34 10m bluish violet 18 12
181 " 15m green 30 25
182 " 30m ultramarine 75 60

Issued to commemorate the tenth anniversary of the signing of the Universal Declaration of Human Rights.

Date Palms and F.A.O. Emblem
A35

1959, Dec. 5 ***Perf. 14*** **Unwmkd.**

183 A35 10m pale violet & black 18 15
184 " 15m bluish green & black 30 25
185 " 45m lt. blue & black 75 70

Issued to commemorate the first International Dates Conference, Tripoli, Dec. 5-11.

Arab League Center, Cairo, and Arms of Libya—A36

Perf. 13x13½

1960, Mar. 22 **Wmk. 328**

186 A36 10m dull green & black 42 25

Issued to commemorate the opening of the Arab League Center and the Arab Postal Museum in Cairo.

Emblems of W.R.Y. and U.N., Arms of Libya
A37

Palm Tree and Radio Mast
A38

1960, Apr. 7 ***Perf. 14*** **Unwmkd.**

187 A37 10m violet & black 30 25
188 " 45m blue & black 1.15 95

Issued to publicize World Refugee Year, July 1, 1959–June 30, 1960.

1960, Aug. 4 Engr. ***Perf. 13x13½***

189 A38 10m violet 18 7
190 " 15m blue green 30 18
191 " 45m dk. car. rose 75 38

Issued to commemorate the Third Arab Telecommunications Conference, Tripoli, Aug. 4.

Emblems Type of 1955
Engraved

1960 ***Perf. 11½*** **Wmk. 310**

Size: 18x21½mm.

192 A30 1m *gray* 4 4
193 " 2m bistre brn., *buff* 4 4
194 " 3m blue, *bluish* 4 4
195 " 4m brn. car., *rose* 4 4
196 " 5m green, *greenish* 25 4
197 " 10m violet, *pale violet* 10 6
198 " 15m brown, *buff* 10 8
199 " 20m orange, *buff* 10 8
200 " 30m red, *pink* 12 12
201 " 40m rose car., *rose* 25 18
202 " 45m blue, *bluish* 25 25
203 " 50m olive, *buff* 50 25

Size: 27½x32½mm.

204 A30 100m dark green & purple, *gray* 70 35
205 " 200m blue & rose carmine, *bluish* 2.10 75
206 " 500m green & orange, *greenish* 12.50 2.50

Size: 26½x32mm.

206A A30 £1 ocher, brown & grn., *brown* 22.50 13.50
Nos. 192-206A (16) 39.63 18.32

Watchtower and Broken Chain
A39

1961, Aug. 9 Photo. **Unwmkd.**

207 A39 5m lt. yellow green & brown 25 12
208 " 15m lt. blue & brown 42 18

Issued for Army Day, Aug. 9, 1961.

Map of Zelten Oil Field and Tanker at Marsa Brega
A40

1961, Oct. 25 ***Perf. 11½***

209 A40 15m olive green & buff 12 12
210 " 50m red brown & pale violet 60 38
211 " 100m ultra. & blue 1.50 50

Opening of first oil pipe line in Libya.

Hands Breaking Chain, Tractor and Cows—A41

Designs: 50m, Modern highways and buildings. 100m, Machinery.

1961, Dec. 24 ***Perf. 11½***

Granite Paper

212 A41 15m pale green, grn. & brn. 12 12
213 " 50m buff & brown 50 38
214 " 100m salmon, violet & brown 1.35 75

Tenth anniversary of independence.

Camel Riders—A42

Designs: 15m, Well. 50m, Oil installations in desert.

1962, Feb. 20 Photo. ***Perf. 12***

215 A42 10m chocolate & orange brown 10 10
216 " 15m plum & yellow green 40 40
217 " 50m emerald & ultramarine 1.50 1.00
a. Souv. sheet of 3 25.00 10.00

Issued to publicize the International Fair at Tripoli, Feb. 20–March 20. No. 217a contains one each of Nos. 215-217, imperf. with marginal inscription and control number. Size: 147½x105mm.

Nos. 215-217 exist imperf. Price about twice that of perf.

Malaria Eradication Emblem and Palm
A43

Ahmed Rafik El Mehdawi
A44

1962, Apr. 7 ***Perf. 11½*** **Unwmkd.**

No.	Type	Description	Unused	Used
218	A43	15m multicolored	45	25
219	"	50m grn., yel. & brn.	70	70

Issued for the World Health Organization drive to eradicate malaria.

Exist imperf. Price about three times that of perf.

Two imperf. souvenir sheets exist, one containing the 15m, the other the 50m. Marginal inscriptions in gray brown and red brown respectively. Size: 68x102mm. Sold for 20m and 70m respectively. Price for both, $6.

1962, July 6 **Engr.** ***Perf. 13x14***

No.	Type	Description	Unused	Used
220	A44	15m green	18	12
221	"	20m brown	42	35

Issued to commemorate the first anniversary of the death of the poet Ahmed Rafik El Mehdawi (1898–1961).

Clasped Hands and Scout Emblem
A45

Drop of Oil with New City, Desert, Oil Wells and Map of Coast Line
A46

Designs: 10m, 30m, Boy Scouts. 15m, 50m, Scout emblem and tents.

1962, July 13 **Photo.** ***Perf. 12***

No.	Type	Description	Unused	Used
222	A45	5m yellow, black & red	12	12
223	"	10m blue, black & & yellow	25	18
224	"	15m multicolored	30	30

Souvenir Sheet
Imperf.

No.	Type	Description	Unused	Used
225	A45	Sheet of three	3.25	2.75
		a. 20m yellow, black & red	65	65
		b. 30m blue, black & yellow	65	65
		c. 50m blue gray, yel., blk. & green	65	65

Third Libyan Scout meeting (Philia).

No. 225 contains three imperf. stamps with blue marginal inscription. Size: 129x95mm.

Nos. 222–224 exist imperf. Price for set, $1.50.

1962, Nov. 25 ***Perf. 11x11½***

No.	Type	Description	Unused	Used
226	A46	15m grn. & vio. blk.	18	12
227	"	50m brown orange & olive	65	50

Issued to commemorate the opening of the Essider Terminal Sidrah pipeline system.

Centenary Emblem
A47

Lithographed and Photogravure

1963, Jan. 1 ***Perf. 11½***

No.	Type	Description	Unused	Used
228	A47	10m rose, black, red & blue	18	12
229	"	15m citron, black, red & blue	25	18
230	"	20m gray, black, red & blue	65	42

Centenary of the International Red Cross.

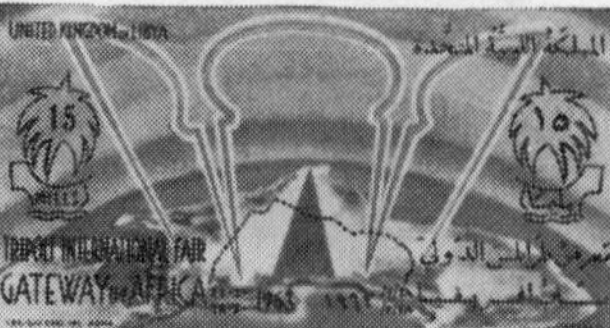

Rainbow and Arches over Map of Africa and Libya—A48

Lithographed

1963, Feb. 28 ***Perf. 13½*** **Unwmkd.**

No.	Type	Description	Unused	Used
231	A48	15m multicolored	30	18
232	"	30m "	55	50
233	"	50m "	85	75

Issued to publicize the Tripoli International Fair "Gateway of Africa," Feb. 28–March 28. Every other horizontal row inverted in sheet of 50 (25 tête bêche pairs).

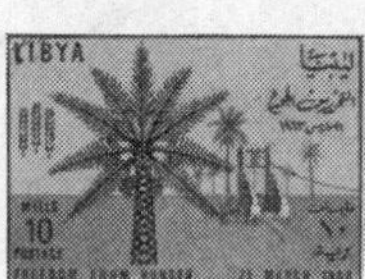

Date Palm and Well
A49

Designs: 15m, Camel and flock of sheep. 45m, Sower and tractor.

1963, Mar. 21 **Photo.** ***Perf. 11½***

No.	Type	Description	Unused	Used
234	A49	10m green, light blue & bister	12	12
235	"	15m purple, light green & bister	18	18
236	"	45m dark blue, salmon & sepia	80	42

Issued for the "Freedom from Hunger" campaign of the U.N. Food and Agriculture Organization.

Man with Whip and Slave Reaching for U.N. Emblem—A50

1963, Dec. 10 ***Perf. 11½*** **Unwmkd.**

No.	Type	Description	Unused	Used
237	A50	5m red brown & blue	12	12
238	"	15m dp. claret & blue	18	12
239	"	50m green & blue	55	38

Issued to commemorate the 15th anniversary of the Universal Declaration of Human Rights.

Exhibition Hall and Finger Pointing to Libya
A51

Photogravure

1964, Feb. 28 ***Perf. 11½*** **Unwmkd.**

No.	Type	Description	Unused	Used
240	A51	10m red brown, gray green & brown	25	12
241	"	15m purple, gray green & brown	50	38
242	"	30m dark blue, gray grn. & brown	1.40	70

Issued to publicize the 3rd International Fair at Tripoli, Feb. 28–March 20, 1964.

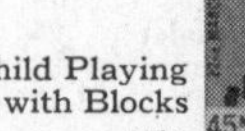

Child Playing with Blocks
A52

Design: 15m, Child in bird's nest.

1964, March 22 ***Perf. 11½***

No.	Type	Description	Unused	Used
243	A52	5m multicolored	12	12
244	"	15m "	18	18
245	"	45m "	55	42
		a. Souv. sheet of 3	2.40	2.40

Issued for Children's Day.

Exist imperf. Price about 1½ times that of perf.

No. 245a contains one each of Nos. 243–245, imperf. Brown marginal inscription. Size: 80x130mm. Sold for 100m.

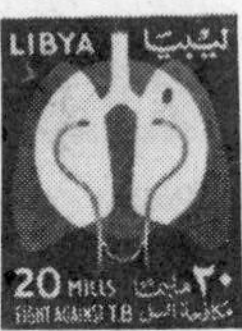

Lungs and Stethoscope
A53

1964, Apr. 7 **Photo.** ***Perf. 13½x14***

No.	Type	Description	Unused	Used
246	A53	20m deep purple	75	38

Campaign against tuberculosis.

Map of Libya—A54

1964, Apr. 27 ***Perf. 11½*** **Unwmkd.**

No.	Type	Description	Unused	Used
247	A54	5m emerald & orge.	12	6
248	"	50m blue & yellow	55	42

First anniversary of Libyan union.

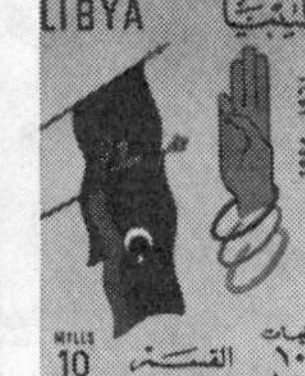

Moth Emerging from Cocoon, Veiled and Modern Women
A55

Hand Giving Scout Sign, Scout and Libyan Flags
A56

1964, June 15 **Engr. & Litho.**

No.	Type	Description	Unused	Used
249	A55	10m vio. bl. & lt. grn.	12	6
250	"	20m violet blue & yel.	18	12
251	"	35m vio. blue & pink	42	30
		a. Souv. sheet of 3	2.40	2.40

Issued to honor Libyan women in a new epoch. No. 251a contains one each of Nos. 249–251. Violet blue marginal inscriptions. Size: 124x106½mm. Sold for 100m.

1964, July 24 **Photo.** ***Perf. 12x11½***

Design: 20m, Libyan Scout emblem and hands.

No.	Type	Description	Unused	Used
252	A56	10m lt. bl. & multi.	42	38
253	"	20m multicolored	80	60
		a. Souv. sheet of 2	3.00	3.00

Issued to commemorate the opening of new Boy Scout headquarters and the installation of Crown Prince Hassan al-Rida el Senussi as Chief Scout. No. 253a contains 2 imperf. stamps similar to Nos. 252–253. Brown Scout emblem and inscription in margin. Size: 119x85mm. Sold for 50m.

Nos. 252–253 exist imperf. Price about 1½ times that of perf.

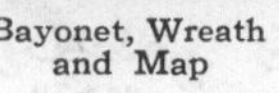

Bayonet, Wreath and Map
A57

Ahmed Bahloul el-Sharef
A58

1964, Aug. 9 **Litho.** ***Perf. 14x13½***

No.	Type	Description	Unused	Used
254	A57	10m yel. grn. & brn.	12	
255	"	20m orange & blk.	38	1

Founding of the Senussi Army.

1964, Aug. 11 **Engraved** ***Perf. 11½***

No.	Type	Description	Unused	Used
256	A58	15m lilac	18	
257	"	20m greenish blue	50	2

Poet Ahmed Bahloul el-Sharef, died 1953.

Soccer—A59

Sports: 10m, Bicycling. 20m, Boxing. 30m, Sprinter. 35m, Woman diver. 50m Hurdling.

1964, Oct. 1 **Litho.** ***Perf. 1***

Black Inscriptions and Gold Olympic Rings

No.	Type	Description	Unused	Used
258	A59	5m bright blue	35	3
259	"	10m dull claret	35	3
260	"	20m brick red	35	3
261	"	30m dull yellow	35	3
262	"	35m dull yel. green	35	3
263	"	50m bright green	35	3
		Block of 6, #258–263	2.10	2.1
		Nos. 258–263 (6)	2.10	2.1

Issued to commemorate the 18th Olympi Games, Tokyo, Oct. 10–25. Nos. 258–26 were printed in same sheet of 48 (6x8 containing 8 blocks of 6. The two block in each double row are inverted in rela tion to the two blocks in the next row providing various tete beche and se-tenar arrangements.

Nos. 258–263 exist imperf. Price fo set, $7.50.

Perf. and imperf. souvenir sheets exis containing six 15m stamps in the design and colors of Nos. 258–263. Sheets sol for 100m. Dull claret marginal inscriptio and black control number. Size: 160x11 mm. Price for both, $13.50.

Arab Postal Union Emblem
A59a

Perf. 11x11½

1964, Dec. 1 **Photo.** **Unwmkd**

No.	Type	Description	Unused	Used
264	A59a	10m yellow & blue	12	
265	"	15m pale violet & orange brown	25	1
266	"	30m lt. yellow green & brown	75	5

Issued to commemorate the 10th anni versary of the Permanent Office of the Ara Postal Union.

International Cooperation Year Emblem—A60

Perf. 14½x14

1965, Jan. 1 Litho. *Perf. 14½x14*

No.	Type	Description	Unused	Used
267	A60	5m violet blue & gold	12	12
268	"	15m rose car. & gold	75	75

International Cooperation Year.

Imperfs. exist. Price about twice that of perfs.

See also Nos. C51–C51a.

European Bee Eater

A61

Birds: 5m, Long-legged buzzard (vert.). 15m, Chestnut-bellied sandgrouse. 20m, Houbara bustard. 30m, Spotted sandgrouse. 40m, Libyan Barbary partridge (vert.).

Granite Paper

1965, Feb. 10 Photo. *Perf. 11½*

Birds in Natural Colors

No.	Type	Description	Unused	Used
269	A61	5m gray & black	5	5
270	"	10m light blue & orange brown	15	6
271	"	15m light green & blk.	22	12
272	"	20m pale lilac & black	30	12
273	"	30m tan & dark brn.	38	18
274	"	40m dull yel. & black	65	18
		Nos. 269–274 (6)	1.75	71

Map of Africa with Libya

A62

1965, Feb. 28 Photo. *Perf. 11½*

Granite Paper

No.	Type	Description	Unused	Used
275	A62	50m multicolored	50	30

Issued to publicize the Fourth International Tripoli Fair, Feb. 28–March 20.

Compass Rose, Rockets, Satellites and Stars—A63

1965, Mar. 23 Lithographed

No.	Type	Description	Unused	Used
276	A63	10m multicolored	6	6
277	"	15m "	18	12
278	"	50m "	50	42

Fifth World Meteorological Day.

ITU Emblem, Old and New Communication Equipment

A64

1965, May 17 Unwmkd.

No.	Type	Description	Unused	Used
279	A64	10m sepia	13	5
280	"	20m red lilac	18	12
281	"	50m lilac rose	38	30

Issued to commemorate the centenary of the International Telecommunication Union.

Library Aflame and Lamp

A65

1965, June Litho. *Perf. 11½*

No.	Type	Description	Unused	Used
282	A65	15m multicolored	18	12
283	"	50m "	55	25

Issued to commemorate the burning of the Library of Algiers, June 7, 1962.

Rose — A66

Jet Plane and Globe — A67

Flowers: 2m, Iris. 3m, Opuntia. 4m, Sunflower.

1965, Aug. Litho. *Perf. 14*

Flowers in Natural Colors

No.	Type	Description	Unused	Used
284	A66	1m pale green & blk.	5	5
285	"	2m yellow & black	5	5
286	"	3m dull lilac & black	12	5
287	"	4m blue & black	25	25

Photogravure

1965, Oct. *Perf. 11½* Unwmkd.

No.	Type	Description	Unused	Used
288	A67	5m multicolored	6	6
289	"	10m "	18	12
290	"	15m "	38	18

Issued to publicize Libyan Airlines.

Forum, Cyrene — A68

Mausoleum at Germa — A69

Designs: 100m, Arch of Trajan. 200m, Temple of Apollo, Cyrene. 500m, Antonine Temple of Jupiter, Sabratha (horiz.). £1, Theater, Sabratha.

Perf. 12x11½, 11½x12

1965, Dec. 24 Engr. Wmk. 310

No.	Type	Description	Unused	Used
291	A68	50m vio. blue & olive	60	18
292	"	100m Prussian blue & deep orange	1.20	42
293	"	200m pur. & Prus. bl.	1.80	60
294	"	500m car. rose & grn.	3.75	1.80
295	"	£1 grn. & dp. org.	11.00	3.75
		Nos. 291–295 (5)	18.35	6.75

Nos. 293–295 with "Kingdom of Libia" in both Arabic and English blocked out with a blue felt-tipped pen were issued June 21, 1970, by the Republic.

Lithographed

1966, Feb. 10 *Perf. 11½* Unwmkd.

No.	Type	Description	Unused	Used
296	A69	70m purple & salmon	50	38

Coat of Arms of Libya and "POLIGRAFICA & CARTEVALORI—NAPLES" printed on back in yellow green. See No. E13.

Globe in Space, Satellites—A70

1966, Feb. 28 *Perf. 12*

No.	Type	Description	Unused	Used
297	A70	15m multicolored	18	6
298	"	45m "	30	30
299	"	55m "	95	50

Issued to publicize the 5th International Fair at Tripoli, Feb. 28–March 20, 1966.

Arab League Center, Cairo, and Emblem

A71

Lithographed & Photogravure

1966, Mar. 22 *Perf. 11*

No.	Type	Description	Unused	Used
300	A71	20m car., emerald & black	18	12
301	"	55m brt. blue, verm. & black	45	38

Issued to publicize the Arab League.

Souvenir Sheet

WHO Headquarters, Geneva, and Emblem—A72

1966, May 3 Litho. *Imperf.*

No.	Type	Description	Unused	Used
302	A72	50m multicolored	2.40	2.40

Inauguration of the World Health Organization headquarters, Geneva. No. 302 has red marginal inscription and black date. Size: 80x69mm. See Nos. C55–C57.

Tuareg and Camel

A73

A74

Three Tuareg Riders—A75

Design: 20m, like 10m, facing left.

1966, June 20 *Perf. 10* Unwmkd.

No.	Type	Description	Unused	Used
303	A73	10m bright red	38	30
304	"	20m ultramarine	60	55
305	A74	50m multicolored	1.40	1.10
		a. Strip of 3 Nos. 303–305)	2.50	2.50

Souvenir Sheet

Imperf.

No.	Type	Description	Unused	Used
306	A75	100m multicolored	3.50	2.50

Nos. 303–305 printed se-tenant in sheets of 15. Each sheet contains 5 No. 305a. No. 306 measures 162x110mm.

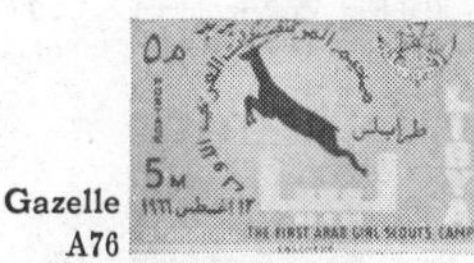

Gazelle

A76

Emblem

A77

Lithographed

1966, Aug. 12 *Perf. 13x11, 11x13*

No.	Type	Description	Unused	Used
307	A76	5m lt. grn., blk. & red	12	12
308	A77	25m multicolored	25	18
309	"	65m "	50	30

No. 307 commemorates the first Arab Girl Scout Camp, Nos. 308–309 the seventh Arab Boy Scout Camp, Good Daim, Libya, Aug. 12, 1966.

UNESCO Emblem

A78

1967, Jan. Litho. *Perf. 10x10½*

No.	Type	Description	Unused	Used
310	A78	15m multicolored	18	12
311	"	25m "	30	25

Issued to commemorate the 20th anniversary (in 1966) of UNESCO (United Nations Educational, Scientific and Cultural Organization).

Castle of Columns, Tolemaide — A79

Fair Emblem — A80

Design: 55m, Sebha Fort (horiz.).

Perf. 13x13½, 13½x13

1966, Dec. 24 Engraved

312 A79 25m lilac, red brown & black 25 18
313 " 55m black, lilac & red brown 50 42

Photogravure

1967, Feb. 28 *Perf. 11½* Unwmkd.

314 A80 15m multicolored 25 7
315 " 55m " 50 30

Issued to publicize the 6th International Fair at Tripoli, Feb. 28–March 20.

Oil Tanker, Marsa Al Hariga Terminal—A81

1967, Feb. 14 Litho. *Perf. 10*

316 A81 60m multicolored 60 35

Opening of Marsa Al Hariga oil terminal.

Tourist Year Emblem—A82

1967, May 1 Litho. *Perf. 10½x10*

317 A82 5m gray, black & bright blue 5 5
318 " 10m lt. blue, black & bright blue 12 6
319 " 45m pink, black & bright blue 38 25

International Tourist Year, 1967.

Map of Mediterranean and Runners
A83

Designs (Map and): 10m, Javelin. 15m, Bicycling. 45m, Soccer. 75m, Boxing.

1967, Sept. 8 Litho. *Perf. 10½*

320 A83 5m org., bl. & black 6 6
321 " 10m dp. brn., bl. & blk. 6 6
322 " 15m vio., bl. & black 18 6
323 " 45m carmine rose, blue & black 25 25
324 " 75m bright green, blue & black 65 38
Nos. 320-324 (5) 1.20 81

Issued to commemorate the 5th Mediterranean Games, Tunis, Sept. 8–17.

Arab League Emblem and Hands Reaching for Knowledge
A84

1967, Oct. 1 Litho. *Perf. 12½x13*

325 A84 5m org. & dk. purple 5 5
326 " 10m bright green & dark purple 6 6
327 " 15m lilac & dk. pur. 12 6
328 " 25m bl. & dk. purple 38 12

Literacy campaign.

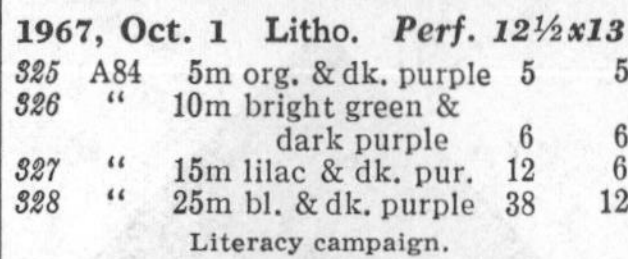

Human Rights Flame
A85

1968, Jan. 15 Litho. *Perf. 13½x14*

329 A85 15m green & verm. 25 6
330 " 60m org. & vio. blue 42 38

International Human Rights Year 1968.

Map, Derrick, Plane and Camel Riders—A86

1968, Feb. 28 Photo. *Perf. 11½*

331 A86 55m car. rose, brown & yellow 65 50

Issued to publicize the 7th International Fair at Tripoli, Feb. 28–March 20.

Arab League Emblem
A87

1968, Mar. 22 Engraved *Perf. 13½*

332 A87 10m bl. gray & car. 12 12
333 " 45m fawn & green 50 38

Issued for Arab League Week.

Children, Statuary Group
A88

Design: 55m, Mother and children.

1968, Mar. 21 Litho. *Perf. 11*

334 A88 25m gray, black & magenta 25 12
335 " 55m gray & multi. 38 30

Issued for Children's Day.

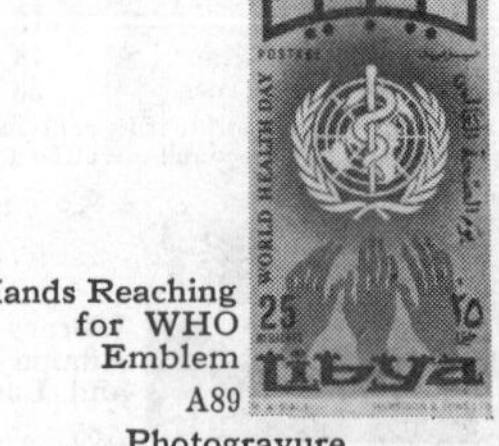

Hands Reaching for WHO Emblem
A89

Photogravure

1968, Apr. 7 *Perf. 13½x14½*

336 A89 25m rose claret, dk. bl. & gray bl. 18 12
337 " 55m blue, blk. & gray 55 30

Issued to commemorate the 20th anniversary of the World Health Organization.

From Oil Field to Tanker
A90

1968, Apr. 23 Litho. *Perf. 11*

338 A90 10m multicolored 12 12
339 " 60m " 50 38

Opening of the Zueitina oil terminal.

Teacher and Crowd
A91

1968, Sept. 8 Litho. *Perf. 13½*

340 A91 5m bright pink 6 6
341 " 10m orange 6 6
342 " 15m blue 12 12
343 " 20m emerald 38 25

Literacy campaign.

Arab Labor Emblem
A92

1968, Nov. 3 Photo. *Perf. 14x13½*

344 A92 10m multicolored 12 12
345 " 15m " 30 18

Issued to publicize the 4th session of the Arab Labor Ministers' Conference, Tripoli, Nov. 3–10.

Wadi el Kuf Bridge and Road Sign
A93

1968, Dec. 25 Litho. *Perf. 11x11½*

346 A93 25m ultra. & multi. 25 18
347 " 60m emerald & multi. 50 30

Opening of the Wadi el Kuf Bridge.

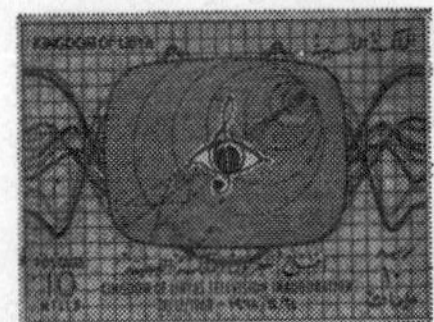

Television Screen and Chart
A94

1968, Dec. 25 Photo. *Perf. 14x13½*

348 A94 10m yellow & multi. 12 6
349 " 30m lilac & multi. 30 25

Issued to commemorate the inauguration of television service, Dec. 24, 1968.

Melons
A95

Designs: 10m, Peanuts. 15m, Lemons. 20m, Oranges. 25m, Peaches. 35m, Pears.

1969, Jan. Photo. *Perf. 11½*

Granite Paper

350 A95 5m black, grn. & yel. 6 6
351 " 10m brown & ocher 6 6
352 " 15m brn., grn. & yel. 12 6
353 " 20m brn., grn. & org. 25 12
354 " 25m brown & multi. 30 12
355 " 35m " " 42 [illegible]
Nos. 350-355 (6) 1.21 [illegible]

Nos. 350–355 with "Kingdom of Libya" in both English and Arabic blocked out with a blue felt-tipped pen were issued in December, 1971, by the Republic.

Tripoli Fair Emblem
A96

1969, Apr. 8 Granite Paper

356 A96 25m silver & multi. 12 12
357 " 35m bronze & multi. 18 12
358 " 40m gold & multi. 42 25

8th International Fair at Tripoli, Mar. 6–26.

Weather Balloon and Observer
A97

1969, Mar. 21 Photo. *Perf. 14x13*

359 A97 60m gray & multi. 60 50

World Meteorological Day, Mar. 23.

Cogwheel and Workers
A98

1969, Mar. 29 Litho. *Perf. 13½*

360 A98 15m blue & multi. 12 12
361 " 55m salmon & multi. 38 30

10th anniversary of Social Insurance.

ILO Emblem
A99

1969, June 1 Photogravure *Perf. 14*

362 A99 10m blue green, black & light olive 12 12
363 " 60m car. rose, black & light olive 50 30

Issued to commemorate the 50th anniversary of the International Labor Organization.

African Tourist Year Emblem
A100

1969, July *Perf. 11½*

Emblem in Emerald, Light Blue & Red

364 A100 15m emerald & silver 12 12
365 " 30m black & gold 38 30

Issued to publicize African Tourist Year.

Libyan Arab Republic

Soldiers, Tanks and Planes
A101

Radar, Flags and Carrier Pigeon
A102

1969, Dec. 7 Photo. *Perf. 12x12½*

366 A101 5m orange & multi. 4 6
367 " 10m ultra. & multi. 15 6
368 " 15m multicolored 25 10
369 " 25m " 40 16
370 " 45m brt. bl. & multi. 70 28
371 " 60m multicolored 95 45
Nos. 366-371 (6) 2.49 1.11

Issued to commemorate the establishment of the Libyan Arab Republic, Sept. 1, 1969. See Nos. 379-384.

1970, Mar. 1 Photo. *Perf. 11½*

Granite Paper

372 A102 15m multicolored 35 15
373 " 20m " 50 20
374 " 25m " 60 25
375 " 40m " 95 38

Map of Arab League Countries, Flag and Emblem—A102a

1970, Mar. 22

376 A102a 10m lt. blue, brown & green 17 12
377 " 15m org., brn. & grn. 25 17
378 " 20m olive, brown & green 32 22

25th anniversary of the Arab League.

Type A101 Redrawn
A103

1970, May 2 Photo. *Perf. 12x12½*

379 A103 5m org. & multi. 12 6
380 " 10m ultra. & multi. 17 8
381 " 15m multicolored 25 10
382 " 25m " 40 16
383 " 45m brt. bl. & multi. 75 30
384 " 60m multicolored 95 38
Nos. 379-384 (6) 2.64 1.08

On Nos. 379-384 the numerals are in black, the bottom inscription is in 2 lines and several other changes.

U.P.U. Headquarters, Bern
A104

1970, May 20 Photo. *Perf. 11½x11*

385 A104 10m multicolored 10 6
386 " 25m " 25 16
387 " 60m " 55 35

Issued to commemorate the inauguration of the new Universal Postal Union Headquarters in Bern.

Arms of Libyan Arab Republic
A105

Flags, Soldiers and Tank
A106

1970, June 20 Photo. *Perf. 11*

388 A105 15m blk. & brt. rose 18 6
389 " 25m vio. blue, yel. & bright rose 30 10
390 " 45m emerald, yel. & bright rose 55 22

Evacuation of U.S. military base in Libya.

1970, Sept. 1 Photo. *Perf. 11x11½*

391 A106 20m multicolored 80 17
392 " 25m " 1.00 20
393 " 30m blue & multi. 1.20 25

Issued to commemorate the first anniversary of the Libyan Arab Republic.

U.N. Emblem, Dove and Scales
A107

1970, Oct. 24 Photo. *Perf. 11x11½*

394 A107 5m orange & multi. 15 5
395 " 10m olive & multi. 30 12
396 " 60m multicolored 1.75 65

25th anniversary of the United Nations.

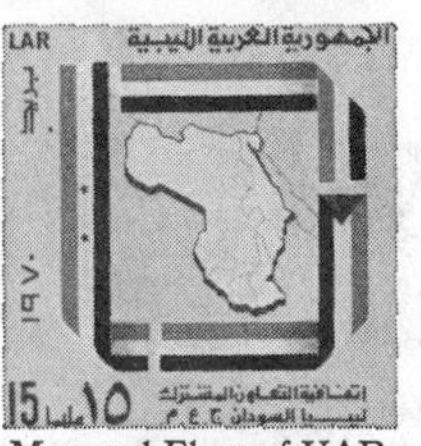

Map and Flags of UAR, Libya, Sudan—A107a

1970, Dec. 27 Photo. *Perf. 11½*

397 A107a 15m lt. green, car. & black 1.50 50

Signing of the Charter of Tripoli affirming the unity of UAR, Libya and the Sudan, Dec. 27, 1970.

U.N. Emblem, Dove and Globe
A108

1971, Jan. 10 Litho. *Perf. 12x11½*

398 A108 15m multicolored 40 9
399 " 20m " 55 12
400 " 60m lt. vio. & multi. 1.65 32

U.N. declaration on granting of independence to colonial countries and peoples, 10th anniversary.

Education Year Fighter—A110

Al Fatah Emblem—A109

1971, Jan. 16

401 A109 5m red, blk. & ocher 12 3
402 " 10m red, black & emerald 30 6
403 " 20m red, black & violet blue 60 10

International Education Year.

1971, Mar. 14 Photo. *Perf. 11*

404 A110 5m olive & multi 7 3
405 " 10m yellow & multi. 15 6
406 " 100m multicolored 1.50 50

Fight for the liberation of Palestine.

Tripoli Fair Emblem
A111

OPEC Emblem
A112

1971, Mar. 18 Litho. *Perf. 14*

407 A111 15m multicolored 17 9
408 " 30m orange & multi. 35 18

9th International Fair at Tripoli.

1971, May 29 Litho. *Perf. 12*

409 A112 10m yellow & brown 12 6
410 " 70m pink & vio. blue 85 30

10th anniversary of OPEC (Oil Producing Countries Association).

Globe and Waves
A113

1971, June 10 *Perf. 14½x13½*

411 A113 25m brt. green, blk. & vio. blue 22 12
412 " 35m gray & multi. 32 17

3rd World Telecommunications Day, May 17, 1971.

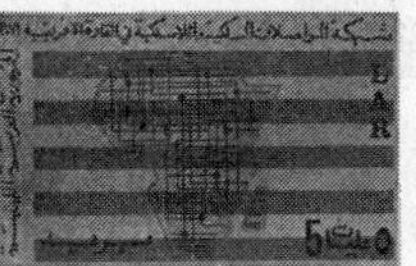

Map of Africa and Telecommunications Network
A114

1971, June 10

413 A114 5m yel., blk. & grn. 6 3
414 " 15m dull bl., black & green 15 8

Pan-African telecommunications system.

Torchbearer and Banner
A115

Ramadan Suehli
A116

1971, June 15 Photo. *Perf. 11½x2*

415 A115 5m yel. & multi. 7 3
416 " 10m org. & multi. 15 6
417 " 15m multicolored 22 10

First anniversary of evacuation of U.S. military base.

1971, Aug. 24 *Perf. 14x14½*

418 A116 15m multicolored 15 5
419 " 55m blue & multi. 60 20

50th anniversary of the death of Ramadan Suehli (1879-1920), freedom fighter.
See also Nos. 422-423, 426-427, 439-440, 479-480.

Date Palm
A117

Gamal Abdel Nasser
A118

1971, Sept. 1
420 A117 5m multicolored 22 8
421 " 15m " 60 20

2nd anniversary of the Sept. 1st (1969) Revolution.

Portrait Type of 1971
Portrait: Omar el Mukhtar.

1971, Sept. 16 *Perf. 14x14½*
422 A116 5m lt. grn. & multi. 4 3
423 " 100m multicolored 1.00 30

Omar el Mukhtar (1858–1931), leader of the Martyrs.

1971, Sept. 28 Photo. *Perf. 11x11½*
424 A118 5m lilac, grn. & blk. 8 3
425 " 15m grn., lilac & blk. 25 12

In memory of Gamal Abdel Nasser (1918–1970), president of Egypt.

Portrait Type of 1971
Portrait: Ibrahim Usta Omar.

1971, Oct. 8 Litho. *Perf. 14x14½*
426 A116 25m vio. bl. & multi. 30 15
427 " 30m multicolored 35 18

Ibrahim Usta Omar (1908–1950), patriotic poet.

Racial Equality Emblem
A119

Arab Postal Union Emblem
A120

1971, Oct. 24 *Perf. 13½x14½*
428 A119 25m multicolored 25 12
429 " 35m " 40 20

International Year Against Racial Discrimination.

1971, Nov. 6 Litho. *Perf. 14½*
Emblem in Black, Yellow and Blue
430 A120 5m red 7 3
431 " 10m violet 13 6
432 " 15m brt. rose lilac 20 10

25th anniversary of the Conference of Sofar, Lebanon, establishing Arab Postal Union.

Postal Union Emblem and Letter
A121

Design: 25m, 55m, African Postal Union emblem, letter and dove.

1971, Dec. Photo. *Perf. 11½x11*
433 A121 10m orange brown, blue & black 12 5
434 " 15m orange, lt. blue & black 17 6
435 " 25m lt. green, orange & black 30 10
436 " 55m lt. brn., yellow & black 65 22

10th anniversary of African Postal Union. Issue dates: 25m, 55m, Dec. 2; 10m, 15m, Dec. 12.

Book Year Emblem
A122

Coat of Arms
A123

1972, Jan. 1 Litho. *Perf. 12½x13*
437 A122 15d ultra., brown, gold & black 22 10
438 " 20d gold, brown, ultra. & black 32 17

International Book Year 1972.

Portrait Type of 1971
Portrait: Ahmed Gnaba.

1972, Jan. 12 *Perf. 14x14½*
439 A116 20m red & multi. 22 15
440 " 35m olive & multi. 40 22

Ahmed Gnaba (1898–1968), poet of unity.

1972, Feb. 10 Photo. *Perf. 14½*
Size: 19x23mm.
441 A123 5m gray & multi. 5 3
442 " 10m lt. olive & multi. 10 4
443 " 15d lilac & multi. 13 5
445 " 25m lt. blue & multi. 22 7
446 " 30m rose & multi. 25 9
447 " 35m lt. olive & multi. 30 10
448 " 40m dull yel. & multi. 35 12
449 " 45m lt. grn. & multi. 40 13
451 " 55m multicolored 50 15
452 " 60m bister & multi. 50 15
453 " 65d multicolored 55 17
454 " 70d lt. vio. & multi. 60 18
455 " 80d ocher & multi. 70 22
456 " 90m blue & multi. 80 25

Size: 27x32mm. *Perf. 14x14½*
457 A123 100d multicolored 90 28
458 " 200d " 1.65 50
459 " 500d " 4.40 1.35
460 " £1 " 8.80 2.50
Nos. 441-460 (18) 21.20 6.38

Numeral
A124

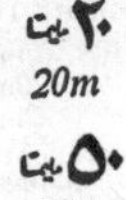
20m
50m

Coil Stamps

1972, July 27 Photo. *Perf. 14½x14*
461 A124 5m slate blue, ocher & black *60* 5
462 " 20m bl., lilac & blk. *2.50* 15
463 " 50m bl., olive & blk. *6.00* 35

See also Nos. 496–498, 575–577.

Tombs at Ghirza
A125

Fair Emblem
A126

Designs: 10m, Kufic inscription, Agedabia (horiz.). 15m, Marcus Aurelius Arch, Tripoli. 25m, Exchange of weapons, mural from Wan Amil Cave. 55m, Garamanthian (Berber) chariot, petroglyph, Wadi Zigza. 70m, Nymph Cyrene strangling a lion, bas-relief, Cyrene.

1972, Feb. 15 Litho. *Perf. 14*
464 A125 5m lilac & multi. 6 3
465 " 10m multicolored 15 10
466 " 15m dp. org. & multi. 25 10
467 " 25m emerald & multi. 40 15
468 " 55m scarlet & multi. 1.00 40
469 " 70m ultra. & multi. 1.10 45
Nos. 464-469 (6) 2.96 1.23

1972, Mar. 1
470 A126 25d gray & multi. 28 10
471 " 35d multicolored 40 12
472 " 50d " 55 17
473 " 70d " 80 22

10th International Fair at Tripoli.

Dissected Arm, and Heart
A127

"Arab Unity"
A128

1972, Apr. 7 *Perf. 14½*
474 A127 15d multicolored 1.00 45
475 " 25d " 1.65 75

"Your heart is your health," World Health Day.

1972, Apr. 17 *Perf. 13½x13*
Litho. & Engr.
476 A128 15d blue, yel. & blk. 20 7
477 " 20d lt. green, yellow & black 28 10
478 " 25d lt. verm., yellow & black 32 13

First anniversary of the Federation of Arab Republics Foundation.

Portrait Type of 1971
Portrait: Suleiman el Baruni.

1972, May 1 Litho. *Perf. 14x14½*
479 A116 10m yellow & multi. 25 6
480 " 70m dp. orange & multi. 1.85 35

Suleiman el Baruni (1870–1940), patriotic writer.

Environment Emblem
A129

Olympic Emblems
A130

1972, Aug. 15 Litho. *Perf. 14½*
481 A129 15m red & multi. 25 7
482 " 55m green & multi. 80 30

U.N. Conference on Human Environment, Stockholm, June 5–16.

1972, Aug. 26
483 A130 25d brt. bl. & multi. 1.25 25
484 " 35d red & multi. 1.75 35

20th Olympic Games, Munich, Aug. 26–Sept. 11.

Emblem and Broken Chain
A131

Dome of the Rock, Jerusalem
A132

1972, Oct. 1 Litho. *Perf. 14x13½*
485 A131 15d blue & multi. 27 10
486 " 25d yellow & multi. 55 18

3rd anniversary of the Libyan Arab Republic.

1972 *Perf. 12½x13*
487 A132 10d multicolored 15 6
488 " 25d " 35 15

Nicolaus Copernicus
A133

Design: 25d, Copernicus in Observatory, by Jan Matejko (horiz.).

1973, Feb. 26
Perf. 14½x13½, 13½x14½
489 A133 15d yellow & multi. 20 10
490 " 25d blue & multi. 35 17

500th anniversary of the birth of Nicolaus Copernicus (1473–1543), Polish astronomer.

Eagle and Fair Buildings
A134

Blind Person, Books, Loom and Basket
A135

1973, Mar. 1 *Perf. 13½x14½*
491 A134 5d dull red & multi. 25 8
492 " 10d bl. grn. & multi. 45 1
493 " 15d vio. bl. & multi. 60 2

11th International Fair at Tripoli.

1973, Apr. 18 Photo. *Perf. 12x11½*
494 A135 20d gray & multi. *3.50* 7
495 " 25d dull yellow & multi. *4.00* 8

Role of the blind in society.

Coil Stamps
Numeral Type of 1972
Denominations in Dirhams

5d 20d 50d

1973, Apr. 26 Photo. *Perf. 14½x14*
496 A124 5d slate bl., ocher & black 17 3
497 " 20d blue, lilac & blk. 60 8
498 " 50d bl., olive & blk. 1.35 2

Map of Africa
A136

1973, May 25 Photo. *Perf. 11x11½*
499 A136 15d yel., grn. & brn. 20 7
500 " 25d lt. yellow green, green & black 35 1

"Freedom in Unity" (Organization for African Unity).

INTERPOL Emblem and General Secretariat, Paris
A138

Lithographed

973, June 30 *Perf. 13½x14½*

01 A138 10d lilac & multi. 18 5
02 " 15d ocher & multi. 22 8
03 " 25d lt. grn. & multi. 38 12

50th anniversary of International Criminal Police Organization (INTERPOL).

Map of Libya, Houses, People, Factories, Tractor
A139

973, July 15 Photo. *Perf. 11½*

4 A139 10d rose red, black & ultra. *1.00* 35
05 " 25d ultra., black & green *2.10* 70
06 " 35d grn., blk. & orange *3.25* 1.10

General census.

UN Emblem
A140

973, Aug. 1 *Perf. 12½x11*

07 A140 5d verm., blk. & bl. 18 7
08 " 10d yel. grn., blk. & bl. 32 15

Centenary of international meteorological cooperation.

Soccer—A141

973, Aug. 10 Photo. *Perf. 11½*

09 A141 5d yellow green & dark brown 15 3
10 " 25d org. & dk. brown 70 15

2nd Palestinian Cup Soccer Tournament.

Torch and Grain
A142

Writing Hand, Lamp and Globe
A143

973, Sept. 1 Litho. *Perf. 14*

11 A142 15d brown & multi. 25 7
12 " 25d emerald & multi. 35 10

4th anniversary of September 1st Revolution.

973, Sept. 8

13 A143 25d multicolored 40 12

Literacy campaign.

Gate of First City Hall
A144

Militia, Flag and Factories
A145

Designs: 25d, Khondok fountain. 35d, Clock tower.

1973, Sept. 18 *Perf. 13*

514 A144 10d blue & multi. 15 5
515 " 25d emerald & multi. 32 5
516 " 35d citron & multi. 45 7

Centenary of Tripoli as a municipality.

1973, Oct. 7 Photo. *Perf. 11½x11*

517 A145 15d yel., blk. & red 18 7
518 " 25d green & multi. 30 10

Libyan Militia.

Revolutionary Proclamation by Mohammed El Gadhafi—A146

Design: 70d, as 25d, with English inscription.

1973, Oct. 15 Litho. *Perf. 12½*

519 A146 25d orange & multi. 20 5
520 " 70d green & multi. 60 15

Proclamation of People's Revolution by Pres. Mohammed El Gadhafi.

FAO Emblem, Camel Pulling Plow
A147

1973, Nov. 1 Photo. *Perf. 11*

521 A147 10d ocher & multi. 10 5
522 " 25d dk. brn. & multi. 20 7
523 " 35d black & multi. 28 10

10th anniversary of World Food Organization.

Human Rights Flame
A148

1973, Dec. 20 Photo. *Perf. 11x11½*

524 A148 25d purple, carmine & dark blue 18 6
525 " 70d lt. green, car. & dark blue 50 18

25th anniversary of the Universal Declaration of Human Rights.

Fish
A149

Designs: Various fish from Libyan waters.

1973, Dec. 31 Photo. *Perf. 14x13½*

526 A149 5d lt. blue & multi. 15 3
527 " 10d " " " 30 7
528 " 15d " " " 45 10
529 " 20d " " " 65 15
530 " 25d " " " 75 18
Nos. 526-530 (5) 2.30 53

1975, Jan. 5

526a A149 5d greenish bl. & multi. 5 3
527a " 10d " " 12 5
528a " 15d " " " 18 5
529a " 20d " " " 25 8
530a " 25d " " " 30 10
Nos. 526a-530a (5) 90 31

Scout, Sun and Scout Signs
A150

Fair Emblem, Flags of Participants
A151

1974, Feb. 1 Litho. *Perf. 11½*

531 A150 5d blue & mutli. 45 8
532 " 20d lt. lilac & multi. 1.75 32
533 " 25d lt. grn. & multi. 2.00 38

Libyan Boy Scouts.

1974, Mar. 1 Litho. *Perf. 12x11½*

534 A151 10d lt. ultra. & multi. 25 5
535 " 25d tan. & multi. 55 12
536 " 35d lt. grn. & multi. 75 15

12th Tripoli International Fair.

Protected Family, WHO Emblem
A152

Minaret and Star
A153

1974, Apr. 7 Litho. *Perf. 12½*

537 A152 5d lt. green & multi. 8 3
538 " 25d red & multi. 32 10

World Health Day.

1974, Apr. 16 *Perf. 11½x11*

539 A153 10d pink & multi. 10 5
540 " 25d yellow & multi. 20 7
541 " 35d orange & multi. 28 10

Inauguration of the City University of Bengazi.

UPU Emblem and Star
A154

Traffic Signs
A156

Lithographed

1974, May 22 *Perf. 13½x14½*

542 A154 25d multicolored *2.00* 40
543 " 70d " *6.00* 1.10

Centenary of Universal Postal Union.

1974, June 8 Photo. *Perf. 11*

547 A156 5d gold & multi. 6 3
548 " 10d " " 12 5
549 " 25d " " 25 7

Automobile and Touring Club of Libya.

Tank, Oil Refinery, Book
A157

Symbolic "5"
A158

1974, Sept. 1 Litho. *Perf. 14*

550 A157 5d red & multi. 5 3
551 " 20d vio. & multi. 12 5
552 " 25d vio. bl. & multi. 15 5
553 " 35d green & multi. 25 8

Souvenir Sheet

Perf. 13

554 A158 55d yel. & maroon 3.00 3.00

5th anniversary of the Revolution of September 1. English inscription on No. 553. No. 554 contains one stamp; black and red margin with eagle emblem and coat of arms. Size: 120x80mm.

WPY Emblem and Crowd
A159

Libyan Woman
A160

1974, Oct. 19 *Perf. 14*

555 A159 25d multicolored 25 8
556 " 35d lt. brn. & multi. 30 10

World Population Year.

1975, Mar. 1 Litho. *Perf. 13x12½*

Libyan Costumes: 10d, 15d, Women. 20d, Old man. 25d, Man riding camel. 50d, Man on horseback.

557 A160 5d org. yel. & multi. 4 3
558 " 10d " " 12 5
559 " 15d " " 18 6
560 " 20d " " 25 8
561 " 25d " " 30 10
562 " 50d " " 60 20
Nos. 557-562 (6) 1.49 52

Congress Emblem
A161

1975, Mar. 4 Litho. *Perf. 12x12½*

563	A161	10d brown & multi.	8	5
564	"	25d violet & multi.	20	7
565	"	35d gray & multi.	28	10

Arab Labor Congress.

Teacher Pointing to Blackboard
A162

1975, Mar. 10 *Perf. 11½*

566	A162	10d gold & multi.	8	5
567	"	25d " "	30	10

Teacher's Day.

Bodies, Globe, Proclamation
A163

Woman and Man in Library
A164

1975, Apr. 7 Litho. *Perf. 12½*

568	A163	20d lilac & multi.	20	7
569	"	25d emerald & multi.	27	10

World Health Day.

1975, May 25 Litho. *Perf. 12½*

570	A164	10d bl. grn. & multi.	7	5
571	"	25d olive & multi.	18	7
572	"	35d lt. vio. & multi.	25	10

Libyan Arab Book Exhibition.

Festival Emblem
A165

Games Emblem and Arms
A166

1975, July 5 Litho. *Perf. 13x12½*

573	A165	20d lt. bl. & multi.	20	7
574	"	25d org. & multi.	25	10

2nd Arab Youth Festival.

Coil Stamps
Redrawn Type of 1973
Without "LAR"

1975, Aug. 15 Photo. *Perf. 14½x14*

575	A124	5d bl., org. & black	10	5
576	"	20d bl., yel. & black	20	5
577	"	50d bl., grn. & black	65	5

1975, Aug. 23 *Perf. 13x12½*

578	A166	10d salmon & multi.	12	5
579	"	25d lilac & multi.	30	5
580	"	50d yellow & multi.	60	10

7th Mediterranean Games, Algiers, Aug. 23–Sept. 6.

Peace Dove, Symbols of Agriculture and Industry
A167

al-Qadhafi's Head over Desert
A168

Design: 70d, Peace dove (different design).

1975, Sept. Litho. *Perf. 13x12½*

581	A167	25d multicolored	20	5
582	"	70d "	70	12

Souvenir Sheet

Litho. & Embossed *Imperf.*

583	A168	100d multicolored	1.75	1.75

6th anniversary of Sept. 1 revolution. No. 583 contains one stamp with simulated perforations; coats of arms and inscriptions in margin. Size: 120x81mm.

Khalil Basha Mosque
A169

Al Kharruba Mosque
A170

Mosques: 10d, Sidi Abdulla El Shaab. 15d, Sidi Ali El Fergani. 25d, Katikhtha. 30d, Murad Agha. 35d, Maulai Mohammed.

1975, Dec. 13 Litho. *Perf. 12½*

584	A169	5d gray & multi.	5	5
585	"	10d purple & multi.	7	5
586	"	15d green & multi.	12	5
587	A170	20d ocher & multi.	15	5
588	"	25d multicolored	20	5
589	"	30d "	25	6
590	"	35d lilac & multi.	27	7
		Nos. 584-590 (7)	1.11	38

Mohammed's 1405th birthday.

Arms of Libya and People
A171

Islamic-Christian Dialogue Emblem
A172

1976, Jan. 15 Photo. *Perf. 13*

591	A171	35d blue & multi.	25	5
592	"	40d multicolored	32	7

General National (People's) Congress.

1976, Feb. 5 Litho. *Perf. 13x12½*

593	A172	40d gold & multi.	25	5
594	"	115d " "	65	13

Seminar of Islamic-Christian Dialogue, Tripoli, Feb. 1–5.

Woman Blowing Horn
A173

National Costumes: 20d, Lancer. 30d, Drummer. 40d, Bagpiper. 100d, Woman carrying jug on head.

1976, Mar. 1 Litho. *Perf. 13x12½*

595	A173	10d multicolored	10	5
596	"	20d "	20	5
597	"	30d pink & multi.	30	5
598	"	40d multicolored	40	7
599	"	100d yel. & multi.	1.00	17
		Nos. 595-599 (5)	2.00	39

14th Tripoli International Fair.

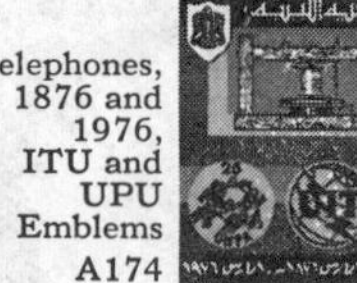

Telephones, 1876 and 1976, ITU and UPU Emblems
A174

Design: 70d, Alexander Graham Bell, telephone, satellites, radar, ITU and UPU emblems.

1976, Mar. 10 Photo. *Perf. 13*

600	A174	40d multicolored	1.00	10
		a. Souvenir sheet	4.00	4.00
601	A174	70d multicolored	1.75	18
		a. Souvenir sheet	6.00	6.00

Centenary of first telephone call by Alexander Graham Bell, Mar. 10, 1876. No. 600a contains 4 No. 600, No. 601a 4 No. 601; multicolored margins showing satellites, radar and emblems. Size: 120x 100mm.

Mother and Child
A175

Hands, Eye and Head
A176

1976, Mar. 21 *Perf. 12*

602	A175	85d gray & multi.	50	15
603	"	110d pink & multi.	65	20

International Children's Day.

1976, Apr. 7 Photo. *Perf. 13½x13*

604	A176	30d multicolored	18	6
605	"	35d "	20	7
606	"	40d "	25	8

World Health Day: "Foresight prevents blindness."

Little Bittern
A177

Birds of Libya: 10d, Great gray shrike. 15d, Songbird. 20d, European bee-eater (vert.). 25d, Hoopoe.

Perf. 13x13½, 13½x13

1976, May 1 Lithographed

607	A177	5d orange & multi.	20	3
608	"	10d ultra. & multi.	40	5
609	"	15d rose & multi.	60	8
610	A177	20d yellow & multi.	80	1
611	"	25d blue & multi.	1.00	1
		Nos. 607-611 (5)	3.00	4

Al Barambekh
A178

Bicycling
A179

Designs: 15d, Whale (horiz.). 30 Lizard (alwaral) (horiz.). 40d, Mastodo skull (horiz.). 70d, Hawk. 115d, Wi mountain sheep.

1976, June 20 Litho. *Perf. 12*

612	A178	10d multicolored	8	
613	"	15d "	12	
614	"	30d "	25	
615	"	40d "	32	
616	"	70d "	55	
617	"	115d "	95	
		Nos. 612-617 (6)	2.27	

Museum of Natural History.

1976, July 17 Litho. *Perf. 12x11*

Designs (Montreal Olympic Emblem and 25d, Boxing. 70d, Soccer. 150d, Vario sports, symbolic.

Granite Paper

618	A179	15d multicolored	10	
619	"	25d "	17	
620	"	70d tan & multi.	50	1

Souvenir Sheet

621	A179	150d multicolored	*9.00*	9.

21st Olympic Games, Montreal, Canad July 17–Aug. 1. No. 621 contains or stamp, black inscription and carmine Mo treal Olympic emblems in margin. Siz 120x78mm.

Tree Growing from Globe
A180

Symbols of Agriculture and Industry
A181

Drummer and Pipeline—A182

1976, Aug. 9 *Perf. 1.*

622	A180	115d multicolored	60	2

5th Conference of Non-Aligned Countries Colombo, Sri Lanka, Aug. 9–19. Multi ple coat of arms printed on back in pal green beneath gum.

1976, Sept. 1 *Perf. 14½x1*

623	A181	30d yel. & multi.	12	
624	"	40d multicolored	18	
625	"	100d "	45	1

Souvenir Sheet
Perf. 13

626 A182 200d multicolored 2.00 2.00

7th anniversary of Sept. 1 Revolution. Size of No. 626: 120x80mm. Nos. 623–626 have multiple coat of arms printed on back in pale green beneath gum.

Sports, Torch and Emblems
A183

Chess Board, Rook, Knight, Emblem
A184

Design: 145d, Symbolic wrestlers and various emblems (horiz.).

1976, Oct. 6 Litho. *Perf. 13*

627	A183	15d multicolored	8	5
628	"	30d "	15	5
629	"	100d "	50	12

Souvenir Sheet

630 A183 145d multicolored 1.25 1.25

5th Arab Games, Damascus, Syria. No. 630 has multicolored marginal inscriptions and emblems. Size: 121x80mm. Nos. 627–630 have multiple coat of arms printed on back in pale green beneath gum.

1976, Oct. 24 Photo. *Perf. 11½*

631	A184	15d pink & multi.	25	5
632	"	30d buff & multi.	55	6
633	"	100d multicolored	1.75	18

The "Against" (protest) Chess Olympiad, Tripoli, Oct. 24–Nov. 15.

A185

Designs: Various local flowers.

1976, Nov. 1 Photo. *Perf. 11½*

Granite Paper

634	A185	15d lilac & multi.	15	5
635	"	20d multicolored	20	5
636	"	35d yel. & multi.	35	5
637	"	40d sal. & multi.	40	5
638	"	70d multicolored	70	6
		Nos. 634-638 (5)	1.80	26

International Archives Council Emblem and Document—A186

1976, Nov. 10 Litho. *Perf. 13x13½*

639	A186	15d brown, orange & buff	10	5
640	"	35d brn., brt. green & buff	22	5
641	A186	70d brown, blue & buff	45	10

Arab Regional Branch of International Council on Archives, Baghdad.

Holy Kaaba and Pilgrims
A187

Numeral
A188

1976, Dec. 12 Litho. *Perf. 14*

642	A187	15d multicolored	6	5
643	"	30d "	12	5
644	"	70d "	28	6
645	"	100d "	40	10

Pilgrimage to Mecca.

Coil Stamps

1977, Jan. 15 Photo. *Perf. 14½x14*

646	A188	5d multicolored	4	3
647	"	20d "	16	5
648	"	50d "	40	10

Covered Basket
A189

Designs: 20d, Leather bag. 30d, Vase. 40d, Embroidered slippers. 50d, Ornate saddle. 100d, Horse with saddle and harness.

1977, Mar. 1 Litho. *Perf. 12½x12*

649	A189	10d multicolored	8	5
650	"	20d "	16	8
651	"	30d "	24	12
652	"	40d "	32	17
653	"	50d "	40	20
		Nos. 649-653 (5)	1.20	62

Souvenir Sheet
Imperf.

654 A189 100d multicolored 1.00 1.00

15th Tripoli International Fair. No. 654 contains one stamp (49x53mm.) with simulated perforations. Multicolored margin shows pair of pistols. Size: 140x100 mm. Nos. 649–654 have multiple coat of arms printed on back in pale green beneath gum.

Girl and Flowers, UNICEF Emblem
A190

Children's Drawings and UNICEF Emblem: 30d, Clothing store. 40d, Farm yard.

1977, Mar. 28 Litho. *Perf. 13x13½*

655	A190	10d multicolored	8	5
656	"	30d "	25	12
657	"	40d "	32	17

Children's Day.

Gun, Fighters, U.N. Headquarters
A191

1977, Mar. 13 *Perf. 13½*

658	A191	15d multicolored	12	6
659	"	25d "	20	10
660	"	70d "	56	28

Battle of Al-Karamah, 9th anniversary.

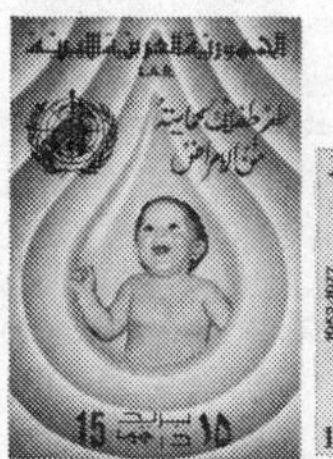

Child, Raindrop, WHO Emblem
A192

APU Emblem
A193

1977, Apr. 7 Litho. *Perf. 13x12½*

661	A192	15d multicolored	12	6
662	"	30d "	25	12

World Health Day.

Nos. 661–662 have multiple coat of arms printed on back in pale green beneath gum.

1977, Apr. 12 *Perf. 13½*

663	A193	15d multicolored	12	6
664	"	30d "	25	12
665	"	40d "	32	16

Arab Postal Union, 25th anniversary.

Maps of Africa and Libya—A194

1977, May 8 Litho. *Perf. 14x13½*

666	A194	40d multicolored	32	17
667	"	70d "	58	30

African Labor Day 1977.

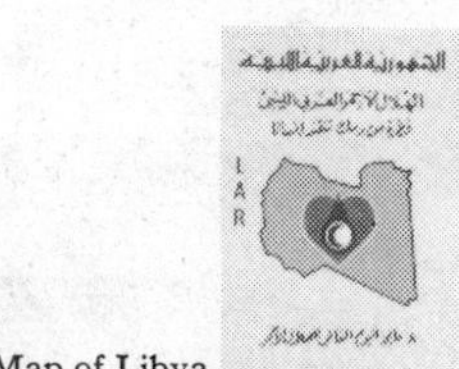

Map of Libya and Heart
A195

1977, May 10 *Perf. 14½x14*

668	A195	5d multicolored	4	3
669	"	10d "	8	5
670	"	30d "	25	12

Libyan Red Crescent Society. Nos. 668–670 have multiple coat of arms printed on back in pale green beneath gum.

Electronic Tree, ITU Emblem, Satellite and Radar
A196

Designs (Electronic Tree, ITU Emblem and): 115d, Communications satellite, Montreal Olympics emblem, boxer on TV screen. 200d, Spacecraft over earth. 300d, Solar system.

1977, May 17 Litho. *Perf. 13½x13*

671	A196	60d multicolored	50	25
672	"	115d "	92	45
673	"	200d "	1.60	80

Souvenir Sheet

674 A196 300d multicolored 2.50 2.50

9th World Telecommunications Day. No. 674 contains one stamp (size: 52x35mm.); multicolored margin shows observatory, satellite, emblems and Olympic runner. Size: 118x88mm.

Plane over Tripoli, Messenger
A197

Designs (UPU Emblem and): 25d, Concorde, messenger on horseback. 150d, Loading transport plane and messenger riding camel. 300d, Graf Zeppelin LZ127 over Tripoli.

1977, May 17 Litho. *Perf. 13½*

675	A197	20d multicolored	16	8
676	"	25d "	20	10
677	"	150d "	1.20	60

Souvenir Sheet

678 A197 300d multicolored

Centenary (in 1974) of the Universal Postal Union. No. 678 contains one stamp (52x35mm.); multicolored margin shows various means of transportation. Size: 119x90mm.

Mosque
A198

Designs: Various Mosques. 50d, 100d, vertical.

1977, June 1 Photo. *Perf. 14*

679	A198	40d multicolored	32	17
680	"	50d "	40	20
681	"	70d "	56	28
682	"	90d "	72	37
683	"	100d "	80	40
684	"	115d "	92	45
		Nos. 679-684 (6)	3.72	1.87

Archbishop Capucci, Map of Palestine
A199

1977, Aug. 18 Litho. *Perf. 13½*

687	A199	30d multicolored	25	12
688	"	40d "	32	17
689	"	115d "	92	45

Palestinian Archbishop Hilarion Capucci, jailed by Israel in 1974.

Raised Hands, Pylons, Wheel, Buildings
A200

Star and Ornament
A201

1977, Sept. 1 Litho. *Perf. 13½x12½*

690	A200 15d multicolored		12	6
691	" 30d	"	25	12
692	" 85d	"	68	35

Souvenir Sheet

Perf. 12½

693	A201 100d gold & multi.	80	80

8th anniversary of Sept. 1 Revolution. No. 693 contains one stamp; light green margin with black inscription and multicolored daisy and rose. Size: 120x80mm. Nos. 690–693 have multiple coat of arms printed on back in pale green beneath gum.

Soccer—A202

Designs (Games' Emblem and): 5d, Swimmers (vert.). 15d, Soccer (vert.). 25d, Table tennis. 40d, Basketball (vert.).

1977, Oct. 8 *Perf. 13½*

694	A202 5d multicolored		4	3
695	" 10d	"	8	5
696	" 15d	"	12	6
697	" 25d	"	20	10
698	" 40d	"	32	17
	Nos. 694–698 (5)		76	41

7th Arab School Games.

Steeplechase
A203

Designs (Show Emblem and): 10d, Bedouin on horseback. 15d, Show emblem (Horse and "7"; vert.). 45d, Steeplechase. 100d, Hurdles. 115d, Bedouins on horseback.

1977, Oct. 10 *Perf. 14½*

699	A203 5d multicolored		4	3
700	" 10d	"	8	6
701	" 15d	"	12	6
702	" 45d	"	38	20
703	" 115d	"	92	45
	Nos. 699–703 (5)		1.54	80

Souvenir Sheet

704	A203 100d multicolored	80	80

7th International Turf Championships, Tripoli, Oct. 1977. No. 704 contains one stamp; multicolored margin with soldier on horseback and coat of arms. Size: 124x 83mm.

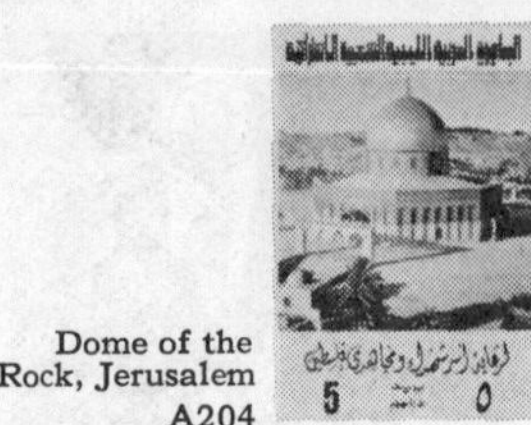

Dome of the Rock, Jerusalem
A204

1977, Oct. 14 *Perf. 14½x14*

705	A204 5d multicolored		4	3
706	" 10d	"	8	5

Palestinian fighters and their families.

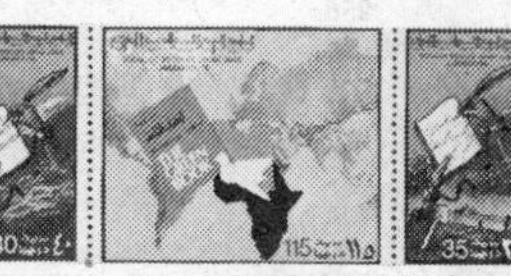

"The Green Book"—A205

Designs: 35d, Hands with broken chain holding hook over citadel. 40d, Hands above chaos. 115d, Dove and Green Book rising from Africa, world map.

1977 Litho. *Perf. 14*

707	A205 Strip of 3	1.65	1.65
	a. 35d multicolored	28	
	b. 40d "	32	
	c. 115d "	92	

The Green Book, by Muammar al Qadhafi outlines Libyan democracy. Green descriptive inscription on back beneath gum, in English on 35d, French on 40d, Arabic on 115d.

Emblems
A206

1977 *Perf. 12½x13*

708	A206 5d multicolored		4	3
709	" 15d	"	12	6
710	" 30d	"	25	12

Standardization Day.
Nos. 708–710 have multiple coat of arms printed on back in pale green beneath gum.

Crocodile and Young
A207

Rock Carvings, Wadi Mathendous, c. 8000 B.C.: 15d, Elephant hunt. 20d, Giraffe (vert.). 30d, Antelope. 40d, Trumpeting elephant.

1978, Jan. 1 *Perf. 12½x13, 13x12½*

711	A207 10d multicolored		8	5
712	" 15d	"	12	6
713	" 20d	"	16	8
714	" 30d	"	25	12
715	" 40d	"	32	17
	Nos. 711–715 (5)		93	48

Silver Pendant
A208

Emblem, Compass and Lightning
A209

Silver Jewelry: 10d, Ornamental plate. 20d, Necklace with pendants. 25d, Crescent-shaped brooch. 115d, Armband.

1978, Mar. 1 Litho. *Perf. 13x12½*

716	A208 5d multicolored		4	3
717	" 10d	"	8	5
718	" 20d	"	16	8
719	" 25d	"	20	10
720	" 115d	"	92	45
	Nos. 716–720 (5)		1.40	71

Tripoli International Fair.

1978, Mar. 10 *Perf. 13½*

721	A209 30d multicolored		25	12
722	" 115d	"	92	45

Arab Cultural Education Organization.

Bride and Attendants
A210

Designs: Children's drawings and UNESCO emblem.

1978, Mar. 21 Multicolored

723	A210 40d *Dancing*	32	16
724	" 40d *Children with posters*	32	16
725	" 40d *Shopping street*	32	16
726	" 40d *Playground*	32	16
727	" 40d *shown*	32	16
	Nos. 723–727 (5)	1.60	80

Children's Day. Nos. 723–727 printed se-tenant.

Clenched Fist, Made of Bricks
A211

1978, Mar. 22

728	A211 30d multicolored		25	12
729	" 115d	"	92	45

Determination of Arab people.

Blood Pressure Gauge, WHO Emblem
A212

1978, Apr. 7 *Perf. 13x12½*

730	A212 30d multicolored		25	12
731	" 115d	"	92	45

World Health Day, drive against hypertension.

Antenna and ITU Emblem
A213

1978, May 17 Photo. *Perf. 13½*

732	A213 30d silver & multi.	25	12
733	" 115d gold & multi.	92	45

10th World Telecommunications Day.

Games Emblem
A214

1978, July 13 Litho. *Perf. 12½*

734	A214 15d multicolored		12	[illegible]
735	" 30d	"	25	12
736	" 115d	"	92	45

3rd African Games, Algiers, 1978.

Tripoli International Airport—A215

Design: 115d, Terminal.

1978, Aug. 10 Litho. *Perf. 13½*

737	A215 40d multicolored		32	[illegible]
738	" 115d	"	92	[illegible]

Inauguration of Tripoli International Airport.

View of Ankara
A216

Soldiers, Jet, Ship
A217

1978, Aug. 17

739	A216 30d multicolored		25	[illegible]
740	" 35d	"	30	[illegible]
741	" 115d	"	92	[illegible]

Turkish-Libyan friendship.

1978, Sept. 1 *Perf. 14½*

Designs: 35d, Tower, Green Book, oil derrick. 100d, View of Tripoli with mosque and modern buildings. 115d, View of Tripoli within cogwheel.

742	A217 30d multicolored	25	[illegible]
743	" 35d org. & multi.	30	[illegible]
744	" 115d blue & multi.	92	[illegible]

Souvenir Sheet

745	A217 100d multicolored	95	[illegible]

9th anniversary of Sept. 1 Revolution. No. 745 contains one stamp (50x41mm.) Lilac, black and red margin. Size: 116x 91mm.

Quarry and Symposium Emblem
A218

Designs: 40d, Oasis lake. 115d, Crater

1978, Sept. 16 *Perf. 13½*

746	A218	30d multicolored		25	12
747	"	40d	"	32	15
748	"	115d	"	92	45

2nd Symposium on Libyan Geology.

Green Book and Three Races
A219

1978, Oct. 18 *Perf. 12½*

749	A219	30d multicolored		25	12
750	"	40d	"	32	15
751	"	115d	"	92	45

International Anti-Apartheid Year. Nos. 749–751 have multiple coat of arms printed on back in pale green beneath gum.

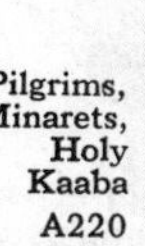

Pilgrims, Minarets, Holy Kaaba
A220

1978, Nov. 9 Photo. *Perf. 12*

752	A220	5d multicolored		4	3
753	"	10d	"	8	5
754	"	15d	"	12	6
755	"	20d	"	16	8

Pilgrimage to Mecca.

Handclasp over Globe
A221

1978, Nov. 10 Litho. *Perf. 13½*

756	A221	30d multicolored		25	12
757	"	40d	"	32	15
758	"	115d	"	92	45

Technical Cooperation Among Developing Countries Conference, Buenos Aires, Argentina, Sept. 1978.

Fists, Guns, Map of Israel
A222

Scales, Globe and Human Rights Flame
A223

Designs: 40d, 115d, Map of Arab countries and Israel, eagle and crowd (horiz.). 145d, like 30d.

1978, Dec. 5 Litho. *Perf. 13½*

759	A222	30d multicolored		25	12
760	"	40d	"	32	16
761	"	115d	"	92	45
762	"	145d	"	1.12	55

Anti-Israel Summit Conference, Baghdad, Dec. 2–8.

1978, Dec. 10

763	A223	15d multicolored		12	6
764	"	30d	"	25	12
765	"	115d	"	92	45

Universal Declaration of Human Rights, 30th anniversary.

Libyan Fort and Horse Racing
A224

1978, Dec. 11

766	A224	20d multicolored		16	8
767	"	40d	"	32	16
768	"	115d	"	92	45

Libyan Study Center.

Lilienthal's Glider, 1896
A225

Designs: 25d, Spirit of St. Louis, 1927. 30d, Adm. Byrd's Polar flight, 1929. 50d, Graf Zeppelin, 1934, hydroplane and storks. 115d, Wilbur and Orville Wright and Flyer A. No. 774, Icarus falling. No. 775, Eagle and Boeing 727.

1978, Dec. 26 Litho. *Perf. 14*

769	A225	20d multicolored		16	8
770	"	25d	"	20	10
771	"	30d	"	25	12
772	"	50d	"	40	20
773	"	115d	"	92	45
		Nos. 769–773 (5)		1.93	95

Souvenir Sheets

774	A225	100d multicolored		80	80
775	"	100d	"	80	80

75th anniversary of 1st powered flight. Nos. 769–773 issued also in sheets of 4 with black marginal inscription and blue border. Size: 105x128mm. Nos. 774–775 have multicolored margins showing various aircraft. Size: 96x102mm.

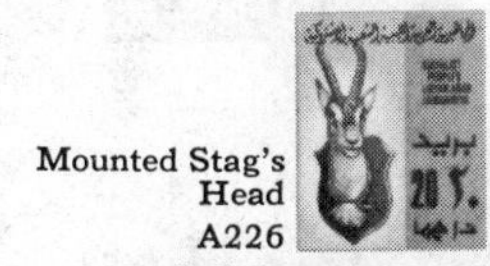

Mounted Stag's Head
A226

Coil Stamps

1979, Jan. 15 Photo. *Perf. 14½x14*

776	A226	5d multicolored		4	3
777	"	20d	"	16	8
778	"	50d	"	40	20

SEMI-POSTAL STAMPS.

Many issues of Italy and Italian Colonies include one or more semipostal denominations. To avoid splitting sets, these issues are generally listed as regular postage, semipostals or airmails, etc.

Semi-Postal Stamps of Italy Overprinted **LIBIA**

Wmkd. Crown. (140)

1915-16 *Perf. 14.*

B1 SP1 10c+5c rose 50 75
B2 SP2 15c+5c slate 2.75 3.00
B3 " 20c+5c orange 75 1.10

No. B2 with Additional Surcharge **20**

1916, Mar.

B4 SP2 20c on 15c+5c slate 2.75 3.00

View of Port, Tripoli
SP1

Designs: B5, B6, View of port, Tripoli. B7, B8, Arch of Marcus Aurelius. B9, B10, View of Tripoli.

1927, Feb. 15 **Lithographed**

B5 SP1 20c+5c brown violet & black 70 1.25
B6 " 25c+5c blue green & black 70 1.25
B7 " 40c+10c black brown & black 70 1.25
B8 " 60c+10c orange brown & black 70 1.25
B9 " 75c+20c red & black 70 1.25
B10 " 1.25 l+20c blue & black 14.00 18.50
Nos. B5-B10 (6) 17.50 24.75

First Sample Fair, Tripoli. Surtax aided fair. See also Nos. EB1-EB2.

View of Tripoli
SP2

Knights of Malta Castle
SP3

Designs: 50c+20c, Date palm. 1.25 l+20c, Camel riders. 2.55 l+50c, View of Tripoli. 5 l+1 l, Traction well.

1928, Feb. 20 *Perf. 14* **Wmk. 140**

B11 SP2 30c+20c maroon & black 1.20 1.85
B12 " 50c+20c blue green & black 1.20 1.85
B13 " 1.25 l+20c red & blk. 1.20 1.85
B14 SP3 1.75 l+20c blue & black 1.20 1.85
B15 " 2.55 l+50c brown & black 1.50 2.40
B16 " 5 l+1 l purple & black 3.25 5.00
Nos. B11-B16 (6) 9.55 14.80

Issued in connection with the Second Sample Fair, Tripoli, 1928. The surtax was for the aid of the Fair.

Olive Tree
SP4

Herding
SP5

Designs: 50c+20c, Dorcas gazelle. 1.25 l+20c, Peach blossoms. 2.55 l+50c, Camel caravan. 5 l+1 l, Oasis with date palms.

1929, Apr. 7

B17 SP4 30c+20c maroon & black 3.75 6.25
B18 " 50c+20c blue grn. & black 3.75 6.25
B19 " 1.25 l+20c scarlet & black 3.75 6.25
B20 SP5 1.75 l+20c blue & black 3.75 6.25
B21 " 2.55 l+50c yellow brown & blk. 3.75 6.25
B22 " 5 l+1 l pur. & black 90.00 120.00
Nos. B17-B22 (6) 108.75 151.25

Issued in connection with the Third Sample Fair, Tripoli, 1929. The surtax was for the aid of the Fair.

Harvesting Bananas
SP6

Water Carriers
SP7

Designs: 50c, Tobacco plant. 1.25 l, Venus of Cyrene. 2.55 l+45c, Black bucks. 5 l+1 l, Motor and camel transportation. 10 l+2 l, Rome pavilion.

1930, Feb. 20 **Photogravure**

B23 SP6 30c dark brown 90 1.25
B24 " 50c violet 90 1.25
B25 " 1.25 l deep blue 90 1.25
B26 SP7 1.75 l+20c scarlet 1.20 1.85
B27 " 2.55 l+45c dp. grn. 9.00 9.00
B28 " 5 l+1 l dp. org. 4.00 6.00
B29 " 10 l+2 l dark violet 12.00 16.00
Nos. B23-B29 (7) 28.90 36.60

Issued in connection with the Fourth Sample Fair at Tripoli, 1930. The surtax was for the aid of the Fair.

Statue of Ephebus
SP8

Exhibition Pavilion
SP9

Designs: 25c, Arab musician. 50c, View of Zeughet. 1.25 l, Snake charmer. 1.75 l+25c, Windmill. 2.75 l+45c, "Zaptie." 5 l+1 l, Mounted Arab.

1931, Mar. 8

B30 SP8 10c black brown 1.20 1.85
B31 " 25c green 1.20 1.85
B32 " 50c purple 1.20 1.85
B33 " 1.25 l blue 1.20 1.85
B34 " 1.75 l+25c car. rose 1.85 3.00
B35 " 2.75 l+45c orange 1.85 3.00
B36 SP8 5 l+1 l dull violet 7.25 11.00
B37 SP9 10 l+2 l brown 27.50 37.50
Nos. B30-B37 (8) 43.25 61.90

Fifth Sample Fair, Tripoli, 1931. Surtax aided fair. See also Nos. C3, EB3.

Papaya Tree
SP10

Dorcas Gazelle
SP12

Ar Tower, Mogadiscio
SP11

Designs: 10c, 50c, Papaya tree. 20c, 30c, Euphorbia abyssinica. 25c, Fig cactus. 75c, Mausoleum, Ghirza. 1.75 l+25c, Lioness. 5 l+1 l, Bedouin with camel.

1932, Mar. 8

B38 SP10 10c olive brown 1.85 2.50
B39 " 20c brown red 1.85 2.50
B40 " 25c green 1.85 2.50
B41 " 30c olive black 1.85 2.50
B42 " 50c dark violet 1.85 2.50
B43 " 75c carmine 3.00 4.25
B44 SP11 1.25 l dark blue 3.00 4.25
B45 " 1.75 l+25c olive brown 15.00 18.50
B46 " 5 l+1 l dp. bl. 19.00 24.00
B47 SP12 10 l+2 l brown violet 72.50 90.00
Nos. B38-B47 (10) 121.75 153.50

Sixth Sample Fair, Tripoli, 1932. Surtax aided fair. See also Nos. C4-C7.

Ostrich
SP13

Arab Musician
SP14

Designs: 25c, Incense plant. 30c, Arab musician. 50c, Arch of Marcus Aurelius. 1.25 l, African eagle. 5 l+1 l, Leopard. 10 l+2.50 l, Tripoli skyline and fasces.

Inscribed: "VII Fiera Campionaria."

1933, Mar. 2 **Photo.** **Wmk. 140**

B48 SP13 10c deep violet 18.50 5.50
B49 " 25c deep green 3.75 1.85
B50 SP14 30c orange brn. 2.40 1.85
B51 SP13 50c purple 3.75 1.85
B52 " 1.25 l dark blue 18.50 7.50
B53 SP14 5 l+1 l olive brown 38.50 47.50
B54 SP13 10 l+2.50 l car. 47.50 67.50
Nos. B48-B54 (7) 132.90 133.55

Seventh Sample Fair, Tripoli, 1932. Surtax aided fair. See also Nos. C8-C13.

Pomegranate Tree
SP15

Designs: 10c+10c, 20c+10c, Pomegranate tree. 50c+10c, 2 l+50c, Musician. 75c+15c, 1.25 l+25c, Tribesman.

1935, Feb. 16

B55 SP15 10c+10c brown 1.40 2.10
B56 " 20c+10c rose red 1.40 2.10
B57 " 50c+10c purple 1.40 2.10
B58 " 75c+15c carmine 1.40 2.10
B59 " 1.25 l+25c dull blue 1.40 2.10
B60 " 2 l+50c olive grn. 1.40 2.10
Nos. B55-B60 (6) 8.40 12.60

Ninth Sample Fair, Tripoli, 1935. Surtax aided fair. See also Nos. C19-C24.

AIR POST STAMPS.

Italy Nos. C3 and C5 Overprinted **Libia**

Wmkd. Crowns. (140)

1928-29 *Perf. 14*

C1 AP2 50c rose red 60 50
C2 " 80c brown violet & brown ('29) 1.50 1.90

Airplane
AP1

1931, Mar. 8 **Photo.** **Wmk. 140**

C3 AP1 50c blue 2.10 3.75

See note after No. B37.

Seaplane over Bedouin Camp
AP2

Designs: 50c, 1 l, Seaplane over Bedouin camp. 2 l+1 l, 5 l+2 l, Seaplane over Tripoli.

1932, Mar. 1 *Perf. 14*

C4 AP2 50c dark blue 1.85 2.40
C5 " 1 l orange brown 1.85 2.40
C6 " 2 l+1 l dark gray 14.00 19.00
C7 " 5 l+2 l carmine 52.50 72.50

See note after No. B47.

Seaplane Arriving at Tripoli
AP3

Designs: 50c, 2 l+50c, Seaplane arriving at Tripoli. 75c, 10 l+2.50 l, Plane over Tagiura. 1 l, 5 l+1 l, Seaplane leaving Tripoli.

1933, Mar. 1

C8 AP3 50c deep green 1.85 3.00
C9 " 75c carmine 2.50 3.75
C10 " 1 l dark blue 2.50 3.75
C11 " 2 l + 50c purple 6.00 9.00
C12 " 5 l + 1 l org. brn. 16.50 25.00
C13 " 10 l + 2.50 l gray black 16.50 25.00
Nos. C8-C13 (6) 45.85 69.50

See note after No. B54.

Seaplane over Tripoli Harbor
AP4

Airplane and Camel
AP5

Designs: 50c, 5 l+1 l, Seaplane over Tripoli harbor. 75c, 10 l+2 l, Plane and minaret.

1934, Feb. 17 Photo. Wmk. 140

C14 AP4 50c slate blue 1.50 2.50
C15 " 75c red orange 1.50 2.50
C16 " 5 l+1 l deep grn. 30.00 50.00
C17 " 10 l+2 l dull vio. 30.00 50.00
C18 AP5 25 l+3 l org. brn. 40.00 60.00
Nos. C14–C18 (5) 103.00 165.00

Eighth Sample Fair, Tripoli. Surtax aided fair. See also Nos. CE1–CE2.

Plane and Ancient Tower
AP6

Camel Train—AP7

Designs: 25c+10c, 3 l+1.50 l, Plane and ancient tower. 50c+10c, 2 l+30c, Camel train. 1 l+25c, 10 l+5 l, Arab watching plane.

1935, Apr. 12

C19 AP6 25c+10c green 75 1.25
C20 AP7 50c+10c slate blue 75 1.25
C21 " 1 l+25c blue 75 1.25
C22 " 2 l+30c rose red 75 1.25
C23 AP6 3 l+1.50 l brown 75 1.25
C24 AP7 10 l+5 l dull vio. 15.00 25.00
Nos. C19–C24 (6) 18.75 31.25

See note after No. B60.

Cyrenaica No. C6
Overprinted in Black **LIBIA**

1936, Oct.

C25 AP2 50c purple 25 7

Same on Tripolitania Nos. C8 and C12.

1937

C26 AP1 50c rose carmine 18 6
C27 AP2 1 l deep blue 42 18

See also Nos. C45–C50.

Ruins of Odeon Theater, Sabrata
AP8

1937, Mar. 15 Photogravure.

C28 AP8 50c dark violet 90 1.00
C29 " 1 l violet black 90 1.50

Issued in commemoration of the opening of a coastal road to the Egyptian frontier.

Nos. C28-C29 Overprinted
"XI FIERA DI TRIPOLI".

1937, Mar. 15

C30 AP8 50c dark violet 3.00 4.25
C31 " 1 l violet black 3.00 4.25

11th Sample Fair, Tripoli.

View of Tripoli
AP9

Eagle Attacking Serpent
AP10

1938, Mar. 12 *Perf. 14*

C32 AP9 50c dark olive green 60 60
C33 " 1 l slate blue 90 1.25

12th Sample Fair, Tripoli.

1938, Apr. 25 Wmk. 140

C34 AP10 50c olive brown 50 42
C35 " 1 l brown violet 60 70

Issued to commemorate the bimillenary of the birth of Augustus Caesar (Octavianus), first Roman emperor.

Arab and Camel
AP11

Design: 50c, Fair entrance.

1939, Apr. 12 Photogravure.

C36 AP11 25c green 25 38
C37 " 50c olive brown 25 38
C38 " 1 l rose violet 38 50

13th Sample Fair, Tripoli.

Plane Over Modern City
AP12

Design: 1 l, 5 l+2.50 l, Plane over oasis.

1940, June 3

C39 AP12 50c brown black 38 50
C40 " 1 l brown violet 38 50
C41 " 2 l+75c indigo 55 75
C42 " 5 l+2.50 l copper brown 55 75

Triennial Overseas Exposition, Naples.

Hitler, Mussolini and Inscription "Two Peoples, One War"
AP13

1941, Apr. 24

C43 AP13 50c slate green 30 5.00

Issued to commemorate the Rome - Berlin Axis.

Cyrenaica No. C9
Overprinted in Black **LIBIA**

1941

C44 AP3 1 l black 1.20 1.90

Same Overprint on Tripolitania
Nos. C9–C11, C13–C15.

C45 AP1 60c red orange 30 50
C46 " 75c deep blue 30 50
C47 " 80c dull violet 30 50
C48 AP2 1.20 l dark brown 30 50
C49 " 1.50 l orange red 30 50
C50 " 5 l green 55 1.00
Nos. C44–C50 (7) 3.25 5.40

United Kingdom of Libya

ICY Type of Regular Issue
Perf. 14½x14

1965, Jan. 1 Litho. Unwmkd.

C51 A60 50m dp. lilac & gold 1.00 1.00
a. Souv. sheet 2.50 2.50

Issued to publicize the United Nations International Cooperation Year. No. C51a contains one stamp. Dark blue margin and gold inscription. Size: 101x76mm. Sheet exists imperf.; same price.

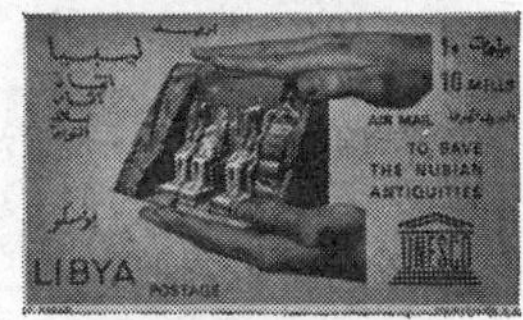

Hands Holding Facade of Abu Simbel—AP14

1966, Jan. 1 Photo. *Perf 11½*
Granite Paper

C52 AP14 10m bis. & dk. brn. 12 5
a. Souv. sheet 1.20 1.20
C53 " 15m gray green & dark brown 25 12
a. Souv. sheet 1.20 1.20
C54 " 40m dull salmon & dark brown 50 42
a. Souv. sheet 3.00 1.80

Issued to publicize the UNESCO world campaign to save historic monuments in Nubia. Each souvenir sheet contains four stamps of identical denomination. Marginal inscription in color of stamp background. Size: 125x87½mm.

WHO Headquarters, Geneva
AP15

Unwmkd.

1966, May 3 Litho. *Perf. 10x10½*

C55 AP15 20m blk., yel. & bl. 12 12
C56 " 50m black, yellow green & red 25 25
C57 " 65m black, salmon & brn. red 50 38

Issued to commemorate the inauguration of the World Health Organization Headquarters, Geneva.

Flag and Globe
AP16

1966, Oct. 1 Photo. *Perf. 11½*
Granite Paper

C58 AP16 25m multicolored 18 12
C59 " 60m " 38 30
C60 " 85m gray & multi. 60 50

Issued to commemorate the first anniversary of the inauguration of Kingdom of Libya Airlines.

AIR POST SPECIAL DELIVERY STAMPS.

APSD1

Photogravure.

1934, Feb. 17 *Perf. 14* Wmk. 140

CE1 APSD1 2.25 l olive blk. 15.00 22.50
CE2 " 4.50 l+1 l gray black 15.00 22.50

Issued in connection with the Eighth Sample Fair at Tripoli. The surtax was for the aid of the Fair.

SPECIAL DELIVERY STAMPS

Special Delivery Stamps of Italy
Overprinted **Libia**

Wmkd. Crowns. (140)

1915, Nov. *Perf. 14*

E1 SD1 25c rose red 3.25 2.10
E2 SD2 30c blue & rose 2.10 2.75

"Italia"
SD3

1921-23 Engraved. *Perf. 13½.*

E3 SD3 30c blue & rose 75 90
E4 " 50c rose red & brn 1.00 1.35
E5 " 60c dark red & brown ('23) 1.75 2.10
E6 " 2 l dark blue & red ('23) 3.25 3.75

Special Delivery Stamps
of 1915 Surcharged:

a b

1922, June 1

E7 SD1 (*a*) 60c on 25c rose red 2.10 2.40
E8 SD2 (*b*) 1.60 l on 30c blue & rose 3.25 4.25

Special Delivery Stamps of 1923
Surcharged in Dark Blue or Red:

70 ٧٠
c
2,50 ٢,٥٠
d

1926, July

E9 SD3 (*c*) 70c on 60c dark red & brown (Bl) 1.75 2.10
E10 " (*d*) 2.50 l on 2 l dk. bl. & red (R) 3.25 3.75

Special Delivery Stamps of 1923
Surcharged in Blue or Red:

LIRE
1,25

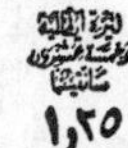

1927–36 *Perf. 11*

E11 SD3 1.25 l on 60c dark red & brn. (Bl) 1.50 30
a. Perf. 14 ('36) 12.00 1.25
b. Black surch. 20,000.00 1500.00
E12 " 2.50 l on 2 l dk. blue & red (R) 18.50 25.00

United Kingdom of Libya

Zuela Saracen Castle
SD4

Lithographed

1966, Feb. 10 *Perf. 11½* **Unwmkd.**

E13 SD4 90m carmine rose & light green 1.00 70

Coat of Arms of Libya and "POLIGRAFICA & CARTEVALORI—NAPLES" printed on back in yellow green.

SEMI-POSTAL SPECIAL DELIVERY STAMPS.

Camel Caravan
SPSD1

Lithographed.

1927, Feb. 15 *Perf. 14* **Wmk. 140**

EB1 SPSD1 1.25 l+30c purple & black 5.50 6.75
EB2 " 2.50 l+1 l yellow & black 6.75 8.00

See note after No. B10.
No. EB2 is inscribed "EXPRES".

War Memorial
SPSD2

1931, Mar. 8 Photogravure

EB3 SPSD2 1.25 l+20c carmine rose 4.25 6.00

See note after No. B37.

AUTHORIZED DELIVERY STAMPS

Italy No. EY1 Overprinted in Black **LIBIA**

Wmkd. Crown. (140)

1929, May 11 *Perf. 14*

EY1 AD1 10c dull blue 8.00 8.00
a. Perf. 11 42.50 45.00

Italy No. EY2 Overprinted in Black **LIBIA**

1941, May *Perf. 14*

EY2 AD2 10c dark brown 2.40 2.40

A variety of No. EY2, with larger "LIBIA" and yellow gum, was prepared in 1942, but not issued. Price 35 cents.

AD1

1942 Litho. **Wmk. 140**

EY3 AD1 10c sepia 20

No. EY3 was not issued.

POSTAGE DUE STAMPS.

Italian Postage Due Stamps, 1870-1903 Overprinted in Black **Libia**

Wmkd. Crown. (140)

1915, Nov. *Perf. 14*

J1 D3 5c buff & magenta 30 42
J2 " 10c " " 38 50
J3 " 20c buff & magenta 60 90
a. Double overprint 25.00 25.00
b. Inverted overprint 35.00 35.00
J4 D3 30c buff & magenta 60 90
J5 " 40c " " 60 90
a. "40" in black 1250.00
J6 " 50c buff & magenta 60 90
J7 " 60c " " 95 1.20
J8 " 1 l blue & magenta 75 40
a. Double ovpt. 1250.00
J9 " 2 l blue & magenta 9.00 11.00
J10 " 5 l " " 11.50 13.50
Nos. J1-J10 (10) 25.28 30.62

1926

J11 D3 60c buff & brown 18.50 27.50

Postage Due Stamps of Italy, 1934, Overprinted in Black **LIBIA**

1934

J12 D6 5c brown 25 30
J13 " 10c blue 25 30
J14 " 20c rose red 38 30
J15 " 25c green 38 38
J16 " 30c red orange 50 55
J17 " 40c black brown 50 55
J18 " 50c violet 60 25
J19 " 60c black 60 75
J20 D7 1 l red orange 60 25
J21 " 2 l green 8.50 1.85
J22 " 5 l violet 25.00 7.50
J23 " 10 l blue 3.00 4.75
J24 " 20 l carmine 3.00 6.00
Nos. J12-J24 (13) 43.56 23.73

In 1942 a set of 11 "Segnatasse" stamps, picturing a camel and rider and inscribed "LIBIA," was prepared but not issued. Price, $4.

United Kingdom of Libya

Postage Due Stamps of Cyrenaica, 1950 Surcharged in Black

-- ليبيا --
٢ ليرة ع.

2 MAL. LIBYA

For Use in Tripolitania.

1951 *Perf. 12½* **Unwmkd.**

J25 D1 1 mal on 2m dk. brn. 6.50 6.50
J26 " 2 mal on 4m dp. grn. 2.25 2.25
J27 " 4 mal on 8m scarlet 8.00 8.00
J28 " 10 mal on 20m orange yellow 16.50 16.50
a. Arabic '20' for '10' 375.00
J29 " 20 mal on 40m deep blue 27.50 27.50
Nos. J25-J29 (5) 60.75 60.75

ليبيا

Cyrenaica Nos. J1-J7 Overprinted in Black

LIBYA

For Use in Cyrenaica.

Overprint 13mm. High.

1952 *Perf. 12½.* **Unwmkd.**

J30 D1 2m dark brown 5.00 5.00
J31 " 4m deep green 5.00 5.00
J32 " 8m scarlet 5.50 5.50
J33 " 10m vermilion 6.75 7.25
J34 " 20m orange yellow 11.00 11.00
J35 " 40m deep blue 22.50 25.00
J36 " 100m dark gray 32.50 35.00
Nos. J30-J36 (7) 88.25 93.75

D1

Castle at Tripoli
D2

1952 Lithographed *Perf. 11½*

J37 D1 2m chocolate 25 25
J38 " 5m blue green 1.20 60
J39 " 10m carmine 2.25 1.00
J40 " 50m violet blue 7.00 3.25

1964, Feb. 1 Photo. *Perf. 14*

J41 D2 2m red brown 25 25
J42 " 6m Prussian green 25 25
J43 " 10m rose red 25 25
J44 " 50m bright blue 75 75

Men in Boat, Birds, Mosaic
D3

Ancient Mosaics: 10d, Head of Medusa. 20d, Peacock. 50d, Fish.

1976, Nov. 15 Litho. *Perf. 14*

J45 D3 5d bister & multi. 4 4
J46 " 10d orange & multi. 8 5
J47 " 20d blue & multi. 15 8
J48 " 50d emerald & multi. 35 17

Nos. J45-J48 have multiple coat of arms printed on back in pale green beneath gum.

OFFICIAL STAMPS.

United Kingdom of Libya

Nos. 135-142 Overprinted in Black

رسمي

Official

1952 *Perf. 11½.* **Unwmkd.**

O1 A27 2m yellow brown 50 40
O2 " 4m gray 50 40
O3 " 5m blue green 3.50 2.50
O4 " 8m vermilion 1.50 1.25
O5 " 10m purple 3.50 2.00
O6 " 12m lilac rose 7.50 4.00
O7 " 20m deep blue 10.00 7.50
O8 " 25m chocolate 13.00 12.00
Nos. O1-O8 (8) 40.00 30.05

PARCEL POST STAMPS.

These stamps were used by affixing them to the way bill so that one half remained on it following the parcel, the other half staying on the receipt given the sender. Most used halves are right halves. Complete stamps were obtainable canceled, probably to order.

Both unused and used prices are for complete stamps.

Italian Parcel Post Stamps, 1914-22, Overprinted **LIBIA**

1915-24 *Perf. 13½* **Wmk. 140**

Q1 PP2 5c brown 38 50
a. Double ovpt. 25.00
Q2 " 10c deep blue 38 50
Q3 " 20c black ('18) 38 50
Q4 " 25c red 60 80
Q5 " 50c orange 1.20 1.50
Q6 " 1 l violet 60 80
Q7 " 2 l green 1.20 1.50
Q8 " 3 l bistre 1.20 1.50
Q9 " 4 l slate 1.20 1.50
Q10 " 10 l rose lilac ('24) 21.50 27.50
Q11 " 12 l red brn. ('24) 30.00 37.50
Q12 " 15 l olive grn. ('24) 30.00 37.50
Q13 " 20 l brn. vio. ('24) 35.00 42.50
Nos. Q1-Q13 (13) 123.64 154.10

Same Overprint on Parcel Post Stamps of Italy, 1927-36.

1927-38

Q14 PP3 10c deep blue ('36) 1.20 1.85
Q15 " 25c red ('36) 90 1.20
Q16 " 30c ultramarine ('29) 18 30
Q17 PP3 50c orange 100.00 115.00
a. Ovpt. 8 3/4x2mm. ('31) 90.00 100.00
Q18 " 60c red ('29) 25 38
Q19 " 1 l lilac ('36) 18.50 25.00
Q20 " 2 l green ('38) 18.50 25.00
Q21 " 3 l bistre 37 60
Q22 " 4 l gray 37 60
Q23 " 10 l rose lilac ('36) 72.50 90.00
Q24 " 20 l brown violet ('36) 72.50 90.00
Nos. Q14-Q24 (11) 285.27 349.93

On No. Q17 the overprint measures 10x1½mm.

Same Overprint on Italy No. Q24.

1939

Q25 PP3 5c brown *11,000.00*

The overprint was applied to the 5c in error. Few copies exist.

OCCUPATION STAMPS.

Issued under French Occupation.

Stamps of Italy and Libya were overprinted in 1943: "FEZZAN Occupation Française" and "R. F. FEZZAN" for use in this region when General Leclerc's forces first occupied it.

Fezzan-Ghadames.

Sebha Fort—OS1

Mosque and Fort Turc Murzuch—OS2

Map of Fezzan-Ghadames, Soldier and Camel—OS3

Engraved.

1946		*Perf. 13*	Unwmkd.	
N1	OS1	10c black	18	25
N2	"	50c rose	18	25
N3	"	1fr brown	18	25
N4	"	1.50fr green	18	25
N5	"	2fr ultramarine	18	25
N6	OS2	2.50fr violet	18	25
N7	"	3fr rose carmine	18	25
N8	"	5fr chocolate	18	25
N9	"	6fr dark green	25	30
N10	"	10fr blue	30	38
N11	OS3	15fr violet	42	50
N12	"	20fr red	50	55
N13	"	25fr sepia	60	65
N14	"	40fr dark green	70	80
N15	"	50fr deep blue	85	1.00
		Nos. N1-N15 (15)	5.06	6.18

Fezzan.

Monument, Djerma Oasis
OS1

Tombs of the Beni-Khettab
OS2

Well at Gorda—OS3

Col. Colonna d'Ornano and Fort at Murzuch
OS4

Philippe F. M. de Hautecloque (Gen. Jacques Leclerc)
OS5

Engraved.

1949		*Perf. 13*	Unwmkd.	
2N1	OS1	1fr black	25	30
2N2	"	2fr lilac pink	25	30
2N3	OS2	4fr red brown	50	60
2N4	"	5fr emerald	50	60
2N5	OS3	8fr blue	50	60
2N6	"	10fr brown	1.25	1.50
2N7	"	12fr dark green	2.75	3.25
2N8	OS4	15fr salmon red	2.75	3.25
2N9	"	20fr brown black	1.25	1.50
2N10	OS5	25fr dark blue	1.25	1.50
2N11	"	50fr copper red	2.25	2.50
		Nos. 2N1-2N11 (11)	13.50	15.90

Camel Raising
OS6

Agriculture—OS7

Well Drilling
OS8

Ahmed Bey
OS9

1951				
2N12	OS6	30c brown	20	25
2N13	"	1fr deep blue	30	35
2N14	"	2fr rose carmine	30	35
2N15	OS7	4fr red	30	35
2N16	"	5fr green	30	35
2N17	"	8fr deep blue	40	50
2N18	OS8	10fr sepia	1.50	1.75
2N19	"	12fr deep green	1.50	1.75
2N20	"	15fr bright red	2.50	3.00
2N21	OS9	20fr black brown & violet brn.	2.50	3.00
2N22	"	25fr dark blue & blue	1.50	1.75
2N23	"	50fr indigo & brown orange	2.75	2.75
		Nos. 2N12-2N23 (12)	14.05	16.15

OCCUPATION SEMI-POSTAL STAMPS.

"The Unhappy Ones"
OSP1 OSP2

Engraved.

1950		*Perf. 13*	Unwmkd.	
2NB1	OSP1	15fr+5fr red brown	2.10	2.10
2NB2	OSP2	25fr+5fr blue	2.10	2.10

The surtax was for charitable works.

OCCUPATION AIR POST STAMPS.

Airport in Fezzan—OAP1

Plane over Fezzan
OAP2

Engraved.

1948		*Perf. 13*	Unwmkd.	
2NC1	OAP1	100fr red	2.50	2.75
2NC2	OAP2	200fr indigo	4.50	5.00

Oasis—OAP3

Murzuch—OAP4

1951				
2NC3	OAP3	100fr dark blue	3.50	4.00
2NC4	OAP4	200fr vermilion	5.50	6.00

OCCUPATION POSTAGE DUE STAMPS.

Oasis of Brak
D1

Engraved.

1950		*Perf. 13.*	Unwmkd.	
2NJ1	D1	1fr brown black	33	45
2NJ2	"	2fr deep green	33	45
2NJ3	"	3fr red brown	55	65
2NJ4	"	5fr purple	55	65
2NJ5	"	10fr red	1.65	2.00
2NJ6	"	20fr deep blue	4.00	4.25
		Nos. 2NJ1-2NJ6 (6)	7.41	8.45

Ghadames.

Cross of Agadem
OS1

Engraved.

1949		*Perf. 13*	Unwmkd.	
3N1	OS1	4fr sepia & red brown	50	60
3N2	"	5fr peacock blue & dark green	50	60
3N3	"	8fr sepia & orange brown	1.50	1.75
3N4	"	10fr black & dark ultramarine	1.50	1.75
3N5	"	12fr vio. & red violet	6.00	6.50
3N6	"	15fr brown & red brown	4.00	4.50
3N7	"	20fr sepia & emerald	4.00	3.50
3N8	"	25fr sepia & blue	4.00	4.50
		Nos. 3N1-3N8 (8)	22.00	23.70

OCCUPATION AIR POST STAMPS.

Cross of Agadem
OAP1

Engraved.

1949		*Perf. 13*	Unwmkd.	
3NC1	OAP1	50fr purple & rose	7.50	8.50
3NC2	"	100fr sepia & pur. brown	10.00	11.00

LIECHTENSTEIN

(lĭk'tĕn·shtīn)

LOCATION — In central Europe southeast of Lake Constance, between Austria and Switzerland.

GOVT.—Principality.

AREA—62 sq. mi.

POP.—24,169 (1976).

CAPITAL—Vaduz.

The Principality of Liechtenstein is a sovereign state consisting of the two counties of Schellenberg and Vaduz. Since 1921 the post office has been administered by Switzerland.

100 Heller = 1 Krone

100 Rappen = 1 Franc (1921)

Austrian Administration of the Post Office.

Prince Johann II

A1

Typographed.

1912 *Perf. 12½x13* **Unwmkd.**

Thick Chalky Paper.

1 A1 5h yellow green 8.00 4.50
2 " 10h rose 60.00 4.50
3 " 25h dark blue 60.00 25.00

1915

Thin Unsurfaced Paper

1a A1 5h yellow green 5.00 5.50
2a " 10h rose 40.00 11.00
3a " 25h dark blue 325.00 100.00
 b. 25h ultramarine 275.00 325.00

Coat of Arms — A2 Prince Johann II — A3

1917–18

4 A2 3h violet 75 90
5 " 5h yellow green 75 90
6 A3 10h claret 75 90
7 " 15h dull red 75 90
8 " 20h dark green 75 90
9 " 25h deep blue 75 90
 Nos. 4-9 (6) 4.50 5.40

Exist imperf.

Prince Johann II

A4

1918

Dates in Upper Corners.

10 A4 20h dark green 90 1.10

Commemorative of the sixtieth anniversary of the accession of Prince Johann II. Exists imperf.

National Administration of the Post Office.

Stamps of 1917–18 Overprinted or Surcharged:

a

b

c

1920

11 A2 (*a*) 5h yellow green 2.50 5.50
 a. Inverted overprint 60.00
 b. Dbl. ovpt. 22.50 55.00
12 A3 (") 10h claret 2.50 5.50
 a. Inverted overprint 60.00
 b. Double overprint 22.50 55.00
 c. Overprint type "c" 16.50 110.00
13 " (") 25h deep blue 2.50 5.50
 a. Inverted overprint 60.00
 b. Dbl. ovpt. 27.50 55.00
14 A2 (*b*) 40h on 3h violet 2.50 5.50
 a. Inverted surcharge 60.00
15 A3 (*c*) 1k on 15h dull red 2.50 5.50
 a. Inverted surcharge 60.00
 b. Overprint type "a" 60.00 225.00
16 " (") 2½k on 20h dark green 2.50 5.50
 a. Inverted surcharge 60.00
 Nos. 11-16 (6) 15.00 33.00

Coat of Arms — A5 Chapel of St. Mamertus — A6

Coat of Arms with Supporters

A15

Designs: 40h, Gutenberg Castle. 50h, Courtyard, Vaduz Castle. 60h, Red Tower, Vaduz. 80h, Old Roman Tower, Schaan. 1k, Castle at Vaduz. 2k, View of Bendern. 5k, Prince Johann I. 7½k, Prince Johann II.

1920 **Engraved.** ***Imperf.***

18 A5 5h olive bistre 15 15
19 " 10h deep orange 15 15
20 " 15h dark blue 15 15
21 " 20h deep brown 15 15
22 " 25h dark green 15 15
23 " 30h gray black 15 15
24 " 40h dark red 15 15
25 A6 1k blue 15 15

Perf. 12½.

32 A5 5h olive bistre 20 25
33 " 10h deep orange 20 25
34 " 15h deep blue 20 25
35 " 20h red brown 20 25
36 A6 25h olive green 20 25
37 A5 30h dark gray 20 25
38 A6 40h claret 20 25
39 " 50h yellow green 20 25
40 " 60h red brown 20 25
41 " 80h rose 20 25
42 " 1k dull violet 20 25
43 " 2k light blue 30 45
44 " 5k black 35 45
45 " 7½k slate 35 45
46 A15 10k ochre 35 45
 Nos. 18-46 (23) 4.75 5.75

Used prices for Nos. 18-46 are for cancelled to order stamps.

Many denominations of Nos. 32-46 are found imperforate, imperforate vertically and imperforate horizontally.

Madonna and Child

A16

1920, Oct. 5

47 A16 50h olive green 35 1.10
 a. Imperf., pair 6.50
48 " 80h brown red 35 1.10
 a. Imperf., pair 6.50
49 " 2k dark blue 35 1.10
 a. Imperf., pair 6.50

80th birthday of Prince Johann II.

Swiss Administration of the Post Office.

Coat of Arms

A17 A18

Engraved.

1921 ***Imperf.*** **Unwmkd.**

51 A17 2rp on 10h dp. org. 1.10 11.00
 a. Double surch. 40.00 110.00
 b. Inverted surcharge 40.00 110.00
 c. Double surch., one inverted 40.00 110.00
52 A18 2rp on 10h dp. org. 25 13.00
 a. Double surch. 40.00 110.00
 b. Inverted " 40.00 110.00
 c. Double surcharge, one inverted 40.00 110.00

Arms with Supporters — A19 Chapel of St. Mamertus — A20

Castle at Vaduz

A21

View of Bendern

A22

Prince Johann II

A23

Old Roman Tower at Schaan

A24

Gutenberg Castle

A25

Red Tower at Vaduz

A26

View of Vaduz

A27

Surface Tinted Paper (#54–61)

1921 ***Perf. 12½***

54 A19 2rp lemon, perf. 9½ 85 7.25
55 " 2½rp black 75 6.50
 a. Perf. 9½ 1.10 40.00
56 " 3rp orange 90 6.50
 a. Perf. 9½ 120.00 3250.00
57 " 5rp olive green 6.00 65
 a. Perf. 9½ 40.00 11.00
58 " 7½rp dark blue 6.00 22.50
 a. Perf. 9½ 150.00 950.00
59 " 10rp yellow green, perf. 9½ 30.00 3.00
 a. Perf. 12½ 37.50 3.75
60 " 13rp brown 6.00 60.00
 a. Perf. 9½ 60.00 1500.00
61 " 15rp dark violet, perf. 9½ 7.50 5.50
 a. Perf. 12½ 11.00 12.00
62 A20 20rp dull violet & black 72.50 1.35
63 A21 25rp rose red & black 2.50 1.65
64 A22 30rp deep green & black 85.00 10.00
65 A23 35rp brown & black, *straw* 3.25 5.50
66 A24 40rp dk. blue & black 1.90 1.90
67 A25 50rp dk. grn. & black 2.50 1.90
68 A26 80rp gray & black 11.00 47.50
69 A27 1fr deep claret & black 13.50 21.00
 Nos. 54-69 (16) 250.15 202.70

Nos. 54–69 exist imperforate; Nos. 54–61, partly perforated. See Nos. 73, 81.

Stamps of 1921 Surcharged in Red **10**

1924

70 A19 5rp on 7½rp dark blue, perf. 12½ 2.25 1.65
 a. Perf. 9½ 9.50 4.25

71 A19 10rp on 13rp brown, perf. 9½ 75 1.10

a. Perf. 12½ 13.50 27.50

Type of 1921.

Wmk. 183

Wmkd. Greek Cross. (183)

1924 Granite Paper ***Perf. 11½***

73 A19 10rp green 11.00 75

Peasant A28

Courtyard, Vaduz Castle A29

Government Palace and Church at Vaduz A30

1924-28 Typographed ***Perf. 11½.***

74 A28 2½rp olive green & red violet ('28) 2.25 4.50

75 " 5rp brown & blue 2.50 1.00

76 " 7½rp blue green & brown ('28) 1.65 4.50

77 " 15rp red brown & blue grn. ('28) 6.50 22.50

Engraved.

78 A29 10rp yellow green 3.50 1.00

79 " 20rp deep red 30.00 1.00

80 A30 1½fr blue 75.00 90.00

Nos. 74-80 (7) 121.40 124.50

1925 Bendern Type of 1921

81 A22 30rp blue & black 11.00 1.00

Prince Johann II A31

Prince Johann II as Boy and Man A32

1928, Nov. 12 Typo. **Wmk. 183**

82 A31 10rp light brown & olive green 2.25 3.75

83 " 20rp orange red & olive green 5.50 7.00

84 " 30rp slate blue & olive green 27.50 25.00

85 " 60rp red violet & olive green 60.00 70.00

Engraved.

Unwmkd.

86 A32 1.20fr ultramarine 70.00 110.00

87 " 1.50fr black brown 100.00 190.00

88 " 2fr dp. carmine 100.00 150.00

89 " 5fr dark green 100.00 200.00

Nos.82-89 (8) 465.25 755.75

Issued to commemorate the 70th year of the reign of Prince Johann II.

Prince Francis I, as a Child A33

Prince Francis I as a Man A34

Princess Elsa A35

Prince Francis and Princess Elsa A36

1929, Dec. 2 Photogravure

90 A33 10rp olive green 75 3.50

91 A34 20rp carmine 1.25 4.00

92 A35 30rp ultramarine 2.00 9.50

93 A36 70rp brown 17.50 100.00

Issued in commemoration of the accession of Prince Francis I, February 11, 1929.

Grape Girl A37

Chamois Hunter A38

Mountain Cattle A39

Courtyard, Vaduz Castle A40

Mt. Naafkopf A41

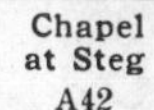

Chapel at Steg A42

Rofenberg Chapel A43

Chapel of St. Mamertus A44

Alpine Hotel, Malbun A45

Gutenberg Castle A46

Schellenberg Monastery A47

Castle at Vaduz A48

Mountain Cottage A49

Prince Francis and Princess Elsa A50

Perf. 10½, 11½, 11½x10½

1930

94 A37 3rp brown lake 90 1.10

95 A38 5rp deep green 1.10 85

96 A39 10rp dark violet 1.25 70

a. Perf. 11½x10½ 6.25 20.00

97 A40 20rp deep rose red 20.00 90

98 A41 25rp black 7.00 19.00

a. Perf. 11½ 75.00 240.00

99 A42 30rp deep ultra. 3.85 1.25

a. Perf. 11½x10½ 625.00 1500.00

100 A43 35rp dark green 3.85 10.00

a. Perf. 11½ 3000.00 5000.00

101 A44 40rp light brown 4.25 3.25

102 A45 50rp black brown 45.00 16.50

a. Perf. 11½ 55.00 120.00

103 A46 60rp olive black 45.00 16.50

104 A47 90rp violet brown 62.50 80.00

105 A48 1.20fr olive brown 57.50 110.00

a. Perf. 11½x10½ 1650.00 3250.00

106 A49 1.50fr black violet 32.50 42.50

107 A50 2fr gray green & red brown 50.00 85.00

a. Perf. 11½x10½ 1250.00 3250.00

Nos. 94-107 (14) 334.70 387.55

Mt. Naafkopf A51

Gutenberg Castle A52

Vaduz Castle A53

1933, Jan. 23 ***Perf. 14½.***

108 A51 25rp red orange 135.00 55.00

109 A52 90rp dark green 11.00 55.00

110 A53 1.20fr red brown 115.00 225.00

Prince Francis I

A54 A55

1933, Aug. 28 ***Perf. 11***

111 A54 10rp purple 25.00 32.50

112 " 20rp brown car. 25.00 32.50

113 " 30rp dark blue 25.00 32.50

80th birthday of Prince Francis I.

1933, Dec. 15 **Engr.** ***Perf. 12½.***

114 A55 3fr violet blue 150.00 225.00

See also No. 152.

Agricultural Exhibition Issue.

Souvenir Sheet.

Arms of Liechtenstein—A56

Granite Paper.

1934, Sept. 29 ***Perf. 12.***

115 A56 5fr brown 2750.00 4000.00

Sheet size: approximately 104x126mm. See No. 131.

Coat of Arms A57

"Three Sisters" (Landmark) A58

Church of Schaan A59

Bendern A60

Rathaus, Vaduz A61

Samina Valley A62

Samina Valley in Winter
A63

Ruin at Schellenberg
A64

Government Palace
A65

Vaduz Castle—A66

Vaduz Castle—A67

Gutenberg Castle—A68

Alpine Hut—A69

Valüna—A70

Princess Elsa—A71

Coat of Arms
A71a

Perf. 11½, 11x11½, 12½.

1934-35 Photogravure.

116	A57	3rp copper red	27	33
117	A58	5rp emerald	1.10	33
118	A59	10rp deep violet	55	33
119	A60	15rp red orange ('35)	70	1.00
120	A61	20rp red ('35)	1.10	33
121	A62	25rp brown ('35)	19.00	25.00
122	A63	30rp dk. blue ('35)	1.65	85
123	A64	35rp gray grn. ('35)	1.10	1.90
124	A65	40rp brown ('35)	1.10	1.90
125	A66	50rp light brown	15.00	10.00
126	A67	60rp claret	1.20	*2.75*
127	A68	90rp deep green	3.25	*8.00*
128	A69	1.20fr deep blue	2.25	*8.00*
129	A70	1.50fr brn. car. ('35)	2.75	*13.50*
		Nos. 116-129 (14)	51.02	*74.22*

Engraved.

130	A71	2fr henna brown ('35)	110.00	190.00
131	A71a	5fr dk. vio. ('35)	750.00	1200.00

No. 131 has the same design as the 5fr in the souvenir sheet, No. 115. See Nos. 226, B14.

Labor Issue

Bridge at Malbun—A72

Constructing Road to Triesenberg—A73

Binnen Canal—A74

Bridge near Planken
A75

1937, June 30 Photogravure

132	A72	10rp bright violet	80	95
133	A73	20rp red	80	95
134	A74	30rp bright blue	1.35	1.65
135	A75	50rp yellow brown	1.35	1.90

Ruin at Schalun
A76

Chapel at Masescha
A77

Knight and Vaduz Castle
A78

Upper Valüna Valley
A79

Wooden Bridge over Rhine, Bendern
A80

Chapel at Steg
A81

Peasant in Rhine Valley
A82

Ruin at Schellenberg
A84

Knight and Gutenberg Castle
A85

Baron von Brandis and Vaduz Castle
A86

"The Three Sisters"
A87

Frontier Stone—A88

Gutenberg Castle and Harpist
A89

Alpine View of Lawena and Schwartzhorn
A90

1937-38

136	A76	3rp yellow brown	18	33
		Pale Buff Shading		
137	A77	5rp emerald	18	22
138	A78	10rp violet	18	15
139	A79	15rp dark slate green	38	65
140	A80	20rp brown orange	38	27
141	A81	25rp chestnut	1.20	1.20
142	A82	30rp blue & gray	1.20	55
144	A84	40rp dark green	1.10	1.90
145	A85	50rp dark brown	1.20	1.90
146	A86	60rp dp. claret ('38)	1.50	1.90
147	A87	90rp gray vio. ('38)	10.00	6.50
148	A88	1fr red brown	2.50	4.25
149	A89	1.20fr dp. brn. ('38)	12.00	18.50
150	A90	1.50fr slate blue ('38)	2.75	*15.00*
		Nos. 136-150 (14)	34.75	*53.32*

Souvenir Sheet.

Josef Rheinberger— A91

1938, July 30 Engraved *Perf. 12.*

151	A91	50(rp) slate gray, sheet of 4	19.00	19.00
		a. Single stamp	3.25	3.25

Issued in connection with the Third Philatelic Exhibition of Liechtenstein. Sheet size: 99¾x135mm.

Francis Type of 1933.
Thick Wove Paper.

1938, Aug. 15 *Perf. 12½*

152	A55	3fr black, *buff*	18.50	*85.00*

Issued in memory of Prince Francis I, who died July 25, 1938. Sheets of 20.

Josef Rheinberger
A92

1939, Mar. 31

153 A92 50(rp) slate green 1.00 3.00

Issued to commemorate the centenary of the birth of Josef Gabriel Rheinberger (1839–1901), German composer and organist. Issued in sheets of 20.

Scene of Homage, 1718
A93

1939, May 29

154 A93 20rp brown lake 1.10 1.90
155 " 30rp slate blue 1.10 1.90
156 " 50rp gray green 1.10 1.90

Issued to honor Prince Franz Joseph II. Sheets of 20.

Cantonal Coats of Arms
A94

Arms of Principality
A95

Prince Franz Joseph II
A96

1939

157 A94 2fr dark green, *buff* 9.00 32.50
158 A95 3fr indigo, *buff* 9.00 32.50
159 A96 5fr brown, *buff* 17.50 27.50
Sheet of 4 75.00 115.00

Nos. 157–158 issued in sheets of 12; No. 159 in sheets of 4.

Prince Johann as a Child
A97

Prince Johann and Tower at Vaduz
A98

Prince Johann and Gutenberg Castle—A99

Prince Johann in 1920 and Vaduz Castle
A100

Memorial Tablet—A101

Prince Johann II
A102

1940 Photo. *Perf. 11½.*

160 A97 20rp henna brown 65 3.50
161 A98 30rp indigo 1.00 5.50
162 A99 50rp dk. slate grn. 2.25 7.50
163 A100 1fr brown violet 12.50 42.50
164 A101 1.50fr violet black 9.00 37.50
165 A102 3fr brown 7.50 22.50
Nos. 160–165 (6) 32.90 119.00

Birth centenary of Prince Johann II. Nos. 160–164 issued in sheets of 25; No. 165 in sheets of 12.

Issue dates: 3fr, Oct. 5; others Aug. 10.

Gathering Corn—A103

Wine Press—A104

Sharpening Scythe—A105

Milkmaid and Cow—A106

Native Costume
A107

1941, Apr. 7

166 A103 10(rp) dull red brown 38 55
167 A104 20(rp) lake 75 1.10
168 A105 30(rp) royal blue 75 1.35
169 A106 50(rp) myrtle green 3.50 8.00
170 A107 90(rp) deep claret 3.50 16.50
Nos. 166–170 (5) 8.88 27.50

Madonna and Child
A108

1941, July 7 Engraved

171 A108 10fr brn. carmine 110.00 175.00

Issued in sheets of 4.

Johann Adam Andreas
A109

Wenzel
A110

Anton Florian
A111

Joseph Adam
A112

1941, Dec. 18 Photogravure

172 A109 20rp brn. carmine 55 65
173 A110 30rp royal blue 55 2.25
174 A111 100rp violet black 2.25 10.00
175 A112 150rp slate green 2.75 12.00

Saint Lucius—A113

Reconstruction of Vaduz Castle
A114

Signing the Treaty of May 3, 1342
A115

Battle of Gutenberg—A116

Scene of Homage, 1718
A117

1942, Apr. 22 Engraved *Perf. 11½*

176 A113 20(rp) brn. org., *buff* 1.90 80
177 A114 30(rp) steel bl., *buff* 1.90 2.50
178 A115 50(rp) dark olive green, *buff* 3.75 6.50
179 A116 1fr dull brn., *buff* 3.75 11.00
180 A117 2fr violet black, *buff* 3.75 12.00
Nos. 176–180 (5) 15.05 32.80

Issued in commemoration of the 600th anniversary of the separation of Liechtenstein from the House of Monfort.

Johann Karl
A118

Franz Joseph I
A119

Alois I
A120

Johann I
A121

1942, Oct. 5 Photogravure.

181 A118 20rp rose 38 1.10
182 A119 30rp bright blue 70 1.65
183 A120 1fr rose lilac 2.25 13.50
184 A121 1.50fr deep brown 2.25 13.50

Prince Franz Joseph II
A122

Countess Georgina von Wilczek
A123

Prince and Princess—A124

1943, Mar. 5

185 A122 10(rp) dp. rose vio. 90 1.35

186 A123 20(rp) henna brown 90 1.35
187 A124 30(rp) slate blue 90 1.35

Issued to commemorate the marriage of Prince Franz Joseph II and Countess Georgina von Wilczek.

Prince Alois II A125 — Prince Johann II A126

Prince Franz Joseph I A127 — Prince Franz Joseph II A128

Photogravure.

1943, July 5 *Perf. 11½.* Unwmkd.

188 A125 20rp copper brown 38 55
189 A126 30rp deep ultra. 70 1.10
190 A127 100rp olive gray 2.00 *9.00*
191 A128 150rp slate green 2.00 *9.00*

Sheets of 20.

Terrain before Reclaiming—A129

Draining the Canal—A130

Plowing Reclaimed Land—A131

Harvesting Crops
A132

1943, Sept. 6

192 A129 10(rp) violet black 32 55
193 A130 30(rp) deep blue 65 *3.25*
194 A131 50(rp) slate green 1.35 *5.00*
195 A132 2fr olive brown 2.75 *11.00*

Vaduz A133 — Gutenberg A134

1943, Dec. 27

196 A133 10(rp) dark gray 60 50
197 A134 20(rp) chestnut brown 85 1.00

Planken A135 — Bendern A136

Designs: 10rp, Triesen. 15rp, Ruggell. 20rp, Vaduz. 25rp, Triesenberg. 30rp, Schaan. 40rp, Balzers. 50rp, Mauren. 60rp, Schellenberg. 90rp, Eschen. 1fr, Vaduz Castle. 120rp, Valuna Valley. 150rp, Lawena.

1944–45

198 A135 3(rp) dark brown & buff 18 32
199 A136 5(rp) slate green & buff 18 18
200 " 10(rp) gray & buff ('45) 38 10
201 " 15(rp) blue gray & buff ('45) 38 *1.00*
202 " 20(rp) orange red & buff 38 28
203 " 25(rp) dark rose violet & buff 38 *1.20*
204 " 30(rp) blue & buff 38 28
205 " 40(rp) brown & buff ('45) 80 1.35
206 " 50(rp) bluish black & pale gray ('45) 80 2.25
207 " 60(rp) green & buff ('45) 3.25 3.25
208 " 90(rp) olive green & buff ('45) 4.00 4.50
209 " 1fr deep claret & buff ('45) 3.25 4.00
210 " 120rp red brown 4.00 4.50
211 " 150rp royal blue 3.50 4.50
Nos. 198-211 (14) 21.86 27.71

See also No. 239.

Crown and Rose
A149

1945, Apr. 9

212 A149 20rp multicolored 1.10 1.35
213 " 30rp " 1.10 2.25
214 " 1fr " 1.40 *8.00*

Issued to commemorate the birth of Prince Johann Adam Pius, Feb. 14, 1945. Sheets of 20.

Prince Franz Joseph II A150 — Princess Georgina A151

Arms of Liechtenstein and Vaduz Castle—A152

1944–45 Photogravure

215 A150 2fr brown, *buff* 7.00 *12.00*
216 A151 3fr dark green 6.00 *12.00*

Engraved.

217 A152 5fr blue gray, *cream* ('45) 12.00 *25.00*

Nos. 215–217 were issued in sheets of 8. See also Nos. 222, 259–260.

Saint Lucius A153

1946, Mar. 14 *Perf. 11½* Unwmkd.

218 A153 10fr gray black, *cream* 32.50 40.00
Sheet of four 140.00 170.00

Issued in sheets measuring 105x130mm.

Red Deer A154 — Varying Hare A155

Capercaillie
A156

1946, Dec. 10 Photogravure

219 A154 20rp henna brown 1.85 2.50
220 A155 30rp greenish bl. 1.85 3.00
221 A156 150rp olive brown 5.00 *14.00*

Arms Type of 1945.

1947, Mar. 20 Engraved

222 A152 5fr henna brown, *cream* 13.00 *32.50*

Issued in sheets of 8.

Chamois A157 — Alpine Marmot A158

Golden Eagle
A159

1947, Oct. 15 Photo. Unwmkd.

223 A157 20rp henna brown 2.75 3.50
224 A158 30rp greenish bl. 2.75 4.50
225 A159 150rp dark brown 3.50 *11.50*

Elsa Type of 1935.

1947, Dec. 10 Engraved *Perf. 14½*

226 A71 2fr black, *yellowish* 3.25 *15.00*

Issued in memory of Princess Elsa, who died Sept. 28, 1947. Sheets of 20.

Portrait of Ginevra dei Benci by Leonardo da Vinci
A160

Designs: 20rp, Girl, Rubens. 30rp, Self-portrait, Rembrandt. 40rp, Canon, Massys. 50rp, Madonna, Memling. 60rp, French Painter, 1456, Fouquet. 80rp, Lute Player, Gentileschi. 90rp, Man, Strigel. 120rp, Man, Raphael.

1949, Mar. 15 Photo. *Perf. 11½*

227 A160 10rp dark green 70 55
228 " 20rp henna brown 70 55
229 " 30rp sepia 2.35 3.25
230 " 40rp blue 3.75 80
231 " 50rp violet 6.50 7.50
232 " 60rp greenish gray 7.25 7.50
233 " 80rp brown orange 4.50 5.50
234 " 90rp olive bistre 6.25 6.00
235 " 120rp claret 4.50 6.50
Nos. 227-235 (9) 36.50 38.15

Issued in sheets of 12.
See No. 238.

No. 198 Surcharged with New Value and Bars in Dark Brown.

1949, Apr. 14

236 A135 5rp on 3(rp) dark brown & buff 35 45

Map, Post Horn and Crown
A161

1949, May 23

237 A161 40(rp) bl. & indigo 3.75 6.50

Issued to commemorate the 75th anniversary of the formation of the Universal Postal Union.

Souvenir Sheet.

A162

Photogravure.

1949, Aug. 6 *Imperf.* Unwmkd.

238 A162 Sheet of three 57.50 *100.00*
a. 10(rp) dull green 13.50 20.00
b. 20(rp) lilac rose 13.50 20.00
c. 40(rp) blue 13.50 20.00

Issued to publicize the 5th Philatelic Exhibition.
Sheet measures 121½x69½mm., with marginal gray inscriptions. Sold for 3 fr.

Scenic Type of 1944

1949, Dec. 1 *Perf. 11½*

239 A136 5(rp) dark brown & buff 7.00 65

Rossauer Castle, Vienna
A163

Church at Bendern
A164

Prince Johann Adam Andreas
A165

1949, Nov. 15 Engraved *Perf. 14½*

240 A163 20rp dark violet 1.50 2.25

241 A164 40rp blue 6.00 9.00

242 A165 150rp brown red 5.00 7.50

Issued to commemorate the 250th anniversary of the purchase of the former dukedom of Schellenberg. Sheets of 20.

Roe Deer—A166

Black Grouse A167 — Badger A168

1950, Mar. 7 Photo. *Perf. 11½*

243 A166 20(rp) red brown 5.75 4.00

244 A167 30(rp) Prus. grn. 8.50 4.00

245 A168 80(rp) dark brn. 28.50 45.00

Issued in sheets of 20.

No. 237 Surcharged with New Value and Bars Obliterating Commemorative Inscriptions in Black.

1950, Nov. 7

246 A161 1fr on 40(rp) blue & indigo 21.00 *57.50*

Boy Cutting Bread
A169

Designs: 10rp, Laborer. 15rp, Cutting hay. 20rp, Harvesting corn. 25rp, Load of hay. 30rp, Wine grower. 40rp, Farmer and scythe. 50rp, Cattle raising. 60rp, Plowing. 80rp, Woman with potatoes. 90rp, Potato cultivation. 1fr, Tractor with potatoes.

Photogravure.

1951, May 3 *Perf. 11½* Unwmkd.

247 A169 5(rp) claret 42 40

248 A169 10(rp) green 65 40

249 " 15(rp) yel. brown 2.10 4.00

250 " 20(rp) olive brown 90 80

251 " 25(rp) rose brown 2.75 3.50

252 " 30(rp) greenish gray 2.10 2.25

253 " 40(rp) deep blue 3.25 4.00

254 " 50(rp) violet brn. 2.65 3.25

255 " 60(rp) brown 3.25 3.50

256 " 80(rp) henna brn. 3.25 3.25

257 " 90(rp) olive green 3.25 3.25

258 " 1fr indigo 35.00 4.00

Nos. 247-258 (12) 59.57 32.60

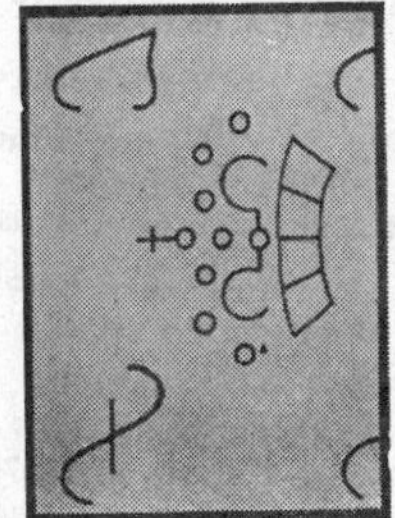

Wmk. 296

Types of 1944, Redrawn.

Wmkd. Crown and Initials. (296)

1951, Nov. 20 Engr. *Perf. 12½x12*

259 A150 2fr dark blue 18.00 *37.50*
a. Perf. 14½ 450.00 225.00

260 A151 3fr dark red brown 90.00 90.00
a. Perf. 14½ 75.00 *250.00*

Issued in sheets of 20.

Portrait, Savolodo
A170

Madonna, Botticelli
A171

Design: 40(rp) St. John, Del Sarto.

Photogravure.

1952, Mar. 27 *Perf. 11½* Unwmkd.

261 A170 20(rp) violet brn. 18.00 6.00

262 A171 30(rp) brn. olive 18.00 6.00

263 A170 40(rp) violet blue 14.00 4.25

Issued in sheets of 12.

Vaduz Castle
A172

Engraved

1952, Sept. 25 *Perf. 14½* Wmk. 296

264 A172 5fr deep green 185.00 165.00

Issued in sheets of 9.

No. 241 Surcharged with New Value and Wavy Lines in Red.

1952, Sept. 25 Unwmkd.

265 A164 1.20fr on 40(rp) bl. 27.50 45.00

Portrait of a Young Man
A173

St. Nicholas by Zeitblom
A174

Designs: 30(rp), St. Christopher by Cranach. 40(rp), Leonhard, Duke of Hag, by Kulmbach.

Photogravure.

1953, Feb. 5 *Perf. 11½* Unwmkd.

266 A173 10(rp) dark olive green 2.00 1.65

267 A174 20(rp) olive brown 6.50 3.85

268 " 30(rp) vio. brown 20.00 8.00

269 A173 40(rp) slate blue 20.00 *40.00*

Issued in sheets of 12.

Lord Baden-Powell
A175

Engraved

1953, Aug. 4 *Perf. 13x13½*

270 A175 10(rp) deep green 1.85 1.65

271 " 20(rp) dark brown 9.00 3.85

272 " 25(rp) red 12.50 25.00

273 " 40(rp) deep blue 5.50 5.50

Issued to publicize the 14th International Scout Conference. Sheets of 20.

Alemannic Disc, 600 A. D.
A176

Prehistoric Settlement of Borscht
A177

Design: 1.20fr, Rössen jug.

1953, Nov. 26 *Perf. 11½*

274 A176 10(rp) org. brown 11.00 *27.50*

275 A177 20(rp) deep gray green 11.00 16.50

276 A176 1.20fr dark blue gray 32.50 25.00

Opening of National Museum, Vaduz.

Soccer Players
A178

Designs: 20(rp), Player kicking ball. 25(rp), Goalkeeper. 40(rp), Two opposing players.

1954, May 18 Photogravure

277 A178 10(rp) dull rose & brown 2.25 2.25

278 " 20(rp) olive green 4.50 3.25

279 " 25(rp) orange brn. 12.50 25.00

280 " 40(rp) lilac gray 7.50 11.00

See also Nos. 289-292, 297-300, 308-311, 320-323.

Nos. B19-B21 Surcharged with New Value and Bars in Color of Stamp.

1954, Sept. 28 *Perf. 11½* Unwmkd.

281 SP15 35(rp) on 10rp+10rp olive green 4.50 6.75

282 SP16 60(rp) on 20rp+10rp dk. violet brn. 11.00 13.50

283 SP15 65(rp) on 40rp+10rp blue 4.50 4.00

Madonna in Wood, 14th Century
A179

1954, Dec. 16 Engraved

284 A179 20(rp) henna brn. 3.75 5.50

285 " 40(rp) gray 12.50 19.00

286 " 1fr dk. brown 12.50 19.00

Prince Franz Joseph II
A180

Princess Georgina
A181

1955, Apr. 5 *Perf. 14½*

Cream Paper

287 A180 2fr dark brown 42.50 35.00

288 A181 3fr dark green 42.50 35.00

Issued in sheets of 9.

Sports Type of 1954.

Designs: 10(rp), Slalom. 20(rp), Mountain climbing. 25(rp), Skiing. 40(rp), Resting on summit.

1955, June 14 Photo. *Perf. 11½*

289 A178 10(rp) aquamarine & brn. violet 1.10 1.00

290 " 20(rp) grn. & olive bistre 2.50 1.25

291 " 25(rp) light ultramarine & sepia 9.00 16.50

292 " 40(rp) olive & pink 7.25 6.00

Prince Johann Adam
A183

Eagle, Crown and Oak Leaves
A184

Portraits: 20(rp), Prince Philipp. 40(rp), Prince Nikolaus. 60(rp), Princess Nora.

1955, Dec. 14 **Granite Paper**

Cross in Red.

293 A183 10(rp) dull violet 70 80
294 " 20(rp) slate green 3.75 3.50
295 " 40(rp) olive brown 4.50 6.50
296 " 60(rp) rose brown 4.50 5.50

Liechtenstein Red Cross, 10th anniversary.

Sports Type of 1954.

Designs: 10rp, Javelin thrower. 20rp, Hurdling. 40rp, Pole vaulting. 1fr, Sprinters.

Photogravure.

1956, June 21 ***Perf. 11½*** **Unwmkd.**

Granite Paper.

297 A178 10rp light red brown & olive green 1.10 1.10
298 " 20rp light olive green & purple 2.50 2.50
299 " 40rp blue & violet brown 4.50 5.50
300 " 1fr orange verm. & olive brown 9.50 14.00

1956, Aug. 21 **Granite Paper**

301 A184 10rp dark brown & gold 1.85 1.35
302 " 120rp slate black & gold 3.25 4.25

150th anniversary of independence.

Prince Franz Joseph II
A185

Prince Johann Adam
A186

1956, Aug. 21

303 A185 10rp dark green 1.65 1.10
304 " 15rp bright ultra. 2.00 3.50
305 " 25rp purple 2.25 2.50
306 " 60rp dark brown 2.50 3.00

Issued to commemorate the 50th birthday of Prince Franz Joseph II.

1956, Aug. 21 **Granite Paper**

307 A186 20rp olive green 1.65 60

Issued to publicize the 6th Philatelic Exhibition, Vaduz, Aug. 25–Sept. 2. Sheets of 9.

Sports Type of 1954.

Designs: 10rp, Somersault on bar. 15rp, Jumping over vaulting horse. 25rp, Exercise on rings. 1.50fr, Somersault on parallel bars.

1957, May 14 Photo. ***Perf. 11½***

308 A178 10rp pale rose & olive green 1.50 1.65
309 " 15rp pale green & dull purple 2.50 5.50
310 " 25rp olive bistre & Prussian grn. 5.00 6.50
311 " 1.50fr lemon & sepia 11.00 16.50

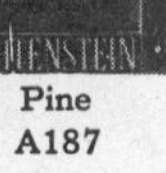

Pine
A187

Lord Baden-Powell
A188

Designs: 20rp, Wild roses. 1fr, Birches.

1957, Sept. 10 ***Perf. 11½***

Granite Paper.

312 A187 10rp dark violet 4.25 3.00
313 " 20rp brown carmine 4.25 1.35
314 " 1fr green 4.25 5.50

See also Nos. 326–328, 332–334, 353–355.

1957, Sept. 10 **Unwmkd.**

Design: 10rp, Symbolical torchlight parade.

315 A188 10rp blue black 1.50 2.25
316 " 20rp dark brown 1.50 2.25
a. Sheet of 12 25.00 32.50

Issued to commemorate the centenary of the birth of Lord Baden-Powell and the 60th anniversary of the Boy Scout movement.

No. 316a contains six each of Nos. 315–316, with Boy Scout emblems and dates in margins.

Chapel of St. Mamertus
A189

Designs: 40rp, Madonna and saints. 1.50fr, Pieta.

1957, Dec. 16 ***Perf. 11½***

317 A189 10rp dark brown 1.10 1.10
318 " 40rp dark blue 6.50 8.50
319 " 1.50fr brown lake 8.50 11.00

Issued in sheets of 20. Sheet inscribed: "Furstentum Liechtenstein" and "Weihnacht 1957" (Christmas 1957).

Sports Type of 1954.

Designs: 15rp, Girl swimmer. 30rp, Fencers. 40rp, Tennis. 90rp, Bicyclists.

1958, Mar. 18 **Photogravure**

Granite Paper.

320 A178 15rp light blue & purple 1.85 2.25
321 " 30rp pale rose lilac & olive gray 5.00 7.50
322 " 40rp salmon pink & slate blue 5.00 7.50
323 " 90rp light olive grn. & violet brn. 2.50 4.25

Relief Map of Liechtenstein
A190

1958, Mar. 18

324 A190 25rp bistre, violet & red 50 70
325 " 40rp blue, violet & red 80 1.10

World's Fair, Brussels, Apr. 17–Oct. 19. Sheets of 25, inscribed: "Furstentum Liechtenstein" and "Weltausstellung Brussel 1958."

Tree-Bush Design of 1957.

Designs: 20rp, Maples at Lawena. 50rp, Holly at Schellenberg. 90rp, Yew at Maurerberg.

1958, Aug. 12 ***Perf. 11½***

Granite Paper

326 A187 20rp chocolate 2.85 1.10
327 " 50rp olive green 5.00 5.50
328 " 90rp violet blue 2.85 3.25

Sts. Moritz and Agatha
A191

"The Good Shepherd"
A192

Designs: 35rp, St. Peter. 80rp, Chapel of St. Peter, Mals-Balzers.

1958, Dec. 14 Photo. **Unwmkd.**

Granite Paper.

329 A191 20rp dark slate grn. 4.00 3.25
330 " 35rp dark blue vio. 2.50 2.75
331 " 80rp dark brown 3.75 2.75

Issued in sheets of 20. Sheet inscribed: "Furstentum Liechtenstein" and "Weihnacht 1958" (Christmas 1958).

Tree-Bush Type of 1957.

Designs: 20rp, Larch in Lawena. 50rp, Holly on Alpila. 90rp, Linden in Schaan.

1959, Apr. 15 ***Perf. 11½***

332 A187 20rp dark violet 3.75 3.25
333 " 50rp henna brown 3.75 2.25
334 " 90rp dark green 3.75 3.25

1959, Apr. 15 **Unwmkd.**

335 A192 30rp rose violet & gold 1.00 1.50

Issued in memory of Pope Pius XII.

Flags and Rhine Valley
A193

Man Carrying Hay
A194

Apple Harvest
A195

Designs: 5rp, Church at Bendern and sheaves. 20rp, Rhine embankment. 30rp, Gutenberg Castle. 40rp, View from Schellenberg. 50rp, Vaduz Castle. 60rp, Naafkopf, Falknis Range. 75rp, Woman gathering sheaves. 90rp, Woman in vineyard. 1fr, Woman in kitchen. 1.30fr, Return from the field. 1.50fr, Family saying grace.

1959–64 **Granite Paper**

336 A193 5rp gray olive ('61) 30 10
337 " 10rp dull violet 15 5
338 " 20rp lilac rose 20 5
339 " 30rp dark red 25 10
340 " 40rp olive grn. ('61) 1.35 70
341 " 50rp deep blue 50 45
342 " 60rp bright greenish blue 70 1.00
343 A194 75rp deep ochre ('60) 1.50 1.35
344 " 80rp olive green ('61) 90 85
345 " 90rp red lilac ('61) 1.10 1.10
346 " 1fr chestnut ('61) 1.25 95
347 A195 1.20fr org. verm. ('60) 1.50 1.35
348 " 1.30fr brt. grn. ('64) 1.25 1.10
349 " 1.50fr brt. blue ('60) 1.60 1.35
Nos. 336–349 (14) 12.55 10.50

Belfry, Bendern Church
A196

Designs: 60rp, Sculpture, bell, St. Theodul's church. 1fr, Sculpture, tower of St. Lucius' church.

1959, Dec. 2 ***Perf. 11½*** **Unwmkd.**

350 A196 5rp dark slate green 75 28
351 " 60rp olive 6.50 6.50
352 " 1fr deep claret 5.00 2.50

Issued in sheets of 20 inscribed: "Furstentum Liechtenstein" and "Weihnacht 1959" (Christmas 1959).

Tree-Bush Type of 1957.

1960, Sept. 19

Designs: 20rp, Beech tree on Gafadura. 30rp, Juniper on Alpila. 50rp, Pine on Sass.

353 A187 20rp brown 3.75 3.25
354 " 30rp deep plum 3.75 3.25
355 " 50rp Prussian grn. 7.25 3.75

Europa Issue, 1960

Honeycomb
A197

1960, Sept. 19 ***Perf. 14***

356 A197 50rp multi. 120.00 75.00

Issued to promote the idea of a united Europe. Sheets of 20.

Princess Gina
A198

Heinrich von Frauenberg
A199

Portraits: 1.70fr, Prince Johann Adam Pius. 3fr, Prince Franz Joseph II.

1960–64 **Engraved** ***Perf. 14***

356A A198 1.70fr violet ('64) 2.00 1.90
b. Imperf., pair 1800.00 1800.00
357 A198 2fr dark blue 2.50 2.50
a. Imperf., pair 1800.00 2250.00
358 A198 3fr deep brown 3.75 2.75

Issued in sheets of 16.

1961–62 **Photogravure** ***Perf. 11½***

Minnesingers: 20rp, King Konradin. 25rp, Ulrich von Liechtenstein. 30rp, Kraft von Toggenburg. 35rp, Ulrich von Gutenberg. 40rp, Heinrich von Veldig. 1fr, Konrad von Alstetten. 1.50fr, Walther von der Vogelweide. 2fr, Tannhäuser. (Designs from 14th century Manesse manuscript.)

359 A199 15rp multicolored 50 55
360 " 20rp multi. ('62) 40 45
361 " 25rp multicolored 50 80
362 " 30rp multi., ('62) 60 65
363 " 35rp multi. 1.25 1.65
364 " 40rp multi., ('62) 1.25 1.10
365 " 1fr multi. 6.25 7.00
366 " 1.50fr multi. 12.00 16.50
367 " 2fr multi., ('62) 3.00 3.25
Nos. 359–367 (9) 25.75 31.95

Issued in sheets of 20. See also Nos. 381–384, 471.

Europa Issue, 1961

Cogwheels
A200

1961, Oct. 3 ***Perf. 13½*** **Unwmkd.**

368 A200 50rp multicolored 35 38

Printed in sheets of 20, with left sheet margin decorated and inscribed.

Souvenir Sheet

Prince Johann II
A201

Portraits: 10rp, Francis I. 25rp, Franz Joseph II.

1962, Aug. 2 Photo. ***Perf. 11½***

369 A201 Souv. sheet of 3 7.00 6.50
a. 5rp gray green 1.50 1.50
b. 10rp deep rose 1.50 1.50
c. 25rp blue 1.50 1.50

Issued to commemorate the 50th anniversary of Liechtenstein's postage stamps and in connection with the Anniversary Stamp Exhibition, Vaduz, Aug. 4–12. No. 369 contains one each of Nos. 369a, b, and c. Dark green marginal inscription. Size: 132x117mm. Sold for 3 fr.

Europa Issue, 1962

Hands
A202

1962, Aug. 2

370 A202 50rp indigo & red 1.25 1.35

Issued in sheets of 20.

30 30
FUERSTENTUM
LIECHTENSTEIN

Malaria Eradication Emblem
A203

Pietà
A204

1962, Aug. 2 **Engraved**

371 A203 50rp turquoise blue 60 55

Issued for the World Health Organization drive to eradicate malaria. Sheets of 20.

1962, Dec. 6 **Photogravure**

Designs: 50rp, Angel with harp, fresco. 1.20fr, View of Mauren.

372 A204 30rp magenta 75 1.10
373 " 50rp deep orange 1.00 1.10
374 " 1.20fr deep blue 1.75 1.65

Issued in sheets of 20 inscribed: "Fürstentum Liechtenstein" and "Weihnacht 1962."

Prince Franz Joseph II
A205

1963, Apr. 3 **Engr.** ***Perf. 13½x14***

375 A205 5fr dull green 5.50 5.00

Issued to commemorate the 25th anniversary of the accession of Prince Franz Joseph II. Sheets of 8.

Exists imperf. Price $1,500.

Angel of the Annunciation
A206

Greek Architectural Elements
A207

Designs: 80rp, Three Kings. 1fr, Family.

Photogravure

1963, Aug. 26 ***Perf. 11½*** **Unwmkd.**

376 A206 20rp multicolored 55 55
377 " 80rp gray, purple & red 1.10 1.10
378 " 1fr multicolored 1.10 1.10

Centenary of the International Red Cross.

Europa Issue, 1963

1963, Aug. 26

379 A207 50rp multicolored 1.75 1.20

Bread and Milk
A208

1963, Aug. 26

380 A208 50rp dk. red, purple & brown 80 80

Issued for the "Freedom from Hunger" campaign of the U.N. Food and Agriculture Organization.

Minnesinger Type of 1961–62

Minnesingers: 25rp, Heinrich von Sax. 30rp, Kristan von Hamle. 75rp, Werner von Teufen. 1.70fr, Hartmann von Aue.

Photogravure

1963, Dec. 5 ***Perf. 11½*** **Unwmkd.**

381 A199 25rp multicolored 55 55
382 " 30rp " 55 55
383 " 75rp " 1.35 1.35
384 " 1.70fr " 2.25 2.25

Issued in sheets of 20.

Olympic Rings, Flags of Austria and Japan—A209

1964, Apr. 15 ***Perf. 11½***

385 A209 50rp Prussian blue, red & black 80 80

Olympic Games 1964. Sheets of 20.

Arms of Counts of Werdenberg-Vaduz
A210

Coats of Arms: 30rp, Barons of Brandis. 80rp, Counts of Sulz. 1.50fr, Counts of Hohenems.

1964, Sept. 1 **Photogravure**

386 A210 20rp multicolored 28 28
387 " 30rp " 40 40
388 " 80rp " 95 95
389 " 1.50fr " 1.50 1.35

See also Nos. 396–399.

Europa Issue, 1964

Roman Castle, Schaan
A211

1964, Sept. 1 ***Perf. 13x14***

390 A211 50rp multicolored 3.25 1.65

Masescha Chapel
A212

Peter Kaiser
A213

Designs: 40rp, Mary Magdalene, altarpiece. 1.30fr, Madonna with Sts. Sebastian and Roch, altarpiece.

1964, Dec. 9 Photo. ***Perf. 11½***

391 A212 10rp violet black 13 13
392 " 40rp dark blue 1.10 1.10
393 " 1.30fr deep claret 1.40 1.40

Issued in sheets of 20 inscribed: "Fürstentum Liechtenstein" and "Weihnacht 1964."

1964, Dec. 9 **Engraved**

394 A213 1fr dk. green, *buff* 1.10 1.00

Issued to commemorate the centenary of the death of Peter Kaiser (1793–1864), historian. Sheets of 20.

Madonna, Wood Sculpture, 18th Century
A214

Alemannic Ornament
A215

Engraved

1965, Apr. 22 ***Perf. 11½*** **Unwmkd.**

395 A214 10fr orange red 12.00 8.50

Issued in sheets of 4.

Arms Type of 1965

Coats of Arms (Lords of): 20rp, Schellenberg. 30rp, Gutenberg. 80rp, Frauenberg. 1fr, Ramschwag.

Photogravure

1965, Aug. 31 ***Perf. 11½*** **Unwmkd.**

396 A210 20rp multicolored 27 27
397 " 30rp " 33 27
398 " 80rp " 95 95
399 " 1fr " 1.00 95

Europa Issue, 1965

1965, Aug. 31

400 A215 50rp vio. blue, gray & brown 1.00 1.00

The design is from a belt buckle, about 600 A.D., found in a man's tomb near Eschen.

The Annunciation by Ferdinand Nigg
A216

Princess Gina and Prince Franz Josef Wenzel
A217

Paintings by Nigg: 30rp, The Three Kings. 1.20fr, Jesus in the Temple (horiz.).

1965, Dec. 7 Photo. ***Perf. 11½***

401 A216 10rp yel. green & dark green 13 13
402 " 30rp org. & red brn. 40 40
403 " 1.20fr ultra. & greenish bl. 1.25 80

Issued to commemorate the centenary of the birth of Ferdinand Nigg (1865–1949), painter.

1965, Dec. 7

404 A217 75rp gray, buff & gold 75 70

Communication Symbols
A218

1965, Dec. 7

405 A218 25rp multicolored 28 28

Issued to commemorate the centenary of the International Telecommunication Union.

Soil Conservation, Tree
A219

Designs: 20rp, Clean air, bird. 30rp, Unpolluted water, fish. 1.50fr, Nature preservation, sun.

1966, Apr. 26 Photo. ***Perf. 11½***

406 A219 10rp bright yellow & green 10 10
407 " 20rp bl. & dk. blue 22 18
408 " 30rp brt. green & ultra. 38 38
409 " 1.50fr yellow & red 1.50 1.10

Issued to publicize nature conservation.

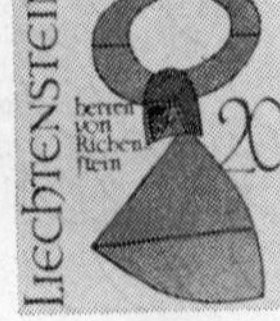

Prince Franz Joseph II
A220

Arms of Barons of Richenstein
A221

1966, Apr. 26

410 A220 1fr gray, gold, buff & dk. brown 1.00 1.00

60th birthday of Prince Franz Joseph II.

1966, Sept. 6 Photo. ***Perf. 11½***

Coats of Arms: 30rp, Vaistli knights. 60rp, Lords of Trisun. 1.20fr, von Schiel.

Light Gray Background

411 A221 20rp multicolored 22 17
412 " 30rp " 33 30
413 " 60rp " 60 55
414 " 1.20fr " 1.25 1.20

Europa Issue, 1966
Common Design Type

1966, Sept. 6 **Photo.** ***Perf. 14x13***

Size: 25x32mm.

415 CD9 50rp ultra., dp. org. & lt. green 75 75

Vaduz Parish Church
A222

St. Florin
A223

Designs: 30rp, Madonna. 1.70fr, God the Father.

1966, Dec. 6 Photo. ***Perf. 11½***

416 A222 5rp org. red & citron 13 13
417 A223 20rp lemon & magenta 22 13
418 " 30rp dull rose & deep blue 33 33
419 " 1.70fr gray & red brown 1.75 1.30

Restoration of the Vaduz Parish Church.

Europa Issue, 1967
Common Design Type

1967, Apr. 20 Photo. ***Perf. 11½***

420 CD10 50rp multicolored 55 55

Folklore Issue, 1967

The Man from Malans and his White Horse
A225

Fairy Tales of Liechtenstein: 30rp, The Treasure of Gutenberg. 1.20fr, The Giant of Guflina slaying the Dragon.

1967, Apr. 20

421 A225 20rp multicolored 22 22
422 " 30rp " 33 33
423 " 1.20fr grn. & multi. 1.25 1.10

See also Nos. 443-445, 458-460.

Common Design Types

pictured in section at front of book.

Souvenir Sheet

Prince Hans Adam and Countess Kinsky
A226

1967, June 26 **Engr.** ***Perf. 14x13½***

424 A226 Souv. sheet of 2 3.25 3.00
a. 1.50fr slate blue (*Prince*) 1.50 1.25
b. 1.50fr red brown (*Countess*) 1.50 1.25

Issued to commemorate the wedding of Prince Hans Adam of Liechtenstein and Marie Aglaë Countess Kinsky of Wchinitz and Tettau, July 30, 1967. No. 424 has gold coats of arms and inscriptions in margin. Size: 85x95mm.

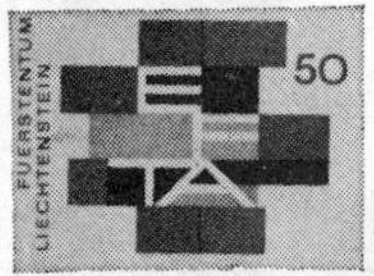

EFTA Emblem
A227

1967, Sept. 28 Photo. ***Perf. 11½***

425 A227 50rp multicolored 65 65

Issued to publicize the European Free Trade Association. See note after Norway No. 501.

Trophaeum (The Victorious Cross)
A228

Christian Symbols: 20rp, Alpha and Omega. 70rp, Chrismon.

1967, Sept. 28

426 A228 20rp rose claret, blk., & gold 25 25
427 " 30rp multicolored 33 30
428 " 70rp dp. ultra., black & gold 85 80

Johann Baptist Büchel
A229

1967, Sept. 28 Engr. & Litho.

429 A229 1fr rose claret & pale green 1.10 90

Issued in memory of Johann Baptist Büchel (1853-1927), priest, educator, historian and poet. Printed on fluorescent paper.

Peter and Paul, Patron Saints of Mauren
A230

Patron Saints: 5rp, St. Joseph, Planken. 10rp, St. Laurentius, Schaan. 30rp, St. Nicholas, Balzers. 40rp, St. Sebastian, Nendeln. 50rp, St. George, Schellenberg Chapel. 60rp, St. Martin, Eschen. 70rp, St. Fridolin, Ruggell. 80rp, St. Gallus, Triesen. 1fr, St. Theodul, Triesenberg. 1.20fr, St. Ann, Vaduz Castle. 1.50fr, St. Mary, Bendern-Gamprin. 2fr, St. Lucius, patron saint of the Principality.

1967-71 Photo. ***Perf. 11½***

430 A230 5rp multi. ('68) 12 8
431 " 10rp " ('68) 12 8
432 " 20rp blue & multi. 28 22
433 " 30rp dk. red & multi. 38 25
433A " 40rp multi. ('71) 55 38
434 " 50rp " ('68) 55 38
435 " 60rp " ('68) 80 55
436 " 70rp " 75 60
437 " 80rp " ('68) 85 75
438 " 1fr " ('68) 1.10 90
439 " 1.20fr violet blue & multi. 1.40 1.20
440 " 1.50fr multi. ('68) 1.60 1.40
441 " 2fr " ('68) 2.10 1.75
Nos. 430-441 (13) 10.60 8.54

Issue dates: 20rp, 30rp, 70rp, 1.20fr, Dec. 7, 1967; 5rp, 1.50fr, Aug. 29, 1968; 40rp, June 11, 1971. 2fr, Dec. 5, 1968. Others Apr. 25, 1968.

Europa Issue, 1968
Common Design Type

1968, Apr. 25

Size: 32½x23mm.

442 CD11 50rp crimson, gold & ultra. 65 65

Folklore Issue, 1968
Type of 1967

Fairy Tales of Liechtenstein: 30rp, The Treasure of St. Mamerten. 50rp, The Goblin from the Bergerwald. 80rp, The Three Sisters. (Denominations at right.)

1968, Aug. 29

443 A225 30rp Prussian blue, yellow & red 33 27
444 " 50rp green, yellow & blue 55 55
445 " 80rp brt. bl., yellow & light blue 95 90

Arms of Liechtenstein and Wilczek
A231

1968, Aug. 29

446 A231 75rp multicolored 1.75 1.50

Silver wedding anniversary of Prince Franz Joseph II and Princess Gina.

Sir Rowland Hill
A232

Coat of Arms
A233

Portraits: 30rp, Count Philippe de Ferrari. 80rp, Carl Lindenberg. 1fr, Maurice Burrus. 1.20fr, Théodore Champion.

1968-69 **Engraved** ***Perf. 14x13½***

447 A232 20rp green 22 22
448 " 30rp red brown 38 38
449 " 80rp dark brown ('69) 85 75
450 " 1fr black 1.15 1.15
451 " 1.20fr dk. bl. ('69) 1.25 1.15
Nos. 447-451 (5) 3.85 3.65

Issued to honor "Pioneers of Philately." Issue dates: 80rp, 1.20fr, Aug. 28, 1969. Others, Dec. 5, 1968.

See Nos. 509-511.

1969, Apr. 24 Engr. ***Perf. 14x13½***

452 A233 3.50fr dark brown 3.75 3.00

Sheets of 16.

Europa Issue, 1969
Common Design Type

1969, Apr. 24 Photo. ***Perf. 14***

Size: 33x23mm.

453 CD12 50rp brn. red, yellow & green 1.25 1.10

"Biology" (Man and DNA Molecule)
A234

Designs: 30rp, "Physics" (man and magnetic field). 50rp, "Astronomy" (man and planets). 80rp, "Art" (artist and Prince Franz Joseph II and Princess Gina).

1969, Aug. 28 Photo. ***Perf. 11½***

454 A234 10rp grn., dk. blue & dp. claret 12 10
455 " 30rp brn. & multi. 33 33
456 " 50rp ultra. & green 55 55
457 " 80rp brn., dk. brn. & yellow 1.00 95

Issued to commemorate the 250th anniversary of the Duchy of Liechtenstein.

Folklore Issue, 1969
Type of 1967

Fairy Tales of Liechtenstein: 20rp, The Cheated Devil. 50rp, The Fiery Red Goat. 60rp, The Grafenberg Treasure (toad). (Denominations at right.)

1969, Dec. 4 Photo. ***Perf. 11½***

458 A225 20rp multicolored 22 17
459 " 50rp yellow & multi. 55 55
460 " 60rp red & multi. 70 70

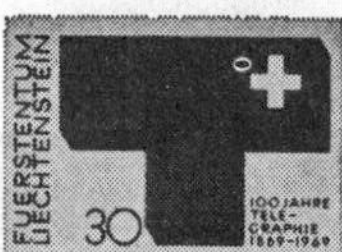

"T" and Arms of Austria-Hungary, Liechtenstein and Switzerland
A235

1969, Dec. 4 ***Perf. 13½***

461 A235 30rp gold & multi. 33 33

Issued to commemorate the centenary of the Liechtenstein telegraph system.

Arms of St. Lucius Monastery, Chur
A236

Prince Wenzel
A237

Arms of Ecclesiastic Patrons: 50rp, Pfäfers Abbey (dove). 1.50fr, Chur Bishopric (stag).

1969, Dec. 4 ***Perf. 11½***

462 A236 30rp multicolored 33 28
463 " 50rp " 55 55
464 " 1.50fr " 1.60 1.50

See Nos. 475–477, 486–488.

1970, Apr. 30 Photo. ***Perf. 11½***

465 A237 1fr sepia & multi. 1.10 1.10

Issued to commemorate the 25th anniversary of the Liechtenstein Red Cross.

Orange Lily
A238

1970, Apr. 30

Native Flowers: 30rp, Bumblebee orchid. 50rp, Glacier crowfoot. 1.20fr, Buck bean.

466 A238 20rp multicolored 22 22
467 " 30rp green & multi. 38 38
468 " 50rp olive & multi. 65 65
469 " 1.20fr multicolored 1.65 1.65

Issued to publicize the European Conservation Year 1970. See also Nos. 481–484, 500–503.

Europa Issue, 1970

Common Design Type

1970, Apr. 30 Litho. ***Perf. 14***

Size: 31½x20½mm.

470 CD13 50rp emerald, dk. blue & yellow 70 70

Minnesinger Type of 1961–62

Souvenir Sheet

Minnesingers: 30rp, Wolfram von Eschenbach. 50rp, Reinmar der Fiedler. 80rp, Hartmann von Starkenberg. 1.20fr, Friedrich von Hausen.

1970, Aug. 27 Photo. ***Perf. 11½***

471 A199 Sheet of 4 3.25 3.00
a. 30rp multicolored 33 28
b. 50rp " 55 50
c. 80rp " 85 80
d. 1.20fr " 1.25 1.20

Issued to commemorate the 800th anniversary of the birth of Wolfram von Eschenbach (1170–1220), German minnesinger (poet). No. 471 contains 4 stamps printed se-tenant. Gold marginal inscription. Size: 72x85mm. Sold for 3fr.

Prince Franz Joseph II

A239

Mother and Child, Sculpture by Rudolf Schädler

A240

Portrait: 2.50fr, Princess Gina.

1970–71 Engraved ***Perf. 14x13½***

472 A239 2.50fr violet blue ('71) 2.60 2.25
473 " 3fr black 3.25 2.65

Issue dates: 2.50fr, June 11, 1971. 3fr, Dec. 3, 1970. Sheets of 16.

Christmas Issue

1970, Dec. 3 Photo. ***Perf. 11½***

474 A240 30rp dk. red & multi. 38 32

Ecclesiastic Arms Type of 1969

Arms of Ecclesiastic Patrons: 20rp, Abbey of St. John in Thur Valley (Lamb of God). 30rp, Ladies' Abbey, Schänis (crown). 75rp, Abbey of St. Gallen (bear rampant).

1970, Dec. 3

475 A236 20rp lt. bl. & multi. 22 22
476 " 30rp gray, red & gold 38 38
477 " 75rp multicolored 90 90

Bronze Boar, La Tène Period
A241

Designs: 30rp, Peacock, Roman, 2nd century. 75rp, Decorated copper bowl, 13th century.

1971, March 11 Photo. ***Perf. 11½***

478 A241 25rp dp. ultra. & bluish black 27 22
479 " 30rp dk. brn. & grn. 33 33
480 " 75rp grn., yel. & brn. 80 80

Opening of the National Museum, Vaduz.

Flower Type of 1970

1971, March 11

Flowers: 10rp, Cyclamen. 20rp, Moonwort. 50rp, Superb pink. 1.50fr, Alpine columbine.

481 A238 10rp multicolored 9 9
482 " 20rp " 22 20
483 " 50rp " 55 55
484 " 1.50fr " 1.65 1.65

Europa Issue, 1971

Common Design Type

1971, June 11 Photo. ***Perf. 13½***

Size: 31x21mm.

485 CD14 50rp greenish blue, yel. & black 65 65

Ecclesiastic Arms Type of 1969

Arms of Ecclesiastic Patrons: 30rp, Knights of St. John, Feldkirch (Latin and moline crosses). 50rp, Weingarten Abbey (grapes). 1.20fr, Ottobeuren Abbey (eagle and cross).

1971, Sept. 2 Photo. ***Perf. 11½***

486 A236 30rp bister & multi. 33 33
487 " 50rp multicolored 55 55
488 " 1.20fr gray & multi. 1.35 1.35

Princely Crown
A242

Design: 70rp, Page from constitution.

1971, Sept. 2

489 A242 70rp grn., gold, black & copper 85 85
490 " 80rp dk. blue, gold, red & plum 1.10 1.10

50th anniversary of the constitution.

Madonna, by Andrea della Robbia

A243

Long-distance Skiing

A244

1971, Dec. 9

491 A243 30rp multicolored 38 38

Christmas 1971.

1971, Dec. 9

Designs (Olympic Rings and): 40rp, Ice hockey. 65rp, Downhill skiing, women's. 1.50fr, Figure skating, women's.

492 A244 15rp lemon & dk. brown 18 18
493 " 40rp multi. 45 45
494 " 65rp " 70 70
495 " 1.50fr " 1.65 1.65

11th Winter Olympic Games, Sapporo, Japan, Feb. 3–13, 1972.

1972, Mar. 16 Photo. ***Perf. 11***

Designs (Olympic Rings and): 10rp, Gymnast. 20rp, High jump. 40rp, Running, women's. 60rp, Discus. (All horiz.).

496 A244 10rp claret, brown & gray 12 12
497 " 20rp olive, brown & yellow 22 22
498 " 40rp red, brn. & gray 45 45
499 " 60rp brown, dark brown & blue 65 65

20th Olympic Games, Munich, Aug. 26–Sept. 10.

Flower Type of 1970.

1972, Mar. 16

Flowers: 20rp, Anemone. 30rp, Turk's cap. 60rp, Alpine centaury. 1.20fr, Reed mace.

500 A238 20rp dk. bl. & multi. 22 22
501 " 30rp olive & multi. 33 33
502 " 60rp multicolored 65 65
503 " 1.20fr " 1.35 1.35

Europa Issue 1972

Common Design Type

1972, Mar. 16

504 CD15 40rp dk. olive, blue green & rose red 80 60

Souvenir Sheet

Bendern and Vaduz Castle—A246

1972, June 8 Engraved ***Perf. 13½***

505 A246 Sheet of 2 3.75 3.75
a. 1fr violet blue 1.10 1.10
b. 2fr carmine 2.25 2.25

8th Liechtenstein Philatelic Exhibition, LIBA 1972, Vaduz, Aug. 18–27. No. 505 has gold marginal inscription and LIBA emblem. Stamp size: 33x22mm.; sheet size: 100x65mm.

Faun, by Rudolf Schädler

A247

Madonna with Angels, by Ferdinand Nigg

A248

Designs: 30rp, Dancer. 1.10fr, Owl.

1972, Sept. 7 Photo. ***Perf. 11½***

506 A247 20rp slate & multi. 22 22
507 " 30rp dp. bl. & multi. 33 33
508 " 1.10fr multicolored 1.35 1.35

Sculptures made of roots and branches by Rudolf Schädler.

Portrait Type of 1968–69

Portraits: 30rp, Emilio Diena. 40rp, André de Cock. 1.30fr, Theodore E. Steinway.

1972, Sept. 7 Engr. ***Perf. 14x13½***

509 A232 30rp Prussian green 33 27
510 " 40rp dk. vio. brown 45 35
511 " 1.30fr violet blue 1.35 1.35

Pioneers of Philately.

1972, Dec. 7 Photo. ***Perf. 11½***

512 A248 30rp blk. & multi. 38 38

Christmas 1972.

Lawena Springs
A249

Nautilus Cup
A250

Landscapes: 5rp, Silum. 15rp, Ruggell Marsh. 25rp, Steg, Kirchlispitz. 30rp, Fields, Schellenberg. 40rp, Rennhof, Mauren. 50rp, Tidrüfe Vaduz. 60rp, Eschner Riet. 70rp, Mittagspitz. 80rp, Three Sisters, Schaan Forest. 1fr, St. Peter's and Tower House, Mäls. 1.30fr, Road, Frommenhaus. 1.50fr, Ox Head Mountain. 1.80fr, Hehlawangspitz. 2fr, Saminaschlucht.

1972–73 Engr. & Litho. ***Perf. 11½***

513 A249 5rp brown, yellow & magenta ('73) 8 8
514 " 10rp slate green & citron 12 12
515 " 15rp red brown & citron 17 17
516 " 25rp dk. violet & pale green ('73) 33 33
517 " 30rp purple & buff ('73) 33 33
518 " 40rp violet & pale salmon ('73) 45 45
519 " 50rp vio. bl. & rose ('73) 55 50
520 " 60rp grn. & yel. ('73) 65 65
521 " 70rp dark & light blue ('73) 75 75
522 " 80rp Prussian green & citron 85 80
523 " 1fr red brown & light green 1.10 1.00
524 " 1.30fr ultra. & lt. grn. ('73) 1.35 1.35
525 " 1.50fr brn. & lt. blue 1.65 1.40
526 " 1.80fr brown & buff ('73) 2.00 2.00
527 " 2fr sepia & pale green ('73) 2.10 2.00
Nos. 513-527 (15) 12.48 11.93

Europa Issue, 1973

Common Design Type

1973, Mar. 8 Photo. ***Perf. 11½***

Size: 33x23mm.

528 CD16 30rp purple & multi. 45 45
529 " 40rp blue & multi. 55 55

1973, June 7 Photo. ***Perf. 11½***

Designs: 70rp, Ivory tankard. 1.10fr, Silver goblet.

530 A250 30rp gray & multi. 38 38
531 " 70rp multicolored 75 75
532 " 1.10fr dk. bl. & multi. 1.25 1.25

Drinking vessels from the Princely Treasury.

Arms of Liechtenstein and Municipalities
A251

Engraved & Photogravure

1973, Sept. 6 *Perf. 14x13½*

533 A251 5fr blk. & multi. 5.50 5.50

Coenonympha Oedippus
A252

Designs: 15rp, Alpine newt. 25rp, European viper (adder). 40rp, Common curlew. 60rp, Edible frog. 70rp, Dappled butterfly. 80rp, Grass snake. 1.10fr, Three-toed woodpecker.

1973–74 Photo. *Perf. 11½*

534 A252 15rp multi. ('74) 17 17
535 " 25rp " ('74) 33 33
536 " 30rp orange & multi. 33 33
537 " 40rp brown & multi. 45 45
538 " 60rp multicolored 65 65
539 " 70rp multi. ('74) 75 75
540 " 80rp " 85 85
541 " 1.10fr " ('74) 1.15 1.15
Nos. 534-541 (8) 4.68 4.68

Virgin and Child, by Bartolomeo di Tommaso
A253

The Vociferant Horseman, by Andrea Riccio
A254

Engraved & Lithographed

1973, Dec. 6 *Perf. 13½*

542 A253 30rp gold & multi. 55 55

Christmas 1973.

Europa Issue, 1974

Design: 40rp, Kneeling Venus, by Antonio Susini.

1974, Mar. 21 Photo. *Perf. 11½*

543 A254 30rp tan & multi. 38 38
544 " 40rp ultra. & multi. 60 60

Chinese Vase, 19th Century
A255

Soccer
A256

Designs: Chinese vases from Princely Treasury.

1974, Mar. 21

Multicolored

545 A255 30rp *shown* 33 33
546 " 50rp *from 1740* 55 50
547 A255 60rp *from 1830* 65 65
548 " 1fr *circa 1700* 1.10 1.10

1974, Mar. 21

549 A256 80rp lemon & multi. 85 85

World Soccer Championships, Munich June 13–July 7.

Post Horn and UPU Emblem
A257

1974, June 6 *Perf. 13½*

550 A257 40rp gold, green & black 45 40
551 " 60rp gold, red & blk. 65 65

Centenary of Universal Postal Union.

Bishop F. A. Marxer
A258

Photogravure and Engraved

1974, June 6 *Perf. 14x13½*

552 A258 1fr multicolored 1.10 1.10

Bicentenary of the death of Bishop Franz Anton Marxer (1703–1775).

Prince Constantin
A259

Prince Hans Adam
A260

Princess Gina and Prince Franz Joseph II—A261

Designs: 80rp, Prince Maximilian. 1.20fr, Prince Alois.

1974–75 Photogravure *Perf. 11½*

553 A259 70rp dk. grn. & gold 75 75
554 " 80rp deep claret & gold 85 85
555 " 1.20fr bluish black & gold 1.35 1.35

Engraved *Perf. 14x13½*

556 A260 1.70fr slate green 1.80 1.80

Photo. and Engr. *Perf. 13½x14*

557 A261 10fr gold & choc. 11.00 11.00

No. 557 printed in sheets of 4; gold margin, multicolored coat of arms and black inscription including signatures of Prince and Princess. Size: 140x164mm.

Issue dates: 1.70fr, Dec. 5, 1974; 10fr, Sept. 5, 1974; others, Mar. 13, 1975.

St. Florian
A262

Designs: 50rp, St. Wendelin. 60rp, Virgin Mary with Sts. Anna and Joachim. 70rp, Nativity.

1974, Dec. 5 Photogravure *Perf. 12*

560 A262 30rp multicolored 33 33
561 " 50rp " 55 55
562 " 60rp " 65 65
563 " 70rp " 90 90

Designs are from 19th century devotional glass paintings. Christmas 1974.

Europa Issue 1975

"Cold Sun," by Martin Frommelt
A263

Design: 60rp, "Village," by Louis Jaeger.

1975, Mar. 13 *Perf. 11½*

564 A263 30rp multicolored 40 40
565 " 60rp " 65 65

Red Cross Activities
A264

Imperial Crown
A266

Coronation Robe—A265

1975, June 5 Photo. *Perf. 11½*

566 A264 60rp dk. bl. & multi. 75 75

30th anniversary of the Liechtenstein Red Cross.

1975 Engr. & Photo. *Perf. 14*

Gold and Multicolored

567 A266 30rp *Imperial cross* 45 45
568 " 60rp *Imperial sword* 80 80
569 " 1fr *Orb* 1.75 1.75
570 A265 1.30fr *shown* 27.50 27.50
571 A266 2fr *shown* 4.00 4.00
Nos. 567-571 (5) 34.50 34.50

Treasures of the Holy Roman Empire from the Treasury of the Hofburg in Vienna, Austria.

Issue dates: No. 570, Sept. 4; others, June 5.

See Nos. 617–620.

St. Mamerten, Triesen
A267

Designs: 50rp, Red House, Vaduz, 14th century. 70rp, Prebendary House, Eschen, 14th century. 1fr, Gutenberg Castle.

1975, Sept. 4 Photo. *Perf. 11½*

572 A267 40rp multicolored 55 55
573 " 50rp " 80 80
574 " 70rp plum & multi. 1.10 1.10
575 " 1fr dk.bl. & multi. 1.65 1.65

European Architectural Heritage Year 1975.

Speed Skating
A268

Designs (Olympic Rings and): 25rp, Ice hockey. 70rp, Downhill skiing. 1.20fr, Slalom.

1975, Dec. 4 Photo. *Perf. 11½*

576 A268 20rp multicolored 27 27
577 " 25rp " 33 33
578 " 70rp " 80 80
579 " 1.20fr yel. & multi. 1.35 1.35

12th Winter Olympic Games, Innsbruck, Austria, Feb. 4–15, 1976.

Daniel in the Lions' Den
A269

River Crayfish
A270

Designs: 60rp, Virgin and Child. 90rp, St. Peter. All designs are after Romanesque sculptured capitals in Chur Cathedral, c. 1208.

Photogravure and Engraved

1975, Dec. 4 *Perf. 14*

580 A269 30rp gold & purple 33 33
581 " 60rp gold & green 65 60
582 " 90rp gold & claret 1.10 1.10

Christmas and Holy Year 1975.

1976, Mar. 11 Photo. *Perf. 11½*

Designs: 40rp, European pond turtle. 70rp, Old-world otter. 80rp, Lapwing.

583 A270 25rp multicolored 45 45
584 " 40rp " 70 70
585 " 70rp " 1.25 1.25
586 " 80rp " 1.50 1.50

World Wildlife Fund.

Europa Issue 1976

Mouflon
A271

Design: 80rp, Pheasant family. Ceramics by Prince Hans von Liechtenstein.

1976, Mar. 11

587	A271	40rp multicolored	55	55
588	"	80rp vio. & multi.	1.00	1.00

Roman Fibula, 3rd Century
A272

1976, Mar. 11

589	A272	90rp vio. blue, green & gold	1.10	1.10

Historical Association of Liechtenstein, 75th anniversary.

Souvenir Sheet

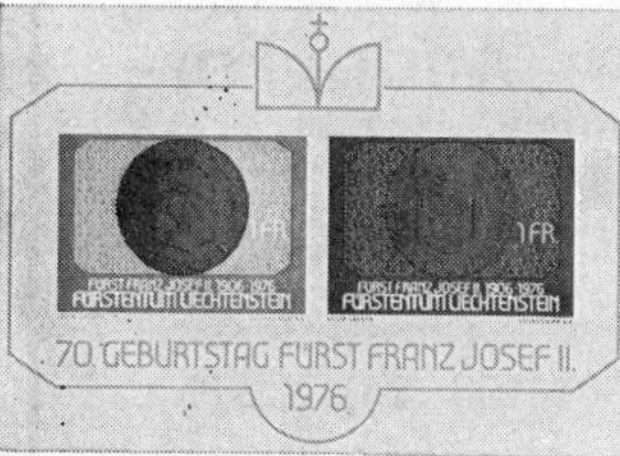

Franz Josef II 50fr-Memorial Coin
A273

1976, June 10 Photo. ***Imperf.***

590	A273	Sheet of 2	2.50	2.50
		a. 1fr blue & multicolored	1.00	90
		b. 1fr red & multicolored	1.00	90

70th birthday of Prince Franz Joseph II of Liechtenstein. No. 590 has blue marginal border and inscription. Size: 101x64 mm.

Judo and Olympic Rings
A274

Rubens' Sons, Albrecht and Nikolas
A275

Designs (Olympic Rings and): 50rp, Volleyball. 80rp, Relay race. 1.10fr, Long jump, women's.

1976, June 10 ***Perf. 11½***

591	A274	35rp multicolored	40	40
592	"	50rp "	55	55
593	"	80rp "	85	85
594	"	1.10fr "	1.20	1.20

21st Olympic Games, Montreal, Canada, July 17–Aug. 1.

1976, Sept. 9 Engr. ***Perf. 13½x14***

Rubens Paintings: 50rp, Singing Angels. 1fr, The Daughters of Cecrops (horiz.). (from Collection of Prince of Liechtenstein).

Size: 24x38mm.

595	A275	50rp gold & multi.	3.75	3.75
596	"	70rp " "	5.00	5.00

Size: 48x38mm.

597	A275	1fr gold & multi.	7.50	7.50

400th anniversary of the birth of Peter Paul Rubens (1577–1640), Flemish painter. Sheets of 8 (2x4).

Pisces
A276

Designs: Zodiac Signs.

1976–78 Photo. ***Perf. 11½***

Multicolored

598	A276	20rp *shown*	27	27
599	"	40rp *Aries*	50	50
600	"	40rp *Cancer* ('77)	55	55
601	"	40rp *Scorpio* ('78)	32	32
602	"	50rp *Sagittarius* ('78)	40	40
603	"	70rp *Leo* ('77)	75	75
604	"	80rp *Taurus*	85	85
605	"	80rp *Virgo* ('77)	85	85
606	"	80rp *Capricorn* ('78)	65	65
607	"	90rp *Gemini*	1.10	1.10
608	"	1.10fr *Libra* ('77)	1.15	1.10
609	"	1.50fr *Aquarius* ('78)	1.20	1.20
		Nos. 598–609 (12)	8.59	8.59

Flight into Egypt
A277

Ortlieb von Brandis, Sarcophagus
A278

Monastic Wax Works: 20rp, Holy Infant of Prague (horiz.). 80rp, Holy Family and Trinity. 1.50fr, Holy Family (horiz.).

1976, Dec. 9 Photo. ***Perf. 11½***

610	A277	20rp multicolored	27	27
611	"	50rp "	55	55
612	"	80rp "	85	80
613	"	1.50fr "	1.65	1.65

Christmas 1976.

Photogravure and Engraved

1976, Dec. 9 ***Perf. 13½x14***

614	A278	1.10fr gold & dark brown	1.20	1.20

Ortlieb von Brandis, Bishop of Chur (1458–1491).

Europa Issue 1977

Map of Liechtenstein, by J. J. Heber, 1721
A279

Design: 80rp, View of Vaduz, by Ferdinand Bachmann, 1815.

1977, Mar. 10 Photo. ***Perf. 12½***

615	A279	40rp multicolored	55	55
616	"	80rp "	1.00	1.00

Treasure Type of 1975

Designs: 40rp, Holy Lance and Particle of the Cross. 50rp, Imperial Evangel of St. Matthew. 80rp, St. Stephen's Purse. 90rp, Tabard of Imperial Herald.

Engraved and Photogravure

1977, June 8 ***Perf. 14***

617	A266	40rp gold & multi.	45	45
618	"	50rp " "	55	55
619	"	80rp " "	85	80
620	"	90rp " "	95	90

Treasures of the Holy Roman Empire from the Treasury of the Hofburg in Vienna.

Emperor Constantius II Coin
A280

Coins: 70rp, Lindau bracteate, c. 1300. 80rp, Ortlieb von Brandis, 1458–1491.

1977, June 8 Photo. ***Perf. 11½***

Granite Paper

621	A280	35rp gold & multi.	38	38
622	"	70rp silver & multi.	75	70
623	"	80rp " "	85	80

Frauenthal Castle
A281

Castles: 50rp, Gross Ullersdorf. 80rp, Liechtenstein Castle near Mödling, Austria. 90rp, Liechtenstein Palace, Vienna.

Engraved and Photogravure

1977, Sept. 8 ***Perf. 13½x14***

624	A281	20rp slate green & gold	22	22
625	"	50rp magenta & gold	55	50
626	"	80rp dark violet & gold	85	80
627	"	90rp dk. blue & gold	95	90

Children
A282

Traditional Costumes: 70rp, Two girls. 1fr, Woman in festival dress.

1977, Sept. 8 Photo. ***Perf. 11½***

Granite Paper

628	A282	40rp multicolored	45	45
629	"	70rp "	75	70
630	"	1fr "	1.05	1.00

Princess Tatjana
A283

1977, Dec. 7 Photo. ***Perf. 11½***

631	A283	1.10fr brn. & gold	1.20	1.20

Angel
A284

Liechtenstein Palace, Vienna
A285

Sculptures by Erasmus Kern: 50rp, St. Rochus. 80rp, Virgin and Child. 1.50fr, God the Father.

1977, Dec. 7

632	A284	20rp multicolored	22	22
633	"	50rp "	55	50
634	"	80rp "	85	80
635	"	1.50fr "	1.65	1.65

Christmas 1977.

Europa Issue 1978

Design: 80rp, Feldsberg Castle.

Photogravure and Engraved

1978, Mar. 2 ***Perf. 14***

636	A285	40rp gold & slate blue	45	40
637	"	80rp gold & claret	85	80

Residential Tower, Balzers-Mäls
A286

Designs: 10rp, Farmhouse, Triesen. 20rp, Houses, Upper Village, Triesen. 35rp, Barns, Balzers. 40rp, Monastery, Bendern. 70rp, Parish house. 80rp, Farmhouse, Schellenberg. 90rp, Parish house, Balzers. 1fr, Rheinberger House, Music School, Vaduz. 1.10fr, Street, Mitteldorf, Vaduz. 1.50fr, Town Hall, Triesenberg. 2fr, National Museum and Administrator's Residence, Vaduz.

1978 Photo. ***Perf. 11½***

638	A286	10rp multicolored	12	12
639	"	20rp "	22	22
640	"	35rp "	38	38
641	"	40rp "	45	45
642	"	50rp "	55	55
643	"	70rp "	75	75
644	"	80rp "	85	85
645	"	90rp "	1.00	1.00
646	"	1fr "	1.10	1.10
647	"	1.10fr "	1.15	1.15
648	"	1.50fr "	1.60	1.60
649	"	2fr "	2.10	2.10
		Nos. 638–649 (12)	10.27	10.27

Vaduz Castle
A287

Vaduz Castle: 50rp, Courtyard. 70rp, Staircase. 80rp, Triptych from High Altar, Castle Chapel.

Engraved and Photogravure

1978, June 1 ***Perf. 13½x14***

650	A287	40rp gold & multi.	45	45
651	"	50rp " "	55	55
652	"	70rp " "	75	75
653	"	80rp " "	85	85

40th anniversary of reign of Prince Franz Joseph II. Sheets of 8.

Prince Karl I, Coin, 1614
A288

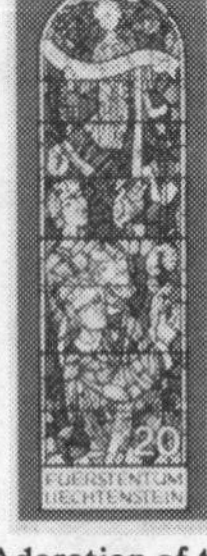

Adoration of the Shepherds
A289

Designs: 50rp, Prince Johann Adam, medal, 1694. 80rp, Prince Josef Wenzel, medal, 1773.

1978, Sept. 7 Photo. ***Perf. 11½***

654	A288	40rp multicolored	45	45
655	"	50rp "	55	55
656	"	80rp "	90	90

1978, Dec. 7 Photo. ***Perf. 11½***

Stained-glass Windows, Triesenberg: 50rp, Holy Family. 80rp, Adoration of the Kings.

657	A289	20rp multicolored	22	22
658	"	50rp "	55	55
659	"	80rp "	90	90

Christmas 1978.

Piebald, by Hamilton and Faistenberger
A290

Golden Carriage of Prince Joseph Wenzel, by Martin von Meytens—A291

Design: 80rp, Black stallion, by Johann Georg von Hamilton.

Perf. 13½x14, 12(1.10fr)

1978, Dec. 7 Photo. & Engr.

660	A290	70rp multicolored	75	75
661	"	80rp "	90	90
662	A291	1.10fr "	1.30	1.30

Sheets of 8.

Europa Issue 1979

Mail Plane over Schaan
A292

Design: 80rp, Zeppelin over Vaduz Castle.

1979, March 8 Photo. ***Perf. 11½***

663	A292	40rp multicolored	45	45
664	"	80rp "	90	90

First airmail service, St. Gallen to Schaan, Aug. 31, 1930, and first Zeppelin flight to Liechtenstein, June 10, 1931.

Child Drinking
A293

Designs: 90rp, Child eating. 1.10fr, Child reading.

1979, March 8

665	A293	80rp silv. & multi.	90	90
666	"	90rp " "	1.00	1.00
667	"	1.10fr " "	1.30	1.30

International Year of the Child.

Ordered Wave Fields
A294

Sun over Continents
A296

Council of Europe
A295

1979, June 7 Litho. ***Perf. 11½***

668	A294	50rp multicolored	55	55

Engraved

669	A295	80rp multicolored	90	90
670	A296	100rp "	1.10	1.10

International Radio Consultative Committee (CCIR) of the International Telecommunications Union, 50th anniversary (50rp); Entry into Council of Europe (80rp); aid to developing countries (100rp).

Heraldic Panel of Carl Ludwig von Sulz
A297

Heraldic Panels of: 70rp, Barbara von Sulz, née zu Staufen. 1.10fr, Ulrich von Ramschwag and Barbara von Hallwil.

Photogravure and Engraved

1979, June 1 ***Perf.***

671	A297	40rp multicolored	45	45
672	"	70rp "	80	80
673	"	1.10fr "	1.30	1.30

SEMI-POSTAL STAMPS.

Prince Johann II
SP1

Coat of Arms
SP2

Wmkd. Greek Cross. (183)

1925, Oct. 5 Engr. ***Perf. 11½***

B1	SP1	10rp yellow green	45.00	8.00
B2	"	20rp deep red	32.50	8.00
B3	"	30rp deep blue	11.00	3.25

Issued in commemoration of the 85th birthday of the Prince Regent. Sold at a premium of 5rp each, the excess being devoted to charities.

1927, Oct. 5 Typographed

B4	SP2	10rp multicolored	13.50	19.00
B5	"	20rp "	13.50	19.00
B6	"	30rp "	8.00	19.00

Commemorating the 87th birthday of Prince Johann II.

These stamps were sold at premiums of 5, 10 and 20rp respectively. The money thus obtained was devoted to charity.

Railroad Bridge Demolished by Flood
SP3

Designs: 10rp+10rp, Inundated Village of Ruggel. 20rp+10rp, Austrian soldiers rescuing refugees. 30rp+10rp, Swiss soldiers salvaging personal effects.

1928, Feb. 6 Litho. **Unwmkd.**

B7	SP3	5rp+5rp brown violet & brown	18.50	22.50
B8	"	10rp+10rp blue green & brown	18.50	22.50
B9	"	20rp+10rp dull red & brown	18.50	22.50
B10	"	30rp+10rp deep blue & brown	18.50	22.50

The surtax on these stamps was used to aid the sufferers from the Rhine floods.

Coat of Arms
SP7

Princess Elsa
SP8

Prince Francis I
SP9

1932, Dec. 21 Photogravure

B11	SP7	10rp(+5rp) olive green	25.00	35.00
B12	SP8	20rp(+5rp) rose red	25.00	35.00
B13	SP9	30rp(+10rp) ultra.	25.00	35.00

The surtax was for the Child Welfare Fund.

Postal Museum Issue.
Souvenir Sheet.

SP10

1936, Oct. 24 Litho. ***Imperf.***

B14	SP10	Sheet of four	19.00	35.00

Sheet contains 2 of No. 120 (20rp red) and 2 of No. 122 (30rp dark blue). Size 160x119mm. Sold for 2 francs.

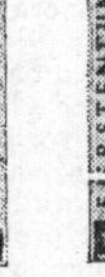

"Protect the Child"
SP11

"Take Care of the Sick"
SP12

"Help the Aged"
SP13

Perf. 11½

1945, Nov. 27 Photo. **Unwmkd.**

Cross in Red.

B15	SP11	10(rp)+10(rp) brown violet & buff	55	*2.75*
B16	SP12	20(rp)+20(rp) henna brown & buff	85	*2.75*
B17	SP13	1(fr)+1.40(fr) slate & buff	8.00	*19.00*

Souvenir Sheet.

Post Coach—SP14

1946, Aug. 10

B18	SP14	Sheet of two	30.00	40.00
		a. 10 (rp) dark violet brown & buff	9.00	16.50

Issued in sheets measuring 82x60½ mm., to commemorate the 25th anniversary of the Swiss-Liechtenstein Postal Agreement.

The sheet sold for 3 francs.

Canal by Albert Cuyp
SP15

Willem van Huythuysen by Frans Hals
SP16

Design: 40rp+10rp, Landscape by Jacob van Ruysdael.

1951, July 24 ***Perf. 11½***

B19	SP15	10rp+10rp olive green	6.25	7.00
B20	SP16	20rp+10rp dark violet brown	9.00	13.50
B21	SP15	40rp+10rp blue	6.50	9.00

Issued in sheets of 12.

World Refugee Year Issue

Nos. 324-325 Surcharged with New Value and Uprooted Oak Emblem.

1960, Apr. 7

B22	A190	30rp+10rp on 40rp blue, violet & red	60	90
B23	"	50rp+10rp on 25rp bistre, vio. & red	1.65	2.50

Issued to publicize World Refugee Year, July 1, 1959–June 30, 1960. The surtax was for aid to refugees.

Growth Symbol
SP17

1967, Dec. 7 Photo. ***Perf. 11½***

B24	SP17	50rp+20rp multi.	1.00	1.25

Surtax was for development assistance.

AIR POST STAMPS.

Airplane over Snow-capped Mountain Peaks
AP1

Airplane above Vaduz Castle
AP2

Airplane over Rhine Valley
AP3

Perf. 10½, 10½x11½

1930, Aug. 12 Photo. **Unwmkd.**

Gray Wavy Lines in Background

C1	AP1	15rp dark brown	7.50	5.50
C2	"	20rp slate	16.50	11.00
C3	AP2	25rp olive brown	8.50	10.00
C4	"	35rp slate blue	22.50	10.00
C5	AP3	45rp olive green	37.50	55.00
C6	"	1fr lake	70.00	50.00
		Nos. C1-C6 (6)	162.50	141.50

Zeppelin Issue.

Zeppelin over Naafkopf, Falknis Range
AP4

Zeppelin over Valüna Valley
AP5

1931, June 1 ***Perf. 11½***

C7	AP4	1fr olive black	80.00	110.00
C8	AP5	2fr blue black	175.00	325.00

Golden Eagle
AP6 AP7

Golden Eagle
AP8

Osprey
AP9

Eagle
AP10

1934–35

C9	AP6	10rp brt. vio. ('35)	11.00	16.50
C10	AP7	15rp red orange ('35)	16.50	25.00
C11	AP8	20rp red ('35)	18.00	27.50
C12	AP9	30rp brt. bl. ('35)	19.00	30.00
C13	AP10	50rp emerald	15.00	22.50
		Nos. C9-C13 (5)	79.50	121.50

No. C6 Surcharged with New Value in Black.

1935, June 24 ***Perf. 10½x11½***

C14	AP3	60rp on 1fr lake	42.50	55.00

Airship "Hindenburg"
AP11

Airship "Graf Zeppelin"
AP12

1936, May 1 ***Perf. 11½***

C15	AP11	1fr rose carmine	50.00	90.00
C16	AP12	2fr violet	35.00	70.00

Barn Swallows
AP13

Black-headed Gulls
AP14

Gulls
AP15

Eagle
AP16

Northern Goshawk
AP17

Lammergeier
AP18

Lammergeier
AP19

1939, Apr. 3 Photogravure

C17 AP13 10(rp) violet 33 45
C18 AP14 15(rp) red orange 80 *2.75*
C19 AP15 20(rp) dark red 55 1.00
C20 AP16 30(rp) dull blue 1.90 1.75
C21 AP17 50(rp) bright grn. 2.75 3.25
C22 AP18 1fr rose car. 3.75 *13.50*
C23 AP19 2fr violet 3.75 *8.00*
Nos. C17-C23 (7) 13.83 *30.70*

Leonardo da Vinci
AP20

Designs: 15rp, Joseph Montgolfier. 20rp, Jacob Degen. 25rp, Wilhelm Kress. 40rp, E. G. Robertson. 50rp, W. S. Henson. 1fr, Otto Lilienthal. 2fr, S. A. Andrée. 5fr, Wilbur Wright. 10fr, Icarus.

1948

C24 AP20 10(rp) dark green 1.80 80
C25 AP20 15(rp) dark violet 1.50 1.90
C26 " 20(rp) brown 1.50 80
a. 20(rp) reddish brown 50.00 3.25
C27 AP20 25(rp) dark red 1.80 *4.00*
C28 " 40(rp) violet blue 3.25 2.25
C29 " 50(rp) Prussian bl. 4.25 3.75
C30 " 1fr chocolate 4.25 5.00
C31 " 2fr rose lake 6.25 6.50
C32 " 5fr olive green 7.50 13.00
C33 " 10fr slate black 32.50 30.00
Nos. C24-C33 (10) 64.60 68.00

Issued in sheets of 9.
Exist imperf. Price, set $6,500.

Helicopter, Bell 47-J
AP21

Planes: 40rp, Boeing 707 jet. 50rp, Convair 600 jet. 75rp, Douglas DC-8.

1960, Apr. 7 *Perf. 11½* **Unwmkd.**

C34 AP21 30rp red orange 2.25 3.00
C35 " 40rp blue black 2.75 3.25
C36 AP21 50rp deep claret 4.00 2.75
C37 " 75rp olive green 1.50 3.75

Issued to commemorate the 30th anniversary of Liechtenstein's air post stamps.

POSTAGE DUE STAMPS.

National Administration of the Post Office.

Numeral of Value
D1

Engraved

1920 *Perf. 12½* **Unwmkd.**

J1 D1 5h rose red 10 15
J2 " 10h " 10 15
J3 " 15h " 10 15
J4 " 20h " 10 15
J5 " 25h " 10 15
J6 " 30h " 10 15
J7 " 40h " 10 15
J8 " 50h " 10 15
J9 " 80h " 10 15
J10 " 1k dull blue 15 30
J11 " 2k " 17 30
J12 " 5k " 17 30
Nos. J1-J12 (12) 1.39 2.25

Nos. J1 to J12 exist imperforate and partly perforated.

Swiss Administration of the Post Office.

Numeral of Value
D2

Post Horn
D3

Granite Paper.
Wmkd. Greek Cross. (183)

1928 **Lithographed.** ***Perf. 11½.***

J13 D2 5(rp) purple & org. 1.65 2.75
J14 " 10(rp) " " 1.65 2.75
J15 " 15(rp) " " 2.75 4.25
J16 " 20(rp) " " 2.25 3.50
J17 " 25(rp) " " 2.75 4.25
J18 " 30(rp) " " 3.50 *8.00*
J19 " 40(rp) " " 5.00 8.50
J20 " 50(rp) " " 6.50 *13.50*
Nos. J13-J20 (8) 26.05 *47.50*

Engr.; Value Typo. in Dark Red.

1940 ***Perf. 11½.*** **Unwmkd.**

J21 D3 5(rp) gray blue 2.25 *5.00*
J22 " 10(rp) " 80 *1.65*
J23 " 15(rp) " 1.35 *3.25*
J24 " 20(rp) " 1.35 2.25
J25 " 25(rp) " 2.25 3.75
J26 " 30(rp) " 3.25 5.00
J27 " 40(rp) " 3.25 5.50
J28 " 50(rp) " 3.25 *7.00*
Nos. J21-J28 (8) 17.75 *33.40*

OFFICIAL STAMPS.

Regular Issue of 1930
Overprinted Crown and
REGIERUNGS DIENSTSACHE
in Various Colors.

Perf. 10½, 11½, 11½x10½.

1932 **Unwmkd.**

O1 A38 5rp dk. grn. (Bk) 18.50 10.00
O2 A39 10rp dk. vio. (R) 50.00 10.00
a. Perf. 11½x10½ *650.00 1000.00*
O3 A40 20rp deep rose red (Bl) 32.50 10.00
a. Perf. 10½ 110.00 45.00
O4 A42 30rp ultra. (R) 9.00 12.00
a. Perf. 10½ 16.50 13.50
O5 A43 35rp dp. grn. (Bk) 11.00 10.00
a. Perf. 11½ *4250.00 6500.00*
O6 A45 50rp black brown (Bl) 65.00 13.50
a. Perf. 11½ 75.00 80.00
O7 A46 60rp olive black (R) 13.50 18.50
O8 A48 1.20fr olive brown (G) 250.00 300.00
Nos. O1-O8 (8) 449.50 384.00

Nos. 108, 110
Overprinted
in Black

REGIERUNGS DIENSTSACHE

1933 ***Perf. 14½.***

O9 A51 25rp red org. 55.00 47.50
O10 A53 1.20fr red brown 72.50 *225.00*

Same Overprint in Various Colors on Regular Issue of 1934–35

1934-36 ***Perf. 11½.***

O11 A58 5rp emerald (R) 38 *90*
O12 A59 10rp dp. violet (Bk) 38 *85*
O13 A60 15rp red orange (V) 38 *1.20*
O14 A61 20rp red (Bk) 38 *1.00*
O15 A62 25rp brown (R) 40.00 52.50
O16 " 25rp brown (Bk) 2.50 *8.00*
O17 A63 30rp dark bl. (R) 1.85 *3.75*
O18 A66 50rp lt. brown (V) 1.85 3.25
O19 A68 90rp deep green (Bk) 2.75 *11.00*
O20 A70 1.50fr brown carmine (Bl) 35.00 *75.00*
Nos. O11-O20 (10) 85.47 *157.45*

Regular Issue of 1937-38
Overprinted in Black,
Red or Blue

1937-41

O21 A77 5rp emerald (Bk) 22 32
O22 A78 10rp violet & buff (R) 22 32
O23 A80 20rp brown orange (Bl) 1.65 1.20
O24 " 20rp brown orange (Bk) ('41) 1.20 1.20
O25 A81 25rp chestnut (Bk) 65 *1.50*
O26 A82 30rp blue & gray (Bk) 65 65
O27 A85 50rp dark brown & buff (R) 65 1.00
O28 A88 1fr red brn. (Bk) 1.10 *3.25*
O29 A90 1.50fr slate blue (Bk) ('38) 2.25 *6.00*
Nos. O21-O29 (9) 8.59 *15.44*

Stamps of 1944-45
Overprinted in Black **DIENSTMARKE**

1947

O30 A136 5rp slate green & buff 45 65
O31 " 10rp gray & buff 45 65
O32 " 20rp orange red & buff 65 65
O33 " 30rp blue & buff 85 1.00
O34 " 50rp bluish blk. & pale gray 1.25 *3.25*
O35 " 1fr deep claret & buff 4.50 *9.00*
O36 " 150rp royal blue 4.50 *9.00*
Nos. O30-O36 (7) 12.65 *24.20*

Crown
O1

Engraved; Value Typographed

1950-68 ***Perf. 11½*** **Unwmkd.**

Buff Granite Paper
Narrow Gothic Numerals

O37 O1 5(rp) red violet & gray 10 12
O38 O1 10(rp) olive green & magenta 12 18
O39 " 20(rp) orange brown & blue 22 32
O40 " 30(rp) dark red brown & orge. red 32 50
O41 " 40(rp) blue & henna brown 45 65
O42 " 55(rp) dark gray green & red 1.75 2.50
a. White paper ('68) 50.00 *175.00*
O43 O1 60(rp) slate & magenta 1.75 2.50
a. White paper ('68) 8.00 *42.50*
O44 O1 80(rp) red orange & gray 85 1.25
O45 " 90(rp) choc. & blue 1.30 1.75
O46 " 1.20fr greenish blue & orange 1.50 2.00
Nos. O37-O46 (10) 8.36 11.77

1968-69 ***Perf. 11½***

White Granite Paper.
Broad Numerals, Varying Thickness

O47 O1 5(rp) olive brown & orange 4 4
O48 " 10(rp) violet & car. 10 10
O49 " 20(rp) vermilion & emerald 22 22
O50 " 30(rp) green & red 33 32
O51 " 50(rp) ultra. & red 55 55
O52 " 60(rp) org. & ultra. 65 65
O53 " 70(rp) maroon & emerald 75 75
O54 " 80(rp) blue green & carmine 85 85
O55 " 95(rp) slate & red ('69) 1.00 1.00
O56 " 1(fr) rose claret & green 1.10 1.10
O57 " 1.20(fr) lt. red brown & green 1.35 1.35
O58 " 2(fr) brown & org. ('69) 2.25 2.25
Nos. O47-O58 (12) 9.19 9.18

Government Building, Vaduz
O2

Engraved, Value Typographed

1976, Dec. 9 ***Perf. 14***

O59 O2 10rp yel. brn. & vio. 10 10
O60 " 20rp car. lake & blue 22 22
O61 " 35rp blue & red 38 38
O62 " 40rp dull pur. & grn. 45 45
O63 " 50rp slate & mag. 55 55
O64 " 70rp violet brown & blue green 75 75
O65 " 80rp green & mag. 85 85
O66 " 90rp vio. & bl. grn. 1.00 1.00
O67 " 1fr olive & mag. 1.10 1.10
O68 " 1.10fr brn. & ultra. 1.20 1.20
O69 " 1.50fr dull grn. & red 1.65 1.65
O70 " 2fr orange & blue 2.25 2.25
Nos. O59-O70 (12) 10.50 10.50

LITHUANIA

(lĭth'ū̇-ā'nĭ-ȧ)

(Lietuva)

LOCATION—In northern Europe bordering on the Baltic Sea.

GOVT.—Former independent republic.

AREA—22,959 sq. mi.

POP.—2,879,070 (1940).

CAPITAL—Vilnius.

Lithuania was under Russian rule when it declared its independence in 1918. The League of Nations recognized it in 1922. In 1940 it became a republic in the Union of Soviet Socialist Republics.

100 Skatiku = 1 Auksinas
100 Centai = 1 Litas (1922)

A1 A2

Type-set.

1918, Dec. 27 *Perf. 11½* **Unwmkd.**

First Vilnius Printing

Thin Figures.

1 A1 10sk black 50.00 30.00
2 " 15sk " 50.00 30.00

1918, Dec. 31

Second Vilnius Printing

Thick Figures

3 A1 10sk black 45.00 30.00
4 " 15sk " 40.00 25.00
5 " 20sk " 4.50 3.50
6 " 30sk " 4.50 3.50
7 A1 40sk black 4.50 3.50
8 " 50sk " 4.50 3.50
Nos. 3-8 (6) 103.00 69.00

1919 First Kaunas Issue.

9 A2 10sk black 5.00 3.00
10 " 15sk black 5.00 3.00
a. "5" for "15" 40.00 35.00
11 " 20sk black 5.00 3.00
12 " 30sk " 5.00 3.00

A3 A4

Second Kaunas Issue.

13 A3 10sk black 1.50 50
14 " 15sk " 1.50 50
15 " 20sk black 1.50 50
a. "astas" for "pastas" 50.00 40.00
16 " 30sk black 1.50 50
17 " 40sk " 1.50 60
18 " 50sk " 1.50 60
19 " 60sk " 1.50 90
Nos. 13-19 (7) 10.50 4.10

Third Kaunas Issue.

20 A4 10sk black 1.25 75
21 " 15sk " 1.25 75
22 " 20sk " 1.25 75
23 " 30sk " 1.25 75
24 " 40sk " 1.25 75
25 " 50sk " 1.25 75
26 " 60sk " 1.25 1.00
Nos. 20-26 (7) 8.75 5.50

Nos. 1 to 26 were printed in sheets of 20 (5x4) which were imperforate at the outer sides, so that only six stamps in each sheet were fully perforated. Prices are for the stamps partly imperforate. The stamps fully perforated sell for about double these prices. There was also a printing of Nos. 19 to 26 in a sheet of 160, composed of blocks of 20 of each stamp. Pairs or blocks with different values se-tenant sell for considerably more than the prices for the stamps singly.

The White Knight "Vytis"

A5 A6

A7 A8

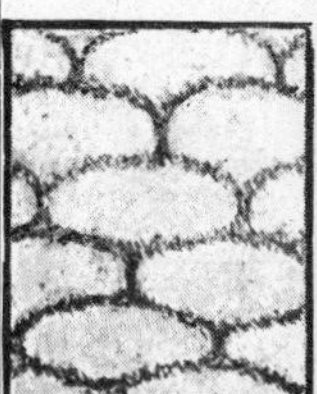

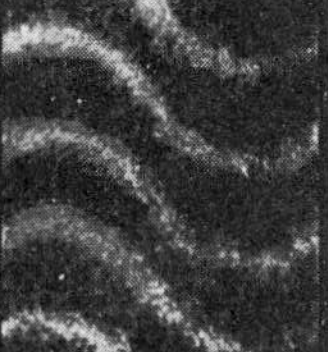

Wmk. 144 Wmk. 145

Perf. 10½ to 14 & Compound

Gray Granite Paper.

1919 Litho. Wmkd. Network. (144)

30 A5 10sk deep rose 15 15
a. Wmk. vert. 12.50 7.50
31 A5 15sk violet 15 15
a. Wmk. vert. 12.50 7.50
32 " 20sk dark blue 15 15
33 " 30sk deep orange 15 15
a. Wmk. vert. 12.50 7.50
34 " 40sk dark brown 15 15
35 A6 50sk blue green 25 15
36 " 75sk orange & dp. rose 20 15
37 A7 1auk gray & rose 30 25
38 " 3auk bistre brown & rose 30 25
39 " 5auk blue green & rose 35 35
Nos. 30-39 (10) 2.15 1.90

Nos. 30a, 31a and 33a are from the first printing with watermark vertical showing points to left; various perforations.

Nos. 30-39 exist imperf. Price in pairs, $40.

Thick White Paper.

1919 Wmkd. Wavy Lines. (145)

40 A5 10sk dull rose 10 10
41 " 15sk violet 10 10
42 " 20sk dark blue 10 10
43 " 30sk orange 10 10
44 " 40sk red brown 10 10
45 A6 50sk green 10 10
46 " 75sk yellow & dp. rose 10 10
47 A7 1auk gray & rose 25 15
48 " 3auk yellow brown & rose, perf. 12½ 25 15
49 " 5auk blue green & rose 30 25
Nos. 40-49 (10) 1.50 1.25

Nos. 40-49 exist imperf. Price in pairs, $40.

Perf. 10½ to 14 & Compound

1919 Thin White Paper

50 A5 10sk red 10 10
51 " 15sk lilac 10 10
52 " 20sk dull blue 10 10
53 " 30sk buff 10 10
54 " 40sk gray brown 10 10
55 A6 50sk light green 10 10
56 " 60sk violet & red 10 10
57 " 75sk bistre & red 10 10
58 A8 1auk gray & red 10 10
59 " 3auk light brown & red 15 10
60 " 5auk blue green & red 25 20
Nos. 50-60 (11) 1.30 1.20

Nos. 50-60 exist imperf. Price in pairs, $40.

See also Nos. 93-96.

"Lithuania" Receiving Benediction — A9

The Spirit of Lithuania Rises — A10

"Lithuania" with Chains Broken — A11

White Knight — A12

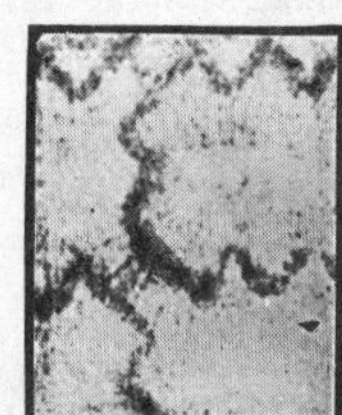

Wmk. 146

Wmkd. Zigzag Lines Forming Rectangles. (146)

1920, Feb. 16 *Perf. 11½*

70 A9 10sk deep rose 2.00 1.50
71 " 15sk light violet 2.00 1.50
72 " 20sk gray blue 2.00 1.50
73 A10 30sk yellow brown 2.00 1.50
74 A11 40sk brown & green 2.00 1.50
75 A10 50sk deep rose 2.00 1.50
76 " 60sk light violet 2.00 1.50
77 A11 80sk purple & red 2.00 1.50
78 " 1auk green & red 2.00 1.50
79 A12 3auk brown & red 2.00 1.50
80 " 5auk green & red 2.00 1.50
a. Right "5" dbl., green and red 75.00 60.00
Nos. 70-80 (11) 22.00 16.50

This issue was to commemorate the anniversary of national independence. The stamps were on sale only three days. Only a limited number of stamps was sold at post offices but 40,000 sets were delivered to the bank of Kaunas.

All values exist imperforate.

White Knight — A13

Grand Duke Vytautas — A14

Grand Duke Gediminas — A15

Sacred Oak and Altar — A16

1920, Aug. 25

81 A13 10sk rose 50 50
a. Imperf., pair 12.00
82 A13 15sk dark violet 50 50
83 A14 20sk grn. & lt. grn. 50 50
84 A13 30sk brown 50 50
85 A15 40sk gray grn. & vio. 50 50
86 A14 50sk brn. & brn. org. 1.00 1.00
87 " 60sk red & orange 1.00 1.00
88 A15 80sk black, drab & red 1.00 1.00
89 A16 1auk orange & black 1.00 1.00
90 " 3auk green & black 1.00 1.00
91 " 5auk gray violet & black 1.50 1.50
Nos. 81-91 (11) 9.00 9.00

Opening of Lithuanian National Assembly. On sale for three days.

Nos. 82 and 84 were printed on the same sheet and are found in pairs, se-tenant. Price for pair, $6.

1920

92 A14 20sk green & lilac 20.00
92A A15 40sk gray green, buff & violet 20.00
92B A14 50sk brown & gray lilac 20.00
92C " 60sk red & green 20.00
92D A15 80sk black, green & red 20.00
Nos. 92-92D (5) 100.00

Nos. 92 to 92D were trial printngs. By order of the Ministry of Posts, 2,000 copies of each were placed on sale at post offices.

Type of 1919 Issue

1920 *Perf. 11½* **Unwmkd.**

93 A5 15sk lilac 5.00 3.00
a. Imperf., pair 6.00 4.00
94 A5 20sk deep blue 4.00 3.00
a. Imperf., pair 6.00 4.00

No. 93 exists with perf. 10½x11 and 14.

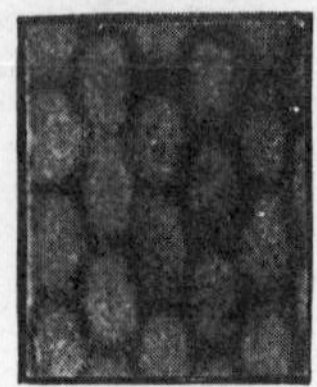

Wmk. 109

Wmkd. Webbing. (109)

1920 *Perf. 11½*

No.	Type	Description	Unused	Used
95	A5	20sk deep blue	2.50	1.25
		a. Imperf., pair	4.00	3.00
96	A5	40sk gray brown	3.50	2.00
		a. Imperf., pair	5.00	5.00

Watermark horizontal on Nos. 95–96. No. 96 exists with perf. 10½x11½.

Sower
A17

Peasant Sharpening Scythe
A18

Prince Kestutis
A19

Black Horseman
A20

1921-22

Perf. 11, 11½ and Compound.

No.	Type	Description	Unused	Used
97	A17	10sk bright rose	30	75
		a. Imperf., pair	20.00	
98	A17	15sk violet	30	75
		a. Imperf., pair	15.00	
99	A17	20sk ultramarine	20	10
		a. Imperf., pair	20.00	
100	A18	30sk brown	75	1.25
		a. Imperf., pair	35.00	
101	A19	40sk red	25	5
102	A18	50sk olive	20	5
		a. Imperf., pair	2.50	
103	A18	60sk green & violet	50	1.25
		a. Imperf., pair	25.00	
104	A19	80sk brown orange & carmine	35	10
		a. Imperf., pair	20.00	
105	A19	1auk brown & green	25	10
		a. Imperf., pair	20.00	
106	A19	2auk gray blue & red	30	10
		a. Imperf., pair	20.00	
107	A20	3auk yellow brown & dark blue	60	75
		a. Imperf., pair	25.00	
108	A17	4auk yellow & dark blue('22)	50	18
109	A20	5auk gray black & rose	75	1.00
		a. Imperf., pair	25.00	
110	A17	8auk green & black ('22)	75	18
		a. Imperf., pair	15.00	
111	A20	10auk rose & violet	1.50	75
112	"	25auk bistre brown & green	1.75	1.00
113	"	100auk dull red & gray black	6.00	6.50
		Nos. 97–113 (17)	15.25	14.86

No. 57 Surcharged **4 AUKSINAI**

Wmkd. Wavy Lines. (145)

1922, May *Perf. 12½x11½*

No.	Type	Description	Unused	Used
114	A6	4auk on 75sk bistre & red	50	25
		a. Inverted surcharge	5.00	4.00

Same with Bars over Original Value.

No.	Type	Description	Unused	Used
115	A6	4auk on 75sk bistre & red	75	35
		a. Double surcharge	8.50	8.50

Povilas Luksis
A20a

Justinas Staugaitis, Antanas Smetona, Stasys Silingas
A20b

Portraits: 40s, Lt. Juozapavicius. 50s, Dr. Basanavicius. 60s, Mrs. Petkeviciute. 1a, Prof. Voldemaras. 2a, Pranas Dovidaitis. 3a, Dr. Slezevicius. 4a, Dr. Galvanauskas. 5a, Kazys Grinius. 6a, Dr. Stulginskis. 8a, Pres. Smetona.

1922, Sept. Litho. **Unwmkd.**

Various Portraits.

No.	Type	Description	Unused	Used
116	A20a	20s black & carmine rose	50	25
116A	"	40s blue green & violet	50	25
116B	"	50s plum & greenish blue	50	25
117	"	60s purple & orge.	50	25
117A	"	1auk car. & lt. blue	50	40
117B	"	2auk deep blue & yellow brn.	50	40
		c. Center inverted	75.00	75.00
118	"	3auk maroon & ultramarine	50	40
118A	"	4auk dark green & red violet	50	50
118B	"	5auk black brown & deep rose	50	50
119	"	6auk dark blue & greenish bl.	50	50
		a. Cliché of 8auk in sheet of 6auk	30.00	30.00
119B	"	8auk ultra. & bistre	1.00	60
119C	A20b	10auk dark violet & blue green	1.50	1.00
		Nos. 116–119C (12)	7.50	5.30

Issued to commemorate the League of Nations' recognition of Lithuania. Sold only on Oct. 1, 1922.

Forty sheets of the 6auk each included eight copies of the 8auk.

Stamps of 1919-22 Surcharged in Black, Carmine or Green

1 CENT **10 CENTU**

On Stamps of 1919.

Gray Granite Paper.

Wmkd. Network. (144)

1922 *Perf. 11½x12.*

No.	Type	Description	Unused	Used
120	A7	3c on 1auk gray & rose	100.00	100.00
121	"	3c on 3auk bistre brown & rose	75.00	75.00
122	"	3c on 5auk blue green & rose	30.00	30.00

Excellent counterfeits exist.

White Paper.

Wmkd. Wavy Lines. (145)

Perf. 14, 11½, 12½x11½.

No.	Type	Description	Unused	Used
123	A5	1c on 10sk red	50	75
124	A5	1c on 15sk lilac	50	75
125	"	1c on 20sk dull blue	50	75
126	"	1c on 30sk orange	60.00	
127	"	1c on 30sk buff	25	30
128	"	1c on 40sk gray brown	50	75
129	A6	2c on 50sk green	50	75
130	"	2c on 60sk violet & red	15	10
131	"	2c on 75sk bistre & red	50	75
132	A8	3c on 1auk gray & red	30	35
133	"	3c on 3auk brown & red	15	25
134	"	3c on 5auk blue green & red	15	25
		Nos. 123–125, 127–134 (11)	4.00	5.75

On Stamps of 1920.

1922 *Perf. 11* **Unwmkd.**

No.	Type	Description	Unused	Used
136	A5	1c on 20sk dp. bl. (C)	1.00	1.50

Wmkd. Webbing. (109)

Perf. 11, 11½.

No.	Type	Description	Unused	Used
138	A5	1c on 20sk deep blue (C)	75	1.25
139	"	1c on 40sk gray brown (C)	2.25	2.50

On Stamps of 1921-22.

No.	Type	Description	Unused	Used
140	A18	1c on 50sk olive (C)	15	10
		a. Imperf., pair	30.00	
		b. Inverted surch.	10.00	
		c. Double surcharge, one inverted		
141	A17	3c on 10sk rose	2.25	2.50
142	"	3c on 15sk violet	20	20
143	"	3c on 20sk ultra.	35	50
144	A18	3c on 30sk brown	1.75	2.00
145	A19	3c on 40sk red	25	25
		a. Imperf., pair		
146	A18	5c on 50sk olive	15	10
147	"	5c on 60sk grn. & vio.	85	1.25
148	A19	5c on 80sk brn. org. & carmine	20	30
		a. Imperf., pair	20.00	20.00

Wmkd. Wavy Lines. (145)

Perf. 12½x11½.

No.	Type	Description	Unused	Used
149	A6	5c on 4auk on 75sk bistre & red (No. 114) (G)	75	1.25
150	"	5c on 4auk on 75sk bistre & red (No. 115) (G)	2.00	3.00

Wmkd. Webbing. (109)

Perf. 11, 11½.

No.	Type	Description	Unused	Used
151	A19	10c on 1auk brown & green	50	25
		a. Inverted surcharge	20.00	
152	"	10c on 2auk blue & red	20	10
		a. Inverted surch.	10.00	
		b. Imperf., pair	20.00	
153	A17	15c on 4auk yellow & dark blue	20	10
		a. Inverted surcharge	5.00	
154	A20	25c on 3auk yel. brn. & dark blue	4.50	5.00
155	"	25c on 5auk gray black & rose	2.50	3.00
156	"	25c on 10auk rose & violet	1.50	2.00
		a. Imperf., pair	25.00	
157	A17	30c on 8auk green & black (C)	50	40
		a. Inverted surch.	10.00	10.00
158	A20	50c on 25auk bistre brown & green	2.25	2.75
160	"	1 l on 100auk red & gray	4.00	4.00
		Nos. 136–160 (23)	29.05	34.30

A21

Ruin
A22

Seminary Church, Kaunas
A23

Wmkd. Webbing. (109)

1923 **Lithographed.** ***Perf. 11.***

No.	Type	Description	Unused	Used
165	A21	10c violet	6.00	5
166	"	15c scarlet	2.50	10
167	"	20c olive brown	2.50	18
168	"	25c deep blue	2.50	10
169	A22	50c yellow green	2.50	10
170	"	60c red	2.50	15
171	A23	1 l org. & green	12.00	15
172	"	3 l red & gray	9.50	40
173	"	5 l brown & blue	14.50	1.50
		Nos. 165–173 (9)	54.50	2.73

See also Nos. 189–209, 281–282.

Memel Coat of Arms
A24

Lithuanian Coat of Arms
A25

Biruta Chapel
A26

Kaunas, War Memorial
A27

Trakai Ruins
A28

Memel Lighthouse
A29

Memel Harbor
A30

Perf. 11, 11½, 12

1923, Aug. Unwmkd.

176 A24 1c rose, grn. & black 1.00 1.00
177 A25 2c dull vio. & black 1.00 1.00
178 A26 3c yellow & black 1.50 1.50
179 A24 5c blue, buff & black 2.00 2.00
180 A27 10c orange & black 2.00 2.00
181 " 15c green & black 2.50 2.50
182 A28 25c brt. violet & black 3.50 3.50
183 A25 30c red violet & black 4.00 4.00
184 A29 60c olive green & blk. 4.00 4.00
185 A30 1 l blue green & black 4.00 4.00
186 A26 2 l red & black 5.00 5.00
187 A28 3 l blue & black 7.50 7.50
188 A29 5 l ultra. & black 7.50 7.50
Nos. 176-188 (13) 45.50 45.50

This series was issued ostensibly to commemorate the incorporation of Memel with Lithuania.

Type of 1923 Issue.

1923 *Perf. 11* **Unwmkd.**

189 A21 5c pale green 3.50 5
190 " 10c violet 4.75 5
a. Imperf., pair 30.00
191 " 15c scarlet 6.00 5
a. Imperf., pair 30.00
193 " 25c blue 9.50 5

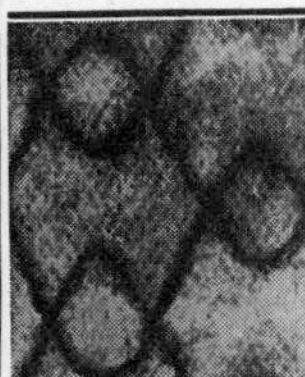
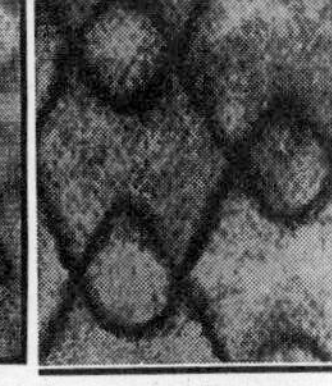

Wmk. 147 Wmk. 198

1923 Wmkd. Parquetry. (147)

196 A21 2c pale brown 1.25 30
197 " 3c olive bistre 1.75 25
198 " 5c pale green 1.75 18
199 " 10c violet 3.50 10
202 " 25c deep blue 9.00 5
a. Imperf., pair 42.50
204 A21 36c orange brown 12.00 75
Nos. 196-204 (6) 29.25 1.63

Wmkd. Intersecting Diamonds. (198)

1923-25

Perf. 11½, 14½, 11½x14½.

207 A21 25c deep blue 200.00 225.00
208 A22 50c deep green ('25) 3.00 5
209 " 60c carmine ('25) 4.25 6

Double-barred Cross A31 — **Dr. Jonas Basanavicius** A32

1927, Jan. *Perf. 11½, 14½.*

210 A31 2c orange 1.25 4
211 " 3c dark brown 1.25 4
212 " 5c green 2.00 5
a. Imperf., pair 17.50
213 A31 10c violet 3.50 5
214 " 15c red 3.00 6
a. Imperf., pair 17.50
215 A31 25c blue 3.00 6
Nos. 210-215 (6) 14.00 30

1927-29 *Perf. 14½.* **Wmk. 147**

216 A31 5c green 15.00 20.00
217 " 30c blue ('29) 15.00 3.00

See also Nos. 233-240, 278-280.

Perf. 11½, 14½x11½.

1927 Unwmkd.

219 A32 15c claret & black 1.00 30
220 " 25c dull bl. & black 1.00 35
221 A32 50c dk. grn. & blk. 2.00 75
222 " 60c dk. vio. & black 3.00 1.25

Issued as a memorial to Dr. Jonas Basanavicius (1851-1927), patriot and folklorist.

National Arms A33

Wmkd. Webbing. (109)

1927, Dec. 23 *Perf. 14½*

223 A33 1 l blue green & gray 1.50 25
224 " 3 l vio. & pale green 5.00 60
225 " 5 l brown & gray 8.50 1.00

President Antanas Smetona A34

Decade of Independence A35

Dawn of Peace—A36

1928, Feb. Wmk. 109

226 A34 5c org. brn. & grn. 50 10
227 " 10c violet & black 50 10
228 " 15c orange & brown 50 20
229 " 25c blue & indigo 1.00 15
230 A35 50c ultra. & dull vio. 1.00 40
231 " 60c carmine & black 1.50 75
232 A36 1 l black brown & drab 1.50 90
Nos. 226-232 (7) 6.50 2.60

Issued in commemoration of the tenth anniversary of Lithuanian independence.

Type of 1926 Issue.

1929-31

233 A31 2c orange ('31) 1.75 15
234 " 5c green 1.75 5
235 " 10c violet ('31) 9.00 15
237 " 15c red 3.00 5
a. Tête bêche pair 9.00 9.00
239 " 30c dark blue 4.75 5

Unwmkd.

240 A31 15c red 10.50 15
Nos. 233-240 (6) 30.75 60

Grand Duke Vytautas A37

Grand Duke, Mounted A38

1930, Feb. 16 *Perf. 14*

242 A37 2c yellow brown & dark brown 50 10
243 " 3c dk. brn. & violet 50 10
244 " 5c yellow green & deep orange 50 10
245 " 10c violet & emerald 50 15
246 " 15c deep rose & violet 50 15
247 " 30c dark blue & brown violet 75 20
248 " 36c brown violet & olive black 75 20
249 " 50c dull grn. & ultra. 75 30
250 " 60c dark blue & rose 75 30
251 A38 1 l blue green, drab & red brown 2.00 40
252 " 3 l dark brown, salmon & dark violet 2.50 1.00
253 " 5 l olive brown, gray & red 5.00 1.20
254 " 10 l multicolored 15.00 10.00
255 " 25 l " 45.00 45.00
Nos. 242-255 (14) 75.00 59.20

Issued in commemoration of the fifth centenary of the death of the Grand Duke Vytautas.

Kaunas, Railroad Station A39

Cathedral at Vilnius A39a

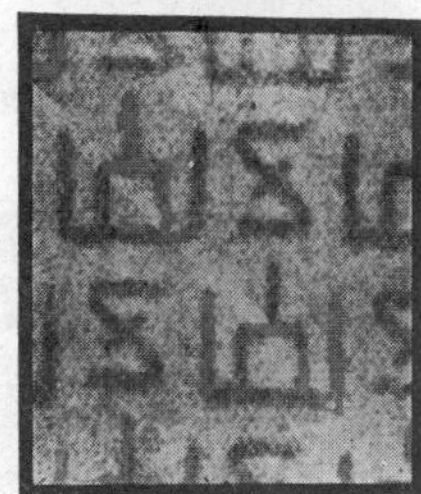

Wmk. 238

Designs: 15c, 25c, Landscape on the Neman River. 50c, Main Post Office, Kaunas.

Wmkd. Multiple Letters. (238)

1932, July 21 *Perf. 14, Imperf.*

256 A39 10c dark red brown & ochre 25 25
257 " 15c dark brown & olive 50 50
258 " 25c dark blue and olive 75 75
259 " 50c gray black & olive 1.50 1.50
260 A39a 1 l dk. blue & olive 3.00 3.00
261 " 3 l red brown & gray green 4.50 4.50

Wmk. 198

262 A39 5c vio. blue & ochre 25 25
263 A39a 60c greenish black & lilac 2.00 2.00
Nos. 256-263 (8) 12.75 12.75

Issued for the benefit of Lithuanian orphans.

In September, 1935, a red overprint was applied to No. 259: "ORO PASTAS / LITUANICA II / 1935 / NEW YORK-KAUNAS". Price $200.

Vytautas Fleeing from Prison, 1382 A40

Wmk. 209

Designs: 15c, 25c, Conversion of Ladislas II Jagello and Vytautas (1386). 50c, 60c, Battle at Tannenberg (1410). 1 l, 3 l, Meeting of the Nobles (1429).

Wmkd. Multiple Ovals. (209)

1932 *Perf. 14, Imperf.*

264 A40 5c red & rose lake 50 50
265 " 10c olive bistre & orange brown 50 50
266 " 15c rose lilac & olive green 60 60
267 " 25c dark violet brown & ochre 1.25 1.25
268 " 50c deep green & bistre brown 1.75 1.75
269 " 60c olive green & brn. carmine 2.25 2.25
270 " 1 l ultramarine & olive green 2.50 2.50
271 " 3 l dark brown & dark green 3.75 3.75
Nos. 264-271 (8) 13.10 13.10

15th anniversary of independence.

A. Visteliauskas A41 — Mother and Child A42

Designs: 15c, 25c, Petras Vileisis. 50c, 60c, Dr. John Sliupas. 1 l, 3 l, Jonas Basanavicius.

1933 *Perf. 14, Imperf.*

272 A41 5c yel. grn. & carmine 30 30
273 " 10c ultra. & carmine 30 30
274 " 15c orange & red 35 35
275 " 25c dark blue & black brown 60 60
276 " 50c olive gray & dark blue 1.10 1.10
277 " 60c orange brown & chestnut 2.50 2.50
277A " 1 l red & vio. brown 3.00 3.00
277B " 3 l turquoise green & violet brown 5.00 5.00
Nos. 272-277B (8) 13.15 13.15

Issued to commemorate the 50th anniversary of the first newspaper "Ausra" in Lithuanian language.

1933, Sept. *Perf. 14, Imperf.*

Designs: 15c, 25c, Boy reading. 50c, 60c, Boy playing with blocks. 1 l, 3 l, Woman and boy at the Spinning Wheel.

277C A42 5c deep yellow green & orange brown 20 20
277D " 10c rose brown & ultramarine 20 20
277E " 15c olive green & plum 30 30

277F A42 25c org. & gray blk. 60 60
277G " 50c olive green & carmine 1.25 1.25
277H " 60c blk. & yel. org. 2.50 2.50
277I " 1 l dark brown & ultramarine 3.00 3.00
277K " 3 l rose lilac & olive green 5.00 5.00
Nos. 277C-277K (8) 13.05 13.05

Issued for the benefit of Lithuanian orphans.

Types of 1923–26 Issues.

1933-34 ***Perf. 14.*** **Wmk. 238**

278 A31 2c orange 20.00 3.00
279 " 10c dark violet 18.00 1.75
280 " 15c red 27.50 60
281 A22 50c green 9.00 1.25
282 " 60c red 12.00 60
Nos. 278-282 (5) 86.50 7.20

Antanas Smetona
A43

Engraved.

1934 ***Perf. 11½*** **Unwmkd.**

283 A43 15c red 4.00 10
284 " 30c green 7.50 20
285 " 60c blue 10.00 45

60th birthday of President Smetona.

Arms
A44 A45

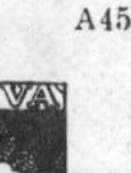

Girl with Wheat
A46

A47

Knight—A48

Wmk. 198; Wmk. 209 (35c, 10 l)

1934-35 **Lithographed** ***Perf. 14***

286 A44 2c rose & dull orange 50 15
287 " 5c blue green & green 50 5
288 A45 10c chocolate 1.50 5
289 A46 25c dark brown & emerald 3.50 10
290 A45 35c carmine 3.50 5
291 A46 50c dark blue & blue 4.50 5
292 A47 1 l salmon & maroon 12.50 10
293 " 3 l grn. & gray grn. 30 10
294 A48 5 l maroon & gray blue 40 30
295 " 10 l choc. & yel. 2.50 75
Nos. 286-295 (10) 29.70 1.70

No. 290 exists imperf. Price $25.

1936-37 ***Perf. 14.*** **Wmk. 238**

Size: 17½x23mm.

296 A44 2c orange ('37) 10 10
297 " 5c green 25 6

President Smetona A49 — Arms A50

1936-37 **Unwmkd.**

298 A49 15(c) carmine 4.00 5
299 " 30(c) green ('37) 7.50 5
300 " 60(c) ultra. ('37) 6.00 5

1937-39 ***Perf. 14.*** **Wmk. 238**

Paper with Gray Network.

301 A50 10c green 2.00 8
302 " 25c magenta 18 5
303 " 35c red 1.00 5
304 " 50c brown 20 5
305 " 1 l deep violet blue ('39) 12 12
Nos. 301-305 (5) 3.50 35

No. 304 exists in two types: I. "50" is fat and broad, with "0" leaning to right. II. "50" is thinner and narrower, with "0" straight.

Jonas Basanavicius Reading Act of Independence
A51

President Antanas Smetona
A52

Perf. 13x13½

1939, Jan. 15 **Engr.** **Unwmkd.**

306 A51 15c dark red 50 10
307 A52 30c deep green 50 20
308 A51 35c red lilac 1.00 40
309 A52 60c dark blue 1.00 30
a. Souvenir sheet 6.00 7.50
b. As "a," imperf. 15.00 20.00

Issued in commemoration of the 20th anniversary of Independence.

Nos. 309a and 309b measure 148x105mm. and contain one each of Nos. 308 and 309, with marginal inscriptions. Sold for 2 l.

Same Overprinted in Blue

1939

310 A51 15c dark red 75 15
311 A52 30c deep green 1.25 30
312 A51 35c red lilac 1.50 50
313 A52 60c dark blue 2.00 75

Recovery of Vilnius.

View of Vilnius—A53

Gediminas
A54

Trakai Ruins—A55

Photogravure.

1940, May 6 ***Perf. 14*** **Unwmkd.**

314 A53 15c brn. & pale brn. 50 10
315 A54 30c dark green & light green 1.00 20
316 A55 60c dark blue & light blue 2.00 60
a. Souvenir sheet, imperf. 7.50 9.00

Issued to commemorate the return of Vilnius to Lithuania, Oct. 10, 1939. Exist imperf.

No. 316a measures 148x105mm. and contains one each of Nos. 314-316, with inscriptions and simulated perforations in gold. Sold for 2 l.

White Knight A56 — Angel A57

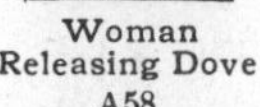

Woman Releasing Dove A58 — Mother and Children A59

Liberty Bell A60 — Mythical Animal A61

1940

317 A56 5c brown carmine 6 10
318 A57 10c green 6 10
319 A58 15c dull orange 6 10
320 A59 25c light brown 6 15
321 A60 30c Prussian green 10 10
322 A61 35c red orange 12 30
Nos. 317-322 (6) 46 85

Nos. 317-322 exist imperf.

SEMI-POSTAL STAMPS.

Regular Issue of 1923–24
Surcharged in Blue, Violet or Black:

a b c

1924, Feb. ***Perf. 11*** **Wmk. 147**

B1 A21 (a) 2c+2c pale brown (Bl) 1.00 1.00
B2 " (") 3c+3c olive bistre (Bl) 1.00 1.00
B3 " (") 5c+5c pale green (V) 1.00 1.00
B4 " (") 10c+10c violet (Bk) 2.00 2.00
B5 " (") 36c+34c orange brown (V) 7.50 7.50

Wmkd. Webbing. (109)

B6 A21 (a) 10c+10c violet (Bk) 10.00 10.00
B7 " (") 15c+15c scarlet (V) 2.25 2.25
B8 " (") 20c+20c olive brown (Bl) 3.00 3.00
B9 " (") 25c+25c blue (Bk) 25.00 25.00
B10 A22 (b) 50c+50c yellow green (V) 7.50 7.50
B11 " (") 60c+60c red (V) 10.00 10.00
B12 A23 (c) 1 l+1 l orange & green (V) 10.00 10.00
B13 " (") 3 l+2 l red & gray (V) 12.50 12.50
B14 " (") 5 l+3 l brown & blue (V) 20.00 20.00

Unwmkd.

B15 A21 (a) 25c+25c deep blue (Bk) 6.00 6.00
Nos. B1-B15 (15) 118.75 118.75

For War Invalids.

Semi-Postal Stamps of 1924
Surcharged.

Surcharged in Gold or Copper

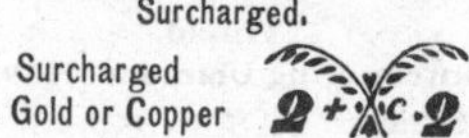

1926, Dec. 3 **Wmk. 147**

B16 A21 1+1c on 2c+2c pale brown (G) 75 75
a. Invtd. surch. 10.00
B17 " 2+2c on 3c+3c olive bistre (C) 1.00 1.00
B19 " 2+2c on 5c+5c pale green (G) 1.00 1.00
a. Double surcharge, one inverted 10.00
B20 " 5+5c on 10c+10c violet (G) 2.00 2.00
B21 " 14+14c on 36c+34c orange brn. (G) 6.00 6.00

Wmkd. Webbing. (109)

B22 A21 5+5c on 10c + 10c violet (G) 12.50 12.50
B23 " 5+5c on 15c+15c scarlet (G) 2.00 2.00
B24 " 10+10c on 20c+20c olive brown (G) 2.00 2.00
B25 " 10+10c on 25c+25c blue (G) 70.00 70.00

Unwmkd.

B26 A21 10+10c on 25c+25c blue (G) 5.00 5.00

Surcharged in Copper or Silver:

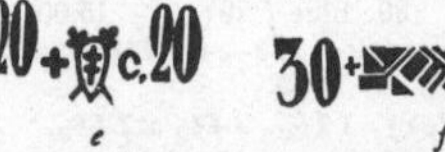

e  f

Wmkd. Webbing. (109)

B27 A22 (e) 20+20c on 50c+50c green (C) 5.00 5.00

B28 A22 (e) 25+25c on 60c+60c red (S) 7.50 7.50
B29 A23 (f) 30+30c on 1l+1l orange & green (S) 10.00 10.00
Nos. B16-B29 (13) 124.75 124.75

For War Orphans.

Surcharged in Gold

Wmkd. Parquetry. (147)

1926, Dec. 3

B30 A21 1+1c on 2c+2c pale brown 1.00 1.00
B31 " 2+2c on 3c+3c olive bistre 1.00 1.00
 a. Inverted surcharge 12.00
B32 " 2+2c on 5c+5c pale green 1.00 1.00
 a. Inverted surcharge
B33 " 5+5c on 10c+10c violet 2.00 2.00
B34 " 19+19c on 36c+34c org. brown 5.00 5.00

Wmkd. Webbing. (109)

B35 A21 5+5c on 10c+10c violet 12.50 12.50
B36 " 10+10c on 15c+15c scarlet 2.00 2.00
B37 " 15+15c on 20c+20c olive brown 2.00 2.00
B38 " 15+15c on 25c+25c blue 75.00 75.00

Unwmkd.

B39 A21 15+15c on 25c+25c blue 5.00 5.00

Surcharged in Gold:

h

i

Wmkd. Webbing. (109)

B40 A22 (h) 25c on 50c+50c green 6.00 6.00
B41 " (") 30c on 60c+60c red 10.00 10.00
B42 A23 (i) 50c on 1l+1l org. & grn. 10.00 10.00
Nos. B30-B42 (13) 132.50 132.50

Archery
SP1

Javelin Throwing
SP2

Diving
SP3

Running
SP4

Photogravure.

1938, July 13 *Perf. 14* **Unwmkd.**

B43 SP1 5(c)+5(c) green & dark green 2.00 2.00
B44 SP2 15(c)+5(c) orange & red orange 3.50 3.50
B45 SP3 30(c)+10(c) blue & dark blue 6.00 6.00
B46 SP4 60(c)+15(c) tan & brown 12.00 10.00

National Olympiad, July 15-20.

Same Overprinted in Red, Blue or Black:

k

l

1938, July 13

B47 SP1 (k) 5(c)+5(c) grn. & dk. grn. (R) 5.00 4.00
B48 SP2 (l) 15(c)+5(c) orange & red orange (Bl) 5.00 4.00
B49 SP3 (") 30(c)+10(c) blue & dark blue (R) 7.50 7.50
B50 SP4 (k) 60(c)+15(c) tan & brn. (Bk) 12.00 10.00

National Scout Jamboree, July 12-14.

Basketball Players
SP6 SP7

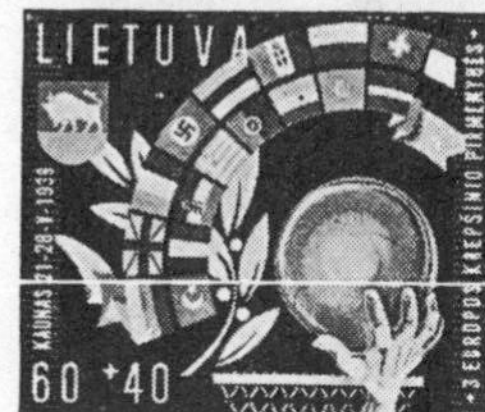

Flags of Competing Nations and Basketball—SP8

1939 Photogravure. *Perf. 14*

B52 SP6 15(c)+10(c) copper brown & brn. 4.00 4.00
B53 SP7 30(c)+15(c) myrtle green & green 6.00 4.00
B54 SP8 60(c)+40(c) blue violet & gray violet 8.00 10.00

Issued to commemorate the 3rd European Basketball Championships held at Kaunas. The surtax was used for athletic equipment. Nos. B52-B54 exist imperf. Price, pair, $150.

AIR POST STAMPS.

Winged Posthorn—AP1

Airplane over Neman River
AP2

Air Squadron—AP3

Plane over Gediminas Castle
AP4

Wmkd. Webbing. (109)

1921 Lithographed. *Perf. 11½.*

C1 AP1 20sk ultramarine 1.25 60
C2 " 40sk red orange 1.00 60
C3 " 60sk green 1.00 60
 a. Imperf., pair 40.00
C4 AP1 80sk light rose 1.00 60
 a. Imperf. vertically, pair 50.00
C5 AP2 1auk green & red 1.75 75
 a. Imperf., pair 20.00
C6 AP3 2auk brown & blue 2.00 1.00
C7 AP4 5auk slate & yellow 3.00 2.00
Nos. C1-C7 (7) 11.00 6.15

Allegory of Flight
AP5

1921, Nov. 6

C8 AP5 20sk org. & gray bl. 1.00 1.00
C9 " 40sk dull bl. & lake 1.00 1.00
C10 " 60sk violet blue & olive green 1.00 1.00
C11 " 80sk ochre & deep green 1.00 1.00
 a. Vertical pair, imperf. between 20.00
C12 AP5 1auk blue green & blue 1.00 1.00
C13 " 2auk gray & brn. org. 1.00 1.00
C14 " 5auk dull lilac & Prussian blue 1.00 1.00
Nos. C8-C14 (7) 7.00 7.00

Opening of airmail service.

Plane over Kaunas—AP6

Black Overprint.

1922, July 16 *Perf. 11, 11½*

C15 AP6 1auk olive brown & red 1.00 75
 a. Imperf., pair 60.00
C16 AP6 3auk violet & grn. 1.00 75
C17 AP6 5auk deep blue & yellow 1.35 1.00

It was the intention to issue Nos. C15 to C17, without overprint, in commemoration of the founding of the Air Post service but they were not put in use at that time. Subsequently the word "ZENKLAS" (stamp) was overprinted over "ISTEIGIMAS" (founding) and the date "1921, VI, 25" was obliterated by short vertical lines.

Plane over Gediminas Castle
AP7

1922, July 22

C18 AP7 2auk blue & rose 1.00 60
C19 " 4auk brn. & rose 1.00 60
C20 " 10auk black & gray blue 2.00 1.00

Air Post Stamps of 1921-22 Surcharged like Regular Issues in Black or Carmine

1922

C21 AP1 10c on 20sk ultra. 2.00 2.50
C22 " 10c on 40sk red org. 2.00 2.50
C23 " 10c on 60sk green 1.50 1.75
 a. Inverted surcharge 20.00
C24 " 10c on 80sk lt. rose 2.00 2.50
C25 AP2 20c on 1auk green & red 5.00 6.00
C26 AP3 20c on 2auk brown & blue 8.00 9.00
 a. Without "CENT" 125.00 125.00
C27 AP7 25c on 2auk blue & rose 1.50 1.00
 a. Inverted surcharge 20.00 20.00
C28 " 30c on 4auk brown & rose (C) 1.50 1.25
 a. Double surch. 20.00 20.00
C29 AP4 50c on 5auk slate & yellow 2.00 1.50
C30 AP7 50c on 10auk black & blue 1.25 1.25
 a. Inverted surcharge 20.00 20.00
C31 AP6 1l on 5auk deep blue & yellow 12.50 15.00
 a. Double surcharge 40.00
Nos. C21-C31 (11) 39.25 44.25

Airplane and Carrier Pigeons
AP8

"Flight"—AP9

Wmkd. Parquetry. (147)

1924, Jan. 28 *Perf. 11*

C32 AP8 20c yellow 2.00 75
 a. Unwmkd. 500.00 500.00
C33 " 40c emerald 2.00 75
 a. Horiz. or vert. pair, imperf. between 50.00
C34 " 60c rose 2.50 1.00
 a. Imperf., pair 90.00
C35 AP9 1l dark brown 3.50 50

Unwmkd.

C36 AP8 60c rose 275.00 275.00

Most, if not all, copies of Nos. C32a, C36 and CB5 show faint traces of watermark, according to experts. Counterfeits lack any trace of watermark.

Swallow
AP10

Wmkd.
Intersecting Diamonds. (198)

1926, June 17 *Perf. 14½*

C37 AP10 20c carmine rose 1.00 60
a. Horiz. or vert. pair, imperf. between 20.00
C38 " 40c violet & red orange 1.00 40
a. Horiz. or vert. pair, imperf. between 20.00
C39 " 60c blue & black 2.00 40
a. Horiz. or vert. pair, imperf. between 20.00
c. Center invtd. 175.00 175.00

Juozas Tubelis
AP11

Vytautas and Airplane over Kaunas
AP12

Vytautas and Antanas Smetona
AP13

1930, Feb. 16 *Perf. 14* **Wmk. 109**

C40 AP11 5c black, bistre & brown 60 30
C41 " 10c dark blue, drab & black 60 30
C42 " 15c maroon, gray & blue 60 30
C43 AP12 20c dk. brown, org. & dull red 60 40
C44 " 40c dark blue, light blue & vio. 1.00 60
C45 AP13 60c blue green, lilac & black 1.25 75
C46 " 1 l dull red, lilac & black 2.00 1.00
Nos. C40–C46 (7) 6.65 3.65

Issued in commemoration of the fifth centenary of the death of the Grand Duke Vytautas.

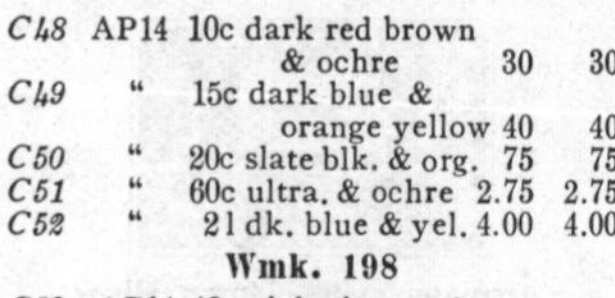

Map of Lithuania, Klaipeda and Vilnius—AP14

Designs: 15c, 20c, Airplane over Neman. 40c, 60c, City Hall, Kaunas. 1 l, 2 l, Church of Vytautas, Kaunas.

Wmk. Multiple Letters (238)

1932, July 21 *Perf. 14, Imperf.*

C47 AP14 5c vermilion & olive green 30 30
C48 AP14 10c dark red brown & ochre 30 30
C49 " 15c dark blue & orange yellow 40 40
C50 " 20c slate blk. & org. 75 75
C51 " 60c ultra. & ochre 2.75 2.75
C52 " 2 l dk. blue & yel. 4.00 4.00

Wmk. 198

C53 AP14 40c violet brown & yellow 2.00 2.00
C54 " 1 l violet brown & green 3.25 3.25
Nos. C47–C54 (8) 13.75 13.75

Issued for the benefit of Lithuanian orphans.

Mindaugas in the Battle of Shauyai, 1236
AP15

Designs: 15c, 20c, Coronation of Mindaugas (1253). 40c, Grand Duke Gediminas and his followers. 60c, Founding of Vilnius by Gediminas (1332). 1 l, Gediminas capturing the Russian Fortifications. 2 l, Grand Duke Algirdas before Moscow (1368).

Perf. 14, Imperf.

1932, Nov. 28 **Wmk. 209**

C55 AP15 5c green & red lilac 20 20
C56 " 10c emerald & rose 25 25
C57 " 15c rose violet & bistre brown 30 30
C58 " 20c rose red & black brown 40 40
C59 " 40c choc. & dk. gray 1.25 1.25
C60 " 60c orange & gray black 1.50 1.50
C61 " 1 l rose vio. & grn. 2.50 2.50
C62 " 2 l deep blue & brown 3.50 3.50
Nos. C55–C62 (8) 9.90 9.90

Issued to commemorate the anniversary of independence.

Nos. C58–C62 exist with overprint "DARIUS-GIRENAS / NEW YORK—1933—KAUNAS" below small plane. The overprint was applied in New York with the approval of the Lithuanian consul general. Lithuanian postal authorities seem not to have been involved in the creation or release of these overprints.

Trakai Castle,
Home of the Grand Duke Kestutis
AP16

Designs: 15c, 20c, Meeting of Kestutis and the Hermit Birute. 40c, 60c, Hermit Birute. 1 l, 2 l, Kestutis and his Brother Algirdas.

Perf. 14, Imperf.

1933, May 6 **Wmk. 209**

C63 AP16 5c olive gray & deep blue 25 25
C64 " 10c gray violet & orange brown 30 30
C65 " 15c deep blue & lilac 30 30
C66 " 20c orange brown & lilac 70 70
C67 " 40c lt. ultra. & lilac 1.50 1.50
C68 " 60c brn. & lt. ultra. 2.75 2.75
C69 " 1 l olive gray & deep blue 3.25 3.25
C70 " 2 l violet gray & yellow green 4.50 4.50
Nos. C63–C70 (8) 13.55 13.55

Issued to commemorate the reopening of air service to Berlin-Kaunas-Moscow, and the 550th anniversary of the death of Kestutis.

Joseph Maironis—AP17

Joseph Tumas-Vaizgantas
AP17a

Designs: 40c, 60c, Vincas Kudirka. 1 l, 2 l, Julia A. Zemaite.

Perf. 14, Imperf.

1933, Sept 15 **Wmk. 209**

C71 AP17 5c crimson & deep blue 20 20
C72 " 10c blue violet & green 20 20
C73 AP17a 15c dark green & chocolate 25 25
C74 " 20c brown carmine & ultramarine 40 40
C75 AP17 40c red brown & olive green 1.10 1.10
C76 " 60c dark blue & chocolate 1.50 1.50
C77 " 1 l citron & indigo 2.25 2.25
C78 " 2 l deep green & red brown 3.25 3.25
Nos. C71–C78 (8) 9.15 9.15

Issued for the benefit of Lithuanian orphans.

Capts. Steponas Darius and Stas. Girenas
AP18

Ill-Fated Plane "Lituanica"
AP19

The Dark Angel of Death
AP20

"Lituanica" over Globe
AP21

"Lituanica" and White Knight
AP22

Engraved

1934, May 18 *Perf. 11½* **Unwmkd.**

C79 AP18 20c scarlet & black 8 5
C80 AP19 40c dp. rose & blue 8 8
C81 AP18 60c dk. vio. & blk. 10 10
C82 AP20 1 l black & rose 60 15
C83 AP21 3 l gray green & orange 1.00 50
C84 AP22 5 l dark brown & blue 2.50 1.50
Nos. C79–C84 (6) 4.36 2.38

Issued to commemorate the death of Capts. Steponas Darius and Stas. Girenas on their New York–Kaunas flight of 1933.

No. C80 exists with diagonal overprint: "F. VAITKUS / nugalejo Atlanta / 21-22-IX-1935". Price, $225.

Felix Waitkus and Map of Transatlantic Flight
AP23

Wmkd. Multiple Letters. (238)

1936, Mar. 24 Litho. *Perf. 14*

C85 AP23 15c brown lake 1.25 35
C86 " 30c dark green 1.50 50
C87 " 60c blue 2.75 1.00

Issued in commemoration of the Transatlantic Flight of the Lituanica II, September 21-22, 1935.

AIR POST SEMI-POSTAL STAMPS.

Air Post Stamps of 1924 Surcharged like Semi-Postal Stamps of 1924 in Red, Violet or Black.

Wmkd. Parquetry. (147)

1924 *Perf. 11.*

CB1 AP8 (*a*) 20c+20c yellow (R) 8.00 8.00
CB2 " (*b*) 40c+40c emerald (V) 8.00 8.00
CB3 " (") 60c+60c rose (V) 8.00 8.00
CB4 AP9 (*c*) 1 l+1 l dark brown (Bk) 10.00 10.00

Unwmkd.

CB5 AP8 (*b*) 60c+60c rose (V) 300.00 300.00

The surtax was for the Red Cross. See note on No. CB5 below No. C36.

South Lithuania

Grodno District

Russian Stamps of 1909-12 Surcharged in Black or Red

Lietuva
Літва.
50
skatikų
грашэй.

Perf. 14, 14½x15.

1919 **Unwmkd.**

L1 A14 50sk on 3k red 60.00 30.00
a. Double surcharge
L2 A14 50sk on 5k claret 30.00 25.00
a. Imperf., pair 300.00 200.00
L3 A15 50sk on 10k dark blue (R) 30.00 25.00

L4 A11 50sk on 15k red brn. & blue 30.00 25.00
a. Imperf., pair 350.00 350.00
L5 A11 50sk on 25k green & gray violet (R) 30.00 25.00
L6 " 50sk on 35k red brn. & green 30.00 25.00
L7 A8 50sk on 50k violet & green 30.00 25.00
L8 A11 50sk on 70k brown & orange 40.00 25.00
Nos. L1-L8 (8) 280.00 205.00

Excellent counterfeits are plentiful.
This surcharge exists on Russia No. 119, the imperf. 1k orange of 1917. Price, unused $90, used $60.

OCCUPATION STAMPS.

Issued under German Occupation.

German Stamps Overprinted in Black **Postgebiet Ob. Ost**

On Stamps of 1905–17.
Wmkd. Lozenges. (125)

1916-17 *Perf. 14, 14½.*

1N1 A22 2½pf gray 12 15
1N2 A16 3pf brown 15 20
1N3 " 5pf green 15 15
1N4 A22 7½pf orange 15 15
1N5 A16 10pf carmine 15 15
1N6 A22 15pf yellow brown 1.50 1.50
1N7 " 15pf dark vio. ('17) 15 20
1N8 A16 20pf ultramarine 45 50
1N9 " 25pf orange & black, *yellow* 15 40
1N10 " 40pf lake & black 65 75
1N11 " 50pf violet & black, *buff* 50 60
1N12 A17 1m carmine rose 3.00 2.75
Nos. 1N1-1N12 (12) 7.12 7.50

These stamps were used in the former Russian provinces of Suvalki, Vilnius, Kaunas, Kurland.

Issued under Russian Occupation.

Lithuanian Stamps of 1937-40 Overprinted in Red or Blue **LTSR 1940 VII 21**

1940 *Perf. 14.* Wmk. 238

2N9 A44 2c orange (Bl) 15 20
2N10 A50 50c brown (Bl) 55 65

Unwmkd.

2N11 A56 5c brn. car. (Bl) 15 20
2N12 A57 10c green (R) 2.25 2.25
2N13 A58 15c dull orange (Bl) 20 25
2N14 A59 25c light brown (R) 25 30
2N15 A60 30c Prus. grn. (R) 50 50
2N16 A61 35c red orange (Bl) 50 60
Nos. 2N9-2N16 (8) 4.55 4.95

The Lithuanian Soviet Socialist Republic was proclaimed July 21, 1940.

LOURENÇO MARQUES

(lô-rĕn'sô mär'kĕs)

LOCATION — In the southern part of Mozambique in Southeast Africa.
GOVT.—Part of Portuguese East Africa Colony.
AREA—28,800 sq. mi. (approx.).
POP.—474,000 (approx.).
CAPITAL—Lourenço Marques.

Stamps of Mozambique replaced those of Lourenço Marques in 1920. See Mozambique.

1000 Reis = 1 Milreis
100 Centavos = 1 Escudo (1913)

King Carlos
A1

Perf. 11½, 12½, 13½.

1895 Typographed. Unwmkd.

1 A1 5r yellow 50 25
2 " 10r reddish violet 50 35
3 " 15r chocolate 80 60
4 " 20r lavender 80 60
5 " 25r blue green 75 30
a. Perf. 11½ 3.25 75
6 " 50r light blue 1.00 75
a. Perf. 13½ 8.50 4.00
b. Perf. 11½
7 " 75r rose 1.75 1.50
8 " 80r yellow green 4.75 3.25
9 " 100r brown, *yellow* 2.00 1.25
a. Perf. 12½ 4.00 3.00
10 " 150r carmine, *rose* 3.75 3.00
11 " 200r dark blue, *blue* 4.00 2.50
12 " 300r dk. bl., *salmon* 4.00 2.50
Nos. 1-12 (12) 24.60 16.85

Saint Anthony of Padua Issue.

Regular Issues of Mozambique, 1886 and 1894, Overprinted in Black
L. MARQUES
—
CENTENARIO
DE
S. ANTONIO
—
MDCCCXCV

1895 Without Gum *Perf. 12½*

On 1886 Issue

13 A2 5r black 10.00 9.00
14 " 10r green 12.00 9.00
15 " 20r rose 16.00 10.00
16 " 25r lilac 18.00 15.00
17 " 40r chocolate 16.00 13.50
18 " 50r blue, perf. 13½ 12.00 10.00
a. Perf. 12½ 37.50 27.50
19 " 100r yellow brown 30.00 25.00
20 " 200r gray violet 25.00 22.50
21 " 300r orange 35.00 35.00

On 1894 Issue
Perf. 11½

22 A3 5r yellow 10.00 8.00
23 " 10r reddish violet 16.50 13.50
24 " 50r light blue 21.00 13.50
a. Perf. 12½
25 " 75r rose, perf. 12½ 30.00 20.00
26 " 80r yellow green 45.00 30.00
27 " 100r brown, *buff* 50.00 45.00
28 " 150r carmine, *rose*, perf. 12½ 35.00 30.00

No. 12 Surcharged in Black **50 réis**

1897, Jan. 2

29 A1 50r on 300r dark blue, *salmon* 160.00 140.00

No. 29 issued mostly wthout gum.

King Carlos
A2

1898–1903 *Perf. 11½.*

Name, Value in Black except 500r

30 A2 2½r gray 25 25
31 " 5r orange 25 25
32 " 10r light green 25 20
33 " 15r brown 1.50 1.25
34 " 15r gray green ('03) 45 40
a. Imperf.
35 " 20r gray violet 60 30
a. Imperf.
36 " 25r sea green 80 40
a. Perf. 13½ 32.50 7.50
b. 25r light green (error) 20.00 20.00
c. Perf. 12½ 80.00 75.00
37 " 25r carmine ('03) 40 30
a. Imperf.
38 " 50r blue 1.40 60
39 " 50r brown ('03) 1.20 1.00
40 " 65r dull blue ('03) 4.75 4.00
41 " 75r rose 2.25 2.00
42 " 75r lilac ('03) 1.60 1.40
a. Imperf.
43 " 80r violet 2.25 1.75
44 A2 100r dark blue, *blue* 1.60 80
a. Perf. 13½ 14.00 3.25
45 " 115r orange brown, *pink* ('03) 4.75 3.75
46 " 130r brown, *straw* ('03) 4.75 4.00
47 " 150r brown, *straw* 2.25 1.75
48 " 200r red lilac, *pinkish* 3.25 1.75
49 " 300r dark blue, *rose* 2.00 1.50
50 " 400r dull blue, *straw* ('03) 7.50 5.00
51 " 500r black & red, *blue* ('01) 4.00 3.00
52 " 700r violet, *yellowish* ('01) 8.75 6.50
Nos. 30-52 (23) 56.80 42.15

Coat of Arms
A3

Surcharged On Upper and Lower Halves of Stamp.

1899 *Imperf.*

53 A3 5r on 10r grn. & brn. 7.50 7.50
54 " 25r on 10r grn. & brn. 7.50 7.50
55 " 50r on 30r grn. & brn. 10.00 10.00
a. Invtd. surch. 30.00
56 " 50r on 800r green & brown 15.00 15.00

The lower half of No. 55 can be distinguished from that of No. 56 by the background of the label containing the word "REIS". The former is plain, while the latter is formed of white intersecting curved horizontal lines over vertical shading of violet brown.
Prices are for undivided stamps. Halves sell for half as much.
Nos. 53–56 issued mostly without gum.

No. 41 Surcharged in Black **50 Réis**

1899 *Perf. 11½*

57 A2 50r on 75r rose 2.75 1.75

No. 57 issued mostly without gum.

Surcharged in Black **65 RÉIS**

On Issue of 1895.

1902 *Perf. 11½, 12½*

58 A1 65r on 5r yellow 2.75 2.25
59 " 65r on 15r chocolate 2.75 2.25
60 " 65r on 20r lavender 2.75 2.25
a. Perf. 12½ 25.00
61 " 115r on 10r red violet 2.75 2.25
62 " 115r on 200r bl., *blue* 2.75 2.25
63 " 115r on 300r blue, *salmon* 2.75 2.25
64 " 130r on 25r green, perf. 12½ 2.50 2.00
a. Perf. 11½ 25.00 17.50
65 " 130r on 80r yel. grn. 2.75 2.25
66 " 130r on 150r car., *rose* 2.75 2.25
67 " 400r on 50r light blue 8.00 4.75
68 " 400r on 75r rose 8.00 5.00
69 " 400r on 100r brn., *buff* 5.00 4.00

On Newspaper Stamp of 1893.

70 N1 65r on 2½r brown 2.75 2.25
Nos. 58-70 (13) 48.25 36.00

Surcharge exists inverted on Nos. 61, 70.

Nos. 64, 67 and 68 have been reprinted on thin white paper with shiny white gum and clean-cut perforation 13½. Price $3 each.

Issue of 1898-1903 Overprinted in Black **PROVISORIO**

1903 *Perf. 11½*

71 A2 15r brown 1.50 1.00
72 " 25r sea green 1.40 1.00
73 " 50r blue 1.75 1.25
74 " 75r rose 3.00 2.00
a. Inverted overprint 15.00 15.00

Surcharged in Black **50 RÉIS**

1905

76 A2 50r on 65r dull blue 2.75 2.25

Regular Issues Overprinted in Carmine or Green **REPUBLICA**

1911

77 A2 2½r gray 30 30
78 " 5r orange 30 30
a. Double overprint 2.75 2.50
b. Inverted overprint 2.75 2.50
79 " 10r light green 45 35
80 " 15r gray green 50 40
a. Inverted overprint 2.00 2.00
81 " 20r dull violet 1.00 60
82 " 25r carmine (G) 35 30
83 " 50r brown 1.00 60
84 " 75r lilac 1.00 60
85 " 100r dark blue, *blue* 1.00 60
86 " 115r orangebrown, *pink* 8.50 3.00
87 " 130r brown, *straw* 75 60
88 " 200r red lilac, *pinkish* 75 50
89 " 400r dull bl., *straw* 1.00 1.00
90 " 500r black & red, *blue* 1.40 1.00
91 " 700r vio., *yellowish* 2.00 1.25
Nos. 77-91 (15) 20.30 11.40

Vasco da Gama Issue of Various Portuguese Colonies Common Design Types Surcharged
REPUBLICA
LOURENCO MARQUES
¼ C.

1913 *Perf. 12½-16*

On Stamps of Macao.

92 CD20 ¼c on ½a bl. green 1.50 1.50
93 CD21 ½c on 1a red 1.50 1.50
94 CD22 1c on 2a red violet 1.50 1.50
95 CD23 2½c on 4a yel. grn. 1.50 1.50
96 CD24 5c on 8a dark blue 1.50 1.50
97 CD25 7½c on 12a violet brown 2.25 2.25
98 CD26 10c on 16a bis. brn. 1.75 1.75
a. Inverted surcharge
99 CD27 15c on 24a bistre 1.75 1.75
Nos. 92-99 (8) 13.25 13.25

On Stamps of Portuguese Africa.

100 CD20 ¼c on 2½r bl. green 1.25 1.25
101 CD21 ½c on 5r red 1.25 1.25
102 CD22 1c on 10r red violet 1.25 1.25
103 CD23 2½c on 25r yel. grn. 1.25 1.25
104 CD24 5c on 50r dark blue 1.25 1.25
105 CD25 7½c on 75r vio. brn. 2.00 2.00
106 CD26 10c on 100r bis. brn. 1.75 1.75
107 CD27 15c on 150r bistre 1.75 1.75
Nos. 100-107 (8) 11.75 11.75

On Stamps of Timor.

108 CD20 ¼c on ½a bl. green 1.75 1.75
109 CD21 ½c on 1a red 1.75 1.75
110 CD22 1c on 2a red violet 1.75 1.75
111 CD23 2½c on 4a yel. grn. 1.75 1.75
112 CD24 5c on 8a dark blue 1.75 1.75
113 CD25 7½c on 12a vio. brn. 3.00 3.00
114 CD26 10c on 16a bis. brn. 2.00 2.00
115 CD27 15c on 24a bistre 2.00 2.00
Nos. 108-115 (8) 15.75 15.75

Ceres
A4

1914 Typographed. *Perf. 15x14.*

Name and Value in Black.

116 A4 ¼c olive brown 12 12
117 " ½c black 12 12
a. Value omitted
118 " 1c blue green 12 12
119 " 1½c lilac brown 12 12
a. Imperf.
120 " 2c carmine 12 12
121 " 2½c light violet 9 9
122 " 5c deep blue 15 12
123 " 7½c yellow brown 15 12
124 " 8c slate 20 12
125 " 10c orange brown 2.00 1.00
126 " 15c plum 35 25
127 " 20c yellow green 2.00 75
128 " 30c brown, *green* 2.25 1.25
129 " 40c brown, *pink* 5.00 5.00
130 " 50c orange, *salmon* 2.75 2.75
131 " 1e green, *blue* 2.75 2.00
Nos. 116–131 (16) 18.29 14.05

Prices of Nos. 116–124 are for stamps on ordinary paper. Those on chalky paper sell for 8 to 12 times as much. Nos. 127–131 issued only on chalky paper.

In 1921 Nos. 117 and 119 were surcharged 10c and 30c respectively, for use in Mozambique as Nos. 230 and 231. These same values, surcharged 5c and 10c respectively, with the addition of the word "PORTEADO," were used in Mozambique as postage dues, Nos. J44 and J45.

Provisional Issue of 1902 Overprinted Locally in Carmine

1914 ***Perf. 11½, 12½***

132 A1 115r on 10r red violet 1.00 60
a. "Republica" inverted
133 " 115r on 200r be., *blue* 1.00 60
134 " 115r on 300r blue, *salmon* 1.00 60
a. Double overprint 10.00 10.00
135 " 130r on 25r green 1.50 1.00
a. Perf. 12½ 3.50 2.00
136 " 130r on 80r yel. grn. 1.00 60
137 " 130r on 150r car., *rose* 1.00 60
Nos. 132–137 (6) 6.50 4.00

No. 135a was issued without gum.

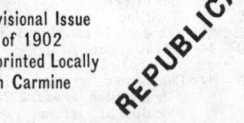

Nos. 78 and 117 Perforated Diagonally and Surcharged in Carmine

¼

¼

1915 ***Perf. 11½***

138 A2 ¼c on half of 5r orange, pair 5.00 5.00
a. Pair without dividing perforation 10.00 10.00

Perf. 15x14

139 A4 ¼c on half of ½c black, pair 7.50 7.50

The added perforation on Nos. 138–139 runs from lower left to upper right corners, dividing the stamp in two. Prices are for pairs, both halves of the stamp.

Provisional Issue of 1902 Overprinted in Carmine

REPUBLICA

1915 ***Perf. 11½, 12½***

140 A1 115r on 10r red violet 80 60
141 " 115r on 200r blue, *blue* 80 60
142 A1 115r on 300r blue, *salmon* 80 60
143 " 130r on 150r car., *rose* 80 60

Nos. 34 and 80 Surcharged

Dois centavos

1915

On Issue of 1903.

144 A2 2c on 15r gray green 80 60

On Issue of 1911.

145 A2 2c on 15r gray green 80 60
a. New value inverted 5.00

Regular Issues of 1898-1903 Overprinted Locally in Carmine

REPUBLICA

1916

146 A2 15r gray green 75 50
147 " 50r brown 2.00 1.75
a. Inverted overprint
148 " 75r lilac 2.25 2.00
149 " 100r blue, *blue* 1.00 1.00
150 " 115r org. brown, *pink* 1.00 1.00
151 " 130r brown, *straw* 7.50 6.00
152 " 200r red lilac, *pinkish* 2.00 1.25
153 " 400r dull blue, *straw* 3.25 2.50
154 " 500r black & red, *blue* 2.50 1.75
155 " 700r violet, *yellowish* 4.00 2.50
Nos. 146–155 (10) 26.25 20.25

Same Overprint on Nos. 67–68

1917

156 A1 400r on 50r light blue 1.50 75
a. Perf. 13½
157 " 400r on 75r rose 3.00 1.25

No. 69 exists with this overprint. It was not officially issued.

Type of 1914 Surcharged in Red

Quatro centavos

1920 ***Perf. 15x14***

159 A4 4c on 2½c violet 1.25 35

Stamps of 1914 Surcharged in Green or Black:

Um quarto de centavo
a

1 Centavo
b

1921

160 A1 (*a*) ¼c on 115r on 10r red vio. (G) 1.00 1.00
161 A4 (*b*) 1c on 2½c violet (Bk) 75 50
a. Invtd. surch. 10.00
162 A4 (*b*) 1½c on 2½c violet (Bk) 1.00 75

Nos. 159–162 were postally valid throughout Mozambique.

SEMI-POSTAL STAMPS.

Regular Issue of 1914 Overprinted or Surcharged:

= + 9-3-18
a

= $20 + 9-3-18
b

= 1$ + 9-3-18
c

1918 ***Perf. 15x14½.***

B1 A4 (*a*) ¼c olive brown 2.00 2.00
B2 " (") ½c black 2.00 2.00
B3 " (") 1c blue green 2.00 2.00
B4 " (") 2½c violet 3.50 3.50
B5 " (") 5c blue 3.50 3.50
B6 " (") 10c orange brn. 4.00 4.00
B7 A4 (*b*) 20c on 1½c lilac brown 4.00 4.00
B8 " (*a*) 30c brn., *green* 4.00 4.00
B9 " (*b*) 40c on 2c carmine 4.00 4.00
B10 " (") 50c on 7½c bistre 7.50 7.50
B11 " (") 70c on 8c slate 7.50 7.50
B12 " (*c*) $1 on 15c magenta 7.50 7.50
Nos. B1–B12 (12) 51.50 51.50

Nos. B1-B12 were used in place of ordinary postage stamps on March 9, 1918.

NEWSPAPER STAMPS.

Numeral of Value
N1

Perf. 11½

1893, July 28 Typo. Unwmkd.

P1 N1 2½r brown 30 75
a. Perf. 12½ 17.50 15.00

Saint Anthony of Padua Issue.

Mozambique No. P6 Overprinted

L. MARQUES
—
CENTENARIO
DE
S. ANTONIO
—
MDCCCXCV

1895, July 1 ***Perf. 11½, 13½***

P2 N3 2½r brown 20.00 15.00
a. Inverted overprint

LUBECK

See German States group preceding Germany.

LUXEMBOURG

(lŭk'sĕm-bûrg)

LOCATION—In western Europe, between southern Belgium, Germany and France.
GOVT.—Grand Duchy.
AREA—999 sq. mi.
POP.—360,000 (est. 1977).
CAPITAL—Luxembourg.

12½ Centimes = 1 Silbergroschen
100 Centimes = 1 Franc

Prices of early Luxembourg stamps vary according to condition. Quotations for Nos. 1–12 are for fine copies. Very fine to superb specimens sell at much higher prices, and inferior or poor copies sell at reduced prices, depending on the condition of the individual specimen.

Grand Duke William III
A1

Wmk. 149

Luxembourg Print.
Wmkd. W (149)

1852, Sept. 15 Engr. *Imperf.*

1 A1 10c gray black 1850.00 30.00
a. 10c black 2100.00 60.00
2 A1 1sg brick red 1200.00 55.00
a. 1sg brown red 1300.00 67.50
b. 1sg orange red 1350.00 80.00
c. 1sg copper red 1200.00 67.50
3 " 1sg rose 1350.00 67.50

Reprints of both values exist on watermarked paper. Some of the reprints show traces of lines cancelling the plates, but others can be distinguished only by an expert.

Coat of Arms
A2 A3

Frankfort Print.

1859-63 Typographed. Unwmkd.

4 A2 1c buff ('63) 100.00 *275.00*
5 " 2c black ('60) 100.00 *300.00*
6 " 4c yellow ('60) 180.00 180.00
a. 4c orange 180.00 180.00
7 A3 10c blue 115.00 9.00
8 " 12½c rose 190.00 150.00
9 " 25c brown 325.00 225.00
10 " 30c rose lilac 265.00 180.00
11 " 37½c green 265.00 180.00
12 " 40c red orange 650.00 250.00

Counterfeits of Nos. 1-12 exist.

1865-71 ***Rouletted.***

13 A2 1c red brown 175.00 210.00
14 " 2c black ('67) 12.00 9.00
15 " 4c yellow ('67) 425.00 200.00
16 " 4c green ('71) 30.00 24.00

Coat of Arms
A4 A5

1865-73 ***Rouletted in Color***

17 A2 1c red brown ('67) 16.50 2.50
18 " 1c orange('69) 12.00 4.50
a. 1c brown orange 65.00 32.50
19 A3 10c lilac 110.00 1.50
a. 10c rose lilac 125.00 1.75
b. 10c gray lilac 125.00 1.50
20 " 12½c carmine 140.00 6.25
a. 12½c rose 160.00 8.00
21 " 20c gray brn. ('67) 110.00 3.00
a. 20c yellow brown ('69) 125.00 10.00
22 " 25c blue ('72) 325.00 16.50
22A " 25c ultra. ('65) 300.00 18.50
23 " 30c lilac rose 450.00 70.00
24 " 37½c bistre ('66) 650.00 275.00
25 " 40c pale org. ('66) 45.00 *90.00*
a. 40c orange red 950.00 45.00
26 A4 1fr on 37½c bistre ('73) 650.00 80.00
a. Surcharge inverted *2250.00*

Luxembourg Print.

1874 Typographed. *Imperf.*

27 A2 4c green 75.00 75.00

1875-79 ***Perf. 13.***

Narrow Margins

29 A2 1c red brown ('78) 30.00 4.50
30 " 2c black 120.00 19.00
31 " 4c green 1.25 *5.50*
32 " 5c yellow ('76) 175.00 16.50
a. 5c org. yellow 325.00 25.00
b. Imperf. 425.00 350.00
33 A3 10c gray lilac 200.00 1.25
b. 10c lilac 700.00 25.00
c. Imperforate 1200.00 1800.00
34 " 12½c lilac rose ('76) 375.00 20.00
35 " 12½c car. rose ('77) 325.00 25.00
36 " 25c blue ('77) 800.00 15.00
37 " 30c dull rose ('78) 800.00 300.00
38 " 40c orange ('79) 90 *4.50*

39 A5 1fr on 37½c bistre ('79) 6.75 15.00
a. "Pranc" 3000.00 3250.00
b. Without surch. 325.00
c. As "b", imperf. 475.00

In the Luxembourg print the perforation is close to the border of the stamp. Excellent forgeries of No. 39a are plentiful, as well as faked cancellations on Nos. 31, 38 and 39.

Nos. 32b and 33c are said to be essays; Nos. 39b and 39c printer's waste.

Haarlem Print.

Perf. 11½x12, 12½x12, 13½.

1880-81 Wide Margins

40 A2 1c yel. brn. ('81) 7.50 5.25
41 " 2c black 6.75 90
42 " 5c yellow ('81) 135.00 80.00
a. Gray yellowish paper, perf. 12½ 4.50
43 A3 10c gray lilac 135.00 80
a. Gray yellowish paper, perf. 12½ 1.75
44 " 12½c rose ('81) 190.00 165.00
a. Gray yellowish paper, perf. 12½ 6.75
45 " 20c gray brown ('81) 45.00 15.00
46 " 25c blue 225.00 2.75
a. Gray yellowish paper, perf. 12½ 2.25
47 " 30c dull rose ('81) 2.25 11.00

Stamps on gray yellowish paper were not regularly issued.

"Industry" and "Commerce"
A6

Grand Duke Adolphe
A7

Perf. 11½x12, 12½x12, 12½, 13½

1882, Dec. 1 Typographed

48 A6 1c gray lilac 27 22
49 " 2c olive gray 25 18
a. 2c olive brown 55 25
50 " 4c olive bistre 80 80
51 " 5c light green 80 25
52 " 10c rose 22.50 25
53 " 12½c slate 4.25 5.50
54 " 20c orange 7.00 1.65
55 " 25c ultramarine 175.00 1.65
56 " 30c gray green 55.00 13.50
57 " 50c bistre brown 1.40 1.65
58 " 1fr pale violet 2.25 3.50
59 " 5fr brown orange 38.50 45.00

Perf. 11, 11½, 11½x11 and 12½.

1891-93 Engraved.

60 A7 10c carmine 50 25
a. Sheet of 25 65.00
61 " 12½c slate green ('93) 1.00 32
a. Booklet pane of 6 45.00
62 " 20c orange ('93) 25.00 40
a. 20c brn. (error) 100.00 150.00
63 " 25c blue 1.00 35
a. Sheet of 25 750.00
64 " 30c olive green ('93) 1.25 60
65 " 37½c green ('93) 2.00 1.60
66 " 50c brown ('93) 12.50 2.00
67 " 1fr dp. violet ('93) 17.50 3.50
68 " 2½fr black ('93) 2.00 3.25
69 " 5fr lake ('93) 60.00 55.00

No. 62a was never on sale at any post office, but exists postally used.

Grand Duke Adolphe
A8

1895, May 4 Typo. *Perf. 12½*

70 A8 1c pearl gray 4.00 25
71 " 2c gray brown 15 15
72 " 4c olive bistre 35 35
73 " 5c green 3.00 15
a. Booklet pane of 6 27.50
74 " 10c carmine 22.50 18

Coat of Arms
A9

Grand Duke William IV
A10

1906-26 Typo. *Perf. 12½*

75 A9 1c gray ('07) 13 10
76 " 2c olive brown ('07) 13 8
77 " 4c bistre ('07) 27 15
78 " 5c green ('07) 40 12
79 " 5c lilac ('26) 10 10
80 " 6c violet ('07) 40 12
81 " 7½c orange ('19) 12 20

Engraved.

Perf. 11, 11½x11

82 A10 10c scarlet 2.50 12
a. Souvenir sheet of ten 375.00 550.00
83 " 12½c slate grn. ('07) 2.50 27
84 " 15c org. brn. ('07) 2.50 65
85 " 20c orange ('07) 4.50 35
86 " 25c ultra. ('07) 100.00 22
87 " 30c olive grn. ('08) 1.50 35
88 " 37½c green ('07) 1.50 60
a. Perf. 12½ 75.00 7.50
89 " 50c brown ('07) 6.25 70
90 " 87½c dk. blue ('08) 3.25 6.50
91 " 1fr violet ('08) 6.00 1.20
92 " 2½fr verm. ('08) 75.00 60.00
93 " 5fr claret ('08) 11.00 15.00
Nos. 75-93 (19) 218.05 86.83

No. 82a was issued to commemorate the accession of Grand Duke William IV to the throne.

Surcharged in Red or Black **62½ cts.**

1912-15

94 A10 62½c on 87½c dark blue (R) 3.00 1.75
95 " 62½c on 2½fr verm. (Bk) ('15) 6.50 5.50
96 " 62½c on 5fr claret (Bk) ('15) 1.25 90

Grand Duchess Marie Adelaide
A11

Grand Duchess Charlotte
A12

Engraved.

1914-17 *Perf. 11½, 11½x11.*

97 A11 10c lake 6 6
98 " 12½c dull green 6 6
99 " 15c sepia 8 8
100 " 17½c deep brown ('17) 20 22
101 " 25c ultramarine 20 5
102 " 30c bistre 30 22
103 " 35c dark blue 20 17
104 " 37½c black brown 20 17
105 " 40c orange 30 17
106 " 50c dark gray 30 22
107 " 62½c blue green 70 70
108 " 87½c orange ('17) 70 90
109 " 1fr orange brown 1.65 90
110 " 2½fr red 1.50 1.50
111 " 5fr dark violet 7.50 7.50
Nos. 97-111 (15) 13.95 12.92

Stamps of 1906-19 Surcharged with New Value and Bars in Black or Red

1916-24

112 A9 2½c on 5c green ('18) 10 10
113 " 3c on 2c olive brown ('21) 10 10
114 " 5c on 1c gray ('23) 10 10
115 " 5c on 4c bistre ('23) 15 15
116 " 5c on 7½c org. ('24) 10 10
117 " 6c on 2c olive brown (R) ('22) 27 15
118 A11 7½c on 10c lake ('18) 15 15
119 " 17½c on 30c bistre 27 30
120 " 20c on 17½c brn. ('21) 18 20
121 A11 25c on 37½c black brown ('23) 20 33
a. Double surcharge 75.00
122 " 75c on 62½c blue green (R) ('22) 20 25
123 " 80c on 87½c orange ('22) 20 25
124 " 87½c on 1fr org. brn. 1.00 1.35
Nos. 112-124 (13) 3.02 3.53

1921, Jan. 6 Engr. *Perf. 11½*

125 A12 15c rose 12 12
a. Sheet of 5, perf. 11 135.00 135.00
b. Sheet of 25, perf. 11½, 11x11½, 12x11½ 4.00 13.50

No. 125a was issued Jan. 6, 1921, the day after Prince Jean, first son of Grand Duchess Charlotte, was born. No. 125 was printed in sheets of 100.

See Nos. 131-148.

Vianden Castle
A13

Foundries at Esch
A14

Adolphe Bridge
A15

1921-34 *Perf. 11, 11x11½, 11½*

126 A13 1fr carmine 20 25
127 " 1fr dark blue ('26) 35 35

Perf. 11½x11; 11½ (#129)

128 A14 2fr indigo 30 35
129 " 2fr dark brn. ('26) 1.85 1.10
130 A15 5fr dark violet 12.50 3.50
a. Perf. 12½ ('34) 20.00 8.50
Nos. 126-130 (5) 15.20 5.55

Charlotte Type of 1921

1921-26 *Perf. 11½.*

131 A12 2c brown 6 8
132 " 3c olive green 6 8
a. Sheet of 25 7.50 15.00
133 " 6c violet 6 8
a. Sheet of 25 7.50 15.00
134 " 10c yellow green 10 8
135 " 10c olive brown ('24) 10 7
136 " 15c brown olive 10 8
137 " 15c pale green ('24) 10 8
138 " 15c deep orange ('26) 10 8
139 " 20c deep orange 10 8
a. Sheet of 25 45.00 70.00
140 " 20c yellow green ('26) 10 8
141 " 25c dark green 10 5
142 " 30c carmine rose 10 5
143 " 40c brown orange 10 8
144 " 50c deep blue 30 20
145 " 50c red ('24) 17 8
146 " 75c red 20 20
a. Sheet of 25 300.00
147 " 75c deep blue ('24) 17 8
148 " 80c black 30 30
a. Sheet of 25 300.00
Nos. 131-148 (18) 2.32 1.83

Philatelic Exhibition Issue.

1922, Aug. 27 *Imperf.*

Laid Paper

149 A12 25c dark green 2.75 3.75
150 " 30c carmine rose 2.75 3.75

Nos. 149 and 150 were sold exclusively at the Luxembourg Philatelic Exhibition, August, 1922. They were, however, available for postage throughout the country.

Souvenir Sheet.

View of Luxembourg—A16

1923, Jan. 3 *Perf. 11*

151 A16 10fr deep green, sheet 1400.00 2500.00

Issued in sheets measuring 79x59 mm. containing one stamp. Issued to commemorate the birth of Princess Elisabeth.

1923, Mar. *Perf. 11½*

152 A16 10fr black 7.50 11.50
a. Perf. 12½ ('34) 5.50 8.00

The Wolfsschlucht near Echternach
A17

1923-34 *Perf. 11½*

153 A17 3fr dk. blue & blue 1.75 1.25
a. Perf. 12½ ('34) 1.10 55

Stamps of 1921-26

Surcharged with New Values and Bars

1925-28

154 A12 5c on 10c yel. green 10 10
155 " 15c on 20c yellow green ('28) 20 30
a. Bars omitted
156 " 35c on 40c brown orange ('27) 22 25
157 " 60c on 75c deep blue ('27) 22 25
158 " 60c on 80c black ('28) 35 55
Nos. 154-158 (5) 1.09 1.45

Grand Duchess Charlotte
A18

1926-35 Engraved *Perf. 12*

159 A18 5c dark violet 6 5
a. Booklet pane of 10 8.50
160 " 10c olive green 5 5
a. Booklet pane of 10 8.50
161 " 15c black ('30) 17 25
162 " 20c orange 12 8
163 " 25c yellow green 12 10
164 " 25c violet brown ('27) 15 18
165 " 30c yellow green ('27) 22 30
166 " 30c gray violet ('30) 45 25
167 " 35c gray violet ('28) 50 12
168 " 35c yellow green ('30) 10 15
a. Booklet pane of 10 8.50
169 " 40c olive gray 10 8
170 " 50c red brown 10 5
171 " 60c blue green ('28) 80 4
172 " 65c black brown 15 20
173 " 70c blue violet ('35) 6 3
a. Booklet pane of 10 8.50
174 " 75c rose 15 12
175 " 75c bistre brown ('27) 13 10
176 " 80c bistre brown 20 25
177 " 90c rose ('27) 55 75
178 " 1fr black 25 25
179 " 1fr rose ('30) 45 30
180 " 1¼fr dark blue 17 20
181 " 1¼fr yellow ('30) 8.00 1.20
182 " 1¼fr blue green ('31) 30 8
183 " 1¼fr rose carmine ('34) 45.00 2.00
184 " 1½fr deep blue ('27) 1.20 75
185 " 1¾fr dark blue ('30) 1.00 38
Nos. 159-185 (27) 60.55 8.31

Stamps of 1926-35,

Surcharged with New Values and Bars.

1928-39

186 A18 10(c) on 30c yellow green ('29) 45 45

187 A18 15c on 25c yel. green 35 38
187A " 30c on 60c blue green ('39) 17 38
188 " 60c on 65c bk. brown 35 60
189 " 60c on 75c rose 35 25
190 " 60c on 80c bis. brown 35 25
191 " 70(c) on 75c bistre brown ('35) 13.00 33
192 " 75(c) on 90c rose ('29) 1.35 27
193 " 1¾(fr) on 1½fr deep blue ('29) 2.75 1.50
Nos. 186-193 (9) 19.12 4.41

The surcharge on No. 187A has no bars.

View of Clervaux—A19

1928-34 ***Perf. 12½.***

194 A19 2fr black ('34) 1.10 30
a. Perf. 11½ ('28) 1.50 45

See also No. B66.

Coat of Arms
A20

1930, Dec. 20 Typo. ***Perf. 12½***

195 A20 5c claret 80 27
196 " 10c olive green 1.35 10

View of the Lower City of Luxembourg
A21

Gate of "Three Towers"
A22

1931, June 20 Engraved

197 A21 20fr deep green 5.00 10.00

1934, Aug. 30 ***Perf. 14x13½***

198 A22 5fr blue green 2.00 4.00

Castle From Our Valley
A23

1935, Nov. 15 ***Perf. 12½x12***

199 A23 10fr green 3.00 5.50

Municipal Palace
A24

Granite Paper.

1936, Aug. 26 Photo. ***Perf. 11½***

200 A24 10c brown 25 40
201 " 35c green 65 1.10
202 " 70c red orange 65 1.10
203 " 1fr carmine rose 2.00 4.00
204 " 1.25fr violet 4.75 10.00
205 " 1.75fr bright ultra. 2.50 5.50
Nos. 200-205 (6) 10.80 22.10

Issued in commemoration of the 11th Congress of International Federation of Philately.

Arms of Luxembourg
A25

William I
A26

William II
A27

William III
A28

Prince Henry
A29

Grand Duke Adolphe
A30

William IV
A31

Regent Marie Anne
A32

Grand Duchess Marie Adelaide
A33

Grand Duchess Charlotte
A34

1939, May 27 Engr. ***Perf. 12½x12***

206 A25 35c bright green 60 95
207 A26 50c orange 60 95
208 A27 70c slate green 17 27
209 A28 75c sepia 60 95
210 A29 1fr red 1.65 2.75
211 A30 1.25fr brown violet 17 27
212 A31 1.75fr dark blue 17 27
213 A32 3fr light brown 50 80
214 A33 5fr gray black 80 1.25
215 A34 10fr copper red 1.60 2.50
Nos. 206-215 (10) 6.86 10.96

Centenary of Independence.

Allegory of Medicinal Baths
A35

1939, Sept. 18 Photo. ***Perf. 11½***

216 A35 2fr brown rose 75 1.75

Issued to commemorate the elevation of Mondorf-les-Bains to the dignity of a town.

Souvenir Sheet.

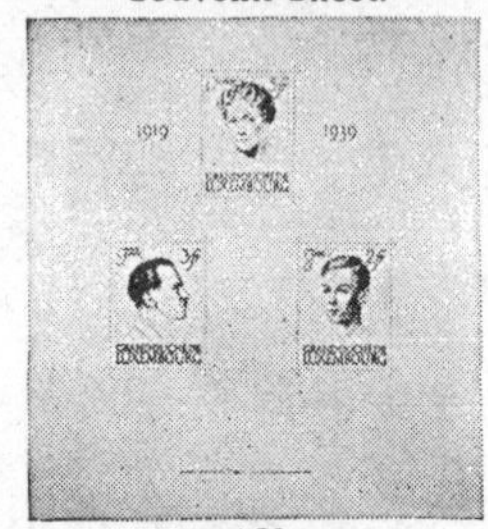

A36

1939, Dec. 20 Engr. ***Perf. 14x13***

217 A36 Sheet of three 42.50 80.00
a. 2fr vermilion, *buff* 10.00 15.00
b. 3fr dark green, *buff* 10.00 15.00
c. 5fr blue, *buff* 10.00 15.00

20th anniversary of the reign of Grand Duchess Charlotte (January 15, 1919) and her marriage to Prince Felix (November 6, 1919). Size: 145x165mm.
See Nos. B98-B103.

Grand Duchess Charlotte
A37

Lion from Duchy Arms
A38

1944-46 ***Perf. 12*** **Unwmkd.**

218 A37 5c brown red 7 13
219 " 10c black 7 13
219A " 20c orange ('46) 7 13
220 " 25c sepia 7 13
220A " 30c carmine ('46) 15 22
221 " 35c green 7 13
221A " 40c dark blue ('46) 15 22
222 " 50c dark violet 7 13
222A " 60c orange ('46) 1.50 50
223 " 70c rose pink 7 13
223A " 70c deep green ('46) 35 45
223B " 75c sepia ('46) 35 22
224 " 1fr olive 7 13
225 " 1¼fr red orange 7 13
226 " 1½fr red orange ('46) 30 10
227 " 1¾fr blue 15 22
228 " 2fr rose car. ('46) 1.20 50
229 " 2½fr dp. violet ('46) 2.25 3.25
230 " 3fr deep yellow green ('46) 45 65
231 " 3½fr bright blue ('46) 60 85
232 " 5fr dark blue green 15 22
233 " 10fr carmine 30 75
234 " 20fr deep blue 60 1.85
Nos. 218-234 (23) 9.13 11.17

1945 Engraved. ***Perf. 14x13.***

235 A38 20c black 8 12
236 " 30c bright green 8 12
237 " 60c deep violet 15 22
238 " 75c brown red 15 22
239 " 1.20fr red 10 15
240 " 1.50fr rose lilac 10 15
241 " 2.50fr light blue 15 22
Nos. 235-241 (7) 81 1.20

Patton's Grave, U.S. Military Cemetery, Hamm—A39

Gen. Patton, Broken Chain and Advancing Tanks
A40

1947, Oct. 24 Photo. ***Perf. 11½***

242 A39 1.50fr dark carmine 18 30
243 A40 3.50fr dull blue 2.10 3.50
244 A39 5fr dk. slate grn. 2.10 3.50
245 A40 10fr chocolate 7.00 13.50

George S. Patton, Jr. (1885-1945), American general.

Oesling Mountain Forts
A41

Luxembourg
A44

Moselle River
A42

Steel Mills
A43

Perf. 11½x11, 11x11½

1948, Aug. 5 Engr. **Unwmkd.**

246 A41 7fr dark brown 14.00 75
247 A42 10fr dark green 1.25 30
248 A43 15fr carmine 1.60 75
249 A44 20fr dark blue 1.60 25

Grand Duchess Charlotte
A45

1948-49 ***Perf. 11½***

250 A45 15c olive brown ('49) 8 10
251 " 25c slate 8 5
252 " 60c brown ('49) 30 15
253 " 80c green ('49) 30 15
254 " 1fr red lilac 45 5

255 A45 1.50fr greenish blue 30 4
256 " 1.60fr slate gray ('49) 50 90
257 " 2fr dark violet brown 45 5
258 " 4fr violet blue 75 25
259 " 6fr bright red violet ('49) 1.75 25
260 " 8fr dull green ('49) 1.75 85
Nos. 250-260 (11) 6.71 2.84

See also Nos. 265-271, 292, 337-340, B151.

Self-Inking Canceller
A46

1949, Oct. 6 Photogravure

261 A46 80c black, Prus. grn. & pale green 60 90
262 " 2.50fr dark brown, brown red & salmon rose 1.60 2.25
263 " 4fr black, blue & pale blue 8.00 13.50
264 " 8fr dark brown, brown & buff 25.00 40.00

Issued to commemorate the 75th anniversary of the formation of the Universal Postal Union.

Charlotte Type of 1948-49.

1951, Mar. 15 Engr. Unwmkd.

265 A45 5c red orange 8 10
266 " 10c ultramarine 8 10
267 " 40c crimson 15 20
268 " 1.25fr dark brown 30 25
269 " 2.50fr red 30 10
270 " 3fr blue 1.25 25
271 " 3.50fr rose lake 1.25 25
Nos. 265-271 (7) 3.41 1.25

Agriculture and Industry
A47

Globe and Scales
A48

Design: 1fr, 3fr, People of Europe and Charter of Freedom.

1951, Oct. 25 Photo. *Perf. 11½*

272 A47 80c deep green 13.00 10.00
273 " 1fr purple 5.00 1.25
274 A48 2fr black brown 26.50 1.25
275 A47 2.50fr dark carmine 40.00 30.00
276 " 3fr orange brown 60.00 42.50
277 A48 4fr blue 120.00 90.00
Nos. 272-277 (6) 264.50 175.00

Issued to promote a united Europe.

Grand Duke William III—A49

Perf. 13½x13

1952, May 24 Engr. Unwmkd.

Dates, Ornaments in Olive Green

278 A49 2fr black 50.00 90.00
279 " 4fr red brown 50.00 90.00

Printed in sheets containing two panes of eight stamps each, alternating the two denominations. Issued to commemorate the centenary of Luxembourg's postage stamps. Price per set, 26fr, which included admission to the CENTILUX exhibition.

See also Nos. C16-C20.

Hurdle Race
A50

Designs: 2fr, Football. 2.50fr, Boxing. fr, Water polo. 4fr, Bicycle racing. 8fr, Fencing.

1952, Aug. 20 Photo. *Perf. 11½*

Designs in Black.

280 A50 1fr pale green 50 42
281 " 2fr brown buff 1.75 42
282 " 2.50fr salmon pink 3.50 1.00
283 " 3fr buff 6.25 1.75
284 " 4fr light blue 26.50 9.00
285 " 8fr lilac 12.50 6.00
Nos. 280-285 (6) 51.00 18.59

Issued to commemorate the XV Olympic Games at Helsinki and the World Bicycling Championships of 1952.

Princess Josephine-Charlotte and Hereditary Grand Duke Jean
A51

1953, Apr. 1

286 A51 80c dull violet 45 50
287 " 1.20fr light brown 45 50
288 " 2fr green 1.25 30
289 " 3fr red lilac 1.85 1.20
290 " 4fr bright blue 7.00 1.50
291 " 9fr brown red 7.00 2.00
Nos. 286-291 (6) 18.00 6.00

Issued to commemorate the wedding of Hereditary Grand Duke Jean of Luxembourg to Princess Josephine-Charlotte of Belgium.

Charlotte Type of 1948-49

1953, May 18 Engraved

292 A45 1.20fr gray 30 12

Radio Luxembourg
A52

Victor Hugo's Home, Vianden
A53

1953, May 18 *Perf. 11½x11*

293 A52 3fr purple 6.25 2.25
294 A53 4fr Prussian blue 4.25 2.25

No. 294 issued to commemorate the 150th anniversary of the birth of Victor Hugo.

St. Willibrord Basilica Restored
A54

Pierre d'Aspelt
A55

Design: 2.50fr, Interior view.

1953, Sept. 18 *Perf. 13x13½*

295 A54 2fr red 6.00 60
296 " 2.50fr dark gray green 8.50 12.50

Issued to commemorate the consecration of St. Willibrord Basilica at Echternach.

1953, Sept.

297 A55 4fr black 10.00 8.00

Issued to commemorate the 700th anniversary of the birth of Pierre d'Aspelt (1250-1320), chancellor of the Holy Roman Empire and Archbishop of Mainz.

Fencing Swords, Mask and Glove
A56

Winged "L" Over Map
A57

1954, May 6 *Perf. 13½x13*

298 A56 2fr red brown & black brown, *gray* 8.50 75

Issued to publicize the World Fencing Championship Matches, Luxembourg, June 10-22, 1954.

1954, May 6 Photo. *Perf. 11½*

299 A57 4fr deep blue, yellow & red 15.00 5.00

Issued to publicize the 6th International Fair, Luxembourg, July 10-25, 1954.

Tulips
A58

Artisan, Wheel and Tools
A59

Flowers: 2fr, Daffodils. 3fr, Hyacinths. 4fr, Parrot tulips.

1955, Apr. 1

300 A58 80c dark brown, rose red & blue green 28 40
301 " 2fr cerise, yellow & green 28 40
302 " 3fr blue green & lilac rose 3.00 4.25
303 " 4fr multicolored 3.50 5.00

Flower festival at Mondorf-les-Bains.
See also Nos. 351-353.

1955, Sept. 1 Engr. *Perf. 13*

304 A59 2fr dark gray & black brown 1.10 32

Issued to commemorate the National Handicraft Exposition at Luxembourg-Limpertsburg, Sept. 3-12, 1955.

Dudelange Television Station
A60

1955, Sept. 1 Unwmkd.

305 A60 2.50fr dark brown & reddish brown 1.10 38

Issued to publicize the installation of the Tele-Luxembourg station at Dudelange.

United Nations Emblem and Children Playing—A61

Designs: 80c, "Charter". 4fr, "Justice" (Sword and Scales). 9fr, "Assistance" (Workers).

1955, Oct. 24 *Perf. 11x11½*

306 A61 80c black & dk. blue 1.10 60
307 " 2fr red & brown 6.75 20
308 " 4fr dark blue & red 4.50 5.75
309 " 9fr dark brown & slate green 1.50 2.00

Issued to commemorate the tenth anniversary of the United Nations, Oct. 24, 1955.

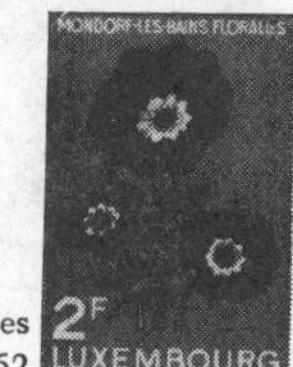

Anemones
A62

Design: 2.50fr, 4fr, Roses. 3fr, Crocuses.

1956 Photogravure. *Perf. 11½*

Flowers in Natural Colors.

310 A62 2fr gray violet 30 25
311 " 2.50fr bright blue 5.75 7.00
312 " 3fr red brown 1.75 2.00
313 " 4fr purple 2.50 3.00

Nos. 310 and 312 were issued to publicize the Flower Festival at Mondorf-les-Bains. Nos. 311 and 313 are inscribed: "Luxembourg-Ville des Roses."

Issue dates: Nos. 310, 312, Apr. 27; Nos. 311, 313, May 30.

Steel Beam and City Emblem
A63

1956, May 30

314 A63 2fr bright greenish blue, red & blk. 1.75 50

50th anniversary of Esch-sur-Alzette.

Bessemer Converter and Blast Furnaces
A64

Steel Beam and Model of City of Luxembourg
A65

"Rebuilding Europe"
A66

Design: 4fr, Six-link chain and miner's lamp.

Perf. 11x11½, 11½x11

1956, Aug. 10 Engraved

315 A64 2fr dull red 18.50 1.00
316 A65 3fr dark blue 22.50 27.50
317 A64 4fr green 3.50 4.00

Issued to commemorate the fourth anniversary of the establishment in Luxembourg of the headquarters of the European Coal and Steel Community.

1956, Sept. 15 *Perf. 13*

318 A66 2fr brown & black 125.00 50
319 " 3fr brick red & carmine 42.50 50.00
320 " 4fr bright blue & deep blue 7.00 7.50

Issued to symbolize the cooperation among the six countries comprising the Coal and Steel Community.

Central Station from Train Window
A67

1956, Sept. 29 *Perf. 13x12½*

321 A67 2fr black & sepia 1.40 40

Electrification of Luxembourg railways.

Ignace de la Fontaine
A68

Design: 7fr, Grand Duchess Charlotte.

1956, Nov. 7 *Perf. 11½*

322 A68 2fr gray brown 4.25 22
323 " 7fr dull purple 7.25 1.10

Centenary of the Council of State.

Lord Baden-Powell and Luxembourg Scout Emblems
A69

Designs: 2.50fr, Lord Baden-Powell and Luxembourg Girl Scout emblems.

1957, June 17 *Perf. 11½x11*

324 A69 2fr olive green & red brown 2.10 75
325 A69 2.50fr dark violet & claret 6.25 7.50

Issued to commemorate the centenary of the birth of Robert Baden-Powell and the 50th anniversary of the founding of the Scout movement.

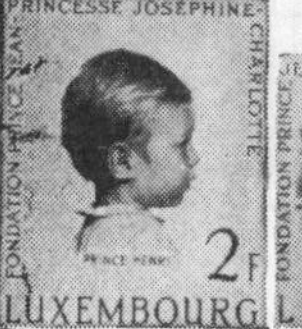

Prince Henry
A70

Children's Clinic
A71

Design: 4fr, Princess Marie-Astrid.

1957, June 17 Photo. *Perf. 11½*

326 A70 2fr brown 70 1.00
327 A71 3fr bluish green 5.25 7.50
328 A70 4fr ultramarine 5.25 7.50

Issued to publicize the Children's Clinic of the Prince Jean-Princess Josephine-Charlotte Foundation.

"United Europe"
A72

Fair Building and Flags
A73

1957, Sept. 16 Engr. *Perf. 12½x12*

329 A72 2fr reddish brown 90 38
330 " 3fr red 17.50 22.50
331 " 4fr rose lilac 13.00 15.00

Issued to publicize a united Europe for peace and prosperity.

Perf. 12x11½

1958, Apr. 16 **Unwmkd.**

332 A73 2fr ultramarine & multicolor 25 20

10th International Luxembourg Fair.

Luxembourg Pavilion, Brussels—A74

1958, Apr. 16

333 A74 2.50fr car. & ultra. 35 32

International Exposition at Brussels.

St. Willibrord
A75

Designs: 1fr, Sts. Willibrord and Irmina from "Liber Aureus." 5fr, St. Willibrord, young man and wine cask.

1958, May 23 Engr. *Perf. 13x13½*

334 A75 1fr red 35 40
335 " 2.50fr olive brown 50 30
336 " 5fr blue 1.25 1.50

Issued to commemorate the 1300th anniversary of the birth of St. Willibrord, apostle of the Low Countries and founder of Echternach Abbey.

Charlotte Type of 1948–49.

1958 *Perf. 11½* **Unwmkd.**

337 A45 20c dull claret 15 10
338 " 30c olive 22 7
339 " 50c deep orange 35 7
340 " 5fr violet 3.25 20

Europa Issue, 1958

Common Design Type

1958, Sept. 13 Litho. *Perf. 12½x13*

Size: 21x34mm.

341 CD1 2.50fr carmine & blue 18 25
342 " 3.50fr green & orange 25 38
343 " 5fr blue & red 85 1.25

Issued to show the European Postal Union at the service of European integration.

Wiltz Open-Air Theater
A76

Vintage, Moselle—A77

1958, Sept. 13 Engr. *Perf. 11x11½*

344 A76 2.50fr slate & sepia 25 15
345 A77 2.50fr light green & sepia 25 10

No. 345 issued to publicize 2,000 years of grape growing in Luxembourg region.

Grand Duchess Charlotte
A78

NATO Emblem
A79

1959, Jan. 15 Photo. *Perf. 11½*

346 A78 1.50fr pale green & dark green 22 25
347 " 2.50fr pink & dark brown 22 20
348 " 5fr light blue & dark blue 70 90

Issued to commemorate the 40th anniversary of the accession to the throne of the Grand Duchess Charlotte.

1959, Apr. 3 *Perf. 12½x12*

349 A79 2.50fr bright olive & blue 25 25
350 " 8.50fr red brown & blue 60 55

Issued to commemorate the 10th anniversary of the North Atlantic Treaty Organization.

Flower Type of 1955, Inscribed "1959"

Flowers: 1fr, Iris. 2.50fr, Peonies. 3fr, Hydrangea.

1959, Apr. 3 *Perf. 11½*

Flowers in Natural Colors

351 A58 1fr dark blue green 75 60
352 " 2.50fr deep blue 35 38
353 " 3fr deep red lilac 75 1.00

Flower festival, Mondorf-les-Bains.

Common Design Types pictured in section at front of book.

Europa Issue, 1959

Common Design Type

Lithographed.

1959, Sept. 19 *Perf. 12½x13½*

Size: 22 x 33mm.

354 CD2 2.50fr olive 50 25
355 " 5fr dark blue 85 1.25

Locomotive of 1859 and Hymn
A80

1959, Sept. 19 Engraved *Perf. 13½*

356 A80 2.50fr red & ultra. 60 25

Centenary of Luxembourg's railroads.

Man and Child Knocking at Door
A81

Holy Family, Flight into Egypt
A82

Perf. 11½x11, 11x11½

1960, Apr. 7 **Unwmkd.**

357 A81 2.50fr orange & slate 18 25
358 A82 5fr purple & slate 50 55

Issued to publicize World Refugee Year, July 1, 1959–June 30, 1960.

Steel Worker Drawing CECA Initials and Map of Member Countries
A83

1960, May 9 *Perf. 11x11½*

359 A83 2.50fr dk. car. rose 42 30

Issued to commemorate the 10th anniversary of the Schumann Plan for a European Steel and Coal Community.

European School and Children
A84

1960, May 9

360 A84 5fr blue & gray blk. 1.20 1.65

Issued to publicize the establishment of the first European school in Luxembourg.

Heraldic Lion and Tools
A85

1960, June 14 Photo. ***Perf. 11½***

361 A85 2.50fr gray, red, blue & black 75 28

Issued to publicize the National Exhibition of Craftsmanship, Luxembourg-Limpertsberg, July 9–18.

Grand Duchess Charlotte
A86

1960–64 Engraved Unwmkd.

No.	Type	Description	Unused	Used
362	A86	10c claret ('61)	15	5
363	"	20c rose red ('61)	18	7
363A	"	25c orange ('64)	18	20
364	"	30c gray olive	10	5
365	"	50c dull green	25	8
366	"	1fr violet blue	32	6
367	"	1.50fr rose lilac	50	12
368	"	2fr blue ('61)	55	7
369	"	2.50fr rose violet	50	10
370	"	3fr vio. brn. ('62)	1.25	7
371	"	3.50fr aqua. ('64)	1.75	2.50
372	"	5fr lt. red brown	85	12
373	"	6fr slate ('64)	1.30	25
		Nos. 362-373 (13)	7.89	3.74

The 50c, 1fr and 3fr were issued in sheets and in coils. Every fifth coil stamp has control number on back.

Europa Issue, 1960
Common Design Type

1960, Sept. 19 ***Perf. 11x11½***
Size: 37x27mm.

374 CD3 2.50fr indigo & emerald 35 25
375 " 5fr maroon & black 55 75

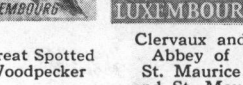

Great Spotted Woodpecker A87 — **Clervaux and Abbey of St. Maurice and St. Maur** A88

Designs: 1.50fr, Cat (horiz.). 3fr, Filly (horiz.). 8.50fr, Dachshund.

1961, May 15 Photo. ***Perf. 11½***

376 A87 1fr multicolored 15 20
377 " 1.50fr " 15 20
378 " 3fr gray, buff & red brown 50 65
379 " 8.50fr lt. green, black & ochre 1.00 85

Issued to publicize animal protection.

1961, June 8 Engr. ***Perf. 11½x11***

380 A88 2.50fr green 20 17

General Patton Monument, Ettelbruck—A89

1961, June 8 ***Perf. 11x11½***

381 A89 2.50fr dark blue & gray 20 17

The monument commemorates the American victory of the 3rd Army under Gen. George S. Patton, Jr., Battle of the Ardennes Bulge, 1944–45.

Europa Issue, 1961
Common Design Type

1961, Sept. 18 ***Perf. 13x12½***
Size: 29½x27mm.

382 CD4 2.50fr red 20 25
383 " 5fr blue 40 50

Cyclist Carrying Bicycle A90 — **St. Laurent's Church, Diekirch** A91

Design: 5fr, Emblem of 1962 championship.

1962, Jan. 22 Photo. ***Perf. 11½***

384 A90 2.50fr light ultra., crimson & black 32 17
385 " 5fr multicolored 80 60

Issued to publicize the International Cross-country Bicycle Race, Esch-sur-Alzette, Feb. 18.

Europa Issue, 1962
Common Design Type

1962, Sept. 17 ***Perf. 11½*** **Unwmkd.**
Size: 32½x23mm.

386 CD5 2.50fr olive bistre, yel. grn. & brown blk. 32 17
387 " 5fr rose lilac, lt. grn. & brn. black 65 50

1962, Sept. 17 Engr. ***Perf. 11½x11***

388 A91 2.50fr brown & black 25 17

Bock Rock Castle, 10th Century A92 — **Gate of Three Towers, 11th Century** A93

Designs (each stamp represents a different century): No. 391, Benedictine Abbey, Munster. No. 392, Great Seal of Luxembourg, 1237. No. 393, Rham Towers. No. 394, Black Virgin, Grund. No. 395, Grand Ducal Palace. No. 396, The Citadel of the Holy Ghost. No. 397, Castle Bridge. No. 398, Town Hall. No. 399, Municipal theater, bridge and European Community Center.

Engraved; Perf. 14x13 (A92),
Photogravure; Perf. 11½ (A93)

1963, Apr. 13 Unwmkd.

No.	Type	Description	Unused	Used
389	A92	1fr slate blue	65	75
390	A93	1fr multicolored	18	20
391	A92	1.50fr dull red brown	65	75
392	A93	1.50fr multicolored	18	20
393	A92	2.50fr gray green	65	75
394	A93	2.50fr multicolored	27	30
395	A92	3fr brown	65	75
396	A93	3fr multicolored	22	25
397	A92	5fr bright violet	90	1.00
398	A93	5fr multicolored	90	1.00
399	A92	11fr blue	1.35	1.00
		Nos. 389-399 (11)	6.60	7.45

Issued to commemorate the millennium of the city of Luxembourg and to publicize MELUSINA International Philatelic Exhibition, Luxembourg, Apr. 13–21. Set sold only at exhibition. Price of 62fr included entrance ticket. Nos. 390, 392, 394 and 396 however were sold without restriction.

Blackboard Showing European School Buildings—A94

1963, Apr. 13 Photo. ***Perf. 11½***

400 A94 2.50fr gray, green & magenta 25 25

Issued to commemorate the 10th anniversary of the European Schools in Luxembourg, Brussels, Varese, Mol and Karlsruhe.

Colpach Castle and Centenary Emblem—A95

1963, May 8 Engraved ***Perf. 13***

401 A95 2.50fr henna brown, gray & red 28 25

Issued to commemorate the centenary of the International Red Cross. Colpach Castle, home of Emile Mayrisch, was donated to the Luxembourg League of the Red Cross for a rest home.

Twelve Stars of Council of Europe A96 — **Brown Trout Taking Bait** A97

1963, June 25 ***Perf. 13x14***

402 A96 2.50fr deep ultra., *gold* 32 35

Issued to commemorate the 10th anniversary of the European Convention of Human Rights.

Europa Issue, 1963
Common Design Type
Photogravure

1963, Sept. 16 ***Perf. 11½*** **Unwmkd.**
Size: 32½x23mm.

403 CD6 3fr blue green, light grn. & orange 33 25
404 CD6 6fr red brn., orange red & org. 50 50

1963, Sept. 16 Engraved ***Perf. 13***

405 A97 3fr indigo 33 18

Issued to publicize the World Fly-Fishing Championship, Wormeldange, Sept. 22.

Map of Luxembourg, Telephone Dial and Stars A98 — **Power House** A99

1963, Sept. 16 Photo. ***Perf. 11½***

406 A98 3fr ultramarine, brt. grn. & blk. 30 20

Completion of telephone automation.

1964, Apr. 17 Engraved ***Perf. 13***

Designs: 3fr, Upper reservoir (horiz.). 6fr, Lohmuhle dam.

407 A99 2fr red brown & slate 20 25
408 " 3fr red, slate green & light blue 30 20
409 " 6fr choc., green & bl. 60 50

Issued to commemorate the inauguration of the Vianden hydroelectric station.

Barge Entering Lock at Grevenmacher Dam—A100

1964, May 26 Unwmkd.

410 A100 3fr indigo & brt. bl. 40 25

Opening of Moselle River canal system.

Europa Issue, 1964
Common Design Type

1964, Sept. 14 Photo. ***Perf. 11½***
Size: 22x38mm.

411 CD7 3fr org. brn., yel. & dark blue 33 20
412 " 6fr yel. green, yel. & dark brown 55 60

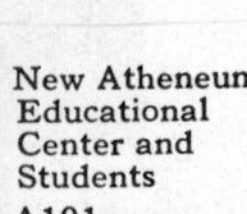

New Atheneum Educational Center and Students
A101

1964, Sept. 14 Unwmkd.

413 A101 3fr dk. bl. grn. & blk. 33 18

Benelux Issue

King Baudouin, Queen Juliana and Grand Duchess Charlotte
A101a

1964, Oct. 12

Size: 45x26mm.

414 A101a 3fr dull blue, yellow & brn. 33 30

Issued to commemorate the 20th anniversary of the customs union of Belgium, Netherlands and Luxembourg.

Grand Duke Jean and Grand Duchess Josephine Charlotte

A102

1964, Nov. 11 Photo. *Perf. 11½*

415	A102	3fr indigo	30	22
416	"	6fr dark brown	50	40

Grand Duke Jean's accession to throne.

Rotary Emblem and Cogwheels

A103

Grand Duke Jean

A104

1965, Apr. 5 Photo. *Perf. 11½*

417 A103 3fr gold, carmine, gray & ultra. 27 17

Rotary International, 60th anniversary.

1965–71 Engraved Unwmkd.

418	A104	25c olive bister ('66)	5	5
419	"	50c rose red	8	5
420	"	1fr ultramarine	6	5
421	"	1.50fr dk. vio. brn. ('66)	8	10
422	"	2fr magenta ('66)	12	10
423	"	2.50fr orange ('71)	20	15
424	"	3fr gray	17	5
425	"	3.50fr brn. org. ('66)	20	25
426	"	4fr vio. brn. ('71)	22	5
427	"	5fr green ('71)	28	10
428	"	6fr purple	33	15
429	"	8fr bl. grn. ('71)	1.40	50
		Nos. 418–429(12)	3.19	1.60

The 50c, 1fr, 2fr, 3fr and 6fr were issued in sheets and in coils. Every fifth coil stamp has control number on back.

See also Nos. 571–575.

ITU Emblem, Old and New Communication Equipment—A105

1965, May 17 Litho. *Perf. 13½*

431 A105 3fr dark purple, claret & black 30 20

Issued to commemorate the centenary of the International Telecommunication Union.

Europa Issue, 1965

Common Design Type

Perf. 13x12½

1965, Sept. 27 Photo. Unwmkd.

Size: 30x23½mm.

432	CD8	3fr green, maroon & black	32	25
433	"	6fr tan, dark blue & green	50	50

WHO Headquarters, Geneva

A106

1966, March 7 Engr. *Perf. 11x11½*

434 A106 3fr green 28 22

Inauguration of World Health Organization Headquarters, Geneva.

Torch and Banner

A107

Key and Arms of City of Luxembourg, and Arms of Prince of Chimay

A108

1966, March 7 Photo. *Perf. 11½*

435 A107 3fr gray & brt. red 28 20

Issued to commemorate the 50th anniversary of the Workers' Federation in Luxembourg.

1966, Apr. 28 Engr. *Perf. 13x14*

Designs: 2fr, Interior of Cathedral of Luxembourg, painting by Juan Martin. 3fr, Our Lady of Luxembourg, engraving by Richard Collin. 6fr, Column and spandrel with sculptured angels from Cathedral.

436	A108	1.50fr green	10	10
437	"	2fr dull red	15	15
438	"	3fr dark blue	35	25
439	"	6fr red brown	45	50

Issued to commemorate the 300th anniversary of the Votum Solemne (Solemn Promise) which made the Virgin Mary Patron Saint of the City of Luxembourg.

Europa Issue, 1966

Common Design Type

Lithographed

1966, Sept. 26 *Perf. 13½x12½*

Size: 25x37mm.

440	CD9	3fr gray & vio. blue	20	25
441	"	6fr olive & dk. grn.	50	50

Diesel Locomotive

A109

Design: 3fr, Electric locomotive.

1966, Sept. 26 Photo. *Perf. 11½*

442	A109	1.50fr multicolored	25	20
443	"	3fr "	33	20

Issued to publicize the 5th International Philatelic Exhibition of Luxembourg Railroad Men, Sept. 30–Oct. 3.

Grand Duchess Charlotte Bridge

A110

1966, Sept. 26 Engraved *Perf. 13*

444 A110 3fr dk. carmine rose 25 15

Tower Building, Kirchberg, Seat of European Community

A111

Design: 13fr, Design for Robert Schuman monument, Luxembourg.

1966, Sept. 26

445	A111	1.50fr dark green	30	25
446	"	13fr deep blue	80	45

"Luxembourg, Center of Europe."

View of Luxembourg, 1850, by Nicolas Liez

A112

Map of Luxembourg Fortress, 1850, by Theodore de Cederstolpe

A113

1967, March 6 Engraved *Perf. 13*

447	A112	3fr blue, violet brown & green	30	20
448	A113	6fr bl., brn. & red	45	40

Issued to commemorate the centenary of the Treaty of London, which guaranteed the country's neutrality after the dismantling of the Fortress of Luxembourg.

Europa Issue, 1967

Common Design Type

1967, May 2 Photo. *Perf. 11½*

Size: 33x22mm.

449	CD10	3fr claret brn., gray & buff	25	25
450	"	6fr dk. brown, vio. gray & lt. blue	50	50

Lion, Globe and Lions Emblem

A115

NATO Emblem and European Community Administration Building

A116

1967, May 2 Photo. *Perf. 11½*

451 A115 3fr multicolored 25 25

Lions International, 50th anniversary.

Canceled to Order

Luxembourg's Office des Timbres, Direction des Postes, was offering, at least as early as 1967, to sell commemorative issues canceled to order.

1967, June 13 Litho. *Perf. 13x12½*

452	A116	3fr lt. grn. & dk. grn.	50	15
453	"	6fr deep rose & dark carmine	80	80

Issued to commemorate the meeting of the NATO Council in Luxembourg, June 13–14.

Youth Hostel, Ettelbruck

A117

Home Gardener

A118

1967, Sept. 14 Photo. *Perf. 11½*

454 A117 1.50fr multicolored 25 17

Luxembourg youth hostels.

1967, Sept. 14

455 A118 1.50fr brt. grn. & org. 22 20

Issued to publicize the 16th Congress of the International Association of Home Gardeners.

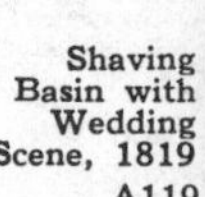

Shaving Basin with Wedding Scene, 1819

A119

Design: 3fr, Ornamental vase, 1820.

1967, Sept. 14

456	A119	1.50fr olive green & multi.	20	15
457	"	3fr ultra. & light gray	40	20

Issued to commemorate the 200th anniversary of the faience industry in Luxembourg.

Wormeldingen on Mosel River

A120

Mertert, Mosel River Port

A121

1967, Sept. 14 Engr. *Perf. 13*

458	A120	3fr dp. blue, claret & olive	20	15
459	A121	3fr vio. bl. & slate	20	15

Swimming
A122

Sport: 1.50fr, Soccer. 2fr, Bicycling. 3fr, Running. 6fr, Walking. 13fr, Fencing.

1968, Feb. 22 Photo. *Perf. 11½*

460 A122 50c blue & greenish blue 12 15
461 " 1.50fr bright green & emerald 12 15
462 " 2fr yel. green & lt. yellow green 17 20
463 " 3fr dp. orange & dull orange 30 20
464 " 6fr greenish blue & pale green 50 25
465 " 13fr rose claret & rose 80 60
Nos. 460-465 (6) 2.01 1.55

Issued to publicize the 19th Olympic Games, Mexico City, Oct. 12–27.

Europa Issue, 1968

Common Design Type

1968, Apr. 29 Photo. *Perf. 11½*

Size: 32½x23mm.

466 CD11 3fr apple grn., blk. & org. brown 25 25
467 " 6fr brn. org., blk. & apple green 50 50

Kind Spring Pavilion
A123

1968, Apr. 29 Photo. *Perf. 11½*

468 A123 3fr multicolored 25 25

Issued to publicize Mondorf-les-Bains.

Fair Emblem
A124

1968, Apr. 29

469 A124 3fr dp. violet, dull blue gold & red 25 25

Issued to publicize the 20th International Fair, Luxembourg City, May 23–June 2.

Children's Village of Mersch
A125

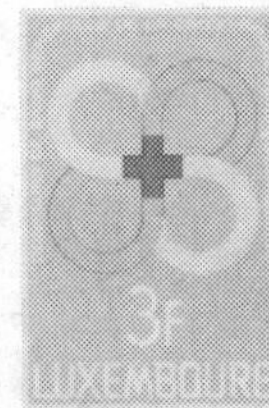

Orphan and Foster Mother
A126

1968, Sept. 18 Engraved *Perf. 13*

470 A125 3fr slate green & dk. red brown 20 20
471 A126 6fr slate blue, black & brown 55 38

Issued to publicize the Mersch children's village. (Modeled after Austrian SOS villages for homeless children.)

Red Cross and Symbolic Blood Transfusion
A127

1968, Sept. 18 Photo. *Perf. 11½*

472 A127 3fr lt. blue & car. 25 20

Issued to honor the voluntary Red Cross blood donors.

Luxair Plane over Luxembourg
A128

1968, Sept. 18 Engraved *Perf. 13*

473 A128 50fr olive, blue & dark blue 3.00 2.10

Issued for tourist publicity.

Souvenir Sheet

"Youth and Leisure"—A129

Designs, 3fr, Doll. 6fr, Ballplayers. 13fr, Book, compass rose and ball.

1969, Apr. 3 Photo. *Perf. 11½*

Granite Paper

474 A129 Sheet of 3 5.00 6.00
a. 3fr ultra., blk. & orange 1.50 1.50
b. 6fr ultra., red & black 1.50 1.50
c. 13fr dull green, red & yellow 1.50 1.50

Issued to publicize the First International Youth Philatelic Exhibition, JUVENTUS 1969, Luxembourg, Apr. 3–8.

No. 474 has black marginal inscription. Size: 110x70mm. It was on sale only at the exhibition Apr. 3–8. Sold only with entrance ticket for 40fr.

Europa Issue, 1969

Common Design Type

1969, May 19 Photo. *Perf. 11½*

Size: 32½x23mm.

475 CD12 3fr gray, brn. & org. 20 25
476 " 6fr vio. gray, black & yellow 50 50

Boy on Hobby-horse, by Joseph Kutter
A130

Design: 6fr, View of Luxembourg, by Joseph Kutter.

1969, May 19 Engraved *Perf. 12x13*

477 A130 3fr multicolored 50 30
a. Green omitted 55.00 45.00
478 A130 6fr multicolored 50 50

75th anniversary of the birth of Joseph Kutter (1894–1941), painter.

ILO Emblem
A131

Photo.; Gold Impressed (Emblem)

1969, May 19 *Perf. 14x14½*

479 A131 3fr bright green, violet & gold 25 20

International Labor Organization, 50th anniversary.

Möbius strip in Benelux Colors
A131a

Perf. 12½x13½

1969, Sept. 8 Lithographed

480 A131a 3fr multicolored 28 25

Issued to commemorate the 25th anniversary of the signing of the customs union of Belgium, Netherlands and Luxembourg.

NATO Emblem
A132

Grain and Mersh Agricultural Center
A133

1969, Sept. 8 *Perf. 13½x12½*

481 A132 3fr orange brown & dark brown 28 25

Issued to commemorate the 20th anniversary of the North Atlantic Treaty Organization.

1969, Sept. 8 Photo. *Perf. 11½*

482 A133 3fr blue green, gray & black 25 18

Issued to publicize agricultural progress.

St. Willibrord's Basilica and Abbey, Echternach
A134

Design: No. 484, Castle and open-air theater, Wiltz.

1969, Sept. 8 Engraved *Perf. 13*

483 A134 3fr dk. blue & indigo 20 12
484 " 3fr slate green & indigo 20 12

Pasqueflower
A135

Design: 6fr, Hedgehog and 3 young.

1970, Mar. 9 Photo. *Perf. 11½*

485 A135 3fr multicolored 30 30
486 " 6fr green & multi. 55 60

European Conservation Year 1970.

Goldcrest
A136

1970, Mar. 9 Engraved *Perf. 13*

487 A136 1.50fr orange, green & blk. brn. 18 15

Issued to commemorate the 50th anniversary of the Luxembourg Society for the protection and study of birds.

Traffic Sign and Street Scene
A137

1970, May 4 Photo. *Perf. 11½*

488 A137 3fr rose magenta, red & black 25 15

Issued to publicize the importance of traffic safety.

Europa Issue, 1970

Common Design Type

1970, May 4 Size: 32½x23mm.

489 CD13 3fr brown & multi. 25 20
490 " 6fr green & multi. 50 55

Empress Kunigunde and Emperor Henry II, Window, Luxembourg Cathedral—A138

1970, Sept. 14 Photo. *Perf. 12*

491 A138 3fr multicolored 33 35

Centenary of the Diocese of Luxembourg.

Census Symbol
A139

1970, Sept. 14 ***Perf. 11½***

492 A139 3fr dk. grn., greenish blue & red 25 15

Issued to publicize the census of Dec. 31, 1970.

Lion, Luxembourg City Hall
A140

1970, Sept. 14

493 A140 3fr bister, lt. blue & dark brown 25 15

Issued to commemorate the 50th anniversary of the City of Luxembourg through the union of 5 municipalities.

U.N. Emblem
A141

Lithographed

1970, Sept. 14 ***Perf. 12½x13½***

494 A141 1.50fr blue & vio. bl. 18 18

25th anniversary of the United Nations.

Monks in Abbey Workshop
A142

Olympic Rings, Arms of Luxembourg
A143

Miniatures Painted at Echternach, about 1040: 3fr, Laborers going to the vineyard (Matthew 20:1–6). 6fr, Laborers toiling in vineyard. 13fr, Workers searching for graves of the saints.

1971, March 15 **Photo.** ***Perf. 12***

495 A142 1.50fr gold & multi. 12 15
496 " 3fr " " 25 25
497 " 6fr " " 50 50
498 " 13fr " " 1.00 1.15

1971, May 3 **Photo.** ***Perf. 12½***

499 A143 3fr ultra. & multi. 38 25

71st session of the International Olympic Committee.

Europa Issue, 1971

Common Design Type

1971, May 3 ***Perf. 12½x13***

Size: 34x25mm.

500 CD14 3fr verm., brown & black 20 20
501 " 6fr brt. green, brn. & black 45 50

A145

1971, May 3 **Litho.** ***Perf. 13x13½***

502 A145 3fr orange, dk. brown & yellow 25 25

50th anniversary of Christian Workers Union.

Artificial Lake, Upper Sure
A146

Designs: No. 504, Water treatment plant, Esch-sur-Sure. 15fr, ARBED Steel Corporation Headquarters, Luxembourg.

1971, Sept. 13 **Engraved** ***Perf. 13***

503 A146 3fr olive, greenish blue & indigo 20 10
504 " 3fr brn., slate grn. & greenish blue 20 10
505 " 15fr indigo & black brown 1.00 40

School Girl with Coin
A147

1971, Sept. 13 **Photo.** ***Perf. 11½***

506 A147 3fr violet & multi. 25 20

School children's savings campaign.

Coins of Luxembourg and Belgium
A148

Bronze Mask
A149

1972, Mar. 6

507 A148 1.50fr lt. grn., silver & black 20 20

Economic Union of Luxembourg and Belgium, 50th anniversary.

1972, Mar. 6

Archaeological Objects, 4th to 1st centuries, B.C.: 1fr, Bronze bowl (horiz.). 8fr, Limestone head. 15fr, Glass jug in shape of head.

508 A149 1fr lemon & multi. 35 20
509 " 3fr multicolored 35 18
510 " 8fr " 90 1.00
511 " 15fr " 1.20 1.25

Europa Issue 1972

Common Design Type

1972, May 2 **Photo.** ***Perf. 11½***

Size: 22x33mm.

512 CD15 3fr rose vio. & multi. 25 20
513 " 8fr gray bl. & multi. 65 60

Archer
A150

1972, May 2

514 A150 3fr crimson, black & olive 35 20

3rd European Archery Championships.

Robert Schuman Medal
A151

The Fox Wearing Tails
A152

1972, May 2 **Engraved** ***Perf. 13***

515 A151 3fr gray & slate grn. 35 25

20th anniversary of the establishment in Luxembourg of the European Coal and Steel Community.

1972, Sept. 11 **Photo.** ***Perf. 11½***

516 A152 3fr scarlet & multi. 25 20

Centenary of the publication of "Renert," satirical poem by Michel Rodange.

National Monument
A153

Court of Justice of European Communities, Kirchberg—A154

1972, Sept. 11 **Engr.** ***Perf. 13***

517 A153 3fr slate green, olive & violet 25 20
518 A154 3fr brown, blue & slate green 32 25

Epona on Horseback
A155

Archaeological Objects: 4fr, Panther killing swan (horiz.). 8fr, Celtic gold stater inscribed Pottina. 15fr, Bronze boar (horiz.).

1973, Mar. 14 **Photo.** ***Perf. 11½***

519 A155 1fr salmon & multi. 18 12
520 " 4fr beige & multi. 55 25
521 " 8fr multicolored 75 75
522 " 15fr " 1.35 1.20

Europa Issue 1973

Common Design Type

1973, Apr. 30 **Photo.** ***Perf. 11½***

Size: 32x22mm.

523 CD16 4fr org., dark violet & light blue 30 25
524 " 8fr olive, vio. black & yellow 70 70

Bee on Honeycomb
A156

Nurse Holding Child
A157

1973, Apr. 30 **Photo.** ***Perf. 11½***

525 A156 4fr ocher & multi. 27 25

Publicizing importance of beekeeping.

1973, Apr. 30

526 A157 4fr multicolored 27 25

Publicizing importance of day nurseries.

Laurel Branch
A158

1973, Sept. 10 **Photo.** ***Perf. 11½***

527 A158 3fr vio. bl. & multi. 25 20

50th anniversary of Luxembourg Board of Labor.

Jerome de Busleyden
A159

National Strike Memorial, Wiltz
A160

1973, Sept. 10 **Engraved** ***Perf. 13***

528 A159 4fr blk., brn. & pur. 27 25

500th anniversary of the Council of Mechelen.

1973, Sept. 10

529 A160 4fr olive bister, slate & slate green 32 20

In memory of the Luxembourg resistance heroes who died during the great strike of 1942.

Capital, Byzantine Hall, Vianden
A161

St. Gregory the Great
A161a

Designs: No. 534, Sts. Cecilia and Valerian crowned by angel, Hollenfels Church. No. 535, Interior, Septfontaines Church. 8fr, Madonna and Child, St. Irmina's Chapel, Rosport. 12fr, St. Augustine Sculptures by Jean-Georges Scholtus from pulpit in Feulen parish church, c. 1734.

Perf. 13x12½, 14 (6fr, 12fr)

1973–77

533 A161 4fr grn. & rose vio. 33 20
534 " 4fr red brn., green & lilac 33 25
535 " 4fr gray, brown & dark violet 33 25
536 A161a 6fr maroon 35 35

537 A161 8fr sepia & vio. blue 75 75
538 A161a 12fr slate blue 70 70
Nos. 533-538 (6) 2.79 2.50

Architecture of Luxembourg: Romanesque, Gothic, Baroque.

Issue dates: No. 533, 8fr, Sept. 10, 1973; Nos. 534-535, Sept. 9, 1974; 6fr, 12fr, Sept. 16, 1977.

Princess Marie Astrid
A162

Torch
A163

1974, Mar. 14 Photo. *Perf. 11½*

540 A162 4fr blue & multi. 32 25

Princess Marie-Astrid, president of the Luxembourg Red Cross Youth Section.

1974, Mar. 14

541 A163 4fr ultra. & multi. 32 25

50th anniversary of Luxembourg Mutual Insurance Federation.

Royal Seal of Henri VII
A164

Designs (Seals from 13th-14th Centuries): 3fr, Equestrian, seal of Jean, King of Bohemia. 4fr, Seal of Town of Diekirch. 19fr, Virgin and Child, seal of Convent of Marienthal.

1974, Mar. 14

542 A164 1fr purple & multi. 10 10
543 " 3fr green & multi. 35 35
544 " 4fr multicolored 45 25
545 " 19fr " 1.40 1.40

Hind, by Auguste Trémont
A165

Winston Churchill, by Oscar Nemon
A166

Europa Issue 1974

Design: 8fr, "Growth," abstract sculpture, by Lucien Wercollier.

1974, Apr. 29 Photo. *Perf. 11½*

546 A165 4fr ocher & multi. 33 30
547 " 8fr brt. bl. & multi. 80 70

1974, Apr. 29

548 A166 4fr lilac & multi. 38 25

Centenary of the birth of Sir Winston Churchill (1874-1965), statesman.

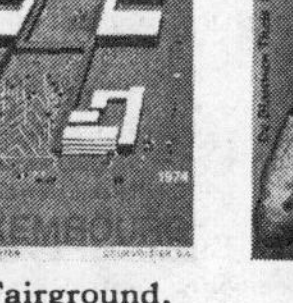

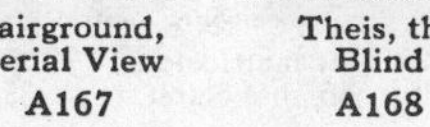

Fairground, Aerial View
A167

Theis, the Blind
A168

1974, Apr. 29

549 A167 4fr silver & multi. 38 25

Publicity for New International Fairground, Luxembourg-Kirchberg.

1974, Apr. 29

550 A168 3fr multicolored 27 25

Sesquicentennial of the death of Mathias Schou, Theis the Blind (1747-1824), wandering minstrel.

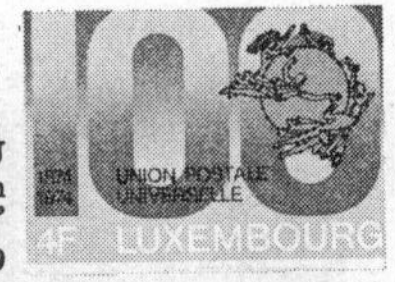

UPU Emblem and "100"
A169

1974, Sept. 9 Photo. *Perf. 11½*

551 A169 4fr multicolored 50 35
552 " 8fr " 1.00 75

Centenary of Universal Postal Union.

"BENELUX"
A170

1974, Sept. 9

553 A170 4fr bl. grn., dk. grn. & light blue 50 25

30th anniversary of the signing of the customs union of Belgium, Netherlands and Luxembourg.

View of Differdange
A171

1974, Sept. 9 Engraved *Perf. 13*

554 A171 4fr rose claret 35 25

Bourglinster
A172

Designs: 1fr, Fish Market, Old Luxembourg (vert.). 4fr, Market Square, Echternach. 19fr, St. Michael's Square, Mersch (vert.).

Perf. 14x13½, 13½x14

1975, Mar. 10 Engraved

555 A172 1fr olive green 25 12
556 " 3fr deep brown 60 30
557 " 4fr dark purple 90 60
558 " 19fr copper red 2.00 1.75

European Architectural Heritage Year.

Joseph Kutter, Self-portrait
A173

Moselle Bridge, Remich, by Nico Klopp
A174

Paintings: 8fr, Still Life, by Joseph Kutter. 20fr, The Dam, by Dominique Lang.

1975, Apr. 28 Photo. *Perf. 11½*

559 A173 1fr multicolored 12 12
560 A174 4fr " 30 25
561 A174 8fr multicolored 70 65
562 A173 20fr " 1.50 1.50

Cultural series. Nos. 560-561 are 1975 Europa Issue.

Robert Schuman, Gaetano Martino, Paul-Henri Spaak Medals—A175

1975, Apr. 28

563 A175 4fr yel. grn., gold & brown 45 30

25th anniversary of Robert Schuman's declaration establishing European Coal and Steel Community.

Albert Schweitzer
A176

1975, Apr. 28 Engr. *Perf. 13*

564 A176 4fr bright blue 45 25

Birth centenary of Albert Schweitzer (1875-1965), medical missionary.

Civil Defense Emblem
A177

Figure Skating
A178

1975, Sept. 8 Photo. *Perf. 11½*

565 A177 4fr multicolored 30 25

Civil Defense Organization for protection and rescue.

1975, Sept. 8 Engr. *Perf. 13*

Designs: 4fr, Water skiing (horiz.). 15fr, Mountain climbing.

566 A178 3fr grn., bl. & lilac 25 22
567 " 4fr dk. brn., grn. & light brown 45 30
568 " 15fr brown, indigo & green 1.25 1.00

Grand Duke Type of 1965-71

1975 Engraved *Perf. 11½*

571 A104 9fr yellow green 60 45
572 " 10fr black 70 60
573 " 12fr brick red 75 60
575 " 20fr blue 1.40 1.00

Grand Duchess Charlotte
A179

Design: No. 580, Prince Henri.

1976, Mar. 8 Litho. *Perf 14x13½*

579 A179 6fr green & multi. 50 30
580 " 6fr dull bl. & multi. 50 30

80th birthday of Grand Duchess Charlotte and 21st birthday of Prince Henri, heir to the throne.

Gold Brooch
A180

Designs: 5fr, Footless beaker (horiz.). 6fr, Decorated vessel (horiz.). 12fr, Gold coin. All designs show excavated items of Franco-Merovingian period.

Perf. 13½x12½, 12½x13½

1976, Mar. 8

581 A180 2fr blue & multi. 15 15
582 " 5fr black & multi. 35 35
583 " 6fr lilac & multi. 50 35
584 " 12fr multicolored 1.00 1.00

Europa Issue 1976

Soup Tureen
A181

Design: 12fr, Deep bowl. Tureen and bowl after pottery from Nospelt, 19th century.

1976, May 3 Photo. *Perf. 11½*

585 A181 6fr lt. vio. & multi. 50 30
586 " 12fr yellow green & multicolored 1.00 70

Independence Hall, Philadelphia
A182

Boomerang
A183

1976, May 3

587 A182 6fr lt. blue & multi. 50 30

American Bicentennial.

1976, May 3

588 A183 6fr bright rose lilac & gold 50 30

21st Olympic Games, Montreal, Canada, July 17-Aug. 1.

"Vibrations of Sound"
A184

1976, May 3

589 A184 6fr red & multi. 50 30

Jeunesses Musicales (Young Music Friends), association to foster interest in music and art.

Alexander Graham Bell
A185

Virgin and Child with St. Anne
A186

1976, Sept. 9 Engr. *Perf. 13*

590 A185 6fr slate green 45 25

Centenary of first telephone call by Alexander Graham Bell, Mar. 10, 1876.

1976, Sept. 9 Photo. *Perf. 11½*

Sculptures: 12fr, Grave of Bernard de Velbruck, Lord of Beaufort.

591 A186 6fr gold & multi. 50 25
592 " 12fr gold, gray & black 90 55

Renaissance art.

Johann Wolfgang von Goethe
A187

Old Luxembourg
A188

Portraits: 5fr, J. M. William Turner. 6fr, Victor Hugo. 12fr, Franz Liszt.

1977, Mar. 14 Engr. *Perf. 13*

593 A187 2fr lake 20 20
594 " 5fr purple 35 35
595 " 6fr slate green 45 45
596 " 12fr violet blue 80 80

Famous visitors to Luxembourg.

Europa Issue 1977

1977, May 3 Photo. *Perf. 11½*

Design: 12fr, Adolphe Bridge and European Investment Bank headquarters.

597 A188 6fr multicolored 45 45
598 " 12fr " 80 80

Esch-sur-Sure
A189

Marguerite de Busbach
A190

Design: 6fr, View of Ehnen.

1977, May 3 Engr. *Perf. 13*

599 A189 5fr Prussian blue 35 30
600 " 6fr deep brown 45 38

1977, May 3 Photo. *Perf. 11½*

Design: No. 602, Louis Braille, by Lucienne Filippi.

601 A190 6fr multicolored 45 38
602 " 6fr " 45 38

Notre Dame Congregation, founded by Marguerite de Busbach, 350th anniversary; Louis Braille (1809–1852), inventor of the Braille system of writing for the blind, 125th death anniversary.

Souvenir Sheet

Luxembourg Nos. 1–2—A191

Engraved and Photogravure

1977, Sept. 15 *Perf. 13½*

603 A191 40fr gray & red brn. 2.40 2.40

125th anniversary of Luxembourg's stamps. No. 603 has gold marginal inscription. Size: 90x60mm.

Head of Medusa, Roman Mosaic, Diekirch, 3rd Century A.D.
A192

1977, Sept. 15 Photo. *Perf. 11½*

604 A192 6fr multicolored 38 38

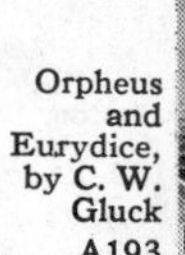

Orpheus and Eurydice, by C. W. Gluck
A193

1977, Sept. 15 *Perf. 11½x12*

605 A193 6fr multicolored 38 38

International Wiltz Festival, 25th anniversary.

Europa Tamed, by R. Zilli, and Map of Europe
A194

1977, Dec. 5 Photo. *Perf. 11½*

606 A194 6fr multicolored 35 35

20th anniversary of the Treaties of Rome, setting up the European Economic Community and the European Atomic Energy Commission.

Souvenir Sheet

Grand Duke and Grand Duchess of Luxembourg—A195

Photogravure and Engraved

1978, Apr. 3 *Perf. 13½x14*

607 A195 Sheet of 2 1.20 1.20
a. 6fr dk. blue & multi. 35 35
b. 12fr dk. red & multi. 70 70

Silver wedding anniversary of Grand Duke Jean and Grand Duchess Josephine Charlotte. No. 607 has silver marginal inscription. Size: 116x66mm.

Souvenir Sheet

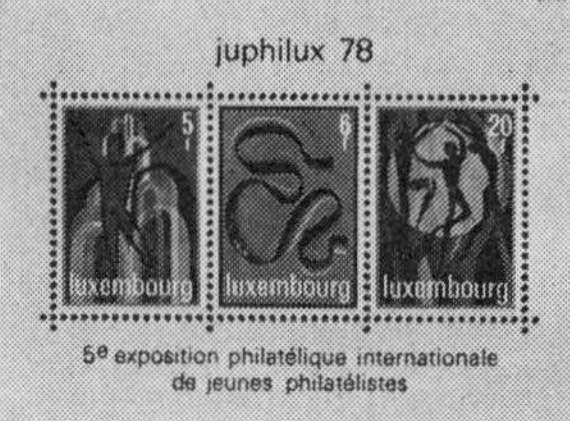

Youth Fountain, Streamer and Dancers—A196

1978, Apr. 3 Photo. *Perf. 11½*

608 A196 Sheet of 3 3.50 3.50
a. 5fr ultra. & multi. 50 50
b. 6fr orange & multi. 60 60
c. 20fr yellow green & multi. 2.00 2.00

Juphilux 78, 5th International Young Philatelists' Exhibition, Luxembourg, Apr. 6–10. No. 608 has yellow green marginal inscription. Size: 102x72mm.

Charles IV, Statue, Charles Bridge, Prague
A197

Emile Mayrish, by Theo Van Rysselberghe
A198

Europa Issue 1978

1978, May 18 Engr. *Perf. 13½*

Design: 12fr, Pierre d'Aspelt, tomb, Mainz Cathedral.

609 A197 6fr dk. violet blue 35 35
610 " 12fr dull rose lilac 70 70

Charles IV (1316–1378), Count of Luxembourg, Holy Roman Emperor, 600th death anniversary. Pierre d'Aspelt (c. 1250–1320), Archbishop of Mainz and Prince-Elector.

1978, May 18 *Perf. 11½*

611 A198 6fr multicolored 35 35

Emile Mayrish (1862–1928), president of International Steel Cartel and promoter of United Europe, 50th death anniversary.

Our Lady of Luxembourg
A199

Trumpeters and Old Luxembourg
A200

1978, May 18 Photo. *Perf. 11½*

612 A199 6fr multicolored 35 35
613 A200 6fr " 35 35

Our Lady of Luxembourg, patroness, 300th anniversary; 135th anniversary of Grand Ducal Military Band.

Starving Child, Helping Hand, Millet
A201

League Emblem, Lungs, Open Window
A202

Open Prison Door
A203

1978, Sept. 11 Photo. *Perf. 11½*

614 A201 2fr multicolored 12 8
615 A202 5fr " 30 20
616 A203 6fr " 35 25

"Terre des Hommes," an association to help underprivileged children; Luxembourg Anti-Tuberculosis League, 70th anniversary; Amnesty International and 30th anniversary of Universal Declaration of Human Rights.

Squared Stone Emerging from Rock, City of Luxembourg—A204

1978, Sept. 11 Engr. *Perf. 13½x13*

617 A204 6fr violet blue 35 25

Masonic Grand Lodge of Luxembourg, 175th anniversary.

Julius Caesar on Denarius, c. 44 B.C.
A205

St. Michael's Church, Mondorf-les-Bains
A206

Roman Coins, Found in Luxembourg: 6fr, Empress Faustina I on Sestertius, 141 A.D. 9fr, Empress Helena on Follis, c. 324–330. 26fr, Emperor Valens on Solidus, c. 367–375.

1979, Mar. 5 Photo. *Perf. 11½*

618 A205 5fr multicolored 30 20
619 " 6fr " 35 25
620 " 9fr " 52 38
621 " 26fr " 1.55 1.05

1979, Mar. 5 Engr. *Perf. 13*

Design: 6fr, Luxembourg Central Station.

622 A206 5fr multicolored 30 20
623 " 6fr rose claret 35 25

SEMI-POSTAL STAMPS.

Clervaux Monastery—SP1

Designs: 15c+10c, View of Pfaffenthal. 25c+10c, View of Luxembourg.

Engraved; Surcharge Typographed in Red or Black

1921, Aug. 2 ***Perf. 11½*** **Unwmkd.**

B1 SP1 10c+5c green (R) 30 60
B2 " 15c+10c orange red 30 1.00
B3 " 25c+10c dp. grn. (R) 30 60

The amount received from the surtax on these stamps was added to a fund for the erection of a monument to the soldiers from Luxembourg who died in World War I.

Nos. B1–B3 with Additional Surcharge in Red or Black

+ 25

× 27 mai 1923 ×

1923, May 27

B4 SP1 10c+5c+25c green (R) 2.75 6.00
B5 " 15c+10c+25c orange red 2.75 6.00
B6 " 25c+10c+25c dp. grn. (R) 2.75 6.00

Issued to commemorate the unveiling of the monument to the soldiers who died in World War I.

CARITAS

Regular Issue of 1914-15 Surcharged in Black or Red

+10c

1924, Apr. 17 ***Perf. 11½x11***

B7 A11 12½c+7½c green 17 30
B8 " 35c+10c dk. bl. (R) 17 30
B9 " 2½fr+1fr red 2.00 3.50
B10 " 5fr+2fr dark vio. 1.00 2.50

Nurse and Patient SP4

Prince Jean SP5

1925, Dec. 21 Litho. ***Perf. 13***

B11 SP4 5c (+5c) dull violet 15 27
B12 " 30c (+5c) orange 15 38
B13 " 50c (+5c) red brown 35 80
B14 " 1fr (+10c) deep blue 50 1.65

1926, Dec. 15 Photo. ***Perf. 12½x12***

B15 SP5 5c (+5c) vio. & blk. 8 27
B16 " 40c (+10) grn. & blk. 12 38
B17 " 50c (+15c) lemon & black 13 38
B18 " 75c (+20c) light red & black 33 95
B19 " 1.50fr(+30c) gray blue & black 45 1.10
Nos. B15-B19 (5) 1.11 3.08

Grand Duchess Charlotte and Prince Felix SP6

1927, Sept. 4 Engr. ***Perf 11½***

B20 SP6 25c deep violet 2.00 3.85
B21 " 50c green 2.75 5.50
B22 " 75c rose lake 2.00 3.85
B23 " 1fr gray black 2.25 3.85
B24 " 1½fr deep blue 2.25 3.85
Nos. B20-B24 (5) 11.25 20.90

Issued to commemorate the seventy-fifth anniversary of the introduction of postage stamps in Luxembourg. These stamps were sold exclusively at the Luxembourg Philatelic Exhibition, September 4-8, 1927, at a premium of 3 francs per set, which was donated to the exhibition funds.

Princess Elisabeth SP7

Princess Marie Adelaide SP8

1927, Dec. 1 Photo. ***Perf. 12½***

B25 SP7 10c(+5c) turquoise blue & black 10 27
B26 " 50c(+10c) dark brown & black 15 38
B27 " 75c(+20c) org. & blk. 15 38
B28 " 1fr(+30c) brown lake & black 30 1.10
B29 " 1½fr(+50c) ultra. & blk. 30 1.10
Nos. B25-B29 (5) 1.00 3.23

The surtax was for Child Welfare societies.

1928, Dec. 12 ***Perf. 12½x12***

B30 SP8 10c(+5c) olive green & brown violet 33 65
B31 " 60c(+10c) brown & olive green 60 1.25
B32 " 75c(+15c) violet rose & blue green 90 1.65
B33 " 1fr(+25c) dark green & brown 1.25 1.90
B34 " 1½fr(+50c) citron & bl. 1.25 3.25
Nos. B30-B34 (5) 4.33 8.70

Princess Marie Gabrielle SP9

Prince Charles SP10

1929, Dec. 14 ***Perf. 13***

B35 SP9 10c(+10c) maroon & deep green 55 1.10
B36 " 35c(+15c) dark green & red brown 1.35 2.75
B37 " 75c(+30c) vermilion & black 1.85 3.50
B38 " 1¼fr(+50c) magenta & blue green 3.25 5.00
B39 " 1¾fr(+75c) Prussian blue & slate 4.00 7.00
Nos. B35-B39 (5) 11.00 19.35

The surtax was for Child Welfare societies.

1930, Dec. 10 ***Perf. 12½***

B40 SP10 10c(+5c) blue green & olive brown 65 1.10
a. Booklet pane of 10 20.00
B41 " 75c(+10c) violet brn. & blue green 1.35 2.25
a. Booklet pane of 10 40.00
B42 " 1fr(+25c) carmine rose & violet 3.75 6.50
B43 " 1¼fr(+75c) olive bis. & dark brown 8.00 14.00
B44 " 1¾fr(+1.50fr) ultra. & red brown 8.00 14.00
Nos. B40-B44 (5) 21.75 37.85

The surtax was for Child Welfare societies.

Princess Alix SP11

Countess Ermesinde SP12

1931, Dec. 10

B45 SP11 10c+5c brown orange& gray 75 1.10
B46 " 75c+10c claret & blue green 3.00 4.25
B47 " 1fr+25c deep green & gray 11.00 16.50
B48 " 1¼fr+75c dark violet & blue green 11.00 16.50
B49 " 1¾fr+1.50fr blue & gray 21.00 32.50
Nos. B45-B49 (5) 46.75 70.85

The surtax was for Child Welfare societies.

1932, Dec. 8

B50 SP12 10c(+5c) olive bistre 75 1.10
B51 " 75c(+10c) deep violet 3.75 5.50
B52 " 1fr(+25c) scarlet 16.00 24.00
B53 " 1¼fr(+75c) red brown 18.00 27.50
B54 " 1¾fr(+1.50fr) deep blue 16.50 25.00
Nos. B50-B54 (5) 55.00 83.10

The surtax was for Child Welfare societies.

Count Henry VII SP13

1933, Dec. 12

B55 SP13 10c(+5c) yel. brn. 1.75 2.75
B56 " 75c(+10c) deep violet 7.25 11.00
B57 " 1fr(+25c) car. rose 22.50 35.00
B58 " 1¼fr(+75c) orange brown 25.00 37.50
B59 " 1¾fr(+1.50fr) bright blue 32.50 50.00
Nos. B55-B59 (5) 89.00 136.25

John the Blind—SP14

1934, Dec. 5

B60 SP14 10c(+5c) dk. vio. 1.00 1.65
B61 " 35c(+10c) deep green 4.00 6.50
B62 " 75c(+15c) rose lake 5.25 8.00
B63 " 1fr(+25c) deep rose 28.50 45.00
B64 " 1¼fr(+75c) org. 32.50 50.00
B65 " 1¾fr(+1.50fr) bright blue 28.50 45.00
Nos. B60-B65 (6) 99.75 156.15

Teacher SP15

Sculptor and Painter SP16

Journalist SP17

Engineer SP18

Scientist SP19

Lawyer SP20

University SP21

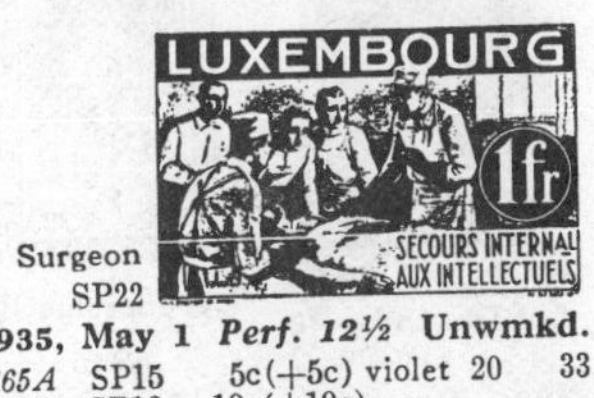

Surgeon SP22

1935, May 1 ***Perf. 12½*** **Unwmkd.**

B65A SP15 5c(+5c) violet 20 33
B65B SP16 10c(+10c) brown red 40 65
B65C SP17 15c(+15c) olive 60 80
B65D SP18 20c(+20c) org. 90 1.10
B65E SP19 35c(+35c) yellow grn. 1.65 2.75
B65F SP20 50c(+50c) gray black 2.75 4.50
B65G SP21 70c(+70c) dark green 4.00 8.00
B65H SP22 1fr(+1fr) carmine red 6.00 11.00
B65J SP19 1.25fr(+1.25fr) turquoise 15.00 25.00
B65K SP18 1.75fr(+1.75fr) blue 23.50 37.50
B65L SP16 2fr(+2fr) light brown 52.50 75.00
B65M SP17 3fr(+3fr) dark brown 67.50 120.00
B65N SP20 5fr(+5fr) light blue 120.00 225.00
B65P SP15 10fr(+10fr) red violet 240.00 350.00

B65Q SP22 20fr(+20fr) dark grn. 240.00 350.00
Nos. B65A-B65Q (15) 775.00 1211.63

Nos. B65A-B65Q were sold at double face value, the surtax going to an international fund to aid professional people.

Philatelic Exhibition Issue.

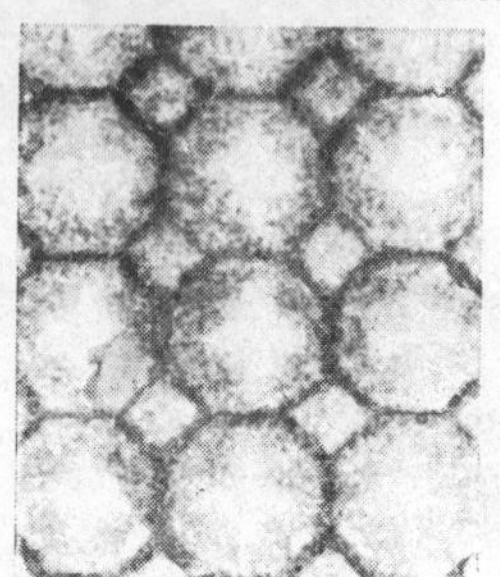

Wmk. 246

Type of Regular Issue of 1928.

Wmkd. Multiple Cross Enclosed in Octagons. (246)

1935, Aug. 15 **Engr.** ***Imperf.***

B66 A19 2fr (+50c) black 13.50 16.50

Issued in connection with a philatelic exhibition held at Esch-sur-Alzette.

Charles I
SP23

1935, Dec. 2 **Photo.** **Unwmkd.**
Perf. 11½

B67 SP23 10c(+5c) violet 32 55
B68 " 35c(+10c) green 80 1.35
B69 " 70c(+20c) dark brown 1.50 2.50
B70 " 1fr(+25c) rose lake 19.00 32.50
B71 " 1.25fr(+75c) org. brown 17.00 29.00
B72 " 1.75fr(+1.50fr) bl. 22.50 38.50
Nos. B67-B72 (6) 61.12 104.40

Wenceslas I, Duke of Luxembourg
SP24

Wenceslas II
SP25

1936, Dec. 1 ***Perf. 11½x13***

B73 SP24 10c+5(c) blk.brn. 25 38
B74 " 35c+10(c) blue green 38 60
B75 " 70c+20(c) black 65 1.00
B76 " 1fr+25(c) rose carmine 2.00 3.85
B77 " 1.25fr+75(c) violet 7.50 13.50
B78 " 1.75fr+1.50(fr) sapphire 5.50 11.00
Nos. B73-B78 (6) 16.28 30.33

1937, Dec. 1 ***Perf. 11½x12½***

B79 SP25 10c+5c carmine & black 15 27
B80 " 35c+10c red violet & green 32 55
B81 " 70c+20c ultra. & red brown 38 80
B82 " 1fr+25c dk. green & scarlet 1.85 3.75
B83 " 1.25fr+75c dk. brown & violet 2.50 5.25
B84 SP25 1.75fr+1.50fr black & ultramarine 4.75 8.50
Nos. B79-B84 (6) 9.95 19.12

Souvenir Sheet.

SP25a

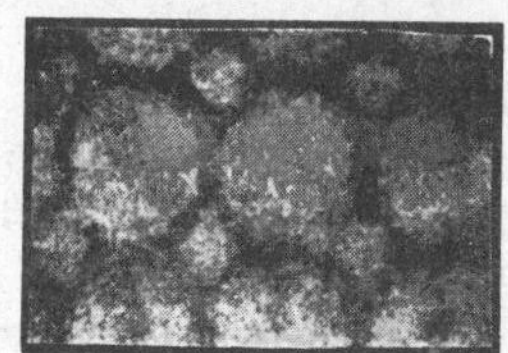

Wmk. 110

Wmkd. Octagons. (110)

1937, July 25 **Engr.** ***Perf. 13***

B85 SP25a 2fr red brown, sheet of two 4.50 12.50
a. Single stamp 2.00 4.25

Issued in commemoration of the National Philatelic Exposition at Dudelange on July 25-26, 1937.

Issued in sheets measuring 125x85mm. Sold for 5fr per sheet, of which 1fr was for the aid of the exposition.

Portrait of St. Willibrord
SP26

The Rathaus at Echternach
SP27

Pavilion in Abbey Park, Echternach
SP28

St. Willibrord, after a Miniature
SP29

Abbey at Echternach
SP30

Dancing Procession in Honor of St. Willibrord
SP31

Perf. 14x13, 13x14.

1938, June 5 **Engr.** **Unwmkd.**

B86 SP26 35c+10c dark blue green 60 1.10
B87 SP27 70c+10c olive gray 1.25 1.10
B88 SP28 1.25fr+25c brown carmine 2.50 2.25
B89 SP29 1.75fr+50c slate blue 3.75 2.75
B90 SP30 3fr+2fr violet brown 15.00 12.00
B91 SP31 5fr+5fr dark violet 16.50 12.00
Nos. B86-B91 (6) 39.60 31.20

Issued in commemoration of the twelfth centenary of the death of St. Willibrord. The surtax was used for the restoration of the ancient Abbey at Echternach.

Grand Duke Sigismond
SP32

1938, Dec. 1 **Photo.** ***Perf. 11½***

B92 SP32 10c+5c lilac & black 12 25
B93 " 35c+10c green & black 30 50
B94 " 70c+20c buff & black 55 1.00
B95 " 1fr+25c red orge. & black 4.00 6.75
B96 " 1.25fr+75c gray blue & black 4.00 6.75
B97 " 1.75fr+1.50fr blue & black 6.00 11.00
Nos. B92-B97 (6) 14.97 26.25

Prince Jean
SP33

Prince Felix
SP34

Grand Duchess Charlotte
SP35

1939, Dec. 1 **Litho.** ***Perf. 14x13***

B98 SP33 10c+5c red brown, *buff* 35 55
B99 SP34 35c+10c slate green, *buff* 50 1.00
B100 SP35 70c+20c black, *buff* 85 1.75
B101 SP33 1fr+25c red org., *buff* 6.00 11.00
B102 SP34 1.25fr+75c violet brown, *buff* 7.50 13.50
B103 SP35 1.75fr+1.50fr light blue, *buff* 12.50 25.00
Nos. B98-B103 (6) 27.70 52.80

See No. 217 (souvenir sheet).

Allegory of Medicinal Baths
SP36

1940, Mar. 1 **Photo.** ***Perf. 11½***

B104 SP36 2fr+50c gray, black & slate green 2.50 *8.00*

Stamps of 1944, type A37, surcharged "+50C," "+5F" or "+15F" in black, were sold only in cancelled condition, affixed to numbered folders. The surtax was for the benefit of Luxembourg evacuees. Price for folder, $15.

Homage to France
SP37

Thanks to Russia
SP38

Thanks to Britannia
SP39

Thanks to America
SP40

1945, Mar. 1 Engr. ***Perf. 13***

B117	SP37	60c+1.40fr deep green	18	18
B118	SP38	1.20fr+1.80fr red	18	18
B119	SP39	2.50fr+3.50fr deep blue	35	33
B120	SP40	4.20fr+4.80fr deep violet	35	33

Issued to honor the Allied Nations. Exist imperf. Price, set $60.

Statue Carried in Procession
SP41

Statue of Our Lady "Patrona Civitatis"
SP42

"Our Lady of Luxembourg"
SP43

Cathedral Façade
SP44

Altar with Statue of Madonna
SP45

1945, June 4

B121	SP41	60c+40c green	18	*40*
B122	SP42	1.20fr+80c red	18	*40*
B123	SP43	2.50fr+2.50r deep blue	35	*1.10*
B124	SP44	5.50fr+6.50fr dark violet	1.60	*6.75*
B125	SP45	20fr+20fr choc.	1.60	*6.75*
		Nos. B121-B125 (5)	3.91	*15.40*

Exist imperf. Price, set $52.50.

Souvenir Sheet.

"Our Lady of Luxembourg"
SP46

1945, Sept. 30 Engr. ***Imperf.***

B126	SP46	50fr+50fr black	2.50	*18.50*

Sheet size: 83x96mm.

Young Fighters
SP47

Refugee Mother and Children
SP48

Political Prisoner
SP49

Executed Civilian
SP50

1945, Dec. 20 Photo. ***Perf. 11½***

B127	SP47	20c+30c slate green & buff	15	*33*
B128	SP48	1.50fr+1fr brown red & buff	15	*38*
B129	SP49	3.50fr+3.50fr blue, dp. bl. & buff	70	*3.25*
B130	SP50	5fr+10fr brn., dk. brown & buff	70	*2.75*

Surtax was for National Welfare Fund.

Souvenir Sheets.

SP51

1946, Jan. 30 ***Perf. 11½*** **Unwmkd.**

B131	SP51	Sheet of four	25.00	*125.00*
		a. 2.50fr+2.50fr slate grn. & buff	4.00	*20.00*
		b. 3.50fr+6.50fr brn. red & buff	4.00	*20.00*
		c. 5fr+15fr blue, deep blue & buff	4.00	*20.00*
		d. 20fr+20fr brn., dk. brn. & buff	4.00	*20.00*

Issued in sheets measuring 100x112mm., to pay tribute to Luxembourg's heroes and martyrs.

The surtax was for the National Welfare Fund.

Old Rolling Mill, Dudelange
SP52

1946, July 28 **Engr. & Typo.**

B132	SP52	50fr brown & dk. bl., *buff*	9.00	16.50

Issued in sheets measuring 100x80mm., in honor of the National Postage Stamp Exhibition, Dudelange, July 28–29, 1946. The sheets sold for 55fr.

Jean l'Aveugle
SP53

1946, Dec. 5 **Photogravure**

B133	SP53	60c+40c dark green	25	*60*
B134	"	1.50fr+50c brown red	50	*1.25*
B135	"	3.50fr+3.50fr dp. bl.	1.65	*3.85*
B136	"	5fr+10fr sepia	80	*2.75*

Issued to commemorate the 600th anniversary of the death of Jean l'Aveugle (John the Blind), Count of Luxembourg.

Ruins of St. Willibrord Basilica
SP54

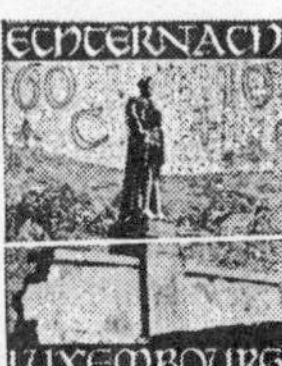

Statue of Abbot Jean Bertels
SP55

Emblem of Echternach Abbey
SP56

Ruins of the Basilica's Interior
SP57

St. Irmine and Pepin of Hersta Holding Model of the Abbey
SP58

Twelfth Century Miniature of St. Willibrord
SP59

Engraved

1947, May 25 ***Perf. 13x14, 14x13***

B137	SP54	20c+10c black	50	70
B138	SP55	60c+10c dark green	85	1.20
B139	SP56	75c+25c dark carmine	1.40	1.90
B140	SP57	1.50fr+50c dark brown	1.80	2.50
B141	SP58	3.50fr+2.50fr dark blue	5.25	7.00
B142	SP59	25fr+25fr dark purple	35.00	50.00
		Nos. B137-B142 (6)	44.80	63.30

The surtax was to aid in restoring the Basilica of Saint Willibrord at Echternach.

Michel Lentz
SP60

Edmond de La Fontaine (Dicks)
SP61

1947, Dec. 4 Photo. ***Perf. 11½***

B143	SP60	60c+40c sepia & buff	70	1.00
B144	"	1.50fr+50c deep plum & buff	70	1.00
B145	"	3.50fr+3.50fr deep blue & gray	7.25	9.50
B146	"	10fr+5fr dk. green & gray	7.25	9.50

1948, Nov. 18

B147	SP61	60c+40c brown & pale bistre	80	1.35
B148	"	1.50fr+50c brown car. & buff	80	1.35
B149	"	3.50fr+3.50fr deep blue & gray	8.00	13.50
B150	"	10fr+5fr dark green & gray	10.00	16.50

Issued to commemorate the 125th anniversary of the birth of Edmond de La Fontaine, poet and composer.

Souvenir Sheet.

Type of Regular Issue of 1948.

1949, Jan. 8 ***Perf. 11½*** **Unwmkd.**

B151	A45	Sheet of three	150.00	110.00
		a. 8fr+3fr blue gray	35.00	25.00
		b. 12fr+5fr green	35.00	25.00
		c. 15fr+7fr brown	35.00	25.00

Issued in sheets measuring 110 x 74 mm., to commemorate the 30th anniversary of Grand Duchess Charlotte's ascension to the throne. Border and dates "1919-1949" in gray.

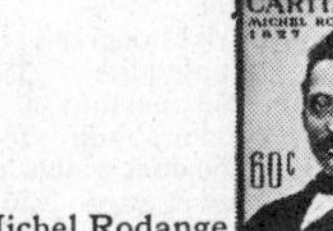

Michel Rodange
SP62

1949, Dec. 5

B152 SP62 60c+40c olive green & gray 1.10 1.65
B153 " 2fr+1fr dark violet & rose 5.25 8.00
B154 " 4fr+2fr slate black & gray 8.00 11.00
B155 " 10fr+5fr brown & buff 10.00 15.00

Wards of the Nation
SP63 SP64

Engraved

1950, June 24 ***Perf. 12½x12***

B156 SP63 60c+15c dark slate blue 1.85 2.75
B157 SP64 1fr+20c dark carmine rose 2.25 3.50
B158 SP63 2fr+30c red brn. 3.25 4.75
B159 SP64 4fr+75c dk. bl. 11.00 22.50
B160 SP63 8fr+3fr black 55.00 90.00
B161 SP64 10fr+5fr lilac rose 55.00 90.00
Nos. B156-B161 (6) 128.35 213.50

The surtax was for child welfare.

Jean A. Zinnen SP65 Laurent Menager SP66

1950, Dec. 5 Photo. ***Perf. 11½***

B162 SP65 60c+10c indigo & grey 55 80
B163 " 2fr+15c cerise & buff 70 1.10
B164 " 4fr+15c violet blue & blue gray 4.25 6.25
B165 " 8fr+5fr dark brown & buff 18.50 27.50

1951, Dec. 5

Gray Background

B166 SP66 60c+10c sepia 35 55
B167 " 2fr+15c dull olive green 55 80
B168 " 4fr+15c blue 2.75 4.00
B169 " 8fr+5fr violet brown 22.50 32.50

Issued to commemorate the 50th anniversary of the death of Laurent Menager, composer.

J. B. Fresez SP67 Candlemas Singing SP68

1952, Dec. 3

B170 SP67 60c+15c dark blue green & pale blue 35 55
B171 " 2fr+25c chestnut brown & buff 70 1.10
B172 " 4fr+25c dark violet blue & gray 3.25 5.00
B173 " 8fr+4.75fr dp. plum & lilac gray 22.50 32.50

1953, Dec. 3

Designs: 80c+20c, 4fr+50c, Procession with ratchets. 1.20fr+30c, 7fr+3.35fr, Breaking Easter eggs.

B174 SP68 25c+15c red orange & deep carmine 25 38
B175 " 80c+20c vio. brn. & blue gray 25 38
B176 " 1.20fr+30c blue green & olive green 80 1.25
B177 " 2fr+25c brown car. & brown 55 80
B178 " 4fr+50c greenish blue & violet blue 4.25 6.25
B179 " 7fr+3.35fr violet & purple 14.00 21.00
Nos. B174-B179 (6) 20.10 30.06

The surtax was for the National Welfare Fund of Grand Duchess Charlotte.

Clay Censer and Whistle SP69 Toys for St. Nicholas Day SP70

Designs: 80c+20c, 4fr+50c, Sheep and bass drum. 1.20fr+30c, 7fr+3.45fr, Merry-go-round horses. 2fr+25c, As No. B180.

1954, Dec. 3

B180 SP69 25c+5c carmine lake & copper brn. 30 38
B181 " 80c+20c dark gray 30 38
B182 " 1.20fr+30c dark blue green & cream 80 1.25
B183 " 2fr+25c brown & ochre 55 80
B184 " 4fr+50c brt. bl. 4.25 6.25
B185 " 7fr+3.45fr pur. 14.00 21.00
Nos. B180-B185 (6) 20.20 30.06

1955, Dec. 5 ***Perf. 11½*** **Unwmkd.**

Designs: 80c+20c, 4fr+50c, Christ child and lamb (Christmas). 1.20fr+30c, 7fr+3.45fr, Star, crown and cake (Epiphany).

B186 SP70 25c+5c salmon & dark carmine 22 35
B187 " 80c+20c gray & gray black 22 35
B188 " 1.20fr+30c olive green & slate green 70 1.10
B189 " 2fr+25c buff & dark brown 65 95
B190 " 4fr+50c light blue & bright blue 3.50 5.50
B191 " 7fr+3.45fr rose vio. & claret 12.50 19.00
Nos. B186-B191 (6) 17.79 27.25

Arms of Echternach
SP71

Arms: 80c + 20c, 4fr + 50c, Esch-sur-Alzette. 1.20fr+30c, 7fr+3.45fr, Grevenmacher.

1956, Dec. 5 Photogravure

Arms in Original Colors.

B192 SP71 25c+5c black & salmon pink 30 45
B193 " 80c+20c ultramarine & yellow 30 45
B194 " 1.20fr+30c ultramarine & gray 55 80
B195 " 2fr+25c black & buff 35 55
B196 " 4fr+50c ultramarine & light blue 3.00 4.50
B197 " 7fr+3.45fr ultra., & pale violet 7.25 11.00
Nos. B192-B197 (6) 11.75 17.75

1957, Dec. 4 ***Perf. 11½*** **Unwmkd.**

Arms: 25c+5c, 2fr+25c, Luxembourg. 80c+20c, 4fr+50c, Mersch. 1.20fr+30c, 7fr+3.45fr, Vianden.

Arms in Original Colors.

B198 SP71 25c+5c ultramarine & orange 20 27
B199 " 80c+20c black & lemon 20 27
B200 " 1.20fr+30c ultra. & lt. blue green 55 95
B201 " 2fr+25c ultra. & pale brown 35 65
B202 " 4fr+50c black & pale vio. blue 1.35 2.25
B203 " 7fr+3.45fr ultra. & rose lilac 6.25 11.00
Nos. B198-B203 (6) 8.90 15.39

1958, Dec. 3 ***Perf 11½***

Arms: 30c+10c, 2.50fr+50c, Capellen. 1fr+25c, 5fr + 50c, Diekirch. 1.50fr + 25c, 8.50fr + 4.60fr, Redange.

Arms in Original Colors.

B204 SP71 30c+10c black & pink 18 27
B205 " 1fr+25c ultramarine & buff 18 27
B206 " 1.50fr+25c ultra. & pale green 35 55
B207 " 2.50fr+50c black & gray 18 27
B208 " 5fr+50c ultra. 90 1.90
B209 " 8.50fr+4.60fr ultramarine & lilac 6.25 11.00
Nos. B204-B209 (6) 8.04 14.26

1959, Dec. 2

Arms: 30c+10c, 2.50fr+50c, Clervaux. 1fr+25c, 5fr+50c, Remich. 1.50fr+25c, 8.50fr+4.60fr, Wiltz.

Arms in Original Colors.

B210 SP71 30c+10c ultramarine & pink 20 27
B211 " 1fr+25c ultramarine & pale lemon 20 27
B212 " 1.50fr+25c black & pale green 40 55
B213 " 2.50fr+50c ultramarine & pale fawn 20 27
B214 " 5fr+50c ultramarine & light blue 1.40 1.90
B215 " 8.50fr+4.60fr black & pale violet 4.75 6.50
Nos. B210-B215 (6) 7.15 9.76

Princess Marie-Astrid SP72 Prince Jean SP73

Designs: 1fr+25c, 5fr+50c, Princess in party dress. 1.50fr+25c, 8.50fr+4.60fr, Princess with book.

1960, Dec. 5 Photo. ***Perf. 11½***

B216 SP72 30c+10c brown & lt. blue 20 27
B217 " 1fr+25c brown & pink 20 27
B218 " 1.50fr+25c brown & lt. blue 40 55
B219 " 2.50fr+50c brown & yellow 20 27
B220 " 5fr+50c brn. & pale lilac 1.80 2.50
B221 " 8.50fr+4.60fr brn. & pale olive 4.00 5.50
Nos. B216-B221 (6) 6.80 9.36

Type of 1960.

Prince Henri: 30c+10c, 2.50fr+50c, Infant in long dress. 1fr+25c, 5fr+50c, Informal portrait. 1.50fr+25c, 8.50fr+4.60fr, In dress suit.

1961, Dec. 4 ***Perf. 11½*** **Unwmkd.**

B222 SP72 30c+10c brown & br. pink 20 27
B223 " 1fr+25c brown & lt. violet 20 27
B224 SP72 1.50fr+25c brown & salmon 30 40
B225 " 2.50fr+50c brown & pale green 30 40
B226 " 5fr+50c brown & citron 80 1.35
B227 " 8.50fr+4.60fr brn. & gray 1.60 2.75
Nos. B222-B227 (6) 3.40 5.44

1962, Dec. 3 Photo. ***Perf. 11½***

Designs: Different portraits of the twins Prince Jean and Princess Margaretha. Nos. B228 and B233 are horizontal.

Inscriptions and Portraits in Dark Brown.

B228 SP73 30c+10c org. yel. 20 27
B229 " 1fr+25c lt. blue 20 27
B230 " 1.50fr+25c pale olive 30 40
B231 " 2.50fr+50c rose 25 33
B232 " 5fr+50c lt. yel. green 50 65
B233 " 8.50fr+4.60fr lilac gray 2.00 2.75
Nos. B228-B233 (6) 3.45 4.67

St. Roch, Patron of Bakers SP74 Three Towers SP75

Patron Saints: 1fr+25c, St. Anne, tailors. 2fr+25c, St. Eloi, smiths. 3fr+50c, St. Michael, shopkeepers. 6fr+50c, St. Bartholomew, butchers. St. Theobald, seven crafts.

1963, Dec. 2 ***Perf. 11½*** **Unwmkd.**

Multicolored Design

B234 SP74 50c+10c pale lilac 20 27
B235 " 1fr+25c tan 20 27
B236 " 2fr+25c light greenish blue 20 27
B237 " 3fr+50c light blue 30 40
B238 " 6fr+50c buff 90 1.25
B239 " 10fr+5.90fr pale yellow green 1.20 1.65
Nos. B234-B239 (6) 3.00 4.11

1964, Dec. 7 Photo. ***Perf. 11½***

Designs (children's paintings): 1fr+25c, 6fr+50c, Grand Duke Adolphe Bridge (horiz.). 2fr+25c, 10fr+5.90fr, The Lower City.

B240 SP75 50c+10c multi. 12 17
B241 " 1fr+25c " 15 18
B242 " 2fr+25c " 20 27
a. Value omitted 300.00
B243 " 3fr+50c multi. 25 35
B244 " 6fr+50c " 60 95
B245 " 10fr+5.90fr " 1.10 1.65
Nos. B240-B245 (6) 2.42 3.57

The Roman Lady of Titelberg
SP76

Fairy Tales of Luxembourg: 1fr+25c, Schäppchen, the Huntsman. 2fr+25c, The Witch of Koerich. 3fr+50c, The Gnomes of Schoenfels. 6fr+50c, Tollchen, Watchman of Hesperange. 10fr+5.90fr, The Old Spinster of Heispelt.

1965, Dec. 6 Photo. ***Perf. 11½***

B246 SP76 50c+10c multi. 20 27
B247 " 1fr+25c " 15 17
B248 " 2fr+25c " 20 27
B249 " 3fr+50c " 25 35
B250 " 6fr+50c " 80 1.10
B251 " 10fr+5.90fr " 1.20 1.65
Nos. B246-B251 (6) 2.80 3.81

Fairy Tale Type of 1965

Fairy Tales of Luxembourg: 50c+10c, The Veiled Matron of Wormeldange. 1.50fr+25c, Jekel, Warden of the Wark. 2fr+25c, The Black Man of Vianden. 3fr+50c, The Gracious Fairy of Rosport. 6fr+1fr, The Friendly Shepherd of Donkolz. 13fr+6.90fr, The Little Sisters of Trois-Vièrges.

1966, Dec. 6 Photo. *Perf. 11½*

B252	SP76	50c+10c multi.	10	13
B253	"	1.50fr+25c "	10	13
B254	"	2fr+25c "	12	17
B255	"	3fr+50c "	25	40
B256	"	6fr+1fr "	55	85
B257	"	13fr+6.90fr "	1.30	2.25
		Nos. B252-B257 (6)	2.42	3.93

Prince Guillaume SP77 — Castle of Berg SP78

Portraits: 1.50fr+25c, Princess Margaretha. 2fr+25c, Prince Jean. 3fr+50c, Prince Henri as Boy Scout. 6fr+1fr, Princess Marie-Astrid.

1967, Dec. 6 Photo. *Perf. 11½*

B258	SP77	50c+10c yel. & brn.	12	17
B259	"	1.50fr+25c gray blue & brown	15	22
B260	"	2fr+25c pale rose & brown	20	27
B261	"	3fr+50c light olive & brown	32	45
B262	"	6fr+1fr light violet & brown	80	1.10
B263	SP78	13fr+6.90fr multi.	1.20	1.65
		Nos. B258-B263 (6)	2.79	3.86

Medico-professional Institute at Cap SP79 — Deaf-mute Child Imitating Bird SP80

Handicapped Children: 2fr+25c, Blind child holding candle. 3fr+50c, Nurse supporting physically handicapped child. 6fr+1fr, Cerebral palsy victim. 13fr+6.90fr, Mentally disturbed child.

1968, Dec. 5 Photo. *Perf. 11½*

Designs and Inscriptions in Dark Brown

B264	SP79	50c+10c lt. blue	12	17
B265	SP80	1.50fr+25c lt. grn.	12	17
B266	"	2fr+25c yellow	15	22
B267	"	3fr+50c blue	20	40
B268	"	6fr+1fr buff	60	95
B269	"	13fr+6.90fr pink	1.20	1.90
		Nos. B264-B269 (6)	2.39	3.81

Vianden Castle SP81

Castles in Luxembourg: 1.50fr+25c, Lucilinburhuc. 2fr+25c, Bourglinster. 3fr+50c, Hollenfels. 6fr+1fr, Ansembourg. 13fr+6.90fr, Beaufort.

1969, Dec. 8 Photo. *Perf. 11½*

B270	SP81	50c+10c multi.	10	13
B271	"	1.50fr+25c "	13	18
B272	SP87	2fr+25c multi.	22	30
B273	"	3fr+50c "	30	40
B274	"	6fr+1fr "	75	1.00
B275	"	13fr+6.90fr "	1.20	1.90
		Nos. B270-B275 (6)	2.70	3.91

Castle Type of 1969

Castles in Luxembourg: 50c+10c, Clervaux. 1.50fr+25c, Septfontaines. 2fr+25c, Bourscheid. 3fr+50c, Esch-sur-Sure. 6fr+1fr, Larochette. 13fr+6.90fr, Brandenbourg.

1970, Dec. 7 Photo. *Perf. 11½*

B276	SP81	50c+10c multi.	12	17
B277	"	1.50fr+25c "	13	18
B278	"	2fr+25c "	20	27
B279	"	3fr+50c "	25	25
B280	"	6fr+1fr "	70	1.20
B281	"	13fr+6.90fr "	1.20	1.75
		Nos. B276-B281 (6)	2.60	3.82

The surtax on Nos. B180-B281 was for charitable purposes.

Children of Bethlehem SP82 — Angel SP83

Wooden Statues from Crèche of Beaufort Church: 1.50fr+25c, Shepherds. 3fr+50c, Nativity. 8fr+1fr, Herdsmen. 18fr+6.50fr, King offering gift.

1971, Dec. 6 Photo. *Perf. 11½*

Sculptures in Shades of Brown

B282	SP82	1fr+25c lilac	12	17
B283	"	1.50fr+25c olive	15	22
B284	"	3fr+50c gray	20	27
B285	"	8fr+1fr lt. ultra.	60	80
B286	"	18fr+6.50fr grn.	2.00	2.75
		Nos. B282-B286 (5)	3.07	4.21

The surtax was for various charitable organizations.

1972, Dec. 4

Stained Glass Windows, Luxembourg Cathedral: 1.50fr+25c, St. Joseph. 3fr+50c, Virgin and Child. 8fr+1fr, People of Bethlehem. 18fr+6.50fr, Angel facing left.

B287	SP83	1fr+25c multi.	12	17
B288	"	1.50fr+25c "	15	22
B289	"	3fr+50c "	25	33
B290	"	8fr+1fr "	60	80
B291	"	18fr+6.50fr "	1.80	2.50
		Nos. B287-B291 (5)	2.92	4.02

Surtax was for charitable purposes.

Sts. Anne and Joachim SP84

Sculptures: 3fr+25c, Mary meeting Elizabeth. 4fr+50c, Virgin and Child and a King. 8fr+1fr, Shepherds. 15fr+7fr, St. Joseph holding candle. Designs from 16th century reredos, Hermitage of Hachiville.

1973, Dec. 5 Photo. *Perf. 11½*

B292	SP84	1fr+25c multi.	12	17
B293	"	3fr+25c "	25	33
B294	"	4fr+50c "	30	40
B295	"	8fr+1fr "	60	80
B296	"	15fr+7fr "	1.60	2.25
		Nos. B292-B296 (5)	2.87	3.95

Annunciation SP85 — Crucifixion SP86

Designs: 3fr+25c, Visitation. 4fr+50c, Nativity. 8fr+1fr, Adoration of the King. 15fr+7fr, Presentation at the Temple. Designs of Nos. B297-B301 are from miniatures in the "Codex Aureus Epternacensis" (Gospel from Echternach Abbey). The Crucifixion is from the carved ivory cover of the Codex, by the Master of Echternach, c. 983-991.

1974, Dec. 5 Photo. *Perf. 11½*

B297	SP85	1fr+25c multi.	10	13
B298	"	3fr+25c "	22	30
B299	"	4fr+50c "	32	55
B300	"	8fr+1fr "	55	80
B301	"	15fr+7fr "	1.50	2.25
		Nos. B297-B301 (5)	2.69	4.03

Souvenir Sheet

Perf. 13½

Photogravure and Engraved

B302	SP86	20fr+10fr multi.	2.25	3.25

50th anniversary of Caritas issues. No. B302 contains one stamp (size: 34x42mm.) Gold marginal inscription. Size: 80x89 mm.

Fly Orchid SP87 — Lilies of the Valley SP88

Flowers: 3fr+25c, Pyramidal orchid. 4fr+50c, Marsh hellebore. 8fr+1fr, Pasqueflower. 15fr+7fr, Bee orchid.

1975, Dec. 4 Photo. *Perf. 11½*

B303	SP87	1fr+25c multi.	10	17
B304	"	3fr+25c "	22	38
B305	"	4fr+50c "	32	55
B306	"	8fr+1fr "	55	95
B307	"	15fr+7fr "	1.40	2.25
		Nos. B303-B307 (5)	2.59	4.30

The surtax on Nos. B303-B317 was for various charitable organizations.

1976, Dec. 6

Flowers: 2fr+25c, Gentian. 5fr+25c, Narcissus. 6fr+50c, Red hellebore. 12fr+1fr, Late spider orchid. 20fr+8fr, Two-leafed squill.

B308	SP87	2fr+25c multi.	20	27
B309	"	5fr+25c "	37	50
B310	"	6fr+50c "	50	65
B311	"	12fr+1fr "	85	1.10
B312	"	20fr+8fr "	1.75	2.25
		Nos. B308-B312 (5)	3.67	4.77

1977, Dec. 5 Photo. *Perf. 11½*

Flowers: 5fr+25c, Columbine. 6fr+50c, Mezereon. 12fr+1fr, Early spider orchid. 20fr+8fr, Spotted orchid.

B313	SP88	2fr+25c multi.	15	17
B314	"	5fr+25c "	30	33
B315	"	6fr+50c "	38	38
B316	"	12fr+1fr "	72	80
B317	"	20fr+8fr "	1.60	1.65
		Nos. B313-B317 (5)	3.15	3.33

The first price column gives the catalogue value of an unused stamp, the second that of a used stamp.

St. Matthew SP89

Behind-glass Paintings, 19th Century: 5fr+25c, St. Mark. 6fr+50c, Nativity. 12fr+1fr, St. Luke. 20fr+8fr, St. John.

1978, Dec. 5 Photo. *Perf. 11½*

B318	SP89	2fr+25c multi.	10	10
B319	"	5fr+25c "	30	27
B320	"	6fr+50c "	38	35
B321	"	12fr+1fr "	75	70
B322	"	20fr+8fr "	1.60	1.50
		Nos. B318-B322 (5)	3.13	2.92

Surtax was for charitable organizations.

AIR POST STAMPS.

Airplane over Luxembourg
AP1

Engraved.

1931–33		*Perf. 12½*	Unwmkd.	
C1	AP1	50c green ('33)	1.40	2.25
C2	"	75c dark brown	80	1.65
C3	"	1fr red	80	1.65
C4	"	1¼fr dark violet	80	1.65
C5	"	1¾fr dark blue	80	1.65
C6	"	3fr gray black ('33)	1.40	3.25
		Nos. C1–C6 (6)	6.00	12.10

Air View of Mosel River
AP2

Wing and View of Luxembourg
AP3

Viandén Castle
AP4

1946, June 7		Photo. *Perf. 11½*		
C7	AP2	1fr dark olive green & gray	40	15
C8	AP3	2fr chestnut brown & buff	40	15
C9	AP4	3fr sepia & brown	60	22
C10	AP2	4fr deep violet & gray violet	35	27
C11	AP3	5fr deep magenta & buff	35	15
C12	AP4	6fr dk. brn. & gray	35	40
C13	AP2	10fr henna brown & buff	1.50	40
C14	AP3	20fr dark blue & cream	1.50	1.90
C15	AP4	50fr dark green & gray	3.00	1.75
		Nos. C7–C15 (9)	8.45	5.39

1852 and 1952
AP5

1952, May 24

Stamps in Gray and Dark Violet Brown.

C16	AP5	80c olive green	1.10	1.65
C17	"	2.50fr bright carmine	1.85	2.75
C18	"	4fr bright blue	4.25	6.50
C19	"	8fr brown red	72.50	120.00
C20	"	10fr dull brown	60.00	100.00
		Nos. C16–C20 (5)	139.70	230.90

Issued to commemorate the centenary of Luxembourg's postage stamps. Nos. C16-C18 were available at face, but complete sets sold for 45.30fr, which included admission to the CENTILUX exhibition.

A particular stamp may be scarce, but if few want it, its market potential may remain relatively low.

POSTAGE DUE STAMPS.

Coat of Arms
D1

Typographed.

1907		*Perf. 12½.*	Unwmkd.	
J1	D1	5c green & black	55	27
J2	"	10c " "	6.50	27
J3	"	12½c " "	2.25	70
J4	"	20c " "	2.25	70
J5	"	25c " "	30.00	1.65
J6	"	50c " "	2.25	1.65
J7	"	1fr " "	80	90
		Nos. J1–J7 (7)	44.60	6.14

Nos. J3, J5 Surcharged **15**

1920				
J8	D1	15c on 12½c	3.00	2.50
J9	"	30c on 25c	3.85	3.25

Arms Type of 1907

1921-35				
J10	D1	5c green & red	25	33
J11	"	10c " "	25	33
J12	"	20c " "	25	33
J13	"	25c " "	30	33
J14	"	30c " "	30	33
J15	"	35c " " ('35)	2.00	25
J16	"	50c " "	30	33
J17	"	60c " " ('28)	75	33
J18	"	70c " " ('35)	2.00	25
J19	"	75c " " ('30)	1.00	27
J20	"	1fr " "	50	50
J21	"	2fr " " ('30)	1.50	2.00
J22	"	3fr " " ('30)	2.00	4.25
		Nos. J10-J22 (13)	11.40	9.83

D2

D3

1946-48		Photogravure.	*Perf. 11½.*	
J23	D2	5c bright green	20	27
J24	"	10c "	20	27
J25	"	20c "	20	27
J26	"	30c "	20	27
J27	"	50c "	20	27
J28	"	70c "	20	27
J29	"	75c " ('48)	20	27
J30	D3	1fr carmine	20	27
J31	"	1.50fr "	20	27
J32	"	2fr "	20	27
J33	"	3fr "	27	27
J34	"	5fr "	50	40
J35	"	10fr "	1.00	1.10
J36	"	20fr "	1.80	3.25
		Nos. J23-J36 (14)	5.57	7.72

OFFICIAL STAMPS.

Forged overprints on Nos. O1–O64 abound.

Regular Issues Overprinted:

Overprinted

Overprint Reads Diagonally Up or Down

Rouletted in Color except 2c

1875		Frankfort Print.	Unwmkd.	
O1	A2	1c red brown	15.00	22.50
		a. Inverted overprint	110.00	150.00
O2	"	2c black	32.50	35.00
		a. Inverted overprint	110.00	135.00
O3	A3	10c lilac	1100.00	1100.00
		a. Invtd. ovpt.	1350.00	1350.00
O4	"	12½c rose	190.00	210.00
		a. Invtd. overprint	375.00	450.00
O5	"	20c gray brown	25.00	35.00
		a. Inverted overprint	25.00	35.00
O6	"	25c blue	240.00	150.00
		a. Inverted overprint	650.00	650.00
O7	"	25c ultramarine	850.00	850.00
		a. Invtd. ovpt.	1000.00	1000.00
O8	"	30c lilac rose	45.00	85.00
		a. Inverted overprint	350.00	425.00
O9	"	40c pale orange	60.00	120.00
		a. 40c org. red, thick paper	135.00	165.00
		b. Inverted overprint (pale orange)	175.00	265.00
		c. As "a," thin paper	1100.00	900.00
O10	A4	1fr on 37½c bistre	110.00	25.00
		a. Invtd. overprint	165.00	32.50

Double overprints exist on Nos. O1–O6, O8–O10.

Overprints reading diagonally down sell for more.

Luxembourg Print.

1875–76			*Perf. 13.*	
O11	A2	1c red brown	4.50	7.50
		a. Inverted overprint	30.00	75.00
O12	"	2c black	9.00	20.00
		a. Inverted overprint	90.00	120.00
O13	"	4c green	75.00	90.00
		a. Inverted overprint	120.00	165.00
O14	"	5c yellow	45.00	90.00
		a. 5c orange yellow	52.50	100.00
		b. Inverted overprint	325.00	400.00
O15	A3	10c gray lilac	60.00	90.00
		a. Inverted overprint	175.00	250.00
O16	"	12½c rose	65.00	100.00
		a. Inverted overprint	275.00	350.00
O17	"	12½c lilac rose	150.00	150.00
		a. Invtd. overprint	300.00	300.00
O18	"	25c blue	11.00	35.00
		a. Inverted overprint	100.00	150.00
O19	A5	1fr on 37½c bistre	30.00	75.00
		a. Inverted overprint	185.00	275.00

Double overprints exist on Nos. O11–O15.

Haarlem Print.

Perf. 11½x12, 12½x12, 13½.

1880				
O22	A3	25c blue	3.25	3.75

Overprinted **OFFICIEL**

Frankfort Print.

1878			*Rouletted in Color.*	
O23	A2	1c red brown	67.50	100.00
		a. Inverted overprint	200.00	250.00
O25	"	20c gray brown	150.00	185.00
		a. Inverted ovpt.	200.00	235.00
O26	"	30c lilac rose	550.00	525.00
		a. Inverted overprint	750.00	600.00
O27	"	40c orange	185.00	200.00
		a. Inverted overprint	300.00	325.00
O28	A4	1fr on 37½c bistre	375.00	90.00
		a. Inverted overprint	350.00	125.00

Luxembourg Print.

1878-80			*Perf. 13.*	
O29	A2	1c red brown	325.00	350.00
		a. Inverted overprint	110.00	175.00
O30	"	2c black	130.00	150.00
		a. Inverted overprint	22.50	30.00
O31	"	4c green	85.00	90.00
		a. Inverted overprint	100.00	120.00
O32	"	5c yellow	400.00	325.00
		a. Inverted overprint		
O33	A3	10c gray lilac	250.00	275.00
		a. Inverted overprint	75.00	90.00
O34	"	12½c rose	60.00	90.00
		a. Invtd. ovpt.	450.00	525.00
O35	"	25c blue	325.00	325.00
		a. Invtd. overprint	700.00	750.00

Overprinted **S. P.**

Frankfort Print.

1881			*Rouletted in Color*	
O39	A3	40c orange	30.00	75.00
		a. Inverted overprint	135.00	175.00

"S.P." are initials of "Service Public."

Luxembourg Print.

Perf. 13.

O40	A2	1c red brown	110.00	125.00
O41	"	4c green	75.00	75.00
		a. Inverted overprint	120.00	
O42	A2	5c yellow	450.00	450.00
O43	A5	1fr on 37½c bistre	22.50	45.00

Haarlem Print

Perf. 11½x12, 12½x12, 13½.

O44	A2	1c yellow brown	6.00	7.50
O45	"	2c black	6.00	7.50
O46	"	5c yellow	90.00	100.00
		a. Invtd. overprint	120.00	
O47	A3	10c gray lilac	90.00	100.00
O48	"	12½c rose	175.00	200.00
O49	"	20c gray brown	32.50	60.00
O50	"	25c blue	32.50	60.00
O51	"	30c dull rose	62.50	90.00

Stamps of the 1881 issue with overprint of type "d" were never issued.

Overprinted **S. P.**
d

1882

Perf. 11½x12, 12½x12, 12½, 13½.

O52	A6	1c gray lilac	65	65
		a. "S" omitted		
O53	"	2c olive gray	65	55
O54	"	4c olive bistre	65	55
O55	"	5c light green	90	65
O56	"	10c rose	20.00	12.50
O57	"	12½c slate	4.50	2.25
O58	"	20c orange	4.50	2.25
O59	"	25c ultramarine	37.50	22.50
O60	"	30c gray green	11.00	11.00
O61	"	50c bistre brown	2.25	1.50
O62	"	1fr pale violet	2.25	1.50
O63	"	5fr brown orange	22.50	17.50

Nos. O52–O63 exist without one or both periods, also with varying space between "S" and "P". Nine denominations exist with double overprint, six with inverted overprint.

Overprinted **S. P.**

1883			*Perf. 13½.*	
O64	A6	5fr brn. orange	1500.00	1200.00

1891-93

Overprinted **S. P.**

Perf. 11, 11½, 11½x11, 12½.

O65	A7	10c carmine	65	45
		a. Sheet of 25	60.00	
O66	"	12½c slate green	20.00	7.50
O67	"	20c orange	22.50	6.00
O68	"	25c blue	65	45
		a. Sheet of 25	60.00	
O69	"	30c olive green	18.50	6.00
O70	"	37½c green	20.00	7.50
O71	"	50c brown	21.00	10.00
O72	"	1fr deep violet	22.50	12.00
O73	"	2½fr black	75.00	30.00
O74	"	5fr lake	75.00	30.00

1895			*Perf. 12½.*	
O75	A8	1c pearl gray	4.50	2.25
O76	"	2c gray brown	4.50	2.25
O77	"	4c olive bistre	4.50	2.25
O78	"	5c green	9.00	3.75
O79	"	10c carmine	60.00	27.50

Nos. O66–O79 exist without overprint and perforated "OFFICIEL" through the stamp. Price for set, $35.

Nos. O65a and O68a were issued to commemorate the coronation of Duke Adolphe.

Scott's editorial staff cannot undertake to identify, authenticate or appraise stamps and postal markings.

Regular Issue of 1906-26 Overprinted *Official* g

1908-26 ***Perf. 11x11½, 12½.***

O80 A9 1c gray 20 20
a. Invtd. ovpt. 100.00
O81 " 2c olive brown 20 20
O82 " 4c bistre 20 20
a. Dbl. ovpt. 120.00
O83 " 5c green 20 20
O84 " 5c lilac ('26) 15 20
O85 " 6c violet 20 20
O86 " 7½c orange ('19) 20 20
O87 A10 10c scarlet 50 50
O88 " 12½c slate green 65 50
O89 " 15c orange brown 85 65
O90 " 20c orange 1.00 85
O91 " 25c ultramarine 85 50
O92 " 30c olive green 8.50 4.25
O93 " 37½c green 1.75 1.00
O94 " 50c brown 2.50 1.75
O95 " 87½c dark blue 7.00 4.00
O96 " 1fr violet 10.00 5.00
O97 " 2½fr vermilion 125.00 75.00
O98 " 5fr claret 110.00 80.00
Nos. O80–O98 (19) 269.95 175.40

Regular Issue of 1914–17 Overprinted Type "g."

1915-17

O99 A11 10c lake 50 50
O100 " 12½c dull green 50 50
O101 " 15c olive black 50 50
O102 " 17½c dp. brown ('17) 50 50
O103 " 25c ultramarine 50 50
O104 " 30c bistre 2.00 2.00
O105 " 35c dark blue 50 50
O106 " 37½c black brown 50 50
O107 " 40c orange 65 65
O108 " 50c dark gray 65 65
O109 " 62½c blue green 85 85
O110 " 87½c orange ('17) 85 85
O111 " 1fr orange brown 85 85
O112 " 2½fr red 65 65
O113 " 5fr dark violet 1.00 1.00
Nos. O99–O113 (15) 11.00 11.00

Regular Issues of 1921–26 Overprinted Type "g" in Black.

Perf. 11½, 11½x11, 12½.

1922-26

O114 A12 2c brown 6 10
O115 " 3c olive green 6 10
O116 " 6c violet 6 10
O117 " 10c yellow green 10 15
O118 " 10c olive green ('24) 13 18
O119 " 15c brown olive 10 15
O120 " 15c pale green ('24) 13 18
O121 " 15c deep orange ('26) 18 25
O122 " 20c deep orange 10 15
O123 " 20c yellow grn. ('26) 18 25
O124 " 25c dark green 10 15
O125 " 30c carmine rose 10 15
O126 " 40c brown orange 10 15
O127 " 50c deep blue 15 22
O128 " 50c red ('24) 13 18
O129 " 75c red 15 22
O130 " 75c deep blue ('24) 13 18
O131 " 80c black 5.25 8.25
O132 A13 1fr carmine 27 45
O133 A14 2fr indigo 3.00 5.00
O134 " 2fr dark brn. ('26) 2.00 3.25
O135 A15 5fr dark violet 18.00 30.00
Nos. O114–O135 (22) 30.48 49.81

Regular Issues of 1921–26 Overprinted Type "g" in Red.

Perf. 11, 11½, 11½x11, 12½

1922–34

O136 A12 80c black, perf. 11½ 15 22
O137 A13 1fr dark blue, perf. 11½ ('26) 40 60
O138 A14 2fr indigo, perf. 11½x11 90 1.30
O139 A17 3fr dk. blue & blue, perf. 11 3.75 3.00
a. Perf. 11½ 1.35 2.00
b. Perf. 12½ 1.65 2.50
O140 A15 5fr dark violet, perf. 11½x11 8.50 12.50
a. Perf. 12½ ('34) 17.50 25.00
O141 A16 10fr blk., perf. 11½ 17.50 22.50
a. Perf. 12½ 27.50 40.00
Nos. O136–O141 (6) 31.20 40.12

Regular Issue of 1926–35 Overprinted Type "g."

1926-27 ***Perf. 12.***

O142 A18 5c dark violet 15 25
O143 " 10c olive green 15 25
O144 " 20c orange 15 25
O145 " 25c yellow green 15 25
O146 " 25c black brown ('27) 50 75
O147 " 30c yel. grn. ('27) 50 75
O148 " 40c olive gray 15 25
O149 " 50c red brown 15 25
O150 " 65c black brown 15 25
O151 " 75c rose 15 25
O152 " 75c bistre brown ('27) 50 75
O153 " 80c bistre brown 15 25
O154 " 90c rose ('27) 50 75
O155 " 1fr black 15 25
O156 " 1¼fr dark blue 15 25
O157 " 1½fr deep blue ('27) 50 75
Nos. O142–O157 (16) 4.15 6.50

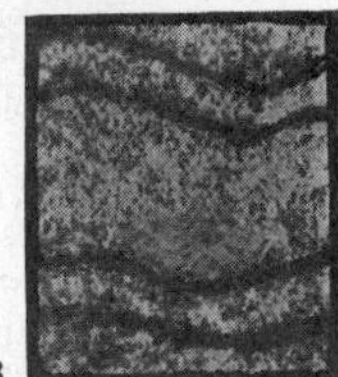
Wmk. 213

Type of Regular Issue of 1926-35 Overprinted *Official* h

Wmkd. Double Wavy Lines. (213)

1928-35

O158 A18 5c dark violet 18 25
O159 " 10c olive green 18 25
O160 " 15c black ('30) 55 90
O161 " 20c orange 50 75
O162 " 25c violet brown 50 75
O163 " 30c yellow green 60 80
O164 " 30c gray violet ('30) 60 90
O165 " 35c yel. grn. ('30) 60 90
O166 " 35c gray violet 60 80
O167 " 40c olive gray 60 80
O168 " 50c red brown 50 75
O169 " 60c blue green 50 75
O170 " 70c blue vio. ('35) 4.25 6.00
O171 " 75c bistre brown 50 75
O172 " 90c rose 60 80
O173 " 1fr black 60 80
O174 " 1fr rose ('30) 60 80
O175 " 1¼fr yellow ('30) 2.00 3.25
O176 " 1¼fr blue green ('31) 2.75 4.25
O177 " 1½fr deep blue 60 80
O178 " 1¾fr dark blue ('30) 55 90
Nos. O158–O178 (21) 18.36 26.95

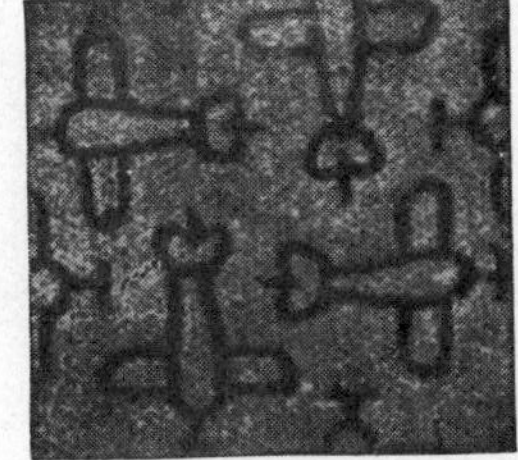
Wmk. 216

Type of Regular Issue of 1928 Overprinted Type "g."

Wmkd. Multiple Airplanes. (216)

1928 ***Perf. 11½***

O179 A19 2fr black 90 1.50

Type of Regular Issue of 1931 Overprinted Type "g."

Wmkd. Octagons. (110)

1931 ***Perf. 12½***

O180 A21 20fr deep green 3.75 5.50

No. 198 Overprinted Type "g."

1934 ***Perf. 14x13½.*** **Unwmkd.**

O181 A22 5fr blue green 3.00 5.25

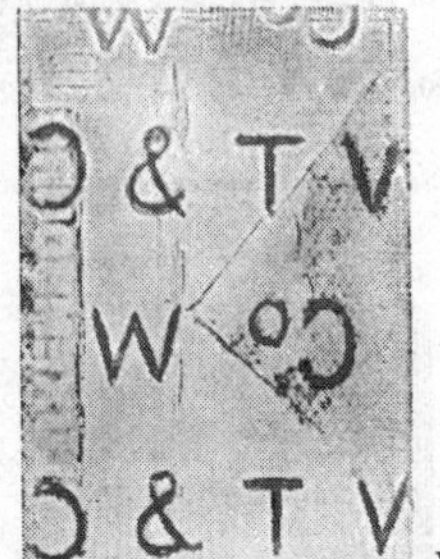
Wmk. 247

Type of Regular Issue of 1935 Overprinted Type "h" in Red.

Wmkd. Multiple Letters. (247)

1935 ***Perf. 12½x12.***

O182 A23 10fr green 3.25 5.00

OCCUPATION STAMPS.

Issued under German Occupation.

Stamps of Germany, 1933-36, Overprinted in Black **Luxemburg**

Wmkd. Swastikas. (237)

1940 ***Perf. 14.***

N1 A64 3(pf) olive bistre 15 33
N2 " 4(pf) dull blue 17 38
N3 " 5(pf) bright green 15 33
N4 " 6(pf) dark green 15 33
N5 " 8(pf) vermilion 15 33
N6 " 10(pf) chocolate 15 33
N7 " 12(pf) deep carmine 15 30
N8 " 15(pf) maroon 30 50
a. Invtd. ovpt. 135.00
N9 " 20(pf) bright blue 35 75
N10 " 25(pf) ultramarine 50 90
N11 " 30(pf) olive green 50 90
N12 " 40(pf) red violet 60 90
N13 " 50(pf) dark green & black 60 1.00
N14 " 60(pf) claret & black 60 1.10
N15 " 80(pf) dk. bl. & blk. 1.25 1.75
N16 " 100(pf) org. & black 1.75 2.25
Nos. N1–N16 (16) 7.52 12.38

Stamps of Luxembourg 1926-39 Surcharged in Black:

❋ ❋

a **4 Rpf**

Perf. 12, 14x13½, 12½x12, 11½.

1940 **Unwmkd.**

N17 A18 (a) 3rpf on 15c blk. 4 17
N18 " (") 4rpf on 20c org. 10 22
N19 " (") 5rpf on 35c yellow green 4 17
N20 " (") 6rpf on 10c olive green 4 17
N21 " (") 8rpf on 25c violet brown 4 17
N22 " (") 10rpf on 40c olive gray 4 17
N23 " (") 12rpf on 60c blue green 4 17
N24 " (") 15rpf on 1fr rose 10 22
N25 " (") 20rpf on 50c red brown 10 25
N26 " (") 25rpf on 5c dark violet 25 65
N27 " (") 30rpf on 70c blue violet 12 33
N28 " (") 40rpf on 75c bistre brown 25 50
N29 " (") 50rpf on 1¼fr blue green 30 33

80 Rpf

—60 Rpf ❋
b c

100 Rpf

❋ ❋
d

N30 A35 (b) 60rpf on 2fr brown rose 3.00 5.25
N31 A22 (c) 80rpf on 5fr blue green 90 1.10
N32 A23 (d) 100rpf on 10fr green 1.10 1.65
Nos. N17–N32 (16) 6.46 11.52

OCCUPATION SEMI-POSTAL STAMPS.

Semi-Postal Stamps of Germany, 1940 Overprinted in Black **Luxemburg**

1941 ***Perf. 14.*** **Unwmkd.**

NB1 SP153 3(pf)+2(pf) dark brown 20 38
NB2 " 4(pf)+3(pf) bluish black 20 38
NB3 " 5(pf)+3(pf) yellow green 20 38
NB4 " 6(pf)+4(pf) dark green 20 38
NB5 " 8(pf)+4(pf) deep orange 20 38
NB6 " 12(pf)+6(pf) car. 20 38
NB7 " 15(pf)+10(pf) dk. violet brn. 33 70
NB8 " 25(pf)+15(pf) deep ultra. 90 1.35
NB9 " 40(pf)+35(pf) red lilac 1.65 2.25
Nos. NB1–NB9 (9) 4.08 6.58

MACAO

(mȧ-kä'ō)

LOCATION—Off the Chinese coast at the mouth of the Canton River.

GOVT.—Portuguese Overseas Territory.

AREA—6 sq. mi.

POP.—280,000 (est. 1977).

CAPITAL—Macao.

The territory includes the two small adjacent islands of Colôane and Taipa.

1000 Reis = 1 Milreis
78 Avos = 1 Rupee (1894)
100 Avos = 1 Pataca (1913)

Portuguese Crown
A1

Perf. 12½, 13½.

1884-85 Typographed. Unwmkd.

1 A1 5r black 3.50 2.50
2 " 10r orange 4.75 3.25
3 " 10r green ('85) 3.50 3.00
a. Perf. 13½ 14.00 11.00
4 " 20r bistre 7.00 5.00
5 " 20r rose ('85) 4.25 4.00
6 " 25r rose 3.00 2.60
7 " 25r violet ('85) 2.75 2.50
a. Perf. 13½ 20.00 15.00
8 " 40r blue 10.00 7.50
a. Perf. 12½ 25.00 7.50
9 " 40r yellow ('85) 5.25 4.00
a. Perf. 13½ 12.00 8.00
10 " 50r green 12.00 8.75
a. Perf. 12½ 42.50 17.50
11 " 50r blue ('85) 2.75 2.00
a. Perf. 13½ 15.00 15.00
12 " 80r gray ('85) 7.00 6.00
13 " 100r red lilac 4.00 3.00
a. 100r lilac 5.25 3.00
14 " 200r orange 7.00 3.50
a. Perf. 12½ 17.50 14.00
15 " 300r chocolate 7.00 6.00
a. Perf. 13½ 25.00 22.50

The reprints of the 1885 issue are printed on smooth, white chalky paper, ungummed and on thin white paper with shiny white gum and clean-cut perforation 13½. Price, $1 each.

No. 13a Surcharged in Black — 80 reis

1884

16 A1 80r on 100r lilac 6.00 5.00
a. Inverted surcharge
b. Without accent on "e" of "reis" 8.50 8.50
c. Perf. 13½ 7.00 7.00

Nos. 16–23, 25 and 27 were issued without gum.

Nos. 6 and 10 Surcharged in Black, Blue or Red:

b

5

c

1885

17 A1 (*b*) 5r on 25r rose, perf. 12½ (Bk) 2.50 1.75
a. With accent on "e" of "Reis" 3.50 3.25
b. Double surcharge
c. Inverted surch. 45.00 20.00
d. Perf. 13½ 25.00 14.00
18 A1 (*b*) 10r on 25r rose (Bl) 5.25 4.00
a. Accent on "e" of "Reis"
b. Pair, one without surcharge 70.00
19 A1 (*b*) 10r on 50r green, perf. 13½ (Bl) 18.50 14.00
a. Perf. 12½ 18.50 16.00
20 A1 (*b*) 20r on 50r green (Bk) 3.50 2.00
a. Double surcharge 40.00
b. Accent on "e" of "Reis"
21 A1 (*b*) 40r on 50r green, perf. 13½ (R) 12.00 10.00
a. Perf. 12½ 14.00 11.00

1885

22 A1 (*c*) 5r on 25r rose (Bk) 2.50 2.00
a. Original value not obliterated
23 A1 (*c*) 10r on 50r green (Bk) 2.75 2.50
a. Inverted surcharge
b. Perf. 12½ 3.50 2.75

Nos. 12, 13a and 14 Surcharged in Black — 5 Reis

1887

24 A1 5r on 80r gray 2.50 2.00
a. "R" of "Reis" 4 mm. high 13.50 14.00
b. Perf. 12½ 10.00 8.00
25 A1 5r on 100r lilac 11.00 7.50
a. Perf. 12½ 10.00 8.00
26 " 10r on 80r gray 3.50 3.25
a. "R" 4mm. high 13.50 14.00
27 " 10r on 200r orange 11.50 6.50
a. "R" 4mm. high 14.00 12.50
b. Perf. 13½ 10.00 7.25
28 " 20r on 80r gray 4.25 3.50
a. "R" 4mm. high 13.50 14.00
b. Perf. 12½

The surcharges with larger "R" (4mm.) have accent on "e". Smaller "R" is 3 mm. high.

Coat of Arms—A6
Red Surcharge.
Without Gum

1887, Oct. 20 *Perf. 12½*

32 A6 5r green & buff 1.75 1.75
a. With labels, 5r on 10r 14.00 12.00
b. With labels, 5r on 20r 14.00 12.00
c. With labels, 5r on 60r 14.00 12.00
33 " 10r green & buff 1.50 1.50
a. With labels, 10r on 10r 14.00 12.00
b. With labels, 10r on 60r 27.50 15.00
34 " 40r green & buff 3.00 3.00
a. With labels, 40r on 20r 14.00 12.00

The 10r also exists with 20r labels, and 40r with 10r labels.

King Luiz A7

King Carlos A9

Typo. and Embossed.
Chalk-surfaced Paper.

1888, Jan. *Perf. 12½, 13½*

35 A7 5r black 2.75 1.50
36 " 10r green 2.75 1.50
a. Perf. 13½ 8.00 7.00
37 " 20r carmine 3.00 2.00
38 " 25r violet 3.50 2.50
39 " 40r chocolate 3.50 2.50
a. Perf. 13½ 6.50 3.50
40 " 50r blue 3.50 2.50
41 " 80r gray 3.50 3.25
a. Imperf. (pair) 80.00
42 " 100r brown 3.50 3.00
43 " 200r gray lilac 6.25 3.75
44 " 300r orange 7.00 5.50

No. 43 Surcharged in Red — 30 30

1892 Without Gum

45 A7 30r on 200r gray lilac 5.00 4.00
a. Inverted surcharge 9.00 9.00

1894, Nov. 15 Typo. *Perf. 11½*

46 A9 5r yellow 1.75 1.25
47 " 10r reddish violet 1.75 1.25
48 " 15r chocolate 2.25 1.75
49 " 20r lavender 2.50 1.65
50 " 25r green 5.00 2.75
51 " 50r light blue 3.50 2.75
a. Perf. 13½ 17.50 15.00
52 " 75r carmine 3.75 2.75
53 " 80r yellow green 5.50 4.50
54 " 100r brown, *buff* 5.00 4.00
55 " 150r carmine, *rose* 6.00 5.00
56 A9 200r dark blue, *blue* 7.00 5.50
57 " 300r dark blue, *salmon* 8.00 7.50

Stamps of 1888 Surcharged in Red, Green or Black

1894 Without Gum *Perf. 12½*

58 A7 1a on 5r black (R) 1.00 70
a. Short "1" 1.00 75
b. Inverted surcharge 5.00 5.00
c. Double surcharge 12.50 12.50
d. Surcharge on back instead of face 17.50 17.50
59 " 3a on 20r car. (G) 2.50 1.00
a. Inverted surcharge 5.00 5.00
60 " 4a on 25r vio. (Bk) 2.75 1.60
a. Inverted surcharge 5.00 5.00
61 " 6a on 40r chocolate (Bk) 2.75 1.50
a. Perf. 13½ 6.00 4.00
62 " 8a on 50r blue (R) 5.00 3.00
a. Double surcharge, one inverted
b. Inverted surcharge 7.00 7.00
c. Perf. 13½ 14.00 11.00
63 " 13a on 80r gray (Bk) 3.50 3.00
a. Double surcharge 8.50 8.50
64 " 16a on 100r brown (Bk) 3.50 3.00
a. Inverted surcharge 7.00 7.00
b. Perf. 13½ 27.50 22.50
65 " 31a on 200r gray lilac (Bk) 7.00 6.00
a. Inverted surcharge 12.00 12.00
b. Perf. 13½ 7.00 6.00
66 " 47a on 300r org. (G) 7.00 6.00
a. Double surcharge 12.00 12.00

The style of type used for the word "PROVISORIO" on Nos. 58 to 66 differs for each value.
A 2a on 10r green was unofficially surcharged and denounced by the authorities.

On No. 45

66B A7 5a on 30r on 200r gray lilac 6.50 5.25

Vasco da Gama Issue.

Common Design Types

1898, Apr. 1 Engr. *Perf. 12½ to 16*

67 CD20 ½a blue green 75 60
68 CD21 1a red 75 60
69 CD22 2a red violet 1.25 80
70 CD23 4a yellow green 1.25 80
71 CD24 8a dark blue 2.25 1.50
72 CD25 12a violet brown 3.50 2.75
73 CD26 16a bistre brown 2.50 1.75
74 CD27 24a bistre 3.50 3.00
Nos. 67–74 (8) 15.75 11.80

King Carlos
A11

Name and Value in Black except No. 103.

1898–1910 Typo. *Perf. 11½*

75 A11 ½a gray 30 25
a. Perf. 12½ 1.00 60
76 A11 1a orange 30 25
a. Perf. 12½ 1.00 60
77 A11 2a yellow green 30 25
78 " 2a gray green ('03) 75 55
79 " 2½a red brown 1.00 80
80 " 3a gray violet 1.00 75
81 " 3a slate ('03) 75 55
a. Diag. half used as 1½a on cover ('10) 3.00
82 A11 4a sea green 1.00 75
83 " 4a carmine ('03) 75 55
84 " 5a gray brown ('00) 1.75 1.00
85 A11 5a pale yellow brown ('03) 75 65
86 " 6a red brown ('03) 1.75 1.75
87 " 8a blue 1.50 1.00
88 " 8a gray brown ('03) 1.75 1.00
89 " 10a slate blue ('00) 1.75 1.00
90 " 12a rose 2.25 2.00
91 " 12a red lilac ('03) 7.25 5.50
92 " 13a violet 2.25 2.00
93 " 13a gray lilac ('03) 2.50 2.50
94 " 15a pale olive green ('00) 9.00 7.00
95 " 16a dark blue, *blue* 2.25 2.00
96 " 18a orange brown, *pink* ('03) 3.50 3.00
97 " 20a brn., *yellowish* ('00) 2.75 1.75
98 " 24a brown, *buff* 2.75 2.50
99 " 31a red lilac 3.00 2.50
100 " 31a red lilac, *pink* ('03) 4.50 4.25
101 " 47a dark blue, *rose* 4.00 3.50
102 " 47a dull blue, *straw* ('03) 6.00 5.00
103 " 78a black & red, *blue* ('00) 7.50 4.00
Nos. 75–103 (29) 74.90 58.60

Issued without gum: Nos. 76a, 77, 79–80, 82, 84, 89, 94, 97 and 103.

Nos. 92, 95, 98–99 Surcharged in Black — 5 PROVISORIO

1900

104 A11 5a on 13a violet 1.40 1.10
105 " 10a on 16a dark blue, *blue* 1.60 1.25
106 " 15a on 24a brn., *buff* 1.60 1.40
107 " 20a on 31a red lilac 1.75 1.75

Regular Issues Surcharged

1902 *Perf. 11½*

On Stamps of 1884–85.
Black Surcharge.

108 A1 6a on 10r orange 2.50 1.75
a. Double surcharge 12.50 12.50
109 " 6a on 10r green 1.50 1.25

On Stamps of 1888.
Perf. 12½, 13½.
Red Surcharge.

110 A7 6a on 5r black 1.00 75
a. Inverted surcharge 13.00 13.00

Black Surcharge.

111 A7 6a on 10r green 1.00 75
112 " 6a on 40r chocolate 1.25 85
a. Double surcharge 13.00 13.00
b. Perf. 13½ 3.50 3.00
113 " 18a on 20r rose 1.75 1.50
a. Double surcharge 13.00 13.00
114 " 18a on 25r violet 12.00 7.00
115 " 18a on 80r gray 15.00 10.00
a. Double surcharge 25.00 25.00
116 " 18a on 100r brown 2.25 2.00
a. Perf. 13½ 9.00 8.25
117 " 18a on 200r gray lilac 15.00 12.50
a. Perf. 12½ 15.00 12.50
118 " 18a on 300r orange 3.50 3.00
a. Perf. 13½ 7.50 7.00

Issued without gum: Nos. 110–118.

Nos. 109 to 118 inclusive, except No. 111, have been reprinted. The reprints have white gum and clean-cut perforation 13½ and the colors are usually paler than those of the originals. Price $1 each.

Common Design Types
pictured in section at front of book.

On Stamps of 1894.

1902–10 *Perf. 11½, 13½*

119 A9 6a on 5r yellow 90 70
a. Inverted surcharge 7.50 7.00
120 " 6a on 10r red violet 90 70
121 " 6a on 15r chocolate 90 70
122 " 6a on 25r green 90 70
123 " 6a on 80r yellow green 90 70
124 " 6a on 100r brown, *buff* 90 70
a. Perf. 11½ 4.25 3.00
125 A9 6a on 200r blue, *blue* 90 70
a. Vert. half used as 3a on cover ('10) 12.50
126 A9 18a on 20r lavender 2.25 1.50
127 " 18a on 50r light blue 2.25 1.50
a. Perf. 13½ 7.50 5.50
128 A9 18a on 75r carmine 2.25 1.50
129 " 18a on 150r car., *rose* 2.25 1.50
130 " 18a on 300r blue, *salmon* 2.25 1.50

On Newspaper Stamp of 1893.

Perf. 12½

131 N3 18a on 2½r brown 2.00 1.50
a. Perf. 13½ 3.50 2.00
b. Perf. 11½ 8.00 5.50
Nos. 108–131 (24) 76.30 55.75

Issued without gum: Nos. 122–130 and 131b.

Stamps of 1898–1900 Overprinted in Black

PROVISORIO

1902 *Perf. 11½*

132 A11 2a yellow green 3.00 2.00
133 " 4a sea green 2.00 1.25
134 " 8a blue 2.00 1.50
135 " 10a slate blue 2.25 1.50
136 " 12a rose 3.50 2.50
Nos. 132–136 (5) 12.75 8.75

Issued without gum: Nos. 133, 135.

Reprints of No. 133 have shiny white gum and clean-cut perforation 13½. Price $1.

No. 91 Surcharged

10 AVOS

1905

141 A11 10a on 12a red lilac 2.50 1.75

MACAU ½ AVO — CONTRIBUIÇÃO INDUSTRIAL ULTRAMAR REIS 5 REIS

Numeral of Value A13 — Coat of Arms A14

Postage Due Stamps of 1904 Overprinted with Bars

1910, Oct. *Perf. 11½x12*

144 A13 ½a gray green 1.00 1.00
a. Ovpt. inverted 3.00 3.00
145 A13 1a yellow green 1.00 1.00
a. Ovpt. inverted 3.00 3.00
146 A13 2a slate 1.00 1.00
a. Ovpt. inverted 7.00 7.00

Stamps of 1898-1903 Overprinted in Carmine or Green

REPUBLICA

Lisbon Overprint

1911, Apr. 2 *Perf. 11½*

147 A11 ½a gray 28 25
a. Inverted overprint
147B " 1a orange 28 25
c. Inverted overprint
148 " 2a gray green 28 25
149 " 3a slate 28 25
150 " 4a carmine (G) 1.00 70
a. 4a pale yellow brown (error) 7.00 7.00
151 A11 5a pale yel. brown 1.00 80
152 " 6a red brown 1.00 80
153 " 8a gray brown 1.00 80
154 " 10a slate blue 1.00 80
155 " 13a gray lilac 1.00 70
156 " 16a dark blue, *blue* 1.25 75
157 " 18a org. brown, *pink* 2.00 1.50
157A " 20a brown, *straw* 2.00 1.75
157B " 31a red lilac, *pink* 2.00 1.75
157C " 47a dull blue, *straw* 2.25 1.75
157D " 78a black & red, *blue* 4.25 3.50
Nos. 147–157D (16) 20.87 16.60

Issued without gum: Nos. 153–157D.

1911 *Perf. 11½x12*

Red Surcharge.

158 A14 1a on 5r brn. & buff 1.50 1.50
a. "1" omitted 10.00 10.00
b. Inverted surcharge 5.00 5.00

Stamps of 1900–03 Surcharged

2 AVOS 2 AVOS

Diagonal Halves

1911 Without Gum *Perf. 11½*

Black Surcharge.

159 A11 2a on half of 4a car. 2.50 2.50
a. "2" omitted 8.50 8.50
b. Inverted surcharge 12.50 12.50
d. Entire stamp 10.00 10.00
159C " 5a on half of 10a slate blue (No. 89) 200.00 200.00

Red Surcharge.

160 A11 5a on half of 10a slate blue (No. 89) 75.00 75.00
a. Inverted surcharge
b. Entire stamp
161 " 5a on half of 10a slate blue (No. 135) 7.00 6.00
a. Inverted surcharge 12.50 12.50
b. Entire stamp 25.00 25.00

MACAU N.° 63 1 avo — Director do Correio.

A15

1911 *Perf. 12x11½*

Laid or Wove Paper.

162 A15 1a black 70.00 60.00
a. "Corrieo" 275.00 250.00
163 " 2a black 75.00 60.00
a. "Corrieo" 275.00 250.00

Surcharged Stamps of 1902 Overprinted in Red or Green

REPUBLICA

Local Overprint

1913 Without Gum *Perf. 11½*

164 A1 6a on 10r green (R) 3.50 3.00

Perf. 12½, 13½

165 A7 6a on 5r black (G) 1.40 1.00
166 " 6a on 10r green (R) 3.50 3.00
167 " 6a on 40r choc. (R) 1.75 1.25
a. Perf. 13½ 5.25 4.00
168 " 18a on 20r car. (G) 2.25 2.00
169 " 18a on 100r brn. (R) 7.50 5.50
a. Perf. 13½ 16.00 12.00
170 " 18a on 300r org. (R) 4.50 3.00
a. Perf. 12½ 5.25 4.00
Nos. 164–170 (7) 24.40 18.75

"Republica" overprint exists inverted on Nos. 164–170. Price, each $7.50.
"Republica" overprint exists double on No. 164.

1913 Without Gum *Perf. 11½, 13½*

171 A9 6a on 10r red vio. (G) 1.50 1.00
172 " 6a on 10r red violet (R) 10.00 4.50
173 " 6a on 15r choc. (R) 1.50 1.00
174 " 6a on 25r green (R) 1.50 1.25
175 " 6a on 80r yellow green (R) 1.50 1.25
176 " 6a on 100r brown, *buff* (R) 1.50 1.25
a. Perf. 11½ 3.50 1.75
177 " 18a on 20r lavender (R) 2.50 1.75
178 " 18a on 50r lt. bl. (R) 2.50 1.75
a. Perf. 13½ 3.50 1.75
179 " 18a on 75r car. (G) 2.50 1.75
180 " 18a on 150r carmine, *rose* (G) 3.50 1.75
181 " 18a on 300r dark blue, *buff* (R) 2.00 1.75

On No. 141

182 A11 10a on 12a red lilac (R) 2.00 2.00
Nos. 171–182 (12) 32.50 21.00

"Republica" overprint exists inverted on Nos. 171–181. Price, $5–$9.

Stamps of Preceding Issue Surcharged

2

1913 Without Gum *Perf. 11½*

183 A9 2a on 18a on 20r lavender (R) 90 70
184 " 2a on 18a on 50r light blue (R) 90 70
a. Perf. 13½ 1.75 1.25
185 " 2a on 18a on 75r carmine (G) 90 70
186 " 2a on 18a on 150r carmine, *rose* (G) 90 70

"Republica" overprint exists inverted on Nos. 183–186. Price, each $5.
The 2a surcharge exists inverted or double on Nos. 183–186. Price, each $7.50.

Vasco da Gama Issue Overprinted or Surcharged:

REPUBLICA

REPUBLICA 10 A.
j k

187 CD20 (j) ½a bl. green 90 70
188 CD21 (") 1a red 90 70
189 CD22 (") 2a red violet 90 70
a. Double overprint one inverted 8.00
190 CD23 (") 4a yel. green 75 75
a. Half used as 2a on cover
191 CD24 (") 8a dark blue 1.00 70
192 CD25 (k) 10a on 12a vio. brown 2.00 2.00
193 CD26 (j) 16a bis. brn. 1.25 1.00
194 CD27 (") 24a bistre 1.75 1.25
Nos. 187–194 (8) 9.45 7.80

Stamps of 1898-1903 Overprinted in Red or Green

REPUBLICA

1913 Without Gum *Perf. 11½*

195 A11 4a carmine (G) 15.00 15.00
196 " 5a yellow brown 2.50 2.50
a. Inverted overprint 4.00
197 " 6a red brown 2.50 2.50
198 " 8a gray brown 20.00 20.00
199 " 13a violet 6.25 6.25
a. Inverted overprint 15.00
200 " 13a gray lilac 3.50 2.50
201 " 16a blue, *blue* 3.50 2.50
202 " 18a orange brown, *pink* 3.50 2.50
203 " 20a brown, *yellowish* 3.00 2.50
204 " 31a red lilac, *pink* 3.00 2.50
205 " 47a dull blue, *straw* 3.00 2.50
Nos. 195–205 (11) 65.75 61.25

Stamps of 1911-13 Surcharged

½ Avo

1913

On Stamps of 1911 With Lisbon "Republica".

206 A11 ½a on 5a yel. brn. (R) 90 60
a. "½ Avo" inverted 4.00
207 " 4a on 8a gray brown (R) 1.00 70
a. "4 Avos" inverted 5.00

On Stamps of 1913 With Local "Republica".

208 A11 1a on 13a violet (R) 20.00 20.00
209 " 1a on 13a gray lilac (R) 90 60
a. "REPUBLICA" omitted

Issued without gum: Nos. 207–209.

REPUBLICA PORTUGUESA — CORREIO — MACAU

"Ceres"
A16

1913-24 *Perf. 12x11½, 15x14.*

Name and Value in Black.

210 A16 ½a olive brown 18 15
a. Inscriptions inverted 10.00
211 " 1a black 25 20
a. Inscriptions inverted 10.00
b. Inscriptions double 10.00
212 " 1½a yellow green ('24) 20 18
213 " 2a blue green 20 18
a. Inscriptions inverted 5.00
214 " 3a orange ('23) 1.50 80
215 " 4a carmine 1.00 35
a. Half used as 2a on cover
216 " 4a lemon ('24) 1.50 75
217 " 5a lilac brown 1.75 1.25
218 " 6a light violet 1.25 75
219 " 6a gray ('23) 5.00 3.00
220 " 8a lilac brown 1.00 70
221 " 10a deep blue 1.25 50
222 " 10a pale blue ('23) 2.50 1.75
223 " 12a yellow brown 1.75 1.00
224 " 14a lilac ('24) 6.00 4.00
225 " 16a slate 2.50 90
226 " 20a orange brown 3.25 1.75
227 " 24a slate green ('23) 3.25 2.50
228 " 32a org. brn. ('24) 3.25 2.50
229 " 40a plum 3.25 1.75
230 " 56a dull rose ('24) 6.00 2.75
231 " 58a brown, *green* 3.50 3.00
232 " 72a brown ('23) 6.00 3.50
233 " 76a brown, *pink* 5.00 3.00
234 " 1p orange, *salmon* 6.75 4.00
235 " 1p orange ('24) 7.25 4.00
236 " 3p green, *blue* 15.00 9.00
237 " 3p pale turquoise ('24) 17.50 14.00
238 " 5p car. rose ('24) 25.00 15.00
Nos. 210–238 (29) 132.83 83.21

Preceding Issues and No. P4 Overprinted in Carmine

REPUBLICA

1915

On Stamps of 1902.

Perf. 11½, 12, 12½, 13½, 11½x12.

239 A7 6a on 10r green 1.00 75
240 A9 6a on 5r yellow 1.00 75
241 " 6a on 10r red violet 1.00 75
242 " 6a on 15r chocolate 75 45
243 " 6a on 25r green 75 60
244 " 6a on 80r yel. green 75 60

245 A9 6a on 100r brown, *buff* 1.75 1.00
246 " 6a on 200r blue, *blue* 65 45
247 " 18a on 20r lavender 1.75 1.25
248 " 18a on 50r light blue 2.25 1.25
249 " 18a on 75r carmine 1.75 1.25
250 " 18a on 150r carmine, *rose* 2.25 1.50
251 " 18a on 300r blue, *salmon* 2.00 1.25
252 N3 18a on 2½r brown 1.25 75

With Additional Overprint PROVISORIO

253 A11 8a blue 80 60
254 " 10a slate blue 75 60
  a. "Provisorio" double 5.00

On Stamp of 1905.

255 A11 10a on 12a red lilac 75 50
Nos. 239-255 (17) 21.20 14.30

Issued without gum: Nos. 243-251 and 255.

No. 217 Surcharged ½ AVO Without Gum

1919-20

256 A16 ½a on 5a lilac brn. 3.25 2.75

Nos. 243 and 244 Surcharged 2

257 A9 2a on 6a on 25r green 7.00 5.00
258 " 2a on 6a on 80r yellow green 5.00 4.00

No. 152 Surcharged 2 avos

258A A11 2a on 6a red brown 6.00 4.75

Issued without gum: Nos. 256-258A.

Stamps of 1913-24 Surcharged 7 avos

1931-33

259 A16 1a on 24a slate green 70 50
260 " 2a on 32a org. brown 75 55
261 " 4a on 12a bistre brown 75 50
262 " 5a on 6a light gray 2.50 1.75
263 " 5a on 6a lt. violet 2.50 1.75
264 " 7a on 8a lilac brown ('31) 1.75 1.10
265 " 12a on 14a lilac ('31) 1.50 1.10
266 " 15a on 16a dark gray 1.50 1.10
267 " 20a on 56a dull rose 2.25 1.50
Nos. 259-267 (9) 14.20 9.85

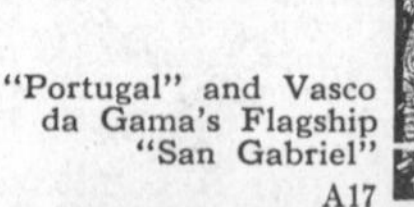

"Portugal" and Vasco da Gama's Flagship "San Gabriel" A17

Wmk. 232

Wmkd. Maltese Cross. (232)

1934, Feb. 1 Typo. *Perf. 11½*

268 A17 ½a bistre 10 10
269 " 1a olive brown 10 10
270 " 2a blue green 12 12
271 " 3a violet 20 18
272 " 4a black 30 20
273 " 5a gray 30 20
274 " 6a brown 30 20
275 " 7a bright rose 45 30
276 " 8a bright blue 45 35
277 " 10a red orange 75 40
278 " 12a dark blue 80 60
279 " 14a olive green 80 60
280 " 15a maroon 80 60
281 " 20a orange 80 60
282 " 30a apple green 2.00 1.00
283 " 40a violet 2.00 1.00
284 " 50a olive bistre 2.00 1.00
285 " 1p light blue 4.75 2.00
286 " 2p brown orange 8.00 4.00
287 " 3p emerald 12.50 6.75
288 " 5p dark violet 20.00 11.50
Nos. 268-288 (21) 57.52 31.80

See also Nos. 316-323.

Common Design Types
Perf. 13½x13

1938, Aug. 1 Engr. **Unwmkd.**

Name and Value in Black.

289 CD34 1a gray green 10 10
290 " 2a orange brown 18 15
291 " 3a dark violet brown 18 15
292 " 4a bright green 18 15
293 CD35 5a dark carmine 20 18
294 " 6a slate 20 18
295 " 8a rose violet 35 30
296 CD36 10a bright red violet 35 30
297 " 12a red 40 30
298 " 15a orange 40 30
299 CD37 20a blue 90 60
300 " 40a gray black 1.75 80
301 " 50a brown 1.75 80
302 CD38 1p brown carmine 3.50 1.50
303 " 2p olive green 7.00 3.00
304 " 3p blue violet 10.50 4.50
305 " 5p red brown 17.50 8.50
Nos. 289-305 (17) 45.44 21.81

Stamps of 1934 Surcharged in Black:

5 avos (a) — 5 avos (b)

1941 *Perf. 11½x12.* **Wmk. 232**

306 A17 (a) 1a on 6a brown 1.50 1.00
307 " (b) 2a on 6a brown 75 50
308 " (") 3a on 6a brown 75 50
309 " (a) 5a on 7a bright rose 27.50 20.00
310 " (b) 5a on 7a brt. rose 75 50
311 " (a) 5a on 8a brt. bl. 2.00 1.60
312 " (b) 5a on 8a brt. blue 80 60
313 " (") 8a on 30a apple green 1.50 1.25
314 " (") 8a on 40a violet 1.50 1.25
315 " (") 8a on 50a olive bistre 1.50 1.25
Nos. 306-315 (10) 38.55 28.45

No. 294 Surcharged in Black: 3 avos

1941 *Perf. 13½x13.* **Unwmkd.**

315A CD35 3a on 6a slate 17.50 12.50

Counterfeits exist.

"Portugal" Type of 1934.

1942 Litho. *Rough Perf. 12*

Thin Paper Without Gum.

316 A17 1a olive brown 55 50
317 " 2a blue green 55 45
318 " 3a violet, perf. 11 2.00 1.75
  a. Perf. 12 3.50 2.25
319 " 6a brown 2.75 1.75
  a. Perf. 10 7.00 4.25
  b. Perf. 11 6.00 4.00
320 " 10a red orange 2.50 90
321 " 20a orange 2.50 1.50
  a. Perf. 11 3.50 2.25
322 A17 30a apple green 3.00 1.75
323 " 40a violet 5.00 2.00
Nos. 316-323 (8) 18.85 10.60

Macao Dwelling A18

Gate of Cerco A19

Designs: 2a, Mountain fort. 3a, View of Macao. 8a, Praia Grande Bay. 10a, Leal Senado Square. 20a, Sao Jeronimo Hill. 30a, Marginal Ave. 50a, Relief of Goddess Ma. 2p, Pagoda of Barra. 3p, Post Office. 5p, Solidao Walk.

1948, Dec. 20 Litho. *Perf. 10½*

324 A18 1a dk. brn. & orange 32 25
325 A19 2a rose brown & rose 25 20
326 A18 3a brn. violet & lilac 55 25
327 " 8a rose car. & rose 32 25
328 " 10a lilac rose & rose 35 30
329 " 20a dark blue & gray 65 35
330 " 30a black & gray 1.35 45
331 " 50a brn. & pale bistre 2.00 50
332 A19 1p emerald & pale green 15.00 5.00
333 " 2p scarlet & rose 12.50 3.50
334 " 3p dull green & gray green 15.00 4.00
335 A18 5p vio. blue & gray 20.00 9.50
Nos. 324-335 (12) 68.29 24.55

See also Nos. 341-347.

Lady of Fatima Issue.
Common Design Type

1949, Feb. 1 *Perf. 14½* **Unwmkd.**

336 CD40 8a scarlet 4.50 3.50

Issued to honor Our Lady of the Rosary at Fatima, Portugal.

Symbols of the U.P.U. A20

Dragon A21

1949, Dec. 24 Litho. **Unwmkd.**

337 A20 32a claret & rose 27.00 15.00

Issued to commemorate the 75th anniversary of the formation of the Universal Postal Union.

Holy Year Issue.
Common Design Types

1950, July 26 *Perf. 13x13½*

339 CD41 32a dark slate gray 2.00 1.00
340 CD42 50a carmine 1.75 1.00

Holy Year, 1950.

Scenic Types of 1948.
Designs as before.

1950-51 *Perf. 14*

341 A18 1a violet & rose 25 18
342 A19 2a olive bistre & yel. 20 18
343 A18 3a orange red & buff 30 25
344 " 8a slate & gray 25 20
345 " 10a red brn. & orange 27 20
346 " 30a vio. blue & blue 1.25 35
347 " 50a olive green & yellow green 1.25 45
347A A19 1p dk. orange brown & orange brown 1.60 50
Nos. 341-347A (8) 5.37 2.31

The 1p was issued in 1950, Nos. 341-347 in 1951.

A 1p ultramarine and violet blue, type A19 and perf. 11, was prepared but not put on sale in the colony. Price $6.

1951 *Perf. 11½x12.*

348 A21 1a org. yel., *lemon* 35 75
349 " 2a dark green, *blue* 35 75
350 " 10a violet brown, *blue* 45 75
351 " 10a bright pink, *blue* 45 75

Holy Year Extension Issue.
Common Design Type

1951, Dec. 3 Litho. *Perf. 14*

352 CD43 60a magenta & pink 2.00 1.25

Extension of the Holy Year into 1951.

Fernão Mendes Pinto—A22

Portraits: 2a and 10a, St. Francis Xavier. 3a and 50a, Jorge Alvares. 6a and 30a, Luis de Camoens.

1951, Aug. 27 *Perf. 11½*

353 A22 1a steel blue & gray blue 10 10
354 " 2a dark brown & olive green 20 20
355 " 3a deep green & green 12 10
356 " 6a purple 30 30
357 " 10a red brown & orange 50 30
358 " 20a brown carmine 75 40
359 " 30a dark brown & olive green 90 50
360 " 50a red & orange 1.50 1.00
Nos. 353-360 (8) 4.37 2.90

Sampan A23

Junk A24

Design: 5p, Junk.

1951, Nov. 1 **Unwmkd.**

361 A23 1p vio. blue & blue 2.25 55
362 A24 3p black & violet 8.50 1.50
363 A23 5p henna brown 16.00 5.00

Medical Congress Issue.
Common Design Type
Design: Sao Rafael Hospital.

1952, June 16 *Perf. 13½* **Unwmkd.**

364 CD44 6a black & purple 50 30

First National Congress of Tropical Medicine, Lisbon, 1952.

Statue of St. Francis Xavier A25

Statue of Virgin Mary A26

St. Francis Xavier Issue

Designs: 16a, Arm of St. Francis. 40a, Tomb of St. Francis.

1952, Nov. 28 Litho. *Perf. 14*

365 A25 3a *greenish gray* 15 12
366 " 16a chocolate, *buff* 60 35
367 " 40a *blue* 1.75 1.00

Issued to commemorate the 400th anniversary of the death of St. Francis Xavier.

1953, Apr. 28 *Perf. 13½* **Unwmkd.**

368 A26 8a chocolate & dull olive 15 15
369 " 10a blue black & buff 35 35
370 " 50a slate green & olive green 1.00 50

Issued to commemorate the Exhibition of Sacred Missionary Art, held at Lisbon in 1951.

Stamp of Portugal and Arms of Colonies
A27

1954, Mar. 9 Photo. *Perf. 13*

Stamp and Arms Multicolored.

371 A27 10a pale yellow green & olive green 70 60

Issued to commemorate the centenary of Portugal's first postage stamps.

Firecracker Flower A28 — Map of Colony A29

Flowers: 3a, Forget-me-not. 5a, Dragon claw. 10a, Nunflower. 16a, Narcissus. 30a, Peach flower. 39a, Lotus flower. 1p, Chrysanthemum. 3p, Cherry blossoms. 5p, Tangerine blossoms.

1953, Sept. 22 *Perf. 11½*

Flowers in Natural Colors.

372 A28 1a dark red 6 6
373 " 3a dark green 9 6
374 " 5a dark brown 20 15
375 " 10a dp. greenish blue 35 20
376 " 16a yellow brown 30 15
377 " 30a dark olive green 30 15
378 " 39a violet blue 45 25
379 " 1p deep plum 3.00 1.25
380 " 3p dark gray 5.00 3.00
381 " 5p deep carmine 8.50 4.00
Nos. 372-381 (10) 18.25 9.27

Sao Paulo Issue.

Common Design Type

1954, Aug. 4 Litho. *Perf. 13½*

382 CD46 39a orange, cream & black 40 20

Sao Paulo founding, 400th anniversary.

Perf. 12½x13½

1956, May 10 Photogravure

Inscriptions and design in brown, red, green, ultramarine and yellow. Buff substituted for yellow on Nos. 386, 388 and 389.

383 A29 1a gray 5 5
384 " 3a pale gray 5 5
385 " 5a pale pink 15 12
386 " 10a buff 12 12
387 " 30a light blue 20 15
388 " 40a pale green 20 15
389 " 90a pale gray 1.00 25
390 " 1.50p pink 1.50 60
Nos. 383-390 (8) 3.27 1.49

Exhibition Emblems and View A30 — Armillary Sphere A31

1958, Nov. 8 Litho. *Perf. 14½*

391 A30 70a multicolored 45 40

World's Fair, Brussels, Apr. 17-Oct. 19.

Tropical Medicine Congress Issue

Common Design Type

Design: Cinnamomum camphora.

1958, Nov. 15 *Perf. 13½*

392 CD47 20a multicolored 2.00 1.50

6th International Congress for Tropical Medicine and Malaria, Lisbon, Sept. 1958.

1960, June 25 Litho. *Perf. 13½*

393 A31 2p multicolored 1.25 1.00

Issued to commemorate the 500th anniversary of the death of Prince Henry the Navigator.

Sports Issue

Common Design Type

Sports: 10a, Field hockey. 16a, Wrestling. 20a, Table tennis. 50a, Motorcycling. 1.20p, Relay race. 2.50p, Badminton.

1962, Feb. 9 *Perf. 13½*

Multicolored Design

394 CD48 10a blue & yel. grn. 8 8
395 " 16a bright pink 60 35
396 " 20a orange 20 15
397 " 50a rose 40 30
398 " 1.20p blue & beige 75 60
399 " 2.50p gray & brown 2.00 1.50
Nos. 394-399 (6) 4.03 2.98

Anti-Malaria Issue

Common Design Type

Design: Anopheles hyrcanus sinensis.

1962, Apr. 7 Litho. *Perf. 13½*

400 CD49 40a multicolored 60 45

Issued for the World Health Organization drive to eradicate malaria.

Bank Building
A32

1964, May 16 *Perf. 13½* **Unwmkd.**

401 A32 20a multicolored 45 35

Issued to commemorate the centenary of the National Overseas Bank of Portugal.

ITU Issue

Common Design Type

1965, May 17 Litho. *Perf. 14½*

402 CD52 10a pale grn. & multi. 60 45

National Revolution Issue

Common Design Type

Design: 10a, Infante D. Henrique School and Count de S. Januario Hospital.

1966, May 28 Litho. *Perf. 11½*

403 CD53 10a multicolored 20 18

40th anniversary, National Revolution.

Drummer, 1548
A32a

Designs: 15a, Soldier with sword, 1548. 20a, Harquebusier, 1649. 40a, Infantry officer, 1783. 50a, Infantry soldier, 1783. 60a, Colonial infantry soldier (Indian), 1902. 1p, Colonial infantry soldier (Chinese), 1903. 3p, Colonial infantry soldier (Chinese) 1904.

1966, Aug. 8 Litho. *Perf. 13*

404 A32a 10a multicolored 30 25
405 " 15a " 45 25
406 " 20a " 45 25
407 " 40a " 75 35
408 " 50a " 75 35
409 A32a 60a multicolored 1.00 35
410 " 1p " 1.00 45
411 " 3p " 3.00 2.50
Nos. 404-411 (8) 7.70 4.75

Navy Club Issue, 1967

Common Design Type

Designs: 10a, Capt. Oliveira E. Carmo and armed launch Vega. 20a, Capt. Silva Junior and frigate Dom Fernando.

1967, Jan. 31 Litho. *Perf. 13*

412 CD54 10a multicolored 20 15
413 " 20a " 25 20

Centenary of Portugal's Navy Club.

Arms of Pope Paul VI and Golden Rose A33 — Cabral Monument, Lisbon A34

1967, May 13 *Perf. 12½x13*

414 A33 50a multicolored 40 30

Issued to commemorate the 50th anniversary of the apparition of the Virgin Mary to three shepherd children at Fatima.

Cabral Issue

Design: 70a, Cabral monument, Belmonte.

1968, Apr. 22 Litho. *Perf. 14*

415 A34 20a multicolored 45 30
416 " 70a " 1.00 60

500th anniversary of the birth of Pedro Alvares Cabral, navigator who took possession of Brazil for Portugal.

Admiral Coutinho Issue

Common Design Type

Design: 20a, Adm. Coutinho with sextant (vert.).

1969, Feb. 17 Litho. *Perf. 14*

417 CD55 20a multicolored 15 12

Church of Our Lady of the Relics, Vidigueira A35 — Bishop D. Belchior Carneiro A36

Vasco da Gama Issue

1969, Aug. 29 Litho. *Perf. 14*

418 A35 1p multicolored 50 35

Issued to commemorate the 500th anniversary of the birth of Vasco da Gama (1469-1524), navigator.

Administration Reform Issue

Common Design Type

1969, Sept. 25 Litho. *Perf. 14*

419 CD56 90a multicolored 40 30

1969, Oct. 16 Litho. *Perf. 13*

420 A36 50a multicolored 30 25

Issued to commemorate the 4th centenary of the founding of the Santa Casa da Misericordia in Macao.

King Manuel I Issue

Portal of Mother Church, Golega
A37

1969, Dec. 1 Lithographed *Perf. 14*

421 A37 30a multicolored 20 15

Issued to commemorate the 500th anniversary of the birth of King Manuel I.

Marshal Carmona Issue

Common Design Type

Design: 5a, Antonio Oscar Carmona in general's uniform.

1970, Nov. 15 Litho. *Perf. 14*

422 CD57 5a multicolored 10 10

Dragon Mask
A38

Design: 10a, Lion mask.

1971, Sept. 30 *Perf. 13½*

423 A38 5a lt. blue & multi. 12 10
424 " 10a pale sal. & multi. 25 25

Lusiads Issue

Portuguese Delegation at Chinese Court
A39

1972, May 25 Litho. *Perf. 13*

425 A39 20a citron & multi. 15 10

4th centenary of publication of The Lusiads by Luiz Camoëns.

Olympic Games Issue

Common Design Type

Design: Hockey and Olympic emblem.

1972, June 20 *Perf. 14x13½*

426 CD59 50a multicolored 30 20

20th Olympic Games, Munich, Aug. 26-Sept. 11.

Lisbon-Rio de Janeiro Flight Issue

Common Design Type

Design: "Santa Cruz" landing in Rio de Janeiro.

1972, Sept. 20 Litho. *Perf. 13½*

427 CD60 5p multicolored 2.75 2.00

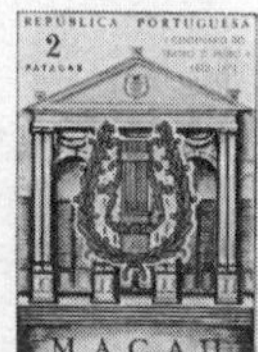

Pedro V Theater and Lyre
A42

1972, Dec. 25 Litho. *Perf. 13½*

428	A42	2p multicolored	1.25	80

Centenary of Pedro V Theater, Macao.

WMO Centenary Issue

Common Design Type

1973, Dec. 15 Litho. *Perf. 13*

429	CD61	20a bl. green & multi.	18	10

Centenary of international meteorological cooperation.

Viscount St. Januario A44

Design: 60a, Hospital, 1874 and 1974.

1974, Jan. 25 Litho. *Perf. 13½*

430	A44	15a multicolored	10	6
431	"	60a "	35	20

Centenary of Viscount St. Januario Hospital, Macao.

George Chinnery, Self-portrait A45

1974, Sept. 23 Litho. *Perf. 14*

432	A45	30a multicolored	20	15

George Chinnery (1774–1852), English painter who lived in Macao.

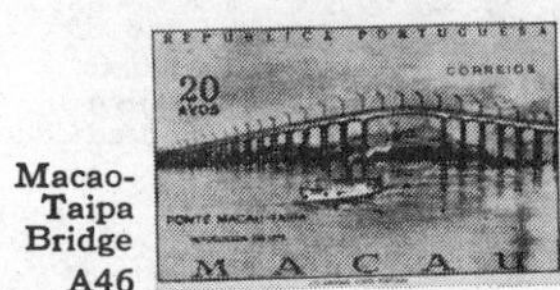

Macao-Taipa Bridge A46

Design: 2.20p, Different view of bridge.

1974, Oct. 7 Litho. *Perf. 14x13½*

433	A46	20a multicolored	15	10
434	"	2.20p "	1.25	55

Inauguration of the Macao-Taipa Bridge.

Man Raising Banner A47

1975, Apr. 25 *Perf. 12*

435	A47	10a ocher & multi.	10	10
436	"	1p multicolored	60	50

Revolution of Apr. 25, 1974, first anniversary.

Pou Chai Pagoda A48

Design: 20p, Tin Hau Pagoda.

1976, Jan. 30 Litho. *Perf. 13½x13*

437	A48	10p multicolored	6.00	1.50
438	"	20p "	12.00	3.00

Macao Cathedral A49

1976, Dec. Litho. *Perf. 13½x13*

439	A49	1p multicolored	50	50

400th anniversary of Diocese of Macao.

"The Law"—A50

1978 Litho. *Perf. 13½*

440	A50	5a blk., dk. & lt. bl.	3	3
441	"	2p blk., org. brn. & buff	1.00	70
442	"	5p black, olive & yellow green	2.50	1.75

Legislative Assembly, Aug. 9, 1976.

A well-informed dealer has services to offer that would be helpful toward building your collection.

Use the Yellow Pages to fulfill your philatelic requirements.

Prices of premium quality never hinged stamps will be in excess of catalogue price.

AIR POST STAMPS.

Stamps of 1934
Overprinted or Surcharged in Black

Avião (a) — Avião 5 avos (b)

1936 *Perf. 11½* Wmk. 232

C1	A17 (a)	2a blue green	1.00	90
C2	" (")	3a violet	1.00	90
C3	" (b)	5a on 6a brown	1.00	90
C4	" (a)	7a bright rose	1.00	90
C5	" (")	8a bright blue	1.00	90
C6	" (")	15a maroon	5.00	3.50
		Nos. C1-C6 (6)	10.00	8.00

Common Design Type
Name and Value in Black.
Perf. 13½x13

1938, Aug. 1 Engraved Unwmkd.

C7	CD39	1a scarlet	30	25
C8	"	2a purple	30	25
C9	"	3a orange	45	45
C10	"	5a ultramarine	90	60
C11	"	10a lilac brown	90	60
C12	"	20a dark green	1.75	1.00
C13	"	50a red brown	2.75	1.50
C14	"	70a rose carmine	3.50	2.00
C15	"	1p magenta	6.00	2.75
		Nos. C7-C15 (9)	16.85	9.40

No. C13 exists with overprint "Exposicao Internacional de Nova York, 1939–1940" and Trylon and Perisphere.

Plane over Bay of Grand Beach
AP1

Designs (Plane above Scene): 76a, Chapel of Penha. 3p, View of Macao. 5p, Bairro de Mong Ha. 10p, Penha and Bay of Grand Beach.

1960, Dec. 11 Litho. *Perf. 14*
Multicolored Centers.

C16	AP1	50a yellow brown	60	30
C17	"	76a pink	1.00	45
C18	"	3p greenish blue	2.00	1.25
C19	"	5p pale lilac	3.50	2.25
C20	"	10p yellow	7.00	4.00
		Nos. C16-C20 (5)	14.10	8.25

POSTAGE DUE STAMPS.

Numeral of Value
D1

Perf. 11½x12

1904, July Typo. Unwmkd.
Name and Value in Black.

J1	D1	½a gray green	25	18
		a. Name & value inverted	6.50	6.50
J2	"	1a yellow green	25	18
J3	"	2a slate	25	18
J4	"	4a pale brown	25	18
J5	"	5a red orange	1.00	60
J6	"	8a gray brown	1.00	60
J7	"	12a red brown	1.00	75
J8	"	20a dull blue	1.75	1.25
J9	"	40a carmine	2.75	2.10
J10	"	50a orange	5.00	4.00
J11	"	1p gray violet	8.00	5.50
		Nos. J1-J11 (11)	21.50	15.52

Issued without gum: Nos. J7–J11.

Issue of 1904
Overprinted in
Carmine or Green

REPUBLICA

1911

J12	D1	½a gray green	18	15
J13	"	1a yellow green	18	15
J14	"	2a slate	18	15
J15	"	4a pale brown	25	25
J16	"	5a orange	25	25
J17	"	8a gray brown	27	27
J18	"	12a red brown	42	35
J19	"	20a dull blue	1.00	75
J20	"	40a carmine (G)	1.85	1.50
J21	"	50a orange	3.50	2.75
J22	"	1p gray violet	4.00	3.25
		Nos. J12-J22 (11)	12.08	9.82

Issued without gum: Nos. J19–J22.

Issue of 1904
Overprinted in
Red or Green

1914

J22A	D1	½a gray green	17.50	12.50
J23	"	1a yellow green	50	50
J24	"	2a slate	50	50
J25	"	4a pale brown	50	50
J26	"	5a orange	60	50
J27	"	8a gray brown	60	50
J28	"	12a red brown	60	50
J29	"	20a dull blue	1.35	1.00
J30	"	40a carmine (G)	3.00	2.50
		a. Double overprint, red and green	4.00	4.00
J31	"	50a orange	3.25	2.50
J32	"	1p gray violet	4.50	3.50
		Nos. J22A-J32 (11)	32.90	25.00

Issued without gum: J28, J30–J32.

D2

Name and Value in Black.

1947 Typographed *Perf. 11½x12.*

J33	D2	1a red violet	1.40	1.00
J34	"	2a purple	1.40	1.00
J35	"	4a dark blue	1.40	1.00
J36	"	5a chocolate	1.40	1.00
J37	"	8a red violet	1.40	1.00
J38	"	12a orange brown	1.40	1.00
J39	"	20a yellow green	2.00	1.50
J40	"	40a bright carmine	3.00	1.75
J41	"	50a orange yellow	4.25	3.25
J42	"	1p blue	4.25	3.25
		Nos. J33-J42 (10)	21.90	15.75

Stamps of 1934 Surcharged
"PORTEADO" and New Values in Carmine

1949, May 1 Wmk. 232

J43	A17	1a on 4a black	1.50	1.25
J44	"	2a on 6a brown	1.50	1.25
J45	"	4a on 8a bright blue	1.50	1.25
J46	"	5a on 10a red org.	1.50	1.25
J47	"	8a on 12a dark blue	2.25	2.00
J48	"	12a on 30a apple grn.	2.50	2.00
J49	"	20a on 40a violet	2.50	2.00
		Nos. J43-J49 (7)	13.25	11.00

Nos. 348, 349 and 351
Overprinted or Surcharged in Black or Carmine

PORTEADO

1951, June 6 Unwmkd.

J50	A21	1a org. yel., *lemon*	35	30
J51	"	2a dark green, *blue* (C)	35	30
J52	"	7a on 10a bright pink, *blue*	35	30

Common Design Type

1952 Photo. & Typo. *Perf. 14*
Numeral in Red; Frame Multicolored.

J53	CD45	1a violet blue	10	10
J54	"	3a chocolate	10	10
J55	"	5a indigo	10	10
J56	"	10a dark red	20	20
J57	"	30a indigo	30	30
J58	"	1p chocolate	1.00	1.00
		Nos. J53-J58 (6)	1.80	1.80

WAR TAX STAMPS.

Victory—WT1

Perf. 15x14

1919, Aug. 11 Unwmkd.
Overprinted in Black or Carmine

MR1	WT1	2a green	1.00	60
MR2	"	11a " (C)	1.50	1.25

Nos. MR1–MR2 were also for use in Timor.
A 9a value was issued for revenue use.

NEWSPAPER STAMPS.

King Luiz
N1 N2

Typo. and Embossed

1892-93 *Perf. 12½, 13½* Unwmkd.
Black Surcharge.

P1	N1	2½r on 40r chocolate	75	60
		a. Inverted surcharge	8.00	8.00
P2	"	2½r on 80r gray	75	60
		a. Inverted surcharge	8.00	8.00
		b. Double surcharge		
		c. Perf. 13½	14.00	10.00
P3	N2	2½r on 10r green ('93)	75	60
		a. Double surcharge		

Numeral of Value
N3 N4

1893-94 Typographed
Perf. 11½, 12½, 13½

P4	N3	2½r brown	40	35
P5	N4	½a on 2½r brown (Bk) ('94)	90	65
		a. Double surcharge		

POSTAL TAX STAMPS.

Pombal Commemorative Issue.
Common Design Types
Perf. 12½

1925, Nov. 3 Engr. Unwmkd.

RA1	CD28	2a red org. & blk.	60	75
RA2	CD29	2a " "	60	75
RA3	CD30	2a " "	60	75

Symbolical of Charity
PT1 PT2

1930, Dec. 25 Litho. *Perf. 11*

RA4	PT1	5a dark brown, *yellow*	16.00	14.00

1945-47 *Perf. 11½, 12, 10*

RA5	PT2	5a black brown *yellow*	16.00	14.00
RA6	"	5a blue, *bluish* ('47)	15.00	11.00
RA7	"	10a green, *citron*	10.50	5.00
RA8	"	15a orange, *buff*	5.00	2.00
RA9	"	20a rose red, *salmon*	20.00	12.50
RA10	"	50a red violet *pinkish*	5.00	5.00

1953-56 *Perf. 10½x11½.*

RA11	PT2	10a blue, *pale green* ('56)	50	25
RA12	"	20a chocolate, *yellow*	6.25	4.25
RA13	"	50a carmine, *pale rose*	3.00	3.00

1958 *Perf. 12x11½*

RA14	PT2	1a gray green, *greenish*	20	12
RA15	"	2a rose lilac, *grayish*	20	12

Type of 1945–47 Redrawn.
Imprint: "Lito. Imp. Nac.-Macau"

1961-66 *Perf. 11*

RA16	PT2	1a gray green, *greenish*	20	10
RA17	"	2a rose lilac, *grayish*	20	10
RA18	"	10a blue, *pale green* ('62)	35	18
RA19	"	20a brn., *yellow* ('66)	65	25

Nos. RA16–RA19 have accent added to "E" in "Assistencia."
Nos. RA4–RA19 were issued without gum.

POSTAL TAX DUE STAMPS.

Pombal Commemorative Issue.
Common Design Types

1925 *Perf. 12½.* Unwmkd.

RAJ1	CD31	4a red org. & blk.	1.00	1.00
RAJ2	CD32	4a " "	1.00	1.00
RAJ3	CD33	4a " "	1.00	1.00

MADAGASCAR

Malagasy Republic

LOCATION—A large island off the coast of southeastern Africa.

GOVT.—Republic.

AREA—229,233 sq. mi.

POP.—8,520,000 (est. 1977).

CAPITAL—Tananarive.

Madagascar became a French protectorate in 1885 and a French colony in 1896 following several years of dispute between Great Britain, France and the native government. The colony administered the former protectorates of Anjouan, Grand Comoro, Mayotte, Diégo-Suarez, Nossi-Bé and Sainte-Marie de Madagascar. Previous issues of postage stamps are listed under these individual headings. The Malagasy Republic succeeded the colony in 1958 and became the Democratic Republic of Madagascar in 1975.

For Madagascar's British Consular Mail Stamps of 1884–1886, see Vol. I.

100 Centimes = 1 Franc
100 Centimes = 1 Ariary (1976)

French Offices in Madagascar

The general issues of French Colonies were used in these offices in addition to the stamps listed here.

Stamps of French Colonies Surcharged in Black:

25 (a) 05 (b)

1889 *Perf. 14x13½.* Unwmkd.

1 A9 (a) 05c on 10c *lavender* 300.00 100.00
a. Inverted surcharge 550.00 350.00
2 " (") 05c on 25c *rose* 300.00 90.00
a. Inverted surcharge 550.00 350.00
b. 25c on 10c lavender (error) 1850.00 1500.00
3 " (") 25c on 40c red, *straw* 275.00 55.00
a. Inverted surcharge 500.00 300.00

1891

4 A9 (b) 05c on 40c red, *straw* 70.00 30.00
5 " (") 15c on 25c *rose* 70.00 30.00
a. Surcharge vertical 70.00 40.00

5 (c)

6 A9 (c) 5c on 10c *lavender* 90.00 40.00
a. Dbl. surch. 200.00
7 " (") 5c on 25c *rose* 90.00 40.00

Forgeries of Nos. 1–7 exist.

A4

1891 Type-set Without Gum *Imperf.*

8 A4 5c *green* 32.50 9.00
9 A4 10c *light blue* 40.00 12.00
10 " 15c ultramarine, *pale blue* 40.00 13.50
11 " 25c brown, *buff* 6.00 5.00
12 " 1fr *yellow* 400.00 135.00
13 " 5fr violet & blk., *lilac* 850.00 400.00

Ten varieties of each. Nos. 12–13 have been extensively forged.

Stamps of France 1876-90, Overprinted in Red or Black — POSTE FRANÇAISE Madagascar

1895 ***Perf. 14x13½.***

14 A15 5c green, *greenish* (R) 4.00 2.00
15 " 10c *lavender* (R) 15.00 11.00
16 " 15c blue (R) 25.00 6.00
17 " 25c *rose* (R) 30.00 7.00
18 " 40c red, *straw* (Bk) 25.00 12.00
19 " 50c rose, *rose* (Bk) 30.00 16.50
20 " 75c deep violet, *orange* (R) 30.00 16.50
21 " 1fr bronze green, *straw* (Bk) 37.50 20.00
22 " 5fr violet, *lavender* (Bk) 45.00 25.00

Majunga Issue.

Stamps of France, 1876–86, Surcharged with New Value

1895

Manuscript Surcharge in Red.

22A A15 0,15c on 25c *rose* *2500.00*
22B " 0,15c on 1fr bronze green, *straw* *2100.00*

Handstamped in Black.

22C A15 15c on 25c *rose* *2500.00*
22D " 15c on 1fr bronze green, *straw* *2500.00*

Three types of "15" were used for No. 22C.

Stamps of France, 1876-84, Surcharged with New Value — 25c

1896

23 A15 5c on 1c *blue* *1850.00 900.00*
24 " 15c on 2c brown, *buff* *1000.00 500.00*
25 " 25c on 3c gray, *grayish* *1100.00 500.00*
26 " 25c on 4c claret, *lavender* *2000.00 850.00*
27 " 25c on 40c red, *straw* *500.00 325.00*

The oval of the 5c and 15c surcharges is smaller than that of the 25c, and it does not extend beyond the edges of the stamp as the 25c surcharge does.
Excellent counterfeits of the surcharges on Nos. 22A to 27 exist.

Issues of the Colony.

Navigation and Commerce
A7

1896–1906 Typographed
Colony Name in Blue or Carmine

28 A7 1c *lilac blue* 40 30
29 " 2c brown, *buff* 40 30
a. Name in blue blk. 1.85 1.85
30 " 4c claret, *lavender* 60 30
31 " 5c green, *greenish* 2.40 50
32 " 5c yellow green ('01) 50 30
33 " 10c *lavender* 3.00 60
34 " 10c red ('00) 50 20
35 " 15c blue, quadrille paper 4.50 20
36 " 15c gray ('00) 50 20
37 " 20c red, *green* 2.00 40
38 " 25c *rose* 2.40 2.00
39 A7 25c blue ('00) 10.00 8.50
40 " 30c brown, *bistre* 3.00 1.25
a. Half used as 15c on cover
41 " 35c *yellow* ('06) 15.00 2.25
42 " 40c red, *straw* 3.00 1.75
43 " 50c carmine, *rose* 4.50 60
44 " 50c brown, *azure* ('00) 12.50 11.00
45 " 75c dp. vio., *orange* 1.00 60
46 " 1fr bronze green *straw* 4.00 1.20
a. Name in bl. ('99) 8.00 6.00
47 " 5fr red lilac, *lavender* ('99) 11.00 9.00
Nos. 28–47 (20) 81.20 41.45

Surcharged in Black — 05

1902

48 A7 05c on 50c carmine, *rose* 2.00 2.00
a. Inverted surcharge 30.00 30.00
49 " 10c on 5fr red lilac, *lavender* 8.00 6.00
a. Inverted surcharge 35.00 35.00
50 " 15c on 1fr olive green, *straw* 2.00 2.00
a. Inverted surcharge 35.00 35.00
b. Double surcharge 80.00 80.00

Surcharged in Black — 0,01

51 A7 0,01 on 2c brown, *buff* 2.50 2.50
a. Inverted surcharge 16.50 16.50
b. "00,1" instead of "0,01" 25.00 25.00
c. Same as "b" inverted
d. Comma omitted 32.50 32.50
e. Name in blue black 2.50 2.50
52 " 0,05 on 30c brown, *bistre* 3.50 3.50
a. Inverted surcharge 16.50 16.50
b. "00,5" instead of "0,05" 22.50 22.50
c. Same as "b" inverted 70.00 70.00
d. Comma omitted 32.50 32.50
53 " 0,10 on 50c carmine, *rose* 3.50 3.50
a. Inverted surcharge 16.50 16.50
b. Comma omitted 35.00 35.00
54 " 0,15 on 75c violet, *orange* 2.50 2.50
a. Inverted surcharge 20.00 20.00
b. Comma omitted 40.00 40.00
55 " 0,15 on 1fr olive green, *straw* 4.00 4.00
a. Inverted surcharge 25.00 25.00
b. Comma omitted 42.50 42.50

Surcharged On Stamps of Diego-Suarez.

56 A11 0,05 on 30c brown, *bistre* 60.00 60.00
a. "00,5" instead of "0,05" 175.00 175.00
b. Inverted surcharge 300.00 300.00
57 " 0,10 on 50c carmine, *rose* *1500.00 1500.00*

Counterfeits of Nos. 56–57 exist with surcharge both normal and inverted.

Surcharged in Black — 0,01

58 A7 0,01 on 2c brown, *buff* 2.50 2.50
a. Inverted surcharge 16.50 16.50
b. Comma omitted 32.50 32.50
59 " 0,05 on 30c brown, *bistre* 3.00 3.00
a. Inverted surcharge 16.50 16.50
b. Comma omitted 32.50 32.50
60 " 0,10 on 50c carmine, *rose* 2.50 2.50
a. Inverted surcharge 16.50 16.50
b. Comma omitted 40.00 40.00

Surcharged On Stamps of Diego-Suarez.

61 A11 0,05 on 30c brown, *bistre* 60.00 60.00
a. Inverted surch. 300.00 300.00
62 A11 0,10 on 50c carmine, *rose* *1500.00 1500.00*

During alleged stamp shortages at several Madagascar towns in 1904, it is claimed that bisects were used. After being affixed to letters, these bisects were handstamped "Affranchissement—exceptionnel—(faute de timbres)" and other inscriptions of similar import. The stamps bisected were 10c, 20c, 30c and 50c denominations of Madagascar type A7 and Diego-Suarez type A11. The editors believe these provisionals were unnecessary and speculative.

Zebu, Traveler's Tree and Lemur
A8

Transportation by Sedan Chair
A9

1903 Engraved. ***Perf. 11½.***

63 A8 1c dark violet 40 40
a. On bluish paper 3.00 2.25
64 " 2c olive brown 40 40
65 " 4c brown 40 40
66 " 5c yellow green 3.00 40
67 " 10c red 3.50 40
68 " 15c carmine 6.00 40
a. On bluish paper 50.00
69 " 20c orange 2.40 70
70 " 25c dull blue 15.00 2.25
71 " 30c pale red 16.50 6.00
72 " 40c gray violet 13.50 1.75
73 " 50c brown orange 22.50 10.00
74 " 75c orange yellow 25.00 10.00
75 " 1fr deep green 25.00 15.00
76 " 2fr slate 32.50 16.50
77 " 5fr gray black 30.00 16.50
Nos. 63–77 (15) 196.10 81.10

Nos. 63–77 exist imperf. Price of set, $500.

Typographed.

1908-28 ***Perf. 13½x14.***

79 A9 1c violet & olive 5 4
80 " 2c red & olive 5 5
81 " 4c olive brn. & brn. 5 5
82 " 5c blue green & olive 5 3
a. Booklet pane of 4 2.00
83 " 5c black & rose ('22) 5 3
a. Booklet pane of 4 2.00
84 " 10c rose & brown 5 3
a. Booklet pane of 4 4.00
85 " 10c blue green & olive green ('22) 6 5
86 " 10c orange brown & violet ('25) 6 6
a. Booklet pane of 4 3.00
87 " 15c dull violet & rose ('16) 10 6
a. Booklet pane of 4 3.75
88 " 15c dull green & light green ('27) 8 5
a. Booklet pane of 4 3.00
89 " 15c dark blue & rose red ('28) 45 40
90 " 20c orange & brown 10 8
91 " 25c blue & black 60 10
92 " 25c vio. & black ('22) 7 5
93 " 30c brown & black 1.00 50
94 " 30c rose red & brown ('22) 6 6
95 " 30c green & red violet ('25) 7 5
96 " 30c deep green & yel. green ('27) 33 33
97 " 35c red & black 20 10
98 " 40c vio. brown & blk. 20 8
99 " 45c blue green & black 15 8
100 " 45c red & vermilion ('25) 8 8
101 " 45c gray lilac & magenta ('27) 25 23
102 " 50c violet & black 15 8
103 " 50c blue & black ('22) 8 8
104 " 50c blk. & org. ('25) 6 5
105 " 60c violet, *pinkish* ('25) 10 10
106 " 65c black & blue ('25) 25 25

107 A9 75c rose red & black 15 10

108 " 85c green & vermilion ('25) 30 30

109 " 1fr brown & olive 15 10

110 " 1fr dull blue ('25) 20 15

111 " 1fr rose & grn. ('28) 2.50 2.25

112 " 1.10fr bistre & blue green ('28) 40 30

113 " 2fr blue & olive 1.40 33

114 " 5fr violet & violet brown 3.50 2.25

Nos. 79-114 (36) 13.40 8.93

Preceding Issues Surcharged in Black or Carmine

05 *e* **10** *f*

1912, Nov. ***Perf. 14x13½***

115 A7 (*e*) 5c on 15c gray (C) 20 20

116 " (") 5c on 20c red, *green* 20 20

a. Inverted surch. 45.00 45.00

117 " (") 5c on 30c brown, *bistre* (C) 30 30

118 " (*f*) 10c on 75c violet, *orange* 3.50 3.50

a. Dbl. surcharge 75.00 75.00

119 A8 (*e*) 5c on 2c olive brown (C) 10 10

120 " (") 5c on 20c orange 20 20

121 " (") 5c on 30c pale red 30 30

122 " (*f*) 10c on 40c gray violet (C) 30 30

123 " (") 10c on 50c brn. org. 1.00 1.00

124 " (") 10c on 75c orange yellow 2.50 2.50

a. Inverted surch. 75.00 75.00

Nos. 115-124 (10) 8.60 8.60

Two spacings between the surcharged numerals are found on Nos. 115 to 118.

Stamps of Anjouan, Grand Comoro Island, Mayotte and Mohéli with similar surcharges were also available for use in Madagascar and the entire Comoro archipelago.

Preceding Issues Surcharged in Red or Black:

0,30 *g* **1 FR.** *h*

1921

On Nos. 98 & 107.

125 A9 (*g*) 30c on 40c violet brown & black (R) 40 30

126 " (") 60c on 75c rose red & black 90 40

On Nos. 45 & 47.

127 A7 (*g*) 60c on 75c violet, *orange* (R) 2.50 2.50

a. Inverted surcharge 55.00 55.00

128 " (*h*) 1fr on 5fr red lilac, *lavender* 30 30

On No. 77.

129 A8 (*h*) 1fr on 5fr black (R) 30.00 30.00

Stamps and Type of 1908-16 Surcharged in Black or Red:

0,25

1 cent. *j* **≡** *k*

130 A9 (*j*) 1c on 15c dull violet & rose 10 10

131 " (*k*) 25c on 35c red & black 1.65 1.25

132 " (") 25c on 35c red & black (R) 6.50 5.00

133 " (") 25c on 40c brown & black 1.65 1.25

134 A9 (*k*) 25c on 45c green & black 1.25 1.00

Nos. 125-134 (10) 45.25 42.10

Stamps and Type of 1908-28 Surcharged with New Value and Bars.

1922-27

135 A9 25c on 15c dull violet & rose ('25) 6 6

a. Double surcharge 22.50

136 " 25c on 2fr blue & olive ('24) 5 5

137 " 25c on 5fr violet & vio. brown ('24) 5 5

138 " 60c on 75c violet, *pinkish* ('22) 6 6

139 " 65c on 75c rose red & black ('25) 10 10

140 " 85c on 45c blue green & black ('25) 12 12

141 " 90c on 75c dull red & rose red ('27) 12 6

142 " 1.25fr on 1fr light blue (R) ('26) 12 10

143 " 1.50fr on 1fr deep blue & dull blue ('27) 12 10

144 " 3fr on 5fr green & violet ('27) 40 40

145 " 10fr on 5fr orange & rose lilac ('27) 2.85 2.25

146 " 20fr on 5fr rose & slate blue ('27) 3.50 2.75

Nos. 135-146 (12) 7.55 6.10

See Nos. 178-179.

Sakalava Chief A10

Hova Woman A12

Hova with Oxen—A11

Bétsiléo Woman—A13

Typographed.

1930-44 ***Perf. 13½x14, 14x13½.***

147 A11 1c dark blue & blue green ('33) 6 6

148 A10 2c brown red & dark brown 6 6

149 " 4c dk. brn. & violet 6 6

150 A11 5c light green & red 6 6

151 A12 10c verm. & dp. grn. 6 6

152 A13 15c deep red 7 6

153 A11 20c yellow brown & dark blue 5 5

154 A12 25c vio. & dk. brn. 6 6

155 A13 30c Prussian blue 8 8

156 A10 40c green & red 18 18

157 A13 45c dull violet 25 18

158 A11 65c olive brn. & vio. 30 17

159 A13 75c dark brown 22 15

160 A11 90c brown red & dark red 32 17

161 A12 1fr yellow brown & dark blue 70 20

162 " 1fr dark red & car. rose ('38) 6 6

163 " 1.25fr deep blue & dark brown ('33) 45 25

164 A10 1.50fr dk. & dp. blue 2.50 35

165 " 1.50fr brown & dark red ('38) 7 7

165A " 1.50fr dark red & brown ('44) 7 7

166 " 1.75fr dark brown & dark red ('33) 1.40 18

167 " 5fr vio. & dk. brn. 15 15

168 " 20fr yellow brown & dark blue 50 50

Nos. 147-168 (23) 7.73 3.23

Colonial Exposition Issue.

Common Design Types

1931 Engraved. ***Perf. 12½.***

Name of Country in Black.

169 CD70 40c deep green 30 20

170 CD71 50c violet 1.00 25

171 CD72 90c red orange 40 30

172 CD73 1.50fr dull blue 1.00 40

General Joseph Simon Galliéni A14

Size: 21½x34½mm.

1931 Engraved. ***Perf. 14.***

173 A14 1c ultramarine 10 10

174 " 50c orange brown 50 10

175 " 2fr deep red 2.50 1.35

176 " 3fr emerald 2.00 60

177 " 10fr deep orange 1.40 70

Nos. 173-177 (5) 6.50 2.85

See also Nos. 180-190.

25c

Nos. 113 and 109 Surcharged

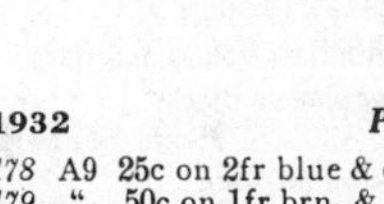

1932 ***Perf. 13½x14***

178 A9 25c on 2fr blue & olive 10 8

179 " 50c on 1fr brn. & olive 10 8

No. 178 has numerals in thick block letters. No. 136 has thin shaded numerals.

Galliéni Type of 1931.

Photogravure.

Size: 21x34mm.

1936-40 ***Perf. 13½, 13x13½.***

180 A14 3c sapphire ('40) 5 4

181 " 45c bright green ('40) 6 6

182 " 50c yellow brown 5 5

183 " 60c bright red lilac ('40) 6 5

184 " 70c bright rose ('40) 8 8

185 " 90c copper brn. ('39) 7 7

186 " 1.40fr orange yel. ('40) 13 12

187 " 1.60fr purple ('40) 13 12

188 " 2fr dark carmine 7 7

189 " 3fr green 1.85 1.00

190 " 3fr olive black ('39) 22 12

Nos. 180-190 (11) 2.77 1.78

Common Design Types

pictured in section at front of book.

Paris International Exposition Issue.

Common Design Types

1937, Apr. 15 Engr. ***Perf. 13***

191 CD74 20c deep violet 45 45

192 CD75 30c dark green 40 40

193 CD76 40c carmine rose 40 40

194 CD77 50c dark brown & black 25 25

195 CD78 90c red 50 50

196 CD79 1.50fr ultramarine 50 50

Nos. 191-196 (6) 2.50 2.50

Colonial Arts Exhibition Issue.

Common Design Type

Souvenir Sheet.

1937 ***Imperf.***

197 CD74 3fr orange red 1.65 1.65

Issued in sheets measuring 118x99mm.

Jean Laborde A15

1938-40 ***Perf. 13.***

198 A15 35c green 20 12

199 " 55c deep purple 20 10

200 " 65c orange red 20 6

201 " 80c violet brown 20 7

202 " 1fr rose carmine 20 8

203 " 1.25fr rose car. ('39) 10 8

204 " 1.75fr dark ultra. 60 12

205 " 2.15fr yellow brown 1.25 45

206 " 2.25fr dark ultra. ('39) 10 8

207 " 2.50fr blk. brn. ('40) 10 6

208 " 10fr dark green ('40) 25 15

Nos. 198-208 (11) 3.40 1.37

Nos. 198 to 202, 204 and 205 were issued in commemoration of the 60th anniversary of the death of Jean Laborde, explorer.

New York World's Fair Issue.

Common Design Type

1939, May 10 Engr. ***Perf. 12½x12***

209 CD82 1.25fr carmine lake 40 40

210 " 2.25fr ultramarine 40 40

Porters Carrying Man in Chair, and Marshal Petain A15a

1941 Engraved ***Perf. 12x12½***

210A A15a 1fr bister brown 18

210B " 2.50fr blue 18

Nos. 210A-210B were issued by the Vichy government and were not placed on sale in the colony.

Type of 1930-44 Surcharged in Black with New Value.

1942 ***Perf. 14x13½.***

211 A11 50c on 65c dark brown & magenta 40 8

V2

Stamps of the design shown above and types A10, A11, A12 and A14, without "RF," were issued in 1942-44 by the Vichy government, but were not placed on sale in the colony.

Stamps of 1927 with additional Overprint in Red or Black **FRANCE LIBRE** *l*

1942 ***Perf. 14x13½.*** **Unwmkd.**

212 A9 (*l*) 1.50fr on 1fr deep blue & dull blue (R) 40 40

213 " (") 10fr on 5fr orange & rose lilac (Bk) 2.00 2.00

214 " (") 20fr on 5fr rose & slate blue (R) 3.00 3.00

Stamps of 1930-40 Overprinted in Black or Red

FRANCE LIBRE *m*

215 A10 (*l*) 2c brown red & dark brown (Bk) 25 25

216 A14 (") 3c sapphire (R) 32.50 32.50

217 A13 (*m*) 15c deep red (Bk) 3.50 3.00

218 A11 (") 65c dark brown & magenta (Bk) 25 25

219 A14 (*l*) 70c bright rose (Bk) 12 12

220 A15 (") 80c violet brown (Bk) 60 60

221 A14 (") 1.40fr orange yellow (Bk) 13 13

222 A10 (") 1.50fr dark blue & deep blue (R) 40 40

223 " (") 1.50fr brown & dark red (Bk) 30 30

224 A14 (") 1.60fr purple (Bk) 15 15

225 A15 (") 2.25fr dark ultramarine (R) 18 18

226 " (") 2.50fr black brown (R) 1.00 1.00

227 " (") 10fr dark green (Bk) 1.40 1.40

228 A10 (") 20fr yel. brn. & dark blue (R) 350.00 350.00

Stamps of 1930-40 Surcharged in Black or Red **FRANCE LIBRE 0,10 ×**

229 A11 5c on 1c dark blue & blue green (Bk) 10 10

230 A15 10c on 55c deep purple (Bk) 30 30

231 " 30c on 65c orange red (Bk) 18 18

232 A14 50c on 90c copper brown (Bk) 7 7

233 A12 1fr on 1.25fr deep blue & dark brown (Bk) 60 60

234 A15 1fr on 1.25fr rose carmine (Bk) 1.65 1.65

235 A10 1.50fr on 1.75fr dark brown & dark red (Bk) 12 12

236 A15 1.50fr on 1.75fr ultramarine (R) 10 10

237 " 2fr on 2.15fr yellow brown (Bk) 25 25

No. 211 with additional Overprint in Black.

239 A11 (*m*) 50c on 65c dark brown & magenta 40 8

New York World's Fair Stamp Overprinted in Red.

Perf. 12½x12.

240 CD82 (*m*) 2.25fr ultra. (R) 12 12

Nos. 212-227, 229-240 (27) 50.07 49.25

Traveler's Tree
A16

Photogravure.

1943 ***Perf. 14x14½.*** **Unwmkd.**

241 A16 5c olive gray 5 5

242 " 10c pale rose violet 5 5

243 " 25c emerald 6 6

244 " 30c deep orange 6 6

245 " 40c slate blue 6 6

246 " 80c dark red brown 8 8

247 " 1fr dull blue 6 6

248 " 1.50fr crimson rose 6 6

249 " 2fr dull yellow 5 5

250 " 2.50fr bright ultra. 8 8

251 " 4fr aqua. & red 10 10

252 " 5fr green & black 22 20

253 " 10fr salmon pink & dark blue 20 10

254 " 20fr dull vio. & brn. 30 22

Nos. 241-254 (14) 1.43 1.23

Nos. 241 and 242 Surcharged with New Values and Bars in Red or Blue.

1944

255 A16 1.50fr on 5c olive gray (R) 20 20

256 " 1.50fr on 10c pale rose vio. (Bl) 30 30

Nos. 229 and 224 Surcharged with New Values and Bars in Red or Black.
Perf. 14x13½, 14.

257 A11 50c on 5c on 1c dark blue & bluegreen (R) 13 13

258 A14 1.50fr on 1.60fr purple (Bk) 7 7

Eboue Issue.
Common Design Type

1945 Engraved ***Perf. 13***

259 CD91 2fr black 10 10

260 " 25fr Prussian green 25 25

Nos. 241, 243 and 250 Surcharged with New Values and Bars in Carmine or Black.

1945 ***Perf. 14x14½***

261 A16 50c on 5c olive gray (C) 5 5

262 " 60c on 5c olive gray (C) 15 15

263 " 70c on 5c olive gray (C) 8 8

264 " 1.20fr on 5c olive gray (C) 8 8

265 " 2.40fr on 25c emerald 8 8

266 " 3fr on 25c emerald 8 8

267 " 4.50fr on 25c emerald 15 15

268 " 15fr on 2.50fr bright ultra. (C) 13 13

Nos. 261-268 (8) 80 80

Southern Dancer
A17

Gen. J. S. Galliéni
A20

Herd of Zebus
A18

Sakalava Man and Woman
A19

Betsimisaraka Mother and Child
A21

General Jacques C. R. A. Duchesne
A22

Marshal Joseph J. C. Joffre
A23

Perf. 13x13½, 13½x13.

1946 Photogravure. **Unwmkd.**

269 A17 10c green 4 3

270 " 30c orange 4 4

271 " 40c brown olive 5 5

272 " 50c violet brown 5 5

273 A18 60c deep ultramarine 6 6

274 " 80c blue green 6 6

275 A19 1fr brown 6 6

276 " 1.20fr green 6 6

276A A20 1.50fr dark red 6 6

277 " 2fr slate black 6 6

278 " 3fr deep claret 6 6

278A A21 3.60fr dk. car. rose 20 20

279 " 4fr deep ultra. 8 5

280 " 5fr red orange 10 4

281 A22 6fr dark greenish blue 8 6

282 " 10fr red brown 17 6

283 A23 15fr violet brown 30 6

284 " 20fr dark violet blue 40 12

285 " 25fr brown 45 6

Nos. 269-285 (19) 2.38 1.24

Military Medal Issue.
Common Design Type
Engraved and Typographed.

1952, Dec. 1 ***Perf. 13*** **Unwmkd.**

286 CD101 15fr multicolored 1.10 75

Centenary of the creation of the French Military Medal.

Tropical Flowers
A24

Long-tailed Ground Roller
A25

1954 **Engraved.**

287 A24 7.50fr indigo & gray green 60 10

288 A25 8fr brown carmine 30 10

289 " 15fr dark green & deep ultra. 85 8

Colonel Lyautey and Royal Palace, Tananarive
A26

1954-55

290 A26 10fr violet blue, indigo & blue ('55) 40 6

291 " 40fr dark slate blue & red brown 90 8

FIDES Issue.
Common Design Type

Designs: 3fr, Tractor and modern settlement. 5fr, Galliéni school. 10fr, Pangalanes Canal. 15fr, Irrigation project.

1956, Oct. 22 Engr. ***Perf. 13x12½***

292 CD103 3fr gray vio. & vio. brown 12 6

293 " 5fr org. brn. & dk. vio. brn. 8 6

294 " 10fr indigo & lilac gray 25 8

295 " 15fr grn. & bl. grn. 30 7

Coffee—A26a

1956, Oct. 22 ***Perf. 13***

296 A26a 20fr red brown & dark brown 25 10

Manioc
A27

Vanilla
A28

Design: 4fr, Cloves.

1957, Mar. 12 ***Perf. 13*** **Unwmkd.**

297 A27 2fr bl., green & sepia 10 6

298 A28 4fr deep green & red 15 10

299 " 12fr dark violet, dull green & sepia 25 15

Malagasy Republic

Human Rights Issue
Common Design Type

1958, Dec. 10 Engr. ***Perf. 13***

300 CD105 10fr brn. & dk. blue 35 20

Universal Declaration of Human Rights, 10th anniversary.
"CF" stands for "Communauté française."

Imperforates

Most Malagasy stamps from 1958 onward exist imperforate in issued and trial colors, and also in small presentation sheets in issued colors.

Flower Issue
Common Design Type

Designs: 6fr, Datura (horiz.) 25fr, Poinsettia.

Perf. 12½x12, 12x12½

1959, Jan. 31 Photogravure

301 CD104 6fr multicolored 15 10

302 " 25fr " 50 10

Flag and Assembly Building
A29

Flag and Map
A30

French and Malagasy Flags and Map
A31

1959, Feb. 28 Engr. *Perf. 13*

303 A29 20fr brown violet, carmine & emerald 35 20
304 A30 25fr gray, red & emerald 45 25

Proclamation of the Malagasy Republic.

1959, Feb. 28

305 A31 60fr multicolored 85 45

Issued to honor the French Community.

Chionaema Pauliani
A32

Ylang-ylang
A33

Designs: 30c, 40c, 50c, 3fr, Various butterflies. 5fr, Sisal. 8fr, Pepper. 10fr, Rice. 15fr, Cotton.

1960 *Perf. 13* Unwmkd.

306 A32 30c multicolored 6 4
307 " 40c emerald, sepia & red brown 6 4
308 " 50c violet brown, black & steel blue 6 4
309 " 1fr indigo, red & dull purple 6 6
310 " 3fr olive, violet black & orange 8 6
311 " 5fr red, brown & emerald 8 6
312 A33 6fr dark green & bright yellow 12 10
313 A32 8fr crimson rose, emerald & blk. 15 10
314 A33 10fr dark green, yellow grn. & lt. brn. 20 10
315 A32 15fr brown & green 27 17
Nos. 306-315 (10) 1.14 77

See also Nos. C61-C66.

Family Planting Trees
A34

1960, Feb. 1 Engraved *Perf. 13*

316 A34 20fr red brown, buff & green 35 20

Issued for the "Week of the Tree," Feb. 1-7.

C.C.T.A. Issue

Common Design Type

1960, Feb. 22

317 CD106 25fr light blue green & plum 60 45

Pres. Philibert Tsiranana and Map—A36

1960, Mar. 25 *Perf. 13* Unwmkd.

318 A36 20fr green & brown 30 10

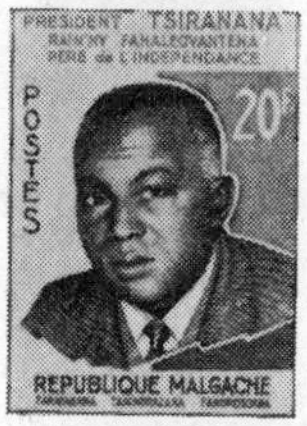

Athletes of Two Races
A37

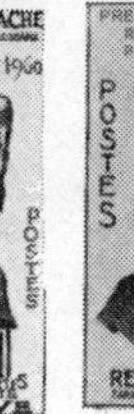

Pres. Philibert Tsiranana
A38

1960 Engraved *Perf. 13*

319 A37 25fr chocolate, orange brown & ultramarine 50 35

First Games of the French Community, Apr. 13-18, at Tananarive.

1960, July 29 *Perf. 13* Unwmkd.

320 A38 20fr red, black & bright green 30 15

Issued to honor Pres. Tsiranana, "Father of Independence." See also No. B18.

Gray Lemur
A39

Designs: 4fr, Ruffed lemur (horiz.). 12fr, Mongoose lemur.

1961, Dec. 9 *Perf. 13*

321 A39 2fr brown & greenish blue 10 8
322 " 4fr brown, green & black 15 12
323 " 12fr green & red brown 30 20

See also Nos. C67-C69.

Pres. Tsiranana Bridge, Sofia River
A40

1962, Jan. 4 *Perf. 13* Unwmkd.

324 A40 25fr bright blue 35 10

First Train Built at Tananarive
A41

1962, Feb. 1

325 A41 20fr dark green 30 10

U.N. and Malagasy Flags over Government Building, Tananarive
A42

1962, March 14 *Perf. 13*

326 A42 25fr multicolored 35 25
327 " 85fr " 1.25 80

Issued to commemorate the Malagasy Republic's admission to the United Nations.

Ranomafana Village
A43

Designs: 30fr, Tritriva crater lake. 50fr, Foulpointe shore. 60fr, Fort Dauphin.

1962, May 7 Engraved *Perf. 13*

328 A43 10fr slate green, greenish blue & claret 12 8
329 " 30fr slate green, claret & greenish blue 35 20
330 " 50fr ultra., claret, & slate green 60 40
331 " 60fr claret, ultra. & slate green 75 50

See also No. C70 and souvenir sheet No. C70a.

African and Malgache Union Issue

Common Design Type

1962, Sept. 8 Photo. *Perf. 12½x12*

332 CD110 30fr grn., bluish grn., red & gold 65 50

Issued to commemorate the first anniversary of the African and Malgache Union.

Arms of Republic and UNESCO Emblem
A44

1962, Sept. 3 Unwmkd.

333 A44 20fr rose, emerald & black 40 30

Issued to publicize the first Conference on Higher Education in Africa, Tananarive, Sept. 3-12.

Power Station
A45

Designs: 8fr, Atomic reactor and atom symbol (horiz.). 10fr, Oil derrick. 15fr, Tanker (horiz.).

Perf. 12x12½, 12½x12

1962, Oct. 18 Lithographed

334 A45 5fr blue, yel. & red 8 6
335 " 8fr blue, red & yel. 12 6
336 " 10fr multicolored 15 8
337 " 15fr blue, red brown & black 22 10

Industrialization of Madagascar.

Factory and Globe
A46

1963, Jan. 7 Typo. *Perf. 14x13½*

338 A46 25fr dp. org. & blk. 35 20

International Fair at Tamatave.

Hertzian Cable, Tananarive-Fianarantsoa
A47

1963, Mar. 7 Photo. *Perf. 12½x12*

339 A47 20fr multicolored 30 20

Madagascar Blue Pigeon
A48

Gastrorchis Humblotii
A49

Birds: 2fr, Blue coua. 3fr, Red fody. 6fr, Madagascar pigmy kingfisher. Orchids: 10fr, Eulophiella Roempleriana. 12fr, Angraecum sesquipedale.

1963 *Perf. 13* **Unwmkd.**

340 A48 1fr multicolored 30 30
341 " 2fr " 30 30
342 " 3fr " 30 30
343 " 6fr " 30 30
344 A49 8fr " 25 20
345 " 10fr " 40 35
346 " 12fr " 40 35
Nos. 340-346, C72-C74(10) 7.25 4.40

Arms of Fianarantsoa
A50

Arms of: 1.50fr, Antsirabe. 5fr, Antalaha. 10fr, Tulear. 15fr, Majunga. 25fr, Tananarive. 50fr, Diégo-Suarez.

Imprint: "R. Louis del. So. Ge. Im."

1963-65 Lithographed *Perf. 13*

Size: 23½x35½mm.

347 A50 1.50fr multi. ('64) 5 5
348 " 5fr " ('65) 6 6
349 " 10fr " ('64) 12 6
350 " 15fr " ('64) 22 15
351 " 20fr " 30 13
352 " 25fr " 35 12
353 " 50fr " ('65) 60 45
Nos. 347-353 (7) 1.70 1.02

See also Nos. 388-390, 434-439.

Map and Centenary Emblem
A51

Globe and Hands Holding Torch
A52

1963, Sept. 2 *Perf. 12x12½*

354 A51 30fr multicolored 85 75

Centenary of the International Red Cross.

1963, Dec. 10 Engraved *Perf. 12½*

355 A52 60fr olive, ocher & car. 75 50

Issued to commemorate the 15th anniversary of the Universal Declaration of Human Rights.

Scouts and Campfire
A53

1964, June 6 Engraved *Perf. 13*

356 A53 20fr dark red, orange & carmine 35 18

Issued to commemorate the 40th anniversary of the Boy Scouts of Madagascar.

Europafrica Issue, 1964

Dove and Globe—A54

1964, July 20 **Engraved**

357 A54 45fr olive green, brown red & black 60 40

First anniversary of economic agreement between the European Economic Community and the African and Malgache Union.

Carved Statue of Woman
A55

University Emblem
A56

Malagasy Art: 30fr, Statue of sitting man.

1964, Oct. 20 *Perf. 13* **Unwmkd.**

358 A55 6fr dark blue, brt. blue & sepia 20 15
359 " 30fr dp. green, olive bis. & dk. brn. 45 30

See also No. C79.

Cooperation Issue

Common Design Type

1964, Nov. 7 Engraved *Perf. 13*

360 CD119 25fr blk., dk. brn. & orge. brn. 40 25

1964, Dec. 5 Litho. *Perf. 13x12½*

361 A56 65fr red, blk. & grn. 75 50

Issued to commemorate the founding of the University of Madagascar, Tananarive. The inscription reads: "Foolish is he who does not do better than his father."

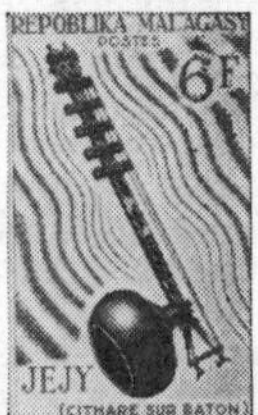

Jejy
A57

Valiha Player
A58

Musical instruments: 3fr, Kabosa (lute). 8fr, Hazolahy (sacred drum).

1965 Engraved *Perf. 13*

Size: 22x36mm.

362 A57 3fr magenta, violet blue & dk. brn. 8 8
363 " 6fr emerald, rose lilac & dk. brn. 12 10
364 " 8fr brn., grn. & blk. 15 10

Photogravure *Perf. 12½x13*

365 A58 25fr multicolored 40 25
Nos. 362-365, C80 (5) 3.50 2.03

PTT Receiving Station, Foulpointe
A59

1965, May 8 Engraved *Perf. 13*

366 A59 20fr red orange, dark green & ocher 25 20

Issued for Stamp Day, 1965.

ITU Emblem, Old and New Telecommunication Equipment
A60

1965, May 17

367 A60 50fr ultra., red & grn. 1.00 60

Issued to commemorate the centenary of the International Telecommunication Union.

Jean Joseph Rabearivelo
A61

Pres. Philibert Tsiranana
A62

1965, June 22 Photo. *Perf. 13x12½*

368 A61 40fr dk. brn. & orge. 55 35

Issued to honor the poet Jean Joseph Rabearivelo (pen name of Joseph Casimir), 1901-37.

1965, Oct. 18 *Perf. 13x12½*

369 A62 20fr multicolored 25 15
a. Souv. sheet of 4 1.10 1.10
370 " 25fr multicolored 30 20
a. Souv. sheet of 4 1.25 1.25

Issued to commemorate the 55th birthday of President Philibert Tsiranana. No. 369a contains four Nos. 369, No. 370a four Nos. 370. Black marginal inscription. Size: 77x120mm.

Mail Coach
A63

History of the Post: 3fr, Early automobile. 4fr, Litter. 10fr, Mail runner (vert.). 12fr, Mail boat. 25fr, Oxcart. 30fr, Old railroad mail car. 65fr, Hydrofoil.

1965-66 Engraved *Perf. 13*

371 A63 3fr vio., dp. bister & sky blue ('66) 8 6
372 " 4fr ultra., green & dk. brn. ('66) 12 8
373 " 10fr multicolored 18 12
374 " 12fr " 22 12
375 " 20fr bister, green & red brown 40 20
376 " 25fr slate grn., dk. brn. & orange 45 22
377 " 30fr peacock blue, red & sepia ('66) 50 30
378 A63 65fr violet, brown & Prus. bl. ('66) 85 50
Nos. 371-378 (8) 2.80 1.60

Leper's Crippled Hands
A64

1966, Jan. 30

379 A64 20fr dk. green, dk. brown & red 40 30

Issued for the 13th World Leprosy Day.

Couple Planting Trees
A65

1966, Feb. 21

380 A65 20fr dk. brown, pur. & blue green 30 20

Reforestation as a national duty.

Tiger Beetle
A66

Insects: 6fr, Mantis. 12fr, Long-horned beetle. 45fr, Weevil.

1966 Photo. *Perf. 12½x12*

Insects in Natural Colors

381 A66 1fr brick red 7 7
382 " 6fr rose claret 7 7
383 " 12fr Prussian blue 20 15
384 " 45fr lt. yellow green 55 30

Stamp of 1903
A67

1966, May 8 Engraved *Perf. 13*

385 A67 25fr red & sepia 40 30

Issued for Stamp Day 1966.

Betsileo Dancers
A68

1966, June 13 Photo. *Perf. 12½x13*

Size: 36x23mm.

386 A68 5fr multicolored 10 5

See also No. C83.

Symbolic Tree and Emblems
A69

1966, June 26

387 A69 25fr multicolored 35 15

Issued to commemorate the conference of the Organisation Commune Africaine et Malgache (OCAM), Tananarive.

No. 387 dated "JUIN 1966," original date "Janvier 1966" obliterated with bar. Exists without overprint "JUIN 1966" and bar. Price $45.

Arms Type of 1963–65

Imprint: "S. Gauthier So. Ge. Im."

Arms: 20fr, Mananjary. 30fr, Nossi-Bé. 90fr, Antsohihy.

1966–68 Lithographed *Perf. 13*

Size: 23½x35½mm.

388 A50 20fr multi. ('67) 13 5
389 " 30fr multicolored 30 18
390 " 90fr multi. ('68) 85 50

Singers and Map of Madagascar
A70

1966, Oct. 14 Engraved *Perf. 13*

392 A70 20fr red brn., green & dk. car. rose 20 10

Issued in honor of the National Anthem.

UNESCO Emblem
A71

1966, Nov. 4

393 A71 30fr red, yel. & slate 40 30

Issued to commemorate the 20th anniversary of UNESCO (United Nations Educational, Scientific and Cultural Organization).

Lions Emblem
A72

1967, Jan. 14 Photo. *Perf. 13x12½*

394 A72 30fr multicolored 40 25

50th anniversary of Lions International.

Rice Harvest
A73

1967, Jan. 27 *Perf. 12½x13*

395 A73 20fr multicolored 25 15

Issued to publicize the International Rice Year under sponsorship of the U.N. Food and Agricultural Organization.

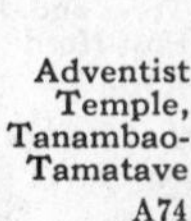

Adventist Temple, Tanambao-Tamatave
A74

Designs: 5fr, Catholic Cathedral, Tananarive (vert.). 10fr, Mosque, Tamatave.

1967, Feb. 20 Engraved *Perf. 13*

396 A74 3fr lt. ultra., green & blister 6 6
397 " 5fr bright rose lilac, green & violet 9 6
398 " 10fr dp. blue, brown & green 15 8

Norbert Raharisoa at Piano
A75

1967, Mar. 23 Photo. *Perf. 12½x12*

399 A75 40fr citron & multi. 50 20

Issued in memory of Norbert Raharisoa (1914–1963), composer.

Jean Raoult Flying Blériot Plane, 1911
A76

Design: 45fr, Barnard-Bougault and hydroplane, 1926.

1967, Apr. 28 Engraved *Perf. 13*

Size: 35½x22mm.

400 A76 5fr gray blue, brown & green 12 6
401 " 45fr brn., steel blue & black 60 35

History of aviation in Madagascar. See No. C84.

Ministry of Equipment and Communications
A77

1967, May 8 Engraved *Perf. 13*

402 A77 20fr ocher, ultra. & green 25 10

Issued for Stamp Day, 1967.

Lutheran Church, Tananarive, Madagascar Map
A78

Map of Madagascar and Emblems
A79

1967, Sept. 24 Photo. *Perf. 12x12½*

403 A78 20fr multicolored 25 10

Issued to commemorate the centenary of the Lutheran Church in Madagascar.

1967, Oct. 16 Engr. *Perf. 13*

404 A79 90fr red brown, blue & dark red 1.00 60

Hydrological Decade (UNESCO), 1965–74.

Dance of the Bilo Sakalavas
A80

Design: 30fr, Atandroy dancers.

1967, Nov. 25 Photo. *Perf. 13x12½*

Size: 22x36mm.

405 A80 2fr lt. grn. & multi. 6 5
406 " 30fr multicolored 40 20

See also Nos. C86–C87.

Woman's Face, Scales and U.N. Emblem—A81

1967, Dec. 16 *Perf. 12½x13*

407 A81 50fr emerald, dk. bl. & brown 55 35

Issued to publicize the United Nations Commission on the Status of Women.

Human Rights Flame
A82

1968, Mar. 16 Litho. *Perf. 13x12½*

408 A82 50fr black, vermilion & green 55 35

International Human Rights Year.

No. 327 Surcharged with New Value and 3 Bars

1968, June 4 Engraved *Perf. 13*

409 A42 20fr on 85fr multi. 25 15

"Industry"
A83

Designs: 20fr, "Agriculture" (mother and child carrying fruit and grain, and cattle) (vert.). 40fr, "Communications and Investments," (train, highway, factory and buildings).

1968, July 15

410 A83 10fr rose car., green & dk. purple 15 10
411 " 20fr dp. car., green & black 25 15
412 " 40fr brown, violet & slate blue 50 25

Completion of Five-year Plan, 1964–68.

Church, Translated Bible, Cross and Map of Madagascar
A84

1968, Aug. 18 Photo. *Perf. 12½x12*

413 A84 20fr multicolored 25 12

Issued to commemorate the sesquicentennial of Christianity in Madagascar.

Isotry-Fitiavana Protestant Church
A85

Designs: 12fr, Catholic Cathedral, Fianarantsoa. 50fr, Aga Khan Mosque, Tananarive.

1968, Sept. 10 Engraved *Perf. 13*

414 A85 4fr red brown, brt. green & dark brown 8 7
415 " 12fr plum, blue & henna brown 18 12
416 " 50fr bright green, blue & indigo 50 30

President and Mrs. Tsiranana
A86

1968, Oct. 14 Photo. *Perf. 12½x12*

417 A86 20fr car., orange & black 20 10
418 " 30fr car., greenish blue & black 30 15
a. Souv. sheet of 4 1.60 1.60

Issued to commemorate the 10th anniversary of the Republic. No. 418a contains 2 stamps each of Nos. 417–418 arranged checkerwise. Black marginal inscription. Size: 160x120mm.

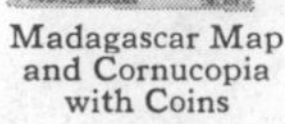

Madagascar Map and Cornucopia with Coins
A87

Striving Mankind
A88

1968, Nov. 3 Photo. *Perf. 12x12½*

419 A87 20fr multicolored 25 10

Issued to commemorate the 50th anniversary of the Malagasy Savings Bank.

1968, Dec. 3 Photo. *Perf. 12½x12*

Design: 15fr, Mother, child and physician (horiz.).

420 A88 15fr ultra., yellow & crimson 15 10
421 " 45fr vio. bl. & multi. 50 35

Completion of Five-Year Plan, 1964–68.

Queen Adelaide Receiving Malagasy Delegation, London, 1836—A89

1969, Mar. 29 Photo. *Perf. 12x12½*

422 A89 250fr multicolored 3.25 2.00

Issued to commemorate the Malagasy delegation visiting London, 1836–1837.

Cogwheels, Wrench and ILO Emblem—A90

1969, Apr. 11 *Perf. 12½x12*

423 A90 20fr green & multi. 25 10

Issued to commemorate the 50th anniversary of the International Labor Organization.

Telecommunications and Postal Building, Tananarive—A91

1969, May 8 Engraved *Perf. 13*

424 A91 30fr blue, brt. green & car. lake 35 20

Issued for Stamp Day 1969.

Steering Wheel, Map, Automobiles

A92

1969, June 1 Photo. *Perf. 12*

425 A92 65fr multicolored 75 40

Issued to commemorate the 20th anniversary of the Automobile Club of Madagascar.

Pres. Philibert Tsiranana

A93

Banana Plants

A94

1969, June 26 Photo. *Perf. 12x12½*

426 A93 20fr multicolored 20 10

Issued to commemorate the 10th anniversary of the inauguration of Pres. Philibert Tsiranana.

1969, July 7 Engraved *Perf. 13*

Design: 15fr, Lichi tree.

427 A94 5fr grn., lt. bl. & brn. 8 6

428 " 15fr yel. green, slate grn. & verm. 20 10

Runners

A95

1969, Sept. 9 Engraved *Perf. 13*

429 A95 15fr yellow green, brown & red 25 18

Issued to commemorate the 19th Olympic Games, Mexico City, Oct. 12–27, 1968.

Malagasy House, Highlands

A96

Carnelian

A97

1969–70 Engraved *Perf. 13*

Designs (Malagasy Houses): No. 430, Betsileo house, Highlands. No. 431, Tsimihety house, West Coast (horiz.). 60fr, Malagasy house, Highlands.

430 A96 20fr blue, olive & verm. ('70) 20 10

431 " 20fr slate, brt. green & red ('70) 20 10

432 " 40fr blk., bl. & dk. red 45 20

433 " 60fr violet blue, deep green & brown 70 30

Issues dates: 40fr, 60fr, Nov. 25, 1969. Others, Nov. 25, 1970.

Arms Type of 1963–65

Arms: 1fr, Maintirano. 10fr, Ambalavao. No. 436, Morondava. No. 437, Ambatondrazaka. No. 438, Fenerive-Est. 80fr, Tamatave.

1970–72 Photogravure *Perf. 13*

434 A50 1fr multi. ('72) 5 5

435 " 10fr " 15 5

436 " 25fr " ('71) 35 20

437 " 25fr " ('71) 35 20

438 " 25fr " ('72) 30 20

439 " 80fr pink & multi. 85 45

Nos. 434–439 (6) 2.05 1.15

The 10fr and 80fr are dated "1970." No. 437 is dated "1971." Nos. 434, 438 are dated "1972."

Sizes: 22x37mm. (Nos. 434, 438); 25½x36mm. (others).

Imprints: "S. Gauthier" on Nos. 434, 438. "S. Gauthier Delrieu" on others.

Perf. 12x12½ (5fr, 20fr), 13 (12fr, 15fr)

1970–71 Photogravure

Semi-precious Stones: 12fr, Yellow calcite. 15fr, Quartz. 20fr, Ammonite.

440 A97 5fr brown, dull rose & yellow 15 12

441 " 12fr multi. ('71) 20 15

442 " 15fr " ('71) 25 15

443 " 20fr green & multi. 30 20

U.P.U. Headquarters Issue

Common Design Type

1970, May 20 Engraved *Perf. 13*

444 CD133 20fr lilac rose, brown & ultramarine 30 12

Inauguration of new Universal Postal Union Headquarters, Bern, Switzerland.

U.N. Emblem and Symbols of Justice

A98

1970, June 26 Engraved *Perf. 13*

445 A98 50fr blk., ultra. & org. 55 30

25th anniversary of the United Nations.

Fruits of Madagascar

A99

1970, Aug. 18 Photo. *Perf. 13*

446 A99 20fr multicolored 20 10

Volute Delessertiana

A100

Shells: 10fr, Murex tribulus. 20fr, Spondylus.

1970, Sept. 9 Photo. *Perf. 13*

447 A100 5fr Prus. bl. & multi. 7 5

448 " 10fr violet & multi. 17 8

449 " 20fr multicolored 30 12

Aye-aye—A101

1970, Oct. 7 Photo. *Perf. 12½*

450 A101 20fr multicolored 35 25

Issued to publicize the International Conference for Nature Conservation, Tananarive, Oct. 7–10.

Pres. Tsiranana

A102

1970, Dec. 30 Photo. *Perf. 12½*

451 A102 30fr grn. & lt. brown 30 15

Sixtieth birthday of Pres. Philibert Tsiranana.

Tropical Soap Factory, Tananarive

A103

Designs: 15fr, Comina chromium smelting plant, Andriamena. 50fr, Textile mill, Majunga.

1971, Apr. 14 Photo. *Perf. 12½x12*

452 A103 5fr multicolored 7 6

Engraved *Perf. 13*

453 A103 15fr vio. blue, black & ocher 17 12

Photogravure *Perf. 13*

454 A100 50fr multicolored 55 30

Economic development.

Globe, Agriculture, Industry, Science

A104

1971, Apr. 22 Photo. *Perf. 12½x12*

455 A104 5fr multicolored 7 5

Extraordinary meeting of the Council of the C.E.E.-E.A.M.A. (Communauté Economique Européen–Etats Africains et Malgache Associés).

Mobile Rural Post Office

A105

1971, May 8 *Perf. 13*

456 A105 25fr multicolored 30 15

Stamp Day.

Gen. Charles de Gaulle

A106

Madagascar Hilton, Tananarive—A107

1971, June 26 Engraved *Perf. 13*

457 A106 30fr ultra., black & rose 60 30

In memory of Charles de Gaulle (1890–1970), President of France.

1971, July 23 Photogravure

Design: 25fr, Hotel Palm Beach, Nossi-Bé.

458 A107 25fr multicolored 30 15

Engraved

459 A107 65fr vio. blue, brown & lt. green 70 40

Trees and Post Horn

A108

1971, Aug. 6 Photo. *Perf. 12½x12*

460 A108 3fr red, yel. & green 10 8

Forest preservation campaign.

House, South West Madagascar
A109

Design: 10fr, House from Southern Madagascar.

1971, Nov. 25 ***Perf. 13x12½***

461 A109 5fr lt. bl. & multi. 5 5
462 " 10fr " " " 10 8

Children Playing, and Cattle
A110

1971, Dec. 11 Litho. ***Perf. 13***

463 A110 50fr green & multi. 60 35

25th anniversary of the United Nations International Children's Fund (UNICEF).

Cable-laying Railroad Car, PTT Emblem
A111

1972, Apr. 8 Engr. ***Perf. 13***

464 A111 45fr slate green, red & choc. 50 35

Coaxial cable connection between Tananarive and Tamatave.

Philibert Tsiranana Radar Station
A112

1972, Apr. 8 Photo. ***Perf. 13½***

465 A112 85fr blue & multi. 1.00 55

Voters and Pres. Tsiranana
A113

1972, May 1 ***Perf. 12½x13***

466 A113 25fr yellow & multi. 60 50

Commemorating the Presidential election, Jan. 30, 1972.

Mail Delivery
A114

1972, May 30 Photo. ***Perf. 12x12½***

467 A114 10fr multicolored 15 10

Stamp Day 1972.

Emblem and Stamps of Madagascar
A115

Design: Stamps shown are Madagascar Nos. 352, 410, 429, 449.

1972, June 26 ***Perf. 13***

468 A115 25fr org. & multi. 20 15
469 " 40fr " " 40 25
470 " 100fr " " 1.00 50
a. Souvenir sheet of 3 2.00 2.00

2nd Malgache Philatelic Exhibition, Tananarive, June 26—July 9. No. 470a contains one each of Nos. 468—470. Black marginal inscription. Size: 150x115mm.

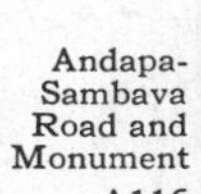

Andapa-Sambava Road and Monument
A116

1972, July 6 ***Perf. 12½x12***

471 A116 50fr multicolored 45 30

Opening of the Andapa-Sambava road.

Diesel Locomotive
A117

1972, July 6 Engraved ***Perf. 13***

472 A117 100fr multicolored 1.00 40

Razafindrahety College
A118

1972, Aug. 6

473 A118 10fr chocolate, blue & red brown 10 5

Sesquicentennial of Razafindrahety College, Tananarive.

Volleyball
A119

1972, Aug. 6 Typo. ***Perf. 12½x13***

474 A119 12fr org., blk. & brn. 15 12

African volleyball championship.

Oil Refinery, Tamatave
A120

1972, Sept. 18 Engr. ***Perf. 13***

475 A120 2fr blue, bister & slate green 6 6

Ravoahangy Andrianavalona Hospital
A121

1972, Oct. 14 Photo. ***Perf. 13x12½***

476 A121 6fr multicolored 6 4

Plowing
A122

1972, Nov. 15 Photo. ***Perf. 13½x14***

477 A122 25fr gold & multi. 20 15

Betsimisaraka Costume
A123

Design: 15fr, Merina costume.

1972, Dec. 30 Photo. ***Perf. 13x12½***

478 A123 10fr blue & multi. 10 7
479 " 15fr brown & multi. 13 12

Farmer and Produce
A124

1973, Feb. 6 Photogravure ***Perf. 13***

480 A124 25fr lt. blue & multi. 25 18

10th anniversary of the Malagasy Committee of "Freedom from Hunger Campaign."

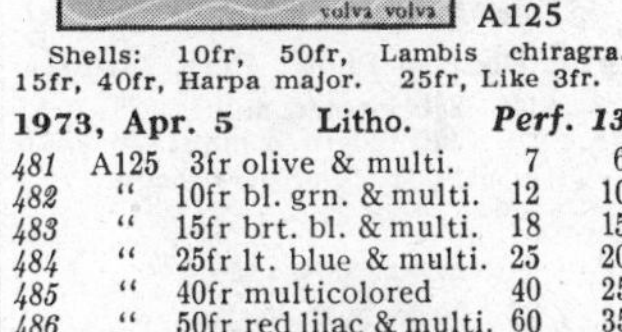

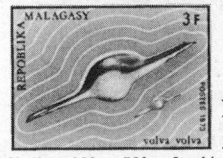

Volva Volva
A125

Shells: 10fr, 50fr, Lambis chiragra. 15fr, 40fr, Harpa major. 25fr, Like 3fr.

1973, Apr. 5 Litho. ***Perf. 13***

481 A125 3fr olive & multi. 7 6
482 " 10fr bl. grn. & multi. 12 10
483 " 15fr brt. bl. & multi. 18 15
484 " 25fr lt. blue & multi. 25 20
485 " 40fr multicolored 40 25
486 " 50fr red lilac & multi. 60 35
Nos. 481-486 (6) 1.62 1.11

Tsimandoa Mail Carrier
A126

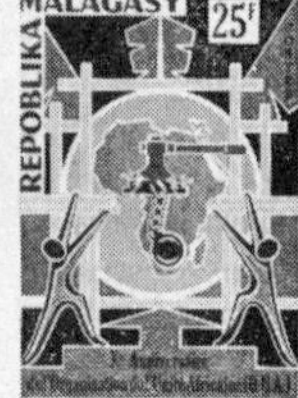

Builders and Map of Africa
A127

1973, May 13 Engraved ***Perf. 13***

487 A126 50fr indigo, ocher & slate green 40 25

Stamp Day 1973.

1973, May 25 Photo. ***Perf. 13***

488 A127 25fr multicolored 20 18

Organization for African Unity, 10th anniversary.

Campani Chameleon
A128

Various Chameleons: 5fr, 40fr, Male nasutus. 10fr, 85fr, Female nasutus. 60fr, Like 1fr.

1973, June 15 Photo. ***Perf. 13x12½***

489 A128 1fr dp. car. & multi. 3 3
490 " 5fr brown & multi. 7 6
491 " 10fr green & multi. 8 6
492 " 40fr red lilac & multi. 33 20
493 " 60fr dk. blue & multi. 55 35
494 " 85fr brown & multi. 75 50
Nos. 489-494 (6) 1.81 1.20

Lady's Slipper
A129

Orchids: 25fr, 40fr, Pitcher plant. 100fr, Like 10fr.

1973, Aug. 6 Photo. ***Perf. 12½***

495 A129 10fr multicolored 10 10
496 " 25fr rose & multi. 25 15
497 " 40fr lt. bl. & multi. 35 20
498 " 100fr multicolored 85 60

No. 480 Surcharged with New Value, 2 Bars, and Overprinted in Ultramarine: "SECHERESSE/SOLIDARITE AFRICAINE"

1973, Aug. 16 ***Perf. 13***

499 A124 100fr on 25fr multi. 85 50

African solidarity in drought emergency.

African Postal Union Issue
Common Design Type

1973, Sept. 12 Engr. ***Perf. 13***

500 CD137 100fr violet, red & slate green 85 50

Greater Dwarf Lemur
A131

Design: 25fr, Weasel lemur (vert.).

1973, Oct. 9 Engraved ***Perf. 13***

501 A131 5fr brt. grn. & multi. 6 5
502 " 25fr ocher & multi. 20 15

Lemurs of Madagascar. See Nos. C117—C118.

25 Fmg

No. 389 Surcharged

1974, Feb. 9 Litho. ***Perf. 13***

503 A50 25fr on 30fr multi. 20 10

Scouts Helping to Raise Cattle
A132

Mother with Children and Clinic
A133

Design: 15fr, Scouts building house; African Scout emblem.

1974, Feb. 14 Engr. *Perf. 13*

504 A132 4fr blue, slate & emerald 5 5
505 " 15fr choc. & multi. 12 8

Malagasy Boy Scouts. See Nos. C122-C123.

1974, May 24 Photo. *Perf. 13*

506 A133 25fr multicolored 20 12

World Population Year.

Rainibetsimi-saraka
A134

1974, July 26 Photogravure *Perf. 13*

507 A134 25fr multicolored 20 15

In memory of Rainibetsimisaraka, independence leader.

Marble Blocks
A135

Design: 25fr, Marble quarry.

1974, Sept. 27 Photo. *Perf. 13*

508 A135 4fr multicolored 6 5
509 " 25fr " 20 15

Malagasy marble.

Europafrica Issue, 1974

Links, White and Black Faces, Map of Europe and Africa
A136

1974, Oct. 17 Engraved *Perf. 13*

510 A136 150fr dark brown & orange 1.25 50

Grain and Hand
A137

1974, Oct. 29

511 A137 80fr lt. blue & ocher 65 40

World Committee against Hunger.

Tuléar Dog
A138

Design: 100fr, Hunting dog.

1974, Nov. 26 Photo. *Perf. 13x13½*

512 A138 50fr multicolored 40 25
513 " 100fr " 80 55

Malagasy Citizens
A139

1974, Dec. 9 *Perf. 13½x13*

514 A139 5fr bl. grn. & multi. 7 5
515 " 10fr multicolored 10 7
516 " 20fr yel. grn. & multi. 15 10
517 " 60fr orange & multi. 50 30

Introduction of "Fokonolona" community organization.

Symbols of Development
A140

1974, Dec. 16 Photo. *Perf. 13x13½*

518 A140 25fr ultra. & multi. 25 15
519 " 35fr bl. grn. & multi. 30 20

National Council for Development.

Woman, Rose, Dove and Emblem
A141

1975, Jan. 21 Engraved *Perf. 13*

520 A141 100fr brn., emerald & orange 80 35

International Women's Year 1975.

Col. Richard Ratsimandrava
A142

1975, Apr. 25 Photo. *Perf. 13*

521 A142 15fr brn. & salmon 13 8
522 " 25fr black, blue & brown 20 12
523 " 100fr black, lt. grn. & brown 85 40

Col. Richard Ratsimandrava (1933-1975), head of state.

Sofia Bridge—A143

1975, May 29 Litho. *Perf. 12½*

524 A143 45fr multicolored 35 20

Count de Grasse and "Randolph"
A144

Design: 50fr, Marquis de Lafayette, "Lexington" and HMS "Edward."

1975, June 30 Litho. *Perf. 11*

525 A144 40fr multicolored 40 20
526 " 50fr " 50 25
Nos. 525-526, C137-C139 (5) 6.30 2.95

American Bicentennial.

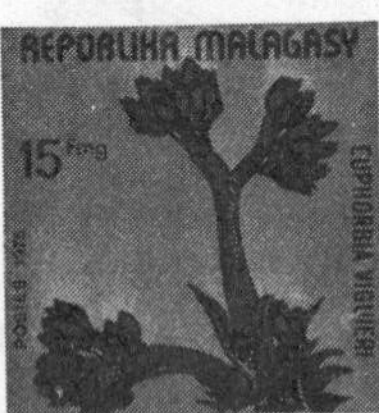

Euphorbia Viguieri
A145

Tropical Plants: 25fr, Hibiscus. 30fr, Plumieria rubra acutifolia. 40fr, Pachypodium rosulatum.

1975, Aug. 4 Photo. *Perf. 12½*

527 A145 15fr lemon & multi. 12 8
528 " 25fr black & multi. 20 12
529 " 30fr org. & multi. 25 15
530 " 40fr dk. red & multi. 33 20
Nos. 527-530, C141 (5) 1.60 90

Brown, White, Yellow and Black Hands Holding Globe
A146

1975, Aug. 26 Litho. *Perf. 12*

531 A146 50fr multicolored 40 25

Namibia Day (independence for South-West Africa).

Woodpecker—A147

Designs: 40fr, Rabbit. 50fr, Frog. 75fr, Tortoise.

1975, Sept. 16 Litho. *Perf. 14x13½*

532 A147 25fr multicolored 25 13
533 " 40fr " 35 18
534 " 50fr " 45 20
535 " 75fr " 65 30
Nos. 532-535, C145 (5) 2.80 1.36

International Exposition, Okinawa.

Lily Waterfall
A148

Design: 40fr, Lily Waterfall, different view.

1975, Sept. 17 Litho. *Perf. 12½*

536 A148 25fr multicolored 20 10
537 " 40fr " 35 20

4-man Bob Sled—A149

Designs: 100fr, Ski jump. 140fr, Speed skating.

1975, Nov. 19 Litho. *Perf. 14*

538 A149 75fr multicolored 60 30
539 " 100fr " 80 35
540 " 140fr " 1.20 45
Nos. 538-540, C149-C150 (5) 6.25 2.90

12th Winter Olympic games, Innsbruck, 1976.

Pirogue
A150

Designs: 45fr, Boutre (Arabian coastal essel).

975, Nov. 20 Photo. *Perf. 12½*

41 A150 8fr multicolored 8 5
42 " 45fr ultra. & multi. 35 20

Canadian Canoe and Kayak—A151

Design: 50fr, Sprint and Hurdles.

976, Jan. 21 Litho. *Perf. 14x13½*

43 A151 40fr multicolored 35 15
44 " 50fr " 45 20
Nos. 543–544, C153–C155 (5) 5.70 2.50

21st Summer Olympic games, Montreal.

Count Zeppelin and LZ-127 over Fujiyama, Japan—A152

Designs (Count Zeppelin and LZ-127 ver): 50fr, Rio de Janeiro, Brazil. 75fr, ew York City. 100fr, Sphinx, Egypt.

976, Mar. 3 *Perf. 11*

45 A152 40fr multicolored 35 12
46 " 50fr " 45 15
47 " 75fr " 70 25
48 " 100fr " 90 30
Nos. 545–548, C158–C159 (6) 6.05 2.52

75th anniversary of the Zeppelin.

Worker, Globe, Eye Chart and Eye—A153

976, Apr. 7 Photo. *Perf. 12½*

49 A153 100fr multicolored 80 50

World Health Day: "Foresight prevents lindness."

Aragonite
A154

Designs: 50fr, Petrified wood. 150fr, Celestite.

1976, May 7 Photo. *Perf. 12½*

550 A154 25fr blue & multi. 20 12
551 " 50fr blue green & multi. 40 20
552 " 150fr org. & multi. 1.25 65

Alexander Graham Bell and First Telephone—A155

Designs: 50fr, Telephone lines, 1911. 100fr, Central office, 1895. 200fr, Cable ship, 1925. 300fr, Radio telephone. 500fr, Telstar satellite and globe.

1976, May 13 Litho. *Perf. 14*

553 A155 25fr multicolored 20 8
554 " 50fr " 40 15
555 " 100fr " 80 32
556 " 200fr " 1.60 55
557 " 300fr " 2.40 80
Nos. 553–557 (5) 5.40 1.90

Souvenir Sheet

558 A155 500fr multicolored 4.00 1.75

Centenary of first telephone call by Alexander Graham Bell, March 10, 1876. No. 558 has multicolored margins showing symbolic expansion of sound and linesman. Size: 132x103½mm.

Children with Books
A156

Design: 25fr, Children with books (vert.).

1976, May 25 Lithographed

559 A156 10fr multicolored 8 4
560 " 25fr " 20 15

Books for children.

Nos. 538–540 Overprinted

a. VAINQUEUR ALLEMAGNE FEDERALE
b. VAINQUEUR KARL SCHNABL AUTRICHE
c. VAINQUEUR SHEILA YOUNG ETATS-UNIS

1976, June 17

561 A149 (a) 75fr multi. 60 32
562 " (b) 100fr " 80 45
563 " (c) 140fr " 1.10 65
Nos. 561–563, C161–C162 (5) 6.15 3.27

12th Winter Olympic games winners.

Nos. 525–526 Overprinted "4 Juillet / 1776–1976"

1976, July 4

564 A144 40fr multicolored 40 20
565 " 50fr " 45 25
Nos. 564–565, C164–C166 (5) 5.75 2.85

American Bicentennial.

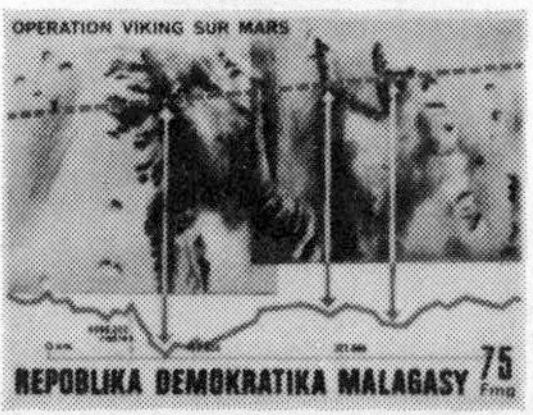

Graph of Projected Landing Spots on Mars—A157

Designs: 100fr, Viking probe in flight. 200fr, Viking probe on Mars. 300fr, Viking probe over projected landing spot. 500fr, Viking probe approaching Mars.

1976, July 17 Litho. *Perf. 14*

566 A157 75fr multicolored 60 25
567 " 100fr " 80 27
568 " 200fr " 1.60 50
569 " 300fr " 2.40 80

Souvenir Sheet

570 A156 500fr multicolored 4.00 1.85

Viking project to Mars. No. 570 has multicolored margin showing Mars in space. Size: 132x89mm.

Nos. 543–544 Overprinted

a. A. ROGOV / V. DIBA
b. H. CRAWFORD / J. SCHALLER

1977, Jan.

571 A151 (*a*) 40fr multi. 40 20
572 " (*b*) 50fr " 50 25
Nos. 571–572, C168–C170 (5) 5.80 2.85

21st Summer Olympic games winners.

Rainandriamampandry
A158

Portrait: No. 574, Rabezavana.

1976–77 Litho. *Perf. 12x12½*

573 A158 5a (25fr) multi. 20 15
574 " 5a (25fr) " 20 15

Rainandriamampandry was Malagasy Foreign Minister who signed treaties in 1896.

Issue dates: No. 573, Oct. 15, 1976. No. 574, Mar. 29, 1977.

Doves, Indian Ocean on Globe
A159

Design: 12a, Globe with Africa and Indian Ocean, doves (vert.).

Perf. 12½x12, 12x12½

1976, Nov. 18

575 A159 12a (60fr) multi. 50 30
576 " 32a (160fr) " 1.35 75

"Indian Ocean—Zone of Peace."

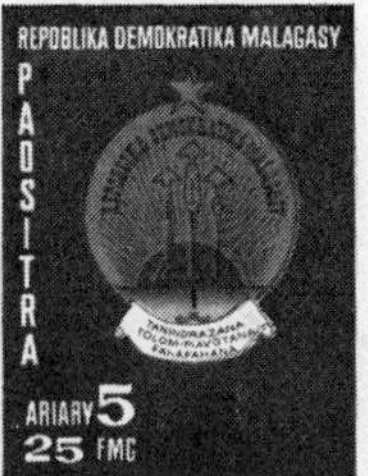

Coat of Arms
A160

1976, Dec. 30 Litho. *Perf. 12*

577 A160 5a (25fr) multi. 20 15

Democratic Republic of Malagasy, first anniversary.

Lt. Albert Randriamaromanana
A161

Portrait: No. 573, Avana Ramanantoanina.

1977, Mar. 29

578 A161 5a (25fr) multi. 20 15
579 " 5a (25fr) multi. 20 15

National Mausoleum—A162

1977, Mar. 29 *Perf. 12½x12*

580 A162 20a (100fr) multi. 75 50

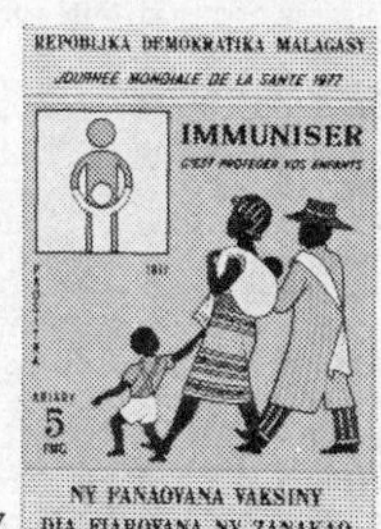

Family
A163

1977, Apr. 7 *Perf. 12x12½*

581 A163 5a yellow & multi. 20 15

World Health Day: Immunization protects the children.

Tananarive Medical School—A164

1977, June 30 Litho. *Perf. 12½x12*

582 A164 50a (250fr) multi. 2.00 1.00

80th anniversary of Tananarive Medical School.

Mail Bus—A165

1977, Aug. 18 Litho. *Perf. 12½x12*

583 A165 7a (35fr) multi. 30 15

Rural mail delivery.

Telegraph Operator—A166

1977, Sept. 13 Litho. *Perf. 12½x12*

584 A166 3a (15fr) multi. 12 6

90th anniversary of telegraph service Tananarive-Tamatave.

Malagasy Art
A167

1977, Sept. 29 *Perf. 12x12½*

585 A167 2a (10fr) multi. 8 4

Malagasy Academy, 75th anniversary.

Lenin and Russian Flag—A168

1977, Nov. 7 Litho. *Perf. 12½x12*

586 A168 5a (25fr) multi. 20 10

60th anniversary of Russian October Revolution.

Raoul Follereau, Map of Malagasy
A169

1978, Jan. 28 Litho. *Perf. 12x12½*

587 A169 5a multicolored 20 10

25th anniversary of Leprosy Day.

Antenna, ITU Emblem
A170

1978, May 17 Litho. *Perf. 12x12½*

588 A170 4a (20fr) multi. 20 8

10th World Telecommunications Day.

Black and White Men Breaking Chains of Africa
A171

1978, June 22 Photo. *Perf. 12½x12*

589 A171 12a (60fr) multi. 60 25

Anti-Apartheid Year.

Boy and Girl, Arch: Pen, Gun and Hoe
A172

Farm Workers, Factory, Tractor
A173

1978, July 28 Litho. *Perf. 12½x12*

590 A172 25a (125fr) multi. 1.25 50

Youth, the pillar of revolution.

1978, Aug. 24

591 A173 5a (25fr) multi. 25 5

Socialist cooperation.

Women
A174

1979, Mar. 8 Litho. *Perf. 12½x12*

592 A174 40fr multicolored 40 15

Women, supporters of the revolution.

SEMI-POSTAL STAMPS

No. 84 Surcharged in Red

Perf. 13½x14

1915, Feb. **Unwmkd.**

B1 A9 10c+5c rose & brown 20 20

Curie Issue

Common Design Type

1938, Oct. 24 ***Perf. 13***

B2 CD80 1.75fr+50c bright ultramarine 4.00 4.00

French Revolution Issue.

Common Design Type

Name and Value Typo. in Black

1939, July 5 Photogravure

B3 CD83 45(c)+25(c) green 3.00 3.00
B4 " 70(c)+30(c) brown 3.00 3.00
B5 " 90(c)+35(c) red orange 3.00 3.00
B6 " 1.25fr+1fr rose pink 3.00 3.00
B7 " 2.25fr+2fr blue 3.00 3.00
Nos. B3-B7 (5) 15.00 15.00

Common Design Type and

Malgache Sharpshooter SP1

Tank Corps-man SP2

1941 Photogravure ***Perf. 13½***

B8 SP1 1fr+1fr red 60
B9 CD86 1.50fr+3fr maroon 60
B10 SP2 2.50fr+1fr blue 60

Nos. B8-B10 were issued by the Vichy government, and were not placed on sale in the colony.

Nos. 162 and 190 surcharged "SECOURS +50c NATIONAL," and Nos. 210A-210B surcharged "OEUVRES COLONIALES" and surtax (including change of denomination of the 2.50fr to 50c) were issued in 1942-44 by the Vichy government, and not placed on sale in the colony.

Red Cross Issue

Common Design Type

1944 ***Perf. 14½x14.*** **Unwmkd.**

B15 CD90 5fr+20fr dark green 25 25

The surtax was for the French Red Cross and national relief.

Gen. J. S. Galliéni and Malagasy Plowing SP3

1946, Nov. **Engraved** ***Perf. 13***

B16 SP3 10fr+5fr dark violet brown 12 12

Issued to commemorate the 50th anniversary of Madagascar's existence as a French Colony.

Tropical Medicine Issue

Common Design Type

1950, May 15

B17 CD100 10fr+2fr dark Prussian green & brn. violet 1.65 1.65

The surtax was for charitable work.

Malagasy Republic

No. 320 Surcharged in Ultramarine with New Value and:

"FETES DE L'INDEPENDANCE."

1960, July 29 **Engr.** ***Perf. 13***

B18 A38 20fr+10fr red, black & bright green 55 40

Anti-Malaria Issue

Common Design Type

1962, Apr. 7 ***Perf. 12½x12***

B19 CD108 25fr+5fr yel. green 65 65

Issued for the World Health Organization drive to eradicate malaria.

Post Office, Tamatave SP4

1962, May 8 **Engr.** ***Perf. 13***

B20 SP4 25fr+5fr slate green, blue & light red brown 40 40

Issued for Stamp Day, 1962.

Freedom from Hunger Issue

Common Design Type

1963, Mar. 21 ***Perf. 13***

B21 CD112 25fr+5fr red orange, plum & brown 50 50

"Freedom from Hunger" campaign of U.N. Food and Agriculture Organization.

Type of 1962

Design: 20fr+5fr, Central Parcel Post Office, Tananarive.

1963, May 8 **Engraved**

B22 SP4 20fr+5fr blue green & red brown 35 35

Issued for Stamp Day, 1963.

Postal Savings and Checking Accounts Building, Tananarive SP5

1964, May 8 ***Perf. 13*** **Unwmkd.**

B23 SP5 25fr+5fr bl., bister & dark green 55 55

Issued for Stamp Day, 1964.

No. 457 Surcharged in Violet Blue

+ 20F
MEMORIAL

1972, June 26 **Engraved** ***Perf. 13***

B24 A106 30fr+20fr multi. 55 55

Charles de Gaulle memorial.

AIR POST STAMPS

Airplane and Map of Madagascar AP1

Perf. 13x13½.

1935-41 **Photogravure.** **Unwmkd.**

C1 AP1 50c yel. grn. & red 20 15
C2 " 90c yellow green & red ('41) 10
C3 " 1.25fr claret & red 12 10
C4 " 1.50fr brt. blue & red 12 10
C5 " 1.60fr bright blue & red ('41) 6 6
C6 " 1.75fr orange & red 4.00 2.00
C7 " 2fr Prus. bl. & red 18 10
C8 " 3fr deep orange & red ('41) 7 7
C9 " 3.65fr olive black & red ('38) 8 8
C10 " 3.90fr peacock green & red ('41) 8 8
C11 " 4fr rose & red 16.00 85
C12 " 4.50fr black & red 10.00 50
C13 " 5.50fr olive black & red ('41) 8 8
C14 " 6fr rose lilac & red ('41) 10 10
C15 " 6.90fr dull violet & red ('41) 8 8
C16 " 8fr rose lilac & red 30 18
C17 " 8.50fr green & red 35 35
C18 " 9fr olive green & red ('41) 10 10
C19 " 12fr violet brn. & red 15 10
C20 " 12.50fr dull violet & red 45 45
C21 " 15fr orange yellow & red ('41) 35 30
C22 " 16fr olive green & red 70 70
C23 " 20fr dark brn. & red 60 60
C24 " 50fr bright ultra. & red ('38) 1.85 1.85
Nos. C1, C3-C24 (23) 36.02 8.98

According to some authorities the 90c was not placed on sale in Madagascar.

V5

Stamps of type AP1, without "RF" monogram, and stamp of design shown above were issued in 1942 to 1944 by the Vichy Government, but were not placed on sale in the colony.

Air Post Stamps of 1935-38 Overprinted in Black

FRANCE LIBRE

1942 ***Perf. 13x13½.***

C28 AP1 1.50fr bright blue & red 1.60 1.60
C28A " 1.75fr org. & red 27.50 27.50
C29 " 8fr rose lilac & red 50 50
C30 " 12fr violet brown & red 1.00 1.00
C31 " 12.50fr dull violet & red 60 60
C32 " 16fr olive green & red 1.50 1.50
C33 " 50fr bright ultra. & red 1.00 1.00

Air Post Stamps of 1935-38 Surcharged in Black

FRANCE LIBRE

1,00 ×

C34 AP1 1fr on 1.25fr claret & red 1.20 1.20
C35 " 3fr on 3.65fr olive black & red 30 30
C36 " 8fr on 8.50fr green & red 30 30
Nos. C28-C36 (10) 35.50 35.50

Common Design Type

1943 **Photo.** ***Perf. 14½x14***

C37 CD87 1fr dark orange 8 8
C38 " 1.50fr bright red 8 7
C39 " 5fr brown red 10 10
C40 " 10fr black 15 15
C41 " 25fr ultramarine 25 15
C42 " 50fr dark green 40 22
C43 " 100fr plum 75 25
Nos. C37-C43 (7) 1.81 1.02

Victory Issue

Common Design Type

Engraved.

1946, May 8 ***Perf. 12½.*** **Unwmkd.**

C44 CD92 8fr brown red 15 13

Issued to commemorate the European victory of the Allied Nations in World War II.

Chad to Rhine Issue

Common Design Types

1946, June 6

C45 CD93 5fr bright blue 40 40
C46 CD94 10fr dk. car. rose 40 40
C47 CD95 15fr gray green 40 40
C48 CD96 20fr brown olive 50 50
C49 CD97 25fr dark violet 55 55
C50 CD98 50fr brown orange 55 55
Nos. C45-C50 (6) 2.80 2.80

Tamatave—AP2

Allegory of Air Mail AP3

Plane over Map of Madagascar AP4

Perf. 13½x12½, 12½x13½.

1946 Photogravure **Unwmkd.**

C51 AP2 50fr blue violet & carmine 65 10
C52 AP3 100fr brn. & car. 1.35 20
C53 AP4 200fr blue green & brown 3.00 70

No. C52 Overprinted in Carmine

TERRE ADÉLIE
DUMONT D'URVILLE
1840

1948, Oct. 26 ***Perf. 12½x13½.***

C54 AP3 100fr brn. & car. 25.00 25.00

Issued to publicize the French claim to Antarctic Adelie Land, discovered by Jules S. C. Dumont d'Urville in 1840.

UPU Issue

Common Design Type

1949, July 4 **Engraved** ***Perf. 13***

C55 CD99 25fr multicolored 1.65 1.25

Issued to commemorate the 75th anniversary of the formation of the Universal Postal Union.

Scene Near Bemananga—AP5

1952, June 30 ***Perf. 13.*** **Unwmkd.**

C56 AP5 500fr brown, black brown & dark green 12.00 2.25

Liberation Issue

Common Design Type

1954, June 6

C57 CD102 15fr violet & vio. brown 1.00 60

10th anniversary of the liberation of France.

Pachypodes—AP6

Designs: 100fr, Antsirabé viaduct. 200fr, Ring-tailed lemurs.

1954, Sept. 20

C58 AP6 50fr dk. blue green & dk. green 1.50 10
C59 " 100fr dp. ultra. & chocolate 2.50 60
C60 " 200fr dark green & sepia 6.00 1.25

Malagasy Republic

Sugar Cane Harvest—AP7

Charaxes Antamboulou—AP8

Designs: 40fr, Tobacco field. 100fr, Chrysiridia Madagascariensis. 200fr, Argema mittrei (vert.). 500fr, Mandrare bridge.

Engraved.

1960 ***Perf. 13*** **Unwmkd.**

C61 AP7 30fr green, violet brown & pale brown 65 15
C62 " 40fr Prussian green & olive gray 1.00 30
C63 AP8 50fr multicolored 1.10 25
C64 " 100fr slate green, emerald & orange 2.25 35
C65 " 200fr pur. & yellow 3.50 90
C66 AP7 500fr Prussian green, bis. & ultra. 8.00 2.25
Nos. C61-C66 (6) 16.50 4.20

Diademed Sifakas—AP9

Lemurs: 85fr, Indri. 250fr, Verreaux's sifaka.

1961, Dec. 9 ***Perf. 13*** **Unwmkd.**

C67 AP9 65fr slate green & red brown 1.00 40
C68 " 85fr olive, black & brown 1.25 50
C69 " 250fr Pruss. grn., blk. & maroon 4.00 1.75

Plane over Nossi-Bé AP10

1962, May 7 **Engraved** ***Perf. 13***

C70 AP10 100fr red brown, blue & dark green 1.35 75
a. Souvenir sheet of 5 3.00 3.00

No. C70a contains one each of Nos. 328–331 and C70 with claret marginal inscription. Size: 150x85mm. The sheet was issued to publicize the first Malagasy Philatelic Exhibition, Tananarive, May 5–13.

Turbojet Airliner, Emblem—AP11

1963, Apr. 18 ***Perf. 13*** **Unwmkd.**

C71 AP11 500fr dark blue, red & grn. 7.00 2.50

Issued to publicize Madagascar commercial aviation.

Helmet Bird—AP12

Birds: 100fr, Pitta-like ground roller. 200fr, Crested wood ibis.

1963, Aug. 12 Photo. ***Perf. 13x12½***

C72 AP12 40fr multicolored 50 40
C73 " 100fr " 1.50 65
C74 " 200fr " 3.00 1.25

African Postal Union Issue

Common Design Type

1963, Sept. 8 ***Perf. 12½***

C75 CD114 85fr green, ocher & red 1.50 1.10

Founding of African and Malagasy Posts and Telecommunications Union (UAMPT).

Map of Madagascar, Jet Plane and U.P.U. Emblem AP13

1963, Nov. 2 **Engraved** ***Perf. 13***

C76 AP13 45fr dk. carmine, greenish blue & ultramarine 60 30
C77 " 85fr dk. carmine, violet & blue 1.10 60

Malagasy Republic's admission to the U.P.U., Nov. 2, 1961.

Meteorological Center, Tananarive and Tiros Satellite—AP14

1964, March 23 **Unwmkd.**

C78 AP14 90fr orange brown, ultra. & grn. 1.75 75

Issued to commemorate the United Nations Fourth World Meteorological Day, March 23.

Zebu, Wood Sculpture AP15

1964, Oct. 20 **Engraved** ***Perf. 13***

C79 AP15 100fr lilac rose, dk. vio. & brn. 1.35 85

Musical Instrument Type of Regular Issue

Design: 200fr, Lokanga bara (stringed instrument).

1965, Feb. 16 ***Perf. 13*** **Unwmkd.**

Size: 26x47mm.

C80 A57 200fr green, orange & chocolate 2.75 1.50

Nurse Weighing Infant, and ICY Emblem—AP16

Design: 100fr, Small boy and girl, child care scenes and ICY emblem.

1965, Sept. 20 **Engraved** ***Perf. 13***

C81 AP16 50fr multicolored 65 40
C82 " 100fr " 1.25 75

International Cooperation Year.

Dance Type of Regular Issue

Design: 250fr, Dance of a young girl, Sakalava (vert.).

1966, June 13 Photo. ***Perf. 13***

Size: 27x49mm.

C83 A68 250fr multicolored 3.00 1.25

Aviation Type of Regular Issue

Design: 500fr, Dagnaux-Dufert and his Bréguet biplane, 1927.

1967, Apr. 28 **Engraved** ***Perf. 13***

Size: 48x27mm.

C84 A76 500fr Prus. blue, blk. & brown 6.00 2.00

History of aviation in Madagascar. No. C84 commemorates the 40th anniversary of the first Majunga-Tananarive flight.

African Postal Union Issue, 1967

Common Design Type

1967, Sept. 9 **Engraved** ***Perf. 13***

C85 CD124 100fr olive bister, red brn. & brt. pink 1.25 50

Dancer Type of Regular Issue

Designs: 100fr, Tourbillon dance (horiz.). 200fr, Male dancer from the South.

1967–68 Photo. ***Perf. 11½***

Size: 38x23mm.

C86 A80 100fr multi. ('68) 1.00 55

Perf. 13

Size: 27x48mm.

C87 A80 200fr multicolored 2.35 1.10

Dates of issue: 100fr, Nov. 25, 1968. 200fr, Nov. 25, 1967.

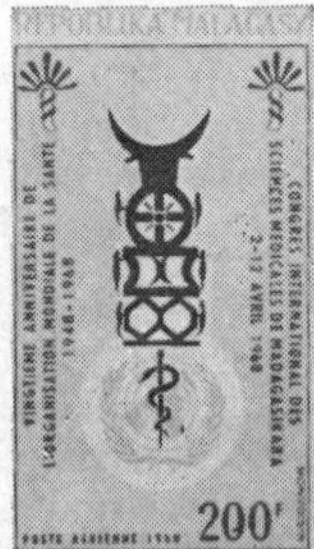

WHO Emblem, Bull's Head Totem and Palm Fan AP17

1968, Apr. 7 Photo. *Perf. 12½x13*

C88 AP17 200fr blue, yellow brn. & red 2.25 1.25

Issued to commemorate the 20th anniversary of the World Health Organization, and to publicize the International Congress of Medical Science, Apr. 2–12.

Tananarive-Ivato International Airport—AP18

1968, May 8 Engraved *Perf. 13*

C89 AP18 500fr lt. red brn., dull bl. & dull green 4.75 2.00

Issued for Stamp Day.

No. C68 Surcharged in Vermilion with New Value and 2 Bars

1968, June 24 Engraved *Perf. 13*

C90 AP9 20fr on 85fr multi. 25 10

PHILEXAFRIQUE Issue

Lady Sealing Letter, by Jean Baptiste Santerre
AP19

1968, Dec. 30 Photo. *Perf. 12½x12*

C91 AP19 100fr lilac & multi. 1.65 90

Issued to publicize PHILEXAFRIQUE Philatelic Exhibition in Abidjan, Feb. 14–23. Printed with alternating lilac label.

2nd PHILEXAFRIQUE Issue

Common Design Type

Design: 50fr, Madagascar No. 274, map of Madagascar and Malagasy emblem.

1969, Feb. 14 Engraved *Perf. 13*

C92 CD128 50fr gray, brn. red & slate grn. 90 50

Issued to commemorate the opening of PHILEXAFRIQUE, Abidjan, Feb. 14.

Sunset over Madagascar Highlands, by Henri Ratovo—AP20

Painting: 100fr, On the Seashore of the East Coast of Madagascar, by Alfred Razafinjohany.

1969, Nov. 5 Photo. *Perf. 12x12½*

C93 AP20 100fr brn. & multi. 1.20 75
C94 " 150fr multicolored 1.80 1.25

Lunar Landing Module and Man on the Moon—AP21

1970, July 20 Engraved *Perf. 13*

C95 AP21 75fr ultra., dk. gray & slate grn. 70 40

Issued to commemorate the first anniversary of man's first landing on the moon.

Boeing 737—AP22

1970, Dec. 18 Engraved *Perf. 13*

C96 AP22 200fr blue, red brn. & green 1.75 1.00

Jean Ralaimongo (1884–1944)
AP23

Portraits: 40fr, René Rakotobe (1918–1971). 65fr, Albert Sylla (1909–1967). 100fr, Joseph Ravoahangy Andrianavalona (1893–1970).

Perf. 12½; 13 (40fr)

1971–72 Photogravure

C97 AP23 25fr red brn., org. & black 25 20
C98 " 40fr dp. claret, ocher & blk., perf. 13 ('72) 35 25
C99 " 65fr green, lt. grn. & black 50 40
C100 " 100fr violet blue, lt. bl. & black 90 50

Famous Malagasy men.

Issue dates: No. C98, July 25, 1972; others, Oct. 14, 1971.

African Postal Union Issue, 1971

"Mpisikidy" by G. Rakotovao and UAMPT Building, Brazzaville, Congo—AP24

1971, Nov. 13 Photo. *Perf. 13x13½*

C105 AP24 100fr bl. & multi. 1.00 65

10th anniversary of African and Malagasy Posts and Telecommunications Union (UAMPT).

Running, Olympic Village
AP25

Design: 200fr, Judo, Olympic Stadium.

1972, Sept. 11 Photo. *Perf. 13½*

C106 AP25 100fr multi. 1.00 50
C107 " 200fr " 1.75 85

20th Olympic Games, Munich, Aug. 26–Sept. 11.

Mohair Goat
AP26

1972, Nov. 15

C108 AP26 250fr multi. 2.75 1.50

Adoration of the Kings, by Andrea Mantegna—AP27

Design: 85fr, Virgin and Child, Florentine School, 15th century (vert.).

1972, Dec. 15 Photo. *Perf. 13*

C109 AP27 85fr gold & multi. 75 40
C110 " 150fr " " 1.35 65

Christmas 1972.

Landing Module, Astronauts and Lunar Rover
AP28

1973, Jan. 25 Engraved *Perf. 13*

C111 AP28 300fr dp. claret, gray & brown 2.75 1.35

Apollo 17 U.S. moon mission, Dec. 7–19, 1972.

The Burial of Christ, by Grunewald—AP29

Design: 200fr, Resurrection, by Mattias Grunewald (horiz.). Both paintings from panels of Issenheim altar.

1973, Mar. 22 Photo. *Perf. 13*

C112 AP29 100fr gold & multi. 90 50
C113 " 200fr " " 1.85 1.00

Easter 1973.

Early Excursion Car—AP30

Design: 150fr, Early steam locomotive.

1973, July 25 Photo. *Perf. 13x12½*

C114 AP30 100fr multi. 90 50
C115 " 150fr " 1.35 75

WMO Emblem, Radar, Map of Madagascar, Hurricane
AP31

Pres. John F. Kennedy, U.S. Flag
AP32

1973, Sept. 3 Engraved *Perf. 13*

C116 AP31 100fr blk., ultra. & orange 90 45

Centenary of international meteorological cooperation.

Lemur Type of Regular Issue

Designs: 150fr, Lepilemur mustelinus (vert.). 200fr, Cheirogaleus major.

1973, Oct. 9 Engraved *Perf. 13*

C117 A131 150fr multi. 1.35 50
C118 " 200fr " 1.85 65

Lemurs of Madagascar.

1973, Nov. 22 Photo. *Perf. 13*

C119 AP32 300fr multi. 2.40 1.50

10th anniversary of the death of John F. Kennedy (1917–63).

Soccer—AP33

1973, Dec. 20 Engraved *Perf. 13*
C120 AP33 500fr lilac rose, dk. brn. & org. brown 4.00 1.50

World Soccer Cup, Munich, 1974.

Copernicus, Skylab and Heliocentric System—AP34

1974, Jan. 22
C121 AP34 250fr multi. 2.00 85

500th anniversary of the birth of Nicolaus Copernicus (1473–1543), Polish astronomer.

Scout Type of Regular Issue

Designs (African Scout Emblem and): 100fr, Scouts bringing sick people to Red Cross tent (horiz.). 300fr, Scouts fishing and fish (horiz.).

1974, Feb. 14 Engr. *Perf. 13*
C122 A132 100fr multi. 85 35
C123 " 300fr " 2.50 1.15

Malagasy Boy Scouts.

Camellia, Hummingbird, Table Tennis Player—AP35

Design: 100fr, Girl player, flower and bird design.

1974, Mar. 19 Engraved *Perf. 13*
C124 AP35 50fr blue & multi. 40 20
C125 " 100fr multi. 80 40

Table Tennis Tournament, Peking.

Autorail Micheline—AP36

Designs (Malagasy Locomotives): 85fr, Track inspection trolley. 200fr, Garratt (steam).

1974, June 7 Engr. *Perf. 13*
C126 AP36 50fr multicolored 40 20
C127 " 85fr " 65 30
C128 " 200fr " 1.60 75

Letters and UPU Emblem—AP37

1974, July 9 Engraved *Perf. 13*
C129 AP37 250fr multi. 2.00 1.00

Centenary of Universal Postal Union.

No. C120 Overprinted:
"R.F.A. 2 / HOLLANDE 1"

1974, Aug. 20 Engraved *Perf. 13*
C130 AP33 500fr multi. 4.00 2.25

World Cup Soccer Championship, 1974, victory of German Federal Republic.

Link-up in Space, Globe, Emblem—AP38

Design: 250fr, Link-up, globe and emblem (different).

1974, Sept. 12
C131 AP38 150fr org., blue & slate grn. 1.25 60
C132 " 250fr blue, brn. & slate grn. 2.00 1.00

Russo-American space cooperation.

No. C129 Overprinted
100 ANS DE COLLABORATION INTERNATIONALE

1974, Oct. 9 Engraved *Perf. 13*
C133 AP37 250fr multi. 2.00 1.00

100 years of international collaboration.

Adoration of the Kings, by J. L. David
AP39

Design: 300fr, Virgin of the Cherries and Child, by Quentin Massys.

1974, Dec. 20 Photo. *Perf. 13*
C134 AP39 200fr gold & multi. 1.65 75
C135 " 300fr gold & multi. 2.40 1.20

Christmas 1974.

U.N. Emblem and Globe—AP40

1975, June 24 Litho. *Perf. 12½*
C136 AP40 300fr green, blue & black 2.40 1.20

United Nations Charter, 30th anniversary.

American Bicentennial Type, 1975

Designs: 100fr, Count d'Estaing and "Languedoc." 200fr, John Paul Jones, "Bonhomme Richard" and "Serapis." 300fr, Benjamin Franklin, "Millern" and "Montgomery." 500fr, George Washington and "Hanna."

1975, June 30 Litho. *Perf. 11*
C137 A144 100fr multi. 90 40
C138 " 200fr " 1.75 85
C139 " 300fr " 2.75 1.25

Souvenir Sheet

C140 A144 500fr multi. 4.50 2.25

American Bicentennial. No. C140 has multicolored margin showing Count d'Estaing and deck scene during battle. Size: 126x90mm.

Flower Type of 1975

Design: 85fr, Turraea sericea.

1975, Aug. 4 Photo. *Perf. 12½*
C141 A145 85fr dp. grn., yel. & orange 70 35

Nos. C131–C132 Overprinted
JONCTION 17 JUILLET 1975

1975, Aug. 5 Engraved *Perf. 13*
C142 AP38 150fr multi. 1.20 60
C143 " 250fr " 2.00 1.00

Apollo Soyuz link-up in space, July 17, 1975.

Bas-relief and Stupas—AP41

1975, Aug. 10 Engraved *Perf. 13*
C144 AP41 50fr blue, carmine & bister 40 25

UNESCO campaign to save Borobudur Temple, Java.

Exposition Type, 1975

Designs: 125fr, Deer. 300fr, Jay.

1975, Sept. 16 Litho. *Perf. 14x13½*
C145 A147 125fr multi. 1.10 55

Souvenir Sheet

C146 A147 300fr multi. 2.50 1.50

International Exposition, Okinawa. No. C146 has multicolored margin showing coastal village. Size: 101x80½mm.

Hurdling and Olympic Rings—AP42

Design: 200fr, Weight lifting and Olympic rings (vert.).

1975, Oct. 9 Litho. *Perf. 12½*
C147 AP42 75fr multi. 60 30
C148 " 200fr " 1.65 80

Pre-Olympic Year 1975.

12th Winter Olympics Type, 1975

Designs: 200fr, Cross-country skiing. 245fr, Down-hill skiing. 450fr, Figure skating, pairs.

1975, Nov. 19 *Perf. 14*
C149 A149 200fr multi. 1.65 80
C150 " 245fr " 2.00 1.00

Souvenir Sheet

C151 A149 450fr multi. 3.75 2.25

12th Winter Olympic games, Innsbruck, 1976. No. C151 has multicolored margin showing slalom skiers. Size: 115x88mm.

Landing Module, Apollo 14 Emblem
AP43

1976, Jan. 18 Engr. *Perf. 13*
C152 AP43 150fr red, green & indigo 1.20 60

Apollo 14 moon landing, 5th anniversary.

21st Summer Olympics Type, 1976

Designs: 100fr, Shot-put and long jump. 200fr, Gymnastics, horse and balance bar. 300fr, Diving, 3-meter and platform. 500fr, Swimming, free-style and breast stroke.

1976, Jan. 21 Litho. *Perf. 13½*
C153 A151 100fr multi. 75 35
C154 " 200fr " 1.65 80
C155 " 300fr " 2.50 1.00

Souvenir Sheet

C156 A151 500fr multi. 4.00 2.25

21st Summer Olympic games, Montreal. No. C156 has multicolored margin showing Olympic emblem, eternal flame and flags. Size: 116x90½mm.

No. C152 Overprinted:
"5e Anniversaire / de la mission / APOLLO XIV"

1976, Feb. 5 Engr. *Perf. 13*
C157 AP43 150fr red, grn. & indigo 1.20 60

Apollo 14 moon landing, 5th anniversary.

Zeppelin Type of 1976

Designs (Count Zeppelin and LZ-127 over): 200fr, Brandenburg Gate, Berlin 300fr, Parliament, London. 450fr, St. Peter's Cathedral, Rome.

1976, Mar. 3 Litho. *Perf. 11*
C158 A152 200fr multi. 1.65 70
C159 " 300fr " 2.00 1.00

Souvenir Sheet

C160 A152 450fr multi. 3.50 1.75

75th anniversary of the Zeppelin. No. C160 has multicolored margin showing LZ-127 and Dürr, Zeppelin and Eckener.

Nos. C149–C151 Overprinted

a. VAINQUEUR IVAR FORMO NORVEGE
b. VAINQUEUR ROSI MITTERMAIER ALLEMAGNE DE L'OUEST
c. VAINQUEUR IRINA RODNINA ALEXANDER ZAITSEV URSS

1976, June 17
C161 A149 (a) 200fr multi. 1.65 85
C162 " (b) 245fr " 2.00 1.00

Souvenir Sheet

C163 A149 (c) 450fr multi. 3.50 2.25

12th Winter Olympic games winners.

Nos. C137–C140 Overprinted
"4 Juillet / 1776–1976"

1976, July 4
C164 A144 100fr multi. 85 40
C165 " 200fr " 1.65 80
C166 " 300fr " 2.40 1.20

Souvenir Sheet

C167 A144 500fr multi. 4.00 2.50

American Bicentennial.

Nos. C153–C156 Overprinted

a. U. BEYER/A. ROBINSON
b. N. ANDRIANOV/N. COMANECI
c. K. DIBIASI/E. VAYTSEKHOVSKAIA,
d. J. MONTGOMERY/H. ANKE

1977, Jan.
C168 A151 (a) 100fr multi. 85 40
C169 " (b) 200fr " 1.65 80
C170 " (c) 300fr " 2.40 1.20

Souvenir Sheet

C171 A151 (d) 500fr multi. 4.00 2.50

21st Summer Olympic games winners.

AIR POST SEMI-POSTAL STAMPS.

French Revolution Issue

Common Design Type

Photogravure.

1939, July 5 *Perf. 13* **Unwmkd.**

Name and Value in Orange.

CB1	CD83	4.50fr+4fr brown black	7.00	7.00

V6

V7

V8

Stamps of the designs shown above, and type of Cameroun V10 inscribed "Madagascar", were issued in 1942 by the Vichy Government, but were not placed on sale in the colony.

POSTAGE DUE STAMPS.

Inscription of Value D1 — Governor's Palace D2

Postage Due Stamps of French Colonies Overprinted in Red or Blue.

1896 *Imperf.* **Unwmkd.**

J1	D1	5c blue (R)	2.50	2.35
J2	"	10c brown (R)	2.50	2.25
J3	"	20c yellow (Bl)	3.00	2.75
J4	"	30c rose red (Bl)	3.00	2.75
J5	"	40c lilac (R)	20.00	17.50
J6	"	50c gray violet (Bl)	4.00	2.75
J7	"	1fr dark green (R)	25.00	20.00
		Nos. J1-J7 (7)	60.00	50.35

1908-24 Typo. *Perf. 13½x14*

J8	D2	2c violet brown	5	5
J9	"	4c violet	5	5
J10	"	5c green	5	5
J11	"	10c deep rose	6	6
J12	"	20c olive green	6	6
J13	"	40c brown, *straw*	6	6
J14	"	50c brown, *blue*	6	6
J15	"	60c orange ('24)	8	8
J16	"	1fr dark blue	20	20
		Nos. J8-J16 (9)	67	67

Type of 1908 Issue Surcharged **60c**

1924-27

J17	D2	60c on 1fr orange	70	70

Surcharged **2f**

J18	D2	2fr on 1fr lilac rose ('27)	25	25
J19	"	3fr on 1fr ultra. ('27)	25	25

Postage Due Stamps of 1908-27 Overprinted or Surcharged in Black **FRANCE LIBRE**

1943 *Perf. 13½x14.*

J20	D2	10c deep rose	35	35
J21	"	20c olive green	35	35
J22	"	30c on 5c green	35	35
J23	"	40c brown, *straw*	35	35
J24	"	50c brown, *blue*	35	35
J25	"	60c orange	35	35
J26	"	1fr dark blue	35	35
J27	"	1fr on 2c vio. brown	1.65	1.65
J28	"	2fr on 1fr lilac rose	35	35
J29	"	2fr on 4c violet	50	50
J30	"	3fr on 1fr ultramarine	35	35
		Nos. J20-J30 (11)	5.30	5.30

D3 — Independence Monument D4

1947 Photogravure *Perf. 13*

J31	D3	10c dark violet	4	4
J32	"	30c brown	4	4
J33	"	50c dark blue green	4	4
J34	"	1fr deep orange	6	6
J35	"	2fr red violet	10	10
J36	"	3fr red brown	10	10
J37	"	4fr blue	15	15
J38	"	5fr henna brown	15	15
J39	"	10fr slate green	15	15
J40	"	20fr violet blue	35	35
		Nos. J31-J40 (10)	1.18	1.18

Malagasy Republic

Engr.; Denomination Typo.

1962, May 7 *Perf. 13* **Unwmkd.**

J41	D4	1fr bright green	5	5
J42	"	2fr copper brown	5	5
J43	"	3fr bright violet	5	5
J44	"	4fr slate	7	7
J45	"	5fr red	8	8
J46	"	10fr yellow green	15	10
J47	"	20fr dull claret	25	15
J48	"	40fr blue	50	30
J49	"	50fr rose red	60	45
J50	"	100fr black	1.25	1.25
		Nos. J41-J50 (10)	3.05	2.55

MADEIRA

(mȧ-dēr'ȧ)

LOCATION—A group of islands in the Atlantic Ocean northwest of Africa.

GOVT. — Part of the Republic of Portugal.

AREA—314 sq. mi.

POP.—150,574 (1900).

CAPITAL—Funchal.

These islands are considered an integral part of Portugal and since 1898 postage stamps of Portugal have been in use. In 1928 a special series of stamps was issued to raise funds for building a museum. (See footnote following No. 65.)

1000 Reis = 1 Milreis

100 Centavos = 1 Escudo (1925)

King Luiz

A1 — A2

Stamps of Portugal Overprinted.

1868, Jan. 1 *Imperf.* **Unwmkd.**

Black Overprint.

2	A1	20r bistre	200.00	150.00
		a. Inverted overprint		
		b. Rouletted		
		c. Lozenge perf.	225.00	
3	"	50r green	225.00	150.00
		a. Lozenge perf.	250.00	
4	"	80r orange	200.00	150.00
		a. Double overprint		
		b. Lozenge perf.	225.00	
5	"	100r lilac	225.00	150.00
		a. Lozenge perf.	200.00	

The 5r black does not exist as a genuinely imperforate original.

Reprints of 1885 are on stout white paper, ungummed. (Also, 5r, 10r and 25r values were overprinted.) Reprints of 1905 are on ordinary white paper with shiny gum and have a wide "D" and "R". Price, $7.50 each.

Overprinted in Red or Black

1868-70 *Perf. 12½.*

6	A1	5r black (R)	15.00	10.00
8	A1	10r yellow	45.00	37.50
9	"	20r bistre	75.00	55.00
10	"	25r rose	35.00	5.00
		a. Inverted overprint	50.00	20.00
11	"	50r green	120.00	100.00
		a. Inverted ovpt.	120.00	100.00
12	"	80r orange	165.00	100.00
13	"	100r lilac	150.00	120.00
		a. Inverted ovpt.	150.00	120.00
14	"	120r blue	87.50	50.00
15	"	240r violet ('70)	300.00	175.00

Two types of 5r differ in the position of the "5" at upper right.

The reprints are on stout white paper, ungummed, with rough perforation 13½, and on thin white paper with shiny white gum and clean-cut perforation 13½. The overprint has the wide "D" and "R" and the first reprints included the 5r with both black and red overprint. Price $7.50 each.

Common Design Types

pictured in section at front of book.

Overprinted in Red or Black

1871-80 *Perf. 12½, 13½.*

16	A2	5r black (R)	4.00	3.00
		a. Inverted ovpt.	18.50	18.50
		b. Double overprint		
		c. Perf. 14	35.00	30.00
18	"	10r yellow	12.50	9.00
19	"	10r bl. green ('79)	35.00	25.00
		a. Perf. 13½	45.00	30.00
20	"	10r yel. green ('80)	17.50	15.00
21	"	15r brown ('75)	7.50	6.00
22	"	20r bistre	12.50	10.00
23	"	25r rose	9.00	3.25
		a. Invtd. overprint	50.00	
24	"	50r green ('72)	15.00	8.00
		a. Double overprint		
		b. Invtd. overprint	60.00	40.00
25	"	50r blue ('80)	52.50	22.50
26	"	80r orange ('72)	40.00	25.00
27	"	100r pale lilac ('73)	25.00	17.50
		a. Perf. 14	250.00	210.00
		b. Perf. 13½	30.00	15.00
28	A2	120r blue	62.50	30.00
29	"	150r blue ('76)	115.00	100.00
		a. Perf. 13½	140.00	100.00
30	"	150r yellow ('79)	210.00	180.00
31	"	240r violet ('74)	450.00	250.00
32	"	300r violet ('76)	42.50	30.00

There are two types of the overprint, the second one having a broad "D".

The reprints have the same characteristics as those of the 1868-70 issues. Price, $2 each.

King Luiz

A4 — A5

1880-81

33	A4	5r black	10.50	7.00
34	A5	25r pearl gray	10.50	7.00
		a. Inverted overprint	30.00	25.00
35	A4	25r lilac	10.00	3.00

No. 35 is overprinted on Portugal type A18.

Nos. 33, 34 and 35 have been reprinted on stout white paper, ungummed, and the last three on thin white paper with shiny white gum. The perforations are as previously described. Price, $1.50 each.

Vasco da Gama Issue.

Common Design Types

1898, Apr. 1 Engraved *Perf. 14-15*

37	CD20	2½r blue green	1.00	60
38	CD21	5r red	1.00	60
39	CD22	10r red violet	3.00	1.75
40	CD23	25r yellow green	1.50	80
41	CD24	50r dark blue	3.00	2.00
42	CD25	75r violet brown	4.50	4.25
43	CD26	100r bistre brown	3.00	2.50
44	CD27	150r bistre	4.25	3.25
		Nos. 37-44 (8)	21.25	15.75

Nos. 37-44 with "REPUBLICA" overprint and surcharges are listed as Portugal Nos. 199-206.

Ceres

A6

Value Typographed in Black.

1928, May 1 Engr. *Perf. 13½*

45	A6	3c deep violet	20	20
46	"	4c orange	20	20
47	"	5c light blue	20	20
48	"	6c brown	20	20
49	"	10c red	20	20
50	"	15c yellow green	20	20
51	"	16c red brown	25	25
52	"	25c violet rose	25	25
53	"	32c blue green	25	25
54	"	40c yellow brown	50	55
55	"	50c slate	50	55
56	"	64c Prussian blue	75	1.00
57	"	80c dark brown	75	1.00

58 A6 96c carmine rose 75 1.00
59 " 1e black 75 1.00
a. Value omitted 10.00
60 " 1.20e light rose 75 1.00
61 " 1.60e ultramarine 75 1.00
62 " 2.40e yellow 75 1.00
63 " 3.36e dull green 1.25 1.50
64 " 4.50e brown red 1.25 1.50
65 " 7e dark blue 2.00 2.50
Nos. 45-65 (21) 12.70 15.55

It was obligatory to use these stamps in place of those in regular use on May 1, June 5, July 1 and Dec. 31, 1928, Jan. 1 and 31, May 1 and June 5, 1929. The amount obtained from this sale was donated to a fund for building a museum.

NEWSPAPER STAMP.

Numeral of Value
N1

Newspaper Stamp of Portugal Overprinted in Black.

Perf. 12½, 13½

1876, July 1 Unwmkd.

P1 N1 2½r olive 1.75 1.50
a. Inverted ovpt. 10.00

The reprints have the same papers, gum, perforations and overprint as the reprints of the regular issues. Price $2.

POSTAL TAX STAMPS.

Pombal Commemorative Issue.

Common Design Types

Engraved.

1925 ***Perf. 12½.*** **Unwmkd.**

RA1 CD28 15c gray & black 55 60
RA2 CD29 15c " " 55 60
RA3 CD30 15c " " 55 60

POSTAL TAX DUE STAMPS.

Pombal Commemorative Issue.

Common Design Types

1925 ***Perf. 12½.*** **Unwmkd.**

RAJ1 CD31 30c gray & blk. 75 1.50
RAJ2 CD32 30c " " 75 1.50
RAJ3 CD33 30c " " 75 1.50

MALAGASY REPUBLIC

(See Madagascar.)

MALI

(mäl·ē)

Federation of Mali

LOCATION—West Africa.
GOVT.—Republic within French Community.
AREA—531,000 sq. mi.
POP.—5,862,000 (est.).
CAPITALS—Dakar and Bamako.

The Federation of Mali, founded Jan. 17, 1959, consisted of the Republic of Senegal and the Sudanese Republic. It broke up in June, 1960. See Senegal.

100 Centimes = 1 Franc

Flag and Map of Mali
A1

Engraved.

1959, Nov. 7 ***Perf. 13*** **Unwmkd.**

1 A1 25fr green, carmine & deep claret 50 50

Issued to commemorate the founding of the Federation of Mali.

Imperforates

Most Mali stamps exist imperforate in issued and trial colors, and also in small presentation sheets in issued colors.

Parrot-fish
A2

Fish: 10fr, Triggerfish. 15fr, Psetta. 20fr, Blepharis crinitus. 25fr, Butterfly-fish. 30fr, Surgeonfish. 85fr, Dentex.

1960, Mar. 5

Fish in Natural Colors.

2 A2 5fr olive 27 13
3 " 10fr brt. greenish blue 32 20
4 " 15fr dark blue 40 25
5 " 20fr gray green 55 30
6 " 25fr slate green 65 40
7 " 30fr dark blue 90 60
8 " 85fr dark green 2.00 1.50
Nos. 2-8 (7) 5.09 3.38

C.C.T.A. Issue

Common Design Type

1960, May 21 ***Perf. 13***

9 CD106 25fr light violet & magenta 1.10 80

Republic of Mali

GOVT.—Republic.
AREA—463,500 sq. mi.
POP.—5,990,000 (est. 1977).
CAPITAL—Bamako.

The Republic of Mali, formerly the Sudanese Republic, proclaimed its independence on June 20, 1960, when the Federation of Mali ceased to exist. See French Sudan.

Nos. 5, 6 and 8 Overprinted "REPUBLIQUE DU MALI" and Bar.

Engraved

1961, Jan. 15 ***Perf. 13*** **Unwmkd.**

Fish in Natural Colors

10 A2 20fr gray green 65 50
11 " 25fr slate green 80 50
12 " 85fr dark green 1.75 1.10

Pres. Mamadou Konate
A3

Design: 25fr, Pres. Modibo Keita.

1961, Mar. 18

13 A3 20fr green & black 22 12
14 " 25fr maroon & black 27 10

For miniature sheet see No. C11a.

Common Design Types

pictured in section at front of book.

Reading Class, Bullock Team and Factory—A4

1961, Sept. 22 ***Perf. 13*** **Unwmkd.**

15 A4 25fr multicolored 50 30

First anniversary of Independence.

Shepherd and Sheep
AP5

Designs: 1fr, 10fr, 40fr, Cattle. 2fr, 15fr, 50fr, Mali Arts Museum. 3fr, 20fr, 60fr, Plowing. 4fr, 25fr, 85fr, Harvester.

Engraved

1961, Dec. 24 ***Perf. 13*** **Unwmkd.**

16 A5 50c carmine rose, black & dk. grn. 3 3
17 " 1fr green, blue & bistre 5 5
18 " 2fr ultra., green & orange red 5 5
19 " 3fr blue, green & brn. 5 5
20 " 4fr blue green, indigo & bistre 6 6
21 " 5fr blue, olive & maroon 10 10
22 " 10fr olive black, blue & sepia 15 6
23 " 15fr ultra., green & bistre brown 15 8
24 " 20fr blue, green & orange red 22 8
25 " 25fr dark blue & yellow brown 30 8
26 " 30fr violet, green & dark brown 35 25
27 " 40fr slate green, blue & orange red 50 18
28 " 50fr ultra., green & rose carmine 45 18
29 " 60fr blue, green & brn. 60 25
30 " 85fr blue, bistre & dk. red brown 90 33
Nos. 16-30 (15) 3.96 1.83

King Mohammed V of Morocco and Map of Africa—A6

1962, Jan. 4 Photogravure ***Perf. 12***

31 A6 25fr multicolored 32 15
32 " 50fr " 55 20

Issued to commemorate the first anniversary of the conference of African heads of state at Casablanca.

Patrice Lumumba—A7

1962, Feb. 12 ***Perf. 12*** **Unwmkd.**

33 A7 25fr chocolate & brown orange 25 17
34 A7 100fr chocolate & emerald 1.00 55

Issued in memory of Patrice Lumumba, Premier of the Congo (Democratic) Republic.

Pegasus and U.P.U. Monument, Bern—A8

1962, Apr. 21 ***Perf. 12½x12***

35 A8 85fr red brown, yellow & bright green 1.00 75

Issued to commemorate the first anniversary of Mali's admission to the Universal Postal Union.

Map of Africa and Post Horn
A8a

1962, Apr. 23 ***Perf. 13½x13***

36 A8a 25fr dark red brown & deep green 27 20
37 " 85fr deep green & orange 90 50

Establishment of African Postal Union.

Sansanding Dam
A9

Cotton Plant
A10

1962, Oct. 27 Photo. ***Perf. 12***

38 A9 25fr dk. gray, ultra. & green 27 13
39 A10 45fr multicolored 65 30

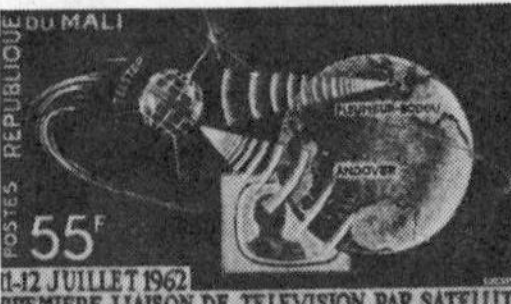

Telstar, Earth and Television Set
A10a

1962, Nov. 24 Engraved ***Perf. 13***

40 A10a 45fr dark carmine, violet & brn. 55 45
41 " 55fr green, violet & olive 80 55

Issued to commemorate the first television connection of the United States and Europe through the Telstar satellite, July 11-12.

Bull, Chemical Equipment, Chicks
A11

1963, Feb. 23 ***Perf. 13*** **Unwmkd.**
42 A11 25fr red brown & greenish blue 35 22

Issued to publicize the Sotuba Zootechnical Institute. See also No. C15.

Tractor
A12

1963, Mar. 21 **Engraved**
43 A12 25fr violet blue, dark brown & black 27 20
44 " 45fr blue green, red brown & green 60 40

Issued for the "Freedom from Hunger" campaign of the U.N. Food and Agriculture Organization.

High Altitude Balloon and World Meteorological Organization Emblem
A13

Winners, 800-meter Race
A14

1963, June 12 **Photo.** ***Perf. 12½***

Green Emblem; Yellow and Black Balloon.

45 A13 25fr ultramarine 30 20
46 " 45fr carmine rose 55 40
47 " 60fr red brown 75 60

Studies of the atmosphere.

1963, Aug. 10 ***Perf. 12*** **Unwmkd.**

Designs: 20fr, Acrobatic dancers (horiz.). 85fr, Soccer (horiz.).

48 A14 5fr multicolored 10 10
49 " 10fr " 13 10
50 " 20fr " 27 20
51 " 85fr " 90 50

Issued to publicize Youth Week.

Centenary Emblem
A15

Kaempferia Aethiopica
A16

1963, Sept. 1 ***Perf. 13½x13***

Emblem in Gray, Yellow and Red

52 A15 5fr lt. olive green & blk. 12 12
53 " 10fr yellow & black 20 15
54 " 85fr red & black 90 60

Centenary of the International Red Cross.

1963, Dec. 23 ***Perf. 13*** **Unwmkd.**

Tropical plants: 70fr, Bombax costatum. 100fr, Adenium Honghel.

55 A16 30fr multicolored 35 18
56 " 70fr " 80 35
57 " 100fr " 1.10 40

Plane Spraying, Locust and Village
A17

Designs (each inscribed "O.I.C.M.A."): 5fr, Head of locust and map of Africa (vert.). 10fr, Locust in flight over map of Mali (vert.).

1964, June 15 **Engraved** ***Perf. 13***
58 A17 5fr orange brown, dull claret & green 15 10
59 " 10fr orange brown, olive & blue green 20 13
60 " 20fr bister, orange brn. & yel. green 30 15

Anti-locust campaign.

Soccer Player and Tokyo Stadium
A18

Designs (stadium in background): 10fr, Boxer (vert.). 15fr, Runner (vert.). 85fr, Hurdler.

1964, June 27 **Unwmkd.**
61 A18 5fr red, bright green & dark purple 10 8
62 " 10fr black, dull blue & orange brown 15 12
63 " 15fr violet & dark red 25 20
64 " 85fr violet, dark brown & slate green 1.00 70
a. Min. sheet of 4 2.00 2.00

18th Olympic Games, Tokyo, Oct. 10–25. No. 64a contains one each of Nos. 61–64. Size: 190x100mm.

IQSY Emblem and Eclipse of Sun
A19

1964, July 27 **Engr.** ***Perf. 13***
65 A19 45fr multicolored 70 30

International Quiet Sun Year, 1964–65.

Map of Viet Nam
A20

Defassa Waterbuck
A21

1964, Nov. 2 **Photo.** ***Perf. 12x12½***
66 A20 30fr multicolored 35 20

Issued to publicize the solidarity of the workers of Mali and those of South Viet Nam.

1965, Apr. 5 **Engraved**

Designs: 5fr, Cape buffalo (horiz.). 10fr, Scimitar-horned oryx. 30fr, Leopard (horiz.). 90fr, Giraffe.

67 A21 1fr chocolate, bright blue & green 5 3
68 " 5fr grn., ocher & choc. 8 5
69 " 10fr grn., brt. pink & bister brown 12 10
70 " 30fr dark red, green & chocolate 33 20
71 " 90fr bister brn., slate & yel. green 90 65
Nos. 67-71 (5) 1.48 1.03

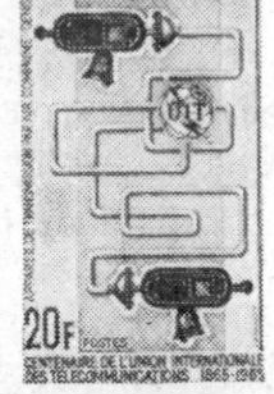

Abraham Lincoln
A22

Denis Compressed Air Transmitter
A23

1965, Apr. 15 **Photo.** ***Perf. 13x12½***
72 A22 45fr black & multi. 60 45
73 " 55fr dp. grn. & multi. 70 60

Centenary of the death of Lincoln.

1965, May 17 **Engraved** ***Perf. 13***

Designs: 30fr, Hughes telegraph system (horiz.). 50fr, Lescurre heliograph.

74 A23 20fr orge., blk. & blue 28 22
75 " 30fr orange, ocher & slate green 35 25
76 " 50fr orge., dark brown & slate green 55 40

Issued to commemorate the centenary of the International Telecommunication Union.

Mobile X-ray Unit and Lungs
A24

Designs: 10fr, Mother and infants. 25fr, Examination of patient at Marchoux Institute and slide. 45fr, Biology laboratory.

1965, July 5 ***Perf. 13*** **Unwmkd.**
77 A24 5fr lake, red & vio. 8 6
78 " 10fr brn. olive, red & slate green 15 10
79 " 25fr dark brown, red & green 27 22
80 " 45fr dark brown, red & slate green 50 35

Issued to publicize the Health Service.

Swimmer
A25

Design: 15fr, Judo.

1965, July 19 **Engraved**
81 A25 5fr multicolored 12 8
82 " 15fr dk. red, brown & bright green 25 17

First African Games, Brazzaville, July 18–25.

Globe, Vase, Quill, Trumpet
A26

Designs: 55fr, Mask, palette and microphones. 90fr, Dancers, mask and printed cloth.

1966, Apr. 4 **Engraved** ***Perf. 13***
83 A26 30fr blk., red & ocher 33 20
84 " 55fr car. rose, emerald & black 55 40
85 " 90fr ultra., orange & dark brown 90 55

Issued to commemorate the International Negro Arts Festival, Dakar, Senegal, Apr. 1–24.

WHO Headquarters, Geneva
A27

1966, May 3 **Photo.** ***Perf. 12½x13***
86 A27 30fr org. yellow, blue & olive green 35 20
87 " 45fr org. yellow, blue & dull red 45 30

Issued to commemorate the inauguration of the World Health Organization Headquarters.

Fishermen with Nets
A28

River Fishing: 4fr, 60fr, Group fishing with large net. 20fr, 85fr, Commercial fishing boats.

1966, May 30 **Engraved** ***Perf. 13***
88 A28 3fr ultra. & brown 5 3
89 " 4fr Prussian blue & orange brown 8 6
90 " 20fr dark brown, ultra. & green 22 10
91 " 25fr dark brown, blue & bright green 28 12
92 " 60fr magenta, brown & bright green 55 25
93 " 85fr dark purple, dull blue & green 75 40
Nos. 88-93 (6) 1.93 96

Initiation of Pioneers
A29

Design: 25fr, Dance and Pioneer emblem.

1966, July 25 **Engraved** ***Perf. 13***
94 A29 5fr multicolored 8 5
95 " 25fr " 27 15

Issued to honor the pioneers of Mali.

Inoculation of Zebu
A30

1967, Jan. 16 **Photo.** ***Perf. 12½x13***
96 A30 10fr deep green, yellow green & brown 10 8
97 " 30fr Prussian blue, blue & brown 32 22

Campaign against cattle plague.

View of Timbuktu and Tourist Year Emblem
A31

1967, May 15 Engraved *Perf. 13*

98 A31 25fr Prus. blue, red lilac & orange 27 13

International Tourist Year, 1967.

Ugada Grandicollis
A32

Insects: 5fr, Chelorrhina polyphemus (vert.). 50fr, Phymateus cinctus.

1967, Aug. 14 Engraved *Perf. 13*

99 A32 5fr brt. blue, slate grn. & brown 10 8
100 " 15fr slate green, dk. brown & red 25 12
101 " 50fr slate grn., dk. brn. & dp. orange 50 30

Teacher and Adult Class
A33

1967, Sept. 8 Photo. *Perf. 12½x13*

102 A33 50fr blk., grn. & car. 50 15

International Literacy Day, Sept. 8.

Europafrica Issue

Birds, New Buildings and Map
A34

1967, Sept. 18 *Perf. 12½x12*

103 A34 45fr multicolored 55 25

Lions Emblem and Crocodile
A35

1967, Oct. 16 Photo. *Perf. 13x12½*

104 A35 90fr yellow & multi. 70 40

50th anniversary of Lions International.

Water Cycle and UNESCO Emblem
A36

1967, Nov. 15 Photo. *Perf. 13*

105 A36 25fr multicolored 25 15

Hydrological Decade (UNESCO), 1965-74.

WHO Emblem
A37

1968, Apr. 8 Engraved *Perf. 13*

106 A37 90fr slate green, dk. carmine rose & blue 55 20

Issued to commemorate the 20th anniversary of the World Health Organization.

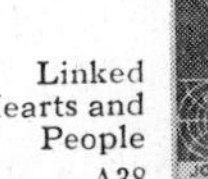

Linked Hearts and People
A38

1968, Apr. 28 Engraved *Perf. 13*

107 A38 50fr slate grn., red & violet blue 33 12

International Day of Sister Communities.

Books, Student, Chart, and Map of Africa
A39

1968, Aug. 12 Engraved *Perf. 13*

108 A39 100fr carmine, olive & black 60 30

Issued to commemorate the 10th anniversary of the International Association for the Development of Libraries and Archives in Africa.

Draisienne, 1809
A40

Designs: 5fr, De Dion-Bouton automobile, 1894 (horiz.). 10fr, Michaux bicycle, 1861. 45fr, Panhard & Levassor automobile, 1914 (horiz.).

1968, Aug. 12

109 A40 2fr green, olive & magenta 8 6
110 " 5fr lemon, black & indigo 10 7
111 " 10fr bright green, indigo & brn. 12 8
112 " 45fr ocher, grey green & blk. 28 17

Tourist Emblem with Map of Africa and Dove
A41

1969, May 12 Photo. *Perf. 12½x13*

113 A41 50fr lt. ultramarine, green & red 28 12

Year of African Tourism.

ILO Emblem and "OIT"
A42

1969, May 12 Engraved *Perf. 13*

114 A42 50fr vio., slate green & bright blue 35 15
115 " 60fr slate, red & olive brown 40 15

Issued to commemorate the 50th anniversary of the International Labor Organization.

Panhard, 1897, and Citroën 24, 1969—A43

Design: 30fr, Citroën, 1923, and Citroën DS 21, 1969.

1969, May 30 Engraved *Perf. 13*

116 A43 25fr black, maroon & lemon 20 12
117 " 30fr black, brt. green & dark green 25 12

See also Nos. C71-C72.

Play Blocks
A44

Toys: 10fr, Mule on wheels. 15fr, Ducks. 20fr, Racing car and track.

1969 Photogravure *Perf. 12½x13*

118 A44 5fr red, gray & yel. 10 5
119 " 10fr red, yel. & olive 12 8
120 " 15fr red, salmon & yellow green 15 8
121 " 20fr red, indigo & org. 20 12

Issued to publicize the International Toy Fair in Nuremberg, Germany.

Ram
A45

Animals: 2fr, Goat. 10fr, Donkey. 35fr, Horse. 90fr, Dromedaries.

1969, Aug. 18 Engraved *Perf. 13*

122 A45 1fr olive, bright green & brown 6 6
123 " 2fr red, gray & brown olive 8 7
124 " 10fr ultra., brn. orange & olive green 12 12
125 " 35fr rose red & dk. gray 33 25
126 " 90fr brt. blue, ultra. & brown orange 80 50
Nos. 122-126 (5) 1.39 1.00

Development Bank Issue
Common Design Type

1969, Sept. 10

127 CD130 50fr brt. lilac, green & ocher 30 20
128 " 90fr olive brown, green & ocher 55 20

Issued to commemorate the 5th anniversary of the African Development Bank.

Boy Being Vaccinated
A46

1969, Nov. 10 Engraved *Perf. 13*

129 A46 50fr brn., indigo & bright green 35 15

Campaign against smallbox and measles.

ASECNA Issue
Common Design Type

1969, Dec. 12 Engraved *Perf. 13*

130 CD132 100fr dk. slate green 60 30

African and Japanese Women
A47

Design: 150fr, Flags and maps of Mali and Japan.

1970, Apr. 13 Engraved *Perf. 13*

131 A47 100fr brown, blue & ocher 65 25
132 " 150fr dk. red, yellow grn. & org. 90 30

Issued to publicize EXPO '70 International Exhibition, Osaka, Japan, Mar. 15-Sept. 13.

Satellite Telecommunications, Map of Africa and ITU Emblem—A48

1970, May 17 Engraved *Perf. 13*

133 A48 90fr car. rose & brn. 60 30

World Telecommunications Day.

U.P.U. Headquarters Issue
Common Design Type

1970, May 20 Engraved *Perf. 13*

134 CD132 50fr dark red, blue green & olive 30 20
135 " 60fr red lilac, ultra. & red brown 40 25

Post Office, Bamako
A49

Public Buildings: 40fr, Chamber of Commerce, Bamako. 60fr, Public Works Ministry, Bamako. 80fr, City Hall, Segou.

1970, Nov. 23 Engraved *Perf. 13*

136 A49 30fr brn., brt. green & olive 15 10
137 " 40fr brn., slate green & dp. claret 20 12
138 " 60fr brn. red, slate green & gray 30 20
139 " 80fr brn., brt. green & emerald 40 25

Gallet 030T, 1882
A50

Old Steam Locomotives: 40fr, Felou 030T, 1882. 50fr, Bechevel 230T, 1882. 80fr, Type 231, 1930. 100fr, Type 141, 1930.

1970, Dec. 14 Engraved *Perf. 13*

140	A50	20fr brt. green, dark car. & black	18	13
141	"	40fr black, dark green & ocher	27	18
142	"	50fr bister brn., bl. green & black	32	20
143	"	80fr car. rose, black & blue green	40	30
144	"	100fr ocher, blue green & black	60	35
		Nos. 140-144 (5)	1.77	1.16

Scout Sounding Retreat—A51

Bambara Mask, San—A52

Designs (Boy Scouts): 5fr, Crossing river (horiz.). 100fr, Canoeing (horiz.).

Perf. 13x12½, 12½x13

1970, Dec. 28 Lithographed

145	A51	5fr multicolored	8	5
146	"	30fr "	20	12
147	"	100fr "	55	27

1971, Jan. 25 Photo. *Perf. 12x12½*

Designs: 25fr, Dogon mask, Bandiagara. 50fr, Kanaga ideogram. 80fr, Bambara ideogram.

148	A52	20fr orange & multi.	12	7
149	"	25fr brt. grn. & multi.	15	10
150	"	50fr dk. pur. & multi.	32	15
151	"	80fr blue & multi.	45	22

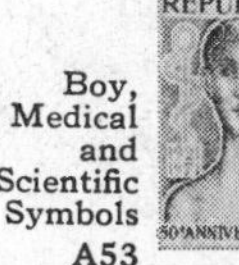

Boy, Medical and Scientific Symbols A53

1971, March 22 Engr. *Perf. 13*

152	A53	100fr dp. car., ocher & green	65	35

50th anniversary of B.C.G. inoculation (Bacillus-Calmette-Guerin) against tuberculosis.

Boy Scouts, Mt. Fuji, Japanese Print A54

1971, Apr. 19

153	A54	80fr lt. ultra., dp. plum & bright green	35	22

13th Boy Scout World Jamboree, Asagiri Plain, Japan, Aug. 2–10.

UNICEF Emblem, Hands and Rose A55

Design: 60fr, UNICEF emblem, women and children (vert.).

1971, May 24 Engraved *Perf. 13*

154	A55	50fr brn. org., car. & dk. brown	25	15
155	A55	60fr violet blue, green & red brown	27	18

25th anniversary of UNICEF (U.N. International Children's Fund).

Mali Farmer A56

Map of Africa with Communications Network A57

Costumes of Mali: 10fr, Mali farm woman. 15fr, Tuareg. 60fr, Embroidered robe, Grand Boubou. 80fr, Ceremonial robe, woman.

1971, June 14 Photo. *Perf. 13*

156	A56	5fr gray & multi.	5	5
157	"	10fr vio. bl. & multi.	8	7
158	"	15fr yellow & multi.	13	8
159	"	60fr gray & multi.	27	13
160	"	80fr tan & multi.	35	25
		Nos. 156-160 (5)	88	58

1971, Aug. 16 Photo. *Perf. 13*

161	A57	50fr blue, vio. blue & orange	30	15

Pan-African telecommunications system.

Hibiscus A58

Flowers: 50fr, Poinsettia. 60fr, Adenium obesum. 80fr, Dogbane. 100fr, Satanocrater berhautii.

1971, Oct. 4 Litho. *Perf. 14x13½*

162	A58	20fr multicolored	10	7
163	"	50fr "	25	12
164	"	60fr "	35	12
165	"	80fr "	40	12
166	"	100fr "	50	20
		Nos. 162-166 (5)	1.60	63

Mother, Child and Bird (Sculpture) A59

1971, Dec. 27 Engr. *Perf. 13x12½*

167	A59	70fr magenta, sepia & blue green	35	15

National Institute of Social Security, 15th anniversary.

ITU Emblem A60

1972, May 17 Photo. *Perf. 13x13½*

168	A60	70fr blue, maroon & black	35	20

4th World Telecommunications Day.

Clay Funerary Statuette A61

Mali Art: 40fr, Female torso, wood. 50fr, Masked figure, painted stone. 100fr, Animals and men, wrought iron.

1972, May 29 *Perf. 12½x13*

169	A61	30fr org. red & multi.	15	12
170	"	40fr yellow & multi.	20	15
171	"	50fr red & multi.	25	15
172	"	100fr lt. grn. & multi.	45	20

Morse and Telegraph A62

1972, June 5 Engraved *Perf. 13*

173	A62	80fr red, emerald & chocolate	35	20

Centenary of the death of Samuel F. B. Morse (1791–1872), inventor of the telegraph.

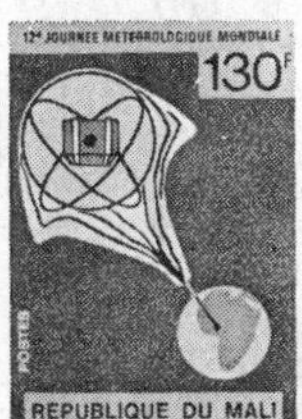

Weather Balloon over Africa A63

1972, July 10 Photo. *Perf. 12½x13*

174	A63	130fr multicolored	60	35

12th World Meteorology Day.

Sarakolé Dance, Kayes A64

People, Book, Pencil A65

Designs: Folk dances.

1972, Aug. 21 Photo. *Perf. 13*

Multicolored

175	A64	10fr *shown*	5	5
176	"	20fr *La Gomba, Bamako*	12	6
177	"	50fr *Hunters' dance, Bougouni*	22	18
178	"	70fr *Koré Duga, Ségou*	27	20
179	"	80fr *Kanaga, Sanga*	32	20
180	"	120fr *Targui, Timbuktu*	40	25
		Nos. 175-180 (6)	1.38	94

1972, Sept. 8 Typo. *Perf. 12½x13*

181	A65	80fr blk. & yel. green	32	15

World Literacy Day, Sept. 8.

"Edison Classique," Mali Instruments A66

1972, Sept. 18 Engr. *Perf. 13*

182	A66	100fr multicolored	45	22

First Anthology of Music of Mali.

Aries A67

Signs of the Zodiac: No. 184, Taurus. No. 185, Gemini. No. 186, Cancer. No. 187, Leo. No. 188, Virgo. No. 189, Libra. No. 190, Scorpio. No. 191, Sagittarius. No. 192, Capricorn. No. 193, Aquarius. No. 194, Pisces.

1972, Oct. 23 Engr. *Perf. 11*

183	A67	15fr lilac & bis. brn.	10	7
184	"	15fr bis. brn. & blk.	10	7
185	"	35fr maroon & indigo	15	10
186	"	35fr emerald & maroon	15	10
187	"	40fr blue & red brn.	20	15
188	"	40fr dark purple & red brown	20	15
189	"	45fr dark blue & maroon	25	15
190	"	45fr maroon & bright green	25	15
191	"	65fr dark violet & indigo	28	20
192	"	65fr dark violet & gray olive	28	20
193	"	90fr bright pink & indigo	35	25
194	"	90fr brt. pink & grn.	35	25
		Nos. 183-194 (12)	2.66	1.84

Arrival of First Locomotive in Bamako, 1906 A68

Designs (Locomotives): 30fr, Thies-Bamako, 1920. 60fr, Thies-Bamako, 1927. 120fr, Two Alsthom BB, 1947.

1972, Dec. 11 Engraved *Perf. 13*

195	A68	10fr indigo, brown & slate green	10	8
196	"	30fr slate green, indigo & brn.	15	12
197	"	60fr slate green, indigo & brn.	30	18
198	"	120fr slate green & chocolate	50	30

High Jump A69

Designs: 270fr, Discus. 280fr, Soccer.

1973, Jan. 15 Photo. *Perf. 12½*

199	A69	70fr yel. grn., blue & dark brown	35	20
200	"	270fr blue, orange & dark brown	1.20	60
201	"	280fr multicolored	1.25	60

2nd African Games, Lagos, Nigeria, Jan. 7–18.

INTER-POL Emblem and Head-quarters
A70

1973, Feb. 28 Photo. *Perf. 13*

202 A70 80fr multicolored 35 20

50th anniversary of International Criminal Police Organization (INTERPOL).

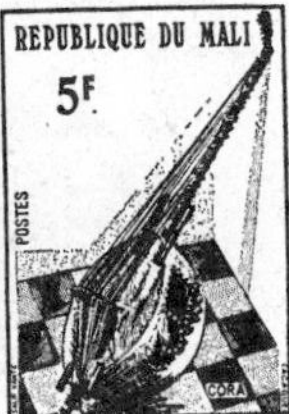

Blind Man and Disabled Boy
A71

Cora
A72

1973, Apr. 24 Engr. *Perf. 12½x13*

203 A71 70fr dk. car., brick red & black 35 15

Help for the handicapped.

No. 166 Surcharged with New Value, 2 Bars, and Overprinted: "SECHERESSE / SOLIDARITE AFRICAINE"

1973, Aug. 16 Litho. *Perf. 13½*

204 A58 200fr on 100fr multi. 80 50

African solidarity in drought emergency.

Perf. 12½x13, 13x12½

1973, Dec. 10 Engraved

Musical Instruments: 10fr, Balafon (horiz.). 15fr, Djembe. 20fr, Guitar. 25fr, N'Djarka. 30fr, M'Bolon. 35fr, Dozo N'Goni. 40fr, N'Tamani.

205 A72 5fr maroon, dark green & brown 3 3
206 " 10fr blue & choc. 5 5
207 " 15fr brown, dark red & yellow 6 6
208 " 20fr maroon & brn. olive 10 6
209 " 25fr org., yel. & blk. 13 6
210 " 30fr vio. blue & blk. 15 8
211 " 35fr dk. red & brown 18 12
212 " 40fr dk. red & choc. 18 15
Nos. 205-212 (8) 88 61

Farmer with Newspaper, Corn
A73

Soccer, Goalkeeper, Symbolic Globe and Net
A74

1974, Mar. 11 Engr. *Perf. 12½x13*

213 A73 70fr multicolored 30 20

2nd anniversary of "Kibaru," rural newspaper.

1974, May 6 Engraved *Perf. 13*

Design: 280fr, Games' emblem, soccer and ball.

214 A74 270fr multicolored 1.20 65
215 A74 280fr multicolored 1.25 65

World Cup Soccer Championship, Munich, June 13–July 7.

Old and New Ships, UPU Emblem
A75

Weaver
A76

Designs: 90fr, Old and new planes, UPU emblem. 270fr, Old and new trains, UPU emblem.

1974, June 2 Engr. *Perf. 12½x13*

216 A75 80fr brown & multi. 35 25
217 " 90fr ultra. & multi. 45 30
218 " 270fr lt. grn. & multi. 1.20 65

Centenary of Universal Postal Union.

Nos. 214-215 Surcharged and Overprinted in Black or Red: "R.F.A. 2 / HOLLANDE 1"

1974, Aug. 28 Engraved *Perf. 13*

219 A74 300fr on 270fr multi. 1.35 70
220 " 330fr on 280fr " (R) 1.40 70

World Cup Soccer Championship, 1974, victory of German Federal Republic.

1974, Sept. 16 Photo. *Perf. 12½x13*

Multicolored

221 A76 50fr *shown* 20 15
222 " 60fr *Potter* 25 15
223 " 70fr *Smiths* 30 15
224 " 80fr *Sculptor* 35 20

Artisans of Mali.

Niger River near Gao
A77

Landscapes: 20fr, The Hand of Fatma (rock formation; vert.). 40fr, Gouina Waterfall. 70fr, Dogon houses (vert.).

Perf. 13x12½, 12½x13

1974, Sept. 23

225 A77 10fr multicolored 5 6
226 " 20fr " 8 6
227 " 40fr " 15 15
228 " 70fr " 30 15

Nos. 216 and 218 Surcharged and Overprinted in Black or Red: "9 OCTOBRE 1974"

1974, Oct. 9 Engraved *Perf. 13*

229 A75 250fr on 80fr multi. 1.35 70
230 " 300fr on 270fr " (R) 1.35 70

UPU Day.

Mao Tse-tung, Flags, Great Wall
A78

1974, Oct. 21 Engraved *Perf. 13*

231 A78 100fr multicolored 40 25

People's Republic of China, 25th anniversary.

Artisans and Lions Emblem—A79

Design: 100fr, View of Samanko and Lions emblem.

1975, Feb. 3 Photo. *Perf. 13*

232 A79 90fr red & multi. 40 25
233 " 100fr blue & multi. 45 30

5th anniversary of lepers' rehabilitation village, Samanko, sponsored by Lions International.

Tetrodon Fahaka
A80

Designs: Fish.

1975, May 12 Engraved *Perf. 13*

Multicolored

234 A80 60fr *shown* 25 15
235 " 70fr *Malopterurus electricus* 30 18
236 " 80fr *Citharinus latus* 30 18
237 " 90fr *Hydrocyon forskali* 35 22
238 " 110fr *Lates niloticus* 40 20
Nos. 234-238 (5) 1.60 93

See Nos. 256-260.

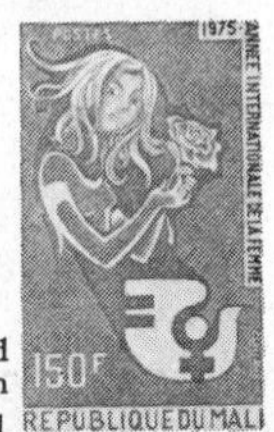

Woman and IWY Emblem
A81

1975, June 9 Engr. *Perf. 13*

239 A81 150fr red & green 60 30

International Women's Year 1975.

Morris "Oxford," 1913
A82

Automobiles: 130fr, Franklin "E," 1907. 190fr, Daimler, 1900. 230fr, Panhard & Levassor, 1895.

1975, June 16

240 A82 90fr blk., olive & lilac 35 20
241 " 130fr violet blue, gray & red 50 28
242 " 190fr bl., grn. & ind. 75 45
243 " 230fr red, ultra. & brown olive 90 55

Carthaginian Tristater, 500 B.C.
A83

Ancient Coins: 170fr, Decadrachma, Syracuse, 413 B.C. 190fr, Acanthe tetradrachma, 400 B.C. 260fr, Didrachma, Eritrea, 480-445 B.C.

1975, Oct. 13 Engr. *Perf. 13*

244 A83 130fr blue, claret & black 50 28
245 " 170fr emerald, brn. & black 65 35
246 " 190fr green, red & black 75 45
247 " 260fr dp. bl., org. & black 1.00 65

UN Emblem and "ONU"—A84

1975, Nov. 10 Engr. *Perf. 13*

248 A84 200fr emerald & bright blue 85 50

30th anniversary of UN.

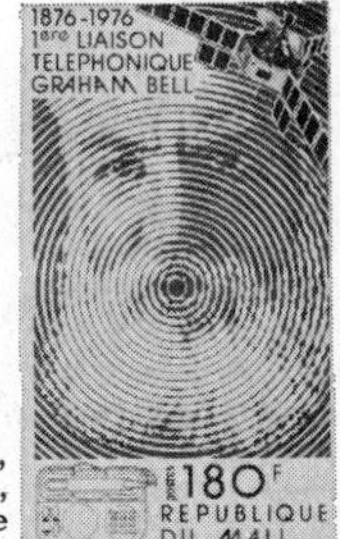

A. G. Bell, Waves, Satellite, Telephone
A85

1976, Mar. 8 Litho. *Perf. 12x12½*

249 A85 180fr brown, ultra. & ocher 75 40

Centenary of first telephone call by Alexander Graham Bell, Mar. 10, 1876.

Chameleon
A86

Reptiles: 30fr, Lizzard. 40fr, Tortoise. 90fr, Python. 120fr, Crocodile.

1976, Mar. 31 Litho. *Perf. 12½*

250 A86 20fr multicolored 8 5
251 " 30fr " 12 5
252 " 40fr " 17 8
253 " 90fr " 35 18
254 " 120fr " 50 32
Nos. 250-254 (5) 1.22 68

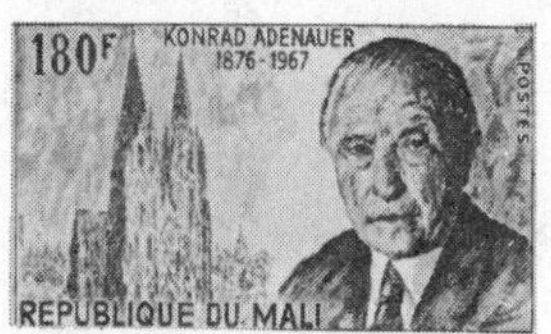

Konrad Adenauer and Cologne Cathedral—A87

1976, Apr. 26 Engr. *Perf. 13*

255	A87	180fr magenta & dark brown	70	40

Konrad Adenauer (1876–1967), German Chancellor, birth centenary.

Fish Type of 1975

1976, June 28 Engr. *Perf. 13*

Multicolored

256	A80	100fr *Heterotis niloticus*	40	25
257	"	120fr *Synodontis budgetti*	50	28
258	"	130fr *Heterobranchus bidorsalis*	55	28
259	"	150fr *Tilapia monodi*	60	32
260	"	220fr *Alestes macrolepidotus*	85	50
		Nos. 256–260 (5)	2.90	1.63

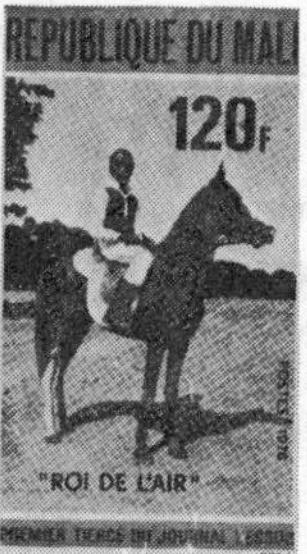

Page from Children's Book A88 — "Le Roi de l'Air" A89

1976, July 19

261	A88	130fr red & multi.	50	30

Books for children.

1976, July 26 Litho. *Perf. 12½x13*

262	A89	120fr multicolored	45	25

First lottery, sponsored by L'Essor newspaper.

"Do not overload scaffold"

A90

1976, Aug. 16 Litho. *Perf. 13*

263	A90	120fr multicolored	45	25

National Insurance Institute, 20th anniversary.

Letters, UPU and UN Emblems—A91

1976, Oct. 4 Engr. *Perf. 13*

264	A91	120fr lilac, orange & green	45	25

United Nations Postal Administration, 25th anniversary.

Moto-Guzzi 254, Italy—A92

Motorcycles: 120fr, BMW 900, Germany. 130fr, Honda-Egli, Japan. 140fr, Motobecane LT-3, France.

1976, Oct. 18 Engr. *Perf. 13*

265	A92	90fr multicolored	35	20
266	"	120fr "	48	28
267	"	130fr "	52	28
268	"	140fr "	55	35

Fishing Boat, Masgat—A93

Designs: 180fr, Coaster, Cochin China. 190fr, Fireboat, Dunkirk, 1878. 200fr, Nile river boat.

1976, Dec. 6 Engr. *Perf. 13*

269	A93	160fr multicolored	65	28
270	"	180fr "	70	35
271	"	190fr "	75	40
272	"	200fr "	80	40

Indigo Finch A94

Birds: 25fr, Yellow-breasted barbet. 30fr, Vitelline masked weaver. 40fr, Bee-eater. 50fr, Senegal parrot.

1977, Apr. 18 Photo. *Perf. 13*

273	A94	15fr multicolored	6	5
274	"	25fr "	10	6
275	"	30fr "	12	8
276	"	40fr "	16	8
277	"	50fr "	20	12
		Nos 273–277 (5)	64	39

See Nos. 298–302.

A particular stamp may be scarce, but if few want it, its market potential may remain relatively low.

Braille Statue, Script and Reading Hands—A95

1977, Apr. 25 Engr. *Perf. 13*

278	A95	200fr multicolored	80	45

Louis Braille (1809–1852), inventor of the reading and writing system for the blind.

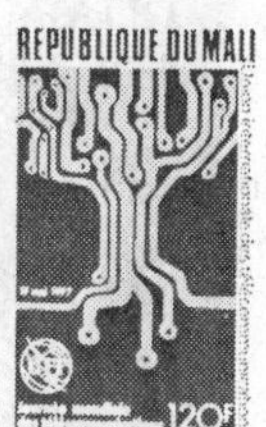

Electronic Tree, ITU Emblem A96

1977, May 17 Photogravure

279	A96	120fr dk. brn. & org.	48	28

World Telecommunications Day.

Dragonfly A97

Insects: 10fr, Praying mantis. 20fr, Tropical wasp. 35fr, Cockchafer. 60fr, Flying stag beetle.

1977, June 15 Photo. *Perf. 13x12½*

280	A97	5fr multicolored	3	3
281	"	10fr "	4	3
282	"	20fr "	8	6
283	"	35fr "	14	10
284	"	60fr "	24	15
		Nos. 280–284 (5)	53	37

Knight and Rook A98

Chess Pieces: 130fr, Bishop and pawn (vert.). 300fr, Queen and King.

1977, June 27 Engr. *Perf. 13*

285	A98	120fr multicolored	50	28
286	"	130fr "	50	28
287	"	300fr "	1.20	70

Europafrica Issue

Symbolic Ship, White and Brown Persons A99

1977, July 18 Litho. *Perf. 13*

288	A99	400fr multicolored	1.60	1.00

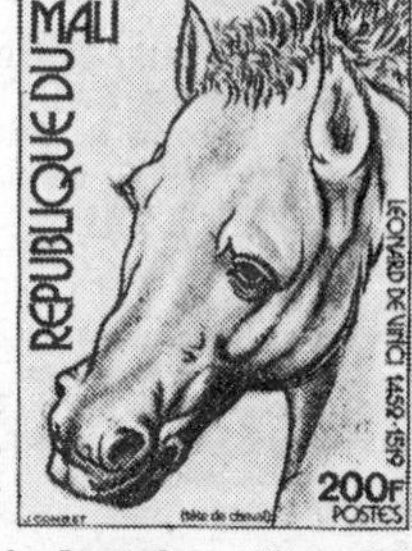

Horse, by Leonardo da Vinci A100

Drawings by Leonardo da Vinci: 300fr, Head of Young Woman. 500fr, Self-portrait.

1977, Sept. 5 Engr. *Perf. 13*

289	A100	200fr dk. brown & black	80	50
290	"	300fr dk. brown & olive	1.20	65
291	"	500fr dk. brown & red	2.00	95

Hotel de l'Amitié, Bamako—A101

1977, Oct. 15 Litho. *Perf. 13x12½*

292	A101	120fr multicolored	50	28

Opening of the Hotel de l'Amitié, Oct. 15.

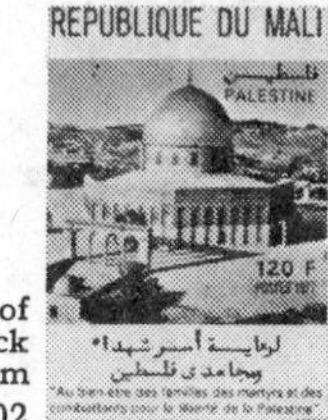

Dome of the Rock Jerusalem A102

1977, Oct. 17 *Perf. 12½*

293	A102	120fr multicolored	50	28
294	"	180fr "	70	40

Palestinian fighters and their families.

Black Man, Chains and UN Emblem A103

Design: 130fr, Statue of Liberty, people and UN emblem. 180fr, Black children and horse behind fence.

1978, Mar. 13 Engr. *Perf. 13*

295	A103	120fr multicolored	50	28
296	"	130fr "	50	28
297	"	180fr "	70	40

International Year against Apartheid.

Bird Type of 1977

Birds: 20fr, Granatine bengala. 30fr, Lagonosticta vinacea. 50fr, Lagonosticta. 70fr, Turtle dove. 80fr, Buffalo weaver.

1978, Apr. 10 Litho. *Perf. 13*

298	A94	20fr multicolored	8	5
299	"	30fr "	12	8
300	"	50fr "	20	12
301	"	70fr "	28	16
302	"	80fr "	32	20
		Nos. 298–302 (5)	1.00	61

Nos. 232–233 Surcharged with New Value, Bar and: "XXe ANNIVERSAIRE DU LIONS CLUB DE BAMAKO 1958–1978"

1978, May 8 **Photogravure**

303	A79	120fr on 90fr multi.	48	25
304	"	130fr on 100fr "	52	27

20th anniversary of Bamako Lions Club.

UPU Emblem, World Map, Country Names—A104

1978, May 15 **Engraved**

305	A104	120fr multicolored	48	25

Centenary of Congress of Paris where General Postal Union became Universal Postal Union. See No. C335.

Wall and Desert—A105

1978, May 18 **Litho.** ***Perf. 13***

306	A105	200fr multicolored	80	40

Hammamet Conference for reclamation of the desert.

Mahatma Gandhi and Roses A106

1978, May 29 **Engraved**

307	A106	140fr black, brown & red	55	28

Mohandas K. Gandhi (1869–1948), Hindu spiritual leader, 30th death anniversary.

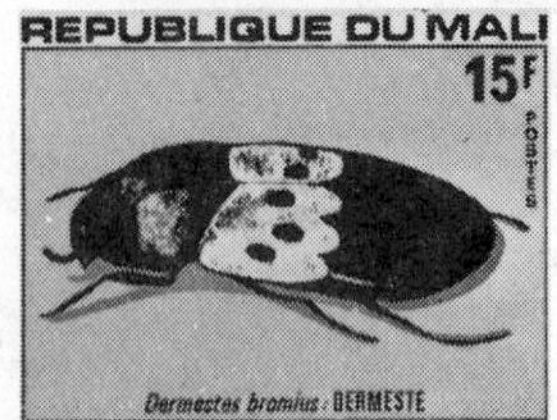

Dermestes—A107

Insects: 25fr, Ground beetle. 90fr, Cricket. 120fr, Ladybird. 140fr, Goliath beetle.

1978, June 12 **Photo.** ***Perf. 13***

308	A107	15fr multicolored	6	4
309	"	25fr "	10	6
310	"	90fr "	35	20
311	"	120fr "	50	28
312	"	140fr "	55	30
		Nos. 308-312 (5)	1.56	88

Bridge—A108

Design: 100fr, Dominoes (vert.).

1978, June 26 **Engraved**

313	A108	100fr multicolored	40	20
314	"	130fr "	52	27

Aristotle A109

1978, Oct. 16 **Engr.** ***Perf. 13***

315	A109	200fr multicolored	80	40

Aristotle (384–322 B.C.), Greek philosopher.

Human Rights and UN Emblems A110

1978, Dec. 11 **Engr.** ***Perf. 13***

316	A110	180fr red, bl. & brn.	72	35

Universal Declaration of Human Rights, 30th anniversary.

SEMI-POSTAL STAMPS

Anti-Malaria Issue

Common Design Type

Perf. 12½x12

1962, Apr. 7 Engraved Unwmkd.

B1 CD108 25fr+5fr pale violet blue 75 75

Issued for the World Health Organization drive to eradicate malaria.

Algerian Family SP1

1962, Dec. 24 Photo. ***Perf. 12x12½***

B2 SP1 25fr+5fr multicolored 35 35

Issued for the national campaign to show the solidarity of the peoples of Mali and Algeria.

AIR POST STAMPS

Federation

Composite View of St. Louis, Senegal AP1

Engraved.

1959, Dec. 11 ***Perf. 13*** **Unwmkd.**

C1 AP1 85fr multicolored 1.50 1.25

Issued to commemorate the tercentenary of the founding of St. Louis, Senegal, and to honor the opening of the 6th meeting of the executive council of the French Community.

Amethyst Starling AP2

Birds: 200fr, Bateleur eagle (horiz.). 500fr, Barbary shrike.

Perf. 12½x13, 13x12½

1960, Feb. 13 Photogravure

Birds in Natural Colors.

C2 AP2 100fr multicolored 2.00 1.50
C3 " 200fr " 4.00 2.25
C4 " 500fr black & blue 10.00 6.75

Republic

Nos. C2-C4 Overprinted or Surcharged "REPUBLIQUE DU MALI" and Bars.

1960, Dec. 18

Birds in Natural Colors

C5 AP2 100fr multicolored 2.00 1.40
C6 " 200fr " 3.50 2.25
C7 AP2 300fr on 500fr black & blue 5.50 4.50
C8 " 500fr black & blue 9.50 6.75

Pres. Modibo Keita AP3

Designs: 200fr, Mamadou Konate.

1961, Mar. 18 Engr. ***Perf. 13***

C9 AP3 200fr claret & gray brown 2.50 1.10
C10 " 300fr grn. & black 3.25 1.35

Flag, Map, U.N. Emblem—AP4

1961, Mar. 18

C11 AP4 100fr multicolored 1.25 90
a. Miniature sheet of 3 2.50 2.50

Proclamation of independence and admission to U.N.

No. C11a contains one each of Nos. 13, 14 and C11. Size: 158x99mm.

Sankore Mosque, Timbuktu AP5

Designs: 200fr, View of Timbuktu. 500fr, Bamako and arms.

1961, Apr. 15 ***Perf. 13*** **Unwmkd.**

C12 AP5 100fr Prussian blue, red brown & gray 1.25 40
C13 " 200fr green, brown & red 2.50 1.25
C14 " 500fr red brown, Prussian blue & dk. green 7.00 2.50

Issued for the inauguration of Timbuktu airport and Air Mali.

Bull, Chemical Equipment and Chicks—AP6

1963, Feb. 23 Engraved

C15 AP6 200fr bister, maroon & greenish blue 2.25 1.10

Sotuba Zootechnical Institute.

Air Ambulance—AP7

Designs: 55fr, National Line plane loading. 100fr, International Line Vickers Viscount in flight.

1963, Nov. 2 ***Perf. 13*** **Unwmkd.**

C16 AP7 25fr dark blue, emerald & red brown 35 20
C17 " 55fr bister, blue & red brown 75 40
C18 " 100fr dk. bl., red brn. & yel. grn. 1.25 65

Issued to publicize Air Mali.

Crowned Crane and Giant Tortoise AP8

1963, Nov. 23 ***Perf. 13*** **Unwmkd.**

C19 AP8 25fr sepia, orange & vermilion 60 40
C20 " 200fr multicolored 2.75 1.85

Animal protection.

U.N. Emblem, Flag, Doves—AP9

1963, Dec. 10 **Engraved**

C21 AP9 50fr light green, yellow & red 60 40

Issued to commemorate the 15th anniversary of the Universal Declaration of Human Rights.

Cleopatra and Ptolemy at Kôm Ombo AP10

1964, March 9 ***Perf. 12*** **Unwmkd.**

C22 AP10 25fr deep claret & bister 50 28
C23 " 55fr deep claret & lt. olive grn. 90 55

Issued to publicize the UNESCO world campaign to save historic monuments in Nubia.

Pres. John F. Kennedy—AP11

1964, Oct. 26 Photo. ***Perf. 12½***

C24 AP11 100fr salmon, red brn. & blk. 1.35 1.10
a. Souv. sheet of 4 6.00 6.00

Issued in memory of Pres. John F. Kennedy (1917-1963). No. C24a contains four No. C24. Dark brown marginal inscription. Size: 119x90mm.

Touracos—AP12

Birds: 200fr, Abyssinian ground hornbills (vert.). 300fr, Egyptian vultures (vert.). 500fr, Goliath herons.

1965, Feb. 15 Engraved ***Perf. 13***

C25 AP12 100fr green, dark blue & red 1.50 80
C26 " 200fr black, red & brt. blue 2.50 1.20
C27 " 300fr black, slate grn. & yel. 4.00 2.00
C28 " 500fr slate green, dk. brn. & claret 6.75 3.50

U.N. Headquarters, New York, and ICY Emblem AP13

1965, Mar. 15 ***Perf. 13*** **Unwmkd.**

C29 AP13 55fr bister, dk. bl. & violet brn. 70 45

International Cooperation Year.

Pope John XXIII AP14

Perf. 12½x13

1965, Sept. 14 Photo. Unwmkd.

C30 AP14 100fr multi. 1.40 85

Issued in memory of Pope John XXIII (1881-1963).

Winston Churchill
AP15

1965, Oct. 11 Engraved ***Perf. 13***

C31 AP15 100fr brn. & indigo 1.40 90

Issued in memory of Sir Winston Spencer Churchill (1874–1965), statesman and World War II leader.

Dr. Albert Schweitzer and Sick Child
AP16

1965, Dec. 20 Photo. ***Perf. 12½***

C32 AP16 100fr multicolored 1.50 85
a. Souv. sheet of 4 6.00 5.00

Issued in memory of Dr. Albert Schweitzer (1875–1965), medical missionary to Gabon, winner of Nobel peace prize. No. C32a contains 4 of No. C32. Ultramarine marginal inscription. Size: 160x140mm.

Major Edward H. White and Gemini 4—AP17

Designs: No. C34, Lt. Col. Alexei A. Leonov. 300fr, Gordon Cooper, Charles Conrad, Alexei Leonov and Pavel Belyayev, Parthenon, Athens, and vase (vert.).

1966, Jan. 10

C33 AP17 100fr violet, yel., lt blue & blk. 1.20 60
C34 " 100fr blue, red, yel. & blk. 1.20 60
C35 " 300fr multicolored 3.25 2.00

Issued to honor achievements in space research and to commemorate the 16th International Astronautical Congress, Athens, Sept. 12–18, 1965.

Papal Arms and U.N. Emblem
AP18

1966, July 11 Engraved ***Perf. 13***

C36 AP18 200fr bright blue, greenish bl. & green 2.40 80

Issued to commemorate the visit of Pope Paul VI to the United Nations, New York, Oct. 4, 1965.

People and UNESCO Emblem
AP19

1966, Sept. 5 Engraved ***Perf. 13***

C37 AP19 100fr dk. car. rose, slate green & ultra. 1.15 65

Issued to commemorate the 20th anniversary of the United Nations Educational, Scientific and Cultural Organization (UNESCO).

Soccer Players, Ball, Globe, and Jules Rimet Cup—AP20

1966, Oct. 31 Photo. ***Perf. 13***

C38 AP20 100fr multicolored 1.15 65

Issued to commemorate the 8th International Soccer Championship Games, Wembley, England, July 11–30.

Crab and Mt. Fuji—AP21

UNICEF Emblem and Children
AP22

1966, Nov. 30 Photo. ***Perf. 13***

C39 AP21 100fr multicolored 1.10 50

Issued to commemorate the 9th International Anticancer Congress, Tokyo, Oct. 23–29.

1966, Dec. 10 Engraved

C40 AP22 45fr deep blue, bister brown & red lilac 55 25

Issued to commemorate the 20th anniversary of UNICEF (United Nations Children's Emergency Fund).

Land Cruisers in Hoggar Mountain Pass—AP23

1967, March 20 Engraved ***Perf. 13***

C41 AP23 200fr multicolored 2.50 1.25

Issued to commemorate the "Black Cruise 1924," which crossed Africa from Beni-Abbes, Algeria to the Indian Ocean and on to Tananarive, Madagascar, Oct. 28, 1924–June 26, 1925.

Diamant Rocket and Francesco de Lana's 1650 Flying Boat
AP24

Designs: 100fr, A-1 satellite and rocket launching adapted from Jules Verne. 200fr, D-1 satellite and Leonardo da Vinci's bird-borne flying machine.

1967, Apr. 17 Engraved ***Perf. 13***

C42 AP24 50fr brt. blue, pur. & green 60 35
C43 " 100fr dk. Prus. blue, dk. carmine & lilac 1.40 70
C44 " 200fr slate bl., olive & purple 2.40 1.00

Issued to honor French achievements in space.

Amelia Earhart and Map of Mali
AP25

1967, May 29 Photo. ***Perf. 13***

C45 AP25 500fr blue & multi. 5.50 2.50

Issued to commemorate the 30th anniversary of Amelia Earhart's stop at Gao, West Africa.

Paul as Harlequin, by Picasso—AP26

Picasso Paintings: 50fr, Bird Cage. 250fr, The Flutes of Pan.

1967, June 16 ***Perf. 12½***

C46 AP26 50fr multicolored 60 33
C47 " 100fr " 1.15 65
C48 " 250fr " 2.75 1.50

See also No. C82.

Jamboree Emblem, Scout Knots and Badges
AP27

Design: 100fr, Scout with portable radio transmitter, tents and Jamboree badge.

1967, July 10 Engraved ***Perf. 13***

C49 AP27 70fr dk. carmine, emerald & blue green 65 35
C50 " 100fr dk. car. lake, slate green & black 1.00 45
a. Strip of 2 + label 2.00 1.75

Issued to publicize the 12th Boy Scout World Jamboree, Farragut State Park, Idaho, Aug. 1–9. No. C50a contains one each of Nos. C49–C50 and label showing emblem in light ultramarine.

Head of Horse, by Toulouse-Lautrec—AP28

Design: 300fr, Cob-drawn gig, by Toulouse-Lautrec (vert.).

Perf. 12x12½, 12½x12

1967, Dec. 11 Photogravure

C51 AP28 100fr multicolored 1.20 80
C52 " 300fr " 3.50 1.50

See Nos. C66–C67.

Grenoble
AP29

Design: 150fr, Bobsled course on Huez Alp.

1968, Jan. 8 Engraved ***Perf. 13***

C53 AP29 50fr blue, yel. brn. & green 40 15
C54 " 150fr brown, vio. bl. & steel bl. 1.00 45

10th Winter Olympic Games, Grenoble, France, Feb. 6–18.

Roses and Anemones, by Van Gogh
AP30

Paintings: 150fr, Peonies in Vase, by Edouard Manet (vert. 36x49mm.). 300fr, Bouquet, by Delacroix (41x42mm). 500fr, Daisies in Vase, by Jean François Millet (horiz. 49x37mm.).

Perf. 13, 12½x12, 12x12½

1968, June 24 Photogravure

C55 AP30 50fr multicolored 40 20
C56 " 150fr grn. & multi. 1.00 45
C57 " 300fr " " 1.75 1.00
C58 " 500fr car. & multi. 3.25 1.40

Martin Luther King, Jr.
AP31

Long Jumper and Satellite
AP32

1968, July 22 ***Perf. 12½***

C59 AP31 100fr rose lilac, sal. pink & black 55 25

Issued in memory of the Rev. Dr. Martin Luther King, Jr. (1929–1968), American civil rights leader.

Bicycle Type of Regular Issue

Designs: 50fr, Bicyclette, 1918. 100fr, Mercedes Benz, 1927 (horiz.).

1968, Aug. 12 Engraved ***Perf. 13***

C60 A40 50fr gray, dk. green & brick red 35 30

C61 " 100fr lemon, indigo & carmine 70 35

1968, Nov. 25 Photo. ***Perf. 12½***

Design: 100fr, Soccer goalkeeper and satellite (horiz.).

C62 AP32 100fr multicolored 65 40

C63 " 150fr " 1.00 50

Issued to commemorate the 19th Olympic Games, Mexico City, Oct. 12–27.

PHILEXAFRIQUE Issue

Editorial Department, by François Marius Granet
AP33

1968, Dec. 23 Photo. ***Perf. 12½x12***

C64 AP33 200fr multicolored 1.30 1.00

Issued to publicize PHILEXAFRIQUE Philatelic Exhibition in Abidjan, Feb. 14–23. Printed with alternating light green label.

See also Nos. C85–C87, C110–C112, C205–C207, C216–C217.

2nd PHILEXAFRIQUE Issue

Common Design Type

Design: 100fr, French Sudan No. 64 and sculpture.

1969, Feb. 14 Engraved ***Perf. 13***

C65 CD128 100fr pur. & multi. 75 75

Issued to commemorate the opening of PHILEXAFRIQUE, Abidjan, Feb. 14.

Painting Type of 1967

Paintings: 150fr, Napoleon as First Consul, by Antoine Jean Gros (vert.). 250fr, Bivouac at Austerlitz, by Louis François Lejeune.

Perf. 12½x12, 12x12½

1969, Feb. 25 Photogravure

C66 AP28 150fr multi. 1.75 1.10

C67 " 250fr " 2.50 1.75

Issued to commemorate the 200th anniversary of the birth of Napoleon Bonaparte (1769–1821).

Concorde—AP34

Designs: 50fr, Montgolfier's balloon. 150fr, Ferber 5, experimental biplane.

1969, Mar. 10 Photo. ***Perf. 13***

C68 AP34 50fr multicolored 40 20

C69 " 150fr " 1.00 40

C70 " 300fr " 2.00 1.10

Issued to commemorate the first flight of the prototype Concorde plane at Toulouse, France, March 1, 1969. Nos. C68–C70 are printed se-tenant.

Auto Type of Regular Issue

Designs: 55fr, Renault, 1898, and Renault 16, 1969. 90fr, Peugeot, 1893, and Peugeot 404, 1969.

1969, May 30 Engraved ***Perf. 13***

C71 A43 55fr rose car., blk. & brt. pink 40 30

C72 " 90fr black, dp. car. & indigo 60 30

Ronald Clark, Australia, 10,000-meter Run, 1965
AP35

World Records: 90fr, Yanis Lusis, USSR, Javelin, 1968. 120fr, Yoshinobu Miyake, Japan, weight lifting, 1967. 140fr, Randy Matson, USA, shot put, 1968. 150fr, Kipchoge Keino, Kenya, 3,000-meter run, 1965.

1969, June 23 Engraved ***Perf. 13***

C73 AP35 60fr bl. & olive brn. 35 20

C74 " 90fr carmine rose & red brown 55 32

C75 " 120fr emerald & gray olive 70 32

C76 " 140fr gray & brown 90 40

C77 " 150fr red org. & blk. 1.00 50

Nos. C73–C77 (5) 3.50 1.74

Issued to honor sports world records.

Nos. C68–C70 Overprinted in Red with Lunar Landing Module and: "L'HOMME SUR LA LUNE / JUILLET 1969 / APOLLO 11"

1969, July 25 Photo. ***Perf. 13***

C78 AP34 50fr multicolored 65 45

C79 " 150fr " 1.65 1.25

C80 " 300fr " 3.25 2.50

Man's first landing on moon, July 20, 1969. U.S. astronauts Neil A. Armstrong and Col. Edwin E. Aldrin, Jr., with Lieut. Col. Michael Collins piloting Apollo 11. Printed se-tenant.

Apollo 8, Moon and Earth
AP35a

Embossed on Gold Foil

1969, July 24 ***Die-cut Perf. 10½***

C81 AP35a 2000fr gold 13.50 13.50

Issued to commemorate the U.S. Apollo 8 mission, the first men in orbit around the moon, Dec. 21–27, 1968.

Painting Type of 1967

Design: 500fr, Mona Lisa, by Leonardo da Vinci.

1969, Oct. 20 Photo. ***Perf. 12½***

C82 AP26 500fr multicolored 4.50 3.25

Mahatma Gandhi
AP36

1969, Nov. 24 Engraved ***Perf. 13***

C83 AP36 150fr brt. bl., olive brown & red brown 1.00 50

Issued to commemorate the centenary of the birth of Mohandas K. Gandhi (1869–1948), leader in India's fight for independence.

Map of West Africa, Post Horns and Lightning Bolts—AP37

1970, Feb. 23 Photo. ***Perf. 12½***

C84 AP37 100fr multicolored 65 40

Issued to commemorate the 11th anniversary of the West African Postal Union (CAPTEAO).

Painting Type of 1968

Paintings: 100fr, Madonna and Child, from Rogier van der Weyden school. 150fr, Nativity, by the master of Flemalle. 250fr, Madonna and Child with St. John, from the Dutch School.

1970, Mar. 2

C85 AP33 100fr multicolored 75 45

C86 " 150fr " 1.10 70

C87 " 250fr " 1.75 1.10

Roosevelt
AP38

Lenin
AP39

1970, Mar. 30 Photo. ***Perf. 12½***

C88 AP38 500fr red, lt. ultra. & black 4.00 2.00

Issued to commemorate the 25th anniversary of the death of Pres. Franklin Delano Roosevelt (1882–1945), 32nd president of the United States.

1970, Apr. 22

C89 AP39 300fr pink, green & black 1.90 80

Issued to commemorate the centenary of the birth of Lenin (1870–1924), Russian communist leader.

Jules Verne and Firing of Moon Rockets—AP40

Designs: 150fr, Jules Verne, rockets, landing modules and moon. 300fr, Jules Verne and splashdown.

1970, May 4

C90 AP40 50fr multicolored 35 18

C91 " 150fr " 1.10 45

C92 " 300fr " 2.10 85

Issued to honor Jules Verne (1828–1905), French science-fiction writer.

Nos. C90–C92 Overprinted in Red or Blue: "APOLLO XIII / EPOPEE SPATIALE / 11–17 AVRIL 1970"

1970, June Photo. ***Perf. 12½***

C93 AP40 50fr multi. (Bl) 40 28

C94 " 150fr " (R) 1.10 45

C95 " 300fr " (Bl) 2.25 1.30

Issued to commemorate the space flight and safe return of Apollo 13, Apr. 11–13, 1970.

Intelsat III—AP41

Telecommunications Through Space: 200fr, Molniya I satellite. 300fr, Radar. 500fr, "Project Symphony" (various satellites).

1970, July 13 Engraved ***Perf. 13***

C96 AP41 100fr gray, brt. bl. & orange 70 40

C97 " 200fr blue, gray & red lilac 1.40 65

C98 " 300fr org., dk. brn. & gray 2.10 95

C99 " 500fr dk. brn., slate & greenish blue 3.50 1.60

Auguste and Louis Lumière, Jean Harlow and Marilyn Monroe—AP42

1970, July 27 Photo. ***Perf. 12½x12***

C100 AP42 250fr multi. 1.40 80

Issued to honor Auguste Lumière (1862–1954), and his brother Louis Jean Lumière (1864–1948), inventors of the Lumière process of color photography and of a motion picture camera.

Soccer—AP43

1970, Sept. 7 Engraved *Perf. 13*

C101	AP43	80fr bl., dp. car. & brown olive	50	25
C102	"	200fr deep carmine, blue green & olive brn.	1.15	65

Issued to commemorate the 9th World Soccer Championships for the Jules Rimet Cup, Mexico City, May 30–June 21, 1970.

Rotary Emblem, Map of Mali and Ceremonial Antelope Heads AP44

Men Holding U.N. Emblem, and Doves AP45

1970, Sept. 21 Photo. *Perf. 12½*

C103	AP44	200fr multi.	1.15	65

Issued to honor Rotary International.

1970, Oct. 5 Engraved *Perf. 13*

C104	AP45	100fr dark purple, red brn. & dark blue	55	35

25th anniversary of the United Nations.

Koran Page, Baghdad, 11th Century AP46

Moslem Art: 200fr, Tree, and lion killing deer, mosaic, Jordan, c. 730 (horiz.). 250fr, Scribe, miniature, Baghdad, 1287.

1970, Oct. 26 Photo. *Perf. 12½x12*

C105	AP46	50fr multicolored	33	20
C106	"	200fr "	90	45
C107	"	250fr "	1.10	55

Nos. C97–C98 Surcharged and Overprinted: "LUNA 16 / PREMIERS PRELEVEMENTS AUTOMATIQUES / SUR LA LUNE / SEPTEMBRE 1970"

1970, Nov. 9 Engraved *Perf. 13*

C108	AP41	150fr on 200fr multi.	90	45
C109	"	250fr on 300fr multi.	1.50	65

Issued to commemorate the unmanned moon probe of the Russian space ship Luna 16, Sept. 12–24.

Painting Type of 1968

Paintings: 100fr, Nativity, Antwerp School, c. 1530. 250fr, St. John the Baptist, by Hans Memling. 300fr, Adoration of the Kings, Flemish School, 17th century.

1970, Dec. 1 Photo. *Perf. 12½x12*

C110	AP33	100fr brn. & multi.	65	33
C111	"	250fr " "	1.30	65
C112	"	300fr " "	1.90	80

Christmas 1970.

Gamal Abdel Nasser AP47

Embossed on Gold Foil.

1970, Nov. 25 *Perf. 12½*

C113	AP47	1000fr gold	7.25	7.25

In memory of Gamal Abdel Nasser (1918–1970), President of Egypt.

Charles de Gaulle AP48

Embossed on Gold Foil

1971, Feb. 8 *Die-cut Perf. 10*

C114	AP48	2000fr gold, red & dp. ultra.	17.50	17.50

In memory of Gen. Charles de Gaulle (1890–1970), President of France.

Alfred Nobel AP49

Tennis, Davis Cup—AP50

1971, Feb. 22 Engraved *Perf. 13*

C115	AP49	300fr claret, brt. green & dk. brown	1.40	90

75th anniversary of the death of Alfred Nobel (1833–1896), inventor of dynamite, sponsor of Nobel Prize.

1971, Mar. 8

Designs: 150fr, Derby at Epsom (horiz.). 200fr, Racing yacht, America's Cup.

C116	AP50	100fr blue, lilac & slate	40	20
C117	"	150fr brn., brt. grn. & olive	55	25
C118	"	200fr brt. bl., olive & brown	1.00	35

The Arabian Nights—AP51

Designs: 180fr, Ali Baba and the 40 Thieves. 200fr, Aladdin's Lamp.

1971, Apr. 5 Photo. *Perf. 13*

C119	AP51	120fr gold & multi.	50	33
C120	"	180fr " "	65	40
C121	"	200fr " "	1.00	55

Olympic Rings and Sports—AP52

1971, June 28 Photo. *Perf. 12½*

C122	AP52	80fr ultra., yellow grn. & brt. magenta	35	18

Pre-Olympic Year.

Mariner 4—AP53

Design: 300fr, Venera 5 in space.

1971, Sept. 13 Engraved *Perf. 13*

C123	AP53	200fr bl., ocher & brt. green	85	45
C124	"	300fr dk. pur., brt. rose lilac & dk. bl.	1.25	65

Space explorations of U.S. Mariner 4 (200fr); and U.S.S.R. Venera 5 (300fr).

Santa Maria, 1492—AP54

Famous Ships: 150fr, Mayflower, 1620. 200fr, Potemkin, 1905. 250fr, Normandie, 1935.

1971, Sept. 27

C125	AP54	100fr brn., bluish grn. & pur.	35	20
C126	"	150fr slate grn., brn. & purple	55	30
C127	"	200fr car., blue & dk. olive	90	50
C128	"	250fr black, blue & red	1.10	65

Symbols of Justice and Maps—AP55

1971, Oct. 18

C129	AP55	160fr maroon, ocher & dk. brn.	75	35

25th anniversary of the International Court of Justice in The Hague, Netherlands.

Statue of Zeus, by Phidias AP56

Nat "King" Cole AP57

The Seven Wonders of the Ancient World: 80fr, Cheops Pyramid and Sphinx. 100fr, Temple of Artemis, Ephesus (horiz.). 130fr, Lighthouse at Alexandria. 150fr, Hanging Gardens of Babylon (horiz.). 270fr, Mausoleum of Halicarnassus. 280fr, Colossus of Rhodes.

1971, Dec. 13

C130	AP56	70fr indigo, dark red & pink	32	18
C131	"	80fr brown, blue & black	35	18
C132	"	100fr orange, indigo & purple	45	25
C133	"	130fr rose lilac, blk. & greenish blue	60	25
C134	"	150fr brown, bright grn. & blue	65	25
C135	"	270fr slate, brown & plum	1.20	32
C136	"	280fr slate lilac & olive	1.25	32
		Nos. C130–C136 (7)	4.82	1.75

1971, Dec. 6 Photo. *Perf. 13x12½*

Famous American Black Musicians: 150fr, Erroll Garner. 270fr, Louis Armstrong.

C137	AP57	130fr black, brown & yellow	60	25
C138	"	150fr black, blue & yellow	65	28
C139	"	270fr black, rose carmine & yellow	1.20	50

Slalom and Japanese Child AP58

Design: 200fr, Ice hockey and character from Noh play.

1972, Jan. 10 Engraved *Perf. 13*

C140	AP58	150fr slate green, dk. brown & red	65	30
C141	"	200fr red, slate green & dk. brown	90	50
		a. Souvenir sheet of 2	2.00	2.00

11th Winter Olympic Games, Sapporo, Japan, Feb. 3–13. No. C141a contains one each of Nos. C140–C141 with brown and red center label showing Olympic rings. Size: 159x100mm.

Santa Maria della Salute, by Ippolito Caffi—AP59

Paintings of Venice, by Ippolito Caffi: 270fr, Rialto Bridge. 280fr, St. Mark's Square (vert.).

1972, Feb. 21 Photo. *Perf. 13*

C142 AP59 130fr gold & multi. 70 32
C143 " 270fr gold & multi. 1.20 65
C144 " 280fr gold & multi. 1.30 80

UNESCO campaign to save Venice.

Hands of 4 Races Holding Scout Flag AP60

1972, Mar. 27 Engr. *Perf. 13*

C145 AP60 200fr dk. red, ocher & olive gray 85 40

World Boy Scout Seminar, Cotonou, Dahomey, March, 1972.

"Your Heart is your Health"—AP61

1972, Apr. 7 Engr. *Perf. 13*

C146 AP61 150fr brt. bl. & red 65 40

World Health Day.

Soccer Player and Frauenkirche, Munich—AP62

Designs (Sport and Munich Landmarks): 150fr, Wrestling and TV Tower (vert.). 200fr, High hurdles and Propylaeum (vert.). 300fr, Runner and Church of the Theatines.

1972, Apr. 17

C147 AP62 50fr ocher, dk. bl. & green 30 12
C148 " 150fr dk. bl., ocher & green 70 32
C149 " 200fr grn., dk. blue & ocher 90 40
C150 " 300fr dk. bl., green & ocher 1.40 55
a. Miniature sheet of 4 4.25 4.25

20th Olympic Games, Munich, Aug. 26–Sept. 10. No. C150a contains one each of Nos. C147–C150. Size: 190x100mm.

Apollo 15, Lunar Rover, Landing Module—AP63

Design: 250fr, Cugnot's steam wagon and Montgolfier's Balloon.

1972, Apr. 27

C151 AP63 150fr verm., slate grn. & rose magenta 80 40
C152 " 250fr ultra., green & rose red 1.20 55

Development of transportation.

Cinderella AP64

Fairy Tales: 80fr, Puss in Boots. 150fr, Sleeping Beauty.

1972, June 19 Engr. *Perf. 13x12½*

C153 AP64 70fr car. rose, slate grn. & olive 40 20
C154 " 80fr choc., brt. grn. & dp. org. 50 28
C155 " 150fr vio., bl. & lilac 80 40

Charles Perrault (1628–1703), French writer.

Astronauts and Lunar Rover on Moon—AP65

1972, July 24 Engr. *Perf. 13*

C156 AP65 500fr olive bister, violet & brt. green 2.50 1.10

U.S. Apollo 16 moon mission, Apr. 15–27.

Book Year Emblem—AP66

1972, Aug. 7 Litho. *Perf. 12½*

C157 AP66 80fr blue, gold & green 40 25

International Book Year 1972.

Bamako Rotary Emblem with Crocodiles AP67

1972, Oct. 9 Engraved *Perf. 13*

C158 AP67 170fr dk. brn., red & ultra. 80 32

10th anniversary of the Bamako Rotary Club.

Hurdler, Olympic Rings, Melbourne Cathedral, Kangaroo—AP68

Designs (Olympic Rings and): 70fr, Boxing, Helsinki Railroad Station, arms of Finland (vert.). 140fr, Running, Colosseum, Roman wolf. 150fr, Weight lifting, Tokyo stadium, phoenix (vert.). 170fr, Swimming, University Library, Mexico City; Aztec sculpture. 210fr, Javelin, Munich Stadium, Arms of Munich. Stamps inscribed with name of gold medal winner of event shown.

1972, Nov. 13 Engr. *Perf. 13*

C159 AP68 70fr red, ocher & indigo 30 20
C160 " 90fr red brn., bl. & slate 40 25
C161 " 140fr brn., brt. grn. & olive gray 60 25
C162 " 150fr dark carmine, emerald & gray olive 65 28
C163 " 170fr red lilac, brn. & Prus. bl. 70 32
C164 " 210fr ultra., emerald & brick red 1.00 50
Nos. C159–C164 (6) 3.65 1.80

Retrospective of Olympic Games 1952–1972.

Nos. C148–C150 and C164 Overprinted:

a. JUDO / RUSKA / 2 MEDAILLES D'OR
b. STEEPLE / KEINO / MEDAILLE D'OR
c. MEDAILLE D'OR / 90m. 48
d. 100m.-200m. / BORZOV / 2 MEDAILLES D'OR

1972, Nov. 27 Engraved *Perf. 13*

C165 AP62 (*a*) 150fr multi. 65 35
C166 " (*b*) 200fr " 85 40
C167 AP68 (*c*) 210fr " 90 45
C168 AP62 (*d*) 300fr " 1.40 65

Gold medal winners in 20th Olympic Games: Wim Ruska, Netherlands, heavyweight judo (C165); Kipchoge Keino, Kenya, 3000m. steeplechase (C166); Klaus Wolfermann, Germany, javelin (C167); Valery Borzov, USSR, 100m., 200m. race (C168).

Emperor Haile Selassie AP69

1972, Dec. 26 Photo. *Perf. 12½*

C169 AP69 70fr green & multi. 35 20

80th birthday of Emperor Haile Selassie of Ethiopia.

Plane, Balloon, Route Timbuktu to Bamako—AP70

Design: 300fr, Balloon, jet and route Timbuktu to Bamako.

1972, Dec. 29 *Perf. 13½*

C170 AP70 200fr multi. 1.00 45
C171 " 300fr bl. & multi. 1.40 65

First postal balloon flight in Mali.

Bishop of 14th Century European Chess Set AP71

Design: 200fr, Knight (elephant), from 18th century Indian set.

1973, Feb. 19 Engraved *Perf. 13*

C172 AP71 100fr dk. car., blue & indigo 60 30
C173 " 200fr black, red & brown 1.00 45

World Chess Championship, Reykjavik, Iceland, July–Sept., 1972.

Postal Union Emblem, Letter and Dove AP72

1973, Mar. 9 Photo. *Perf. 11½x11*

C174 AP72 70fr bl., blk. & org. 35 25

10th anniversary (in 1971) of African Postal Union.

No. C20, Collector's Hand and Philatelic Background AP73

1973, Mar. 12 Engraved *Perf. 13*

C175 AP73 70fr multicolored 45 25

Stamp Day, 1973.

Astronauts and Lunar Rover on Moon AP74

1973, Mar. 26

C176 AP74 250fr blue, indigo & bister 1.10 65

Souvenir Sheet

C177 AP74 350fr chocolate, violet blue & ultra. 1.65 1.65

Apollo 17 U.S. moon mission, Dec. 7–19, 1972. No. C177 contains one stamp. Apollo 17 badge and inscription in violet blue in margin. Size: 129x100mm.

Nicolaus Copernicus—AP75

1973, Apr. 9 **Engr.** ***Perf. 13***

C178 AP75 300fr brt. blue & magenta 1.50 75

500th anniversary of the birth of Nicolaus Copernicus (1473–1543), Polish astronomer.

Dr. Armauer G. Hansen and Leprosy Bacillus—AP76

1973, May 7 **Engraved** ***Perf. 13***

C179 AP76 200fr blk., yel. grn. & red 1.00 60

Centenary of the discovery of the Hansen bacillus, the cause of leprosy.

Bentley and Alfa Romeo, 1930—AP77

Designs: 100fr, Jaguar and Talbot, 1953. 200fr, Matra and Porsche, 1972.

1973, May 21 **Engr.** ***Perf. 13***

C180 AP77 50fr blue, orange & green 25 12
C181 " 100fr green, ultra. & carmine 50 20
C182 " 200fr indigo, green & carmine 1.00 40

50th anniversary of the 24-hour automobile race at Le Mans, France.

Camp Fire, Fleur-de-Lis
AP78

Designs (Fleur-de-Lis and): 70fr, Scouts saluting flag (vert.). 80fr, Scouts with flags. 130fr, Lord Baden-Powell (vert.). 270fr, Round dance and map of Africa.

1973, June 4

C183 AP78 50fr dk. red, ultra. & chocolate 25 15
C184 " 70fr slate grn., dk. brown & red 35 20
C185 " 80fr mag., slate grn. & olive 40 20
C186 " 130fr brn., ultra. & slate green 70 30
C187 " 270fr mag., gray & violet blue 1.35 70
Nos. C183–C187 (5) 3.05 1.55

Mali Boy and Girl Scouts and International Scouts Congress.

Swimming, US and "Africa" Flags
AP79

Designs (US, Africa Flags and): 80fr, Discus and javelin (vert.). 330fr, Runners.

1973, July 30 **Engraved** ***Perf. 13***

C188 AP79 70fr red, slate grn. & blue 35 20
C189 " 80fr vio. blue, dk. olive & red 45 25
C190 " 330fr red & violet blue 1.50 65

First African-United States Sports Meet.

Head and City Hall, Brussels
AP80

Perseus, by Benvenuto Cellini
AP81

1973, Sept. 17 **Engraved** ***Perf. 13***

C191 AP80 70fr brt. ultra., olive & vio. 35 20

Africa Weeks, Brussels, Sept. 15–30, 1973.

1973, Sept. 24

Famous Sculptures: 150fr, Pietá, by Michelangelo. 250fr, Victory of Samothrace, Greek 1st century B.C.

C192 AP81 100fr dk. carmine & slate grn. 50 32
C193 " 150fr dk. car. & dp. claret 70 40
C194 " 250fr dk. car. & dk. olive 1.25 65

Stephenson's Rocket and Buddicom Engine—AP82

Locomotives: 150fr, Union Pacific, 1890, and Santa Fe, 1940. 200fr, Mistral and Tokaido, 1970.

1973, Oct. 8 **Engraved** ***Perf. 13***

C195 AP82 100fr brown, blue & black 45 22
C196 " 150fr red, bright ultra. & dk. car. 70 32
C197 " 200fr ocher, blue & indigo 1.00 45

Canceled-to-order stamps are often from remainders. Most collectors of canceled stamps prefer postally used specimens.

Apollo XI on Moon
AP83

Designs: 75fr, Landing capsule, Apollo XIII. 100fr, Astronauts and equipment on moon, Apollo XIV. 280fr, Rover, landing module and astronauts on moon, Apollo XV. 300fr, Lift-off from moon, Apollo XVII.

1973, Oct. 25

C198 AP83 50fr vio., orange & slate green 25 15
C199 " 75fr slate, red & bl. 35 20
C200 " 100fr slate, blue & olive brown 50 25
C201 " 280fr vio. bl., red & slate green 1.25 55
C202 " 300fr slate, red & slate green 1.50 70
Nos. C198–C202 (5) 3.85 1.85

Apollo U.S. moon missions.

Pablo Picasso
AP84

John F. Kennedy
AP85

1973, Nov. 7 **Litho.** ***Perf. 12½***

C203 AP84 500fr multi. 2.50 1.25

Pablo Picasso (1881–1973), painter.

1973, Nov. 12

C204 AP85 500fr gold, bright rose lilac & black 2.50 1.25

10th anniversary of the death of President John F. Kennedy (1917–1963).

Painting Type of 1968

Paintings: 100fr, Annunciation, by Vittore Carpaccio (horiz.). 200fr, Virgin of St. Simon, by Federigo Baroccio. 250fr, Flight into Egypt, by Andrea Solario.

Perf. 13x12½, 12½x12, 12½x13

1973, Nov. 30 **Lithographed**

C205 AP33 100fr blk. & multi. 45 30
C206 " 200fr " " 1.00 45
C207 " 250fr " " 1.25 60

Christmas 1973.

Soccer Player and Ball
AP86

Designs: 250fr, Goalkeeper and ball. 500fr, Frauenkirche, Munich, Arms of Munich and soccer ball (horiz.).

1973, Dec. 3 **Engraved** ***Perf. 13***

C208 AP86 150fr emerald, ol. brn. & red 75 40
C209 " 250fr emerald, vio. blue & ol. brown 1.25 55

Souvenir Sheet

C210 AP86 500fr bl. & multi. 2.50 2.50

World Soccer Cup, Munich. No. C210 contains one stamp. Red marginal inscription and border. Size: 109x84mm.

Musicians, Mosaic from Pompeii
AP87

Designs (Mosaics from Pompeii): 250fr, Alexander the Great in battle (vert.). 350fr, Bacchants (vert.).

1974, Jan. 21 **Engraved** ***Perf. 13***

C211 AP87 150fr slate blue, olive & rose 70 40
C212 " 250fr mag., olive & ocher 1.25 65
C213 " 350fr olive, deep brn. & ocher 1.85 95

Winston Churchill
AP88

1974, Mar. 18 **Engraved** ***Perf. 13***

C214 AP88 500fr black 2.50 1.65

Centenary of the birth of Sir Winston Churchill (1874–1965), statesman.

Chess Game—AP89

1974, Mar. 25 **Engraved** ***Perf. 13***

C215 AP89 250fr multi. 1.35 65

21st Chess Olympic Games, Nice 1974.

Painting Type of 1968

Paintings: 400fr, Crucifixion, Alsatian School, c. 1380 (vert.). 500fr, Burial of Christ, by Titian.

Perf. 12½x13, 13x12½

1974, Apr. 12 **Photogravure**

C216 AP33 400fr multi. 1.85 1.00
C217 " 500fr " 2.25 1.10

Easter 1974.

Lenin—AP90

1974, Apr. 22 Engraved *Perf. 13*

C218	AP90	150fr vio. bl. & lake	60	30

50th anniversary of the death of Lenin.

Women's Steeplechase—AP91

1974, May 20 Engraved *Perf. 13*

C219	AP91	130fr blue, lilac & brown	60	35

World Horsewomen's Championship, La Baule, France, June 30–July 7.

Skylab Docking in Space—AP92

Design: 250fr, Skylab over globe with Africa.

1974, July 1 Engraved *Perf. 13*

C220	AP92	200fr blue, slate & org.	85	45
C221	"	250fr lilac, slate & org.	1.00	55

Skylab's flight over Africa, 1974.

Nos. C184–C185 Surcharged in Violet Blue with New Value, Two Bars and:

a. 11e JAMBOREE ARABE / AOUT 1974 LIBAN

b. CONGRES PANARABE LIBAN / AOUT 1974

1974, July 8 Engraved *Perf. 13*

C222	AP78	(*a*) 130fr on 70fr	60	40
C223	"	(*b*) 170fr on 80fr	85	60

11th Pan-Arab Jamboree and Pan-Arab Congress, Batrun, Lebanon, Aug. 1974.

Nos. C200–C201 Surcharged in Red with New Value, Two Bars and:

c. 1er DEBARQUEMENT / SUR LA LUNE / 20-VII-69

d. 1er PAS SUR LA / LUNE 21-VII-69

1974, July 15

C224	AP83	(*c*) 130fr on 100fr	55	40
C225	"	(*d*) 300fr on 280fr	1.25	65

First manned moon landing, July 20, 1969, and first step on moon, July 21, 1969.

1906 and 1939 Locomotives—AP93

Locomotives: 120fr, Baldwin, 1870, and Pacific, 1920. 210fr, Al., 1925, and Buddicom, 1847. 330fr, Hudson, 1938, and La Gironde, 1839.

1974, Oct. 7 Engraved *Perf. 13*

C226	AP93	90fr dk. carmine & multi.	40	25
C227	"	120fr ocher & multi.	50	30
C228	"	210fr org. & multi.	85	45
C229	"	330fr grn. & multi.	1.35	65

Skier, Winter Sports and Olympic Rings AP94

1974, Oct. 7

C230	AP94	300fr multi.	1.25	65

Holy Family, by Hans Memling AP95

Designs: 310fr, Virgin and Child, Bourgogne School. 400fr, Adoration of the Kings, by Martin Schongauer.

1974, Nov. 4 Photo. *Perf. 12½*

C231	AP95	290fr multi.	1.25	55
C232	"	310fr "	1.25	65
C233	"	400fr "	1.65	80

Christmas 1974.

See Nos. C238–C240, C267–C269.

Raoul Follereau AP96

1974, Nov. 18 Engraved *Perf. 13*

C234	AP96	200fr bright blue	85	50

Raoul Follereau (1903–1977), apostle to the lepers and educator of the blind.

Europafrica Issue

Train, Jet, Cogwheel, Grain, Maps of Africa and Europe—AP97

1974, Dec. 27 Engr. *Perf. 13*

C235	AP97	100fr brn., green & indigo	40	25
C236	"	110fr ocher, vio. bl. & purple	45	30

Painting Type of 1974

Designs: 200fr, Christ at Emmaus, by Phillipe de Champaigne (horiz.). 300fr, Christ at Emmaus, by Paolo Veronese (horiz.). 500fr, Christ in Majesty, Limoges, 13th century.

Perf. 13x12½, 12½x13

1975, Mar. 24 Lithographed

C238	AP95	200fr multicolored	85	50
C239	"	300fr "	1.25	65
C240	"	500fr "	2.00	1.10

Easter 1975.

"Voyage to the Center of the Earth"—AP99

Jules Verne's Stories: 170fr, "From Earth to Moon" and Verne's portrait. 190fr, "20,000 Leagues under the Sea." 220fr, "A Floating City."

1975, Apr. 7 Engraved *Perf. 13*

C241	AP99	100fr multicolored	40	28
C242	"	170fr "	70	40
C243	"	190fr "	80	45
C244	"	220fr "	90	55

Jules Verne (1828–1905), French science fiction writer.

Dawn, by Michelangelo AP100

Design: 500fr, Moses, by Michelangelo.

1975, Apr. 28 Photo. *Perf. 13*

C245	AP100	400fr multi.	1.65	1.00
C246	"	500fr "	2.00	1.25

500th birth anniversary of Michelangelo Buonarroti (1475–1564), Italian sculptor, painter and architect.

Astronaut on Moon AP101

Designs: 300fr, Constellations Virgo and Capricorn. 370fr, Statue of Liberty, Kremlin, Soyuz and Apollo spacecraft.

1975, May 19 Engraved *Perf. 13*

C247	AP101	290fr multi.	1.25	55
C248	"	300fr "	1.25	65
C249	"	370fr "	1.50	80

Russo-American space cooperation.

Boy Scout, Globe, Nordjamb 75 Emblem AP103

Designs (Globe, Nordjamb 75 Emblem and): 150fr, Boy Scout giving Scout sign. 290fr, Scouts around campfire.

1975, June 23 Engr. *Perf. 13*

C251	AP103	100fr claret, brn. & blue	40	25
C252	"	150fr red, brown & green	60	32
C253	"	290fr blue, brown & claret	1.25	65

Nordjamb 75, 14th Boy Scout Jamboree, Lillehammer, Norway, July 29–Aug. 7.

Battle Scene and Marquis de Lafayette—AP104

Designs: 300fr, Battle scene and George Washington. 370fr, Battle of Chesapeake Bay and Count de Grasse.

1975, July 7 Engr. *Perf. 13*

C254	AP104	290fr lt. bl. & indigo	1.25	65
C255	"	300fr lt. bl. & indigo	1.25	65
C256	"	370fr lt. bl. & indigo	1.40	80
		Strip of 3, # C254–C256	4.00	2.75

Bicentenary of the American Revolution. Nos. C254–C256 printed se-tenant in continuous design.

Schweitzer, Bach and Score AP105

Designs: No. C257, Albert Einstein (1879–1955), theoretical physicist. No. No. C258, André-Marie Ampère (1775–1836), French physicist. 100fr, Clément Ader (1841–1925), French aviation pioneer. No. C260, Dr. Albert Schweitzer (1875–1965), Medical missionary and musician. No. C261, Sir Alexander Fleming (1881–1955), British bacteriologist, discoverer of penicillin.

1975 Engraved *Perf. 13*

C257	AP105	90fr multicolored	35	25
C258	"	90fr purple, org. & bister	35	20
C259	"	100fr blue, red & lilac	40	25
C260	"	150fr grn., blue & dk. green	60	32
C261	"	150fr lilac, blue & brick red	60	32
		Nos. C257–C261 (5)	2.30	1.34

Issue dates: No. C257, May 26. No. C258, Sept. 23. 100fr, Dec. 8. No C260, Jan. 14. No. C261, July 21.

Olympic Rings and Globe—AP106

Design: 400fr, Montreal Olympic Games' emblem.

1975, Oct.

C262	AP106	350fr pur. & bl.	1.40	80
C263	"	400fr blue	1.65	95

Pre-Olympic Year 1975.

Nos. C247–C249 Overprinted: "ARRIMAGE / 17 Juil. 1975"

1975, Oct. 20 Engr. *Perf. 13*

C264	AP101	290fr multi.	1.25	55
C265	"	300fr "	1.25	65
C266	"	370fr "	1.50	80

Apollo-Soyuz link-up in space, July 17, 1975.

Painting Type of 1974

Designs: 290fr, Visitation, by Ghirlandaio. 300fr, Nativity, Fra Filippo Lippi school. 370fr, Adoration of the Kings, by Velazquez.

1975, Nov. 24 Litho. *Perf. 12½x13*

C267	AP95	290fr multi.	1.25	55
C268	"	300fr "	1.25	65
C269	"	370fr "	1.50	80

Christmas 1975.

Concorde—AP107

1976, Jan. 12 Litho. *Perf. 13*

C270	AP107	500fr multi.	2.00	1.35

Concorde supersonic jet, first commercial flight, Jan. 21, 1976.

Figure Skating AP108

Designs (Games Emblem and): 420fr, Ski Jump. 430fr, Slalom.

1976, Feb. 16 Litho. *Perf. 13*

C271	AP108	120fr grn., lt. grn. & black	50	25
C272	"	420fr brn., rose & black	1.65	90
C273	"	430fr ultra., lt. blue & black	1.75	90

12th Winter Olympic Games, Innsbruck, Austria, Feb. 4–15.

Eye Examination, WHO Emblem AP109

1976, Apr. 5 Litho. *Perf. 12½*

C274	AP109	130fr multi.	50	28

World Health Day: "Foresight prevents blindness."

Space Ship with Solar Batteries—AP110

Design: 300fr, Astronaut working on orbital space station (vert.).

1976, May 10 Engr. *Perf. 13*

C275	AP110	300fr org., dk. & lt. blue	1.25	65
C276	"	400fr magenta, dk. bl. & org.	1.65	95

Futuristic space achievements.

American Eagle, Flag and Liberty Bell—AP111

Designs: 400fr, Revolutionary War naval battle and American eagle. 440fr, Indians on horseback and American eagle (vert.).

1976, May 24 Litho. *Perf. 12½*

C277	AP111	100fr multi.	40	25
C278	"	400fr "	1.65	1.00
C279	"	440fr "	1.85	1.10

American Bicentennial. Nos. C278–C279 also commemorate Interphil 76, International Philatelic Exhibition, Philadelphia, Pa, May 29–June 6.

Running AP112

Designs (Olympic Rings and): 250fr, Swimming. 300fr, Field ball. 440fr, Soccer.

1976, June 7 Engr. *Perf. 13*

C280	AP112	200fr red brown & black	85	40
C281	"	250fr multi.	1.00	55
C282	"	300fr "	1.25	65
C283	"	440fr "	1.85	95

21st Olympic Games, Montreal, Canada, July 17–Aug. 1.

Cub Scout and Leader AP113

Designs: 180fr, Scouts tending sick animal (horiz.). 200fr, Night hike.

1976, June 14 Engr. *Perf. 13*

C284	AP113	140fr ultra. & red brn.	55	45
C285	"	180fr dk. brn. & multi.	70	50
C286	"	200fr brn. org. & vio. bl.	85	55

First African Boy Scout Jamboree, Nigeria.

Mohenjo-Daro, Bull from Wall Relief—AP114

Design: 500fr, Man's head, animals, wall and UNESCO emblem.

1976, Sept. 6 Engr. *Perf. 13*

C287	AP114	400fr blk., bl. & purple	1.60	80
C288	"	500fr dk. red, bl. & green	2.00	1.20

UNESCO campaign to save Mohenjo-Daro excavations.

Europafrica Issue

Freighter, Plane, Map of Europe and Africa—AP115

1976, Sept. 20

C289	AP115	200fr vio. brown & blue	80	50

Nativity, by Taddeo Gaddi—AP116

Paintings: 300fr, Adoration of the Kings, by Hans Memling. 320fr, Nativity, by Carlo Crivelli.

1976, Nov. 8 Litho. *Perf. 13x12½*

C290	AP116	280fr multi.	1.10	55
C291	"	300fr "	1.20	65
C292	"	320fr "	1.30	70

Christmas 1976.

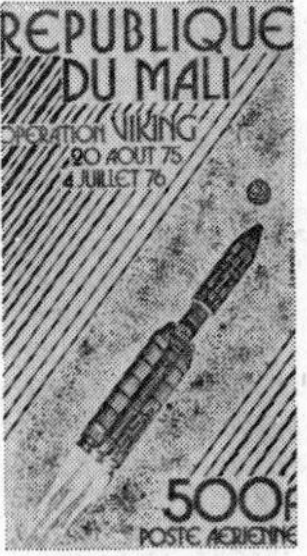

Viking Flying to Mars AP117

Design: 1000fr, Viking landing craft on Mars.

1976, Dec. 8 Engr. *Perf. 13*

C293	AP117	500fr red, brown & blue	2.00	95
C294	"	1000fr multi.	4.00	2.00
		a. Miniature sheet of 2	6.50	3.75

Operation Viking, U.S. Mars mission, No. C294a contains 2 stamps similar to Nos. C293–C294 in changed colors. Size: 119x 90mm.

Pres. Giscard d'Estaing, Village and Bambara Antelope—AP118

1977, Feb. 13 Photo. *Perf. 13*

C295	AP118	430fr multi.	1.75	80

Visit of Pres. Valéry Giscard d'Estaing of France, Feb. 13–15.

Elizabeth II and Prince Philip AP119

Designs: 200fr, Charles de Gaulle (vert.). 250fr, Queen Wilhelmina (vert.). 300fr, King Baudouin and Queen Fabiola. 480fr, Coronation of Queen Elizabeth II (vert.).

1977, Mar. 21 Litho. *Perf. 12*

C296	AP119	180fr multicolored	70	40
C297	"	200fr "	80	50
C298	"	250fr "	1.00	55
C299	"	300fr "	1.20	70
C300	"	480fr "	2.00	1.00
		Nos. C296–C300 (5)	5.70	3.15

Personalities involved in de-colonization.

Newton, Rocket and Apple—AP120

1977, May 7 Engr. *Perf. 13*

C301	AP120	400fr grn., brn. & red	1.65	80

Isaac Newton (1643–1727), natural philosopher and mathematician, 250th death anniversary.

Charles Lindbergh and Spirit of St. Louis—AP121

Design: 430fr, Spirit of St. Louis flying over clouds.

1977, Apr. 4 **Litho.** ***Perf. 12***

C302	AP121	420fr orange & purple	1.60	80
C303	"	430fr multi.	1.65	80

Charles A. Lindbergh's solo transatlantic flight from New York to Paris, 50th anniversary.

Sassenage Castle, Grenoble—AP122

1977, May 21 **Litho.** ***Perf. 12½***

C304	AP122	300fr multi.	1.20	65

10th anniversary of International French Language Council.

Zeppelin No. 1, 1900—AP123

Designs: 130fr, Graf Zeppelin, 1924. 350fr, Hindenburg aflame at Lakehurst, N.J., 1937. 500fr, Ferdinand von Zeppelin and Graf Zeppelin.

1977, May 30 **Engr.** ***Perf. 13***

C305	AP123	120fr multi.	50	28
C306	"	130fr "	50	28
C307	"	350fr "	1.40	80
C308	"	500fr "	2.00	1.00

History of the Zeppelin.

Martin Luther King, American and Swedish Flags AP124

Design: 600fr, Henri Dunant, Red Cross, Swiss and Swedish flags.

1977, July 4 **Engr.** ***Perf. 13***

C309	AP124	600fr multi.	2.40	1.25
C310	"	700fr "	2.80	1.40

Nobel Peace Prize recipients.

The only foreign revenue stamps listed in this Catalogue are those authorized for prepayment of postage.

Soccer—AP125

Designs: 200fr, 3 soccer players (vert.). 420fr, 3 soccer players.

1977, Oct. 3 **Engr.** ***Perf. 13***

C311	AP125	180fr multi.	70	40
C312	"	200fr "	80	50
C313	"	420fr "	1.75	90

World Soccer Cup Elimination Games.

Mao Tse-tung and COMATEX Hall, Bamako—AP126

1977, Nov. 7 **Engr.** ***Perf. 13***

C314	AP126	300fr dull red	1.20	65

Chairman Mao Tse-tung (1893–1976), first death anniversary.

No. C270 Overprinted in Violet Blue: "PARIS NEW-YORK 22.11.77"

1977, Nov. 22 **Litho.** ***Perf. 13***

C315	AP107	500fr multi.	5.00	2.75

Concorde, first commerical transatlantic flight, Paris to New York.

Virgin and Child, by Rubens AP127

Rubens Paintings: 400fr, Adoration of the Kings. 600fr, Detail from Adoration of the Kings (horiz.).

1977, Dec. 5 ***Perf. 12½x12, 12x12½***

C316	AP127	400fr gold & multi.	1.60	95
C317	"	500fr gold & multi.	2.00	1.20
C318	"	600fr gold & multi.	2.40	1.40

Christmas 1977, and 400th birth anniversary of Peter Paul Rubens (1577–1640).

Battle of the Amazons, by Rubens—AP128

Rubens Paintings: 300fr, Return from the fields. 500fr, Hercules fighting the Nemean Lion (vert.).

Perf. 12x12½, 12½x12

1978, Jan. 16 **Lithographed**

C319	AP128	200fr multi.	80	50
C320	AP128	300fr multi.	1.20	75
C321	"	500fr "	2.00	1.25

Peter Paul Rubens, 400th birth anniversary.

Schubert Composing "Winterreise"—AP129

Design: 300fr, Schubert and score (vert.).

1978, Feb. 13

C322	AP129	300fr multi.	1.20	75
C323	"	420fr "	1.75	90

Franz Schubert (1797–1828), Austrian composer, death sesquicentennial.

Capt. Cook Receiving Hawaiian Delegation—AP130

Design: 300fr, Cook landing on Hawaii. Designs after sketches by John Webber.

1978, Feb. 27 **Engr.** ***Perf. 13***

C324	AP130	200fr multi.	80	50
C325	"	300fr "	1.20	65

Capt. James Cook (1728–1779), bicentenary of his arrival in Hawaii.

Soccer AP131

Designs: 250fr, One player. 300fr, Two players (horiz.).

1978, Mar. 20

C326	AP131	150fr multi.	60	35
C327	"	250fr "	1.00	60
	a. "REPUPLIQUE"		1.00	60
C328	AP131	300fr multi.	1.20	65
	a. Miniature sheet of 3		2.75	2.25
	b. As "a" (#C326, C327a, C328)			

World Soccer Cup Championships, Argentina, 1978, June 1–25. No. C328a contains Nos. C326–C328 and blue label with Argentina '78 emblem. Size: 190x100mm.

Nos. C327 and C328a were issued in July to correct the spelling error.

Jesus with Crown of Thorns, by Dürer AP132

Design: 430fr, Resurrection, by Albrecht Dürer.

1978, Mar. 28

C329	AP132	420fr multi.	1.70	1.00
C330	"	430fr "	1.75	1.00

Easter 1978. See Nos. C359–C361.

Citroen, C3-Trefle, 1922—AP133

Citroen Cars: 130fr, Croisiere Noire, 1924, tractor. 180fr, B14G, 1927. 200fr, "11" Tractor Avant, 1934.

1978, Apr. 24 **Engr.** ***Perf. 13***

C331	AP133	120fr multi.	48	30
C332	"	130fr "	52	32
C333	"	180fr "	72	40
C334	"	200fr "	80	45

Andre Citroen (1878–1935), automobile designer and manufacturer.

UPU Type of 1978

Design: 130fr, UPU emblem, globe and names of member countries.

1978, May 15

C335	A104	130fr red, green & emerald	52	32

Centenary of Congress of Paris where General Postal Union became the Universal Postal Union.

Europafrica Issue

Ostrich Incubating Eggs, Syrian Manuscript, 14th Century—AP134

Design: 110fr, Zebra, Miniature by Mansur, Jehangir School, 1620.

1978, July 24 **Litho.** ***Perf. 13x12½***

C336	AP134	100fr multi.	40	25
C337	"	110fr "	45	28

Nos. C326–C328a Overprinted in Black:

a. CHAMPION / 1978 / ARGENTINE
b. 2e HOLLANDE
c. 3e BRESIL / 4e ITALIE

1978, Aug. 7 **Engraved** ***Perf. 13***

C338	AP131	(*a*) 150fr multi.	60	35
C339	"	(*b*) 250fr "	1.00	60
C340	"	(*c*) 300fr "	1.20	65
	a. Souvenir sheet of 3		2.25	2.25

Winners, World Soccer Cup Championship, Argentina. Overprints on No. C340a are green including label overprint: FINALE / ARGENTINA 3 HOLLANDE 1.

Elizabeth II in Coronation Robes AP135

Design: 500fr, Coronation coach.

Lithographed

1978, Sept. 18 *Perf. 12½x12*

C341	AP135	500fr multi.	2.00	1.25
C342	"	1000fr "	4.00	2.50

25th anniversary of coronation of Queen Elizabeth II.

U.S. No. C3a and Douglas DC-3
AP136

Designs: 100fr, Belgium No. 252 and Stampe SV-4. 120fr, France No. C48 and Ader's plane No. 3. 130fr, Germany No. C2 and Junker Ju-52. 320fr, Japan No. C25 and Mitsubishi A-6M "Zero".

1978, Oct. 16 Engr. *Perf. 13*

C343	AP136	80fr multi.	32	20
C344	"	100fr "	40	28
C345	"	120fr "	48	32
C346	"	130fr "	52	35
C347	"	320fr "	1.30	85
	Nos. C343-C347 (5)		3.02	2.00

History of aviation.

REPUBLIQUE DU MALI
POSTE AERIENNE 420F
NOEL 1978 A. DURER
L'ANNONCIATION

Annunciation, by Dürer
AP137

Etchings by Dürer: 430fr, Virgin and Child. 500fr, Adoration of the Kings.

1978, Nov. 6

C348	AP137	420fr blk. & rose carmine	1.70	95
C349	"	430fr olive green & brn.	1.75	1.00
C350	"	500fr black & red	2.00	1.25

Christmas 1978 and 450th death anniversary of Albrecht Dürer (1471–1528), German painter.

Rocket and Trajectory Around Moon
AP138

Design: 300fr, Spaceship circling moon.

1978, Nov. 20 Engr. *Perf. 13*

C351	AP138	200fr multi.	80	55
C352	"	300fr "	1.20	85

10th anniversary of 1st flight around moon. Nos. C351–C352 printed se-tenant with label between showing earth, moon and U.S. astronauts' names.

Condition is the all-important factor of price. Prices quoted are for stamps in fine condition.

Ader's Plane and Concorde—AP139

Designs: 130fr, Wright Flyer A and Concorde. 200fr, Spirit of St. Louis and Concorde.

1979, Jan. 25 Litho. *Perf. 13*

C353	AP139	120fr multi.	48	32
C354	"	130fr "	52	35
C355	"	200fr "	80	55

Third anniversary of 1st supersonic commercial flight.

Philexafrique II—Essen Issue
Common Design Types

Designs: No. C356, Dromedary and Mali No. C26. No. C357, Bird and Lubeck No. 1.

1979, Jan. 29 Litho. *Perf. 13x12½*

C356	CD138	200fr multi.	80	55
C357	CD139	200fr "	80	55

Nos. C356–C357 printed se-tenant.

No. C257 Surcharged

"1879-1979"
130 F

1979, Mar. 26 Engr. *Perf. 13*

C358	AP105	130fr on 90fr multi.	52	35

Centenary of the birth of Albert Einstein (1879–1955).

Easter Type of 1978

Dürer Etchings: 400fr, Jesus Carrying Cross. 430fr, Crucified Christ. 480fr, Pietà.

1979, Apr. 9

C359	AP132	400fr bl. & blk.	1.60	1.10
C360	"	430fr red & black	1.72	1.20
C361	"	480fr ultra. & black	1.90	1.35

Easter 1979.

POSTAGE DUE STAMPS

Bambara Headpiece D1

Perf. 14x13½

1961, Mar. 18 Engraved Unwmkd.

J1	D1	1fr black	5	5
J2	"	2fr bright ultramarine	5	4
J3	"	5fr red lilac	20	17
J4	"	10fr orange	25	18
J5	"	20fr bright green	30	20
J6	"	25fr red brown	35	27
		Nos. J1-J6 (6)	1.20	91

Polyptychus Roseus—D2

Designs: No. J8, Deilephila Nerii. No. J9, Gynanisa maja. No. J10, Bunaea alcinoe. No. J11, Teracolus eris. No. J12, Colotis antevippe. No. J13, Charaxes epijasius. No. J14, Manatha microcera. No. J15, Hypokopelates otraeda. No. J16, Lipaphnaeus leonina. No. J17, Gonimbrasia hecate. No. J18, Lobounaea christyi. No. J19, Hypolimnas misippus. No. J20, Catopsilia florella.

1964, June 1 Photo. *Perf. 11*

Butterflies and Moths in Natural Colors

J7	D2	1fr olive green	5	5
J8	"	1fr orange & brown	5	5
J9	"	2fr emerald & brown	5	5
J10	"	2fr " " "	5	5
J11	"	3fr rose lilac & brn.	20	20
J12	"	3fr " " "	20	20
J13	"	5fr black & rose	10	10
J14	"	5fr green	10	10
J15	"	10fr yel., orge. & blk.	15	15
J16	"	10fr blue	15	15
J17	"	20fr light blue & brn.	35	35
J18	"	20fr " " "	35	35
J19	"	25fr green & yellow	45	45
J20	"	25fr deep grn. & black	45	45
		Nos. J7-J20 (14)	2.70	2.70

The two stamps of the same denomination are printed together in the sheet, se-tenant at the base.

OFFICIAL STAMPS

Dogon Mask O1

Mali Coat of Arms O2

Perf. 14x13½

1961, Mar. 18 Engraved Unwmkd.

O1	O1	1fr gray	4	4
O2	"	2fr red orange	5	5
O3	"	3fr black	5	5
O4	"	5fr light blue	10	8
O5	"	10fr bistre brown	15	10
O6	"	25fr bright ultra.	30	15
O7	"	30fr carmine rose	40	15
O8	"	50fr Prussian green	70	27
O9	"	85fr red brown	1.00	60
O10	"	100fr emerald	1.25	70
O11	"	200fr red lilac	2.40	1.50
		Nos. O1-O11 (11)	6.44	3.69

1964, June 1 Photo. *Perf. 12½*

National Colors and Arms in Multicolor, Background in Light Green.

O12	O2	1fr green	3	3
O13	"	2fr light violet	3	3
O14	O2	3fr gray	3	3
O15	"	5fr lilac rose	6	6
O16	"	10fr bright blue	10	10
O17	"	25fr ocher	25	25
O18	"	30fr dark green	28	28
O19	"	50fr orange	40	40
O20	"	85fr dark brown	60	60
O21	"	100fr red	75	60
O22	"	200fr dk. violet blue	1.60	60
		Nos. O12-O22 (11)	4.13	2.98

MANCHUKUO

(män'jō'kwō'; -chōō'kwō')

LOCATION—Covering Manchuria, or China's three northeastern provinces — Fengtien, Kirin and Heilungkiang—plus Jehol province.

GOVT. — A former independent state under Japanese influence.

AREA—503,013 sq. mi. (estimated).

POP.—43,233,954 (estimated 1940).

CAPITAL—Hsinking (Changchun).

Manchukuo was formed in 1932 with the assistance of Japan. In 1934 Henry Pu-yi, Chief Executive, was enthroned as Emperor Kang Teh. In 1945, when Japan surrendered to the Allies, the terms included the return of Manchukuo to China. The puppet state was dissolved.

100 Fen = 1 Yuan

Pagoda at Liaoyang A1

Chief Executive Henry Pu-yi A2

Five characters in top label.

Inscription reads "Manchu State Postal Administration."

Lithographed; White Paper.

Perf. 13x13½

1932, July 26 Unwmkd.

1	A1	½f gray brown	50	25
2	"	1f dull red	50	25
3	"	1½f lilac	1.75	75
4	"	2f slate	1.50	15
5	"	3f dull brown	2.00	70
6	"	4f olive green	65	20
7	"	5f green	85	25
8	"	6f rose	2.50	30
9	"	7f gray	85	25
10	"	8f ochre	3.00	1.50
11	"	10f orange	2.25	20
12	A2	13f dull brown	2.25	1.50
13	"	15f rose	4.25	60
14	"	16f turquoise green	6.00	1.75
15	"	20f gray brown	2.25	50
16	"	30f orange	2.00	60
17	"	50f olive green	4.25	1.10
18	"	1y violet	8.00	1.75
		Nos. 1-18 (18)	45.35	12.60

A local provisional overprint of a horizontal line of four characters in red or black, reading "Chinese Postal Administration," was applied to Nos. 1-18 by followers of Gen. Su Ping-wen, who rebelled against the Manchukuo government in September, 1932. Many counterfeits exist.

See also Nos. 23-31.

Flags, Map and Wreath A3

Old State Council Building A4

1933, Mar. 1 *Perf. 12½*

19	A3	1f orange	2.50	1.75
20	A4	2f dull green	3.50	2.50
21	A3	4f light red	2.50	1.75
22	A4	10f deep blue	6.00	4.00

Issued in commemoration of the first anniversary of the establishing of the State. Nos. 19-22 were printed in sheets of 100 with a special printing in sheets of 20.

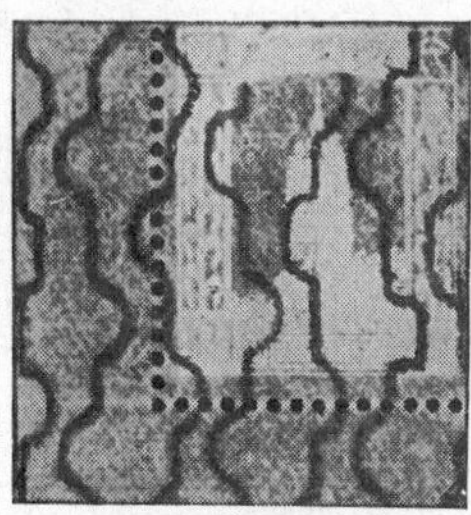

Wmk. 239

Type of 1932.

Granite Paper.

Wmkd. Curved Wavy Lines. (239)

1934, Feb. Engr. *Perf. 13x13½*

23	A1	½f dark brown	50	30
24	"	1f red brown	50	25
25	"	1½f dark violet	75	35
26	"	2f slate	1.00	25
27	"	3f brown	75	15
28	"	4f olive brown	7.00	1.00
29	"	10f deep orange	1.50	20
30	A2	15f rose	200.00	65.00
31	"	1y violet	4.75	3.00
		Nos. 23-31 (9)	216.75	70.50

Emperor's Palace A5

Phoenix A6

1934, Mar. 1 *Perf. 12½*

32	A5	1½f orange brown	75	75
33	A6	3f carmine	1.25	1.25
34	A5	6f green	4.00	3.00
35	A6	10f dark blue	8.00	3.00

Issued to commemorate the enthronement of Emperor Kang Teh. Nos. 32-35 were printed in sheets of 100, with a special printing in sheets of 20.

No. 6 Surcharged in Black

壹暫
分作

White Paper.

1934 *Perf. 13x13½* Unwmkd.

36	A1	1f on 4f olive green	85	60
		a. Brown surcharge	10.00	7.50
		b. Upper left character of surcharge omitted		
		c. Inverted surcharge	35.00	35.00

Pagoda at Liaoyang A7

Emperor Kang Teh A8

Six characters in top label instead of five as in 1932-34 issues.

Inscription reads "Manchu Empire Postal Administration".

Engraved.

Granite Paper.

1934-36 *Perf. 13x13½* Wmk. 239

37	A7	½f brown	20	15
38	A7	1f red brown	20	15
39	"	1½f dark violet	35	20
		a. Booklet pane of 6	10.00	
41	"	3f brown ('35)	25	15
		a. Booklet pane of 6	17.50	
42	"	5f dark blue ('35)	2.25	30
43	"	5f gray ('36)	60	50
44	"	6f rose ('35)	75	20
45	"	7f dark gray ('36)	1.00	35
47	"	9f red orange ('35)	60	20
50	A8	15f vermilion ('35)	75	30
51	"	18f Prus. green ('35)	9.00	1.00
52	"	20f dark brown ('35)	1.00	25
53	"	30f org. brown ('35)	1.00	25
54	"	50f olive green ('35)	2.00	40
55	"	1y dark violet ('35)	5.00	2.25
		a. 1y violet	5.00	3.00
		Nos. 37-55 (15)	24.95	6.65

4f and 8f, type A7, were prepared but not issued.

Wmk. 242

Wmkd. Characters (242)

1935 *Perf. 13x13½.*

57	A7	10f deep blue	1.25	15
58	A8	13f light brown	1.25	75

Nos. 6 and 28 Surcharged in Black

三暫
分作

1935 White Paper. Unwmkd.

59	A1	3f on 4f olive green	12.50	12.50

1935 Granite Paper. Wmk. 239

60	A1	3f on 4f olive brown	1.25	1.10

Similar Surcharge on No. 14.

1935 White Paper. Unwmkd.

61	A2	3f on 16f turq. grn.	5.00	2.75

Orchid Crest of Manchukuo A9

Sacred White Mountains and Black Waters A10

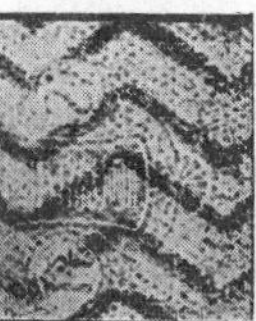

Wmk. 141

Wmkd. Horizontal Zigzag Lines. (141)

1935, Jan. 1 Lithographed

Granite Paper

62	A9	2f green	1.25	40
63	A10	4f dull olive green	50	30
64	A9	8f ochre	1.25	1.00
65	A10	12f brown red	2.50	2.25

Nos. 62-65 exist imperforate.

1935 Wmk. 242

66	A9	2f yellow green	1.00	40
68	"	8f ochre	1.25	50
70	A10	12f brown red	2.50	1.25

Nos. 62-70 issued primarily to pay postage to China, but valid for any postal use.

See also Nos. 76, 78, 113, 115, 158.

Mt. Fuji A11 — Phoenix A12

Perf. 11, 12½ and Compound.

1935, Apr. 1 Engr. Wmk. 242

No.	Type	Description	Unused	Used
71	A11	1½f dull green	90	90
72	A12	3f orange	90	90
		a. 3f red orange	6.00	6.00
73	A11	6f dark carmine	1.25	1.25
		a. Horizontal pair, imperf. between	100.00	
		b. Perf.11x12½	15.00	15.00
74	A12	10f dark blue	1.85	1.85
		a. Perf. 12½x11	12.50	7.50
		b. Perf. 12½	15.00	

Issued in April in commemoration of the visit of the Emperor of Manchukuo to Tokyo in 1935.

Orchid Crest A13

Types of A9 & A10 Redrawn and Engraved.

1936 *Perf. 13x13½* Wmk. 242

No.	Type	Description	Unused	Used
75	A13	2f light green	25	15
76	A10	4f olive green	50	25
77	A13	8f ochre	35	15
78	A10	12f orange brown	9.00	5.00

Unbroken lines of shading in the background of Nos. 76 and 78. Shading has been removed from right and left of the mountains. Nearly all lines have been removed from the lake. There are numerous other alterations in the design.

Issued primarily to pay postage to China, but valid for any postal use.

See also No. 112.

Wild Goose over Sea of Japan A14 — Communications Building at Hsinking A15

Perf. 12x12½, 12½x12

1936, Jan. 26 Wmk. 242

No.	Type	Description	Unused	Used
79	A14	1½f black brown	70	70
80	A15	3f rose lilac	70	70
81	A14	6f carmine rose	2.50	2.50
82	A15	10f blue	2.75	2.75

Postal convention with Japan.

New State Council Building A16 — Carting Soybeans A17

North Mausoleum at Mukden A18

Summer Palace at Chengteh A19

1936-37 *Perf. 13x13½* Wmk. 242

No.	Type	Description	Unused	Used
83	A16	½f brown	15	10
84	"	1f red brown	15	10
85	"	1½f violet	1.50	80
		a. Booklet pane of 6	17.50	
86	A17	2f light green ('37)	15	10
		a. Booklet pane of 6	2.50	
87	A16	3f chocolate	15	10
		a. Booklet pane of 6	5.00	
88	A18	4f lt. olive grn. ('37)	15	10
		a. Booklet pane of 6	5.00	
89	A16	5f gray black	3.50	75
90	A17	6f carmine	18	10
91	A18	7f brown black	25	10
92	"	9f red orange	30	15
93	A19	10f blue	25	10
94	A18	12f deep orange ('37)	25	12
95	"	13f brown	7.50	2.25
96	"	15f carmine	40	25
97	A17	20f dark brown	40	40
98	A19	30f chestnut brown	40	30
99	A17	50f olive green	60	60
100	A19	1y violet	1.25	30
		Nos. 83-100 (18)	17.53	6.72

Nos. 83, 84, 86, 88 and 93 are known imperforate but were not regularly issued. See also Nos. 159-163.

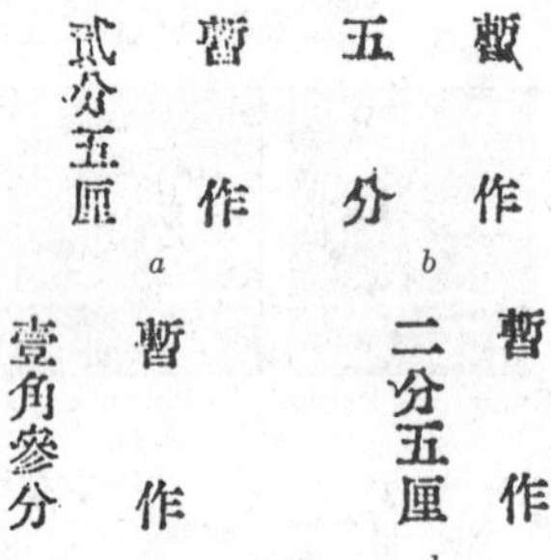

1937

No.	Type	Description	Unused	Used
101	A9	(*a*) 2½f on 2f yellow green	80	80

Surcharged on Nos. 75, 76 and 78.

No.	Type	Description	Unused	Used
102	A13	(*a*) 2½f on 2f lt. green	80	80
103	A10	(*b*) 5f on 4f olive green	1.35	1.35
104	"	(*c*) 13f on 12f orange brown	4.00	4.00

Surcharged in Black on Nos. 75, 76 and 70

Space between bottom characters of surcharge 4½ mm.

No.	Type	Description	Unused	Used
105	A13	(*d*) 2½f on 2f lt. grn.	80	80
		a. Inverted surcharge	60.00	40.00
		b. Vert. pair, one without surch.	50.00	
106	A10	(*b*) 5f on 4f olive green	1.00	1.00
107	"	(*c*) 13f on 12f brn. red	3.50	3.50

Surcharged on No. 70.

Space between characters 6½ mm.

No.	Type	Description	Unused	Used
108	A10	(*c*) 13f on 12f brown red	60.00	50.00

Same Surcharge on No. 63.

Space between characters 4½ mm

Wmk. 141

No.	Type	Description	Unused	Used
109	A10	(*b*) 5f on 4f dull olive green	3.00	1.50
		Nos. 101-109 (9)	75.25	63.75

Nos. 101-109 were issued primarily to pay postage to China, but were valid for any postal use.

Rising Sun over Manchurian Plain A20 — Composite Picture of Manchurian City A21

Perf. 12½

1937, Mar. 1 Litho. Unwmkd.

No.	Type	Description	Unused	Used
110	A20	1½f carmine rose	1.00	65
111	A21	3f blue green	85	65

Issued in commemoration of the fifth anniversary of the founding of the State of Manchukuo.

Types of 1936.

Engraved.

1937 *Perf. 13x13½.* Wmk. 242

No.	Type	Description	Unused	Used
112	A13	2½f dark violet	40	20
113	A10	5f black	12	10
115	"	13f dark red brown	25	20

Issued primarily to pay postage to China, but were valid for any postal use.

Pouter Pigeon A22 — National Flag and Buildings A23

Perf. 12x12½

1937, Sept. 16 Unwmkd.

No.	Type	Description	Unused	Used
116	A22	2f dark violet	50	40
117	A23	4f rose carmine	50	40
118	A22	10f dark green	1.50	1.25
119	A23	20f dark blue	1.85	1.50

Issued in commemoration of the completion of the national capital, Hsinking, under the first Five-Year Construction Plan.

Map A24 — Department of Justice Building A27

Japanese Residents' Association Building A25

Postal Administration Building A26

Perf. 12x12½, 13.

1937, Dec. 1 Litho. Unwmkd.

No.	Type	Description	Unused	Used
121	A24	2f dark carmine	25	25
122	A25	4f green	50	50
123	"	8f orange	1.25	1.25
124	A26	10f blue	1.75	1.75
125	A27	12f light violet	2.00	2.00
126	A26	20f lilac brown	2.50	2.50
		Nos. 121-126 (6)	8.25	8.25

Issued in commemoration of the abolition of extraterritorial rights within Manchukuo.

New Year Greetings A28 — Map and Cross A29

1937, Dec. 15 Engr. *Perf. 12x12½*

No.	Type	Description	Unused	Used
127	A28	2f dark bl. and red	1.10	40
		a. Double impression of border		

Issued to pay postage on New Year's greeting cards.

Lithographed.

1938, Oct. 15 *Perf. 13* Wmk. 242

No.	Type	Description	Unused	Used
128	A29	2f lake & scarlet	45	45
129	"	4f slate green & scarlet	45	45

Issued in commemoration of the founding of the Red Cross Society in Manchukuo.

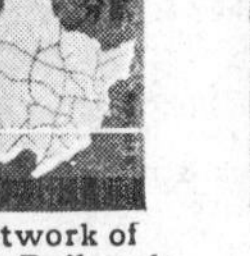

Network of State Railroads in Manchukuo A30 — Express Train "Asia" A31

1939, Oct. 21

No.	Type	Description	Unused	Used
130	A30	2f dark orange, black & deep blue	25	25
131	A31	4f deep blue & indigo	50	50

Issued in commemoration of the attainment of 10,000 kilometers in the railway mileage in Manchuria.

Stork Flying above Mast of Imperial Flagship A32

1940 Photogravure Unwmkd.

No.	Type	Description	Unused	Used
132	A32	2f bright red violet	15	15
133	"	4f bright green	20	20

Issued in commemoration of the second visit of Emperor Kang Teh to Emperor Hirohito of Japan.

Census Taker and Map of Manchukuo A33 — Census Form A34

1940, Sept. 10 Litho. Wmk. 242

No.	Type	Description	Unused	Used
134	A33	2f vio. brown & orange	15	15
135	A34	4f black & green	20	20
		a. Double impression of green	20.00	

National census starting Oct. 1.

Message of Congratulation from Premier Chang Ching-hui
A35

Dragon Dance—A36

1940, Sept. 18 Engraved

136	A35	2f carmine	12	15
137	A36	4f indigo	18	20
		a. Imperf., pair	60.00	

Issued in commemoration of the 2600th anniversary of the birth of the Japanese Empire.

Soldier
A37

1941, May 25 Photo. Unwmkd.

138	A37	2f deep carmine	12	10
139	"	4f bright ultramarine	18	15

Issued to commemorate the Conscription Law, effective June 1, 1941.

Nos. 86 and 88 Overprinted in Red or Blue

Perf. 13x13½

1942, Feb. 16 Wmk. 242

140	A17	2f light green (R)	12	12
141	A18	4f lt. olive green (Bl)	18	18

Issued to commemorate the "Return of Singapore to East Asia, 9th year of Kang Teh."

Kengoku Shrine A38 Map of Manchukuo A39

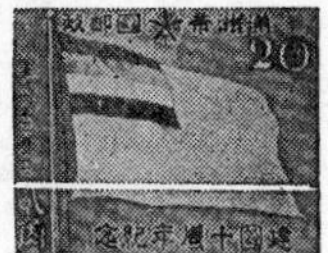

Flag of Manchukuo
A40

Perf. 12x12½, 12½x12

1942, Mar. 1 Engraved

142	A38	2f carmine	12	12
143	"	4f lilac	12	12
144	A39	10f red, *yellow*	20	20
145	A40	20f indigo, *yellow*	20	20

Issued to commemorate "the 10th anniversary of Manchukuo, March 1, 1942".

Allegory of National Harmony A41 Women of Five Races, Dancing A42

1942, Sept. 15

146	A41	3f orange	20	20
147	A42	6f light green	30	30

Issued to commemorate "the 10th anniversary of the founding of Manchukuo, September 15, 1942."

Nos. 87 and 90 Overprinted in Green or Blue

1942, Dec. 8 *Perf. 13x13½*

148	A16	3f chocolate (G)	12	12
149	A17	6f carmine (Bl)	18	18

Issued to commemorate the first anniversary of the "Greater East Asia War."

The overprint reads "Asiatic Prosperity Began This Day December 8, 1941."

Nos. 87 and 90 Overprinted in Red or Blue

1943, May 1

150	A16	3f chocolate (R)	12	12
151	A17	6f carmine (Bl)	18	18

Proclamation of the labor service law.

Red Cross Nurse Carrying Stretcher A43 Smelting Furnace A44

1943, Oct. 1 Photogravure

152	A43	6f green	18	18

Issued to commemorate the 5th anniversary of the founding of the Red Cross Society of Manchukuo, October 1, 1938.

1943, Dec. 8 *Perf. 13* Unwmkd.

153	A44	6f red brown	18	18

Issued to commemorate the 2nd anniversary of the "Greater East Asia War".

"Japan's Progress Is Manchukuo's Progress" (Chinese Characters) A45 "Japan's Progress Is Manchukuo's Progress" (Japanese Characters) A46

Lithographed.

1944 *Perf. 13x13½* Wmk. 242

154	A45	10f rose	50	50
		a. Imperf. (vertical pair Nos. 154 + 155)	2.50	2.50
155	A46	10f rose	50	50
156	A45	40f gray green	1.25	1.25
		a. Imperf. (vertical pair Nos. 156+157)	5.00	5.00
		b. 40f with 10f vignette, perf.	30.00	30.00
		c. 40f with 10f vignette, imperf.	75.00	
157	A46	40f gray green	1.25	1.25

Issued as propaganda for the close relationship of Japan and Manchukuo. Sheets contain alternate horizontal rows of stamps with Chinese and Japanese inscriptions.

Frames of the 10f vignettes have rounded corners; those of the 40f vignettes have indented corners.

Types of 1935 and 1936-37.

1944–45 Lithographed

158	A10	5f gray black	30	30
		a. Imperf. (pair)	2.00	
159	A17	6f crimson rose	35	35
160	A19	10f light blue	35	35
161	A17	20f brown	50	50
162	A19	30f buff	75	75
163	"	1y dull lilac	1.00	1.00
		Nos. 158-163 (6)	3.25	3.25

"One Heart, One Soul"
A47

1945, May 2

164	A47	10f red	18	18
		a. Imperf. (pair)	1.50	1.50

Issued to commemorate the 10th anniversary of the emperor's edict issued May 2, 1935.

AIR POST STAMPS.

Sheep Grazing AP1 Railroad Bridge AP2

Granite Paper.

Wmkd. Characters. (242)

1936-37 Engraved. *Perf. 13x13½.*

C1	AP1	18f green	3.00	1.25
C2	"	19f blue green ('37)	2.00	75
C3	AP2	38f blue	3.00	1.25
C4	"	39f deep blue ('37)	75	50

MARIANA ISLANDS

(mä'rē·ä'nä ī'ləndz)

LOCATION—A group of 14 islands in the West Pacific Ocean, about 1500 miles east of the Philippines.

GOVT.—Former possession of Spain, then of Germany.

AREA—246 sq. mi.

POP.—44,025 (1935).

CAPITAL—Saipan.

Until 1899 this group belonged to Spain but in that year all except Guam were ceded to Germany.

100 Centavos = 1 Peso

100 Pfennig = 1 Mark (1899)

Issued under Spanish Dominion.

King Alfonso XIII
A1

Stamps of the Philippines Handstamped Vertically in Blackish Violet, Reading Up or Down.

1899, Sept. *Perf. 14* Unwmkd.

1	A1	2c dk. blue green	425.00	100.00
2	"	3c dark brown	400.00	100.00
3	"	5c carmine rose	425.00	90.00
4	"	6c dark blue	1350.00	500.00
5	"	8c gray brown	275.00	100.00
6	"	15c slate green	850.00	525.00

Overprint forgeries of Nos. 1–6 exist.

Issued under German Dominion.

Stamps of Germany, 1889-90, Overprinted in Black at 56° Angle.

Marianen

Perf. 13½x14½

1900, May Unwmkd.

11	A9	3pf dark brown	12.00	*32.50*
12	"	5pf green	16.50	*32.50*
13	A10	10pf carmine	19.00	*45.00*
14	"	20pf ultramarine	27.50	*150.00*
15	"	25pf orange	80.00	*185.00*
		b. Invtd. surch.	*1100.00*	
16	"	50pf red brown	80.00	*225.00*
		Nos. 11-16 (6)	235.00	*670.00*

Forged cancellations exist on Nos. 11–16, 17–29.

Overprinted at 48° Angle.

1899, Nov. 18

11a	A9	3pf light brown	*1900.00*	*1900.00*
12a	"	5pf green	*2500.00*	*1400.00*
13a	A10	10pf carmine	275.00	275.00
14a	"	20pf ultramarine	275.00	275.00
15a	"	25pf orange	*2750.00*	*2750.00*
16a	"	50pf red brown	*2750.00*	*2750.00*

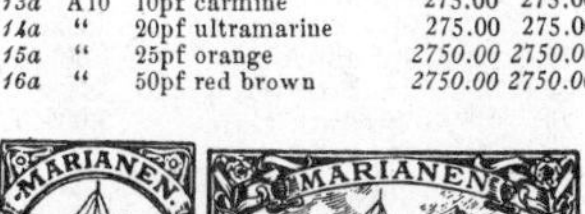

Kaiser's Yacht "Hohenzollern"
A4 A5

1901, Jan. Typographed *Perf. 14*

17	A4	3pf brown	1.10	1.10
18	"	5pf green	1.10	1.10
19	"	10pf carmine	1.10	*4.50*
20	"	20pf ultramarine	1.40	*10.00*
21	"	25pf orange & black, *yellow*	1.65	*19.00*
22	"	30pf orange & black, *salmon*	1.65	*19.00*
23	"	40pf lake & black	1.90	*19.00*
24	"	50pf purple & black, *salmon*	2.25	*22.50*
25	"	80pf lake & blk., *rose*	3.25	*32.50*

Engraved.

Perf. 14½x14

26	A5	1m carmine	3.85	*95.00*
27	"	2m blue	7.50	*110.00*
28	"	3m black violet	11.00	*165.00*
29	"	5m slate & car.	225.00	*600.00*
		Nos. 17-29 (13)	262.75	

Wmkd. Lozenges. (125)

1916–19 Typographed *Perf. 14*

30	A4	3pf brown ('19)	1.10	

Engraved.

Perf. 14½x14

31	A5	5m slate & carmine	32.50	

Nos. 30 and 31 were never placed in use.

The first price column gives the catalogue value of an unused stamp, the second that of a used stamp.

MARIENWERDER

(mä·rē′ĕn·vĕr′dĕr)

LOCATION — In northeastern Germany, bordering on Poland.

GOVT. — A former district of West Prussia.

By the Versailles Treaty the greater portion of West Prussia was ceded to Poland but the district of Marienwerder was allowed a plebiscite which was held in 1920 and resulted in favor of Germany.

100 Pfennig = 1 Mark

Plebiscite Issues.

Symbolical of Allied Supervision of the Plebiscite

A1

Lithographed.

1920	***Perf. 11½.***		**Unwmkd.**	
1	A1	5pf green	50	38
2	"	10pf rose red	42	33
3	"	15pf gray	60	50
4	"	20pf brown orange	35	28
5	"	25pf deep blue	85	70
6	"	30pf orange	1.30	1.00
7	"	40pf brown	85	70
8	"	50pf violet	70	55
9	"	60pf red brown	4.25	3.25
10	"	75pf chocolate	1.40	1.10
11	"	1m brown & green	1.00	80
12	"	2m dark violet	5.00	3.85
13	"	3m red	5.50	4.25
14	"	5m blue & rose	27.50	22.50
		Nos. 1-14 (14)	50.22	40.19

These stamps occasionally show parts of two papermakers' watermarks, consisting of the letters "O. B. M." with two stars before and after, or "P. & C. M."

Nos. 1–14 exist imperf.; price for set, $300. Nearly all exist part perf.

Stamps of Germany, 1905–19, Overprinted

Commission
Interalliée
Marienwerder

Wmkd. Lozenges. (125)

1920		***Perf. 14, 14½***		
24	A16	5pf green	21.00	32.50
		a. Invert. ovpt.	200.00	275.00
26	"	20pf blue violet	8.50	13.50
		a. Invtd. overprint	125.00	165.00
		b. Double overprint	140.00	190.00
28	"	50pf violet & black, *buff*	350.00	600.00
29	"	75pf green & black	5.25	8.00
		a. Inverted ovpt.	125.00	165.00
30	"	80pf lake & black, *rose*	85.00	135.00
31	A17	1m carmine rose	85.00	135.00
		a. Invtd. overprint	300.00	400.00
		Nos. 24-31 (6)	554.75	924.00

Trial impressions were made in red, green and lilac, and with 2¼ mm. instead of 3 mm. space between the lines of the overprint. These were printed on the 75pf and 80pf. The 1 mark was overprinted with the same words in three lines of large sans-serif capitals. All these are essays. Some of them were passed through the post, apparently with speculative intent.

Stamps of Germany, 1905–18, Surcharged

1 Mark 1
Commission
Interalliée
Marienwerder

32	A22	1m on 2pf gray	21.00	32.50
33	"	2m on 2½pf gray	10.00	16.50
		a. Inverted surcharge	80.00	110.00
34	A16	3m on 3pf brown	10.00	16.50
		a. Double surcharge	80.00	110.00
		b. Inverted surch.	80.00	110.00
35	A22	5m on 7½pf orange	10.00	16.50
		a. Inverted surcharge	80.00	110.00
		b. Double surcharge	80.00	110.00

There are two types of the letters "M", "C", "i" and "e" and of the numerals "2" and "5" in these surcharges.

Counterfeits exist of Nos. 24–35.

Stamps of Germany, 1920, Overprinted

Commission
Interalliée
Marienwerder

1920, July		***Perf. 15x14½***		
36	A17	1m red	3.50	6.50
37	"	1.25m green	3.50	6.50
38	"	1.50m yellow brown	5.25	11.00
39	A21	2.50m lilac rose	3.50	6.50

A2

1920	***Perf. 11½***		**Unwmkd.**	
40	A2	5pf green	3.00	2.50
41	"	10pf rose red	3.00	2.50
42	"	15pf gray	11.00	8.50
43	"	20pf brown orange	2.50	2.00
44	"	25pf deep blue	11.00	8.50
45	"	30pf orange	1.25	1.00
46	"	40pf brown	75	60
47	"	50pf violet	1.90	1.50
48	"	60pf red brown	4.25	3.25
49	"	75pf chocolate	6.25	5.00
50	"	1m brown & green	1.00	80
51	"	2m dark violet	1.40	1.10
52	"	3m light red	1.75	1.35
53	"	5m blue & rose	1.90	1.50
		Nos. 40-53 (14)	50.95	40.10

MARSHALL ISLANDS

(mär′shăl ī′lăndz)

LOCATION—Two chains of islands in the West Pacific Ocean, northwest of the Gilbert and Ellice group

GOVT.—Former German possession.

AREA—176 sq. mi.

POP.—15,179 (1913).

CAPITAL—Jaluit.

100 Pfennig = 1 Mark

Issued under German Dominion.

A1

A2

Stamps of Germany
Overprinted "Marschall-Inseln" in Black.

1897	***Perf. 13½x14½***		**Unwmkd.**	
1	A1	3pf dark brown	190.00	*385.00*
		a. 3pf light brown	*3500.00*	*2250.00*
2	A1	5pf green	165.00	*325.00*
3	A2	10pf carmine	55.00	*85.00*
4	"	20pf ultramarine	55.00	*85.00*
5	"	25pf orange	165.00	*650.00*
6	"	50pf red brown	165.00	*650.00*

Nos. 5 and 6 were not placed in use, but canceled copies exist.

A small quantity of the 3pf, 5pf, 10pf and 20pf were issued at Jaluit. These have yellowish, dull gum. Later overprintings of Nos. 1–6 were sold only at Berlin, and have white, smooth, shiny gum. No. 1a belongs to the Jaluit issue.

Forged cancellations are found on almost all Marshall Islands stamps.

Overprinted "Marshall-Inseln".

1899–1900				
7	A1	3pf dk. brown ('00)	4.75	3.25
		a. 3pf light brown	165.00	*325.00*
8	"	5pf green	12.00	6.50
9	A2	10pf carmine ('00)	16.50	16.50
10	"	20pf ultra. ('00)	22.50	22.50
11	"	25pf orange	27.50	32.50
12	"	50pf red brown	45.00	45.00
		Nos. 7-12 (6)	128.25	126.25

Kaiser's Yacht "Hohenzollern"
A3 A4

Typographed.

1901	***Perf. 14***		**Unwmkd.**	
13	A3	3pf brown	1.10	*1.65*
14	"	5pf green	1.10	*1.65*
15	"	10pf carmine	1.10	*6.50*
16	"	20pf ultramarine	1.35	*13.50*
17	"	25pf org. & blk., *yel.*	1.65	*25.00*
18	"	30pf org. & blk., *sal.*	1.65	*25.00*
19	"	40pf lake & black	1.65	*25.00*
20	"	50pf pur. & blk., *sal.*	2.25	*32.50*
21	"	80pf lake & blk., *rose*	3.85	*40.00*

Engraved.

Perf. 14½x14

22	A4	1m carmine	5.25	*85.00*
23	"	2m blue	7.50	*120.00*
24	"	3m black violet	12.00	*185.00*
25	"	5m slate & car.	165.00	*650.00*
		Nos. 13-25 (13)	205.45	

Wmkd. Lozenges. (125)

1916	**Typographed**		***Perf. 14***
26	A3	3pf brown	1.10

Engraved.

Perf. 14½x14

27	A4	5m slate & carmine	27.50

Nos. 26 and 27 were never placed in use.

The stamps of Marshall Islands overprinted "G. R. I." and new values in British currency were all used in New Britain and are, therefore, listed among the issues for that country, in Volume I of the Standard Postage Stamp Catalogue.

MARTINIQUE

(mär′ti·nēk′)

LOCATION—An island in the West Indies, southeast of Puerto Rico.

GOVT.—Former French Colony.

AREA—385 sq. mi.

POP.—261,595 (1946).

CAPITAL—Fort-de-France.

Formerly a French colony, Martinique became an integral part of the Republic, acquiring the same status as the departments in metropolitan France, under a law effective Jan. 1, 1947.

100 Centimes = 1 Franc

Stamps of French Colonies 1881–86 Surcharged in Black:

MARTINIQUE 5 — *a*

MARTINIQUE 5c — *b*

MQE 15 c. — *c*

MQE 15 c. — *d*

MARTINIQUE 01 — *e*

MARTINIQUE 01c. — *f*

1886–91	***Perf. 14x13½.***		**Unwmkd.**		
1	A9	(*a*)	5 on 20c red, *green*	20.00	18.50
			a. Double surcharge	175.00	175.00
2	"	(*b*)	5c on 20c red, *green*	*4000.00*	*4000.00*
3	"	(*c*)	15c on 20c red, *green* ('87)	80.00	80.00
			a. Inverted surcharge	500.00	500.00
4	"	(*d*)	15c on 20c red, *green* ('87)	35.00	30.00
			a. Inverted surcharge	400.00	400.00
5	"	(*e*)	01 on 20c red, *green* ('88)	4.75	3.75
			a. Inverted surcharge	100.00	100.00
6	"	(")	05 on 20c red, *green*	2.50	2.00
7	"	(*a*)	15 on 20c red, *grn.* ('88)	60.00	50.00
			a. Slanting "5"	70.00	60.00
			b. Double surcharge	75.00	60.00
			c. Inverted surcharge	175.00	175.00
8	"	(*e*)	015 on 20c red, *green* ('87)	18.50	16.50
			a. Inverted surcharge	185.00	165.00
9	"	(*f*)	01c on 2c brown, *buff* ('88)	85	75
			a. Double surcharge	90.00	90.00
10	"	(")	01c on 4c claret, *lavender* ('88)	2.50	1.00
11	"	(")	05c on 4c claret, *lavender* ('88)	500.00	450.00
			a. Slanting "5"	*850.00*	*850.00*
12	"	(")	05c on 10c *lavender* ('90)	25.00	15.00
			a. Slanting "5"	50.00	45.00
13	"	(")	05c on 20c red, *green* ('88)	6.00	5.00
			a. Slanting "5"	50.00	45.00
			b. Inverted surcharge	100.00	80.00
14	"	(")	05c on 30c brown, *bistre* ('91)	9.00	8.00
			a. Slanting "5"	50.00	45.00
15	"	(")	05c on 35c deep violet, *orange* ('91)	5.00	4.00
			a. Slanting "5"	35.00	35.00
			b. Inverted surcharge	70.00	65.00
16	"	(")	05c on 40c red, *straw* ('91)	16.50	14.00
			a. Slanting "5"	65.00	65.00
17	"	(")	15c on 4c claret, *lavender* ('88)	*3750.00*	*3250.00*
18	"	(")	15c on 20c red, *green* ('87)	40.00	30.00
19	"	(")	15c on 25c *rose* ('90)	5.00	4.00
			a. Slanting "5"	35.00	35.00
			b. Inverted surcharge	90.00	85.00
20	"	(")	15c on 75c carmine, *rose* ('91)	55.00	45.00
			a. Slanting "5"	90.00	85.00

French Colonies No. 47 Surcharged

TIMBRE-POSTE 01c. MARTINIQUE — *g*

1891				
21	A9	01c on 2c brn., *buff*	2.50	2.50

French Colonies Nos. J5–J9 Surcharged

TIMBRE-POSTE 05c. MARTINIQUE

h

Black Surcharge.

1891-92 *Imperf.*

22 D1 (h) 05c on 5c black ('92) 4.00 4.00
a. Slanting "5" 18.50 17.50
23 " (") 05c on 15c black 3.00 2.75
a. Without "TIMBRE-POSTE" 7.50
b. Slanting "5" 18.50 17.50
24 " (") 15c on 20c black 4.00 3.00
a. Inverted surcharge 70.00 70.00
b. Double surch. 70.00 70.00
25 " (") 15c on 30c black 4.00 3.75
a. Inverted surcharge 70.00 70.00
b. Slanting "5" 18.50 17.50

Red Surcharge.

26 D1 (h) 05c on 10c black 2.50 2.50
a. Inverted surcharge 70.00 70.00
27 " (") 05c on 15c black 4.00 4.00
28 " (") 15c on 20c black 12.00 10.00
a. Inverted surcharge 85.00 85.00

French Colonies No. 54 Surcharged in Black:

1892 MARTINIQUE 05c.

j

1892 05c. MARTINIQUE

k

1892 *Perf. 14x13½.*

29 A9 (j) 05c on 25c *rose* 16.50 16.50
a. Slanting "5" 70.00 70.00
30 " (") 15c on 25c *rose* 7.00 7.00
a. Slanting "5" 70.00 70.00
31 " (k) 05c on 25c *rose* 15.00 13.50
a. "1882" instead of "1892" 120.00 100.00
b. "95" instead of "05" 140.00 120.00
c. Slanting "5" 70.00 70.00
32 " (") 15c on 25c *rose* 7.00 7.00
a. "1882" instead of "1892" 110.00 100.00
b. Slanting "5" 35.00 35.00

Navigation and Commerce
A15

1892–1906 Typographed

Name of Colony in Carmine or Blue

33 A15 1c *lilac blue* 40 40
a. Name in blue 125.00 125.00
34 " 2c brown, *buff* 40 40
35 " 4c claret, *lavender* 40 40
36 " 5c green, *greenish* 60 30
37 " 5c yel. green ('99) 80 20
38 " 10c *lavender* 2.25 30
39 " 10c red ('99) 1.25 20
40 " 15c blue, quadrille paper 8.00 1.85
41 " 15c gray ('99) 3.00 40
42 " 20c red, *green* 5.00 1.40
43 " 25c *rose* 6.00 60
44 " 25c blue ('99) 4.00 3.25
45 " 30c brown, *bistre* 10.00 4.00
46 " 35c *yellow* ('06) 5.00 2.00
47 " 40c red, *straw* 10.00 4.00
48 " 50c carmine, *rose* 9.00 5.00
49 " 50c brown, *azure* ('99) 10.00 8.00
50 " 75c dp. vio., *orange* 9.00 5.50
51 " 1fr bronze green, *straw* 7.00 4.00
52 " 2fr violet, *rose* ('04) 27.50 27.50
53 A15 5fr lilac, *lavender* ('03) 32.50 32.50
Nos. 33-53 (21) 152.10 102.20

Stamps of 1892–1903 Surcharged in Black 10c

1904

54 A15 10c on 30c brown, *bistre* 2.50 2.50
a. Double surch. 35.00 35.00
55 " 10c on 5fr lilac, *lavender* 4.00 4.00

Surcharged 1904 0f10

56 A15 10c on 30c brown, *bistre* 5.00 5.00
57 " 10c on 40c red, *straw* 5.00 5.00
a. Double surch. 110.00 110.00
58 " 10c on 50c car., *rose* 5.00 5.00
59 " 10c on 75c deep violet, *orange* 4.50 4.50
60 " 10c on 1fr bronze green, *straw* 5.00 5.00
a. Double surcharge 65.00 65.00
61 " 10c on 5fr lilac, *lavender* 70.00 70.00
Nos. 54-61 (8) 101.00 101.00

Martinique Woman
A16

Girl Bearing Pineapple in Cane Field
A18

View of Fort-de-France
A17

1908–30 Typographed

62 A16 1c red brn. & brn. 6 6
63 " 2c olive grn. & brn. 6 6
64 " 4c vio. brn. & brown 8 5
65 " 5c green & brown 10 6
66 " 5c org. & brn. ('22) 5 5
67 " 10c carmine & brown 15 8
68 " 10c blue green & green ('22) 10 10
69 " 10c brown violet & rose ('25) 6 6
70 " 15c brown violet & rose ('17) 10 5
71 " 15c blue green & gray green ('25) 7 7
72 " 15c deep blue & red orange ('27) 20 20
73 " 20c violet & brown 25 20
74 A17 25c blue & brown 25 5
75 " 25c org. & brn. ('22) 10 6
76 " 30c brn. org. & brn. 30 20
77 " 30c dull red & brown ('22) 6 6
78 " 30c rose & vermilion ('24) 5 5
79 " 30c olive brown & brown ('25) 5 5
80 " 30c slate blue & blue green ('27) 15 15
81 " 35c violet & brown 15 15
82 " 40c gray grn. & brn. 20 10
83 " 45c dk. brn. & brown 15 15
84 " 50c rose & brown 25 20
85 " 50c bl. & brn. ('22) 25 20
86 " 50c org. & grn. ('25) 10 5
87 A17 60c dark blue & lilac rose ('25) 10 5
88 " 65c violet & olive brown ('27) 40 40
89 " 75c slate & brown 20 15
90 " 75c indigo & dark blue ('25) 10 8
91 " 75c orange brown & light blue ('27) 65 65
92 " 90c brown red & brt. red ('30) 1.20 1.20
93 A18 1fr dull bl. & brn. 15 10
94 " 1fr dark blue ('25) 10 8
95 " 1fr vermilion & olive grn. ('27) 40 40
96 " 1.10fr violet & dark brown ('28) 70 70
97 " 1.50fr indigo & ultra. ('30) 1.50 1.50
98 " 2fr gray & brown 85 30
99 " 3fr red violet ('30) 1.85 1.85
100 " 5fr org. red & brn. 3.25 3.00
Nos. 62-100 (39) 14.79 12.97

Nos. 63 and 64 exist on both ordinary and chalky paper.

Nos. 41, 43, 47 and 53 Surcharged in Carmine or Black

05 a 10 b

1912, Aug.

101 A15 (a) 5c on 15c gray (C) 15 15
102 " (") 5c on 25c *rose* (C) 40 40
103 " (b) 10c on 40c red, *straw* 45 45
104 " (") 10c on 5fr lilac, *lavender* 50 50

Two spacings between the surcharged numerals are found on Nos. 101 to 104.

Nos. 62, 63, 70 Surcharged 05

1920, June 15

105 A16 5c on 1c red brown & brown 45 45
a. Double surcharge 8.00 8.00
b. Inverted surcharge 8.00 8.00
106 " 10c on 2c olive green & brown 35 35
a. Inverted surcharge 8.00 8.00
107 " 25c on 15c brown violet & rose 30 30
a. Double surcharge 10.00 10.00
b. Inverted surch. 10.00 10.00

No. 70 Surcharged ≡ 0,01 ≡ in Various Colors

1922, Dec.

108 A16 1c on 15c brown violet & rose (Bk) 6 6
109 " 2c on 15c brown violet & rose (Bl) 6 6
110 " 5c on 15c brown violet & rose (R) 6 6
a. Imperf., pair 30.00

Types of 1908-30 Surcharged 60

1923–25

111 A17 60c on 75c blue & rose 10 10
112 " 65c on 45c olive brown & brown ('25) 30 30
113 " 85c on 75c black & brown (R) ('25) 25 25

Nos. 63, 73, 76–77, 84–85 Surcharged 0,01 in Brown.

1924, Feb. 14

114 A16 1c on 2c olive green & brown 55 55
a. Double surch. 90.00 90.00
b. Inverted surcharge 16.50 16.50
115 " 5c on 20c violet & brown 65 65
a. Inverted surcharge 15.00 15.00
116 A17 15c on 30c brown org. & brn. 3.50 3.50
a. Inverted surch. 8.00 8.00
117 " 15c on 30c dull red & brown 4.00 4.00
118 " 25c on 50c rose & brown 100.00 90.00
119 " 25c on 50c blue & brown 1.50 1.50
Nos. 114-119 (6) 110.20 100.20

Stamps and Types of 1908-30 Surcharged with New Value and Bars

1924-27

120 A16 25c on 15c brown violet & rose ('25) 7 7
121 A18 25c on 2fr gray & brown 7 7
122 " 25c on 5fr orange red & brown (Bl) 20 20
123 A17 90c on 75c brown red & red ('27) 75 65
124 A18 1.25fr on 1fr dark blue ('26) 10 7
125 " 1.50fr on 1fr dark blue & ultra. ('27) 30 28
126 " 3fr on 5fr dull red & green ('27) 50 45
127 " 10fr on 5fr dull green & dp. red ('27) 3.00 2.75
128 " 20fr on 5fr orange brown & red violet ('27) 4.50 4.00
Nos. 120-128 (9) 9.49 8.54

Colonial Exposition Issue.

Common Design Types

1931, Apr. 13 Engr. *Perf. 12½*

Name of Country in Black.

129 CD70 40c deep green 1.10 1.10
130 CD71 50c violet 1.10 1.10
131 CD72 90c red orange 1.10 1.10
132 CD73 1.50fr dull blue 1.10 1.10

Village of Basse-Pointe
A19

Government Palace, Fort-de-France
A20

Martinique Women
A21

1933–40 Photo. *Perf. 13½*

133 A19 1c red, *pink* 4 4
134 A20 2c dull blue 6 6
135 " 3c sepia ('40) 6 6
136 A19 4c olive green 6 6
137 A20 5c deep rose 6 6
138 A19 10c black, *pink* 6 6
139 A20 15c black, *orange* 6 6
140 A21 20c orange brown 5 5
141 A19 25c brown violet 7 7
142 A20 30c green 7 7
143 " 30c light ultra. ('40) 5 5
144 A21 35c dull green ('38) 5 5
145 " 40c olive brown 5 5
146 A20 45c dark brown 38 38
147 " 45c green ('40) 10 10
148 " 50c red 5 5
149 A19 55c brown red ('38) 15 15

150 A19 60c light blue ('40) 10 10
151 A21 65c red, *green* 10 10
152 " 70c bright red violet ('40) 7 7
153 A19 75c dark brown 18 18
154 A20 80c violet ('38) 10 10
155 A19 90c carmine 45 45
156 " 90c bright red violet ('39) 10 10
157 A20 1fr black, *green* 45 30
158 " 1fr rose red ('38) 12 12
159 A21 1.25fr dark violet 12 12
160 " 1.25fr deep rose ('39) 12 12
161 A19 1.40fr lt. ultra. ('40) 12 12
162 A20 1.50fr deep blue 5 5
163 " 1.60fr chestnut ('40) 15 15
164 A21 1.75fr olive green 2.50 1.00
165 " 1.75fr deep blue ('38) 12 12
166 A19 2fr dark blue, *green* 8 8
167 A21 2.25fr blue ('39) 10 10
168 A19 2.50fr sepia ('40) 10 10
169 A21 3fr brown violet 7 7
170 " 5fr red, *pink* 30 10
171 A19 10fr dark blue, *blue* 13 13
172 A20 20fr red, *yellow* 20 20
Nos. 133-172 (40) 7.25 5.40

Landing of Bélain d'Esnambuc
A22

Freed Slaves Paying Homage to Victor Schoelcher
A23

1935, Oct. 22 Engr. *Perf. 13*

173 A22 40c black brown 65 65
174 " 50c dull red 65 65
175 " 1.50fr ultramarine 5.25 4.75
176 A23 1.75fr lilac rose 4.75 4.75
177 " 5fr brown 4.75 4.75
178 " 10fr blue green 3.00 3.00
Nos. 173-178 (6) 19.05 18.55

Tercentenary of French possessions in the West Indies.

Colonial Arts Exhibition Issue.
Souvenir Sheet.
Common Design Type

1937 *Imperf.*

179 CD74 3fr bright green 1.65 1.65

Issued in sheets measuring 118x99mm. containing one stamp.

Paris International Exposition Issue.
Common Design Types

1937, Apr. 15 *Perf. 13*

180 CD74 20c deep violet 40 40
181 CD75 30c dark green 40 40
182 CD76 40c carmine rose 40 40
183 CD77 50c dk. brn. & blk. 40 40
184 CD78 90c red 40 40
185 CD79 1.50fr ultramarine 40 40
a. Name omitted
Nos. 180-185 (6) 2.40 2.40

Common Design Types
pictured in section at front of book.

New York World's Fair Issue.
Common Design Type

1939, May 10 *Perf. 12½x12*

186 CD82 1.25fr carmine lake 35 35
187 " 2.25fr ultramarine 35 35

View of Fort-de-France and Marshal Pétain
A23a

1941 Engraved *Perf. 12½x12*

188 A23a 1fr dull lilac 12
189 " 2.50fr blue 12

Nos. 188-189 were issued by the Vichy government, and were not placed on sale in Martinique.

Nos. 134, 135, 136 and 151 Surcharged with New Values and Bars or Wavy Lines in Red, Black or Blue.

1945 *Perf. 13½, 13x13½.*

190 A20 1fr on 2c dull bl. (R) 8 8
191 A19 2fr on 4c olive green 10 10
192 A20 3fr on 2c dull blue (R) 12 12
193 A21 5fr on 65c red, *green* 25 25
194 " 10fr on 65c red, *green* 20 20
195 A20 20fr on 3c sepia (Bl) 30 30
Nos. 190-195 (6) 1.05 1.05

Eboue Issue.
Common Design Type

1945 Engraved. *Perf. 13*

196 CD91 2fr black 8 8
197 " 25fr Prussian green 25 25

Victor Schoelcher and View of Town of Schoelcher
A24

Lithographed.

1945 *Perf. 11½* Unwmkd.

198 A24 10c deep blue violet & ultramarine 4 4
199 " 30c dark orange brown & light orange brown 4 4
200 " 40c greenish blue & pale blue 5 5
201 " 50c carmine brown & rose lilac 6 6
202 " 60c org. yel. & yellow 6 6
203 " 70c brown & pale brown 6 6
204 " 80c light blue green & pale green 8 8
205 " 1fr blue & light blue 6 6
206 " 1.20fr rose violet & rose lilac 8 8
207 " 1.50fr red orange & orange 8 8
208 " 2fr black & gray 10 10
209 " 2.40fr red & pink 30 30
210 " 3fr pink & pale pink 8 8
211 " 4fr ultramarine & lt. ultra. 10 7
212 " 4.50fr yellow green & light green 18 12
213 " 5fr orange brown & lt. org. brn. 10 10
214 " 10fr dark violet & lilac 30 15
215 " 15fr rose carmine & lilac rose 30 15
216 " 20fr olive green & light olive green 40 30
Nos. 198-216 (19) 2.47 1.98

Martinique Girl
A25

Mountains
A30

Cliffs—A26

Gathering Sugar Cane
A27

Mount Pelée—A28

Tropical Fruit—A29

Engraved

1947, June 2 *Perf. 13* Unwmkd.

217 A25 10c red brown 6 6
218 " 30c deep blue 5 5
219 " 50c olive brown 5 5
220 A26 60c dark green 5 5
221 " 1fr red brown 8 8
222 " 1.50fr purple 7 6
223 A27 2fr blue green 30 30
224 " 2.50fr black brown 30 25
225 " 3fr deep blue 25 20
226 A28 4fr dark brown 25 25
227 " 5fr dark green 25 25
228 " 6fr lilac rose 20 15
229 A29 10fr indigo 30 20
230 " 15fr red brown 50 40
231 " 20fr black brown 65 55
232 A30 25fr violet 70 50
233 " 40fr blue green 70 55
Nos. 217-233 (17) 4.76 3.95

SEMI-POSTAL STAMPS

Regular Issue of 1908 Surcharged in Red ✚ 5c

Perf. 13½x14

1915, May 15 Unwmkd.

B1 A16 10c+5c car. & brown 60 50

Curie Issue
Common Design Type

1938, Oct. 24 *Perf. 13*

B2 CD80 1.75fr+50c bright ultramarine 3.25 3.25

French Revolution Issue.
Common Design Type
Name and Value Typographed in Black

1939, July 5 Photogravure

B3 CD83 45(c)+25(c) green 2.25 2.25
B4 " 70(c)+30(c) brown 2.25 2.25
B5 " 90(c)+35(c) red orange 2.25 2.25
B6 " 1.25fr+1fr rose pink 2.25 2.25
B7 " 2.25fr+2fr blue 2.25 2.25
Nos. B3-B7 (5) 11.25 11.25

Common Design Type and

Colonial Infantry with Machine Gun—SP1

Naval Rifleman
SP2

1941 Photogravure *Perf. 13½*

B8 SP1 1fr+1fr red 25
B9 CD86 1.50fr+3fr maroon 25
B10 SP2 2.50fr+1fr blue 25

Nos. B8-B10 were issued by the Vichy government, and were not placed on sale in Martinique.

Nos. 188-189 were surcharged "OEUVRES COLONIALES" and surtax (including change of denomination of the 2.50fr to 50c). These were issued in 1944 by the Vichy government, and were not placed on sale in Martinique.

Red Cross Issue
Common Design Type

1944 *Perf. 14½x14.*

B11 CD90 5fr+20fr dark purple 25 25

The surtax was for the French Red Cross and national relief.

AIR POST STAMPS.
Common Design Type
Photogravure.

1945 *Perf. 14½x14* Unwmkd.

C1 CD87 50fr dark green 20 20
C2 " 100fr plum 30 30

Two other values, 8.50fr orange and 18fr red brown, were prepared but not issued. Price, $50 each.

Victory Issue
Common Design Type

1946, May 8 Engraved *Perf. 12½*

C3 CD92 8fr indigo 45 45

Issued to commemorate the European victory of the Allied Nations in World War II.

Chad to Rhine Issue
Common Design Types

1946, June 6

C4 CD93 5fr orange 15 15
C5 CD94 10fr slate green 20 20
C6 CD95 15fr carmine 20 20
C7 CD96 20fr chocolate 20 20
C8 CD97 25fr deep blue 35 35
C9 CD98 50fr gray black 40 40
Nos. C4-C9 (6) 1.50 1.50

Seaplane and Beach Scene—AP1

Plane over Tropic Shore
AP2

Albatross—AP3

1947, June 2 *Perf. 13*

C10	AP1	50fr dk. brn. vio.	1.25	1.10
C11	AP2	100fr dk. bl. green	1.75	1.60
C12	AP3	200fr violet	10.00	7.50

AIR POST SEMI-POSTAL STAMPS.

Stamps similar to French Guiana type V6 inscribed "Martinique" and stamp of Cameroun type V10 inscribed "Martinique" were issued in 1942 by the Vichy Government, but were not placed on sale in Martinique.

POSTAGE DUE STAMPS.

The set of 14 French Colonies postage due stamps (Nos. J1-14) overprinted "MARTINIQUE" diagonally in red in 1887 was not an official issue.

Postage Due Stamps of France, 1893–1926

Overprinted **MARTINIQUE**

1927, Oct. 10 *Perf. 14x13½*

J15	D2	5c light blue	40	40
J16	"	10c brown	60	60
J17	"	20c olive green	60	60
J18	"	25c rose	1.00	1.00
J19	"	30c red	1.00	1.00
J20	"	45c green	1.00	1.00
J21	"	50c brown violet	2.00	2.00
J22	"	60c blue green	2.00	2.00
J23	"	1fr red brown	2.50	2.50
J24	"	2fr bright violet	3.00	3.00
J25	"	3fr magenta	4.00	4.00
		Nos. J15-J25 (11)	18.10	18.10

Tropical Fruit
D3

Map
D4

1933, Feb. 15 Photo. *Perf. 13½*

J26	D3	5c dark blue, *green*	5	5
J27	"	10c orange brown	8	8
J28	"	20c dark blue	30	30
J29	"	25c red, *pink*	30	30
J30	"	30c dark violet	22	22
J31	"	45c red, *yellow*	10	10
J32	"	50c dark brown	22	22
J33	"	60c dull green	25	25
J34	"	1fr black, *orange*	45	45
J35	"	2fr deep rose	20	20
J36	D3	3fr dark blue, *blue*	30	30
		Nos. J26-J36 (11)	2.47	2.47

Stamps of type D3 without the "RF" monogram were issued in 1943 by the Vichy Government, but were not placed on sale in Martinique.

1947, June 2 Engr. *Perf. 14x13*

J37	D4	10c ultramarine	6	6
J38	"	30c bright blue green	5	5
J39	"	50c slate gray	8	8
J40	"	1fr orange red	10	10
J41	"	2fr dark violet brown	15	15
J42	"	3fr lilac rose	17	17
J43	"	4fr dark brown	25	25
J44	"	5fr red	30	30
J45	"	10fr black	45	45
J46	"	20fr olive green	40	40
		Nos. J37-J46 (10)	2.01	2.01

PARCEL POST STAMPS.

Postage Due Stamp of French Colonies Surcharged in Black

TIMBRE POSTE
5 F.
MARTINIQUE
COLIS POSTAUX

1903, Oct. *Imperf.* **Unwmkd.**

Q1	D1	5fr on 60c brn., *buff*	185.00	185.00
		a. Inverted surch.	250.00	250.00

MAURITANIA

(mô'rĭ·tā'nĭ·ȧ)

LOCATION—In northwestern Africa, bordering on the Atlantic Ocean.

GOVT.—Republic; former French Colony.

AREA—415,900 sq. mi.

POP.—1,481,000 (est. 1977).

CAPITAL—Nouakchott (formerly St. Louis).

100 Centimes = 1 Franc

Ouguiya ("um") (1973)

The Islamic Republic of Mauritania was proclaimed Nov. 28, 1958.

Stamps of French West Africa were used in the period between the issues of the colony and the republic.

General Louis Faidherbe
A1

Oil Palms
A2

Dr. Noel Eugène Ballay
A3

Perf. 14x13½

1906-07 Typo. **Unwmkd.**

"Mauritanie" in Red or Blue.

1	A1	1c slate	10	8
2	"	2c chocolate	25	20
3	"	4c chocolate, *gray blue*	40	25
4	"	5c green	30	12
5	"	10c carmine (B)	2.50	1.65
7	A2	20c *azure*	6.00	5.00
8	"	25c blue, *pinkish*	2.35	2.00
9	"	30c chocolate, *pinkish*	32.50	25.00
10	"	35c *yellow*	2.25	1.50
11	"	40c car., *azure* (B)	2.25	1.50
12	"	45c choc., *greenish* ('07)	2.00	1.85
13	"	50c deep violet	1.85	1.75
14	"	75c blue, *orange*	1.85	1.75
15	A3	1fr *azure*	5.00	5.00
16	"	2fr blue, *pink*	12.00	10.00
17	"	5fr car., *straw* (B)	47.50	47.50
		Nos. 1-17 (16)	119.10	105.15

Crossing Desert—A4

1913-38

18	A4	1c brn. vio. & brn.	6	6
19	"	2c black & blue	6	6
20	"	4c violet & black	6	6
21	"	5c yellow green & blue green	6	6
		a. Booklet pane of 4	2.00	
22	"	5c brown violet & rose ('22)	5	5
23	"	10c rose & red orange	25	25
		a. Booklet pane of 4	3.50	
24	"	10c yellow green & blue green ('22)	5	5
		a. Booklet pane of 4	3.50	
25	"	10c lilac rose, *bluish* ('25)	5	5
26	"	15c dark brown & black ('17)	5	5
		a. Booklet pane of 4	3.50	
27	"	20c bis. brn. & org.	10	10
28	"	25c blue & violet	35	35
29	"	25c green & rose ('22)	6	6
30	"	30c blue green & rose	20	20
31	"	30c rose & red orange ('22)	25	25
32	"	30c black & yellow ('26)	6	6
33	"	30c blue green & yel. green ('28)	40	40
34	"	35c brown & violet	15	15
35	"	35c deep green & light green ('38)	10	10
36	"	40c gray & blue green	65	65
37	"	45c org. & bis. brn.	20	20
38	"	50c brn. vio. & rose	20	20
39	"	50c dark blue & ultramarine ('22)	10	10
40	"	50c gray green & deep blue ('26)	15	15
41	"	60c violet, *pinkish* ('26)	10	10
42	"	65c yellow brown & light blue ('26)	20	20
43	"	75c ultra. & brown	25	20
44	"	85c myrtle green & light brown ('26)	30	30
45	"	90c brown red & rose ('30)	40	40
46	"	1fr rose & black	15	10
47	"	1.10fr violet & vermilion ('28)	3.00	3.00
48	"	1.25fr dark blue & black brown ('33)	45	45
49	"	1.50fr light blue & deep blue ('30)	10	10
50	"	1.75fr blue green & brown red ('33)	10	10
51	"	1.75fr dark blue & ultramarine ('38)	10	10
52	"	2fr red orange & violet	55	40
53	"	3fr red violet ('30)	35	35
54	"	5fr violet & blue	65	40
		Nos. 18-54 (37)	10.36	9.86

Stamps and Type of 1913-38 Surcharged

60 **60**

1922-25

55	A4	60c on 75c violet, *pinkish*	15	15
56	"	65c on 15c dark brown & black ('25)	45	45
57	"	85c on 75c ultramarine & brown ('25)	45	45

Stamp and Type of 1913-38 Surcharged with New Value and Bars.

1924-27

58	A4	25c on 2fr red orange & violet	30	30
59	"	90c on 75c brown red & cerise ('27)	60	60
60	"	1.25fr on 1 fr dk. blue & ultra. ('26)	10	10
61	"	1.50fr on 1fr blue & deep blue ('27)	40	40
62	"	3fr on 5fr olive brown & red violet ('27)	2.35	2.35
63	"	10fr on 5fr magenta & blue green ('27)	2.00	2.00
64	"	20fr on 5fr blue violet & dp. orange ('27)	2.35	2.35
		Nos. 58-64 (7)	8.10	8.10

Colonial Exposition Issue.

Common Design Types
Name of Country
Typographed in Black.

1931, Apr. 13 Engr. *Perf. 12½*

65	CD70	40c deep green	1.50	1.50
66	CD71	50c violet	1.25	1.25
67	CD72	90c red orange	1.25	1.25
68	CD73	1.50fr dull blue	1.25	1.25

Paris International Exposition Issue.

Common Design Types

1937, Apr. 15 *Perf. 13*

69	CD74	20c deep violet	35	25
70	CD75	30c dark green	35	30
71	CD76	40c carmine rose	35	30
72	CD77	50c dk. brn. & black	25	25
73	CD78	90c red	30	30
74	CD79	1.50fr ultramarine	30	30
		Nos. 69-74 (6)	1.90	1.70

Colonial Arts Exhibition Issue.

Souvenir Sheet.
Common Design Type

1937 *Imperf.*

75	CD76	3fr dark blue	1.35	1.35

Size: 118x99mm.

Camel Rider
A5

Mauri Couple
A8

Mauris on Camels—A6

Family before Tent—A7

1938-40 *Perf. 13.*

76 A5 2c violet black 5 5
77 " 3c deep ultramarine 6 6
78 " 4c rose violet 5 5
79 " 5c orange red 5 5
80 " 10c brown carmine 5 5
81 " 15c dark violet 5 5
82 A6 20c red 5 5
83 " 25c deep ultramarine 6 6
84 " 30c deep brown 6 6
85 " 35c Prussian green 7 7
86 " 40c rose carmine('40) 7 7
87 " 45c Prus. green ('40) 10 10
88 " 50c purple 10 10
89 A7 55c rose violet 15 15
90 " 60c violet ('40) 12 12
91 " 65c deep green 20 20
92 " 70c red ('40) 20 20
93 " 80c deep blue 45 45
94 " 90c rose violet ('39) 15 15
95 " 1fr red 45 45
96 " 1fr deep green ('40) 15 15
97 " 1.25fr rose carmine('39) 30 30
98 " 1.40fr deep blue ('40) 25 25
99 " 1.50fr violet 20 20
99A " 1.50fr red brn. ('40) 25.00 25.00
100 " 1.60fr black brown('40) 30 30
101 A8 1.75fr deep ultramarine 25 25
102 " 2fr rose violet 30 30
103 " 2.25fr dull ultra. ('39) 15 15
104 " 2.50fr black brown ('40) 20 20
105 " 3fr deep green 15 15
106 " 5fr scarlet 22 22
107 " 10fr deep brown 45 45
108 " 20fr brown carmine 45 45
Nos. 76–108 (34) 30.91 30.91

Nos. 91 and 109 surcharged with new values are listed under French West Africa.

Caillie Issue.

Common Design Type

Perf. 12½x12

1939, Apr. 5 Engraved

109 CD81 90c org. brn. & orange 50 50
110 " 2fr bright violet 55 55
111 " 2.25fr ultramarine & dark blue 50 50

Centenary of the death of René Caillié (1799–1838), French explorer.

New York World's Fair Issue.

Common Design Type

1939, May 10

112 CD82 1.25fr carmine lake 25 25
113 " 2.25fr ultramarine 25 25

Caravan and Marshal Pétain A9

1941

114 A9 1fr green 10
115 " 2.50fr deep blue 10

Nos. 114–115 were issued by the Vichy government, and were not placed on sale in the colony. This also holds true for six stamps of types A5–A7 without "RF," issued in 1943–44.

Common Design Types

pictured in section at front of book.

Islamic Republic

Camel and Hands Raising Flag A10

Engraved.

1960, Jan. 20 *Perf. 13* Unwmkd.

116 A10 25fr multi., *pink* 50 32

Issued to commemorate the proclamation of the Islamic Republic of Mauritania.

Imperforates

Most Mauritania stamps from 1960 onward exist imperforate in issued and trial colors, and also in small presentation sheets in issued colors.

C.C.T.A. Issue

Common Design Type

1960, May 16

117 CD106 25fr bluish green & ultramarine 55 35

Flag and Map A11

1960, Dec. 15 Engr. *Perf. 13*

118 A11 25fr orange brown, emerald & sepia 35 25

Issued to commemorate the proclamation of independence, Nov. 28, 1960.

Pastoral Well A12

Scimitar-horned Oryx A15

Spotted Hyena A13

Ore Train and Camel Riders A14

Designs: 50c, 1fr, Well. 2fr, Date harvesting. 3fr, Aoudad. 4fr, Fennecs. 5fr, Millet harvesting. 10fr, Shoemaker. 15fr, Fishing boats. 20fr, Nomad school. 25fr, 30fr, Seated dance. No. 130, Religious student. 60fr, Metalworker.

1960–62 *Perf. 13* Unwmkd.

119 A12 50c magenta, yel. & brown ('61) 4 3
120 " 1fr brown, yellow brown & green 5 4
121 A12 2fr dark brown, blue & green 6 4
122 A13 3fr blue green, red brown & gray ('61) 6 6
123 " 4fr yellow green & ochre ('61) 8 7
124 A12 5fr red, dark brown & yellow brn. 10 5
125 A14 10fr dk. bl. & orange 20 8
126 " 15fr vermilion, dark brown, green & blue 30 8
127 " 20fr grn., slate green & red brown 35 10
128 A12 25fr ultramarine & gray green ('61) 40 7
129 " 30fr lilac, bistre & indigo 45 8
130 " 50fr orange brown & green 90 32
131 A14 50fr red brown, bl. & olive ('62) 80 55
132 A12 60fr green, claret & purple 1.00 32
133 A15 85fr blue, brown & black ('61) 1.50 75
Nos. 119–133 (15) 6.29 2.64

An overprint, "Jeux Olympiques/Rome 1960 · Tokyo 1964," the 5-ring Olympic emblem and a 75fr surcharge were applied to Nos. 126–127 in 1962.

An overprint, "Aide aux Réfugiès" with uprooted oak emblem, was applied in 1962 to No. 132 and to pink-paper printings of Nos. 129–130.

Other overprints, applied to airmail stamps, are noted after No. C16.

1963, July 6

Designs: 50c, Striped hyena. 1.50fr, Cheetah. 2fr, Guinea baboons. 5fr, Dromedaries. 10fr, Leopard. 15fr, Bongo antelopes. 20fr, Aardvark. 25fr, Patas monkeys. 30fr, Crested porcupine. 50fr, Dorcas gazelle. 60fr, Common chameleon.

134 A15 50c slate green, black & orge. brown 6 3
135 A13 1fr ultramarine, black & yel. 6 3
136 A15 1.50fr olive green, brn. & bister 6 3
137 A13 2fr dk. brn., grn. & deep orge. 10 7
138 A15 5fr brown, ultra. & bister 15 7
139 A13 10fr blk. & bister 20 10
140 " 15fr vio. blue & red brown 25 10
141 " 20fr dk. red brn., dk. bl. & bister 27 10
142 A15 25fr brt. grn., red brown & olive bister 45 15
143 A13 30fr dark brown, dark blue & olive bister 60 20
144 A15 50fr green, ocher & brown 85 40
145 A13 60fr dark blue, emerald & ocher 1.20 70
Nos. 134–145 (12) 4.25 1.98

U.N. Headquarters, New York, and View of Nouakchott A15a

1962, June 1 Engraved *Perf. 13*

167 A15a 15fr black, ultra. & copper red 25 20
168 " 25fr copper red, slate green & ultramarine 40 35
169 " 85fr dark blue, dull purple & copper red 1.25 1.00

Issued to commemorate Mauritania's admission to the United Nations.

African-Malagasy Union Issue

Common Design Type

1962, Sept. 8 Photo. *Perf. 12½x12*

170 CD110 30fr multicolored 50 45

First anniversary of African and Malagasy Union.

Organization Emblem and View of Nouakchott—A16

1962, Oct. 15 *Perf. 12½*

171 A16 30fr dk. red brown, ultramarine & bright green 40 35

Issued to commemorate the 8th Conference of the Organization to Fight Endemic Diseases, Nouakchott, Oct. 15–18.

Map, Mechanized and Manual Farm Work—A17

1962, Nov. 28 Engraved *Perf. 13*

172 A17 30fr black, green & violet brown 45 35

2nd anniversary of independence.

People in European and Mauritanian Clothes—A18

1962, Dec. 24 Unwmkd.

173 A18 25fr multicolored 35 25

First anniversary of Congress for Unity.

Weather and WMO Symbols A20

1964, March 23 *Perf. 13* Unwmkd.

175 A20 85fr dark brown, dark blue & orange 1.25 90

Issued to commemorate the United Nations Fourth World Meteorological Day, March 23.

IQSY Emblem—A21

1964, July 3 Engraved

176 A21 25fr dk. bl., red & grn. 35 25

International Quiet Sun Year, 1964–65

Striped Mullet—A22

Designs: 5fr, Mauritanian lobster (vert.). 10fr, Royal lobster (vert.). 60fr, Maigre fish.

1964, Oct. 5 Engraved *Perf. 13*

177 A22 1fr orge. brn., dark blue & green 5 5
178 " 5fr orge. brn., slate grn. & choc. 13 10
179 " 10fr dk. bl., bister & slate green 30 20
180 " 60fr dk. brn., dp. grn. & dull blue 90 70

Cooperation Issue

Common Design Type

1964, Nov. 7 *Perf. 13* Unwmkd.

181 CD119 25fr magenta, slate green & dk. brown 40 30

Water Lilies
A23

Tropical Plants: 10fr, Acacia (vert.). 20fr, Adenium obesum. 45fr, Caralluma retrospiciens (vert.).

1965, Jan. 11 Engraved *Perf. 13*

182 A23 5fr green, dark blue & pink 12 10
183 " 10fr grn., dull pur. & bister 15 12
184 " 20fr dk. car., dk. brn. & pale brown 22 20
185 " 45fr plum, dk. slate grn. & Prus. bl. 50 40

Hardine
A24

Musical Instruments: 8fr, Tobol (drums). 25fr, Tidinit (stringed instruments). 40fr, Musicians.

1965, Mar. 8 *Perf. 13*

186 A24 2fr red brown, bright blue & sepia 8 5
187 " 8fr red brown, red & brown 15 10
188 " 25fr red brown, emerald & black 30 15
189 " 40fr violet blue, plum & black 45 27

Abraham Lincoln
A25

1965, Apr. 23 Photo. *Perf. 13x12½*

190 A25 50fr lt. ultra. & multi. 75 40

Centenary of death of Abraham Lincoln.

Palms at Adrar
A26

Designs: 4fr, Chinguetti mosque (vert.). 15fr, Clay pit and donkeys. 60fr, Decorated door, Oualata.

1965, June 14 Engraved *Perf. 13*

191 A26 1fr brn., blue & grn. 6 5
192 " 4fr dk. red, bl. & brn. 8 6
193 " 15fr multicolored 17 10
194 " 60fr grn., dark brown & red brown 80 50

Issued for tourist publicity.

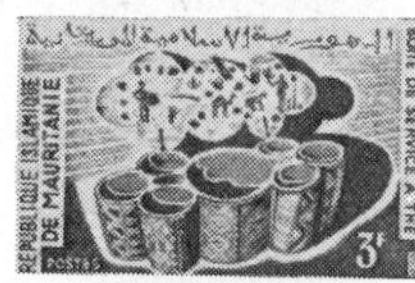

Tea Service in Inlaid Box—A27

Designs: 7fr, Tobacco pouch and pipe (vert.). 25fr, Dagger (vert.). 50fr, Mederdra ornamental chest.

1965, Sept. 13 *Perf. 13* Unwmkd.

195 A27 3fr gray, chocolate & ocher 6 5
196 " 7fr red lilac, Prus. blue & orange 8 8
197 " 25fr black, org. red & brown 25 15
198 " 50fr brt. green, brn. org. & maroon 50 32

Choum Railroad Tunnel
A28

Designs: 10fr, Nouakchott wharf, ships and anchor (horiz.). 85fr, Nouakchott hospital and caduceus (horiz.).

1965, Oct. 18 Engraved *Perf. 13*

199 A28 5fr dark brown & bright green 8 7
200 " 10fr dk. violet blue, brown red & Prussian blue 13 7
201 " 30fr brown red, red & red brown 40 15
202 " 85fr deep blue, rose claret & lilac 1.00 60

Sculptured Heads
A29

Designs: 30fr, "Music and Dance." 60fr, Movie camera and huts.

1966, Apr. Engraved *Perf. 13*

203 A29 10fr brt. green, black & brown 15 15
204 " 30fr brt. blue, red lilac & black 40 25
205 " 60fr red, orange & dark brown 85 50

Issued to commemorate the International Negro Arts Festival, Dakar, Senegal, Apr. 1–24.

Mimosa
A30

Myrina Silenus
A31

Flowers: 15fr, Schouwia purpurea. 20fr, Ipomea asarifolia. 25fr, Grewia bicolor. 30fr, Pancratium trianthum. 60fr, Blepharis linariifolia.

1966, Aug. 8 Photo. *Perf. 13x12½*

Flowers in Natural Colors

206 A30 10fr dull bl. & dk. bl. 12 6
207 " 15fr dk. brown & buff 18 10
208 " 20fr greenish blue & light blue 30 12
209 " 25fr brown & buff 35 15
210 " 30fr lilac & violet 45 18
211 " 60fr grn. & pale grn. 75 40
Nos. 206-211 (6) 2.15 1.01

1966, Oct. 3 Photo. *Perf. 12x12½*

Various Butterflies

212 A31 5fr buff & multi. 10 10
213 " 30fr bl. green & multi. 50 15
214 " 45fr yel. grn. & multi. 75 25
215 " 60fr dull bl. & multi. 1.00 45

Hunter, Petroglyph from Adrar
A32

Designs: 3fr, Two men fighting, petroglyph from Tenses (Adrar). 30fr, Copper jug, Le Mreyer (Adrar). 50fr, Camel caravan.

1966, Oct. 24 Engraved *Perf. 13*

216 A32 2fr dk. brn. & brn. org. 6 5
217 " 3fr blue & brn. orange 8 8
218 " 30fr slate green & dark red 45 20
219 " 50fr magenta, slate grn. & brown 75 50

Issued for tourist publicity.

UNESCO Emblem
A33

1966, Dec. 5 Litho. *Perf. 12½x13*

220 A33 30fr multicolored 45 20

Issued to commemorate the 20th anniversary of UNESCO (United Nations Educational, Scientific and Cultural Organization).

Plaza of Three Cultures, Mexico City
A34

Olympic Village, Grenoble
A35

Designs: 40fr, Olympic torch and skating rink. 100fr, Olympic Stadium, Mexico City.

1967, Mar. 11 Engraved *Perf. 13*

221 A34 20fr dull blue, brn. & slate grn. 30 15
222 A35 30fr dull bl., brown & green 45 15
223 A34 40fr brt. bl., dk. brn. & sepia 55 25
224 A35 100fr brn., emerald & black 1.10 65

Nos. 221 and 223 publicize the 19th Olympic Games, Mexico City; Nos. 222 and 224 the 10th Winter Olympic Games, Grenoble.

Prosopis Tree
A36

1967 Jamboree Emblem and Campsite
A37

Trees: 15fr, Jujube. 20fr, Date palm. 25fr, Peltophorum. 30fr, Baobab.

1967, May 15 Engraved *Perf. 13*

225 A36 10fr brown, blue & slate green 12 8
226 " 15fr dk. brn., vio. bl. & slate green 18 12
227 " 20fr slate green, blue & dark brown 25 15
228 " 25fr brn. & slate grn. 33 15
229 " 30fr verm., slate grn. & yel. brown 40 20
Nos. 225-229 (5) 1.28 70

1967, June 5

Design: 90fr, 1967 Jamboree emblem and Mauritanian Boy Scouts (horiz.).

230 A37 60fr brown, ultra. & slate green 85 40
231 " 90fr dull red, blue & slate green 1.25 55

Issued to publicize the 12th Boy Scout World Jamboree, Farragut State Park, Idaho, Aug. 1–9.

Weavers
A38

Designs: 10fr, Embroiderer (vert.). 20fr, Nurse, mother and infant. 30fr, Laundress (vert.). 50fr, Seamstresses.

1967, July 3 Engraved *Perf. 13*

232 A38 5fr plum, black & claret 8 7
233 " 10fr plum, brt. green & black 10 6
234 " 20fr brt. blue, plum & black 20 15
235 " 30fr dk. blue, brown & black 30 17
236 " 50fr plum, slate & black 50 25
Nos. 232-236 (5) 1.18 70

Progress made by working women.

Cattle and Hypodermic Syringe
A39

1967, Aug, 21 Engraved *Perf. 13*

237 A39 30fr slate grn., brt. bl. & rose claret 30 20

Campaign against cattle plague.

Monetary Union Issue

Common Design Type

1967, Nov. 4 Engraved *Perf. 13*

238 CD125 30fr gray & orange 45 15

Issued to commemorate the 5th anniversary of the West African Monetary Union.

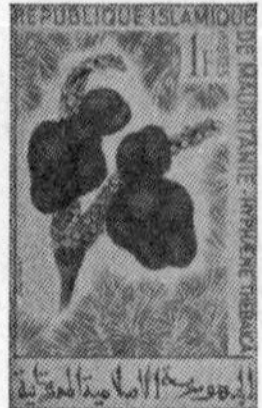

Fruit of Doom Palm
A40

Human Rights Flame
A41

Fruit: 2fr, Bito (horiz.). 3fr, Baobab. 4fr, Jujube (horiz.). 5fr, Date.

1967, Dec. 4 Engraved *Perf. 13*

239 A40 1fr brt. grn., bister & red brown 5 5
240 " 2fr brn. red, yellow & brt. green 5 5
241 " 3fr purple, bright green & olive 6 5
242 " 4fr dk. brn., brt. grn. & dk. car. rose 8 7
243 " 5fr emerald, orange & brown 10 8
Nos. 239-243 (5) 34 30

1968, Jan. 8 Photo. *Perf. 13x12½*

244 A41 30fr brt. grn., black & yellow 40 15
245 " 50fr brn. org., black & yellow 60 28

International Human Rights Year 1968.

Nouakchott Mosque—A42

Designs: 45fr, Amogjar Pass. 90fr, Cavaliers' Towers.

1968, Apr. 1 Photo. *Perf. 12½x13*

246 A42 30fr multicolored 30 15
247 " 45fr " 40 20
248 " 90fr " 80 40

UPU Building, Bern, Globe and Map of Africa
A43

1968, June 3 Engraved *Perf. 13*

249 A43 30fr vermilion, ultra. & olive 30 20

Issued to commemorate Mauritania's admission to the Universal Postal Union.

Symbolic Water Cycle
A44

1968, June 24

250 A44 90fr car. lake, green & slate green 80 45

Issued to publicize the Hydrological Decade (UNESCO), 1965–74.

Land Yacht Racing
A45

Donkey and Foal
A46

Designs: 40fr, Three land yachts racing (horiz.). 60fr, Crew changing wheel of land yacht.

1968, Oct. 7 Engraved *Perf. 13*

251 A45 30fr ultra., orange & ocher 30 15
252 " 40fr ultra., dp. orange & plum 40 20
253 " 60fr brt. green, deep org. & ocher 60 28

1968, Dec. 16 Photo. *Perf. 13*

Domestic Animals: 10fr, Ewe and lamb. 15fr, Camel and calf. 30fr, Mare and foal. 50fr, Cow and calf. 90fr, Goat and kid.

254 A46 5fr ocher & multi. 6 5
255 " 10fr multicolored 10 5
256 " 15fr " 15 10
257 " 30fr " 30 15
258 " 50fr purple & multi. 45 22
259 " 90fr multicolored 80 45
Nos. 254-259 (6) 1.86 1.02

ILO Emblem and Map
A47

Desert Monitor
A48

1969, Apr. 14 Photo. *Perf. 13x12½*

260 A47 50fr dk. & lt. blue, pur. & orange 65 25

Issued to commemorate the 50th anniversary of the International Labor Organization.

1969, May 5 Photo. *Perf. 13x12½*

Reptiles: 10fr, Horned viper. 30fr, Common spitting cobra. 60fr, Rock python. 85fr, African crocodile.

261 A48 5fr brn., pink & yel. 15 10
262 " 10fr brown, lt. green & yellow 25 15
263 " 30fr dk. brown, pink & yellow 40 22
264 " 60fr dk. brown, lt. bl. & yellow 70 40
265 " 85fr dk. brown, yellow & red 1.00 70
Nos. 261-265 (5) 2.50 1.57

Palm Weevil
A49

1969, May 26 Engraved *Perf. 13*

266 A49 30fr indigo, green & maroon 40 20

Protection of date palms.

Development Bank Issue
Common Design Type

1969, Sept. 10 Engraved *Perf. 13*

267 CD130 30fr Prus. blue, green & ocher 35 15

Issued to commemorate the 5th anniversary of the African Development Bank.

Pendant
A50

Design: 20fr, Rahla headdress (horiz.).

1969, Oct. 13 Engraved *Perf. 13*

268 A50 10fr dark brown, lilac & brown 12 6
269 " 20fr black, Prus. blue & magenta 25 10

Desalination Plant
A51

Designs: 15fr, Fishing harbor, Nouadhibou. 30fr, Meat refrigeration plant, Kaedi.

1969, Dec. 1 Engraved *Perf. 13*

270 A51 10fr brt. rose lilac, dk. blue & red brn. 10 6
271 " 15fr dark car., black & deep blue 15 12
272 " 30fr black, dk. blue & rose brown 30 18

Issued to publicize economic progress.

Lenin
A52

Sternocera Interrupta
A53

1970, Feb. 16 Photo. *Perf. 12x12½*

273 A52 30fr car., lt. bl. & blk. 35 15

Issued to commemorate the centenary of the birth of Lenin (1870–1924), Russian Communist leader.

1970, Mar. 16 Engraved *Perf. 13*

Insects: 10fr, Anoplocnemis curvipes. 20fr, Julodis aequinoctialis. 30fr, Thermophilum sexmaculatum marginatum. 40fr, Plocaederus denticornis.

274 A53 5fr red brown, buff & black 8 5
275 " 10fr red brown, yellow & brown 10 7
276 " 20fr red brown, lilac & dark olive 20 10
277 " 30fr red brown, green & violet 30 15
278 " 40fr red brown, light blue & brown 40 25
Nos. 274-278 (5) 1.08 62

Soccer Players and Hemispheres
A54

Designs: Hemispheres and various views of soccer play.

1970, May 11 Engraved *Perf. 13*

279 A54 25fr blue, vio. blue & dark brown 25 12
280 " 30fr vio. blue, brn. & olive brown 30 15
281 " 70fr brt. pink, maroon & dark brown 60 35
282 " 150fr brn. red, green & dark brown 1.40 75

Issued to publicize the 9th World Soccer Championships for the Jules Rimet Cup, Mexico City, May 29–June 21.

U.P.U. Headquarters Issue
Common Design Type

1970, May 20 Engraved *Perf. 13*

283 CD133 30fr grn, dk. brown & red brown 30 20

Woman Wearing 'Boubou'
A55

Various Traditional Costumes: 30fr, 70fr, Men. 40fr, 50fr, Women.

1970, Sept. 21 Engr. *Perf. 12½x13*

284 A55 10fr red brown & org. 10 6
285 " 30fr olive, red brown & indigo 25 15
286 " 40fr red brn., plum & dark brown 40 20
287 " 50fr dark brown & bright blue 45 25
288 " 70fr blue, brown & dark brown 60 30
Nos. 284-288 (5) 1.80 96

People of Various Races—A55a

Design: 40fr, Outstretched hands (vert.).

1971, Mar. 22 Engraved *Perf. 13*

288A A55a 30fr brn. vio., olive & brt. blue 30 15
288B " 40fr brn. red, blue & black 35 20

International year against racial discrimination.

Gen. Charles de Gaulle
A56

Design: 100fr, De Gaulle as President.

1971, June 18 Photo. *Perf. 13*

289 A56 40fr gold, black & greenish blue 75 45
290 " 100fr lt. blue, gold & black 2.10 1.20
a. Souvenir sheet of 2 3.25 3.25

In memory of Charles de Gaulle (1890–1970), President of France. No. 290a contains one each of Nos. 289–290. Black marginal inscription. Size: 140x160mm.

Iron Ore Freight Train of Miferma Mines
A57 A58

1971, Nov. 8 Photo. *Perf. 12½x12*

291 A57 35fr blue & multi. 38 22
292 A58 100fr " " 1.10 60

Nos. 291–292 printed se-tenant.

UNICEF Emblem and Child
A59

1971, Dec. 11 Litho. *Perf. 13½*

293 A59 35fr lt. ultra., black & brown 35 18

25th anniversary of the United Nations International Children's Fund (UNICEF).

Samuel F. B. Morse and Telegraph
A60

Designs: 40fr, Relay satellite over globes. 75fr, Alexander Graham Bell.

1972, May 17 Engraved *Perf. 13*

294 A60 35fr lilac, indigo & violet 40 18
295 " 40fr bl., ocher & choc. 42 25
296 " 75fr grn., olive grn. & Prussian blue 70 40

4th World Telecommunications Day.

Fossil Spirifer Shell—A61

1972, July 31 Litho. *Perf. 12½*

Multicolored

297 A61 25fr *shown* 25 18
298 " 75fr *Gryphaea shell* 65 45

Fossil shells.

West African Monetary Union Issue

Common Design Type

1972, Nov. 2 Engraved *Perf. 13*

299 CD136 35fr brown, yellow green & gray 35 20

10th anniversary of West African Monetary Union.

Mediterranean Monk Seal and Pup
A63

1973, Feb. 28 Litho. *Perf. 13*

300 A63 40fr multicolored 45 25

See No. C130.

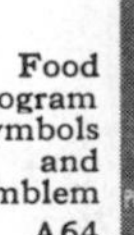

Food Program Symbols and Emblem
A64

1973, Apr. 30 Photo. *Perf. 12x12½*

301 A64 35fr gray bl. & multi. 35 20

World Food Program, 10th anniversary.

UPU Monument and Globe
A65

1973, May 28 Engraved *Perf. 13*

302 A65 100fr green, ocher & blue 1.00 75

Universal Postal Union Day.

Currency Change to Ouguiya ("um")

No. 258 Surcharged with New Value, 2 Bars, and Overprinted: "SECHERESSE / SOLIDARITE / AFRICAINE"

1973, Aug. 16 Photo. *Perf. 13*

303 A46 20um on 50fr multi. 90 55

African solidarity in drought emergency.

African Postal Union Issue

Common Design Type

1973, Sept. 12 Engraved *Perf. 13*

304 CD137 20um org., brown & ocher 90 55

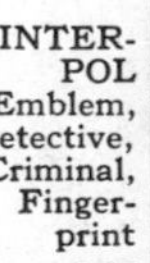

INTERPOL Emblem, Detective, Criminal, Fingerprint
A66

1973, Sept. 24

305 A66 15um brown, verm. & violet 75 45

50th anniversary of International Criminal Police Organization (INTERPOL).

Nos. 297–298, 300 and 268–269 Surcharged with New Value and Two Bars in Ultramarine, Red or Black

1973–74 Lithographed *Perf. 12½*

306 A61 5um on 25fr multi. (U) ('74) 25 12
307 A63 8um on 40fr multi. (R) 40 20
308 A61 15um on 75fr " (U) ('74) 70 40

Engraved *Perf. 13*

309 A50 27um on 10fr multi. (B) ('74) 1.10 55
310 " 28um on 20fr multi. (R) ('74) 1.20 65
Nos. 306–310 (5) 3.65 1.92

Nos. 274–278 Surcharged with New Value and Two Bars in Violet Blue or Red

1974, July 29 Engraved *Perf. 13*

Multicolored

311 A53 5um on 5fr 25 10
312 " 7um on 10fr 35 15
313 " 8um on 20fr 35 25
314 " 10um on 30fr (R) 50 30
315 " 20um on 40fr 1.00 60
Nos. 311–315 (5) 2.45 1.40

UPU Emblem and Globes—A67

1974, Aug. 5 Photo. *Perf. 13*

316 A67 30um multicolored 1.40 1.00
317 " 50um " 2.25 1.40

Centenary of Universal Postal Union.

5-Ouguiya Coin and Bank Note
A68

Designs: 8um, 10-ouguiya coin. 20um, 20-ouguiya coin. Each design includes picture of different bank note.

1974, Aug. 12 Engraved

318 A68 7um black, ultra. & green 30 12
319 " 8um blk., slate grn. & magenta 35 15
320 " 20um blk., red & bl. 90 50

First anniversary of currency reform.

Nos. 316–317 Overprinted in Red: "9 OCTOBRE / 100 ANS D'UNION POSTALE / INTERNATIONALE"

1974, Oct. 9 Photogravure *Perf. 13*

321 A67 30um multicolored 1.40 75
322 " 50um " 2.25 1.00

Centenary of Universal Postal Union.

Nos. 239–243 Surcharged with New Value and Two Bars in Black or Violet Blue

1975, Feb. 14 Engraved *Perf. 13*

323 A40 1um on 5fr multi. (B) 6 5
324 " 2um on 4fr " (VB) 10 6
325 " 3um on 2fr " (B) 12 6
326 " 10um on 1fr " (B) 45 20
327 " 12um on 3fr " (VB) 50 22
Nos. 323–327 (5) 1.23 59

Hunters, Rock Carvings
A69

Rock Carvings from Zemmour Cave: 5um, Ostrich. 10um, Elephant (horiz.).

1975, May 26 Engraved *Perf. 13*

328 A69 4um lt. brn. & car. 20 6
329 " 5um red lilac 25 10
330 " 10um blue 45 25

White and Black Men, Map of Europe and Africa
A70

Europafrica Issue

1975, July 7 Engr. *Perf. 13*

331 A70 40um dk. brn. & red 1.75 1.10

Nos. 247–248 Surcharged in Red or Black

15UM

SECHERESSE SOLIDARITE AFRICAINE

1975, Aug. 25 Photo. *Perf. 12½x13*

Multicolored

332 A42 15um on 45fr (R) 65 45
333 " 25um 90fr 1.10 75

African solidarity in drought emergency.

Map of Africa with Mauritania, Akjoujt Blast Furnace, Camel
A71

Fair Emblem
A72

Design: 12um, Snim emblem, furnace, dump truck, excavator.

1975, Sept. 22 Engr. *Perf. 13*

334 A71 10um brt. bl., choc. & orange 45 25
335 " 12um brt. bl. & multi. 55 32

Mining and industry: Somima (Société Minière de Mauritanie) and Snim (Société Nationale Industrielle et Minière).

1975, Oct. 5 Litho. *Perf. 12*

336 A72 10um multicolored 45 22

National Nouakchott Fair, Nov. 28–Dec. 7.

Commemorative Medal—A73

Design: 12um, Map of Mauritania (vert.).

1975, Nov. 28 Litho. *Perf. 12*

337 A73 10um silver & multi. 45 22
338 " 12um grn., yel. & brn. 55 30

15th anniversary of independence.

Docked Space Ships and Astronauts—A74

Design (Docked Space Ships and): 10um, Soyuz rocket launch.

1975, Dec. 29 Litho. *Perf. 14*

339 A74 8um multicolored 40 20
340 " 10um " 50 25
Nos. 339-340, C156-C158 (5) 6.80 3.05

Apollo Soyuz space test project, Russo-American cooperation, launched July 15, link-up July 17, 1975.

French Legion Infantryman A75

Uniform: 10um, Green Mountain Boy.

1976, Jan. 26 *Perf. 13½x14*

341 A75 8um multicolored 40 15
342 " 10um " 45 20
Nos. 341-342, C160-C162 (5) 7.35 2.95

American Bicentennial.

10e ANNIVERSAIRE DE LA CHARTE ARABE DU TRAVAIL

No. 296 Surcharged

12UM

1976, Mar. 1 Engr. *Perf. 13*

343 A60 12um on 75fr multi. 50 25

Arab Labor Charter, 10th anniversary.

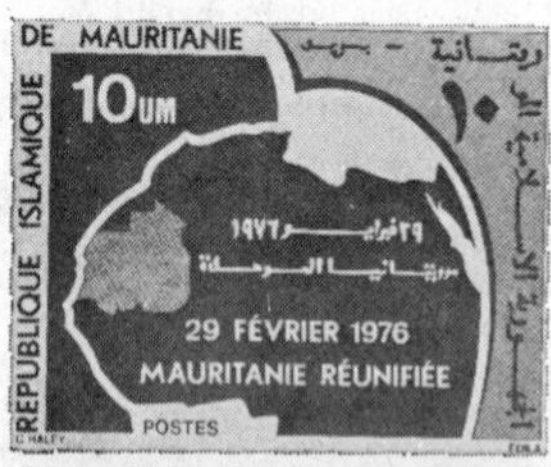

Map of Mauritania with Spanish Sahara Incorporated—A76

1976, Mar. 15 Litho. *Perf. 13x12½*

344 A76 10um grn. & multi. 45 25

Reunified Mauritania, Feb. 29, 1976.

Stamps not listed in this Catalogue or mentioned in "For the Record" (unless recent issues) usually are revenues, locals or labels.

LZ-4 over Hangar—A77

Designs: 10um, Dr. Hugo Eckener and "Schwaben" (LZ-10). 12um, "Hansa" (LZ-13) over Heligoland. 20um, "Bodensee" (LZ-120) and Dr. Ludwig Dürr.

1976, June 28 Litho. *Perf. 11*

345 A77 5um multicolored 25 12
346 " 10um " 50 20
347 " 12um " 60 25
348 " 20um " 1.00 32
Nos. 345-348, C167-C168 (6) 6.95 2.54

75th anniversary of the Zeppelin.

Mohenjo-Daro—A78

1976, Sept. 6 Litho. *Perf. 12*

349 A78 15um multicolored 65 32

UNESCO campaign to save Mohenjo-Daro excavations, Pakistan.

A. G. Bell, Telephone and Satellite A79

1976, Oct. 11 Engraved *Perf. 13*

350 A79 10um bl., car. & red 45 25

Centenary of first telephone call by Alexander Graham Bell, Mar. 10, 1876.

Mohammed Ali Jinnah—A80

1976, Dec. 25 Litho. *Perf. 13*

351 A80 10um multcolored 45 25

Mohammed Ali Jinnah (1876-1948), Governor General of Pakistan, birth centenary.

NASA Control Room, Houston—A81

Design: 12um, Viking components (vert.).

1977, Feb. 28 *Perf. 14*

352 A81 10um multicolored 45 15
353 " 12um " 55 20
Nos. 352-353, C173-C175 (5) 6.35 2.25

Viking Mars project.

Jackals A82

Designs: 5um, Wild rabbits. 12um, Warthogs. 14um, Lions. 15um, Elephants.

1977, Mar. 14 Litho. *Perf. 12½*

354 A82 5um multicolored 20 8
355 " 10um " 45 25
356 " 12um " 55 32
357 " 14um " 60 32
358 " 15um " 70 32
Nos. 354-358 (5) 2.50 1.29

Irene and Frederic Joliot-Curie, Chemistry—A83

Design: 15um, Emil A. von Bering, medicine.

1977, Apr. 29 Litho. *Perf. 14*

359 A83 12um multicolored 55 20
360 " 15um " 65 25
Nos. 359-360, C177-C179 (5) 7.05 2.40

Nobel prize winners.

APU Emblem, Member's Flags A84

1977, May 30 Photo. *Perf. 13*

361 A84 12um multicolored 55 32

Arab Postal Union, 25th anniversary.

Oil Lamp A85

Tegdaoust Pottery: 2um, 4-handled pot. 5um, Large jar. 12um, Jug with filter.

1977, June 13 Engr. *Perf. 13*

362 A85 1um multicolored 5 3
363 " 2um " 10 6
364 " 5um " 20 10
365 " 12um " 55 28

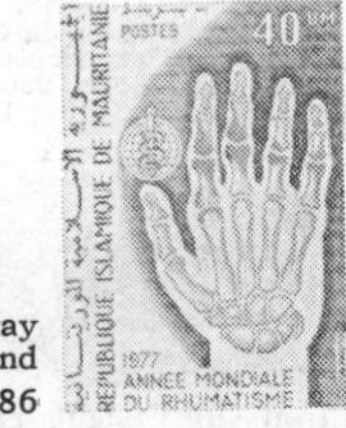

X-ray of Hand A86

1977, June 27 Engr. *Perf. 12½x13*

366 A86 40um multicolored 1.75 1.00

World Rheumatism Year.

Charles Lindbergh and "Spirit of St. Louis"—A87

Designs: 14um, Clement Ader and "Eole!" 15um, Louis Bleriot over channel. 55um, Italo Balbo and seaplanes. 60um, Concorde. 100um, Charles Lindbergh and "Spirit of St. Louis."

1977, Sept. 19

367 A87 12um multicolored 55 20
368 " 14um " 60 25
369 " 15um " 65 28
370 " 55um " 2.50 80
371 " 60um " 2.75 90
Nos. 367-371 (5) 7.05 2.43

Souvenir Sheet

372 A87 100um multicolored 4.50 2.00

History of aviation. No. 372 has multicolored margin showing "Spirit of St. Louis" in flight and various early planes. Size: 117x91mm.

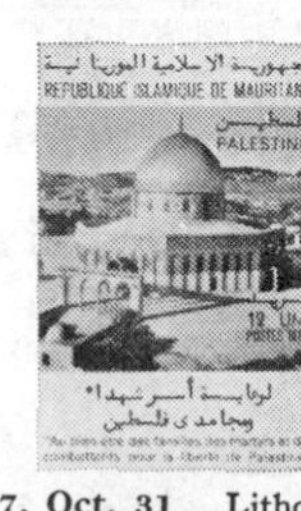

Dome of the Rock, Jerusalem A88

1977, Oct. 31 Litho. *Perf. 12½*

373 A88 12um multicolored 55 32
374 " 14um " 60 35

Palestinian fighters and their families.

Soccer and Emblems—A89

Designs (Emblems and): 14um, Alf Ramsey and stadium. 15um, Players and goalkeeper.

1977, Dec. 19 Litho. *Perf. 13½*

375 A89 12um multicolored 55 20
376 " 14um " 60 25

377	A89	15um multicolored	65	25
		Nos. 375-377, C182-C183 (5)	6.40	2.30

Elimination Games for World Cup Soccer Championship, Argentina, 1978.

Helen Fourment and her Children, by Rubens
A90

Rubens Paintings: 14um, Knight in armor. 67um, Three Burghers. 69um, Landscape (horiz.). 100um, Rubens with wife and son.

1977, Dec. 26

378	A90	12um multicolored	55	20
379	"	14um "	65	28
380	"	67um "	3.00	95
381	"	69um "	3.00	95

Souvenir Sheet

382	A90	100um gold & multi.	4.50	2.00

Peter Paul Rubens (1577-1640), painter, 400th birth anniversary. No. 382 has multicolored margin showing entire painting. Size: 91x116mm.

Sable Antelope and Wildlife Fund Emblem—A91

Endangered Animals: 12um, Gazelles (vert.). 14um, Manatee. 55um, Aoudad (vert.). 60um, Elephant. 100um, Ostrich (vert.).

1978, Feb. 28 Litho. *Perf. 13½x14*

383	A91	5um multicolored	25	8
384	"	12um "	55	20
385	"	14um "	60	25
386	"	55um "	2.50	80
387	"	60um "	2.75	85
388	"	100um "	4.50	1.50
		Nos. 383-388 (6)	11.15	3.68

Soccer and Games' Emblem
A92

Designs: 14um, Rimet Cup. 20um, Soccer ball and F.I.F.A. flag. 50um, Soccer ball and Rimet Cup (horiz.).

1978, June 26 Photo. *Perf. 13*

389	A92	12um multicolored	60	25
390	"	14um "	70	30
391	"	20um "	1.00	40

Souvenir Sheet

392	A92	50um multicolored	2.60	1.50

11th World Cup Soccer Championship, Argentina, June 1-25. No. 392 has black marginal inscription. Size: 82x70mm.

Raoul Follereau and St. George Slaying Dragon—A93

1978, Sept. 4 Engr. *Perf. 13*

393	A93	12um brn. & dp. grn.	60	25

25th anniversary of the Raoul Follereau Anti-Leprosy Foundation.

Anti-Apartheid Emblem, Fenced-in People—A94

Design: 30um, Anti-Apartheid emblem and free people (vert.).

1978, Oct. 9

394	A94	25um blue, red & brown	1.25	55
395	"	30um grn., blue & brown	1.50	65

Anti-Apartheid Year.

Charles de Gaulle
A95

Portraits: 14um, King Baudouin. 55um, Queen Elizabeth II.

1978, Oct. 16 Litho. *Perf. 12½x12*

396	A95	12um multicolored	60	25
397	"	14um "	70	30
398	"	55um "	2.75	1.25

Rulers who helped in de-colonization. No. 398 also commemorates 25th anniversary of coronation of Queen Elizabeth II.

Nos. 375-377 Overprinted in Arabic and French in Silver:
"ARGENTINE - / PAY BAS 3-1"

1978, Dec. 11 Litho. *Perf. 13½*

399	A89	12um multicolored	60	25
400	"	14um "	70	30
401	"	15um "	75	32
		Nos. 399-401, C187-C188 (5)	7.55	3.12

Argentina's victory in World Cup Soccer Championship 1978.

View of Nouakchott—A96

1978, Dec. 18 Litho. *Perf. 12*

402	A96	12um multicolored	60	25

20th anniversary of Nouakchott (formerly St. Louis).

Flame Emblem
A97

1978, Dec. 26 *Perf. 12½*

403	A97	55um ultra. & red	2.75	1.20

30th anniversary of Universal Declaration of Human Rights.

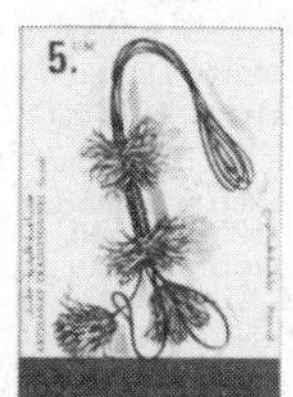

Leather Key Holder
A98

Leather Craft: 7um, Toothbrush case. 10um, Knife holder.

1979, Feb. 5 Litho. *Perf. 13½x14*

404	A98	5um multicolored	25	12
405	"	7um "	35	18
406	"	10um "	50	25

Help us serve you better. Please fill out the questionnaire at the front of this book.

SEMI-POSTAL STAMPS.

Nos. 23 and 26 Surcharged in Red ✚5c

1915–18 *Perf. 14x13½* **Unwmkd.**

B1 A4 10c+5c rose & red orange 35 35
B2 " 15c+5c dark brown & black ('18) 25 25
a. Inverted surcharge 2.50 2.50

Curie Issue
Common Design Type

1938, Oct. 24 *Perf. 13*

B3 CD80 1.75fr+50c bright ultramarine 3.00 3.00

French Revolution Issue.
Common Design Type

1939, July 5 Photo. **Unwmkd.**
Name and Value Typo. in Black.

B4 CD83 45(c)+25(c) green 2.50 2.50
B5 " 70(c)+30(c) brown 2.50 2.50
B6 " 90(c)+35(c) red org. 2.50 2.50
B7 " 1.25fr+1fr rose pink 2.50 2.50
B8 " 2.25fr+2fr blue 2.50 2.50
Nos. B4-B8 (5) 12.50 12.50

Stamps of 1938 Surcharge in Red or Black **SECOURS + 1 fr. NATIONAL**

1941

B9 A6 50c+1fr purple (R) 40 40
B10 A7 80c+2fr deep blue (R) 2.25 2.25
B11 " 1.50fr+2fr violet (R) 2.25 2.25
B12 A8 2fr+3fr rose violet (Bk) 2.25 2.25

Common Design Type and

Moorish Goumier SP1

White Goumier SP2

1941 Photogravure. *Perf. 13½.*

B13 SP1 1fr+1fr red 30
B14 CD86 1.50fr+3fr claret 30
B15 SP2 2.50fr+1fr blue 25

Nos. B13–B15 were issued by the Vichy government, and were not placed on sale in the colony.
Nos. 114–115 were surcharged "OEUVRES COLONIALES" and surtax (including change of denomination of the 2.50fr to 50c). These were issued in 1944 by the Vichy government and were not placed on sale in the colony.

Islamic Republic

Anti-Malaria Issue
Common Design Type

1962, Apr. 7 Engr. *Perf. 12½x12*

B16 CD108 25fr+5fr light olive green 60 60

Issued for the World Health Organization drive to eradicate malaria.

Freedom from Hunger Issue
Common Design Type

1963, Mar. 21 *Perf. 13* **Unwmkd.**

B17 CD112 25fr+5fr dp. claret, dp. bl. & ocher 50 50

Nurse Tending Infant SP3

1972, May 8 Photo. *Perf. 12½x13*

B18 SP3 35fr+5fr green, red & brown 40 40

Surtax was for Mauritania Red Crescent Society.

AIR POST STAMPS.

Common Design Type
Perf. 12½x12.

1940, Feb. 8 Engraved **Unwmkd.**

C1 CD85 1.90fr ultramarine 10 10
C2 " 2.90fr dark red 10 10
C3 " 4.50fr dk. gray grn. 15 15
C4 " 4.90fr yellow bistre 35 35
C5 " 6.90fr deep orange 30 30
Nos. C1-C5 (5) 1.00 1.00

Common Design Types

1942

C6 CD88 50c carmine & blue 8
C7 " 1fr brown & black 10
C8 " 2fr dark green & red brown 12
C9 " 3fr dark blue & scarlet 20
C10 " 5fr violet & brown red 30

Frame Engraved, Center Typographed.

C11 CD89 10fr ultramarine, indigo & henna 20
a. Center inverted 500.00
C12 " 20fr rose carmine, magenta & buff 25
C13 " 50fr yellow green, dull green & orange 35 60
Nos. C6-C13 (8) 1.60

There is doubt whether Nos. C6–C12 were officially placed in use.

Islamic Republic

Flamingoes AP1

Designs: 200fr, African spoonbills. 500fr, Slender-billed gull (horiz.).

Engraved

1961, June 30 *Perf. 13* **Unwmkd.**

C14 AP1 100fr red orange, brown & ultra. 2.10 1.40
C15 " 200fr red orange, sepia & slate green 4.50 2.75
C16 " 500fr red orange, gray & blue 10.00 5.50

An overprint, "Europa/CECA/MIFERMA," was applied in carmine to No. C16 in 1962.
The anti-malaria emblem, including slogan "Le Monde contre le Paludisme," was overprinted on Nos. C14–C15 in 1962.

Air Afrique Issue
Common Design Type

1962, Feb. 17

C17 CD107 100fr slate green, chocolate & bistre 1.50 1.00

Founding of Air Afrique (African Airlines).

U.N. Headquarters, New York; View of Nouakchott—AP2

1962, Oct. 27 Engr. *Perf. 13*

C18 AP2 100fr bluish green, dark bl. & org. brn. 1.50 1.10

Issued to commemorate Mauritania's admission to the United Nations.

Plane, Nouakchott Airport—AP3

1963, May 3 *Perf. 13* **Unwmkd.**

C19 AP3 500fr deep blue, golden brown & slate green 7.50 4.25

Miferma Open-pit Mine at Zouerate—AP4

Design: 200fr, Ore transport at Port Etienne.

Photogravure

1963, June 15–16 *Perf. 13x12*

C20 AP4 100fr multicolored 1.30 70
C21 " 200fr " 3.00 1.50

African Postal Union Issue
Common Design Type

1963, Sept. 8 *Perf. 12½* **Unwmkd.**

C22 CD114 85fr black brown, ocher & red 1.15 60

Globe and Telstar—AP5

Design: 150fr, Relay satellite and stars.

1963, Oct. 7 Engraved *Perf. 13*

C23 AP5 50fr yel. grn., pur. & red brown 70 50
C24 " 150fr red brown & slate green 2.25 1.40

Communication through space.

Tiros Satellite and Emblem of World Meteorological Organization AP6

U.N. Emblem, Doves and Sun AP7

1963, Nov. 4

C25 AP6 200fr ultra., brn. & green 3.00 1.75

Issued to publicize space research for meteorology and navigation.

1963 Air Afrique Issue
Common Design Type

1963, Nov. 19 Photo. *Perf. 13x12*

C26 CD115 25fr multicolored 45 28

First anniversary of Air Afrique and inauguration of DC-8 service.

1963, Dec. 10 Engraved *Perf. 13*

C27 AP7 100fr violet, brown, & dark blue 1.50 85

15th anniversary of the Universal Declaration of Human Rights.

Symbols of Agriculture and Industry AP8

Lichtenstein's Sand Grouse AP9

Europafrica Issue

1964, Jan. 6 Photogravure

C28 AP8 50fr multicolored 1.20 75

Signing of economic agreement between the European Economic Community and the African and Malgache Union at Yaoundé, Cameroun, July 20, 1963.

1964, Feb. 3 Engraved *Perf. 13*

Birds: 200fr, Long-tailed cormorant. 500fr, Chanting goshawk.

C29 AP9 100fr ocher, olive & dark brown 1.50 60
C30 " 200fr black, dark blue & brn. 2.75 1.25
C31 " 500fr rose red, grn. & slate 7.00 3.00

Isis, Temple at Philae and Trajan's Kiosk—AP10

1964, March 8 ***Perf. 13*** **Unwmkd.**

C32 AP10 10fr red brn., Pruss. blue & blk. 40 28
C33 " 25fr red brn., indigo & Pruss. bl. 60 45
C34 " 60fr black brown, Prussian blue & red brn. 1.20 90

Issued to publicize the UNESCO world campaign to save historic monuments in Nubia.

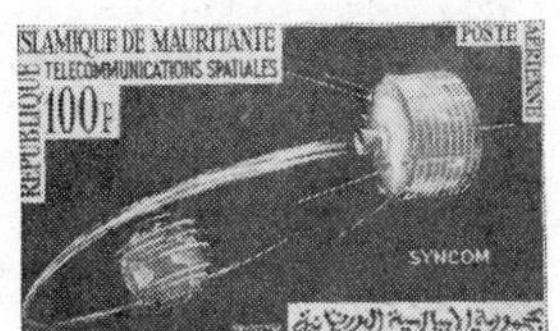

Syncom Satellite, Globe—AP11

1964, May 4 **Engraved**

C35 AP11 100fr red, red brn. & ultra. 1.50 90

Issued to publicize space communications.

Horse Race on Bowl—AP12

Sport Designs from Ancient Pottery: 50fr, Runner (vert.). 85fr, Wrestlers (vert.). 100fr, Charioteer.

1964, Sept. 27 ***Perf. 13*** **Unwmkd.**

C36 AP12 15fr olive bister & chocolate 25 15
C37 " 50fr bl. & orge. brn. 75 45
C38 " 85fr crimson & brn. 1.25 75
C39 " 100fr emerald & dk. red brn. 1.50 90
a. Min. sheet of 4 4.50 4.50

Issued to commemorate the 18th Olympic Games, Tokyo, Oct. 10–25. No. C39a contains one each of Nos. C36–C39. Size: 190x100mm.

Pres. John F. Kennedy
AP13

1964, Dec. 7 **Photo.** ***Perf. 12½***

C40 AP13 100fr red brn., blue grn. & dk. brown 1.50 1.25
a. Souv. sheet of 4 6.25 6.25

Issued in memory of Pres. John F. Kennedy (1917–63). No. C40a contains four No. C40. Red brown marginal inscription. Size: 90x130mm.

ITU Emblem, Induction Telegraph and Relay Satellite—AP14

1965, May 17 **Engraved** ***Perf. 13***

C41 AP14 250fr multicolored 3.75 2.50

Issued to commemorate the centenary of the International Telecommunication Union.

Fight Against Cancer
AP15

Winston Churchill
AP16

1965, July 19 ***Perf. 13*** **Unwmkd.**

C42 AP15 100fr bister, Prus. bl. & red 1.50 65

Issued to publicize the fight against cancer.

1965, Dec. 6 **Photo.** ***Perf. 13***

C43 AP16 200fr multicolored 3.00 1.20

Issued in memory of Sir Winston Spencer Churchill (1874–1965), statesman and World War II leader.

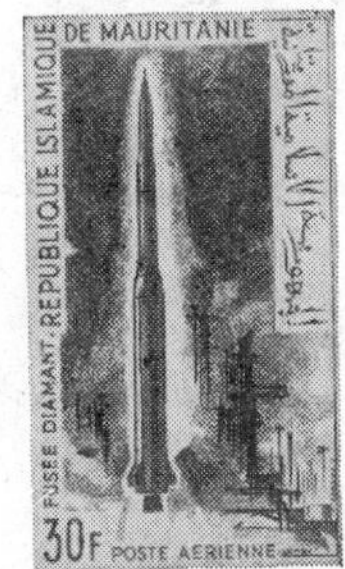

Diamant Rocket Ascending
AP17

Designs: 60fr, Satellite A-1 and earth (horiz.). 90fr, Scout rocket and satellite FR-1 (horiz.).

1966, Feb. 7 **Engraved** ***Perf. 13***

C44 AP17 30fr dp. blue, red & green 45 25
C45 " 60fr maroon, Prus. grn. & blue 90 40
C46 " 90fr dp. blue, rose claret & vio. 1.35 65

French achievements in space.

Dr. Albert Schweitzer and Clinic
AP18

1966, Feb. 21 **Photo.** ***Perf. 12½***

C47 AP18 50fr multicolored 75 35

Issued in memory of Dr. Albert Schweitzer (1875–1965), medical missionary to Gabon, theologian and musician.

Thomas P. Stafford, Walter M. Schirra and Gemini 6
AP19

Designs: 100fr, Frank A. Borman, James A. Lovell, Jr., and Gemini 7. 200fr, Pavel Belyayev, Alexei Leonov, Voskhod 2.

1966, March 7 **Photo.** ***Perf. 12½***

C48 AP19 50fr multicolored 75 32
C49 " 100fr " 1.35 70
C50 " 200fr " 3.00 1.20

Issued to honor achievements in space.

Map of Africa and Dove
AP20

D-1 Satellite over Earth
AP21

1966, May 9 **Photo.** ***Perf. 13***

C51 AP20 100fr red brn., slate & yel. grn. 1.35 55

Organization for African Unity.

1966, June 6 **Engraved**

C52 AP21 100fr bl., dk. purple & ocher 1.35 65

Issued to commemorate the launching of the D-1 satellite at Hammaguir, Algeria, Feb. 17, 1966.

Bréguet 14
AP22

Planes: 100fr, Goliath Farman, and camel caravan. 150fr, Couzinet "Arc-en-Ciel." 200fr, Latécoère 28 hydroplane.

1966, July 4 **Engraved** ***Perf. 13***

C53 AP22 50fr slate bl., dull green & olive bister 75 28
C54 " 100fr brt. bl., dk. green & dk. red brown 1.35 45
C55 " 150fr dull brown, Prus. blue & sapphire 2.00 70
C56 " 200fr dark red brn., bl. & indigo 3.00 1.10

Air Afrique Issue, 1966
Common Design Type

1966, Aug. 31 **Photo.** ***Perf. 13***

C57 CD123 30fr red, black & gray 45 15

Issued to commemorate the introduction of DC-8F planes by Air Afrique.

"The Raft of the Medusa," by Théodore Géricault—AP23

1966, Sept. 5 **Photo.** ***Perf. 12½***

C58 AP23 500fr multicolored 7.50 4.00

Issued to commemorate the sinking of the frigate "Medusa" off Mauritania, July 2, 1816.

Symbols of Agriculture and Industry
AP24

1966, Nov. 7 **Photo.** ***Perf. 13x12***

C59 AP24 50fr multicolored 65 25

Third anniversary, economic agreement between the European Economic Community and the African and Malgache Union.

Crowned Crane
AP25

Eye, Globe and Rockets
AP26

Birds: 200fr, Common egret. 500fr, Ostrich.

1967, Apr. 3 ***Perf. 12½x13***

C60 AP25 100fr multicolored 1.00 60
C61 " 200fr " 2.00 90
C62 " 500fr " 5.00 2.50

1967, May 2 **Engraved** ***Perf. 13***

C63 AP26 250fr brown, Prus. bl. & black 3.00 1.50

Issued to commemorate EXPO '67 International Exhibition, Montreal, Apr. 28–Oct. 27, 1967.

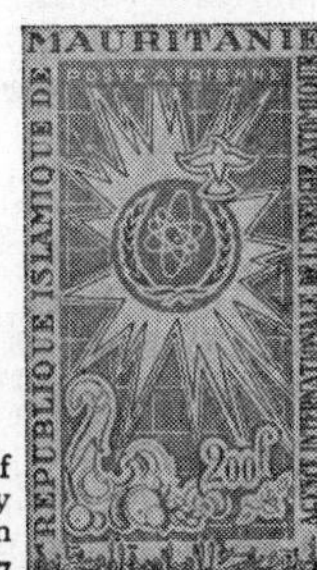

Emblem of Atomic Energy Commission
AP27

1967, Aug. 7 Engr. *Perf. 13*

C64 AP27 200fr dk. red, brt. green & ultra. 2.50 1.10

International Atomic Energy Commission.

African Postal Union Issue, 1967

Common Design Type

1967, Sept. 9 Engraved *Perf. 13*

C65 CD124 100fr brn. org., vio. brown & brt. green 1.35 60

Francesca da Rimini, by Ingres

AP28

Paintings by and of Ingres: 100fr, Young man's torso. 150fr, "The Iliad" (seated woman). 200fr, Ingres in his Studio, by Alaux. 250fr, "The Odyssey" (seated woman).

1967-68 Photo. *Perf. 12½*

C66	AP28	90fr multicolored	1.35	65
C67	"	100fr multi. ('68)	1.25	70
C68	"	150fr " ('68)	2.00	1.00
C69	"	200fr "	3.00	1.40
C70	"	250fr " ('68)	3.25	1.75
		Nos. C66-C70 (5)	10.85	5.50

Issued to commemorate the centenary of the death of Jean Dominique Ingres (1780-1867), French painter.

Issue dates: Oct. 2, 1967, 90fr, 200fr. Sept. 2, 1968, others.

See also No. C79.

Konrad Adenauer

AP29

Gymnast

AP30

1968, Feb. 5 Photo. *Perf. 12½*

C71 AP29 100fr org. brown, lt. bl. & blk. 1.50 70

a. Souv. sheet of 4 6.00 5.00

Issued in memory of Konrad Adenauer (1876-1967), chancellor of West Germany (1949-63). No. C71a contains 4 No. 71. Margin with black inscription and 1967 CEPT (Europa) emblem. Size: 120x160mm.

1968, Mar. 4 Engraved *Perf. 13*

Sports: 20fr, Slalom (horiz.). 50fr, Ski jump. 100fr, Hurdling (horiz.).

C72	AP30	20fr plum, black & blue	25	12
C73	"	30fr dull pur., brt. grn. & brown	35	15
C74	"	50fr Prus. bl., bister & bl. green	60	28
C75	"	100fr brown, green & verm.	1.25	50

1968 Olympic Games.

WHO Emblem, Man and Insects

AP31

1968, May 2 Engraved *Perf. 13*

C76 AP31 150fr red lilac, dp. blue & org. red 1.75 90

Issued to commemorate the 20th anniversary of the World Health Organization.

Martin Luther King

AP32

Design: No. C78, Mahatma Gandhi.

1968, Nov. 4 Photo. *Perf. 12½*

C77 AP32 50fr slate blue, citron & blk. 50 28

C78 " 50fr slate blue, lt. blue & black 50 28

a. Souv. sheet of 4 2.25 2.25

Issued to honor two apostles of peace. No. C78a contains 2 each of Nos. C77-C78 arranged checkerwise. Black marginal inscription. Size: 120x160mm.

PHILEXAFRIQUE Issue

Painting Type of 1967

Design: 100fr, The Surprise Letter, by Charles Antoine Coypel.

1968, Dec. 9 Photo. *Perf. 12½*

C79 AP28 100fr multi. 1.50 1.50

Issued to publicize PHILEXAFRIQUE, Philatelic Exhibition in Abidjan, Feb. 14-23. Printed with alternating brown red label.

2nd PHILEXAFRIQUE Issue

Common Design Type

Design: 50fr, Mauritania No. 89 and family on jungle trail.

1969, Feb. 14 Engraved *Perf. 13*

C80 CD128 50fr slate green, violet brown & red brown 85 85

Issued to commemorate the opening of PHILEXAFRIQUE, Abidjan, Feb. 14.

Napoleon Installed in Council of State, by Louis Charles Couder—AP33

Paintings: 50fr, Napoleon at Council of the 500, by F. Bouchot. 250fr, Farewell at Fontainebleau, by Horace Vernet.

1969, Feb. 24 Photo. *Perf. 12½*

C81	AP33	50fr pur. & multi.	1.25	1.00
C82	"	90fr multicolored	1.75	1.50
C83	"	250fr "	5.00	3.50

Issued to commemorate the 200th anniversary of the birth of Napoleon Bonaparte (1769-1821).

Camel, Gazelles, and Tourist Year Emblem—AP34

1969, June 9 Engraved *Perf. 13*

C84 AP34 50fr org., dk. brown & lt. blue 65 35

Year of African Tourism, 1969.

Dancers and Temple Ruins, Baalbek

AP35

1969, June 16

C85 AP35 100fr Prus. bl., olive brn. & rose carmine 1.00 50

International Baalbek Festival, Lebanon.

Apollo 8 and Moon Surface

AP36

Embossed on Gold Foil

1969 *Die-cut Perf. 10*

C86 AP36 1000fr gold 13.50 13.50

Issued to commemorate man's first flight around the moon, Dec. 21-28, 1968 (U.S. astronauts Col. Frank Borman, Capt. James Lovell and Maj. William Anders).

Mamo Wolde, Ethiopia, Marathon

AP37

Designs: 70fr, Bob Beamon, USA, broad jump. 150fr, Vera Caslavska, Czechoslovakia, gymnastics.

1969, July 7 Engraved *Perf. 13*

C87	AP37	30fr multicolored	30	15
C88	"	70fr "	65	32
C89	"	150fr "	1.40	80

Issued to honor gold medal winners in the 19th Olympic Games, Mexico City.

Map of London-Istanbul Route

AP38

Designs: 20fr, Map showing Ankara to Teheran route, and compass rose. 50fr, Map showing Kandahar to Bombay route, arms of Afghanistan and elephant. 70fr, Map of Australia with Perth to Sydney route, and kangaroo.

1969, Aug. 14 Engraved *Perf. 13*

C90	AP38	10fr brt. lilac, blue & brn. orange	10	5
C91	"	20fr brt. lilac, brn. org. & blue	20	10
C92	"	50fr brn. org., blue & brt. lilac	50	22
C93	"	70fr brt. lilac, blue & brn. org.	60	28
		a. Min. sheet of 4	2.00	2.00

Issued to commemorate the London to Sydney automobile rally. No. C93a contains one each of Nos. C90-C93. Size: 129x100mm.

Palette with World Map, Geisha and EXPO '70 Emblem

AP39

Designs (EXPO '70 Emblem and): 75fr, Fan and fireworks. 150fr, Stylized bird, map of Japan and boat.

1970, June 15 Photo. *Perf. 12½*

C94	AP39	50fr multicolored	55	25
C95	"	75fr "	75	40
C96	"	150fr "	1.60	70

Issued to publicize EXPO '70 International Exhibition, Osaka, Japan, Mar. 15-Sept. 13.

U.N. Emblem, Balloon, Rocket, Farm Woman, Tractor, Old and New Record Players

AP40

1970, June 22 Engraved *Perf. 13*

C97 AP40 100fr ultra., dark brn. & grn. 1.10 65

25th anniversary of the United Nations.

Elliott See (1927–1966), American Astronaut
AP41

Apollo 13 Capsule with Parachutes
AP42

Portraits: No. C99, Vladimir Komarov (1927–1967). C100, Yuri Gagarin (1934–1968). No. C101, Virgil Grissom (1926–1967). No. C102, Edward White (1930–1967). No. C103, Roger Chaffee (1935–1967).

1970 Engraved *Perf. 13*

Portrait in Brown

C98 AP41 150fr gray & brt. blue 1.50 65
C99 " 150fr gray & org. 1.50 65
C100 " 150fr gray & org. 1.50 65
a. Souvenir sheet of 3 4.50 4.50
C101 AP41 150fr ultra. & greenish blue 1.50 65
C102 " 150fr ultramarine & orange 1.50 65
C103 " 150fr ultra. & greenish blue 1.50 65
a. Souvenir sheet of 3 4.50 4.50
Nos. C98–C103 (6) 9.00 3.90

Issued in memory of American and Russian astronauts who died in space explorations. No. C100a contains one each of Nos. C98–C100 with marginal inscription in dark brown. No. C103a contains one each of Nos. C101–103 with marginal inscription in dark brown. Size: 129x99 mm.

Gold Embossed

1970, Aug. 17 *Perf. 12½*

C104 AP42 500fr gold, crimson & blue 6.00 6.00

Safe return of Apollo 13 crew.

Parliament, Nouakchott, and Coat of Arms
AP43

1970, Nov. 28 Photo. *Perf. 12½*

C105 AP43 100fr multi. 1.00 50

10th anniversary of Independence.

Hercules Wrestling Antaeus—AP44

1971, Mar. 8 Engraved *Perf. 13*

C106 AP44 100fr red lilac, brn. & ultra. 1.20 75

Pre-Olympic Year. Design from a vase decoration by Euphronius.

Gamal Abdel Nasser—AP46

1971, May 10 Photo. *Perf. 12½*

C109 AP46 100fr gold & multi. 90 45

In memory of Gamal Abdel Nasser (1918–1970), President of U.A.R.

Boy Scout, Emblem and Map of Mauritania
AP47

1971, Aug. 16 Photo. *Perf. 12½*

C110 AP47 35fr yel. & multi. 30 18
C111 " 40fr pink & multi. 35 25
C112 " 100fr multi. 90 50

13th Boy Scout World Jamboree, Asagiri Plain, Japan, Aug. 2–10.

African Postal Union Issue, 1971

Common Design Type

Design: 100fr, Women musicians and UAMPT building, Brazzaville, Congo.

1971, Nov. 13 Photo. *Perf. 13x13½*

C113 CD135 100fr bl. & multi. 1.00 65

Letter and Postal Emblem
AP48

1971, Dec. 2 *Perf. 13*

C114 AP48 35fr bister & multi. 35 20

10th anniversary of African Postal Union.

Mosul Monarch, from Book of Songs, c. 1218
AP49

Designs from Mohammedan Miniatures: 40fr, Prince holding audience, Egypt, 1334. 100fr, Pilgrim caravan, from "Maquamat," Baghdad, 1237.

1972, Jan. 10 Photo. *Perf. 13*

C115 AP49 35fr gold & multi. 35 25
C116 " 40fr gray & multi. 40 30
C117 " 100fr buff & multi. 1.00 65

Grand Canal, by Canaletto—AP50

Designs: 45fr, Venice Harbor, by Carlevaris (vert.). 250fr, Santa Maria della Salute, by Canaletto.

1972, Feb. 14

C118 AP50 45fr gold & multi. 40 25
C119 " 100fr " " 90 50
C120 " 250fr " " 2.50 1.20

UNESCO campaign to save Venice.

Hurdles and Olympic Rings—AP51

1972, Apr. 27 Engraved *Perf. 13*

C121 AP51 75fr org., vio. brn. & black 70 32
C122 " 100fr Prus. bl., vio. brn. & brn. 1.00 50
C123 " 200fr lake, vio. brn. & black 2.00 80
a. Min. sheet of 3 3.75 3.75

20th Olympic Games, Munich, Aug. 26–Sept. 11. No. C123a contains one each of Nos. C121–C123. Size: 190x99mm.

Luna 17 on Moon—AP52

Design: 75fr, Luna 16 take-off from moon (vert.).

1972, Oct. 9

C124 AP52 75fr vio. bl., bister & green 70 32
C125 " 100fr dull pur., slate & ol. bis. 1.00 50

Russian moon missions, Luna 16, Sept. 12–14, 1970; and Luna 17, Nov. 10–17, 1970.

Nos. C121–C123 Overprinted in Violet Blue or Red:

a. 110m HAIES / MILBURN MEDAILLE D'OR
b. 400m HAIES / AKII-BUA MEDAILLE D'OR
c. 3.000m STEEPLE / KEINO MEDAILLE D'OR

1972, Oct. 16

C126 AP51 (*a*) 75fr multi. (VB) 70 32
C127 " (*b*) 100fr multi. (R) 1.00 50
C128 " (*c*) 200fr multi. (VB) 2.00 80

Gold medal winners in 20th Olympic Games: Rod Milburn, U.S.A., John Akii-Bua, Uganda, and Kipchoge Keino, Kenya.

No. C62 Surcharged with New Value, Two Bars and: "Apollo XVII / December 1972"

1973, Jan. 29 Photo. *Perf. 12½x13*

C129 AP25 250fr on 500fr multi. 3.00 1.25

Apollo 17 U.S. moon mission, Dec. 7–19, 1972.

Seal Type of Regular Issue

Design: 135fr, Seal's head.

1973, Feb. 28 Litho. *Perf. 13*

C130 A63 135fr multi. 1.75 1.10

Lion Eating Caiman, by Delacroix—AP53

Painting: 250fr, Lion Eating Boar, by Delacroix.

1973, Mar. 26 Photo. *Perf. 13x12½*

C131 AP53 100fr blk. & multi. 1.25 65
C132 " 250fr " " 3.00 1.60

Villagers Observing Solar Eclipse
AP54

Designs: 40fr, Rocket take-off and Concord (vert.). 140fr, Scientists with telescopes observing eclipse.

1973, June 20 Engraved *Perf. 13*

C133 AP54 35fr grn. & pur. 35 15
C134 " 40fr ultra., purple & scarlet 40 20
C135 " 140fr scarlet & purple 1.40 80
a. Souvenir sheet of 3 3.00 3.00

Solar eclipse, June 30, 1973. No. C135a contains 3 stamps similar to Nos. C133–C135 in changed colors (35fr, 140fr in magenta and violet blue; 40fr in magenta, violet blue and orange). Marginal inscription in violet blue. Size: 119x99mm.

Soccer
AP55

1973, Dec. 24 Photo. *Perf. 13*

C136 AP55 7um multicolored 35 20
C137 " 8um " 35 20
C138 " 20um " 1.00 65

Souvenir Sheet

C139 AP55 30um multi. 1.65 1.65

World Soccer Cup, Munich, 1974. No. C139 contains one stamp. Dark green and yellow green ornamental margin with vermilion inscription. Size: 119x104mm.

Nos. C115–C117, C130 and C133–C135 Surcharged with New Value and Two Bars in Red, Black or Ultramarine

1973–74 Photo., Litho. or Engr.

C140 AP49 7um on 35fr multi. (R) ('74) 35 20
C141 AP54 7um on 35 fr multi. (B) 40 20
C142 " 8um on 40fr multi. (B) 40 25
C143 AP49 8um on 40fr multi. (U) ('74) 40 25

C144 AP49 20um on 100fr multi. (R) ('74) 1.10 65
C145 A63 27um on 135fr multi. (R) 1.25 75
C146 AP54 28um on 140fr multi. (B) 1.35 80
Nos. C140-C146 (7) 5.25 3.10

Churchill—AP56 Lenin—AP57

1974, June 3 Engraved *Perf. 13*
C147 AP56 40um blk. brown & henna brown 1.50 90

Centenary of the birth of Winston Churchill (1874-1965), statesman.

Nos. C131-C132 Surcharged with New Value and Two Bars in Red

1974, July 15 Photo. *Perf. 13x12½*
C148 AP53 20um on 100fr multi. 90 55
C149 " 50um on 250fr multi. 2.35 1.40

1974, Sept. 16 Engr. *Perf. 13*
C150 AP57 40um slate green & red 1.50 90

50th anniversary of the death of Lenin (1870-1924).

Women, IWY Emblem AP58

Design: 40um, Woman's head and IWY emblems.

1975, June 16 Engr. *Perf. 13*
C151 AP58 12um multicolored 55 32
C152 " 40um dk. brn., lt. brn. & bl. 1.85 1.00

International Women's Year 1975.

Schweitzer and Patients Arriving AP59

1975, Aug. 4 Engraved *Perf. 13*
C153 AP59 60um multicolored 2.50 1.50

Albert Schweitzer (1875-1965), medical missionary, birth centenary.

Javelin and Olympic Emblem—AP60

Design: 52um, Running and Olympic emblem.

1975, Nov. 17 Engr. *Perf. 13*
C154 AP60 50um slate green, red & ol. 2.25 1.25
C155 " 52um car., ocher & ultra. 2.35 1.25

Pre-Olympic Year 1975.

Apollo Soyuz Type, 1975

Designs (Docked Space Ships and): 20um, Apollo rocket launch. 50um, Handshake in linked-up cabin. 60um, Apollo splash-down. 100um, Astronauts and Cosmonauts.

1975, Dec. 29 Litho. *Perf. 14*
C156 A74 20um multi. 90 40
C157 " 50um " 2.25 1.00
C158 " 60um " 2.75 1.20

Souvenir Sheet
C159 A74 100um multi. 4.50 2.50

Apollo Soyuz space test project, Russo-American cooperation, launched July 15, link-up July 17, 1975. No. C159 has multicolored margin showing handclasp and launch pads. Size: 103x76mm.

American Bicentennial Type, 1976

Uniforms: 20um, French Hussar officer. 50um, 3rd Continental Artillery officer. 60um, French infantry regiment grenadier. 100um, American infantryman.

1976, Jan. 26
C160 A75 20um multi. 1.00 40
C161 " 50um " 2.50 1.00
C162 " 60um " 3.00 1.20

Souvenir Sheet
C163 A75 100um multi. 4.50 2.50

American Bicentennial. No. C163 has multicolored margin showing sword and pistols. Size: 100x12mm.

Running and Olympic Rings AP61

Designs (Olympic Rings and): 12um, High jump. 52um, Fencing.

1976, June 14 Engr. *Perf. 13*
C164 AP61 10um pur., green & brown 45 25
C165 " 12um pur., green & brown 55 32
C166 " 52um pur., green & brown 2.25 1.20

21st Olympic Games, Montreal, Canada, July 17-Aug. 1.

Zeppelin Type, 1976

Designs: 50um, "Graf Zeppelin" (LZ-127) over U.S. Capitol. 60um, "Hindenburg" (LZ-130) over Swiss Alps. 100um, "Führersland" (LZ-129) over 1936 Olympic stadium.

1976, June 28 Litho. *Perf. 11*
C167 A77 50um multi. 2.10 75
C168 " 60um " 2.50 90

Souvenir Sheet
C169 A77 100um multi. 4.25 2.00

75th anniversary of the Zeppelin. No. C169 has multicolored margin showing balloon, cabin of "Führersland" and Count Ferdinand von Zeppelin. Size: 129x104 mm.

Marabou Storks—AP62

African Birds: 50um, Sacred ibis (vert.). 200um, Long-crested eagles (vert.).

1976, Sept. 20 Litho. *Perf. 13½*
C170 AP62 50um multi. 2.25 95
C171 " 100um " 4.50 2.00
C172 " 200um " 8.50 3.50

Viking Type, 1977

Designs: 20um, Viking orbiter in flight to Mars. 50um, Viking "B" in descent to Mars. 60um, Various phases of descent. 100um, Viking lander using probe.

1977, Feb. 28 *Perf. 14*
C173 A81 20um multi. 85 30
C174 " 50um " 2.00 75
C175 " 60um " 2.50 85

Souvenir Sheet
C176 A81 100um multi. 4.00 1.50

Viking Mars project. No. C176 has multicolored margin showing Viking orbiter in flight. Size: 104x77½mm.

Nobel Prize Type, 1977

Designs: 14um, George Bernard Shaw, literature. 55um, Thomas Mann, literature. 60um, International Red Cross Society, peace. 100um, George C. Marshall, peace.

1977, Apr. 29 Litho. *Perf. 14*
C177 A83 14um multi. 60 25
C178 " 55um " 2.50 80
C179 " 60um " 2.75 90

Souvenir Sheet
C180 A83 100um multi. 4.50 2.00

Nobel prize winners. No. C180 has multicolored margin showing allegorical figures of music and learning. Size: 118x80mm.

Holy Kaaba AP63

1977, July 25 Litho. *Perf. 12½*
C181 AP63 12um multicolored 55 32

Pilgrimage to Mecca.

Soccer Type of 1977

Designs (Emblems and): 50um, Soccer ball. 60um, Eusebio Ferreira. 100um, Players holding pennants.

1977, Dec. 19 Litho. *Perf. 13½*
C182 A89 50um multicolored 2.10 70
C183 " 60um " 2.50 90

Souvenir Sheet
C184 A89 100um multi. 4.50 2.00

Elimination Games for World Cup Soccer Championship, Argentina, 1978. No. C184 has multicolored margin showing Mauritanian flag and Elimination Games' emblem. Size: 119x80mm.

Philexafrique II—Essen Issue
Common Design Types

Designs: No. C185, Hyena and Mauritania No. C60. No. C186, Wading bird and Hamburg No. 1.

1978, Nov. 1 Litho. *Perf. 12½*
C185 CD138 20um multi. 1.00 50
C186 CD139 20um " 1.00 50

Nos. C185-C186 printed se-tenant.

Nos. C182-C184 Overprinted in Arabic and French in Silver: "ARGENTINE - / PAY BAS 3-1"

1978, Dec. 11 Litho. *Perf. 13½*
C187 A89 50um multi. 2.50 1.00
C188 " 60um " 3.00 1.25

Souvenir Sheet
C189 A89 100um multi. 5.25 2.25

Argentina's victory in World Cup Soccer Championship 1978.

Flyer A and Prototype Plane—AP64

Design: 40um, Flyer A and supersonic jet.

1979, Jan. 29 Engr. *Perf. 13*
C190 AP64 15um multicolored 65 30
C191 " 40um " 1.60 80

75th anniversary of first powered flight.

AIR POST SEMI-POSTAL STAMPS.

Stamps of Dahomey types V1, V2, V3 and V4 inscribed "Mauritanie" were issued in 1942 by the Vichy Government, but were not placed on sale in the colony.

Prices of premium quality never hinged stamps will be in excess of catalogue price.

POSTAGE DUE STAMPS.

Natives D1 — Numeral of Value D2

Typographed

1906-07 ***Perf. 14x13½*** **Unwmkd.**

J1	D1	5c green, *greenish*	85	85
J2	"	10c red brown	1.25	1.25
J3	"	15c dark blue	3.00	2.50
J4	"	20c *yellow*	3.50	3.00
J5	"	30c red, *straw*	4.50	4.00
J6	"	50c violet	5.00	5.00
J7	"	60c *buff*	4.50	4.00
J8	"	1fr *pinkish*	5.50	5.50
		Nos. J1-J8 (8)	28.10	26.10

Issue dates: 20c, 1906; others 1907.
Regular postage stamps canceled "T" in a triangle were used for postage due.

1914

J9	D2	5c green		5
J10	"	10c rose	5	5
J11	"	15c gray	5	5
J12	"	20c brown	6	6
J13	"	30c blue	6	6
J14	"	50c black	40	40
J15	"	60c orange	25	25
J16	"	1fr violet	25	25
		Nos. J9-J16 (8)	1.17	1.17

Type of 1914 Issue Surcharged **2F.**

1927, Oct. 10

J17	D2	2fr on 1fr lilac rose	80	80
J18	"	3fr on 1fr orange brown	80	80

Islamic Republic

Oualata Motif
D3

Perf. 14x13½

1961, July 1 **Typo.** **Unwmkd.**

Denominations in Black

J19	D3	1fr plum & org. yel.	7	7
J20	"	2fr red & gray	8	8
J21	"	5fr maroon & pink	10	10
J22	"	10fr dk. green & grn.	20	20
J23	"	15fr olive & brn. org.	25	20
J24	"	20fr red brn. & lt. bl.	30	25
J25	"	25fr green & verm.	50	40
		Nos. J19-J25 (7)	1.50	1.30

Vulture (Ruppell's Griffon)—D4

Birds: No. J27, Eurasian crane. No. J28, Pink-backed pelican. No. J29, Garganey teal. No. J30, European golden oriole. No. J31, Variable sunbird. No. J32, Shoveler ducks. No. J33, Great snipe. No. J34, Vulturine guinea fowl. No. J35, Black stork. No. J36, Gray heron. No. J37, White stork. No. J38, Red-legged partridge. No. J39, Paradise whydah. No. J40, Sandpiper (little stint). No. J41, Sudan bustard.

1963, Sept. 7 **Engraved** ***Perf. 11***

J26	D4	50c black, yellow orange & red	5	5
J27	"	50c black, yellow, orange & red	5	5
J28	"	1fr blk., red & yel.	5	5
J29	D4	1fr blk., red & yel.	5	5
J30	"	2fr black, blue green & yellow	8	8
J31	"	2fr black, blue green & yellow	8	8
J32	"	5fr black, green & red brown	12	12
J33	"	5fr black, green & red brown	12	12
J34	"	10fr blk., red & tan	18	18
J35	"	10fr blk., red & tan	18	18
J36	"	15fr black, emerald & red	25	25
J37	"	15fr black, emerald & red	25	25
J38	"	20fr black, yellow green & red	40	40
J39	"	20fr black, yellow green & red	40	40
J40	"	25fr black, yellow green & brown	60	60
J41	"	25fr black, yellow green & brown	60	60
		Nos. J26-J41 (16)	3.46	3.46

Ornament
D5

1976, May 10 **Litho.** ***Perf. 12½x13***

J42	D5	1um buff & multi.	7	5
J43	"	3um " "	13	10
J44	"	10um " "	45	30
J45	"	12um " "	50	35
J46	"	20um " "	85	60
		Nos. J42-J46 (5)	2.00	1.40

OFFICIAL STAMPS

Islamic Republic

Cross of Trarza
O1

Perf. 14x13½

1961, July 1 **Typo.** **Unwmkd.**

O1	O1	1fr violet & lilac	5	5
O2	"	3fr red & slate	7	7
O3	"	5fr green & brown	10	10
O4	"	10fr grn. & vio. blue	15	10
O5	"	15fr blue & orange	20	15
O6	"	20fr slate green & emerald	25	20
O7	"	25fr red orange & maroon	30	30
O8	"	30fr maroon & grn.	40	35
O9	"	50fr dark red & dark brown	80	60
O10	"	100fr orange & blue	1.50	1.10
O11	"	200fr green & red orange	2.75	2.00
		Nos. O1-O11 (11)	6.57	5.02

Ornament
O2

1976, May 3 **Litho.** ***Perf. 12½x13***

O12	O2	1um black & multi.	7	5
O13	"	2um " "	13	5
O14	"	5um " "	25	10
O15	"	10um " "	45	30
O16	"	12um " "	50	40
O17	"	40um " "	1.85	1.35
O18	"	50um " "	2.25	1.50
		Nos. O12-O18 (7)	5.50	3.75

MAYOTTE

(mȧ'yôt')

LOCATION — One of the Comoro Islands situated in the Mozambique Channel midway between Madagascar and Mozambique (Africa).

GOVT.—Former French Colony.

AREA—140 sq. mi.

POP.—13,783 (1914).

CAPITAL—Dzaoudzi.

See Comoro Islands.

100 Centimes = 1 Franc

Navigation and Commerce
A1

Perf. 14x13½.

1892-1907 Typographed. Unwmkd.

Name of Colony
in Blue or Carmine.

1 A1 1c *lilac blue* 20 20
2 " 2c brown, *buff* 30 30
a. Name double 90.00 90.00
3 " 4c claret, *lavender* 50 40
4 " 5c green, *greenish* 90 50
5 " 10c *lavender* 1.10 75
6 " 10c red ('00) 14.00 11.00
7 " 15c blue, quadrille paper 4.00 2.50
8 " 15c gray ('00) 27.50 25.00
9 " 20c red, *green* 3.00 2.50
10 " 25c *rose* 2.00 2.00
11 " 25c blue ('00) 2.50 2.00
12 " 30c brown, *bistre* 4.50 3.00
13 " 35c *yellow* ('06) 2.00 1.75
14 " 40c red, *straw* 4.00 3.00
15 " 45c *gray green* ('07) 4.00 2.75
16 " 50c carmine, *rose* 5.50 4.00
17 " 50c brown, *azure* ('00) 4.50 4.50
18 " 75c dp. vio., *orange* 7.00 4.00
19 " 1fr bronze green, *straw* 5.00 4.00
20 " 5fr red lilac, *lavender* ('99) 30.00 25.00
Nos. 1-20 (20) 122.50 99.15

Issues of 1892-1907 Surcharged in Black or Carmine **05** *a* **10** *b*

1912

22 A1 5c on 2c brn., *buff* 40 40
23 " 5c on 4c claret, *lavender* (C) 30 30
24 " 5c on 15c blue (C) 25 25
25 " 5c on 20c red, *green* 30 30
26 " 5c on 25c *rose* (C) 30 30
a. Double surcharge 60.00
27 " 5c on 30c brown, *bistre* (C) 30 30
28 " 10c on 40c red, *straw* 30 30
a. Double surcharge 60.00
29 " 10c on 45c *gray green* (C) 15 15
a. Double surcharge 60.00
30 " 10c on 50c car., *rose* 70 70
31 " 10c on 75c dp. vio., *org.* 50 50
32 " 10c on 1 fr bronze green, *straw* 50 50
Nos. 22-32 (11) 4.00 4.00

Two spacings between the surcharged numerals are found on Nos. 22 to 32.

Nos. 22 to 32 were available for use in Madagascar and the entire Comoro archipelago.

Stamps of Mayotte were replaced successively by those of Madagascar, Comoro Islands and France.

MECKLENBURG-SCHWERIN

MECKLENBURG-STRELITZ

See German States group preceding Germany.

MEMEL

(mā'mĕl)

LOCATION — In northern Europe, bordering on the Baltic Sea.

GOVT. — Special commission (see below).

AREA—1099 sq. mi.

POP.—151,960.

Following World War I this territory was detached from Germany and by Treaty of Versailles assigned to the government of a commission of the Allied and Associated Powers (not the League of Nations), which administered it until January, 1923, when it was forcibly occupied by Lithuania. In 1924 Memel became incorporated as a semi-autonomous district of Lithuania with the approval of the Allied Powers and the League of Nations.

100 Pfennig = 1 Mark
100 Centu = 1 Litas (1923)

Stamps of Germany, 1905-20, Overprinted **Memel-gebiet**

Wmkd. Lozenges. (125)

1920, Aug. 1 ***Perf. 14, 14½***

1 A16 5pf green 40 40
2 " 10pf carmine rose 3.50 5.25
3 " 10pf orange 35 35
4 A22 15pf violet brown 4.00 5.25
5 A16 20pf blue violet 20 20
6 " 30pf orange & black, *buff* 1.60 1.60
7 " 30pf dull blue 25 35
8 " 40pf lake & black 14 15
9 " 50pf purple & black, *buff* 20 20
10 " 60pf olive green 80 1.50
11 " 75pf green & black 3.25 5.00
12 " 80pf blue violet 1.60 2.50

Overprinted **Memelgebiet**

13 A17 1m carmine rose 50 55
14 " 1.25m green 18.00 20.00
15 " 1.50m yellow brown 5.50 7.25
16 A21 2m blue 2.50 3.25
17 " 2.50m red lilac 14.00 16.00
Nos. 1-17 (17) 56.79 69.80

A1

A2

Stamps of France, Surcharged in Black.

1920 ***Perf. 14x13½.*** **Unwmkd.**

18 A1 5pf on 5c green 15 16
19 " 10pf on 10c red 12 15
20 " 20pf on 25c blue 14 18
21 " 30pf on 30c orange 14 20
22 " 40pf on 20c red brown 12 20
23 " 50pf on 35c violet 25 35
24 A2 60pf on 40c red & pale blue 45 50
25 " 80pf on 45c green & blue 25 27
26 " 1m on 50c brown & lavender 17 25
27 " 1m 25(pf) on 60c vio. & ultra. 1.75 2.00
28 " 2m on 1fr claret & olive green 22 25
29 A2 3m on 5fr blue & buff 18.00 18.00
Nos. 18-29 (12) 21.76 22.51

French Stamps of 1900-20 Surcharged like Nos. 24 to 29 in Red or Black.

FOUR MARKS :

4 Type I. **4** Type II.

1920-21 ***Perf. 14x13½*** **Unwmkd.**

30 A2 3m on 2fr orange & pale bl. (R) 15.00 22.50
31 " 4m on 2fr orange & pale blue (I) (Bk) 30 35
a. 4m on 2fr orange & pale blue (II) 110.00 125.00
32 " 10m on 5fr blue & buff (R) 3.00 4.00
33 " 20m on 5fr blue & buff (R) 40.00 50.00

1921

New Value with Initial Capital

39 A2 60Pf on 40c red & pale blue 3.25 4.75
40 " 3M on 60c violet & ultramarine 80 80
41 " 10M on 5fr bl. & buff 1.00 1.25
42 " 20M on 45c grn. & bl. 3.25 4.00

The surcharged value on No. 40 is in italics.

Stamps of 1920 Surcharged with Large Numerals in Dark Blue or Red.

1921-22

43 A1 15pf on 10pf on 10c red 25 32
a. Inverted surcharge 50.00 50.00
44 " 15pf on 20pf on 25c blue 35 45
a. Inverted surcharge 50.00 50.00
45 " 15pf on 50pf on 35c violet (R) 27 45
a. Inverted surcharge 50.00 50.00
46 " 60pf on 40pf on 20c red brown 15 20
a. Inverted surcharge 50.00 50.00
47 A2 75pf on 60pf on 40c red & pale blue 65 90
48 " 1.25m on 1m on 50c brown & lavender 27 33
49 " 5.00m on 2m on 1fr claret & olive green 90 90
a. Inverted surcharge 225.00 225.00
Nos. 43-49 (7) 2.84 3.55

A3

A4

Black or Red Surcharge.

1922

50 A3 5pf on 5c orange 8 12
51 " 10pf on 10c red 90 1.35
52 " 10pf on 10c green 12 12
53 " 15pf on 10c green 22 45
54 " 20pf on 20c red brn. 4.00 6.00
55 " 20pf on 25c blue 4.00 6.00
56 " 25pf on 5c orange 8 10
57 " 30pf on 30c red 65 1.80
58 " 35pf on 35c violet 10 22
59 " 50pf on 50c dull blue 15 20
60 " 75pf on 15c green 12 22
61 " 75pf on 35c violet 12 20
62 " 1m on 25c blue 12 22
63 " 1¼m on 30c red 12 22
64 " 3m on 5c orange 10 33
65 " 6m on 15c green (R) 15 33
66 " 8m on 30c red 22 60
67 A4 40pf on 40c red & pale blue 9 18
68 " 80pf on 45c grn. & blue 12 20
69 " 1m on 40c red & pale blue 12 20
70 A4 1.25m on 60c violet & ultra. (R) 12 22
71 " 1.50m on 45c green & blue (R) 12 22
72 " 2m on 45c grn. & bl. 12 22
73 " 2m on 1fr claret & olive green 16 22
74 " 2¼m on 40c red & pale blue 12 22
75 " 2½m on 60c violet & ultramarine 30 45
76 " 3m on 60c violet & ultra. (R) 65 80
77 " 4m on 45c grn. & bl. 12 22
78 " 5m on 1fr claret & olive green 33 38
79 " 6m on 60c violet & ultramarine 12 22
80 " 6m on 2fr orange & pale blue 33 38
81 " 9m on 1fr claret & olive green 20 33
82 " 9m on 5fr blue & buff (R) 45 50
83 " 10m on 45c green & blue (R) 25 33
84 " 12m on 40c red & pale blue 20 33
85 " 20m on 40c red & pale blue 25 33
86 " 20m on 2fr orange & pale blue 20 33
87 " 30m on 60c violet & ultramarine 25 33
88 " 30m on 5fr dark blue & buff 3.25 5.00
89 " 40m on 1fr claret & olive green 25 33
90 " 50m on 2fr orange & pale blue 8.00 10.00
91 " 80m on 2fr orange & pale blue (R) 25 33
92 " 100m on 5fr blue & buff 35 45
Nos. 50-92 (43) 27.97 41.20

Nos. 59, 60 and 65 are on France type A20.

A 500m on 5fr dark blue and buff was prepared, but not officially issued. Price $500.

Stamps of 1922 Surcharged "Mark."

1922-23

93 A3 10m on 10pf on 10c green 80 1.80
a. Double surch. 50.00 50.00
94 " 20m on 20pf on 20c red brown 60 65
95 A4 40m on 40pf on 40c red & pale blue ('23) 60 90
96 A3 50m on 50pf on 50c dull blue 1.60 2.75

No. 96 is on France Type A20.

Stamps of 1922 Surcharged with New Values in Red or Black.

97 A4 10(m) on 2m on 45c grn.& bl. (R) 1.10 1.40
98 A3 25(m) on 1m on 25c blue (R) 1.10 1.40
99 A4 80(m) on 1.25m on 60c violet & ultra. (Bk) ('23) 60 90

AIR POST STAMPS.

Regular Issues of 1920-21 Overprinted in Dark Blue

Perf. 14x13½

1921, July 6 **Unwmkd.**

C1 A2 60pf on 40c red & pale blue 45.00 52.50
C2 " 80pf on 45c green & blue 3.25 4.75
C3 " 1m on 50c brown & lavender 2.50 3.25
C4 " 2m on 1fr claret & olive green 3.25 4.75
a. "Flugpost" inverted 200.00 250.00

C5 A2 4m on 2fr orange & pale blue (I) 4.00 8.00
 a. 4m on 2fr orange & pale blue (II) 200.00 225.00

New Value with Initial Capital.

C6 A2 60Pf on 40c red & pale blue 4.00 6.50
 a. "Flugpost" inverted 200.00 225.00
C7 " 3M on 60c violet & ultramarine 3.25 4.75
 a. "Flugpost" inverted 200.00 225.00
 Nos. C1-C7 (7) 65.25 84.50

The surcharged value on No. C7 is in italics.

Regular Issue of 1922 Overprinted in Dark Blue

1922, May 12

C8 A4 40pf on 40c red & pale blue 55 90
C9 " 80pf on 45c grn. & bl. 55 90
C10 " 1m on 40c red & pale blue 55 90
C11 " 1.25m on 60c violet & ultramarine 90 1.60
C12 " 1.50m on 45c green & blue 90 1.60
C13 " 2m on 1fr claret & olive green 90 1.60
C14 " 3m on 60c violet & ultramarine 90 1.60
C15 " 5m on 1fr claret & olive green 1.00 1.80
C16 " 6m on 2fr orange & pale blue 1.00 1.80
C17 " 9m on 5fr bl. & buff 1.00 1.80

Same Overprints On Regular Issue of 1920-21.

C18 A2 3m on 60c violet & ultra. 150.00 *375.00*
C19 " 4m on 2fr orange & pale blue 90 1.60
 Nos. C8-C17, C19 (11) 9.15 16.10

Regular Issue of 1922 Overprinted in Black or Red **FLUGPOST**

1922, Oct. 17

C20 A4 40pf on 40c red & pale blue 1.00 2.75
C21 " 1m on 40c red & pale blue 1.00 2.75
C22 " 1.25m on 60c violet & ultra. (R) 1.00 2.75
C23 " 1.50m on 45c green & blue (R) 1.00 2.75
C24 " 2m on 1fr claret & olive green 1.00 2.75
C25 " 3m on 60c violet & ultra. (R) 1.00 2.75
C26 " 4m on 2fr orange & pale blue 1.00 2.75
C27 " 5m on 1fr claret & olive green 1.00 2.75
C28 " 6m on 2fr orange & pale blue 1.00 2.75
C29 " 9m on 5fr blue & buff (R) 1.00 2.75
 Nos. C20-C29 (10) 10.00 27.50

No. C26 is not known without the "FLUGPOST" overprint.

OCCUPATION STAMPS.

Issued under Lithuanian Occupation.

"Vytis"
O1 O2

Lithographed
1923 *Perf. 11* **Unwmkd.**

Memel Printing.
Surcharged in Various Colors.

N1 O1 10m on 5c blue (Bk) 1.00 1.10
 a. "Memel" and bars omitted 7.50 12.50
N2 " 25m on 5c blue (R) 1.00 1.10
N3 " 50m on 25c red (Bk) 1.00 1.10
N4 " 100m on 25c red (G) 1.00 1.10
N5 " 400m on 1 l brn. (R) 1.10 1.65
N6 " 500m on 1 l brn. (Bl) 1.10 1.65
 Nos. N1-N6 (6) 6.20 7.70

Nos. N1 and N3-N6 exist with double surcharge. Price $50 each.

Kaunas Printing.
Black Surcharge.

N7 O2 10m on 5c blue 50 75
N8 " 25m on 5c blue 50 75
N9 " 50m on 25c red 50 75
N10 " 100m on 25c red 75 1.00
N11 " 400m on 1 l brown 1.25 1.75
 Nos. N7-N11 (5) 3.50 5.00

No. N8 has the value in "Markes", others of the group have it in "Markiu."

O3

Surcharged in Various Colors.

1923

N12 O3 10m on 5c blue (R) 90 1.25
 a. "Markes" instead of "Markiu" 17.50 25.00
N13 " 20m on 5c blue (R) 90 1.25
N14 " 25m on 25c red (Bl) 90 1.25
N15 " 50m on 25c red (Bl) 1.00 1.75
 a. Invtd. surcharge 50.00
N16 " 100m on 1 l brn. (Bk) 1.25 2.25
 a. Invtd. surcharge 50.00
N17 " 200m on 1 l brn. (Bk) 1.25 2.25
 Nos. N12-N17 (6) 6.20 10.00

No. N14 has the value in "Markes", others of the group have it in "Markiu."

O4 O5

1923, Mar.

N18 O4 10m light brown 25 30
N19 " 20m yellow 25 30
N20 " 25m orange 25 30
N21 " 40m violet 25 30
N22 " 50m yellow green 75 85
N23 O5 100m carmine 40 45
N24 " 300m olive green 3.75 *20.00*
N25 " 400m olive brown 55 65
N26 " 500m lilac 3.75 *20.00*
N27 " 1000m blue 75 85
 Nos. N18-N27 (10) 10.95 *44.00*

No. N20 has the value in "Markes".

No. 99 Surcharged in Green — Klaipėda 400 M

1923, Apr. 13

N28 A4 100m on No. 99 5.00 6.00
N29 " 400m on No. 99 5.00 6.00
N30 " 500m on No. 99 5.00 6.00

The normal position of the green surcharge is sideways, with the top at the left. It exists reversed on the three stamps.

Ship O7 — Seal O8 — Lighthouse O9

1923, Apr. 12 **Lithographed**

N31 O7 40m olive green 3.75 7.00
N32 " 50m brown 3.75 7.00
N33 " 80m green 3.75 7.00
N34 " 100m red 3.75 7.00
N35 O8 200m deep blue 3.75 7.00
N36 " 300m brown 3.75 7.00
N37 " 400m lilac 3.75 7.00
N38 " 500m orange 3.75 7.00
N39 " 600m olive green 3.75 7.00
N40 O9 800m deep blue 3.75 7.00
N41 " 1000m lilac 3.75 7.00
N42 " 2000m red 3.75 7.00
N43 " 3000m green 3.75 7.00
 Nos. N31-N43 (13) 48.75 91.00

Union of Memel with Lithuania. Forgeries exist.

Stamps of 1922 Surcharged in Various Colors — 3 CENTŲ

1923 **Thin Figures**

N44 O5 2c on 300m olive grn. (R) 5.00 7.50
N45 " 3c on 300m olive grn. (R) 5.00 7.50
N46 O4 10c on 25m org. (Bk) 5.00 7.50
 a. Double surcharge 50.00
N47 " 15c on 25m org. (Bk) 5.00 7.50
N48 O5 20c on 500m lilac (Bl) 6.00 9.00
N49 " 30c on 500m lilac (Bk) 5.00 7.50
N50 " 50c on 500m lilac (G) 10.00 15.00
 a. Inverted surcharge 50.00
 Nos. N44-N50 (7) 41.00 61.50

Surcharged:

2 CENT. — 1 LITAS

N51 O4 2c on 20m yellow 3.00 4.50
N52 " 2c on 50m yellow grn. 3.00 4.50
N53 " 3c on 40m violet 3.75 5.00
 a. Double surcharge 60.00
N54 O5 3c on 300m olive grn. 3.00 4.25
 a. Double surcharge 60.00
N55 " 5c on 100m carmine 3.75 4.25
N56 " 5c on 300m olive green (R) 3.50 5.00
N57 " 10c on 400m olive brn. 7.50 8.00
N58 " 30c on 500m lilac 3.75 7.00
N59 " 1 l on 1000m blue 15.00 20.00
 Nos. N51-N59 (9) 46.25 62.50

There are several types of the numerals in these surcharges. Nos. N56 and N58 have "CENT" in short, thick letters, as on Nos. N44 to N50.

Surcharged — 2 CENT.

Thick Figures.

N60 O4 2c on 10m lt. brown 1.75 *2.50*
N61 " 2c on 20m yellow 15.00 *30.00*
N62 O4 2c on 50m yel. green 3.50 *5.00*
N63 " 3c on 10m lt. brown 3.50 *5.00*
 a. Double surcharge 50.00
N64 O4 3c on 40m violet 22.50 *40.00*
N65 O5 5c on 100m carmine 3.50 *5.00*
 a. Double surcharge 50.00
N66 " 10c on 400m olive brown 125.00 *200.00*
N67 O4 15c on 25m orange 125.00 *200.00*
N68 O5 50c on 1000m blue 3.50 *5.00*
 a. Double surcharge 50.00
N69 " 1 l on 1000m blue 7.50 *12.50*
 a. Double surcharge 90.00
 Nos. N60-N69 (10) 310.75 *505.00*

No. N69 is surcharged like type "b" in the following group.

Nos. N31-N43 Surcharged:

30 a CENT. — 1 LITAS b

N70 O7 (a) 15c on 40m olive green 6.25 *8.00*
N71 " (") 30c on 50m brown 5.00 *7.00*
N72 " (") 30c on 80m green 6.25 *8.00*
N73 " (") 30c on 100m red 5.00 *7.00*
N74 O8 (") 50c on 200m deep blue 6.25 *8.00*
N75 " (") 50c on 300m brn. 5.00 *7.00*
N76 " (") 50c on 400m lilac 6.25 *8.00*
N77 " (") 50c on 500m org. 5.00 *7.00*
N78 " (b) 1 l on 600m olive green 6.25 *8.00*
N79 O9 (") 1 l on 800m deep blue 6.25 *8.00*
N80 " (") 1 l on 1000m lilac 6.25 *8.00*
N81 " (") 1 l on 2000m red 6.25 *8.00*
N82 " (") 1 l on 3000m grn. 6.25 *8.00*
 Nos. N70-N82 (13) 76.25 *100.00*

These stamps are said to have been issued to commemorate the institution of autonomous government.

Double or inverted surcharges exist on Nos. N71, N75-N77. Price, each $50.

Commemorative Issue of 1923 Surcharged in Green — 25 CENT.

1923

N83 O7 15c on 50m brown 200.00 *550.00*
N84 " 25c on 100m red 125.00 *400.00*
N85 O8 30c on 300m brn. 175.00 *475.00*
N86 " 60c on 500m org. 115.00 *375.00*

Surcharges on Nos. N83-N86 are of two types, differing in width of numerals. Prices are for stamps with narrow numerals, as illustrated. Stamps with wide numerals sell for two to four times as much.

Provisional Issue of 1923 Surcharged in Red or Green — 15 Centų

N87 O2 10c on 25m on 5c blue (R) 22.50 *30.00*
N88 " 15c on 100m on 25c red (G) 32.50 *60.00*
 a. Inverted surcharge 100.00
N89 O2 30c on 400m on 1 l brown (R) 7.50 *11.00*
N90 O1 60c on 50m on 25c red (G) 37.50 *50.00*

Stamps of 1923 Surcharged in Green or Red — 15 Centų

N91 O4 15c on 10m lt. brn. 9.00 *18.00*
N92 " 15c on 20m yellow 5.00 *10.00*

N93	O4	15c on 25m orange	6.00	*12.00*
N94	"	15c on 40m violet	5.00	*10.00*
N95	"	15c on 50m yellow green (R)	3.75	*7.50*
N96	"	25c on 10m light brown	7.00	*14.00*
N97	"	25c on 20m yellow	5.00	*10.00*
N98	"	25c on 25m orange	6.00	*12.00*
N99	"	25c on 40m violet	5.00	*10.00*
N100	"	25c on 50m yellow green (R)	3.75	*7.50*
N101	"	30c on 10m light brown	9.00	*18.00*
N102	"	30c on 20m yellow	5.00	*10.00*
N103	"	30c on 25m orange	6.00	*12.00*
N104	"	30c on 40m violet	5.00	*10.00*
N105	"	30c on 50m yellow green (R)	3.75	*7.50*
		Nos. N91-N105 (15)	84.25	*168.50*

Nine stamps between Nos. N95 and N114 exist with inverted surcharge. No. 102 exists with double surcharge.

Surcharged in Green or Red

15 Centu

N106	O5	15c on 100m carmine	3.75	*7.50*
N107	"	15c on 400m olive brown	3.25	*6.50*
N108	"	15c on 1000m blue (R)	75.00	*150.00*
N109	"	25c on 100m carmine	3.75	*7.50*
N110	"	25c on 400m olive brown	3.25	*6.50*
N111	"	25c on 1000m blue (R)	80.00	*160.00*
N112	"	30c on 100m car.	3.75	*7.50*
N113	"	30c on 400m olive brown	3.25	*6.50*
N114	"	30c on 1000m blue (R)	75.00	*150.00*
		Nos. N106-N114 (9)	251.00	*502.00*

Nos. N96 to N100 and N109 to N111 are surcharged "Cental", the others "Centu".

Excellent counterfeits of all Memel issues exist.

MEXICO

(mĕk'sĭ-kō)

LOCATION—In the extreme southern part of the North American Continent, south of the United States.

GOVT.—Republic.

AREA—758,259 sq. mi.

POP.—64,590,000 (est. 1977).

CAPITAL—Mexico, D. F.

8 Reales = 1 Peso
100 Centavos = 1 Peso

> Prices of early Mexico stamps vary according to condition. Quotations for Nos. 1-104 are for fine copies. Very fine to superb specimens sell at much higher prices, and inferior or poor copies sell at reduced prices, depending on the condition of the individual specimen.

District Overprints

Nos. 1-149 are overprinted with names of various districts, and sometimes also with district numbers and year dates. Some of the district overprints are rare and command high prices. Prices given for Nos. 1-149 are for the commoner district overprints.

Miguel Hidalgo y Costilla
A1

Handstamped with District Name.

Engraved.

1856 ***Imperf.*** **Unwmkd.**

1	A1	½r blue	18.00	7.00
		a. 1½r dark blue	18.00	7.00
		b. Without ovpt.	10.00	13.00
2	A1	1r yellow	10.00	1.75
		a. 1r deep yellow	10.00	1.75
		b. Half used as ½r on cover		360.00
		c. Without ovpt.	8.00	6.50
3	A1	2r yellow green	8.00	1.25
		a. 2r blue green	65.00	10.00
		b. 2r emerald	100.00	19.00
		c. Half used as 1r on cover		275.00
		d. Without ovpt.	11.00	5.50
		e. Printed on both sides (yellow green)	125.00	150.00
4	A1	4r red	85.00	40.00
		a. Half used as 2r on cover		110.00
		b. Quarter used as 1r on cover		165.00
		c. Without ovpt.	55.00	75.00
5	A1	8r red lilac	125.00	85.00
		a. 8r violet	125.00	85.00
		b. Without ovpt.	85.00	125.00
		c. Eighth used as 1r on cover		850.00
		d. Quarter used as 2r on cover		120.00
		e. Half used as 4r on cover		190.00
		f. Three-quarters used as 6r on cover		750.00

The 1r and 2r were printed in sheets of 60 with wide spacing between stamps, and in sheets of 190 or 200 with narrow spacing.

All values have been reprinted, some of them several times. The reprints usually show signs of wear and the impressions are often smudgy. The paper is usually thicker than that of the originals. Reprints are usually on very white paper. Reprints are found with and without overprints and with cancellations made both from the original handstamps and from forged ones.

1861

6	A1	½r *buff*	20.00	16.50
		a. Without overprint	15.00	19.00
7	"	1r *green*	10.00	2.50
		a. Impression of 2r on back		225.00
		b. Without overprint	3.00	4.00
		c. Printed on both sides		200.00
		d. 1r *pink* (error)		
		e. Half used as ½r on cover		
8	"	2r *pink*	5.50	1.75
		a. Impression of 1r on back	250.00	
		b. Half used as 1r on cover		200.00
		c. Without overprint	2.00	3.00
		d. Printed on both sides		275.00
		e. 2r *green* (error)		
9	"	4r *yellow*	60.00	35.00
		a. Half used as 2r on cover		140.00
		b. Without overprint	22.50	45.00
		c. Quarter used as 1r on cover		175.00
10	"	4r dull rose, *yellow*	82.50	25.00
		a. Half used as 2r on cover		250.00
		b. Without overprint	55.00	65.00
		c. Printed on both sides		*700.00*
		d. Quarter used as 1r on cover		325.00
11	"	8r *red brown*	150.00	110.00
		a. Eighth used as 1r on cover		*700.00*
		b. Quarter used as 2r on cover		120.00
		c. Half used as 4r on cover		175.00
		d. Without overprint	50.00	90.00
		e. Three quarters used as 6r on cover		
12	"	8r grn., *red brown*	150.00	70.00
		a. Half used as 4r on cover		
		b. Without overprint	85.00	110.00
		c. Quarter used as 2r on cover		

Nos. 6, 9, 10, 11 and 12 have been reprinted. Most reprints of the ½r, 4r and 8r are on vertically grained paper. Originals are on horizontally grained paper. The original ½r stamps are much worn but the reprints are unworn. The paper of the 4r is too deep and rich in color and No. 10 is printed in too bright red. Reprints of the 8r can only be told by experts. All these reprints are found in fancy colors and with overprints and cancellations as in the 1856 issue.

Hidalgo—A3 Coat of Arms—A4

With District Name.

1864 ***Perf. 12.***

14	A3	1r red	*300.00*	*650.00*
		a. Without District Name	20	
15	A3	2r blue	*250.00*	*550.00*
		a. Without District Name	25	
16	A3	4r brown	*600.00*	*1200.00*
		a. Without District Name	50	
		b. Vert. pair, imperf. between		
17	A3	1p black	*1000.00*	
		a. Without District Name	1.00	

Nos. 14 to 17 were not issued without district overprint. Counterfeit cancellations are plentiful. The 1r red with "½" surcharge is bogus.

Overprint of District Name, etc.

1864-66 ***Imperf.***

Five types of overprints:

I. District name only.
II. District name, consignment number and "1864" in large figures.
III. District name, number and "1864" in small figures.
IV. District name, number and "1865."
V. District name, number and "1866."

18	A4	3c brown (IV, V)	850.00	*1600.00*
		a. Without ovpt.	400.00	
		b. Laid paper	*2750.00*	*3500.00*
19	"	½r brown (I)	225.00	160.00
		a. Type II	800.00	700.00
		b. Without ovpt.	110.00	240.00
20	"	½r lilac (IV)	40.00	35.00
		a. Type III	45.00	40.00
		b. Type II	90.00	85.00
		c. Type V		700.00
		d. ½r gray (V)	45.00	45.00
		e. Without ovpt.	3.50	
21	"	1r blue (IV, V)	8.50	5.00
		a. Type III	9.50	5.50
		b. Without ovpt.	1.35	
		c. Half used as ½r on cover		900.00
22	"	1r ultra. (I, II)	40.00	17.50
		a. Type III	45.00	19.00
		b. Without ovpt.	80.00	85.00
23	"	2r org. (III, IV, V)	3.00	1.75
		a. Type II	10.00	2.25
		b. Type I	25.00	3.50
		c. 2r deep orange, without ovpt., early plate	100.00	35.00
		d. Without ovpt., late plate	1.10	
		e. Half used as 1r on cover		650.00
24	"	4r grn. (III, IV, V)	65.00	45.00
		a. Types I, II	90.00	55.00
		b. 4r dark green, without ovpt.	3.00	*85.00*
		d. Half used as 2r on cover		700.00
25	"	8r red (IV, V)	100.00	60.00
		a. Types II, III	120.00	70.00
		b. Type I	275.00	85.00
		c. 8r dark red, without ovpt.	4.00	*175.00*
		e. Half used as 4r on cover		1500.00
		f. Quarter used as 2r on cover		1100.00

The 2r printings from the early plates are 25½mm. high; those from the late plate, 24½mm.

Varieties listed as "Without ovpt." in unused condition are remainders.

Besides the overprints of district name, number and date, Nos. 18-34 often received, in the district offices, additional overprints of numbers and sometimes year dates. Copies with these "sub-consignment numbers" sell for more than stamps without them.

Faked quarterlings and bisects of 1856-64 are plentiful.

The 3c has been reprinted from a die on which the words "TRES CENTAVOS", the outlines of the serpent and some of the background lines have been retouched.

> The indexes in each volume of the Scott Catalogue contain many listings which help to identify stamps.

Emperor Maximilian
A5

Lithographed.

Overprinted with District Name, Number and Date 1866 or 866; also with Number and Date only, or with Name only.

1866

26	A5	7c lilac gray	40.00	70.00
		a. 7c deep gray	42.50	70.00
27	"	13c blue	12.50	12.50
28	"	25c buff	5.25	4.25
29	"	25c orange	5.25	4.25
		a. 25c red orange	10.00	8.00
30	"	50c green	12.50	12.50
		a. Half used as 25c on cover		700.00

Engraved

Overprinted with District Name, Number and Date 866 or 867; also with Number and Date only.

31	A5	7c lilac	250.00	*2500.00*
		a. Without overprint	2.75	
32	"	13c blue	3.75	5.25
		a. Without overprint	75	
33	"	25c orange brown	2.75	4.25
		a. Without overprint	75	
34	"	50c green	135.00	37.50
		a. Without overprint	1.25	

See "sub-consignment" note after No. 25.

Stamps of 1856-61 Overprinted **Mexico**

1867

35	A1	½r *buff*	750.00	650.00
36	"	1r *green*	21.00	6.25
		a. 1r *pink* (error)		
37	"	2r *pink*	7.50	2.75
		a. Printed on both sides		80.00
38	"	4r red, *yellow*	75.00	10.00
		a. Printed on both sides		125.00
39	"	4r red		135.00
		a. Printed on both sides		550.00
40	"	8r *red brown*	700.00	145.00
41	"	8r green, *red brown*		1350.00

Dangerous counterfeits exist of the "Mexico" overprint.

Wmk. 151

Same Overprint.

Thin Gray Blue Paper.

Wmkd. R. P. S. in the Sheet. (151)

(R.P.S. stands for "Rente Papel Sellado")

42	A1	½r gray	145.00	120.00
		a. Without ovpt.	120.00	120.00
43	"	1r blue	225.00	40.00
		a. Half used as ½r on cover		
		b. Without ovpt.		47.50
44	"	2r green	30.00	6.25
		a. Printed on both sides		450.00
		b. Without ovpt.	45.00	12.00

45 A1 4r rose 525.00 42.50
a. Without ovpt. 50.00

Some reprints are on thin bluish wove paper without watermark. The ½r is unworn while the originals show signs of wear. The 4r is printed in red instead of rose. It is doubtful if the 1r and 2r have been reprinted.

The ½r and 8r have also been reprinted in gray on thick grayish wove paper, unwatermarked.

Hidalgo
A6

Thin Figures of Value, without Period

6 CENT. 12 CENT.
25 CENT. 50 CENT.
100 CENT.

Overprinted with District Name, Number and Abbreviated Date.

Lithographed

1868 ***Imperf.*** **Unwmkd.**

46 A6 6c *buff* 9.50 7.00
47 " 12c *green* 9.00 6.25
a. Period after "12" 18.50
48 " 25c blue, *pink* 14.00 4.00
a. Without ovpt. 60.00
49 " 50c *yellow* 90.00 22.50
a. Half used as 25c on cover 300.00
50 " 100c *brown* 175.00 55.00
a. Quarter used as 25c on cover 400.00
b. Half used as 50c on cover 475.00
51 " 100c brown, *brown* 500.00 175.00
a. Half used as 50c on cover
b. Quarter used as 25c on cover

Perf.

52 A6 6c *buff* 8.00 5.75
a. Without ovpt. 50.00
53 " 12c *green* 5.75 2.00
a. Period after "12" 35.00 12.00
b. Very thick paper 12.00 8.00
c. Without ovpt. 40.00
54 " 25c blue, *pink* 8.50 1.75
a. Half used as 12c on cover
b. Without ovpt. 60.00
55 " 50c *yellow* 55.00 11.00
a. Half used as 25c on cover 275.00
56 " 100c *brown* 100.00 35.00
a. Half used as 50c on cover 400.00
b. Quarter used as 25c on cover 300.00
c. Without ovpt. 140.00
57 " 100c brown, *brown* 350.00 150.00
a. Printed on both sides 525.00 525.00

Four kinds of perforation are found in the 1868 issue: serrate, square, pin and regular.

Thick Figures of Value with Period

6.CENT. 12.CENT
25.CENT. 50.CENT.
100.CENT

Overprinted with District Name, Number and Abbreviated Date.

Imperf.

58 A6 6c *buff* 6.50 4.00
a. Pelure paper 7.00 4.25
59 " 12c *green* 1.75 1.25
a. Very thick paper 3.75
b. Pelure paper 5.50 3.25
c. 12c *buff* (error) 250.00 250.00
61 " 25c blue, *pink* 3.50 1.00
a. No period after "25" 40.00
b. Pelure paper 11.50 2.75
c. Very thick paper 10.00 2.75

62 A6 50c *yellow* 60.00 12.00
a. No period after "50" 62.50 12.50
b. 50c blue, *light pink* (error) 1900.00 1250.00
c. Half used as 25c on cover 275.00
d. Very thick paper
64 " 100c *brown* 45.00 30.00
a. No period after "100" 47.50 32.50
b. Very thick paper

Perf.

65 A6 6c *buff* 10.00 7.00
a. Very thick paper 11.00 8.00
66 " 12c *green* 1.75 1.75
a. Very thick paper 10.00 2.75
b. 12c *buff* (error) 300.00 300.00
68 " 25c blue, *pink* 8.00 80
a. No period after "25" 40.00
b. Pelure paper 22.50 3.00
c. Thick paper 5.00
69 " 50c *yellow* 55.00 9.00
a. No period after "50" 57.50 9.50
b. 50c blue, *light pink* (error) 1650.00 1200.00
c. Half used as 25c on cover 275.00
70 " 100c *brown* 42.50 25.00
a. No period after "100" 45.00 27.50
b. Very thick paper

Stamps of 1868
Handstamped

Overprinted with District Name, Number and Abbreviated Date. Thick Figures with Period.

1872 ***Imperf.***

71 A6 6c *buff* 100.00 100.00
72 " 12c *green* 20.00 20.00
73 " 25c blue, *pink* 10.00 8.00
74 " 50c *yellow* 300.00 125.00
a. No period after "50" 325.00 135.00
75 " 100c *brown* 600.00 350.00
a. No period after "100" 625.00 375.00

Perf.

76 A6 6c *buff* 110.00 120.00
77 " 12c *green* 30.00 30.00
78 " 25c blue, *pink* 8.00 12.00
a. Pelure paper 20.00 15.00
79 " 50c *yellow* 300.00 125.00
a. No period after "50" 325.00 135.00
80 " 100c *brown* 600.00 350.00
a. No period after "100" 625.00 375.00

The stamps of the 1872 issue are found perforated with square holes, pin-perf. 13, 14 or 15, and with serrate perforation.

The 1868, 12c buff, 50c and 100c (both colors) have been reprinted. The reprints are apparently from new plates. The impressions are clear and sharp and there are more lines in the shading of the face than on the original stamps. The reprints exist with both thin and thick numerals of value, imperforate and perforated and with the "Anotado" overprint.

Hidalgo
A8

Wmk. 150

Moiré on White Back. Overprinted with District Name, Number and Abbreviated Date.

Wmkd. PAPEL SELLADO in Sheet. (150)

White Wove Paper.

1872 **Lithographed** ***Imperf.***

81 A8 6c green 47.50 30.00
82 " 12c blue 27.50 18.00
a. Laid paper
83 " 25c red 60.00 14.00
a. Laid paper
84 " 50c yellow 325.00 140.00
a. 50c blue (error) 750.00
b. Laid paper
c. As "a," without ovpt. 50.00
86 " 100c gray lilac 210.00 110.00

Wmkd. "LA + F"

81a A8 6c green 135.00 75.00
82b " 12c blue 100.00 35.00
83b " 25c red 115.00 27.50
84d " 50c yellow 750.00 550.00
86a " 100c gray lilac 550.00 375.00

1872 ***Pin-perf.*** **Wmk. 150**

87 A8 6c green 150.00 130.00
88 " 12c blue 32.50 27.50
89 " 25c red 80.00 15.00
b. Laid paper
90 " 50c yellow 325.00 150.00
a. 50c blue (error) 400.00 500.00
b. Same as "a" without overprint 50.00
92 " 100c gray lilac 175.00 125.00

Wmkd. "LA+F"

87a A8 6c green 250.00 200.00
88a " 12c blue 75.00 75.00
89a " 25c red 160.00 45.00
90c " 50c yellow 650.00 500.00
92a " 100c gray lilac 500.00 350.00

The watermark "LA+F" stands for La Croix Frères, the paper manufacturers, and is in double-lined block capitals 13mm. high. A single stamp will show only part of this watermark.

1872 ***Imperf.*** **Unwmkd.**

93 A8 6c green 7.00 7.00
a. Without moiré on back 27.50 40.00
b. Vertically laid paper 1000.00
c. Bottom label retouched 55.00 50.00
d. Very thick paper 20.00
94 " 12c blue 1.25 1.00
a. Without moiré on back 11.00 22.50
b. Vertically laid paper 225.00 140.00
c. Thin gray blue paper of 1867 (Wmk. 151)
95 " 25c red 3.75 90
a. Without moiré on back 11.00 22.50
b. Vertically laid paper 325.00 125.00
c. Thin gray blue paper of 1867 (Wmk. 151)
96 " 50c yellow 70.00 17.50
a. 50c orange 70.00 17.50
b. Without moiré on back 16.00 42.50
c. Vertically laid paper 1100.00
d. 50c blue (error) 450.00
e. Same as "d" without overprint 30.00
f. Same as "e" without moiré on back 50.00
g. Half used as 25c on cover 325.00

98 A8 100c gray lilac 50.00 25.00
a. 100c lilac 55.00 25.00
b. Without moiré on back 30.00 75.00
c. Vertically laid paper 500.00
d. Quarter used as 25c on cover 350.00
e. Half used as 50c on cover 400.00

The reprints of these stamps are 24½ mm. high instead of 24mm. The moire pattern on the back is printed in gray blue instead of bright blue and is blurred and indistinct. Some authorities claim these are not reprints but counterfeits.

Pin-perf. and Serrate Perf.

99 A8 6c green 30.00 20.00
100 " 12c blue 1.75 1.40
a. Vertically laid paper 175.00
b. Imperf. vertically 50.00 50.00
c. Vert. pair, imperf. between
101 " 25c red 2.10 80
a. Vertically laid paper 275.00
b. Imperf. vertically 50.00 50.00
102 " 50c yellow 70.00 25.00
a. 50c orange 70.00 25.00
b. 50c blue (error) 200.00
c. Same as "b" without overprint 15.00
104 " 100c lilac 65.00 35.00
a. 100c gray lilac 55.00 35.00

Hidalgo
A9 A10

A11 A12

A13

A14

Engraved.

Overprinted with District Name and Number and Date; also with Number and Date only.

Thick Wove Paper, Some Showing Vertical Ribbing

1874-80 ***Perf. 12.*** **Unwmkd.**

105 A9 4c orange ('80) 9.00 8.00
a. Vertical pair, imperf. between 35.00
b. Without overprint 5.50 5.00
106 A10 5c brown 2.00 1.75
a. Horizontally laid paper 32.50 22.50
b. Imperf., pair 35.00
c. Horizontal pair, imperf. between 25.00
d. Vertical pair, imperf. between 60.00 60.00
e. Without overprint 20.00 17.50
f. Wmkd. "LA+F" 100.00 100.00

107 A11 10c black 1.25 1.10
- *a.* Horizontally laid paper 1.50 1.50
- *b.* Horizontal pair, imperf. between 30.00 30.00
- *c.* Without overprint 15.00 15.00
- *d.* Half used as 5c on cover 100.00
- *e.* Imperf., pair 17.50
- *f.* Wmkd. "LA+F" 37.50 27.50

108 " 10c orange ('78) 1.25 1.10
- *a.* 10c yel. bister 4.00 2.75
- *b.* Imperf., pair 45.00 45.00
- *c.* Without overprint 30.00 30.00
- *d.* Half used as 5c on cover 75.00

109 A12 25c blue 50 40
- *a.* Close horizontally laid paper 3.00 2.00
- *b.* Wide horizontally laid paper 1.45 1.45
- *c.* Imperf., pair 25.00 17.50
- *d.* Without ovpt. 17.50 12.00
- *e.* Horiz. pair, imperf. between 30.00 30.00
- *f.* As "b," imperf. vert., pair 25.00
- *g.* Wmkd. "LA+F" 17.50 15.00

110 A13 50c green 8.00 7.00
- *a.* Without overprint 30.00 30.00
- *b.* Half used as 25c on cover 100.00

111 A14 100c carmine 11.00 9.00
- *a.* Imperf., pair 100.00
- *b.* Without overprint 30.00 30.00
- *c.* Half used as 50c on cover 150.00

Nos. 105-111 (7) 33.00 28.35

The "LA+F" watermark of La Croix Freres is described in note following No. 92a.

Wmkd. PAPEL SELLADO in Sheet. (150)

1875-77

112 A10 5c brown 15.00 15.00
113 A11 10c black 16.50 16.50
114 A12 25c blue 13.00 11.00
115 A13 50c green 100.00 100.00
116 A14 100c carmine 70.00 70.00

Thin Wove Paper

1881 **Unwmkd.**

117 A9 4c orange 25.00 17.00
- *a.* Without overprint 7.00 7.00

118 A10 5c brown 3.50 2.75
- *a.* Without overprint 30
- *b.* Imperf. horiz., pr. 60.00 60.00

119 A11 10c orange 2.25 1.40
- *a.* Imperf.
- *b.* Imperf. horiz., pair 25.00 25.00
- *c.* Without overprint 40
- *d.* Vertical pair, imperf. between 25.00 25.00

120 A12 25c blue 1.25 90
- *a.* Imperf.
- *b.* Without overprint 30
- *c.* Double impression 10.00

121 A13 50c green 19.00 14.00
- *a.* Without overprint 2.00

122 A14 100c carmine 25.00 18.00
- *a.* Without overprint 3.00

Nos. 117-122 (6) 76.00 54.05

The stamps of 1874-81 are found with number and date wide apart, close together or omitted, and in various colors.

Benito Juárez
A15

Overprinted with District Name and Number and Date; also with Number and Date only. Thick Wove Paper, Some Showing Vertical Ribbing

1879 ***Perf. 12***

123 A15 1c brown 2.25 2.00
- *a.* Without overprint 37.50

124 " 2c dark violet 2.15 1.80
- *a.* Without overprint 30.00
- *b.* Printed on both sides

125 " 5c orange 1.50 1.00
- *a.* Without overprint 27.50

126 " 10c blue 2.00 1.70
- *a.* Without overprint 27.50
- *b.* 10c ultra. 70.00 70.00

127 " 25c rose 6.75 6.25
- *a.* Without overprint 1.50

128 " 50c green 9.00 7.00
- *a.* Without overprint 1.00
- *b.* Printed on both sides 135.00

129 " 85c violet 13.00 11.00
- *a.* Without overprint 2.00

130 " 100c black 15.00 12.00
- *a.* Without overprint 2.25

Nos. 123-130 (8) 51.65 42.75

1882 **Thin Wove Paper.**

131 A15 1c brown 13.00 9.00
- *a.* Without overprint 65.00

132 " 2c dark violet 11.50 9.00
- *a.* 2c slate 16.00 11.00
- *b.* Without overprint 35.00

133 " 5c orange 3.25 1.75
- *a.* Without overprint 75

134 " 10c blue 3.25 1.85
- *a.* Without overprint 75

135 " 10c brown 4.00
- *a.* Imperf., pair 2.00

136 " 12c brown 3.00 2.50
- *a.* Without overprint 1.50

137 " 18c org. brown 3.50 3.00
- *a.* Horizontal pair, imperf. between 35.00 35.00
- *b.* Without overprint 1.00 2.00

138 " 24c violet 3.25 3.00
- *a.* Without overprint 1.00

139 " 25c rose 16.00 14.00
- *a.* Without overprint 2.50

140 " 25c orange brown 2.25

141 " 50c green 16.00 14.00
- *a.* Without overprint 4.00 4.00

142 " 50c yellow 37.50 37.50
- *a.* Without overprint 70.00

143 " 85c red violet 17.50

144 " 100c black 18.00 16.00
- *a.* Without overprint 3.00
- *b.* Vertical pair, imperf. between 60.00 60.00

145 " 100c orange 37.50 37.50
- *a.* Without overprint 70.00

Nos. 131-145 (15) 189.50

No. 135, 140 and 143 exist only without overprint. They were never placed in use.

Used prices for 50c, 85c and 100c of type A15 (Juarez) are for privately canceled copies. Postally used examples sell for several times as much.

Numeral of Value
A16

Hidalgo
A17

Overprinted with District Name, Number and Abbreviated Date.

1882-83

146 A16 2c green 3.00 2.25
- *a.* Without overprint 5.00 3.00

147 " 3c carmine lake 2.50 1.75
- *a.* Without overprint 1.25 1.25

148 " 6c blue ('83) 6.00 5.00
- *a.* Without overprint 7.00 6.00

149 A16 6c ultramarine 2.25 1.35
- *a.* Without overprint 75
- *b.* Imperf. (pair) 22.50

Wove or Laid Paper.

1884 ***Perf. 11, 12.***

150 A17 1c green 80 20
- *a.* Imperf. (pair) 10.00
- *b.* 1c blue (error) 225.00 225.00

151 " 2c green 1.75 35
- *a.* Imperf. (pair) 15.00 15.00

152 " 3c green 3.25 50
- *a.* Imperf. (pair) 30.00 30.00
- *b.* Horiz. pair, imperf. vert. 15.00

153 " 4c green 3.50 45
- *a.* Imperf. (pair) 20.00 20.00
- *b.* Diagonal half used as 2c on cover 35.00

154 " 5c green 3.00 40
- *a.* Imperf. (pair) 35.00 35.00

155 " 6c green 5.00 55
- *a.* Imperf. (pair) 25.00 25.00

156 " 10c green 2.75 20
- *a.* Imperf. (pair) 10.00 10.00

157 " 12c green 7.00 1.00
- *a.* Vert. pair, imperf. between 20.00 20.00
- *b.* Half used as 6c on cover 25.00

158 " 20c green 13.00 45
- *a.* Diagonal half used as 10c on cover 20.00
- *b.* Imperf. (pair) 30.00 30.00

159 " 25c green 22.50 90
- *a.* Imperf. (pair) 50.00 50.00

160 " 50c green 75 40
- *a.* Imperf. (pair) 10.00 10.00

161 " 1p blue 75 30
- *a.* Imperf. (pair) 20.00 20.00
- *b.* Vert. pair, imperf. between

162 " 2p blue 75 35
- *a.* Imperf. (pair) 25.00 25.00

163 " 5p blue 150.00 75.00
164 " 10p blue 190.00 100.00

Nos. 150-162 (13) 64.80 6.05

Imperforate varieties should be purchased in pairs or larger. Single imperforates are usually trimmed perforated stamps.

1885

165 A17 1c pale green 6.50 1.25

166 " 2c carmine 4.50 1.15
- *a.* Diagonal half used as 1c on cover 30.00

167 " 3c orange brown 6.50 1.10
- *a.* Imperf. (pair) 35.00 35.00

168 " 4c red orange 9.00 5.00
169 " 5c ultramarine 5.50 1.00

170 " 6c dark brown 8.00 1.25
- *a.* Half used as 3c on cover 30.00

171 " 10c orange 5.50 55
- *a.* 10c yellow 5.00 55
- *b.* Horizontal pair, imperf. between 30.00 30.00

172 " 12c olive brown 11.00 2.75
173 " 25c greenish blue 45.00 8.00

Nos. 165-173 (9) 101.50 22.05

Numeral of Value
A18

1886 ***Perf. 11, 12.***

174 A18 1c blue green 50 15
- *a.* 1c yellow green 50 15
- *b.* Horizontal pair, imperf. between 15.00 7.50
- *c.* Perf. 11 5.00 5.00

175 " 2c carmine 65 25
- *a.* Horizontal pair, imperf. between 10.00
- *b.* Vert. pair, imperf. between 10.00 10.00
- *c.* Perf. 11 5.00 5.00

176 " 3c lilac 2.10 80
177 " 4c " 3.50 50

178 " 5c ultramarine 30 12
- *a.* 5c blue 30 12

179 " 6c lilac 3.25 55

180 " 10c " 2.50 20
- *a.* Perf. 11 5.50 5.00

181 " 12c lilac 4.00 1.00
182 " 20c " 50.00 22.50
183 A18 25c lilac 12.00 2.25

Nos. 174-183 (10) 78.80 28.32

The 2c is known with blue surcharge "Vale 1 Cvo.", but was not regularly issued.

The 20c has been reprinted in a darker shade and on watermarked paper.

1887

184 A18 3c scarlet 50 15
- *a.* Imperf., pair

185 A18 4c scarlet 1.25 30

186 " 6c " 1.50 35
- *a.* Horiz. pair, imperf. between 15.00

187 A18 10c scarlet 85 10
- *a.* Imperf., pair
- *b.* Horiz. pair, imperf. between 10.00

188 A18 20c scarlet 3.00 40
- *a.* Horiz. pair, imperf. between 20.00

189 A18 25c scarlet 3.00 60

Nos. 184-189 (6) 10.10 1.90

Perf. 6.

190 A18 1c blue green 1.75 1.00
191 " 2c brown carmine 2.50 85
191A " 3c scarlet *50.00* 15.00

192 " 5c ultramarine 1.50 50
- *a.* 5c blue 1.50 50

193 " 10c lilac 1.25 40
193A " 10c brown lilac 1.25 25
194 " 10c scarlet 2.25 1.50

Perf. 6x12.

194A A18 1c blue green 6.00 5.00
194B " 2c brown carmine 7.00 5.00
194C " 3c scarlet 20.00
194D " 5c ultramarine 6.00 4.00
194E " 10c lilac 6.00 6.00
194F " 10c scarlet 6.00 4.50
194G " 10c brown lilac 6.00 4.00

Paper ruled with blue lines on face or reverse of stamp.

1887 ***Perf. 12.***

195 A18 1c green 3.00 1.50
196 " 2c brown carmine 3.00 1.50
196A " 3c scarlet
198 " 5c ultramarine 3.00 1.25
199 " 10c scarlet 2.00 1.00

Perf. 6.

201 A18 1c green 2.50 1.00
202 " 2c brown carmine 2.50 1.10
204 " 5c ultramarine 1.50 60
205 " 10c brown lilac 1.50 50
206 " 10c scarlet 6.00 2.50

Perf. 6x12.

207 A18 1c green 7.00 5.00
208 " 2c brown carmine 6.00 5.00
209 " 5c ultramarine 4.00 3.00
210 " 10c brown lilac 6.00 4.00
211 " 10c scarlet 14.00 11.00

Wmk. 152

Wmkd. "CORREOS E. U. M." on Every Horizontal Line of Ten Stamps. (152)

1890-95 ***Perf. 11 and 12.***

Wove or Laid Paper.

212 A18 1c yellow green 12 6
- *a.* 1c blue green 12 6
- *b.* Horizontal pair, imperf. between 5.00
- *c.* Laid paper

213 " 2c brown carmine 25 15
- *a.* 2c carmine 25 15
- *b.* Laid paper

214 " 3c vermilion 20 12
- *a.* Laid paper 50
- *b.* Horiz. pair, imperf. between 5.00

215 " 4c vermilion 60 20
- *a.* Horiz. pair, imperf. between

216 " 5c ultramarine 12 8
- *a.* 5c dull blue 20 12
- *b.* Laid paper

217 A18 6c vermilion 60 30
a. Horizontal pair, imperf. between 6.00
218 " 10c vermilion 10 8
a. Laid paper
b. Horizontal pair, imperf. between 6.00
219 " 12c vermilion ('95) 3.50 3.50
220 " 20c " 75 30
221 " 25c " 85 35
Nos. 212-221 (10) 7.09 5.14

No. 219 has been reprinted in slightly darker shade than the original.

1892 Change of Colors.

222 A18 3c orange 1.00 45
223 " 4c " 1.10 65
224 " 6c " 1.75 45
225 " 10c " 7.00 40
226 " 20c " 10.00 1.25
227 " 25c " 5.00 1.00
Nos. 222-227 (6) 25.85 4.20

1892

228 A18 5p carmine 375.00 325.00
229 " 10p " 800.00 425.00
230 A17 5p blue green 900.00 650.00
231 " 10p " 2750.00 1500.00

1894 *Perf. 5½, 6.*

232 A18 1c yellow green 60 60
232A " 2c brown carmine
233 " 3c vermilion 2.00 2.00
234 " 4c " 7.00 6.00
235 " 5c ultramarine 1.50 75
236 " 10c vermilion 1.25 60
236A " 20c " 20.00 20.00
237 " 25c " 10.00 10.00

Perf. 5½x11, 11x5½ and Compound.

238 A18 1c yellow green 1.35 1.35
238A " 2c brown carmine 2.75 2.75
238B " 3c vermilion 5.50 4.50
238C " 4c " 7.50 7.50
239 " 5c ultramarine 1.50 1.25
a. 5c blue 1.50 1.25
239C " 6c vermilion 9.00 9.00
240 " 10c " 2.75 1.50
240A " 20c " 45.00 22.50
241 " 25c " 7.00 4.00

The stamps of the 1890 to 1895 issues are also to be found unwatermarked, as part of the sheet frequently escaped the watermark.

Letter Carrier A20

Mounted Courier with Pack Mule A21

Statue of Cuauhtémoc A22

Mail Coach A23

Mail Train A24

Wove or Laid Paper.

Wmkd. "CORREOS E. U. M."(152)

1895 *Regular or Pin Perf. 12*

242 A20 1c green 35 15
a. Vert. pair, imperf. horiz. 30.00
243 " 2c carmine 50 20
a. Half used as 1c on cover 10.00
244 " 3c orange brown 50 15
a. Vert. pair, imperf. horiz. 35.00
246 A21 4c orange 1.75 45
a. 4c orange red 1.75 45
247 A22 5c ultramarine 85 10
a. Imperf. (pair) 15.00 15.00
b. Horiz. or vert. pair, imperf. between 15.00 15.00
248 A23 10c lilac rose 75 18
a. Horiz. or vert. pair, imperf. between
b. Half used as 5c on cover 25.00
249 A21 12c olive brown 10.00 4.00
251 A23 15c bright blue 5.00 60
252 " 20c brown rose 5.00 60
253 " 50c purple 15.00 3.50
a. Half used as 25c on cover 50.00
254 A24 1p brown 30.00 11.00
255 " 5p scarlet 100.00 55.00
256 " 10p deep blue 170.00 110.00
Nos. 242-256 (13) 339.70 185.93

Perf. 6.

242b A20 1c green 22.50 11.00
243b " 2c carmine 40.00 20.00
244b " 3c orange brown 27.50 13.50
247c A22 5c ultramarine 27.50 13.50
248c A23 10c lilac rose 40.00 20.00
249a A21 12c olive brown 22.50

Perf. 6x12, 12x6 & Compound

242c A20 1c green 11.00 9.00
244c " 3c orange brown 11.00 9.00
246b A21 4c orange 27.50 16.50
247d A22 5c ultramarine 22.50 16.50
248d A23 10c lilac rose 12.00 9.00
249b A21 12c olive brown 22.50 13.50
251a A23 15c bright blue 22.50 16.50
252a " 20c brown rose 30.00 16.50
253b " 50c purple 60.00 32.50

Wmk. 153

Wmkd. "R M" Interlaced. (153)

1896-97 *Perf. 12*

257 A20 1c green 1.25 25
258 " 2c carmine 1.50 30
a. Horizontal pair, imperf. vertically
259 " 3c orange brown 1.60 35
260 A21 4c orange 2.75 40
261 A22 5c ultramarine 1.50 15
a. Imperf., pair 15.00
b. Vert. pair, imperf. between 25.00
262 A21 12c olive brown 25.00 15.00
263 A23 15c bright blue 22.50 2.50
264 " 20c brown rose 160.00 75.00
265 " 50c purple 30.00 25.00
266 A24 1p brown 75.00 35.00
267 " 5p scarlet 225.00 140.00
268 " 10p deep blue 350.00 175.00
Nos. 257-268 (12) 896.10 468.95

Perf. 6.

257a A20 1c green 6.50 6.50
259a " 3c orange brown 7.50 5.50
260a A21 4c orange
261c A22 5c ultramarine 40.00 25.00
263a A23 15c bright blue 30.00 10.00

Perf. 6x12, 12x6 and Compound.

257b A20 1c green 5.50 4.50
258b " 2c carmine 9.00 6.50
259b A20 3c orange brown 9.00 5.50
260b A21 4c orange 14.00 5.50
261d A22 5c ultramarine 7.75 4.50
262a A21 12c olive brown 52.50 32.50
263b A23 15c bright blue 60.00 32.50
264a " 20c brown rose
265a " 50c purple

Wmk. 154

Wmkd. Eagle and R. M. (154)

1897-98 *Perf. 12*

269 A20 1c green 2.00 40
270 " 2c scarlet 3.75 70
271 A21 4c orange 7.00 65
a. Horiz. pair, imperf. vert.
272 A22 5c ultramarine 4.00 35
a. Imperf., pair 25.00
273 A21 12c olive brown 20.00 6.50
275 A23 15c bright blue 35.00 20.00
276 " 20c brown rose 25.00 2.50
277 " 50c purple 40.00 15.00
278 A24 1p brown 70.00 30.00
278A " 5p scarlet 5000.00 3500.00
Nos. 269-278 (9) 206.75 76.10

Perf. 6.

269a A20 1c green 6.50 4.50
270a " 2c scarlet 6.50 3.25
272b A22 5c ultramarine 30.00 12.00
273a A21 12c olive brown 55.00 40.00
276a A23 20c brown rose 50.00

Perf. 6x12, 12x6 and Compound.

269b A20 1c green 9.00 3.00
270b " 2c scarlet 12.00 3.75
271b A21 4c orange 20.00 6.50
272c A22 5c ultramarine 13.00 5.50
273b A21 12c olive brown 60.00 22.50
275a A23 15c bright blue 70.00 20.00
276b " 20c brown rose 50.00 10.00
277a " 50c purple 75.00 30.00

1898 *Perf. 12.* **Unwmkd.**

279 A20 1c green 25 10
a. Horiz. pair, imperf. vert.
b. Imperf., pair 35.00
280 " 2c scarlet 75 25
a. 2c green (error) 175.00
281 " 3c orange brown 60 15
a. Imperf., pair 50.00
b. Pair, imperf. between 20.00
282 A21 4c orange 3.00 1.00
283 A22 5c ultramarine 40 6
a. Imperf. (pair) 15.00 15.00
b. Pair, imperf. between 25.00
284 A23 10c lilac rose 85.00 50.00
285 A21 12c olive brown 11.00 5.00
a. Imperf., pair 75.00
286 A23 15c bright blue 30.00 1.60
287 " 20c brown rose 9.00 1.10
a. Imperf. (pair) 75.00
288 " 50c purple 25.00 10.00
289 A24 1p brown 35.00 16.00
290 " 5p carmine rose 200.00 120.00
291 " 10p deep blue 325.00 160.00
Nos. 279-291 (13) 725.00 365.26

Perf. 6.

279c A20 1c green 25.00 6.50
280b " 2c scarlet 22.50 4.50
281c " 3c orange brown 22.50 5.50
283c A22 5c ultramarine 22.50 5.50
287b A23 20c brown rose 55.00 25.00

Perf. 6x12, 12x6 and Compound.

279d A20 1c green 11.00 3.25
280c " 2c scarlet 12.00 4.50
281d " 3c orange brown 5.50 3.25
282a A21 4c orange 20.00 5.50
283d A22 5c ultramarine 5.50 2.75
284a A23 10c lilac rose 100.00 75.00
286a " 15c bright blue 50.00 11.00
287c " 20c brown rose 30.00 15.00

Forgeries of the 6 and 6x12 perforations of 1895-98 are plentiful. Some experts doubt that genuine examples exist.

Coat of Arms

A25 A26

A27 A28

A29 A30

Juanacatlán Falls

A31 A32

View of Mt. Popocatépetl

A33

Cathedral, Mexico, D. F.—A34

Wmk. 155

Wmkd.

SERVICIO POSTAL DE LOS ESTADOS UNIDOS MEXICANOS. (155)

1899 *Perf. 14, 15.*

294 A25 1c green 1.10 12
295 A26 2c vermilion 2.50 20
296 A27 3c orange brown 1.50 10
297 A28 5c dark blue 2.85 8
298 A29 10c violet & orange 3.50 30
299 A30 15c lavender & claret 4.00 25
300 A31 20c rose & dark blue 4.50 35

301 A32 50c red lilac & black 20.00 1.50
 a. 50c lilac & black 25.00 1.50
302 A33 1p blue & black 40.00 2.25
303 A34 5p car. & black 150.00 8.00
 Nos. 294–303 (10) 229.95 13.15

A35

1903

304 A25 1c violet 75 10
 a. Booklet pane of 6 12.00
305 A26 2c green 1.10 10
 a. Booklet pane of 6 12.00
306 A35 4c carmine 2.50 30
307 A28 5c orange 65 6
 a. Booklet pane of 6 12.00
308 A29 10c blue & orange 2.00 25
309 A32 50c carmine & blk. 30.00 3.00
 Nos. 304–309 (6) 37.00 3.81

Independence Issue.

Josefa Ortiz
A36

Leona Vicario
A37

López Rayón
A38

Juan Aldama
A39

Miguel Hidalgo
A40

Ignacio Allende
A41

Epigmenio González
A42

Mariano Abasolo
A43

Declaration of Independence
A44

Mass on the Mount of Crosses
A45

Capture of Granaditas
A46

1910 ***Perf. 14***

310 A36 1c dull violet 10 8
 a. Booklet pane of 4 5.00
311 A37 2c green 12 10
 a. Booklet pane of 8 5.00
312 A38 3c orange brown 45 12
313 A39 4c carmine 80 18
314 A40 5c orange 10 5
 a. Booklet pane of 8 8.00
315 A41 10c blue & orange 75 12
316 A42 15c gray blue & claret 5.50 40
317 A43 20c red & blue 3.25 25
318 A44 50c red brown & black 8.00 1.25
319 A45 1p blue & black 11.00 1.75
320 A46 5p carmine & blk. 35.00 5.00
 Nos. 310–320 (11) 65.07 9.30

Commemorative of the centenary of the independence of Mexico from Spain.

CIVIL WAR ISSUES.

During the 1913–16 Civil War, provisional issues with various handstamped overprints were circulated in limited areas.

Sonora.

A47

A48

Typeset in a row of five varieties. Two impressions placed tête bêche (foot to foot) constitute a sheet. The settings show various wrong font and defective letters, "!" for "1" in "1913," etc. The paper occasionally has a manufacturer's watermark.

a *b* *c* *d*

Four Types of the Numerals.

a. Wide, heavy-faced numerals.
b. Narrow Roman numerals.
c. Wide Roman numerals.
d. Gothic or sans-serif numerals.

Embossed "CONSTITUCIONAL"

1913 ***Perf. 12.*** **Unwmkd.**

321 A47 (*a*) 5c black & red 600.00 275.00
 a. "CENTAVOB" *750.00* *325.00*

Colorless Roulette.

322 A47 (*b*) 1c black & red 6.00 7.00
 a. With green seal *250.00* *200.00*
323 " (*a*) 2c black & red 5.00 5.00
 a. With green seal *300.00* *300.00*
324 " (*c*) 2c black & red 27.50 27.50
 a. With green seal *750.00* *750.00*
325 " (*a*) 3c black & red 37.50 15.00
 a. With green seal *200.00* *200.00*
326 " (") 5c black & red 110.00 25.00
 a. "CENTAVOB" 135.00 37.50
327 " (*d*) 5c black & red 150.00 125.00
 a. With green seal 250.00
328 " (*b*) 10c black & red 11.00 13.00

Black Roulette.

329 A47 (*d*) 5c black & red 40.00 22.50
 a. "MARO" 50.00 27.50

Stamps are known with the embossing double or omitted.

The varieties with green seal are from a few sheets embossed "Constitucional" which were in stock at the time the green seal control was adopted.

With Green Seal.

Colorless Roulette.

336 A48(*b*) 1c black, red & green 3.50 3.50
337 " (*a*) 3c black, red & green 3.00 3.00
 a. Imperf. 50.00
338 " (") 5c black, red & green 300.00 115.00
 a. "CENTAVOB" *350.00* *135.00*
339 " (*b*) 10c black, red & green 2.50 2.50

Colored Roulette.

340 A48(*d*) 5c brownish black, red & green 1.75 1.50
 a. 5c lilac brown, red & green 15.00 3.50
 b. Double seal 250.00 150.00
 c. Red printing omitted 175.00

1913–14 ***Black Roulette***

With Green Seal

341 A48(*a*) 1c black, red & grn. 1.00 75
 a. Without seal 15.00 15.00
 b. "erano" ('14) 15.00 15.00
342 " (*d*) 2c black, red & grn. 1.00 70
 a. "erano" ('14) 10.00 10.00
 b. Without seal ('14) 10.00
343 " (*a*) 3c black, red & grn. 1.50 1.25
 a. "CENTAVO" 5.00 5.00
 b. "erano" ('14) 10.00 10.00
 c. "TRSS" ('14) 30.00
 d. Without seal 50.00
344 " (*d*) 5c black, red & grn. 1.50 90
 a. Without seal 50.00
 b. Heavy black penetrating roulette 2.00 1.50
 c. As "b," "MARO" 4.00 3.00

On Nos. 341–344 the rouletting cuts the paper slightly or not at all. On Nos. 344b–344c the rouletting is heavy, cutting deeply into the paper.

1914

345 A48 (*a*) 5c black, red & green 1.75 1.50
346 " (*b*) 10c black, red & green 1.00 1.00

Coat of Arms
A49

Revenue Stamps Used for Postage

1913 **Litho.** ***Rouletted 14, 14x7***

347 A49 1c yellow green 1.25 1.25
 a. With coupon 2.50 2.50
348 " 2c violet 2.50 2.50
 a. With coupon 5.00 5.00
349 " 5c brown 35 35
 a. With coupon 50 45
350 " 10c claret 1.75 1.75
 a. With coupon 2.75 2.75
351 A49 20c gray green 2.00 2.50
 a. With coupon 7.00 7.00
352 " 50c ultramarine 5.00 7.50
 a. With coupon 12.50 12.50
353 " 1p orange 35.00 35.00
 a. With coupon 80.00 60.00
 Nos. 347–353 (7) 47.85 50.85

For a short time these stamps (called "Ejercitos") were used for postage with coupon attached. Later this was required to be removed unless they were to be used for revenue purposes.

Denominations higher than 1p were used for revenue. Several denominations exist imperf.

Use of typeset Sonora revenue stamps for postage was not authorized or allowed.

Coat of Arms
A50 A51

5c (A50): "CINCO CENTAVOS" 14x2mm.

1914 ***Rouletted 9½x14***

354 A50 1c deep blue 30 25
355 " 2c yellow green 40 25
 a. 2c green 1.00 1.00
356 " 4c blue violet 4.50 1.75
 a. Horizontal pair, imperf. between 25.00
357 " 5c gray green 5.50 1.00
 a. Horizontal pair imperf. between 15.00
358 " 10c red 25 25
359 " 20c yellow brown 35 50
 a. 20c deep brown 1.50 1.50
 b. Horizontal pair, imperf. between 30.00
360 " 50c claret 1.25 1.50
 a. Horizontal pair, imperf. between 30.00
361 " 1p bright violet 9.00 9.00
 a. Horizontal pair, imperf. between 30.00
 Nos. 354–361 (8) 21.55 14.50

Nos. 354–361 (called "Transitorios") exist imperf. and imperf. horizontally, but were not regularly issued in that condition. See also No. 369.

Overprinted in Black

Victoria de
TORREON
ABRIL 2-1914

1914

362 A50 1c deep blue 75.00 60.00
363 " 2c yellow green 90.00 60.00
364 " 4c blue violet 100.00 100.00
365 " 5c gray green 15.00 18.00
 a. Horizontal pair, imperf. between 175.00
366 " 10c red 50.00 60.00
367 " 20c yellow brown *650.00* *650.00*
368 " 50c claret *750.00* *750.00*

Excellent counterfeits of this overprint exist.

1914 **Redrawn** ***Perf. 12***

369 A51 5c gray green 12 12
 a. Imperf., pair 50

In type A51, "CINCO CENTAVOS" measures 16x2½mm.

Regular Issue of 1910 Overprinted in Violet, Magenta, Black or Green

1914 ***Perf. 14.*** **Wmk. 155**

370 A36 1c dull violet 40 40
 a. Booklet pane of 4 10.00
371 A37 2c green 60 60
 a. Booklet pane of 8 10.00
372 A38 3c orange brown 40 35
373 A39 4c carmine 75 50
374 A40 5c orange 25 15
 a. Booklet pane of 8 10.00
375 A41 10c blue & orange 1.00 75
376 A42 15c gray bl. & claret 1.50 1.25
377 A43 20c red & blue 2.40 2.00
378 A44 50c red brn. & blk. 3.50 3.00
379 A45 1p blue & black 6.50 4.00

380 A46 5p car. & black 40.00 30.00
Nos. 370–380 (11) 57.30 43.00

Overprinted
On Postage Due Stamps of 1908.

381 D1 1c blue 5.50 6.50
382 " 2c " 5.50 6.50
383 " 4c " 5.50 6.50
384 " 5c " 5.50 6.50
385 " 10c " 5.50 6.50
Nos. 381–385 (5) 27.50 32.50

This overprint is found double, inverted, sideways and in pairs with and without the overprint.
There are two or more types of this overprint.
The Postage Due Stamps and similar groups of them which follow were issued and used as regular postage stamps.
Counterfeits abound.

A52

A53

Lithographed.

1914 *Perf. 12* Unwmkd.

386 A52 1c pale blue 35 35
387 " 2c light green 30 30
388 " 3c orange 50 30
389 " 5c deep rose 50 25
390 " 10c rose 60 60
391 " 15c rose lilac 1.00 1.00
392 " 50c yellow 1.50 1.25
a. 50c ochre 1.50
393 " 1p violet 4.00 3.00
Nos. 386–393 (8) 8.75 7.05

Nos. 386–393, except 392, are known imperforate.
This set is usually called the Denver Issue because it was printed there.

Revenue Stamps Used for Postage

1914, July *Perf. 12*

393A A53 1c rose 4.00
393B " 2c light green 3.00
393C " 3c light orange 5.00
393D " 5c red 2.00
393E " 10c gray green 6.00
393F " 25c light green 10.00

Nos. 393A–393F were used in the northeast. Prices are for examples with postal cancellations.

Background as A55.
A54

A55

1914 *Imperf.*

Values and Inscriptions in Black.

Inscribed "SONORA".

394 A54 1c blue & red 20 20
a. Double seal
b. Without seal 10.00
395 " 2c green & orange 25 25
a. Without seal 15.00
396 " 5c yellow & green 25 25
a. 5c orange & green 1.25 1.00
b. Without seal 25.00
397 " 10c light blue & red 3.00 1.50
a. Blue & red 10.00 4.00
398 " 20c yellow & green 1.00 1.00
399 " 20c orange & blue 12.00 12.00
a. Network on back
400 " 50c green & orange 75 60
Nos. 394–400 (7) 17.45 15.80

Stamps of type A54 are usually termed the "Coach Seal Issue".

Inscribed
"DISTRITO SUR DE LA BAJA CAL."

401 A54 1c yellow & blue 50 10.00
a. Without seal 15.00
402 " 2c gray & olive green 70 10.00
403 " 5c olive & rose 50 10.00
a. Without seal 15.00
404 " 10c pale red & dull violet 50 10.00
a. Without seal 15.00

Counterfeit cancellations exist.

Inscribed "SONORA".

405 A55 1c blue & red 3.50
a. Without seal 20.00
406 " 2c green & orange 50
407 " 5c yellow & green 50 2.50
a. Without seal 12.00
408 " 10c blue & red 50 2.50
409 " 20c yellow & green 15.00
a. Without seal 25.00
b. Double seal 30.00
Nos. 405–409 (5) 19.50

With "PLATA" added to the inscription.

410 A55 1c blue & red 1.00
a. "PLATA" invtd. 20.00
b. Pair, one without "PLATA" 6.00
411 " 10c blue & red 50
412 " 20c yellow & green 2.00
a. "PLATA" double 10.00
413 " 50c gray green & orange 1.75
a. Without seal 75
b. As "a" "P" of "PLATA" missing 20.00

Stamps of type A55 are termed the "Anvil Seal Issue".
Nos. 394–413 were issued without gum.

Oaxaca.

Coat of Arms
A56

Typographed.

5c: Type I. Thick numerals, 2mm. wide.
Type II. Thin numerals, 1½mm. wide.

1915 *Perf. 8½ to 14* Unwmkd.

414 A56 1c dull violet 50 1.00
a. 1c bright violet 50 1.25
b. Imperf., pair 12.00
c. Imperf. vert., pair 8.00
d. Imperf. horiz., pair 8.00
e. Printed on both sides 20.00
415 " 2c emerald 65 1.25
a. Inverted numeral 12.00
b. Imperf., pair 15.00
c. Horizontal pair, imperf. between 15.00
d. Imperf. vert., pair 10.00
416 " 3c red brown 1.15 1.75
a. 3c orange brown 1.25 1.75
b. Inverted numeral 15.00
c. Imperf., pair 12.00
417 " 5c orange (type I) 17.00 15.00
a. Tête bêche pair 40.00
b. Imperf., pair 30.00
c. As "a", imperf. vertically 35.00
418 " 5c orange (type II) 70 1.50
a. Types I and II in pair 40.00
b. Imperf., pair 15.00
c. Imperf. horiz., pair 10.00
d. Imperf. vert., pair 10.00
e. Invtd. numeral 10.00
419 " 10c blue & carmine 1.25 2.00
a. Paper ruled with blue lines 4.00 5.00
b. Numerals inverted
c. Imperf., pair 25.00
d. Numerals omitted 15.00
e. Numerals reversed 12.00
Nos. 414–419 (6) 21.25 22.50

Nos. 414 to 419 were printed on the backs of post-office receipt forms.

Regular ssues of 1899-1910 Overprinted in Black — GOBIERNO $ CONSTITUCIONALISTA

1914 *Perf. 14* Wmk. 155

On Issues of 1899-1903.

420 A28 5c orange 55.00 65.00
421 A30 15c lavender & claret 100.00 60.00
422 A31 20c rose & dk. blue 170.00 125.00

On Issue of 1910.

423 A36 1c dull violet 15 15
424 A37 2c green 20 20
425 A38 3c orange brown 35 35
426 A39 4c carmine 45 50
427 A40 5c orange 10 10
428 A41 10c blue & orange 20 20
429 A42 15c gray blue & claret 60 50
430 A43 20c red & blue 65 60

Overprinted GOBIERNO Y CONSTITUCIONALISTA

431 A44 50c red brown & blk. 1.50 1.25
432 A45 1p blue & black 5.00 3.50
433 A46 5p carmine & blk. 25.00 15.00
Nos. 423–433 (11) 34.20 22.35

In the first setting of the overprint on 1c to 20c, the variety "GONSTITUCIONALISTA" occurs 4 times in each sheet of 100. In the second setting it occurs on the last stamp in each row of 10.
The overprint exists reading downward on Nos. 423–430; inverted on Nos. 431–433; double on Nos. 424–425 and 427; etc.

Postage Due Stamps of 1908 Overprinted — GOBIERNO $ CONSTITUCIONALISTA

434 D1 1c blue 1.50 1.50
435 " 2c " 1.75 1.75
436 " 4c " 10.00 10.00
437 " 5c " 10.00 10.00
438 " 10c " 2.25 2.25
a. Double overprint
Nos. 434–438 (5) 25.50 25.50

Preceding Issues Overprinted

This is usually called the "Villa" monogram. Counterfeits abound.

1915 On Issue of 1899.

439 A25 1c green
440 A26 2c vermilion
441 A27 3c orange brown
442 A28 5c dark blue
443 A29 10c violet & orange
444 A30 15c lavender & claret 15.00
445 A31 20c rose & blue 15.00
446 A32 50c red lilac & black
447 A33 1p blue & black
448 A34 5p car. & black 150.00

On Issue of 1903.

449 A25 1c violet
450 A26 2c green
451 A35 4c carmine
452 A28 5c orange
a. Inv. ovpt.
453 A29 10c blue & orange 50.00
454 A32 50c car. & black 75.00

Manipulation and unauthorized reprinting characterized the overprint on Nos. 439–454. Only 5 denominations were obtainable at the post office (one in a quantity of 4), it is stated. These are believed to have been sold to a favored few. The status of Nos. 439–443, 446–447 and 449–452 is dubious.

On Issue of 1910.

455 A36 1c dull violet 40 35
456 A37 2c green 30 30
457 A38 3c orange brown 30 30
458 A39 4c carmine 1.50 1.50
459 A40 5c orange 12 12
460 A41 10c blue & orange 3.00 3.00
461 A42 15c gray blue & claret 1.25 1.25
462 A43 20c red & blue 1.50 1.50
463 A44 50c red brn. & blk. 3.00 2.50
464 A45 1p blue & black 4.00 4.00
465 A46 5p car. & black 40.00
Nos. 455–464 (10) 15.37 14.82

Nos. 455–465 are known with overprint inverted, double and other variations. Their status is questionable.

Overprinted
On Postage Due Stamps of 1908.

466 D1 1c blue 3.50 3.50
467 " 2c " 3.50 3.50
468 " 4c " 3.50 3.50
469 " 5c " 3.50 3.50
470 " 10c " 3.50 3.50
Nos. 466–470 (5) 17.50 17.50

Nos. 466 to 470 are known with inverted overprint.

Issues of 1899–1910 Overprinted

This is called the "Carranza" or small monogram. Counterfeits abound.

On Issues of 1899-1903.

482 A28 5c orange 10.00 10.00
483 A30 15c lavender & claret 40.00 40.00

On Issue of 1910.

484 A36 1c dull violet 60 60
485 A37 2c green 60 50
486 A38 3c orange brown 70 75
487 A39 4c carmine 1.00 1.10
488 A40 5c orange 25 25
489 A41 10c blue & orange 1.25 1.25
a. Double overprint, one inverted 7.50
490 A42 15c gray blue & claret 1.25 1.25
491 A43 20c red & blue 1.25 1.25
492 A44 50c red brn. & blk. 7.00 5.00
493 A45 1p blue & black 10.00 7.00
494 A46 5p car. & black 40.00 35.00
Nos. 484–494 (11) 63.90 53.95

All values are known with inverted overprint and all except the 5 pesos with double overprint.

Overprinted
On Postage Due Stamps of 1908.

495 D1 1c blue 5.00 4.00
496 " 2c " 5.00 4.00
497 " 4c " 5.00 4.00
498 " 5c " 5.00 4.00
499 " 10c " 5.00 4.00
Nos. 495–499 (5) 25.00 20.00

Nos. 495–499 exist with inverted overprint.
It is stated that, in parts of Mexico occupied by the revolutionary forces, instructions were given to apply a distinguishing overprint to all stamps found in the post offices. This overprint was usually some arrangement or abbreviation of "Gobierno Constitucionalista". Such overprints as were specially authorized or were in general use in large sections of the country are listed. Numerous other handstamped overprints were used in one town or locality. They were essentially military faction control marks necessitated in most instances by the chaotic situation following the split between Villa and Carranza. The fact that some were often struck in a variety of colors and positions suggests the influence of philatelists.

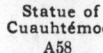

Coat of Arms
A57

Statue of Cuauhtémoc
A58

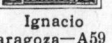

Ignacio Zaragoza—A59

José María Morelos—A60

Francisco Madero A61 — Benito Juárez A62

Lithographed.

1915 *Rouletted 14.* **Unwmkd.**

No.	Type	Description	Unused	Used
500	A57	1c violet	12	12
501	A58	2c green	20	15
502	A59	3c brown	18	18
503	A60	4c carmine	25	20
504	A61	5c orange	25	20
505	A62	10c ultramarine	18	15
		Nos. 500–505 (6)	1.18	1.00

Nos. 500–505 exists imperf.; some exist imperf. vertically or horizontally; some with rouletting and perforation combined. These probably were not regularly issued in these forms.

See also Nos. 506–511.

Map of Mexico A63

Veracruz Lighthouse A64

Post Office, Mexico, D.F. A65

TEN CENTAVOS.

Type I. Size 19½x24mm. Crossed lines on coat.
Type II. Size 19x23½mm. Diagonal lines only on coat.

1915-16 *Perf. 12.*

No.	Type	Description	Unused	Used
506	A57	1c violet	15	15
507	A58	2c green	15	15
508	A59	3c brown	25	15
509	A60	4c carmine	25	20
		a. "CEATRO"	3.50	3.50
510	A61	5c orange	30	15
511	A62	10c ultra., type I	30	20
		a. 10c ultra., II	20	15

Engraved.

No.	Type	Description	Unused	Used
512	A63	40c slate	45	40
513	A64	1p brown & black	60	40
		a. Inverted center	50.00	
514	A65	5p claret & ultra-marine ('16)	6.00	5.00
		a. Inverted center	100.00	
		Nos. 506–514 (9)	8.45	6.80

Nos. 507 to 514, except 509, are known imperforate and Nos. 513 and 514 with inverted center and imperforate. It is doubtful that any of these varieties were regularly issued.

See also Nos. 625–628, 647.

Issues of 1899–1910 Overprinted in Blue, Red or Black

1916 *Perf. 14* **Wmk. 155**

On Issues of 1899-1903.

No.	Type	Description	Unused	Used
515	A28	5c orange (Bl)	50.00	40.00
516	A30	15c lavender & claret (Bl)	200.00	200.00

On Issue of 1910.

No.	Type	Description	Unused	Used
517	A36	1c dull violet (R)	1.00	1.50
518	A37	2c green (R)	45	30
519	A38	3c org. brn. (Bl)	50	30
		a. Dbl. ovpt.	100.00	100.00
520	A39	4c carmine (Bl)	4.00	3.00
521	A40	5c orange (Bl)	20	12
		a. Double overprint	35.00	
522	A41	10c blue & org. (R)	1.00	90
523	A42	15c gray blue & claret (Bk)	1.25	1.00
524	A43	20c red & blue (Bk)	1.25	1.00
525	A44	50c red brown & black (R)	7.50	4.00
526	A45	1p blue & blk. (R)	12.00	5.50
527	A46	5p carmine & black (R)	60.00	35.00
		Nos. 517–527 (11)	89.15	52.62

Nos. 518–524 exist with this overprint (called the "Corbata") reading downward and Nos. 525–527 with it inverted.

With Additional Overprint

GOBIERNO $ CONSTITUCIONALISTA

No.	Type	Description	Unused	Used
528	A36	1c dull violet (R)	1.25	1.25
529	A37	2c green (R)	60	50
530	A38	3c org. brn. (Bl)	50	50
531	A39	4c carmine (Bl)	50	50
532	A40	5c orange (Bl)	80	25
533	A41	10c blue & orange (R)	60	50
534	A42	15c gray blue & claret (Bk)	65	65
535	A43	20c red & blue (Bk)	65	65

With Additional Overprint

GOBIERNO
Y
CONSTITUCIONALISTA

No.	Type	Description	Unused	Used
536	A44	50c red brown & black (R)	6.00	3.50
537	A45	1p blue & black (R)	10.00	7.50
538	A46	5p carmine & black (R)	60.00	40.00
		Nos. 528–538 (11)	81.55	55.80

Nos. 529 to 535 are known with the overprint reading downward and Nos. 536 to 538 with it inverted.

With Additional Overprint

On Issue of 1903.

No.	Type	Description	Unused	Used
539	A28	5c orange (Bl)	20.00	20.00

On Issue of 1910.

No.	Type	Description	Unused	Used
540	A36	1c dull violet (R)	1.75	2.00
541	A37	2c green (R)	50	50
		a. Monogram inverted	20.00	
542	A38	3c org. brown (Bl)	45	40
543	A39	4c carmine (Bl)	2.50	2.50
544	A40	5c orange (Bl)	75	20
545	A41	10c bl. & orange (R)	1.20	1.20
546	A42	15c gray blue & claret (Bk)	1.00	50
		a. Tablet double	50.00	50.00
		b. Monogram double		50.00
547	A43	20c red & blue (Bk)	1.00	90
548	A44	50c red brown & black (R)	6.00	4.00
		a. Monogram inverted	20.00	
549	A45	1p blue & black (R)	11.00	8.50
		a. Tablet double	35.00	
		b. Monogram inverted	20.00	
		Nos. 539–549 (11)	46.15	40.70

Nos. 542 to 547 are known with the overprint reading downward. A few 5 peso stamps were overprinted for the Post Office collection but were not regularly issued to the public.

With Additional Overprint

On Issue of 1903.

No.	Type	Description	Unused	Used
550	A28	5c orange (Bl)	35.00	*35.00*

On Issue of 1910.

No.	Type	Description	Unused	Used
551	A36	1c dull violet (R)	6.00	*6.00*
552	A37	2c green (R)	1.25	70
553	A38	3c org. brown (Bl)	2.00	*2.00*
554	A39	4c carmine (Bl)	7.00	*7.00*
555	A40	5c orange (Bl)	2.00	*2.00*
556	A41	10c blue & org. (R)	5.00	*5.00*
		a. Monogram inverted	20.00	
557	A42	15c gray blue & claret (Bk)	5.00	*5.00*
		a. Monogram inverted	20.00	
558	A43	20c red & blue (Bk)	5.00	*5.00*
		a. Monogram inverted	20.00	
		Nos. 550–558 (9)	68.25	*67.70*

Stamps of 50c, 1p and 5p were overprinted for the Post Office collection but were not regularly issued.

Issues of 1914 Overprinted

On "Transitorio" Issue.

Unwmkd.

Rouletted 9½x14.

No.	Type	Description	Unused	Used
559	A50	1c deep blue (R)	12.00	
560	"	2c yellow green (R)	7.50	
561	"	4c blue violet (R)	125.00	100.00
562	"	10c red (Bl)	1.20	1.20
		a. Vertical overprint	30.00	
563	"	20c yellow brn. (Bl)	1.50	1.50
564	"	50c claret (Bl)	10.00	
565	"	1p violet (Bl)	12.00	10.00
		a. Horizontal pair, imperf. between		

Overprinted in Blue.

On "Denver" Issue.

Perf. 12.

No.	Type	Description	Unused	Used
566	A52	1c pale blue	2.50	
567	"	2c light green	2.50	
568	"	3c orange	50	
569	"	5c deep rose	50	
570	"	10c rose	50	
571	"	15c rose lilac	50	
572	"	50c yellow	1.25	
573	"	1p violet	10.00	
		Nos. 566–573 (8)	18.25	

Many of the foregoing stamps exist with the "G. P. DE M." overprint printed in other colors than those listed. These "trial color" stamps were not regularly on sale at post offices but were available for postage and used copies are known.

There appears to have been speculation in Nos. 516, 517, 520, 528, 539, 540, 543, 566, and 567. A small quantity of each of these stamps was sold at post offices but subsequently they could be obtained only from officials or their agents at advanced prices.

Venustiano Carranza A66 — Coat of Arms A67

1916, June 1 **Engraved.** ***Perf. 12***

No.	Type	Description	Unused	Used
574	A66	10c blue	90	55
		a. Imperf., pair	17.50	
575	"	10c lilac brown	8.00	8.00
		a. Imperf., pair	35.00	35.00

Commemorative of the entry of General Carranza into Mexico, D. F.

Stamps of type A66 with only horizontal lines in the background of the oval are essays.

1916

No.	Type	Description	Unused	Used
576	A67	1c lilac	15	15

Issue of 1910 Surcharged in Various Colors

This overprint is called the "Barril."

1916 ***Perf. 14.*** **Wmk. 155**

No.	Type	Description	Unused	Used
577	A36	5c on 1c dull violet (Br)	15	15
		a. Vertical surcharge	1.00	1.00
		b. Double surcharge	50.00	
578	"	10c on 1c dull violet (Bl)	20	20
579	A40	20c on 5c orange (Br)	15	15
		a. Double surcharge	50.00	
580	"	25c on 5c orange (G)	25	25
581	A37	60c on 2c green (R)	13.50	12.00
		Nos. 577–581 (5)	14.25	12.75

With Additional Overprint

GOBIERNO $ CONSTITUCIONALISTA

No.	Type	Description	Unused	Used
582	A36	5c on 1c dull violet (Br)	20	20
		a. Double tablet, one vertical	50.00	
		b. Invtd. tablet	150.00	150.00
583	"	10c on 1c dull violet (Bl)	50	50
584	A40	25c on 5c orange (G)	30	30
		a. Invtd. tablet	100.00	100.00
585	A37	60c on 2c grn. (R)	125.00	125.00

The variety "GONSTITUCIONALISTA" is found on Nos. 582 to 585.

With Additional Overprint

No.	Type	Description	Unused	Used
586	A40	25c on 5c orange (G)	15	12

With Additional Overprint

No.	Type	Description	Unused	Used
587	A36	5c on 1c dull violet (Br)	7.50	6.00
		a. Vertical tablet	50.00	50.00
588	"	10c on 1c dull violet (Bl)	2.50	2.50
589	A40	25c on 5c orange (G)	75	75
		a. Invtd. tablet	90.00	
590	A37	60c on 2c grn. (R)	120.00	

Surcharged on "Denver" Issue of 1914.

1916 ***Perf. 12.*** **Unwmkd.**

No.	Type	Description	Unused	Used
591	A52	60c on 1c pale blue (Br)	2.50	3.00
592	"	60c on 2c light green (Br)	2.50	3.00
		a. Invtd. surch.	90.00	

Postage Due Stamps Surcharged

1916 ***Perf. 14.*** **Wmk. 155**

No.	Type	Description	Unused	Used
593	D1	5c on 1c blue (Br)	1.00	
594	"	10c on 2c blue (V)	1.00	
595	"	20c on 4c blue (Br)	1.00	
596	"	25c on 5c blue (G)	1.35	
597	"	60c on 10c blue (R)	60	
598	"	1p on 1c blue (C)	70	
599	"	1p on 2c blue (C)	60	
600	"	1p on 4c blue (C)	50	50
601	"	1p on 5c blue (C)	80	
602	"	1p on 10c blue (C)	90	
		Nos. 593–602 (10)	8.45	

There are numerous "trial colors" and "essays" of the overprints and surcharges on Nos. 577 to 602. They were available for postage though not regularly issued.

Postage Due Stamps Surcharged

$2.50

1916

603 D1 2.50p on 1c blue 50 50
604 " 2.50p on 2c blue 6.00
605 " 2.50p on 4c bl. 5.00
606 " 2.50p on 5c bl. 6.00
607 " 2.50p on 10c bl. 6.00
Nos. 603-607 (5) 23.50

Regular Issue.

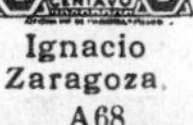

Ignacio Zaragoza. A68 — Ildefonso Vázquez A69

M. J. Pino Suárez A70 — Jesús Carranza A71

Maclovio Herrera A72 — F. I. Madero A73

Belisario Domínguez A74  — Aguiles Serdán A75

Rouletted 14½

1916-20 Engraved **Unwmkd.**

Thick Paper.

608 A68 1c dull violet 30 12
609 " 1c gray ('20) 75 25
a. 1c lilac gray ('20) 75 25
610 A69 2c gray green 40 10
611 A70 3c bistre brown 40 8
612 A71 4c carmine 75 25
613 A72 5c ultramarine 1.00 15
a. Horizontal pair, imperf. between 25.00
614 A73 10c blue 1.75 10
a. Without imprint 2.50 15
615 A74 20c rose 10.00 50
a. 20c brown rose 12.00 40
616 A75 30c gray brown 30.00 30
617 " 30c gray black ('20) 30.00 50
Nos. 608-617 (10) 75.35 2.35

Perf. 12.

Thick or Medium Paper

618 A68 1c dull violet 10.00 8.00
619 A69 2c gray green 3.50 2.50
620 A70 3c bistre brown ('17) 85.00 70.00
621 A71 4c carmine 250.00 150.00
622 A72 5c ultramarine 1.50 15

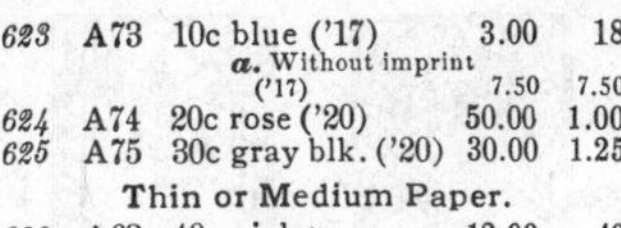

623 A73 10c blue ('17) 3.00 18
a. Without imprint ('17) 7.50 7.50
624 A74 20c rose ('20) 50.00 1.00
625 A75 30c gray blk. ('20) 30.00 1.25

Thin or Medium Paper.

626 A63 40c violet 12.00 40
a. Without imprint
627 A64 1p blue & black 15.00 50
a. With center of 5p 200.00
b. 1p blue & dark blue (error) 475.00 35.00
628 A65 5p green & black 11.00 7.50
a. With control number 35.00 6.00
b. With center of 1p 200.00
Nos. 618-628 (11) 471.00 241.48

The 1, 2, 3, 5 and 10c are known on thin paper perforated. It is stated they were printed for Postal Union and "specimen" purposes.

All values of the 1916-20 issue exist imperforate but it is not certain that they were regularly issued in that condition.

The stamps of this issue, with the exception of the 3c, normally have an imprint at the foot.

Meeting of Iturbide and Guerrero
A77

Entering City of Mexico
A78

1921

632 A77 10c blue & brown 6.00 1.00
a. Center inverted 2500.00
633 A78 10p black brown & black 20.00 17.50

Commemorating the meeting of Augustin de Iturbide and Vincente Guerrero and the entry into City of Mexico in 1821.

"El Salto de Agua," Public Fountain
A79

Pyramid of the Sun at Teotihuacán A80 — Chapultepec Castle A81

Columbus Monument A82 — Juárez Colonnade, Mexico, D. F. A83

Monument to Josefa de Dominguez Ortiz A84 — Cuauhtémoc Monument A85

1923 *Rouletted 14½.* **Unwmkd.**

634 A79 2c scarlet 1.00 10
635 A80 3c bistre brown 1.25 15
636 A81 4c green 1.50 30
637 A82 5c orange 3.00 10
638 A83 10c brown 2.50 8
639 A85 10c claret 2.00 5
640 A84 20c dark blue 22.50 75
641 A85 30c dark green 22.50 1.25
Nos. 634-641 (8) 56.25 2.78

See also Nos. 642-646, 650-657, 688-692, 727A, 735A, 736.

Communications Building
A87

Palace of Fine Arts (National Theater)
A88

Wmk. 156

Two types of 1p:
I. Eagle on palace dome.
II. Without eagle.

Wmkd. CORREOS MEXICO. (156)

1923 *Perf. 12*

642 A79 2c scarlet 3.00 3.50
a. Bklt. pane of 3 15.00
b. Bklt. pane of 2 15.00
643 A81 4c green 80 15
644 A82 5c orange 3.00 3.50
a. Bklt. pane of 3 12.50
645 A85 10c brown lake 3.00 3.00
a. Bklt. pane of 3 12.50
646 A83 30c dark green 70 15
647 A63 40c violet 75 20
648 A87 50c olive brown 40 12
649 A88 1p red brown & blue (I) 1.25 35
a. Type II 20.00 8.00
Nos. 642-649 (8) 12.90 10.97

Most of Nos. 642-649 are known imperforate or part perforate but probably were not regularly issued.

1923-34 *Rouletted 14½*

650 A79 2c scarlet 20 6
651 A80 3c bistre brown ('27) 25 8
652 A81 4c green 9.00 4.50
653 A82 4c green ('27) 20 6
654 " 5c orange 20 6
655 A85 10c lake 25 3
656 A84 20c deep blue 50 12
657 A83 30c dark green ('34) 2.50 1.25
Nos. 650-657 (8) 13.10 6.16

Nos. 650 to 657 inclusive exist imperforate.

Medallion A90 — Map of Americas A91

Francisco García y Santos A92  — Post Office, Mexico, D. F. A93

1926 *Perf. 12*

658 A90 2c red 35 25
659 A91 4c green 75 60
660 A90 5c orange 45 35
661 A91 10c brown red 2.25 30
662 A92 20c dark blue 2.25 75
663 " 30c dark green 2.00 1.25
664 " 40c violet 4.00 1.25
665 A93 1p brown & blue 12.00 5.00
Nos. 658-665 (8) 24.05 9.75

Pan-American Postal Congress.

Nos. 658-665 were also printed in black, on unwatermarked paper, for presentation to delegates to the Universal Postal Congress at London in 1929. Remainders were overprinted in 1929 for use as airmail official stamps, and are listed as Nos. CO3-CO10.

Benito Juárez
A94

1926 *Rouletted 14½*

666 A94 8c orange 25 8
a. 8c yellow 20.00 5.00

Nos. 658-665 Overprinted

HABILITADO 1930

1930 *Perf. 12*

667 A90 2c red 2.50 1.50
a. Reading down 10.00
668 A91 4c green 2.50 1.50
a. Reading down 10.00
669 A90 5c orange 2.50 1.50
a. Reading down 10.00
670 A91 10c brown red 4.00 1.75
a. Reading down 10.00
671 A92 20c dark blue 6.00 2.00
672 " 30c dark green 5.00 3.00
a. Reading down 5.50
673 " 40c violet 7.50 5.00
a. Reading down 30.00
674 A93 1p red brown & blue 7.50 5.00
a. Double overprint 75.00
Nos. 667-674 (8) 37.50 21.25

Overprint horizontal on 1p.

Arms of Puebla
A95

1931, May 1 **Engraved**

675 A95 10c dark blue & dark brown 2.00 45

400th anniversary of Puebla.

Nos. 658–665 Overprinted **HABILITADO 1931**

1931

675A A90 2c red *50.00*
676 A91 4c green *20.00*
677 A90 5c orange *3.50*
678 A91 10c brown red *3.50*
679 A92 20c dark blue *6.00*
680 " 30c dark green *10.00*
681 " 40c violet *12.00*
682 A93 1p brown & blue *15.00*
Nos. 675A–682 (8) *120.00*

Overprint horizontal on 1p.
Nos. 676 and 682 are not known to have been sold to the public through post offices.

Bartolomé de las Casas
A96

Emblem of Mexican Society of Geography and Statistics
A97

1933, Mar. 3 Engr. ***Rouletted 14½***

683 A96 15c dark blue 15 6

1933, Oct. ***Rouletted 14½***

684 A97 2c deep green 1.25 40
685 " 5c dark brown 1.50 50
686 " 10c dark blue 60 12
687 " 1p dark violet 30.00 30.00

Issued in commemoration of the XXI International Congress of Statistics and the first centenary of the Mexican Society of Geography and Statistics.

Types of 1923 and PT1.

1934 ***Perf. 10½, 11 (4c)***

687A PT1 1c brown 60 30
688 A79 2c scarlet 30 15
689 A82 4c green 30 15
690 A85 10c brown lake 30 15
691 A84 20c dark blue 1.00 1.00
692 A83 30c dark blue green 5.00 5.00
Nos. 687A–692 (6) 7.50 6.75

See second note after Postal Tax stamp No. RA3.

Indian Mother and Child
A98

Indian Archer
A99

Indian
A100

Woman Decorating Pottery
A101

Peon
A102

Potter
A103

Sculptor
A104

Craftsman
A105

Offering to the Gods
A106

Worshiper
A107

1934, Sept. 1 ***Perf. 10½*** **Wmk. 156**

697 A98 1c dull orange 25 5
698 A99 5c dark green 1.00 25
699 A100 10c brown lake 1.50 40
700 A101 20c ultramarine 5.00 2.50
701 A102 30c black 10.00 8.00
702 A103 40c black brown 17.50 7.50
703 A104 50c dull blue 35.00 25.00
704 A105 1p brown lake & black 40.00 32.50
705 A106 5p brown black & red brown 175.00 150.00
706 A107 10p brown & vio. 750.00 650.00
a. Unwatermarked *1750.00*
Nos. 697–706 (10) 1035.25 876.20

National University.
See also Nos. C54–C61.

Yalalteca Indian
A108

Tehuana Indian
A109

Arch of the Revolution
A110

Tower of Los Remedios
A111

Cross of Palenque
A112

Independence Monument
A113

Monument, Puebla Independence Building, Mexico, D. F.
A114

Monument to the Heroic Cadets
A115

Stone of Tizoc
A116

Ruins of Mitla
A117

Coat of Arms
A118

Cowboy
A119

Imprint: "Oficina Impresora de Hacienda-Mexico"

Wmkd. CORREOS MEXICO. (156)

1934–40 Size: 20x26mm. ***Perf. 10½***

707 A108 1c orange 30 6
a. Unwmkd. 275.00
708 A109 2c green 30 8
a. Unwmkd. 2.00 1.50
709 A110 4c carmine 50 18
710 A111 5c olive brown 35 5
a. Unwmkd. 300.00 275.00
711 A112 10c dark blue 25 5
712 " 10c violet ('35) 15 3
a. Unwmkd. 140.00 25.00
713 A113 15c light blue 75 15
714 A114 20c gray green 50 10
a. 20c olive green 50 10
715 A114 20c ultra. ('35) 50 7
a. Unwmkd. 80.00
716 A115 30c lake 30 7
a. Unwmkd. 250.00
716B A115 30c light ultra. ('40) 30 7
717 A116 40c red brown 25 6
718 A117 50c greenish black 30 5
a. Imperf. (pair) 60.00
b. Unwmkd. 250.00
719 A118 1p dk. brn. & org. 60 10
a. Imperf. (pair) 60.00
720 A119 5p orange & violet 3.00 60
Nos. 707–720 (15) 8.35 1.72

No. 718a was not regularly issued.
See also Nos. 729–733, 733B, 735, 784–788, 795A–800A, 837–838, 840–841, 844, 846–851.

Tractor
A120

1935, Apr. 1 ***Perf. 10½*** **Wmk. 156**

721 A120 10c violet 2.50 35

Industrial census of Apr. 10, 1935.

Arms of Chiapas
A121

Emiliano Zapata
A122

1935, Sept. 14

722 A121 10c dark blue 35 15
a. Unwmkd. 60.00 50.00

The 111th anniversary of the joining of the state of Chiapas with the federal republic of Mexico. See No. 734.

1935, Nov. 20 **Wmk. 156**

723 A122 10c violet 40 12

25th anniversary of the Plan of Ayala.

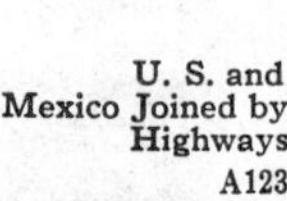

U. S. and Mexico Joined by Highways
A123

Matalote Bridge
A124

View of Nuevo Laredo Highway
A125

Wmk. 248

Wmkd. SECRETARIA DE HACIENDA MEXICO. (248)

1936 ***Perf. 14***

725 A123 5c blue grn. & rose 15 10
726 A124 10c slate blue & black 35 15
727 A125 20c brn. & dk. grn. 50 50

Issued to commemorate the opening of the Nuevo Laredo Highway. See Nos. C77–C79.

Monument Type of 1923. Engraved.

1936 ***Perf. 10½.*** **Wmk. 248**

727A A85 10c brown lake 350.00 250.00

No. 712 Overprinted in Green **PRIMER CONGRESO NAL. DE HIGIENE Y MED. DEL TRABAJO**

1936, Dec. **Wmk. 156**

728 A112 10c violet 30 30

Issued in commemoration of the First National Congress of Industrial Hygiene and Medicine.

Types of 1934.
Redrawn size 17½x21mm.
Imprint: "Talleres de Imp. de Est. y Valores-Mexico"
Wmk. 156

1937 Photogravure. *Perf. 14.*

729	A108	1c orange	35	3
		a. Imperf. (pair)	10.00	
730	A109	2c dull green	35	3
		a. Imperf. (pair)	10.00	
731	A110	4c carmine	50	6
		a. Imperf. (pair)	10.00	
732	A111	5c olive brown	50	3
		a. Unwmkd.		75.00
733	A112	10c violet	30	3
		a. Imperf. (pair)	10.00	
		Nos. 729–733 (5)	2.00	18

The imperfs were not regularly issued.

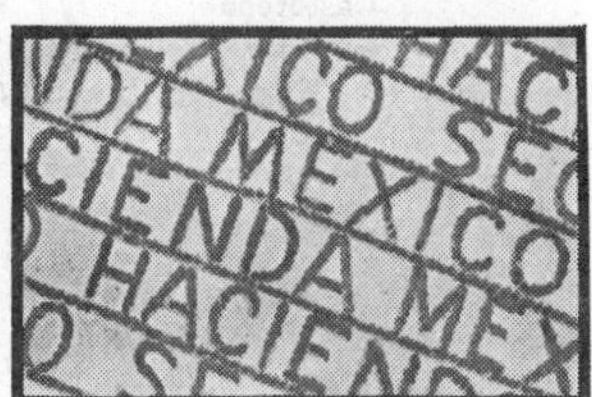

Wmk. 260

Types of 1934–35.
Wmkd.
Lines and SECRETARIA DE HACIENDA MEXICO. (260)

1937

Size: 17½x21mm.

733B	A111	5c olive brown	300.00	90.00

1937 Engraved *Perf. 10½*

734	A121	10c dark blue	12.00	5.00

1937

Size: 20x26mm.

735	A112	10c violet	100.00	20.00

Types of 1923.

1935–37 *Perf. 10½* Wmk. 260

735A	A79	2c scarlet		1800.00
735B	A85	10c brown lake		

Rouletted 14½.

736	A85	10c claret ('37)	550.00	185.00

Blacksmith A126

Revolutionary Soldier A127

Revolutionary Envoy A128

Wmkd. CORREOS MEXICO. (156)

1938, Mar. 26 Photo. *Perf. 14*

737	A126	5c black & brown	35	10
738	A127	10c red brown	15	8
739	A128	20c maroon & orange	3.50	75

Issued to commemorate the 25th anniversary of the Plan of Guadalupe. See also Nos. C82–C84.

Arch of the Revolution—A129

National Theater A130

Liberty Monument A131

1938, July 1

740	A129	5c bistre brown	70	35
741	"	5c red brown	1.25	1.00
742	A130	10c orange	3.50	2.50
743	"	10c chocolate	25	10
744	A131	20c brown lake	2.00	1.50
745	"	20c black	5.00	3.00
		Nos. 740–745 (6)	12.70	8.45

Issued to commemorate the 16th International Congress of Planning and Housing. See also Nos. C85–C90.

Arch of the Revolution—A132

1939, May 1

746	A132	10c Prussian blue	50	15

New York World's Fair. See also Nos. C91–C93.

Indian—A133

1939, May 17

747	A133	10c red orange	35	8

Issued to commemorate the Tulsa World Philatelic Convention. See also Nos. C94–C96.

Juan Zumárraga A134

First Printing Shop in Mexico, 1539 A135

Design: 10c, Antonio de Mendoza.

1939, Sept. 1 Engraved *Perf. 10½*

748	A134	2c brown black	50	25
749	A135	5c green	50	15
750	A134	10c red brown	15	8

Issued to commemorate the 400th anniversary of printing in Mexico. See also Nos. C97–C99.

View of Taxco A137

Allegory or Agriculture A138

Design: 10c, Two hands holding symbols of commerce.

1939, Oct. 1 Photo. *Perf. 12x13*

751	A137	2c dark carmine	75	20
752	A138	5c slate green & gray green	15	5
753	"	10c orange brown & buff	10	5

Census Taking. See Nos. C100–C102.

"Penny Black" of 1840 A140

Roadside Monument A141

1940, May *Perf. 14*

754	A140	5c black & lemon	80	50
755	"	10c dark violet	20	8
756	"	20c light blue & carmine	30	10
757	"	1p gray & red orange	6.00	3.50
758	"	5p black & Pruss. blue	45.00	35.00
		Nos. 754–758 (5)	52.30	39.18

Issued to commemorate the centenary of the postage stamp. See also Nos. C103–C107.

1940 Wmk. 156

759	A141	6c deep green	40	10

Issued to commemorate the opening of the highway between Mexico, D. F., and Guadalajara. See also No. 789, 842.

Vasco de Quiroga A142

Melchor Ocampo A143

College Seal A144

1940, July 15 Engraved *Perf. 10½*

760	A142	2c violet	1.00	50
761	A143	5c copper red	75	20
762	A144	10c olive bistre	75	15
		a. Imperf. (pair)	60.00	

Issued to commemorate the 400th anniversary of the founding of the National College of San Nicolas de Hidalgo. See also Nos. C108–C110.

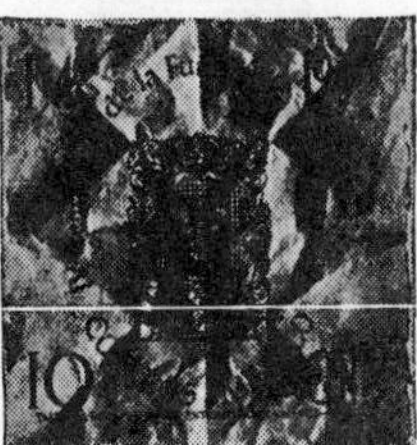

Coat of Arms of Campeche A145

1940, Aug. 7 Photo. *Perf. 12x13*

763	A145	10c bistre brown & dk. carmine	2.50	1.00

Issued to commemorate the 400th anniversary of the founding of Campeche. See also Nos. C111–C113.

Man at Helm—A146

1940, Dec. 1

764	A146	2c red orange & black	1.00	50
765	"	5c peacock blue & red brown	3.00	1.00
766	"	10c slate green & dark brown	1.35	40

Issued to commemorate the inauguration of Pres. Manuel Avila Camacho. See also Nos. C114–C116.

Javelin Thrower—A147

1941, Nov. 4 ***Perf. 14***

767 A147 10c dull yellow green 3.00 50

Issued to commemorate the National Athletic Games of the Revolution, Nov. 4–20, 1941.

Serpent Columns, Chichén Itzá A148 — Mayan Sculpture A149

Coat of Arms of Merída—A150

1942, June 30

768	A148	2c dk. olive bistre	1.00	60
769	A149	5c deep orange	1.50	60
770	A150	10c dark violet	1.25	25

Issued to commemorate the 400th anniversary of the founding of Merida. See also Nos. C117–C119.

Independence Monument to Hidalgo A151

Government Palace A152 — View of Guadalajara A153

1942, Aug. 8 Engr. ***Perf. 10x10½***

771	A151	2c blue violet & violet brown	40	30
772	A152	5c black & copper red	1.00	50
773	A153	10c red orange & ultramarine	80	40

Issued to commemorate the 400th anniversary of the founding of Guadalajara. See also Nos. C120–C122.

Black Cloud in Orion

A154

Designs: 5c, Total solar eclipse. 10c, Spiral galaxy in the "Hunting Dogs."

1942, Feb. 17 Photo. ***Perf. 12x13***

774	A154	2c light violet & indigo	1.75	1.00
775	"	5c blue & indigo	10.00	1.50
776	"	10c red orange & indigo	10.00	50

Issued to commemorate the Astrophysics Congress and the inauguration of an observatory at Tonanzintla, Feb. 17, 1942. See also Nos. C123–C125.

"Mother Earth"

A157

Sowing Wheat

A158

Western Hemisphere Carrying Torch

A159

1942, July 1

777	A157	2c chestnut	50	35
778	A158	5c turquoise blue	1.50	80
779	A159	10c red orange	75	35

Issued to commemorate the 2nd Inter-American Agricultural Conference. See also Nos. C126–C128.

Fuente Academy

A160

1942, Nov. 16 ***Perf. 14***

780 A160 10c greenish black 1.00 25

75th anniversary of Fuente Academy.

Las Monjas Church

A161

Generalissimo Ignacio José de Allende

A163

Design: 5c, San Miguel Church.

1943, May 11

781	A161	2c intense blue	75	35
782	"	5c deep brown	85	30
783	A163	10c dull black	2.25	75

Issued to commemorate the 400th anniversary of the founding of San Miguel de Allende. See also Nos. C129–C131.

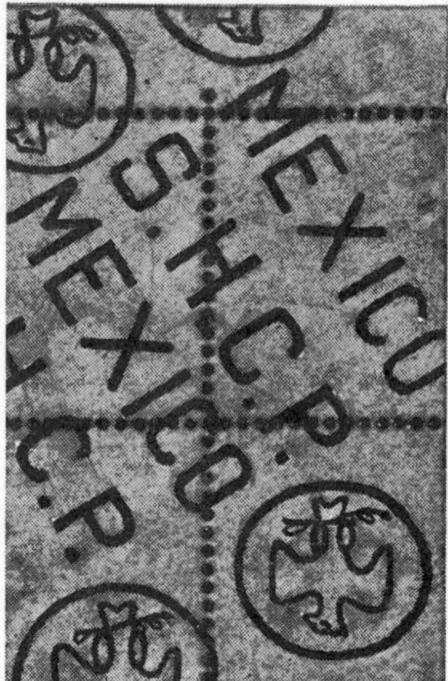

Wmk. 272

Types of 1937.

Wmkd. "S. H. C. P. MEXICO" and Eagle in Circle. (272)

1944 Photogravure.

784	A108	1c orange	35	5
785	A109	2c dull green	25	5
786	A110	4c carmine	60	12
787	A111	5c olive brown	50	8
788	A112	10c violet	25	3

Type of 1940

789	A141	6c green	50	8
		Nos. 784–789 (6)	2.45	41

"Liberty"

A164

1944 Photogravure

790 A164 12c violet brown 20 5

See also No. 845.

Juan M. de Castorena

A165

1944, Oct. 12 Engraved ***Perf. 10***

791 A165 12c dark brown 40 15

Third Book Fair. See also No. C142.

Hands Holding Globe Showing Western Hemisphere

A166

1945, Feb. 27 Photo. ***Perf. 12x13***

792	A166	12c dark carmine	35	10
793	"	1p slate green	50	25
794	"	5p olive brown	5.00	3.00
795	"	10p black	7.50	4.00

Issued to commemorate the Inter-American Conference held at Chapultepec, February 1945. See also Nos. C143–C147.

Types of 1934-40.

Engraved.

1945–46 ***Perf. 10½*** **Wmk. 272**

795A	A113	15c light greenish blue ('46)	125.00	20.00
796	A114	20c gray green	1.00	10
797	A115	30c light ultra.	1.50	10
798	A116	40c brown	1.00	20
799	A117	50c greenish blk.	1.00	15
800	A118	1p dark brown & orange	1.50	15
800A	A119	5p orange & violet ('46)	7.50	2.00
		Nos. 795A–800A (7)	138.50	22.70

Theater of Peace, San Luis Potosi — Fountain of Diana, the Huntress

A167 — A168

1945, July 27 Photo. ***Perf. 12x13***

801	A167	12c black & vio. brn.	25	10
802	"	1p black & blue gray	35	25
803	"	5p blk. & brn. lake	4.00	1.75
804	"	10p black & greenish blue	9.00	7.00

Issued to commemorate the reconstruction of the Peace Theater (Teatro de la Paz), San Luis Potosi. See also Nos. C148–C152.

1945 *Perf. 14*

805	A168	3c violet blue	35	10

See also No. 839.

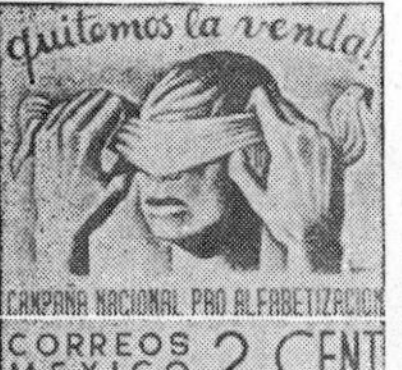

Removing Blindfold
A169

M. E. Irrigoya
A170

1945, Nov. 2 *Perf. 12x13*

806	A169	2c bluish green	20	15
807	"	6c orange	30	15
808	"	12c ultramarine	30	10
809	"	1p olive	40	20
810	"	5p gray & pale rose	2.00	1.50
811	"	10p blue & yel. grn.	12.50	6.00
		Nos. 806-811 (6)	15.70	8.10

Issued to publicize the national literacy campaign. See also Nos. C153-C157.

1946 *Perf. 14.*

812	A170	8c black	1.25	15

Issued to honor Martines Enriques Irrigoya, founder of the Mexican posts. See also No. 843.

Allegory of World Peace
A171

1946, Apr. 10 *Perf. 12x13*

813	A171	2c dark olive bistre	20	15
814	"	6c red brown	20	10
815	"	12c Prussian green	12	7
816	"	1p light green	35	25
817	"	5p dull red violet	3.00	1.25
818	"	10p light ultra.	15.00	7.00
		Nos. 813-818 (6)	18.87	8.82

United Nations. See Nos. C158-C162.

Arms of Zacatecas
A173

Monument to Gen. Gonzalez Ortega
A174

Ramón Lopez Velarde
A175

Francisco Garcia Salinas
A176

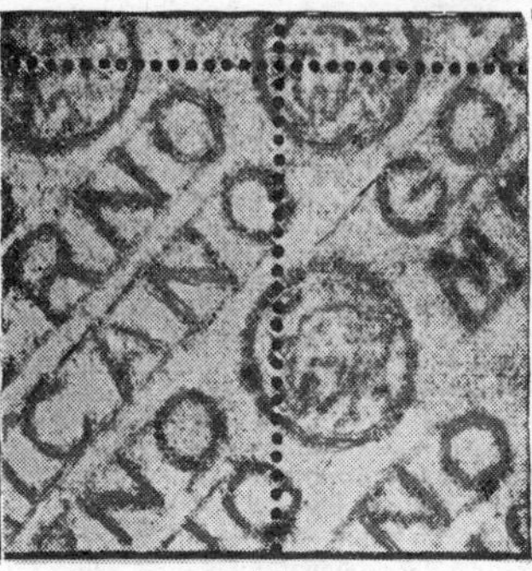

Wmk. 279

Wmkd. GOBIERNO MEXICANO and Eagle in Circle. (279)

1946, Sept. 1 Photo. *Perf. 14*

820	A173	2c orange brown	40	10
821	"	12c Prussian blue	15	10

Engraved

Perf. 10x10½

822	A174	1p lilac rose	50	20
823	A175	5p red	4.00	3.00
824	A176	10p dk. blue & black	12.50	7.00
		Nos. 820-824 (5)	17.55	10.40

Issued to commemorate the 400th anniversary of the founding of the city of Zacatecas. See also Nos. C163-C166.

Postman
A177

1947 Photogravure *Perf. 14*

825	A177	15c greenish blue	15	4
		a. Imperf., pair	100.00	

Franklin D. Roosevelt and Stamp of First Mexican Issue
A178

Arms of Mexico and Stamp of First U.S. Issue
A179

1947, May 16

826	A178	10c yellow brown	1.00	60
827	A179	15c green	15	7

Issued to honor the Centenary International Philatelic Exhibition, New York, May 17-25, 1947.
See also Nos. C167-C169.

Justo Sierra
A180

Communications Building
A181

Perf. 10x10½, 10½x10.

1947 Engraved **Wmk. 279**

828	A180	10p brown & dull green	85.00	22.50
829	A181	20p dark green & lilac	7.00	5.00

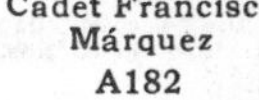

Cadet Francisco Márquez
A182

Gen. Manuel Rincón
A186

Flag of San Blas Battalion
A188

Designs: 5c, Cadet Fernando Montes de Oca. 10c, Cadet Juan Escutia. 15c, Cadet Agustin Melgar. 1p, Gen. Lucas Balderas.

1947, Sept. 8 Photo. *Perf. 14*

830	A182	2c brown black	30	7
831	"	5c red orange	15	5
832	"	10c dark brown	15	7
833	"	15c dk. Pruss. green	15	6
834	A186	30c dull olive green	20	8

Engraved

Perf. 10x10½.

835	A186	1p aquamarine	35	20
836	A188	5p dark blue & claret	1.65	90
		Nos. 830-836 (7)	2.95	1.43

Issued to commemorate the centenary of the battles of Chapultepec, Churubusco and Molino del Rey. See Nos. C180-C184.

Types of 1934-46.

Photogravure

1947-50 *Perf. 14* **Wmk. 279**

837	A108	1c orange	50	25
		a. Imperf., pair	80.00	
838	A109	2c dark green	50	6
839	A168	3c violet blue	50	6
840	A110	4c dull red	60	7
841	A111	5c olive brown	75	7
842	A141	6c deep green	30	5
		a. Imperf., pair	60.00	
843	A170	8c black	20	7
844	A112	10c violet	1.50	7
845	A164	12c violet brown	6.00	25

Types A108 to A112 are in the redrawn size of 1937.

Engraved.

Size: 19x25 mm.

Perf. 10½.

846	A114	20c olive green	1.00	12
847	A115	30c light ultra.	7.50	30
848	A116	40c red brown	1.00	10
849	A117	50c green	1.50	12
		a. Imperf., pair	75.00	
850	A118	1p dark brown & orange	12.00	1.00
851	A119	5p orange & violet ('50)	15.00	2.00
		Nos. 837-851 (15)	48.85	4.59

Puebla Cathedral
A189

Designs: 3c, Modernistic church, Nuevo Leon. 5c, Modern building, Mexico City. 10c, Convent, Morelos. 15c, Benito Juarez. 30c, Indian dancer, Michoacan. 40c, Stone head, Tabasco. 50c, Carved head, Veracruz. 1p, Convent and carved head, Hidalgo. 5p, Galleon, arms of Campeche. 10p, Francisco I. Madero. 20p, Modern building, Mexico City.

Photogravure.

1950-52 *Perf. 14.* **Wmk. 279**

856	A189	3c blue violet ('51)	20	4
857	"	5c dark red brown	20	5
858	"	10c dark green	40	4
859	"	15c dark green ('51)	50	6
860	"	20c blue violet	50	5
861	"	30c red	25	3
862	"	40c red orange ('51)	40	7
863	"	50c blue	40	4

Engraved.

864	A189	1p dull brown	40	4
865	"	5p ultramarine & blue green	7.00	75
866	"	10p black & deep ultra. ('52)	8.00	1.50
867	"	20p purple & green ('52)	7.50	3.50
		Nos. 856-867 (12)	25.75	6.17

See also Nos. 875-885, 928-931, 943-952, 1003-1004, 1054-1055, 1072, 1076, 1081, 1090-1091, 1094-1102.

Highway Bridge
A190

Symbolical of Construction in 1950
A191

Railroad Laborer
A192

Perf. 10½x10, 10x10½

1950, May 5 Photogravure

868	A190	15c purple	20	6
869	A191	20c deep blue	30	20

Issued to commemorate the completion of the International Highway between Ciudad Juarez and the Guatemala border. See Nos. C199-C200.

Inscribed:

"Ferrocarril del Sureste 1950."

Design: 20c, Map and locomotive.

1950, May 24 *Perf. 10x10½*

870	A192	15c chocolate	15	5
871	"	20c deep carmine	25	10

Issued to commemorate the opening of the Southeastern Railroad between Veracruz, Coatzocoalcos and Yucatan, 1950. See also Nos. C201-C202.

Postal Service A193 — Miguel Hidalgo y Costilla A194

1950, June 25 *Perf. 10x10½*

872 A193 50c purple 25 12

75th anniversary (in 1949) of Universal Postal Union.
See also Nos. C203–C204.

Wmk. 300

Wmkd. MEX— MEX and Eagle in Circle, Multiple. Letters 6mm. (300)

1953, May 8 *Perf. 14*

873 A194 20c greenish blue & dk. brown 1.50 20

Bicentenary of birth of Miguel Hidalgo y Costilla. See also Nos. C206–C207.

Type of 1950–52.

Designs as before.
Two types of 5p:
I. Imprint ½mm. high and blurred.
II. Imprint ¾mm. high and clear.

1954–67 Photogravure *Perf. 14*

875 A189 5c red brown 15 3
876 " 10c dark green 40 4
a. 10c grn., redrawn 40 8
877 " 15c dark green 20 4
878 " 20c dark blue 20 4
a. 20c bluish blk., white paper, colorless gum ('67) 20 3
879 " 30c brown red 30 5
a. 30c reddish brown 30 5
880 " 40c red orange 40 6
881 " 50c light blue 30 5

Engraved.

882 A189 1p olive brown 4.50 7
a. 1p olive green 6.00 7
b. As "a," perf. 11, vert. wmk. ('58) 10.00 25
883 A189 5p ultra. & bl. grn., I 3.50 25
a. Type II 300.00 2.00
884 A189 10p slate & deep ultra. ('56) 6.00 1.50
a. 10p slate green & ultra. 20.00 3.00
885 A189 20p purple & green 10.00 2.50
a. 20p brn. violet & yel. green 20.00 4.00
Nos. 875–885 (11) 25.95 4.63

Nos. 875–881 come only with watermark vertical, and in various shades.
On No. 876a, imprint extends full width of stamp.

Aztec Messenger of the Sun A195

Symbolizing Adoption of National Anthem A196

1954, Mar. 6

886 A195 20c rose & blue gray 65 12

Issued to publicize the 7th Central American and Caribbean Games. See Nos. C222–C223.

1954, Sept. 16 Photogravure

887 A196 5c rose lilac & dark bl 60 12
888 " 20c yel. brn. & brn. vio. 75 12
889 " 1p gray green & cerise 35 25

Issued to commemorate the centenary of the adoption of Mexico's National Anthem. See Nos. C224–C226.

Torch-Bearer and Stadium A197 — "Motion" A198

1955, Mar. 12 *Perf. 14* **Wmk. 300**

890 A197 20c dark green & red brown 60 20

Issued to publicize the second Pan American Games, 1955. See also Nos. C227–C228.

1956, Aug. 1

Aztec Designs: 10c, Bird. 30c, Flowers. 50c, Corn. 1p, Deer. 5p, Man.

891 A198 5c orange brown & bright green 40 10
892 " 10c lilac gray & deep blue 40 10
893 " 30c red & dk. purple 25 6
894 " 50c aquamarine & henna brown 30 10
895 " 1p emerald & black 40 15
896 " 5p dull yellow & dark brown 1.50 90
a. Souvenir sheet, imperf. 12.50 12.50
Nos. 891–896 (6) 3.25 1.41

Centenary of Mexico's first postage stamps.
No. 896a contains one each of Nos. 891–896. It measures 190x148mm. and sold for 15 pesos.
See also Nos. C229–C234.

Stamp of 1856 A199

Francisco Zarco A200

1956, Aug. 1

897 A199 30c brown & intense blue 55 15

Issued to commemorate the Centenary International Philatelic Exhibition, Mexico City, Aug. 16, 1956.

1956–63

Portraits: 25c, 45c, Guillermo Prieto. 60c, Ponciano Arriaga.

897A A200 25c dark brn. ('63) 60 12
898 " 45c dk. blue green 20 10
899 " 60c red lilac 20 10
900 " 70c violet blue 25 7

Centenary of the constitution (in 1957). See also Nos. C236–C237A, C289, 1071, 1075, 1092–1093.

"Mexico" A201 — Mexican Eagle and Oil Derrick A202

Design: 1p, National Assembly.

1957, Aug. 31 Photo. *Perf. 14*

901 A201 30c maroon & gold 20 7
902 " 1p pale brown & metallic green 30 15

Issued to commemorate the centenary of the constitution. See Nos. C239–C240.

1958, Aug. 30 *Perf. 14* **Wmk. 300**

Design: 5p, Map of Mexico and refinery.

903 A202 30c light blue & black 20 7
904 " 5p henna brown & Prus. green 1.25 85

Issued to commemorate the 20th anniversary of the nationalization of Mexico's oil industry. See also Nos. C243–C244.

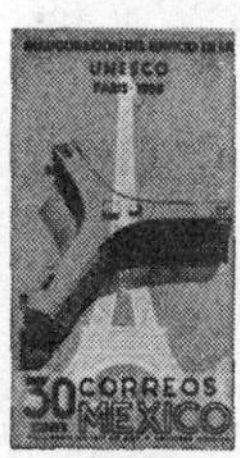
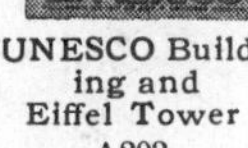
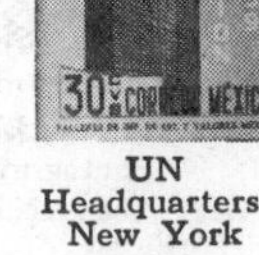

UNESCO Building and Eiffel Tower A203 — UN Headquarters, New York A204

1959, Jan. 20

905 A203 30c dull lilac & blk. 20 6

Issued to commemorate the opening of UNESCO (U. N. Educational, Scientific and Cultural Organization) Headquarters in Paris, Nov. 9.

1959, Sept. 7 Litho. *Perf. 14*

906 A204 30c orange yellow & blue 20 6

Issued to commemorate the meeting of the United Nations Economic and Social Council.

Pres. Venustiano Carranza A205 — Alexander von Humboldt Statue A206

1960, Jan. 15 Photo. **Wmk. 300**

907 A205 30c pale grn. & plum 20 7

Issued to commemorate the birth centenary of Pres. Venustiano Carranza. See No. C246.

1960, Mar. 16 *Perf. 14* **Wmk. 300**

908 A206 40c bis. brn. & green 20 7

Issued to commemorate the centenary of the death (in 1859) of Alexander von Humboldt, German naturalist and geographer.

Type of 1950–52 Inscribed: "HOMENAJE AL COLECCIONISTA DEL TIMBRE DE MEXICO—JUNIO 1960"

Design: 10p, Francisco I. Madero.

1960, June 8 Engr. Wmk. 300

909 A189 10p lilac, brown & green 45.00 45.00

Issued to commemorate the 25th anniversary visit of the Elmhurst (Ill.) Philatelic Society of Mexico Specialists to Mexico. See also No. C249.

Independence Bell A207 — Independence Monument A208

Designs: 5p, Bell of Dolores and Miguel Hidalgo.

Perf. 14

1960, Sept. 15 Photo. **Wmk. 300**

910 A207 30c green & rose red 25 8
911 A208 1p dull green & dark brown 30 15
912 " 5p maroon & dark blue 1.25 90

Issued to commemorate the 150th anniversary of Mexican independence. See United States No. 1157. See Mexico Nos. C250–C252.

Agricultural Reform A209

Symbols of Health Education A210

Designs: 20c, Sailor and Soldier, 1960, and Fighter of 1910. 30c, Electrification. 1p, Political development (schools). 5p, Currency stability (Bank and money).

1960–61 Photogravure *Perf. 14*

913 A209 10c slate green, blk. & red org. 40 15
914 A210 15c green & orange brown 2.00 25
915 " 20c bright blue & lt. brown ('61) 75 10
916 " 30c violet brown & sepia 25 7
917 " 1p reddish brown & slate 35 15
918 " 5p maroon & gray 1.75 1.25
Nos. 913–918 (6) 5.50 1.97

Issued to commemorate the 50th anniversary (in 1960) of the Mexican Revolution. See Nos. C253–C256.

Tunnel
A211

Microscope, Mosquito and Globe
A212

1961, Dec. *Perf. 14* Wmk. 300

919 A211 40c black & bright green 25 7

Issued to commemorate the opening of the railroad from Chihuahua to the Pacific Ocean. See Nos. C258–C259.

1962, Apr. 6

920 A212 40c dull blue & maroon 30 10

Issued for the World Health Organization drive to eradicate malaria.

President Joao Goulart of Brazil
A213

Mexican Indian at Marker for Battle of Puebla
A214

Photogravure

1962, Apr. 11 *Perf. 14* Wmk. 300

921 A213 40c brown olive 60 15

Issued to commemorate the visit of Joao Goulart, president of Brazil, to Mexico.

1962, May 5

922 A214 40c sepia & dark green 30 10

Issued to commemorate the centenary of the Battle of May 5 at Puebla and the defeat of French forces by Gen. Ignacio Zaragoza. See No. C260.

Draftsman and Surveyor
A215

Plumbline
A216

1962, June 11

923 A215 40c slate green & dark blue 65 15

Issued to commemorate the 25th anniversary of the National Polytechnic Institute. See No. C261.

1962, June 21

924 A216 20c dp. blue & blk. 85 20

Issued to publicize the importance of mental health.

"Space Needle" and Gear Wheels
A217

Globe
A218

1962, July 6

925 A217 40c dk. grn. & gray 30 10

Issued to publicize the "Century 21" International Exposition, Seattle, Wash., Apr. 21–Oct. 12.

1962, Oct. 1 *Perf. 14*

926 A218 40c gray & brown 30 10

Issued to commemorate the 1962 meeting of the Inter-American Economic and Social Council. See No. C263.

Pres. Alessandri of Chile
A219

Pres. Betancourt of Venezuela
A220

1962, Dec. 20 *Perf. 14* Wmk. 300

927 A219 20c olive black 60 15

Issued to commemorate the visit of President Jorge Alessandri Rodriguez of Chile to Mexico, Dec. 17–20.

Type of 1950–52

Designs as Before

Wmk. 300, Vertical

1962–74 Photogravure *Perf. 14*

928 A189 1p olive gray ('67) 50 10
929 " 5p dull blue & dark green 3.00 50
a. 5p bluish gray & dark green, white paper ('67) 3.00 35
930 A189 10p gray & bl. ('63) 6.00 1.25
a. 10p green & deep blue ('74) 6.00 1.25
931 A189 20p lilac & black ('63) 7.50 3.50

No. 928 is on thick, luminescent paper. No. 929 is 20½mm. high; No. 929a, 20¾mm.

1963, Feb. 28 Wmk. 300

932 A220 20c slate 50 15

Issued to commemorate the visit of President Romulo Betancourt of Venezuela to Mexico.

Congress Emblem
A221

Wheat Emblem
A222

1963, Apr. 22 *Perf. 14* Wmk. 300

933 A221 40c terra cotta & black 60 12

Issued to commemorate the 19th International Chamber of Commerce Congress. See No. C271.

1963, June 17 *Perf. 14* Wmk. 300

934 A222 40c crimson & dk. bl. 60 15

Issued for the "Freedom from Hunger" campaign of the U.N. Food and Agriculture Organization.

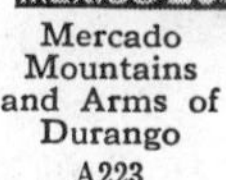

Mercado Mountains and Arms of Durango
A223

Belisario Dominguez
A224

1963, July 13 Photogravure

935 A223 20c dk. bl. & choc. 55 12

Issued to commemorate the 400th anniversary of the founding of Durango.

1963, July 13 Photogravure

936 A224 20c dk. grn. & olive gray 55 12

Issued to commemorate the centenary of the birth of Belisario Dominguez, revolutionary leader.

Stamp of 1956
A225

Wmkd. MEX and Eagle in Circle, Multiple. Letters 8-9mm. (350)

1963, Oct. 9 *Perf. 14*

937 A225 1p intense bl. & brn. 1.40 40

Issued to commemorate the 77th Annual Convention of the American Philatelic Society, Mexico City, Oct. 7–13. See No. C274.

Tree of Life
A226

José Morelos
A227

1963, Oct. 26 *Perf. 14* Wmk. 350

938 A226 20c dull blue green & carmine 40 12

Issued to commemorate the centenary of the International Red Cross. See No. C277.

1963, Nov. 9

939 A227 40c green & dark slate green 55 15

Issued to commemorate the 150th anniversary of the first congress of Anahuac.

Pres. Victor Paz Estenssoro
A228

Arms of Sinaloa University
A229

1963, Nov. 9 *Perf. 14* Wmk. 350

940 A228 40c dark brown & dark red brown 60 15

Issued to commemorate the visit of President Victor Paz Estenssoro of Bolivia.

1963 Photogravure

941 A229 40c slate green & olive bister 60 15

Issued to commemorate the 90th anniversary of the founding of the University of Sinaloa.

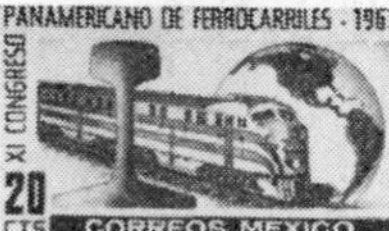

Diesel Train, Rail Cross Section and Globe
A230

1963, Nov. 29 Photogravure

942 A230 20c black & dark brn. 60 20

Issued to commemorate the 11th Pan-American Railroad Congress. See No. C279.

Type of 1950–52

Designs as Before

Photogravure

1963–66 *Perf. 14* Wmk. 350

943 A189 5c red brown ('65) 25 4
944 " 10c dark green ('64) 30 4
945 " 15c dark green ('66) 40 5
946 " 20c dark blue 40 4
948 " 40c red orange 50 6
949 " 50c blue ('64) 1.00 5
950 " 1p olive green ('64) 60 7
951 " 5p dull bl. & dark green ('66) 35.00 2.00
952 " 10p gray & Pruss. blue ('65) 30.00 3.50
Nos. 943-952 (9) 68.45 5.85

The 20c is redrawn; clouds almost eliminated and other slight variations.

"F.S.T.S.E." Emblem
A231

Academy of Medicine Emblem
A232

1964, Feb. 15

954 A231 20c red orange & dark brown 40 10

Issued to commemorate the 25th anniversary (in 1963) of the Civil Service Statute affecting federal employees.

1964, May 18 *Perf. 14* Wmk. 350

955 A232 20c gold & black 40 10

Issued to commemorate the centenary of the National Academy of Medicine.

José Rizal
A233

View of Zacatecas
A234

Design: 40c, Miguel Lopez de Legaspi, Spanish navigator.

1964, Nov. 10 Photo. ***Perf. 14***

956 A233 20c dk. bl. & dp. grn. 50 15
957 " 40c dk. bl. & brt. vio. 60 15

Issued to honor 400 years of Mexican—Philippine friendship. See Nos. C300–C301.

1964, Nov. 10 **Wmk. 350**

958 A234 40c slate grn. & red 55 15

Issued to commemorate the 50th anniversary of the capture of Zacatecas.

Col. Gregorio Mendez
A235

Morelos Theater, Aguascalientes
A236

1964, Nov. 10

959 A235 40c grayish black & dk. brown 50 12

Issued to commemorate the centenary of the Battle of Jahuactal, Tabasco.

1965, Jan. 9 Photo. ***Perf. 14***

960 A236 20c dull claret & dark gray 30 10

Issued to commemorate the 50th anniversary of the Aguascalientes Convention, Oct. 1–Nov. 9, 1914.

Andrés Manuel del Río
A237

1965, Feb. 19 ***Perf. 14*** **Wmk. 350**

961 A237 30c gray 35 10

Issued to commemorate the bicentenary of the birth of Andrés Manuel del Rio, founder of the National School of Mining and discoverer of vanadium.

José Morelos and Constitution
A238

1965, Apr. 24 Photo. ***Perf. 14***

962 A238 40c bright green & dark red brown 50 15

Issued to commemorate the sesquicentennial (in 1964) of the first Mexican constitution.

Trees
A239

1965, July 14 ***Perf. 14*** **Wmk. 350**

963 A239 20c blue & green 25 10

Issued to commemorate Tree Day, July 8.

ICY Emblem
A240

1965, Sept. 13 Photogravure

964 A240 40c olive gray & slate green 35 10

International Cooperation Year, 1965.

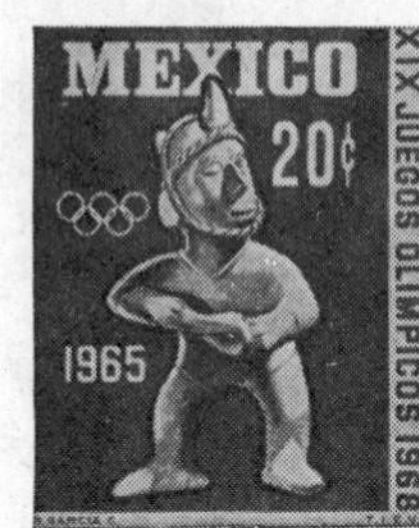

Athlete with Sling, Clay Figure
A241

Design: 40c, Batter. Clay figures on 20c and 40c found in Colima, period 300–650 A.D.

1965, Dec. 17 ***Perf. 14*** **Wmk. 350**

965 A241 20c olive & vio. bl. 1.00 15
966 " 40c pink & black 35 10

Issued to publicize the 19th Olympic Games, Mexico, 1968. For souvenir sheet see No. C310a. See also Nos. C309–C311.

José Morelos by Diego Rivera
A242

Emiliano Zapata
A243

1965, Dec. 22

967 A242 20c lt. vio. bl. & blk. 45 12

Issued to publicize the 19th Olympic of the birth of José Maria Morelos y Pavon (1765–1815), priest and patriot in 1810 revolution against Spain.

1966, Jan. 10 Photogravure

Design: 20c, Corn, cotton, bamboo, wheat and cow.

968 A243 20c carmine rose 35 7
969 " 40c black 40 12

Issued to commemorate the 50th anniversary of the Agrarian Reform Law.

Mexican Postal Service Emblem
A244

Bartolomé de Las Casas
A245

1966, June 24 ***Perf. 14*** **Wmk. 300**

970 A244 40c brt. grn. & black 35 10

Issued to publicize the Congress of the Postal Union of the Americas and Spain, UPAE, Mexico City, June 24–July 23. See also Nos. C314–C315.

1966, Aug. 1 Photo. **Wmk. 300**

971 A245 20c black & buff 35 10

Issued to commemorate the 400th anniversary of the death of Bartolomé de Las Casas (1474–1566), "Apostle of the Indies."

Mechanical Drawings and Cogwheels
A246

1966, Aug. 15 Photo. ***Perf. 14***

972 A246 20c gray & green 35 10

Issued to commemorate the 50th anniversary of the founding of the School of Mechanical and Electrical Engineering (ESIME).

FAO Emblem
A247

1966, Sept. 30 ***Perf. 14*** **Wmk. 300**

973 A247 40c green 35 10

Issued to publicize the International Rice Year sponsored by the United Nations Food and Agricultural Organization.

Running and Jumping, by Diego Rivera
A248

Design: 40c, Wrestling.

1966, Oct. 15 Size: 35x21mm.

974 A248 20c vio. bl. & blk. 75 15
975 " 40c dark carmine 35 10
a. Souv. sheet 2.00 2.00

Issued to publicize the 19th Olympic Games, Mexico City, D.F., 1968. No. 975a contains 2 imperf. stamps similar to Nos. 974–975 with simulated perforations, black marginal inscription and control number. Size: 100x60mm. Sold for 90c.

See also Nos. C318–C320.

First Page of Constitution
A249

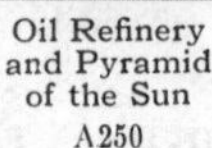

Oil Refinery and Pyramid of the Sun
A250

Photogravure

1967, Feb. 5 ***Perf. 14*** **Wmk. 300**

976 A249 40c black 45 15

Issued to commemorate the 50th anniversary of the Constitution. See No. C322.

1967, Apr. 2 ***Perf. 14*** **Wmk. 300**

977 A250 40c lt. blue & black 35 10

Issued to publicize the 7th International Oil Congress, Mexico City, September, 1967.

Nayarit Indian
A251

Photogravure

1967, May 1 ***Perf. 14*** **Wmk. 300**

978 A251 20c pale grn. & blk. 40 10

50th anniversary of Nayarit State.

Degollado Theater, Guadalajara
A252

Photogravure

1967, June 12 ***Perf. 14*** **Wmk. 300**

979 A252 40c pink & black 50 15

Issued to commemorate the centenary of the founding of the Degollado Theater, Guadalajara.

Mexican Eagle over Imperial Crown
A253

Perf. 10x10½

1967, June 19 Litho. **Wmk. 350**

980 A253 20c black & ocher 40 12

Issued to commemorate the centenary of the victory of the Mexican republican forces and of the execution of Emperor Maximilian I.

Canoeing
A254

Designs: 40c, Basketball. 50c, Hockey. 80c, Bicycling. 2p, Fencing.

Photogravure

1967, Oct. 12 *Perf. 14* Wmk. 300

981 A254 20c blue & black 45 12
982 " 40c brick red & blk. 35 10
983 " 50c brt. yellow green & black 35 10
a. Souv. sheet of 3 2.00 2.00
984 " 80c brt. pur. & black 50 12
985 " 2p orange & black 75 25
a. Souv. sheet of 2 2.75 2.75
Nos. 981–985 (5) 2.40 69

Issued to publicize the 19th Olympic Games, Mexico City, Oct. 12–27, 1968.
No. 983a contains 3 imperf. stamps similar to Nos. 981–983, sold for 1.50p; No. 985a contains 2 imperf. stamps similar to Nos. 984–985, sold for 3.50p. Both sheets have black marginal inscriptions, control numbers and watermark 350. Size: 130x98mm.
See also Nos. 990–995, C328–C331, C335–C338.

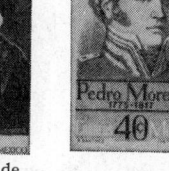

Artemio de Valle-Arizpe
A255

Pedro Moreno
A256

1967, Nov. 1 Photogravure

986 A255 20c brown & slate 45 12

Issued to commemorate the centenary of the Ateneo Fuente, a college at Saltillo, Coahuila.

1967, Nov. 18 *Perf. 14* Wmk. 300

987 A256 40c black & lt. blue 45 12

Issued to commemorate the 150th anniversary of the death of Pedro Moreno (1775–1817), revolutionary leader.

Gabino Barreda
A257

Staircase, Palace of Mining
A258

1968, Jan. 27 Photo. *Perf. 14*

988 A257 40c dk. blue & rose claret 45 10
989 A258 40c blk. & bl. gray 45 12

Issued to commemorate the centenary of the founding of the National Preparatory and Engineering Schools.

Type of Olympic Issue, 1967

Designs: 20c, Wrestling. 40c, Pentathlon. 50c, Water polo. 80c, Gymnastics. 1p, Boxing. 2p, Pistol shoot.

1968, Mar. 21 *Perf. 14* Wmk. 300

990 A254 20c olive & black 45 10
991 " 40c red lilac & black 40 12
992 " 50c brt. grn. & blk. 45 12
a. Souv. sheet of 3 2.00 2.00
993 " 80c brt. pink & blk. 45 15
994 " 1p org. brn. & blk. 2.50 50
995 A254 2p gray & black 2.50 75
a. Souv. sheet of 3 4.00 4.00
Nos. 990–995 (6) 6.75 1.74

Issued to publicize the 19th Olympic Games, Mexico City, Oct. 12–27. No. 992a contains 3 imperf. stamps similar to Nos. 990–992, sold for 1.50p; No. 995a contains 3 imperf. stamps similar to Nos. 993–995, sold for 5p. Both sheets have black marginal inscriptions, control numbers and watermark 350. Size: 105x70mm.
See also Nos. C335–C338.

Map of Mexico, Peace Dove
A259

Arms of Veracruz
A261

Symbols of Cultural Events
A260

Designs: 40c, University City Olympic stadium. 50c, Telecommunications tower. 2p, Sports Palace. 10p, Pyramid of the Sun, Teotihuacan, and Olympic torch.

Photogravure

1968, Oct. *Perf. 14* Wmk. 350

996 A259 20c blue, yel. & grn. 30 10
997 " 40c multicolored 40 12
998 " 50c " 40 12
a. Souv. sheet of 3 6.00 6.00
999 A260 2p multicolored 65 30
1000 " 5p silver & black 2.00 85
a. Souv. sheet of 2 5.00 5.00
1001 A259 10p multicolored 3.00 1.75
Nos. 996–1001 (6) 6.75 3.24

Nos. 996–1000 commemorate the 19th Olympic Games, Mexico City, Oct. 12–27. No. 1001 commemorates the arrival of the Olympic torch in Veracruz.
No. 998a contains 3 imperf. stamps similar to Nos. 996–998. Sold for 1.50p. No. 1000a contains 2 imperf. stamps similar to Nos. 999–1000. Sold for 9p. Sheets have black marginal inscriptions and control numbers. Size of sheets: 105x70 mm.
See also Nos. C340–C344a.

1969, May 20 *Perf. 14* Wmk. 350

1002 A261 40c multicolored 35 10

Issued to commemorate the 450th anniversary of the founding of Veracruz.

Type of 1950–52
Coil Stamps
Photogravure

1969 *Perf. 11 Vert.* Wmk. 300

1003 A189 20c dark blue 80 20
1004 " 40c red orange 1.00 25

Subway Train—A262

1969, Sept. 4 *Perf. 14* Wmk. 350

1005 A262 40c multicolored 45 10

Inauguration of Mexico City subway.

Honeycomb, Bee and ILO Emblem
A263

Gen. Allende, by Diego Rivera
A264

1969, Oct. 18 Photo. *Perf. 14*

1006 A263 40c multicolored 25 8

Issued to commemorate the 50th anniversary of the International Labor Organization.

1969, Nov. 15 *Perf. 14* Wmk. 350

1007 A264 40c multicolored 25 8

Issued to commemorate the bicentenary of the birth of Gen. Ignacio Allende Unzaga (1769–1811), father of Mexican independence.

Tourist Issue

Pyramid of Niches at El Tajin, Veracruz, and Dancers Swinging from Pole
A265

Anthropology Museum, Mexico City
A266

Deer Dance, Sonora
A267

Designs: No. 1010, View of Puerto Vallarta, Jalisco. No. 1011, Puebla Cathedral. No. 1012, Calle Belaunzaran, Guanajuato. No. 1014, Ocotlan Cathedral, Tlaxcala (horiz.).

1969–73 Photogravure Wmk. 350
Multicolored

1008 A265 40c *shown* 55 15
1009 A266 40c " ('70) 55 15
1010 " 40c *Jalisco* ('70) 55 15
1011 " 40c *Puebla* ('70) 55 15
1012 " 40c *Guanajuato* ('70) 55 15

Wmk. 300

1013 A267 40c *shown* ('73) 25 10
1014 " 40c *Tlaxcala* ('73) 25 10
Nos. 1008–1014 (7) 3.25 95

No. 1010 is inscribed "1970" below the design. Copies inscribed "1969" are from an earlier, unissued printing.
See Nos. C354–C358.

Luminescence

Fluorescent stamps include Nos. 1013–1014, 1035, 1038, 1041, 1043–1045, 1047–1050, 1054–1059. (See Luminescence note over No. C527.)

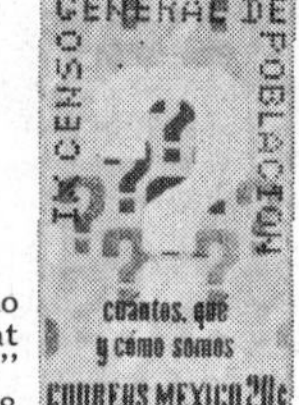

"How Many, Who and What are We?"
A268

Design: 40c, "What, How and How Much do we produce?" (horse's head and symbols of agriculture).

1970, Jan. 26 *Perf. 14* Wmk. 350

1024 A268 20c multicolored 40 10
1025 " 40c blue & multi. 35 10

Issued to publicize the 1970 census.

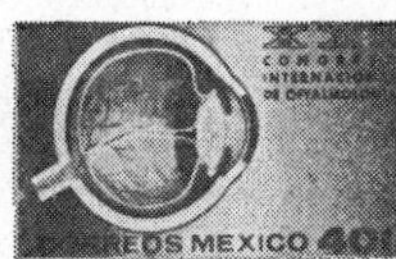

Human Eye and Spectrum
A269

1970, Mar. 8 Photo. Wmk. 350

1026 A269 40c multicolored 20 8

Issued to publicize the 21st International Congress of Ophthalmology, Mexico City, Mar. 8–14.

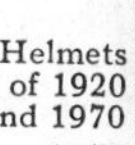

Helmets of 1920 and 1970
A270

1970, Apr. 11 *Perf. 14* Wmk. 350

1027 A270 40c dk. car. rose, blk. & lt. brn. 20 8

50th anniversary of the Military College.

José Maria Pino Suarez
A271

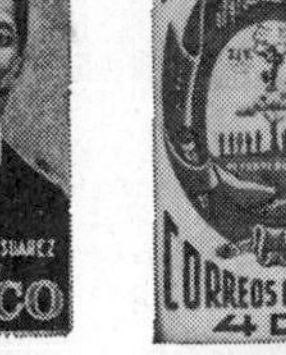

Coat of Arms of Celaya
A272

1970, Apr. 25 Photogravure

1028 A271 40c black & multi. 20 8

Issued to commemorate the centenary of the birth of José Maria Pino Suarez (1869–1913), lawyer, poet and Vice President of Mexico.

1970, Oct. 12 Photo. *Perf. 14*

1029 A272 40c black & multi. 20 8

City of Celaya, 400th anniversary.

Eclipse of Sun
A273

1970, Nov. 11 *Perf. 14* Wmk. 350

1030 A273 40c black & gray 25 8

Total eclipse of the sun, March 7, 1970.

Spheres with Dates 1970–1770
A274

1971, June 26 Photo. *Perf. 14*
1031 A274 40c emerald & blk. 35 8
Bicentenary of National Lottery.

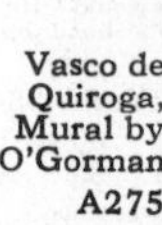

Vasco de Quiroga, Mural by O'Gorman
A275

1971, July 10 Photogravure
1032 A275 40c multicolored 20 8
500th anniversary of the birth of Vasco de Quiroga (1470–1565), Archbishop of Michoacan, founder of hospitals and schools.

Amado Nervo
A276

1971, Aug. 7 *Perf. 14* **Wmk. 350**
1033 A276 40c multicolored 20 8
Centenary of the birth of Amado Nervo (1870–1919), poet.

Waves and Transformer
A277

1971, Oct. 9
1034 A277 40c black, lt. blue & lt. green 30 8
50th anniversary of Mexican radio.

Lazaro Cardenas
A278

1971, Oct. 19 **Wmk. 300**
1035 A278 40c blk. & pale lilac 30 8
Anniversary of the death of Pres. Lazaro Cardenas (1895–1970).

Keyboard and Lara's Signature
A279

1971, Nov. 6 **Wmk. 350**
1036 A279 40c black, buff & pale blue 30 8
In memory of Agustín Lara (1900–1970), composer.

Arms of Monterrey
A280

Cardiology Institute and WHO Emblems
A281

1971, Dec. 18
1037 A280 40c black & multi. 30 8
375th anniversary of the founding of Monterrey.

1972, Apr. 8 **Wmk. 300**
1038 A281 40c multicolored 25 8
"Your heart is your health," World Health Day 1972. See No. C395.

Gaceta de Mexico, Jan. 1, 1722
A282

1972, June 24 **Wmk. 350**
1039 A282 40c multicolored 25 8
250th anniversary of 1st Mexican newspaper.

Lions International Emblem
A283

Sailing Ship Zaragoza
A284

1972, June 28
1040 A283 40c black & multi. 25 8
55th Lions International Convention.

1972, July 1 **Wmk. 360**
1041 A284 40c blue & multi. 25 8
75th anniversary of the Naval School of Veracruz.

Olive Tree and Branch
A285

1972, July 18 *Perf. 14* **Wmk. 350**
1042 A285 40c lt. green, gold & black 25 8
Centenary of Chilpancingo as capital of Guerrero State.

Margarita Maza de Juárez
A286

Design: 40c, Benito Juárez, by Diego Rivera.

1972, Sept. 15 Photo. **Wmk. 300**
1043 A286 20c pink & multi. 25 7
1044 " 40c dp. yel. & multi. 25 8
Nos. 1043–1044, C403–C405 (5) 1.90 72
Centenary of the death of Benito Juárez (1806–1872), revolutionary leader and president of Mexico.

Emperor Justinian I, Mosaic
A287

1972, Sept. 30 **Wmk. 300**
1045 A287 40c multicolored 25 8
Mexican Bar Association, 50th anniversary.

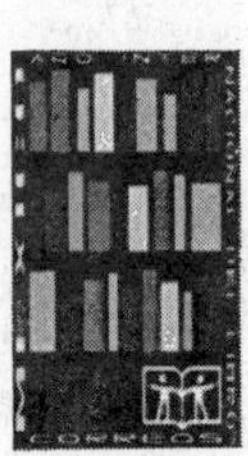

Caravel
A288

Library, Book Year Emblem
A290

Olympic Emblems
A289

1972, Oct. 12 **Wmk. 350**
1046 A288 80c buff, purple & ocher 45 15
Stamp Day of The Americas.

1972, Dec. 9 **Wmk. 300**
1047 A289 40c multicolored 25 8
20th Olympic Games, Munich, Aug. 26–Sept. 11. See Nos. C410–C411.

1972, Dec. 16
1048 A290 40c black & multi. 25 8
International Book Year 1972.

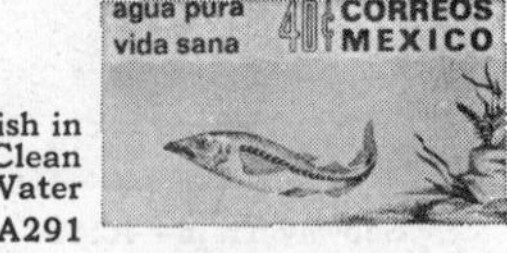

Fish in Clean Water
A291

1972, Dec. 16
1049 A291 40c blk. & lt. blue 25 8
Anti-pollution campaign. See No. C412.

Metlac Railroad Bridge—A292

1973, Feb. 2 *Perf. 14*
1050 A292 40c multicolored 30 8
Centenary of Mexican railroads.

Cadet
A293

1973, Oct. 11 Photo. **Wmk. 300**
1051 A293 40c black & multi. 25 8
Sesquicentennial of Military College.

Madero, by Diego Rivera
A294

Antonio Narro
A295

1973, Nov. 9 *Perf. 14* **Wmk. 350**
1052 A294 40c multicolored 25 8
Centenary of the birth of Pres. Francisco I. Madero (1873–1913).

1973, Nov. 9 Photogravure
1053 A295 40c steel gray 25 8
50th anniversary of the Antonio Narro Agriculture School in Saltillo.

Type of 1950–52

Designs as before.

1973 *Perf. 14* **Unwmkd.**
1054 A189 20c blue violet 1.80 50
1055 " 40c red orange 1.80 50
Fluorescent printing on back (or on front of 40c) consisting of beehive pattern and diagonal inscription.

Hydrocarbon Molecule
A296

Perf. 14

1973, Dec. 7 Photo. **Wmk. 300**
1056 A296 40c blk., dk. carmine & yellow 25 7

Pointing Hand Emblem of Foreign Trade Institute
A297

1974, Jan. 11 Photo. Wmk. 300
1057 A297 40c dk. grn. & black 20 5
Export promotion.

A298

1974, Jan. 18 Litho. Wmk. 300
1058 A298 40c black 10 5
EXMEX 73 Philatelic Exhibition, Cuernavaca, Apr. 7–15. See No. C424.

Manuel M. Ponce at Keyboard
A299

1974, Jan. 18 Photo. Wmk. 300
1059 A299 40c gold & multi. 10 5
Manuel M. Ponce (1882–1948), composer.

Silver Statuette of Mexican Woman
A300

1974, Mar. 23 Photo. *Perf. 14*
1060 A300 40c red & multi. 10 5
First World Silver Fair.

Mariano Azuela
A301

1974, Apr. 10 *Perf. 14* Wmk. 300
1061 A301 40c multicolored 10 5
Mariano Azuela (1873–1952), writer.

Dancing Dogs, Pre-Columbian
A302

1974, Apr. 10
1062 A302 40c multicolored 10 5
6th Traveling Dog Exhibition, Mexico City, Nov. 23–Dec. 1.

Aqueduct, Tepotzotlan—A303

1974, July 10 Photo. Wmk. 300
1063 A303 40c brt. bl. & blk. 10 5
National Engineers' Day, July 1.

Dr. Rodolfo Robles
A304

1974, July 19 *Perf. 14*
1064 A304 40c bister & grn. 10 5
25th anniversary of the World Health Organization (in 1973).

EXFILMEX 74 Emblem
A305

1974, July 26 *Perf. 13x12*
1065 A305 40c buff, grn. & blk. 10 5
EXFILMEX 74, Fifth Inter-American Philatelic Exhibition honoring centenary of Universal Postal Union, Mexico City, Oct. 26–Nov. 3. See No. C429.

Demosthenes
A306

1974, Aug. 2 Photo. *Perf. 14*
1066 A306 20c grn. & brn. 10 5
2nd Spanish-American Congress for Reading and Writing Studies, Mexico City, May 7–14.

Map of Chiapas and Head
A307

1974, Sept. 14 *Perf. 14* Wmk. 300
1067 A307 20c black & green 10 5
Centenary of Chiapas statehood.

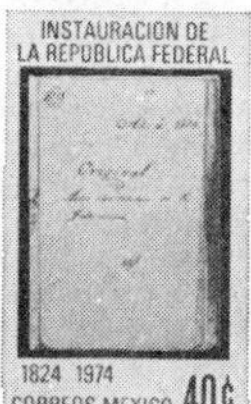

Law of 1824
A308

Sebastian Lerdo de Tejada
A309

1974, Oct. 11 Wmk. 300
1068 A308 40c gray & green 10 5
Sesquicentennial of the establishment of the Federal Republic of Mexico.

1974, Oct. 11 Photogravure
1069 A309 40c blk. & lt. blue 10 5
Centenary of the restoration of the Senate.

UPU Monument, Bern
A310

1974, Dec. 13 *Perf. 14* Wmk. 300
1070 A310 40c ultra. & org. brn. 10 5
Centenary of Universal Postal Union. See Nos. C437–C438.

Types of 1950–56

Designs (as 1951–56 issues): 60c, Ponciano Arriaga. 2p, Convent, Morelos. 2.30p, Guillermo Prieto. 3p, Modernistic church, Nuevo Leon. 50p, Benito Juarez.

Perf. 14

1975 Photogravure Wmk. 300

1071	A200	60c red lilac	3.75	30
1072	A189	80c green	40	10
1075	A200	2.30p dp. vio. blue	75	15
1076	A189	3p brick red	80	15
1081	"	50p org. & grn.	10.00	4.00
		Nos. 1071-1081 (5)	15.70	4.70

Gov. José Maria Mora
A312

1975, Feb. 21 Photo. Wmk. 300
1084 A312 20c yellow & multi. 3 3
Sesquicentennial (in 1974) of establishment of the State of Mexico.

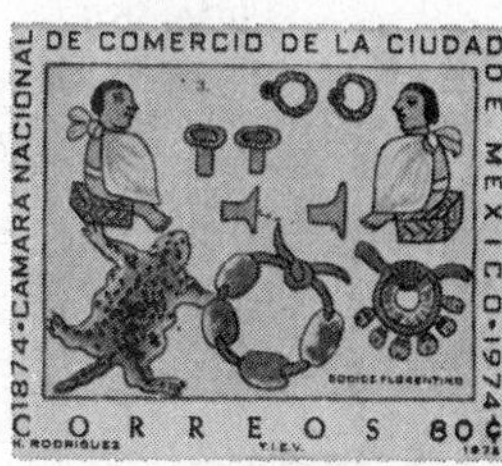

Merchants with Pre-Columbian Goods—A313

1975, Apr. 18 Photo. Unwmkd.
1085 A313 80c multicolored 8 5
Centenary (in 1974) of the National Chamber of Commerce in Mexico City. Design from Florentine Codex.

Juan Aldama, by Diego Rivera
A314

1975, June 6 *Perf. 14*
1086 A314 80c multicolored 8 5
Juan Aldama (1774–1811), officer and patriot, birth bicentenary.

Indians and Eagle on Cactus Destroying Serpent, from Duran Codex
A315

1975, Aug. 1 Photo. Unwmkd.
1087 A315 80c multicolored 8 5
650th anniversary of Tenochtitlan (Mexico City).

Julián Carrillo
A316

Academy Emblem
A317

1975, Sept. 12 Photo. Unwmkd.
1088 A316 80c bright green & red brown 8 5
Julián Carrillo (1875–1965), violinist and composer, birth centenary.

1975, Sept. 13 *Perf. 14*

1089 A317 80c brown & ocher 8 5

Centenary of Mexican Academy of Languages.

Types of 1950–56

Designs (as 1950–56 issues): 40c, Stone head, Tabasco. 50c, Carved head, Veracruz. 60c, Ponciano Arriaga. 70c, Francisco Zarco. 80c, Indian dancer, Michoacan. 1p, Convent and carved head, Hidalgo. 2p, Convent, Morelos. 3p, Modernistic Church, Nuevo Leon. 5p, Galleon, arms of Campeche. 10p, Francisco I. Madero. 20p, Modern building, Mexico City.

1975–76 **Photogravure** **Unwmkd.**

No.	Type	Description	Unused	Used
1090	A189	40c orange	20	6
1091	"	50c blue	25	6
1092	A200	60c red lilac	30	7
1093	"	70c violet blue	30	7
1094	A189	80c green	30	8
1095	"	1p olive green	35	8
1096	"	2p scarlet	75	15
1097	"	3p brick red	1.10	20
1099	"	5p gray bl. & grn.	1.50	25
1101	"	10p green & dp. ultra. ('76)	3.25	75
1102	"	20p lilac & black ('76)	6.50	1.50
		Nos. 1090–1102 (11)	14.80	3.27

University of Guadalajara—A318

1975, Oct. 1 **Photo.** *Perf. 14*

1107 A318 80c multicolored 8 5

University of Guadalajara, 50th anniversary.

Road Workers A139

1975, Oct. 17 **Photo.** **Unwmkd.**

1108 A319 80c gray green, grn. & black 8 5

50 years of road building for progress.

Pistons—A320

Designs (Export Emblem and): 5c, Steel pipes. 20c, Chemistry flasks. 40c, Cup of coffee. 80c, Meat cuts marked on steer. 1p, Electrical conductor. 2p, Sea shell. 3p, Men's shoes. 5p, Minerals (chemical formula). 10p, Tequila production. 20p, Wrought iron.

Perf. 14

1975–78 **Photo.** **Unwmkd.**

No.	Type	Description	Unused	Used
1109	A320	5c gray blue ('77)	5	4
1111	"	20c black ('76)	6	4
1114	"	40c dk. brown ('76)	6	4
1115	"	50c dull blue	6	4
		a. 50c slate blue	6	4
1118	A320	80c brt. carmine	8	6
		a. Perf. 11	8	6
1119	A320	1p violet blue & orange ('78)	10	6
1121	"	2p brt. grn. & blue	20	10
1123	"	3p brown	30	12
1125	A320	5p gray olive ('78)	50	15
1126	"	10p dark & light green ('78)	1.00	30
1128	"	20p black ('78)	2.00	60
		Nos. 1109–1128 (11)	4.41	1.55

See No. 1170.

Aguascalientes Cathedral A323

Jaime Torres Bodet A324

1975, Nov. 28

1140 A323 50c bl. grn. & black 6 3

400th anniversary of Aguascalientes.

1975, Nov. 28

1141 A324 80c blue & brown 8 5

Jaime Torres Bodet (1920–1974), writer, director general of UNESCO (1958–1962).

Allegory, by José Clemente Orozco—A325

1975, Dec. 9 *Perf. 14*

1142 A325 80c multicolored 8 5

Sesquicentennial of Supreme Court.

The Death of Cuauhtemoc, by Chavez Morado A326

1975, Dec. 12 **Photogravure**

1143 A326 80c multicolored 8 5

450th anniversary of the death of Cuauhtemoc (1495?–1525), last Aztec emperor.

Netzahualcoyotl (Water God)—A327

1976, Jan. 9 *Perf. 14* **Unwmkd.**

1144 A327 80c bl. & vio. blue 8 5

50th anniversary of Mexican irrigation projects.

Arch, León A328

1976, Jan. 20

1145 A328 80c dark brown & ocher 8 5

400th anniversary of Léon, Guanajuato.

Forest Fire A329

1976, July 8 **Photo.** *Perf. 14*

1146 A329 80c blk., grn. & red 8 5

Prevent fires!

Hat and Scout Emblem A330

Exhibition Emblem A331

1976, Aug. 24 **Photo.** **Unwmkd.**

1147 A330 80c olive & red brown 8 5

Mexican Boy Scout Association, 50th anniversary.

1976, Sept. 2

1148 A331 80c black, red & green 8 5

Mexico Today and Tomorrow Exhibition.

New Building, Military College A332

1976, Sept. 13 *Perf. 14*

1149 A332 50c red brown & ocher 6 3

Military College, new installations.

Dr. Ricardo Vertiz A333

1976, Sept. 24 **Photo.** *Perf. 14*

1150 A333 80c blk. & reddish brown 8 5

Our Lady of Light Ophthalmological Hospital, centenary.

National Basilica of Guadeloupe A334

1976, Oct. 12

1151 A334 50c black & ocher 6 3

Inauguration of the new National Basilica of Our Lady of Guadeloupe.

Listings of stamps issued since this Catalogue went to press will be found in Scott's Monthly Stamp Journal.

"40" and Emblem A335

1976, Oct. 28 **Photo.** *Perf. 14*

1152 A335 80c blk., lt. green & carmine 8 5

National Polytechnic Institute, 40th anniversary.

Blast Furnace A336

1976, Nov. 4

1153 A336 50c multicolored 6 3

Inauguration of the Lazaro Cardenas Steel Mill, Las Truchas.

Saltillo Cathedral A337

Electrification A338

1977, July 25 **Photo.** *Perf. 14*

1154 A337 80c yel. & dk. brn. 14 5

400th anniversary of the founding of Saltillo.

1977, Aug. 14 **Photo.** *Perf. 14*

1155 A338 80c multicolored 8 5

40 years of Mexican development program.

Flags of Spain and Mexico A339

1977, Oct. 8 **Photo.** **Wmk. 300**

No.	Type	Description	Unused	Used
1156	A339	50c multicolored	6	3
1157	"	80c "	8	5
		Nos. 1156–1157, C537–C539 (5)	93	54

Resumption of diplomatic relations with Spain.

Aquiles Serdan
A340

1977, Nov. 18 Photo. *Perf. 14*

158 A340 80c lt. & dk. green & black 8 5

Aquiles Serdan (1877–1910), martyr of the revolution, birth centenary.

Poinsettia
A341

1977, Dec. 2 *Perf. 14* **Wmk. 300**

159 A341 50c multicolored 6 3

Christmas 1977.

Old and
New Telephones
A342

1978, Mar. 15 Photo. *Perf. 14*

160 A342 80c salmon & maroon 8 5

Centenary of first telephone in Mexico.

Oil
Derrick
A343

1978, Mar. 18

1161 A343 80c deep orange & maroon 8 5

40th anniversary of nationalization of oil industry. See Nos. C556–C557.

Institute
Emblem
A344

1978, July 21 Photo. *Perf. 14*

1162 A344 80c blue & black 8 5

Pan-American Institute for Geography and History, 50th anniversary. See Nos. C574–C575.

Scott's editorial staff cannot undertake to identify, authenticate or appraise stamps and postal markings.

Dahlias
A345

Decorations
and
Candles
A346

Design: 80c, Frangipani.

1978, Sept. 29 Photo. **Wmk. 300**

1163 A345 50c multicolored 5 3

1164 " 80c " 8 5

1978, Nov. 22 Photo. *Perf. 14*

1165 A346 50c multicolored 6 3

Christmas 1978.

Export Type of 1975

Perf. 14

1979 Photo. **Wmk. 300**

1170 A320 80c brt. carmine 8 6

Hermosillo
Coat of Arms
A347

Photogravure

1979, Apr. 26 *Perf. 14* **Wmk. 300**

1177 A347 80c multicolored 8 5

Centenary of Hermosillo, Sonora.

SEMI-POSTAL STAMPS.

Regular Issue of 1916

Surcharged ✚ 3 ¢ in Red.

1918, Dec. 25 *Perf. 12* **Unwmkd.**

B1 A72 5c+3c ultra. 12.50 10.00

Rouletted.

B2 A73 10c+5c blue 12.50 10.00

AIR POST STAMPS.

Eagle
AP1

Engraved

1922–29 *Perf. 12* **Unwmkd.**

C1 AP1 50c blue & red brown 60.00 32.50
a. 50c dark blue & claret ('29) 90.00 80.00

Wmkd. CORREOS MEXICO. (156)

1927-29

C2 AP1 50c dark blue & red brown 50 25
a. 50c dark blue and claret ('29) 50 25
b. Vertical strip of 3, imperf. between 2000.00

1928

C3 AP1 25c brown carmine & gray brown 40 15
C4 " 25c dark green & gray brown 40 20

On May 3rd, 1929, certain proofs or essays were sold at the post office in Mexico, D. F. They were printed in different colors from those of the regularly issued stamps. There were seven varieties perforated and two imperforate and a total of 225 copies. They were sold with the understanding that they were for collections but the buyers used the majority of them on air mail sent out that day.

Capt. Emilio Carranza and his Airplane "México Excelsior"
AP2

1929, June 19

C5 AP2 5c olive green & sepia 80 50
C6 " 10c sepia & brown red 1.00 60
C7 " 15c violet & dark green 2.25 1.10
C8 " 20c brown & black 1.00 75
C9 " 50c brown red & black 2.25 2.00
C10 " 1p black & brown 5.00 2.50
Nos. C5–C10 (6) 12.30 7.45

First anniversary of death of Capt. Emilio Carranza (1905–1928).

Coat of Arms and Airplane
AP3

1929-34 *Perf. 11½, 12.*

C11 AP3 10c violet 25 15
C12 " 15c carmine 1.10 20
C13 " 20c brown olive 7.50 18
C14 " 30c gray black 25 25
C15 " 35c blue green 25 25
a. Imperf. (pair) 450.00
C16 " 50c red brn. ('34) 1.00 65
C17 " 1p black & dark blue 1.00 65
C18 AP3 5p claret & deep blue 4.25 3.50
C19 " 10p violet & olive brown 7.00 6.50
Nos. C11–C19 (9) 22.60 12.33

1930-32 ***Rouletted 13, 13½.***

C20 AP3 5c light blue ('32) 20 7
C21 " 10c violet 20 6
C22 " 15c carmine 30 5
a. 15c rose carmine 35 5
C23 " 20c brown olive 60 5
a. 20c brown 50 5
b. 20c yellow brown 50 8
C24 " 25c violet 75 65
C25 " 50c red brown 70 55
Nos. C20–C25 (6) 2.75 1.43

Trial impressions of No. C20 were printed in orange but were never sold at post offices.

See also Nos. C62–C64, C75.

Plane over Plaza, Mexico City
AP4

1929, Dec. 10 *Perf. 12* **Wmk. 156**

C26 AP4 20c black violet 1.00 75
C27 " 40c slate green 75.00 75.00

Aviation Week, Dec. 10–16.

No. C21 Over-printed in Red: **Primer Congreso Nacional de Turismo. México. Abril 20-27 de 1930.**

1930, Apr. 20 ***Rouletted 13, 13½***

C28 AP3 10c violet 1.50 1.10

Issued to commemorate the National Tourism Congress at Mexico, D. F., April 20–27, 1930.

Nos. C5 and C7 Overprinted: **HABILITADO 1930**

1930, Sept. 1 ***Perf. 12***

C29 AP2 5c olive green & sepia 3.00 3.00
a. Double ovpt. 150.00
C30 " 15c violet & dark green 5.00 5.00

Nos. C5 to C10 Overprinted: **HABILITADO Aéreo 1930-1931**

1930, Dec. 18

C31 AP2 5c olive green & sepia 4.50 4.00
C32 " 10c sepia & brn. red 2.50 2.00
C33 " 15c violet & dark green 4.50 4.00
C34 " 20c brown & black 5.00 4.00
C35 " 50c brn. red & blk. 8.50 7.00
C36 " 1p black & brown 2.50 1.75
Nos. C31–C36 (6) 27.50 22.75

Plane over Flying Field—AP5

1931, May 15 **Engraved.** ***Perf. 12***

C37 AP5 25c lake 2.50 2.50
a. Imperf. (pair) 35.00 35.00

Issued to commemorate the Aeronautic Exhibition of the Aero Club of Mexico. Of the 25c face value, 15c paid air mail postage and 10c went to a fund to improve the Mexico City airport.

Nos. C13 and C23 Surcharged in Red: **HABILITADO Quince centavos**

1931

C38 AP3 15c on 20c brown olive 20.00 20.00

Rouletted 13, 13½.

C39 AP3 15c on 20c brown olive 20 8
a. Inverted surcharge 40.00
b. Double surcharge 40.00
c. Pair, one without surcharge 150.00

Nos. C5 to C9 Overprinted: **HABILITADO AEREO-1932**

1932, July 13 ***Perf. 12***

C40 AP2 5c olive green & sepia 3.00 2.50
a. Imperf. (pair) 75.00 75.00
C41 " 10c sepia & brown red 3.00 2.50
a. Imperf. (pair) 75.00 75.00
C42 " 15c violet & dark green 3.00 2.50
a. Imperf. (pair) 75.00 75.00
C43 " 20c brown & black 3.50 3.00
a. Imperf. (pair) 75.00 75.00
C44 " 50c brown red & black 25.00 25.00
a. Imperf. (pair) 75.00 75.00
Nos. C40–C44 (5) 37.50 35.50

Issued to commemorate the fourth anniversary of the death of Capt. Emilio Carranza.

No. C37 Surcharged

1932

C45 AP5 20c on 25c lake 50 30
a. Imperf. (pair) 35.00 35.00

No. C13 Surcharged

C46 AP3 30c on 20c brown olive 17.50 17.50

Similar Surcharge on Nos. C3 and C4.

C47 AP1 40c on 25c brown carmine & gray brown 60 75
a. Inverted surcharge 500.00
C48 AP1 40c on 25c dark green & gray brown 25.00 25.00

Surcharged on Nos. C23 and C24.

Rouletted 13, 13½.

C49 AP3 30c on 20c brown olive 25 12
a. Inverted surcharge 1500.00
C50 AP3 80c on 25c dull vio. 1.25 1.00

Palace of Fine Arts—AP6

1933, Oct. 1 **Engraved.** ***Perf. 12***

C51 AP6 20c dark red & dull violet 3.00 1.25
C52 " 30c dark brown & dull violet 6.00 4.00
C53 " 1p greenish black & dull violet 55.00 55.00

Issued in commemoration of the twenty-first International Congress of Statistics and the centenary of the Mexican Society of Geography and Statistics.

National University Issue.

Nevado de Toluca—AP7

Pyramids of the Sun and Moon
AP8

View of Ajusco—AP9

Volcanoes Popocatepetl and Iztaccíhuatl
AP10

Bridge over Tepecayo—AP11

Chapultepec Fortress
AP12

Orizaba Volcano (Citlaltépetl)
AP13

Mexican Girl and Aztec Calendar Stone
AP14

Perf. 10½

1934, Sept. 1 **Wmk. 156**

C54 AP7 20c orange 5.00 3.00
C55 AP8 30c red lilac & violet 9.00 6.00
C56 AP9 50c olive green & bistre brown 10.00 7.50

C57 AP10 75c black & yel. grn. 11.00 9.00
C58 AP11 1p black & peacock blue 4.00 12.00
C59 AP12 5p bistre brown & dark blue 85.00 85.00
C60 AP13 10p indigo & maroon 175.00 175.00
C61 AP14 20p brn. & brn. lake 1000.00 1000.00
Nos. C54-C61 (8) 1309.00 1297.50

Type of 1929-34.

1934-35 ***Perf. 10½, 10½x10.***

C62 AP3 20c olive green 35 15
a. 20c slate 100.00 75.00
C63 AP3 30c slate 40 35
C64 " 50c red brn. ('35) 1.75 1.75

Symbols of Air Service
AP15

Tláloc, God of Water (Quetzalcóatl Temple)
AP16

Orizaba Volcano (Citlaltépetl)
AP17

"Eagle Man"—AP18

Symbolical of Flight
AP19

Aztec Bird-Man
AP20

Natives Looking at Airplane and Orizaba Volcano
AP23

Allegory of Flight and Pyramid of the Sun—AP21

"Eagle Man" and Airplanes
AP22

Imprint: "Oficina Impresora de Hacienda-Mexico."

Perf. 10½x10, 10x10½

1934-35 **Wmk. 156**

C65 AP15 5c black 30 8
C66 AP16 10c red brown 50 10
C67 AP17 15c gray green 60 15
a. Imperf., pair 275.00
C68 AP18 20c brn. carmine 30 6
a. 20c lake 1.00 6
C69 AP19 30c brown olive 35 8
C70 AP20 40c blue ('35) 85 8
C71 AP21 50c green 1.50 10
a. Imperf., pair 175.00
C72 AP22 1p gray green & red brown 1.50 10
C73 AP23 5p dk. car. & blk. 4.00 50
Nos. C65-C73 (9) 9.90 1.25

The 15c, 20c and 50c exist imperforate. See also Nos. C76A, C80, C81, C132-C140, C170-177A.

No. C68 Overprinted in Violet

AMELIA EARHART
VUELO DE BUENA VOLUNTAD
MEXICO
1935

1935, April 16

C74 AP18 20c lake *3500.00 3500.00*

Issued to commemorate Amelia Earhart's good-will flight to Mexico.

Arms-Plane Type of 1929-34.
Wmkd. SECRETARIA DE HACIENDA MEXICO. (248)

1935 ***Perf. 10½x10***

C75 AP3 30c slate 5.00 5.00

Francisco I. Madero
AP24

1935, Nov. 20 **Wmk. 156**

C76 AP24 20c scarlet 30 15

Issued to commemorate the 25th anniversary of the Plan of San Luis. See also No. C76B.

Eagle Man Type of 1934-35.
Wmkd. Lines and SECRETARIA DE HACIENDA MEXICO. (260)

1936

C76A AP18 20c lake *4000.00* 75.00

Madero Type of 1935.

C76B AP24 20c scarlet *8500.00*

Tasquillo Bridge—AP25

Corona River Bridge
AP26

Bridge on Nuevo Laredo Highway
AP27

Photogravure.

1936, July 1 ***Perf. 14*** **Wmk. 248**

C77 AP25 10c slate blue & light blue 25 15
C78 AP26 20c dull violet & orange 30 15
C79 AP27 40c dark blue & dark green 70 50

Opening of Nuevo Laredo Highway.

Eagle Man Type of 1934-35.

Perf. 10½x10

1936, June 18 **Engr.** **Unwmkd.**

C80 AP18 20c brown carmine 2.75 2.75

Imprint:
"Talleres de Imp. de Est. y Valores-Mexico"
Photogravure.

1937 ***Perf. 14.*** **Wmk. 156**

C81 AP18 20c rose red 60 5
a. 20c brn. carmine 60 5
b. 20c dark carmine 60 5
c. Imperf. (pair) 10.00

There are two sizes of watermark 156. No. C81c was not regularly issued.

Cavalryman—AP28

Early Biplane over Mountains.
AP29

Venustiano Carranza on Horseback
AP30

1938, Mar. 26

C82 AP28 20c orange red & blue 35 20
C83 AP29 40c blue & orange red 55 30
C84 AP30 1p blue & bistre brown 3.50 2.25

Plan of Guadalupe, 25th anniversary.

The Zócalo and Cathedral, Mexico City—AP31

Designs: Nos. C87, C88, Reconstructed edifices of Chichén Itzá. Nos. C89, C90, View of Acapulco.

1938, July 1

C85 AP31 20c carmine rose 50 25
C86 " 20c purple 10.00 8.00
C87 " 40c bright green 6.00 4.00
C88 " 40c dark green 6.00 4.00
C89 " 1p light blue 6.00 4.00
C90 " 1p slate blue 6.00 4.00
Nos. C85-C90 (6) 34.50 24.25

16th International Congress of Planning and Housing.

Statue of José María Morelos
AP34

CORREOS MEXICO-1939 AEREO
20 CENT
TULSA OKLA
CONMEMORATIVO

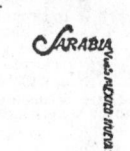

Statue of Pioneer Woman, Ponca City, Oklahoma
AP35

1939 **Engraved** ***Perf. 10½***

C91 AP34 20c green 1.00 50
C92 " 40c red violet 2.50 1.25
C93 " 1p violet brown & carmine 2.00 1.00

Issued to commemorate the New York World's Fair. Released in New York May 2, in Mexico May 24.

Type of 1939 Overprinted in Cerise

SARABIA

1939, May 23

C93A AP34 20c blue & red 350.00 350.00

Issued for the flight of Francisco Sarabia from Mexico City to New York on May 25.

1939, May 17

C94 AP35 20c gray brown 1.00 40
C95 " 40c slate green 1.75 1.25
C96 " 1p violet 1.65 90

Tulsa World Philatelic Convention.

First Engraving Made in Mexico, 1544
AP36

First Work of Legislation Printed in America, 1563
AP37

Designs: 1p, Reproduction of oldest preserved Mexican printing.

Wmkd. CORREOS MEXICO. (156)

1939, Sept. 7 Engraved. *Perf. 10½*

C97 AP36 20c slate blue 20 7
a. Unwmkd. 30.00 10.00
C98 AP37 40c slate green 55 15
a. Imperf. (pair) 400.00
C99 " 1p dk. brn. & car. 1.00 65

Issued in commemoration of the 400th anniversary of printing in Mexico.

Transportation—AP39

Designs: 40c, Finger counting and factory. 1p, "Seven Censuses."

Photogravure

1939, Oct. 2 *Perf. 12x13, 13x12*

C100 AP39 20c dark blue & blue 75 20
C101 " 40c red orange & orange 75 25
a. Unwmkd. 50.00 25.00
C102 " 1p indigo & violet blue 1.80 75

National Census of 1939–40.

Penny Black Type of Regular Issue, 1940

1940, May *Perf. 14*

C103 A140 5c black & dark green 1.00 60
C104 " 10c bistre brown & deep blue 90 25
C105 " 20c carmine & blue violet 40 10
C106 " 1p carmine & chocolate 5.00 4.50
C107 " 5p gray green & red brown 70.00 67.50
Nos. C103–C107 (5) 77.30 72.95

Centenary of the postage stamp. Nos. C103–C106 were issued May 2; No. C107, May 15.

Part of Original College at Pátzcuaro—AP43

College at Morelia (18th Century) AP44

College at Morelia (1940) AP45

1940, July 15 Engraved. *Perf. 10½*

C108 AP43 20c bright green 50 15
C109 AP44 40c orange 60 20
C110 AP45 1p dark purple, red brn. & orange 1.40 90

Issued in commemoration of the 400th anniversary of the founding of the National College of San Nicolas de Hidalgo.

Pirate Ship—AP46

Designs: 40c, Castle of San Miguel. 1p, Temple of San Francisco.

Photogravure.

1940, Aug. 7 *Perf. 12x13, 13x12*

C111 AP46 20c red brown & bistre brn. 1.15 45
C112 " 40c black & slate green 1.40 50
C113 " 1p violet blue & black 3.75 2.00

400th anniversary of Campeche.

Inauguration Type of Regular Issue, 1940

1940, Dec. 1 *Perf. 12x13*

C114 A146 20c gray black & red orange 1.75 70
C115 " 40c chestnut brown & dark slate green 2.25 1.25
C116 " 1p bright violet blue & rose 3.50 1.50

Issued in commemoration of the inauguration of President Manuel Avila Camacho.

Tower of the Convent of the Nuns—AP50

Casa de Montejo—AP51

Campanile of Cathedral at Merída—AP52

1942, Jan. 2 *Perf. 14*

C117 AP50 20c Prussian blue 1.50 50
C118 AP51 40c greenish black (C) 2.25 1.00
a. Without overprint 6.00 6.00
C119 AP52 1p carmine 2.25 1.25

400th anniversary of Merída.
No. C118 bears the overprint "Servicio Aereo" in carmine.

Church of Zapopán—AP53

Our Lady of Guadalupe Church AP54

Guadalajara Arms—AP55

1942, Feb. 11 Engr. *Perf. 10½x10*

C120 AP53 20c green & blk. 2.00 75
C121 AP54 40c olive & yellow green 2.25 1.00
C122 AP55 1p purple & sepia 2.00 1.15

400th anniversary of Guadalajara.

Astrophysics Type of Regular Issue, 1942

Designs: 20c, Spiral Galaxy NGC 4594. 40c, Planetary Nebula in Lyra. 1p, Russell Diagrams.

1942, Feb. 17 Photo. *Perf. 12x13*

C123 A154 20c dark green & indigo 13.50 2.00
C124 " 40c carmine lake & indigo 11.50 3.50
C125 " 1p orange & black 11.50 4.00

Issued in commemoration of the Astrophysics Congress and the inauguration of an observatory at Tonanzintla, February 17, 1942.

Corn AP59

Designs: 40c, Coffee. 1p, Bananas.

1942, July 1

C126 AP59 20c green 2.00 50
C127 " 40c brown 1.50 50
C128 " 1p violet 2.75 1.35

Issued in commemoration of the 2nd Inter-American Agricultural Conference.

View of San Miguel de Allende—AP62

Designs: 40c, Birthplace of Allende. 1p, Church of Our Lady of Health.

1943, May 18 *Perf. 14*

C129 AP62 20c dk. slate green 1.10 60
C130 " 40c purple 1.50 60
C131 " 1p deep carmine 2.60 1.50

Issued to commemorate the 400th anniversary of the founding of San Miguel de Allende.

Types of 1934-35.

Wmkd. "S. H. C. P. MEXICO" and Eagle in Circle. (272)

1944 Photogravure.

C132 AP18 20c brown carmine 75 15

Perf. 10½x10

1944-46 Engraved Wmk. 272

C133 AP15 5c black 40 6
C134 AP16 10c red brn. ('45) 1.10 6
C135 AP17 15c gray green ('45) 75 7
C136 AP19 30c brown olive ('45) 11.00 60
C137 AP20 40c gray bl. ('45) 1.00 20
C138 AP21 50c green 75 15
C139 AP22 1p gray green & red brown ('45) 3.50 40
C140 AP23 5p dark carmine & black ('46) 4.00 1.00
Nos. C133–C140 (8) 22.50 2.54

Symbol of Flight AP65

Microphone, Book and Camera AP66

1944 Photogravure *Perf. 14*

C141 AP65 25c chestnut brown 30 12

See also No. C185.

1944, Nov. 8 Wmk. 272

C142 AP66 25c dull slate green 50 12

Issued to commemorate the third Book Fair.

Globe-in-Hands Type of Regular Issue, 1945

1945, Feb. 27 *Perf. 12x13*

C143 A166 25c red orange 30 10
C144 " 1p bright green 45 30
C145 " 5p indigo 2.50 2.00
C146 " 10p bright rose 6.00 3.75
C147 " 20p brt. vio. bl. 10.00 10.00
Nos. C143–C147 (5) 19.25 16.15

Issued to commemorate the Inter-American Conference held at Chapultepec, February 1945.

Theater Type of Regular Issue, 1945

1945, July 27

C148 A167 30c slate & olive 20 10
C149 " 1p slate & lilac 40 40
C150 " 5p slate & black 3.00 1.50
C151 " 10p slate & light ultramarine 5.00 3.25
C152 " 20p black & gray green 8.50 7.00
Nos. C148–C152 (5) 17.10 12.25

Issued to commemorate the reconstruction of the Peace Theater (Teatro de la Paz), San Luis Potosi.

Blindfold Type of Regular Issue, 1945

1945, Nov. 21

C153 A169 30c slate green 20 20
C154 " 1p brown red 40 30
C155 " 5p red brown & pale blue 3.00 1.50
C156 " 10p slate black & pale lilac 5.00 3.50

C157 A169 20p green & light brown 16.00 15.00
Nos. C153–C157 (5) 24.60 20.50

Issued to publicize the National Education Campaign.

Torch, Laurel and Flag-decorated ONU
AP70

1946, Apr. 10

C158 AP70 30c chocolate 20 15
C159 " 1p slate green 35 35
C160 " 5p chestnut & dark green 1.75 1.40
C161 " 10p dark brown & chestnut 5.00 3.00
C162 " 20p slate green & orange red 10.00 7.00
Nos. C158–C162 (5) 17.30 11.90

Issued to honor the United Nations.

Father Margil de Jesus and Plane over Zacatecas
AP71

Designs (Zacatecas scene and): 1p, Genaro Codina. 5p, Gen. Enrique Estrada. 10p, Fernando Villalpando.

Perf. 10½x10

1946, Sept. 13 Engr. Wmk. 279

C163 AP71 30c gray 20 12
C164 " 1p brown & Prussian green 40 40
C165 " 5p red & olive 2.00 1.50
C166 " 10p Prussian green & dark brown 8.50 5.00

400th anniversary of Zacatecas.

Franklin D. Roosevelt and Stamp of First Mexican Issue
AP72

Arms of Mexico and Stamp of First U. S. Issue
AP73

1947, May 16 Photo. *Perf. 14*

C167 AP72 25c lt. violet blue 75 40
C168 AP73 30c gray black 50 20
a. Imperf., pair 200.00
C169 AP72 1p bl. & carmine 1.00 35

Issued to honor the Centenary International Philatelic Exhibition, New York, May 17-25, 1947.

Types of 1934-35.

Perf. 10½x10, 10x10½.

1947 Engraved Wmk. 279

C170 AP15 5c black 30 8
C171 AP16 10c red brown 40 8
C172 AP17 15c olive green 50 8
C173 AP19 30c brown olive 40 8
C174 AP20 40c blue gray 40 10
C175 AP21 50c green 3.25 25
a. Imperf., pair 250.00
C176 AP22 1p gray green & red brown 80 15
a. Imperf., pair 250.00
C177 AP23 5p red & black 5.00 1.00

Photogravure

Perf. 14

C177A AP18 20c brn. carmine 75 10
b. Imperf., pair 200.00
Nos. C170–C177A (9) 11.80 1.92

Emilio Carranza—AP74

Douglas DC-4—AP75

1947, June 25 Engr. *Perf. 10½x10*

C178 AP74 10p red & dk. brown 5.00 3.50
C179 AP75 20p blue & red brown 6.00 4.00

Cadet Vincente Suárez
AP76

Chapultepec Castle
AP78

Designs: 30c, Lieut. Juan de la Barrera. 1p, Gen. Pedro M. Anaya. 5p, Gen. Antonio de Leon.

1947, Sept. 8 Photo. *Perf. 14*

C180 AP76 25c dull violet 20 10
C181 " 30c blue 20 15

Engraved

Perf. 10x10½.

C182 AP78 50c deep green 30 10
C183 " 1p violet 40 10
C184 " 5p aqua. & brn. 1.80 1.35
Nos. C180–C184 (5) 2.90 1.80

Issued to commemorate the centenary of the battles of Chapultepec, Churubusco and Molino del Rey.

Flight Symbol Type of 1944

Photogravure.

1947 *Perf. 14* Wmk. 279

C185 AP65 25c chestnut brown 25 12
a. Imperf., pair 150.00

Puebla, Dance of the Half Moon
AP81

Designs: 5c, Guerrero, Acapulco waterfront. 10c, Oaxaca, dance. 20c, Chiapas, musicians (Mayan). 25c, Michoacan, masks. 30c, Cuauhtemoc. 35c, Guerrero, view of Taxco. 40c, San Luis Potosi, head. 50c, Chiapas, bas-relief profile, Mayan culture. 80c, Mexico City University Stadium. 5p, Queretaro, architecture. 10p, Miguel Hidalgo. 20p, Modern building.

Two types of 20p:
I. Blue gray part 21¼mm. wide. Child's figure touching left edge.
II. Blue gray part 21¾mm. wide; "LQ" at lower left corner. Child's figure 1mm. from left edge.

Imprint: "Talleres de Impresion de Estampillas y Valores-Mexico"

Engraved.

1950–52 *Perf. 10½x10* Wmk. 279

C186 AP81 5c aqua. ('51) 40 10
C187 " 10c brn. org. ('51) 1.00 30
C188 " 20c carmine 80 15
C189 " 25c reddish brown 60 7
C190 " 30c olive bistre 45 8
C191 " 35c violet 30 12
a. Retouched die 1.50 20
b. As "a", imperf. pair 150.00
C192 " 40c dark gray blue ('51) 1.50 15
a. Imperf., pair 165.00
C193 " 50c green 2.10 8
C194 " 80c claret ('52) 1.00 40
a. Imperf., pair 165.00
C195 " 1p blue gray 1.00 8
C196 " 5p dark brown & orange ('51) 5.00 75
a. Imperf., pair
C197 " 10p black & aqua. ('52) 45.00 10.00
C198 " 20p carmine & blue gray, I ('52) 8.00 8.00
a. Type II 300.00 40.00
Nos. C186–C198 (13) 67.15 20.28

No. C191a: A patch of heavy shading has been added at right of "MEXICO;" lines in sky increased and strengthened.

Many shades exist of Nos. C186–C198.

See also Nos. C208–C221, C265–C268, C285–C288, C290–298, C347–C349, C422, C444, C446–C450, C471–C480.

Pres. Aleman and Highway Bridging Map of Mexico—AP82

Design: 35c, Pres. Juarez and map.

1950, May 21 Engraved

C199 AP82 25c lilac rose 40 20
C200 " 35c deep green 30 15

Issued to commemorate the completion of the International Highway between Ciudad Juarez and the Guatemala border.

Trains Crossing Isthmus of Tehuantepec—AP83

Design: 35c, Pres. Aleman and bridge.

1950, May 24

C201 AP83 25c green 40 20
C202 " 35c ultramarine 30 18

Issued to commemorate the opening of the Southeastern Railroad between Veracruz, Coatzocoalcos and Yucatan, 1950.

Aztec Courier, Plane, Train—AP84

Design: 80c, Symbols of universal postal service.

1950, June 15

C203 AP84 25c red orange 30 12
C204 " 80c blue 30 25

Issued to commemorate the 75th anniversary (in 1949) of the formation of the Universal Postal Union.

Miguel Hidalgo—AP86

Design: 35c, Hidalgo and Mexican Flag.

Photogravure.

1953, May 8 *Perf. 14* Wmk. 300

C206 AP86 25c gray blue & dark red brown 65 10
C207 " 35c slate green 45 20

Bicentenary of birth of Miguel Hidalgo y Costilla (1753–1811), priest and revolutionist.

Type of 1950–52.

Designs as Before.

Imprint: "Talleres de Impresion de Estampillas y Valores-Mexico."

Wmk. 300, Horizontal

1953–56 Engr. *Perf. 10½x10*

C208 AP81 5c aquamarine 40 8
C209 " 10c orange brown 2.50 30
a. 10c orange 6.00 75
C210 " 30c gray olive 10.00 50
C211 " 40c gray bl. ('56) 11.00 40
C212 " 50c green 300.00 100.00
C213 " 80c claret 50.00 5.00
C214 " 1p blue gray 3.50 20
C215 " 5p dk. brn. & org. 3.00 40
C216 " 10p black & aqua. 4.50 1.00
C217 " 20p car. & bl. gray (II) ('56) 40.00 5.00
Nos. C208–C211, C213–C217 (9) 124.90 12.88

Printed in sheets of 30.

Type of 1950–52.

Designs as in 1950–52. 2p, Guerrero, view of Taxco. 2.25p, Michoacan, masks.

Two types of 2p:
I. No dots after "Colonial". Frame line at right broken near top.
II. Three dots in a line after "Colonial". Right frame line unbroken.

Wmk. 300, Vertical

1955–65 *Perf. 11½x11*

C218 AP81 5c bluish grn. ('56) 10 6
C219 " 10c orange brown, perf. 11 ('60) 30 15
a. Perf. 11½x11 65 35
C220 AP81 20c carmine, perf. 11 ('60) 15 5
k. Perf. 11½x11 ('57) 20 5
C220A AP81 25c violet brown 65 10
C220B " 30c olive gray, perf. 11 ('60) 15 5
l. Perf. 11½x11 25 6
C220C AP81 35c dark violet 40 15
C220D " 40c slate blue, perf. 11 ('60) 20 8
m. Perf. 11½x11 75 10
C220E AP81 50c green 30 6
n. Perf. 11 ('60) 30 6
C220F AP81 80c claret, perf. 11 ('60) 3.00 25
o. Perf. 11½x11 4.50 45
C220G AP81 1p grn. gray, perf. 11 ('60) 1.00 20
p. Perf. 11½x11 5.00 20
C220H AP81 2p dk. org. brn., II, perf. 11 ('63) 1.00 40
i. 2p lt. org. brn., perf. 11½x11 ('65) 225.00 30.00
j. 2p org. brn., I, perf. 11 10.00 1.00
C221 AP81 2.25p maroon, perf. 11 ('63) 80 60
Nos. C218–C221 (12) 8.05 2.15

Printed in sheets of 50. Nos. C218–C221 have been re-engraved.

No. C218 has been redrawn and there are many differences. "CTS" measures 7mm.; it is 5½mm. on No. C208.

Nos. C208–C221 exist in various shades.

No. C220n was privately overprinted in red: "25vo Aniversario / Primer Cohete Internacional / Reynosa, Mexico—McAllen, U.S.A. / 1936–1961".

Mayan Ball Court and Player
AP87

Design: 35c, Modern Stadium, Mexico.

1954, Mar. 6 Photo. *Perf. 14*

C222 AP87 25c brown & dark blue green 85 30
C223 " 35c dull slate green & lilac rose 60 20

Issued to publicize the 7th Central American and Caribbean Games.

Allegory—AP88

1954, Sept. 15

C224 AP88 25c red brown & deep blue 60 20
C225 " 35c dark blue & violet brown 25 12
C226 " 80c black & blue green 30 20

Centenary of national anthem.

Aztec God Tezcatlipoca and Map
AP89

Design: 35c, Stadium and map.

1955, Mar. 12

C227 AP89 25c dark Prussian green & red brown 65 20
C228 " 35c carmine & brown 65 20

2nd Pan American Games, 1955.

Ornaments and Mask, Archeological Era—AP90

Designs: 10c, Virrey Enriquez de Almanza, bell tower and coach, colonial era. 50c, Jose Maria Morelos and cannon, heroic Mexico. 1p, Woman and child and horseback rider, revolutionary Mexico. 1.20p, Sombrero and spurs, popular Mexico. 5p, Pointing hand and school, modern Mexico.

Perf. 11½x11

1956, Aug. 1 Engraved. Wmk. 300

C229 AP90 5c black 40 10
C230 " 10c light blue 40 10
C231 " 50c violet brown 25 8
C232 " 1p blue gray 40 15
C233 " 1.20p magenta 50 20
C234 " 5p blue green 1.50 90
a. Souv. sheet of 6 15.00 15.00
Nos. C229-C234 (6) 3.45 1.53

Centenary of Mexico's first postage stamps.

No. C234a contains one each of Nos. C229-C234, perf. 10½x10, measuring 190x148mm. It sold for 15 pesos.

Paricutin Volcano—AP91

1956, Sept. 5 Photogravure. *Perf. 14*

C235 AP91 50c dark violet blue 30 10

20th International Geological Congress, Mexico City.

Valentin Gomez Farias and Melchor Ocampo—AP92

Design: 1.20p, Leon Guzman and Ignacio Ramirez.

1956-63 *Perf. 14* Wmk. 300

C236 AP92 15c intense blue 30 7
C237 " 1.20p dark green & purple 65 30
C237A " 2.75p purple ('63) 85 65

Centenary of the constitution (in 1957). See also Nos. C289, C445, C451.

Map
AP93

1956, Dec. 1

C238 AP93 25c gray & dark blue 25 8

Issued to publicize the 4th Inter-American Regional Tourism Congress of the Gulf of Mexico and the Caribbean (in 1955).

Eagle Holding Scales
AP94

Design: 1p, Allegorical figure writing the law.

1957, Aug. 31 Photogravure *Perf. 14*

C239 AP94 50c metallic red brown & green 25 10
C240 " 1p metallic lilac & ultramarine 35 20

Centenary of 1857 Constitution.

Globe, Weights and Measure
AP95

1957, Sept. 21

C241 AP95 50c metallic blue & black 30 10

Issued to commemorate the centenary of the adoption of the metric system in Mexico.

Death of Jesus Garcia
AP96

1957, Nov. 7 *Perf. 14* Wmk. 300

C242 AP96 50c carmine rose & dark violet 25 10

Issued to commemorate the 50th anniversary of the death of Jesus Garcia, hero of Nacozari.

Oil Industry Symbols
AP97

Design: 1p, Derricks at night.

1958, Aug. 30

C243 AP97 50c emerald & black 25 10
C244 " 1p carmine & bluish black 35 10

Issued to commemorate the 20th anniversary of the nationalization of Mexico's oil industry.

Independence Monument Figure
AP98

1958, Dec. 15 Engraved *Perf. 11*

C245 AP98 50c gray blue 25 10

Issued to commemorate the tenth anniversary of the signing of the Universal Declaration of Human Rights.

Pres. Venustiano Carranza
AP99

1960, Jan. 15 Photogravure. *Perf. 14*

C246 AP99 50c salmon & dark blue 25 10

Issued to commemorate the centenary of the birth of President Venustiano Carranza.

Alberto Braniff's 1910 Plane, Douglas DC-7 and Mexican Airlines Map
AP100

1960, May 15 *Perf. 14* Wmk. 300

C247 AP100 50c light brown & violet 40 8
C248 " 1p light brown & blue green 35 20

Issued to commemorate the 50th anniversary of Mexican aviation.

Type of 1950-52 inscribed: "HOMENAJE AL COLECCIONISTA DEL TIMBRE DE MEXICO—JUNIO 1960"

Design: 20p, Modern building.

Engraved

1960, June 8 *Perf. 10½x10*

C249 AP81 20p lilac, brown & lt. green 75.00 75.00

See note below No. 909.

Flag—AP101

Designs: 1.20p, Bell of Dolores and eagle. 5p, Dolores Church.

Photogravure

1960, Sept. 16 *Perf. 14* Wmk. 300

C250 AP101 50c deep green & brt. red 25 8
C251 " 1.20p greenish blue & dk.brn. 35 20
C252 " 5p sepia & green 1.50 1.00

150th anniversary of independence.

Aviation (Douglas DC-8 Airliner)
AP102

Designs: 1p, Oil industry. 1.20p, Road development. 5p, Water power (dam).

1960, Nov. 20 Photogravure *Perf. 14*

C253 AP102 50c gray blue & black 25 10
C254 " 1p dk. green & rose car. 35 15
C255 " 1.20p dk. green & sepia 35 25
C256 " 5p blue & lilac 1.50 1.00

50th anniversary of Mexican Revolution.

Count de Revilla Gigedo
AP103

1960, Dec. 23

C257 AP103 60c dk. carmine & black 40 10

Issued to publicize the 80th census and to honor Juan Vicente Güémez Pacheco de Padilla Horcasitas, Count de Revilla Gigedo, who conducted the first census in America, 1793.

Railroad Tracks and Map
AP104

Design: 70c, Railroad bridge.

1961, Nov. *Perf. 14* Wmk. 300

C258 AP104 60c chalky blue & dk. green 30 15
C259 " 70c dk. blue & gray 30 15

Issued to commemorate the opening of the railroad from Chihuahua to the Pacific Ocean.

Gen. Ignacio Zaragoza and View of Puebla—AP105

1962, May 5

C260 AP105 1p gray green & slate grn. 40 15

Issued to commemorate the centenary of the Battle of May 5 at Puebla and the defeat of French forces by Gen. Ignacio Zaragoza.

Laboratory—AP106

1962, June 11

C261 AP106 1p olive & violet blue 40 15

Issued to commemorate the 25th anniversary of the National Polytechnic Institute.

Pres. John F. Kennedy
AP107

1962, June 29

C262 AP107 80c br. blue & car. 2.00 35

Issued to commemorate the visit of President John F. Kennedy to Mexico, June 29–30.

Globe—AP108

1962, Oct. 20

C263 AP108 1.20p violet & dk. brn. 40 20

Inter-American Economic and Social Council meeting.

Balloon over Mexico City, 1862
AP109

1962, Dec. 21 *Perf. 14* Wmk. 300

C264 AP109 80c lt. bl. & blk. 1.65 50

Issued to commemorate the centenary of the first Mexican balloon ascension by Joaquin de la Cantolla y Rico.

Type of 1950–52

Imprint: "Talleres de Imp. de Est. y Valores-Mexico"

Designs as Before.

Wmk. 300, Vertical

1962–72 Photogravure *Perf. 14*

Two sizes of 80c:
I. 35½x20mm.
II. 37x20½mm.

C265 AP81 80c claret, I ('63) 1.00 20
a. Perf. 11½x11, size II ('63) 3.00 30
b. Perf. 11, size II ('63) 2.50 25
c. Perf. 11, size I ('72) 50 15
C266 AP81 5p dark brown & yel. orge. 3.00 75
C267 " 10p black & lt. grn. ('63) 5.00 2.50
C268 " 20p carmine & blue gray 6.00 3.50

ALALC Emblem—AP110

1963, Feb. 15 Wmk. 300

C269 AP110 80c orange & dull purple 80 20

Issued to commemorate the second general session of the Latin American Free Trade Association (ALALC), held in 1962.

Mexican Eagle and Refinery
AP111

1963, Mar. 23

C270 AP111 80c red orange & slate 40 15

25th anniversary of the nationalization of the oil industry.

Polyconic Map—AP112

1963, Apr. 22 Photo. *Perf. 14*

C271 AP112 80c blue & black 75 25

Issued to commemorate the 19th International Chamber of Commerce Congress.

EXMEX Emblem and Postmark
AP113

1963, Oct. 9 *Perf. 14* Wmk. 300

C274 AP113 5p rose red 2.75 1.50

Issued to commemorate the 77th Annual Convention of the American Philatelic Society, Mexico City, Oct. 7–13.

Marshal Tito—AP114

1963, Oct. 15 *Perf. 14* Wmk. 350

C275 AP114 2p dark green & violet 1.50 60

Visit of Marshal Tito of Jugoslavia.

Modern Architecture
AP115

1963, Oct. 19

C276 AP115 80c dk. bl. & gray 60 20

Issued to publicize the International Architects' Convention, Mexico City.

Dove—AP116

1963, Oct. 26

C277 AP116 80c dull bl. grn. & carmine 85 30

Centenary of the International Red Cross.

Don Quixote by
José Guadalupe Posada
AP117

1963, Nov. 9 Engraved *Perf. 10½*

C278 AP117 1.20p black 1.50 40

Issued to commemorate the 50th anniversary of the death of José Guadalupe Posada, satirical artist and Mexican independence hero.

Horse-drawn Rail Coach,
Old and New Trains
AP118

Photogravure

1963, Nov. 29 *Perf. 14* Wmk. 350

C279 AP118 1.20p vio. bl. & bl. 80 30

11th Pan-American Railroad Congress.

Eleanor Roosevelt, Flame
and U.N. Emblem
AP119

1964, Feb. 22 *Perf. 14* Wmk. 350

C280 AP119 80c light ultra. & red 60 15

Issued to commemorate the 15th anniversary (in 1963) of the Universal Declaration of Human Rights and to honor Eleanor Roosevelt.

Gen. Charles de Gaulle
AP120

1964, Mar. 16 Photogravure

C281 AP120 2p dull violet blue & brown 2.00 60

Issued to commemorate the visit of President Charles de Gaulle of France to Mexico, March 16–18.

Pres. John F. Kennedy and
Pres. Adolfo López Mateos
and Map—AP121

1964, Apr. 11 Photogravure

C282 AP121 80c vio. bl. & gray 65 20

Issued to commemorate the ratification of the Chamizal Treaty, returning the Chamizal area of El Paso, Texas, to Mexico, July 18, 1963.

Queen Juliana—AP122

1964, May 8 *Perf. 14* Wmk. 350

C283 AP122 80c bister & vio. blue 95 20

Visit of Queen Juliana of the Netherlands.

Lt. José Azueta and Cadet
Virgilio Uribe—AP123

1964, June 18 *Perf. 14* Wmk. 350

C284 AP123 40c dk. brn. & blk. 45 15

50th anniversary of the defense of Veracruz (against U.S. Navy).

Types of 1950–62

Designs as Before

Engr.; Photo. (C296–C298)

Perf. 11 (20c, 40c, 50c, 80c, 2p); 14

1964–73 Wmk. 350

C285 AP81 20c car. ('71) 5.00 5.00
C286 " 40c gray blue ('71) 125.00 *50.00*
C287 " 50c green ('71) 40 15
C288 " 80c claret, I ('73) 50 20
C289 AP92 1.20p dark green & purple 5.00 50
C290 AP81 2p red brn., II ('71) 1.35 45
C296 " 5p brn. & org. ('66) 6.00 1.35
C297 " 10p black & aqua. 15.00 3.00
C298 " 20p carmine & bl. gray 25.00 5.00
Nos. C285–C290, C296–C298 (9) 183.25 *65.65*

National Emblem, Cahill's Butterfly
World Map, Sword and Scales
of Justice—AP124

1964, July 29 Photogravure

C299 AP124 40c sepia & dp. bl. 60 15

Issued to commemorate the 10th conference of the International Bar Association, Mexico City, July 27–31.

Galleon
AP125

Map Showing 16th Century Voyages Between Mexico and Philippines—AP126

1964, Nov. 10 *Perf. 14* **Wmk. 350**

C300 AP125 80c ultramarine & indigo 2.00 35
C301 AP126 2.75p brt. yellow & black 2.50 75
a. Yel. omitted

Issued to honor 400 years of Mexican—Philippine friendship.

Netzahualcoyotl Dam, Grijalva River AP127

1965, Feb. 19 Photo. *Perf. 14*

C302 AP127 80c violet gray & dk. brn. 70 15

Radio-electric Unit of San Benito, Chiapas AP128

Design: 80c, Microwave tower, Villahermosa, Tabasco.

1965, June 19 *Perf. 14* **Wmk. 350**

C303 AP128 80c light blue & dark blue 90 30
C304 " 1.20p dk. green & black 1.00 30

Issued to commemorate the centenary of the International Telecommunication Union.

Campfire, Tent and Scout Emblem AP129

1965, Sept. 27 Photo. *Perf. 14*

C305 AP129 80c light ultra. & violet blue 90 25

Issued to publicize the 20th World Scout Conference, Mexico City, Sept. 27–Oct. 3.

King Baudouin, Queen Fabiola and Arms of Belgium AP130

1965, Oct. 18 *Perf. 14* **Wmk. 350**

C306 AP130 2p slate green & dull blue 1.50 40

Visit of the King and Queen of Belgium.

Mayan Antiquities and Unisphere AP131

1965, Nov. 9 Photogravure

C307 AP131 80c lemon & emerald 75 20

Issued for the N.Y. World's Fair, 1964–65.

Dante by Raphael AP132

Engraved

1965, Nov. 23 *Perf. 10½* **Wmk. 350**

C308 AP132 2p henna brown 1.75 50

Issued to commemorate the 700th anniversary of the birth of Dante Alighieri.

Runner in Starting Position, Terra Cotta Found in Colima, 300–650 A.D.—AP133

Designs: 1.20p, Chin cultic disk, ball game scoring stone with ball player in center, Mayan culture, c. 500 A.D., found in Chiapas. 2p, Clay sculpture of ball court, players, spectators and temple. Pieces on 80c and 2p from 300–650 A.D.

1965, Dec. 17 Photo. *Perf. 14*

Size: 35x21mm.

C309 AP133 80c orge. & slate 50 20
C310 " 1.20p bl. & vio. bl. 75 25
a. Souv. sheet of 4 2.00 2.00

Size: 43x36mm.

C311 AP133 2p bright blue & dark brn. 65 25
a. Souv. sheet 2.00 2.00

Issued to publicize the 19th Olympic Games, Mexico, 1968. No. C310a contains four imperf. stamps similar to Nos. 965–966 and C309–C310. Black marginal inscription and control number. Sold for 3.90p. Size: 140x89mm. No. C311a contains one imperf. stamp similar to No. C311. Black marginal inscription and control number. Sold for 3p. Size: 71x91 mm.

Nos. C310a and C311a have large watermark of national arms (diameter 54mm.) and "SECRETARIA DE HACIENDA Y CREDITO PUBLICO." Issued without gum.

Ruben Dario AP134

1966, March 17 *Perf. 14* **Wmk. 350**

C312 AP134 1.20p sepia 80 30

Issued to commemorate the 50th anniversary of the death of Ruben Dario (pen name of Felix Ruben Garcia Sarmiento, 1867–1916), Nicaraguan poet, newspaper correspondent and diplomat.

Father Andres de Urdaneta and Compass Rose AP135

Perf. 10½x10

1966, June 4 Engraved **Wmk. 350**

C313 AP135 2.75p bluish blk. 1.75 60

Issued to commemorate the fourth centenary of Father Urdaneta's return trip from the Philippines.

UPAE Type of Regular Issue

Designs: 80c, Pennant and post horn. 1.20p, Pennant and UPAE emblem (horiz.).

Photogravure

1966, June 24 *Perf. 14* **Wmk. 300**

C314 A244 80c magenta & black 40 15
C315 " 1.20p lt. ultra. & blk. 50 20

Issued to publicize the Congress of the Postal Union of the Americas and Spain, UPAE, Mexico City, June 24–July 23.

U Thant and U. N. Emblem AP136

1966, Aug. 24. Photo. **Wmk. 300**

C316 AP136 80c blk. & ultra. 75 20

Issued to commemorate the visit of U Thant, Secretary General of the United Nations.

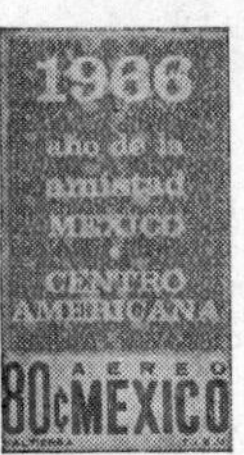

AP137

1966, Aug. 26 *Perf. 14*

C317 AP137 80c green & red 35 12

Issued to publicize the year of friendship between Mexico and Central America.

Olympic Type of Regular Issue, 1966

Designs by Diego Rivera: 80c, Obstacle race. 2.25p, Football. 2.75p, Lighting Olympic torch.

1966, Oct. 15 *Perf. 14* **Wmk. 300**

Size: 57x21mm.

C318 A248 80c org. brn. & blk. 35 15
C319 " 2.25p green & blk. 65 35
C320 " 2.75p dp. pur. & blk. 1.50 50
a. Souv. sheet of 3 4.00 4.00

Issued to publicize the 19th Olympic Games, Mexico City, D.F., 1968. No. C320a contains 3 imperf. stamps similar to Nos. C318–C320 with simulated perforations, black marginal inscription and control number. Size: 125x70mm. Sold for 8.70p.

UNESCO Emblem AP138

Lithographed and Engraved

1966, Nov. 4 *Perf. 11* **Wmk. 300**

C321 AP138 80c blk., car., brt. grn. & org. 65 15

Issued to commemorate the 20th anniversary of UNESCO (United Nations Educational, Scientific and Cultural Organization).

Venustiano Carranza AP139 — Tyros Satellite over Earth AP140

Photogravure

1967, Feb. 5 *Perf. 14* **Wmk. 300**

C322 AP139 80c dk. red brown & ocher 50 15

Issued to commemorate the 50th anniversary of the constitution. Venustiano Carranza (1859–1920), was president of Mexico 1917–20.

1967, March 23 Photo. **Wmk. 300**

C323 AP140 80c blk. & dk. bl. 60 25

World Meteorological Day, Mar. 23.

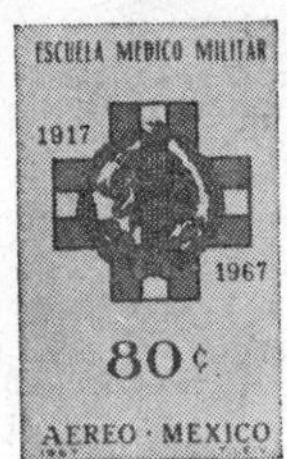

Medical School Emblem AP141 — Captain Horacio Ruiz Gaviño AP142

1967, July 10 *Perf. 14* **Wmk. 300**

C324 AP141 80c blk. & ocher 50 20

Issued to commemorate the 50th anniversary of the Mexican Military Medical School.

1967, July 17 Photogravure

Design: 2p, Biplane (horiz.).

C325 AP142 80c blk. & brown 40 15
C326 " 2p " " " 70 25

Issued to commemorate the 50th anniversary of the first Mexican air post flight, from Pachuca to Mexico City, July 6, 1917.

Marco Polo and ITY Emblem AP143

1967, Sept. 9 *Perf. 14* **Wmk. 300**

C327 AP143 80c rose claret & black 30 12

Issued for International Tourist Year, 1967.

Olympic Games Type of Regular Issue, 1967.

Designs: 80c, Diving. 1.20p, Runners. 2p, Weight lifters. 5p, Soccer.

1967, Oct. 12 Photo. *Perf. 14*

C328 A254 80c dp. lilac rose & black 30 15
C329 " 1.20p bright green & black 40 20
a. Souvenir sheet of 2 2.50 2.50
C330 A254 2p yel. & black 1.50 40
C331 " 5p olive & black 2.00 75
a. Souvenir sheet of 2 5.00 5.00

Issued to publicize the 19th Olympic Games, Mexico City, Oct. 12–27, 1968.

No. C329a contains 2 imperf. stamps similar to Nos. C328–C329, sold for 2.50p; No. C331a contains 2 imperf. stamps similar to Nos. C330–C331, sold for 9p. Both sheets have black marginal inscriptions, control numbers and watermark 350. Size: 130x98mm.

Heinrich Hertz and James Clerk Maxwell
AP144

1967, Nov. 15 Photo. Wmk. 300

C332 AP144 80c bright green & black 40 15

Issued to commemorate the Second International Telecommunications Plan Conference, Mexico City, Oct. 30–Nov. 15.

EFIMEX Emblem, Showing Official Stamp of 1884
AP145

1968, Feb. 24 *Perf. 14* Wmk. 300

C333 AP145 80c black & green 75 25
C334 " 2p black & verm. 70 40

Issued to publicize EFIMEX '68, International Philatelic Exhibition, Mexico City, Nov. 1–9, 1968.

Olympic Games Type of Regular Issue, 1967

Designs: 80c, Sailing. 1p, Rowing. 2p, Volleyball. 5p, Equestrian.

1968, Mar. 21 Photo. *Perf. 14*

C335 A254 80c ultra. & black 30 12
C336 " 1p brt. bl. green & black 40 15
a. Souv. sheet 1.75 1.75
C337 " 2p yel. & black 1.00 30
C338 " 5p red brn. & blk. 1.60 1.00
a. Souv. sheet 4.00 4.00

Issued to publicize the 19th Olympic Games, Mexico City, Oct. 12–27. No. C336a contains 2 imperf. stamps similar to Nos. C335–C336, sold for 2.40p; No. C338a contains 2 imperf. stamps similar to Nos. C337–C338, sold for 9p. Both sheets have black marginal inscriptions, control numbers and watermark 350. Size: 105x70 mm.

Martin Luther King, Jr.
AP146

1968, June 8 Photo. Wmk. 300

C339 AP146 80c blk. & gray 50 15

Issued in memory of the Rev. Dr. Martin Luther King, Jr. (1929–1968), American civil rights leader.

Olympic Types of Regular Issue, 1968

Designs: 80c, Peace dove and Olympic rings. 1p, Discobolus. 2p, Olympic medals. 5p, Symbols of Olympic sports events. 10p, Symbolic design for Mexican Olympic Games.

1968, Oct. 12 *Perf. 14* Wmk. 350

C340 A259 80c green, lilac & orange 30 12
C341 " 1p green, blue & black 40 15
C342 " 2p multicolored 1.00 35
a. Souv. sheet of 3 2.00 2.00
C343 A260 5p multicolored 2.50 1.25
C344 " 10p blk. & multi. 4.00 2.25
a. Souv. sheet of 2 7.50 7.50
Nos. C340–C344 (5) 8.20 4.12

Issued to commemorate the 19th Olympic Games, Mexico City, Oct. 12–27. No. C342a contains 3 imperf. stamps similar to Nos. C340–C342. Sold for 5p. No. C344a contains 2 imperf. stamps similar to Nos. C343–C344. Sold for 20p. Sheets have black marginal inscriptions and control numbers. Size: 105x70mm.

Souvenir Sheet

EFIMEX Emblem
AP147

1968, Nov. 1 Photo. *Imperf.*

C345 AP147 5p blk. & ultra. 3.00 3.00

Issued to commemorate EFIMEX '68 International philatelic exhibition, Mexico City, Nov. 1–9. No. C345 contains one stamp with simulated perforations. Orange margin with black inscription, control number and emblems of various international philatelic societies. Size: 99x69mm.

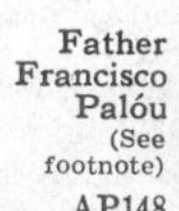

Father Francisco Palóu (See footnote)
AP148

1969, July 16 *Perf. 14* Wmk. 350

C346 AP148 80c multicolored 50 15

Issued to honor Father Junipero Serra (1713–1784), Franciscan missionary, founder of San Diego, Calif. The portrait was intended to be that of Father Serra. By error the head of Father Palóu, his coworker, was taken from a painting (c. 1785) by Mariano Guerrero which also contains a Serra portrait.

Type of 1950–52 Redrawn
Coil Stamps
Perf. 11 Vert.

1969 Photo. Wmk. 300 Vert.

Imprint: "T.I.E.V."

C347 AP81 20c carmine 1.35 30

Imprint: "Talleres de Est. y Valores-Mexico"

C348 AP81 80c claret 1.50 30

Imprint: "T.I.E.V."

C349 AP81 1p gray green 1.75 50

Soccer Ball
AP149

Design: 2p, Foot and soccer ball.

1969, Aug. 16 *Perf. 14* Wmk. 350

C350 AP149 80c red & multi. 35 15
C351 " 2p grn. & multi. 60 25

Issued to publicize the 9th World Soccer Championships for the Jules Rimet Cup, Mexico City, May 30–June 21, 1970.

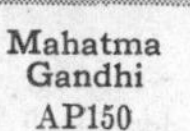

Mahatma Gandhi
AP150

Astronaut's Footprint
AP151

1969, Sept. 27 Photo. *Perf. 14*

C352 AP150 80c multicolored 30 15

Issued to commemorate the centenary of the birth of Mohandas K. Gandhi (1869–1948), leader in India's fight for independence.

1969, Oct. 29 Photogravure

C353 AP151 2p black 60 30

Issued to commemorate man's first landing on the moon, July 20, 1969. See note after U.S. No. C76.

Tourist Issue
Type of Regular Issue, 1969–73 and

"Sound and Light" at Pyramid, Teotihuacan
AP152

Designs: No. C355, Acapulco Bay. No. C356, El Caracol Observatory, Yucatan. No. C357, Dancer with fruit basket, Oaxaca. No. C358, Sports fishing, Lower California (horiz.).

1969–73 *Perf. 14* Wmk. 350

Multicolored

C354 AP152 80c *shown* 1.00 25
C355 " 80c *Acapulco* 1.00 25
C356 " 80c *Yucatan* 1.00 25

Wmk. 300

C357 A267 80c *Dancer, Oaxaca* 40 20
C358 " 80c *Sports fishing, Lower California* 40 15
Nos. C354–C358 (5) 3.80 1.10

Issue dates: Nos. C354–C356, Nov. 1, 1969. Nos. C357–C358, Mar. 16, 1973.

Red Crosses
AP154

1969, Nov. 8 Photo. Wmk. 350

C370 AP154 80c blk. & multi. 35 12

Issued to commemorate the 50th anniversary of the League of Red Cross Societies.

Radar Satellite Ground Station
AP155

1969, Dec. 6 *Perf. 14* Wmk. 350

C371 AP155 80c multicolored 40 15

Issued to publicize the installation of the ground station for communications by satellite at Tulancingo, Hidalgo.

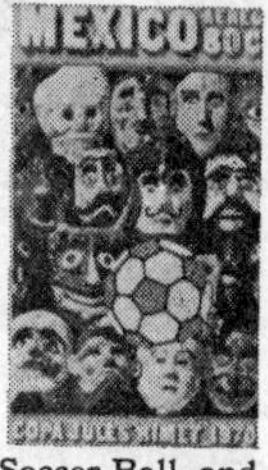

Soccer Ball, and Mexican Masks
AP156

Design: 2p, Pre-Columbian sculptured heads and soccer ball.

1970, May 31 *Perf. 14* Wmk. 350

C372 AP156 80c blue & multi. 35 15
C373 " 2p multicolored 60 30

Issued to publicize the World Soccer Championships for the Jules Rimet Cup, Mexico City, May 30–June 21, 1970. The design of Nos. C372–C373 is continuous.

SPORTMEX '70 Emblem
AP157

1970, June 19 *Rouletted 13*

C374 AP157 2p gray & car. 5.00 1.50

Issued to publicize SPORTMEX '70 philatelic exposition devoted to sports, especially soccer, on stamps. Mexico City, June 19–28. The 2p stamp of No. C374 is imperf.; multicolored emblems of philatelic groups organizing SPORTMEX and black control number in margin. Size: 60x 50mm.

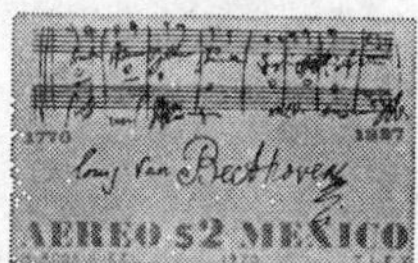

Ode to Joy and Beethoven's Signature—AP158

1970, Sept. 26 *Perf. 14* Wmk. 350

C375 AP158 2p multicolored 60 35

Issued to commemorate the 200th anniversary of the birth of Ludwig van Beethoven (1770–1827), composer.

U.N. General Assembly Floor Plan
AP159

1970, Oct. 24 Photo. *Perf. 14*

C376 AP159 80c multicolored 35 15

25th anniversary of United Nations.

Isaac Newton
AP160

1971, Feb. 27 ***Perf. 14*** **Wmk. 350**

Multicolored

C377	AP160	2p *shown*	60	30
C378	"	2p *Galileo*	60	30
C379	"	2p *Johannes Kepler*	60	30

Mayan Warriors, Dresden Codex
AP161

Designs: No. C381, Sister Juana, by Miguel Cabrera (1695–1768). No. C382, José Maria Velasco (1840–1912), self-portrait. No. C383, El Paricutin (volcano), by Gerardo Murillo ("Dr. Atl," 1875–1964). No. C384, Detail of mural, Man in Flames, by José Clemente Orozco (1883–1949).

Imprint includes "1971"

1971, Apr. 24 **Photo.** **Wmk. 350**

C380	AP161	80c multicolored	40	15
C381	"	80c "	40	15
C382	"	80c "	40	15
C383	"	80c "	40	15
C384	"	80c "	40	15
		Nos. C380-C384 (5)	2.00	75

Mexican art and science through the centuries. See Nos. C396–C400, C417–C421, C439–C443, C513–C517, C527–C531.

Stamps of Venezuela, Mexico and Colombia
AP162

1971, May 22 **Photo.** **Wmk. 350**

C385	AP162	80c multicolored	40	15

EXFILCA 70, 2nd Interamerican Philatelic Exhibition, Caracas, Venezuela, Nov. 27–Dec. 6, 1970.

Francisco Javier Clavijero
AP163

1971, July 10 ***Perf. 14*** **Wmk. 350**

C386	AP163	2p lt. olive bister & dk. brown	70	30

Francisco Javier Clavijero (1731–1786), Jesuit and historian, whose remains were returned from Italy to Mexico in 1970.

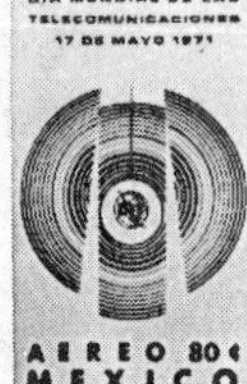

Waves
AP164

Mariano Matamoros, by Diego Rivera
AP165

1971, Aug. 7 ***Perf. 14*** **Wmk. 350**

C387	AP164	80c multicolored	30	12

3rd World Telecommunications Day, May 17.

1971, Aug. 28 **Photogravure**

C388	AP165	2p multicolored	60	30

Bicentenary of the birth of Mariano Matamoros (1770–1814), priest and patriot.

Vicente Guerrero
AP166

Circles
AP167

1971, Sept. 27

C389	AP166	2p multicolored	60	30

Vicente Guerrero (1783–1831), independence leader, president of Mexico. Painting by Juan O'Gorman.

1971, Nov. 4 **Wmk. 300**

C390	AP167	80c greenish bl., dark blue & black	45	18

25th anniversary of United Nations Educational, Scientific and Cultural Organization (UNESCO).

Stamps of Venezuela, Mexico, Colombia and Peru
AP168

1971, Nov. 4

C391	AP168	80c multicolored	40	15

EXFILIMA '71, 3rd Interamerican Philatelic Exhibition, Lima, Peru, Nov. 6–14.

Faces and Hand
AP169

1971, Nov. 29

C392	AP169	2p black, dk. blue & pink	60	30

5th Congress of Psychiatry, Mexico City, Nov. 28–Dec. 4.

Ex Libris by Albrecht Dürer
AP170

1971, Dec. 18

C393	AP170	2p black & buff	60	30

500th anniversary of the birth of Albrecht Dürer (1471–1528), German painter and engraver.

Retort, Pulley and Burner
AP171

Scientists and WHO Emblem
AP172

1972, Feb. 26 ***Perf. 14*** **Wmk. 300**

C394	AP171	2p lilac, black & yellow	60	25

Anniversary of the National Council on Science and Technology.

1972, Apr. 8

C395	AP172	80c multicolored	35	12

World Health Day 1972. Stamp shows Willem Einthoven and Frank Wilson.

Art and Science Type of 1971

Designs: No. C396, King Netzahuacoyotl (1402–1472) of Texcoco, art patron. No. C397, Juan Ruiz de Alarcon (c. 1580–1639), lawyer. No. C398, José Joaquin Fernandez de Lizardi (1776–1827), author. No. C399, Ramon Lopez Velarde (1888–1921), writer. No. C400, Enrique Gonzalez Martinez (1871–1952), poet.

1972, Apr. 15 **Wmk. 350**

Imprint includes "1972"

Black Inscriptions

C396	AP161	80c ocher	35	12
C397	"	80c green	35	12
C398	"	80c brown	35	12
C399	"	80c carmine	35	12
C400	"	80c gray blue	35	12
		Nos. C396-C400 (5)	1.75	60

Mexican art and science through the centuries.

Rotary Emblem
AP173

1972, Apr. 5

C401	AP173	80c multicolored	35	12

Rotary International in Mexico, 50th anniversary.

Tire Treads
AP174

1972, May 11 **Wmk. 300**

C402	AP174	80c gray & black	25	12

74th Assembly of the International Tourism Alliance, Mexico City, May 8–11.

Benito Juárez
AP175

Design: 80c, Page of Civil Register. 1.20p, Juárez, by Pelegrin Clavé.

1972 **Photo.** ***Perf. 14***

C403	AP175	80c gray bl. & blk.	25	12
C404	"	1.20p multicolored	45	15
C405	"	2p yel. & multi.	70	30

Centenary of the death of Benito Juárez (1806–1872), revolutionary leader and president of Mexico.

Issue dates: 80c, 2p, July 18; 1.20p, Sept. 15.

Atom Symbol, Olive Branch
AP176

"Over the Waves," by Juventina Rosas
AP177

1972, Oct. 3 **Photo.** **Wmk. 300**

C406	AP176	2p gray, blue & black	50	25

16th Conference of the Atomic Energy Commission, Mexico City, Sept. 26.

1972, Oct. 16 ***Perf. 14***

C407	AP177	80c olive bister	25	15

28th International Congress of the Societies of Authors and Composers, Mexico City, Oct. 16–21.

Child with Doll, by Guerrero Galvan, UNICEF Emblem—AP178

1972, Nov. 4

C408	AP178	80c multicolored	35	15

25th anniversary (in 1971) of the United Nations International Children's Fund (UNICEF).

Pedro de Gante, by Rodriguez y Arangorti
AP179

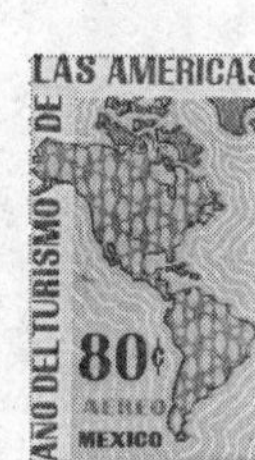

Map of Americas with Tourists' Footprints
AP180

1972, Nov. 22 ***Perf. 14***

C409 AP179 2p multicolored 60 25

400th anniversary of the death of Brother Pedro de Gante (Pedro Moor or van der Moere; 1480 ?–1572), Franciscan brother who founded first school in Mexico, and writer.

Olympic Games Type of Regular Issue, 1972

Designs: 80c, Olympic emblems and stylized soccer game. 2p, Olympic emblems (vert.).

1972, Dec. 9 **Photo.** **Wmk. 300**

C410 A289 80c green & multi. 35 15
C411 " 2p yellow green, black & blue 65 30

20th Olympic Games, Munich, Aug. 26–Sept. 11.

Anti-pollution Type of Regular Issue

Design: 80c, Bird sitting on ornamental capital (vert.).

1972, Dec. 16

C412 A291 80c lt. blue & black 25 12

Anti-pollution campaign.

1972, Dec. 23

C413 AP180 80c black, yellow & green 35 12

Tourism Year of the Americas.

Mexico #O1, Brazil #992, Colombia #130, Venezuela #22, Peru #C320
AP181

1973, Jan. 19 ***Perf. 14***

C414 AP181 80c multicolored 35 12

4th Interamerican Philatelic Exhibition, EXFILBRA 72, Rio de Janeiro, Brazil, Aug. 26–Sept. 2, 1972.

Aeolus, God of Winds
AP182

1973, Sept. 14 **Photo.** **Wmk. 300**

C415 AP182 80c brt. pink, blk. & blue 35 12

Centenary of international meteorological cooperation.

Nicolaus Copernicus
AP183

San Martin Monument
AP184

Perf. 14

1973, Oct. 10 **Photo.** **Wmk. 300**

C416 AP183 80c slate green 30 12

500th anniversary of the birth of Nicolaus Copernicus (1473–1543), Polish astronomer.

Art and Science Type of 1971

Designs: No. C417, Aztec calendar stone. No. C418, Carlos de Sigüenza y Gongora (1645–1700), mathematician, astronomer. No. C419, Francisco Diaz Covarrubias (1833–1889), topographer. No. C420, Joaquin Gallo (1882–1965), geographer, astronomer. No. C421, Luis Enrique Erro (1897–1955), founder of Tonanzintla Observatory.

Imprint includes "1973"

1973, Nov. 21 **Wmk. 350**

C417 AP161 80c carmine & slate green 25 15
C418 " 80c multicolored 25 15
C419 " 80c " 25 15
C420 " 80c " 25 15
C421 " 80c " 25 15
Nos. C417-C421 (5) 1.25 75

Type of 1950–52

Design: 80c, Mexico City University Stadium.

Imprint: "Talleres de. Imp. de Est. y Vallores—Mexico"

1973 ***Perf. 11*** **Unwmkd.**

C422 AP81 80c claret, I 1.50 35

Fluorescent printing on front or back of stamps consisting of beehive pattern and diagonal inscription.

Perf. 14

1973, Nov. 9 **Photo.** **Wmk. 350**

C423 AP184 80c org., indigo & yellow 25 12

Erection of a monument to San Martin in Mexico City, a gift of Argentina.

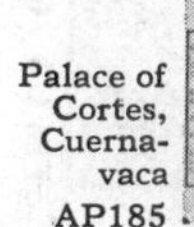

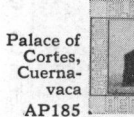

Palace of Cortes, Cuernavaca
AP185

Lithographed.

1974, Jan. 18 ***Perf. 14*** **Wmk. 300**

C424 AP185 80c blk. & multi. 15 10

EXMEX 73 Philatelic Exhibition, Cuernavaca, Apr. 7–15.

Gold Brooch, Mochica Culture
AP186

1974, Mar. 6 **Photo.** **Wmk. 300**

C425 AP186 80c gold & multi. 20 12

Exhibition of Peruvian gold treasures, Mexico City, 1973–74.

Luggage
AP187

1974, Mar. 22 ***Perf. 14***

C426 AP187 80c multicolored 15 10

16th Convention of the Federation of Latin American Tourist Organizations (COTAL), Acapulco, May 1974.

CEPAL Emblem
AP188

1974, Mar. 22

C427 AP188 80c blk. & multi. 15 10

25th anniversary (in 1973) of the Economic Commission for Latin America (CEPAL).

"The Enameled Casserole," by Picasso—AP189

1974, Mar. 29 **Wmk. 300**

C428 AP189 80c multicolored 15 10

Pablo Ruiz Picasso (1881–1973), painter and sculptor.

EXFILMEX Type of 1974

1974, July 26 ***Perf. 13x12***

C429 A305 80c buff, red brn. & black 15 10

See note after No. 1065.

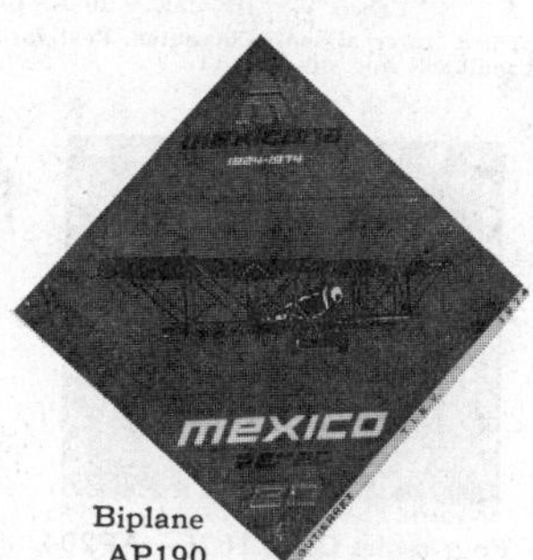

Biplane
AP190

Design: 2p, Jet plane.

Perf. 13x12

1974, Aug. 20 **Photo.** **Wmk. 300**

C430 AP190 80c brt. bl., blk. & rose 15 10
C431 " 2p multicolored 30 15

50th anniversary of Mexican Airlines (MEXICANA).

Transmitter and Waves Circling Globe—AP191

1974, Oct. 4 ***Perf. 14*** **Wmk. 300**

C432 AP191 2p multicolored 25 15

First International Congress of Electric and Electronic Communications, Sept. 17–21.

Volleyball
AP192

1974, Oct. 12 ***Perf. 13x12***

C433 AP192 2p org., bister & black 25 15

8th World Volleyball Championship. Perforation holes are of two sizes.

Souvenir Sheet

Mexico #O1, Colombia #130, Venezuela #22, Peru #C320, Brazil #992, Mexico #123—AP193

Imperf.

1974, Oct. 28 **Photo.** **Wmk. 300**

C434 AP193 10p multi. 2.50 2.00

EXFILMEX 74, 5th Inter-American Philatelic Exhibition, Mexico City, Oct. 26–Nov. 3. Size: 105x70mm.

Felipe Carrillo Puerto
AP194

1974, Nov. 8 ***Perf. 14***

C435 AP194 80c green & golden brn. 15 10

Birth centenary of Felipe Carrillo Puerto (1874–1924), politician and journalist.

Mask, Bat and Catcher's Mitt
AP195

1974, Nov. 29 ***Perf. 14*** **Wmk. 350**

C436 AP195 80c multicolored 15 10

Mexican Baseball League, 50th anniversary.

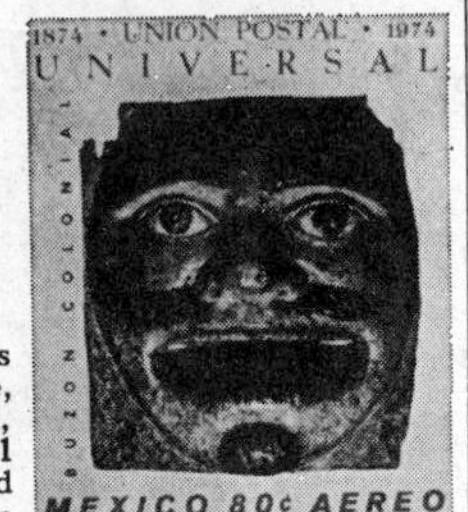

Man's Face, Mailbox, Colonial Period
AP196

Design: 2p, Heinrich von Stephan, contemporary engraving.

1974, Dec. 13 Photo. Wmk. 300

C437 AP196 80c multicolored 15 10
C438 " 2p green & ocher 25 15

Centenary of Universal Postal Union.

Art and Science Type of 1971

Designs: No. C439, Mayan mural (8th century), Bonampak, Chiapas. No. C440, First musical score printed in Mexico, 1556. No. C441, Miguel Lerdo de Tejada (1869–1941), composer. No. C442, Silvestre Revueltas (1899–1940), composer (bronze bust). No. C443, Angela Peralta (1845–1883), singer.

Imprint includes "1974"

1974, Dec. 20 Wmk. 300

C439 AP161 80c multicolored 15 10
C440 " 80c " 15 10
C441 " 80c " 15 10
C442 " 80c " 15 10
C443 " 80c " 15 10
Nos. C439-C443 (5) 75 50

Mexican art and science through the centuries.

Types of 1950–56

Designs (as 1950–56 issues): 40c, San Luis Potosi, head. 60c, Leon Guzman and Ignacio Ramirez. 1.60p, Chiapas, Mayan bas-relief. 1.90p, Guerrero, Acapulco waterfront. 4.30p, Oaxaca, dance. 5.20p, Guerrero, view of Taxco. 5.60p, Michoacan, masks. 50p, Valentin Gomez Farias and Melchor Ocampo.

Engr. (40c), Photo.
Perf. 11 (40c, 1.60p), 14

1975 Wmk. 300

C444 AP81 40c bluish gray 20 4
C445 AP92 60c yellow green 40 6
C446 AP81 1.60p red 90 10
C447 " 1.90p rose red 1.10 15
C448 " 4.30p ultramarine 1.60 20
C449 " 5.20p purple 1.90 25
C450 " 5.60p blue green 2.00 35
C451 AP92 50p dark blue & brick red 12.00 3.00
Nos. C444-C451 (8) 20.10 4.15

Women's Year Emblem
AP199

1975, Jan. 3 *Perf. 14* Wmk. 300

C456 AP199 1.60p bright pink & black 20 12

International Women's Year 1975.

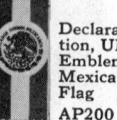

Declaration, UN Emblem, Mexican Flag
AP200

1975, Feb. 7 Photo. Wmk. 300

C457 AP200 1.60p multi. 20 12

Declaration of Economic Rights and Duties of Nations.

Balsa Raft "Acali"—AP201

1975, Mar. 7 *Perf. 14* Wmk. 300

C458 AP201 80c multicolored 15 10

Trans-Atlantic voyage of the "Acali" from Canary Islands to Yucatan, May–Aug. 1973.

Dr. Miguel Jimenez, by I. Ramirez
AP202

Miguel de Cervantes
AP203

1975, Mar. 24 *Perf. 14* Unwmkd.

C459 AP202 2p multicolored 25 12

Fifth World Gastroenterology Congress.

1975, Apr. 26 Photo. Unwmkd.

C460 AP203 1.60p bl. blk. & dk. car. 20 10

Third International Cervantes Festival, Guanajuato, Apr. 26–May 11.

Four-reales Coin, 1675—AP204

1975, May 2

C461 AP204 1.60p blue, gold & black 20 10

International Numismatic Convention, Mexico City, Mar. 28–30, 1974, and 300th anniversary of first coin struck by Mexico City Mint.

Salvador Novo, by Roberto Montenegro
AP205

1975, May 9

C462 AP205 1.60p multi. 20 10

Salvador Novo (1904–1974), author.

Mural, Siqueiros—AP206

1975, May 16

C463 AP206 1.60p multi. 18 10

David Alfaro Siqueiros (1896–1974), painter.

UN and IWY Emblems
AP207

1975, June 19

C464 AP207 1.60p ultramarine & pink 20 10

International Women's Year World Conference, Mexico City, June 19–July 2.

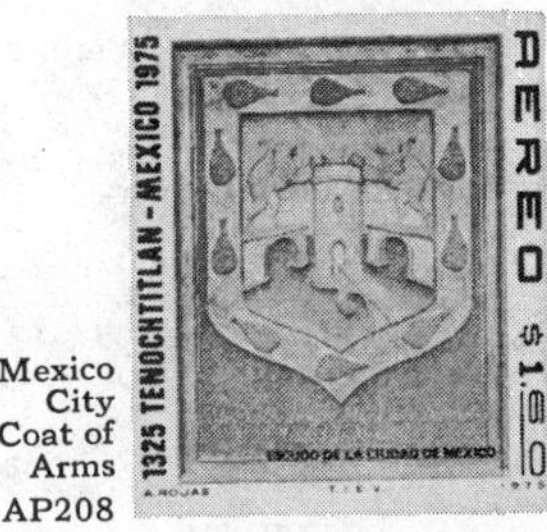

Mexico City Coat of Arms
AP208

Perf. 14

1975, Aug. 1 Photo. Unwmkd.

C465 AP208 1.60p multi. 20 10

650th anniversary of Tenochtitlan (Mexico City).

Domingo F. Sarmiento
AP209

Teachers' Monument
AP210

Perf. 14

1975, Aug. 9 Photo. Unwmkd.

C466 AP209 1.60p brown & slate grn. 20 10

1st International Congress of Third World Educators, Acapulco, Aug. 5–9. Domingo Faustino Sarmiento (1811–1888), Argentinian statesman, writer and educator.

1975, Aug. 9

C467 AP210 4.30p green & ocher 45 20

Mexican-Lebanese friendship. The monument in Mexico City, by I Naffa al Rozzi, shows Cadmus, a mythical Phoenician, teaching the alphabet.

7th Pan American Games' Emblem
AP211

1975, Aug. 29

C468 AP211 1.60p multi. 20 12

Pan American Games, Mexico City, Oct. 13–26.

Dr. Atl, Self-portrait
AP212

Perf. 14

1975, Oct. 3 Photo. Unwmkd.

C469 AP212 4.30p multi. 45 20

Geraldo Murillo ("Dr. Atl," 1875–1924), painter and writer, birth centenary.

Globe and Traffic Circle
AP213

1975, Oct. 12

C470 AP213 1.60p bl., blk. & gray 20 12

15th World Road Congress, Mexico City, Oct. 12–26.

Type of 1950–52

Designs: 40c, San Luis Potosi, head. 80c, Mexico City University stadium. 1p, Puebla, Half Moon dance. 1.60p, Chiapas, Mayan bas-relief. 5p, Queretaro, architecture. 5.60p, Michoacan, masks. 10p, Miguel Hidalgo. 20p, Modern building.

Engr. (40c, 1p), Photo.
Perf. 11 (40c, 80c, 1p, 1.60p), 14

1975–76 Unwmkd.

C471 AP81 40c bluish gray 35 4
C472 " 80c claret, II 70 6
C473 " 1p grayish grn. 1.00 7
C474 " 1.60p red 1.50 12
C476 " 5p dk. brown & org. ('76) 1.20 25
C477 " 5.60p bluish green ('76) 5.00 30
C479 " 10p blk. & grn. 3.50 50
C480 " 20p red & dull grn. ('76) 6.50 75
Nos. C471-C480 (8) 19.75 2.09

Stamps not listed in this Catalogue or mentioned in "For the Record" (unless recent issues) usually are revenues, locals or labels.

Bicycle and Export Emblem AP214

Designs: 30c, Vase, copper industry. 80c, Overalls. 1.90p, Valves, oil industry. 2p, Books. 4.30p, Strawberry. 5p, Automobiles. 5.20p, Farm machinery. 5.60p, Cotton.

Photogravure

1975–76 *Perf. 14* Unwmkd.

C486 AP214 30c copper ('76) 8 4
C489 " 80c dull bl. ('76) 12 4
C491 " 1.60p blk. & org. 20 6
C492 " 1.90p verm. & dk. green 25 10
C493 " 2p ultra. & gold ('76) 30 10
C496 " 4.30p brt. pink & olive 60 25
C497 " 5p dark blue & ocher ('76) 75 25
C498 " 5.20p red & blk. ('76) 80 30
C499 " 5.60p yel. grn. & org. ('76) 85 30
Nos. C486–C499 (9) 3.95 1.44

Art and Science Type of 1971

Designs: No. C513, Title page of "Medical History of New Spain," by Francisco Hernandez, 1628. No. C514, Alfonso L. Herrera (1868–1942), biologist. No. C515, Title page, Aztec Herbal, 1552. No. C516, Arturo S. Rosenblueth (1900–1970). No. C517, Alfredo Augusto Duges (1826–1910) French-born naturalist.

Imprint includes "1975"

1975, Nov. 21 *Perf. 14* Unwmkd.

C513 AP161 1.60p buff, red & black 20 12
C514 " 1.60p violet blue & multi. 20 12
C515 " 1.60p black & multi. 20 12
C516 " 1.60p gray & multi. 20 12
C517 " 1.60p green & multi. 20 12
Nos. C513–C517 (5) 1.00 60

Mexican art and science through the centuries.

Telephone AP216

60-peso Gold Coin, Oaxaca, 1917 AP217

1976, Mar. 10 Photogravure

C518 AP216 1.60p gray & blk. 20 12

Centenary of first telephone call by Alexander Graham Bell, Mar. 10, 1876.

1976, Mar. 25 Photo. Unwmkd.

C519 AP217 1.60p blk., ocher & yellow 20 12

4th International Numismatic Convention, Mexico City, March 1976.

Rain God Tlaloc and Calles Dam AP218

1976, Mar. 29 *Perf. 14*

C520 AP218 1.60p vio.brn. & dk. grn. 20 12

12th International Great Dams Congress, Mar. 29–Apr. 2.

Perforation Gauge—AP219

1976, May 7 Photo. Unwmkd.

C521 AP219 1.60p black, red & blue 20 12

Interphil 76 International Philatelic Exhibition, Philadelphia, Pa., May 29–June 6.

Rainbow over City AP220

1976, May 31 *Perf. 14* Unwmkd.

C522 AP220 1.60p black & multi. 20 12

Habitat, U.N. Conference on Human Settlements, Vancouver, Canada, May 31– June 11.

Liberty Bell AP221 **"Peace" AP222**

1976, July 4 Photo. *Perf. 14*

C523 AP221 1.60p ultra. & red 20 12

American Bicentennial.

1976, Aug. 3 Photo. *Perf. 14*

Design: "Peace" written in Chinese, Japanese, Hebrew, Hindi and Arabic.

C524 AP222 1.60p multi. 20 21

30th International Congress of Science and Humanities of Asia and North Africa, Mexico, Aug. 3–8.

Television Screen AP223

1976, Aug. 24 Photo. Unwmkd.

C525 AP223 1.60p multi. 20 12

1st Latin-American Forum on Children's Television.

Luminescence

Fluorescent airmail stamps include Nos. C265, C265c, C288, C357–C358, C390–C415, C422–C423.

Airmail stamps issued on both ordinary and fluorescent paper include Nos. C220, C220D–C220E, C220G–C220H, C265b, C266–C268, C286.

Sky, Sun, Water and Earth AP224

1976, Nov. 8 Photo. *Perf. 14*

C526 AP224 1.60p multi. 20 12

World Conservation Day.

Art and Science Type of 1971

Designs: No. C527, Coatlicue, Mother of Earth, Aztec sculpture. No. C528, El Caballito, statue of Charles IV of Spain, by Manuel Tolsá. No. C529, Chief Tlahuicole, bronze statue by Manuel Vilar. No. C530, Today's God, Money, seated ceramic figure, by L. Ortiz Monasterio. No. C531, Signal, abstract sculpture by Angela Gurria.

1976, Dec. 10 Photo. *Perf. 14*

C527 AP161 1.60p blk. & yel. 20 12
C528 " 1.60p blk. & red brown 20 12
C529 " 1.60p black & multi. 20 12
C530 " 1.60p carmine & multi. 20 12
C531 " 1.60p carmine & black 20 12
Nos. C527–C531 (5) 1.00 60

Mexican art and science through the centuries.

Score for El Pesebre by Casals AP225

1976, Dec. 29

C532 AP225 4.30p lt. bl., blk. & brown 45 20

Pablo Casals (1876–1973), cellist and composer, birth centenary.

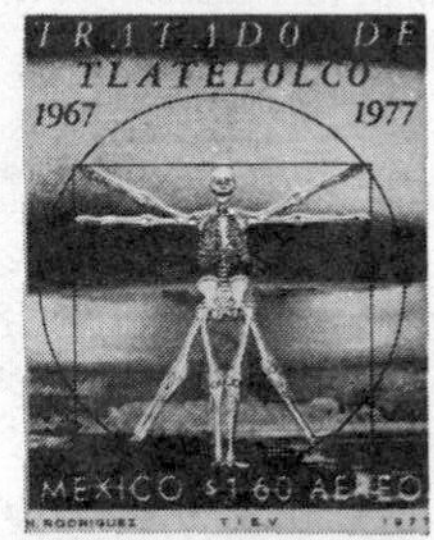

Mankind Destroyed by Nuclear Power—AP226

1977, Feb. 14 Photo. *Perf. 14*

C533 AP226 1.60p multicolored 20 12

10th anniversary of the Agreement of Tlatelolco, banning nuclear arms in Latin America.

Soccer AP227

Anniversary Emblem AP228

1977, Aug. 23 *Perf. 14* Wmk. 300

C534 AP227 1.60p multi. 16 12
C535 AP228 4.30p black, blue & yellow 45 25

Mexican Soccer Federation, 50th anniversary.

Hands and Scales AP229

1977, Sept. 28 Photo. *Perf. 14*

C536 AP229 1.60p org., brown & black 16 12

Federal Council of Reconciliation and Arbitration, 50th anniversary.

Arms of Mexico and Spain AP230

Designs: 1.90p, Maps of Mexico and Spain. 4.30p, Pres. José Lopez Portillo and King Juan Carlos.

1977, Oct. 8 *Perf. 14*

C537 AP230 1.60p dull blue & black 16 12
C538 " 1.90p lt. green & maroon 18 14
C539 " 4.30p tan, green & brown 45 25

Resumption of diplomatic relations with Spain.

Tlaloc, the Rain God AP231

Ludwig van Beethoven AP232

Perf. 14

1977, Nov. 4 Photo. Wmk. 300

C540 AP231 1.60p multi. 16 12

National Central Observatory, centenary.

1977, Nov. 12 Photogravure

C541 AP232 1.60p brt. grn. & brown 16 12
C542 " 4.30p lilac rose & blue 45 25

Ludwig van Beethoven (1770–1827), composer, 150th death anniversary.

Tractor and Dam—AP233

1977, Nov. 25 Photo. *Perf. 14*

C543 AP233 1.60p multi. 16 12

United Nations Desertification Conference.

Mexico City-Cuernavaca Highway—AP234

1977, Nov. 30

C544 AP234 1.60p multi. 16 12

25th anniversary of first national highway.

Arms of Campeche AP235

1977, Dec. 3

C545 AP235 1.60p multi. 16 12

200th anniversary of the naming of Campeche.

Congress Emblem AP236

1977, Dec. 9

C546 AP236 1.60p multi. 16 12

20th World Congress for Education, Hygiene and Recreation, July 18–24, 1977.

Freighter Navimex AP237

1977, Dec. 16

C547 AP237 1.60p multi. 16 12

60th anniversary of National Merchant Marine.

Mayan Dancer, Jaina AP238

Pre-Columbian Sculptures: No. C549, Aztec dance god. No. C550, Snake dancer, bas-relief. No. C551, Monte Alban, bas-relief. No. C552, Totonaca figurine.

1977, Dec. 26 *Perf. 14*

C548 AP238 1.60p salmon, blk. & car. 16 12

C549 AP238 1.60p lt. & dark bl. & blk. 16 12

C550 " 1.60p yel., black & gray 16 12

C551 " 1.60p bl. green, blk. & grn. 16 12

C552 " 1.60p gray, black & red brn. 16 12

Nos. C548–C552 (5) 80 60

Mexican art.

Tumor Clinic, by David A. Siqueiros AP239

Design: 4.30p, La Raza Medical Center, by Diego Rivera.

1978, Jan. 19 Photo. **Wmk. 300**

C553 AP239 1.60p multi. 16 12

C554 " 4.30p " 45 25

35th anniversary of Mexican Social Security Institute.

Moorish Fountain—AP240

1978, Mar. 1 Photo. *Perf. 14*

C555 AP240 1.60p multi. 16 12

450th anniversary of the founding of Chiapa de Corzo, Chiapas.

Oil Industry Type of 1978

Designs: 1.60p, Gen. Lazaro Cardenas. 4.30p, Offshore oil rig.

Wmk. 300

1978, Mar. 18 Photo. *Perf. 14*

C556 A343 1.60p brt. blue & lilac rose 16 10

C557 " 4.30p bl., brt. bl. & black 45 25

40th anniversary of nationalization of oil industry.

Arms of Diego de Mazariegos AP241

Wmk. 300

1978, Apr. 3 Photo. *Perf. 14*

C558 AP241 1.60p pink, black & purple 16 10

400th anniversary of the founding of San Cristobal de las Casas, Chiapas, by Diego de Mazariegos.

Blood Pressure Gauge, Map of Mexico AP242

Globe, Snake, Hand Holding Stethoscope AP243

1978, Apr. 30

C559 AP242 1.60p dk. blue & carmine 16 10

C560 AP243 4.30p org. & dk. blue 45 20

Drive against hypertension and World Health Day.

X-ABC1 Plane AP244

1978, Apr. 15

C561 AP244 1.60p ultra. & multi. 16 10

C562 " 4.30p ultra. & multi. 45 20

First Mexican airmail route, 50th anniversary.

Globe, Cogwheel, U.N. Emblem—AP245

Design: 4.30p, Globe, flags, cogwheel, U.N. emblem.

1978, Apr. 21

C563 AP245 1.60p multi. 16 10

C564 " 4.30p " 45 20

World Conference on Technical Cooperation of Underdeveloped Countries.

Soccer AP246

Designs: 1.90p, Goalkeeper catching ball. 4.30p, Soccer player.

Wmk. 300

1978, June 1 Photo. *Perf. 14*

C565 AP246 1.60p multi. 16 10

C566 " 1.90p " 20 12

C567 " 4.30p " 42 20

11th World Cup Soccer Championship, Argentina, June 1–25.

A little time given to study of the arrangement of the Scott Catalogue can make it easier to use effectively.

Francisco (Pancho) Villa AP247

1978, June 5

C568 AP247 1.60p multi. 16 10

Pancho Villa (1878–1923), revolutionary leader, birth centenary.

Mexico No. C6, Independence Monument, Washington Obelisk AP248

1978, June 11

C569 AP248 1.60p olive gray & red 16 10

50th anniversary of flight Mexico to Washington by Emilio Carranza (1905–1928).

Woman and Calendar Stone AP249

Photogravure

1978, July 15 *Perf. 14* **Wmk. 300**

C570 AP249 1.60p rose, black & brown 16 10

C571 " 1.90p brt. green, black & brown 20 12

C572 " 4.30p orange, blk. & brown 42 20

Miss Universe contest, Acapulco, July 1978.

Alvaro Obregón AP250

1978, July 17

C573 AP250 1.60p multi. 16 10

Alvaro Obregón (1880–1928), president of Mexico.

Geographical Institute Type of 1978

Designs: Institute emblem in different arrangements.

1978, July 21 Photo. **Wmk. 300**

C574 A344 1.60p emerald & black 16 10

C575 " 4.30p ocher & blk. 42 20

Pan-American Institute for Geography and History, 50th anniversary.

Sun Rising over Obregón
AP251

1978, Aug. 4 *Perf. 14*

C576 AP251 1.60p multi. 16 10

50th anniversary of the founding of Obregón.

Mayan Figure, Castle and Pawn
AP252

Aristotle
AP253

1978, Aug. 19 Photo. *Perf. 14*

C577 AP252 1.60p multi. 16 10
C578 " 4.30p " 42 20

World Youth Team Chess Championship, Ajedrez, Aug. 19–Sept. 7.

1978, Aug. 25

Design: 4.30p, Statue of Aristotle.

C579 AP253 1.60p multi. 16 10
C580 " 4.30p " 42 20

Aristotle (384–322 B.C.), philosopher.

Mule Deer
AP254

Man's Head, Dove, UN Emblem
AP255

Design: No. C582, Ocelot.

1978, Sept. 8 Photo. **Wmk. 300**

C581 AP254 1.60p multi. 16 10
C582 " 1.60p " 16 10

Protected animals.

1978, Sept. 22 *Perf. 14*

Design: 4.30p, Woman's head, dove, UN emblem.

C583 AP255 1.60p verm., gray & black 16 10
C584 " 4.30p lilac, gray & black 42 20

Anti-Apartheid Year.

Emblem
AP256

Wmk. 300

1978, Oct. 23 Photo. *Perf. 14*

C585 AP256 1.60p multi. 16 10

13th Congress of International Union of Architects, Mexico City, Oct. 23–27.

Dr. Rafael Lucio (1819–1886)
AP257

Franz Schubert, "Death and the Maiden"
AP258

1978, Nov. 13 **Wmk. 350**

C586 AP257 1.60p yel. green 16 10

11th International Anti-Leprosy Congress.

1978, Nov. 19 Photo. *Perf. 14*

C587 AP258 4.30p brn., grn. & black 42 20

Franz Schubert (1797–1828), Austrian composer.

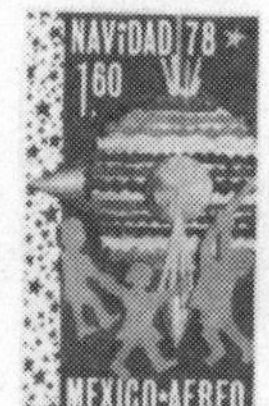
Children, Christmas Decorations
AP259

Antonio Vivaldi
AP260

Perf. 14

1978, Nov. 22 Photo. **Wmk. 350**

C588 AP259 1.60p multi. 16 10

Christmas 1978.

1978, Dec. 1

C589 AP260 4.30p multi. 42 20

Antonio Vivaldi (1675–1741), Italian violinist and composer.

Wright Brothers' Flyer
AP261

Design: 4.30p, Flyer, different view.

1978, Dec. 17

C590 AP261 1.60p multi. 16 10
C591 " 4.30p " 42 20

75th anniversary of 1st powered flight.

Einstein and his Equation
AP262

Wmk. 300

1979, Apr. 20 Photo. *Perf. 14*

C592 AP262 1.60p multi. 16 10

Albert Einstein (1879–1955), theoretical physicist.

Rowland Hill
AP263

1979, Apr. 27

C593 AP263 1.60p multi. 16 10

Sir Rowland Hill (1795–1879), originator of penny postage.

AIR POST OFFICIAL STAMPS.

Nos. C4 and C3 Overprinted in Black or Red **OFICIAL.**

1929 *Perf. 12.* **Wmk. 156**

CO1 AP1 25c dark green & gray brown 1.50 1.50
a. Without period 4.00 3.50
CO2 " 25c dark green & gray brown (R) 1.75 1.75
a. Without period 7.50 7.00
CO2B " 25c brown carmine & gray brown 3.50 3.50
c. Without period 10.00 10.00

Types of Regular Issue of 1926 Overprinted in Red **HABILITADO Servicio Oficial Aereo**

1929, Oct. 15 **Unwmkd.**

CO3 A90 2c black 40.00 40.00
CO4 A91 4c " 40.00 40.00
CO5 A90 5c " 40.00 40.00
CO6 A91 10c " 40.00 40.00
CO7 A92 20c " 40.00 40.00
CO8 " 30c " 40.00 40.00
CO9 " 40c " 40.00 40.00
Nos. CO3–CO9 (7) 280.00 280.00

Horizontal Overprint.

CO10 A93 1p black *1150.00 1150.00*

Nos. CO3–CO9 also exist with overprint reading up.

No. C26 Overprinted in Black **OFICIAL.**

1930 **Wmk. 156**

CO11 AP4 20c black violet 50 50
a. Without period 5.00 5.00
b. Inverted overprint 5.00 5.00
c. Inverted overprint without period 65.00

No. CO11 with red overprint is believed not to have been issued for postal purposes.

Plane over Mexico City—OA1

1930 Engraved

CO12 OA1 20c gray black 2.50 2.50
CO13 " 35c light violet 70 70
CO14 " 40c olive brown & deep blue 80 80
CO15 " 70c violet & olive gray 80 80

No. CO12 Surcharged in Red
HABILITADO
Quince centavos

1931

CO16 OA1 15c on 20c gray blk. 50 50
a. Inverted surch. 40.00
b. Double surch. 40.00

No. C20 Overprinted **OFICIAL.**

1932 *Rouletted 13, 13½.*

CO17 AP3 5c light blue 50 30

Air Post Stamps of 1927–32 Overprinted
SERVICIO OFICIAL
On Stamp No. C1a.

1932 *Perf. 12.* **Unwmkd.**

CO18 AP1 50c dark blue & claret 550.00 550.00

On Stamp No. C2.
Wmkd. CORREOS MEXICO. (156)

CO19 AP1 50c dark blue & red brown 75 75

On Stamps Nos. C11 and C12.

1932 *Perf. 12.*

CO20 AP3 10c violet 10.00 10.00
CO21 " 15c carmine 75.00 75.00

On Stamps Nos. C21 to C23.
Rouletted 13, 13½.

CO22 AP3 10c violet 30 30
CO23 " 15c carmine 1.00 90
CO24 " 20c brown olive 1.00 80

Nos. C20, C21 C23 and C25 Overprinted **SERVICIO OFICIAL**

1933-34 *Rouletted 13½.*

CO25 AP3 5c light blue 30 30
CO26 " 10c violet ('34) 30 30
CO27 " 20c brown olive 70 70
CO28 " 50c red brown ('34) 90 90

On Air Post Stamp No. C2.
Perf. 12.

CO29 AP1 50c dark blue & red brown 85 85

On Air Post Stamp No. C11.
Perf. 12.

CO30 AP3 10c violet ('34) 35.00 35.00

SPECIAL DELIVERY STAMPS.

Motorcycle Postman
SD1

Engraved

1919 *Perf. 12.* **Unwmkd.**

E1 SD1 20c red & black 10.00 1.25

Wmkd. CORREOS MEXICO. (156)

1923

E2 SD1 20c dk. car. & black 40 15

Toltec Messenger with Quipu
SD2

1934

E3 SD2 10c brown red & blue 50 40

Indian Archer
SD3

Imprint: "Oficina Impresora de Hacienda Mexico."

1934 *Perf. 10x10½*

E4 SD3 10c black violet 1.00 30

Redrawn design.
Imprint: "Talleres de Imp. de Est. y Valores-Mexico."

1938–41 Photogravure *Perf. 14*

E5 SD3 10c slate violet 60 20
E6 " 20c orange red ('41) 60 15

Imperforate copies of No. E6 were not regularly issued.

No. E2 Overprinted "1940" in Violet.

1940 Engraved *Perf. 12*

E7 SD1 20c red & black 50 15

Redrawn Archer Type of 1941
Photogravure.

1944–47 *Perf. 14* **Wmk. 272**

E8 SD3 20c orange red 1.00 35

Wmk. 279

E9 SD3 20c orange red ('47) 80 20

Special Delivery Messenger
SD4

Messengers' Hands Transferring Letter
SD5

1950–51 Photo. **Wmk. 279**

E10 SD4 25c bright red 30 8
E11 SD5 60c dark blue green ('51) 2.00 75

Redrawn.

1951

E12 SD4 25c bright red 15.00 1.50

Sharper impression, heavier shading; motorcycle sidecar ½ mm. from "s" of "centavos;" imprint wider, beginning under "n" of "inmediata."

Second Redrawing.

1952

E13 SD4 25c bright red 4.00 25

Design 35½ mm. wide (33 mm. on Nos. E10 and E12); finer lettering at left, and height of letters in imprint reduced 50 per cent; three distinct lines in tires.

Redrawn Type of 1951.

1954 **Wmk. 300**

E14 SD4 25c red orange 40 10

1954 Type of 1951

E15 SD5 60c dark blue green 35 15

Hands and Pigeon
SD6

Plane Circling Globe
SD7

Photogravure

1956 *Perf. 14* **Wmk. 300**

E16 SD6 35c red lilac 25 10
E17 SD7 80c henna brown 35 25

1962

E18 SD6 50c green 35 8
E19 SD7 1.20p dark purple 55 30

1964 **Wmk. 350**

E20 SD6 50c green 25 10
E21 SD7 1.20p dark purple 75 30

1973 **Unwmkd.**

E22 SD6 50c green 5.00 50

Fluorescent printing on front or back consists of beehive pattern and diagonal inscription.

1975 **Wmk. 300**

E23 SD6 2p orange 25 15
E24 SD7 5p violet blue 2.00 50

1976 **Unwmkd.**

E25 SD6 2p red orange 25 15
E26 SD7 5p dark violet blue 60 30

Watch
SD8

Photogravure

1976 *Perf. 14* **Unwmkd.**

E27 SD8 2p orange & black 20 12

INSURED LETTER STAMPS.

Insured Letters
IL1

Registered Mailbag
IL2

Safe
IL3

Wmkd. CORREOS MEXICO. (156)

1935 Engraved. *Perf. 10½.*

G1 IL1 10c vermilion 75 35
G2 IL2 50c dark blue 45 25
G3 IL3 1p turquoise green 65 45

Nos. G1 and G4 were issued both with and without imprint.

Perf. 10x10½.

1944-45 **Wmk. 272**

G4 IL1 10c vermilion ('45) 2.00 50
G5 IL2 50c dark blue 50 25
G6 IL3 1p turquoise green 1.00 50

1947 *Perf. 10x10½.* **Wmk. 279**

G7 IL1 10c vermilion 1.00 30
G8 IL2 50c dark blue 50 25
G9 IL3 1p turquoise green 60 35

Vault—IL4

1950-51 Photogravure *Perf. 14*

G10 IL4 20c blue 40 10
G11 " 40c purple 30 15
G12 " 1p yel. green ('51) 90 30
G13 " 5p dark blue & gray green ('51) 1.25 85
G14 " 10p carmine & ultramarine ('51) 2.50 1.50
Nos. G10-G14 (5) 5.35 2.90

1954-71 **Wmk. 300**

G15 IL4 20c blue ('56) 25 8
G16 " 40c lt. purple ('56) 25 10
G17 " 1p yellow green 35 15
a. Size 37x20½mm. ('71) 1.50 35
G18 IL4 5p blue & green ('59) 1.10 10
G19 " 10p carmine & ultra. ('63) 4.00 2.00
Nos. G15-G19 (5) 5.95 2.93

No. G17 measures 35x19½mm. Vertical measurement excludes imprint.

1967 *Perf. 14* **Wmk. 350**

G21 IL4 40c light purple 1.50 30
G22 " 1p yellow green 1.50 35

1975 Photogravure **Wmk. 300**

G23 IL4 2p lilac rose 20 12
G24 " 20p orange & gray 2.00 1.50

Padlock
IL5

Photogravure

1976 *Perf. 14* **Unwmkd.**

G25 IL5 40c black & blue 5 3
G26 " 1p " " 10 6
G27 " 5p " " 50 25
G28 " 10p " " 1.00 75

POSTAGE DUE STAMPS.

D1

Wmkd.

SERVICIO POSTAL DE LOS ESTADOS UNIDOS MEXICANOS. (155)

1908 Engraved *Perf. 14*

J1 D1 1c blue 2.00 2.00
J2 " 2c " 2.00 2.00
J3 " 4c " 2.00 2.00
J4 " 5c " 2.00 2.00
J5 " 10c " 2.00 2.00
Nos. J1-J5 (5) 10.00 10.00

PORTE DE MAR STAMPS.

These stamps were used to indicate the amount of cash to be paid to the captains of the mail steamers taking outgoing foreign mail.

PM1

PM2

PM3

Lithographed.

1875 *Imperf.* **Unwmkd.**

JX1 PM1 10c *yellow* 1.50
JX2 " 25c " 2.00
JX3 " 35c " 2.00
JX4 " 50c " 2.00
JX5 " 60c " 3.25
JX6 " 75c " 4.00
JX7 " 85c " 3.25
JX8 PM1 100c *yellow* 4.00
Nos. JX1-JX8 (8) 22.00

Nos. JX1 to JX8 were never put to use. All were printed in same sheet of 49 (7x7). Sheet consists of 14 of 10c; 7 of 25c, 35c and 50c; 4 of 60c and 85c; 3 of 75c and 100c. There are four varieties of 10c, two of 25c, 35c and 50c.

JX9 PM2 2c black 40 *1.25*
a. "5" added to make 25c 4.00 *12.50*
JX10 " 10c black 50 *1.25*
JX11 " 12c " 50 *1.50*
JX12 " 20c " 60 *1.50*
JX13 " 25c " 2.50 *5.00*
JX14 " 35c " 2.50 *5.00*
JX15 " 50c " 2.25 *5.00*
JX16 " 60c " 2.25 *6.00*
JX17 " 75c " 2.75 *6.00*
JX18 " 85c " 2.50 *6.00*
JX19 " 100c " 3.00 *10.00*
Nos. JX9-JX19 (11) 19.75 *48.50*

Same, Numerals Larger.

JX20 PM2 5c black 60 *5.00*
JX21 " 25c " 1.25 *3.50*
JX22 " 35c " 100.00 100.00
JX23 " 50c " 70 *5.00*
JX24 " 60c " 40.00 40.00
JX25 " 100c " 50 *6.00*
Nos. JX20-JX25 (6) 143.05 159.50

In Nos. JX9 to JX19 the figures of value are 7 mm. high and "CENTAVOS" is 7½ mm. long. On Nos. JX20 to JX25 the figures of value are 8 mm. high and "CENTAVOS" is 9½ mm. long.

Nos. JX9-JX25 exist with overprints of district names.

Counterfeits exist of Nos. JX9-JX31.

1879

JX26 PM3 2c brown 45
JX27 " 5c yellow 45
JX28 " 10c red 45
JX29 " 25c blue 45
JX30 " 50c green 45
JX31 " 100c violet 45
Nos. JX26-JX31 (6) 2.70

Nos. JX26 to JX31 were never put in use.

OFFICIAL STAMPS

Hidalgo
O1

Engraved.

Wove or Laid Paper.

1884-93 *Perf. 11, 12* **Unwmkd.**

O1 O1 red 50 35
a. Vertical pair, imperf. between 50.00
O2 O1 olive brown ('87) 30 15
a. Blue ruled lines on paper
O3 O1 orange 75 30
a. Vertical pair, imperf. between 50.00
O4 O1 blue green ('93) 50 25
a. Imperf., pair

Pin-perf. 6.

O5 O1 olive brown 7.50 4.50

Wmkd.

"Correos E. U. M." on every Vertical Line of Ten Stamps. (152)

1894 *Perf. 5½*

O6 O1 ultramarine 1.25 1.00
a. Imperf. horiz., pair 12.50
b. Imperf., pair 20.00

Perf. 11 and 12

O7 O1 ultramarine 75 60
O8 " carmine

Perf. 5½x11, 11x5½.

O9 O1 ultramarine 2.00 2.00

Regular Issues with Handstamped Overprint in Black **OFICIAL**

1895 *Perf. 12.*

O10 A20 1c green 1.00 1.00
O11 " 2c carmine 1.25 1.00
O12 A20 3c orange brown 1.50 1.00
O13 A21 4c orange 1.75 1.50
O14 A22 5c ultramarine 2.25 2.00
O15 A23 10c lilac rose 2.00 80
O16 A21 12c olive brown 9.00 5.00
O17 A23 15c bright blue 5.00 3.00
O18 " 20c brown rose 5.00 3.00
O19 " 50c purple 10.00 7.50
O20 A24 1p brown 30.00 15.00
O21 " 5p scarlet 100.00 50.00
O22 " 10p deep blue 175.00 100.00
Nos. O10-O22 (13) 343.75 190.80

Similar stamps with red overprint were not officially placed in use.

Black Overprint.

Wmkd. "R. M." Interlaced. (153)

1896-97

O23 A20 1c green 6.00 3.00
O24 " 2c carmine 6.00 3.00
O25 " 3c orange brown 6.00 3.00
O26 A21 4c orange 8.00 3.50
O27 A22 5c ultramarine 6.00 3.00
O28 A21 12c olive brown 17.50 7.00
O29 A23 15c bright blue 20.00 10.00
O29A " 50c purple 80.00 35.00
Nos. O23-O29A (8) 149.50 67.50

Black Overprint.

1897 **Wmkd. Eagle and R. M. (154)**

O30 A20 1c green 17.50 7.00
O31 " 2c scarlet 17.50 7.00
O33 A21 4c orange 30.00 13.00
O34 A22 5c ultramarine 20.00 7.00
O35 A21 12c olive brown 30.00 10.00
O36 A23 15c bright blue 35.00 10.00
O37 " 20c brown rose 20.00 5.00
O38 " 50c purple 30.00 8.00
O39 A24 1p brown 70.00 30.00
Nos. O30-O39 (9) 270.00 97.00

1898 Black Overprint. **Unwmkd.**

O40 A20 1c green 5.00 2.00
O41 " 2c scarlet 5.50 2.00
O42 " 3c orange brown 6.00 2.00
O43 A21 4c orange 8.00 2.00
O44 A22 5c ultramarine 10.00 4.00
O45 A23 10c lilac rose 100.00 65.00
O46 A21 12c olive brown 30.00 7.00
O47 A23 15c bright blue 25.00 7.00
O48 " 20c brown rose 35.00 10.00
O48A " 50c purple 60.00 30.00
Nos. O40-O48A (10) 284.50 131.00

Black Overprint.

Wmkd.

SERVICIO POSTAL, etc. (155)

1900 *Perf. 14, 15.*

O49 A25 1c green 6.00 85
O50 A26 2c vermilion 7.00 85
O51 A27 3c yellow brown 7.00 75
O52 A28 5c dark blue 7.00 1.25
O53 A29 10c vio. & orange 11.00 1.50
O54 A30 15c lavender & claret 11.00 1.50
O55 A31 20c rose & dk. blue 12.00 60
O56 A32 50c red lilac & blk. 20.00 6.00
O57 A33 1p blue & black 50.00 5.00
O58 A34 5p car. & black 150.00 15.00
Nos. O49-O58 (10) 281.00 33.30

1903 Black Overprint.

O59 A25 1c violet 6.00 85
O60 A26 2c green 7.00 85
O61 A35 4c carmine 12.00 60
O62 A28 5c orange 10.00 2.00
O63 A29 10c blue & orange 12.00 85
O64 A32 50c car. & black 30.00 5.00
Nos. O59-O64 (6) 77.00 10.15

Regular Issues Overprinted **OFICIAL**

1910 On Issues of 1899-1903.

O65 A26 2c green 35.00 1.50
O66 A27 3c orange brown 35.00 1.00
O67 A35 4c carmine 45.00 2.00
O68 A28 5c orange 35.00 8.00
O69 A29 10c blue & orange 40.00 1.00
O70 A30 15c lavender & claret 45.00 1.50
O71 A31 20c rose & dark blue 50.00 85
O72 A32 50c car. & black 80.00 7.00
O73 A33 1p blue & black 135.00 20.00
O74 A34 5p car. & black 150.00 25.00
Nos. O65-O74 (10) 650.00 67.85

1911 On Issue of 1910.

O75	A36	1c violet	1.00	60
O76	A37	2c green	1.00	60
O77	A38	3c orange brown	1.50	60
O78	A39	4c carmine	2.00	60
O79	A40	5c orange	3.00	2.00
O80	A41	10c blue & orange	1.75	60
O81	A42	15c gray blue & claret	3.50	2.50
O82	A43	20c red & blue	3.00	60
O83	A44	50c red brown & black	9.00	4.00
O84	A45	1p blue & black	14.00	5.00
O85	A46	5p car. & black	40.00	15.00
		Nos. O75-O85 (11)	79.75	32.10

Nos. 500 to 505 Overprinted **OFICIAL**

1915 ***Rouletted 14½.*** **Unwmkd.**

O86	A57	1c violet	40	50
O87	A58	2c green	40	50
O88	A59	3c brown	50	60
O89	A60	4c carmine	40	50
O90	A61	5c orange	40	50
O91	A62	10c ultramarine	50	60
		Nos. O86-O91 (6)	2.60	3.20

All values are known with inverted overprint. All values exist imperforate and part perforate but were not regularly issued in these forms.

On Nos. 506 to 514.

1915-16 ***Perf. 12.***

O92	A57	1c violet	30	40
O93	A58	2c green	30	40
O94	A59	3c brown	35	40
O95	A60	4c carmine	35	40
O96	A61	5c orange	35	40
O97	A62	10c ultra., type II	35	40
O98	A63	40c slate	1.25	1.50
		a. Inverted overprint	6.00	
		b. Double overprint	9.00	
O99	A64	1p brown & black	2.00	2.50
		a. Inverted overprint	7.00	
O100	A65	5p claret & ultra.	10.00	12.00
		a. Inverted overprint	17.50	
		Nos. O92-O100 (9)	15.25	18.40

Nos. O98 and O99 exist imperforate but probably were not issued in that form.

Preceding Issues Overprinted in Red, Blue or Black G.P.DE M.

On No. O74.

1916 **Wmk. 155**

O101	A34	5p carmine & black (R)	300.00	

On Nos. O75 to O85.

O102	A36	1c violet (R)	1.75	
O103	A37	2c green (R)	45	
O104	A38	3c orange brown (Bl)	60	
O105	A39	4c carmine (Bl)	2.00	
O106	A40	5c orange (Bl)	60	
O107	A41	10c blue & orange (R)	60	
O108	A42	15c gray blue & claret (Bk)	60	
O109	A43	20c red & blue (Bk)	70	
O110	A44	50c red brown & black (R)	30.00	
O111	A45	1p blue & black (R)	2.50	
O112	A46	5p carmine & black (R)	*900.00*	
		Nos. O102-O111 (10)	39.80	

No. O102 with blue overprint is a trial color. Counterfeits exist of No. O112.

Nos. 608, 610 to 612, 615 and 616 Overprinted **OFICIAL** Vertically in Red or Black.

Thick Paper.

1918 ***Rouletted 14½.*** **Unwmkd.**

O113	A68	1c violet (R)	12.00	6.00
O114	A69	2c gray green (R)	15.00	7.00
O115	A70	3c bistre brown (R)	12.00	6.00
O116	A71	4c carmine (Bk)	12.00	7.00
O117	A74	20c rose (Bk)	17.50	12.00
O118	A75	30c gray brown (R)	27.50	20.00

On Nos. 621 and 622.

Medium Paper.

Perf. 12.

O119	A72	5c ultramarine (R)	6.00	4.00
O120	A73	10c blue (R)	6.00	3.00
		a. Double overprint		
		Nos. O113-O120 (8)	108.00	65.00

Overprinted Horizontally in Red **OFICIAL**

On Nos. 625, 626 and 628.

Thin Paper.

O121	A63	40c violet (R)	7.00	5.00
O122	A64	1p blue & black (R)	17.50	15.00
O123	A65	5p green & black (R)	125.00	75.00

Nos. 608 and 610 to 615 Overprinted **OFICIAL** Vertically in Red or Black.

Thick Paper.

1919 ***Rouletted 14½.***

O124	A68	1c dull violet (R)	1.50	1.25
O125	A69	2c gray green (R)	1.75	1.15
O126	A70	3c bistre brown (R)	3.00	1.50
O127	A71	4c carmine (Bk)	6.00	4.00
O127A	A72	5c ultramarine	10.00	7.00
O128	A73	10c blue (R)	2.50	60
O129	A74	20c rose (Bk)	12.00	8.00

On Nos. 618 and 621.

Perf. 12.

O130	A68	1c dull violet (R)	8.00	6.00
O131	A72	5c ultramarine (R)	8.00	6.00

Overprinted Horizontally On Nos. 625 and 626.

Thin Paper.

O132	A63	40c violet (R)	9.00	7.00
O133	A64	1p blue & black (R)	7.00	5.00
		Nos. O124-O133 (11)	68.75	47.50

Nos. 608 to 615 and 617 Overprinted **OFICIAL** Vertically in Black, Red or Blue

Size: 17½x3mm.

1921 ***Rouletted 14½.***

O134	A68	1c gray (Bk)	4.00	2.00
		a. 1c dull vio. (Bk)	4.00	2.00
O135	A69	2c gray green (R)	1.00	75
O136	A70	3c bistre brown (R)	1.50	85
O137	A71	4c carmine (Bk)	3.00	2.00
O138	A72	5c ultramarine (R)	4.00	2.50
O139	A73	10c blue (R)	7.00	3.00
O140	A74	20c rose (Bl)	9.00	4.00
O141	A75	30c gray black (R)	6.00	3.50

Overprinted Horizontally On Nos. 625, 626 and 628.

Perf. 12.

O142	A63	40c violet (R)	8.00	8.00
O143	A64	1p blue & black (R)	5.00	5.00
O144	A65	5p green & black (Bk)	95.00	85.00
		Nos. O134-O144 (11)	143.50	116.60

Nos. 609 to 615 Overprinted Vertically in Black

OFICIAL.

1921-30 ***Rouletted 14½.***

O145	A68	1c gray	30	20
		a. 1c lilac gray	30	25
O146	A69	2c gray green	25	20
O147	A70	3c bistre brown	30	20
		a. "OFICAL"	7.00	7.00
		b. "OIFCIAL"	7.00	7.00
		c. Double overprint	25.00	
O148	A71	4c carmine	2.50	40
O149	A72	5c ultramarine	35	20
O150	A73	10c blue	35	20
		a. "OIFCIAL"	8.00	
O151	A74	20c brown rose	1.00	50
		a. 20c rose	1.00	50

On No. 624.

Perf. 12.

O152	A75	30c gray black	4.00	1.00

Overprinted Horizontally On Nos. 625 and 628.

O153	A63	40c violet	2.00	1.00
		a. "OFICAL"	9.00	9.00
		b. "OICIFAL"	9.00	9.00
		c. Invtd. ovpt.	17.50	
O154	A65	5p green & black ('30)	40.00	30.00
		Nos. O145-O154 (10)	51.05	33.90

Overprinted Vertically in Red On Nos. 609, 610, 611, 613 and 614.

1921-24 ***Rouletted 14½.***

O155	A68	1c lilac	45	30
O156	A69	2c gray green	35	25
O157	A70	3c bistre brown	1.00	30
O158	A72	5c ultramarine	45	25
O159	A73	10c blue	4.00	65
		a. Double ovpt.		

On Nos. 623 and 624.

Perf. 12.

O160	A74	20c rose	1.00	40
O161	A75	30c gray black	1.75	1.25

Overprinted Horizontally On Nos. 625, 626 and 628.

O162	A63	40c violet	1.75	1.50
O163	A64	1p blue & black	7.00	5.00
O164	A65	5p green & black	40.00	30.00

Overprinted Vertically in Blue on No. 612.

Rouletted 14½

O165	A71	4c carmine	2.00	1.00
		Nos. O155-O165 (11)	59.75	40.90

Same Overprint Vertically in Red or Blue On Nos. 635 and 637.

1926-27 ***Rouletted 14½.***

O166	A80	3c bistre brown, ovpt. horiz. (R)	2.00	2.00
O167	A82	5c orange (R)	5.50	5.50

On Nos. 650, 651, 655 and 656.

Wmkd. CORREOS MEXICO. (156)

O168	A79	2c scarlet (Bl)	3.50	3.50
O169	A80	3c bistre brown, ovpt. horiz. (R)	1.00	1.00
O170	A85	10c claret (Bl)	5.00	2.50
O171	A84	20c deep blue (R)	2.50	2.50

Overprinted Horizontally On Nos. 643, 646 to 649.

Perf. 12.

O172	A81	4c green (R)	1.75	1.75
O173	A83	30c dark green (R)	1.25	1.25
O174	A63	40c violet (R)	3.00	3.00
		a. Inverted overprint	10.00	
O175	A87	50c olive brown (R)	60	60
O176	A88	1p red brown & blue (R)	5.00	4.00
		Nos. O168-O176 (9)	23.60	20.10

Same Overprint Horizontally on No. RA3, Vertically on Nos. 650-651, 653-656, 666.

1927-31 ***Rouletted 14½***

O177	PT1	1c brown ('31)	25	25
O178	A79	2c scarlet	25	25
		a. "OFICAIL"	6.00	6.00
O179	A80	3c bistre brown, ovpt. horiz.	60	40
		a. "OFICAIL"	6.00	6.00
O180	A82	4c green	60	45
		a. "OFICAIL"	6.00	6.00
O181	"	5c orange	75	60
O182	A94	8c orange	2.00	1.50
O183	A85	10c lake	60	60
O184	A84	20c dark blue	2.50	2.00
		a. "OFICAIL"	7.50	7.50
		Nos. O177-O184 (8)	7.55	6.05

Overprinted Horizontally On Nos. 643 and 645 to 649.

1927-33 ***Perf. 12***

O185	A81	4c green	1.50	1.00
		a. Inverted overprint	8.00	5.00
O186	A85	10c brown lake	7.00	7.00
O187	A83	30c dark green	40	25
		a. Inverted overprint	6.00	3.00
		b. Pair, tête bêche overprints	7.50	
		c. "OFICAIL"	7.00	7.00
O188	A63	40c violet	3.50	2.50
O189	A87	50c olive brown ('33)	1.00	1.00
O190	A88	1p red brown & blue	7.00	7.00
		Nos. O185-O190 (6)	20.40	18.75

The overprint on No. O186 is vertical.

Nos. 320, 628, 633 Overprinted Horizontally **OFICIAL**

On Stamp No. 320.

1927-28 ***Perf. 14, 15.*** **Wmk. 155**

O191	A46	5p carmine & black (R)	40.00	35.00
O192	"	5p carmine & black (Bl)	35.00	30.00

Perf. 12. **Unwmkd.**

O193	A65	5p green & black (Bk)	35.00	22.50
		a. Inverted overprint	55.00	55.00
O194	A78	10p black brown & black (Bl)	65.00	50.00

No. 320 Overprinted Horizontally **OFICIAL.**

Perf. 14 **Wmk. 155**

O195	A46	5p car. & black	45.00	

Nos. 650 and 655 Overprinted Horizontally **OFICIAL**

Size: 16x2½mm.

Wmkd. CORREOS MEXICO. (156)

1928-29 ***Rouletted 14½.***

O196	A79	2c dull red	5.00	4.50
O197	A85	10c rose lake	6.00	4.25

Nos. RA1, 650-651, 653-656 Overprinted **SERVICIO OFICIAL**

1932-33

O198	PT1	1c brown	25	25
O199	A79	2c dull red	20	20
O200	A80	3c bistre brown	60	60
O201	A82	4c green	2.00	2.00
O202	"	5c orange	1.50	1.00
O203	A85	10c rose lake	1.00	75
O204	A84	20c dark blue	2.50	1.50
		a. Double ovpt.	10.00	
		Nos. O198-O204 (7)	8.05	6.30

Nos. 651, 646-649 Overprinted Horizontally **SERVICIO OFICIAL**

1933 ***Rouletted 14½***

O205	A80	3c bistre brown	60	60

Perf. 12.

O206	A83	30c dark green	85	85
O207	A63	40c violet	1.75	1.75
O208	A87	50c olive brown	60	60
		a. Overprinted "OFICIAL OFICIAL"	6.00	6.00
O209	A88	1p red brn. & bl.	75	50

Overprinted Vertically On No. 656.

Rouletted 14½.

O210	A84	20c dark blue	4.00	2.50
		Nos. O205-O210 (6)	8.55	6.80

Nos. RA1, 651, 653, 654, 683 Overprinted Horizontally

OFICIAL

Size: 13x2mm

1934–37 *Rouletted 14½*

O211 PT1 1c brown 1.00 1.00
O212 A80 3c bistre brown 20 20
O213 A82 4c green 2.00 2.00
O214 " 5c orange 20 20
O215 A96 15c dark blue ('37) 35 35
Nos. O211–O215 (5) 3.75 3.75
See also No. O217a.

Same Overprint on Nos. 687A–692.

1934–37 *Perf. 10½*

O216 PT1 1c brown ('37) 35 35
O217 A79 2c scarlet 25 25
a. On No. 650 (error) 10.00
O218 A82 4c green ('35) 35 35
O219 A85 10c brown lake 30 30
O220 A84 20c dark blue ('37) 40 40
O221 A83 30c dark blue green ('37) 75 75

On Nos. 647 and 649.
Perf. 12, 11½x12.

O222 A63 40c violet 1.00 1.00
O223 A88 1p red brn. & bl. 1.50 1.50
Nos. O216–O223 (8) 4.90 4.90

On Nos. 707 to 709, 712, 715, 716, 717, 718 and 719.

O224 A108 1c orange 65 65
a. Unwmkd. 12.00
O225 A109 2c green 40 40
O226 A110 4c carmine 40 30
O227 A112 10c violet 40 40
O228 A114 20c ultramarine 50 50
O229 A115 30c lake 75 75
O230 A116 40c red brown 75 75
O231 A117 50c black 1.00 1.00
O232 A118 1p dk. brn. & org. 1.25 1.25
Nos. O224–O232 (9) 6.10 6.00

PARCEL POST STAMPS.

Railroad Train—PP1

Wmkd. CORREOS MEXICO. (156)

1941 Photogravure *Perf. 14*

Q1 PP1 10c bright rose 1.25 12
Q2 " 20c dark violet blue 1.00 20

1944–46 **Wmk. 272**

Q3 PP1 10c bright rose 85 20
Q4 " 20c dark violet blue ('46) 1.00 30

1947–49 **Wmk. 279**

Q5 PP1 10c bright rose 75 25
Q6 " 20c dark violet blue ('49) 1.00 35

Streamlined Locomotive
PP2

1951

Q7 PP2 10c rose pink 60 15
Q8 " 20c blue violet 1.10 25

1954 **Wmk. 300**

Q9 PP2 10c rose pink 1.00 15
Q10 " 20c blue violet 1.00 15

POSTAL TAX STAMPS.

Morelos Monument
PT1

Engraved.

Wmkd. CORREOS MEXICO. (156)

1925 *Rouletted 14½.*

RA1 PT1 1c brown 25 10
a. Imperf. 20.00

1926 *Perf. 12*

RA2 PT1 1c brown 60 *3.00*
a. Booklet pane of 2 9.00

1925 *Rouletted 14½* **Unwmkd.**

RA3 PT1 1c brown 11.00 5.00

It was obligatory to add a stamp of type PT1 to the regular postage on every article of domestic mail matter. The money obtained from this source formed a fund to combat a plague of locusts.

In 1931, 1c stamps of type PT1 were discontinued as Postal Tax stamps. It was subsequently used for the payment of postage on drop letters (announcement cards and unsealed circulars) to be delivered in the city of cancellation. See No. 687A.

PT2

Mother and Child
PT3

1929 Red Overprint. **Wmk. 156**

RA4 PT2 1c brown 25 10
a. Ovpt. reading down 30.00 30.00

There were two settings of this overprint. They may be distinguished by the two lines being spaced 4 mm. or 6 mm. apart.

The money from sales of this stamp was devoted to child welfare work.

1929 Litho. *Rouletted 13, 13½*

RA5 PT3 1c violet 15 8

PT4

PT5

1929 **Unwmkd.**

Size: 18x24½mm.

RA6 PT4 2c deep green 25 10
RA7 " 5c brown 15 8

1929

Size: 19x25¼mm.

Two types of 1c:
Type I: Background lines continue through lettering of top inscription. Denomination circle hangs below second background line. Paper and gum white.
Type II: Background lines cut away behind some letters. Circle rests on second background line. Paper and gum yellowish.

RA8 PT5 1c violet, type I 10 6
a. Booklet pane of 4 7.00
b. Booklet pane of 2 14.00
c. Type II 10 6
RA9 " 2c deep green 25 10
a. Imperf. (pair) 8.00

The use of these stamps, in addition to the regular postage, was compulsory. The money obtained from their sale was used for child welfare work.

Postal Tax Stamps of 1929 Surcharged

HABILITADO
$0.01

1930

RA10 PT4 1c on 2c deep green 50 20
RA11 " 1c on 5c brown 40 20
RA12 PT5 1c on 2c deep green 60 20

PT6

Mosquito Attacking Man
PT7

1931, Jan. 30 *Perf. 14* **Wmk. 155**

RA13 PT6 1c dull violet 20 15
a. "PRO INFANCIA" double 35.00

Wmkd. CORREOS MEXICO. (156)

1939 Photogravure.

RA14 PT7 1c Prussian blue 1.00 6
a. Imperf. 2.50 1.50

This stamp was obligatory on all mail, the money being used to aid in a drive against malaria.

Miguel Hidalgo y Costilla
PT8

1941

RA15 PT8 1c bright carmine 35 5

Type of 1939.

1944 *Perf. 14.* **Wmk. 272**

RA16 PT7 1c Prussian blue 75 8

Learning Vowels
PT9

Wmkd. GOBIERNO MEXICANO and Eagle in Circle. (279)

1946 Photogravure. *Perf. 14.*

RA17 PT9 1c black brown 20 6

1947 **Wmk. 272**

RA18 PT9 1c black brown 25.00 1.00

Type of 1939.
Wmk. 279

RA19 PT7 1c Prussian blue 2.00 10

Certain countries cancel stamps in full sheets and sell them (usually with gum) for less than face value. Dealers generally sell "CTO" (canceled to order) stamps for much less than postally used copies.

PROVISIONAL ISSUES.

During the struggle led by Juarez to expel the Emperor Maximilian, installed June, 1864 by Napoleon III and French troops, a number of towns when free of Imperial forces issued provisional postage stamps. Maximilian was captured and executed June 19, 1867, but provisional issues continued current for a time pending re-establishment of Republican Government.

Campeche

(käm·pä'chā)

A southern state in Mexico, comprising the western part of the Yucatan peninsula.

A1

White Paper.
Numerals in Black.

1876 Handstamped *Imperf.*

1 A1 5c gray blue & blue *1600.00*
2 " 25c " " *850.00*
3 " 50c " " *3250.00*

The stamps printed in blue-black and blue on yellowish paper, formerly listed as issued in 1867, are now known to be an unofficial production of later years. They are reprints, but produced without official sanction.

Chiapas

(chē·ä'päs)

A southern state in Mexico, bordering on Guatemala and the Pacific Ocean.

A1

1866 Typeset

1 A1 ½r *gray blue* 1600.00 1000.00
2 " 1r *light green* 550.00
3 " 2r *rose* 550.00
4 " 4r *light buff* 1600.00
a. Vertical half used as 2r on cover 2250.00
5 " 8r *rose* 8500.00
a. Quarter used as 2r on cover 3250.00
b. Half used as 4r on cover 3750.00

Chihuahua

(chē·wä'wä)

A city of northern Mexico and capital of the State of Chihuahua.

A1

1872 Handstamped

1 A1 12(c) black *1000.00*
2 " 25(c) " *750.00*

Cuautla

A town in the state of Morelos.

A1

1867 Handstamped

1 A1 (2r) black *1000.00*

Cuernavaca

(kwĕr′nä·vä′kä)

A city of Mexico, just south of the capital, and the capital of the State of Morelos.

A1

1867 Handstamped

1 A1 (2r) black *1200.00*

Counterfeits exist.

Guadalajara

(gwä′thä·lä·hä′rä)

A city of Mexico and capital of the State of Jalisco.

A1

Handstamped in Black
Dated "1867"
1st Printing
Medium Wove Paper

1867 ***Imperf.***

1 A1 Medio r *white* 95.00 70.00
2 " un r *gray blue* 60.00
3 " un r *dark blue* 60.00
4 " un r *white* 50.00
5 " 2r *dark green* 30.00 12.00
6 " 2r *white* 40.00
7 " 4r *rose* 80.00 50.00
a. Half used as 2r on cover 175.00
8 A1 4r *white* 75.00
9 " un p *lilac* 100.00 75.00

Serrate Perf.

10 A2 un r *gray blue* 100.00
11 " 2r *dark green* 50.00
12 " 4r *rose* 60.00

2nd Printing
No Period after "2" or "4"
Thin Quadrille Paper
Imperf.

13 A1 2r *green* 20.00 12.00
a. Half used as 1r on cover 175.00

Serrate Perf.

14 A1 2r *green* 35.00

Thin Laid Batonné Paper
Imperf.

15 A1 2r *green* 30.00 15.00

Serrate Perf.

16 A1 2r *green* 35.00

3rd Printing
Capital "U" in "Un" on 1r, 1p
Period after "2" and "4"
Thin Wove Paper
Imperf.

17 A1 Un r *blue* 40.00
17A " Un r *lilac* 60.00
18 " 2r *rose* 35.00

Serrate Perf.

19 A1 Un r *blue* 70.00

Thin Quadrille Paper
Imperf.

20 A1 2r *rose* 27.50 27.50
21 " 4r *blue* 10.00 20.00
22 " 4r *white* 45.00
23 " Un p *lilac* 10.00 30.00
24 " Un p *rose* 45.00

Serrate Perf.

25 A1 Un p *lilac* 100.00
25A " Un p *rose* 100.00

Thin Laid Batonné Paper
Imperf.

26 A1 Un r *green* 15.00 12.00
27 " 2r *rose* 17.50 15.00
28 " 4r *blue* 12.00 30.00
29 " 4r *white* 45.00
30 " Un p *lilac* 20.00 35.00
31 " Un p *rose* 45.00

Serrate Perf.

32 A1 Un r *green* 45.00
33 " 2r *rose* 50.00
34 " 4r *blue* 75.00

Thin Oblong Quadrille Paper
Imperf.

35 A1 Un r *blue* 15.00
36 " 4r *blue* 110.00

Serrate Perf.

37 A1 Un r *blue* 55.00

4th Printing
Dated "1868"
Wove Paper

1868 ***Imperf.***

38 A1 2r *lilac* 20.00 10.00
a. Half used as 1r on cover 200.00
39 A1 2r *rose* 35.00 45.00

Serrate Perf.

40 A1 2r *lilac* 35.00
41 " 2r *rose* 60.00

Laid Batonné Paper
Imperf.

42 A1 un r *green* 8.00 8.00
a. "nu" instead of "un" 40.00
43 A1 2r *lilac* 8.00 8.00

Serrate Perf.

44 A1 un r *green* 50.00 35.00

Quadrille Paper.
Imperf.

45 A1 2r *lilac* 15.00 10.00

Serrate Perf.

46 A1 2r *lilac* 45.00 40.00

Laid Paper.
Imperf.

47 A1 un r *green* 8.00 11.00
a. "nu" instead of "un" 40.00
48 A1 2r *lilac* 22.50 22.50
49 " 2r *rose* 27.50 27.50

Serrate Perf.

50 A1 un r *green* 37.50
51 " 2r *rose* 75.00

Counterfeits of Nos. 1–51 abound.

A particular stamp may be scarce, but if few want it, its market potential may remain relatively low.

Merida

(mä′rē·thä)

A city of southeastern Mexico, capital of the State of Yucatan.

Mexico No. 521 Surcharged **25**

1916 ***Perf. 14*** **Wmk. 155**

1 A40 25(c) on 5c orange, on cover *125.00*

The G.P.DE.M. overprint reads down.

Authorities consider the Monterrey, Morelia and Patzcuaro stamps to be bogus.

Tlacotalpan

(tlä′ko·täl′pän)

A village in the state of Veracruz.

A1

1856, Oct. Handstamped

1 A1 ½(r) black *6000.00*

REVOLUTIONARY ISSUES.

Sinaloa

(sē′nä·lō′ä)

A northern state in Mexico, bordering on the Pacific Ocean. Stamps were issued by a provisional government.

Coat of Arms
A1
Lithographed.

1929 ***Perf. 12.*** **Unwmkd.**

1 A1 10c black, red & blue 1.25
a. Tête bèche pair 20.00
2 " 20c black, red & gray 1.25

Just as Nos. 1 and 2 were ready to be placed on sale the state was occupied by the Federal forces and the stamps could not be used. At a later date a few copies were cancelled by favor.

Yucatan

(yōō′kä·tän′)

A southeastern state of Mexico.

Mayan Altar Support—A1

"Casa de Monjas"—A2

Temple of the Tigers
A3
Lithographed.

1924 ***Imperf.*** **Unwmkd.**

1 A1 5c violet 8.50 8.50
2 A2 10c carmine 22.50 22.50
3 A3 50c olive green 60.00

Perf. 12.

4 A1 5c violet 12.00 12.00
5 A2 10c carmine 27.50 27.50
6 A3 50c olive green 75.00

Nos. 3 and 6 were not regularly issued.

MIDDLE CONGO

(mĭd″l kŏng′gō)

LOCATION—In western Africa at the Equator, bordering on the Atlantic Ocean.

GOVT.—Former French Colony.

AREA—166,069.

POP.—746,805 (1936).

CAPITAL—Brazzaville.

In 1910 Middle Congo, formerly a part of French Congo, was declared a separate colony. It was grouped with Gabon and the Ubangi-Shari and Chad Territories and officially designated French Equatorial Africa. This group became a single administrative unit in 1934. See Gabon.

See Congo Republic (ex-French) for issues of 1959 onward.

100 Centimes = 1 Franc

Leopard
A1

Bakalois Woman
A2

Coconut Grove
A3

Perf. 14x13½

1907–22 Typographed **Unwmkd.**

1 A1 1c olive gray & brown 5 5
2 " 2c violet & brown 8 8
3 " 4c blue & brown 8 8
4 " 5c dark green & blue 12 10
5 " 5c yellow & blue ('22) 15 15
6 " 10c carmine & blue 17 12
7 " 10c deep green & blue green ('22) 65 65
8 " 15c brown violet & rose 35 22
9 " 20c brown & blue 1.00 70
10 A2 25c blue & green 15 12
11 " 25c bl. grn. & gray ('22) 25 25
12 " 30c scarlet & green 35 32
13 " 30c deep rose & rose ('22) 25 25
14 " 35c violet brown & blue 30 30
15 " 40c dull green & brown 25 25
16 " 45c violet & red 1.50 1.00
17 " 50c blue green & red 30 30

18 A2 50c blue & green ('22) 25 25
19 " 75c brown & blue 2.50 1.75
20 A3 1fr dp. green & violet 3.00 2.65
21 " 2fr violet & gray green 2.00 2.00
22 " 5fr blue & rose 8.00 7.00
Nos. 1-22 (22) 21.75 18.59

For stamps of types A1-A3 in changed colors, see Chad, French Congo and Ubangi-Shari.

Stamps and Types of 1907-22 Overprinted in Black, Blue or Red **AFRIQUE EQUATORIALE FRANÇAISE**

1924-30
23 A1 1c olive gray & brown 6 6
24 " 2c violet & brown 6 6
25 " 4c blue & brown 6 6
26 " 5c yellow & blue 7 7
27 " 10c green & blue green (R) 10 10
28 " 10c car. & gray ('25) 7 6
29 " 15c brown violet & rose (Bl) 12 12
a. Double surch. 22.50
30 " 20c brown & blue 8 8
31 " 20c blue green & yellow green ('26) 8 8
32 " 20c deep brown & rose lilac ('27) 15 10

Overprinted **AFRIQUE EQUATORIALE FRANÇAISE**

33 A2 25c blue green & gray 12 12
34 " 30c rose & pale rose (Bl) 17 12
35 " 30c gray & blue violet (R) ('25) 10 8
36 " 30c dark green & green ('27) 40 30
37 " 35c chocolate & blue 10 10
38 " 40c olive green & brown 20 17
39 " 45c violet & pale red (Bl) 20 18
a. Inverted ovpt. 25.00 25.00
40 " 50c blue & green (R) 10 10
41 " 50c org. & blk. ('25) 10 8
a. Without ovpt. 50.00
42 " 65c orange brown & blue ('27) 90 85
43 " 75c brown & blue 12 12
44 " 90c brown red & pink ('30) 1.00 1.00
45 A3 1fr green & violet 25 20
a. Double ovpt. 65.00 60.00
46 " 1.10fr vio. & brn. ('28) 90 80
47 " 1.50fr ultramarine & blue ('30) 2.00 1.65
48 " 2fr violet & gray green 30 25
49 " 3fr red violet ('30) 2.50 2.50
50 " 5fr blue & rose 1.00 70
Nos. 23-50 (28) 11.31 10.11

Nos. 48 and 50 Surcharged with New Values.

1924
51 A3 25c on 2fr violet & gray green 15 15
52 " 25c on 5fr blue & rose (Bl) 15 15

Types of 1924-27 Surcharged with New Values in Black or Red.

1925-27
53 A3 65c on 1fr red orange & olive brown 25 25
54 " 85c on 1fr red orange & olive brown 25 25
55 A2 90c on 75c brown red & rose red ('27) 25 25
56 A3 1.25fr on 1fr dull blue & ultramarine (R) 10 10
57 " 1.50fr on 1fr ultra. & blue ('27) 45 35
a. New value omitted 35.00
58 " 3fr on 5fr orange brown & dull red ('27) 70 50
a. New value omitted 60.00
59 A3 10fr on 5fr vermilion & blue green ('27) 3.50 2.75
60 " 20fr on 5fr org. brn. & vio. ('27) 3.50 3.00
Nos. 53-60 (8) 9.00 7.45

Bars cover old values on Nos. 56-60.

Colonial Exposition Issue.
Common Design Types

1931 Engraved. ***Perf. 12½.***
Name of Country in Black.
61 CD70 40c deep green 1.50 1.10
62 CD71 50c violet 50 50
63 CD72 90c red orange 85 70
64 CD73 1.50fr dull blue 1.25 70

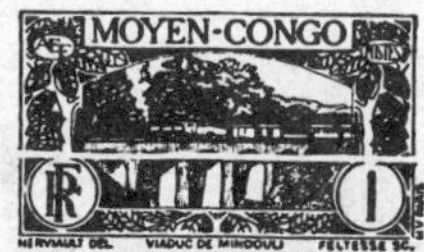

Viaduct at Mindouli
A4

Pasteur Institute at Brazzaville
A5

Government Building, Brazzaville—A6

1933 Photogravure. ***Perf. 13½.***
65 A4 1(c) light brown 5 5
66 " 2(c) dull blue 6 6
67 " 4(c) olive green 8 8
68 " 5(c) red violet 10 10
69 " 10(c) slate 10 10
70 " 15(c) dark violet 13 13
71 " 20(c) red, *pink* 2.50 1.85
72 " 25(c) orange 15 12
73 " 30(c) yellow green 60 50
74 A5 40(c) orange brown 40 35
75 " 45(c) *green* 60 40
76 " 50(c) black violet 25 25
77 " 65(c) brn. red, *green* 30 27
78 " 75(c) *pink* 3.00 2.50
79 " 90(c) carmine 35 35
80 " 1fr dark red 30 15
81 " 1.25fr Prussian blue 45 45
82 " 1.50fr dark blue 2.25 1.00
83 A6 1.75fr dark violet 60 55
84 " 2fr greenish black 50 40
85 " 3fr *orange* 1.00 1.00
86 " 5fr slate blue 4.50 4.50
87 " 10fr black 13.50 9.00
88 " 20fr dark brown 9.00 6.00
Nos. 65-88 (24) 40.77 30.16

SEMI-POSTAL STAMPS

No. 6 Surcharged in Black **+ 5c**

1916 ***Perf. 14x13½*** **Unwmkd.**
B1 A1 10c+5c car. & blue 30 25
a. Double surcharge 25.00 25.00
b. Inverted surcharge 25.00 25.00

A printing with the surcharge placed lower and more to the left was made and used in Ubangi.

Common Design Types
pictured in section at front of book.

No. 6 Surcharged in Red **+ 5c**

B2 A1 10c+5c carmine & blue 20 20

POSTAGE DUE STAMPS.

Postage Due Stamps of France Overprinted **MOYEN-CONGO** **A. E. F.**

1928 ***Perf. 14x13½.*** **Unwmkd.**
J1 D2 5c light blue 12 12
J2 " 10c gray brown 13 13
J3 " 20c olive green 20 20
J4 " 25c bright rose 20 20
J5 " 30c light red 20 20
J6 " 45c blue green 30 30
J7 " 50c brown violet 40 40
J8 " 60c yellow brown 45 45
J9 " 1fr red brown 65 65
J10 " 2fr orange red 75 75
J11 " 3fr bright violet 1.60 1.60
Nos. J1-J11 (11) 5.00 5.00

Village on Ubangi, Dance Mask
D3

Steamer on Ubangi River
D4

1930 **Typographed.**
J12 D3 5c deep blue & olive 25 25
J13 " 10c deep red & brown 45 45
J14 " 20c green & brown 1.20 1.20
J15 " 25c light blue & brown 1.20 1.20
J16 " 30c bistre brown & Prussian blue 1.85 1.65
J17 " 45c Prussian blue & olive 1.85 1.65
J18 " 50c red violet & brown 1.85 1.75
J19 " 60c gray lilac & blue black 2.50 2.25
J20 D4 1fr bistre brown & blue black 3.00 2.65
J21 " 2fr violet & brown 3.00 2.65
J22 " 3fr dark red & brown 3.00 2.65
Nos. J12-J22 (11) 20.15 18.35

Rubber Trees and Djoué River
D5

1933 Photogravure ***Perf. 13½***
J23 D5 5(c) apple green 20 20
J24 " 10(c) dark blue, *blue* 20 20
J25 " 20(c) red, *yellow* 25 25
J26 " 25(c) chocolate 25 25
J27 " 30(c) orange red 30 30
J28 " 45(c) dark violet 30 30
J29 " 50(c) gray black 80 80
J30 " 60(c) *orange* 1.00 1.00
J31 " 1fr brown rose 1.40 1.40
J32 " 2fr orange yellow 1.85 1.85
J33 " 3fr Prussian blue 2.50 2.50
Nos. J23-J33 (11) 9.05 9.05

MODENA

See Italian States group preceding Italy.

MOHELI

(mô'â'lē')

LOCATION—One of the Comoro Islands, situated in the Mozambique Channel midway between Madagascar and Mozambique (Africa).
GOVT.—Former French Colony.
AREA—89 sq. mi.
POP.—4,000.
CAPITAL—Fomboni.
See Comoro Islands.

100 Centimes = 1 Franc

Navigation and Commerce
A1

Perf. 14x13½.
1906-07 **Typographed** **Unwmkd.**
Name of Colony in Blue or Carmine
1 A1 1c *lilac blue* 60 60
2 " 2c brown, *buff* 70 60
3 " 4c claret, *lavender* 85 85
4 " 5c yellow green 90 60
5 " 10c carmine 1.25 85
6 " 20c red *green* 2.50 1.50
7 " 25c blue 2.50 1.50
8 " 30c brown, *bistre* 5.00 3.00
9 " 35c *yellow* 2.00 1.00
10 " 40c red, *straw* 4.00 2.75
11 " 45c *gray green* ('07) 18.50 15.00
12 " 50c brown, *azure* 7.00 4.00
13 " 75c dp. vio., *orange* 7.00 7.00
14 " 1fr bronze green, *straw* 7.00 4.00
15 " 2fr violet, *rose* 11.00 9.00
16 " 5fr lilac, *lavender* 40.00 37.50
Nos. 1-16 (16) 110.80 89.75

Issue of 1906-07 Surcharged in Carmine or Black **05** *a* **10** *b*

1912
17 A1 5c on 4c claret, *lavender* (C) 30 30
18 " 5c on 20c red, *green* 1.00 1.00
19 " 5c on 30c brown, *bistre* (C) 40 40
20 " 10c on 40c red, *straw* 30 30
21 " 10c on 45c *gray green* (C) 35 35
a. "Moheli" double 72.50
b. "Moheli" triple 72.50
22 " 10c on 50c brown, *azure* (C) 55 55
Nos. 17-22 (6) 2.90 2.90

Two spacings between the surcharged numerals are found on Nos. 17 to 22.

The stamps of Mohéli were supposed to have been superseded by those of Madagascar, January, 1908. However, Nos. 17-22 were surcharged in 1912 to use up remainders. These were available for use in Madagascar and the entire Comoro archipelago. In 1950 stamps of Comoro Islands came into use.

MONACO

(mŏn′ȧ·kō)

LOCATION—On the southern coast of France, bordering on the Mediterranean Sea.

GOVT.—Principality.

AREA—0.575 sq. mi.

POP.—30,000 (est. 1977).

CAPITAL—Monaco.

100 Centimes = 1 Franc

Prince Charles III
A1

Prince Albert I
A2

Typographed.

1885 *Perf. 14x13½.* **Unwmkd.**

No.	Type	Description	Unused	Used
1	A1	1c olive green	6.00	6.00
2	"	2c dull lilac	15.00	12.00
3	"	5c blue	22.50	18.50
4	"	10c brown, *straw*	27.50	18.50
5	"	15c rose	95.00	7.50
6	"	25c green	250.00	25.00
7	"	40c slate, *rose*	26.50	20.00
8	"	75c *rose*	62.50	32.50
9	"	1fr *yellow*	600.00	275.00
10	"	5fr rose, *green*	1750.00	1200.00

1891-1921

No.	Type	Description	Unused	Used
11	A2	1c olive green	30	30
12	"	2c dull violet	30	30
13	"	5c blue	17.50	1.50
14	"	5c yellow green ('01)	30	25
15	"	10c brown, *straw*	52.50	7.50
16	"	10c carmine ('01)	50	40
17	"	15c rose	60.00	2.00
18	"	15c violet brown, *straw* ('01)	1.00	60
19	"	15c gray green ('21)	1.50	1.50
20	"	25c green	135.00	13.00
21	"	25c deep blue ('01)	2.50	60
22	"	40c slate, *rose* ('94)	2.50	1.25
23	"	50c violet, *orange*	3.00	2.00
24	"	75c violet brown, *buff* ('94)	10.00	6.00
		a. 75c lilac brn., *buff*	12.00	6.00
25	"	75c olive brown, *buff* ('21)	6.00	5.00
26	"	1fr *yellow*	6.75	5.00
27	"	5fr rose, *green*	50.00	30.00
28	"	5fr dull violet ('21)	120.00	110.00
29	"	5fr dark green ('21)	16.00	16.00
		Nos. 11-29 (19)	485.65	203.20

The handstamp "OL" in a circle of dots is a cancellation, not an overprint.

Stamps of 1901–21 Overprinted or Surcharged:

28
DÉCEMBRE
1920
a

28
DÉCEMBRE
1920
2f
b

1921, Mar. 5

No.	Type	Description	Unused	Used
30	A2	(a) 5c light green	40	40
31	"	(") 75c brown, *buff*	4.00	4.00
32	"	(b) 2fr on 5fr dull violet	27.50	27.50

Issued to commemorate the birth of Princess Antoinette, daughter of Princess Charlotte and Prince Pierre, Comte de Polignac.

Stamps and Type of 1891–1921 Surcharged

25c.

1922

No.	Type	Description	Unused	Used
33	A2	20c on 15c gray grn.	1.25	1.00
34	"	25c on 10c rose	70	60
35	"	50c on 1fr *yellow*	6.00	4.75

Prince Albert I
A5

Oceanographic Museum
A6

"The Rock" of Monaco
A7

Royal Palace
A8

1922-24 **Engraved.** *Perf. 11.*

No.	Type	Description	Unused	Used
40	A5	25c olive brown	4.00	4.00
41	A6	30c dark green	1.00	1.00
42	"	30c scarlet ('23)	40	40
43	"	50c ultramarine	4.50	4.50
44	A7	60c black brown	20	20
45	"	1fr *yellow*	20	20
46	"	2fr scarlet	40	40
47	A8	5fr red brown	32.50	32.50
48	"	5fr dk. grn., *lilac* ('24)	5.00	5.00
49	"	10fr carmine	11.00	8.50
		Nos. 40-49 (10)	59.20	56.70

Nos. 40-49 exist imperf.

Prince Louis II
A9 A10

St. Dévote Viaduct
("Bridge of Suicides")
A11

1923-24 **Engraved**

No.	Type	Description	Unused	Used
50	A9	10c deep green	40	40
51	"	15c carmine rose ('24)	70	70
52	"	20c red brown	40	40
53	"	25c violet	35	35
		a. Without engraver's name	1.50	1.50
54	A11	40c org. brown ('24)	40	40
55	A10	50c ultramarine	35	35
		Nos. 50-55 (6)	2.60	2.60

The 25c comes in 2 types, one with larger "5" and "c" touching frame of numeral tablet.

Stamps of the 1922-24 issues sometimes show parts of the letters of a papermaker's watermark.

The engraved stamps of type A11 measure 31x21½ mm. The typographed stamps of that design measure 36x21½mm.

Stamps and Type of 1891–1921 Surcharged

45

1924, Aug. 5 *Perf. 14x13½*

No.	Type	Description	Unused	Used
57	A2	45c on 50c brown olive, *buff*	70	70
		a. Double surch.	400.00	400.00
58	A2	75c on 1fr *yellow*	50	50
		a. Double surch.	325.00	325.00
59	"	85c on 5fr dark green	50	50
		a. Double surch.	350.00	350.00

Grimaldi Family Coat of Arms
A12

Prince Louis II
A13

Louis II
A14

View of Monaco
A15

1924-33 **Typographed.**

No.	Type	Description	Unused	Used
60	A12	1c gray black	10	10
61	"	2c red brown	15	15
62	"	3c brt. violet ('33)	1.35	30
63	"	5c orange ('26)	30	30
64	"	10c blue	20	20
65	A13	15c apple green	20	20
66	"	15c dull violet ('29)	1.75	1.00
67	"	20c violet	20	10
68	"	20c rose	35	20
69	"	25c rose	15	10
70	"	25c red, *yellow*	30	20
71	"	30c orange	20	20
72	"	40c black brown	15	10
73	"	40c light blue, *bluish*	25	20
74	"	45c gray black ('26)	75	40
75	A14	50c myrtle green ('25)	32	25
76	A13	50c brown, *orange*	20	10
77	A14	60c yel. brown ('25)	20	20
78	A13	60c olive green, *greenish*	20	10
79	"	75c olive green, *greenish* ('26)	25	20
80	"	75c carmine, *straw* ('26)	25	20
81	"	75c slate	60	30
82	"	80c red, *yellow* ('26)	40	30
83	"	90c rose, *straw* ('27)	65	50
84	"	1.25fr blue, *bluish* ('26)	20	20
85	"	1.50fr bl., *bluish* ('27)	1.00	75

Size: 36x21½mm.

No.	Type	Description	Unused	Used
86	A11	1fr *orange*	20	20
87	"	1.05fr red violet ('26)	20	20
88	"	1.10fr blue grn. ('27)	8.00	4.00
89	A15	2fr violet & olive brown ('25)	1.10	90
90	"	3fr rose & ultra., *yellow* ('27)	5.50	4.00
91	"	5fr green & rose ('25)	5.50	3.50
92	"	10fr yellow brown & blue ('25)	9.00	6.50
		Nos. 60-92 (33)	40.17	26.15

Nos. 60 to 74 and 76 exist imperforate.

Type of 1924–33
Surcharged with New Value and Bars

1926-31

No.	Type	Description	Unused	Used
93	A13	30c on 25c rose	25	20
94	"	50c on 60c olive green, *greenish* ('28)	65	25
95	A11	50c on 1.05fr red violet ('28)	50	40
		a. Double surcharge		
96	"	50c on 1.10fr blue green ('31)	2.50	1.50
97	A13	50c on 1.25fr blue, *bluish* (R) ('28)	60	40
98	"	1.25fr on 1fr blue, *bluish*	50	30
99	A15	1.50fr on 2fr violet & olive brn. ('28)	2.00	1.00
		Nos. 93-99 (7)	7.00	4.05

Princes Charles III, Louis II and Albert I—A17

1928, Feb. 18 **Engraved** *Perf. 11*

No.	Type	Description	Unused	Used
100	A17	50c dull carmine	1.20	1.20
101	"	1.50fr dark blue	1.20	1.20
102	"	3fr dark violet	1.20	1.20

Nos. 100 to 102 were sold exclusively at the International Philatelic Exhibition at Monte Carlo, February, 1928. One set was sold to each purchaser of a ticket of admission to the exhibition which cost 5 francs.

Exist imperf. Price, set $20.

Old Watchtower—A20

Royal Palace
A21

Church of St. Dévote
A22

Prince Louis II
A23

"The Rock" of Monaco
A24

Gardens of Monaco
A25

Fortifications and Harbor
A26

1932-37 *Perf. 13, 14x13½.*

No.	Type	Description	Unused	Used
110	A20	15c lilac rose	60	20
111	"	20c orange brown	60	20
112	A21	25c olive black	85	40
113	A22	30c yellow green	1.00	40
114	A23	40c dark brown	1.65	1.00
115	A24	45c brown red	2.50	60
		a. 45c red	185.00	185.00

No.	Type	Description	Unused	Used
116	A23	50c purple	1.40	50
117	A25	65c blue green	2.50	40
118	A26	75c deep blue	3.00	1.85
119	A23	90c red	3.00	1.50
120	A22	1fr red brn.('33)	10.00	6.00
121	A26	1.25fr rose lilac	4.00	3.00
122	A23	1.50fr ultramarine	12.00	6.00
123	A21	1.75fr rose lilac	18.50	3.00
124	"	1.75fr car. rose ('37)	15.00	3.00
125	A24	2fr dark blue	6.00	3.00
126	A20	3fr purple	8.00	4.00
127	A21	3.50fr orange ('35)	40.00	20.00
128	A22	5fr red violet	18.50	12.00
129	A21	10fr deep blue	60.00	37.50
130	A25	20fr black	110.00	65.00
		Nos. 110-130 (21)	319.10	169.55

Postage Due Stamps of 1925-32 Surcharged or Overprinted in Black:

POSTES
=5
a

POSTES
b

1937-38 *Perf. 14x13*

No.	Type	Description	Unused	Used
131	D3 (*a*)	5c on 10c violet	70	70
132	" (*b*)	10c violet	70	70
133	" (*a*)	15c on 30c bistre	70	70
134	" (")	20c on 30c bistre	70	70
135	" (")	25c on 60c red	1.10	1.00
136	" (*b*)	30c bistre	1.85	1.65
137	" (*a*)	40c on 60c red	1.50	1.20
138	" (")	50c on 60c red	2.00	1.20
139	" (")	65c on 1fr lt. bl.	1.50	1.25
140	" (")	85c on 1fr lt. bl.	3.00	2.50
141	" (*b*)	1fr light blue	3.00	2.50
142	" (*a*)	2.15fr on 2fr dull red	4.50	4.00
143	" (")	2.25fr on 2fr dull red ('38)	6.00	5.00
144	" (")	2.50fr on 2fr dull red ('38)	8.00	7.00
		Nos. 131-144 (14)	35.25	30.10

Grimaldi Arms
A27

Prince Louis II
A28

1937-43 **Engraved.**

No.	Type	Description	Unused	Used
145	A27	1c dark violet brown ('38)	5	5
146	"	2c emerald	7	5
147	"	3c bright red violet	8	6
148	"	5c red	15	10
149	"	10c ultramarine	8	8
149A	"	10c black ('43)	5	5
150	"	15c violet ('39)	75	60
150A	"	30c dull green ('43)	15	15
150B	"	40c rose carmine ('43)	8	8
150C	"	50c bright violet ('43)	8	8
151	A28	55c red brown ('38)	2.00	1.00
151A	A27	60c Pruss. bl. ('43)	8	8
152	A28	65c violet ('38)	14.00	6.00
153	"	70c red brown ('39)	15	15
153A	A27	70c red brown ('43)	8	10
154	A28	90c violet ('39)	8	10
155	"	1fr rose red ('38)	3.25	2.00
156	"	1.25fr rose red ('39)	30	25
157	"	1.75fr ultra. ('38)	5.75	3.25
158	"	2.25fr ultramarine ('39)	30	22
		Nos. 145-158 (20)	27.53	14.45

Nos. 151, 152, 155 and 157 exist imperforate.

Souvenir Sheet.

Prince Louis II
A29

1938, Jan. 17 *Imperf.* **Unwmkd.**

No.	Type	Description	Unused	Used
159	A29	10fr magenta	22.50	20.00

"Fête Nationale" January 17, 1938. Size: 99x120mm.

Cathedral of Monaco
A30

St. Nicholas Square
A31

Palace Gate
A32

Palace of Monaco
A34

Panorama of Monaco
A33

Harbor of Monte Carlo
A35

1939-46 *Perf. 13*

No.	Type	Description	Unused	Used
160	A30	20c rose lilac	20	20
161	A31	25c golden brown	40	25
162	A32	30c dark blue green	30	25
162A	"	30c brown red ('40)	25	20
163	A31	40c henna brown	60	40
164	A33	45c bright red violet	25	25
165	A34	50c dark blue green	25	20
166	A32	60c rose carmine	40	30
166A	"	60c dark green ('40)	30	25
166B	A35	70c bright red violet ('41)	25	20
167	"	75c dark green	25	20
167A	A30	80c dull green ('43)	10	10
168	A34	1fr brown black	25	20
168A	A33	1fr claret ('43)	10	10
168B	A35	1.20fr ultra. ('46)	20	20
168C	A34	1.30fr brn. blk. ('41)	25	20
168D	A31	1.50fr ultra. ('46)	20	20
169	"	2fr rose violet	30	25
169A	A35	2fr lt. ultra. ('43)	10	10
169B	A34	2fr green ('46)	15	15
170	A33	2.50fr red	15.00	8.50
171	"	2.50fr deep blue ('40)	70	30
172	A35	3fr brown red	35	20
172A	A31	3fr black ('43)	10	10
172B	A30	4fr rose lilac ('46)	35	35
172C	A34	4.50fr brt. vio. ('43)	15	15
173	A30	5fr Prussian blue	1.00	40
173A	A32	5fr deep green ('43)	15	15
173B	A34	6fr light violet ('46)	50	50
174	A33	10fr green	1.25	35
174A	A30	10fr deep blue ('43)	15	15
174B	A35	15fr rose pink ('43)	30	25
175	A32	20fr bright ultra.	1.50	40
175A	A33	20fr sepia ('43)	30	25
175B	A35	25fr bl. grn. ('46)	1.10	80
		Nos. 160-175B (35)	28.00	17.05

See also Nos. 214-221, 228-232, 274-275, 319-320, 407-408 and 423, 426, 428-429.

Louis II Stadium
A36

1939, Apr. 23 **Engraved**

No.	Type	Description	Unused	Used
176	A36	10fr dark green	110.00	100.00

Inauguration of Louis II Stadium.

Louis II Stadium
A37

1939, Aug. 15

No.	Type	Description	Unused	Used
177	A37	40c dull green	1.25	1.25
178	"	70c brown black	1.35	1.35
179	"	90c dark violet	1.65	1.65
180	"	1.25fr copper red	1.65	1.65
181	"	2.25fr dark blue	2.75	2.75
		Nos. 177-181 (5)	8.65	8.65

8th International University Games.

Imperforates

Nearly all Monaco stamps from 1940 onward exist imperforate. Officially 20 sheets, ranging from 25 to 100 subjects, were left imperforate.

Prince Louis II
A38 A39

1941-46 *Perf. 14x13.*

No.	Type	Description	Unused	Used
182	A38	40c brown carmine	15	15
183	"	80c deep green	15	15
184	"	1fr rose violet	15	15
185	"	1.20fr green ('42)	10	10
186	"	1.50fr rose	10	10
187	"	1.50fr violet ('42)	10	10
187A	"	2fr light green ('46)	25	25
188	"	2.40fr red ('42)	10	10
189	"	2.50fr deep ultramarine	35	35
190	"	4fr blue ('42)	10	10
		Nos. 182-190 (10)	1.55	1.55

1943 *Perf. 13*

No.	Type	Description	Unused	Used
191	A39	50fr purple	75	75

Prince Louis II
A40 A41

Engraved.

1946 *Perf. 14x13* **Unwmkd.**

No.	Type	Description	Unused	Used
192	A40	2.50fr dark blue green	8	7
193	"	3fr bright red violet	12	10
194	"	6fr bright red	15	12
195	"	10fr bright ultra.	15	12

Perf. 13

No.	Type	Description	Unused	Used
196	A41	50fr dp. Prus. grn.	2.00	1.65
197	"	100fr red	3.00	2.50
		Nos. 192-197 (6)	5.50	4.56

Nos. 196-197 exist imperforate.
See also Nos. 222-227, 233-236.

Franklin D. Roosevelt
A42

Harbor of Monte Carlo
A43

Palace of Monaco
A44

Map of Monaco
A45

Prince Louis II
A46

1946, Dec. 13 *Perf. 13* **Unwmkd.**

No.	Type	Description	Unused	Used
198	A42	10c red violet	20	20
199	A43	30c deep blue	20	20
200	A44	60c blue black	20	20
201	A45	1fr sepia	50	50
202	"	3fr light violet	85	85
		Nos. 198-202, B93, C14-C15, CB6 (9)	4.55	4.25

Issued in tribute to the memory of Franklin D. Roosevelt.

1947, May 15

No.	Type	Description	Unused	Used
203	A46	10fr dk. blue green	1.75	1.75

See No. C20a.

Hurdler
A47

Runner
A48

Designs: 2fr, Discus thrower. 2.50fr, Basketball. 4fr, Swimmer.

1948, July 1 *Perf. 13*

No.	Type	Description	Unused	Used
204	A47	50c blue green	20	20

205	A48	1fr rose brown	20	20
206	"	2fr greenish blue	50	50
207	"	2.50fr vermilion	60	50
208	"	4fr slate gray	75	60
		Nos. 204-208, CB7-CB10 (9)	40.25	40.00

Issued to publicize Monaco's participation in the 1948 Olympic Games held at Wembley, England, during July and August.

Nymph Salmacis
A49

Hercules
A50

Aristaeus
A51

Hyacinthus
A52

François J. Bosio and Louis XIV Statue
A53

1948, July 12

209	A49	50c dark green	15	15
210	A50	1fr red	15	15
211	A51	2fr deep ultra.	20	20
212	A52	2.50fr deep violet	30	30
213	A53	4fr purple	50	50
		Nos. 209-213, CB11-CB14 (9)	21.30	20.80

Issued to honor François J. Bosio (1768-1845), sculptor. No. 213 inscribed "J F Bosio."

Scenic Types of 1939.

1948 **Engraved.**

214	A30	50c sepia	20	20
215	A31	60c rose pink	20	20
216	A32	3fr violet rose	40	30
217	A31	4fr emerald	40	30
218	A34	8fr red brown	1.40	85
219	"	10fr brown red	2.00	70
220	A33	20fr carmine rose	1.00	20
221	A35	25fr gray black	14.00	5.50
		Nos. 214-221 (8)	19.60	8.25

Louis II Type of 1946.

1948, July ***Perf. 14x13***

222	A40	30c black	20	10
223	"	5fr orange brown	40	20
224	"	6fr purple	1.00	45
225	"	10fr orange	20	20
226	"	12fr deep carmine	2.50	75
227	"	18fr dark blue	3.75	2.50
		Nos. 222-227 (6)	8.05	4.20

Scenic Types of 1939.

1949 ***Perf. 13***

228	A33	5fr blue green	40	20
229	A35	10fr orange	80	10
230	A32	25fr blue	9.00	4.50
231	A30	40fr brown red	4.50	2.50
232	"	50fr purple	2.75	80
		Nos. 228-232 (5)	17.45	8.10

Louis II Type of 1946.

1949, Mar. 10 ***Perf. 14x13***

233	A40	50c olive	20	12
234	"	1fr dark violet blue	20	18
235	"	12fr dark slate green	3.50	2.50
236	"	15fr brown carmine	3.50	2.50

Hirondelle I
A54

Cactus Plants
A55

Designs: 4fr, Oceanographic Museum. 5fr, Princess Alice II at Spitzbergen. 6fr, Albert I Monument. 10fr, Hirondelle II. 12fr, Albert I whaling. 18fr, Bison.

1949, Mar. 5 ***Perf. 13***

237	A54	2fr bright blue	20	20
238	A55	3fr dark green	25	25
239	A54	4fr black brn. & blue	25	25
240	"	5fr crimson	25	25
241	A55	6fr dark violet	50	50
242	A54	10fr black brown	45	45
243	"	12fr bright red violet	60	60
244	"	18fr dark brown & orange brown	2.00	2.00
		Nos. 237-244 (8)	4.50	4.50

See also Nos. C21-C26.

Palace, Globe and Pigeon
A56

1949-50 **Engraved** **Unwmkd.**

245	A56	5fr blue green	25	25
245A	"	10fr orange ('50)	2.50	2.50
246	"	15fr carmine	30	30
		Nos. 245-246, C30-C33 (7)	8.60	8.05

Issued to commemorate the 75th anniversary of the formation of the Universal Postal Union.

Nos. 245, 245A and 246 exist imperf.

Prince Rainier III
A57 A58

1950, Apr. 11

247	A57	10c red & black brown	15	15
248	"	50c dp. yel. & dk. brn.	15	15
249	"	1fr purple	15	15
250	"	5fr dark green	65	65
251	"	15fr carmine	1.10	1.10
252	"	25fr ultramarine, olive grn. & indigo	1.85	1.85
		Nos. 247-252, C34-C35 (8)	10.05	9.05

Enthronement of Prince Rainier III.

1950, Apr. **Engraved** ***Perf. 14x13***

253	A58	50c purple	10	8
254	"	1fr orange brown	15	12
255	"	8fr blue green	1.50	1.00
256	"	12fr blue	65	50
257	"	15fr crimson	1.00	50
		Nos. 253-257 (5)	3.40	2.20

1951, Apr. 31 **Typographed**

258	A58	5fr emerald	2.65	2.25
259	"	10fr orange	5.00	3.75

See also Nos. 276-279.

Statue of Prince Albert I
A59

1951, Apr. 11 **Engraved** ***Perf. 13***

260	A59	15fr deep blue	5.00	5.00

Edmond and Jules de Goncourt
A60

1951, Apr. 11

261	A60	15fr violet brown	5.00	5.00

Issued to commemorate the 50th anniversary of the foundation of Goncourt Academy.

St. Vincent de Paul
A61

Judgment of St. Dévote
A62

Symbolizing Monaco's Adoption of Catholicism
A63

Blessed Rainier of Westphalia
A65

Mosaic of the Immaculate Conception—A64

Designs: 50c, Pope Pius XII. 12fr, Prince Rainier III at Prayer. 15fr, St. Nicholas de Patare. 20fr, St. Roman. 25fr, St. Charles Borromée. 40fr, Cross, arms and Roman Coliseum. 50fr, Chapel of St. Dévote.

Inscribed: "Anno Santo."

1951, June 4 ***Perf. 13*** **Unwmkd.**

262	A61	10c ultra. & red	25	25
263	"	50c dark rose lake & purple	25	25
264	A62	1fr brn. & dk. grn.	30	30
265	A63	2fr violet brown & vermilion	50	50
266	A64	5fr blue green	50	50
267	A63	12fr rose violet	70	70
268	"	15fr vermilion	3.00	3.00
269	"	20fr red brown	4.00	4.00
270	"	25fr ultramarine	4.50	4.50
271	"	40fr dark carmine rose & purple	5.00	5.00
272	"	50fr olive green & dk. vio. brn.	5.00	5.00
273	A65	100fr dk. vio. brn.	16.50	16.50
		Nos. 262-273 (12)	40.50	40.50

Issued to commemorate the Holy Year, 1951.

Scenic Types of 1939-46.

1951, Dec. 22 ***Perf. 13***

274	A31	3fr dp. turq. grn.	60	30
275	A32	30fr slate black	4.00	2.25

Rainier Type of 1950.

1951, Dec. 22 ***Perf. 14x13***

276	A58	6fr blue green	45	35
277	"	8fr orange	60	35
278	"	15fr indigo	65	25
279	"	18fr crimson	2.00	1.10

Radio Monte Carlo
A66

Knight in Armor
A67

1951, Dec. 22 ***Perf. 13***

280	A66	1fr blue, car. & org.	25	20
281	"	15fr purple, carmine & rose violet	1.00	30
282	"	30fr indigo & red brn.	1.75	1.00

1951, Dec. 22

283	A67	1fr purple	50	40
284	"	5fr gray black	2.00	80
285	"	8fr deep carmine	3.00	1.85
286	"	15fr emerald	3.50	3.00
287	"	30fr slate black	5.00	3.00
		Nos. 283-287 (5)	14.00	9.05

See also Nos. 328-332.

Nos. B96-B99a Surcharged with New Values and Bars in Black.

1951, Dec. ***Perf. 13½x13, Imperf.***

Cross Typographed in Red.

288	SP51	1fr on 10fr+5fr red brown	5.50	5.50
289	SP52	3fr on 15fr+5fr bright red	5.50	5.50
290	"	5fr on 25fr+5fr violet blue	5.50	5.50

291 SP51 6fr on 40fr+5fr dull green 5.50 5.50
b. Block of 4, 1 each of Nos. 288-291 25.00 25.00

Gallery of Hercules, Royal Palace
A68

1952, Apr. 26 Engraved *Perf. 13*

292 A68 5fr red brown & brown 55 50
293 " 15fr purple & lilac rose 65 20
294 " 30fr indigo & ultra. 80 70

Issued on the occasion of the opening of a philatelic museum at the royal palace, April 26, 1952.

Basketball—A69

Designs: 2fr, Soccer. 3fr, Sailing. 5fr, Cyclist. 8fr, Gymnastics. 15fr, Louis II Stadium.

1953, Feb. 23 *Perf. 11* Unwmkd.

295 A69 1fr dark purple & magenta 35 30
296 " 2fr dark green & slate blue 35 30
297 " 3fr blue & light blue 35 30
298 " 5fr dark brown & greenish black 1.00 50
299 " 8fr brn. lake & red 1.40 90
300 " 15fr blue, brown black & dark green 1.10 70
Nos. 295-300, C36-C39 (10) 38.55 33.00

Issued to publicize Monaco's participation in the Helsinki Olympic Games.

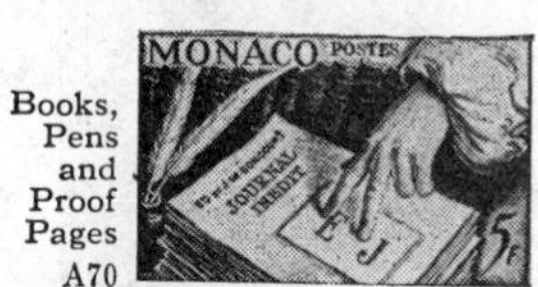

Books, Pens and Proof Pages
A70

1953, June 29 *Perf. 13*

301 A70 5fr dark green 60 45
302 " 15fr red brown 1.00 65

Issued to publicize the publication of a first edition of the unexpurgated diary of Edmond and Jules Goncourt.

Physalia and Laboratory Ship Hirondelle II
A71

1953, June 29

303 A71 2fr Prussian green, purple & chocolate 20 15
304 " 5fr deep magenta, red & Prussian green 45 35
305 A71 15fr ultra., vio. brn. & Prussian green 1.85 1.40

Issued to commemorate the 50th anniversary of the discovery of anaphylaxis by Charles Richet and Paul Portier.

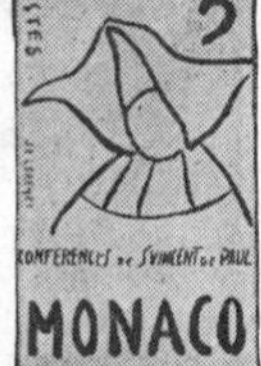

Frederic Ozanam A72 — Nun A73

1954, Apr. 12 Engraved *Perf. 13*

306 A72 1fr bright red 10 10
307 A73 5fr dark blue 45 45
308 A72 15fr black 90 90

Issued to commemorate the centenary of the death of Frederic Ozanam, founder of the Society of Saint Vincent de Paul.

Jean Baptiste de la Salle
A74 A75

1954, Apr. 12

309 A74 1fr dark carmine 10 10
310 A75 5fr black brown 45 45
311 A74 15fr bright ultramarine 90 90

Issued to honor Jean Baptiste de la Salle, founder of the Christian Brothers Institute and saint.

A76

A77

Grimaldi Arms A78 — Knight in Armor A79

Perf. 13½x14, 14x13½

1954, Apr. 12 Typographed

Various Forms of Grimaldi Arms in Black and Red or Black, Red and Deep Plum (5fr.)

312 A76 50c black & magenta 6 6
313 A77 70c black & aquamarine 6 6
314 A76 80c blk., red & dk. grn. 6 6
315 A77 1fr violet blue 6 6
316 " 2fr black & deep orange 8 6
317 " 3fr black & green 12 8
318 A78 5fr black & light green 20 12
Nos. 312-318 (7) 64 50

Scenic Types of 1939-46.

1954, Apr. 12 Engraved *Perf. 13*

319 A34 25fr bright red 1.25 50
320 A31 75fr dark green 10.00 4.50

1954, Apr. 12 *Perf. 13* Unwmkd.

321 A79 4fr dark red 60 20
322 " 8fr dark green 55 40
323 " 12fr dark purple 1.00 70
324 " 24fr dark maroon 2.50 1.85

Nos. 321-324 were issued precanceled only. Prices for precanceled stamps in first column are for those which have not been through the post and have original gum. Prices in the second column are for postally used, gumless stamps.

See also Nos. 400-404, 430-433, 466-469.

Lambarene Landing, Gabon
A80

Dr. Albert Schweitzer—A81

Design: 15fr, Lambarene hospital.

1955, Jan. 14 *Perf. 11x11½*

325 A80 2fr olive green, blue green & indigo 20 20
326 A81 5fr dark greenish blue & green 80 80
327 " 15fr dark blue green, deep claret & brown black 2.00 2.00

Issued to honor Dr. Albert Schweitzer, medical missionary. See No. C40.

Knight Type of 1951

1955, Jan. 14 *Perf. 13*

328 A67 5fr purple 1.75 70
329 " 6fr red 1.65 1.10
330 " 8fr red brown 1.75 1.35
331 " 15fr ultramarine 4.00 2.35
332 " 30fr dark green 5.00 3.00
Nos. 328-332 (5) 14.15 8.50

Automobile and Representation of Eight European Cities
A82

Prince Rainier III
A83

1955, Jan. 14 Unwmkd.

333 A82 100fr dk. brn. & red 47.50 47.50

25th Monte Carlo Automobile Rally.

1955, June 7 Engraved *Perf. 13*

334 A83 6fr green & vio. brn. 20 10
335 " 8fr red & violet 25 10
336 " 12fr carmine & green 30 10
337 " 15fr purple & blue 50 25
338 " 18fr orange & blue 60 45
339 A83 30fr ultramarine & gray 3.50 2.00
Nos. 334-339 (6) 5.35 3.00

See also Nos. 405-406, 424-425, 427, 462-465, 586, 603-604A, 725-728, 730, 789, 791.

"Five Weeks in a Balloon"
A84

"A Floating City" and Jules Verne—A85

"Michael Strogoff"
A86

"Around the World in 80 Days"
A87

USS Nautilus and Verne—A88

Designs (Scenes from Jules Verne's Books): 3fr, The House of Vapors. 6fr, The 500 Millions of the Begum. 8fr, The Magnificent Orinoco. 10fr, A Journey to the Center of the Earth. 25fr, Twenty Thousand Leagues under the Sea.

1955, June 7

340 A84 1fr red brown & blue gray 12 10
341 A85 2fr blue, indigo & brown 12 10
342 " 3fr red brown, gray & slate 15 10
343 A86 5fr car. & blk. brown 15 10
344 A84 6fr black brown & bluish gray 40 25
345 A86 8fr olive green & aquamarine 50 35

346 A85 10fr indigo, turquoise & brown 1.25 1.00

347 A87 15fr rose brown & vermilion 1.10 1.00

348 A85 25fr blue green, green & gray 1.85 1.50

349 A88 30fr violet, turquoise & black 4.50 4.50

Nos. 340-349, C45 (11) 40.14 39.00

Issued to commemorate the 50th anniversary of the death of Jules Verne.

Virgin by Francois Brea—A89

Blessed Rainier—A90

Design: 10fr, Pieta by Louis Brea.

1955, June 7

350 A89 5fr violet brown, gray & dark green 45 45

351 " 10fr violet brown, gray & dark green 45 45

352 A90 15fr black brown & orange brown 60 60

Issued to commemorate the Marian Year.

Rotary Emblem, World Map—A91

1955, June 7

353 A91 30fr blue & orange 1.10 1.10

Issued to commemorate the 50th anniversary of the founding of Rotary International.

George Washington A92

Dwight D. Eisenhower A94

Franklin D. Roosevelt—A93

Palace of Monaco, c. 1790—A95

Palace of Monaco, c. 1750—A96

Designs: 3fr, Abraham Lincoln. 30fr, Columbus landing in America. 40fr, Prince Rainier III. 100fr, Early Louisiana scene.

1956, Apr. 3 Engraved *Perf. 13*

354 A92 1fr dark purple 10 10

355 A93 2fr claret & dk. pur. 10 10

356 " 3fr vio. & dp. ultra. 15 10

357 A94 5fr brown lake 35 35

358 A95 15fr brown black & violet brown 70 70

359 " 30fr indigo, black & ultramarine 1.25 1.25

360 A94 40fr dark brown & violet brown 1.25 1.10

361 A96 50fr vermilion 1.50 1.25

362 " 100fr Prussian green 2.00 2.00

a. Strip of 3 (1 each of Nos. 360-362) 5.00 5.00

Nos. 354-362 (9) 7.40 6.95

Issued to publicize the Fifth International Philatelic Exhibition (FIPEX) in New York City, April 28-May 6, 1956.

Ski Jump, Cortina d'Ampezzo

A97

Design: 30fr, Olympic Scenes.

1956, Apr. 3

363 A97 15fr brn. vio., brown & dark green 1.25 1.00

364 " 30fr red orange 2.25 2.25

Issued to publicize Monaco's participation in the 1956 Olympic Games.

"Glasgow to Monte Carlo"—A98

1956, Apr. 3 Unwmkd.

365 A98 100fr red brn. & red 17.50 17.50

The 26th Monte Carlo Automobile Rally.

See also Nos. 411, 437, 460, 483, 500, 539, 549, 600, 629.

Princess Grace and Prince Rainier III

A99

1956, Apr. 19 Engraved *Perf. 13*

Portraits in Black.

366 A99 1fr dark green 4 4

367 " 2fr dark carmine 5 5

368 " 3fr ultramarine 6 6

369 " 5fr bright yellow green 6 6

370 " 15fr reddish brown 40 35

Nos. 366-370, C46-C48 (8) 4.71 4.66

Issued to commemorate the wedding of Prince Rainier III to Grace Kelly, April 19, 1956.

Nos. J41-J47, J50-J56 Overprinted with Bars and Surcharged in Indigo, Red or Black.

Engraved.

1956, Apr. 3 *Perf. 11* Unwmkd.

Designs: Early Transportation.

371 D6 2fr on 4fr dark brown & Prussian green (I) 30 30

372 " 3fr Prussian green & brown lake (R) 30 30

373 " 5fr on 4fr dark brown & Prussian green 60 60

374 " 10fr on 4fr dark brown & Prussian green (R) 70 70

375 " 15fr on 5fr ultramarine & purple (I) 1.25 1.25

376 " 20fr indigo & purple (R) 1.65 1.65

377 " 25fr on 20fr indigo & purple 2.50 2.50

378 " 30fr on 10fr deep ultramarine & dark blue (I) 2.75 2.75

379 " 40fr on 50fr red & dark brown (R) 3.00 3.00

380 " 50fr on 100fr violet brown & deep green 4.50 4.50

Designs: Modern Transportation.

381 D7 2fr on 4fr Prussian green & dark brown (I) 30 30

382 " 3fr brown lake & Prussian grn. (R) 30 30

383 " 5fr on 4fr Prussian grn. & dk. brown 60 60

384 " 10fr on 4fr Prussian green & dark brown (R) 70 70

385 " 15fr on 5fr purple & ultramarine (I) 1.25 1.25

386 " 20fr purple & indigo (R) 1.65 1.65

387 " 25fr on 20fr purple & indigo 2.50 2.50

388 D7 30fr on 10fr dark blue & deep ultramarine (I) 2.75 2.75

389 " 40fr on 50fr dark brn. & red (R) 3.00 3.00

390 " 50fr on 100fr deep green & violet brown 4.50 4.50

Nos. 371-390, C49-C50 (22) 55.10 55.10

The two types of each value in Nos. 371-390 were printed tête bêche, se-tenant at the base.

Princess Grace

A100

1957, May 11 Engraved *Perf. 13*

391 A100 1fr blue violet 5 5

392 " 2fr light olive green 5 5

393 " 3fr yellow brown 4 4

394 " 5fr magenta 10 5

395 " 15fr pink 15 10

396 " 25fr Prussian blue 30 20

397 " 30fr purple 30 25

398 " 50fr scarlet 35 30

399 " 75fr orange 65 65

Nos. 391-399 (9) 1.99 1.69

Birth of Princess Caroline of Monaco.

Knight Type of 1954.

1957 *Perf. 13* Unwmkd.

400 A79 5fr dark blue 25 15

401 " 10fr yellow green 25 15

402 " 15fr bright orange 60 50

403 " 30fr bright blue 90 60

404 " 45fr crimson 1.20 85

Nos. 400-404 (5) 3.20 2.25

Nos. 400-404 were issued precanceled only. See note after No. 324.

Types of 1955 and 1939-46.

1957

405 A83 20fr greenish blue 65 50

406 " 35fr red brown 2.50 1.00

407 A33 65fr bright violet 3.50 3.00

408 A30 70fr orange yellow 4.00 3.00

Princesses Grace and Caroline

A101

1958, May 15 Engraved *Perf. 13*

409 A101 100fr bluish black 3.50 2.50

Issued to commemorate the birth of Prince Albert Alexander Louis, March 14.

Order of St. Charles

A102

1958, May 15

410 A102 100fr carmine, green & bistre 2.25 2.25

Issued to commemorate the centenary of the National Order of St. Charles.

Rally Type of 1956

Design: 100fr, "Munich to Monte Carlo."

1958, May 15

411 A98 100fr red, green & sepia 5.50 4.50

27th Monte Carlo Automobile Rally.

Virgin Mary, Popes Pius IX and XII—A103

Bernadette Soubirous A104

Tomb of Bernadette, Nevers A105

Designs: 3fr, Shepherdess Bernadette at Bartres. 5fr, Bouriette kneeling (first miracle). 8fr, Stained glass window showing apparition. 10fr, Empty grotto at Lourdes. 12fr, Grotto with statue and altar. 20fr, Bernadette praying. 35fr, High Altar at St. Peter's during canonization of Bernadette. 50fr, Bernadette, Pope Pius XI, Mgr. Laurence and Abbe Peyramale.

1958, May 15 **Unwmkd.**

412 A103 1fr lilac gray & violet brown 6 6
413 A104 2fr blue & violet 6 6
414 " 3fr green & sepia 8 5
415 " 5fr gray brown & violet blue 15 6
416 " 8fr black, olive bistre & indigo 35 25
417 A105 10fr multicolored 25 20
418 " 12fr indigo, olive bis. & olive green 35 25
a. Strip of 3 (1 each of Nos. 416-418) 1.00 1.00
419 A104 20fr dark slate green & rose 45 35
420 " 35fr olive, gray olive & dark slate green 65 55
421 A103 50fr lake, olive green & indigo 80 70
422 A105 65fr indigo & greenish blue 1.25 1.00
Nos. 412-422, C51-C52 (13) 9.95 8.53

Centenary of the apparition of the Virgin Mary at Lourdes.

Nos. 413-415 and 419-420 measure 26x36mm. No. 416 measures 22x36mm. Nos. 417-418 measure 48x36mm. No. 422 measures 36x26mm.

Types of 1939-46 and 1955.

1959 **Engraved** ***Perf. 13***

423 A32 5fr copper red 45 40
424 A83 25fr orange & black 45 40
425 " 30fr dark violet 90 50
426 A34 35fr dark blue 2.00 1.00
427 A83 50fr blue green & rose claret 1.00 70
428 A31 85fr dk. car. rose 3.25 2.00
429 A33 100fr bright greenish blue 3.00 2.50
Nos. 423-429 (7) 11.05 7.50

Knight Type of 1954

1959

430 A79 8fr deep magenta 45 25
431 " 20fr bright green 70 60
432 " 40fr chocolate 1.00 80
433 " 55fr ultramarine 2.00 1.00

Nos. 430-433 were issued precanceled only. See note after No. 324.

Princess Grace Polyclinic—A106

1959, May 16

434 A106 100fr gray, brown & green 1.25 1.00

Opening of Princess Grace Hospital.

UNESCO Building, Paris, and Cultural Emblems—A107

Design: 50fr, UNESCO Building and children of various races.

1959, May 16

435 A107 25fr multicolored 35 30
436 " 50fr olive, blue green & black brown 65 60

Issued to commemorate the opening of UNESCO (U. N. Educational, Scientific and Cultural Organization) Headquarters in Paris, Nov. 3, 1958.

Rally Type of 1956

Design: 100fr, "Athens to Monaco."

1959, May 16

437 A98 100fr violet blue, red & slate green, *blue* 5.50 5.50

28th Monte Carlo Automobile Rally.

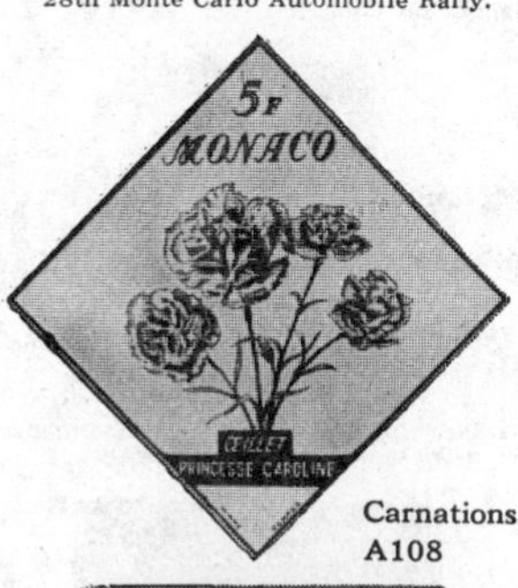

Carnations A108

Bougainvillea—A109

Flowers: 10fr on 3fr, Princess Grace Carnations. 15fr on 1fr, Mimosa (vert.). 25fr on 6fr, Geranium (vert.). 35fr, Oleander. 50fr, Jasmine. 85fr on 65fr, Lavender. 100fr, Grace de Monaco Rose.

1959, May 16

438 A108 5fr brown, Prussian green & rose carmine 20 15
439 " 10fr on 3fr brown, green & rose 25 20
440 A109 15fr on 1fr dark green & citron 25 20
441 " 20fr olive green & magenta 45 40
442 " 25fr on 6fr yellow green & red 65 45
443 " 35fr dark green & pink 90 60
444 " 50fr dark brown & dark green 1.10 60
445 " 85fr on 65fr olive green & gray violet 1.50 1.00
446 A108 100fr green & pink 1.75 1.40
Nos. 438-446 (9) 7.05 5.00

Nos. 439-440, 442 and 445 were not issued without surcharge.

View of Monaco and Uprooted Oak Emblem A110

1960, June 1 ***Perf. 13*** **Unwmkd.**

447 A110 25c blue, olive green & sepia 25 25

Issued to publicize World Refugee Year, July 1, 1959–June 30, 1960.

Entrance to Oceanographic Museum A111

Museum and Aquarium—A112

Designs: 15c, Museum conference room. 20c, Arrival of equipment, designed by Prince Albert I. 25c, Research on electrical qualities of cephalopodes. 50c, Albert I and vessels Hirondelle I and Princesse Alice.

1960, June 1 **Engraved** ***Perf. 13***

448 A111 5c blue, sepia & claret 35 25
449 A112 10c multicolored 55 35
450 " 15c sepia, ultra. & bister 40 30
451 " 20c rose lilac, black & blue 70 50
452 A112 25c greenish blue 1.40 1.20
453 " 50c light ultra. & brown 1.65 1.40
Nos. 448-453 (6) 5.05 4.00

Issued to commemorate the 50th anniversary of the inauguration of the Oceanographic Museum of Monaco. See No. 475.

Horse Jumping—A113

Sports: 10c, Women swimmers. 15c, Broad jumper. 20c, Javelin thrower. 25c, Girl figure skater. 50c, Skier.

1960, June 1

454 A113 5c dark brown, carmine & emerald 30 30
455 " 10c red brown, blue & green 30 30
456 " 15c dull red brown, olive & magenta 30 30
457 " 20c black, blue & green 2.50 2.50
458 " 25c dark green & dull purple 90 90
459 " 50c dark blue, greenish blue & dull purple 1.25 1.25
Nos. 454-459 (6) 5.55 5.55

Nos. 454—457 issued to commemorate the 17th Olympic Games, Rome, Aug. 25–Sept. 11; Nos. 458–459 commemorate the 8th Winter Olympic Games, Squaw Valley, Feb. 18–29.

Rally Type of 1956

1960, June 1

Design: 25c, "Lisbon to Monte Carlo."

460 A98 25c blue, brn. & car., *bluish* 1.75 1.75

29th Monte Carlo Automobile Rally.

Stamps of Sardinia and France, 1860, and Stamp of Monaco, 1885—A114

1960, June 1 **Engr. & Embossed**

461 A114 25c violet, blue & olive 1.35 1.25

Issued to commemorate the 75th anniversary of postage stamps of Monaco.

Prince Rainier Type of 1955

1960 **Engraved** ***Perf. 13***

462 A83 25c orange & black 15 10
463 " 30c dark violet 30 10
464 " 50c blue green & rose lilac 50 20
465 " 65c yellow brown & slate 1.25 45

Knight Type of 1954

1960

466 A79 8c deep magenta 60 25
467 " 20c bright green 80 25
468 " 40c chocolate 80 45
469 " 55c ultramarine 1.20 55

Nos. 466-469 were issued precanceled only. See note after No. 324.

Sea Horse A115 — Palace of Monaco A116

Designs: Nos. 471 Cactus (Cereanee). No. 472, Cactus (Nopalea dejecta). No. 473, Scorpion fish (horiz.).

1960, June 1

470 A115 15c orange brown & slate green 35 22
471 " 15c olive green, yel. & brown 35 15
472 " 20c maroon & olive green 35 20
473 " 20c brown, red brn., red & olive 30 20

See also Nos. 581–584.

Type of 1960 and A116

1960, June 1 Engraved

Designs: 10c, Type A111 without inscription. 45c, Aerial view of Palace. 85c, Honor court. 1fr, Palace at night.

474 A116 5c green & sepia 8 6
475 A111 10c dark blue & violet brown 50 30
476 A116 45c dark blue, sepia & green 40 30
477 " 85c slate, gray & bistre 1.00 60
478 " 1fr dk. blue, red brn. & slate green 90 35
Nos. 474–478 (5) 2.88 1.61

See also Nos. 585, 602, 729, 731, 731A, 790, 792.

Sphinx of Wadi-es-Sebua—A117

1961, June 3 *Perf. 13* Unwmkd.

479 A117 50c chocolate, dark blue & ochre 1.20 1.20

Issued as publicity to save historic monuments in Nubia.

Murena, Starfish, Sea Urchin, Sea Cucumber and Coral A118 — Medieval Town and Leper A119

1961, June 3

480 A118 25c violet buff & dark red 30 25

Issued to commemorate the World Congress of Aquariology, Monaco, Nov. 1960.

1961, June 3

481 A119 25c olive gray, ochre & car. 30 25

Issued to honor the Sovereign Order of the Knights of Malta.

Hand and Ant A120

1961, June 3

482 A120 25c magenta & deep carmine 30 25

Issued to publicize "Respect for Life."

Rally Type of 1956

Design: 1fr, "Stockholm to Monte Carlo."

1961, June 3

483 A98 1fr multicolored 2.25 2.25

30th Monte Carlo Automobile Rally.

Turcat-Mery, 1911 Winner, and 1961 Car—A121

1961, June 3

484 A121 1fr orange brown, violet & rose red 2.00 1.75

Issued to commemorate the 50th anniversary of the founding of the Monte Carlo Automobile Rally.

Chevrolet, 1912 A122

Automobiles (pre-1912): 2c, Peugeot. 3c, Fiat. 4c, Mercedes. 5c, Rolls Royce. 10c, Panhard-Levassor. 15c, Renault. 20c, Ford. 25c, Rochet-Schneider. 30c, FN-Herstal. 45c, De Dion Bouton. 50c, Buick. 65c, Delahaye. 1fr, Cadillac.

1961, June 13 Engraved

485 A122 1c orange brown, dark brown & green 15 15
486 " 2c orange red, dark blue & brown 15 15
487 " 3c multicolored 15 15
488 " 4c " 15 15
489 " 5c olive bistre, slate green & carmine 15 15
490 " 10c brown, slate & red 25 25
491 " 15c greenish blue & dark slate green 25 25
492 " 20c purple, black & red 30 30
493 " 25c dark brown lilac & red 40 40
494 A122 30c olive green & dull purple 60 60
495 " 45c multicolored 1.25 1.25
496 " 50c brown black, red & ultra. 1.25 1.25
497 " 65c multicolored 1.25 1.25
498 " 1fr bright purple, indigo & red 2.00 2.00
Nos. 485–498 (14) 8.30 8.30

See also Nos. 648–661.

Bugatti, First Winner, and Course A123

1962, June 6 *Perf. 13* Unwmkd.

499 A123 1fr lilac rose 2.00 1.60

20th Automobile Grand Prix of Monaco.

Rally Type of 1956

Design: 1fr, "Oslo to Monte Carlo."

1962, June 6

500 A98 1fr multicolored 1.75 1.50

31st Monte Carlo Automobile Rally.

Louis XII and Lucien Grimaldi A124

Designs: 50c, Document granting sovereignty. 1fr, Seals of Louis XII and Lucien Grimaldi.

1962, June 6 Engraved

501 A124 25c verm., black & violet blue 50 40
502 " 50c dk. blue, brn. & magenta 40 35
503 " 1fr dark brown, green & car. 80 70

Issued to commemorate the 450th anniversary of Monaco's reception of sovereignty from Louis XII.

Mosquito and Swamp A125

1962, June 6

504 A125 1fr brown olive & light green 90 80

Issued for the World Health Organization drive to eradicate malaria.

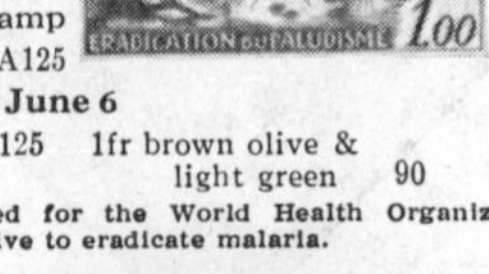

Aquatic Stadium at Night A126

1962, June 6

505 A126 10c dk. blue, indigo & green 12 8

Sun, Flowers and Hope Chest A127

1962, June 6

506 A127 20c multicolored 30 25

Issued to publicize the National Multiple Sclerosis Society of New York.

Europa Issue, 1962

Wheat Harvest—A128

1962, June 6

507 A128 25c dark blue, red brn. & brn. 30 30
508 " 50c indigo, olive bistre & dark blue green 45 45
509 " 1fr red lilac & olive bistre 80 80

See also No. C61.

Blood Donor's Arm and Globe A129

1962, Nov. 15 Engr. *Perf. 13*

510 A129 1fr dark red, black & orange 80 70

3rd International Blood Donors' Congress, Nov. 15–18 at Monaco.

Yellow Wagtails A130

Birds: 10c, European robins. 15c, European goldfinches. 20c, Blackcaps. 25c, Great spotted woodpeckers. 30c, Nightingale. 45c, Barn owls. 50c, Common starlings. 85c, Red crossbills. 1fr, White storks.

1962, Dec. 12 Unwmkd.

511 A130 5c green, sepia & yellow 10 10
512 " 10c bister, dk. pur. & red 15 15
513 " 15c multicolored 20 20
514 " 20c magenta, green & black 30 25
515 " 25c multicolored 40 30
516 " 30c brown, slate green & blue 40 35
517 " 45c violet & golden brown 60 55
518 " 50c blue green, black & yel. 85 70

519 A130 85c multicolored 90 80
520 " 1fr blk., grn. & red 1.10 1.00
Nos. 511-520 (10) 5.00 4.40

Issued to publicize protection of useful birds.

Divers
A131

Designs: 10c, Galeazzi's turret (vert.). 25c, Williamson's photosphere, 1914 and bathyscape "Trieste," 1962. 45c, Diving suits. 50c, Diving chamber. 85c, Fulton's "Nautilus," 1800 and modern submarine. 1fr, Alexander the Great's underwater chamber and bathysphere of the New York Zoological Society.

1962, Dec. 12

521 A131 5c bluish green, violet & black 12 12
522 " 10c multicolored 18 18
523 " 25c bister, bluish green & slate green 25 25
524 " 45c green, indigo & black 55 55
525 " 50c citron & dk. bl. 55 55
526 " 85c Prussian green & dk. vio. bl. 1.00 1.00
527 " 1fr dk. bl., dk. brn. & dk. green 1.10 1.10
Nos. 521-527 (7) 3.75 3.75

Issued in connection with an exhibition at the Oceanographic Museum "Man Under Water," showing ancient and modern methods of under-water exploration.

Dancing Children and U.N. Emblem
A132

Children on Scales—A133

Designs: 10c, Bird feeding nestlings (vert.). 20c, Sun shining on children of different races (vert.). 25c, Mother and child (vert.). 50c, House and child. 95c, African mother and child (vert.). 1fr, Prince Albert and Princess Caroline.

1963, May 3 ***Perf. 13*** **Unwmkd.**

528 A132 5c ocher, dark red & ultramarine 8 5
529 A133 10c vio. bl., emerald & olive gray 12 10
530 " 15c ultra., red & grn. 20 15
531 " 20c multicolored 25 20
532 " 25c blue. brn. & pink 30 30
533 " 50c multicolored 55 50
534 " 95c multicolored 75 75
535 A132 1fr greenish blue, dull purple & rose red 1.00 1.00
Nos. 528-535 (8) 3.25 3.05

Issued to publicize the United Nations Children's Charter.

Figurehead with Red Cross, Red Crescent and Red Lion and Sun—A134

Design: 1fr, Centenary emblem, Gustave Moynier, Henri Dunant and Gen. Henri Dufour (horiz.).

1963, May 3 **Engraved**

536 A134 50c bluish green, red & red brown 60 60
537 " 1fr blue, slate green & red 90 90

Centenary of International Red Cross.

Racing Cars on Monte Carlo Course and Map of Europe
A135

1963, May 3

538 A135 50c multicolored 70 65

European Automobile Grand Prix.

Rally Type of 1956

Design: 1fr, "Warsaw to Monte Carlo."

1963, May 3

539 A98 1fr multicolored 1.40 1.20

32nd Monte Carlo Auto Race.

Lions International Emblem
A136

1963, May 3

540 A136 50c bister, light violet & blue 60 60

Issued to commemorate the founding of the Lions Club of Monaco, March 24, 1962.

Hôtel des Postes, Paris, and UPU Allegory—A137

1963, May 3

541 A137 50c multicolored 65 65

Issued to commemorate the centenary of the first International Postal Conference, Paris, 1863.

Globe and Telstar—A138

1963, May 3

542 A138 50c green, dark purple & maroon 75 75

Issued to commemorate the first television connection of the United States and Europe through the Telstar satellite, July 11-12, 1962.

Holy Spirit over St. Peter's and World—A139

1963, May 3

543 A139 1fr green, red brown & blue 70 70

Issued to commemorate Vatican II, the 21st Ecumenical Council of the Roman Catholic Church.

Wheat Emblem and Dove Feeding Nestlings—A140

1963, May 3 **Engraved**

544 A140 1fr multicolored 70 70

Issued for the "Freedom from Hunger" campaign of the U.N. Food and Agriculture Organization.

Henry Ford and 1903 Model A
A141

1963, Dec. 12 ***Perf. 13*** **Unwmkd.**

545 A141 20c slate green & lilac rose 40 35

Issued to commemorate the centenary of the birth of Henry Ford, American automobile manufacturer.

Bicyle Racer in Town—142

Design: 50c, Bicyclist on country road.

1963, Dec. 12

546 A142 25c blue, slate grn. & red brown 25 20
547 " 50c blue, gray grn. & blk. brown 40 35

Issued to commemorate the 50th anniversary of the Bicycle Tour de France.

Pierre de Coubertin and Myron's Discobolus—A143

1963, Dec. 12

548 A143 1fr dp. claret, carm. & ocher 75 75

Issued to commemorate the centenary of the birth of Baron Pierre de Coubertin, organizer of the modern Olympic Games.

Rally Type of 1956

Design: 1fr, "Paris to Monte Carlo."

1963, Dec. 12

549 A98 1fr multicolored 1.20 1.20

33rd Monte Carlo Automobile Rally.

Children with Stamp Album and UNESCO Emblem—A144

1963, Dec. 12

550 A144 50c dp. ultramarine, red & violet 50 45

Issued to publicize the International Philatelic and Educational Exposition, Monaco, Nov.-Dec., 1963.

Europa Issue, 1963

Woman, Dove and Lyre—A145

1963, Dec. 12

551 A145 25c brown, green & carmine 30 30
552 " 50c dark brown, blue & carm. 50 50

Wembley Stadium and British Football Association Emblem
A146

Overhead Kick—A147

Calcio Game, Florence, 16th Century—A148

Tackle—A149

Designs: 3c, Goalkeeper. 4c, Louis II Stadium and emblem of Sports Association of Monaco, with black overprint: "Championnat/1962–1963/Coupe de France." 15c, Soule Game, Brittany, 19th century. 20c, Soccer, England, 1827. 25c, Soccer, England, 1890. 50c, Clearing goal area. 95c, Heading the ball. 1fr, Kicking the ball.

1963, Dec. 12

553	A146	1c green, violet & dark red	8	8
554	A147	2c blk., red & grn.	8	8
555	"	3c gray olive, orange & red	8	8
556	A146	4c blue, red, green, purple & blk.	10	10
557	A148	10c dk. blue, carm. & sepia	12	12
558	"	15c sepia & carm.	15	15
559	"	20c sepia & dk. blue	20	20
560	"	25c sepia & lilac	20	20
		a. Block of four	80	80
561	A149	30c grn., sepia & red	35	35
562	"	50c sepia, grn. & red	45	45
563	"	95c sepia, grn. & red	1.00	1.00
564	"	1fr sepia, grn. & red	1.25	1.25
		a. Block of four	5.00	5.00
		Nos. 553-564 (12)	4.06	4.06

Issued to commemorate the centenary of British Football Association (organized soccer). No. 556 also commemorates the successes of the soccer team of Monaco, 1962–63 (overprint typographed). No. 556 was not regularly issued without overprint. Price $225.

Nos. 557–560 and 561–564 printed in sheets of 40, containing 10 blocks of 4 each: Nos. 560a and 564a respectively. The 4 stamps of No. 560a are connected by an 1863 soccer ball in red brown; the stamps of No. 564a by a modern soccer ball.

Design from 1914 Rally Post Card A150

Farman Biplane over Monaco A151

Designs: 3c, Nieuport monoplane. 4c, Breguet biplane. 5c, Morane-Saulnier monoplane. 10c, Albatros biplane. 15c, Deperdussin monoplane. 20c, Vickers-Vimy biplane and map (Ross Smith's flight London-Port Darwin, 1919). 25c, Douglas Liberty biplane (first American around-the-world flight. 4 planes, 1924). 30c, Savoia S-16 hydroplane (De Pinedo's Rome-Australia-Japan-Rome flight, 1925). 45c, Trimotor Fokker F-7 monoplane (first aerial survey of North Pole, Richard E. Byrd and James Gordon Bennett, 1925). 50c, Spirit of St. Louis (first crossing of Atlantic, New York-Paris, Charles Lindbergh, 1927). 65c, Breguet 19 (Paris-New York, Coste and Bellonte, 1930). 95c, Laté 28 hydroplane (first South Atlantic airmail route, Dakar-Natal, 1930). 1fr, Dornier DO-X, (Germany-Rio de Janeiro, 1930).

1964, May 22 Engraved *Perf. 13*

565	A150	1c grn., bl. & olive	8	8
566	A151	2c blue, bister & red brown	8	8
567	"	3c olive, grn. & bl.	10	8
568	"	4c red brn., blue & Prussian grn.	10	8
569	"	5c gray olive, vio. & magenta	10	8
570	"	10c vio., bl. & olive	15	10
571	"	15c bl., org. & brn.	20	15
572	"	20c bright green, black & blue	25	20
573	"	25c red, blue & olive	30	25
574	"	30c bl., slate green & dp. claret	40	35
575	"	45c red brown, greenish blue & black	70	65
576	"	50c purple, olive & bister	75	75
577	"	65c steel blue, black & red	80	80
578	"	95c ocher, slate grn. & red	1.25	1.10
579	"	1fr slate green, blue & vio. brn.	1.25	1.25
		Nos. 565-579, C64 (16)	12.01	11.00

Issued to commemorate the 50th anniversary of the first airplane rally of Monte Carlo. Nos. 565–571 show planes which took part in the 1914 rally, Nos. 572–579 and C64 show important flights from 1919 to 1961.

Ancient Egyptian Message Transmitters and Rocket A152

1964, May 22 Unwmkd.

580	A152	1fr dk. blue, indigo & orge. brn.	1.20	1.20

Issued to publicize "PHILATEC", International Philatelic and Postal Techniques Exhibition, Paris, June 5–21, 1964.

Types of 1955–60.

Designs: 1c, Crab (Macrocheira Kampferi) (horiz.). 2c, Flowering cactus (Selenicereus Gr.). 12c, Shell (Fasciolaria trapezium). 18c, Aloe ciliaris. 70c, Honor court of palace (like No. 477). 95c, Prince Rainier III.

1964, May 19 *Perf. 13*

581	A115	1c bl. grn. & dk. red	4	4
582	"	2c dk. grn. & multi.	5	5
583	"	12c violet & brn. red	20	6
584	"	18c green, yel. & car.	25	13
585	A116	70c light green, choc. & red orange	60	35
586	A83	95c ultramarine	90	35
		Nos. 581-586 (6)	2.04	98

Rainier III Aquatic Stadium A153

1964–67 Engraved *Perf. 13*

587	A153	10c dk. car. rose, blue & black	90	6
587A	"	15c dk. car. rose, brt. bl. & blk. ('67)	50	6
588	"	25c dull grn., dark blue & black	50	10
589	"	50c lilac, blue green & black	80	18

Nos. 587–589 were issued precanceled only. See note after No. 324. The "1962" date has been obliterated with 2 bars. See also Nos. 732–734, 793–796, 976–979.

Europa Issue, 1964

Common Design Type

1964, Sept. 12

Size: 22x34½mm.

590	CD7	25c brt. red, bright grn. & dk. grn.	35	35
591	"	50c ultra., olive bister & dark red brown	75	75

Weight Lifter—A154

Sport: 2c, Judo. 3c, Pole vault. 4c, Archery.

1964, Dec. 3 *Perf. 13* Unwmkd.

592	A154	1c dk. red, brown & ultra.	10	8
593	"	2c olive, dark red & Prus. green	10	8
594	"	3c red brown, blue & brown	10	8
595	"	4c brown red, olive & Prus. green	10	8

Issued to commemorate the 18th Olympic Games, Tokyo, Oct. 10–25. See No. C65.

Pres. John F. Kennedy and Mercury Capsule—A155

1964, Dec. 3

596	A155	50c brt. bl. & indigo	1.20	1.00

Issued in memory of Pres. John F. Kennedy (1917–63).

Television Set and View of Monte Carlo—A156

1964, Dec. 3

597	A156	50c dk. carm. rose, dk. bl. & brn.	50	50

Fifth International Television Festival.

Common Design Types pictured in section at front of book.

Frédéric Mistral—A157

1964, Dec. 3 Engraved

598	A157	1fr gray olive & brown red	75	75

Issued to commemorate the 50th anniversary of the death of Frederic Mistral, (1830–1914), Provençal poet.

Scales of Justice and Code A158

1964, Dec. 3

599	A158	1fr golden brown & slate green	75	75

Universal Declaration of Human Rights.

Rally Type of 1956

Design: 1fr, "Minsk to Monte Carlo."

1964, Dec. 3

600	A98	1fr blue green, ocher & brown	1.00	90

34th Monte Carlo Automobile Rally.

International Football Association Emblem—A159

1964, Dec. 3

601	A159	1fr red, blue & olive bister	1.10	1.10

Issued to commemorate the 60th anniversary of FIFA, the Federation Internationale de Football (soccer).

Types of 1955 and 1960

Designs: 40c, Aerial view of palace. 60c, 1.30fr, 2.30fr, Prince Rainier III.

1965–66 Engraved *Perf. 13*

602	A116	40c slate green, dull claret & bright green	40	22
603	A83	60c slate green & black	50	25
604	"	1.30fr dk. red & blk.	1.50	75
604A	"	2.30fr org. & rose lilac ('66)	1.40	45

Telstar and Pleumeur-Bodou Relay Station—A160

Alexander Graham Bell and Telephone A161

Designs (ITU Emblem and): 5c, Syncom II and Earth. 10c, Echo II and Earth. 12c, Relay satellite and Earth (vert.). 18c, Lunik III and Moon. 50c, Samuel Morse and telegraph. 60c, Edouard Belin, belinograph and newspaper. 70c, Roman signal towers and Chappe telegraph. 95c, Cable laying ships; "The Great Eastern" (British, 1858) and "Alsace" (French, modern). 1fr, Edouard Branly, Guglielmo Marconi and map of English Channel.

1965, May 17

605 A161 5c violet blue & slate green 10 10
606 " 10c dk. bl. & sepia 10 10
607 " 12c gray, brown & dark carmine 20 20
608 " 18c indigo, dark carmine & plum 25 25
609 A160 25c violet, olive & rose brown 30 30
610 A161 30c dark brown, olive & bister brn. 40 40
611 " 50c green & indigo 45 45
612 " 60c dull red brown & bright blue 50 50
613 A160 70c brown blk., org & dark blue 70 70
614 " 95c indigo, blk. & bl. 85 85
615 " 1fr brown, black & ultra. 1.20 1.20
Nos. 605-615, C66 (12) 12.05 12.05

Issued to commemorate the centenary of the International Telecommunication Union.

Europa Issue, 1965
Common Design Type

1965, Sept. 25 Engraved *Perf. 13*
Size: 36x22mm.

616 CD8 30c red brn. & grn. 25 25
617 " 60c vio. & dk. car. 50 45

Palace of Monaco, 18th Century
A162

Views of Palace: 12c, From the Bay, 17th century. 18c, Bay with sailboats, 18th century. 30c, From distance, 19th century. 60c, Close-up, 19th century. 1.30fr, Aerial view, 20th century.

1966, Feb. 1 Engraved *Perf. 13*

618 A162 10c vio., dull grn. & indigo 15 15
619 " 12c blue, bister brn. & dk. brown 15 15
620 " 18c blk., grn. & bl. 25 25
621 " 30c vio. blue, sepia & red brn. 30 30
622 " 60c blue, green & brown 40 40
623 " 1.30fr dk. grn. & red brown 1.00 1.00
Nos. 618-623 (6) 2.25 2.25

750th anniversary of Palace of Monaco.

Dante Alighieri—A163

Designs: 60c, Dante facing Panther of Envy. 70c, Dante and Virgil boating across muddy swamp of 5th Circle. 95c, Dante watching the arrogant and Cross of Salvation. 1fr, Invocation of St. Bernard; Dante and Beatrice.

1966, Feb. 1

624 A163 30c crimson & dp. green 60 60
625 " 60c dull green, Prus. bl. & indigo 1.20 1.20
626 " 70c black, sepia & carmine 1.20 1.20
627 " 95c red lilac & blue 2.50 2.50
628 " 1fr ultra. & bluish green 2.50 2.50
Nos. 624-628 (5) 8.00 8.00

Issued to commemorate the 700th anniversary (in 1965) of the birth of Dante (1265-1321), poet.

Rally Type of 1956
Design: 1fr, "London to Monte Carlo."

1966, Feb. 1

629 A98 1fr pur., red & indigo 90 90

The 35th Monte Carlo Automobile Rally.

Nativity by Gerard van Honthorst
A164

1966, Feb. 1

630 A164 30c brown 30 30

Issued to honor the World Association for the Protection of Children.

Casino, Monte Carlo
A165

View of La Condamine, 1860, and François Blanc—A166

Designs: 12c, Prince Charles III (vert.). 40c, Charles III monument, Bowling Green Gardens. 60c, Seaside Promenade and Rainier III. 70c, René Blum, Sergei Diaghilev and "Petroushka." 95c, Jules Massenet and Camille Saint-Saens. 1.30fr, Gabriel Fauré and Maurice Ravel.

1966, June 1 Engraved *Perf. 13*

631 A165 12c dp. bl., black & magenta 20 20
632 " 25c multicolored 25 25
633 A166 30c blue, plum, green & org. 30 30
634 A165 40c multicolored 35 35
635 A166 60c " 45 45
636 " 70c rose claret & indigo 45 45
637 A165 95c purple & black 90 90
638 " 1.30fr brn. org., olive bister & brn. 1.10 1.10
Nos. 631-638, C68 (9) 7.50 7.50

Centenary of founding of Monte Carlo.

Europa Issue, 1966
Common Design Type

1966, Sept. 26 Engraved *Perf. 13*
Size: 21½x35½mm.

639 CD9 30c orange 25 25
640 " 60c light green 55 55

Prince Albert I, Yachts Hirondelle I and Princesse Alice—A167

1966, Dec. 12 Engraved *Perf. 13*

641 A167 1fr ultra. & dark violet brown 90 80

Issued to commemorate the first International Congress of the History of Oceanography, Monaco, Dec. 12-17. Issued in sheets of 10.

Red Chalk Drawing by Domenico Zampieri
A168

Television Screen and Cross over Monaco
A169

1966, Dec. 12

642 A168 30c bright rose & dark brown 20 20
643 " 60c bright blue & yellow brown 40 40

Issued to commemorate the 20th anniversary of UNESCO (United Nations Educational, Scientific and Cultural Organization).

1966, Dec. 12

644 A169 60c dk. car. rose, lilac & red 40 30

Issued to commemorate the 10th meeting of "UNDA" the International Catholic Association for Radio and Television.

Precontinent III and Divers on Ocean Floor—A170

1966, Dec. 12

645 A170 1fr Prus. blue, yel. & dk. brown 60 55

Issued to commemorate the first anniversary of the submarine research station Precontinent III.

WHO Headquarters, Geneva
A171

1966, Dec. 12

646 A171 30c dp. bl., olive brn. & dp. bl. grn. 20 15
647 " 60c dk. grn., crimson & dk. brown 35 30

Issued to commemorate the opening of World Health Organization Headquarters, Geneva.

Automobile Type of 1961

Automobiles (Previous Winners): 1c, Bugatti, 1931. 2c, Alfa Romeo, 1932. 5c, Mercedes, 1936. 10c, Maserati, 1948. 18c, Ferrari, 1955. 20c, Alfa Romeo, 1950. 25c, Maserati, 1957. 30c, Cooper-Climax, 1958. 40c, Lotus-Climax, 1960. 50c, Lotus-Climax, 1961. 60c, Cooper-Climax, 1962. 70c, B.R.M., 1963-66. 1fr, Walter Christie, 1907. 2.30fr, Peugeot, 1910.

1967, Apr. 28 Engr. *Perf. 13x12½*

648 A122 1c indigo, red & brt. blue 8 5
649 " 2c grn., red & blk. 8 5
650 " 5c red, indigo & gray 12 10
651 " 10c violet, red & indigo 12 10
652 " 18c indigo & red 20 18
653 " 20c dk. green, red & indigo 20 20
654 " 25c ultra., red & indigo 25 20
655 " 30c brown, indigo & green 30 25
656 " 40c carmine rose, indigo & grn. 30 30
657 " 50c lilac, indigo & green 40 35
658 " 60c car., indigo & green 55 50
659 " 70c dull yellow, bl. grn. & indigo 55 50
660 " 1fr brn. red, black & gray 85 80
661 " 2.30fr multicolored 1.50 1.40
Nos. 648-661, C73 (15) 7.75 6.98

25th Grand Prix of Monaco, May 7.

Dog, Egyptian Statue
A172

1967, Apr. 28 *Perf. 12½x13*

662 A172 30c dk. green, brown & black 30 25

Issued to commemorate the congress of the International Dog Fanciers Federation, Monaco, Apr. 5-9.

View of Monte Carlo—A173

1967, Apr. 28 *Perf. 13*

663 A173 30c slate grn., brt. blue & brown 25 20

International Tourist Year, 1967.

Chessboard and Monte Carlo Harbor—A174

1967, Apr. 28

664 A174 60c brt. bl., dk. pur. & black 70 65

International Chess Championships, Monaco, Mar. 19-Apr. 1.

Melvin Jones, View of Monte Carlo and Lions Emblem—A175

1967, Apr. 28

665 A175 60c ultra., slate blue & chocolate 45 40

50th anniversary of Lions International.

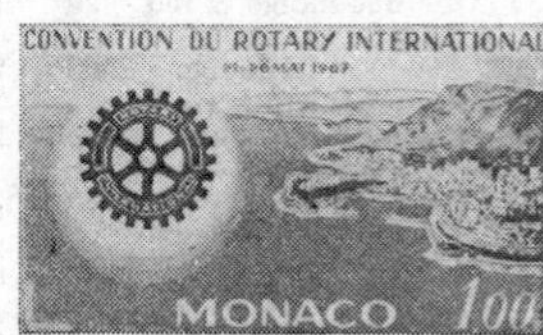

Rotary Emblem and View of Monte Carlo—A176

1967, Apr. 28

666 A176 1fr brt. blue & lt. olive green 60 55

Issued to publicize the Rotary International Convention, Monaco, May 21-26.

EXPO '67 Monaco Pavilion A177

1967, Apr. 28

667 A177 1fr multicolored 60 50

Issued to commemorate EXPO '67, International Exhibition, Montreal, Apr. 28–Oct. 27, 1967.

Map of Europe A178

1967, Apr. 28

668 A178 1fr chocolate, lemon & Prus. blue 55 40

Issued to publicize the International Committee for European Migration, CIME.

Europa Issue, 1967

Common Design Type

1967, Apr. 28 ***Perf. 12½x13***

669 CD10 30c bright carmine, rose lilac & bright violet 25 20

670 " 60c green olive & blue green 35 30

Skier and Olympic Emblem—A179

1967, Dec. 7 **Engraved** ***Perf. 13***

671 A179 2.30fr red brn., gray & brt. bl. 1.50 1.25

Issued to commemorate the 10th Winter Olympic Games, Grenoble, France, Feb. 6–18, 1968.

Sounding Line and Map—A180

1967, Dec. 7

672 A180 1fr dark blue, green & olive 60 50

Issued to commemorate the 9th International Hydrographic Conference, Monte Carlo, April–May, 1967.

Marie Curie, Chemical Apparatus and Atom Symbol—A181

1967, Dec. 7

673 A181 1fr brown, ultra. & olive 60 55

Issued to commemorate the centenary of the birth of Marie Curie (1867–1934), discoverer of radium and polonium.

Princes of Monaco Issue

Rainier I, by Eugene Charpentier A182

Design: No. 675, Lucien Grimaldi, by Ambrogio di Predis.

1967, Dec. 7 ***Perf. 12x13***

674 A182 1fr multicolored 2.00 1.50

675 " 1fr " 2.00 1.50

See Nos. 710–711, 735–736, 774–775, 813–814, 860–861, 892–893, 991–992, 1035–1036, 1093, 1135–1136.

Shot Put A183

Sport: 30c, High jump. 60c, Gymnast on rings. 70c, Water polo. 1fr, Wrestling. 2.30fr, Gymnast.

1968, Apr. 29 **Engraved** ***Perf. 13***

676 A183 20c brt. blue, grn. & brown 25 25

677 " 30c vio. blue, sepia & brn. violet 30 30

678 " 60c car., brt. rose lilac & dp. bl. 45 45

679 " 70c ocher, brn. org. & Prus. blue 50 50

680 " 1fr brown orange, brn. & indigo 70 70

681 " 2.30fr dk. car., vio. blue & olive 1.50 1.50

Nos. 676-681, C74 (7) 5.95 5.70

Issued to publicize the 19th Olympic Games, Mexico City, Oct. 12–27.

St. Martin and the Beggar A184

1968, Apr. 29

682 A184 2.30fr brn. red, Prus. blue & blk. brn. 1.50 1.40

Red Cross of Monaco, 20th anniversary.

Anemones, by Raoul Dufy A185

1968, Apr. 29 **Photo.** ***Perf. 12x13***

683 A185 1fr lt. blue & multi. 80 60

Issued to publicize the International Flower Show in Monte Carlo. See Nos. 766, 776, 815–816, 829, 865.

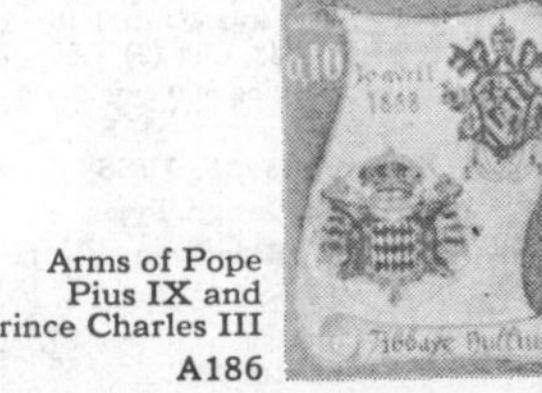

Arms of Pope Pius IX and Prince Charles III A186

St. Nicholas A187

Designs: 30c, St. Benedict. 60c, Benedictine Monastery, Subiaco (Italy). 1fr, Church of St. Nicholas, Monaco, 13th century (horiz.).

Engraved

1968, Apr. 29 ***Perf. 12½x13, 13x12½***

684 A186 10c red & brown 10 10

685 A187 20c slate grn., ocher & carmine 25 20

686 " 30c ultramarine & olive green 30 25

687 " 60c lt. blue, brown & dk. green 40 40

688 " 1fr indigo, blue & olive bister 65 65

Nos. 684-688 (5) 1.70 1.60

Issued to commemorate the centenary of the elevation of St. Nicholas Church to an Abbey *Nullius*, directly subject to the Holy See.

Europa Issue, 1968

Common Design Type

1968, Apr. 29 ***Perf. 13***

Size: 36x22mm.

689 CD11 30c dp. org. & car. 25 20

690 " 60c car. & ultra. 30 25

691 " 1fr grn. & red brn. 70 60

Locomotive 030, 1868—A188

Locomotives and Views: 30c, Type "C"-220, 1898. 60c, Type 230-"C", 1910. 70c, Type 231-"F," 1925. 1fr, Type 241-"A," 1932. 2.30fr, Type "BB," 1968.

1968, Dec. 12 **Engraved** ***Perf. 13***

692 A188 20c violet blue, brn. & black 20 15

693 " 30c dk. olive green, blue & black 25 20

694 " 60c blue, bister & black 35 30

695 " 70c violet, red brn. & black 40 35

696 " 1fr blue, brown red & black 55 50

697 " 2.30fr sal. pink, brt. blue & blk. 1.60 1.50

Nos. 692-697 (6) 3.35 3.00

Centenary of the Nice-Monaco Railroad.

Chateaubriand and Combourg Castle A189

Scenes from Chateaubriand Novels: 20c, The Genius of Christianity. 25c, René. 30c, The Last Abencerage. 60c, The Martyrs. 2.30fr, Atala.

1968, Dec. 12

698 A189 10c dk. grn., green & purple 15 10
699 " 20c brt. blue, violet & magenta 25 20
700 " 25c slate, purple & brown 30 25
701 " 30c dp. brn., brn. & purple 35 30
702 " 60c brown red, blue green & dark brown 45 35
703 " 2.30fr dk. blue, olive & magenta 1.50 1.40
Nos. 698-703 (6) 3.00 2.60

Issued to commemorate the 200th anniversary of the birth of Vicomte François René de Chateaubriand (1768–1848), novelist and statesman.

"France" and "Fidelity" by Bosio
A190

François Joseph Bosio
A191

Designs: 25c, Henri IV as a boy. 60c, Louis XIV on horseback, Place des Victoires. 2.30fr, Busts of Louis XVIII, Napoleon I and Charles X.

1968, Dec. 12

704 A190 20c brown 15 .10
705 A191 25c salmon pink & dark brown 20 15
706 " 30c slate & vio. bl. 25 20
707 " 60c dk. olive green & gray green 40 35
708 A190 2.30fr black & slate 1.35 1.25
Nos. 704-708 (5) 2.35 2.05

Issued to commemorate the 200th anniversary of the birth of Francois Joseph Bosio (1768–1845), sculptor.

WHO Emblem
A192

1968, Dec. 12 Photogravure

709 A192 60c multicolored 35 30

Issued to commemorate the 20th anniversary of the World Health Organization.

Princes of Monaco Type of 1967

Designs: 1fr, Charles II (1581–89). 2.30fr, Jeanne Grimaldi (1596–1620).

1968, Dec. 12 Engr. *Perf. 12x13*

710 A182 1fr multicolored 70 70
711 " 2.30fr " 1.50 1.50

Faust and Mephistopheles
A193

Scenes from "Damnation of Faust" by Berlioz: 10c, Rakoczy March. 25c, Auerbach's Cellar. 30c, Dance of the Sylphs. 40c, Dance of the Sprites. 50c, Faust and Marguerite. 70c, Woods and Meadows. 1fr, The Ride to the Abyss. 1.15fr, Heaven.

1969, Apr. 26 Engraved *Perf. 13*

712 A193 10c bl. green, pur. & org. brown 10 10
713 " 20c magenta, dark olive & light brown 15 10
714 " 25c indigo, brown & magenta 20 15
715 " 30c yel. green, slate & black 25 20
716 " 40c orange red, slate & black 30 25
717 " 50c olive, plum & slate 40 30
718 " 70c dp. grn., slate & lt. brown 50 45
719 " 1fr magenta, black & olive bister 60 60
720 " 1.15fr Prus. blue, blk. & ultra. 80 80
Nos. 712-720, C75 (10) 4.70 4.20

Issued to commemorate the centenary of the death of Hector Berlioz (1803–1869), French composer.

St. Elizabeth and Husband, Louis IV, Landgrave of Thuringia
A194

1969, Apr. 26

721 A194 3fr dark red, slate & gray 2.00 2.00

Issued for the Red Cross.
See Nos. 767, 812, 830, 905, 963, 1037, 1094.

Europa Issue, 1969
Common Design Type

1969, Apr. 26

Size: 36x26mm.

722 CD12 40c scarlet & purple 25 20
723 " 70c brt. blue & black 45 30
724 " 1fr yel. bister, brown & blue 60 50

Prince Rainier Type of 1955 and Palace Type of 1960.

Designs: 80c, Aerial view of Palace. 1.15fr, 1.30fr, Honor Court.

1969–70 Engraved *Perf. 13*

725 A83 40c ol. & rose red 20 10
726 " 45c slate & ocher 30 15
727 " 50c ocher & maroon 35 15
728 " 70c dk. purple & brt. vio. bl. 45 20
729 A116 80c blue, red brn. & green 60 40
730 A83 85c dk. violet & brt. green 60 40
731 A116 1.15fr black, blue & maroon 80 60
731A A116 1.30fr ol. brn., lt. bl. & dull grn. ('70) 75 40
Nos. 725-731A (8) 4.05 2.40

Aquatic Stadium Type of 1964–67, "1962" Omitted

1969 Engraved *Perf. 13*

732 A153 22c chocolate, brt. blue & black 30 10
733 " 35c Prus. blue, brt. blue & black 30 15
734 " 70c black & vio. blue 50 25

Nos. 732–734 were issued precanceled only. See note after No. 324.

Princes of Monaco Type of 1967

Designs: 1fr, Honoré II (1604–1662), by Philippe de Champaigne. 3fr, Louise-Hippolyte (1697–1731), by Pierre Gobert.

1969, Nov. 25 Engraved *Perf. 12x13*

735 A182 1fr multicolored 80 80
736 " 3fr " 2.00 2.00

Woman's Head, by Leonardo da Vinci
A195

Drawings by Leonardo da Vinci: 40c, Self-portrait. 70c, Head of old man. 80c, Study for head of St. Magdalene. 1.15fr, Man's head. 3fr, Professional soldier.

1969, Nov. 25 *Perf. 13*

737 A195 30c dull brown 20 15
738 " 40c brn. & rose red 25 20
739 " 70c gray green 40 30
740 " 80c dark brown 45 35
741 " 1.15fr orange brown 80 70
742 " 3fr olive brown 1.65 1.50
Nos. 737-742 (6) 3.75 3.20

Issued to commemorate the 450th anniversary of the death of Leonardo da Vinci (1452–1519), Florentine painter, sculptor and scientist.

Alphonse Daudet and Scenes from "Letters from My Windmill"
A196

Various Scenes from "Letters from My Windmill" (Lettres de Mon Moulin).

1969, Nov. 25

743 A196 30c bl. grn. & multi. 30 30
744 " 40c brown, violet blue & olive 50 50
745 " 70c purple, brn. & olive gray 55 55
746 " 80c slate grn., vio. bl. & maroon 65 65
747 " 1.15fr ocher, sepia & black 80 80
Nos. 743-747 (5) 2.80 2.80

Centenary of publication of "Letters from My Windmill," by Alphonse Daudet (1840–1897).

ILO Emblem
A197

1969, Nov. 25 *Perf. 13x12½*

748 A197 40c dk. bl. & dk. pur. 30 30

Issued to commemorate the 50th anniversary of the International Labor Organization.

World Map and JCI Emblem
A198

1969, Nov. 25

749 A198 40c olive, dark blue & blue 30 30

Issued to commemorate the 25th anniversary of the Junior Chamber of Commerce in Monaco.

Television Camera and View of Monte Carlo
A199

1969, Nov. 25

750 A199 40c red brown, lilac & blue 30 30

Issued to publicize the 10th International Television Festival in 1970.

King Alfonso XIII, Prince Albert I and Underwater Scene
A200

1969, Nov. 25 *Perf. 12½x13*

751 A200 40c dk. brown, blk. & greenish bl. 30 30

Issued to commemorate the 50th anniversary of the International Commission for the Scientific Exploration of the Mediterranean.

Congress Building, Princes Albert I and Rainier III
A201

1970, Feb. 21 Engraved *Perf. 13*

752 A201 40c gray & carmine 30 25

Issued to commemorate the meeting of the Interparliamentary Union, Monaco, Mar. 30–Apr. 5

EXPO '70 Emblem, Japanese Scroll
A202

Designs (EXPO '70 Emblem and): 30c, Ibis. 40c, Torii. 70c, Cherry blossoms (horiz.) 1.15fr, Palace and arms of Monaco, Osaka Castle and arms (horiz.).

1970, Mar. 16

753 A202 20c brn., yel. grn. & carmine 15 15
754 " 30c brn., yel. grn. & buff 25 25
755 " 40c olive bister & purple 30 30
756 " 70c lt. gray & red 65 65
757 " 1.15fr red & multi. 85 85
Nos. 753-757 (5) 2.20 2.20

Issued to publicize EXPO '70 International Exposition, Osaka, Japan, Mar. 15-Sept. 13.

Harbor Seal Pup—A203

1970, Mar. 16

758 A203 40c red lilac, blue & gray 35 30

Protection of seal pups.

Doberman Pinscher
A204

1970, Apr. 25

759 A204 40c ocher & black 30 25

International Dog Show, Monte Carlo, Apr. 25. See also No. 996.

Basque Ponies
A205

Designs: 30c, Parnassius Apollo butterfly. 50c, Harbor seal in Somme Bay. 80c, Pyrenean chamois (vert.). 1fr, White-tailed sea eagles (vert.). 1.15fr, European otter (vert.).

1970, May 4

760 A205 30c Prussian blue & multi. 25 20
761 " 40c blue & multi. 30 25
762 " 50c greenish blue, bister & brown 35 25
763 " 80c gray green, slate blue & brown 55 40
764 " 1fr gray, brown & bister 75 50
765 A205 1.15fr dark brown, light blue & yel. green 80 60
Nos. 760-765 (6) 3.00 2.20

Issued to commemorate the 20th anniversary of the International Federation of Animal Protection.

Flower Type of 1968

Design: 3fr, Roses and Anemones, by Vincent van Gogh.

1970, May 4 Photo. ***Perf. 12x13***

766 A185 3fr black & multi. 2.00 2.00

International Flower Show, Monte Carlo.

Red Cross Type of 1969

Design: 3fr, St. Louis giving alms to the poor.

1970, May 4 Engraved *Perf. 13*

767 A194 3fr dark gray, olive gray & slate green 2.00 2.00

Issued for the Red Cross.

Europa Issue, 1970
Common Design Type

1970, May 4 Size: 26x36mm.

768 CD13 40c deep rose lilac 30 15
769 " 80c bright green 50 20
770 " 1fr deep blue 60 40

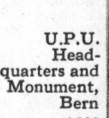

U.P.U. Headquarters and Monument, Bern
A206

1970, May 4

771 A206 40c brn. olive, gray & blue green 30 25

Issued to commemorate the opening of the new Universal Postal Union Headquarters in Bern.

Plaque and Flag on the Moon, Presidents Kennedy and Nixon
A207

Design: 80c, Astronauts and landing module on moon, and Apollo 11 emblem.

1970, May 4 **Photogravure**

772 A207 40c multicolored 35 30
773 " 80c " 70 50

Man's first landing on moon, July 20, 1969. U.S. astronauts Neil A. Armstrong and Col. Edwin E. Aldrin, Jr., with Lt. Col. Michael Collins piloting Apollo 11.

Princes of Monaco Type of 1967

Designs: 1fr, Louis I (1662-1701), by Jean Francois de Troy. 3fr, Charlotte de Gramont (1639-1678), by Sebastian Bourdon.

1970, Dec. 15 **Engr.** ***Perf. 12x13***

774 A182 1fr multicolored 70 70
775 " 3fr " 2.00 2.00

Painting Type of 1968

Design: 3fr, Portrait of Dédie, by Amedeo Modigliani (1884-1920).

1970, Dec. 15

776 A185 3fr multicolored 2.00 1.85

Beethoven and "Ode to Joy"
A208

1970, Dec. 15

777 A208 1.30fr brown & maroon 1.00 90

Bicentenary of the birth of Ludwig van Beethoven (1770-1827), composer.

Dumas and Scene from "Three Musketeers"—A209

Designs: 40c, Henri Rougier and biplane over Monaco. 80c, Alphonse de Lamartine and scenes from his works.

1970, Dec. 15

778 A209 30c bl., brn. & gray 20 15
779 " 40c bl., sepia & gray 30 20
780 " 80c multicolored 50 35

Nos. 778-780 commemorate: Centenary of the death of Alexandre Dumas, père (1802-1870), novelist; 60th anniversary of first flight over the Mediterranean by Henri Rougier; 150th anniversary of the publication of "Méditations Poétiques" by Alphonse de Lamartine (1790-1869), poet.

Camargue Horse
A210

Horses: 20c, Anglo-Arabian thoroughbred. 30c, French saddle horse. 40c, Lippizaner. 50c, Trotter. 70c, English thoroughbred. 85c, Arabian. 1.15fr, Barbary.

1970, Dec. 15 Engraved *Perf. 13*

781 A210 10c bl., olive bister & dark blue 10 8
782 " 20c vio. bl., brown & olive 15 12
783 " 30c bl., brn. & grn. 25 15
784 " 40c gray, indigo & olive bister 30 25
785 " 50c bl., dk. brown & olive 40 30
786 " 70c dk. green, olive brown & red brown 55 55
787 " 85c dk. green, olive & slate 65 55
788 " 1.15fr blue, emerald & black 80 70
Nos. 781-788, C77 (9) 5.45 4.20

Prince Rainier Type of 1955 and Palace Type of 1960

Designs: 90c, Honor Court. 1.40fr, Aerial view of Palace.

1971 **Engraved** ***Perf. 13***

789 A83 60c plum & black 45 30
790 A116 90c dk. car., ultra. & black 70 50
791 A83 1.10fr gray & ultra. 75 55
792 A116 1.40fr purple, orange & green 1.10 75

Aquatic Stadium Type of 1964-67, "1962" Omitted

1971

793 A153 26c pur., ultra. & blk. 30 6
794 " 30c copper red, bl., lilac & black 30 10
795 " 45c slate grn., violet blue & black 30 15
796 " 90c olive, Prussian blue & black 70 25

Nos. 793-796 were issued precanceled only. See note after No. 324.

Europa Issue, 1971
Common Design Type

1971, Sept. 6

797 CD14 50c carmine rose 30 20
798 " 80c bright blue 50 30
799 " 1.30fr slate green 80 40

Old Bridge at Sospel—A211

Designs: 80c, Roquebrune Castle. 1.30fr, Grimaldi Castle. 3fr, Roman Monument, La Turbie (vert.). All views in Alpes-Maritimes Department, France.

1971, Sept. 6

800 A211 50c slate grn., blue & olive brn. 30 20
801 " 80c slate green, slate & brn. 50 25
802 " 1.30fr brn., slate grn. & red 70 50
803 " 3fr brt. blue, slate & olive 1.75 1.20

Protection of historic monuments.

Theodolite, Underwater Scene and Coast Line—A212

1971, Sept. 6

804 A212 80c bl. grn. & multi. 50 40

50th anniversary of International Hydrographical Bureau.

Sea Bird Covered with Oil
A213

1971, Sept. 6

805 A213 50c dp. bl. & indigo 40 30

Against pollution of the seas.

"Arts" (Organ Pipes and Michelangelo's Creation of Adam)—A214

"Science" (Alchemist, Radar and Rocket) A215 — Prince Pierre of Monaco A216

Design: 80c, "Culture" (medieval scholar, book, film and television).

1971, Sept. 6 Engr. *Perf. 13*

806 A214 30c brt. blue, purple & brown 25 10
807 A215 50c slate & brn. org. 35 20
808 A214 80c emerald & brn. 55 30

Photo. *Perf. 12½x13*

809 A216 1.30fr gray green 80 60

25th anniversary of United Nations Educational, Scientific and Cultural Organization (UNESCO).

Cocker Spaniel A217

1971, Sept. 6 *Perf. 13x12½*

810 A217 50c multicolored 45 35

International Dog Show. See Nos. 826, 879, 910.

Hand Holding Blood Donor Emblem A218

1971, Sept. 6 Engraved *Perf. 13*

811 A218 80c red, vio. & gray 50 40

7th International Blood Donors Congress, Monaco, Oct. 21–24.

Red Cross Type of 1969

Design: 3fr, St. Vincent de Paul appearing to prisoners.

1971, Sept. 6

812 A194 3fr bl. grn., olive grn. & deep green 2.00 1.75

For the Red Cross

Princes of Monaco Type of 1967

Designs: 1fr, Antoine I (1701–1731), by Hyacinthe Rigaud. 3fr, Marie de Lorraine (1674–1724), French School.

1972, Jan. 18 *Perf. 12x13*

813 A182 1fr multicolored 65 55
814 " 3fr " 2.00 1.60

Painting Type of 1968

Designs: 2fr, The Cradle, by Berthe Morisot. 3fr, Clown, by Jean Antoine Watteau.

1972, Jan. 18

815 A185 2fr green & multi. 1.35 90
816 " 3fr multicolored 2.00 1.60

No. 815 issued for 25th anniversary (in 1971) of the United Nations International Children's Fund (UNICEF).

Christ Before Pilate, by Dürer A219

1972, Jan. 18 *Perf. 13*

817 A219 2fr lt. brn. & black 1.35 90

500th anniversary of the birth of Albrecht Dürer (1471–1528), German painter and engraver.

La Fontaine and Animals A220

Saint-Saens and "Samson et Dalila"—A221

Design: 1.30fr, Charles Baudelaire, nudes and cats.

1972, Jan. 18

818 A220 50c brn., green & slate green 35 20
819 A221 90c dk. brown & yel. brown 60 35
820 A220 1.30fr black, red & vio. brown 85 70

350th anniversary of the birth of Jean de La Fontaine (1621–1695), fabulist (50c); 50th anniversary of the death of Camille Saint-Saens (1835–1921), composer (90c); 150th anniversary of the birth of Charles Baudelaire (1821–1867), poet (1.30fr).

Father Christmas A222

1972, Jan. 18

821 A222 30c bister, slate blue & red 20 10
822 " 50c violet brown, green & red 35 20
823 " 90c ocher, indigo & red 55 35

Christmas 1971.

Battle of Lepanto—A223

1972, Jan. 18

824 A223 1fr dull blue, red & brown 70 50

400th anniversary of the Battle of Lepanto against the Turks.

Steam and Diesel Locomotives, UIC Emblem—A224

1972, Apr. 27 Engr. *Perf. 13*

825 A224 50c dk. car., lilac & chocolate 30 20

50th anniversary of the founding of the International Railroad Union (UIC).

Dog Type of 1971

Design: Great Dane.

1972, Apr. 27 Photo. *Perf. 13x12½*

826 A217 60c multicolored 45 35

International Dog Show.

Serene Landscape, Pollution, Destruction—A225

1972, Apr. 27 Engr. *Perf. 13*

827 A225 90c grn., brn. & blk. 65 40

Anti-pollution fight.

Ski Jump, Sapporo '72 Emblem A226

1972, Apr. 27

828 A226 90c blue green, dark red & black 70 50

11th Winter Olympic Games, Sapporo, Japan, Feb. 3–13.

Flower Type of 1968

Design: 3fr, Flowers in Vase, by Paul Cezanne.

1972, Apr. 27 Photo. *Perf. 12x13*

829 A185 3fr multicolored 1.65 1.20

International Flower Show, Monte Carlo.

Red Cross Type of 1969

Design: 3fr, St. Francis of Assisi comforting poor man.

1972, Apr. 27 Engr. *Perf. 13*

830 A194 3fr dk. pur. & brn. 2.00 1.65

For the Red Cross.

Europa Issue 1972

Common Design Type

1972, Apr. 27 *Perf. 12½x13*

Size: 26x36mm.

831 CD15 50c vio. blue & org. 30 20
832 " 90c violet blue & emerald 60 40

Church of Sts. John and Paul (detail), by Canaletto A227

Designs: 60c, Church of St. Peter of Castello, by Francesco Guardi. 2fr, St. Mark's Square, by Bernardo Bellotto.

1972, Apr. 27 *Perf. 13*

Sizes: 36x48mm. (30c, 2fr); 26½x48mm. (60c)

833 A227 30c rose red 40 30
834 " 60c bright purple 45 35
835 " 2fr Prussian blue 1.35 1.00

UNESCO campaign to save Venice.

Dressage A228

Designs (Equestrian Events): 90c, Jump over fences. 1.10fr, Jump over wall. 1.40fr, Jump over gates.

1972, Apr. 27

836 A228 60c rose car., vio. blue & brn. 60 55
837 " 90c vio. blue, rose car. & brn. 1.00 90
838 " 1.10fr brn., rose car. & vio. blue 1.20 1.10
839 " 1.40fr vio. blue, rose car. & brn. 1.75 1.65
a. Block of 4+2 labels 5.00 5.00

20th Olympic Games, Munich, Aug. 26–Sept. 10. Nos. 836–839 printed se-tenant in sheets of 24 stamps and 6 labels.

Auguste Escoffier and his Birthplace
A229

1972, May 6 Engraved *Perf. 13*

840 A229 45c black & olive 35 25

125th anniversary of the birth of Georges Auguste Escoffier (1846–1935), French chef.

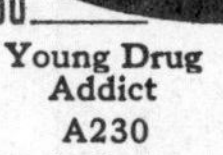

Young Drug Addict
A230

Congress Emblem, Birds and Animals
A231

1972, July 3

841 A230 50c carmine, sepia & orange 35 20
842 " 90c slate green, sepia & indigo 55 40

Fight against drug abuse.

1972, Sept. 25

Designs: 50c, Congress emblem, Neptune, sea, earth and land creatures (horiz.). 90c, Globe, land, sea and air creatures.

843 A231 30c olive, brt. grn. & carmine 20 15
844 " 50c ocher, brown & org. brown 35 25
845 " 90c orange brown, blue & olive 60 50

17th International Zoology Congress, Monaco, Sept. 24–30.

Arrangement of Lilies and Palm
A232

Designs: Floral arrangements.

1972, Nov. 13 Photogravure *Perf. 13*

846 A232 30c org. red & multi. 20 10
847 " 50c multicolored 35 25
848 " 90c black & multi. 55 30

International Flower Show, Monte Carlo, May, 1973. See also Nos. 894–896.

Child and Adoration of the Kings
A233

1972, Nov. 13 Engraved

849 A233 30c gray, vio. blue & bright pink 20 10
850 " 50c deep carmine, lilac & brown 30 15
851 " 90c vio. bl. & purple 55 35

Christmas 1972.

Louis Bleriot and his Monoplane
A234

Designs: 50c, Roald Amundsen and Antarctic landscape. 90c, Louis Pasteur and laboratory.

1972, Dec. 4

852 A234 30c choc. & brt. bl. 20 12
853 " 50c Prussian blue & indigo 35 25
854 " 90c choc. & ocher 60 50

Anniversaries of the births of: Louis Bleriot (1872–1936), French aviation pioneer (30c); Roald Amundsen (1872–1928), Norwegian polar explorer (50c); Louis Pasteur (1822–1895), French chemist and bacteriologist (90c).

Gethsemane, by Giovanni Canavesio
A235

Frescoes by Canavesio, 15th century, Chapel of Our Lady of Fountains at La Brique: 50c, Christ Stripped of His Garments. 90c, Christ Carrying the Cross. 1.40fr, Resurrection. 2fr, Crucifixion.

1972, Dec. 4

855 A235 30c bright rose 25 15
856 " 50c indigo 45 35
857 " 90c slate green 60 55
858 " 1.40fr bright red 80 75
859 " 2fr purple 1.40 1.20
Nos. 855–859 (5) 3.50 3.00

Protection of historic monuments.

Princes of Monaco Type of 1967

Designs: 1fr, Jacques I, by Nicolas de Largillière. 3fr, Louise Hippolyte (1697–1731), by Jean Baptiste Vanloo.

1972, Dec. 4 *Perf. 12x13*

860 A182 1fr multicolored 80 60
861 " 3fr " 2.00 1.60

Girl, Syringe, Addicts
A236

1973, Jan. 5 Engraved *Perf. 13*

862 A236 50c brt. bl., claret & slate green 30 15
863 " 90c org., lilac & emerald 60 35

Fight against drug abuse.

Souvenir Sheet

Sts. Barbara, Dévote and Agatha, by Louis Brea—A237

1973, Apr. 30

864 A237 5fr dull red 14.00 14.00

Red Cross of Monaco, 25th anniversary. No. 864 contains one stamp; red decorative margin. Size: 100x149mm.

Flower Type of 1968

Design: 3.50fr, Flowers in Vase, by Ambrosius Bosschaert.

1973, Apr. 30 Photo. *Perf. 12x13*

865 A185 3.50fr multicolored 2.25 1.65

International Flower Show, Monte Carlo.

Europa Issue 1973
Common Design Type

1973, Apr. 30 Engraved *Perf. 13*

Size: 36x26mm.

866 CD16 50c orange 30 20
867 " 90c blue green 60 30

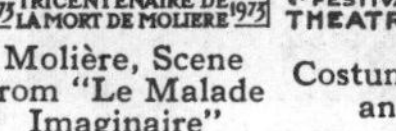

Molière, Scene from "Le Malade Imaginaire"
A238

Costumed Players and Mask
A239

1973, Apr. 30

868 A238 20c red, violet blue & brown 30 20

Tricentenary of the death of Molière (1622–1673), French actor and writer.

1973, Apr. 30

869 A239 60c red, lilac & bl. 45 25

5th International Amateur Theater Festival.

Virgin Mary, St. Teresa, Lisieux Basilica—A240

1973, Apr. 30

870 A240 1.40fr indigo, ultra. & brown 1.00 75

Centenary of the birth of St. Teresa of Lisieux (Thérèse Martin, 1873–1897), Carmelite nun.

Charles Peguy and Cathedral of Chartres—A241

1973, Apr. 30

871 A241 50c dp. claret, olive brn. & slate 40 25

Centenary of the birth of Charles Pierre Peguy (1873–1914), French writer.

Colette, Books and Cat
A242

Designs: No. 873, Eugene Ducretet and transmission from Eiffel Tower to Pantheon. 45c, Jean Henri Fabre and insects. 50c, Blaise Pascal (vert.). 60c, Radar installation and telegraph wire insulators. No. 877, William Webb Ellis and rugby. No. 878, Sir George Cayley and early model plane.

1973, Apr. 30

872 A242 30c dp. org., blk. & dark blue 35 20
873 " 30c brown. & multi. 30 20
874 " 45c dp. bl. & multi. 30 20
875 " 50c vio. bl., lilac & dark purple 30 20
876 " 60c brn., bl. black & bright blue 40 25
877 " 90c brn. & car. rose 65 45
878 " 90c red & multi. 60 50
Nos. 872–878 (7) 2.90 2.00

Various anniversaries: Centenary of the birth of Colette (1873–1954), French writer (No. 872); 75th anniversary of first Hertzian wave transmission (No. 873); sesquicentennial of birth of Fabre (1823–1915), entomologist (45c); 350th birth anniversary of Pascal (1623–1662), scientist and philosopher (50c); 5th International Telecommunications Day (60c); Sesquicentennial of the invention of rugby (No. 877); Sesquicentennial of the birth of Cayley (1821–1895), aviation pioneer (No. 878).

Dog Type of 1971

Design: German shepherd.

1973, Apr. 30 Photo. *Perf. 13x12½*

879 A217 45c multicolored 35 20

International Dog Show.

The First Crèche, by Giotto—A243

Paintings of the Nativity by: 45c, School of Filippo Lippi. 50c, Giotto. 1fr, 15th century miniature (vert.). 2fr, Fra Angelico (vert.).

Engraved

1973, Nov. 12 *Perf. 13x12, 12x13*

880 A243 30c purple 30 25
881 " 45c rose magenta 35 30
882 " 50c brown orange 40 35
883 " 1fr slate green 75 70
884 " 2fr olive green 1.50 1.40
Nos. 880–884, C78 (6) 5.55 4.50

750th anniversary of the first crèche assembled by St. Francis of Assisi.

Picnic and View of Monte Carlo
A244

Designs: 20c, Dance around maypole (vert.). 30c, "U Brandi" folk dance. 45c, Dance around St. John's fire. 50c, Blessing of the Christmas bread. 60c, Blessing of the sea. 1fr, Good Friday procession.

1973, Nov. 12 ***Perf. 13***

885 A244 10c slate green, dark blue & sepia 15 15
886 " 20c bl., olive & lilac 20 20
887 " 30c lt. green, blue & brown 25 25
888 " 45c dk. brn., violet & red brown 40 40
889 " 50c black, brown & vermilion 40 40
890 " 60c blue, magenta & violet blue 50 50
891 " 1fr indigo, violet & olive bister 80 80
Nos. 885-891 (7) 2.70 2.70

Monegasque customs.

Princes of Monaco Type of 1967.

Paintings of Charlotte Grimaldi, by Pierre Gobert, 1733: No. 892, in court dress, No. 893, in nun's habit.

1973, Nov. 12 ***Perf. 12x13***

892 A182 2fr multicolored 1.75 1.50
893 " 2fr " 1.75 1.50

Flower Type of 1972

Designs: Floral arrangements.

1973, Nov. 12 Photo. ***Perf. 13***

894 A232 45c vio. bl. & multi. 30 20
895 " 60c dk. brn. & multi. 50 40
896 " 1fr brn. org. & multi. 70 55

International Flower Show, Monte Carlo, May 1974.

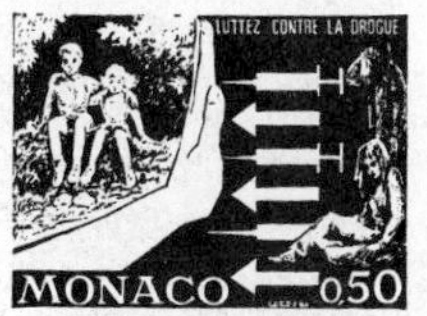

Children, Syringes, Drug Addicts—A245

1973, Nov. 12 Engraved

897 A245 50c bl., grn. & brn. 35 30
898 " 90c red, brown & indigo 60 50

Fight against drug abuse.

Souvenir Sheet

1949  1974

RAINIER III
PRINCE DE MONACO

Prince Rainier III—A246

1974, May 8 Engraved ***Imperf.***

899 A246 10fr black 11.00 11.00

25th anniversary of the accession of Prince Rainier III. No. 899 has red inscription and Monegasque coat of arms in margin. Size: 99x129mm.

Art from Around the World
A247

King of Rome (Napoleon's Son), by Bosio
A248

Designs (UPU Emblem and): 70c, Hands holding letters. 1.10fr, Famous buildings, Statue of Liberty and Sphinx.

1974, May 8 ***Perf. 13***

900 A247 50c chocolate & org. brown 30 25
901 " 70c aquamarine & multicolored 50 40
902 " 1.10fr indigo & multi. 90 70

Centenary of the Universal Postal Union.

Europa Issue, 1974

Design: 1.10fr, Madame Elisabeth (sister of Louis XVI), by Francois Josef Bosio.

1974, May 8

903 A248 45c slate green & sepia 60 50
904 " 1.10fr brown & olive brown 1.00 80
a. Souvenir sheet of 10 16.50 16.50

No. 904a contains 5 each of Nos. 903-904 with gutter inscribed in brown. Size: 168x129mm.

Red Cross Type of 1969

Design: St. Bernard of Menthon rescuing mountain traveler.

1974, May 8

905 A194 3fr Prussian blue & violet brown 2.00 1.65

For the Red Cross.

Henri Farman and Farman Planes
A249

Designs: 40c, Guglielmo Marconi, circuit diagram and ships which conducted first tests. 45c, Ernest Duchesne and penicillin. 50c, Fernand Forest and 4-cylinder motor.

1974, May 8

906 A249 30c multicolored 25 15
907 " 40c " 30 20
908 " 45c " 35 20
909 " 50c " 30 20

Centenary of the birth of Henri Farman (1874-1934), French aviation pioneer (30c); centenary of the birth of Guglielmo Marconi (1874-1937), Italian inventor (40c); centenary of the birth of Ernest Duchesne (1874-1912), French biologist (45c); 60th anniversary of the death of Fernand Forest (1851-1914), inventor (50c).

Dog Type of 1971

Design: Schnauzer.

1974, May 8 Photo. ***Perf. 13x12½***

910 A217 60c multicolored 40 25

International Dog Show, Monte Carlo, Apr. 6-7.

Ronsard and Scenes from his Sonnet à Hélène—A250

1974, May 8 Engraved ***Perf. 13***

911 A250 70c chocolate & dark carmine 50 30

450th anniversary of the birth of Pierre de Ronsard (1524-1585), French poet.

Winston Churchill
A251

1974, May 8

912 A251 1fr gray & brown 75 45

Centenary of the birth of Sir Winston Churchill (1874-1965), statesman.

Palaces of Monaco and Vienna—A252

1974, May 8

913 A252 2fr multicolored 1.20 80

60th anniversary of the first International Police Congress, Monaco, Apr. 1914.

The Box, by Auguste Renoir
A253

Rising Sun, by Claude Monet
A254

Impressionist Paintings: No. 915, Dancing Class, by Edgar Degas. No. 917, Entrance to Voisins Village, by Camille Pissarro. No. 918, House of the Hanged Man, by Paul Cezanne. No. 919, The Flooding of Port Marly, by Alfred Sisley.

Engraved

1974, Nov. 12 ***Perf. 12x13, 13x12***

914 A253 1fr multicolored 65 40
915 " 1fr " 65 40
916 A254 2fr " 1.35 75
917 " 2fr " 1.35 75
918 " 2fr " 1.35 75
919 " 2fr " 1.35 75
Nos. 914-919 (6) 6.70 3.80

Trainer and Tigers
A255

Prancing Horses
A256

Perf. 13x12½, 12½x13

1974, Nov. 12

Multicolored

920 A255 2c *shown* 5 5
921 A256 3c *shown* 10 8
922 A255 5c *Elephants* 10 8
923 A256 45c *Equestrian act* 30 18
924 A255 70c *Clowns* 60 45
925 A256 1.10fr *Jugglers* 85 65
926 " 5fr *Trapeze act* 3.00 2.00
Nos. 920-926 (7) 5.00 3.49

International Circus Festival.

Honoré II Coin
257

1974, Nov. 12 ***Perf. 13***

927 A257 60c rose red & black 40 30

350th anniversary of coins of Monaco.

Underwater Fauna and Flora—A258

Designs: 45c, Fish, and marine life. 1.10fr, Coral.

1974, Nov. 12 Photo. ***Perf. 13x12½***

Size: 35x25mm.

928 A258 45c multicolored 30 20

Size: 48x27mm. ***Perf. 13***

929 A258 70c multicolored 45 25
930 " 1.10fr " 65 40

Congress of the International Commission for the Scientific Exploration of the Mediterranean, Monaco, Dec. 6-14.

Floral Arrangements
A259 A260

1974, Nov. 12 ***Perf. 13x12½***

931	A259	70c multicolored	50	30
932	A260	1.10fr "	75	40

International Flower Show, Monte Carlo, May 1975. See Nos. 1003–1004, 1084–1085.

Prince Rainier III
A261

1974–79 **Engraved** ***Perf. 13***

933	A261	60c slate green	30	15
934	"	80c red	40	20
935	"	80c brt. green	35	8
936	"	1fr brown	50	25
937	"	1fr scarlet	45	8
938	"	1fr slate green	50	25
939	"	1.20fr violet blue	60	30
940	"	1.20fr red	60	30
941	"	1.25fr blue	55	12
942	"	1.50fr black	75	38
943	"	1.70fr deep blue	85	42
944	"	2fr dark purple	90	60
945	"	2.10fr olive bister	1.05	50
946	"	2.50fr indigo	1.10	40
947	"	9fr brt. violet	4.50	2.25
		Nos. 933–947 (15)	13.40	6.28

Issue dates: Nos. 933, 934, 936, 939, 944, Dec. 23, 1974. Nos. 935, 937, 941, 946, Jan. 10, 1977. Nos. 938, 940, 942, 943, 945, 947, Aug. 18, 1978.

Monte Carlo Beach
A262

Clock Tower—A263

Prince Albert I Statue and Museum—A264

1974–77

Multicolored

948	A262	25c *shown*	20	15
949	A263	50c *shown*	25	15
950	A262	1.10fr *shown* ('77)	50	20
951	A264	1.40fr *shown*	70	40
952	A262	1.70fr *All Saints' Tower*	85	60
953	A263	3fr *Fort Antoine*	1.50	90
954	A262	5.50fr *La Condamine (view)*	2.50	1.75
		Nos. 948–954 (7)	6.50	4.15

See Nos. 1005–1008, 1030–1033, 1069–1072, 1148–1152.

Haageocereus
A265

1974, Dec. 23 **Photo.** ***Perf. 12½x13***

Multicolored

955	A265	10c *shown*	5	3
956	"	20c *Matucana*	10	4
957	"	30c *Parodia*	15	6
958	"	85c *Mediolobivia*	42	15
959	"	1.90fr *Matucana*	90	40
960	"	4fr *Echinocereus*	1.85	90
		Nos. 955–960 (6)	3.47	1.58

Plants from Monaco Botanical Gardens.

Europa Issue 1975

Sailor, by Philibert Florence
A266

St. Dévote, by Ludovic Brea
A267

1975, May 13 **Engraved** ***Perf. 13***

961	A266	80c brt. red lilac	50	30
962	A267	1.20fr bright blue	75	40
	a.	Souvenir sheet of 10	7.00	7.00

No. 962a contains 5 each of Nos. 961–962 with gutter inscribed in bister. Size: 168x130mm.

Red Cross Type of 1969

Design: St. Bernardino of Siena (1380–1444) burying the dead.

1975, May 13

963	A194	4fr pur. & Prus. bl.	2.50	1.75

For the Red Cross.

Carmen, at the Tavern—A268

Scenes from Carmen: 30c, Prologue (vert.). 80c, The smugglers' hide-out. 1.40fr, Entrance to bull ring.

1975, May 13

964	A268	30c multicolored	20	12
965	"	60c "	35	18
966	"	80c "	50	25
967	"	1.40fr "	90	50

Centenary of first performance of opera Carmen by George Bizet (1838–1875).

Louis de Saint-Simon
A269

Albert Schweitzer
A270

1975, May 13

968	A269	40c bluish black	30	20
969	A270	60c blk. & dull red	35	25

300th birth anniversary of Louis de Saint-Simon (1675–1755), statesman and writer, and birth centenary of Albert Schweitzer (1875–1965), medical missionary.

ARPHILA 75 Emblem
G Clef—A271

1975, May 13

970	A271	80c sepia & org. brn.	60	40

ARPHILA 75 International Philatelic Exhibition, Paris, June 6–16.

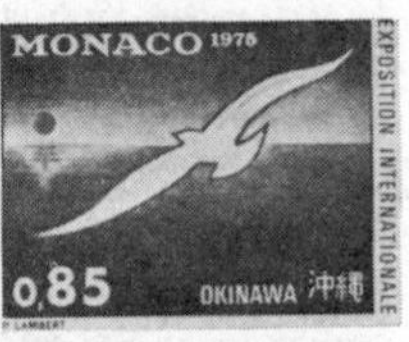

Seagull and Rising Sun
A272

1975, May 13 **Photogravure**

971	A272	85c multicolored	60	45

Oceanexpo 75, International Exhibition, Okinawa, July 20, 1975–Jan. 1976.

Charity Label and "1f" Destroying Cancer
A273

1975, May 13 **Engraved**

972	A273	1fr multicolored	60	30

Fight against cancer.

Jesus with Crown of Thorns, Holy Year Emblem
A274

1975, May 13

973	A274	1.15fr lilac, bis. & indigo	70	40

Holy Year 1975.

Villa Sauber, by Charles Garnier
A275

1975, May 13

974	A275	1.20fr multicolored	75	50

European Architectural Heritage Year 1975.

Woman, Globe, IWY Emblem
A276

1975, May 13

975	A276	1.20fr multicolored	75	50

International Women's Year.

Nos. 793–796 Surcharged

1975, Apr. 1 **Engr.** ***Perf. 13***

976	A153	42c on 26c multi.	30	15
977	"	48c on 30c "	35	20
978	"	70c on 45c "	45	40
979	"	1.35fr on 90c "	80	60

Nos. 976–979 were issued precanceled only. See note after No. 324.

Rolls Royce "Silver Ghost" 1907
A277

1975, Nov. **Engr.** ***Perf. 13***

Multicolored

980	A277	5c *shown*	5	3
981	"	10c *Hispano Suiza, 1926*	8	6
982	"	20c *Isotta Fraschini, 1928*	12	8
983	"	30c *Cord L. 29*	25	10
984	"	50c *Voisin, 1930*	30	12
985	"	60c *Duesenberg, 1933*	35	15
986	"	80c *Bugatti, 1938*	45	25
987	"	85c *Delahaye, 1940*	50	30
988	"	1.20fr *Cisitalia, 1946*	60	45
989	"	1.40fr *Mercedes Benz, 1955*	80	45
990	"	5.50fr *Lamborghini, 1974*	2.50	1.50
		Nos. 980–990 (11)	6.00	3.49

Development of the automobile.

Princes of Monaco Type of 1967.

Paintings (Unknown Artists): 2fr, Prince Honoré III (1733–1795). 4fr, Princess Catherine de Brignole (1759–1813).

1975, Nov.

991	A182	2fr multicolored	1.20	75
992	"	4fr "	2.40	1.20

Caged Dog
A278

Designs: 80c, Cat chased up a tree (vert.). 1.20fr, Horses pulling heavy load.

1975, Nov.

993	A278	60c blk. & brown	35	20
994	"	80c blk., gray & brown	45	25
995	"	1.20fr magenta & slate green	70	40

125th anniversary of the Grammont (J. P. Delmas Grammont) Law against cruelty to animals.

Dog Type of 1970

Design: Poodle.

1975, Nov.

996	A204	60c lilac rose & black	35	20

International Dog Show, Monte Carlo.

Maurice Ravel A279 — Clown A280

Design: 1.20fr, Johann Strauss and dancers.

1975, Nov.

No.	Type	Description	Unused	Used
997	A279	60c maroon & sepia	35	20
998	"	1.20fr maroon & indigo	70	30

Maurice Ravel (1875–1937), birth centenary, and Johann Strauss (1804–1849), sesquicentennial of birth, composers.

1975, Nov. Photo. *Perf. 12½x13*

No.	Type	Description	Unused	Used
999	A280	80c multicolored	50	25

2nd International Circus Festival, Monte Carlo, Dec. 1975.

Honoré II Florin, 1640—A281

1975, Nov. Engr. *Perf. 13*

No.	Type	Description	Unused	Used
1000	A281	80c slate & gray	50	25

See Nos. 1040, 1088.

Ampère and Ampère Balance A282

1975, Nov.

No.	Type	Description	Unused	Used
1001	A282	85c ultra. & indigo	50	25

André Marie Ampère (1775–1836), physicist, birth bicentennial.

Lamentation for the Dead Christ, by Michelangelo A283

1975, Nov.

No.	Type	Description	Unused	Used
1002	A283	1.40fr blk. & olive gray	80	55

Michelangelo Buonarroti (1475–1564), Italian sculptor, painter and architect, 500th anniversary of birth.

Flower Types of 1974

Designs: Floral arrangements.

1975, Nov. Photo. *Perf. 13x12½*

No.	Type	Description	Unused	Used
1003	A259	60c multicolored	30	15
1004	A260	80c "	50	25

International Flower Show, Monte Carlo, May 1976.

Clock Tower Type, 1974

1976, Jan. 26 Engr. *Perf. 13*

No.	Type	Description	Unused	Used
1005	A263	50c brown lake	25	10
1006	"	60c olive green	30	15
1007	"	90c purple	45	22
1008	"	1.60fr bright blue	80	30

Nos. 1005–1008 were issued precanceled only. See note after No. 324.

Prince Pierre A284

André Maurois and Colette—A285

Portraits: 25c, Jean and Jerome Tharaud. 30c, Emile Henriot, Marcel Pagnol, Georges Duhamel. 50c, Philippe Heriat, Jules Supervielle, L. Pierard. 60c, Roland Dorgeles, M. Achard, G. Bauer. 80c, Franz Hellens, A. Billy, Msgr. Grente. 1.20fr, Jean Giono, L. Pasteur-Vallery-Radot, M. Garcon.

1976, May 3 Engr. *Perf. 13*

No.	Type	Description	Unused	Used
1009	A284	10c black	5	5
1010	A285	20c red & slate	10	8
1011	"	25c red, dk. blue & black	15	13
1012	"	30c brown	15	15
1013	"	50c brown, red & violet blue	25	20
1014	"	60c green, brown & lt. brown	30	25
1015	"	80c black & magenta	40	25
1016	"	1.20fr black, violet & claret	60	40
		Nos. 1009–1016 (8)	2.00	1.51

Literary Council of Monaco, 25th anniversary.

Dachshunds—A286

1976, May 3 Photogravure

No.	Type	Description	Unused	Used
1017	A286	60c multicolored	35	25

International Dog Show, Monte Carlo.

Bridge Table, Coast A287

1976, May 3 Engraved

No.	Type	Description	Unused	Used
1018	A287	60c multicolored	35	25

Fifth Bridge Olympiade, Monte Carlo.

A. G. Bell, Telephone, 1876, Radar A288

1976, May 3

No.	Type	Description	Unused	Used
1019	A288	80c multicolored	40	25

Centenary of first telephone call by Alexander Graham Bell, Mar. 10, 1876.

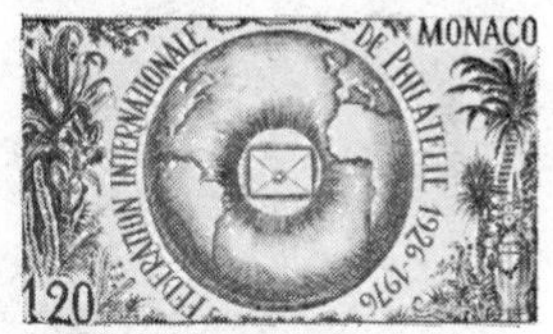

Federation Emblem—A289

1976, May 3

No.	Type	Description	Unused	Used
1020	A289	1.20fr multicolored	60	30

International Federation of Philately (F.I.P.), 50th anniversary.

U.S. Liberty Bell Type of 1926 A290

1976, May 3

No.	Type	Description	Unused	Used
1021	A290	1.70fr car. & black	85	45

American Bicentennial.

Fritillaria, by Vincent van Gogh A291

1976, May 3 Photo. *Perf. 12x13*

No.	Type	Description	Unused	Used
1022	A291	3fr multicolored	1.60	1.20

International Flower Show, Monte Carlo, May 1976.

Europa Issue 1976

Plate with Lemon Branch A292

Design: 1.20fr, The Peddler, 19th century figurine, and CEPT emblem.

1976, May 3 *Perf. 12½x13*

No.	Type	Description	Unused	Used
1023	A292	80c sal. & multi.	40	20
1024	"	1.20fr ultramarine & multi.	60	40
		a. Souvenir sheet of 10	6.00	6.00

No. 1024a contains 5 each of Nos. 1023–1024 with gutter inscribed in salmon. Size: 170x140mm.

Diving A293

Designs (Olympic Rings and): 80c, Athlete on parallel bars. 85c, Hammer throw. 1.20fr, Rowing (horiz.). 1.70fr, Boxing (horiz.).

1976, May 3 Engr. *Perf. 13*

No.	Type	Description	Unused	Used
1025	A293	60c multicolored	35	20
1026	"	80c "	40	25
1027	"	85c "	45	30
1028	"	1.20fr "	60	35
1029	"	1.70fr "	85	50
		a. Souvenir sheet of 5	2.80	2.80
		Nos. 1025–1029 (5)	2.65	1.60

21st Olympic Games, Montreal, Canada, July 17–Aug. 1. No. 1029a contains one each of Nos. 1025–1029; marginal inscription in red brown; dark blue Olympic rings. Size: 150x143mm.

Clock Tower Type, 1974

1976, Sept. 1 Engraved *Perf. 13*

No.	Type	Description	Unused	Used
1030	A263	52c bister	26	15
1031	"	62c red lilac	31	20
1032	"	95c scarlet	48	30
1033	"	1.70fr blue green	85	55

Nos. 1030–1033 were issued precanceled only. See note after No. 324.

Princes of Monaco Type of 1967

Paintings: 2fr, Honoré IV (1815–1819), by Francois Lemoyne. 4fr, Louise d'Aumont-Mazarin (1750–1826), by Marie Verroust.

1976, Nov. 9 *Perf. 12½x13*

No.	Type	Description	Unused	Used
1035	A182	2fr violet brown	1.00	70
1036	"	4fr multicolored	2.00	1.60

Red Cross Type of 1969

Design: St. Louise de Marillac and children.

1976, Nov. 9 *Perf. 13*

No.	Type	Description	Unused	Used
1037	A194	4fr green, gray & plum	2.00	1.50

St. Vincent de Paul, View of Monaco A294

1976, Nov. 9

No.	Type	Description	Unused	Used
1038	A294	60c multicolored	30	20

St. Vincent de Paul Conference, Monaco, July 31, 1876, centenary.

Marquise de Sevigné A295

1976, Nov. 9

No.	Type	Description	Unused	Used
1039	A295	80c multicolored	40	20

Marie de Rabutin-Chantal, Marquise de Sevigné (1626–1696), writer.

Coin Type of 1975

Design: 80c, Honoré II 2-gros coin.

1976, Nov. 9

No.	Type	Description	Unused	Used
1040	A281	80c grn. & steel bl.	40	25

Richard E. Byrd, Roald Amundsen, North Pole—A296

1976, Nov. 9

No.	Type	Description	Unused	Used
1041	A296	85c ol., blk. & bl.	45	25

First flights over the North Pole, 50th anniversary.

Gulliver Holding King, Queen and Enemy Fleet
A297

1976, Nov. 9

No.	Type	Description	Unused	Used
1042	A297	1.20fr indigo, blue & brown	60	35

250th anniversary of the publication of Gulliver's Travels, by Jonathan Swift.

Child and Christmas Decorations
A298

1976, Nov. 9 *Perf. 13x12½*

No.	Type	Description	Unused	Used
1043	A298	60c multicolored	30	20
1044	"	1.20fr "	60	30

Christmas 1976.

"Trapped by Drugs"
A299

1976, Nov. 9

No.	Type	Description	Unused	Used
1045	A299	80c green, ultra. & orange	40	25
1046	"	1.20fr red brn., vio. & carmine	60	35

Fight against drug abuse.

Floral Arrangement
A300

Clown and Circus Acts
A301

Design: 1fr, Floral arrangement. Designs by Princess Grace.

1976, Nov. 9 Photo. *Perf. 13½x13*

No.	Type	Description	Unused	Used
1047	A300	80c yellow green & multi.	40	20
1048	"	1fr lt. bl. & multi.	50	30

International Flower Show, Monte Carlo, May 1977. See Nos. 1124–1125.

1976, Nov. 9

No.	Type	Description	Unused	Used
1049	A301	1fr multicolored	50	30

3rd International Circus Festival, Dec. 26–30.

L'Hirondelle I—A302

Prince Albert I
A303

Designs (Gouaches by Louis Tinayre): 30c, Crew of L'Hirondelle. 80c, L'Hirondelle in Storm. 1fr, The Helmsman (vert.). 1.25fr, L'Hirondelle in Storm. 1.40fr, Shrimp Fishermen in Boat. 1.90fr, Hauling in the Net (vert.). 2.50fr, Catching Opah Fish.

1977, May 3 Engr. *Perf. 13*

No.	Type	Description	Unused	Used
1050	A302	10c multicolored	5	5
1051	A303	20c "	12	8
1052	A302	30c "	22	15
1053	"	80c "	40	27
1054	"	1fr "	55	30
1055	"	1.25fr "	65	45
1056	"	1.40fr "	75	50
1057	"	1.90fr "	95	60
1058	"	2.50fr "	1.40	1.10
		Nos. 1050-1058 (9)	5.09	3.50

75th anniversary of publication of "The Career of a Sailor," by Prince Albert I. See Nos. 1073–1081.

Pyreneean Mountain Dogs—A304

1977, May 3 Photogravure

No.	Type	Description	Unused	Used
1059	A304	80c multicolored	40	25

International Dog Show, Monte Carlo.

Motherhood, by Mary Cassatt
A305

1977, May 3 Engraved

No.	Type	Description	Unused	Used
1060	A305	80c multicolored	40	25

World Association of the Friends of Children.

Archers, Target and Monte Carlo—A306

1977, May 3

No.	Type	Description	Unused	Used
1061	A306	1.10fr multicolored	55	30

10th International Rainier III Archery Championships.

Spirit of St. Louis and Lindbergh—A307

1977, May 3

No.	Type	Description	Unused	Used
1062	A307	1.90fr multi.	1.00	60

50th anniversary of first transatlantic flight by Charles Lindbergh.

The Dock at Deauville, by Dufy—A308

1977, May 3 Photogravure

No.	Type	Description	Unused	Used
1063	A308	2fr multicolored	1.00	60

Raoul Dufy (1877–1953), painter, birth centenary.

Young Girl, by Rubens
A309

Helmet Tower, Monaco
A310

Rubens Paintings: 1fr, Duke of Buckingham. 1.40fr, Rubens' son Nicolas, 2 years old.

1977, May 3 Engraved

No.	Type	Description	Unused	Used
1064	A309	80c multicolored	40	25
1065	"	1fr "	50	30
1066	"	1.40fr "	70	40

Peter Paul Rubens (1577–1640), 400th birth anniversary.

Europa Issue 1977

1977, May 3

Design: 1.40fr, St. Michael's Church, Menton.

No.	Type	Description	Unused	Used
1067	A310	1fr multicolored	50	20
1068	"	1.40fr "	70	35
		a. Souvenir sheet of 10	6.25	6.25

No. 1068a contains 5 each of Nos. 1067–1068 with gutter inscribed in brown. Size: 168x129mm.

Unused prices are for stamps that have been hinged.

Clock Tower Type of 1974

1977, Apr. 1 Engr. *Perf. 13*

No.	Type	Description	Unused	Used
1069	A263	54c brt. green	30	25
1070	"	68c orange	40	35
1071	"	1.05fr olive	60	50
1072	"	1.85fr brown	1.20	90

Nos. 1069–1072 were issued precanceled only. See note after No. 324.

Career of a Sailor Types of 1977

Designs (Gouaches by Louis Tinayre): 10c, Yacht Princess Alice II, Kiel harbor. 20c, Laboratory on board ship. 30c, Yacht amidst ice floes. 80c, Crew in arctic outfits. 1fr, Yacht in polar region. 1.25fr, Yacht in snow storm. 1.40fr, Building camp on ice. 1.90fr, Yacht under steam amidst ice floes. 3fr, Yacht passing iceberg.

1977, Nov. Engr. *Perf. 13*

No.	Type	Description	Unused	Used
1073	A302	10c blk. & brt. blue	5	3
1074	"	20c Prus. blue	10	6
1075	"	30c blk. & brt. blue	15	10
1076	A303	80c multicolored	40	20
1077	A302	1fr brt. grn. & black	50	25
1078	"	1.25fr vio., sepia & black	62	35
1079	"	1.40fr olive, blue & purple	70	40
1080	"	1.90fr blk. & brt. blue	95	50
1081	"	3fr dark green, olive & brt. blue	1.50	80
		Nos. 1073-1081 (9)	4.97	2.69

75th anniversary of publication of "The Career of a Sailor," by Prince Albert I.

Santa Claus
A311

1977, Nov.

No.	Type	Description	Unused	Used
1082	A311	80c multicolored	40	20
1083	"	1.40fr "	70	30

Christmas 1977.

Flowers Types of 1974

Designs: 80c, Snapdragons and bellflowers. 1fr, Ikebana arrangement.

1977, Nov. Photo. *Perf. 13½x13*

No.	Type	Description	Unused	Used
1084	A259	80c multicolored	40	20
1085	A260	1fr "	50	25

International Flower Show, Monte Carlo, May 1978.

Face (Van Gogh), Syringe, Hallucination Pattern
A312

Clown, Flags of Participants
A313

1977, Nov. Engr. *Perf. 13*

No.	Type	Description	Unused	Used
1086	A312	1fr multicolored	50	25

Fight against drug abuse.

1977, Nov. Photo. *Perf. 13½x13*

No.	Type	Description	Unused	Used
1087	A313	1fr multicolored	50	25

Fourth International Circus Festival. Monte Carlo, December 1977.

Coin Type of 1975

Design: 80c, Doubloon of Honoré II, 1648.

1977, Nov. Engr. *Perf. 13*

1088 A281 80c lilac & brown 40 20

Mediterranean Landscape and Industrial Pollution—A314

1977, Nov.

1089 A314 1fr multicolored 50 25

Protection of the Mediterranean. Meeting of the U.N. Mediterranean Environmental Protection Group, Monte Carlo, Nov. 28–Dec. 6.

Men Spreading Tar, Dr. Guglielminetti, 1903 Car—A315

1977, Nov.

1090 A315 1.10fr multicolored 55 28

75th anniversary of first tarred roads, invented by Swiss Dr. Guglielminetti.

View of Monaco and Tennis Emblem—A316

First Match at Wimbledon and Stadium—A317

1977, Nov.

1091 A316 1fr multicolored 50 25
1092 A317 1.40fr " 70 30

50th anniversary of the Lawn Tennis Federation of Monaco and centenary of first international tennis match at Wimbledon.

Prince of Monaco Type of 1967

Painting: 6fr, Honoré V (1819–1841), by Marie Verroust.

1977, Nov. *Perf. 12½x13*

1093 A182 6fr multicolored 3.00 1.50

Red Cross Type of 1969

Design: 4fr, St. John Bosco and boys.

1977, Nov. *Perf. 13*

1094 A194 4fr multicolored 2.00 1.00

Nos. 1069–1072 Surcharged

1978, Jan. 17

1095 A263 58c on 54c brt. green 25 10
1096 " 73c on 68c org. 32 15
1097 A263 1.15fr on 1.05fr olive 55 30
1098 " 2fr on 1.85fr brown 95 45

See note after No. 324.

The Abandoned Ship, from "Mysterious Island"
A318

Illustrations, Novels by Jules Verne: 5c, Shipwreck. 30c, Secret of the Island. 80c, Robur, the Conqueror. 1fr, Master Zacharius. 1.40fr, The Castle in the Carpathians. 1.70fr, The Children of Capt. Grant. 5.50fr, Jules Verne and allegories.

1978, May 2 Engraved *Perf. 13*

1099	A318	5c multicolored		5	5
1100	"	25c	"	12	5
1101	"	30c	"	15	8
1102	"	80c	"	40	20
1103	"	1fr	"	50	25
1104	"	1.40fr	"	70	35
1105	"	1.70fr	"	85	40
1106	"	5.50fr	"	2.75	1.10
	Nos. 1099–1106 (8)			5.52	2.48

Jules Verne (1828–1905), science fiction writer, birth sesquicentennial.

Congress Center and Monte Carlo
A319

Design: 1.40fr, Congress Center, view from the sea.

1978, May 2

1107 A319 1fr multicolored 50 25
1108 " 1.40fr " 70 35

Inauguration of Monaco Congress Center.

Soccer Players and Globe—A320

1978, May 2

1109 A320 1fr multicolored 50 25

11th World Soccer Cup Championship, Argentina, June 1–25.

Vivaldi and St. Mark's Place, Venice
A321

Control Ship and Grimaldi Palace
A322

1978, May 2

1110 A321 1fr dk. brn. & red 50 25

Antonio Vivaldi (1675?–1741), Italian violinist and composer.

1978, May 2

Design: 1fr, Map of coastal area and city emblems (horiz.).

Size: 26x36mm.

1111 A322 80c multicolored 40 15

Size: 48x27mm.

1112 A322 1fr multicolored 50 25

Protection of the environment, signing of "Ra Mo Ge" agreement for the protection of the Mediterranean Coast between Saint-Raphael, France, and Genoa, Italy (including Monaco).

Europa Issue 1978

Monaco Cathedral
A323

Design: 1.40fr, View of Principality from East.

1978, May 2

1113 A323 1fr multicolored 50 25
1114 " 1.40fr " 70 35
a. Souv. sheet of 10 7.00 7.00

No. 1114a contains 5 each of Nos. 1113–1114 with gutter inscribed in black. Size: 171x144mm.

Cinderella—A324

Mother Goose Tales: 25c, Puss in Boots. 30c, Sleeping Beauty. 80c, Fairy tale princess. 1fr, Little Red Riding Hood. 1.40fr, Bluebeard. 1.70fr, Tom Thumb. 1.90fr, Riquet with the Tuft of Hair. 2.50fr, The Fairies.

1978, Nov. 8 Engraved *Perf. 13*

1115	A324	5c multicolored		3	3
1116	"	25c	"	12	6
1117	"	30c	"	15	8
1118	"	80c	"	40	15
1119	"	1fr	"	50	25
1120	"	1.40fr	"	70	35
1121	"	1.70fr	"	85	42
1122	"	1.90fr	"	95	48
1123	"	2.50fr	"	1.25	65
	Nos. 1115–1123 (9)			4.95	2.47

Charles Perrault (1628–1703), compiler of Mother Goose Tales.

Flower Type of 1976

Van Gogh Paintings: 1fr, Sunflowers. 1.70fr, Iris.

1978, Nov. 8 Photo. *Perf. 12½x13*

1124 A300 1fr multicolored 50 25
1125 " 1.70fr " 85 42

International Flower Show, Monte Carlo, May 1979, and 125th birth anniversary of Vincent van Gogh (1853–1890), Dutch painter.

Afghan Hound
A325

Design: 1.20fr, Russian wolfhound.

1978, Nov. 8 *Perf. 13x12½*

1126 A325 1fr multicolored 50 25
1127 " 1.20fr " 60 30

International Dog Show, Monte Carlo.

Child Holding Gift of Shoes
A326

1978, Nov. 8 Engr. *Perf. 12½x13*

1128 A326 1fr multicolored 50 25

Christmas 1978.

Catherine and William Booth, Salvation Army Band—A327

1978, Nov. 8 Engr. *Perf. 13*

1129 A327 1.70fr multicolored 85 42

Centenary of founding of Salvation Army.

Trained Seals
A328

Designs: 1fr, Lions (vert.). 1.40fr, Equestrian act. 1.90fr, Monkey music band. 2.40fr, Trapeze act.

1978, Nov. 8 *Perf. 13x12½*

1130	A328	80c multicolored		40	20
1131	"	1fr	"	50	25
1132	"	1.40fr	"	70	35
1133	"	1.90fr	"	95	48
1134	"	2.40fr	"	1.20	60
	Nos. 1130–1134 (5)			3.75	1.88

5th International Circus Festival, Monte Carlo.

Princes of Monaco Type of 1967

Paintings: 2fr, Florestan I (1841–1856), by G. Dauphin. 4fr, Caroline Gilbert de Lametz (1793–1879), by Marie Verroust.

1978, Nov. 8 Engr. *Perf. 12½x13*

1135 A182 2fr multicolored 1.00 50
1136 " 4fr " 2.00 1.00

Souvenir Sheet

Henri Dunant and Battle Scene—A329

1978, Nov. 8 Engr. *Perf. 13*

1137 A329 5fr multicolored 2.50 1.25

Henri Dunant (1828–1910), founder of Red Cross. Marginal inscription in dark brown with red crosses. Size: 100x130mm.

View Types of 1974

1978, Aug. 18

Multicolored

1148 A262 25c *All Saints' Tower* 12 6
1149 " 65c *Monte Carlo Beach* 32 16
1150 A263 1.30fr *Cathedral* 65 32

1151	A262	1.80fr *La Condamine*	90	45
1152	"	6.50fr *Monte Carlo Auditorium*	3.25	1.60
		Nos. 1148–1152 (5)	5.24	2.59

Convention Center, Monte Carlo
A330

1978–79

1157	A330	61c vermilion	30	12
1158	"	64c green	32	10
1159	"	78c dp. rose lilac	40	15
1160	"	83c violet blue	42	18
1161	"	1.25fr brown	62	22
1162	"	1.30fr purple	65	22
1163	"	2.10fr violet blue	1.05	60
1164	"	2.25fr brn. orange	1.10	62
		Nos. 1157–1164 (8)	4.86	2.21

Nos. 1157–1164 were issued precanceled only. See note after No. 324.

Issue dates: Nos. 1157, 1159, 1161 and 1163, July 10, 1978. Others, Jan. 15, 1979.

Souvenir Sheet

Prince Albert
A331

1979, Apr. 30 Engr. *Perf. 12½x13*

1166	A331	10fr multicolored	5.00	5.00

21st birthday of Hereditary Prince Albert. Prince Albert's initials and birthdate in rose carmine in margin. Size: 80x150mm.

The Juggler of Notre Dame, by Jules Massenet—A332

Designs: 1.20fr, Hans, the Flute Player, by Gaston L. Ganne. 1.50fr, Don Quichotte, by Massenet. 1.70fr, L'Aiglon, by Jacques Ibert and Arthur Honegger (vert.). 2.10fr, The Child and the Sorcerer, by Maurice Ravel. 3fr, Monte Carlo Opera and Charles Garnier, architect.

1979, Apr. 30 *Perf. 13*

1167	A332	1fr multicolored	50	25
1168	"	1.20fr "	60	30
1169	"	1.50fr "	75	38
1170	"	1.70fr "	85	42
1171	"	2.10fr "	1.05	50
1172	"	3fr "	1.50	75
		Nos. 1167–1172 (6)	5.25	2.60

Centenary of the Salle Garnier, Monte Carlo Opera.

Flower, Bird, Butterfly, IYC Emblem—A333

Children's Drawings (IYC Emblem and): 1fr, Horse and child. 1.20fr, Children shaking hands, and heart. 1.50fr, Children of the world for peace. 1.70fr, Children against pollution.

1979, Apr. 30

1173	A333	50c multicolored	25	12
1174	"	1fr "	50	25
1175	"	1.20fr "	60	30
1176	"	1.50fr "	75	38
1177	"	1.70fr "	85	42
		Nos. 1173–1177 (5)	2.95	1.47

International Year of the Child.

Europa Issue

Armed Messenger, 15th–16th Centuries—A334

Designs (similar to 1960 postage dues); 1.50fr, Felucca, 18th century. 1.70fr, Arrival of first train, Dec. 12, 1868.

1979, Apr. 30

1178	A334	1.20fr multicolored	60	30
1179	"	1.50fr "	75	38
1180	"	1.70fr "	85	42
		a. Souvenir sheet of 6	4.50	4.50

No. 1180a contains 2 each of Nos. 1178–1180. Sepia marginal inscription. Size: 130x150mm.

SEMI-POSTAL STAMPS.

No. 16 Surcharged in Red **+5c**

Perf. 14x13½

1914, Oct. **Unwmkd.**

B1	A2	10c+5c carmine	3.50	2.50

View of Monaco
SP2

1919, Sept. 20 **Typographed**

B2	SP2	2c+3c lilac	10.00	10.00
B3	"	5c+5c green	8.00	8.00
B4	"	15c+10c rose	8.00	8.00
B5	"	25c+15c blue	19.00	19.00
B6	"	50c+50c brown, *buff*	80.00	80.00
B7	"	1fr+1fr *yellow*	275.00	275.00
B8	"	5fr+5fr dull red	850.00	850.00
		Nos. B2-B8 (7)	1250.00	1250.00

Semi-Postal Stamps of 1919 Surcharged

20 mars
1920
2c + 3c

1920, Mar. 20

B9	SP2	2c+3c on 15c+10c rose	24.00	24.00
		a. "c" of "3c" inverted	*1250.00*	*1250.00*
B10	"	2c+3c on 25c+15c bl.	24.00	24.00
		a. "c" of "3c" inverted	*1250.00*	*1250.00*
B11	"	2c+3c on 50c+50c brn., *buff*	24.00	24.00
		a. "c" of "3c" inverted	*1250.00*	*1250.00*
B12	"	5c+5c on 1fr+1fr *yellow*	24.00	24.00
B13	"	5c+5c on 5fr+5fr red	22.50	22.50

Overprinted

20 mars
1920

B14	SP2	15c+10c rose	15.00	15.00
B15	"	25c+15c blue	7.00	7.00
B16	"	50c+50c brn., *buff*	30.00	30.00
B17	"	1fr+1fr *yellow*	30.00	30.00
B18	"	5fr+5fr red	*4500.00*	*4500.00*
		Nos. B9-B17 (9)	200.50	200.50

Issued to commemorate the marriage of Princess Charlotte to Prince Pierre, Comte de Polignac.

Palace Gardens—SP3

"The Rock" of Monaco
SP4

Bay of Monaco—SP5

Prince Louis II
SP6

1937, Apr. **Engraved** ***Perf. 13***

B19	SP3	50c+50c green	2.00	2.00
B20	SP4	90c+90c carmine	2.00	2.00
B21	SP5	1.50fr+1.50fr blue	4.00	4.00
B22	SP6	2fr+2fr violet	5.00	5.00
B23	"	5fr+5fr brown red	57.50	57.50
		Nos. B19-B23 (5)	70.50	70.50

The surtax was used for welfare work.

Pierre and Marie Curie
SP7

Monaco Hospital, Date Palms
SP8

1938, Nov. 15 ***Perf. 13***

B24	SP7	65c+25c deep blue green	5.50	5.50
B25	SP8	1.75fr+50c deep ultramarine	6.00	6.00

B24 and B25 exist imperforate.
The surtax was for the International Union for the Control of Cancer.

Lucien
SP9

Honoré II
SP10

Louis I
SP11

Charlotte de Gramont
SP12

Antoine I
SP13

Marie de Lorraine
SP14

Jacques I
SP15

Louise-Hippolyte
SP16

Honoré III
SP17

"The Rock," 18th Century
SP18

1939, June 26

B26	SP9	5c+5c brn. blk	1.00	1.00
B27	SP10	10c+10c rose violet	1.00	1.00
B28	SP11	45c+15c bright green	2.00	2.00
B29	SP12	70c+30c bright red violet	4.50	4.50
B30	SP13	90c+35c violet	4.50	4.50
B31	SP14	1fr+1fr ultra.	13.50	13.50
B32	SP15	2fr+2fr brown orange	15.00	15.00
B33	SP16	2.25fr+1.25fr Prus. blue	22.50	22.50
B34	SP17	3fr+3fr deep rose	32.50	32.50
B35	SP18	5fr+5fr red	62.50	62.50
		Nos. B26-B35 (10)	159.00	159.00

Types of Regular Issue, 1939 Surcharged in Red

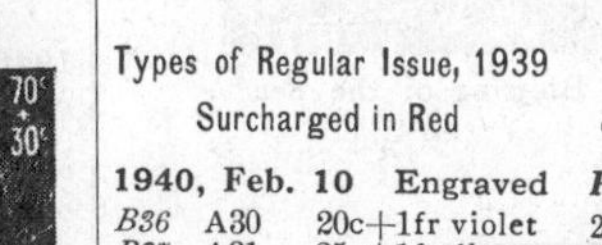

+
+1f

1940, Feb. 10 **Engraved** ***Perf. 13***

B36	A30	20c+1fr violet	2.50	2.50
B37	A31	25c+1fr dk. grn.	2.50	2.50
B38	A32	30c+1fr brn. red	2.50	2.50
B39	A31	40c+1fr dk. blue	2.50	2.50
B40	A33	45c+1fr rose carmine	2.50	2.50
B41	A34	50c+1fr brown	3.00	3.00
B42	A32	60c+1fr dk. grn.	3.00	3.00
B43	A35	75c+1fr brn. blk.	3.00	3.00
B44	A34	1fr+1fr scarlet	3.00	3.00
B45	A31	2fr+1fr indigo	3.50	3.50
B46	A33	2.50fr+1fr dk. grn.	7.00	7.00
B47	A35	3fr+1fr dk. blue	9.00	9.00
B48	A30	5fr+1fr brn. blk.	10.00	10.00
B49	A33	10fr+5fr lt. blue	12.00	12.00
B50	A32	20fr+5fr brn. vio.	14.00	14.00
		Nos. B36-B50 (15)	80.00	80.00

The surtax was used to purchase ambulances for the French government.

Symbol of Charity and View of Monaco
SP19

Symbol of Charity and View of Monaco
SP20

1941, May 15

B51	SP19	25c+25c bright red violet	1.40	1.40
B52	SP20	50c+25c dark brown	1.40	1.40
B53	"	75c+50c rose violet	1.75	1.75
B54	SP19	1fr+1fr dk. bl.	1.75	1.75
B55	SP20	1.50fr+1.50fr rose red	2.25	2.25
B56	SP19	2fr+2fr Pruss. green	2.25	2.25
B57	SP20	2.50fr+2fr bright ultra.	2.25	2.25
B58	SP19	3fr+3fr dull red brown	2.25	2.25
B59	SP20	5fr+5fr dark blue green	3.00	3.00
B60	SP19	10fr+8fr brown black	5.00	5.00
		Nos. B51-B60 (10)	23.30	23.30

The surtax was for various charities.

Rainier Grimaldi
SP21

Charles II
SP22

Jeanne Grimaldi
SP23

Charles-August Goyon de Matignon
SP24

Jacques I
SP25

Louise-Hippolyte
SP26

Charlotte Grimaldi
SP27

Marie-Charles Grimaldi
SP28

Honoré III
SP29

Honoré IV
SP30

Honoré V
SP31

Florestan I
SP32

Charles III
SP33

Albert I
SP34

Marie-Victoire—SP35

1942, Dec. 10

B61	SP21	2c+3c ultra.	20	20
B62	SP22	5c+5c orange vermilion	20	20
B63	SP23	10c+5c black	20	20
B64	SP24	20c+10c brt. grn.	20	20
B65	SP25	30c+30c brn. vio.	20	20
B66	SP26	40c+40c rose red	20	20
B67	SP27	50c+50c violet	20	20
B68	SP28	75c+75c bright red violet	20	20
B69	SP29	1fr+1fr dk. grn.	20	20
B70	SP30	1.50fr+1fr carmine brown	20	20
B71	SP31	2.50fr+2.50fr pur.	1.20	1.20
B72	SP32	3fr+3fr turquoise blue	1.40	1.40
B73	SP33	5fr+5fr sepia	1.40	1.40
B74	SP34	10fr+5fr rose lilac	1.40	1.40
B75	SP35	20fr+5fr ultra.	1.60	1.60
		Nos. B61-B75 (15)	9.00	9.00

Saint Dévote
SP36

Procession
SP37

Procession—SP38

Church of St. Dévote
SP39

Burning of Symbolic Boat
SP40

Blessing of the Sea
SP41

Church of St. Dévote
SP42

Trial of St. Barbara
SP43

Arrival of St. Dévote at Monaco
SP44

1944, Jan. 27 *Perf. 13* Unwmkd.

B76	SP36	50c+50c sepia	25	25
B77	SP37	70c+80c dp. ultra.	25	25
B78	SP38	80c+70c green	20	20
B79	SP39	1fr+1fr rose vio.	20	20
B80	SP40	1.50fr+1.50fr red	40	40
B81	SP41	2fr+2fr brn. vio.	40	40
B82	SP42	5fr+2fr violet	40	40
B83	SP43	10fr+40fr royal blue	40	40
B84	SP44	20fr+60fr chalky blue	4.00	4.00
		Nos. B76-B84 (9)	6.50	6.50

Issued in honor of St. Dévote.

Type SP43 is inscribed "Jugement de Sainte Dévote," but actually shows the trial of St. Barbara in 235 A.D.

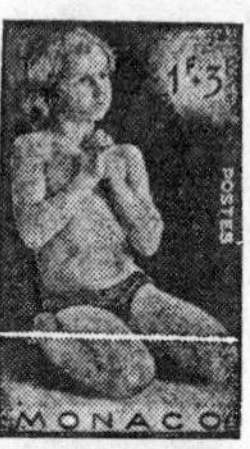

Needy Child
SP45

Nurse and Child
SP46

1946, Feb. 18 Engraved

B85	SP45	1fr+3fr deep blue green	25	25
B86	"	2fr+4fr rose pink	25	25
B87	"	4fr+6fr dark blue	25	25
B88	"	5fr+40fr dark violet	40	40
B89	"	10fr+60fr brown red	40	40
B90	"	15fr+100fr indigo	65	65
		Nos. B85-B90 (6)	2.20	2.20

The surtax was for child welfare.

1946, Feb. 18

B91	SP46	2fr+8fr bright blue	15	15

The surtax was used for prevention of tuberculosis.

19th Century Steamer and Map
SP47

1946

B92	SP47	3fr+2fr deep blue	15	15

Stamp Day, June 23, 1946.

Harbor of Monte Carlo
SP48

1946, Dec. 13

B93	SP48	2fr+3fr dark bluish green	60	60

Issued in tribute to the memory of Franklin D. Roosevelt. The surtax was for a fund to erect a monument in his honor.

Souvenir Sheet.

SP49

Engraved.

1947, May 15 *Imperf.* Unwmkd.

B94	SP49	200fr+300fr dark red & chocolate	6.50	6.50

Issued in sheets measuring 83½ x 98 mm., to commemorate the 25th anniversary of the reign of Prince Louis II.

Prince Charles III
SP50

1948, Mar. 6 *Perf. 14x13*

B95	SP50	6fr+4fr dark blue green, *light blue*	24	24

Issued for Stamp Day, Mar. 6.

Princess Charlotte
SP51

Prince Rainier III
SP52

Perf. 13½x13, Imperf.

1949, Dec. 27 Engraved

Cross Typographed in Red.

B96	SP51	10fr+5fr red brn.	5.50	5.50
B97	SP52	15fr+5fr brt. red	5.50	5.50
B98	"	25fr+5fr dark violet blue	5.50	5.50
B99	SP51	40fr+5fr dull grn.	5.50	5.50
		a. Block of 4, 1 each of Nos. B96 to B99	25.00	25.00

Printed in sheets measuring 151 x 173mm., perforated and imperforate, containing four of No. B99a, together with arms in red brown and crosses and inscriptions in red.

The surtax was for the Red Cross.

AIR POST STAMPS.

No. 91 Surcharged in Black

1F50

Perf. 14x13½

1933, Aug. 22 Unwmkd.

C1 A15 1.50fr on 5fr green & rose 15.00 11.50
 a. Imperf., pair 200.00

Plane over Monaco
AP1

Plane Propeller and Buildings
AP2

Pegasus—AP3

Sea Gull—AP4

Plane, Globe and Arms of Monaco
AP5

1942, Apr. 15 Engraved *Perf. 13*

C2 AP1 5fr blue green 25 25
C3 " 10fr ultramarine 25 25
C4 AP2 15fr sepia 25 25
C5 AP3 20fr henna brown 45 45
C6 AP4 50fr red violet 2.25 1.65
C7 AP5 100fr red & violet brown 2.25 1.25
 Nos. C2–C7 (6) 5.70 4.10

Nos. 196–197 Overprinted in Blue

POSTE AÉRIENNE

1946, May 20

C8 A41 50fr dp. Prussian green 1.20 1.20
C9 A41 100fr red 1.75 1.75
 a. Invtd. ovpt. 5500.00
 b. Double ovpt. 300.00

Douglas DC-3 and Arms
AP6

1946, May 20

C10 AP6 40fr red 75 50
C11 " 50fr red brown 1.00 65
C12 " 100fr dp. blue grn. 1.60 1.00
C13 " 200fr violet 2.25 1.40

Nos. C8–C13 exist imperforate. See also Nos. C27–C29.

Harbor of Monte Carlo
AP7

Map of Monaco
AP8

1946, Dec. 13

C14 AP7 5fr carmine rose 55 50
C15 AP8 10fr violet black 45 40

Issued in tribute to the memory of Franklin D. Roosevelt.

Franklin D. Roosevelt Examining his Stamp Collection
AP9

Main Post Office, New York City
AP10

Oceanographic Museum, Monaco
AP11

Harbor of Monte Carlo—AP12

Statue of Liberty and New York City Skyline—AP13

1947, May 15 Unwmkd.

C16 AP9 50c violet 25 25
C17 AP10 1.50fr rose violet 30 30
C18 AP11 3fr henna brown 35 35
C19 AP12 10fr deep blue 1.35 1.35
C20 AP13 15fr rose carmine 1.60 1.65
 a. Strip of 3, Nos. C20+203 +C19 5.50 5.50
 Nos. C16–C20 (5) 3.85 3.90

Issued to commemorate the principality's participation in the Centenary International Philatelic Exhibition, New York, May, 1947.

Crowd Acclaiming Constitution of 1911
AP14

Anthropo-logical Museum
AP15

Designs: 25fr, Institute of Human Paleontology, Paris. 50fr, Albert I. 100fr, Oceanographic Institute, Paris. 200fr, Albert I medal.

1949, Mar. 5 Engraved *Perf. 13*

C21 AP14 20fr brown red 1.00 1.00
C22 " 25fr indigo 1.00 1.00
C23 AP15 40fr blue green 1.00 1.00
C24 " 50fr black, brown & green 1.50 1.50
C25 " 100fr cerise 3.00 3.00
C26 AP14 200fr deep orange 7.00 7.00
 Nos. C21–C26 (6) 14.50 14.50

Plane-Arms Type of 1946

1949, Mar. 10

C27 AP6 300fr deep ultra. & indigo 45.00 32.50
C28 " 500fr greenish black & blue green 30.00 25.00
C29 " 1000fr black & red violet 55.00 40.00

Palace, Globe and Pigeon
AP16

1949–50

C30 AP16 25fr deep blue 70 70
C31 " 40fr red brown & sepia ('50) 1.00 90
C32 " 50fr dark green & ultra. ('50) 1.35 1.00
C33 " 100fr dk. car. & dk. green ('50) 2.50 2.40

Issued to commemorate the 75th anniversary of the formation of the Universal Postal Union.

Nos. C30 to C33 exist imperforate, also No. C30 in deep plum and violet, imperforate.

Rainier Type of Regular Issue

1950, Apr. 11 Unwmkd.

C34 A57 50fr black & red brown 2.50 2.00
C35 " 100fr red brown, sepia & indigo 3.50 3.00

Enthronement of Prince Rainier III.

Runner—AP18

Designs: 50fr, Fencing. 100fr, Target Shooting. 200fr, Olympic Torch.

1953, Feb. 23 *Perf. 11*

C36 AP18 40fr black 7.00 6.00
C37 " 50fr bright purple 8.00 7.00
C38 " 100fr dk. slate grn. 9.00 8.00
C39 " 200fr deep carmine 10.00 9.00

Issued to publicize Monaco's participation in the Helsinki Olympic Games.

Dr. Albert Schweitzer and Ogowe River Scene, Gabon
AP19

1955, Jan. 14 *Perf. 13*

C40 AP19 200fr slate black, dark blue green & blue 17.50 15.00

Issued to honor Dr. Albert Schweitzer, medical missionary.

Mediterranean Sea Swallows
AP20

Birds: 200fr, Sea gulls. 500fr, Albatross. 1000fr, Great cormorants.

1955–57 *Perf. 11*

C41 AP20 100fr deep blue & indigo 15.00 8.00
a. Perf. 13 ('57) 14.00 7.00
C42 " 200fr blue & blk. 17.50 10.00
a. Perf. 13 ('57) 140.00 30.00
C43 " 500fr gray & dark green 18.50 15.00
C44 " 1000fr dark blue green & black brown 140.00 120.00
a. Perf. 13 ('57) 55.00 35.00

"From the Earth to the Moon" and Jules Verne
AP21

1955, June 7 **Unwmkd.**

C45 AP21 200fr deep blue & slate 30.00 30.00

Issued to commemorate the 50th anniversary of the death of Jules Verne.

Princess Grace and Prince Rainier III
AP22

1956, April 19 **Engraved**

Portraits in Brown.

C46 AP22 100fr purple 60 60
C47 " 200fr carmine 1.00 1.00
C48 " 500fr gray violet 2.50 2.50

Issued to commemorate the wedding of Prince Rainier III to Grace Kelly, April 19, 1956.

Nos. J45 and J54 Surcharged and Overprinted "Poste Aerienne" and bars.

1956, April *Perf. 11*

C49 D6 100fr on 20fr indigo & purple 10.00 10.00
a. Dbl. surch. *500.00 500.00*
C50 D7 100fr on 20fr purple & indigo 10.00 10.00
a. Dbl. surch. *500.00 500.00*

See footnote after No. 390.

Basilica of Lourdes—AP23

Design: 200fr, Pope Pius X and underground basilica.

1958, May 15 *Perf. 13* **Unwmkd.**

C51 AP23 100fr dark blue, green & gray 2.25 2.00
C52 " 200fr red brown & sepia 3.25 3.00

Issued to commemorate the centenary of the apparition of the Virgin Mary at Lourdes.

A little time given to study of the arrangement of the Scott Catalogue can make it easier to use effectively.

Prince Rainier III and Princess Grace
AP24

1959, May 16

C53 AP24 300fr dark purple 5.00 4.00
C54 " 500fr blue 8.00 6.50

St. Dévote
AP25

1960, June 1 **Engraved** *Perf. 13*

C55 AP25 2fr green, blue & violet 2.00 1.25
C56 AP24 3fr dark purple 20.00 10.00
C57 " 5fr blue 20.00 15.00
C58 AP25 10fr grn. & brown 6.00 5.00

1961, June 3

C59 AP25 3fr ultra., green & gray olive 3.00 1.75
C60 " 5fr rose carmine 4.00 3.00

Europa Issue, 1962

Mercury over Map of Europe
AP26

1962, June 6 *Perf. 13* **Unwmkd.**

C61 AP26 2fr dark green, slate green & brown 1.85 1.50

Oceanographic Museum, Atom Symbol and Princes Albert I and Rainier III
AP27

C62 AP27 10fr violet, blue & bistre 12.00 11.00

Issued to commemorate the establishment of a scientific research center by agreement with the International Atomic Energy Commission.

Roland Garros—AP28

1963, Dec. 12 **Engraved** *Perf. 13*

C63 AP28 2fr dark blue & dark brown 1.85 1.35

Issued to commemorate the 50th anniversary of the first airplane crossing of the Mediterranean by Roland Garros (1888–1918).

Type of Regular Issue, 1964

Design: 5fr, Convair B-58 Hustler (New York-Paris in 3 hours, 19 minutes, 41 seconds, Maj. William R. Payne, USAF, 1961).

1964, May 22 *Perf. 13* **Unwmkd.**

C64 A151 5fr brn., blk. & bl. 5.50 5.00

Issued to commemorate the 50th anniversary of the first airplane rally of Monte Carlo.

Bob-sledding
AP29

1964, Dec. 3 **Engraved** *Perf. 13*

C65 AP29 5fr multicolored 3.50 3.50

Issued to commemorate the 9th Winter Olympic Games, Innsbruck, Austria, Jan. 29–Feb. 9, 1964.

ITU Type of Regular Issue

Design: 10fr, ITU Emblem and Monte Carlo television station on Mount Agel (vert.).

1965, May 17 **Engraved** *Perf. 13*

C66 A161 10fr bister brown, slate green & blue 7.00 7.00

Issued to commemorate the centenary of the International Telecommunication Union.

Princess Grace with Albert Alexander Louis, Caroline and Stephanie—AP30

1966, Feb. 1 **Engraved** *Perf. 13*

C67 AP30 3fr pur., red brn. & Prus. blue 2.85 2.25

Issued to commemorate the birth of Princess Stephanie, Feb. 1, 1965.

Opera House Interior
AP31

1966, June 1 **Engraved** *Perf. 13*

C68 AP31 5fr Prus. bl., bister & dark car. rose 3.50 3.50

Centenary of founding of Monte Carlo.

Prince Rainier III and Princess Grace
AP32

1966–71 **Engraved** *Perf. 13*

C69 AP32 2fr pink & slate 1.35 50
C70 " 3fr emerald & slate 3.25 1.00
C71 " 5fr lt. bl. & slate 3.50 1.50
C72 " 10fr lemon & slate ('67) 6.00 4.00
C72A " 20fr org. & brown ('71) 17.50 8.00
Nos. C69–C72A (5) 31.60 15.00

Issue dates: 10fr, Dec. 7, 1967; 20fr, Sept. 6, 1971. Others, Dec. 12, 1966.

Panhard-Phenix, 1895—AP33

1967, Apr. 28 **Engraved** *Perf. 13*

C73 AP33 3fr Prussian blue & black 2.25 2.00

25th Grand Prix of Monaco.

Olympic Games Type of Regular Issue

Sport: 3fr, Field hockey.

1968, Apr. 29 **Engraved** *Perf. 13*

C74 A183 3fr emerald, vio. bl. & Prus. blue 2.25 2.00

Issued to publicize the 19th Olympic Games, Mexico City, Oct. 12–27.

Berlioz Monument, Monte Carlo
AP34

1969, Apr. 26 **Engraved** *Perf. 13*

C75 AP34 2fr green, black & ultra. 1.40 1.25

Issued to commemorate the centenary of the death of Hector Berlioz (1803–1869), French composer.

Napoleon, by Paul Delaroche
AP35

1969, Apr. 26 Photo. *Perf. 12x13*

C76 AP35 3fr multicolored 2.25 2.00

Bicentenary of birth of Napoleon I.

Horses, Prehistoric Drawing from Lascaux Cave—AP36

1970, Dec. 15 Engraved *Perf. 13*

C77 AP36 3fr multicolored 2.25 1.50

Nativity Type of Regular Issue

Design: 3fr, Nativity, Flemish School, 15th century (vert.).

1973, Nov. 12 Engr. *Perf. 12x13*

C78 A243 3fr Prussian green 2.25 1.50

750th anniversary of the first crèche assembled by St. Francis of Assisi.

Prince Rainier III
AP37

1974, Dec. 23 Engr. *Perf. 12½x13*

C81 AP37 10fr dark purple 4.50 2.00
C82 " 15fr henna brown 6.75 3.00
C83 " 20fr ultramarine 9.00 4.00

AIR POST SEMI-POSTAL STAMPS.

Types of 1942
Air Post Stamps Surcharged with New Values and Bars in Black.

Perf. 13

1945, Mar. 27 Engr. Unwmkd.

CB1 AP1 1fr+4fr on 10fr rose red 18 18
CB2 AP2 1fr+4fr on 15fr red brown 18 18
CB3 AP3 1fr+4fr on 20fr sepia 18 18
CB4 AP4 1fr+4fr on 50fr ultramarine 18 18
CB5 AP5 1fr+4fr on 100fr bright red violet 18 18
Nos. CB1-CB5 (5) 90 90

The surtax was for the benefit of prisoners of war.

Franklin D. Roosevelt
SPAP1

1946, Dec. 13

CB6 SPAP1 15fr+10fr red 1.00 80

Issued in tribute to the memory of Franklin D. Roosevelt. The surtax was for a fund to erect a monument in his honor.

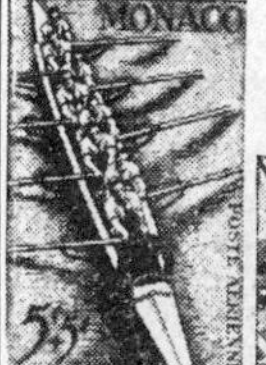

Rowing SPAP2 — Sailboat Race SPAP3

1948, July

CB7 SPAP2 5fr+5fr sepia 6.50 6.50
CB8 " 6fr+9fr violet (*Skiing*) 8.00 8.00
CB9 " 10fr+15fr carmine rose (*Tennis*) 9.50 9.50
CB10 SPAP3 15fr+25fr dark blue 14.00 14.00

Issued to publicize Monaco's participation in the 1948 Olympic Games held at Wembley, England, during July and August.

Salmacis Nymph
SPAP4

Designs Similar to Regular Issue

1948, July

CB11 A50 5fr + 5fr black blue 4.00 3.50
CB12 A51 6fr + 9fr dark green 4.00 4.00
CB13 A52 10fr + 15fr crimson 5.00 5.00
CB14 SPAP4 15fr + 25fr red brown 7.00 7.00

Issued to honor François J. Bosio (1769–1845), sculptor.

POSTAGE DUE STAMPS.

D1 — Prince Albert I D2

Typographed.

1905-43 *Perf. 14x13½* Unwmkd.

J1 D1 1c olive green 35 35
J2 " 5c green 55 35
J3 " 10c rose 25 25
J4 " 10c brown ('09) 300.00 100.00
J5 D1 15c violet brown, *straw* 1.40 60
J6 " 20c bistre brown, *buff* ('26) 12 12
J7 " 30c blue 25 25
J8 " 40c red violet ('26) 15 15
J9 " 50c brown, *orange* 2.50 1.75
J10 " 50c blue green ('27) 15 15
J11 " 60c gray black ('26) 40 40
J12 " 60c bright vio. ('34) 8.00 8.00
J13 " 1fr red brown, *straw* ('26) 15 15
J14 " 2fr red orange ('27) 35 35
J15 " 3fr magenta ('27) 35 35
J15A " 5fr ultramarine ('43) 35 35
Nos. J1-J15A (16) 315.32 113.57

1910

J16 D2 1c olive green 20 20
J17 " 10c light violet 25 25
J18 " 30c bistre 180.00 150.00

In January, 1917, regular postage stamps overprinted "T" in a triangle were used as postage due stamps.

Nos. J17 and J18 Surcharged **20c.**

1918

J19 D2 20c on 10c lt. violet 1.25 1.00
a. Double surch. 300.00
J20 " 40c on 30c bistre 1.25 1.00

D3

1925-32

J21 D3 1c gray green 15 15
J22 " 10c violet 20 20
J23 " 30c bistre 20 20
J24 " 60c red 30 30
J25 " 1fr light blue ('32) 80.00 60.00
J26 " 2fr dull red ('32) 100.00 70.00
Nos. J21-J26 (6) 180.85 130.85

Nos. J25 and J26 have the numerals of value double-lined.

"Recouvrements" stamps were used to recover charges due on undelivered or refused mail which was returned to the sender.

No. J9 Surcharged **1 franc à percevoir**

1925

J27 D1 1fr on 50c brown, *orange* ('25) 40 35
a. Dbl. surcharge 250.00

D4 — D5

1946-57 Engraved *Perf. 14x13, 13*

J28 D4 10c sepia 20 20
J29 " 30c dark violet 20 20
J30 " 50c deep blue 20 20
J31 " 1fr dark green 20 20
J32 " 2fr yellow brown 20 20
J33 " 3fr bright red violet 30 30
J34 " 4fr carmine 40 40
J35 D5 5fr chocolate 30 30
J36 " 10fr deep ultramarine 45 45
J37 " 20fr greenish blue 55 55
J38 " 50fr red violet & red ('50) 6.00 5.00
J38A " 100fr dark green & red ('57) 4.00 4.00
Nos. J28-J38A (12) 13.00 12.00

Sailing Vessel—D6

Early Postal Transport: 1fr, Carrier pigeons. 3fr, Old railroad engine. 4fr, Old monoplane. 5fr, Steam automobile. 10fr, daVinci's flying machine. 20fr, Balloon. 50fr, Post rider. 100fr, Old mail coach.

1953-54 *Perf. 11.*

J39 D6 1fr dark green & bright red ('54) 10 10
J40 " 2fr deep ultramarine & blue green 10 10
J41 " 3fr Prussian green & brown lake 15 15
J42 " 4fr dark brown & Prussian green 20 20
J43 " 5fr ultra. & purple 40 40
J44 " 10fr deep ultramarine & dark blue 5.00 5.00
J45 " 20fr indigo & purple 1.50 1.50
J46 " 50fr red & dark brown 4.50 4.50
J47 " 100fr violet brown & deep green 8.00 8.00

The two types of each value in Nos. J39–J56 (early and modern transportation) were printed tête bêche, se-tenant at the base.

S. S. United States—D7

Modern Postal Transport: 1fr, Sikorsky S-51 helicopter. 3fr, Modern locomotive. 4fr, Comet airliner. 5fr, Sabre sports car. 10fr, Rocket. 20fr, Graf Zeppelin. 50fr, Motorcyclist. 100fr, Railroad mail car.

J48 D7 1fr bright red & dark green ('54) 10 10
J49 " 2fr blue green & deep ultramarine 10 10
J50 " 3fr brown lake & Prussian green 15 15
J51 " 4fr Prussian green & dark brown 20 20
J52 " 5fr purple & ultra. 40 40
J53 " 10fr dark blue & deep ultramarine 5.00 5.00
J54 " 20fr purple & indigo 1.50 1.50
J55 " 50fr dark brown & red 4.50 4.50
J56 " 100fr deep green & violet brown 8.00 8.00
Nos. J39–J56 (18) 39.90 39.90

See note following No. J47.

Felucca, 18th Century
D8

Designs: 2c, Paddle steamer La Palmaria, 19th century. 5c, Arrival of first train. 10c, Armed messenger, 15th–16th century. 20c, Monaco-Nice courier, 18th century. 30c, "Charles III," 1866. 50c, Courier on horseback, 17th century. 1fr, Diligence, 19th century.

1960-69 Engraved *Perf. 13*

J57 D8 1c blue green, bistre brown & blue 35 35
J58 " 2c slate green, sepia & ultramarine 10 10
J59 " 5c greenish blue, gray & red brown 10 10
J60 " 10c violet blue, black & green 10 10
J61 " 20c blue, brown & green 30 30
J62 " 30c brn., brt. green & brt. bl. ('69) 15 15
J63 " 50c dark blue, brown & slate green 45 45
J64 " 1fr slate green, blue & brown 60 60
Nos. J57–J64 (8) 2.15 2.15

MONGOLIA

(mŏng·gō′lĭ·ȧ)

Mongolian People's Republic

(Outer Mongolia)

LOCATION — In central Asia, bounded on the north by Siberia, on the west by Sinkiang, on the south and east by China proper and Manchuria.

GOVT.—Republic.

AREA—604,000 sq. mi.

POP.—1,530,000 (est. 1977).

CAPITAL—Ulan Bator (formerly Urga).

Outer Mongolia, which had long been under Russian influence although nominally a dependency of China, voted at a plebiscite Oct. 20, 1945, to sever all ties with China and become an independent nation. See Tannu Tuva.

100 Cents = 1 Dollar
100 Mung = 1 Tugrik (1926)

Scepter of Indra A1 A2

1924 Lithographed. **Unwmkd.**

Perf. 10, 13½ and Compound.

Surface Tinted Paper.
Inscriptions in Black.

1	A1	1c buff, gray brown, gray, *bistre*	2.00	2.00
2	"	2c red brown, yellow brown, drab, dull blue, *brownish*	2.00	2.00
		a. Perf. 13½	12.50	12.50
3	"	5c gray, rose brown, yellow	20.00	20.00
		a. Perf. 10	20.00	20.00
4	"	10c blue, dull blue, brown, *gray blue*	5.00	3.50
		a. Perf. 10	6.00	3.50
5	"	20c gray blue, dull blue, drab, *gray*	10.00	6.00
6	"	50c dull red, orange, drab, *salmon*	17.50	10.00
7	"	$1 buff, light brown, drab, red, *yellow*	20.00	20.00
		b. Perf. 10	60.00	60.00
		Nos. 1-7 (7)	76.50	63.50

These stamps vary in size from 19x25 mm (1c) to 30x39mm ($1). They also differ in details of the design.

Errors of perforating and printing exist.

Some quantities of Nos. 1-2, 4-7 were defaced with horizontal perforation across the center.

Revenue Stamps Handstamp
Overprinted "POSTAGE" in Violet

Sizes: 1c to 20c: 22x36 mm.
50c, $1: 26x43½ mm.
$5: 30x45½ mm.

1926 ***Perf. 11.***

16	A2	1c blue	4.50	4.00
17	"	2c orange	4.50	4.00
18	"	5c plum	4.50	4.00
19	"	10c green	4.50	4.00
20	"	20c yellow brown	4.50	4.00
21	"	50c brown & olive green	*100.00*	*100.00*
22	"	$1 brn. & salmon	*300.00*	*300.00*
23	"	$5 red, yellow & gray	*175.00*	*175.00*
		Nos. 16-23 (8)	*597.50*	*595.00*

Black Overprint

16a	A2	1c blue	7.50	7.50
17a	"	2c orange	7.50	7.50
18a	"	5c plum	7.50	6.00
19a	"	10c green	7.50	6.00
20a	"	20c yellow brown	7.50	6.00
21a	"	50c brown & ol. green	*130.00*	*130.00*
22a	"	$1 brown & salmon	*275.00*	*275.00*
23a	"	$5 red, yellow & gray	*185.00*	*185.00*
		Nos. 16a-23a (8)	*627.50*	*623.00*

Red Overprint

16b	A2	1c blue	*25.00*	*25.00*
17b	"	2c orange	*25.00*	*25.00*
18b	"	5c plum	*25.00*	*25.00*
19b	"	10c green	*25.00*	*25.00*
20b	"	20c yellow brown	*25.00*	*25.00*
		Nos. 16b-20b (5)	*125.00*	*125.00*

Blue Overprint

16c	A2	1c blue	*35.00*	*35.00*
17c	"	2c orange	*35.00*	*35.00*
18c	"	5c plum	*35.00*	*35.00*
20c	"	20c yellow brown	*35.00*	*35.00*

The preceding handstamped overprints may be found inverted, double, etc. Counterfeits abound.

Yin Yang and other Symbols
A3 A4

TYPE I. The pearl above the crescent is solid. The devices in the middle of the stamp are not outlined.

TYPE II. The pearl is open. The devices and panels are all outlined in black.

1926-29 ***Perf. 11***

Type I.

Size: 22x28mm.

32	A3	5m lilac & black	2.00	2.00
33	"	20m blue & black	1.75	1.75

Type II.

Size: 22x29mm.

34	A3	1m yellow & black	40	30
35	"	2m brn. org. & black	60	40
36	"	5m lilac & black	1.20	90
37	"	10m light blue & black	85	60
		a. Imperf.		
38	"	20m deep blue & black ('29)	6.00	4.00
		a. Imperf.		
39	"	25m yellow green & black	1.20	1.00
		a. Imperf.		

Size: 26x34mm.

40	A3	40m lemon & black	1.85	1.75
41	"	50m buff & black	2.75	2.00

Size: 28x37mm.

42	A4	1t brn., grn. & black	8.50	6.00
43	"	3t red, yel. & black	22.50	16.50
44	"	5t brown violet, rose & black	35.00	35.00
		Nos. 32-44 (13)	84.60	72.20

In 1929 a change was made in the perforating machine. Every fourth pin was removed, which left the perforation holes in groups of three with blank spaces between the groups. Nos. 38 and 44A have only this interrupted perforation. Nos. 37 and 39 are found with both perforations.

Yin Yang and other Symbols
A5

1929

44A	A5	5m lilac & black	6.50	6.50

See note after No. 44.

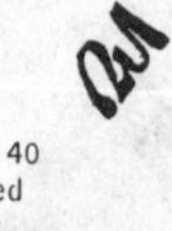

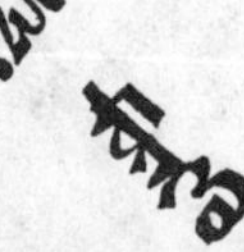

Nos. 34, 35, 40 Handstamped With New Values in Black

1930

45	A3	10m on 1m yellow & black	14.00	14.00
46	"	20m on 2m brown orange & black	14.00	14.00
47	"	25m on 40m lemon & black	14.00	14.00

Symbols of Government
A6 A7

1931

Violet Overprint, Handstamped

48	A6	1c blue	6.00	5.00
		a. Blue ovpt.	10.00	5.00
49	"	2c orange	8.50	5.00
50	"	5c brown violet	8.50	6.50
		a. Blue ovpt.	12.50	7.50
51	"	10c green	12.00	7.50
		a. Blue ovpt.	15.00	12.50
52	"	20c bistre brown	15.00	7.50
53	"	50c brown & olive yellow	65.00	50.00
54	"	$1 brown & salmon	90.00	75.00
55	"	$5 scarlet & olive yellow	185.00	185.00
		Nos. 48-55 (8)	390.00	341.50

Revenue Stamps Surcharged in Black, Red or Blue.

1931

59	A7	5m on 5c brown violet (Bk)	13.50	6.00
		a. Invtd. surch.		20.00
		b. Imperf., pair	30.00	30.00
60	"	10m on 10c green (R)	22.50	12.00
		a. Invtd. surch.	16.50	12.00
		b. Imperf., pair	50.00	50.00
61	"	20m on 20c bistre brown (Bl)	32.50	16.50
		a. Invtd. surch.		16.50
		b. Imperf., pair	70.00	70.00

On Nos. 59-61, "Postage" is always diagonal, and may read up or down.

Weaver at Loom—A8

Telegrapher
A9

Sukhe Bator
A10

Lake and Mountains
A11

Wmk. 170

Designs: 5m, Mongol at lathe. 10m, Government building, Ulan Bator. 15m, Young Mongolian revolutionary. 20m, Studying Latin alphabet. 25m, Mongolian soldier. 50m, Monument to Sukhe Bator. 3t, Sheep shearing. 5t, Camel caravan. 10t, Chasing wild horses.

Wmkd.

Greek Border and Rosettes. (170)

1932 Photogravure. ***Perf. 12½x12.***

62	A8	1m brown	60	30
63	A9	2m red violet	60	30
64	A8	5m indigo	40	20
65	"	10m dull green	40	20
66	A9	15m deep brown	40	20
67	"	20m rose red	40	20
68	"	25m dull violet	40	20
69	A10	40m gray black	50	40
70	"	50m dull blue	35	25

Perf. 11x12.

71	A11	1t dull green	50	50
72	"	3t dull violet	1.25	1.25
73	"	5t brown	3.50	3.50
74	"	10t ultramarine	6.00	6.00
		Nos. 62-74 (13)	15.30	13.50

Marshal Kharloin Choibalsan
A21

1945 ***Perf. 12½*** **Unwmkd.**

83	A21	1t black brown	4.00	4.00

Choibalsan
A22

Victory Medal
A24

Sukhe Bator and Choibalsan
A23

Designs: No. 86, Choibalsan as young man. No. 87, Choibalsan University, Ulan Bator. 1t, Anniversary medal. 2t, Sukhe Bator.

1946, July Photo. *Perf. 12½*

84	A22	30m olive bister	2.00	2.00
85	A23	50m dull purple	3.00	3.00
86	A24	60m black	3.00	3.00
87	A23	60m orange brown	3.50	3.50
88	A24	80m dk. org. brown	4.00	4.00
89	"	1t indigo	8.50	8.50
90	"	2t deep brown	10.00	10.00
		Nos. 84-90 (7)	34.00	34.00

25th anniversary of independence.

New Housing
A25

School Children—A26

Mongolian Arms and Flag
A27

Sukhe Bator
A28

Flags of Communist Countries—A29

Lenin
A30

Designs: 15m, Altai Hotel. No. 94, State Store. No. 95, Like 30m. 25m, University. 40m, National Theater. 50m, Pedagogical Institute. 60m, Sukhe Bator monument. Sizes of type A25: Nos. 91, 93-94, 98-99, 32½x22mm. 25m, 55x26mm.

1951

91	A25	5m brown, *pink*	1.00	1.00
92	A26	10m dp. blue, *pink*	1.00	1.00
93	A25	15m green, *greenish*	1.25	1.25
94	"	20m red orange	1.30	1.30
95	A27	20m dk. bl. & multi.	2.00	2.00
96	A25	25m blue, *bluish*	2.00	2.00
97	A27	30m red & multi.	2.00	2.00
98	A25	40m purple, *pink*	2.25	2.25
99	"	50m brown, *grayish*	6.00	6.00
100	A28	60m brown black	6.00	6.00
101	A29	1t multicolored	6.00	6.00
102	A28	2t dark brown & orange brown	8.00	8.00
103	A30	3t multicolored	9.00	9.00
		Nos. 91-103 (13)	47.80	47.80

30th anniversary of independence.

Choibalsan
A31

Choibalsan and Farmer
A32

Choibalsan and Sukhe Bator
A33

Designs: No. 108, 30m, Choibalsan and factory worker (47x33mm). 50m, Choibalsan and Young Pioneer. No. 112, 2t, Choibalsan in uniform.

1953, Dec. Photogravure *Perf. 12½*

104	A31	15m dull blue	1.25	1.25
105	A32	15m dull green	1.50	1.50
106	A31	20m dull green	2.00	2.00
107	A32	20m sepia	2.25	2.25
108	"	20m violet blue	2.25	2.25
109	"	30m dark brown	2.50	2.50
110	A33	50m orange brown	2.25	2.25
111	"	1t carmine rose	3.00	3.00
112	A31	1t sepia	3.00	3.00
113	"	2t red	2.50	2.50
114	A33	3t sepia	3.00	3.00
115	A33	5t red	4.50	4.50
		Nos. 104-115 (12)	30.00	30.00

First anniversary of death of Marshal Karloin Choibalsan (1895-1952).

Arms of Mongolia
A34

1954, Mar. Litho. *Perf. 12½*

116	A34	10m carmine	3.00	2.00
117	"	20m "	5.00	2.00
118	"	30m "	3.50	2.00
119	"	40m "	4.50	2.00
120	"	60m "	4.00	2.00
		Nos. 116-120 (5)	20.00	10.00

Sukhe Bator and Choibalsan
A35

Guard with Dog
A37

Lake Hubsugul
A36

Designs: No. 122, Lenin Statue, Ulan Bator. 50m, Choibalsan University. 1t, Arms and flag of Mongolia.

1955, June Photo. *Perf. 12½*

121	A35	30m green	30	10
122	"	30m orange vermilion	40	10
123	A36	30m bright blue	30	10
124	A37	40m dp. red lilac	50	20
125	A36	50m ocher	75	45
126	A37	1t red & multi.	2.25	1.00
		Nos. 121-126 (6)	4.50	1.95

35th anniversary of independence.

1955

Design: 2t, Lenin.

127	A35	2t bright blue	2.75	1.25

85th anniversary of birth of Lenin.

Flags of Communist Countries
A38

Arms of Mongolia
A39

1955

128	A38	60m blue & multi.	1.25	80

Fight for peace.

1956 Photo. *Perf. 12½*

129	A39	20m dark brown	25	15
130	"	30m dark olive	30	20
131	"	40m bright blue	40	30
132	"	60m blue green	50	35
133	"	1t deep carmine	80	35
		Nos. 129-133 (5)	2.25	1.35

Kremlin, Moscow, Train and Sukhe Bator Monument
A40

Design: 2t, Flags of Mongolia and USSR.

1956

134	A40	1t dk. blue & multi.	1.50	1.00
135	"	2t red & multi.	3.00	1.50

Establishment of railroad connection between Moscow and Ulan Bator.

Mongolian Arms and Flag
A41

Hunter with Golden Eagle
A42

Wrestlers
A43

Designs: No. 138, Three children (33x26½mm.).

1956, July Typo. *Perf. 9*

136	A41	30m blue	3.00	3.00
137	A42	30m pale brown	10.00	7.50
138	"	60m orange	12.00	10.00
139	A43	60m yellow green	12.00	10.00

35th anniversary of independence.

Types A41 and A43 without "XXXV"

1958

140	A41	20m red	75	75
141	A43	50m brown, *pink*	3.75	3.75

Nos. 140-143 were issued both with and without gum.

Poster
A44

Globe and Dove
A45

1958, March Litho. *Perf. 9*

142	A44	30m maroon & sal.	2.75	2.00

13th Congress of Mongolian People's Party.

1958, May

143	A45	60m deep blue	2.50	1.25

4th Congress of International Democratic Women's Federation, Vienna, June, 1958. Nos. 142-143 exist imperf.

Yak
A46

Designs: No. 144, Pelicans (vert.). No. 145, Siberian ibex (vert.). No. 147, Yak. No. 148, Camels.

1958, July Typo. *Perf. 9*

144	A46	30m light blue	1.00	50
145	"	30m bright green	1.00	50
146	"	60m orange	1.50	1.00
147	"	1t blue	3.50	2.00
148	"	1t rose	3.50	2.00
		Nos. 144-148 (5)	10.50	6.00

Shades exist.

Canceled to Order

From Nos. 149–158 onward, almost all stamps were printed by the Hungarian State Printing Office, Budapest. A few issues (as noted) were printed by the State Printing Works, Ulan Bator.

Canceling to order was done at Budapest to some quantity of all issues printed there, except Nos. 296–303, the anti-malaria set.

Used prices are for canceled to order stamps. Postally used specimens sell for considerably more.

Stallion
A47

Designs: 5m, 40m, Goat. 10m, 30m, Ram. 15m, 60m, Stallion. 20m, 50m, Bull. 25m, 1t, Bactrian camel.

Lithographed

1958, Nov. 11 ***Perf. 10½x11½***

No.	Type	Description	Unused	Used
149	A47	5m yellow & brown	6	5
150	"	10m lt. grn. & brown	6	5
151	"	15m lilac & brown	6	5
152	"	20m lt. blue & brown	10	7
153	"	25m rose & brown	12	9
154	"	30m lilac & purple	14	10
155	"	40m lt. & dk. green	16	12
156	"	50m salmon & brown	25	15
157	"	60m lt. bl. & indigo	30	20
158	"	1t yellow & brown	75	40
		Nos. 149–158 (10)	2.00	1.28

Holy Flame (Tulaga)
A48

1959, May 1 **Litho.** ***Perf. 9***

No.	Type	Description	Unused	Used
159	A48	1t multicolored	2.50	1.00

See No. C36.

Archer
A49

Mongol Sports: 5m, Taming wild horse. 10m, Wrestlers. 15m, Horseback riding. 25m, Horse race. 30m, Archers. 70m, Hunting wild horse. 80m, Proclaiming a champion.

1959, June 6 **Photo.** ***Perf. 11***

No.	Type	Description	Unused	Used
160	A49	5m multicolored	6	5
161	"	10m "	6	5
162	"	15m "	15	5
163	"	20m "	18	10
164	"	25m "	25	12
165	"	30m "	25	20
166	"	70m "	50	25
167	"	80m "	75	40
		Nos. 160–167 (8)	2.20	1.22

Young Wrestlers A50

Youth Festival Emblem A51

Designs: 5m, Young musician (horiz.). 20m, Boy on horseback. 25m, Two opera singers. 40m, Young Pioneers with flags (horiz.).

Photogravure; Lithographed (30m)

1959, July ***Perf. 12, 11 (30m)***

No.	Type	Description	Unused	Used
168	A50	5m vio. bl. & rose car.	5	5
169	"	10m bl. green & brn.	6	5
170	"	20m claret & green	20	10
171	"	25m green & vio. bl.	25	15
172	A51	30m lilac & light blue	25	20
173	A50	40m green & purple	50	30
		Nos. 168–173 (6)	1.31	85

Mongolian Youth Festival.

The 30m was printed by State Printing Works, Ulan Bator.

Issue dates: 30m, July 11; others July 10.

"Mongol" in Stylized Uighur Script
A52

"Mongol" in Various Scripts: 40m, Soyombo. 50m, Kalmuck. 60m, Square (Pagspa). 1t, Cyrillic.

Printed by State Printing Works, Ulan Bator.

1959, Sept. 1 **Litho.** ***Perf. 11***

Size: 29x42½mm.

No.	Type	Description	Unused	Used
174	A52	30m black & multi.	2.00	2.00
175	"	40m " "	2.00	2.00
176	"	50m " "	3.00	3.00
177	"	60m " "	5.00	5.00

Size: 21x31mm. ***Perf. 9***

No.	Type	Description	Unused	Used
178	A52	1t blk. & multi.	7.50	7.50
		Nos. 174–178 (5)	19.50	19.50

First International Mongolian Language Congress.

Battle Emblem
A53

Battle Monument
A54

1959, Sept. 15 **Photo.** ***Perf. 12½x12***

No.	Type	Description	Unused	Used
179	A53	40m yel., brn. & car.	35	15
180	A54	50m multicolored	40	15

Battle of Ha-lo-hsin (Khalka) River, 20th anniversary.

Congress Emblem
A55

Printed by State Printing Works, Ulan Bator.

1959, Dec. **Lithographed** ***Perf. 11***

No.	Type	Description	Unused	Used
181	A55	30m green	2.00	2.00

2nd meeting of rural economy cooperatives of Mongolia.

Sable
A56

Pheasants—A57

Photogravure

1959, Dec. 21 ***Perf. 15, 11x13***

Multicolored

No.	Type	Description	Unused	Used
182	A56	5m *shown*	5	4
183	A57	10m *shown*	6	5
184	A56	15m *Muskrat*	15	10
185	A57	20m *Otter*	15	12
186	A56	30m *Argali*	24	15
187	A57	50m *Saigas*	50	40
188	"	1t *Musk deer*	1.00	75
		Nos. 182–188 (7)	2.15	1.61

Lunik 3
A58

Design: 50m, Lunik 3 with path around moon (horiz.).

1959, Dec. 30 **Photo.** ***Perf. 12***

No.	Type	Description	Unused	Used
189	A58	30m vio. & yel. grn.	40	20
190	"	50m red, dk. bl. & grn.	50	25

Lunik 3 Russian moon mission, Oct. 7, 1959.

Motherhood Badge
A59

Flower Emblem
A60

1960, Mar. 8 ***Perf. 11, 12½x11½***

No.	Type	Description	Unused	Used
191	A59	40m blue & bister	50	15
192	A60	50m blue, grn. & yel.	70	25

International Women's Day.

Lenin A61

Jacob's-ladder A62

1960, Apr. 22 **Photo.** ***Perf. 11½x12***

No.	Type	Description	Unused	Used
193	A61	40m dk. rose carmine	40	15
194	"	50m rose violet	60	20

90th anniversary, birth of Lenin.

1960, May 31 ***Perf. 11½x12***

Multicolored

No.	Type	Description	Unused	Used
195	A62	5m *Larkspur*	5	5
196	"	10m *Tulips*	8	5
197	"	15m *shown*	10	5
198	"	20m *Globeflowers*	12	8
199	"	30m *Bellflowers*	15	12
200	"	40m *Parnassia*	25	15
201	"	50m *Geranium*	35	20
202	"	1t *Begonia*	1.00	40
		Nos. 195–202 (8)	2.10	1.10

Equestrian—A63

Running
A64

1960, Aug. 1 ***Perf. 15, 11***

Multicolored

No.	Type	Description	Unused	Used
203	A63	5m *shown*	6	4
204	A64	10m *shown*	10	4
205	A63	15m *Diving*	15	6
206	A64	20m *Wrestling*	20	8
207	A63	30m *Hurdling*	30	12
208	A64	50m *Gymnastics, women's*	50	16
209	A63	70m *High jump*	60	20
210	A64	1t *Discus, women's*	1.00	40
		Nos. 203–210 (8)	2.91	1.10

17th Olympic Games, Rome, Aug. 25–Sept. 11.

Red Cross
A65

1960, Aug. 29 — *Perf. 11*

211	A65	20m bl., red & yellow	25	18

Red Cross.

Newspaper "Unen" (Truth)
A66

1960, Dec. 19 — *Perf. 12x11½*

212	A66	20m red, yellow & slate green	20	12
213	"	30m grn., yel. & red	30	18

40th anniversary of Mongolian press.

Golden Orioles
A67

Songbirds: 5m, Rose-colored starling. 10m, Hoopoe. 20m, Black-billed capercaillie. 50m, Oriental broad-billed roller. 70m, Tibetan sandgrouse. 1t, Mandarin duck. (Triangle points down on 5m, 50m, 70m, 1t.)

1961, Jan. 3 — *Perf. 11*

214	A67	5m multicolored	6	5
215	"	10m "	6	5
216	"	15m "	15	10
217	"	20m "	20	15
218	"	50m "	40	20
219	"	70m "	50	25
220	"	1t "	75	35
		Nos. 214-220 (7)	2.12	1.15

Federation Emblem
A68

Design: 30m, Worker and emblem (vert.).

Perf. 11½x12, 12x11½

1961, Jan. 29 — Photogravure

221	A68	30m dk. gray & rose	20	10
222	"	50m ultra. & red	30	18

World Federation of Trade Unions, 15th anniversary.

Patrice Lumumba
A69

1961, Apr. 8 — *Perf. 11½x12*

223	A69	30m brown	1.00	40
224	"	50m violet gray	1.90	60

Patrice Lumumba (1925–1961), premier of Congo.

Bridge
A70

Designs: 10m, Shoemaker. 15m, Department Store, Ulan Bator. 20m, Government building. 30m, State Theater, Ulan Bator. 50m, Machinist. 1t, Modern and old buildings.

1961, Apr. 30 — *Perf. 11½x12, 15*

Sizes: 31½x21mm., 59x20mm. (20m).

225	A70	5m emerald	6	5
226	"	10m blue	8	5
227	"	15m rose red	12	8
228	"	20m brown	15	10
229	"	30m blue	25	15
230	"	50m olive green	40	25
231	"	1t violet	50	35
		Nos. 225-231 (7)	1.56	1.03

40th anniversary of independence; modernization of Mongolia.

Yuri Gagarin and Globe—A71

Designs: 20m, Gagarin with rocket (vert.). 50m, Gagarin making parachute descent (vert.). 1t, Gagarin wearing helmet; globe.

1961, May 31 — *Perf. 15*

232	A71	20m multicolored	25	15
233	"	30m "	40	20
234	"	50m "	75	35
235	"	1t "	1.00	75

Yuri A. Gagarin, first man in space, Apr. 12, 1961.

Postman on Reindeer
A72

Designs: 15m, No. 241a, Postman on camel. 10m, 20m, Postman with yaks. 25m, No. 241c, Postman with ship. 30m, 50m, Diesel train.

1961, June 5 — *Perf. 15*

236	A72	5m multicolored	8	5
237	"	15m "	15	10
238	"	20m "	16	12
239	"	25m "	20	15
240	"	30m "	30	25
		Nos. 236-240, C1-C3 (8)	1.85	1.37

Souvenir Sheet

Perf. 11

241	A72	Sheet of 4	1.50	1.50
	a.	5m lt. blue & brown	35	35
	b.	10m green, brown & blue	35	35
	c.	15m green, violet & brown	35	35
	d.	50m violet, green & black	35	35

40th anniversary of independence; postal modernization. No. 241 has gold margin. Size: 114x90mm. See No. C4b for 25m, perf. 11.

Souvenir Sheet

Ornamental Column—A73

1961, June 20 — *Perf. 12*

242	A73	Souvenir sheet of 2	3.00	3.00
	a.	2t blue, red & gold	1.25	1.25

40th anniversary of the Mongolian People's Revolution. No. 242 contains two No. 242a and label, imperf. between. Blue inscription and gold border. Size: 117x127mm.

Herdsman and Oxen—A74

Designs: Herdsmen and domestic animals (except 1t and No. 252a).

1961, July 10 — *Perf. 13*

Multicolored

243	A74	5m *Rams*	6	5
244	"	10m *shown*	8	5
245	"	15m *Camels*	15	10
246	"	20m *Pigs and geese*	16	12
247	"	25m *Angora goats*	20	15
248	"	30m *Horses*	25	20
249	"	40m *Sheep*	30	20
250	"	50m *Cows*	35	25
251	"	1t *Combine harvester*	60	45
		Nos. 243-251 (9)	2.15	1.57

Souvenir Sheets

Perf. 12

252	A74	Sheet of 3	1.25	1.25
	a.	5m *Combine harvester*	30	30
	b.	15m *Angora goats*	30	30
	c.	40m *Oxen*	30	30
253	A74	Sheet of 3	1.25	1.25
	a.	10m *Pigs and geese*	30	30
	b.	20m *Horses*	30	30
	c.	30m *Cows*	30	30
254	A74	Sheet of 3	1.25	1.25
	a.	25m *Camels*	30	30
	b.	50m *Rams*	30	30
	c.	1t *Sheep*	30	30

40th anniversary of independence. Nos. 252–254 each contain 3 stamps imperf. between. No. 252 has bright green, No. 253 brown, and No. 254 red ornamental border. Size: 104x150mm.

Horseback Riders
A75

Designs: 5m, Young wrestlers and instructor. 15m, Camel and pony riders. 20m, Falconers. 30m, Skier. 50m, Archers. 1t, Male dancers.

1961, Aug. 10 — *Perf. 11*

255	A75	5m multicolored	6	3
256	A75	10m multicolored	7	3
257	"	15m "	12	4
258	"	20m "	15	10
259	"	30m "	25	15
260	"	50m "	50	20
261	"	1t "	75	35
		Nos. 255-261 (7)	1.90	90

40th anniversary of independence; Mongolian youth sports.

Statue of Sukhe Bator
A76

Arms of Mongolia
A77

Designs: 5m, Mongol youth. 10m, Mongol chieftain. 20m, Singer. 30m, Dancer. 50m, Dombra player. 70m, Musicians. 1t, Gymnast. (5m, 10m, 70m, 1t, horiz.).

Perf. 12x11½, 11½x12

1961, Sept. 16

262	A76	5m bright green & red lilac	6	5
263	"	10m red & dk. blue	8	5
264	"	15m blue & lt. brn.	15	6
265	"	20m pur. & brt. grn.	16	8
266	"	30m vio. bl. & car.	20	12
267	"	50m olive & violet	35	20
268	"	70m brt. lilac rose & olive	50	25
269	"	1t dk. bl. & verm.	75	40
		Nos. 262-269 (8)	2.25	1.21

40th anniversary of independence; Mongolian culture.

1961, Nov. 17 — *Perf. 11½x12*

270	A77	5m multicolored	8	5
271	"	10m "	10	5
272	"	15m "	15	8
273	"	20m "	20	8
274	"	30m "	25	12
275	"	50m "	30	20
276	"	70m "	40	25
277	"	1t "	75	40
		Nos. 270-277 (8)	2.23	1.23

Congress Emblem
A78

1961, Dec. 4 — Litho. — *Perf. 11½*

278	A78	30m violet blue, yellow & red	25	15
279	"	50m brn., yel. & red	35	25

5th World Congress of Trade Unions, Moscow, Dec. 4–16.

U.N. Emblem and Arms of Mongolia—A79

Designs: 10m, Globe, map of Mongolia and dove. 50m, Flags of U.N. and Mongolia. 60m, U.N. Headquarters, New York and Parliament, Ulan Bator. 70m, U.N. assembly, U.N. and Mongolian flags.

1962, Mar. 15 Photo. *Perf. 11*

280 A79 10m gold & multi. 5 4
281 " 30m " " 15 10
282 " 50m " " 30 15
283 " 60m " " 45 25
284 " 70m " " 75 50
Nos. 280-284 (5) 1.70 1.04

Mongolia's admission to U.N.

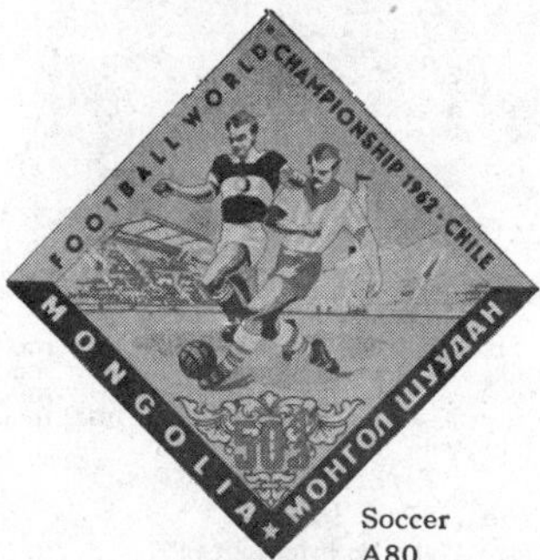

Soccer
A80

Designs: 10m, Soccer ball, globe and flags. 50m, Soccer players, globe and ball. 60m, Goalkeeper. 70m, Stadium.

1962, May 15 Litho. *Perf. 10½*

285 A80 10m multicolored 7 4
286 " 30m " 18 6
287 " 50m " 25 15
288 " 60m " 50 30
289 " 70m " 75 40
Nos. 285-289 (5) 1.75 95

World Soccer Championship, Chile, May 30-June 17.

D. Natsagdorji
A81

Solidarity Emblem
A82

1962, May 15 Photo. *Perf. 15x14½*

290 A81 30m brown 20 12
291 " 50m bluish green 30 18

Mongolian writers' congress.

Lithographed

1962, May 22 *Perf. 11½x10½*

292 A82 20m yel. grn. & multi. 20 12
293 " 30m blue & multi. 30 18

Afro-Asian Peoples' solidarity.

Flags of USSR and Mongolia
A83

Lithographed

1962, June 25 *Perf. 11½x10½*

294 A83 30m brown & multi. 20 12
295 " 50m vio. bl. & multi. 30 18

Mongol-Soviet friendship.

Nos. 195-202 Overprinted

1962, July 20 Photo. *Perf. 11½x12*

296 A62 5m multicolored 20 20
297 " 10m " 20 20
298 " 15m " 30 30
299 " 20m " 30 30
300 " 30m " 40 40
301 " 40m " 50 50
302 " 50m " 75 75
303 " 1t " 1.00 1.00
Nos. 296-303 (8) 3.65 3.65

World Health Organization drive to eradicate malaria.

Military Field Emblem
A84

Designs: 30m, Tablets with inscriptions. 50m, Stone column. 60m, Genghis Khan.

1962, July 20 *Perf. 11½x12*

304 A84 20m blue & multi. 60 60
305 " 30m red & multi. 90 90
306 " 50m pink, brown & black 1.50 1.50
307 " 60m blue & multi. 2.50 2.50

800th anniversary of birth of Genghis Khan (1162-1227), Mongol conqueror.

River Perch
A85

1962, Dec. 28 *Perf. 11*

Multicolored

308 A85 5m *shown* 6 5
309 " 10m *Burbot* 8 5
310 " 15m *Arctic grayling* 15 8
311 " 20m *Shorthorn sculpin* 16 8
312 " 30m *Marine zander* 25 10
313 " 50m *Siberian sturgeon* 30 15
314 " 70m *Waleck's chub minnow* 50 25
315 " 1.50t *Cottocomephorid* 80 45
Nos. 308-315 (8) 2.30 1.21

Sukhe Bator
A86

1963, Feb. 2 Photo. *Perf. 11½x12*

316 A86 30m blue 20 12
317 " 60m rose carmine 30 18

70th anniversary of birth of Sukhe Bator (1893-1923), national hero.

Laika and Rocket—A87

Designs: 15m, Rocket launching (vert.). 25m, Lunik 2 (vert.). 70m, Andrian G. Nikolayev and Pavel R. Popovich. 1t, Mars rocket.

1963, Apr. 1 Litho. *Perf. 12½x12*

Size: 46x32mm.

318 A87 5m multicolored 6 4

Size: 20x68mm.

319 A87 15m multicolored 15 10
320 " 25m " 34 16

Size: 46x32mm.

321 A87 70m multicolored 55 30
322 " 1t " 75 45
Nos. 318-322 (5) 1.85 1.05

Soviet space explorations.

Blood Transfusion
A88

1963, Aug. 15 *Perf. 10½*

Multicolored

323 A88 20m *Packing Red Cross parcels* 10 5
324 " 30m *shown* 20 10
325 " 50m *Vaccination* 35 15
326 " 60m *Ambulance service* 45 25
327 " 1t *Centenary emblem* 65 35
Nos. 323-327 (5) 1.75 90

Red Cross centenary.

Karl Marx
A89

Mongolian Woman
A90

1963, Sept. 16 Photo. *Perf. 11½x12*

328 A89 30m blue 20 12
329 " 60m dk. carmine rose 30 18

145th anniversary of birth of Karl Marx.

1963, Sept. 26

330 A90 30m blue & multi. 25 10

5th International Women's Congress, Moscow, June 24-29.

Inachis
A91

Designs: Mongolian butterflies.

1963, Nov. 7 Litho. *Perf. 11½*

Multicolored

331 A91 5m *shown* 6 4
332 " 10m *Gonepteryx rhamni* 9 4
333 " 15m *Aglais urticae* 15 12
334 " 20m *Parnassius apollo* 20 12
335 " 30m *Papilio machaon* 30 20
336 " 60m *Agrodiaetus damon* 50 30
337 " 1t *Limenitis populi* 70 40
Nos. 331-337 (7) 2.00 1.22

UNESCO Emblem, Globe and Scales—A92

1963, Dec. 10 Photo. *Perf. 12*

338 A92 30m multicolored 25 10
339 " 60m " 40 18

Universal Declaration of Human Rights, 15th anniversary.

Coprinus Comatus
A93

Designs: Mushrooms.

1964, Jan. 1 Litho. *Perf. 10½*

Multicolored

340 A93 5m *shown* 5 4
341 " 10m *Lactarius torminosus* 6 4
342 " 15m *Psalliota campestris* 14 6
343 " 20m *Russula delica* 20 8
344 " 30m *Ixocomus granulatus* 30 18
345 " 50m *Lactarius scrobiculatus* 35 25
346 " 70m *Lactarius deliciosus* 50 30
347 " 1t *Ixocomus variegatus* 75 40
Nos. 340-347 (8) 2.35 1.35

Souvenir Sheet

Skier
A94

1964, Feb. 12 Photo. *Perf. 12x11½*

348 A94 4t gray 2.40 2.40

9th Winter Olympic Games, Innsbruck, Jan. 29–Feb. 9. No. 348 contains one stamp; dark red and gray ornamental margin. Size: 86x71mm.

Lenin
A95

1964 Photo. *Perf. 11½x12*

349 A95 30m salmon & multi. 55 8
350 " 50m blue & multi. 65 15

60th anniversary of Communist Party. Nos. 349–350 printed with alternating label showing Lenin quotation.

Javelin
A96

1964, Apr. 30 Litho. *Perf. 10½*

Multicolored

351 A96 5m *Gymnastics, women's* 5 3
352 " 10m *shown* 6 5
353 " 15m *Wrestling* 12 10
354 " 20m *Running, women's* 15 12
355 " 30m *Equestrian* 25 18
356 " 50m *Diving, women's* 35 25
357 " 60m *Bicycling* 45 30
358 " 1t *Olympic Games emblem* 75 45
Nos. 351-358 (8) 2.18 1.48

Souvenir Sheet

Perf. 12x11½

359 A96 4t *Wrestling* 2.75 2.75

18th Olympic Games, Tokyo, Oct. 10–25. No. 359 contains one horizontal stamp, 37x27½mm. Multicolored margin with Olympic emblem and inscription. Size: 85x76½mm. Issued Sept. 1.

Congress Emblem
A97

1964, Sept. 30 Photo. *Perf. 11*

360 A97 30m multicolored 30 12

4th Mongolian Women's Congress.

Lunik 1—A98

Russian Space Research: 10m, Vostok 1 and 2. 15m, Tiros weather satellite (vert.). 20m, Cosmos circling earth (vert.). 30m, Mars probe (vert.). 60m, Luna 4 (vert.). 80m, Echo 2. 1t, Radar and rockets.

1964, Oct. 30

361 A98 5m multicolored 8 4
362 " 10m " 10 5
363 " 15m " 18 5
364 " 20m " 20 6
365 " 30m " 30 10
366 " 60m " 35 15
367 " 80m " 45 30
368 " 1t " 75 45
Nos. 361-368 (8) 2.41 1.20

Rider Carrying Flag
A99

1964, Nov. 26 Photo. *Perf. 11½x12*

369 A99 25m multicolored 25 12
370 " 50m " 40 18

40th anniversary of Mongolian constitution.

Weather Balloon
A100

Designs: 5m, Oceanographic exploration. 60m, Northern lights and polar bears. 80m, Geomagnetism. 1t, I.Q.S.Y. emblem and Mercator map.

1965, May 15 Photo. *Perf. 13½*

371 A100 5m gray & multi. 8 5
372 " 10m green & multi. 8 6
373 " 60m bl., blk. & pink 30 15
374 " 80m citron & multi. 50 25
375 " 1t brt. green & multicolored 85 50
Nos. 371-375, C6-C8 (8) 2.44 1.43

International Quiet Sun Year.

Horses—A101

Designs: Mongolian horses.

1965, Aug. 25 *Perf. 11*

Multicolored

376 A101 5m *shown* 6 3
377 " 10m *Falconers* 6 3
378 " 15m *Taming wild horse* 15 10
379 " 20m *Horse race* 18 12
380 " 30m *Hurdles* 25 15
381 " 60m *Wolf hunt* 30 20
382 " 80m *Milking a mare* 40 30
383 " 1t *Mare and foal* 65 45
Nos. 376-383 (8) 2.05 1.38

Girl Holding Lambs
A102

1965, Oct. 10 Photo. *Perf. 11*

Multicolored

384 A102 5m *shown* 10 4
385 " 10m *Boy and girl drummers* 10 6
386 " 20m *Camp fire* 20 10
387 " 30m *Wrestlers* 40 20
388 " 50m *Emblem* 55 40
Nos. 384-388 (5) 1.35 80

40th anniversary of Mongolian Youth Organization.

Chinese Perch
A103

1965, Nov. 25

Multicolored

389 A103 5m *shown* 5 4
390 " 10m *Lenok trout* 10 6
391 " 15m *Siberian sturgeon* 20 8
392 " 20m *Amur salmon* 20 10
393 " 30m *Bagrid catfish* 25 15
394 " 60m *Silurid catfish* 35 20
395 " 80m *Northern pike* 50 25
396 " 1t *River perch* 75 40
Nos. 389-396 (8) 2.40 1.28

Marx and Lenin
A104

1965, Dec. 15 *Perf. 11½x12*

397 A104 10m red & black 15 6

6th Conference of Postal Ministers of Communist Countries, Peking, June 21–July 15.

Sable—A105

1966, Feb. 15 Photo. *Perf. 12½*

Multicolored

398 A105 5m *shown* 5 4
399 " 10m *Fox* 6 4
400 " 15m *Otter* (vert.) 14 6
401 " 20m *Cheetah* (vert.) 15 6
402 " 30m *Pallas's cat* 25 15
403 " 60m *Stone marten* 35 20
404 " 80m *Ermine* (vert.) 45 30
405 " 1t *Woman in mink coat* (vert.) 75 40
Nos. 398-405 (8) 2.20 1.25

W.H.O. Headquarters
A106

1966, May 3 Photo. *Perf. 12x11½*

406 A106 30m blue green, blue & gold 20 8
407 " 50m red, bl. & gold 40 15

Opening of World Health Organization Headquarters, Geneva.

Soccer
A107

Designs: 30m, 60m, 80m, Various soccer plays. 1t, British flag and World Soccer Cup emblem. 4t, Wembley Stadium (horiz.).

1966, May 31 Photo. *Perf. 11*

408 A107 10m multicolored 5 3
409 " 30m " 15 10
410 " 60m " 30 15
411 " 80m " 40 25
412 " 1t " 50 40
Nos. 408-412 (5) 1.40 93

Souvenir Sheet

Perf. 12½, Imperf.

413 A107 4t gray & brown 2.50 2.50

World Soccer Championship for Jules Rimet Cup, Wembley, England, July 11–30. No. 413 contains one stamp (61x83mm.). Gold marginal inscription; gold and brown ornaments. Size: 122x83mm.

Sukhe Bator, Parliament Building, Ulan Bator
A108

1966, June 7 Litho. *Perf. 12x12½*

414 A108 30m red, blue & brn. 30 8

15th Congress of Mongolian Communist Party.

Wrestling
A109

Designs: Various wrestling holds.

1966, June 15 Photo. *Perf. 11½x12*

415	A109	10m multicolored	5	3
416	"	30m "	10	8
417	"	60m "	35	16
418	"	80m "	40	25
419	"	1t "	50	40
		Nos. 415–419 (5)	1.40	92

World Wrestling Championship, Toledo, Spain.

Emblem and Map of Mongolia
A110

Sukhe Bator, Grain and Factories
A111

Perf. 11½x12, 12x11½

1966, July 11 Lithographed

420	A110	30m red & multi.	25	15
421	A111	50m " "	40	25

45th anniversary of independence.

Lilium Tenuifolium
A112

1966, Oct. 15 Photo. *Perf. 12x11½*

Multicolored

422	A112	5m *Physochlaena physaloides*	10	3
423	"	10m *Allium polyrrchizum*	10	5
424	"	15m *shown*	15	6
425	"	20m *Thermopsis lanceolata*	20	8
426	"	30m *Amygdalus mongolica*	30	15
427	"	60m *Caryopteris mongolica*	40	20
428	"	80m *Piptanthus mongolicus*	50	30
429	"	1t *Iris bungei*	75	45
		Nos. 422–429 (8)	2.50	1.32

Nos. 290–291 Overprinted: "1906/1966"

1966, Oct. 26 Photo. *Perf. 15x14½*

430	A81	30m brown	40	12
431	"	50m bluish green	50	20

60th anniversary of birth of D. Natsagdorji, writer.

Child with Dove
A113

Perf. 11½x12, 12x11½

1966, Dec. 2

Multicolored

432	A113	10m *shown*	8	5
433	"	15m *Children with reindeer*	10	8
434	"	20m *Boys wrestling* (vert.)	20	10
435	"	30m *Horseback riding*	30	15
436	"	60m *Children riding camel* (vert.)	35	25
437	"	80m *Child with sheep*	50	30
438	"	1t *Boy archer* (vert.)	75	50
		Nos. 432–438 (7)	2.28	1.43

Children's Day.

Proton 1—114

Perf. 11½x12½, 12½x11½

1966, Dec. 28 Photogravure

Multicolored

439	A114	5m *Vostok 2* (vert.)	5	3
440	"	10m *shown*	10	6
441	"	15m *Telstar 1* (vert.)	15	8
442	"	20m *Molnija 1* (vert.)	20	12
443	"	30m *Syncom 3* (vert.)	25	18
444	"	60m *Luna 9*	35	24
445	"	80m *Luna 12* (vert.)	50	32
446	"	1t *Mariner 4*	75	40
		Nos. 439–446 (8)	2.35	1.43

Space exploration.

Tarbosaurus
A115

1967, Mar. 31 *Perf. 12x11½*

Multicolored

447	A115	5m *shown*	5	3
448	"	10m *Talarurus*	10	6
449	"	15m *Proceratops*	15	12
450	"	20m *Indricotherium*	25	15
451	"	30m *Saurolophus*	30	18
452	"	60m *Mastodon*	35	24
453	"	80m *Mongolotherium*	50	32
454	"	1t *Mammoth*	75	40
		Nos. 447–454 (8)	2.45	1.50

Prehistoric animals.

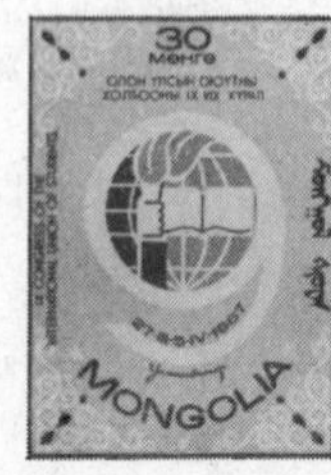

Congress Emblem
A116

1967, June 9 Litho. *Perf. 12*

455	A116	30m lt. bl. & multi.	20	8
456	"	50m pink & multi.	30	15

9th Youth Festival for Peace and Friendship, Sofia.

Sukhe Bator and Soldiers
A117

Design: 60m, Lenin and soldiers.

1967, Oct. 25 Litho. *Perf. 11½x12*

457	A117	40m red & multi.	30	20
458	"	60m " "	40	25

50th anniversary of the Russian October Revolution.

Ice Hockey and Olympic Rings
A118

1967, Dec. 29 *Perf. 12x12½*

Multicolored

459	A118	5m *Figure skating*	5	3
460	"	10m *Speed skating*	10	6
461	"	15m *shown*	15	8
462	"	20m *Ski jump*	20	12
463	"	30m *Bobsledding*	30	18
464	"	60m *Figure skating, pair*	40	30
465	"	80m *Slalom*	60	40
		Nos. 459–465 (7)	1.80	1.17

Souvenir Sheet

Perf. 12

466	A118	4t *Women's figure skating*	3.00	3.00

10th Winter Olympic Games, Grenoble, France, Feb. 6–18. No. 466 contains one stamp. Blue margin with Grenoble Olympics emblem and snowflake design. Size: 91x91mm.

Bactrian Camels
A119

1968, Jan. 15 Photo. *Perf. 12*

Multicolored

467	A119	5m *shown*	10	3
468	"	10m *Yak*	20	5
469	"	15m *Lamb*	25	8
470	"	20m *Foal*	30	10
471	"	30m *Calf*	35	15
472	"	60m *Bison*	40	20
473	"	80m *Roe deer*	55	25
474	"	1t *Reindeer*	80	40
		Nos. 467–474 (8)	2.95	1.26

Young animals.

Black Currants
A120

Berries: 5m, Rosa acicularis. 15m, Gooseberries. 20m, Malus. 30m, Strawberries. 60m, Ribes altissimum. 80m, Blueberries. 1t, Hippophaë rhamnoides.

1968, Feb. 15 Litho. & Engr.

475	A120	5m blue & ultra.	8	5
476	"	10m buff & brown	8	5
477	"	15m lt. grn. & green	15	8
478	"	20m yellow & red	20	12
479	"	30m pink & carmine	30	18
480	"	60m sal. & org. brn.	35	20
481	"	80m pale & dull blue	50	30
482	"	1t lt. yel. & red	75	45
		Nos. 475–482 (8)	2.41	1.43

Nos. 406–407 Overprinted

ДЭХБ
20 ЖИЛ
WHO

1968, Apr. 16 Photo. *Perf. 12x11½*

483	A106	30m blue green, blue & gold	20	12
484	"	50m red, bl. & gold	30	20

World Health Organization, 20th anniversary.

Human Rights Flame
A121

1968, June 20 Litho. *Perf. 12*

485	A121	30m turq. & vio. bl.	20	12

International Human Rights Year.

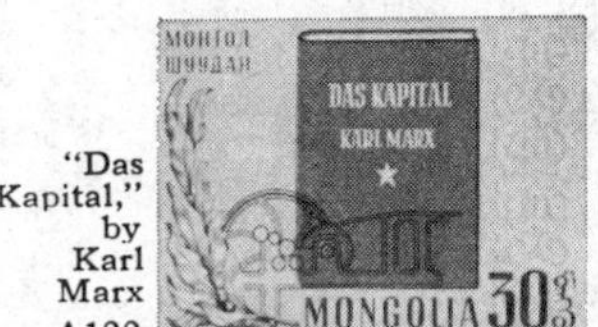

"Das Kapital," by Karl Marx
A122

Design: 50m, Karl Marx.

1968, July 1 Litho. *Perf. 12*

486	A122	30m blue & multi.	20	12
487	"	50m red & multi.	30	18

Sesquicentennial of the birth of Karl Marx (1818–1883).

Artist, by A. Sangatzohyo
A123

Paintings: 10m, On Remote Roads, by Sangatzohyo. 15m, Camel calf, by B. Avarzad. 20m, Milk, by Avarzad. 30m, The Bowman, by B. Gombosuren. 80m, Girl Sitting on Yak, by Sangatzohyo. 1.40t, Cagan Dara Eke, by Janaivajara. 4t, Meeting, by Sangatzohyo (horiz.).

1968, July 11 Litho. *Perf. 12*

488	A123	5m brn. & multi.		10	4
489	"	10m "	"	10	6
490	"	15m "	"	20	8
491	"	20m "	"	35	16
492	"	30m "	"	45	25
493	"	80m "	"	60	30
494	"	1.40t "	"	90	50
		Nos. 488-494 (7)		2.70	1.39

Miniature Sheets

Perf. 11½, Imperf.

495	A123	4t brn. & multi.	2.75	2.75

Paintings from national museum, Ulan Bator. No. 495 contains one stamp (54x84 mm.). Gray and carmine margin. Size: 119x84mm.

Volleyball A124

Sports (Olympic Rings and): 10m, Wrestling. 15m, Bicycling. 20m, Javelin, women's. 30m, Soccer. 60m, Running. 80m, Gymnastics, women's. 1t, Weight lifting. 4t, Equestrian.

1968, Sept. 1 Litho. *Perf. 12*

496	A124	5m multicolored	5	3
497	"	10m "	10	5
498	"	15m "	15	8
499	"	20m "	20	12
500	"	30m "	25	15
501	"	60m "	35	20
502	"	80m "	40	30
503	"	1t "	75	40
		Nos. 496-503 (8)	2.25	1.33

Souvenir Sheets

Perf. 11½, Imperf.

504	A124	4t org. & multi.	2.75	2.75

19th Olympic Games, Mexico City, Oct. 12–27. No. 504 contains one stamp (size: 52x44mm.). Blue and yellow margin with Olympic rings and inscription. Size: 90x 91mm.

Hammer, Spade & Cogwheel A125

1968, Sept. 17 Litho. *Perf. 11½*

505	A125	50m blue & verm.	20	12

Industrial development in town of Darhan.

Maxim Gorki A126

1968, Nov. 6 Litho. *Perf. 12*

506	A126	60m turq. & sepia	25	15

Birth centenary of Maxim Gorki (1868–1936), Russian writer.

Madonna and Child, by Boltraffio A127

Paintings: 10m, St. Roch Healed by an Angel, by Brescia. 15m, Madonna and Child with St. Anne, by Macchietti. 20m, St. John on Patmos, by Cano. 30m, Lady with Viola da Gamba, by Kupetzky. 80m, Boy, by Amerling. 1.40t, Death of Adonis, by Furini. 4t, Portrait of a Lady, by Renoir.

1968, Nov. 20 Litho. *Perf. 12*

507	A127	5m gray & multi.		5	4
508	"	10m "	"	15	8
509	"	15m "	"	20	12
510	"	20m "	"	30	15
511	"	30m "	"	40	20
512	"	80m "	"	60	30
513	"	1.40t "	"	70	40
		Nos. 507-513 (7)		2.40	1.29

Miniature Sheet

514	A127	4t gray & multi.	2.40	2.40

22nd anniversary of the United Nations Educational, Scientific and Cultural Organization (UNESCO). No. 514 contains one stamp with gray and brown margin. Size: 84x119mm.

Jesse Owens, USA A128

Olympic Gold Medal Winners: 5m, Paavo Nurmi, Finland. 15m, Fanny Blankers-Koen, Netherlands. 20m, Laszlo Papp, Hungary. 30m, Wilma Rudolph, USA. 60m, Boris Sahlin, USSR. 80m, Donald Schollander, USA. 1t, Akinori Nakayama, Japan. 4t, Jigjidin Munhbat, Mongolia.

1969, Mar. 25 Litho. *Perf. 12*

515	A128	5m multicolored	5	4
516	"	10m "	10	5
517	"	15m "	15	10
518	"	20m "	25	12
519	"	30m "	30	18
520	"	60m "	30	20
521	"	80m "	40	30
522	"	1t "	70	40
		Nos. 515-522 (8)	2.25	1.39

Souvenir Sheet

523	A128	4t grn. & multi.	2.40	2.40

No. 523 contains one stamp with multicolored margin showing Mongolian flag bearer. Size: 110x80mm.

Bayit Woman A129

Regional Costumes: 10m, Torgut man. 15m, Dzakhachin woman. 20m, Khalkha woman. 30m, Dariganga woman. 60m, Mingat woman. 80m, Khalkha man. 1t, Bargut woman.

1969, Apr. 20 Litho. *Perf. 12*

524	A129	5m multicolored	5	3
525	"	10m "	10	5
526	"	15m "	15	8
527	"	20m "	20	10
528	"	30m "	25	15
529	"	60m "	35	24
530	"	80m "	40	30
531	"	1t "	65	40
		Nos. 524-531 (8)	2.15	1.35

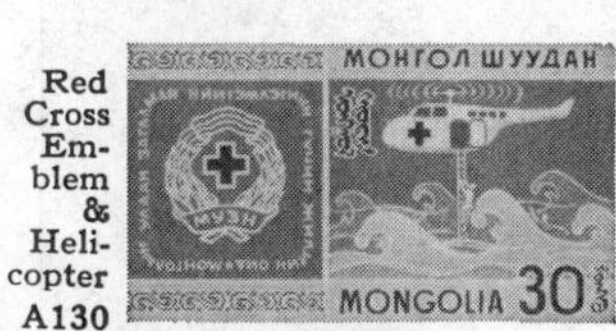

Red Cross Emblem & Helicopter A130

Design: 50m, Emblem, Red Cross car and shepherd.

1969, May 15 Litho. *Perf. 12*

532	A130	30m multicolored	20	12
533	"	50m "	30	20

30th anniversary of Mongolian Red Cross.

Landscape and Edelweiss—A131

Designs: Mongolian landscapes and flowers.

1969, May 20

Multicolored

534	A131	5m *shown*	5	3
535	"	10m *Pinks*	10	5
536	"	15m *Dianthus superbus*	15	8
537	"	20m *Geranium*	20	10
538	"	30m *Dianthus ramosissimus*	25	15
539	"	60m *Globeflowers*	35	24
540	"	80m *Delphinium*	40	32
541	"	1t *Haloxylon*	65	45
		Nos. 534-541 (8)	2.15	1.42

Bull Fight, by Tsewegdjaw—A132

Paintings from National Museum: 10m, Fighting Colts, by O. Tsewegdjaw. 15m, Horseman and Herd, by A. Sangatzohyo. 20m, Camel Caravan, by D. Damdinsuren. 30m, On the Steppe, by N. Tsultem. 60m, Milking Mares, by Tsewegdjaw. 80m, Going to School, by B. Avarzad. 1t, After Work, by G. Odon. 4t, Horses, by Damdinsuren.

1969, July 11 Litho. *Perf. 12*

542	A132	5m multicolored	5	4
543	"	10m "	5	5
544	"	15m "	15	10
545	"	20m "	20	12
546	"	30m "	25	15
547	"	60m "	35	18
548	"	80m "	40	30
549	"	1t "	65	40
		Nos. 542-549 (8	2.10	1.34

Souvenir Sheet

550	A132	4t multicolored	2.00	2.00

10th anniversary of cooperative movement. No. 550 contains one stamp (65x42 mm.). Design of painting extends into margin. Size: 120x85mm.

Mongolian Flag and Emblem A133

1969, Sept. 20 Litho. *Perf. 12*

551	A133	50m multicolored	25	12

Battle of Ha-lo-hsin (Khalka) River, 30th anniversary.

Nos. 420-421 Overprinted

ВНМАУ-ыг
түнхагласны
45
жилийн ой
1969–XI–26

Perf. 11½x12, 12x11½

1969, Nov. 26 Photogravure

552	A110	30m red & multi.	20	12
553	A111	50m " "	30	20

45th anniversary of Mongolian People's Republic.

Mercury 7—A134

Designs: 5m, Sputnik 3. 10m, Vostok 1. 20m, Voskhod 2. 30m, Apollo 8. 60m, Soyuz 5. 80m, Apollo 12.

1969, Dec. 6 Photo. *Perf. 12x11½*

554	A134	5m multicolored	10	3
555	"	10m "	10	5
556	"	15m "	15	8
557	"	20m "	20	10
558	"	30m "	30	15
559	"	60m "	45	30
560	"	80m "	70	40
		Nos. 554-560 (7)	2.00	1.11

Souvenir Sheet

561	A134	4t multicolored	3.50	3.50

Space achievements of US and USSR. No. 561 contains one stamp. Lilac margin with earth and moon. Size: 109x77mm.

Wolf—A135

Designs: 10m, Brown bear. 15m, Lynx. 20m, Wild boar. 30m, Moose. 60m, Bobac marmot. 80m, Argali. 1t, Old wall carpet showing hunter and dog.

1970, Mar. 25 Photo. *Perf. 12*

562	A135	5m multicolored	5	3
563	"	10m "	5	3
564	"	15m "	15	6
565	"	20m "	20	8
566	"	30m "	20	10
567	"	60m "	30	18

568	A135	80m multicolored	45	25
569	"	1t "	60	40
		Nos. 562-569 (8)	2.00	1.13

Lenin and Mongolian Delegation, by Sangatzohyo—A136

Designs: 20m, Lenin, embroidered panel, by Cerenhuu (vert.). 1t, Lenin, by Mazhig (vert.).

Photogravure & Lithographed

1970, Apr. 22 ***Perf. 12***

570	A136	20m multicolored	5	3
571	"	50m "	25	15
572	"	1t lt. bl., blk. & red	60	35

Centenary of the birth of Lenin.

Souvenir Sheet

EXPO '70 Pavilion of Matsushita Electric Co. and Time Capsule A137

1970, May 26 **Photo.** ***Perf. 12½***

573	A137	4t gold & multi.	3.00	3.00

EXPO '70 International Exposition, Osaka, Japan, Mar. 15-Sept. 13. No. 573 contains one stamp. Multicolored margin shows Sun Tower, USSR pavilion and EXPO '70 emblem. Size: 110x81mm.

Sumitomo Fairy Tale Pavilion A138

1970, June 5 **Photo.** ***Perf. 12x11½***

574	A138	1.50t multicolored	75	75

EXPO '70 International Exposition, Osaka. No. 574 printed in sheets of 20 (5x4) with alternating horizontal rows of tabs showing various fairy tales and EXPO '70 emblem.

Soccer, Rimet Cup—A139

Designs: Soccer players of various teams in action.

1970, June 20 ***Perf. 12½x11½***

575	A139	10m multicolored	10	5
576	"	20m "	10	8
577	"	30m "	15	12
578	"	50m "	20	15
579	"	60m "	30	20
580	"	1t "	60	40
581	"	1.30t "	75	55
		Nos. 575-581 (7)	2.20	1.55

Souvenir Sheet

Perf. 12½

582	A139	4t multicolored	3.00	2.50

World Soccer Championship for Jules Rimet Cup, Mexico City, May 30-June 21. No. 582 contains one stamp (51x37mm.). Multicolored margin shows Mexico City Stadium. Size: 120x95mm.

Old World Buzzard A140

Birds of Prey: 20m, Tawny owls. 30m, Northern goshawk. 50m, White-tailed sea eagle. 60m, Peregrine falcon. 1t, Old world kestrel. 1.30t, Black kite.

1970, June 30 **Litho.** ***Perf. 12***

583	A140	10m blue & multi.	10	4
584	"	20m pink & multi.	10	6
585	"	30m yellow green & multi.	20	10
586	"	50m blue & multi.	25	15
587	"	60m yellow & multi.	30	18
588	"	1t green & multi.	50	35
589	"	1.30t blue & multi.	75	40
		Nos. 583-589 (7)	2.20	1.28

Russian War Memorial, Berlin A141

1970, July 11 **Litho.** ***Perf. 12***

590	A141	60m blue & multi.	25	15

25th anniversary of end of World War II.

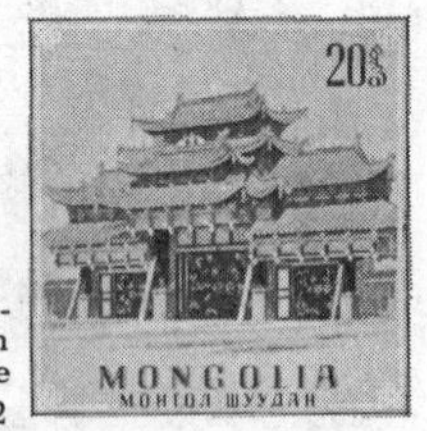

Bogdo-Gegen Palace A142

Designs: 10m, Archer. 30m, Horseman. 40m, "White Mother" Goddess. 50m, Girl in national costume. 60m, Lion statue. 70m, Dancer's mask. 80m, Detail from Bogdo-Gegen Palace, Ulan Bator.

1970, Sept. 20 **Litho.** ***Perf. 12***

591	A142	10m multicolored	10	10
592	"	20m "	15	15
593	"	30m "	25	25
594	"	40m "	30	30
595	"	50m "	40	40
596	"	60m "	50	50
597	"	70m "	60	60
598	"	80m "	75	75
		Nos. 591-598 (8)	3.05	3.05

Nos. 595-598 printed se-tenant in blocks of 4, in sheets of 40.

Souvenir Sheet

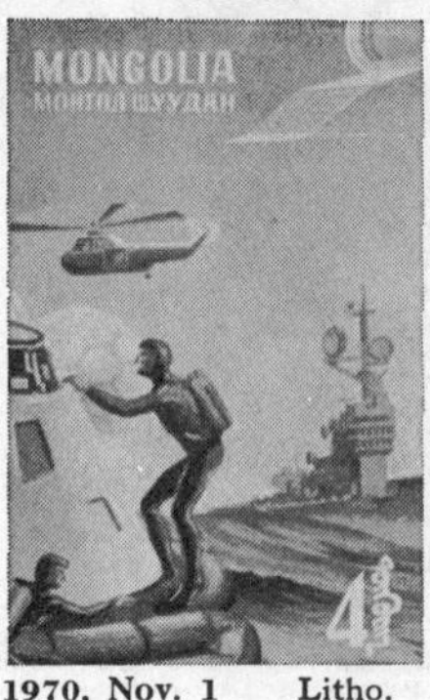

Recovery of Apollo 13 Capsule A143

1970, Nov. 1 **Litho.** ***Perf. 12***

599	A143	4t blue & multi.	2.75	2.75

Space missions of Apollo 13, Apr. 11-17, and Soyuz 9, June 1-10, 1970. No. 599 contains one stamp. Multicolored margin and black control number. Size: 109x80 mm.

Mongolian Flag, UN and Education Year Emblems A144

1970, Nov. 7

600	A144	60m multicolored	60	30

International Education Year.

Mounted Herald A145

1970, Nov. 7 **Litho.** ***Perf. 12***

601	A145	30m gold & multi.	20	12

50th anniversary of newspaper Unen (Truth).

Apollo 11 Lunar Landing Module A146

Designs: 10m, Vostok 2 and 3. 20m, Voskhod 2 and space walk. 30m, Gemini 6 and 7 capsules. 50m, Soyuz 4 and 5 docking in space. 60m, Soyuz 6, 7 and 8 group flight. 1t, Apollo 13 with damaged capsule. 1.30t, Luna 16 unmanned moon landing. 4t, Radar ground tracking station.

1971, Feb. 25 **Litho.** ***Perf. 12***

602	A146	10m multicolored	10	3
603	"	20m "	15	5
604	"	30m "	20	8
605	"	50m "	30	12
606	"	60m "	35	16
607	"	80m "	40	24
608	"	1t "	60	30
609	"	1.30t "	75	42
		Nos. 602-609 (8)	2.85	1.40

Souvenir Sheet

610	A146	4t vio. blue & multi.	3.00	3.00

US and USSR space explorations. No. 610 contains one stamp. Multicolored margin with rockets and parachuting capsule. Size: 120x90mm.

Rider with Mongolian Flag—A147

Designs: 30m, Party meeting. 90m, Lenin with Mongolian leader. 1.20t, Marchers, pictures of Lenin and Marx.

1971, Mar. 1 **Photo.** ***Perf. 12½***

611	A147	30m gold & multi.	15	6
612	"	60m " "	20	10
613	"	90m " "	25	20
614	"	1.30t " "	50	40

50th anniversary of Mongolian Revolutionary Party.

Souvenir Sheet

Lunokhod 1 on Moon A148

Design: No. 615b, Apollo 14 on moon.

1971, Apr. 15 **Photo.** ***Perf. 14***

615	A148	Sheet of 2	2.50	2.50
		a. 2t gold & multicolored	1.20	1.20
		b. 2t "	1.20	1.20

Luna 17 unmanned automated moon mission, Nov. 10-17, 1970, and Apollo 14 moon landing, Jan. 31-Feb. 9, 1971. No. 615 has gold frame, black marginal inscription and control number. Size: 112x95mm.

Dancer's Mask A149

Designs: Various masks for dancers.

1971, Apr. 25 **Litho.** ***Perf. 12***

616	A149	10m gold & multi.	10	3
617	"	20m " "	15	6
618	"	30m " "	20	12
619	"	50m " "	25	15
620	"	60m " "	30	20
621	"	1t " "	65	45
622	"	1.30t " "	85	50
		Nos. 616-622 (7)	2.50	1.51

Red Flag and Emblems A150

1971, May 31 Photo. *Perf. 12x11½*

623	A150	60m blue, red & gold	25	12

16th Congress of Mongolian Revolutionary Party.

Steam Locomotive—A151

1971, July 11 Litho. *Perf. 12*

Multicolored

624	A151	20m *shown*	10	6
625	"	30m *Diesel locomotive*	18	12
626	"	40m *Truck*	24	16
627	"	50m *Automobile*	30	20
628	"	60m *Biplane PO-2*	36	24
629	"	80m *AN-24 plane*	48	32
630	"	1t *Fishing boat*	60	40
		Nos. 624-630 (7)	2.26	1.50

50th anniversary of modern transportation.

Arms of Mongolia and Soldier A152

Design: 1.50t, Arms, policeman and child.

1971, July 11 Litho. *Perf. 12*

631	A152	60m multicolored	25	12
632	"	1.50t "	65	25

50th anniversary of the people's army and police.

Mongolian Flag and Emblem A153

1971, Aug. 25 Photo. *Perf. 12x11½*

633	A153	60m lt. bl. & multi.	25	12

International Year Against Racial discrimination.

Flag of Youth Organization—A154

1971, Aug. 25 Litho. *Perf. 12*

634	A154	60m org. & multi.	30	12

50th anniversary of Mongolian revolutionary youth organization.

The Woodsman and the Tiger A155

Designs: Various Mongolian fairy tales.

1971, Sept. 15 Litho. *Perf. 12*

635	A155	10m gold & multi.	10	4
636	"	20m " "	10	6
637	"	30m " "	15	10
638	"	50m " "	20	14
639	"	60m " "	30	18
640	"	80m " "	35	24
641	"	1t " "	45	35
642	"	1.30t " "	55	45
		Nos. 635-642 (8)	2.20	1.56

Bactrian Camel A156

1971, Nov. 1 Litho. *Perf. 12½*

Multicolored

643	A156	20m *Yaks*	10	6
644	"	30m *shown*	15	12
645	"	40m *Sheep*	15	15
646	"	50m *Goats*	25	18
647	"	60m *Cattle*	40	30
648	"	80m *Horses*	50	35
649	"	1t *White horse*	65	45
		Nos. 643-649 (7)	2.20	1.61

Mongolian livestock breeding.

Cross-country Skiing—A157

Designs (Sapporo Olympic Emblem and): 20m, Bobsledding. 30m, Women's figure skating. 50m, Slalom. 60m, Speed skating. 80m, Downhill skiing. 1t, Ice hockey. 1.30t, Figure skating, pairs. 4t, Ski jump.

Photogravure

1972, Jan. 20 *Perf. 12½x11½*

650	A157	10m multicolored	10	4
651	"	20m olive & multi.	10	5
652	"	30m ultra. & multi.	15	8
653	"	50m brt. bl. & multi.	20	15
654	"	60m multicolored	30	20
655	"	80m green & multi.	35	28
656	"	1t blue & multi.	45	35
657	"	1.30t vio. & multi.	55	45
		Nos. 650-657 (8)	2.20	1.60

Souvenir Sheet

Perf. 12½

658	A157	4t lt. bl. & multi.	2.75	2.75

11th Winter Olympic Games, Sapporo, Japan, Feb. 3-13. No. 658 contains one stamp. Gray and multicolored margin with Olympic rings and torch. Size: 110x89 mm.

Taming Wild Horse A158

Paintings: 20m, Mythological animal in winter. 30m, Lancer on horseback. 50m, Athletes. 60m, Waterfall and horses. 80m, The Wise Musician, by Sarav. 1t, Young musician. 1.30t, Old sage with animals.

1972, Apr. 15 Litho. *Perf. 12*

659	A158	10m multicolored	10	4
660	"	20m "	10	5
661	"	30m "	15	8
662	"	50m "	20	15
663	"	60m "	30	20
664	"	80m "	35	28
665	"	1t "	45	35
666	"	1.30t "	55	45
		Nos. 659-666 (8)	2.20	1.60

Paintings by contemporary artists in Ulan Bator Museum.

Calosoma Fischeri A159

Designs: Various insects.

1972, Apr. 30 Litho. *Perf. 12*

667	A159	10m multicolored	10	4
668	"	20m "	10	5
669	"	30m "	15	10
670	"	50m "	20	15
671	"	60m "	35	20
672	"	80m "	40	28
673	"	1t "	50	35
674	"	1.30t "	60	45
		Nos. 667-674 (8)	2.40	1.62

UN Emblem A160

1972, Aug. 30 Photo. *Perf. 12*

675	A160	60m multicolored	30	12

25th anniversary of the U.N. Economic Commission for Asia and the Far East (ECAFE).

Slow Lizard—A161

Designs: 15m, Radd's toad. 20m, Pallas's viper. 25m, Toad-headed agamid. 30m, Siberian wood frog. 60m, Przwalski's lizard. 80m, Taphrometopon lineolatum (snake). 1t, Stoliczka's agamid.

1972, Sept. 5 Litho. *Perf. 12*

676	A161	10m multicolored	10	4
677	"	15m "	10	5
678	"	20m "	15	10
679	"	25m "	20	15
680	"	30m "	25	20
681	"	60m "	40	28
682	"	80m "	50	35
683	"	1t "	60	45
		Nos. 676-683 (8)	2.30	1.62

Symbols of Technical Knowledge A162

Design: 60m, University of Mongolia.

1972, Sept. 25

684	A162	50m org. & multi.	25	12
685	"	60m lilac & multi.	30	18

30th anniversary of Mongolian State University.

Virgin and Child with St. John, by Bellini—A163

Paintings by Venetian Masters: 20m, Transfiguration, by Bellini (vert.). 30m, Virgin and Child, by Bellini (vert.). 50m, Presentation in the Temple, by Bellini. 60m, St. George, by Mantegna (vert.). 80m, Departure of St. Ursula, by Carpaccio (vert.). 1t, Departure of St. Ursula, by Carpaccio.

1972, Oct. 1

686	A163	10m multicolored	10	8
687	"	20m "	10	8
688	"	30m "	20	12
689	"	50m "	30	24
690	"	60m "	50	30
691	"	80m "	60	35
692	"	1t "	80	45
		Nos. 686-692 (7)	2.60	1.62

Save Venice campaign. See No. B3.

Manlay Bator Ramdinsuren A164

Designs: 20m, Ard Ayus (horiz.). 50m, Hatan Bator Magsarzhav. 60m, Has Bator (horiz.). 1t, Sukhe Bator.

1972, Oct. 20 Litho. *Perf. 12*

693 A164 10m gold & multi. 10 8
694 " 20m " " 20 12
695 " 50m " " 30 20
696 " 60m " " 45 35
697 " 1t " " 60 50
Nos. 693-697 (5) 1.65 1.25

Paintings of national heroes.

Spasski Tower, Moscow
A165

1972, Nov. 7 Photo. *Perf. 11*

698 A165 60m multicolored 25 15

50th anniversary of USSR. Printed with small label showing arms of USSR.

Mark Spitz, USA, Gold Medal
A166

Designs (Medal and): 10m, Ulrike Meyfarth, Germany. 20m, Sawao Kato, Japan. 30m, András Balczó, Hungary. 60m, Lasse Viren, Finland. 80m, Shane Gould, Australia. 1t, Anatoli Bondarchuk, USSR. 4t, Khorloo Baianmunk, Mongolia.

1972, Dec. 15 Photo. *Perf. 12½*

699 A166 5m green & multi. 10 5
700 " 10m verm. & multi. 10 8
701 " 20m blue & multi. 20 15
702 " 30m multicolored 30 18
703 " 60m lt. vio. & multi. 40 25
704 " 80m olive & multi. 50 35
705 " 1t lemon & multi. 60 50
Nos. 699-705 (7) 2.20 1.56

Souvenir Sheet

706 A166 4t red & multi. 2.75 2.75

Winners in 20th Olympic Games, Munich. No. 706 contains one stamp. Blue and multicolored margin with flags, Olympic emblems and flame. Size: 110x90mm.

Chimpanzee on Bicycle
A167

Circus Scenes: 10m, Seal playing ball. 15m, Bear riding wheel. 20m, Woman acrobat on camel. 30m, Woman equestrian. 50m, Clown playing flute. 60m, Woman gymnast. 1t, Circus building, Ulan Bator (horiz.).

1973, Jan. 29 Litho. *Perf. 12*

707 A167 5m multicolored 10 5
708 " 10m " 15 8
709 " 15m " 20 10
710 " 20m " 25 12
711 " 30m " 30 16
712 " 50m " 35 20
713 " 60m " 50 24
714 " 1t " 70 40
Nos. 707-714 (8) 2.55 1.35

Postrider
A168

Designs: 60m, Diesel locomotive. 1t, Truck.

1973, Jan. 31 Photo. *Perf. 12*

715 A168 50m brown 35 10
716 " 60m green 45 15
717 " 1t rose claret 75 30

See No. C34.

Sukhe Bator and Merchants
A169

Paintings of Sukhe Bator: 20m, With elders. 50m, Leading partisans. 60m, With revolutionary council. 1t, Receiving deputation (horiz.).

1973, Feb. 2 Photo. *Perf. 11½x12*

718 A169 10m gold & multi. 10 5
719 " 20m " " 20 10
720 " 50m " " 30 20
721 " 60m " " 40 30
722 " 1t " " 65 50
Nos. 718-722 (5) 1.65 1.15

80th anniversary of birth of Sukhe Bator (1893-1923).

Nicolaus Copernicus
A170

Marx and Lenin
A171

Designs: 60m, 2t, Copernicus in laboratory, by Jan Matejko (horiz.; 55x35mm.). 1t (No. 725, 726b), Portrait. 1t (No. 726a), like 50m.

1973, Mar. Litho. *Perf. 12*

723 A170 50m gold & multi. 30 18
724 " 60m " " 40 20
725 " 1t " " 60 30

Souvenir Sheet

726 A170 Sheet of 3 3.00 3.00
a. 1t multicolored 50 50
b. 1t " 50 50
c. 2t " 1.00 1.00

500th anniversary of the birth of Nicolaus Copernicus (1473-1543), Polish astronomer. No. 726 shows heliocentric system in multicolored margin. Size: 149x114mm.

1973, July 15 Photo. *Perf. 11½x12*

727 A171 60m gold, carmine & ultramarine 40 20

9th meeting of postal administrations of socialist countries, Ulan Bator.

Common Shelducks—A172

Designs: Aquatic birds.

1973, Aug. 10 Litho. *Perf. 12x11*

Multicolored

728 A172 5m *shown* 10 5
729 " 10m *Arctic loons* 10 8
730 " 15m *Bar-headed geese* 20 12
731 " 30m *Great crested grebe* 25 15
732 " 50m *Mallards* 35 25
733 " 60m *Mute swans* 45 35
734 " 1t *Greater scaups* 80 50
Nos. 728-734 (7) 2.25 1.50

1973, Aug. 25 Litho. *Perf. 12x11*

Designs: Fur-bearing animals.

Multicolored

735 A172 5m *Siberian weasel* 10 5
736 " 10m *Siberian chipmunk* 10 8
737 " 15m *Flying squirrel* 15 10
738 " 20m *Eurasian badger* 15 12
739 " 30m *Eurasian red squirrel* 20 16
740 " 60m *Wolverine* 40 30
741 " 80m *Mink* 50 35
742 " 1t *White hare* 60 45
Nos. 735-742 (8) 2.20 1.61

1973, Dec. 15 Litho. *Perf. 12x11*

Designs: Flowers.

Multicolored

743 A172 5m *Alpine aster* 10 5
744 " 10m *Mongolian silene* 10 8
745 " 15m *Rosa davurica* 15 10
746 " 20m *Mongolian dandelion* 15 12
747 " 30m *hododendron dahuricum* 25 16
748 " 50m *Clematis tangutica* 30 20
749 " 60m *Siberian primula* 45 30
750 " 1t *Pasqueflower* 70 45
Nos. 743-750 (8) 2.20 1.46

Globe and Red Flag Emblem
A173

1973, Dec. 10 Photo. *Perf. 12x12½*

751 A173 60m gold, red & blue 40 10

15th anniversary of the review "Problems of Peace and Socialism," published in Prague.

Limenitis Populi
A174

Butterflies: 10m, Arctia hebe. 15m, Rhyparia purpurata. 20m, Catocala pacta. 30m, Isoceras kaszabi. 50m, Celerio costata. 60m, Arctia caja. 1t, Diacrisia sannio.

1974, Jan. 15 Litho. *Perf. 11*

752 A174 5m lilac & multi. 10 5
753 " 10m brown & multi. 10 8
754 " 15m blue & multi. 15 10
755 " 20m brn. org. & multi. 15 10
756 " 30m lt. vio. & multi. 20 14
757 " 50m dull red & multi. 30 24
758 " 60m yel. grn. & multi. 40 35
759 " 1t ultra. & multi. 60 45
Nos. 752-759 (8) 2.00 1.51

"Hehe Namshil" by L. Merdorsh
A175

Designs (Various Scenes from): 20m, "Sive Hiagt," by D. Luvsansharav. 25m, 80m, 1t, "Edre," by D. Namdag. 30m, "The 3 Khans of Sara-Gol" (legend). 60m, "Amarsana," by B. Damdinsuren. 20m and 30m horizontal.

1974, Feb. 20 Litho. *Perf. 12*

760 A175 15m silver & multi. 15 8
761 " 20m " " 15 10
762 " 25m " " 20 15
763 " 30m " " 30 16
764 " 60m " " 45 28
765 " 80m " " 60 35
766 " 1t " " 70 45
Nos. 760-766 (7) 2.25 1.57

Mongolian operas and dramas.

Government Building and Sukhe Bator
A176

1974, Mar. 1 Photo. *Perf. 11*

767 A176 60m gold & multi. 40 18

50th anniversary of renaming capital Ulan Bator.

Juggler
A177

Designs: 10m, Dressage (horiz.). 30m, Trained elephant. 40m, Yak pushing ball (horiz.). 60m, Acrobats with ring. 80m, Woman acrobat on unicycle.

1974, May 4 Litho. *Perf. 12*

768	A177	10m multicolored	6	5
769	"	20m "	12	8
770	"	30m "	18	12
771	"	40m "	24	18
772	"	60m "	36	28
773	"	80m "	48	35
		Nos. 768-773, C65 (7)	2.14	1.51

Mongolian Circus. No. 773 has se-tenant label, with similar design.

Girl on Bronco—A178

Children's Activities: 20m, Boy roping calf. 30m, 40m, Boy taming horse (different designs). 60m, Girl with doves. 80m, Wrestling. 1t, Dancing.

1974, June 2 Litho. *Perf. 12*

774	A178	10m dull yel. & multi.	6	3
775	"	20m lt. blue & multi.	12	8
776	"	30m green & multi.	18	14
777	"	40m yellow & multi.	30	18
778	"	60m pink & multi.	45	24
779	"	80m blue & multi.	60	35
780	"	1t dull bl. & multi.	80	45
		Nos. 774-780 (7)	2.51	1.47

Children's Day.

Archer
A179

National Sports: 20m, Two horsemen fighting for goatskin. 30m, Archer on horseback. 40m, Horse race. 60m, Riding wild horse. 80m, Rider chasing riderless horse. 1t, Boys wrestling.

1974, July 11 Photo. *Perf. 11*

781	A179	10m vio. bl. & multi.	6	4
782	"	20m yel. & multi.	12	8
783	"	30m lilac & multi.	18	12
784	"	40m multicolored	25	18
785	"	60m "	40	24
786	"	80m "	60	36
787	A179	1t multicolored	80	48
		Nos. 781-787 (7)	2.41	1.50

Nadam, Mongolian national festival.

Grizzly Bear
A180

1974, July Lithographed *Perf. 12*

Multicolored

788	A180	10m *shown*	6	4
789	"	20m *Common panda*	12	8
790	"	30m *Giant panda*	18	12
791	"	40m *Two brown bears*	25	18
792	"	60m *Sloth bear*	40	28
793	"	80m *Asiatic black bears*	60	36
794	"	1t *Giant brown bear*	80	48
		Nos. 788-794 (7)	2.41	1.54

Stag in Zuun Araat Wildlife Preserve—A181

1974, Sept. Litho. *Perf. 12*

Multicolored

795	A181	10m *shown*	6	4
796	"	20m *Beaver*	12	8
797	"	30m *Leopard*	18	12
798	"	40m *Great black-backed gull*	25	16
799	"	60m *Deer*	40	28
800	"	80m *Mouflon*	60	36
801	"	1t *Deer and entrance to Bogd-uul Preserve*	80	48
		Nos. 795-801 (7)	2.41	1.52

Protected fauna in Mongolian wildlife preserves.

Buddhist Temple, Bogdo Gegen Palace—A182

Mongolian Architecture: 15m, Buddhist Temple, now Museum. 30m, Entrance to Charity Temple, Ulan Bator. 50m, Mongolian yurta. 80m, Gazebo in convent yard.

1974, Oct. 15 Lithographed *Perf. 12*

802	A182	10m blue & multi.	6	4
803	"	15m multicolored	10	5
804	"	30m green & multi.	20	15
805	"	50m multicolored	40	25
806	"	80m yel. & multi.	60	45
		Nos. 802-806 (5)	1.36	94

Spasski Tower, Sukhe Bator Statue
A183

1974, Nov. 26 Photo. *Perf. 11½x12*

807	A183	60m multicolored	40	15

Visit of General Secretary Brezhnev and a delegation from the USSR to participate in celebration of 50th anniversary of People's Republic of Mongolia.

Sukhe Bator Proclaiming Republic
A184

1974, Nov. 28 Lithographed

Designs: No. 808, "First Constitution," symbolic embroidery. No. 809, Flag over landscape, lane and communications tower.

808	A184	60m multicolored	40	15
809	"	60m "	40	15
810	"	60m "	40	15

50th anniversary of People's Republic of Mongolia.

Decanter
A185

Designs: 20m, Silver jar. 30m, Night lamp. 40m, Tea jug. 60m, Candelabra. 80m, Teapot. 1t, Silver bowl on 3-legged stand.

1974, Dec. 1 Photogravure

811	A185	10m blue & multi.	6	4
812	"	20m claret & multi.	12	8
813	"	30m multicolored	18	10
814	"	40m dp. bl. & multi.	25	15
815	"	60m multicolored	40	25
816	"	80m green & multi.	60	35
817	"	1t lilac & multi.	80	50
		Nos. 811-817 (7)	2.41	1.47

Mongolian 19th century goldsmiths' work.

Lapwing (plover)
A186

1974, Dec. Lithographed *Perf. 11*

Multicolored

818	A186	10m *shown*	6	4
819	"	20m *Fish*	12	8
820	"	30m *Marsh marigolds*	18	12
821	"	40m *White pelican*	30	20
822	"	60m *Perch*	40	30
823	"	80m *Mink*	60	40
		Nos. 818-823, C66 (7)	2.46	1.59

Water and nature protection.

American Mail Coach, UPU Emblem—A187

Designs (UPU Emblem and): 20m, French two-wheeled coach. 30m, Changing horses, Russian coach. 40m, Swedish caterpillar mail truck. 50m, First Hungarian mail truck. 60m, German Daimler-Benz mail truck. 1t, Mongolian dispatch rider.

1974, Dec. Litho. *Perf. 12*

824	A187	10m multicolored	6	4
825	"	20m "	12	8
826	"	30m "	18	12
827	"	40m "	30	20
828	"	50m "	40	25
829	"	60m "	50	30
830	"	1t "	80	50
		Nos. 824-830 (7)	2.36	1.49

See note after No. C68.

Mongolian Flag, Broken Swastika
A188

1975, May 9 Photo. *Perf. 11½x12*

832	A188	60m multicolored	40	18

30th anniversary of the end of World War II and victory over fascism.

Mongolian Woman
A189

1975, May

833	A189	60m multicolored	40	18

International Women's Year 1975.

Zygophyllum Xanthoxylon—A190

Medicinal Plants: 20m, Ingarvillea potaninii. 30m, Lancea tibetica. 40m, Jurinea mongolica. 50m, Saussurea involucrata. 60m, Allium mongolicum. 1t, Adonis mongolica.

1975, May 24 Photo. *Perf. 11x11½*

834	A190	10m dp. org. & multi.	6	3
835	"	20m green & multi.	12	8
836	"	30m yellow & multi.	18	12
837	"	40m violet & multi.	25	18
838	"	50m brown & multi.	40	25
839	"	60m blue & multi.	50	30
840	"	1t multicolored	80	50
		Nos. 834-840 (7)	2.31	1.46

12th International Botanists' Conference.

Shepherd A191

Puppet Theater: 20m, Boy on horseback. 30m, Boy and disobedient bull calf. 40m, Little orphan camel's tale. 50m, Boy and obedient little yak. 60m, Boy riding swan. 1t, Children's choir.

1975, June 30 Lithographed *Perf. 12*

841	A191	10m multicolored	6	3
842	"	20m "	12	8
843	"	30m "	18	12
844	"	40m "	25	18
845	"	50m "	40	25
846	"	60m "	50	30
847	"	1t "	80	50
		Nos. 841-847 (7)	2.31	1.46

Pioneers Tending Fruit Tree A192

Designs: 60m, Pioneers studying, and flying model plane. 1t, New emblem of Mongolian Pioneers.

1975, July 15 *Perf. 12x11½*

848	A192	50m multicolored	40	12
849	"	60m "	50	18
850	"	1t "	80	35

Mongolian Pioneers, 50th anniversary.

Nos. 624-630 Overprinted

Тээвэр—50
1975—7—15

1975, July 15 Litho. *Perf. 12*

850A	A151	20m multi.	1.00	1.00
850B	"	30m "	1.00	1.00
850C	"	40m "	1.25	1.25
850D	"	50m "	1.50	1.50
850E	"	60m "	1.75	1.75
850F	"	80m "	2.00	2.00
850G	"	1t "	3.00	3.00
		Nos. 850A-850G (7)	11.75	11.75

Fifty years of communication.

Golden Eagle Hunting Fox—A193

Hunting Scenes: 20m, Dogs treeing lynx (vert.). 30m, Hunter stalking marmots. 40m, Hunter riding reindeer (vert.). 50m, Boar hunt. 60m, Trapped wolf (vert.). 1t, Bear hunt.

1975, Aug. 25 Litho. *Perf. 12*

851	A193	10m multicolored	15	3
852	"	20m "	22	6
853	"	30m "	30	12
854	"	40m "	35	18
855	"	50m "	45	25
856	"	60m "	55	30
857	"	1t "	1.00	50
		Nos. 851-857 (7)	3.02	1.44

Hunting in Mongolia.

Mesocottus Haitej—A194

Various Fish: 20m, Pseudaspius lepto cephalus. 30m, Oreoleuciscus potanini. 40m, Tinca tinca. 50m, Coregonus lavaretus pidschian. 60m, Erythroculter mongolicus. 1t, Carassius auratus.

1975, Sept. 15 Photo. *Perf. 11*

858	A194	10m multicolored	6	3
859	"	20m "	12	8
860	"	30m "	18	10
861	"	40m blue & multi.	25	18
862	"	50m grn. & multi.	40	25
863	"	60m lilac & multi.	50	30
864	"	1t vio. bl. & multi.	80	50
		Nos. 858-864 (7)	2.31	1.44

Neck and Bow of Musical Instrument (Morin Hur) A195

National Handicraft: 20m, Saddle. 30m, Silver headgear. 40m, Boots. 50m, Tasseled Woman's cap. 60m, Pipe and tobacco pouch. 1t, Sable cap.

1975, Oct. 10 Litho. *Perf. 11½x12½*

865	A195	10m multicolored	6	3
866	"	20m "	12	6
867	"	30m "	18	12
868	"	40m "	25	18
869	"	50m "	40	25
870	"	60m "	50	30
871	"	1t "	80	50
		Nos. 865-871 (7)	2.31	1.44

Revolutionists with Flags A196

1975, Nov. 15 Litho. *Perf. 11½x12*

872	A196	60m multicolored	40	18

70th anniversary of Russian Revolution.

Ski Jump, Olympic Games Emblem A197

Designs (Winter Olympic Games Emblem and): 20m, Ice hockey. 30m, Skiing. 40m, Bobsled. 50m, Biathlon. 60m, Speed skating. 1t, Figure skating, women's. 4t, Skier carrying torch.

1975, Dec. 20 Litho. *Perf. 11½x12½*

873	A197	10m multicolored	6	3
874	"	20m "	12	6
875	"	30m brn. & multi.	18	12
876	"	40m grn. & multi.	25	18
877	"	50m multicolored	40	25
878	"	60m olive & multi.	50	30
879	"	1t multicolored	80	50
		Nos. 873-879 (7)	2.31	1.44

Souvenir Sheet

880	A197	4t multicolored	3.25	3.25

12th Winter Olympic Games, Innsbruck, Austria, Feb. 4-15, 1976. No. 880 has multicolored margin showing mountain range and Winter Olympic Games emblem. Size: 110x70mm.

Taming Wild Horse A198

Paintings: 20m, Camel caravan (horiz.). 30m, Man playing lute. 40m, Woman adjusting headdress (horiz.). 50m, Woman wearing ceremonial costume. 60m, Women fetching water. 1t, Woman musician. 4t, Warrior on horseback.

1975, Nov. 30 *Perf. 12*

881	A198	10m brn. & multi.	6	3
882	"	20m blue & multi.	12	6
883	"	30m olive & multi.	18	12
884	"	40m lilac & multi.	25	18
885	"	50m blue & multi.	40	25
886	"	60m lilac & multi.	50	30
887	"	1t silver & multi.	80	50
		Nos. 881-887 (7)	2.31	1.44

Souvenir Sheet

888	A198	4t blue & multi.	3.00	3.00

Mongolian paintings. No. 888, multicolored margin showing palette and horseback rider. Size: 110x90mm.

House of Young Technicians A199

Designs: 60m, Hotel Ulan Bator. 1t, Musem of the Revolution.

1975 Photo. *Perf. 12x11½*

893	A199	50m ultramarine	40	15
894	A199	60m blue green	50	20
895	"	1t brick red	80	35

Issue date: Dec. 30.

Camels in Gobi Desert—A200

Designs: 20m, Horse taming. 30m, Horseback riding. 40m, Pioneers' camp. 60m, Young musician. 80m, Children's festival. 1t, Mongolian wrestling.

1976, June 1 Litho. *Perf. 12*

896	A200	10m multicolored	6	3
897	"	20m "	12	5
898	"	30m "	18	10
899	"	40m "	30	18
900	"	60m "	40	25
901	"	80m "	60	40
902	"	1t "	80	50
		Nos. 896-902 (7)	2.46	1.51

International Children's Day.

Red Star A201

1976, May 1 Photo. *Perf. 11x12½*

903	A201	60m red, maroon & silver	45	10

17th Congress of the Mongolian People's Revolutionary Party, June 14.

Archery, Montreal Games' Emblem, Canadian Flag—A202

Designs (Montreal Olympic Games' Emblem, Canadian Flag and): 20m, Judo. 30m, Boxing. 40m, Vaulting. 60m, Weight lifting. 80m, High Jump. 1t, Target shooting.

1976, May 20 Litho. *Perf. 12½x11½*

904	A202	10m yellow & multi.	6	3
905	"	20m " "	12	5
906	"	30m " "	18	10
907	"	40m " "	30	18
908	"	60m " "	50	25
909	"	80m " "	60	40
910	"	1t " "	80	50
		Nos. 904-910 (7)	2.56	1.51

21st Olympic Games, Montreal, Canada, July 17-Aug. 1. See No. C81.

Partisans A203

Fighter and Sojombo Independence Symbol
A204

Perf. 12x11½, 11½x12

1976, June 15 **Lithographed**

911 A203 60m multicolored 50 20
912 A204 60m " 60 20

55th anniversary of Mongolia's independence. See No. C82.

Souvenir Sheet

Sukhe Bator Medal—A205

1976, July 11 ***Perf. 11½***

913 A205 4t multicolored 3.00 3.00

Mongolian honors medals. No. 913 has ultramarine and multicolored margin showing various Mongolian medals. Size: 115x76mm.

Osprey—A206

Protected Birds: 20m, Griffon vulture. 30m, Bearded lammergeier. 40m, Marsh harrier. 60m, Black vulture. 80m, Golden eagle. 1t, Tawny eagle.

1976, Aug. 16 **Litho.** ***Perf. 12***

914 A206 10m multicolored 6 3
915 " 20m " 12 5
916 " 30m " 18 10
917 " 40m " 30 18
918 " 60m " 50 25
919 " 80m " 60 40
920 " 1t " 80 50
Nos. 914-920 (7) 2.56 1.51

"Nadom" Military Game—A207

Paintings by O. Cevegshava: 10m, Taming Wild Horse (vert.). 30m, Hubsugul Lake Harbor. 40m, The Steppe Awakening. 80m, Wrestlers. 1.60t, Yak Descending in Snow (vert.).

1976, Sept. **Litho.** ***Perf. 12***

921 A207 10m multicolored 6 3
922 " 20m " 12 5
923 A207 30m multicolored 20 10
924 " 40m " 30 18
925 " 80m " 60 40
926 " 1.60t " 80 50
Nos. 921-926 (6) 2.08 1.26

Interlocking Circles, Industry and Transport
A208

1976, Oct. 15 **Photo.** ***Perf. 12x11½***

927 A208 60m brn., bl. & red 50 25

Soviet-Mongolian friendship.

John Naber, US Flag, Gold Medals
A209

Designs: 20m, Nadia Comaneci, Romanian flag. 30m, Kornelia Ender, East German flag. 40m, Mitsuo Tsukahara, Japanese flag. 60m, Gregor Braun, German flag. 80m, Lasse Viren, Finnish flag. 1t, Nikolai Andrianov, Russian flag.

1976, Nov. 30 **Litho.** ***Perf. 12***

928 A209 10m multicolored 6 3
929 " 20m " 12 5
930 " 30m " 20 10
931 " 40m " 30 18
932 " 60m " 50 25
933 " 80m " 60 40
934 " 1t " 80 50
Nos. 928-934 (7) 2.58 1.51

Gold medal winners, 21st Olympic Games, Montreal. See No. C83.

Stone Tablet on Tortoise
A210

Carved Tablet, 6th-8th Centuries
A211

1976, Dec. 15 **Litho.** ***Perf. 11½x12***

935 A210 50m brn. & lt. blue 40 20
936 A211 60m gray & bright green 50 25

International Archaeological Conference, Ulan Bator.

R-1 Plane—A212

Designs: Various Mongolian planes.

1976, Dec. 22 ***Perf. 12***

937 A212 10m multicolored 8 3
938 " 20m " 15 5
939 A212 30m multicolored 20 10
940 " 40m " 25 15
941 " 60m " 50 25
942 " 80m " 60 35
943 " 1t " 70 45
Nos. 937-943 (7) 2.48 1.38

Dancers—A213

Folk Dances: 20m, 13th century costumes. 30m, West Mongolian dance. 40m, "Ekachi," or horse-dance. 60m, "Bielge," West Mongolian trunk dance. 80m, "Hodak," or friendship dance. 1t, "Dojarka."

1977, Mar. 20 **Litho.** ***Perf. 12½***

944 A213 10m multicolored 8 3
945 " 20m " 15 8
946 " 30m " 20 10
947 " 40m " 25 18
948 " 60m " 50 25
949 " 80m " 60 40
950 " 1t " 70 50
Nos. 944-950 (7) 2.48 1.54

Miniature Sheet

Path of Pioneer from Earth to Jupiter, deflected by Mars—A214

Isaac Newton
A215

1977, Mar. 31 **Litho.** ***Perf. 11½x12***

Green and Multicolored

951 Sheet of 9 3.00 1.50
a. A214 60m *shown* 30 15
b. A215 60m *Apple tree* 30 15
c. A214 60m *Sextant and planets* 30 15
d. " 60m *Astronauts in space* 30 15
e. A215 60m *shown* 30 15
f. A214 60m *Prism and spectrum* 30 15
g. " 60m *Rain falling on earth* 30 15
h. A215 60m *Motion of celestial bodies* 30 15
i. A214 60m *Pioneer 10 over Jupiter* 30 15

Sir Isaac Newton (1642-1727), English natural philosopher and mathematician, 250th death anniversary. Nos. 951a-951i arranged in 3 rows of 3. Nos. 951d and 951i inscribed AIR MAIL. Size of sheet: 170x139mm.

D. Natsagdorji, Writer, and Quotation—A216

Design: No. 953, Grazing horses, landscape, ornament and quotation.

1977 ***Perf. 11½x12***

952 A216 60m multicolored 50 25
953 " 60m " 50 25

D. Natsagdorji, founder of modern Mongolian literature. Label and vignette separated by simulated perforations.

Primitive Tortoises—A217

Prehistoric Animals: 20m, Ungulate (titanothere). 30m, Flying lizard. 40m, Entelodon (swine). 60m, Antelope. 80m, Hipparion. 1t, Aurochs.

1977, May 7 **Photo.** ***Perf. 12½***

954 A217 10m multicolored 8 4
955 " 20m " 15 5
956 " 30m " 20 10
957 " 40m " 25 18
958 " 60m " 50 25
959 " 80m " 60 40
960 " 1t " 70 50
Nos. 954-960 (7) 2.48 1.52

Souvenir Sheet

Mongolia, Type A2 and Netherlands No. 1—A218

1977, May 20

961 A218 4t multicolored 3.00

AMPHILEX '77 International Philatelic Exhibition, Amsterdam, May 27-June 5. No. 961 contains one stamp (37x52mm.); multicolored margin shows clipper ship. Size: 100x76mm.

Boys on Horseback—A219

Designs: 20m, Girl on horseback. 30m, Hunter on horseback. 40m, Grazing horses. 60m, Mare and foal. 80m, Grazing horse and student. 1t, White stallion.

1977, June 15 **Litho.** ***Perf. 12***

962 A219 10m multicolored 8 4
963 " 20m " 15 5
964 " 30m " 20 10
965 " 40m " 30 18
966 " 60m " 50 25
967 " 80m " 60 40
968 " 1t " 80 50
Nos. 962-968 (7) 2.63 1.52

The lack of a price for a listed item does not necessarily indicate rarity.

Copper and Molybdenum Plant, Vehicles
A220

1977, June 15 Litho. ***Perf. 12***

969 A220 60m multicolored 50 25

Erdenet, a new industrial town.

Bucket Brigade Fighting Fire—A221

Fire Fighting: 20m, Horse-drawn fire pump. 30m, Horse-drawn steam pump. 40m, Men in protective suits fighting forest fire. 60m, Modern foam extinguisher. 80m, Truck and ladder. 1t, Helicopter fighting fire on steppe.

1977, Aug. Litho. ***Perf. 12***

970 A221 10m multicolored 8 4
971 " 20m " 15 5
972 " 30m " 20 10
973 " 40m " 30 18
974 " 60m " 50 25
975 " 80m " 60 40
976 " 1t " 80 50
Nos. 970-976 (7) 2.63 1.52

Radar and Molnya Satellite on TV Screen
A222

1977, Sept. 12 Photo. ***Perf. 12x11½***

977 A222 60m gray, bl. & blk. 50 25

40th anniversary of Technical Institute.

Lenin Museum, Ulan Bator
A223

1977, Oct. 1 Litho. ***Perf. 12***

978 A223 60m multicolored 50 25

Inauguration of Lenin Museum in connection with the 60th anniversary of the Russian October Revolution.

Dove, Globe, Decree of Peace
A224

Designs: 50m, Cruiser Aurora and Russian flag (vert.). 1.50t, Globe and "Freedom."

Perf. 11½x12, 12x11½

1977, Oct. 1 Photogravure

979 A224 50m gold & multi. 40 22
980 " 60m " " 50 25
981 " 1.50t " " 1.20 68

60th anniversary of the Russian Revolution.

Aporia Crataegi—A225

Moths: 20m, Gastropacha quercifolia. 30m, Colias chrysoteme. 40m, Dasychira fascelina. 60m, Malocosoma neustria. 80m, Diacrisia sanno. 1t, Heodes virgaureae.

1977, Sept. 25 Photo. ***Perf. 12½***

982 A225 10m multicolored 8 4
983 " 20m " 15 5
984 " 30m " 20 10
985 " 40m " 30 18
986 " 60m " 50 25
987 " 80m " 60 40
988 " 1t " 80 50
Nos. 982-988 (7) 2.63 1.52

Giant Pandas—A226

Pandas: 10m, Eating bamboo (vert.). 30m, Female and cub in washtub (vert.). 40m, Male and cub playing with bamboo. 60m, Female and cub (vert.). 80m, Family. 1t, Male (vert.).

1977, Nov. 25 Litho. ***Perf. 12***

989 A226 10m multicolored 8 4
990 " 20m " 15 5
991 " 30m " 20 10
992 " 40m " 30 18
993 " 60m " 50 25
994 " 80m " 60 40
995 " 1t " 80 50
Nos. 989-995 (7) 2.63 1.52

Souvenir Sheet

Helen Fourment and her Children, by Rubens—A227

1977, Dec. 5 ***Perf. 11½x10½***

996 A227 4t multicolored 3.00 3.00

Peter Paul Rubens (1577-1640), 400th birth anniversary. No. 996 has silver and multicolored margin showing entire painting. Size: 51x36mm.

Ferrari Racing Car—A228

Experimental Racing Cars: 30m, Ford McLaren. 40m, Madi, USSR. 50m, Mazda. 60m, Porsche. 80m, Russian model car. 1.20t, The Blue Flame, U.S. speed car.

1978, Jan. 28 Litho. ***Perf. 12***

997 A228 20m multicolored 15 5
998 " 30m " 20 5
999 " 40m " 30 18
1000 " 50m " 40 25
1001 " 60m " 50 30
1002 " 80m " 60 40
1003 " 1.20t " 1.00 55
Nos. 997-1003 (7) 3.15 1.78

Boletus Variegatus—A229

Mushrooms: 30m, Russula cyanoxantha. 40m, Boletus aurantiacus. 50m, Boletus scaber. 60m, Russula flava. 80m, Lactarius resimus. 1.20t, Flammula spumosa.

1978, Feb. 28 Photo. ***Perf. 11x11½***

1004 A229 20m yel. & multi. 15 5
1005 " 30m " " 20 5
1006 " 40m " " 30 18
1007 " 50m " " 40 25
1008 " 60m " " 50 30
1009 " 80m " " 60 40
1010 " 1.20t " " 1.00 55
Nos. 1004-1010 (7) 3.15 1.78

Young Couple with Youth Flag
A230

1978, Apr. Litho. ***Perf. 11½x12***

1011 A230 60m multicolored 50 25

17th Congress of Mongolian Youth Organization, Ulan Bator, Apr. 1978.

Soccer, Sugar Loaf Mountain, Rio de Janeiro, Brazil 1950 Emblem—A231

Designs (Various Soccer Scenes and): 30m, Old Town Tower, Bern, Switzerland, 1954. 40m, Town Hall, Stockholm, Sweden, 1958. 50m, University of Chile, Chile, 1962. 60m, Parliament and Big Ben, London, 1966. 80m, Degolladeo Theater, Guadalajara, Mexico, 1970. 1.20t, Town Hall and TV Tower, Munich, Germany.

1978, Apr. 15 ***Perf. 12***

1012 A231 20m multicolored 15 5
1013 " 30m " 20 10
1014 " 40m " 30 18
1015 A231 50m multicolored 40 25
1016 " 60m " 50 30
1017 " 80m " 60 40
1018 " 1.20t " 1.00 55
Nos. 1012-1018 (7) 3.15 1.83

11th World Cup Soccer Championship, Argentina, June 1-25. See No. C109.

Capex Emblem, Eurasian Beaver and Canada No. 336—A232

Designs: 30m, Tibetan sand grouse and Canada No. 478. 40m, Red-throated loon and Canada No. 369. 50m, Argali and Canada No. 324. 60m, Eurasian brown bear and Canada No. 322. 80m, Moose and Canada No. 323. 1.20t, Great black-backed gull and Canada No. 343.

1978, June Litho. ***Perf. 12***

1019 A232 20m multicolored 15 5
1020 " 30m " 20 10
1021 " 40m " 30 18
1022 " 50m " 40 25
1023 " 60m " 50 30
1024 " 80m " 60 40
1025 " 1.20t " 1.00 55
Nos. 1019-1025 (7) 3.15 1.83

CAPEX '78 International Philatelic Exhibition, Montreal, June 9-18. See No. C110.

Marx, Engels and Lenin
A233

1978, July 11 Photo. ***Perf. 12x11½***

1026 A233 60m gold, blk. & red 50 25

50th anniversary of publication in Prague of "Problems of Peace and Socialism."

Souvenir Sheet

Outdoor Rest, by Amgalan
A234

Paintings by D. Amgalan: No. 1027b, Winter Night (dromedary and people in snow). No. 1027c, Saddling up.

1978, Aug. 10 Lithographed ***Perf. 12***

1027 Sheet of 3 *6.00*
a. A234 1.50t multicolored 1.20
b. " 1.50t " 1.20
c. " 1.50t " 1.20

Philatelic cooperation between Hungary and Mongolia, 20th anniversary. No. 1027 contains 3 stamps and 3 labels showing War Memorial, Ulan Bator; commemorative inscription; Elizabeth Bridge and Liberation Monument, Budapest. Blue and silver margin. Size: 100x133mm.

Papillon—A235

Dogs: 20m, Black Mongolian sheepdog. 30m, Puli. 40m, St. Bernard. 50m, German shepherd. 60m, Mongolian watchdog. 70m, Samoyed. 80m, Laika (1st dog in space) and rocket. 1.20t, Cocker spaniels and poodle.

1978, Sept. 25 **Litho.** ***Perf. 12***

1028	A235	10m multicolored	8	4
1029	"	20m "	15	5
1030	"	30m "	20	10
1031	"	40m "	30	15
1032	"	50m "	40	18
1033	"	60m "	50	25
1034	"	70m "	55	30
1035	"	80m "	60	35
1036	"	1.20t "	1.00	50
		Nos. 1028-1036 (9)	3.78	1.92

Open Book and Pen
A236

1978, Oct. 20 **Photo.** ***Perf. 12x11½***

1037	A236	60m car. & ultra.	50	25

Mongolian Writers' Association, 50th anniversary.

Souvenir Sheets

Clothed Maya, by Goya—A237

Melancholy, by Dürer
A238

Paintings: No. 1038b, "Ta Matete," by Gauguin. No. 1038c, Bridge at Arles, by Van Gogh.

1978, Oct. 30 **Litho.** ***Perf. 12***

1038		Sheet of 3+ 3 labels	4.00
	a.	A237 1.50t multicolored	1.20
	b.	" 1.50t "	1.20
	c.	" 1.50t "	1.20

Perf. 11½

1039	A238	4t black	3.25

Anniversaries of European painters: Francisco Goya (1746–1828); Paul Gauguin (1848–1903); Vincent van Gogh (1853–1890). Albrecht Dürer (1471–1528). Labels of No. 1038 show portraits of painters; gold, silver and black margin. Size: 100x130mm. Margin of No. 1039 shows entire etching. Size: 104x131mm.

Camel and Calf
A239

Bactrian Camels: 30m, Young camel. 40m, Two camels. 50m, Woman leading pack camel. 60m, Old camel. 80m, Camel pulling cart. 1.20t, Race.

1978, Nov. 30 **Litho.** ***Perf. 12***

1040	A239	20m multicolored	14	3
1041	"	30m "	20	8
1042	"	40m "	25	12
1043	"	50m "	32	15
1044	"	60m "	40	18
1045	"	80m "	52	25
1046	"	1.20t "	80	35
		Nos. 1040-1046 (7)	2.63	1.16

Flags of Comecon Members, Globe
A240

1979, Jan. 2 **Litho.** ***Perf. 12***

1047	A240	60m multicolored	40	15

30th anniversary of the Council of Mutual Assistance (Comecon).

Silver Tabby
A241

Domestic Cats: 30m, White Persian. 50m, Red Persian. 60m, Cream Persian. 70m, Siamese. 80m, Smoky Persian. 1t, Burmese.

1979, Feb. 10

1048	A241	10m multicolored	8	3
1049	"	30m "	20	8
1050	"	50m "	32	15
1051	"	60m "	40	18
1052	"	70m "	45	20
1053	"	80m "	52	25
1054	"	1t "	65	30
		Nos. 1048-1054 (7)	2.62	1.19

Potaninia Mongolica
A242

Flowers: 30m, Sophora alopecuroides. 50m, Halimodendron halodendron. 60m, Forget-me-nots. 70m, Pincushion flower. 80m, Leucanthemum Sibiricum. 1t, Edelweiss.

1979, Mar. 10 **Litho.** ***Perf. 12***

1055	A242	10m multicolored	8	3
1056	"	30m "	20	8
1057	"	50m "	32	15
1058	"	60m "	40	18
1059	"	70m "	45	20
1060	"	80m "	52	25
1061	"	1t "	65	30
		Nos. 1055-1061 (7)	2.62	1.19

Finland-Czechoslovakia, Finnish Flag—A243

Ice Hockey Games and 1980 Olympic Emblems: 30m, German Fed. Rep.–Sweden, German flag. 50m, USA–Canada, US flag. 60m, USSR–Sweden, Russian flag. 70m, Canada–USSR, Canadian flag. 80m, Swedish goalie and flag. 1t, Czechoslovakia–USSR, Czechoslovak flag.

1979, Apr. 10 **Litho.** ***Perf. 12***

1062	A243	10m multicolored	8	3
1063	"	30m "	20	8
1064	"	50m "	32	15
1065	"	60m "	40	18
1066	"	70m "	45	20
1067	"	80m "	52	25
1068	"	1t "	65	30
		Nos. 1062-1068 (7)	2.62	1.19

Ice Hockey World Championship, Moscow, Apr. 14–27.

Lambs—A244

Paintings: 30m, Milking, camels. 50m, Plane bringing supplies in winter. 60m, Herdsmen and horses. 70m, Milkmaids (vert.). 80m, Summer Evening (camels). 1t, Landscape with herd. 4t, After the Storm.

Perf. 12x11½, 11½x12

1979, May 3 **Lithographed**

1069	A244	10m multicolored	8	3
1070	"	30m "	20	8
1071	"	50m "	32	15
1072	"	60m "	40	18
1073	"	70m "	45	20
1074	"	80m "	52	25
1075	"	1t "	65	30
		Nos. 1069-1075 (7)	2.62	1.19

Souvenir Sheet

1076	A244	4t multicolored	2.75

20th anniversary of first agricultural cooperative. No. 1076 has multicolored margin showing grazing horses. Size: 86x70 mm.

SEMI-POSTAL STAMPS

Vietnamese Mother and Child
SP1

1967, Dec. 22 **Photo.** ***Perf. 12x11½***

B1	SP1	30m+20m multi.	20	12
B2	"	50m+30m "	30	20

Solidarity with Vietnam.

Souvenir Sheet

Save Venice Type of Regular Issue

Design: 3t+1t, Departure of St. Ursula, by Carpaccio.

1972, Oct. 1 **Litho.** ***Perf. 12***

B3	A163	3t+1t multi.	2.50	2.50

Save Venice Campaign. No. B3 contains one horizontal stamp. Multicolored margin with waterfront scene, gold border and black control number. Size: 90x110mm.

Girl Feeding Lambs
SP2

Designs (UNICEF Emblem and): 20+5m, Boy playing flute and dancing girl. 30+5m, Girl chasing butterflies. 40+5m, Girl with ribbon. 60+5m, Girl with flowers. 80+5m, Girl carrying bucket. 1t+5m, Boy going to school.

1977, June 1 **Litho.** ***Perf. 12***

B4	SP2	10m+5m multi.	10	4
B5	"	20m+5m "	18	5
B6	"	30m+5m "	30	18
B7	"	40m+5m "	40	25
B8	"	60m+5m "	60	30
B9	"	80m+5m "	70	40
B10	"	1t+5m "	90	55
		Nos. B4-B10 (7)	3.18	1.77

Surtax was for Mongolian Children's Village. See No. CB1.

Boys on Horseback
SP3

Mongolian Children and IYC Emblem: 30+5m, Raising chickens. 50+5m, With deer. 60+5m, With flowers. 70+5m, Planting tree. 80+5m, Studying space project. 1t+5m, Dancing. 4t+50m, Girl on horseback.

1979, Jan. 10

B11	SP3	10m+5m multi.	10	5
B12	"	30m+5m "	20	5
B13	"	50m+5m "	35	10
B14	"	60m+5m "	40	15
B15	"	70m+5m "	50	25
B16	"	80m+5m "	60	35
B17	"	1t+5m "	80	45
		Nos. B11-B17 (7)	2.95	1.40

Souvenir Sheet

B18	SP3	4t+50m multi.	3.50	3.50

International Year of the Child. No. B18 has multicolored margin showing boys on horseback. Size: 78x99mm.

AIR POST STAMPS

Postal Modernization Type of Regular Issue

Designs: 10m, 20m, Postman with horses. 25m, Postman with reindeer. 30m, 50m, Plane over map of Mongolia. 1t, Post horn and flag of Mongolia.

1961, June 5 Photo. ***Perf. 15***

C1	A72	10m multicolored	6	5
C2	"	50m "	30	20
C3	"	1t "	60	45

Souvenir Sheet

Perf. 11

C4	A72	Sheet of 4	1.50	1.50
		a. 20m lt. blue green. & multi.	35	35
		b. 25m lt. blue & multicolored	35	35
		c. 30m lt. green & multicolored	35	35
		d. 1t rose carmine & multi.	35	35

40th anniversary of independence; postal modernization. No. C4 has gold border with coat of arms. Size: 114x88mm. No. C4b is not inscribed Airmail.

Souvenir Sheet

Austria Type SP55, Austrian and Mongolian Stamps Circling Globe—AP1

1965, May 1 Engraved ***Perf. 11½***

C5	AP1	4t brown carmine	3.50	3.00

Vienna International Philatelic Exhibition, WIPA, June 4-13. No. C5 contains one stamp (size: 61x38mm.). WIPA emblem, Mongolian child and commemorative inscription in margin. Size: 90x128mm.

Weather Satellite AP2

Designs: 20m, Antarctic exploration. 30m, Space exploration.

1965, May 15 Photo. ***Perf. 13½***

C6	AP2	15m lilac, gold & blk.	18	10
C7	"	20m blue & multi.	20	12
C8	"	30m rose & multi.	25	20

International Quiet Sun Year, 1964-65.

ITU Emblem AP3

1965, Dec. 20 ***Perf. 11½x12***

C9	AP3	30m blue & bister	15	10
C10	"	50m red & bister	30	15

Souvenir Sheet

Design: 4t, Communications satellite.

Perf. 11, Imperf.

C11	AP3	4t gold, bl. & blk.	2.75	2.75

Centenary of International Communications Union. No. C11 contains one stamp, 38x51mm. Commemorative inscription and ITU emblem in margin. Size: 86x130 mm.

Souvenir Sheet

Luna 10, Moon and Earth AP4

1966, July 10 Photo. ***Imperf.***

C12	AP4	4t multicolored	3.25	2.50

Luna 10 Russian moon mission, Apr. 3, 1966. No. C12 contains one stamp. Gold border and dull blue marginal inscription. Size: 84x128mm.

Souvenir Sheet

Astronaut and Landing Module AP5

1969, Aug. 20 Litho. ***Perf. 11½***

C13	AP5	4t ultra. & multi.	2.75	2.75

Apollo 11 US moon mission, first man landing on moon. No. C13 contains one stamp. Multicolored margin showing moon, earth and space. Commemorative inscription and brown control number. Size: 85x120mm.

Souvenir Sheet

Apollo 16—AP6

Photogravure

1972, Apr. 16 ***Perf. 12½x11½***

C14	AP6	4t multicolored	3.00	3.00

Apollo 16 moon mission, Apr. 15-27. No. C14 contains one stamp. Multicolored margin with gold commemorative inscription and black control number. Size 110x91 mm.

Souvenir Sheet

Mongolian Horse—AP7

1972, May 10 Photo. ***Perf. 12½***

C15	AP7	4t multicolored	2.75	2.75

Centenary of the discovery of the Przewalski wild horse, bred in captivity in Berlin Zoo. No. C15 contains one stamp. Light yellow green margin with brown inscription and black control number. Size: 114x88mm.

Telecommunication—AP8

Designs: 30m, Horse breeding. 40m, Train and plane. 50m, Corn and farm machinery. 60m, Red Cross ambulance and hospital. 80m, Actors. 1t, Factories.

1972, July 11 Litho. ***Perf. 12***

C16	AP8	20m olive & multi.	10	5
C17	"	30m vio. & multi.	10	8
C18	"	40m rose & multi.	20	12
C19	"	50m red & multi.	30	18
C20	"	60m multicolored	50	24
C21	"	80m lt. bl. & multi.	50	32
C22	"	1t grn. & multi.	60	48
		Nos. C16-C22 (7)	2.30	1.47

Mongolian Achievements.

Mongolian Flag, Globe and Radar AP9

Photogravure

1972, July 20 ***Perf. 12½x11½***

C23	AP9	60m olive & multi.	40	25

International Telecommunications Day, May 17, 1972.

Running and Olympic Rings—AP10

Designs (Olympic Rings and): 15m, Boxing. 20m, Judo. 25m, High jump. 30m, Rifle shooting. 60m, Wrestling. 80m, Weight lifting. 1t, Mongolian flag and sport emblem. 4t, Woman archer (vert.).

Photogravure

1972, July 30 ***Perf. 12½x11½***

C24	AP10	10m multicolored	10	5
C25	"	15m "	10	5
C26	"	20m "	15	10
C27	"	25m "	20	12
C28	"	30m "	25	18
C29	"	60m "	35	28
C30	"	80m "	45	36
C31	"	1t "	70	48
		Nos. C24-C31 (8)	2.30	1.62

Souvenir Sheet

Perf. 11½x12½

C32	AP10	4t org. & multi.	3.00	3.00

20th Olympic Games, Munich, Aug. 26-Sept. 11. No. C32 contains one stamp. Blue margin with gold inscription and Olympic emblems. Size: 89x110mm.

Dragon and Mariner 2—AP11

1972, Dec. 4 Photo. *Perf. 12*

Bright Blue & Multicolored

C33	AP11	Sheet of 12	5.00	3.00

Size: 55x35mm.

a.	60m *Snake; Mars 1*	36	20
b.	60m *shown*	36	20
c.	60m *Hare; Soyuz 5*	36	20
d.	60m *Monkey; Explorer 6*	36	20
e.	60m *Cock; Venus 1*	36	20
f.	60m *Rat; Apollo 15*	36	20

Size: 35x35mm.

g.	60m *Horse; Apollo 8*	36	20
h.	60m *Boar; Cosmos 110*	36	20
i.	60m *Tiger; Gemini 7*	36	20
j.	60m *Sheep; Electron 2*	36	20
k.	60m *Dog; Ariel 2*	36	20
l.	60m *Ram; Venus 4*	36	20

Space achievements of US and USSR, and signs of Eastern Calendar.

Airliner AP12

1973, Jan. Photogravure *Perf. 12*

C34	AP12	1.50t blue	1.00	30

Weather Satellite, Earth Station, WMO Emblem—AP13

1973, Feb. Photo. *Perf. 12x11½*

C35	AP13	60m multicolored	40	18

Centenary of international meteorological cooperation.

Holy Flame Type of 1959

Souvenir Sheet

1973, Apr. 15 Photo. *Perf. 12½*

C36	A48	4t gold & multi.	3.00	3.00

IBRA München 1973 International Stamp Exhibition, Munich, May 11–20. No. C36 contains one stamp (size: 40x63mm.) in redrawn design of A48 with simulated perforations and wide gold margin. Multicolored sheet margin shows deity and clouds. Size: 81x115m.

Russia No. 3100 AP14

Designs: Stamps (with mail-connected designs) of participating countries.

1973, July 31 Litho. *Perf. 12½*

Multicolored

C37	AP14	30m *shown*	30	20
C38	"	30m *Mongolia No. 236*	30	20
C39	"	30m *Bulgaria No. 1047*	30	20
C40	"	30m *Hungary No. B202*	30	20
C41	"	30m *Czechoslovakia No. C72*	30	20
C42	"	30m *German Dem. Rep. No. 369*	30	20
C43	"	30m *Cuba No. C31*	30	20
C44	"	30m *Romania No. 2280*	30	20
C45	"	30m *Poland No. 802*	30	20
		Nos. C37–C45 (9)	2.70	1.80

Conference of Permanent Committee for Posts and Telecommunications of Council for Economic Aid (COMECON), Ulan Bator, Aug. 1973.

Launching of Soyuz Spacecraft AP15

1973, Oct. 26 Litho. *Perf. 12½*

Multicolored

C46	AP15	5m *shown*	10	5
C47	"	10m *Apollo 8*	10	8
C48	"	15m *Soyuz 4 & 5 docking*	15	10
C49	"	20m *Apollo 11 lunar module*	15	12
C50	"	30m *Apollo 14 splash-down*	30	16
C51	"	50m *Soyuz 6, 7 & 8*	40	24
C52	"	60m *Apollo 16 moon rover*	50	40
C53	"	1t *Lunokhod 1 on moon*	80	55
		Nos. C46–C53 (8)	2.50	1.70

Souvenir Sheet

C54	AP15	4t *Soyuz and Apollo*	2.50	2.50

American and Russian achievements in space. No. C54 contains one stamp. Violet margin with multicolored design showing flags of US and USSR, sky, earth and moon. Size: 110x90mm.

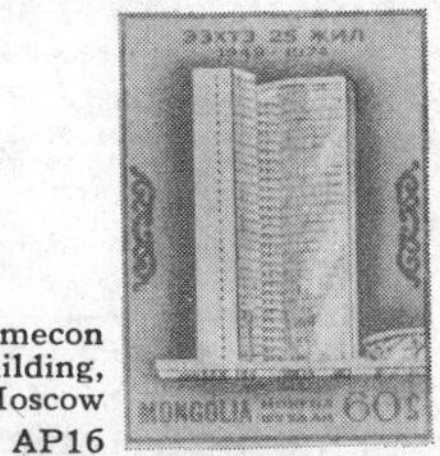

Comecon Building, Moscow AP16

1974, Feb. 28 Photo. *Perf 11½x12*

C55	AP16	60m blue & multi.	40	18

25th anniversary of the Council of Mutual Economic Assistance.

Unused prices are for stamps that have been hinged.

Souvenir Sheet

Mongolia No. 4—AP17

1974, Mar. 15 Photo. *Perf. 12½*

C56	AP17	4t multicolored	2.50	2.50

50th anniversary of first stamps of Mongolia. No. C56 has ultramarine and multicolored margin showing flag, postrider, mountains and plane. Size: 130x85 mm.

Postrider and UPU Emblem—AP18

Designs: UPU emblem and means of transportation.

1974, Apr. Lithographed *Perf. 12*

Multicolored

C57	AP18	50m *shown*	40	25
C58	"	50m *Reindeer post*	40	25
C59	"	50m *Mail coach*	40	25
C60	"	50m *Balloon post*	40	25
C61	"	50m *Steamship and AN-2 plane*	40	25
C62	"	50m *Train, truck and city*	40	25
C63	"	50m *Rocket over North Pole*	40	25
		Nos. C57–C63 (7)	2.80	1.75

Souvenir Sheet

C64	AP18	4t *Globe and post horn* (vert.)	3.50	3.50

Centenary of Universal Postal Union. No. C64 contains one stamp; bright magenta margin showing various means of transportation. Size: 100x90mm.

Circus Type of 1974

Design: 1t, Two women contortionists.

1974, May 4 Litho. *Perf. 12*

C65	A177	1t multicolored	70	45

Mongolian Circus. No. C65 has se-tenant label, with similar design.

Nature Type of Regular Issue

Designs: 1t, Scientist checking water, globe. 4t, Wild rose.

1974, Dec. Lithographed *Perf. 11*

C66	A186	1t multicolored	80	45

Souvenir Sheet

Perf. 12½

C67	A186	4t multicolored	3.00	3.00

Water and nature protection. No. C67 contains one stamp with multicolored margin showing sun, clouds and water. Size: 83x117mm.

UPU Type of 1974

Souvenir Sheet

Design: UPU Emblem (vert.).

1974, Dec. *Perf. 11½x12*

C68	A187	4t multicolored	3.50	3.50

Centenary of Universal Postal Union and for Stockholmia 74, International Philatelic Exhibition, Stockholm, Sept. 21–29. No. C68 contains one stamp; multicolored margin shows Stockholm Town Hall, Stockholmia 74 emblem, and Sweden No. 1. Size: 111x90mm.

Soyuz on Launching Pad, Project Emblem—AP19

Designs (Project Emblem and): 20m, Radar and Apollo. 30m, Apollo, Soyuz and earth. 40m, Spacecraft before docking. 50m, Spacecraft after docking. 60m, Soyuz circling earth. 1t, Spacecraft, space station and earth. 4t, Russian and American astronauts.

1975, June 14 Litho. *Perf. 12*

C69	AP19	10m blue & multi.	10	3
C70	"	20m multicolored	15	6
C71	"	30m sepia & multi.	20	12
C72	"	40m silver & multi.	25	18
C73	"	50m multicolored	40	30
C74	"	60m "	60	40
C75	"	1t "	80	55
		Nos. C69–C75 (7)	2.50	1.64

Souvenir Sheet

C76	AP19	4t blk. & multi.	4.00	3.50

Apollo Soyuz space test project (Russo-American space cooperation), launching July 15; link-up July 17. No. C76 contains one stamp; multicolored margin shows capsule interior. Size: 105x85mm.

Mongolian Mountain Sheep AP20

1975, Aug. 4 Litho. *Perf. 12*

C77	AP20	1.50t multicolored	1.20	45

South Asia Tourism Year 1975. No. C77 printed se-tenant with label showing modern hotel, map and stone turtle.

Satellite over Weather Map of Mongolia AP21

1976, Mar. 20 *Perf. 12x11½*

C78	AP21	60m blue & yellow	45	25

40th anniversary of meteorological service.

Souvenir Sheet

Girl with Books and Flowers—AP22

1976, Mar. 30 *Perf. 12*

C79	AP22	4t multicolored	3.00	3.00

30th anniversary of UNESCO (United Nations Educational, Scientific and Cultural Organization). No. C79 has orange margin with yellow and gray design. Size: 99½x 85mm.

Souvenir Sheet

The Wise Musician, by Sarav
AP23

1976, May 3 Litho. *Perf. 11½x12½*

C80 AP23 4t multicolored 3.00 3.00

Interphil 76 Philatelic Exhibition, Philadelphia, Pa., May 29–June 6. No. C80 has multicolored margin showing world map with Philadelphia. Size: 96x70mm.

Olympic Games Type of 1976
Souvenir Sheet

Design: 4t, Wrestling.

1976, May 20 *Perf. 12½x11½*

C81 A202 4t gold & multi. 3.00 3.00

21st Olympic Games, Montreal, Canada, July 17–Aug. 1. No. C81 contains one stamp, violet blue and ultramarine margin with space design, Montreal Games emblem and Canadian flag. Size: 104x78mm.

Independence Type of 1976

Design: 60m, Progress in agriculture and industry.

1976, June 20 Litho. *Perf. 12x11½*

C82 A203 60m multicolored 50 25

55th anniversary of Mongolia's independence.

Olympic Medalists Type, 1976
Souvenir Sheet

Design: 4t, Oidov Zeveg, Mongolian flag.

1976, Nov. 30 Litho. *Perf. 11x11½*

C83 A209 4t multicolored 3.00 3.00

Gold medal winner, 21st Olympic Games, Montreal. No. C83 contains one stamp; Prussian blue and multicolored margin with satellite, Montreal emblem, Canadian flag and Moscow 1980 emblem. Size: 104x78 mm.

Mounting Carrier Rocket with Bell-shaped Gear—AP24

Designs: 20m, Launching of Intercosmos 3. 30m, Marine Observatory Gagarin (ship). 40m, Satellite observation of lunar eclipse. 60m, Observatory with multiple antenna system. 80m, Examination of Van Allen Zone, magnetosphere. 1t, Meteorological earth satellite. 4t, Intercosmos satellite with lines showing participating countries on globe.

1977, June 20 Litho. *Perf. 12*

C84	AP24	10m	multicolored	8	4
C85	"	20m	"	15	5
C86	"	30m	"	20	13
C87	"	40m	"	30	18
C88	"	60m	"	50	30
C89	"	80m	"	60	42
C90	"	1t	"	80	55
	Nos. C84-C90 (7)			2.63	1.67

Souvenir Sheet
Perf. 12½

C91 AP24 4t multicolored 3.00 3.00

11th anniversary of Intercosmos program, cooperation of 9 socialist countries for space research. No. C91 contains one stamp (58x37mm.); multicolored margin shows Konstantin E. Tsiolkovsky and various spacecraft. Size: 125x90mm.

Trade Union Emblem, Factory and Sheep
AP25

1977, June *Perf. 12x11½*

C92 AP25 60m multicolored 50 25

11th Congress of Mongolian Trade Unions, May 12.

Montgolfier's Balloon—AP26

Dirigibles: 30m, Zeppelin over North Pole, 1931. 40m, Osoaviahim, Russian Arctic cargo. 50m, North, Russian heavy duty cargo. 60m, Aeron-340, Russian planned. 80m, Machinery transport, Russian planned. 1.20t, Flying crane, French planned. 4t, Russia No. C26 (stamp) and Sukhe Bator statue.

1977, Dec. Litho. *Perf. 12*

C93	AP26	20m	multicolored	15	5
C94	"	30m	"	20	10
C95	"	40m	"	30	18
C96	"	50m	"	40	22
C97	"	60m	"	50	25
C98	"	80m	"	60	35
C99	"	1.20t	"	85	55
	Nos. C93-C99 (7)			3.00	1.70

Souvenir Sheet
Perf. 12½x11½

C100 AP26 4t multicolored 3.00 3.00

History of airships. No. C100 has light and dark green margin showing portraits of Montgolfier brothers and Count Zeppelin. Size: 105x75mm.

A. F. Mozhaiski and his Plane, 1884—AP27

Designs: 30m, Henry Farman and his plane, 1909. 40m, Geoffrey de Havilland and D. H. 66 Hercules, 1920's. 50m, Charles A. Lindbergh, Spirit of St. Louis and route New York to Paris, 1927. 60m, Mongolian pilots Shagdarsuren and Demberel and plane over Altai Mountains, 1935. 80m, Soviet aviators Chkalov, Baidukov, Beliakov, plane and route Moscow to Vancouver, 1937. 1.20t, A. N. Tupolev, supersonic plane TU 154, route Moscow to Alma-Ata, 1968. 4t, Wilbur and Orville Wright and their plane.

1978, Mar. 25 Litho. *Perf. 12½x11*

C101	AP27	20m	multicolored	15	5
C102	"	30m	"	20	10
C103	"	40m	"	30	18
C104	"	50m	"	40	22
C105	"	60m	"	50	25
C106	"	80m	"	60	35
C107	"	1.20t	"	1.00	55
	Nos. C101-C107 (7)			3.15	1.70

Souvenir Sheet

C108 AP27 4t multicolored 3.50

75th anniversary of first powered flight, Wright brothers, 1903. No. C108 contains one stamp; multicolored margin shows various flight commemorative stamps and portrait of Mongolian flier Shagdarsuren. Size: 110x75mm.

Souvenir Sheet
Soccer Type of 1978

Design: 4t, Two soccer players.

1978, Apr. 15 *Perf. 11½*

C109 A231 4t multicolored 3.50

World Soccer Championships, Argentina 78, June 1–25. No. C109 contains one stamp (45x38mm.). Multicolored margin shows globe with South America, satellites and Argentina 1978 emblem. Size: 105x 70mm.

Souvenir Sheet

Canada No. 553 and Mongolia No. 549—AP28

1978, June Litho. *Perf. 12½*

C110 AP28 4t multicolored 3.50

CAPEX '78, International Philatelic Exhibition, Montreal, June 9–18.

No. C110 has multicolored margin showing Montreal and TV tower. Size: 100x80 mm.

Map of Cuba, Ship, Plane and Festival Emblem—AP29

1978, July 28 Litho. *Perf. 12*

C111 AP29 1t multicolored 80 35

11th World Youth Festival, Havana, July 28–Aug. 5.

Souvenir Sheet

Aleksei Gubarev and Vladimir Remek, PRAGA '78 Emblem—AP30

1978, Sept. 5 Lithographed *Perf. 12*

C112 AP30 4t multicolored 3.50

PRAGA '78 International Philatelic Exhibition, Prague, Sept. 8–17, and Russian-Czechoslovak space cooperation, Intercosmos.

No. C112 has multicolored margin showing various spacecraft. Size: 109x89mm.

AIR POST SEMI-POSTAL STAMP

UNICEF Type of 1977
Souvenir Sheet

Design: 4t+50m, Balloon with Mongolian flag, children and UNICEF emblem.

1977, June 1 Litho. *Perf. 12*

CB1 SP2 4t+50m multi. 3.50 3.50

First balloon flight in Mongolia. Surtax was for Children's Village. No. CB1 contains one stamp; multicolored margin shows children and balloons. Size: 83x71mm.

MONTENEGRO

(mŏn′tē-nē′grō)

LOCATION — In Southern Europe, bordering on the Adriatic Sea.

GOVT.—A former Kingdom.

AREA—5,603 sq. mi.

POP.—516,000 (estimated).

CAPITAL—Cetinje.

This kingdom, formerly a Turkish Protectorate, later became independent. On December 1, 1918, Montenegro united with Serbia, Bosnia and Herzegovina, Croatia, Dalmatia and Slovenia to form the Kingdom of the Serbs, Croats and Slovenes which became Jugoslavia in 1929.

100 Novcic = 1 Florin
100 Helera = 1 Kruna (1902)
100 Para = 1 Kruna (1907)
100 Para = 1 Perper (1910)

Canceled to Order

Used prices are for canceled to order stamps. Postally used specimens sell for considerably more.

Prince Nicholas I
A1

Wmk. 91

Wmkd. "ZEITUNGS-MARKEN" in Double-lined Capitals across the Sheet. (91)

1874-93 Typographed

Third Printing (1893)

Perf. 10½, 11, 11½.

Small holes, broad teeth.

(Perf. 11½ also with pointed teeth.)

No.	Type	Description	Unused	Used
1	A1	2n yellow	1.75	1.50
		c. Perf. 11 ('91)	14.00	12.50
2	"	3n green	85	60
3	"	5n red	70	50
4	"	7n rose	70	50
		f. Perf. 11 ('91)	4.00	3.50
5	"	10n blue	1.20	1.25
6	"	15n brown	1.20	1.00
7	"	25n brown violet	1.00	1.00
		Nos. 1-7 (7)	7.40	6.35

Nos. 1-7 exist imperforate, but experts believe these to be printer's waste.

First Printing (1874)

Perf. 10½

Large holes, pointed teeth.

Narrow spacing, 2 to 2½mm.

No.	Type	Description	Unused	Used
1a	A1	2n yellow	22.50	20.00
2a	"	3n green	35.00	27.50
3a	"	5n rose red	25.00	20.00
4a	"	7n light lilac	30.00	22.50
5a	"	10n blue	70.00	55.00
6a	"	15n yellow bistre	85.00	75.00
7a	"	25n lilac gray	150.00	125.00

Second Printing (1880)

Perf. 12, 13 and Compound (also with 10½).

Narrow spacing, 2 to 2½mm.

No.	Type	Description	Unused	Used
1b	A1	2n yellow	6.50	5.00
		d. Perf. 12-13x10½	125.00	125.00
2b	"	3n green	6.00	3.75
3b	"	5n red	5.00	4.25
4b	"	7n rose lilac	6.00	3.00
		c. 7n lilac	20.00	15.00
5b	"	10n blue	7.75	5.00
		c. Perf. 12-13x10½	150.00	150.00
6b	"	15n bistre brown	15.00	9.00
7b	"	25n gray lilac	15.00	12.00

Types of 1874-93 Overprinted

Прослава
1493
1893
Штампарије

1893 ***Perf. 10½, 11, 11½***

Black Overprint.

No.	Type	Description	Unused	Used
8	A1	2n yellow	12.50	3.00
9	"	3n green	2.00	1.50
10	"	5n red	1.00	75
11	"	7n rose	1.00	1.50
		a. Perf. 12	45.00	35.00
		b. Red ovpt.	7.00	5.00
12	"	10n blue	1.00	1.50
13	"	15n brown	1.00	1.50
		a. 15n bistre brown, perf. 12	45.00	40.00
14	"	25n brown violet	1.25	2.50

Red Overprint.

No.	Type	Description	Unused	Used
15	A1	10n blue	3.00	3.00
16	"	15n grayish brown	1500.00	1500.00
17	"	25n brown violet	75	2.00
		a. 25n gray lilac, perf. 12½	75.00	75.00

Introduction of printing to Montenegro, 400th anniversary.

This overprint had three settings. Several values exist with "1494" or "1495" instead of "1493", or with missing letters or numerals due to wearing of the clichés. Double and inverted overprints exist. Some printings were made after 1893 to supply a philatelic demand, but were available for postage.

Wmkd. "ZEITUNGS-MARKEN" in Double-lined Capitals across the Sheet. (91)

1894-98 ***Perf. 10½, 11½.***

No.	Type	Description	Unused	Used
18	A1	1n gray blue	20	18
19	"	2n emerald ('98)	25	20
20	"	3n carmine rose ('98)	20	18
21	"	5n orange ('98)	60	30
22	"	7n gray lilac ('98)	25	20
23	"	10n magenta ('98)	22	15
24	"	15n red brown ('98)	25	20
25	"	20n brown orange	20	18
26	"	25n dull blue ('98)	25	18
27	"	30n maroon	20	18
28	"	50n ultramarine	35	30
29	"	1fl deep green	50	45
30	"	2fl red brown	75	75
		Nos. 18-30 (13)	4.20	3.45

Nos. 18, 24-25, 27-30 exist imperforate but experts believe these to be printer's waste.

Monastery at Cetinje (Royal Mausoleum)—A3

Perf. 10½, 11½

1896, Sept. 1 **Litho.** **Unwmkd.**

No.	Type	Description	Unused	Used
31	A3	1n dark blue & bistre	20	20
32	"	2n magenta & yellow	20	20
33	"	3n orange brown & yellow green	20	20
34	"	5n blue green & bistre	20	20
35	"	10n yellow & ultra.	20	20
36	"	15n dark blue & green	20	20
		a. Perf. 11½	25.00	25.00
37	A3	20n bl. green & ultra.	20	20
38	"	25n dk. blue & yellow	20	20
39	"	30n magenta & bistre	20	20
40	"	50n red brown & gray blue	20	20
41	"	1fl rose & gray blue	50	50
42	"	2fl brown & black	50	50
		Nos. 31-42 (12)	3.00	3.00

Issued to commemorate the bicentenary of the ruling dynasty, founded by the Vladika, Danilo Petrovich of Nyegosh.

Several varieties with inverted centers and other errors exist, but experts believe these to be printer's waste.

Counterfeits exist.

Prince Nicholas I
A4 A5

Perf. 13x13½ (2h-5k), 13x12½ (2h, 5h, 50h, 2k, 5k), 12½ (1h, 25h)

1902, July 12

No.	Type	Description	Unused	Used
44	A4	1h ultramarine	12	12
45	"	2h rose lilac	15	12
46	"	5h green	12	12
47	"	10h rose	30	12
48	"	25h dull blue	20	20
49	"	50h gray green	30	20
50	"	1k chocolate	25	25
51	"	2k pale brown	35	30
52	"	5k buff	50	50
		Nos. 44-52 (9)	2.29	1.93

All values except the 1k and 2k are known imperforate. These are remainders. A 2h black brown and 25h indigo were never placed in use.

Constitution Issue.

Same Overprinted in Red or Black

УСТАВ
Constitution
Никољдан
1905

1905, Dec. 5

No.	Type	Description	Unused	Used
53	A4	1h ultramarine (R)	18	18
54	"	2h rose lilac	18	18
55	"	5h green (R)	18	18
56	"	10h rose	18	18
57	"	25h dull blue (R)	18	18
58	"	50h gray green (R)	18	18
59	"	1k chocolate (R)	24	24
60	"	2k pale brown (R)	30	30
61	"	5k buff	45	45
		Nos. 53-61 (9)	2.07	2.07

There were two settings of this overprint, one of which contained four varieties of "YCTAB" and two spelling errors: "Constitutton" and "Coustitution". Nearly all values exist with double, inverted and misplaced overprint. There are also numerous errors in the color of the overprint. Most of these probably were not sold at time of issue but came from remainders.

1907, June 1 **Engr.** ***Perf. 12½***

No.	Type	Description	Unused	Used
62	A5	1pa ochre	5	5
63	"	2pa black	5	5
64	"	5pa yellow green	6	4
65	"	10pa rose red	6	4
66	"	15pa ultramarine	6	6
67	"	20pa red orange	8	6
68	"	25pa indigo	8	8
69	"	35pa bistre brown	12	12
70	"	50pa dull violet	20	15
71	"	1kr carmine rose	20	20
72	"	2kr green	20	20
73	"	5kr red brown	30	30
		Nos. 62-73 (12)	1.46	1.37

Exist imperf. Some experts believe these to be printer's waste.

King Nicholas I as a Youth
A6

King Nicholas I and Queen Milena
A7

King Nicholas I in 1910
A8

King Nicholas I (the Prince) in 1878
A9

King and Queen—A10

King Nicholas I
A11

Prince Nicholas
A12

1910, Aug. 28 **Engraved**

No.	Type	Description	Unused	Used
74	A6	1pa black	9	4
75	A7	2pa purple brown	9	4
76	A8	5pa dark green	15	8
77	"	10pa carmine	15	4
78	A9	15pa slate blue	12	10
79	A10	20pa olive green	12	10
80	A8	25pa deep blue	15	12
81	"	35pa chestnut	25	25
82	A11	50pa violet	15	15
83	"	1per lake	15	15
84	"	2per yellow green	20	20
85	A12	5per pale blue	35	35
		Nos. 74-85 (12)	1.97	1.62

Issued in commemoration of the Proclamation of Montenegro as a kingdom, the fiftieth anniversary of the reign of King Nicholas and the golden wedding celebration of the King and Queen.

King Nicholas I
A13

1913, Apr. 1 **Typographed**

No.	Type	Description	Unused	Used
86	A13	1pa orange	4	4
87	"	2pa plum	4	4
88	"	5pa deep green	4	4
89	"	10pa deep rose	4	4
90	"	15pa blue gray	4	4
91	"	20pa dark brown	15	15
92	"	25pa deep blue	15	10
93	"	35pa vermilion	25	20
94	"	50pa pale blue	15	15
95	"	1per yellow brown	15	15
96	"	2per gray violet	20	20
97	"	5per yellow green	20	20
		Nos. 86-97 (12)	1.45	1.35

ACKNOWLEDGMENT OF RECEIPT STAMPS.

Prince Nicholas I
AR1 AR2

Perf. 10½, 11½

1895 Lithographed **Wmk. 91**

H1 AR1 10n ultramarine & rose 40 40

1902 *Perf. 12½* **Unwmkd.**

H2 AR2 25h orange & carmine 50 50

Constitution Issue.

УСТАВ Constitution Никољдан 1905

No. H2 Overprinted in Black

1905

H3 AR2 25h orange & carmine 25 25

See note after No. 61.

Nicholas I

AR3 AR4

1907 **Engraved**

H4 AR3 25pa olive 20 20

1913 **Typographed**

H5 AR4 25pa olive green 20 20

POSTAGE DUE STAMPS.

Numeral of Value

D1 D2

Wmkd. "ZEITUNGS-MARKEN" In Double-lined Capitals across the Sheet. (91)

1894 Litho. ***Perf. 10½, 11, 11½***

J1 D1 1n red 1.00 75
J2 " 2n yellow green 15 12
J3 " 3n orange 18 15
J4 " 5n olive green 10 10
J5 " 10n violet 12 12
J6 " 20n ultramarine 12 12
J7 " 30n emerald 12 12
J8 " 50n pale gray green 12 12
Nos. J1-J8 (8) 1.91 1.60

1902 ***Perf. 12½.*** **Unwmkd.**

J9 D2 5h orange 10 10
J10 " 10h olive green 12 10
J11 " 25h dull lilac 12 10
J12 " 50h emerald 12 10
J13 " 1k pale gray green 15 15
Nos. J9-J13 (5) 61 55

Nos. J9, J11-J13 exist imperf.

Constitution Issue.

УСТАВ Constitution Никољдан 1905

Postage Due Stamps of 1902 Overprinted in Black or Red

1905

J14 D2 5h orange 12 12
J15 " 10h olive green (R) 15 12
J16 D2 25h dull lilac 15 15
J17 " 50h emerald 15 15
J18 " 1k pale gray green 18 18
Nos. J14-J18 (5) 75 72

Note after No. 61 applies also to No. J15.

D3 D4

1907 Typographed ***Perf. 13x13½***

J19 D3 5pa red brown 12 12
J20 " 10pa violet 12 12
J21 " 25pa rose 12 12
J22 " 50pa green 12 12

Nos. J19-J22 exist imperf.

1913 ***Perf. 12½.***

J23 D4 5pa gray 27 27
J24 " 10pa violet 12 12
J25 " 25pa blue gray 12 12
J26 " 50pa lilac rose 15 15

OCCUPATION STAMPS.

Issued under Austrian Occupation.

Austrian Military Stamps of 1917 Overprinted

K.U.K.MILIT. VERWALTUNG MONTENEGRO

1917 ***Perf. 12½*** **Unwmkd.**

1N1 M1 10h blue 8.00 5.00
1N2 " 15h carmine rose 8.00 5.00

Austrian Military Stamps of 1917 Overprinted **Montenegro**

1918

1N3 M1 10h blue 40.00
1N4 " 15h carmine rose 2.00

Nos. 1N3 and 1N4 were never placed in use.

Issued under Italian Occupation

Jugoslavia Nos. 142, 144-154 Overprinted

Montenegro Црна Гора 17-IV-41-XIX

Typographed.

1941 ***Perf. 12½*** **Unwmkd.**

2N1 A16 25p black 20 25
2N2 " 1d yellow green 20 25
2N3 " 1.50d red 20 25
2N4 " 2d deep magenta 20 25
2N5 " 3d dull red brown 20 25
2N6 " 4d ultramarine 20 25
2N7 " 5d dark blue 80 1.00
2N8 " 5.50d dk. vio. brown 80 1.00
2N9 " 6d slate blue 80 1.00
2N10 " 8d sepia 90 1.10
2N11 " 12d bright violet 80 1.00
2N12 " 16d dull violet 80 1.00
2N13 " 20d blue 175.00 200.00
2N14 " 30d bright pink 75.00 100.00
Nos. 2N1-2N14 (14) 256.10 307.60

The 25p, 1d, 3d, 6d and 8d exist with inverted overprint.

Stamps of Italy, 1929, Overprinted in Red or Black ЦРНА ГОРА

1941 ***Perf. 14.*** **Wmk. 140**

2N15 A90 5c olive brown (R) 8 8
2N16 A92 10c dark brown 8 8
2N17 A93 15c slate green (R) 8 8
2N18 A91 20c rose red 8 8
2N19 A94 25c deep green 8 8
2N20 A95 30c olive brn. (R) 8 8
2N21 " 50c purple (R) 8 8
2N22 A94 75c rose red 8 8
2N23 " 1.25l deep blue (R) 8 8
Nos. 2N15-2N23 (9) 72 72

Jugoslavia Nos. 144-145, 147-148, 148B, 149-152 Overprinted in Red

Governatorato del Montenegro Valore LIRE

Typographed

1942 ***Perf. 12½*** **Unwmkd.**

2N24 A16 1d yellow green 50 60
a. Black overprint 50 65
2N25 " 1.50d red 25.00 30.00
a. Black overprint 20.00 25.00
N26 " 3d dull red brn. 50 60
a. Black overprint 50 65
2N27 " 4d ultramarine 50 60
a. Black overprint 50 65
2N28 " 5.50d dk. vio. brown 50 60
a. Black overprint 50 65
2N29 " 6d slate blue 50 6
a. Black overprint 50 65
2N30 " 8d sepia 50 60
a. Black overprint 50 65
2N31 " 12d bright violet 50 60
a. Black overprint 50 65
2N32 " 16d dull violet 50 60
a. Black overprint 50 65
Nos. 2N24-2N32 (9) 29.00 34.80
Nos. 2N24a-2N32a (9) 24.00 30.20

Jugoslavia Nos. 142 and 146 with this overprint in red were not officially issued.

Peter Nyegosh and Mt. Lovchen View

OS1

Mt. Lovchen Scene

OS2

Mountain Church, Eve of Trinity Feast

OS3

Peter Petrovich Nyegosh

OS10

Designs: 20c, Chiefs at Cetinje Monastery. 25c, Folk Dancing at Cetinje Monastery. 50c, Eagle dance. 1.25l, Chiefs taking loyalty oath. 2l, Moslem wedding procession. 5l, Group sitting up with injured standard bearer.

Photogravure.

1943, May 9 ***Perf. 14.*** **Unwmkd.**

2N33 OS1 5c deep violet 20 25
2N34 OS2 10c dull olive green 20 25
2N35 OS3 15c brown 20 25
2N36 " 20c dull orange 20 25
2N37 " 25c dull green 20 25
2N38 " 50c rose pink 20 25
2N39 " 1.25l sapphire 25 30
2N40 " 2l blue green 35 45
2N41 OS2 5l dark red, *salmon* 1.75 2.00
2N42 OS10 20l dark violet, *gray* 8.00 9.00
Nos. 2N33-2N42 (10) 11.55 13.25

Quotations from national poem on backs of stamps.

OCCUPATION AIR POST STAMPS.

Jugoslavia Nos. C7-C14 Overprinted

Montenegro Црна Гора 17-IV-41-XIX

Perf. 12½, 11½x12½, 12½x11½.

1941 **Photogravure.** **Unwmkd.**

2NC1 AP6 50p brown 5.50 6.50
2NC2 AP7 1d yel. green 2.50 2.75
2NC3 AP8 2d blue gray 2.50 2.75
2NC4 AP9 2.50d rose red 5.50 6.50
2NC5 AP6 5d brn. vio. 50.00 50.00
2NC6 AP7 10d brown lake 50.00 50.00
2NC7 AP8 20d dk. green 75.00 75.00
2NC8 AP9 30d ultra. 50.00 50.00
Nos. 2NC1-2NC8 (8) 241.00 243.50

Italy No. C13 Overprinted in Red ЦРНА ГОРА

1941 ***Perf. 14*** **Wmk. 140**

2NC9 AP3 50c olive brown 10 20

Jugoslavia Nos. C7-C14 Overprinted in Black

Governatorato del Montenegro Valore in Lire
a

Governatorato del Montenegro Valore in Lire
b

Perf. 12½, 11½x12½, 12½x11½

1942, Jan. 9 **Unwmkd.**

2NC10 AP6 (*a*) 50p brown 1.00 1.00
2NC11 AP7 (") 1d yel. grn. 1.00 1.00
2NC12 AP8 (*b*) 2d bl. gray 1.00 1.00
2NC13 AP9 (") 2.50d rose red 1.00 1.00
2NC14 AP6 (*a*) 5d brn. vio. 1.00 1.00
2NC15 AP7 (") 10d brown lake 1.00 1.00

2NC16 AP8 (*b*) 20d dark green 165.00 165.00
2NC17 AP9 (") 30d ultra. 55.00 55.00
Nos. 2NC10–2NC17 (8) 226.00 226.00

Nos. 2NC10–2NC17 exist with red overprints. Price, each $80 unused, $90 used.

Governatorato del Montenegro

c

Overprints *a*, *b* or *c* were applied in 1941–42 to the following Jugoslavia stamps under Italian occupation:
a. or *b*. Nos. B120–B123 (4 val). in black and in red.
c. Nos. B116–B119 (4 val.) in black and in red.

Cetinje
AP1

Mt. Durmitor
AP6

Designs: 1l, Seacoast. 2l, Budua. 5l, Mt. Lovchen. 10l, Rieka River.

Photogravure.

1943 *Perf. 14.* **Unwmkd.**

2NC18 AP1 50c brown 20 25
2NC19 " 1 l ultramarine 20 25
2NC20 " 2 l rose pink 20 25
2NC21 " 5 l green 20 35
2NC22 " 10 l lake, *rose buff* 3.00 3.50
2NC23 AP6 20 l indigo, *rose* 11.00 12.00
Nos. 2NC18–2NC23 (6) 14.80 16.60

OCCUPATION POSTAGE DUE STAMPS.

Jugoslavia Nos. J28–J32 Overprinted

Montenegro
Црна Гора
17-IV-41-XIX

Typographed.

1941 *Perf. 12½* **Unwmkd.**

2NJ1 D4 50p violet 30 40
2NJ2 " 1d deep magenta 30 40
2NJ3 " 2d deep blue 30 40
2NJ4 " 5d orange 20.00 25.00
2NJ5 " 10d chocolate 1.50 1.75
Nos. 2NJ1–2NJ5 (5) 22.40 27.95

Postage Due Stamps of Italy, 1934, Overprinted in Black **ЦРНА ГОРА**

1942 *Perf. 14.* **Wmk. 140**

2NJ6 D6 10c blue 6 8
2NJ7 " 20c rose red 8 10
2NJ8 " 30c red orange 12 15
2NJ9 " 50c violet 15 20
2NJ10 D7 1 l red orange 30 50
Nos. 2NJ6–2NJ10 (5) 71 1.03

Issued under German Occupation.

Jugoslavia Nos. 147–148 Surcharged

Deutsche Militaer-Verwaltung Montenegro
0.50 LIRE

Typographed

1943 *Perf. 12½* **Unwmkd.**

3N1 A16 50c on 3d dull red brown 2.50 3.00
3N2 " 1 l on 3d dull red brown 2.50 3.00
3N3 " 1.50 l on 3d dull red brown 2.50 3.00
3N4 " 2 l on 3d dull red brown 4.50 6.00
3N5 " 4 l on 3d red dull brown 3.00 4.00
3N6 " 5 l on 4d ultra. 5.00 6.00
3N7 " 8 l on 4d " 5.00 7.50
3N8 " 10 l on 4d " 15.00 17.50
3N9 " 20 l on 4d " 22.50 30.00
Nos. 3N1–3N9 (9) 62.50 80.00

Montenegro Nos. 2N37–2N41 Ovptd.

Nationaler Verwaltungsausschuss
10.XI.1943

b

1943 Photogravure *Perf. 14*

3N10 OS3 25c dull green 3.00 5.00
3N11 " 50c rose pink 3.00 5.00
3N12 " 1.25 l sapphire 3.00 5.00
3N13 " 2 l blue green 3.00 5.00
3N14 OS2 5 l dark red, *salmon* 200.00 250.00
Nos. 3N10–3N14 (5) 212.00 270.00

Counterfeits exist.

SEMI-POSTAL STAMPS

Jugoslavia Nos. 147–148 Surcharged

Flüchtlingshilfe Montenegro
0.15+0.85 RM.

Typographed

1944 *Perf. 12½* **Unwmkd.**

3NB1 A16 15pf+85pf on 3d dull red brn. 9.00 11.00
3NB2 " 15pf+85pf on 4d ultra. 9.00 11.00

Montenegro Nos. 2N37–2N40 Surcharged

Flüchtlingshilfe Montenegro

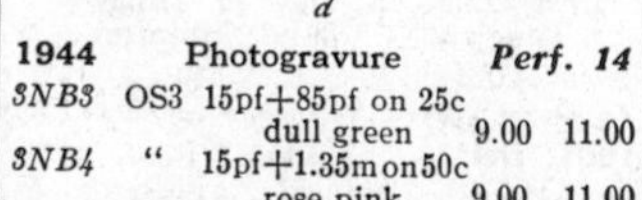

d

1944 Photogravure *Perf. 14*

3NB3 OS3 15pf+85pf on 25c dull green 9.00 11.00
3NB4 " 15pf+1.35m on 50c rose pink 9.00 11.00
3NB5 OS3 25pf+1.75m on 1.25 l sapphire 9.00 11.00
3NB6 " 25pf+1.75m on 2 l blue green 9.00 11.00
Nos. 3NB1–3NB6 (6) 54.00 66.00

Surtax on Nos. 3NB1–6 aided refugees.

Montenegro Nos. 2N37–2N38 Surcharged

Crveni krst Montenegro
0.25+1.75 RM.

e

1944

3NB7 OS3 15pf+85pf on 25c dull green 6.00 7.50
3NB8 " 15pf+1.35m on 50c rose pink 6.00 7.50

Jugoslavia Nos. 147–148 Surcharged

Crveni krst Montenegro

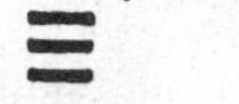

Typographed *Perf. 12½*

3NB9 A16 50pf+2.50m on 3d dull red brn. 6.00 7.50
3NB10 " 50pf+2.50m on 4d ultra. 6.00 7.50

The surtax on Nos. 3NB7–3NB10 aided the Montenegro Red Cross.

AIR POST STAMPS

Montenegro Nos. 2NC18–2NC22 Overprinted Type "b".

Photogravure

1943 *Perf. 14* **Unwmkd.**

3NC1 AP1 50c brown 4.00 6.00
3NC2 " 1 l ultramarine 4.00 6.00
3NC3 " 2 l rose pink 4.00 6.00
3NC4 " 5 l green 4.00 6.00
3NC5 " 10 l lake, *rose buff* *2250.00 2500.00*

Counterfeits exist.

AIR POST SEMI-POSTAL STAMPS

Montenegro Nos. 2NC18–2NC20 Surcharged Type "d".

Photogravure

1944 *Perf. 14* **Unwmkd.**

3NCB1 AP1 15pf+85pf on 50c brown 9.00 11.00
3NCB2 " 25pf+1.25m on 1 l ultra. 9.00 11.00
3NCB3 " 50pf+1.50m on 2 l rose pink 9.00 11.00

The surtax aided refugees.

Same Surcharged Type "e".

1944

3NCB4 AP1 25pf+1.75m on 50c brown 6.00 7.50
3NCB5 " 25pf+2.75m on 1 l ultra. 6.00 7.50
3NCB6 " 50pf+2m on 2 l rose pink 6.00 7.50

The surtax aided the Montenegro Red Cross.

MOROCCO

(mô·rŏk'ō)

LOCATION — Northwest coast of Africa.
GOVT.—Kingdom.
AREA—171,953 sq. mi.
POP.—18,240,000 (est. 1977).
CAPITAL—Rabat.

In 1956 the three zones of Morocco—French, Spanish and Tangier—were united to form an independent nation.

Nos. 1–24 and C1–C3 were intended for use only in the Southern (French currency) Zone.

Issues of the Northern Zone (Spanish currency) are listed after Postage Due stamps.

For earlier issues, see French Morocco and Spanish Morocco.

100 Centimes = 1 Franc
100 Francs = 1 Dirham (1962)

Sultan Mohammed V
A1

Men Reading
A2

Engraved.

1956–1957 *Perf. 12* **Unwmkd.**

1 A1 5fr bright blue & indigo 15 6
2 " 10fr bis. brn. & choc. 20 6
3 " 15fr deep green & magenta 25 6
4 " 25fr purple ('57) 70 6
5 " 30fr green ('57) 70 6
6 " 50fr rose red ('57) 1.50 20
7 " 70fr dark brown & brown red ('57) 2.00 15
Nos. 1–7 (7) 5.50 65

1956, Nov. 5

Designs: 15fr, Girls reading. 20fr, Instructor and pupils. 30fr, Old man and child reading. 50fr, Girl pointing out poster.

8 A2 10fr purple & violet 1.65 1.35
9 " 15fr carmine & rose lake 1.85 1.50
10 " 20fr blue green & grn. 2.50 1.75
11 " 30fr rose lake & bright red 3.25 2.50
12 " 50fr deep blue & blue 5.00 4.00
Nos. 8–12 (5) 14.25 11.10

Campaign against illiteracy.

Sultan Mohammed V
A3

Prince Moulay el Hassan
A4

1957, Mar. 2 Photo. *Perf. 13½x13*

13 A3 15fr blue green 1.65 1.40
14 " 25fr gray olive 1.65 1.40
15 " 30fr deep rose 2.75 2.25

Anniversary of independence.

1957, July 9 *Perf. 13*

16 A4 15fr blue 1.20 1.00
17 " 25fr green 1.65 1.40

18 A4 30fr carmine rose 1.85 1.65

Issued to commemorate the designation of Prince Moulay el Hassan as heir to the throne.

King Mohammed V
A5

1957, Nov. ***Perf. 12½***

19 A5 15fr blk. & brt. green 80 70
20 " 25fr black & rose red 90 80
21 " 30fr black & violet 1.10 1.00

30th anniversary of enthronement of Mohammed V.

Morocco Pavilion, Brussels World's Fair
A6

1958, Apr. 20 **Engr.** ***Perf. 13***

22 A6 15fr bright greenish blue 30 25
23 " 25fr carmine 35 30
24 " 30fr indigo 45 35

World's Fair, Brussels.

UNESCO Building, Paris, and King Mohammed V—A7

1958, Nov. 23

25 A7 15fr green 30 25
26 " 25fr lake 35 30
27 " 30fr blue 45 35

Issued to commemorate the opening of UNESCO (U.N. Educational, Scientific and Cultural Organization) Headquarters in Paris, Nov. 3.

Ben Smin Sanatorium
A8

1959, Jan. 18 ***Perf. 13*** **Unwmkd.**

28 A8 50fr dark brown, carmine & slate green 50 40

Issued to honor the Red Cross—Red Crescent Society.

King Mohammed V
A9

Princess Lalla Amina
A10

1959, Aug. 18 **Engr.** ***Perf. 13***

29 A9 15fr dark carmine rose 50 35
30 " 25fr bright blue 60 45
31 " 45fr dark green 70 60

50th birthday of King Mohammed V.

1959, Nov. 17

32 A10 15fr blue 40 30
33 " 25fr green 45 35
34 " 45fr rose lilac 55 45

Issued for International Children's Week.

Map of Africa and Symbols of Agriculture, Industry and Commerce
A11

1960, Jan. 31 ***Perf. 13***

35 A11 45fr violet, ochre & emerald 90 75

Issued to publicize the meeting of the Economic Commission for Africa, Tangier.

Refugees and Uprooted Oak Emblem—A12

Design: 45fr, Refugee family and uprooted oak emblem.

1960, Apr. 7 ***Perf. 13*** **Unwmkd.**

36 A12 15fr ochre, black & green 30 25
37 " 45fr black & green 50 40

Issued to publicize World Refugee Year, July 1, 1959–June 30, 1960.

Marrakesh—A13

1960, Apr. 25 **Engr.** ***Perf. 13***

38 A13 100fr green, blue & red brown 1.25 1.00

900th anniversary of Marrakesh.

Lamp
A14

Designs: 25fr, Fountain and arched door. 30fr, Minaret. 35fr, Ornamented wall. 45fr, Moorish architecture.

1960, May 12 ***Perf. 13½***

39 A14 15fr rose lilac 40 35
40 " 25fr dark blue 50 40
41 " 30fr orange red 70 45
42 " 35fr black 90 70
43 A14 45fr yellow green 1.20 90
Nos. 39-43 (5) 3.70 2.80

1,100th anniversary of Karaouiyne University, Fes.

Arab League Center, Cairo and Mohammed V—A15

1960, June 28 **Photo.** ***Perf. 12½***

44 A15 15fr green & black 25 25

Issued to commemorate the opening of the Arab League Center and the Arab Postal Museum, Cairo.

Wrestlers
A16

Sports: 10fr, Gymnast. 15fr, Bicyclist. 20fr, Weight lifter. 30fr, Runner. 40fr, Boxers. 45fr, Sailboat. 70fr, Fencers.

1960, Sept. 26 **Engr.** ***Perf. 13***

45 A16 5fr olive, violet blue & plum 12 8
46 " 10fr orange brown, blue & brown 22 12
47 " 15fr emerald, blue & orange brown 30 20
48 " 20fr ultramarine, olive & brown 35 30
49 " 30fr violet blue, maroon & sepia 45 40
50 " 40fr greenish blue, dark purple & red brown 50 40
51 " 45fr green, plum & ultramarine 70 55
52 " 70fr dark brown, blue & gray 85 65
Nos. 45-52 (8) 3.49 2.70

Issued to commemorate the 17th Olympic Games, Rome, Aug. 25–Sept. 11.

Runner—A17

1961, Aug. 30 ***Perf. 13*** **Unwmkd.**

53 A17 20fr dark green 25 15
54 " 30fr dk. carmine rose 35 20
55 " 50fr bright blue 60 45

3rd Pan-Arabic Games, Casablanca.

Post Office, Tangier
A18

View of Tangier and Gibraltar
A19

Design: 30fr, Telephone operator.

1961, Dec. 8 **Litho.** ***Perf. 12½***

56 A18 20fr red violet 45 40
57 A18 30fr green 55 50
57A A19 90fr light blue & violet blue 1.00 70

Issued to commemorate the conference of the African Postal and Telecommunications Union, Tangier.

Mohammed V and Map of Africa
A20

Patrice Lumumba and Map of Congo
A21

1962, Jan. 4 ***Perf. 11½*** **Unwmkd.**

58 A20 20fr buff & violet brown 25 25
59 " 30fr lt. & dark blue 35 35

Issued to commemorate the first anniversary of the conference of African heads of state at Casablanca.

1962, Feb. 12 ***Perf. 12½***

60 A21 20fr bistre & black 25 25
61 " 30fr dull red brown & black 40 35

Issued to commemorate the first anniversary of the death of Patrice Lumumba, Premier of Congo Democratic Republic.

Moroccan Students
A22

Arab League Building, Cairo
A23

1962, March 5 **Engraved**

62 A22 20fr multicolored 40 30
63 " 30fr " 50 40
64 " 90fr gray green, indigo & brown 90 70

Issued to honor the nation's students.

1962, Mar. 22 **Photo.** ***Perf. 13½x13***

65 A23 20fr red brown 25 20

Arab Propaganda Week, Mar. 22–28.
See No. 146.

Malaria Eradication Emblem and Swamp—A24

Design: 50fr, Dagger stabbing mosquito (vert.).

1962, Sept. 3 **Engraved** ***Perf. 13***

66 A24 20fr dark green & greenish black 25 20
67 " 50fr dk. grn. & magenta 55 35

Issued for the World Health Organization drive to eradicate malaria.

Fish and Aquarium
A25

Design: 30fr, Moray eel.

1962, Nov. 5 ***Perf. 13*** **Unwmkd.**

68 A25 20fr grn., blue & red brown 35 25
69 " 30fr bister, dk. green & blue green 45 35

Casablanca Aquarium.

Courier and Sherifian Stamp of 1912
A26

Designs: 30fr, Courier on foot and round Sherifian cancellation. 50fr, Sultan Hassan I and octagonal cancellation.

1962, Dec. 15 **Unwmkd.**

70 A26 20fr Prussian green & reddish brown 50 40
71 " 30fr dark carmine rose & black 60 50
72 " 50fr blue & bister 90 70

Issued for Stamp Day and for the First National Stamp Exhibition, Dec. 15–23. The issue also commemorates the 75th anniversary of the Sherifian Post and the 50th anniversary of its reorganization.

Boy Scout
A27

King Hassan II
A28

1962, Aug. 8 **Litho.** ***Perf. 11½***

73 A27 20fr vio. brn. & lt. bl. 25 20

5th Arab Boy Scout Jamboree, Rabat.

1962 **Engraved** ***Perf. 13½x13***

75	A28	1fr gray olive	3	3
76	"	2fr violet	3	3
77	"	5fr black	5	3
78	"	10fr brown orange	10	3
79	"	15fr Prussian green	17	4
80	"	20fr purple	20	5
81	"	30fr deep yellow green	30	6
82	"	50fr violet brown	45	5
83	"	70fr deep blue	80	15
84	"	80fr magenta	90	20
		Nos. 75-84 (10)	3.03	67

See also Nos. 110–114. "Mazelin" (designer-engraver) reads down on Nos. 75–84.

King Moulay Ismail
A29

Al Idrissi, Geographer
A30

1963, Mar. 3 ***Perf. 12½***

85 A29 20fr sepia 30 30

Tercentenary of Meknes as Ismaili capital.

1963–66 **Engraved**

Portraits: Nos. 87, 88A, Ibn Batota, explorer. No. 88, Ibn Khaldoun, historian and sociologist.

86	A30	20fr dark slate green	30	30
87	"	20fr dark carmine rose	40	40
88	"	20fr black	30	30
88A	"	40fr dk. vio. blue ('66)	35	20

Issued to honor famous medieval men of Morocco (Maghreb). No. 88A also marks the inauguration of the ferryboat "Ibn Batota" connecting Tangier and Malaga. Issue dates: Nos. 86–88, May 7, 1963. No. 88A, July 15, 1966.

Sugar Beet and Sugar Refinery, Sidi Slimane—A31

Design: 50fr, Tuna fisherman (vert.).

1963, June 10 ***Perf. 13*** **Unwmkd.**

89 A31 20fr blk., grn. & brn. 30 30
90 " 50fr black, brown & dark blue 55 40

Issued for the "Freedom from Hunger" campaign of the U.N. Food and Agriculture Organization.

Heads of Ramses II, Abu Simbel
A32

Designs: 30fr, Isis, Kalabsha Temple (vert.). 50fr, Temple of Philae.

Engraved

1963, July 15 ***Perf. 11½*** **Unwmkd.**

91 A32 20fr black 25 20
92 " 30fr violet, *grayish* 35 30
93 " 50fr maroon, *buff* 50 40

Campaign to save historic monuments in Nubia.

Agadir Before Earthquake
A33

Designs: 30fr, Like 20fr with "29 Février 1960" and crossed bars added. 50fr, Agadir rebuilt.

Engr.; Engr. & Photo. (No. 95)

1963, Oct. 10 ***Perf. 13½x13***

94 A33 20fr blue & brn. red 40 35
95 " 30fr blue, brown red & red 60 40
96 " 50fr blue & brn. red 60 50

Issued to publicize the rebuilding of Agadir.

Centenary Emblem and Plan of Agadir Hospital—A34

1963, Oct. 28 **Photo.** ***Perf. 12½x13***

97 A34 30fr black, deep carmine & silver 30 30

Centenary of the International Red Cross.

Arms of Morocco and Rabat
A35

Flag
A37

Hands Breaking Chain—A36

1963, Nov. 18 ***Perf. 13x12½***

98 A35 20fr gold, red, black & emerald 30 30

Installation of Parliament.

1963, Dec. 10 **Engraved** ***Perf. 13***

99 A36 20fr dark brown, green & orange 30 30

15th anniversary of the Universal Declaration of Human Rights.

Perf. 13x12½

1963, Dec. 25 **Photo.** **Unwmkd.**

100 A37 20fr black, deep carm. & green 35 30

Evacuation of all foreign military forces from Moroccan territory.

Moulay Abd-er-Rahman, by Delacroix—A38

1964, March 3 **Engr.** ***Perf. 12x13***

101 A38 1d multicolored 3.25 2.25

Issued to commemorate the third anniversary of the coronation of King Hassan II.

Weather Map of Africa and U.N. Emblem
A39

Children on Vacation
A40

Designs: 30fr, World map and barometer trace (horiz.).

1964, Mar. 23 **Photo.** ***Perf. 11½***

Granite Paper

102 A39 20fr multicolored 30 25
103 " 30fr " 40 35

Issued to commemorate the United Nations Fourth World Meteorological Day, Mar. 23. See also No. C10.

1964, July 6 **Litho.** ***Perf. 12½***

Design: 30c, Heads of boy and girl, buildings.

104 A40 20fr multicolored 25 20
105 " 30fr " 40 35

Issued for vacation camps for children of P.T.T. employees.

Olympic Torch
A41

Cape Spartel Lighthouse, Sultan Mohammed ben Abd-er-Rahman
A42

1964, Sept. 22 **Engraved** ***Perf. 13***

106 A41 20fr car. lake, dark purple & green 30 25
107 " 30fr blue, dark green & red brown 35 30
108 " 50fr green, red & brn. 55 50

18th Olympic Games, Tokyo, Oct. 10–25.

1964, Oct. 15 **Photo.** ***Perf. 12½x11½***

109 A42 25fr multicolored 30 20

Centenary of the Cape Spartel lighthouse.

King Type of 1962

1964–65 **Engraved** ***Perf. 12½x13***

Size: 17x23mm.

110 A28 20fr purple (redrawn) 40 10

Perf. 13½x13

Size: 18x22mm.

111	A28	25fr rose red ('65)	25	5
112	"	35fr slate ('65)	35	10
113	"	40fr ultra. ('65)	40	5
114	"	60fr red lilac ('65)	55	7
		Nos. 110-114 (5)	1.95	37

The Arabic inscription touches the frame on No. 110. "Mazelin" (designer-engraver) reads up on No. 110, down on Nos. 111–114. No. 110 is a coil stamp with red control numbers on the back of some copies.

Iris
A43

King Mohammed V Arriving by Plane
A44

Flowers: 40fr, Gladiolus segetum. 60fr, Capparis spinosa (horiz.).

1965 **Photo.** ***Perf. 11½***

Granite Paper

115 A43 25fr multicolored 35 30
116 " 40fr green, citron & violet 40 35
117 " 60fr multicolored 65 55

Printed in sheets of 10. Five tête-bêche pairs in every sheet; vertical stamps arranged 5x2, horizontal stamps 2x5.
See also Nos. 129–131.

1965, Mar. 15 **Litho.** ***Perf. 12½***

118 A44 25fr lt. bl. & dk. grn. 30 25

10th anniversary of the return of King Mohammed V from exile and the restoration of the monarchy.

ITU Emblem, Punched-Tape Writer and Telegraph Wires
A45

Design: 40fr, ITU emblem, Syncom satellite, radio waves and "ITU" in Morse code.

Typographed

1965, May 17 *Perf. 13x14* **Unwmkd.**

119 A45 25fr multicolored 25 25
120 " 40fr lt. blue, deep blue & bister 45 40

Issued to commemorate the centenary of the International Telecommunication Union.

ICY Emblem
A46

1965, June 14 Engraved *Perf. 13*

121 A46 25fr slate green 35 25
122 " 60fr dark carm. rose 60 55

International Cooperation Year, 1965.

Triton Shell
A47

Designs: No. 124, Varnish shell (pitaria chione). No. 125, Great voluted shell (cymbium neptuni). No. 126, Helmet crab (vert.). 40fr, Mantis shrimp (vert.). 1d, Royal prawn.

1965 Photogravure *Perf. 11½*

Granite Paper

123 A47 25fr violet & multi. 35 25
124 " 25fr light blue & multicolored 35 25
125 " 25fr orange & multi. 45 25
126 " 25fr lt. grn. & multi. 45 25
127 " 40fr blue & multi. 70 50
128 " 1d yellow & multi. 1.20 90
Nos. 123-128 (6) 3.50 2.40

Printed in sheets of 10. Nos. 126–127 (5x2); others (2x5). Five tête bêche pairs in every sheet.

Flower Type of 1965

Orchids: 25fr, Ophrys speculum. 40fr, Ophrys fusca. 60fr, Ophrys tenthredinifera (front and side view; horiz.).

1965, Dec. 13 Photo. *Perf. 11½*

Granite Paper

129 A43 25fr yel. & multi. 30 25
130 " 40fr dull rose & multi. 50 35
131 " 60fr lt. bl. & multi. 70 50

Note on tête bêche pairs after No. 117 also applies to Nos. 129–131.

Grain
A48

Designs: 40fr, Various citrus fruit. 60fr, Olives (horiz.).

1966 Photogravure *Perf. 11½*

Granite Paper

133 A48 25fr black & bister 25 20
136 " 40fr multicolored 40 12
137 " 60fr gray & multi. 50 27

Flag, Map and Dove—A49

1966, March 2 Typo. *Perf. 14x13*

139 A49 25fr brt. grn. & red 25 20

Tenth anniversary of Independence.

King Hassan II—A50

1966, March 2 Engraved *Perf. 13*

140 A50 25fr red, brt. green & indigo 25 20

Issued to commemorate the fifth anniversary of the coronation of King Hassan II.

Cross-country Runner—A51

1966, March 20 Engraved *Perf. 13*

141 A51 25fr blue green 25 20

53rd International Cross-country Race.

WHO Headquarters from West
A52

Design: 40fr, WHO Headquarters from the East.

1966, May 3 Engraved *Perf. 13*

142 A52 25fr rose lilac & black 25 20
143 " 40fr dp. blue & black 35 30

Issued to commemorate the inauguration of the World Health Organization Headquarters, Geneva.

Crown Prince Hassan Kissing Hand of King Mohammed V
A53

Design: 25fr, King Hassan II and parachutist.

Perf. 12½x12

1966, May 14 Photo. **Unwmkd.**

144 A53 25fr gold & black 40 30
145 " 40fr " " 50 40
a. Strip of 2 + label 1.00 1.00

Issued to commemorate the tenth anniversary of the Royal Armed Forces. No. 145a contains Nos. 144–145 and label between inscribed: "Xème ANNIVERSAIRE DES FORCES ARMÉES ROYALES" and Arabic inscription.

Type of 1962 Inscribed: "SEMAINE DE LA PALESTINE"

1966, May 16 *Perf. 11x11½*

146 A23 25fr slate blue 25 20

Issued for Palestine Week.

Train
A54

Designs: 40fr, Ship. 1d, Autobus.

1966, Dec. 19 Photo. *Perf. 13½*

147 A54 25fr multicolored 25 20
148 " 40fr " 30 20
149 " 1d " 65 25

Twaite Shad
A55

Fish: 40fr, Plain bonito. 1d, Bluefish (vert.).

1967, Feb. 1 Photo. *Perf. 11½*

Granite Paper

150 A55 25fr yellow & multi. 30 25
151 " 40fr multicolored 45 30
152 " 1d lt. grn. & multi. 80 50

Printed tête bêche in sheets of 10. Nos. 150–151 (2x5); No. 152 (5x2).

Ait Aadel Dam
A56

1967, March 3 Engraved *Perf. 13*

153 A56 25fr slate grn., Prus. blue & gray 30 18
154 " 40fr Prussian blue & lt. brown 40 25

Inauguration of Ait Aadel Dam.

Rabat Hilton Hotel, Map of Morocco and Roman Arch
A57

1967, Mar. 3

155 A57 25fr brt. blue & blk. 30 20
156 " 1d brt. blue & pur. 70 25

Opening of the Rabat Hilton Hotel.

Torch, Globe, Town and Lions Emblem—A58

1967, Apr. 22 Photo. *Perf. 12½*

157 A58 40fr gold & sapphire blue 30 20
158 " 1d gold & slate grn. 70 30

Lions International, 50th anniversary.

Three Hands Holding Pickax
A59

1967, July 9 Engraved *Perf. 13*

159 A59 25fr slate green 25 15

Community Development Campaign.

ITY Emblem
A60

1967, Aug. 9 Photo. *Perf. 12½*

160 A60 1d lt. ultra. & dk. bl. 65 40

International Tourist Year, 1967.

Arrow and Map of Mediterranean
A61

1967, Sept. 8 *Perf. 13x12*

161 A61 25fr dk. blue, ultra., red & tan 30 20
162 " 40fr blk., bl. green, red & tan 40 20

Mediterranean Games, Tunis, Sept. 8–17.

Steeplechase
A62

1967, Oct. 14 Photo. *Perf. 12½*

163 A62 40fr lt. yel. grn., blk. & brt. rose lilac 40 25
164 " 1d lt. ultra., blk. & brt. rose lilac 60 45

International Horseshow.

Cotton A63 — Human Rights Flame A64

1967, Nov. 15 Photo. *Perf. 12½*

165 A63 40fr lt. bl., grn. & yel. 35 20

1968, Jan. 10 Engraved *Perf. 13*

166 A64 25fr gray 30 30
167 " 1d rose claret 50 40

International Human Rights Year 1968.

King Hassan II
A65

1968 Lithographed *Perf. 13*

Portrait in Magenta, Brown and Black

Size: 23x30mm.

170 A65 1fr cream & black 3 3
171 " 2fr lt. greenish blue & black 5 3
172 " 5fr light olive green & black 7 3
173 " 10fr pale rose & blk. 10 3
174 " 15fr gray blue & blk. 15 4
175 " 20fr pink & black 17 5
176 " 25fr black 18 5
177 " 30fr pale rose & blk. 25 5
178 " 35fr blue & black 30 15
179 " 40fr gray & black 30 7
180 " 50fr lt. blue & black 35 8
181 " 60fr salmon & black 40 8
182 " 70fr gray & black 60 18
183 " 80fr ocher & black 65 25

Perf. 13½x14

Size: 26x40mm.

184 A65 90fr light blue green & black 90 25
185 " 1d tan & black 1.10 30
186 " 2d lt. ultra. & blk. 1.40 50
187 " 3d bluish lilac & black 2.25 80
188 " 5d apple green & black 4.75 1.75
Nos. 170-188 (19) 14.00 4.72

Nurse and Child A66 — Pendant A67

1968, Apr. 8 Engraved *Perf. 13*

189 A66 25fr ultra., red & olive 25 15
190 A66 40fr slate, red & olive 30 20

Issued to commemorate the 20th anniversary of the World Health Organization.

1968, May 15 Photo. *Perf. 11½*

Design: 40fr, Bracelet.

191 A67 25fr dk. olive bister & multi. 50 40
192 " 40fr ultra. & multi. 70 60

Issued to honor the Moroccan Red Crescent Society.

Nos. 191-192 were printed se-tenant in sheets of 10 (5x2) arranged vertically tête bêche, with marginal inscriptions and control number.

See Nos. 373-374.

Map of Morocco and Rotary Emblem—A68

1968, May 23 *Perf. 13*

193 A68 40fr multicolored 35 25
194 " 1d ultra. & multi. 65 40

Issued to publicize the Rotary International District Conference, Casablanca, May 24-25.

Ornamental Design
A69

Designs: Various patterns used for sashes.

1968, July 12 Photo. *Perf. 11½*

195 A69 25fr multicolored 60 40
196 " 40fr " 80 50
197 " 60fr " 1.00 60
198 " 1d " 1.65 90

Berber (Riff), North Morocco A70 — Princess Lalla Meryem A71

Regional Costumes: 10f, Man from Ait Moussa ou Ali. 15fr, Woman from Ait Mouhad. No. 200, Bargeman from Rabat Salé. No. 201, Citadin man. 40fr, Citadin woman. 60fr, Royal Mokhazni. No. 204, Zemmours man. No. 204A, Man from Meknassa. No. 206, Msouffa woman, Sahara.

1968-74 Litho. *Perf. 13x12½*

198A A70 10fr multi. ('69) 25 20
199 " 15fr yel. & multi. ('69) 20 20
200 " 25fr bister & multi. 25 20
201 " 25fr tan & multi. ('69) 30 20
202 " 40fr lt. blue & multi. 30 20
203 " 60fr emerald & multi. 55 30
204 " 1d lt. blue & multi. 70 45
204A " 1d gray & multi. ('69) 60 30

Perf. 15

205 A70 1d bister & multi. 90 60
206 " 1d green & multi. 90 60
a. Souv. sheet of 10 ('70) 10.00 10.00
b. As "a" with red ovpt. & surch. ('74) 14.00 14.00
Nos. 198A-206 (10) 4.95 3.25

No. 206a contains one each of Nos. 198A-206, but perf. 13. Black marginal inscription, control number and greenish emblem. Issued June 30, 1970, to commemorate the opening of the National P.T.T. Museum, Rabat. Size: 244x120 mm. Sold for 10d.

No. 206b issued Nov. 22, 1974, to commemorate the 8th Congress of the International Federation of Blood Donors. Each stamp overprinted vertically "8eme Congres de la F.I.O.D.S." and blood container emblem. Black marginal inscription partially obliterated with lines, new Arabic inscription and price added. Sold for 20d.

1968, Oct. 7 Litho. *Perf. 13½*

Designs: 40fr, Princess Lalla Asmaa. 1d, Crown Prince Sidi Mohammed.

207 A71 25fr red & multi. 35 25
208 " 40fr yellow & multi. 40 30
209 " 1d lt. blue & multi. 65 40

Issued for Children's Week.

Wrestling, Aztec Calendar Stone and Olympic Rings—A72

Sports: 20fr, Basketball. 25fr, Bicycling. 40fr, Boxing. 60fr, Running. 1d, Soccer.

1968, Oct. 25 Photo. *Perf. 12x11½*

210 A72 15fr yel. grn. & multi. 20 20
211 " 20fr dull yel. & multi. 20 20
212 " 25fr salmon & multi. 20 20
213 " 40fr multicolored 30 17
214 " 60fr gray & multi. 50 22
215 " 1d lt. ultra. & multi. 60 30
Nos. 210-215 (6) 2.00 1.29

Issued to commemorate the 19th Olympic Games, Mexico City, Oct. 12-27.

10 Dirham Coin of Tetuan, 1780
A73

Coins: 25fr, Dirham, Agmat, c. 1138 A.D. 40fr, Dirham, El Alya (Fes), c. 840 A.D. 60fr, Dirham, Marrakesh, c. 1248 A.D.

1968, Dec. 17 Photo. *Perf. 11½*

Granite Paper

216 A73 20fr deep plum, silver & black 30 25
217 " 25fr dark rose brown, gold & black 40 35
218 " 40fr dark green, silver & black 55 45
219 " 60fr dark red, gold & black 75 55

See also Nos. C16-C17.

Women from Zagora
A74

Design: 25fr, Women from Ait Adidou.

1969, Jan. 21 Litho. *Perf. 12*

220 A74 15fr multicolored 30 25
221 " 25fr " 35 30

See No. C15.

Painting by Belkahya A75 — King Hassan II A76

1969, Mar. 27 Litho. *Perf. 11½x12*

222 A75 1d lt. greenish blue, black & brown 60 30

International Day of the Theater.

1969, July 9 Photo. *Perf. 11½*

223 A76 1d gold & multi. 70 30

40th birthday of King Hassan II.

A souvenir sheet contains one of No. 223. Size: 75x105mm. Sold for 2.50d.

No. 185 Overprinted

مؤتمر القمة الاسلامي
الرباط ١٠ رجب 1389

1969, Sept. 22 Litho. *Perf. 13*

224 A65 1d tan & multi. 4.00 3.50

First Arab Summit Conference, Rabat.

Mahatma Gandhi
A77

1969, Oct. 16 Photo. *Perf. 11½*

225 A77 40fr pale violet, black & gray 30 20

Mohandas K. Gandhi (1869-1948), leader in India's struggle for independence.

ILO Emblem
A78

1969, Oct. 29

226 A78 50fr multicolored 30 20

Issued to commemorate the 50th anniversary of the International Labor Organization.

King Hassan II on Way to Prayer
A79

1969, Nov. 20 Photo. *Perf. 11½*

227 A79 1d multicolored 80 45

Issued to commemorate the first Arab Summit Conference, Rabat, September 1969.

Spahi Horsemen, by Haram al Glaoui
A80

1970, Jan. 23 Engraved *Perf. 12x13*

228 A80 1d multicolored 80 40

Main Sewer, Fes
A81

Guedra Dance, by P. C. Beaubrun
A82

1970, Mar. 23 Litho. *Perf. 12*

229 A81 60fr multicolored 40 25

Issued to publicize the 50th Congress of Municipal Engineers, Rabat, March, 1970.

1970, Apr. 15

230 A82 40fr multicolored 40 25

Folklore Festival, Marrakesh, May 1970.

No. 137 Overprinted "1970", "Census" in Arabic in Red and Surcharged "0, 25" and Wavy Bars in Black

1970 احصاء 0,25

1970, July 9 Photo. *Perf. 11½*

231 A48 25fr on 60fr multi. 25 15

Issued to publicize the 1970 census.

Radar Station at Souk El Arba des Sehoul, and Satellite—A83

Ruddy Shelduck
A84

1970, Aug. 20

232 A83 1d lt. ultra. & multi. 60 40

Revolution of King and People, 17th anniversary.

1970, Sept. 25 Photo. *Perf. 11½*

Design: 40fr, Houbara bustard.

233 A84 25fr multicolored 30 20
234 " 40fr " 40 25

Campaign to save Moroccan wildlife.

Man Reading Book, Education Year Emblem—A85

1970, Oct. 20 Litho. *Perf. 12x11½*

235 A85 60fr dull yel. & multi. 40 25

International Education Year.

Symbols of Peace, Justice and Progress
A86

1970, Oct. 27 *Perf. 13½*

236 A86 50fr multicolored 30 20

United Nations, 25th anniversary.

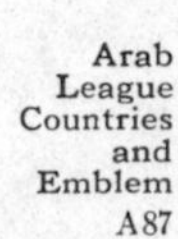

Arab League Countries and Emblem
A87

1970, Nov. 13 Photo. *Perf. 11½*

237 A87 50fr multicolored 35 20

Arab League, 25th anniversary.

Olive Grove, Tree and Branch
A88

1970, Dec. 3 Litho. *Perf. 12*

238 A88 50fr red brn. & green 35 25

International Olive Year.

Es Sounna Mosque, Rabat
A89

1971, Jan. 5 Engraved *Perf. 13*

239 A89 60fr olive bister, blue & slate green 40 20

Restoration of Es Sounna Mosque, Rabat, built in 1785.

Heart and Horse
A90

1971, Feb. 23 Photo. *Perf. 12x12½*

240 A90 50fr black & multi. 35 25

European heart research week, Feb. 21–28.

Dam and Hassan II
A91

1971, Mar. 3 *Perf. 11½*

241 A91 25fr multicolored 20 15
a. Souv. sheet of 4 1.75 1.75

10th anniversary of accession of King Hassan II.

No. 241a contains 4 No. 241. Black marginal inscription and control number. Size: 115x99mm. Issued Mar. 24. Sold for 2.50d.

Black and White Hands with Dove and Emblem
A92

1971, June 16 Photo. *Perf. 13*

242 A92 50fr brown & multi. 30 20

International Year against Racial Discrimination.

Children Around the World
A93

Shah Mohammed Riza Pahlavi of Iran
A94

1971, Oct. 4 Litho. *Perf. 13x14*

243 A93 40fr emerald & multi. 30 20

International Children's Day.

1971, Oct. 11 Photo. *Perf. 11½*

244 A94 1d blue & multi. 50 40

2500th anniversary of the founding of the Persian empire by Cyrus the Great.

Mausoleum of Mohammed V—A95

Designs: 50fr, Mausoleum, close-up view, and Mohammed V. 1d, Decorated interior wall (vert.).

1971, Nov. 10 Litho. *Perf. 14*

245 A95 25fr multicolored 20 20
246 " 50fr " 30 25
247 " 1d " 60 30

Soccer Ball and Games Emblem
A96

Design: 60fr, Runner and games emblem.

1971, Nov. 30 Photo. *Perf. 13x13½*

248 A96 40fr multicolored 25 20
249 " 60fr red & multi. 35 20

Mediterranean Games, Izmir, Turkey, Oct. 6–17.

Arab Postal Union Emblem
A97

1971, Dec. 23 Litho. *Perf. 13x12½*

250 A97 25fr dk. & light blue & orange 20 10

25th anniversary of the Conference of Sofar, Lebanon, establishing Arab Postal Union.

Sun over Cultivated Sand Dunes
A98

Torch and Book Year Emblem
A99

1971, Dec. 30 Photo. *Perf. 12½*

251 A98 70fr black, bl. & yel. 40 25

Sherifian Phosphate Office (fertilizer production and export), 50th anniversary.

1972, Jan. 12 *Perf. 11½*

252 A99 1d silver & multi. 55 30

International Book Year 1972.

National Lottery A100 — Bridge of Sighs A101

1972, Feb. 7 Photo. *Perf. 13*
253 A100 25fr tan, blk. & gold 20 18
Creation of a national lottery.

1972, Feb. 25
Designs: 50fr, St. Mark's Basilica and waves (horiz.). 1d, Lion of St. Mark.
254 A101 25fr multicolored 20 20
255 " 50fr red, blk. & buff 30 20
256 " 1d lt. bl. & multi. 60 30
UNESCO campaign to save Venice.

Bridge, Road, Map of Africa—A102

1972, Apr. 21 *Perf. 13*
257 A102 75fr blue & multi. 45 25
2nd African Road Conference, Rabat, Apr. 17–22.

Morocco No. 223 A103

1972, Apr. 27 *Perf. 11½*
258 A103 1d lt. ultra. & multi. 55 30
Stamp Day 1972.

The Engagement of Imilchil, by Tayeb Lahlou A104

1972, May 26 Litho. *Perf. 13x13½*
259 A104 60fr black & multi. 40 25
Folklore Festival, Marrakesh, May 26–June 4.

Map of Africa, Dove and OAU Emblem A105

1972, June 12 Photo. *Perf. 11½*
260 A105 25fr multicolored 20 20
9th Summit Conference of Organization of African Unity, Rabat, June 12–15.

Landscape, Environment Emblem A106

1972, July 20 Photo. *Perf. 12½x12*
261 A106 50fr blue & multi. 30 20
U.N. Conference on Human Environment, Stockholm, June 5–16

Olympic Emblems, Running A107

Designs (Olympic Emblems and): 50fr, Wrestling. 75fr, Soccer. 1d, Bicycling.

1972, Aug. 29 Photo. *Perf. 13x13½*
262 A107 25fr red brown, pink & black 20 20
263 " 50fr vio., lilac & blk. 25 20
264 " 75fr green, yellow green & black 40 30
265 " 1d blue, lt. blue & black 50 40
20th Olympic Games, Munich, Aug. 26–Sept. 11.

Sow Thistle A108 — Mountain Gazelle A109

Design: 40fr, Amberboa crupinoides.

1972, Sept. 15 Litho. *Perf. 14*
266 A108 25fr lt. grn. & multi. 20 20
267 " 40fr multicolored 30 20

1972, Sept. 29 Photo. *Perf. 11½*
Design: 40fr, Barbary sheep.
268 A109 25fr multicolored 20 20
269 " 40fr " 30 20
Nos. 266–269 issued for nature protection.

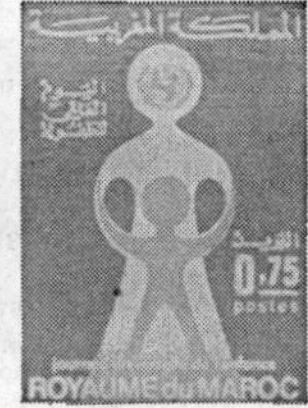

Rabat Rug A110 — Child and UNICEF Emblem A111

Designs: 25fr, High Atlas rug. 70fr, Tazenakht rug. 75fr, Rabat rug, different pattern.

Perf. 13½ (25fr, 70fr), 11½
1972–73 Photogravure
270 A110 25fr multi. ('73) 20 15
270A " 50fr multicolored 35 25
271 A110 70fr multi. ('73) 40 30
271A " 75fr " 45 35
Issue dates: 50fr, 75fr, Oct. 27, 1972; 25fr, 70fr, Dec. 28, 1973.
See Nos. 326–327.

1972, Dec. 20 Photo. *Perf. 13½x13*
272 A111 75fr brt. grn. & blue 45 25
International Children's Day.

Symbolic Letter Carrier and Stamp A112

1973, Jan. 30 Photo. *Perf. 13x13½*
273 A112 25fr brown & multi. 20 10
Stamp Day 1973.

Weather Map, Northern Hemisphere A113

1973, Feb. 23 Photo. *Perf. 13*
274 A113 70fr silver & multi. 45 30
Centenary of international meteorological cooperation.

King Hassan II, Coat of Arms A114

1973–76 Photogravure *Perf. 14*
275 A114 1fr pale yel. & multi. 3 3
276 " 2fr pale bl. & multi. 3 3
277 " 5fr pale olive & multi. 5 3
278 " 10fr brn. org. & multi. 6 3
279 " 15fr vio. gray & multi. 9 5
280 " 20fr pink & multi. 12 6
281 " 25fr pale bl. & multi. 15 5
282 " 30fr rose & multi. 15 5
283 " 35fr org. yel. & multi. 19 17
284 " 40fr lt. gray & multi. 20 5
285 " 50fr ultra. & multi. 27 10
286 " 60fr salmon & multi. 30 10
287 " 70fr yel. grn. & multi. 33 10
288 " 75fr lemon & multi. 35 10
289 " 80fr multicolored 40 33
290 " 90fr brt. grn. & multi. 50 10
291 " 1d beige & multi. 80 25
292 " 2d gray & multi. 2.00 30
293 " 3d lt. lilac & multi. 2.50 60
294 " 5d lt. brn. & multi. ('75) 3.00 1.25
294A " 5d pink & multi. ('76) 2.25 1.00
Nos. 275–294A (21) 13.77 4.78

مناظرة
الساحة
1973

Nos. B26–B27 Surcharged to Obliterate Surtax

1973, Mar. 13 *Perf. 11½*
295 SP1 25fr multicolored 1.50 1.50
296 " 70fr " 1.50 1.50
Tourism Conference 1973. Arabic overprint and date on one line on No. 296.
See se-tenant note below No. B11.
See Nos. 351–352.

Holy Ka'aba, Mecca, Mosque and Minaret, Rabat A115

1973, May 3 Photo. *Perf. 13½x14*
297 A115 25fr lt. blue & multi. 20 15
Mohammed's 1,403rd birthday.

Roses and M'Gouna A116

1973, May 14 *Perf. 13*
298 A116 25fr blue & multi. 20 15
Rose Festival of M'Gouna.

Hands, Torch, OAU Emblem A117

1973, May 25 Photo. *Perf. 14x13*
299 A117 70fr deep claret & multi. 40 20
Organization for African Unity, 10th anniversary.

Dancers with Tambourines A118

Design: 1d, Dancer with handbells, Marrakesh Minaret, Atlas Mountain.

1973, May 30 *Perf. 12½x13*
300 A118 50fr multicolored 30 20
301 " 1d " 50 35
Folklore Festival, Marrakesh.

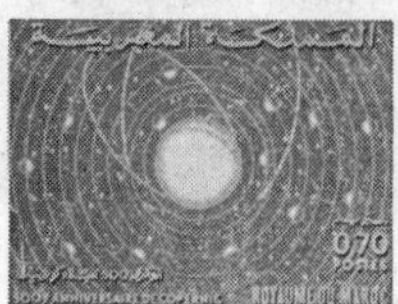

Heliocentric System A119

1973, June 29 *Perf. 13x13½*
302 A119 70fr dk. bl. & multi. 40 25
500th anniversary of the birth of Nicolaus Copernicus (1473–1543), Polish astronomer.

Microscope, WHO Emblem, World Map A120

1973, July 16 Photo. *Perf. 13x12½*
303 A120 70fr multicolored 40 25
World Health Organization, 25th anniversary.

INTERPOL Emblem, Fingerprint
A121

1973, Sept. 12 Photo. *Perf. 13x13½*
304 A121 70fr brn., silver & bl. 40 30
50th anniversary of International Criminal Police Organization (INTERPOL).

Flower Type of 1972

Designs: 25fr, Daisies (horiz.). 1d, Thistle.

1973, Oct. 12 Litho. *Perf. 14*
305 A108 25fr ocher & multi. 20 10
306 " 1d yellow & multi. 55 35
Nature protection.

Berber Hyena
A122

Design: 50fr, Eleonora's falcon (vert.).

1973, Nov. 23 Photo. *Perf. 14*
307 A122 25fr multicolored 20 20
308 " 50fr " 35 20
Nature protection.

Map and Colors of Morocco, Algeria and Tunisia
A123

1973, Dec. 7 *Perf. 13x13½*
309 A123 25fr gold & multi. 20 15
Maghreb Committee for Coordination of Posts and Telecommunications.

Fairway and Drive over Water Hazard
A124

Map of Africa, Scales, Human Rights Flame
A125

1974, Feb. 8 Photo. *Perf. 14x13*
310 A124 70fr multicolored 45 30
International Golf Grand Prix for the Hassan II Morocco trophy.

No. 227 Overprinted in Red المؤتمر الاسلامي - لاهور
1394

1974, Feb. 25 *Perf. 11½*
311 A79 1d multicolored 1.20 50
Islamic Conference, Lahore, India, 1974.

1974, Mar. 15 Photo. *Perf. 14x13½*
312 A125 70fr gold & multi. 40 25
25th anniversary of the Universal Declaration of Human Rights.

Vanadinite
A126

Minaret, Marrakesh Mosque, Rotary Emblem
A127

1974–75 Photogravure *Perf. 13*
Multicolored
313 A126 25fr *shown* 20 20
313A " 50fr *Aragonite* 30 20
314 " 70fr *Erythrine* 40 25
314A " 1d *Agate* 50 25
Issue dates: 25fr, 70fr, Apr. 30, 1974; 50fr, 1d, Feb. 14, 1975.

1974, May 11 Photo. *Perf. 14*
315 A127 70fr multicolored 40 30
District 173 Rotary International annual meeting, Marrakesh, May 10–12.

UPU Emblem, Congress Dates
A128

Drummer and Dancers
A129

Design: 1d, Scroll with UPU emblem, Lausanne coat of arms and 17th UPU Congress emblem (horiz.).

1974, May 30 Photogravure
316 A128 25fr lt. grn., orange & black 20 15
317 " 1d dark green & multi. 50 35
Centenary of Universal Postal Union.

1974, June 7 Photo. *Perf. 14*
Design: 70fr, Knife juggler and women.
318 A129 25fr multicolored 25 15
319 " 70fr " 45 25
National folklore festival, Marrakesh.

Environment Emblem, Polution, Clean Water and Air—A130

1974, June 25 *Perf. 13*
320 A130 25fr multicolored 20 15
World Environment Day.

Simulated Stamps, Cancel and Magnifier
A131

1974, Aug. 2 Photogravure *Perf. 13*
321 A131 70fr silver & multi. 40 30
Stamp Day 1974.

No. J5 Surcharged الاحصاء الفلاحي

1,00

1974, Sept. 25 Photo. *Perf. 14*
322 D2 1d on 5fr multi. 1.20 1.00
Agricultural census.

World Soccer Cup
A132

Double-spurred Francolin
A133

1974, Oct. 11
323 A132 1d brt. bl. & multi. 60 45
World Cup Soccer Championship, Munich, June 13–July 7.
A stamp similar to No. 323, also issued Oct. 11, has gold inscription: "CHAMPION: R.F.A." in French and Arabic, honoring the German Federal Republic as championship winner. Price $25.

Perf. 14x13½, 13½x14

1974, Dec. 5 Photogravure
Design: 70fr, Leopard (horiz.).
324 A133 25fr multicolored 20 15
325 " 70fr " 40 35
Nature protection.

Zemmour Rug
A134

Columbine
A135

Design: 1d, Beni Mguilo rug.

1974, Dec 20 *Perf. 13*
326 A134 25fr multicolored 20 15
327 " 1d " 50 30
See Nos. 349-350, 398-400.

1975 Photogravure *Perf. 13½*
Flowers: 10fr, Daisies. 35fr, Orange lilies. 50fr, Anemones. 60fr, White starflower. 70fr, Poppies. 90fr, Carnations. 1d, Pansies.

328	A135	10fr multicolored		15	15
329	"	25fr	"	15	10
330	"	35fr	"	20	15
331	"	50fr	"	25	15
332	"	60fr	"	30	20
333	"	70fr	"	35	20
334	"	90fr	"	50	25
335	"	1d	"	50	40
		Nos. 328-335 (8)		2.40	1.60

Issue dates: 25fr, 35fr, 70fr, 90fr, Jan. 10; others, Apr. 29.

Water Carrier, by Feu Tayeb Lahlou
A136

1975, Apr. 3 *Perf. 13*
338 A136 1d multicolored 50 25

Stamp Collector, Carrier Pigeon, Globe
A137

Musicians and Dancers
A138

1975, May 21 Photo. *Perf. 13*
339 A137 40fr gold & multi. 25 15
Stamp Day 1975.

1975, June 12 Photo. *Perf. 14x13½*
340 A138 1d multicolored 50 30
16th Folklore Festival, Marrakesh, May 30–June 15.

Guitar and Association for the Blind Emblem
A139

1975, July 8 *Perf. 13x13½*
341 A139 1d purple & multi. 50 30
Week of the Blind.

Animals in Forest
A140

1975, July 25 Photo. *Perf. 13x13½*
342 A140 25fr multicolored 20 10
Children's Week.

Games' Emblem, Runner, Weight Lifter—A141

1975, Sept. 4 Photo. ***Perf. 13***
343 A141 40fr gold, maroon & buff 20 10

7th Mediterranean Games, Algiers, Aug. 23–Sept. 6.

Bald Ibis A142

Design: 1d, Persian lynx (vert.).

1975, Oct. 21 Photo. ***Perf. 13***
344 A142 40fr multicolored 20 15
345 " 1d " 50 35

Nature protection.

King Mohammed V Greeting Crowd, Prince Moulay Hassan at Left—A143

King Hassan II A144

Design: No. 348, King Mohammed V wearing fez.

1975, Nov. 21 Photo. ***Perf. 13½***
346 A143 40fr black, silver & dark blue 20 12
347 A144 1d black, gold & dark blue 45 30
348 " 1d black, gold & dark blue 45 30
a. Sheet of 3 15.00 15.00

20th anniversary of independence.
No. 348a contains one each of Nos. 346–348; silver stars and black coat of arms in margin. Size: 187x96mm.

Rug Type of 1974

Designs: 25fr, Ouled Besseba rug. 1d, Ait Ouaouzguid rug.

1975, Dec. 11
349 A134 25fr red & multi. 20 10
350 " 1d org. & multi. 45 30

المسيرة الخضراء
1975

Nos. B29–B30 Surcharged in Green

1975 ***Perf. 11½***
351 SP1 25fr blue & multi. 1.10 90
352 " 70fr org. & multi. 1.65 1.35

March of Moroccan people into Spanish Sahara, Dec. 1975.
See se-tenant note after No. B11.

"Green March of the People" A145
Copper Coin, Fes, 1883–84 A146

1975, Dec. 30 Photo. ***Perf. 13½x13***
353 A145 40fr multicolored 20 15

March of Moroccan people into Spanish Sahara, Dec. 1975.

1976 Photo. ***Perf. 14x13½***

Coins: 15fr, 50fr, Silver coin, Rabat, 1774–75. 35fr, 65fr, Gold coin, Sabta, 13th–14th centuries. 1d, Square coin, Sabta, 12th–13th centuries. 40fr, as 5fr.

354 A146 5fr dull rose & multicolored 6 5
355 " 15fr brown & multi. 8 4
356 " 35fr gray & multi. 20 10
357 " 40fr ocher & multi. 18 12
358 " 50fr ultra. & black 22 13
359 " 65fr yel. & multi. 30 20
360 " 1d multicolored 45 30
Nos. 354-360 (7) 1.49 94

Issue dates: Nos. 354–356, Apr. 26. Nos. 357–360, Jan. 20.
See Nos. 403–406.

1976, Sept. 9

Designs: Various Moroccan coins.

361 A146 5fr green & multi. 6 5
362 " 15fr deep rose & multicolored 10 8
363 " 20fr light blue & multicolored 13 6
364 " 30fr lilac rose & multicolored 15 8
365 " 35fr green & multi. 20 13
366 " 70fr orange & multi. 35 20
Nos. 361-366 (6) 99 60

Family A147

Arch, Ibn Zaidoun Mosque A148

1976, Feb. 12 ***Perf. 14x13½***
367 A147 40fr multicolored 20 12

Family planning.

Perf. 13½x14, 14x13½

1976, Feb. 12 Photogravure

Design: 40fr, Hall, Ibn Zaidoun Mosque (horiz.).

368 A148 40fr multicolored 20 15
369 " 65fr " 30 20

Ibn Zaidoun Mosque, millennium.

Medersa bou Anania, Fes A149

1976, Feb. 26 ***Perf. 13x14½***
370 A149 1d multicolored 40 25

Boro-budur Temple A150

Design: 40fr, Bas-relief, Borobudur.

1976, Mar. 11 Photo. ***Perf. 13***
371 A150 40fr multicolored 20 15
372 " 1d " 45 25

UNESCO campaign to save Borobudur Temple, Java.

Jewelry Type of 1968

Designs: 40fr, Pendant. 1d, Breastplate.

1976, June 29 Photo. ***Perf. 14x13½***
373 A67 40fr blue & multi. 20 15
374 " 1d olive & multi. 45 30

Moroccan Red Crescent Society.
Nos. 373–374 were printed se-tenant in sheets of 10 (5x2) arranged vertically tête-bêche.

Bicentennial Emblem, Flags and Map of U.S. and Morocco—A152

Design: 1d, George Washington, King Hassan, Statue of Liberty and Royal Palace, Rabat (vert.).

1976, July 27 Photo. ***Perf. 14***
375 A152 40fr multicolored 30 20
376 " 1d " 60 45

American Bicentennial.

Wrestling A153

Designs (Montreal Olympic Games Emblem and): 40fr, Bicycling. 50fr, Boxing. 1d, Running.

1976, Aug. 11 ***Perf. 13x13½***
377 A153 35fr multicolored 15 10
378 " 40fr " 20 15
379 " 50fr red & multi. 25 20
380 " 1d purple & multi. 50 30

21st Olympic Games, Montreal, Canada, July 17–Aug. 1.

Old and New Telephones, Radar A154

1976, Sept. 29 Photo. ***Perf. 14***
381 A154 1d gold & multi. 55 35

Centenary of first telephone call by Alexander Graham Bell, Mar. 10, 1876.

Blind Person's Identification A155

1976, Oct. 12 Photo. ***Perf. 13½x14***
382 A155 50fr multicolored 25 15

Week of the Blind.

Chanting Goshawk A156

Design: 1d, Purple gallinule.

1976, Oct. 29 ***Perf. 13x13½***
383 A156 40fr multicolored 20 15
384 " 1d " 45 30

Nature protection.

King Hassan, Star, Torch, Map of Morocco A157

1976, Nov. 19 Photo. ***Perf. 12½x13***
385 A157 40fr multicolored 20 12

First anniversary of Green March into Spanish Sahara.

Nos. B34–B35 Overprinted with 2 Bars over Surcharge and 4-line Arabic Inscription.

1976, Nov. 29 Photo. ***Perf. 13½***
386 SP1 25fr ultra., black & orange 50 40
387 " 70fr red, blk. & org. 1.50 1.20

5th African Tuberculosis Conference, Rabat.

Globe and Dove A158

1976, Dec. 16 ***Perf. 13***
388 A158 1d blue, blk. & red 45 30

5th Summit Meeting of Non-aligned Countries, Colombo, Aug. 9–19, and 25th anniversary of Organization of Non-aligned Countries.

Africa Cup A159

1976, Dec. 29 Photo. *Perf. 14*
389 A159 1d multicolored 45 30
African Soccer Cup.

Letters Circling Globe, Postmark
A160

1977, Jan. 24 Photo. *Perf. 13½*
390 A160 40fr multicolored 20 12
Stamp Day 1977.

Aeonium Arboreum
A161

Malope Trifida
A162

Design: 1d, Hesperolaburnum platyclarpum.

Perf. 13x13½, 14 (A162)

1977, Feb. 22
391 A161 40fr multicolored 20 10
392 A162 50fr " 25 20
393 A161 1d " 45 30

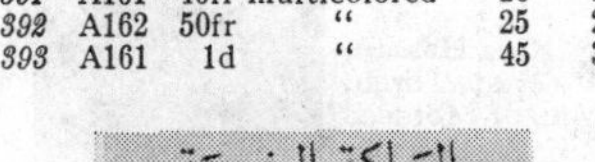

Ornamental Lamps, View of Salé
A163

1977, Mar. 24 Photo. *Perf. 14*
394 A163 40fr multicolored 20 12
Candle procession of Salé.

موسم حب الملوك
1977

No. J6 Surcharged in Orange

0,40

1977, May 11 Photo. *Perf. 14*
395 D2 40fr on 10fr multi. 55 35
Cherry Festival 1977.

Map of Arab Countries, Emblem
A164

1977, June 2 Photo. *Perf. 14*
396 A164 50fr multicolored 22 15
5th Congress of Organization of Arab Cities.

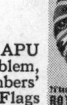

APU Emblem, Members' Flags
A165

1977, June 20
397 A165 1d multicolored 45 30
Arab Postal Union, 25th anniversary.

Rug Type of 1974

Designs: 35fr, No. 399A, Marmoucha rug (diff.). No. 399, Ait Haddou rug. 1d, Salé rug.

Perf. 11½x12, 13½ (#399A)

1977–79 Photogravure
398 A134 35fr multicolored 15 10
399 " 40fr " 15 10
399A " 40fr " 20 12
400 " 1d " 45 35

Issue dates: No. 399A, Mar. 8, 1979, others, July 21, 1977.

Cithara
A166

Ali Jinnah and Map of Pakistan
A167

1977, Aug. 18 Photo. *Perf. 14*
401 A166 1d multicolored 45 30
Week of the Blind.

1977, Oct. 10 Photo. *Perf. 13½x13*
402 A167 70fr multicolored 30 20
Mohammed Ali Jinnah (1876–1948), first Governor General of Pakistan.

Coin Type of 1976

Designs: Various Moroccan coins.

1977–78 *Perf. 14x13½*
403 A146 10fr gray & multi. 5 5
404 " 60fr dk. red & multi. ('78) 25 20
405 " 75fr citron & multi. 30 20
406 " 2d yellow green & multi. 90 55

Marcher with Flag, Map of Morocco and Spanish Sahara
A168

1977, Nov. 6 Photo. *Perf. 14*
407 A168 1d multicolored 45 30
Second anniversary of Green March into Spanish Sahara.

Chamber of Representatives—A169

1977, Nov. 6 *Perf. 13½*
408 A169 1d multicolored 45 30
a. Souvenir sheet 2.00 2.00

Opening of Chamber of Representatives. No. 408a contains one No. 408; multicolored margin with black control number. Size: 122x86mm. Sold for 3d.

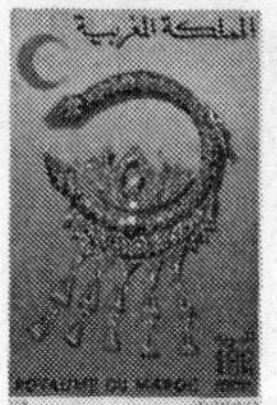

Enameled Silver Brooch
A170

Copper Vessel
A171

1977, Dec. 14 Photo. *Perf. 11½*
409 A170 1d multicolored 45 30
Moroccan Red Crescent Society.

1978, Jan. 5 Photo. *Perf. 13*
Design: 1d, Standing filigree copper bowl with cover.
410 A171 40fr gold & multi. 15 10
411 " 1d " " 45 30

Printed se-tenant in sheets of 10 (5x2) arranged vertically tête bêche.

Map of Sahara, Cogwheel Emblem
A172

Covered Jar
A173

Design: 1d, Map of North Africa, fish in net, camels (horiz.).

1978, Feb. 27 Photo. *Perf. 14*
412 A172 40fr multicolored 15 10
413 " 1d " 45 30
Promotion of the Sahara.

1978, Mar. 27 *Perf. 13½x13*
Design: No. 415, Vase.
414 A173 1d multicolored 45 30
415 " 1d " 45 30
Week of the Blind.

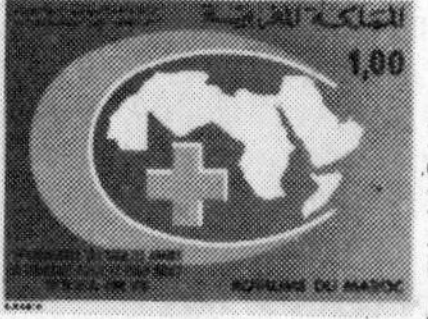

Red Crescent, Red Cross, Arab Countries
A174

1978, Apr. 14 *Perf. 13x13½*
416 A174 1d multicolored 45 30
10th Conference of Arab Red Crescent and Red Cross Societies, Apr. 10–15.

View of Fes, Rotary Emblem
A175

1978, Apr. 22 Photo. *Perf. 14*
417 A175 1d multicolored 50 30
Rotary International Meeting, Fes, District 173.

Dome of the Rock, Jerusalem
A176

Folk Dancers and Flutist
A177

1978, May 29 *Perf. 14½*
418 A176 5fr multicolored 3 3
419 " 10fr " 5 3
Palestinian fighters and their families.

1978, June 15 *Perf. 13½x13*
420 A177 1d multicolored 50 30
National Folklore Festival, Marrakesh.

Sugar Cane Field, and Conveyor Belt—A178

1978, July 24 Photo. *Perf. 13*
421 A178 40fr multicolored 20 12
Sugar industry.

Games Emblem
A179

Bird, Tree, Tent, Scout Emblem
A180

1978, Aug. 25
422 A179 1d multicolored 50 30
World sailing championships.

1978, Sept. 26 Photo. *Perf. 13*
423 A180 40fr multicolored 20 12
Pan-Arab Scout Jamboree, Rabat.

View of Fes
A181

1978, Oct. 10
424 A181 40fr multicolored 20 12
Moulay Idriss the Great, Festival, Fes.

Flame Emblem
A182

1978, Dec. 21 Photo. *Perf. 14*

425	A182	1d multicolored	50	30

30th anniversary of Universal Declaration of Human Rights.

Houses, Agadir
A183

Design: 1d, Old Fort, Marrakesh.

1979, Jan. 25 Photo. *Perf. 12*

426	A183	40fr multicolored	20	12
427	"	1d "	50	30

Soccer and Cup
A184

1979, Mar. 2 *Perf. 13*

428	A184	40fr multicolored	20	12

Mohammed V Soccer Cup.

SEMI-POSTAL STAMPS

+10f

Nos. 1-5 Surcharged

اغاثة ضحايا
الزيوت المسممة
اكتوبر 1959

Engraved

1960, Mar. *Perf. 13* Unwmkd.

B1	A1	5fr+10fr bright blue & indigo	50	45
B2	"	10fr+10fr bistre brown & chocolate	70	65
B3	"	15fr+10fr deep green & magenta	1.00	90
B4	"	25fr+15fr purple	1.35	1.10
B5	"	30fr+20fr green	1.50	1.35
		Nos. B1-B5 (5)	5.05	4.45

The surtax aided families whose members consumed adulterated cooking oil with crippling or fatal results.

French Morocco Nos. 321 and 322 Surcharged

اسبوعا
التضامن
1380
1960
15+3

1960, Sept. 12

B6	A71	15fr+3fr on 18fr dark green	40	40
B7	"	20fr+5fr brown lake	60	60

Nos. 1 and 6 Surcharged in Red or Black

فيضانات
1
9
6
3

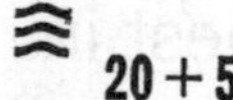

Engraved

1963, Jan. 28 *Perf. 13* Unwmkd.

B8	A1	20fr+5fr on 5fr bright blue & indigo (R)	50	45
B9	"	30fr+10fr on 50fr rose red	70	65

The surtax was for flood victims.

Moroccan Brooch
SP1

Design: 40fr+10fr, Brooch with pendants.

1966, May 23 Photo. *Perf. 11½*

Granite Paper

B10	SP1	25fr+5fr ultra., silver, blk. & red	35	30
B11	"	40fr+10fr magenta, silver, black, ultra. & blue	55	50

Issued to commemorate the meeting in Morocco of the Middle East and North African Red Cross-Red Crescent Seminar. The surtax was for the Moroccan Red Crescent Society.

Nos. B10-B11 were printed se-tenant in sheets of 10 (5x2) arranged vertically tête bêche.

See also Nos. B12-B13, B15-B16, B19-B22, B26-B27, B29-B30, B34-B35.

1967, May 15 Granite Paper

Designs: 60fr+5fr, Two brooches linked by silver drapery. 1d+10fr, Two bracelets.

B12	SP1	60fr+5fr yel. bis. & multicolored	60	60
B13	"	1d+10fr emerald & multicolored	1.20	1.20

The surtax was for the Moroccan Red Crescent Society. Each value printed tête bêche in sheets of 10 (5x2).

Hands Reading Braille and Map of Morocco—SP2

1969, Mar. 21 Photo. *Perf. 12½*

B14	SP2	25fr+10fr multi.	25	20

Week of the Blind, Mar. 21-29.

Jewelry Type of 1966

Designs: 25fr+5fr, Silver earrings. 40fr+10fr, Gold ear pendant.

1969, May 9 Photo. *Perf. 11½*

Granite Paper

B15	SP1	25fr+5fr gray green & multicolored	35	30
B16	"	40fr+10fr tan & multicolored	55	50

50th anniversary of the League of Red Cross Societies. Surtax was for Moroccan Red Crescent Society.

See se-tenant note after No. B11.

Nos. 173-174 Surcharged

+0 25
فيضانات 1970

1970, Feb. 26 Litho. *Perf. 13*

B17	A65	10fr+25fr multi.	3.25	3.25
B18	"	15fr+25fr "	3.25	3.25

The surtax was for flood victims.

Jewelry Type of 1966

Designs: 25fr+5fr Necklace with pendants. 50fr+10fr, Earring with 5 pendants.

1970, May 25 Photo. *Perf. 11½*

Granite Paper

B19	SP1	25fr+5fr gray & multicolored	30	30
B20	"	50fr+10fr brt. violet & multicolored	60	60

Surtax for Moroccan Red Crescent Society.

See se-tenant note after No. B11.

1971, May 10

Designs: 25fr+5fr, Brooch. 40fr+10fr, Stomacher.

Granite Paper

B21	SP1	25fr+5fr gray & multicolored	30	30
B22	"	40fr+10fr yellow & multicolored	40	40

See se-tenant note after No. B11.

Globe and Map of Palestine
SP3

1971, Apr. 30 *Perf. 13*

B23	SP3	25fr+10fr multi.	30	25

Palestine Week, May 3-8.

Banjo and Cross-bow
SP4

1971, June 28 Photo. *Perf. 12*

B24	SP4	40fr+10fr multi.	30	30

Week of the Blind.

Mizmar (Double Flute)
SP5

1972, Mar. 31 Photo. *Perf. 13x13½*

B25	SP5	25fr+10fr multi.	25	25

Week of the Blind.

Jewelry Type of 1966

Designs: 25fr+5fr, Jeweled bracelets. 70fr+10fr, Rectangular pendant with ball drop.

1972, May 8 Photo. *Perf. 11½*

Granite Paper

B26	SP1	25fr+5fr brown & multicolored	30	30
B27	"	70fr+10fr dp. grn. & multicolored	50	50

See se-tenant note after No. B11.

Drums
SP6

1973, Mar. 30 Photo. *Perf. 13x14*

B28	SP6	70fr+10fr multi.	50	45

Week of the Blind.

Jewelry Type of 1966

Designs: 25fr+5fr, Silver box pendant. 70fr+10fr, Bracelet.

1973, June 15 Photo. *Perf. 11½*

B29	SP1	25fr+5fr bl. & multi.	30	30
B30	"	70fr+10fr orange & multicolored	50	50

Moroccan Red Crescent Society. See 2nd note after No. B11.

Pistol
SP7

Erbab (Fiddle)
SP8

Design: 70fr+10fr, Decorated antique powder box.

1974, July 8 Photo. *Perf. 14x13½*

B31	SP7	25fr+5fr multi.	30	30
B32	"	70fr+10fr "	65	65

Moroccan Red Crescent Society. See se-tenant note after B11.

1975, Jan. 10 Photo. *Perf. 13*

B33	SP8	70fr+10fr multi.	40	35

Week of the Blind.

Jewelry Type of 1966

Designs: 25fr+5fr, Silver pendant. 70fr+10fr, Earring.

1975, Mar. 13 Photo. *Perf. 13½*

B34	SP1	25fr+5fr multi.	25	25
B35	"	70fr+10fr "	45	40

Moroccan Red Crescent Society. See se-tenant note after No. B11.

AIR POST STAMPS

Sultan's Star over Casablanca AP1 — King Hassan II AP2

Engraved.

1957, May 4 ***Perf. 13*** **Unwmkd.**

No.	Type	Description	Unused	Used
C1	AP1	15fr car. & brt. green	90	90
C2	"	25fr bright greenish blue	90	90
C3	"	30fr red brown	1.20	1.20

Issued to publicize the International Fair at Casablanca, May 4-19, 1957.

1962

No.	Type	Description	Unused	Used
C5	AP2	90fr black	60	15
C6	"	1d rose red	1.00	20
C7	"	2d deep blue	1.25	85
C8	"	3d dull blue green	2.00	1.35
C9	"	5d purple	3.75	1.50
		Nos. C5-C9 (5)	8.60	4.05

Type of Regular Issue

Design: 90fr, Anemometer and globe.

1964, Mar. 23 **Photo.** ***Perf. 11½***

Granite Paper

No.	Type	Description	Unused	Used
C10	A39	90fr multicolored	75	60

Issued to commemorate the United Nations Fourth World Meteorological Day, March 23.

Casablanca Fair AP3

1964, Apr. 30 **Photo.** ***Perf. 12½***

No.	Type	Description	Unused	Used
C11	AP3	1d bl., bister & orge.	75	60

Issued to commemorate the 20th anniversary of the International Fair at Casablanca.

Moroccan Pavilion and Unisphere AP4

1964, May 25 ***Perf. 12½*** **Unwmkd.**

No.	Type	Description	Unused	Used
C12	AP4	1d dk. grn., red & bl.	1.00	80

New York World's Fair, 1964-65.

Ramses II and UNESCO Emblem AP5

Lithographed and Engraved

1966, Oct. 3 ***Perf. 12x11½***

No.	Type	Description	Unused	Used
C13	AP5	1d magenta, *yellow*	90	60

Issued to commemorate the 20th anniversary of UNESCO (United Nations Educational, Scientific and Cultural Organization).

Jet Plane—AP6

Photogravure

1966, Dec. 19 ***Perf. 12½x13½***

No.	Type	Description	Unused	Used
C14	AP6	3d multicolored	2.50	1.20

Costume Type of Regular Issue

Design: 1d, Women from Ait Ouaouzguit.

1969, Jan. 21 **Litho.** ***Perf. 12***

No.	Type	Description	Unused	Used
C15	A74	1d multicolored	1.00	60

Coin Type of Regular Issue, 1968

Coins: 1d, King Mohammed V, 1960. 5d, King Hassan II, 1965.

1969, Mar. 3 **Photo.** ***Perf. 11½***

Granite Paper

No.	Type	Description	Unused	Used
C16	A73	1d bright blue, silver & black	1.50	1.20
C17	"	5d violet black, silver & black	6.50	4.00

POSTAGE DUE STAMPS

D1 — Oranges D2

Typographed

1965 ***Perf. 14x13½*** **Unwmkd.**

No.	Type	Description	Unused	Used
J1	D1	5fr green	10	5
J2	"	10fr bister brown	10	5
J3	"	20fr red	20	8
J4	"	30fr brown black	25	13

1974-78 **Photo.** ***Perf. 14***

Multicolored

No.	Type	Description	Unused	Used
J5	D2	5fr *shown*	6	3
J6	"	10fr *Cherries*	10	5
J7	"	20fr *Grapes*	20	10
J8	"	30fr *Peaches* (horiz.)	25	15
J9	"	40fr *Grapes* ('78)	15	10
J10	"	60fr *Peaches* (horiz.) ('78)	30	20
J11	"	80fr *Oranges* ('78)	35	25
		Nos. J5-J11 (7)	1.41	88

Northern Zone

100 Centimos = 1 Peseta

Sultan Mohammed V A1

Villa Sanjurjo Harbor A2

Designs: 25c, Polytechnic school. 50c, 10p, Institute of Culture, Tetuan.

Perf. 13x12½, 12½x13

1956, Aug. 23 **Photo.** **Unwmkd.**

No.	Type	Description	Unused	Used
1	A1	10c deep rose	8	7
2	A2	15c yellow brown	8	8
3	"	25c dark blue gray	8	8
4	A1	50c dark olive	38	38
5	"	80c bright green	38	38
6	A2	2p bright red lilac	3.00	2.50
7	"	3p bright blue	6.00	4.50
8	A1	10p green	21.00	18.00
		Nos. 1-8 (8)	31.00	25.99

Sultan Mohammed V A3 — A4

1957, Mar. 2 ***Perf. 13½x13***

No.	Type	Description	Unused	Used
9	A3	80c blue green	60	45
10	"	1.50p gray olive	1.80	1.50
11	"	3p deep rose	5.00	4.50

Issued to commemorate the first anniversary of independence. See Morocco Nos. 13-15.

1957 **Engraved.** ***Perf. 13***

No.	Type	Description	Unused	Used
12	A4	30c bright blue & indigo	15	8
13	"	70c bis. brown & choc.	30	8
14	"	80c bright violet	75	22
15	"	1.50p deep green & magenta	45	15
16	"	3p green	60	22
17	"	7p rose red	2.50	75
		Nos. 12-17 (6)	4.75	1.50

Prince Moulay el Hassan A5 — King Mohammed V A6

1957, July 15 **Photo.** ***Perf. 13***

No.	Type	Description	Unused	Used
18	A5	80c blue	45	45
19	"	1.50p green	1.25	1.10
20	"	3p carmine rose	3.50	3.00

Nos. 13 and 15 Surcharged in Carmine or Black

بسيطة 1'20 PESETAS

1957 **Engraved.**

No.	Type	Description	Unused	Used
21	A4	15c on 70c bistre brown & chocolate (C)	50	38
22	"	1.20p on 1.50p deep green & magenta	1.20	50

The surcharge is in two lines on No. 21.

1957, Nov. **Photo.** ***Perf. 12½***

No.	Type	Description	Unused	Used
23	A6	1.20p black & brt. green	60	60
24	"	1.80p black & rose red	65	65
25	"	3p black & violet	1.50	1.20

30th anniversary of the enthronement of Mohammed V.

AIR POST STAMPS.

Plane over Lau Dam AP1

Design: 1.40p, 4.80p, Plane over Nekor bridge.

Perf. 12½x13

1956, Dec. 17 **Photo.** **Unwmkd.**

No.	Type	Description	Unused	Used
C1	AP1	25c rose violet	15	15
C2	"	1.40p lilac rose	22	22
C3	"	3.40p org. vermilion	2.25	2.00
C4	"	4.80p dull violet	3.25	3.00

MOZAMBIQUE,

People's Republic of

(mō'zăm·bēk')

LOCATION — In southeastern Africa, bordering on the Mozambique Channel.

GOVT.—Independent state.

POP.—9,680,000 (est. 1977).

AREA—297,731 sq. mi.

CAPITAL—Maputo (Lourenço Marques).

Formerly a Portuguese colony, Mozambique, or Portuguese East Africa, was divided into eight districts: Lourenço Marques, Inhambane, Quelimane, Tete, Mozambique, Zambezia, Nyassa and the Manica and Sofala region formerly administered by the Mozambique Company. At various times the districts issued their own stamps which were eventually replaced by those inscribed "Mocambique."

Mozambique achieved independence June 25, 1975, taking the name People's Republic of Mozambique.

1000 Reis = 1 Milreis
100 Centavos = 1 Escudo (1913)

Portuguese Crown
A1

King Luiz
A2

Perf. 12½, 13½.

1877-85 Typographed Unwmkd.

1 A1 5r black 1.00 75
a. Perf. 13½ 2.25 2.00
2 " 10r yellow 5.50 4.25
3 " 10r green ('81) 1.25 90
4 " 20r bistre 1.40 90
a. Perf. 13½ 3.00 1.75
5 " 20r rose ('85) 200.00 100.00
6 " 25r rose 70 50
a. Perf. 13½ 7.50 1.25
7 " 25r violet ('85) 3.25 2.00
8 " 40r blue 15.00 11.00
9 " 40r yellow buff ('81) 2.25 2.00
a. Perf. 12½ 3.75 3.00
10 " 50r green 50.00 17.50
a. Perf. 13½ 87.50 55.00
11 " 50r blue ('81) 90 70
12 " 100r lilac 1.00 70
13 " 200r orange 3.50 2.00
a. Perf. 12½ 5.00 3.50
14 " 300r chocolate 3.25 2.25

The reprints of the 1877-85 issues are printed on a smooth white chalky paper, ungummed, with rough perforation 13½, also on thin white paper, with shiny white gum and clean-cut perforation 13½. Price $1 each.

Typo. and Embossed

1886 ***Perf. 12½, 13½***

15 A2 5r black 1.40 90
a. Perf. 13½ 4.50 3.25
16 A2 10r green 1.40 90
a. Perf. 13½ 5.25 3.50
17 A2 20r rose 1.65 1.25
a. Perf. 13½ 11.00 6.00
18 A2 25r dull lilac 11.00 1.50
a. Perf. 13½ 19.50 5.50
19 A2 40r chocolate 2.00 1.25
a. Perf. 13½ 7.50
20 A2 50r blue 2.00 90
a. Perf. 13½ 12.50 3.00
21 A2 100r yellow brown 2.25 1.00
22 " 200r gray violet 4.50 3.00
a. Perf. 13½ 14.00 12.50
23 A2 300r orange 5.50 3.50

Nos. 15, 18, 19, 20, 21 and 23 have been reprinted. The reprints have shiny white gum and clean-cut perforation 13½. Many of the colors are paler than those of the originals. Price $1 each.

No. 19 Surcharged in Black

PROVISORIO
5 5

1893, Jan. ***Perf. 12½***

Without Gum

23A A2 5r on 40r chocolate 32.50 25.00

There are three varieties of No. 23A:
I. "PROVISORIO" 19mm. long, numerals 4½mm. high.
II. "PROVISORIO" 19½mm. long, numerals 5mm. high.
III. "PROVISORIO" 19½mm. long, numerals of both sizes.

King Carlos I
A3

Typographed.

1894 ***Perf. 11½, 12½***

24 A3 5r yellow 75 50
25 " 10r red lilac 75 50
26 " 15r red brown 1.00 75
27 " 20r gray lilac 1.25 75
28 " 25r blue green 1.00 30
29 " 50r light blue 4.50 60
a. Perf. 12½ 6.25 2.00
30 " 75r rose 2.00 1.75
31 " 80r yellow green 4.50 2.00
32 " 100r brown, *buff* 2.00 1.50
33 " 150r carmine, *rose* 11.00 6.00
a. Perf. 11½
34 " 200r dark blue, *blue* 4.50 3.25
35 " 300r dark blue, *salmon* 6.25 4.00

Nos. 28 and 31-33 have been reprinted with shiny white gum and clean-cut perforation 13½. Price of Nos. 28 and 31, each $1; Nos. 32-33, each $30.

Stamps of 1886 Overprinted in Red or Black

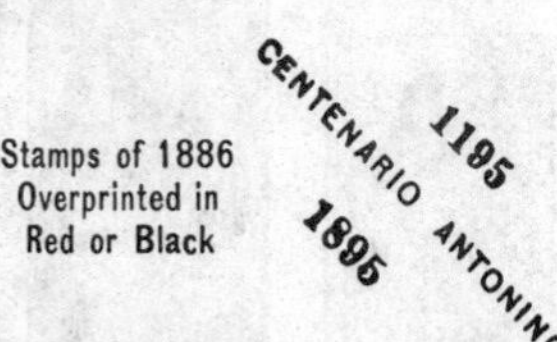

1895, July 1 ***Perf. 12½***

Without Gum

36 A2 5r black (R) 8.00 7.00
37 " 10r green 9.00 8.00
38 " 20r rose 10.00 8.00
39 " 25r violet 10.00 8.00
a. Double overprint
40 " 40r chocolate 10.00 9.00
41 " 50r blue 10.00 9.00
a. Perf. 13½ 60.00 45.00
42 " 100r yellow brown 10.00 10.00
43 " 200r gray violet 25.00 15.00
a. Perf. 13½ 60.00 45.00
44 " 300r orange 25.00 17.50

Commemorating the seventh centenary of the birth of Saint Anthony of Padua.

No. 35 Surcharged in Black

50
réis

1897, Jan. 2 ***Perf. 12½***

Without Gum

45 A3 50r on 300r dark blue, *salmon* 140.00 75.00

Nos. 17, 19 Surcharged

MOCAMBIQUE 2 ½ REIS *a*
MOCAMBIQUE 2½ RÉIS *b*
MOÇAMBIQUE 5 RÉIS *c*

1898 Without Gum

46 A2 (a) 2½r on 20r rose 17.50 15.00
47 " (b) 2½r on 20r rose 15.00 12.50
a. Inverted surcharge 30.00 30.00
48 " (c) 5r on 40r choc. 15.00 12.50
a. Inverted surcharge 35.00 35.00

King Carlos I
A4

Name and Value in Black except 500r.

1898-1903 Typographed. ***Perf. 11½***

49 A4 2½r gray 25 20
50 " 5r orange 25 20
51 " 10r light green 27 25
52 " 15r brown 2.75 1.50
53 " 15r gray green ('03) 90 70
54 " 20r gray violet 1.00 60
55 " 25r sea green 1.00 50
56 " 25r carmine ('03) 1.00 40
57 " 50r dark blue 1.25 50
58 " 50r brown ('03) 2.50 2.00
59 " 65r dull blue ('03) 6.50 5.50
60 " 75r rose 3.75 2.75
61 " 75r red lilac ('03) 2.50 1.90
62 " 80r violet 3.75 2.75
63 " 100r dark blue, *blue* 2.50 1.00
64 " 115r orange brown, *pink* ('03) 4.50 3.50
65 " 130r brn., *straw* ('03) 4.75 3.75
66 " 150r brown, *straw* 4.00 2.75
67 " 200r red lilac, *pinkish* 2.75 2.00
68 " 300r dark blue, *rose* 3.50 2.75
69 " 400r dull blue, *straw* ('03) 7.00 5.50
70 " 500r black & red, *blue* ('01) 7.50 5.50
71 " 700r violet, *yellowish* ('01) 12.00 9.00
Nos. 49-71 (23) 76.17 55.50

Stamps of 1886-94 Surcharged

65
RÉIS

1902 ***Perf. 12½, 13½***

On Stamps of 1886

Red Surcharge.

72 A2 115r on 5r black 2.50 1.75

Black Surcharge.

73 A2 65r on 20r rose 4.00 3.00
a. Double surcharge 10.00 10.00
74 " 65r on 40r chocolate 5.50 4.75
75 " 65r on 200r violet 4.00 2.00
76 " 115r on 50r blue 1.60 1.40
77 " 130r on 25r red violet 2.40 1.25
78 " 130r on 300r orange 2.00 1.25
79 " 400r on 10r green 6.50 4.00
80 A2 400r on 100r yellow brown 25.00 12.50

The reprints of Nos. 74, 75, 76, 77, 79 and 80 have shiny white gum and clean-cut perforation 13½. Price $1 each.

On Stamps of 1894.

Perf. 11½

81 A3 65r on 10r red lilac 3.00 2.50
82 " 65r on 15r red brown 3.25 2.75
a. Pair, one without surcharge
83 " 65r on 20r gray lilac 3.25 2.75
84 " 115r on 5r yellow 3.25 2.75
a. Inverted surcharge
85 " 115r on 25r blue green 3.25 2.75
86 " 130r on 75r rose 3.25 2.75
87 " 130r on 100r brown, *buff* 6.00 5.50
88 " 130r on 150r car., *rose* 3.25 2.75
89 " 130r on 200r blue, *blue* 4.75 4.50
90 " 400r on 50r light blue 1.50 1.00
91 " 400r on 80r yel. green 1.50 1.00
92 " 400r on 300r blue, *salmon* 1.50 1.00

On Newspaper Stamp of 1893.

Perf. 13½

93 N3 115r on 2½r brown 3.00 2.50

Reprints of No. 87 have shiny white gum and clean-cut perforation 13½. Price, $1 each.

Overprinted in Black PROVISORIO

On Stamps of 1898.

Perf. 11½

94 A4 15r brown 1.50 1.00
95 " 25r sea green 1.50 1.00
96 " 50r blue 2.25 2.00
97 " 75r rose 4.00 2.50

No. 59 Surcharged in Black

50
RÉIS

1905

98 A4 50r on 65r dull blue 2.50 2.25

Stamps of 1898-1903 Overprinted in Carmine or Green

REPUBLICA

1911

99 A4 2½r gray 30 25
a. Inverted overprint 2.10 2.10
100 " 5r orange 30 25
101 " 10r light green 1.25 75
102 " 15r gray green 30 25
103 " 20r gray violet 75 60
104 " 25r carmine (G) 25 20
a. 25r gray violet (error) 11.00 9.00
105 " 50r brown 30 25
106 " 75r red lilac 75 60
107 " 100r dark blue, *blue* 75 60
108 " 115r org. brown, *pink* 1.25 1.00
109 " 130r brown, *straw* 1.25 1.00
a. Double overprint
110 " 200r red lilac, *pinkish* 1.75 1.00
111 " 400r dull blue, *straw* 1.50 1.00
112 " 500r black & red, *blue* 1.50 1.00
113 " 700r violet, *straw* 1.50 1.00
Nos. 99-113 (15) 13.70 9.75

King Manoel
A5

Overprinted in Carmine or Green.

1912 ***Perf. 11½x12***

114 A5 2½r violet 20 18
115 " 5r black 20 18

116 A5 10r gray green 30 25
117 " 20r carmine (G) 35 35
118 " 25r violet brown 15 10
119 " 50r deep blue 50 35
120 " 75r bistre brown 50 35
121 " 100r brown, *light green* 40 35
122 " 200r dark green, *salmon* 80 40
123 " 300r *azure* 80 40

Perf. 14x15

124 A5 500r olive green & violet brown 1.25 1.00
Nos. 114-124 (11) 5.45 3.91

Vasco da Gama Issue of Various Portuguese Colonies Common Design Types Surcharged

REPUBLICA MOCAMBIQUE ¼ C.

1913

On Stamps of Macao.

125 CD20 ¼c on ½a bl. green 1.60 1.60
126 CD21 ½c on 1a red 1.60 1.60
127 CD22 1c on 2a red violet 1.60 1.60
128 CD23 2½c on 4a yel. green 1.60 1.60
a. Double surch. 20.00 20.00
129 CD24 5c on 8a dark blue 3.50 3.50
130 CD25 7½c on 12a vio. brn. 2.50 2.50
131 CD26 10c on 16a bistre brown 1.60 1.60
132 CD27 15c on 24a bistre 1.75 1.75
Nos. 125-132 (8) 15.75 15.75

On Stamps of Portuguese Africa.

133 CD20 ¼c on 2½r bl. green 1.25 1.25
134 CD21 ½c on 5r red 1.25 1.25
135 CD22 1c on 10r red violet 1.25 1.25
a. Inverted surch. 9.00 9.00
136 CD23 2½c on 25r yellow green 1.25 1.25
137 CD24 5c on 50r dk. blue 1.25 1.25
138 CD25 7½c on 75r violet brown 2.00 2.00
139 CD26 10c on 100r bistre brown 1.40 1.40
140 CD27 15c on 150r bistre 1.40 1.40
Nos. 133-140 (8) 11.05 11.05

On Stamps of Timor.

141 CD20 ¼c on ½a bl. green 1.60 1.60
142 CD21 ½c on 1a red 1.60 1.60
143 CD22 1c on 2a red violet 1.60 1.60
144 CD23 2½c on 4a yellow green 1.60 1.60
145 CD24 5c on 8a dark blue 1.60 1.60
146 CD25 7½c on 12a violet brown 3.00 3.00
147 CD26 10c on 16a bistre brown 1.60 1.60
148 CD27 15c on 24a bistre 1.75 1.75
Nos. 141-148 (8) 14.35 14.35

Ceres A6

Typographed.

1914-26 ***Perf. 15x14, 12x11½***

Name and Value in Black.

149 A6 ¼c olive brown 10 10
150 " ½c black 10 10
151 " 1c blue green 10 10
152 " 1½c lilac brown 10 10
153 " 2c carmine 10 10
154 " 2c gray ('26) 18 18
155 " 2½c light violet 10 10
156 " 3c orange ('21) 10 8
157 " 4c pale rose ('21) 10 8
158 " 4½c gray ('21) 10 8
159 " 5c deep blue 10 10
160 " 6c lilac ('21) 8 6
a. Name and value printed twice
161 " 7c ultramarine ('21) 15 8
162 " 7½c yellow brown 10 10
163 " 8c slate 10 10
164 " 10c orange brown 12 12
165 A6 12c gray brown ('21) 20 15
166 " 12c blue green ('22) 20 15
167 " 15c plum 2.00 1.50
a. Perf. 12x11½ ('30) 40 25
168 " 15c brown rose ('22) 15 10
169 " 20c yellow green 18 10
170 " 24c ultramarine ('26) 5.50 1.40
171 " 25c chocolate ('26) 50 40
172 " 30c brown, *green* 1.50 90
173 " 30c deep green ('21) 25 15
174 " 30c gray blue, *pink* ('21) 75 40
175 " 40c brown, *pink* 1.25 80
176 " 40c turquoise bl. ('22) 40 30
177 " 50c orange, *salmon* 1.50 1.00
178 " 50c light violet ('26) 25 15
179 " 60c red brown, *pink* ('21) 75 65
180 " 60c dark blue ('22) 35 25
181 " 60c rose ('26) 35 25
182 " 80c dark brown, *blue* ('21) 65 25
183 " 80c bright rose ('22) 35 20
184 " 1e green, *blue*, perf. 12x11½ ('21) 80 35
a. Perf. 15x14 15.00 3.25
185 " 1e rose ('21) 1.60 35
186 " 1e blue ('26) 75 35
187 " 2e bright violet, *pink* (21) 2.00 15
188 " 2e dark violet ('22) 1.00 25
189 " 5e buff ('26) 4.00 1.75
190 " 10e pink ('26) 10.00 4.50
191 " 20e pale turq. ('26) 22.50 11.00
Nos. 149-191 (43) 61.46 29.38

Stamps of 1902 Overprinted Locally in Carmine **REPUBLICA**

1915

On Provisional Stamps of 1902.

192 A2 115r on 5r black 20.00 18.00
193 A3 115r on 5r yellow 80 50
194 " 115r on 25r blue green 80 50
195 " 130r on 75r rose 80 50
196 " 130r on 100r brn., *buff* 80 50
197 " 130r on 150r carmine, *rose* 80 50
198 " 130r on 200r blue, *blue* 80 50
199 N3 115r on 2½r brown 80 50

On No. 97.

200 A4 75r rose 1.50 75
Nos. 192-200 (9) 27.10 22.25

Stamps of 1902-05 Overprinted in Carmine **REPUBLICA**

1915

On Provisional Stamps of 1902.

201 A3 115r on 5r yellow 55 45
202 " 115r on 25r blue green 55 45
203 " 130r on 75r rose 55 45
204 " 130r on 150r car., *rose* 55 45
205 " 130r on 200r blue, *blue* 55 45
206 N3 115r on 2½r brown 55 45

On No. 96.

207 A4 50r blue 55 45

On No. 98.

208 A4 50r on 65r dull blue 55 45
Nos. 201-208 (8) 4.40 3.60

Stamps of 1898-1903 Overprinted Locally in Carmine **REPUBLICA**

1917

209 A4 2½r gray 14.00 10.00
210 " 15r gray green 10.00 6.00
211 A4 20r gray violet 10.00 7.50
212 " 50r brown 10.00 7.50
213 " 75r red lilac 22.50 20.00
214 " 100r blue, *blue* 2.50 1.75
215 " 115r org. brown, *pink* 2.50 1.75
216 " 130r brown, *straw* 2.50 1.75
217 " 200r red lilac, *pinkish* 2.50 1.75
218 " 400r dull blue, *straw* 2.50 2.00
219 " 500r black & red, *blue* 2.50 2.00
220 " 700r violet, *yellowish* 3.25 3.00
Nos. 209-220 (12) 84.75 65.00

War Tax Stamps of 1916-18 Surcharged **2½ CENTAVOS**

1918 ***Rouletted 7***

221 WT2 2½c on 5c rose 1.00 60

Perf. 11, 12.

222 WT2 2½c on 5c red 1.00 60
a. "PETRIA" 2.00 2.00
b. "PEPUBLICA" 2.00 2.00
c. "1910" for "1916" 5.00 3.00

War Tax Stamps of 1916-18 Surcharged **"CORREIOS" 1 C.**

1919 ***Perf. 11***

224 WT1 1c on 1c gray green 50 30
a. "PEPUBLICA" 2.50 2.00
b. Rouletted 7 75.00 60.00

Perf. 12

225 WT2 1½c on 5c red 60 40
a. "PETRIA" 2.50 2.00
b. "PEPUBLICA" 2.50 2.00
c. "1910" for "1916" 3.00 2.00
d. Rouletted 7 150.00 125.00

Stamps of 1902 Overprinted Locally in Carmine **REPUBLICA**

1920

226 A3 400r on 50r light blue 75 55
227 " 400r on 80r yel. green 75 55
228 " 400r on 300r blue, *salmon* 75 55

War Tax Stamp of 1918 Surcharged in Green **SEIS CENTAVOS**

Perf. 12.

229 WT2 6c on 5c red 60 35
a. "1910" for "1916" 5.00 3.25
b. "PETRIA" 2.00 1.50
c. "PEPUBLICA" 2.00 1.50

Lourenco Marques Nos. 117, 119 Surcharged in Red or Bue **10 c.**

1921 ***Perf. 15x14***

230 A4 10c on ½c black (R) 50 50
231 " 30c on 1½c brown (Bl) 50 50

Common Design Types pictured in section at front of book.

Same Surcharge on Mozambique Nos. 150, 152, 155 in Red, Blue or Green.

232 A6 10c on ½c black (R) 60 60
233 " 30c on 1½c brown (Bl) 60 60
234 " 60c on 2½c vio. (G) 1.00 1.00
Nos. 230-234 (5) 3.20 3.20

War Tax Stamp of 1918 Surcharged in Green **2$00**

1921 ***Perf. 12***

235 WT2 2e on 5c red 1.00 40
a. "PETRIA" 2.00 2.00
b. ,,PEPUBLIA" 3.50 2.75
c. "1910" for "1916" 6.00 4.75

No. 157 Surcharged **50 c.**

1923 ***Perf. 12x11½***

236 A6 50c on 4c pale rose 60 40

No. 183 Overprinted in Green **Vasco da Gama 1924**

1924

237 A6 80c bright rose 60 35

To commemorate the fourth centenary of the death of Vasco da Gama.

Nos. 90 and 91 Surcharged **República 40 C.**

1925 ***Perf. 11½***

238 A3 40c on 400r on 50r light blue 60 30
239 " 40c on 400r on 80r yellow green 60 40
a. "a" omitted 30.00 30.00

Postage Due Stamp of 1917 Overprinted **CORREIOS** in Black and Bars in Red.

1929, Jan. ***Perf. 12***

247 D1 50c gray 50 30

No. 188 Surcharged **70 C.**

1931 ***Perf. 11½***

249 A6 70c on 2e dark violet 50 45
250 " 1.40e on 2e dark violet 75 45

"Portugal" Holding Volume of the "Lusiads" A7

Wmkd. Maltese Cross. (232)

1933, July 13 **Typo.** ***Perf. 14***

Value in Red or Black.

251 A7 1c bistre brown (R) 5 4
252 " 5c black brown 5 4
253 " 10c deep violet 5 4
254 " 15c black (R) 5 4
255 " 20c light gray 6 4
256 " 30c slate gray 10 6
257 " 40c orange red 12 10
258 " 45c bright blue 20 17
259 " 50c dark brown 15 10
260 " 60c olive green 30 15

No.	Type	Description	Unused	Used
261	A7	70c orange brown	30	15
262	"	80c emerald	30	15
263	"	85c deep rose	80	50
264	"	1e red brown	75	15
265	"	1.40e dark blue (R)	6.00	60
266	"	2e dark violet	1.50	30
267	"	5e apple green	2.50	40
268	"	10e olive bistre	4.50	75
269	"	20e orange	22.50	1.00
		Nos. 251–269 (19)	40.28	4.78

See also Nos. 298 and 299.

Common Design Types

Perf. 13½x13

1938, Aug. Engr. Unwmkd.

Name and Value in Black.

No.	Type	Description	Unused	Used
270	CD34	1c gray green	6	10
271	"	5c orange brown	6	6
272	"	10c dark carmine	6	6
273	"	15c dark violet brown	10	6
274	"	20c slate	12	6
275	CD35	30c rose violet	15	12
276	"	35c bright green	25	18
277	"	40c brown	40	20
278	"	50c bright red violet	40	20
279	CD36	60c gray black	40	20
280	"	70c brown violet	40	20
281	"	80c orange	75	20
282	"	1e red	50	25
283	CD37	1.75e blue	1.60	40
284	"	2e brown carmine	1.75	30
285	"	5e olive green	3.50	50
286	CD38	10e blue violet	9.00	1.00
287	"	20e red brown	22.50	1.25
		Nos. 270–287 (18)	42.00	5.34

No. 258 Surcharged in Black

40 centavos

Perf. 14

1938, Jan. 16 Wmk. 232

No.	Type	Description	Unused	Used
288	A7	40c on 45c brt. blue	1.50	60

Map of Africa
A7a

Perf. 11½x12

1939, July 17 Litho. Unwmkd.

No.	Type	Description	Unused	Used
289	A7a	80c violet, *pale rose*	3.00	2.50
290	"	1.75e blue, *pale blue*	9.50	4.00
291	"	3e green, *yellow green*	15.00	7.50
292	"	20e brown, *buff*	75.00	37.50

Presidential visit.

New Cathedral,
Lourenço Marques
A8

Railroad Station
A9

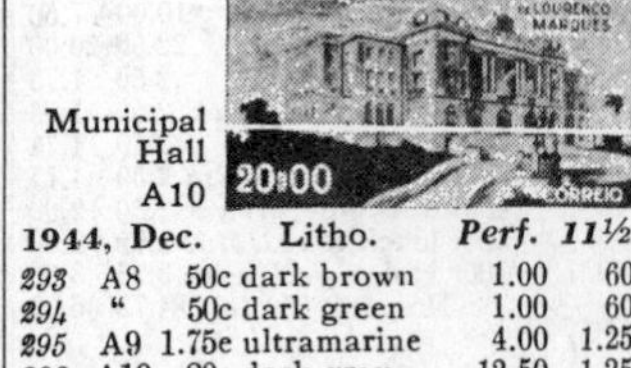

Municipal Hall
A10

1944, Dec. Litho. *Perf. 11½*

No.	Type	Description	Unused	Used
293	A8	50c dark brown	1.00	60
294	"	50c dark green	1.00	60
295	A9	1.75e ultramarine	4.00	1.25
296	A10	20e dark gray	12.50	1.25

Issued to commemorate the 4th centenary of the founding of Lourenço Marques. See also No. 302.

No. 283 Surcharged in Carmine

60 CENTAVOS

1946 Engraved. *Perf. 13½x13.*

No.	Type	Description	Unused	Used
297	CD37	60c on 1.75e blue	90	35

Lusiads Type of 1933.
Typographed.

1947 *Perf. 14.* Wmk. 232

Value in Black.

No.	Type	Description	Unused	Used
298	A7	35c yellow green	2.00	75
299	"	1.75e deep blue	2.00	75

No. 296 Surcharged in Pink

2$00

1946 *Perf. 11½* Unwmkd.

No.	Type	Description	Unused	Used
300	A10	2e on 20e dark gray	1.50	45

No. 273 Surcharged with New Value and Wavy Lines

Perf. 13½x13.

No.	Type	Description	Unused	Used
301	CD34	10c on 15c dark violet brown	75	40
		a. Inverted surch.	9.00	

Cathedral Type of 1944.
Commemorative Inscription Omitted.

1948 Lithographed. *Perf. 11½.*

No.	Type	Description	Unused	Used
302	A8	4.50e bright vermilion	2.00	55

Antonio Enes
A11

1948, Oct. 4 *Perf. 14*

No.	Type	Description	Unused	Used
303	A11	50c black & cream	1.75	42
304	"	5e violet brown & cream	7.50	90

Birth centenary of Antonio Enes.

Gogogo Peak
A12

Zambezi River
Bridge—A13

Zumbo
River
A14

Waterfall
at Nhanhangare
A15

Lourenço
Marques
A16

Plantation,
Baixa
A17

Pungwe River
at Beira
A18

Polana Beach
A19

Lourenço
Marques
A20

Malema River
A21

Perf. 13½x13, 13x13½.

1948–49 Typographed Unwmkd.

No.	Type	Description	Unused	Used
305	A12	5c orange brown	25	20
306	A13	10c violet brown	25	15
307	A14	20c dark brown	25	15
308	A12	30c plum	25	15
309	A14	40c dull green	25	15
310	A16	50c slate	25	15
311	A15	60c brown carmine	25	15
312	A16	80c violet black	25	15
313	A17	1e carmine	50	25
314	A13	1.20e slate gray	50	25
315	A18	1.50e dark purple	50	25
316	A19	1.75e dk. blue ('49)	1.10	35
317	A18	2e brown	75	25
318	A20	2.50e dk. slate ('49)	3.00	30
319	A19	3e gray olive ('49)	2.00	30
320	A15	3.50e olive gray	2.50	30
321	A17	5e blue green	2.50	30
322	A20	10e choc. ('49)	4.75	50
323	A21	15e dp. car. ('49)	11.00	2.00
324	"	20e orange ('49)	22.50	1.75
		Nos. 305–324 (20)	53.60	8.05

Lady of Fatima Issue.

Common Design Type

1948, Oct. Litho. *Perf. 14½*

No.	Type	Description	Unused	Used
325	CD40	50c blue	3.25	1.50
326	"	1.20e red violet	7.50	3.00
327	"	4.50e emerald	25.00	9.00
328	"	20e chocolate	47.50	12.50

Symbols of the U.P.U.
A21a

1949, Apr. 11 *Perf. 14*

No.	Type	Description	Unused	Used
329	A21a	4.50e ultramarine & pale gray	2.00	1.00

75th anniversary of U.P.U.

Holy Year Issue.

Common Design Types

1950, May *Perf. 13x13½*

No.	Type	Description	Unused	Used
330	CD41	1.50e red orange	1.00	35
331	CD42	3e bright blue	1.35	40

Issued to commemorate the Holy Year, 1950.

Spotted Triggerfish A22 — Pennant Coral Fish A22a

Fish: 10c, Golden butterflyfish. 15c, Orange butterflyfish. 20c, Lionfish. 30c, Sharpnose puffer. 40c, Porky filefish. 50c, Dark brown surgeonfish. 1.50e Rainbow wrasse. 2e, Orange-spottted grayskin. 2.50e, Kasmir snapper. 3e, Convict fish. 3.50e, Stellar triggerfish. 4e, Cornetfish. 4.50e, Vagabond butterflyfish. 5e, Mail-cheeked fish. 6e, Pinnate batfish. 8e, Moorish idol. 9e, Triangulate boxfish. 10e, Flying gurnard. 15e, Redtooth triggerfish. 20e, Striped triggerfish. 30e, Horned cowfish. 50e, Spotted cowfish.

Photogravure and Lithographed.

1951 *Perf. 14x14½.* Unwmkd.

Fish in Natural Colors

No.	Type	Description	Unused	Used
332	A22	5c deep yellow	35	30
333	"	10c light blue	20	20
334	"	15c yellow	85	60
335	"	20c pale olivine	40	25
336	"	30c gray	35	25
337	"	40c pale green	25	18
338	"	50c pale buff	25	18
339	A22a	1e aquamarine	25	18
340	A22	1.50e olive	20	15
341	"	2e blue	30	25
342	"	2.50e brownish lilac	75	25
343	"	3e aquamarine	75	25
344	"	3.50e olive green	60	25
345	"	4e blue gray	1.00	1.00
346	"	4.50e green	1.00	1.00
347	"	5e buff	1.00	25
348	A22a	6e salmon pink	1.00	30
349	"	8e gray blue	1.00	35
350	A22	9e lilac rose	1.50	45
351	"	10e gray lilac	16.50	3.25
352	"	15e gray	52.50	17.50
353	"	20e lemon	25.00	7.50
354	"	30e yellow green	20.00	7.00
355	"	50e gray violet	45.00	15.00
		Nos. 332–355 (24)	171.00	56.89

Holy Year Extension Issue.
Common Design Type

1951, Oct. Litho. *Perf. 14*
356 CD43 5e carmine & rose 2.50 1.50

Extension of the Holy Year into 1951. See note after Macao No. 352.

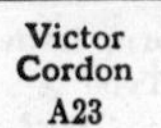

Victor Cordon
A23

Plane and Ship
A24

1951, Oct. *Perf. 11½*
357 A23 1e dark brown 90 35
358 " 5e black & slate 6.50 1.00

Issued to commemorate the centenary of the birth of Victor Cordon, explorer.

Medical Congress Issue.
Common Design Type
Design: Miguel Bombarda Hospital.

1952, June 19 Litho. *Perf. 13½*
359 CD44 3e dk.bl.& brn.buff 1.25 30

National Congress of Tropical Medicine, Lisbon, 1952.

1952, Sept. 15 **Unwmkd.**
360 A24 1.50e multicolored 55 30

4th African Tourism Congress.

Missionary
A25

Papilio Demodocus
A26

1953
361 A25 10c red brown & pale violet 6 6
362 " 1e red brown & pale yellow green 30 15
363 " 5e blk. & lt. blue 1.10 25

Issued to commemorate the Exhibition of Sacred Missionary Art, held at Lisbon in 1951.

Canceled to Order

Certain issues, including Nos. 364–383, were canceled to order under Republican administration.

Photogravure and Lithographed.
1953, May 28 *Perf. 13x14*
Various Butterflies and Moths in Natural Colors.

364 A26 10c light blue 5 5
365 " 15c cream 10 5
366 " 20c yellow green 10 6
367 " 30c light violet 10 6
368 " 40c brown 10 6
369 " 50c bluish gray 10 6
370 " 80c bright blue 15 8
371 " 1e gray blue 20 8
372 " 1.50e ochre 25 12
373 " 2e orange brown 6.75 75
374 " 2.30e blue 4.25 50
375 " 2.50e citron 9.50 50
376 " 3e lilac rose 2.25 22
377 " 4e light blue 35 15
378 " 4.50e orange 40 15
379 " 5e green 40 15
380 " 6e pale violet 50 20
381 " 7.50e buff 4.00 45
382 " 10e pink 8.50 1.10
383 " 20e greenish gray 12.00 1.00
Nos. 364–383 (20) 50.05 5.79

Stamps of Portugal and Mozambique
A27

Stamp of Portugal and Arms of Colonies
A27a

1953, July 23 Litho. *Perf. 14*
384 A27 1e multicolored 90 45
385 " 3e " 3.00 75

Issued in connection with the Lourenço Marques philatelic exhibition, July 1953.

Stamp Centenary Issue.

1953 Photogravure. *Perf. 13.*
Stamp and Arms Multicolored
386 A27a 50c pale orange & brown orange 1.00 75

Map
A28

1954, Oct. 15 Lithographed
Colors (except Colony) on map: Gray, Light Blue, Blue, Carmine and Black.

387 A28 10c pale rose lilac 6 5
388 " 20c pale yellow 6 5
389 " 50c lilac 6 4
390 " 1e orange yellow 25 5
391 " 2.30e white 65 25
392 " 4e pale salmon 90 30
393 " 10e light green 2.75 30
394 " 20e brown buff 3.50 60
Nos. 387-394 (8) 8.23 1.64

Sao Paulo Issue
Common Design Type

1954, July 2
395 CD46 3.50e dark gray, cream & olive 45 15

400th anniversary of Sao Paulo.

Arms of Beira
A29

Mousinho de Albuquerque
A30

Paper with network as in parenthesis

1954, Dec. 1 *Perf. 13x13½*
Arms in Silver, Gold, Red and Pale Green
396 A29 1.50e dk. bl. (*blue*) 30 15
397 " 3.50e brown (*buff*) 55 25

Issued to publicize the first philatelic exhibition of Manica and Sofala.

1955, Feb. 1 Litho. *Perf. 11½x12*
Design: 2.50e, Statue of Mousinho de Albuquerque.
398 A30 1e gray, black & buff 25 15
399 " 2.50e olive bistre, black & blue 35 15

Issued to commemorate the 100th anniversary of the birth of Mousinho de Albuquerque, statesman.

Eight Races Holding Arms of Portugal
A31

View of Beira
A32

1956, Aug. 4 *Perf. 14½* **Unwmkd.**
Central Design in Multicolor
400 A31 1e pale yellow 30 20
401 " 2.50e light blue 75 30

Issued to commemorate the visit of President Antonio Oscar de Fragoso Carmona.

1957, Aug. 15 **Lithographed**
402 A32 2.50e multicolored 90 30

50th anniversary of the city of Beira.

Brussels Fair Issue

Exhibition Emblems and View
A32a

1958, Oct. 8 *Perf. 14½* **Unwmkd.**
403 A32a 3.50e black, green, yellow, red & blue 45 30

Tropical Medicine Congress Issue
Common Design Type
Design: Strophanthus grandiflorus.

1958, Sept. 14 *Perf. 13½*
404 CD47 1.50e salmon brown, green & red 1.75 1.00

6th International Congress of Tropical Medicine and Malaria, Lisbon, Sept. 1958.

Caravel
A33

Technical Instruction
A34

1960, June 25 Litho. *Perf. 13½*
405 A33 5e multicolored 75 30

Issued to commemorate the 500th anniversary of the death of Prince Henry the Navigator.

1960, Nov. 21 *Perf. 14½* **Unwmkd.**
406 A34 3e multicolored 45 30

Issued to commemorate the 10th anniversary of the Commission for Technical Co-operation in Africa South of the Sahara (C.C.T.A.).

Arms of Lourenço Marques
A35

Arms of various cities of Mozambique.

1961, Jan. 30 Litho. *Perf. 13½*
Arms in Original Colors; Black, Ultramarine and Red Inscriptions.

407 A35 5c salmon 6 6
408 " 15c pale green 6 6
409 " 20c light violet gray 15 9
410 " 30c buff 9 6
411 " 50c bluish gray 9 6
412 " 1e pale olive 45 10
413 " 1.50e light blue 45 10
414 " 2e pale pink 65 10
415 " 2.50e lt. blue green 1.25 12
416 " 3e beige 90 30
417 " 4e yellow 55 15
418 " 4.50e pale gray 55 15
419 " 5e pale bluish grn. 1.25 15
420 " 7.50e rose 1.50 33
a. "CORREIOS 7$50" omitted
421 " 10e lt. yel. green 1.75 35
422 " 20e beige 4.25 75
423 " 50e gray 8.00 1.50
Nos. 407-423 (17) 22.00 4.43

Sports Issue
Common Design Type

Sports: 50c, Water skiing. 1e, Wrestling. 1.50e, Woman gymnast. 2.50e, Field hockey. 4.50e, Women's basketball. 15e, Speedboat racing.

1962, Feb. 10 *Perf. 13½* **Unwmkd.**
Multicolored Designs
424 CD48 50c gray green 10 4
425 " 1e dark gray 75 27
426 " 1.50e pink 40 10
427 " 2.50e buff 60 15
428 " 4.50e gray 85 25
429 " 15e gray green 2.25 1.10
Nos. 424-429 (6) 4.95 1.91

Anti-Malaria Issue
Common Design Type
Design: Anopheles funestus.

1962, Apr. 5 *Perf. 13½*
430 CD49 2.50e multicolored 90 30

Issued for the World Health Organization drive to eradicate malaria.

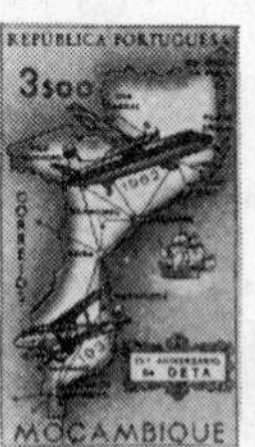

Planes over Mozambique
A36

Lourenço Marques 1887 and 1962
A37

1962, Oct. 15 Litho. *Perf. 14½*
431 A36 3e multicolored 60 25

25th anniversary of DETA airlines.

1962, Nov. 1 *Perf. 13*
432 A37 1e multicolored 60 25

75th anniversary of Lourenço Marques.

Vasco da Gama Statue and Arms
A38

1963, Apr. 25 *Perf. 14½* **Unwmkd.**

433	A38	3e multicolored	60	25

Issued to commemorate the 200th anniversary of the founding of Mozambique City.

Airline Anniversary Issue
Common Design Type

1963, Oct. 21 Litho. *Perf. 14½*

434	CD50	2.50e bright pink & multicolored	45	25

Issued to commemorate the 10th anniversary of Transportes Aéreos Portugueses.

Barque, 1430 — A39 Caravel, 1436 — A40

Development of Sailing Ships: 30c, Lateen-rigged caravel, 1460. 50c, "Sao Gabriel," 1497. 1e, Dom Manuel's ship, 1498. 1.50e, Warship, 1500. 2e, "Flor de la Mar," 1511. 2.50e, Redonda caravel, 1519. 3.50e, 800-ton ship, 1520. 4e, Portuguese India galley, 1521. 4.50e, "Santa Tereza," 1639. 5e, "Nostra Senhora da Conceiçao," 1716. 6e, "Nostra Senhora do Bom Sucesso," 1764. 7.50e, Launch with mortar, 1788. 8e, Brigantine, 1793. 10e, Corvette, 1799. 12.50e, Schooner "Maria Teresa," 1820. 15e, "Vasco da Gama," 1841. 20e, Frigate "Dom Fernando II," 1843. 30e, Training Ship "Sagres," 1924.

1963, Dec. 1 Litho. *Perf. 14½*

435	A39	10c	multicolored	5	5
436	A40	20c	"	5	5
437	"	30c	"	5	5
438	"	50c	"	10	5
439	"	1e	"	50	12
440	"	1.50e	"	25	12
441	"	2e	"	35	12
442	A39	2.50e	"	75	12
443	A40	3.50e	"	55	42
444	A39	4e	"	65	20
445	A40	4.50e	"	1.00	25
446	"	5e	"	5.00	25
447	A39	6e	"	1.00	30
448	"	7.50e	"	1.35	35
449	"	8e	"	1.35	40
450	"	10e	"	1.75	60
451	"	12.50e	"	2.00	75
452	"	15e	"	2.00	75
453	A40	20e	"	3.00	1.00
454	"	30e	"	4.50	1.75
			Nos. 435-454 (20)	26.25	7.70

National Overseas Bank Issue

Modern Bank Building, Luanda
A40a

1964, May 16 *Perf. 13½*

455	A40a	1.50e blue, yellow gray & green	30	10

Issued to commemorate the centenary of the National Overseas Bank of Portugal.

Pres. Americo Rodrigues Thomaz
A41

1964, July 23 Litho. *Perf. 13½x12½*

456	A41	2.50e multicolored	35	15

Issued to commemorate the visit of Pres. Americo Rodrigues Thomaz of Portugal to Mozambique, in July.

Royal Barge of King John V, 1728
A42

Designs: 35c, Barge of Dom Jose I, 1753. 1e, Customs barge, 1768. 1.50e, Sailor, 1780 (vert.). 2.50e, Royal barge, 1780. 5e, Barge of Dona Carlota Joaquina, 1790. 9e, Barge of Dom Miguel, 1831.

1964, Dec. 18 Litho. *Perf. 14½*

457	A42	15c multicolored	5	5
458	"	35c lt. bl. & multi.	8	8
459	"	1e gray & multi.	60	10
460	"	1.50e gray & multi.	75	8
461	"	2.50e multicolored	25	10
462	"	5e "	75	25
463	"	9e "	1.00	75
		Nos. 457-463 (7)	3.48	1.41

ITU Issue
Common Design Type

1965, May 17 *Perf. 14½* **Unwmkd.**

464	CD52	1e yellow & multi.	55	25

Issued to commemorate the centenary of the International Telecommunication Union.

National Revolution Issue
Common Design Type

Design: 1e, Beira Railroad Station, and Antonio Enes School.

1966, May 28 Litho. *Perf. 11½*

465	CD53	1e multicolored	20	10

40th anniversary of National Revolution.

Harquebusier, 1560
A42a

Designs: 30c, Harquebusier, 1640. 40c, Infantry soldier, 1777. 50c, Infantry officer, 1777. 80c, Drummer, 1777. 1e, Infantry sergeant, 1777. 2e, Infantry major, 1784. 2.50e, Colonial officer, 1788. 3e, Infantry soldier, 1789. 5e, Colonial bugler, 1801. 10e, Colonial officer, 1807. 15e, Colonial infantry soldier, 1817.

1967, Jan. 12 Photo. *Perf. 14*

466	A42a	20c	multicolored	15	12
467	"	30c	"	15	12
468	"	40c	"	15	12
469	"	50c	"	15	12
470	"	80c	"	55	25
471	"	1e	"	55	10
472	"	2e	"	55	15
473	"	2.50e	"	1.00	25
474	"	3e	"	50	15
475	"	5e	"	85	25
476	"	10e	"	1.10	40
477	"	15e	"	1.65	75
			Nos. 466-477 (12)	7.35	2.78

Navy Club Issue
Common Design Type

Designs: 3e, Capt. Azevedo Coutinho and gunboat (stern-wheeler) Tete. 10e, Capt. Joao Roby and gunboat (paddle steamer) Granada.

1967, Jan. 31 Litho. *Perf. 13*

478	CD54	3e multicolored	50	20
479	"	10e "	1.25	75

Centenary of Portugal's Navy Club.

Virgin's Crown, Presented by Portuguese Women
A43

1967, May 13 Litho. *Perf. 12½x13*

480	A43	50c multicolored	20	6

Issued to commemorate the 50th anniversary of the appearance of the Virgin Mary to 3 shepherd children at Fatima.

Cabral Issue

Raising the Cross at Porto Seguro
A44

Designs: 1.50e, First mission to Brazil. 3e, Grace Church, Santarem (vert.).

1968, Apr. 22 Litho. *Perf. 14*

481	A44	1e multicolored	20	4
482	"	1.50e "	60	10
483	"	3e "	75	25

500th anniversary of the birth of Pedro Alvares Cabral, navigator who took possession of Brazil for Portugal.

Admiral Coutinho Issue
Common Design Type

Design: 70c, Adm. Coutinho and Adm. Gago Coutinho Airport.

1969, Feb. 17 Litho. *Perf. 14*

484	CD55	70c multicolored	20	10

Luiz Vaz de Camoëns — A45 Sailing Ship, 1553 — A46

Designs: 1.50e, Map of Mozambique, 1554. 2.50e, Chapel of Our Lady of Baluarte, 1552. 5e, Excerpt from Lusiads about Mozambique (1st Song, 14th Stanza).

Perf. 12½x13, 13x12½

1969, June 10 Lithographed

485	A45	15c	multicolored	15	5
486	A46	50c	"	5	5
487	A45	1.50e	"	18	10
488	A46	2.50e	"	40	15
489	A45	5e	"	50	40
			Nos. 485-489 (5)	1.28	75

Issued to commemorate the 400th anniversary of the visit to Mozambique of Luiz Vaz de Camoëns (1524-1580), poet.

Vasco da Gama Issue

Map Showing Voyage to Mozambique and India
A47

1969, Aug. 29 Litho. *Perf. 14*

490	A47	1e multicolored	20	5

Issued to commemorate the 500th anniversary of the birth of Vasco da Gama (1469-1524), navigator.

Administration Reform Issue
Common Design Type

1969, Sept. 25 Litho. *Perf. 14*

491	CD56	1.50e multicolored	15	10

Issued to commemorate the centenary of the administration reforms of the overseas territories.

King Manuel I Issue

Illuminated Miniature of King's Arms
A48

1969, Dec. 1 Litho. *Perf. 14*

492	A48	80c multicolored	15	10

Issued to commemorate the 500th anniversary of the birth of King Manuel I.

Marshal Carmona Issue
Common Design Type

Design: 5e, Antonio Oscar Carmona in marshal's uniform.

1970, Nov. 15 Litho. *Perf. 14*

493	CD57	5e multicolored	45	25

Birth centenary of Marshal Antonio Oscar Carmona de Fragoso (1869-1951), president of Portugal.

Fossil Fern
A49

Fossils and Minerals: 50c, Fossil snail. 1e, Stibnite. 1.50e, Pink beryl. 2e, Dinosaur. 3e, Tantalocolumbite. 3.50e, Verdelite. 4e, Zircon. 10e, Petrified wood.

1971, Jan. 15 Litho. *Perf. 13*

494	A49	15c gray & multi.	6	3
495	"	50c lt. ultra. & multi.	6	3
496	"	1e green & multi.	10	5
497	"	1.50e multicolored	15	8
498	"	2e "	18	10
499	"	3e lt. blue & multi.	30	15
500	"	3.50e lilac & multi.	40	20
501	"	4e multicolored	45	20
502	"	10e dull red & multi.	1.10	45
		Nos. 494-502 (9)	2.80	1.29

Mozambique Island
A49a

1972, May 25 Litho. *Perf. 13*

503 A49a 4e ultra. & multi. 38 20

4th centenary of publication of The Lusiads by Luiz Camoëns.

Olympic Games Issue
Common Design Type

Design: 3e, Hurdles and swimming, Olympic emblem.

1972, June 20 *Perf. 14x13½*

504 CD59 3e multicolored 35 15

20th Olympic Games, Munich, Aug. 26–Sept. 11.

Lisbon-Rio de Janeiro Flight Issue
Common Design Type

Design: 1e, "Santa Cruz" over Recife harbor.

1972, Sept. 20 Litho. *Perf. 13½*

505 CD60 1e multicolored 10 5

Sailboats
A50

Designs: Various sailboats.

1973, Aug. 21 Litho. *Perf. 12x11½*

506 A50 1e multicolored 10 5
507 " 1.50e " 15 10
508 " 3e " 35 20

World Sailing Championships, Vauriens Class, Lourenço Marques, Aug. 21–30.

WMO Centenary Issue
Common Design Type

1973, Dec. 15 Litho. *Perf. 13*

509 CD61 2e rose red & multi. 25 15

Centenary of international meteorological cooperation.

Radar Station
A51

1974, June 25 Litho. *Perf. 13*

510 A51 50c multicolored 10 5

Establishment of satellite communications network via Intelsat among Portugal, Angola and Mozambique.

"Bird" Made of Flags of Portugal and Mozambique
A52

1975, Jan. Litho. *Perf. 14½*

511 A52 1e pink & multi. 10 10
512 " 1.50e yellow & multi. 25 10
513 " 2e gray & multi. 25 15
514 " 3.50e lemon & multi. 40 25
515 A52 6e lt. bl. & multi. 70 45
a. Souvenir sheet of 5 3.75
Nos. 511-515 (5) 1.70 1.05

Lusaka Agreement, Sept. 7, 1974, which gave Mozambique independence from Portugal, effective June 25, 1975.

No. 515a contains one each of Nos. 511–515 and label with black inscription. Size: 150x75mm. Sold for 25e.

Republic

Issues of 1953–74 Overprinted in Red or Black:

a

INDEPENDÊNCIA
25 JUN 75

b

1975, June 25
Multicolored

516 A28 (a) 10c (R; #387)
517 A26 (") 40c (R; #368)
518 A51 (b) 50c (B; #510)
519 A50 (") 1e (B; #506)
520 " (") 1.50e (B; #507)
521 CD61 (a) 2e (B; #509)
522 CD48 (b) 2.50e (B; #427)
523 CD59 (a) 3e (B; #504)
524 A50 (b) 3e (B; #508)
525 A49 (") 3.50e (B; #500)
526 CD48 (") 4.50e (B; #428)
527 A26 (a) 7.50e (R; #381)
528 A49 (b) 10e (B; #502)
529 CD48 (") 15e (B; #429)
530 A28 (a) 20e (R; #394)
Nos. 516-530, C35-C38 (19) 20.00

Workers, Farmers and Children
A53

Designs: 30c, 50c, 2.50e, like 20c. 4.50e, 5e, 10e, 50e, Dancers, workers, armed family.

1975 Litho. *Perf. 12x11½*

531 A53 20c pink & multi. 3 3
532 " 30c bister & multi. 5 5
533 " 50c blue & multi. 8 8
534 " 2.50e green & multi. 38 38
535 " 4.50e brown & multi. 68 68
536 " 5e bister & multi. 75 75
537 " 10e blue & multi. 1.50 1.50
538 " 50e yel. & multi. 7.50
a. Souvenir sheet of 8 15.00 15.00
Nos. 531-538 (8) 10.97

No. 538a contains 8 stamps similar to Nos. 531–538 with simulated perforation. Buff and brown margin showing dancers and white inscription commemorating independence. Size: 132x179mm. Sold for 75e.

Farm Woman
A54

Designs: 1.50e, Teacher. 2.50e, Nurse. 10e, Mother.

1976, Apr. 7 Litho. *Perf. 14½*

539 A54 1e yel. grn. & blk. 15 15
540 " 1.50e tan & multi. 24 24
541 " 2.50e lt. ultra. & multicolored 38 38
542 " 10e red & multi. 1.50 1.50

Day of the Mozambique Woman, Apr. 7.

Nos. 513–515 Overprinted in Red:
"PRESIDENTE KENNETH KAUNDA / PRIMEIRA VISITA 20/4/1976"

1976, Apr. 20 Litho. *Perf. 14½*

543 A52 2e gray & multi. 25 25
544 " 3.50e lemon & multi. 45 45
545 " 6e lt. bl. & multi. 75 75

Visit of President Kaunda of Zambia.

Pres. Machel's Arrival at Maputo
A55

Mozambique No. 1
A56

Designs: 1e, Independence proclamation ceremony. 2.50e, Pres. Samora Moises Machel taking office. 7.50e, Military parade. 20e, Flame of Unity and festival.

1976, June 25

546 A55 50c multicolored 10 10
547 " 1e " 15 15
548 " 2.50e " 30 30
549 " 7.50e " 95 45
550 " 20e " 2.50 2.50
Nos. 546-550 (5) 4.00 4.00

First anniversary of independence.

1976, July *Perf. 11½x12*

551 A56 1.50e ocher & multi. 25 25
552 " 6e red & multi. 95 95

Centenary of Mozambique postage stamps.

Flag and Weapons
A57

1976, Sept. 25 Litho. *Perf. 14½*

553 A57 3e multicolored 35 35

Army Day 1976.

No. 534 Overprinted in Silver: "FACIM"

1976 Litho. *Perf. 12x11½*

554 A53 2.50e multicolored 45 45

FACIM, Industrial Fair.

Bush Baby
A58

Animals: 1e, Honey badger. 1.50e, Pangolin. 2e, Steinbok. 2.50e, Guenon (monkey). 3e, Cape hunting dog. 4e, Cheetah. 5e, Spotted hyena. 7.50e, Wart hog. 8e, Hippopotamus. 10e, Rhinoceros. 15e, Sable antelope. 1e, 2e, 3e, 4e, 7.50e, 8e, 10e horiz.

1977, Jan. Litho. *Perf. 14½*

555 A58 50c multicolored 5 5
556 " 1e " 10 10
557 " 1.50e " 15 15
558 " 2e " 20 20
559 " 2.50e " 25 25
560 " 3e " 30 30
561 " 4e " 40 40
562 " 5e " 50 50
563 " 7.50e " 75 75
564 " 8e " 80 80
565 " 10e " 1.00 1.00
566 " 15e " 1.50 1.50
Nos. 555-566 (12) 6.00 6.00

Congress Emblem
A59

Monument in Maputo
A60

Design: 3.50e, Monument in Machaje, site of 2nd Frelimo Congress (horiz.).

1977, Feb. 7 *Perf. 14½*

567 A59 3e multicolored 30 30

Perf. 12x11½, 11½x12

568 A60 3.50e multicolored 40 40
569 " 20e " 2.25 2.25

3rd FRELIMO Party Congress, Maputo, Feb. 3–7.

Women, Child's Design
A61

Worker and Farmer
A62

1977, Apr. 7 Litho. *Perf. 14½*

570 A61 5e dp. org. & multi. 55 55
571 " 15e lt. grn. & multi. 1.65 1.65

Mozambique Women's Day 1977.

1977, May 1 Litho. *Perf. 14½*

572 A62 5e red, blk. & yellow 55 55

Labor Day.

People, Flags and Rising Sun
A63

1977, June 25 Litho. *Perf. 11½x12*

573 A63 50c multicolored 5 5
574 " 1.50e " 15 15
575 " 3e " 30 30
576 " 15e " 1.50 1.50

2nd anniversary of independence.

Bread Palm
A64

Design: 10e, Nyala.

1977, Dec. 21 Litho. *Perf. 12x11½*

577	A64	1e multicolored	10	10
578	"	10e "	1.00	1.00

Nature protection and Stamp Day.

Chariesthes Bella Rufoplagiata
A65

Violet-crested Touraco
A66

Beetles: 1e, Tragocephalus variegata. 1.50e, Monochamus leuconotus. 3e, Prosopocera lactator meridionalis. 5e, Dinocephalus ornatus. 10e, Tragiscoschema nigroscriptum maculata.

1978, Jan. 20 Litho. *Perf. 11½x12*

579	A65	50c multicolored	5	5
580	"	1e "	10	10
581	"	1.50e "	15	15
582	"	3e "	30	30
583	"	5e "	50	50
584	"	10e "	1.00	1.00
		Nos. 579-584 (6)	2.10	2.10

1978, Mar. 20 Litho. *Perf. 11½*

Birds of Mozambique: 1e, Lilac-breasted roller. 1.50e, Weaver. 2.50e, Violet-backed starling. 3e, Peter's twinspot. 15e, European bee-eater.

585	A66	50c multicolored	5	5
586	"	1e "	10	10
587	"	1.50e "	15	15
588	"	2.50e "	25	25
589	"	3e "	30	30
590	"	15e "	1.50	1.50
		Nos. 585-590 (6)	2.35	2.35

Mother and Child, WHO Emblem
A67

1978, Apr. 17 *Perf. 12*

591	A67	15e multicolored	1.50	1.50

Smallpox eradication campaign.

Crinum Delagoense
A68

Mozambique No. 1, Canada No. 1
A69

Flowers of Mozambique: 1e, Gloriosa superba. 1.50e, Eulophia speciosa. 3e, Erithrina humeana. 5e, Astripomoea malvacea. 10e, Kigelia africana.

1978, May 16 *Perf. 11½x12*

592	A68	50c multicolored	5	5
593	"	1e "	10	10
594	"	1.50e "	15	15
595	"	3e "	30	30
596	"	5e "	50	50
597	"	10e "	1.00	1.00
		Nos. 592-597 (6)	2.10	2.10

1978, June 9

598	A69	15e multicolored	1.50	1.50

CAPEX Canadian International Philatelic Exhibition, Toronto, Ont., June 9-18.

National Flag
A70

Soldiers, Festival Emblem
A71

Designs: 1.50e, Coat of arms. 7.50e, Page of Constitution and people. 10e, Music band and national anthem.

1978, June 25 *Perf. 11½x12*

599	A70	1e multicolored	10	10
600	"	1.50e "	15	15
601	"	7.50e "	75	75
602	"	10e "	1.00	1.00
		a. Souvenir sheet of 4	3.25	

3rd anniversary of proclamation of independence. No. 602a contains 4 stamps similar to Nos. 599-602 with simulated perforations. Multicolored margin shows reading of proclamation. Size: 130x100 mm. Sold for 30e.

1978, July 28

Designs (Festival Emblem and): 2.50e, Student. 7.50e, Farmworkers.

603	A71	2.50e multicolored	25	25
604	"	3e "	30	30
605	"	7.50e "	75	75

11th World Youth Festival, Havana, July 28-Aug. 5.

Czechoslovakia No. B126 and PRAGA '78 Emblem—A72

1978, Sept. 8 Litho. *Perf. 12x11½*

606	A72	15e multicolored	1.50	1.50
		a. Souvenir sheet	3.00	

PRAGA '78 International Philatelic Exhibition, Prague, Sept. 8-17.

No. 606a contains one stamp with simulated perforations. Multicolored margin shows mosque and PRAGA '78 emblem. Size: 135x109mm. Sold for 30e.

Soccer
A73

Designs: 1.50e, Shotput. 3e, Hurdling. 7.50e, Fieldball. 12.50e, Swimming. 25e, Roller skate hockey.

1978, Dec. 21 Litho. *Perf. 12x11½*

607	A73	50c multicolored	5	5
608	"	1.50e "	15	15
609	"	3e "	30	30
610	"	7.50e "	75	75
611	"	12.50e "	1.25	1.25
612	A73	25e multicolored	2.50	2.50
		Nos. 607-612 (6)	5.00	5.00

Stamp Day 1978.

Carrier Pigeon, UPU Emblem
A74

1979, Jan. 1 Litho. *Perf. 11x11½*

613	A74	20e multicolored	2.00	2.00

Membership in Universal Postal Union.

Soldier Giving Gourd to Woman—A75

Edward Chivambo Mondlane
A76

Designs: 3e, Frelimo soldiers. 7.50e, Mozambique children in school.

1979, Feb. 3 *Perf. 11½x11, 11x11½*

614	A75	1e multicolored	10	10
615	"	3e "	30	30
616	"	7.50e "	75	75
617	A76	12.50e "	1.25	1.25

10th anniversary of death of Dr. Edward Chivambo Mondlane (1920-1969), educator, founder of Frelimo Party.

Shaded Silver Cat
A77

Cats: 1.50e, Manx. 2.50e, English blue. 3e, Turkish. 12.50e, Long-haired Mid-East tabby. 20e, African wild cat.

1979, Mar. 27 Litho. *Perf. 11*

618	A77	50c multicolored	5	5
619	"	1.50e "	15	15
620	"	2.50e "	25	25
621	"	3e "	30	30
622	"	12.50e "	1.25	1.25
623	"	20e "	2.00	2.00
		Nos. 618-623 (6)	4.00	4.00

Wrestling and Moscow '80 Emblem
A78

Sport and Moscow '80 Emblem: 2e, Running. 3e, Equestrian. 5e, Canoeing. 10e, High jump. 15e, Archery.

1979, Apr. 24 Litho. *Perf. 11*

624	A78	1e gray grn. & blk.	10	10
625	"	2e brt. bl. & black	20	20
626	"	3e lt. brn. & black	30	30
627	"	5e multicolored	50	50
628	"	10e green & black	1.00	1.00
629	"	15e lilac rose & blk.	1.50	1.50
		Nos. 624-629 (6)	3.60	3.60

22nd Olympic Games, Moscow, July 19-Aug. 3, 1980.

SEMI-POSTAL STAMPS.

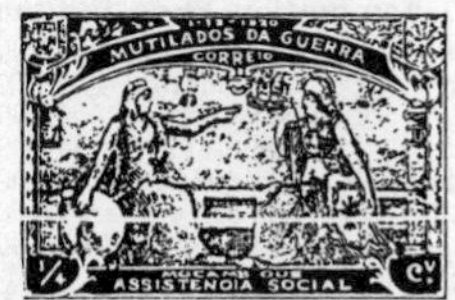

"History" Pointing out to "the Republic" Need for Charity
SP1

Nurse Leading Wounded Soldiers
SP2

Veteran Relating Experiences
SP3

Perf. 11½

1920, Dec. 1 Litho. Unwmkd.

B1	SP1	¼c olive	2.50	2.00
B2	"	½c olive black	2.50	2.00
B3	"	1c deep bistre	2.50	2.00
B4	"	2c lilac brown	2.50	2.00
B5	"	3c lilac	2.50	2.00
B6	"	4c green	2.50	2.00
B7	SP2	5c greenish blue	2.50	2.00
B8	"	6c light blue	2.50	2.00
B9	"	7½c red brown	2.50	2.00
B10	"	8c lemon	2.50	2.00
B11	"	10c gray lilac	2.50	2.00
B12	"	12c pink	2.50	2.00
B13	SP3	18c rose	2.50	2.00
B14	"	24c violet brown	2.50	2.00
B15	"	30c pale olive green	2.50	2.00
B16	"	40c dull red	2.50	2.00
B17	"	50c yellow	2.50	2.00
B18	"	1e ultramarine	2.50	2.00
		Nos. B1-B18 (18)	45.00	36.00

Nos. B1-B18 were used Dec. 1, 1920, in place of ordinary stamps. The proceeds were for war victims.

AIR POST STAMPS.

Common Design Type

Perf. 13½x13

1938, Aug. Engraved Unwmkd.

Name and Value in Black.

C1	CD39	10c scarlet	40	30
C2	"	20c purple	40	30
C3	"	50c orange	38	25
C4	"	1e ultramarine	55	35
C5	"	2e lilac brown	1.00	40
C6	"	3e dark green	1.65	50
C7	"	5e red brown	2.50	90
C8	"	9e rose carmine	4.50	1.00
C9	"	10e magenta	6.00	1.50
		Nos. C1-C9 (9)	17.38	5.50

No. C7 exists with overprint "Exposicao Internacional de Nova York, 1939–1940" and Trylon and Perisphere.

No. C7 Surcharged in Black

3$00

1946, Nov. 2 *Perf. 13½x13*

C10	CD39	3e on 5e red brn.	6.50	3.00
		a. Inverted surch.		

Plane
AP1

1946, Nov. 2 Typo. *Perf. 11½*

Denomination in Black.

C11	AP1	1.20e carmine	1.65	1.25
C12	"	1.60e blue	2.00	1.35
C13	"	1.70e plum	3.50	2.00
C14	"	2.90e brown	4.50	2.75
C15	"	3e green	3.75	2.50
		Nos. C11-C15 (5)	15.40	9.85

Inscribed "Taxe perçue" and Denomination in Brown Carmine or Black.

1947, May 20

C16	AP1	50c black (BrC)	90	60
C17	"	1e pink	90	60
C18	"	3e green	2.25	1.00
C19	"	4.50e yellow green	4.50	1.50
C20	"	5e red brown	3.75	1.65
C21	"	10e ultramarine	12.50	4.50
C22	"	20e violet	27.50	11.00
C23	"	50e orange	50.00	22.50
		Nos. C16-C23 (8)	102.30	43.35

Dangerous counterfeits exist.

Planes Circling Globe
AP2

1949, Mar.

C24	AP2	50c sepia	45	20
C25	"	1.20e violet	75	45
C26	"	4.50e dull blue	2.50	1.00
C27	"	5e blue green	4.00	1.00
C28	"	20e chocolate	8.25	2.00
		Nos. C24-C28 (5)	15.95	4.65

Oil Refinery, Sonarep
AP3

Designs: 2e, Salazar High School, Lourenço Marques. 3.50e, Lourenço Marques harbor. 4.50e, Salazar dam. 5e, Trigo de Morais bridge. 20e, Marcelo Caetano bridge.

1963, Mar. 5 Litho. *Perf. 13*

C29	AP3	1.50e multicolored	1.00	20
C30	"	2e "	60	15
C31	"	3.50e "	1.00	30
C32	"	4.50e "	60	30
C33	"	5e "	60	15
C34	"	20e "	2.50	90
		Nos. C29-C34 (6)	6.30	2.00

Republic

Nos. C31–C34 Overprinted in Red

INDEPENDÊNCIA
25 JUN 75

1975, June 25 Litho. *Perf. 13*

C35	AP3	3.50e multicolored		
C36	"	4.50e "		
C37	"	5e "		
C38	"	20e "		

POSTAGE DUE STAMPS.

D1

Typographed.

1904 *Perf. 11½x12* **Unwmkd.**

Name and Value in Black.

J1	D1	5r yellow green	35	30
J2	"	10r slate	35	30
J3	"	20r yellow brown	35	30
J4	"	30r orange	75	60
J5	"	50r gray brown	1.00	60
J6	"	60r red brown	2.25	1.35
J7	"	100r red lilac	2.00	1.25
J8	"	130r dull blue	90	70
J9	"	200r carmine	2.00	85
J10	"	500r violet	2.00	1.00
		Nos. J1-J10 (10)	11.95	7.25

Same Overprinted in Carmine or Green

REPUBLICA

1911

J11	D1	5r yellow green	25	20
J12	"	10r slate	30	25
J13	"	20r yellow brown	33	30
J14	"	30r orange	33	30
J15	"	50r gray brown	33	30
J16	"	60r red brown	60	33
J17	"	100r red lilac	45	40
J18	"	130r dull blue	45	40
J19	"	200r carmine (G)	75	60
J20	"	500r violet	75	60
		Nos. J11-J20 (10)	4.54	3.68

Nos. J1–J10 Overprinted Locally in Carmine

REPUBLICA

1916

J21	D1	5r yellow green	2.50	2.00
J22	"	10r slate	3.50	3.00
J23	"	20r yellow brown	45.00	30.00
J24	"	30r orange	7.50	6.50
J25	"	50r gray brown	35.00	30.00
J26	"	60r red brown	27.50	27.50
J27	"	100r red lilac	45.00	32.50
J28	"	130r dull blue	1.50	1.25
J29	"	200r carmine	1.50	1.25
J30	"	500r violet	3.50	3.00
		Nos. J21-J30 (10)	172.50	137.00

War Tax Stamps of 1916 Overprinted Diagonally

PORTEADO

1918 *Rouletted 7*

J31	WT1	1c gray green	70	60
J32	WT2	5c rose	70	60
		a. Inverted overprint	1.50	1.25

Perf. 11.

J33	WT1	1c gray green	70	60
		a. "PEPUBLICA"	4.00	3.50

Type of 1904 Issue With Value in Centavos.

1917 *Perf. 12.*

J34	D1	½c yellow green	12	12
J35	"	1c slate	12	12
J36	"	2c orange brown	12	12
J37	"	3c orange	12	12
J38	"	5c gray brown	12	12
J39	"	6c pale brown	12	12
J40	"	10c red violet	12	12
J41	"	13c deep blue	12	12
J42	"	20c rose	12	12
J43	"	50c gray	25	25
		Nos. J34-J43 (10)	1.33	1.33

Lourenco Marques Nos. 117, 119 Surcharged in Red

10 C.
PORTEADO

1921

J44	A4	5c on ½c black	1.50	1.00
J45	"	10c on 1½c brown	1.50	1.00

Same Surcharge on Mozambique Nos. 151, 155, 157 in Red or Green.

J46	A6	6c on 1c blue green (R)	75	60
J47	"	20c on 2½c violet (R)	75	60
J48	"	50c on 4c rose (G)	75	60
		Nos. J44-J48 (5)	5.25	3.80

Regular Issues of 1921-22 Surcharged in Black or Red

Porteado
50 C.

1924 *Perf. 12x11½*

J49	A6	20c on 30c olive green (Bk)	50	25
		a. Perf. 15x14	17.50	4.50
J50	A6	50c on 60c dk. bl. (R)	50	45

Common Design Type

Photogravure and Typographed.

1952 *Perf. 14.* **Unwmkd.**

Numeral in Red Orange or Red; Frame Multicolored.

J51	CD45	10c carmine (RO)	15	10
J52	"	30c black brown	10	10
J53	"	50c black	10	10
J54	"	1e violet blue	10	10
J55	"	2e olive green	30	20
J56	"	5e orange brown	75	40
		Nos. J51-J56 (6)	1.50	1.00

WAR TAX STAMPS.

Coats of Arms of Portugal and Mozambique on Columns, Allegorical Figures of History of Portugal and the Republic Holding Scroll with Date of Declaration of War
WT1

Prow of Galley of Discoveries. Left, "Republic" Teaching History of Portugal; Right "History" with Laurels (Victory) and Sword (Symbolical of Declaration of War)
WT2

Lithographed.

1916 *Rouletted 7* **Unwmkd.**

MR1	WT1	1c gray green	60	40
		a. Imperf. (pair)		
MR2	WT2	5c rose	60	40
		a. Imperf. (pair)		

1918 *Perf. 11, 12.*

MR3	WT1	1c gray green	60	40
		a. "PEPUBLICA"	3.00	2.50

MR4 WT2 5c red 60 50
- *a.* "PETRIA" 1.75 1.60
- *b.* "PEPUBLICA" 2.25 1.50
- *c.* "1910" for "1916" 3.50 3.00
- *d.* Imperf. (pair)

See also Nos. 221–225, 229, 235, J31–J33.

NEWSPAPER STAMPS.

No. 19 Surcharged in Black, Red or Blue:

JORNAES

2 1/2 REIS

a

JORNAES

2½ 2½

b

Perf. 11½, 12½, 13½.

1893 **Unwmkd.**

P1	A2 (*a*) 2½r on 40r choc. (Bk)		62.50	45.00
P2	" (") 5r on 40r choc. (Bk)		60.00	50.00
P3	" (") 5r on 40r choc. (R)		70.00	52.50
P4	" (") 5r on 40r choc. (Bl)		70.00	52.50
P5	" (*b*) 2½r on 40r choc. (Bk)		20.00	15.00

Nos. P1–P5 exist with double surcharge, Nos. P2–P4 with inverted surcharge.

N3

1893 Typo. ***Perf. 11½, 13½***

P6 N3 2½r brown 35 30

No. P6 has been reprinted on thick, chalk-surfaced paper with clean-cut perforation 13½. Price, 50 cents.

POSTAL TAX STAMPS.

Pombal Commemorative Issue.

Common Design Types

1925 Engraved ***Perf. 12½***

RA1	CD28 15c brown & blk.		40	35
RA2	CD29 15c " "		40	35
RA3	CD30 15c " "		40	35

Seal of Local Red Cross Society

PT7 PT8

Surcharged in Various Colors.

1925 **Typographed.** ***Perf. 11½***

RA4 PT7 50c slate & yellow (Bk) 1.50 1.50

1926

RA5	PT8 40c slate & yellow (Bk)	2.00	2.00
RA6	" 50c slate & yellow (R)	2.00	2.00
RA7	" 60c slate & yellow (V)	2.00	2.00
RA8	" 80c slate & yellow (Br)	2.00	2.00
RA9	" 1e slate & yellow (Bl)	2.00	2.00
RA10	" 2e slate & yellow (G)	2.00	2.00
	Nos. RA5–RA10 (6)	12.00	12.00

Obligatory on mail certain days of the year. The tax benefited the Cross of the Orient Society.

Type of 1926 Issue.

1927 Black Surcharge.

RA11	PT8 5c red & yellow	1.50	1.50
RA12	" 10c grn. & yellow	1.50	1.50
RA13	" 20c gray & yel.	2.00	2.00
RA14	" 30c lt. bl. & yel.	2.00	2.00
RA15	" 40c violet & yel.	2.00	2.00
RA16	" 50c car. & yel.	2.00	2.00
RA17	" 60c brown & yel.	2.00	2.00
RA18	" 80c blue & yellow	2.00	2.00
RA19	" 1e olive & yellow	2.00	2.00
RA20	" 2e yel. brn. & yel.	2.50	2.50
	Nos. RA11–RA20 (10)	19.50	19.50

See note after No. RA10.

PT9

1928 **Lithographed.**

RA21	PT9 5c green, yellow & black	3.50	3.50
RA22	" 10c slate blue, yel. & black	3.50	3.50
RA23	" 20c gray black, yel. & black	3.50	3.50
RA24	" 30c brown rose, yel. & black	3.50	3.50
RA25	" 40c claret brown, yel. & black	3.50	3.50
RA26	" 50c red orange, yel. & black	3.50	3.50
RA27	" 60c brown, yellow & black	3.50	3.50
RA28	" 80c dark brown, yel. & black	3.50	3.50
RA29	" 1e gray, yellow & black	3.50	3.50
RA30	" 2e red, yel. & blk.	3.50	3.50
	Nos. RA21–RA30 (10)	35.00	35.00

See note after RA10.

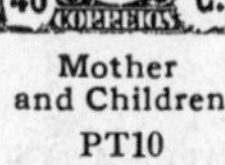

Mother and Children — PT10

Mousinho de Albuquerque — PT11

1929 **Photogravure** ***Perf. 14***

RA31 PT10 40c ultramarine, claret & blk. 2.00 2.00

The use of this stamp was compulsory on all correspondence to Portugal and Portuguese Colonies for eight days beginning July 24th, 1929.

1930-31 ***Perf. 14½x14.***

	Inscribed: "MACONTENE".		
RA32	PT11 50c lake, red & gray	6.50	6.50
	Inscribed: "COOLELA".		
RA33	PT11 50c red violet, red brown & gray	6.50	6.50
	Inscribed: "MUJENGA".		
RA34	PT11 50c orange red, red & gray	6.50	6.50
	Inscribed: "CHAIMITE".		
RA35	PT11 50c dp. grn., bl. grn. & gray	6.50	6.50
	Inscribed: "IBRAHIMO".		
RA36	PT11 50c dark blue, blk. & gray	6.50	6.50
	Inscribed: "MUCUTO-MUNO".		
RA37	PT11 50c ultramarine, blk. & gray	6.50	6.50
	Inscribed: "NAGUEMA".		
RA38	PT11 50c dk. vio., lt. vio. & gray	6.50	6.50
	Nos. RA32–RA38 (7)	45.50	45.50

The portrait is that of Mousinho de Albuquerque, the celebrated Portuguese warrior, and the names of seven battles in which he took part appear at the foot of the stamps. The stamps were issued for the memorial fund bearing his name and their use was obligatory on all correspondence posted on eight specific days in the year.

Type of 1929 Issue.

Denominations in Black.

1931 ***Perf. 14.***

RA39 PT10 40c rose & vio. 4.00 4.00

1932

RA40 PT10 40c olive green & violet 4.00 4.00

1933

RA41 PT10 40c bistre brown & rose 4.00 4.00

1934 **Without Denomination.**

RA42 PT10 bl. green & rose 4.00 4.00

Denominations in Black

1936

RA43 PT10 40c org. & ultra. 4.00 4.00

1937

RA44 PT10 40c chocolate & ultra. 4.00 4.00

1938

RA45 PT10 40c green & brown carmine 6.00 6.00

1939

RA46 PT10 40c yel. & blk. 6.00 6.00

1940

RA47 PT10 40c gray brown 6.00 6.00

Allegory of Charity — PT12

White Pelican — PT13

Lithographed.

1942 ***Perf. 11½*** **Unwmkd.**

Denomination in Black

RA48 PT12 50c rose car. 10.00 1.75

1943-51 ***Perf. 11½, 14.***

Denomination Typo. in Black.

RA49	PT13 50c rose car.	15.00	45
RA50	" 50c emerald	10.00	45
RA51	" 50c purple	12.00	45
RA52	" 50c blue	10.00	45
RA53	" 50c red brown	15.00	45
RA54	" 50c olive bistre	10.00	45
	Nos. RA49–RA54 (6)	72.00	2.70

There are two sizes of the numeral on No. RA49.

Inscribed: "Provincia de Mocambique"

1954-56 ***Perf. 14½x14***

RA55	PT13 50c orange	2.00	40
RA56	" 50c olive green ('56)	2.00	40
RA57	" 50c brown ('56)	2.00	40

No. RA57 Surcharged with New Value and Wavy Lines.

1956

RA58 PT13 30c on 50c brown 60 40

Pelican Type of 1954–56.

1958 **Litho.** ***Perf. 14***

Denomination in Black

RA59	PT13 30c yellow	60	40
RA60	" 50c salmon	60	40

Imprint: "Imprensa Nacional de Mocambique"

1963–64

Denomination Typo. in Black

RA61	PT13 30c yellow ('64)	35	20
RA62	" 50c salmon	30	20

Women and Children — PT14

Lineman on Pole and Map of Mozambique — PT15

1963 **Litho.** ***Perf. 14***

RA63 PT14 50c black, bister & red 40 20

1965 **Litho.** ***Perf. 14***

RA64 PT14 50c black, pink & red 40 20

1965, Apr. 1 ***Perf. 14*** **Unwmkd.**

Design: 30c, Telegraph poles and map of Mozambique.

Size: 23x30mm.

RA65 PT15 30c black, salmon & lilac 10 5

Size: 19x36mm.

RA66	PT15 50c black, blue & sepia	25	18
RA67	" 1e blk., yel. & org.	25	10

The tax was for improvement of the telecommunications system. Obligatory on inland mail. A 2.50e in the design of the 30c was issued for use on telegrams.

Type of 1963

1967, June 29 **Litho.** ***Perf. 14***

RA68 PT14 50c blk., lt. yel. grn. & red 40 25

1969

RA69 PT14 50c black, lt. blue & red 40 25

1970

RA70 PT14 50c black, buff & bright red 40 25

1972-73

RA71 PT14 30c black, light green & red 10 5
RA72 " 50c blk., gray & red ('73) 1.50 25
RA73 " 1e blk., bister & red ('73) 25 12

1974-75

RA74 PT14 50c bl., yel. & red 20 10
RA75 " 1e black, gray & vermilion 40 20
RA76 " 1e blk., lilac rose & red ('75) 40 20

POSTAL TAX DUE STAMPS.

Pombal Commemorative Issue.

Common Design Types

1925 ***Perf. 12½.*** **Unwmkd.**

RAJ1 CD31 30c brown & blk. 75 90
RAJ2 CD32 30c " " 75 90
RAJ3 CD33 30c " " 75 90

MOZAMBIQUE COMPANY

LOCATION — Comprises the territory of Manica and Sofala of the Mozambique Colony in southeastern Africa.

GOVT. — A part of the Portuguese Colony of Mozambique.

AREA—51,881 sq. mi.

POP.—368,447 (1939).

CAPITAL—Beira.

The Mozambique Company was chartered by Portugal in 1891 for 50 years. The territory was under direct administration of the Company until July 18, 1941.

1000 Reis = 1 Milreis

100 Centavos = 1 Escudo (1916)

Mozambique Nos. 15-23 Overprinted in Carmine or Black

COMP.^A DE MOÇAMBIQUE

1892 ***Perf. 12½, 13½.*** **Unwmkd.**

1 A2 5r black (C) 40 35
a. Pair, one without overprint 10.00 10.00
2 " 10r green 75 35
3 " 20r rose 1.00 60
a. Perf. 13½ 20.00 16.50
4 " 25r violet 1.00 60
a. Double ovpt. 6.50
5 " 40r chocolate 75 50
a. Double ovpt. 5.00
6 " 50r blue 65 40
7 " 100r yellow brown 65 45
8 " 200r gray violet 1.25 60
9 " 300r orange 1.35 80
Nos. 1-9 (9) 7.80 4.65

Nos. 1 to 6, 8-9 were reprinted in 1905. These reprints have white gum and clean-cut perf. 13½ and the colors are usually paler than those of the originals. Price, $1 each.

Company Coat of Arms
A2

Perf. 11½, 12½, 13½.

Black or Red Numerals.

1895-1907 Typographed.

10 A2 2½r olive yellow 25 25
11 " 2½r gray ('07) 90 50
12 " 5r orange 30 25
a. Value omitted 2.00
b. Perf. 13½ 1.75 1.00
13 " 10r red lilac 45 30
14 " 10r yel. green ('07) 1.25 60
a. Value inverted at top of stamp 5.00 3.00
15 " 15r red brown 75 40
16 " 15r dark green ('07) 1.25 60
17 " 20r gray lilac 1.00 40
18 " 25r green 75 40
a. Perf. 13½ 2.00 1.35
19 " 25r carmine ('07) 1.50 70
a. Value omitted 5.00 5.00
20 " 50r blue 1.00 40
21 " 50r brown ('07) 1.35 65
a. Value omitted 5.00
22 " 65r slate blue ('02) 50 35
23 " 75r rose 55 40
24 " 75r red lilac ('07) 2.00 1.50
25 " 80r yellow green 50 35
26 " 100r brown, *buff* 50 33
27 " 100r dark blue, *blue* ('07) 2.00 1.25
28 " 115r carm., *pink* ('04) 65 50
29 " 115r orange brown, *pink* ('07) 2.25 1.75
30 " 130r green, *pink* ('04) 80 60
31 " 130r brn., *yellow* ('07) 2.25 2.00
32 " 150r org. brown, *pink* 45 33
33 " 200r dark blue, *blue* 45 33
a. Perf. 13½ 2.00 1.75
34 A2 200r red lilac, *pink* ('07) 2.25 2.00
35 " 300r dark blue, *salmon* 45 35
a. Perf. 13½ 3.50 2.00
36 " 400r brown, *blue* ('04) 65 50
37 " 400r dull blue, *yellow* ('07) 2.75 2.25
38 " 500r black & red 65 50
39 " 500r black & red, *blue* ('07) 3.00 2.25
a. 500r purple & red, *yellow* (error)
40 " 700r slate, *buff* ('04) 1.65 1.50
41 " 700r purple, *yellow* ('07) 3.00 2.25
42 " 1000r violet & red 75 65
Nos. 10-42 (33) 38.80 27.39

Nos. 12b, 18a, 33a and 35a were issued without gum.

Nos. 25 and 6 Surcharged or Overprinted in Red:

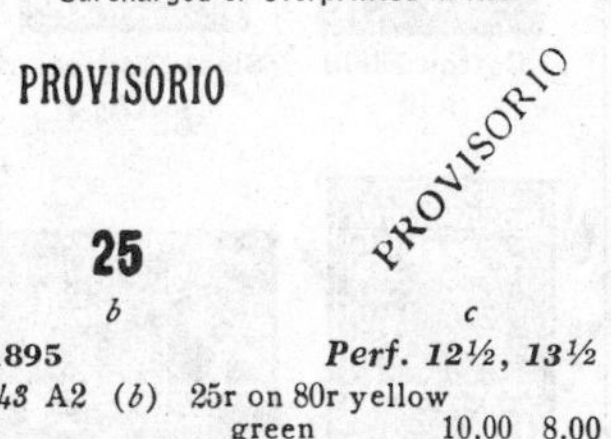

b c

1895 ***Perf. 12½, 13½***

43 A2 (b) 25r on 80r yellow green 10.00 8.00
44 " (c) 50r blue 3.00 2.50

Overprint "c" on No. 44 also exists reading from upper left to lower right.

Stamps of 1895 Overprinted in Bister, Orange, Violet, Green, Black or Brown

1498
Centenario da India
1898

1898 ***Perf. 12½, 13½***

Without Gum

45 A2 2½r olive yel. (Bi) 1.25 1.00
a. Double overprint 8.00 8.00
b. Red overprint 10.00 10.00
46 " 5r orange (O) 1.35 1.00
47 " 10r red lilac (V) 1.35 1.00
48 " 15r red brown (V) 3.00 1.75
a. Red overprint 7.50 7.50
49 " 20r gray lilac (V) 2.25 1.50
50 " 25r green (G) 3.25 1.75
a. Invtd. ovpt. 12.50 10.00
51 " 50r blue (Bk) 2.50 2.00
a. Invtd. ovpt. 12.50 12.50
52 " 75r rose (V) 3.75 3.25
a. Invtd. ovpt. 15.00 15.00
b. Red overprint 15.00 15.00
53 " 80r yellow grn. (G) 4.00 2.75
a. Invtd. ovpt.
54 " 100r brn., *buff* (Br) 4.25 3.25
55 " 150r orange brown, *pink* (O) 4.25 3.25
a. Invtd. ovpt. 12.50 12.50
b. Double overprint
56 " 200r dark blue, *blue* (Bk) 5.00 4.00
57 " 300r dark blue, *salmon* (Bk) 6.75 5.00
a. Invtd. ovpt. 12.50 12.50
b. Green overprint
Nos. 45-57 (13) 42.95 31.50

Vasco da Gama's discovery of route to India, 400th anniversary.

No. 57b was prepared but not issued.

Nos. 45 and 49 were also issued with gum.

The "Centenario" overprint on stamps perf. 11½ is forged.

See "Special Notices" at the front of this volume for data on the listing methods of this Catalogue, abbreviations, condition, prices and examination.

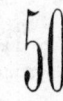

Surcharged in Black, Carmine or Violet

25 PROVISORIO
e

25 Réis
f

50 RÉIS
g

1899 ***Perf. 12½***

59 A2 (e) 25r on 75r rose (Bk) 3.00 1.50

1900 ***Perf. 12½, 12½x11½***

60 A2 (f) 25r on 5r org. (C) 1.50 1.00
61 " (g) 50r on half of 20r gray lilac (V) 1.25 1.00
b. Entire stamp 5.00 5.00

No. 61b is perf. 11½ vertically through center.

Stamps of 1895-1907 Overprinted Locally in Carmine or Green

1911 ***Perf. 11½, 13½***

61A A2 2½r gray (C) 90 60
62 " 5r orange (G) 1.35 90
63 " 10r yellow green (C) 1.00 75
64 " 15r dark green (C) 1.00 75
a. Double overprint 4.00 4.00
65 " 20r gray lilac (G) 1.25 38
a. Perf. 13½ 1.00 75
66 " 25r carmine (G) 1.25 85
67 " 50r brown (G) 1.00 60
68 " 75r red lilac (G) 1.25 60
69 " 100r dk. bl., *blue* (C) 1.35 60
70 " 115r orange brown, *pink* (G) 1.50 75
71 " 130r brn., *yellow* (G) 2.00 85
72 " 200r red lilac, *pink* (G) 2.00 85
73 " 400r dull blue, *yellow* (C) 2.00 85
74 " 500r blk. & red, *bl.* (C) 2.25 1.15
75 " 700r pur., *yellow* (G) 2.25 1.15
Nos. 61A-75 (15) 22.35 11.63

Nos. 63, 67 and 71 exist with inverted overprint; Nos. 63, 72 and 75 with double overprint.

Overprinted in Lisbon in Carmine or Green

REPUBLICA

1911 ***Perf. 11½, 12½***

75B A2 2½r gray 50 25
76 " 5r orange 50 20
77 " 10r yellow green 35 20
78 " 15r dark green 50 20
79 " 20r gray lilac 40 20
80 " 25r carmine (G) 50 10
a. Value inverted at top of stamp 7.50
81 " 50r brown 50 20
82 " 75r red lilac 50 20
a. Value omitted 5.00
83 " 100r dark blue, *blue* 75 15
84 " 115r org. brn., *pink* 1.00 20
85 " 130r brown, *yellow* 1.35 20
a. Double overprint 5.00
86 " 200r red lilac, *pink* 60 20
87 " 400r dull blue, *yellow* 1.00 40
88 " 500r black & red, *blue* 1.00 25
89 " 700r purple, *yellow* 1.25 25
Nos. 75B-89 (15) 10.70 3.20

Second Issue of 1911 Surcharged **1/4 C**

1916			*Perf. 11½*	
90	A2	¼c on 2½r gray	25	25
91	"	½c on 5r orange	25	25
		a. "½c" double	5.00	
92	"	1c on 10r yellow green	60	30
93	"	1½c on 15r dark green	60	30
		a. Imperf. (pair)	6.00	
94	"	2c on 20r gray lilac	75	30
95	"	2½c on 25r carmine	1.00	25
96	"	5c on 50r brown	60	30
		a. Imperf. (pair)	6.00	
97	"	7½c on 75r red lilac	75	25
98	"	10c on 100r dk. bl., *bl.*	45	35
		a. Inverted surcharge	7.50	5.00
99	"	11½c on 115r orange brown, *pink*	1.50	45
		a. Inverted surcharge	9.00	7.50
100	"	13c on 130r brown, *yellow*	1.75	45
101	"	20c on 200r red lilac, *pink*	1.00	50
102	"	40c on 400r dull blue, *yellow*	1.50	50
103	"	50c on 500r black & red, *blue* (R)	1.75	55
104	"	70c on 700r purple, *yellow*	2.25	90
		Nos. 90-104 (15)	15.00	5.90

Nos. 87 to 89 Surcharged **1/2 Cent.**

1918			*Perf. 11½*	
105	A2	½c on 700r purple, *yellow*	75	75
106	"	2½c on 500r black & red, *blue* (Bl)	75	60
107	"	5c on 400r dull blue, *yellow*	75	60

Native and Village
A9

Man and Ivory Tusks
A10

Corn
A11

Tapping Rubber Tree
A12

Sugar Refinery
A13

Buzi River Scene
A14

Tobacco Field
A15

View of Beira
A16

Coffee Plantation
A17

Orange Tree
A18

Cotton Field
A19

Sisal Plantation
A20

Scene on Beira R. R.
A21

Court House at Beira
A22

Coconut Palm
A23

Mangroves
A24

Cattle
A25

Company Arms
A26

1918–31	Engr.		*Perf. 14, 15, 12½*	
108	A9	¼c brn. & yel. green	20	20
109	"	¼c olive green & black ('25)	12	12
110	A10	½c black	20	20
111	A11	1c green & black	20	20
112	A12	1½c black & green	20	20
113	A13	2c carmine & black	20	20
114	"	2c olive black & black ('25)	20	20
115	A14	2½c lilac & black	20	20
116	A11	3c ocher & blk. ('23)	30	20
117	A15	4c green & brn. ('21)	30	20
118	"	4c red & black ('25)	25	20
119	A9	4½c gray & black ('23)	30	25
120	A16	5c blue & black	27	25
121	A17	6c claret & blue ('21)	75	40
122	"	6c lilac & black ('25)	25	20
123	A21	7c ultra. & blk. ('23)	1.00	65
124	A18	7½c orange & green	65	35
125	A19	8c violet & black	30	27
126	A20	10c red orange & black	30	20
128	A19	12c brn. & blk. ('23)	1.00	50
129	"	12c blue green & black ('25)	60	35
130	A21	15c carmine & black	40	25
131	A22	20c deep green & blk.	50	25
132	A23	30c red brown & blk.	2.50	1.00
133	"	30c gray green & black ('25)	1.25	27
134	A23	30c blue green & blk. ('31)	2.50	30
135	A24	40c yel. grn. & blk.	1.25	75
136	"	40c greenish blue & black ('25)	1.00	40
137	A25	50c orange & black	1.75	1.25
138	"	50c light violet & black ('25)	1.75	35
139	"	60c rose & brown ('23)	75	30
140	A20	80c ultramarine & brown ('23)	1.75	1.00
141	"	80c car. & blk. ('25)	75	30
142	A26	1e dark grn. & blk.	1.75	50
143	"	1e bl. & blk. ('25)	1.50	40
144	A16	2e rose & vio. ('23)	2.75	60
145	"	2e lilac & blk. ('25)	2.00	35
		Nos. 108-145 (37)	31.94	13.81

Shades exist of several denominations.

Stamps of 1918 Surcharged with New Values in Red, Blue, Violet or Black:

Um e meio Centavo
h

4 Cent.
i

Seis Centavos
j

1920			*Perf. 14, 15*	
146	A23 (*h*)	½c on 30c red brown & black (Bk)	4.50	4.50
147	A26 (")	½c on 1e dark green & black (R)	4.50	4.50
148	A14 (")	1½c on 2½c violet & black (Bl)	1.75	1.75
149	A16 (")	1½c on 5c blue & black (V)	3.00	3.00
150	A14 (")	2c on 2½c violet & black (R)	1.75	1.75
151	A22 (*i*)	4c on 20c green & black (V)	4.50	4.50
152	A24 (")	4c on 40c yel. grn. & black (V)	4.50	4.50
153	A19 (*j*)	6c on 8c dk. vio. & black (R)	4.50	4.50
154	A25 (")	6c on 50c orange & black (Bk)	4.50	4.50
		Nos. 146-154 (9)	33.50	33.50

The surcharge on No. 148 is placed vertically between two bars. On No. 154 the two words of the surcharge are 13mm. apart.

Native
A27

View of Beira
A28

Tapping Rubber Tree
A29

Picking Tea
A30

Zambezi River
A31

1925–31		Engr.	*Perf. 12*	
155	A27	24c ultra. & black	75	50
156	A28	25c choc. & ultra.	75	50
157	A27	85c brown red & black ('31)	75	40
158	A28	1.40e dull blue & black ('31)	65	35
159	A29	5e yellow brown & ultramarine	1.50	30
160	A30	10e rose & black	2.00	75
161	A31	20e green & black	3.00	75
		Nos. 155-161 (7)	9.40	3.55

Ivory Tusks
A32

Panning Gold
A33

1931		Lithographed.	*Perf. 14.*	
162	A32	45c light blue	2.00	45
163	A33	70c yellow brown	2.00	45

Zambezi Railroad Bridge—A34

1935		Engraved	*Perf. 12½*	
164	A34	1e dark blue & black	2.00	1.35

Issued to commemorate the opening of a new bridge over the Zambezi River.

Airplane over Beira—A35

1935				
165	A35	5c blue & black	65	50
166	"	10c red orange & black	65	50
		a. Square pair, imperf. between	20.00	
167	"	15c red & black	65	50
		a. Square pair, imperf. between	20.00	
168	"	20c yel. green & black	65	50
169	"	30c green & black	65	50
170	"	40c gray blue & black	65	50
171	"	45c blue & black	65	50
172	"	50c violet & black	65	50
		a. Square pair imperf. between	35.00	
173	"	60c carmine & brown	65	50
174	"	80c carmine & black	65	50
		Nos. 165-174 (10)	6.50	5.00

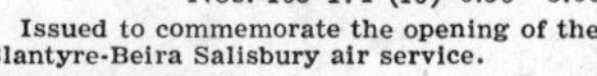

Issued to commemorate the opening of the Blantyre-Beira Salisbury air service.

Giraffe
A36

Thatched Huts
A37

Rock Python—A41

Coconut Palms
A50

Zambezi Railroad Bridge
A52

Sena Gate A53 — Company Arms A54

Designs: 10c, Dhow. 15c, St. Caetano Fortress, Sofala. 20c, Zebra. 40c, Black rhinoceros. 45c, Lion. 50c, Crocodile. 60c, Leopard. 70c, Mozambique woman. 80c, Hippopotami. 85c, Vasco da Gama's flagship. 1e, Man in canoe. 2e, Greater kudu.

1937, May 16 *Perf. 12½.*

175 A36 1c yellow green & violet 5 *30*
176 A37 5c blue & yellow green 10 6
177 A36 10c verm. & ultra. 10 6
178 A37 15c carmine & black 10 6
179 A36 20c green & ultra. 10 10
180 A41 30c dark green & indigo 15 *40*
181 " 40c gray blue & black 15 *40*
182 " 45c blue & brown 15 *40*
183 " 50c dark violet & emerald 15 *40*
184 A37 60c carmine & blue 15 12
185 A36 70c yellow brown & pale green 15 12
186 A37 80c car. & pale grn. 35 25
187 A41 85c org. red & blk. 75 60
188 " 1e deep blue & black 30 15
189 A50 1.40e dark blue & pale green 25 15
190 A41 2e pale lilac & brn. 25 15
191 A52 5e yellow brown & blue 60 *1.00*
192 A53 10e carmine & black 1.25 *2.50*
193 A54 20e green & brown violet 2.25 *4.00*
Nos. 175-193 (19) 7.35 *11.22*

Stamps of 1937 Overprinted in Red or Black

28-VII-1939

Visita Presidencial

1939, Aug. 28

194 A41 30c dark green & indigo (R) 1.25 50
195 " 40c gray bl. & black (R) 1.25 75
196 " 45c bl. & brown (Bk) 1.25 75
197 " 50c dark violet & emerald (R) 1.25 75
198 " 85c orange red & black (Bk) 1.25 50
199 " 1e deep blue & black (R) 1.25 50
200 " 2e pale lilac & brown (Bk) 1.25 1.00
Nos. 194-200 (7) 8.75 4.75

Visit of the President of Portugal to Beira in 1939.

King Alfonso Henriques
A55

King John IV
A56

Typographed

1940, Feb. 16 *Perf. 11½x12.*

201 A55 1.75e bl. & light blue 1.00 50

Issued in commemoration of the 800th anniversary of Portuguese independence.

1941 Engraved *Perf. 12½*

202 A56 40c gray green & black 35 25
203 " 50c dark violet & bright green 35 25
204 " 60c bright carmine & deep blue 35 25
205 " 70c brown orange & dark green 35 25
206 " 80c car. & dp. green 35 25
207 " 1e dark blue & black 35 25
Nos. 202-207 (6) 2.10 1.50

Issued in commemoration of the 300th anniversary of the restoration of the Portuguese Monarchy.

Mozambique Company's charter terminated July 18th, 1941 after which date its stamps were superseded by those of the territory of Mozambique.

SEMI-POSTAL STAMPS.

Lisbon Issue of 1911 Overprinted in Red

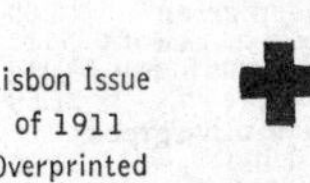

1917 *Perf. 11½.* **Unwmkd.**

B1 A2 2½r gray 5.00 5.00
a. Double overprint 20.00 20.00
B2 " 10r yellow green 5.00 5.00
B3 " 20r gray lilac 5.00 5.00
B4 " 50r brown 5.00 5.00
B5 " 75r red lilac 20.00 15.00
B6 " 100r dark blue, *blue* 20.00 15.00
B7 " 700r purple, *yellow* 50.00 50.00
Nos. B1-B7 (7) 110.00 100.00

Nos. B1-B7 were used on July 31, 1917, in place of ordinary stamps. The proceeds were given to the Red Cross.

AIR POST STAMPS.

Airplane over Beira
AP1

Engraved.

1935 *Perf. 12½* **Unwmkd.**

C1 AP1 5c blue & black 7 7
C2 " 10c orange red & black 8 8
C3 " 15c red & black 8 8
C4 " 20c yel. grn. & black 8 8
C5 " 30c green & black 8 8
C6 " 40c gray blue & black 8 8
C7 " 45c blue & black 8 8
C8 " 50c dk. violet & black 8 8
C9 " 60c carmine & brown 8 8
C10 " 80c carmine & black 8 8
C11 " 1e blue & black 8 8
C12 AP1 2e mauve & black 8 8
C13 " 5e bis. brn. & blue 60 30
C14 " 10e carmine & black 1.00 65
C15 " 20e blue grn. & blk. 2.00 90
Nos. C1-15 (15) 4.55 2.80

POSTAGE DUE STAMPS.

D1

Typographed.

1906 *Perf. 11½x12* **Unwmkd.**

Denominations in Black.

J1 D1 5r yellow green 35 25
J2 " 10r slate 35 25
J3 " 20r yellow brown 35 25
J4 " 30r orange 50 35
J5 " 50r gray brown 50 35
J6 " 60r red brown 3.75 3.25
J7 " 100r red lilac 1.25 1.00
J8 " 130r dull blue 6.25 4.00
J9 " 200r carmine 5.00 2.00
J10 " 500r violet 5.00 2.00
Nos. J1-J10 (10) 23.30 13.70

Postage Due Stamps of 1906 Overprinted in Carmine or Green

REPUBLICA

1911

J11 D1 5r yellow green 20 20
J12 " 10r slate 20 20
J13 " 20r yellow brown 20 20
J14 " 30r orange 30 20
J15 " 50r gray brown 45 30
J16 " 60r red brown 45 30
J17 " 100r red lilac 45 30
J18 " 130r dull blue 70 50
J19 " 200r carmine (G) 75 50
J20 " 500r violet 1.10 70
Nos. J11-J20 (10) 4.80 3.40

D2

Company Arms
D3

1916 Typographed.

With Value in Centavos in Black

J21 D2 ½c yellow green 15 15
J22 " 1c slate 20 15
J23 " 2c orange brown 20 15
J24 " 3c orange 25 20
J25 " 5c gray brown 30 20
J26 " 6c pale brown 25 20
J27 " 10c red lilac 30 25
J28 " 13c gray blue 70 45
J29 " 20c rose 75 50
J30 " 50c gray 1.25 1.00
Nos. J21-J30 (10) 4.35 3.25

Perf. 11½, 13½, 14 to 15½

1919 Engraved

J31 D3 ½c green 15 15
J32 " 1c slate 15 15
J33 " 2c red brown 15 15
J34 " 3c orange 15 15
J35 " 5c gray brown 30 20
J36 " 6c light brown 50 45
J37 " 10c lilac rose 50 45
J38 " 13c dull blue 50 45
J39 " 20c rose 50 45
J40 " 50c gray 50 45
Nos. J31-J40 (10) 3.40 3.05

NEWSPAPER STAMP.

Newspaper Stamp of Mozambique Overprinted Like Nos. 1-9

1894 *Perf. 11½* **Unwmkd.**

P1 N3 2½r brown 50 45
a. Invtd. opt. 3.00 3.00
b. Perf. 12½ 1.00 75

Reprints are on stout white paper with clean-cut perf. 13½. Price $1.

POSTAL TAX STAMPS.

No. 116a Surcharged in black

1932 *Perf. 12½*

RA1 A11 2c on 3c orange & black 2.00 *3.00*

Charity
PT2

1933 Lithographed *Perf. 11*

RA2 PT2 2c magenta & blk. 2.00 *3.00*

PT3

PT4

1940 *Perf. 10½* **Unwmkd.**

RA3 PT3 2c blk. & ultra. 12.50 *15.00*

1941

RA4 PT4 2c blk. & brt. red 12.50 *15.00*

NEJD

(See Saudi Arabia, Vol. IV.)

NETHERLANDS

(nĕth'ẽr-lăndz)

(Holland)

LOCATION—Northwestern Europe, bordering on North Sea.
GOVT.—Kingdom.
AREA—13,203 sq. mi.
POP.—13,850,000 (est. 1977).
CAPITAL — Amsterdam (constitutional), The Hague (legislative).

100 Cents = 1 Gulden
(Guilder or Florin)

Prices of early Netherlands stamps vary according to condition. Quotations for Nos. 1-12 are for fine copies (with original gum if unused). Very fine to superb specimens sell at much higher prices, and inferior or poor copies sell at reduced prices, depending on the condition of the individual specimen.

A1

A2

King William III

Wmk. 158

1852 Engraved *Imperf.*

1 A1 5c blue 1200.00 40.00
  a. 5c light blue 1200.00 40.00
  b. 5c steel blue 2150.00 160.00
  c. 5c dark blue 1275.00 45.00
2 " 10c lake 1500.00 35.00
3 " 15c orange 2000.00 165.00

In 1895 the 10c was privately reprinted in several colors on unwatermarked paper by Joh. A. Moesman, whose name appears on the back.

Perf. 12½x12

1864, May 12 **Unwmkd.**

4 A2 5c blue 500.00 30.00
5 " 10c lake 625.00 12.50
6 " 15c orange 1150.00 125.00
  a. 15c yellow 1200.00 125.00

The paper varies considerably in thickness. It is sometimes slightly bluish, also vertically ribbed.

William III
A3

Coat of Arms
A4

1867

Perf. 12½x12, 13, 13½, 14 and Compound.

7 A3 5c ultramarine 100.00 1.30
  a. Imperf., pair 400.00
  b. Bluish paper 100.00 1.30
8 " 10c lake 160.00 2.50
  a. Imperf., pair 400.00
  b. Bluish paper 160.00 2.50
9 " 15c orange brown 625.00 45.00
  a. Imperf., pair 700.00
  b. Bluish paper 650.00 45.00
10 " 20c dark green 525.00 27.50
  a. Imperf., pair 700.00
  b. Bluish paper 575.00 27.50
11 " 25c dark violet 1250.00 120.00
  a. Imperf., pair 1350.00
  b. Bluish paper *6000.00*
12 " 50c gold 2250.00 225.00
  a. Imperf. pair 2500.00
  b. Bluish paper *8000.00*

Two varieties of numerals in each value, differing chiefly in the thickness.

Imperforate varieties of Nos. 7–12 are not known to have been regularly issued.

1869 *Perf. 10½x10.*

7c A3 5c ultramarine 190.00 10.00
8c " 10c lake 275.00 4.25
9c " 15c orange brown *3250.00* 700.00
  d. Bluish paper *3250.00* 700.00
10c " 20c dark green *1500.00* 170.00
  d. Bluish paper *1500.00* 170.00

Typographed.

1869-71 *Perf. 13, 13½, 14.*

17 A4 ½c red brown ('71) 32.50 2.65
  a. Imperf., pair 450.00
  b. Bluish paper 32.50 3.00
  c. Perf. 14 *3000.00* *1000.00*
18 " 1c black 275.00 100.00
  a. Imperf., pair 550.00
19 " 1c green 13.50 1.25
  a. Imperf., pair 450.00
  b. Bluish paper 19.00 1.50
  c. Perf. 14 35.00 7.50
20 " 1½c rose 200.00 100.00
  a. Imperf., pair 450.00
  b. Perf. 14 210.00 100.00
21 " 2c buff 67.50 13.50
  a. Imperf., pair 450.00
  b. Bluish paper 67.50 13.50
  c. Perf. 14 70.00 13.50
22 " 2½c violet ('71) 650.00 80.00
  a. Imperf., pair 600.00
  b. Bluish paper 650.00 80.00
  c. Perf. 14 1100.00 525.00

A5 A6

1872-88

Perf. 12½, 13, 13½, 14, 12½ x12 and 11½x12.

23 A5 5c ultramarine 15.00 25
  a. 5c blue 15.00 25
  b. Imperf., pair 125.00
24 " 7½c red brown ('88) 42.50 24.00
25 " 10c rose 72.50 1.20
  a. Imperf., pair 900.00
26 " 12½c gray ('75) 65.00 1.85
27 " 15c brown orange 450.00 5.25
  a. Imperf., pair 900.00
28 " 20c green 525.00 5.25
  a. Imperf., pair 1000.00
29 " 22½c dark green ('88) 90.00 62.50
30 " 25c dull violet 650.00 4.25
  a. Imperf., pair 1000.00
31 " 50c bistre 750.00 12.00
  a. Imperf., pair 1200.00
32 " 1g gray vio. ('88) 600.00 37.50
33 A6 2g 50c rose & ultra. 1000.00 135.00
  a. Imperf., pair 1600.00

Numeral of Value
A7

HALF CENT

Type I. Fraction bar 8 to 8½mm. long.
Type II. Fraction bar 9mm. long and thinner.

1876–94

34 A7 ½c rose, II 4.25 15
  a. ½c rose, I 15.00 25
  b. Imperf., pair 125.00
  c. Laid paper 65.00
  d. Perf. 14, I 1800.00 825.00
35 A7 1c emerald green ('94) 3.00 15
  a. Imperf., pair 125.00
  b. Laid paper 90.00 7.00
  c. 1c green 11.00 25
36 A7 2c olive yel. ('94) 42.50 3.25
  a. 2c yellow 95.00 3.25
  b. Imperf., pair 125.00
37 A7 2½c violet ('94) 18.50 25
  a. Imperf., pair 125.00
  b. 2½c dk. violet ('94) 24.00 60
  c. 2½c lilac 120.00 80

Imperforate varieties of Nos. 17 to 37 are not known to have been regularly issued.

Queen Wilhelmina
A8 A9

1891–94 *Perf. 12½*

40 A8 3c orange ('94) 10.00 1.40
  a. 3c org. yel. ('92) 16.00 1.25
41 " 5c lt. ultra. ('94) 5.00 20
  a. 5c dull blue 6.00 50
  b. 5c orange (error) *12,500.00* *9500.00*
42 " 7½c brown ('94) 24.00 5.00
  a. 7½c red brown 45.00 6.00
43 " 10c bright rose ('94) 35.00 90
  a. 10c brick red 100.00 4.75
44 " 12½c bluish gray ('94) 30.00 90
  a. 12½c gray 42.50 1.10
45 " 15c yel. brn. ('94) 65.00 5.00
  a. 15c org. brown 125.00 5.00
46 " 20c green ('94) 75.00 2.50
  a. 20c yel. green 135.00 4.00
47 " 22½c dk. green ('94) 45.00 17.50
  a. 22½c deep blue green 75.00 17.50

48 A8 25c dull vio. ('94) 120.00 4.00
  a. 25c dark violet 120.00 4.00
49 " 50c yel. brn. ('94) 575.00 24.00
  a. 50c bistre 625.00 40.00
50 " 1g gray violet 800.00 75.00

The paper used in 1891–93 was white, rough and somewhat opaque. In 1894, a thinner, smooth and sometimes transparent paper was introduced.

1891–96 *Perf. 11½x11*

51 A9 50c emerald & yel. brown ('96) 110.00 12.00
  a. Perf. 11 *3750.00* 300.00
52 " 1g brown & olive green ('96) 275.00 45.00
  a. Perf. 11 350.00 55.00
53 " 2g 50c bright rose & ultra. 800.00 200.00
  a. 2g 50c lilac rose & ultra., perf. 11 825.00 225.00
  b. Perf. 11½ 875.00 275.00
54 " 5g bronze green & red brn., perf. 11 ('96) 1200.00 575.00

Numeral of Value
A10

Queen Wilhelmina
A11

1898–1924

Perf. 12½, 11, 11½x11.

55 A10 ½c violet 70 10
56 " 1c red 1.50 10
  a. Bklt. pane of 6 90.00
  b. Imperf., pair *5500.00*
57 " 1½c ultra. ('08) 3.75 1.00
  a. Bklt. pane of 6 90.00
58 " 1½c deep blue ('13) 6.00 25
  a. Bklt. pane of 6 90.00
59 " 2c yellow brown 6.00 15
  a. Bklt. pane of 6 100.00
60 " 2½c deep green 6.00 15
  a. Bklt. pane of 6 75.00
  b. Imperf., pair *8000.00*
61 A11 3c orange 27.50 5.00
62 " 3c pale olive green ('01) 1.60 10
  a. Bklt. pane of 6 75.00
63 " 4c claret ('21) 2.25 1.25
64 " 4½c violet ('19) 5.25 5.50
65 " 5c carmine rose 2.25 8
  a. Bklt. pane of 6 75.00
66 " 7½c brown 80 10
  a. Tête bêche pair ('24) 110.00 125.00
  b. Booklet pane 125.00
67 " 10c gray lilac 10.00 10
  a. Bklt. pane of 6 125.00
68 " 12½c blue 5.00 25
  a. Bklt. pane of 6 125.00
69 " 15c yellow brown 135.00 4.00
70 " 15c bl. & car. ('08) 6.00 20
71 " 17½c violet ('06) 77.50 16.50
73 " 17½c ultramarine & brown ('10) 25.00 80
74 " 20c yellow green 150.00 90
75 " 20c olive green & gray ('08) 15.00 25
76 " 22½c brn. & olive grn. 11.00 30
77 " 25c carmine & blue 11.00 25
78 " 30c lilac & violet brown ('17) 35.00 25
79 " 40c grn. & org. ('20) 55.00 90
80 " 50c bronze green & red brown 110.00 1.20
81 " 50c gray & violet ('14) 135.00 80
  a. Perf. 11½x11 135.00 15.00
82 " 60c olive green & green ('20) 55.00 1.35
  a. Perf. 11½ 325.00 40.00
  Nos. 55–82 (27) 899.10 41.83

See also Nos. 107–112.

A12

Type I.

Type II.

Type I. The figure "I" is 3¾mm. high and 2¾mm. wide.

Type II. The figure "1" is 3½mm. high and 2½mm. wide, it is also thinner than in type I.

Perf. 11, 11x11½, 11½, 11½x11

1898–1905 **Engraved**

83 A12 1g dark green (type II) ('99) 62.50 40
  a. 1g dark green (type I) ('98) 325.00 115.00
84 " 2½g brn. lilac ('99) 165.00 4.25
85 " 5g claret ('99) 400.00 6.75
86 " 10g orange ('05) 1550.00 1300.00

Admiral M. A. de Ruyter and Fleet
A13

King William I
A14

Perf. 12x12½

1907, Mar. 23 **Typographed**

87 A13 ½c blue 95 1.10
88 " 1c claret 3.75 3.25
89 " 2½c vermilion 15.00 3.25

Issued to commemorate the tercentenary of the birth of Adm. Michiel A. de Ruyter (1607–1676), naval hero.

Perf. 11½, 11½x11

1913, Nov. 29 **Engraved**

Designs: 2½c, 12½c, 1g, King William I. 3c, 20c, 2½g, King William II. 5c, 25c, 5g, King William III. 10c, 50c, 10g, Queen Wilhelmina.

90 A14 2½c green, *green* 75 80
91 " 3c buff, *straw* 1.10 1.25
92 " 5c rose red, *salmon* 95 65
93 " 10c gray black 5.25 2.50
94 " 12½c deep blue, *blue* 3.25 2.40
95 " 20c orange brown 18.50 10.50
96 " 25c pale blue 18.50 10.50
97 " 50c yellow green 40.00 40.00
98 " 1g claret 72.50 22.50
  a. Perf. 11½ 100.00 22.50
99 " 2½g dull violet 190.00 77.50
100 " 5g yel., *straw* 475.00 72.50
101 " 10g red, *straw* 1500.00 1400.00
  Nos. 90–101 (12) 2325.80 1641.10

Centenary of Dutch independence.

No. 78 Surcharged in Red or Black

Veertig Cent (a) Zestig Cent (b)

1919, Dec. 1 *Perf. 12½*

102 A11 (*a*) 40c on 30c lilac & violet brown (R) 42.50 6.75
103 " (*b*) 60c on 30c lilac & violet brown (Bk) 40.00 6.50

Nos. 86 and 101 Surcharged in Black

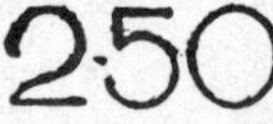

1920, Aug. 17 *Perf. 11, 11½*

104 A12 2.50g on 10g org. 300.00 275.00
105 A14 2.50g on 10g red, *straw* 325.00 165.00

No. 64 Surcharged in Red

—4C—

1921, Mar. 1 *Perf. 12½*
106 A11 4c on 4½c violet 3.25 1.40

A17

1921, Aug. 5 **Typo.** *Perf. 12½*
107 A17 5c green 19.00 18
108 " 12½c vermilion 22.50 2.75
109 " 20c blue 45.00 25
a. Booklet pane of 6 600.00

Queen Type of 1898–99, 10c Redrawn

1922–23 *Perf. 12½*
110 A11 10c gray 55.00 10

Imperf.

111 A11 5c car. rose ('23) 11.00 11.00
112 " 10c gray ('23) 12.50 12.50

In redrawn 10c the horizontal lines behind the Queen's head are wider apart.

Orange Tree and Lion of Brabant
A18

Post Horn and Lion
A19

Numeral of Value
A20

1923, Mar. *Perf. 12½*
113 A18 1c dark violet 70 80
114 " 2c orange 10.00 12
115 A19 2½c bluish green 2.35 80
116 A20 4c deep blue 1.85 80

Stamps of 1898–1913 Surcharged in Various Colors

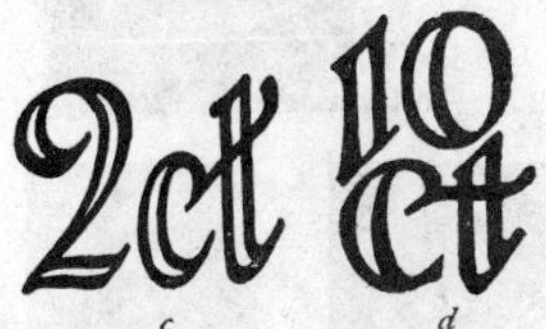

c d

Perf. 12½, 11½x11, 11½

1923, Aug.
117 A10 (*c*) 2c on 1c red (Bl) 70 25
118 " (") 2c on 1½c bl. (Bk) 70 25
119 A11 (*d*) 10c on 3c olive green (Br) 7.00 15
120 " (") 10c on 5c carmine rose (Bk) 13.00 50
121 " (") 10c on 12½c blue (R) 12.00 75
122 " (") 10c on 17½c ultra. & brn. (R) 4.75 5.00
a. Perf. 11½ 2250.00 1500.00
b. Perf. 11½x11 4.25 4.50
123 " (") 10c on 22½c brn.& ol. grn. (R) 4.75 5.00
a. Perf. 11½ 4.25 4.50
b. Perf. 11½x11 4.25 4.50
Nos. 117–123 (7) 42.90 11.90

Queen Wilhelmina
A21 A22

Perf. 11, 11½, 12, 12½ and Compound.

1923, Aug. 31 **Engraved**
124 A22 2c myrtle green 12 10
a. Vertical pair, imperf. between 2250.00
125 A21 5c green 25 18
a. Vert. pair, imperf. between 2250.00
126 A22 7½c carmine 30 12
127 " 10c vermilion 40 10
a. Vert. pair, imperf. between 800.00 900.00
128 " 20c ultramarine 4.00 65
129 " 25c yellow 5.50 65
130 " 35c orange 6.75 2.75
131 " 50c black 22.50 20
132 A21 1g red 45.00 8.00
133 " 2½g black 385.00 350.00
134 " 5g dark blue 360.00 275.00
Nos. 124–134 (11) 829.82 637.75

Issued to commemorate the 25th anniversary of the assumption of the Government of the Netherlands by Queen Wilhelmina at the age of 18.

Nos. 73, 119 Overprinted in Red "DIENSTZEGEL PORTEN AANTEEKENRECHT; No. 119 with New Value in Blue

e

1923 *Perf. 12½*
135 A11 (*d*) 10c on 3c olive green (Br) 1.35 1.50
136 " (*e*) 1g on 17½c ultramarine & brown (Bl) 100.00 25.00
a. Perf. 11½ 135.00 47.50
b. Perf. 11½x11 110.00 35.00

The stamps with the red surcharge were prepared for use as Officials but were not issued.

International Philatelic Exhibition Issue.

Queen Wilhelmina
A23

1924, Sept. 6 **Photo.** *Perf. 12½*
137 A23 10c slate green 70.00 80.00
138 " 15c gray black 90.00 100.00
139 " 35c brown orange 70.00 80.00

These stamps were available solely to visitors to the International Philatelic Exhibition at The Hague and were not obtainable at regular post offices.

Ship in Distress
A23a

Lifeboat
A23b

1924, Sept. 15 **Litho.** *Perf. 11½*
140 A23a 2c black brown 2.00 2.50
141 A23b 10c orange brown 10.00 1.65

Centenary of Royal Dutch Lifeboat Society

Type A23 and

Gull
A24

1924–26 *Perf. 12½*
142 A24 1c deep red 70 90
b. Bklt. pane of 6 60.00
143 " 2c red orange 3.50 12
b. Bklt. pane of 6 60.00
144 " 2½c deep green 4.25 80
145 " 3c yel. green ('25) 18.00 1.15
146 " 4c deep ultra. 4.25 65

Photogravure

147 A23 5c dull green 8.00 1.00
b. Bklt. pane of 6 60.00
148 " 6c orange brn. ('25) 1.35 70
149 " 7½c orange ('25) 45 12
150 " 9c orange red & black ('26) 2.35 2.00
151 " 10c red 2.00 12
b. Bklt. pane of 6 60.00
152 " 12½c deep rose 2.75 60
153 " 15c ultramarine 9.50 60
b. Bklt. pane of 6 90.00
154 " 20c deep blue ('25) 18.00 85
155 " 25c olive bis. ('25) 37.50 80
156 " 30c violet 22.50 80
157 " 35c olive brown ('25) 52.50 10.00
158 " 40c deep brown 47.50 85
159 " 50c bl. green ('25) 100.00 85
160 " 60c dark vio. ('25) 47.50 95
Nos. 142–160 (19) 382.60 23.86

Syncopated Perforations

Type A

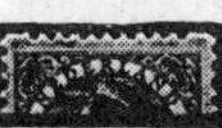

Type C

Type B

These special "syncopated" or "interrupted" perforations, devised for coil stamps, are found on Nos. 142–156, 158–160, 164–166, 168–185, 187–193 and certain semipostals of 1925–33, between Nos. B9 and B69. There are four types:

A. On two shorter sides, groups of four holes separated by blank spaces equal in width to two or three holes.

B. As "A," but on all four sides.

C. On two shorter sides, end holes are omitted.

D. Four-hole sequence on horiz. sides, three-hole on vert. sides.

Syncopated, Type A

(2 Sides)

1925–26
142a A24 1c deep red 80 80
143a " 2c red orange 5.50 4.50
144a " 2½c deep green 4.25 75
145a " 3c yellow green 42.50 42.50
146a " 4c deep ultramarine 3.50 2.75
147a A23 5c dull green 8.50 2.50
148a " 6c orange brown 200.00 190.00
149a " 7½c orange 1.65 1.25
150a " 9c orange red & black 2.50 1.75
151a " 10c red 32.50 5.00
152a " 12½c deep rose 2.50 1.50
153a " 15c ultramarine 150.00 14.00
154a " 20c deep blue 19.00 6.50
155a " 25c olive bister 110.00 100.00
156a " 30c violet 35.00 15.00
158a " 40c deep brown 100.00 62.50

159a A23 50c blue green 125.00 22.50
160a " 60c dark violet 60.00 16.00
Nos. 142a-160a (18) 903.20 489.80

A25

1925–27 **Engr.** *Perf. 11½, 12½*
161 A25 1g ultramarine 12.50 40
162 " 2½g carmine ('27) 150.00 6.75
163 " 5g gray black 285.00 4.00

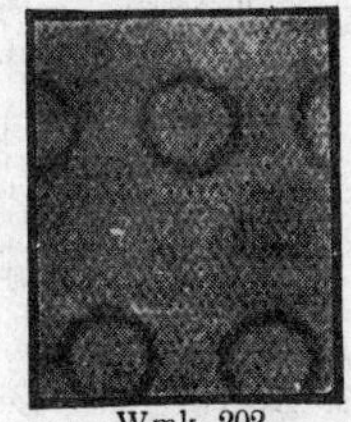

Wmk. 202

Types of 1924-26 Issue.
Lithographed.

Perf. 12½, 13½x12½, 12½x13½

1926–39 **Wmkd. Circles. (202)**
164 A24 ½c gray ('28) 1.25 1.25
165 " 1c deep red ('27) 10 7
c. Booklet pane of 6
166 " 1½c red violet ('28) 1.85 7
c. "CEN" for "CENT" 400.00 500.00
d. Bklt. pane of 6 25.00
167 " 1½c gray ('35) 12 7
a. 1½c dark gray 12 7
b. Bklt. pane of 6 12.50
168 " 2c deep orange 10 7
a. 2c red orange 12 8
e. Bklt. pane of 6 12.50
169 " 2½c green ('27) 3.75 7
c. Booklet pane of 6
170 " 3c yel. green ('27) 10 7
d. Bklt. pane of 6 12.50
171 " 4c dp. ultra. ('27) 10 10
d. Bklt. pane of 6 110.00

Photogravure

172 A23 5c deep green 20 7
d. Bklt. pane of 6 20.00
173 " 6c org. brown ('27) 20 7
d. Booklet pane of 6
174 " 7½c dk. violet ('27) 5.50 10
d. Booklet pane of 6
175 " 7½c red ('28) 25 7
b. Booklet pane of 6
176 " 9c orange red & black ('28) 15.00 13.50
b. Value omitted 17,500.00
177 " 10c red 1.75 7
178 " 10c dull violet ('29) 3.75 10
179 " 12½c dp. rose ('27) 72.50 5.25
180 " 12½c ultramarine ('28) 35 10
b. Bklt. pane of 6 30.00
181 " 15c ultramarine 11.00 30
182 " 15c orange ('29) 1.10 10
183 " 20c dp. blue ('28) 11.00 15
184 " 21c olive brown ('31) 37.50 1.00
185 " 22½c olive brn. ('27) 10.00 2.00
186 " 22½c dp. org. ('39) 20.00 21.00
187 " 25c olive bis. ('27) 6.00 18
188 " 27½c gray ('28) 6.00 85
189 " 30c violet 8.00 15
190 " 35c olive brown 100.00 22.50
191 " 40c deep brown 16.00 25
192 " 50c blue green 8.25 25
193 " 60c black ('29) 45.00 1.35
Nos. 164–193 (30) 386.72 71.18

See also Nos. 243A–243Q.

Syncopated, Type A

(2 Sides)

1926–27
168b A24 2c deep orange 60 50
170a " 3c yellow green 1.00 60
171a " 4c deep ultramarine 90 90
172a A23 5c deep green 1.50 1.35
173a " 6c orange brown 75 75
174a " 7½c dark violet 8.00 3.00

177a A23 10c red 1.85 1.25
181a " 15c ultramarine 14.00 3.75
185a " 22½c olive brown 14.00 5.25
187a " 25c olive bister 35.00 30.00
189a " 30c violet 22.50 15.00
190a " 35c olive brown 110.50 35.00
191a " 40c deep brown 90.00 90.00
Nos. 168b–191a (13) 300.10 182.35

Syncopated, Type B

(4 Sides)

1928

164a A24 ½c gray 80 50
165a " 1c deep red 50 30
166a " 1½c red violet 25 15
168c " 2c deep orange 1.50 1.50
169a " 2½c green 3.50 30
170b " 3c yellow green 1.00 75
171b " 4c deep ultramarine 1.00 75
172b A23 5c deep green 1.60 1.00
173b " 6c orange brown 1.00 75
174b " 7½c dark violet 8.00 3.00
175a " 7½c red 30 25
176a " 9c orange red & black 11.00 11.00
178a " 10c dull violet 11.00 10.00
179a " 12½c deep rose 125.00 140.00
180a " 12½c ultramarine 2.25 60
181b " 15c ultramarine 14.00 3.50
182a " 15c orange 1.15 50
183a " 20c deep blue 11.00 5.25
187b " 25c olive bister 24.00 16.00
188a " 27½c gray 6.50 3.00
189b " 30c violet 25.00 15.00
191b " 40c deep brown 70.00 35.00
192a " 50c blue green 90.00 85.00
193a " 60c black 75.00 47.50
Nos. 164a–193a (24) 485.35 381.60

Syncopated, Type C

(2 Sides, Corners Only)

1930

164b A24 ½c gray 80 50
165b " 1c deep red 1.25 75
166b " 1½c red violet 40 20
168d " 2c deep orange 1.15 90
169b " 2½c green 3.50 40
170c " 3c yellow green 1.75 90
171c " 4c deep ultramarine 75 35
172c A23 5c deep green 1.25 90
173c " 6c orange brown 1.00 90
178b " 10c dull violet 16.00 15.00
183b " 20c deep blue 11.00 6.25
184a " 21c olive brown 37.50 15.00
189c " 30c violet 22.00 15.00
192b " 50c blue green 82.50 80.00
Nos. 164b–192b (14) 180.85 137.05

Syncopated, Type D

(3 Holes Vert., 4 Holes Horiz.)

1927

174c A23 7½c dark violet 5500.00 5000.00

No. 185 Surcharged in Red **21**

1929, Nov. 11 *Perf. 12½*

194 A23 21(c) on 22½c olive brown 35.00 1.75

Queen Wilhelmina A26

Photogravure.

1931, Oct. *Perf. 12½*

195 A26 70c dark blue & red 35.00 65
a. Perf. 14¾x13½ ('39) 40.00 6.50

Arms of the House of Orange A27

William I, Portrait by Goltzius A28

Designs: 6c, Portrait of William I by Van Key. 12½c, Portrait attributed to Moro.

Engraved.

1933, Apr. 1 *Perf. 12½* **Unwmkd.**

196 A27 1½c black 75 20
197 A28 5c dark green 2.75 25
198 " 6c dull violet 5.50 12
199 " 12½c deep blue 30.00 5.50

Issued in commemoration of the 400th anniversary of the birth of William I, Count of Nassau and Prince of Orange, frequently referred to as William the Silent.

Star, Dove and Sword A31

Queen Wilhelmina and Ships A32

1933, May 18 Photo. **Wmk. 202**

200 A31 12½c deep ultra. 17.50 40

1933, July 26 *Perf. 14½x13½*

201 A32 80c Prussian blue & red 165.00 4.50

Tercentenary of Curacao.

Willemstad Harbor—A33

Van Walbeeck's Ship A34

Perf. 14x12½

1934, July 2 Engr. **Unwmkd.**

202 A33 6c violet black 7.50 18
203 A34 12½c dull blue 37.50 5.50

Minerva—A35

Design: 12½c, Gisbertius Voetius.

Wmkd. Circles. (202)

1936, May 15 Photo. *Perf. 12½*

204 A35 6c brown lake 4.00 35
205 " 12½c indigo 7.00 6.50

Issued in commemoration of the 300th anniversary of the founding of the University at Utrecht.

Boy Scout Emblem A37

"Assembly" A38

Mercury A39

1937, Apr. 1 *Perf. 14x13*

206 A37 1½c green & black 25 12
207 A38 6c red brown & blk. 3.25 12
208 A39 12½c blue & black 6.00 1.65

Fifth Boy Scout World Jamboree, Vogelenzang, Netherlands, July 31–Aug. 13, 1937.

Queen Wilhelmina A40

St. Willibrord A41

1938, Aug. 27 *Perf. 12½x12*

209 A40 1½c black 25 12
210 " 5c red orange 40 12
211 " 12½c royal blue 6.00 1.65

Issued in commemoration of the 40th anniversary of the reign of Queen Wilhelmina.

Perf. 12½x13½

1939, June 15 Engr. **Unwmkd.**

Design: 12½c, St. Willibrord as older man.

212 A41 5c dk. slate green 1.35 18
213 " 12½c slate blue 8.00 4.00

Issued in commemoration of the 12th centenary of the death of St. Willibrord.

Wood-burning Engine A43

Queen Wilhelmina A45

Design: 12½c, Streamlined electric car.

Perf. 14x13½

1939, Sept. 1 Photo. **Wmk. 202**

214 A43 5c dark slate green 1.60 25
215 " 12½c dark blue 12.50 5.25

Centenary of Dutch Railroads.

1940–47 *Perf. 13½x12½*

216 A45 5c dark green 7 7
a. Bklt. pane of 6 12.00
216B " 6c henna brown ('47) 40 15
217 " 7½c bright red 7 7
a. Bklt. pane of 6 17.50
218 " 10c bright red violet 10 7
219 " 12½c sapphire 12 10
a. Bklt. pane of 6 17.50
220 " 15c light blue 18 12
220B " 17½c slate blue ('46) 2.00 80
221 " 20c purple 25 15
222 " 22½c olive green 95 95
223 " 25c rose brown 30 12
224 " 30c bistre 90 25
225 " 40c bright green 1.60 50
225A " 50c orange ('46) 13.00 75
225B " 60c pur. brn. ('46) 11.00 3.50
Nos. 216–225B (14) 30.94 7.60

Imperf. copies of Nos. 216, 218–220 were released through philatelic channels during the German occupation, but were never issued at any post office. Price, set, $1.

Type of 1924-26 Surcharged in Black or Blue

Wmkd. Circles. (202)

1940, Oct. Photo. *Perf. 12½x13½*

226 A24 2½(c) on 3c verm. 1.50 20
227 " 5(c) on 3c light green 12 10
a. Bklt. pane of 6 11.00
228 A24 7½(c) on 3c vermilion 12 10
a. Bklt. pane of 6 14.00
229 A24 10(c) on 3c light green 18 10
230 " 12½(c) on 3c lt. bl. (Bl) 30 40
a. Bklt. pane of 6 14.00
231 A24 17½(c) on 3c light green 60 65
232 " 20(c) on 3c " 30 12
233 " 22½(c) on 3c " 1.10 1.10
234 " 25(c) on 3c " 45 25
235 " 30(c) on 3c " 60 40
236 " 40(c) on 3c " 75 65
237 " 50(c) on 3c " 1.10 40
238 " 60(c) on 3c " 1.85 1.00
239 " 70(c) on 3c " 3.50 2.00
240 " 80(c) on 3c " 5.25 5.25
241 " 1 (g) on 3c " 50.00 55.00
242 " 2.50(g) on 3c " 50.00 55.00
243 " 5(g) on 3c " 50.00 55.00
Nos. 226–243 (18) 167.72 177.72

Nos. 226 and 228 were issued se-tenant.

Gull Type of 1924–26.

1941

243A A24 2½c dark green 1.30 10
b. Booklet pane of 6 3.50
243C " 5c bright green 7 10
d. Booklet pane of 6 3.50
243E " 7½c henna 10 10
f. Booklet pane of 6 4.00
243G " 10c bright violet 20 10
243H " 12½c ultramarine 15 15
i. Booklet pane of 6 6.00
243J " 15c light blue 20 18
243K " 17½c red orange 15 18
243L " 20c light violet 30 18
243M " 22½c dark olive green 18 25
243N " 25c lake 20 18
243O " 30c olive 8.00 20
243P " 40c emerald 20 20
243Q " 50c orange brown 15 20
Nos. 243A–243Q (13) 11.20 2.12

Nos. 243A and 243E were issued se-tenant for vending machines.

Post Horn and Lion A46

Gold Surcharge.

1943, Jan. 15 Photo. *Perf. 12½x12*

244 A19 10c on 2½c yellow 10 15
a. Surch. omitted 10,000.00 12,500.00

Issued to commemorate the founding of the European Union of Posts and Telegraphs at Vienna, Oct. 19, 1942. Surcharge reads: "Europeesche P T T Vereeniging 19 October 1942 10 Cent" in capitals.

Sea Horse A47

Triple-crown Tree A48

Admiral M. A. de Ruyter A54

Designs: 2c, Swans. 2½c, Tree of Life. 3c, Tree with snake roots. 4c, Man on horseback. 5c, Prancing white horses. 10c, Johan Evertsen. 12½c, Martin Tromp. 15c, Piet Hein. 17½c, Willem van Ghent. 20c, Witte de With. 22½c, Cornelis Evertsen. 25c, Tjerk de Vries. 30c, Cornelis Tromp. 40c, Cornelis Evertsen De Jongste.

Perf. 12x12½, 12½x12

1943–44 **Photogravure** **Wmk. 202**

245 A47 1c black 5 10
246 A48 1½c rose lake 5 7

247 A47 2c dark blue 5 10
248 A48 2½c dark blue green 5 7
249 A47 3c copper red 5 10
250 A48 4c black brown 5 10
251 A47 5c dull yellow green 5 7

Unwmkd.

252 A54 7½c henna brown 7 7
a. Thinner numerals and letters ('44) 7 7
253 " 10c dark green 7 7
254 " 12½c blue 8 20
255 " 15c dull lilac 8 18
256 " 17½c slate ('44) 7 18
257 " 20c dull brown 7 12
258 " 22½c orange red 8 25
259 " 25c violet rose ('44) 50 65
260 " 30c cobalt blue ('44) 7 20

Engraved.

261 A54 40c bluish black 18 22
Nos. 245–261 (17) 1.62 2.75

In 1944, 200,000 copies of No. 247 were privately punched with a cross and printed on the back with a number and the words "Prijs 15 Cent toeslag ten bate Ned. Roode Kruis." These were sold at an exhibition, the surtax going to the Red Cross. The Dutch post office tolerated these stamps.

Soldier
A64

S. S. "Nieuw Amsterdam"
A65

Pilot
A66

Cruiser "De Ruyter"
A67

Queen Wilhelmina
A68

Engraved.

1944–46 *Perf. 12, 12½* Unwmkd.

262 A64 1½c black 12 12
263 A65 2½c yellow green 12 12
264 A66 3c dull red brown 12 12
265 A67 5c dark blue 12 12
266 A68 7½c vermilion 12 12
267 " 10c yellow orange 15 15
268 " 12½c ultramarine 15 15
269 " 15c dull red brown ('46) 4.25 4.50
270 " 17½c gray grn. ('46) 2.60 2.50
271 " 20c violet 25 30
272 " 22½c rose red ('46) 1.00 1.25
273 " 25c brn. org. ('46) 6.00 3.50
274 " 30c blue green 25 25
275 " 40c dark violet brown ('46) 5.25 5.50
276 " 50c red vio. ('46) 3.25 2.00
Nos. 262–276 (15) 23.75 20.70

These stamps were used on board Dutch war and merchant ships until Netherlands' liberation.

Lion and Dragon
A69

Queen Wilhelmina
A70

1945, July 15 *Perf. 12½x14*

277 A69 7½c red orange 7 7

Issued to commemorate Netherlands' liberation or "rising again."

1946 Engraved *Perf. 13½x14*

278 A70 1g dark blue 1.00 35
279 " 2½g brick red 225.00 9.00
280 " 5g dk. olive grn. 225.00 37.50
281 " 10g dark purple 225.00 37.50

A71

Photogravure.

1946–47 *Perf. 12x13½* Wmk. 202

282 A71 1c dark red 7 7
283 " 2c ultramarine 7 7
a. Booklet pane of 6 7.50
284 " 2½c dp. orange ('47) 21.00 1.85
285 " 4c olive green 55 7

The 1c was reissued in 1969 on phosphorescent paper in booklet pane No. 345b. The 4c was reissued on fluorescent paper in 1962.

The 2c was issued in coils in 1972. Every fifth stamp has black control number on back.

See Nos. 340–343A, 404–406.

Queen Wilhelmina
A72 A73

1947–48 *Perf. 13½x12½*

286 A72 5c olive green ('48) 75 5
287 " 6c brown black 12 5
288 " 7½c dp. red brn. ('48) 12 12
289 " 10c bright red violet 65 7
a. Bklt. pane of 6 15.00
290 " 12½c scarlet ('48) 50 50
291 " 15c purple 3.25 12
292 " 20c deep blue 5.25 12
293 " 22½c olive brown ('48) 80 70
294 " 25c ultramarine 22.50 12
295 " 30c deep orange 9.50 25
296 " 35c dark blue green 8.00 38
297 " 40c henna brown 32.50 38

Engraved.

298 A73 45c deep blue ('48) 32.50 19.00
299 " 50c brown ('48) 32.50 20
300 " 60c red ('48) 32.50 2.50
Nos. 286–300 (15) 181.44 24.56

Type of 1947.

1948 Photogravure

301 A72 6c gray blue 40 7

Queen Wilhelmina
A74

Queen Juliana
A75

Perf. 13x14

1948, Aug. 30 Engraved Unwmkd.

302 A74 10c vermilion 12 10
303 " 20c deep blue 2.50 2.50

Issued to commemorate the 50th anniversary of the reign of Queen Wilhelmina.

Perf. 14x13

1948, Sept. 7 Photo. Wmk. 202

304 A75 10c dark brown 1.50 7
305 " 20c ultramarine 3.75 80

Investiture of Queen Juliana, Sept. 6, 1948.

Queen Juliana
A76 A77

1949 *Perf. 13½x12½*

306 A76 5c olive green 70 7
307 " 6c gray blue 28 7
308 " 10c deep orange 28 7
a. Bklt. pane of 6 30.00
309 " 12c orange red 70 1.10
310 " 15c olive brown 3.25 12
311 " 20c bright blue 3.25 12
312 " 25c orange brown 11.00 12
313 " 30c violet 5.25 12
314 " 35c gray 11.00 15
315 " 40c red violet 21.00 20
316 " 45c red orange 1.25 90
317 " 50c blue green 7.00 18
318 " 60c red brown 10.00 18
Nos. 306–318 (13) 74.96 3.40

See also No. 325-327.

Engraved.

1949 *Perf. 12½x12* Unwmkd.

319 A77 1g rose red 5.25 15
320 " 2½g black brown 200.00 2.00
321 " 5g org. brown 475.00 5.25
322 " 10g dk. vio. brn. 400.00 25.00

Two types exist of No. 321.

Post Horns Entwined
A78

Janus Dousa
A79

Perf. 11½x12½

1949, Oct. 1 Photo. Wmk. 202

323 A78 10c brown red 12 12
324 " 20c dull blue 7.25 3.25

Issued to commemorate the 75th anniversary of the formation of the Universal Postal Union.

Juliana Type of 1949

1950–51 *Perf. 13½x12½.*

325 A76 12c scarlet ('51) 8.00 40
326 " 45c violet brown 40.00 30
327 " 75c car. rose ('51) 65.00 1.10

1950, Oct. 3 *Perf 11½x13*

328 A79 10c olive brown 5.75 10
329 " 20c deep blue (*Jan van Hout*) 5.75 2.00

Issued to commemorate the 375th anniversary of the founding of the University of Leyden.

No. 288 Surcharged with New Value.

1950 *Perf. 13½x12½*

330 A72 6(c) on 7½c deep red brown 2.65 12

Miner
A80

Perf. 12x12½

1952, Apr. 16 Engr. Unwmkd.

331 A80 10c dark blue 3.00 10

Issued to commemorate the 50th anniversary of the founding of Netherlands' mining and chemical industry.

Telegraph Poles and Train of 1852
A81

Designs: 6c, Radio towers. 10c, Mail Delivery 1852. 20c, Modern postman.

1952, June 28 *Perf. 13x14*

332 A81 2c gray violet 55 12
333 " 6c vermilion 65 12
334 " 10c green 85 12
335 " 20c gray blue 11.00 3.00

Issued to commemorate the centenary of Dutch postage stamps and of the telegraph service.

1952, June 28

336 A81 2c chocolate 32.50 25.00
337 " 6c dark bluish grn. 32.50 25.00
338 " 10c brown carmine 32.50 25.00
339 " 20c violet blue 32.50 25.00

Nos. 336 to 339 sold for 1.38g, which included the price of admission to the International Postage Stamp Centenary Exhibition, Utrecht.

Numeral Type of 1946–47.

Photogravure.

1953–57 *Perf. 12½x13½* Wmk. 202

340 A71 3c dp. orange brown 12 7
341 " 5c orange 7 7
342 " 6c gray ('54) 35 12
343 " 7c red orange 20 7
343A " 8c bright lilac ('57) 20 7
Nos. 340-343A (5) 94 40

The 5c and 7c perf. on 3 sides, and with watermark vertical, are from booklet panes Nos. 346a–346b. The 5c perf. on 3 sides, with wmk. horiz., is from No. 349a.

In 1972 the 5c was printed on phosphorescent paper.

Queen Juliana
A82 A83

Perf. 13½x12½

1953–71 Wmk. 202

344 A82 10c dark red brown 12 4
a. Bklt. pane of 6 (1 # 344+5 # 346C) ('65) 8.50
345 A82 12c dark Prussian green ('54) 12 4
a. Blkt. pane of 7+label (5 No. 345+2 No. 347) ('67) 7.00
b. Bklt. pane of 12 (4 # 282+8 # 345) ('69) 16.00
346 A82 15c deep carmine 15 4
a. Bklt. pane of 8 (2 No. 341 in vert. pair+6 No. 346) ('64) 16.50
b. Bklt. pane of 12 (10 No. 343+2 No. 346) ('64) 16.00
e. Bklt. pane of 8 (2 # 341 in horiz. pair+6 # 346) ('70) 12.50
346C A82 18c dull blue ('65) 40 4
d. Bklt. pane of 10 (8 No. 343A+2 No. 346C) ('65) 8.25
347 A82 20c dark gray 25 4
b. Bklt. pane of 5+label ('66) 15.00
347A A82 24c olive ('63) 60 15
348 " 25c deep blue 25 4
349 " 30c deep orange 1.00 4
a. Bklt. pane of 5+label (2 No. 341+3 No. 349) ('71) 25.00
350 A82 35c dark olive brown ('54) 1.85 4

351 A82 37c aqua. ('58) 1.50 15
352 " 40c dark slate 60 4
353 " 45c scarlet 75 4
354 " 50c dark olive green 65 4
355 " 60c brown bistre 75 4
356 " 62c dull red lilac ('58) 12.50 6.00
357 " 70c blue ('57) 1.00 4
358 " 75c deep plum 1.00 4
359 " 80c brt. violet ('58) 1.25 10
360 " 85c brt. bl. grn. ('56) 2.00 10
360A " 95c org. brown ('67) 5.00 30
Nos. 344-360A (20) 31.75 7.36

Coils of the 12, 15, 20, 25, 30, 40, 45, 50, 60, 70, 75 and 80c were issued in 1972. Black control number on back of every fifth stamp.

Watermark is vertical on some stamps from booklet panes.

Some booklet panes—Nos. 344a, 347b, 349a, etc.—have a large selvage the size of four or six stamps, with printed inscription and sometimes illustration.

Phosphorescent paper was introduced in 1967 for the 12, 15, 20 and 45c; in 1969 for the 25c, and in 1971 for the 30, 40, 50, 60, 70, 75 and 80c.

Of the booklet panes, Nos. 345a, 345b, 346d, 346e and 347b were issued on both ordinary and phosphorescent paper, and No. 349a only on phosphorescent paper.

See also No. 407.

Engraved.

1954-57 ***Perf. 12½x12*** **Unwmkd.**

361 A83 1g vermilion 15.00 7
362 " 2½g dk. green ('55) 45.00 10
363 " 5g black ('55) 8.00 30
364 " 10g vio. blue ('57) 62.50 1.25

St. Boniface
A84

Flaming Sword
A85

1954, June 16

365 A84 10c blue 3.00 10

Issued to commemorate the 1200th anniversary of the death of St. Boniface.

Charter of the Kingdom Issue

Type of Netherlands Antilles, 1954, with "Nederland" above portrait.

Perf. 13½

1954, Dec. 15 Photo. **Wmk. 202**

366 A48 10c scarlet 65 10

Issued to publicize the Charter of the Kingdom, adopted December 15, 1954.

1955, May 4 ***Perf. 12½x12***

367 A85 10c crimson 1.00 10

Issued to commemorate the 10th anniversary of Netherlands' liberation.

"Rebuilding Europe"
A86

Admiral M. A. de Ruyter
A87

Europa Issue.

Perf. 13x14

1956, Sept. 15 **Unwmkd.**

368 A86 10c rose brown & blk. 1.25 10
369 " 25c brt. bl. & black 45.00 3.25

Issued to symbolize the cooperation among the six countries comprising the Coal and Steel Community.

1957, July 2 Engr. ***Perf. 12½x12***

Design: 30c, Flagship "De Zeven Provincien."

370 A87 10c orange 55 10
371 " 30c dark blue 4.75 2.65

Issued to commemorate the 350th anniversary of the birth of Adm. M. A. de Ruyter (1607–1676).

"United Europe"
A88

Photogravure

1957, Sept. 16 ***Perf. 13x14***

372 A88 10c black, gray & ultramarine 25 10
373 " 30c dull grn. & ultra. 3.75 2.50

United Europe for peace and prosperity.

No. 344 Surcharged in Silver with New Value and Bars.

Perf. 13½x12½

1958, May 16 Photo. Wmk. 202

374 A82 12c on 10c dark red brown 1.85 12
a. Double surch. 600.00 600.00
b. Inverted surch. 600.00 600.00

Europa Issue, 1958

Common Design Type

Perf. 13x14

1958, Sept. 13 Litho. Unwmkd.

Size: 22x33mm.

375 CD1 12c orange vermilion & blue 25 10
376 " 30c blue & red 1.50 1.25

NATO Emblem
A89

1959, Apr. 3 ***Perf. 12½x12***

377 A89 12c yel. org. & blue 12 10
378 " 30c red & blue 1.10 1.00

Issued to commemorate the 10th anniversary of the North Atlantic Treaty Organization.

Europa Issue, 1959.

Common Design Type

1959, Sept. 19 ***Perf. 13x14***

Size : 22 x 33 mm.

379 CD2 12c crimson 55 10
380 " 30c yellow green 3.25 2.75

Douglas DC-8 and World Map
A90

J. C. Schroeder van der Kolk
A91

Design: 30c, Douglas DC-8 in flight.

1959, Oct. 5 Engr. ***Perf. 14x13***

381 A90 12c carmine & ultramarine 25 10
382 " 30c deep blue & deep green 2.00 1.65

Issued to commemorate the 40th anniversary of the founding of KLM, Royal Dutch Airlines.

Perf. 12½x12

1960, July 18 **Unwmkd.**

Design: 30c, Johannes Wier.

383 A91 12c red 12 10
384 " 30c dark blue 4.00 3.25

Issued to publicize Mental Health Year and to honor Schroeder van der Kolk and Johannes Wier, pioneers of mental health.

Europa Issue, 1960

Common Design Type

1960, Sept. 19 Photo. ***Perf. 12x12½***

Size: 27x21mm.

385 CD3 12c carmine rose & orange 25 10
386 " 30c dk. blue & yel. 3.50 3.25

First anniversary of C.E.P.T. (Conference of European Postal and Telecommunications Administrations). Spokes symbolize 19 founding members of Conference.

Europa Issue, 1961

Common Design Type

1961, Sept. 18 ***Perf. 14x13***

Size: 32½x21½mm.

387 CD4 12c golden brown 10 10
388 " 30c Prussian blue 30 35

Queen Juliana and Prince Bernhard
A92

Telephone Dial
A93

Photogravure

1962, Jan. 7 ***Perf. 14x13*** **Unwmkd.**

389 A92 12c dark red 25 10
390 " 30c dark green 1.65 1.35

Issued to commemorate the silver wedding anniversary of Queen Juliana and Prince Bernhard.

1962, May 22 ***Perf. 13x14, 14x13***

Designs: 12c, Map showing telephone network. 30c, Arch and dial (horiz.).

391 A93 4c brown red & blk. 20 10
392 " 12c brn. olive & blk. 35 10
393 " 30c black, bistre & Prussian blue 2.25 2.25

Issued to commemorate the completion of the automation of the Netherlands telephone network.

Europa Issue, 1962

Common Design Type

1962, Sept. 17 ***Perf. 14x13***

Size: 33x22mm.

394 CD5 12c lemon, yel. & black 12 10
395 " 30c blue, yel. & blk. 1.25 1.10

Polder with Canals and Windmills
A94

Design: 4c, Cooling towers, Limburg State Coal Mines. 10c, Dredging in Delta.

Photogravure

1962–66 ***Perf. 12½x13½*** **Wmk. 202**

399 A94 4c dark blue ('63) 20 8
401 " 6c grn. & dk. green 75 12
403 A94 10c deep claret ('63) 12 8
a. Bklt. pane of 10 ('66) 11.50

The 10c was issued in coils in 1972. Every fifth stamp has black control number on back.

See also No. 461b.

Types of 1946 and 1953

1962–73 **Unwmkd.**

Phosphorescent Paper

404 A71 4c olive green 25 12
405 " 5c orange ('73) 7 5
406 " 8c bright lilac 9.00 8.00
407 A82 12c dk. Prussian grn. 25 12

See Nos. 460d, 461c, 461d and 463a.

Wheat Emblem and Globe
A95

Inscription in Circle
A96

1963, Mar. 21 Photo. ***Perf. 14x13***

413 A95 12c dull blue, dark blue & yellow 12 10
414 " 30c dull car., rose & yellow 1.85 1.65

Issued for the "Freedom from Hunger" campaign of the U.N. Food and Agriculture Organization.

Lithographed

1963, May 7 ***Perf. 13x14*** **Unwmkd.**

415 A96 30c brt. bl., blk. & green 2.00 1.85

Issued to commemorate the centenary of the first International Postal Conference, Paris, 1963.

Europa Issue, 1963

Common Design Type

1963, Sept. 16 Photo. ***Perf. 14x13***

Size: 33x22mm.

416 CD6 12c red brn. & yel. 12 10
417 " 30c Prussian green & yellow 2.00 1.90

Prince William of Orange Landing at Scheveningen
A97

Designs: 12c, G. K. van Hogendorp, A. F. J. A. Graaf van der Duyn van Maasdam and L. Graaf van Limburg Stirum, Dutch leaders, 1813. 30c, Prince William taking oath of allegiance.

1963 **Photo.** ***Perf. 12x12½***

Size: 27½x27½mm.

418 A97 4c dull bl., blk. & brn. 7 10
419 " 5c dk. grn., blk. & red 14 10
420 " 12c olive & black 10 10
421 " 30c maroon & black 65 60

Issued to commemorate the 150th anniversary of the founding of the Kingdom of the Netherlands.

Knights' Hall, The Hague
A98

Arms of Groningen University
A99

1964, Jan. 9 *Perf. 14x13*
422 A98 12c olive & black 15 10

Issued to commemorate the 500th anniversary of the meeting of the States-General (Parliament).

1964, June 16 Engr. *Perf. 12½x12*

Design: 30c, Initials "AG" and crown.

423 A99 12c slate 12 10
424 " 30c yellow brown 25 25

Issued to commemorate the 350th anniversary of the University of Groningen.

Railroad Light Signal
A100

Design: 40c, Electric locomotive.

1964, July 28 Photo. *Perf. 14x13*
425 A100 15c blk. & brt. green 28 10
426 " 40c black & yellow 1.10 1.10

Issued to commemorate the 125th anniversary of the Netherlands railroads.

Bible, Chrismon and Dove
A101

1964, Aug. 25 **Unwmkd.**
427 A101 15c brown red 18 10

Issued to commemorate the 150th anniversary of the founding of the Netherlands Bible Society.

Europa Issue, 1964
Common Design Type
1964, Sept. 14 Photo. *Perf. 13x14*
Size: 22x33mm.

428 CD7 15c dp. olive green 15 10
429 " 20c yellow brown 45 40

Benelux Issue

King Baudouin, Queen Juliana and Grand Duchess Charlotte
A101a

1964, Oct. 12 *Perf. 14x13*
Size: 33x22mm.

430 A101a 15c purple & buff 15 10

Issued to commemorate the 20th anniversary of the signing of the customs union of Belgium, Netherlands and Luxembourg.

Queen Juliana
A102

"Killed in Action" and "Destroyed Town"
A103

1964, Dec. 15 Photo. *Perf. 13x14*
431 A102 15c green 15 8

Issued to commemorate the 10th anniversary of the Charter of the Kingdom of the Netherlands.

1965, Apr. 6 Photo. *Perf. 12x12½*

Statues: 15c, "Docker" Amsterdam, and "Killed in Action" Waalwijk. 40c, "Destroyed Town" Rotterdam, and "Docker" Amsterdam.

432 A103 7c blk. & dk. red 10 10
433 " 15c blk. & dk. olive 16 10
434 " 40c blk. & dk. red 1.10 1.10

Resistance movement of World War II.

Knight Class IV, Order of William
A104

ITU Emblem
A105

1965, Apr. 29 *Perf. 13x14*
435 A104 1g gray 95 80

Issued to commemorate the 150th anniversary of the establishment of the Military Order of William.

1965, May 17 Litho. *Perf. 14x13*
436 A105 20c dull bl. & tan 32 25
437 " 40c tan & dull bl. 65 50

Issued to commemorate the centenary of the International Telecommunication Union.

Europa Issue, 1965
Common Design Type
Perf. 14x13
1965, Sept. 27 Photo. **Unwmkd.**
Size: 33x22mm.

438 CD8 18c org. brown, dk. red & black 22 10
439 " 20c sapphire, brown & black 30 35

Marines of 1665 and 1965
A106

1965, Dec. 10 Engraved *Perf. 13x14*
440 A106 18c dk. violet blue & carmine 12 10

Issued to commemorate the 300th anniversary of the Netherlands Marine Corps.

Europa Issue, 1966
Common Design Type
Photogravure
1966, Sept. 26 *Perf. 13x14*
Size: 22x33mm.

441 CD9 20c citron 20 10
442 " 40c dull blue 40 30

Assembly Hall, Delft University
A107

1967, Jan. 5 Litho. *Perf. 14x13*
443 A107 20c lemon & sepia 22 10

Issued to commemorate the 125th anniversary of the founding of the Delft University of Technology.

Europa Issue, 1967
Common Design Type
Photogravure
1967, May 2 *Perf. 13x14* **Unwmkd.**
Ordinary Paper
Size: 22x32½mm.

444 CD10 20c dull blue 40 10
445 " 45c dull vio. brown 70 65

Wmk. 202

446 CD10 20c dull blue 80 30
447 " 45c dull vio. brown 1.10 1.10

Nos. 446–447 are on phosphorescent paper.

Stamp of 1852, No. 1
A108

Designs: 25c, Stamp of 1864, No. 5. 75c, Stamp of 1867, No. 10.

1967, May 8 Engraved **Unwmkd.**
448 A108 20c blk. & steel bl. 5.00 4.50
449 " 25c black & dull red brown 5.00 4.50
450 " 75c black & green 5.00 4.50

Issued to publicize AMPHILEX 67, Amsterdam, May 11–21. Sold only in complete sets together with a 2.50g admission ticket to Amsterdam Philatelic Exhibition. Issued in sheets of 10 (5x2).

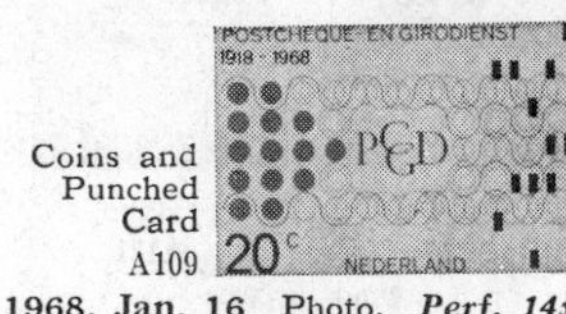

Coins and Punched Card
A109

1968, Jan. 16 Photo. *Perf. 14x13*
451 A109 20c vermilion, black & dull yellow 32 10

Issued to commemorate the 50th anniversary of the postal checking service.

Luminescence

All commemorative issues from No. 451 to No. 511 are printed on phosphorescent paper except No. 478 which is printed with phosphorescent ink, and Nos. 490–492. Some later issues are tagged.

Europa Issue, 1968
Common Design Type
1968, Apr. 29 Photo. *Perf. 14x13*
Size: 32½x22mm.

452 CD11 20c deep blue 40 10
453 " 45c crimson 1.35 1.35

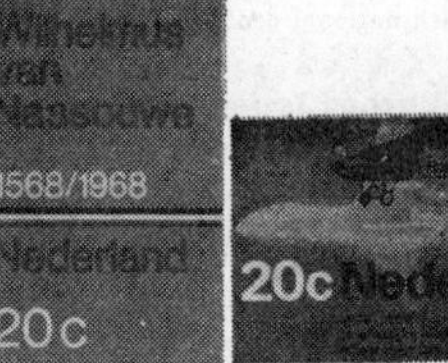

National Anthem
A110

Fokker F.2, 1919, and Friendship F.29
A111

1968, Aug. 27 Litho. *Perf. 13x14*
454 A110 20c gray, org., car. & dark blue 55 10

Issued to commemorate the 400th anniversary of the national anthem "Wilhelmus van Nassouwe."

1968, Oct. 1 *Perf. 14x13*

Planes: 12c, Wright A, 1909, and Cessna sports plane. 45c, De Haviland DH-9, 1919, and Douglas DC-9.

455 A111 12c crimson, pink & black 28 15
456 " 20c brt. green, blue green & black 28 10
457 " 45c brt. blue, light grn. & black 1.90 1.90

Issued to commemorate the 50th anniversaries of the founding in 1919 of Royal Dutch Airlines and the Royal Netherlands Aircraft Factories Fokker, and the 60th anniversary in 1967 of the Royal Netherlands Aeronautical Association.

"iao"
A112

Design is made up of 28 minute lines, each reading "1919 internationale arbeidsorganisatie 1969".

1969, Feb. 25 Engraved *Perf. 14x13*
458 A112 25c brick red & black 80 10
459 " 45c ultra. & blue 1.50 1.35

International Labor Organization, 50th anniversary.

Queen Juliana
A113 A114

Perf. 13½ horiz. x 12½ on one vert. side.

1969–75 Photogravure
460 A113 25c org. vermilion 4.00 12
a. Bklt. pane of 4+2 labels 50.00
460B A113 25c dull red ('73) 1.25 12
c. Booklet pane of 6 (#460B + 5 #461A) 40.00
d. Booklet pane of 12 (5 #405 + 7 #460B) 17.50

Perf. 13x12½

461 A113 30c chocolate ('72) 35 3
d. Bklt. pane of 10 (4 #405+6 #461+2 labels) ('74) 8.50
461A A113 35c greenish blue ('72) 38 3
b. Bklt. pane of 5 (3 #403, 2 #461A + label) ('72) 16.50
c. Bklt. pane of 10 (5 #405+5 #461A+2 labels) ('75) 2.50
462 A113 40c car. rose ('72) 42 3
a. Bklt. pane of 5 + label ('73) 5.50
463 A113 45c ultra. ('72) 45 3
a. Bktl. pane of 8 (4 #405+4 #463) ('74) 2.50
464 A113 50c lilac ('72) 50 3
a. Bklt. pane of 4+2 labels ('75) 2.25
465 A113 60c slate blue ('72) 55 8
466 " 70c bister ('72) 70 8
467 " 75c green ('72) 75 8
468 " 80c red orange ('72) 80 8
468A " 90c gray ('75) 90 8

Perf. 13x14

469 A114 1g yellow green 1.00 5
470 " 1.25g maroon 1.25 5
471 " 1.50g yel. bis. ('71) 1.50 8
471A " 2g deep rose lilac ('72) 2.00 15
472 " 2.50g greenish blue 2.50 8

473 A114 5g gray ('70) 5.00 50
474 " 10g vio. blue ('70) 10.00 4.00
Nos. 460-474 (19) 34.30 5.70

Both 25c stamps issued only in booklets. No. 464 is on phosphorescent paper. No. 460 was printed on both ordinary and phosphorescent paper. Nos. 461c, 461d, 463a and 464a are on ordinary paper.

Coil printings were issued later for Nos. 461, 462-471. Black control number on back of every fifth stamp.

Booklet panes have a large selvage the size of four or six stamps, with printed inscription.

See No. 546.

Europa Issue, 1969
Common Design Type

1969, Apr. 28 Photo. ***Perf. 14x13***
Size: 33½x22mm.

475 CD12 25c dark blue 1.35 10
476 " 45c red 3.00 2.40

Möbius Strip in Benelux Colors
A114a

1969, Sept. 8 Photo. ***Perf. 13x14***

477 A114a 25c multicolored 55 10

Issued to commemorate the 25th anniversary of the signing of the customs union of Belgium, Netherlands and Luxembourg.

Desiderius Erasmus
A115

Photogravure and Engraved

1969, Sept. 30 ***Perf. 13x14***

478 A115 25c yellow green & maroon 55 10

Issued to commemorate the 500th anniversary of the birth of Desiderius Erasmus (1469-1536), scholar.

Queen Juliana and Rising Sun
A116

1969, Dec. 15 Photo. ***Perf. 14x13***

479 A116 25c blue & multi. 55 10

Issued to commemorate the 15th anniversary of the Charter of the Kingdom of the Netherlands.

Prof. E. M. Meijers
A117

1970, Jan. 13 Photo. ***Perf. 14x13***

480 A117 25c blue, violet blue & green 55 10

Issued to publicize the new Civil Code and to honor Prof. Meijers, who prepared it.

Dutch Pavilion, EXPO '70
A118

1970, Mar. 16 Photo. ***Perf. 14x13***

481 A118 25c multicolored 55 10

Issued to publicize EXPO '70 International Exposition, Osaka, Japan, Mar. 15-Sept. 13.

"V" for Victory
A119

1970, Apr. 21 Photo. ***Perf. 13x14***

482 A119 12c red, ultra., brown olive & lt. blue 35 10

Issued to commemorate the 25th anniversary of the liberation from the Germans.

Europa Issue, 1970
Common Design Type

1970, May 4 Photo. ***Perf. 14x13***
Size: 32½x21½mm.

483 CD13 25c carmine 50 10
484 " 45c dark blue 2.50 1.35

Panels
A120

Globe
A121

Perf. 13x14

1970, June 23 Photogravure

485 A120 25c gray, black & brt. yel. green 75 10
486 A121 45c ultra., black & purple 1.60 1.35

No. 485 publicizes the meeting of the Interparliamentary Union; No. 486 commemorates the 25th anniversary of the United Nations.

Punch Cards
A122

1971, Feb. 16 Photo. ***Perf. 14x13***

487 A122 15c deep rose lilac 28 10

14th national census, 1971.

Europa Issue, 1971
Common Design Type

1971, May 3 Photo. ***Perf. 14x13***
Size: 33x22mm.

488 CD14 25c lilac rose, yellow & black 42 10
489 " 45c ultra., yellow & black 2.35 1.50

No. 488 was issued in coils and sheets. In the coils every fifth stamp has a black control number on the back.

Prince Bernhard, Fokker F27, Boeing 747 B
A123

Designs: 15c, Stylized carnation (Prince Bernhard Fund). 20c, Giant Panda (World Wildlife Fund).

1971, June 29 Photo. ***Perf. 13x14***

490 A123 15c black & yellow 25 12
491 " 20c multicolored 42 25
492 " 25c " 65 12

60th birthday of Prince Bernhard. See No. B475.

Map of Delta
A124

1972, Feb. 15 Photo. ***Perf. 14x13***

493 A124 20c blue, green, black & red 42 10

Publicity for the Delta plan, a project to shorten the coastline and to build roads.

Europa Issue 1972
Common Design Type

1972, May 2 Photo. ***Perf. 13x14***
Size: 22x33mm.

494 CD15 30c blue & bister 1.00 10
495 " 45c orange & bister 2.00 1.65

No. 494 was issued in coils and sheets. In the coils every fifth stamp has a black control number on the back.

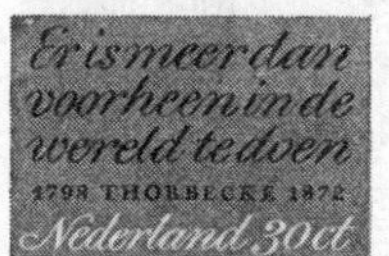

Thorbecke Quotation
A126

1972, May 30 Photo. ***Perf. 14x13***

496 A126 30c lt. ultra. & blk. 60 10

Centenary of the death of Jan Rudolf Thorbecke (1798-1872), statesman, who said: "There is more to be done in the world than ever before."

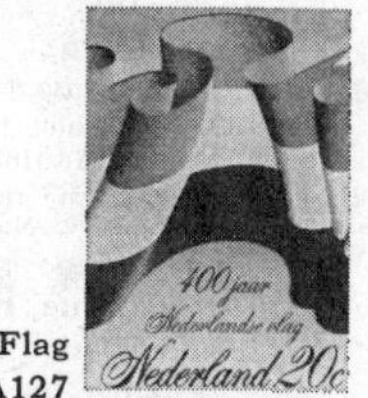

Dutch Flag
A127

1972 ***Perf. 13x14***

497 A127 20c blue & multi. 1.00 15
498 " 25c " " 1.00 12

400th anniversary of the Dutch flag. Issue dates: 20c, July 4; 25c, Nov. 1.

Woman Hurdler
A128

Designs: 30c, Woman swimmer. 45c, Bicycling.

1972, July 11 ***Perf. 14x13***

499 A128 20c multicolored 25 15
500 " 30c crimson & multi. 42 10
501 " 45c violet & multi. 1.25 1.25

20th Olympic Games, Munich, Aug. 26-Sept. 11.

Red Cross
A129

1972, Aug. 15 Photo. ***Perf. 13x14***

502 A129 5c red 10 10
Nos. 502, B485-B488 (5) 4.50 3.95

Netherlands Red Cross.

Tulips
A130

1973, Mar. 20 Photo. ***Perf. 14x13***

503 A130 25c rose, bright green & black 45 10

Dutch flower and bulb exports.

Europa Issue 1973
Common Design Type

1973, May 1 Photo. ***Perf. 14x13***
Size: 32½x22mm.

504 CD16 35c bright blue 70 12
505 " 50c purple 1.50 1.25

Hockey
A132

Woman Gymnast
A133

Antenna, Burum
A134

Rainbow, Measures
A135

Photo. (25c, 35c); Litho. (30c, 50c)
Perf. 13x14, 14x13

1973, July 31

506 A132 25c black & green 55 12
507 A133 30c gray & multi. 70 55
508 A134 35c blue & multi. 70 12
509 A135 50c " " 1.15 1.00

Netherlands Hockey Association, 75th anniversary (25c); Rythmical Gymnastics World Championship, Rotterdam (30c); inauguration of satellite ground station at Burum (35c); centenary of international meteorological cooperation (50c).

Queen Juliana, Dutch and House of Orange Colors
A136

Engraved & Lithographed

1973, Sept. 4 ***Perf. 13x12***

510 A136 40c silver & multi. 70 15

25th anniversary of reign of Queen Juliana.

Chain with Open Link
A137

Perf. 13x14

1973, Oct. 16 Photogravure

511 A137 40c green, black, gold & silver 1.00 10

Development Corporation.

Nature and Environment—A138

1974, Feb. 19 Photo. ***Perf. 13x14***

Multicolored

512 A138 Strip of 3 4.50 3.00
- *a.* 25c *Bird of prey* 1.10 25
- *b.* 25c *Tree* 1.10 25
- *c.* 25c *Fisherman in boat and frog* 1.10 25

75th anniversary of the Netherlands Association for the Protection of Birds and of the State Forestry Service. No. 512 printed se-tenant in sheets of 90.

Soccer Ball
A139

Tennis Ball
A140

Perf. 14x13, 13x14

1974, June 5 Photogravure

513 A139 25c multicolored 50 10
514 A140 40c " 65 10

World Cup Soccer Championship, Munich, June 13–July 7 (25c) and 75th anniversary of the Royal Dutch Lawn Tennis Association (40c).

Cattle
A141

Pierced Crab under Lens
A142

Shipwreck Seen Through Binoculars
A143

1974, July 30 ***Perf. 13x14***

515 A141 25c multicolored 10.00 1.00
516 A142 25c salmon pink & multi. 25 25
517 A143 40c dk. vio. & multi. 40 10

Centenary of the Netherlands Cattle Herdbook Society (No. 515); 25th anniversary of Queen Wilhelmina Fund (for cancer research) (No. 516); sesquicentennial of Royal Dutch Lifeboat Society (No. 517).

BENELUX Issue

"BENELUX"—A143a

1974, Sept. 10 Photo. ***Perf. 14x13***

518 A143a 30c bl. grn., dk. grn. & light blue 55 12

30th anniversary of the signing of the customs union of Belgium, Netherlands and Luxembourg.

Council of Europe Emblem
A144

NATO Emblem and Sea Gull
A145

1974, Sept. 10 ***Perf. 13x14***

519 A144 45c blk., bl. & yel. 60 12
520 A145 45c dk. bl. & silver 60 12

25th anniversaries of Council of Europe (No. 519) and of North Atlantic Treaty Organization (No. 520).

Letters and Hands, Papier-maché Sculpture
A146

521 A146 60c pur. & multi. 1.00 70

Centenary of Universal Postal Union.

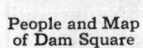

People and Map of Dam Square
A147

Brain with Window Symbolizing Free Thought
A148

Design: No. 523, Portuguese Synagogue and map of Mr. Visser Square. 35c, No. 526, like No. 522.

1975 Photogravure ***Perf. 13x14***

522 A147 30c multicolored 55 12
523 " 30c " 55 22
524 " 35c " 50 10
525 A148 45c dp. bl. & multi. 55 12

Coil Stamps

Perf. 13 Horiz.

526 A147 30c multicolored 55 30
527 " 35c " 65 25

700th anniversary of Amsterdam (No. 522); 300th anniversary of the Portuguese Synagogue in Amsterdam (No. 523) and 400th anniversary of the founding of the University of Leyden and the beginning of higher education in the Netherlands (No. 525).

Issue dates: Nos. 522–523, 525–526, Feb. 26; Nos. 524, 527, Apr. 1.

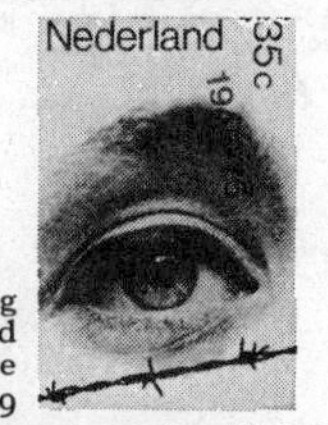

Eye Looking over Barbed Wire
A149

1975, Apr. 29 Photo. ***Perf. 12½x13½***

528 A149 35c blk. & carmine 50 12

Liberation of the Netherlands from Nazi occupation, 30th anniversary.

Company Emblem and "Stad Middelburg"
A150

1975, May 21 Photo. ***Perf. 14x13***

529 A150 35c multicolored 55 12

Zeeland Steamship Company, centenary.

Albert Schweitzer in Boat
A151

1975, May 21

530 A151 50c multicolored 70 12

Albert Schweitzer (1875–1965), medical missionary.

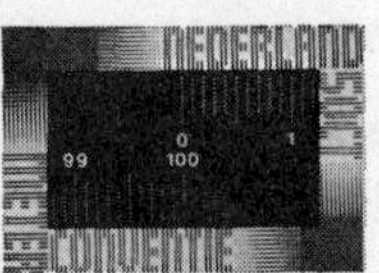

Symbolic Metric Scale
A152

1975, July 29 Litho. ***Perf. 14x13***

531 A152 50c multicolored 70 12

Centenary of International Meter Convention, Paris, 1875.

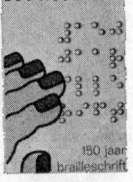

Playing Card with Woman, Man, Pigeons, Pens
A153

Fingers Reading Braille
A154

1975, July 29 ***Perf. 13x14***

532 A153 35c multicolored 55 12

International Women's Year 1975.

1975, Oct. 7 Photo. ***Perf. 13x14***

533 A154 35c multicolored 55 12

Sesquicentennial of the invention of Braille system of writing for the blind by Louis Braille (1809–1852).

Rubbings of 25¢ Coins
A155

1975, Oct. 7 ***Perf. 14x13***

534 A155 50c grn., blk. & blue 70 12

To publicize the importance of saving.

Lottery Ticket, 18th Century
A156

1976, Feb. 3 Photo. ***Perf. 14x13***

535 A156 35c multicolored 45 12

250th anniversary of National Lottery.

Queen Type of 1969 and

Numeral
A157

1976 Photo. ***Perf. 12½x13½***

536 A157 5c gray 8 3
- *a.* Bklt. pane of 8 (3 #536, 2 #537, 3 #546) 2.00
- *b.* Bklt. pane of 10 (4 #536, 2 #537, 4 #543) 2.00
- *c.* Bklt. pane of 8 (#536, 2 #537, 5 #546) 3.00
- *d.* Bklt. pane of 11 (4 #536, 7 #543 + label) 3.00

537 A157 10c ultramarine 16 3
541 " 25c violet 25 3
543 " 40c sepia 40 3
544 " 45c bright blue 45 3
546 A113 55c carmine 55 4
Nos. 536-546 (6) 1.89 19

The 55c was issued in sheets and coils. Nos. 536c and 536d have inscribed selvages the size of 4 and 6 stamps respectively.

Coil Stamps

1976–79 ***Perf. 13½ Vert.***

548 A157 5c gray 8 3
549 " 10c ultramarine 10 3
550 " 25c violet 25 3
551 " 40c sepia ('77) 40 3
552 " 45c bright blue 45 3
553 " 50c bright rose ('79) 50 4
Nos. 548-553 (6) 1.78 19

Nos. 548–553 and the coil printings of No. 546 have black control number on back of every 5th stamp.

De Ruyter Statue, Flushing
A158

1976, Apr. 22 Photo. ***Perf. 14x13***

555 A158 55c multicolored 70 12

Adm. Michiel Adriaenszon de Ruyter (1607–1676), Dutch naval hero, 300th death anniversary.

Van Prinsterer and Page
A159

1976, May 19 Photo. ***Perf. 14x13***

556 A159 55c multicolored 70 12

Guillaume Groen van Prinsterer (1801–1876), statesman and historian.

Women Waving American Flags
A160

Design is from a 220-year old permanent wooden calendar from Ameland Island.

1976, May 25

557 A160 75c multicolored 1.00 55

American Bicentennial.

Marchers
A161

1976, June 15 Photo. ***Perf. 14x13***

558 A161 40c multicolored 45 16

Nijmegen 4-day march, 60th anniversary.

Runners
A162

1976, June 15 Tagged

559 A162 55c multicolored 75 12

Royal Dutch Athletic Society, 75th anniversary.

Printing: One Communicating with Many
A163

1976, Sept. 2 Photo. ***Perf. 13x14***

560 A163 45c blue & red 65 12

Netherlands Printers Organization, 75th anniversary.

Sailing Ship and City
A164

Design: 75c, Sea gull over coast.

1976, Sept. 2 Litho. ***Perf. 14x13***

Tagged

561 A164 40c bis., red & blue 55 12
562 " 75c ultramarine, yellow & red 90 42

Zuider Zee Project, the conversion of water areas into land.

Radiation of Heat and Light
A165

Ballot and Pencil
A166

Perf. 13x14, 14x13

1977, Jan. 25 Photogravure

563 A165 40c multicolored 45 12
564 A166 45c black, red & ocher 50 12

Coil Stamps

Perf. 13 Horiz.

565 A165 40c multicolored 45 12

Perf. 13 Vert.

566 A166 45c multicolored 50 12

Publicity for wise use of energy (40c) and forthcoming elections (45c). Nos. 565–566 have black control number on back of every 5th stamp.

Spinoza
A167

1977, Feb. 21 Photo. ***Perf. 13x14***

567 A167 75c multicolored 90 28

Baruch Spinoza (1632–1677), philosopher, 300th death anniversary.

Delft Bible Text, Old Type, Electronic "a"
A168

1977, Mar. 8 ***Perf. 14x13***

568 A168 55c ocher & black 65 12

Delft Bible (Old Testament), oldest book printed in Dutch, 500th anniversary. Printed in sheets of 50 se-tenant with label inscribed with description of stamp design and purpose.

No. 564 Overprinted in Blue

25 MEI'77

1977, Apr. 15 Photo. ***Perf. 14x13***

569 A166 45c multicolored 50 12

Elections of May 25.

Kaleidoscope of Activities
A169

1977, June 9 Litho. ***Perf. 13x14***

570 A169 55c multicolored 40 18

Netherlands Society for Industry and Commerce, bicentenary.

Man in Wheelchair Looking at Obstacles
A170

Engineer's Diagram of Water Currents
A171

Teeth, Dentist's Mirror
A172

1977, Sept. 6 Litho. ***Perf. 14x13***

571 A170 40c multicolored 45 15
572 A171 45c " 50 15

Perf. 13x14

573 A172 55c multicolored 65 15

50th anniversaries of AVO (Actio vincit omnia), an organization to help the handicapped (40c), and of Delft Hydraulic Laboratory (45c); centenary of Dentists' Training in the Netherlands (55c).

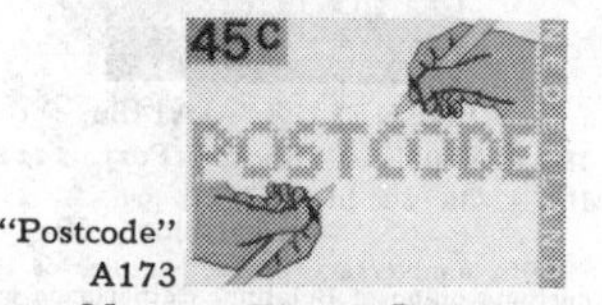

"Postcode"
A173

1978, Mar. 14 Photo. ***Perf. 14x13***

574 A173 40c dk. blue & red 45 10
575 " 45c red, dk. & lt. bl. 50 10

Introduction of new postal code.

European Human Rights Treaty
A174

Haarlem Town Hall
A175

1978, May 2 Photo. ***Perf. 13x14***

576 A174 45c gray, bl. & blk. 50 10

European Treaty of Human Rights, 25th anniversary.

Europa Issue

1978, May 2

577 A175 55c multicolored 65 15

Stamps not listed in this Catalogue or mentioned in "For the Record" (unless recent issues) usually are revenues, locals or labels.

Chess Board and Move Diagram
A176

Korfball
A177

1978, June 1 Photo. ***Perf. 13x14***

578 A176 40c multicolored 45 10
579 A177 45c red & vio. blue 50 10

18th IBM Chess Tournament, Amsterdam, July 12, and 75th anniversary of korfball in the Netherlands.

Man Pointing to his Kidney
A178

Heart, Torch, Gauge and Clouds
A179

1978, Aug. 22

580 A178 40c multicolored 45 10
581 A179 45c " 50 10

Importance of kidney transplants and drive against hypertension.

Epaulettes, Military Academy
A180

1978, Sept. 12 Litho. ***Perf. 13x14***

582 A180 55c multicolored 65 15

Royal Military Academy, sesquicentennial. Printed in continuous design in sheets of 100 (10x10).

Verkade as Hamlet
A181

1978, Oct. 17 Photo. ***Perf. 14x13***

583 A181 45c multicolored 50 15

Eduard Rutger Verkade (1878–1961), actor and producer.

Clasped Hands and Arrows
A182

1979, Jan. 23 Engr. ***Perf. 13x13½***

584 A182 55c blue 65 15

Union of Utrecht, 400th anniversary.

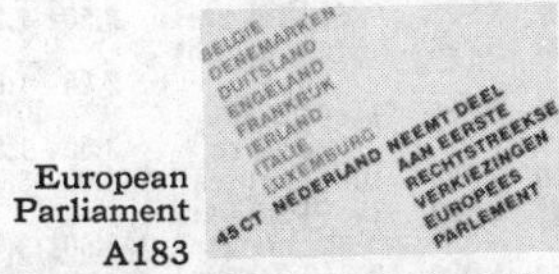

European Parliament A183

1979, Feb. 20 Litho. ***Perf. 13½x13***

585	A183	45c bl., blk. & red	50	10

European Parliament, first direct elections, June 7-10.

Queen Juliana A184

1979, Mar. 13 Photo. ***Perf. 13½***

586	A184	55c multicolored	65	15

70th birthday of Queen Juliana.

SEMI-POSTAL STAMPS.

Design Symbolical of the Four Chief Means for Combating Tuberculosis: Light, Water, Air and Food
SP1

Perf. 12½

1906, Dec. 21 Typo. Unwmkd.

B1 SP1 1c (+1c) rose red 4.25 4.25
B2 " 3c (+3c) pale olive green 47.50 37.50
B3 " 5c (+5c) gray 47.50 11.00

The surtax aided the Society for the Prevention of Tuberculosis.
Nos. B1-3, canceled-to-order "AMSTERDAM 31. JAN. 07 10-12N," sell at $1.35 a set.

Symbolical of Charity
SP2

SP3

1923, Dec. 16 ***Perf. 11½***

B4 SP2 2c (+5c) violet blue 32.50 35.00
B5 SP3 10c (+5c) orange red 35.00 35.00

The surtax was for the benefit of charity.

Allegory, Charity Protecting Child
SP6

1924, Dec. 15 Photo. ***Perf. 12½***

B6 SP6 2c (+2c) emerald 1.25 2.00
B7 " 7½c (+3½c) dark brn. 8.50 10.00
B8 " 10c (+2½c) vermilion 8.50 1.15

These stamps were sold at a premium over face value for the benefit of Child Welfare Societies.

Arms of North Brabant
SP7

Arms of Gelderland
SP8

Arms of South Holland
SP9

Perf. 12½ and Syncopated

1925, Dec. 17

B9 SP7 2c (+2c) green & orange 1.30 1.85
a. Perfs. type A 19.00 19.00
B10 SP8 7½c (+3½c) violet & blue 6.75 7.25
a. Perfs. type A 55.00 55.00
B11 SP9 10c (+2½c) red & orange 5.25 50
a. Perfs. type A 150.00 115.00

Surtax went to Child Welfare Societies. See note after No. 141.

Arms of Utrecht
SP10

Arms of Zeeland
SP11

Arms of North Holland
SP12

Arms of Friesland
SP13

Perf. 12½ and Syncopated.

1926, Dec. 1 Wmkd. Circles. (202)

B12 SP10 2c (+2c) silver & red 80 65
a. Perfs. type A 6.75 6.75
B13 SP11 5c (+3c) green & gray blue 2.50 1.40
a. Perfs. type A 15.00 13.00
B14 SP12 10c (+3c) red & gold 4.00 20
a. Perfs. type A 30.00 15.00
B15 SP13 15c (+3c) ultra. & yellow 11.50 11.00
a. Perfs. type A 37.50 35.00

The surtax on these stamps was devoted to Child Welfare Societies.

Red Cross Issue

King William III
SP14

Red Cross and Doves
SP18

Designs: 3c, Queen Emma. 5c, Prince Consort Henry. 7½c, Queen Wilhelmina.

Perf. 11½, 11½x12.

1927, June Unwmkd.

B16 SP14 2c(+2c) scarlet 2.65 2.65
a. Bklt. pane of 4 40.00

Engraved.

B17 SP14 3c(+2c) deep grn. 9.00 12.00
a. Bklt. pane of 4 40.00
B18 SP14 5c(+3c) slate blue 70 45
a. Bklt. pane of 4 40.00
b. Bklt. pane of 10 135.00

Photogravure.

B19 SP14 7½c(+3½c) ultra. 7.00 2.00
a. Bklt. pane of 4 40.00
b. Bklt. pane of 10 125.00
B20 SP18 15c(+5c) ultra. & red 17.50 17.00
a. Bklt. pane of 4 100.00
b. Bklt. pane of 10 250.00

Nos. B16-B20 (5) 36.85 34.10

Issued to commemorate the sixtieth anniversary of the Netherlands Red Cross Society. The surtaxes in parentheses were for the benefit of the Society.

Arms of Drenthe
SP19

Arms of Groningen
SP20

Arms of Limburg
SP21

Arms of Overijssel
SP22

Perf. 12½ and Syncopated.

1927, Dec. 15

Wmkd. Circles. (202)

B21 SP19 2c (+2c) deep rose & violet 50 50
a. Perfs. type A 4.00 2.50
B22 SP20 5c (+3c) olive grn. & yellow 2.10 2.00
a. Perfs. type A 8.00 3.75
B23 SP21 7½c (+3½c) red & black 5.25 25
a. Perfs. type A 9.50 3.75
B24 SP22 15c (+3c) ultra. & org. brown 9.50 9.00
a. Perfs. type A 22.50 16.00

The surtax on these stamps was for the benefit of Child Welfare Societies.

Olympic Games Issue.

Rowing
SP23

Fencing
SP24

Soccer
SP25

Yachting
SP26

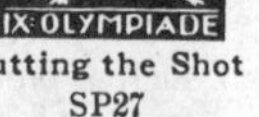

Putting the Shot
SP27

Running
SP28

Riding
SP29

Boxing
SP30

Perf. 11½, 12, 11½x12, 12x11½

1928, Mar. 27 Lithographed

B25 SP23 1½c(+1c) dark green 1.50 1.00
B26 SP24 2c(+1c) red violet 2.50 1.40
B27 SP25 3c(+1c) green 2.50 1.20
B28 SP26 5c(+1c) light blue 2.75 1.00
B29 SP27 7½c(+2½c) orange 3.50 1.50
B30 SP28 10c(+2c) scarlet 11.00 8.00
B31 SP29 15c(+2c) dark blue 8.50 3.75
B32 SP30 30c(+3c) dark brown 50.00 47.50

Nos. B25-B32 (8) 82.25 65.35

The surtax on these stamps was used to help defray the expenses of the Olympic Games of 1928.

Jean Pierre Minckelers
SP31

Child on Dolphin
SP35

Designs: 5c, Hermann Boerhaave. 7½c, Hendrik Antoon Lorentz. 12½c, Christian Huygens.

1928, Dec. 10 Photo. ***Perf. 12x12½***

B33 SP31 1½c(+1½c) violet 60 35
B34 " 5c(+3c) green 1.15 1.00
B35 " 7½c(+3½c) verm., perf. 12 3.50 35
a. Perf. 12x12½ 7.50 50
B36 " 12½c(+3½c) ultra., perf. 12 19.00 12.00
a. Perf. 12x12½ 125.00 15.00

The surtax on these stamps was for the benefit of Child Welfare Societies.

Perf. 12½ and Syncopated.

1929, Dec. 10 Lithographed

B37 SP35 1½c(+1½c) gray 2.50 50
a. Perfs. type B 3.75 1.25
B38 " 5c(+3c) blue green 5.00 1.25
a. Perfs. type B 8.50 1.25
B39 " 6c(+4c) scarlet 3.25 25
a. Perfs. type B 7.00 1.25
B40 " 12½c(+3½c) dark blue 27.50 19.00
a. Perfs. type B 32.50 21.00

Surtax for child welfare.

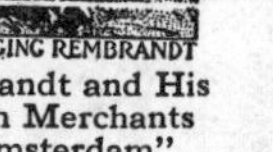

Rembrandt and His "Cloth Merchants of Amsterdam"
SP36

"Spring"
SP37

Perf. 11½

1930, Feb. 15 Engr. Unwmkd.

B41 SP36 5c(+5c) blue grn. 12.00 11.50
B42 " 6c(+5c) gray blk. 7.00 2.50
B43 " 12½c(+5c) deep blue 19.00 20.00

The surtax on these stamps was for the benefit of the Rembrandt Society.

Perf. 12½ and Syncopated

1930, Dec. 10

Designs: 5c, Summer. 6c, Autumn. 12½c, Winter.

B44 SP37 1½c(+1½c) light red 1.85 35
a. Perfs. type C 5.25 2.50
B45 " 5c(+3c) gray green 2.85 85
a. Perfs. type C 5.25 2.50
B46 " 6c(+4c) claret 3.25 25
a. Perfs. type C 5.25 2.50
B47 " 12½c(+3½c) light ultramarine 27.50 17.50
a. Perfs. type C 37.50 27.50

Surtax was for Child Welfare work.

Stained Glass Window and Detail of Repair Method
SP41

Deaf Mute Learning Lip Reading
SP43

Design: 6c, Gouda Church and repair of window frame.

Perf. 12½

1931, Oct. 1 Photo. Wmk. 202

B48	SP41	1½c(+1½c) blue green	25.00	25.00
B49	"	6c(+4c) carmine rose	50.00	47.50

Design: 6c, Gouda Church and repair of window frame.

Perf. 12½ and Syncopated.

1931, Dec. 10

Designs: 5c, Imbecile child. 6c, Blind girl learning to read Braille. 12½c, Child victim of malnutrition.

B50	SP43	1½c(+1½c) verm. & ultramarine	2.00	50
		a. Perfs. type C	3.75	3.00
B51	"	5c(+3c) Prussian blue & vio.	3.25	1.75
		a. Perfs. type C	10.00	3.00
B52	"	6c(+4c) violet & green	2.75	25
		a. Perfs. type C	10.00	3.00
B53	"	12½c(+3½c) ultra. & dp. org.	42.50	35.00
		a. Perfs. type C	55.00	40.00

The surtax was for Child Welfare work.

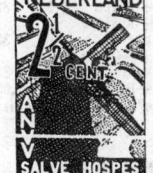

Windmill and Dikes
SP47

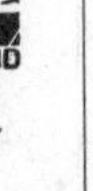

Furze and Boy
SP51

Designs: 6c, Council House, Zierikzee. 7½c, Drawbridge. 12½c, Flower fields.

1932, May 23 *Perf. 12½*

B54	SP47	2½c(+1½c) turq. green & black	8.00	3.75
B55	"	6c(+4c) gray black & black	14.00	3.75
B56	"	7½c(+3½c) bright red & black	70.00	47.50
B57	"	12½c(+2½c) ultra. & black	75.00	47.50

The surtax was for the benefit of the National Tourist Association.

Perf. 12½ and Syncopated.

1932, Dec. 10

Designs (Heads of children and flowers typifying the seasons): 5c, Cornflower. 6c, Sunflower. 12½c, Christmas rose.

B58	SP51	1½c(+1½c) brown & yellow	3.25	50
		a. Perfs. type C	5.25	2.50
B59	"	5c(+3c) red orange & ultramarine	3.25	1.25
		a. Perfs. type C	6.75	2.50
B60	"	6c(+4c) dark green & ochre	3.25	25
		a. Perfs. type C	6.75	2.50
B61	"	12½c(+3½c) ochre & ultra.	50.00	37.50
		a. Perfs. type C	62.50	42.50

The surtax aided Child Welfare Societies.

Monument at Den Helder
SP55

The "Hope," A Church and Hospital Ship
SP56

Lifeboat in a Storm
SP57

Dutch Sailor and Sailors' Home
SP58

1933, June 10 *Perf. 14x13½*

B62	SP55	1½c(+1½c) deep red	5.00	1.50
B63	SP56	5c(+3c) bl. green & red orange	25.00	3.50
B64	SP57	6c(+4c) deep green	30.00	2.75
B65	SP58	12½c(+3½c) ultramarine	37.50	35.00

The surtax was for the aid of Sailors' Homes.

Child Carrying the Star of Hope, Symbolical of Christmas Cheer
SP59

Perf. 12½ and Syncopated

1933, Dec. 10

B66	SP59	1½c(+1½c) slate & orange brown	2.00	50
		a. Perfs. type C	3.75	1.40
B67	"	5c(+3c) dark brn. & ochre	2.75	75
		a. Perfs. type C	5.25	1.65
B68	"	6c(+4c) blue green & gold	3.25	25
		a. Perfs. type C	6.50	1.65
B69	"	12½c(+3½c) dark bl. & silver	45.00	30.00
		a. Perfs. type C	55.00	35.0

The surtax aided Child Welfare Societies.

Queen Wilhelmina
SP60

Princess Juliana
SP61

Perf. 12½

1934, Apr. 30 Engr. Unwmkd.

B70	SP60	5c(+4c) dk. violet	19.00	3.50
B71	SP61	6c(+5c) blue	21.00	6.50

The surtax was for the benefit of the Anti-Depression Committee.

Dowager Queen Emma
SP62

Poor Child
SP63

1934, Oct. 1 *Perf. 13x13½*

B72	SP62	6c(+2c) blue	21.00	1.85

Photogravure.

Wmkd. Circles. (202)

1934, Dec. 10 *Perf. 13½x12½*

B73	SP63	1½c(+1½c) olive	2.00	75
B74	"	5c(+3c) rose red	3.25	1.50
B75	"	6c(+4c) blue green	3.25	25
B76	"	12½c(+3½c) ultramarine	40.00	32.50

Henri D. Guyot
SP64

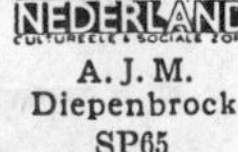

A. J. M. Diepenbrock
SP65

F. C. Donders
SP66

J. P. Sweelinck
SP67

Perf. 12½x12, 12.

1935, June Engr. Unwmkd.

B77	SP64	1½c(+1½c) dark carmine	2.50	3.50
B78	SP65	5c(+3c) black brown	7.00	7.00
B79	SP66	6c(+4c) myrtle green	8.50	40
B80	SP67	12½c(+3½c) deep blue	50.00	7.00

Netherlands Map, DC-3 Planes' Shadows
SP68

Girl Picking Apple
SP69

Perf. 14x12½

1935, Oct. 16 Photo. Wmk. 202

B81	SP68	6c(+4c) brown	40.00	4.75

1935, Dec. 4 *Perf. 14x13*

B82	SP69	1½c(+1½c) crimson	75	35
B83	"	5c(+3c) dark yellow green	2.50	1.50
B84	"	6c(+4c) black brown	2.25	35
B85	"	12½c(+3½c) ultramarine	38.50	12.00

H. Kamerlingh Onnes
SP70

Dr. A. S. Talma
SP71

Msgr. Hjam Schaepman
SP72

Desiderius Erasmus
SP73

Perf. 12½x12

1936, May 1 Engr. Unwmkd.

B86	SP70	1½c(+1½c) brn. black	2.00	1.40
B87	SP71	5c(+3c) dull green	8.50	7.50
B88	SP72	6c(+4c) dk. red	3.25	35
B89	SP73	12½c(+3½c) dull blue	27.50	4.25

Cherub
SP74

Perf. 14½x13½

1936, Dec. 1 Photo. Wmk. 202

B90	SP74	1½c(+1½c) lilac gray	1.00	25
B91	"	5c(+3c) turquoise green	3.75	1.00
B92	"	6c(+4c) deep red brown	3.75	25
B93	"	12½c(+3½c) indigo	25.00	8.50

Summer Help Issue.

Jacob Maris
SP75

Franciscus de la Boe Sylvius
SP76

Joost van den Vondel
SP77

Anthony van Leeuwenhoek
SP78

Perf. 12½x12

1937, June 1 Engr. Unwmkd.

B94	SP75	1½c(+1½c) black brown	60	75
B95	SP76	5c(+3c) dull green	7.00	7.00
B96	SP77	6c(+4c) brown violet	1.60	25
B97	SP78	12½c(+3½c) dull blue	15.00	1.75

"The Laughing Child" after Frans Hals
SP79

Perf. 14x13½

1937, Dec. 1 Photo. Wmk. 202

B98	SP79	1½c(+1½c) black	25	20
B99	"	3c(+2c) green	1.40	2.60
B100	"	4c(+2c) henna brown	75	60
B101	"	5c(+3c) blue green	60	12
B102	"	12½c(+3½c) dark blue	13.50	2.75
		Nos. B98-B102 (5)	16.50	6.27

Marnix de Sint Aldegonde
SP80

Otto Gerhard Heldring
SP81

Maria Tesselschade
SP82

Harmenszoon Rembrandt van Rijn
SP83

Hermann Boerhaave
SP84

Perf. 12½x12

1938, May 16 Engr. Unwmkd.

B103	SP80	1½c(+1½c) sepia	70	1.15
B104	SP81	3c(+2c) dark green	90	35
B105	SP82	4c(+2c) rose lake	2.85	3.75
B106	SP83	5c(+3c) dark slate grn.	3.50	25
B107	SP84	12½c(+3½c) dull blue	16.50	1.85
		Nos. B103-B107 (5)	24.45	7.35

The surtax was for the benefit of cultural and social relief.

Child with Flowers, Bird and Fish
SP85

Perf. 14x13½

1938, Dec. 1 Photo. Wmk. 202

B108	SP85	1½c(+1½c) black	18	18
B109	"	3c(+2c) maroon	60	25
B110	"	4c(+2c) dark blue green	1.25	1.00
B111	"	5c(+3c) henna brown	50	12
B112	"	12½c(+3½c) deep blue	14.00	3.50
		Nos. B108-B112 (5)	16.53	5.05

Mathijs Maris
SP86

Anton Mauve
SP87

Gerard van Swieten
SP88

Nikolaas Beets
SP89

Peter Stuyvesant
SP90

Perf. 12½x12

1939, May 1 Engr. Unwmkd.

B113	SP86	1½c(+1½c) sepia	75	75
B114	SP87	2½c(+2½c) gray green	7.25	5.00
B115	SP88	3c(+3c) verm.	1.25	1.50
B116	SP89	5c(+3c) dark slate green	3.50	25
B117	SP90	12½c(+3½c) indigo	13.50	1.50
		Nos. B113-B117 (5)	26.25	9.00

The surtax was for the benefit of cultural and social relief.

Child Carrying Cornucopia
SP91

Perf. 14x13

1939, Dec. 1 Photo. Wmk. 202

B118	SP91	1½c(+1½c) black	24	20
B119	"	2½c(+2½c) dark olive grn.	8.50	4.25
B120	"	3c(+3c) henna brown	80	25
B121	"	5c(+3c) dark green	1.50	12
B122	"	12½c(+3½c) dark blue	5.50	2.00
		Nos. B118-B122 (5)	16.54	6.82

The surtax was used for destitute children.

Vincent van Gogh
SP92

E. J. Potgieter
SP93

Petrus Camper
SP94

Jan Steen
SP95

Joseph Scaliger
SP96

1940, May 11 Engr. *Perf. 12½x12*

B123	SP92	1½c+1½c brown black	2.00	50
B124	SP93	2½c+2½c dark green	5.50	1.75
B125	SP94	3c+3c carmine	3.50	1.50
B126	SP95	5c+3c deep green	7.25	40
		a. Bklt. pane of 4	250.00	
B127	SP96	12½c+3½c deep blue	6.75	1.20

Type of 1940 Surcharged in Black **7½+2½**

1940, Sept. 7

B128	SP95	7½(c)+2½(c) on 5c+3c dark red	65	50
		Nos. B123-B128 (6)	25.65	5.85

Child with Flowers and Doll
SP97

1940, Dec. 2 Photo. *Perf. 14x13½*

B129	SP97	1½c+1½c dull blue gray	1.00	25
B130	"	2½c+2½c deep olive	3.50	90
B131	"	4c+3c royal bl.	3.25	1.00
B132	"	5c+3c dark blue green	3.25	25
B133	"	7½c+3½c henna	1.00	25
		Nos. B129-B133 (5)	12.00	2.65

The surtax was used for destitute children.

Dr. Antonius Mathijsen
SP98

Dr. Jan Ingenhousz
SP99

Aagje Deken
SP100

Johannes Bosboom
SP101

A. C. W. Staring
SP102

1941, May 29 Engr. *Perf. 12½x12*

B134	SP98	1½(c)+1½c black brown	1.50	32
B135	SP99	2½(c)+2½c dark slate green	1.35	32
B136	SP100	4(c)+3c red	1.25	32
B137	SP101	5(c)+3c slate green	1.65	32
B138	SP102	7½(c)+3½c rose violet	1.65	32
		Nos. B134-B138 (5)	7.40	1.60

The surtax was for cultural and social relief.

Rembrandt's Painting of Titus, His Son
SP103

Perf. 14x13½

1941, Dec. 1 Photo. Wmk. 202

B139	SP103	1½c+1½c vio. blk.	32	25
B140	"	2½c+2½c dk. olive	32	25
B141	"	4c+3c royal blue	32	25
B142	"	5c+3c deep green	32	25
B143	"	7½c+3½c deep henna brown	32	25
		Nos. B139-B143 (5)	1.60	1.25

The surtax aided child welfare.

Legionary
SP104 SP105

Perf. 12½x12, 12x12½

1942, Nov. 1

B144 SP104 7½c+2½c dk. red 40 28
a. Sheet of 10 90.00 75.00
B145 SP105 12½c+87½c ultra. 9.50 10.00
a. Sheet of 4 75.00 90.00

The surtax aided the Netherlands Legion.
Nos. B144a and B145a measure 155x111mm. and 94x94mm. respectively, with inscription in bottom margin.

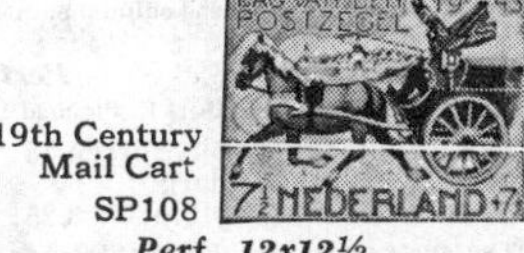

19th Century Mail Cart
SP108

Perf. 12x12½

1943, Oct. 9 **Unwmkd.**

B148 SP108 7½c+7½c henna brown 7 7

Issued to commemorate Stamp Day.

Child and House
SP109

Mother and Child
SP110

Mother and Children
SP111

Child Carrying Sheaf of Wheat
SP112

Mother and Children
SP113

Perf. 12½x12

1944, Mar. 6 **Wmk. 202**

B149 SP109 1½c+3½c dull black 18 20
B150 SP110 4c+3½ rose lake 18 20
B151 SP111 5c+5c dark blue green 18 20
B152 SP112 7½c+7½c deep henna brown 18 20
B153 SP113 10c+40c royal bl. 18 20
Nos. B149-B153 (5) 90 1 00

The surtax aided National Social Service and winter relief.

Child
SP114

Fortuna
SP115

1945, Dec. 1 Photo. *Perf. 14x13½*

B154 SP114 1½c+2½c gray 25 25
B155 " 2½c+3½c dark blue green 25 25
B156 " 5c+5c brown red 25 25
B157 " 7½c+4½c red 25 25
B158 " 12½c+5½c brt. blue 25 25
Nos. B154-B158 (5) 1.25 1.25

The surtax was for Child Welfare.

Perf. 12½x12

1946, May 1 **Engr.** **Unwmkd.**

B159 SP115 1½(c)+3½(c) brown black 75 40
B160 " 2½(c)+5(c) dull green 90 65
B161 " 5(c)+10(c) dark violet 1.35 90
B162 " 7½(c)+15(c) carmine lake 75 40
B163 " 12½(c)+37½(c) dark blue 1.50 80
Nos. B159-B163 (5) 5.25 3.15

The surtax was for victims of World War II.

Princess Irene
SP116

Princess Margriet
SP117

Princess Beatrix
SP118

Child on Merry-go-round
SP119

1946, Sept. 16

B164 SP116 1½(c)+1½(c) blk brown 1.00 75
B165 SP117 2½(c)+1½(c) bl. green 1.00 75
B166 SP116 4(c)+2(c) magenta 1.25 90
B167 SP117 5(c)+2(c) brn. 1.25 75
B168 SP118 7½(c)+2½(c) red 1.00 25
B169 " 12½(c)+7½(c) dark blue 1.00 90
Nos. B164-B169 (6) 6.50 4.30

The surtax was for child welfare and anti-tuberculosis work.

1946, Dec. 2 Photo. **Wmk. 202**

B170 SP119 2(c)+2c lilac gray 90 65
B171 " 4(c)+2c dark green 90 65
B172 " 7½(c)+2½c brt. red 90 65
B173 " 10(c)+5c deep plum 90 25
B174 " 20(c)+5c dp. blue 1.10 90
Nos. B170-B174 (5) 4.70 3.10

The surtax was for child welfare.

Dr. Hendrik van Deventer
SP120

Peter Cornelisz Hooft
SP121

Johan de Witt
SP122

Jean F. van Royen
SP123

Hugo de Groot
SP124

1947, Aug. 1 **Engr.** **Unwmkd.**

B175 SP120 2c+2c dark red 1.25 75
B176 SP121 4c+2c dk. green 3.00 1.00
B177 SP122 7½c+2½c dark purple brown 4.00 1.00
B178 SP123 10c+5c brown 3.00 20
B179 SP124 20c+5c dk. blue 2.00 1.00
Nos. B175-B179 (5) 13.25 3.95

The surtax was for social and cultural purposes.

Children
SP125

Infant
SP126

1947, Dec. 1 Photo. *Perf. 13x14*

B180 SP125 2c+2c red brn. 12 12
B181 SP126 4c+2c bl. green 2.75 90
B182 " 7½c+2½c sepia 2.75 1.00
B183 " 10c+5c dark red 2.75 12
B184 SP125 20c+5c blue 2.75 1.35
Nos. B180-B184 (5) 11.12 3.49

The surtax was for child welfare.

Hall of Knights, The Hague
SP127

Boy in Kayak
SP128

Designs: 6c+4c, Royal Palace, Amsterdam. 10c+5c, Kneuterdyk Palace, The Hague. 20c+5c, New Church, Amsterdam.

1948, June 17 **Engr.** *Perf. 13x14*

B185 SP127 2c+2c dk. brown 3.75 35
B186 " 6c+4c green 3.75 65
B187 " 10c+5c bright red 2.25 25
B188 " 20c+5c deep blue 3.75 1.75

The surtax was for cultural and social purposes.

1948, Nov. 15 **Photogravure**

Designs: 5c+3c, Swimming. 6c+4c, Sledding. 10c+5c, Swinging. 20c+8c, Figure skating.

B189 SP128 2c+2c yel. green 12 12
B190 " 5c+3c dark blue green 4.25 1.15
B191 " 6c+4c gray 1.50 25
B192 " 10c+5c red 12 12
B193 " 20c+8c blue 4.50 1.35
Nos. B189-B193 (5) 10.49 2.99

The surtax was for child welfare.

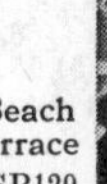

Beach Terrace
SP129

Boy and Girl Hikers
SP130

Campers
SP131

Reaping—SP132

Sailboats
SP133

Perf. 13½x12½

1949, May 2 **Wmk. 202**

B194 SP129 2c+2c blue & org. yellow 2.00 25
B195 SP130 5c+3c blue & yellow 3.50 2.50
B196 SP131 6c+4c dark blue green 3.50 75
B197 SP132 10c+5c blue & org. yellow 5.50 12
B198 SP133 20c+5c blue 4.50 2.75
Nos. B194-B198 (5) 19.00 6.37

The surtax was for cultural and social purposes.

Hands Reaching for Sunflower
SP134

"Autumn"
SP135

Perf. 14x13½

1949, Aug. 1 Photo. **Unwmkd.**

Flower in Yellow.

B199 SP134 2c+3c gray 3.00 40
B200 " 6c+4c red brown 2.00 65
B201 " 10c+5c brt. blue 7.00 40
B202 " 30c+10c dk. brn. 15.00 4.25

The surtax was for the Red Cross and for Indonesia Relief work.

1949, Nov. 14 **Engr.** *Perf. 13x14*

Designs: 5c+3c, "Summer." 6c+4c, "Spring." 10c+5c, "Winter." 20c+7c, "New Year."

B203 SP135 2c+3c brown 12 10
B204 " 5c+3c red 6.50 1.75

B205 SP135 6c+4c dull green 2.00 30
B206 " 10c+5c gray 25 10
B207 " 20c+7c blue 6.50 1.75
Nos. B203-B207 (5) 15.37 4.00

The surtax was for child welfare.

Figure from PTT Monument, The Hague
SP136

Combine Harvester
SP137

Designs: 4c+2c, Dike repairs. 5c+3c, Apartment House, Rotterdam. 10c+5c, Bridge section being towed. 20c+5c, Canal freighter.

Perf. 12½x12, 12x12½

1950, May 2

B208 SP136 2c+2c dk. brown 2.50 1.50
B209 " 4c+2c dk. green 22.50 16.50
B210 " 5c+3c sepia 12.50 4.00
B211 SP137 6c+4c purple 5.25 1.00
B212 " 10c+5c blue gray 7.00 25
B213 " 20c+5c dp. blue 25.00 17.50
Nos. B208-B213 (6) 74.75 40.75

The surtax was for social and cultural works.

Church Ruins and Good Samaritan
SP138

Baby and Bees
SP139

1950, July 17 **Photogravure**

B214 SP138 2c+2c olive brn. 5.00 2.00
B215 " 5c+3c brn. red 30.00 16.00
B216 " 6c+4c dp. grn. 16.50 2.50
B217 " 10c+5c bright lilac rose 19.00 50
B218 " 20c+5c ultra. 47.50 32.50
Nos. B214-B218 (5) 118.00 53.50

The surtax was for the restoration of ruined churches.

1950, Nov. 13 ***Perf. 13x12***

Designs: 5c+3c, Boy and rooster. 6c+4c, Girl feeding birds. 10c+5c, Boy and fish. 20c+7c, Girl, butterfly and toad.

B219 SP139 2c+3c carmine 12 12
B220 " 5c+3c olv. grn. 12.50 4.25
B221 " 6c+4c dark blue green 2.25 80
B222 " 10c+5c lilac 12 25
B223 " 20c+7c blue 23.50 14.00
Nos. B219-B223 (5) 38.49 19.42

The surtax was to aid needy children.

Hillenraad Castle
SP140

Bergh Castle
SP141

Castles: 6c+4c, Hernen. 10c+5c, Rechteren. 20c+5c, Moermond.

Perf. 12x12½, 12½x12

1951, May 15 **Engr.** **Unwmkd.**

B224 SP140 2c+2c purple 5.25 1.50
B225 SP141 5c+3c dk. red 14.00 9.50
B226 SP140 6c+4c dk. brn. 2.50 95
B227 SP141 10c+5c dk. grn. 5.25 25
B228 " 20c+5c dp. bl 14.00 10.00
Nos. B224-B228 (5) 41.00 22.20

The surtax was for cultural, medical and social purposes.

Girl and Windmill
SP142

Jan van Riebeeck
SP143

Designs: 5c+3c, Boy and building construction. 6c+4c, Fisherboy and net. 10c+5c, Boy, chimneys and steelwork. 20c+7c, Girl and apartment house.

1951, Nov. 12 **Photo.** ***Perf. 12½x14***

B229 SP142 2c+3c deep green 25 12
B230 " 5c+3c slate vio. 11.00 4.00
B231 " 6c+4c dk. brn. 13.50 90
B232 " 10c+5c red brown 25 12
B233 " 20c+7c dp. blue 13.50 12.50
Nos. B229-B233 (5) 38.50 17.64

The surtax was for child welfare.

1952, Mar. ***Perf. 12½x12***

B234 SP143 2c+3c dark gray 7.00 4.00
B235 " 6c+4c dark blue green 13.50 8.00
B236 " 10c+5c brt. red 16.00 5.25
B237 " 20c+5c brt. blue 6.75 4.00

Tercentenary of Van Riebeeck's landing in South Africa. Surtax was for Van Riebeeck monument fund.

Scotch Rose
SP144

Girl and Dog
SP145

Designs: 5c+3c, Marsh marigold. 6c+4c, Tulip. 10c+5c, Ox-eye daisy. 20c+5c, Cornflower.

1952, May 1

B238 SP144 2c+2c cerise & dull green 1.50 85
B239 " 5c+3c deep green & yellow 2.00 1.50
B240 " 6c+4c red & dull green 2.25 60
B241 " 10c+5c orange yellow & dull green 3.25 25
B242 " 20c+5c blue & dull green 28.50 16.50
Nos. B238-B242 (5) 37.50 19.70

The surtax was for social, cultural and medical purposes.

Perf. 12x12½

1952, Nov. 17 **Unwmkd.**

Designs: 2c+3c, Boy and goat. 5c+3c, Girl on donkey. 10c+5c, Boy and kitten. 20c+7c, Boy and rabbit.

Design in Black.

B243 SP145 2c+3c olive 12 10
B244 " 5c+3c dp. rose 1.50 1.00
B245 " 6c+4c aqua. 3.50 60
B246 " 10c+5c org. yel. 12 10
B247 " 20c+7c blue 16.50 10.00
Nos. B243-B247 (5) 21.74 11.80

The surtax was for child welfare.

No. 308 Surcharged in Black

19 53
10c +10
WATERSNOOD

Perf. 13½x12½

1953, Feb. 10 **Wmk. 202**

B248 A76 10c+10(c) org. yel. 50 10

The surtax was for flood relief.

Hyacinth
SP146

Red Cross on Shield
SP147

Designs: 5c+3c, African Marigold. 6c+4c, Daffodil. 10c+5c, Anemone. 20c+5c, Iris.

1953, May 1 ***Perf. 12*** **Unwmkd.**

B249 SP146 2c+2c vio. & grn. 1.00 50
B250 " 5c+3c deep orange & green 1.90 1.60
B251 " 6c+4c grn. & yel. 1.75 60
B252 " 10c+5c dark red & green 5.50 25
B253 " 20c+5c dp. ultra. & green 30.00 20.00
Nos. B249-B253 (5) 40.15 22.95

The surtax was for social, cultural and medical purposes.

1953, Aug. 24 **Engraved**

Designs: 6c+4c, Man holding lantern. 7c+5c, Worker and ambulance at flood. 10c+5c, Nurse giving blood transfusion. 25c+8c, Red Cross flags.

Cross in Red.

B254 SP147 2c+3c dk. olive 50 55
B255 " 6c+4c dk. vio. brn. 5.50 4.00
B256 " 7c+5c dark gray green 1.00 65
B257 " 10c+5c red 75 7
B258 " 25c+8c dp. blue 16.00 7.00
Nos. B254-B258 (5) 23.75 12.27

The surtax was for the Red Cross.

Spade, Flag, Bucket and Girl's Head
SP148

Designs: Head of child and: 5c+3c, Apple. 7c+5c, Pigeon. 10c+5c, Sailboat. 25c+8c, Tulip.

1953, Nov. 16 **Litho.** ***Perf. 12x12½***

B259 SP148 2c+3c yellow & blue gray 12 12
B260 " 5c+3c apple green & brown carmine 1.60 1.00
B261 " 7c+5c light blue & sepia 6.75 1.25
B262 " 10c+5c olive bistre & lilac 15 10
B263 " 25c+8c pink & blue green 27.50 16.50
Nos. B259-B263 (5) 36.12 18.97

The surtax was for child welfare.

Martinus Nijhoff, Poet
SP149

Boy Flying Model Plane
SP150

Portraits: 5c+3c, Willem Pijper, composer. 7c+5c, H. P. Berlage, architect. 10c+5c, Johan Huizinga, historian. 25c+8c, Vincent van Gogh, painter.

1954, May 1 **Photo.** ***Perf. 12½x12***

B264 SP149 2c+3c dp. blue 3.00 2.50
B265 " 5c+3c olive brown 75 75
B266 " 7c+5c dark red 3.75 2.00
B267 " 10c+5c dull grn. 13.50 25
B268 " 25c+8c plum 24.00 21.50
Nos. B264-B268 (5) 45.00 27.00

The surtax was for social and cultural purposes.

1954, Aug. 23 ***Perf. 12***

Portrait: 10c+4c, Albert E. Plesman.

B269 SP150 2c+2c olive green 75 1.10
B270 " 10c+4c dark gray blue 3.25 75

The surtax was for the Netherlands Aviation Foundation.

Children Making Paper Chains
SP151

Girl Brushing Teeth
SP152

Designs: 7c+5c, Boy sailing toy boat. 10c+5c, Nurse drying child. 25c+8c, Young convalescent, drawing.

Perf. 12x12½, 12½x12

1954, Nov. 15

B271 SP151 2c+3c brown 10 8
B272 SP152 5c+3c olive green 1.00 75
B273 " 7c+5c gray bl. 1.25 60
B274 " 10c+5c brn. red 15 7
B275 SP151 25c+8c dp. blue 16.00 9.00
Nos. B271-B275 (5) 18.50 10.50

The surtax was for child welfare.

Factory, Rotterdam
SP153

Amsterdam Stock Exchange
SP154

Designs: 5c+3c, Post office, The Hague. 10c+5c, Town hall, Hilversum. 25c+8c, Office building, The Hague.

1955, Apr. 25 **Engr.** ***Perf. 12x12½***

B276 SP153 2c+3c brownish bistre 2.50 1.50
B277 " 5c+3c blue green 50 50
B278 SP154 7c+5c rose brn. 2.00 1.50
B279 SP153 10c+5c steel blue 2.50 25
B280 " 25c+8c choc. 27.50 15.00
Nos. B276-B280 (5) 35.00 18.75

The surtax was for social and cultural purposes.

Microscope and Crab
SP155

Willem van Loon by Dirck Santvoort
SP156

1955, Aug. 15 **Photo.** ***Perf. 12½x12***

Crab in Red

B281 SP155 2c+3c dark gray 85 85
B282 " 5c+3c dark green 50 50
B283 " 7c+5c dk. violet 1.10 1.00

B284 SP155 10c+5c dark blue 1.00 12
B285 " 25c+8c olive 15.00 11.00
Nos. B281-B285 (5) 18.45 13.47

The surtax was for cancer research.

1955, Nov. 14 **Unwmkd.**

Portraits: 5+3c, Boy by Jacob Adriaanszoon Backer. 7+5c, Girl by unknown artist. 10+5c, Philips Huygens by Adriaan Hanneman. 25+8c, Constantijn Huygens by Adriaan Hanneman.

B286 SP156 2c+3c dark green 12 7
B287 " 5c+3c dp. car. 75 75
B288 " 7c+5c dull red brown 3.75 1.15
B289 " 10c+5c deep blue 15 7
B290 " 25c+8c purple 18.00 11.50
Nos. B286-B290 (5) 22.77 13.54

The surtax was for child welfare.

Farmer Wearing High Cap
SP157

Sailboat
SP158

Rembrandt Etchings: 5c+3c, Young Tobias with Angel. 7c+5c, Persian Wearing Fur Cap. 10c+5c, Old Blind Tobias. 25c+8c, Self-portrait of 1639.

1956, Apr. 23 **Engr.** ***Perf. 13½x14***

B291 SP157 2c+3c bluish blk. 5.00 6.50
B292 " 5c+3c olive green 2.50 2.00
B293 " 7c+5c brown 7.50 7.50
B294 " 10c+5c dk. green 35.00 50
B295 " 25c+8c reddish brown 40.00 27.50
Nos. B291-B295 (5) 90.00 44.00

Issued to commemorate the 350th anniversary of the birth of Rembrandt van Rijn.

1956, Aug. 27 **Litho.** ***Perf. 12½x12***

Designs: 5c+3c, Woman runner. 7c+5c, Amphora depicting runners. 10c+5c, Field hockey. 25c+8c, Waterpolo player.

B296 SP158 2c+3c brt. bl. & blk. 50 50
B297 " 5c+3c dull yellow & black 50 50
B298 " 7c+5c red brown & black 2.00 1.50
B299 " 10c+5c gray & blk. 3.00 1.00
B300 " 25c+8c bright green & black 12.50 12.50
Nos. B296-B300 (5) 18.50 16.00

Issued to publicize the forthcoming 16th Olympic Games at Melbourne, Nov. 22-Dec. 8, 1956.

The surtax was for the benefit of the Netherlands Olympic Committee.

Boy by Jan van Scorel
SP159

Motor Freighter
SP160

Children's Portraits: 5c+3c, Boy, 1563. 7c+5c, Girl, 1563. 10c+5c, Girl, 1590. 25c+8c, Eechie Pieters, 1592.

Perf. 12½x12

1956, Nov. 12 **Unwmkd.**

B301 SP159 2c+3c black violet 12 7
B302 " 5c+3c olive green 65 65
B303 " 7c+5c brn. vio. 4.25 1.85
B304 " 10c+5c deep red 15 7
B305 " 25c+8c dk. blue 14.00 6.50
Nos. B301-B305 (5) 19.17 9.14

The surtax was for child welfare.

1957, May 13 **Photo.** ***Perf. 14x13***

Ships: 6+4c, Coaster. 7+5c, "Willem Barendsz." 10+8c, Trawler. 30+8c, S. S. "Nieuw Amsterdam."

B306 SP160 4c+3c brt. blue 2.00 2.00
B307 " 6c+4c brt. violet 1.00 1.00
B308 " 7c+5c dk. car. rose 2.00 1.50
B309 " 10c+8c green 3.75 12
B310 " 30c+8c chocolate 9.50 10.00
Nos. B306-B310 (5) 18.25 14.62

The surtax was for social and cultural purposes.

White Pelican Feeding Young
SP161

Girl by B. J. Blommers
SP162

Designs: 6c+4c, Vacation ship, "Castle of Staverden." 7c+5c, Cross and dates: 1867-1957. 10c+8c, Cross and laurel wreath. 30c+8c, Globe and Cross.

1957, Aug. 19 **Lithographed**

Cross in Red.

B311 SP161 4c+3c blue & red 1.50 1.25
B312 " 6c+4c dark green 90 75
B313 " 7c+5c dark green & pink 1.50 90
B314 " 10c+8c yel. orange 1.50 10
B315 " 30c+8c violet blue 6.25 6.00
Nos. B311-B315 (5) 11.65 9.00

Issued for the 90th anniversary of the founding of the Netherlands Red Cross.

1957, Nov. 18 ***Perf. 12½x12***

Girls' Portraits by: 6c+4c, William B. Tholen. 8c+4c, Jan Sluyters. 12c+9c, Matthijs Maris. 30c+9c, Cornelis Kruseman.

B316 SP162 4c+4c dp. carmine 12 12
B317 " 6c+4c olive green 3.00 1.25
B318 " 8c+4c gray 4.25 2.50
B319 " 12c+9c deep claret 10 7
B320 " 30c+9c dark blue 15.00 13.00
Nos. B316-B320 (5) 22.47 16.94

The surtax was for child welfare.

Woman from Walcheren, Zeeland
SP163

Girl on Stilts and Boy on Tricycle
SP164

Regional Costumes: 6c+4c, Marken. 8c+4c, Scheveningen. 12c+9c, Friesland. 30c+9c, Volendam.

Perf. 12½x12

1958, Apr. 28 **Photo.** **Unwmkd.**

B321 SP163 4c+4c blue 60 90
B322 " 6c+4c bistre 1.00 1.15
B323 " 8c+4c dark carmine rose 4.50 2.50
B324 " 12c+9c org. brn. 1.35 20
B325 " 30c+9c violet 11.00 8.00
Nos. B321-B325 (5) 18.45 12.75

The surtax was for social and cultural purposes.

1958, Nov. 17 **Lithographed**

Children's Games: 6c+4c, Boy and girl on scooters. 8c + 4c, Leapfrog. 12c + 9c, Roller skating. 30c+9c, Boy in toy car and girl jumping rope.

B326 SP164 4c+4c light blue 12 12
B327 " 6c+4c deep red 2.50 1.50
B328 " 8c+4c bright blue green 2.50 1.50
B329 " 12c+9c red orange 12 12
B330 " 30c+9c dk. blue 9.00 7.25
Nos. B326-B330 (5) 14.24 10.49

The surtax was for child welfare.

Tugs and Caisson
SP165

Designs: 6c + 4c, Dredger. 8c + 4c, Laborers making fascine mattresses. 12c + 9c, Grab cranes. 30c + 9c, Sand spouter.

1959, May 11 ***Perf. 14x13***

B331 SP165 4c+4c dark blue, *blue green* 1.50 1.50
B332 " 6c+4c red orange, *gray* 1.50 1.50
B333 " 8c+4c blue violet, *light blue* 2.50 2.00
B334 " 12c+9c blue green, *brt. yellow* 5.25 25
B335 " 30c+9c dark brown, *brick red* 12.00 12.00
Nos. B331-B335 (5) 22.75 17.25

Issued to publicize the endless struggle to keep the sea out and the land dry.

Child in Playpen
SP166

Refugee Woman
SP167

Designs: 6c+4c, Playing Indian. 8c+4c, Child feeding geese. 12c + 9c, Children crossing street. 30c+9c, Doing homework.

Perf. 12½x12

1959, Nov. 16 **Unwmkd.**

B336 SP166 4c+4c deep rose & dark blue 12 12
B337 " 6c+4c red brown & emerald 2.50 2.00
B338 " 8c+4c red & bl. 3.00 2.25
B339 " 12c+9c greenish blue, orange & gray 12 12
B340 " 30c+9c yellow & blue 6.00 4.50
Nos. B336-B340 (5) 11.74 8.99

The surtax was for child welfare.

1960, Apr. 7 **Photo.** ***Perf. 13x14***

B341 SP167 12c+8c dp. claret 50 25
B342 " 30c+10c dark olive green 3.25 3.00

Issued to publicize World Refugee Year, July 1, 1959-June 30, 1960. The surtax was for aid to refugees.

Tulip
SP168

Girl from Marken
SP169

Flowers: 6c+4c, Gorse. 8c+4c, White waterlily (horiz.). 12c+8c, Red poppy. 30c+10c, Blue sea holly.

Perf. 12½x12, 12x12½

1960, May 23 **Unwmkd.**

B343 SP168 4c+4c gray, green & red 75 75
B344 " 6c+4c salmon, green & yel. 45 45
B345 " 8c+4c multi. 2.00 1.85
B346 " 12c+8c dull org., red & grn. 2.25 40
B347 " 30c+10c yellow, grn. & ultra. 7.50 7.00
Nos. B343-B347 (5) 12.95 10.45

The surtax was for social and cultural purposes.

1960, Nov. 14 ***Perf. 12½x12***

Regional Costumes: 6c+4c, Volendam. 8c+4c, Bunschoten. 12c+9c, Hindeloopen. 30c+9c, Huizen.

B348 SP169 4c+4c multi. 12 12
B349 " 6c+4c " 2.00 1.50
B350 " 8c+4c " 5.50 2.50
B351 " 12c+9c " 12 12
B352 " 30c+9c " 9.00 7.25
Nos. B348-B352 (5) 16.74 11.49

The surtax was for child welfare.

Herring Gull
SP170

St. Nicholas on his Horse
SP171

Birds: 6c+4c, Oystercatcher (horiz.). 8c+4c, Curlew. 12c+8c, Avocet (horiz.). 30c+10c, Lapwing.

Perf. 12½x12, 12x12½

1961, Apr. 24 **Litho.** **Unwmkd.**

B353 SP170 4c+4c yellow & greenish gray 2.00 1.75
B354 " 6c+4c terra cotta & black 50 50
B355 " 8c+4c olive & red brown 1.75 1.75
B356 " 12c+8c light blue & gray 3.25 50
B357 " 30c+10c green & black 6.50 5.75
Nos. B353-B357 (5) 14.00 10.25

The surtax was for social and cultural purposes.

1961, Nov. 13 ***Perf. 12½x12***

Holiday folklore: 6c+4c, Epiphany. 8c+4c, Palm Sunday. 12c+9c, Whitsun bride, Pentecost. 30c+9c, Martinmas.

B358 SP171 4c+4c br. red 12 10
B359 " 6c+4c br. blue 2.10 1.50
B360 " 8c+4c olive 2.10 1.75
B361 " 12c+9c dp. green 12 10
B362 " 30c+9c dp. org. 4.25 3.50
Nos. B358-B362 (5) 8.69 6.95

The surtax was for child welfare.

Christian Huygens' Pendulum Clock by van Ceulen
SP172

Children Cooking
SP173

Designs: 4c+4c, Cat, Roman sculpture (horiz.). 6c+4c, Fossil Ammonite. 12c+8c, Figurehead from admiralty ship model. 30c+10c, Guardsmen Hendrick van Berckenrode and Jacob van Lourensz, by Frans Hals (horiz.).

Perf. 14x13, 13x14

1962, Apr. 27 **Photogravure**

B363 SP172 4c+4c olive green 1.75 1.65
B364 " 6c+4c gray 1.00 85
B365 " 8c+4c deep claret 1.85 1.85
B366 " 12c+8c olive bistre 1.85 1.50
B367 " 30c+10c bl. blk. 2.35 2.10
Nos. B363-B367 (5) 8.80 7.95

The surtax was for social and cultural purposes. Issued to publicize the International Congress of Museum Experts, July 4-11.

1962, Nov. 12 *Perf. 12½x12*

Children's Activities: 6c+4c, Bicycling. 8c+4c, Watering flowers. 12c+9c, Feeding chickens. 30c+9c, Music making.

B368 SP173 4c+4c red 12 12
B369 " 6c+4c yel. bis. 1.20 75
B370 " 8c+4c ultra. 2.50 1.65
B371 " 12c+9c dp. green 12 12
B372 " 30c+9c dk. car. rose 5.00 4.00
Nos. B368-B372 (5) 8.94 6.64

The surtax was for child welfare.

Gallery Windmill
SP174

Roadside First Aid Station
SP175

Windmills: 6c+4c, North Holland polder mill. 8c+4c, South Holland polder mill (horiz.). 12c+8c, Post mill. 30c+10c, Wip mill.

Perf. 13x14, 14x13

1963, Apr. 24 Litho. Unwmkd.

B373 SP174 4c+4c dk. blue 1.10 1.20
B374 " 6c+4c dk. pur. 2.00 2.00
B375 " 8c+4c dk. grn. 2.50 2.50
B376 " 12c+8c black 2.75 50
B377 " 30c+10c dk. car. 3.25 3.50
Nos. B373-B377 (5) 11.60 9.70

The surtax was for social and cultural purposes.

1963, Aug. 20 Photo. *Perf. 14x13*

Designs: 6c+4c, Book collection box. 8c+4c, Crosses. 12c+9c, International aid to Africans. 30c+9c, First aid team.

B378 SP175 4c+4c dk. blue & red 65 65
B379 " 6c+4c dull pur. & red 40 40
B380 " 8c+4c black & red 1.50 1.15
B381 " 12c+9c red brn. & red 65 25
B382 " 30c+9c yel. grn. & red 2.25 1.75
Nos. B378-B382 (5) 6.45 4.20

Issued to commemorate the centenary of the International Red Cross. The surtax went to the Netherlands Red Cross.

"Aunt Lucy Sat on a Goosey"
SP176

Seeing-Eye Dog
SP177

Nursery Rhymes: 6c+4c, "In the Hague there lives a count." 8c+4c, "One day I passed a puppet's fair." 12c+9c, "Storky, storky, Billy Spoon." 30c+9c, "Ride on in a little buggy."

1963, Nov. 12 Litho. *Perf. 13x14*

B383 SP176 4c+4c greenish bl. & dk. bl. 12 12
B384 " 6c+4c org. red & slate grn. 1.10 90
B385 " 8c+4c dull grn. & dk. brn. 1.50 90
B386 " 12c+9c yel. & dk. purple 12 12
B387 " 30c+9c rose & dark blue 2.25 2.00
Nos. B383-B387 (5) 5.09 4.04

The surtax was for mentally and physically handicapped children.

1964, Apr. 21 *Perf. 14x13*

Designs: 8c+5c, Three red deer. 12c+9c, Three kittens. 30c+9c, European bison and young.

B388 SP177 5c+5c gray olive, red & blk. 40 35
B389 " 8c+5c dark red, pale brn. & blk. 40 35
B390 " 12c+9c dull yel., black & gray 40 25
B391 " 30c+9c blue, gray & black 70 70

The surtax was for social and cultural purposes.

Child Painting
SP178

View of Veere
SP179

"Artistic and Creative Activities of Children": 10c+5c, Ballet dancing. 15c+10c, Girl playing the flute. 20c+10c, Little Red Riding Hood (masquerading children). 40c+15c, Boy with hammer at work bench.

Perf. 13x14

1964, Nov. 17 Photo. Unwmkd.

B392 SP178 7c+3c lt. olive green & blue 50 50
B393 " 10c+5c red, brt. pink & green 80 75
B394 " 15c+10c yel. bis., blk. & yellow 12 7
B395 " 20c+10c brt. pink, brown & red 70 75
B396 " 40c+15c blu e & yellow grn. 1.10 85
Nos. B392-B396 (5) 3.22 2.92

The surtax was for child welfare.

1965, June 1 Litho. *Perf. 14x13*

Views: 10c+6c, Thorn. 18c+12c, Dordrecht. 20c+10c, Staveren. 40c+10c, Medemblik.

B397 SP179 8c+6c yel. & blk. 30 20
B398 " 10c+6c greenish blue & black 35 35
B399 " 18c+12c sal. & blk. 30 20
B400 " 20c+10c bl. & blk. 40 40
B401 " 40c+10c apple green & black 65 50
Nos. B397-B401 (5) 2.00 1.65

The surtax was for social and cultural purposes.

Child
SP180

Designs by Children: 10c+6c, Ship. 18c+12c, Woman (vert.). 20c+10c, Child, lake and swan. 40c+10c, Tractor.

1965, Nov. 16 Photo. *Perf. 14x13*

Gray Frame

B402 SP180 8c+6c multi. 14 12
B403 " 10c+6c " 70 70
B404 " 18c+12c " 25 12
a. Min. sheet of 11 7.50 8.00
B405 " 20c+10c multi. 80 80
B406 " 40c+10c " 90 80
Nos. B402-B406 (5) 2.79 2.54

The surtax was for child welfare. No. B404a contains five No. B402, six No. B404 and one label. Size: 141x124mm.

"Help them to a safe haven"
SP181

1966, Jan. 31 Photo. *Perf. 14x13*

B407 SP181 18c+7c black & org. yellow 40 45
B408 " 40c+20c black & red 60 30
a. Min. sheet of 3 1.75 1.10

The surtax was for the Intergovernmental Committee for European Migration (ICEM). The message on the stamps was given and signed by Queen Juliana. No. B408a contains one No. B407 and two Nos. B408. Size: 117x43mm.

Inkwell, Goose Quill and Book
SP182

Designs: 12c+8c, Fragment of Gysbert Japicx manuscript. 20c+10c, Knight on horseback, miniature from "Roman van Walewein" manuscript, 1350. 25c+10c, Initial "D" from "Ferguut" manuscript, 1350. 40c+20c, Print shop, 16th century woodcut.

1966, May 3 *Perf. 13x14*

B409 SP182 10c+5c multi. 55 40
B410 " 12c+8c multi. 55 40
B411 " 20c+10c " 70 50
B412 " 25c+10c " 85 75
B413 " 40c+20c " 85 70
Nos. B409-B413 (5) 3.50 2.75

Issued to commemorate the 300th anniversary of the death of Gysbert Japicx (1603-1666), Friesian poet, and the 200th anniversary of the founding of the Netherlands Literary Society.

The surtax was for social and cultural purposes.

Infant
SP183

Designs: 12c+8c, Daughter of the painter S. C. Lixenberg. 20c+10c, Boy swimming. 25c+10c, Dominga Blazer, daughter of Carel Blazer, photographer of this set. 40c+20c, Boy and horse.

1966, Nov. 15 Photo. *Perf. 14x13*

B414 SP183 10c+5c dp. org. & blue 20 15
B415 " 12c+8c apple grn. & red 20 15
B416 " 20c+10c brt. bl. & red 30 15
a. Min. sheet of 12 4.00 4.25
B417 " 25c+10c brt. rose lilac & dk. bl. 1.15 1.15
B418 " 40c+20c dp. car. & dk. green 1.15 1.15
Nos. B414-B418 (5) 3.00 2.75

The surtax was for child welfare. No. B416a contains four No. B414, five No. B415 and three No. B416. Size: 133x125mm.

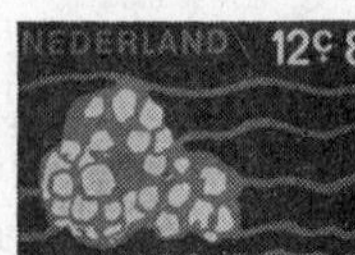

Whelk Eggs
SP184

Designs: 15c+10c, Whelk. 20c+10c, Mussel with acorn shells. 25c+10c, Jellyfish. 45c+20c, Crab.

Lithographed

1967, Apr. 11 *Perf. 14x13* Unwmkd.

B419 SP184 12c+8c olive grn. & tan 50 50
B420 SP184 15c+10c lt. blue, ultra. & black 50 50
B421 " 20c+10c gray, black & red 50 50
B422 " 25c+10c brn. car., plum & olive brown 1.00 1.00
B423 " 45c+20c multi. 1.00 1.00
Nos. B419-B423 (5) 3.50 3.50

Red Cross and Dates Forming Cross
SP185

"Lullaby for the Little Porcupine"
SP186

Designs (Red Cross and): 15c+10c, Crosses. 20c+10c, Initials "NRK" forming cross. 25c+10c, Maltese cross and crosses. 45c+20c, "100" forming cross.

1967, Aug. 8 *Perf. 14x13*

B424 SP185 12c+8c dull blue & red 50 40
B425 " 15c+10c red 65 65
B426 " 20c+10c olive & red 50 25
B427 " 25c+10c olive green & red 65 65
B428 " 45c+20c gray & red 1.00 1.00
Nos. B424-B428 (5) 3.30 2.95

Centenary of the Dutch Red Cross.

1967, Nov. 7 Litho. *Perf. 13x14*

Nursery Rhymes: 15c+10c, "Little Whistling Kettle." 20c+10c, "Dikkertje Dap and the Giraffe." 25c+10c, "The Nicest Flowers." 45c+20c, "Pippeljoentje, the Little Bear."

B429 SP186 12c+8c multi. 15 12
B430 " 15c+10c " 25 12
B431 " 20c+10c " 25 12
a. Min. sheet of 10 5.00 5.25
B432 " 25c+10c multi. 1.50 1.50
B433 " 45c+20c " 1.50 1.50
Nos. B429-B433 (5) 3.65 3.36

The surtax was for child welfare. No. B431a contains three No. B429, four No. B430 and three No. B431. Size: 149x108 mm.

St. Servatius Bridge, Maastricht
SP187

Bridges: 15c+10c, Narrow Bridge, Amsterdam. 20c+10c, Railroad Bridge, Culenborg. 25c+10c, Van Brienenoord Bridge, Rotterdam. 45c+20c, Zeeland Bridge, Schelde Estuary.

1968, Apr. 9 Photo. *Perf. 14x13*

B434 SP187 12c+8c green 1.10 1.00
B435 " 15c+10c olive brown 1.85 1.85
B436 " 20c+10c rose red 1.60 60
B437 " 25c+10c gray 1.60 1.60
B438 " 45c+20c ultra. 2.10 2.00
Nos. B434-B438 (5) 8.25 7.05

Goblin
SP188

Fairy Tale Characters: 15c+10c, Giant. 20c+10c, Witch. 25c+10c, Dragon. 45c+20c, Magician.

1968, Nov. 12 Photo. ***Perf. 14x13***

B439 SP188 12c+8c green, pink & black 40 18
B440 " 15c+10c blue, pink & black 55 18
B441 " 20c+10c blue, emerald & blk. 55 18
a. Min. sheet of 10 9.00 9.50
B442 " 25c+10c org. red, org. & black 4.00 3.75
B443 " 45c+20c yellow, org. & black 4.00 4.00
Nos. B439-B443 (5) 9.50 8.29

The surtax was for child welfare. No. B441a contains three No. B439, four No. B440 and three No. B441. Size: 107½x150mm.

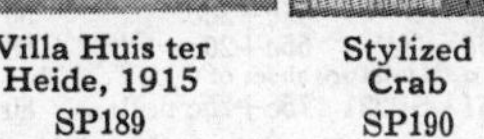

Villa Huis ter Heide, 1915
SP189

Stylized Crab
SP190

Contemporary Architecture: 15c+10c, House, Utrecht, 1924. 20c+10c, First open-air school, Amsterdam, 1960. 25c+10c, Burgweeshuis (orphanage), Amsterdam, 1960. 45c+20c, Netherlands Congress Building, The Hague, 1969.

1969, Apr. 15 Photo. ***Perf. 14x13***

B444 SP189 12c+8c lt. brown & slate 1.85 1.90
B445 " 15c+10c blue, gray & red 1.85 1.9
B446 " 20c+10c violet & black 1.85 2.25
B447 " 25c+10c green & gray 2.75 75
B448 " 45c+20c gray, bl. & yellow 3.75 3.75
Nos. B444-B448 (5) 12.05 10.55

1969, Aug. 12 Photo. ***Perf. 13x14***

B449 SP190 12c+8c violet 2.00 2.50
B450 " 25c+10c orange 3.00 75
B451 " 45c+20c bl. grn. 5.00 5.00

Issued to commemorate the 20th anniversary of the Queen Wilhelmina Fund. The surtax was for cancer research.

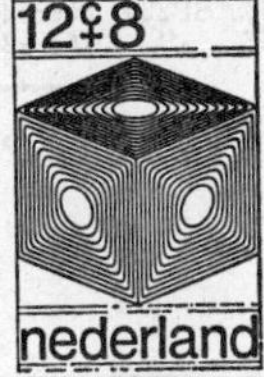

Child with Violin
SP191

Isometric Projection from Circle to Square
SP192

Designs: 12c+8c, Child with flute. 20c+10c, Child with drum. 25c+10c, Three children singing (horiz.). 45c+20c, Two girls dancing (horiz.).

Perf. 13x14, 14x13

1969, Nov. 11 Photogravure

B452 SP191 12c+8c ultra., blk. & yellow 30 15
B453 " 15c+10c black & red 35 20
B454 " 20c+10c red, black & yel. 5.75 5.00
B455 " 25c+10c yellow, black & red 40 15
a. Min. sheet of 10 10.00 10.00
B456 SP191 45c+20c green, black & red 5.75 5.00
Nos. B452-B456 (5) 12.55 10.50

The surtax was for child welfare. No. B455a contains 4 No. B452, 4 No. B453 and 2 No. B455. Size: 150x98mm.

Lithographed and Engraved

1970, Apr. 7 ***Perf. 13x14***

Designs made by Computer: 15c+10c, Parallel planes in a cube. 20c+10c, Two overlapping scales. 25c+10c, Transition phases of concentric circles with increasing diameters. 45c+20c, Four spirals.

B457 SP192 12c+8c yellow & black 2.65 2.65
B458 " 15c+10c silver & black 2.65 2.65
B459 " 20c+10c black 2.65 2.65
B460 " 25c+10c brt. blue & black 2.65 2.00
B461 " 45c+20c silver & white 3.00 3.00
Nos. B457-B461 (5) 13.60 12.95

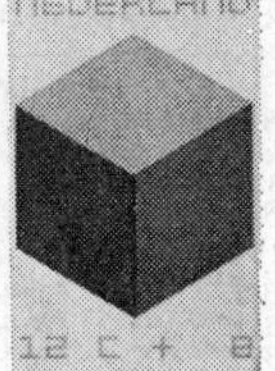

Bleeding Heart
SP193

Toy Block
SP194

1970, July 28 Photo. ***Perf. 13x14***

B462 SP193 12c+8c orange yellow, red & black 1.35 1.40
B463 " 25c+10c pink, red & black 1.35 80
B464 " 45c+20c bright green, red & black 1.35 1.40

The surtax was for the Netherlands Heart Foundation.

1970, Nov. 10 Photo. ***Perf. 13x14***

B465 SP194 12c+8c bl., violet blue & green 30 12
B466 " 15c+10c green, blue & yel. 2.75 2.25
B467 " 20c+10c lilac rose, red & vio. blue 3.00 3.00
B468 " 25c+10c red, yel. & lilac rose 60 12
a. Miniature sheet of 11 12.50 12.50
B469 SP194 45c+20c gray & black 5.00 4.75
Nos. B465-B469 (5) 11.65 10.24

The surtax was for child welfare. No. B468a contains nine No. B465, two No. B468 and a label with commemorative inscription. Size: 126x145mm.

St. Paul
SP195

Detail from Borobudur
SP196

Designs: 15c+10c, "50" and people. 25c+10c, Joachim and Ann. 30c+15c, John the Baptist and the Scribes. 45c+20c, St. Anne. The sculptures are wood, 15th century, and in Dutch museums.

1971, Apr. 20 Litho. ***Perf. 13x14***

B470 SP195 15c+10c multi. 2.50 2.50

Lithographed and Photogravure

B471 SP195 20c+10c gray, grn. & black 2.50 2.50
B472 SP195 25c+10c buff, org. & black 3.00 1.20
B473 " 30c+15c gray, blue & black 3.25 3.25
B474 " 45c+20c pink, verm. & blk 3.25 3.25
Nos. B470-B474 (5) 14.50 12.70

50th anniversary of the Federation of Netherlands Universities for Adult Education.

1971, June 29 Litho. ***Perf. 13x14***

B475 SP196 45c+20c purple, yel. & black 5.25 5.00

60th birthday of Prince Bernhard. Surtax for Save Borobudur Temple Fund.

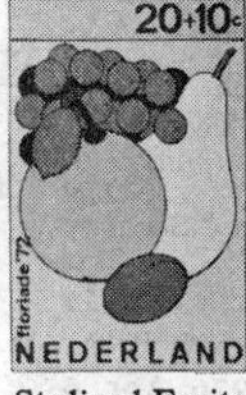

"Earth"
SP197

Stylized Fruits
SP198

Designs: 20c+10c, "Air" (butterfly). 25c+10c, "Sun" (horiz.). 30c+15c, "Moon" (horiz.). 45c+20c, "Water" (child looking at reflection).

Perf. 13x14, 14x13

1971, Nov. 9 Photogravure

B476 SP197 15c+10c black, lilac & orange 40 20
B477 " 20c+10c yel., blk. & rose lilac 1.00 80
B478 " 25c+10c multi. 85 30
a. Miniature sheet of 9 7.50 7.50
B479 SP197 30c+15c blue, blk. & purple 3.00 1.25
B480 " 45c+20c green, black & blue 4.50 4.75
Nos. B476-B480 (5) 9.75 7.30

The surtax was for child welfare. No. B478a contains 6 No. B476, one No. B477 and 2 No. B478. Size: 100x143mm.

Luminescence

Some semipostal issues from Nos. B481-B484 onward are tagged.

1972, Apr. 11 Litho. ***Perf. 13x14***

Multicolored

B481 SP198 20c+10c *shown* 2.25 2.50
B482 " 25c+10c *Flower* 2.50 2.75
B483 " 30c+15c *"Sunlit Landscape"* 2.25 1.00
B484 " 45c+25c *"Music"* 2.75 2.75

Summer festivals: Nos. B481-B482 publicize the Floriade, flower festival; Nos. B483-B484 the Holland Festival of Arts.

Red Cross, First Aid
SP199

Prince Willem-Alexander
SP200

Designs (Red Cross and): 25c+10c, Blood bank. 30c+15c, Disaster relief. 45c+25c, Child care.

1972, Aug. 15 Photo. ***Perf. 13x14***

B485 SP199 20c+10c bright pink & red 90 85
B486 " 25c+10c orange & red 90 1.00
B487 SP199 30c+15c black & red 1.20 50
B488 " 45c+25c ultra. & red 1.40 1.50

The surtax was for the Netherlands Red Cross.

Perf. 13x14, 14x13

1972, Nov. 7 Photogravure

Photographs of Dutch Princes: 30c+10c, Johan Friso. 35c+15c, Constantijn. 50c+20c, Johan Friso, Constantijn and Willem-Alexander. All are horizontal.

B489 SP200 25c+15c multi. 75 30
B490 " 30c+10c " 2.00 2.00
B491 " 35c+15c " 2.00 20
a. Miniature sheet of 7 9.50 9.50
B492 SP200 50c+20c " 3.50 3.50

Surtax was for child welfare. No. B491a contains 4 No. B489, 1 No. B490, 2 No. B491 and a label. Size: 124½x108mm.

"W. A. Scholten," 1874
SP201

Ships: 25c+15c, Flagship "De Seven Provincien," 1673 (vert.). 35c+15c, "Veendam," 1923. 50c+20c, Zuider Zee fish well boat, 17th century (vert.).

1973, Apr. 10 Lithographed

B493 SP201 25c+15c multi. 2.50 2.50
B494 " 30c+10c " 2.50 2.50
B495 " 35c+15c " 2.50 1.25
B496 " 50c+20c " 2.50 2.50

Tercentenary of the Battle of Kijkduin and centenary of the Holland-America Line.

nederland

25+15 cent

Chessboard
SP202

Games: 30c+10c, Tick-tack-toe. 40c+20c, Labyrinth. 50c+20c, Dominoes.

1973, Nov. 13 Photo. ***Perf. 13x14***

B497 SP202 25c+15c multi. 1.00 25
B498 " 30c+10c " 1.85 1.40
B499 " 40c+20c " 1.65 15
a. Miniature sheet of 6 9.00 9.00
B500 SP202 50c+20c multi. 3.50 3.50

Surtax was for child welfare. No. B499a contains 2 No. B497, 1 No. B498 and 3 No. B499. Size: 75x144mm.

Music Bands
SP203

Herman Heijermans
SP204

Designs: 30c+10c, Ballet dancers and traffic lights. 50c+20c, Kniertje, the fisher woman, from play by Heijermans.

1974, Apr. 23 Photo. ***Perf. 13x14***

B501 SP203 25c+15c multi. 1.00 1.00
B502 " 30c+10c " 1.00 1.00
B503 SP204 40c+20c " 1.25 60
B504 " 50c+20c " 1.25 1.40

Surtax was for various social and cultural institutions.

Boy with Hoop
SP205

Designs: 35c+20c, Girl and infant. 45c+20c, Two girls. 60c+20c, Girl sitting on balustrade. Designs are from turn-of-the-century photographs.

1974, Nov. 12 Photo. *Perf. 13x14*

B505	SP205	30c+15c black & brown	60	25
B506	"	35c+20c maroon	85	1.10
B507	"	45c+20c blk.brn.	1.10	25
		a. Miniature sheet of 6	5.00	5.00
B508	SP205	60c+20c indigo	1.75	1.75

Surtax was for child welfare. No. B507a contains 4 No. B505, one No. B506 and one No. B507. Size: 74x143mm.

Beguinage, Amsterdam
SP206

Cooper's Gate, Middelburg
SP207

Designs: 35c+20c, St. Hubertus Hunting Lodge (horiz.). 60c+20c, Orvelte Village (horiz.).

Perf. 14x12½, 12½x14

1975, Apr. 4 Lithographed

B509	SP206	35c+20c multi.	85	85
B510	"	40c+15c "	85	85
B511	SP207	50c+20c "	1.10	1.10
B512	"	60c+20c "	1.35	1.35

European Architectural Heritage Year 1975. Surtax was for various social and cultural institutions.

Orphans, Sculpture, 1785
SP208

Designs: 40c+15c, Milkmaid, 17th century. 50c+25c, Aymon's 4 sons on steed Bayard, 17th century. 60c+25c, Life at orphanage, 1557. All designs are after ornamental stones from various buildings.

1975, Nov. 11 Photo. *Perf. 14x12½*

B513	SP208	35c+15c multi.	85	85
B514	"	40c+15c "	85	85
B515	"	50c+25c "	1.10	1.10
		a. Miniature sheet of 5	3.50	3.50
B516	SP208	60c+25c multi.	1.35	1.35

Surtax was for child welfare. No. B515a contains 3 No. B513, 2 No. B515 and label with black inscription. Size: 143x74mm.

Hedgehog
SP209

Book with "ABC" and Grain; Open Field
SP210

Green Frog and Spawn
SP212

People and Initials of Social Security Acts
SP211

Perf. 14x12½, 12½x14

1976, Apr. 6 Lithographed

B517	SP209	40c+20c multi.	85	85
B518	SP210	45c+20c "	85	85
B519	SP211	55c+20c "	1.10	1.10
B520	SP212	75c+25c "	1.35	1.35

Surtax was for various social and cultural institutions. Nos. B517, B520 are for wildlife protection; No. B518 commemorates centenary of agricultural education and 175th anniversary of elementary education legislation; No. B519 commemorates 75th anniversary of social legislation and the Social Insurance Bank.

Patient Surrounded by Caring Hands
SP213

Netherlands No. 41
SP214

1976, Sept. 2 Litho. *Perf. 13x14*

B521	SP213	55c+25c multi.	1.35	1.10

Dutch Anti-Rheumatism Association, 50th anniversary.

1976, Oct. 8 Litho. *Perf. 13x14*

Designs: No. B523, Netherlands No. 64. No. B524, Netherlands No. 155. No. B525, Netherlands No. 294. No. B526, Netherlands No. 220.

B522	SP214	55c+55c multi.	1.35	1.35
B523	"	55c+55c "	1.35	1.35
B524	"	55c+55c "	1.35	1.35
B525	"	75c+75c "	1.65	1.65
B526	"	75c+75c "	1.65	1.65
		Nos. B522-B526 (5)	7.35	7.35

Amphilex 77 Philatelic Exhibition, Amsterdam, May 26–June 5, 1977. Nos. B522–B524 printed se-tenant in sheets of 90; Nos. B525–B526 printed checkerwise in sheets of 100.

Soccer
SP215

Designs (Children's Drawings): 45c+20c, Sailboat. 55c+20c, Elephant. 75c+25c, Mobile home.

1976, Nov. 16 Photo. *Perf. 14x13*

B527	SP215	40c+20c multi.	85	85
B528	"	45c+20c "	85	85
B529	SP215	55c+20c multi.	1.10	1.10
		a. Miniature sheet of 6	4.50	4.50
B530	SP215	75c+25c multi.	1.35	1.35

Surtax was for child welfare. No. B529a contains 2 each of Nos. B527–B529. Size: 144x75mm.

Hot Room, Thermal Bath, Heerlen
SP216

Designs: 45c+20c, Altar of Goddess Nehalennia, 200 A.D., Eastern Scheldt. 55c+20c, Part of oaken ship, Zwammerdam. 75c+25c, Helmet with face, Waal River at Nijmegen.

1977, Apr. 19 Photo. *Perf. 14x12½*

B531	SP216	40c+20c multi.	85	85
B532	"	45c+20c "	85	85
B533	"	55c+20c "	1.10	1.10
B534	"	75c+25c "	1.35	1.35

Archaeological finds of Roman period.

Type of 1976

Designs: No. B535, Netherlands No. 83. No. B536, Netherlands No. 128. No. B537, Netherlands No. 211. No. B538, Netherlands No. 302.

1977, May 26 Litho. *Perf. 13x14*

B535	SP214	55c+45c multi.	1.10	1.10
B536	"	55c+45c "	1.10	1.10
B537	"	55c+45c "	1.10	1.10
B538	"	55c+45c "	1.10	1.10
		a. Souvenir sheet of 2	1.75	1.75

Amphilex 77 International Philatelic Exhibition, Amsterdam May 26–June 5. Nos. B535–B536 and B537–B538 each printed se-tenant in sheets of 100. No. B538a contains one each of Nos. B535 and B538, gray margin with dark gray inscription. Size: 100x72mm. No. B538a sold at Exhibition only.

Risk of Drowning
SP217

Childhood Dangers: 45c+20c, Poisoning. 55c+20c, Following ball into street. 75c+25c, Playing with matches.

1977, Nov. 15 Photo. *Perf. 13x14*

B539	SP217	40c+20c multi.	60	60
B540	"	45c+20c "	65	65
B541	"	55c+20c "	75	75
		a. Miniature sheet of 6	4.25	4.25
B542	SP217	75c+25c multi.	1.00	1.00

Surtax was for child welfare. No. B541a contains 2 each of Nos. B539–B541. Size: 144x75mm.

Anna Maria van Schuurman
SP218

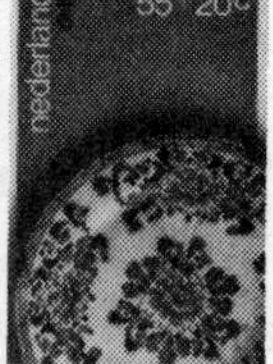

Delft Plate
SP219

Designs: 45c+20c, Part of letter written by author Belle van Zuylen (1740–1805). 75c+25c, Makkum dish with dog.

1978, Apr. 11 Litho. *Perf. 13x14*

B543	SP218	40c+20c multi.	45	20
B544	"	45c+20c "	50	25
B545	SP219	55c+20c "	58	30
B546	"	75c+25c "	80	35

Dutch authors and pottery products.

Red Cross and World Map
SP220

1978, Aug. 22 Photo. *Perf. 14x13*

B547	SP220	55c+25c multi.	65	32
		a. Souvenir sheet of 3	2.25	2.25

Surtax was for Dutch Red Cross. No. B547a has silver margin with black inscription. Size: 144x50mm.

Boy Ringing Doorbell
SP221

Designs: 45c+20c, Child reading book. 55c+20c, Boy writing "30x Children for Children" (vert.). 75c+25c, Girl at blackboard, arithmetic lesson.

Perf. 14x13, 13x14

1978, Nov. 14 Photogravure

B548	SP221	40c+20c multi.	45	20
B549	"	45c+20c "	50	25
B550	"	55c+20c "	58	30
		a. Miniature sheet of 6	3.25	3.25
B551	SP221	75c+25c multi.	80	35

Surtax was for child welfare. No. B550a contains 2 each of Nos. B548–B550. Size: 75x143mm.

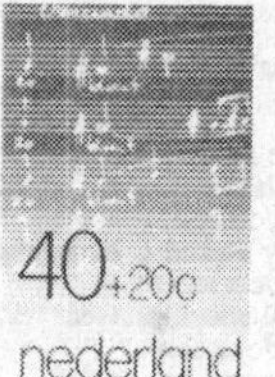

Psalm Trilogy, by Jurriaan Andriessen
SP222

Birth of Christ (detail) Stained-glass Window
SP223

Designs: 45c+20c, Amsterdam Toonkunst Choir. 75c+25c, William of Orange, stained-glass window, 1603. Windows from St. John's Church, Gouda.

1979, Apr. 5 Litho. *Perf. 13x14*

B552	SP222	40c+20c multi.	60	30
B553	"	45c+20c "	65	32
B554	SP223	55c+20c "	75	38
B555	"	75c+25c "	1.00	50

AIR POST STAMPS

Stylized Seagull
AP1

Typographed.

1921, May 1 *Perf. 12½* **Unwmkd.**
C1 AP1 10c red 2.65 1.40
C2 " 15c yellow green 10.00 2.75
C3 " 60c deep blue 27.50 25

Nos. C1–C3 were used to pay airmail fee charged by the carrier, KLM.

Lt. G. A. Koppen AP2 — Capt. Jan van der Hoop AP3

Wmkd. Circles. (202)

1928, Aug. 20 Litho. *Perf. 12*
C4 AP2 40c orange red 40 45
C5 AP3 75c blue green 40 45

Mercury AP4 — Queen Wilhelmina AP5

Engraved.

1929, July 16 *Perf. 11½* **Unwmkd.**
C6 AP4 1½g gray 3.75 2.50
C7 " 4½g carmine 2.25 5.00
C8 " 7½g blue green 50.00 6.50

Perf. 12½, 14x13½.

1931, Sept. 21 Photo. **Wmk. 202**
C9 AP5 36c orange red & dark blue 16.50 50

Fokker Pander—AP6

1933 *Perf. 12½.*
C10 AP6 30c dark green 45 75

Nos. C10–C12 were issued for use on special flights.

Crow in Flight—AP7

1938-53 *Perf. 13x14.*
C11 AP7 12½c dark blue & gray 20 40
C12 " 25c dark blue & gray ('53) 75 1.10

Seagull AP8 — Airplane AP9

Perf. 13x14

1951, Nov. 12 Engraved Unwmkd.
C13 AP8 15g gray 350.00 175.00
C14 " 25g blue gray 350.00 175.00

Lithographed

1966, Sept. 24 *Perf. 14x13*
C15 AP9 25c gray, blk. & blue 30 38

Issued for use on special flights.

MARINE INSURANCE STAMPS.

Floating Safe Attracting Gulls MI 1 — Floating Safe with Night Flare MI 2

Fantasy of Floating Safe
MI 3

Engraved.

1921 *Perf. 11½* **Unwmkd.**
GY1 MI 1 15c slate green 10.00 *100.00*
GY2 " 60c car. rose 10.00 *100.00*
GY3 " 75c gray brn. 15.00 *125.00*
GY4 MI 2 1.50g dark blue 225.00 *750.00*
GY5 " 2.25g org. brn. 500.00 *1000.00*
GY6 MI 3 4½g black 500.00 *1200.00*
GY7 " 7½g red 550.00 *1600.00*
Nos. GY1–GY7 (7) 1810.00 *4875.00*

POSTAGE DUE STAMPS.

Postage due types of Netherlands were also used for Curacao, Netherlands Indies and Surinam in different colors.

Numeral of Value
D1 — D2

Perf. 12½x12, 13 to 14

1870 Typographed Unwmkd.
J1 D1 5c brown, *orange* 70.00 14.00
a. Imperf., pair 500.00
J2 " 10c violet, *blue* 165.00 18.50
a. Imperf., pair 300.00

Type I. 34 loops. "T" of "BETALEN" over center of loop; top branch of "E" of "TE" shorter than lower branch.

Type II. 33 loops. "T" of "BETALEN" between two loops.

Type III. 32 loops. "T" of "BETALEN" slightly to the left of loop; top branch of first "E" of "BETALEN" shorter than lower branch.

Type IV. 37 loops. Letters of "PORT" larger than in the other three types.

Perf. 11½x12, 12½x12, 12½, 13½.

1881-87 Value in Black
J3 D2 1c light blue (III) 12.50 15.00
a. 1c light blue (I) 16.50 22.50
b. 1c light blue (II) 21.00 24.00
c. 1c light blue (IV 55.00 67.50
J4 " 1½c light blue (III) 15.00 18.00
a. 1½c light blue (I) 18.50 22.50
b. 1½c light blue (II) 25.00 30.00
c. 1½c light blue (IV) 80.00 90.00
J5 " 2½c light blue (III) 37.50 3.25
a. 2½c light blue (I) 45.00 4.00
b. 2½c light blue (II) 57.50 4.75
c. 2½c lt. blue (IV) 225.00 110.00
J6 " 5c light blue (III) ('87) 125.00 3.00
a. 5c light blue (I) 150.00 4.00
b. 5c light blue (II) 165.00 4.50
c. 5c lt. blue (IV) 2000.00 325.00
J7 " 10c lt. bl. (III) ('87) 140.00 3.25
a. 10c light blue (I) 175.00 4.25
b. 10c light blue (II) 185.00 4.75
c. 10c lt. blue (IV) 3000.00 375.00
J8 " 12½c light blue (III) 110.00 25.00
a. 12½c lt. blue (I) 130.00 35.00
b. 12½c lt. blue (II) 150.00 37.50
c. 12½c lt. blue (IV) 425.00 125.00
J9 " 15c lt. blue (III) 125.00 3.25
a. 15c light blue (I) 150.00 4.25
b. 15c light blue (II) 165.00 4.75
c. 15c lt. blue (IV) 190.00 27.50
J10 " 20c light blue (III) 28.00 3.25
a. 20c light blue (I) 40.00 4.25
b. 20c light blue (II) 45.00 5.50
c. 20c lt. blue (IV) 175.00 27.50
J11 " 25c lt. blue (III) 300.00 2.50
a. 25c light blue (I) 325.00 2.50
b. 25c lt. blue (II) 375.00 4.50
c. 25c lt. blue (IV) 650.00 175.00

Value in Red.
J12 D2 1g light blue (III) 100.00 22.50
a. 1g light blue (I) 110.00 30.00
b. 1g light blue (II) 135.00 35.00
c. 1g light blue (IV) 225.00 75.00

1894-1910 *Perf. 12½.*

Value in Black.
J13 D2 ½c dark blue (I) ('01) 12 15
J14 " 1c dark blue (I) 2.00 20
a. 1c dark blue (III) 3.25 3.25
J15 " 1½c dark blue (I) 70 25
a. 1½c dark blue (III 3.25 2.75
J16 " 2½c dark blue (I) 2.10 25
a. 2½c dark blue (III) 3.50 40
J17 " 3c dark blue (I) ('10) 2.00 1.35
J18 " 4c dark blue (I) ('09) 2.25 2.50
J19 " 5c dark blue (I) 16.00 20
a. 5c dark blue (III) 21.00 30
J20 " 6½c dark blue (I) ('07) 47.50 50.00
J21 " 7½c dark blue (I) ('04) 1.60 70
J22 " 10c dark blue (I) 42.50 35
a. 10c dark blue (III) 60.00 1.65
J23 " 12½c dark blue (I) 27.50 1.15
a. 12½c dark blue (III) 50.00 3.50
J24 " 15c dark blue (I) 42.50 90
a. 15c dark blue (III) 60.00 90
J25 " 20c dk. blue (I) ('96) 22.50 10.00
a. 20c dark blue (III) 22.50 10.00
J26 " 25c dark blue (I) 50.00 75
a. 25c dark blue (III) 55.00 75
Nos. J13–J26 (14) 259.27 68.75

Surcharged in Black **50 CENT**

1906 *Perf. 12½*
J27 D2 50c on 1g light blue (III) 165.00 165.00
a. 50c on 1g light blue (I) 175.00 175.00
b. 50c on 1g light blue (II) 185.00 185.00

Surcharged in Red **6½**

J28 D2 6½c on 20c dark blue (I) 6.00 6.25

1907

Nos. 87–89 Surcharged **PORTZEGEL**

CENT

J29 A13 ½c on 1c claret 1.75 2.00
J30 " 1c on 1c " 50 50
J31 " 1½c on 1c " 65 65
J32 " 2½c on 1c " 1.50 1.50
J33 A13 5c on 2½c verm. 1.65 50
J34 " 6½c on 2½c " 4.00 4.00
J35 " 7½c on ½c blue 2.25 1.50
J36 " 10c on ½c " 2.00 85
J37 " 12½c on ½c " 6.25 6.25
J38 " 15c on 2½c verm. 8.00 4.75
J39 " 25c on ½c blue 12.50 11.00
J40 " 50c on ½c " 55.00 50.00
J41 " 1g on ½c " 80.00 75.00
Nos. J29–J41 (13) 176.05 158.50

Two printings of the above surcharges were made. Some values show differences in the setting of the fractions; others are practically impossible to distinguish.

No. J20 Surcharged in Red

1909
J42 D2 4c on 6½c dark blue 7.25 8.00

No. J12, Surcharged in Black **3 CENT**

1910
J43 D2 3c on 1g light blue, type III 35.00 42.50
a. Type I 37.50 45.00
b. Type II 40.00 42.50

TYPE I.

1912-21 *Perf. 12½, 13½x13.*

Value in Color of Stamp.
J44 D2 ½c pale ultra. 7 10
J45 " 1c " ('13) 7 10
J46 " 1½c " ('15) 1.35 1.50
J47 " 2½c " 10 10
J48 " 3c " 50 50
J49 " 4c " ('13) 10 20
J50 " 4½c " ('16) 5.50 5.75
J51 " 5c " 10 10
J52 " 5½c " ('16) 5.50 5.75
J53 " 7c " ('21) 2.75 3.00
J54 " 7½c " ('13) 2.50 1.25
J55 " 10c " ('13) 12 10
J56 " 12½c " ('13) 20 20
J57 " 15c " ('13) 20 12
J58 " 20c " ('20) 25 12
J59 " 25c " ('17) 110.00 1.00
J60 " 50c " ('20) 55 20
Nos. J44–J60 (17) 129.86 20.09

D3

Typographed

1921-38 *Perf. 12½, 13½x12½*
J61 D3 3c pale ultra. ('28) 12 15
J62 " 6c " ('27) 15 15
J63 " 7c " ('28) 18 20
J64 " 7½c " ('26) 30 30
J65 " 8c " ('38) 18 20
J66 " 9c " ('30) 30 30
J67 " 11c ultramarine ('21) 14.00 4.25
J68 " 12c " ('28) 15 15
J69 " 25c " ('25) 20 12
J70 " 30c pale ultra. ('35) 30 12
J71 " 1g vermilion ('21) 85 15
Nos. J61–J71 (11) 16.73 6.09

Stamps of 1912–21 Surcharged

1923 *Perf. 12½*
J72 D2 1c on 3c ultramarine 30 50
J73 " 2½c on 7c " 30 35
J74 " 25c on 1½c " 11.00 45
J75 " 25c on 7½c " 11.00 25

D4 — D5

1924

J76	D4	4c on 3c olive grn.	1.20	1.50
J77	"	5c on 1c red	40	15
		a. Inverted surcharge	750.00	650.00
J78	"	10c on 1½c blue	90	18
		a. Tête bêche pair	11.00	11.00
J79	"	12½c on 5c carmine	90	22
		a. Tête bêche pair	12.50	12.50

The basic stamps of Nos. J76 and J79 are type A11; those of J77–J78 are type A10.

Stamps of type D4 of denominations of 11c on 22½c and 15c on 17½c exist. These were used by the postal service for accounting of parcel post fees.

Photogravure.

1947-58 *Perf. 13½x12½.* **Wmk. 202**

J80	D5	1c light blue	('48)	7	7
J81	"	3c "	('48)	7	14
J82	"	4c "		27.50	1.00
J83	"	5c "	('48)	7	7
J84	"	6c "	('50)	15	18
J85	"	7c "		15	12
J86	"	8c "	('48)	15	12
J87	"	10c "		15	7
J88	"	11c "		25	25
J89	"	12c "	('48)	30	25
J90	"	14c "	('53)	50	55
J91	"	15c "		35	7
J92	"	16c "		75	65
J93	"	20c "		35	7
J94	"	24c "	('57)	90	75
J95	"	25c "	('48)	35	7
J96	"	26c "	('58)	90	75
J97	"	30c "	('48)	65	7
J98	"	35c "		75	10
J99	"	40c "		90	7
J100	"	50c "	('48)	1.00	7
J101	"	60c "	('58)	1.35	30
J102	"	85c "	('50)	32.50	50
J103	"	90c "	('56)	3.25	35
J104	"	95c "	('57)	3.25	35
J105	"	1g carmine	('48)	2.50	7
J106	"	1.75g "	('57)	6.50	20
		Nos. J80–J106 (27)		85.61	7.26

OFFICIAL STAMPS.

Regular Issues of 1898–1908

Overprinted **ARMENWET**

1913 *Perf. 12½.* **Unwmkd.**

O1	A10	1c red	6.50	2.75
O2	"	1½c ultramarine	2.00	2.00
O3	"	2c yellow brown	11.00	10.00
O4	"	2½c deep green	22.50	16.00
O5	A11	3c olive green	6.50	1.00
O6	"	5c carmine rose	6.75	6.50
O7	"	10c gray lilac	80.00	72.50
		Nos. O1–O7 (7)	135.25	110.75

1918

Same Overprint in Red on No. 58

O8	A10	1½c dp. blue (R)	190.00	190.00

Nos. O1 to O8 were used to defray the postage on matter relating to the Poor Laws. Counterfeit overprints exist.

For the International Court of Justice.

Regular Issue of 1926–33 Overprinted in Gold

COURPER MANENTE DJUSTICE EJ INTER NATIONALE

Wmkd. Circles. (202)

1934 *Perf. 12½*

O9	A24	1½c red violet	80
O10	"	2½c deep green	80
O11	A23	7½c red	1.25
O12	A31	12½c deep ultramarine	35.00
O13	A23	15c orange	1.50
O14	"	30c violet	2.50
		a. Perf. 13½x12½	2.50
		Nos. O9–O14 (6)	41.85

Same Overprint on No. 180 in Gold.

1937 *Perf. 13x12½.*

O15	A23	12½c ultramarine	12.50

Nos. O9–O15 were sold to the public only canceled. Uncanceled, they were obtainable only by favor of an official.

Same on Regular Issue of 1940 Overprinted in Gold.

1940 *Perf. 13½x12½.*

O16	A45	7½c bright red	30.00	12.50
O17	"	12½c sapphire	30.00	12.50
O18	"	15c light blue	30.00	12.50
O19	"	30c bistre	30.00	12.50

Nos. 217 to 219, 221 and 223 Overprinted in Gold

COUR INTERNATIONALE DE JUSTICE

1947

O20	A45	7½c bright red	70
O21	"	10c bright red violet	70
O22	"	12½c sapphire	70
O23	"	20c purple	70
O24	"	25c rose brown	70
		Nos. O20–O24 (5)	3.50

O1

Photogravure

1950 *Perf. 14½x13½* **Unwmkd.**

O25	O1	2c ultramarine	1100.00	3.50
O26	"	4c olive green	1100.00	3.50

Palace of Peace, The Hague

O2

Queen Juliana

O3

1951-58 *Perf. 12½x12*

O27	O2	2c red brown	30
O28	"	3c ultramarine ('53)	20
O29	"	4c deep green	20
O30	"	5c olive brown ('53)	20
O31	"	6c olive green ('53)	25
O32	"	7c red ('53)	20

Engraved.

O33	O3	6c brown violet	3.00
O34	"	10c dull green	12
O35	"	12c rose red	15
O36	"	15c rose brown ('53)	15
O37	"	20c dull blue	20
O38	"	25c violet brown	50
O39	"	30c rose lilac ('58)	60
O40	"	1g slate gray	80
		Nos. O27–O40 (14)	6.87

1977, May Photo. *Perf. 12½x12*

O41	O2	40c brt. greenish blue	30
O42	"	45c brick red	35
O43	"	50c brt. rose lilac	40

Note after No. O15 also applies to Nos. O20–O43.

See "Special Notices" at the front of this volume for data on the listing methods of this Catalogue, abbreviations, condition, prices and examination.

NETHERLANDS ANTILLES (Curaçao)

(kōō'rä-sä'ō; kū'rȧ-sō')

LOCATION—Two groups of islands lying 500 miles apart in the West Indies, north of Venezuela.

AREA—393 sq. mi.

POP.—240,000 (est. 1976).

CAPITAL—Willemstad.

Formerly a colony named Curacao, Netherlands Antilles became an integral part of the Kingdom of the Netherlands under the Constitution of 1954.

100 Cents = 1 Gulden

King William III

A1

Numeral

A2

Regular Perf. 11½, 12½, 11½x12, 12½x12, 13½x13, 14.

1873 Typographed **Unwmkd.**

1	A1	2½c green	4.00	8.25
		a. Bluish paper	8.00	13.00
		b. Perf. 14, small holes	11.00	16.00
2	"	3c bistre	47.50	150.00
		a. Bluish paper	50.00	135.00
		b. Perf. 14, small holes	52.50	165.00
3	"	5c rose	6.25	7.50
		a. Bluish paper	7.00	10.50
		b. Perf. 14, small holes	10.00	16.00
4	"	10c ultramarine	52.50	15.00
		a. Bluish paper	55.00	60.00
		b. Perf. 14, small holes	57.50	80.00
5	"	25c brown orange	37.50	7.50
		a. Bluish paper	40.00	40.00
		b. Perf. 14, small holes	57.50	47.50
6	"	50c violet	1.75	3.25
		a. Bluish paper	25.00	27.50
		b. Perf. 14, small holes	27.50	37.50
7	"	2.50g bistre & purple	25.00	25.00

The gulden denominations, Nos. 7 and 12, are of larger size.

Perf. 11½, 12½, 12½x12, 13½.

1886-89

8	A1	12½c yellow	75.00	37.50
9	"	15c olive	20.00	14.00
10	"	30c pearl gray	32.50	45.00
11	"	60c olive bistre	35.00	14.00
12	"	1.50g lt. & dk. blue	100.00	90.00

Nos. 1–12 were issued without gum until 1890. Imperfs. exist.

1889 *Perf. 12½*

13	A2	1c gray	1.00	1.10
14	"	2c violet	65	1.30
15	"	2½c green	4.00	2.25
16	"	3c bistre	4.00	4.50
17	"	5c rose	16.50	1.20

King William III

A3

Queen Wilhelmina

A4

Black Surcharge, Handstamped

Without Gum

1891 *Perf. 12½x12*

18	A3	25c on 30c pearl gray	15.00	18.00

No. 18 exists with double surcharge, price $225, and with inverted surcharge, price $275.

1892-93 *Perf. 12½*

19	A4	10c ultramarine	1.00	1.30
20	"	12½c green	32.50	7.50
21	"	15c rose	3.00	3.25
22	"	25c brown orange	90.00	7.00
23	"	30c gray	3.00	13.00

King William III

A5 A6

Perf. 12½, 13½

Magenta Surcharge, Handstamped

1895

25	A5	2½c on 10c ultra.	12.00	7.75

Perf. 12½x12

Black Surcharge, Handstamped

26	A6	2½c on 30c gray	135.00	6.50

Nos. 25–26 exist with surcharge double or inverted. Prices: No. 25, double $275 and $200; inverted $350 and $250. No. 26, double $275, inverted $550.

No. 26 and No. 25, perf. 13½, were issued without gum.

Queen Wilhelmina

A7 A8

1901 *Perf. 12½, 11½x11*

Black Surcharge.

27	A7	25c on 25c car. & bl.	1.25	1.25
28	A8	1.50(g) on 2.50g brown lilac	20.00	25.00

1902 *Perf. 12½*

29	A7	12½c on 12½c blue	32.50	9.50

A9

A10

1903-08

30	A9	1c olive green	1.40	90
31	"	2c yellow brown	16.00	4.75
32	"	2½c blue green	4.75	40
		a. Booklet pane of 6		
33	"	3c orange	9.50	4.75
34	"	5c rose red	8.50	40
35	"	7½c gray ('08)	40.00	8.50
36	A10	10c slate	15.00	4.75
37	"	12½c deep blue	1.50	22
		a. Booklet pane of 6		
38	"	15c brown	20.00	13.50
39	"	22½c brown & olive ('08)	20.00	11.00
40	"	25c violet	20.00	2.50
41	"	30c brown orange	50.00	19.00
42	"	50c red brown	40.00	12.50
		Nos. 30-42 (13)	246.65	83.07

Queen Wilhelmina

A11

1906 Without Gum *Perf. 11½*

No.	Type	Description	Unused	Used
43	A11	1½g red brown	50.00	32.50
44	"	2½g slate blue	50.00	32.50

A12

Queen Wilhelmina
A13 A14

Perf. 12½, 11½, 11x11½, 11

1915–33 Typographed

No.	Type	Description	Unused	Used
45	A12	½c lilac ('20)	65	1.00
46	"	1c olive green	25	20
47	"	1½c blue ('20)	20	18
48	"	2c yellow brown	1.75	1.75
		a. Diagonal half used as 1c on cover		6.50
49	"	2½c green	1.25	22
		a. Diagonal half used as 1c on cover		12.50
50	"	3c yellow	1.75	1.90
51	"	3c green ('26)	2.75	3.25
52	"	5c rose	1.75	18
53	"	5c green ('22)	3.25	3.75
54	"	5c lilac ('26)	1.40	20
55	"	7½c drab	2.75	2.25
56	"	7½c bistre ('20)	1.50	18
		a. Booklet pane of 6		
57	"	10c lilac ('22)	5.50	6.00
58	"	10c rose ('26)	5.50	1.75
59	A13	10c carmine rose	16.50	3.75
60	"	12½c blue	2.10	75
61	"	12½c red ('22)	1.85	2.00
		a. Booklet pane of 6		
62	"	15c olive green	70	1.00
63	"	15c light blue ('26)	4.25	3.25
		a. Booklet pane of 6		
64	"	20c blue ('22)	8.50	3.75
		a. Booklet pane of 6		
65	"	20c olive green ('26)	2.40	3.25
66	"	22½c orange	1.85	3.25
67	"	25c red violet	4.00	1.25
68	"	30c slate	4.00	1.90
69	"	35c slate & red ('22)	3.75	5.75

Engraved.

Perf. 11½x11, 11½, 12½, 11

No.	Type	Description	Unused	Used
70	A14	50c green	3.50	30
71	"	1½g violet	18.50	15.00
72	"	2½g carmine	30.00	30.00
		a. Perf. 12½ ('33)	200.00	450.00
		Nos. 45-72 (28)	132.15	98.01

Some stamps of 1915 were issued without gum.

A15

Laid Paper, without Gum.

1918, July 16 Typo. *Perf. 12*

No.	Type	Description	Unused	Used
73	A15	1c *buff*	7.50	4.25

"HAW" are the initials of Postmaster H. A. Willemsen.

No. 60 Surcharged in Black — 5 CENT

1918, Sept. 1

No.	Type	Description	Unused	Used
74	A13	5c on 12½c blue	6.25	3.00
		a. "5" 2⅓mm. wide	70.00	37.50
		b. Double surch.		600.00

The "5" of No. 74 is 3mm. wide. Illustration shows No. 74a surcharge.

Queen Wilhelmina
A16 A17

1923 Engr. *Perf. 11½, 11x11½*

No.	Type	Description	Unused	Used
75	A16	5c green	90	2.50
76	"	7½c olive green	1.10	2.00
77	"	10c carmine rose	1.50	2.50
78	"	20c indigo	2.60	4.50
		a. Perf. 11x11½	3.75	5.25
79	"	1g brown violet	40.00	27.50
80	"	2½g gray black	100.00	*250.00*
81	"	5g brown	125.00	*300.00*
		a. Perf. 11x11½	1000.00	1000.00
		Nos. 75-81 (7)	271.10	*589.00*

Issued to commemorate the 25th anniversary of the assumption of the government of the Netherlands by Queen Wilhelmina, at the age of 18.

Types of Netherlands Marine Insurance Stamps, Inscribed "CURACAO" Surcharged in Black — FRANKEER = ZEGEL = 10 CENT

1927, Oct. 3

No.	Type	Description	Unused	Used
87	MI 1	3c on 15c dk. grn.	25	33
88	"	10c on 60c carmine rose	30	40
89	"	12½c on 75c gray brown	33	40
90	MI 2	15c on 1.50g dk. bl.	4.25	4.25
		a. Double surch.	*600.00*	
91	"	25c on 2.25g orange brown	9.00	9.00
92	MI 3	30c on 4½g black	16.50	15.00
93	"	50c on 7½g red	10.00	10.00
		Nos. 87-93 (7)	40.63	39.38

Nos. 90, 91 and 92 have "FRANKEERZEGEL" in one line of small capitals. Nos. 90 and 91 have a heavy bar across the top of the stamp.

1928–30 Engr. *Perf. 11½, 12½.*

No.	Type	Description	Unused	Used
95	A17	6c orange red ('30)	2.00	38
		a. Booklet pane of 6		
96	"	7½c orange red	90	75
97	"	10c carmine	2.10	65
98	"	12½c red brown	2.10	1.75
		a. Booklet pane of 6		
99	"	15c dark blue	2.00	50
		a. Booklet pane of 6		
100	"	20c blue black	7.50	1.00
101	"	21c yel. grn. ('30)	13.00	14.00
102	"	25c brown violet	4.75	2.50
103	"	27½c black ('30)	16.50	17.50
104	"	30c deep green	7.50	1.00
105	"	35c brownish black	2.75	3.50
		Nos. 95-105 (11)	61.10	43.53

No. 96 Surcharged in Black — 6 ct. — Bars over original value.

1929, Nov. 1

No.	Type	Description	Unused	Used
106	A17	6c on 7½c org. red	1.65	1.25
		a. Inverted surcharge	375.00	350.00

No. 51 Surcharged in Red — 2½

1931, Mar. 1 *Perf. 12½*

No.	Type	Description	Unused	Used
107	A12	2½c on 3c green	1.25	1.50

No. 49 Surcharged in Red — 1½

1932

No.	Type	Description	Unused	Used
108	A12	1½c on 2½c green	3.75	4.00

Prince William I, Portrait by Van Key
A18

1933 *Perf. 12½*

No.	Type	Description	Unused	Used
109	A18	6c deep orange	2.25	1.75

Issued in commemoration of the 400th anniversary of the birth of Prince William I, Count of Nassau and Prince of Orange, frequently referred to as William the Silent.

Willem Usselinx A19 — Frederik Hendrik A20

Jacob Binckes—A21 — Van Walbeeck's Ship—A22

Cornelis Evertsen the Younger A23 — Louis Brion A24

1934, Jan. 1 Engr. *Perf. 12½*

No.	Type	Description	Unused	Used
110	A19	1c black	1.50	1.75
111	"	1½c dull violet	1.15	50
112	"	2c orange	1.50	1.75
113	A20	2½c dull green	1.25	1.85
114	"	5c black brown	1.25	1.25
115	"	6c violet blue	1.15	38
116	A21	10c lake	3.00	1.40
117	"	12½c bistre brown	9.00	9.00
118	"	15c blue	2.50	1.50
119	A22	20c black	4.50	3.00
120	"	21c brown	17.50	22.50
121	"	25c dull green	16.00	15.00
122	A23	27½c brown violet	22.50	25.00
123	"	30c scarlet	16.00	6.50
124	"	50c orange	16.00	9.50
125	A24	1.50g indigo	90.00	87.50
126	"	2.50g yellow green	95.00	62.50
		Nos. 110-126 (17)	299.80	250.88

Issued in commemoration of the third centenary of the founding of the colony.

Numeral A25 — Queen Wilhelmina A26

1936 Photo. *Perf. 13½x12½*

Size: 18x22mm.

No.	Type	Description	Unused	Used
127	A25	1c brown black	25	25
128	"	1½c deep ultramarine	28	20
129	"	2c orange	35	38
130	"	2½c green	30	30
131	"	5c scarlet	30	12

Engraved *Perf. 12½*

Size: 20¼x30½mm.

No.	Type	Description	Unused	Used
132	A26	6c brown violet	75	12
133	"	10c orange red	1.50	25
134	"	12½c dk. blue green	2.25	1.30
135	"	15c dark blue	1.65	70
136	"	20c orange yellow	1.65	80
137	"	21c dark gray	3.25	3.25
138	"	25c brown lake	2.25	1.25
139	"	27½c violet brown	3.75	3.75
140	"	30c olive brown	90	25

Perf. 12½x14

Size: 22x33mm.

No.	Type	Description	Unused	Used
141	A26	50c dull yel. green	4.25	30
		a. Perf. 14	55.00	30
142	"	1.50g black brown	30.00	25.00
		a. Perf. 14	55.00	27.50
143	"	2.50g rose lake	17.50	11.50
		a. Perf. 14	17.50	11.50
		Nos. 127-143 (17)	71.18	49.72

See also Nos. 147-151.

Queen Wilhelmina
A27

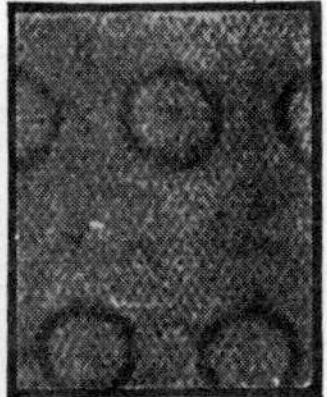

Wmk. 202

Wmkd. Circles. (202)

1938, Aug. 27 Photo. *Perf. 12½x12*

No.	Type	Description	Unused	Used
144	A27	1½c dull purple	25	38
145	"	6c red orange	1.00	1.00
146	"	15c royal blue	1.75	1.75

Issued in commemoration of the 40th anniversary of the reign of Queen Wilhelmina.

Numeral Type of 1936 and

Queen Wilhelmina
A28

Typographed.

1941–42 *Perf. 12½* **Unwmkd.**

Thick Paper.

Size: 17¾x22mm.

No.	Type	Description	Unused	Used
147	A25	1c gray brn. ('42)	1.00	1.25
148	"	1½c dull blue ('42)	10.00	25
149	"	2c lt. orange ('42)	5.50	5.00
150	"	2½c green ('42)	50	50
151	"	5c crimson ('42)	50	50

Photo. *Perf. 12½, 13*

Size: 18½x23mm.

No.	Type	Description	Unused	Used
152	A28	6c rose violet	3.00	4.50
153	"	10c red orange	1.75	1.25
154	"	12½c light green	2.60	90
155	"	15c bright ultra.	5.25	2.75
156	"	20c orange	50	65
157	"	21c gray	2.50	2.00
158	"	25c brown lake	2.75	2.25
159	"	27½c deep brown	3.50	4.25
160	"	30c olive bistre	13.50	4.25

Size: 21x26½mm.

No.	Type	Description	Unused	Used
161	A28	50c olive grn. ('42)	15.00	20
162	"	1½g gray olive ('42)	18.50	1.25
163	"	2½g rose lake ('42)	16.50	1.50
		Nos. 147-163 (17)	102.85	33.25

See also Nos. 174-187.

Bonaire
A29

St. Eustatius
A30

Designs: 2c, View of Saba. 2½c, St. Maarten. 5c, Aruba. 6c, Curacao.

Perf. 13x13½, 13½x13.

1943 Engraved. Unwmkd.

164	A29	1c rose violet & orange brown	12	15
165	A30	1½c deep blue & yellow green	20	20
166	A29	2c slate black & orange brown	75	40
167	"	2½c green & orange	30	35
168	"	5c red & slate black	1.15	28
169	"	6c rose lilac & light blue	75	90
		Nos. 164-169 (6)	3.27	2.28

Royal Family
A35

1943, Nov. 2 ***Perf. 13½x13***

170	A35	1½c deep orange	8	8
171	"	2½c red	18	20
172	"	6c black	1.00	80
173	"	10c deep blue	1.15	1.10

Issued in honor of Princess Margriet Francisca of the Netherlands.

Wilhelmina Type of 1941.

1947 Photogravure. ***Perf. 13½x12½***

Size: 18x22mm.

174	A28	6c brown violet	1.75	2.75
175	"	10c orange red	1.75	2.75
176	"	12½c dark blue green	1.75	2.75
177	"	15c dark blue	1.75	2.75
178	"	20c orange yellow	1.75	4.25
179	"	21c dark gray	2.25	3.00
180	"	25c brown lake	25	20
181	"	27½c chocolate	1.75	2.00
182	"	30c olive bistre	2.00	1.15
183	"	50c dull yel. green	2.50	20

Engraved

Perf. 13½.

Size: 25x31¼mm.

184	A28	1½g dark brown	1.25	75
185	"	2½g rose lake	30.00	8.00
186	"	5g olive green	150.00	175.00
187	"	10g red orange	180.00	275.00
		Nos. 174-187 (14)	378.75	480.55

Used prices for Nos. 186-187 are for genuinely canceled copies clearly dated before the end of 1949.

Queen Wilhelmina
A36 A37

Photogravure.

1948 ***Perf. 13½x12½.*** **Unwmkd.**

188	A36	6c dark vio. brown	1.25	1.50
189	"	10c scarlet	1.25	2.00
190	"	12½c dark blue green	1.25	1.25
191	"	15c deep blue	1.25	1.50
192	"	20c red orange	1.25	2.60
193	"	21c black	1.25	2.60
194	"	25c bright red violet	50	18
195	"	27½c henna brown	25.00	25.00
196	"	30c olive brown	20.00	1.25
197	"	50c olive green	20.00	33

Engraved.

Perf. 12½x12.

198	A37	1.50g chocolate	30.00	6.25
		Nos. 188-198 (11)	103.00	44.46

Queen Wilhelmina Queen Juliana
A38 A39

1948, Aug. 30 ***Perf. 13x14***

199	A38	6c vermilion	75	75
200	"	12½c deep blue	75	75

Issued to commemorate the 50th anniversary of the reign of Queen Wilhelmina.

Perf. 14x13

1948, Oct. 18 Photo. Wmk. 202

201	A39	6c red brown	90	65
202	"	12½c dark green	90	65

Investiture of Queen Juliana, Sept. 6, 1948. Nos. 201-202 were issued in Netherlands Sept. 6.

Ship of Ojeda Alonso de Ojeda
A40 A41

Perf. 14x13, 13x14

1949, July Photo. Unwmkd.

203	A40	6c olive green	6.75	3.00
204	A41	12½c brown red	8.50	5.25
205	A40	15c ultramarine	9.00	3.75

Issued to commemorate the 450th anniversary of the discovery of Curacao by Alonso de Ojeda, 1499.

Post Horns Entwined
A42

1949, Oct. 3 ***Perf. 11½x12½***

206	A42	6c brown red	5.00	4.00
207	"	25c dull blue	6.25	1.75

Issued to commemorate the 75th anniversary of the formation of the Universal Postal Union.

A43

Queen Juliana
A44 A45

1950-79 Photo. ***Perf. 12½x13½***

208	A43	1c red brown	12	15
209	"	1½c blue	8	6
210	"	2c orange	15	10
211	"	2½c green	1.50	25
212	"	3c purple	15	10
212A	"	4c yellow green ('59)	55	55
213	"	5c dark red	12	6

Perf. 13½x12½

214	A44	6c deep plum	1.00	10
215	"	7½c red brown ('54)	5.50	10
216	"	10c red	1.65	12
		a. Redrawn ('79)	15	4
217	A44	12½c dark green	2.00	15
218	"	15c deep blue	2.00	18
		a. Redrawn ('79)	22	6
219	A44	20c orange	2.50	18
		a. Redrawn ('79)	30	8
220	A44	21c black	2.75	2.10
221	"	22½c bl. green ('54)	7.25	10
222	"	25c violet	2.25	12
		a. Redrawn ('79)	38	10
223	A44	27½c henna brown	4.00	2.75
224	"	30c olive brown	4.00	15
225	"	50c olive green	4.25	10

Engraved.

Perf. 12½x12.

226	A45	1½g slate green	13.00	35
227	"	2½g black brown	22.50	1.35
228	"	5g rose red	60.00	15.00
229	"	10g dark violet brown	115.00	60.00
		Nos. 208-229 (23)	252.32	84.12

Nos. 216a, 218a, 219a and 222a are from booklets Nos. 427a and 428a. Background design is sharper and stamps have one or two straight edges.

Fort Beekenburg
A46

Perf. 13x12½

1953, June 16 Unwmkd.

230	A46	22½c olive brown	3.75	65

Issued to commemorate the 250th anniversary of the founding of Fort Beekenburg.

Beach at Aruba—A47

1954, May 1 ***Perf. 11x11½***

231	A47	15c dark blue, salmon & deep blue	4.75	3.50

Issued to publicize the third congress of the Caribbean Tourist Association, Aruba, May 3-6, 1954.

Queen Juliana—A48

1954, Dec. 15 ***Perf. 13½***

232	A48	7½c olive green	1.00	1.00

Issued to publicize the Charter of the Kingdom, adopted December 15, 1954. See also Netherlands No. 366 and Surinam No. 264.

Beach—A49

Petroleum Refinery, Aruba
A50

1955, Dec. 5 Litho. ***Perf. 12***

233	A49	15c chestnut, blue & emerald	3.75	3.25
234	A50	25c chestnut, blue & emerald	4.25	3.75

Caribbean Commission, 21st meeting, Aruba.

St. Annabaai Harbor and Flags
A51

Perf. 14x12½

1956, Dec. 6 Unwmkd.

235	A51	15c light blue, black & red	60	50

Caribbean Commission, 10th anniversary.

Man Watching Rising Sun
A52

1957, Mar. 14 Photo. ***Perf. 11x11½***

236	A52	15c brn., blk. & yel.	60	55

Issued to publicize the First Caribbean Mental Health Conference, Aruba, March 14-19, 1957.

Saba
A53

Views: 15c, St. Maarten. 25c, St. Eustatius.

1957, July 1 Litho. ***Perf. 14x12½***

237	A53	7½c multicolored	75	75
238	"	15c "	75	75
239	"	25c "	75	75

Issued to publicize these islands as tourist attractions.

Curacao Intercontinental Hotel
A54

1957, Oct. 12 *Perf. 14x13*

240 A54 15c light ultramarine 55 50

Issued to mark the opening of the Intercontinental Hotel, Willemstad.

Map of Curacao
A55

1957, Dec. 10 *Perf. 14x13½*

241 A55 15c indigo & lt. blue 1.25 1.25

International Geophysical Year.

Flamingoes, Bonaire—A56

Designs: 7½c, 8c, 25c, 1½g, Old buildings, Curacao. 10c, 5g, Extinct volcano and palms, Saba. 15c, 30c, 1g, Fort Willem III, Aruba. 20c, 35c, De Ruyter obelisk, St. Eustatius. 12c, 40c, 2½g, Town Hall, St. Maarten.

Lithographed.

1958-59 *Perf. 14x13* **Unwmkd.**

Size: 33x22mm.

242 A56 6c light olive green & pink 15.00 12
243 " 7½c red brn. & orange 12 15
244 " 8c dark blue & orange ('59) 12 20
245 " 10c gray & org. yellow 16 6
246 " 12c bluish green & gray ('59) 20 25
247 " 15c green & light ultramarine 25 12
a. 15c green & lilac 25 12
248 A56 20c crimson & gray 32 12
249 " 25c Prussian blue & yellow green 40 12
250 " 30c brn. & blue grn. 48 15
251 " 35c gray & rose ('59) 55 30
252 " 40c magenta & green 65 15
253 " 50c grayish brown & pink 80 15
254 " 1g bright red & gray 1.60 25
255 " 1½g rose violet & pale brown 2.40 30
256 " 2½g blue & citron 4.00 50
257 " 5g light red brown & rose lilac 8.00 1.50
Nos. 242-257 (16) 35.05 4.44

See also Nos. 340-348, 400-403.

Globe—A57

1958, Oct. 16 *Perf. 11x11½*

258 A57 7½c blue & lake 38 45
259 " 15c red & ultramarine 65 50

Issued to commemorate the 50th anniversary of the Netherlands Antilles Radio and Telegraph Administration.

Hotel Aruba Caribbean
A58

1959, July 18 *Perf. 14x13*

260 A58 15c multicolored 55 50

Issued to mark the opening of the Hotel Aruba Caribbean, Aruba.

Sea Water Distillation Plant
A59

1959, Oct. 16 Photo. *Perf. 14x13*

261 A59 20c bright blue 75 75

Opening of sea water distillation plant at Balashi, Aruba.

Netherlands Antilles Flag
A60

1959, Dec. 14 Litho. *Perf. 13½*

262 A60 10c ultra. & red 50 50
263 " 20c ultra., yel. & red 65 75
264 " 25c ultramarine, green & red 65 50

Issued to commemorate the 5th anniversary of the new constitution (Charter of the Kingdom).

Fokker "Snip" and Map of Caribbean
A61

Designs: 20c, Globe showing route flown, and plane. 25c, Map of Atlantic ocean and view of Willemstad. 35c, Map of Atlantic ocean and plane on Aruba airfield.

Perf. 14x13

1959, Dec. 22 **Unwmkd.**

265 A61 10c yellow, light & dark blue 50 65
266 " 20c yellow, light & dark blue 75 65
267 " 25c yellow, light & dark blue 75 38
268 " 35c yellow, light & dark blue 75 90

25th anniversary of Netherlands-Curacao air service.

Msgr. Martinus J. Niewindt
A62

1960, Jan. 12 Photo. *Perf. 13x13½*

269 A62 10c deep claret 65 65
270 " 20c deep violet 80 90
271 " 25c olive green 85 65

Issued to commemorate the centenary of the death of Monsignor Niewindt, first apostolic vicar for Curacao.

Worker, Flag and Factories
A63

1960, Apr. 29 *Perf. 12½x13*

272 A63 20c multicolored 75 65

Issued for Labor Day, May 1, 1960.

U.S. Brig "Andrew Doria" and Gun at Fort Orange, St. Eustatius—A64

1961, Nov. 16 Litho. *Perf. 14x13*

273 A64 20c blue, red, green & black 1.25 1.10

185th anniversary of first salute by a foreign power to the U.S. flag flown by an American ship.

Silver Wedding Issue
Type of Netherlands, 1962

1962, Jan. 31 Photo. *Perf. 14x13*

274 A92 10c deep orange 30 30
275 " 25c deep blue 70 70

Issued to commemorate the silver wedding anniversary of Queen Juliana and Prince Bernhard.

Benta Player
A65

Designs: 6c, Corn masher. 20c, Petji kerchief. 25c, "Jaja" (nurse) with child, sculpture.

1962, Mar. 14 Photo. *Perf. 12½*

276 A65 6c red brown & yel. 25 25
277 " 10c multicolored 33 25
278 " 20c crimson, indigo & bright green 55 50
279 " 25c bright green, brown & gray 65 50
a. Souv. sheet of 4 2.75 3.25

No. 279a contains one each of Nos. 276-279 with deep blue marginal inscription. Size: 108x134mm.

Emblem of Family Relationship
A66

Design: 25c, Emblem of mental health (cross).

1963, Apr. 17 Litho. *Perf. 14x13*

280 A66 20c dk bl. & ocher 75 75
281 " 25c blue & red 90 1.00

Fourth Caribbean Conference for Mental Health, Curacao, Apr. 17-23.

Dove with Olive Branch
A67

1963, July 1 **Unwmkd.**

282 A67 25c orange yellow & dark brown 70 70

Centenary of emancipation of the slaves.

Hotel Bonaire
A68

1963, Aug. 31 *Perf. 14x13*

283 A68 20c dk. red brown 50 50

Opening of Hotel Bonaire on Bonaire.

Prince William of Orange Taking Oath of Allegiance
A69

1963, Nov. 21 Photo. *Perf. 13x13½*

284 A69 25c green, blk. & rose 55 65

Issued to commemorate the 150th anniversary of the founding of the Kingdom of the Netherlands.

Chemical Equipment
A70

1963, Dec. 10 Litho. *Perf. 13½x13*

285 A70 20c blue green, brt. yel. grn. & red 1.00 1.25

Opening of chemical factories on Aruba.

Airmail Letter and Wings
A71

Design: 25c, Map of Caribbean, Miami-Curacao route and planes of 1929 and 1964.

1964, June 22 Photo. *Perf. 11x11½*

286 A71 20c light blue, red & ultramarine 75 75
287 " 25c light green, blue, red & black 75 90

Issued to commemorate the 35th anniversary of the first regular Curacao airmail service.

Map of the Caribbean
A72

1964, Nov. 30 Photo. Unwmkd.

288 A72 20c ultra., org. & dark red 55 65

Issued to commemorate the fifth meeting of the Caribbean Council, Curacao, Nov. 30–Dec. 4.

Netherlands Antilles Flags, Map of Curacao and Crest—A73

1964, Dec. 15 Litho. *Perf. 11½x11*

289 A73 25c lt. blue & multi. 65 65

Issued to commemorate the 10th anniversary of the Charter of the Kingdom of the Netherlands. The flags, shaped like seagulls, represent the six islands comprising the Netherlands Antilles.

Princess Beatrix
A74

Perf. 13½x14

1965, Feb. 22 Photo. Unwmkd.

290 A74 25c brick red 90 90

Visit of Princess Beatrix of Netherlands.

ITU Emblem, Old and New Communication Equipment
A75

1965, May 17 Litho. *Perf. 13½*

291 A75 10c brt. bl. & dk. blue 38 38

Issued to commemorate the centenary of the International Telecommunication Union.

Shell Refinery, Curacao
A76

Designs: 10c, Catalytic cracking installation (vert.). 25c, Workers operating manifold, primary distillation plant (vert.).

Perf. 13x14, 14x13

1965, June 22 Photogravure

292 A76 10c blk., red & yel. 40 40
293 " 20c multicolored 40 40
294 " 25c " 50 50

Issued to commemorate the 50th anniversary of the oil industry in Curacao.

Floating Market, Curacao
A77

Designs (flag and): 2c, Divi-divi tree and Haystack Mountain, Aruba. 3c, Lace, Saba. 4c, Flamingoes, Bonaire. 5c, Church ruins, St. Eustatius. 6c, Lobster, St. Maarten.

Perf. 14x13

1965, Aug. 25 Litho. Unwmkd.

295 A77 1c light green, ultra. & red 12 12
296 " 2c yel., ultra. & red 10 10
297 " 3c chalky blue, ultra. & red 10 10
298 " 4c org., ultra. & red 12 12
299 " 5c light blue, ultra. & red 10 10
300 " 6c pink, ultra. & red 12 10
Nos. 295-300 (6) 66 64

Marine Guarding Beach
A78

1965, Dec. 10 Photo. *Perf. 13x10½*

301 A78 25c multicolored 50 55

Issued to commemorate the 300th anniversary of the Netherlands Marine Corps.

Budgerigars, Wedding Rings and Initials
A79

1966, March 10 Photo. *Perf. 13x14*

302 A79 25c gray & multi. 50 55

Issued to commemorate the marriage of Princess Beatrix and Claus van Amsberg.

M. A. de Ruyter and Map of St. Eustatius
A80

1966, July 19 Photo. *Perf. 13x13½*

303 A80 25c violet, ocher & light blue 50 55

Visit of Adm. Michiel Adriaanszoon de Ruyter (1607–1676) to St. Eustatius, 1666.

Liberal Arts and Grammar
A81

Designs: 10c, Rhetoric and dialectic. 20c, Arithmetic and geometry. 25c, Astronomy and music.

Perf. 13x12½

1966, Sept. 19 Litho. Unwmkd.

304 A81 6c yel., bl. & black 15 12
305 " 10c yellow green, red & black 20 22
306 " 20c bl., yel. & black 35 40
307 " 25c red, yellow green & black 40 40

25th anniversary of secondary education.

Cruiser
A82

Ships: 10c, Sailing ship. 20c, Tanker. 25c, Passenger ship.

Perf. 13x14

1967, Mar. 29 Litho. Unwmkd.

308 A82 6c lt. & dark green 20 20
309 " 10c orange & brown 20 20
310 " 20c sepia & brown 30 30
311 " 25c chalky blue & dark blue 35 35

Issued to commemorate the 60th anniversary of *Onze Vloot* (Our Fleet), an organization which publicizes the Dutch navy and merchant marine and helps seamen.

Manuel Carlos Piar
A83

Discobolus after Myron
A84

1967, Apr. 26 Photo. *Perf. 14x13*

312 A83 20c red & black 40 45

Issued to commemorate the 150th anniversary of the death of Manuel Carlos Piar (1777–1817), independence hero.

1968, Feb. 19 Litho. *Perf. 13x14*

Designs: 10c, Hand holding torch, and Olympic rings. 25c, Stadium, doves and Olympic rings.

313 A84 10c multicolored 50 50
314 " 20c dark brown, olive & yellow 65 50
315 " 25c bl., dk. blue & brt. yel. green 65 65

Issued to commemorate the 19th Olympic Games, Mexico City, Oct. 12–27.

Map of Bonaire, Radio Mast and Waves
A85

Code of Law
A86

1969, Mar. 6 Litho. *Perf. 14x13*

316 A85 25c blue, emerald & black 55 60

Issued to publicize the opening of the relay station of the Dutch World Broadcasting System on Bonaire.

1969, May 19 Photo. *Perf. 12½x13*

Designs: 25c, Scales of Justice.

317 A86 20c dk. green, yellow green & gold 50 55
318 A86 25c violet blue, blue & gold 50 55

Court of Justice, centenary.

ILO Emblem, Cactus and House
A87

1969, Aug. 25 Litho. *Perf. 14x12½*

319 A87 10c blue & black 38 38
320 " 25c dk. red & black 65 65

ILO, 50th anniversary.

Charter, 15th Anniversary Issue

Type of Netherlands

1969, Dec. 15 Photo. *Perf. 14x13*

321 A116 25c blue & multi. 70 70

Issued to commemorate the 15th anniversary of the Charter of the Kingdom of the Netherlands. Phosphorescent paper.

Radio Bonaire Studio and Transmitter
A88

Design: 15c, Radio waves and cross set against land, sea and air.

1970, Feb. 5 Photo. *Perf. 12½x13*

322 A88 10c multicolored 38 38
323 " 15c " 38 38

Issued to commemorate the 5th anniversary of the opening of the Trans World Missionary Radio Station, Bonaire.

Altar, St. Anna's Church, Otraband 1752
A89

Designs: 20c, Interior, Synagogue at Punda, 1732 (horiz.). 25c, Pulpit, Fort Church, Fort Amsterdam, 1769.

Perf. 13½x14, 14x13½

1970, May 12 Photogravure

324 A89 10c gold & multi. 38 38
325 " 20c " " 50 50
326 " 25c " " 65 50

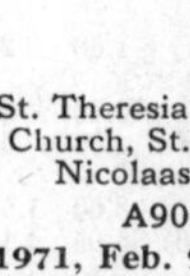

St. Theresia Church, St. Nicolaas
A90

1971, Feb. 9 Litho. *Perf. 14x13½*

327 A90 20c dull blue, gray & rose 70 70

40th anniversary of the Parish of St. Theresia at St. Nicolaas, Aruba.

Lions Emblem
A91

1971, Feb. 24 *Perf. 13½*

328 A91 25c dk. blue & multi. 90 90

Lions Club in the Netherlands Antilles, 25th anniversary.

Prince Bernhard Type of Netherlands

1971, June 29 Photo. *Perf. 13x14*

329 A123 45c multicolored 1.35 1.35

60th birthday of Prince Bernhard.

Pedro Luis Brion
A92

1971, Sept. 27 Photo. *Perf. 13x12½*

330 A92 40c multicolored 90 80

Sesquicentennial of the death of Admiral Pedro Luis Brion (1782–1821), naval commander in fight for South American independence.

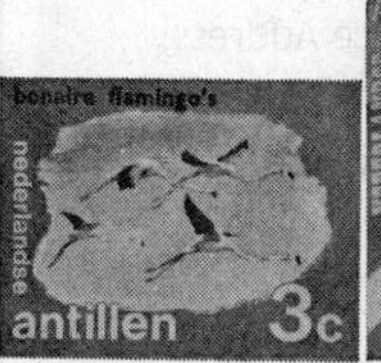

Flamingoes, Bonaire
A93

Ship in Dry Dock
A94

Designs: 1c, Queen Emma Bridge, Curaçao. 2c, The Bottom, Saba. 4c, Water tower, Aruba. 5c, Fort Amsterdam, St. Maarten. 6c, Fort Orange, St. Eustatius.

1972, Jan. 17 Litho. *Perf. 13½x14*

331 A93 1c yellow & multi. 10 10
332 " 2c yel. grn. & multi. 10 10
333 " 3c dp. org. & multi. 10 10
334 " 4c brt. bl. & multi. 10 10
335 " 5c red org. & multi. 10 10
336 " 6c lilac rose & multi. 10 10
Nos. 331–336 (6) 60 60

1972, Apr. 7 *Perf. 14x13½*

337 A94 30c bl. gray & multi. 75 65

Inauguration of large dry dock facilities in Willemstad.

Juan Enrique Irausquin
A95

Costa Gomez
A96

1972, June 20 Photo. *Perf. 12½x14*

338 A95 30c deep orange 75 70

10th anniversary of the death of Juan Enrique Irausquin (1904–1962), financier and patriot.

1972, Oct. 27 Litho. *Perf. 12½x14*

339 A96 30c yel. grn. & blk. 75 70

65th anniversary of the birth of Moises Frumencio da Costa Gomez (1907–1966), lawyer, legislator, patriot.

Island Series Type of 1958–59

Designs: 45c, 85c, Extinct volcano and palms, Saba. 55c, 90c, De Ruyter obelisk, St. Eustatius. 65c, 75c, 10g, Flamingoes, Bonaire. 70c, Fort Willem III, Aruba. 95c, Town Hall, St. Maarten.

1973, Feb. 12 Litho. *Perf. 14x12½*

Size: 33x22mm.

340 A56 45c vio. bl. & lt. blue 70 12
341 " 55c dk. carmine rose & emerald 85 15
342 " 65c green & pink 1.10 15
343 " 70c gray vio. & org. 1.15 16
344 " 75c brt. lilac & sal. 1.20 18
345 " 85c brown olive & apple green 1.40 18
346 " 90c blue & ocher 1.45 20
347 " 95c orange & yellow 1.50 25
348 " 10g bright ultra. & salmon 16.00 6.00
Nos. 340–348 (9) 23.35 7.39

Mailman
A97

Designs: 15c, King William III from 1873 issue. 30c, Emblem of Netherlands Antilles postal service.

1973, May 23 Photo. *Perf. 12½x14*

349 A97 15c lilac, gold & vio. 50 40
350 " 20c dk. grn. & multi. 50 50
351 " 30c orange & multi. 50 50

Centenary of first stamps of Netherlands Antilles.

Cable Linking Aruba, Curacao and Bonaire
A98

Designs: 30c, 6 stars symbolizing the islands, and cable. 45c, Saba, St. Maarten and St. Eustatius linked by cable.

1973, June 20 Litho. *Perf. 14x12½*

352 A98 15c multicolored 50 40
353 " 30c " 65 65
354 " 45c " 75 75
a. Souvenir sheet of 3 2.25 2.10

Inauguration of the inter-island submarine cable. No. 354a contains one each of Nos. 352–354. Prussian blue marginal inscription. Size: 144x50mm.

Queen Juliana Type of Netherlands

Design: 15c, Queen Juliana, Netherlands Antilles and House of Orange colors.

Engraved & Lithographed

1973, Sept. 4 *Perf. 13x12*

355 A136 15c silver & multi. 75 65

25th anniversary of reign of Queen Juliana.

Jan Hendrik Albert Eman
A99

Lionel Bernard Scott
A100

1973, Oct. 17 Litho. *Perf. 12½x14*

356 A99 30c light yellow green & black 70 65

Jan Hendrik Albert Eman (1888–1957), founder of the People's Party in Aruba, member of Antillean Parliament.

1974, Jan. 28 *Perf. 12½x14*

357 A100 30c lt. blue & multi. 70 65

Lionel Bernard Scott (1897–1966), architect and statesman.

Family at Supper
A101

Designs: 12c, Parents watching children at play. 15c, Mother and daughter sewing, father and son gardening.

1974, Feb. 18 Litho. *Perf. 12½x14*

358 A101 6c blue & multi. 12 10
359 " 12c bister & multi. 38 32
360 " 15c brt. grn. & multi. 40 40

Planned parenthood and World Population Year.

Desulphurization Plant, Lago
A102

Designs: 30c, Distillation plant. 45c, Lago refinery at night.

1974, Aug. 12 Litho. *Perf. 14x12½*

361 A102 15c lt. blue, black & yellow 50 50
362 " 30c lt. blue, black & yellow 65 50
363 " 45c dk. brn. & multi. 65 65

Oil industry in Aruba, 50th anniversary.

UPU Emblem
A103

1974, Oct. 9 Litho. *Perf. 12½x14*

364 A103 15c yel. grn., blk. & gold 50 50
365 " 30c bl., blk. & gold 65 65

Centenary of Universal Postal Union.

Queen Emma Bridge
A104

Willemstad Bridges: 30c, Queen Juliana Bridge. 40c, Queen Wilhelmina Bridge.

1975, Feb. 5 Litho. *Perf. 14x12½*

366 A104 20c ultra. & multi. 75 65
367 " 30c " " 75 75
368 " 40c " " 75 75

Dedication of new Queen Juliana Bridge spanning Curacao Harbor.

Salt Crystals
A105

Designs: 20c, Solar salt pond. 40c, Map of Bonaire and location of solar salt pond (vert.).

Perf. 14x12½, 12½x14

1975, Apr. 24 Lithographed

369 A105 15c multicolored 50 40
370 " 20c " 65 65
371 " 40c " 65 65

Bonaire's salt industry.

Aruba Airport, 1935 and Fokker F-18
A106

Designs: 30c, Aruba Airport, 1950, and Douglas DC-9. 40c, New Princess Beatrix Airport and Boeing 727.

1975, June 19 Litho. *Perf. 14x13*

372 A106 15c violet & multi. 40 40
373 " 30c black & multi. 65 50
374 " 40c yellow & multi. 65 65

40th anniversary of Aruba Airport.

International Women's Year Emblem
A107

Designs: 12c, "Women's role in social development." 20c, Embryos within female and male symbols.

1975, Aug. 1 Photo. *Perf. 14x13*

375 A107 6c multicolored 25 25
376 " 12c " 50 40
377 " 20c " 50 50

International Women's Year 1975.

Beach, Aruba
A108

Designs: No. 379, Beach pavilion and boat, Bonaire. No. 380, Table Mountain and Spanish Water, Curacao.

1976, June 21 Litho. *Perf. 14x13*

378 A108 40c blue & multi. 75 75
379 " 40c " " 90 75
380 " 40c " " 90 75

Tourist publicity.

Julio Antonio Abraham
A109

Dike and Produce
A110

1976, Aug. 10 Photo. *Perf. 13x14*

381 A109 30c tan & claret 55 50

Julio Antonio Abraham (1909–1960), founder of Democratic Party of Bonaire.

1976, Sept. 21 Lithographed

Designs: 35c, Cattle. 45c, Fish.

382 A110 15c multicolored 38 25
383 " 35c car. & black 65 65
384 " 45c yel., org. & blk. 75 75

Agriculture, husbandry and fishing in Netherlands Antilles.

Plaque, Fort Oranje Memorial
A111

Designs: 40c, Andrew Doria in St. Eustatius harbor receiving salute. 55c, Johannes de Graaff, Governor of St. Eustatius, holding Declaration of Independence.

1976, Nov. 16 Litho. *Perf. 14x12½*

385 A111 25c multicolored 65 50
386 " 40c " 75 65
387 " 55c " 90 1.00

First gun salute to U.S. flag, St. Eustatius, Nov. 16, 1776.

Dancer with Cactus Headdress — A112
Bird Petroglyph, Aruba — A113

Designs: 35c, Woman in feather costume. 40c, Woman in pompadour costume.

1977, Jan. 20 Litho. *Perf. 12½x14*

388 A112 25c multicolored 50 50
389 " 35c " 65 50
390 " 40c " 65 65

Carnival.

1977, Mar. 29 Litho. *Perf. 12½x14*

Indian Petroglyphs: 35c, Loops and spiral, Savonet Plantation, Curacao. 40c, Tortoise, Onima, Bonaire.

391 A113 25c red & multi. 38 38
392 " 35c brn. & multi. 50 50
393 " 40c yellow & multi. 65 65

Cordia Sebestena — A114
Chimes, Spritzer & Fuhrmann Building — A115

Tropical Trees: 40c, East Indian walnut (vert.). 55c, Tamarind.

Perf. 14x13, 13x14

1977, July 20 Lithographed

394 A114 25c black & multi. 50 50
395 " 40c " " 65 65
396 " 55c " " 90 90

1977, Sept. 27 Litho. *Perf. 13½x14*

Designs: 40c, Globe with Western Hemisphere and sun over Curacao. 55c, Diamond ring and flag of Netherlands Antilles.

397 A115 20c brt. green & multicolored 50 50
398 " 40c yellow & multi. 65 65
399 " 55c blue & multi. 90 90

Spritzer & Fuhrmann, jewelers of Netherlands Antilles, 50th anniversary.

Type of 1958–59

Designs: 20c, 35c, 55c, De Ruyter obelisk, St. Eustatius. 40c, Town Hall, St. Maarten.

1977, Nov. 30 *Perf. 13½ Horiz.*

Size: 39x22mm

400 A56 20c crimson & gray 40 30
a. Bklt. pane of 6 (2 #400, 4 #402) 4.00
401 A56 35c gray & rose 75 50
a. Bklt. pane of 4 (1 #401, 3 #403) 3.25
402 A56 40c magenta & grn. 40 30
403 " 55c dk. carmine rose & emerald 82 70

Nos. 400–403 issued in booklets only. No. 400a has label with red inscription in size of 3 stamps; No. 401a has label with dark carmine rose inscription in size of 2 stamps.

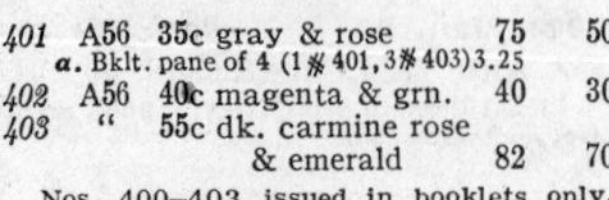

Winding Road, Map of Saba
A116

Designs: 35c, Ruins of Synagogue, map of St. Eustatius. 40c, Greatbay, Map of St. Maarten.

1977, Nov. 30 Litho. *Perf. 14x13*

404 A116 25c multicolored 38 25
405 " 35c " 52 40
406 " 40c " 60 48

Tourist publicity.

Treasure Chest
A117

Designs: 20c, Logo of Netherlands Antilles Bank. 40c, Safe deposit door.

1978, Feb. 7 Litho. *Perf. 14x13*

407 A117 15c brt. & dk. blue 22 15
408 " 20c orange & gold 30 20
409 " 40c brt. & dk. grn. 60 45

Bank of Netherlands Antilles, 150th anniversary.

Flamboyant — A118
Polythysana Rubrescens — A119

Flowers: 25c, Erythrina velutina. 40c, Guaiacum officinale (horiz.). 55c, Gliricidia sepium (horiz.).

Perf. 13x14, 14x13

1978, May 31 Lithographed

410 A118 15c multicolored 22 18
411 " 25c " 38 28
412 " 40c " 60 42
413 " 55c " 82 60

1978, June 20 *Perf. 13x14*

Butterflies: 25c, Caligo eurilochus. 35c, Prepona omphale amesis. 40c, Morpho aega.

414 A119 15c multicolored 22 18
415 " 25c " 38 28
416 " 35c " 52 38
417 " 40c " 60 42

"Conserve Energy"
A120

1978, Aug. 31 Litho. *Perf. 13x14*

418 A120 15c orange & black 22 15
419 " 20c dp. grn. & blk. 30 22
420 " 40c dk. red & black 60 42

Morse Ship-to-Shore Service
A121

Designs: 40c, Ship-to-shore telex service. 55c, Future radar-satellite service (vert.).

Perf. 14x13, 13x14

1978, Oct. 16 Lithographed

421 A121 20c multicolored 30 20
422 " 40c " 60 42
423 " 55c " 82 60

70th anniversary of ship-to-shore communications.

Villa Maria Waterworks
A122

Designs: 35c, Leonard B. Smith (vert.). 40c, Opening of Queen Emma Bridge, Willemstadt, 1888.

1978, Dec. 13

424 A122 25c multicolored 38 28
425 " 35c " 52 38
426 " 40c " 60 42

Leonard B. Smith, engineer, 80th death anniversary.

Queen Juliana Type of 1950.

Perf. 13½x12½

1979, Jan. 11 Photogravure

427 A44 5c deep yellow 8 3
a. Bklt. pane of 10 (4 #427, 1 #216a, 2 #222a, 3 #429) 3.25
428 A44 30c brown 45 10
a. Bklt. pane of 10 (1 #428, 4 #218a, 3 #219a, 2 #222a) 3.25
429 A44 40c bright blue 60 15

Nos. 427–429 issued in booklets only. Nos. 427a–428a have 2 labels and selvages the size of 6 stamps. Background design of booklet stamps sharper than 1950 issue. All stamps have 1 or 2 straight edges.

Goat and Conference Emblem
A123

Designs: 75c, Horse and map of Curacao. 150c, Cattle, Netherlands Antilles flag, U.N. and Conference emblems.

1979, Apr. 18 Litho. *Perf. 14x13*

437 A123 50c multicolored 75 75
438 " 75c " 1.15 1.15
439 " 150c " 2.25 2.25
a. Souvenir sheet of 3 4.30 4.30

12th Inter-American Meeting at Ministerial Level on Foot and Mouth Disease and Zoonosis Control, Curacao, Apr. 17–20. No. 439a contains Nos. 437–439.

SEMI-POSTAL STAMPS

NIWIN

Nos. 132, 133 and 135 Surcharged in Black

1½ ct. + 2½ ct.

1947 *Perf. 12½* **Unwmkd.**

B1	A26	1½c+2½c on 6c brown violet	1.00	1.10
B2	"	2½c+5c on 10c orange red	1.00	1.10
B3	"	5c+7½c on 15c dark blue	1.00	1.10

The surtax was for the National Inspanning Welzijnszorg in Nederlandsch Indie, relief organization for Netherlands Indies.

Curaçao Children

SP1 SP2

SP3

1948 Photogravure *Perf. 12½x12*

B4	SP1	6c+10c olive brn.	2.75	2.10
B5	SP2	10c+15c bright red	2.75	2.10
B6	SP3	12½c+20c Prus. grn.	2.75	2.25
B7	SP1	15c+25c brt. blue	2.75	2.50
B8	SP2	20c+30c red brown	2.75	2.75
B9	SP3	25c+35c purple	2.75	2.75
		Nos. B4-B9 (6)	16.50	14.45

The surtax was for crippled children.

Leapfrog SP4 — Ship and Gull SP5

Designs: 5c+2½c, Flying kite. 6c+2½c, Girls swinging. 12½c+5c, "London Bridge." 25c+10c, Rolling hoops.

1951 *Perf. 14x13.* **Unwmkd.**

B10	SP4	1½c+1c purple	2.50	3.00
B11	"	5c+2½c brown	10.00	6.50
B12	"	6c+2½c blue	10.00	6.50
B13	"	12½c+5c red	10.00	6.50
B14	"	25c+10c dull grn.	10.00	6.00
		Nos. B10-B14 (5)	42.50	28.50

The surtax was for child welfare.

1952 *Perf. 12½x13½.*

Designs: 6c+4c, Sailor and lighthouse. 12½c+7c, Prow of sailboat. 15c+10c, Ships. 25c+15c, Ship, compass and anchor.

Inscribed: "Zeemanswelvaren."

B15	SP5	1½c+1c dark grn.	1.25	1.50
B16	"	6c+4c chocolate	8.50	4.50
B17	"	12½c+7c red violet	8.50	5.00
B18	"	15c+10c dp. blue	10.00	5.75
B19	"	25c+15c red	10.00	4.50
		Nos. B15-B19 (5)	38.25	21.25

The surtax was for the seamen's welfare fund.

No. 226 Surcharged in Black

22½ Ct. +7½ Ct. WATERSNOOD NEDERLAND 1953

1953

B20	A45	22½c+7½c on 1½g slate green	1.50	1.65

The surtax was for flood relief in the Netherlands.

Tribulus Cistoides SP6

Flowers: 7½c + 5c, Yellow hibiscus. 15c + 5c, Oleander. 22½c+7½c, Cactus. 25c+10c, Red hibiscus.

1955 Photogravure *Perf. 14x12½*

Flowers in Natural Colors

B21	SP6	1½c+1c blue green & dark blue	60	65
B22	"	7½c+5c deep ultramarine	4.00	3.00
B23	"	15c+5c olive green	4.00	3.25
B24	"	22½c+7½c dark blue	4.00	3.00
B25	"	25c+10c indigo & gray	4.00	3.25
		Nos. B21-B25 (5)	16.60	13.15

The surtax was for child welfare.

Prince Bernhard and Queen Juliana

SP7

1955 *Perf. 11x11½*

B26	SP7	7½(c)+2½(c) rose brown	25	38
B27	"	22½(c)+7½(c) deep blue	1.75	1.50

Issued to commemorate the royal visit to the Netherlands Antilles, October 1955.

Lord Baden-Powell SP8

1957, Feb. 22 *Perf. 13½x13*

B28	SP8	6c+1½c org. yellow	90	75
B29	"	7½c+2½c deep green	90	1.00
B30	"	15c+5c red	1.00	1.00

Issued to commemorate the 50th anniversary of the Boy Scout movement.

Soccer Player SP9

Map of Central America and the Caribbean

SP10

Designs: 15c+5c, Goalkeeper catching ball. 22½c+7½c, Men playing soccer.

1957 *Perf. 11½x11, 11x11½*

B31	SP9	6c+2½c orange	90	1.00
B32	SP10	7½c+5c dark red	1.50	1.40
B33	SP9	15c+5c bright blue green	1.65	1.65
B34	"	22½c+7½c brt. blue	1.65	1.50

Issued to publicize the Eighth Central American and Caribbean Soccer Championships, Aug. 11-25.

American Kestrel SP11 — Flag and Map SP12

Birds: 7½+1½c, Yellow oriole. 15+2½c, Common ground doves. 22½+2½c, Brown-throated parakeet.

1958, Apr. 15 Photo. *Perf. 13x13½*

B35	SP11	2½+1c multicolored	38	38
B36	"	7½+1½c "	1.25	1.10
B37	"	15+2½c "	1.40	1.50
B38	"	22½+2½c "	1.50	1.50

The surtax was for child welfare.

1958, Dec. 1 **Unwmkd.**

Cross in Red

B39	SP12	6c+2c red brown	65	65
B40	"	7½c+2½c bl. green	1.00	90
B41	"	15c+5c org. yellow	90	75
B42	"	22½c+7½c blue	1.00	1.00

The surtax was for the Red Cross.

Community House, Zeeland

SP13

Designs (historic buildings): 7½c+2½c, Molenplein. 15c+5c, Saba (vert.). 22½c+7½c, Scharlooburg. 25c+7½c, Community House, Brievengat.

Perf. 13½x13, 13x13½

1959, Sept. 16 **Lithographed**

B43	SP13	6c+1½c multi.	1.50	1.25
B44	"	7½c+2½c "	1.50	1.50
B45	"	15c+5c "	1.50	1.50
B46	"	22½c+7½c "	1.50	1.50
B47	"	25c+7½c "	1.50	1.50
		Nos. B43-B47 (5)	7.50	7.25

The surtax went to the Foundation for the Preservation of Historical Monuments.

Fish—SP14

Designs: 10c+2c, Skin diver with spear-gun (vert.). 25c+5c, Two fish.

1960, Aug. 24 **Photogravure**

B48	SP14	10c+2c sapphire	1.60	1.60
B49	"	20c+3c multi.	1.90	1.90
B50	"	25c+5c black, bright pink & dark blue	1.90	1.90

The surtax was for the fight against cancer.

Infant

SP15

Designs: 10c+3c, Girl and doll. 20c+6c, Boy on beach. 25c+8c, Children in school.

Lithographed

1961, July 24 *Perf. 13x13½*

Designs in Black.

B51	SP16	6c+2c lt. yellow green	65	50
B52	"	10c+3c rose red	80	75
B53	"	20c+6c yellow	80	90
B54	"	25c+8c orange	90	90

The surtax was for child welfare.

Globe and Knight

SP16

1962, May 2 *Perf. 13x14*

B55	SP16	10c+5c green	1.10	1.10
B56	"	20c+10c carmine	1.20	1.10
B57	"	25c+10c dark blue	1.20	1.10

Issued to commemorate the International Candidates Chess Tournament, Willemstad, May–June.

No. 248 Surcharged

TEGEN DE HONGER

+10c

1963, Mar. 21 *Perf. 13½x13*

B58	A56	20c+10c crim. & gray	1.25	1.35

Issued for the "Freedom from Hunger" campaign of the U.N. Food and Agriculture Organization.

Child and Flowers SP17 — Bougainvillea SP18

Designs: 6c+3c, Three girls and flowers (horiz.). 10c+5c, Girl with ball and trees (horiz.). 20c+10c, Three boys with flags (horiz.). 25c+12c, Singing boy.

Perf. 14x13, 13x14

1963, Oct. 23 Photo. **Unwmkd.**

B59	SP17	5c+2c multi.	50	65
B60	"	6c+3c "	50	65
B61	"	10c+5c "	65	65

B62	SP17	20c+10c multi.	65	80
B63	"	25c+12c "	75	90
		Nos. B59-B63 (5)	3.05	3.65

The surtax was for the Antillean Youth Federation.

1964, Oct. 21 ***Perf. 14x13***

Designs: 10c+5c, Wild rose. 20c+10c, Chalice flower. 25c+11c, Bellisima.

Flowers in Natural Colors

B64	SP18	6c+3c blue violet & black	50	50
B65	"	10c+5c yel. brown, yellow & black	60	90
B66	"	20c+10c dull red & black	65	75
B67	"	25c+11c citron & brown	75	90

The surtax was for child welfare.

Sea Anemones and Star Coral
SP19

Corals: 6c+3c, Blue cup sponges. 10c+5c, Green cup sponges. 25c+11c, Basket sponge, knobbed brain coral and reef fish.

1965, Nov. 10 Photo. ***Perf. 14x13***

B68	SP19	6c+3c multi.	30	38
B69	"	10c+5c "	45	65
B70	"	20c+10c "	50	65
B71	"	25c+11c "	75	1.00

The surtax was for child welfare.

ICEM Issue

Type of Netherlands, 1966

1966, Jan. 31 Photo. ***Perf. 14x13***

B72	SP181	35c+15c brn. & dull yellow	1.00	1.10

The surtax was for the Intergovernmental Committee for European Migration (ICEM). The message on the stamps was given and signed by Queen Juliana.

Girl Cooking
SP20

Helping Hands Supporting Women
SP21

Youth at Work: 10c+5c, Nurse's aide with infant. 20c+10c, Young metalworker. 25c+11c, Girl ironing.

1966, Nov. 15 ***Perf. 13x13½***

B73	SP20	6c+3c multicolored	18	20
B74	"	10c+5c "	35	30
B75	"	20c+10c "	50	65
B76	"	25c+11c "	60	65

The surtax was for child welfare.

1967, July 4 Litho. ***Perf. 13x14***

B77	SP21	6c+3c blue & blk.	30	25
B78	"	10c+5c brt. pink & black	33	38
B79	"	20c+10c lilac	50	50
B80	"	25c+11c dark blue	50	65

The surtax was for various social and cultural institutions.

Nanzi the Spider and the Tiger
SP22

Nanzi Stories (Folklore): 6c+3c, Princess Longnose (vert.). 10c+5c, The Turtle and the Monkey. 25c+11c, Adventure of Shon Arey.

1967, Nov. 15 ***Perf. 14x13, 13x14***

B81	SP22	6c+3c dark red, pink & orange	25	25
B82	"	10c+5c vio. bl. & org.	38	38
B83	"	20c+10c green & org.	65	50
B84	"	25c+11c bright blue & orange	65	65

The surtax was for child welfare.

Lintendans (Dance) and Koeoekoe House
SP23

1968, May 29 Litho. ***Perf. 14x13***

B85	SP23	10c+5c multi.	40	35
B86	"	15c+5c "	42	45
B87	"	20c+10c "	60	65
B88	"	25c+10c "	70	75

The surtax was for various social and cultural institutions.

Boy and Pet Cat
SP24

Designs: 6c+3c, Boy and goat. 10c+5c, Girl and poodle. 25c+11c, Girl and duckling.

1968, Nov. 13 Photo. ***Perf. 13½x13***

B89	SP24	6c+3c multi.	25	30
B90	"	10c+5c "	30	35
B91	"	20c+10c "	55	60
B92	"	25c+11c "	65	75

The surtax was for child welfare.

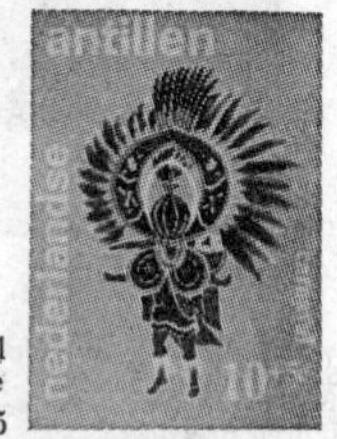

Carnival Headpiece
SP25

Designs (Folklore): 15c+5c, Harvest-home festival. 20c+10c, Feast of St. John (dancers and cock). 25c+10c, "Dande" New Year's celebration.

1969, July 23 Litho. ***Perf. 13x13½***

B93	SP25	10c+5c multi.	90	90
B94	"	15c+5c "	90	90
B95	"	20c+10c "	1.00	90
B96	"	25c+10c "	1.00	90

The surtax was for various social and cultural institutions.

Boy Playing Guitar
SP26

Designs: 10c+5c, Girl with English flute. 20c+10c, Boy playing the marimula. 25c+11c, Girl playing the piano.

1969, Nov. 3 Litho. ***Perf. 14x13***

B97	SP26	6c+3c org. & vio.	38	50
B98	"	10c+5c yellow & bright green	65	65
B99	"	20c+10c blue & car.	90	90
B100	"	25c+11c pink & brown	90	1.00

The surtax was for child welfare.

Printing Press and Quill
SP27

Mother and Child
SP28

Designs (Mass Media): 15c+5c, Filmstrip and reels. 20c+10c, Horn and radio mast. 25c+10c, Television antenna and eye focused on globe.

1970, July 14 Litho. ***Perf. 13x13½***

B101	SP27	10c+5c multi.	1.50	1.40
B102	"	15c+5c "	1.50	1.40
B103	"	20c+10c "	1.65	1.40
B104	"	25c+10c "	1.65	1.40

The surtax was for various social and cultural institutions.

1970, Nov. 16 Litho. ***Perf. 13½x14***

Designs: 10c+5c, Girl holding piggy bank. 20c+10c, Boys wrestling (Judokas). 25c+11c, Youth carrying small boy on his shoulders.

B105	SP28	6c+3c multi.	1.40	1.25
B106	"	10c+5c "	1.40	1.25
B107	"	20c+10c "	1.50	1.4
B108	"	25c+11c "	1.50	1.40

The surtax was for child welfare.

Charcoal Burner
SP29

Kitchen Utensils: 15c+5c, Earthenware vessel for water. 20c+10c, Baking oven. 25c+10c, Soup plate, stirrer and kneading stick.

1971, May 12 Photo. ***Perf. 14x13½***

B109	SP29	10c+5c multi.	1.25	1.25
B110	"	15c+5c "	1.25	1.25
B111	"	20c+10c "	1.40	1.25
B112	"	25c+10c "	1.40	1.25

Surtax was for various social and cultural institutions.

Homemade Dolls and Comb
SP30

Homemade Toys: 20c+10c, Cars. 30c+15c, Musical top made from calabash.

1971, Nov. 15 Litho. ***Perf. 13½x14***

B113	SP30	15c+5c multi.	1.00	90
B114	"	20c+10c "	1.00	90
B115	"	30c+15c "	1.00	1.00

Surtax was for child welfare.

Steel Band
SP31

Designs: 20c+10c, Harvest festival (Seu). 30c+15c, Tambu dancers.

1972, May 16 Litho. ***Perf. 13x13½***

B116	SP31	15c+5c multi.	1.15	1.00
B117	"	20c+10c "	1.15	1.15
B118	"	30c+15c "	1.25	1.25

Surtax was for various social and cultural institutions.

Child at Play on Ground
SP32

Designs: 20c+10c, Child playing in water. 30c+15c, Child throwing ball into air.

1972, Nov. 14 Litho. ***Perf. 14x12½***

B119	SP32	15c+5c multi.	1.50	1.50
B120	"	20c+10c "	1.65	1.50
B121	"	30c+15c "	1.65	1.50

Surtax was for child welfare.

Pedestrian Crossing, Traffic Sign
SP33

Designs: 15c+7c, School crossing. 40c+20c, Traffic light, road and car.

1973, Apr. 9 Litho. ***Perf. 12½x13½***

B122	SP33	12c+6c multi.	1.15	1.00
B123	"	15c+7c "	1.15	1.15
B124	"	40c+20c "	1.25	1.15

Surtax was for various social and cultural institutions.

"1948–73"
SP34

Designs: 20c+10c, Children. 30c+15c, Mother and child.

1973, Nov. 19 Litho. ***Perf. 14x12½***

B125	SP34	15c+ 5c multi.	1.25	1.25
B126	"	20c+10c "	1.40	1.25
		a. Miniature sheet of 4	4.50	4.25
B127	SP34	30c+15c multi.	1.40	1.25

25th anniversary of first Child Welfare semi-postal stamps. No. B126a contains 2 each of Nos. B125-B126. Size: 108x75mm.

Girl Combing her Hair
SP35

Designs: 15c+7c, Young people listening to rock music. 40c+20c, Drummer, symbolizing rock music.

1974, Apr. 9 Litho. ***Perf. 14x12½***

B128	SP35	12c+6c multi.	1.50	1.40
B129	"	15c+7c "	1.50	1.40
B130	"	40c+20c "	1.50	1.50

Surtax was for various social and cultural institutions.

Child, Saw and Score
SP36

Designs: 20c+10c, Footprints in circle. 30c+15c, Moon and sun. Each design includes score of a children's song.

1974, Nov. 12 Litho. *Perf. 12½x14*

B131	SP36	15c+5c	multi.	1.15	1.00
B132	"	20c+10c	"	1.15	1.00
B133	"	30c+15c	"	1.15	1.00

Surtax was for child welfare.

Carved Stone Grid, Flower Pot
SP37

Jewish Tombstone, Mordecai's Procession
SP38

Design: 40c+20c, Ornamental stone from facade of Jewish House, 1728.

1975, Mar. 21 Litho. *Perf. 12½x14*

B134	SP37	12c+6c	multi.	1.00	90
B135	SP38	15c+7c	"	1.00	90
B136	SP37	40c+20c	"	1.00	1.00

Surtax was for various social and cultural institutions.

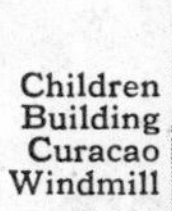

Children Building Curacao Windmill
SP39

Designs: 20c+10c, Girl molding clay animal. 30c+15c, Children drawing picture.

1975, Nov. 12 Litho. *Perf. 14x12½*

B137	SP39	15c+5c	multi.	1.15	1.00
B138	"	20c+10c	"	1.25	1.15
B139	"	30c+15c	"	1.25	1.15

Surtax was for child welfare.

Carrying a Child
SP40

Designs: Different ways of carrying a child. 40c+18c is vertical.

Perf. 14x12½, 12½x14

1976, Oct. 4 Lithographed

B140	SP40	20c+10c	multi.	75	65
B141	"	25c+12c	"	1.00	90
B142	"	40c+18c	"	1.00	1.00

Surtax was for child welfare.

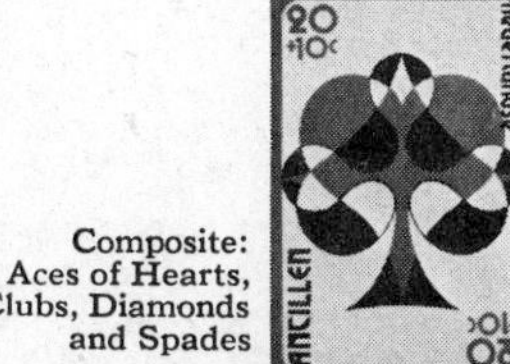

Composite: Aces of Hearts, Clubs, Diamonds and Spades
SP41

Designs: 25c+12c, "King" and inscription. 40c+18c, Hand holding cards; map of Aruba as ace of hearts (horiz.).

Perf. 13x14, 14x13

1977, May 6 Lithographed

B143	SP41	20c+10c	red & black	60	50
B144	"	25c+12c	multi.	80	65
	a. Miniature sheet of 4			3.00	2.25
B145	SP41	40c+18c	multi.	1.20	90

Central American and Caribbean Bridge Championships, Aruba. No. B144a contains 2 each of Nos. B143–B144. Size: 75x107mm.

Souvenir Sheet

1977, May 26 *Perf. 14x13*

B146	SP41	Sheet of 3	2.75	2.75

Amphilex 77 International Philatelic Exhibition, Amsterdam, May 26–June 5. No. B146 contains 3 stamps similar to Nos. B143–B145 with bright green background. Green, black and red margin shows bridge hands and names of participants in final game of Central and Caribbean Bridge Championships. Size: 175x105mm.

Children and Toys
SP42

Designs: Children playing with fantasy animals.

1977, Oct. 25 Litho. *Perf. 14x13*

B147	SP42	15c+5c	multi.	38	38
B148	"	20c+10c	"	65	65
B149	"	25c+12c	"	70	70
B150	"	40c+18c	"	85	85
	a. Miniature sheet of 4			3.00	3.00

Surtax was for child welfare.
No. B150a contains 2 each of Nos. B148 and B150. Size: 108x75mm.

Water Skiing
SP43

Designs: 20c+10c, Sailing. 25c+12c, Soccer. 40c+18c, Baseball.

1978, Mar. 31 Litho. *Perf. 13x14*

B151	SP43	15c+5c	multi.	20	20
B152	"	20c+10c	"	30	30
B153	"	25c+12c	"	38	38
B154	"	40c+18c	"	65	65

Surtax was for sports.

Red Cross
SP44

1978, Sept. 19 Litho. *Perf. 14x13*

B155	SP44	55c+25c	red & black	1.20	1.20
	a. Souvenir sheet of 3			3.75	3.75

Henri Dunant (1828–1910), founder of Red Cross. No. B155a contains 3 No. B155; red and black marginal inscription. Size: 143x50mm.

Roller Skating
SP45

Children's Activities: 20c+10c, Kite flying. 25c+12c, Playing marbles. 40c+18c, Bicycling.

1978, Nov. 7 Litho. *Perf. 13x14*

B156	SP45	15c+5c	multi.	30	30
B157	"	20c+10c	"	45	45
	a. Miniature sheet of 4			1.50	
B158	SP45	25c+12c	"	55	55
B159	"	40c+18c	"	85	85

Surtax was for child welfare.
No. B157a contains 2 each of Nos. B156–B157. Size: 75x108mm.

Carnival King
SP46

Design: 75c+20c, Carnival Queen and coat of arms.

1979, Feb. 20 Litho. *Perf. 13x14*

B160	SP46	40c+10c	multi.	75	75
B161	"	75c+20c	"	1.45	1.45

25th Aruba Carnival.

Regatta Emblem
SP47

Designs: 35c+10c, Race. 40c+15c, Globe and yacht (horiz.). 55c+25c, Yacht, birds and sun.

Perf. 12½x14, 14x12½

1979, May 16 Lithographed

B162	SP47	15c+5c	multi.	30	30
B163	"	35c+10c	"	65	65
B164	"	40c+15c	"	80	80
B165	"	55c+25c	"	1.15	1.15
	a. Souvenir sheet of 4			3.00	

12th International Sailing Regatta, Bonaire.
No. B165a contains Nos. B162–B165; orange marginal inscription. Size: 125x72 mm.

AIR POST STAMPS

Regular Issues of 1915-22 Surcharged in Black

1929, July 6 *Perf. 12½* **Unwmkd.**

C1	A13	50c on 12½c red	15.00	17.50
C2	"	1g on 20c blue	15.00	17.50
C3	"	2g on 15c olive green	62.50	70.00

Excellent forgeries exist.

Allegory, "Flight"
AP1

1931-39 **Engraved.**

C4	AP1	10c Prussian green ('34)	20	15
C5	"	15c dull blue ('38)	25	25
C6	"	20c red	1.00	25
C7	"	25c gray ('38)	55	50
C8	"	30c yellow ('39)	38	35
C9	"	35c dull blue	1.15	1.00
C10	"	40c green	80	35
C11	"	45c orange	3.25	3.00
C12	"	50c lake ('38)	55	75
C13	"	60c brown violet	90	50
C14	"	70c black	9.00	3.00
C15	"	1.40g brown	6.50	7.00
C16	"	2.80g bistre	7.00	7.50
		Nos. C4-C16 (13)	31.53	24.60

No. C6 Surcharged in Black **10 CT**

1934, Aug. 25

C17	AP1	10c on 20c red	28.50	22.50

Map of the Atlantic
AP2

Plane over Islands
AP3

Map of Curaçao, Aruba and Bonaire
AP4

Planes
AP5

Plane
AP6

1942, Oct. 20 *Perf. 13x13½*

C18	AP2	10c green & blue	25	15
C19	AP3	15c rose carmine & yellow green	35	18
C20	AP4	20c red brn. & grn.	40	20
C21	AP5	25c dp. ultra. & org. brown	25	25
C22	AP6	30c red & light violet	50	40
C23	AP2	35c dark violet & olive green	75	40
C24	AP3	40c gray olive & chestnut	90	55
C25	AP4	45c dk. red & blk.	65	30
C26	AP5	50c violet & blk.	1.15	20
C27	AP6	60c lt. yel. brown & dull blue	1.15	90
C28	AP2	70c red brown & Prussian bl.	1.25	90
C29	AP3	1.40g blue violet & slate green	6.25	1.90
C30	AP4	2.80g intense blue & light blue	7.50	3.75
C31	AP5	5g rose lake & slate green	16.00	16.00
C32	AP6	10g green & red brown	24.00	24.00
		Nos. C18-C32 (15)	61.35	50.08

Plane and Post Horn
AP7

DC-4 above Waves
AP8

1947 **Photogravure.** *Perf. 12½x12.*

C32A	AP7	6c gray black	18	12
C33	"	10c deep red	20	20
C33A	"	12½c plum	35	18
C34	"	15c deep blue	30	30
C35	"	20c dull yellow green	35	35
C36	"	25c orange yellow	35	22
C37	"	30c lilac gray	40	42
C38	"	35c orange red	50	75
C39	"	40c blue green	60	75
C40	"	45c bright violet	70	1.10
C41	"	50c carmine	60	25
C42	"	60c bright blue	90	75
C43	"	70c brown	2.00	1.50

Engraved.
Perf. 12x12½

C44	AP8	1.50g black	1.50	80
C45	"	2.50g dk. carmine	13.00	4.25
C46	"	5g green	27.50	10.00
C47	"	7.50g dark blue	85.00	85.00
C48	"	10g dk. red vio.	55.00	20.00
C49	"	15g red orange	100.00	100.00
C50	"	25g chocolate	95.00	85.00
		Nos. C32A-C50 (20)	384.43	311.94

Friendship 500
AP9

Designs: 20c, Beechcraft Queen Air. 25c, Friendship and DC-9.

1968, Dec. 3 **Litho.** *Perf. 14x12½*

C51	AP9	10c dull yellow, blk. & bright blue	50	50
C52	"	20c tan, black & bright blue	50	50
C53	"	25c sal. pink, black & bright blue	50	50

Issued to publicize Dutch Antillean Airlines (ALM).

AIR POST SEMI-POSTAL STAMPS.

Flags of the Netherlands and the House of Orange with Inscription "Netherlands Shall Rise Again"
SPAP1

Engraved and Lithographed.

1941, Dec. 11 *Perf. 12* **Unwmkd.**

CB1	SPAP1	10c+10c multi.	5.00	4.50
CB2	"	15c+25c "	25.00	20.00
CB3	"	20c+25c "	25.00	20.00
CB4	"	25c+25c "	25.00	20.00
CB5	"	30c+50c "	25.00	20.00
CB6	"	35c+50c "	25.00	20.00
CB7	"	40c+50c "	25.00	20.00
CB8	"	50c+100c "	25.00	20.00
		Nos. CB1-CB8 (8)	180.00	144.50

The surtax was used by the Prince Bernhard Committee to purchase war material for the Netherlands' fighting forces in Great Britain.

Air Post Stamps of 1942 Surcharged in Black

Voor Krijgsgevangenen

50 ct. + 75 ct

1943, Dec. 1 *Perf. 13x13½*

CB9	AP3	40c+50c on 1.40g blue violet & slate green	8.00	6.50
CB10	AP4	45c+50c on 2.80g intense blue & light blue	8.00	6.00
CB11	AP5	50c+75c on 5g rose lake & slate green	8.00	6.00
CB12	AP6	60c+100c on 10g green & red brown	8.00	6.00

The surtax was for the benefit of prisoners of war. These stamps were not sold to the public in the normal manner. All were sold in sets by advance subscription, the majority to philatelic speculators.
On No. CB9 overprint reads: "Voor / Krijgsgevangenen".

Princess Juliana
SPAP2

The frame is printed in carmine and deep blue, the cross in carmine.

1944, Aug. 16 *Perf. 12*

CB13	SPAP2	10c+10c light brown	3.00	2.50
CB14	"	15c+25c turquoise green	2.75	2.50
CB15	"	20c+25c dark olive gray	2.75	2.50
CB16	"	25c+25c slate	2.75	2.50
CB17	"	30c+50c sepia	2.75	2.50
CB18	"	35c+50c chestnut	2.75	2.50
CB19	"	40c+50c green	2.75	2.50
CB20	"	50c+100c dark violet	3.00	2.75
		Nos. CB13-CB20 (8)	22.50	20.25

The surtax was for the Red Cross.

Map of Netherlands Indies
SPAP3

Map of Netherlands
SPAP4

Photogravure and Typographed

1946, July 1 *Perf. 11x11½*

Denomination in Black.

CB21	SPAP3	10c+10c purple, pale violet & buff	1.50	1.65
CB22	"	15c+25c dark blue, blue & buff	1.50	1.65
CB23	"	20c+25c deep plum, rose & brown orange	1.50	1.65
CB24	"	25c+25c olive green, pale green & buff	1.50	1.65
CB25	"	30c+50c deep violet, violet & gray	1.50	2.00
		a. Double impression of denomination	400.00	400.00
CB26	"	35c+50c dark green, pale grn. & yel. orange	1.50	2.00
CB27	"	40c+75c carmine, rose & gray	1.75	2.25
CB28	"	50c+100c gray, pale gray & orange	1.75	2.25
CB29	SPAP4	10c+10c slate, gray & org.	1.50	1.65
CB30	"	15c+25c carmine, rose & gray	1.50	1.65
CB31	"	20c+25c dk. grn., pale green & yel. orange	1.50	1.65
CB32	"	25c+25c deep vio., vio. & gray	1.50	1.65
CB33	"	30c+50c olive green, pale green & buff	1.50	2.00
CB34	"	35c+50c deep plum, rose & brn. orge.	1.50	2.00
CB35	"	40c+75c dark blue, blue & buff	1.75	2.25
CB36	"	50c+100c dark purple, violet & buff	1.75	2.25
		Nos. CB21-CB36 (16)	25.00	30.20

The surtax on Nos. CB21 to CB36 was for the National Relief Fund.

POSTAGE DUE STAMPS.

D1 D2

Type I. 34 loops. "T" of "*BETALEN*" over center of loop, top branch of "E" of "*TE*" shorter than lower branch.

Type II. 33 loops. "T" of "*BETALEN*" over center of two loops.

Type III. 32 loops. "T" of "*BETALEN*" slightly to the left of loop, top of first "E" of "*BETALEN*" shorter than lower branch.

Typographed.
Value in Black.

1889 *Perf. 12½* **Unwmkd.**

J1	D1	2½c green (III)	2.10	3.25
		a. 2½c green (I)	2.75	3.75
		b. 2½c green (II)	3.75	4.00
J2	"	5c green (III)	1.10	1.60
		a. 5c green (I)	37.50	32.50
		b. 5c green (II)	210.00	160.00
J3	"	10c green (III)	25.00	27.50
		a. 10c green (I)	30.00	32.50
		b. 10c green (II)	35.00	37.50
J4	"	12½c green (III)	350.00	175.00
		a. 12½c green (I)	375.00	190.00
		b. 12½c green (II)	400.00	225.00
J5	"	15c green (III)	14.00	16.00
		a. 15c green (I)	16.00	17.00
		b. 15c green (II)	19.00	19.00
J6	"	20c green (III)	5.25	6.00
		a. 20c green (I)	75.00	75.00
		b. 20c green (II)	600.00	600.00
J7	"	25c green (III)	160.00	115.00
		a. 25c green (I)	675.00	475.00
		b. 25c green (II)	*2000.00*	*2000.00*
J8	"	30c green (III)	5.25	6.00
		a. 30c green (I)	75.00	75.00
		b. 30c green (II)	600.00	600.00
J9	"	40c green (III)	5.25	6.00
		a. 40c green (I)	75.00	75.00
		b. 40c green (II)	600.00	600.00
J10	"	50c green (III)	32.50	35.00
		a. 50c green (I)	35.00	37.50
		b. 50c green (II)	40.00	42.50

Nos. J1 to J10 were issued without gum.

Value in Black.

1892-98 *Perf. 12½.*

J11	D2	2½c green (III)	25	20
		a. 2½c green (I)	50	50
		b. 2½c green (II)	25.00	25.00
J12	"	5c green (III)	65	45
		a. 5c green (I)	2.65	2.65
		b. 5c green (II)	1.00	1.00
J13	"	10c green (III)	80	38
		a. 10c green (I)	2.00	2.00
		b. 10c green (II)	1.00	1.00
J14	"	12½c green (III)	90	45
		a. 12½c green (I)	1.30	1.30
		b. 12½c green (II)	8.00	8.00
J15	"	15c green (III) ('95)	1.15	90
J16	"	20c green (I) ('95)	1.65	1.00
J17	"	25c green (III)	1.00	75
		a. 25c green (I)	1.40	1.40
		b. 25c green (II)	11.00	11.00
J18	"	30c green (I) ('95)	14.00	11.00
J19	"	40c green (I) ('95)	16.00	12.50
J20	"	50c green (I) ('95)	17.50	12.50

Type I.
On Yellowish or White Paper.
Value in Color of Stamp.

Perf. 11½, 12½, 13½x12, 13½x12½

1915-44

J21	D2	2½c green	75	75
J22	"	5c "	75	75
J23	"	10c green	65	65
		a. 10c yel. grn., perf. 11½ ('44)	16.50	21.50
J24	D2	12½c green	90	90
		a. 12½c yel. grn., perf. 11½ ('44)	15.00	10.00
J25	D2	15c green	1.40	1.65
J26	"	20c "	75	1.40
J27	"	25c green	25	12
		a. 25c yel. grn., perf. 11½ ('44)	35.00	1.60
J28	D2	30c green	3.25	3.75
J29	"	40c "	3.25	3.75
J30	"	50c "	2.75	3.00
		Nos. J21-J30 (10)	14.70	16.72

Type of 1915
Typographed.
Type I.
Value in Color of Stamp.

1948-49 *Perf. 13½x12½.* **Unwmkd.**

J31	D2	2½c blue grn. ('48)	50	1.25
J32	"	5c " ('48)	50	1.25
J33	"	10c "	11.00	12.50
J34	"	12½c "	11.00	2.50
J35	"	15c "	18.00	20.00
J36	"	20c "	16.00	20.00
J37	"	25c "	1.50	50
J38	"	30c "	16.00	30.00
J39	"	40c "	16.00	30.00
J40	"	50c "	16.00	20.00
		Nos. J31-J40 (10)	106.50	138.00

D3

1953-59 Photogravure.

J41	D3	1c dk. bl. grn. ('59)	10	10
J42	"	2½c "	75	75
J43	"	5c "	12	12
J44	"	6c " ('59)	50	50
J45	"	7c " ('59)	50	50
J46	"	8c " ('59)	50	50
J47	"	9c " ('59)	50	50
J48	"	10c "	30	25
J49	"	12½c "	30	25
J50	"	15c "	38	30
J51	"	20c "	45	50
J52	"	25c "	55	12
J53	"	30c "	1.50	1.50
J54	"	35c " ('59)	1.50	1.50
J55	"	40c "	1.50	1.50
J56	"	45c " ('59)	1.50	1.50
J57	"	50c "	1.50	1.15
		Nos. J41-J57 (17)	12.45	11.54

NETHERLANDS INDIES

(Dutch Indies, Indonesia)

LOCATION—East Indies.

GOVT.—Former Dutch colony.

AREA—735,268 sq. mi.

POP.—76,000,000 (estimated 1949).

CAPITAL.—Jakarta (formerly Batavia).

Netherlands Indies consisted of the islands of Sumatra, Java, the Lesser Sundas, Madura, two thirds of Borneo, Celebes, the Moluccas, western New Guinea and many small islands.

Netherlands Indies changed its name to Indonesia in 1948. Holland transferred sovereignty on Dec. 28, 1949, to the Republic of the United States of Indonesia (see "Indonesia"), except for the western part of New Guinea (see "Netherlands New Guinea"). The Republic of Indonesia was proclaimed Aug. 15, 1950.

100 Cents = 1 Gulden
100 Sen = 1 Rupiah (1949)

King William III
A1 A2

Engraved

1864 *Imperf.* **Unwmkd.**

1 A1 10c lake 325.00 125.00

1868 *Perf. 12½x12.*

2 A1 10c lake 1200.00 210.00

Privately perforated examples of No. 1 sometimes are mistaken for No. 2.

Typographed.

ONE CENT.
Type I. "CENT" 6 mm. long.
Type II. "CENT" 7½ mm. long.

Perf. 11½x12, 12½, 12½x12, 13x14, 13½, 14.

1870-88

3 A2 1c slate green, type I 7.00 6.25
4 " 1c slate green, type II 2.65 1.65
5 " 2c red brown 6.00 3.75
a. 2c fawn 6.00 3.75
6 " 2c violet brown 110.00 90.00
7 " 2½c orange 35.00 25.00
8 " 5c pale green 62.50 4.00
a. Perf. 14, small holes 67.50 4.25
b. Perf. 13x14, small holes 62.50 6.00
9 " 10c orange brown 15.00 12
a. Perf. 14, small holes 27.50 80
b. Perf. 13x14, small holes 45.00 1.10
10 " 12½c gray 3.00 1.25
a. Perf. 12½x12 750.00
11 " 15c bistre 20.00 75
a. Perf. 13x14, small holes 27.50 2.00
12 " 20c ultramarine 110.00 2.25
a. Perf. 14, small holes 115.00 2.35
b. Perf. 13x14, small holes 115.00 2.75
13 " 25c dark violet 20.00 65
b. Perf. 13x14, small holes 27.50 2.00
c. Perf. 14, large holes 385.00 90.00
14 " 30c green 30.00 3.00
15 " 50c carmine 16.50 90
a. Perf. 14, small holes 21.00 90
b. Perf. 13x14, small holes 16.50 1.10
c. Perf. 14, large holes 27.50 2.00
16 A2 2.50g grn. & violet 100.00 15.00
b. Perf. 14, small holes 100.00 15.00
c. Perf. 14, large holes 100.00 15.00

Imperforate examples of Nos. 3-16 are proofs. The 1c red brown and 2c yellow are believed to be bogus.

Numeral of Value — A3
Queen Wilhelmina — A4

1883-90 ***Perf. 12½***

17 A3 1c slate green ('88) 65 20
a. Perf. 12½x12 1.60 90
18 " 2c brown ('84) 65 20
a. Perf. 12½x12 90 40
b. Perf. 11½x12 75.00 25.00
19 " 2½c yellow 90 90
a. Perf. 12½x12 1.65 1.00
b. Perf. 11½x12 16.50 6.50
20 " 3c lilac ('90) 1.00 20
21 " 5c green ('87) 27.50 18.50
22 " 5c ultramarine ('90) 9.00 20

1892-97 ***Perf. 12½***

23 A4 10c orange brown 4.50 25
24 " 12½c gray 9.00 19.00
25 " 15c bistre 13.50 90
26 " 20c ultramarine 30.00 1.00
27 " 25c violet 30.00 1.40
28 " 30c green 42.50 2.00
29 " 50c carmine 26.50 75
30 " 2.50g orange brown & ultra. 125.00 35.00

Queen Wilhelmina
A5

Stamps of Netherlands, 1898-99 Surcharged in Black.

1900

31 A5 10c on 10c gray lilac 1.80 12
32 " 12½c on 12½c blue 2.50 75
33 " 15c on 15c yel. brn. 2.50 25
34 " 20c on 20c yel. grn. 16.50 65
35 " 25c on 25c car. & bl. 16.50 75
36 " 50c on 50c bronze grn. & red brn. 27.50 1.00

Netherlands No. 84, Surcharged in Black

NED.-INDIË

Perf. 11½x11

37 A12 2.50g on 2½g brown lilac 55.00 10.50
a. Perf. 11 57.50 12.50
Nos. 31-37 (7) 122.30 14.02

A6

1902-09 ***Perf. 12½***

38 A6 ½c violet 40 12
39 " 1c olive green 40 12
a. Booklet pane of 6
40 A6 2c yellow brown 3.25 25
41 " 2½c green 2.10 12
a. Booklet pane of 6
42 " 3c orange 2.00 1.50
43 " 4c ultra. ('09) 12.50 11.00
44 " 5c rose red 5.50 12
a. Booklet pane of 6
45 " 7½c gray ('09) 2.75 40
Nos. 38-45 (8) 28.90 13.63

A7 A8

1902

46 A7 ½c on 2c yellow brown 25 25
a. Double surcharge 235.00 235.00
47 A8 2½c on 3c violet 30 30

Queen Wilhelmina
A9 A10

1902-08

48 A9 10c slate 1.15 10
a. Booklet pane of 6
49 " 12½c deep blue 1.90 12
a. Booklet pane of 6
50 " 15c chocolate 10.00 2.25
a. Ovptd. with 2 horiz. bars 1.90 90
51 " 17½c bistre ('08) 3.25 20
52 " 20c greenish slate 2.10 2.00
53 " 20c olive green 27.50 15
54 " 22½c brown & olive green ('08) 4.75 18
55 " 25c violet 11.00 15
56 " 30c orange brown 35.00 15
57 " 50c red brown 22.50 15
Nos. 48-57 (10) 119.15 5.45

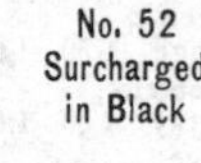

No. 52 Surcharged in Black

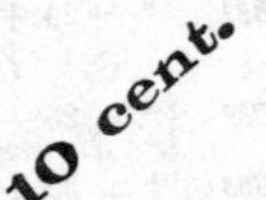

1905

58 A9 10c on 20c greenish slate 2.50 1.50

1905-12 **Engraved** ***Perf. 11x11½***

59 A10 1g dull lilac ('05) 60.00 30
a. Perf. 11½x11 60.00 50
b. Perf. 11 75.00 4.50
60 " 1g dull lilac, *blue* ('12) 60.00 8.00
a. Perf. 11 70.00 67.50
61 " 2½g slate blue ('05) 75.00 2.00
a. Perf. 11½ 80.00 2.10
b. Perf. 11½x11 80.00 2.10
c. Perf. 11 900.00
62 " 2½g slate blue, *blue* ('12) 90.00 40.00
a. Perf. 11 100.00 110.00

Previous Issues Overprinted

1908

63 A6 ½c violet 25 25
a. Ovpt. reading down 65 4.00
64 " 1c olive green 38 25
a. Ovpt. reading down 50 3.25
65 A6 2c yellow brown 1.90 3.00
a. Ovpt. reading down 2.75 7.50
66 " 2½c green 75 25
a. Ovpt. reading down 1.00 3.50
67 " 3c orange 65 1.25
a. Ovpt. reading down 17.50 60.00
68 " 5c rose red 2.50 50
a. Ovpt. reading down 1.35 3.25
69 " 7½c gray 2.75 3.00
70 A9 10c slate 65 12
a. Ovpt. reading down 80 2.35
71 " 12½c deep blue 10.00 3.00
a. Ovpt. reading down 5.50 10.00
72 " 15c choc. (#50a) 4.75 2.50
a. Ovpt. reading down 25.00 90.00
73 " 17½c bistre 1.65 1.25
74 " 20c olive green 8.50 1.85
a. Ovpt. reading down 5.00 10.00
75 " 22½c brown & olive green 7.00 4.75
a. Ovpt. reading down 1350.00 1350.00
76 " 25c violet 5.50 38
a. Ovpt. reading down 5.00 10.00
77 " 30c orange brown 19.00 2.50
a. Ovpt. reading down 12.50 20.00
78 " 50c red brown 8.50 90
a. Ovpt. reading down 9.00 10.00
79 A10 1g dull lilac 70.00 3.50
a. Ovpt. reading down 225.00 250.00
80 " 2½g slate blue 100.00 80.00
a. Ovpt. reading down 2750.00 3250.00
Nos. 63-80 (18) 244.73 109.25

The above stamps were overprinted for use in the territory outside of Java and Madura, stamps overprinted "Java" being used in these latter places.

The 15c is overprinted, in addition, with two horizontal lines, 2¼ mm. apart.

Overprinted **JAVA.**

1908

81 A6 ½c violet 20 25
a. Inverted overprint 65 2.75
b. Double overprint 425.00
82 " 1c olive green 22 22
a. Inverted overprint 50 3.25
83 " 2c yellow brown 2.25 2.25
a. Inverted overprint 1.75 7.00
84 " 2½c green 1.00 15
a. Invtd. overprint 2.50 4.00
85 " 3c orange 80 1.00
a. Inverted overprint 21.00 27.50
86 " 5c rose red 2.75 15
a. Inverted overprint 1.85 3.00
87 " 7½c gray 2.35 2.25
88 A9 10c slate 65 12
a. Inverted overprint 65 2.10
89 " 12½c deep blue 3.25 75
a. Inverted ovpt. 3.25 6.00
b. Dbl. ovpt. one inverted 130.00 140.00
90 " 15c chocolate (on No. 50a) 3.25 3.00
a. Inverted ovpt. 3.25 11.00
91 " 17½c bistre 2.10 90
92 " 20c olive green 11.00 75
a. Inverted ovpt. 10.00 11.50
93 " 22½c brown & olive green 5.50 2.75
94 " 25c violet 4.75 25
a. Inverted ovpt. 5.00 11.00
95 " 30c orange brown 32.50 2.75
a. Inverted ovpt. 22.50 32.50
96 " 50c red brown 20.00 75
a. Inverted overprint 15.00 25.00
97 A10 1g dull lilac 55.00 3.00
a. Inverted overprint 175.00 175.00
b. Perf. 11 60.00 5.00
98 " 2½g slate blue 85.00 57.50
a. Inverted overprint 2750.00 3250.00
Nos. 81-98 (18) 232.57 78.79

A11

Queen Wilhelmina
A12 A13

1912–40 Typographed *Perf. 12½*

101 A11 ½c light violet 12 10
102 " 1c olive green 18 10
103 " 2c yellow brown 40 10
104 " 2c gray black ('30) 45 10
105 " 2½c green 1.40 10
106 " 2½c light red ('22) 30 10
107 " 3c yellow 45 10
108 " 3c green ('29) 90 12
109 " 4c ultramarine 65 25
110 " 4c deep green ('28) 1.40 20
111 " 4c yellow ('30) 10.00 5.50
112 " 5c rose 1.00 10
113 " 5c green ('22) 1.10 10
114 " 5c chalky blue ('28) 50 10
114A " 5c ultra. ('40) 1.00 10
115 " 7½c bister 45 10
116 " 10c lilac ('22) 1.10 10
117 A12 10c carmine rose('14) 65 10
118 " 12½c dull blue ('14) 1.00 10
119 " 12½c red ('22) 1.00 10
120 " 15c blue ('29) 9.00 15
121 " 17½c red brown ('15) 90 10
122 " 20c green ('15) 1.75 10
123 " 20c blue ('22) 1.75 10
124 " 20c orange ('32) 16.50 12
125 " 22½c orange ('15) 1.50 65
126 " 25c red violet ('15) 1.65 10
127 " 30c slate ('15) 1.75 10
128 " 32½c violet & red ('22) 1.75 18
129 " 35c org. brn. ('29) 10.00 65
130 " 40c green ('22) 1.75 10

Engraved.
Perf. 11½

131 A13 50c green ('13) 4.00 10
a. Perf. 11x11½ 4.25 12
b. Perf. 12½ 5.00 25
132 " 60c deep blue ('22) 4.25 10
133 " 80c orange ('22) 4.75 15
134 " 1g brown ('13) 3.75 10
a. Perf. 11x11½ 4.25 15
135 " 1.75g dk. violet('31) 17.50 2.75
136 " 2½g carmine ('13) 15.00 50
a. Perf. 11x11½ 16.00 90
b. Perf. 12½ 17.50 70
Nos. 101–136 (37) 121.60 13.72

Water Soluble Ink

Some values of types A11 and A12 and late printings of types A6 and A9 are in soluble ink and the design disappears when immersed in water.

No. 105 Surcharged **1/2**

1917 *Perf. 12½.*

137 A11 ½c on 2½c green 25 25

Nos. 109 and 54 Surcharged

1 **17½**
a *b*

1918

138 A11 (*a*) 1c on 4c ultra. 50 65
139 A9 (*b*) 17½c on 22½c brown & olive grn. 1.00 50
a. Inverted surcharge 400.00 500.00

No. 59 Surcharged **30 CENT**

Perf. 11x11½.

140 A10 30c on 1g dull lilac 8.50 1.90
a. Perf. 11½x11 130.00 65.00

Nos. 121 and 125 Surcharged in Red or Blue.

A14

1921 *Perf. 12½*

144 A14 12½c on 17½c red brown (R) 35 10
145 " 12½c on 22½c orange (R) 55 10
146 " 20c on 22½c orange (Bl) 55 10

Nos. 131 and 134 Surcharged with New Value in Blue or Red

40 CENT

Two types of 32½c on 50c:
I. Surcharge bars spaced as in illustration.
II. Bars more closely spaced.

Perf. 11½, 11x11½

147 A13 32½c on 50c green (Bl) (I, perf. 11½) 2.00 10
a. Type II, perf. 11½ 12.50 12
b. Type I, perf. 11x11½ 325.00 8.50
c. Type II, perf. 11x11½ 27.50 1.75
148 " 40c on 50c grn. (R) 5.50 65
149 " 60c on 1g brn. (Bl) 10.00 50
150 " 80c on 1g brn. (R) 11.00 1.15
Nos. 144–150 (7) 29.95 2.70

Stamps of 1912–22 Overprinted in Red, Blue, Green or Black

3de N.I. JAARBEURS
BANDOENG 1922
a

3de N. I. JAARBEURS
BANDOENG 1922
b

1922 Typographed *Perf. 12½*

102a A11 (*a*) 1c olive green (R) 7.50 6.50
103a " (") 2c yellow brn. (Bl) 7.50 6.50
106a " (") 2½c light red (G) 90.00 80.00
107a " (") 3c yellow (R) 7.50 7.50
109a " (") 4c ultramarine (R) 55.00 47.50
113a " (") 5c green (R) 16.50 12.50
115a " (") 7½c drab (Bl) 10.50 6.50
116a " (") 10c lilac (Bk) 100.00 100.00
145a A14 (*b*) 12½c on 22½c orange (Bl) 10.50 7.50
121a A12 (*b*) 17½c red brown (Bk) 7.50 6.50
123a " (") 20c blue (Bk) 10.50 6.50
Nos. 102a–123a (11) 323.00 287.50

Issued to publicize the 3rd Netherlands Indies Industrial Fair at Bandoeng, Java. On No. 145a the overprint is vertical.

Nos. 102a–123a were sold at a premium for 3, 4, 5, 6, 8, 9, 10, 12½, 15, 20 and 22½ cents respectively.

Queen Wilhelmina
A15

Prince William I Portrait by Van Key
A16

1923 *Perf. 11½*

151 A15 5c myrtle green 20 15
a. Perf. 11½x11 375.00 185.00
b. Perf. 11x11½ 6.00 70
152 " 12½c rose 20 18
a. Perf. 11x11½ 2.00 20
b. Perf. 11½x11 2.00 30
153 " 20c dark blue 38 18
a. Perf. 11½x11 4.50 45
154 A15 50c red orange 1.75 75
a. Perf. 11x11½ 8.50 1.50
b. Perf. 11½x11 2.50 1.00
c. Perf. 11 5.50 1.00
155 " 1g brown violet 4.00 50
a. Perf. 11½x11 9.50 1.00
156 " 2½g gray black 32.50 12.50
157 " 5g org. brown 115.00 125.00
Nos. 151–157 (7) 154.03 139.26

Issued to commemorate the 25th anniversary of the assumption of the government of the Netherlands by Queen Wilhelmina, at the age of 18.

No. 123 Surcharged **12½**

1931 *Perf. 12½*

158 A12 12½c on 20c blue (R) 38 10
a. Inverted surcharge 350.00 550.00

1933 Photogravure

163 A16 12½c deep orange 1.75 25

Issued in commemoration of the 400th anniversary of the birth of Prince William I, Count of Nassau and Prince of Orange, frequently referred to as William the Silent.

Rice Field Scene
A17

Queen Wilhelmina
A18

Queen Wilhelmina
A19

1933–37 *Perf. 11½x12½* Unwmkd.

164 A17 1c lilac gray ('34) 30 12
165 " 2c plum ('34) 30 12
166 " 2½c bistre ('34) 30 12
167 " 3c yel. grn. ('34) 30 20
168 " 3½c dark gray ('37) 20 20
169 " 4c dark olive ('34) 90 15
170 " 5c ultra. ('34) 25 10
171 " 7½c violet ('34) 1.50 10
172 " 10c vermilion ('34) 2.25 15
173 A18 10c vermilion ('37) 38 10
174 " 12½c deep orange 38 10
a. 12½c light orange, perf. 12½ 6.25 30
175 " 15c ultra. ('34) 38 10
176 " 20c plum ('34) 50 10
177 " 25c blue green ('34) 2.00 12
178 " 30c lilac gray ('34) 3.25 12
179 " 32½c bistre ('34) 8.00 8.00
180 " 35c violet ('34) 5.75 1.25
181 " 40c yel. grn. ('34) 2.75 12
182 " 42½c yellow ('34) 2.75 18

Perf. 12½

183 A19 50c lilac gray ('34) 4.25 18
184 " 60c ultra. ('34) 5.25 50
185 " 80c vermilion ('34) 5.25 65
186 " 1g violet ('34) 8.00 38
187 " 1.75g yel. grn. ('34) 19.00 15.00
188 " 2.50g plum ('34) 25.00 1.50
Nos. 164–188 (25) 99.19 29.66

See also Nos. 200–225, 272–275.

Water Soluble Ink

Nos. 164–188 and the first printing of No. 163 have soluble ink and the design disappears when immersed in water.

Air Post Stamps of 1928–31 Surcharged in Black:

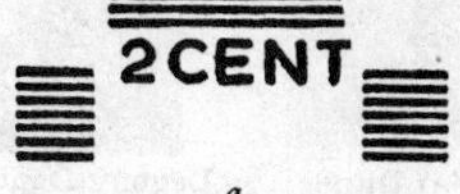

a

b

1934 *Perf. 12½x11½, 12½*

189 AP1 (*a*) 2c on 10c red violet 38 65
190 " (") 2c on 20c brown 25 25
191 AP3 (*b*) 2c on 30c red violet 50 90
192 AP1 (*a*) 42½c on 75c grn. 6.00 38
193 " (") 42½c on 1.50g orange 6.00 50
Nos. 189–193 (5) 13.13 2.68

Nos. 127–128 Surcharged with New Value in Red or Black

1937 *Perf. 12½*

194 A12 10c on 30c slate (R) 3.00 30
a. Dbl. surch. 1100.00
195 " 10c on 32½c violet & red (Bk) 3.00 30

Queen Wilhelmina
A20

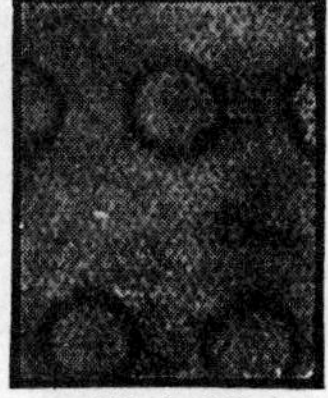

Wmk. 202

Wmkd. Circles. (202)

1938 *Perf. 12½x12.*

196 A20 2c dull purple 12 20
197 " 10c carmine lake 25 18
198 " 15c royal blue 2.00 1.00
199 " 20c red orange 90 38

Issued in commemoration of the 40th anniversary of the reign of Queen Wilhelmina.

Types of 1933–37.

1938–40 Photo. *Perf. 12½x11½*

200 A17 1c lilac gray ('39) 40 1.10
201 " 2c plum ('39) 12 18
202 " 2½c bistre ('39) 65 65
203 " 3c yel. green ('39) 1.65 1.50
205 " 4c gray olive ('39) 1.65 1.50
206 " 5c ultramarine ('39) 12 8
a. Perf. 11½x12½ 2.00 12
207 " 7½c violet ('39) 3.00 1.25
208 A18 10c vermilion ('39) 10 8
210 " 15c ultramarine ('39) 15 10
211 " 20c plum ('39) 25 10
a. Perf. 11½x12½ 1.60 18
212 " 25c bl. green ('39) 32.50 27.50
213 " 30c lilac gray ('39) 8.00 1.00
215 " 35c violet ('39) 4.00 90
216 " 40c deep yellow green ('40) 5.50 20

Perf. 12½.

218 A19 50c lilac gray ('40) 500.00
219 " 60c ultra. ('39) 15.00 1.40
220 " 80c vermilion ('39) 80.00 32.50
221 " 1g violet ('39) 37.50 1.00
223 " 2g Prussian green 37.50 18.50
225 " 5g yellow brown 35.00 7.50
Nos. 200–216, 219–225 (19) 263.09 97.04

The note following No. 188 applies also to this issue.

The 50c was sold only at the philatelic window in Amsterdam.

War Dance of Nias Island
A23

Legong Dancer of Bali
A24

Wayang Wong Dancer of Java
A25

Padjogé Dancer, Southern Celebes
A26

Dyak Dancer of Borneo
A27

1941 *Perf. 12½* **Unwmkd.**

228	A23	2½c rose violet	25	25
229	A24	3c green	30	55
230	A25	4c olive green	23	50
231	A26	5c blue	8	10
232	A27	7½c dark violet	80	15
		Nos. 228-232 (5)	1.66	1.55

See also Nos. 279–280, 293, N38.

The 2c carmine, No. N38, was prepared for this series. It was issued in 1945, not by the Netherlands Indies authorities, who do not recognize its validity, but by the "Indonesian Republic." See No. N38.

Queen Wilhelmina
A28 A28a

1941–42 *Perf. 12½*

Size: 18x22¾mm.

233	A28	10c red orange	25	8
235	"	15c ultramarine	2.10	1.50
236	"	17½c orange	65	80
237	"	20c plum	32.50	40.00
238	"	25c Prussian green ('42)	47.50	65.00
239	"	30c olive bistre	3.00	1.25
240	"	35c purple ('42)	165.00	*400.00*
241	"	40c yellow green	13.00	3.00

Perf. 13½

Size: 20½x26mm.

242	A28	50c carmine lake	3.00	90
243	"	60c ultramarine	1.65	75
244	"	80c red orange	2.10	1.15
245	"	1g purple	2.35	38
246	"	2g Prus. green	13.50	1.25
247	"	5g bistre, perf. 12½ ('42)	400.00	*700.00*
248	"	10g green	47.50	17.50

Size: 26x32mm.

249	A28a	25g orange	300.00	200.00
		Nos. 233-249 (16)	1034.10	*1433.56*

Nos. 242 to 246 come also with Pin-perf. 13½.

Rice Fields
A29

Barge on Java Lake
A30

University of Medicine, Batavia
A31

Palms on Shore
A32

Plane over Bromo Volcano
A33

Queen Wilhelmina
A34 A35

1945 Engraved *Perf. 12*

250	A29	1c green	30	18
251	A30	2c rose lilac	30	40
252	A31	2½c dull lilac	30	17
253	A32	5c blue	20	12
254	A33	7½c olive gray	65	12
255	A34	10c red brown	10	7
256	"	15c dark blue	12	10
257	"	17½c rose lake	20	20
258	"	20c sepia	20	10
259	"	30c slate gray	38	10
260	A35	60c gray black	80	15
261	"	1g blue green	1.25	15
262	"	2½g red orange	4.00	65
		Nos. 250-262 (13)	8.80	2.51

Railway Viaduct Near Soekaboemi
A36

Dam and Power Station
A37

Palm Tree and Menangkabau House
A38

Huts on Piles
A39

Buddhist Stupas
A40

Wmk. 228

Wmkd. Small Crown and C. of A. Multiple. (228)

1946 Typographed. *Perf. 14½x14.*

263	A36	1c dark green	10	10
264	A37	2c black brown	10	10
265	A38	2½c scarlet	22	18
266	A39	5c indigo	10	7
267	A40	7½c ultramarine	22	12
		Nos. 263-267 (5)	74	57

Stamps of 1946 Surcharged with New Value in Black.

1947

268	A38	3(c) on 2½c scarlet	10	12
269	A40	3(c) on 7½c ultra.	10	12
		a. Double surch.	150.00	150.00
270	A36	4(c) on 1c dark green	20	18

No. 184 Surcharged with New Value and Bars in Red.

1947 *Perf. 12½.* **Wmk. 202**

271	A19	45(c) on 60c ultra.	1.50	1.35

Nos. 212, 218 and 220 Overprinted "1947" in Red or Black

1947 *Perf. 11½x12, 12½*

272	A18	25c blue green (R)	25	12
		a. Unwmkd.		175.00
273	A19	50c lilac gray (R)	75	38
274	"	80c vermilion	1.00	85
		a. Unwmkd.	600.00	175.00

Bar above "1947" on No. 274.

Nos. 174, 241, 246 and 247 Overprinted "1947" in Black.

1947 *Perf. 12½* **Unwmkd.**

275	A18	12½c deep orange	10	8
276	A28	40c yellow green	40	10
277	"	2g Prussian green	4.50	50
278	"	5g bistre	12.00	7.50

The overprint is vertical on Nos. 276 to 278.

Dancer Types of 1941, 1945

1948 Lithographed

279	OS21	3c rose red	15	15
280	A24	4c dull olive green	15	15

Queen Wilhelmina
A41

1948 Photogravure *Perf. 12½*

Size: 18x22mm.

281	A41	15c red orange	75	75
282	"	20c bright blue	15	12
283	"	25c dark green	18	12
284	"	40c dp. yellow green	25	12
285	A41	45c plum	50	65
286	"	50c red brown	33	12
287	"	80c bright red	45	15

Perf. 13.

Size: 20½x26mm.

288	A41	1g deep violet	40	12
		a. Perf. 12½x12	1.10	50
289	"	10g green	32.50	6.50
290	"	25g orange	70.00	57.50
		Nos. 281-290 (10)	105.51	66.15

Wilhelmina Type of 1948 Inscribed: "1898 1948."

1948 *Perf. 12½x12*

Size: 21x26½mm.

291	A41	15c orange	30	18
292	"	20c ultramarine	30	15

Issued to commemorate the 50th anniversary of the reign of Queen Wilhelmina.

Dancer Type of 1941.

1948 Photogravure *Perf. 12½*

293	A27	7½c olive bistre	90	90

Juliana Type of Netherlands 1948

1948 *Perf. 14x13.* **Wmk. 202**

293A	A75	15c red orange	30	25
293B	"	20c deep ultramarine	30	15

Issued to commemorate the investiture of Queen Juliana, September 6, 1948.

Indonesia.

Nos. 281 to 287 Overprinted in Black

INDONESIA

Two types of overprint:
I. Shiny ink, bar 1.8mm. wide. By G. C. T. van Dorp & Co.
II. Dull ink, bar 2.2mm. By G. Kolff & Co.

1948–49 *Perf. 12½*

294	A41	15c red orange (I)	90	18
		a. Type II	75	10
295	"	20c bright blue (I)	23	10
		a. Type II	25	12
296	"	25c dark green (I)	28	18
		a. Type II	18	10
297	"	40c deep yellow green (I)	30	10
298	"	45c plum ('49) (II)	1.15	75
299	"	50c red brown ('49) (II)	25	10
300	"	80c bright red (I)	95	15
		a. Type II	95	15

Nos. 288 to 290 Overprinted in Black

INDONESIA

Two or Three Bars.

Perf. 13.

301	A41	1g deep violet, perf. 12½x12	75	10
		a. Perf. 13	1.35	20
302	"	10g green ('49)	65.00	5.50
303	"	25g orange ('49)	75.00	55.00
		Nos. 294-303 (10)	144.81	62.16

Same Surcharge in Black on No. 262.

1949 *Perf. 12.*

Bars 28½ mm. Long.

304	A35	2½g red orange	19.00	8.00

Numeral
A42

Tjandi Puntadewa Temple Entrance, East Java
A43

Detail, Temple of the Dead, Bedjuning, Bali
A44

Menangkabau House, Sumatra
A45

Toradja House, Celebes
A46

Designs: 5r, 10r, 25r, Temple entrance.

Photogravure.

1949 ***Perf. 12½, 11½.*** **Unwmkd.**

307 A42 1s gray 22 15
308 " 2s claret 28 10
a. Perf. 11½ 3.75 9.00
309 " 2½s olive brown 22 10
310 " 3s rose pink 28 10
a. Perf. 11½ 1.20 90
311 " 4s green 38 40
312 " 5s blue 12 10
a. Perf. 11½ 90 12
313 " 7½s dark green 42 10
a. Perf. 11½ 70 50
314 " 10s violet 20 10
a. Perf. 11½ 450.00
315 " 12½s bright red 38 10
a. Perf. 11½ 3.00 2.00
316 A43 15s rose red 33 10
317 " 20s gray black 33 10
318 " 25s ultramarine 33 10
319 A44 30s bright red 33 10
320 " 40s gray green 38 10
321 " 45s claret 38 30
a. Perf. 12½ 2.00 35
322 A45 50s orange brown 38 10
323 " 60s brown 45 10
324 " 80s scarlet 38 10
a. Perf. 12½ 2.75 20

Perf. 12½

325 A46 1r purple 25 7
326 " 2r gray green 2.75 6
327 " 3r red violet 22.50 12
328 " 5r dark brown 22.50 12
329 " 10r gray 45.00 25
330 " 25r orange brown 25 25
Nos. 307-330 (24) 99.04 3.22

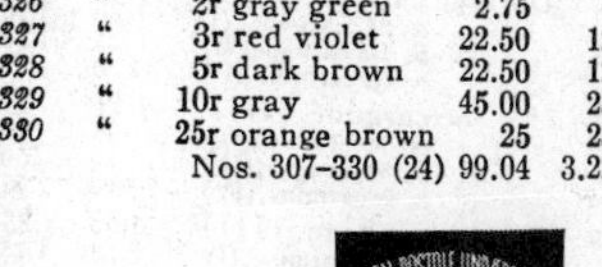

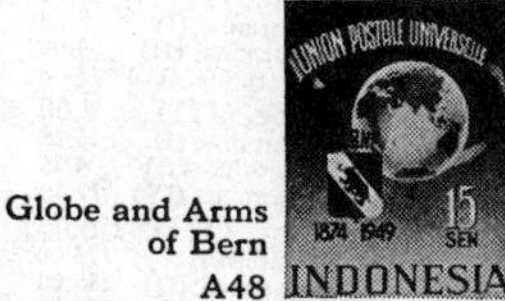

Globe and Arms of Bern
A48

1949 ***Perf. 12½***

331 A48 15s bright red 75 40
332 " 25s ultramarine 75 30

75th anniversary of Universal Postal Union.

See Indonesia (republic) for subsequent listings.

SEMI-POSTAL STAMPS.

Regular Issue of 1912-14 Surcharged in Carmine

1915 ***Perf. 12½*** **Unwmkd.**

B1 A11 1c+5c olive green 5.50 4.50
B2 " 5c+5c rose 7.00 6.00
B3 A12 10c+5c rose 11.50 9.50

Bali Temple
SP1

Watchtower
SP2

Menangkabau Compound
SP3

Borobudur Temple, Java
SP4

Photogravure.

1930 ***Perf. 11½x11, 11x11½.***

B4 SP1 2c(+1c) violet & brown 1.25 1.00
B5 SP2 5c(+2½c) dark green & brown 5.00 3.00
B6 SP3 12½c(+2½c) dp. red & brown 3.50 65
B7 SP4 15c(+5c) ultramarine & brown 7.00 6.75

Farmer and Carabao
SP5

Designs: 5c, Fishermen. 12½c, Dancers. 15c, Musicians.

1931 **Typographed** ***Perf. 12½***

B8 SP5 2c(+1c) olive bistre 3.25 2.25
B9 " 5c(+2½c) blue green 5.25 4.00
B10 " 12½c(+2½c) dp. red 3.25 65
B11 " 15c(+5c) dull blue 12.00 9.50

The surtax was for the aid of the Leper Colony at Salatiga.

Weaving—SP9

Designs: 5c, Plaiting rattan. 12½c, Woman batik dyer. 15c, Coppersmith.

1932 **Photogravure.** ***Perf. 13.***

B12 SP9 2c(+1c) deep violet & bistre 65 50
B13 " 5c(+2½c) dp. green & bistre 4.25 2.75
B14 " 12½c(+2½c) bright rose & bistre 1.25 38
B15 " 15c(+5c) blue & bistre 5.75 4.50

The surtax was donated to the Salvation Army.

Woman and Lotus
SP13

Designs: 5c, "The Light that Shows the Way." 12½c, YMCA emblem. 15c, Jobless man.

1933 ***Perf. 12½.***

B16 SP13 2c(+1c) red violet & olive bistre 1.25 38
B17 " 5c(+2½c) green & olive bistre 3.75 2.50
B18 " 12½c(+2½c) vermilion & olive bistre 4.25 38
B19 " 15c(+5c) blue & olive bistre 5.50 2.75

The surtax was for the Amsterdam Young Men's Society for Relief of the Poor.

Dowager Queen Emma
SP17

A Pioneer at Work
SP18

1934 ***Perf. 13x13½.***

B20 SP17 12½c(+2½c) black brown 2.10 65

Issued in memory of the late Dowager Queen Emma of Netherlands. The surtax was for the Anti-Tuberculosis Society.

1935 ***Perf. 12½***

Designs: 5c, Cavalryman rescuing wounded native. 12½c, Artilleryman under fire. 15c, Bugler.

B21 SP18 2c(+1c) plum & olive bistre 2.50 1.85
B22 " 5c(+2½c) green & olive bis. 6.00 3.75
B23 " 12½c(+2½c) red orange & olive bistre 6.00 38
B24 " 15c(+5c) bright blue & olive bistre 8.00 8.00

The surtax was for the Indian Committee of the Christian Military Association for the East and West Indies.

Child Welfare Work
SP22

Boy Scouts
SP23

Size: 23x20mm.

1936

B25 SP22 2c(+1c) plum 2.00 90

Size: 30x26½mm.

B26 SP22 5c(+2½c) gray violet 2.25 1.50
B27 " 7½c(+2½c) dark violet 2.25 2.00
B28 " 12½c(+2½c) red orange 2.25 38
B29 " 15c+(5c) bright blue 3.75 2.75
Nos. B25-B29 (5) 12.50 7.53

Surtax for Salvation Army.

1937

B30 SP23 7½c+2½c dark olive brown 2.25 1.50
B31 SP23 12½c+2½c rose carmine 2.25 75

Fifth Boy Scout World Jamboree, Vogelenzang, Netherlands, July 31–Aug. 13, 1937. Surtax for local Scout association, De Padvindersbond.

Sifting Rice
SP24

Designs: 3½c, Mother and children. 7½c, Plowing with carabao team. 10c, Carabao team and cart. 20c, Native couple.

1937

B32 SP24 2c+(1c) dark brown & orange 1.75 1.15
B33 " 3½c+(1½c) gray 1.75 1.15
B34 " 7½c+(2½c) Prussian green & orange 2.00 1.25
B35 " 10c+(2½c) carmine & orange 2.25 25
B36 " 20c+(5c) brt. blue 2.25 1.75
Nos. B32-B36 (5) 10.00 5.55

Nun and Child
SP29 SP30

Designs: 7½c, Nurse examining child's arm. 10c, Nurse bathing baby. 20c, Nun bandaging child's head.

1938 **Wmkd. Circles. (202)**

Perf. 12

B37 SP29 2c(+1c) violet 1.00 65

Perf. 11½x12

B38 SP30 3½c(+1½c) bright green 1.65 1.50

Perf. 12x11½

B39 SP30 7½c(+2½c) copper red 1.25 1.25
B40 " 10c(+2½c) verm. 1.50 25
B41 " 20c(+5c) bright ultramarine 1.85 1.25
Nos. B37-B41 (5) 7.25 4.90

The surtax was for the Central Mission Bureau in Batavia.

Social Workers
SP34

Indonesian Nurse Tending Patient
SP35

European Nurse Tending Patient
SP36

Photogravure.

1939 ***Perf. 13x11½, 11½x13.***

B42 SP34 2c(+1c) purple 38 22
B43 SP35 3½c(+1½c) blue green & pale blue green 60 35
B44 SP34 7½c(+2½c) copper brown 38 25
B45 SP35 10c(+2½c) scarlet & pink 2.25 1.15
B46 SP36 10c(+2½c) scarlet 2.25 1.15
B47 " 20c(+5c) dark blue 70 50
Nos. B42-B47 (6) 6.56 3.62

No. B44 shows native social workers.
Nos. B45 and B46 were issued se-tenant vertically and horizontally. The surtax was used for the Bureau of Social Service.

No. 174
Surcharged in Brown

✚
10+5 ct

1940 ***Perf. 11½x12.*** **Unwmkd.**

B48 A18 10c+5c on 12½c deep orange 1.25 55

Netherlands Coat of Arms and Inscription "Netherlands Shall Rise Again"
SP37

1941 **Typographed.** ***Perf. 12½.***

B49 SP37 5c+5c deep orange, ultra. & blk. 18 18
B50 " 10c+10c scarlet, ultra. & blk. 20 20
B51 " 1g+1g gray & ultramarine 15.00 10.00

The surtax was used to purchase bombing planes for Dutch pilots fighting with the Royal Air Force in Great Britain.

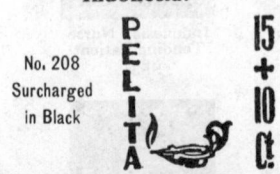

Doctor and Child
SP38

Designs: 3½c, Rice eater. 7½c, Nurse and patient. 10c, Nurse and children. 15c, Basket weaver.

1941 **Photogravure.**

B52 SP38 2c(+1c) yel. grn. 75 75
B53 " 3½c(+1½c) violet brown 4.50 4.25
B54 " 7½c(+2½c) violet 3.50 3.25
B55 " 10c(+2½c) dk. red 1.25 25
B56 " 15c(+5c) sapphire 12.50 6.50
Nos. B52-B56 (5) 22.50 15.00

The surtax was used for various charities.

Indonesia.

No. 208
Surcharged
in Black

PELITA
15 + 10 Ct

1948 ***Perf. 12½x11½.*** **Wmk. 202**

B57 A18 15c+10c on 10c vermilion 10 10
a. Inverted surcharge 265.00 275.00

The surtax was for war victims and other charitable purposes.

AIR POST STAMPS.

LUCHTPOST

Regular Issues of 1913-1923 Surcharged and New Values in Black or Blue.

Perf. 12½, 11½.

1928, Sept. 20 **Unwmkd.**

C1 A12 10c on 12½c red 1.25 1.25
C2 " 20c on 25c red violet 3.00 3.00
C3 A13 40c on 80c orange 2.50 1.75
C4 " 75c on 1g brown (Bl) 1.25 55
C5 " 1½g on 2½g carmine 9.00 6.75
Nos. C1-C5 (5) 17.00 13.30

On Nos. C4 and C5 there are stars over the original values and the airplane is of different shape. On No. C3 there are no bars under "OST".

Planes over Temple
AP1

1928, Dec. 1 Litho. ***Perf. 12½x11½***

C6 AP1 10c red violet 40 20
C7 " 20c brown 1.25 75
C8 " 40c rose 1.50 75
C9 " 75c green 3.00 20
C10 " 1.50g orange 6.00 65
Nos. C6-C10 (5) 12.15 2.55

No. C8 Surcharged in Black or Green

1930-32

C11 AP1 30c on 40c rose 1.15 20
C12 " 30c on 40c rose (G) ('32) 1.40 18

Pilot at Controls of Plane
AP2

1931, Apr. 1 **Photo.** ***Perf. 12½***

C13 AP2 1g blue & brown 17.50 17.50

Issued for the first air mail flight from Java to Australia.

Landscape and Garudas
AP3

1931, May

C14 AP3 30c red violet 4.00 18
C15 " 4½g bright blue 14.00 3.75
C16 " 7½g yellow green 16.50 4.00

No. C10 Surcharged in Blue

1932 ***Perf. 12½x11½.***

C17 AP1 50c on 1.50g org. 5.25 50
a. Inverted surcharge 1750.00 2250.00

Airplane—AP4

1933 ***Perf. 12½.***

C18 AP4 30c deep blue 1.65 1.75

AIR POST SEMI-POSTAL STAMPS.

Modern Plane
SPAP1

Design: 20c, Plane nose facing left.

Wmkd. Circles. (202)

1938 **Photogravure.** ***Perf. 12½.***

CB1 SPAP1 17½c+(5c) olive brown 1.40 1.25
CB2 " 20c+(5c) slate 1.40 75

Issued in commemoration of the 10th anniversary of the Dutch East Indies Royal Air Lines. (K. N. I. L. M.)

MARINE INSURANCE STAMPS.

Floating Safe Attracting Gulls
MI1

Floating Safe with Night Flare
MI2

Artistic Fantasy of Floating Safe
MI3

Engraved.

1922 ***Perf. 11½*** **Unwmkd.**

GY1 MI1 15c slate green 3.00 *40.00*
GY2 " 60c rose 8.00 *60.00*
GY3 " 75c gray brown 8.00 *65.00*
GY4 MI2 1.50g dark blue 47.50 *325.00*
GY5 " 2.25g org. brown 55.00 *400.00*
GY6 MI3 4½g black 100.00 *675.00*
GY7 " 7½g red 115.00 *1100.00*
Nos. GY1-GY7 (7) 336.50 *2665.00*

POSTAGE DUE STAMPS.

Aangebragt per Land-Mail.
Te betalen port duiten.
BATAVIA,

D1

Aangebragt per Land-Mail.
Te betalen port *f* koper.
BATAVIA,

D2

Typeset

1845-46 ***Imperf.*** **Unwmkd.**

Bluish Paper.

J1 D1 black ('46) 1900.00
J2 D2 black 1900.00
a. "Maill" instead of "Mail" 3750.00

D3

Perf. 12½x12, 13x14

1874 **Typographed**

J3 D3 5c ochre 225.00 250.00
J4 " 10c green, *yellow* 115.00 95.00
J5 " 15c ochre, *orange* 25.00 16.00
a. Perf. 11½x12 55.00 50.00
J6 " 20c green, *blue* 42.50 6.50
a. Perf. 11½x12 90.00 20.00

D4 D5

Type I. 34 loops. "T" of "Betalen" over center of loop, top branch of "E" of "Te" shorter than lower branch.
Type II. 33 loops. "T" of "Betalen" over center of two loops.
Type III. 32 loops. "T" of "Betalen" slightly to the left of loop, top branch of first "E" of "Betalen" shorter than lower branch.
Type IV. 37 loops and letters of "PORT" larger than in the other three types.

Value in Black.

Perf. 11½x12, 12½, 12½x12, 13½.

1882-88

J7 D4 2½c carmine, (III) 45 1.15
a. 2½c carmine, (I) 50 1.30
b. 2½c carmine, (II) 55 1.60
c. 2½c carmine, (IV) 2.50 4.25
J8 " 5c carmine, (III) 25 45
a. 5c carmine, (I) 25 50
b. 5c carmine, (II) 30 50
c. 5c carmine, (IV) 1.00 2.25
J9 " 10c carmine, (III) 3.00 3.25
a. 10c carmine, (I) 3.50 4.75
b. 10c carmine, (II) 4.00 5.25
c. 10c carmine, (IV) 23.50 35.00
J10 " 15c carmine, (III) 3.50 3.50
a. 15c carmine, (I) 3.75 4.25
b. 15c carmine, (II) 4.25 4.75
c. 15c carmine, (IV) 17.50 20.00
J11 " 20c carmine, (III) 110.00 45
a. 20c carmine, (I) 125.00 50
b. 20c carmine, (II) 135.00 65
c. 20c carmine, (IV) 225.00 6.00
J12 " 30c carmine, (III) 2.10 3.00
a. 30c carmine, (I) 3.50 4.50
b. 30c carmine, (II) 7.00 9.00
J13 " 40c carmine, (III) 1.40 2.75
a. 40c carmine, (I) 1.60 2.35
b. 40c carmine, (II) 1.75 3.00
c. 40c carmine, (IV) 2.75 5.00
J14 " 50c dp. sal., (III) 60 60
a. 50c carmine, (I) 70 65
b. 50c carmine, (II) 80 90
c. 50c carmine, (IV) 11.00 20.00
J15 " 75c carmine, (III) 45 55
a. 75c carmine, (I) 45 60
b. 75c carmine, (II) 70 65
c. 75c carmine, (IV) 1.50 2.50

1892-95

J16 D5 10c carmine, (I) 2.00 35
a. 10c dull red, (III) 3.25 2.50
b. 10c dull red, (II) 16.50 16.50
J17 " 15c car., (I) ('95) 11.50 2.00
J18 " 20c carmine, (I) 2.35 17
a. 20c dull red, (III) 5.00 1.65
b. 20c dull red, (II) 25.00 9.00

1906-09 Type I.

J19 D5 2½c carmine ('08) 65 38
J20 " 5c " ('09) 3.00 18
J21 " 30c " ('06) 18.00 6.50
J22 " 40c " ('09) 11.50 1.50
J23 " 50c " ('09) 8.50 1.00
J24 " 75c " ('09) 17.50 4.00
Nos. J19-J24 (6) 59.15 13.56

Value in Color of Stamp.

1913-39 *Perf. 12½.*

J25 D5 1c salmon ('39) 8 *1.25*
J26 " 2½c " 12 10
J27 " 3½c " ('39) 8 *1.25*
J28 " 5c " 12 10
J29 " 7½c " ('22) 12 10
J30 " 10c " 12 10
J31 " 12½c " ('22) 3.75 12
J32 " 15c " 3.75 15
J33 " 20c " 20 10
J34 " 25c " ('22) 20 10
J35 " 30c " 25 25
J36 " 37½c " ('30) 18.00 15.00
J37 " 40c " 25 18
J38 " 50c " 1.75 12
J39 " 75c " 3.25 18
Nos. J25-J39 (15) 32.04 *19.10*

Thick White Paper.
Invisible Gum.
Numerals Slightly Larger.

1941 *Perf. 12½.*

J25a D5 1c light red 75 2.50
J28a " 5c " 85 1.25
J30a " 10c " 14.00 14.00
J32a " 15c " 1.25 1.25
J33a " 20c " 1.00 1.00
J35a " 30c " 1.50 1.25
J37a " 40c " 1.25 1.00
Nos. J25a-J37a(7) 20.60 22.25

No. J36 Surcharged with New Value.

1937 *Perf. 12½.* **Unwmkd.**

J40 D5 20c on 37½c salmon 30 40

D6

D7

1939-40

J41 D6 1g salmon 5.50 7.50
J42 " 1g blue ('40) 25 *3.25*

Thick Paper.
Invisible Gum.

1941

J42a D6 1g light blue 90 90

Nos. 233, 237 and 241 Surcharged or Overprinted in Black

TE BETALEN

PORT

1946 *Perf. 12½.* **Unwmkd.**

J43 A28 2½c on 10c red org. 65 65
J44 " 10c red orange 1.20 1.20
J45 " 20c plum 3.50 3.50
J46 " 40c yellow green 47.50 47.50

Typographed.

1946 *Perf. 14½x14.* **Wmk. 228**

J47 D7 1c purple 75 1.00
J48 " 2½c brown orange 2.00 2.00
J49 " 3½c ultramarine 75 1.00
J50 " 5c red orange 1.00 1.00
J51 " 7½c Prussian green 1.00 1.10
J52 " 10c deep magenta 1.00 1.10
J53 " 20c light ultra. 1.00 1.25
J54 " 25c olive 1.10 1.25
J55 " 30c red brown 1.10 1.40
J56 " 40c yellow green 1.40 1.50
J57 " 50c yellow 1.50 1.65
J58 D7 75c aquamarine 1.50 1.65
J59 " 100c apple green 1.50 1.65
Nos. J47-J59 (13) 15.60 17.55

1948 *Perf. 12½.* **Unwmkd.**

J59A D7 2½c brown orange 70 1.00

OFFICIAL STAMPS.

Regular Issues of 1883-1909 Overprinted

1911 *Perf. 12½.* **Unwmkd.**

O1 A6 ½c violet 12 40
a. Inverted overprint 50.00 *165.00*
O2 " 1c olive green 18 18
a. Inverted overprint 2.75 *25.00*
O3 " 2c yellow brown 15 15
a. Inverted overprint 2.75 *25.00*
O4 A3 2½c yellow 80 80
O5 A6 2½c blue green 1.25 1.50
a. Inverted overprint 10.00 *37.50*
O6 " 3c orange 50 38
a. Invtd. ovpt. 165.00 52.50
O7 " 4c ultramarine 20 12
O8 " 5c rose red 1.00 1.00
a. Inverted overprint 2.75 *25.00*
b. Double overprint 325.00
O9 " 7½c gray 3.25 3.50
O10 A9 10c slate 20 10
a. Inverted overprint 2.75 *8.50*
O11 " 12½c deep blue 2.50 3.00
a. Inverted overprint 37.50 72.50
O12 " 15c chocolate 80 75
a. Overprinted with two bars 45.00
b. As "a," "Dienst." inverted 55.00
O13 " 17½c bistre 3.50 3.00
O14 " 20c olive green 80 65
a. Invtd. ovpt. 300.00 85.00
O15 " 22½c brown & olive green 4.25 3.50
O16 " 25c violet 2.65 2.25
a. Inverted overprint 1500.00 1400.00
O17 " 30c orange brown 1.10 65
a. Inverted ovpt. 250.00 165.00
O18 " 50c red brown 16.50 10.00
a. Inverted overprint 35.00 40.00
O19 A10 1g dull lilac 3.75 1.50
a. Inverted ovpt. 700.00 1100.00
O20 " 2½g slate blue 37.50 40.00
a. Invtd. ovpt. 275.00 *850.00*
Nos. O1-O20 (20) 81.00 73.43

The overprint reads diagonally downward on Nos. 01-03 and 05-09.

Regular Issue of 1892-1894 Overprinted

1911

O21 A4 10c orange brown 1.25 75
a. Inverted overprint 11.00 *37.50*
O22 " 12½c gray 3.00 5.75
a. Inverted overprint 350.00 350.00
O23 " 15c bistre 3.00 3.00
a. Inverted overprint 350.00 350.00
O24 " 20c blue 2.00 1.00
a. Inverted ovpt. 100.00 100.00
O25 " 25c lilac 10.00 10.50
a. Inverted overprint 500.00 500.00
O26 " 50c carmine 1.25 1.00
a. Inverted overprint 11.00 *100.00*
O27 " 2.50g orange brown & blue 55.00 60.00
a. Inverted ovpt. 650.00 1100.00
Nos. O21-O27 (7) 75.50 82.00

OCCUPATION STAMPS.

Issued under Japanese Occupation.

大日本

During the Japanese occupation of the Netherlands Indies, 1942-45, the occupation forces applied a great variety of overprints to supplies of Netherlands Indies stamps of 1933-42. A few typical examples are shown above.

Most of these overprinted stamps were for use in limited areas, such as Java, Sumatra, Bangka and Billiton, etc. The anchor overprints were applied by the Japanese naval authorities for areas under their control.

For a time, stamps of Straits Settlements and some of the Malayan states, with Japanese overprints, were used in Sumatra and the Riouw archipelago. Stamps of Japan without overprint were also used in the Netherlands Indies during the occupation.

For Use in Java and Sumatra.

100 Sen (Cents) = 1 Rupee (Gulden)

Globe Showing Japanese Empire
OS1

Farmer Plowing Rice Field
OS2

Mt. Semeru, Java's Highest Active Volcano
OS3

Bantam Bay, Northwest Java
OS4

Values in Sen.
Lithographed.

1943 *Perf. 12½.* **Unwmkd.**

N1 OS1 2s red brown 40 60
N2 OS2 3½s carmine 15 15
N3 OS3 5s green 30 30
N4 OS4 10s light blue 3.50 30

Issued to mark the anniversary of Japan's "Victory" in Java.

For Use in Java.
(also Sumatra, Borneo and Malaya.)

Javanese Dancer
OS5

Javanese Puppet
OS6

Buddha Statue, Borobudur
OS7

Map of Java
OS8

Sacred Dancer of Djokja Palace, and Borobudur
OS9

Bird of Vishnu, Map of Java and Mt. Semeru
OS10

Plowing with Carabao
OS11

Terraced Rice Fields
OS12

Values in Cents, Sen or Rupees.

1943-44 *Perf. 12½.* **Unwmkd.**

N5 OS5 3½c rose red 10 15
N6 OS6 5s yellow green 10 20
N7 OS7 10c dark blue 10 10
N8 OS8 20c gray olive 25 25
N9 OS9 40c rose lilac 1.50 45
N10 OS10 60c red orange 80 25
N11 OS11 80s fawn ('44) 2.00 90
N12 OS12 1r violet ('44) 3.25 75
Nos. N5-N12 (8) 8.10 3.05

Indies Soldier—OS13

1943

N13 OS13 3½c rose 10.00 2.00
N14 " 10c blue 10.00 75

Issued to commemorate reaching the postal savings goal of 5,000,000 gulden.

For Use in Sumatra.

Batta Tribal House
OS14

Menangkabau House
OS15

Plowing with Carabao
OS16

Nias Island Scene
OS17

Carabao Canyon
OS18

1943		*Perf. 12½.*		**Unwmkd.**
N15	OS14	1c olive green	7	7
N16	"	2c brt. yel. green	8	8
N17	"	3c bluish green	12	12
N18	OS15	3½c rose red	15	15
N19	"	4c ultramarine	20	15
N20	"	5c red orange	15	15
N21	OS16	10c blue gray	25	25
N22	"	20c orange brown	50	40
N23	OS17	30c red violet	50	50
N24	"	40c dull brown	3.25	1.75
N25	OS18	50c bistre brown	3.25	1.50
N26	"	1r lt. bl. violet	11.00	2.25
		Nos. N15–N26 (12)	19.52	7.37

For Use in the Lesser Sunda Islands, Molucca Archipelago and Districts of Celebes and South Borneo Controlled by the Japanese Navy.

Japanese Flag and Island Scene
OS19

Mt. Fuji, Kite, Flag and Map of East Indies
OS20

Values in Cents and Gulden.

Typographed.

1943		*Perf. 13*		**Wmk. 257**
N27	OS19	2c brown	5	5
N28	"	3c yellow green	8	8
N29	"	3½c brown orange	75	75
N30	"	5c blue	10	10
N31	"	10c carmine	5	5
N32	"	15c ultramarine	12	12
N33	"	20c dull violet	15	15
		Engraved.		
N34	OS20	25c orange	2.00	3.00
N35	"	30c blue	2.00	1.25
N36	"	50c slate green	2.00	1.25
N37	"	1g brown lilac	12.00	7.00
		Nos. N27–N37 (11)	19.30	13.80

Issued under Nationalist Occupation

Menari Dancer of Amboina
OS21

1945		*Perf. 12½.*		**Unwmkd.**
N38	OS21	2c carmine	10	20

This stamp was prepared in 1941 or 1942 by Netherlands Indies authorities as an addition to the 1941 "dancers set," but was issued in 1945 by the Nationalists (Indonesian Republic). It was not recognized by the Dutch.

No. N38 exists imperforate.

NETHERLANDS NEW GUINEA

(Dutch New Guinea)

LOCATION—Western half of New Guinea, southwest Pacific Ocean.

GOVT.—Former Overseas Territory of the Netherlands.

AREA—151,789 sq. mi.

POP.—730,000 (est. 1958).

CAPITAL—Hollandia.

Netherlands New Guinea came under temporary United Nations administration Oct. 1, 1962, when stamps of this territory overprinted "UNTEA" were introduced to replace issues of Netherlands New Guinea. See West New Guinea (West Irian) in Vol. IV.

100 Cents = 1 Gulden

Numeral
A1

A2

A3

Queen Juliana

Photogravure.

1950–52		*Perf. 12½x13½*		**Unwmkd.**
1	A1	1c slate blue	15	15
2	"	2c deep orange	17	15
3	"	2½c olive brown	17	15
4	"	3c deep plum	2.00	1.75
5	"	4c blue green	2.00	1.50
6	"	5c ultramarine	4.25	20
7	"	7½c orange brown	50	25
8	"	10c purple	2.25	25
9	"	12½c crimson	2.25	2.00
		Perf. 13½x12½.		
10	A2	15c brown orange	1.75	70
11	"	20c blue	50	12
12	"	25c orange red	50	12
13	"	30c deep blue ('52)	3.25	38
14	"	40c blue green	1.00	15
15	"	45c brown ('52)	3.25	75
16	"	50c deep orange	1.00	15
17	"	55c brown black ('52)	5.00	75
18	"	80c purple	7.50	3.75
		Engraved.		
		Perf. 12½x12		
19	A3	1g red	15.00	15
20	"	2g yellow brown ('52)	14.00	2.00
21	"	5g dark olive green	14.00	1.50
		Nos. 1–21 (21)	80.49	16.92

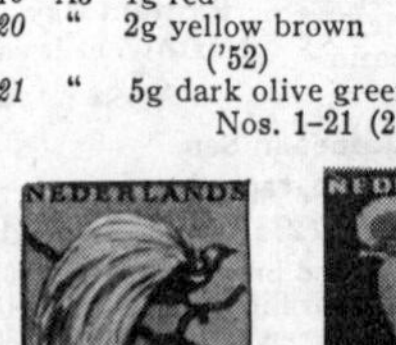

Bird of Paradise
A4

Queen Victoria Crowned Pigeon
A5

Queen Juliana
A6

Designs: 10c, 15c and 20c, Bird of Paradise with raised wings.

Photogravure;

Lithographed (Nos. 24, 26, 28)

1954–60			*Perf. 12½x12*	
22	A4	1c verm. & yel. ('58)	8	8
23	"	5c chocolate & yellow	12	10
24	A5	7c orange red, blue & brown vio. ('59)	25	50
25	A4	10c aquamarine & red brown	20	10
26	A5	12c green, blue & brown violet ('59)	25	50
27	A4	15c deep yellow & red brown	30	10
28	A5	17c brown violet & blue ('59)	25	35
29	A4	20c light blue green & red brn. ('56)	1.00	65
30	A6	25c red	25	15
31	"	30c deep blue	25	20
32	"	40c deep orange ('60)	2.50	3.50
33	"	45c dark olive ('58)	85	1.25
34	"	55c dark blue green	60	12
35	"	80c dull gray violet	1.00	40
36	"	85c dark violet brown ('56)	1.00	60
37	"	1g plum ('59)	6.00	3.00
		Nos. 22–37 (16)	14.90	11.60

Stamps overprinted "UNTEA" are listed under West New Guinea in Vol. IV.

Papuan Watching Helicopter
A7

Mourning Woman
A8

1959		Photogravure	*Perf. 11½x11*	
38	A7	55c red brown & bl.	1.65	1.25

Issued to honor the 1959 expedition to the Star Mountains of New Guinea.

1960		*Perf. 13x14*		**Unwmkd.**
39	A8	25c blue	60	75
40	"	30c yellow bistre	75	1.00

Issued to publicize World Refugee Year, July 1, 1959–June 30, 1960.

Council Building—A9

1961		Lithographed	*Perf. 11x11½*	
41	A9	25c bluish green	40	50
42	"	30c rose	40	50

Inauguration of the New Council.

School Children Crossing Street
A10

Design: 30c, Men looking at traffic sign.

1962, Mar. 16		Photo.	*Perf. 14x13*	
43	A10	25c deep blue & red	40	50
44	"	30c brt. green & red	40	50

Need for road safety.

Silver Wedding Issue

Type of Netherlands, 1962

1962, Apr. 28		*Perf. 14x13*	**Unwmkd.**	
45	A92	55c olive brown	50	60

Issued to commemorate the silver wedding anniversary of Queen Juliana and Prince Bernhard.

Tropical Beach—A11

Design: 30c, Palm trees on beach.

1962, July 18			*Perf. 14x13½*	
46	A11	25c multicolored	38	55
47	"	30c "	38	55

Issued to commemorate the fifth South Pacific Conference, Pago Pago, July 1962.

SEMI-POSTAL STAMPS.

Regular Issue of 1950-52 Surcharged in Black

		Perf. 13½x12½, 12½x13½.		
1953				**Unwmkd.**
B1	A1	5c+5c ultramarine	16.50	14.00
B2	A2	15c+10c brown org.	16.50	14.00
B3	"	25c+10c orange red	16.50	14.00

The tax was for flood relief work in the Netherlands.

Nos. 23, 25, 27 Surcharged in Red

1955			*Perf. 12½x12*	
B4	A4	5c+5c choc. & yel.	1.50	1.50
B5	"	10c+10c aquamarine & red brn.	1.50	1.50
B6	"	15c+10c deep yellow & red brown	1.50	1.50

The surtax was for the Red Cross.

Leprosarium
SP1

Papuan Girl and Beach Scene
SP2

Design: 10c+5c, 30c+10c, Young Papuan and huts.

Photogravure

1956		*Perf. 12x12½*		**Unwmkd.**
B7	SP1	5c+5c dark slate green	1.50	1.40
B8	"	10c+5c brown violet	1.50	1.40
B9	"	25c+10c bright blue	1.50	1.40
B10	"	30c+10c ochre	1.50	1.40

The surtax was for the fight against leprosy.

1957			*Perf. 12½x12*	

Design: 10c+5c, 30c+10c, Papuan boy and pile dwelling.

B11	SP2	5c+5c maroon	1.50	1.40
B12	"	10c+5c slate green	1.50	1.40
B13	"	25c+10c brown	1.50	1.40
B14	"	30c+10c dark blue	1.50	1.40

The surtax was to fight infant mortality.

Ancestral Image, North Coast New Guinea
SP3

Bignonia
SP4

Design: 10c+5c, 30c+10c, Bowl in form of human figure, Asmat-Papua.

1958 Lithographed *Perf. 12½x12*

B15	SP3	5c+5c blue, black & red	1.40	1.40
B16	"	10c+5c rose lake, black, red & yellow	1.40	1.40
B17	"	25c+10c blue green, black & red	1.40	1.40
B18	"	30c+10c olive gray, black, red & yellow	1.40	1.40

The surtax was for the Red Cross.

1959 Photogravure *Perf. 12½x13*

Flowers: 10c+5c, Orchid. 25c+10c, Rhododendron. 30c+10c, Gesneriaceae.

B19	SP4	5c+5c carmine rose & green	75	75
B20	"	10c+5c olive, yellow & lilac	75	75
B21	"	25c+10c red, orange & green	75	75
B22	"	30c+10c violet & green	75	75

Birdwing
SP5

Various Butterflies

Lithographed

1960 *Perf. 13x12½* Unwmkd.

B23	SP5	5c+5c light blue, black, emerald & yellow	1.00	1.00
B24	"	10c+5c salmon, black & blue	1.00	1.00
B25	"	25c+10c yellow, black & org. red	1.00	1.00
B26	"	30c+10c light green, brown & yellow	1.00	1.00

Rhinoceros Beetle and Coconut Palm Leaf—SP6

Designs (beetles and leaves of host plants): 10c+5c, Ectocemus 10-maculatus Montri, a primitive weevil. 25c+10c, Stag beetle. 30c+10c, Tortoise beetle.

1961, Sept. 15 *Perf. 13x12½*

Beetles in Natural Colors.

B27	SP6	5c+5c deep orange	38	45
B28	"	10c+5c light ultra.	38	45
B29	"	25c+10c citron	45	50
B30	"	30c+10c green	55	60

Crab
SP7

Designs: 10c+5c, Lobster (vert.). 25c+10c, Spiny lobster (vert.). 30c+10c, Shrimp.

Perf. 13½x13, 13x13½

1962, Sept. 17 Unwmkd.

B31	SP7	5c+5c red, green, brown & yel.	25	25
B32	"	10c+5c Prussian blue & yellow	25	30
B33	"	25c+10c multi.	38	38
B34	"	30c+10c blue, org. red & yellow	38	45

The surtax on Nos. B19–B34 went to various social works organizations.

POSTAGE DUE STAMPS.

Type of Netherlands Antilles, 1953

1957 *Perf. 13½x12½* Unwmkd.

J1	D3	1c vermilion	8	25
J2	"	5c "	55	1.50
J3	"	10c "	1.60	3.00
J4	"	25c "	2.40	1.00
J5	"	40c "	2.50	1.15
J6	"	1g blue	3.00	5.00
		Nos. J1–J6 (6)	10.13	11.90

NEW CALEDONIA

(nū'kăl'ē·dō'nĭ·ȧ)

LOCATION—An island in the South Pacific Ocean, east of Queensland, Australia.

GOVT.—French Overseas Territory.

POP.—138,000 (est. 1975).

AREA—7,374 sq. mi.

CAPITAL—Nouméa.

Dependencies of New Caledonia are the Loyalty Islands, Isle of Pines, Huon Islands and Chesterfield Islands.

100 Centimes = 1 Franc

Napoleon III
A1

Lithographed

1859 *Imperf.* Unwmkd.

Without Gum.

1	A1	10c black	100.00

Fifty varieties. Counterfeits abound. See No. 315.

1881-83

Type of French Colonies, 1877 Surcharged in Black:

NCE 5 — *a*

NCE 5 — *b*

2	A8 (*a*)	5c on 40c red, *straw* ('82)	150.00	125.00
		a. Inverted surcharge	300.00	300.00
3	" (")	05c on 40c red, *straw* ('83)	11.00	11.00
4	" (")	25c on 35c deep violet, *yellow*	120.00	100.00
		a. Inverted surcharge	250.00	250.00
5	" (")	25c on 75c rose carmine, *rose* ('82)	140.00	120.00
		a. Inverted surcharge	250.00	250.00

1883-84

6	A8 (*b*)	5c on 40c red, *straw* ('84)	7.00	7.00
		a. Inverted surcharge	5.00	5.00
7	" (")	5c on 75c rose car., *rose* ('83)	15.00	15.00
		a. Inverted surcharge	13.50	13.50

In type "a" surcharge, the narrower-spaced letters measure 14½mm., and an early printing of No. 4 measures 13½mm. Type "b" letters measure 18mm.

French Colonies No. 59 Surcharged in Black:

N.C.E. 5c. — *c*

N.C.E. 5c. — *d*

1886 *Perf. 14x13½*

8	A9 (*c*)	5c on 1fr bronze green, *straw*	8.00	8.00
		a. Inverted surcharge	10.00	10.00
9	" (*d*)	5c on 1fr bronze green, *straw*	8.00	8.00
		b. Inverted surcharge	12.00	12.00

French Colonies No. 29 Surcharged.

Imperf.

10	A8 (*d*)	5c on 1fr bronze green, *straw*	3750.00	3750.00

Types of French Colonies, 1877-86, Surcharged in Black:

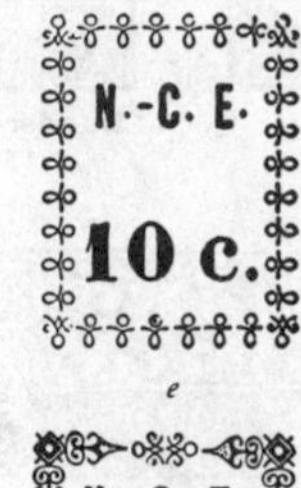

e

f

1891–92 *Imperf.*

11	A8 (*e*)	10c on 40c red, *straw* ('92)	9.00	8.00
		a. Inverted surcharge	10.00	10.00
		b. Double surcharge	17.50	17.50
		c. No period after "10c"	10.00	10.00

Perf. 14x13½.

12	A9 (*f*)	10c on 30c brn., *bistre*	4.00	4.00
		a. Inverted surcharge	4.00	4.00
		b. Double surcharge	12.00	12.00
		c. Double surcharge, inverted	10.00	10.00
13	" (*e*)	10c on 40c red, *straw* ('92)	4.00	4.00
		a. Inverted surcharge	4.00	4.00
		b. No period after "10c"	4.00	4.00
		c. Dbl. surch.	12.00	12.00

Variety "double surcharge, one inverted" exists on Nos. 11–13. Price same as for "double surcharge."

Types of French Colonies, 1877–86, Handstamped in Black

g

1892 *Imperf.*

16	A8	20c red, *green*	140.00	14.00
17	"	35c violet, *orange*	20.00	18.50
18	"	40c red, *straw*		
19	"	1fr bronze green, *straw*	100.00	100.00

The 1c, 2c, 4c and 75c of type A8 are believed not to have been officially made or actually used.

1892 *Perf. 14x13½*

23	A9	5c green, *greenish*	5.00	4.00
24	"	10c *lavender*	40.00	22.50
25	"	15c blue	32.50	12.00
26	"	20c red, *green*	30.00	20.00
27	"	25c yellow, *straw*	7.00	5.00
28	"	25c *rose*	32.50	5.00
29	"	30c brown, *bistre*	22.50	20.00
30	"	35c violet, *orange*	65.00	60.00
32	"	75c carmine, *rose*	70.00	60.00
33	"	1fr bronze green, *straw*	60.00	40.00

The note following No. 19 also applies to the 1c, 2c, 4c and 40c of type A9.

Surcharged in Blue or Black

h

1892-93 *Imperf.*

34	A8	10c on 1fr bronze grn., *straw* (Bl)	1650.00	1400.00

Perf. 14x13½.

35	A9	5c on 20c red, *green* (Bk)	7.50	4.50
		a. Inverted surcharge	30.00	30.00
		b. Double surcharge inverted		
36	"	5c on 75c carmine, *rose* (Bk)	4.50	3.00
		a. Inverted surcharge	30.00	30.00
37	"	5c on 75c carmine, *rose* (Bl)	3.50	2.50
		a. Inverted surcharge	30.00	30.00
38	"	10c on 1fr bronze green, *straw* (Bk)	3.50	3.00
		a. Inverted surcharge	140.00	140.00
39	"	10c on 1fr bronze green, *straw* (Bl)	5.50	5.50
		a. Inverted surcharge	30.00	30.00

Navigation and Commerce
A12

1892–1904 Typographed

Name of Colony in Blue or Carmine.

40	A12	1c *blue*	35	20
41	"	2c brown, *buff*	50	40
42	"	4c claret, *lavender*	80	60
43	"	5c green, *greenish*	80	40
44	"	5c yellow green ('00)	50	40
45	"	10c *lavender*	2.65	1.25
46	"	10c rose red ('00)	2.50	60
47	"	15c blue, quadrille paper	8.00	60
48	"	15c gray ('00)	3.00	50
49	"	20c red, *green*	5.00	3.00
50	"	25c *rose*	6.00	1.40
51	"	25c blue ('00)	4.00	2.50
52	"	30c brown, *bistre*	6.00	3.25
53	"	40c red, *straw*	6.00	4.00
54	"	50c carmine, *rose*	16.50	7.00

55 A12 50c brown, *azure* (name in carmine) ('00) 28.50 26.50
56 " 50c brown, *azure* (name in blue) ('04) 16.50 13.50
57 " 75c violet, *orange* 8.00 6.00
58 " 1fr bronze green, *straw* 10.00 6.00
Nos. 40-58 (19) 125.60 78.10

Stamps of 1892 Surcharged in Black:

N-C.E. N.-C.E.

j

k

1900-01

59 A12 (*h*) 5c on 2c brown, *buff* ('01) 6.00 5.00
a. Dbl. surch. 32.50 32.50
b. Invtd. surch. 32.50 32.50
60 " (") 5c on 4c claret, *lavender* 1.00 1.00
a. Inverted surcharge 15.00 15.00
b. Double surcharge 15.00 15.00
61 " (*j*) 15c on 30c brown, *bistre* 1.50 1.50
a. Inverted surcharge 13.50 13.50
b. Dbl. surch. 13.50 13.50
62 " (") 15c on 75c violet, *orge.* ('01) 5.00 3.50
a. Pair, one without surcharge
b. Inverted surcharge 32.50 32.50
c. Double surcharge 32.50 32.50
63 " (") 15c on 1fr bronze green, *straw* ('01) 7.50 7.00
a. Double surcharge 40.00 40.00
b. Inverted surcharge 40.00 40.00
Nos. 59-63 (5) 21.00 18.00

1902

64 A12 (*k*) 5c on 30c brown, *bistre* 3.25 2.75
a. Inverted surcharge 10.00 10.00
65 " (") 15c on 40c red, *straw* 2.50 2.25
a. Inverted surcharge 10.00 10.00

Jubilee Issue.

Stamps of 1892-1900 Overprinted in Blue, Red, Black or Gold

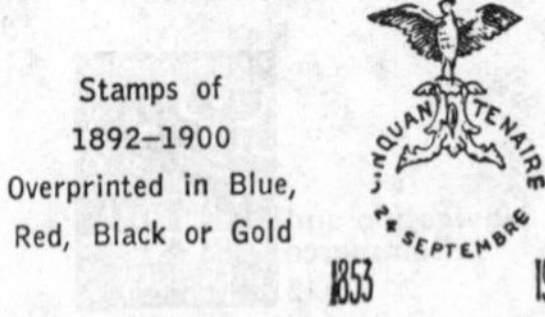

1903

66 A12 1c *lilac blue* (Bl) 60 60
a. Invtd. overprint 45.00 45.00
67 " 2c brown, *buff* (Bl) 1.40 1.00
68 " 4c claret, *lavender* (Bl) 1.50 1.00
a. Double overprint 60.00 60.00
69 " 5c dark green, *greenish* (R) 2.00 1.00
70 " 5c yellow green (R) 3.00 2.50
71 " 10c *lavender* (R) 5.00 3.50
72 " 10c *lavender* (double, G & Bk) 2.85 3.00
73 " 15c gray (R) 3.00 1.75
74 " 20c red, *green* (Bl) 6.00 5.00
75 " 25c *rose* (Bl) 6.00 5.00
a. Double overprint
76 " 30c brown, *bistre* (R) 7.00 5.75
77 " 40c red, *straw* (Bl) 11.00 7.00
78 A12 50c carmine, *rose* (Bl) 13.00 7.50
a. Pair, one without overprint
79 " 75c violet, *orange* (Bk) 22.50 16.50
a. Double overprint in black and red 135.00 135.00
80 " 1fr bronze green, *straw* (Bl) 26.50 24.00
a. Double overprint, one in red 135.00 135.00
Nos. 66-80 (15) 111.35 85.60

With Additional Surcharge of New Value in Blue.

81 A12 1c on 2c brown, *buff* (Bl) 25 25
a. Numeral double 25.00 25.00
b. Numeral only
82 " 2c on 4c claret, *lavender* (Bl) 55 55
83 " 4c on 5c dark green (R) 60 60
a. Small "4" 200.00 200.00
84 " 4c on 5c yel.grn. (R) 1.00 1.00
a. Pair, one without numeral
85 " 10c on 15c gray (R) 1.00 1.00
86 " 15c on 20c red, *green* (Bl) 1.00 1.00
87 " 20c on 25c *rose* (Bl) 1.65 1.65
Nos. 81-87 (7) 6.05 6.05

50 years of French occupation.

Surcharge on Nos. 81-83, 85-86 is horizontal, reading down.

There are three types of numeral on No. 83. The numeral on No. 84 is identical with that of No. 83a except that its position is upright.

Nos. 66-87 are known with "I" of "TENAIRE" missing.

Kagu
A16

Landscape
A17

Ship—A18

1905-28 Typo. *Perf. 14x13½*

88 A16 1c *green* 4 4
89 " 2c red brown 6 4
90 " 4c blue, *orange* 6 6
91 " 5c pale green 8 8
92 " 5c dull blue ('21) 6 6
93 " 10c carmine 20 7
94 " 10c green ('21) 12 12
95 " 10c red, *pink* ('25) 8 8
96 " 15c violet 8 8
97 A17 20c brown 6 6
98 " 25c blue, *green* 6 6
99 " 25c red, *yellow* ('21) 8 8
100 " 30c brown, *orange* 8 8
101 " 30c deep rose ('21) 25 25
102 " 30c orange ('25) 8 8
103 " 35c *yellow* 7 7
104 " 40c carmine, *green* 15 10
105 " 45c violet brown, *lavender* 10 10
106 " 50c carmine, *orange* 60 55
107 " 50c dark blue ('21) 20 20
108 " 50c gray ('25) 8 8
109 " 65c deep blue ('28) 7 7
110 " 75c olive green, *straw* 8 8
111 " 75c blue, *bluish* ('25) 8 8
112 " 75c violet ('27) 10 10
113 A18 1fr blue, *yellow green* 13 13
114 " 1fr deep blue ('25) 10 10
115 " 2fr carmine, *blue* 45 45
116 " 5fr *straw* 1.75 1.75
Nos. 88-116 (29) 5.35 5.10

See Nos. 311, 317a.

Stamps of 1892-1904 Surcharged in Carmine or Black

05 10
n *o*

1912

117 A12 5c on 15c gray (C) 20 20
a. Inverted surch. 40.00 40.00
118 " 5c on 20c red, *green* 15 15
119 " 5c on 30c brown, *bistre* (C) 25 25
120 " 10c on 40c red, *straw* 50 50
121 " 10c on 50c brown, *azure* (C) 55 55
Nos. 117-121 (5) 1.65 1.65

Two spacings between the surcharged numerals are found on Nos. 117 to 121.

No. 96 Surcharged in Brown

5
CENTIMES

1918

122 A16 5c on 15c violet 35 35
a. Double surcharge 18.50 18.50
b. Inverted surcharge 9.00 9.00

The color of the surcharge on No. 122 varies from red to dark brown.

No. 96 Surcharged

0,05

1922

123 A16 5c on 15c vio. (R) 13 13
a. Double surch. 16.50 16.50

Stamps and Types of 1905-28 Surcharged New Value and Bars in Red or Black

60

1924-27

124 A16 25c on 15c vio. ('25) 10 10
a. Double surch. 15.00
125 A18 25c on 2fr carmine, *blue* ('24) 10 10
126 " 25c on 5fr *straw* ('24) 20 20
a. Double surch. 25.00 25.00
127 A17 60c on 75c blue green (R) 7 7
128 " 65c on 45c red brown ('25) 25 25
129 " 85c on 45c red brown ('25) 25 25
130 " 90c on 75c deep rose ('27) 20 20
131 A18 1.25fr on 1fr deep blue (R) ('26) 12 12
132 " 1.50fr on 1fr deep blue, *blue* ('27) 30 30
133 " 3fr on 5fr red violet ('27) 30 30
134 " 10fr on 5fr olive, *lavender* (R) ('26) 2.00 2.00
135 " 20fr on 5fr violet rose, *orange* ('27) 3.75 3.75
Nos. 124-135 (12) 7.64 7.64

Bay of Palétuviers Point
A19

Landscape with Chief's House
A20

Admiral de Bougainville and Count de La Pérouse—A21

1928-40 **Typographed.**

136 A19 1c brown violet & indigo 4 4
137 " 2c dark brown & yellow green 4 4
137B " 3c brown violet & indigo ('40) 4 4
138 " 4c orange & Prussian green 5 5
139 " 5c Prussian blue & deep olive 5 5
140 " 10c gray lilac & dark brown 5 5
141 " 15c yellow brown & deep blue 5 5
142 " 20c brown red & dark brown 5 5
143 " 25c dark green & dark brown 7 7
144 A20 30c gray green & blue green 6 6
145 " 35c black & bright violet ('33) 6 6
146 " 40c bright red & olivine 6 6
147 " 45c deep blue & red orange 10 10
147A " 45c blue green & dull green ('40) 8 8
148 " 50c violet & brown 6 6
149 " 55c violet blue & carmine ('38) 70 35
150 " 60c violet blue & carmine ('40) 8 8
151 " 65c orange brown & blue 20 20
152 " 70c deep rose & brown ('33) 10 10
153 " 75c Prussian blue & olive gray 45 10
154 " 80c red brown & green ('38) 10 6
155 " 85c green & brown ('33) 40 25
156 " 90c deep red & bright red 20 15
157 " 90c olive green & rose red ('39) 10 10
158 A21 1fr deep olive & salmon red 1.25 65
159 " 1fr rose red & dark carmine ('38) 40 40
160 " 1fr brown red & green ('40) 6 6
161 " 1.10fr deep green & brown 3.00 2.75
162 " 1.25fr brown red & green ('33) 20 20
163 " 1.25fr rose red & dk. car. ('39) 15 15
164 " 1.40fr dark blue & red org. ('40) 15 15
165 " 1.50fr dp. blue & blue 10 10
166 " 1.60fr deep green & brown ('40) 25 25
167 " 1.75fr dark blue & red orange ('33) 20 20
168 " 1.75fr violet blue ('38) 20 20
169 " 2fr red org. & brn. 10 10
170 " 2.25fr violet blue ('39) 13 13
171 " 2.50fr brown & light brown ('40) 15 15
172 " 3fr magenta & brown 15 10
173 " 5fr dk. blue & brn. 15 10
174 " 10fr violet & brown, *pinkish* 35 35
175 " 20fr red & brown, *yellow* 60 50
Nos. 136-175 (42) 10.78 8.79

The 35c in Prussian green and dark green without overprint is listed as Wallis and Futuna No. 53a.

Colonial Exposition Issue.

Common Design Types

1931 Engraved. *Perf. 12½*

Country Name Typo. in Black

No.	Type	Description	Unused	Used
176	CD70	40c deep green	1.25	1.25
177	CD71	50c violet	1.25	1.25
178	CD72	90c red orange	1.25	1.25
179	CD73	1.50fr dull blue	1.25	1.25

Paris-Nouméa Flight Issue.

Regular Issue of 1928 Overprinted:

1932 *Perf. 14x13½.*

No.	Type	Description	Unused	Used
180	A20	40c bright red & olivine	180.00	180.00
181	"	50c violet & brown	180.00	180.00

Issued to commemorate the arrival on April 5, 1932 at Nouméa, of the French aviators, Verneilh, Dévé and Munch.

Excellent forgeries exist of Nos. 180 and 181.

Types of 1928-33 Overprinted in Black or Red:

PARIS-NOUMÉA
Première liaison aérienne
5 Avril 1932

1933

No.	Type	Description	Unused	Used
182	A19	1c red violet & dull blue	2.25	2.25
183	"	2c dark brown & yellow green	2.25	2.25
184	"	4c dull orange & Prus. blue	2.25	2.25
185	"	5c Prussian green & olive (R)	2.25	2.25
186	"	10c gray lilac & dark brown (R)	2.25	2.25
187	"	15c yellow brown & deep blue (R)	2.25	2.25
188	"	20c brown red & dark brown	2.25	2.25
189	"	25c dark green & dark brown (R)	2.25	2.25
190	A20	30c gray green & blue green (R)	2.25	2.25
191	"	35c black & light violet	2.25	2.25
192	"	40c bright red & olivine	2.25	2.25
193	"	45c deep blue & red orange	2.25	2.25
194	"	50c violet & brown	2.25	2.25
195	"	70c deep rose & brown	2.25	2.25
196	"	75c Prussian blue & olive gray (R)	2.25	2.25
197	"	85c green & brown	2.25	2.25
198	"	90c deep red & bright red	2.25	2.25
199	A21	1fr deep olive & salmon red	2.25	2.25
200	"	1.25fr brown red & green	2.25	2.25
201	"	1.50fr deep blue & blue (R)	2.25	2.25
202	"	1.75fr dark blue & red orange	2.25	2.25
203	"	2fr red orange & brown	2.25	2.25
204	"	3fr magenta & brown	2.25	2.25
205	"	5fr dark blue & brown (R)	2.25	2.25
206	"	10fr violet & brown, *pinkish*	2.25	2.25
207	A21	20fr red & brown, *yellow*	2.25	2.25
		Nos. 182-207 (26)	58.50	58.50

Commemorating the first anniversary of the Paris to Nouméa flight.

The airplane is centered horizontally on Nos. 190 to 207.

Paris International Exposition Issue.

Common Design Types

1937 Engraved. *Perf. 13.*

No.	Type	Description	Unused	Used
208	CD74	20c deep violet	30	30
209	CD75	30c dark green	30	30
210	CD76	40c carmine rose	30	30
211	CD77	50c dark brown & blue	30	30
212	CD78	90c red	40	40
213	CD79	1.50fr ultramarine	40	40
		Nos. 208-213 (6)	2.00	2.00

Colonial Arts Exhibition Issue.

Souvenir Sheet.

Common Design Type

1937 *Imperf.*

No.	Type	Description	Unused	Used
214	CD78	3fr sepia	1.35	1.35

Issued in sheets measuring 118x99mm. containing one stamp.

New York World's Fair Issue.

Common Design Type

1939 *Perf. 12½x12.*

No.	Type	Description	Unused	Used
215	CD82	1.25fr carmine lake	22	22
216	"	2.25fr ultramarine	28	28

Nouméa Roadstead and Marshal Pétain
A21a

1941 Engraved *Perf. 12½x12*

No.	Type	Description	Unused	Used
216A	A21a	1fr bluish green	15	
216B	"	2.50fr dark blue	15	

Nos. 216A-216B were issued by the Vichy government and were not placed on sale in the colony.

A 10c, type A19, without "RF," and a 60c, type A20, without "REPUBLIQUE FRANCAISE," were also issued by the Vichy government and not placed on sale in New Caledonia.

Types of 1928-40 Overprinted in Black **France Libre**

1941 *Perf. 14x13½.*

No.	Type	Description	Unused	Used
217	A19	1c red violet & dull blue	6.00	6.00
218	"	2c dark brown & yellow green	6.00	6.00
219	"	3c brown violet & indigo	6.00	6.00
220	"	4c dull orange & Prussian blue	6.00	6.00
221	"	5c Prussian blue & deep olive	6.00	6.00
222	"	10c gray lilac & dark brown	6.00	6.00
223	"	15c yellow brown & deep blue	6.00	6.00
224	"	20c brown red & dark brown	6.00	6.00
225	"	25c dark green & dark brown	6.00	6.00
226	A20	30c gray green & blue green	6.00	6.00
227	"	35c black & bright violet	6.00	6.00
228	"	40c bright red & olivine	6.00	6.00
229	"	45c blue green & dull green	6.00	6.00
230	"	50c violet & brown	6.00	6.00
231	"	55c violet blue & carmine	6.00	6.00
232	"	60c violet blue & carmine	6.00	6.00
233	A20	65c orange brown & blue	6.00	6.00
234	"	70c dp. rose & brn.	6.00	6.00
235	"	75c Prussian blue & olive gray	6.00	6.00
236	"	80c red brown & green	6.00	6.00
237	"	85c green & brown	6.00	6.00
238	"	90c deep red & bright red	6.00	6.00
239	A21	1fr rose red & dark carmine	6.00	6.00
240	"	1.25fr brown red & green	6.00	6.00
241	"	1.40fr dark blue & red orange	6.00	6.00
242	"	1.50fr dp. bl. & blue	6.00	6.00
243	"	1.60fr deep green & brown	6.00	6.00
244	"	1.75fr dark blue & red orange	6.00	6.00
245	"	2fr red orange & brown	6.00	6.00
246	"	2.25fr violet blue	6.00	6.00
247	"	2.50fr brown & light brown	8.00	8.00
248	"	3fr magenta & brown	8.00	8.00
249	"	5fr dark blue & brown	8.00	8.00
250	"	10fr violet & brown, *pinkish*	8.00	8.00
251	"	20fr red & brown, *yellow*	8.00	8.00
		Nos. 217-251 (35)	220.00	220.00

Issued to note this colony's affiliation with the "Free France" movement.

Kagu
A22

1942 Photo. *Perf. 14½x14*

No.	Type	Description	Unused	Used
252	A22	5c brown	8	8
253	"	10c dark gray blue	8	8
254	"	25c emerald	8	8
255	"	30c red orange	8	8
256	"	40c dark slate green	10	10
257	"	80c dull red brown	10	10
258	"	1fr rose violet	10	10
259	"	1.50fr red	10	10
260	"	2fr gray black	17	17
261	"	2.50fr bright ultra.	25	25
262	"	4fr dull violet	20	20
263	"	5fr bistre	25	25
264	"	10fr deep brown	40	40
265	"	20fr deep green	50	50
		Nos. 252-265 (14)	2.49	2.49

Stamps of 1942 Surcharged in Carmine or Black **60 c. =**

1945-46 *Perf. 14½x14* **Unwmkd.**

No.	Type	Description	Unused	Used
266	A22	50c on 5c brown (C) ('46)	20	20
267	"	60c on 5c brown (C)	20	20
268	"	70c on 5c brown (C)	20	20
269	"	1.20fr on 5c brown (C)	15	15
270	"	2.40fr on 25c emerald	15	15
271	"	3fr on 25c emerald ('46)	15	15
272	"	4.50fr on 25c emerald	30	30
273	"	15fr on 2.50fr bright ultramarine (C)	40	40
		Nos. 266-273 (8)	1.75	1.75

Eboue Issue.

Common Design Type

1945 Engraved *Perf. 13*

No.	Type	Description	Unused	Used
274	CD91	2fr black	15	15
275	"	25fr Prussian green	40	40

Kagus—A23

Ducos Sanatorium—A24

Porcupine Isle—A25

Nickel Foundry—A26

"Towers of Notre Dame"
A27

Chieftain's House
A28

Photogravure

1948 *Perf. 13½x13* **Unwmkd.**

No.	Type	Description	Unused	Used
276	A23	10c yellow & brown	6	6
277	"	30c green & brown	6	6
278	"	40c orange & brown	6	6
279	A24	50c pink & brown	6	6
280	"	60c yellow & brown	8	8
281	"	80c light green & blue green	8	8
282	A25	1fr brown, purple & orange	12	10
283	"	1.20fr pale gray, brown & blue	12	12
284	"	1.50fr cream, dark blue & yellow	12	10
285	A26	2fr peacock green & brown	20	6
286	"	2.40fr vermilion & deep rose	15	15
287	"	3fr org. & purple	1.75	25
288	"	4fr blue & dark blue	30	15
289	A27	5fr verm. & purple	45	25
290	"	6fr yellow & brown	45	20
291	"	10fr org. & dk. blue	55	12
292	A28	15fr brown & gray	75	45
293	"	20fr purple & yellow	85	35
294	"	25fr dark blue & orange	90	60
		Nos. 276-294 (19)	7.11	3.30

Military Medal Issue.

Common Design Type

Engraved and Typographed.

1952 *Perf. 13.* **Unwmkd.**

No.	Type	Description	Unused	Used
295	CD101	2fr multicolored	1.00	90

Common Design Types

pictured in section at front of book.

Admiral Bruni d'Entrecasteaux and his Two Frigates

A29

Designs: 2fr, Msgr. Douarre and Cathedral of Nouméa. 6fr, Admiral Dumont d'Urville and map. 13fr, Admiral Auguste Febvrier-Despointes and Nouméa roadstead.

1953, Sept. 24 Engraved

296 A29 1.50fr orange brown & deep claret 2.50 1.75
297 " 2fr indigo & aqua. 1.50 1.20
298 " 6fr dark brown, blue & carmine 3.00 1.50
299 " 13fr blue green & dark greenish blue 3.50 2.50

Issued to commemorate the centenary of the presence of the French in New Caledonia.

"Towers of Notre Dame"

A30

Coffee

A31

1955, Nov. 21 *Perf. 13* **Unwmkd.**

300 A30 2.50fr dark brown, ultra. & green 50 30
301 " 3fr green, ultra. & red brown 3.00 1.75
302 A31 9fr violet blue & indigo 50 30

FIDES Issue.

Common Design Type

Design: 3fr, Dumbea Dam.

1956, Oct. 22 Engr. *Perf. 13x12½*

303 CD103 3fr ultra. & green 50 30

Flower Issue

Common Design Type

Designs: 4fr, Xanthostemon. 15fr, Hibiscus.

1958, July 7 Photo. *Perf. 12x12½*

304 CD104 4fr multicolored 1.00 40
305 " 15fr grn., red & yel. 1.75 50

Imperforates

Most stamps of New Caledonia from 1958 onward exist imperforate, in trial colors, or in small presentation sheets in which the stamps are printed in changed colors.

Human Rights Issue

Common Design Type

1958, Dec. 10 Engraved *Perf. 13*

306 CD105 7fr car. & dk. blue 60 50

Universal Declaration of Human Rights, 10th anniversary.

Brachyrus Zebra

A32

Lienardella Fasciata

A33

Designs: 10fr, Claucus and Spirographe. 26fr, Fluorescent corals.

1959, Mar. 21 Engraved *Perf. 13*

307 A32 1fr lilac gray & red brown 20 15
308 A33 3fr blue, green & red 30 20
309 A32 10fr dark brown, Prussian blue & orange brown 70 45
310 A33 26fr multicolored 2.00 1.20

Types of 1859, 1905 and

Girl Operating Check Writer

A34

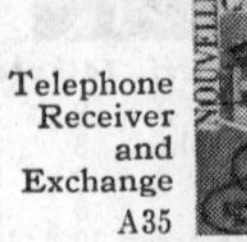

Telephone Receiver and Exchange

A35

Port-de-France (Nouméa) in 1859

A36

Designs: 9fr, Wayside mailbox and mail bus (vert.). 33fr, Like 19fr without stamps.

Perf. 13½x13, 13

1960, May 20 **Unwmkd.**

311 A16 4fr red 55 20
312 A34 5fr claret & orange brown 60 30
313 A36 9fr dk. grn. & brown 65 40
314 A35 12fr blue & black 70 40
315 A1 13fr slate blue 1.60 1.00
316 A36 19fr blue green, dull green & red 1.60 70
317 " 33fr Prussian blue & dull red 2.35 1.50
a. Souvenir sheet of 3 + label 5.50 5.50
Nos. 311-317 (7) 8.05 4.50

Issued to commemorate the centenary of postal service and stamps in New Caledonia.

No. 317a contains one each of Nos. 315, 311 and 317 with commemorative inscription on label between 4fr and 33fr stamps. Size: 155x81mm.

Melanesian Sailing Canoes— A37

Designs: 4fr, Spear fisherman (vert.). 5fr, Sail Rock and sailboats, Noumea.

1962, July 2 Engraved *Perf. 13*

318 A37 2fr slate green, ultra. & brown 30 20
319 " 4fr brown, carmine & green 35 25
320 " 5fr sepia, green & blue 40 30

See also Nos. C29-C32.

Map of Australia and South Pacific—A37a

1962, July 18 Photo. *Perf. 13x12*

321 A37a 15fr multicolored 1.20 70

Issued to commemorate the Fifth South Pacific Conference, Pago Pago, 1962.

Air Currents over Map of New Caledonia and South Pacific, Barograph and Compass Rose

A38

1962, Nov. 5 *Perf. 12x12½*

322 A38 50fr multicolored 4.00 3.00

Issued to commemorate the 3rd regional assembly of the World Meteorological Association, Noumea, November 1962.

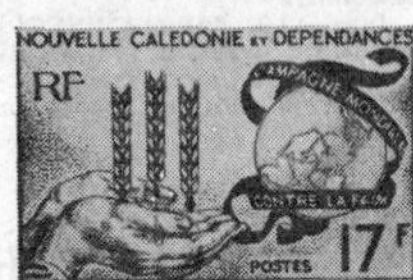

Wheat Emblem and Globe

A38a

1963, Mar. 21 Engr. *Perf. 13*

323 A38a 17fr choc. & dk. blue 1.35 75

Issued for the "Freedom from Hunger" campaign of the U.N. Food and Agriculture Organization.

Relay Race

A39

Designs: 7fr, Tennis. 10fr, Soccer. 27fr, Throwing the javelin.

Photogravure

1963, Aug. 29 *Perf. 12½* **Unwmkd.**

324 A39 1fr dark gray & dull red 30 20
325 " 7fr dull blue & orange brown 60 35
326 A39 10fr green & brown 85 55
327 " 27fr dk. plum & ultra. 2.00 1.50

Issued to publicize the South Pacific Games, Suva, Aug. 29–Sept. 7.

Red Cross Centenary Issue

Common Design Type

1963 Sept. 2 Engraved *Perf. 13*

328 CD113 37fr bl., gray & car. 2.75 2.75

Centenary of the International Red Cross.

Human Rights Issue

Common Design Type

1963, Dec. 10 *Perf. 13* **Unwmkd.**

329 CD117 50fr slate green & deep claret 3.50 3.00

Bikkia Fritillarioides

A40

Sea Squirts

A41

Flowers: 1fr, Freycinettia Sp. 3fr, Xanthostemon Francii. 4fr, Psidiomyrtus locellatus. 5fr, Callistemon suberosum. 7fr, Montrouziera sphaeroidea (horiz.). 10fr, Ixora collina (horiz.). 17fr, Deplanchea speciosa.

Photo.; Litho. (2fr, 3fr)

1964-65 *Perf. 13x12½*

330 A40 1fr multicolored 25 20
331 " 2fr " 30 25
332 " 3fr " 50 25
333 " 4fr " ('65) 70 40
334 " 5fr " ('65) 70 30
335 " 7fr " 1.25 45
336 " 10fr " 1.20 65
337 " 17fr " 2.00 1.00
Nos. 330-337 (8) 6.90 3.50

1964-65 Engraved *Perf. 13*

Design: 10fr, Alcyonium catalaY. 17fr, Shrimp (hymenocera elegans).

338 A41 7fr dark blue, orange & brn. 60 30
339 " 10fr dk. red & dark vio. blue ('65) 70 40
340 " 17fr dark blue, magenta & green 1.35 70

Nouméa Aquarium. See Nos. C41-C43.

Philatec Issue

Common Design Type

1964, Apr. 9 *Perf. 13* **Unwmkd.**

341 CD118 40fr dark violet, green & choc. 3.25 3.25

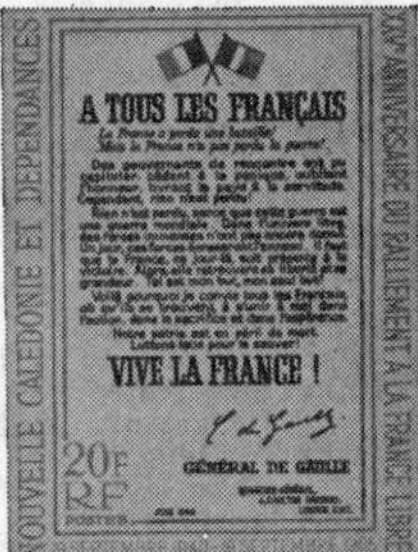

De Gaulle's 1940 Poster "A Tous les Francais"

A42

1965, Sept. 20 Engraved *Perf. 13*

342 A42 20fr red, bl. & black 3.75 2.25

Issued to commemorate the 25th anniversary of the rallying of the Free French.

Amedee Lighthouse
A43

Games' Emblem
A44

1965, Nov. 25
343 A43 8fr dark violet blue, bister & green 50 25
Centenary of the Amedee lighthouse.

1966, Feb. 28 Engraved *Perf. 13*
344 A44 8fr dk. red, brt. blue & black 50 30
Issued to publicize the Second South Pacific Games, Nouméa, December, 1966.

Red-throated Parrot Finch
A45
Design: 3fr, Giant imperial pigeon.

1966, Oct. 10 Litho. *Perf. 13x12½*
Size: 22x37mm.
345 A45 1fr green & multi. 40 20
346 " 3fr citron & multi. 60 30
See also Nos. 361-366, 380-381, C48-C49A, C70-C71.

Dancers and UNESCO Emblem
A46

1966, Nov. 4 Engraved *Perf. 13*
347 A46 16fr purple, ocher & green 90 50
Issued to commemorate the 20th anniversary of UNESCO (United Nations Educational, Scientific and Cultural Organization).

High Jump and Games' Emblem
A47
Designs: 20fr, Hurdling. 40fr, Running. 100fr, Swimming.

1966, Dec. 8 Engraved *Perf. 13*
348 A47 17fr maroon, violet & green 1.00 75
349 " 20fr maroon, lilac & blue green 2.00 1.00
350 " 40fr maroon, slate grn. & vio. 2.50 1.25
351 " 100fr maroon, bl. grn. & lilac 5.50 3.00
a. Souvenir sheet of 4 12.00 12.00
Issued to commemorate the Second South Pacific Games, Nouméa, Dec. 8-18.
No. 351a contains one each of Nos. 348-351 and label with Games' emblem. Size: 149x100mm.

Lekine Cliffs
A48

1967, Jan. 14 Engraved *Perf. 13*
352 A48 17fr brt. grn., ultra. & slate green 90 55

Magenta Stadium, Nouméa
A49
Design: 20fr, Fish hatchery, Nouméa.

1967, June 5 Photo. *Perf. 12x13*
353 A49 10fr multicolored 70 30
354 " 20fr " 1.10 70

ITY Emblem, Beach at Nouméa
A50

1967, June 19 Engraved *Perf. 13*
355 A50 30fr multicolored 1.85 90
Issued for International Tourist Year, 1967.

19th Century Mailman
A51

1967, July 12
356 A51 7fr dark car., blue green & brown 50 35
Issued for Stamp Day.

Papilio Montrouzieri
A52
Butterflies: 9fr, Polyura clitarchus. 13fr, 15fr, Hypolimnas bolina, male and female respectively.

1967-68 Engraved *Perf. 13*
Size: 36x22mm.
357 A52 7fr lt. green, black & ultra. 60 40
358 " 9fr brown, lilac & indigo ('68) 80 45
359 " 13fr vio. bl., brn. org. & dark brown 1.20 75
360 " 15fr dk. brn., bl. & yel. 1.40 80
Nos. 357-360, C51-C53 (7) 11.35 6.45
Issue dates: 9fr, Mar. 26, 1968. Others, Aug. 10, 1967.

Bird Type of 1966
Birds: 1fr, New Caledonian grass warbler. 2fr, New Caledonia whistler. 3fr, New Caledonia white-throated pigeon. 4fr, Kagus. 5fr, Crested parakeet. 10fr, Crow honey-eater.

1967-68 Photo. *Perf. 13x12½*
Size: 22x37mm.
361 A45 1fr multicolored ('68) 30 20
362 " 2fr " ('68) 40 25
363 " 3fr " ('68) 40 40
364 " 4fr green & multi. 60 45
365 " 5fr lt. yel. & multi. 80 55
366 " 10fr pink & multi. 1.85 90
Nos. 361-366 (6) 4.35 2.75
Issue dates: Nos. 364-366, Dec. 16, 1967. Others May 14, 1968.

WHO Anniversary Issue
Common Design Type

1968, May 4 Engraved *Perf. 13*
367 CD126 20fr maroon, vio. & dk. bl. green 1.10 70
Issued for the 20th anniversary of the World Health Organization.

Ferrying Mail Truck Across Tontouta River, 1900
A53

1968, July 1 Engraved *Perf. 13*
368 A53 9fr dk. red brown, green & ultra. 60 35
Issued for Stamp Day, 1968.

Human Rights Year Issue
Common Design Type

1968, Aug. 10 Engraved *Perf. 13*
369 CD127 12fr slate green, deep car. & org. yel. 70 55

Conus Geographus
A54

1968, Nov. 9 Engraved *Perf. 13*
Size: 36x22mm.
370 A54 10fr dk. brown, brt. blue & gray 65 35
See Nos. C58-C60.

Car on Road
A55

1968, Dec. 26 Engraved *Perf. 13*
371 A55 25fr deep blue, slate green & henna brown 1.65 70
2nd Automobile Safari of New Caledonia.

Cattle Dip
A56
Design: 25fr, Cattle branding.

1969, May 10 Engraved *Perf. 13*
Size: 36x22mm.
372 A56 9fr slate green, ultra. & brown 50 30
373 " 25fr grn., brn. & lilac 1.50 65
Issued to publicize cattle breeding in New Caledonia. See No. C64.

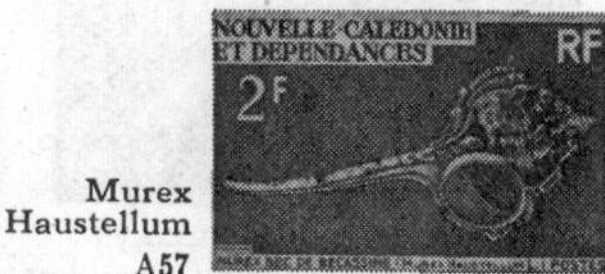
Murex Haustellum
A57
Sea Shells: 5fr, Venus comb. 15fr, Murex ramosus.

1969, June 21 Engraved *Perf. 13*
Size: 35½x22mm.
374 A57 2fr verm., bl. & brn. 30 25
375 " 5fr dull red, purple & beige 50 30
376 " 15fr vermilion, dull green & gray 1.20 55
See No. C65.

Judo
A58
Design: 20fr, Boxers.

1969, Aug. 7 Engraved *Perf. 13*
Size: 36x22mm.
377 A58 19fr verm., blue & violet brown 1.20 50
378 " 20fr bright green, red & black 1.20 60
Issued to publicize the 3rd South Pacific Games, Port Moresby, Papua and New Guinea, Aug. 13-23. See Nos. C66-C67.

ILO Issue
Common Design Type

1969, Nov. 24 Engraved *Perf. 13*
379 CD131 12fr orange, brown violet & brown 50 30

Bird Type of 1966
Birds: 15fr, Friarbird. 30fr, Sacred kingfisher.

1970, Feb. 19 Photo. *Perf. 13*
Size: 22x37mm.
380 A45 15fr yel. grn. & multi. 1.20 60
381 " 30fr pale sal. & multi. 2.25 85
See Nos. C70-C71.

U.P.U. Headquarters Issue
Common Design Type

1970, May 20 Engraved *Perf. 13*
382 CD133 12fr brown, gray & dark carmine 55 35

Porcelain Sieve Shell
A59
Designs: 1fr, Strombus epidromis linne (vert.). No. 385, Strombus variabilis swainson (vert.). 21fr, Mole porcelain shell.

1970 Size: 22x36, 36x22mm.
383 A59 1fr brt. grn. & multi. 20 20
384 " 10fr rose & multi. 60 35
385 " 10fr black & multi. 70 40
386 " 21fr bl. green, brown & dk. brown 1.40 75
Nos. 383-386, C73-C76 (8) 10.50 5.25
See Nos. 395-396, C89-C90.

Packet Ship "Natal," 1883
A60

1970, July 23 Engraved *Perf. 13*
387 A60 9fr Prus. blue, black & bright green 55 35
Issued for Stamp Day.

Dumbea Railroad Post Office
A61

1971, March 13 Engraved *Perf. 13*

388 A61 10fr red, slate green & black 70 40

Stamp Day, 1971.

Racing Yachts—A62

1971, Apr. 17 Engraved *Perf. 13*

389 A62 16fr bl., Prus. blue & slate green 1.00 60

Third sailing cruise from Whangarei, New Zealand, to Nouméa.

Morse Recorder, Communications Satellite
A63

1971, May 17 Engraved *Perf. 13*

390 A63 19fr red, lake & org. 90 45

3rd World Telecommunications Day.

Weight Lifting
A64

Design: 23fr, Basketball.

1971, June 24 Engraved *Perf. 13*

391 A64 11fr dk. brown & rose red 80 40
392 " 23fr blue & multi. 1.40 70

4th South Pacific Games, Papeete, French Polynesia, Sept. 8–19. See Nos. C82–C83.

De Gaulle Issue
Common Design Type

Designs: 34fr, Gen. de Gaulle, 1940. 100fr, Pres. de Gaulle, 1970.

1971, Nov. 9

393 CD134 34fr dk. pur. & blk. 2.25 90
394 " 100fr " " " 5.00 2.25

First anniversary of the death of Charles de Gaulle (1890–1970), president of France.

Sea Shell Type of 1970

Designs: 1fr, Scorpion conch (vert.). 3fr, Common spider conch. (vert.).

1972, Mar. 4 Engraved *Perf. 13*
Size: 22x36mm.

395 A59 1fr violet & dk. brown 15 12
396 " 3fr green & ocher 20 12

See Nos. C89–C90.

Carved Wooden Pillow
A66

1972–73 Photo. *Perf. 12½x13*
Multicolored

397 A66 1fr *Doorpost, Goa* ('73) 20 10
398 " 2fr *shown* 30 20
399 " 5fr *Monstrance* 40 30
400 " 12fr *Tchamba mask* 70 40
Nos. 397-400, C102–C103 (6) 3.60 2.15

Objects from Nouméa Museum.

Chamber of Commerce Emblem
A67

1972, Dec. 16

401 A67 12fr black, yellow & bright blue 60 30

10th anniversary of the Junior Chamber of Commerce.

Tchamba Mask
A68

1973, Mar. 15 Engraved *Perf. 13*

402 A68 12fr lilac 70 40
a. Booklet pane of 5 3.50

No. 402 issued in booklets only. See No. C99.

Black-back Butterflyfish (Day)
A69

1973, June 23 Photo. *Perf. 13x12½*
Multicolored

403 A69 8f *shown* 40 25
404 " 14fr *same fish (night)* 60 40

Nouméa Aquarium. See No. C105.

Emblem
A70

1973, July 21 *Perf. 13*

405 A70 20fr green, yellow & violet blue 65 35

School Coordinating Office, 10th anniversary.

"Nature Protection"—A72

1974, June 22 Photo. *Perf. 13x12½*

406 A72 7fr multicolored 30 15

Scorched Landscape
A73

Calanthe Veratrifolia
A74

1975, Feb. 3 Photo. *Perf. 13*

407 A73 20fr multicolored 50 35

"Prevent brush fires."

1975, May 30 Photo. *Perf. 13*

Design: 11fr, Liperanthus gigas.

408 A74 8fr purple & multi. 30 20
409 " 11fr dk. bl. & multi. 40 30

Orchids. See Nos. 425–426, C125.

Festival Emblem
A75

1975, Sept. 6 Photo. *Perf. 12½x13*

410 A75 12fr ultra., org. & yel. 30 20

Melanesia 2000 Festival.

Birds in Flight
A76

Georges Pompidou
A77

1975, Oct. 18 Photo. *Perf. 13½x13*

411 A76 5fr ocher, yel. & blk. 15 10

Nouméa Ornithological Society, 10th anniversary.

1975, Dec. 6 Engr. *Perf. 13*

412 A77 26fr dk. grn., blk. & slate 65 40

Georges Pompidou (1911–1974), president of France

Brown Booby
A78

Sea Birds: 2fr, Blue-faced booby. 8fr, Red-footed booby (vert.).

Perf. 13x12½, 12½x13

1976, Feb. 21 Photogravure

413 A78 1fr multicolored 10 10
414 A78 2fr multicolored 10 10
415 " 8fr " 40 30

Festival Emblem
A79

1976, Mar. 13 Litho. *Perf. 12½*

416 A79 27fr bl., org. & blk. 65 40

Rotorua 1976, South Pacific Arts Festival, New Zealand.

Lion and Lions Emblem
A80

1976, Mar. 13 Photo. *Perf. 12½x13*

417 A80 49fr multicolored 1.00 80

Lions Club of Nouméa, 15th anniversary.

Music Pavilion—A81

Design: 30fr, Fountain (vert.).

1976, July 3 Litho. *Perf. 12½*

418 A81 25fr multicolored 50 25
419 " 30fr blue & multi. 60 35

Old Nouméa.

Polluted Shore—A82

1976, Aug. 21 Photo. *Perf. 13*

420 A82 20fr dp. bl. & multi. 40 30

Nature protection.

South Pacific People
A83

1976, Oct. 23 Photo. ***Perf. 13***
421 A83 20fr blue & multi. 50 30

16th South Pacific Commission Conference, Nouméa, Oct. 1976.

Giant Grasshopper A84

Design: 31fr, Beetle and larvae.

1977, Feb. 21 Engr. ***Perf. 13***
422 A84 26fr multicolored 55 30
423 " 31fr " 65 40

Ground Satellite Station, Nouméa—A85

1977, Apr. 16 Litho. ***Perf. 13***
424 A85 29fr multicolored 65 40

Orchid Type of 1975

Designs: 22fr, Phajus daenikeri. 44fr, Dendrobium finetianum.

1977, May 23 Photo. ***Perf. 13***
425 A74 22fr brown & multi. 50 35
426 " 44fr blue & multi. 1.00 75

Mask, Palms, "Stamps"—A86

1977, June 25 Photo. ***Perf. 13***
427 A86 35fr multicolored 75 55

Philately in school, Philatelic Exhibition, La Perouse Lyceum, Nouméa.

Trees A87

1977, July 16 Photo. ***Perf. 13***
428 A87 20fr multicolored 45 35

Nature protection.

Congress Emblem—A88

1977, Aug. 6 Photo. ***Perf. 13***
429 A88 200fr multicolored 4.50 3.00

French Junior Economic Chambers Congress, Nouméa.

Young Frigate Bird A89

Designs: 22fr, Terns (horiz.). 40fr, Sooty terns (horiz.).

1977, Sept. 17 Photo. ***Perf. 13***
430 A89 16fr multicolored 35 25
431 " 22fr " 50 35
432 " 40fr " 90 65

Issue dates: 16fr, Sept. 17, 1977. 22fr, 40fr, Feb. 11, 1978.
See No. C138.

Mare and Foal A90

1977, Nov. 19 Engr. ***Perf. 13***
433 A90 5fr multicolored 10 8

10th anniversary of the Society for Promotion of Caledonian Horses.

Araucaria Montana A91

Halityle Regularis A92

Design: 42fr, Amyema scandens (horiz.).

Perf. 12½x13, 13x12½

1978, Mar. 17 Photogravure
434 A91 16fr multicolored 35 25
435 " 42fr " 1.00 35

1978, May 20 Photo. ***Perf. 13***
436 A92 10fr violet blue & multicolored 25 15

Nouméa Aquarium.

Stylized Turtle and Globe A93

1978, May 20
437 A93 30fr multicolored 70 40

Protection of the turtle.

Flying Fox—A94

1978, June 10
438 A94 20fr multicolored 50 30

Nature protection.

Maurice Leenhardt A95

Soccer Player, League Emblem A96

1978, Aug. 16 Engr. ***Perf. 13***
439 A95 37fr multicolored 85 60

Pastor Maurice Leenhardt (1878–1954).

1978, Nov. 4 Photo. ***Perf. 13***
440 A96 26fr multicolored 65 40

New Caledonia Soccer League, 50th anniversary.

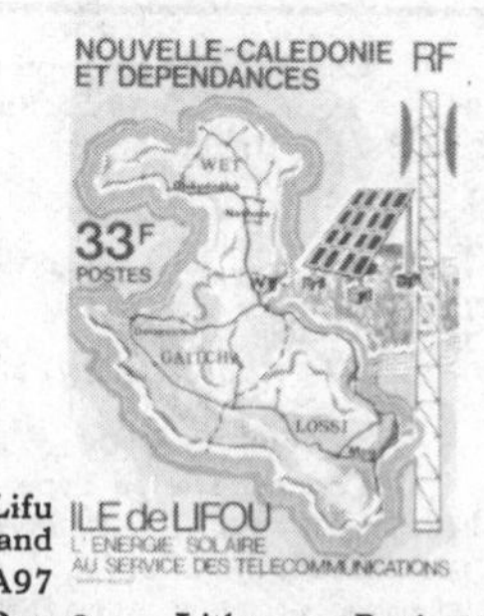

Lifu Island A97

1978, Dec. 9 Litho. ***Perf. 13***
441 A97 33fr multicolored 75 45

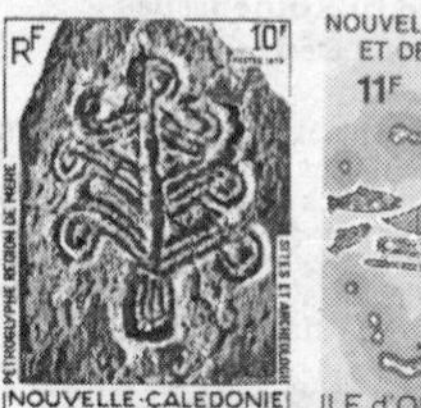

Petroglyph, Mère A98

Map of Ouvea A99

1979, Jan. 27 Engr. ***Perf. 13***
442 A98 10fr brick red 25 15

Perf. 12½x13, 13x12½

1979, Feb. 17 Photogravure

Design: 31fr, Map of Mare Island (horiz.).

443 A99 11fr multicolored 28 18
444 " 31fr " 70 40

SEMI-POSTAL STAMPS

SP1

1915 *Perf. 14x13½.* **Unwmkd.**

B1 SP1 10c+5c carmine 35 35
  a. Inverted surch. 10.00 10.00
  b. Cross omitted

Regular Issue of 1905 Surcharged ✚5c

1917

B2 A16 10c+5c rose 25 25
  a. Double surcharge 15.00 15.00
B3 " 15c+5c violet 25 25

Curie Issue
Common Design Type

1938, Oct. 24 *Perf. 13*

B4 CD80 1.75fr+50c bright ultramarine 3.75 3.75

French Revolution Issue.
Common Design Type

1939, July 5 Photogravure
Name and Value Typo. in Black.

B5 CD83 45(c)+25(c) green 2.25 2.25
B6 " 70(c)+30(c) brown 2.25 2.25
B7 " 90(c)+35(c) red orange 2.25 2.25
B8 " 1.25fr+1fr rose pink 2.25 2.25
B9 " 2.25fr+2fr blue 2.25 2.25
  Nos. B5-B9 (5) 11.25 11.25

Common Design Type and

Dumont d'Urville's ship, "Zélée" SP2

New Caledonian Militiaman SP3

1941 Photogravure *Perf. 13½*

B10 SP2 1fr+1fr red 30
B11 CD86 1.50fr+3fr maroon 30
B12 SP3 2.50fr+1fr dk. blue 30

Nos. B10–B12 were issued by the Vichy government and were not placed on sale in the colony.

In 1944 Nos. 216A–216B were surcharged "OEUVRES COLONIALES" and surtax (including change of denomination of the 2.50fr to 50c). These were issued by the Vichy government and not placed on sale in New Caledonia.

Red Cross Issue
Common Design Type

1944 *Perf. 14½x14*

B13 CD90 5fr+20fr brt. scarlet 30 30

The surtax was for the French Red Cross and national relief.

Tropical Medicine Issue
Common Design Type

1950, May 15 Engraved *Perf. 13*

B14 CD100 10fr+2fr red brown & sepia 1.20 1.20

The surtax was for charitable work.

AIR POST STAMPS

Seaplane Over Pacific Ocean AP1

Engraved.

1938-40 *Perf. 13.* **Unwmkd.**

C1 AP1 65c deep violet 25 25
  a. "65c" omitted 45.00
C2 " 4.50fr red 30 30
C3 " 7fr dark blue green ('40) 20 20
C4 " 9fr ultramarine 85 85
C5 " 20fr dk. orange ('40) 55 55
C6 " 50fr black ('40) 65 65
  Nos. C1-C6 (6) 2.80 2.80

V4

Stamps of type AP1, without "RF" monogram, and stamp of the design shown above were issued in 1942 to 1944 by the Vichy Government, but were not placed on sale in the colony.

Common Design Type

1942 *Perf. 14½x14.* **Unwmkd.**

C7 CD87 1fr dark orange 15 15
C8 " 1.50fr bright red 15 15
C9 " 5fr brown red 25 20
C10 " 10fr black 30 30
C11 " 25fr ultramarine 35 35
C12 " 50fr dark green 40 40
C13 " 100fr plum 60 45
  Nos. C7-C13 (7) 2.20 2.00

Victory Issue
Common Design Type

1946, May 8 Engraved *Perf. 12½.*

C14 CD92 8fr bright ultra. 35 35

European victory of Allied Nations in World War II.

Chad to Rhine Issue
Common Design Types

1946, June 6

C15 CD93 5fr black 40 40
C16 CD94 10fr carmine 40 40
C17 CD95 15fr dark blue 40 40
C18 CD96 20fr orange brown 40 40
C19 CD97 25fr olive green 60 60
C20 CD98 50fr dk. rose violet 80 80
  Nos. C15-C20 (6) 3.00 3.00

St. Vincent Bay—AP2

Planes over Islands AP3

View of Nouméa—AP4

Perf. 13x12½, 12½x13.

1948, Mar. 1 Photo. **Unwmkd.**

C21 AP2 50fr orange & rose violet 1.75 1.50
C22 AP3 100fr blue green & slate blue 3.00 1.85
C23 AP4 200fr brown & yel. 7.00 3.25

U. P. U. Issue
Common Design Type

1949, July 4 Engraved. *Perf. 13.*

C24 CD99 10fr multicolored 2.00 1.65

Liberation Issue
Common Design Type

1954, June 6

C25 CD102 3fr indigo & ultra. 2.00 1.75

10th anniversary of the liberation of France.

Conveyor for Nickel Ore—AP5

1955, Nov. 21 *Perf. 13* **Unwmkd.**

C26 AP5 14fr indigo & sepia 1.10 40

Rock Formations, Bourail—AP6

1959, Mar. 23

C27 AP6 200fr light blue, brown & green 11.00 6.25

Yaté Dam AP7

1959, Sept. 20 Engraved

C28 AP7 50fr green, bright blue & sepia 2.75 1.65

Dedication of Yaté Dam.

Fisherman with Throw-net AP8

Skin Diver Shooting Bumphead Surgeonfish—AP9

Designs: 20fr, Nautilus shell. 100fr, Yaté rock.

1962 *Perf. 13* **Unwmkd.**

C29 AP8 15fr red, Prussian grn. & sepia 1.35 60
C30 AP9 20fr dk. slate green & org. verm. 2.00 1.10
C31 " 25fr red brown, gray & blue 2.50 1.10
C32 " 100fr dk. brn., dk. blue & slate green 6.50 2.75

Telstar Issue
Common Design Type

1962, Dec. 4 *Perf. 13* **Unwmkd.**

C33 CD111 200fr dk. bl., choc. & greenish bl. 12.00 8.00

Nickel Mining, Houailou AP10

1964, May 14 Photogravure

C34 AP10 30fr multicolored 1.50 90

Isle of Pines—AP11

1964, Dec. 7 Engr. *Perf. 13*

C35 AP11 50fr dk. bl., slate grn. & choc. 2.50 1.50

Phyllobranchus—AP12

Design: 27fr, Paracanthurus teuthis (fish).

1964, Dec. 17 Photogravure

C36 AP12 27fr red brn., yel., dp. bl. & blk. 1.85 1.10
C37 " 37fr bl., brn. & yel. 3.50 1.60

Issued to publicize the Nouméa Aquarium.

Greco-Roman Wrestling—AP13

1964, Dec. 28 Engraved

C38 AP13 10fr bright green, pink & blk. 7.25 6.00

18th Olympic Games, Tokyo, Oct. 10–25.

Nimbus Weather Satellite over New Caledonia
AP14

1965, Mar. 23 Photo. *Perf. 13x12½*

C39 AP14 9fr multicolored 1.75 1.25

Fifth World Meteorological Day.

ITU Issue
Common Design Type

1965, May 17 Engraved *Perf. 13*

C40 CD120 40fr lt. blue, lilac rose & lt. brn. 4.50 3.25

Issued to commemorate the centenary of the International Telecommunication Union.

Coris Angulata (Young Fish)—AP15

Coris Angulata: 15fr, Adolescent fish. 25fr, Adult fish.

1965, Dec. 6 Engraved *Perf. 13*

C41 AP15 13fr red org., olive bis. & blk. 1.00 60

C42 " 15fr indigo, slate grn. & bis. 1.25 70

C43 " 25fr indigo & yel. green 2.25 1.25

Issued to publicize the Nouméa Aquarium.

French Satellite A-1 Issue
Common Design Type

Designs: 8fr, Diamant rocket and launching installations. 12fr, A-1 satellite.

1966, Jan. 10 Engraved *Perf. 13*

C44 CD121 8fr rose brn., ultra. & Prus. blue 1.25 75

C45 " 12fr ultra., Prus. bl. & rose brown 1.65 1.10

a. Strip of 2 + label 3.00 2.25

Issued to commemorate the launching of France's first satellite, Nov. 26, 1965. No. C45a contains one each of Nos. C44–C45 and rose brown label with commemorative inscription. Each sheet contains 16 triptychs (2x8).

French Satellite D-1 Issue
Common Design Type

1966, May 16 Engraved *Perf. 13*

C46 CD122 10fr dull blue, ocher & sepia 1.50 1.00

Issued to commemorate the launching of the D-1 satellite, Hammaguir, Algeria, Feb. 17, 1966.

Port-de-France, 1866—AP16

1966, June 2

C47 AP16 30fr dark red, blue & indigo 1.75 1.10

Issued to commemorate the centenary of Port-de-France changing name to Nouméa.

Bird Type of Regular Issue

Designs: 27fr, Uvea crested parakeet. 37fr, Scarlet honey eater. 50fr, Two cloven-feathered doves.

1966–68 Photogravure *Perf. 13*

Size: 26x46mm.

C48 A45 27fr pink & multi. 1.50 75

C49 " 37fr green & multi. 2.25 1.25

Size: 27x48mm.

C49A A45 50fr multi. ('68) 2.75 1.50

Issue dates: 50fr, May 14, 1968. Others, Oct. 10, 1966.

Sailboats and Map of New Caledonia-New Zealand Route
AP17

1967, Apr. 15 Engr. *Perf. 13*

C50 AP17 25fr brt. green, dp. ultra. & red 1.35 90

Issued to commemorate the 2nd sailboat race from Whangarei, New Zealand, to Nouméa, New Caledonia.

Butterfly Type of Regular Issue

Butterflies: 19fr, Danaus plexippus. 29fr, Hippotion celerio. 85fr, Delias elipsis.

1967–68 Engraved *Perf. 13*

Size: 48x27mm.

C51 A52 19fr multi. ('68) 1.25 80

C52 " 29fr " ('68) 1.85 1.00

C53 " 85fr red, dk. brown & yellow 4.25 2.25

Issue dates: 85fr, Aug. 10, 1967. Others, Mar. 26, 1968.

Jules Garnier, Garnierite and Mine
AP18

1967, Oct. 9 Engraved *Perf. 13*

C54 AP18 70fr bl. gray, brn. & yel. green 2.75 1.50

Issued to commemorate the centenary of the discovery of garnierite (nickel ore).

Lifu Island—AP19

1967, Oct. 28 Photo. *Perf. 13*

C55 AP19 200fr multi. 8.00 4.00

Skier, Snowflake and Olympic Emblem—AP20

1967, Nov. 16 Engraved *Perf. 13*

C56 AP20 100fr brn. red, slate green & brt. blue 5.00 3.00

Issued to publicize the 10th Winter Olympic Games, Grenoble, France, Feb. 6–18, 1968.

Sea Shell Type of Regular Issue

Designs: 39fr, Conus lienardi. 40fr, Conus cabriti. 70fr, Conus coccineus.

1968, Nov. 9 Engraved *Perf. 13*

C58 A54 39fr blue green, brn. & gray 1.75 1.00

C59 " 40fr black, brown red & olive 2.25 1.25

C60 " 70fr brown, purple & gray 4.00 2.25

Maré Dancers
AP21

1968, Nov. 20 Engraved *Perf. 13*

C61 AP21 60fr grn., ultra. & henna brn. 2.50 1.50

World Map and Caudron C 600 "Aiglon"—AP22

1969, Mar. 24 Engraved *Perf. 13*

C62 AP22 29fr lilac, dk. blue & dk. car. 2.00 1.00

Issued for Stamp Day and to commemorate the first flight from Nouméa to Paris of Henri Martinet and Paul Klein, March 24, 1939.

Concorde Issue
Common Design Type

1969, Apr. 17 Engraved *Perf. 13*

C63 CD129 100fr slate green & brt. green 9.00 6.75

Cattle Type of Regular Issue

Design: 50fr, Cowboy and herd.

1969, May 10 Engraved *Perf. 13*

Size: 48x27mm.

C64 A56 50fr slate green, dk. brown & red brown 1.75 1.00

Cattle breeding in New Caledonia.

Shell Type of Regular Issue, 1969

Design: 100fr, Black murex.

1969, June 21 Engraved *Perf. 13*

Size: 48x27mm.

C65 A57 100fr lake, bl. & blk. 7.00 3.00

Sports Type of 1969

Designs: 30fr, Woman diver. 39fr, Shot put (vert.).

1969, Aug. 7 Engraved *Perf. 13*

Size: 48x27, 27x48mm.

C66 A58 30fr dk. brown, blue & black 1.40 75

C67 " 39fr dark olive, brt. green & olive 2.25 1.20

Napoleon in Coronation Robes, by François P. Gerard
AP23

1969, Oct. 2 Photo. *Perf. 12½x12*

C68 AP23 40fr lilac & multi. 4.50 3.00

Issued to commemorate the 200th anniversary of the birth of Napoleon Bonaparte (1769–1821).

Air France Plane over Outrigger Canoe—AP24

1969, Oct. 2 Engraved *Perf. 13*

C69 AP24 50fr slate green, sky bl. & choc. 2.25 1.40

Issued to commemorate the 20th anniversary of the inauguration of the Nouméa to Paris airline.

Bird Type of Regular Issue, 1966.

Birds: 39fr, Emerald doves. 100fr, Whistling kite.

1970, Feb. 19 Photo. *Perf. 13*

Size: 27x48mm.

C70 A45 39fr multicolored 2.25 1.35

C71 " 100fr lt. bl. & multi. 4.50 2.50

Planes Circling Globe and Paris-Nouméa Route—AP25

1970, May 6 Engraved *Perf. 13*

C72 AP25 200fr vio., org. brn. & greenish blue 7.00 4.00

Issued to commemorate the 10th anniversary of the Paris to Nouméa flight: "French Wings Around the World."

Shell Type of Regular Issue

Designs: 22fr, Strombus sinuatus humphrey (vert.). 33fr, Argus porcelain shell. 34fr, Strombus vomer (vert.). 60fr, Card porcelain shell.

1970 Engraved *Perf. 13*

Size: 27x48, 48x27mm.

C73 A59 22fr blue & multi. 1.10 60

C74 " 33fr brown & gray blue 1.75 80

C75 " 34fr pur. & multi. 1.75 80

C76 " 60fr light green & brown 3.00 1.35

See Nos. C89–C90.

Bicyclists on Map of New Caledonia
AP26

1970, Aug. 20 Engraved *Perf. 13*

C77 AP26 40fr blue, ultra. & chocolate 1.65 85

The 4th Bicycling Race of New Caledonia.

Mt. Fuji and Monorail Train
AP27

Design: 45fr, Map of Japan and Buddha statue.

1970, Sept. 3 Photo. *Perf. 13x12½*

C78 AP27 20fr blk., blue & yellow green 85 50

C79 " 45fr maroon, lt. blue & olive 1.65 90

EXPO '70 International Exposition, Osaka, Japan, Mar. 15–Sept. 13.

Racing Yachts
AP28

1971, Feb. 23 Engraved *Perf. 13*

C80 AP28 20fr green, black & vermilion 1.00 60

First challenge in New Zealand waters for the One Ton Cup ocean race.

Lt. Col. Broche and Map of Mediterranean—AP29

1971, May 5 Photo. *Perf. 12½*

C81 AP29 60fr multicolored 2.50 1.25

30th anniversary of Battalion of the Pacific.

Pole Vault—AP30

Design: 100fr, Archery.

1971, June 24 Engraved *Perf. 13*

C82 AP30 25fr bl. grn. & red 1.20 60

C83 AP30 100fr yel. grn., dk. blue & red 4.50 2.35

4th South Pacific Games, Papeete, French Polynesia, Sept. 8–19.

Port de Plaisance, Nouméa—AP31

1971, Sept. 27 Photo. *Perf. 13*

C84 AP31 200fr multicolored 7.50 4.00

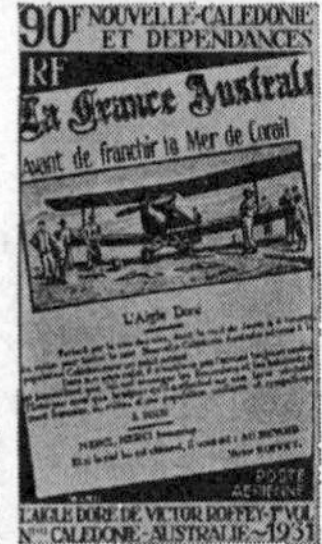

Golden Eagle and Pilot's Leaflet
AP32

1971, Nov. 20 Engraved *Perf. 13*

C85 AP32 90fr dk. brn., org. & indigo 3.25 1.75

40th anniversary of the first flight from New Caledonia to Australia with Victor Roffey piloting the Golden Eagle.

Skiing and Sapporo '72 Emblem—AP33

1972, Jan. 22 Engraved *Perf. 13*

C86 AP33 50fr brt. blue, car. & slate grn. 1.85 90

11th Winter Olympic Games, Sapporo, Japan, Feb. 3–13.

South Pacific Commission Headquarters, Nouméa—AP34

1972, Feb. 5 Photogravure

C87 AP34 18fr blue & multi. 65 35

South Pacific Commission, 25th anniversary.

St. Mark's Basilica, Venice—AP35

1972, Feb. 5 Engraved

C88 AP35 20fr lt. green, blue & brown 1.10 50

UNESCO campaign to save Venice.

Shell Type of Regular Issue, 1970

Designs: 25fr, Orange spider conch. (vert.). 50fr, Chiragra spider conch. (vert.).

1972, Mar. 4 Engraved *Perf. 13*

Size: 27x48mm.

C89 A59 25fr deep carmine & dark brown 1.50 85

C90 " 50fr green, brown & rose carmine 2.50 1.25

Breguet F-ALMV and Globe—AP36

1972, Apr. 5 Engraved *Perf. 13*

C91 AP36 110fr brt. rose lilac, bl. & grn. 5.00 3.00

40th anniversary of the first Paris-Nouméa flight, Mar. 9–Apr. 5, 1932.

Round House and Festival Emblem
AP37

1972, May 13

C92 AP37 24fr org., bl. & brn. 1.00 50

South Pacific Festival of Arts, Fiji, May 6–20.

Hurdles and Olympic Rings—AP38

1972, Sept. 2 Engr. *Perf. 13*

C93 AP38 72fr violet, blue & red lilac 2.75 1.10

20th Olympic Games, Munich, Aug. 26–Sept. 11.

New Post Office, Noumea—AP39

1972, Nov. 25 Engraved *Perf. 13*

C94 AP39 23fr brown, bright blue & green 75 35

Molière and Scenes from Plays—AP40

1973, Feb. 24 Engraved *Perf. 13*

C95 AP40 50fr multicolored 2.00 1.00

300th anniversary of the death of Molière (Jean Baptiste Poquelin, 1622–1673), French actor and playwright.

Woodlands—AP41

Designs: 18fr, Palm trees on coast (vert.). 21fr, Waterfall (vert.).

1973, Feb. 24 Photogravure

C96 AP41 11fr gold & multi. 50 20

C97 " 18fr " " 75 35

C98 " 21fr " " 1.10 50

Concorde
AP42

1973, Mar. 15 Engraved *Perf. 13*

C99 AP42 23fr blue 1.50 75

a. Booklet pane of 5 7.50

No. C99 issued in booklets only.

El Kantara in Panama Canal—AP43

1973, Mar. 24 Engraved *Perf. 13*

C100 AP43 60fr brown, yellow grn. & blk. 2.50 1.20

50th anniversary of steamship connection Marseilles to Nouméa through Panama Canal.

Sun, Earth, Wind God and Satellite—AP44

1973, Mar. 24

C101 AP44 80fr multicolored 2.50 1.25

Centenary of international meteorological cooperation and 13th World Meteorological Day.

Museum Type of Regular Issue

Designs: 16fr, Carved arrows and arrowhead. 40fr, Carved entrance to chief's house.

1973, Apr. 30 Photo. *Perf. 12½x13*

C102	A66	16fr multicolored	60	40
C103	"	40fr "	1.40	75

Nouméa Museum.

DC-10 over Map of Route Paris to Nouméa—AP45

1973, May 19 Engraved *Perf. 13*

C104 AP45 100fr brn., ultra. & slate green 3.25 1.50

First direct flight by DC-10, Nouméa to Paris.

Fish Type of Regular Issue

Design: 32fr, Old and young olive surgeonfish.

1973, June 23 Photo. *Perf. 13x12½*

C105 A69 32fr multicolored 1.25 75

Nouméa Aquarium.

Coach, 1880—AP46

1973, Sept. 22 Engraved *Perf. 13*

C106 AP46 15fr choc., blue & slate green 55 40

Stamp Day 1973.

Landscape—AP47

West Coast Landscapes: 8fr, Rocky path (vert.). 26fr, Trees on shore.

1974, Feb. 23 Photo. *Perf. 13*

C107	AP47	8fr gold & multi.	30	15
C108	"	22fr " "	60	30
C109	"	26fr " "	80	40

Anse-Vata, Scientific Center, Nouméa—AP48

1974, Mar. 23 Photo. *Perf. 13x12½*

C110 AP48 50fr multi. 1.25 80

Ovula Ovum AP49

1974, Mar. 23

Multicolored

C111	AP49	3fr *shown*	12	8
C112	"	32fr *Hydatina*	85	50
C113	"	37fr *Dolium perdix*	1.20	60

Nouméa Aquarium.

Capt. Cook, Map of Grande Terre and "Endeavour"—AP50

Designs: 25fr, Jean F. de la Perouse, his ship and map of Grande Terre. 28fr, French sailor, 18th century, on board ship (vert.). 30fr, Antoine R. J. d'Entrecasteaux, ship and map. 36fr, Dumont d'Urville, ship and map of Loyalty Islands.

1974, Sept. 4 Engraved *Perf. 13*

C114	AP50	20fr multicolored	50	30
C115	"	25fr "	60	35
C116	"	28fr "	70	40
C117	"	30fr "	85	45
C118	"	36fr "	90	50
		Nos. C114-C118 (5)	3.55	2.00

Discovery and exploration of New Caledonia and Loyalty Islands.

UPU Emblem and Symbolic Design—AP51

1974, Oct. 9 Engraved *Perf. 13*

C119 AP51 95fr multicolored 2.85 1.50

Centenary of Universal Postal Union.

Abstract Design—AP52

1974, Oct. 26 Photo. *Perf. 13*

C120 AP52 80fr blue, black & orange 2.00 1.15

ARPHILA 75, Philatelic Exhibition, Paris, June 6–16, 1975.

Hôtel Chateau-Royal, Nouméa—AP53

1975, Jan. 20 Photo. *Perf. 13*

C121 AP53 22fr multicolored 50 30

Cricket—AP54

Designs: 25fr, Bougna ceremony (food offering). 31fr, Pilou dance.

1975, Mar. 24 Photo. *Perf. 13*

C122	AP54	3fr blue & multi.	12	8
C123	"	25fr olive green & multi.	65	32
C124	"	31fr yellow green & multi.	85	40

Tourist publicity.

Orchid Type of 1975

Design: 42fr, Eriaxis rigida.

C125 A74 42fr green & multi. 1.10 60

Globe as "Flower" with "Stamps" as Leaves AP55

1975, June 7 Engr. *Perf. 13*

C126 AP55 105fr multi. 2.50 1.40

ARPHILA 75 International Philatelic Exhibition, Paris, June 6–16.

Discus and Games' Emblem—AP56

Design: 50fr, Volleyball and Games' emblem.

1975, Aug. 23 Photo. *Perf. 13x12½*

C127	AP56	24fr emerald, pur. & dk. blue	60	35
C128	"	50fr multicolored	1.10	60

5th South Pacific Games, Guam, Aug. 1–10.

Concorde—AP57

1976, Jan. 21 Engr. *Perf. 13*

C129 AP57 147fr carmine & ultra. 4.00 2.75

First commercial flight of supersonic jet Concorde, Paris-Rio de Janeiro, Jan. 21.

Telephones 1876 and 1976, Satellite AP58

1976, Mar. 10 Photo. *Perf. 13*

C130 AP58 36fr multicolored 70 45

Centenary of first telephone call by Alexander Graham Bell, Mar. 10, 1876.

Battle Scene—AP59

1976, June 14 Engr. *Perf. 13*

C131 AP59 24fr red brown & vermilion 50 30

American Bicentennial.

Runners and Maple Leaf AP60

1976, July 24 Engr. *Perf. 13*

C132 AP60 33fr car., violet & brown 65 40

21st Olympic Games, Montreal, Canada, July 17–Aug. 1.

Whimsical Bird as Student and Collector AP61

1976, Aug. 21 Photogravure

C133 AP61 42fr multicolored 1.00 60

Philately in School, Philatelic Exhibition in La Perouse Lyceum, Nouméa.

Old City Hall, Nouméa—AP62

Design: 125fr, New City Hall, Nouméa.

1976, Oct. 22 **Photo.** ***Perf. 13***

C134	AP62	75fr multi.	1.50	90
C135	"	125fr "	2.50	1.40

Lagoon, Women and Festival Symbols AP63

1977, Jan. 15 **Photo.** ***Perf. 13x12½***

C136	AP63	11fr multicolored	25	15

Summer Festival 1977, Nouméa.

Training Children in Toy Cars AP64

1977, Mar. 12 **Litho.** ***Perf. 13***

C137	AP64	50fr multicolored	1.10	80

Road safety training.

Bird Type of 1977

Design: 42fr, Male frigate bird (horiz.).

1977, Sept. 17 **Photo.** ***Perf. 13***

138	CA89	42fr multicolored	95	70

Magenta Airport and Routes—AP65

Design: 57fr, La Tontouta airport.

1977, Oct. 22 **Litho.** ***Perf. 13***

C139	AP65	24fr multicolored	55	40
C140	"	57fr "	1.25	90

No. C129 Surcharged in Violet Blue: "22.11.77 PARIS NEW YORK"

1977, Nov. 22 **Engr.** ***Perf. 13***

C141	AP57	147fr carmine & ultra.	3.50	2.25

Concorde, first commercial flight Paris to New York.

Old Nouméa, by H. Didonna—AP66

Valley of the Settlers, by Jean Kreber—AP67

1977, Nov. 26 **Photo.** ***Perf. 13***

C142	AP66	41fr gold & multi.	90	65

Engraved

C143	AP67	42fr yel. brn. & dk. brn.	95	70

"Underwater Carnival," Aubusson Tapestry—AP68

1978, June 17 **Photo.** ***Perf. 13***

C144	AP68	105fr multi.	3.00	2.00

"The Hare and the Tortoise"—AP69

1978, Aug. 19 **Photo.** ***Perf. 13x13½***

C145	AP69	35fr multi.	1.00	60

School philately.

Bourail School Children, Map and Conus Shell—AP70

1978, Sept. 30 **Engr.** ***Perf. 13***

C146	AP70	41fr multi.	1.10	70

Promotion of topical philately in Bourail public schools.

Old and New Candles AP71

1978, Oct. 21 **Photo.** ***Perf. 13***

C147	AP71	36fr multi.	1.00	60

Third Caledonian Senior Citizens' Day.

Scott's editorial staff cannot undertake to identify, authenticate or appraise stamps and postal markings.

Faubourg Blanchot, by Lacouture AP72

1978, Nov. 25 **Photo.** ***Perf. 13***

C148	AP72	24fr multicolored	65	40

Orbiting Weather Satellites, WMO Emblem AP73

1979, Mar. 24 **Photo.** ***Perf. 13***

C149	AP73	53fr multi.	1.55	1.10

First world-wide satellite system in the atmosphere.

Ships and Emblem AP74

1979, Mar. 31 **Engraved**

C150	AP74	49fr multi.	1.50	1.00

Chamber of Commerce and Industry, centenary.

Child's Drawing, IYC Emblem AP75

1979, Apr. 21 **Photo.** ***Perf. 13***

C151	AP75	35fr multi.	1.10	70

International Year of the Child.

AIR POST SEMI-POSTAL STAMP.

French Revolution Issue
Common Design Type
Photogravure.

1939, July 5 *Perf. 13.* **Unwmkd.**
Name and Value Typo. in Orange.

CB1 CD83 4.50fr+4fr brown black 6.00 6.00

V5

Stamps of the design shown above and stamp of Cameroun type V10 inscribed "Nlle Calédonie" were issued in 1942 by the Vichy Government, but were not placed on sale in the colony.

POSTAGE DUE STAMPS.

For a short time in 1894, 5, 10, 15, 20, 25 and 30c postage stamps (Nos. 43, 45, 47, 49, 50 and 52) were overprinted with a "T" in an inverted triangle and used as Postage Due stamps.

French Colonies Postage Due Stamps Overprinted in Carmine, Blue or Silver

1853 1903

1903 *Imperf.* **Unwmkd.**

J1 D1 5c blue (C) 60 60
J2 " 10c brown (C) 3.00 2.00
J3 " 15c yellow green (C) 6.50 2.50
J4 " 30c carmine (Bl) 4.50 3.50
J5 " 50c violet (Bl) 20.00 5.00
J6 " 60c brn., *buff* (Bl) 55.00 20.00
J7 " 1fr rose, *buff* (S) 5.00 4.50
J8 " 2fr red brown (Bl) 300.00 300.00
Nos. J1-J8 (8) 394.60 338.10

Nos. J1 to J8 are known with the "I" in "TENAIRE" missing.
Commemorating fifty years of French occupation.

Men Poling Boat
D2

1906 Typographed. *Perf. 13½x14.*

J9 D2 5c ultramarine, *azure* 10 10
J10 " 10c violet brown, *buff* 15 15
J11 " 15c green, *greenish* 20 20
J12 " 20c *yellow* 25 25
J13 " 30c carmine 30 30
J14 " 50c ultramarine, *buff* 35 35
J15 " 60c brown, *azure* 40 40
J16 " 1fr dark green, *straw* 45 45
Nos. J9-J16 (8) 2.20 2.20

Type of 1906 Issue Surcharged **2F.**

1926-27

J17 D2 2fr on 1fr violet 80 80
J18 " 3fr on 1fr orange brown 80 80

Malayan Sambar
D3 D4

1928 Typographed.

J19 D3 2c slate blue & deep brown 6 6
J20 " 4c brown red & blue green 5 5
J21 " 5c red orange & blue black 8 8
J22 " 10c magenta & Prussian blue 8 8
J23 " 15c dull green & scarlet 10 10
J24 " 20c maroon & olive green 30 30
J25 " 25c bistre brown & slate blue 18 18
J26 " 30c blue green & olive green 20 20
J27 " 50c light brown & dark red 35 35
J28 " 60c magenta & bright rose 30 30
J29 " 1fr dull blue & Prussian green 50 50
J30 " 2fr dark red & olive green 40 40
J31 " 3fr violet & brown 60 60
Nos. J19-J31 (13) 3.20 3.20

Photogravure.

1948 *Perf. 13.* **Unwmkd.**

J32 D4 10c violet 3 3
J33 " 30c brown 3 3
J34 " 50c blue green 6 6
J35 " 1fr orange 5 5
J36 " 2fr red violet 10 10
J37 " 3fr red brown 10 10
J38 " 4fr dull blue 15 15
J39 " 5fr henna brown 30 20
J40 " 10fr slate green 35 30
J41 " 20fr violet blue 85 75
Nos. J32-J41 (10) 2.02 1.77

MILITARY STAMPS.

Stamps of the above types, although issued by officials, were unauthorized and practically a private speculation.

OFFICIAL STAMPS

Ancestor Pole — Carved Wooden Pillow
O1 O2
Various carved ancestor poles.

Typographed.

1959 *Perf. 14x13* **Unwmkd.**

O1 O1 1fr orange yellow 15 7
O2 " 3fr light blue green 20 10
O3 " 4fr purple 25 12
O4 " 5fr ultramarine 40 22
O5 " 9fr black 45 25
O6 O1 10fr bright violet 50 25
O7 " 13fr yellow green 60 35
O8 " 15fr light blue 75 60
O9 " 24fr red lilac 90 65
O10 " 26fr deep orange 1.10 80
O11 " 50fr green 2.25 1.40
O12 " 100fr chocolate 3.50 2.25
O13 " 200fr red 6.00 3.00
Nos. O1-O13 (13) 17.05 10.06

1973-76 Photogravure *Perf. 13*
Green Vignette, Black Inscriptions

O14 O2 1fr yellow 5 5
O15 " 3fr tan 12 10
O16 " 4fr pale violet 18 10
O17 " 5fr lilac rose 20 15
O18 " 9fr light blue 30 20
O19 " 10fr orange 30 25
O20 " 11fr bright lilac 20 10
O21 " 12fr blue green 45 35
O22 " 15fr green 30 10
O23 " 20fr rose 40 10
O24 " 24fr Prussian blue 50 15
O25 " 26fr yellow 55 25
O26 " 36fr deep lilac rose 70 30
O27 " 42fr bister 85 50
O28 " 50fr blue 1.00 75
O29 " 100fr red 2.00 1.35
O30 " 200fr orange 4.00 2.00
Nos. O14-O30 (17) 12.10 6.80

Issue dates: Nos. O14-O19, O21, July 1, 1973. Others, Dec. 1, 1976.

PARCEL POST STAMPS.

Type of Regular Issue of 1905-28 Surcharged or Overprinted

50
Colis Postaux

1926 *Perf. 14x13½.* **Unwmkd.**

Q1 A18 50c on 5fr olive, *lavender* 30 30
Q2 " 1fr deep blue 60 60
Q3 " 2fr carmine, *bluish* 60 60

Regular Issue of 1928 Overprinted:

Colis Postaux

1930

Q4 A20 50c violet & brown 25 25
Q5 A21 1fr deep olive & salmon red 25 25
Q6 " 2fr red org. & brn. 50 50

NEW HEBRIDES

(nū' hĕb'rĭ·dēz)

LOCATION—A group of islands in the South Pacific Ocean lying north of New Caledonia.
GOVT.—Condominium under the joint administration of Great Britain and France.
AREA—5,790 sq. mi.
POP.—100,000 (est. 1976).
CAPITAL—Port-Vila (Vila).

Postage stamps are issued by both Great Britain and France. In 1911 a joint issue was made bearing the coats of arms of both countries. The British stamps bore the coat of arms of Great Britain and the value in British currency on the right and the French coat of arms and values at the left. On the French stamps the positions were reversed. This resulted in some confusion when the value of the French franc decreased following World War I but the situation was corrected by arranging that both series of stamps be sold for their value as expressed in French currency.

12 Pence = 1 Shilling
100 Centimes = 1 Franc
New Hebrides Franc (FNH)—1977

See Vol. I for British issues.

French Issues.

Stamps of New Caledonia, 1905, Overprinted in Black or Red **NOUVELLES HÉBRIDES**

1908 *Perf. 14x13½* **Unwmkd.**

1 A16 5c green 1.10 1.10
2 " 10c rose 1.50 1.50
3 A17 25c bl., *greenish* (R) 2.00 2.00
4 " 50c carmine, *orange* 2.50 2.50

Overprinted
NOUVELLES-HEBRIDES

5 A18 1fr blue, *yellow green* (R) 6.00 6.00
Nos. 1-5 (5) 13.10 13.10

Stamps of 1908 with Additional Overprint **CONDOMINIUM**

1910

6 A16 5c green 45 45
7 " 10c rose 45 45
8 A17 25c blue, *greenish* (R) 50 50
9 " 50c carmine, *orange* 1.65 1.65
10 A18 1fr blue, *yellow green* (R) 6.00 6.00
Nos. 6-10 (5) 9.05 9.05

A2

Wmkd.
Multiple Crown and C. A. (3)

1911, July 12 Engraved *Perf. 14*

11 A2 5c pale green 25 25
12 " 10c red 25 25
13 " 20c gray 1.25 1.00
14 " 25c ultramarine 1.35 1.10
15 " 30c violet, *yellow* 1.35 1.10
16 " 40c red, *yellow* 1.75 1.50
17 " 50c olive green 1.75 1.50
18 " 75c brown orange 2.50 2.50
19 " 1fr brown red, *blue* 1.35 1.35
20 " 2fr violet 2.75 2.75
21 " 5fr brown red, *green* 5.25 5.25
Nos. 11-21 (11) 19.80 18.55

1912 **Wmkd. R F in Sheet**

22 A2 5c pale green 90 90

23	A2	10c red	90	90
24	"	20c gray	1.40	1.40
25	"	25c ultramarine	1.40	1.40
26	"	30c violet, *yellow*	1.40	1.40
27	"	40c red, *yellow*	9.00	9.00
28	"	50c olive green	5.00	5.00
29	"	75c brown orange	5.00	5.00
30	"	1fr brown red, *blue*	2.50	2.50
31	"	2fr violet	4.00	4.00
32	"	5fr brn. red, *green*	8.50	8.50
		Nos. 22-32 (11)	40.00	40.00

In the watermark, "R F" (République Française initials) are large double-lined Roman capitals, about 120mm. high. About one-fourth of the stamps in each sheet show parts of the watermark. The other stamps are without watermark.

Nos. 9 and 8 Surcharged **5c.**

1920 *Perf. 14x13½.* **Unwmkd.**

33	A17	5c on 50c red, *org.*	1.25	1.25
34	"	10c on 25c blue, *greenish*	50	50

Same Surcharge on No. 4

35	A17	5c on 50c red, *orange*	475.00	475.00

British Issue No. 21 and French Issue No. 15 Surcharged **10c.**

1921 *Perf. 14* **Wmk. 3**

36	A1	10c on 5p olive green	5.00	5.00
37	A2	20c on 30c vio., *yel.*	5.00	5.00

Nos. 27 and 26 Surcharged **05c.**

1921 **Wmkd. R F in Sheet**

38	A2	5c on 40c red, *yellow*	12.50	12.50
39	"	20c on 30c violet, *yellow*	5.00	5.00

Stamps of 1910-12 Surcharged with New Values as in 1920-21

1924

40	A2	10c on 5c pale green	40	40
41	"	30c on 10c red	35	35
42	"	50c on 25c ultramarine	1.00	1.00

Wmk. 3

43	A2	50c on 25c ultramarine	2.00	2.00

A4

The values at the lower right denote the currency and amount for which the stamps were to be sold. The stamps could be purchased at the French post office and used to pay postage at the English rates.

Wmkd. R F in Sheet.

1925 Engraved.

44	A4	5c (⅛p) black	50	50
45	"	10c (1p) green	25	25
46	"	20c (2p) greenish gray	25	25
47	"	25c (2½p) brown	25	25
48	"	30c (3p) carmine	25	25
49	"	40c (4p) car., *org.*	45	45
50	"	50c (5p) ultramarine	45	45
51	"	75c (7½p) bistre brn.	70	70
52	"	1fr (10p) car., *blue*	1.25	1.25
53	"	2fr (1sh 8p) gray violet	1.25	1.25
54	"	5fr (4sh) carmine, *greenish*	3.00	3.00
		Nos. 44-54 (11)	8.60	8.60

Beach Scene A6

1938 *Perf. 12.*

55	A6	5c green	30	30
56	"	10c dark orange	30	30
57	"	15c violet	30	30
58	"	20c rose red	30	30
59	"	25c brown	45	45
60	"	30c dark blue	45	45
61	"	40c olive green	65	65
62	"	50c brown violet	65	65
63	"	1fr dk. car., *green*	1.25	1.25
64	"	2fr blue, *green*	3.50	3.50
65	"	5fr red, *yellow*	9.00	9.00
66	"	10fr violet, *blue*	18.50	18.50
		Nos. 55-66 (12)	35.65	35.65

Stamps of 1938 Overprinted in Black

France Libre

1941

67	A6	5c green	4.00	4.00
68	"	10c dark orange	4.00	4.00
69	"	15c violet	4.00	4.00
70	"	20c rose red	4.00	4.00
71	"	25c brown	5.50	5.50
72	"	30c dark blue	5.50	5.50
73	"	40c olive green	5.50	5.50
74	"	50c brown violet	5.50	5.50
75	"	1fr dark carmine, *green*	6.00	6.00
76	"	2fr blue, *green*	6.00	6.00
77	"	5fr red, *yellow*	8.00	8.00
78	"	10fr violet, *blue*	10.00	10.00
		Nos. 67-78 (12)	68.00	68.00

U.P.U. Monument, Bern
A7

Wmkd. RF in Sheet

1949 Engraved *Perf. 13½x14*

79	A7	10c red orange	85	85
80	"	15c violet	1.00	1.00
81	"	30c violet blue	1.25	1.25
82	"	50c rose violet	2.50	2.50

Issued to commemorate the 75th anniversary of the formation of the Universal Postal Union.

Some stamps in each sheet show part of the watermark; others show none.

Outrigger Canoes with Sails A8

Designs: 5c, 10c, 15c, 20c, Canoes with sails. 25c, 30c, 40c, 50c, Native carving. 1fr, 2fr, 5fr, Natives.

1953 *Perf. 12½*

83	A8	5c green	10	10
84	"	10c red	20	20
85	"	15c yellow	25	25
86	"	20c ultramarine	45	45
87	"	25c olive	45	45
88	"	30c light brown	85	85
89	"	40c black brown	85	85
90	"	50c violet	85	85
91	"	1fr deep orange	2.00	2.00
92	"	2fr red violet	6.00	6.00
93	"	5fr scarlet	8.00	8.00
		Nos. 83-93 (11)	20.00	20.00

Discovery of New Hebrides, 1606
A9

Designs: 20c, 50c, Britannia, Marianne, Flags and Mask.

Photogravure.

1956 *Perf. 14½x14* **Unwmkd.**

94	A9	5c emerald	75	75
95	"	10c crimson	75	75
96	"	20c ultramarine	85	85
97	"	50c purple	2.50	2.50

Issued to commemorate the 50th anniversary of the establishment of the Anglo-French Condominium.

Port Vila and Iririki Islet
A10

Designs: 25c, 30c, 40c, 50c, Tropical river and spear fisherman. 1fr, 2fr, 5fr, Woman drinking from coconut (inscribed: "Alliance Franco-Britannique 4 Mars 1947").

Wmkd. RF in Sheet.

1957 Engraved. *Perf. 13½x13*

98	A10	5c green	10	10
99	"	10c red	20	20
100	"	15c orange yellow	40	40
101	"	20c ultramarine	40	40
102	"	25c olive	40	40
103	"	30c light brown	85	85
104	"	40c sepia	85	85
105	"	50c violet	90	90
106	"	1fr orange	2.00	2.00
107	"	2fr rose lilac	5.00	5.00
108	"	5fr black	6.00	6.00
		Nos. 98-108 (11)	17.10	17.10

Wheat Emblem and Globe
A10a

1963, Sept. 2 *Perf. 13* **Unwmkd.**

109	A10a	60c orange brown & slate green	1.65	1.65

"Freedom from Hunger" campaign of the U.N. Food and Agriculture Organization.

Centenary Emblem
A11

1963, Sept. 2 **Unwmkd.**

110	A11	15c org., gray & car.	60	60
111	"	45c bis., gray & car.	1.20	1.20

Centenary of International Red Cross.

Copra Industry
A12

Designs: 5c, Manganese loading, Forari Wharf. 10c, Cacao. 20c, Map of New Hebrides, tuna, marlin and ships. 25c, Striped triggerfish. 30c, Nautilus. 40c, 60c, Turkeyfish (pterois volitans). 50c, Lined tang (fish). 1fr, Cardinal honey-eater and hibiscus. 2fr, Buff-bellied fly-catcher. 3fr, Thicket warbler. 5fr, White-collared kingfisher.

Photo. (10c, 20c, 40c, 60c, 3fr); Engraved (others).

Perf. 12½ (10c, 20c, 40c, 60c); 14 (3fr); 13 (others).

1963-67 **Unwmkd.**

112	A12	5c Prussian blue & claret ('66)	25	25
113	"	10c brt. grn., org. brn. & dk. brn. ("RF" at left) ('65)	90	70
114	"	15c dark purple, yellow & brn.	30	30
115	"	20c bright blue, gray & citron ("RF" at left) ('65)	1.85	1.35
116	"	25c vio., rose lilac & org. brown ('66)	60	60
117	"	30c lilac, brown & citron	60	60
118	"	40c dk. blue & verm. ('65)	2.75	2.00
119	"	50c Prussian blue, yellow & green	70	70
119A	"	60c dk. bl. & verm. ('67)	60	60
120	"	1fr blue green, black & red ('66)	1.40	1.20
121	"	2fr olive, black & brown	3.00	3.00
122	"	3fr org. brn., brt. grn. & black ("RF" at left) ('65)	8.00	5.00
123	"	5fr indigo, dp. blue & gray ('67)	5.00	5.00
		Nos. 112-123 (13)	25.95	21.30

See also Nos. 146-148.

Telegraph, Syncom Satellite and ITU Emblem—A13

1965, May 17 *Perf. 13* **Unwmkd.**

124	A13	15c dk. red brn., brt. blue & emerald	1.25	85
125	"	60c Prussian green, magenta & slate	2.50	2.25

Issued to commemorate the centenary of the International Telecommunication Union.

ICY Emblem—A14

1965, Oct. 24 **Litho.** *Perf. 14½*

126	A14	5c blue grn. & claret	20	20
127	"	55c lt. violet & green	75	75

International Cooperation Year, 1965.

Churchill Memorial Issue

Winston Churchill and St. Paul's, London, During Air Attack
A15

1966, Jan. 24 Photo. *Perf. 14*

Design in Black, Gold and Carmine Rose

128	A15	5c bright blue	25	25
129	"	15c green	35	35
130	"	25c brown	60	60
131	"	30c violet	70	70

Issued in memory of Winston Churchill (1874–1965), British statesman.

Soccer Player and Rimet Cup A16

1966, July 1 Litho. *Perf. 14*

132	A16	20c multicolored	40	40
133	"	40c "	60	60

Issued to publicize the World Cup Soccer Championship, Wembley, England, July 11–30.

WHO Headquarters, Geneva A17

1966, Sept. 20 Litho. *Perf. 14*

134	A17	25c multicolored	40	40
135	"	60c "	70	70

Issued to commemorate the inauguration of World Health Organization Headquarters, Geneva.

"Education"—A18

Designs: 30c, "Science" (retort and grain). 45c, "Culture" (lyre and columns).

1966, Dec. 1 Litho. *Perf. 14*

136	A18	15c dp. orange, yellow & dull violet	30	30
137	"	30c vio., dk. olive grn. & yellow	40	40
138	"	45c yellow, magenta & black	50	50

Issued to commemorate the 20th anniversary of UNESCO (United Nations Educational, Scientific and Cultural Organization).

U.S. Marine, Australian Soldier and Map of South Pacific War Zone—A19

Designs: 15c, The coast watchers. 60c, Australian cruiser Canberra. 1fr, Flying fortress taking off from Bauer Field, and view of Vila.

Perf. 14x13

1967, Sept. 26 Photo. Unwmkd.

139	A19	15c lt. blue & multi.	30	30
140	"	25c yellow & multi.	45	45
141	"	60c multicolored	85	85
142	"	1fr pale sal. & multi.	1.25	1.25

Issued to commemorate the 25th anniversary of the Allied Forces' campaign in the South Pacific War Zone.

L. A. de Bougainville, Ship's Figurehead and Bougainvillea A20

Designs: 15c, Globe and world map. 25c, Ships La Boudeuse and L'Etoile and map of Bougainville Strait.

1968, May 23 Engraved *Perf. 13*

143	A20	15c verm., emerald & dull violet	25	25
144	"	25c ultra., olive & brown	40	40
145	"	60c magenta, green & brown	70	70

Issued to commemorate the 200th anniversary of Louis Antoine de Bougainville's (1729–1811) voyage around the world.

Type of 1963–67 Redrawn, "E II R" at left, "RF" at Right.

Designs as before

1968, Aug. 5 Photo. *Perf. 12½*

146	A12	10c brt. grn., org. brn. & dark brown	15	15
147	"	20c bright blue, gray & citron	25	25

Perf. 14

148	A12	3fr org. brown, brt. grn. & black	2.75	2.75

On Nos. 113, 115 and 122 "RF" is at left and "E II R" is at right.

Concorde Supersonic Airliner A21

Design: 25c, Concorde seen from above.

Perf. 14x13½

1968, Oct. 9 Litho. Unwmkd.

149	A21	25c violet blue, red & light blue	2.50	2.00
150	"	60c red, ultra. & black	4.50	4.00

Issued to commemorate the development of the Concorde supersonic airliner, a joint Anglo-French project to produce a high speed plane.

Kauri Pine A22

1969, June 30 *Perf. 14½x14*

151	A22	20c brown & multi.	30	30

Issued to publicize the New Hebrides timber industry. Issued in sheets of 9 (3x3) on simulated wood grain background.

Relay Race, British and French Flags—A23

Design: 1fr, Runner at right.

1969, Aug. 13 Photo. *Perf. 12½x13*

152	A23	25c multicolored	35	35
153	"	1fr "	1.10	1.10

Issued to publicize the 3rd South Pacific Games, Port Moresby, Papua and New Guinea, Aug. 13–23.

Land Diver at Start, Pentecost Island A24

Designs: 25c, Diver in mid-air. 1fr, Diver nearing ground.

1969, Oct. 15 Litho. *Perf. 12½*

154	A24	15c yellow & multi.	25	25
155	"	25c pink & multi.	40	40
156	"	1fr gray & multi.	1.85	1.85

Issued to publicize the land divers of Pentecost Island.

U.P.U. Headquarters and Monument, Bern A25

1970, May 20 Engraved *Perf. 13*

157	A25	1.05fr orange, lilac & slate	1.10	1.10

Issued to commemorate the opening of the new Universal Postal Union Headquarters, Bern.

Charles de Gaulle A26

1970, July 20 Photo. *Perf. 13*

158	A26	65c brown & multi.	90	90
159	"	1.10fr deep blue & multi.	1.85	1.85

Issued to commemorate the 30th anniversary of the rallying of the Free French.

No. 147 Surcharged

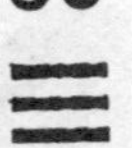

1970, Oct. 15 Photo. *Perf. 12½*

160	A12	35c on 20c multi.	40	40

Virgin and Child, by Giovanni Bellini A27

Design: 50c, Virgin and Child, by Giovanni Cima.

1970, Nov. 30 Litho. *Perf. 14½x14*

161	A27	15c tan & multi.	25	20
162	"	50c lt. grn. & multi.	75	60

Christmas 1970. See Nos. 186–187.

Nos. 158–159 Overprinted "1890–1970 / IN MEMORIAM / 9-11-70" in Gold, 2 Vert. Bars in Black

1971, Jan. 19 Photo. *Perf. 13*

163	A26	65c brown & multi.	70	60
164	"	1.10fr dp. bl. & multi.	1.75	1.40

In memory of Gen. Charles de Gaulle (1890–1970), President of France.

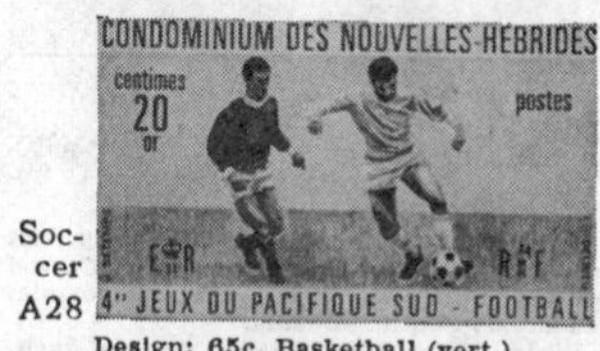

Soccer A28

Design: 65c, Basketball (vert.).

1971, July 13 Photo. *Perf. 12½*

165	A28	20c multicolored	30	25
166	"	65c "	80	75

4th South Pacific Games, Papeete, French Polynesia, Sept. 8–19.

Breadfruit Tree and Fruit, Society Arms A29

Perf. 14½x14

1971, Sept. 7 Litho. Unwmkd.

167	A29	65c multicolored	65	50

Expedition of the Royal Society of London for the Advancement of Science to study vegetation and fauna, July 1–October.

Adoration of the Shepherds, by Louis Le Nain A30

Design: 50c, Adoration of the Shepherds, by Jacopo Tintoretto.

1971, Nov. 23 *Perf. 14x13½*

168	A30	25c lt. grn. & multi.	40	30
169	"	50c lt. blue & multi.	60	50

Christmas 1971.

Drover Mk III
A31

Airplanes: 25c, Sandringham seaplane. 30c, Dragon Rapide. 65c, Caravelle.

1972, Feb. 29 Photo. *Perf. 13½x13*

170	A31	20c lt. green & multi.	35	25
171	"	25c ultra. & multi.	40	30
172	"	30c orange & multi.	40	35
173	"	65c dk. blue & multi.	75	60

Headdress, South Malekula
A32

Baker's Pigeon
A33

Designs: Artifacts; 15c, Slit gong and carved figure, North Ambrym. 1fr, Carved figures, North Ambrym. 3fr, Ceremonial headdress, South Malekula.

Birds: 20c, Red-headed parrot-finch. 35c, Chestnut-bellied kingfisher. 2fr, Green palm lorikeet.

Sea Shells; 25c, Cribraria fischeri. 30c, Oliva rubrolabiata. 65c, Strombus plicatus. 5fr, Turbo marmoratus.

1972, July 24 Photo. *Perf. 12½x13*

174	A32	5c plum & multi.	10	10
175	A33	10c blue & multi.	15	15
176	A32	15c red & multi.	20	20
177	A33	20c org. brn. & multi.	25	25
178	A32	25c dp. blue & multi.	30	30
179	"	30c dk. grn. & multi.	40	30
180	A33	35c gray bl. & multi.	50	40
181	A32	65c dk. grn. & multi.	85	60
182	"	1fr orange & multi.	1.35	1.00
183	A33	2fr multicolored	2.50	1.75
184	A32	3fr yellow & multi.	3.50	3.00
185	"	5fr pink & multi.	8.00	6.00
		Nos. 174-185 (12)	18.10	14.05

Christmas Issue

Type of 1970

Designs: 25c, Adoration of the Magi (detail), by Bartholomaeus Spranger. 70c, Virgin and Child, by Jan Provoost.

1972, Sept. 25 Litho. *Perf. 14x13½*

186	A27	25c lt. green & multi.	35	25
187	"	70c lt. blue & multi.	65	50

Queen Elizabeth II and Prince Philip—A34

Wmkd. Mult. St. Edward's Crown and CA (314)

1972, Nov. 20 Photo. *Perf. 14x14½*

188	A34	35c vio. blk. & multi.	40	30
189	"	65c olive & multi.	70	55

25th anniversary of the marriage of Queen Elizabeth II and Prince Philip.

Dendrobium Teretifolium
A35

New Wharf, Vila
A36

Orchids: 30c, Ephemerantha comata. 35c, Spathoglottis petri. 65c, Dendrobium mohlianum.

Lithographed

1973, Feb. 26 *Perf. 14* Unwmkd.

190	A35	25c bl. violet & multi.	25	25
191	"	30c multicolored	35	30
192	"	35c violet & multi.	45	40
193	"	65c dk. green & multi.	65	50

1973, May 14 Litho. *Perf. 14*

Design: 70c, New Wharf (horiz.).

194	A36	25c multicolored	35	25
195	"	70c "	70	50

New wharf at Vila, completed Nov. 1972.

Wild Horses, Tanna
A37

Design: 70c, Yasur Volcano, Tanna.

1973, Aug. 13 Photo. *Perf. 13x13½*

196	A37	35c multicolored	35	25
197	"	70c "	65	50

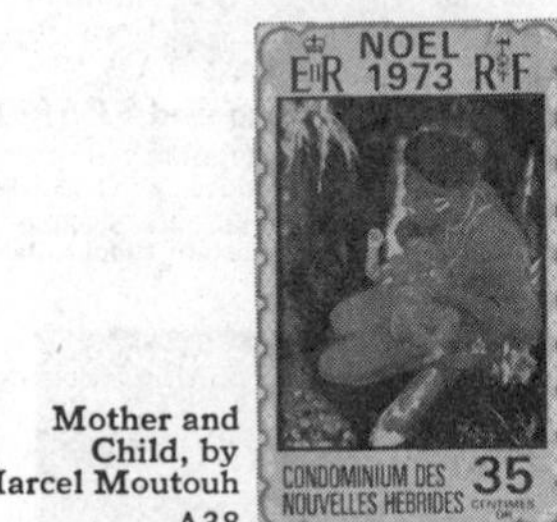

Mother and Child, by Marcel Moutouh
A38

Design: 70c, Star over Lagoon, by Tatin D'Avesnieres.

1973, Nov. 19 Litho. *Perf. 14x13½*

198	A38	35c tan & multi.	40	30
199	"	70c lilac rose & multi.	70	60

Christmas 1973.

Nos. 180, 183 Overprinted in Red or Black: "VISITE ROYALE / 1974"

1974, Feb. 11 Photo. *Perf. 12½x13*

200	A33	35c multi. (R)	40	30
201	"	2fr " (B)	2.00	1.75

Visit of British Royal Family, Feb. 15–16.

Pacific Dove
A39

Designs: 35c, Night swallowtail. 70c, Green sea turtle. 1.15fr, Flying fox.

1974, Feb. 11 *Perf. 13x12½*

202	A39	25c gray & multi.	25	20
203	"	35c " "	35	25
204	"	70c " "	65	50
205	"	1.15fr " "	1.00	85

Nature conservation.

Old Post Office, Vila—A40

Design: 70c, New Post Office.

Photogravure

1974, May 6 *Perf. 12* Unwmkd.

206	A40	35c blue & multi.	40	30
207	"	70c red & multi.	70	60

Opening of New Post Office, May, 1974. Nos. 206–207 printed se-tenant at the base in sheets of 50.

Capt. Cook and Tanna Island
A41

Designs: No. 209, William Wales and boat landing on island. No. 210, William Hodges painting islanders and landscape. 1.15fr, Capt. Cook, "Resolution" and map of New Hebrides.

1974, Aug. 1 Litho. *Perf. 13*

Size: 40x25mm.

208	A41	35c multicolored	35	30
209	"	35c "	35	30
210	"	35c "	35	30

Size: 58x34mm. *Perf. 11*

211	A41	1.15fr lilac & multi.	1.00	75

Bicentenary of the discovery of the New Hebrides by Capt. James Cook.

Nos. 208–210 printed se-tenant in continuous design in sheets of 30 (6x5).

Exchange of Letters, UPU Emblem
A42

1974, Oct. 9 Photo. *Perf. 13x12½*

212	A42	70c multicolored	65	60

Centenary of Universal Postal Union.

Nativity, by Gerard Van Honthorst—A43

Design: 35c, Adoration of the Kings, by Velazquez (vert.).

1974, Nov. 14 Litho. *Perf. 13½*

213	A43	35c multicolored	35	25
214	"	70c "	65	55

Christmas 1974.

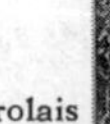

Charolais Bull
A44

1975, Apr. 29 Engraved *Perf. 13*

215	A44	10fr multicolored	8.00	5.50

Nordjamb Emblem, Kayaks
A45

Pitti Madonna, by Michelangelo
A46

1975, Aug. 5 Litho. *Perf. 14x13½*

Multicolored

216	A45	25c *shown*	30	20
217	"	35c *Camp cooks*	40	30
218	"	1fr *Map makers*	85	70
219	"	5fr *Fishermen*	4.00	3.00

Nordjamb 75, 14th Boy Scout Jamboree, Lillehammer, Norway, July 29–Aug. 7.

1975, Nov. 11 Litho. *Perf. 14½x14*

Designs (After Michelangelo): 70c, Bruges Madonna. 2.50fr, Taddei Madonna.

220	A46	35c multicolored	40	30
221	"	70c brn. & multi.	70	60
222	"	2.50fr blue & multi.	2.25	1.85

Christmas 1975.

Concorde, Air France Colors and Emblem—A47

Perf. 13

1976, Jan. 30 Typo. Unwmkd.

223	A47	5fr blue & multi.	4.00	3.50

First commercial flight of supersonic jet Concorde from Paris to Rio de Janeiro, Jan. 21.

Telephones, 1876 and 1976
A48

Designs: 70c, Alexander Graham Bell. 1.15fr, Nouméa Earth Station and satellite.

1976, Mar. 31 Photo. *Perf. 13*

224	A48	25c blk., car. & bl.	25	20
225	"	70c blk. & multi.	55	35
226	"	1.15fr blk., org. & violet blue	90	60

Centenary of first telephone call by Alexander Graham Bell, Mar. 10, 1876.

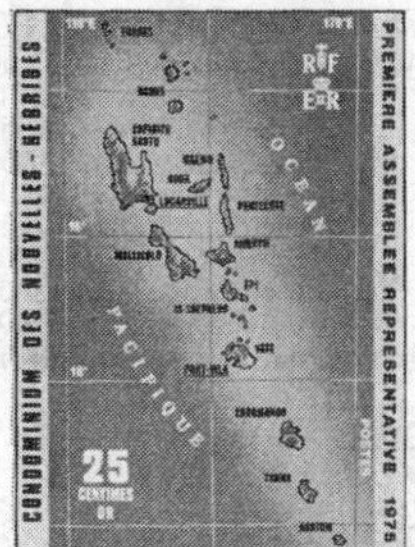

Map of New Hebrides
A49

View of Luganville (Santo)
A50

Design: 2fr, View of Vila.

1976, June 29 Photo. *Perf. 13*

227	A49	25c blue & multi.	25	20
228	A50	1fr multicolored	75	55
229	"	2fr "	1.75	1.10

Opening of first Representative Assemby, June 29, 1976 (25c); first Luganville (Santo) Municipal Council (1fr); first Vila Municipal Council (2fr).

Nos. 228–229 exist with lower inscription reading "Premiere Assemblée Representative 1975" instead of "Premiere Municipalite de Luganville" on 1fr and "Premiere Municipalite de Port-Vila" on 2fr.

Flight into Egypt, by Francisco Vieira Lusitano
A51

Portuguese 16th Century Paintings: 70c, Adoratiion of the Shepherds. 2.50fr, Adoration of the Kings.

1976, Nov. 8 Litho. *Perf. 14*

230	A51	35c pur. & multi.	30	20
231	"	70c blue & multi.	55	40
232	"	2.50fr multicolored	2.00	1.65

Christmas 1976.

Queen's Visit, 1974
A52

Designs: 70c, Imperial State crown. 2fr, The blessing.

1977, Feb. 7 Litho. *Perf. 14x13½*

233	A52	35c lt. grn. & multi.	30	20
234	"	70c blue & multi.	60	40
235	"	2fr pink & multi.	1.65	1.25

25th anniversary of the reign of Queen Elizabeth II.

Nos. 174–185, 215 Surcharged with New Value, "FNH" and Bars

1977, July 1 Photo. *Perf. 12½x13*

236	A32	5fr on 5c multi.	10	10
237	A33	10fr on 10c "	25	25
238	A32	15fr on 15c "	35	35
239	A33	20fr on 20c "	50	50
240	A32	25fr on 25c "	60	60
241	"	30fr on 30c "	75	75
242	A33	35fr on 35c "	85	85
243	A32	40fr on 65c "	1.00	1.00
244	"	50fr on 1fr "	1.40	1.40
245	A33	70fr on 2fr "	2.00	2.00
246	A32	100fr on 3fr "	2.75	2.75
247	"	200fr on 5fr "	5.50	5.50

Engr. *Perf. 13*

248	A44	500fr on 10fr multi.	14.00	14.00
		Nos. 236–248 (13)	30.05	30.05

Nos. 236–248 were surcharged in Paris. Later all denominations except 20fr and 70fr were surcharged in Vila with slightly larger, different letters and different bars. Of these 11 surcharges, the 50fr and 100fr were reported to have been sold only at the philatelic bureau.

Espiritu Santo and Cattle
A53

Designs: 5fr, Erromango Island and Kaori tree. 10fr, Archipelago and man making copra. 20fr, Efate Island and Post Office, Vila. 25fr, Malakula Island and headdresses. 30fr, Aoba and Maewo Islands and pig tusks. 35fr, Pentecost Island and land diving. 40fr, Tanna Island and Prophet John Frum's Red Cross. 50fr, Shepherd Island and canoe with sail. 70fr, Banks Island and dancers. 100fr, Ambrym Island and carvings. 200fr, Aneityum Island and decorated baskets. 500fr, Torres Islands and fishing with bow and arrow.

1977–78 Litho. *Perf. 14*

258	A53	5fr multicolored	10	10
259	"	10fr "	25	20
260	"	15fr "	35	25
261	"	20fr "	50	35
262	"	25fr "	60	40
263	"	30fr "	75	50
264	"	35fr "	85	60
265	"	40fr "	1.00	70
266	"	50fr "	1.25	90
267	"	70fr "	1.75	1.25
268	"	100fr "	2.75	1.85
269	"	200fr "	5.00	3.50
270	"	500fr "	12.00	9.50
		Nos. 258-270 (13)	27.15	20.10

Issue dates: 5fr, 20fr, 50fr, 100fr, 200fr, Sept. 7; 15fr, 25fr, 30fr, 40fr, Nov. 23, 1977; 10fr, 35fr, 70fr, 500fr, May 9, 1978.

Tempi Madonna, by Raphael
A54

Designs: 15fr, Virgin and Child, by Gerard David. 30fr, Virgin and Child, by Pompeo Batoni.

1977, Dec. 8 Litho. *Perf. 12*

271	A54	10fr multicolored	25	20
272	"	15fr "	35	30
273	"	30fr "	75	60

Christmas 1977.

British Airways Concorde over New York—A55

Designs: 20fr, British Airways Concorde over London. 30fr, Air France Concorde over Washington. 40fr, Air France Concorde over Paris.

1978, May 9 Litho. *Perf. 14*

274	A55	10fr multicolored	25	20
275	"	20fr "	50	40
276	"	30fr "	75	60
277	"	40fr "	1.00	80

Souvenir Sheet

White Horse of Hanover
A56

Elizabeth II
A57

Design: No. 278c, Gallic cock.

1978, June 2 Litho. *Perf. 15*

278	Sheet of 6	7.00	7.00
	a. A56 40fr greenish bl. & multi.	1.10	1.10
	b. A57 40fr greenish bl. & multi.	1.10	1.10
	c. A56 40fr greenish bl. & multi.	1.10	1.10

25th anniversary of coronation of Queen Elizabeth II. No. 278 contains 2 se-tenant strips of Nos. 278a–278c, separated by horizontal gutter with commemorative and descriptive inscriptions and showing central part of coronation procession with coach. Size: 100x135mm.

Virgin and Child, by Dürer
A58

Dürer Paintings: 15fr, Virgin and Child with St. Anne. 30fr, Virgin and Child with Goldfinch. 40fr, Virgin and Child with Pear.

1978, Dec. 1 Litho. *Perf. 14x13½*

279	A58	10fr multicolored	25	20
280	"	15fr "	38	30
281	"	30fr "	75	60
282	"	40fr "	1.00	80

Christmas 1978 and 450th death anniversary of Albrecht Dürer (1471–1528), German painter.

Type of 1976 Surcharged with New Value, Bars over Old Denomination and Inscription at Right. Longitude changed to "166E."

1979, Jan. 11 Photo. *Perf. 13*

283	A49	10fr on 25c blue & multicolored	25	20
284	"	40fr on 25c lt. green & multi.	1.00	80

First anniversary of Internal Self-Government.

POSTAGE DUE STAMPS.

French Issues

Regular Issue of 1925 Overprinted
CHIFFRE TAXE

Wmkd. R F in Sheet.

1925 *Perf. 14.*

J1	A4	10c green	18.50	1.85
J2	"	20c gray	18.50	1.85
J3	"	30c carmine	18.50	1.85
J4	"	50c ultramarine	18.50	1.85
J5	"	1fr carmine, *blue*	18.50	1.85
		Nos. J1–J5 (5)	92.50	9.25

Regular Stamps of 1938
Overprinted in Black **CHIFFRE TAXE**

1938 *Perf. 12.*

J6	A6	5c green	35	35
J7	"	10c dark orange	45	45
J8	"	20c rose red	60	60
J9	"	40c olive green	1.40	1.40
J10	"	1fr dark carmine, *green*	2.25	2.25
		Nos. J6–J10 (5)	5.05	5.05

Postage Due Stamps of 1938
Overprinted **France Libre**

1941

J11	A6	5c green	3.75	3.25
J12	"	10c dark orange	3.75	3.25
J13	"	20c rose red	3.75	3.25
J14	"	40c olive green	3.75	3.25
J15	"	1fr dark car., *green*	3.75	3.25
		Nos. J11–J15 (5)	18.75	16.25

Regular Stamps of 1953
Overprinted "TIMBRE-TAXE"

1953 *Perf. 12½* Unwmkd.

J16	A8	5c green	20	20
J17	"	10c red	25	25
J18	"	20c ultramarine	45	45
J19	"	40c black brown	1.25	1.25
J20	"	1fr deep orange	3.00	3.00
		Nos. J16–J20 (5)	5.15	5.15

Regular Stamps of 1957 Overprinted
"TIMBRE-TAXE"

Wmkd. R F in Sheet

1957 Engraved *Perf. 13½x13*

J21	A10	5c green	20	20
J22	"	10c red	30	30
J23	"	20c ultramarine	40	40
J24	"	40c sepia	85	85
J25	"	1fr orange	3.50	3.50
		Nos. J21–J25 (5)	5.25	5.25

NICARAGUA

(nĭk'ȧ-rä'gwȧ)

LOCATION—In Central America, between Honduras and Costa Rica.

GOVT.—Republic.

AREA—57,143 sq. mi. (estimated).

POP.—2,310,000 (est. 1977).

CAPITAL—Managua.

100 Centavos = 1 Peso

100 Centavos = 1 Córdoba (1913)

Liberty Cap on Mountain Peak; From Seal of Country
A1

A2

A3

Engraved.

1862, Dec. 2 *Perf. 12.* Unwmkd.

Yellowish Paper

No.	Type	Description	Unused	Used
1	A1	2c dark blue	20.00	15.00
2	"	5c black	60.00	60.00

Nos. 1–2 were canceled only by pen. See No. C509.

1869-71 White Paper.

No.	Type	Description	Unused	Used
3	A1	1c bister ('71)	5.00	2.50
4	"	2c blue	5.00	2.00
5	"	5c black	25.00	1.50
6	A2	10c vermilion	7.50	3.00
7	A3	25c green	10.00	5.00

1878–80 *Rouletted 8½*

No.	Type	Description	Unused	Used
8	A1	1c brown	3.00	2.50
9	"	2c blue	3.50	2.00
10	"	5c black	20.00	1.50
11	A2	10c vermilion ('80)	4.00	3.00
12	A3	25c green ('79)	5.00	5.00

Nos. 3–12 were reprinted in 1892. The corresponding values of the two series are printed in the same shades which is not usually true of the originals. They are, however, similar to some of the original shades and the only certain test is comparison. Originals have thin white gum; reprints have rather thick yellowish gum. Price 50c each.

Seal of Nicaragua
A4

Locomotive and Telegraph Key
A5

1882 Engraved *Perf. 12*

No.	Type	Description	Unused	Used
13	A4	1c green	15	25
14	"	2c carmine	15	25
15	"	5c blue	15	25
16	"	10c dull violet	20	75
17	"	15c yellow	50	2.50
18	"	20c slate gray	75	5.00
19	"	50c dull violet	1.00	10.00
		Nos. 13–19 (7)	2.90	

Used Prices

of Nos. 13–120 are for stamps with genuine cancellations applied while the stamps were valid. Various counterfeit cancellations exist.

1890 Engraved

No.	Type	Description	Unused	Used
20	A5	1c yellow brown	15	30
21	"	2c vermilion	15	30
22	"	5c deep blue	15	25
23	"	10c lilac gray	15	30
24	"	20c red	15	1.75
25	"	50c purple	15	5.00
26	"	1p brown	20	8.50
27	"	2p dark green	20	11.00
28	"	5p lake	20	17.50
29	"	10p orange	20	25.00
		Nos. 20–29 (10)	1.70	

The issues of 1890–1899 were printed by the Hamilton Bank Note Co., New York, to the order of N. F. Seebeck who held a contract for stamps with the government of Nicaragua. Reprints were made, for sale to collectors, of the 1896, 1897 and 1898, postage, postage due and official stamps. See notes following those issues.

Goddess of Plenty
A6

Columbus Sighting Land
A7

1891 Lithographed

No.	Type	Description	Unused	Used
30	A6	1c yellow brown	20	30
31	"	2c red	20	30
32	"	5c dark blue	20	20
33	"	10c slate	20	50
34	"	20c plum	20	2.00
35	"	50c purple	20	5.00
36	"	1p black brown	20	5.00
37	"	2p green	20	8.50
38	"	5p brown red	20	11.00
39	"	10p orange	20	16.50
		Nos. 30–39 (10)	2.00	

1892 Engraved

No.	Type	Description	Unused	Used
40	A7	1c yellow brown	20	25
41	"	2c vermilion	20	20
42	"	5c dark blue	20	20
43	"	10c slate	20	30
44	"	20c plum	20	2.00
45	"	50c purple	20	7.00
46	"	1p brown	20	7.00
47	"	2p blue green	20	8.50
48	"	5p rose lake	20	15.00
49	"	10p orange	20	20.00
		Nos. 40–49 (10)	2.00	

Commemorative of the 400th anniversary of the discovery of America by Columbus.

Stamps of the 1892 design were printed in other colors than those listed and overprinted "Telegrafos". The 1c blue, 10c orange, 20c slate, 50c plum and 2p vermilion are telegraph stamps which did not receive the overprint.

Arms
A8

"Victory"
A9

1893 Engraved

No.	Type	Description	Unused	Used
51	A8	1c yellow brown	20	20
52	"	2c vermilion	20	20
53	"	5c dark blue	20	20
54	"	10c slate	20	30
55	"	20c dull red	20	1.75
56	"	50c violet	20	4.00
57	"	1p dark brown	20	7.00
58	"	2p blue green	20	8.50
59	"	5p rose lake	20	11.00
60	"	10p orange	20	13.50
		Nos. 51–60 (10)	2.00	

The 1c blue and 2c dark brown are telegraph stamps which did not receive the "Telegrafos" overprint.

1894 Engraved

No.	Type	Description	Unused	Used
61	A9	1c yellow brown	20	30
62	"	2c vermilion	20	30
63	"	5c deep blue	20	25
64	"	10c slate	20	30
65	"	20c lake	20	1.75
66	"	50c purple	20	4.00
67	"	1p brown	20	7.00
68	"	2p green	20	12.50
69	"	5p brown red	20	15.00
70	"	10p orange	20	20.00
		Nos. 61–70 (10)	2.00	

Specialists believe the 25c yellow green, type A9, is a telegraph denomination never issued for postal purposes. Stamps in other colors are telegraph stamps without the usual "Telegrafos" overprint.

Coat of Arms
A10

Map of Nicaragua
A11

1895 Engraved

No.	Type	Description	Unused	Used
71	A10	1c yellow brown	20	30
72	"	2c vermilion	20	30
73	"	5c deep blue	20	25
74	"	10c slate	20	30
75	"	20c claret	20	75
76	"	50c dull violet	20	2.50
77	"	1p dark brown	20	5.00
78	"	2p deep green	20	8.00
79	"	5p brown red	20	11.00
80	"	10p orange	20	16.50
		Nos. 71–80 (10)	2.00	

Frames of Nos. 71–80 differ for each denomination.

A 50c blue exists. Its status is questioned.

1896 Engraved

No.	Type	Description	Unused	Used
81	A11	1c violet	30	1.00
82	"	2c blue green	30	50
83	"	5c bright rose	30	30
84	"	10c blue	50	50
85	"	20c bistre brown	3.00	4.00
86	"	50c blue gray	60	8.00
87	"	1p black	60	11.00
88	"	2p claret	60	15.00
89	"	5p deep blue	60	15.00
		Nos. 81–89 (9)	6.80	

See italic note after No. 109M.

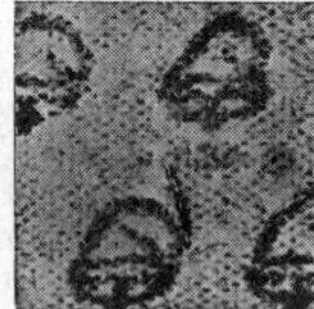

Wmk. 117

Wmkd. Liberty Cap. (117)

No.	Type	Description	Unused	Used
89A	A11	1c violet	3.00	75
89B	"	2c blue green	3.00	1.00
89C	"	5c bright rose	12.00	25
89D	"	10c blue	20.00	75
89E	"	20c bistre brown	3.00	3.50
89F	"	50c blue gray	35.00	7.50
89G	"	1p black	30.00	10.00
89H	"	2p claret		15.00
89I	"	5p deep blue		32.50

Same, dated 1897.

1897 Engraved Unwmkd.

No.	Type	Description	Unused	Used
90	A11	1c violet	40	40
91	"	2c blue green	40	50
92	"	5c bright rose	40	25
93	"	10c blue	5.00	60
94	"	20c bistre brown	2.00	3.00
95	"	50c blue gray	7.00	7.50
96	"	1p black	7.00	12.50
97	"	2p claret	16.00	15.00
98	"	5p deep blue	16.00	35.00
		Nos. 90–98 (9)	54.20	74.75

See italic note after No. 109M.

Wmkd. Liberty Cap. (117)

No.	Type	Description	Unused	Used
98A	A11	1c violet	11.00	40
98B	"	2c blue green	11.00	40
98C	"	5c bright rose	16.50	30
98D	"	10c blue	17.50	75
98E	"	20c bistre brown	3.00	4.00
98F	"	50c blue gray	18.50	6.50
98G	"	1p black	20.00	13.00
98H	"	2p claret	20.00	20.00
98I	"	5p deep blue	95.00	40.00
		Nos. 98A–98I (9)	212.50	85.35

Coat of Arms of "Republic of Central America"
A12

1898 Engraved Wmk. 117

No.	Type	Description	Unused	Used
99	A12	1c brown	20	30
100	"	2c slate	20	30
101	"	4c red brown	20	40
102	"	5c olive green	32.50	18.50
103	"	10c violet	12.00	50
104	"	15c ultramarine	25	1.50
105	"	20c blue	8.00	1.50
106	"	50c yellow	8.00	7.50
107	"	1p violet blue	25	12.50
108	"	2p brown	15.00	17.50
109	"	5p orange	20.00	25.00
		Nos. 99–109 (11)	96.60	85.50

Unwmkd.

No.	Type	Description	Unused	Used
109A	A12	1c brown	1.00	25
109B	"	2c slate	1.00	1.00
109D	"	4c red brown	1.75	50
109E	"	5c olive green	20.00	10
109G	"	10c violet	20.00	50
109H	"	15c ultramarine	20.00	
109I	"	20c blue	20.00	
109J	"	50c yellow	20.00	
109K	"	1p deep ultra.	20.00	
109L	"	2p olive brown	20.00	
109M	"	5p orange	20.00	

The paper of Nos. 109A to 109M is slightly thicker and more opaque than that of Nos. 81 to 89 and 90 to 98. The 5c and 10c also exist on very thin, semi-transparent paper.

Many reprints of Nos. 81–109M are on thick, porous paper, with and without watermark. The watermark is sideways. Paper of the originals is thinner for Nos. 81–109 but thicker for Nos. 109A–109M. Price 15 cents each.

In addition, reprints of Nos. 81–89 and 90–98 exist on thin paper, but with shades differing slightly from those of originals.

"Justice"
A13

Mt. Momotombo
A14

1899 Lithographed

No.	Type	Description	Unused	Used
110	A13	1c gray green	15	35
111	"	2c brown	10	30
112	"	4c deep rose	35	40
113	"	5c deep blue	20	30
114	"	10c buff	20	30
115	"	15c chocolate	20	65
116	"	20c dark green	35	75
117	"	50c bright rose	20	3.00
118	"	1p red	20	8.50
119	"	2p violet	20	20.00
120	"	5p light blue	20	25.00
		Nos. 110–120 (11)	2.35	59.55

Nos. 110–120 exist imperf. and in horizontal pairs imperf. between.

Imprint: "American Bank Note Co. NY"

1900, Jan. 1 Engraved

No.	Type	Description	Unused	Used
121	A14	1c plum	25	12
122	"	2c vermilion	35	15
123	"	3c green	35	25
124	"	4c olive green	50	25
125	"	5c dark blue	2.00	20

126 A14 6c carmine rose 10.00 3.00
127 " 10c violet 5.00 25
128 " 15c ultramarine 5.00 50
129 " 20c brown 5.00 50
130 " 50c lake 4.00 1.00
131 " 1p yellow 9.00 2.75
132 " 2p salmon 7.00 1.75
133 " 5p black 8.00 2.50
Nos. 121–133 (13) 56.45 13.22

See also Nos. 159–161.

Nos. 131–133 Surcharged in Black or Red

1901

2 Cent.

1901, Mar. 5
134 A14 2c on 1p yellow 3.00 2.25
a. Bar below date 10.00 6.00
b. Invtd. surcharge 12.00
c. Double surcharge 20.00
135 " 10c on 5p black (R) 3.75 2.75
a. Bar below date 10.00 6.00
136 " 20c on 2p salmon 5.00 5.00
a. Bar below date 10.00 7.00

A 2c surcharge on No. 121, the 1c plum, was not put on sale, nor postally used.

The 2c on 1p yellow without ornaments is a reprint.

Correos

Postage Due Stamps of 1900 Overprinted in Black or Gold

1901

1901, Mar.
137 D3 1c plum 3.25 2.75
138 " 2c vermilion 3.25 2.75
139 " 5c dark blue 4.00 2.75
140 " 10c purple (G) 5.00 3.50
a. Double overprint 10.00 10.00
141 " 20c orange brown 6.50 5.00
142 " 30c dark green 6.50 5.00
143 " 50c lake 5.00 2.50
a. "1091" for "1901" 12.50 12.50
b. "Correo" 27.50
Nos. 137–143 (7) 33.50 24.25

In 1904 an imitation of this overprint was made to fill a dealer's order. The date is at top and "Correos" at bottom. The overprint is printed in black, sideways on the 1c and 2c and upright on the 5c and 10c. Some copies of the 2c were further surcharged "1 Centavo". None of these stamps was ever regularly used.

3 Cent.

Nos. 126, 131–133 Surcharged

1901

Black Surcharge.

1901, Oct. 20
144 A14 3c on 6c rose 3.50 2.50
a. Bar below value 4.25 3.50
b. Inverted surcharge 5.00 5.00
c. Double surcharge 5.00 5.00
d. Double surcharge, one inverted 18.50 18.50
145 " 4c on 6c rose 3.25 2.25
a. Bar below value 4.00 3.25
b. "1 cent" instead of "4 cent" 6.00 6.00
c. Double surcharge 15.00 15.00
146 " 5c on 1p yellow 3.00 2.00
a. Three bars below value 4.00 3.00
b. Ornaments at each side of "1901" 4.00 3.00
c. Double surcharge, one in red 10.00 10.00
147 " 10c on 2p salmon 3.50 2.50
a. Inverted surcharge 9.00 9.00
b. Double surcharge

Blue Surcharge.

148 A14 3c on 6c rose 3.25 2.50
a. Bar below value 4.25 3.75
Double surcharge 6.00 6.00
149 A14 4c on 6c rose 3.25 2.75
a. Bar below value 4.25 4.25
b. "1 cent" instead of "4 cent" 6.50 6.50
c. Inverted surcharge 15.00 15.00

Red Surcharge.

150 A14 5c on 1p yellow 5.00 4.00
a. Three bars below value 6.00 5.00
b. Ornaments at each side of "1901" 6.00 5.00
c. Inverted surcharge 8.00 8.00
d. Double surcharge, inverted 13.50 13.50
151 " 20c on 5p black 3.00 2.50
a. Invtd. surcharge 12.00 12.00
b. Double surcharge 18.50 18.50
c. Triple surcharge
Nos. 144–151 (8) 27.75 21.00

In 1904 a series was surcharged as above, but with "Centavos" spelled out. About the same time No. 122 was surcharged "1 cent." and "1901", "1902" or "1904". All of these surcharges were made to fill a dealer's order and none of the stamps was regularly issued or used.

1901

Postage Due Stamps of 1900 Overprinted in Black

Correos

1901, Oct.
152 D3 1c red violet 55 25
a. Ornaments at each side of the stamp 55 50
b. Ornaments at each side of "1901" 50 50
c. "Correos" in italics 1.00 1.00
d. Double overprint 10.00 10.00
153 " 2c vermilion 40 25
a. Double overprint 6.00 4.00
154 " 5c dark blue 60 35
a. Double ovpt., one inverted
b. Double overprint 5.00 5.00
155 " 10c purple 60 35
b. Double overprint 7.00 7.00
c. Double overprint, one inverted 9.00 9.00
156 " 20c orange brown 90 1.00
b. Double overprint 5.00 5.00
157 " 30c dark green 65 1.00
a. Double overprint 7.00 7.00
b. Inverted overprint 15.00 15.00
158 " 50c lake 65 1.00
a. Triple overprint 20.00 20.00
b. Double overprint 13.00 13.00
Nos. 152–158 (7) 4.35 4.20

One stamp in each group of twenty-five has the second "o" of "Correos" italic.

Momotombo Type of 1900.
Without Imprint

1902 Lithographed. *Perf. 14.*
159 A14 5c blue 25 15
a. Imperf., pair 2.50
160 " 5c carmine 25 12
a. Imperf., pair 2.50
161 " 10c violet 25 12
a. Imperf., pair 2.50

No. 161 was privately surcharged 6c, 1p and 5p in black in 1903.

15 cvos.

Nos. 121 and 122 Surcharged in Black

1902

1902, Oct. *Perf. 12*
162 A14 15c on 2c vermilion 1.25 50
a. Double surcharge 25.00
b. Blue surcharge 75.00
163 " 30c on 1c plum 50 2.50
a. Double surcharge 7.00
b. Inverted surcharge 20.00

President José Santos Zelaya
A15

1903, Jan. Engraved
167 A15 1c emerald & black 30 50
168 " 2c rose & black 60 50
169 " 5c ultra. & black 30 50
170 " 10c yellow & black 30 1.00
171 " 15c lake & black 45 2.00
172 " 20c violet & black 45 2.00
173 " 50c olive & black 45 5.00
174 " 1p red brn. & black 45 6.00
Nos. 167–174 (8) 3.30 17.50

Tenth anniversary of first election of President Zelaya.

The so-called color errors—1c orange yellow and black, 2c ultramarine and black, 5c lake and black and 10c emerald and black—were also delivered to postal authorities. They were intended for official use though not issued as such.

A16

A17

No. 161 Surcharged with New Values in Blue.

1904–05
175 A16 5c on 10c violet ('05) 1.00 15
a. Inverted surcharge 1.25 1.00
b. Without ornaments 1.25 50
c. Character for "cents" inverted 35 25
d. Same as "b" inverted
e. Same as "c" inverted 2.00 2.00
f. Double surcharge 6.00 6.00
g. "5" omitted 2.00 2.00
176 " 15c on 10c violet ('05) 20 20
a. Inverted surcharge 1.00 1.00
b. Without ornaments 1.00 1.00
c. Character for "cents" inverted 75 50
d. Same as "b" inverted
e. Same as "c" inverted 1.25 1.25
f. Imperf. 5.00
h. Same as "a" imperf. 7.00 7.00
i. Double surcharge 10.00 10.00
177 A17 15c on 10c violet 3.00 2.50
a. Inverted surcharge 3.50 3.50
b. "Centcvos" 3.50 3.00
c. "5" of "15" omitted 5.00
d. Same as "b" inverted 6.00 6.00
e. Double surcharge 8.00 8.00
f. Double surcharge, inverted 10.00 10.00
g. Imperf., pair 7.00 7.00

There are two settings of the surcharge on No. 175. In the first the character for "cents" and the figure "5" are 2mm. apart and in the second 4mm.

The 2c vermilion, No. 122, with surcharge "1 cent. / 1904" was not issued.

No. 161 Surcharged in Black 5 CENTS.

1905, June
178 A14 5c on 10c violet 40 25
a. Inverted surcharge 2.00 2.00
b. Double surcharge 3.00 3.00
c. Surch. in blue 10.00

Coat of Arms
A18

Imprint:
"American Bank Note Co. NY"

1905, July 25 Engr. *Perf. 12*
179 A18 1c green 15 15
180 " 2c carmine rose 15 15
181 " 3c violet 20 20
182 " 4c orange red 20 20
183 " 5c blue 20 10
184 " 6c slate 30 30
185 " 10c yellow brown 40 15
186 " 15c brown olive 40 20
187 " 20c lake 30 20
188 " 50c orange 1.50 1.50
189 " 1p black 1.00 2.00
190 " 2p dark green 1.00 2.25
191 A18 5p violet 1.00 2.50
Nos. 179–191 (13) 6.80 9.90

See also Nos. 202–208, 237–248.

Nos. 179–184 and 191 Surcharged in Black or Red Reading Up or Down

1906–08
193 A18 10c on 2c carmine rose (up) 4.00 3.00
a. Surcharge reading down 10.00 10.00
194 " 10c on 3c violet (up) 25 12
a. "¢" normal 2.00 1.00
b. Double surcharge 3.00 3.00
c. Double surcharge, up and down 4.50 3.50
d. Pair, one without surcharge 7.00
e. Surcharge reading down 20 12
195 " 10c on 4c orange red (up) ('08) 27.50 16.50
a. Surcharge reading down 25.00 17.50
196 " 15c on 1c green (up) 30 18
a. Double surcharge 5.00 5.00
b. Double surcharge, one reading down 7.50 7.50
c. Surcharge reading down 25 15
197 " 20c on 2c carmine rose (down) ('07) 35 20
a. Double surcharge 10.00 10.00
b. Surcharge reading up 30.00 25.00
c. "V" omitted 7.00 7.00
198 " 20c on 5c blue (down) 35 35
a. Surcharge reading up 27.50
199 " 50c on 6c slate (R) (down) 30 30
a. Double surcharge
b. Surcharge reading up 22.50 22.50
c. Yel. brn. surch. 30 30
200 " 1p on 5p violet (down) ('07) 32.50 18.00

There are several settings of these surcharges and many varieties in the shapes of the figures, the spacing, etc.

Surcharged **Vale 35 cts.** in Red Vertically Reading Up.

1908, May
201 A18 35c on 6c slate 2.00 1.75
a. Dbl. surch. (R) 20.00
b. Double surcharge (R + Bk) 50.00
c. Carmine surch. 2.00 2.00

Arms Type of 1905.

Imprint: "Waterlow & Sons, Ltd."

1907, Feb. *Perf. 14 to 15*
202 A18 1c green 25 20
203 " 2c rose 25 16
204 " 4c brown orange 1.00 20
205 " 10c yellow brown 1.50 15
206 " 15c brown olive 2.00 50
207 " 20c lake 3.00 1.00
208 " 50c orange 5.00 2.50
Nos. 202–208 (7) 13.00 4.71

Nos. 202–204, 207–208 Surcharged in Black or Blue (Bl) Reading Down

1907–08
212 A18 10c on 2c rose 1.00 40
a. Double surcharge 7.50
b. "Vale" only 15.00
c. Surcharge reading up 10.00 5.00
213 " 10c on 4c brn. org. (up) ('08) 1.50 65
a. Double surcharge 7.50
b. Surcharge reading down 5.00 3.50

214 A18 10c on 20c lake ('08) 2.00 1.25
b. Surcharge reading up 60.00

215 " 10c on 50c orange (Bl) ('08) 1.25 35

216 " 15c on 1c grn. ('08) 25.00 3.00
Nos. 212–216 (5) 30.75 5.65

Several settings of this surcharge provide varieties of numeral font, spacing, etc.

Revenue Stamps Overprinted "CORREO—1908"

A19

1908, June

217 A19 5c yellow & black 35 30
a. "CORROE" 2.00 2.00
b. Overprint reading down 5.00
c. Double overprint 10.00

218 " 10c light blue & black 25 15
a. Double overprint 3.00 3.00
b. Overprint reading down 25 15
c. Double overprint, up and down 10.00 10.00

219 " 1p yellow brown & black 10 *2.00*
a. "CORROE" 6.00 6.00

220 " 2p pearl gray & black 10 *2.50*
a. "CORROE" 7.50 7.50

Remainders of Nos. 219–220 were sold.

Revenue Stamps Surcharged Vertically Reading Up

CORREO–1908

VALE 2 ₵

in Red, Blue, Green or Orange

221 A19 1c on 5c yellow & black (R) 25 20
a. "1008" 1.00 1.00
b. "8908" 1.00 1.00
c. Surcharge reading down 3.00 3.00
d. Double surcharge 3.00 3.00

222 " 2c on 5c yellow & black (Bl) 25 20
b. "ORREO" 1.25 1.25
c. "1008" 1.25 1.25
d. "8908" 1.25 1.25
f. Double surcharge 5.00 5.00
g. Double surcharge, one inverted 5.00 5.00
h. Surcharge reading down 7.50 7.50

223 " 4c on 5c yellow & black (G) 45 20
a. "ORREO" 2.00 2.00
b. "1008" 1.50 1.50
c. "8908" 1.50 1.50

224 " 15c on 50c olive & black (R) 30 25
a. "1008" 3.00 3.00
b. "8908" 3.00 3.00
c. Surcharge reading down 8.00 8.00

225 " 35c on 50c olive & black (O) 2.50 60
a. Double surcharge, one inverted 10.00 10.00
b. Surcharge reading down 10.00 10.00
c. Double surcharge, one in black
Nos. 221–225 (5) 3.75 1.45

Revenue Stamps Surcharged Vertically Reading Up

CORREOS–1908

VALE 2 ₵

in Blue, Black or Orange

1908, Nov.

225D A19 2c on 5c yellow & black (Bl) 12.00 9.00
e. "9c" instead of "2c" 75.00 75.00

225F A19 10c on 50c olive & black (Bk) *700.00 225.00*
g. Double surcharge *400.00*

225H " 35c on 50c olive & black (O) 12.00 9.00

In this setting there are three types of the character for "cents".

A20

A20a

Surcharged in Black, Blue or Green

1908, Dec.

226 A20 2c orange (Bk) 2.25 1.25
a. Double overprint 5.00 5.00
b. Overprint reading up 4.00 4.00

227 A20a 4c on 2c org. (Bk) 1.00 60
a. Surcharge reading up 4.00 4.00
b. Blue surch. 70.00 70.00

228 " 5c on 2c orange (Bl) 85 40
a. Surcharge reading up 4.50 4.50

229 " 10c on 2c orange (G) 80 18
a. "1988" for "1908" 3.00 2.00
b. Surcharge reading up 4.00 4.00
c. "¢" inverted 3.00 3.00
d. Double surcharge 6.00

Two printings of No. 229 exist. In the first, the initial of "VALE" is a small capital, and in the second a large capital.

The overprint "Correos—1908." 35mm. long, handstamped on 1c blue revenue stamp of type A20, is private and fraudulent.

Revenue Stamps Surcharged in Various Colors

CORREOS 1909
VALE 10 ₵

1909, Feb.

230 A19 1c on 50c olive & black (V) 2.25 1.25

231 " 2c on 50c olive & black (Br) 3.50 1.50

232 " 4c on 50c olive & black (G) 3.50 1.50

233 " 5c on 50c olive & black (C) 2.00 1.00
a. Double surcharge 12.50 12.50

234 " 10c on 50c olive & black (Bk) 75 60
Nos. 230–234 (5) 12.00 5.85

Nos. 230 to 234 are found with three types of the character for "cents".

Nos. 190 and 191 Surcharged in Black

VALE 10 ₵

1909, Mar. ***Perf. 12***

235 A18 10c on 2p dk. green 13.50 8.50

236 " 10c on 5p violet *67.50 55.00*

There are three types of the character for "cents."

Arms Type of 1905. Imprint: "American Bank Note Co. NY"

1909, Mar.

237 A18 1c yellow green 25 15
238 " 2c vermilion 25 15
239 A18 3c red orange 25 15
240 " 4c violet 25 15
241 " 5c deep blue 25 15
242 " 6c gray brown 1.25 1.00
243 " 10c lake 55 10
244 " 15c black 55 15
245 " 20c brown olive 55 15
246 " 50c deep green 60 35
247 " 1p yellow 60 35
248 " 2p carmine rose 60 35
Nos. 237–248 (12) 5.95 3.20

Nos. 239, 244 and 245, Surcharged in Black or Red

VALE 2 ¢

1910, July

249 A18 2c on 3c red orange (Bk) 2.00 1.00

250 " 10c on 15c black (R) 55 18
a. "VLEA" 2.50 1.50
b. Double surcharge 15.00 15.00

There are two types of the character for "cents".

Surcharged in Black or Red

VALE 2 C

1910

252 A18 2c on 3c red orange (Bk) 80 80
a. Double surcharge 5.00 5.00
b. Pair, one without surcharge
c. "Vale" omitted 10.00 10.00

254 " 5c on 20c brown olive (R) 25 20
a. Dbl. surch. (R) 5.00 4.00
b. Invtd. surch. (R) 3.00 2.00
c. Black surch. 90.00
d. Dbl. surch. (Bk) 125.00
e. Invtd. surch. (Bk) 100.00

255 " 10c on 15c black (Bk) 45 20
a. "c" omitted 1.50 1.00
b. "10c" omitted 2.00 1.25
c. Inverted surcharge 3.00 3.00
d. Double surcharge 5.00 5.00
e. Double surcharge, one inverted 10.00

There are several minor varieties in this setting, such as italic "L" and "E" and fancy "V" in "VALE", small italic "C", and italic "I" for "1" in "10".

Nos. 239, 244, 246 and 247, Surcharged in Black

Vale
2 cts.

1910, Dec. 10

256 A18 2c on 3c red orange 50 30
a. Without period 75 50
b. Inverted surcharge 5.00 5.00
c. Double surcharge 5.00 5.00

257 " 10c on 15c black 1.25 50
a. Without period 2.50 1.00
b. Double surcharge 2.50 2.50
c. Inverted surcharge 3.75 3.75

258 " 10c on 50c deep green 75 30
a. Without period 1.00 50
b. Double surcharge 2.50 2.50
c. Inverted surcharge 2.50 2.50

259 " 10c on 1p yellow 50 30
a. Without period 1.00 60
b. Double surcharge 2.50 2.50

259C " 15c on 50c deep green

Nos. 240, 244–248 Surcharged in Black

Vale
2 cts.

Surcharge as on Nos. 256–259c, but lines wider apart.

1911, Mar.

260 A18 2c on 4c violet 18 15
a. Without period 20 20
b. Double surcharge 2.00 2.00
c. Double surcharge, inverted 3.00 3.00
d. Double surcharge, one inverted 2.50 2.50
e. Inverted surcharge 6.00 6.00

261 " 5c on 20c brown olive 18 15
a. Without period 50 40
b. Double surcharge 2.00 2.00
c. Inverted surcharge 2.00 1.50
d. Double surcharge, one inverted 5.00 5.00

262 A18 10c on 15c black 25 15
a. Without period 75 35
b. "Yale" 10.00 10.00
c. Double surcharge 2.50 2.50
d. Inverted surcharge 2.50 2.50
e. Double surcharge, one inverted 4.00 3.50
f. Double surcharge, both inverted 10.00 10.00

263 " 10c on 50c deep green 15 15
a. Without period 75 40
b. Double surcharge 2.50 2.00
c. Double surcharge, one inverted 4.00 3.00
d. Inverted surcharge 4.00 4.00

264 " 10c on 1p yellow 1.00 30
a. Without period 1.50 1.00
b. Double surcharge 3.00 3.00
c. Double surcharge, one inverted *6.00*

265 " 10c on 2p carmine rose 35 35
a. Without period 1.75 1.25
b. Double surcharge 2.00 2.00
c. Double surcharge, one inverted 5.00 5.00
d. Inverted surcharge 5.00 5.00
Nos. 260–265 (6) 2.11 1.25

Revenue Stamps Surcharged in Black

Correos
02 cts
1911

1911, Apr. 10 ***Perf. 14 to 15***

266 A19 2c on 5p dull blue 50 1.00
a. Without period 75 1.25
b. Double surcharge 2.00 2.00

267 " 2c on 5p ultramarine 35 40
a. Without period 75 1.25
b. Double surcharge *3.50*

268 " 5c on 10p pink 50 30
a. Without period 1.25 75
b. "cte" for "cts" 1.25 75
c. Double surcharge 3.00 3.00
d. Inverted surcharge 2.00 2.00

269 " 10c on 25c lilac 25 18
a. Without period 75 50
b. "cte" for "cts" 1.00 75
c. Inverted surcharge 3.00 3.00
d. Double surcharge 2.00 2.00
e. Double surcharge, one inverted 3.00 3.00

270 " 10c on 2p gray 25 20
a. Without period 75 50
b. "cte" for "cts" 1.00 75
c. Double surcharge 4.00 4.00
d. Double surcharge, one inverted 3.00 2.50

271 " 35c on 1p brown 25 25
a. Without period 75 50
b. "cte" for "cts" 1.00 75
c. "Corre" 1.25 1.25
d. Double surcharge 2.00 2.00
e. Double surcharge, one inverted 2.00 2.00
f. Double surcharge inverted 2.50 2.50
g. Inverted surcharge *4.00*
Nos. 266–271 (6) 2.10 2.33

These surcharges are in settings of twenty-five. One stamp in each setting has a large square period after "cts" and two have no period. One of the 2c has no space between "02" and "cts" and one 5c has a small thin "s" in "Correos".

Surcharged in Black

CORREOS
05 cts.
1911

1911, June

272 A19 5c on 2p gray 85 85
a. Inverted surcharge 5.00 4.00

In this setting one stamp has a large square period and another has a thick upright "c" in "cts".

Surcharged in Black

VALE
05 cts
POSTAL
de 1911

1911, June 12

273 A19 5c on 25c lilac 75 75
274 " 5c on 50c olive green 3.50 3.50

275 A19 5c on 5p dull blue 6.00 6.00
276 " 5c on 5p ultramarine 6.00 6.00
a. Inverted surcharge
277 " 5c on 50p vermilion 3.50 3.50
278 " 10c on 50c olive green 60 45
Nos. 273–278 (6) 20.35 20.20

This setting has the large square period and the thick "c" in "cts". Many of the stamps have no period after "cts". Owing to broken type and defective impressions letters sometimes appear to be omitted.

A21

Revenue Stamps
Surcharged on the Back in Black:

vale / 05 cts. / CORREO / DE 1911 — a
Vale / 05 cts / CORREO / DE 1911 — b

Railroad coupon tax stamps (1c red and 2c blue) are the basic stamps of Nos. 279–294. They were first surcharged for revenue use in 1903 in two types: I. "Timbre Fiscal" and "ctvs." II. "TIMBRE FISCAL" and "cents" (originally intended for use in Bluefields).

1911, July

279 A21 (a) 2c on 5c on 2c blue 15 25
a. New value in yellow on face 5.00 5.00
b. New value in black on face 4.00 4.00
c. New value in red on face 50.00
d. Inv. surch. 50
e. Double surcharge, one inverted 6.50 6.50
f. "TIMBRE FISCAL" in black 60 60
280 " (b) 2c on 5c on 2c blue 15 20
a. New value in yellow on face 50 50
b. New value in black on face 3.50 3.50
c. New value in red on face 50.00
d. Inv. surch. 60 85
e. Double surcharge, one inverted 6.00 6.00
f. "TIMBRE FISCAL" in black 75 75
281 " (a) 5c on 5c on 2c blue 12 12
a. Inverted surcharge 35 25
b. "TIMBRE FISCAL" in black 75 75
c. New value in yellow on face
282 " (b) 5c on 5c on 2c blue 15 12
a. Inverted surcharge 25 25
b. "TIMBRE FISCAL" in black 75 75
283 " (a) 10c on 5c on 2c blue 12 15
a. Inverted surcharge 50 40
b. "TIMBRE FISCAL" in black 75 75
c. New value in yellow on face 50.00
284 " (b) 10c on 5c on 2c blue 12 15
a. Inverted surcharge 40 35
b. "TIMBRE FISCAL" in black 75 75
c. Double surcharge 5.00 5.00
d. New value in yellow on face 60.00
285 " (a) 15c on 10c on 1c red 15 20
a. Inv. surch. 75 1.00
b. "Timbre Fiscal" double 4.00
286 " (b) 15c on 10c on 1c red 20 25
a. Inv. surch. 75 75
b. "Timbre Fiscal" double 4.00
Nos. 279–286 (8) 1.16 1.44

These surcharges are in settings of 20. For listing, they are separated into small and large figures, but there are many other varieties due to type and arrangement.

Surcharged on the Face in Black — CORREO / 02 centavos

1911, Oct.

287 A21 2c on 10c on 1c red 5.00 5.00
a. Inverted surcharge 50 50
b. Double surcharge 7.50 7.50
288 " 20c on 10c on 1c red 3.00 3.00
a. Inverted surcharge 4.00 4.00
289 " 50c on 10c on 1c red 4.00 4.00
a. Inverted surcharge 7.50 7.50

There are two varieties of the figures "2" and "5" in this setting.

Surcharged on the Back in Black — Vale / 10 cts. / CORREO DE / 1911

1911, Nov.

289B A21 5c on 10c on 1c red 30.00
c. Inverted surcharge 15.00
289D " 10c on 10c on 1c red 10.00
e. Inverted surcharge 20.00

Surcharged on the Face — Correo / Vale / 2 cts. / 1911

1911, Dec.

Dark Blue Postal Surcharge.

290 A21 2c on 10c on 1c red 15 15
a. Inverted surcharge 2.00 2.00
b. Double surcharge 4.00 4.00
291 " 5c on 10c on 1c red 20 15
a. Double surcharge 2.00 2.00
b. Inverted surcharge 2.00 2.00
292 " 10c on 10c on 1c red 20 15
a. Inverted surcharge 2.00 2.00
b. Double surcharge 2.00 2.00
c. "TIMBRE FISCAL" on back 3.00 3.00

Black Postal Surcharge.

293 A21 10c on 10c on 1c red 75 50
a. Inverted surcharge 5.00 5.00
b. New value surcharged on back 10.00 10.00

Red Postal Surcharge.

293C A21 5c on 5c on 2c blue 1.00 1.00
d. "TIMBRE FISCAL" in black 2.00 1.50
e. "5" omitted 3.00 3.00
f. Inverted surcharge 4.00 4.00
Nos. 290–293C (5) 2.30 1.95

Bar Overprinted on No. O234 in Dark Blue — Correo ~~oficial~~ / Vale / 10 cts. / 1911

294 A21 10c on 10c on 1c red 75 75
a. Inverted surcharge 2.50 2.50
b. Bar at foot of stamp 5.00 5.00

Nos. 290 to 294 each have three varieties of the numerals in the surcharge.

"Liberty"
A22

Coat of Arms
A23

1912, Jan. Engraved *Perf. 14, 15*

295 A22 1c yellow green 15 12
296 " 2c carmine 15 12
297 " 3c yellow brown 15 15
298 " 4c brown violet 15 12
299 " 5c blue & black 12 12
300 " 6c olive bistre 15 1.00
301 " 10c red brown 12 12
302 " 15c violet 12 12
303 " 20c red 15 12
304 " 25c bl. green & black 15 15
305 A23 35c green & chestnut 90 1.50
306 A22 50c light blue 40 25
307 " 1p orange 65 2.00
308 " 2p dark blue green 65 2.50
309 " 5p black 1.50 3.50
Nos. 295–309 (15) 5.51 11.89

No. 305 Surcharged in Violet — Vale 15 cts. / Correos-1913.

1913, Mar.

310 A23 15c on 35c green & chestnut 25 15
a. "ats" for "cts" 5.00 5.00

Stamps of 1912 Surcharged in Red or Black — VALE / medio / centavo / de córdoba / 1913

1913–14

311 A22 ½c on 3c yellow brown (R) 30 25
a. "Córóoba" 2.00 2.00
b. "do" for "de" 2.00 2.00
c. Inverted surcharge 20.00
d. Black surch. 45.00
312 " ½c on 15c violet (R) 15 15
a. "Córóoba" 75 75
b. "do" for "de" 1.00 1.00
c. Black surch. 22.50
313 " ½c on 1p orange 15 15
a. "VALB" 1.25 75
b. "ALE" 3.50 3.00
c. "LE" 5.00 4.00
d. "VALE" omitted 3.00 3.00
314 " 1c on 3c yel. brown 50 50
315 " 1c on 4c brown violet 15 15
316 " 1c on 50c light blue 15 15
317 " 1c on 5p black 15 15
318 " 2c on 4c brown violet 20 20
a. "do" for "de" 1.00 1.00
319 " 2c on 20c red 2.50 4.00
a. "do" for "de" 15.00 10.00
320 " 2c on 25c blue green & black 20 15
a. "do" for "de" 3.00 2.00
321 A23 2c on 35c green & chestnut 15 50
a. "9131" 2.50 1.50
b. "do" for "de" 2.00 1.50
322 A22 2c on 50c light blue 15 15
a. "do" for "de" 1.00 1.00
323 " 2c on 2p dark blue green 12 10
a. "VALB" 1.00 50
b. "ALE" 2.00 1.00
c. "VALE" omitted 5.00
d. "VALE" and "dos" omitted 5.00
324 " 3c on 6c olive bistre 12 12
a. "VALB" 30.00

Surcharged on Zelaya Issue of 1912.

325 Z2 ½c on 2c vermilion 30 30
a. "Coróoba" 1.00 1.00
b. "do" for "de" 1.00 1.00
326 " 1c on 3c orange brown 20 15
327 " 1c on 4c carmine 20 15
328 " 1c on 6c red brown 20 15
329 " 1c on 20c dark violet 20 15
330 " 1c on 25c green & black 20 15
331 " 2c on 1c yel. grn. ('14) 3.00 1.00
a. "Ccntavos" 5.00 1.25
332 " 2c on 25c grn. & blk. 1.50 3.00
a. "9131" 10.00
b. "do" for "de" 10.00
333 " 5c on 35c brn. & black 20 15
334 " 5c on 50c olive green 20 15
a. Double surcharge 20.00
335 " 6c on 1p orange 20 15
336 " 10c on 2p orange brown 20 15
337 " 1p on 5p dk. bl. green 20 30
Nos. 325–337 (13) 6.80 5.95

On No. 331 the surcharge has a space of 2½mm. between "Vale" and "dos".

Space between "Vale" and "dos" 2½mm. instead of 1mm. "de Cordoba" in different type.

1914, Feb.

337A A22 2c on 4c brown violet 15.00 2.75
b. "Ccntavos" 10.00
337C " 2c on 20c red 7.50 75
d. "Ccntavos" 3.50
337E " 2c on 25c blue green 4.50
f. "Ccntavos" 10.00
337G A23 2c on 35c green & chestnut 5.00
h. "Ccntavos" 12.50
337I A22 2c on 50c light blue 12.50 2.50
j. "Ccntavos" 9.00

No. 310 with Additional Surcharge — medio / cvo. Córdoba

1913, Dec.

337K A23 ½c on 15c on 35c green & chestnut 40.00

The word "Medio" is usually in heavy-faced, shaded letters. It is also in thinner, unshaded letters and in letters from both fonts mixed.

No. 310 Surcharged in Black and Violet — ½ ct. Cordoba / Correos 1913.

338 A23 ½c on 15c on 35c green & chestnut 10 10
a. Double surcharge 3.00
b. Inverted surcharge 3.00
c. Surcharged on No. 305 10.00
339 " 1c on 15c on 35c green & chestnut 15 15
a. Double surcharge 3.50

Official Stamps of 1912 Surcharged — VALE / ₡ 0.01

1914, Feb.

340 A22 1c on 25c light blue 25 20
a. Double surcharge 7.50
341 A23 1c on 35c light blue 25 20
a. "0.10" for "0.01" 2.00 2.00
341B A22 1c on 50c lt. blue 100.00
342 " 1c on 1p light blue 15 15
342A " 2c on 20c lt. blue 110.00 85.00
b. "0.12" for "0.02"
343 " 2c on 50c light blue 25 15
a. "0.12" for "0.02" 60.00
344 " 2c on 2p light blue 25 15
345 " 2c on 5p lt. blue 125.00
346 " 5c on 5p light blue 15 15

Red Surcharge.

347 A22 5c on 1p lt. blue 50.00
348 " 5c on 5p lt. blue 250.00

National Palace, Managua
A24

León Cathedral
A25

Various Frames.

1914, May 13 Engraved *Perf. 12*

349 A24 ½c light blue 40 15
350 " 1c dark green 40 12
351 A25 2c red orange 40 10
352 A24 3c red brown 60 20
353 A25 4c scarlet 70 20
354 A24 5c gray black 20 10
355 A25 6c black brown 5.50 4.00
356 " 10c orange yellow 40 15
357 A24 15c deep violet 3.00 1.65
358 A25 20c slate 6.00 4.00
359 A24 25c orange 75 25

360 A25 50c pale blue 75 30
Nos. 349-360 (12) 19.10 11.22

No. 359 measures 26x22½mm. No. 662 measures 27x22¾mm.

No. 356 with overprint "Union Panamericana 1890-1940" in green is of private origin.

See also Nos. 408-415, 483-495, 513-523, 652-664.

No. 355 Surcharged in Black — VALE 5 cts de Córdoba 1915

1915, Sept.

361 A25 5c on 6c black brown 1.00 35
a. Double surcharge 6.00 6.00

Stamps of 1914 Surcharged in Black or Red — Vale 1 centavo de córdoba

New Value in Figures.

1918-19

362 A24 1c on 3c red brown 4.00 1.75
a. Double surcharge, one inverted 10.00
363 A25 2c on 4c scarlet 20.00 15.00
364 A24 5c on 15c deep violet (R) 5.00 1.25
a. Double surcharge 10.00
364C " 5c on 15c deep violet 240.00

Surcharged in Black — VALE por 2 centavos de Córdoba

365 A25 2c on 20c slate 22.50 11.00
a. "ppr" for "por" 100.00
b. Double surcharge 75.00 25.00
c. "Cordobo" 125.00 100.00
365D " 5c on 20c slate 200.00 95.00
e. Double surcharge (Bk+R) 225.00
f. "Cordobo" 175.00

The surcharge on No. 365 is in blue black, and that on No. 365D usually has an admixture of red.

Surcharged in Black, Red or Violet — Vale medio centavo de córdoba

New Value in Words.

366 A25 ½c on 6c blk. brn. 2.50 1.25
a. "Meio" 12.50
b. Double surcharge 10.00
367 " ½c on 10c yellow 1.25 20
a. "Val" for "Vale" 2.50
b. "Codoba" 2.50
c. Inverted surcharge 4.00
d. Double surch., one inverted 8.00
368 A24 ½c on 15c dp. vio. 1.35 45
a. Double surcharge 6.00
b. "Codoba" 3.00
c. "Meio" 5.00
369 " ½c on 25c orange 3.25 1.25
a. Double surcharge 7.00
b. Double surcharge one inverted 5.00
370 A25 ½c on 50c pale blue 1.25 20
a. "Meio" 4.50
b. Double surcharge 3.50
c. Double surcharge, one inverted 5.00
371 " ½c on 50c pale blue (R) 2.50 1.25
a. Double surcharge 8.00
372 A24 1c on 3c red brown 1.50 20
a. Double surcharge 2.50
373 A25 1c on 6c blk. brn. 7.00 2.50
a. Double surcharge 7.50
374 " 1c on 10c yellow 13.00 6.00
a. "nu" for "un" 20.00
375 A24 1c on 15c dp. vio. 2.25 60
a. Double surcharge 9.00
b. "Codoba" 4.00
376 A25 1c on 20c slate 70.00 45.00
a. Black surcharge, normal and red surcharge inverted 65.00
b. Double surcharge, red and black 75.00
c. Blue surcharge 100.00
377 " 1c on 20c slate (V) 70.00 45.00
a. Double surcharge (V+Bk) 65.00
378 A25 1c on 20c slate (R) 1.35 20
a. Double surcharge, one inverted
b. "Val" for "Vale" 2.50 2.50
379 A24 1c on 25c orange 2.50 75
a. Double surcharge 10.00
380 A25 1c on 50c pale blue 8.00 4.00
a. Double surcharge 15.00
381 " 2c on 4c scarlet 1.75 20
a. Double surcharge 9.00
b. "centavo" 4.00
c. "Val" for "Vale"
382 " 2c on 6c blk. brn. 14.00 6.50
a. "Centavoss"
b. "Cordobas"
383 " 2c on 10c yellow 14.00 3.50
a. "centavo"
384 " 2c on 20c slate (R) 7.50 2.50
a. "pe" for "de" 12.50
b. Double surcharge, red and black 25.00
c. "centavo" 10.00
d. Double surcharge (R) 15.00
385 A24 2c on 25c orange 3.00 30
a. "Vle" for "Vale" 6.00
b. "Codoba" 6.00
c. Inverted surcharge 9.00
386 A25 5c on 6c blk. brn. 5.50 4.50
a. Double surcharge 12.00
387 A24 5c on 15c dp. violet 1.75 50
a. "cincoun" for "cinco" 12.50
b. "Vle" for "Vale" 10.00
c. "Codoba" 10.00
Nos. 366-387 (22) 235.20 126.85

No. 378 is surcharged in light red and brown red: the latter color is frequently offered as the violet surcharge (No. 377).

Official Stamps of 1915 Surcharged in Black or Blue — Vale dos centavos de cordoba

1919-21

388 A24 1c on 25c light blue 90 20
a. Double surcharge 8.50
b. Inverted surcharge 10.00
389 A25 2c on 50c light blue 90 20
a. "centavo" 3.00 3.00
b. Double surcharge 10.00
390 " 10c on 20c light blue 1.00 40
a. "centovos" 4.00 4.00
b. Double surcharge 7.00
390F " 10c on 20c lt. blue (Bl) 45.00

There are numerous varieties of omitted, inverted and italic letters in the foregoing surcharges.

No. 358 Surcharged in Black — VALE 5 Centavos

Types of the numerals:

2 2 2
I II III

2 2 2 2 2
IV V VI VII VIII

5 5 5 5
I II III IV

5 5 5 5
V VI VII VIII

1919, May

391 A25 2c on 20c slate (I) 100.00 95.00
a. Type II
b. Type III
c. Type IV
d. Type VI
e. Type VIII
392 " 5c on 20c slate (I) 70.00 30.00
a. Type II 75.00 35.00
b. Type III 80.00 45.00
c. Type IV 85.00 45.00
d. Type V 100.00 50.00
e. Type VI 100.00 50.00
f. Type VII 150.00 100.00
h. Double surcharge one inverted

No. 358 Surcharged in Black — VALE 2 Cents

393 A25 "2 Cents" on 20c slate (I) 95.00
a. Type II
b. Type III
c. Type IV
d. Type V
e. Type VI
f. Type VII
393G " "5 Cents." on 20c slate, type VIII 75.00 30.00

No. 351 Surcharged in Black — Vale un centavo de córdoba

1920, Jan.

394 A25 1c on 2c red orange 70 15
a. Inverted surcharge
b. Double surcharge

Official Stamps of 1912 Overprinted in Carmine — «Particular»

1921, Mar.

395 A22 1c light blue 75 50
a. "Parricular" 4.50 4.50
b. Inverted overprint 8.00
396 " 5c light blue 75 35
a. "Parricular" 4.50 4.50

Official Stamps of 1915 Surcharged in Carmine — Vale un centavo de córdoba

397 A25 ½c on 2c light blue 25 15
a. "Mddio" 2.00 2.00
398 " ½c on 4c light blue 60 15
a. "Mddio" 2.00 2.00
399 A24 1c on 3c light blue 60 20

No. 354 Surcharged in Red — Vale medio centavo

1921, Aug.

400 A24 ½c on 5c gray black 30 15

Trial printings of this stamp were surcharged in yellow, black and red, and yellow and red. Some of these were used for postage.

Gen. Manuel José Arce A26

José Cecilio del Valle A27

Miguel Larreinaga A28

Gen. Fernando Chamorro A29

Gen. Máximo Jérez A30

Gen. Pedro Joaquín Chamorro A31

Rubén Darío A32

1921, Sept. Engraved

401 A26 ½c light blue & black 25 25
402 A27 1c green & black 25 25
403 A28 2c rose red & black 25 25
404 A29 5c ultra. & black 25 25
405 A30 10c orange & black 25 25
406 A31 25c yellow & black 25 25
407 A32 50c violet & black 25 25
Nos. 401-407 (7) 1.75 1.75

Centenary of independence.

Types of 1914 Issue.

1922 Various Frames.

408 A24 ½c green 10 8
409 " 1c violet 10 8
410 A25 2c carmine rose 10 6
411 A24 3c olive gray 15 12
411A A25 4c vermilion 20 20
412 " 6c red brown 15 12
413 A24 15c brown 20 12
414 A25 20c bistre brown 30 15
415 " 1cor black brown 50 30
Nos. 408-415 (9) 1.80 1.23

No. 356 Surcharged in Black — Vale 0.01 de córdoba

1922, Nov.

416 A25 1c on 10c org. yel. 60 25
417 " 2c on 10c org. yel. 60 20

Nos. 354 and 356 Surcharged in Red — Vale 2 centavos de córdoba

1923, Jan.

418 A24 1c on 5c gray black 65 15
419 A25 2c on 10c org. yel. 65 15
a. Inverted surcharge

Nos. 401 and 402 Overprinted in Red — Sello Postal

1923

420 A26 ½c lt. blue & black 3.50 4.00
421 A27 1c green & black 40 25
a. Double overprint 5.00

Francisco Hernández de Córdoba A33

1924 Engraved.

422 A33 1c deep green 75 25
423 " 2c carmine rose 75 25
424 " 5c deep blue 50 25
425 " 10c bistre brown 50 50

400th anniversary of the founding of León and Granada.

Stamps of 1914-22 Overprinted — Resello 1927

Black, Red or Blue Overprint.

1927, May 3

427 A24 ½c green (Bk) 15 15
428 " 1c violet (R) 10 10
a. Double overprint 2.50
428B " 1c violet (Bk) 50.00 40.00
429 A25 2c car. rose (Bk) 10 10
a. Inverted overprint 3.50
b. Double overprint 3.50

430 A24 3c olive gray (Bk) 75 75
a. Inverted overprint 4.00
b. Double overprint 5.00
c. Double overprint, one inverted 7.50 6.00
430D " 3c olive gray (Bl) 5.00 2.25
431 A25 4c vermilion (Bk) 10.00 10.00
a. Inverted overprint 25.00
432 A24 5c gray black (R) 75 20
a. Inverted overprint 6.00
432B " 5c gray black (Bk) 40 20
c. Double overprint, one inverted 6.00
d. Double overprint 6.00
433 A25 6c red brown (Bk) 7.50 7.50
a. Inverted overprint 15.00
b. Double overprin:
434 " 10c yellow (Bl) 50 30
a. Double overprint 10.00
b. Double overprint, one inverted 8.00
435 A24 15c brown (Bk) 4.00 2.00
436 A25 20c bis. brn. (Bk) 4.00 2.00
a. Double overprint 15.00
437 A24 25c orange (Bk) 15.00 3.00
438 A25 50c pale blue (Bk) 5.00 2.50
439 " 1cor blk. brn. (Bk) 10.00 8.00

Most stamps of this group exist with tall "1" in "1927". Counterfeits exist of normal stamps and errors of Nos. 427-478.

Violet Overprint.

1927, May 19
440 A24 ½c green 8 8
a. Inv. ovpt. 1.50 1.50
b. Double overprint 1.50 1.50
441 " 1c violet 10 10
a. Double overprint 1.50 1.50
442 A25 2c carmine rose 10 6
a. Double overprint 1.50 1.50
b. "1927" double 4.00
d. Double overprint, one inverted 1.50 1.50
443 A24 3c olive gray 15 12
a. Inverted overprint 5.00
b. Overprinted "1927" only 10.00
c. Double overprint, one inverted 7.50
444 A25 4c vermilion 20.00 20.00
a. Inv. ovpt. 60.00
445 A24 5c gray black 60 20
a. Double overprint, one inverted 5.00
446 A25 6c red brown 20.00 20.00
a. Inv. ovpt. 60.00
447 " 10c yellow 20 15
a. Double overprint 1.50 1.50
448 A24 15c brown 50 25
a. Double overprint 4.00
b. Double overprint, one inverted 7.00
449 A25 20c bistre brown 20 15
a. Double overprint
450 A24 25c orange 25 15
451 A25 50c pale blue 20 15
a. Double overprint, one inverted 3.00 3.00
452 " 1cor black brown 50 15
a. Double overprint 2.50
b. "1927" double 4.00
c. Double overprint, one inverted 5.00
Nos. 440-452 (13) 42.88 41.56

Stamps of 1914-22 Overprinted in Violet — **Resello 1928**

1928, Jan. 3
453 A24 ½c green 15 15
a. Double overprint 2.50
b. Double overprint, one inverted 3.50
454 " 1c violet 8 8
a. Inverted overprint 1.50
b. Double overprint 1.50
c. Double overprint, one inverted 1.50
d. "928" for "1928" 2.00
455 A25 2c carmine rose 12 12
a. Inverted overprint 1.50
b. Double overprint 1.50
c. "1928" omitted 4.00
d. "928" for "1928" 2.00
e. Same as "d" inverted
f. "19" for "1928"
456 A24 3c olive gray 25 12
457 A25 4c vermilion 12 12
458 A24 5c gray black 12 12
a. Double overprint 4.00
b. Double overprint, one inverted 4.00
459 A25 6c red brown 12 12
460 " 10c yellow 15 12
a. Double overprint 2.00
Inverted overprint

461 A24 15c brown 20 20
462 A25 20c bistre brown 30 20
a. Double overprint
463 A24 25c orange 40 20
a. Double overprint, one inverted 3.00
464 A25 50c pale blue 75 12
465 " 1cor black brown 1.00 25
Nos. 453-465 (13) 3.76 1.92

Stamps of 1914-22 Overprinted in Violet — **Correos 1928**

1928, June 11
466 A24 ½c green 12 12
467 " 1c violet 10 8
a. "928" omitted
469 " 3c olive gray 50 20
a. Double overprint 5.00
470 A25 4c vermilion 20 12
471 A24 5c gray black 15 15
a. Double overprint 3.00
472 A25 6c red brown 25 15
a. Double overprint 4.00
473 " 10c yellow 30 15
474 A24 15c brown 1.35 15
a. Double overprint
475 A25 20c bistre brown 1.35 15
476 A24 25c orange 1.35 20
a. Double overprint, one inverted 5.00
477 A25 50c pale blue 1.35 20
478 " 1cor black brown 3.00 2.00
a. Double overprint 8.00
Nos. 466-478 (12) 10.02 3.67

No. 410 with above overprint in black was not regularly issued.

No. 470 with Additional Surcharge in Violet — **Vale 2 Cts.**

1928
479 A25 2c on 4c vermilion 1.00 25
a. Double surcharge 7.50

A34

Inscribed: "Timbre Telegrafico"

Red Surcharge

1928
480 A34 1c on 5c blue & blk. 18 15
a. Double surcharge 4.00
b. Double surcharge, one inverted
481 " 2c on 5c blue & blk. 18 15
a. Double surcharge 4.00
482 " 3c on 5c blue & blk. 18 15

Stamps similar to Nos. 481-482, but with surcharge in black and with basic stamp inscribed "Timbre Fiscal," are of private origin.

Types of 1914 Issue.
Various Frames.

1928
483 A24 ½c orange red 25 12
484 " 1c orange 25 12
485 A25 2c green 25 12
486 A24 3c deep violet 25 18
487 A25 4c brown 25 18
488 A24 5c yellow 25 15
489 A25 6c light blue 25 20
490 " 10c dark blue 50 15
491 A24 15c carmine rose 75 40
492 A25 20c dark green 75 40
493 A24 25c black brown 17.50 5.00
494 A25 50c bistre brown 2.00 75
495 " 1cor dull violet 4.00 2.50
Nos. 483-495 (13) 27.25 10.27

No. 425 Overprinted in Violet — **Correos 1928**

1929
499 A33 10c bistre brown 50 50

No. 408 Overprinted in Red — **Correos 1929**

1929
500 A24 ½c green (R) 15 15
a. Inverted overprint 2.00
b. Double overprint 2.00
c. Double overprint, one inverted 3.00

A36

A37

Overprinted Horizontally in Black "R. de T." Surcharged Vertically in Red.

1929
504 A36 1c on 5c blue & black (R) 15 15
a. Inverted surcharge 2.50
b. Surcharged "0.10" for "0.01" 2.50
c. "0.0" instead of "0.01" 4.00
509 " 2c on 5c blue & black (R) 15 12
a. Double surcharge 2.00
b. Double surcharge, one inverted 3.00
c. Inverted surcharge 3.50

Overprinted Horizontally in Black "R. de C." Surcharged Vertically in Red.

510 A36 2c on 5c blue & black (R) 12.00 75
a. Dbl. surcharge, one inverted 17.50

Surcharged in Red.

511 A37 1c on 10c dark green & black (R) 15 15
a. Double surcharge
512 " 2c on 5c blue & black (R) 15 12

The varieties tall "1" in "0.01" and "O$" for "C$" are found in this surcharge.

Nos. 500, 504, 509-512 and RA38 were surcharged in red and sold in large quantities to the public. Surcharges in various other colors were distributed only to a favored few and not regularly sold at the post offices.

Types of 1914 Issue.

1929-31 **Various Frames.**
513 A24 1c olive green 10 6
514 " 3c light blue 15 12
515 A25 4c dark blue ('31) 15 15
516 A24 5c olive brown 20 12
517 A25 6c bistre brown ('31) 25 25
518 " 10c light brown ('31) 35 15
519 A24 15c orange red ('31) 50 20
520 A25 20c orange ('31) 70 30
521 A24 25c dark violet 12 10
522 A25 50c green ('31) 25 15
523 " 1cor yellow ('31) 2.75 1.10
Nos. 513-523 (11) 5.52 2.70

New Post Office at Managua
A38

1930, Sept. 15 **Engraved**
525 A38 ½c olive gray 75 75
526 " 1c carmine 75 75
527 " 2c red orange 50 50
528 " 3c orange 1.00 1.00
529 " 4c yellow 1.00 1.00
530 " 5c olive green 1.25 1.25
531 " 6c blue green 1.25 1.25
532 A38 10c black 1.50 1.50
533 " 25c deep blue 3.25 3.00
534 " 50c ultramarine 5.50 4.50
535 " 1cor deep violet 15.00 10.00
Nos. 525-535 (11) 31.75 25.50

Opening of the new general post office at Managua. The stamps were on sale on day of issuance and for an emergency in April, 1931.

No. 499 Surcharged in Black and Red — **₡ 0.02 1931**

1931, May 29
536 A33 2c on 10c bistre brown 40 2.50
a. Red surcharge omitted 3.00
b. Red surcharge double 6.00
c. Red surcharge inverted 4.00
d. Red surcharge double, one inverted

Types of 1914-31 Issue Overprinted — **1931**

1931, June 11
540 A24 ½c green 30 10
a. Double overprint 1.00
b. Double overprint, one inverted 1.50
c. Inverted overprint 1.00
541 " 1c olive green 30 10
a. Double overprint 1.00
b. Double overprint, one inverted 1.50
c. Inverted overprint
542 A25 2c carmine rose 30 7
a. Double overprint 1.00
b. Double overprint, both inverted 3.00
c. Inverted overprint 1.50
543 A24 3c light blue 30 12
a. Double overprint 1.00
b. Double overprint, one inverted 1.50
c. Inverted overprint 1.50
544 " 5c yellow 3.00 3.00
545 " 5c olive brown 1.00 18
a. Double overprint 1.50
b. Inverted overprint 1.50
546 " 15c orange red 1.10 45
a. Double overprint 4.00
547 " 25c black brown 10.00 9.00
a. Double overprint 12.00 10.00
b. Invtd. overprint 12.00 10.00
548 " 25c dark violet 3.50 3.50
a. Double overprint 8.00
Nos. 540-548 (9) 19.80 16.52

Counterfeits exist of the scarcer values. The 4c brown and 6c light blue with this overprint are bogus.

Managua P.O. Before and After Earthquake
A40

Soft porous paper. Without gum.

1932, Jan. 1 **Litho.** ***Perf. 11½***
556 A40 ½c emerald 2.25
557 " 1c yellow brown 2.75
558 " 2c deep carmine 2.25
559 " 3c ultramarine 2.25
560 " 4c deep ultramarine 2.25
561 " 5c yellow brown 3.00
562 " 6c gray brown 3.00
563 " 10c yellow brown 5.00
564 " 15c dull rose 7.00
565 " 20c orange 5.00
566 " 25c dark violet 5.00
567 " 50c emerald 5.00
568 " 1cor yellow 10.00
Nos. 556-568 (13) 54.75

Issued in commemoration of the earthquake at Managua, March 31, 1931. The stamps were on sale on January 1, 1932, only. The money received from this sale was for the reconstruction of the Post Office building and for the improvement of the postal service. Many shades exist. Sheets of 10. See also Nos. C20-C24.

Reprints are on thin hard paper, and sometimes have fake cancels. Price 75 cents each.

Rivas Railroad Issue.

"Fill" at El Nacascolo
A41

Designs: 1c, Wharf at San Jorge. 5c, Rivas Station. 10c, San Juan del Sur. 15c, Train at Rivas Station.

Soft porous paper.

1932, Dec. 17 Litho. *Perf. 12*

570 A41 1c yellow 12.50
a. 1c ochre 20.00
571 " 2c carmine 12.50
572 " 5c black brown 12.50
573 " 10c chocolate 12.50
574 " 15c yellow 12.50
a. 15c deep orange 20.00
Nos. 570-574 (5) 62.50

Inauguration of the railroad from San Jorge to San Juan del Sur. On sale only on Dec. 17, 1932.

Sheets of four, without gum. See also Nos. C67-C71.

Reprints exist on thin hard paper. Price $2.50 each.

Leon-Sauce Railroad Issue.

Bridge No. 2 at Santa Lucia
A42

Designs: 1c, Environs of El Sauce. 5c, Santa Lucia. 10c, Works at Km. 64. 15c, Rock cut at Santa Lucia.

Soft porous paper.

1932, Dec. 30 *Perf. 12*

575 A42 1c orange 12.50
576 " 2c carmine 12.50
577 " 5c black brown 12.50
578 " 10c brown 12.50
579 " 15c orange 12.50
Nos. 575-579 (5) 62.50

Inauguration of the railroad from Leon to El Sauce. On sale only on Dec. 30, 1932.

Sheets of 4, without gum. See also Nos. C72-C76.

Reprints exist on thin hard paper. Price $2.50 each.

Nos. 514-515, 543 Surcharged in Red — **Vale un centavo**

1932, Dec. 10

580 A24 1c on 3c lt. blue (514) 30 15
a. Double surcharge 4.00
581 " 1c on 3c light blue (543) 4.00 4.00
582 A25 2c on 4c dk. blue (515) 25 15
a. Double surcharge 3.00

Nos. 514, 516, 545 and 518 Surcharged in Black or Red — **Resello 1933 Vale Un Centavo**

1933

583 A24 1c on 3c light blue (Bk) (514) 15 12
a. "Censavo" 5.00 3.00
b. Double surcharge, one inverted 5.00
584 " 1c on 5c olive brown (R) (516) 15 12
a. Inverted surcharge
b. Double surcharge
585 A24 1c on 5c olive brown (R) (545) 6.50 6.50
a. Red surch. double 15.00
586 A25 2c on 10c lt. brown (Bk) (518) 15 15
a. Double surcharge 5.00 3.00
b. Inverted surcharge 4.00 4.00
c. Double surcharge, one inverted 5.00 3.00

No. 583 with green surcharge and No. 586 with red surcharge are bogus.

Flag of the Race Issue.

Flag with Three Crosses for Three Ships of Columbus
A43

Without gum.

1933, Aug. 3 Litho. *Rouletted 9*

587 A43 ½c emerald 2.50 2.50
588 " 1c green 2.00 2.00
589 " 2c red 2.00 2.00
590 " 3c deep rose 2.00 2.00
591 " 4c orange 2.00 2.00
592 " 5c yellow 2.50 2.50
593 " 10c deep brown 2.50 2.50
594 " 15c dark brown 2.50 2.50
595 " 20c violet blue 2.50 2.50
596 " 25c dull blue 2.50 2.50
597 " 30c violet 6.00 6.00
598 " 50c red violet 6.00 6.00
599 " 1cor olive brown 6.00 6.00
Nos. 587-599 (13) 41.00 41.00

Commemorating the raising of the symbolical "Flag of the Race"; also commemorating the 441st anniversary of the sailing of Columbus for the New World, Aug. 3, 1492. Printed in sheets of 10.

See also Nos. C77-C87, O320-O331.

Reprints of Nos. 587-599 exist.

In October, 1933, various postage, airmail and official stamps of current issues were overprinted with facsimile signatures of the Minister of Public Works and the Postmaster-General. These overprints are control marks.

Nos. 410 and 513 Overprinted in Black — **Resello 1935**

1935 *Perf. 12.*

600 A24 1c olive green 10 8
a. Inverted overprint 1.50 1.50
b. Double overprint 1.50 1.50
c. Double overprint, one inverted 2.00 2.00
601 A25 2c carmine rose 12 8
a. Inverted overprint 2.00
b. Double overprint 2.00
c. Double overprint, one inverted 2.00
d. Double overprint, both inverted 3.00 3.00

No. 517 Surcharged in Red as in 1932.

1936, June

602 A25 ½c on 6c bistre brown 30 15
a. "Ccentavo" 1.00 1.00
b. Double surcharge 4.00 4.00

Regular Issues of 1929-35 Overprinted in Blue — **RESELLO-1935**

1935, Dec.

603 A25 ½c on 6c bistre brown 65 12
604 A24 1c olive green (600) 80 12
605 A25 2c carmine rose (601) 80 12
a. Black overprint inverted 7.50
606 A24 3c light blue 75 25
607 " 5c olive brown 1.00 30
608 A25 10c light brown 1.50 1.00
Nos. 603-608 (6) 5.50 1.91

Same Overprint in Red.

1936, Jan.

609 A24 ½c dark green 15 15
610 A25 ½c on 6c bistre brown (602) 12 12
a. Surch. dbl., one inverted 8.00 8.00
611 A24 1c olive green (513) 20 7
612 " 1c olive green (600) 25 7
613 A25 2c car. rose (410) 40 7
614 " 2c carmine rose (601) 25 7
a. Black overprint inverted 3.00 3.00
b. Black overprint double, one inverted 4.00 4.00
615 A24 3c light blue 25 12
616 A25 4c dark blue 25 15
617 A24 5c olive brown 20 7
618 A25 6c bistre brown 25 12
619 " 10c light brown 45 20
620 A24 15c orange red 12 8
621 A25 20c orange 75 25
622 A24 25c dark violet 25 15
623 A25 50c green 30 25
624 " 1cor yellow 40 40
Nos. 609-624 (16) 4.59 2.34

Nos. 603-624 may have script control mark. Red or blue "Resello 1935" overprint may be found inverted or double. Red and blue overprints on same stamp are bogus.

Regular Issues of 1922-29 Overprinted in Carmine — **RESELLO-1935**

1936, May

625 A24 ½c green 12 8
626 " 1c olive green 15 7
627 A25 2c carmine rose 45 7
628 A24 3c light blue 15 15

Nos. 514, 516 Surcharged in Black — **Resello 1936 Vale Un Centavo**

1936, June

629 A24 1c on 3c light blue 12 10
a. "1396" for "1936" 1.25 1.25
b. "Un" omitted 1.50 1.50
c. Inverted surcharge 2.00 2.00
d. Double surcharge 2.00 2.00
630 " 2c on 5c olive brown 12 10
a. "1396" for "1936" 1.50 1.50
b. Double surcharge 4.00 4.00

Regular Issues of 1929-31 Surcharged in Black or Red — **1936 Vale Un Centavo**

1936

631 A24 ½c on 15c orange red (R) 15 15
a. Double surcharge 5.00
632 A25 1c on 4c dark blue (Bk) 20 15
633 A24 1c on 5c olive brown (Bk) 20 20
634 A25 1c on 6c bistre brown (Bk) 35 20
a. "1939" instead of "1936" 3.00 2.00
635 A24 1c on 15c orange red (Bk) 20 20
a. "1939" instead of "1936" 3.00 2.00
636 A25 1c on 20c org. (Bk) 15 15
a. "1939" instead of "1936" 3.00 2.00
b. Double surcharge 5.00
637 " 1c on 20c orange (R) 15 15
638 " 2c on 10c light brown (Bk) 25 20
639 A24 2c on 15c orange red (Bk) 1.00 1.00
640 A25 2c on 20c orange (Bk) 40 40
641 A24 2c on 25c dark violet (R) 30 15
642 " 2c on 25c dark violet (Bk) 30 15
a. "1939" instead of "1936" 3.00 2.00
643 A25 2c on 50c green (Bk) 30 30
a. "1939" instead of "1936" 3.00 2.00
644 " 2c on 1 cor yellow (Bk) 30 30
a. "1939" instead of "1936" 3.00 2.00
645 A25 3c on 4c dark blue (Bk) 60 60
a. "1939" instead of "1936" 3.00 2.00
b. "s" of "Centavos" omitted and "r" of "Tres" inverted 3.00
Nos. 631-645 (15) 4.85 4.30

Nos. 629-645 may bear script control mark.

Regular Issues of 1929-31 Overprinted in Black — **Resello 1936**

1936, Aug.

646 A24 3c light blue 30 25
647 " 5c olive brown 25 15
648 A25 10c light brown 50 50

No. 648 bears script control mark.

A44

Surcharged in Red.

1936, Oct. 19

649 A44 1c on 5c grn. & blk. 18 5
650 " 2c on 5c grn. & blk. 18 5

Types of 1914.

1937, Jan. 1 Engraved

652 A24 ½c black 10 7
653 " 1c carmine rose 10 7
654 A25 2c deep blue 10 7
655 A24 3c chocolate 10 10
656 A25 4c yellow 12 12
657 A24 5c orange red 10 10
658 A25 6c dull violet 12 12
659 " 10c olive green 15 15
660 A24 15c green 10 10
661 A25 20c red brown 20 15
662 A24 25c orange 20 7
663 A25 50c brown 25 15
664 " 1cor ultramarine 45 25
Nos. 652-664 (13) 2.09 1.52

See note after No. 360.

Mail Carrier
A45

Designs: 1c, Mule carrying mail. 2c, Mail coach. 3c, Sailboat. 5c, Steamship. 7½c, Train.

1937, Dec. Litho. *Perf. 11*

665 A45 ½c green 15 15
666 " 1c magenta 15 10
667 " 2c brown 15 12
668 " 3c purple 15 10
669 " 5c blue 15 12
670 " 7½c red orange 70 30
Nos. 665-670 (6) 1.45 89

75th anniversary of the postal service in Nicaragua.

Nos. 665-670 were also issued in sheets of 4, price, set of sheets, $7.

The minature sheets are ungummed, and also exist imperf. and part-perf.

Nos. 662, 663 and 664 Surcharged in Red — **Vale Tres Centavos 1938**

1938 *Perf. 12.*

671 A24 3c on 25c orange 12 10

672 A25 5c on 50c brown 12 10
a. "e" of "Vale" omitted 2.50 1.50
673 " 6c on 1cor ultramarine 12 12

On No. 672 the surcharge is in three lines.

Darío Park
A46

1939, Jan. Engraved *Perf. 12½*

674 A46 1½c yellow green 8 6
675 " 2c deep rose 8 8
676 " 3c bright blue 8 6
677 " 6c brown orange 15 15
678 " 7½c deep green 12 10
679 " 10c black brown 25 15
680 " 15c orange 25 12
681 " 25c light violet 25 15
682 " 50c brt. yel. green 20 20
683 " 1cor yellow 70 65
Nos. 674-683 (10) 2.16 1.72

Nos. 660 and 661 Surcharged in Red
Vale un Centavo
1939

1939 *Perf. 12.*

684 A24 1c on 15c green 10 10
a. Inverted surcharge 3.00 3.00
685 A25 1c on 20c red brown 10 10

No. C236 Surcharged in Carmine
Servicio ordinario
Vale Diez Centavos
de Córdoba

1941 *Perf. 12.* Unwmkd.

686 AP14 10c on 1c bright green 15 10
a. Double surcharge 4.00 4.00
b. Inverted surch. 4.00 4.00

Rubén Darío
A47

1941, Dec. Engraved *Perf. 12½*

687 A47 10c red 30 18
Nos. 687, C257-C260 (5) 2.55 1.43

25th anniversary of the death of Rubén Darío, poet and writer.

No. C236 Surcharged in Carmine
Servicio Ordinario
Vale Diez Centavos

1943 *Perf. 12.*

688 AP14 10c on 1c bright green 15 8
a. Inverted surch. 2.50
b. Double surch. 2.50

"Victory"
A48

Columbus and Lighthouse
A49

1943, Dec. 8 Engraved

689 A48 10c violet & cerise 6 5
690 " 30c orange brown & cerise 15 10

Issued to commemorate the second anniversary of Nicaragua's declaration of war against the Axis. See Nos. C261-C262.

1945, Sept. 1 *Perf. 12½* Unwmkd.

691 A49 4c dark green & black 20 15
692 " 6c orange & black 25 15
693 " 8c deep rose & black 35 25
694 " 10c blue & black 40 30
Nos. 691-694, C266-C271 (10) 6.35 5.22

Issued in honor of the discovery of America by Columbus and the Columbus Lighthouse near Ciudad Trujillo, Dominican Republic.

Franklin D. Roosevelt, Philatelist—A50

Roosevelt Signing Declaration of War Against Japan
A51

Designs: 8c, F. D. Roosevelt and Winston Churchill. 16c, Gen. Henri Giraud, Roosevelt, Gen. Charles de Gaulle and Churchill. 32c, Stalin, Roosevelt and Churchill. 50c, Sculptured head of Roosevelt.

Engraved, Center Photogravure.
Frame in Black.

1946, June 15 *Perf. 12½* Unwmkd.

695 A50 4c slate green 20 20
696 " 8c violet 35 35
697 A51 10c ultramarine 40 40
698 A50 16c rose red 50 50
699 " 32c orange brown 35 35
700 A51 50c gray 35 35
Nos. 695-700 (6) 2.15 2.15

Issued to honor U.S. Pres. Franklin D. Roosevelt (1882-1945). See Nos. C272-C276.

Metropolitan Cathedral, Managua—A56

Designs: 5c, Sanitation Building. 6c, Municipal Building. 10c, Projected Provincial Seminary. 75c, Communications Building.

1947, Jan. 10 Frame in Black

701 A56 4c carmine 15 12
702 " 5c blue 20 15
703 " 6c green 25 20
704 " 10c olive 25 20
705 " 75c golden brown 35 35
Nos. 701-705 (5) 1.20 1.02

Issued to commemorate the centenary of the founding of the city of Managua. See Nos. C277-C282.

San Cristóbal Volcano
A61

Designs: 3c, Tomb of Rubén Darío. 4c, Grandstand. 5c, Soldiers' monument. 6c, Sugar cane. 8c, Tropical fruit. 10c, Cotton industry. 20c, Horse race. 30c, Nicaraguan coffee. 50c, Steer. 1cor, Agriculture.

Engraved, Center Photogravure.

1947, Aug. 29

Frame in Black.

706 A61 2c orange 10 10
707 " 3c violet 8 8
708 " 4c gray 14 12
709 " 5c rose carmine 35 18
710 " 6c green 20 12
711 " 8c orange brown 25 12
712 " 10c red 35 18
713 " 20c bright ultra. 1.20 40
714 " 30c rose lilac 1.00 40
715 " 50c deep claret 2.00 1.00
716 " 1cor brown orange 75 50
Nos. 706-716 (11) 6.42 3.20

The frames differ for each denomination.

Softball
A62

Boy Scout, Badge and Flag
A63

Designs: 3c, Pole vault. 4c, Diving. 5c, Bicycling. 10c, Proposed stadium. 15c, Baseball. 25c, Boxing. 35c, Basketball. 40c, Regatta. 60c, Table tennis. 1cor, Soccer. 2cor, Tennis.

1949, July 15 Photo. *Perf. 12*

717 A62 1c henna brown 10 10
718 A63 2c ultramarine 75 20
719 " 3c blue green 30 10
720 A62 4c deep claret 20 10
721 A63 5c orange 50 12
722 A62 10c emerald 50 15
723 " 15c cerise 75 18
724 A63 25c bright blue 75 20
725 " 35c olive green 1.25 25
726 A62 40c violet 1.75 30
727 " 60c olive gray 2.00 50
728 " 1cor scarlet 2.50 1.50
729 " 2cor red violet 4.50 3.00
Nos. 717-729 (13) 15.85 6.70

Issued to publicize the tenth World Series of Amateur Baseball, 1948.

Each denomination was also issued in a souvenir sheet containing four stamps and marginal inscriptions. Price, set of 13 sheets, $100.

See also Nos. C296-C308.

Rowland Hill
A64

Designs: 25c, Heinrich von Stephan. 75c, U. P. U. Monument. 80c, Congress medal, obverse. 4cor, as 80c, reverse.

1950, Nov. 23 Engraved *Perf. 13*

Frame in Black.

730 A64 20c carmine lake 10 10
731 " 25c yellow green 20 18
732 " 75c ultramarine 65 25
733 " 80c green 30 30
734 " 4cor blue 1.25 1.25
Nos. 730-734 (5) 2.50 2.08

Issued to commemorate the 75th anniversary (in 1949) of the formation of the Universal Postal Union.

Each denomination was also issued in a souvenir sheet containing four stamps and marginal inscriptions. Size: 115x123mm. Price, set of 5 sheets, $30.

See also Nos. C309-C315, CO45-CO50.

Queen Isabella I
A65

Ships of Columbus
A66

Designs: 98c, Santa Maria. 1.20cor, Map. 1.76cor, Portrait facing left.

1952, June 25 *Perf. 11½*

735 A65 10c lilac rose 10 10
736 A66 96c deep ultra. 45 45
737 A65 98c carmine 45 45
738 " 1.20cor brown 50 50
739 " 1.76cor red violet 70 70
a. Souvenir sheet of 5 2.50 2.50
Nos. 735-739 (5) 2.20 2.20

Issued to commemorate the 500th anniversary of the birth of Queen Isabella I of Spain.

No. 739a measures 160x128mm., and contains one each of Nos. 735-739 with marginal inscriptions typographed in black.

See also Nos. C316-C320.

ODECA Flag
A67

Designs: 5c, Map of Central America. 6c, Arms of ODECA. 15c, Presidents of Five Central American Republics. 50c, ODECA Charter and Flags.

1953, Apr. 15 *Perf. 13½x14*

740 A67 4c dark blue 5 5
741 " 5c emerald 10 6
742 " 6c light brown 10 8
743 " 15c light olive green 15 10
744 " 50c black brown 20 15
Nos. 740-744 (5) 60 44

Issued to commemorate the founding of the Organization of the Central American States (ODECA). See also Nos. C321-C325.

Pres. Carlos Solorzano
A68

Presidents: 6c, Diego Manuel Chamorro. 8c, Adolfo Diaz. 15c, Gen. Anastasio Somoza. 50c, Gen. Emiliano Chamorro.

Engraved (frames); Photo. (heads).

1953, June 25 *Perf. 12½*

Heads in Gray Black

745 A68 4c dark carmine rose 5 4
746 " 6c deep ultramarine 6 5
747 " 8c brown 10 8
748 " 15c carmine rose 15 12
749 " 50c blue green 25 15
Nos. 745-749 (5) 61 44

See also Nos. C326-C338.

Sculptor and U. N. Emblem
A69

Capt. Dean L. Ray, USAF
A70

Designs: 4c, Arms of Nicaragua. 5c, Globe. 15c, Candle and Charter. 1cor, Flags of Nicaragua and U. N.

Perf. 13½

1954, Apr. 30 Engraved Unwmkd.

750	A69	3c olive	4	4
751	"	4c olive green	6	6
752	"	5c emerald	25	15
753	"	15c deep green	1.25	25
754	"	1cor blue green	1.00	50
		Nos. 750-754 (5)	2.60	1.00

Issued to honor the United Nations Organization. See also Nos. C339-C345.

Engraved; Center Photogravure.

1954, Nov. 5 ***Perf. 13***

Designs: 2c, Sabre jet plane. 3c, Plane, type A-20. 4c, B-24 bomber. 5c, Plane, type AT-6. 15c, Gen. Anastasio Somoza. 1cor, Air Force emblem.

Frame in Black

755	A70	1c gray	5	5
756	"	2c gray	6	6
757	"	3c dark gray green	5	5
758	"	4c orange	5	5
759	"	5c emerald	12	10
760	"	15c aquamarine	15	10
761	"	1cor purple	30	15
		Nos. 755-761 (7)	78	56

Issued to honor the National Air Force. See also Nos. C346-C352.

Rotary Slogans and Wreath
A71

Map of the World and Rotary Emblem
A72

Designs: 20c, Handclasp, Rotary emblem and globe. 35c, Flags of Nicaragua and Rotary. 90c, Paul P. Harris.

Granite Paper.

1955, Aug. 30 Photo. ***Perf. 11½***

762	A71	15c deep orange	10	10
763	"	20c reseda	15	15
764	"	35c red violet	15	15
765	A72	40c carmine	20	20
766	A71	90c black & gray	30	30
		a. Souvenir sheet of 5	3.00	3.00
		Nos. 762-766 (5)	90	90

Issued to commemorate the 50th anniversary of Rotary International.

No. 766a contains one each of Nos. 762-766 and is inscribed in blue: "Conmemoracion de las Bodas de Oro de Rotary International 1905-1955."

See also Nos. C353-C362.

Issues of 1947-55 Surcharged in Various Colors

Conmemoración
Exposición Nacional
Febrero 4-16, 1956
$ 0.15

Engraved, Photogravure.

Perf. 13½x14, 12½, 11½, 13

1956, Feb. 4 Unwmkd.

767	A67	5c on 6c light brown	6	6
768	A68	5c on 6c ultramarine & gray black (Ult)	6	6
769	A61	5c on 8c black & orange brown	6	6
770	A71	15c on 35c red violet (G)	15	10
771	A64	15c on 80c blk. & grn.	15	10
772	A71	15c on 90c black & gray (Bl)	15	10
		Nos. 767-772 (6)	63	48

Spacing of surcharge varies to fit shape of stamps.

Issued to commemorate the National Exhibition, Feb. 4-16, 1956. See also Nos. C363-C366.

Gen. Máximo Jerez
A73

Battle of San Jacinto
A74

Designs: 10c, Gen. Fernando Chamorro. 25c, Burning of Granada. 50c, Gen. José Dolores Estrada.

Perf. 12½x12, 12, 12½

1956, Sept. 14 Engraved

773	A73	5c brown	6	6
774	"	10c dark carmine rose	8	6
775	A74	15c blue gray	15	8
776	"	25c bright red	25	18
777	A73	50c bright red violet	30	20
		Nos. 773-777 (5)	84	58

Issued to commemorate the centenary of the National War. See also Nos. C367-C371.

Boy Scout
A75

Pres. Luis A. Somoza
A76

Designs: 15c, Cub Scout. 20c, Boy Scout. 25c, Lord Baden-Powell. 50c, Joseph A. Harrison.

Perf. 13½x14

1957, Apr. 9 Photo. Unwmkd.

778	A75	10c violet & olive	10	6
779	"	15c deep plum & gray black	15	10
780	"	20c ultra. & brown	20	12
781	"	25c dull red brown & deep bluish green	20	15
782	"	50c red & olive	30	25
		a. Souvenir sheet of 5	2.00	2.00
		Nos. 778-782 (5)	95	68

Issued to commemorate the centenary of the birth of Lord Baden-Powell, founder of the Boy Scouts.

No. 782a contains one each of Nos. 778-782, imperf., and is inscribed in black: "Hoja Souvenir—Conmemoracion del Primer Centenario del Nacimento del Fundador del Escultismo Mundial Lord Robert Baden Powell 1856-1956."

See also Nos. C377-C386.

1957, July 2 ***Perf. 14x13½***

Portrait in Dark Brown

783	A76	10c bright red	5	5
784	"	15c deep blue	8	6
785	"	35c rose violet	15	10
786	"	50c brown	20	15
787	"	75c gray green	45	45
		Nos. 783-787 (5)	93	81

Issued to honor President Luis A. Somoza. See also Nos. C387-C391.

Managua Cathedral
A77

Bishop Pereira y Castellon
A78

Designs: 15c, Archbishop Lezcano y Ortega. 20c, Leon Cathedral. 50c, De la Merced Church, Granada. 1cor, Father Mariano Dubon.

Perf. 13½x14, 14x13½

1957, July 12

Centers in Olive Gray.

788	A77	5c dull green	6	5
789	A78	10c dark purple	8	6
790	"	15c dark blue	10	6
791	A77	20c dark brown	12	8
792	"	50c dark slate green	25	16
793	A78	1cor dark violet	45	40
		Nos. 788-793 (6)	1.06	81

Issued in honor of the Catholic Church in Nicaragua. See Nos. C392-C397.

M. S. Honduras
A79

Designs: 5c, Gen. Anastasio Somoza and freighter. 6c, M. S. Guatemala. 10c, M. S. Salvador. 15c, Ship between globes. 50c, Globes and ship.

1957, Oct. 15 Litho. ***Perf. 14***

794	A79	4c green, blue & black	6	5
795	"	5c multicolored	6	5
796	"	6c red, blue & black	5	5
797	"	10c brown, blue green & black	10	6
798	"	15c dark carmine, ultramarine & olive brown	18	8
799	"	50c violet, blue & maroon	30	20
		Nos. 794-799 (6)	75	49

Issued to honor Nicaragua's Merchant Marine. See also Nos. C398-C403.

Melvin Jones and Lions Emblem
A80

Designs: 5c, Arms of Central American Republics. 20c, Dr. Teodoro A. Arias. 50c, Edward G. Barry. 75c, Motto and emblem. 1.50 cor, Map of Central America.

1958, May 8 ***Perf. 14*** **Unwmkd.**

Emblem in Yellow, Red and Blue.

800	A80	5c blue & multicolor	8	6
801	"	10c blue & orange	6	6
802	"	20c blue & olive	12	8
803	"	50c blue & lilac	25	20
804	"	75c blue & pink	35	25
805	A80	1.50cor blue, gray olive & salmon	60	45
		a. Souvenir sheet of 6	2.00	2.00
		Nos. 800-805 (6)	1.46	1.10

Issued to commemorate the 17th convention of Lions International of Central America, May, 1958.

No. 805a measures 154x89mm. and contains one each of Nos. 800-805. Marginal inscriptions in dark blue.

See also Nos. C410-C415.

St. Jean Baptiste De La Salle
A81

U. N. Emblem and Globe
A82

Designs: 5c, Arms of La Salle. 10c, School, Managua (horiz.). 20c, Bro. Carlos. 50c, Bro. Antonio. 75c, Bro. Julio. 1cor, Bro. Argeo.

1958, July 13 Photo. ***Perf. 14***

806	A81	5c carmine, blue & yellow	5	5
807	"	10c emerald, black & ultramarine	6	6
808	"	15c red brown, bistre & black	8	8
809	"	20c carmine, bistre & black	12	10
810	"	50c orange, bistre & brown black	20	15
811	"	75c blue, light green & dark brown	30	25
812	"	1cor violet, bistre & greenish black	40	40
		Nos. 806-812 (7)	1.21	1.09

Issued to honor the Christian Brothers. See also Nos. C416-C423.

1958, Dec. 15 Litho. ***Perf. 11½***

Designs: 15c, UNESCO building. 25c, 45c, "UNESCO." 40c, UNESCO building and Eiffel tower.

813	A82	10c bright pink & blue	6	6
814	"	15c blue & bright pink	10	6
815	"	25c green & brown	12	8
816	"	40c red org. & black	18	12
817	"	45c dark blue & rose lilac	20	13
818	"	50c brown & green	20	15
		a. Miniature sheet of six	85	85
		Nos. 813-818 (6)	86	60

Issued to commemorate the opening of UNESCO (U.N. Educational, Scientific and Cultural Organization) Headquarters in Paris, Nov. 3. See also Nos. C424-C429.

No. 818a contains one each of Nos. 813-818.

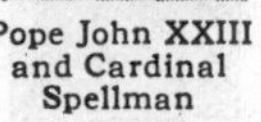

Pope John XXIII and Cardinal Spellman
A83

Abraham Lincoln
A84

Designs: 10c, Spellman coat of arms. 15c, Cardinal Spellman. 20c, Human rosary and Cardinal (horiz.). 25c, Cardinal with Ruben Dario order.

1959, Nov. 26 ***Perf. 12½*** **Unwmkd.**

819	A83	5c greenish blue & brown	6	5
820	"	10c yellow, blue & carmine	5	5
821	"	15c dark green, black & dark carmine	6	5

822 A83 20c yel., dk. bl. & grn. 10 6
823 " 25c ultramarine, violet & magenta 15 8
a. Miniature sheet of 5 40 40
Nos. 819-823 (5) 42 29

Issued to commemorate Cardinal Spellman's visit to Managua, Feb. 1958. See also Nos. C430-C436.

No. 823a contains one each of Nos. 819-823, perf. or imperf. Size: 125½x97mm.

1960, Jan. Engraved *Perf. 13x13½*

Center in Black.

824 A84 5c deep carmine 6 5
825 " 10c green 8 5
826 " 15c deep orange 10 6
827 " 1cor plum 40 30
828 " 2cor ultramarine 70 60
a. Souvenir sheet of five, imperf. 1.25 1.25
Nos. 824-828 (5) 1.34 1.06

Issued to commemorate the 150th anniversary of the birth of Abraham Lincoln. See also Nos. C437-C442.

No. 828a contains one each of Nos. 824-828, imperf. with black Nicaragua coat of arms and Spanish Lincoln quotation in margin. Size: 152x116mm.

Nos. 824-828 Overprinted in Red ✠ Resello

1960, Sept. 19 Center in Black

829 A84 5c deep carmine 5 5
830 " 10c green 6 5
831 " 15c deep orange 8 5
832 " 1cor plum 35 30
833 " 2cor ultramarine 75 65
Nos. 829-833 (5) 1.29 1.10

Issued for the Red Cross to aid earthquake victims in Chile. See Nos. C446-C451.

Gen. Tomas Martinez and Pres. Luis A. Somoza
A85

Arms of Nueva Segovia
A86

Designs: 5c, Official decrees. 10c, Two envelopes.

Lithographed

1961, Aug. 29 *Perf. 13½* Unwmkd.

834 A85 5c greenish blue & lt. brown 6 6
835 " 10c green & lt. brn. 8 8
836 " 15c pink & brown 10 8

Issued to commemorate the centenary (in 1960) of the postal rates regulation.

1962, Nov. 22 *Perf. 12½x13*

Coats of Arms: 3c, León. 4c, Managua. 5c, Granada. 6c, Rivas.

Arms in Original Colors; Black Inscriptions

837 A86 2c pink 3 3
838 " 3c light blue 4 4
839 " 4c pale lilac 4 4
840 " 5c yellow 5 5
841 " 6c buff 6 5
Nos. 837-841 (5) 22 21

See Nos. C510-C514.

No. RA73 Overprinted in Red: "CORREOS"

1964 Photogravure *Perf. 11½*

842 PT13 5c gray, red & orge. 10 5
a. Inverted overprint

Nos. RA66-RA75 Overprinted

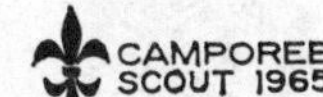

1965 Photogravure *Perf. 11½*

Orchids in Natural Colors

843 PT13 5c pale lilac & grn. 25
844 " 5c yellow & green 25
845 " 5c pink & green 25
846 " 5c pale vio. & green 25
847 " 5c lt. greenish blue & red 25
848 " 5c buff & lilac 25
849 " 5c yel. grn. & brown 25
850 " 5c gray & red 25
851 " 5c lt. bl. & dk. blue 25
852 " 5c lt. green & brown 25
Nos. 843-852 (10) 2.50

Issued to commemorate the 7th Central American Scout Camporee at El Coyotete. This overprint was also applied to each stamp on souvenir sheet No. C386a.

Use of Nos. 843-852 for postage was authorized by official decree.

Nos. 746 and 841 Surcharged with New Value and "RESELLO"

1968, May Engraved *Perf. 12½*

853 A68 5c on 6c dp. ultra. & gray black 3 3

Lithographed *Perf. 12½x13*

854 A86 5c on 6c multicolored 3 3

Nos. RA66-RA67, RA69 and RA71 Overprinted **CORREO**

1969 Photogravure *Perf. 11½*

Orchids in Natural Colors

855 PT13 5c pale lilac & green 3 3
856 " 5c yel. & green 3 3
857 " 5c pale vio. & green 3 3
858 " 5c buff & lilac 3 3

Nos. RA66-RA75 Overprinted **O. I. T. 1919 - 1969**

1969 Photo. *Perf. 11½*

Orchids in Natural Colors

859 PT13 5c pale lilac & green 3 3
860 " 5c yellow & green 3 3
861 " 5c pink & green 3 3
862 " 5c pale vio. & green 3 3
863 " 5c lt. greenish blue & red 3 3
864 " 5c buff & lilac 3 3
865 " 5c yel. green & brn. 3 3
866 " 5c gray & red 3 3
867 " 5c lt. & dark blue 3 3
868 " 5c lt. green & brown 3 3
Nos. 859-868 (10) 30 30

Issued to commemorate the 50th anniversary of the International Labor Organization.

Pelé, Brazil
A87

Soccer Players: 10c, Ferenc Puskás, Hungary. 15c, Sir Stanley Matthews, England. 40c, Alfredo di Stefano, Argentina. 2cor, Giacinto Facchetti, Italy. 3cor, Lev Yashin, USSR. 5cor, Franz Beckenbauer, West Germany.

1970, May 11 Litho. *Perf. 13½*

869 A87 5c multicolored 5 5
870 " 10c " 5 5
871 " 15c " 5 5
872 A87 40c multicolored 20 15
873 " 2cor " 75 60
874 " 3cor " 1.00 90
875 " 5cor " 1.00 1.25
Nos. 869-875, C712-C716 (12) 6.95 5.85

Issued to honor the winners of the 1970 poll for the International Soccer Hall of Fame. Names of players and their achievements printed in black on back of stamps.

No. 766 Surcharged with New Value and Overprinted "RESELLO" and Bar Through Old Denomination.

1971, March Photogravure *Perf. 11*

876 A71 30c on 90c blk. & gray 20 15

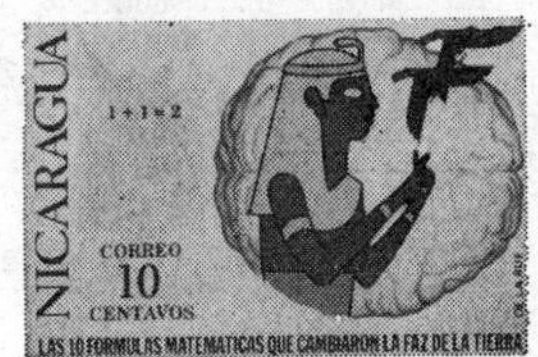

Egyptian Using Fingers to Count—A88

Symbolic Designs of Scientific Formulas: 15c, Newton's law (gravity). 20c, Einstein's theory (relativity). 1cor, Tsiolkovski's law (speed of rockets). 2cor, Maxwell's law (electromagnetism).

1971, May 15 Litho. *Perf. 13½*

877 A88 10c lt. blue & multi. 5 5
878 " 15c " " " 5 5
879 " 20c " " " 10 10
880 " 1cor " " " 35 30
881 " 2cor " " " 75 60
Nos. 877-881, C761-C765 (10) 2.80 2.15

Mathematical equations which changed the world. On the back of each stamp is a descriptive paragraph.

Symbols of Civilization, Peace Emblem with Globe—A89

1971, Sept. 6 Litho. *Perf. 14*

882 A89 10c black & blue 5 3
883 " 15c violet blue, blue & black 5 4
884 " 20c brn. bl. & blk. 10 6
885 " 40c emerald, blue & black 15 10
886 " 50c magenta, blue & black 20 12
887 " 80c org., bl. & blk. 30 20
888 " 1cor olive, bl. & blk. 40 25
889 " 2cor vio., bl. & blk. 75 50
Nos. 882-889 (8) 2.00 1.30

"Is there a formula for peace?" issue.

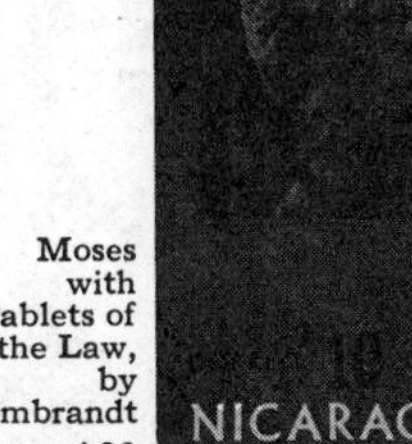

Moses with Tablets of the Law, by Rembrandt
A90

The Ten Commandments (Paintings): 15c, Moses and the Burning Bush, by Botticelli (I). 20c, Jephthah's Daughter, by Degas, (II, horiz.). 30c, St. Vincent Ferrer Preaching in Verona, by Domenico Morone (III). 35c, The Nakedness of Noah, by Michelangelo (IV, horiz.). 40c, Cain and Abel, by Francesco Trevisani (V, horiz.). 50c, Potiphar's wife, by Rembrandt (VI). 60c, Isaac Blessing Jacob, by Gerbrand van den Eeckhout (VII, horiz.). 75c, Susanna and the Elders, by Rubens (VIII, horiz.).

1971, Nov. 1 *Perf. 11*

890 A90 10c ocher & multi. 3 3
891 " 15c " " 4 3
892 " 20c " " 6 4
893 " 30c " " 8 6
894 " 35c " " 10 8
895 " 40c " " 11 10
896 " 50c " " 14 12
897 " 60c " " 21 18
898 " 75c " " 35 25
Nos. 890-898, C776-C777 (11) 1.96 1.64

Descriptive inscriptions printed in gray on back of stamps.

Nos. 873-874 Surcharged

OLIMPIADAS
MUNICH 1972

1972, Mar. 20 Litho. *Perf. 13¼*

899 A87 40c on 2cor multi. 15 12
900 " 50c on 3cor " 20 15
Nos. 899-900, C786-C788 (5) 2.15 1.75

20th Olympic Games, Munich, Aug. 26-Sept. 10.

Nos. RA66-RA69, RA71-RA74 Overprinted in Blue **CORREO**

1972, July 29 Photo. *Perf. 11½*

Granite Paper

901 PT13 5c multi. (RA66) 30 10
902 " 5c " (RA67) 30 10
903 " 5c " (RA68) 30 10
904 " 5c " (RA69) 30 10
905 " 5c " (RA71) 30 10
906 " 5c " (RA72) 30 10
907 " 5c " (RA73) 30 10
908 " 5c " (RA74) 30 10
Nos. 901-908 (8) 2.40 80

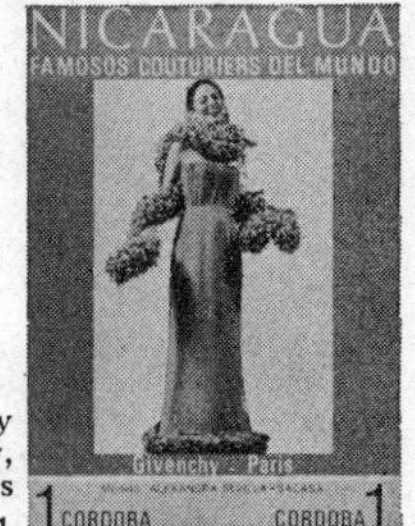

Gown by Givenchy, Paris
A91

1973, July 26 Litho. *Perf. 13½*

Multicolored

909 A91 1cor *shown* 30 25
910 " 2cor *Hartnell, London* 55 50
911 " 5cor *Balmain, Paris* 1.40 1.25
Nos. 909-911, C839-C844 (9) 2.81 2.50

Gowns by famous designers, modeled by Nicaraguan women. Inscriptions on back printed on top of gum give description of gown in Spanish and English.

See also Nos. C839-C844.

Nos. 909-911 in perf. 11, see No. C844a.

Certain unlisted issues of Nicaragua, starting in 1973, are mentioned and briefly described in "For the Record" at the back of this volume.

Hollyhocks
A95

Wild Flowers and Cacti: 3c, Paguira insignis. 4c, Morning glory. 5c, Pereschia autumnalis. 10c, Cultivated morning glory. 15c, Hibiscus. 20c, Pagoda tree blossoms.

1974, June 11		Litho.	*Perf. 14*	
932	A95	2c green & multi.	3	3
933	"	3c " "	3	3
934	"	4c " "	3	3
935	"	5c " "	3	3
936	"	10c " "	3	3
937	"	15c " "	4	3
938	"	20c " "	6	5
		Nos. 932–938, C854–C855 (9)	1.38	1.23

Four-toed Anteater
A97

Designs: 2c, Puma. 3c, Raccoon. 4c, Ocelot. 5c, Kinkajou. 10c, Coypu. 15c, Peccari. 20c, Tapir.

1974, Sept. 10		Litho.	*Perf. 14½*	
946	A97	1c multicolored	3	3
947	"	2c "	3	3
948	"	3c "	3	3
949	"	4c "	3	3
950	"	5c "	3	3
951	"	10c "	3	3
952	"	15c "	4	3
953	"	20c "	6	5
		Nos. 946–953, C857–C858 (10)	2.53	2.26

Wild animals from San Diego and London Zoos.

Prophet Zacharias, by Michelangelo
A98

Works of Michelangelo: 2c, The Last Judgment. 3c, The Creation of Adam (horiz.). 4c, Sistine Chapel. 5c, Moses. 10c, Mouscron Madonna. 15c, David. 20c, Doni Madonna.

1974, Dec. 15				
954	A98	1c dp. rose & multi.	3	3
955	"	2c yellow & multi.	3	3
956	"	3c salmon & multi.	3	3
957	"	4c blue & multi.	3	3
958	"	5c tan & multi.	3	3
959	"	10c multicolored	3	3
960	"	15c "	4	3
961	"	20c blue & multi.	6	5
		Nos. 954–961, C859–C862 (12)	2.59	2.31

Christmas 1974 and 500th birth anniversary of Michelangelo Buonarroti (1475–1564), Italian painter, sculptor and architect.

Giovanni Martinelli, Othello
A99

Opera Singers and Scores: 2c, Tito Gobbi, Simone Boccanegra. 3c, Lotte Lehmann, Der Rosenkavalier. 4c, Lauritz Melchior, Parsifal. 5c, Nellie Melba, La Traviata. 15c, Jussi Bjoerling, La Bohème. 20c, Birgit Nilsson, Turandot.

1975, Jan. 22			*Perf. 14x13½*	
962	A99	1c rose lilac & multi.	5	5
963	"	2c brt. bl. & multi.	5	5
964	"	3c yellow & multi.	5	5
965	"	4c dull bl. & multi.	5	5
966	"	5c orange & multi.	5	5
967	"	15c lake & multi.	5	5
968	"	20c gray & multi.	10	10
		Nos. 962–968, C863–C870 (15)	4.35	2.86

Famous opera singers.

Jesus Condemned
A100

The Spirit of 76, by Archibald M. Willard
A101

Stations of the Cross: 2c, Jesus Carries the Cross. 3c, Jesus falls the first time. 4c, Jesus meets his mother. 5c, Simon of Cyrene carries the Cross. 15c, St. Veronica wipes Jesus' face. 20c, Jesus falls the second time. 25c, Jesus meets the women of Jerusalem. 35c, Jesus falls the third time. Designs from Leon Cathedral.

1975, Mar. 20			*Perf. 14½*	
969	A100	1c ultra. & multi.	3	3
970	"	2c " "	3	3
971	"	3c " "	3	3
972	"	4c " "	3	3
973	"	5c " "	3	3
974	"	15c " "	4	3
975	"	20c " "	6	5
976	"	25c " "	8	6
977	"	35c " "	10	8
		Nos. 969–977, C871–C875 (14)	2.62	2.29

Easter 1975.

1975, Apr. 16 *Perf. 14*

Designs: 2c, Pitt Addressing Parliament, by K. A. Hickel. 3c, The Midnight Ride of Paul Revere (horiz.). 4c, Statue of George III Demolished, by W. Walcutt (horiz.). 5c, Boston Massacre. 10c, Colonial coin and seal (horiz.). 15c, Boston Tea Party (horiz.). 20c, Thomas Jefferson, by Rembrandt Peale. 25c, Benjamin Franklin, by Charles Willson Peale. 30c, Signing Declaration of Independence, by John Trumbull (horiz.). 35c, Surrender of Cornwallis, by Trumbull (horiz.).

978	A101	1c tan & multi.	3	3
979	"	2c " "	3	3
980	"	3c " "	3	3
981	"	4c " "	3	3
982	"	5c " "	3	3
983	"	10c " "	3	3
984	"	15c " "	4	3
985	"	20c " "	6	5
986	"	25c " "	8	6
987	"	30c " "	8	6
988	"	35c " "	10	8
		Nos. 978–988, C876–C879 (15)	2.76	2.43

American Bicentennial.

Scouts Saluting Flag, Scout Emblems
A102

Designs (Scout and Nordjamb Emblems and): 2c, Two-men canoe. 3c, Scouts of various races shaking hands. 4c, Scout cooking. 5c, Entrance to Camp Nicaragua. 20c, Group discussion.

1975, Aug. 15			*Perf. 14½*	
989	A102	1c multicolored	3	3
990	"	2c "	3	3
991	"	3c "	3	3
992	"	4c "	3	3
993	"	5c "	3	3
994	"	20c "	6	5
		Nos. 989–994, C880–C883 (10)	3.46	3.13

Nordjamb 75, 14th World Boy Scout Jamboree, Lillehammer, Norway, July 29–Aug. 7.

Pres. Somoza, Map and Arms of Nicaragua
A103

1975, Sept. 10			*Perf. 14*	
995	A103	20c multicolored	6	5
996	"	40c orange & multi.	12	10
		Nos. 995–996, C884–C886 (5)	8.71	7.90

Reelection of Pres. Anastasio Somoza D.

King's College Choir, Cambridge
A104

Famous Choirs: 2c, Einsiedeln Abbey. 3c, Regensburg. 4c, Vienna Choir Boys. 5c, Sistine Chapel. 15c, Westminster Cathedral. 20c, Mormon Tabernacle.

1975, Nov. 15			*Perf. 14½*	
997	A104	1c silver & multi.	3	3
998	"	2c " "	3	3
999	"	3c " "	3	3
1000	"	4c " "	3	3
1001	"	5c " "	3	3
1002	"	15c " "	4	3
1003	"	20c " "	6	5
		Nos. 997–1003, C887–C890 (11)	2.64	2.35

Christmas 1975.

The Chess Players, by Ludovico Carracci
A105

Designs: 2c, Arabs Playing Chess, by Delacroix. 3c, Cardinals Playing Chess, by Victor Marais-Milton. 4c, Albrecht V of Bavaria and Anne of Austria Playing Chess, by Hans Muelich (vert.). 5c, Chess Players, Persian manuscript, 14th century. 10c, Origin of Chess, Indian miniature, 17th century. 15c, Napoleon Playing Chess at Schönbrunn, by Antoni Uniechowski (vert.). 20c, The Chess Game, by J. E. Hummel.

1976, Jan. 8			*Perf. 14½*	
1004	A105	1c brn. & multi.	5	5
1005	"	2c lt. vio. & multi.	5	5
1006	"	3c ocher & multi.	5	5
1007	"	4c multicolored	5	5
1008	"	5c "	5	5
1009	"	10c "	5	5
1010	"	15c blue & multi.	5	5
1011	"	20c ocher & multi.	10	10
		Nos. 1004–1011, C891–C893 (11)	2.85	2.28

History of Chess.

Olympic Rings, Danish Crew, 1964—A107

Winners, Rowing and Sculling Events: 2c, East Germany, 1972. 3c, Italy, 1968. 4c, Great Britain, 1936. 5c, France, 1952. 35c, United States, 1920 (vert.).

1976, Sept. 7		Litho.	*Perf. 14*	
1022	A107	1c blue & multi.	5	5
1023	"	2c " "	5	5
1024	"	3c " "	5	5
1025	"	4c " "	5	5
1026	"	5c " "	5	5
1027	"	35c " "	15	10
		Nos. 1022–1027, C902–C905 (10)	7.20	5.95

The Smoke Signal, by Frederic Remington—A108

Designs (American Bicentennial Emblem and): No. 1029, Space Signal Monitoring Center. No. 1030, Candlelight. No. 1031, Edison's laboratory and light bulb. No. 1032, Agriculture, 1776. No. 1033, Agriculture, 1976. No. 1034, Harvard College, 1726. No. 1035, Harvard University, 1976. No. 1036, Horse-drawn carriage. No. 1037, Boeing 747.

1976, May 25		Litho.	*Perf. 13½*	
1028	A108	1c gray & multi.	10	5
1029	"	1c " "	10	5
1030	"	2c " "	10	5
1031	"	2c " "	10	5
1032	"	3c " "	10	5
1033	"	3c " "	10	5
1034	"	4c " "	10	5
1035	"	4c " "	10	5
1036	"	5c " "	10	5
1037	"	5c " "	10	5
		Nos. 1028–1037, C907–C912 (16)	6.20	4.30

American Bicentennial, 200 years of progress. Stamps of same denomination printed se-tenant.

Mauritius No. 2—A109

Rare Stamps: 2c, Western Australia No. 3a. 3c, Mauritius No. 1. 4c, Jamaica No. 83a. 5c, United States No. C3a. 10c, Basel No. 3L1. 25c, Canada No. 387a.

1976, Dec.			*Perf. 14*	
1038	A109	1c multicolored	3	3
1039	"	2c "	3	3
1040	"	3c "	3	3

No.	Type	Description	Unused	Used
1041	A109	4c multicolored	3	3
1042	"	5c "	3	3
1043	"	10c "	3	3
1044	"	25c "	8	9
		Nos. 1038-1044, C913-C917 (12)	5.42	4.82

Back inscriptions printed on top of gum describe illustrated stamp.

Zeppelin in Flight
A110

Designs: 1c, Zeppelin in hangar. 3c, Giffard's dirigible airship, 1852. 4c, Zeppelin on raising stilts coming out of hangar. 5c, Zeppelin ready for take-off.

1977, Oct. 31 Litho. *Perf. 14½*

No.	Type	Description	Unused	Used
1045	A110	1c multicolored	5	5
1046	"	2c "	5	5
1047	"	3c "	5	5
1048	"	4c "	5	5
1049	"	5c "	5	5
		Nos. 1045-1049, C921-C924 (9)	4.45	3.75

75th anniversary of Zeppelin.

Lindbergh, Map of Nicaragua
A111

Designs: 2c, Spirit of St. Louis, map of Nicaragua. 3c, Lindbergh (vert.). 4c, Spirit of St. Louis and New York-Paris route. 5c, Lindbergh and Spirit of St. Louis. 20c, Lindbergh, New York-Paris route and plane.

1977, Nov. 30

No.	Type	Description	Unused	Used
1050	A111	1c multicolored	5	5
1051	"	2c "	5	5
1052	"	3c "	5	5
1053	"	4c "	5	5
1054	"	5c "	5	5
1055	"	20c "	10	8
		Nos. 1050-1055, C926-C929 (10)	4.35	3.63

Charles A. Lindbergh's solo transatlantic flight from New York to Paris, 50th anniversary.

Clara and Snowflakes
A112

Nutcracker Suite: 1c, Christmas party. 2c, Dancing dolls. 4c, Snowflake and prince. 5c, Snowflake dance. 15c, Sugarplum fairy and prince. 40c, Waltz of the flowers. 90c, Chinese tea dance. 1cor, Bonbonnière. 10cor, Arabian coffee dance.

1977, Dec. 12

No.	Type	Description	Unused	Used
1056	A112	1c multicolored	3	3
1057	"	2c "	3	3
1058	"	3c "	3	3
1059	"	4c "	3	3
1060	"	5c "	3	3
1061	"	15c "	3	3
1062	"	40c "	12	8
1063	"	90c "	25	22
1064	"	1cor "	28	25
1065	"	10cor "	2.80	2.50
		Nos. 1056-1065 (10)	3.63	3.23

Christmas 1977. See No. C931.

Mr. and Mrs. Andrews, by Gainsborough—A113

Paintings: 2c, Giovanna Bacelli, by Gainsborough. 3c, Blue Boy by Gainsborough. 4c, Francis I, by Titian. 5c, Charles V in Battle of Muhlberg, by Titian. 25c, Sacred Love, by Titian.

1978, Jan. 11 Litho. *Perf. 14½*

No.	Type	Description	Unused	Used
1066	A113	1c multicolored	3	3
1067	"	2c "	3	3
1068	"	3c "	3	3
1069	"	4c "	3	3
1070	"	5c "	3	3
1071	"	25c "	8	5
		Nos. 1066-1071, C932-C933 (8)	4.43	3.95

Thomas Gainsborough (1727-1788), 250th birth anniversary; Titian (1477-1576), 500th birth anniversary.

Gothic Portal, Lower Church, Assisi
A114

Designs: 2c, St. Francis preaching to the birds. 3c, St. Francis, painting. 4c, St. Francis and Franciscan saints, 15th century tapestry. 5c, Portiuncola, cell of St. Francis, now in church of St. Mary of the Angels, Assisi. 15c, Blessing of St. Francis for Brother Leo (parchment). 25c, Stained-glass window, Upper Church of St. Francis, Assisi.

1978, Feb. 23 Litho. *Perf. 14½*

No.	Type	Description	Unused	Used
1072	A114	1c red & multi.	3	3
1073	"	2c brt. grn. & multicolored	3	3
1074	"	3c blue green & multicolored	3	3
1075	"	4c ultra. & multi.	3	3
1076	"	5c rose & multi.	3	3
1077	"	15c yellow & multi.	3	3
1078	"	25c ocher & multi.	7	6
		Nos. 1072-1078, C935-C936 (9)	3.27	2.90

St. Francis of Assisi (1182-1266), 750th anniversary of his canonization, and in honor of Our Lady of the Immaculate Conception, patron saint of Nicaragua.

Passenger and Freight Locomotives
A115

Locomotives: 2c, Lightweight freight. 3c, American. 4c, Heavy freight Baldwin. 5c, Light freight and passenger Baldwin. 15c, Presidential coach.

1978, Apr. 7 Litho. *Perf. 14½*

No.	Type	Description	Unused	Used
1079	A115	1c lilac & multi.	3	3
1080	"	2c rose lilac & multicolored	3	3
1081	"	3c blue & multi.	3	3
1082	"	4c olive & multi.	3	3
1083	"	5c yel. & multi.	3	3
1084	"	15c dp. orange & multicolored	3	3
		Nos. 1079-1084, C938-C940 (9)	4.20	3.76

Centenary of Nicaraguan railroads.

Michael Strogoff, by Jules Verne—A116

Designs (Jules Verne Books): 2c, The Mysterious Island. 3c, Journey to the Center of the Earth (battle of the sea monsters). 4c, Five Weeks in a Balloon.

1978, Aug. Litho. *Perf. 14½*

No.	Type	Description	Unused	Used
1085	A116	1c multicolored	3	3
1086	"	2c "	3	3
1087	"	3c "	3	3
1088	"	4c "	3	3
		Nos. 1085-1088, C942-C943 (6)	3.17	2.78

Jules Verne (1828-1905), science fiction writer.

Montgolfier Balloon
A117

Designs: 1c, Icarus (horiz.). 3c, Wright Brothers' Flyer A (horiz.). 4c, Orville Wright at control of Flyer, 1908.

1978, Sept. 29 Litho. *Perf. 14½*

No.	Type	Description	Unused	Used
1089	A117	1c multicolored	3	3
1090	"	2c "	3	3
1091	"	3c "	3	3
1092	"	4c "	3	3
		Nos. 1089-1092, C945-C946 (6)	3.08	2.72

History of aviation and 75th anniversary of first powered flight.

Ernst Ocwirk and Alfredo Di Stefano
A118

St. Peter, by Goya
A119

Soccer Players: 25c, Ralf Edstroem and Oswaldo Piazza.

1978, Oct. 25 Litho. *Perf. 13½x14*

No.	Type	Description	Unused	Used
1093	A118	20c multicolored	6	4
1094	"	25c "	7	4

11th World Soccer Cup Championship, Argentina, June 1-25. See Nos. C948-C950.

1978, Dec. 12 Litho. *Perf. 13½x14*

Paintings: 15c, St. Gregory, by Goya.

No.	Type	Description	Unused	Used
1095	A119	10c multicolored	3	3
1096	"	15c "	4	3

Christmas 1978. See Nos. C951-C953.

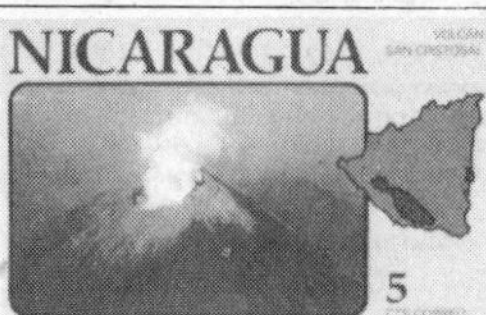

San Cristobal Volcano and Map
A120

Designs: No. 1098, Lake Cosiguina. No. 1099, Telica Volcano. No. 1100, Lake Jiloa.

1978, Dec. 29 *Perf. 14x13½*

No.	Type	Description	Unused	Used
1097	A120	5c multicolored	3	3
1098	"	5c "	3	3
1099	"	20c "	6	4
1100	"	20c "	6	4
		Nos. 1097-1100, C954-C961 (12)	7.04	5.02

Volcanos, lakes and their locations. Stamps of same denomination printed se-tenant in sheets of 40.

AIR POST STAMPS.

Counterfeits exist of almost all scarce surcharges among Nos. C1–C66.

Regular Issues of 1914-28 Overprinted in Red

Correo Aéreo 1929 P.A.A.

1929, May 15 Perf. 12 Unwmkd.

C1 A24 25c orange 1.50 1.50
- a. Double overprint, one inverted 12.50
- b. Inverted overprint 12.50
- c. Double overprint 12.50

C2 " 25c black brown 2.00 2.00
- a. Double overprint, one inverted 12.50
- b. Double overprint 12.50
- c. Inverted overprint 12.50

There are numerous varieties in the setting of the overprint. The most important are: Large "1" in "1929" and large "A" in "Aereo" and "P. A. A."

Similar Overprint on Regular Issue of 1929 in Red.

C3 A24 25c dark violet 1.00 90
- a. Double overprint 9.00
- b. Inverted overprint 9.00
- c. Double overprint, one inverted 15.00

The stamps in the bottom row of the sheet have the letters "P. A. A." larger than usual.

Airplanes over Mt. Momotombo

AP1

1929, Dec. 15 Engraved

C4 AP1 25c olive black 50 40
C5 " 50c black brown 75 60
C6 " 1cor orange red 1.00 85

See also Nos. C18–C19, C164–C168.

No. C4 Surcharged in Red or Black

Vale C$ 0.15

1930, May 15

C7 AP1 15c on 25c olive black (R) 50 45
- a. "$" inverted 3.00
- b. Double surcharge (R + Bk) 6.00
- c. Red surcharge, normal and black surcharge inverted 6.00
- d. Double red surcharge, one inverted 6.00

C8 " 20c on 25c olive black (Bk) 65 60
- a. "$" inverted 6.00
- b. Invtd. surch. 12.00

Nos. C1, C2 and C3 Surcharged in Green

Vale ₵ 0.15 1931

1931, June 7

C9 A24 15c on 25c orange 65.00 65.00
- a. "1391" 200.00
- b. "1921" 200.00

C10 " 15c on 25c black brown 175.00 175.00
- a. "1391" 250.00
- b. "1921" 250.00

C11 A24 15c on 25c dark violet 14.00 14.00
- a. "1391" 50.00
- b. "1921" 50.00
- c. Invtd. surch 17.50
- d. As "a," invtd. 250.00
- e. As "b," invtd. 250.00

C12 " 20c on 25c dark violet 12.00 12.00
- a. "1391" 25.00
- b. "1921" 25.00
- c. Invtd. surch. 17.50
- d. Dbl. surcharge 15.00
- e. As "a," invtd. 250.00
- f. As "b," invtd. 250.00
- g. As "a," double 250.00
- h. As "b," double 250.00

C13 " 20c on 25c black brown *600.00*
- a. "1391"
- b. "1921"

Nos. C4 to C6 Surcharged in Blue

1931 ₵ 0.15

1931, June

C14 AP1 15c on 20c on 25c olive black 12.00 12.00
- a. "1391" 50.00
- b. Blue surcharge inverted 20.00
- c. "$" in black, surcharge inverted 15.00
- d. Blue surcharge double, one inverted 20.00

C15 " 15c on 25c olive black 7.50 7.50
- a. "1391" 25.00
- b. Blue surcharge inverted 15.00
- c. Double surcharge, one inverted 20.00

C16 " 15c on 50c black brown 55.00 55.00
- a. "1391" 100.00

C17 " 15c on 1cor orange red 200.00 200.00
- a. "1391" 300.00

Momotombo Type of 1929.

1931, July 8

C18 AP1 15c deep violet 25 10
C19 " 20c deep green 70 65

Managua Post Office Before and After Earthquake

AP2

Without gum. Soft porous paper.

1932, Jan. 1 Litho. Perf. 11

C20 AP2 15c lilac 2.25
- a. 15c violet 35.00
- c. Vertical pair, imperf. between 35.00

C21 " 20c emerald 2.75
- b. Horizontal pair, imperf. between 40.00

C22 " 25c yellow brown 10.00
- b. Vertical pair, imperf. between 90.00

C23 " 50c yellow brown 12.50

C24 " 1cor deep carmine 20.00
- a. Vert. or horiz. pair, imperf. btwn. 125.00

Nos. C20–C24 (5) 47.50

Sheets of 10. See note after No. 568.

Reprints are on thin hard paper, often with fake cancels. Price $1 each.

Nos. C5 and C6 Surcharged in Red or Black

Vale ₵ 0.30

1932, July 12 Perf. 12

C25 AP1 30c on 50c black brown (Bk) 1.50 1.50
- a. "Valc" 6.00
- b. Double surcharge 5.00
- c. Double surcharge, one inverted 5.00
- d. Period omitted after "O" 6.00
- e. Var. "a" double 37.50

C26 " 35c on 50c black brown (R) 1.50 1.50
- a. "Valc" 6.00
- b. Double surcharge 5.00
- c. Double surcharge, one inverted 5.00
- d. Var. "a" double 37.50

C27 " 35c on 50c black brown (Bk) 30.00 30.00
- a. "Valc" 70.00

C28 " 40c on 1cor orange red (Bk) 1.50 1.50
- a. "Valc" 6.00
- b. Double surcharge 6.00
- c. Double surcharge, one inverted 6.00
- d. Inverted surcharge 6.00
- e. Var. "a" inverted 22.50
- f. Var. "a" double 22.50

C29 " 55c on 1cor orange red (R) 1.50 1.50
- a. "Valc" 6.00
- b. Double surcharge 5.00
- c. Double surcharge, one inverted 5.00
- d. Inverted surcharge 5.00
- e. Var. "a" inverted 22.50
- f. Var. "a" double 22.50

Nos. C25–C29 (5) 36.00 36.00

No. C18 Overprinted in Red

Semana Correo Aéreo Internacional 11-17 Septiembre 1932

1932, Sept. 11

C30 AP1 15c deep violet 20.00 20.00
- a. "Aerreo" 75.00 75.00
- b. Inverted "m" in "Septiembre" 50.00

International Air Mail Week.

No. C6 Surcharged

Inauguracion Interior 12 Octubre 1932 Vale ₵ 0.08

1932, Oct. 12

C31 AP1 8c on 1cor org. red 15.00 15.00
- a. "1232" 25.00 25.00
- b. Second "u" of "Inauguration" inverted 25.00 25.00

Issued for the inauguration of airmail service to the interior.

Regular Issue of 1932 Overprinted in Red

Correo Aéreo Interior 1932

Without Gum

1932, Oct. 24 Perf. 11½

C32 A40 1c yellow brown 20.00 20.00
- a. Inverted overprint 40.00 40.00

C33 " 2c carmine 20.00 20.00
- a. Inverted overprint 40.00 40.00
- b. Double overprint 35.00 35.00

C34 " 3c ultramarine 9.00 9.00
- a. Inverted overprint 40.00 40.00
- b. Vertical pair, imperf. between 100.00

C35 " 4c deep ultra. 9.50 9.50
- a. Inverted overprint 40.00 40.00
- b. Double overprint 25.00 25.00
- c. Vert. or horiz. pair, imperf. btwn. 75.00

C36 " 5c yellow brown 9.00 9.00
- a. Inverted overprint 40.00 40.00
- b. Vertical pair, imperf. between 75.00

C37 A40 6c gray brown 9.00 9.00
- a. Inverted overprint 25.00 25.00

C38 " 50c green 9.00 9.00
- a. Invtd. ovpt. 27.50 27.50

C39 " 1cor yellow 9.00 9.00
- a. Invtd. ovpt. 30.00 30.00
- b. Horizontal pair, imperf. between 75.00

Nos. C32–C39 (8) 94.50 94.50

Nos. C20 and C21 exist overprinted as C32–C39. The editors believe they were not regularly issued.

Surcharged in Red

Correo Aéreo Interior 1932 Vale ₵ 0.16

C40 A40 8c on 10c yellow brown 9.50 9.50
- a. Inverted surcharge 30.00 30.00

C41 " 16c on 20c orange 9.00 9.00
- a. Inverted surcharge 30.00 30.00

C42 " 24c on 25c deep violet 9.00 9.00
- a. Inverted surcharge 30.00 30.00
- b. Imperf. vertically (pair) 75.00

Surcharged in Red as No. C40 but without the word "Vale".

C43 A40 8c on 10c yellow brown 47.50 47.50
- a. Inverted surcharge 95.00 95.00
- b. Imperf. vertically (pair) 200.00

No. C22 Overprinted in Red

Interior—1932

C44 AP2 25c yellow brown 9.50 9.50
- a. Inverted overprint 25.00 25.00

Nos. C23 and C24 Surcharged in Red

Interior—1932 Vale ₵ 0.32

C45 AP2 32(c) on 50c yellow brown 9.00 9.00
- a. Inverted surcharge 25.00 25.00
- b. "Interior-1932" inverted 30.00 30.00
- c. "Vale $0.32" inverted 30.00 30.00
- d. Horizontal pair, imperf. between 75.00

C46 " 40(c) on 1cor carmine 7.50 7.50
- a. Inverted surcharge 30.00 30.00
- b. "Vale $0.40" inverted 35.00 35.00

Nos. 557–558 Overprinted in Black like Nos. C32 to C39.

1932, Nov. 16

C47 A40 1c yellow brown 25.00 22.50
- a. "1232" 27.50 27.50
- b. Inverted overprint 30.00 30.00
- c. Double overprint, one inverted 30.00 30.00
- d. Var. "a" inverted 125.00

C48 " 2c deep carmine 25.00 22.50
- a. "1232" 27.50 27.50
- b. Inverted overprint 30.00 30.00
- c. As "a," inverted 150.00

Excellent counterfeits exist of Nos. C27, C30–C48. Forged overprints and surcharges as on Nos. C32–C48 exist on reprints of Nos. C20–C24.

Regular Issue of 1914-32 Surcharged in Black

Correo Aéreo Interior-1932 Vale ₵ 0.01

1932 Perf. 12

C49 A25 1c on 2c bright rose 50 45
C50 A24 2c on 3c light blue 50 45
C51 A25 3c on 4c dark blue 50 45

C52 A24 4c on 5c gray brown 50 45
C53 A25 5c on 6c olive brn. 50 45
C54 " 6c on 10c lt. brown 50 45
a. Double surcharge 6.00
C55 A24 8c on 15c org. red 50 45
C56 A25 16c on 20c orange 50 50
C57 A24 24c on 25c dk. vio. 2.00 1.85
C58 " 25c on 25c dk. vio. 2.00 1.85
a. Double surcharge 3.00
C59 A25 32c on 50c green 2.00 1.85
C60 " 40c on 50c green 2.50 2.35
C61 " 50c on 1cor yellow 3.50 3.50
C62 " 1cor on 1cor yellow 4.50 4.50
Nos. C49–C62 (14) 20.50 19.55

Nos. C49–C62 exist with inverted surcharge.

In addition to C49 to C62, four other stamps, Type A25, exist with this surcharge.

40c on 50c bistre brown, black surcharge.
1cor on 2c bright rose, black surcharge.
1cor on 1cor yellow, red surcharge.
1cor on 1cor dull violet, black surcharge.

The editors believe they were not regularly issued.

Surcharged on Nos. 548, 547

1932

C65 A24 24c on 25c dk. vio. 50.00 50.00
C66 " 25c on 25c blk. brn. 60.00 60.00

Counterfeits of Nos. C65 and C66 are plentiful.

Rivas Railroad Issue.

La Chocolata Cut
AP3

El Nacascola
AP4

Designs: 25c, Cuesta cut. 50c, Mole of San Juan del Sur. 1cor, View of El Estero.

Soft porous paper.

1932, Dec. **Lithographed**

C67 AP3 15c dark violet 20.00
C68 AP4 20c blue green 20.00
C69 " 25c dark brown 20.00
C70 " 50c black brown 20.00
C71 " 1cor rose red 20.00
Nos. C67–C71 (5) 100.00

Issued in commemoration of the inauguration of the railroad from San Jorge to San Juan del Sur December 18, 1932. Printed in sheets of four, without gum.

Reprints exist on thin or thick paper. Price $3 each.

Demand as well as supply determine a stamp's market value. The first is as important as the other.

Leon-Sauce Railroad Issue.

"Fill" at Santa Lucia River
AP5

Designs: 15c, Bridge at Santa Lucia. 25c, Malpaicillo Station. 50c, Panoramic view. 1cor, San Andres.

1932, Dec. 30 **Soft porous paper**

C72 AP5 15c purple 20.00
C73 " 20c blue green 20.00
C74 " 25c dark brown 20.00
C75 " 50c black brown 20.00
C76 " 1cor rose red 20.00
Nos. C72–C76 (5) 100.00

Issued to commemorate the inauguration of the railroad from Leon to El Sauce, Dec. 30, 1932. Sheets of 4, without gum.

Reprints exist on thin or thick paper. Price $3 each.

Flag of the Race Issue.

Flag with Three Crosses
AP6

1933, Aug. 3 **Litho.** ***Rouletted 9***
Without gum.

C77 AP6 1c dark brown 2.25 2.25
C78 " 2c red violet 2.25 2.25
a. Imperf. (pair) 20.00
C79 " 4c violet 3.50 3.50
a. Imperf. (pair) 15.00
C80 " 5c dull blue 3.50 3.50
C81 " 6c violet blue 3.50 3.50
a. Imperf. (pair) 15.00
C82 " 8c deep brown 1.15 1.15
a. Imperf. (pair) 15.00
C83 " 15c olive brown 1.15 1.10
a. Imperf. (pair) 15.00
C84 " 20c yellow 3.50 3.50
a. Horizontal pair imperf. between 22.50
b. Imperf. vertically (pair) 22.50
C85 " 25c orange 3.50 3.50
C86 " 50c rose 3.50 3.50
C87 " 1cor green 16.50 16.00
a. Imperf. (pair) 45.00
Nos. C77–C87 (11) 44.30 43.75

See note after No. 599. Printed in sheets of 10. Reprints exist.

AP7

1933, Nov. ***Perf. 12***

C88 AP7 10c bistre brown 2.25 2.25
a. Vert. pair, imperf. between 50.00
C89 " 15c violet 2.25 2.25
a. Vert. pair, imperf. between 55.00
C90 " 25c red 2.25 2.25
a. Horiz. pair, imperf. between 35.00
C91 " 50c deep blue 2.25 2.25

Issued to commemorate International Air Post Week, Nov. 6–11, 1933. Printed in sheets of 4. Counterfeits exist.

Stamps and Types of 1928-31 Surcharged in Black — **Correo Aéreo Interior Vale ₡ 0.01**

1933, Nov. 3

C92 A25 1c on 2c green 15 12
C93 A24 2c on 3c olive gray 15 12
C94 A25 3c on 4c car. rose 15 12
C95 A24 4c on 5c light blue 15 12
C96 A25 5c on 6c dark blue 20 20
C97 " 6c on 10c olive brown 12 10
C98 A24 8c on 15c bis. brn. 30 18
C99 A25 16c on 20c brown 25 20
C100 A24 24c on 25c vermilion 15 15
C101 " 25c on 25c orange 35 25
C102 A25 32c on 50c violet 30 30
C103 " 40c on 50c green 30 20
C104 " 50c on 1cor yellow 25 20
C105 " 1cor on 1cor orange red 50 40
Nos. C92–C105 (14) 3.32 2.66

Nos. C92 to C105 exist with or without script control mark.

Type of Air Post Stamps of 1929 Surcharged in Black — **Vale ₡ 0.30**

1933, Oct. 28

C106 AP1 30c on 50c orange red 35 15
C107 " 35c on 50c light blue 40 25
C108 " 40c on 1cor yellow 60 25
C109 " 55c on 1cor green 45 40

No. C19 Surcharged in Red — **Servicio Centroamericano Vale 10 centavos**

1934, Mar. 31

C110 AP1 10c on 20c green 45 45
a. Inverted surcharge 3.00
b. Double surcharge, one inverted 3.00
c. "Ceutroamericano" 1.50

No. C110 with black surcharge is believed to be of private origin.

No. C4 Surcharged in Red — **Servicio Centroamericano Vale 10 centavos**

1935, Aug.

C111 AP1 10c on 25c olive black 45 45
a. Small "v" in "vale" (R) 1.50
b. "centrvos" (R) 1.50
c. Double surcharge (R) 4.00
d. Inverted surcharge (R) 3.00
g. As "a," inverted 15.00
h. As "a," double 15.00

No. C111 with blue surcharge is believed to be private origin.

The editors do not recognize the Nicaraguan air post stamps overprinted in red "VALIDO 1935" in two lines and with or without script control marks as having been issued primarily for postal purposes.

Nos C4-C6, C18-C19 Overprinted Vertically in Blue, Reading Up: **RESELLO - 1935**

1935–36

C112 AP1 15c deep violet 1.50 1.50
C113 " 20c deep green 2.50 2.50
C114 " 25c olive black 2.75 2.75
C115 " 50c black brown 8.00 8.00
C116 " 1cor orange red 60.00 60.00
Nos. C112–C116 (5) 74.75 74.75

Same Overprint on Nos. C106–C109 Reading Up or Down.

C117 AP1 30c on 50c orange red 2.25 2.00
C118 AP1 35c on 50c light blue 10.00 10.00
C119 " 40c on 1cor yel. 10.00 10.00
C120 " 55c on 1cor grn. 10.00 10.00

Same Overprint in Red on Nos. C92-C105.

1936

C121 A25 1c on 2c green 15 15
C122 A24 2c on 3c olive gray 25 25
C123 A25 3c on 4c carmine rose 25 25
C124 A24 4c on 5c light blue 25 25
C125 A25 5c on 6c dark blue 25 25
C126 " 6c on 10c olive brown 30 30
C127 A24 8c on 15c bistre brown 25 25
C128 A25 16c on 20c brown 40 40
C129 A24 24c on 25c vermilion 50 40
C130 " 25c on 25c orange 35 35
C131 A25 32c on 50c violet 25 25
C132 " 40c on 50c green 85 75
C133 " 50c on 1cor yellow 60 50
C134 " 1cor on 1cor orange red 2.00 1.25
Nos. C121–C134 (14) 6.65 5.60

Nos. C121 to C134 are handstamped with script control mark.

Overprint Reading Down on No. C110.

C135 AP1 10c on 20c green 500.00 500.00

This stamp has been extensively counterfeited.

Overprinted in Red on Nos. C4 to C6, C18 and C19.

C136 AP1 15c deep violet 80 15
C137 " 20c deep green 1.00 90
C138 " 25c olive black 1.00 85
C139 " 50c black brown 1.00 85
C140 " 1cor orange red 1.75 80

On Nos. C106 to C109.

C141 AP1 30c on 50c orange red 1.00 90
C142 " 35c on 50c light blue 1.00 75
C143 " 40c on 1cor yellow 1.00 85
C144 " 55c on 1cor green 1.00 90

Same Overprint in Red or Blue on No. C111 Reading Up or Down.

C145 AP1 10c on 25c olive black (R), down 80 70
a. "Centrvos" 4.00
C146 " 10c on 25c olive black (Bl), up 1.75 1.50
a. "Centrvos" 4.00
Nos. C136–C146 (11) 12.10 9.15

Overprint on No. C145 is at right, on No. C146 in center.

Nos. C92, C93 and C98 Overprinted in Black — **Resello 1936**

1936

C147 A25 1c on 2c green 30 25
C148 A24 2c on 3c olive gray 15 15
a. "Resello 1936" double, one inverted 4.00
C149 " 8c on 15c bis. brn. 35 35

With script control handstamp.

Nos. C5 and C6 Surcharged in Red — **1936 Vale Quince Centavos**

C150 AP1 15c on 50c blk. brn. 30 30
C151 " 15c on 1cor org. red 30 30

Nos. C18 and C19 Overprinted in Carmine — **RESELLO - 1935**

C152 AP1 15c deep violet 50 30
C153 " 20c deep green 50 40

Overprint reading up or down.

No. C4 Surcharged and Overprinted in Red

Servicio Centroamericano Vale diez centavos and RESELLO - 1935

C154 AP1 10c on 25c olive black 45 45
a. Surcharge and overprint inverted 5.00

Same Overprint in Carmine on Nos. C92 to C99.

C155 A25 1c on 2c green 15 15
C156 A24 2c on 3c olive gray 1.00 1.00
C157 A25 3c on 4c car. rose 15 15
C158 A24 4c on 5c light blue 15 15
C159 A25 5c on 6c dark blue 15 15
C160 " 6c on 10c olive brown 15 15
C161 A24 8c on 15c bis. brn. 20 20
C162 A25 16c on 20c brown 18 18
Nos. C155-C162 (8) 2.13 2.13

No. 518 Overprinted in Black

Correo Aéreo Centro-Americano Resello 1936

C163 A25 10c light brown 25 25
a. Overprint inverted 3.50
b. Double ovpt. 3.50

Two fonts are found in the sheet of No. C163.

Momotombo Type of 1929

1937

C164 AP1 15c yellow orange 12 8
C165 " 20c orange red 15 15
C166 " 25c black 20 15
C167 " 50c violet 35 10
C168 " 1cor orange 85 18
Nos. C164-C168 (5) 1.67 66

Surcharged in Black Vale ₡ 0.30

1937

C169 AP1 30c on 50c carmine rose 25 10
C170 " 35c on 50c olive green 30 12
C171 " 40c on 1cor green 35 10
C172 " 55c on 1cor blue 30 30

No. C168 Surcharged in Violet

Servicio Centroamericano Vale Diez Centavos

1937 *Perf. 12.* Unwmkd.

C173 AP1 10c on 1cor orange 25 20
a. "Centauos" 15.00

No. C98 with Additional Overprint "1937".

C174 A24 8c on 15c bis. brn. 70 20
a. "1937" double 10.00

Nos. C92-C102 with Additional Overprint in Blue reading "HABILITADO 1937".

C175 A25 1c on 2c green 10 8
a. Blue overprint double 4.00
C176 A24 2c on 3c olive gray 10 8
a. Double surcharge, one inverted 4.00
C177 A25 3c on 4c car. rose 10 8
C178 A24 4c on 5c light blue 10 10
C179 A25 5c on 6c dark blue 12 10
C180 " 6c on 10c olive brown 10 8
C181 A24 8c on 15c bis. brn. 10 10
a. "Habilitado 1937" double 5.00
C182 A25 16c on 20c brown 25 25
a. Double surcharge 4.00
C183 A24 24c on 25c vermilion 25 25
C184 " 25c on 25c orange 35 30
C185 A25 32c on 50c violet 35 35
Nos. C175-C185 (11) 1.92 1.77

Map of Nicaragua AP8

For Foreign Postage.

1937, July 30 Engraved

C186 AP8 10c green 20 8
C187 " 15c deep blue 20 10
C188 " 20c yellow 30 25
C189 " 25c blue violet 30 25
C190 " 30c rose carmine 35 30
C191 " 50c orange yellow 50 30
C192 " 1cor olive green 1.10 1.00
Nos. C186-C192 (7) 2.95 2.28

Presidential Palace AP9

For Domestic Postage.

C193 AP9 1c rose carmine 15 10
C194 " 2c deep blue 15 10
C195 " 3c olive green 15 10
C196 " 4c black 15 10
C197 " 5c dark violet 15 10
C198 " 6c chocolate 15 10
C199 " 8c blue violet 18 10
C200 " 16c orange yellow 35 30
C201 " 24c yellow 25 18
C202 " 25c yellow green 40 30
Nos. C193-C202 (10) 2.03 1.48

No. C201 with green overprint "Union Panamericana 1890-1940" is of private origin.

Managua AP10

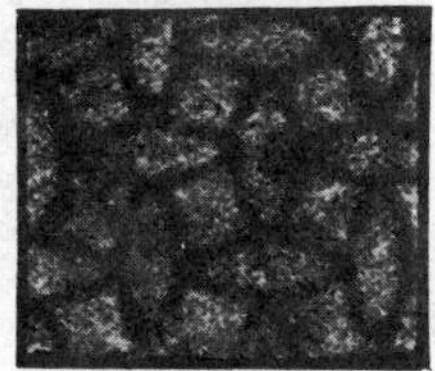

Wmk. 209

Designs: 15c, Presidential Palace. 20c, Map of South America. 25c, Map of Central America. 30c, Map of North America. 35c, Lagoon of Tiscapa, Managua. 40c, Road Scene. 45c, Park. 50c, Another park. 55c, Scene in San Juan del Sur. 75c, Tipitapa River. 1cor, Landscape.

Wmkd. Multiple Ovals. (209)

1937, Sept. 17 Typo. *Perf. 11*

Center in Dark Blue

C203 AP10 10c yellow green 2.50 2.00
C204 " 15c orange 2.50 2.00
C205 " 20c red 1.50 1.50
C206 " 25c violet brown 1.50 1.50
C207 " 30c blue green 1.50 1.50
a. Great Lakes omitted 50.00 50.00
C208 " 35c lemon 75 70
C209 " 40c green 60 55
C210 " 45c bright violet 60 50
C211 " 50c rose lilac 60 50
a. Vertical pair, imperf. between 200.00
C212 " 55c light blue 60 50
C213 " 75c gray green 60 50

Center in Brown Red

C214 AP10 1cor dark blue 1.50 75
Nos. C203-C214 (12) 14.75 12.50

Issued in commemoration of the 150th anniversary of the Constitution of the United States of America.

Diriangen—AP11

Designs: 4c, 10c, Nicarao. 5c, 15c, Bartolomé de Las Casas. 8c, 20c, Columbus.

For Domestic Postage.

Without gum.

1937, Oct. 12 *Perf. 11* Unwmkd.

C215 AP11 1c green 12 10
a. Imperf. (pair) 25 25
C216 " 4c brown carmine 15 12
a. Imperf. (pair) 30 30
C217 " 5c dark violet 20 18
a. Without imprint 60
b. Imperf. (pair) 30 30
C218 " 8c deep blue 12 12
a. Without imprint 75
b. Imperf. (pair) 30

For Foreign Postage.

With gum.

Wmkd. Multiple Ovals. (209)

C219 AP11 10c light brown 15 12
a. Imperf. (pair) 30 30
C220 " 15c pale blue 15 12
a. Without imprint 1.50
b. Imperf. (pair) 35 35
C221 " 20c pale rose 25 20
a. Imperf. (pair) 50 50
Nos. C215-C221 (7) 1.14 96

Nos. C215-C221 were printed in sheets of 4.

Gen. Tomas Martinez—AP11a

Design: 10c, 15c, 25c, 50c, Gen. Anastasio Somoza.

For Domestic Postage.

Without Gum.

Perf. 11½, Imperf.

1938, Jan. 18 Typo. Unwmkd.

Center in Black.

C221B AP11a 1c orange 30 30
C221C " 5c red violet 30 30
C221D " 8c dark blue 35 35
C221E " 16c brown 40 40
f. Sheet of 4 1.85 1.85

For Foreign Postage.

C221G AP11a 10c green 35 30
C221H " 15c dark blue 40 40
C221J " 25c violet 65 60
C221K " 50c carmine 75 70
m. Sheet of 4 3.00 3.00
Nos. C221B-C221K (8) 3.50 3.35

Nos. C221B-C221m were issued to commemorate the 75th anniversary of postal service in Nicaragua. Printed in sheets of four: No. C221f contains one each of the 1c, 5c, 8c and 16c; No. C221m contains one of the 10c, 15c, 25c and 50c.

Stamps of type AP11a exist in changed colors and with inverted centers, double centers and frames printed on the back. These varieties were private fabrications.

Lake Managua AP12

President Anastasio Somoza AP13

For Domestic Postage.

Engraved

1939 *Perf. 12½.* Unwmkd.

C222 AP12 2c deep blue 10 10
C223 " 3c green 10 10
C224 " 8c pale lilac 10 10
C225 " 16c orange 20 15
C226 " 24c yellow 20 20
C227 " 32c dark green 25 20
C228 " 50c deep rose 25 20

For Foreign Postage.

C229 AP13 10c dark brown 15 12
C230 " 15c dark blue 15 12
C231 " 20c orange yellow 20 15
C232 " 25c dark purple 20 20
C233 " 30c lake 25 25
C234 " 50c deep orange 40 30
C235 " 1cor dark olive green 60 50
Nos. C222-C235 (14) 3.15 2.69

For Domestic Postage.

Will Rogers and View of Managua AP14

Designs: 2c, Rogers standing beside plane. 3c, Leaving airport office. 4c, Rogers and U. S. Marines. 5c, Managua after earthquake.

1939, Mar. 31 Engraved *Perf. 12*

C236 AP14 1c bright green 8 8
C237 " 2c orange red 8 6
C238 " 3c light ultramarine 6 6
C239 " 4c dark blue 12 8
C240 " 5c rose carmine 8 6
Nos. C236-C240 (5) 42 34

Issued in commemoration of Will Rogers' flight to Managua after the earthquake, March 31, 1931.

Pres. Anastasio Somoza in U. S. House of Representatives AP19

President Somoza and U.S. Capitol—AP20

President Somoza, Tower of the Sun and Trylon and Perisphere
AP21

For Domestic Postage.

1940, Feb. 1

No.	Type	Description	Unused	Used
C241	AP19	4c red brown	15	10
C242	AP20	8c black brown	12	8
C243	AP19	16c greenish blue	15	8
C244	AP20	20c bright plum	75	45
C245	AP21	32c scarlet	25	25

For Foreign Postage.

No.	Type	Description	Unused	Used
C246	AP19	25c deep blue	30	15
C247	"	30c black	30	10
C248	AP20	50c rose pink	70	55
C249	AP21	60c green	75	45
C250	AP19	65c dk. vio. brn.	75	30
C251	"	90c olive green	1.00	45
C252	AP21	1cor violet	1.50	1.00
		Nos. C241-C252 (12)	6.72	3.96

Visit of Pres. Somoza to U.S. in 1939.

L. S. Rowe, Statue of Liberty, Nicaraguan Coastline, Flags of 21 American Republics, United States Shield and Arms of Nicaragua—AP22

1940, Aug. 2 Engr. *Perf. 12½*

No.	Type	Description	Unused	Used
C253	AP22	1.25cor multi.	1.00	90

50th anniversary of Pan American Union.

First Nicaraguan Postage Stamp and Sir Rowland Hill—AP23

1941, Apr. 4

No.	Type	Description	Unused	Used
C254	AP23	2cor brown	4.00	1.50
C255	"	3cor dark blue	16.00	2.00
C256	"	5cor carmine	35.00	5.00

Centenary of the first postage stamp.
Nos. C254-C256 imperf. are proofs.

Rubén Darío
AP24

1941, Dec. 23

No.	Type	Description	Unused	Used
C257	AP24	20c pale lilac	35	20
C258	"	35c yellow green	40	25
C259	"	40c orange yellow	50	35
C260	"	60c light blue	1.00	45

Issued to commemorate the 25th anniversary of the death of Rubén Dario, poet and writer.

"Victory"
AP25

1943, Dec. 8 *Perf. 12*

No.	Type	Description	Unused	Used
C261	AP25	40c dark blue green & cerise	20	6
C262	"	60c light blue & cerise	30	8

Issued to commemorate the second anniversary of Nicaragua's declaration of war against the Axis.

Red Cross
AP26

Cross and Globes
AP27

Red Cross Workers
AP28

1944, Oct. 12 Engraved.

No.	Type	Description	Unused	Used
C263	AP26	25c red lilac & carmine	1.00	45
C264	AP27	50c olive brown & carmine	1.35	80
C265	AP28	1cor dk. bl. green & carmine	2.75	2.50

Issued to commemorate the 80th anniversary of the International Red Cross Society.

Caravels of Columbus and Columbus Lighthouse
AP29

Landing of Columbus
AP30

1945, Sept. 1 *Perf. 12½*

No.	Type	Description	Unused	Used
C266	AP29	20c deep green & gray	15	12
C267	"	35c dark carmine & black	35	30
C268	"	75c olive green & rose pink	45	40
C269	"	90c brick red & aquamarine	80	75
C270	"	1cor black & pale blue	90	30
C271	AP30	2.50cor dark blue & carmine rose	2.50	2.50
		Nos. C266-C271 (6)	5.15	4.37

Issued in honor of the discovery of America by Columbus and the Columbus Lighthouse near Cindad Trujillo, Dominican Republic.

Franklin D. Roosevelt and Winston Churchill
AP31

Roosevelt Signing Declaration of War Against Japan
AP32

Designs: 1cor, Gen. Henri Giraud, Roosevelt, Gen. Charles de Gaulle and Churchill. 3cor, Stalin, Roosevelt and Churchill. 5cor, Sculptured head of Roosevelt.

Engraved, Center Photogravure.

1946, June 15 *Perf. 12½*

Frame in Black.

No.	Type	Description	Unused	Used
C272	AP31	25c orange	12	12
		a. Horizontal pair, imperf. between	225.00	
		b. Imperf., pair	175.00	
C273	AP32	75c carmine	25	25
		a. Imperf., pair	175.00	
C274	AP31	1cor dark green	40	40
C275	"	3cor violet	3.75	3.75
C276	AP32	5cor greenish blue	5.00	5.00
		Nos. C272-C276 (5)	9.52	9.52

Issued to honor Franklin D. Roosevelt.

Projected Provincial Seminary
AP36

Designs: 20c, Communications Building. 35c, Sanitation Building. 90c, National Bank. 1cor, Municipal Building. 2.50cor, National Palace.

1947, Jan. 10 Frame in Black

No.	Type	Description	Unused	Used
C277	AP36	5c violet	10	8
		a. Imperf., pair	125.00	
C278	"	20c gray green	15	15
C279	"	35c orange	20	18
C280	"	90c red lilac	40	30
C281	"	1cor brown	60	45
C282	"	2.50cor rose lilac	1.75	1.50
		Nos. C277-C282 (6)	3.20	2.66

City of Managua centenary.

Rubén Darío Monument—AP42

Designs: 6c, Tapir. 8c, Stone Highway. 10c, Genizaro Dam. 20c, Detail of Dario Monument. 25c, Sulphurous Lake of Nejapa. 35c, Mercedes Airport. 50c, Prinzapolka River delta. 1cor, Tipitapa Spa. 1.50cor, Tipitapa River. 5cor, United States Embassy. 10cor, Indian fruit vendor. 25cor, Franklin D. Roosevelt Monument.

Engraved, Center Photogravure.

1947, Aug. 29 *Perf. 12½* Unwmkd.

No.	Type	Description	Unused	Used
C283	AP42	5c dark blue green & rose carmine	6	6
C284	"	6c black & yellow	8	6
C285	"	8c carmine & olive	8	6
C286	"	10c brown & blue	15	10
C287	"	20c bl. vio. & org.	25	18
C288	"	25c brown red & emerald	30	20
C289	"	35c gray & bistre	25	20
C290	"	50c purple & sepia	20	15
C291	"	1cor black & lilac rose	60	35
C292	"	1.50cor red brown & aquamarine	65	65
C293	"	5cor chocolate & carmine rose	5.00	4.50
C294	"	10cor violet & dark brown	4.00	3.50
C295	"	25cor dark blue green & yellow	9.00	9.00
		Nos. C283-C295 (13)	20.60	19.01

The frames differ for each denomination.

Tennis
AP43

Designs: 2c, Soccer. 3c, Table tennis. 4c, Proposed stadium. 5c, Regatta. 15c, Basketball. 25c, Boxing. 30c, Baseball. 40c, Bicycling. 75c, Diving. 1cor, Pole vault. 2cor, Boy Scouts. 5cor, Softball.

1949, July Photo. *Perf. 12*

No.	Type	Description	Unused	Used
C296	AP43	1c cerise	12	6
C297	"	2c olive gray	12	6
C298	"	3c scarlet	12	8
C299	"	4c dark blue gray	8	8
C300	"	5c aquamarine	30	10
C301	"	15c blue green	90	12
C302	"	25c red violet	2.00	30
C303	"	30c red brown	1.75	30
C304	"	40c violet	45	30
C305	"	75c magenta	4.50	2.75
C306	"	1cor light blue	5.00	1.35
C307	"	2cor brown olive	2.75	2.00
C308	"	5cor light green	2.50	2.50
		Set of 13 souvenir sheets of 4	150.00	150.00
		Nos. C296-C308 (13)	20.59	10.00

Issued to publicize the tenth World Series of Amateur Baseball, 1948.

Rowland Hill
AP44

Designs: 20c, Heinrich von Stephan. 25c, First U. P. U. Bldg. 30c, U. P. U. Bldg., Bern. 85c, U. P. U. Monument. 1.10cor, Congress medal, obverse. 2.14 cor, as 1.10cor, reverse.

1950, Nov. 23 Engraved *Perf. 13*

Frames in Black.

No.	Type	Description	Unused	Used
C309	AP44	16c cerise	15	12
C310	"	20c orange	15	12
C311	"	25c gray	20	20
C312	"	30c cerise	30	12
C313	"	85c dark blue green	65	65
C314	"	1.10cor chestnut brown	50	45
C315	"	2.14cor olive green	2.25	2.25
		Set of 7 souvenir sheets of 4	35.00	35.00
		Nos. C309-C315 (7)	4.20	3.91

Issued to commemorate the 75th anniversary (in 1949) of the formation of the Universal Postal Union.

Each denomination was also issued in a souvenir sheet containing four stamps and marginal inscriptions. Size: 126x114mm. Price, set of 7 sheets, $35.

Queen Isabella I
AP45

Columbus' Ships
AP46

Designs: 2.80cor, Map. 3cor, Santa Maria. 3.60cor, Portrait facing right.

1952, June 25 *Perf. 11½* Unwmkd.

C316	AP45	2.30cor rose car.	1.50	1.50
C317	"	2.80cor red org.	1.35	1.35
C318	"	3cor green	1.50	1.50
C319	AP46	3.30cor lt. blue	1.50	1.50
C320	AP45	3.60cor yellow green	1.65	1.65
		a. Souvenir sheet of 5	7.50	7.50
		Nos. C316-C320 (5)	7.50	7.50

Issued to commemorate the 500th anniversary of the birth of Queen Isabella I of Spain.

No. C320a measures 160x128mm., and contains one each of Nos. C316-C320 with marginal inscriptions typographed in black.

Arms of ODECA
AP47

Designs: 25c, ODECA Flag. 30c, Presidents of five Central American countries. 60c, ODECA Charter and Flags. 1cor, Map of Central America.

1953, Apr. 15 *Perf. 13½x14*

C321	AP47	20c red lilac	12	12
C322	"	25c light blue	15	15
C323	"	30c sepia	20	15
C324	"	60c dk. bl. green	30	25
C325	"	1cor dark violet	70	65
		Nos. C321-C325 (5)	1.47	1.32

Issued to commemorate the founding of the Organization of Central American States (ODECA).

Leonardo Arguello
AP48

Presidents: 5c, Gen. Jose Maria Moncada. 20c, Juan Bautista Sacasa. 25c, Gen. Jose Santos Zelaya. 30c, Gen. Anastasio Somoza. 35c, Gen. Tomas Martinez. 40c, Fernando Guzman. 45c, Vicente Cuadra. 50c, Pedro Joaquin Chamorro. 60c, Gen. Joaquin Zavala. 85c, Adan Cardenas. 1.10cor, Evaristo Carazo. 1.20cor, Roberto Sacasa.

Engraved (frames); Photo. (heads).

1953, June 25 *Perf. 12½*

Heads in Gray Black

C326	AP48	4c deep carmine	6	6
C327	"	5c deep orange	6	6
C328	"	20c dk. Prus. blue	10	8
C329	"	25c blue	12	8
C330	"	30c red brown	12	8
C331	"	35c deep green	25	25
C332	"	40c dk. vio. brn.	30	25
C333	"	45c olive	30	30
C334	"	50c carmine	35	20
C335	"	60c ultramarine	40	30
C336	"	85c brown	50	45
C337	"	1.10cor purple	60	60
C338	"	1.20cor olive bistre	60	60
		Nos. C326-C338 (13)	3.76	3.31

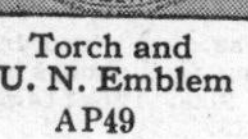

Torch and U. N. Emblem
AP49

Capt. Dean L. Ray, USAF
AP50

Designs: 4c, Raised hands. 5c, Candle and charter. 30c, Flags of Nicaragua and U. N. 2cor, Globe. 3cor, Arms of Nicaragua. 5cor, Type A69 inscribed "Aereo."

1954, Apr. 30 Engr. *Perf. 13½*

C339	AP49	3c rose pink	8	8
C340	"	4c deep orange	8	8
C341	"	5c red	15	8
C342	"	30c cerise	1.00	20
C343	"	2cor magenta	1.35	1.00
C344	"	3cor orange brown	2.50	1.75
C345	"	5cor brown violet	3.00	2.75
		Nos. C339-C345 (7)	8.16	5.94

Issued to honor the United Nations Organization.

Engraved; Center Photogravure.

1954, Nov. 5 *Perf. 13*

Designs: 15c, Sabre jet plane. 20c, Air Force emblem. 25c, National Air Force hangars. 30c, Gen. A. Somoza. 50c, AT-6's in formation. 1cor, Plane, type P-38.

Frame in Black

C346	AP50	10c gray	8	5
C347	"	15c gray	12	6
C348	"	20c claret	15	10
C349	"	25c red	15	10
C350	"	30c ultramarine	20	8
C351	"	50c blue	65	65
C352	"	1cor green	50	35
		Nos. C346-C352 (7)	1.85	1.39

Issued to honor the National Air Force.

Paul P. Harris—AP51

Map of the World and Rotary Emblem
AP52

Designs: 2c, 50c, Handclasp, Rotary emblem and globe. 4c, 30c, Rotary slogans and wreath. 5c, 25c, Flags of Nicaragua and Rotary.

Granite Paper.

Photogravure.

1955, Aug. 30 *Perf. 11½* Unwmkd.

C353	AP51	1c vermilion	5	5
C354	"	2c ultramarine	5	5
C355	AP52	3c peacock green	5	5
C356	AP51	4c violet	5	5
C357	"	5c orange brown	10	8
C358	"	25c brt. greenish blue	20	18
C359	"	30c dull purple	15	12
C360	AP52	45c lilac rose	35	30
C361	AP51	50c lt. bl. green	25	20
C362	"	1 cor ultramarine	35	35
		a. Souvenir sheet of 5	7.00	7.00
		Nos. C353-C362 (10)	1.60	1.43

Rotary International, 50th anniversary.

No. C362a contains one each of Nos. C358-C362 and is inscribed in red: "Conmemoracion de las Bodas de Oro de Rotary International 1905—1955."

Issues of 1953-55 Surcharged in Green or Black

Conmemoración
Exposición Nacional
Febrero 4-16, 1956
¢ 0.15

Engraved, Photogravure.

1956, Feb. 4 *Perf. 13½x13, 11½*

C363	AP48	30c on 35c deep green & gray black (G)	20	18
C364	AP48	30c on 45c olive & gray black (G)	20	18
C365	AP52	30c on 45c lilac rose	20	12
C366	AP49	2cor on 5cor brown violet	80	75

National Exhibition, Feb. 4-16, 1956.
See note after No. 772.

Gen. Jose D. Estrada
AP53

The Stoning of Andres Castro
AP54

Designs: 1.50 cor, Emanuel Mongalo. 2.50 cor, Battle of Rivas. 10 cor, Com. Hiram Paulding.

1956, Sept. 14 Engraved *Perf. 12½*

C367	AP53	30c dark carmine rose	10	10
C368	AP54	60c chocolate	20	18
C369	AP53	1.50cor green	45	45
C370	AP54	2.50cor dark ultra.	75	75
C371	AP53	10cor red orange	3.50	3.50
		Nos. C367-C371 (5)	5.00	4.98

Centenary of the National War.

President Somoza
AP55

1957, Feb. 1 Photo. *Perf. 14x13½*

Various Frames: Centers in Black

C372	AP55	15c gray black	12	12
C373	"	30c indigo	20	20
C374	"	2cor purple	1.00	1.00
C375	"	3cor dark green	2.00	2.00
C376	"	5cor dark brown	3.25	3.25
		Nos. C372-C376 (5)	6.57	6.57

Issued in tribute to President Anastasio Somoza, 1896-1956.

Type of Regular Issue and

Handshake and Globe
AP56

Designs: 4c, Scout emblem, globe and Lord Baden-Powell. 5c, Cub Scout. 6c, Crossed flags and Scout emblem. 8c, Scout symbols. 30c, Joseph A. Harrison. 40c, Pres. Somoza receiving decoration at first Central American Camporee. 75c, Explorer Scout. 85c, Boy Scout. 1cor, Lord Baden-Powell.

Perf. 13½x14

1957, Apr. 9 Unwmkd.

C377	AP56	3c red orange & olive	15	15
C378	A75	4c dark brown & dark Prussian green	15	15
C379	"	5c green & brown	15	15
C380	"	6c purple & olive	15	15
C381	"	8c greenish black & red	15	15
C382	"	30c Prussian green & gray	20	20
C383	AP56	40c dark blue & grayish black	20	20
C384	A75	75c maroon & brn.	30	30
C385	"	85c red & gray	35	35
C386	"	1cor dull red brown & slate green	45	40
		a. Souvenir sheet of 5	3.50	3.50
		Nos. C377-C386 (10)	2.25	2.20

Issued to commemorate the centenary of the birth of Lord Baden-Powell, founder of the Boy Scouts.

No. C386a contains one each of Nos. C382-C386, imperf., and is inscribed in black: "Hoja Souvenir—Conmemoracion del Primer Centenario del Nacimiento del Fundador del Escultismo Mundial Lord Robert Baden-Powell 1856-1956."

No. C386a with each stamp overprinted "CAMPOREE SCOUT 1965" was issued in 1965 along with Nos. 843-852.

Pres. Luis A. Somoza
AP57

1957, July 2 *Perf. 14x13½*

Portrait in Dark Brown.

C387	AP57	20c deep blue	12	10
C388	"	25c lilac rose	15	12
C389	"	30c black brown	15	15
C390	"	40c greenish blue	20	20
C391	"	2cor bright violet	1.25	1.25
		Nos. C387-C391 (5)	1.87	1.82

Issued to honor President Luis A. Somoza.

Types of Regular Issue, 1957.

Designs: 30c, Archbishop Lezcano y Ortega. 60c, Managua Cathedral. 75c, Bishop Pereira y Castellon. 90c, Leon Cathedral. 1.50cor, De la Merced Church, Granada. 2cor, Father Mariano Dubon.

1957, July 16 Unwmkd.

Centers in Olive Gray.

C392	A78	30c dark green	12	12
C393	A77	60c chocolate	20	20
C394	A78	75c dark blue	30	30
C395	A77	90c bright red	40	40
C396	"	1.50cor Prus. green	60	60
C397	A78	2cor bright purple	90	90
		Nos. C392-C397 (6)	2.52	2.52

Issued in honor of the Catholic Church in Nicaragua.

1957, Oct. 24 Litho. *Perf. 14*

Designs: 25c, M. S. Managua. 30c, Ship's wheel and map. 50c, Pennants. 60c, M. S. Costa Rica. 1 cor, M. S. Nicarao. 2.50 cor, Flag, globe & ship.

C398	A79	25c ultramarine, grayish blue & gray	12	12
C399	"	30c red brown, gray & yellow	15	10
C400	"	50c violet, olive gray & blue	25	25
C401	"	60c lake, greenish blue & black	30	25
C402	"	1cor crimson, bright blue & black	40	40
C403	"	2.50cor black, blue & red brown	1.20	1.10
		Nos. C398-C403 (6)	2.42	2.22

Issued to honor Nicaragua's Merchant Marine.

Fair Emblem
AP58

Designs: 30c, 2cor, Arms of Nicaragua. 45c, 10cor, Pavilion of Nicaragua, Brussels.

1958, Apr. 17 *Perf. 14* **Unwmkd.**

C404 AP58 25c bluish green, black & yellow 12 12
C405 " 30c multicolored 15 15
C406 " 45c bistre, blue & black 18 18
C407 " 1cor pale brn., lt. bl. & black 35 35
C408 " 2cor multicolored 65 65
C409 " 10cor pale blue, lilac & brown 3.25 1.25
a. Souvenir sheet of 6 15.00 15.00
Nos. C404-C409 (6) 4.70 2.70

World's Fair, Brussels, Apr. 17-Oct. 19.
No. C409a contains one each of Nos. C404-C409. Size: 128x118½mm.

Type of Regular Issue, 1958.

Designs: 30c, Dr. Teodoro A. Arias. 60c, Arms of Central American Republics. 90c, Edward G. Barry. 1.25cor, Melvin Jones. 2cor, Motto and emblem. 3cor, Map of Central America.

1958, May 8 **Lithographed**
Emblem in Yellow, Red and Blue.

C410 A80 30c blue & orange 12 12
C411 " 60c multicolored 25 20
C412 " 90c blue 35 30
C413 " 1.25cor blue & olive 45 40
C414 " 2cor blue & green 80 70
C415 " 3cor blue, lilac & pink 1.35 1.25
a. Souvenir sheet of 6 4.00 4.00
Nos. C410-C415 (6) 3.32 2.97

Issued to commemorate the 17th convention of Lions International of Central America, May, 1958.
No. C415a measures 154x89mm. and contains one each of Nos. C410-C415. Marginal inscriptions in dark blue.

Type of Regular Issue, 1958.

Designs: 30c, Arms of La Salle. 60c, School, Managua (horiz.) 85c, St. Jean Baptiste De La Salle. 90c, Bro. Carlos. 1.25cor, Bro. Julio. 1.50cor, Bro. Antonio. 1.75cor, Bro. Argeo. 2cor, Bro. Eugenio.

1958, July 13 **Photo.** *Perf. 14*

C416 A81 30c blue, carmine & yellow 12 10
C417 " 60c gray, brown & lilac 35 30
C418 " 85c red, blue & greenish black 40 35
C419 " 90c olive green, ochre & black 50 45
C420 " 1.25cor carmine, ochre & black 70 65
C421 " 1.50cor light green, gray & violet black 80 70
C422 " 1.75cor brown, blue & greenish black 90 80
C423 " 2cor olive green, gray & violet black 1.25 1.25
Nos. C416-C423 (8) 5.02 4.60

Issued to honor the Christian Brothers.

UNESCO Building, Paris
AP59

Designs: 75c, 5cor, "UNESCO." 90c, 3cor, UNESCO building and Eiffel tower. 1cor, Emblem and globe.

Lithographed.

1958, Dec. 15 *Perf. 11½* **Unwmkd.**

C424 AP59 60c bright pink & blue 30 20
C425 " 75c green & red brown 30 25
C426 " 90c light brown & green 35 30
C427 " 1cor ultramarine & bright pink 40 40
C428 " 3cor gray & orange 1.25 1.25
C429 AP59 5cor rose lilac & dark blue 2.00 1.85
a. Miniature sheet of six 5.00 5.00
Nos. C424-C429 (6) 4.60 4.25

Issued to commemorate the opening of UNESCO (U. N. Educational, Scientific and Cultural Organization) Headquarters in Paris, Nov. 3.
No. C429a contains one each of Nos. C424-C429.

Type of Regular Issue, 1959 and

Nicaraguan, Papal and U. S. Flags
AP60

Designs: 35c, Pope John XXIII and Cardinal Spellman. 1 cor, Spellman coat of arms. 1.05 cor, Cardinal Spellman. 1.50 cor, Human rosary and Cardinal (horiz.). 2 cor, Cardinal with Ruben Dario order.

1959, Nov. 26 *Perf. 12½*

C430 AP60 30c violet blue, yellow & red 10 10
C431 A83 35c deep orange & greenish black 12 12
C432 " 1cor yellow, blue & carmine 35 35
C433 " 1.05cor red, black & dark carmine 40 40
C434 " 1.50cor dark blue & yellow 45 45
C435 " 2cor multicolored 60 60
C436 AP60 5cor " 1.75 1.75
a. Miniature sheet of 7 4.00 4.00
Nos. C430-C436 (7) 3.77 3.77

Issued to commemorate the visit of Cardinal Spellman to Managua, Feb. 1958.
No. C436a contains one each of Nos. C430-C436, perf. or imperf. Size: 115x130mm.

Type of Lincoln Regular Issue and

AP61

1960, Jan. 21 **Engraved** **Unwmkd.**
Perf. 13x13½, 13½x13
Portrait in Black

C437 A84 30c indigo 10 8
C438 " 35c bright carmine 15 12
C439 " 70c plum 30 30
C440 " 1.05cor emerald 45 45
C441 " 1.50cor violet 60 60
C442 AP61 5cor intense black & bistre 1.75 1.75
a. Souvenir sheet of six 4.00 4.00
Nos. C437-C442 (6) 3.35 3.30

Issued to commemorate the 150th anniversary of the birth of Abraham Lincoln.
No. C442a contains one each of Nos. C437-C442, imperf. with black Nicaragua coat of arms and Spanish Lincoln quotation in margin. Size: 152x116 mm.

Nos. C343, C370 and C318 Overprinted: "X Aniversario Club Filatelico S.J.—C.R."

1960, July 4 **Engraved**

C443 AP49 2cor magenta 1.00 80
C444 AP54 2.50cor dk. ultra. 1.00 90
C445 AP45 3cor green 1.25 1.25

Issued to commemorate the 10th anniversary of the Philatelic Club of San Jose, Costa Rica.

Nos. C437-C442 Overprinted in Red ✠ Resello

Perf. 13x13½, 13½x13

1960, Sept. 19 **Unwmkd.**
Center in Black

C446 A84 30c indigo 30 25
C447 " 35c brt. carmine 25 15
C448 " 70c plum 25 25
C449 " 1.05cor emerald 35 35
C450 " 1.50cor violet 55 50
C451 AP61 5cor intense black & bistre 1.65 1.65
Nos. C446-C451 (6) 3.35 3.15

Issued for the Red Cross to aid earthquake victims in Chile. The overprint on No. C451 is horizontal and always inverted.

People and World Refugee Year Emblem
AP62

Design: 5cor, Crosses, globe and WRY emblem.

1961, Jan. 2 **Litho.** *Perf. 11x11½*

C452 AP62 2cor multicolored 90 90
C453 " 5cor " 2.00 2.00
a. Souv. sheet of 2 5.00 5.00

Issued to commemorate World Refugee Year, July 1, 1959-June 30, 1960.
No. C453a contains one each of Nos. C452-C453 with blue marginal inscription. Size: 101x71mm.

Consular Service Stamps Surcharged "Correo Aéreo" and New Denomination in Red, Black or Blue

AP63

Engraved

1961, Feb. 21 *Perf. 12* **Unwmkd.**
Red Marginal Number

C454 AP63 20c on 50c deep blue (R) 15 12
C455 " 20c on 1cor greenish black (R) 15 12
C456 " 20c on 2cor green (R) 15 12
C457 " 20c on 3cor dark carmine 15 12
C458 " 20c on 5cor orange (Bl) 15 12
C459 " 20c on 10cor violet (R) 15 12
C460 " 20c on 20cor red brown (R) 15 12
C461 " 20c on 50cor brown (R) 15 12
C462 " 20c on 100cor magenta 15 12
Nos. C454-C462 (9) 1.35 1.08

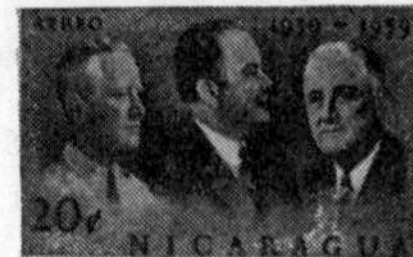

Charles L. Mullins, Anastasio Somoza and Franklin D. Roosevelt—AP64

Standard Bearers with Flags of Nicaragua and Academy
AP65

Designs: 25c, 70c, Flags of Nicaragua and Academy. 30c, 1.05cor, Directors of Academy: Fred T. Cruse, LeRoy Bartlett, Jr., John F. Greco, Anastasio Somoza Debayle, Francisco Boza, Elias Monge. 40c, 2cor, Academy Emblem. 45c, 5cor, Anastasio Somoza Debayle and Luis Somoza Debayle.

Perf. 11x11½, 11½x11

1961, Feb. 24 **Litho.** **Unwmkd.**

C463 AP64 20c rose lilac, gray & buff 10 8
C464 AP65 25c blue, red & black 15 15
C465 AP64 30c blue, gray & yellow 12 10
C466 AP65 35c multi. 15 12
C467 " 40c " 18 15
C468 AP64 45c pink, gray & buff 15 15
a. Miniature sheet of 6 1.10 1.10
C469 AP64 60c brn., gray & buff 20 20
C470 AP65 70c multi. 30 30
C471 AP64 1.05cor lilac, gray & yellow 40 40
C472 AP65 1.50cor multi. 50 50
C473 " 2cor " 70 65
C474 AP64 5cor gray & buff 1.75 1.75
a. Miniature sheet of 6 5.00 5.00
Nos. C463-C474 (12) 4.70 4.55

Issued to commemorate the 20th anniversary (in 1959) of the founding of the Military Academy of Nicaragua.
No. C468a contains one each of Nos. C463-C468, imperf. No. C474a contains one each of Nos. C469-C474, imperf. Size: 160x100mm.
In 1977, Nos. C468a and C474a were overprinted in black: "1927-1977 50 ANIVERSARIO / Guardia Nacional de Nicaragua." Price, $4.

Emblem of Junior Chamber of Commerce
AP66

Designs: 2c, 15c, Globe showing map of Americas (horiz.). 4c, 35c, Globe and initials (horiz.). 5c, 70c, Chamber credo. 6c, 1.05cor, Handclasp. 10c, 5cor, Regional map.

Perf. 11x11½, 11½x11

1961, May 16 **Unwmkd.**

C475 AP66 2c multicolored 5 5
C476 " 3c yellow & black 5 5
C477 " 4c multicolored 5 5
C478 " 5c crimson & black 5 5
C479 " 6c brown, yellow & black 5 5
C480 " 10c red orange, black & blue 6 6
C481 " 15c blue, black & green 6 6
C482 " 30c blue & black 10 10
C483 " 35c multicolored 15 12
C484 " 70c yellow, black & crimson 30 25

C485 AP66 1.05cor multicolored 45 40
C486 " 5cor " 1.65 1.65
Nos. C475-C486 (12) 3.02 2.89

Issued to commemorate the 13th Regional Congress of the Junior Chamber of Commerce of Nicaragua and the International Junior Chamber of Commerce.

The imperforates of Nos. C475-C486 were not authorized.

Rigoberto Cabezas
AP67

Map of Mosquito Territory and View of Cartago—AP68

Designs: 45c, Newspaper. 70c, Building. 2cor, Cabezas quotation. 10cor, Map of lower Nicaragua with Masaya area.

1961, Aug. 29 Litho. *Perf. 13½*

C487 AP67 20c orange & dk. blue 12 12
C488 AP68 40c lt. blue & claret 25 25
C489 " 45c citron & brown 20 20
C490 " 70c beige & grn. 30 25
C491 " 2cor pink & dk. blue 80 55
C492 " 10cor greenish blue & claret 3.50 3.50
Nos. C487-C492 (6) 5.17 4.87

Issued to commemorate the centenary of the birth of Rigoberto Cabezas, who acquired the Mosquito Territory (Atlantic Littoral) for Nicaragua.

No. C253 Overprinted in Red: "Convención Filatélica-Centro-América-Panama-San Salvador-27 Julio 1961."

1961, Aug. 23 Engr. *Perf. 12½*

C493 AP22 1.25cor multi. 85 85
a. Invtd. ovpt. 150.00

Central American Philatelic Convention, San Salvador, July 27.

Nos. C424-C429 Overprinted in Red: "Homenaje a Hammarskjold Sept. 18—1961"

1961 Lithographed *Perf. 11½*

C494 AP59 60c bright pink & blue 50 50
C495 " 75c green & red brown 55 55
C496 " 90c light brown & green 60 60
C497 " 1cor ultramarine & br. pink 65 65
C498 " 3cor gray & orange 1.25 1.25
C499 " 5cor rose lilac & dark blue 3.50 3.50
Nos. C494-C499 (6) 7.05 7.05

Issued in memory of Dag Hammarskjold, Secretary General of the United Nations, 1953-61.

RESELLO

Nos. C314 and C440 Surcharged in Red:

₡ 1.00

Engraved

1962, Jan. 20 *Perf. 13x13½, 13*

C500 A84 1cor on 1.05 cor emerald 40 35
C501 AP44 1cor on 1.10 cor black & chestnut brown 40 35

UNESCO Emblem and Crowd
AP69

Design: 5cor, UNESCO and U.N. Emblems.

Photogravure

1962, Feb. 26 *Perf. 12* Unwmkd.

C502 AP69 2cor multicolored 70 65
C503 " 5cor " 1.65 1.65
a. Souv. sheet of 2 2.50 2.50

Issued to commemorate the 15th anniversary (in 1961) of UNESCO (U.N. Educational, Scientific and Cultural Organization).

No. C503a contains one each of Nos. C502-C503, imperf., with black marginal inscription. Size: 90x65mm.

Nos. C480 and C483-C486 Overprinted

Perf. 11x11½, 11½x11

1962, July Lithographed

C504 AP66 10c red orange, blk. & blue 45 40
C505 " 35c multi. 60 40
C506 " 70c yel., blk. & crimson 75 60
C507 " 1.05cor multi. 1.00 90
C508 " 5cor " 1.75 2.75
Nos. C504-C508 (5) 4.55 5.05

Issued for the World Health Organization drive to eradicate malaria.

Souvenir Sheet

Stamps and Postmarks of 1862
AP69a

1962, Sept. 9 Litho. *Imperf.*

C509 AP69a 7cor multicolored 5.00 5.00

Issued to commemorate the centenary of Nicaraguan postage stamps. Size: 85x95mm.

Arms Type of Regular Issue, 1962.

Coats of Arms: 30c, Nueva Segovia. 50c, León. 1cor, Managua. 2cor, Granada. 5cor, Rivas.

1962, Nov. 22 *Perf. 12½x13*

Arms in Original Colors; Black Inscriptions.

C510 A86 30c rose 10 8
C511 " 50c salmon 15 12
C512 " 1cor light green 30 25
C513 " 2cor gray 65 55
C514 " 5cor light blue 1.65 1.50
Nos. C510-C514 (5) 2.85 2.50

Liberty Bell
AP70

1963, May 15 Litho. *Perf. 13x12*

C515 AP70 30c lt. bl., blk. & olive bister 20 8

Issued to commemorate the sesquicentennial of the first Nicaraguan declaration of Independence (in 1961).

Paulist Brother Comforting Boy
AP71

Map of Central America
AP72

Designs: 60c, Nun comforting girl. 2cor, St. Vincent de Paul and St. Louisa de Marillac (horiz.).

1963, May 15 Photo. *Perf. 13½*

C516 AP71 60c gray & ocher 20 15
C517 " 1cor salmon & blk. 35 30
C518 " 2cor crimson & blk. 70 65

Issued to commemorate the 300th anniversary of the deaths of St. Vincent de Paul and St. Louisa de Marillac (in 1960).

Lithographed and Engraved

1963, Aug. 2 *Perf. 12* Unwmkd.

C519 AP72 1cor blue & yel. 40 30

Issued to honor the Federation of Central American Philatelic Societies.

Cross over World
AP73

Wheat and Map of Nicaragua
AP74

1963, Aug. 6

C520 AP73 20c yellow & red 15 8

Issued to commemorate Vatican II, the 21st Ecumenical Council of the Roman Catholic Church.

1963, Aug. 6

Design: 25c, Dead tree on parched earth.

C521 AP74 10c lt. grn. & green 10 8
C522 " 25c yel. & dk. brn. 15 10

Issued for the "Freedom from Hunger" campaign of the U.N. Food and Agriculture Organization.

Boxing
AP75

Flags of Central American States
AP75a

Lithographed and Engraved

1963, Dec. 12 *Perf. 12* Unwmkd.

Multicolored

C523 AP75 2c *shown* 5 5
C524 " 3c *Running* 5 5
C525 " 4c *Underwater fishing* 10 6
C526 " 5c *Soccer* 10 6
C527 " 6c *Baseball* 15 8
C528 " 10c *Tennis* 25 8
C529 " 15c *Bicycling* 25 10
C530 " 20c *Motorcycling* 25 10
C531 " 35c *Chess* 40 15
C532 " 60c *Deep-sea fishing* 50 25
C533 " 1cor *Table tennis* 75 50
C534 " 2cor *Basketball* 1.25 75
C535 " 5cor *Golf* 3.50 2.00
Nos. C523-C535 (13) 7.60 4.23

Publicizing the 1964 Olympic Games.

Central American Independence Issue

1964, Sept. 15 Litho. *Perf. 13x13½*

Size: 27x43mm.

C536 AP75a 40c multicolored 20 15

Nos. C479, C430, C437 and C416 Surcharged in Black or Red

Resello ₡ 0.15
a

RESELLO ₡ 0.20
b

1964 Litho. *Perf. 11½x11*

C537 AP66 5c on 6c brown, yel. & blk. 50 8

Perf. 12½

C538 AP60 10c on 30c vio. bl., yel. & red 1.00 10

Engr. *Perf. 13x13½*

C539 A84 15c on 30 indigo & black (R) 1.25 12

Photo. *Perf. 14*

C539A A81 20c on 30c blue, car. & yellow 20 10

Floating Red Cross Station
AP76

Designs: 5c, Alliance for Progress emblem (vert.). 15c, Highway. 20c, Plowing with tractors, and sun. 25c, Housing development. 30c, Presidents Somoza and Kennedy and World Bank Chairman Eugene Black. 35c, Adult education. 40c, Smokestacks.

1964, Oct. 15 Litho. *Perf. 12*

C540 AP76 5c yel., brt. bl., grn. & gray 8 5
C541 " 10c multicolored 10 6
C542 " 15c " 10 5
C543 " 20c orge. brown, yel. & blk. 12 6
C544 " 25c multicolored 15 10
C545 " 30c dk. bl., black & brown 20 10
C546 " 35c lilac rose, dk. red & black 25 15

C547 AP76 40c dp. carmine, blk. & yel. 30 20
Nos. C540-C547 (8) 1.30 77

Alliance for Progress.

Map of Central America and Central American States
AP77

Designs (Map of Central America and): 25c, Grain. 40c, Cogwheels. 50c, Heads of cattle.

1964, Nov. 30 Litho. *Perf. 12*

C548 AP77 15c ultra. & multi. 6 6
C549 " 25c multicolored 10 8
C550 " 40c " 15 12
C551 " 50c " 20 15

Central American Common Market.

Nos. C523-C525, C527 and C533-C534 Overprinted:
"OLIMPIADAS / TOKYO — 1964"

Lithographed and Engraved

1964, Dec. 19 *Perf. 12* Unwmkd.

C553 AP75 2c multicolored 6 6
C554 " 3c " 6 6
C555 " 4c " 6 6
C556 " 6c " 6 6
C557 " 1cor " 2.00 2.00
C558 " 2cor " 4.00 4.00
Nos. C553-C558 (6) 6.24 6.24

18th Olympic Games, Tokyo, Oct. 10-25.

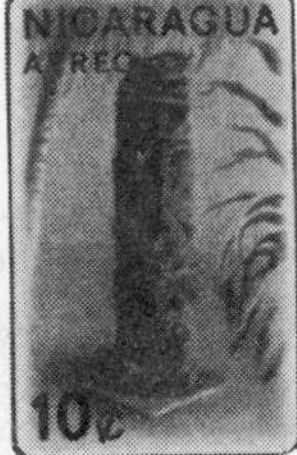

Blood Transfusion AP78 **Stele AP79**

Designs: 20c, Volunteers and priest rescuing wounded man. 40c, Landscape during storm. 10cor, Red Cross over map of Nicaragua.

1965, Jan. 28 Litho. *Perf. 12*

C559 AP78 20c yel., blk. & red 10 8
C560 " 25c red, black & olive bister 15 12
C561 " 40c grn., blk. & red 20 15
C562 " 10cor multicolored 4.00 4.00

Issued to commemorate the centenary (in 1963) of the International Red Cross.

Perf. 13½x13, 13x13½

1965, Mar. 24 Litho. Unwmkd.

Black Margin and Inscription

Antique Indian artifacts: 5c, Three jadeite statuettes (horiz.). 15c, Dog (horiz.). 20c, Talamanca pendant. 25c, Decorated pottery bowl and vase (horiz.). 30c, Stone pestle and mortar on animal base. 35c, Three statuettes (horiz.). 40c, Idol on animal pedestal. 50c, Decorated pottery bowl and vase. 60c, Vase and metate (tripod bowl; horiz.). 1cor, Metate.

C563 AP79 5c yel. & multi. 5 5
C564 " 10c multicolored 5 5
C565 " 15c " 5 5
C566 " 20c salmon & dk. brown 6 6
C567 " 25c lilac & multi. 8 8
C568 " 30c lt. grn. & multi. 10 8
C569 " 35c multicolored 10 8
C570 " 40c citron & multi. 15 8
C571 " 50c ocher & multi. 20 10
C572 AP79 60c multicolored 30 12
C573 " 1cor car. & multi. 60 20
Nos. C563-C573 (11) 1.74 95

Pres. John F. Kennedy
AP80

Photogravure & Lithographed

1965, Apr. 28 *Perf. 12½x13½*

C574 AP80 35c black & brt. green 20 12
C575 " 75c black & brt. pink 35 20
C576 " 1.10cor blk. & dk. bl. 50 35
C577 " 2cor black & yel. brn. 1.25 75
Set of 4 souvenir sheets 10.00 10.00

Issued in memory of Pres. John F. Kennedy (1917-63). Nos. C574-C577 each exist in separate imperf. souvenir sheets, each containing one imperf. block of four. Black marginal inscription. Size: 88x115 mm.

Andrés Bello
AP81

1965, Oct. 15 Litho. *Perf. 14*

C578 AP81 10c dark brown & red brn. 6 6
C579 " 15c indigo & lt. bl. 8 8
C580 " 45c black & dull lilac 15 12
C581 " 80c blk. & yel. grn. 25 20
C582 " 1cor dk. brn. & yel. 35 30
C583 " 2cor black & gray 65 60
Nos. C578-C583 (6) 1.54 1.36

Issued to commemorate the centenary of the death of Andrés Bello (1780?-1864), Venezuelan writer and educator.

Winston Churchill AP82 **Pope John XXIII AP83**

Winston Churchill: 35c, 1cor, Broadcasting (horiz.). 60c, 3cor, On military inspection. 75c, As young officer.

1966, Feb. 7 *Perf. 14* Unwmkd.

C584 AP82 20c cerise & black 10 8
C585 " 35c dk. olive grn. & black 15 12
C586 " 60c brown & black 25 20
C587 " 75c rose red 30 25
C588 " 1cor violet black 40 35
C589 " 2cor lilac & black 85 75
a. Souv. sheet of 4 2.25 2.25
C590 " 3cor indigo & blk. 1.25 1.10
Nos. C584-C590 (7) 3.30 2.85

Issued in memory of Sir Winston Spencer Churchill (1874-1965), statesman and World War II leader. No. C589a contains four imperf. stamps similar to Nos. C586-C589 with simulated perforations. Rose red border, black inscription and green emblems in margin. Size: 99x95mm.

1966, Dec. 15 Litho. *Perf. 13*

Designs: 35c, Pope Paul VI. 1cor, Archbishop Gonzalez y Robleto. 2cor, St. Peter's, Rome. 3cor, Arms of Pope John XXIII and St. Peter's.

C591 AP83 20c multicolored 10 10
C592 " 35c " 15 15
C593 " 1cor " 42 35
C594 " 2cor " 85 70
C595 " 3cor " 1.25 1.00
Nos. C591-C595 (5) 2.77 2.30

Issued to commemorate the closing of the Ecumenical Council, Vatican II.

RESELLO

Nos. C571-C572 Surcharged in Red

₡ 0.10

1967 *Perf. 13x13½, 13½x13*

C596 AP79 10c on 50c multi. 6 6
C597 " 15c on 60c " 8 6

Rubén Dario and Birthplace—AP84

Portrait and: 10c, Monument, Managua. 20c, Leon Cathedral, site of Dario's tomb. 40c, Centaurs. 75c, Swans. 1cor, Roman triumphal march. 2cor, St. Francis and the Wolf. 5cor, "Faith" defeating "Death."

1967, Jan. 18 Litho. *Perf. 13*

C598 AP84 5c lt. brown, tan & black 5 5
C599 " 10c org., pale org. & black 6 6
C600 " 20c vio., lt. blue & black 8 6
C601 " 40c grn., dk. grn. & black 20 12
a. Souv. sheet of 4 75 75
C602 " 75c ultra., pale bl. & black 30 25
C603 " 1cor red, pale red & black 35 30
C604 " 2cor rose pink, car. & black 65 55
C605 " 5cor dp. ultra., vio. bl., & blk. 1.50 1.35
a. Souv. sheet of 4 6.00 6.00
Nos. C598-C605 (8) 3.19 2.74

Issued to commemorate the centenary of the birth of Rubén Dario (pen name of Felix Rubén Garcia Sarmiento, 1867-1916), poet, newspaper correspondent and diplomat.

No. C601a contains one each of Nos. C598-C601; No. C605a contains one each of Nos. C602-C605. Black and red inscription and light blue border. Size: 130x107mm. Sheets were issued perf. and imperf.

Megalura Peleus—AP85

Designs: Various butterflies. 5c, 10c, 30c, 35c, 50c and 1cor are vertical.

1967, Apr. 20 Litho. *Perf. 14*

C606 AP85 5c multicolored 5 5
C607 " 10c " 8 6
C608 " 15c " 8 6
C609 " 20c " 8 6
C610 " 25c " 10 8
C611 " 30c " 12 8
C612 AP85 35c multicolored 15 10
C613 " 40c " 18 12
C614 " 50c " 22 15
C615 " 60c " 25 18
C616 " 1cor " 45 30
C617 " 2cor " 80 60
Nos. C606-C617 (12) 2.56 1.84

Com. James McDivitt and Maj. Edward H. White—AP86

Gemini 4 Space Flight: 10c, 40c, Rocket launching and astronauts. 15c, 75c, Edward H. White walking in space. 20c, 1cor, Recovery of capsule.

1967, Sept. 20 Litho. *Perf. 13*

C618 AP86 5c red & multi. 6 6
C619 " 10c orange & multi. 8 8
C620 " 15c multicolored 8 8
C621 " 20c " 10 10
C622 " 35c olive & multi. 12 12
C623 " 40c ultra. & multi. 15 15
C624 " 75c brn. & multi. 30 30
C625 " 1cor multicolored 35 35
Nos. C618-C625 (8) 1.24 1.24

Saquanjoche, National Flower of Nicaragua AP87 **Presidents of Nicaragua and Mexico AP88**

National Flowers: No. C626, White nun orchid, Guatemala. No. C627, Rose, Honduras. No. C629, Maquilishuat, Salvador. No. C630, Purple guaria orchid, Costa Rica.

1967, Nov. 22 Litho. *Perf. 13½*

C626 AP87 40c multicolored 18 10
C627 " 40c " 18 10
C628 " 40c " 18 10
C629 " 40c " 18 10
C630 " 40c " 18 10
Nos. C626-C630 (5) 90 50

Issued to commemorate the 5th anniversary of the General Treaty for Central American Economic Integration. Nos. C626-C630 are printed se-tenant in horizontal rows of 5 in sheet of 25 (5x5). Sheet has marginal inscription and control number. Price $5.

1968, Feb. 28 Litho. *Perf. 12½*

Designs: 40c Pres. Gustavo Diáz Ordaz of Mexico and Pres. René Schick of Nicaragua signing statement (horiz.). 1cor, President Diáz.

C631 AP88 20c black 14 6
C632 " 40c slate green 25 10
C633 " 1cor deep brown 45 25

Issued to commemorate the visit of the President of Mexico, Gustavo Diáz Ordaz.

Nos. C479, C527, C242, C440 and C434 Surcharged "Resello" and New Value in Black, Red or Yellow

1968, May Lithographed; Engraved

C634 AP66 5c on 6c multi. 5
C635 AP75 5c on 6c " 5 5
C636 AP20 5c on 8c blk. brn. 5 5
C637 A84 1cor on 1.05cor emerald & black (R) 30 25
C638 A83 1cor on 1.50cor dk. blue & yel. (Y) 30 25
Nos. C634-C638 (5) 75 65

Mangos
AP89

1968, May 15 Litho. *Perf. 14*

Multicolored

C639	AP89	5c *shown*	4	4
C640	"	10c *Pineapples*	5	5
C641	"	15c *Orange*	6	6
C642	"	20c *Papaya*	10	8
C643	"	30c *Bananas*	12	10
C644	"	35c *Avocado*	15	10
C645	"	50c *Watermelon*	20	12
C646	"	75c *Cashews*	35	20
C647	"	1cor *Sapodilla*	50	30
C648	"	2cor *Cacao*	1.00	60
		Nos. C639–C648 (10)	2.57	1.65

The Last Judgment, by Michelangelo
AP90

Paintings: 10c, The Crucifixion, by Fra Angelo (horiz.). 35c, Madonna with Child and St. John, by Raphael. 2cor, The Disrobing of Christ, by El Greco. 3cor, The Immaculate Conception, by Murillo. 5cor, Christ of St. John of the Cross, by Salvador Dali.

1968, July 22 Litho. *Perf. 12½*

C649	AP90	10c gold & multi.	8	8
C650	"	15c " "	10	10
C651	"	35c " "	18	15
C652	"	2cor " "	90	80
C653	"	3cor " "	1 25	1.10
		Nos. C649–C653 (5)	2.51	2.23

Miniature Sheet

C654	AP90	5cor gold & multi.	4.50	4.50

No. C654 contains one stamp, black marginal inscription and control number on the back. Size: 100x80mm.

Nos. C649–C652 Overprinted:
"Visita de S.S. Paulo VI
C.E. de Bogota 1968"

1968, Oct. 25 Litho. *Perf. 12½*

C655	AP90	10c gold & multi.	7	7
C656	"	15c " "	8	8
C657	"	35c " "	12	10
C658	"	2cor " "	75	65

Issued to commemorate the visit of Pope Paul VI to Bogota, Colombia, Aug. 22–24. The overprint has 3 lines on the 10c stamp and 5 lines on others.

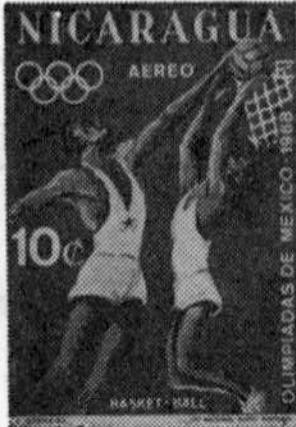

Basketball
AP91

Sports: 15c, Fencing (horiz.). 20c, Diving. 35c, Running. 50c, Hurdling (horiz.). 75c, Weight lifting. 1cor, Boxing (horiz.). 2cor, Soccer.

1968, Nov. 28 Litho. *Perf. 14*

C659	AP91	10c multicolored	5	4
C660	"	15c orange red, blk. & gray	5	5
C661	"	20c multicolored	10	5
C662	"	35c "	12	8
C663	"	50c "	18	10
C664	"	75c "	30	20
C665	"	1cor yel. & multi.	50	25
C666	"	2cor gray & multi.	1.25	50
		a. Souv. sheet of 4	2.75	2.75
		Nos. C659–C666 (8)	2.55	1.27

Issued to commemorate the 19th Olympic Games, Mexico City, Oct. 12–27. No. C666a contains one each of Nos. C663–C666, Marginal inscription and blue border. Size: 100x119mm.

Cichlasoma Citrinellum—AP92

Fish: 15c, Cichlasoma nicaraguensis. 20c, Carp. 30c, Gar (lepisosteus tropicus). 35c, Swordfish. 50c, Phylipnus dormitor (vert.). 75c, Tarpon atlanticus (vert.). 1cor, Eulamia nicaraguensis (vert.). 2cor, Sailfish (vert.). 3cor, Sawfish (vert.).

Perf. 13½x13, 13x13½

1969, Mar. 12 Lithographed

C667	AP92	10c vio. bl. & multi.	4	4
C668	"	15c orange & multi.	5	5
C669	"	20c green & multi.	6	5
C670	"	30c pur. & multi.	13	8
C671	"	35c yel. & multi.	13	8
C672	"	50c brn. & multi.	20	10
C673	"	75c ultra. & multi.	25	18
C674	"	1cor org. & multi.	40	20
C675	"	2cor dk. bl. & multi.	80	50
C676	"	3cor multicolored	1.25	85
		a. Min. sheet of 4	2.50	2.50
		Nos. C667–C676 (10)	3.31	2.13

No. C676a contains one each of Nos. C673–C676. Size: 82x136mm.

Nos. C544, C549, C567 and C439
Surcharged in Black or Red

RESELLO
C$ 0.10

Lithographed

1969, Mar. *Perf. 12, 13½x13*

C677	AP76	10c on 25c multi.	5	5
C678	AP77	10c on 25c "	5	5
C679	AP79	15c on 25c "	5	5

Engraved

C680	A84	50c on 70c plum & black (R)	15	12

Size of 50c surcharge: 11½x9mm.

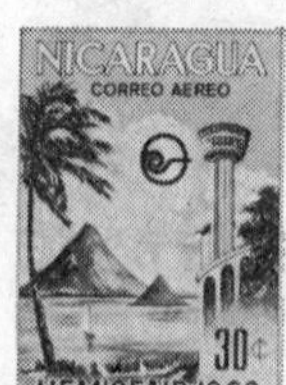

View, Exhibition Tower and Emblem
AP93

1969, May 30 Litho. *Perf. 13½x13*

C681	AP93	30c dk. violet blue & red	10	8
C682	"	35c black & red	12	10
C683	"	75c car. rose & violet blue	20	18
C684	"	1cor deep plum & black	40	25
C685	"	2cor dk. brn. & blk.	75	55
		a. Souv. sheet of 4	2.50	2.50
		Nos. C681–C685 (5)	1.57	1.16

Issued to commemorate the HEMISFAIR 1968 Exhibition. No. C685a contains one each of Nos. C681–C682, C684–C685. Multicolored margin with inscription and coat of Arms. Size: 75x111mm.

Nos. C410, C482, C567–C569, C399,
C465, C546 Surcharged in Black or Red

RESELLO
C$ 0.20

Perf. 14, 11x11½, 13½x13, 13x13½, 12

1969 Lithographed

C686	A80	10c on 30c multi.	4	4
C687	AP66	10c on 30c bl. & black (R)	4	4
C688	AP79	10c on 25c multi.	4	4
C689	"	10c on 30c "	4	4
C690	"	15c on 35c " (R)	4	4
C691	A79	20c on 30c "	6	6
C692	AP64	20c on 30c "	6	6
C693	AP76	20c on 35c "	6	6
		Nos. C686–C693 (8)	38	38

Fishing
AP94

Products of Nicaragua: 5c, Minerals (miner). 15c, Bananas. 20c, Timber (truck). 35c, Coffee. 40c, Sugar cane. 60c, Cotton. 75c, Rice and corn. 1cor, Tobacco. 2cor, Meat.

1969, Sept. 22 Litho. *Perf. 13x13½*

C694	AP94	5c gold & multi.	5	3
C695	"	10c " "	5	3
C696	"	15c " "	6	4
C697	"	20c " "	9	6
C698	"	35c " "	13	8
C699	"	40c " "	18	10
C700	"	60c " "	25	12
C701	"	75c " "	30	18
C702	"	1cor " "	40	25
C703	"	2cor " "	85	50
		Nos. C694–C703 (10)	2.36	1.39

Woman Carrying Jar, Conference Emblem
AP95

1970, Feb. 26 Litho. *Perf. 13½x14*

C704	AP95	10c multicolored	3	3
C705	"	15c green & multi.	6	4
C706	"	20c ultra. & multi.	9	6
C707	"	35c multicolored	12	8
C708	"	50c "	20	10
C709	"	75c "	25	18
C710	"	1cor lilac & multi.	45	25
C711	"	2cor multicolored	85	50
		Nos. C704–C711 (8)	2.05	1.24

Issued to publicize the 8th Inter-American Conference on Savings and Loans.

Soccer Type of Regular Issue and

Flags of Participating Nations, World Cup, 1970
AP96

Soccer Players: 20c, Djalma Santos, Brazil. 80c, Billy Wright, England. 4cor, Jozef Bozsik, Hungary. 5cor, Bobby Charlton, England.

1970, May 11 Litho. *Perf. 13½*

C712	A87	20c multicolored	15	10
C713	"	80c "	25	20
C714	AP96	1cor "	30	25
C715	A87	4cor "	1.25	1.00
C716	"	5cor "	1.50	1.25
		Nos. C712–C716 (5)	3.45	2.80

Issued to honor the winners of the 1970 poll for the International Soccer Hall of Fame. No. C714 also publicizes the 9th World Soccer Championships for the Jules Rimet Cup, Mexico City, May 30–June 21, 1970.

Names of players and their achievements printed in black on back of stamps.

EXPO Emblem, Mt. Fuji and Torii
AP97

1970, July 5 Litho. *Perf. 13½x14*

C717	AP97	25c multi.	10	6
C718	"	30c "	15	8
C719	"	35c "	15	8
C720	"	75c "	30	18
C721	"	1.50cor "	55	38
C722	"	3cor "	1.00	75
		a. Souvenir sheet of 3	2.00	2.00
		Nos. C717–C722 (6)	2.25	1.53

Issued to publicize EXPO '70 International Exhibition, Osaka, Japan, Mar. 15–Sept. 13, 1970. No. C722a contains 3 imperf. stamps similar to Nos. C720–C722, gray margin with commemorative inscription and red control number. Size: 108½x78½mm.

Moon Landing, Apollo 11 Emblem and Nicaragua Flag
AP98

Designs (Apollo 11 Emblem, Nicaragua Flag and): 40c, 75c, Moon surface and landing capsule. 60c, 1cor, Astronaut planting U.S. flag.

1970, Aug. 12 Litho. *Perf. 14*

C723	AP98	35c multicolored	15	8
C724	"	40c "	15	10
C725	"	60c pink & multi.	25	15
C726	"	75c yel. & multi.	30	18
C727	"	1 cor vio. & multi.	50	25
C728	"	2 cor org. & multi.	90	50
		Nos. C723–C728 (6)	2.25	1.26

Issued to commemorate man's first landing on the moon, July 20, 1969. See note after U.S. No. C76.

Franklin D. Roosevelt—AP99

Annunciation, by Matthias Grunewald AP100

Roosevelt Portraits: 15c, 1cor, as stamp collector. 20c, 50c, 2cor, Full face.

1970, Oct. 12

C729 AP99 10c black & bluish black 4 3
C730 " 15c blk. & brown violet 7 4
C731 " 20c black & olive green 8 5
C732 " 35c blk. & brown violet 13 8
C733 " 50c brown 18 12
C734 " 75c blue 28 18
C735 " 1cor rose red 37 25
C736 " 2cor black 75 50
Nos. C729–C736 (8) 1.90 1.25

Issued to commemorate the 25th anniversary of the death of Franklin Delano Roosevelt (1882–1945), 32nd president of the U.S.

1970, Dec. 1 Litho. *Perf. 14*

Paintings: No. C737, like 15c. No. C738, 20c, Nativity, by El Greco. No. C739, 35c, Adoration of the Magi, by Albrecht Dürer. No. C740, 75c, Virgin and Child, by J. van Hemessen. No. C741, 1cor, Holy Shepherd, Portuguese School, 16th century.

C737 AP100 10c multicolored 5 3
C738 " 10c " 5 3
C739 " 10c " 5 3
C740 " 10c " 5 3
C741 " 10c " 5 3
C742 " 15c " 8 4
C743 " 20c " 10 5
C744 " 35c " 17 8
C745 " 75c " 35 18
C746 " 1cor " 45 25
Nos. C737–C746 (10) 1.40 75

Christmas 1970. Nos. C737–C741 printed se-tenant.

RESELLO
C$ 0.15

Issues of 1947–1967 Surcharged

1971, March Multicolored

C747 A83 10c on 1.05cor (# C433) 10 8
C748 AP64 10c on 1.05cor (# C471) 10 8
C749 AP66 10c on 1.05cor (#C485) 10 8
C750 AP42 15c on 1.50cor (#C292) 15 10
C751 AP53 15c on 1.50cor (# C369) 15 10
C752 A83 15c on 1.50cor (# C434) 15 10
C753 A84 15c on 1.50cor (#C441) 15 10
C754 A75 20c on 85c (# C385) 15 10
C755 A81 20c on 85c (# C418) 15 10
C756 A81 25c on 90c (#C419) 20 15
C757 AP48 30c on 1.10cor (# C337) 20 15
C758 AP44 40c on 1.10cor (# C314) 25 20
C759 AP65 40c on 1.50cor (# C472) 25 20
C760 AP80 1cor on 1.10cor (#C576) 60 50
Nos. C747–C760 (14) 2.70 2.04

The arrangement of the surcharge differs on each stamp.

Mathematics Type of Regular Issue

Symbolic Designs of Scientific Formulae: 25c, Napier's law (logarithms). 30c, Pythagorean theorem (length of sides of right-angled triangle). 40c, Boltzman's equation (movement of gases). 1cor, Broglie's law (motion of particles of matter). 2cor, Archimedes' principle (displacement of mass).

1971, May 15 Litho. *Perf. 13½*

C761 A88 25c lt. blue & multi. 10 8
C762 " 30c " " " 10 8
C763 " 40c " " " 15 14
C764 " 1cor " " " 40 25
C765 " 2cor " " " 75 50
Nos. C761–C765 (5) 1.50 1.05

Mathematical equations which changed the world. On the back of each stamp is a descriptive paragraph.

Montezuma Oropendola AP101

Birds: 15c, Turquoise-browed motmot. 20c, Magpie-jay. 25c, Scissor-tailed flycatchers. 30c, Spot-breasted oriole (horiz.). 35c, Rufous-naped wren. 40c, Great kiskadee. 75c, Red-legged honeycreeper (horiz.). 1cor, Great-tailed grackle (horiz.). 2cor, Belted kingfisher.

1971, Oct. 15 Litho. *Perf. 14*

C766 AP101 10c multicolored 5 3
C767 " 15c " 7 4
C768 " 20c gray & multi. 10 5
C769 " 25c multicolored 12 6
C770 " 30c " 14 6
C771 " 35c " 17 8
C772 " 40c " 18 10
C773 " 75c yel. & multi. 37 18
C774 " 1cor org. & multi. 45 25
C775 " 2cor multicolored 95 50
Nos. C766–C775 (10) 2.60 1.35

Ten Commandments Type of Regular Issue

Designs: 1cor, Bathsheba at her Bath, by Rembrandt (IX). 2cor, Naboth's Vineyard, by James Smetham (X).

1971, Nov. 1 *Perf. 11*

C776 A90 1cor ocher & multi. 30 25
C777 " 2cor " " 55 50

Descriptive inscriptions printed in gray on back of stamps.

U Thant, Anastasio Somoza, U.N. Emblem AP102

1972, Feb. 15 *Perf. 14x13½*

C778 AP102 10c pink & maroon 5 3
C779 " 15c green 7 3
C780 " 20c blue 8 4
C781 " 25c rose claret 12 6
C782 " 30c org. & brown 14 6
C783 " 40c gray & slate green 18 10
C784 " 1cor olive green 45 25
C785 " 2cor brown 90 50
Nos. C778–C785 (8) 1.99 1.07

25th anniversary of the United Nations (in 1970).

Nos. C713, C715, C716 Surcharged or Overprinted Like Nos. 899–900.

1972, Mar. 20 Litho. *Perf. 13½*

C786 A87 20c on 80c multi. 10 8
C787 " 60c on 4cor multi. 20 15
C788 " 5cor multi. 1.50 1.25

20th Olympic Games, Munich, Aug. 26–Sept. 11.

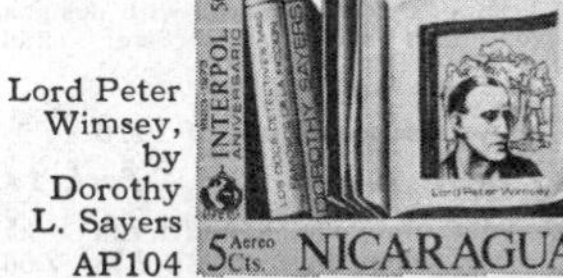

Ceramic, Figure, Map of Nicaragua AP103

Designs: Pre-Columbian ceramics (700–1200A.D.) found at sites indicated on map of Nicaragua.

1972, Sept. 16 Litho. *Perf. 14x13½*

C789 AP103 10c blue & multi. 5 3
C790 " 15c " " 5 4
C791 " 20c " " 10 5
C792 " 25c " " 10 6
C793 " 30c " " 10 6
C794 " 35c " " 10 8
C795 " 40c " " 15 10
C796 " 50c " " 15 12
C797 " 60c " " 20 13
C798 " 80c " " 25 20
C799 " 1cor " " 40 25
C800 " 2cor " " 75 50
Nos. C789–C800 (12) 2.40 1.62

Lord Peter Wimsey, by Dorothy L. Sayers AP104

Designs (Book and): 10c, Philip Marlowe, by Raymond Chandler. 15c, Sam Spade, by Dashiell Hammett. 20c, Perry Mason, by Erle S. Gardner. 25c, Nero Wolfe, by Rex Stout. 35c, Auguste Dupin, by Edgar Allan Poe. 40c, Ellery Queen, by Frederick Dannay and Manfred B. Lee. 50c, Father Brown, by G. K. Chesterton. 60c, Charlie Chan, by Earl Derr Biggers. 80c, Inspector Maigret, by Georges Simenon. 1cor, Hercule Poirot, by Agatha Christie. 2cor, Sherlock Holmes, by A. Conan Doyle.

1972, Nov. 13 Litho. *Perf. 14x13½*

C801 AP104 5c blue & multi. 3 3
C802 " 10c " " 3 3
C803 " 15c " " 4 4
C804 " 20c " " 6 5
C805 " 25c " " 7 6
C806 " 35c " " 10 8
C807 " 40c " " 11 10
C808 " 50c " " 14 12
C809 " 60c " " 16 13
C810 " 80c " " 23 20
C811 " 1cor " " 28 25
C812 " 2cor " " 56 50
Nos. C801–C812 (12) 1.81 1.59

50th anniversary of INTERPOL, international police organization. Designs show famous fictional detectives. Inscriptions on back, printed on top of gum, give thumbnail sketch of character and author.

Shepherds Following Star AP105

Legend of the Christmas Rose: 15c, Adoration of the kings and shepherds. 20c, Shepherd girl alone crying. 35c, Angel appears to girl. 40c, Christmas rose (Helleborus niger). 60c, Girl thanks angel. 80c, Girl and Holy Family. 1cor, Girl presents rose to Christ Child. 2cor, Adoration.

1972, Dec. 20

C813 AP105 10c gold & multi. 3 3
C814 " 15c " " 4 4
C815 " 20c " " 6 5
C816 " 35c " " 10 8
C817 " 40c " " 11 10
C818 " 60c " " 16 13
C819 " 80c " " 23 20
C820 " 1cor " " 28 25
C821 AP105 2cor gold & multi. 56 50
a. Souvenir sheet of 9 2.00 2.00
Nos. C813–C821 (9) 1.57 1.38

Christmas 1972. No. C821a contains one each of Nos. C813–C821. Legend of the Christmas rose in margin. Size: 131½x133mm.

No. C821a exists with red marginal overprint, "TERREMOTO DESASTRE," commemorating the Managua earthquake of Dec. 22–23, 1972. It was sold abroad, starting in January 1973.

Sir Walter Raleigh, Patent to Settle New World—AP106

Events and Quotations from Contemporary Illustrations: 15c, Mayflower Compact, 1620. 20c, Acquittal of Peter Zenger, 1735 (vert.). 25c, William Pitt, 1766 (vert.). 30c, British revenue stamp for use in America No. RM31 (vert.). 35c, "Join or Die" serpent, 1768. 40c, Boston Massacre and State House, 1770 (vert.). 50c, Boston Tea Party and 3p coin, 1774. 60c, Patrick Henry, 1775 (vert.). 75c, Battle scene ("Our cause is just, our union is perfect," 1775). 80c, Declaration of Independence, 1776. 1cor, Liberty Bell, Philadelphia. 2cor, Seal of United States, 1782 (vert.).

1973, Feb. 22 Photo. *Perf. 13½*

C822 AP106 10c olive & multi. 5 5
C823 " 15c " " 5 5
C824 " 20c " " 10 10
C825 " 25c " " 10 10
C826 " 30c " " 10 10
C827 " 35c olive, gold & black 15 10
C828 " 40c olive & multi. 15 10
C829 " 50c " " 15 15
C830 " 60c " " 20 15
C831 " 75c " " 25 20
C832 " 80c " " 25 20
C833 " 1cor " " 40 25
C834 " 2cor " " 75 50
Nos. C822–C834 (13) 2.70 2.05

Inscriptions on back, printed on top of gum, give brief description of subject and event.

NICARAGUA AMIGA '72
XX CAMPEONATO MUNDIAL DE BEISBOL AFICIONADO

Baseball, Player and Map of Nicaragua AP107

1973, May 25 Litho. *Perf. 13½x14*

C835 AP107 15c lilac & multi. 5 4
C836 " 20c multicolored 10 5
C837 " 40c " 15 10
C838 " 10cor " 3.00 2.50
a. Souvenir sheet of 4 4.00 4.00

20th International Baseball Championships, Managua, Nov. 15–Dec. 5, 1972. No. C838a contains 4 stamps similar to Nos. C835–C838 with changed background colors (15c, olive; 20c, gray; 40c, lt. green; 10cor, lilac), and 5 labels with commemorative inscriptions and list of participating countries; gold margin. Size: 105x134mm.

Fashion Type of 1973

1973, July 26 Litho. *Perf. 13½*

Multicolored

C839 A91 10c *Lourdes, Nicaragua* 3 3
C840 " 15c *Halston, New York* 4 4
C841 " 20c *Pino Lancetti, Rome* 6 5
C842 " 35c *Madame Grés, Paris* 10 8

C843 A91 40c *Irene Galitzine, Rome* 11 10
C844 " 80c *Pedro Rodriguez, Barcelona* 22 20
a. Souvenir sheet of 9+3 labels 3.50 3.50
Nos. C839-C844 (6) 56 50

Gowns by famous designers, modeled by Nicaraguan women. Inscriptions on back printed on top of gum give description of gown in Spanish and English. No. C844a contains one each of Nos. 909-911, C839-C844, Perf. 11, and 3 labels showing orchids. Ocher margin with black inscription in four languages. Size: 170x 170mm.

Type of Air Post Semi-Postal Issue.

Design: 2cor, Pediatric surgery.

1973, Sept. 25

C845 SPAP1 2cor multi. 55 50
Nos. C845, CB1-CB11 (12) 2.25 2.01

Planned Children's Hospital. Inscription on back, printed on top of gum gives brief description of subject shown.

Certain unlisted issues of Nicaragua, starting in 1973, are mentioned and briefly described in "For the Record" at the back of this volume.

Flower Type of 1974

Wild Flowers and Cacti: 1 cor, Centrosema. 3 cor, Night-blooming cereus.

1974, June 11 Litho. *Perf. 14*

C854 A95 1cor green & multi. 28 25
C855 " 3cor " " 85 75

Animal Type of 1974

Designs: 3cor, Colorado deer. 5cor, Jaguar.

1974, Sept. 10 Litho. *Perf. 14½*

C857 A97 3cor multicolored 85 75
C858 " 5cor " 1.40 1.25

Wild animals from San Diego Zoo.

Christmas Type of 1974

Works of Michelangelo: 40c, Madonna of the Stairs. 80c, Pitti Madonna. 2cor, Pietà. 5cor, Self-portrait.

1974, Dec. 15

C859 A98 40c multicolored 12 10
C860 " 80c " 24 20
C861 " 2cor " 55 50
C862 " 5cor " 1.40 1.25

Christmas 1974 and 500th birth anniversary of Michelangelo Buonarroti (1475-1564). An imperf. souvenir sheet exists containing 2cor and 5cor stamps.

Opera Type of 1975

Opera Singers and Scores: 25c, Rosa Ponselle, Norma. 35c, Giuseppe de Luca, Rigoletto. 40c, Joan Sutherland, La Figlia del Reggimento. 50c, Ezio Pinza, Don Giovanni. 60c, Kirsten Flagstad, Tristan and Isolde. 80c, Maria Callas, Tosca. 2cor, Fyodor Chaliapin, Boris Godunov. 5cor, Enrico Caruso, La Juive.

1975, Jan. 22 *Perf. 14x13½*

C863 A99 25c green & multi. 10 6
C864 " 35c multicolored 10 8
C865 " 40c " 15 10
C866 " 50c org. & multi. 15 12
C867 " 60c rose & multi. 25 15
C868 " 80c lake & multi. 35 20
C869 " 2cor sepia & multi. 85 50
C870 " 5cor multicolored 2.00 1.25
a. Souvenir sheet of 3 3.50
Nos. C863-C870 (8) 3.95 2.46

Famous opera singers.

No. C870a contains one each of Nos. C869-C870 and a 1cor with design and colors of No. C868. Size: 134x117mm. Exists imperf.

Easter Type of 1975

Stations of the Cross: 40c, Jesus stripped of his clothes. 50c, Jesus nailed to the Cross. 80c, Jesus dies on the Cross. 1cor, Descent from the Cross. 5cor, Jesus laid in the tomb.

1975, Mar. 20 *Perf. 14½*

C871 A100 40c ultra. & multi. 12 10
C872 " 50c " " 15 12
C873 " 80c " " 24 20
C874 " 1cor " " 28 25
C875 " 5cor " " 1.40 1.25
Nos. C871-C875 (5) 2.19 1.92

Easter 1975.

American Bicentennial Type of 1975

Designs: 40c, Washington's Farewell, 1783. 50c, Washington Addressing Continental Congress by J. B. Stearns. 2cor, Washington Arriving for Inauguration. 5cor, Statue of Liberty and flags of 1776 and 1976. 40c, 50c, 2cor, horiz.

1975, Apr. 16 *Perf. 14*

C876 A101 40c tan & multi. 12 10
C877 " 50c " " 15 12
C878 " 2cor " " 55 50
C879 " 5cor " " 1.40 1.25

American Bicentennial. 7cor perf. and imperf. souvenir sheets exist.

Nordjamb 75 Type of 1975

Designs (Scout and Nordjamb Emblems and): 35c, Camp. 40c, Scout musicians. 1cor, Campfire. 10cor, Lord Baden-Powell.

1975, Aug. 15 *Perf. 14½*

C880 A102 35c multicolored 10 8
C881 " 40c " 12 10
C882 " 1cor " 28 25
C883 " 10cor " 2.75 2.50

Nordjamb 75, 14th World Boy Scout Jamboree, Lillehammer, Norway, July 29-Aug. 7.

Two airmail souvenir sheets of 2 exist. One, perf., contains 2cor and 3cor with designs of Nos. 992 and 990. The other, imperf., contains 2cor and 3cor with designs of Nos. 993 and C882. Size: 125x 101mm.

Pres. Somoza Type of 1975

1975, Sept. 10 *Perf. 14*

C884 A103 1cor vio. & multi. 28 25
C885 " 10cor bl. & multi. 2.75 2.50
C886 " 20cor multicolored 5.50 5.00

Reelection of Pres. Anastasio Somoza D.

Choir Type of 1975

Famous Choirs: 50c, Montserrat Abbey. 1cor, St. Florian Choir Boys. 2cor, Choir Boys of the Wooden Cross (vert.). 5cor, Boys and Pope Paul VI (Pueri Cantores International Federation).

1975, Nov. 15 *Perf. 14½*

C887 A104 50c silver & multi. 15 12
C888 " 1cor " " 28 25
C889 " 2cor " " 56 50
C890 " 5cor " " 1.40 1.25

Christmas 1975. A 10cor imperf. souvenir sheet exists (Oberndorf Memorial Chapel Choir and score of "Holy Night-Silent Night").

Chess Type of 1976

Designs: 40c, The Chess Players, by Thomas Eakins. 2cor, Bobby Fischer and Boris Spasski in Reykjavik, 1972. 5cor, Shakespeare and Ben Johnson Playing Chess, by Karel van Mander.

1976, Jan. 8 *Perf. 14½*

C891 A105 40c multicolored 15 8
C892 " 2cor vio. & multi. 75 50
C893 " 5cor multicolored 1.50 1.25

History of chess. A souvenir sheet contains one each of Nos. C892-C893, perf. and imperf. Size: 143x67mm.

Olympic Winner Type 1976

Winners, Rowing and Sculling Events: 55c, U.S.S.R., 1956, 1960, 1964 (vert.). 70c, New Zealand, 1972 (vert.). 90c, New Zealand, 1968. 20cor, U.S.A., 1956.

1976, Sept. 7 Litho. *Perf. 14*

C902 A107 55c blue & multi. 25 15
C903 " 70c " " 25 20
C904 " 90c " " 30 25
C905 " 20cor " " 6.00 5.00

Souvenir Sheet

Design: 10cor, Women's rowing crew, U.S.A., 1976 (vert.).

C906 A107 10cor multi. 3.25

No. C906 commemorates the first participation of women in Olympic rowing events: multicolored margin. Size of stamp: 37x50 mm., size of sheet: 156x110mm.

The overprint "Republica Democratica Alemana Vencedor en 1976" was applied in 1976 to No. C905 in black in 3 lines and to the margin of No. C906 in gold in 2 lines.

Bicentennial Type of 1976

Designs (American Bicentennial Emblem and): No. C907, Philadelphia, 1776. No. C908, Washington, 1976. No. C909, John Paul Jones' ships. No. C910, Atomic submarine. No. C911, Wagon train. No. C912, Diesel train.

1976, May 25 Litho. *Perf. 13½*

C907 A108 80c multi. 35 15
C908 " 80c " 35 15
C909 " 2.75cor " 1.00 75
C910 " 2.75cor " 1.00 75
C911 " 4cor " 1.25 1.00
C912 " 4cor " 1.25 1.00
Nos. C907-C912 (6) 5.20 3.80

American Bicentennial, 200 years of progress. Stamps of same denomination printed se-tenant. A souvenir sheet contains two 10cor stamps showing George Washington and Gerald R. Ford with their families. Black marginal inscription, red and blue border and Bicentennial emblem. Size: 140x111mm.

Rare Stamps Type of 1976

Rare Stamps: 40c, Hawaii No. 1. 1cor, Great Britain No. 1. 2cor, British Guiana No. 13. 5cor, Honduras No. C12. 10cor, Newfoundland No. C1.

1976, Dec. *Perf. 14*

C913 A109 40c multicolored 12 8
C914 " 1cor " 28 25
C915 " 2cor " 56 50
C916 " 5cor " 1.40 1.25
C917 " 10cor " 2.80 2.50
Nos. C913-C917 (5) 5.16 4.58

Inscriptions on back printed on top of gum give description of illustrated stamp. A 4cor imperf. souvenir sheet shows 1881 Great Britain-Nicaragua combination cover. Blue margin with black inscription. Size: 140x101mm.

Olga Nuñez de Saballos—AP108

Designs: 1cor, Josefa Toledo de Aguerri. 10cor, Hope Portocarrero de Somoza.

1977, Feb. Litho. *Perf. 13½*

C918 AP108 35c multi. 12 8
C919 " 1cor red & multi. 28 25
C920 " 10cor multi. 2.80 2.50

Famous Nicaraguan women and for International Women's Year (in 1975).

Zeppelin Type of 1977

Designs: 35c, Ville de Paris airship. 70c, Zeppelin "Schwaben." 3cor, Zeppelin in flight. 10cor, Vickers "Mayfly" before take-off. 20cor, Zeppelin with leadlines extended.

1977, Oct. 31 Litho. *Perf. 14½*

C921 A110 35c multicolored 15 10
C922 " 70c " 20 15
C923 " 3cor " 85 75
C924 " 10cor " 3.00 2.50

Souvenir Sheet

C925 A110 20cor multi. 6.00 6.00

75th anniversary of Zeppelin. No. C925 has gray and black margin showing airships. Size: 102x65mm.

Lindbergh Type of 1977

Designs: 55c, Lindbergh's plane approaching Nicaraguan airfield, 1928. 80c, Spirit of St. Louis and map of New York-Paris route. 2cor, Plane flying off Nicaragua's Pacific Coast. 10cor, Lindbergh flying past Momotombo Volcano on way to Managua. 20cor, Spirit of St. Louis.

1977, Nov. 30

C926 A111 55c multicolored 15 10
C927 " 80c " 25 20
C928 " 2cor " 60 50
C929 " 10cor " 3.00 2.50

Souvenir Sheet

C930 A111 20cor multi. 6.00 6.00

Charles A. Lindbergh's solo transatlantic flight, 50th anniversary. No. C930 has multicolored border showing Lindbergh, plane and map of Nicaragua. Size: 124x80 mm.

Souvenir Sheet

Christmas Type of 1977

Design: 20cor, Finale of Nutcracker Suite.

1977, Dec. 12

C931 A112 20cor multi. 6.00 6.00

Christmas 1977. No. C931 has multicolored margin showing stage with snow-covered trees. Size: 130x108mm.

Painting Type of 1978

Rubens Paintings: 5cor, Hippopotamus and Crocodile Hunt. 10cor, Duke de Lerma on Horseback. 20cor, Self-portrait.

1978, Jan. 11 Litho. *Perf. 14½*

C932 A113 5cor multi. 1.40 1.25
C933 " 10cor " 2.80 2.50

Souvenir Sheet

C934 A113 20cor multi. 6.00 6.00

Peter Paul Rubens (1577-1640), 400th birth anniversary. No. C934 has multicolored margin showing painting of Rubens and Isabella Brant (from which portrait on stamp was taken). Size: 130x105mm.

St. Francis Type of 1978

Designs: 80c, St. Francis and the wolf. 10cor, St. Francis, painting. 20cor, Our Lady of Conception, statue in Church of El Viejo.

1978, Feb. 23 Litho. *Perf. 14½*

C935 A114 80c lt. brown & multi. 22 16
C936 " 10cor bl. & multi. 2.80 2.50

Souvenir Sheet

C937 A114 20cor deep rose & multi. 5.75

St. Francis of Assisi (1182-1226), 750th anniversary of his canonization, and in honor of Our Lady of Conception, patron saint of Nicaragua. No. C937 has multicolored margin showing portal of Our Lady of Conception Church, El Viejo. Size: 121x105mm.

Railroad Type of 1978

Locomotives: 35c, Light-weight American. 4cor, Heavy Baldwin. 10cor, Juniata, 13-ton. 20cor, Map of route system.

1978, Apr. 7 Litho. *Perf. 14½*

C938 A115 35c lt. grn. & multi. 12 8
C939 " 4cor dp. org. & multi. 1.10 1.00
C940 " 10cor citron & multi. 2.80 2.50

Souvenir Sheet

C941 A115 20cor multi. 5.75

Century of Nicaraguan railroads.

No. C941 has multicolored margin showing map of Nicaragua and 19th century train. Size: 143x108mm.

Jules Verne Type of 1978

Designs: 90c, 20,000 Leagues under the Sea. 10cor, Around the World in 80 Days. 20cor, From the Earth to the Moon.

1978, Aug. Litho. *Perf. 14½*

C942 A116 90c multicolored 25 16
C943 " 10cor " 2.80 2.50

Souvenir Sheet

C944 A116 20cor multi. 5.75

Jules Verne (1828-1905), science fiction writer. No. C944 has multicolored margin showing Jules Verne, and various scenes from his books. Size: 113x87mm.

Aviation History Type of 1978

Designs: 55c, Igor Sikorsky in his helicopter, 1913 (horiz.). 10cor, Space shuttle (horiz.). 20cor, Flyer III (horiz.).

1978, Sept. 29 Litho. *Perf. 14½*

C945 A117 55c multicolored 16 10
C946 " 10cor " 2.80 2.50

Souvenir Sheet

C947	A117	20cor multi.	5.75	

History of aviation and 75th anniversary of first powered flight. No. C947 has multicolored margin showing modern control panel, early flying attempt, and Concorde. Size: 142x115mm.

Soccer Type of 1978

Soccer Players: 50c, Denis Law and Franz Beckenbauer. 5cor, Dino Zoff and Pelé. 20cor, Dominique Rocheteau and Johan Neeskens.

1978, Oct. 25 Litho. ***Perf. 13½x14***

C948	A118	50c multicolored	14	8
C949	"	5cor "	1.40	1.25

Souvenir Sheet

C950	A118	20cor multi.	5.75	

11th World Cup Soccer Championship, Argentina, June 1–25. No. C950 has multicolored margin showing Stadium and Argentina '78 emblem. Size: 103x78mm.

Christmas Type of 1978

Paintings: 3cor, Apostles John and Peter, by Dürer. 10cor, Apostles Paul and Mark, by Dürer. 20cor, Virgin and Child with Garlands, by Dürer.

1978, Dec. 12 Litho. ***Perf. 13½x14***

C951	A119	3cor multi.	90	60
C952	"	10cor "	2.80	2.50

Souvenir Sheet

C953	A119	20cor multi.	5.75	

Christmas 1978. No. C953 has multicolored margin showing portraits of Albrecht Dürer and Francisco Goya. Size: 143x103mm.

Volcano Type of 1978

Designs: No. C954, Cerro Negro Volcano. No. C955, Lake Masaya. No. C956, Momotombo Volcano. No. C957, Lake Asososca. No. C958, Mombacho Volcano. No. C959, Lake Apoyo. No. C960, Concepcion Volcano. No. C961, Lake Tiscapa.

1978, Dec. 29 ***Perf. 14x13½***

C954	A120	35c multi.	10	8
C955	"	35c "	10	8
C956	"	90c "	25	16
C957	"	90c "	25	16
C958	"	1cor "	28	20
C959	"	1cor "	28	20
C960	"	10cor "	2.80	2.00
C961	"	10cor "	2.80	2.00
		Nos. C954-C961 (8)	6.86	4.88

Volcanos, lakes and their locations. Stamps of same denomination printed se-tenant in sheets of 40.

Bernardo O'Higgins
AP109

1979, Mar. 7 Litho. ***Perf. 14***

C962	AP109	20cor multi.	5.50	4.00

Bernardo O'Higgins (1778–1842), Chilean soldier and statesman.

AIR POST SEMI-POSTAL STAMPS

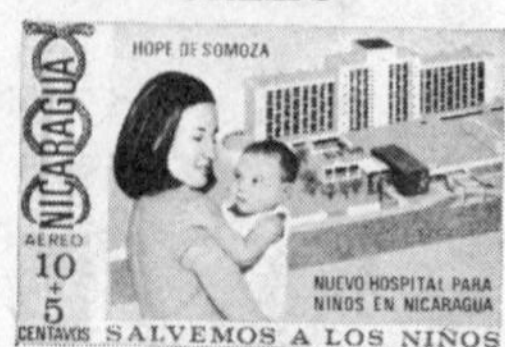

Mrs. Somoza and Children's Hospital—SPAP1

Designs: 5c+5c, Children and weight chart. 15c+5c, Incubator and Da Vinci's "Child in Womb." 20c+5c, Smallpox vaccination. 30c+5c, Water purification. 35c+5c, 1cor+50c, like 10c+5c. 50c+10c, Antibiotics. 60c+15c, Malaria control. 70c+10c, Laboratory. 80c+20c, Gastroenteritis (sick and well babies).

1973, Sept. 25 Litho. *Perf. 13½x14*

CB1	SPAP1	5c+5c	multi.	3	3
CB2	"	10c+5c	"	4	4
CB3	"	15c+5c	"	6	5
CB4	"	20c+5c	"	7	6
CB5	"	30c+5c	"	10	8
CB6	"	35c+5c	"	12	10
CB7	"	50c+10c	"	16	14
CB8	"	60c+15c	"	20	18
CB9	"	70c+10c	"	22	20
CB10	"	80c+20c	"	28	25
CB11	"	1cor+50c	"	42	38
		Nos. CB1–CB11 (11)		1.70	1.51

The surtax was for hospital building fund. See No. C845. Inscriptions on back, printed on top of gum give brief description of subjects shown.

AIR POST OFFICIAL STAMPS

OA1

"Typewritten" Overprint.

1929, Aug. *Perf. 12* Unwmkd.

CO1	OA1	25c orange	50.00	45.00

Excellent counterfeits of No. CO1 are plentiful.

Official Stamps of 1926 Overprinted in Dark Blue

Correo Aéreo

1929, Sept. 15

CO2	A24	25c orange	50	50
		a. Inv. ovpt.	6.00	
		b. Double overprint	6.00	
CO3	A25	50c pale blue	75	75
		a. Inv. ovpt.	4.00	
		b. Double overprint	6.00	
		c. Double overprint, one inverted	8.00	

Nos. 519–523 Overprinted in Black

Correo Aéreo
OFICIAL

1932, Feb.

CO4	A24	15c orange red	60	60
		a. Inv. ovpt.	6.00	
		b. Double overprint	6.00	
		c. Double overprint, one inverted	6.00	
CO5	A25	20c orange	70	70
		a. Double overprint	6.00	
CO6	A24	25c dark violet	70	70
CO7	A25	25c green	80	80
CO8	"	1cor yellow	1.50	1.50
		Nos. CO4–CO8 (5)	4.30	4.30

Nos. CO4-CO8 exist with and without script control mark.

Overprinted on Stamp No. 547.

CO9	A24	25c black brown	50.00	50.00

The varieties "OFICAL", "OFIAIAL" and "CORROE" occur in the setting and are found on each stamp of the series.

Counterfeits of No. CO9 are plentiful.

Stamp No. CO4 with overprint "1931" in addition is believed to be of private origin.

Type of Regular Issue of 1914 Overprinted

Correo Aéreo
OFICIAL

1933

CO10	A24	25c olive	20	20
CO11	A25	50c olive green	33	33
CO12	"	1cor orange red	60	60

On Stamps of 1914–28.

CO13	A24	15c deep violet	13	13
CO14	A25	20c deep green	15	15
		Nos. CO10–CO14 (5)	1.41	1.41

Nos. CO10 to CO14 sometimes have script control mark in addition to the overprint.

Air Post Official Stamps of 1932–33 Overprinted in Blue

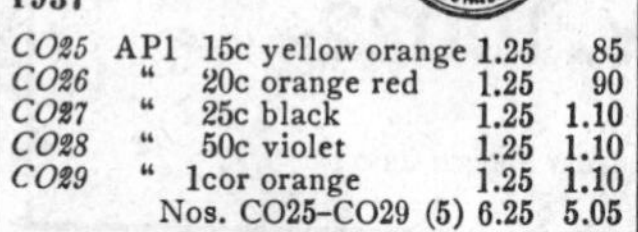

1935

CO15	A24	15c deep violet	1.50	1.25
CO16	A25	20c deep green	3.00	2.50
CO17	A24	25c olive	4.25	4.00
CO18	A25	50c olive green	42.50	42.50
CO19	"	1cor orange red	50.00	50.00
		Nos. CO15–CO19 (5)	101.25	100.25

Overprinted in Red.

CO20	A24	15c deep violet	40	35
CO21	A25	20c deep green	40	35
CO22	A24	25c olive	40	40
CO23	A25	50c olive green	1.25	1.25
CO24	"	1cor orange red	1.25	1.25
		Nos. CO20–CO24 (5)	3.70	3.60

Nos. CO15 to CO24 are handstamped with script control mark. Counterfeits of blue overprint are plentiful.

The editors do not recognize the Nicaraguan air post Official stamps overprinted in red "VALIDO 1935" in two lines and with or without script control marks as having been issued primarily for postal purposes.

Nos. C164-C168 Overprinted in Black

SERVICIO OFICIAL

1937

CO25	AP1	15c yellow orange	1.25	85
CO26	"	20c orange red	1.25	90
CO27	"	25c black	1.25	1.10
CO28	"	50c violet	1.25	1.10
CO29	"	1cor orange	1.25	1.10
		Nos. CO25–CO29 (5)	6.25	5.05

Pres. Anastasio Somoza
OA2

1939, Feb. 7 Engraved *Perf. 12½*

CO30	OA2	10c brown	40	40
CO31	"	15c dark blue	40	40
CO32	"	20c yellow	40	40
CO33	"	25c dark purple	40	40
CO34	"	30c lake	40	40
CO35	"	50c deep orange	1.00	1.00
CO36	"	1cor dk. olive grn.	1.75	1.75
		Nos. CO30–CO36 (7)	4.75	4.75

Mercedes Airport—OA3

Designs: 10c, Sulphurous Lake of Nejapa. 15c, Ruben Dario Monument. 20c, Tapir. 25c, Genizaro Dam. 50c, Tipitapa Spa. 1cor, Stone Highway. 2.50cor, Franklin D. Roosevelt Monument.

Engraved, Center Photogravure.
Various Frames in Black.

1947, Aug. 29

CO37	OA3	5c orange brown	10	10
CO38	"	10c blue	20	20
CO39	"	15c violet	10	10
CO40	"	20c red orange	20	10
CO41	"	25c blue	15	15
CO42	"	50c carmine rose	20	20
CO43	"	1cor slate	45	45
CO44	"	2.50cor red brown	1.25	1.25
		Nos. CO37–CO44 (8)	2.65	2.55

Rowland Hill
OA4

Designs: 10c, Heinrich von Stephan. 25c, First U. P. U. Bldg. 50c, U. P. U. Bldg., Bern. 1cor, U. P. U. Monument. 2.60cor, Congress medal, reverse.

1950, Nov. 23 Engraved *Perf. 13*

Frames in Black.

CO45	OA4	5c rose violet	10	8
CO46	"	10c deep green	10	10
CO47	"	25c rose violet	10	10
CO48	"	50c deep orange	15	15
CO49	"	1cor ultramarine	40	40
CO50	"	2.60cor gray black	3.50	3.25
		Nos. CO45–CO50 (6)	4.35	4.08

Issued to commemorate the 75th anniversary (in 1949) of the formation of the Universal Postal Union.

Each denomination was also issued in a souvenir sheet containing four stamps and marginal inscriptions. Price, set of 6 sheets, $35. Size: 121x96mm.

Consular Service Stamps Surcharged "Oficial Aéreo" and New Denomination in Red, Black or Blue.

Type AP63 illustrated above No. C454.

Engraved

1961, Nov. *Perf. 12* Unwmkd.

Red Marginal Number

CO51	AP63	10c on 1cor greenish black (R)	8	8
CO52	"	15c on 20cor red brown (R)	15	12
CO53	"	20c on 100cor magenta	15	12
CO54	"	25c on 50c deep blue (R)	10	10
CO55	"	35c on 50cor brown (R)	15	15
CO56	"	50c on 3cor dk. carmine	15	15
CO57	"	1cor on 2cor green (R)	30	30
CO58	"	2cor on 5cor orange (Bl)	65	65
CO59	"	5cor on 10 cor violet (R)	1.50	1.50
		Nos. CO51–CO59 (9)	3.23	3.17

POSTAGE DUE STAMPS.

D1

D2

Engraved.

1896 *Perf. 12.* Unwmkd.

J1	D1	1c orange	50	*1.25*
J2	"	2c "	50	*1.25*
J3	"	5c "	50	*1.25*
J4	"	10c "	50	*1.25*
J5	"	20c "	50	*1.25*
J6	"	30c "	50	*1.25*
J7	"	50c "	50	*1.50*
		Nos. J1–J7 (7)	3.50	*9.00*

Wmkd. Liberty Cap. (117)

J8	D1	1c orange	1.00	*1.50*
J9	"	2c "	1.00	*1.50*
J10	"	5c "	1.00	*1.50*
J11	"	10c "	1.00	*1.50*
J12	"	20c "	1.25	*1.50*
J13	"	30c "	1.00	*1.50*
J14	"	50c "	1.00	*1.50*
		Nos. J8–J14 (7)	7.25	*10.50*

1897 Unwmkd.

J15	D1	1c violet	50	*1.50*
J16	"	2c "	50	*1.50*
J17	"	5c "	50	*1.50*
J18	"	10c "	50	*1.50*
J19	"	20c "	1.25	*2.00*
J20	"	30c "	50	*1.50*
J21	"	50c "	50	*1.50*
		Nos. J15–J21 (7)	4.25	*11.00*

Wmkd. Liberty Cap. (117)

J22	D1	1c violet	50	*1.50*
J23	"	2c "	50	*1.50*
J24	"	5c "	50	*1.50*
J25	"	10c "	50	*1.50*
J26	"	20c "	1.00	*2.00*
J27	"	30c "	50	*1.50*
J28	"	50c "	50	*1.50*
		Nos. J22–J28 (7)	4.00	*11.00*

Reprints of Nos. J1–J28 are on thick, porous paper. Color of 1896 reprints, reddish orange; or 1897 reprints, reddish violet. On watermarked reprints, liberty cap is sideways. Price 25c each.

1898 Lithographed. Unwmkd.

J29	D2	1c blue green	15	*2.00*
J30	"	2c "	15	*2.00*
J31	"	5c "	15	*2.00*
J32	"	10c "	15	*2.00*
J33	"	20c "	15	*2.00*
J34	"	30c "	15	*2.00*
J35	"	50c "	15	*2.00*
		Nos. J29–J35 (7)	1.05	*14.00*

1899

J36	D2	1c carmine	10	*2.00*
J37	"	2c "	10	*2.00*
J38	"	5c "	10	*2.00*
J39	"	10c "	10	*2.00*
J40	"	20c "	10	*2.00*
J41	"	50c "	10	*2.00*
		Nos. J36–J41 (6)	60	*12.00*

Some denominations are found in se-tenant pairs.

Various counterfeit cancellations exist on Nos. J1–J41.

D3

1900 Engraved

J42	D3	1c plum	1.00
J43	"	2c vermilion	1.00
J44	"	5c dark blue	1.00
J45	"	10c purple	1.00
J46	"	20c orange brown	1.00
J47	"	30c dark green	2.00
J48	"	50c lake	2.00
		Nos. J42–J48 (7)	9.00

Nos. J42–J48 were not issued without postage overprint. See Nos. 137–143, 152–158.

OFFICIAL STAMPS.

Types of Postage Stamps Overprinted in Red Diagonally Reading up

FRANQUEO
OFICIAL

Engraved.

1890 *Perf. 12* Unwmkd.

O1	A5	1c ultramarine	15	*35*
O2	"	2c ultramarine	15	*35*
O3	"	5c ultramarine	15	*35*
O4	"	10c ultramarine	15	*50*

O5	A5	20c ultramarine	15	*75*
O6	"	50c ultramarine	15	*75*
O7	"	1p ultramarine	15	*1.25*
O8	"	2p ultramarine	15	*1.50*
O9	"	5p ultramarine	15	*2.50*
O10	"	10p ultramarine	15	*4.00*
		Nos. O1–O10 (10)	1.50	*12.30*

All values of the 1890 issue are known without overprint and most of them with inverted or double overprint, or without overprint and imperforate. There is no evidence that they were issued in these forms.

Official stamps of 1890–1899 are scarce with genuine cancellations. Forged cancellations are plentiful.

Overprinted Vertically Reading Up

1891 Lithographed

O11	A6	1c green	15	*35*
O12	"	2c green	15	*35*
O13	"	5c green	15	*35*
O14	"	10c green	15	*35*
O15	"	20c green	15	*75*
O16	"	50c green	15	*1.25*
O17	"	1p green	15	*1.50*
O18	"	2p green	15	*1.50*
O19	"	5p green	15	*2.50*
O20	"	10p green	15	*4.00*
		Nos. O11–O20 (10)	1.50	*12.90*

All values of this issue except the 2c and 5p exist without overprint and several with double overprint. They are not known to have been issued in this form.

Many of the denominations may be found in se-tenant pairs.

Overprinted in Dark Blue — FRANQUEO OFICIAL

1892 Engraved

O21	A7	1c yellow brown	15	*35*
O22	"	2c yellow brown	15	*35*
O23	"	5c yellow brown	15	*35*
O24	"	10c yellow brown	15	*35*
O25	"	20c yellow brown	15	*75*
O26	"	50c yellow brown	15	*1.00*
O27	"	1p yellow brown	15	*1.50*
O28	"	2p yellow brown	15	*2.00*
O29	"	5p yellow brown	15	*3.00*
O30	"	10p yellow brown	15	*4.00*
		Nos. O21–O30 (10)	1.50	*13.65*

The 2c and 1p are known without overprint and several values exist with double or inverted overprint. These probably were not regularly issued.

Commemorative of the 400th anniversary of the discovery of America by Christopher Columbus.

Overprinted in Red — FRANQUEO OFICIAL

1893 Engraved

O31	A8	1c slate	15	*35*
O32	"	2c slate	15	*35*
O33	"	5c slate	15	*35*
O34	"	10c slate	15	*35*
O35	"	20c slate	15	*50*
O36	"	25c slate	15	
O37	"	50c slate	15	*1.00*
O38	"	1p slate	15	*1.50*
O39	"	2p slate	15	*2.00*
O40	"	5p slate	15	*3.00*
O41	"	10p slate	15	*4.00*
		Nos. O31–O41 (11)	1.65	

The 2, 5, 10, 20, 25, 50c and 5p are known without overprint but probably were not regularly issued. Some values exist with double or inverted overprints.

Overprinted in Black — FRANQUEO OFICIAL

1894

O42	A9	1c orange	15	*35*
O43	"	2c "	15	*35*
O44	"	5c "	15	*35*
O45	"	10c "	15	*35*
O46	"	20c "	15	*50*
O47	"	50c "	15	*75*
O48	"	1p "	15	*1.50*
O49	"	2p "	15	*2.00*
O50	"	5p "	15	*3.00*
O51	"	10p "	15	*4.00*
		Nos. O42–O51 (10)	1.50	*13.15*

1895 Overprinted in Blue.

O52	A10	1c green	15	*35*
O53	A10	2c green	15	*35*
O54	"	5c "	15	*35*
O55	"	10c "	15	*35*
O56	"	20c "	15	*50*
O57	"	50c "	15	*1.00*
O58	"	1p "	15	*1.50*
O59	"	2p "	15	*2.00*
O60	"	5p "	15	*3.00*
O61	"	10p "	15	*4.00*
		Nos. O52–O61 (10)	1.50	*13.40*

Wmkd. Liberty Cap. (117)

O62	A10	1c green	15	*35*
O63	"	2c "	15	*35*
O64	"	5c "	15	*40*
O65	"	10c "	15	*50*
O66	"	20c "	15	*50*
O67	"	50c "	15	*75*
O68	"	1p "	15	*1.00*
O69	"	2p "	15	*1.50*
O70	"	5p "	15	*3.00*
O71	"	10p "	15	*4.00*
		Nos. O62–O71 (10)	1.50	*12.35*

Postage Due Stamps of Same Date Handstamped in Violet — *Franqueo Oficial*

1896 Unwmkd.

O72	D1	1c orange	5.50
O73	"	2c "	5.50
O74	"	5c "	4.00
O75	"	10c "	4.00
O76	"	20c "	4.00
		Nos. O72–O76 (5)	23.00

Wmkd. Liberty Cap. (117)

O77	D1	1c orange	5.50
O78	"	2c "	5.50
O79	"	5c "	4.00
O80	"	10c "	4.00
O81	"	20c "	4.00
		Nos. O77–O81 (5)	23.00

Nos. O72 to O81 were handstamped in rows of five. Several handstamps were used, one of which had the variety "Oftcial". Most varieties are known inverted and double.

Types of Postage Stamps Overprinted in Red

1896 Unwmkd.

O82	A11	1c red	2.50	3.00
O83	"	2c "	2.50	3.00
O84	"	5c "	2.50	3.00
O85	"	10c "	2.50	3.00
O86	"	20c "	3.00	3.00
O87	"	50c "	5.00	*5.00*
O88	"	1p "	12.00	*12.00*
O89	"	2p "	12.00	*12.00*
O90	"	5p "	16.00	*16.00*
		Nos. O82–O90 (9)	58.00	*60.00*

Wmkd. Liberty Cap. (117)

O91	A11	1c red	3.00	3.50
O92	"	2c "	3.00	3.50
O93	"	5c "	3.00	3.50
O94	"	10c "	3.00	5.00
O95	"	20c "	5.00	5.00
O96	"	50c "	3.00	*5.00*
O97	"	1p "	14.00	*14.00*
O98	"	2p "	16.50	*16.50*
O99	"	5p "	25.00	*25.00*
		Nos. O91–O99 (9)	75.50	*81.00*

Same, Dated 1897.

1897 Unwmkd.

O100	A11	1c red	3.00	3.00
O101	"	2c "	3.00	3.00
O102	"	5c "	3.00	2.50
O103	"	10c "	3.00	3.00
O104	"	20c "	3.00	4.00
O105	"	50c "	5.00	*5.00*
O106	"	1p "	12.00	*12.00*
O107	"	2p "	12.00	*12.00*
O108	"	5p "	16.00	*16.00*
		Nos. O100–O108 (9)	60.00	*60.50*

Wmkd. Liberty Cap. (117)

O109	A11	1c red	5.00	5.00
O110	"	2c "	5.00	5.00
O111	"	5c "	5.00	5.00
O112	"	10c "	10.00	10.00
O113	"	20c "	10.00	10.00
O114	"	50c "	12.00	*12.00*
O115	"	1p "	20.00	*20.00*
O116	A11	2p red	20.00	*20.00*
O117	"	5p "	20.00	*20.00*
		Nos. O109–O117 (9)	107.00	*107.00*

Overprinted in Blue

1898 Unwmkd.

O118	A12	1c carmine	4.00	4.00
O119	"	2c "	4.00	4.00
O120	"	4c "	4.00	4.00
O121	"	5c "	2.50	2.50
O122	"	10c "	4.00	4.00
O123	"	15c "	6.00	6.00
O124	"	20c "	6.00	6.00
O125	"	50c "	8.50	*8.50*
O126	"	1p "	11.00	*11.00*
O127	"	2p "	11.00	*11.00*
O128	"	5p "	11.00	*11.00*
		Nos. O118–O128 (11)	72.00	*72.00*

Stamps of this set with sideways watermark 117 or with black overprint are reprints. Price 25c each.

Reprints of Nos. O82–O117 are described in notes after No. 109M. Price 15c each.

Overprinted in Dark Blue — FRANQUEO OFICIAL

1899

O129	A13	1c gray green	10	*1.00*
O130	"	2c bistre brown	10	*1.00*
O131	"	4c lake	10	*1.00*
O132	"	5c dark blue	10	*50*
O133	"	10c buff	10	*1.00*
O134	"	15c chocolate	10	*2.00*
O135	"	20c dark green	10	*3.00*
O136	"	50c carmine rose	10	*3.00*
O137	"	1p red	10	*10.00*
O138	"	2p violet	10	*10.00*
O139	"	5p light blue	10	*15.00*
		Nos. O129–O139 (11)	1.10	*47.50*

Counterfeit cancellations on Nos. O129–O139 are plentiful.

"Justice" O5

1900 Engraved.

O140	O5	1c plum	60	60
O141	"	2c vermilion	50	50
O142	"	4c olive green	60	60
O143	"	5c dark blue	1.25	45
O144	"	10c purple	1.25	35
O145	"	20c brown	90	35
O146	"	50c lake	1.25	50
O147	"	1p ultramarine	3.50	2.50
O148	"	2p brown orange	4.00	4.00
O149	"	5p greenish black	5.00	5.00
		Nos. O140–O149 (10)	18.85	14.85

Nos. 123, 161 Surcharged in Black — 1 1 OFICIAL 1 **Centavo**

1903 *Perf. 12, 14.*

O150	A14	1c on 10c violet	25	30
		a. "Centovo"	1.00	
		b. "Contavo"	1.00	
		c. With ornaments	30	
		d. Invtd. surcharge	1.00	
		e. "1" omitted at upper left	2.00	
O151	"	2c on 3c green	30	40
		a. "Centovos"	1.00	
		b. "Contavos"	1.00	
		c. With ornaments	35	
		d. Inverted surcharge	1.00	
O152	"	4c on 3c green	1.25	1.25
		a. "Centovos"	2.50	
		b. "Contavos"	2.50	
		c. With ornaments	2.50	
		d. Inverted surcharge		
O153	A14	4c on 10c violet	1.25	1.25
		a. "Centovos"	2.50	
		b. "Contavos"	2.50	
		c. With ornaments	2.00	
		d. Inverted surcharge		
O154	"	5c on 3c green	15	18
		a. "Centovos"	1.00	
		b. "Contavos"	1.00	
		c. With ornaments	30	
		d. Double surcharge	2.00	
		e. Inverted surcharge		
		Nos. O150–O154 (5)	3.20	3.38

These surcharges are set up to cover twenty-five stamps. Some of the settings have bars or pieces of fancy border type below "OFICIAL". There are five varieties on No. O150, three on No. O151, and one each on Nos. O152, O153 and O154.

In 1904 No. O151 was reprinted to fill a dealer's order. This printing lacks the small figure at the upper right. It includes the variety "OFICILA". At the same time the same setting was printed in carmine on official stamps of 1900, 1c on 10c violet and 2c on 1p ultramarine. Also the 1, 2 and 5 pesos official stamps of 1900 were surcharged with new values and the dates 1901 or 1902 in various colors, inverted, etc. It is doubtful if any of these varieties were ever in Nicaragua and certain that none of them ever did legitimate postal duty.

No. O145 Surcharged in Black — **10 10 10 Ctvs.**

1904 *Perf. 12*

O155	O5	10c on 20c brown	20	20
		a. No period after "Ctvs"	1.00	75
O156	"	30c on 20c brown	20	20
O157	"	50c on 20c brown	50	35
		Lower "50" *a.* omitted	2.50	2.50
		b. Upper figures omitted	2.50	2.50
		c. Top left and lower figures omitted	3.50	3.50

Coat of Arms O6

1905, July 25 Engraved

O158	O6	1c green	25	25
O159	"	2c rose	25	25
O160	"	5c blue	25	25
O161	"	10c yellow brown	25	25
O162	"	20c orange	25	25
O163	"	50c brown olive	25	25
O164	"	1p lake	25	25
O165	"	2p violet	25	25
O166	"	5p gray black	25	25
		Nos. O158–O166 (9)	2.25	2.25

Surcharged Vertically Up or Down — **Vale 10c**

1907

O167	O6	10c on 1c green	75	75
O168	"	10c on 2c rose	22.50	17.50
O169	"	20c on 2c rose	20.00	13.50
O170	"	50c on 1c green	1.50	1.50
O171	"	50c on 2c rose	20.00	10.00

Surcharged — **Vale $1.00**

O172	O6	1p on 2c rose	1.50	1.50
O173	"	2p on 2c rose	1.50	1.50
O174	"	3p on 2c rose	1.50	1.50
O175	"	4p on 2c rose		*225.00*
O176	"	4p on 5c blue	2.00	2.00

The setting for this surcharge includes various letters from wrong fonts, the figure "1" for "l" in "Vale" and an "l" for "1" in "$1.00".

Surcharged **Vale 20 cts**

O177 O6 20c on 1c green 1.00 1.00
a. Double surcharge 5.00 5.00
Nos. O167–O174, O176–O177 (10) 72.25 50.75

The preceding surcharges are vertical, reading both up and down.

O7

Revenue Stamps Surcharged.

1907 *Perf. 14 to 15*

O178 O7 10c on 2c orange (Bk) 15 15
O179 " 35c on 1c blue (R) 15 15
a. Inverted surcharge 3.00 3.00
O180 " 70c on 1c blue (V) 15 15
a. Inverted surcharge 3.00 3.00
O181 " 70c on 1c blue (O) 15 15
a. Inverted surcharge 3.00 3.00
O182 " 1p on 2c orange (G) 15 15
a. Inverted surcharge 2.50 2.50
O183 " 2p on 2c orange (Br) 15 15
O184 " 3p on 5c brown (Bl) 15 15
O185 " 4p on 5c brown (G) 20 20
a. Double surcharge 3.00 3.00
O186 " 5p on 5c brown (G) 20 20
a. Inverted surcharge 3.50 3.50
Nos. O178–O186 (9) 1.45 1.45

Letters and figures from several fonts were mixed in these surcharges.

No. 202 Surcharged OFICIAL — 10 cvs —

1907, Nov.

Black or Blue Black Surcharge.

O187 A18 10c on 1c green (Bk) 8.00 7.50
O188 " 15c on 1c " 8.00 7.50
O189 " 20c on 1c " 8.00 7.50
O190 " 50c on 1c " 8.00 7.50

Red Surcharge.

O191 A18 1 (un) p on 1c green 7.50 7.50
O192 " 2 (dos) p on 1c green 7.50 7.50
Nos. O187–O192 (6) 47.00 45.00

No. 181 Surcharged *OFICIAL* VALE 10 ₡

1908 Yellow Surcharge. *Perf. 12.*

O193 A18 10c on 3c violet 9.00 8.00
O194 " 15c on 3c " 9.00 8.00
O195 " 20c on 3c " 9.00 8.00
O196 " 35c on 3c " 9.00 8.00
O197 " 50c on 3c " 9.00 8.00
Nos. O193–O197 (5) 45.00 40.00

Black Surcharge.

O198 A18 35c on 3c violet 50.00 30.00

Revenue Stamps Surcharged like 1907 Issue. Dated "1908".

1908 *Perf. 14 to 15.*

O199 O7 10c on 1c blue (V) 75 50
a. Inverted surcharge 3.50 3.50
O200 " 35c on 1c blue (Bk) 75 50
a. Inverted surcharge 3.50 3.50
b. Double surcharge 4.00 4.00
O201 " 50c on 1c blue (R) 75 50
O202 " 1p on 1c blue (Br) 32.50 32.50
a. Inverted surcharge 60.00 60.00
O203 " 2p on 1c blue (G) 90 75
O204 " 10c on 2c orge. (Bk) 1.10 65
O205 " 35c on 2c orange (R) 1.10 65
a. Double surcharge 3.50
O206 " 50c on 2c org. (Bk) 1.10 65
O207 " 70c on 2c orange (Bl) 1.10 65
O208 " 1p on 2c orange (G) 1.10 65
O209 " 2p on 2c orange (Br) 1.10 65
Nos. O199–O209 (11) 42.25 38.65

There are several minor varieties in the figures, etc., in these surcharges.

Nos. 243–248 Overprinted in Black OFICIAL

1909 *Perf. 12.*

O210 A18 10c lake 20 12
a. Double overprint 2.50 2.50
O211 " 15c black 60 50
O212 " 20c brown olive 1.00 75
O213 " 50c deep green 1.50 1.00
O214 " 1p yellow 1.75 1.25
O215 " 2p carmine rose 3.00 2.00
Nos. O210–O215 (6) 8.05 5.62

Overprinted in Black OFICIAL

1910

O216 A18 15c black 1.50 1.25
a. Double overprint 4.00 4.00
O217 " 20c brown olive 2.50 2.00
O218 " 50c deep green 2.50 2.00
O219 " 1p yellow 3.00 2.50
a. Inverted overprint 7.50 7.50
O220 " 2p carmine rose 4.00 3.00
Nos. O216–O220 (5) 13.50 10.75

Nos. 239–240 Surcharged in Black OFICIAL *Vale* 10 *cts.*

1911

O221 A18 5c on 3c red orange 6.00 6.00
O222 " 10c on 4c violet 5.00 5.00
a. Double surcharge 10.00 10.00
b. Pair, one without new value 20.00

Railroad Stamps Surcharged in Black Correo oficial Vale 10 cts.

1911, Nov. *Perf. 14 to 15*

O223 A21 10c on 1c red 3.00 3.00
a. Inverted surcharge 4.50
b. Double surcharge 4.50
O224 " 15c on 1c red 3.00 3.00
a. Inverted surcharge 5.00
b. Double surcharge 4.50
O225 " 20c on 1c red 3.00 3.00
a. Inverted surcharge 5.00
O226 " 50c on 1c red 4.00 4.00
a. Inverted surcharge 4.50
O227 " 1p on 1c red 5.00 7.00
a. Inverted surcharge 6.00
O228 " 2p on 1c red 6.00 10.00
a. Inverted surcharge 7.50
b. Double surcharge 7.50
Nos. O223–O228 (6) 24.00 30.00

Surcharged in Black CORREO OFICIAL 15 centavos

1911, Nov.

O229 A21 10c on 1c red 20.00
O230 " 15c on 1c " 20.00
O231 " 20c on 1c " 20.00
O232 " 50c on 1c " 15.00

Surcharged in Black Correo oficial Vale 5 cts. 1911

1911, Dec.

O233 A21 5c on 1c red 3.50 5.00
a. Double surcharge 6.00
b. Inverted surcharge 6.00
c. "5" omitted 5.00
O234 " 10c on 1c red 4.00 5.50
O235 " 15c on 1c " 4.50 6.00
O236 " 20c on 1c " 5.00 7.00
O237 " 50c on 1c " 5.50 8.00
Nos. O233–O237 (5) 22.50 31.50

Nos. O233 to O237 have a surcharge on the back like Nos. 285 and 286 with "15 cts" obliterated by a heavy bar.

Surcharged Vertically in Black Correo Oficial 1912 85 cvs.

1912

O238 A21 5c on 1c red 6.00 5.00
O239 " 10c on 1c " 6.00 5.00
O240 " 15c on 1c " 6.00 5.00
O241 " 20c on 1c " 6.00 5.00
O242 " 35c on 1c " 6.00 5.00
O243 " 50c on 1c " 6.00 5.00
O244 " 1p on 1c " 6.00 5.00
Nos. O238–O244 (7) 42.00 35.00

Nos. O238 to O244 are printed on Nos. 285 and 286 but the surcharge on the back is obliterated by a vertical bar.

Types of Regular Issue of 1912 Overprinted in Black OFICIAL

1912 *Perf. 12.*

O245 A22 1c light blue 5 5
O246 " 2c " 5 5
O247 " 3c " 8 8
O248 " 4c " 8 8
O249 " 5c " 8 8
O250 " 6c " 10 10
O251 " 10c " 12 12
O252 " 15c " 12 12
O253 " 20c " 12 12
O254 " 25c " 20 20
O255 A23 35c " 25 25
O256 A22 50c " 1.50 1.50
O257 " 1p " 30 30
O258 " 2p " 35 35
O259 " 5p " 50 50
Nos. O245–O259 (15) 3.90 3.90

On the 35c the overprint is 15½ mm. wide, on the other values it is 13 mm.

Types of Regular Issue of 1914 Overprinted in Black OFICIAL

1915, May

O260 A24 1c light blue 12 12
O261 A25 2c " 12 12
O262 A24 3c " 20 12
O263 A25 4c " 12 12
O264 A24 5c " 12 12
O265 A25 6c " 12 15
O266 " 10c " 15 15
O267 A24 15c " 20 20
O268 A25 20c " 20 20
O269 A24 25c " 30 30
O270 A25 50c " 60 60
Nos. O260–O270 (11) 2.25 2.20

Regular Issues of 1914-22 Overprinted in Red Oficial

1925

O271 A24 ½c deep green 12 12
a. Double overprint 2.50 2.50
O272 " 1c violet 10 10
O273 A25 2c carmine rose 12 12
O274 A24 3c olive green 12 10
O275 A25 4c vermilion 12 12
a. Double overprint 2.50 2.50
O276 A24 5c black 12 10
a. Double overprint 2.50 2.50
O277 A25 6c red brown 25 25
O278 " 10c yellow 35 35
a. Double overprint 3.50 3.50
O279 A24 15c red brown 40 40
O280 A25 20c bistre brown 50 50
O281 A24 25c orange 60 60
a. Inverted overprint 4.00 4.00
O282 A25 50c pale blue 75 75
a. Double overprint 5.00 5.00
Nos. O271–O282 (12) 3.55 3.51

There are two types of the overprint on Nos. O271-O282.

Regular Issues of 1914–22 Overprinted in Black OFICIAL

1926

O283 A24 ½c dark green 7 7
O284 " 1c deep violet 7 7
O285 A25 2c carmine rose 7 7
O286 A24 3c olive gray 7 7
O287 A25 4c vermilion 7 7
O288 A24 5c gray black 10 10
O289 A25 6c red brown 10 10
O290 " 10c yellow 10 10
O291 A24 15c deep brown 10 10
O292 A25 20c bistre brown 12 12
O293 A24 25c orange 18 18
O294 A25 50c pale blue 25 25
Nos. O283–O294 (12) 1.30 1.30

No. 499 Surcharged in Black OFICIAL ₡ 0.05 1931

1931

O295 A33 5c on 10c bistre brown 30 30

Nos. 517–518 Overprinted in Red OFICIAL

1931

O296 A25 6c bistre brown 30 30
O297 " 10c light brown 30 30

Nos. 541, 543, 545 With Additional Overprint in Black 1931

O298 A24 1c olive green 25 25
O299 " 3c light blue 25 25
a. "OFICIAL" inverted 1.25 1.25
O300 " 5c gray brown 25 25
a. "1931" double 1.25 1.25

Regular Issues of 1914–31 Overprinted in Black OFICIAL

1932, Feb. 6

O301 A24 1c olive green 8 8
a. Double overprint 2.00 2.00
O302 A25 2c bright rose 10 10
a. Double overprint 2.00 2.00
O303 A24 3c light blue 15 10
a. Double overprint 75 75
O304 A25 4c dark blue 18 10
O305 A24 5c olive brown 20 15
O306 A25 6c bistre brown 30 10
a. Double overprint 3.00 3.00
O307 " 10c light brown 45 30
O308 A24 15c orange red 60 35
a. Double overprint 3.50 3.50
O309 A25 20c orange 1.00 50
O310 A24 25c dark violet 3.00 75
O311 A25 50c green 15 15
O312 " 1cor yellow 30 30
Nos. O301–O312 (12) 6.51 2.98

With Additional Overprint in Black 1931

1932, Feb. 6

O313 A24 1c olive green 8.00 8.00
O314 A25 2c bright rose 9.00 9 00
a. Double overprint 12.00 12.00
O315 A24 3c light blue 8.00 8.00
O316 " 5c olive brown 8.00 8.00
O317 " 15c orange red 1.00 1.00
O318 " 25c black brown 1.00 1.00
O319 " 25c dark violet 2.50 2.50
Nos. O313–O319 (7) 37.50 37.50

The variety "OFIAIAL" occurs once in each sheet of Nos. O301 to O319 inclusive.

Flag of the Race Issue.

O8

Without gum.

1933, Aug. 9 Litho. *Rouletted 9*

O320 O8 1c orange 1.50 1.50
O321 " 2c yellow 1.50 1.50
O322 " 3c dark brown 1.50 1.50
O323 " 4c deep brown 1.50 1.50
O324 " 5c gray brown 1.50 1.50
O325 " 6c dp. ultramarine 1.75 1.75
O326 " 10c deep violet 1.75 1.75
O327 " 15c red violet 1.75 1.75
O328 " 20c deep green 1.75 1.75
O329 " 25c green 3.25 3.25
O330 " 50c carmine 3.75 3.75
O331 " 1cor red 6.00 6.00
Nos. O320–O331 (12) 27.50 27.50

See note after No. 599.
Reprints of Nos. O320–O331 exist.
A 25c dull blue exists. Its status is questioned.

Regular Issue of 1914-31
Overprinted in Red **OFICIAL**

1933, Nov. *Perf. 12*

O332 A24 1c olive green 4 4
O333 A25 2c bright rose 4 4
O334 A24 3c light blue 8 8
O335 A25 4c dark blue 4 4
O336 A24 5c olive brown 4 4
O337 A25 6c bistre brown 5 5
O338 " 10c light brown 5 5
O339 A24 15c red orange 5 5
O340 A25 20c orange 6 6
O341 A24 25c dark violet 15 15
O342 A25 50c green 25 25
O343 " 1cor yellow 50 30
Nos. O332–O343 (12) 1.35 1.15

Nos. O332 to O343 exist with or without script control mark in addition to the overprint.

Official Stamps of 1933
Overprinted in Blue

1935, Dec.

O344 A24 1c olive green 1.00 75
O345 A25 2c bright rose 1.00 75
O346 A24 3c light blue 2.50 75
O347 A25 4c dark blue 2.50 75
O348 A24 5c olive brown 2.50 75
O349 A25 6c bistre brown 4.00 1.00
O350 " 10c light brown 4.00 1.00
O351 A24 15c orange red 40.00 40.00
O352 A25 20c orange 40.00 40.00
O353 A24 25c dark violet 40.00 40.00
O354 A25 50c green 40.00 40.00
O355 " 1cor yellow 40.00 40.00
Nos. O344–O355 (12) 217.50 205.75

Nos. O344–O355 are handstamped with script control marks. Counterfeits of overprint abound.

Same Overprinted in Red.

1936, Jan.

O356 A24 1c olive green 8 8
O357 A25 2c bright rose 8 8
O358 A24 3c light blue 10 10
a. Double overprint
O359 A25 4c dark blue 10 10
O360 A24 5c olive brown 12 12
O361 A25 6c bistre brown 15 15
O362 " 10c light brown 18 18
O363 A24 15c orange red 20 20
O364 A25 20c orange 20 20
O365 A24 25c dark violet 8 8
O366 A25 50c green 25 25
O367 " 1cor yellow 50 50
Nos. O356–O367 (12) 2.04 2.04

Handstamped with script control marks.

Nos. 653 to 655, 657, 659
660, 662 to 664
Overprinted in Black

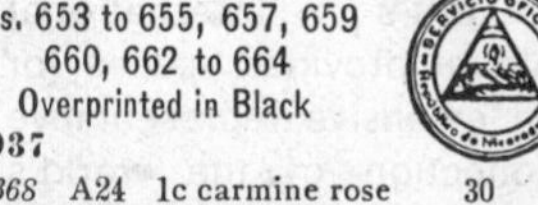

1937

O368 A24 1c carmine rose 30 25
O369 A25 2c deep blue 30 25
O370 A24 3c chocolate 40 35
O371 A24 5c orange red 50 40
O372 A25 10c olive green 1.00 60
O373 A24 15c green 1.25 75
O374 " 25c orange 1.50 1.00
O375 A25 50c brown 2.00 1.25
O376 " 1cor ultramarine 4.00 1.75
Nos. O368–O376 (9) 11.25 6.60

Islands of the Great Lake
O9

1939, Jan. Engraved *Perf. 12½*

O377 O9 2c rose red 15 15
O378 " 3c light blue 15 15
O379 " 6c brown orange 15 15
O380 " 7½c deep green 15 15
O381 " 10c black brown 15 15
O382 " 15c orange 20 20
O383 " 25c dark violet 40 40
O384 " 50c brt. yellow green 60 60
Nos. O377–O384 (8) 1.95 1.95

POSTAL TAX STAMPS.

Official Stamps of 1915
Surcharged in Black

Vale
un centavo
R de C

1921, July *Perf. 12* Unwmkd.

RA1 A24 1c on 5c light blue 1.35 50
RA2 A25 1c on 6c light blue 65 20
a. Double surcharge, one inverted
RA3 " 1c on 10c light blue 90 25
a. Double surcharge 3.00 3.00
RA4 A24 1c on 15c light blue 1.50 25
a. Double surcharge, one inverted 5.00 5.00

"R de C" signifies "Reconstruccion de Comunicaciones." The stamps were intended to provide a fund for rebuilding the General Post Office which was burned in April, 1921. One stamp was required on each letter or parcel, in addition to the regular postage. In the setting of one hundred there are five stamps with antique "C" and twenty-one with "R" and "C" smaller than in the illustration. One or more stamps in the setting have a dotted bar, as illustrated over No. 388, instead of the double bar.
The use of the "R de C" stamps for the payment of regular postage was not permitted.

Official Stamp of 1915
Overprinted in Black

«Particular»
R de C

RA5 A24 1c light blue 5.50 2.00

This stamp is known with the dotted bar as illustrated over No. 388, instead of the double bar.

Coat of Arms
PT1 PT2

1921, Sept. Red Surcharge.

RA6 PT1 1c on 1c vermilion & black 15 10
RA7 " 1c on 2c green & black 15 10
a. Double surcharge 3.00 3.00
b. Double surcharge, one inverted 4.00 4.00
RA8 " 1c on 4c orange & black 15 10
a. Double surcharge 4.00 4.00
RA9 " 1c on 15c dark blue & black 15 10
a. Double surcharge 3.00 3.00

1922, Feb.

Black Surcharge.

RA10 PT2 1c on 10c yellow 15 12
a. Period after "de" 50 40
b. Double surcharge 2.00 2.00
c. Double inverted surcharge 4.00 4.00
d. Inverted surcharge 3.00 3.00
e. Without period after "C" 1.00 1.00

No. 409 Overprinted in Black **R. de C.**

RA11 A24 1c violet 12 10
a. Double overprint 2.00 2.00

This stamp with the overprint in red is a trial printing.

Nos. 402, 404–407
Surcharged in Black

R. de C.
Vale
un centavo

1922, June

RA12 A27 1c on 1c green & black 75 60
RA13 A29 1c on 5c ultramarine & black 75 75
RA14 A30 1c on 10c orange & black 75 40
RA15 A31 1c on 25c yellow & black 75 30
a. Invtd. surch. 5.00 5.00
RA16 A32 1c on 50c violet & black 30 25
a. Dbl. surch. 4.00 4.00
Nos. RA12–RA16 (5) 3.30 2.30

PT3

Surcharge in Red or Dark Blue

1922, Oct. *Perf. 11½*

RA17 PT3 1c yellow (R) 12 10
a. No period after "C" 1.00 1.00
RA18 PT3 1c violet (DBl) 12 10
a. No period after "C" 1.00 1.00

Surcharge is inverted on 22 out of 50 of No. RA17, 23 out of 50 of No. RA18.

Nos. 403-407
Surcharged in Black

R. de C.
Vale
un centavo
de córdoba

1923 *Perf. 12.*

RA19 A28 1c on 2c rose red & black 45 45
RA20 A29 1c on 5c ultramarine & black 50 15
RA21 A30 1c on 10c orange & black 20 20
RA22 A31 1c on 25c yellow & black 30 30
RA23 A32 1c on 50c violet & black 20 15
Nos. RA19–RA23 (5) 1.65 1.25

The variety no period after "R" occurs twice on each sheet.

Wmkd. Coat of Arms in Sheet.

Red Surcharge.
Perf. 11½.

RA24 PT3 1c pale blue 12 10

Unwmkd.

Type of 1921 Issue.
Without Surcharge of New Value.

RA25 PT1 1c vermilion & black 15 10
a. Double overprint, one inverted 3.00 3.00

No. 409
Overprinted in Blue

R. de C.
1924

1924

RA26 A24 1c violet 15 10
a. Double overprint 8.00 8.00

There are two settings of the overprint on No. RA26, with "1924" 5½ mm. or 6½ mm. wide.

No. 409
Overprinted in Blue

R. de C.
1925

1925

RA27 A24 1c violet 15 12

No. 409
Overprinted in Blue **R. de C.**

1926

RA28 A24 1c violet 25 10

No. RA28
Overprinted
in Various Colors

Resello
1927

1927

RA29 A24 1c violet (R) 15 10
a. Double overprint (R) 2.00 2.00
b. Inverted overprint (R) 3.00 3.00
RA30 " 1c violet (V) 15 12
a. Double overprint 2.50 2.50
b. Inverted overprint 2.50 2.50
RA31 " 1c violet (Bl) 15 12
a. Double overprint 5.00 5.00
RA32 " 1c violet (Bk) 15 12
a. Double overprint, one inverted 4.00 4.00
b. Dbl. ovpt. 4.00 4.00

Same Overprint on No. RA27.

RA33 A24 1c violet (Bk) 13.00 8.00
Nos. RA29–RA33 (5) 13.60 8.46

No. RA28
Overprinted in Violet

Resello
1928

1928

RA34 A24 1c violet 12 12
a. Double overprint 2.00 2.00
b. "928" 1.00 1.00

Similar to No. RA34 but 8mm. space between "Resello" and "1928".
Black Overprint.

RA35 A24 1c violet 40 15
a. "1828" 2.00 2.00

PT4

Stamp Inscribed "Timbre Telegrafico".
Horizontal Surcharge in Black,
Vertical Surcharge in Red.

RA36 PT4 1c on 5c blue & black 60 15
a. Comma after "R" 1.25 1.25
b. No period after "R" 1.25 1.25
c. No periods after "R" and "C" 1.25 1.25

Numeral of Value ("CORREOS" at right)

PT5 PT6

1928 Engraved. *Perf. 12.*

RA37 PT5 1c plum 25 10

1929 Surcharged in Red.

RA38 PT6 1c on 5c blue & black 15 12
- *a.* Inverted surcharge 3.00 3.00
- *b.* Double surcharge 2.00 2.00
- *c.* Double surcharge, one inverted 2.00 2.00
- *d.* Period after "de" 1.25 1.25
- *e.* Comma after "R" 1.25 1.25

See note after No. 512.

Regular Issue of 1928 Overprinted in Blue **R. de C.**

RA39 A24 1c red orange 12 10

No. RA39 exists both with and without script control mark.

An additional overprint, "1929" in black or blue on No. RA39, is fraudulent.

No. 513 Overprinted in Red R. de C.

1929

RA40 A24 1c olive green 20 12
- *a.* Double overprint 75 75

No. RA40 is known with overprint in black, and with overprint inverted. These varieties were not regularly issued, but copies have been cancelled by favor.

Type of 1928 Issue. Inscribed at right "COMUNICACIONES".

1930-37

RA41 PT5 1c carmine 30 8
RA42 " 1c orange ('33) 20 10
RA43 " 1c green ('37) 15 10

No. RA39 Overprinted in Black 1931

1931

RA44 A24 1c red orange 12 8
- *a.* "1931" double overprint 50 50
- *b.* "1931" double overprint, one inverted 65 65

No. RA42 Overprinted Vertically, up or down, in Black Resello 1935

1935

RA45 PT5 1c orange 15 10
- *a.* Double overprint 1.50 1.50
- *b.* Dbl., one inverted

No. RA45 and RA45a Overprinted Vertically, Reading Down, in Blue

RA46 PT5 1c orange 75 12
- *a.* Black overprint double 3.00 3.00

Same Overprint in Red on Nos. RA39, RA42 and RA45.

RA47 A24 1c red orange (RA39) 50.00
RA48 PT5 1c org. (RA42) 30 12
RA49 PT5 1c org. (RA45) 30 12
- *a.* Black overprint double 1.25 1.25

Overprint is horizontal on No. RA47 and vertical, reading down, on Nos. RA48–49.

No. RA42 Overprinted Vertically, Reading Down, in Carmine

1935 *Perf. 12* Unwmkd.

RA50 PT5 1c orange 30 15

No. RA45 with Additional Overprint "1936", Vertically, Reading Down, in Red.

1936

RA51 PT5 1c orange 75 25

No. RA39 with Additional Overprint "1936" in Red.

RA52 A24 1c red orange 75 25

No. RA52 exists only with script control mark.

PT7

Vertical Surcharge in Red.

1936

RA53 PT7 1c on 5c green & black 15 12
- *a.* "Cenavo" 2.00 2.00
- *b.* "Centavos" 2.00 2.00

Horizontal Surcharge in Red.

RA54 PT7 1c on 5c green & black 20 12
- *a.* Double surcharge 2.00 2.00

Baseball Player

PT8

1937 Typographed *Perf. 11*

RA55 PT8 1c carmine 50 12
- *a.* Tête bêche pair 1.00 1.00

RA56 " 1c yellow 50 18
- *a.* Tête bêche pr. 1.00 1.00

RA57 " 1c blue 50 18
- *a.* Tête bêche pr. 1.00 1.00

RA58 " 1c green 50 18
- *a.* Tête bêche pair 1.00 1.00
- *b.* Sheet of four 4.50 4.50

Issued for the benefit of the Central American Caribbean Games of 1937.

Control mark in red is variously placed. See dark oval below "OLIMPICO" in illustration.

No. RA58b measures 134x90mm. and contains one each of Nos. RA55–58.

Proposed National Stadium, Managua

PT9 PT10

1949 Photogravure *Perf. 12*

RA60 PT9 5c greenish blue 25 4
- *a.* Souvenir sheet of 4 4.00 4.00

Issued to publicize the tenth World Series of Amateur Baseball, 1948. The tax was used toward the erection of a national stadium at Managua.

No. RA60a contains four of No. RA60 and has marginal inscriptions. Size: 87x96mm.

Type Similar to 1949, with "Correos" omitted.

1952

RA61 PT9 5c magenta 25 4

The tax was used toward the erection of a national stadium at Managua.

1956 Engraved. *Perf. 12½x12*

RA62 PT10 5c dp. ultramarine 10 4

The tax was used for social welfare.

Jesus and Children

PT11 PT12

Surcharged in Red or Black.

1959 *Perf. 12.* Unwmkd.

Red Marginal Number.

RA63 PT11 5c on 50c violet blue (R) 12 4
RA64 " 5c on 50c violet blue (B) 12 4

Nos. RA63–RA64 are surcharged on consular revenue stamps. Surcharge reads "Sobre Tasa Postal CO.05." Vertical surcharge on No. RA63, horizontal on No. RA64.

1959 Photogravure. *Perf. 16*

RA65 PT12 5c ultramarine 15 5

Hexisia Bidentata

PT13

Orchids: No. RA67, Schomburgkia tibicinus. No. RA68, Stanhopea ecornuta. No. RA69, Lycaste macrophylla. No. RA70, Maxillaria tenuifolia. No. RA71, Cattleya skinneri. No. RA72, Cycnoches egertonianum. No. RA73, Bletia roezlii. No. RA74, Sobralia pleiantha. No. RA75, Oncidium cebolleta and ascendens.

Granite Paper

1962, Feb. Photo. *Perf. 11½*

Orchids in Natural Colors

RA66 PT13 5c pale lilac & green 6 6
RA67 " 5c yel. & grn. 6 6
RA68 " 5c pink & green 6 6
RA69 " 5c pale violet & green 6 6
RA70 " 5c lt. greenish blue & red 6 6
RA71 " 5c buff & lilac 6 6
RA72 " 5c yel. grn. & brn. 6 6
RA73 " 5c gray & red 6 6
RA74 " 5c light blue & dark blue 6 6
RA75 " 5c light green & brown 6 6
Nos. RA66–RA75 (10) 60 60

Nos. RA66–RA75 overprinted "Camporee Scout 1965" are listed as Nos. 843–852.

PROVINCE OF ZELAYA

(så·lä′yä)

(Bluefields)

A province of Nicaragua lying along the eastern coast. Special postage stamps for this section were made necessary because for a period two currencies, which differed materially in value, were in use in Nicaragua. Silver money was used in Zelaya and Cabo Gracias a Dios while the rest of Nicaragua used paper money. Later the money of the entire country was placed on a gold basis.

Dangerous counterfeits exist of most of the Bluefields overprints.

Regular Issues of 1900-05 Handstamped in Black

B
Dpto Zelaya.

1904-05 *Perf. 12, 14.* Unwmkd.

On Engraved Stamps of 1900.

1L1 A14 1c plum 1.00 50
1L2 " 2c vermilion 1.00 50
1L3 " 3c green 1.25 1.00
1L4 " 4c olive green 7.50 7.50
1L5 " 15c ultramarine 2.00 1.25
1L6 " 20c brown 2.00 1.25
1L7 " 50c lake 6.50 5.00
1L8 " 1p yellow 12.50
1L9 " 2p salmon 17.50
1L10 " 5p black 20.00

On Lithographed Stamps of 1902.

1L11 A14 5c blue 2.00 50
1L12 " 5c carmine 1.25 60
1L13 " 10c violet 1.00 50

On Postage Due Stamps Overprinted "1901 Correos"

1L14 D3 20c brown (No. 156) 3.00 1.25
1L15 " 50c lake (No. 158) *225.00*

On Surcharged Stamps of 1904-05.

1L16 A16 5c on 10c violet on No. 175 1.00 75
1L17 A14 5c on 10c violet on No. 178 2.75 1.00
1L18 A16 15c on 10c violet 1.00 1.00
1L19 A17 15c on 10c violet 9.00 3.00

On Surcharged Stamp of 1901.

1L20 A14 20c on 5p black 11.00 1.75

On Regular Issue of 1905.

1906-07 *Perf. 12.*

1L21 A18 1c green 20 20
1L22 " 2c carmine rose 20 20
1L23 " 3c violet 20 20
1L24 " 4c orange red 30 30
1L25 " 5c blue 15 15
1L26 " 10c yellow brown 2.00 1.00
1L27 " 15c brown olive 3.00 1.20
1L28 " 20c lake 6.00 5.00
1L29 " 50c orange 22.50 20.00
1L30 " 1p black 17.50 17.50
1L31 " 2p dark green 20.00
1L32 " 5p violet 27.50
Nos. 1L21–1L30 (10) 52.05 45.75

On Surcharged Stamps of 1906-08.

1L33 A18 10c on 3c violet 25 25
1L34 " 15c on 1c green 35 35
1L35 " 20c on 2c rose 2.25 2.25
1L36 " 20c on 5c blue 1.00 1.00
1L37 " 50c on 6c slate(R) 1.00 2.00
Nos. 1L33–1L37 (5) 4.85 5.85

Four or more types exist of the foregoing overprints.

B **B**

Dpto. Zelaya **Dto. Zelaya**

Stamps with the above overprints were made to fill dealers' orders but were never regularly issued or used. Stamps with similar overprints handstamped are bogus.

Surcharged Stamps of 1906 Overprinted in Red, Black or Blue — **B** **Dpto. Zelaya**

1L38 A18 15c on 1c green(R) 1.75 1.75
a. Red overprint inverted
1L39 " 20c on 2c rose (Bk) 1.25 1.25
1L40 " 20c on 5c blue (R) 2.00 2.00
1L41 " 50c on 6c slate (Bl) 8.50 8.50

Stamps of the 1905 issue overprinted as above No. 1L38 or similarly overprinted but with only 2½mm. space between "B" and "Dpto. Zelaya" were made to fill dealers' orders but not placed in use.

No. 205 Handstamped in Black — **B** **Dpto Zelaya.**

Perf. 14 to 15.

1L42 A18 10c yellow brown 15.00 15.00

Stamps of 1907 Overprinted in Red or Black — **B** **Dpto Zelaya**

1L43 A18 15c brown olive (R) 2.25 1.25
1L44 " 20c lake 60 60
a. Invtd. ovpt. 7.50 7.50

With Additional Surcharge — **5 cent.**

1L45 A18 5c on 4c brn. org. 35 30
a. Invtd. surch. 5.00 5.00

With Additional Surcharge — **5 cent.**

1L46 A18 5c on 4c brown orange 7.00 7.00

On Provisional Postage Stamps of 1907-08.

1L47 A18 10c on 2c rose (Bl) 3.00 3.00
1L48 " 10c on 2c rose (Bk) *500.00*
1L48A " 10c on 4c brn. org. (Bk) *600.00*
1L49 " 10c on 20c lake (Bk) 2.00 2.00
1L50 " 10c on 50c orange (Bl) 2.00 1.50

Arms Type of 1905 Overprinted in Black or Violet — **"COSTA ATLANTICA" B.**

1907

1L51 A18 1c green 20 15
1L52 " 2c rose 20 15
1L53 " 3c violet 25 25
1L54 " 4c brown orange 30 30
1L55 " 5c blue 3.00 1.50
1L56 " 10c yellow brown 25 20
1L57 " 15c brown olive 50 25
1L58 " 20c lake 50 30
1L59 " 50c orange 1.50 1.00
1L60 " 1p black (V) 1.50 1.00
1L61 " 2p dark green 1.50 1.25
1L62 " 5p violet 2.50 1.50
Nos. 1L51–1L62 (12) 12.20 7.85

Nos. 217–225 Overprinted in Green — **B** **Dpto. Zelaya**

1908

1L63 A19 1c on 5c yellow & black (R) 30 25
1L64 " 2c on 5c yellow & black (Bl) 30 25
1L65 " 4c on 5c yellow & black (G) 30 25
a. Ovpt. reading down 7.50 7.50
b. Double overprint, reading up and down 12.00 12.00
1L66 " 5c yellow & black 30 30
a. "CORROE" 3.00
b. Double overprint 7.50 7.50
c. Double overprint, reading up and down 12.50 12.50
d. "CORREO 1908" double 10.00 10.00
1L67 " 10c lt. blue & black 30 30
a. Ovpt. reading down 35 35
b. "CORREO 1908" triple 25.00
1L68 " 15c on 50c olive & black (R) 60 60
a. "1008" 3.00
b. "8908" 3.00
1L69 " 35c on 50c olive & black 90 90
1L70 " 1p yel. brn. & blk. 1.25 1.25
a. "CORROE" 8.00 8.00
1L71 " 2p pearl gray & black 1.50 1.50
a. "CORROE" 10.00 10.00
Nos. 1L63–1L71 (9) 5.75 5.60

Overprinted Horizontally in Black or Green.

1L72 A19 5c yellow & black 6.00 5.00
1L72A " 2p pearl gray & black (G) *100.00*

On Nos. 1L72–1L72A, space between "B" and "Dpto. Zelaya" is 13mm.

Nos. 237–248 Overprinted in Black — **B** **Dpto. Zelaya**

Imprint:
"American Bank Note Co. NY"

1909 *Perf. 12*

1L73 A18 1c yellow green 15 15
1L74 " 2c vermilion 15 15
a. Inverted overprint
1L75 " 3c red orange 15 15
1L76 " 4c violet 15 15
1L77 " 5c deep blue 20 15
a. Invtd. ovpt. 6.00 6.00
b. "B" inverted 5.00 5.00
c. Double overprint 8.00 8.00
1L78 " 6c gray brown 3.00 2.00
1L79 " 10c lake 20 18
a. "B" inverted 6.00 6.00
1L80 " 15c black 30 25
a. "B" inverted 7.50 7.50
b. Invtd. ovpt. 8.00 8.00
c. Double overprint 9.00 9.00
1L81 " 20c brown olive 35 35
a. "B" inverted 12.50 12.50
1L82 " 50c deep green 1.00 1.00
1L83 " 1p yellow 1.50 1.50
1L84 " 2p carmine rose 2.00 2.00
a. Double ovpt. 17.50 17.50
Nos. 1L73–1L84 (12) 9.15 8.03

One stamp in each sheet has the "o" of "Dpto." sideways.

Overprinted in Black — **B** **Dpto. Zelaya**

1910

1L85 A18 3c red orange 25 25
1L86 " 4c violet 25 25
a. Invtd. ovpt. 9.00 9.00
1L87 " 15c black 3.00 1.50
1L88 " 20c brown olive 15 20
1L89 " 50c deep green 18 25
1L90 A18 1p yellow 20 30
a. Invtd. ovpt. 5.00
1L91 " 2p carmine rose 25 50
Nos. 1L85–1L91 (7) 4.28 3.25

Z1

Black Ovpt., Green Surch., Carmine Block-outs

1910

1L92 Z1 5c on 10c lake 2.50 2.00

There are three types of the letter "B". It is stated that this stamp was used exclusively for postal purposes and not for telegrams.

No. 247 Surcharged in Black — **B Vale 5 cts.**

1911

1L93 A18 5c on 1p yellow 50 50
a. Double surcharge 9.00
1L94 " 10c on 1p yellow 1.00 1.00
1L95 " 15c on 1p yellow 50 50
a. Inverted surcharge 6.00
b. Double surcharge 6.00
c. Double surcharge, one inverted 9.00

Revenue Stamps Surcharged in Black — **B CORREOS 05 cts. 1911**

Perf. 14 to 15.

1L96 A19 5c on 25c lilac 50 75
a. Without period 1.00 1.00
b. Inverted surcharge 6.00 6.00
1L97 " 10c on 1p yel. brn. 75 50
a. Without period 1.25 1.25
b. "01" for "10" 6.00 5.00
c. Inverted surcharge 9.00 9.00

Surcharged in Black — **VALE 05 cts. POSTAL B de 1911**

1L98 A19 5c on 1p yellow brown 1.00 1.00
a. Without period 1.50
b. "50" for "05" 9.00 9.00
c. Inverted surcharge 10.00 10.00
1L99 " 5c on 10p pink 1.00 1.00
a. Without period 1.50 1.50
b. "50" for "05" 7.50 7.50
1L100 " 10c on 1p yellow brown 50.00 50.00
a. Without period 60.00 60.00
1L101 " 10c on 25p green 50 50
a. Without period 1.50 1.50
b. "1" for "10" 5.00
1L102 " 10c on 50p vermilion 8.00 8.00
a. Without period 10.00
b. "1" for "10" 15.00
Nos. 1L98–1L102 (5) *60.50 60.50*

With Additional Overprint "1904".

1L103 A19 5c on 10p pink 10.00 10.00
a. Without period 15.00 15.00
b. "50" for "05" 75.00 75.00
1L104 A19 10c on 2p gray 50 50
a. Without period 1.25
b. "1" for "10" 5.00
1L105 " 10c on 25p green 50.00
a. Without period 65.00
1L106 " 10c on 50p vermilion 5.00 5.00
a. Without period 9.00
b. "1" for "10" 12.00
c. Inverted surcharge

The surcharges on Nos. 1L96 to 1L106 are in settings of twenty-five. One stamp in each setting has a large square period after "cts" and another has a thick upright "c" in that word. There are two types of "1904".

No. 293C Overprinted — **B** **Dpto. Zelaya**

1911

1L107 A21 5c on 5c on 2c blue (R) 15.00
a. "5" omitted 17.50
b. Red overprint inverted 20.00
c. Varieties "a" and "b" combined 25.00

Same Overprint On Nos. 290, 291, 292 and 289D with Lines of Surcharge spaced 2½ mm. apart Reading Down.

1L107D A21 2c on 10c on 1c red *50.00*
e. Ovpt. reading up *100.00*
1L107F " 5c on 10c on 1c red *50.00*
1L107G " 10c on 10c on 1c red (on No. 292) *85.00*
1L108 " 10c on 10c on 1c red (on No. 289D) *75.00*

Locomotive Z2

1912 Engraved *Perf. 14*

1L109 Z2 1c yellow green 50 50
1L110 " 2c vermilion 35 25
1L111 " 3c orange brown 50 45
1L112 " 4c carmine 50 30
1L113 " 5c deep blue 50 45
1L114 " 6c red brown 2.50 2.10
1L115 " 10c slate 50 30
1L116 " 15c dull lilac 40 60
1L117 " 20c blue violet 40 60
1L118 " 25c green & black 60 80
1L119 " 35c brown & black 75 1.00
1L120 " 50c olive green 75 1.00
1L121 " 1p orange 1.00 1.50
1L122 " 2p orange brown 2.50 3.00
1L123 " 5p dark blue green 5.00 6.00
Nos. 1L109–1L123 (15) 16.75 18.85

The stamps of this issue were for use in all places on the Atlantic Coast of Nicaragua where the currency was on a silver basis.

OFFICIAL STAMPS.

Regular Issue of 1909 Overprinted in Black — **Oficial B**

1909 *Perf. 12.* **Unwmkd.**

1LO1 A18 20c brown olive 10.00 7.50
a. Double overprint 12.50

Official Stamp of 1909 Overprinted in Black — **B**

1LO2 A18 15c black 10.00 7.50

Same Overprint on Official Stamp of 1911

1911

1LO3 A18 5c on 3c red org. 15.00 12.50

CABO GRACIAS A DIOS

(kä'bō grä'sē-äs ä dyōs')

A cape and seaport town in the extreme northeast of Nicaragua. The name was coined by Spanish explorers who had great difficulty finding a landing place along the Nicaraguan coast and when eventually locating this harbor expressed their relief by designating the point "Cape Thanks to God". Special postage stamps came into use for the same reasons as the Zelaya issues. (See Zelaya.)

Dangerous counterfeits exist of most of the Cabo Gracias a Dios overprints.

Regular Issues of 1900-04 Handstamped in Violet **CABO**

On Engraved Stamps of 1900.

1904-05 *Perf. 12, 14.* **Unwmkd.**

2L1	A14	1c plum	1.50	75
2L2	"	2c vermilion	3.00	85
2L3	"	3c green	4.00	3.00
2L4	"	4c olive green	6.00	6.00
2L5	"	15c ultramarine	20.00	17.50
2L6	"	20c brown	2.00	1.50
		Nos. 2L1-2L6 (6)	36.50	29.60

On Lithographed Stamps of 1902.

2L7	A14	5c blue	15.00	15.00
2L8	"	10c violet	2.00	50

On Surcharged Stamps of 1904.

2L9	A16	5c on 10c violet	15.00	15.00
2L10	"	15c on 10c violet	*175.00*	*125.00*

On Postage Due Stamps.

Violet Handstamp.

2L11	D3	20c orange brown (No. 141)	3.00	75
2L12	"	20c orange brown (No. 156)	2.00	75
2L13	"	30c dark green (No. 157)	8.50	8.50
2L14	"	50c lake (No. 158)	2.50	50

Black Handstamp.

2L15	D3	30c dark green (No. 157)	15.00	15.00

Stamps of 1900-05 Handstamped in Violet *Cabo*

On Engraved Stamps of 1900.

2L16	A14	1c plum	1.75	1.25
2L17	"	2c vermilion	17.50	15.00
2L18	"	3c green	22.50	17.50
2L19	"	4c olive green	25.00	22.50
2L20	"	15c ultramarine	27.50	27.50
		Nos. 2L16-2L20 (5)	94.25	83.75

On Lithographed Stamps of 1902.

2L22	A14	5c dark blue	60.00	30.00
2L23	"	10c violet	17.50	15.00

On Surcharged Stamp of 1904.

2L24	A16	5c on 10c violet		

On Postage Due Stamp.

2L25	D3	20c orange brown (No. 141)		*300.00*

Cabo

The editors can find no evidence that stamps with this handstamp were used.

Stamps of 1900-08 Handstamped in Violet **CÂBO**

1905 On Stamps of 1905.

2L26	A18	1c green	75	75
		a. Magenta handstamp	2.50	2.00
2L27	"	2c carmine rose	1.00	1.00
		a. Magenta handstamp	2.00	1.75
2L28	A18	3c violet	1.00	1.00
		a. Magenta handstamp	2.50	2.00
2L29	"	4c orange red	2.50	2.50
2L30	"	5c blue	1.00	75
		a. Magenta handstamp	5.00	4.00
2L31	"	6c slate	2.50	2.50
2L32	"	10c yellow brown	2.00	1.25
2L33	"	15c brown olive	3.00	3.00
		a. Magenta handstamp	9.00	7.50
2L34	"	1p black	12.50	12.50
2L35	"	2p dark green	20.00	20.00
		Nos. 2L26-2L35 (10)	46.25	45.25

On Stamps of 1900-04.

2L36	A16	5c on 10c violet	10.00	10.00
2L37	A14	10c violet		
2L38	"	20c brown	7.50	7.50
2L39	"	20c on 5p black		60.00

On Postage Due Stamps Overprinted "Correos".

2L40	D3	20c orange brown (No. 141)	5.00	5.00
2L41	"	20c orange brown (No. 156)	3.50	2.50

On Surcharged Stamps of 1906-08.

2L42	A18	10c on 3c violet		
2L43	"	20c on 5c blue	5.00	5.00
2L44	"	50c on 6c slate	15.00	15.00

On Stamps of 1907.

Perf. 14 to 15.

2L44A	A18	2c rose		
2L45	"	10c yellow brown	*65.00*	*45.00*
2L46	"	15c brown olive	*55.00*	*45.00*

On Provisional Stamp of 1908 in Magenta

2L47	A19	5c yel. & black	5.00	5.00

Stamps with the above large handstamp in black instead of violet, are bogus. There are also excellent counterfeits in violet.

The foregoing overprints being handstamped are found in various positions, especially the last type.

Stamps of 1905-07, Type A18 Overprinted in Black or Violet **"COSTA ATLANTICA" C.**

1907

2L48	A18	1c green	20	20
2L49	"	2c rose	20	20
2L50	"	3c violet	20	20
		a. Vertical pair, imperf. between	10.00	
2L51	"	4c brown orange	25	25
2L52	"	5c blue	35	35
2L53	"	10c yellow brown	25	25
2L54	"	15c brown olive	50	50
2L55	"	20c lake	50	50
2L56	"	50c orange	1.25	1.00
2L57	"	1p black (V)	1.50	1.25
2L58	"	2p dark green	2.00	1.50
2L59	"	5p violet	3.00	2.50
		Nos. 2L48-2L59 (12)	10.20	8.70

Nos. 237-248 Overprinted in Black **C** **Dpto. Zelaya**

Imprint: American Bank Note Co.

1909 *Perf. 12.*

2L60	A18	1c yellow green	20	25
2L61	"	2c vermilion	20	25
2L62	"	3c red orange	20	25
2L63	"	4c violet	20	25
2L64	"	5c deep blue	25	40
2L65	"	6c gray brown	3.50	3.50
2L66	"	10c lake	35	50
2L67	"	15c black	50	60
2L68	"	20c brown olive	60	75
2L69	"	50c deep green	1.50	1.50
2L70	"	1p yellow	2.50	2.50
2L71	"	2p carmine rose	3.50	3.50
		Nos. 2L60-2L71 (12)	13.50	14.25

No. 199 Overprinted Vertically **CABO**

2L72	A18	50c on 6c slate (R)	6.00	6.00

OFFICIAL STAMPS.

Official Stamps of 1907 Overprinted in Red or Violet **CÂBO**

1907

2LO1	A18	10c on 1c green		*55.00*
2LO2	"	15c on 1c "		*70.00*
2LO3	"	20c on 1c "		*90.00*
2LO4	"	50c on 1c "		*110.00*

NIGER

(nī'jẽr)

LOCATION—In northern Africa, directly north of Nigeria.

GOVT.—Republic; former French Colony.

AREA—494,500 sq. mi.

POP.—4,860,000 (est. 1977).

CAPITAL—Niamey.

The colony, formed in 1922, was originally a military territory. The Republic of the Niger was proclaimed Dec. 19, 1958. In the period between issues of the colony and the republic, stamps of French West Africa were used.

100 Centimes = 1 Franc

Camel and Rider

A1

Stamps of Upper Senegal and Niger Type of 1914, Overprinted.

Perf. 13½x14.

1921-26 **Unwmkd.**

1	A1	1c brn. vio. & violet	6	6
2	"	2c dark gray & dull violet	6	6
3	"	4c black & blue	7	7
4	"	5c olive brown & dark brown	10	10
5	"	10c yellow green & blue green	30	30
6	"	10c magenta, *bluish* ('26)	8	8
7	"	15c red brown & org.	10	10
8	"	20c brn. vio. & black	8	8
9	"	25c black & blue grn.	8	8
10	"	30c red orange & rose	20	20
11	"	30c blue green & red orange ('26)	10	10
12	"	35c rose & violet	10	10
13	"	40c gray & rose	15	15
14	"	45c blue & olive brown	15	15
15	"	50c ultramarine & blue	15	15
16	"	50c dark gray & blue violet ('25)	12	12
17	"	60c orange red ('26)	20	20
18	"	75c yel. & olive brn.	25	25
19	"	1fr dark brown & dull violet	25	25
20	"	2fr green & blue	35	35
21	"	5fr violet & black	60	60
		Nos. 1-21 (21)	3.55	3.55

Stamps and Type of 1921 Surcharged New Value and Bars in Black or Red **60 = 60**

1922-26

22	A1	25c on 15c red brown & orange ('25)	7	7
		a. Triple surch.	30.00	
		b. "25c" inverted	30.00	
23	"	25c on 2fr green & blue (R) ('24)	10	10
24	"	25c on 5fr violet & black (R) ('24)	10	10
		a. Double surch.	30.00	
25	A1	60c on 75c violet, *pinkish*	7	7
26	"	65c on 45c blue & olive brown ('25)	55	55
27	"	85c on 75c yellow & olive brown ('25)	55	55
28	"	1.25fr on 1fr deep blue & light blue (R) ('26)	7	7
		a. Surcharge omitted	50.00	
		Nos. 22-28 (7)	1.51	1.51

Nos. 22-24 are surcharged "25c", No. 28, "1f25". Nos. 25-27 are surcharged like illustration.

Drawing Water from Well

A2

Zinder Fortress

A4

Boat on Niger River

A3

Perf. 13x14, 13½x14, 14x13, 14x13½.

1926-40 Typographed.

29	A2	1c lilac rose & olive	4	4
30	"	2c dark gray & dull red	6	6
31	"	3c red violet & olive gray ('40)	4	4
32	"	4c umber & gray	8	7
33	"	5c verm. & yel. grn.	10	10
34	"	10c deep blue & Prussian blue	6	6
35	"	15c gray green & yellow green	7	7
36	"	15c gray lilac & light red ('28)	12	12
37	A3	20c Prussian green & olive brown	8	7
38	"	25c black & dull red	8	6
39	"	30c blue green & yellow green	15	10
40	"	30c yellow & red violet ('40)	5	5
41	"	35c brown orange & turquoise blue, *bluish*	8	7
42	"	35c blue green & dull green ('38)	8	8
43	"	40c red brown & slate	7	7
44	"	45c yellow & red vio.	20	20
45	"	45c blue green & dull green ('40)	10	10
46	"	50c scarlet & green, *greenish*	10	7
47	"	55c dark carmine & brown ('38)	20	20
48	"	60c dark carmine & brown ('40)	8	8
49	"	65c olive green & rose	10	8
50	"	70c olive green & rose ('40)	25	25
51	"	75c green & violet, *pink*	35	30
52	"	80c claret & olive green ('38)	30	30
53	"	90c brn. red & verm.	20	15
54	"	90c bright rose & yellow green ('39)	25	25
55	A4	1fr rose & yel. grn.	2.50	1.85
56	"	1fr dark red & red orange ('38)	25	20
57	"	1fr green & red ('40)	10	10
58	"	1.10fr olive brown & green	1.00	85
59	"	1.25fr green & red ('33)	30	30

60 A4 1.25fr dark red & red orange ('39) 10 10
61 " 1.40fr red violet & dark brown ('40) 10 10
62 " 1.50fr deep blue & pale blue 7 5
63 " 1.60fr olive brown & green ('40) 25 25
64 " 1.75fr red violet & dark brown ('33) 70 65
65 " 1.75fr dark blue & violet blue ('38) 20 20
66 " 2fr red orange & olive brown 8 8
67 " 2.25fr dark blue & violet blue ('39) 12 12
68 " 2.50fr black brown ('40) 15 15
69 " 3fr dull violet & black ('27) 12 12
70 " 5fr violet brown & black, *pink* 15 15
71 " 10fr chalky blue & magenta 35 35
72 " 20fr yellow green & red orange 45 45
Nos. 29-72 (44) 10.28 9.11

Colonial Exposition Issue.
Common Design Types

1931 Typographed. ***Perf. 12½.***

Name of Country in Black.

73 CD70 40c deep green 1.35 1.10
74 CD71 50c violet 1.35 1.10
75 CD72 90c red orange 1.40 1.35
76 CD73 1.50fr dull blue 1.40 1.35

Paris International Exposition Issue.
Common Design Types

1937 ***Perf. 13.***

77 CD74 20c deep violet 30 30
78 CD75 30c dark green 30 30
79 CD76 40c carmine rose 30 30
80 CD77 50c dark brown 30 30
81 CD78 90c red 30 30
82 CD79 1.50fr ultramarine 30 30
Nos. 77-82 (6) 1.80 1.80

Colonial Arts Exhibition Issue.
Souvenir Sheet.
Common Design Type

1937 ***Imperf.***

83 CD74 3fr magenta 1.50 1.50

Issued in sheets measuring 118x99 mm. containing one stamp.

Caillie Issue.
Common Design Type

1939 ***Perf. 12½x12.***

84 CD81 90c org. brn. & org. 25 25
85 " 2fr bright violet 25 25
86 " 2.25fr ultra. & dk. blue 25 25

Issued to commemorate the centenary of the death of René Caillié, French explorer.

New York World's Fair Issue.
Common Design Type

1939, May 10

87 CD82 1.25fr carmine lake 30 30
88 " 2.25fr ultramarine 30 30

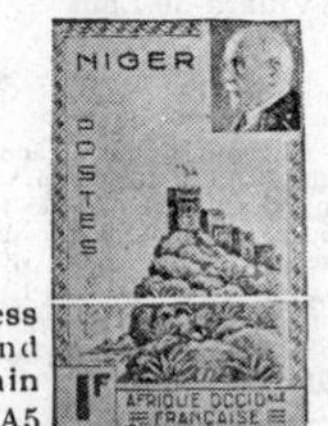

Zinder Fortress and Marshal Pétain
A5

Engraved.

1941 ***Perf. 12x12½.*** **Unwmkd.**

89 A5 1fr green 10
90 " 2.50fr dark blue 10

Nos. 89-90 were issued by the Vichy government and were not placed on sale in the colony.

Republic of the Niger

Giraffes
A6

Designs: 1fr, 2fr, Crested cranes. 5fr, 7fr, Saddle-billed storks. 15fr, 20fr, Barbary sheep. 25fr, 30fr, Giraffes. 50fr, 60fr, Ostriches. 85fr, 100fr, Lion.

Engraved

1959-60 ***Perf. 13*** **Unwmkd.**

91 A6 1fr multicolored 5 5
92 " 2fr " 5 5
93 " 5fr black, carmine & olive 8 8
94 " 7fr grn., black & red 10 8
95 " 15fr greenish blue & dark brown 30 8
96 " 20fr violet, black & indigo 35 8
97 " 25fr multicolored 40 10
98 " 30fr " 50 25
99 " 50fr indigo & orange brown 90 45
100 " 60fr dark brown & emerald 1.10 65
101 " 85fr orange brown & bistre 1.40 70
102 " 100fr bistre & yellow green 1.75 90
Nos. 91-102 (12) 6.98 3.47

No. 97 was issued in 1959; Nos. 91-96 and 98-102 in 1960.

Imperforates

Most stamps of the republic exist imperforate in issued and trial colors, and also in small presentation sheets in issued color.

No. 102 Surcharged with New Value and: "Indépendance 3-8-60."

1960

103 A6 200fr on 100fr orange brown & bistre 7.50 7.50

Issued to commemorate Niger's independence.

C.C.T.A. Issue
Common Design Type

1960 Engraved ***Perf. 13***

104 CD106 25fr buff & red brown 65 55

Emblem of the Entente—A6a

1960 Photogravure ***Perf. 13x13½***

105 A6a 25fr multicolored 65 50

Issued to commemorate the first anniversary of the Entente (Dahomey, Ivory Coast, Niger and Upper Volta).

Common Design Types
pictured in section at front of book.

President Diori Hamani
A7

1960, Dec. 18 Engraved ***Perf. 13***

106 A7 25fr olive bistre & black 40 25

Issued to commemorate the second anniversary of the proclamation of the Republic of the Niger.

Manatee
A8

1962, Jan. 29 ***Perf. 13*** **Unwmkd.**

107 A8 50c green & dark slate green 5 5
108 " 10fr red brown & dark green 25 10

Abidjan Games Issue
Common Design Type

Designs: 25fr, Basketball and Soccer. 85fr, Track (horiz.).

1962, May 26 Photo. ***Perf. 12x12½***

109 CD109 15fr multicolored 20 15
110 " 25fr " 40 25
111 " 85fr " 1.25 70

Abidjan Games, Dec. 24-31, 1961.

African-Malgache Union Issue
Common Design Type

1962, Sept. 8 ***Perf. 12½x12***

112 CD110 30fr multicolored 55 40

Issued to commemorate the first anniversary of the African and Malgache Union.

Pres. Diori Hamani and Map of Niger in Africa—A10

1962, Dec. 18 Photo. ***Perf. 12½x12***

113 A10 25fr multicolored 40 35

Woman Runner
A11

Woodworker
A12

Designs: 15fr, Swimming (horiz.). 45fr, Volleyball.

Engraved

1963, Apr. 11 ***Perf. 13*** **Unwmkd.**

114 A11 15fr bright blue & dark brown 25 15
115 " 25fr dk. brown & red 40 22
116 " 45fr green & black 70 45

Friendship Games, Dakar, Apr. 11-21.

Perf. 12x12½, 12½x12

1963, Aug. 30 Photogravure

Designs: 10fr, Tanners (horiz.). 25fr, Goldsmith. 30fr, Mat makers (horiz.). 85fr, Decoy maker.

117 A12 5fr brn. & multi. 10 8
118 " 10fr dk. grn. & multi. 15 13
119 " 25fr black & multi. 40 22
120 " 30fr violet & multi. 50 27
121 " 85fr dk. bl. & multi. 1.25 70
Nos. 117-121, C26 (6) 3.90 2.15

Berberi (Nuba) Woman's Costume
A13

Costume Museum, Niamey—A14

Costumes: 20fr, Hausa woman. 25fr, Tuareg woman. 30fr, Tuareg man. 60fr, Djerma woman.

Perf. 12x12½, 12½x12

1963, Oct. 15 Photogravure

122 A13 15fr multicolored 25 12
123 " 20fr black & blue 35 15
124 " 25fr multicolored 45 20
125 " 30fr " 50 25
126 " 60fr " 1.10 65
127 A14 85fr " 1.35 75
Nos. 122-127 (6) 4.00 2.12

Man, Globe and Scales
A15

Parkinsonia Aculeata
A16

Engraved

1963, Dec. 10 ***Perf. 13*** **Unwmkd.**

128 A15 25fr light olive green, ultra. & brown orange 42 30

Issued to commemorate the 15th anniversary of the Universal Declaration of Human Rights.

1964-65 Photo. ***Perf. 13½x13***

Flowers: 10fr, Russelia equisetiformis. 15fr, Red sage (lantana). 20fr, Argyreia nervosa. 25fr, Luffa cylindrica. 30fr, Hibiscus rosa sinensis. 45fr, Red jasmine (frangipani). 50fr, Catharanthus roseus. 60fr, Caesalpinia pulcherrima.

129 A16 5fr dark red, green & yellow 45 20
130 " 10fr multicolored 35 20
131 " 15fr " 50 25
132 " 20fr " 50 25
133 " 25fr " 50 25
134 " 30fr " 70 25
135 " 45fr multi. ('65) 90 45
136 " 50fr dk. red, brt. pink & green ('65) 90 45
137 " 60fr multi. ('65) 1.35 65
Nos. 129-137 (9) 6.15 2.95

Solar Flares and IQSY Emblem
A17

1964, May 12 Engraved *Perf. 13*

138 A17 30fr deep orange, violet & black 55 40

International Quiet Sun Year, 1964–65.

Mobile Medical Unit
A18

Designs: 30fr, Mobile children's clinic. 50fr, Mobile women's clinic. 60fr, Outdoor medical laboratory.

1964, May 26

139 A18 25fr blue, org. & olive 45 20
140 " 30fr multicolored 50 25
141 " 50fr vio., org. & blue 75 30
142 " 60fr greenish blue, org. & dk. brn. 90 40

Issued to publicize the Nigerian mobile health education organization, OMNES (Organisation Médicale Mobile Nigérienne d'Education Sanitaire).

Cooperation Issue
Common Design Type

1964, Nov. 7 *Perf. 13* Unwmkd.

143 CD119 50fr vio., dk. brn. & orange 75 45

See note after Madagascar No. 360.

Tuareg Tent of Azawak
A19

Designs: 20fr, Songhaï house. 25fr, Wogo and Kourtey tents. 30fr, Djerma house. 60fr, Huts of Sorkawa fishermen. 85fr, Hausa town house.

1964–65 Engraved

144 A19 15fr ultra., dull grn. & red brown 20 20
145 " 20fr multicolored 30 20
146 " 25fr Pruss. blue, dk. brn. & org. brown 35 20
147 " 30fr multi. ('65) 40 27
148 " 60fr red, green & bister ('65) 75 30
149 " 85fr multi. ('65) 1.10 55
Nos. 144-149 (6) 3.10 1.72

Leprosy Examination
A20

Abraham Lincoln
A21

1964, Dec. 15 Photo. *Perf. 13x12½*

150 A20 50fr multicolored 65 55

Issued to publicize the fight against leprosy.

1965, Apr. 3 *Perf. 13x12½*

151 A21 50fr violet blue, blk., & ocher 75 60

Centenary of death of Abraham Lincoln.

Teaching with Radio and Pictures
A22

Designs: 25fr, Woman studying arithmetic: "A better life through knowledge." 30fr, Adult education class. 50fr, Map of Niger and 5 tribesmen, "Literacy for adults."

1965, Apr. 16 Engraved *Perf. 13*

152 A22 20fr dk. blue, dark brn. & ocher 35 20
153 " 25fr slate green, brn. & olive brn. 45 15
154 " 30fr red, slate green & vio. brown 50 25
155 " 50fr dp. blue, brown & vio. brown 80 38

Issued to promote adult education and "a better life through knowledge."

Ader Portable Telephone
A23

Runner
A24

Designs: 30fr, Wheatstone telegraph interrupter. 50fr, Early telewriter.

1965, May 17 *Perf. 13* Unwmkd.

156 A23 25fr red brown, dark green & indigo 42 20
157 " 30fr lilac, slate green & red 50 30
158 " 50fr red, slate green & purple 75 45

Issued to commemorate the centenary of the International Telecommunication Union.

1965, July 1 Engraved *Perf. 13*

Designs: 10fr, Hurdler (horiz.). 20fr, Pole vaulter (horiz.). 30fr, Long jumper.

159 A24 10fr brn., ocher & blk. 25 8
160 " 15fr gray, brn. & red 30 12
161 " 20fr dk. grn., brown & violet blue 35 15
162 " 30fr maroon, brown & green 50 20

African Games, Brazzaville, July 18–25.

Radio Interview and Club Emblem
A25

Designs (Club Emblem and): 45fr, Recording folk music (vert.). 50fr, Group listening to broadcast (vert.). 60fr, Public debate.

1965, Oct. 1 Engraved *Perf. 13*

163 A25 30fr bright violet, emerald & red brown 45 18
164 " 45fr black, car. & buff 65 28
165 " 50fr dk. car., blue & light brown 70 32
166 A25 60fr bister, ultra. & brown 80 40

Issued to promote radio clubs.

Water Cycle
A26

1966, Feb. 28 Engraved *Perf. 13*

167 A26 50fr vio., ocher & bl. 75 40

Hydrological Decade, 1965–74.

Carvings, Mask and Headdresses
A27

Designs: 50fr, Carvings and wall decorations. 60fr, Carvings and arch. 100fr, Architecture and handicraft.

1966, Apr. 12

168 A27 30fr red brown, black & brt. green 45 25
169 " 50fr bright blue, ocher & purple 75 35
170 " 60fr car. lake, dull pur. & yellow brown 90 45
171 " 100fr brt. red, bl. & blk. 1.50 65

Issued to commemorate the International Negro Arts Festival, Dakar, Senegal, Apr. 1–24.

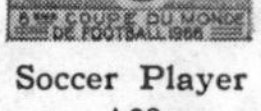

Soccer Player
A28

Color Guard
A29

Designs: 50fr, Goalkeeper (horiz.). 60fr, Player kicking ball.

1966, June 17 Engraved *Perf. 13*

172 A28 30fr dk. brn., brt. bl. & rose red 50 20
173 " 50fr blue, chocolate & emerald 75 28
174 " 60fr bl., lilac & brn. 90 40

Issued to commemorate the 8th World Soccer Cup Championship, Wembley, England, July 11–30.

Perf. 12½x13, 13x12½

1966, Aug. 23 Photogravure

Designs: 20fr, Parachutist (horiz.). 45fr, Tanks (horiz.).

175 A29 20fr multicolored 35 15
176 " 30fr " 45 20
177 " 45fr " 65 40

Issued to commemorate the 5th anniversary of the National Armed Forces.

Cow Receiving Injection
A30

1966, Sept. 26 Litho. *Perf. 12½x13*

178 A30 45fr org. brn., blue & black 65 30

Campaign against cattle plague.

UNESCO Emblem
A31

1966, Nov. 4 Litho. *Perf. 13x12½*

179 A31 50fr multicolored 90 30

20th anniversary of UNESCO.

Cement Works Malbaza
A32

Designs: 10fr, Furnace (vert.). 20fr, Electric center. 50fr, Handling of raw material.

1966, Dec. 17 Engraved *Perf. 13*

180 A32 10fr indigo, brown & orange 15 8
181 " 20fr dk. olive green & dull blue 40 12
182 " 30fr blue, gray & red brown 50 15
183 " 50fr indigo, bl. & brn. 70 28

Red-billed Hornbill
A33

Birds: 2fr, Pied kingfisher. 30fr, Barbary shrike. 45fr, Little weaver and nest. 70fr, Two chestnut-bellied sandgrouse.

1967 Engraved *Perf. 13*

184 A33 1fr red, slate green & dk. brown 5 3
185 " 2fr brn., brt. green & black 5 3
186 " 30fr multicolored 45 20
187 " 45fr " 55 30
188 " 70fr " 80 55
Nos. 184-188 (5) 1.90 1.11

Issue dates: 45fr, 70fr, Nov. 18. Others, Feb. 8. See No. 237.

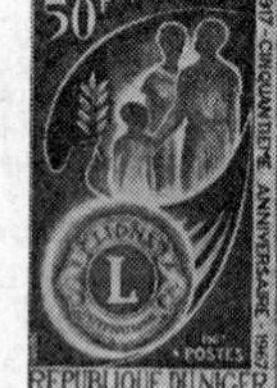

Villard-de-Lans and Olympic Emblem
A34

Lions Emblem and Family
A35

Olympic Emblem and Mountains: 45fr, Autrans and ski jump. 60fr, Saint Nizier du Moucherotte and ski jump. 90fr, Chamrousse and course for downhill and slalom races.

1967, Feb. 24

190 A34 30fr grn., ultra., brn. 40 20
191 " 45fr " " " 60 35
192 " 60fr " " " 80 40
193 " 90fr " " " 1.20 60

Issued to publicize the 10th Winter Olympic Games, Grenoble, 1968.

1967, March 4

194 A35 50fr dk. green, brn. red & ultra. 75 40

Lions International, 50th anniversary.

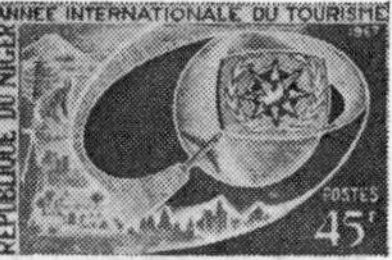

ITY Emblem, Views, Globe and Plane
A36

1967, Apr. 28 Engraved *Perf. 13*

195 A36 45fr vio., brt. green & red lilac 65 40

International Tourist Year, 1967.

1967 Jamboree Emblem and Scouts
A37

Red Cross Aides Carrying Sick Man
A38

Designs (Jamboree Emblem and): 45fr, Scouts gathering from all directions (horiz.). 80fr, Campfire.

1967, May 25 Engraved *Perf. 13*

196 A37 30fr maroon, Prus. blue & olive 40 20
197 " 45fr org., vio. blue & brn. olive 60 35
198 " 80fr multicolored 1.10 60

Issued to publicize the 12th Boy Scout World Jamboree, Farragut State Park, Idaho, Aug. 1–9.

1967, July 13 Engraved *Perf. 13*

Designs: 50fr, Nurse, mother and infant. 60fr, Physician examining woman.

199 A38 45fr blk., grn. & car. 60 25
200 " 50fr grn., blk. & car. 70 30
201 " 60fr blk., grn. & car. 80 35

Issued for the Red Cross.

Europafrica Issue, 1967

Map of Europe and Africa
A39

1967, July 20 Photo. *Perf. 12½x12*

202 A39 50fr multicolored 75 40

Women and U.N. Emblem
A40

1967, Oct. 21 Engraved *Perf. 13*

203 A40 50fr brn., brt. blue & yellow 70 40

U.N. Commission on Status of Women.

Monetary Union Issue
Common Design Type

1967, Nov. 4 Engraved *Perf. 13*

204 CD125 30fr grn. & dk. gray 40 20

Issued to commemorate the 5th anniversary of the West African Monetary Union.

Human Rights Flame, Globe, People and Statue of Liberty
A41

1968, Feb. 19 Engraved *Perf. 13*

205 A41 50fr brown, indigo & bright blue 65 35

International Human Rights Year.

Woman Dancing and WHO Emblem
A42

1968, Apr. 8 Engraved *Perf. 13*

206 A42 50fr brt. blue, black & red brown 65 40

Issued to commemorate the 20th anniversary of the World Health Organization.

Gray Hornbill
A43

Birds: 10fr, Woodland kingfisher. 15fr, Senegalese coucal. 20fr, Rose-ringed parakeets. 25fr, Abyssinian roller. 50fr, Cattle egret.

Dated "1968"

1968, Nov. 15 Photo. *Perf. 12½x13*

207 A43 5fr dk. green & multi. 6 6
208 " 10fr green & multi. 12 8
209 " 15fr bl. violet & multi. 18 15
210 " 20fr pink & multi. 24 17
211 " 25fr olive & multi. 30 15
212 " 50fr purple & multi. 55 30
Nos. 207-212 (6) 1.45 91

See Nos. 233–236, 316.

ILO Emblem and "Labor Supporting the World"
A44

1969, Apr. 22 Engraved *Perf. 13*

213 A44 30fr yellow green & dark carmine 40 20
214 " 50fr dark carmine & yellow green 65 40

Issued to commemorate the 50th anniversary of the World Labor Organization.

Red Crosses, Mother and Child
A45

Designs: 50fr, People, globe, red crosses (horiz.). 70fr, Man with gift parcel and red crosses.

1969, May 5 Engraved *Perf. 13*

215 A45 45fr blue, red & brown olive 55 30
216 " 50fr dark green, red & gray 60 30
217 " 70fr ocher, red & dark brown 80 50

Issued to commemorate the 50th anniversary of the League of Red Cross Societies.

Mouth and Ear
A46

1969, May 20 Photo. *Perf. 12½x12*

218 A46 100fr multicolored 1.25 75

First (cultural) Conference of French-speaking Community at Niamey.

National Administration College
A47

1969, July 8 Photo. *Perf. 12½x12*

219 A47 30fr emerald & deep orange 30 20

Issued to publicize the National Administration College.

Development Bank Issue
Common Design Type

1969, Sept. 10 Engraved *Perf. 13*

220 CD130 30fr purple, green & ocher 35 20

Issued to commemorate the 5th anniversary of the African Development Bank.

ASECNA Issue
Common Design Type

1969, Dec. 12 Engraved *Perf. 12*

221 CD132 100fr carmine rose 1.20 75

Classical Pavilion, National Museum
A48

Pavilions, National Museum: 45fr, Temporary exhibitions. 50fr, Audio-visual. 70fr, Nigerian musical instruments. 100fr, Craftsmanship.

1970, Feb. 23 Engraved *Perf. 13*

222 A48 30fr brt. bl., slate grn. & brown 35 20
223 " 45fr emerald, Prus. blue & brown 50 25
224 " 50fr slate green, vio. blue & brown 60 25
225 " 70fr brn., slate grn. & light blue 85 45
226 " 100fr slate green, vio. blue & brown 1.20 65
Nos. 222-226 (5) 3.50 1.80

Map of Africa and Vaccination Gun
A49

1970, Mar. 31 Engraved *Perf. 13*

227 A49 50fr ultra., dp. yellow grn. & magenta 55 30

Issued to commemorate the 100 millionth smallpox vaccination in West Africa.

Mexican Figurine and Soccer Player
A50

Designs: 70fr, Figurine, globe and soccer ball. 90fr, Figurine and 2 soccer players.

1970, Apr. 25

228 A50 40fr dk. brn., red lilac & emerald 50 30
229 " 70fr red brown, blue & plum 75 50
230 " 90fr black & red 1.10 75

Issued to publicize the 9th World Soccer Championship for the Jules Rimet Cup, Mexico City, May 29–June 21.

U.P.U. Headquarters Issue
Common Design Type

1970, May 20 Engraved *Perf. 13*

231 CD133 30fr brown, dk. gray & dark red 40 20
232 " 60fr violet blue, dark car. & violet 65 30

Bird Types of 1967–68

Birds: 5fr, Gray hornbill. 10fr, Woodland kingfisher. 15fr, Senegalese coucal. 20fr, Rose-ringed parakeets. 40fr, Red bishop.

Dated "1970"

1970–71 Photogravure *Perf. 13*

233 A43 5fr multi. ('71) 6 4
234 " 10fr " ('71) 10 5
235 " 15fr " ('71) 25 15
236 " 20fr " ('71) 35 15

Engraved

237 A33 40fr multicolored 55 40
Nos. 233-237 (5) 1.31 79

Issue dates 40fr, Dec. 9, 1970; others Jan. 4, 1971.

World Map with Niamey in Center
A51

1971, Mar. 3 Photo. *Perf. 12½x12*

238 A51 40fr brown & multi. 50 25

First anniversary of founding of the cooperative agency of French-speaking countries.

Scout Emblem, Merit Badges, Mt. Fuji, Japanese Flag—A52

Designs: 40fr, Boy Scouts and flags (vert.). 45fr, Map of Japan, Boy Scouts and compass rose (vert.). 50fr, Tent and "Jamboree."

1971, July 5 Engraved *Perf. 13*

239 A52 35fr rose lilac, deep car. & orange 40 20
240 " 40fr dk. purple, grn. & maroon 45 20
241 " 45fr ultra., copper red & green 50 30
242 " 50fr multicolored 55 30

13th Boy Scout World Jamboree, Asagiri Plain, Japan, Aug. 2–10.

Maps of Europe and Africa—A53

1971, July 29 Photo. *Perf. 13x12*

243 A53 50fr lt. blue & multi. 65 30

2nd anniversary of the renewal of the agreement on economic association between Europe and Africa.

Broad-tailed Whydah

A54

1971, Aug. 17 *Perf. 12½x12*

244 A54 35fr yellow green & multi. 60 35

See No. 443.

Garaya, Haoussa A55

UNICEF Emblem, Children of 4 Races A56

Stringed Instruments of Niger: 25fr, Gouroumi, Haoussa. 30fr, Molo, Djerma. 40fr, Godjie, Djerma-Sonrai. 45fr, Inzad, Tuareg. 50fr, Kountigui, Sonrai.

1971–72 Engr. *Perf. 13*

245 A55 25fr red, emerald & brown ('72) 30 12

246 " 30fr emerald, purple & brown ('72) 35 13

247 " 35fr brn. red, emerald & indigo 30 20

248 " 40fr emerald, org. & dark brown 35 20

249 " 45fr Prussian blue, grn. & bister 45 30

250 " 50fr black, red & brown ('72) 60 35

Nos. 245-250 (6) 2.35 1.30

Issue dates: 35fr, 40fr, 45fr, Oct. 13, 1971; others, June 16, 1972.

1971, Dec. 11 Photo. *Perf. 11*

251 A56 50fr multicolored 60 45

25th anniversary of United Nations International Children's Fund (UNICEF).

Star with Globe, Book, UNESCO Emblem

A57

Design: 40fr, Boy reading, UNESCO emblem, sailing ship, plane, mosque.

1972, Mar. 27 Engraved *Perf. 13*

252 A57 35fr magenta & emerald 40 20

253 " 40fr dk. carmine & Prussian blue 45 20

International Book Year 1972.

Cattle Egret

A58

1972, July 31 Photo. *Perf. 12½x12*

254 A58 50fr tan & multi. 70 40

See No. 425.

Cattle at Salt Pond of In-Gall

A59

1972, Aug. 25 *Perf. 13*

Multicolored

255 A59 35fr *shown* 40 20

256 " 40fr *Cattle wading in pond* 45 20

Salt cure for cattle.

Lottery Drum

A60

1972, Sept. 18

257 A60 35fr multicolored 40 25

6th anniversary of the national lottery.

West African Monetary Union Issue

Common Design Type

Design: 40fr, African couple, city, village and commemorative coin.

1972, Nov. 2 Engraved *Perf. 13*

258 CD136 40fr brn., lilac & gray 45 20

10th anniversary of West African Monetary Union.

Dromedary Race

A61

Design: 40fr, Horse race.

1972, Dec. 15 Engraved *Perf. 13*

259 A61 35fr bright blue, dark red & brown 40 22

260 " 40fr slate green, maroon & brn. 50 28

Pole Vault, Map of Africa A62

Knight, Pawn, Chessboard A63

Designs (Map of Africa and): 40fr, Basketball. 45fr, Boxing. 75fr, Soccer.

1973, Jan. 15 Engraved *Perf. 13*

261 A62 35fr claret & multi. 35 25

262 " 40fr green & multi. 40 25

263 A62 45fr red & multi. 45 30

264 " 75fr dk. blue & multi. 70 45

2nd African Games, Lagos, Nigeria, Jan. 7-18.

1973, Feb. 16 Engraved *Perf. 13*

265 A63 100fr dull red, slate grn. & blue 1.00 60

World Chess Championship, Reykjavik, Iceland, July-Sept. 1972.

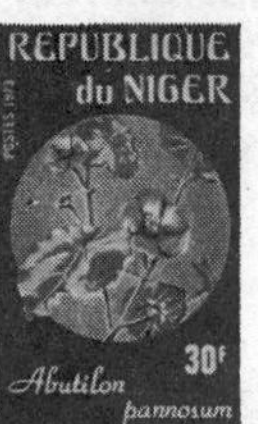

Abutilon Pannosum A64

Interpol Emblem A65

Rare African Flowers: 45fr, Crotalaria barkae. 60fr, Dichrostachys cinerea. 80fr, Caralluma decaisneana.

1973, Feb. 26 Photo. *Perf. 12x12½*

266 A64 30fr dk. vio. & multi. 30 20

267 " 45fr red & multi. 45 28

268 " 60fr ultra. & multi. 60 40

269 " 80fr ocher & multi. 75 45

1973, Mar. 13 Typo. *Perf. 13x12½*

270 A65 50fr brt. grn. & multi. 45 25

50th anniversary of International Criminal Police Organization (INTERPOL).

Dr. Hansen, Microscope and Petri Dish A66

Nurse Treating Infant, UN and Red Cross Emblems A67

1973, Mar. 29 Engraved *Perf. 13*

271 A66 50fr violet blue, slate green & dark brown 50 25

Centenary of the discovery by Dr. Armauer G. Hansen of the Hansen bacillus, the cause of leprosy.

1973, Apr. 3 Engraved *Perf. 13*

272 A67 50fr red, blue & brn. 45 25

25th anniversary of the World Health Organization.

Crocodile

A68

Animals from W National Park: 35fr, Elephant. 40fr, Hippopotamus. 80fr, Wart hog.

1973, June 5 Typo. *Perf. 12½x13*

273 A68 25fr gray & black 30 15

274 " 35fr blk., gold & gray 40 20

275 " 40fr red, lt. bl. & blk. 45 20

276 " 80fr multicolored 75 40

Eclipse over Mountains

A69

1973, June 21 Engraved *Perf. 13*

277 A69 40fr dk. violet blue 40 30

Solar eclipse, June 30, 1973.

Palominos—A70

Horses: 75fr, French trotters. 80fr, English thoroughbreds. 100fr, Arabian thoroughbreds.

1973, Aug. 1 Photo. *Perf. 13x12½*

278 A70 50fr ultra. & multi. 50 28

279 " 75fr gray & multi. 70 35

280 " 80fr emerald & multicolored 80 45

281 " 100fr ocher & multi. 1.00 55

No. 255 Surcharged with New Value, 2 Bars, and Overprinted in Ultramarine: "SECHERESSE/SOLIDARITE AFRICAINE"

1973, Aug. 16 *Perf. 13*

282 A59 100fr on 35fr multi. 90 65

African solidarity in drought emergency.

Diesel Engine and Rudolf Diesel

A71

Designs: Various Diesel locomotives.

1973, Sept. 7 *Perf. 13x12½*

283 A71 25fr gray, choc. & Prussian blue 25 15

284 " 50fr slate bl., gray & dark green 45 28

285 " 75fr red lilac, slate blue & gray 70 50

286 " 125fr brt. grn., vio. blue & car. 1.10 70

60th anniversary of the death of Rudolf Diesel (1858-1913), inventor of an internal combustion engine, later called Diesel engine.

African Postal Union Issue

Common Design Type

1973, Sept. 12 Engr. *Perf. 13*

287 CD137 100fr olive, dk. car. & slate grn. 1.00 65

TV Set, Map of Niger, Children

A72

1973, Oct. 1 Engraved *Perf. 13*

288 A72 50fr carmine, ultra. & brown 45 32

Educational television.

Type of 1971 Overprinted

3e CONFERENCE DE LA FRANCOPHONIE
LIEGE
OCTOBRE 1973

1973, Oct. 12 Photo. *Perf. 13*

289 A51 40fr red & multi. 45 25

3rd Conference of French-speaking countries, Liège, Sept. 15–Oct. 14.

Apollo of Belvedère
A73

Classic Sculpture: No. 291, Venus of Milo. No. 292, Hercules. No. 293, Atlas.

1973, Oct. 15 Engraved

290 A73 50fr brn. & slate green 60 35
291 " 50fr rose car. & purple 60 35
292 " 50fr red brown & dark brown 60 35
293 " 50fr red brn. & black 60 35

Beehive, Bees and Globes
A74

1973, Oct. 31 Engraved *Perf. 13*

294 A74 40fr dull red, ocher & dull blue 40 25

World Savings Day.

Tcherka Songhai Blanket—A75

Design: 35fr, Kounta Songhai blanket (vert.).

Perf. 12½x13, 13x12½

1973, Dec. 17 Photogravure

295 A75 35fr brown & multi. 35 25
296 " 40fr " " 45 28

Textiles of Niger.

WPY Emblem, Infant and Globe
A76

1974, Mar. 4 Engraved *Perf. 13*

297 A76 50fr multicolored 45 25

World Population Year 1974.

Locomotives, 1938 and 1948—A77

1974, May 24 Engraved *Perf. 13*

Multicolored

298 A77 50fr *shown* 45 32
299 " 75fr *Locomotive, 1893* 65 40
300 " 100fr *Locomotives, 1866 and 1939* 90 65
301 " 150fr *Locomotives, 1829* 1.35 1.00

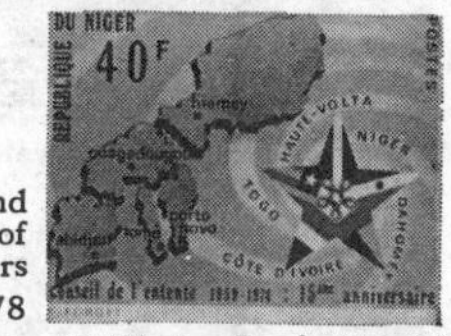

Map and Flags of Members
A78

1974, May 29 Photo. *Perf. 13x12½*

302 A78 40fr blue & multi. 35 20

15th anniversary of the Council of Accord.

Marconi Sending Radio Signals to Australia—A79

1974, July 1 Engraved *Perf. 13*

303 A79 50fr pur., blue & dark brown 45 30

Centenary of the birth of Guglielmo Marconi (1874–1937), Italian inventor and physicist.

Hand Holding Sapling
A80

Camel Saddle
A81

1974, Aug. 2 Engraved *Perf. 13*

304 A80 35fr multicolored 30 15

National Tree Week.

1974, Aug. 20 Engraved *Perf. 13*

Design: 50fr, Three sculptured horses (horiz.).

305 A81 40fr olive brn., blue & red 35 15
306 " 50fr olive brn., blue & red 45 20

Chopin and Polish Eagle
A82

Design: No. 308, Ludwig van Beethoven and allegory of Ninth Symphony.

1974

307 A82 100fr multicolored 90 50
308 " 100fr " 90 50

125th anniversary of the death of Frederic Chopin (1810–1849), composer and 150th anniversary of Beethoven's Ninth Symphony, composed 1823.

Issue dates: No. 307, Sept. 4; No. 308, Sept. 19.

Don-Don Drum
A83

1974, Nov. 12 Engraved *Perf. 13*

309 A83 60fr multicolored 55 30

Tenere Tree, Compass Rose and Caravan—A84

1974, Nov. 24 Engraved *Perf. 13*

310 A84 50fr multicolored 50 35

Tenere tree, a landmark in Sahara Desert, first death anniversary.

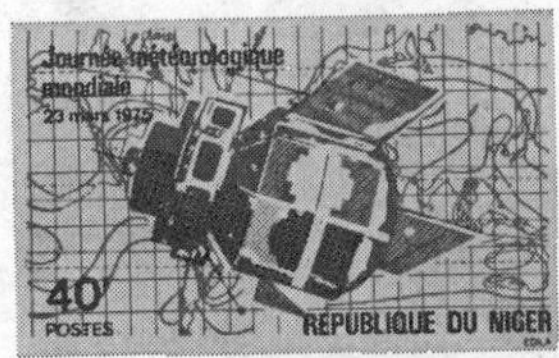

Satellite over World Weather Map—A85

1975, Mar. 23 Litho. *Perf. 13*

311 A85 40fr bl., blk. & red 35 20

World Meteorological Day, Mar. 23, 1975.

"City of Truro," English, 1903
A86

Locomotives and Flags: 75fr, "5.003," Germany, 1937. 100fr, "The General," United States, 1863. 125fr, "Electric BB 15.000," France, 1971.

1975, Apr. 24 Typographed *Perf. 13*

312 A86 50fr orange & multi. 45 30
313 " 75fr yel. grn. & multi. 65 40
314 " 100fr lt. bl. & multi. 90 60
315 " 125fr multicolored 1.25 75

Bird Type of 1968 Dated "1975"

1975, Apr. Photo. *Perf. 13*

316 A43 25fr olive & multi. 20 10

Zabira Leather Bag
A87

Handicrafts: 40fr, Damier tapestry. 45fr, Vase. 60fr, Gourd flask.

1975, May 28 Litho. *Perf. 12½*

317 A87 35fr dp. bl. & multi. 30 20
318 " 40fr dp. grn. & multi. 35 24
319 " 45fr brown & multi. 40 28
320 " 60fr dp. org. & multi. 50 32

Mother and Child, IWY Emblem
A88

1975, June 9 Engr. *Perf. 13*

321 A88 50fr claret, brn. & bl. 45 30

International Women's Year 1975.

Dr. Schweitzer and Lambarene Hospital—A89

1975, June 23 Engr. *Perf. 13*

322 A89 100fr brown, green & black 80 50

Dr. Albert Schweitzer (1875–1965), medical missionary.

Peugeot, 1892—A90

Early Autos: 75fr, Daimler, 1895. 100fr, Fiat, 1899. 125fr, Cadillac, 1903.

1975, July 16 Engr. *Perf. 13*

323 A90 50fr rose & vio. bl. 40 25
324 " 75fr bl. & vio. brn. 60 38
325 " 100fr brt. grn. & magenta 75 50
326 " 125fr brick red & brt. green 1.00 55

Sun, Tree and Earth
A91

Boxing
A92

1975, Aug. 2 Engraved *Perf. 13*

327 A91 40fr multicolored 35 24

National Tree Week.

1975, Aug. 25 Engr. *Perf. 13*

Designs: 35fr, Boxing (horiz.). 45fr, Wrestling (horiz.). 50fr, Wrestling.

328 A92 35fr blk., org. & brn. 30 20
329 " 40fr bl. grn., brown & black 35 24
330 " 45fr black, brt. blue & brown 40 28
331 " 50fr red, brn. & blk. 45 30

Lion's Head Tetradrachma, Leontini, 460 B.C.
A93

Greek Coins: 75fr, Owl tetradrachma, Athens, 500 B.C. 100fr, Crab diadrachma, Himera, 480 B.C. 125fr, Minotaur tetradrachma, Gela, 460 B.C.

1975, Sept. 12 Engr. *Perf. 13*

332 A93 50fr red, dull blue & black 40 25
333 " 75fr lilac, brt. blue & black 60 40
334 " 100fr blue, orange & black 80 50
335 " 125fr green, purple & black 1.00 60

Starving Family
A94

Designs: 45fr, Animal skeletons. 60fr, Truck bringing food.

1975, Oct. 21 Engr. *Perf. 13x12½*

336 A94 40fr multicolored 35 20
337 " 45fr ultra. & brown 40 25
338 " 60fr grn., org. & dk. blue 50 27

Fight against drought.

Niger River Crossing—A95

Designs: 45fr, Entrance to Boubon camp. 50fr, Camp building.

1975, Nov. 10 Litho. *Perf. 12½*

339 A95 40fr multicolored 32 20
340 " 45fr " 38 20
341 " 50fr " 40 25

Tourist publicity.

Teacher and Pupils
A96

Designs: Each stamp has different inscription in center.

1976, Jan. 12 Photo. *Perf. 13*

342 A96 25fr olive & multi. 20 12
343 " 30fr vio. bl. & multi. 25 13
344 " 40fr multicolored 30 15
345 " 50fr " 40 25
346 " 60fr " 45 30
Nos. 342-346 (5) 1.60 95

Literacy campaign 1976.

Ice Hockey—A97

Designs: 50fr, Luge. 150fr, Ski jump.

1976, Feb. 20 Litho. *Perf. 14x13½*

347 A97 40fr multicolored 30 12
348 " 50fr " 40 20
349 " 150fr " 1.20 60
Nos. 347-349, C266-C267 (5) 6.15 2.82

12th Winter Olympic games, Innsbruck.

Satellite, Telephone, ITU Emblem
A98

1976, Mar. 10 Litho. *Perf. 13*

350 A98 100fr org., blue & violet blue 80 50

Centenary of first telephone call by Alexander Graham Bell, Mar. 10, 1876.

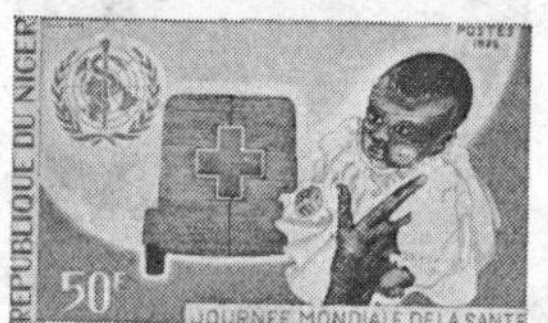

WHO Emblem, Red Cross Truck, Infant—A99

1976, Apr. 7 Engr. *Perf. 13*

351 A99 50fr multicolored 40 25

World Health Day 1976.

Statue of Liberty and Washington Crossing the Delaware—A100

Design: 50fr, Statue of Liberty and call to arms.

1976, Apr. 8 Litho. *Perf. 14x13½*

352 A100 40fr multicolored 30 15
353 " 50fr " 40 18
Nos. 352-353, C269-C271 (5) 5.90 2.63

American Bicentennial.

The Army Helping in Development
A101

Design: 50fr, Food distribution (vert.).

Perf. 12½x13, 13x12½

1976, Apr. 15 Lithographed

354 A101 50fr multicolored 40 25
355 " 100fr " 80 50

National Armed Forces, 2nd anniversary of take-over.

Europafrica Issue 1976

Maps, Concorde, Ship and Grain
A102

1976, June 9 Litho. *Perf. 13*

356 A102 100fr multicolored 80 50

Road Building
A103

Design: 30fr, Rice cultivation.

1976, June 26 *Perf. 12½*

357 A103 25fr multicolored 20 13
358 " 30fr " 25 18

Community labor.

Motobecane 125, France—A104

Motorcycles: 75fr, Norton Challenge, England. 100fr, BMW 90 S, Germany. 125fr, Kawasaki 1000, Japan.

1976, July 16 Engr. *Perf. 13*

359 A104 50fr violet blue & multi. 40 25
360 " 75fr deep green & multi. 60 45
361 " 100fr dk. brown & multi. 80 60
362 " 125fr slate & multi. 1.00 65

Boxing
A105

Designs: 50fr, Basketball. 60fr, Soccer. 80fr, Cycling (horiz.). 100fr, Judo (horiz.).

1976, July 17 Litho. *Perf. 14*

363 A105 40fr multicolored 35 15
364 " 50fr " 40 17
365 " 60fr " 50 20
366 " 80fr " 65 25
367 " 100fr " 80 32
Nos. 363-367 (5) 2.70 1.09

21st Summer Olympic games, Montreal. See No. C279.

Map of Niger, Planting Seedlings
A106

Designs: 50fr, Woman watering seedling (vert.). 60fr, Women planting seedlings (vert.).

1976, Aug. 1 Litho. *Perf. 12½x13*

368 A106 40fr org. & multi. 30 20
369 " 50fr yellow & multi. 40 30
370 " 60fr green & multi. 50 30

Reclamation of Sahel Region.

Nos. 342-346 Overprinted: "JOURNEE / INTERNATIONALE / DE L'ALPHABETISATION"

1976, Sept. 8 Photo. *Perf. 13*

371 A96 25fr olive & multi. 20 12
372 " 30fr vio. bl. & multi. 25 12
373 " 40fr multicolored 35 20
374 " 50fr " 40 25
375 " 60fr " 50 28
Nos. 371-375 (5) 1.70 97

Literacy campaign.

Hairdresser—A107

Designs: 40fr, Woman weaving straw (vert.). 50fr, Women potters (vert.).

1976, Oct. 6 *Perf. 13*

376 A107 40fr buff & multi. 30 18
377 " 45fr blue & multi. 35 25
378 " 50fr red & multi. 40 25

Niger Women's Association.

Rock Carvings
A108

Designs: 50fr, Neolithic sculptures. 60fr, Dinosaur skeleton.

1976, Nov. 15 Photo. *Perf. 13x12½*

379 A108 40fr black, slate & yellow 30 18

380 A108 50fr black, red & bister 40 25
381 " 60fr bister, black & brown 50 25

Archaeology.

Benin Head
A109

Weaver, Dancers and Musicians—A110

1977, Jan. 15 Engr. *Perf. 13*

382 A109 40fr dark brown 35 20
383 A110 50fr gray blue 40 25

2nd World Black and African Festival, Lagos, Nigeria, Jan. 15–Feb. 12.

First Aid, Student, Blackboard and Plow A111 **Midwife A112**

Designs: Inscriptions on blackboard differ on each denomination.

1977, Jan. 23 Photo. *Perf. 12½x13*

384 A111 40fr multicolored 30 18
385 " 50fr " 40 25
386 " 60fr " 50 25

Literacy campaign.

1977, Feb. 23 Litho. *Perf. 13*

Design: 50fr, Midwife examining newborn.

387 A112 40fr multicolored 30 18
388 " 50fr " 40 25

Village health service.

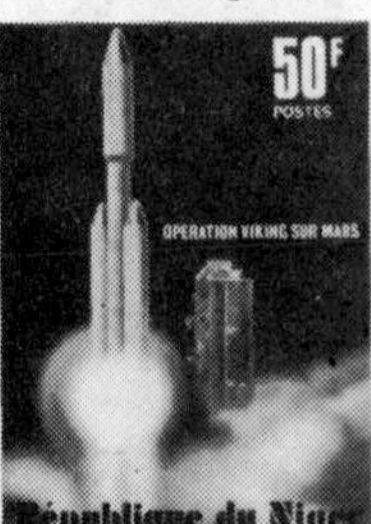

Titan Rocket Launch A113

Design: 80fr, Viking orbiter near Mars (horiz.).

1977, Mar. 15 Litho. *Perf. 14*

389 A113 50fr multicolored 40 18
390 " 80fr " 65 25
Nos. 389-390, C283-C285 (5) 4.65 1.70

Viking Mars project.

Marabous A114

Design: 90fr, Harnessed antelopes.

1977, Mar. 18 Engr. *Perf. 13*

391 A114 80fr multicolored 70 40
392 " 90fr " 75 45

Nature protection.

Weather Map, Satellite, WMO Emblem A115

1977, Mar. 23

393 A115 100fr multicolored 75 50

World Meteorological Day.

Group Gymnastics—A116

Designs: 50fr, High jump. 80fr, Folk singers.

1977, Apr. 7 Litho. *Perf. 13x12½*

394 A116 40fr dull yellow & multicolored 35 20
395 " 50fr blue & multi. 40 25
396 " 80fr org. & multi. 65 32

2nd Tahoua Youth Festival, Apr. 7–14.

Red Cross, WHO Emblems and Children—A117

1977, Apr. 25 Engr. *Perf. 13*

397 A117 80fr lilac, org. & red 65 40

World Health Day: "Immunization means protection of your children."

Eye with WHO Emblem, and Sword Killing Fly—A118

1977, May 7

398 A118 100fr multicolored 80 50

Fight against onchocerciasis, a roundworm infection, transmitted by flies, causing blindness.

Guirka Tahoua Dance A119

Dances: 50fr, Mailfilafili Gaya. 80fr, Naguihinayan Loga.

1977, June 7 Photo. *Perf. 13x12½*

399 A119 40fr multicolored 30 20
400 " 50fr " 40 25
401 " 80fr " 65 32

Popular arts and traditions.

Cavalry—A120

Designs: Traditional chief's cavalry, different groups.

1977, July 7 Litho. *Perf. 13x12½*

402 A120 40fr multicolored 30 20
403 " 50fr " 40 25
404 " 60fr " 50 28

Planting and Cultivating—A121

1977, Aug. 10

405 A121 40fr multicolored 30 18

Reclamation of Sahel Region.

Albert John Luthuli, Peace—A122

Designs: 80fr, Maurice Maeterlinck, literature. 100fr, Allan L. Hodgkin, medicine. 150fr, Albert Camus, literature. 200fr, Paul Ehrlich, medicine.

1977, Aug. 20 Litho. *Perf. 14*

406 A122 50fr multicolored 40 18
407 " 80fr " 60 25
408 " 100fr " 80 28
409 " 150fr " 1.20 40
410 " 200fr " 1.60 55
Nos. 406-410 (5) 4.60 1.66

Nobel prize winners. See No. C287.

Mao Tse-tung A123

1977, Sept. 9 Engr. *Perf. 13*

411 A123 100fr black & red 80 50

Chairman Mao Tse-tung (1893–1976), Chinese communist leader, first death anniversary.

Argentina '78 Emblem, Soccer Players and Coach, Vittorio Pozzo, Italy
A124

Designs (Argentina '78 emblem, soccer players and coach): 50fr, Vincente Feola, Spain. 80fr, Aymore Moreira, Portugal. 100fr, Sir Alf Ramsey, England. 200fr, Helmut Schoen, Germany. 500fr, Sepp Herberger, Germany.

1977, Oct. 12 Litho. *Perf. 13½*

412 A124 40fr multicolored 30 12
413 " 50fr " 40 18
414 " 80fr " 60 25
415 " 100fr " 80 32
416 " 200fr " 1.60 55
Nos. 412-416 (5) 3.70 1.42

Souvenir Sheet

417 A124 500fr multicolored 4.00 1.65

World Cup Soccer championship, Argentina '78. No. 417 has multicolored margin showing World Cup in gold. Size: 117x79mm.

Horse's Head, Parthenon and UNESCO Emblem—A125

1977, Nov. 12 Engr. *Perf. 13*

418 A125 100fr multicolored 80 50

United Nations, Educational, Scientific and Cultural Organization.

Woman Carrying Water Pots
A126

Design: 50fr, Women pounding corn.

1977, Nov. 23 Photo. *Perf. 12½x13*

419 A126 40fr multicolored 30 18
420 " 50fr red & multi. 40 20

Nigerian Women's Association.

Crocodile's Skull, 100 Million Years Old—A127

Design: 80fr, Neolithic flint tools.

1977, Dec. 14 *Perf. 13*

421 A127 50fr multicolored 40 25
422 " 80fr " 65 40

Raoul Follereau and Lepers A128

Design: 40fr, Raoul Follereau and woman leper (vert.).

1978, Jan. 28 Engr. *Perf. 13*

423 A128 40fr multicolored 30 20
424 " 50fr " 40 25

25th anniversary of Leprosy Day. Follereau (1903–1977) was "Apostle to the Lepers" and educator of the blind.

Bird Type of 1972 Redrawn

1978, Feb. Photo. *Perf. 13*

425 A58 50fr tan & multi. 40 18

No. 425 is dated "1978" and has only designer's name in imprint. No. 254 has printer's name also.

Assumption, by Rubens A129

Rubens Paintings: 70fr, Rubens and Friends (horiz.). 100fr, History of Marie de Medici. 150fr, Alathea Talbot and Family. 200fr, Marquise de Spinola. 500fr, Virgin and St. Ildefonso.

1978, Feb. 25 Litho. *Perf. 14*

426 A129 50fr multicolored 40 18
427 " 70fr " 50 20
428 " 100fr " 80 28
429 " 150fr " 1.20 45
430 " 200fr " 1.65 55
Nos. 426–430 (5) 4.55 1.66

Souvenir Sheet

Perf. 13½

431 A129 500fr gold & multi. 4.00 1.75

Peter Paul Rubens (1577–1640), 400th birth anniversary. No. 431 has multicolored margin showing entire painting. Size: 85x110mm.

Shot Put A130

Designs: 50fr, Volleyball. 60fr, Long jump. 100fr, Javelin.

1978, Mar. 22 Photo. *Perf. 13*

432 A130 40fr multicolored 30 20
433 " 50fr " 40 25
434 " 60fr " 50 28
435 " 100fr " 80 50

National University Games' Championships.

First Aid and Red Crosses A131

1978, May 13 Lithographed

436 A131 40fr red & multi. 30 20

Nigerian Red Cross.

Goudel Earth Station A132

1978, May 23

437 A132 100fr multicolored 80 50

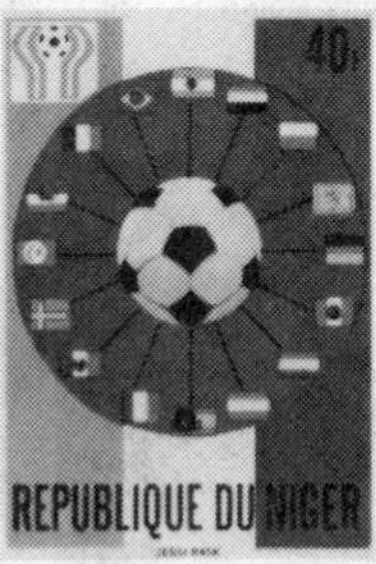

Soccer Ball, Flags of Participants A133

Designs (Argentina '78 Emblem and): 50fr, Ball in net. 100fr, Globe with South America, Soccer field. 200fr, Two players (horiz.). 300fr, Player and globe.

1978, June 18 Litho. *Perf. 13½*

438 A133 40fr multicolored 30 20
439 " 50fr " 40 25
440 " 100fr " 80 50
441 " 200fr " 1.60 1.00

Souvenir Sheet

442 A133 300fr multicolored 2.50 1.75

11th World Cup Soccer Championship, Argentina, June 1–25. No. 442 has multicolored margin showing Jules Rimet Cup and soccer players. Size: 104x77mm.

Bird Type of 1971 Redrawn

1978, June Photogravure *Perf. 13*

443 A54 35fr blue & multi. 30 15

No. 443 has no year date, nor Delrieu imprint.

Post Office, Niamey—A134

Design: 60fr, Post Office, different view.

1978, Aug. 12 Lithographed

444 A134 40fr multicolored 30 20
445 " 60fr " 50 28

Goudel Water Works A135

1978, Sept. 25 Photo. *Perf. 13*

446 A135 100fr multicolored 80 50

Giraffe A136

Animals and Wildlife Fund Emblem: 50fr, Ostrich. 70fr, Cheetah. 150fr, Oryx (horiz.). 200fr, Addax (horiz.). 300fr, Hartebeest (horiz.).

1978, Nov. 20 Litho. *Perf. 15*

447 A136 40fr multicolored 30 20
448 " 50fr " 40 25
449 " 70fr " 55 35
450 " 150fr " 1.20 75
451 " 200fr " 1.60 1.00
452 " 300fr " 2.40 1.50
Nos. 447–452 (6) 6.45 4.05

Endangered species.

Nos. 412–417 Overprinted in Silver

a. "EQUIPE QUATRIEME:ITALIE"
b. "EQUIPE TROISIEME:BRESIL"
c. "EQUIPE / SECONDE: / PAYS BAS"
d. "EQUIPE VAINQUEUR:ARGENTINE"
e. "ARGENTINE – PAYS BAS 3 – 1"

1978, Dec. 1 *Perf. 13½*

453 A124 (*a*) 40fr multi. 30 20
454 " (*b*) 50fr " 40 25
455 " (*c*) 80fr " 60 40
456 " (*d*) 100fr " 80 50
457 " (*e*) 200fr " 1.60 1.00
Nos. 453–457 (5) 3.70 2.35

Souvenir Sheet

458 A124 (*e*) 500fr multi. 4.00 1.75

Winners, World Soccer Cup Championship, Argentina, June 1–25.

Tinguizi A137

Musicians: No. 460, Dan Gourmou. No. 461, Chetima Ganga (horiz.).

1978, Dec. 11 Litho. *Perf. 13*

459 A137 100fr multicolored 80 50
460 " 100fr " 80 50
461 " 100fr " 80 50

Virgin Mary, by Dürer A138

Paintings: 50fr, The Homecoming, by Honoré Daumier. 150fr, 200fr, 500fr, Virgin and Child, by Albrecht Dürer (different).

1979, Jan. 31 Litho. *Perf. 13½*

462 A138 50fr multicolored 40 25
463 " 100fr " 80 50
464 " 150fr " 1.20 75
465 " 200fr " 1.60 1.00
466 " 500fr " 4.00 1.75

Honoré Daumier (1808–1879), and Albrecht Dürer (1471–1528).

No. 466 contains one stamp (38x50mm.); gold margin. Size: 103x78mm.

Solar Panels and Tank—A139

Design: 40fr, Tank and panels on roof (vert.).

Perf. 12½x12, 12x12½

1979, Feb. 28

467 A139 40fr multicolored 32 20
468 " 50fr " 40 25

Hot water from solar heat.

Children with Building Blocks—A140

Children and IYC Emblem: 100fr, Reading books. 150fr, With model plane.

1979, Apr. 10 Litho. *Perf. 13½*

469 A140 40fr multicolored 32 20
470 " 100fr " 80 50
471 " 150fr " 1.20 75

International Year of the Child.

SEMI-POSTAL STAMPS

Curie Issue

Common Design Type

Engraved.

1938 *Perf. 13.* **Unwmkd.**

B1 CD80 1.75fr+50c bright ultramarine 6.00 6.00

French Revolution Issue.

Common Design Type

1939 Photogravure. *Perf. 13.*

Name and Value Typo. in Black.

B2 CD83 45(c)+25(c) green 2.25 2.25
B3 " 70(c)+30(c) brown 2.25 2.25
B4 " 90(c)+35(c) red orange 2.25 2.25
B5 " 1.25fr+1fr rose pink 2.25 2.25
B6 " 2.25fr+2fr blue 2.25 2.25
Nos. B2-B6 (5) 11.25 11.25

Stamps of 1926-38, Surcharged in Black **SECOURS + 1 fr. NATIONAL**

1941 *Perf. 14x13½, 13½x14*

B7 A3 50c+1fr scarlet & green, *greenish* 20 20
B8 " 80c+2fr claret & olive green 1.85 1.85
B9 A4 1.50fr+2fr deep blue & pale blue 2.50 2.50
B10 " 2fr+3fr red orange & olive brown 2.50 2.50

Common Design Type and

Colonial Cavalry SP1

Soldiers and Tank SP2

Photogravure.

1941 *Perf. 13½* **Unwmkd.**

B11 SP1 1fr+1fr red 30
B12 CD86 1.50fr+3fr claret 30
B13 SP2 2.50fr+1fr blue 30

Nos. B11-B13 were issued by the Vichy government and were not placed on sale in the colony.

Nos. 89-90 were surcharged "OEUVRES COLONIALES" and surtax (including change of denomination of the 2.50fr to 50c). These were issued in 1944 by the Vichy government and were not placed on sale in the colony.

Republic of the Niger

Anti-Malaria Issue

Common Design Type

Perf. 12½x12

1962, Apr. 7 **Engraved** **Unwmkd.**

B14 CD108 25fr+5fr brown 60 60

Issued for the World Health Organization drive to eradicate malaria.

Freedom from Hunger Issue

Common Design Type

1963, Mar. 21 *Perf. 13*

B15 CD112 25fr+5fr gray olive, red lilac & brn. 60 60

"Freedom from Hunger" campaign of the U.N. Food and Agriculture Organization.

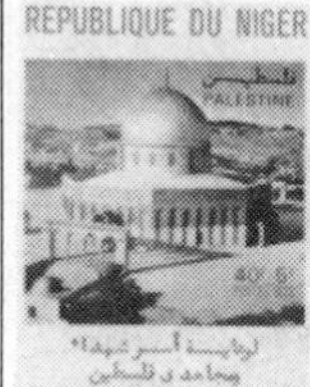

Dome of the Rock SP3

1978, Dec. 11 **Litho.** *Perf. 12½*

B16 SP3 40fr+5fr multi. 36 36

Surtax was for Palestinian fighters and their families.

AIR POST STAMPS.

Common Design Type

Engraved.

1940 *Perf. 12½x12.* **Unwmkd.**

C1 CD85 1.90fr ultramarine 12 12
C2 " 2.90fr dark red 13 13
C3 " 4.50fr dark gray green 45 45
C4 " 4.90fr yellow bistre 25 25
C5 " 6.90fr deep orange 25 25
Nos. C1-C5 (5) 1.20 1.20

Common Design Types

1942

C6 CD88 50c carmine & blue 5
C7 " 1fr brown & black 8
C8 " 2fr multicolored 7
C9 " 3fr " 10
C10 " 5fr vio. & brn. red 12

Frame Engraved, Center Typographed.

C11 CD89 10fr multicolored 18
C12 " 20fr " 20
C13 " 50fr " 45 45
Nos. C6-C13 (8) 1.25

There is doubt whether Nos. C6-C12 were officially placed in use. They were issued by the Vichy government.

Republic of the Niger

Wild Animals, W National Park AP1

1960, Apr. 11 **Engraved** *Perf. 13*

C14 AP1 500fr multicolored 6.50 3.25

Nubian Carmine Bee-eater—AP2

1961, Dec. 18 *Perf. 13* **Unwmkd.**

C15 AP2 200fr multicolored 3.25 1.75

U.N. Headquarters and Emblem, Niger Flag and Map—AP3

1961, Dec. 16

C20 AP3 25fr multicolored 40 25
C21 " 100fr " 1.50 90

Niger's admission to the United Nations.

Air Afrique Issue

Common Design Type

1962, Feb. 17 *Perf. 13* **Unwmkd.**

C22 CD107 100fr multicolored 1.50 90

Founding of Air Afrique (African Airlines).

Mosque at Agadez and UPU Emblem—AP4

Designs: 85fr, Gaya Bridge. 100fr, Presidential Palace, Niamey.

1963, June 12 Photo. *Perf. 12½*

C23 AP4 50fr multicolored 90 32
C24 " 85fr " 1.35 65
C25 " 100fr " 1.50 1.00

2nd anniversary of Niger's admission to the Universal Postal Union.

Type of Regular Issue, 1963

Design: 100fr, Building boats (kadei), (horiz.).

1963, Aug. 30 *Perf. 12½x12*

Size: 47x27mm.

C26 A12 100fr multicolored 1.50 75

African Postal Union Issue

Common Design Type

1963, Sept. 8 *Perf. 12½*

C27 CD114 85fr multicolored 1.25 65

Nos. C20-C21 Overprinted "Centenaire de la Croix-Rouge" and Cross in Red

1963, Sept. 30 **Engraved** *Perf. 13*

C28 AP3 25fr multicolored 60 40
C29 " 100fr " 1.80 1.00

Centenary of International Red Cross.

White and Black before Rising Sun AP5

1963, Oct. 25 Photo. *Perf. 12x13*

C30 AP5 50fr multicolored 1.25 90

See note after Mauritania No. C28.

Peanut Cultivation—AP6

Designs: 45fr, Camels transporting peanuts to market. 85fr, Men closing bags. 100fr, Loading bags on truck.

1963, Nov. 5 **Engraved** *Perf. 13*

C31 AP6 20fr green, blue & red brown 30 18
C32 " 45fr red brown, blue & green 65 35
C33 " 85fr multicolored 1.25 55
C34 " 100fr red brn., olive bister & bl. 1.50 70
a. Souv. sheet of 4 4.00 4.00

To publicize Niger's peanut industry. No. C34a contains one each of Nos. C31-C34. Size: 130x100mm.

1963 Air Afrique Issue

Common Design Type

1963, Nov. 19 Photo. *Perf. 13x12*

C35 CD115 50fr multicolored 75 50

Telstar and Capricornus and Sagittarius Constellations AP7

Design: 100fr, Relay satellite and Leo and Virgo constellations.

1964, Feb. 11 **Engraved** *Perf 13*

C36 AP7 25fr olive gray & vio. 40 25
C37 " 100fr green & rose claret 1.35 1.00

Ramses II Holding Crook and Flail, Abu Simbel

AP8

1964, March 9

C38 AP8 25fr bister brown & dull bl. green 60 45
C39 " 30fr dark blue & orge. brown 70 50
C40 " 50fr deep claret & dark blue 1.25 90

Issued to publicize the UNESCO world campaign to save historic monuments in Nubia.

Tiros I Weather Satellite over Globe and WMO Emblem

AP9

1964, March 23 *Perf. 13* **Unwmkd.**

C41 AP9 50fr emerald, dark blue & choc. 1.25 75

4th World Meteorological Day, Mar. 23.

Rocket, Stars and "Stamp"—AP10

1964, June 5 Engraved

C42 AP10 50fr dark blue & magenta 1.00 65

Issued to publicize "PHILATEC," International Philatelic and Postal Techniques Exhibition, Paris, June 5–21, 1964.

Europafrica Issue, 1963

Common Design Type

Design: 50fr, European and African shaking hands, emblems of industry and agriculture.

1964, July 20 Photo. *Perf. 12x13*

C43 CD116 50fr multicolored 75 40

John F. Kennedy AP11 — Discobolus and Discus Thrower AP12

Photogravure

1964, Sept. 25 *Perf. 12½* Unwmkd.

C44 AP11 100fr multi. 1.50 1.10
 a. Souvenir sheet of 4 6.00 5.00

Issued in memory of President John F. Kennedy (1917–1963). No. C44a contains four No. C44. Dark blue marginal inscription. Size: 90x129mm.

1964, Oct. 10 Engraved *Perf. 13*

Designs: 60fr, Water polo (horiz.). 85fr, Relay race (horiz.). 250fr, Torch bearer and Pierre de Coubertin.

C45 AP12 60fr red brown & slate green 75 55
C46 " 85fr ultra. & red brown 1.25 70
C47 " 100fr brt. grn., dk. red & slate 1.35 85
C48 " 250fr yel. brn., brt. grn. & slate 3.25 2.25
 a. Miniature sheet of 4 6.50 6.50

Issued to commemorate the 18th Olympic Games, Tokyo, Oct. 10–25. No. C48a contains one each of Nos. C45–C48. Size: 190x100mm.

Pope John XXIII AP13

1965, June 3 Photo. *Perf. 12½x13*

C49 AP13 100fr multi. 1.40 1.00

Issued in memory of Pope John XXIII (1881–1963).

Hand Crushing Crab AP14 — Sir Winston Churchill AP15

1965, July 15 Engraved *Perf. 13*

C50 AP14 100fr yellow green, blk. & brn. 1.50 80

Issued to publicize the fight against cancer.

Perf. 12½x13

1965, Sept. 3 Photo. Unwmkd.

C51 AP15 100fr multicolored 1.50 80

Issued in memory of Sir Winston Spencer Churchill (1875–1965), statesman and World War II leader.

Symbols of Agriculture, Industry, Education AP16 — Flags and Niamey Fair AP17

1965, Oct. 24 Engraved *Perf. 13*

C52 AP16 50fr henna brown, black & olive 75 40

International Cooperation Year, 1965.

1965, Dec. 10 Photo. *Perf. 13x12½*

C53 AP17 100fr multicolored 1.40 80

International Fair at Niamey.

Dr. Schweitzer, Crippled Hands and Symbols of Medicine, Religion and Music—AP18

1966, Jan. 4 Photo. *Perf. 12½x13*

C54 AP18 50fr multicolored 75 45

Issued in memory of Dr. Albert Schweitzer (1875–1965), medical missionary, theologian and musician.

Weather Survey Frigate and WMO Emblem—AP19

1966, March 23 Engraved *Perf. 13*

C55 AP19 50fr brt. rose lilac, dull green & dk. violet blue 75 45

6th World Meteorological Day, Mar. 23.

Edward H. White Floating in Space and Gemini IV—AP20

Design: No. C57, Alexei A. Leonov and Voskhod II.

1966, March 30

C56 AP20 50fr dk. red brown, black & brt. green 75 50
C57 " 50fr purple, slate & orange 75 50

Issued to honor astronauts Edward H. White and Alexei A. Leonov.

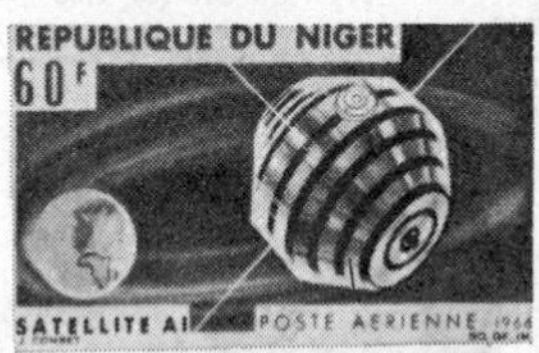

A-1 Satellite and Earth AP21

Designs: 45fr, Diamant rocket and launching pad (vert.). 90fr, FR-1 satellite. 100fr, D-1 satellite.

1966, May 12 Photo. *Perf. 13*

C58 AP21 45fr multicolored 70 45
C59 " 60fr " 90 50
C60 " 90fr " 1.35 70
C61 " 100fr " 1.60 90

French achievements in space.

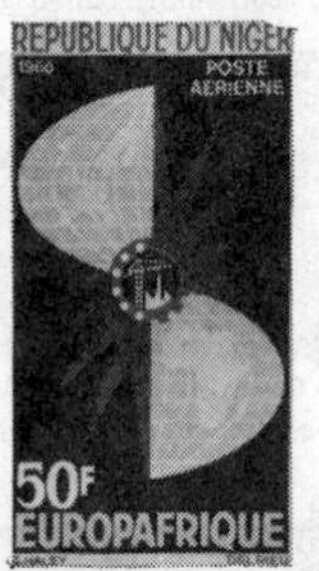

Maps of Europe and Africa and Symbols of Industry AP22

1966, July 20 Photo. *Perf. 12x13*

C62 AP22 50fr multicolored 75 50

Third anniversary of economic agreement between the European Economic Community and the African and Malgache Union.

Air Afrique Issue, 1966

Common Design Type

1966, Aug. 31 Photo. *Perf. 13*

C63 CD123 30fr gray, yellow green & blk. 40 28

Issued to commemorate the introduction of DC-8F planes by Air Afrique.

Gemini 6 and 7—AP23

Design: 50fr, Voskhod 1 (vert.).

1966, Oct. 14 Engraved *Perf. 13*

C64 AP23 50fr red brn., slate & ultra. 75 40
C65 " 100fr red brn., blue & purple 1.50 70

Issued to commemorate Russian and American achievements in space.

Torii and Atom Destroying Crab AP24

1966, Dec. 2 Photo. *Perf. 13*

C66 AP24 100fr dp. claret, brn., violet & bl. grn. 1.40 80

Issued to commemorate the 9th International Anticancer Congress, Tokyo, Oct. 23–29.

New Mosque, Niamey—AP25

1967, Jan. 11 Engraved *Perf. 13*

C67 AP25 100fr grn. & brt. bl. 1.35 70

Albrecht Dürer, Self-portrait AP26

Self-portraits: 100fr, Jacques Louis David. 250fr, Ferdinand Delacroix.

1967, Jan. 27 Photo. ***Perf. 12½***

C68 AP26 50fr multicolored 85 55
C69 " 100fr " 1.50 1.10
C70 " 250fr " 3.50 2.00

See also No. C98.

Maritime Weather Station AP27

1967, Apr. 28 Engraved ***Perf. 13***

C71 AP27 50fr brt. bl., dk. car. rose & blk. 75 45

7th World Meteorological Day.

View of EXPO '67, Montreal AP28

1967, Apr. 28 Engraved ***Perf. 13***

C72 AP28 100fr lilac, brt. bl. & black 1.35 65

Issued for EXPO '67, International Exhibition, Montreal, Apr. 28–Oct. 27, 1967.

Audio-visual Center, Stylized Eye and People—AP29

1967, June 22 Engraved ***Perf. 13***

C73 AP29 100fr bright blue, pur. & grn. 1.35 65

National Audio-Visual Center.

Konrad Adenauer AP30

1967, Aug. 11 Photo. ***Perf. 12½***

C74 AP30 100fr dk. blue, gray & sepia 1.50 80
a. Souv. sheet of 4 6.00 5.00

Issued in memory of Konrad Adenauer (1876–1967), chancellor of West Germany (1949–63). No. C74a contains 4 No. C74 with dark blue marginal inscription. Size: 119x160mm.

African Postal Union Issue, 1967

Common Design Type

1967, Sept. 9 Engraved ***Perf. 13***

C75 CD124 100fr emerald, red & brt. lilac 1.35 65

Jesus Teaching in the Temple, by Ingres—AP31

Design: 150fr, Jesus Giving the Keys to St. Peter, by Ingres (vert.).

1967, Oct. 2 Photo. ***Perf. 12½***

C76 AP31 100fr multicolored 2.00 1.25
C77 " 150fr " 3.00 2.00

Issued to commemorate the centenary of the death of Jean Dominique Ingres (1780–1867), French painter.

Children and UNICEF Emblem AP32

1967, Dec. 11 Engraved ***Perf. 13***

C78 AP32 100fr blue, brown & green 1.35 65

Issued to commemorate the 21st anniversary of UNICEF (United Nations International Children's Emergency Fund).

O.C.A.M. Emblem—AP33

1968, Jan. 12 Engr. ***Perf. 13***

C79 AP33 100fr brt. blue, green & org. 1.35 65

Issued to publicize the conference of the Organization Communitée Afrique et Malgache (OCAM) held in Niamey, January 1968.

Vincent van Gogh, Self-portrait AP34

Self-portraits: 50fr, Jean Baptiste Camille Corot. 150fr, Francisco de Goya.

1968, Jan. 29 Photo. ***Perf. 12½***

C80 AP34 50fr multicolored 90 40
C81 " 150fr " 2.25 1.00
C82 " 200fr " 3.00 1.50

See No. C98.

Breguet 27—AP35

Planes: 80fr, Potez 25 on the ground. 100fr, Potez 25 in the air.

1968, Mar. 14 Engraved ***Perf. 13***

C83 AP35 45fr indigo, carmine & dk. green 65 40
C84 " 80fr indigo, blue & brown 1.10 55
C85 " 100fr sky blue, brown black & dk. green 1.35 65

Issued to commemorate the 25th anniversary of air mail service between France and Niger.

Splendid Glossy Starling—AP36

Design: 100fr, Amethyst starling (vert.).

1968–69 Photogravure ***Perf. 13***

C86 AP36 100fr gold & multi. ('69) 1.25 50

Engraved

C87 AP36 250fr magenta, slate green & brt. blue 2.75 1.35

See No. C255.

Dandy Horse, 1818, and Racer, 1968—AP37

1968, May 17 Engraved ***Perf. 13***

C88 AP37 100fr bl. grn. & red 1.25 65

Issued to commemorate the 150th anniversary of the invention of the bicycle.

Sheet Bend Knot A37a

1968, July 20 Photogravure ***Perf. 13***

C89 A37a 50fr gray, black, red & green 70 40

Fifth anniversary of economic agreement between the European Economic Community and the African and Malgache Union.

Fencing—AP38

Designs: 100fr, Jackknife dive (vert.). 150fr, Weight lifting (vert.). 200fr, Equestrian.

1968, Sept. 10 Engraved ***Perf. 13***

C90 AP38 50fr purple & blk. 60 32
C91 " 100fr chocolate, ultra. & black 1.20 50
C92 " 150fr chocolate & orange 1.75 80
C93 " 200fr brn., emerald & indigo 2.40 1.25
a. Min. sheet of 4 6.75 6.75

Issued to publicize the 19th Olympic Games, Mexico City, Oct. 12–27.

No. C93a contains one each of Nos. C90–C93. It is folded down the vertical gutter separating Nos. C90–C91 se-tenant at left and Nos. C92–C93 se-tenant at right. Size: 235x102mm.

Robert F. Kennedy AP39

Designs: No. C94, John F. Kennedy. No. C95, Rev. Dr. Martin Luther King, Jr. No. C96, Mahatma Gandhi.

1968, Oct. 4 Photo. ***Perf. 12½***

C94 AP39 100fr black & dull orange 1.25 50
C95 " 100fr blk. & aqua. 1.25 50
C96 " 100fr blk. & gray 1.25 50
C97 " 100fr blk. & yel. 1.25 50
a. Souv. sheet of 4 5.50 4.50

Issued to honor proponents of non-violence. No. C97a contains one each of Nos. C94–C97. Black marginal inscription. Size: 119x160mm.

PHILEXAFRIQUE Issue

Painting Type of 1968

Design: 100fr, Interior Minister Paré, by J. L. La Neuville (1748–1826).

1968, Oct. 25 Photo. ***Perf. 12½***

C98 AP34 100fr multicolored 1.50 1.50

Issued to publicize PHILEXAFRIQUE, Philatelic Exhibition in Abidjan, Feb. 14–23, 1969. Printed with alternating light blue label.

Arms and Flags of Niger—AP40

1968, Dec. 17 Litho. ***Perf. 13***

C99 AP40 100fr multicolored 1.20 50

Issued to commemorate the 10th anniversary of the proclamation of the Republic.

Bonaparte as First Consul, by Ingres
AP41

Paintings: 100fr, Napoleon Visiting the Plague House in Jaffa, by Antoine Jean Gros. 150fr, Napoleon on the Imperial Throne, by Jean Auguste Dominique Ingres. 200fr, Napoleon's March Through France, by Jean Louis Ernest Meissonier (horiz.).

Perf. 12½x12, 12x12½

1969, Jan. 20 **Photogravure**

C100 AP41 50fr multicolored 1.50 1.10
C101 " 100fr grn. & multi. 2.50 1.65
C102 " 150fr pur. & multi. 3.25 2.25
C103 " 200fr brn. & multi. 4.75 3.00

Issued to commemorate the 200th anniversary of the birth of Napoleon Bonaparte (1769–1821).

2nd PHILEXAFRIQUE Issue
Common Design Type

Design: 50fr, Niger No. 41 and giraffes.

1969, Feb. 14 **Engraved** ***Perf. 13***

C104 CD128 50fr slate, brown & orange 75 65

Issued to commemorate the opening of PHILEXAFRIQUE, Abidjan, Feb. 14.

Weather Observation Plane in Storm and Anemometer
AP42

1969, Mar. 23 **Engraved** ***Perf. 13***

C105 AP42 50fr blk., brt. blue & green 65 30

9th World Meteorological Day.

Panhard Levassor, 1900—AP43

Early Automobiles: 45fr, De Dion Bouton 8, 1904. 50fr, Opel, 1909. 70fr, Daimler, 1910. 100fr, Vermorel 12/16, 1912.

1969, Apr. 15 **Engraved** ***Perf. 13***

C106 AP43 25fr gray, lt. grn. & blue green 35 18
C107 " 45fr gray, blue & violet 45 28
C108 " 50fr gray, yel. bis. & brown 75 38
C109 " 70fr gray, brt. pink & bright lilac 1.00 50
C110 " 100fr gray, lemon & slate green 1.35 65
Nos. C106-C110 (5) 3.90 1.99

Apollo 8 Trip around Moon
AP44

Embossed on Gold Foil

1969, Mar. 31 ***Die-cut Perf. 10½***

C111 AP44 1000fr gold 13.50 13.50

Issued to commemorate the U.S. Apollo 8 mission, which put the first men into orbit around the moon, Dec. 21–27, 1968.

No. C14 Overprinted in Red with Lunar Landing Module and: "L'HOMME / SUR LA LUNE / JUILLET 1969 / APOLLO 11"

1969, July 25 **Engraved** ***Perf. 13***

C112 AP1 500fr multi. 6.75 6.75

See note after Mail No. C80.

Toys—AP45

1969, Oct. 13 **Engraved** ***Perf. 13***

C113 AP45 100fr blue, red brn. & green 1.25 55

International Nuremberg Toy Fair.

Europafrica Issue

Links—AP46

1969, Oct. 30 **Photogravure**

C114 AP46 50fr violet, yellow & black 65 30

Camels and Motor Caravan Crossing Desert—AP47

Designs: 100fr, Motor caravan crossing mountainous region. 150fr, Motor caravan in African village. 200fr, Map of Africa showing tour, Citroen B-2 tractor, African and European men shaking hands.

1969, Nov. 22 **Engraved** ***Perf. 13***

C115 AP47 50fr lilac, pink & brown 60 28
C116 " 100fr dk. car. rose, light blue & violet blue 1.20 50
C117 " 150fr multicolored 1.75 80
C118 " 200fr slate green, blue & blk. 2.35 1.10

Issued to commemorate the Black Tour across Africa from Colomb-Bechar, Algeria, to Mombassa, Dar es Salaam, Mozambique, Tananarive and the Cape of Good Hope.

EXPO '70 at Osaka
AP48

1970, Mar. 25 **Photo.** ***Perf. 12½***

C119 AP48 100fr multi. 1.25 55

Issued to publicize EXPO '70 International Exhibition, Osaka, Japan, Mar. 15–Sept. 13.

Education Year Emblem and Education Symbols—AP49

1970, Apr. 6 **Engraved** ***Perf. 13***

C120 AP49 100fr plum, red & gray 1.25 55

Issued for International Education Year.

Rotary Emblem, Globe and Niamey Club Emblem—AP50

1970, Apr. 30 **Photo.** ***Perf. 12½***

C121 AP50 100fr gold & multi. 1.25 55

65th anniversary of Rotary International.

Modern Plane, Clement Ader and his Flying Machine—AP51

Designs: 100fr, Joseph and Jacques Montgolfier, rocket and balloon. 150fr, Isaac Newton, planetary system and trajectories. 200fr, Galileo Galilei, spaceship and trajectories. 250fr, Leonardo da Vinci, his flying machine, and plane.

1970, May 11 **Engraved** ***Perf. 13***

C122 AP51 50fr bl., copper red & slate 60 28
C123 " 100fr copper red, bl. & slate 1.10 55
C124 " 150fr brn., green & ocher 1.60 85
C125 " 200fr dk. carmine rose, deep violet & bister 2.25 1.10
C126 " 250fr copper red, gray & purple 3.00 1.50
Nos. C122-C126 (5) 8.55 4.28

Pioneers of space research.

Bay of Naples, Buildings, Mt. Vesuvius and Niger No. 97
AP52

1970, May 5 **Photo.** ***Perf. 12½***

C127 AP52 100fr multi. 1.25 50

Issued to publicize the 10th Europa Philatelic Exhibition, Naples, Italy, May 2–10.

TV Tube, Books, Microscope, Globe and ITU Emblem
AP53

1970, May 16 **Engraved** ***Perf. 13***

C128 AP53 100fr green, brown & red 1.20 50

Issued for World Telecommunications Day.

Nos. C123 and C125 Overprinted: "Solidarité Spatiale / Apollo XIII / 11–17 Avril 1970"

1970, June 6 **Engraved** ***Perf. 13***

C129 AP51 100fr multi. 1.20 55
C130 " 200fr " 2.10 1.00

Issued to commemorate the abortive flight of Apollo 13, Apr. 11–17, 1970.

U.N. Emblem, Man, Woman and Doves—AP54

1970, June 26 **Photo.** ***Perf. 12½***

C131 AP54 100fr brt. blue, dk. bl. & org. 1.10 50
C132 " 150fr multicolored 2.00 80

25th anniversary of the United Nations.

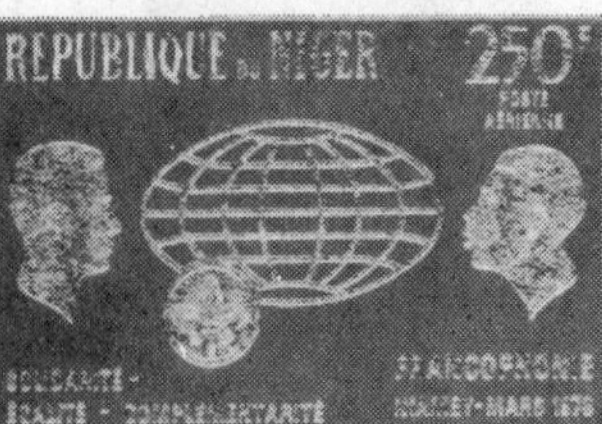

European and African Men, Globe and Fleur-de-lis—AP55

Litho.; Embossed on Gold Foil

1970, July 22 ***Perf. 12½***

C133 AP55 250fr gold & ultra. 3.00 3.00

Issued to commemorate the French Language Congress in Niamey, March 1970.

Europafrica Issue

European and African Women
AP56

1970, July 29 Engraved *Perf. 13*

C134 AP56 50fr slate green & dull red 60 35

EXPO Emblem, Geisha and Torii
AP57

Design: 150fr, EXPO emblem, exhibition at night and character from Noh play.

1970, Sept. 16 Engraved *Perf. 13*

C135 AP57 100fr multi. 1.10 50
C136 " 150fr blue, dk. brn. & green 1.60 80

Issued to commemorate EXPO '70 International Exhibition, Osaka, Japan, Mar. 15–Sept. 13.

Gymnast on Parallel Bars
AP58

Beethoven and Piano
AP59

Sports: 100fr, Vaulting (horiz.). 150fr, Flying jump (horiz.). 200fr, Rings.

1970, Oct. 26 Engraved *Perf. 13*

C137 AP58 50fr bright blue 60 35
C138 " 100fr bright green 1.20 65
C139 " 150fr bright rose lilac 1.80 90
C140 " 200fr red orange 2.40 1.25

Issued to publicize the 17th World Gymnastics Championships, Ljubljana, Oct. 22–27.

Nos. C124 and C126 Surcharged and Overprinted:

"LUNA 16—Sept. 1970 / PREMIERS PRELEVEMENTS / AUTOMATIQUES SUR LA LUNE"

1970, Nov. 5

C141 AP51 100fr on 150fr multi. 1.25 55
C142 " 200fr on 250fr multi. 2.40 1.00

Issued to commemorate the unmanned moon probe of the Russian space ship Luna 16, Sept. 12–24.

1970, Nov. 18 Photo. *Perf. 12½*

Design: 150fr, Beethoven and dancers with dove, symbolic of Ode to Joy.

C143 AP59 100fr multi. 1.25 50
C144 " 150fr " 1.75 75

Issued to commemorate the bicentenary of the birth of Ludwig van Beethoven (1770–1827), composer.

John F. Kennedy Bridge, Niamey
AP60

1970, Dec. 18 Photo. *Perf. 12½*

C145 AP60 100fr multi. 1.10 40

Proclamation of the Republic, 12th anniversary.

Gamal Abdel Nasser
AP61

Design: 200fr, Nasser with raised arm.

1971, Jan. 5 Photo. *Perf. 12½*

C146 AP61 100fr blk., org. brn. & green 1.00 40
C147 " 200fr grn., org. & blk. brn. 2.00 1.10

In memory of Gamal Abdel Nasser (1918–70), President of Egypt.

Charles de Gaulle
AP62

Embossed on Gold Foil

1971, Jan. 22 *Die-cut Perf. 10*

C148 AP62 1000fr gold 27.50 27.50

In memory of Gen. Charles de Gaulle (1890–1970), President of France.

Olympic Rings and "Munich"—AP63

1971, Jan. 29 Engraved *Perf. 13*

C149 AP63 150fr dark blue, rose lilac & green 1.65 80

Publicity for 1972 Summer Olympic Games in Munich.

Landing Module over Moon
AP64

Masks of Hate
AP65

1971, Feb. 5 Engraved *Perf. 13*

C150 AP64 250fr ultra., slate green & orange 2.75 1.35

Apollo 14 mission, Jan. 31–Feb. 9.

1971, March 20 Engr. *Perf. 13*

Design: 200fr, People and 4-leaf clover (symbol of unity).

C151 AP65 100fr red, slate & brt. blue 1.20 50
C152 " 200fr slate, red & green 2.00 1.00

International Year against Racial Discrimination.

Map of Africa and Telecommunications System—AP66

1971, Apr. 6 Photo. *Perf. 12½*

C153 AP66 100fr grn. & multi. 1.10 40

Pan-African telecommunications system.

African Mask and Japan No. 580
AP67

Design: 100fr, Japanese actors, stamps of Niger, No. 95 on cover and No. 170.

1971, Apr. 23 Engraved *Perf. 13*

C154 AP67 50fr dark brown, emerald & black 60 30
C155 " 100fr brn. & multi. 1.20 50

Philatokyo 71, Tokyo Philatelic Exposition, Apr. 19–29.

Longwood, St. Helena, by Carle Vernet—AP68

Design: 200fr, Napoleon's body on camp bed, by Marryat.

1971, May 5 Photo. *Perf. 13*

C156 AP68 150fr gold & multi. 1.80 80
C157 " 200fr gold & multi. 2.40 1.10

Sesquicentennial of the death of Napoleon Bonaparte (1769–1821).

Satellite, Waves and Earth
AP69

Olympic Rings, Athletes and Torch
AP70

1971, May 17 Engraved *Perf. 13*

C158 AP69 100fr org., ultra. & dk. brn. 1.10 55

3rd World Telecommunications Day.

1971, June 10

Designs: 50fr, Pierre de Coubertin, discus throwers (horiz.). 150fr, Runners (horiz.).

C159 AP70 50fr red & slate 60 25
C160 " 100fr slate, brown & green 1.20 40
C161 " 150fr plum, blue & rose lilac 1.80 80

75th anniversary of modern Olympic Games.

Astronauts and Landing Module on Moon
AP71

Charles de Gaulle
AP72

1971, July 26 Engraved *Perf. 13*

C162 AP71 150fr red brn., pur. & slate 1.60 75

U.S. Apollo 15 moon mission, July 26–Aug. 7, 1971.

1971, Nov. 9 Photo. *Perf. 12½x12*

C163 AP72 250fr multi. 4.00 2.50

First anniversary of the death of Charles de Gaulle (1890–1970), president of France.

African Postal Union Issue, 1971

Common Design Type

Design: 100fr, Water carrier, cattle and UAMPT headquarters, Brazzaville, Congo.

1971, Nov. 13 Photo. *Perf. 13x13½*

C164 CD135 100fr bl. & multi. 1.10 50

Al Hariri Holding Audience, Baghdad, 1237—AP73

Designs from Mohammedan Miniatures: 150fr, Archangel Israfil, late 14th century (vert.). 200fr, Horsemen, 1210.

1971, Nov. 25 ***Perf. 13***

C165 AP73 100fr multi. 1.00 50
C166 " 150fr " 1.50 80
C167 " 200fr " 2.00 1.10

Louis Armstrong AP74

Design: 150fr, Armstrong with trumpet.

1971, Dec. 6

C168 AP74 100fr multi. 1.10 50
C169 " 150fr " 1.65 80

Louis Armstrong (1900–1971), American jazz musician.

Adoration of the Kings, by Di Bartolo—AP75

Paintings: 150fr, Nativity, by Domenico Ghirlandaio (vert.). 200fr, Adoration of the Shepherds, by Il Perugino.

1971, Dec. 24 **Photo.** ***Perf. 13***

C170 AP75 100fr blk. & multi. 1.20 50
C171 " 150fr " " 1.80 80
C172 " 200fr " " 2.40 1.10

Christmas 1971. See Nos. C210–C212, C232–C234.

Presidents Pompidou and Diori Hamani, Flags of Niger and France—AP76

1972, Jan. 22

C173 AP76 250fr multi. 4.00 2.75

Visit of President Georges Pompidou of France, Jan. 1972.

Snowflakes, Olympic Torch and Emblem—AP77

Design: 100fr, Torii made of ski poles and skis, and dwarf tree (vert.).

1972, Jan. 27 **Engraved**

C174 AP77 100fr dk. vio., grn. & car. 1.00 45
C175 " 150fr dk. vio., lilac & red 1.60 75
a. Souvenir sheet of 2 3.00 3.00

11th Winter Olympic Games, Sapporo, Japan, Feb. 3–13. No. C175a contains one each of Nos. C174–C175, dark violet inscription. Size: 130x100mm.

The Masked Ball, by Guardi—AP78

Designs: 50fr, 100fr, 150fr, Details from "The Masked Ball," by Francesco Guardi (1712–1793); all vertical.

1972, Feb. 7 **Photogravure**

C176 AP78 50fr gold & multi. 60 28
C177 " 100fr " " 1.20 55
C178 " 150fr " " 1.80 80
C179 " 200fr " " 2.40 1.10

UNESCO campaign to save Venice. See also Nos. C215–C216.

Johannes Brahms and "Lullaby" AP79 **Scout Sign and Tents AP80**

1972, Mar. 17 **Engraved** ***Perf. 13***

C180 AP79 100fr brt. grn., car. rose & slate grn. 1.20 50

75th anniversary of death of Johannes Brahms (1833–1897), German composer.

1972, Mar. 22

C181 AP80 150fr pur., org. & slate blue 1.50 55

World Boy Scout Seminar, Cotonou, Dahomey, March 1972.

Surgical Team, Heart-shaped Globe and Emblem—AP81

1972 **Engraved** ***Perf. 13***

C182 AP81 100fr dp. brn. & carmine 1.20 50

"Your heart is your health," World Health Day.

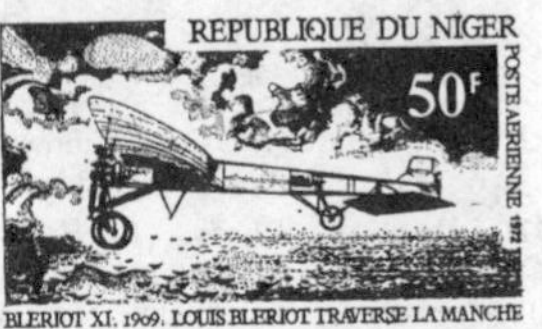

Bleriot XI Crossing English Channel—AP82

Famous Aircraft: 75fr, Spirit of St. Louis crossing Atlantic. 100fr, First flight of Concorde supersonic jet.

1972, Apr. 24

C183 AP82 50fr dk. vio. blue, brown & magenta 65 35
C184 " 75fr brn. red, blue & indigo 1.00 55
C185 " 100fr deep ultra., magenta & greenish bl. 1.40 85

ITU Emblem, Satellite, Stars and Earth—AP83

1972, May 17 **Engraved** ***Perf. 13***

C186 AP83 100fr purple, car. & black 1.10 50

4th World Telecommunications Day.

Boxing and Opera House—AP84

Designs: 100fr, Broad jump and City Hall (vert.). 150fr, Soccer and Church of the Theatines (vert.). 200fr, Running and Propylaeum.

1972, May 26

C187 AP84 50fr blue & brown 55 25
C188 " 100fr yellow green & dk. brown 1.10 45
C189 " 150fr orange red & dk. brown 1.60 70
C190 " 200fr violet & dk. brown 2.25 90
a. Miniature sheet of 4 6.00 5.00

20th Olympic Games, Munich, Aug. 26–Sept. 10. No. C190a contains one each of Nos. C187–C190. Size: 199x99mm.

Alexander Graham Bell, Telephone—AP85

1972, July 7

C191 AP85 100fr car., dk. pur. & slate 1.10 45

50th anniversary of the death of Alexander Graham Bell (1847–1922), inventor of the telephone.

Europafrica Issue

Stylized Maps of Africa and Europe AP86

1972, July 29 **Engraved** ***Perf. 13***

C192 AP86 50fr red brown, bl. & green 55 25

Mail Runner, UPU Emblem—AP87

Designs: 100fr, Mail truck, UPU emblem. 150fr, Mail plane, UPU emblem.

1972, Oct. 9 **Engr.** ***Perf. 13***

C193 AP87 50fr red brown, slate green & dk. brown 55 30
C194 " 100fr red brn., ultra. & Prussian green 1.10 55
C195 " 150fr red brown, purple & slate grn. 1.60 80

Universal Postal Union Day.

Nos. C187–C190 Overprinted in Red or Violet Blue

a. WELTER / CORREA / MEDAILLE D'OR
b. TRIPLE SAUT / SANEEV / MEDAILLE D'OR
c. FOOTBALL / POLOGNE / MEDAILLE D'OR
d. MARATHON / SHORTER / MEDAILLE D'OR

1972, Nov. 10

C196 AP84 (*a*) 50fr multi. (R) 55 25
C197 " (*b*) 100fr multi. (R) 1.10 45
C198 " (*c*) 150fr multi. (VBl) 1.90 70
C199 " (*d*) 200fr multi. (R) 2.50 90

Gold medal winners in 20th Olympic Games: Emilio Correa, Cuba, welterweight boxing (C196); Victor Saneev, USSR, triple jump (C197); Poland, soccer (C198); Frank Shorter, USA, marathon (C199).

The Crow and The Fox—AP88

Fables: 50fr, The Lion and the Mouse. 75fr, The Monkey and the Leopard.

1972, Nov. 23

C200 AP88 25fr emerald, blk. & brown 30 18
C201 " 50fr brt. pink, bl. grn. & brn. 60 28

C202 AP88 75fr lt. brn., grn. & dk. brown 90 50

Jean de La Fontaine (1621–1695), French fabulist.

Astronauts on Moon—AP89

1972, Dec. 12 Photo. ***Perf. 13***

C203 AP89 250fr multi. 2.75 1.25

Apollo 17 U.S. moon mission, Dec. 7–19.

Young Athlete AP90

Design: 100fr, Head of Hermes.

1973, Feb. 7 Engraved ***Perf. 13***

C204 AP90 50fr dark carmine 50 25
C205 " 100fr purple 1.00 45

Treasures of antiquity.

Boy Scouts and Radio Transmission—AP91

Designs: 50fr, Red Cross, first aid. 100fr, Scout and gazelle. 150fr, Scouts with gazelle and bird.

1973, Mar. 21 Engraved ***Perf. 13***

C206 AP91 25fr slate green, chocolate & dark red 25 10
C207 " 50fr green, red & chocolate 50 25
C208 " 100fr maroon, slate green & chocolate 1.00 50
C209 " 150fr multicolored 1.50 65

Nigerian Boy Scouts.

Christmas Type of 1971

Paintings: 50fr, Crucifixion, by Hugo van der Goes (vert.). 100fr, Burial of Christ, by Cima da Conegliano. 150fr, Pietà, by Giovanni Bellini.

1973, Apr. 20 Photo. ***Perf. 13***

C210 AP75 50fr gold & multi. 60 28
C211 " 100fr " " 1.20 60
C212 " 150fr " " 1.75 80

Easter 1973.

Air Afrique Plane and Mail Truck AP92

1973, Apr. 30 Engraved ***Perf. 13***

C213 AP92 100fr brt. grn., choc. & car. 1.10 55

Stamp Day 1973.

WMO Emblem, Pyramids with Weather Symbols, Satellite—AP93

1973, May 7

C214 AP93 100fr ol. brn., brt. grn. & brt. magenta 1.10 55

Centenary of international meteorological cooperation.

Painting Type of 1972

Paintings by Delacroix: 150fr, Prowling lioness. 200fr, Tigress and cub.

1973, May 22 Photo. ***Perf. 13x12½***

C215 AP78 150fr blk. & multi. 1.65 75
C216 " 200fr " " 2.25 1.10

175th anniversary of the birth of Ferdinand Delacroix (1798–1863), French painter.

Nos. C208–C209 Overprinted: "24 · Conference Mondiale / du Scoutisme / NAIROBI 1973"

1973, July 19 Engraved ***Perf. 13***

C217 AP91 100fr multi. 1.00 50
C218 " 150fr " 1.50 65

Boy Scout 24th World Jamboree, Nairobi, Kenya, July 16–21.

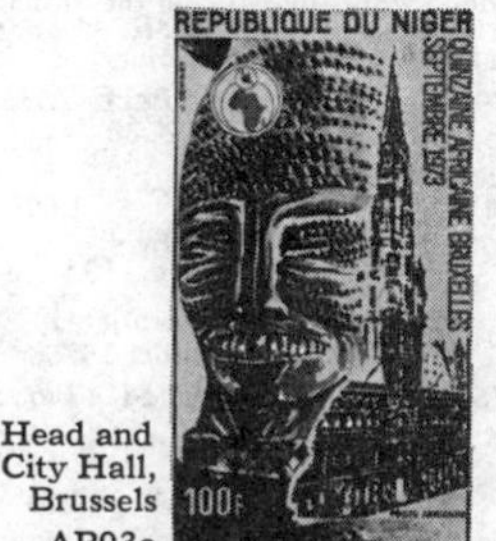

Head and City Hall, Brussels AP93a

1973, Sept. 17 Engraved ***Perf. 13***

C219 AP93a 100fr dk. purple, magenta & vio. bl. 1.10 50

Africa Weeks, Brussels, Sept. 15–30, 1973.

Men Emptying Cornucopia, FAO Emblem, People AP94

1973, Nov. 2 Engraved ***Perf. 13***

C220 AP94 50fr ultra., purple & vermilion 55 28

10th anniversary of the World Food Program.

Copernicus, Sputnik 1, Heliocentric System AP95

1973, Nov. 12

C221 AP95 150fr magenta, vio. bl. & brn. 1.60 80

500th anniversary of the birth of Nicolaus Copernicus (1473–1543), Polish astronomer.

John F. Kennedy AP96

1973, Nov. 22 Photo. ***Perf. 12½***

C222 AP96 100fr reddish brn. & multi. 1.10 55

Souvenir Sheet

Perf. 13

C223 AP96 200fr dp. ultra. & multi. 2.10 2.10

10th anniversary of the death of Pres. John F. Kennedy (1917–63). No. C223 contains one stamp, ultramarine marginal inscription. Size: 79x100mm.

Barge on Niger River—AP97

Design: 75fr, Tug Baban Maza.

1974, Jan. 18 Engraved ***Perf. 13***

C224 AP97 50fr maroon, violet blue & green 45 28
C225 " 75fr yel. grn., blue & lilac rose 70 35

First anniversary of the upstream voyage of the Flotilla of Hope.

Lenin AP98

1974, Jan. 21

C226 AP98 50fr dk. red brown 45 28

50th anniversary of the death of Lenin (1870–1924), Russian Communist leader.

Skiers AP99

1974, Feb. 8 Engr. ***Perf. 11½x11***

C227 AP99 200fr blue, sepia & car. 2.00 1.00

50th anniversary of the first Winter Olympic Games, Chamonix, France.

Soccer and Emblem—AP100

Designs: Various views of soccer game.

1974, Apr. 8 Engraved ***Perf. 13***

C228 AP100 75fr vio. & blk. 70 40
C229 " 150fr brn., lt. & slate grn. 1.35 75
C230 " 200fr Prus. blue, grn. & brn. 1.85 1.25

Souvenir Sheet

C231 AP100 250fr yel. grn., brn. & ol. brn. 2.75 2.75

World Soccer Championship, Munich, June 13–July 7. No. C231 contains one stamp; olive brown inscription and soccer player design in margin. Size: 129½x100 mm.

Christmas Type of 1971

Paintings: 50fr, Crucifixion, by Matthias Grunewald. 75fr, Avignon Pietà, attributed to Enguerrand Quarton. 125fr, Burial of Christ, by G. Isenmann.

1974, Apr. 12 Litho. ***Perf. 13x12½***

C232 AP75 50fr blk. & multi. 50 25
C233 " 75fr " " 70 35
C234 " 125fr " " 1.20 60

Easter 1974.

Chess Knights AP101

Design: 75fr, Kings.

1974, June 3 Engraved ***Perf. 13***

C235 AP101 50fr multicolored 50 25
C236 " 75fr 70 40

21st Chess Olympiad, Nice, June 6–30.

Astronaut and Apollo 11 Badge AP102

1974, July 20 Engraved ***Perf. 13***

C237 AP102 150fr multi. 1.35 75

5th anniversary of the first manned moon landing.

Europafrica Issue

The Rhinoceros, by Pietro Longhi
AP103

1974, Aug. 10 Photo. *Perf. 12½x13*

C238 AP103 250fr multi. 2.50 1.60

Souvenir Sheet

No. C231 Overprinted in Red: "R.F.A. 2 / HOLLANDE 1"

1974, Sept. 27 Engraved *Perf. 13*

C239 AP100 250fr multi. 2.50 2.50

World Cup Soccer Championship, Munich, 1974, victory of German Federal Republic. No. C239 has additional red inscription in margin: "7 JUILLET 1974 / VAINQUEUR REPUBLIQUE FEDERALE ALLEMANDE".

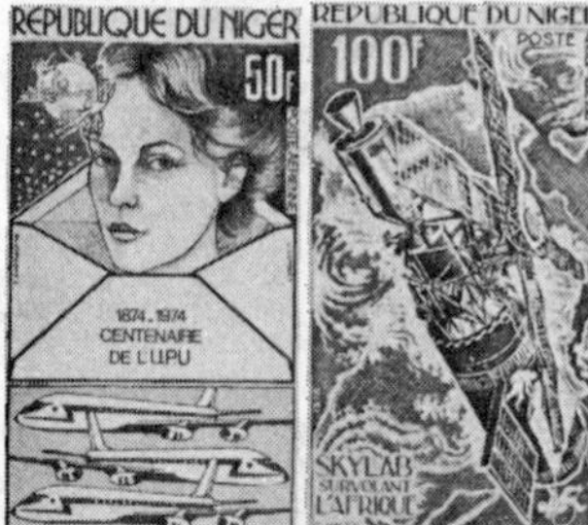

Caucasian Woman, Envelope, UPU Emblem and Jets
AP104

Skylab over Africa
AP105

Designs (UPU emblem, Envelope and): 100fr, Oriental woman and trains. 150fr, Indian woman and ships. 200fr, Black woman and buses.

1974, Oct. 9 Engraved *Perf. 13*

C240 AP104 50fr multicolored 50 25
C241 " 100fr " 90 50
C242 " 150fr bl. & multi. 1.35 75
C243 " 200fr multi. 1.75 1.10

Centenary of Universal Postal Union.

1974, Nov. 4 Engraved *Perf. 13*

C244 AP105 100fr multi. 90 55

Virgin and Child, by Correggio
AP106

Paintings: 150fr, Virgin and Child with St. Hilary, by Filippo Lippi. 200fr, Virgin and Child, by Murillo.

1974, Dec. 24 Litho. *Perf. 12½x13*

C245 AP106 100fr multi. 1.00 40
C246 " 150fr " 1.40 75
C247 " 200fr " 2.00 1.10

Christmas 1974. See Nos. C252–C254, C260–C262, C280–C282.

Apollo and Emblem
AP107

Designs (Emblem of Soyuz-Apollo Space Docking): 100fr, Docking in space over earth. 150fr, Soyuz in space.

1975, Jan. 31 Engraved *Perf. 13*

C248 AP107 50fr bl. & multi. 45 25
C249 " 100fr multi. 85 50
C250 " 150fr " 1.40 75

Russo-American space cooperation.

Europafrica Issue

European and African Women, Globe
AP108

1975, Feb. 28 Engraved *Perf. 13*

C251 AP108 250fr brn., lilac & red 2.25 1.35

Painting Type of 1974

Designs: 75fr, Jesus in Garden of Olives, by Delacroix (horiz.). 125fr, Crucifixion, by El Greco. 150fr, Resurrection, by Leonard Limosin.

Perf. 13x12½, 12½x13

1975, Mar. 27 Lithographed

C252 AP106 75fr multicolored 70 28
C253 " 125fr " 1.10 60
C254 " 150fr " 1.40 75

Easter 1975.

Bird Type of 1968–69 Dated "1975"

Design: 100fr, Cinnyricinclus leucogaster (vert.).

1975, Apr. Photo. *Perf. 13*

C255 AP36 100fr gold & multi. 80 45

Lt. Col. Seyni Kountche
AP109

1975, Apr. 15 Litho. *Perf. 12½x13*

C256 AP109 100fr multi. 80 50

Military Government, first anniversary.

Shot Put, Maple Leaf, Montreal Olympic Emblem
AP110

Design: 200fr, Gymnast on rings, Canadian flag, Montreal Olympic emblem.

1975, Oct. 6 Engr. *Perf. 13*

C257 AP110 150fr blk. & red 1.20 65
C258 " 200fr red & blk. 1.65 1.00

Pre-Olympic Year 1975.

U.N. Emblem and Dove—AP111

1975, Nov. 26 Engr. *Perf. 13*

C259 AP111 100fr grn. & bl. 85 50

United Nations, 30th anniversary.

Painting Type of 1974

Paintings: 50fr, Virgin of Seville, by Murillo. 75fr, Adoration of the Shepherds, by Tintoretto (horiz.). 125fr, Virgin with Angels, Florentine, 15th century.

1975, Dec. 24 Litho. *Perf. 12½x13*

C260 AP106 50fr multi. 40 28
C261 " 75fr " 60 45
C262 " 125fr " 1.00 75

Christmas 1975.

Nos. C248–C250 Overprinted: "JONCTION / 17 Juillet 1975"

1975, Dec. 30 Engraved *Perf. 13*

C263 AP107 50fr bl. & multi. 40 28
C264 " 100fr multi. 85 55
C265 " 150fr multi. 1.25 80

Apollo-Soyuz link-up in space, July 17, 1975.

12th Winter Olympic Games Type, 1976

Designs: 200fr, Women's figure skating. 300fr, Biathlon. 500fr, Speed skating.

1976, Feb. 20 Litho. *Perf. 14x13½*

C266 A97 200fr multicolored 1.75 80
C267 " 300fr " 2.50 1.10

Souvenir Sheet

C268 A97 500fr multicolored 4.00 2.00

12th Winter Olympic games, Innsbruck. No. C268 has multicolored margin showing Austrian Alps and skiers. Size: 116x77½mm.

American Bicentennial Type, 1976

Design (Statue of Liberty and): 150fr, Joseph Warren, martyr at Bunker Hill. 200fr, John Paul Jones on the bridge of the "Bonhomme Richard." 300fr, Molly Pitcher, Monmouth battle heroine. 500fr, Start of the fighting.

1976, Apr. 8

C269 A100 150fr multi. 1.20 40
C270 " 200fr " 1.60 80
C271 " 300fr " 2.40 1.10

Souvenir Sheet

C272 A100 500fr multi. 4.00 2.00

American Bicentennial. No. C272 has multicolored margin showing Declaration of Independence and Captain Parker's orders to the Minute Men. Size: 128x96mm.

Unused prices are for stamps that have been hinged.

LZ-129 over Lake Constance—AP112

Designs: 50fr, LZ-3 over Würzburg. 150fr, LZ-9 over Friedrichshafen. 200fr, LZ-2 over Rothenburg (vert.). 300fr, LZ-130 over Essen. 500fr, LZ-127 over the Swiss Alps.

1976, May 18 Litho. *Perf. 11*

C273 AP112 40fr multi. 30 15
C274 " 50fr " 40 15
C275 " 150fr " 1.20 50
C276 " 200fr " 1.60 55
C277 " 300fr " 2.40 80
Nos. C273–C277 (5) 5.90 2.15

Souvenir Sheet

C278 AP112 500fr multi. 4.00 2.00

75th anniversary of the Zeppelin. No. C278 has multicolored margin showing scenes from 8 cities visited by "Graf Zeppelin." Size: 127½x103mm.

Olympic Games Type, 1976

Souvenir Sheet

Design: 150fr, Sprint.

1976, July 17 Litho. *Perf. 14*

C279 A105 150fr multi. 1.40 70

21st Summer Olympic games, Montreal. No. C279 has multicolored margin showing runner and Montreal Olympic stadium. Size: 103½x78mm.

Christmas Type of 1974

Paintings: 50fr, Nativity, by Rubens. 100fr, Virgin and Child, by Correggio. 150fr, Adoration of the Kings, by Gerard David (horiz.).

1976, Dec. 24 Litho. *Perf. 12½*

C280 AP106 50fr multi. 40 25
C281 " 100fr " 85 50
C282 " 150fr " 1.25 65

Christmas 1976.

Viking Mars Project Type, 1977

Designs: 100fr, Viking lander and probe (horiz.). 150fr, Descent phases of Viking lander. 200fr, Titan rocket start for Mars. 400fr, Viking orbiter in flight.

1977, Mar. 15 Litho. *Perf. 14*

C283 A113 100fr multi. 80 32
C284 " 150fr " 1.20 40
C285 " 200fr " 1.60 55

Souvenir Sheet

C286 A113 400fr multi. 3.25 1.50

Viking Mars project. No. C286 has multicolored margin showing Houston control room. Size: 103½x78mm.

Nobel Prize Type, 1977

Souvenir Sheet

Design: 500fr, Theodore Roosevelt, peace.

1977, Aug. 20 Litho. *Perf. 14*

C287 A122 500fr multi. 4.00 1.75

Nobel prize winners. No. C287 has multicolored margin showing profile of Nobel and Swedish flag. Size: 117x80mm.

Games' Emblem, Wheels and Colors
AP113

Design: 150fr, Rings, colors and Games' emblem.

1978, July 13 Litho. *Perf. 12½x13*

C288	AP113	40fr multi.	32	20
C289	"	150fr "	1.20	75

Third African Games, Algiers, July 13–28.

Emblem AP114

1978, Oct. 6 Litho. *Perf. 13*

C290	AP114	150fr multi.	1.20	75

Niger Broadcasting Company, 20th anniversary.

Philexafrique II—Essen Issue
Common Design Types

Designs: No. C291, Giraffes and Niger No. 92. No. C292, Eagle and Oldenburg No. 7.

1978, Nov. 1 Litho. *Perf. 13x12½*

C291	CD138	100fr multi.	80	50
C292	CD139	100fr "	80	50

Nos. C291–C292 printed se-tenant.

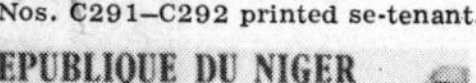

View of Campus and Laying Cornerstone—AP115

1978, Dec. 11 Litho. *Perf. 12½*

C293	AP115	100fr multi.	80	50

Islamic University of Niger.

AIR POST SEMI-POSTAL STAMPS.

Stamps of Dahomey types V1, V2, V3 and V4 inscribed "Niger" were issued in 1942 by the Vichy Government, but were not placed on sale in the colony.

POSTAGE DUE STAMPS.

D1

D2

Postage Due Stamps of Upper Senegal and Niger, 1914, Overprinted.

1921 *Perf. 14x13½* Unwmkd.

J1	D1	5c green	20	20
J2	"	10c rose	20	20
J3	"	15c gray	25	25
J4	"	20c brown	25	25
J5	"	30c blue	25	25
J6	"	50c black	35	35
J7	"	60c orange	45	45
J8	"	1fr violet	55	55
		Nos. J1-J8 (8)	2.50	2.50

1927 Typographed.

J9	D2	2c dark blue & red	5	5
J10	"	4c vermilion & black	8	8
J11	"	5c orange & violet	10	10
J12	"	10c red brown & black violet	12	12
J13	"	15c green & orange	15	15
J14	"	20c cerise & olive brown	20	20
J15	"	25c blk. & olive brn.	20	20
J16	"	30c dull violet & black	40	40
J17	"	50c deep red, *greenish*	20	20
J18	"	60c gray violet & orange, *bluish*	20	20
J19	"	1fr indigo & ultramarine, *bluish*	25	25
J20	"	2fr rose red & violet	25	25
J21	"	3fr orange brown & ultramarine	30	30
		Nos. J9-J21 (13)	2.50	2.50

Republic of the Niger

Cross of Agadez—D3

Designs (Native metalcraft): 3fr, 5fr, 10fr, Cross of Iferouane. 15fr, 20fr, 50fr, Cross of Tahoua.

Photogravure

1962, July 1 *Perf. 12½* Unwmkd.

J22	D3	50c emerald	5	5
J23	"	1fr violet	5	5
J24	"	2fr slate green	5	5
J25	"	3fr lilac rose	5	5
J26	"	5fr green	6	6
J27	"	10fr orange	8	8
J28	"	15fr deep blue	15	15
J29	"	20fr carmine	28	28
J30	"	50fr chocolate	60	60
		Nos. J22-J30 (9)	1.37	1.37

OFFICIAL STAMPS

Djerma Girl Carrying Jug
O1

Perf. 14x13½

1962–71 Typo. Unwmkd.

Denomination in Black

O1	O1	1fr dark purple	5	5
O2	"	2fr yellow green	5	5
O3	"	5fr bright blue	8	8
O4	"	10fr deep red	13	10
O5	"	20fr violet blue	25	20
O6	"	25fr orange	30	25
O7	"	30fr lt. blue ('65)	35	30
O8	"	35fr pale grn. ('71)	45	35
O9	"	40fr brown ('71)	55	45
O10	"	50fr black	55	45
O11	"	60fr rose red	70	60
O12	"	85fr blue green	1.00	50
O13	"	100fr red lilac	1.25	50
O14	"	200fr dark blue	2.40	1.00
		Nos. O1-O14 (14)	8.11	4.88

NORTH INGERMANLAND

(nôrth in'gĕr·mȧn·lănd')

LOCATION — In Northern Russia lying between the River Neva and Finland.

CAPITAL—Kirjasalo.

In 1920 the residents of this territory revolted from Russian rule and set up a provisional government. The new State existed only a short period as the revolution was quickly quelled by Soviet troops.

100 Pennia = 1 Markka

Arms
A1

Lithographed.

1920 *Perf. 11½.* **Unwmkd.**

1 A1 5p green 2.00 2.50
a. Imperf., pair 8.00
2 A1 10p rose red 2.00 2.50
a. Imperf., pair 8.00
3 A1 25p bistre 2.00 2.50
a. Imperf., pair 8.00
4 A1 50p dark blue 2.00 2.50
a. Imperf., pair 8.00
5 A1 1m carmine & blk. 22.50 25.00
a. Imperf., pair 55.00
6 A1 5m lilac & black 90.00 100.00
a. Imperf., pair 225.00
7 A1 10m brown & black 160.00 175.00
a. Imperf., pair 400.00
Nos. 1-7 (7) 280.50 310.00

Arms
A2

Peasant
A3

Plowing
A4

Milking
A5

Planting
A6

Ruins of Church
A7

Peasants Playing Zithers
A8

1920

8 A2 10p gray green & ultramarine 3.50 6.00
9 A3 30p buff & gray grn. 3.50 6.00
10 A4 50p ultra. & red brn. 3.50 6.00
11 A5 80p claret & slate 3.50 6.00
12 A6 1m red & slate 18.00 27.50
13 A7 5m dark violet & dull rose 10.00 14.00
14 A8 10m brown & violet 10.00 14.00
a. Center inverted 300.00
Nos. 8-14 (7) 52.00 79.50

Counterfeits abound.
Nos. 8-14 exist imperf. Price for set in pairs, $150.

NORWAY

(nôr'wā)

LOCATION—In the western half of the Scandinavian Peninsula in northern Europe.

GOVT.—Kingdom.

AREA—124,556 sq. mi.

POP.—4,040,000 (estimated 1977).

CAPITAL—Oslo.

120 Skilling = 1 Specie Daler
100 Öre = 1 Krone (1877)

Coat of Arms
A1

King Oscar I
A2

Wmk. 159

Wmkd. Lion. (159)

1855 Typographed *Imperf.*

1 A1 4s blue *4500.00* 110.00
a. Double foot on right hind leg of lion 2500.00

Only a few genuine unused copies of No. 1 exist. Specimens often offered have had pen-markings removed. The unused catalogue price is for a specimen without gum. Copies with original gum sell for much more.

No. 1 was reprinted in 1914 and 1924 unwatermarked. Lowest priced reprint, $50.

Rouletted Reprints

1963: Nos. 1, 2–5 and 15. Price each $14.
1965: Nos. 57, 70a, 100, 152, J1 and O1. Price each $10.
1969: Nos. 69, 92, 107, 114, 128 and J12. Price each $8.

1856-57 *Perf. 13* **Unwmkd.**

2 A2 2s yellow ('57) 325.00 120.00
3 " 3s lilac ('57) 250.00 65.00
4 A2 4s blue 175.00 10.00
a. Imperf. *4000.00*
b. Half used as 2s on cover *2000.00*
5 " 8s dull lake 650.00 40.00

Nos. 2–5 were reprinted in 1914 and 1924, perf. 10. Lowest priced reprint, $50 each.

A3

A4

Lithographed.

1863-66 *Perf. 14½x13½*

6 A3 2s yellow ('65) 375.00 190.00
7 " 3s gray lilac ('66) 500.00 300.00
8 " 4s blue 70.00 8.00
9 " 8s rose 425.00 40.00
10 " 24s brown 35.00 45.00

There are four types of the 2, 3, 8 and 24 skilling and eight types of the 4 skilling. See note on used price of No. 10 following No. 21.

1867-68 Typographed.

11 A4 1s black ('68) 85.00 35.00
12 " 2s orange 16.00 20.00
13 " 3s dull lilac ('68) 250.00 62.50
14 " 4s blue 55.00 4.50
15 " 8s carmine rose 275.00 40.00
a. 8s rose, clear impression 425.00 225.00

See note on used price of No. 12 following No. 21.
No. 15 was reprinted in 1914 and 1924, perf. 13½. Lowest priced reprint, $50.

Post Horn and Crown
A5

Wmk. 160

1872-75 Wmkd. Post Horn. (160)

16 A5 1s yellow green ('75) 7.50 11.00
a. 1s deep green ('73) 110.00 37.50
b. "E.EN" 30.00 40.00
17 " 2s ultramarine ('73) 16.00 18.00
a. 2s Prussian blue 2000.00 1400.00
b. 2s gray blue 14.00 18.00
18 " 3s rose 50.00 4.00
a. 3s carmine 50.00 4.00
b. 3s carmine, *bluish*, thin paper 120.00 13.00
19 " 4s lilac 16.00 20.00
a. 4s dk. violet 275.00 100.00
b. 4s brown violet 275.00 110.00
20 " 6s org. brn. ('75) 275.00 65.00
21 " 7s red brown 40.00 45.00

In this issue there are 12 types each of Nos. 16, 17, 18 and 19; 15 types of No. 20 and 22 types of No. 21. The differences are in the words of value.

Used prices of Nos. 10, 12, 16–17, 19 and 21 are for specimens canceled in later period, 1888–1908. Those canceled before 1888 are usually worth considerably more. These six stamps were used until Mar. 31, 1908.

Post Horn
A6

King Oscar II
A7

"NORGE" in Sans-serif Capitals, Ring of Post Horn Shaded.

1877-78

22 A6 1ö drab 4.50 3.50
23 " 3ö orange 80.00 18.00
24 A6 5ö ultramarine 45.00 5.00
a. 5ö dull blue 100.00 8.00
b. 5ö bright blue 100.00 10.00
c. No period after "Postfrim" 67.50 7.50
d. Retouched plate 72.50 7.00
e. Same as "c", retouched plate 110.00 10.00
25 " 10ö rose 55.00 1.00
a. No period after "Postfrim" 60.00 1.75
b. Retouched plate 55.00 1.00
26 " 12ö light green 100.00 18.00
27 " 20ö orange brown 250.00 10.00
28 " 25ö lilac 250.00 120.00
29 " 35ö blue green ('78) 13.00 9.00
a. Retouched plate 90.00 90.00
30 " 50ö maroon 32.50 9.00
31 " 60ö dark blue ('78) 32.50 9.00
32 A7 1kr gray green & green ('78) 30.00 9.00
33 " 1.50kr ultramarine & blue ('78) 72.50 42.50
34 " 2kr rose & maroon ('78) 45.00 27.50

There are 6 types each of Nos. 22, 26 and 28 to 34; 12 types each of Nos. 23, 24, 25 and 27. The differences are in the numerals.

The retouch on 5ö, 10ö and 35ö shows as a thin white line between crown and post horn.

Post Horn
Ring of Horn Unshaded
A8

"NORGE" in San-serif Capitals
Perf. 14½x13½.

1882-93 **Wmk. 160**

35 A8 1ö black brown ('91) 15.00 15.00
a. No period after "Postfrim" 85.00 85.00
b. Small "N" in "NORGE" 85.00 85.00
36 A8 1ö gray ('93) 9.00 9.00
37 " 2ö brown ('90) 1.75 1.75
38 " 3ö orange ('83) 60.00 2.50
a. 3ö yellow 60.00 2.50
b. Perf. 13½x12½ 1250.00
39 A8 5ö blue green ('83) 45.00 85
a. 5ö gray green 62.50 2.00
b. 5ö emerald ('88) 150.00 5.00
c. 5ö yellow green ('91) 45.00 85
d. Perf. 13½x12½ 550.00
40 A8 10ö rose 45.00 60
a. 10ö rose red 45.00 60
b. 10ö carmine 50.00 60
c. Imperf., pair 750.00 750.00
41 A8 12ö green ('84) 800.00 350.00
42 " 12ö yel. brown ('84) 22.50 15.00
a. 12ö bister brown 40.00 22.50
43 A8 20ö brown 90.00 9.00
44 " 20ö blue ('83) 60.00 90
a. 20ö ultramarine 90.00 4.00
b. No period after "Postfrim" 300.00 12.00
c. Imperf., pair 750.00 750.00
45 A8 25ö dull violet ('84) 14.00 10.00

Dies vary from 20 to 21mm. high. Numerous types exist due to different production methods, including separate handmade dies for value figures. Many shades exist.

No. 42 and 42a Surcharged in Black **2 Øre.**

1888 *Perf. 14½x13½.*

46 A8 2ö on 12ö yel. brown 1.75 1.75
a. 2ö on 12ö bister brown 1.75 1.75

Post Horn
A10

"NORGE" in Roman instead of Sans-serif capitals.
Perf. 14½x13½.

1893-1908 **Wmk. 160**

Size: 16x20mm.

47 A10 1ö gray ('99) 2.50 1.00
48 " 2ö pale brown ('98) 2.50 1.00
49 " 3ö orange yellow 1.75 20
50 " 5ö deep green ('98) 7.00 15
b. Bklt. pane of 6
51 " 10ö car. rose ('98) 14.00 15
b. Bklt. pane of 6

52 A10 15ö brown ('08) 52.50 3.00
53 " 20ö deep ultra. 35.00 25
b. Bklt. pane of 6
54 " 25ö red violet ('01) 67.50 2.75
55 " 30ö slate gray ('07) 52.50 1.75
56 " 35ö dk. bl. grn. ('98) 14.00 4.50
57 " 50ö maroon ('01) 65.00 1.40
58 " 60ö dark blue ('05) 75.00 14.00
Nos. 47-58 (12) 389.25 30.15

Two dies exist of each except 2, 25 and 60ö.

See also Nos. 74-95, 162-166, 187-191, 193, 307-309, 325-326, 416-419, 606, 709-714.

Perf. 13½x12½.

1893-98 **Wmk. 160**

47a A10 1ö gray 12.00 10.00
49a " 3ö orange 50.00 3.25
50a " 5ö green 35.00 70
51a " 10ö carmine 35.00 70
c. 10ö rose 50.00 80
53a " 20ö dull ultramarine 90.00 2.25
54a " 25ö red violet ('98) 125.00 22.50
56a " 35ö dk. blue green ('95) 125.00 25.00
57a " 50ö maroon ('94) 175.00 18.00

No. 12 Surcharged in Green, Blue or Carmine **Kr. 1.00**

1905 ***Perf. 14½x13½.*** **Unwmkd.**

59 A4 1kr on 2s org. (G) 40.00 37.50
60 " 1.50kr on 2s org. (Bl) 80.00 80.00
61 " 2kr on 2s org. (C) 60.00 55.00

Nos. 19 and 21 Surcharged in Black **30 ØRE**

1906-08 ***Perf. 14½x13½*** **Wmk. 160**

62 A5 15ö on 4s lilac ('08) 3.75 3.00
a. 15ö on 4s violet ('08) 10.00 7.00
63 A5 30ö on 7s red brown 8.50 7.00

King Haakon VII
A11

Die A. Background of ruled lines. The coils at the sides are ornamented with fine cross-lines and small dots. Stamps 20¾ mm. high.

Die B. Background of ruled lines. The coils are ornamented with large white dots and dashes. Stamps 21¼ mm. high.

Die C. Solid background. The coils are without ornamental marks. Stamps 20¾ mm. high.

1907 **Typo.** ***Perf. 14½x13½***

Die A.

64 A11 1kr yellow green 65.00 37.50
65 " 1.50kr ultramarine 135.00 95.00
66 " 2kr rose 170.00 75.00

1909-10 **Die B.**

67 A11 1kr green 210.00 110.00
68 " 1.50kr ultramarine 180.00 *350.00*
69 " 2kr rose 250.00 5.00

1911-18 **Die C.**

70 A11 1kr light green 1.00 15
a. 1kr dark green 55.00 50
71 " 1.50kr ultramarine 2.50 45
72 " 2kr rose ('15) 3.50 45
73 " 5kr dk. vio. ('18) 6.00 5.00

Post Horn Type Redrawn.

Original Redrawn

In the redrawn stamps the white ring of the post horn is continuous instead of being broken by a spot of color below the crown. On the 3 and 30 öre the top of the figure "3" in the oval band is rounded instead of flattened.

1910-29 ***Perf. 14½x13½.***

74 A10 1ö pale olive 30 15
75 A10 2ö pale brown 30 15
76 " 3ö orange 35 12
77 " 5ö green 4.00 8
a. Bklt. pane of 6 72.50
78 " 5ö magenta ('22) 45 8
79 " 7ö green ('29) 45 15
80 " 10ö carmine rose 5.00 8
a. Booklet pane of 6 75.00
81 " 10ö green ('22) 9.00 25
82 " 12ö purple ('17) 60 40
83 " 15ö brown 5.00 15
a. Booklet pane of 6 47.50
84 " 15ö indigo ('20) 4.50 20
85 " 20ö deep ultra. 11.00 15
a. Bklt. pane of 6 150.00
86 " 20ö olive green ('21) 9.00 20
87 " 25ö red lilac 40.00 25
88 " 25ö car. rose ('22) 9.00 1.30
89 " 30ö slate gray 12.00 25
90 " 30ö light blue ('27) 9.00 4.75
91 " 35ö dark olive ('20) 12.50 25
92 " 40ö olive green ('17) 4.25 25
93 " 40ö deep ultra. ('22) 22.50 40
94 " 50ö claret 22.50 25
95 " 60ö deep blue 30.00 25
Nos. 74-95 (22) 211.70 10.11

Constitutional Assembly of 1814
A12

1914, May 10 **Engr.** ***Perf. 13½***

96 A12 5ö green 1.20 35
97 " 10ö carmine rose 2.50 35
98 " 20ö deep blue 15.00 6.00

Issued to commemorate the centenary of Norway's Constitution of May 17, 1814.

No. 87 Surcharged **5 ØRE**

1922, Mar. 1 ***Perf. 14½x13½***

99 A10 5ö on 25ö red lilac 45 45

Lion Rampant
A13

Polar Bear and Airplane
A14

"NORGE" in Roman capitals, Line below "Ore"

1922-24 **Typo.** ***Perf. 14½x13½***

100 A13 10ö dp. green ('24) 14.00 35
101 " 20ö deep violet 22.50 10
102 " 25ö scarlet ('24) 37.50 1.00
103 " 45ö blue ('24) 2.50 70

1925, Apr. 1

104 A14 2ö yellow brown 2.00 2.00
105 " 3ö orange 3.50 3.50
106 " 5ö magenta 6.00 6.00
107 " 10ö yellow green 10.00 10.00
108 " 15ö dark blue 9.00 9.00
109 " 20ö plum 17.50 17.50
110 " 25ö scarlet 2.50 2.50
Nos. 104-110 (7) 50.50 50.50

Issued to help finance Roald Amundsen's attempted flight to the North Pole.

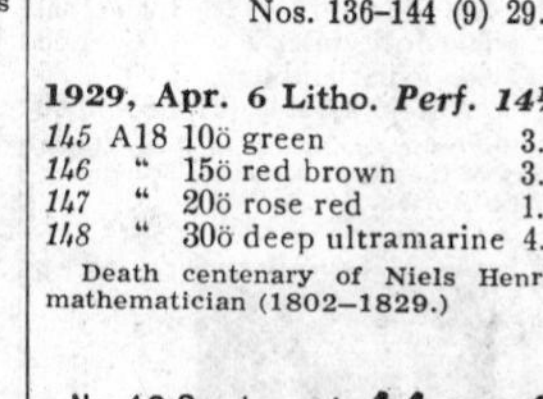

A15 A16

1925, Aug. 19

111 A15 10ö yellow green 6.50 6.00
112 " 15ö indigo 4.50 2.50
113 " 20ö plum 8.50 1.00
114 " 45ö dark blue 6.50 4.50

Annexation of Spitsbergen (Svalbard).

"NORGE" in Sans-serif Capitals, No Line below "Ore"

Size: 16x19½mm.

1926-34 **Wmk. 160**

115 A16 10ö yellow green 1.20 10
116 " 14ö dp. orange ('29) 2.00 1.40
117 " 15ö olive gray 1.20 15
118 " 20ö plum 27.50 15
119 " 20ö scarlet ('27) 1.00 8
a. Booklet pane of 6 50.00
120 " 25ö red 12.50 2.00
121 " 25ö org. brown ('27) 1.20 15
122 " 30ö dull blue ('28) 1.30 15
123 " 35ö olive brn. ('27) 62.50 15
124 " 35ö red violet ('34) 3.25 15
125 " 40ö dull blue 3.75 50
126 " 40ö slate ('27) 2.50 15
127 " 50ö claret ('27) 2.50 15
128 " 60ö Prus. blue ('27) 2.50 15
Nos. 115-128 (14) 124.90 5.43

See also Nos. 167-176, 192, 194-202A, 212-219, 225, 227-234, 302-303.

Nos. 103 and 114 Surcharged **30**

1927, June 13

129 A13 30ö on 45ö blue 17.50 1.00
130 A15 30ö on 45ö dk. blue 2.50 2.50

No. 120 Surcharged **20**

1928

131 A16 20ö on 25ö red 2.50 1.10

See also Nos. 302-303.

Henrik Ibsen
A17

Niels Henrik Abel
A18

1928, Mar. 20 **Lithographed**

132 A17 10ö yellow green 9.00 2.25
133 " 15ö chestnut brown 4.00 2.50
134 " 20ö carmine 3.75 50
135 " 30ö dp. ultramarine 4.50 3.50

Birth centenary of Henrik Ibsen (1828-1906), dramatist.

Postage Due Stamps of 1889-1923 Overprinted:

Post Frimerke (a) **POST** (b)

1929, Jan.

136 D1 (a) 1ö gray 40 40
137 " (") 4ö lilac rose 40 40
138 " (") 10ö green 1.80 1.50
139 " (b) 15ö brown 3.00 3.00
140 " (") 20ö dull violet 1.80 1.10
141 " (") 40ö deep ultra. 2.50 1.10
142 " (") 50ö maroon 8.00 5.50
143 " (a) 100ö org. yellow 4.00 2.25
144 " (b) 200ö dark violet 8.00 5.00
Nos. 136-144 (9) 29.90 20.25

1929, Apr. 6 **Litho.** ***Perf. 14½x13½***

145 A18 10ö green 3.50 90
146 " 15ö red brown 3.50 2.00
147 " 20ö rose red 1.60 45
148 " 30ö deep ultramarine 4.00 3.00

Death centenary of Niels Henrik Abel, mathematician (1802-1829.)

No. 12 Surcharged **14 ØRE 14**

Perf. 14½x13½

1929, July 1 **Unwmkd.**

149 A4 14ö on 2s orange 2.50 2.50

Saint Olaf
A19

Trondheim Cathedral
A20

Death of Olaf in Battle of Stiklestad—A21

Perf. 14½x13½

Typo.; Litho. (15ö)

1930, Apr. 1 **Wmk. 160**

150 A19 10ö yellow green 10.00 45
151 A20 15ö brown & black 1.40 50
152 A19 20ö scarlet 1.40 30

Engr. ***Perf. 13½***

153 A21 30ö deep blue 5.00 4.00

Issued to commemorate the 900th anniversary of the death of King Olaf Haraldsson (995-1030), patron saint of Norway.

Björnson
A22

Ludvig Holberg
A23

1932, Dec. 8 ***Perf. 14½x13½***

154 A22 10ö yellow green 12.00 45
155 " 15ö black brown 1.40 1.00
156 " 20ö rose red 1.40 25
157 " 30ö ultramarine 4.00 3.25

Birth centenary of Björnstjerne Björnson (1832-1910), novelist, poet and dramatist.

1934, Nov. 23

158 A23 10ö yellow green 1.75 35
159 " 15ö brown 1.00 75
160 " 20ö rose red 16.00 30
161 " 30ö ultramarine 3.75 3.00

250th anniversary of birth of Ludvig Holberg (1684-1754), Danish man of letters.

Types of 1893-1900, 1926-34.
Second Redrawing.
Size: 17x21mm.
Photogravure.

1937 ***Perf. 13x13½*** **Wmk. 160**

162 A10 1ö olive 60 55
163 " 2ö yellow brown 60 55
164 " 3ö deep orange 1.20 1.20
165 " 5ö rose lilac 60 10
a. Bklt. pane of 6 27.50
166 A10 7ö bright green 1.00 35
167 A16 10ö bright green 50 10
a. Bklt. pane of 6 27.50
168 A16 14ö deep orange 2.75 2.75
169 " 15ö olive bistre 1.60 25
170 " 20ö scarlet 1.50 10
a. Bklt. pane of 6 27.50
171 A16 25ö dk. org. brown 8.50 30
172 " 30ö ultramarine 4.75 25
173 " 35ö bright violet 3.00 30
174 " 40ö dk. slate green 4.75 25
175 " 50ö deep claret 5.50 60
176 " 60ö Prussian blue 2.50 25
Nos. 162-176 (15) 39.35 7.90

Nos. 162 to 166 have a solid background inside oval. Nos. 74, 75, 76, 78, 79 have background of vertical lines.

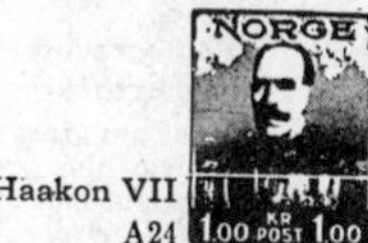

King Haakon VII
A24

1937-38

177 A24 1kr dark green 15 25
178 " 1.50kr sapphire ('38) 1.50 2.00
179 " 2kr rose red ('38) 1.50 4.25
180 " 5kr dull violet ('38) 9.50 32.50

False cancellations exist.

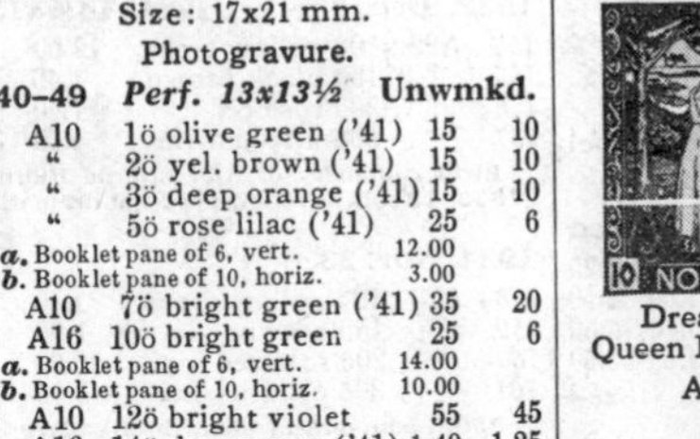

Reindeer A25 — Borgund Church A26

Jolster in Sunnfiord A27

Perf. 13x13½, 13½x13

1938, Apr. 20 Wmk. 160

181 A25 15ö olive brown 80 60
182 A26 20ö copper red 8.50 35
183 A27 30ö bright ultra. 6.50 2.00

1939 Unwmkd.

184 A25 15ö olive brown 60 30
185 A26 20ö copper red 80 20
186 A27 30ö bright ultramarine 70 35

Types of 1937.
Size: 17x21 mm.
Photogravure.

1940-49 *Perf. 13x13½* Unwmkd.

187 A10 1ö olive green ('41) 15 10
188 " 2ö yel. brown ('41) 15 10
189 " 3ö deep orange ('41) 15 10
190 " 5ö rose lilac ('41) 25 6
a. Booklet pane of 6, vert. 12.00
b. Booklet pane of 10, horiz. 3.00
191 A10 7ö bright green ('41) 35 20
192 A16 10ö bright green 25 6
a. Booklet pane of 6, vert. 14.00
b. Booklet pane of 10, horiz. 10.00
193 A10 12ö bright violet 55 45
194 A16 14ö dp. orange ('41) 1.40 1.25
195 " 15ö olive bistre 25 8
a. Booklet pane of 10 30.00
196 A16 20ö red 45 6
a. Booklet pane of 6, vert. 22.50
b. Booklet pane of 10, horiz. 22.50
197 A16 25ö dk. org. brown 1.10 12
197A " 25ö scarlet ('46) 55 6
b. Booklet pane of 10 12.00
198 A16 30ö brt. ultra. ('41) 1.25 25
198A " 30ö gray ('49) 8.00 25
199 " 35ö brt. violet ('41) 1.75 8
200 " 40ö dark slate green ('41) 1.10 10
200A " 40ö dp. ultra. ('46) 1.75 10
201 " 50ö dp. claret ('41) 1.10 10
201A " 55ö dp. org. ('46) 22.50 20
202 " 60ö Prus. blue ('41) 1.00 10
202A " 80ö dark orange brown ('46) 3.25 10
Nos. 187-202A (21) 47.30 3.92

Lion Rampant
A28 A29

Photogravure.

1940 *Perf. 13x13½* Unwmkd.

203 A28 1kr bright green 1.25 10
204 " 1½kr deep blue 1.75 25
205 " 2kr bright red 2.25 1.00
206 " 5kr dull purple 5.00 2.50

Stamps of 1937-41, Overprinted "V" in Black.

1941 *Perf. 13x13½.* Wmk. 160

207 A10 1ö olive 70 2.25
208 " 2ö yellow brown 70 2.25
209 " 3ö orange 2.25 4.50
210 " 5ö rose lilac 1.20 1.75
211 " 7ö bright green 1.20 2.25
212 A16 10ö bright green 2.00 3.50
213 " 14ö deep orange 1.50 2.75
214 " 15ö olive bistre 50 1.00
215 " 30ö ultramarine 1.75 1.10
216 " 35ö bright violet 1.75 1.00
217 " 40ö dark slate green 7.50 6.50
218 " 50ö deep claret 325.00 375.00
219 " 60ö Prussian blue 1.20 1.00
Nos. 207-219 (13) 347.25 404.85

Unwmkd.

220 A10 1ö olive 35 1.75
221 " 2ö yellow brown 35 1.75
222 " 3ö deep orange 35 1.75
223 " 5ö rose lilac 35 65
224 " 7ö bright green 1.20 3.25
225 A16 10ö bright green 30 35
226 A10 12ö bright violet 80 2.50
227 A16 15ö olive bistre 3.00 6.00
228 " 20ö red 40 25
a. Inverted ovpt. 400.00 475.00
229 " 25ö dk. org. brown 50 40
230 " 30ö bright ultra. 60 75
231 " 35ö bright violet 60 60
232 " 40ö dark slate green 60 60
233 " 50ö deep claret 1.20 1.75
234 " 60ö Prussian blue 80 75
235 A28 1kr bright green 85 45
236 " 1½kr deep blue 3.50 4.75
237 " 2kr bright red 8.00 18.00
238 " 5kr dull purple 20.00 37.50

Coil Stamp

239 A29 10ö bright green 1.00 5.00
Nos. 220-239 (20) 44.75 88.80

Dream of Queen Ragnhild A30 — Snorri Sturluson A32

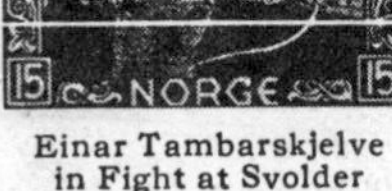

Einar Tambarskjelve in Fight at Svolder
A31

Designs: 30ö, King Olaf sailing in wedding procession to Landmerket. 50ö, Sylpdag's sons and followers going to Hall of Seven Kings. 60ö, Before Battle of Stiklestad.

1941 *Perf. 13½x13, 13x13½.*

240 A30 10ö bright green 30 20
241 A31 15ö olive brown 45 45
242 A32 20ö dark red 30 15
243 A31 30ö blue 1.00 1.00
244 " 50ö dull violet 1.00 1.00
245 " 60ö Prussian blue 1.00 80
Nos. 240-245 (6) 4.05 3.60

Issued in commemoration of the 700th anniversary of the death of Snorri Sturluson, writer and historian.

University of Oslo
A36

1941, Sept. 2 *Perf. 13x13½*

246 A36 1kr dk. olive green 42.50 45.00

Centenary of cornerstone laying of University of Oslo building.

Richard Nordraak—A37

"Broad Sails Go over the North Sea"—A38

View of Coast and Lines of National Anthem
A39

1942, June 12 *Perf. 13*

247 A37 10ö deep green 1.25 1.25
248 A38 15ö deep brown 1.25 1.25
249 A37 20ö rose red 1.25 1.25
250 A39 30ö sapphire 1.25 1.25

To commemorate the centenary of the birth of Richard (Rikard) Nordraak (1842-66), composer.

Johan Herman Wessel
A40

1942, Oct. 6

251 A40 15ö dull brown 20 20
252 " 20ö henna 20 20

To commemorate the bicentenary of the birth of the author, J. H. Wessel (1742-85).

Designs of 1942 and 1855 Stamps of Norway
A41

1942, Oct. 12

253 A41 20ö henna 40 65
254 " 30ö sapphire 50 1.00

To commemorate the European Postal Congress at Vienna, October, 1942.

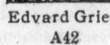

Edvard Grieg A42 — Destroyer Sleipner A43

1943, June 15

255 A42 10ö deep green 45 30
256 " 20ö henna 45 30
257 " 40ö greenish black 45 45
258 " 60ö dk. greenish blue 55 30

To commemorate the centenary of the birth of the composer, Edvard Hagerup Grieg (1843-1907).

Engraved.

1943-45 *Perf. 12½.* Unwmkd.

Designs: 5ö, 10ö, "Sleipner." 7ö, 30ö, Convoy under midnight sun. 15ö, Plane and pilot. 20ö, "We will win." 40ö, Ski troops. 60ö, King Haakon VII.

259 A43 5ö rose violet ('45) 20 20
260 " 7ö greenish blk. ('45) 20 20
261 " 10ö dark blue green 20 15
262 " 15ö dark olive green 60 60
263 " 20ö rose red 20 15
264 " 30ö dp. ultramarine 1.10 1.10
265 " 40ö olive black 85 85
266 " 60ö dark blue 85 85
Nos. 259-266 (8) 4.20 4.10

Nos. 261-266 were used for correspondence carried on Norwegian ships until after the liberation of Norway, when they became regular postage stamps.

Nos. 261-266 exist with overprint "London 17-5-43" and serial number. Price for set, unused, $700; used $800.

Gran's Plane and Map of His North Sea Flight Route
A49

1944, July 30 *Perf. 13*

267 A49 40ö dark greenish blue 50 1.75

To commemorate the 20th anniversary of the first flight over the North Sea, made by Tryggve Gran on July 30, 1914.

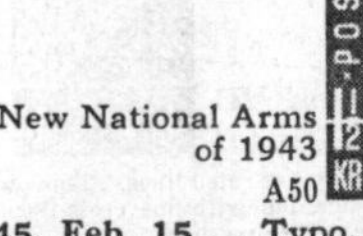

New National Arms of 1943
A50

1945, Feb. 15 Typo. *Perf. 13*

268 A50 1½kr dark blue 1.75 65

Henrik Wergeland A51 — Lion Rampant A52

1945, July 12 Photogravure

269 A51 10ö dark olive green 30 30
270 " 15ö dark brown 1.20 1.20
271 " 20ö dark red 40 25

Issued to commemorate the centenary of the death of Henrik Wergeland, poet and playwright.

1945, Dec. 19

272 A52 10ö dark olive green 30 25
273 " 20ö red 50 25

Issued to commemorate the 50th anniversary of the founding of the Norwegian Folklore Museum.

Pilot and Mechanic
A53

1946, Mar. 22 Engr. *Perf. 12*

274 A53 15ö brown rose 50 55

Issued in honor of Little Norway, training center in Canada for Norwegian pilots.

King Haakon VII
A54

1946, June 7 Photo. *Perf. 13*

275 A54 1kr bright green 1.25 10
276 " 1½kr Prussian blue 2.50 10
277 " 2kr henna brown 25.00 10
278 " 5kr violet 7.50 35

Hannibal Sehested
A55

Designs: 10ö, Letter carrier, 1700. 15ö, Adm. Peter W. Tordenskjold. 25ö, Christian Magnus Falsen. 30ö, Cleng Peerson and "Restaurationen." 40ö, Post ship "Constitution." 45ö, First Norwegian locomotive. 50ö, Sven Foyn and whaler. 55ö, Fridtjof Nansen and Roald Amundsen. 60ö, Coronation of King Haakon VII and Queen Maud, 1906. 80ö, Return of King Haakon, June 7, 1945.

Photogravure.

1947, Apr. 15 *Perf. 13* Unwmkd.

279 A55 5(ö) red lilac 15 8
280 " 10(ö) green 15 8
281 " 15(ö) brown 20 8
282 " 25(ö) orange red 20 6
283 " 30(ö) gray 55 18
284 " 40(ö) blue 65 10
285 " 45(ö) violet 1.40 40
286 " 50(ö) orange brown 85 20
287 " 55(ö) orange 6.00 30
288 " 60(ö) slate gray 2.50 60
289 " 80(ö) dark brown 1.25 55
Nos. 279-289 (11) 13.90 2.63

Issued to commemorate the 300th anniversary of the establishment of the Norwegian Post Office.

Petter Dass
A66

King Haakon VII
A67

1947, July 1

290 A66 25ö bright red 75 55

Issued to commemorate the 300th anniversary of the birth of Petter Dass, poet.

1947, Aug. 2

291 A67 25ö orange red 75 55

Issued to commemorate the 75th anniversary of the birth of King Haakon.

Axel Heiberg
A68

Alexander L. Kielland
A69

1948, June 15

292 A68 25ö deep carmine 75 30
293 " 80ö deep red brown 1.50 25

Issued to commemorate the 50th anniversary of the Norwegian Society of Forestry and the centenary of the birth of Axel Heiberg, its founder.

1949, May 9

295 A69 25ö rose brown 85 20
296 " 40ö greenish blue 85 30
297 " 80ö orange brown 1.25 50

Issued to commemorate the centenary of the birth of Alexander L. Kielland, author.

Symbols of U. P. U. Members
A70

Stylized Pigeons and Globe
A71

Symbolical of the U.P.U.—A72

1949, Oct. 9 *Perf. 13*

299 A70 10ö dk. grn. & blk. 1.10 80
300 A71 25ö scarlet 75 35
301 A72 40ö dull blue 75 45

Issued to commemorate the 75th anniversary of the formation of the Universal Postal Union.

Nos. 196 and 200A Surcharged with New Value and Bar in Black.

1949 *Per. 13x13½*

302 A16 25ö on 20ö red 60 12
303 " 45ö on 40ö dp. ultra. 2.50 25

King Harald Haardraade and Oslo City Hall
A73

1950, May 15 Photo. *Perf. 13*

304 A73 15ö green 75 70
305 " 25ö red 70 40
306 " 45ö ultramarine 1.00 70

900th anniversary of Oslo.

Redrawn Post Horn Type of 1937.

1950-51 Photo. *Perf. 13x13½*

Size: 17x21mm.

307 A10 10ö greenish gray 35 6
a. Booklet pane of 10 4.00
308 " 15ö dark green 1.00 20
a. Booklet pane of 10 11.00
309 " 20ö chestnut brn. ('51) 3.75 1.50

King Haakon VII
A74

Arne Garborg
A75

Photogravure.

1950-51 *Perf. 13x13½* Unwmkd.

310 A74 25ö dark red ('50) 80 6
a. Bklt. pane of 10 17.50
311 " 30ö gray 5.00 35
312 " 35ö red brown 16.00 12
313 " 45ö bright blue 1.60 80
314 " 50ö olive brown 1.20 12
315 " 55ö orange 1.60 80
316 " 60ö gray blue 1.30 10
317 " 80ö chestnut brown 1.20 10
Nos. 310-317 (8) 28.70 2.45

See also Nos. 322-324, 345-352.

1951, Jan. 25 *Perf. 13*

318 A75 25ö red 40 40
319 " 45ö dull blue 85 85
320 " 80ö brown 1.10 55

Issued to commemorate the centenary of the birth of Arne Garborg, poet.

No. 310 Surcharged with New Value in Black.

1951 *Perf. 13x13½*

321 A74 30ö on 25ö dark red 50 10

Haakon Type of 1950-51.

1951-52 Photogravure.

322 A74 25ö gray 17.50 10
323 " 30ö dark red ('52) 70 6
a. Bklt. pane of 10 10.00
324 " 55ö blue ('52) 1.20 20

Redrawn Post Horn Type of 1937.

1952, June 3 *Perf. 13x13½*

325 A10 15ö orange brown 40 8
a. Bklt. pane of 10 4.50
326 " 20ö green 40 6

King Haakon VII
A76

Medieval Sculpture, Nidaros Cathedral
A77

1952, Aug. 3 *Perf. 13* Unwmkd.

327 A76 30ö red 50 20
328 " 55ö deep blue 85 85

80th birthday of King Haakon VII.

No. 308 Surcharged with New Value.

1952, Nov. 18 *Perf. 13x13½*

329 A10 20(ö) on 15ö dk. green 40 20

1953, July 15 *Perf. 13*

330 A77 30ö henna brown 50 20

Issued to commemorate the 800th anniversary of the creation of the Norwegian Archbishopric of Nidaros.

Train of 1854 and Horse-Drawn Sled
A78

Carsten T. Nielsen
A79

Designs: 30ö, Diesel train. 55ö, Engineer.

1954, Apr. 30 Photogravure

331 A78 20ö green 50 30
332 " 30ö red 60 15
333 " 55ö ultramarine 85 65

Issued to commemorate the centenary of the inauguration of the first Norwegian railway.

1954, Dec. 10

Designs: 30ö, Government radio towers. 55ö, Lineman and telegraph poles in snow.

334 A79 20ö olive grn. & blk. 50 30
335 " 30ö bright red 60 15
336 " 55ö blue 85 65

Issued to commemorate the centenary (in 1955) of the inauguration of the first Norwegian public telegraph line.

Norway No. 1—A80

Stamp Reproductions: 30ö, Post horn type A5. 55ö, Lion type A13.

1955, Jan. 3 *Perf. 13*

337 A80 20ö deep green & gray blue 45 20
338 " 30ö red & carmine 45 15
339 " 55ö gray blue & deep blue 85 65

Centenary of Norway's first postage stamp.

Nos. 337-339 Overprinted in Black

OSLO NORWEX

1955, June 4

340 A80 20ö deep green & gray blue 10.00 11.00
341 " 30ö red & carmine 10.00 11.00
342 " 55ö gray blue & deep blue 10.00 11.00

Issued to publicize the Norway Philatelic Exhibition, Oslo, 1955. Sold at exhibition post office for face value plus 1kr admission fee.

King Haakon VII and Queen Maud in Coronation Robes
A81

1955, Nov. 25 Photo. *Perf. 13*

343 A81 30(ö) rose red 50 15
344 " 55(ö) ultramarine 60 50

Issued in honor of Haakon's 50th anniversary as King of Norway.

Haakon Type of 1950-51.

1955-57 *Perf. 13x13½* Unwmkd.

345 A74 25ö dark green ('56) 1.00 8
346 " 35ö brn. red ('56) 2.50 6
a. Bklt. pane of 10 25.00
347 " 40ö pale purple 1.20 15
a. Bklt. pane of 10 20.00
348 " 50ö bistre ('57) 1.20 8
349 " 65ö ultra. ('56) 1.75 18
350 " 70ö brn. olive ('56) 7.00 12
351 " 75ö maroon ('57) 1.75 10
352 " 90ö dp. orange 1.75 10
Nos. 345-352 (8) 18.15 87

Northern Countries Issue.

Whooper Swans
A81a

1956, Oct. 30 Engr. *Perf. 12½*

353 A81a 35ö rose red 1.60 45
354 " 65ö ultramarine 1.00 90

Issued to emphasize the close bonds connecting the northern countries: Denmark, Finland, Iceland, Norway and Sweden.

Jan Mayen Island—A82

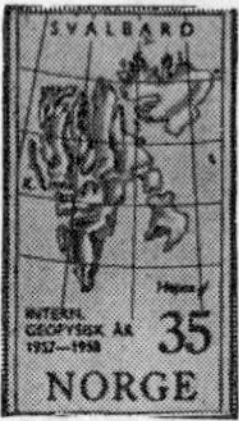

Map of Spitsbergen A83 — King Haakon VII A84

Design: 65ö, Map of South Pole with Queen Maud Land.

Perf. 12½x13, 13x12½

1957, July 1 Photo. Unwmkd.

355 A82 25ö slate green 45 30
356 A83 35ö dark red & gray 70 15
357 " 65ö dark green & blue 60 45

Issued to publicize the International Geophysical Year, 1957-58.

1957, Aug. 2 ***Perf. 13***

358 A84 35ö dark red 25 12
359 " 65ö ultramarine 75 75

85th birthday of King Haakon VII.

King Olav V
A85 A86

1958-60 Photo. ***Perf. 13x13½***

360 A85 25ö emerald 70 6
  a. Bklt. pane of 4 12.50
361 " 30ö purple ('59) 70 10
361A " 35ö brown carmine ('60) 70 6
362 " 40ö dark red 80 6
  a. Bklt. pane of 10 32.50
363 " 45ö scarlet 1.10 6
  a. Bklt. pane of 10 12.50
364 " 50ö bistre ('59) 1.10 10
365 " 55ö dark gray ('59) 1.40 30
366 " 65ö blue 1.40 25
367 " 80ö org. brown ('60) 1.40 18
368 " 85ö olive bwn. ('59) 1.40 15
369 " 90ö orange ('59) 1.60 10
Nos. 360-369 (11) 12.30 1.42

See also Nos. 408-412.

1959, Jan. 12

370 A86 1kr green 75 6
371 " 1.50kr dark blue 1.75 6
372 " 2kr crimson 1.50 6
373 " 5kr lilac 4.50 10
374 " 10kr deep orange 6.00 25
Nos. 370-374 (5) 14.50 53

See Phosphorescence note following No. 430.

Asbjörn Kloster A87

Agricultural Society Medal A88

1959, Feb. 2

375 A87 45ö violet brown 70 18

Issued to commemorate the centenary of the founding of the Norwegian Temperance Movement and to honor Asbjörn Kloster, its founder.

1959, May 26

376 A88 45ö red & ochre 70 20
377 " 90ö blue & gray 2.25 1.25

Issued to commemorate the 150th anniversary of the Royal Agricultural Society of Norway.

Sower A89 — Society Seal A90

Design: 90ö, Grain (vert.).

1959, Oct. 1 Photo. ***Perf. 13***

378 A89 45ö ochre & black 45 18
379 " 90ö blue & black 1.25 1.00

Issued to commemorate the centenary of the Agricultural College of Norway.

1960, Feb. 26 Unwmkd.

380 A90 45ö carmine 70 18
381 " 90ö dark blue 1.25 1.00

Issued to commemorate the bicentenary of the Royal Norwegian Society of Sciences, Trondheim.

Viking Ship A91

Designs: 25ö, Caravel and fish. 45ö, Sailing ship and nautical knot. 55ö, Freighter and oil derricks. 90ö, Passenger ship and Statue of Liberty.

1960, Aug. 27 ***Perf. 12½x13***

382 A91 20ö gray & black 90 50
383 " 25ö yel. grn. & black 90 50
384 " 45ö verm. & black 90 15
385 " 55ö ochre & black 2.00 1.75
386 " 90ö Prussian blue & black 1.70 70
Nos. 382-386 (5) 6.40 3.60

Norwegian shipping industry.

Europa Issue, 1960.
Common Design Type

1960, Sept. 19 ***Perf. 13***
Size: 27x21mm.

387 CD3 90ö blue 85 55

DC-8 Airliner A91a — Javelin Thrower A92

1961, Feb. 24 Photo. ***Perf. 13***

388 A91a 90ö dark blue 85 45

10th anniversary of the Scandinavian Airlines System, SAS.

Common Design Types

pictured in section at front of book.

1961, March 15

Designs: 25ö, Skater. 45ö, Ski jumper. 90ö, Sailboat.

389 A92 20ö ochre 80 40
390 " 25ö blue green 80 40
391 " 45ö crimson 90 15
392 " 90ö plum 1.10 55

Norwegian Sports Federation centenary.

Haakonshallen A93

1961, May 25 ***Perf. 12½x13***

393 A93 45ö maroon & gray 80 15
394 " 1kr gray grn. & gray 1.25 45

The 700th anniversary of Haakonshallen, castle in Bergen.

Domus Media, Oslo University A94

1961, Sept. 2 Photo. ***Perf. 12½x13***

395 A94 45ö dark red 70 15
396 " 1.50kr Prus. blue 1.50 45

150th anniversary of Oslo University.

Fridtjof Nansen A95

1961, Oct. 10 ***Perf. 13***

397 A95 45ö orange red & gray 70 15
398 " 90ö chalky blue & gray 1.25 45

Issued to commemorate the centenary of the birth of Fridtjof Nansen, explorer.

Roald Amundsen—A96

Design: 90ö, Explorers and tent at Pole.

1961, Nov. 10 ***Perf. 13*** **Unwmkd.**

399 A96 45ö dull red brown & gray 90 15
400 " 90ö dk. & lt. blue 1.25 75

Issued to commemorate the 50th anniversary of Roald Amundsen's arrival at the South Pole.

Frederic Passy, Henri Dunant A97 — Vilhelm Bjerknes A98

1961, Dec. 9 Photogravure

401 A97 45ö henna brown 50 15
402 " 1k yellow green 1.20 45

Issued to honor the winners of the first Nobel Peace prize. Frederic Passy, a founder of the Interparliamentary Union, and Henri Dunant, founder of the International Red Cross.

1962, Mar. 14 ***Perf. 13***

403 A98 45ö dk. red & gray 50 15
404 " 1.50k dk. bl. & gray 1.50 45

Issued to commemorate the centenary of the birth of Vilhelm Bjerknes (1862-1951), physicist, mathematician, meteorologist, etc.

German Rumpler Taube over Oslo Fjord—A99

1962, June 1 Photogravure

405 A99 1.50k dull blue & black 1.60 45

50th anniversary of Norwegian aviation.

Fir Branch and Cone A100

1962, June 15

406 A100 45ö salmon & black 50 40
407 " 1k pale grn. & blk. 2.25 45

Olav Type of 1958-60.

1962 ***Perf. 13x13½*** **Unwmkd.**

408 A85 25ö slate green 70 6
  a. Booklet pane of 4 20.00
  b. Booklet pane of 10 5.00
409 A85 35ö emerald 80 6
410 " 40ö gray 1.10 40
411 " 50ö scarlet 1.10 6
  a. Booklet pane of 10 18.00
412 A85 60ö violet 1.30 25
Nos. 408-412 (5) 5.00 83

Europa Issue, 1962
Common Design Type

1962, Sept. 17 Photo. ***Perf. 13***
Size: 37x21mm.

414 CD5 50ö deep rose & maroon 50 20
415 " 90ö blue & dk. blue 1.25 1.00

Post Horn Type of 1893-1908 Redrawn and

Rock Carvings A101 — Boatswain's Knot A102

Designs: 30ö, 55ö, 85ö, Rye and fish. 65ö, 80ö, Stave church and northern lights.

1962-63 Engraved ***Perf. 13x13½***

416 A10 5ö rose claret 3 3
  a. Booklet pane of 4, vert. 20
  b. Booklet pane of 10, horiz. 3.50
417 A10 10ö slate 5 3
  a. Booklet pane of 10 5.50
418 A10 15ö orange brown 6 3
419 " 20ö green 12 3
  a. Booklet pane of 4 50
420 A101 25ö gray green ('63) 50 5
  a. Booklet pane of 4 5.00
  b. Booklet pane of 10 10.00
421 A101 30ö olive brown ('63) 1.00 50
422 A102 35ö brt. green ('63) 50 5
423 A101 40ö lake ('63) 50 5
424 A102 50ö vermilion 50 5
  a. Booklet pane of 10 12.50
425 A101 55ö org. brown ('63) 60 35
426 A102 60ö dark greenish gray ('63) 1.00 20
427 " 65ö dark blue ('63) 1.00 8
  a. Booklet pane of 10 12.50
428 A102 80ö rose lake ('63) 1.00 35
429 A101 85ö sepia ('63) 1.20 15

430 A101 90ö blue ('63) 90 12
Nos. 416-430 (15) 8.96 2.07

Nos. 416-419 have been redrawn and are similar to 1910-29 issue, with vertical lines inside oval and horizontal lines in oval frame. See also Nos. 462-470, 608-615.

Phosphorescence

Nos. 370-372, 416-419, 423, 425, 428, 430, 462, 466, O65-O69, O75, O78-O82, O84 and O88 have been issued on both ordinary and phosphorescent paper.

Nos. 463-465, 467-468, 510 to last number assigned, O86 and O89-O93 have been issued only on phosphorescent paper.

Camilla Collett
A103

1963, Jan. 23 Photo. *Perf. 13*
431 A103 50ö red brn. & tan 50 15
432 " 90ö slate & gray 1.00 85

Issued to commemorate the 150th anniversary of the birth of Camilla Collett (1813-95), author.

Girl in Boat Loaded with Grain
A104

Still Life
A105

1963, Mar. 21 *Perf. 13* Unwmkd.
433 A104 25ö yellow brown 25 20
434 " 35ö dark green 45 25
435 A105 50ö dark red 40 15
436 " 90ö dark blue 1.00 85

Issued for the "Freedom from Hunger" campaign of the U.N. Food and Agriculture Organization.

River Boat—A106

Design: 90ö, Northern sailboat.

1963, May 20 *Perf. 13* Unwmkd.
437 A106 50ö brown red 1.60 15
438 " 90ö blue 1.60 1.25

Issued to commemorate the tercentenary of regular postal service between Northern and Southern Norway.

Ivar Aasen—A107

1963, Aug. 5 Photogravure
439 A107 50ö dk. red & gray 50 10
440 " 90ö dk. bl. & gray 1.20 85

Issued to commemorate the sesquicentennial of the birth of Ivar Aasen, poet and philologist.

Europa Issue, 1963
Common Design Type

1963, Sept. 14 *Perf. 13* Unwmkd.
Size: 27x21½mm.
441 CD6 50ö dull rose & org. 75 18
442 " 90ö bl. & yel. grn. 1.20 1.00

Patterned Fabric—A108

1963, Sept. 24
443 A108 25ö olive & olive green 40 30
444 " 35ö Prussian blue & dark blue 60 50
445 " 50ö dark carmine rose & plum 50 18

Issued to commemorate the 150th anniversary of the Norwegian textile industry.

"Loneliness" A109 Eilert Sundt A110

Paintings by Munch: 25ö, Self-portrait (vert.). 35ö, "Fertility." 90ö, "Girls on Bridge" (vert.).

1963, Dec. 12 Litho. *Perf. 13*
446 A109 25ö black 40 20
447 " 35ö dark green 40 20
448 " 50ö deep claret 50 18
449 " 90ö gray blue & dark blue 1.20 1.00

Issued to commemorate the centenary of the birth of Edvard Munch (1863-1944), painter.

1964, Feb. 17 Photogravure
Design: 50ö, Beehive, Workers' Society emblem.
450 A110 25ö dark green 30 20
451 " 50ö dark red brown 40 15

Centenary of the Oslo Workers' Society.

Cato M. Guldberg and Peter Waage by Stinius Fredriksen—A111

1964, March 11 *Perf. 13* Unwmkd.
452 A111 35ö olive green 80 30
453 " 55ö bister 1.25 1.00

Issued to commemorate the centenary of the presentation of the Law of Mass Action (chemistry) by Professors Cato M. Guldberg and Peter Waage in the Oslo Scientific Society.

Eidsvoll Building
A112

Design: 90ö, Storting (Parliament House).

1964, May 11 Photogravure
454 A112 50ö henna brown & black 50 20
455 " 90ö Prussian blue & dark blue 1.10 1.00

Issued to commemorate the 150th anniversary of Norway's constitution.

Church and Ships in Harbor—A113

1964, Aug. 17 *Perf. 13*
456 A113 25ö dark slate green & buff 30 15
457 " 90ö dk. blue & gray 1.10 1.00

Issued to commemorate the centenary of the Norwegian Seamen's Mission, which operates 32 stations around the world.

Europa Issue, 1964
Common Design Type

1964, Sept. 14 Photo. *Perf. 13*
458 CD7 90ö dark blue 90 80

Herman Anker and Olaus Arvesen
A114

1964, Oct. 31 Litho. Unwmkd.
459 A114 50ö rose 40 15
460 " 90ö blue 1.10 1.00

Issued to commemorate the centenary of the founding of Norwegian schools of higher education (Folk High Schools).

Types of Regular Issue, 1962-63

Designs: 30ö, 45ö, Rye and fish. 40ö, 100ö, Rock carvings. 50ö, 60ö, 65ö, 70ö, Boatswain's knot.

Two types of 60ö:
I. Four twists across bottom of knot.
II. Five twists.

1964-70 Engraved *Perf. 13x13½*
462 A101 30ö dull green 50 10
463 " 40ö lt. bl. green ('68) 50 5
464 " 45ö lt. yel. grn. ('68) 50 40
465 A102 50ö indigo ('68) 50 5
466 " 60ö brick red, II 75 15
a. Booklet pane of 10 11.00
b. Type I ('75) 90 20
467 A102 65ö lake ('68) 45 5
a. Booklet pane of 10 7.50
468 A102 70ö brown ('70) 35 4
a. Booklet pane of 10 7.00
469 A101 100ö vio. blue ('70) 50 12
Nos. 462-469 (8) 4.05 96

See Phosphorescence note following No. 430.

Coil Stamp

1965 *Perf. 13½ Horiz.*
470 A101 30ö dull green 1.00 25

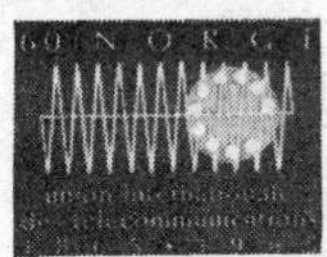

Telephone Dial and Waves
A115

Design: 90ö, Television mast and antenna.

1965, Apr. 1 Engraved *Perf. 13*
471 A115 60ö reddish brn. 35 15
472 " 90ö slate 1.10 1.00

Issued to commemorate the centenary of the International Telecommunication Union.

Mountain Scene
A116

Design: 90ö, Coastal view.

1965, June 4 *Perf. 13* Unwmkd.
473 A116 60ö brn. blk. & car. 35 20
474 " 90ö slate bl. & car. 1.10 1.00

Centenary of the Norwegian Red Cross.

Europa Issue, 1965
Common Design Type

1965, Sept. 25 Photo. *Perf. 13*
Size: 27x21mm.
475 CD8 60ö brick red 35 15
476 " 90ö blue 1.10 1.00

St. Sunniva and Buildings of Bergen
A117

Rondane Mountains by Harold Sohlberg
A118

Design: 90ö, St. Sunniva and stylized view of Bergen (horiz.).

1965, Oct. 25 *Perf. 13*
477 A117 30ö dk. grn. & blk. 50 25
478 " 90ö blue & black 1.00 85

Issued to commemorate the bicentenary of Bergen's philharmonic society "Harmonien."

1965, Nov. 29 Photo. *Perf. 13*
484 A118 1.50k dark blue 1.20 20

Rock Carving of Skier, Rodoy Island, c. 2000 B.C.
A120

Designs: 55ö, Ski jumper. 60ö, Cross country skier. 90ö, Holmenkollen ski jump (vert.).

1966, Feb. 8 Engraved *Perf. 13*
486 A120 40ö sepia 75 35
487 " 55ö dull green 1.50 1.25
488 " 60ö dull red 55 18
489 " 90ö blue 1.00 70

Issued to publicize the World Ski Championships, Oslo, Feb. 17-27.

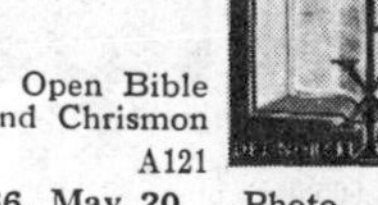

Open Bible and Chrismon
A121

1966, May 20 Photo. *Perf. 13*
490 A121 60ö dull red 35 15
491 " 90ö slate blue 1.00 50

Issued to commemorate the 150th anniversary of the Norwegian Bible Society.

Engine-turned Bank Note Design
A122

Bank of Norway
A123

1966, June 14 Engraved
492 A122 30ö green 35 20
493 A123 60ö dk. carmine rose 65 15

150th anniversary of Bank of Norway.

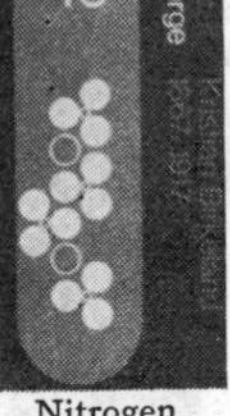

Johan Sverdrup
A124

Nitrogen Molecule in Test Tube
A125

1966, July 30 Photo. *Perf. 13*

494 A124 30ö green 40 20
495 " 60ö rose lake 55 12

Issued to commemorate the 150th anniversary of the birth of Johan Sverdrup (1816–92), Prime Minister of Norway (1884–89).

Canceled to Order

The Norwegian philatelic agency began in 1966 to sell commemorative and definitive issues canceled to order at face value.

Europa Issue, 1966

Common Design Type

1966, Sept. 26 Engraved *Perf. 13*

Size: 21x27mm.

496 CD9 60ö dark carmine 40 15
497 " 90ö blue gray 1.10 1.00

1966, Oct. 29 Photo. *Perf. 13x12½*

Design: 55ö, Wheat and laboratory bottle.

498 A125 40ö blue & dp. blue 40 30
499 " 55ö red, orange & lilac rose 65 60

Issued to commemorate the centenary of the birth of Kristian Birkeland (1867–1917), and of Sam Eyde (1866–1940), who together developed the production of nitrates.

EFTA Emblem
A126

1967, Jan. 16 Engraved *Perf. 13*

500 A126 60ö rose red 55 15
501 " 90ö dark blue 1.10 1.00

Issued to publicize the European Free Trade Association. Tariffs were abolished Dec. 31, 1966, among EFTA members: Austria, Denmark, Finland, Great Britain, Norway, Portugal, Sweden, Switzerland.

Sabers, Owl and Oak Leaves
A127

1967, Feb. 16 Engraved *Perf. 13*

502 A127 60ö chocolate 75 35
503 " 90ö black 1.25 1.10

150th anniversary of higher military training in Norway.

Europa Issue, 1967

Common Design Type

1967, May 2 Photo. *Perf. 13*

Size: 21x27mm.

504 CD10 60ö magenta & plum 45 15
505 " 90ö bl. & dk. vio. bl. 90 65

Johanne Dybwad, by Per Ung
A128

1967, Aug. 2 Photo. *Perf. 13*

506 A128 40ö slate blue 40 20
507 " 60ö dk. carmine rose 55 12

Centenary of the birth of Johanne Dybwad (1867–1950), actress.

Missionary L. O. Skrefsrud
A129

Ebenezer Church, Benagaria, Santal
A130

1967, Sept. 26 Engraved *Perf. 13*

508 A129 60ö red brown 55 15
509 A130 90ö blue gray 1.00 60

Issued to commemorate the centenary of the Norwegian Santal (India) mission.

Mountaineers
A131

Designs: 60ö, Mountain view. 90ö, Glitretind mountain peak.

1968, Jan. 22 Engr. *Perf. 13*

510 A131 40ö sepia 90 20
511 " 60ö brown red 60 15
512 " 90ö slate blue 1.10 80

Centenary of the Norwegian Mountain Touring Association.

Two Smiths
A132

1968, Mar. 30 Photo. *Perf. 12½x13*

513 A132 65ö dk. carmine rose & brown 50 15
514 " 90ö blue & brown 1.10 80

Issued to honor Norwegian craftsmen.

A. O. Vinje
A133

Cross and Heart
A134

1968, May 21 Engraved *Perf. 13*

515 A133 50ö sepia 50 20
516 " 65ö maroon 50 15

Issued to commemorate the 150th anniversary of the birth of Aasmund Olafsson Vinje (1818–1870), poet, journalist and language reformer.

1968, Sept. 16 Photogravure

517 A134 40ö bright green & brown red 2.00 40
518 A134 65ö brown red & violet blue 50 15

Issued to commemorate the centenary of the Norwegian Lutheran Home Mission Society.

Cathinka Guldberg
A135

1968, Oct. 31 Engraved *Perf. 13*

519 A135 50ö bright blue 35 20
520 " 65ö dull red 50 15

Issued to honor the nursing profession and to commemorate the centenary of Deaconess House in Oslo. Cathinka Guldberg was a pioneer of Norwegian nursing and the first deaconess.

Klas P. Arnoldson and Fredrik Bajer
A136

1968, Dec. 10 Engraved *Perf. 13*

521 A136 65ö red brown 45 15
522 " 90ö dark blue 75 40

Issued to commemorate the 60th anniversary of the awarding of the Nobel Peace prize to Klas P. Arnoldson (1844–1916), Swedish writer and statesman, and to Fredrik Bajer (1837–1922), Danish writer and statesman.

Nordic Cooperation Issue

Five Ancient Ships
A136a

1969, Feb. 28 Engraved *Perf. 13*

523 A136a 65ö red 45 15
524 " 90ö blue 65 40

Nordic Society's 50th anniversary and centenary of postal cooperation among the northern countries: Denmark, Finland, Iceland, Norway and Sweden.

Ornament from Urnes Stave Church
A137

Traena Island
A138

1969 Engraved *Perf. 13*

526 A137 1.15k sepia 1.00 40
529 A138 3.50k bluish black 1.40 20

Issue dates: 1.15k, Jan. 23, 3.50k, June 18.

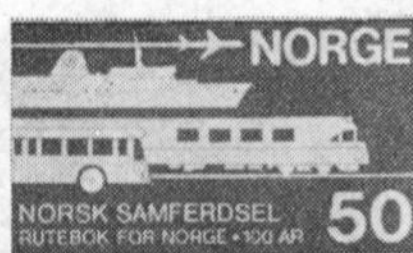

Plane, Train, Ship and Bus
A139

Child Crossing Street
A140

1969, Mar. 24 Photo. *Perf. 13*

531 A139 50ö green 40 20
532 A140 65ö slate green & dark red 50 15

No. 531 issued to commemorate the centenary of the publication of "Rutebok of Norway" (Communications of Norway); No. 532 publicizes traffic safety.

Europa Issue, 1969

Common Design Type

1969, Apr. 28 Size: 37x21mm.

533 CD12 65ö dk. red & gray 45 15
534 " 90ö chalky blue & gray 70 40

Johan Hjort
A141

King Olav V
A142

Design: 90ö, different emblem.

1969, May 30 Engraved *Perf. 13*

535 A141 40ö brown & blue 1.10 25
536 " 90ö blue & green 1.10 60

Issued to commemorate the centenary of the birth of Johan Hjort (1869–1948), zoologist and oceanographer.

1969–70 Engraved *Perf. 13*

537 A142 1k lt. olive grn. ('70) 40 10
538 " 1.50k dark blue ('70) 60 10
539 " 2k dark red ('70) 80 10
540 " 5k vio. blue ('70) 2.00 12
541 " 10k org. brn. ('70) 4.00 45
542 " 20k brown 8.00 60
Nos. 537–542 (6) 15.80 1.47

Man, Woman and Child, by Vigeland
A143

Design: 65ö, Mother and Child, by Gustav Vigeland.

1969, Sept. 8 Photo. *Perf. 13*

545 A143 65ö car. rose & black 50 15
546 " 90ö blue & black 70 40

Issued to commemorate the centenary of the birth of Gustav Vigeland (1869–1943), sculptor.

People
A144

Design: 65ö, Punched card.

1969, Oct. 10

547 A144 65ö red, org. & lilac 50 15
548 " 90ö dk. blue, red & bright blue 70 40

Issued to commemorate the 200th anniversary of the first Norwegian census.

Queen Maud
A145

Pulsatilla Vernalis
A146

1969, Nov. 26 Engraved *Perf. 13*

549 A145 65ö dark carmine 45 15
550 " 90ö violet blue 70 35

Issued to commemorate the centenary of the birth of Queen Maud (1869–1938), wife of King Haakon VII.

1970, Apr. 10 Photo. *Perf. 13*

Designs: 40ö, Wolf. 70ö, Vøringsfossen (waterfall). 100ö, White-tailed sea eagle (horiz.).

551 A146 40ö sepia & pale blue 50 20
552 " 60ö lt. brown & gray 65 30
553 " 70ö pale bl. & brown 70 15
554 " 100ö pale bl. & brn. 1.25 45

Issued to publicize the European Nature Conservation Year, 1970.

"V" for Victory A147 — "Citizens" A148

Design: 100ö, Convoy (horiz.).

Perf. 13x12½, 12½x13

1970, May 8 Photogravure

555 A147 70ö red & lilac 1.50 20
556 " 100ö violet blue & brt. green 1.25 40

Norway's liberation from the Germans, 25th anniversary.

1970, June 23 Engraved *Perf. 13*

Designs: 70ö, "The City and the Mountains." 100ö, "Ships."

557 A148 40ö green 1.00 25
558 " 70ö rose claret 1.75 20
559 " 100ö violet blue 1.20 45

City of Bergen, 900th anniversary.

Olive Wreath and Hands Upholding Globe A149 — Georg Ossian Sars (1837–1927) A150

1970, Sept. 15 Engr. *Perf. 13*

560 A149 70ö dk. car. rose 1.60 20
561 " 100ö steel blue 1.20 50

25th anniversary of the United Nations.

1970, Oct. 15 Engraved *Perf. 13*

Portraits: 50ö, Hans Strøm (1726–1797). 70ö, Johan Ernst Gunnerus (1718–1773). 100ö, Michael Sars (1805–1869).

562 A150 40ö brown 50 20
563 " 50ö dull purple 50 20
564 " 70ö brown red 1.20 12
565 " 100ö bright blue 90 40

Issued to honor Norwegian zoologists.

Leapfrog A151

Design: 50ö, Ball game (vert.).

1970, Nov. 17 Photo. *Perf. 13*

566 A151 50ö dk. blue & sepia 50 20
567 " 70ö red & dk. brn. 1.00 12

Issued to commemorate the centenary of the Central School of Gymnastics in Oslo.

Seal of Tønsberg A152

1971, Jan. 20 Photo. *Perf. 13*

568 A152 70ö dark red 65 12
569 " 100ö blue black 85 30

City of Tønsberg, 1,100th anniversary.

Parliament A153

1971, Feb. 23

570 A153 70ö red brn. & lilac 55 12
571 " 100ö dark blue & slate green 85 40

Centenary of annual sessions of Norwegian Parliament.

Hand, Heart and Eye A154

1971, March 26 Photo. *Perf. 13*

572 A154 50ö emerald & black 50 18
573 " 70ö scarlet & black 65 15

Joint northern campaign for the benefit of refugees.

"Haugianerne" by Adolph Tiedemand A155

1971, Apr. 27 Photo. *Perf. 13*

574 A155 60ö dark gray 50 18
575 " 70ö brown 65 15

200th anniversary of the birth of Hans Nielsen Hauge (1771–1824), church reformer.

Worshippers Coming to Church A156

Design: 70ö, Building first church (vert.).

1971, May 21

576 A156 70ö black & dk. red 65 15
577 " 1k black & blue 85 40

900th anniversary of the Bishopric of Oslo.

Roald Amundsen, Antarctic Treaty Emblem A157 — The Farmer and the Woman A158

1971, June 23 Engraved *Perf. 13*

578 A157 100ö blue & org. red 1.80 80

Tenth anniversary of the Antarctic Treaty pledging peaceful uses of and scientific cooperation in Antarctica.

1971, Nov. 17 Photo. *Perf. 13*

Designs: 50ö, The Preacher and the King (vert.). 70ö, The Troll and the Girl. Illustrations for legends and folk tales by Erik Werenskiold.

579 A158 40ö olive & black 40 20
580 " 50ö blue & black 40 20
581 " 70ö magenta & blk. 1.00 15

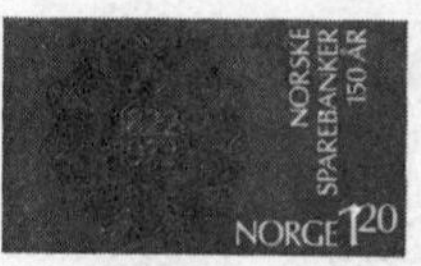

Engine Turning A159

1972, Apr. 10 Photo. *Perf. 13*

582 A159 80ö red & gold 65 15
583 " 1.20k ultra. & gold 75 40

Norwegian Savings Bank sesquicentennial.

Norway No. 18 A160 — Dragon's Head, Oseberg Viking Ship A161

Design: 1k, Norway No. 17.

Engraved and Photogravure

1972, May 6 *Perf. 12*

584 A160 80ö lt. brown & rose 65 15
585 " 1k dull violet & Prussian blue 75 30
a. Souvenir sheet of 2 4.00 4.25

Centenary of the post horn stamps. No. 585a contains one each of Nos. 584–585. Light gray marginal inscription and border. Size: 121x71mm. Sold for 2.50k.

1972, June 7 Engraved *Perf. 13*

Ancient Artifacts: 50ö, Horseman from Stone of Alstad. 60ö, Horseman, wood carving, stave church, Hemsedal. 1.20k, Sword hilt, found at Lodingen.

586 A161 50ö yellow green 50 20
587 " 60ö brown 50 25
588 " 80ö dull red 70 15
589 " 1.20k ultramarine 85 40

1,100th anniversary of unification.

King Haakon VII A162 — "Joy" A163

1972, Aug. 3 Engr. *Perf. 13*

590 A162 80ö brown orange 50 15
591 " 1.20k Prussian blue 70 35

Centenary of the birth of King Haakon VII (1872–1957).

1972, Aug. 15 Photo. *Perf. 13x13½*

Design: 1.20k, "Solidarity."

592 A163 80ö bright magenta 60 15
593 " 1.20k Prussian blue 85 40

2nd International Youth Stamp Exhibition, INTERJUNEX 72, Kristiansand, Aug. 25–Sept. 3.

Same Overprinted "INTERJUNEX 72"

1972, Aug. 25

594 A163 80ö brt. magenta 3.50 3.75
595 " 1.20k Prussian blue 3.50 3.75

Opening of INTERJUNEX 72. Sold at exhibition only together with 3k entrance ticket.

"Maud" A164 — "Little Man" A165

Polar Exploration Ships: 80ö, "Fram." 1.20k, "Gjoa."

1972, Sept. 20 *Perf. 13½x13*

596 A164 60ö olive & green 65 40
597 " 80ö red & black 1.25 20
598 " 1.20k bl. & red brn. 1.10 60

1972, Nov. 15 Litho. *Perf. 13½x13*

Designs: 60o, The Troll who wondered how old he was. 80o, The princess riding the polar bear.

599 A165 50ö green & black 60 18
600 " 60ö blue & black 60 18
601 " 80ö pink & black 60 15

Illustrations for folk tales by Theodor Kittelsen (1857–1914).

Dr. Armauer G. Hansen and Leprosy Bacillus Drawing A166

Design: 1.40k, Dr. Hansen and leprosy bacillus, microscopic view.

1973, Feb. 28 Engr. *Perf. 13x13½*

602 A166 1k henna brn. & bl. 85 15
603 " 1.40k dark blue & deep orange 1.00 35

Centenary of the discovery of the Hansen bacillus, the cause of leprosy.

Europa Issue 1973

Common Design Type

1973, Apr. 30 Photo. *Perf. 12½x13*

Size: 37x20mm.

604 CD16 1k red, org. & lilac 80 15
605 " 1.40k dk. green, green & blue 60 35

Types of 1893 and 1962–63

Designs: 75ö, 85ö, Rye and fish. 80ö, 140ö, Stave church. 100ö, 110ö, 120ö, 125ö, Rock carvings.

1972–75 Engraved *Perf. 13x13½*

606 A10 25ö ultra. ('74) 10 3
a. Booklet pane of 4 1.00
608 A101 75ö green ('73) 30 4
609 A102 80ö red brown 35 4
a. Booklet pane of 10 7.00
610 A101 85ö bister ('74) 35 4
611 " 100ö red ('73) 40 4
a. Booklet pane of 10 6.00
612 A101 110ö rose car. ('74) 45 4
613 " 120ö gray blue 50 4
614 " 125ö red ('75) 50 4
a. Booklet pane of 10 6.00
615 A102 140ö dk. blue ('73) 60 15
Nos. 606–615 (9) 3.55 46

Nordic Cooperation Issue 1973

Nordic House, Reykjavik—A167

1973, June 26 Engr. *Perf. 12½*

617 A167 1k multicolored 80 15
618 " 1.40k " 90 35

A century of postal cooperation among Denmark, Finland, Iceland, Norway and Sweden. Issued also in connection with the Nordic Postal Conference, Reykjavik, Iceland.

King Olav V
A168

Jacob Aall
A169

1973, July 2 Engraved *Perf. 13*

619 A168 1k car. & org. brn. 60 15
620 " 1.40k blue & org. brn. 60 40

70th birthday of King Olav V.

1973, Aug. 22 Engraved *Perf. 13*

621 A169 1k deep claret 40 15
622 " 1.40k dark blue gray 60 40

Bicentenary of the birth of Jacob Aall (1773–1844), mill owner and industrial pioneer.

Blade Decoration
A170

Viola Biflora
A171

Designs: 1k, Textile pattern. 1.40k, Decoration made of tin.

1973, Oct. 9 Photo. *Perf. 13x12½*

623 A170 75ö blk. brn. & buff 45 25
624 " 1k dp. car. & buff 75 15
625 " 1.40k blk. & dull blue 70 40

Handicraft from Lapland.

1973, Nov. 15 Litho. *Perf. 13*
Multicolored

626 A171 65ö *shown* 65 20
627 " 70ö *Speedwell* 65 25
628 " 1k *Mountain heath* 90 15

Surveyor in Northern Norway, 1907
A172

Design: 1.40k, Map of South Norway Mountains, 1851.

1973, Dec. 14 Engr. *Perf. 13*

629 A172 1k red orange 65 15
630 " 1.40k slate blue 60 40

Bicentenary of Geographical Survey of Norway.

Lindesnes
A173

Design: 1.40k, North Cape.

1974, Apr. 25 Photo. *Perf. 13*

631 A173 1k olive 65 15
632 " 1.40k dark blue 90 40

Ferry in Hardanger Fjord, by A. Tidemand and H. Gude—A174

Design: 1.40k, Stugunoset from Filefjell, by Johan Christian Dahl.

1974, May 21 Litho. *Perf. 13*

633 A174 1k multicolored 90 15
634 " 1.40k " 60 40

Classical Norwegian paintings.

Gulating Law Manuscript, 1325
A175

King Magnus VI Lagaböter
A176

1974, June 21 Engraved

635 A175 1k red & brown 90 15
636 A176 1.40k ultra. & brn. 90 40

700th anniversary of the National Code given by King Magnus VI Lagaböter (1238–80).

Saw Blade and Pines
A177

J.H.L. Vogt
A178

Design: 1k, Cog wheel and guard.

1974, Aug. 12 Photo. *Perf. 13*

637 A177 85ö green, olive & dark green 65 50
638 " 1k orange, plum & dark red 90 15

Safe working conditions.

1974, Sept. 4 Engraved *Perf. 13*

Geologists: 85ö, V. M. Goldschmidt. 1k, Theodor Kjerulf. 1.40k, Waldemar C. Brøgger.

639 A178 65ö olive & red brn. 40 15
640 " 85ö magenta & red brown 50 25
641 " 1k org. & red brn. 65 15
642 " 1.40k bl. & red brn. 60 35

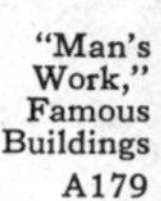

"Man's Work," Famous Buildings
A179

Design: 1.40k, "Men, our brethren," people of various races.

1974, Oct. 9 Photogravure *Perf. 13*

643 A179 1k grn. & brown 70 15
644 " 1.40k brown & greenish bl. 60 35

Centenary of Universal Postal Union.

Horseback Rider
A180

Flowers
A181

1974, Nov. 15 Litho. *Perf. 13*

645 A180 85ö multicolored 35 20
646 A181 1k " 50 15

Norwegian folk art, rose paintings from furniture decorations.

Woman Skier, c. 1900
A182

Design: 1.40k, Telemark turn.

1975, Jan. 15 Lithographed *Perf. 13*

647 A182 1k verm. & green 85 15
648 " 1.40k vio. bl. & ocher 60 35

"Norway, homeland of skiing."

Women
A183

Nusfjord Fishing Harbor
A184

Design: Detail from wrought iron gates of Vigeland Park, Oslo.

1975, Mar. 7 Litho. *Perf. 13*

649 A183 1.25k brt. rose lilac & dark blue 70 20
650 " 1.40k bl. & dk. blue 60 35

International Women's Year 1975.

1975, Apr. 17 Litho. *Perf. 13*

Designs: 1.25k, Street in Stavanger. 1.40k, View of Roros.

651 A184 1k yellow green 80 20
652 " 1.25k dull red 50 18
653 " 1.40k blue 60 35

European Architectural Heritage Year 1975.

Norwegian Krone, 1875
A185

Ole Jacob Broch
A186

1975, May 20 Engraved *Perf. 13*

654 A185 1.25k dark carmine 50 20
655 A186 1.40k blue 60 35

Centenary of Monetary Convention of Norway, Sweden and Denmark (1.25k); and of International Meter Convention, Paris, 1875. Ole Jacob Broch (1818–1889) was first director of International Bureau of Weights and Measures.

Scouting in Summer
A187

Design: 1.40k, Scouting in winter (skiers).

1975, June 19 Litho. *Perf. 13*

656 A187 1.25k multicolored 50 18
657 " 1.40k " 60 35

Nordjamb 75, 14th Boy Scout Jamboree, Lillehammer, July 29–Aug. 7.

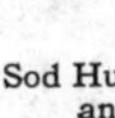

Sod Hut and Settlers
A188

Cleng Peerson and Letter from America, 1874
A189

1975, July 4

658 A188 1.25k red brown 1.10 18
659 A189 1.40k bluish black 60 35

Sesquicentennial of Norwegian emigration to America.

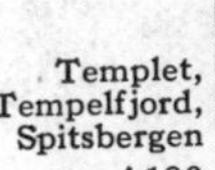

Templet, Tempelfjord, Spitsbergen
A190

Miners Leaving Coal Pit
A191

Design: 1.40k, Polar bear.

1975, Aug. 14 Engr. *Perf. 13*

660 A190 1k olive black 65 20
661 A191 1.25k maroon 50 18
662 " 1.40k Prus. blue 1.10 60

50th anniversary of union of Spitsbergen (Svalbard) with Norway.

Microphone with Ear Phones
A192

Radio Tower and Houses
A193

Designs after children's drawings.

1975, Oct. 9 Litho. *Perf. 13*

663 A192 1.25k multicolored 50 18
664 A193 1.40k " 60 35

50 years of broadcasting in Norway.

Annunciation
A194

Nativity
A195

Designs: 1k, Visitation. 1.40k, Adoration of the Kings. Designs are from painted vault of stave church of Al, 13th century.

1975, Nov. 14

665 A194 80ö red & multi. 32 12
666 " 1k " " 40 15
667 A195 1.25k " " 50 18
668 " 1.40k " " 60 35

Sigurd and Regin — A196

Halling, Hallingdal Dance — A197

1976, Jan. 20 Engr. *Perf. 13*

669 A196 7.50k brown 3.00 50

Norwegian folk tale, Sigurd the Dragon-killer. Design from portal of Hylestad stave church, 13th century.

1976, Feb. 25 Litho. *Perf. 13*

Folk Dances: 1k, Springar, Hordaland region. 1.25k, Gangar, Setesdal.

670 A197 80ö blk. & multi. 32 12
671 " 1k " " 40 15
672 " 1.25k " " 50 18

Silver Sugar Shaker, Stavanger, c. 1770 — A198

Design: 1.40k, Goblet, Nostetangen glass, c. 1770.

1976, Mar. 25 Engr. *Perf. 13*

673 A198 1.25k multicolored 50 18
674 " 1.40k " 55 30

Oslo Museum of Applied Art, centenary.

Europa Issue 1976

Ceramic Bowl Shaped Like Bishop's Mitre — A199

Design: 1.40k, Plate and CEPT emblem. Both designs after faience works from Herrebo Potteries, c. 1760.

1976, May 3 Litho. *Perf. 13*

675 A199 1.25k rose magenta & brown 50 18
676 " 1.40k brt. blue & violet blue 55 30

The Pulpit, Lyse Fjord — A200

Gulleplet (Peak), Sogne Fjord — A201

Perf. 13 on 3 Sides

1976, May 20 Lithographed

677 A200 1k multicolored 40 15
a. Booklet pane of 10 4.00
678 A201 1.25k multicolored 50 18
a. Booklet pane of 10 5.00

Nos. 677–678 issued only in booklets.

Graph Paper, Old and New Subjects — A202

Design: 2k, Graph of national product.

1976, July 1 Engr. *Perf. 13*

679 A202 1.25k red brown 50 18
680 " 2k dark blue 80 45

Central Bureau of Statistics, centenary.

Olav Duun on Dun Mountain — A203

1976, Sept. 10 Engr. *Perf. 13*

681 A203 1.25k multicolored 50 18
682 " 1.40k " 55 30

Olav Duun (1876–1939), novelist, birth centenary.

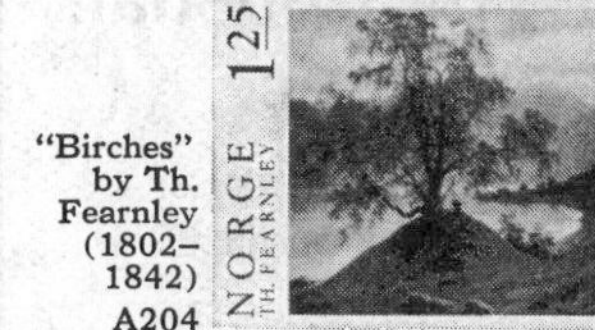

"Birches" by Th. Fearnley (1802–1842) — A204

Design: 1.40k, "Gamle Furutraer" (trees), by L. Hertervig (1830–1902).

1976, Oct. 8 Litho. *Perf. 13*

683 A204 1.25k multicolored 50 18
684 " 1.40k " 55 30

"April" — A205

"May" — A206

Baldishol Tapestry—A207

Design: 80ö, 1k, Details from 13th century Baldishol tapestry, found in Baldishol stave church.

1976, Nov. 5 Litho. *Perf. 13*

685 A205 80ö multicolored 32 12
686 A206 1k " 40 15
687 A207 1.25k " 50 18

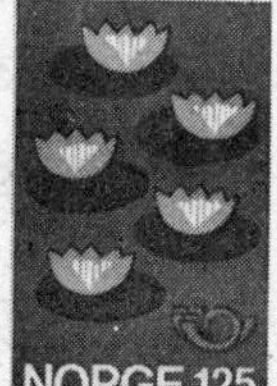

Five Water Lilies — A208

Photogravure and Engraved

1977, Feb. 2 *Perf. 12½*

688 A208 1.25k multicolored 50 18
689 " 1.40k " 55 30

Nordic countries cooperation for protection of the environment and 25th Session of Nordic Council, Helsinki, Feb. 19.

Akershus Castle, Oslo — A209

Steinviksholm Fort, Asen Fjord — A210

Torungen Lighthouses, Arendal — A211

1977, Feb. 24 Engr. *Perf. 13*

690 A209 1.25k red 50 5
691 A210 1.30k olive brown 52 5
692 A211 1.80k blue 72 8

Europa Issue 1977

Hamnoy, Lofoten, Fishing Village — A212

Huldre Falls, Loen — A213

Perf. 13 on 3 Sides

1977, May 2 Lithographed

693 A212 1.25k multicolored 50 18
a. Booklet pane of 10 5.00
694 A213 1.80k multicolored 72 35
a. Booklet pane of 10 7.20

Nos. 693–694 issued only in booklets.

Spruce — A214

Norwegian Trees: 1.25k, Fir. 1.80k, Birch.

1977, June 1 Engr. *Perf. 13*

695 A214 1k olive green 40 15
696 " 1.25k rose lake 50 18
697 " 1.80k slate 72 35

"Constitutionen" at Arendal — A215

Designs: 1.25k, "Vesteraalen" off Bodø, 1893. 1.30k, "Kong Haakon," 1904 and "Dronningen," 1893, off Stavanger. 1.80k, "Nordstjernen" and "Harald Jarl" at pier, 1970. "Constitutionen" was Norway's first steamship.

1977, June 22

698 A215 1k brown 40 15
699 " 1.25k red 50 18
700 " 1.30k green 52 20
701 " 1.80k blue 72 35

Norwegian ships serving coastal routes.

Fishermen and Boats — A216

Fish and Fishhooks — A217

1977, Sept. 22 Engr. *Perf. 13*

702 A216 1.25k buff, lt. brn. & dark brown 50 18
703 A217 1.80k lt. bl., blue & dark blue 72 35

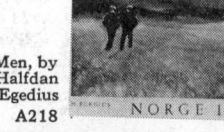

Men, by Halfdan Egedius — A218

Landscape, by August Cappelen — A219

1977, Oct. 7 Litho. *Perf. 13*

704 A218 1.25k multicolored 50 18
705 A219 1.80k " 72 35

Norwegian classical painting.

David with the Bells — A220

Designs: 1k, Singing Friars. 1.25k, Virgin and Child (horiz.). Designs from Bible of Bishop Aslak Bolt, 13th century.

1977, Nov. 10 Litho. *Perf. 13*

Size: 21x27mm.

706 A220 80ö multicolored 32 12
707 " 1k " 40 15

Size: 34x27mm.

708 A220 1.25k multicolored 50 15

Christmas 1977.

Post Horn Type of 1893 and

Austrat Manor, 1650 — A221

Designs: 1.10k, Trondenes Church, early 13th century. 1.40k, Ruins of Hamar Cathedral, 12th century.

1978 Engr. *Perf. 13x13½*

709 A10 40ö olive 16 3
710 " 50ö dull purple 20 3
711 " 60ö vermilion 24 3
712 " 70ö orange 28 3
713 " 80ö red brown 32 4
714 " 90ö brown 36 5
715 A221 1k green 40 6
716 " 1.10k rose magenta 44 6
717 " 1.40k dark purple 55 8
Nos. 709-717 (9) 2.95 41

Issue dates: Nos. 709–714, Feb. 15; Nos. 715–717, Apr. 12.

Peer Gynt, and Reindeer by Per Krogh — A222

Henrik Ibsen, by Erik Werenskiold, 1895 — A223

1978, Mar. 10 Litho. *Perf. 13*

725	A222 1.25k buff & black	50	15
726	A223 1.80k multicolored	72	35

Henrik Ibsen (1828–1906), poet and dramatist, birth sesquicentennial.

Heddal Stave Church, c. 1250 — A224

Lenangstindene and Jaegervasstindene — A225

Europa Issue 1978

Design: 1.80k, Borgund stave church.

1978, May 2 Engr. *Perf. 13*

727	A224 1.25k dk. brn. & red	50	15
728	" 1.80k slate green & blue	72	35

Perf. 13 on 3 Sides

1978, June 1 Lithographed

Design: 1.25k, Gaustatoppen, mountain, Telemark.

729	A225 1k multicolored	40	12
	a. Booklet pane of 10	4.00	
730	A225 1.25k multicolored	50	15
	a. Booklet pane of 10	5.00	

Nos. 729–730 issued only in booklets.

Olav V Sailing — A226

Design: 1.80k, King Olav delivering royal address in Parliament (vert.).

1978, June 30 Engr. *Perf. 13*

731	A226 1.25k red brown	50	15
732	" 1.80k violet blue	72	28

75th birthday of King Olav V.

Norway No. 107 — A227

Perf. 13 on 3 Sides

1978, Sept. 19 Lithographed

Multicolored

733	Booklet pane of 8	6.00	6.50
	a. A227 1.25k *shown*	75	80
	b. " 1.25k *No. 108*	75	80
	c. " 1.25k *No. 109*	75	80
	d. " 1.25k *No. 110*	75	80
	e. " 1.25k *No. 111*	75	80
	f. " 1.25k *No. 112*	75	80
	g. " 1.25k *No. 113*	75	80
	h. " 1.25k *No. 114*	75	80

NORWEX '80 Philatelic Exhibition, Oslo, June 13–22, 1980. Booklet sold for 15k; the additional 5k went for financing the exhibition.

Willow Pipe Player — A228

Musical Instruments: 1.25k, Norwegian violin. 1.80k, Norwegian zither. 7.50k, Ram's horn.

1978, Oct. 6 Engr. *Perf. 13*

734	A228 1k deep green	40	12
735	" 1.25k dk. rose car.	50	15
736	" 1.80k dk. vio. blue	72	28
737	" 7.50k gray	3.00	90

Wooden Doll, 1830 — A229

Ski Jump, Huseby Hill, c. 1900 — A230

Designs: 1k, Toy town 1896–97. 1.25k, Wooden horse from Torpo in Hallingdal.

1978, Nov. 10 Lithographed

738	A229 80ö multicolored	32	12
739	" 1k "	40	12
740	" 1.25k "	50	15

Christmas 1978.

1979, March 2 Engr. *Perf. 13*

Designs: 1.25k, Crown Prince Olav, Holmenkollen ski jump competition, 1922. 1.80k, Cross-country race, Holmenkollen, 1976.

741	A230 1k green	40	12
742	" 1.25k red	50	15
743	" 1.80k blue	72	28

Huseby Hills and Holmenkollen ski competitions, centenary.

Girl, by Mathias Stoltenberg — A231

Road to Briksdal Glacier — A232

Portrait: 1.80k, Boy, by H. C. F. Hosenfelder.

1979, Apr. 26 Litho. *Perf. 13*

744	A231 1.25k multicolored	50	15
745	" 1.80k "	72	28

International Year of the Child.

1979, June 13 *Perf. 13 on 3 Sides*

Design: 1.25k, Boat on Skjernoysund, near Mandal.

746	A232 1k multicolored	40	12
	a. Booklet pane of 10	4.00	
747	A232 1.25k multicolored	50	15
	a. Booklet pane of 10	5.00	

Nos. 746–747 issued only in booklets.

SEMI-POSTAL STAMPS.

North Cape Issue.

North Cape
SP1

Wmkd. Post Horn. (160)

Photogravure

1930, June 28 *Perf. 13½x14*

Size: 33¼ x 21½ mm.

B1 SP1 15ö+25ö black brown 1.75 1.75
B2 " 20ö+25ö carmine 22.50 22.50
B3 " 30ö+25ö ultramarine 80.00 80.00

The surtax was given to the Tourist Association. See also Nos. B9–B10, B28–B30, B54–B56, B59–B61.

Radium Hospital
SP2

1931, Apr. 1 *Perf. 14½x13½*

B4 SP2 20ö+10ö carmine 10.00 3.50

The surtax aided the Norwegian Radium Hospital.

Fridtjof Nansen
SP3

1935, Dec. 13 *Perf. 13½*

B5 SP3 10ö+10ö green 2.00 2.00
B6 " 15ö+10ö red brown 5.50 5.50
B7 " 20ö+10ö crimson 1.75 1.50
B8 " 30ö+10ö bright ultramarine 8.00 8.00

The surtax aided the International Nansen Office for Refugees.

North Cape Type of 1930

Perf. 13x13½

1938, June 20 **Wmk. 160**

Size: 27x21 mm.

B9 SP1 20ö+25ö brn. car. 6.00 6.00
B10 " 30ö+25ö deep ultramarine 12.50 12.50

The surtax was given to the Tourist Association.

Queen Maud
SP4

Fridtjof Nansen
SP5

Perf. 13x13½

1939, July 24 Photo. **Unwmkd.**

B11 SP4 10(ö)+5ö brt. grn. 85 4.75
B12 " 15(ö)+5ö red brown 85 4.75
B13 " 20(ö)+5ö scarlet 85 4.75
B14 " 30(ö)+5ö bright ultramarine 85 4.75

The surtax was used for charities.

1940, Oct. 21

B15 SP5 10(ö)+10(ö) dark green 2.50 2.50
B16 " 15(ö)+10(ö) henna brown 3.75 3.75
B17 SP5 20(ö)+10(ö) dk. red 1.25 1.25
B18 " 30(ö)+10(ö) ultra. 2.50 2.50

The surtax was used for war relief work.

Ancient Sailing Craft off Lofoten Islands
SP6

1941, May 16

B19 SP6 15(ö)+10(ö) dp. blue 85 2.25

Haalogaland Exposition. Surtax for relief fund for families of lost fishermen.

Colin Archer and Lifeboat
SP7

Lifeboat
SP8

Perf. 13x13½, 13½x13

1941, July 9

B20 SP7 10(ö)+10(ö) yellow green 1.00 1.00
B21 " 15(ö)+10(ö) dark olive brown 1.20 1.20
B22 SP8 20(ö)+10(ö) bright red 75 75
B23 " 30(ö)+10(ö) ultramarine 3.75 3.75

Issued in commemoration of the 50th anniversary of the Norwegian Lifeboat Society.

Legionary, Norwegian and Finnish Flags
SP9

Vidkun Quisling
SP10

1941, Aug. 1 *Perf. 13½x13*

B24 SP9 20(ö)+80(ö) scarlet vermilion 60.00 80.00

The surtax was for the Norwegian Legion.

1942, Feb. 1

B25 SP10 20(ö)+30(ö) henna 3.50 10.00

Overprinted in Red **1–2–1942**

B26 SP10 20(ö)+30(ö) henna 3.50 10.00

To commemorate the inauguration of Quisling as prime minister.

Vidkun Quisling
SP11

Frontier Guardsmen Emblem
SP12

1942, Sept. 26 *Perf. 13*

B27 SP11 20(ö)+30(ö) henna 50 2.50

To commemorate the 8th annual meeting of Nasjonal Samling, Quisling's party. The surtax aided relatives of soldiers killed in action.

North Cape Type of 1930.

1943, Apr. 1 Size: 27x21mm.

B28 SP1 15ö+25ö olive brown 1.00 1.00
B29 " 20ö+25ö dk. carmine 1.50 1.50
B30 " 30ö+25ö chalky blue 2.50 2.50

The surtax aided the Tourist Association.

1943, Aug. 2 **Unwmkd.**

B31 SP12 20(ö)+30(ö) henna 75 3.00

The surtax aided the Frontier Guardsmen (Norwegian Nazi Volunteers).

Fishing Village
SP13

Drying Grain
SP14

Barn in Winter
SP15

1943, Nov. 10

B32 SP13 10(ö)+10(ö) gray green 1.40 3.25
B33 SP14 20(ö)+10(ö) henna 1.40 3.25
B34 SP15 40(ö)+10(ö) greenish blk. 1.40 3.25

The surtax was for winter relief.

The Baroy Sinking
SP16

Sanct Svithun Aflame
SP17

Design: 20ö +10ö, "Irma" sinking.

1944, May 20

B35 SP16 10(ö)+10(ö) gray green 1.00 3.25
B36 SP17 15(ö)+10(ö) dark olive 1.00 3.25
B37 SP16 20(ö)+10(ö) henna 1.00 3.25

The surtax aided victims of wartime ship sinkings, and their families.

Spinning
SP19

Plowing
SP20

Tree Felling
SP21

Child Care
SP22

1944, Dec. 1

B38 SP19 5(ö)+10(ö) deep magenta 70 2.25
B39 SP20 10(ö)+10(ö) dark yellow green 70 2.25
B40 SP21 15(ö)+10(ö) choc. 70 2.25
B41 SP22 20(ö)+10(ö) henna 70 2.25

The surtax was for National Welfare.

Red Cross Nurse
SP23

Crown Prince Olav
SP24

1945, Sept. 22

B42 SP23 20(ö)+10(ö) red 80 60

Issued to commemorate the 80th anniversary of the founding of the Norwegian Red Cross. The surtax was for the benefit of that institution.

1946, Mar. 4 **Unwmkd.**

B43 SP24 10(ö)+10(ö) olive green 40 40
B44 " 15(ö)+10(ö) olive brown 40 40
B45 " 20(ö)+10(ö) dk. red 40 40
B46 " 30(ö)+10(ö) bright blue 1.75 1.75

The surtax was for war victims.

No. B42 Surcharged with New Value and Bar in Black.

1948, Dec. 1

B47 SP23 25(ö)+5(ö) on 20(ö)+10(ö) red 75 75

The surtax was for Red Cross relief work.

Child Picking Flowers
SP25

1950, Aug. 15 Photo. *Perf. 13*

B48 SP25 25(ö)+5(ö) brt. red 1.25 1.10
B49 " 45(ö)+5(ö) deep blue 5.00 5.00

The surtax was for poliomyelitis victims.

Skater—SP26

Winter Scene—SP27

Design: 30(ö)+10(ö), Ski jumper.

1951, Oct. 1

B50 SP26 15(ö)+5(ö) olive green 1.75 1.75
B51 " 30(ö)+10(ö) red 1.75 1.75
B52 SP27 55(ö)+20(ö) blue 7.00 7.00

Issued to publicize the Olympic Winter Games Oslo, Feb. 14-29, 1952.

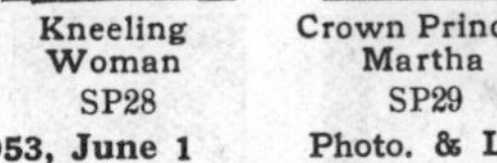

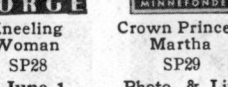

Kneeling Woman SP28 — Crown Princess Martha SP29

1953, June 1 Photo. & Litho.

B53 SP28 30(ö)+10(ö) red & cream 1.10 1.10

The surtax was for cancer research.

North Cape Type of 1930.

1953, June 15 Photogravure

Size: 27x21mm.

B54 SP1 20ö+10ö green 4.50 4.50
B55 " 30ö+15ö red 5.00 5.00
B56 " 55ö+25ö gray blue 9.00 9.00

The surtax aided the Tourist Association.

1956, Mar. 28 *Perf. 13*

B57 SP29 35(ö)+10(ö) dark red 1.50 1.50
B58 " 65(ö)+10(ö) dark blue 3.25 3.25

The surtax was for the Crown Princess Martha Memorial Fund.

North Cape Type of 1930.

1957, May 6 Size: 27x21mm.

B59 SP1 25ö+10ö green 2.75 2.75
B60 " 35ö+15ö red 2.75 2.75
B61 " 65ö+25ö gray blue 2.75 2.75

The surtax aided the Tourist Association.

White Anemone SP30 — Mother, Child, WRY Emblem SP31

Design: 90ö+10ö, Hepatica.

1960, Jan. 12 Litho. *Perf. 13*

B62 SP30 45ö+10ö bright red & green 1.75 1.50
B63 " 90ö+10ö blue, org. & green 5.50 5.50

The surtax was for anti-tuberculosis work.

1960, Apr. 7 Photo. Unwmkd.

B64 SP31 45ö+25ö rose & black 5.00 5.00
B65 " 90ö+25ö blue & black 9.00 9.00

Issued to publicize World Refugee Year, July 1, 1959–June 30, 1960. The surtax was for aid to refugees.

Severed Chain and Dove
SP32

Design: 60ö+10ö, Norwegian flags.

1965, May 8 Photo. *Perf. 13*

B66 SP32 30ö+10ö green, black & tan 80 70
B67 " 60ö+10ö red & dark blue 90 50

20th anniversary of liberation from the Germans. The surtax was for war cripples.

AIR POST STAMPS

Airplane over Akershus Castle
AP1 AP2

Wmkd. Post Horn. (160)

1927-34 Typo. *Perf. 13½x14½*

C1 AP1 45ö lt. blue, strong frame line ('34) 4.50 1.75
a. Faint or broken frame line 15.00 3.00

1937, Aug. 18 Photo. *Perf. 13*

C2 AP2 45ö Prussian blue 1.20 50

1941, Nov. 10 Unwmkd.

C3 AP2 45ö indigo 55 25

POSTAGE DUE STAMPS.

Numeral of Value
D1

Wmkd. Post Horn. (160)

1889-1914 Typo. *Perf. 14½x13½*

Inscribed "at betale".

J1 D1 1ö gray 65 65
J2 " 4ö magenta 1.20 80
J3 " 10ö carmine rose 5.00 50
a. 10ö rose red 52.50 10.00
J4 " 15ö brown ('14) 1.40 50
J5 " 20ö ultramarine 2.50 50
a. Perf. 13½x12½ 225.00 80.00
J6 " 50ö maroon 5.00 1.80
Nos. J1-J6 (6) 15.75 4.75

1922-23

Inscribed "a betale".

J7 D1 4ö lilac rose 7.50 7.50
J8 " 10ö green 2.25 1.50
J9 " 20ö dull violet 4.25 3.50
J10 " 40ö deep ultra. 7.50 75
J11 " 100ö orange yellow 37.50 14.00
J12 " 200ö dark violet 90.00 30.00
Nos. J7-J12 (6) 149.00 57.25

OFFICIAL STAMPS

Coat of Arms
O1 O2

Wmkd. Post Horn. (160)

1926 Typo. *Perf. 14½x13½*

O1 O1 5ö rose lilac 40 40
O2 " 10ö yellow green 40 15
O3 " 15ö indigo 90 90
O4 " 20ö plum 25 12
O5 " 30ö slate 2.50 2.50
O6 " 40ö deep blue 1.00 40
O7 " 60ö Prussian blue 2.75 2.75
Nos. O1-O7 (7) 8.20 7.22

Official Stamp of 1926 Surcharged **2 2**

1929, July 1

O8 O1 2ö on 5ö magenta 40 40

Perf. 14½x13½.

1933-34 Lithographed Wmk. 160

Size: 35x19¼mm.

O9 O2 2ö ochre 50 35
O10 " 5ö rose lilac 1.75 1.60
O11 O2 7ö orange 10.00 7.50
O12 " 10ö green 15.00 55
O13 " 15ö olive 50 25
O14 " 20ö vermilion 11.00 25
O15 " 25ö yellow brown 50 25
O16 " 30ö ultramarine 50 25
O18 " 40ö slate 16.00 50
O19 " 60ö blue 5.50 50
O20 " 70ö olive brown 1.50 1.10
O21 " 100ö violet 1.50 1.10
Nos. O9-O16, O18-O21 (12) 64.25 14.20

On the lithographed stamps, the lion's left leg is shaded.

Typographed.

Size: 34x18¾mm.

O10a O2 5ö rose lilac 75 55
O11a " 7ö orange 5.00 4.50
O12a " 10ö green 45 20
O13a " 15ö olive 16.00 14.00
O14a " 20ö vermilion 50 20
O17 " 35ö red violet ('34) 50 20
O18a " 40ö slate 50 15
O19a " 60ö blue 70 25
Nos. O10a-O14a, O17, O18a-O19a (8) 24.40 20.05

Coat of Arms O3 — Norwegian Nazi Party Emblem O4

1937-38 Photo. *Perf. 13½x13*

O22 O3 5ö rose lilac ('38) 35 20
O23 " 7ö deep orange 35 30
O24 " 10ö bright green 20 12
O25 " 15ö olive bistre 25 25
O26 " 20ö carmine ('38) 35 25
O27 " 25ö red brown ('38) 50 50
O28 " 30ö ultramarine 50 30
O29 " 35ö red violet ('38) 50 25
O30 " 40ö Prus. green ('38) 35 20
O31 " 60ö Prussian blue ('38) 50 25
O32 " 100ö dark violet ('38) 90 30
Nos. O22-O32 (11) 4.75 2.92

1939-47 Unwmkd.

O33 O3 5ö dp. red lilac ('41) 12 10
O34 " 7ö dp. orange ('41) 12 10
O35 " 10ö brt. green ('41) 12 10
O36 " 15ö olive ('45) 25 10
O37 " 20ö carmine 12 10
O38 " 25ö red brown 50 40
O38A " 25ö scarlet ('46) 25 10
O39 " 30ö ultramarine 60 30
O39A " 30ö dark gray ('47) 25 15
O40 " 35ö bright lilac ('41) 25 15
O41 " 40ö greenish black ('41) 30 10
O41A " 40ö dp. ultra. ('46) 30 10
O42 " 60ö Prussian blue ('41) 40 10
O43 " 100ö dark violet ('41) 60 15
Nos. O33-O43 (14) 4.18 2.05

1942-44

O44 O4 5ö magenta 35 70
O45 " 7ö yellow orange 35 70
O46 " 10ö emerald 15 15
O47 " 15ö olive ('44) 1.50 3.25
O48 " 20ö bright red 15 15
O49 " 25ö red brown ('43)) 3.00 4.50
O50 " 30ö brt. ultra. ('44 1.50 3.00
O51 " 35ö brt. pur. ('43) 1.50 4.50
O52 " 40ö greenish black ('43) 25 20
O53 " 60ö indigo ('43) 1.50 2.50
O54 " 1k blue violet ('43) 1.50 4.00
Nos. O44-O54 (11) 11.75 23.65

Type of 1937

1947, Nov. 1

O55 O3 50ö deep magenta 35 12
O56 " 200ö orange 2.50 25

No. O37 Surcharged with New Values and Bars in Black.

1949, Mar. 15

O57 O3 25ö on 20ö carmine 25 12

Norway Coat of Arms
O5 O6

Photogravure.

1951-52 *Perf. 13.* Unwmkd.

O58 O5 5ö rose lilac 15 15
O59 " 10ö dark gray 15 10
O60 " 15ö deep orange brown ('52) 15 10
O61 " 30ö scarlet 20 8
O62 " 35ö red brown ('52) 30 15
O63 " 60ö blue gray 40 10
O64 " 100ö violet blue ('52) 70 20
Nos. O58-O64 (7) 2.05 88

1955-61

O65 O6 5ö rose lilac 3 3
O66 " 10ö slate 4 3
O67 " 15ö orange brown 5 3
O68 " 20ö blue green ('57) 7 3
O69 " 25ö emerald ('59) 18 10
O70 " 30ö scarlet 25 8
O71 " 35ö brown red 25 8
O72 " 40ö blue lilac 25 10
O73 " 45ö scarlet ('58) 30 8
O74 " 50ö golden brn. ('57) 30 8
O75 " 60ö greenish blue 25 10
O76 " 70ö brown olive 60 15
O77 " 75ö maroon ('57) 1.10 1.00
O78 " 80ö org. brn. ('58) 35 10
O79 " 90ö orange ('58) 35 10
O80 " 1k violet ('57) 40 10
O81 " 2k gray green ('60) 80 11
O82 " 5k red lilac ('61) 2.00 60
Nos. O65-O82 (18) 7.57 2.90

See Phosphorescence note after No. 430.

1962-74 Photogravure

O83 O6 30ö green ('64) 14 6
O84 " 40ö olive green ('68) 15 10
O85 " 50ö scarlet 30 8
O86 " 50ö slate ('69) 18 5
O87 " 60ö dark red ('64) 35 8
O88 " 65ö dark red ('68) 30 6
O89 " 70ö dark red ('70) 30 6
O90 " 75ö light green ('73) 30 20
O91 " 85ö ocher ('74) 1.25 55
O92 " 1k dp. org. ('73) 40 8
O93 " 1.10k carmine lake ('74) 45 18
Nos. O83-O93 (12) 4.12 1.50

Shades exist of several values of type O6.

1975-77 Lithographed

O94 O6 25ö yellow green 10 3
O95 " 50ö greenish gray ('76) 20 5
O96 " 60ö dk. greenish bl. 25 8
O97 " 80ö red brown ('76) 32 10
O98 " 1.25k dull red 55 12
O99 " 2k dk. gray green 80 15
O100 " 5k light violet 2.00 60
O101 " 5k blue ('77) 2.00 60
Nos. O94-O101 (8) 6.22 1.73

NOSSI-BE

(nô'sē' bā')

LOCATION — An island in the Indian Ocean, off the northwest coast of Madagascar.

GOVT.—A former French Protectorate.

AREA—130 sq. mi.

POP.—9,000 (approx. 1900).

CHIEF TOWN—Hellville.

In 1896 the island was placed under the authority of the Governor-General of Madagascar and postage stamps of Madagascar were placed in use.

100 Centimes = 1 Franc

Stamps of French Colonies Surcharged in Blue:

25 (a) 25 c (b) 5 c (c)

1889 *Imperf.* Unwmkd.

1 A8 (*a*) 25 on 40c red, *straw* 900.00 450.00
a. Double surcharge 500.00
2 " (*b*) 25c on 40c red, *straw* 1200.00 800.00

Perf. 14x13½.

3 A9 (*b*) 5c on 10c *lavender* 1000.00 450.00
4 " (") 5c on 20c red, *green* 1200.00 800.00
5 " (*c*) 5c on 10c *lavender* 1100.00 600.00
6 " (") 5c on 20c red, *green* 1100.00 600.00
7 " (*a*) 15 on 20c red, *green* 1000.00 500.00
a. 15 on 30c brn, *bistre* (error) 7500.00 7000.00
8 " (") 25 on 30c brn., *bistre* 800.00 400.00
9 " (") 25 on 40c verm., *straw* 800.00 350.00

N S B 0 25 (d) N S B 25 c. (f)

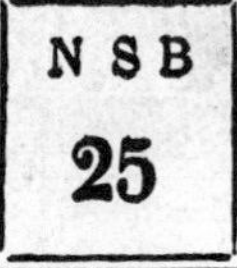

g

Black Surcharge.

1890

10 A9 (*d*) 0.25 on 20c red, *green* 175.00 110.00
11 " (") 0.25 on 75c car., *rose* 175.00 110.00
12 " (") 0.25 on 1fr bronze green, *straw* 175.00 110.00
a. Without ornament
16 " (*f*) 25c on 20c red, *green* 175.00 110.00
17 " (") 25c on 75c car., *rose* 175.00 110.00
18 " (") 25c on 1fr bronze green, *straw* 175.00 110.00
19 " (*g*) 25 on 20c red *green* 375.00 250.00
20 " (") 25 on 75c car., *rose* 375.00 250.00
21 A9 (*g*) 25 on 1fr bronze green, *straw* 375.00 250.00

The 25c on 20c with surcharge composed of "25 c." as in "f", "N S B" as in "d", and frame as in "g" is an essay.

Surcharged or Overprinted in Black, Carmine, Vermilion or Blue:

Nossi-Bé 25 (j)

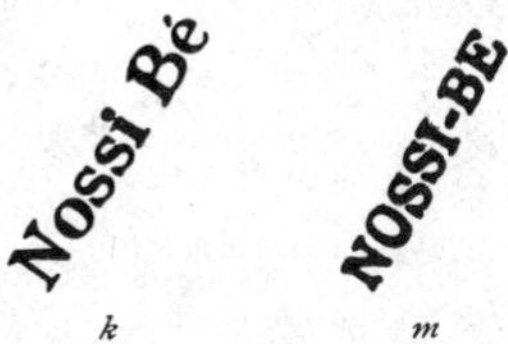

k m

1893

23 A9 (*j*) 25 on 20c red, *green* (Bk) 15.00 12.00
24 " (") 50 on 10c *lavender* (Bk) 17.50 12.00
a. Inverted surcharge 80.00 75.00
25 " (") 75 on 15c blue (Bk) 100.00 72.50
26 " (") 1fr on 5c green, *greenish* (Bk) 40.00 30.00
a. Inverted surcharge 90.00 90.00
27 " (*k*) 10c *lavender* (C) 5.50 4.50
a. Inverted overprint 32.50 27.50
28 " (") 10c *lavender* (V) 5.50 4.50
29 " (") 15c blue (Bk) 5.50 4.50
a. Inverted overprint 32.50 27.50
30 " (") 20c red, *green* (Bk) 165.00 13.50
a. Dbl. ovpt.
31 " (*m*) 20c red, *green* (Bl) 25.00 12.00
a. Inverted overprint 40.00 30.00

Counterfeits exist of surcharges and overprints on Nos. 1–31.

Navigation and Commerce A14

1894 **Typographed.**

Name of Colony in Blue or Carmine.

32 A14 1c *lilac blue* 60 60
33 " 2c brown, *buff* 85 60
34 " 4c claret, *lavender* 1.00 60
35 " 5c green, *greenish* 1.25 85
36 " 10c *lavender* 2.00 1.40
37 " 15c blue, quadrille paper 2.50 1.50
38 " 20c red, *green* 3.50 1.85
39 " 25c *rose* 4.50 3.25
40 " 30c brown, *bistre* 4.00 4.00
41 " 40c red, *straw* 6.00 4.50
42 " 50c carmine, *rose* 6.00 4.00
43 " 75c deep violet, *orange* 13.50 12.50
44 " 1fr bronze green, *straw* 5.00 5.00
Nos. 32-44 (13) 50.70 40.65

Examination

The Catalogue editors cannot undertake to appraise, identify or pass upon genuineness or condition of stamps.

POSTAGE DUE STAMPS.

Stamps of French Colonies Surcharged in Black:

Nossi-Bé chiffre-taxe 0.20 A PERCEVOIR (n) Nossi-Bé chiffre-taxe 0.35 A PERCEVOIR (o)

1891 *Perf. 14x13½.* Unwmkd.

J1 A9 (*n*) 20 on 1c *lilac blue* 165.00 120.00
a. Inverted surcharge 225.00 175.00
b. Surcharged vertically 175.00 175.00
c. Surcharged on reverse of stamp
J2 " (") 30 on 2c brown, *buff* 165.00 120.00
a. Inverted surcharge 225.00 175.00
b. Surcharged on reverse of stamp
J3 " (") 50 on 30c brown, *bistre* 50.00 45.00
a. Inverted surcharge 185.00 150.00
b. Surcharged on reverse of stamp 90.00 90.00
J4 " (*o*) 35 on 4c claret, *lavender* 165.00 120.00
a. Inverted surcharge 225.00 175.00
b. Surcharged on reverse of stamp
c. Pair, one without surcharge
J5 " (") 35 on 20c red, *green* 165.00 120.00
a. Inverted surch. 225.00 175.00
J6 " (") 1fr on 35c violet, *orange* 110.00 75.00
a. Inverted surcharge 175.00 150.00
b. Surcharged on reverse of stamp

Nossi-Bé 5 C. A PERCEVOIR (p) Nossi-Bé 5 C. A PERCEVOIR (q)

Nossi-Bé 0.10 A PERCEVOIR (r)

1891

J7 A9 (*p*) 5c on 20c red, *green* 100.00 100.00
a. Inverted surcharge 120.00 120.00
J8 " (*q*) 5c on 20c red, *green* 100.00 100.00
a. Inverted surcharge 100.00 100.00
J9 " (*r*) 0.10c on 5c green, *greenish* 7.00 6.00
J10 " (*p*) 10c on 15c blue 100.00 100.00
a. Inverted surcharge 120.00 120.00
J11 " (*q*) 10c on 15c blue 100.00 100.00
a. Inverted surcharge 100.00 100.00
J12 " (*p*) 15c on 10c *lavender* 55.00 55.00
a. Inverted surcharge 100.00 100.00
J13 " (*q*) 15c on 10c *lavender* 55.00 55.00
a. Inverted surcharge 100.00 100.00
J14 " (*r*) 0.15c on 20c red, *green* 8.00 8.00
a. 25c on 20c red, grn. (error) 10,000.00 8500.00
J15 A9 (*p*) 25c on 5c green, *greenish* 55.00 55.00
a. Inverted surcharge 100.00 100.00
J16 " (*q*) 25c on 5c green, *greenish* 55.00 55.00
a. Inverted surcharge 100.00 100.00
J17 " (*r*) 0.25c on 75c carmine, *rose* 225.00 200.00
a. Inverted surcharge 450.00 400.00

Stamps of Nossi-Bé were superseded by those of Madagascar.

Counterfeits exist of surcharges on Nos. J1–J17.

NYASSA

(nyä'sä ; nī-äs'ȧ)

LOCATION — In the northern part of Mozambique in southeast Africa.

GOVT. — Part of Portuguese East Africa Colony.

AREA—73,292 sq. mi.

POP.—3,000,000 (estimated).

CHIEF TOWN—Porto Amelia.

The district formerly administered by the Nyassa Company is now a part of Mozambique. Postage stamps of Mozambique are used.

1000 Reis = 1 Milreis
100 Centavos = 1 Escudo (1919)

Mozambique Nos. 24–35 Overprinted in Black NYASSA

Perf. 11½, 12½

1898 Unwmkd.

1 A3 5r yellow 2.00 1.75
2 " 10r reddish violet 2.00 1.75
3 " 15r chocolate 2.00 1.75
4 " 20r gray violet 2.00 1.75
5 " 25r blue green 2.00 1.75
6 " 50r light blue 2.00 1.75
a. Inverted overprint 7.50
b. Perf. 12½ 8.00 6.50
7 " 75r rose 2.50 2.25
8 " 80r yellow green 2.50 2.25
9 " 100r brown, *buff* 2.50 2.25
10 " 150r carmine, *rose* 6.50 6.00
11 " 200r dark blue, *blue* 3.50 3.25
12 " 300r dark blue, *salmon* 3.50 3.25
Nos. 1-12 (12) 33.00 29.75

Reprints of Nos. 1, 5, 8, 9, 10 and 12 have white gum and clean-cut perforation 13½. Price of No. 9, $15; others $2 each.

Same Overprint on Mozambique Issue of 1898.

1898 *Perf. 11½.*

13 A4 2½r gray 1.50 1.25
14 " 5r orange 1.50 1.25
15 " 10r light green 1.50 1.25
16 " 15r brown 1.75 1.50
17 " 20r gray violet 1.75 1.50
18 " 25r sea green 1.75 1.50
19 " 50r blue 1.75 1.50
20 " 75r rose 2.00 1.25
21 " 80r violet 2.50 1.75
22 " 100r dark blue, *blue* 2.50 1.75
23 " 150r brown, *straw* 2.75 1.75
24 " 200r red lilac, *pinkish* 2.75 1.75
25 " 300r dark blue, *rose* 2.75 1.75
Nos. 13-25 (13) 26.75 19.75

Giraffe A3

Camels A4

Perf. 13½–15 & Compound

1901 — Engraved

No.	Type	Description	Unused	Used
26	A3	2½r blk.&red brown	1.00	65
27	"	5r black & violet	1.00	65
28	"	10r blk. & dp. green	1.00	65
29	"	15r blk. & org. brown	1.00	65
30	"	20r blk. & orange red	1.00	65
31	"	25r black & orange	1.00	65
32	"	50r black & dull blue	1.00	65
33	A4	75r blk. & car. lake	1.25	65
34	"	80r black & lilac	1.25	65
35	"	100r blk. & brn. bister	1.25	65
36	"	150r blk. & dp. org.	1.75	1.00
37	"	200r blk. & greenish bl.	1.50	80
38	"	300r black & yel. green	1.50	1.00
		Nos. 26–38 (13)	15.50	9.30

Nos. 26 to 38 are known with inverted centers but are believed to be purely speculative and never regularly issued. Price $7.50 each.

Stamps of 1901 Surcharged **65 REIS**

1903

No.	Type	Description	Unused	Used
39	A4	65r on 80r blk. & lilac	1.00	75
40	"	115r on 150r black & deep orange	1.00	75
41	"	130r on 300r black & yellow green	1.00	75

Overprinted **PROVISORIO**

No.	Type	Description	Unused	Used
42	A3	15r black & org. brn.	1.00	75
43	"	25r black & orange	1.00	75

Surcharged **65 réis**

No.	Type	Description	Unused	Used
44	A4	65r on 80r black & lilac	25.00	20.00
45	"	115r on 150r black & deep orange	25.00	20.00
46	"	130r on 300r black & yellow green	25.00	20.00

Overprinted PROVISORIO

No.	Type	Description	Unused	Used
47	A3	15r blk. & org. brn.	125.00	100.00
48	"	25r black & orange	125.00	100.00

Forgeries exist of Nos. 44–48.

Nos. 26, 35 Surcharged **5 REIS PROVISORIO**

1910

No.	Type	Description	Unused	Used
49	A3	5r on 2½r black & red brown	1.00	75
50	A4	50r on 100r black & brown bistre	1.00	75
		a. "50 REIS" omitted	100.00	

Reprints of Nos. 49–50, made in 1921, have 2mm. space between surcharge lines, instead of 1½mm. Price, each 25 cents.

Camels A5

Zebra A6

Giraffe and Palms A7

Vasco da Gama's Flagship "San Gabriel" A8

1911 — Red Overprint.

No.	Type	Description	Unused	Used
51	A5	2½r blk. & dull violet	1.25	75
52	"	5r black	1.25	75
53	"	10r blk. & gray green	1.25	75
54	A6	20r black & car. lake	1.25	75
55	"	25r black & vio. brn.	1.25	75
56	"	50r black & dp. blue	1.25	75
57	A7	75r black & brown	1.25	75
58	"	100r blk. & brn., *green*	1.25	75
59	"	200r black & deep green, *salmon*	1.50	1.25
60	A8	300r *blue*	2.50	2.25
61	"	400r blk. & dk. brown	3.00	2.50
		a. Pair, one without overprint		
62	"	500r olive & vio. brn.	3.25	2.75
		Nos. 51–62 (12)	20.25	14.75

Nos. 51–62 exist without overprint but were not issued in that condition. Price $4 each.

Stamps of 1901-03 Surcharged **REPUBLICA 1½C.**

1918

On Nos. 26–38.

No.	Type	Description	Unused	Used
63	A3	¼c on 2½r black & red brown	62.50	50.00
64	"	½c on 5r black & violet	62.50	50.00
65	"	1c on 10r black & deep green	62.50	50.00
66	"	1½c on 15r black & orange brown	5.00	3.50
67	"	2c on 20r black & orange red	3.00	3.00
68	"	3½c on 25r black & orange	3.00	3.00
69	"	5c on 50r black & dull blue	3.00	3.00
70	A4	7½c on 75r black & carmine lake	3.00	3.00
71	"	8c on 80r blk. & lilac	3.00	3.00
72	"	10c on 100r black & brown bistre	3.00	3.00
73	"	15c on 150r black & deep orange	5.00	3.50
74	"	20c on 200r black & greenish blue	5.00	3.50
75	"	30c on 300r black & yellow green	7.50	6.00

On Nos. 39–41.

No.	Type	Description	Unused	Used
76	A4	40c on 65r on 80r black & lilac	25.00	20.00
77	"	50c on 115r on 150r black & deep orange	7.50	6.00
78	"	$1 on 130r on 300r black & yellow green	7.50	6.00

On Nos. 42–43.

No.	Type	Description	Unused	Used
79	A3	1½c on 15r black & orange brown	30.00	25.00
80	"	3½c on 25r black & orange	7.50	6.00

On Nos. 70–78 there is less space between "REPUBLICA" and the new value than on the other stamps of this issue.

On Nos. 76–78 the 1903 surcharge is cancelled by a bar.

The surcharge exists inverted on Nos. 64, 66–70, 72, 76 and 78–80, and double on Nos. 64, 67 and 69.

Stamps of 1911 Surcharged in Black or Red **7½ Centavos**

1921 — Lisbon Surcharges.

Numerals: The "1" (large or small) is thin, sharp-pointed, and has thin serifs. The "2" is italic, with the tail thin and only slightly wavy. The "3" has a flat top. The "4" is open at the top. The "7" has thin strokes.

Centavos: The letters are shaded, i.e., they are thicker in some parts than in others. The "t" has a thin cross bar ending in a downward stroke at the right. The "s" is flat at the bottom and wider than in the next group.

No.	Type	Description	Unused	Used
81	A5	¼c on 2½r black & dull violet	10.00	10.00
83	"	½c on 5r black (R)	10.00	10.00
		a. ½c on 2½r black & dull vio. (R) (error)	100.00	100.00
84	A5	1c on 10r black & gray green	10.00	10.00
		a. Pair, one without surcharge		
85	A8	1½c on 300r *blue* (R)	15.00	15.00
86	A6	2c on 20r black & carmine lake	10.00	10.00
87	"	2½c on 25r black & violet brown	15.00	15.00
88	A8	3c on 400r black & dark brown	10.00	10.00
		a. "Republica" omitted		
89	A6	5c on 50r black & deep blue	15.00	15.00
90	A7	7½c on 75r black & brown	10.00	10.00
91	"	10c on 100r black & brown, *green*	15.00	15.00
92	A8	12c on 500r olive & violet brown	10.00	10.00
93	A7	20c on 200r black & grn., *salmon*	15.00	15.00
		Nos. 81–93 (12)	145.00	145.00

The surcharge exists inverted on Nos. 83–85, 87–88 and 92, and double on Nos. 81, 83 and 86.

Forgeries exist of Nos. 81–93.

London Surcharges.

Numerals: The "1" has the vertical stroke and serifs thicker than in the Lisbon printing. The "2" is upright and has a strong wave in the tail. The small "2" is heavily shaded. The "3" has a rounded top. The "4" is closed at the top. The "7" has thick strokes.

Centavos: The letters are heavier than in the Lisbon printing and are of even thickness throughout. The "t" has a thick cross bar with scarcely any down stroke at the end. The "s" is rounded at the bottom and narrower than in the Lisbon printing.

No.	Type	Description	Unused	Used
94	A5	¼c on 2½r black & dull violet	1.35	1.35
95	"	½c on 5r black (R)	1.35	1.35
96	"	1c on 10r black & gray green	1.35	1.35
97	A8	1½c on 300r *blue* (R)	1.35	1.35
98	A6	2c on 20r black & carmine lake	1.35	1 35
99	"	2½c on 25r black & violet brown	1.35	1.35
100	A8	3c on 400r black & dark brown	1.35	1.35
101	A6	5c on 50r black & deep blue	1.35	1.35
102	A7	7½c on 75r blk. & brn.	1.35	1.35
		a. Inverted surcharge		
103	"	10c on 100r black & brown, *green*	1.35	1.35
104	A8	12c on 500r olive & violet brown	1.35	1.35
105	A7	20c on 200r black & green, *salmon*	1.35	1.35
		Nos. 94–105 (12)	16.20	16.20

A9

Vasco da Gama A10

"San Gabriel" A11

Zebra and Warrior A12

Dhow and Warrior A13

Perf. 12½, 13½–15 & Compound

1921–23 — Engraved

No.	Type	Description	Unused	Used
106	A9	¼c claret	1.00	1.00
107	"	½c steel blue	1.00	1.00
108	"	1c green & black	1.00	1.00
109	"	1½c black & ochre	1.00	1.00
110	A10	2c red & black	1.00	1.00
111	"	2½c blk. & olive grn.	1.00	1.00
112	"	4c black & orange	1.00	1.00
113	"	5c ultra. & black	1.00	1.00
114	"	6c black & violet	1.00	1.00
115	A11	7½c blk. & blk. brn.	1.00	1.00
116	"	8c blk. & olive grn.	1.00	1.00
117	"	10c black & red brn.	1.00	1.00
118	"	15c black & carmine	1.00	1.00
119	"	20c black & pale bl.	1.25	1.25
120	A12	30c black & bistre	1.25	1.25
121	"	40c black & gray bl.	1.25	1.25
122	"	50c black & green	1.25	1.25
123	"	1e black & red brn.	1.25	1.25
124	A13	2e red brown & black ('23)	3.25	3.25
125	"	5e ultramarine & red brn. ('23)	3.50	3.50
		Nos. 106–125 (20)	26.00	26.00

POSTAGE DUE STAMPS.

Giraffe—D1

Designs: ½c, 1c, Giraffe. 2c, 3c, Zebra. 5c, 6c, 10c, "San Gabriel." 20c, 50c, Vasco da Gama.

Engraved.

1924 — *Perf. 14.* — Unwmkd.

No.	Type	Description	Unused	Used
J1	D1	½c deep green	2.00	1.75
J2	"	1c gray	2.00	1.75
J3	"	2c red	2.00	1.75
J4	"	3c red orange	2.00	1.75
J5	"	5c dark brown	2.00	1.75
J6	"	6c orange brown	2.00	1.75
J7	"	10c brown violet	2.00	1.75
J8	"	20c carmine	2.00	1.75
J9	"	50c lilac gray	2.00	1.75
		Nos. J1–J9 (9)	18.00	15.75

NEWSPAPER STAMP.

Mozambique No. P6 Overprinted in Black **NYASSA**

1898 — *Perf. 13½.* — Unwmkd.

No.	Type	Description	Unused	Used
P1	N3	2½r brown	1.75	1.50

Reprints have white gum and clean-cut perf. 13½. Price $1.

POSTAL TAX STAMPS.

Pombal Issue

Mozambique Nos. RA1-RA3 Overprinted "NYASSA" in Red

1925	*Perf. 12½*		Unwmkd.	
RA1	CD28	15c brn. & blk.	4.50	4.50
RA2	CD29	15c " "	4.50	4.50
RA3	CD30	15c " "	4.50	4.50

POSTAL TAX DUE STAMPS.

Pombal Issue

Mozambique Nos. RAJ1-RAJ3 Overprinted "NYASSA" in Red

1925	*Perf. 12½*		Unwmkd.	
RAJ1	CD31	30c brown & black	17.50	17.50
RAJ2	CD32	30c brown & black	17.50	17.50
RAJ3	CD33	30c brown & black	17.50	17.50

OBOCK

(ō'bŏk')

LOCATION — A seaport in eastern Africa on the Gulf of Aden, directly opposite Aden.

Obock was the point of entrance from which French Somaliland was formed. The port was acquired by the French in 1862 but was not actively occupied until 1884 when Sagallo and Tadjoura were ceded to France. In 1888 Djibouti was made into a port and the seat of government moved from Obock to the latter city. In 1902 the name Somali Coast was adopted on the postage stamps of Djibouti, these stamps superseding the individual issues of Obock. See Somali Coast in Vol. IV.

100 Centimes = 1 Franc

Counterfeits exist of Nos. 1–31.

Stamps of French Colonies Handstamped in Black:

OBOCK

a

1892	*Perf. 14x13½.*		Unwmkd.	
1	A9	1c *lilac blue*	12.00	11.00
2	"	2c brown, *buff*	12.00	11.00
3	"	4c claret, *lavender*	165.00	165.00
4	"	5c green, *greenish*	9.00	8.00
5	"	10c *lavender*	25.00	15.00
6	"	15c blue	22.50	20.00
7	"	25c *rose*	30.00	25.00
8	"	35c vio., *orange*	185.00	185.00
9	"	40c red, *straw*	175.00	175.00
10	"	75c car., *rose*	185.00	185.00
11	"	1fr bronze green, *straw*	185.00	185.00

No. 3 has been reprinted. On the reprints the second "O" of "OBOCK" is 4mm. high instead of 3½mm. Price $7.50.

OBOCK

b

1892				
12	A9	4c claret, *lavender*	8.00	7.00
13	"	5c green, *greenish*	8.00	7.00
14	"	10c *lavender*	9.00	8.00
15	"	15c blue	9.00	8.00
16	"	20c red, *green*	14.00	12.00
17	"	25c *rose*	7.00	5.50
18	"	40c red, *straw*	17.50	14.00
19	"	75c carmine, *rose*	135.00	100.00
20	"	1fr bronze green, *straw*	24.00	20.00

This handstamped overprint may be found double on all denominations.

Nos. 14, 15, 17, 20 with Additional Surcharge Handstamped in Red, Blue or Black:

1 5F

c *d*

1892					
21	A9	(*c*)	1c on 25c *rose*	4.00	4.00
22	"	(")	2c on 10c *lavender*	20.00	16.50
23	"	(")	2c on 15c blue	5.00	4.00
24	"	(")	4c on 15c blue (Bk)	5.00	4.00
25	"	(")	4c on 25c *rose* (Bk)	6.50	5.00
26	"	(")	5c on 25c *rose*	7.50	6.00
27	"	(")	20c on 10c *lavender*	37.50	30.00
28	"	(")	30c on 10c *lavender*	45.00	40.00
29	"	(")	35c on 25c *rose*	32.50	27.50
			a. "3" instead of "35"	325.00	325.00
30	A9	(*c*)	75c on 1fr bronze green, *straw*	40.00	35.00
			b. "57" instead of "75"	*2500.00*	*2500.00*
			c. "55" instead of "75"	*2500.00*	*2500.00*
31	A9	(*d*)	5fr on 1fr bronze green, *straw* (Bl)	375.00	375.00

This handstamped surcharge is found inverted on most denominations.

Navigation and Commerce A4

1892		Typographed		
		"Obock" in Red (1c, 5c, 15c, 25c, 75c, 1fr) or Blue		
32	A4	1c *lilac blue*	1.25	88
33	"	2c brown, *buff*	40	40
34	"	4c claret, *lavender*	1.10	85
35	"	5c green, *greenish*	1.35	85
36	"	10c *lavender*	2.00	1.20
37	"	15c bl., quadrille paper	5.00	3.00
38	"	20c red, *green*	10.00	7.00
39	"	25c *rose*	9.00	7.00
40	"	30c brown, *bistre*	6.00	5.00
41	"	40c red, *straw*	6.00	4.00
42	"	50c carmine, *rose*	8.00	5.00
43	"	75c violet, *orange*	9.00	5.00
		a. Name double	80.00	80.00
		b. Name inverted	*850.00*	*850.00*
44	"	1fr bronze green, *straw*	11.00	8.00

Camel and Rider—A5

1893			*Imperf.*	
		Quadrille Lines Printed on Paper		
		Size: 32mm. at base.		
44A	A5	2fr bronze green	20.00	18.50
		Size: 45mm. at base.		
45	A5	5fr red	40.00	37.50

Methods and style of listing are detailed in "Special Notices" at the front of this volume.

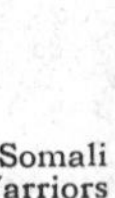

Somali Warriors A7

A8

1894			*Imperf.*	
		Quadrille Lines Printed on Paper.		
46	A7	1c black & rose	80	80
47	"	2c vio. brown & green	90	90
48	"	4c brn. vio. & org.	80	80
49	"	5c bl. green & brn.	1.00	80
50	"	10c black & green	4.00	3.50
		a. Half used as 5c on cover		12.00
51	"	15c blue & rose	3.75	3.00
52	"	20c brown orange & maroon	4.00	3.00
		a. Half used as 10c on cover		10.00
53	"	25c black & blue	4.00	3.50
		a. Half used on cover		10.00
54	"	30c bis. & yel. green	9.00	6.50
		a. Half used as 15c on cover		325.00
55	"	40c red & blue green	5.00	3.50
56	"	50c rose & blue	4.50	3.50
		a. Half used as 25c on cover		650.00
57	"	75c gray lilac & org.	5.00	3.50
58	"	1fr olive green & maroon	5.00	4.00
		Size: 37mm. at base.		
60	A8	2fr vio. & orange	45.00	40.00
		Size: 42mm. at base.		
61	A8	5fr rose & blue	35.00	30.00
		Size: 46mm. at base.		
62	A8	10fr orange & red violet	65.00	60.00
63	"	25fr brown & blue	300.00	300.00
64	"	50fr red violet & green	350.00	350.00

Counterfeits exist of Nos. 63–64.

Stamps of Obock were replaced in 1901 by those of Somali Coast. The 5c on 75c, 5c on 25fr and 10c on 50fr of 1902 are listed under Somali Coast.

POSTAGE DUE STAMPS.

Postage Due Stamps of French Colonies Handstamped Type "a" or "b"

1892			*Imperf.*	Unwmkd.	
J1	D1	(*a*)	5c black	*3000.00*	
J2	"	(")	10c "	80.00	80.00
J3	"	(")	30c "	125.00	125.00
J4	"	(")	60c "	135.00	135.00
J5	"	(*b*)	1c black	13.50	12.00
J6	"	(")	2c black	12.00	10.00
J7	"	(")	3c black	12.00	10.00
J8	"	(")	4c black	10.00	9.00
J9	"	(")	5c black	3.00	2.50
J10	"	(")	10c black	9.00	8.00
J11	"	(")	15c black	6.50	5.50
J12	"	(")	20c black	7.00	5.50
J13	"	(")	30c black	10.00	8.50
J14	"	(")	40c black	16.50	15.00
J15	"	(")	60c "	20.00	18.00
J16	"	(")	1fr brown	65.00	60.00
J17	"	(")	2fr "	65.00	60.00
J18	"	(")	5fr "	150.00	150.00

These handstamped overprints may be found double or inverted on some values. Counterfeits exist of Nos. J1–J18.

No. J1 has been reprinted. The overprint on the original measures 12½x3¾ mm. and on the reprint 12x3¼mm. Price, $120.

OLDENBURG

See German States group preceding Germany.

OLTRE GIUBA

(ōl'trȧ jōō'bä)

(Italian Jubaland)

LOCATION—A strip of land, 50 to 100 miles in width, west of and parallel to the Juba River in East Africa.

GOVT.—Former Italian Protectorate.

AREA—33,000 sq. mi.

POP.—12,000.

CHIEF TOWN—Kismayu.

Oltre Giuba was ceded to Italy by Great Britain in 1924 and in 1926 was incorporated with Italian Somaliland. In 1936 it became part of Italian East Africa.

100 Centesimi = 1 Lira

Wmk. 140

Italian Stamps of 1901-23 Overprinted **OLTRE GIUBA**

Wmkd. Crown. (140)

1925, July 29			*Perf. 14*	
1	A42	1c brown	50	65
		a. Inverted overprint	70.00	
2	A43	2c yellow brown	50	65
3	A48	5c green	25	30
4	"	10c claret	25	30
5	"	15c slate	25	30
6	A50	20c brown orange	25	30
7	A49	25c blue	30	40
8	"	30c orange brown	30	40
9	"	40c brown	40	45
10	"	50c violet	50	65
11	"	60c carmine	65	75
12	A46	1 l brown & green	90	1.10
13	"	2 l dk. grn. & org.	8.50	9.50
14	"	5 l blue & rose	14.00	16.00
15	A51	10 l gray green & red	2.50	3.25
		Nos. 1-15 (15)	30.05	35.00

Italian Stamps of 1925-26 Overprinted **OLTRE GIUBA**

1925-26				
16	A49	20c green	50	60
17	"	30c gray	60	75
18	A46	75c dark red & rose ('26)	4.75	6.00
19	"	1.25 l blue & ultra. ('26)	6.00	7.25
20	"	2.50 l dark green & orange ('26)	7.25	8.50
		Nos. 16-20 (5)	19.10	23.10

Victor Emmanuel Issue

Italian Stamps of 1925 Overprinted **OLTRE GIUBA**

1925-26	*Perf. 11*		Unwmkd.	
21	A78	60c brown carmine	27	45
		a. Perf. 13½	*2250.00*	
22	"	1 l dark blue	27	45
		a. Perf. 13½	100.00	135.00
23	"	1.25 l dark blue ('26)	90	1.75
		a. Perf. 13½	90	1.75

Saint Francis of Assisi Issue.
Italian Stamps and Type of 1926
Overprinted OLTRE GIUBA

1926, Apr. 12 *Perf. 14* Wmk. 140

24	A79	20c gray green	50	75
25	A80	40c dark violet	50	75
26	A81	60c red brown	50	75

Overprinted in Red **Oltre Giuba**
Unwmkd.

27	A82	1.25 l dk. bl., perf. 11	50	75
28	A83	5 l+2.50 l olive grn., perf. 13½	2.50	3.25
		Nos. 24-28 (5)	4.50	6.25

Map of Oltre Giuba
A1

Wmkd. Crowns. (140)
1926, Apr. 21 Typographed

29	A1	5c yellow brown	25	40
30	A1	20c blue green	25	40
31	"	25c olive brown	25	40
32	"	40c dull red	25	40
33	"	60c brown violet	25	40
34	"	1 l blue	25	40
35	"	2 l dark green	25	40
		Nos. 29-35 (7)	1.75	2.80

Oltre Giuba was incorporated with Italian Somaliland on July 1, 1926, and stamps inscribed "Oltre Giuba" were discontinued.

SEMI-POSTAL STAMPS.

Note preceding Italy semi-postals applies to No. 28.

Colonial Institute Issue.

"Peace" Substituting Spade for Sword
SP1

Wmkd. Crowns. (140)
1926, June 1 Typo. *Perf. 14*

B1	SP1	5c+5c brown	20	40
B2	"	10c+5c olive green	20	40
B3	SP1	20c+5c blue green	20	40
B4	"	40c+5c brown red	20	40
B5	"	60c+5c orange	20	40
B6	"	1 l+5c blue	20	40
		Nos. B1-B6 (6)	1.20	2.40

Surtax for Italian Colonial Institute.

SPECIAL DELIVERY STAMPS.
Special Delivery Stamps of Italy
Overprinted OLTRE GIUBA

1926 *Perf. 14* Wmk. 140

E1	SD1	70c dull red	4.25	4.75
E2	SD2	2.50 l blue & red	6.00	7.25

POSTAGE DUE STAMPS.
Italian Postage Due Stamps of 1870-1903
Overprinted OLTRE GIUBA
Wmkd. Crown. (140)

1925, July 29 *Perf. 14* Wmk. 140

J1	D3	5c buff & magenta	5.25	6.00
J2	"	10c " "	65	75
J3	"	20c " "	65	75
J4	"	30c " "	65	75
J5	"	40c " "	90	1.25
J6	"	50c " "	1.25	1.50
J7	"	60c buff & brown	1.50	1.85
J8	"	1 l blue & magenta	2.25	2.50
J9	"	2 l " "	8.00	10.00
J10	"	5 l " "	11.00	12.50
		Nos. J1-J10 (10)	32.10	37.85

PARCEL POST STAMPS.

These stamps were used by affixing them to the waybill so that one half remained on it following the parcel, the other half staying on the receipt given the sender. Most used halves are right halves. Complete stamps were obtainable canceled, probably to order.

Both unused and used prices are for complete stamps.

Italian Parcel Post Stamps of 1914-22
Overprinted OLTRE GIUBA
Wmkd. Crown. (140)

1925, July 29 *Perf. 13½*

Q1	PP2	5c brown	6.50	6.50
Q2	"	10c blue	50	65
Q3	"	20c black	50	65
Q4	"	25c red	50	65
Q5	"	50c orange	1.25	1.50
Q6	"	1 l violet	50	65
		a. Double overprint	60.00	
Q7	"	2 l green	85	1.00
Q8	"	3 l bistre	90	1.25
Q9	"	4 l slate	2.25	2.50
Q10	"	10 l rose lilac	7.00	8.50
Q11	"	12 l red brown	27.50	30.00
Q12	"	15 l olive green	13.00	14.00
Q13	"	20 l brown violet	15.00	16.00
		Nos. Q1-Q13 (13)	76.25	83.85

Halves Used

Q1	50	*Q8*	20
Q2	15	*Q9*	28
Q3	15	*Q10*	50
Q4	15	*Q11*	1.50
Q5	15	*Q12*	1.20
Q6	15	*Q13*	1.50
Q7	20		

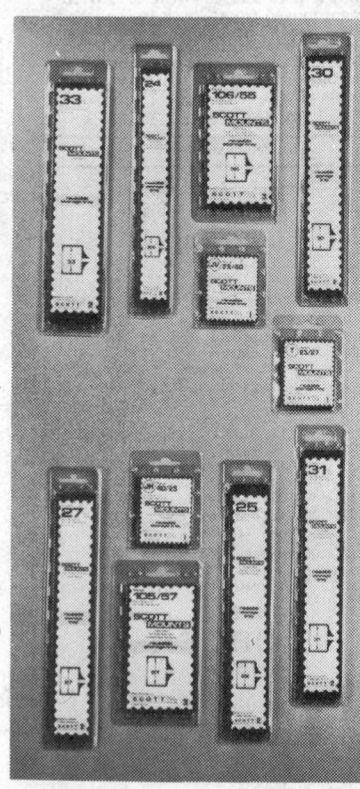

Addenda

For the Record

Index

Number Changes

Advertisements

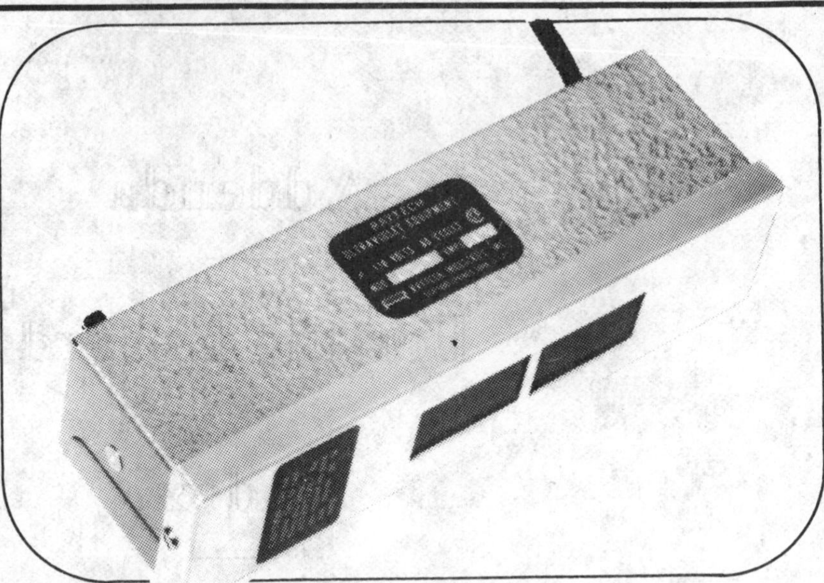

SCOTT ULTRA-VIOLET LIGHT

An invaluable tool to detect flaws, repairs, and alterations.

Lightweight, compact, portable; 7¼″ x 1¾″ x 2⅛″, Only 16 ounces, Scott UV light has shortwave ultra violet (2537 Angstron) for tagged stamps and longwave for fluorescent papers and ink.

Model LS-2 available exclusively from Scott. Individually boxed. Complete instructions included.

Scott Stock #ACC150 Price: $39.95

Available from your dealer or by mail from **Scott Publishing Co.** 3 E. 57th St. New York, N.Y. 10022

Circle No. 77 on Reader Service Card

ADDENDA

These stamps were received too late for inclusion in their proper places in the Catalogue. Later issues will be found listed in Scott's Chronicle of New Issues which appears in Scott's Monthly Stamp Journal. U.S. and Canada subscription price $8.50 for 1 year (12 issues); 2 years $15.50; 3 years $22. $10 per year additional for subscriptions outside U.S. and Canada (by air). Cash with order.

Address Scott's Monthly Stamp Journal, Subscription Dept., P.O. Box 925, Farmingdale, N. Y. 11737.

GABON

Arms Type of 1969

Coats of Arms: 5fr, Ogowe-Maritime. 10fr, Lastoursville. 15fr, M'Bigou.

1979, Mar. 21 Photo. *Perf. 12*

410	A67	5fr multicolored	5	3
411	"	10fr "	10	7
412	"	15fr "	15	8

Equestrian, Kremlin Tower, Olympic Emblem, Ancestral Figure—A123

Designs (Kremlin Towers, Olympic Emblem, Ancestral Figure and): 80fr, Long jump (vert.). 100fr, Yachts.

1979, May 15 Engr. *Perf. 13*

424	A123	60fr multicolored	60	40
425	"	80fr "	80	50
426	"	100fr "	1.00	60
		a. Miniature sheet of 3	2.40	2.40

Pre-Olympic Year. No. 426a contains Nos. 424–426. Size: 180x100mm.

GERMANY

German Democratic Republic

Miniature Sheet

Horch 8, 1911
A605

Design: 35pf, Trabant 601S de luxe, 1978.

1979, Apr. 3 Litho. *Perf. 14*

2000	Sheet of 2 + label	*2.25*
	a. A605 20pf multicolored	*80*
	b. " 35pf "	*1.40*

Sachsenring automobile plant, Zwickau. Label between stamps shows plant. Size of No. 2000: 131x55mm.

Self-Propelled Car
A606

DDR Railroad Cars: 10pf, Self-unloading freight car Us-y. 20pf, Diesel locomotive BR 110. 35pf, Laaes automobile carrier.

1979, Apr. 17 Litho. *Perf. 13*

2001	A606	5pf multicolored	
2002	"	10pf "	
2003	"	20pf "	
2004	"	35pf "	
		Nos. 2001–2004 (4)	*1.90*

Durga, 18th Century
A607

Indian Miniatures in Berlin Museums: 35pf, Mahavira, 15th–16th centuries. 50pf, Todi Ragini, 17th century. 70pf, Asavari Ragini, 17th century.

1979, May 8 Photo. *Perf. 14x13½*

2005	A607	20pf multicolored	
2006	"	35pf "	
2007	"	50pf "	
2008	"	70pf "	
		Nos. 2005–2008 (4)	*4.50*

GREECE

Wheat with Members' Flags, Greek Coins
A419

European Parliament, Strasbourg
A420

Perf. 13x14, 14x13

1979, May 28 Lithographed

1301	A419	7d multicolored	35	35
1302	A420	30d "	1.50	1.50

Greece's entry into European Economic Community and Parliament.

GREENLAND

Queen Margrethe Type of 1973

1979 Engraved *Perf. 13*

98	A28	80ö sepia	28	25
104	"	1.30k red	45	40
104A	"	1.60k blue	55	45

GUATEMALA

AIR POST STAMPS

Tree Planting
AP130

Designs (FAO Emblem and): 8c, Burnt forest. 9c, Watershed, river and trees. 10c, Sawmill. 26c, Forests, river and cultivated terraces.

1979, Apr. 16 Litho. *Perf. 13½*

C670	AP130	6c multicolored	12	3
C671	"	8c "	16	4
C672	"	9c "	18	5
C673	"	10c "	20	5
C674	"	26c "	52	15
		a. Souvenir sheet of 5	1.30	
		Nos. C670–C674 (5)	1.18	32

Forest protection. No. C674a contains Nos. C670–C674 and label showing Guatemalan Institute for Reforestation emblem and emblem of U.N. Food and Agriculture Organization. Size: 140x100mm.

HAITI

Mother Feeding Child
A156

1979, May 11 Photo. *Perf. 11½*

717	A156	25c multicolored	10	8
718	"	50c "	20	16
		Nos. 717–718, C474–C476 (5)	2.00	1.52

30th anniversary of CARE (Cooperative for American Relief Everywhere).

AIR POST STAMPS

Haitians Spinning Cotton, CARE Workshop
AP51

1979, May 11 Photo. *Perf. 11½*

C474	AP51	1g multicolored	40	30
C475	"	1.25g "	50	38
C476	"	2g "	80	60

30th anniversary of CARE.

HONDURAS

AIR POST STAMPS

UPU Emblem—AP105

Designs: 2c, Postal emblem of Honduras. 25c, Dr. Ramon Rosa (vert.). 50c, Pres. Marco Aurelio Soto (vert.).

1979, Apr. 1 Litho. *Perf. 12*

C668	AP105	2c multicolored	3
C669	"	15c "	15
C670	"	25c "	25
C671	"	50c "	50

Centenary of Honduras joining Universal Postal Union.

HUNGARY

Soldiers of the Red Army, by Bela Uitz—A635

1979, Mar. 21 Litho. *Perf. 12*

2569	A635	1fo silver, black & red	20	10

60th anniversary of Hungarian Soviet Republic.

Calvinistic Church, Nyirbator
A636

1979, Mar. 28 *Perf. 11*

2570	A636	1fo brn. & yellow	20	10

700th anniversary of Nyirbator.

Alexander Nevski Cathedral, Sofia, Bulgaria No. 1—A638

NEW FROM SCOTT

FIRST DAY COVER ALBUM

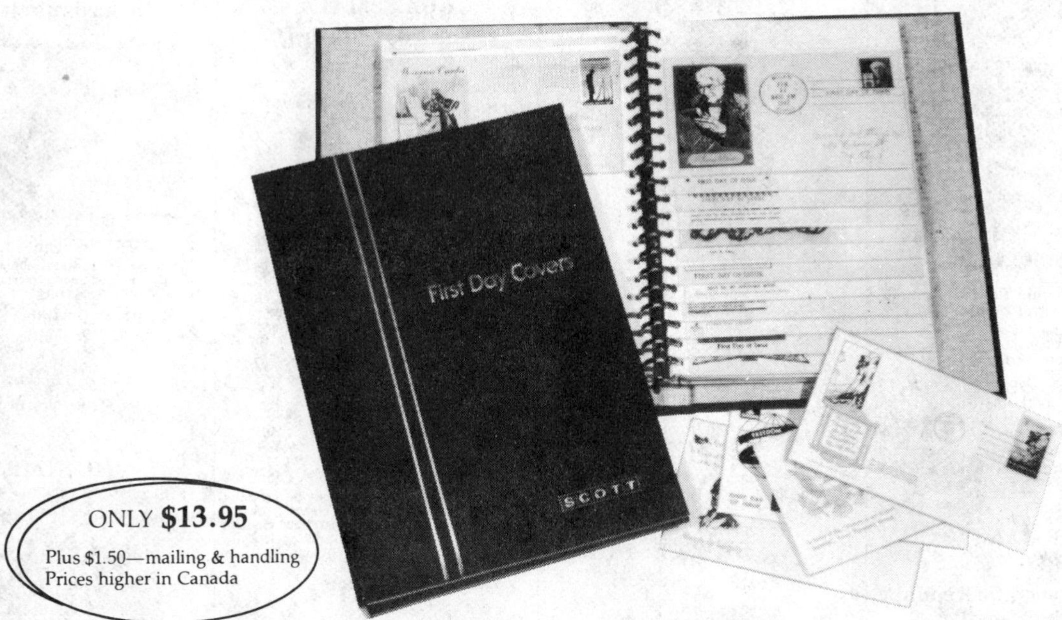

ONLY **$13.95**
Plus $1.50—mailing & handling
Prices higher in Canada

with individual transparent protectors
FOR UNITED STATES COVERS

Protect your valuable first day covers permanently in this handsome, long lasting simulated leather album. Sturdy trigger-action multi-ring construction. Size of pocket—3⅞"x7". Basic album holds 84 covers.
Brown or Green. Individually boxed.

To increase your album to its 140 cover capacity, buy Scott FDC refills at $2.50 each.

If your dealer doesn't know about this product, have him send this ad to us on his letterhead.

Circle No. 78 on Reader Service Card

® SCOTT Serving collectors since 1863.

Available from your dealer or by mail from:
SCOTT PUBLISHING CO.
DEPT. AFD
3 East 57th Street, N.Y., N.Y. 10022

1979, May 18 Litho. *Perf. 11½x12*

2572 A638 3fo multicolored 60 60

Philaserdica '79 Philatelic Exhibition, Sofia, Bulgaria, May 18–27. No. 2572 issued in sheets of 3 stamps and 3 labels showing Philaserdica emblem and arms of Sofia. Size: 105x125mm.

SEMI-POSTAL STAMP

Girl Reading Book, by Ferenc Kovacs
SP152

1979, Mar. 31 Litho. *Perf. 12*

B320 SP152 3fo+1.50fo black & ultramarine 90 55

Surtax was for Junior Stamp Exhibition, Bekescsaba.

ICELAND

Europa Issue 1979

Telephone, c. 1900
A156

Design: 190k, Post horn and satchel.

1979, Apr. 30 Photo. *Perf. 11½*

515 A156 110k multicolored 88 88
516 " 190k " 1.55 1.55

INDONESIA

R. A. Kartini and Girls' School
A229 A230

1979, Apr. 21 Photo. *Perf. 12½*

1053 A229 100r olive & brown 60 32
1054 A230 100r " " 60 32

Mrs. R. A. Kartini, educator, birth centenary. Nos. 1053–1054 printed se-tenant in sheets of 100.

Bureau of Education, UNESCO Emblems
A231

1979, May 25 Photo. *Perf. 12½*

1055 A231 150r multicolored 90 48

50th anniversary of the statutes of the International Bureau of Education.

IRAN

Kurdistani Man Rose
A536 A537

Design: 5r, Kurdistani woman.

1979, Mar. 17

1997 A536 3r multicolored 10 3
1998 " 5r " 15 4

1979, Mar. 17

1999 A537 2r multicolored 6 3

Novrooz, Iranian New Year.

Demonstrators
A538

Designs: 3r, Demonstrators. 5r, Hands holding rose, gun and torch breaking through newspaper. 20r, Hands breaking prison bars, and dove (vert.).

1979, Apr. 20 *Perf. 10½*

2000 A538 3r multicolored 10 3
2001 " 5r " 15 4
2002 " 10r " 30 8
2003 " 20r " 60 15

Islamic revolution.

Type of 1978 Overprinted

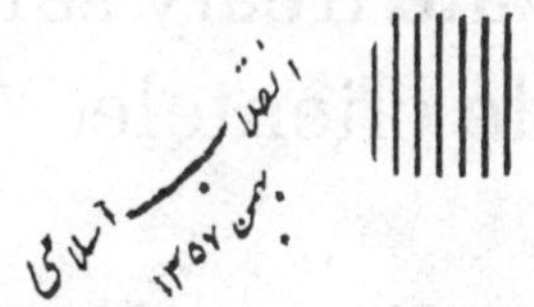

Designs: 15r, Warriors on horseback, basrelief, Naqsh-Rostan. 19r, Chehel Sotoon Palace, Isfahan.

1979, Apr. 26 *Perf. 13x13½*

2006 A520 15r red lilac 45 12
2007 " 19r slate green 58 15

Overprint means Islamic revolution. Nos. 2006–2007 not issued without overprints.

ITALY

Type of 1978

1979 Engr. *Perf. 14x13½*

1304 A674 1500 l multi. 3.00
1305 " 2000 l " 4.00

Issue dates: 2000 l, Apr. 12; 1500 l, May 14.

Carlo Maderno (1556–1629), Architect
A695

Famous Italians: No. 1362, Lazzaro Spallanzani (1729–1799), physiologist. No. 1363, Ugo Foscolo (1778–1827), writer. No. 1364, Massimo Bontempelli (1878–1960), journalist. No. 1365, Francesco Severi (1879–1961), mathematician.

1979, Apr. 23 Engr. *Perf. 14x13½*

1361 A695 170 l multicolored 35 15
1362 " 170 l " 35 15
1363 " 170 l " 35 15
1364 " 170 l " 35 15
1365 " 170 l " 35 15
Nos. 1361–1365 (5) 1.75 75

Europa Issue 1979

Telegraph
A696

Design: 220 l, Carrier pigeons.

1979, Apr. 30 Photo. *Perf. 14*

1366 A696 170 l multicolored 35 15
1367 " 220 l " 45 20

Flags and "E"
A697

1979, May 5 *Perf. 14x13½*

1368 A697 170 l multicolored 35 15
1369 " 220 l " 45 20

European Parliament, first direct elections, June 7–10.

IVORY COAST

Globe and Emblem Child Riding Dove
A173 A174

1979, Apr. 1 Litho. *Perf. 12x12½*

499 A173 60fr multicolored 60 48
500 A174 65fr " 65 52
501 A173 100fr " 1.00 80
502 A174 500fr " 5.00 4.00

International Year of the Child.

Rural Mail Delivery—A175

1979, Apr. 7 *Perf. 12½*

503 A175 60fr multicolored 60 48

Stamp Day 1979.

Korhogo Cathedral—A176

1979, Apr. 9 *Perf. 13*

504 A176 60fr multicolored 60 48

75th anniversary of arrival of Catholic missionaries.

JAPAN

Sketch of Man, by Leonardo da Vinci
A945

Photogravure and Engraved

1979, Apr. 7 *Perf. 13*

1355 A945 50y multicolored 40 12

Centenary of, promulgation of State Medical Act, initiating modern medicine.

Standing Beauties, Middle Edo Period
A946 A947

1979, Apr. 20 Photogravure

1356 A946 50y multicolored 40 12
1357 A947 50y " 40 12

Philatelic Week, Apr. 16–22. Printed se-tenant in sheets of 10.

Mt. Horaiji and Maple
A948

1979, May 26 Photo. *Perf. 13*

1358 A948 50y multicolored 40 12

National land afforestation campaign.

JUGOSLAVIA

Type of 1975

Design: 20p, Church and bridge, Bohinj.

1978 Litho. *Perf. 13*

1242A A323 20p purple ('78) 3 3

Sabre, Mace, Koran Pouch—A394

Old Weapons: 3.40d, Pistol and ramrod, Montenegro. 4.90d, Short carbine and powder horn, Slovenia and Croatia. 10d, Oriental rifle and cartridge pouch.

1979, Mar. 26 Photo. *Perf. 14*

1419	A394	2d multicolored	25	15
1420	"	3.40d "	40	25
1421	"	4.90d "	60	35
1422	"	10d "	1.20	70

5-Pointed Star, Hammer and Sickle A395

1979, Apr. 20 Photo. *Perf. 13½*

1423	A395	2d multicolored	25	15
1424	"	4.90d "	60	35

Communist and Communist Youth Leagues, 60th anniversary.

Cyril and Methodius University and Emblem A396

1979, Apr. 24 Lithographed

1425	A396	2d multicolored	25	15

Sts. Cyril and Methodius University, Skopje, 30th anniversary.

Europa Issue 1979

19th Century Belgrade, by C. Goebel A397

Design: 10d, Postilion and Ljubljana, 17th century, by Jan van der Heyden.

1979, Apr. 30 Photo. *Perf. 11½*

1426	A397	4.90d multicolored	60	35
1427	"	10d "	1.20	70

KOREA

Children on Swing A572a

1979, May 7 Photo. *Perf. 13½x13*

1093	A572a	20w green & orange ('79)	12	10

Nature Conservation Issue.

Mandarin Ducks A616 **Neofinettia Orchid A617**

1979, May 20 *Perf. 13x13½*

1151	A616	20w multicolored	12	10
1152	A617	20w "	12	10

Hand Holding Tools, Gun and Grain A626 **Temple A627**

Women, Silk Screen—A628

1979, Apr. 1 *Perf. 13x13½*

1161	A626	20w multicolored	12	10

Strengthening national security.

1979, Apr. 1

Art Treasures: No. 1163, Statue. No. 1164, Crown. No. 1165, Celadon Vase.

1162	A627	20w gray bl.& multi.	12	10
1163	"	20w bister & multi.	12	10
1164	"	20w vio. & multi.	12	10
1165	"	20w brt. grn. & multi.	12	10
1166	A628	60w multicolored	35	30
		a. Souvenir sheet of 2	90	
		Nos. 1162–1166 (5)	83	70

5000 years of Korean art. No. 1166a has black marginal inscription. Size: 90x126mm.

Pulguk-sa Temple and PATA Emblem A629

1979, Apr. 16 *Perf. 13½x13*

1167	A629	20w multicolored	12	10

28th Pacific Area Travel Association (PATA) Conference, Seoul, Apr. 16–18, and Gyeongju, Apr. 20–21.

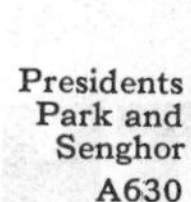

Presidents Park and Senghor A630

1979, Apr. 22 *Perf. 13½x13*

1168	A630	20w multicolored	12	10
		a. Souvenir sheet of 2	30	

Visit of Pres. Leopold Sedar Senghor of Senegal. No. 1168a has black and ultramarine marginal inscription. Size: 90x60 mm.

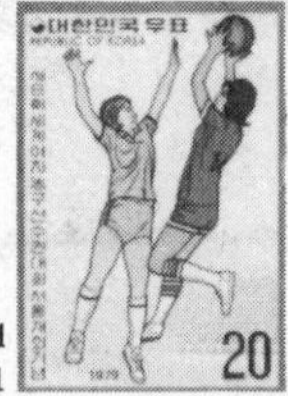

Basketball A631

1979, Apr. 29 *Perf. 13x13½*

1169	A631	20w multicolored	12	10

8th World Women's Basketball Championship, Seoul, Apr. 29–May 13.

Children and IYC Emblem A632

1979, May 5 Photo. *Perf. 13½x13*

1170	A632	20w multicolored	12	10
		a. Souvenir sheet of 2	30	

International Year of the Child. No. 1170a has black marginal inscription. Size: 90x60mm.

LIBERIA

Presidents Gardner and Tolbert, and Post Office, Monrovia—A266

Design: 35c, Anthony W. Gardner, William R. Tolbert, Jr. and UPU emblem.

1979, Apr. 2 Litho. *Perf. 13½x14*

836	A266	5c multicolored	10	10
837	"	35c "	70	70

Centenary of Liberia's joining Universal Postal Union.

LIBYA

Carpobrotus Acinaciformis A227

Flora of Libya: 15d, Caralluma europaea. 20d, Arum cirenaicum. 35d, Lavatera arborea. 40d, Capparis spinosa. 50d, Ranunculus asiaticus.

1979 Litho. *Perf. 14*

779	A227	10d multicolored	8	4
780	"	15d "	12	6
781	"	20d "	16	8
782	"	35d "	30	12
783	"	40d "	32	15
784	"	50d "	40	20
		Nos. 779–784 (6)	1.38	65

LUXEMBOURG

Europa Issue 1979

Trois-vièrges Stage-coach A207

Design: 12fr, Early wall telephone (vert.).

1979, Apr. 30 Photo. *Perf. 11½*

624	A207	6fr multicolored	35	25
625	"	12fr "	70	50

Michel Pintz Facing Jury A208

1979, Apr. 30 Engr. *Perf.*

626	A208	2fr rose lilac	12	10

180th anniversary of peasant uprising against French occupation.

Antoine Meyer A209 **Abundance Crowning Work and Thrift, by Auguste Vinet A210**

Design: 6fr, Sidney Gilchrist Thomas.

1979, Apr. 30

627	A209	5fr carmine	30	20
628	"	6fr light blue	35	25
629	A210	9fr black	50	35

Antoine Meyer (1801–1857), mathematician and first national poet; centenary of acquisition of Thomas process for production of high-quality steel; 50th anniversary of Luxembourg Stock Exchange.

European Parliament A211

1979, June 7 Photo. *Perf. 11½*

630	A211	6fr multicolored	35	25

European Parliament, first direct elections, June 7–10.

MALI

Manatee A111

Endangered Wildlife: 120fr, Chimpanzee. 130fr, Damaliscus antelope. 180fr, Oryx. 200fr, Derby's eland.

1979, Apr. 23 Litho. *Perf. 12½*

No.	Type	Denomination	Color	Unused	Used
317	A111	100fr	multicolored	40	22
318	"	120fr	"	48	25
319	"	130fr	"	52	28
320	"	180fr	"	72	40
321	"	200fr	"	80	45
	Nos. 317-321 (5)			2.92	1.60

Boy Praying and IYC Emblem
A112

Designs (IYC emblem and): 200fr, Girl and Boy Scout holding bird. 300fr, IYC emblem, boys with calf.

1979, May 7 Engr. *Perf. 13*

No.	Type	Denomination	Color	Unused	Used
322	A112	120fr	multicolored	48	32
323	"	200fr	"	80	45
324	"	300fr	"	1.20	68

International Year of the Child.

Judo and Notre Dame, Paris—A113

1979, May 14 Engr. *Perf. 13*

325 A113 200fr multicolored 80 45

World Judo Championship, Paris.

Tele-communications A114 — Wood Carving A115

1979, May 17 Lithographed

326 A114 120fr multicolored 48 25

11th Telecommunications Day.

1979, May 18 *Perf. 13x12½*

Sculptures from National Museum: 120fr, Ancestral figures. 130fr, Animal heads, and kneeling woman.

No.	Type	Denomination	Color	Unused	Used
327	A115	90fr	multicolored	36	25
328	"	120fr	"	48	25
329	"	130fr	"	52	28

International Museums Day.

Rowland Hill and Mali No. 15
A116

Designs: 130fr, Zeppelin and Saxony No. 1. 180fr, Concorde and France No. 3. 200fr, Stagecoach and U.S. No. 2. 300fr, UPU emblem and Penny Black.

1979, May 21 Engr. *Perf. 13*

No.	Type	Denomination	Color	Unused	Used
330	A116	120fr	multicolored	48	25
331	"	130fr	"	52	28
332	"	180fr	"	72	40
333	"	200fr	"	80	45
334	"	300fr	"	1.20	70
	Nos. 330-334 (5)			3.72	2.08

Sir Rowland Hill (1795-1879), originator of penny postage.

AIR POST STAMPS

Basketball and St. Basil's Cathedral, Moscow
AP140

Design: 430fr, Soccer and Kremlin.

1979, Apr. 17 Litho. *Perf. 13*

No.	Type	Denomination	Color	Unused	Used
C362	AP140	420fr	multi.	1.70	1.10
C363	"	430fr	"	1.75	1.20

Pre-Olympic Year.

MAURITANIA

Farmers at Market, by Dürer
A99

Dürer Engravings: 14um, Young Peasant and Wife. 55um, Mercenary with flag. 60um, St. George Slaying Dragon. 100um, Mercenaries (horiz.).

Litho.; Red Foil Embossed

1979, May 3 *Perf. 13½x14*

No.	Type	Denomination	Color	Unused	Used
407	A99	12um	black, *buff*	60	32
408	"	14um	" "	70	35
409	"	55um	" "	2.75	1.40
410	"	60um	" "	3.00	1.60

Souvenir Sheet

Perf. 14x13½

411 A99 100um black, *buff* 5.25 2.50

Albrecht Dürer (1471-1528), German painter. No. 411 shows entire etching from which stamp design was taken. Size: 114x118mm.

MEXICO

Export Type of 1975

Designs as before.

Perf. 14

1979, May Photo. Wmk. 300

No.	Type	Denomination	Color	Unused	Used
1171	A320	2p	brt. grn. & bl.	20	8
1173	"	3p	brown	30	20
1175	"	10p	dk. & lt. grn.	1.00	30

AIR POST STAMPS

Export Type of 1975

Perf. 14

1979, May Photo. Wmk. 300

C596 AP214 1.60p blk. & org. 16 10

Children, Child's Drawing—AP264

1979, May 16

C604 AP264 1.60p multi. 16 10

International Year of the Child.

INSURED LETTER STAMPS

Padlock Type of 1976

Perf. 14

1979 Photo. Wmk. 300

No.	Type	Denomination	Color	Unused	Used
G31	IL5	5p	black & blue	50	25
G32	"	10p	" "	1.00	50

MONGOLIA

Mongolia No. 4, Bulgaria No. 1, Philaserdica Emblem—A245

Designs (Rowland Hill and): No. 1077b, American mail coach. No. 1077c, Mail car, London-Birmingham railroad, 1838. 1077d, Packet leaving Southampton, Sept. 24, 1842, opening Indian mail service.

1979, May 15 Litho. *Perf. 12*

No.	Type	Denomination	Color	Unused	Used
1077		Sheet of 4, multi.		2.75	
a.	A245	1t	dk. red, gray & blk.	65	
b.	"	1t	" " "	65	
c.	"	1t	" " "	65	
d.	"	1t	" " "	65	

Philaserdica '79, Sofia, May 18-27, and death centenary of Rowland Hill (1795-1879), originator of penny postage. No. 1077 has gray marginal inscription and design. Size: 125x94mm.

MOROCCO

Vase A185 — Procession A186

1979, Mar. 29 Photo. *Perf. 14*

429 A185 1d multicolored 50 30

Week of the Blind.

Perf. 13x13½, 13½x13

1979, Apr. 18

Design: 1d, Festival, by Mohamed Ben Ali Rbati (horiz.).

No.	Type	Denomination	Color	Unused	Used
430	A186	40fr	multicolored	20	12
431	"	1d	"	50	30

NETHERLANDS

Europa Issue 1979

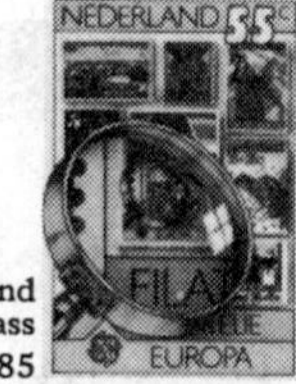

Dutch Stamps and Magnifying Glass
A185

Design: 75c, Hand on Morse key, and ship at sea.

1979, May 2 Litho. *Perf. 13x13½*

No.	Type	Denomination	Color	Unused	Used
587	A185	55c	multicolored	55	30
588	"	75c	"	75	35

NEW CALEDONIA

House at Artillery Point—A100

1979, Apr. 28 Photo. *Perf. 13*

445 A100 20fr multicolored 60 40

AIR POST STAMPS

Surf Casting
AP76

Design: 30fr, Swordfish fishing.

1979, May 26 Litho. *Perf. 12½*

No.	Type	Denomination	Color	Unused	Used
C152	AP76	29fr	multicolored	90	60
C153	"	30fr	"	90	60

NICARAGUA

AIR POST STAMPS

Red Ginger and Ruby-throated Hummingbird—AP110

Designs: 55c, Orchid. 70c, Poinsettia. 80c, Flower and bees. 2cor, Lignum vitae and blue morpho butterfly. 4cor, Cattleya.

1979, Apr. 6 Litho. *Perf. 14x13½*

No.	Type	Denomination	Color	Unused	Used
C963	AP110	50c	multicolored	15	10
C964	"	55c	"	16	10
C965	"	70c	"	22	15
C966	"	80c	"	25	16
C967	"	2cor	"	55	40
C968	"	4cor	"	1.10	80
	Nos. C963-C968 (6)			2.43	1.71

NIGER

The Langa, Traditional Sport
A141

Design: 50fr, The langa (diff.).

1979, Apr. 10 Litho. ***Perf. 12½x12***

472	A141	40fr multicolored	32	20
473	"	50fr "	40	25

FOR THE RECORD

The items recorded here appeared on the stamp market in the 1960's and '70s, and have not been listed in the Scott Standard Catalogue. They are arranged chronologically and briefly described. Completeness is not claimed.

CONTENTS

GABON

1970

Dornier, Claude, 1st death anniversary. *Dec. 5.* 2 miniature sheets of 8: 15, 25, 40, 60, 80, 125, 150, 200fr, perf.; 10, 20, 30, 50, 75, 100, 125, 150fr, imperf. Souvenir sheet of 4 (200, 300, 400, 500fr) perf., imperf. Souvenir sheet, 1000fr imperf.

1971

Apollo 14, *Feb. 19* Perf., imperf. airmail 15, 25, 40, 55, 75, 120fr (6v). Souvenir sheet of 2 (100fr x 2). Same with gold border and black control number.

GUINEA

1971

13th World Boy Scout Jamboree, Japan. Silver foil, 90fr x 4 (se-tenant).

John F. and Robert F. Kennedy and Martin Luther King. Silver foil, airmail 300fr, gold foil, airmail, 1500fr.

1972

Pres. Nixon's China Visit. *Apr.* Silver foil, airmail 90fr x 4 (se-tenant). Gold foil, airmail 290fr x 4 (se-tenant). Gold foil, airmail, 1200fr.

Jules Verne. Airmail, silver foil, 300 fr x 2; gold foil, 1200fr.

GUINEA-BISSAU

1976

American Bicentennial, Generals and Battles. *Mar. 5.* Perf., imperf. 5, 10, 15, 20e; airmail, 30, 40e (6v). Same miniature sheets of 1, perf., imperf. Airmail souvenir sheet, 50e, perf., imperf.

Dance Masks. *May 10.* 2, 3, 5p; airmail, 10, 15, 20p (6v). Airmail souvenir sheet, 50p.

U.P.U. Centenary. Mask set overprinted. *June 8.* Perf., imperf. 2, 3, 5p; airmail, 10, 15, 20p (6v). Same miniature sheets of 1, perf., imperf. Airmail souvenir sheet, 50p, perf., imperf. All exist with red or black overprint.

Apollo Soyuz Space Cooperation. *Oct. 4.* Airmail, 5, 10, 15, 20, 30, 40p (6v). Souvenir sheet, 50p.

Telephone Centenary. *Oct. 18.* 2, 3, 5p; airmail, 10, 15, 20p (6v). Airmail souvenir sheet, 50p.

Winter Olympics, Innsbruck. *Nov. 3.* 1, 3, 5p; airmail, 10, 20, 30p (6v). Airmail souvenir sheet, 50p.

Summer Olympics, Montreal. *Nov. 24.* 1, 3, 5, 10, 20, 30p (6v). Souvenir sheet, 50p.

1977

American Bicentennial, Crispus Attucks, Martin Luther King. *Jan. 27.* 3.50, 5p (2v).

Viking Mars Project, *Jan. 27.* 25, 35p (2v).

Zeppelin, 75th anniversary. *Feb. 27.* 3.50, 5, 10, 20p; airmail, 25, 30p (6v). Airmail souvenir sheet, 50p.

World Soccer Cup, Argentina, June 1–25. *Mar. 15.* 3.50, 5, 10, 20, 25, 30p (6v). Souvenir sheet, 50p.

Nobel Prize Winners. 3.50, 5, 6, 30p; airmail, 35, 40p (6v). Airmail souvenir sheet, 50p.

Postal Progress, 100th anniversary. 3.50, 5, 6, 30p; airmail, 35, 40p (6v). Airmail souvenir sheet, 50p.

Queen Elizabeth II, Silver Jubilee. 3.50, 5, 10, 20p; airmail, 25, 30p (6v). Airmail souvenir sheet. 50p.

1978

History of Aviation. 3.50, 10, 15p; airmail, 20, 25, 30p (6v). Airmail souvenir sheet, 50p (Concorde).

Queen Elizabeth II Coronation, 25th anniversary. *Sept.* 3.50, 5, 10, 20p; airmail, 25, 30p (6v). Airmail souvenir sheet, 50p. Gold foil embossed, 100p, airmail souvenir sheet, 100p.

Endangered Species. *Sept.* 3.50, 5, 6, 30p; airmail, 35, 40p (6v). Airmail souvenir sheet 50p.

Albrecht Durer, 450th death anniversary. 3.50, 5, 6, 30p; airmail, 35, 40p (6v). Airmail souvenir sheet, 50p.

HAITI

1968

10th Winter Olympics, Grenoble. 5, 10, 20, 25, 50c, 1.50g; airmail, 2g (7v). Souvenir sheet, 4g perf., imperf.

Pres. Francois Duvalier. *Sept. 22.* Gold foil airmail 30g.

1969

Olympic Marathon Winners, Summer games 1896–1968. *May 16.* 5, 10, 15, 20c x 2, 25c x 3, Airmail 30, 50, 60, 75c x 2, 90c, 1, 1.25g (16v). 4 souvenir sheets, 1.50, 2g, perf., imperf.

Apollo 11. *Aug. 29.* Nos. C326-C329 overprinted.

Apollo 7, 8. *Oct. 6.* Perf., imperf. 10, 15, 20, 25c; airmail, 70c, 1, 1.25, 1.50g (8v). Same with changed background colors (8v). 2 souvenir sheets, 1.75, 2g. perf., imperf.

1970

Apollo 12. *Sept.* Perf., imperf. 5, 10, 15, 20, 25, 30, 40, 50c; airmail, 25, 30, 40, 50, 75c, 1, 1.25, 1.50g (16v). Same with changed colors (16v).

1971

Apollo 13. Apollo 12 issue of 1970 overprinted in red or gold "Apollo XIII Retour/Sur la Terre." (16v). Same with silver overprint (16).

1973

Gold Medalists, 1972 Munich Olympics. *Jan.* 5, 10, 20, 25, 50c; airmail, 50, 75c, 1.50, 2.50, 5g (10v).

U.S. and Russian Space Explorations. *May 30.* 5, 10, 20, 25, 50c, 2.50, 5g; airmail 50, 75c, 1.50, 2.50, 5g (12v).

Apollo 17. *May 30.* U.S. and Russian Space issue

of 1973 overprinted with Apollo 17 emblem in silver, 50c, 2.50, 5g (3v).

Israeli Athletes (assassinated in Munich, 1972). *June 5.* 2 airmail souvenir sheets, 2.50, 5g.

1974

UPU centenary. U.S. and Russian Space Exploration issue of 1973 overprinted "Centenaire/de/ L'U.P.U./1874 1974." (12v).

1975

Birds (paintings by John James Audubon). 5c x 3, 10c x 4, 25c x 3, 50c x 2, 75c x 5, 1.50g x 3, 2.50g, 5g x 2 (23v).

IVORY COAST

1970

Independence, 10th anniversary, Presidents de Gaulle and Houphouet-Boigny. Embossed on gold and silver foil, souvenir sheets, 300fr x 2 silver, 1000fr x 2 gold. Airmail 300fr silver, 1200fr gold. (6 sheets)

LAOS

1975

Peace Treaty, 1st anniversary. Souvenir sheet, 2000k, gold foil center.

UPU centenary. *July 7.* 10, 15, 30, 40k; airmail, 1000, 1500k (6v). Perf., imperf. 2 souvenir sheets, 1000, 1500k, perf., imperf. Miniature sheets of six values with brown borders. Embossed on gold foil, airmail 2500 (Moonbuggy), 3000k (Concorde) perf., imperf. Same, 2 miniature sheets of 2 (2500, 3000k). Also perf., imperf. 2v airmail, 2500K (mail coach), 3000k (railroad, zeppelin). Same, 2 miniature sheets of 2 (2500, 3000k) perf., imperf.

Apollo-Soyuz Project. *July 7.* 125, 150, 200, 300k, airmail 450, 700k (6v). Same, 6 values in miniature sheets.

American Bicentennial, Presidents. *July 30.* 10, 15, 40, 50, 100, 125, 150, 200k, airmail 1000, 1500k (10v).

NICARAGUA

1973

Christmas. *Nov. 15.* 2, 3, 4, 5, 15, 20c; airmail, 1, 2, 4cor (9v). Airmail souvenir sheet of 3 (1, 2, 4cor).

1974

Churchill, birth centenary. *Apr. 30.* 2, 3, 4, 5, 10c; airmail, 5, 6cor (7v). 2 souvenir sheets of 1, 4cor.

World Cup Soccer Championship, Munich. *May 8.* 1, 2, 3, 4, 5, 10, 15, 20, 25c; airmail, 10cor (10v). 2 airmail souvenir sheets, 4, 5cor.

Victory of German Federal Republic. *July 12.* 10cor overprinted "Triumfador / Alemania / Occidental".

UPU centenary. *July 10.* 2, 3, 4, 5, 10, 20c; airmail; 40c; 3, 5cor (9v). Airmail souvenir sheet of 3 (1, 2, 4cor) imperf.

1975

21st Olympic Games, Montreal. Decathlon Winners 1912–1972. *Aug. 15.* Se-tenant sheet of 16. Airmail, 1, 2, 4, 25cor x 13 (gold foil embossed margins) (16v). 3 airmail souvenir sheets, 20 cor, imperf. with gold foil embossed margins.

INDEX and IDENTIFIER

See also Addenda and For the Record

NUMERICAL INDEX OF WATERMARKS

VOL. III

* Page indicates where illustration may be found.

NUMBER CHANGES

in Scott's 1980 Standard Catalogue, Vol. III

No. in 1979 Cat.	No. in 1980 Cat.
GERMANY	
1176–1182	1177–1183
1183	1185
1232–1236	1234–1238
1237–1238	1240–1240A
Berlin	
9N365–9N371	9N366–9N372
9N372	9N374
9N393–9N397	9N394–9N398
9N398–9N399	9N400–9N401
GUINEA-BISSAU	
350–355	354–359
HAITI	
C426–C431	C421–C426
RAC20	deleted
RAC23	RAC20
HONDURAS	
C597	CE6
C598–C600	C597–C599
IRAN	
1966–1968	1961–1963
1970	1964
1983–1992	1973–1982
1993	1984
O91	O93
ISRAEL	
694	694a
694a	694
ITALY	
Aegean Islds., Rhodes	
BE1–BE2	EB1–EB2
IVORY COAST	
446–454	447–455
KOREA	
1117–1119	1118–1120
LUXEMBOURG	
536	537
537	536
MAURITANIA	
375–380	383–388
MEXICO	
248c	248b
249a–249b	deleted
256A–256C	242b, 243b, 244b
256E–256G	247c, 248c, 249a
256H–256P	242c, 244c, 246b, 247d, 248d, 249b, 251a, 252a, 253b
268A–268N	257a, 259a, 260a, 261c, 263a, 257b, 258b, 259b, 260b, 261d, 262a, 263b, 264a, 265a
273a	deleted
278B–278F	269a, 270a, 272b, 273a, 276a
MEXICO (cont.)	
278H–278I	269b, 270b
278K–278L	271b, 272c
278N–278Q	273b, 275a, 276b, 277a
291A–291C	279c, 280b, 281c
292–292A	283c, 287b
293–293G	279d, 280c, 281d, 282a, 283d, 284a, 286a, 287c
620A	621
621–626	622–627
MONACO	
937–941	933–937
942	939
943	941
945	946
NETHERLANDS	
550–554	548–552
NORWAY	
O94	O98